THE AUTHORITY SINCE 1868

THE WORLD ALMANAC®

AND BOOK OF FACTS

1999

WORLD ALMANAC BOOKS
A PRIMEDIA Company

THE WORLD ALMANAC®
AND BOOK OF FACTS
1999

The editors acknowledge with thanks the many letters of helpful comment and criticism from readers of THE WORLD ALMANAC. Because of the volume of mail directed to the editorial offices, it is not possible to reply to each letter writer. However, every communication is read by the editors and all comments and suggestions receive careful attention. THE WORLD ALMANAC's e-mail address is Walmanac@aol.com.

THE WORLD ALMANAC does not decide wagers.

The first edition of THE WORLD ALMANAC, a 120-page volume with 12 pages of advertising, was published by the New York World in 1868. Annual publication was suspended in 1876. Joseph Pulitzer, publisher of the New York World, revived THE WORLD ALMANAC in 1886 with the goal of making it a "compendium of universal knowledge." It has been published annually since then.

THE WORLD ALMANAC and BOOK OF FACTS 1999

Library of Congress Catalog Card Number 4-3781
International Standard Serial Number (ISSN) 0084-1382
ISBN (softcover) 0-88687-832-2
ISBN (hardcover) 0-88687-833-0
Microform Edition: University Microfilms Intl.
Printed in the United States of America
The softcover and hardcover editions are distributed to the book trade by St. Martin's Press; the paperback edition is distributed to the magazine trade by Hearst Distribution Group.

WORLD ALMANAC BOOKS
An Imprint of PRIMEDIA Reference Inc.
One International Boulevard, Suite 444
Mahwah, New Jersey 07495-0017

CONTENTS

GENERAL INDEX

Note: Page numbers in **boldface** indicate key references. Page numbers in *italics* indicate photos.

The World Almanac

and Book of Facts 1999

THE TOP 10 NEWS STORIES OF 1998

The U.S. House of Representatives, voting largely along party lines on Oct. 8, authorized a House committee inquiry into the possible impeachment of Pres. Bill Clinton. Earlier, on Sept. 9, a report from independent counsel Kenneth Starr had detailed what it called "substantial and credible information" that the president had lied under oath, obstructed justice, and abused powers of his office in an effort to cover up a relationship with former White House intern Monica Lewinsky.

In a surprise turnaround in off-year U.S. elections on Nov. 3, Republicans failed to make any gains in Congress; in fact, Democrats picked up a net gain of 5 seats in the House of Representatives (including 1 seat projected but not final), for a total of 211 out of 435, while the balance of power in the Senate remained unchanged at 55 for the Republicans and 45 for the Democrats. Democrats won key Senate races in New York and California, as well as the California governorship. Republicans defeated the Democratic Senate incumbent in Illinois, while former Pres. George Bush's two sons, Republicans George W. Bush and Jeb Bush, easily won governors' races in Texas and Florida, respectively.

Representatives of Catholic and Protestant groups in Northern Ireland and of the Irish Republic and the United Kingdom signed a major peace accord, Apr. 10. The accord, ratified by the people of Northern Ireland and the Irish Republic in referenda May 22, retained British rule in Northern Ireland but provided mechanisms for limited self-rule and consultation between Northern Ireland and the Irish Republic. David Trimble and John Hume, heads of major Protestant and Catholic parties in Northern Ireland, respectively, won a Nobel Peace Prize for their efforts in the negotiations.

India exploded underground nuclear devices in a desert area May 11 and 13; Pakistan, a neighboring state, followed suit, with nuclear tests May 28 and 30. Both actions prompted international concern, with the U.S. and some other countries applying economic sanctions against the two rival states.

Bombs exploded minutes apart, Aug. 7, outside U.S. embassies in Nairobi, Kenya, and Dar-es-Salaam, Tanzania. A total of 224 people (213 of them in Nairobi) were killed, including 12 Americans. The U.S. government responded Aug. 20 by firing missiles at suspected terrorist training centers in Afghanistan and at a factory in Sudan that the U.S. said was linked to terrorism.

The rippling effects of continuing economic turmoil in Southeast Asia helped depress the Japanese economy and increase volatility in stock markets around the world, and in late August, a severe financial crisis in Russia caused a global plunge in stocks, with the Dow Jones industrial average falling 512 points on one day, Aug. 31.

The weather phenomenon known as El Niño, in which warm ocean currents near the Pacific coast of Peru cause abnormal storm or drought conditions, continued to affect climate in many parts of the world in early 1998. Among other effects, tornadoes hit Florida in February, killing more than 40 people. In California, torrential rains in late February killed 9 people, caused flooding, and destroyed many homes. South America was also hard hit in February. Peru, Bolivia, and Ecuador suffered through storms and mudslides, and Colombia experienced a severe drought.

St. Louis Cardinals slugger Mark McGwire hit his 62d home run of the season, Sept. 8, to surpass the record of 61 set by Roger Maris in 1961; a spectacular home run race ensued between McGwire and Sammy Sosa of the Chicago Cubs, who also surpassed Maris's 61; McGwire ended the season Sept. 27 with a record 70 home runs, 4 ahead of Sosa's 66.

Palestinian leader Yasir Arafat and Israeli Prime Min. Benjamin Netanyahu signed a new peace agreement, Oct. 23, in Washington, DC, reached with the encouragement of Pres. Bill Clinton and Jordan's King Hussein. The pact called for Israel to withdraw troops from another 13% of the West Bank and for Palestinians to step up efforts against terrorism and remove from the Palestinian National Charter language calling for Israel's destruction.

On Mar. 24 in Jonesboro, AR, 2 boys aged 11 and 13 fatally shot 4 students and a teacher and wounded 10 others outside their middle school. On May 21 in Springfield, OR, a 15-year-old high school student allegedly shot his parents, then went to school and fired into the cafeteria, killing 1 student and wounding 23, 1 of whom died the next day. These incidents were among the most notable in a small wave of school shootings by students.

Election '98

By Donald Young

Donald Young is a freelance writer and editor who writes on current affairs.

In the 1998 midterm elections on Nov. 3, the Republican Party failed to increase its margin in the Senate and lost seats in the House. Republicans retained control of both houses of Congress and also held on to a substantial majority of the nation's governorships. However, their failure to make the gains traditional for an off-year election caused consternation in Republican ranks and appeared to take some steam out of impeachment proceedings against Pres. Bill Clinton for actions relating to his relationship with former White House intern Monica Lewinsky.

In Senate elections, the Democrats won 18 contests and the Republicans 16, leaving the breakdown unchanged at 55–45 in favor of the GOP. In the House, where all 435 seats were up for election, unofficial returns showed Republicans winning 223 seats to 211 for the Democrats (counting an Oregon seat where the Democrat was leading), with 1 seat going to an independent.

Democrat Charles E. Schumer, a U.S. representative from Brooklyn, defeated Alfonse D'Amato, the 3-term U.S. senator from New York, in the year's most acrimonious contest. After a campaign marked by negative advertising and heavy spending by both major candidates, D'Amato, the powerful chairman of the Senate Banking Committee, lost by more than 400,000 votes.

Lauch Faircloth of North Carolina was the only other incumbent Republican senator to lose. He was defeated by the telegenic John Edwards, a trial lawyer, who at 45 was 25 years younger and had never held public office. Faircloth, a harsh critic of the president, had run ads suggesting that Clinton and Edwards shared "a habit of stretching the truth."

A 3d Democratic pickup in the Senate came in Indiana, where a former governor, Evan Bayh, was elected to the open seat being vacated by Dan Coats. Bayh, in defeating Fort Wayne Mayor Paul Helmke, took the seat once held by his father, Birch Bayh.

The only Democratic senator to be defeated was Carol Moseley-Braun of Illinois, who in 1992 had been the first black woman elected to the Senate. Moseley-Braun, who had admitted making several ethical missteps, lost to State Sen. Peter G. Fitzgerald, a social conservative. Republicans also picked up 2 open seats. In Ohio, Gov. George V. Voinovich was elected to succeed John Glenn, the once and present astronaut who was orbiting the earth even as the votes were cast. In Kentucky, in a contest between 2 former star athletes, both members of the House, Jim Bunning defeated Scotty Baesler by only about 7,000 votes.

Democratic incumbents who won included Barbara Boxer (CA), who turned back a strong challenge from State Treasurer Matthew Fong; Patty Murray (WA), who won a tough race against U.S. Rep. Linda Smith; and Ernest Hollings (SC), who defeated U.S. Rep. Bob Inglis. In Nevada, the incumbent Sen. Harry Reid (D) held onto a narrow lead to defeat U.S. Rep. John Ensign (R) by a few hundred votes.

Other Democratic incumbents who kept their seats included Christopher J. Dodd (CT), Bob Graham (FL), John B. Breaux (LA), Barbara Ann Mikulski (MD), and Minority Leader Tom Daschle. Leading Republicans returned to the Senate included Charles Grassley (IA), Don Nickles (OK), and Arlen Specter (PA).

Both sponsors of the McCain-Feingold bill to reform campaign financing were returned to office. Sen. John McCain (R) won big in Arizona, and Sen. Russ Feingold (D) survived a strong challenge from a conservative, Mark W. Neumann, in Wisconsin. Feingold, who had denounced the influence of so-called soft money, objected when the national Democratic Party began running negative ads in his behalf.

Although Moseley-Braun lost, the ranks of Democratic women were augmented when Blanche Lambert Lincoln won the open Arkansas Senate seat.

In the voting for the U.S. House, for the first time since 1934, the party that controlled the White House managed to pick up seats in a midterm election. Republican expectations of a gain faded as almost all incumbents in both parties, aided by a strong economy and the usual advantages of incumbency, retained their seats.

In California, former Rep. Robert Dornan (R), a hardline conservative who had narrowly lost his seat in 1996 to Loretta Sanchez, was defeated by her again by a big margin. Among prominent family names, Tom Udall (D), whose father was former Interior Sec. Stewart L. Udall, won election in New Mexico, and his cousin Mark Udall (D), son of former U.S. Rep. Morris Udall, succeeded in Colorado.

In New Jersey, Mike Pappas, a Republican who had strongly backed impeachment proceedings against Clinton, was unseated by Democrat Rush Holt. Also, challenger Jay Inslee (D), running in a suburban Seattle (WA) district, defeated his opponent, Rep. Rich White (R), after criticizing the latter's support of the impeachment process.

The nation's 8 most populous states elected governors, and the Republicans won all but one of these races. Two sons of former Pres. George Bush were elected: George W. Bush, regarded as a possible contender for the GOP presidential nomination in 2000, easily captured a second term in Texas, and Jeb Bush, on his second try, prevailed in Florida. Both brothers demonstrated remarkable success in winning Hispanic support and also did well, by Republican standards, among blacks. On the other hand, in California, where Republicans had become identified with restraints on immigration and opposition to quotas in college admissions, Hispanics and blacks voted heavily for Democrats. A major beneficiary was Lt. Gov. Gray Davis, who took the statehouse for his party after 16 years of Republican occupancy. Davis would be influential in the redistricting process after the 2000 census, when California was expected to have as many as 58 House districts.

In other major governors' races, Republican incumbents won easily in the states of Michigan (John Engler), New York (George E. Pataki), and Pennsylvania (Tom Ridge). Republicans also won open governorships in Illinois (George H. Ryan) and Ohio (Bob Taft, great-grandson of Pres. William Howard Taft). Republican success in these big-state elections was attributed to effective administration and tax-cutting by moderate governors who avoided divisive social issues.

Perhaps the most astonishing story of the night was the victory in Minnesota of Reform Party candidate Jesse ("The Body") Ventura, a former professional wrestler who had been mayor of a Minneapolis suburb before running for governor. Debating his major-party opponents—including Atty. Gen. Hubert H. Humphrey III (D), son of the former vice president, who had been favored to win after obtaining a big settlement with tobacco companies—Ventura articulated straightforward opinions on state issues.

The Democrats, who had become a minority party in the Cotton Belt, once their bastion, staged a partial comeback, unseating GOP governors in South Carolina (David Beasley) and Alabama (Fob James Jr.). The winners, respectively, were Jim Hodges and Don Siegelman. Both had urged the approval of state lotteries to raise money for education. James's loss was a defeat for social conservatives. Roy E. Barnes won the governor's race in Georgia, preserving that state's record of electing only Democratic governors since Reconstruction.

In Maryland, Parris Glendening, a Democrat, won a second term by again defeating his 1994 opponent, Ellen Sauerbrey. Running in a heavily Democratic state, Glendening had been criticized by blacks for ignoring their concerns. After Clinton admitted his relationship with Lewinsky, Glendening canceled a fund-raiser with the president, then agreed to appear with Clinton a month later.

Although the president generally limited his campaigning to fund-raisers held indoors, First Lady Hillary Rodham Clinton, whose popularity was at a peak, and Vice Pres. Al Gore campaigned energetically.

One early analysis showed that about 38% of eligible voters went to the polls, about the same as in recent off-year elections. Turnout was said to be relatively high among African-Americans, regarded as likely Clinton supporters. But exit polling suggested that strong opinions for and against Clinton may have just about canceled each other out at the ballot boxes. One exit poll showed education—typically an issue favoring Democrats—to be the top issue for voters.

In state referenda, 5 states (Alaska, Arizona, Nevada, Oregon, and Washington) approved the use of marijuana for medicinal purposes, and 2 states (Alaska and Hawaii) approved measures against same-sex marriages. Legalizing doctor-assisted suicide was rejected by Michigan voters.

Results at a Glance

The following table shows how the 1998 elections affected the balance of power between parties.

SENATE	Before	After	Change	HOUSE	Before	After	Change	GOVERNORS	Before	After	Change
Rep.	55	55	0	Rep.	228	223	−5	Rep.	32	31	−1
Dem.	45	45	0	Dem.	206	211*	+5*	Dem.	17	17	0
Other	0	0	0	Other	1	1	0	Other	1	2	+1

*Assumes Democratic win in Oregon's 1st District, where Democrat was leading.

Clinton Impeachment Inquiry

By Geoffrey M. Horn

Geoffrey M. Horn is a freelance writer and editor who often writes on political and cultural topics.

In 1998, for only the 3d time in history, the House of Representatives voted to launch presidential impeachment proceedings. On Oct. 8, after mostly partisan debate, 31 Democrats joined 227 Republicans to pass a resolution authorizing the Judiciary Committee, chaired by Henry J. Hyde (R, IL), to investigate "whether sufficient grounds exist for the House of Representatives to exercise its constitutional power to impeach William Jefferson Clinton."

The Republican-sponsored resolution imposed no restrictions on the scope or duration of the committee's work. The House had defeated by 236-198 a Democrat-sponsored measure proposing a more limited inquiry.

The Starr Report

The event that prompted House action was the submission by independent counsel Kenneth Starr of a "referral" concerning Clinton's relationship with former White House intern Monica Lewinsky. The 117,000-word document, commonly known as the Starr report, arrived at the Capitol at 4 PM on Sept. 9, accompanied by 36 boxes of supporting materials. Both the report and a preliminary White House rebuttal were posted on the Internet.

The Starr report cited what it called "substantial and credible information" that the president lied under oath, obstructed justice, and misused the powers of his office to cover up his sexual activities with Lewinsky, which were described in detail. Clinton's defenders generally conceded that the president had done wrong but insisted that his offense amounted to at most lying about sex and did not meet constitutional standards for impeachment.

Clinton-Lewinsky Liaisons

Lewinsky began as an unpaid intern in July 1995, shortly before her 22d birthday, and graduated to a paying job at the White House before year's end. According to her testimony, months of flirtation with Clinton blossomed into their first sexual encounter by Nov. 15 (the president acknowledged no "inappropriate, intimate contact" between them until early 1996). Their liaisons, usually in a private study, hallway, or bathroom near the Oval Office, reportedly did not include sexual intercourse but did include oral sex. Clinton aides, concerned that Lewinsky was spending too much time with the president, arranged for her reassignment to the Pentagon in Apr. 1996. Intimate physical contact ceased, except for a brief interval early in 1997.

After securing immunity from prosecution, Lewinsky provided investigators in 1998 with details of dozens of phone conversations and meetings with the president and of gifts they exchanged. Prosecutors were able to corroborate much of her story by using White House logs, Secret Service testimony, and tape recordings of telephone calls between Lewinsky and a friend, Linda Tripp, made by Tripp without Lewinsky's knowledge.

The Jones Case

Even as Clinton and Lewinsky pursued their relationship, a sexual harassment lawsuit filed against Clinton by Paula Corbin Jones was targeting other instances of alleged sexual misconduct. Jones claimed that on May 8, 1991, while Clinton was governor of Arkansas and she was a state employee, he summoned her to his hotel room and asked her to perform oral sex on him, but that she refused. In fall 1997, Jones's legal team sought to bolster their case by seeking testimony from women rumored to have had illicit sexual contact with Clinton. Acting on tips from Tripp and her friend Lucianne Goldberg, a literary agent, the lawyers identified Lewinsky as a potential witness.

Lewinsky's name appeared on a witness list Dec. 5; she was subpoenaed 2 weeks later. The Starr report documents a series of contacts in late 1997 and early 1998 involving Clinton, Lewinsky, Clinton's personal secretary Betty Currie, and his friend Vernon Jordan. The witnesses differed in their specific recollections, but certain facts appeared clear. Jordan, an influential lawyer, got Lewinsky a job offer from a cosmetics firm; gifts given by Clinton were retrieved from Lewinsky and hidden in a box under Currie's bed; and Lewinsky executed an affidavit stating she "never had a sexual relationship with the president."

Tripped Up

Starr, meanwhile, had been investigating Clinton's involvement in the Whitewater land deal and other scandals since Aug. 1994. A well-connected Republican with an impressive résumé, he was no stranger to the Jones case, having advised her legal team before he became independent counsel. Starr's office believed Clinton had impeded the Whitewater inquiry by encouraging his friends, including Jordan, to arrange lucrative contracts to buy the silence of a key witness, former Associate Attorney Gen. Webster Hubbell. So when Tripp offered her tapes to Starr's office in Jan. 1998, it was the involvement of Jordan in seeking a job for Lewinsky that provided the main rationale for an expansion of Starr's mandate. On Jan. 13, at the urging of prosecutors, Tripp wore a recording device while meeting with Lewinsky, to gain further evidence.

Tripp also briefed Jones's lawyers before they were scheduled to take sworn testimony from Clinton. When asked about Lewinsky in his deposition on Jan. 17, Clinton appeared to many to be evasive, relying on quibbles and contorted definitions to convey the misleading impression that he and Lewinsky were little more than casual acquaintances. Possibly alarmed by how much the Jones team knew, he summoned Currie to the White House the next day (a Sunday) and went over his version of events ("You were always there when she was there, right?"). Starr's report accused him of coaching a potential witness.

Defiance and Repentance

Soon after the scandal broke in the *Washington Post* on Jan. 21, the White House began crafting a hard-line response. Clinton made a vehement, finger-wagging denial and sent out cabinet members and top aides to back up his story. His lawyers sought to shield potential witnesses by making extensive claims of presidential privilege, most of which the courts rejected. Meanwhile, Clinton's high job approval rating allowed the White House to shift the focus to Starr's alleged prosecutorial excesses and portray Starr and his staff as right-wing zealots. On Apr. 1, U.S. District Court Judge Susan Webber Wright threw out the Jones case, but an appeal was filed and both sides were exploring a possible settlement.

The impetus toward an impeachment inquiry built in the summer, after word leaked that Lewinsky had given prosecutors a dress with a semen stain—physical evidence that could prove she and the president had sexual contact. Clinton acknowledged on Aug. 17 that he had misled his family, his staff, the public, and Jones's lawyers, although he insisted that his testimony had been "legally correct" and his tone in videotaped testimony before a grand jury convened by Starr, and in a televised speech the same day, seemed to some to be more combative than contrite. On later occasions he expressed his regret more strongly, but said he would tell his lawyers to mount a "vigorous defense" in upcoming proceedings.

SPECIAL SECTION: THE COMING MILLENNIUM

The new millennium has nearly arrived. What will it be like? How will it compare to the past? How are people going to celebrate? *The World Almanac and Book of Facts 1999* addresses these and other millennial questions in this special section. In the following pages, former astronaut Sally K. Ride describes her vision of how scientific breakthroughs will impact people's lives in the 21st century, while historian Eric Foner relates America's future to its past. Also included is a calendar of millennial events.

Other special features and Millennium Fact Boxes throughout *The World Almanac* highlight intriguing facts and accomplishments in the past century or millennium. For example, in the Sports section sportscaster Bob Costas gives his list of the 25 most dramatic moments in sports in the 20th century, and in the Historical Figures chapter Pulitzer-Prize-winning historian Arthur M. Schlesinger Jr. offers a list of the 10 most influential people of the 2d millennium. Other topics range from the American Film Institute's choice of America's 100 best movies (Arts and Media chapter) to the most popular first names of the 20th century (Language chapter), to trends in immigration to the United States since the 1820s (United States History chapter), to dramatic changes in death rates from killer diseases (Vital Statistics chapter).

Today's Dreams, Tomorrow's Realities: Science in the New Millennium

By Sally K. Ride

Former astronaut Sally K. Ride became the first American woman in space when she flew aboard the space shuttle Challenger *in 1983. She flew in space a second time in 1984. Since 1989 she has been a physics professor at the University of California at San Diego. She is a member of the Presidential Committee of Advisors on Science and Technology.*

We are lucky to be living at the very moment in history when humanity is taking its first careful steps off the planet. As we become a spacefaring species, our perceptions of our world and place in the universe are changing profoundly. Our entry into the Space Age is changing our way of life on Earth, as well. Our day-to-day world is becoming smaller and smaller, as satellites circling the globe link all parts of the planet by telephone, television, and the Internet. But even as the global community is shrinking, our horizons are expanding. Space probes traveling to other planets and telescopes orbiting above Earth's atmosphere are extending our presence and opening new windows on the universe.

The technological and scientific advances of the Space and Information Ages are revolutionizing human society, enabling us to communicate and to gather and share information like never before. Today it is possible to send e-mail to friends and colleagues around the world, make airline reservations on the World Wide Web, and view images beamed just minutes before from the surface of Mars. The Olympics are watched as they happen by billions of people the world over, wars are covered live on CNN, and the Academy Awards presentations can be seen from nearly anywhere in the world.

We are only just beginning to realize the potential of these powerful technologies. The next century will see an explosion in space, communications, and information technologies that will create advances as great as that from the slide rule to the supercomputer.

The Impact of Space and Information Technologies

When I was orbiting the Earth in the Space Shuttle, I looked down at Africa and saw the stark golden deserts, the long winding Nile, and the great rift valleys, but the boundaries between nations were invisible. The view from space makes it vividly clear that the human-made borders separating one group of people from another are artificial. Space and information technologies are beginning to erase these and other boundaries for everyone.

Communications and information now regularly flow across national boundaries. Satellite technology has greatly accelerated that flow. Early satellites were crude compared to their modern descendants. The first communications satellite was nothing more than a huge balloon with a reflective coating; signals were simply bounced off its surface and reflected back down to Earth. The first weather satellite was little more than a camera sent into orbit, but when the photographs were put together into a time-lapse movie it gave weather forecasters their first view of global cloud systems. The first spy satellites carried cameras to keep close watch on adversaries, but their reconnaissance photographs were not transmitted down to satellite dishes. Instead, a capsule containing the exposed film was sent back to Earth, snatched out of the air by an airplane, and then taken to a lab to be developed. Though the early satellites were simple, together they demonstrated the potential for worldwide communication, weather forecasting, accurate positioning, and global monitoring of military movements and intentions.

Advances in satellite technology have been remarkable and rapid. Today, communication satellites carry television signals and telephone conversations all over the world. Weather satellites monitor global weather systems, track storms, and save thousands of lives. Navigation satellites provide precise locations to airplanes, oil tankers, and mountain climbers around the world. Surveillance satellites help keep the peace by watching for troop movements, missile launches, and warhead detonations.

Even more dramatic advances are on the horizon. New constellations of satellites will provide coverage to every square meter of the planet; combinations of telecommunications technologies will make high bandwidth available everywhere. These advances will draw us closer and closer together as we all become part of a global society, able to communicate at the speed of light. Soon, our voices, images, and ideas may be carried as digitized signals—nearly instantaneously—across national, cultural, and economic boundaries to any place on Earth. Soon, the information accessible in downtown Manhattan will also be accessible in rural Madagascar. Soon, wristwatch-size TVs with instant access to the Internet will allow us to stay connected to family and co-workers anytime, anywhere.

Navigation satellites may be the next to affect daily life. These satellites instantly provide a user's precise location any place on Earth. Small receivers may soon be standard equipment in every car and every pager, and be found in every hiker's backpack. Learning the most direct route to a new restaurant, or where (exactly) your children are playing after school, will be as quick as a few keystrokes.

Today, only a small fraction of Earth's roughly 6 billion inhabitants have access to communication and information technologies. The most important outcome of the explosion in these technologies may be the entry of billions of people into the Information Age. Villages in underdeveloped countries will gain access to basic information about clean drinking water and basic sanitation. Young mothers in rural and poverty-stricken regions of developed countries will have access to information about neonatal care and infant nutrition. Remote parts of the world will no longer be unprepared for natural disasters, as weather forecasters will be able to transmit hurricane advisories to places where storms still hit without warning and claim thousands of lives.

As people from all parts of the world gain access to humanity's knowledge base, and to immediate and constant communication, they will be able to make more informed decisions about their lives, their communities, and their planet. With access to the latest information about health and medicine, billions of people will have the opportunity to live healthier lives. With access to information about their local environment, people can make more thoughtful decisions about the natural resources in their communities. With access to information about regional and remote education, more people will be able to learn basic skills and raise their standard of living. And with access to information about different parts of the world, and the ability to communicate with other cultures, more people will gain an appreciation for the splendid diversity of the human family. The future of these technologies appears to be boundless; they will most certainly have an enormous impact on society in the 21st century.

Stepping Into the Solar System

Before the Space Age, scientific instruments were chained to Earth's surface. Telescopes strained to gather light from distant planets. Even the most powerful produced only fuzzy images that did not reveal much about the mysterious worlds they were studying. In the absence of science fact, science fiction flourished. As recently as the 1950s, scientists and writers alike speculated about civilizations on Mars and jungles on Venus.

Now we send spacecraft through the vast expanse of interplanetary space to give us a close-up view of these alien worlds. Though astronauts have never traveled beyond our own moon, humankind can now see the magnificent rings of Saturn, the majestic canyons of Mars, and the stormy atmosphere of Neptune through the eyes of robot spacecraft. These probes have visited every planet except Pluto. They wander the dusty, red surface of Mars; sample the toxic, roiling atmosphere of Venus; and witness volcanoes erupting on Jupiter's moon Io.

New Perspectives From Space

As these robot explorers radio images and data back to Earth, they are changing our view of the solar system. We are learning that today's Mars is a dry, desolate planet, without water or life on its surface; Venus is an inhospitable inferno, with temperatures hot enough to melt lead; and Jupiter's moon Europa has ice-covered oceans that some speculate might harbor life. The exploration of our solar neighborhood is teaching us that each of these worlds is complex and unique. It is also teaching us that each holds important clues to Earth's origin and evolution. In the coming decades, scientists will examine these worlds in detail and learn what they can tell us about our own planet.

The new perspective from space is also revolutionizing our understanding of Earth. Until Yuri Gagarin rocketed into history and became the first human to orbit the planet, no one had ever seen Earth from above. When the *Apollo* astronauts first showed us our magnificent blue planet suspended in space, our perspective as a species changed forever. But today we still know surprisingly little about our own planet. We are only beginning to understand the exquisite interdependence of Earth's land, air, water, and living things; we are only beginning to appreciate the global scale of their interactions and to realize we have the power to throw these systems irreparably out of balance. In the coming decades, fleets of satellites will study the Earth's atmosphere, oceans, and biosphere, and civilization's influence on them.

As more data are gathered and fed into increasingly sophisticated computer models, scientists will come to understand the detailed workings of the planet. They will understand natural effects, like El Niño, that dramatically alter weather patterns and affect the economies and living conditions of billions of people around the globe. They will understand the implications of human-induced changes, like global warming and ozone destruction, which threaten to alter the delicate planetary balance that sustains civilization. This detailed understanding of Earth's systems may be our most important scientific advance in the next century.

In the next millennium, enormous solar sails will unfurl to power planetary spacecraft, and lightweight, miniature instruments will explore every corner of the solar system. Some will return with scoops of comet dust, ice cores from the far side of the moon, and rocks from Mars. A few of the spacecraft launched decades ago are finally about to cross the boundary of the solar system and become our first emissaries into interstellar space. They inspire us to dream of sending spacecraft to other stars. But that grand voyage will have to wait for quantum leaps in technology. *Voyager 1* is traveling at over 35,000 miles per hour, yet it will not reach the nearest star for 40,000 years! Though our technology cannot yet match the "warp speed" of *Star Trek*, this past century has seen modes of travel advance from the horse and buggy to the Space Shuttle, so we can only wonder what marvels the next century will bring.

One of the most intriguing scientific and philosophical questions yet to be answered is whether or not life exists beyond our own planet. In a universe so vast, with countless other galaxies and billions of stars like our sun, it seems likely that other planets exist with the conditions necessary for life to evolve. But no one knows. In the next decades, telescopes will be able to detect Earth-size planets (if there are any) around the nearest stars. But even in our own solar system there are worlds that might harbor life. Future missions may find microscopic living things in underground hot springs on Mars, or in the waters beneath Europa's icy shroud. In the next century we can expect to answer one of our most fundamental questions: Are we alone in the universe? Or will life develop anywhere conditions are right?

Our robot explorers allow us to imagine what it would be like to visit an alien world and are paving the way for human explorers to follow. When Yuri Gagarin and John Glenn squeezed into their tiny capsules and blasted into space, they broke humanity's bond with Earth, and lifted us beyond Earth's boundaries and into orbit with them. Now, as we enter the new millennium, the Space Shuttle routinely carries astronauts and instruments into space. The Space Shuttle and fleets of Russian rockets are launching pieces of the International Space Station, an enormous orbiting laboratory nearly the size of a football field. Astronauts will set up long-term housekeeping there, spending months at a time testing new technologies, studying how people and materials respond to weightlessness, and conducting other experiments impossible on Earth.

Future Explorers

With the Space Station, we will establish a foothold in space, and create a stepping-stone for future exploration. Sometime in the next century, we will extend humanity's presence farther still. Astronauts will return to the moon, this time to stay, and establish a scientific outpost and possibly a launch pad for further exploration. The moon is our nearest neighbor in space—just a 2- or 3-day rocket ride from Earth. Mars, on the other hand, is a long way away! With today's technology, it will take 8 to 10 months to get to the Red Planet. But astronauts will almost certainly embark on an expedition to Mars, the planet most like our own, within the first few decades of the 21st century. Humanity's first visit to another planet will be an historic undertaking. The attention of the world will be focused on the modern pioneers as they travel over 100 million miles through interplanetary space to explore this alien world.

In the 21st century, space travel will become more commonplace. As technologies mature, travel agencies will begin booking passages on commercial "spaceliners" and adventurous travelers will enjoy vacations in orbit around Earth. As they rise above Earth's atmosphere, these space travelers will experience the transforming view of their home planet's oceans and land, wrapped in a thin cocoon of air, set against the velvety blackness of space.

Every day, astronauts floating in orbit gaze back at Earth; orbiting telescopes send us images of the universe unobscured by Earth's atmosphere; and distant spacecraft radio information from faraway worlds. We are literally learning new things about our planet, and its place in the universe, every day. In the future, an understanding of the intricacies of Earth's atmosphere, oceans, and biosphere will enable us to manage the world's natural resources, and avoid disrupting the conditions that make Earth the habitable planet it is today.

Every day, communications satellites relay billions of conversations around the globe, weather satellites track our planet's severe storms, and millions of computers exchange data and information worldwide. We are literally becoming more of a global community every day. In the future, the accelerating advances in telecommunications, space, and information technologies will likely affect the very structure of our society. As these technologies reach all corners of the world, the importance of political, cultural, and economic boundaries will slowly fade.

As we enter the new millennium, no one really knows where our scientific and technological innovations will lead. But our past reminds us that what we dare to dream today often becomes reality tomorrow.

Can America Predict Its Future?

By Eric Foner

Eric Foner, professor of history at Columbia University since 1982, has written numerous books on American history, including The Story of American Freedom *(1998) and* Reconstruction: America's Unfinished Revolution 1863-1877 *(1988), for which he won the Bancroft Prize and the Los Angeles Times Book Award.*

"No man can have in his mind a conception of the future," wrote the 17th-century philosopher Thomas Hobbes, "for the future is not yet. But of our conceptions of the past, we make a future." Hobbes's subject was politics, not prognostication—his point being that deeply-rooted traditional values can in the right circumstances (in this case the English Civil War of the mid-17th century) beget revolutions. But his remark can also be taken as a comment on what we now call futurology—the art, science, or harmless diversion of forecasting events to come. As the world approaches a new century and a new millennium, predictions of all kinds abound. Yet few take into account, as Hobbes reminds us, how powerfully the past informs and shapes the future.

America's View of the Future

Efforts to predict the future, through oracles, crystal balls, or computer programs, are as old as civilization itself. But the obsession with milestones like the year 2000 is a relatively recent phenomenon. For most of human history, people assumed that the future would be much like the past. Until the idea of progress took hold during the Enlightenment, history was generally viewed as a tale of endlessly recurring cycles. Change was impermanent and decline as common as improvement.

Americans have always had a highly ambiguous attitude toward their own past and, therefore, toward the future. On the one hand, they have always tended to adopt rosier views of the future than other peoples. For Americans, as the writer Ambrose Bierce put it, the future seems always to be a time when "our affairs prosper, our friends are true, and our happiness is assured."

From the beginning, after all, the New World has been the site of idealized hereafters, beginning with Sir Thomas More's 1516 satire *Utopia*, which initiated the futurist genre, and continuing in 17th-century writings promoting colonization—which promised European settlers a society in which all would be made equal by the bounty of nature.

The American Revolution greatly enhanced Americans' sense of a future constantly improving and infinitely malleable. "We have it in our power to begin the world over again," wrote Thomas Paine in *Common Sense* (1776), his clarion call for American independence. "The birthday of a new world is at hand." To Paine and his 19th-century progeny, history was a burden to be discarded, not a guide to the future. "The past," wrote the novelist Herman Melville, "is the textbook of tyrants; the future is the Bible of the free." History meant Europe, with its wars, monarchies, and rigid class divisions; progress meant leaving all that behind. Other peoples might ground their sense of national identity on a common experience dating back over the centuries. America's identity rested on a shared future—the destiny of spreading the blessings of liberty to all humanity.

To the founding fathers, however, the future, when viewed through the "lamp of experience," suggested danger as well as limitless possibility. An uneasy amalgam of optimism and pessimism hovered over the creation of the American republic. James Madison, the "father" of the constitution, and his friend and mentor Thomas Jefferson believed that the Revolution had opened a new era for the human race, in which political democracy and unhampered commerce would bring Americans an unprecedented prosperity. Yet, simultaneously, these thinkers were apprehensive about the social and political consequences of economic change.

Convinced that democratic government required an economically independent citizenry, they feared that progress would inevitably produce a society with a wealthy aristocracy akin to the upper classes of Europe, and a nonpropertied majority easily incited by demagogues to use their political power to despoil the rich. In such circumstances, democracy could not flourish. Westward expansion, they hoped, could forestall this day of reckoning by guaranteeing that the United States would remain a society of landowning farmers and independent artisans for generations to come. But eventually, the continent would be filled, the promise of economic autonomy eroded, and the republic endangered.

This same combination of optimism and foreboding affected their views on the most serious internal problem confronting the new nation, slavery. Jefferson and Madison, like many of the founders, were certain that slavery would and should be abolished (even though both owned slaves). "Nothing is more certainly written in the book of fate," Jefferson wrote, "than that these people are to be free." But, he added, it was equally certain that blacks and whites could never live together in harmony or equality. Paralyzed by this conviction, the founders left the contradiction of chattel slavery in a self-proclaimed "empire of liberty" to future generations to solve.

The 19th Century

The 19th century, of course, proved to be an era of unprecedented economic transformation, spurred by the industrial revolution, the railroad, and the advent, via the telegraph, of virtually instantaneous communication. So rapid was the pace of change that when Charles Francis Adams returned to America in 1868 after having served for 8 years as ambassador to Great Britain, his family felt as strange as if they had been "Tyrian traders of the year BC 1000, landing from a galley fresh from Gibraltar." Not only new technologies, but the destruction of slavery reinforced the idea of history as a narrative of unending progress.

Yet the late 19th century also confronted the fact that the consequences of change were complex and contradictory. That era of recurrent economic depressions, violent labor conflict, and agrarian unrest raised anew the question that had concerned Jefferson and Madison—could democratic institutions survive in the face of immense inequalities of wealth and economic power? Why, wondered Henry George in the era's greatest best-seller, did "progress and poverty" always seem to accompany each other? The country's bitter social conflict helped to frame visions of the future as the 20th century approached.

One gets the impression that the years 1700 and 1800 did not produce an outpouring of prognostications about the coming century. But the end of the 19th century certainly did. The most popular, Edward Bellamy's *Looking Backward* (1888) and Ignatius Donnelly's *Caesar's Column* (1891), each projected contemporary trends into the future, but with starkly different results. In Bellamy's novel, the protagonist falls asleep in the late 19th century only to awaken in the year 2000, in a world where inequality has been banished and social harmony achieved. The process of economic concentration, evident in the rise of corporate enterprise in the 1870s and 1880s, had culminated in the creation of a single Great Trust, now controlled by society at large, for whom all citizens worked in an Industrial Army. Equal rights and an adequate income were now guaranteed to all Americans, women as well as men.

From today's vantage point, Bellamy's technocratic utopia seems a chilling blueprint for a world of coerced uniformity. Yet it had an immense impact on social thought and inspired thousands to try to make a reality of Bellamy's social vision. For Bellamy held out the prospect of retaining the material abundance made possible by industrial capitalism while restoring an imagined past of broad equality. Far more disturbing to contemporaries was Donnelly's anti-utopian novel, in which industrial progress produces a degraded, impoverished working class that rises up in violent revolution. Civilization perishes in an immense mound of dead bodies (the "column" of the book's title), while Donnelly's hero implausibly finds sanctuary in Uganda (the New World seeking refuge in the Old).

Americans in 1900 also had to grapple with the same problem of race relations the founders had failed to solve. The abolition of slavery brought with it a "new birth of freedom," as Lincoln called it, but did not produce anything resembling racial justice, except for a brief period after the Civil War when African-Americans enjoyed equality before the law and manhood suffrage. By the turn of the century, a new system of inequality, resting on segregation, disenfranchisement, a labor market rigidly segmented along racial lines, and the threat of lynching for those who challenged the new status quo, was well on its way to being consolidated in the South, with the acquiescence of the rest of the nation. The road to reunion after the Civil War was paved with the shattered dreams of black Americans. Yet few who sought to predict the future around 1900 made much mention of race relations. One exception was the scholar and activist W. E. B. DuBois, whose comment that the "color line" would turn out to be "the problem of the twentieth century" was one of the era's more prescient forecasts.

The 20th Century and Beyond

Not even DuBois, of course, really anticipated the colossal changes in every aspect of human life that have marked the 20th century. Indeed, most of the pivotal events of the century now drawing to a close have come as complete surprises. World wars, the Great Depression, the social upheaval known as the 1960s (which, among other things, overthrew what DuBois had called the "color line"), the rise and fall of the Soviet Union—so much of what has happened to 20th-century men and women was neither expected nor predicted by them. The record of predictions in this century ought to instill modesty among those attempting to forecast the next.

Today, while one can encounter anticipations of impending disaster—the earth consumed by a "population bomb" or the environment destroyed by heedless economic growth—most prognostication remains decidedly optimistic. Even though the 20th century, with its world wars, crimes against humanity, and the social costs of scientific advances like the splitting of the atom, has thrown the idea of progress into disarray, predictions of the next century tend to assume that new technology will solve our problems. Today, cyberspace is hailed as the site of a new, egalitarian utopia, where individuals can reinvent themselves to their heart's desire. Once they turn off their computers, however (and, increasingly, on-line as well), people encounter the same material world, with its opportunities and discontents. What is important about technology, moreover, is not simply how it advances, but who controls it and to what ends.

I would like to propose the heretical idea that in thinking about the future, we pay less attention to predicting what changes will take place and more to the implications of different possible changes for existing values and institutions. If anything is constant in history, it is change. Yet the same issues that preoccupied the men who created the American republic—about the social foundations of democratic government and about the possibility of racial justice in a heterogeneous society—continue to shape American life and, I believe, will do so in the future.

Will progress produce a widely-shared abundance or a continued widening of the gap between social classes (or, more precisely, on the evidence of the 1990s, between the rich and everyone else)? Will democratic self-government survive the next century or will the continuing internationalization of economic relations render the nation-state essentially irrelevant? Will the growing racial and ethnic diversity of the American population promote greater toleration and harmony or will it produce fragmentation and bitterness as the affluent (mostly white) wall themselves off from the increasingly nonwhite groups at the bottom of the social order?

History suggests that such issues will help to shape life in America of the 21st century. The answers to the questions defy accurate forecast, for they rest on the decisions of innumerable men and women about how to order their lives. If history proves anything, it is that life, fortunately, is unpredictable. But these are some of the issues upon which the future will hinge.

A Millennium Calendar

(Dates and details subject to change.)

1999

The Beacon Millennium Festival, an international fund-raiser, begins with the Great Walk, in communities worldwide at noon on **Jan. 1**; the Great World Party takes place **Aug. 15**; and the finale, the Momentous Celebration, happens **Dec. 31**, when beacons are lit at midnight around the world.

First Night International meets in Atlanta, **Apr. 21-25**, to coordinate more than 200 alcohol-free community celebrations for New Year's Eve 1999.

A global peace conference convenes **May 11** at The Hague, Netherlands. In Berlin the restored Reichstag officially reopens **May 23** with the election of Germany's federal president.

After 150 years under Portuguese sovereignty, Macau becomes a special administrative region of China, **Dec. 20**.

From **Dec. 24** through the end of the following year, the Vatican expects more than 13 million tourists to visit sacred sites in Italy for Holy Year 2000.

The U.S. transfers control over the Panama Canal to Panama, **Dec. 31**.

Ceremonies mark the opening of the huge Millennium Dome at Greenwich, England, **Dec. 31**. Worldwide, tens of millions of people gather in cities to celebrate what, for most people, is the dawn of the new millennium. A 24-hour television special, involving networks in more than 40 countries, shows the start of the 21st century in each of the 24 successive time zones. The World Millennium Snapshot project plans to make a massive interactive "holomorph" from photographs taken at the stroke of midnight.

2000

As revelers ring in the New Year, **Jan. 1**, programmers anxiously check whether their computers have survived the switch from 1999 to 2000—the dreaded "millennium bug."

Some 4 million pilgrims are expected to visit Bethlehem, Nazareth, Jerusalem, and other sacred places in Israel and the West Bank for Holy Land 2000, **Jan. 1-Dec. 31**.

Odyssey 2000, a round-the-world bicycle trek, has enlisted about 250 participants to cycle 20,000 miles across some 54 countries during the year 2000.

The Year of the Dragon, year 4698 on the Chinese lunar calendar, begins **Feb. 5**.

New Zealand hosts the America's Cup 2000 championship yacht races, **Feb. 19-Mar. 4**. (Challenger round-robin eliminations start **Oct. 25, 1999**.)

The first centesimal leap year since 1600 adds a day to the calendar, **Feb. 29**.

Apr. 6 marks the 1st full day of the year 1421 on the Islamic calendar.

Organizers hope to enlist more than 300 million people to participate **Apr. 22** in the largest Earth Day ever.

The Expo 2000 world's fair opens, **June 1** (see below).

Participation by more than 30 million people is the goal for the global March for Jesus, **June 10**, with prayer and worship processions in over 2,000 cities.

Up to 30,000 spectator vessels join a flotilla of tall ships for OpSail 2000 in New York harbor, **July 3-9**.

The Holy Shroud of Turin, Italy, is on public display, **Aug. 26-Oct. 22**.

The XXVII Olympiad is held in Sydney, Australia, **Sept. 15-Oct. 1**. Sydney also hosts the Games of the XI Paralympiad for athletes with disabilities, **Oct. 18-29**, and "Harbour of Life," an Olympic arts festival.

On **Sept. 30**, Rosh Hashanah, a Jewish holy day, marks the 1st full day of the year 5761 on the Hebrew calendar.

The U.S. elects its 1st president of the 3d millennium, **Nov. 7**.

New Millennium's Eve, **Dec. 31**. Most authorities say the 3d millennium technically begins **Jan. 1, 2001**.

Some Websites Relating to the Millennium

America's Cup 2000: http://www.americascup2000.org
Beacon Millennium Festival: http://www.zeep.co.uk/beacon
Everything 2000: http://www.everything2000.com
Greenwich 2000: http://millennium.greenwich2000.com
Holy See: http://www.vatican.va/jubilee_2000/pju_en.htm
Jubilee 2000: http://www.xibalba.com/solt/jubilee
Millennium Alliance: http://www.cgv.org/millennium/events/index.html
Sydney 2000: http://www.sydney.olympic.org
White House Millennium Program: http://www.whitehouse.gov/Initiatives/Millennium
Year 2000 Conversion: http://www.y2k.gov

Some Major World's Fairs and Expositions

Source: Bureau of International Expositions, Paris, France; World Almanac research

LOCATION	NAME	DATES	VISITORS
London, England	Crystal Palace Exposition	Apr. 1-Oct. 11, 1851	6,039,195
Paris, France	Paris Universal Exposition	Apr. 1-Nov. 3, 1867	15,000,000
Philadelphia, PA	Centennial Exposition	May 10-Nov. 10, 1876	10,000,000
Paris, France	Paris Universal Exposition	May 20-Nov. 10, 1878	16,156,626
Paris, France	Paris Universal Exposition	May 5-Oct. 31, 1889	32,250,297
Chicago, IL	World's Columbian Exposition	May 1-Oct. 3, 1893	27,500,000
Paris, France	Universal and International Exposition of Paris	Apr. 15-Nov. 12, 1900	50,860,801
Saint Louis, MO	Universal Exposition of Saint Louis	Apr. 3-Dec. 1, 1904	19,694,855
Brussels, Belgium	Universal Expositon of Brussels	Apr. 23-Nov. 7, 1910	13,000,000
San Francisco, CA	Panama-Pacific International Exposition	Feb. 2-Dec. 4, 1915	19,000,000
Chicago, IL	A Century of Progress International Exposition	May 27-Nov. 12, 1933; June 1-Oct. 31, 1934	38,872,000
Brussels, Belgium	Universal Exposition of Brussels	1935	20,000,000
Paris, France	Intl. Exposition of Arts and Techniques in Modern Life	May 25-Nov. 25, 1937	31,040,955
New York, NY	New York World's Fair	Apr. 3-Oct. 31, 1939; May 11-Oct. 27, 1940	44,955,997
Brussels, Belgium	Universal and International Exposition of Brussels	Apr. 17-Oct. 19, 1958	41,454,412
Seattle, WA	Century 21 Exposition	Apr. 21-Oct. 21, 1962	9,609,969
New York, NY	New York World's Fair	Apr. 22-Oct. 18, 1964; Apr. 21-Oct. 17, 1965	51,500,000
Montreal, Canada	Expo 67	Apr. 28-Oct. 27, 1967	50,306,648
Osaka, Japan	Expo 70	Mar. 15-Sept. 13, 1970	64,218,770
Spokane, WA	International Exposition on the Environment	May 1-Nov. 1, 1974	5,600,000
Knoxville, TN	The Knoxville International Energy Exposition	May 1-Oct. 31, 1982	11,127,780
New Orleans, LA	The 1984 Louisiana World Exposition	May 12-Nov. 11, 1984	7,335,000
Tsukuba, Japan	International Exposition	Mar. 17-Sept. 16, 1985	20,334,727
Vancouver, Canada	Expo 86	May 2-Oct. 13, 1986	20,111,578
Brisbane, Australia	International Exposition on Leisure	Apr. 3-Oct. 3, 1988	18,560,447
Seville, Spain	Universal Exposition of Seville	Apr. 2-Oct. 12, 1992	40,000,000
Taejon, S. Korea	The Taejon International Exposition	Aug. 7-Nov. 7, 1993	14,005,808
Lisbon, Portugal	Specialty Exposition: The Oceans	May 22-Sept. 30, 1998	NA
Hannover, Germany	Expo 2000	June 1-Oct. 31, 2000	—

NA = not available.

CHRONOLOGY OF THE YEAR'S EVENTS

Reported Month by Month, Oct. 16, 1997, to Oct. 31, 1998

OCTOBER 16-31, 1997

National

Inflation Remains Low—The Labor Dept. reported, **Oct. 16**, that consumer prices had risen 0.2% in September, sustaining perceptions that inflation was under control. The Commerce Dept. reported, **Oct. 21**, that the trade deficit stood at $10.36 billion in August, a 3.4% rise from the revised July deficit. The department also said, **Oct. 31**, that gross domestic product grew at an annual rate of 3.5% in the 3d quarter—considered vigorous by analysts.

Senate Fund-Raising Inquiry Suspended—The White House, **Oct. 24**, said that Pres. Bill Clinton would decline an invitation to testify before the Senate committee investigating campaign-finance abuses that allegedly occurred in 1996. Sen. Fred Thompson (R, TN), chairman of the committee, who had invited Clinton, announced, **Oct. 31**, that he was suspending public hearings. No concrete evidence had emerged from the hearings that Clinton, Vice Pres. Al Gore, or White House staff members had committed illegal acts. However, it was shown that, at a minimum, Clinton and Gore had been aggressive in soliciting money and that some contributors had gained access to them after making donations. Thompson's inquiry was handicapped because several figures central to the alleged abuse either invoked the 5th Amendment or avoided testifying by leaving the country.

International

Congo-Brazzaville Government Overthrown—One day after rebel militia forces in the Congo Republic seized the capital, Brazzaville, they claimed victory, **Oct. 16**, in a civil war against the government of Pres. Pascal Lissouba. The rebel leader, former Pres. Denis Sassou-Nguesso, after being sworn in as the nation's new leader, said **Oct. 25**, he would appoint a transition council to oversee reconstruction of the country. He also promised new elections. The rebels had been supported by the armed forces of Angola.

Clinton Has "Town Meeting" in Buenos Aires—Touring Latin America, Pres. Bill Clinton, participated, **Oct. 16**, in a "town hall meeting" in Buenos Aires, answering questions from his mostly youthful audience about policy on drugs, free trade, and immigration. Speaking to Argentine women, **Oct. 16**, First Lady Hillary Rodham Clinton called for increased opportunities for women and greater access to family planning programs. Pres. Clinton met with Argentine Pres. Carlos Saúl Menem, **Oct. 18**.

Asian Crisis Impacts World Equity Prices—A decline in the value of Asian currencies that began during the summer led in late October to a rush to dump stocks around the world, as questions were raised about the financial stability of some countries. The solvency of banks, even in Japan, came into doubt. Over a 4-day period, **Oct. 20-23**, Hong Kong's primary stock index fell 23.3%. In apparent reaction, stock prices on **Oct. 23** fell sharply in Japan, Germany, the United States, and elsewhere.

Although stocks snapped back in Hong Kong on **Oct. 24**, values in the United States continued to slide. On **Oct. 27**, the Dow Jones industrial average fell 554.26 points, the largest 1-day point decline ever, and closed at 7161.15, 1,100 points below its August high. (The 1-day percentage decline—7.18%—was, however, only the 12th highest on record.) Trading was stopped twice with the hope that markets would quiet down. In an effort to calm U.S. investors, Treasury Sec. Robert Rubin stated, **Oct. 27**, that "the fundamentals of the U.S. economy are strong." Meanwhile, stocks in Argentina, Brazil, and Mexico showed double-digit declines on **Oct. 27**. On **Oct. 28**, even as the Hong Kong market was falling again, the Dow rebounded on record volume of 1.2 billion shares traded, surging 337.17 points, the largest-ever single-day advance in points. U.S. stock indexes then continued on a generally upward path.

The International Monetary Fund, **Oct. 31**, announced a 3-year, $33 billion loan package for Indonesia, one of the largest Asian economies. The Indonesian government said it would introduce reforms, with an emphasis on the nation's reputedly corrupt banking industry, although many observers doubted the government's commitment.

Chinese Pres. Jiang Visits U.S.—Pres. Jiang Zemin of China made a 9-day visit to the United States, beginning **Oct. 26**. One source of contention eased prior to the trip, on **Oct. 17**, when China made public an agreement in principle to stop providing nuclear energy assistance to Iran. China also said it would no longer sell cruise missiles to Iran. Pres. Bill Clinton predicted, **Oct. 24**, that China's move toward a market economy would eventually bring positive political change as well.

Jiang arrived in Hawaii, **Oct. 26**, then visited Williamsburg, VA, **Oct. 27**. He met with Pres. Clinton in Washington, DC, **Oct. 29**, in the first summit between leaders of the 2 countries since 1989. Clinton announced at a joint news conference that, as a result of China's commitment on Iran, the United States would no longer ban the sale of nuclear technology to China. The 2 leaders announced as well that China would buy 50 jet aircraft from the Boeing Co. At their news conference, Jiang defended China's record on human rights against criticisms from Clinton. While Clinton and Jiang were meeting, hundreds of people across from the White House protested China's human rights record. On **Oct. 29**, 30 top corporate executives attended a White House state dinner for Jiang at the White House.

Iraq Rebuffs UN Arms Inspectors—Iraq continued to prevent UN arms inspectors from examining sites that potentially harbored weapons of mass destruction forbidden to Iraq after its defeat in the Gulf War in 1991. On **Oct. 27**, Iraq's parliament recommended that the inspectors be turned back until the UN agreed to a timetable for ending the international trade embargo imposed on Iraq in 1990. Deputy Prem. Tariq Aziz, in a letter **Oct. 29**, claimed that the UN Special Commission (UNSCOM) was influenced by hostile and illegal U.S. objectives. He also called for an end to U.S. surveillance flights over Iraq. On **Oct. 29**, Iraq ordered all U.S. inspectors on the UN team to leave the country within 7 days. Six of the approximately 100 inspectors were Americans. Iraq prevented 3 U.S. inspectors from entering the country, **Oct. 30**.

General

Florida Marlins Win World Series—The Florida Marlins made baseball history **Oct. 26**, when they defeated the Cleveland Indians, 3-2, in extra innings in the 7th and deciding game of the World Series. An expansion team, the Marlins had begun play in 1993 and won the Series title faster than any other expansion team. Florida rookie pitcher Livan Hernandez, 22, who had defected from Cuba in 1995, was named the Most Valuable Player of the Series.

Au Pair's Conviction in Baby's Death Overturned—A British au pair was convicted of murder **Oct. 30** in the death of an infant, then was freed by the judge in a Massachusetts court. The victim, 8-month-old Matthew Eappen, had been in the care of Louise Woodward, 19. He died in February several days after being taken to a hospital. Woodward was then indicted. At the trial, starting **Oct. 7**, the prosecution contended that she had shaken the child violently and struck his head against a hard surface. Woodward denied having mistreated the baby, and her defense team, **Oct. 27**, prevented the jury, in Middlesex County Superior Court, from considering a lesser manslaughter conviction. The jurors found her guilty of 2d-degree murder, **Oct. 30**, triggering protests outside the courthouse and in England. On **Oct. 31**, Judge Hiller B. Zobel sentenced Woodward to life in prison. But on **Nov. 10** he reduced the conviction to involuntary manslaughter and reduced her sentence to time served—279 days. Zobel said that the baby may have had a preexisting blood clot that was affected by rough handling, and that Woodward's actions had not been prompted by malice, precluding a verdict of murder.

NOVEMBER 1997

National

GOP Wins Big Races in Off-Year Elections—Republicans won the most important contests at stake **Nov. 4** in scattered off-year elections. In New Jersey, Gov. Christine Todd Whitman (R) barely won a 2d term over her Democratic challenger, James E. McGreevey, the mayor of Woodbridge and a former state senator. Her bare margin of 1 percentage point was attributed to a lack of enthusiasm for her candidacy by conservatives and to unhappiness with high auto insurance and property tax rates. In Virginia, former Attorney Gen. James S. Gilmore III (R) defeated his Democratic opponent, Lt. Gov. Donald S. Beyer Jr., by 56% to 43%. Gilmore's major issue was a promise to repeal a personal property tax on auto and truck ownership. In New York City, Mayor Rudolph W. Giuliani (R) defeated Ruth W. Messinger (D) by 57% to 41%. The incumbent benefited from 2 strong issues—a good economy and a significant decline in crime.

In Miami, neither Mayor Joe Carollo (R) nor former Mayor Xavier Suarez (I) won an outright majority in the **Nov. 4** election, forcing a **Nov. 13** runoff, which Suarez won with 53% of the vote. Elsewhere, Democratic mayors kept their seats in elections in Boston, Cleveland, Detroit, Minneapolis, and Pittsburgh. In a nonpartisan runoff election **Nov. 25**, Bill Campbell (D) won a 2d term as mayor of Atlanta.

Clinton Retreats on "Fast Track" Trade Bill—Pres. Bill Clinton, **Nov. 10**, conceded temporary defeat in his effort to get legislation for so-called fast track authority to negotiate trade agreements with other countries. This authority, which Congress had granted to all previous presidents since Gerald Ford, provides that deals can only be accepted or rejected as a whole by Congress, without being subject to amendments; thus, other countries know that the provisions agreed to are more likely to remain intact. Labor unions opposed fast track, fearing administrations would make deals that send jobs out of the United States to cheaper labor markets abroad. Environmentalists feared that goods elsewhere would be produced without sufficient environmental safeguards. Most Democrats in the House opposed fast track. In pulling the bill, Clinton said he hoped to revive it in 1998.

"Mastermind" in New York Bombing Convicted—Two more Islamic militants were convicted, **Nov. 12**, of conspiracy and other charges in the 1993 bombing of the World Trade Center in New York City. Four other men had already been convicted in the explosion, which killed 6 people and injured 1,000. Ramzi Ahmed Yousef, described by prosecutors as the mastermind of the bombing, was sentenced, **Jan. 8, 1998**, to life in prison. Eyad Ismoil, charged with driving the van with the bomb into a parking lot underneath the Trade Center, was sentenced to 240 years in prison.

Clinton Justice Dept. Nominee Rebuffed—Pres. Bill Clinton failed to gain approval for his nomination of Bill Lann Lee to be assistant attorney general for civil rights. In testimony in October before the Senate Judiciary Committee, Lee had said he would include affirmative action, as permitted by law, in his search for "pragmatic solutions" to exclusion and discrimination. Sen. Orrin Hatch (R, UT), the committee chairman, indicated, **Nov. 13**, that this approach was not acceptable to Republicans, and Congress adjourned for the year on that day, without committee action on the nomination, effectively ending it. On **Dec. 15**, Clinton named Lee to the civil rights position in an acting capacity.

Teamsters President Denied Right to Run Again—Ron Carey, president of the International Brotherhood of Teamsters, was barred **Nov. 17** from being a candidate in a special 1998 election for president. In 1996, Carey had won another term as president, narrowly defeating James P. Hoffa. But in August 1997, an overseer appointed by the federal government annulled the election when it was reported that Carey supporters had been involved in illegal fund-raising. In his **Nov. 17** report, another overseer, Kenneth Conboy, concluded that Carey had known of the illegal activities and had "broadly and intentionally violated" union rules. Carey denied any wrongdoing and filed an appeal. The Teamsters, **Nov. 24**, agreed to let an independent, federally appointed financial auditor oversee union expenditures and contracts. Carey announced, **Nov. 25**, that he was taking an unpaid leave of absence.

FBI Ends Inquiry on TWA Disaster—The Federal Bureau of Investigation, **Nov. 18**, ruled out criminal sabotage as a possible cause of the disintegration and crash of TWA Flight 800 off Long Island, NY, in July 1996, citing a lack of evidence. The National Transportation Safety Board, whose inquiry was continuing, had previously concluded that vapors of unknown origin ignited in the central fuel tank, causing an explosion.

Trade Deficit Increase Blamed on Financial Crisis—An $11.07 billion trade deficit was reported for September by the Commerce Dept. **Nov. 20**, and was linked by some analysts to the slowdown of economies in Asia. In other news, the Conference Board (a business-research organization) said, **Nov. 4**, that leading economic indicators had risen 0.2% in September. The Labor Dept., **Nov. 7**, said the unemployment rate had fallen to 4.7% in October—the lowest level since October 1973. The department reported, **Nov. 18**, that consumer prices had gone up 0.2%.

International

Asian Countries Focus on Financial Crisis—Financial problems, including falling currencies and rising debt, occupied the attention of a number of Asian countries. In Thailand, Prem. Chavalit Yongchaiyudh announced, **Nov. 3**, that he would resign; there had been widespread complaints about economic upheaval following devaluation of the Thai currency in July. Chavalit was succeeded, **Nov. 9**, by former Prem. Chuan Leekpai, whose policies had been popular with economists and business leaders.

In South Korea, the Bank of Korea, **Nov. 17**, indicated that it would no longer attempt to prop up the won, which then fell in value to a level of more than 1,000 per the U.S. dollar. South Korea's president, Kim Young Sam, dismissed his finance minister, **Nov. 19**, and named Lim Chang Yuel to the office. Lim immediately announced financial reforms and said, **Nov. 21**, that Korea would ask the International Monetary Fund for $20 billion in loans to deal with its short-term foreign debts. Pres. Kim, **Nov. 22**, apologized to the country in a televised address for having to seek IMF assistance. He also indicated, **Nov. 27**, that more aid would be needed. Meanwhile, the financial leaders of 18 nations, at the Asia-Pacific Economic Cooperation (APEC) meeting **Nov. 18-19** in Manila, approved an agreement that would permit a major role by the IMF in the rescue of Asian economies.

Pres. Bill Clinton, **Nov. 24**, urged Japan to strengthen its economy by helping to increase domestic demand for foreign goods and by strengthening its banks. Japan's Sanyo Securities Co. had closed, **Nov. 3**, and the Hokkaido Takushoku Bank, on **Nov. 17**. One of the largest securities firms, Yamaichi Securities Co., announced, **Nov. 24**, that it would close its doors, and the Tokuyo City Bank followed suit, **Nov. 25**.

The APEC heads of government held their annual trade meeting in Vancouver, British Columbia, **Nov. 24-25**, and displayed optimism, stressing the IMF role and internal reforms that they said were under way or planned.

Iraq Confronts U.S., Then Backs Down—Nine times between **Nov. 3** and **12**, Iraq prevented U.S. weapons inspectors from participating in UN Special Commission inspections. U.S. spy plane surveillance of Iraq resumed, **Nov. 10**, despite an Iraqi threat to shoot down the planes. The UN Security Council, **Nov. 12**, banned foreign travel by Iraqi officials who supported Iraq's hard line. On **Nov. 13**, Iraq expelled 6 U.S. inspectors from the country; they arrived at the Jordanian border after an overnight drive of 400 miles. Most other members of the UN team then left by air for Bahrain, **Nov. 14**. Russia worked out an agreement with Iraq, announced **Nov. 20**, in which Iraq said all the UN inspectors were free to return.

Chinese Free Dissident, Who Goes to U.S.—The Chinese government granted medical parole to one of its most prominent political dissidents, **Nov. 15**. Wei Jingsheng had spent most of the past 18 years in prison, currently as a result of a conviction for sedition in 1995. The Chinese put him on a flight to the United States. On his arrival, **Nov. 16**, in Detroit, Wei entered a hospital for examination.

Militants Kill 58 Foreign Tourists in Egypt—Islamic fundamentalists killed 58 foreign tourists and 4 Egyptians **Nov. 17**, in the worst act of terrorism yet in the militants' 5-year campaign to force the collapse of the secular government. The 6 assailants struck in the morning at the Temple of Queen Hatshepsut, a 3,400-year-old structure in the Luxor area, one of the country's most popular tourist destinations. They used explosives, semiautomatic weapons, hand grenades, and knives, and also killed a guard at the temple entrance. Leaving the scene in a hijacked bus, one militant was killed at a checkpoint, and the others were slain by police after fleeing into nearby hills.

Congress Party Brings Down Indian Government—The United Front government of India collapsed after the Congress (I) Party pulled out of the ruling coalition **Nov. 28**. A Tamil party, Dravida Munnetra Kazagham—one of 14 parties in the ruling coalition—had been linked to a Tamil separatist group implicated in the 1991 assassination of former Prime Min. Rajiv Gandhi. On **Nov. 24**, Prime Min. Inder Kumar Gujral had declined a Congress Party demand that DMK be dropped from the ruling coalition. The Congress Party then withdrew. Gujral continued as prime minister, pending elections set for February.

General

Septuplets Born in Iowa—On **Nov. 19**, Bobbi McCaughey, 29, a seamstress, delivered 7 children by cesarean section in Des Moines, IA. The 4 boys and 3 girls, who were described as surprisingly healthy, ranged in weight from 2.3 pounds to 3.25 pounds. McCaughey had been taking fertility drugs, and she and her husband, Kenny, already had one daughter. Iowa businesses pledged financial support for the family, which lives in Carlisle. The McCaughey septuplets were the second known septuplets to be born alive (and the first to survive for more than a month). On **Jan. 14, 1998**, a Saudi woman, Hasna Mohammed Humair, gave birth to live septuplets—4 boys and 3 girls. She had also taken a fertility drug.

DECEMBER 1997

National

Independent Counsel Rejected for Clinton, Gore—Attorney Gen. Janet Reno, **Dec. 2**, announced that she would not request appointment of an independent counsel to investigate alleged violations of a federal fund-raising law by Pres. Bill Clinton and Vice Pres. Al Gore. The Pendleton Act (1883) prohibits federal employees from soliciting contributions on federal property. Reno found that on 3 occasions Clinton had called donors from the White House, but from the residential area, where the Pendleton Act did not apply. She found that Gore had made 45 calls from his White House office to donors, but said these were permitted because they had been made to raise so-called soft money for party building, rather than hard money for direct campaign use. FBI Director Louis Freeh had recommended an independent counsel, and Republicans strongly criticized her failure to appoint one.

Reno also announced that she would not recommend an independent counsel to investigate former Energy Sec. Hazel O'Leary. Reno said there was no evidence that O'Leary had been personally involved in soliciting a donation for a charity from Johnny Chung, a major Democratic Party donor who was already under investigation.

Economy Does Well, Stocks Show Steep Advance—The economy continued to grow at a moderate pace, with inflation under control. The Conference Board (a business-research organization) reported, **Dec. 2**, that the leading economic indicators had risen 0.2% in October. The Labor Dept. said, **Dec. 5**, that the unemployment rate had declined in November by 0.1 percentage point, to 4.6%, the lowest rate since October 1973. The Commerce Dept. reported, **Dec. 14**, that personal income in November rose 0.8%—the biggest rise since June 1996. In another development, the Commerce Dept., **Dec. 18**, reported that the October trade deficit narrowed to $9.69 billion—a 13.7% decrease from September.

At year's end, figures showed that Wall Street stocks had continued an unprecedented climb. The Dow Jones industrial average closed **Dec. 31** at 7908.25, up by 1459.98 points for the year, in itself a 22.6% advance. The Dow had also posted gains of 33.5% in 1995 and 26% in 1996; an increase in the Dow of more than 20% in 3 consecutive years had never previously been recorded.

Houston Elects First Black Mayor—In a runoff election **Dec. 6**, Houston voters chose a black mayor for the first time. The winner in the nonpartisan election was Lee Brown (D), who defeated businessman Robert Mosbacher Jr. (R). Brown had been chief of police in Atlanta, Houston, and New York City and had served as director of national drug control policy from 1993 to 1996.

Ambassador's Remains Removed From Cemetery—The remains of a financial supporter of Pres. Bill Clinton were removed, **Dec. 11**, from Arlington National Cemetery in Virginia, intended for decorated veterans of the armed services. Republicans in Congress had been investigating reports that the administration had promised cemetery plots in return for contributions. Of 69 persons buried at Arlington since Clinton took office, M. Larry Lawrence was the only one who had been a major donor—of about $200,000 to Clinton's 1992 campaign. Lawrence, a former ambassador to Switzerland, who died in 1996, had claimed he was serving in the merchant marine in 1945, but no evidence could be found of this. Lawrence's widow wrote Clinton, **Dec. 8**, asking that his body be moved.

Injunction Filed Against Microsoft—In the first ruling in an antitrust suit brought, Oct. 20, against software giant Microsoft by the Justice Dept., a preliminary injunction was filed against the company, **Dec. 11**, ordering it to stop "bundling" its Windows 95 operating system with its Internet Explorer browser (a practice that requires computer manufacturers to install both products). The injunction was issued by U.S. District Judge Thomas Penfield Jackson in Washington, DC. Microsoft—claiming that the most current version of Windows would work only with Internet Explorer—said, **Dec. 15**, that it would appeal the ruling but comply in the interim by offering the bundled product or an older version of Windows without Internet Explorer. On **Dec. 19**, Judge Jackson announced that he had personally removed the browser from the most recent version of Windows without any problems. The Justice Dept., **Dec. 29**, asked the judge to find Microsoft in contempt of court.

Separation of Military Recruits Advised—Separation of male and female recruits during much of their basic training in the U.S. armed forces was recommended in a report released **Dec. 16**. Defense Sec. William Cohen had commissioned the panel that drew up the report in the wake of incidents involving improper relations between male trainers and female recruits. The report also called for tighter screening and better preparation of trainers, higher physical requirements for all recruits, and hiring of more women as recruiters and trainers.

Unabomber Trial Moves Toward Opening—A jury was seated, **Dec. 22**, in Sacramento, CA, for the trial of Theodore Kaczynski, charged with being the so-called Unabomber who sent deadly explosives through the mail. On **Dec. 29**, his attorneys told Federal District Judge Garland Burrell Jr., that they would no longer pursue the defense that Kaczynski was a paranoid schizophrenic.

2d Defendant Convicted in Oklahoma Bombing—Terry Nichols was found guilty on some counts and was acquitted on others, **Dec. 23**, in connection with the 1995 bombing of the Murrah Federal Building in Oklahoma City in 1995. The prosecution, in Federal District Court in Denver, concluded its case on **Dec. 2**. Prosecutor Larry Mackey offered both physical and circumstantial evidence tying Nichols to materials used in the bomb. The defense, which concluded its case **Dec. 11**, sought to show that the evidence was weak and the witnesses unreliable. In the split verdict, Nichols was found guilty of 1 count of conspiracy to use a weapon of mass destruction and of 8 counts of involuntary manslaughter of federal agents—but not of murder. He was found not guilty of using a weapon of mass destruction or of causing destruction by an explosive. It appeared that the jury did not believe Nichols had continued to participate in the plot through to its conclusion.

International

Emissions Limits Set at Global Warming Summit—Representatives of more than 150 countries convened in Kyoto, Japan, **Dec. 1**, to consider a treaty to limit emissions of carbon dioxide and other so-called greenhouse gases. Heavy buildups of these gases are widely believed to be responsible for trapping of energy in the Earth's atmosphere that causes temperatures to rise, which may eventually produce a devastating effect on humans, plants, and wildlife. Carbon dioxide comes principally from the burning of fossil fuels, such as coal and crude oil. A principal stumbling block to agreement was the question of how much of the burden of reducing the gases should be borne by developing countries. Industrial nations, led by the United States, emitted most of the world's gases, but the developing world was beginning to catch up.

The final protocol, approved **Dec. 11**, provided that by the year 2012 industrial nations would reduce their gas emissions to 6-8% below 1990 levels. Developing countries, however, were left free to reduce emissions on their own, without being subject to a quota. Achievement of the Kyoto goals would require a significant shift in energy sources, with fossil fuels used far less and renewable sources such as solar and wind power getting greater attention. U.S. Senate approval of the treaty was in doubt.

South Korea Accepts $57 Billion IMF Rescue Terms—South Korea, **Dec. 3**, accepted terms for a $57 billion financial rescue worked out with the International Monetary Fund. The assistance included $21 billion in IMF credits, $10 billion in World Bank loans, and $4 billion from the Asian Development Bank. Several countries would together loan the remaining $22 billion. The size of the rescue package exceeded the previous record, $48 billion for Mexico in 1994. South Korea agreed to cut public spending, discourage expansion by its dominant conglomerates, close weak banks, open markets to outsiders, and raise interest rates.

South Korea said, **Dec. 8**, that its short-term foreign debt exceeded $100 billion, much higher than previously estimated, and that foreign exchange reserves had plunged from $30.5 billion to $6 billion in 2 months. The IMF made $5.5 billion available to South Korea on reaching its agreement, and $3.5 billion more was released **Dec. 18**.

Figures from the Dow Jones World Stock Index showed, **Dec. 31**, that stock valuations during 1997 had plunged around 70% in South Korea, Thailand, and Malaysia—3 countries hardest hit by the financial crisis. Stocks in Japan had fallen 30%.

121 Nations Sign Treaty Banning Land Mines—In Ottawa, **Dec. 3-4**, representatives of 121 nations signed a treaty banning the use and manufacture of land mines. The United States did not sign because of its support for the use of land mines on South Korea's border with North Korea. The treaty does not go into effect until 6 months after 40 countries have ratified it. Signatories agree to destroy their mine stockpiles within 4 years and clear all mines in their territories within 10 years.

UN Renews Program Letting Iraq Sell Some Oil—In a unanimous vote, the UN Security Council, **Dec. 4**, extended a program that permitted Iraq to sell $2 billion worth of oil for another 6 months so that it could obtain food, medicine, and other necessities. After some disagreement on specific terms, Iraq announced, **Dec. 27**, that it expected to resume oil shipments shortly under a new arrangement with the UN on food and medicine distribution.

Terrorism Condemned at Islamic Summit—The Organization of the Islamic Conference opened its summit meeting in Tehran, **Dec. 9**. Speakers from the host country sent different signals in speeches, **Dec. 9**. Iran's supreme leader, Ayatollah Sayyed Ali Khamenei, denounced Western civilization in general and deplored what he saw as U.S. efforts to dominate Middle East peace negotiations. Iranian Pres. Mohammad Khatami, however, indicated a willingness to broaden communications with the West. In a declaration adopted **Dec. 11**, the conference condemned terrorism as incompatible with Islam, noting, in apparent reference to the November 1997 murder of 58 foreign tourists at Luxor, Egypt, that Islam forbids the killing of innocent people. At a news conference **Dec. 14**, Khatami said he hoped to reestablish a "thoughtful dialogue" with the "great people of the United States."

Talks on Peace in Korea Begin—Long-awaited talks aimed at creating a permanent peace on the Korean Peninsula got under way in Geneva, **Dec. 9-10**. The Korean War ended with an armistice in 1953, and no peace treaty had since then been signed. Participants in Geneva included diplomats from both North and South Korea and officials from China and the United States.

Opposition Leader Elected South Korean President—Kim Dae Jung, a longtime dissident, was elected president of South Korea, **Dec. 18**. Kim (40.4%) edged out the candidate of the ruling party, Lee Hoi Chang (38.6%), and a 3d candidate. The campaign unfolded against an explosive debt crisis in South Korea, accompanied by an erratic stock market. The candidates agreed to carry out the reforms required in the bailout agreement with the International Monetary Fund. Kim, 72, had run unsuccessfully for president in 1971 as an advocate of democracy. Abducted by government agents in 1973, he was nearly executed at that time. Kim was sentenced to death in 1980 because of support for pro-democracy demonstrations, but the sentence was commuted to life in prison, and he went into U.S. exile after being freed in 1982. Returning, he was an unsuccessful candidate for president in 1987 and 1992.

With Kim Dae Jung's agreement, incumbent Pres. Kim Young Sam, still in office **Dec. 22**, pardoned 2 former presidents, Chun Doo Hwan and Roh Tae Woo, who had been sentenced to prison in 1996 for taking bribes and for their roles in a military coup and the deaths of pro-democracy demonstrators.

Clinton Visits Capital of Bosnia—Pres. Bill Clinton acknowledged, at a news conference on **Dec. 18**, that he had erred in setting a firm date for withdrawal of U.S. troops from Bosnia. As of then, some 8,000 U.S. troops, down from 27,000, remained in Bosnia as part of the international peacekeeping force. The deadline for withdrawal had initially been December 1996, and was now June 1998, and Clinton said he supported in principle keeping troops there even longer. Clinton and his wife and daughter—joined by former Sen. Robert Dole (R, KS) and his wife, and 11 members of the House and Senate—visited Sarajevo, the capital of Bosnia-Herzegovina, **Dec. 22**, as well as other sites.

45 Massacred in Mexican Village—Men armed with machine guns and machetes struck at the Tzotzil Indian village of Acteal, in the state of Chiapas, **Dec. 22**, killing 45 people and wounding 25. Fifteen of those killed were children. The villagers were thought to sympathize with the Zapatista National Liberation Army, which had launched an armed revolt on behalf of Indian rights in Chiapas. The gunmen were linked to the local Institutional Revolutionary Party (PRI). By Dec. 27, 40 people had been charged in connection with the attack.

"Jackal" Gets Life Term in Killing of French Agents—"Carlos the Jackal," one of the world's most notorious terrorists, was sentenced to life in prison by a Paris court, **Dec. 24**, after being found guilty of murdering 2 French intelligence agents and a Lebanese informant in 1975. The Venezuelan-born defendant's real name is Ilich Ramirez Sanchez. He was linked to various terrorist acts, including the 1975 kidnapping of 11 OPEC oil ministers and the 1976 hijacking of an Air France flight. In 1992 he had been tried in absentia and convicted of murdering 2 other police officers. In 1994 he was arrested in Sudan and then extradited to France.

President of Kenya Reelected—Kenyan Pres. Daniel arap Moi was reelected in voting that took place **Dec. 29-30**. His leading challenger, Mwai Kibaki, charged during the campaign that Moi's government had stolen tax income revenues and international aid money. The voting was chaotic, and a number of people were reported killed in clashes prior to and during the election.

Death Toll Rises in Algerian Violence—The Algerian government reported, **Dec. 31**, that more than 400 persons had died during the last 9 days of December because of incidents perpetrated by Muslim extremists. Massacres had been occurring for some time; more than 500 had died in August and September 1997. On **Dec. 30-31**, at the onset of the Islamic holy month of Ramadan, 78 people were massacred in 3 villages.

General

3 Killed at Kentucky High School—A 14-year-old boy, Michael Carneal, was arrested **Dec. 1** for killing 3 girls and injuring 5 other students that day at Heath High School in West Paducah, KY. Carneal opened fire on a group of students holding a prayer meeting before school; he finally stopped after being restrained by one of the students. Carneal, originally charged as a juvenile, was charged as an adult, **Dec. 12**.

Pro Basketball Player Assaults Coach—Latrell Sprewell, a guard for the NBA's Golden State Warriors, assaulted his coach, P. J. Carlesimo, at a team practice, **Dec. 1**. The Warriors, **Dec. 3**, terminated Sprewell' 4-year, $32 million contract, and NBA Commissioner David Stern announced, **Dec. 4**, that he had been suspended for one year. The player appealed the suspension, **Dec. 5**, and on **Dec. 9**, apologized for his actions. On **Mar. 4, 1998**, an arbitrator ordered the Warriors to reinstate Sprewell's contract and ruled that his suspension would end July 1, 1998. Sprewell, however, would lose $6.4 million for missed games.

JANUARY 1998

National

Clinton's Relationship With Intern Investigated—A serious scandal threatened Pres. Bill Clinton, when it was revealed that Kenneth Starr, the independent counsel investigating the Whitewater scandal, was also looking into a possible sexual relationship between the president and a former White House intern, Monica Lewinsky. It appeared that Starr's focus included possible attempts by Clinton and his associates to cover up the relationship, which could lead to obstruction of justice charges.

In July 1995, Lewinsky, then 21 years old and a recent college graduate, began working at the White House as an unpaid intern. She went on the payroll in the Office of Legislative Affairs in December 1995 but in April 1996 was transferred to the Dept. of Defense at the Pentagon, reportedly after some White House officials became concerned that she was near the president too often. Meanwhile, a civil suit against the president by Paula Corbin Jones, a former Arkansas state employee, was moving forward. Jones charged that Clinton had made an unwanted sexual overture toward her in 1991, while he was Arkansas governor. Her attorneys set out to show that Clinton had had improper relationships with other women.

On **Jan. 7**, at a time when her association with the president was not yet public, Lewinsky reportedly denied in an affidavit filed in the Jones case that she had had an affair with him. However, Lewinsky had become friends at the Pentagon with former White House employee Linda Tripp, telling her, in conversations tape-recorded by Tripp, that she had been involved in a sexual relationship with Clinton beginning in November 1995. On **Jan. 12**, Tripp turned over to Starr tapes containing 20 hours of conversation. Since the legality of these tapes was unclear, Starr arranged through the FBI to obtain new evidence by wiring Tripp, who met with Lewinsky at an Arlington, VA, hotel, **Jan. 13**.

On **Jan. 16**, the 3-judge panel overseeing special prosecutors approved the expansion of Starr's inquiry to encompass possible obstruction of justice in the Jones case. The same day, Attorney Gen. Janet Reno approved the broader mandate for Starr. Also on **Jan. 16**, Starr's investigators questioned Lewinsky for several hours. Clinton, deposed by Jones's lawyers **Jan. 17**, reportedly denied an affair with Lewinsky. In the same sworn deposition he reportedly acknowledged having had sexual relations with Gennifer Flowers. During the 1992 presidential campaign, Clinton had denied her claim that she had had a long-term relationship with him.

The story about Lewinsky became public knowledge when newspapers reported it **Jan. 21**. On that day, Clinton, in previously scheduled interviews, at times using careful wording, appeared to deny having had a sexual relationship with Lewinsky and denied having asked her to lie about the relationship. In a statement **Jan. 22**, he reiterated that he would "never ask anybody to do anything other than tell the truth." He expressed a desire to cooperate with investigators and give "as many answers as we can, at the appropriate time." He added, "I'd like for you to have more rather than less, sooner rather than later."

At a separate press conference that same day, Vernon Jordan, a prominent lawyer and Clinton friend, said he had helped Lewinsky find a job outside government (she had resigned from the Pentagon in late December 1997). But he said Lewinsky had told him she had not had an affair with

Clinton, and he denied having ever said or suggested that Lewinsky should lie under oath. Starr, meanwhile, began serving subpoenas for White House documents that might shed light on the issue.

Lewinsky's attorney, William Ginsburg, said, **Jan. 26**, that he had made a legal "proffer" to Starr stating what Lewinsky would be prepared to say about Clinton if she were to be granted immunity from prosecution. In his most strongly worded statement to date, Clinton, **Jan. 26**, said: "I did not have sexual relations with that woman, Miss Lewinsky. I never told anybody to lie, not a single time—never." First Lady Hillary Rodham Clinton, in a **Jan. 27** television interview, charged that Starr's investigation was part of a "vast right-wing conspiracy that has been conspiring against my husband since the day he announced for president." Rejecting her assertion, Starr said, **Jan. 27**, that he had begun the investigation after receiving "credible evidence of serious federal crimes."

Betty Currie, the president's private secretary, testified before the grand jury on **Jan. 27**. Her desk was near the Oval Office, and packages Lewinsky had sent to the White House listed Currie's extension as a contact number. Former White House Chief of Staff Leon Panetta, after testifying the following day, told reporters he did not know of any improper relationship between Clinton and Lewinsky.

Susan Webber Wright, the federal judge presiding over the Jones trial in Little Rock, AR, ruled, **Jan. 29**, that Jones's attorneys could not admit evidence concerning Lewinsky, because that might interfere with the Starr investigation. Wright also held, **Jan. 30**, that Secret Service agents could not be required to testify in this case about what they might have seen while guarding Clinton.

Tripp said, **Jan. 30**, that she had been with Lewinsky on one occasion when Clinton phoned. She also said that she had seen gifts the pair had exchanged and heard tapes Lewinsky had made of conversations with Clinton. Tripp said she had contacted Starr because she was concerned about being involved in a cover-up.

Nichols Won't Face Death in Oklahoma Bombing—A federal jury in Denver, **Jan. 7**, was unable to agree on a penalty for Terry Nichols, who had been convicted in December 1997 in connection with the 1995 bombing of the Murrah Federal Building in Oklahoma City. Determination of the penalty was therefore left to the judge, who was, however, excluded from imposing the death penalty.

Prices Charged by Producers Declined in 1997—On **Jan. 8**, final Labor Dept. figures showed that prices charged by manufacturers and farmers for finished goods had declined 1.2% during 1997. The department reported **Jan. 13** that consumer prices had risen 0.1% in December and only 1.7% for all of 1997, the lowest inflation rate since 1986. On **Jan. 11**, the department said that the unemployment rate stood at 4.7% in December 1997, significantly lower than the 5.3% rate at the end of 1996. The Commerce Dept., **Jan. 21**, put the November 1997 trade deficit at $8.04 billion. The department said, **Jan. 30**, that the nation's gross domestic product had grown at an annual rate of 3.8% in 1997, up from 3.2% in 1996 and 1.6% in 1995.

Tobacco Companies Settle Suit by Texas—The tobacco industry and the state of Texas reached an agreement, **Jan. 16**, in a lawsuit brought by the state for Medicaid funds it had paid to treat Texans suffering from smoking-related illnesses. The tobacco companies agreed to pay $15.3 billion over 25 years. The tobacco companies had settled similar suits in Mississippi and Florida.

Plea Bargain Sends Unabomber to Prison for Life—The case of the so-called Unabomber was settled **Jan. 22** when the defendant pleaded guilty. Theodore Kaczynski had been indicted in connection with California and New Jersey bombings that had killed 3 people and injured 2 others. Investigators believed that he was responsible for sending 16 mail bombs over 17 years. On **Jan. 20**, Kaczynski was found competent to stand trial, though the prison psychiatrist concluded that he was a paranoid schizophrenic. After Judge Garland Burrell Jr. denied the defendant's request to represent himself, Kaczynski pleaded guilty in federal court in Sacramento to all the counts lodged against him in California and New Jersey. He also admitted planting or mailing 11 other bombs. As the sole condition of the plea-bargain agreement, Kaczynski was spared the death penalty. On **May 4** he was sentenced to 4 life terms in prison plus 30 years.

Clinton Delivers State of the Union Address, Gains in Popularity—In his State of the Union address to a joint session of Congress, **Jan. 27**, Pres. Bill Clinton hailed the fact that the federal government would have a balanced budget in 1999—the first in 30 years. He urged that the surplus income be put in a reserve until Congress enacted legislation ensuring that Social Security was on solid ground. He also endorsed expanding Medicare to serve persons from ages 55 to 65. The president claimed that the decline in the crime rate across the country could be credited in part to his administration's initiative to add 100,000 officers to the nation's police forces. In his speech Clinton warned Pres. Saddam Hussein of Iraq that the United States would not allow his country to rebuild its weapons of mass destruction. Clinton also urged Congress to continue to support the presence of U.S. troops in Bosnia-Herzegovina.

In the Republican response to the president, Senate Majority Leader Trent Lott (MS) called for tax cuts and a simplification of the tax code. He warned Saddam Hussein that no controversy in the United States would prevent Congress from supporting U.S. interests abroad.

Despite predictions to the contrary, the president's speech attracted considerable enthusiasm and appeared to bolster his popularity. On **Jan. 28**, his approval rating reached an all-time high of 73% in a CBS poll.

Friend of Clinton Indicted—Yah Lin (Charlie) Trie, a longtime friend of Pres. Bill Clinton, was indicted **Jan. 28**, along with a 2d man, Yuan Pei (Antonio) Pan. The men were accused of getting people to act as conduits for contributions to the Democratic National Committee, while the funds really came from foreign nationals who were barred by law from making such contributions. Trie had fled the country in late 1996, but on **Feb. 3** he surrendered to federal agents at Dulles International Airport near Washington, DC. Pan's whereabouts were unknown. On **Feb. 5**, Trie pleaded not guilty in federal court.

Bomb Kills Guard at Alabama Abortion Clinic—A security guard at an abortion clinic was killed, **Jan. 29**, when a bomb exploded outside the clinic in Birmingham, AL. A nurse was seriously injured. Federal investigators said, **Feb. 2**, that a group called the Army of God had claimed responsibility. Letters from people claiming the same affiliation had said the group was also responsible for the 1997 bombings in Atlanta of a gay nightclub and an abortion clinic. On **Feb. 14**, prosecutors named Eric Robert Rudolph, whose truck had been seen near the clinic, as a key suspect.

International

Algerian Civil War Death Toll Put at Over 26,000—The new year brought continued bloodletting in Algeria. On **Jan. 6**, some 300 persons were reported to have been massacred during the previous several days. One newspaper reported that several hundred had been burned alive in one village. One hundred more were killed in 2 villages on **Jan. 11**. The government estimated, **Jan. 21**, that 26,536 had died during the 6-year-long civil war. Other estimates ran as high as 75,000.

Ripples from Asian Financial Crisis Continue—Peregrine Investments Holdings Ltd., Hong Kong's largest investment bank, plagued by bad loans in Indonesia and elsewhere, closed its doors, **Jan. 12**, after it was unable to sell a minority stake to Zurich Group of Switzerland. Zurich pulled out after market conditions deteriorated in Asia.

In South Korea, a committee of business, government, and labor union leaders issued a report, **Jan. 20**, that blamed the government and corporate conglomerates for the country's financial woes. Unions and business leaders committed themselves to working together to overcome the crisis. On **Jan. 28**, international creditor banks worked out a deal with South Korean banks to renegotiate $24 billion in short-term foreign-currency loans.

UN Conflict With Iraq Flares Again—On **Jan. 13**, Iraq, for the 2d time in 2 months, forbade United Nations inspectors from searching for chemical and biological weapons. Iraqi officials claimed William Scott Ritter Jr., an American who headed the inspection team, was a spy. The UN Security Council protested Iraq's action.

Progress Toward Peace Slows in Middle East—The Israeli cabinet, **Jan. 13**, announced conditions that the Palestinians must meet before Israel would withdraw further from the West Bank and charged that the Palestinians were not complying with the peace accords. On **Jan. 14** the cabinet declared that Israel planned to annex more of the West Bank. On **Jan. 15**, Palestinian leaders rejected Israel's conditions for a withdrawal. In Washington, DC, Pres. Bill Clinton met with Israeli Prime Min. Benjamin Netanyahu, **Jan. 20**, and with Palestinian National Authority Pres. Yasir Arafat, **Jan. 22**, but little progress was reported.

Pope Speaks Bluntly on Historic Visit to Cuba—Pope John Paul II visited Cuba for the first time, drawing large and enthusiastic crowds in the officially Communist country. He was welcomed upon his arrival, **Jan. 21**, by Pres. Fidel Castro. During his visit the pontiff criticized Communism but also deplored capitalist policies elsewhere that hurt the poor; he specifically called for an end to U.S. economic sanctions against Cuba. In his first outdoor mass, in Santa Clara, **Jan. 22**, the pope criticized Cuba's education system and also denounced abortion (in Cuba there were some 60 abortions for every 100 live births). After a mass in Santiago de Cuba, **Jan. 24**, he appealed for the release of Cuba's political prisoners. Some 250,000 persons attended the final outdoor papal mass in Havana, **Jan. 25**.

Endeavour* Launches Last U.S. Astronaut to Join Russian Crew on *Mir—Dr. Andrew Thomas became the 7th and last American astronaut to join the Russian crew on the space station *Mir*. The U.S. shuttle *Endeavour* was launched from Cape Canaveral, FL, **Jan. 22**; it docked with *Mir* on **Jan. 24**. Thomas replaced another American, Dr. David Wolf, who had been on the Russian station 4 months. The 2 craft separated **Jan. 29**. On **Jan. 31** a Russian Soyuz spacecraft brought 3 new crew members to *Mir*. *Endeavour* landed in Florida on **Jan. 31**.

U.S. Troops Help Seize Bosnian Serb Suspect—For the first time, **Jan. 22**, U.S. troops led NATO soldiers in the seizure of a suspected war criminal in Bosnia-Herzegovina. The arrested man, Goran Jelisic, was a Bosnian Serb who had been indicted in 1995 by the United Nations war crimes tribunal. Jelisic, **Jan. 26**, pleaded not guilty to the charges.

General

2 Schools Share NCAA Football Title—The universities of Nebraska and Michigan emerged as cowinners of the unofficial college football title for the 1997 season. Both Michigan (12-0) and Nebraska (13-0) had perfect records. Michigan, **Jan. 1**, added the Rose Bowl championship to its Big Ten title by defeating Washington State, 21-16. In the Orange Bowl, **Jan. 2**, the Nebraska Cornhuskers trounced Tennessee, 42-17, with a powerful running game that scored all 6 touchdowns on the ground. On **Jan. 3** the Associated Press poll of media representatives named Michigan as the No. 1 team, but the *USA Today*/ESPN poll of coaches put Nebraska in first place.

2 Prominent Americans Die in Ski Accidents—U.S. Rep. Sonny Bono (R, CA) died **Jan. 5** after hitting a tree while skiing at South Lake Tahoe, CA. Bono, along with his former wife Cher, had had a successful career as a pop singer, and he had served as mayor of Palm Springs before being elected to Congress in 1994. Earlier, on **Dec. 31, 1997**, Michael Kennedy, a son of the late Sen. Robert F. Kennedy, suffered fatal injuries when he struck a tree on a ski slope in Aspen, CO. He and family members had been tossing a football back and forth while descending the slope. Kennedy was head of Citizens Energy Corp., a non-profit organization that provided heating energy to the poor, and had been investigated for allegedly having an affair with an underage babysitter.

Elway Leads Denver to Super Bowl Upset—Years of frustration for the Denver Broncos and their star quarterback, John Elway, finally ended with their upset 31-24 victory over the defending National Football League champions, the Green Bay Packers, in Super Bowl XXXII on **Jan. 25**. Denver had won the American Football Conference title, **Jan. 11**, by defeating the Pittsburgh Steelers, 24-21. Green Bay, **Jan. 11**, had taken the National Football Conference title for the 2d year in a row, defeating the San Francisco 49ers, 23-10.

FEBRUARY 1998

National

Clinton's 1999 Budget Has Small Surplus—On **Feb. 2**, for the first time in nearly 3 decades, a U.S. president submitted a balanced federal budget. The last federal budget that was actually balanced was in 1969, and no president since Richard Nixon in 1971 had even proposed one. In his $1.73 trillion budget for the 1999 fiscal year, Pres. Bill Clinton showed a surplus of $9.5 billion. He said this money should go toward saving the Social Security system. Clinton projected that annual surpluses would rise to more than $250 billion per year within 10 years. This assumed that the economy would grow at a modest annual rate of 2% for the next 5 years.

Clinton proposed new spending of up to $150 billion. He called for an extension of Medicare coverage to Americans as young as 55 if they had lost company health coverage. He advocated restoring food stamps for legal immigrants. He also proposed money to subsidize child care, hire 100,000 new schoolteachers, and build more schools. Much of the revenue would be generated by an anticipated increase in the federal tax on cigarettes. Republicans, **Feb. 2**, opposed Clinton's plans to spend money in new areas.

Texas Executes First Female in 135 Years—In a controversial case, the state of Texas, **Feb. 3**, executed its first female convict in 135 years. Karla Faye Tucker, 38, had confessed to committing 2 pickax murders with her boyfriend, Daniel Ryan Garrett, in 1983. She and Garrett were both sentenced to death; he died in prison before his execution date. Meanwhile, Tucker—a drug addict at an early age—became a born-again Christian shortly after her arrest and repeatedly expressed remorse for her actions. Numerous sympathizers, including Pope John Paul II and other religious leaders, made pleas to the state to commute her death sentence, but the Texas Board of Pardons and Paroles unanimously turned down her request for clemency, **Feb. 2**. The next day, both Gov. George W. Bush (R) and the U.S. Supreme Court refused her requests for a reprieve, and Tucker was put to death by lethal injection at the state prison in Huntsville. She became only the 2d woman to be executed in the United States since the Supreme Court reinstated the death penalty in 1976.

On **Mar. 30**, Florida executed Judy Buenoano, 54, the first woman that state had put to death since 1948. She had been convicted of murdering her husband and son and had collected $200,000 in insurance money for their deaths.

More Charges Traded in Clinton-Intern Matter—*The New York Times* reported, **Feb. 3**, that former White House intern Monica Lewinsky had been cleared to enter the White House 37 times after leaving her job there in April 1996.

Clinton said in a news conference, **Feb. 6**, that he would never consider resigning because of the controversy. His supporters and independent counsel Kenneth Starr traded accusations, **Feb. 6**, on who might be illegally leaking secret grand-jury testimony. The *Times*, **Feb. 8**, printed the text of a "talking points" memorandum Lewinsky had reportedly given to her friend Linda Tripp, in which the unknown writer advised Tripp in detail on what to say in an affidavit in connection with another incident. That incident involved a 1993 meeting in the Oval Office between Clinton and Kathleen Willey, a former campaign worker in need of a full-time paid job. Tripp reportedly saw Willey near the Oval Office at that time in a disheveled condition. Willey had later testified in the Paula Corbin Jones sexual harassment suit against Clinton that the president had made improper overtures to her. The memo advised Tripp to testify that, among other things, she did not believe this claim.

Marcia Lewis, Lewinsky's mother, testified before the grand jury, **Feb. 10-11**. According to the transcript of a conversation taped by Tripp, she had known of a relationship between Clinton and her daughter. Lewis cut short the 2d day of her testimony and left the courthouse visibly distraught. Lewinsky's lead lawyer, William Ginsburg, charged, **Feb. 13**, that Starr had abused his power in forcing her mother to testify. A retired Secret Service security guard, Lewis Fox, appeared before the grand jury, **Feb. 17**, after a compromise was reached under which he would not be questioned on matters pertaining to Secret Service procedures. Clinton's lawyers, **Feb. 17**, moved in Little Rock, AR, to dismiss the Jones lawsuit, contending that Jones had not shown that her career had suffered because of the alleged incident.

In a new development in the Whitewater investigation, which had been overshadowed by the Lewinsky story, former Arkansas Gov. Jim Guy Tucker (D) pleaded guilty in U.S. District Court in Little Rock, **Feb. 20**, to 1 count of conspiracy in a tax case. Though that was unrelated to Whitewater, Tucker agreed to cooperate with Starr's Whitewater investigation in return for a reduced sentence.

Starr, angered by what he saw as an organized effort to spread misinformation about his staff, on **Feb. 24** subpoenaed Sidney Blumenthal, an adviser to the president, and Terry Lenzer, a private investigator for the president. Starr also subpoenaed any documents Blumenthal had referring to the Starr investigation. Blumenthal and Lenzer went to the federal courthouse **Feb. 24**, and Lenzer appeared before the grand jury. On **Feb. 24** and **25**, the grand jury heard from 5 current or former members of the White House staff. After testifying **Feb. 26**, Blumenthal said prosecutors had asked him which reporters he had talked with and what he had told them about the investigation.

Annual Trade Deficit at 10-Year High—The Conference Board (a business-research organization) reported, **Feb. 3**, that the index of leading economic indicators remained unchanged in December 1997, and the Labor Dept. said, **Feb. 6**, that 358,000 nonfarm jobs had been created in January, more than expected. The unemployment rate had remained at 4.7%. As for consumer prices, they were unchanged in January, the Labor Dept. said, **Feb. 24**. But the trade deficit remained a problem. The Commerce Dept. said, **Feb. 19**, that the December 1997 trade deficit was $10.79 billion, up 24% from the November gap. For the entire year, the deficit was $113.7 billion, the largest of any year since 1988. Meanwhile, on Wall Street, the Dow Jones industrial average closed **Feb. 27** at an all-time high of 8545.72, the first time it closed over 8,500.

Office of Surgeon General Is Filled—After being vacant for more than 3 years, the office of surgeon general was filled when the administration's latest candidate won Senate confirmation, **Feb. 10**. The nominee, Dr. David Satcher, director of the federal Centers for Disease Control and Prevention (CDC), had come under criticism for his support of abortion rights and for a CDC study of needle-exchange programs aimed at curtailing the spread of the AIDS virus among drug addicts. The Senate halted a filibuster, led by John Ashcroft (R, MO), that had sought to kill the nomination, and confirmed Satcher's nomination, 63-35. He was sworn in on **Feb. 13**.

Interior Secretary Faces Investigation—Interior Sec. Bruce Babbitt became the subject of an investigation after Attorney Gen. Janet Reno, **Feb. 11**, recommended that an independent counsel look into allegations against him. Republicans had charged that in 1985 he had turned down an application from Chippewa Indians in Wisconsin for a gambling casino because of political considerations and that he had testified falsely to Congress concerning his actions. The license sought for the casino was opposed by other Native American groups in Wisconsin and Minnesota that ran gambling activities in the area and that in 1996 were big contributors to Democratic candidates. An independent counsel was named **Mar. 19**.

New Line-Item Veto Rebuffed by Judge—U.S. District Judge Thomas Hogan, **Feb. 12**, declared that the 1996 Line-Item Veto Act was unconstitutional. The ruling came in a suit consolidating 2 cases. New York City and city hospitals had challenged Pres. Bill Clinton's veto of a provision of a bill that would have given more Medicaid money to New York State. Idaho potato growers had challenged the veto of a provision of another bill on tax breaks. Hogan held that because the Constitution vested all legislative powers in Congress, a president could not amend a duly enacted law. As provided under the law itself, the ruling was appealed directly to the Supreme Court.

Campaign Finance Reform Thwarted Again—Once again the Senate failed to act on a proposal to change the way money was raised for political campaigns. The legislation being considered, the McCain-Feingold bill, would ban the unlimited large donations to parties known as soft money. It had already been considered in the fall of 1997, without being approved. Senate opponents, all of whom were Republicans, contended that the bill limited free speech and was unconstitutional. On **Feb. 24**, the bill's supporters prevailed, 51-48, on a motion to kill the bill. However, the bill's progress was blocked **Feb. 26**, at least for the present, when supporters fell 9 votes short of the total (60) needed to overcome a threatened filibuster.

Prominent Republican to Leave House—Bill Paxon (NY), regarded as one of the rising stars of the Republican Party in the U.S. House of Representatives, announced, **Feb. 25**, that he would not seek reelection. In 1997, Paxon, while serving in the 5th-ranking position in the GOP House hierarchy, had been linked to an effort to remove Newt Gingrich (R, GA) as Speaker. Gingrich later removed Paxon from his leadership position. In early 1998, Paxon had reportedly considered challenging the reelection of Richard Armey (TX) as House majority leader.

Oprah Winfrey Defeats Suit by Ranchers—Oprah Winfrey, one of the nation's preeminent television personalities, prevailed, **Feb. 26**, in a lawsuit brought against her by cattle ranchers. During a 1996 telecast of her talk show, a guest had warned against the consumption of beef, saying that a person eating beef could contract a fatal brain disease related to the so-called mad cow disease that had claimed several lives in Britain. Winfrey exclaimed on the show, "It has just stopped me cold from eating another burger!" Some Texas cattle ranchers then sued Winfrey, the guest, and the show for $12 million in damages, claiming that beef prices had fallen and that Winfrey had violated the state's False Disparagement of Perishable Food Products Act. In federal court in Amarillo, TX, Winfrey testified, **Feb. 4**, that viewers had taken her comments as a personal opinion, not fact. Judge Mary Lou Robinson, **Feb. 17**, ruled that the Texas law cited did not apply, but allowed the case to continue under laws protecting companies from defamation. The jury subsequently found Winfrey not guilty.

International

Iraq Backs Down, Averting Military Conflict—Just when it seemed that the United States was ready to launch a military operation against Iraq to force Iraq to allow United Nations inspectors to investigate sites possibly containing weapons of mass destruction, the regime of Pres. Saddam Hussein pulled back from the brink. On **Feb. 1**, Sec. of State Madeleine Albright, in Kuwait, won that country's support for an attack on its larger neighbor, but Albright found that other Arab countries favored continuing diplomacy instead, as did France, Russia, and China. Pres. Bill Clinton said in a television address, **Feb. 17**, that he was prepared to order air attacks on Iraqi weapons sites. But doubts were cast on American public support for such strikes and the administration was put in an awkward position, **Feb. 18**, when Albright, Defense Sec. William Cohen, and National Security Adviser Samuel Berger came under harsh questioning during a town meeting at Ohio State University that was televised around the world.

UN Sec. Gen. Kofi Annan and Iraq's deputy premier, Tariq Aziz, signed an agreement, **Feb. 22**, that appeared to defuse the crisis. The UN restated its commitment to respect the sovereignty and territorial integrity of Iraq, and it agreed that diplomats would accompany inspectors visiting 8 so-called presidential palaces that had come under suspicion. Iraq dropped its demand that these sites be closed to UN inspectors. Russian Pres. Boris Yeltsin, **Feb. 23**, quickly supported the plan; the United States and Britain were more cautious. Clinton said, **Feb. 23**, that U.S. forces in the Persian Gulf region would remain there until Iraq had fully implemented the agreement. The UN Security Council, **Mar. 2**, unanimously approved the accord.

Meanwhile, the UN Security Council, in a humanitarian gesture, on **Feb. 20** approved a large increase (from $2.14 billion to $5.2 billion) in the quota of oil sales allowed Iraq under the oil-for-food program. The Council noted that Iraq's population was facing a serious nutritional problem.

Plane Cuts Cable; 20 in Ski Lift Fall to Death—A U.S. military aircraft, flying low over mountains in Italy, severed a ski lift cable, **Feb. 3**, causing 20 riders in a cable car to plunge some 300 feet to their deaths. The U.S. Marine Corps plane, an EA-6B Prowler surveillance jet, which was on a training mission, sustained little damage, and the crew of 4 was uninjured. For some time, local officials had complained about U.S. and Italian planes flying low through the Dolomite Mountains. The crews of the planes trained at flying at low altitudes to avoid enemy radar. An investigation of the tragedy was begun.

Cuba Frees Political Prisoners—During his January visit to Cuba, Pope John Paul II had called on the regime to free political prisoners, and Vatican representatives had given the Cuban government the names of some 300 such prisoners. The government said, **Feb. 12**, that it would free at least 200 on humanitarian grounds. It said that 106 prisoners on the Vatican list had been freed before the pope's visit. The official government news agency said, **Feb. 13**, that 70 on the list would not be released because of national security considerations or the seriousness of their crimes. On **Feb. 13** and **14**, 299 prisoners, including 75 more on the list, were freed. Canada said, **Feb. 26**, that it would admit 19 political prisoners and their families who were reportedly on the Vatican list. These opponents of the Communist regime would be freed provided that they left Cuba at once.

Nigerian Troops Overthrow Sierra Leone Junta—The military government that had ruled Sierra Leone since ousting the democratically elected government in May 1997 was itself overthrown **Feb. 13**. After his successful power grab 9 months earlier, Lt. Col. Johnny Paul Koromah and his regime had been subjected to international diplomatic and economic sanctions. Peacemakers from the alliance of West African nations known as ECOMOG had entered Sierra Leone, and Koromah had accepted an ECOMOG plan to hand over power to civilians, but had failed to follow through. The Nigerian-led peacemakers opened an attack on the junta, **Feb. 5**, and captured its headquarters in Freetown, the capital, **Feb. 12**. The Koromah government gave up the following day. The fighting cost the lives of more than 100 people.

South Korea's New President Inaugurated—Kim Dae Jung, longtime opposition leader in South Korea, was sworn in as president **Feb. 25**, 2 months after his electoral victory. This was the first time that power had passed from the ruling party. In his inauguration speech, Kim warned that the country faced economic problems, and he asked for the support of the Grand National Party, which retained a majority in Parliament. He also said he was ready for a summit meeting with the leader of North Korea, Kim Jong Il.

General

1997-98 El Niño Creates Chaos—The weather phenomenon called El Niño, starting late in 1997, appeared to reach a culmination in early 1998. El Niño begins with a periodic warming of ocean currents near the Pacific coast of Peru, which ultimately affects climatic conditions elsewhere to a greater or lesser degree, bringing about unusual storm or drought conditions. In Peru, Bolivia, and Ecuador, by early 1998, storms attributed to El Niño had killed more than 450 and left 180,000 homeless. Property damage in Peru alone was put at $700 million. Colombia, meanwhile, suffered from a severe drought. In the United States, in Florida, tornadoes struck on **Feb. 2** and **3** and again on **Feb. 22** and **23**. The Feb. 23 assaults, with winds up to 206 miles an hour, killed 42 people and injured 260. In California, the heaviest winter rainfalls ever reported in Los Angeles and San Francisco were topped off with torrential rains on **Feb. 23** and **24** that washed out roadways and caused mudslides that destroyed many homes. Damage was put at $475 million, and 9 people were killed.

Japan Is Host to Winter Olympics—Nearly 2,500 athletes from 72 nations participated in the XVIII Winter Olympics in Nagano, Japan, which began on **Feb. 7**.

Ross Rebagliati of Canada won the men's snowboarding giant slalom, **Feb. 8**, but the International Olympic Committee took away his gold medal, **Feb. 11**, after he tested positive for a minute amount of marijuana. He blamed secondhand smoke. An arbitration panel restored his medal, **Feb. 13**, declaring that IOC rules on marijuana were not clear. Among many other winners, Hermann Maier of Austria won the men's super giant slalom **Feb. 16** and the giant slalom **Feb. 19**. In the first-ever women's Olympic ice hockey competition, the United States, **Feb. 17**, took the gold medal by defeating Canada, 3-1. Making the longest ski jumps ever in Olympic competition, Takanobu Okabe and Masahiko Harada, **Feb. 17**, led Japan to the gold medal in team ski jumping. On **Feb. 20**, Tara Lipinski of the United States, at age 15, became the youngest person ever to win Olympic gold in figure skating. Michelle Kwan, 17, also from the United States and the favorite, received the silver.

Men's ice hockey was a major disappointment for the United States. For the first time, players in the National Hockey League were eligible to compete. The U.S. team had only a 1-3 record, and also caused $3,000 in damages to their living quarters after being eliminated from the medal round. The Czech Republic, **Feb. 22**, won the gold medal by defeating Russia, 1-0.

When the Games ended, **Feb. 22**, Germany won the most gold medals, 12, and had the highest overall medal count, 29. Norway was 2d in both categories, with 10 golds and 25 medals overall; Russia was 3d, with 9 golds and 18 medals overall. The United States won 6 gold medals, 3 silvers, and 4 bronzes—6th in overall total.

Judge Allows Disabled Golfer to Use Cart—In a legal case concluded **Feb. 11** in Eugene, OR, a golfer who had difficulty walking was allowed to use a cart to compete in tournaments sponsored by the Professional Golfers Association. Casey Martin suffers from a circulatory disorder that causes swelling and pain in his right leg when he stands up and especially when he walks. In his ruling, U.S. District Court Judge Thomas Coffin held that Martin was covered by the Americans With Disabilities Act, which prohibits discrimination against the disabled. Coffin said the fatigue Martin suffered as a result of his ailment was "easily greater" than that which golfers experience while walking the course.

MARCH 1998

National

2 Cases Against Clinton Move Forward—Vernon Jordan, a friend of Pres. Bill Clinton who had helped find a job for Monica Lewinsky, the former White House intern, appeared before the Whitewater grand jury on **Mar. 3** and **5**. Jordan had also arranged for Lewinsky to meet a lawyer who helped her prepare an affidavit for Paula Corbin Jones's lawyers reportedly stating that she (Lewinsky) had not had an affair with Clinton. Jordan told reporters **Mar. 5** that he had kept Clinton informed about what he was doing. He also said his efforts on Lewinsky's behalf "were not a quid pro quo for the affidavit that she signed." Kathleen Willey, who reportedly had said that Clinton had made unwanted overtures toward her during a White House meeting in 1993, testified **Mar. 10**.

Jones's lawyers filed documents in U.S. District Court in Little Rock, AR, **Mar. 13**, in response to Clinton's February motion to have the case dismissed. The documents included sworn testimony from 4 women—including Jones and Willey but not Lewinsky—who claimed to have had sexual contact with Clinton. Jones's lawyers sought, in other documents, to establish that Jones had suffered discrimination in her state job after refusing to have sex with Clinton and that she had suffered emotional distress. A deposition taken from Clinton in January was among papers filed **Mar. 13**. Also included was an affidavit in which Lewinsky denied a sexual relationship with Clinton. She said her White House visits after leaving her job there were for official functions or related to her Pentagon job and that she was never alone with the president.

On **Mar. 15**, Willey appeared on the television program *60 Minutes*, giving her first public account of the 1993 incident. Clinton said, **Mar. 16**, that he was "mystified and disappointed" by her accusations.

In Washington, DC, in U.S. District Court, **Mar. 20**, Clinton's lawyers reportedly invoked executive privilege and attorney-client privilege to protect 2 aides from testifying before the Whitewater grand jury.

Economy Remains Strong—The Conference Board (a business-research organization) reported, **Mar. 3**, that the leading economic indicators remained unchanged in January. The Labor Dept., **Mar. 6**, reported that, for the 4th consecutive month, 300,000 or more new nonfarm jobs—310,000 in February—had been created. The unemployment rate edged down to 4.6% in February. The Labor Dept also said, **Mar. 19**, that consumer prices had risen just 0.1% in February. However, in a sign that the Asian financial crisis was having an effect on the U.S. economy, the Commerce Dept. said, **Mar. 19**, that the trade deficit rose to $12.04 billion in January, the highest since late 1987.

Former Business Partner of Clintons Dies in Jail—James McDougal, who with his then-wife Susan had been business partners with then-Gov. Bill Clinton and Hillary Clinton, died of cardiac arrest **Mar. 8** while serving a prison term at the Federal Medical Center in Ft. Worth, TX. While James McDougal was running a savings and loan, the 2 couples had invested in the Whitewater Development Corp. Investigation into the tangled finances of the corporation had resulted in convictions and jail terms for both McDougals, who had divorced, and in ongoing scrutiny of the Clintons. James McDougal had agreed to cooperate with prosecutors in exchange for less time in jail, and his death was considered a blow to Kenneth Starr, the independent counsel investigating the Clintons.

Rep. Joseph Kennedy to Retire—On **Mar. 13**, Rep. Joseph Kennedy 2d (D, MA)—the oldest son of the late Sen. Robert Kennedy—said that because of personal reasons, he would not seek reelection. He said he would run the company he had founded in 1979, Citizens Energy Corp. In recent years, the company had been led by his brother Michael Kennedy, who was killed in a skiing accident in December 1997. The company provides services in the areas of energy and health care.

Army's Ex-Top Sergeant Acquitted of Sex Charges—Sgt. Maj. Gene McKinney, the first black to ever serve as sergeant major of the Army, was acquitted by a military jury, **Mar. 13**, of most charges that had been filed against him. Six women, all in the military, had accused him of sexual misconduct, and McKinney was eventually charged on 19 counts. Prior to trial, he lost his title. McKinney, however, was acquitted of all 18 sex counts. His only conviction came on a count of coaching a witness who was 1 of his accusers. For that offense, McKinney, **Mar. 16**, was reduced 1 rank and reprimanded.

Democratic Contributor Pleads Guilty—Johnny Chung, a California businessman and key figure in the investigation into Democratic Party fundraising practices during the 1996 campaign, pleaded guilty, **Mar. 16**, to bank fraud, conspiracy, and tax evasion. Chung had given $20,000 to the Clinton-Gore campaign, far more than the legal limit of $1,000, by having an employee persuade 20 people to give $1,000 each; they were then reimbursed by Chung. He used a similar ploy to give $8,000 to the campaign of Sen. John Kerry (D, MA).

Boys 11, 13 Held in Killing of 5 at School—Two boys who were only 11 and 13 years old were arrested, **Mar. 24**, in the slaying of 4 schoolgirls and a teacher outside Westside Middle School in Jonesboro, AR. Teachers and students had gone outside in response to a false fire alarm that one of the boys may have set, when shots were fired from a nearby woods. Eight other girls, a boy, and another teacher were wounded. Police seized Mitchell Johnson, 13, and Andrew Golden, 11, as they ran through the woods. On **Mar. 25**, the county prosecutor said he would charge the boys with 5 counts of murder and 10 counts of battery. Arkansas law required that defendants under 14 be tried as juveniles; the boys, if convicted, would be released at age 18. Golden's grandfather said, **Mar. 25** and **26**, that the boys had stolen some of the guns used in the shooting from him and some from Johnson's stepfather.

First Legal Doctor-Assisted Suicide Reported—The first known physician-assisted suicide to be legal under state law was reported **Mar. 25**. Earlier, on **Mar. 14**, a lawyer for Dr. Jack Kevorkian said that on the previous day in Michigan he had assisted in a suicide for the 100th time. These actions were not sanctioned by law. In Oregon, however, voters in 1997 reaffirmed a law allowing doctors in that state to prescribe drugs in lethal doses to patients who were terminally ill. On **Mar. 25**, the group Compassion in Dying, which advocates assisted suicide, reported that, in accordance with the new law, a Portland woman who had terminal breast cancer had taken her life with a prescribed overdose of barbiturates.

International

Protests by Albanians in Serbia Turn Violent—Unrest in the Serbian province of Kosovo became violent. About 90% of the people in the province are of Albanian descent, and a separatist movement had formed in 1989 after Kosovo was stripped of its status as an autonomous region within Serbia. In early 1998 the Kosovo Liberation Army had occupied several towns and attacked police stations and Serb leaders. Violent clashes in late February and early March claimed some 75 lives. Serbian police used clubs and tear gas, **Mar. 2**, to turn back 30,000 demonstrators in Pristina, the capital of Kosovo. The United States and the European Union, **Mar. 2**, condemned the police crackdown. On **Mar. 6**, Serbian police attacked villages in the Drenica Valley with mortars, armored vehicles, and helicopter gunships.

The United States and 5 European nations, **Mar. 9**, announced they would impose sanctions on Yugoslavia (consisting of Serbia and Montenegro) if the government did not take steps to end the violence. They also agreed to establish a peacekeeping force in neighboring Macedonia after the forces sent there by the United Nations left in August. The 6 nations on **Mar. 25** said they would delay a decision on sanctions for a month. NATO said, **Mar. 27**, that it would send advisers to Albania to train border guards along its border with Yugoslavia. One task of the guards would be to handle refugees fleeing Kosovo. The UN Security Council, **Mar. 31**, voted to impose an arms embargo on Yugoslavia.

Suharto Reelected Amid Stress in Indonesia—Pres. Suharto was elected to a 7th term **Mar. 10**, amid ongoing financial crisis in Indonesia. The International Monetary Fund, citing Suharto's failure to dismantle industrial monopolies that favored his family and friends, had announced, **Mar. 6**, that it would postpone paying an installment of a $40 billion rescue package. Despite this controversy, the People's Consultative Assembly, **Mar. 9**, voted to broaden Suharto's powers in ways not made public, and the following day the assembly reelected him unanimously. Public unrest over the financial crisis, including the collapse of the nation's currency, continued to grow. Thousands of university students, **Mar. 11**, demonstrated against Suharto and burned him in effigy.

Vatican Issues Statement on Holocaust—Ever since the end of World War II, the question of whether the Roman Catholic Church could have done more to prevent the Holocaust had been debated. In a 14-page statement issued **Mar. 16**, the Vatican apologized to Jews for not having taken more decisive steps to prevent the deaths of millions of Jews under the German Nazi regime. In a statement preceding the document, "We Remember: A Reflection on the Shoah," Pope John Paul II said that the Shoah, or Holocaust, "remains an indelible stain on the history of the century. . . ." The document acknowledged that anti-Semitism among Christians contributed to the climate in which the persecution unfolded. It defended the conduct of Pope Pius XII, who was the pontiff during the war, noting that he had, for example, warned against the deification of the state. Cardinal Edward Idris Cassidy, in presenting the statement, called it "an act of repentance." Elan Steinberg of the World Jewish Congress praised parts of the document but objected, **Mar. 16**, to what he called its "gratuitous defense of the silence" of Pius XII.

New President Elected in Armenia—Armenia elected a new president, following the forced resignation in February of Pres. Levon Ter-Petrosian, who had incurred the displeasure of the military. Survivors of a first round of presidential voting, **Mar. 16**, were Prem. Robert Kocharian and Karen Demirchyan, who had led Armenia in its days as a Soviet republic. On **Mar. 30**, in a runoff monitored by the Organization for Security and Cooperation in Europe, Kocharian won with 59% of the vote. Viewed as a reformer, Kocharian was also expected to stand firmly against threats from an antagonistic neighbor, Azerbaijan.

New Premier Elected in China—On **Mar. 17**, the Chinese parliament formally chose Vice Prem. Zhu Rongji as the successor to Prem. Li Peng. Li had served 10 years as premier, the legal limit. Zhu, holder of a degree in electrical engineering, had been a vocal critic of economic policy in the 1950s and 1960s and had suffered banishment twice. Rehabilitated, he became mayor and party secretary in Shanghai in the late 1980s. During student prodemocracy protests in Shanghai in 1989, Zhu succeeded in getting demonstrators to disperse without bloodshed. He became a vice premier in 1991, and as the government's leader in economic policy he succeeded in slashing inflation.

Hindu Nationalist Heads New Indian Government—Atal Bihari Vajpayee became prime minister of India a 2d time **Mar. 19**; he had held the office for 2 weeks in 1996. Parliamentary elections that were concluded on **Feb. 28** had proved inconclusive. Sonia Gandhi, widow of the late Prime Min. Rajiv Gandhi, was elected new leader of the Congress (I) party, **Mar. 14**, then sought to form a majority in the badly divided parliament, but failed. Vajpayee then put together a majority, though some of his coalition partners opposed his advocacy of Hindu nationalism. An author and poet, Vajpayee has a master's degree in political science. In 1996, his belief that Hindu religion and culture should be the basis of national policy had prevented him from establishing a firm parliamentary majority.

Israel Rejects U.S. Plan on West Bank Pullback—The Israeli cabinet, **Mar. 22**, turned down a U.S. proposal that Israel withdraw from an additional 13.1% of the West Bank in the second stage of its withdrawal. The peace process had been stalled for a year because of Palestinian objections to increased Israeli settlement activity in the West Bank and because of Israeli government complaints about the failure of the Palestinians to prevent terrorist acts.

Kiriyenko Named Russian Premier at Age 35—Russia got a young premier after Pres. Boris Yeltsin dismissed his entire cabinet on **Mar. 23**. Yeltsin said he wanted more energy and more results from his cabinet. No significant change in policy was expected. Prem. Viktor Chernomyrdin was among those dismissed. The energy minister, Sergei Kiriyenko, also lost his job but he got a new one: acting premier. Then, on **Mar. 27**, Yeltsin nominated Kiriyenko, who was 35, to be premier, and said he would dissolve parliament if Kiriyenko was not confirmed. Chernomyrdin said, **Mar. 28**, that he would run for president in 2000. Yeltsin, said, **Mar. 30**, that he himself would not.

Clintons Visit 6 Nations in Africa—During an 11-day visit to 6 African nations by Pres. Bill Clinton, accompanied by First Lady Hillary Rodham Clinton, the president emphasized the U.S. need for more trade with and investment in Africa. Clinton spoke to 200,000 people in Accra, Ghana, **Mar. 23**. Meeting with Pres. Jerry Rawlings, **Mar. 23**, he promised more foreign aid. In a speech to schoolchildren near Kampala, Uganda, **Mar. 24**, Clinton said that the enslavement of Africans by the United States had been wrong. Visiting Rwanda briefly, **Mar. 25**, the Clintons remained at the airport for security reasons. The president said that the United States and the world had not done enough to prevent mass killings there in recent years.

In a historic occasion, **Mar. 26**, Clinton became the first U.S. president to visit South Africa. During a joint news conference with Pres. Nelson Mandela, **Mar. 27**, the latter defended his country's continuing ties with radical regimes in Cuba, Iran, and Libya, which had been supportive of the overthrow of white domination in South Africa. The 2 presidents, **Mar. 27**, visited the cell where Mandela had spent 18 of 27 years in prison. In Botswana, **Mar. 29**, Clinton spoke at the residence of Pres. Ketumile Masire, and then he and Mrs. Clinton took a 2-day safari. The Clintons arrived in Senegal, **Mar. 31**, and concluded their trip **Apr. 2** in Dakar, the capital, at a meeting with political activists from a number of countries.

General

Ice Found Near North and South Poles of Moon—The National Aeronautics and Space Administration said, **Mar. 5**, that ice mixed with soil had been found around the moon's north and south poles. Data from the *Lunar Prospector*, an unmanned spacecraft, had shown the presence of hydrogen, a component of water. The amount of ice was estimated at as much as 6 billion tons. Scientists believed the ice could have come from comets that had struck the moon.

***Titanic* Wins 11 Motion Picture Academy Awards**—The motion picture *Titanic* tied a record, **Mar. 23**, when it won 11 Academy Awards, including best picture of 1997. Nominated for 14 Oscars, *Titanic* equaled the total won by *Ben-Hur* in 1959. Directed by James Cameron, *Titanic* presented a fictional love story aboard the doomed ocean liner, which struck an iceberg and sank during its maiden voyage in 1912, claiming 1,503 lives. For the picture, Cameron built a ship nearly as long as the original, and his insistence on historical fidelity and graphic portrayal of the sinking ship sent the movie's budget to $200 million. However, by the time of the awards *Titanic* had already grossed $1.2 billion worldwide, the highest for any movie ever. Cameron was named best director. Jack Nicholson and Helen Hunt won awards for their leading roles in *As Good as It Gets*. Ben Affleck and Matt Damon shared the award for best original screenplay for *Good Will Hunting*, in which they also appeared.

Kentucky Reclaims NCAA Basketball Title—The University of Kentucky Wildcats won the collegiate basketball title for the 2d time in 3 years and for the 7th time overall. They defeated the University of Utah, 78-69, on **Mar. 30** in San Antonio, TX. In each of its last 3 tournament games, the Wildcats overcame deficits of 10 or more points to win. Guard Jeff Sheppard was named Most Valuable Player of the Final Four.

APRIL 1998

National

Harassment Suit Against Clinton Thrown Out—A federal judge, **Apr. 1**, dismissed the sexual harassment suit brought against Pres. Bill Clinton by Paula Corbin Jones. She had claimed that in 1991 then-Gov. Clinton made an unwanted sexual advance toward her in a Little Rock, AR, hotel room, that this incident caused her emotional distress, and that her rejection of his overture damaged her career as a state employee. In her ruling in federal district court in Little Rock, Judge Susan Webber Wright held that even if Jones's account of the incident was true and Clinton's behavior "boorish and offensive," Jones did not show she had suffered distress or detriment to her career. Jones, **Apr. 29**, appealed Wright's ruling. Meanwhile, the White House and Jones's lawyers pursued negotiations aimed at a possible settlement. On **Oct. 31**, real estate developer Abe Hirschfeld offered Jones $1 million if she agreed to settle the case.

The relationship between Clinton and former White House intern Monica Lewinsky remained a matter of legal maneuvering. It was reported on **Apr. 29** that Judge Norma Holloway Johnson rejected Lewinsky's claim to have an enforceable immunity agreement with the office of Kenneth Starr, the independent counsel investigating Whitewater and other matters related to the president.

Asked at a news conference **Apr. 30** about a poll showing declining public regard for his moral values, Clinton said his political opponents were spending a lot of time and money to damage his presidency, adding, "They can affect my reputation. They can do nothing, for good or ill, to affect my character."

Bill in Senate Would Greatly Boost Cost of Cigarettes—The Senate Commerce Committee voted **Apr. 1** to toughen an agreement reached in 1997 between leading tobacco companies and state attorneys general seeking to recover costs of diseases linked to tobacco. The 1997 settlement, which required congressional approval, would have raised the price of a cigarette pack by 62 cents; the industry, in return for payments totaling $368.5 billion, would have gotten immunity from class-action lawsuits and punitive damages for past conduct. However, the Senate committee voted, 19-1, to increase the companies' payments to $506 billion (to a government trust fund over 25 years) and to boost the price of a pack by $1.10 over 5 years as a way of putting cigarettes beyond the means of teenagers. Protection from future class actions and punitive damages was dropped, and the annual limit on compensatory damages was raised from $5 billion to $6.5 billion. Heavy additional penalties would be imposed if tobacco use by young people did not decline. The tobacco companies announced, **Apr. 8**, that they would no longer work to reach an agreement on a bill and said the Senate bill would bankrupt them.

Economy Still Strong—The Conference Board (a business-research organization) reported, **Apr. 1**, that the leading economic indicators had risen again in February, the biggest advance in a year, despite the Asian financial crisis. Meanwhile, on Wall Street, the Dow Jones Industrial Average, **Apr. 6**, closed above 9,000 for the first time, and continued to climb. The Labor Dept. said, **Apr. 3**, that the number of nonfarm jobs had declined by 36,000 in March, the first monthly drop in more than 2 years, but unemployment continued to hold in its recent narrow range, standing at 4.7%. The department also said, **Apr. 14**, that consumer prices had remained unchanged in March.

The Commerce Dept. said, **Apr. 30**, that gross domestic product grew at an annual rate of 4.2% during the first quarter. On the negative side, the department announced, **Apr. 17**, that the trade deficit soared to $12.11 billion in February—the highest in a decade.

"Republic of Texas" Leaders Convicted—A confrontation that began with state troopers in 1997 ended in Dallas in federal court when 8 members of the self-proclaimed Republic of Texas separatist group were convicted, **Apr. 14**, on fraud charges. Richard McLaren, the group's leader, was convicted on 26 counts for writing bad checks totaling millions of dollars. He was already in state prison on a kidnapping conviction.

Clinics Providing Abortions Awarded Damages—A federal jury in Chicago, **Apr. 20**, awarded $85,926 in damages to 2 clinics that provided health services to women, including abortions. The National Organization for Women and the 2 clinics, located in Wilmington, DE, and Milwaukee, WI, had filed a class-action suit asserting that abortion opponents had utilized threats and extortion in an attempt to shut down the clinics. The jury concluded that 3 defendants, all associated with the Pro-Life Action League, had conspired against the clinics. Another defendant, Randall Terry of Operation Rescue, had settled out of court in January.

Hillary Rodham Clinton Testifies; Close Clinton Friend Indicted—On **Apr. 25**, First Lady Hillary Rodham Clinton provided more videotaped testimony at the White House for the Little Rock, AR, grand jury in the Whitewater case. The grand jury viewed the testimony **Apr. 29**. David Kendall, a lawyer for the Clintons, said she had refused to answer 2 questions, citing the principle that spouses were not obliged to testify against each other.

A grand jury in Washington, DC, indicted Webster Hubbell and his wife, Suzanna, **Apr. 30**, for allegedly attempting to conceal income while they owed back taxes and penalties. The Hubbells' accountant and lawyer were indicted for conspiracy. After resigning as associate U.S. attorney general in 1994, Hubbell, a close friend and associate of the Clintons, had pleaded guilty to embezzling money from the Little Rock law firm where Hillary Clinton also had worked. Hubbell, **Apr. 30**, denounced the prosecution team led by Kenneth Starr, the independent counsel, saying, "They think by indicting my wife and my friends that I will lie about the president and the first lady. I will not do so."

International

IMF, Indonesia Reach New Agreement on Aid—For the 3d time in recent months, the International Monetary Fund and Indonesia worked out an agreement by which the latter would receive a financial aid package of about $40 billion, offered to Indonesia in late 1997. Pres. Suharto had not implemented the terms of the 2 previous agreements. This time, on **Apr. 8**, the IMF dropped the requirement that the Indonesian government cease to subsidize food and fuel. The public had demonstrated against a prospective end to the subsidies. Indonesia's troubles were exacerbated by a drought, which brought on extensive brushfires with haze that had sickened thousands. Thousands more had reportedly died from starvation and malaria.

Britain, Ireland Reach Accord on Ulster—The long and bloody dispute over the future of Northern Ireland apparently came closer to an end when an important accord was announced **Apr. 10**.

Northern Ireland, or Ulster, is a part of Great Britain, but the Irish and Roman Catholic minority there had long pressed for unification with the Republic of Ireland. Violence, instigated by the Provisional Irish Republican Army (IRA) and by extreme Protestant Unionists, had taken 3,248 lives over the past 29 years. Participants in the peace talks that produced the accord included the prime ministers of Britain and Ireland, Tony Blair and Bertie Ahern, as well as David Trimble, head of the Ulster Unionist Party, Northern Ireland's largest Protestant Party; John Hume, head of the (Catholic) Social Democratic and Labor Party; and Gerry Adams, head of Sinn Fein, political wing of the Irish Republican Army. An American, former Senate Majority Leader George Mitchell, served as chairman of the negotiations.

Under the agreement, British rule would continue, but a new provincial assembly would have jurisdiction over many local issues. The assembly would often work with the Irish government on a new North-South Ministerial Council. Another new body, the Council of the Isles, would address matters in which Britain and Ireland had a mutual interest. The terms of the accord had to be approved by the people of Ireland and Northern Ireland in referenda and by the parliaments of Britain and Ireland. In addition, it would be necessary to change the statement in the Irish constitution that the republic embraced the entire island.

In an attempt to increase support for the accord among Catholics, the Irish government released 9 members of the IRA from prison on **Apr. 14**. The predominantly Protestant Ulster Unionist Party approved the plan **Apr. 18**. The Dail, the parliament of Ireland, backed it, **Apr. 22**. The IRA gave qualified support, **Apr. 30**, though refusing to surrender its arms as provided in the agreement.

Cambodian Despot Pol Pot Dies—Pol Pot, who presided over a reign of terror in Cambodia in the late 1970s, died **Apr. 15** in a jungle outpost near the Cambodia-Thailand border. Pol Pot had been the leader of the Khmer Rouge, a Communist guerrilla army that seized power in 1975 and imposed a radical overhaul of society. Religion and education were abolished, and millions were forced from cities into rural communes (later called killing fields). It is believed that more than a million people were executed as threats to the Khmer Rouge, or died of starvation or enforced hardship. Ousted from power in 1979 by the Vietnamese, the Khmer Rouge remained in operation in the jungles, but Pol Pot fell into disfavor. After he ordered the killing of Khmer Rouge cofounder Son Sen in 1997, he was put on trial by his comrades and condemned to house arrest—detention in a hut.

Amid speculation that Pol Pot had been killed by the Khmer Rouge or that reports of his death were a ruse, Thai officials examined the body, **Apr. 17**. They confirmed that it was that of Pol Pot. His remains were burned on a pyre of rubber tires, household articles, and debris, **Apr. 18**.

Hemisphere Leaders Back Free-Trade Zone—Presidents, premiers, and prime ministers from 34 nations in the Western Hemisphere attended the 2d Summit of the Americas in Santiago, Chile. On the opening day, **Apr. 18**, Pres. Bill Clinton vowed he would get fast-track authority to negotiate trade agreements, which Congress had denied him in 1997; fast-track authority denies Congress the right to amend trade agreements that the president presents for approval. In a declaration signed **Apr. 19**, the leaders agreed that formal negotiations would begin in 1998 aimed at creating, by 2005, a free-trade zone encompassing the entire hemisphere. The leaders also agreed to take new measures to combat drug trafficking.

China Frees Leading Prodemocracy Dissident—On **Apr. 19**, China freed Wang Dan, one of the leaders of the prodemocracy movement in 1989 that had been suppressed brutally in or around Beijing's Tiananmen Square and elsewhere. Wang had spent most of the past decade in prison. China agreed to free him after the United States refrained from condemning China's record on human rights before the United Nations Human Rights Commission. Released on medical parole, Wang immediately flew to Detroit and entered a hospital for a medical examination.

Yugoslav Assets Frozen in Dispute over Kosovo—A resolution of the confrontation between the Serbian leadership of Yugoslavia and the ethnic Albanian population of Kosovo province remained elusive. Voters in the Republic of Serbia, **Apr. 23**, overwhelmingly rejected foreign mediation of the dispute, which had claimed 120 lives since February. On **Apr. 29**, the 6 nations monitoring the dispute announced that Yugoslavia's foreign assets had been frozen. They insisted that Yugoslavia withdraw police forces from Kosovo and begin negotiations with the ethnic Albanians.

Rwanda Executes 22 for Genocide—The government of Rwanda, **Apr. 24**, executed 22 people convicted of genocide in the 1994 civil war. During one 3-month period in 1994, under a radical Hutu regime, some 500,000 Tutsis and moderate Hutus had been killed. The executions left about 125,000 suspected war criminals still awaiting trial in Rwanda. Earlier, on **Apr. 16**, 2 Roman Catholic priests were convicted in connection with the 1994 murder of 2,000 Tutsis who had taken refuge in a church, and reportedly sentenced to death. A UN tribunal was also trying Rwandans suspected of participating in the 1994 violence.

Russian Parliament Approves Premier—After threats from Pres. Boris Yeltsin and 2 negative votes, the Russian parliament, **Apr. 24**, approved Yeltsin's nomination of Sergei Kiriyenko as the nation's premier. Kiriyenko had been rejected in votes taken **Apr. 10** and **17**. Had a 3d rejection occurred, Yeltsin could have dissolved the Duma and ordered new elections. However, in the 3d vote, a secret ballot, Kiriyenko was approved, 251-25.

U.S. Senate Approves 3 New Nations in NATO—Three former members of the Soviet bloc moved closer to membership in the North Atlantic Treaty Organization on **Apr. 30**, when the U.S. Senate, voting 80-19, approved their application. All 16 current members of NATO had to approve the applications of the 3 countries—the Czech Republic, Hungary, and Poland; U.S. approval brought the number of approving countries up to 5.

General

U.S. Says Drug Prevents Breast Cancer—Tamoxifen, a synthetic hormone, was found to be able to prevent breast cancer in women at high risk. Federal health officials reported, **Apr. 6**, that the drug, which blocks the effects on the breast of the female hormone estrogen, had been tested in a study of 13,388 women who had breast cancer risk factors; half of them took the drug, and half took a placebo. There were 45% fewer breast cancer cases among women who took tamoxifen. However, the drug was determined to have dangerous side effects, including increased risk of uterine cancer and blood clots in the lungs. On **Oct 30** the Food and Drug Administration approved the use of tamoxifen to help prevent breast cancer in healthy women at high risk of developing it. Tamoxifen was already in use to prevent breast cancer recurrence.

Tornadoes Take Heavy Toll in South—The weather phenomenon called El Niño continued to cause loss of life and widespread property destruction. Tornadoes and storms hit Alabama, Georgia, and Mississippi, **Apr. 8** and **9**, taking 39 lives. Of these, 34 were in Alabama, where more than 1,000 homes were destroyed. Tornadoes killed 10 people in Arkansas, Kentucky, and Tennessee, **Apr. 16**. A tornado in northeast Georgia, **Mar. 20**, had killed 12 people and injured at least 120.

New Impotence Drug Becomes Top Seller—A new prescription drug to treat male impotence, Viagra, went on the market **Apr. 10** and became one of the top-selling new drugs of all time. The U.S. Food and Drug Administration had approved the pill, manufactured by Pfizer Inc., **Mar. 27**. Since patients need only to take a pill 1 hour before sexual activity, Viagra is simpler to use than other impotence treatments. Each Viagra pill cost about $10. As a result of the drug's huge popularity, a number of insurance companies began to require proof of a medical cause of a patient's impotence and to set limits on reimbursements for Viagra. Some users reported side effects such as headaches, blurred vision, and upset stomach. Patients wishing to use Viagra need to inform the physician of any other medications they are taking. Viagra cannot be taken by any patient using drugs known as nitrates (such as nitroglycerin often prescribed for chest pain related to heart disease). On **May 28**, Pfizer announced that 6 people had died after taking Viagra, from cardiovascular stress or from combining the drug with nitrate heart medications.

MAY 1998

National

Judge's Rulings Go Against Clinton—In a ruling issued under seal, **May 4**, U.S. District Judge Norma Holloway Johnson held that Pres. Bill Clinton could not invoke executive privilege or attorney-client privilege to prevent aides from testifying in the inquiry involving a former White House intern. She concluded that the executive-privilege claim was outweighed by the need of independent counsel Kenneth Starr to gather information.

Meanwhile, Starr's grand jury in Washington, DC, continued to hear testimony concerning Clinton's relationship with former intern Monica Lewinsky and related allegations of a cover-up and obstruction of justice. Additional testimony was provided by Vernon Jordan (**May 5**), a friend of the president who had helped Lewinsky try to find a new job, and Betty Currie (**May 6-7**), the president's private secretary.

On **May 22**, Judge Johnson held that members of the U.S. Secret Service could be required to testify before the grand jury. The Justice Dept. had argued that such a requirement would damage the relationship of trust between the Secret Service and anyone they were protecting. The Secret Service contended that the president might be in mortal danger if he distanced himself from agents to prevent them from observing his actions or overhearing his words. But Johnson held that agents, as law enforcement officers, could be required to testify in criminal inquiries.

Whitewater Figure Indicted Again—Susan McDougal, a partner of then-Gov. Bill Clinton and Hillary Rodham Clinton in the Whitewater land deal in Arkansas, was indicted again **May 4** for criminal contempt and obstruction of justice. She had completed 1 term for civil contempt for refusing to testify before a Little Rock grand jury, and was currently in prison for bank fraud in connection with the Whitewater case. In April, she had again declined to answer questions before the grand jury,

More Major Corporate Mergers Announced—The surge in major corporate mergers continued. On **May 7**, Daimler-Benz AG and the Chrysler Corp. announced plans to merge. Daimler, the largest industrial corporation in Germany, produced the Mercedes-Benz luxury automobile, as well as trucks and other vehicles, and was also involved in the aerospace and defense industries. Chrysler, 3d in size of the U.S. "Big 3" automakers, produced cars under the names Chrysler, Dodge, and Plymouth, in addition to recreational vehicles. The new DaimlerChrysler would be the world's 5th-largest automaker, and Chrysler would be the largest U.S. company ever acquired by a foreign company. The transaction was valued at about $40 billion.

In what would be the 2d-largest merger in corporate history, valued at about $70 billion, SBC Communications, Inc., **May 11**, said it would acquire Ameritech Corp. SBC provided local telephone service in parts of the West and Midwest. Ameritech served phone customers in the Midwest. The deal would make SBC the largest local-telephone service provider in the United States.

Tobacco Industry Settles 4th State Suit—The tobacco industry, which had previously settled lawsuits with Mississippi, Florida, and Texas, reached an agreement with Minnesota and with Blue Cross & Blue Shield of Minnesota, **May 8**. Te state and Blue Cross had sought compe n-satory damages for costs of treating smoking-related diseases, as well as punitive damages. This was the first state suit to go to trial; the settlement came after 15 weeks of testimony, just as the case was about to go to the jury. The 4 defendant companies agreed to pay the state $6.1 billion over 25 years. Blue Cross would get $469 million over 5 years, and the plaintiffs' lawyers would get $427 million from the defendants. The defendants agreed not to market their products to minors, and a state ban was imposed on billboard advertising of tobacco products and on marketing of products bearing cigarette logos.

Unemployment Rate Drops Again—The Labor Dept. reported, **May 8**, that unemployment in April had declined to 4.3%, the lowest level in 28 years. Prices showed something of an upward trend. The Labor Dept. reported, **May 13**, that producer prices had risen 0.2% in April, ending 5 straight months of decline. The department said, **May 14**, that consumer prices had also risen 0.2% in April, the largest advance in 6 months. Meanwhile, the Commerce Dept. said, **May 20**, that the trade deficit in March had reached $13 billion, a record.

Charges in Shooting at Ruby Ridge Dismissed—A lingering legal case in connection with a deadly shootout at Ruby Ridge, ID, came to an end in May. In 1992, during a siege by law enforcement officials at a cabin occupied by white separatist Randy Weaver, Weaver's wife and son and a deputy U.S. marshall were shot to death. An Idaho prosecutor had charged a former FBI agent, Lon Horiuchi, with involuntary manslaughter in the death of Weaver's wife, Vicki. On **May 14**, U.S. District Judge Edward Lodge in Boise, ID, dismissed the charges, finding that in firing his shots, Horiuchi had acted within the scope of his duties.

Gifts to Democrats Tied to Chinese Government—*The New York Times* reported, **May 15**, that Johnny Chung, a California businessman, told federal investigators that money from a Chinese military officer was given to the Democratic Party for the 1996 campaign. The Democrats had previously returned all money raised by Chung in their behalf, and in March, Chung had pleaded guilty to making illegal campaign contributions. According to the *Times*, nearly $100,000 that Chung gave to the Democrats came from Lt. Col. Liu Chaoying, an executive with the state-owned China Aerospace Corp. and the daughter of China's top military commander. In all, Chung said he had received $300,000 from Col. Liu between July and September 1996; the rest of the money was not accounted for.

Chung's admission added fuel to a controversy involving U.S. satellites and the Chinese. In February 1996, Pres. Bill Clinton had granted waivers to U.S. aerospace companies to launch satellites from Chinese rockets. The head of a leading U.S. satellite company, Bernard Schwartz of Loral Space and Communications, Ltd., had been the biggest individual donor to the Democrats' 1996 campaign. According to the *Times*, U.S. Defense Dept. investigators concluded that engineers—sent to China by 2 U.S. companies to investigate the failure of a Chinese launch of a U.S. satellite—had jeopardized U.S. national security by providing the Chinese with missile technology. Clinton denied, **May 17**, that his waivers had been influenced by political contributions. Loral, **May 18**, denied getting political favors from the administration, and the Chinese government and China Aerospace, **May 19**, denied making contributions to the Democrats.

Parents, 2 Students Shot to Death in Oregon—A 15-year-old student was arrested in Springfield, OR, **May 21**, and charged on **May 22** with 4 counts of murder. Police said the youth, Kipland Kinkel, had shot his parents to death and then gone to his high school, where he fired into a cafeteria, killing 1 student and wounding 23 others, 1 of whom died the next day. Kinkel allegedly used a .22-caliber semiautomatic rifle. Several students, including 1 who had been wounded, had subdued Kinkel. Since October 1997, 2 teachers and 12 students had been killed in shootings by male students across the United States.

Congress Approves $216 Billion Transport Bill—On **May 22**, the Senate, 88-5, and the House, 297-86, approved a $216 billion surface-transportation bill. Some $173 billion would be spent on highways, $41 billion on mass transit, and $2 billion would be allocated for highway-safety programs over a 6-year period.

3d Man Sentenced in Oklahoma City Bombing—Michael Fortier, who had testified in the trials of 2 men convicted in connection with responsibility for the 1995 bombing of a federal building in Oklahoma City, was sentenced **May 27** to 12 years in prison and fined $200,000. Fortier, in a deal with prosecutors, had admitted withholding prior knowledge of a plot to bomb the building. He testified against Timothy McVeigh and Terry Nichols.

International

Ex-Premier of Rwanda Admits Genocide—Jean Kambanda, interim premier of Rwanda in 1994, pleaded guilty, **May 1**, to genocide. His admission represented the 1st conviction for the UN International Criminal Tribunal for Rwanda, which was operating in Tanzania. Kambanda, a radical Hutu, had been charged with chairing cabinet meetings at which massacres were planned and with installing a regional Hutu governor who presided over the massacre of thousands of Tutsis. Some 500,000 people were thought to have been killed in Rwanda's 1994 civil war.

Suharto Falls in Indonesia—The long and autocratic rule of Pres. Suharto in Indonesia came to an end in May. On **May 2**, college students across the country demonstrated in behalf of political and economic reform. As a condition for receiving critical loans from the International Monetary Fund, the Suharto regime, **May 4**, announced it would end government subsidies, thereby increasing gas prices by 71%, diesel fuel prices by 58%, and electricity rates by 20%. This brought renewed and more violent protests. Six people were reported dead and 100 injured in Medan, **May 6**, by gunfire from police or in buildings set afire by rioters. Ethnic Chinese merchants were targets of the rioters' attacks.

Riot police killed 6 student demonstrators at Trisakti Univ. in Jakarta, **May 12**. Between **May 13** and **15**, some 500 died in violence in Jakarta, many in buildings burned by rioters. Suharto returned early from a trip to Egypt, **May 15**, and restored the fuel subsidies. The military stood by, **May 18**, as thousands of students occupied the parliament building. Opponents of the regime rejected promises of cabinet changes and early elections, and on **May 20** the Speaker of Parliament said impeachment proceedings would begin in 2 days if Suharto did not resign.

Suharto, first elected president in 1968, resigned **May 21**. He was succeeded by Vice Pres. Bacharuddin Jusuf (B. J.) Habibie, regarded as a Suharto protege. Habibie named his cabinet **May 22**, retaining 15 of 36 Suharto appointees in the same posts, while reassigning 4. Among those replaced was Suharto's daughter, and Suharto's son-in-law was ousted as commander of an elite armed forces unit. Troops removed 2,000 students from the parliament building **May 22-23**. On **May 25** the new government freed 2 prominent jailed dissidents and promised to review the records of others, while Habibie said he would hold new elections before the scheduled end of his term in 2003.

Voters in Ireland Support Peace Plan—On **May 10**, at a conference in Dublin, the new peace agreement on the future of Northern Ireland received strong backing from Sinn Fein, political wing of the Provisional Irish Republican Army; Sinn Fein also agreed to participate in the projected new legislature for Northern Ireland. On **May 22**, 94% of those voting in the Republic of Ireland and 71% of those voting in Northern Ireland approved the peace plan. A survey indicated that 96% of Catholic voters in Northern Ireland and 55% of Protestant voters supported the accord. Protestant objections to the accord related to the planned early release of prisoners linked to paramilitary groups and to the condition that these groups did not have to immediately surrender their weapons.

Philippines Elects New President—The Philippines, **May 11**, elected a president, vice president, members of Congress, and provincial and local officials. The incumbent president, Fidel Ramos, was not eligible for a 2d term. The new president, officially declared elected **May 29**, was Vice Pres. Joseph Estrada, a populist and former film actor who served as mayor of San Juan and in the Senate. The Lakas party, the party of Ramos but not of Estrada, elected its candidate for vice president and won a majority in the lower house of Congress.

India and Pakistan Conduct Nuclear Tests—India and Pakistan, 2 neighbors and longtime adversaries, alarmed the world in May by conducting nuclear tests. On **May 11** and **13**, India conducted 5 underground tests in the Thar Desert in the state of Rajasthan. The tests were enthusiastically welcomed in India. Prime Min. Atal Bihari Vajpayee—who had taken office in March at the head of a Hindu nationalist government—wrote to Pres. Bill Clinton, **May 11**, saying he was concerned about China, especially its military aid to Pakistan, India's Muslim neighbor. He said, **May 12**, that there was no release of radioactivity into the atmosphere from the tests. Clinton announced, **May 13**, that he would impose economic sanctions against India, as required by the 1994 Nuclear Proliferation Prevention Act. A number of other leading donor countries indicated they would cut aid to India.

On **May 28**, Pakistan conducted 5 underground nuclear tests at its Chagai Hills test sites in the southwest. Prime Min. Nawaz Sharif said no radiation had entered the atmosphere. As with India, many countries deplored the testing. On **May 28**, Clinton imposed economic sanctions on Pakistan, and some leading nations announced, **May 28**, that they would cut back economic aid. Pakistan conducted another nuclear test, **May 30**.

Group of 8 Leaders Hold Annual Summit—Heads of government of major world powers, now referred to collectively as the Group of 8, opened their 24th annual meeting **May 15**, in Birmingham, England. Russia was a formal participant for the 1st time. Recent crucial events in Asia monopolized the attention of the leaders. On **May 15**, they condemned India for its testing of nuclear weapons. The G-8 leaders appealed to Pakistan not to respond to India's action by conducting its own nuclear tests. The summit leaders also urged Pres. Suharto of Indonesia to take peaceful steps to end massive public protests.

General

12-Billion-Year-Old Cosmic Explosion Observed—Astronomers from several countries reported, **May 6**, that they had seen evidence of an enormous and intense explosion that occurred 12 billion years ago at the far edge of the universe. In December 1997, 2 satellite observatories had recorded a burst of gamma rays coming from the direction of the constellation Ursa Major. As the rays faded, observers at the California Institute of Technology saw a previously unknown galaxy where the explosion had occurred. Astronomers suggested the explosion might have been caused when a black hole collided with another black hole or with a neutron star.

Singer Frank Sinatra Dies—Fans worldwide mourned the death of Frank Sinatra—regarded as one of the greatest popular singers and most successful entertainers of all time—who died at 82 after suffering a heart attack, **May 14**, in Los Angeles. Sinatra gained fame as a crooner in the early 1940s. His popularity declined amid allegations of associations with organized-crime figures, but he reemerged in the 1950s and 1960s, reinventing himself as a sophisticated swinger, the hard-drinking tough guy with a romantic streak who led Hollywood's "Rrat Pack." Besides performing and recording numerous albums and songs that became standards—including "All the Way," "It Was a Very Good Year," "My Way," and "Strangers in the Night"—he appeared in 58 motion pictures, winning an Oscar for supporting actor in the 1953 film *From Here to Eternity*.

TV Hit *Seinfeld* Ends—The NBC television show *Seinfeld*, on since 1991, aired its final episode **May 14**. The tightly plotted comedy—by far the most popular TV sitcom of the 1990s—revolved around the lives of 4 neurotic New York City friends. The final show was seen by an estimated 76 million people, though its audience rating of 41.3 (percent of TV households tuned in) was well behind many high-rated programs in TV history.

Photo Seems to Show Planet Outside Solar System—Digitized pictures taken by the Hubbell Space Telescope appeared to include an image of a planet outside the solar system, astronomers announced **May 28**. The planet, named TMR-1C, appeared near 2 stars, in the constellation Taurus, that were circling each other. Dr. Susan Tereby, head of the discovery team, said the trail of light from the double star to the planet indicated that the planet was hurtling away from the stars. Up to 8 extrasolar planetary systems had been identified in the previous 3 years, but no image had been made of a planet before. TMR-1C was found to be very hot, several times larger than Jupiter, and unlikely to support life. The double star and the planet are 450 light years from Earth.

JUNE 1998

National

Supreme Court Rebuffs Prosecutor in Intern Case—A legal confrontation between Pres. Bill Clinton and Kenneth Starr, the independent counsel investigating his association with former White House intern Monica Lewinsky and other matters, continued in June. Clinton, **June 1**, did back off on one point, deciding not to carry his claim of executive privilege to the Supreme Court, although he was continuing to press his claim of attorney-client privilege in an attempt to prevent White House lawyers from testifying in Starr's probe. Starr, **June 2**, asked the Supreme Court to expedite its review of both the attorney-client and Secret Service privileges that had been claimed by Clinton; he was turned down **June 4**. Lewinsky, **June 2**, dropped her lawyer, William Ginsburg, a specialist in medical malpractice, and retained 2 criminal lawyers, Jacob Stein and Plato Cacheris. On **June 9**, they began discussions with Starr's office aimed at obtaining immunity from prosecution in return for her testimony before Starr's grand jury.

Starr, in a magazine article released **June 13**, said he and one of his deputies had given reporters information about his investigation. Clinton's lawyers had argued that Starr had violated grand jury secrecy rules by leaking information to reporters. Starr contended that the information they provided was not actual grand jury testimony. Meanwhile, Linda Tripp, who had taped conversations in which Lewinsky extensively described an affair with Clinton, made her first appearance before the grand jury on **June 30**.

Big-Spending Candidates Lose in California—Two wealthy Democratic candidates who had spent a great deal of their own money were defeated in the open primary for governor of California, **June 2**. They were Al Checchi, a businessman, and U.S. Rep. Jane Harman, who received 12.7% and 12.3% of the vote, respectively. Checchi had put up $40 million of his own money, much of it for negative TV ads, and Harman had spent $16 million, most of it her own. The 2 top vote-getters were Lt. Gov. Gray Davis, a Democrat (34.9%), and Attorney Gen. Dan Lungren, a Republican (33.6%), who would now face each other in the November general election.

In other California results, Sen. Barbara Boxer (D) received 44.1% of the vote in the open primary for Senate, to oppose the top Republican vote-getter, State Treasurer Matt Fong (22%), in November. Former Gov. Jerry Brown was elected mayor of Oakland. In a referendum, voters, 61% to 39%, eliminated the state's bilingual education system, which critics said stunted the opportunities for immigrant children to find jobs requiring English skills.

Nichols Gets Life in Oklahoma Bombing—Terry Nichols, convicted in 1997 of conspiracy in connection with the 1995 bombing of a federal building in Oklahoma City, was sentenced **June 4** to life in prison without the possibility of parole. U.S. District Judge Richard Matsch also sentenced Nichols to 8 consecutive 6-year terms for his conviction for manslaughter in the deaths of 8 federal agents in the bombing. Nichols's lawyer, **June 4**, filed a motion seeking a new trial because of alleged juror misconduct.

Unemployment Rate Remains Low—The Labor Dept. reported, **June 5**, that the unemployment rate had been unchanged in May at 4.3%. Alan Greenspan, chairman of the Federal Reserve Board, said, **June 10**, that the economy was in good shape and that there was no need to raise interest rates to check inflation. There were warning signs, though, of a possible acceleration of inflation. The Labor Dept. said, **June 12**, that prices charged by manufacturers and farmers for finished goods had risen by 0.2% in May. It also reported, **June 16**, that consumer prices had risen 0.3% in May, the largest jump in 17 months. Meanwhile, the Commerce Dept. said, **June 18**, that the trade deficit had climbed to $14.46 billion in April, another record high. The decline in the value of the yen against the dollar had left U.S. goods more expensive for the Japanese to buy.

Senate Defeats $516 Billion Tobacco Bill—The Senate in June effectively killed the tobacco bill that had been the subject of intense negotiations and debate for a year. In 1997, the attorneys general of a number of states had reached a settlement with the tobacco companies that aimed to recoup state medical-insurance costs for smoking-related illnesses and also reduce smoking by teenagers. At that time the cost to the companies had been put at $368.5 billion over 25 years. In April 1998, a Senate committee adopted a tougher bill, with the projected cost to the industry rising to $516 billion. Under the new provisions, the U.S. Food and Drug Administration could regulate tobacco products, and the federal tax on a pack of cigarettes would reach $1.10 over 5 years. The Senate adopted several amendments that had seemed likely to improve the bill's chances of passage. For example, on **June 10**, the Senate approved an amendment providing that one-third of higher tax revenues from cigarettes go to tax breaks for married couples and the self-employed. On **June 17**, the Senate voted, 57-42, in favor of cutting off debate on the bill and bringing it to a vote, but this was 3 votes short of the 60 required. Supporters of the bill then failed in an effort to prevent the bill from being returned to committee.

On **June 10**, a jury in Jacksonville, FL, found Brown & Williamson Tobacco Corp. to be liable in the death of a smoker who had lung cancer. The jury awarded his family $950,000, including $450,000 in punitive damages, the 1st such assessment in a smoking-related lawsuit.

Another Telecommunications Merger Announced—AT&T, **June 24**, announced its plan to acquire Tele-Communications, Inc., a cable TV company. The companies would unite by means of a stock transaction valued at $37.3 billion. AT&T could now utilize TCI cable lines to compete in the local telephone-service market.

Supreme Court Strikes Down Line-Item Veto—The Supreme Court, **June 25**, ruled that the 1996 Line-Item Veto Act, which allowed the president to eliminate specific items from a spending or tax bill, was unconstitutional. The Court's 6-3 ruling came in the case of *Clinton* v. *City of New York*, which consolidated challenges to 2 line-item vetoes Pres. Bill Clinton had issued in 1997. The justices held that the act upset the constitutionally prescribed balance of power between the executive and legislative branches of government. Since 1997, Clinton had used the veto in an attempt to eliminate 82 items in 11 laws.

Whitewater Figure Freed From Prison—Susan McDougal, a former business partner of then-Gov. Bill Clinton and Hillary Rodham Clinton who had been convicted of bank fraud in connection with their Whitewater investment, was freed from prison, **June 25**. She had served 18 months for refusing to testify before a grand jury looking into the Whitewater affair, and had served 2 months of her 2-year sentence for fraud. She had been indicted again in May for refusing to cooperate with the Whitewater investigation headed by Kenneth Starr. In releasing McDougal, U.S. District Judge George Howard Jr. said that she suffered from curvature of the spine, which had been aggravated during her confinement. She was placed under home detention for 3 months.

"Unknown Soldier" Identified—A casualty of the Vietnam War, who had been buried at the Tomb of the Unknown Soldier in Arlington, VA, in 1984, was identified **June 30**. A Defense Dept. report had concluded that the serviceman was likely 1 of 9 reported missing near An Loc, South Vietnam, in 1972. The remains were removed from the tomb and underwent a form of DNA testing not available until 1995. Defense Sec. William Cohen then announced that the remains had been identified as those of Air Force Lt. Michael Blassie of St. Louis. The remains were returned to his family for burial on **July 11**.

International

Economic Fallout From Nuclear Blasts Continues—International sanctions imposed in May against India and Pakistan after they exploded nuclear devices had an ongoing impact in June. The Karachi Stock Exchange fell more than 12% on **June 1**, for a cumulative decline of almost 40% since India had conducted its first test 3 weeks earlier. World Bank directors said, **June 2**, that they would delay $206 million in loans to India. Retired U.S. Adm. David Jeremiah issued a report, **June 2**, on the failure of the U.S. intelligence community to foresee the nuclear tests by India. He said the CIA and other agencies had few spies in India and relied too much on machines, rather than people, to gather information. The 5 major nuclear powers (the United States, Russia, China, France, and Great Britain), **June 4**, renewed their appeal for India and Pakistan to stop development of nuclear arms and offered to help the 2 antagonists resolve their confrontation over the disputed Kashmir region.

Pakistan, **June 11**, announced a moratorium on future nuclear testing, and Prime Min. Nawaz Sharif announced austerity measures to contend with the international sanctions. He said the government would take 1 million acres of farmland from the wealthy and redistribute it to the poor. Ministers of leading industrial nations met in London, **June 12**, and agreed to continue pressuring financial institutions to withhold loans to India and Pakistan.

NATO Warns Serbia on Kosovo Violence—The North Atlantic Treaty Organization signaled its displeasure in June with the level of violence that the Yugoslav republic of Serbia was directing at its rebellious province of Kosovo. The fighting in Kosovo sent up to 10,000 ethnic Albanians fleeing from Kosovo into neighboring Albania in late May and early June. More than 200 people had been killed in the province in fighting since February. The ethnic Albanian leader Ibrahim Rugova met with UN Sec. Gen. Kofi Annan in New York City, **June 1**. The ethnic Albanian delegates pulled out of peace talks with Serbia, **June 5**, because of the ongoing crackdown on Kosovo by Serb police units. On **June 8**, the United States and the European Union banned investments in Serbia and froze Serbian and Yugoslav assets in accounts outside Yugoslavia. EU foreign ministers, **June 8**, urged NATO and the UN to consider military action against the Serbs in Kosovo. On **June 15**, about 80 military aircraft from 13 NATO countries flew over Albania and Macedonia, within 15 miles of the Yugoslav border. Later that day, Russia criticized the display of force. On **June 16**, Pres. Slobodan Milosevic of Yugoslavia indicated a willingness to resume talks with Rugova, and he agreed to allow international relief groups to enter battered areas of Kosovo.

New South Korean President Tours U.S.—Pres. Kim Dae Jung of South Korea began a 9-day tour of the United States, **June 6**, aimed especially at promoting investment. He met with Pres. Bill Clinton in Washington, DC, **June 9**, and in a joint press conference urged flexibility in relations with North Korea, advocating incentives to help open up the reclusive and impoverished Communist regime. Addressing Congress, **June 10**, he again called for an easing of sanctions against North Korea.

Gen. Abacha, Ruler of Nigeria, Dies—Gen. Sani Abacha, who had ruled Nigeria with an iron hand since seizing power in a military coup in 1993, died, **June 8**, at age 54, reportedly of a heart attack. Although Nigeria contains large oil reserves, the economy had declined since 1997, ironically because of an internal oil shortage caused by mismanagement and corruption. The Abacha regime's execution of 9 advocates of reform in 1995 had prompted international denunciations. Opponents of Abacha, **June 8**, called for the installation of Moshood Abiola, among political rivals imprisoned by Abacha, as head of a civilian government. Abiola apparently won a 1993 presidential election but was barred from taking office. Gen. Abdulsalam Abubakar, who was sworn in as Nigeria's new military ruler, **June 9**, promised a transition to democracy. On **June 15**, he ordered the release from prison of 9 of Abacha's political opponents.

Clinton-Jiang Summit Held in Beijing—The much-debated visit to China by Pres. Bill Clinton began in late

June, not long after evidence emerged that China may have sought to influence the result of the 1996 presidential election. Clinton argued, **June 11**, that isolating China would harm the cause of human rights there. On **June 24**, Clinton said the Chinese had erred in denying visas to 3 journalists who were to cover the trip for Radio Free Asia.

Clinton arrived in China, **June 25**. Before attending a summit meeting with Pres. Jiang Zemin, **June 27**, he was welcomed by an honor guard in Tiananmen Square, a site associated with bloody repression of prodemocracy demonstrators in 1989. After the 2 met in the Great Hall of the People, they held a joint news conference broadcast live on Chinese television. Clinton criticized the 1989 crackdown, while Jiang contended that routing the demonstrators, mostly students, had ensured China's current stability. Replying to an appeal by Clinton, Jiang said he would be willing to talk with the Dalai Lama, the exiled spiritual leader of Tibet, if the latter would accept Tibet and Taiwan as parts of China. Jiang denied that China had backed the Democratic Party financially in 1996. The presidents announced that they had agreed not to aim nuclear weapons at each other, and both promised not to sell India and Pakistan missiles that could deliver nuclear weapons. China said that the U.S. could inspect facilities to ensure that high-tech equipment sold to China was not being diverted to military use.

First Lady Hillary Rodham Clinton, **June 27**, met with women's rights activists. U.S. and Chinese representatives, **June 29**, announced business deals involving sales to China by Boeing, IBM, and General Electric. Clinton spoke at Beijing University, **June 29**, and his appeal for liberty and human rights was carried live on Chinese television. In Shanghai, he answered questions from callers on a radio talk show, **June 30**.

Opposition Leader Wins Colombian Presidency—On **June 21**, Andrés Pastrana Arango of the Conservative Party was elected president of Colombia by a narrow margin. Neither Pastrana nor Liberal Party candidate Horacio Serpa Uribe had won a majority in **May 31** elections, necessitating the June runoff. The new president had studied international affairs at Harvard, served as mayor of Bogotá, and won election to the Senate in 1991. After losing the 1994 presidential election to Pres. Ernesto Samper Pizano, Pastrana had produced tapes indicating that Samper had received $6 million in campaign funds from the Cali drug cartel. In his campaign, Pastrana promised to hold talks with leftist rebels, cut the fiscal deficit, and lower the value-added tax.

General

Bulls Beat Jazz Again for NBA Title—The Chicago Bulls won their 6th NBA title in 8 years and 3d in a row **June 14**, defeating the Utah Jazz in the championship round for the 2d year in a row. Earlier, the Bulls had reached the finals by outlasting the Indiana Pacers in a 7-game series, and Utah had advanced by sweeping the Los Angeles Lakers. Michael Jordan of the Bulls, who had been named Most Valuable Player for the regular season, was also named MVP for the playoffs.

Detroit Sweeps to Victory—The Detroit Red Wings, **June 16**, won the National Hockey League's Stanley Cup for the 2d straight year by completing a 4-game sweep of the Washington Capitals, with a score of 4-1 in the final game. It was also the team's 2d consecutive sweep in the finals. Steve Yzerman, the Red Wings' captain, was named MVP for the playoffs.

Africa Bears Brunt of AIDS Epidemic—Statistics released, **June 23**, by the UN showed that HIV, the virus that causes AIDS, was by far most prevalent in Africa, a continent that was home to 2 of every 3 of those infected. In 1997, some 21 million infected people lived in Africa, out of a world total of 30.6 million. In Botswana and Zimbabwe, 1 of every 4 adults was infected. In 1997, 5.8 million people worldwide were newly infected, and 2.3 million died of AIDS-related diseases. Since the epidemic began, about 11.7 million people worldwide had died. A later report released **Oct. 28** noted that in the 29 hardest-hit African countries, average life expectancy was now abut 47 years—7 years less than would have been expected in the absence of AIDS.

JULY 1998

National

Hubbell Indictment Thrown Out—Kenneth Starr, the independent counsel investigating the Whitewater affair, suffered a rebuff, **July 1**, when U.S. District Court Judge James Robertson threw out an indictment of Webster Hubbell, a friend of Pres. Bill Clinton and Hillary Rodham Clinton. Hubbell, who had served as associate attorney general in 1993-94, had been convicted of embezzlement in 1994, and in April, Starr had indicted him, his wife, and 2 advisers on new tax evasion charges. Robertson held that Starr was on a "quintessential fishing expedition" and that the tax charges were outside Starr's mandate to investigate the Clintons' financial dealings. The judge also held that the new indictment was invalid because it was based on information Hubbell had supplied under an improper subpoena from Starr. The judge also threw out indictments of the 3 others.

Secret Service Agents Testify About Intern—U.S. Secret Service agents testified in July before a grand jury concerning a possible relationship between Pres. Bill Clinton and former White House intern Monica Lewinsky. The Secret Service had sought to establish a new privilege against testifying, but a 3-judge panel of the U.S. Court of Appeals for the District of Columbia, **July 7**, upheld a ruling in May by U.S. District Judge Norma Holloway Johnson that its agents may be required to do so. Independent counsel Kenneth Starr subpoenaed a number of Secret Service agents, **July 14**. The same day, Attorney Gen. Janet Reno sought a hearing on the issue before the full Court of Appeals. This was rejected **July 16**, after which the Justice Dept. filed 2 motions with the Supreme Court.

Starr, **July 16**, stated in a filing to the Supreme Court that he had "information that Secret Service personnel may have observed . . . crimes . . . in and around the White House complex." U.S. Chief Justice William Rehnquist, **July 17**, did not bar agents from testifying, though he indicated that the high court would likely consider the case in the fall. The subpoenaed agents did testify, starting on **July 17**.

The same day, Starr issued a subpoena to Clinton to appear before the grand jury. No sitting president had ever been subpoenaed to appear before a federal grand jury. Starr impaneled a 2d grand jury in Washington, and it began hearing testimony, **July 23**. On **July 29**, Starr agreed to withdraw Clinton's subpoena so the president could say he cooperated voluntarily. It was agreed that Clinton would provide videotaped testimony at the White House, with his lawyers present. On **July 30**, Starr gave the FBI a dress that Lewinsky had given to him that she reportedly said had traces of Clinton's semen. The FBI, **July 31**, confirmed that genetic tests were being done on the dress.

A 3-judge panel of the U.S. Court of Appeals for the District of Columbia, **July 27**, denied, 2-1, Clinton's claim of attorney-client privilege.

Lewinsky, **July 27**, met with members of the prosecution team, and on **July 28** she agreed to testify before the grand jury in return for immunity. The prosecution also granted immunity to her mother, Marcia Lewis, in whom she reportedly confided. Linda Tripp, Lewinsky's former friend who had secretly taped their phone conversations, appeared for her 8th and final day of testimony, **July 29**.

Breast-Implant Lawsuit Close to Resolution—A tentative settlement was reported **July 8** between Dow Corning Corp. and lawyers for 170,000 women who claimed they had become ill from the company's silicone breast implants. The company was reorganizing under bankruptcy proceedings brought on by the lawsuits. Dow, while denying that the implants caused disease, agreed to an outline of a settlement under which it would pay women alleging injuries some $3.2 billion, usually from $12,000 to $60,000 each. Meanwhile, a panel of British scientists reported, **July 14**, they had found no evidence that the implants cause disease. The implants were still available in Great Britain, though not in the United States.

Four "Freemen" Convicted of Fraud—Four leaders of the Montana Freemen were convicted, **July 8**, in U.S. District Court in Billings, MT, of conspiring to defraud 4 banks. The antigovernment, antitax organization had gained notoriety in 1996 during an 81-day confrontation with authorities at their compound near Jordan, MT. Prosecutors charged that 12 defendants had tried to pass 3,432 bogus checks for $15.5 billion, as part of an effort to disrupt the U.S. banking system. The jury did not reach a verdict on 8 other defendants.

IRS Reform Bill Becomes Law—The Senate passed a bill on **July 9** to reform the way the Internal Revenue Service operates. (The House had approved the bill on **June 25**.) Congress acted in response to widespread complaints of alleged abuse of taxpayers by the IRS, many of them expressed in testimony at congressional hearings. The bill created a 9-member oversight board. In many cases, the burden of proof in civil tax cases would now shift from the taxpayer to the IRS. Accountants and tax advisers were to be covered by the attorney-client privacy privilege. Taxpayers would now be able to sue the government for IRS negligence. The bill, which also liberalized the capital gains tax, was signed by the president **July 22**.

Stocks Continue Advance—The Dow Jones Industrial Average, **July 17**, closed at an all-time high of 9337.97, its 28th record finish in 1998. The economy continued to be fairly strong. However, unemployment rose from May's 28-year low to 4.5% in June, as reported by the Labor Dept., **July 2**. And the Commerce Dept. said, **July 31**, that gross domestic product had grown at an annual rate of only 1.4% in the 2d quarter, a sharp decline from the revised first-quarter rate of 5.5%. The Labor Dept. said, **July 10**, that producer prices had resumed a downward trend in June, declining 0.1%. It also said, **July 14**, that consumer prices had risen only a modest 0.1%.

Clinton Vetoes Savings for School Costs—Pres. Bill Clinton, **July 21**, vetoed a bill that would have allowed parents to put $2,000 per child per year into special savings accounts that would accrue tax-free interest and could be used to pay private-school tuition, buy school books, and meet other school expenses. Clinton, in his veto message, contended that 70% of the benefits of the bill would have gone to the wealthiest 20% of Americans.

Two Police Officers Shot to Death in Capitol—Two U.S. Capitol Police officers were killed by a gunman, **July 24**, at the Capitol in Washington, DC. Entering the building at a visitors' entrance in midafternoon, the gunman set off a metal detector. He then shot Officer Jacob Chestnut in the head and ran to the suite of Rep. Tom DeLay (R, TX), the House Majority Whip, where he exchanged shots with Special Agent John Gibson. Both police officers were fatally wounded. Police then apprehended the gunman, identified as Russell E. Weston Jr.; Sen. Bill Frist (R, TN), a doctor, provided aid to Weston, who underwent surgery later in the day and survived. A tourist also was wounded in the shooting. Weston had been diagnosed as a paranoid schizophrenic and had spent time in a mental hospital. On **July 27**, he was charged with murder in U.S. District Court in Washington. Gibson and Chestnut were buried with military honors in Arlington National Cemetery, **July 30** and **31**, respectively.

Bell Atlantic and GTE Agree to Merge—In another proposed merger in the telecommunications industry, Bell Atlantic Corp. announced, **July 28**, that it planned to absorb GTE Corp. Bell Atlantic was one of the "Baby Bells" granted regional monopolies after the breakup of AT&T in 1984. GTE was a major independent provider of phone service. Together, Bell Atlantic and GTE had more than 250,000 employees and combined 1997 revenues of $53 billion. They would control one-third, or 63 million, of the nation's local telephone access links. The merger was subject to federal approval.

General Motors, Workers Reach Settlement—A costly 54-day strike against General Motors by 2 locals of the United Auto Workers union came to an end **July 29**. Some 9,200 workers in 2 plants in Flint, MI, had struck in June, ostensibly over health and safety concerns but apparently also because of fear of layoffs and plant closings. A ripple effect caused 27 GM assembly plants to close, with nearly 200,000 workers idle at one time or another. Losses to GM were put at $12 billion in sales. Negotiators for GM and the UAW locals announced a settlement, **July 28**. GM agreed not to close 3 plants in Flint and Dayton, OH, and to fulfill a commitment to invest $180 million in a Flint metal-stamping plant. The UAW agreed to an increase in the production quota at that plant. The locals voted to ratify the agreement, **July 29**.

International

Clinton Completes Visit to China—Continuing his tour of China, Pres. Bill Clinton was interviewed by China's state-run television network during a visit to the Shanghai Stock Exchange, **July 1**. In Guilin, **July 2**, he said the United States would give financial aid to help China monitor air quality and develop clean energy sources. Beginning the first visit ever to Hong Kong by an incumbent president, Clinton landed at the new Chek Lap Kok airport, **July 2**. On **July 3**, he praised Chinese Pres. Jiang Zemin and Prem. Zhu Rongji for being committed to reform. The president and his wife and daughter, who had accompanied him, left for the United States **July 3**.

Renewed Irish Violence Fatal to 3 Brothers—A dispute over the route of a parade planned for **July 5** led to widespread violence in Northern Ireland. British authorities, **June 29**, had barred the (Protestant) Orange Order from passing through a Catholic neighborhood during its annual parade in Portadown. The parade, scheduled for **July 5**, celebrated the anniversary of a 1690 military victory by Protestants over Catholics. Violence broke out on **July 5** during the parade, and within the next 4 days, 44 police officers were wounded during hundreds of incidents initiated by angry Protestants. In Ballymoney, **July 12**, a firebomb thrown at a public-housing complex killed 3 Catholic brothers, ages 9 to 11. Police said, **July 13**, that they had arrested 2 men in connection with the attack. Orange Order members held their annual parades in Belfast and elsewhere, **July 13**. An additional man was charged in the deaths of the brothers, **July 21**.

Nigerian Opposition Leader Dies in Prison—Moshood Abiola, a leader of the opposition in Nigeria, died **July 7**, just a month after the death of Nigeria's military ruler, Gen. Sani Abacha. In 1993 Abiola had appeared about to win the presidential election, but the country's military rulers annulled it and put him in prison. On **July 1**, UN Sec. Gen. Kofi Annan had met with Abiola, who reportedly promised to renounce his claim to the presidency upon release from prison. Instead, while meeting with U.S. diplomats, Abiola collapsed, dying several hours later. Members of his Yoruba tribe, suspecting foul play, engaged in violent demonstrations, and within 3 days, 45 people had died in Lagos. Gen. Abdulsalam Abubakar, **July 8**, appealed for calm and promised to establish a democratic government. He dissolved his cabinet, **July 8**, leaving Nigeria in the hands of a Provisional Ruling Council, also military-controlled. Doctors from Western countries performed an autopsy on Abiola and announced the conclusion, **July 11**, that he had died from heart disease.

Abubakar, **July 15**, dismantled the structure Abacha had set up to accomplish his supposed transition to civilian rule. On **July 20**, he canceled the result of regional elections that he said lacked credibility, dissolved 5 legal political parties that had dutifully nominated Abacha for president, said he would free all political prisoners jailed by the previous regime, and said new parties could nominate candidates for national elections in 1999. Abubakar promised to pay $630 million that the country owed international oil corporations doing business there.

Ex-Premier of Italy Convicted Twice More—Silvio Berlusconi, premier of Italy for 7 months in 1994, was convicted, **July 7**, by a jury in Milan of bribing government inspectors in order to gain favorable tax audits of his businesses. He was sentenced to 2 years and 9 months in prison. Berlusconi had also been found guilty of violating campaign-finance laws in 1997. In a separate case, on **July 13** in Milan, he was convicted for illegally giving $12 million to then-Prem. Bettino Craxi in 1991; for this, he drew 2 years and 4 months in prison and fined $5.6 million. Craxi, who was in Tunisia, was convicted, **July 13**, in absentia for his role in handling the funds.

Economic Woes End Premier's Rule in Japan—Japan's Prem. Ryutaro Hashimoto resigned **July 13** a day after voters dealt his Liberal Democratic Party a setback in elections to the upper house of the Diet. The LDP won only 44 of the 126 seats at stake in the House of Councillors. With another 126 seats not up for election, the LDP still held a plurality over other parties. The LDP also held a majority in the lower house of the Diet, which chose the premier, but Hashimoto decided to step down. Japan's economy had been in a long slump.

As a stepping-stone to the premiership, Foreign Min. Keizo Obuchi was elected president of the LDP, **July 24**. Obuchi, **July 29**, said Kiichi Miyazawa, a former premier, would serve as finance minister; he named the rest of his cabinet **July 30**, the day that he was named premier by the Diet. The new premier, who has a degree in English literature, had served in the Diet since 1963.

Congress Eases Sanctions on India, Pakistan—The United States in July made a major exception to sanctions imposed on India and Pakistan after they tested nuclear devices in May. The House and Senate, by voice vote, **July 14**, approved a bill to allow U.S. farmers to win a contract on 385,000 tons of wheat for Pakistan. Both India and Pakistan were major purchasers of U.S. wheat, and the current contract was valued at more than $40 million. Going a step farther, the Senate, **July 15**, approved a bill allowing Pres. Bill Clinton to waive any other sanctions on the 2 countries that were required under a 1994 law.

Serbs Open New Offensive in Kosovo—Serbs opened a new military push against Kosovo, **July 24**, and occupied several former rebel strongholds. As many as 30,000 ethnic Albanians fled from their homes. Yugoslav Pres. Slobodan Milosevic said, **July 30**, that the offensive was over, though fighting was still reported.

Cambodia Leader's Party Wins Election—The party of Hun Sen, the leader of Cambodia, won an election for seats in the National Assembly. UN observers of the election said, **July 25**, that during the campaign there had been hundreds of murders and beatings of voters supporting opposition candidates. In the voting, **July 26**, Hun Sen's Cambodian People's Party won 41% of the vote and 64 of 122 seats in the assembly. The Funcinpec party led by Prince Norodom Ranariddh, whom Hun Sen had forced from power in 1997, received 32% and about 43 seats. Hun Sen, **July 30**, asked both Ranariddh and Sam Rainsy, leader of the 3d-place party, which gained 15 seats, to join him in a coalition government.

General

Sampras, Novotna Win Wimbledon Titles—Pete Sampras of the United States and Jana Novotna of the Czech Republic won the singles tennis titles at Wimbledon in July. Novotna, seeded 3d and reaching the final for the 3d time, won her first women's title, **July 4**, by defeating Nathalie Tauziat of France, 6-4, 7-6. The top-seeded Sampras won his 5th men's title, **July 5**, equaling the record of Bjorn Borg. He defeated Goran Ivanisevic of Croatia, 6-7, 7-6, 6-4, 3-6, 6-2.

Man Found Guilty of Killing Cosby's Son—Mikail Markhasev, 19, was found guilty of first-degree murder by a Los Angeles jury, **July 7**, in the killing of Ennis Cosby, son of comedian Bill Cosby. Markhasev, a Russian immigrant, was also found guilty of attempted robbery. Cosby, 27, had been changing a tire on a Los Angeles freeway exit ramp in January 1997 when he was fatally shot.

France Wins World Cup in Upset—France won the World Cup soccer tournament, **July 12**, with a 3-0 upset of defending champion Brazil before a stadium crowd of 80,000 and an estimated worldwide TV audience of 1.7 billion. France, which had never won the world championship before, played host to the 1998 tournament. The title game was played in the Paris suburb of St.-Denis. In the elimination rounds involving 16 teams, France had barely survived until the final game, defeating Paraguay, 1-0, in overtime; Italy, 4-3, on penalty kicks after neither team scored during the regular game; and Croatia, 2-1. Against Brazil, a perennial soccer power, France led 2-0, at halftime on 2 goals by midfielder Zinedine Zidane. France's team, coached by Aime Jacquet, included players from the home country as well as players of African, Arab, and Caribbean origins.

AUGUST 1998

National

Economic Indicators Decline; Dow Drops—The Conference Board (a business-research organization) reported, **Aug. 4**, that the leading economic indicators had declined slightly in June for the 2d consecutive month. The Labor Dept. said, **Aug. 7**, that unemployment had held steady at 4.5% in July but that only 66,000 new jobs had been created—the lowest monthly expansion in 2 ½ years. The department also reported that consumer prices had risen 0.2% in July. The Commerce Dept. reported that the trade deficit had narrowed to $14.15 billion in June. On **Aug. 31**, the Dow Jones Industrial Average fell 512.61 points, the 2d-biggest 1-day point drop yet, and closed at 7539.07, almost 1,800 points below its July peak.

Biggest Oil Industry Merger Announced—British Petroleum PLC announced, **Aug. 11**, that it would merge with Amoco Corp., in what was, in effect, the largest takeover ever of a U.S. company by a foreign company. If approved, the $54.3 billion merger would be the largest ever in the oil industry.

Young Boys Found Guilty of Killing 5—On **Aug. 11**, 2 schoolboys were found to be "delinquent," or guilty, on charges of murder and capital battery in the fatal March shootings of 4 students and a teacher in Jonesboro, AR. Ten others had been wounded in a barrage of gunfire from trees near their middle school. The defendants, Mitchell Johnson and Andrew Golden, had been 13 and 11, respectively, at the time of the shootings. The judge sent them to a juvenile detention center; the length of their sentences was in the discretion of the state agency operating the center.

Clinton Testifies, Admits Inappropriate Behavior—In testimony provided to a grand jury, and in a television address to the nation, Pres. Bill Clinton acknowledged, **Aug.**

17, that he had had an inappropriate relationship with a former White House intern, Monica Lewinsky. Clinton was the first president to testify before a grand jury investigating potential criminal actions by a president.

Clinton, **Aug. 17**, testified from the Map Room of the White House, while the grand jury watched via live closed-circuit television. His testimony was also recorded on videotape. Although questions posed by the prosecution team and Clinton's answers were not made public at that time, it was known that Starr wanted to ascertain whether Clinton had committed or suborned perjury or obstructed justice to conceal his relationship with Lewinsky.

On the evening of **Aug. 17**, Clinton addressed the American people. In reference to his January deposition in the sexual harassment suit brought by Paula Corbin Jones, a former Arkansas state employee, he claimed he had given "legally accurate" answers to questions about Lewinsky, and merely "did not volunteer information." He said, "I did have a relationship with Miss Lewinsky that was not appropriate. In fact, it was wrong. It constituted a critical lapse in judgment and a personal failure . . . for which I am solely and completely responsible." He acknowledged that he had misled people, including his wife, but asserted that he had not attempted to conceal evidence or asked anyone else to do so. He said he was motivated by a desire to protect himself from embarrassment and to protect his family. Clinton also chastised the Starr investigation, arguing that the inquiry had "gone on too long, cost too much, and hurt too many innocent people." He said it was time "to move on."

Earlier, on **Aug. 3**, a 3-judge panel of the U.S. Court of Appeals for the District of Columbia held that Judge Norma Holloway Johnson could go ahead with an inquiry into whether the office of independent counsel Kenneth Starr had improperly leaked grand jury testimony. On **Aug. 6**, Lewinsky (who had been granted immunity) testified before the grand jury in Washington, DC. Although the proceedings were secret, it was reported that she had testified that she and the president had had an affair in the White House. Johnson, **Aug. 7**, unsealed a ruling in which she ordered Starr's office to show that it had not been leaking grand jury proceedings.

Many administration officials, White House aides, and Democratic officeholders who had supported Clinton's denials of an affair were reported to be embarrassed and angry by Clinton's disclosure. Sen. Orrin Hatch (R, UT), chairman of the Senate Judiciary Committee, said **Aug. 17** that Starr was not the party responsible for the length of the investigation. On **Aug. 18**, Rep. Paul McHale (D, PA) called for Clinton to resign; some Republicans and more than 100 daily newspapers did the same. First Lady Hillary Rodham Clinton said through a spokesperson, **Aug. 18**, that she was "committed to her marriage." The Clintons began a vacation on Martha's Vineyard, **Aug. 18**. Lewinsky testified again, **Aug. 20**.

Preliminary Inquiry of Vice President Begun—Attorney Gen. Janet Reno, **Aug. 26**, asked for a 90-day preliminary investigation into telephone calls made by Vice Pres. Al Gore from the White House. Gore said he thought the calls were to raise so-called soft money that could be used for general party-building activities. He had denied knowing that some of the money he had raised, on federal property, went into "hard money" accounts for use in the 1996 campaign, in violation of an 1883 law. Earlier, on **Aug. 6**, the House Government Reform and Oversight Committee recommended, in a vote along party lines, that Reno be held in contempt of court. The committee—which was also investigating fund-raising endeavors, principally by the Clinton administration—had subpoenaed memorandums sent to Reno by FBI director Louis Freeh and Charles LaBella (who had conducted a Justice Dept. investigation of fund-raising activities) urging Reno to appoint a special prosecutor to look into Democratic fund-raising. Reno had declined to do so and also declined to honor the subpoena. Reno said, **Aug. 6**, that the House committee was interfering in the Justice Dept.'s investigation for political reasons.

International

Iraq Calls Halt to Weapons Inspections—Talks broke down, **Aug. 3**, between Iraqi officials and Richard Butler, head of the United Nations team overseeing the dismantling of Iraq's missiles and chemical and biological weapons. Iraq said, **Aug. 5**, that it would no longer cooperate with UN weapons inspectors and demanded that UN sanctions imposed since 1991 come to an end. The UN Security Council, **Aug. 6**, rejected Iraq's demand but took no other action. That day, Butler reported to the Security Council on a document that the Iraqi government said was a complete disclosure of its biological weapons program. An evaluation by biological experts had found that Iraq's "disclosure" could not be the basis of reliable information. On **Aug. 26**, William Scott Ritter resigned as an American weapons inspector in Iraq. He said failure to be more aggressive in the inspections constituted "a surrender to Iraqi leadership."

Embassy Bombs Kill 224 in Africa; U.S. Strikes Back—Bombs set off by terrorists outside U.S. embassy buildings **Aug. 7** killed 224 people in 2 African countries. At about 10:35 AM, a bomb exploded at the embassy in Nairobi, capital of Kenya. Within a few minutes, a 2d bomb went off at the embassy in Dar-es-Salaam, capital of Tanzania. On **Aug. 8**, Israel sent 170 soldiers trained in rescue operations to Nairobi, but only a few people were brought out alive.

An embassy guard in Nairobi said later that a man had gotten out of a truck at the rear gate and demanded that the guard open the gate. After the man threw something at him that exploded, the latter attempted to alert U.S. Marine guards. The truck then exploded, wrecking the back of the 5-story embassy, demolishing buses and cars on the adjacent avenue, and leveling a building containing offices and a secretarial school. The death toll in Nairobi eventually reached 213, including 12 Americans; more than 540 were hospitalized, and thousands of others were treated and released. Consul Gen. Julian Bartley Sr. and his son were among the Americans killed.

The Dar-es-Salaam bombing, which severely damaged a corner of the 3-story embassy building, claimed 11 lives, all Tanzanians who worked in the building. At least 70 were injured. The means of delivery of the bomb was uncertain.

U.S. antiterrorist investigators began arriving in the 2 capitals on **Aug. 8**. U.S. officials believed that the mastermind of the latest assaults was Osama bin Laden, a wealthy Saudi living in Afghanistan who was suspected of bombing American military facilities in Saudi Arabia in 1995 and 1996. Tanzanian and Kenyan authorities both reported arrests in connection with the bombings. On **Aug. 15**, Pakistan handed over to Kenya a suspect, Mohammed Saddiq Odeh, who reportedly had confessed to involvement; Odeh, an engineer by training, reportedly said that bin Laden led an international force of up to 5,000 Muslim militants armed with missiles, artillery, and tanks. Militant Islamic groups threatened, **Aug. 19**, that the United States would be the target of more attacks.

On **Aug. 20**, the U.S. Navy fired missiles at sites in Afghanistan and Sudan said to be linked with terrorists. Missiles from ships in the Red Sea struck at the Al Shifa Pharmaceutical Industries factory in Khartoum. U.S. officials said they believed components of chemical weapons were manufactured there; Sudan denounced the attack and said the factory produced only medical drugs. From the Arabian Sea, ships fired missiles at targets in a compound in Afghanistan believed part of a terrorist training facility and weapons center. Pres. Bill Clinton announced the strikes in a televised message from the White House. He said that the United States had strong evidence that bin Laden was responsible for the bombings in Africa and that Afghanistan and Sudan had long harbored terrorists.

A suspect arrested by Kenya, Mohamed Rashed Daoud al-Owhali, was flown to New York on **Aug. 27** and arraigned in U.S. District Court on murder and other charges. The complaint charged that al-Owhali had thrown the explosive at the security guard in Nairobi. Odeh was also brought to New York from Kenya and on **Aug. 28** was arraigned on the same charges.

Swiss Banks Settle Holocaust Claims—The 2 largest Swiss banks and representatives of Holocaust survivors and their heirs announced an agreement, **Aug. 12**, on a settlement of claims against the banks. The banks, doubling a previous offer, agreed to compensate Holocaust victims $1.25 billion. That figure represented money deposited in the banks before and during World War II, either by Jews who later were killed or by Nazis who had seized their assets. As part of the agreement, threats of lawsuits and economic sanctions against the banks would be dropped. Most of the money would be paid out to survivors or heirs who could prove that the money was rightfully theirs, and the rest would be provided as reparations for Holocaust survivors worldwide.

Bomb in Northern Ireland Kills 29—An explosion in Omagh, Northern Ireland, **Aug. 15**, initially killed 28 people and injured more than 300; an injured man died in September, bringing the death to 29. Two phoned warnings had said an explosion would occur near the courthouse in Omagh; the actual detonation, however, occurred several hundred yards from the courthouse, where people had gathered after being evacuated from its immediate vicinity. The attack was the worst in 29 years of paramilitary attacks in Northern Ireland and cast a shadow over the peace settlement currently being implemented. Gerry Adams, leader of Sinn Fein, the political wing of the Irish Republican Army, condemned the bombing, **Aug. 16**. Five men were arrested in connection with it, **Aug. 17**. On **Aug. 18**, a splinter group, the Real IRA, claimed responsibility.

Economic Crisis Sinks Another Russian Premier—Pres. Boris Yeltsin of Russia removed his reformist premier Sergei Kiriyenko on **Aug. 23** as the country slipped deeper into economic turmoil. The current phase of the crisis had been precipitated by the sharp decline in the price of oil, the nation's leading export, and by a ripple effect from the Asian downturn that prompted foreign investors to pull back. On **Aug. 17**, the government of Kiriyenko, fearing a run on the banks, decided to allow the ruble to float within a range of 6 to 9.5 to the U.S. dollar, in effect devaluing the ruble. The government also set a 90-day moratorium on the repayment of foreign debt by banks and companies and said it would restructure $60 billion in domestic debt. On **Aug. 20**, the government said it would insure all private bank deposits.

On **Aug. 23**, Yeltsin dismissed Kiriyenko and brought back Viktor Chernomyrdin as acting premier pending the approval of parliament. Powerful business interests, fearing another round of reforms that might cause leading concerns to fail, welcomed Kiriyenko's fall, as did the Communists. As the ruble continued to fall in value, the central bank, **Aug. 26**, stopped trying to prop it up and on **Aug. 27** halted trading in the currency. That day the stock-market index fell by one-sixth. Since the beginning of 1998 it had declined by 84%. As the currency decline reduced the assets of banks, several large banks began to merge.

In the last days of August, equity markets in many countries began to slide, in large part in reaction to the turmoil in Russia and fears of its impact on Latin American economics. Japan's Nikkei index stood at a 12-year low on **Aug. 28**. By **Aug. 31**, U.S. blue chip stocks were off almost 20% from July highs.

On **Aug. 31**, the Duma, Russia's lower house of parliament, rejected Yeltsin's nomination of Chernomyrdin, 251-94. Yeltsin immediately renominated him in hopes of obtaining approval.

SEPTEMBER 1998

National

Justice Dept. Opens Inquiry on Clinton Fund-Raising—Atty. Gen. Janet Reno, **Sept. 8**, set in motion a 90-day preliminary inquiry into Pres. Bill Clinton's participation in a 1996 Democratic advertising campaign. A preliminary audit by the Federal Election Commission had pointed to the possible use of $42 million in "soft" money (supposed to be used for general party-building) to directly support the Clinton-Gore reelection effort. The Justice Dept. inquiry, which concentrated on Clinton's involvement in advertising bought with the money, could lead to the appointment of an independent counsel.

Earlier, on **Sept. 2**, Reno let congressional leaders see parts of a confidential memorandum from Charles LaBella, head of a Justice Dept. inquiry into Democratic fund-raising practices, calling for appointment of an independent counsel to probe further. Reno had initially rejected the recommendation. She had also initially declined to release the memo, which prompted a recommendation by a House committee that she be held in contempt of Congress.

Starr Presents Case for Impeachment of Clinton—On **Sept. 9**, independent counsel Kenneth Starr sent to the House what he called "substantial and credible information . . . that may constitute grounds" for impeaching Pres. Bill Clinton. The 445-page report, which was released by the House, detailed the president's relationship with former White House intern Monica Lewinsky and his alleged perjury and obstruction of justice in seeking to cover it up. The report contained a mass of detail, some of it sexually explicit. Critics of the report denounced the inclusion of such material; defenders argued that such details were needed to clarify whether Clinton had perjured himself in his account of the events in the Paula Corbin Jones deposition and before the grand jury convened by Starr.

Earlier, on **Sept. 2**, while on a visit to Russia, Clinton expressed "profound regret to all who were hurt and to all who were involved." On **Sept. 3**, Sen. Joseph Lieberman (D, CT), a friend of Clinton's for many years, strongly criticized the president for "behavior [that] is not just inappropriate, it is immoral." He added that Clinton's conduct was harmful because it sent a message to Americans, including children, that it was acceptable. After Lieberman's speech, some other Democratic leaders became more direct in their criticism of Clinton. On **Sept. 4**, in Ireland, Clinton said for the first time that he was "sorry" about what he had done. On **Sept. 5**, Gov. Parris Glendening (D, MD) canceled a fund-raising event with Clinton.

On **Sept. 9**, 2 vans from Starr's office arrived on Capitol Hill with 36 boxes of documents, including the report itself and supporting materials. David Kendall, Clinton's lawyer, objected that the president's lawyers had not had a chance to see the materials before they went to the House. Meeting with Democratic leaders in Congress, **Sept. 9** and **10**, and with his cabinet **Sept. 10**, Clinton expressed emotional apologies for having misled them. The House voted, 363-63, on **Sept. 11** to release to the public the text of Starr's report. Speaking to religious leaders, **Sept. 11**, Clinton said he had sinned.

Although Starr had been investigating Clinton for more than 4 years, his report said almost nothing about several other major inquiries. Instead, it concentrated on the Lewinsky story, which had come to his attention only in January 1998.

The report, which was published in many newspapers and on the Internet, spelled out 11 possible grounds for impeachment—allegations that Clinton had committed perjury, obstructed justice, tampered with a witness, and abused his power. It began with a narrative of the relationship between Clinton and Lewinsky, citing 9 occasions when, according to her grand jury testimony, she performed oral sex on him—twice while he talked on the phone. The two reportedly had 10 sexual contacts between 1995 and 1997 near the Oval Office of the White House. The report said that a dress Lewinsky had worn on one occasion had been tested by the FBI and found to contain a trace of Clinton's semen. Lewinsky told the grand jury that the two never had sexual intercourse. The report said the two had talked about 50 times on the phone, sometimes with sexual content, and had exchanged nearly 50 gifts.

The report included the testimony of Betty Currie, the president's private secretary, that the president had asked her and other staff members to find a job for Lewinsky. The latter also said that she had asked Clinton to ask his friend Vernon Jordan to help her get a job. Some of these efforts by Jordan and others took place after the White House was informed that Lewinsky was on a list of witnesses to be called in the case of Paula Corbin Jones, who, to bolster her sexual harassment charges against Clinton, sought to establish that Clinton had engaged in a pattern of misconduct with women.

At one point, according to Lewinsky's testimony, Clinton suggested that she say she was visiting the West Wing of the White House to see Currie. The report said that on one occasion Currie retrieved gifts that Clinton had given to Lewinsky and held them at her own house. After giving a deposition in the Jones case, **Jan. 17**, that appeared to rule out a sexual relationship with Lewinsky, Clinton, according to Currie, called Currie to the White House on Sunday, **Jan. 18**, and asked her leading questions such as "You were always there when she was there, right?" Starr cited this as an example of witness tampering.

Clinton's lawyers, **Sept. 12**, characterized the report as a smear and said the president's conduct, while wrong, fell short of impeachable offenses. The House Judiciary Committee then voted, **Sept. 18**, along party lines, to release the tape of Clinton's grand-jury testimony and 2,800 pages of documents submitted by Starr.

Clinton's videotaped grand jury testimony was shown on television, **Sept. 21**, and lasted more than 4 hours. He repeatedly argued with prosecutors over the meaning of terms, declined to go into details about his conduct with Lewinsky, and stuck by his claim that he had not lied during his January deposition in the Jones case. The president said, "My goal in this deposition was to be truthful, but not particularly helpful." He dismissed suggestions that he had misused his office or suborned perjury. Even as the grand jury tape of his testimony was being shown, Clinton was at the United Nations, where he received a robust standing ovation before making a speech urging greater efforts to fight international terrorism.

In the documents released **Sept. 22**, it was revealed that Lewinsky told the grand jury, "No one ever asked me to lie." She testified that at times she herself had told lies to Linda Tripp, who taped many of their conversations. The Judiciary Committee, **Sept. 25**, voted to release edited texts of the tapes of the Lewinsky-Tripp conversations.

2 Giant Mergers Completed—In the 3d-largest telecommunications merger in U.S. history, WorldCom Inc. purchased MCI communications, **Sept. 14**, to form MCI WorldCom Inc. The deal, first announced in Oct. 1997, was valued at $43.4 billion. On **Sept. 30**, BankAmerica Corp. merged with NationsBank Corp. in a $61.6 billion stock transfer. The new corporation's $572 billion in total assets made it the largest bank in the U.S.

Political Primary Season Nears an End—Several primary elections were held on **Sept. 15**. In the District of Columbia, Anthony Williams, a former chief financial officer for Washington, DC, won the Democratic primary for mayor. In New York, Rep. Charles Schumer won the Democratic nomination for the U.S. Senate, with 51% of the vote. Geraldine Ferraro, the original favorite, who received 26%, said she would not seek office again. Ferraro had been the Democratic nominee for vice president in 1984. Schumer went on to oppose Sen. Alfonse D'Amato, the Republican incumbent. On the same day, Hubert H. Humphrey 3d, son of the former vice president, won the nomination for governor in Minnesota. Humphrey, the state attorney general, ran against St. Paul mayor Norm Coleman, the Republican candidate, and Reform Party candidate Jesse Ventura, a former professional wrestler and former mayor of Brooklyn Park.

Economy Continues to Expand—The Federal Reserve Board said, **Sept. 16**, that the U.S. economy was continuing to expand moderately. The Conference Board (a business-research organization) had reported, **Sept. 1**, that the leading economic indicators rose 0.4% in July. The Labor Dept. said, **Sept. 4**, that unemployment had remained steady at 4.5% in August, with an impressive 365,000 payroll jobs created. On **Sept. 17**, the Commerce Dept. reported a July trade deficit of $13.92 billion and the Labor Dept. reported that consumer prices rose 0.2% in August.

Ban on Late-Term Abortion Procedure Fails—The Senate, **Sept. 18**, sustained a veto by Pres. Bill Clinton of a prohibition on a late-term abortion procedure sometimes called partial-birth abortion. This was the 2d time the Senate had failed to override a veto of the ban. The Senate vote was 64-36, 3 short of the two-thirds needed to override.

House Backs $80 Billion Tax Cut—The House of Representatives, in a 229-195 vote that was largely along party lines **Sept. 26**, approved an $80 billion tax cut, to be paid for out of anticipated federal-budget surpluses. It would give a tax break to middle-income married couples, cut inheritance taxes, and eliminate taxes on some dividend and interest income. While Republicans argued that taxpayers should benefit from any revenue surplus, Pres. Bill Clinton and the Democrats argued that it should go to shoring up Social Security.

The first of a series of projected surpluses became official, **Sept. 30**, the last day of the fiscal year, when Clinton announced a surplus of $70 billion, the first since 1969.

International

Russia Experiences Economic and Political Turmoil—At a summit, **Sept. 1** and **2** in Moscow, between Pres. Boris Yeltsin and Pres. Bill Clinton, Clinton gave little concrete support to Russia in its economic crisis but held out the promise of financial help if Russia stayed on the path of free-market reform. Although the 2 presidents signed minor agreements on nuclear weapons, a deadlock over the Strategic Arms Reduction Treaty (START II) was not resolved. The Russian parliament (Duma) had not ratified the treaty.

Meanwhile, the ruble continued to fall, standing at 13.46 to the dollar on **Sept. 3**. On **Sept. 7**, the Duma rejected, for the 2d time, Yeltsin's nomination of Viktor Chernomyrdin as prime minister, 273-138. Yeltsin then turned to nominating former Foreign Minister Yevgeny Primakov, and on **Sept. 11**, the Duma approved him, 317-63. The son of Jews, he was born in Ukraine, then a part of the Soviet Union, in 1929. He rose through the ranks of the Communist Party and was named foreign minister in 1996. Primakov, **Sept. 11**, named 2 Communists, who he said were now independent of the party, as deputy premier for economic affairs and chairman of the central bank. Primakov's vow to put together a strong economic-policy team ran afoul of several key resignations and the ouster, **Sept. 28**, of Boris Fydorov, the government's leading policy-maker, also seen as the leading reformer.

Clintons Visit Northern Ireland—Pres. Bill Clinton and First Lady Hillary Rodham Clinton traveled to Northern Ireland and the Republic of Ireland. On **Sept. 1**, Gerry

Adams, leader of Sinn Fein, the political wing of the Irish Republican Army, said that Sinn Fein believed that violence in Northern Ireland was "a thing of the past." On **Sept. 3** the president met with leaders of the Northern Ireland Assembly, created under the peace accord signed in April. In Omagh, **Sept. 3**, the Clintons, accompanied by British Prime Min. Tony Blair and his wife, Cherie Booth, met with victims of the August bombing and their relatives. Clinton, who had been instrumental in adoption of the peace accord, was well received during his visit. The extremist "Real IRA," which had broken off from the IRA and claimed responsibility for the bombing, declared a permanent cease-fire, **Sept. 8**. On **Sept. 10**, Adams met for face-to-face talks for the first time with David Trimble, leader of the Protestant Unionists.

Swissair Jet Crashes, Killing 229—On **Sept. 2**, Swissair Flight 111 crashed into the Atlantic Ocean about 5 miles off the coast of Nova Scotia, Canada, killing all 229 on board. The flight had been en route to Geneva, Switzerland, from New York City. Sixteen minutes before the crash, the pilot had radioed air controllers that there was smoke in the cabin from an unidentified source. FBI investigators, **Sept. 3**, reported finding no evidence of sabotage. Canadian investigators, **Sept. 10**, said the retrieved data recorder indicated that many of the plane's electrical systems had malfunctioned shortly before the crash.

Turmoil in World Equity Markets Continues—Stock markets in various nations continued to rise and fall sharply. Alan Greenspan, chairman of the U.S. Federal Reserve Board, said, **Sept. 4**, that the Federal Open Market Committee he headed would seek to stimulate investor optimism and lift corporate profits. He seemed to hold out the possibility that interest rates would be cut. On **Sept. 8**, the next trading day in the U.S., the Dow Jones industrial average surged nearly 5%, or 380.53 points, to close at 8020.78. But it gave up that gain in just 2 days, and on **Sept. 10** stocks in Brazil fell 15% on fears that the currency would be devalued. Stock values in other major Latin American countries quickly declined as well.

U.S. short-term interest rates were cut by the Federal Reserve Board, **Sept. 29**, with the federal funds rate dropping from 5.5% to 5.25%. The objective was to insulate the U.S. economy from the world financial turmoil. On Wall Street, stocks closed at 7842.62 on **Sept. 30**, ending a month of wild swings.

Iran Lifts Threat to Kill Author—At the United Nations, **Sept. 24**, Iranian Foreign Minister Kamal Kharrazi announced that Iran had dropped its 1989 call for the death of British author Salman Rushdie. Rushdie had written a book, *The Satanic Verses,* containing references to Muhammad that many Muslims found blasphemous. The Ayatollah Ruhollah Khomeini had called for Rushdie to be killed, and a large monetary reward had been offered. Great Britain promptly announced that it would resume diplomatic relations with Iran.

German Voters End Kohl's 16-Year Rule—Gerhard Schröder led the Social Democratic Party to victory in the German parliamentary election, **Sept. 27**. The result brought an end to 16 years in power by Chancellor Helmut Kohl and his Christian Democratic Party. Kohl had led the unification of Germany after the collapse of the Berlin Wall and Communism in 1989. However, the East, where the economy remained weak, had not been fully assimilated, and high unemployment and taxes were issues across the country. Schröder emphasized his comparative youth—he was 54 and Kohl 68—and the need for a change of leadership. Schröder needed the votes of the pro-environment Green Party in order to govern. They held 47 seats, while the Social Democrats held 298 seats, in the 656-seat Parliament. In the popular vote, the Social Democrats got 41%, the Christian Democrats 35%, and the Greens 7%. Kohl lost his own seat.

Born in poverty, Schröder became a Marxist student leader and obtained a law degree. He later moved toward the political center and was elected premier of Lower Saxony in 1990. Divorced 3 times, he was married to his 4th wife. Schröder was installed **Oct. 27**, after winning support from Parliament in a 351-287 vote.

General

Davenport, Rafter Win U.S. Open—Lindsay Davenport of the United States, seeded 2d, defeated the defending champion and top seed, Martina Hingis of Switzerland, in the final of the U.S. Open, 6-3, 7-5, on **Sept. 12**. It was Davenport's 1st Grand Slam tennis title. Patrick Rafter of Australia, the 3d seed, successfully defended his title, **Sept. 13**, beating unseeded fellow Australian Marc Philippoussis, 6-3, 3-6, 6-2, 6-0.

Hurricane Devastates Caribbean—Hurricane Georges caused more than $2 billion in damage in Puerto Rico alone, as it pounded the U.S. territory and the island of Hispaniola, home of Haiti and the Dominican Republic, **Sept. 21-23**. The death toll in the Caribbean was put at more than 600 people, with at least 200 of these in the Dominican Republic alone. Many others were reported missing. In the Dominican Republic, large numbers of people were left homeless, and without food or water for days. The storm crossed Cuba **Sept. 24** and battered the Florida Keys **Sept. 25** with 105-miles-per-hour winds. Some 1.4 million people in Florida were ordered to evacuate; 1.5 million were asked to move out in the New Orleans area. The hurricane struck the Gulf Coast **Sept. 27**, spawning tornadoes, then moved east over land, bringing heavy rains and floods to parts of the South. Four U.S. fatalities were reported.

McGwire Sets New Home Run Record of 70—Mark McGwire of the St. Louis Cardinals, **Sept. 27,** set an all-time major-league season home-run record, his total of 70 well surpassing the 61 hit by Roger Maris in 1961. Sammy Sosa, a Chicago Cubs outfielder, also slammed 4-baggers at a record pace, and the competition between the 2 players provided a big lift to baseball attendance. McGwire hit his 61st home run **Sept. 7**, on his father's 61st birthday. He then broke the record with No. 62 against the Cubs **Sept. 8** in St. Louis. Sosa tied McGwire in Chicago, **Sept. 13**, hitting 2 homers for a total of 62. After falling behind again, Sosa homered twice **Sept. 22** to tie McGwire at 65 each. In separate games, **Sept. 25**, first Sosa and then McGwire hit a 66th home run. McGwire closed out the home-run contest **Sept. 26** and **27**, hitting 2 in each of his final 2 games in St. Louis against Montreal. Sosa added none to his total.

In other baseball news, Cal Ripken Jr. of the Baltimore Orioles chose not to play on **Sept. 20**, thus ending his record streak of playing in 2,632 consecutive games.

OCTOBER 1998

National

House Approves Clinton Impeachment Hearings—On **Oct. 8**, the House of Representatives voted on beginning impeachment hearings against Pres. Bill Clinton. Rep. Henry Hyde (R, IL), chairman of the Judiciary Committee, had called for approval of the resolution, saying that it represented the beginning of a "search for truth"; the vote in favor was 258-176, with 31 Democrats voting yes. A Democratic proposal, which was rejected, was for the Judiciary Committee to complete its investigation by Dec. 31, 1998, unless the House extended it. Clinton, after the final vote, said the process was in the hands of Congress, the people, and God, and added, "There is nothing I can do."

Earlier, on **Oct. 2**, the House had released 4,600 more pages of documents sent by the independent counsel, Kenneth Starr. The edited documents included the texts of taped conversations between Monica Lewinsky, with whom Clinton had become involved, and Linda Tripp, in whom Lewinsky had confided. The documents, which also included testimony by dozens of Clinton's staff members and associates, did not contain any major new disclosures.

At a meeting of the House Judiciary Committee, **Oct. 5**, David Schippers, investigative counsel for the Republicans, outlined 15 possible grounds for impeaching Clinton, including obstruction of justice, lying under oath, and witness tampering. The committee then voted, 21-16 along party lines, to recommend to the full House that the investigation proceed.

Gay College Student Is Beaten to Death in Wyoming—Matthew Shepard, a 21-year-old student at the University of Wyoming, died **Oct. 12** from injuries he received in a beating **Oct. 7**. Shepard, who was openly gay, had been kidnapped, robbed, and beaten and then tied to a ranch fence, where he was found 18 hours later. Although Laramie, WY, police said robbery was a major motive for the attack, it was investigated as a bias crime. Two men, Russell Henderson and Aaron McKinney, were charged **Oct. 9** with kidnapping, aggravated robbery, and attempted first-degree murder, and were charged with murder **Oct. 12**. The suspects' girlfriends were charged as accessories to the crime.

Interest Rates Cut; Market Volatility Continues—The Federal Reserve Board, **Oct. 15**, announced a cut in short-term interest rates. The surprise move, made outside the regularly scheduled meetings of the board, suggested a need to act quickly amid signs that the domestic economy might be buckling under the weight of the international financial crisis. The Federal Funds Rate, the overnight lending rate between banks, was cut by 0.25% to 5%, and the discount rate on loans to banks from the Reserve was cut 0.25% to 4.75%. Wall Street reacted by sending stock prices up 330.58 points **Oct. 15** and a further 117.40 points **Oct. 16**.

Earlier, stocks on Wall Street had been fluctuating widely, and the pattern was repeated in other countries. A late-September slide continued **Oct. 1**, with the Dow Jones industrial average falling 210.09 points to 7632.53. Also on **Oct. 1**, stocks fell sharply in Brazil, Germany, France, Great Britain, and Japan, where the Nikkei average stood at a 12-year low.

The Labor Dept. said, **Oct. 2**, that the unemployment rate had edged upward to 4.6% during September and that only 69,000 new payroll jobs had been created. The department said, **Oct. 15**, that prices paid to producers and farmers for finished goods had risen 0.3% in September and reported, **Oct. 16**, that consumer prices had remained unchanged in the same month. The declining ability of people in other nations to buy U.S. products was reflected in the trade-deficit report issued **Oct. 20**. The Commerce Dept. said the deficit stood at $16.77 billion in August, up $2.2 billion from July.

On Wall Street, markets continued to recover; on **Oct. 23**, after 7 straight daily advances, the Dow Jones industrial average closed at 8533.14. The Commerce Department reported, **Oct. 30**, that the economy had grown at a robust annual rate of 3.3% during the 3d quarter. The Dow Jones average rose 97.07 points, **Oct. 30**, to close the month at 8592.10.

Clinton, Congress Agree on a Budget—Pres. Bill Clinton and leaders of the Republican-controlled Congress reached an agreement, **Oct. 15**, on the remaining unfinished part of the $1.7 trillion 1999 federal budget. Despite the prospect of a big surplus, the Republicans gave up on their bid for a tax cut. Clinton had insisted that the surplus go toward protecting Social Security until a final settlement could be worked out on the future of that system. The Republicans, however, won Clinton's concurrence in the largest peacetime increase in military spending since 1985, while the Democrats won their fight to hire 100,000 elementary schoolteachers. The budget also provided money for significant relief for farmers, for American troops in Bosnia, and for reserves for the International Monetary Fund, among many other items. The House (333-95 on **Oct. 20**) and the Senate (65-29 on **Oct. 21**) approved the bill, and Clinton signed it, **Oct. 21**.

Doctor Who Performed Abortions Shot Dead—Dr. Barnett Slepian, an obstetrician who performed abortions, was shot to death in his home in the Buffalo (NY) suburb of Amherst, **Oct. 23**. He was killed by a sniper who fired a bullet through a window. Slepian, who had been a target of anti-abortion demonstrators for years, was the third doctor who performed the procedure to be killed in the United States since 1993.

John Glenn Returns to Space at Age 77—John Glenn, who in 1962 was the first U.S. astronaut to orbit the earth, returned to space **Oct. 29** aboard the shuttle *Discovery*. His 1962 solo flight had lasted 5 hours. The current trip was scheduled for 9 days, and 7 astronauts were on board, including 1 each from Japan and Spain.

Since his first trip, Glenn had gone on to serve in the U.S. Senate, from which he was retiring in Jan. 1999. Glenn, who was 77, would be the subject of numerous experiments relating to the effects of space travel on older persons. Pres. Bill Clinton and First Lady Hillary Rodham Clinton were among 250,000 people who watched the lift-off from the Kennedy Space Center in Florida. On **Oct. 30**, the crew deployed a small communications satellite.

International

Serb Agreement on Pullback Averts NATO Military Response—The United Nations Security Council, **Oct. 1**, condemned atrocities committed in the Yugoslav province of Kosovo, where Serb military forces were massacring ethnic Albanian civilians. Thousands of civilians had fled from government security forces. UN Secretary General Kofi Annan, **Oct. 1**, denounced the Serbs and said that international relief organizations must be given access to needy refugees.

It was reported, **Oct. 4**, that Pres. Slobodan Milosevic of Yugoslavia, in order to head off the threat of Western military retaliation, had ordered a withdrawal of army forces in Kosovo. However, after meeting with Milosevic **Oct. 7**, U.S. envoy Richard Holbrooke said he had been unable to get any concessions on a pullback or on the refugees. While some units were being withdrawn, others were entering Kosovo. The United States, **Oct. 8**, informed Milosevic that his "cosmetic gestures" would not prevent NATO air strikes.

After another meeting with Milosevic, Holbrooke announced, **Oct. 13**, an agreement that would open Kosovo to 2,000 international observers. NATO surveillance flights would also play a role in monitoring the withdrawal of Serbian troops. In announcing the agreement, Milosevic stressed that no foreign troops would be stationed in Kosovo. On **Oct. 26**, just one day before threatened NATO air strikes were to begin, Serbian soldiers and police began a significant pullback from their positions in Kosovo. Albanian rebels quickly began to occupy their positions. NATO representatives in Brussels, **Oct. 27**, voted to postpone indefinitely the deadline they had imposed for air strikes. They concluded that Milosevic was in "substantial compliance" with NATO demands.

Russian Economic Crisis Continues—Russia's new premier, Yevgeny Primakov, took the unusual step, **Oct. 1**, of announcing that he had not been able to develop a plan for dealing with the nation's deepening economic crisis. He and his top aides were continuing to discuss the situation. Communists and trade unionists staged a nationwide strike,

Oct. 7, and called on Pres. Boris Yeltsin to resign, but work stoppages were only sporadic, and the number of protestors fell below expectations. Russia, which was also suffering from a bad harvest, appealed, **Oct. 9**, for international humanitarian aid, including food.

President of Brazil Reelected—Pres. Fernando Henrique Cardoso of Brazil was reelected **Oct. 4**, narrowly winning a majority of votes and thus avoiding a runoff. The country's finances were in turmoil; the stock market was down 40% in 1998, and the withdrawal of international investment money was further jeopardizing the economy. The government was negotiating a rescue from the International Monetary Fund. On **Oct. 28**, the government took bold steps. It proposed $11 billion in savings coming from tax increases in 1999, combined with an additional $7 billion from spending cuts. Pensions would be cut, and states and cities would be pressured to reduce spending.

Iranians, Afghans Square Off at Border—Iran said its troops had inflicted heavy casualties on Afghan forces during a border skirmish on **Oct. 8**, but a spokesman for the Taliban-led regime in Afghanistan denied any armed clash had occurred. Although the government of Iran and Afghanistan's new Taliban rulers were both Islamic, their religious views were nonetheless disparate, and tensions between the 2 nations had been increasing. In August, at least 8 Iranian diplomats had been killed in Afghanistan. The Taliban admitted to the killings and promised to punish those responsible, but Iran threatened retaliation. Subsequently, Iran massed 270,000 troops along the 2 countries' common border.

2 in Northern Ireland Share Nobel Peace Prize—David Trimble, a Protestant, and John Hume, a Roman Catholic, both leaders of political parties in Northern Ireland, were named, **Oct. 16**, as co-winners of the 1998 Nobel Peace Prize. The 2 men were honored for their efforts in behalf of the April accord that attempted to bring peace to the province of Ulster (Northern Ireland) and end the violence that had claimed more than 3,200 lives over the past 3 decades.

Chilean Dictator Pinochet Arrested in London—After a request by Spanish authorities, in a highly unusual move, Gen. Augusto Pinochet Ugarte, former dictator of Chile, was arrested by British police in London **Oct. 17**, for questioning for "crimes of genocide and terrorism that include murder." On **Oct. 28**, however, Britain's High Court ruled in favor of Pinochet's claim that he was immune from arrest and extradition because he was president of Chile when the alleged crimes were committed. An appeal to decide whether to extradite the 82-year-old Pinochet to face charges in Spain was expected. It has been estimated that human rights violations claimed more than 3,000 lives during Pinochet's 17-year rule.

Former Communist Heads Italian Government—Massimo D'Alema, a former Communist, became Italy's prime minister, **Oct. 21**, ending the hiatus caused when his predecessor, Romano Prodi, lost on a vote of confidence by a single vote in parliament. D'Alema's cabinet was an ideological mix, and included 6 women. D'Alema became the first former Communist to head a major Western European government.

Peru, Ecuador End Conflict—Pres. Jamil Mahuad Witt of Ecuador and Pres. Alberto K. Fujimori of Peru signed a peace treaty **Oct. 26**, officially ending decades of bitter conflict between the 2 countries. According to the agreement, 4 guarantor nations—Argentina, Brazil, Chile, and the United States—would outline Peru's and Ecuador's ill-defined borders. The accord would allow Ecuador access to the Amazon River, as well as the right to build 2 ports in Peru and a monument to its war dead in Peruvian territory atop the Condor Mts.

Agreement Revives Middle East Peace Effort—Prime Min. Benjamin Netanyahu of Israel and Palestinian leader Yasir Arafat came to the United States and, after 9 days of tense negotiations, signed an agreement on **Oct. 23** that revived the peace process in the Middle East.

Negotiations had essentially been stalled since the onset of an increase in Jewish settlement activity in the West Bank in 1997. On **Oct. 7, 1998**, however, Arafat and Netanyahu had dined together for the first time and exchanged gifts during a meeting at Erez, in Gaza. U.S. Sec. of State Madeleine Albright, who also attended, announced a forthcoming U.S. trip by the 2 leaders. On **Oct. 9**, Netanyahu named a longtime hard-liner, Ariel Sharon, as his foreign minister. As defense minister in an earlier government, Sharon had strongly promoted West Bank Jewish settlements. However, the peace process was now proceeding.

Clinton sporadically joined Netanyahu and Arafat for summit negotiations at the Wye Conference Center near Queenstown, MD, **Oct. 15**. With Clinton leaving and then returning, talks stretched beyond their original 4-day timetable. On **Oct. 20**, King Hussein of Jordan, who was suffering from cancer, nevertheless traveled to Washington to join the talks.

The new agreement, while significant, was seen not as a major breakthrough but as a means of getting the peace process back on track. In part, the agreement simply affirmed commitments made in the Oslo accords in 1993 and 1995. The Palestinians agreed to delete a call for the destruction of Israel from their charter, and promised a greater effort against terrorism. Israel agreed to withdraw from an additional 13% of the West Bank, bringing to 40% the proportion that the Palestinians controlled wholly or in part. About 14% of the area that was now under joint control would come under full Palestinian control. Israel also agreed to release 750 Palestinian prisoners, and the Palestinians were to be allowed to build an airport in Gaza.

Negotiations were stalled briefly at the last minute when Netanyahu asked Clinton to free Jonathan Pollard, an American spy for Israel who had been imprisoned in the United States since 1985. Clinton agreed only to look into the matter. In the days after the signing, some Israelis and Palestinians who were opposed to the agreement engaged in violent demonstrations.

General

Yankees Win World Series in a Sweep—The New York Yankees completed a 4-game sweep of the San Diego Padres to win the World Series, **Oct. 21**. The Series opened in Yankee Stadium, **Oct. 17**. In the opener the Yanks, down by 3 runs, scored 7 times in the 7th inning, including a go-ahead grand-slam home run by Tino Martinez, and won 9-6. They won again, 9-3, **Oct. 18**. On **Oct. 20**, in San Diego, third baseman Scott Brosius hit 2 home runs, one with 2 Yankees on base, as New York prevailed again, 5-4. The sweep was completed, **Oct. 21** in San Diego, with a 3-0 New York victory. The shutout was pitched by Andy Pettitte (7⅓ innings), Jeff Nelson, and Mariano Rivera. Brosius was named the Most Valuable Player in the series. The Yankee manager was Joe Torre, who also managed the 1996 Yankee champions. In adding 11 post-season victories to their regular-season total, the Yankees had won a record 125 games altogether.

Hurricane Devastates Central America—Hurricane Mitch, one of the strongest Atlantic storms ever recorded, struck Central America, **Oct. 29-Nov. 3**. According to early estimates, at least 10,000 deaths resulted from the storm itself and from the flooding and mudslides it triggered. Thousands more were missing in villages buried under mud. In Honduras and Nicaragua, the 2 hardest-hit countries, hundreds of thousands were forced to flee their homes. El Salvador, Mexico, Costa Rica, Belize, Guatemala, Cuba, and Panama also reported hundreds of deaths and extensive damage. The European Union approved $7.7 million in aid **Nov. 3**, the United States $2 million, and Canada $1 million.

Notable Supreme Court Decisions, 1997-98

The U.S. Supreme Court term that began Oct. 6, 1997, and ended June 26, 1998, produced signed opinions in 91 cases, 11 more than in 1996-97. In 43 of those cases, the full Court ruled unanimously.

As he has for most of the decade, Associate Justice Anthony M. Kennedy defined the Court's ideological center, casting the fewest dissenting votes (5) in nonunanimous decisions. In most of the 15 cases decided by a 5-4 vote, Kennedy and Associate Justice Sandra Day O'Connor joined the Court's 3 most conservative members—Chief Justice William H. Rehnquist and Associate Justices Antonin Scalia and Clarence Thomas—to form the majority. Associate Justice John Paul Stevens, a moderate liberal, was once again the Court's principal dissenter, casting 22 dissenting votes, followed by Scalia with 19.

Following the conclusion of the 1997-98 term, Chief Justice Rehnquist rejected requests from the Clinton administration to block subpoenas from independent counsel Kenneth Starr compelling Secret Service agents (July 17) and White House lawyers (Aug. 4) to testify about President Bill Clinton's relationship with former White House intern Monica Lewinsky.

Former Associate Justice Lewis F. Powell Jr., 90, died at his home in Richmond, VA, on Aug. 25. Powell, a moderate, served on the Court from 1972 until his retirement in 1987.

Attorney-Client Privilege: In a case stemming from the 1993 dismissal of White House travel office employees, a 6-3 majority held that lawyers may not be compelled to reveal their clients' confidences even after a client dies and even if a prosecutor can show that the information is relevant to a criminal inquiry (*Swidler & Berlin* v. *U.S.*; June 25). The Court rejected a claim by independent counsel Starr that he needed to examine notes made by a lawyer for Vincent Foster shortly before the deputy White House counsel committed suicide in July 1993.

Criminal Procedure: Ruling unanimously, the justices declared that police who take part in high-speed car chases are not liable for consequent injuries to the fleeing suspects or to bystanders unless the police acted "with a purpose to cause harm" (*County of Sacramento* v. *Lewis*; May 26). In his majority opinion, Associate Justice David H. Souter wrote that police pursuing actual or suspected lawbreakers are constitutionally protected unless their behavior is so egregious that it "shocks the conscience."

By an 8-1 margin, the Court ruled that because of lingering doubts about the validity of lie-detector tests, a defendant does not have a constitutional right to present polygraph evidence at trial (*U.S.* v. *Scheffer*; Mar. 31).

Disabilities: The Court held, 5-4, that people who test positive for HIV are covered under the federal Americans with Disabilities Act (1990), even if they exhibit no AIDS symptoms (*Bragdon* v. *Abbott*; June 25). In a unanimous ruling, the justices also extended the law's antidiscrimination provisions to state prison inmates (*Pennsylvania Dept. of Corrections* v. *Yeskey*; June 15).

Ellis Island: The Court resolved a long-standing interstate sovereignty dispute by awarding the landfilled portion of Ellis Island—nearly 90% of the total area—to New Jersey (*New Jersey* v. *New York*; May 26). The importance of the 6-3 decision was more symbolic than practical, since the island, a gateway for millions of immigrants between 1892 and 1954, is federally administered.

First Amendment Rights: By an 8-1 majority, the Court upheld legislation enacted by Congress in 1990 that instructed the National Endowment for the Arts to apply "general standards of decency" in awarding federal arts grants (*NEA* v. *Finley*; June 25).

The Court held that fringe or minor-party candidates may be excluded from broadcasts of political debates by government-owned television stations (*Arkansas Educational Television Comm.* v. *Forbes*; May 18). The 6-3 verdict overturned a 1996 appellate court ruling that a state-owned TV network was required to open the debate to all candidates who had qualified for the ballot, no matter how minuscule their chances of winning.

Line-Item Veto: In a landmark ruling (*Clinton* v. *City of New York*; June 25), the Court struck down the Line-Item Veto Act (1996). Writing for a 6-3 majority, Justice Stevens held that Congress had acted unconstitutionally when it gave the president the "unilateral power to change the text of duly enacted statutes."

Sexual Harassment: In two landmark cases, each decided by a 7-2 vote, the Court sought to clarify the standards governing sexual harassment lawsuits (*Faragher* v. *City of Boca Raton* and *Burlington Industries, Inc.* v. *Ellerth*; June 26). Guidelines issued by the Court held that private employers are liable for misconduct by their supervisory employees. Such liability is absolute if the harassment resulted in some "tangible employment action," such as demotion or dismissal; when no such action occurred, a firm may defend itself by proving that it took "reasonable care" to prevent and correct harassing behavior, or that the employee "unreasonably failed to take advantage" of the remedies the company provided. The Court applied a much more restrictive standard in *Gebser* v. *Lago Vista Independent School District* (June 22), holding by a 5-4 majority that a student who had been sexually harassed by a teacher could not sue the school district unless a district official actually knew of the harassment and did nothing to stop it.

In a unanimous ruling, the Court held that sexual harassment statutes apply even when harasser and victim are the same sex (*Oncale* v. *Sundowner Offshore Services, Inc.*; Mar. 4). Writing for the majority, Justice Scalia noted, "common sense, and an appropriate sensitivity to social context, will enable courts and juries to distinguish between simple teasing or roughhousing . . . and conduct which a reasonable person . . . would find severely hostile or abusive."

The 1998 Nobel Prizes

The 1998 Nobel Prize winners were announced Oct. 8-16. Each prize consisted of a large solid gold medal and a cash award worth 7.6 million Swedish kronor (nearly $1 million).

Chemistry: Walter Kohn, an Austrian-born American, and John A. Pople, British, shared the prize for applying computational methods based on quantum mechanics to the study of molecular properties and chemical processes.

Memorial Prize in Economic Science: Amartya Sen of India received the award for contributions to welfare economics, including studies of poverty, inequality, social choice, and the economic mechanism underlying famines.

Literature: Portuguese writer José Saramago, whose novels include *Baltasar and Blimunda*, *The Stone Raft*, and *Blindness*, was cited for writing that "continually enables us once again to apprehend an elusory reality."

Peace: Political leaders John Hume and David Trimble shared the prize for their efforts to resolve the Northern Ireland conflict, culminating in the peace agreement signed Good Friday, Apr. 10, 1998.

Physics: Three professors at American universities—Robert B. Laughlin, the German-born Horst L. Störmer, and the Chinese-born Daniel C. Tsui—were jointly honored for their discovery that electrons acting together at low temperatures in extremely strong magnetic fields can condense to form a kind of "quantum fluid."

Physiology or Medicine: The American pharmacologists Robert F. Furchgott, Louis J. Ignarro, and Ferid Murad shared the prize for discovering the role of nitric oxide as a signaling molecule in the cardiovascular system. Their work paved the way for several medical breakthroughs, including the anti-impotence drug Viagra.

Major Actions of the 105th Congress

When the 105th Congress convened on Jan. 7, 1997, Republicans held 227 seats in the House of Representatives (Democrats had 207 and there was 1 Independent) and 55 seats in the Senate (Democrats held 45). Newt Gingrich (R, GA) was sworn in as House speaker and Trent Lott (R, MS) as Senate majority leader. Gingrich was reprimanded for ethics violations on Jan. 21, 1997, but allowed to remain as speaker; an attempt by some Republicans to force him to relinquish his leadership post failed in July.

The 1997 session produced landmark budget and tax legislation. In 1998, however, election-year partisanship, White House scandal, and divisions within both the Republican and Democratic parties contributed to a session that deadlocked on many important measures, including bills dealing with campaign finance reform, tobacco, patients' rights, product liability, and fast-track trade negotiating authority. Pres. Bill Clinton vetoed measures that would have banned an abortion method known as late-term or partial-birth abortion, and the Senate killed a bill to raise the hourly minimum wage to $6.15 by Jan. 2000.

Two police officers, Jacob Chestnut and John Gibson, were killed July 24, 1998, when a lone gunman, Russell E. Weston Jr., burst through a public entrance near the offices of House Majority Whip Tom DeLay (R, TX); the shooting was the first in the Capitol since 1954. Congress adjourned for the 1998 election on Oct. 21, but the House Judiciary Committee was expected to begin presidential impeachment hearings in mid-November.

The following is a summary of major actions of the 105th Congress, during Clinton's 5th and 6th years as president. Measures that have become law are identified by their Public Law (PL) number. Detailed legislative information may be accessed via the Internet at http://thomas.loc.gov/home/thomas2.html

1997

Gingrich Reprimand. Adopts the report of the Select Committee on Ethics, reprimanding Speaker Gingrich and fining him $300,000 for using tax-exempt funds for political purposes and supplying false information to the committee. Passed by the House Jan. 21, 395-28.

Assisted Suicide. Bars the use of federal funds for physician-assisted suicide. Passed by the House Apr. 10, 398-16; passed by the Senate Apr. 16, 99-0; signed by Pres. Clinton Apr. 30 (PL 105-12).

Chemical Weapons Ban. Ratifies, subject to certain conditions, the international Convention on the Prohibition of Development, Production, Stockpiling and Use of Chemical Weapons and on Their Destruction, signed by the U.S. on Jan. 13, 1993. Passed by the Senate Apr. 24, 74-26.

Balanced Budget Act. Establishes a timetable to balance the federal budget by 2002, chiefly through savings in Medicare and Medicaid. Funds health care services for indigent children. Restores benefits to elderly and disabled legal immigrants. Passed by the House July 30, 346-85; passed by the Senate July 31, 85-15; signed by Pres. Clinton Aug. 5 (PL 105-33).

Taxpayer Relief Act. Provides for a tax credit of up to $500 per child, tax credits for college tuition and expenses, reductions in capital gains and estate taxes, expansion of Individual Retirement Accounts, and an increase in cigarette taxes. Passed by the House July 31, 389-43; passed by the Senate July 31, 92-8; signed by Pres. Clinton Aug. 5 (PL 105-34).

Congressional Pay Raise. Allows an automatic 2.3% raise in members' salaries as of Jan. 1998, from $133,600 to $136,700 (for the speaker, from $171,500 to $175,400), through a legislative maneuver, stripping from the Treasury and General Government Appropriations Act an annual provision that would have barred such an increase. Act passed by the House Sept. 30, 220-207; passed by the Senate Oct. 1, 55-45; signed by Pres. Clinton Oct. 10 (PL 105-61).

Adoption and Safe Families Act. Facilitates the removal of children from abusive families and provides financial incentives for states to transfer abused or neglected children from foster homes into adoption. Passed by the House Apr. 30, 416-5; passed by the Senate by unanimous consent, Nov. 8; signed by Pres. Clinton Nov. 19 (PL 105-89).

Food and Drug Administration. Accelerates the federal approval process for new drugs and medical devices and makes it easier for doctors and patients to use experimental therapies while FDA approval is still pending. Passed in the House and Senate by voice vote Nov. 9; signed by Pres. Clinton Nov. 21 (PL 105-115).

1998

NATO Expansion. Ratifies enlargement of the North Atlantic Treaty Organization to include the Czech Republic, Hungary, and Poland. Passed by the Senate Apr. 30, 80-19.

Transportation Projects. Authorizes more than $210 billion over 6 years period for highway construction, mass transit, highway safety programs, and other public works projects. Revises the funding formula to alleviate regional disparities. Passed by the House May 22, 297-86; passed by the Senate May 22, 88-5; signed by Pres. Clinton June 9 (PL 105-178).

Internal Revenue Service. Revamps IRS management and policies to curb collection abuses and augment taxpayers' rights. Shifts the burden of proof in civil tax-court cases from the taxpayer to the IRS. Aids investors by shortening the holding period for long-term capital gains. Passed by the House June 25, 402-8; passed by the Senate July 9, 96-2; signed by Pres. Clinton July 22 (PL 105-206).

Workforce Investment Partnership Act. Consolidates about 70 federal job training and vocational education programs into a system of block grants to state and local governments. Passed by the House without objection July 31; passed by the Senate by unanimous consent July 30; signed by Pres. Clinton Aug. 7 (PL 105-220).

Higher Education. Expands Pell Grant program for college students, lowers interest rates on student loans, and provides funds for teacher training and recruitment. Passed by the House Sept. 28 by voice vote; passed by the Senate Sept. 29, 96-0; signed by Pres. Clinton Oct. 7 (PL 105-244).

Clinton Impeachment Inquiry. Authorizes the House Judiciary Committee to investigate whether Pres. Clinton should be impeached. Passed by the House Oct. 8, 258-176.

Omnibus Appropriations Bill. For the fiscal year beginning Oct. 1, appropriates an estimated $520 billion for 10 cabinet departments, the foreign aid budget, the International Monetary Fund, and numerous other programs, including military readiness and overseas contingency operations, antiterrorism activities, antidrug efforts, upgrading of computer systems to deal with the year 2000 (Y2K) problem, and renewal of the tax credit for research and development, as well as many education programs, construction, water, and energy projects, and the like around the U.S. Includes, among other measures, the Foreign Affairs Reform and Restructuring Act, which provides for the State Department to absorb the Arms Control and Disarmament Agency and the U.S. Information Agency; the Child Online Protection Act, which bars commercial websites from providing graphic sexual material to minors; and the Internet Tax Freedom Act, which bans states and localities from taxing Internet access or commerce for a 3-year period. Passed by the House Oct. 20, 333-95; passed by the Senate Oct. 21, 65-29; signed by Pres. Clinton Oct. 21 (PL 105-277).

Digital Millennium Copyright Act. Extends copyright protection to works transmitted over the Internet by making it illegal to crack the encryption systems used to protect such works. Passed by the House Oct. 12 by voice vote; passed by the Senate Oct. 8 by unanimous consent; signed by Pres. Clinton Oct. 28 (PL 105-304).

OBITUARIES

Deaths, Oct. 16, 1997—Oct. 31, 1998

A

Abacha, Sani, 54, president of Nigeria since a 1993 coup; Abuja, Nigeria, June 8, 1998.

Abiola, Moshood, 60, jailed Nigerian opposition leader, denied the presidency by the ruling dictatorship in 1993; Abuja, Nigeria, July 7, 1998.

Abzug, Bella, 77, outspoken feminist and U.S. representative from New York (1970-76); New York, NY, Mar. 31, 1998.

Adams, Johnny, 67, jazz and blues singer known for his 1960s single "Release Me"; Baton Rouge, LA, Sept. 14, 1998.

Aldridge, Lionel, 56, former star defensive end (mostly with the Green Bay Packers, 1963-71); later afflicted with mental illness; found dead, Milwaukee, WI, Feb. 12, 1998.

Alioto, Joseph L., 81, Democratic mayor of San Francisco (1968-76); San Francisco, CA, Jan. 29, 1998.

Ambler, Eric, 89, British author of classic novels of suspense and intrigue, such as *A Coffin for Dimitrios* (1939); London, England, Oct. 22, 1998.

Amory, Cleveland, 81; writer, TV critic, and animal rights advocate; New York, NY, Oct. 14, 1998.

Arcaro, Eddie, 81, only jockey to win racing's Triple Crown twice (1941, 1948); Miami, FL, Nov. 14, 1997.

Autry, Gene, 91, singing cowboy who starred in films and TV, recorded hit songs ("Rudolph the Red-Nosed Reindeer"), and became a millionaire businessman; Los Angeles, CA, Oct. 2, 1998.

B

Banda, Hastings Kamuzu, 99(?), prime minister and later president of Malawi (1964-94), which he led to independence; Johannesburg, South Africa, Nov. 25, 1997.

Barton, Sir Derek H. R., 79, British-born chemist who shared a 1979 Nobel Prize for "conformational analysis"; College Station, TX, Mar. 16, 1998.

Belanger, Mark, 54, Gold Glove-winning shortstop for the Baltimore Orioles (1965-81); New York, NY, Oct. 6, 1998.

Berlin, Sir Isaiah, 88, Russian-born Oxford philosopher-historian; Oxford, England, Nov. 5, 1997.

Bettmann, Otto, 94, photo curator who fled Nazi Germany in 1935 and founded the Bettmann Archive; Boca Raton, FL, May 1, 1998.

Bono, Sonny (Salvatore), 62, singer-songwriter who with his former wife made up the pop duo Sonny and Cher; elected to Congress from California (1994); died in a skiing accident; South Lake Tahoe, CA, Jan. 5, 1998.

Bradley, Tom, 80, sharecropper's son who became the 1st black mayor of Los Angeles (1973-93); West Los Angeles, CA, Sept. 29, 1998.

Bridges, Lloyd, 85, actor who starred in TV's *Sea Hunt* (1957-61) and films ranging from *High Noon* (1952) to *Airplane* (1980); Los Angeles, CA, Mar. 10, 1998.

Buscaglia, Leo, 74, TV personality, lecturer, and author who preached love and self-acceptance; Lake Tahoe, NV, June 12, 1998.

C

Calderone, Mary S., 94, physician and widely influential advocate of sex education; Kennett Square, PA, Oct. 24, 1998.

Campanis, Al, 81, Los Angeles Dodgers executive fired in 1987 for making racial comments on TV; Fullerton, CA, June 21, 1998.

Caray, Harry, 78, Chicago Cubs baseball announcer whose colorful style delighted fans for over 50 years; Rancho Mirage, CA, Feb. 18, 1998.

Carter, Betty, 69, innovative jazz singer, composer, and arranger; Brooklyn, NY, Sept. 26, 1998.

Castenada, Carlos, 72(?), reclusive writer of best-sellers exploring the mystical, including *The Teachings of Don Juan* (1968); Los Angeles, CA, Apr. 27, 1998.

Chaplin, Saul, 85, Oscar-winning songwriter who collaborated with Sammy Cahn on such hits as "Please Be Kind" (1938); Los Angeles, CA, Nov. 15, 1997.

Cleaver, Eldridge, 62, activist who wrote the prison memoir *Soul on Ice* (1968) and led the radical Black Panther Party; later became an evangelical Christian; Pomona, CA, May 1, 1998.

Clifford, Clark, 91, top adviser to Presidents Truman, Kennedy, Johnson, and Carter; Bethesda, MD, Oct. 10, 1998.

Comack, Allan MacLeod, 74, South African-born physicist who shared a 1979 Nobel Prize for helping to invent the CAT scan; Winchester, MA, May 7, 1998.

Commager, Henry Steele, 95, distinguished historian whose books include *The Growth of the American Republic* (1930); Amherst, MA, Mar. 2, 1998.

D

Denning, Richard, 84, actor best known for his TV roles in *Mr. and Mrs. North* and *Hawaii Five-O*; Escondido, CA, Oct. 11, 1998.

Derek, John, 71, Hollywood actor; husband and manager of Bo Derek; Santa Maria, CA, May 22, 1998.

Dickerson, Nancy, 70, TV reporter who in 1960 became the 1st woman network correspondent; New York, NY, Oct. 18, 1997.

Drury, Allen, 80, political novelist who wrote *Advise and Consent* (1959); San Francisco, CA, Sept. 2, 1998.

Duncan, Todd, 95, baritone who originated the role of Porgy in *Porgy and Bess* (1935); Washington, DC, Feb. 28, 1998.

E

Edmonds, Walter D., 94, author of historical novels, including *Drums Along the Mohawk* (1936); Concord, MA, Jan. 24, 1998.

F

Farley, Chris, 33, comedian who starred in TV's *Saturday Night Live* (1990-95); found dead, Chicago, IL, Dec. 18, 1997.

Faye, Alice, 86(?), Hollywood singer who starred in such films as *Alexander's Ragtime Band* (1938), and *Tin Pan Alley* (1940). Rancho Mirage, CA, May 9, 1998.

Fowler, Gene, 80, director of the 1957 cult classic *I Was a Teenage Werewolf;* Hollywood Hills, CA, May 11, 1998.

Frann, Mary, 55, actress who played Bob Newhart's wife on TV's *Newhart* in the 80s; Los Angeles, CA, Sept. 23, 1998.

Friendly, Fred W., 82, CBS News producer and executive who was a pioneer in TV news coverage; New York, NY, Mar. 3, 1998.

Fukui, Kenichi, 79, Japanese chemist who shared a 1981 Nobel Prize for exploring chemical reactions using quantum mechanics; Kyoto, Japan, Jan. 9, 1998.

Fuller, Samuel, 85, director and producer of low-budget cult films, including *The Big Red One* (1980); Hollywood Hills, CA, Oct. 30, 1997.

G

Gellhorn, Martha Ellis, 89, veteran war correspondent; married to Ernest Hemingway in the 40s; London, England, Feb. 15, 1998.

Gill, Brendan, 83, man of letters who wrote for *The New Yorker*; New York, NY, Dec. 27, 1997.

Goizueta, Roberto C., 65, Cuban refugee who became chairman and CEO of the Coca-Cola Co.; Atlanta, GA, Oct. 18, 1997.

Goldwater, Barry M., 89, Arizona senator who lost the 1964 presidential election in a landslide but spearheaded the modern conservative movement; Paradise Village, AZ, May 29, 1998.

Grappelli, Stéphane, 89, French jazz violinist known for his masterful improvisations; Paris, France, Dec. 1, 1997.

Griffith Joyner, Florence ("FloJo"), 38, flamboyant record-setting sprinter; won 3 gold medals at the 1988 Olympics; Mission Viejo, CA, Sept. 21, 1998.

H

Hartman, Phil, 49, Canadian-born comic actor who starred in TV's *Saturday Night Live* and *NewsRadio;* shot apparently by his wife in a murder-suicide; Encino, CA, May 28, 1998.

Hawkes, John, 72, experimental novelist whose postmodern works include *The Blood Oranges* (1971) and *Death, Sleep and the Traveler* (1974); Providence, RI, May 15, 1998.

Herbert, Zbigniew, 73, Polish poet and essayist whose works stressed moral values; Warsaw, Poland, July 28, 1998.

Hickson, Joan, 92, British actress who played Agatha Christie's Miss Marple on a BBC TV series (1984-92); Colchester, England, late Oct. 1998.

Hitchings, George H., 92, biochemist who shared a 1988 Nobel Prize for research that led to drugs for malaria, leukemia, and AIDS; Chapel Hill, NC, Feb. 27, 1998.

Holliman, John, Jr., 49; CNN national correspondent; in an auto accident; Snellville, GA, Sept. 12, 1998.

Holub, Miroslav, 74, distinguished Czech poet and immunologist; Prague, Czech Republic, July 14, 1998.

Hughes, Ted, 68, British poet; poet laureate since 1984; married to poet Sylvia Plath before her 1963 suicide; North Tawton, England, Oct. 28, 1998.

Hutchence, Michael, 37, lead singer of the Australian rock band INXS; committed suicide; Sydney, Australia, Nov. 22, 1997.

I

Innes, Hammond, 84, British author of adventure and suspense best-sellers, including *The Wreck of the Mary Deare* (1956); Kersey, England, June 10, 1998.

Itami, Juzo, 64, Japanese director of subtle, witty films, including *Tampopo* (1986) and *Funeral* (1984); committed suicide; Tokyo, Japan, Dec. 20, 1997.

J

Jones, Grandpa, 84, country music performer and banjo player featured on TV's *Hee Haw* (1968-93); Nashville, TN, Feb. 19, 1998.

Jünger, Ernst, 102, right-wing German writer best known for works on war and heroism, such as *Storm of Steel* (1920); Wilflingen, Germany, Feb. 17, 1998.

K

Karamanlis, Constantine, 91, Greek prime minister (1955-63, 1974-80) and later president; restored democracy in the 70s; Athens, Greece, Apr. 23, 1998.

Kaye, Stubby, 79, singer-comedian who played Nicely-Nicely Johnson in the 50s musical *Guys and Dolls*; Rancho Mirage, CA, Dec. 14, 1997.

Kazin, Alfred, 83, eloquent memoirist and critic of American literature in such works as *On Native Grounds* (1942); New York, NY, June 5, 1998.

Kennedy, Michael, 39, 6th child of the late Sen. Robert Kennedy; headed Boston's Citizens Energy Corp.; killed in skiing accident; Aspen, CO, Dec. 31, 1997.

Kurosawa, Akira, 88, Japanese director of acclaimed epics, including *Rashomon* (1950), *Seven Samurai* (1954), and *Ran* (1985); Tokyo, Japan, Sept. 6, 1998.

L

Laughlin, James, 83, publisher and poet who founded the innovative house New Directions in 1936; Norfolk, CT, Nov. 12, 1997.

Laxness, Halldor, 95, Icelandic writer known for his epic works and reinterpretations of folklore; won a 1955 Nobel Prize; Reykjavik, Iceland, Feb. 8, 1998.

Leonard, Buck, 90, regarded as the greatest 1st baseman in the Negro Leagues (1934-50); inducted into the Baseball Hall of Fame in 1972; Rocky Mount, NC, Nov. 27, 1997.

Levertov, Denise, 74, British-born poet of emotionally intense works; Seattle, WA, Dec. 20, 1997.

Lewis, Shari, 65, puppeteer who entertained children for 40 years with Lamb Chop, Hush Puppy, and Charlie Horse; Los Angeles, CA, Aug. 2, 1998.

Lindley, Audra, 79, actress who played Mrs. Roper on TV's *Three's Company* in the 70s; Los Angeles, CA, Oct. 16, 1997.

Link, Arthur S., 77, Princeton historian regarded as the foremost authority on Woodrow Wilson; Advance, NC, Mar. 26, 1998.

Lord, Jack, 77(?), actor who starred in TV's *Hawaii Five-O* (1968-80); Honolulu, HI, Jan. 21, 1998.

Luckman, Sid, 81, star quarterback for the Chicago Bears (1939-50); inducted into the Pro Football Hall of Fame in 1965; North Miami Beach, FL, July 5, 1998.

M

Manzo, Luis Aguilar, 79, debonair Mexican actor and singer who appeared in some 150 Spanish-language films; Mexico City, Mexico, Oct. 24, 1997.

Marshall, E. G., 84, prolific character actor best known for TV's *The Defenders* (1961-65); Mt. Kisco, NY, Aug. 24, 1998.

McCartney, Linda Eastman, 56, rock-music photographer of the 60s, married to rock superstar Paul McCartney since 1969; Tucson, AZ, Apr. 17, 1998.

McDougal, James, 57, former Arkansas business partner of Bill and Hillary Clinton; convicted of fraud in the Whitewater investigation; imprisoned since June 1997; Fort Worth, TX, Mar. 8, 1998.

McDowall, Roddy, 70, ubiquitous British-born actor whose films included *Lassie Come Home* (1943) and *Planet of the Apes* (1968); Los Angeles, CA, Oct. 3, 1998.

Mehrtens, Warren, 77, jockey who won racing's Triple Crown atop Assault in 1946; Sarasota, FL, Dec. 30, 1997.

Merrill, Bob, 74, prolific songwriter of upbeat tunes like "How Much Is That Doggie in the Window?"; committed suicide; Los Angeles, CA, Feb. 17, 1998.

Michener, James, 90, best-selling author of historical fiction, including *Tales of the South Pacific* (1947), *Hawaii* (1959), *The Source* (1965), and *Texas* (1985); Austin, TX, Oct. 16, 1997.

Middlecoff, Cary, 77, dentist who became a top pro golfer (1945-67); Memphis, TN, Sept. 1, 1998.

Mifune, Toshiro, 77, Japanese actor who played heroic samurai loners in such films as *Rashomon* (1950); Mitaka, Japan, Dec. 24, 1997.

Milburn, Rod, Jr., 47, track star who won in the 110-meter hurdles at the 1972 Olympics; killed in a workplace accident; Port Hudson, LA, Nov. 11, 1997.

Monahan, Jay, 42, legal analyst for NBC and husband of *Today* show coanchor Katie Couric; New York, NY, Jan. 24, 1998.

Morris, Wright, 88, author whose writings and photographs explored his native Nebraska prairie; Mill Valley, CA, Apr. 25, 1998.

N

Nitschke, Ray, 61, linebacker with the Green Bay Packers (1958-72); elected to the Pro Football Hall of Fame in 1978; Venice, FL, Mar. 8, 1998.

O'Sullivan, Maureen, 87, Irish-born actress best known as Jane in *Tarzan* movies of the 30s and 40s; mother of actress Mia Farrow; Scottsdale, AZ, June 23, 1998.

P

Parks, Lillian Rogers, 100, White House maid and seamstress who wrote *My Thirty Years Backstairs at the White House* (1961); Washington, DC, Nov. 6, 1997.

Pasmore, Victor, 89, English painter of abstract art; Malta, Jan. 23, 1998.

Pastrano, Willie, 62, light-heavyweight boxing champion (1963-65); New Orleans, LA, Dec. 6, 1997.

Paz, Octavio, 84, Mexico's leading man of letters; won a 1990 Nobel Prize; his works include essays collected in *The Labyrinth of Solitude* (1950) and the epic poem *Sunstone* (1957); Mexico City, Mexico, Apr. 19, 1998.

Perkins, Carl, 65, influential rockabilly singer-songwriter who wrote "Blue Suede Shoes"; Jackson, TN, Jan. 19, 1998.

Pilatus, Rob, 32, member of the German pop duo Milli Vanilli, forced to relinquish a 1990 Grammy for not singing on their records; found dead, Frankfurt, Germany, Apr. 4, 1998.

Pol Pot, 73(?), Khmer Rouge leader who as ruler of Cambodia (1975-79) was responsible for the deaths of over 1 million people; near the Dangrek Mts., Cambodia, Apr. 15, 1998.

Porsche, Ferdinand, Jr., 88, Austrian-born car designer who created the luxury sports car bearing his name; Zell am See, Austria, Mar. 27, 1998.

Povich, Shirley, 92, renowned sports columnist for *The Washington Post*; Washington, DC, June 4, 1998.

Powell, Lewis, 90, Supreme Court justice (1972-87) who became a key tiebreaker and centrist; Richmond, VA, Aug. 25, 1998.

Prelog, Vladimir, 91, Swiss chemist who shared a 1975 Nobel Prize for work on stereochemistry; Zurich, Switzerland, Jan. 7, 1998.

Pyle, Denver, 77, character actor best known as Uncle Jesse on TV's *The Dukes of Hazzard* (1979-85); Burbank, CA, Dec. 25, 1997.

Q

Qabbani, Nizar, 75, Syrian diplomat who became one of the Arab world's greatest poets; London, England, Apr. 30, 1998.

Questel, Mae, 89, voice of Betty Boop, Olive Oyl, and other cartoon characters; New York, NY, Jan. 4, 1998.

Quisenberry, Dan, 45, star relief pitcher (1979-90), mostly with the Kansas City Royals; Kansas City, MO, Sept. 30, 1998.

R

Rabb, Ellis, 67, actor-director who brought diverse plays to stages across the U.S.; Memphis, TN, Jan. 11, 1998.

Rabbitt, Eddie, 56, singer-songwriter whose hits include "I Love a Rainy Night"; Nashville, TN, May 7, 1998.

Randolph, Jennings, 96, veteran West Virginia Democrat who served in the House (1933-46) and Senate (1958-85); St. Louis, MO, May 8, 1998.

Ray, James Earl, 70, convicted killer of Martin Luther King Jr.; pleaded guilty to the 1968 assassination but then said he had been framed and repeatedly sought a new trial; Nashville, TN, Apr. 23, 1998.

Raymond, Gene, 89, dashing actor whose films credits include *Flying Down to Rio* (1933) and *Smilin' Through* (1941); Los Angeles, CA, May 3, 1998.

Rebozo, Charles (Bebe), 85, self-made Florida millionaire who became a loyal friend of Richard Nixon; Miami, FL, May 8, 1998.

Reines, Frederick, 80, Nobel Prize-winning physicist (1995) who discovered the neutrino; Orange, CA, Aug. 26, 1998.

Ribicoff, Abraham, 87, powerful Connecticut Democrat who was a U.S. representative (1949-52), governor (1955-61), and senator (1963-81); New York, NY, Feb. 22, 1998.

Robbins, Jerome, 79, masterful choreographer for both ballet and Broadway; his works include *Fancy Free* (1944), *The King and I* (1951), and *West Side Story* (1957); New York, NY, July 29, 1998.

Rogers, Roy, 86, singing cowboy who starred in some 90 movies and TV's *Roy Rogers Show* (1951-57); Apple Valley, CA, July 6, 1998.

Rosario, Edwin, 34, 3-time world lightweight boxing champion in the 80s; Toa Baja, Puerto Rico, Dec. 1, 1997.

Rysanek, Leonie, 71, renowned Austrian operatic soprano; Vienna, Austria, Mar. 7, 1998.

S

Sanders, Lawrence, 78, best-selling author of suspense thrillers such as *The First Deadly Sin* (1973); Pompano Beach, FL, Feb. 7, 1998.

Sanford, Terry, 80, North Carolina Democrat who as governor (1961-65) and senator (1986-92), fought racial discrimination and promoted education; Durham, NC, Apr. 18, 1998.

Schnittke, Alfred, 63, Russian composer of symphonies, film scores, and the opera *Life With an Idiot* (1992); Hamburg, Germany, Aug. 3, 1998.

Schultz, Theodore, 95, Univ. of Chicago economist awarded a 1979 Nobel Prize for work in agricultural economics; Evanston, IL, Feb. 26, 1998.

Seraphim, Archbishop, 84, leader since 1974 of the Greek Orthodox Church; Athens, Greece, Apr. 10, 1998.

Shepard, Alan, 74, Mercury astronaut who was the 1st American to fly in space (1961); also walked on the moon in 1971; Monterey, CA, July 21, 1998.

Shevchenko, Arkady, 67, top Soviet diplomat who defected to the U.S. in 1978; Bethesda, MD, Feb. 28, 1998.

Sinatra, Frank, 82, extraordinarily popular singer who began as a crooner in the 40s, becoming a sophisticated swinger in the 50s and 60s; his best-known songs include "All the Way," "My Way," and "Strangers in the Night"; also appeared in 58 films and won an Oscar for *From Here to Eternity* (1953); Los Angeles, CA, May 14, 1998.

Smith, "Buffalo Bob," 80, star of TV's *Howdy Doody Show* (1947-60); Henderson, NC, July 30, 1998.

Spock, Benjamin, 94, pediatrician whose book *Baby and Child Care* (1946) became one of the best-sellers of all time; San Diego, CA, Mar. 15, 1998.

Stans, Maurice, 90, commerce secretary under Richard Nixon; raised funds in the 1972 reelection campaign that helped pay for Watergate dirty tricks; Pasadena, CA, Apr. 14, 1998.

Steel, Dawn, 51, chair of Columbia Pictures (1987-91) and the 1st woman to head a major movie studio; Los Angeles, CA, Dec. 20, 1997.

Stephens, Woody, 84, legendary trainer of champion racehorses; Miami Lakes, FL, Aug. 22, 1998.

Stickney, Dorothy, 101, actress who starred on Broadway in *Life With Father* (1939-44); New York, NY, June 2, 1998.

Sullivan, Billy, 86, businessman who in 1960 founded the New England Patriots; Atlantis, FL, Feb. 23, 1998.

T

Taylor, Telford, 90, attorney who became chief prosecutor at the Nuremberg trials after World War II; New York, NY, May 23, 1998.

Thompson, Kay, 90s, author of the *Eloise* books, about a precocious child living in New York City's Plaza Hotel; New York, NY, July 2, 1998.

Tippett, Sir Michael, 93, British composer known for musical experimentation and large-scale works, including the oratorio *A Child of Our Time* (1939); London, England, Jan. 8, 1998.

U

Ulanova, Galina, 88, lyrical Russian prima ballerina with the Bolshoi (1944-60); one of the greatest 20th-century dancers; Moscow, Russia, Mar. 21, 1998.

W

Walker, Doak, 71, legendary college football player for Southern Methodist; won the Heisman Trophy in 1948; Steamboat Springs, CO, Sept. 27, 1998.

Wallace, George, 79, 4-term Alabama governor who championed segregation in the 60s and 70s, for which he later apologized; paralyzed when shot during the 1972 presidential campaign; Montgomery, AL, Sept. 13, 1998.

Weidman, Jerome, 85, prolific novelist (*I Can Get It for You Wholesale,* 1937) and playwright (*Fiorello!,* 1959); New York, NY, Oct. 6, 1998.

Wells, Junior, 63, harmonica player and singer; a leading figure in Chicago's blues scene; Chicago, IL, Jan. 15, 1998.

Wethered, Joyce, 96, elegant champion woman golfer of the 20s; London, England, Nov. 18, 1997.

Williams, Wendy O., 48, punk rock singer who led the 80s band the Plasmatics; committed suicide; Storrs, CT, Apr. 6, 1998.

Wills Moody, Helen, 92, tennis player who in 15 years won 31 Grand Slam tournaments; Carmel, CA, Jan. 1, 1998.

Wilson, Carl, 51, cofounder and lead guitarist of the Beach Boys; Los Angeles, CA, Feb. 7, 1998.

Wilson, Lionel, 82, 1st black mayor of Oakland, CA (1977-91); Oakland, CA, Jan. 23, 1998.

Wynette, Tammy, 55, country music queen who recorded more than 50 albums and had 20 No. 1 hits, including "Stand by Your Man" (1968); Nashville, TN, Apr. 6, 1998.

Y

Yankovic, Frank, 83, singer and accordionist known as the Polka King; New Port Richey, FL, Oct. 14, 1998.

Yorty, Sam, 88, blunt-talking Democratic mayor of Los Angeles (1961-73); Studio City, CA, June 5, 1998.

Young, Coleman A., 79, combative politician who was the 1st black mayor of Detroit, serving a record 20 years (1974-93); Detroit, MI, Nov. 29, 1997.

Young, Robert, 91, actor who portrayed the wise dad on *Father Knows Best* in the 50s and the caring family doctor on *Marcus Welby, M.D.* (1969-76); Westlake Village, CA, July 21, 1998.

Youngman, Henny, 91, Borscht Belt comedian known as king of the one-liners; New York, NY, Feb. 24, 1998.

Z

Zhivkov, Todor, 86, Communist leader of Bulgaria (1954-89); Sofia, Bulgaria, Aug. 5, 1998.

Historical Anniversaries

1899 — 100 Years Ago

Pres. William McKinley signs the Treaty of Paris, **Feb. 10,** officially ending the Spanish-American War.

Miners on strike in Wardner, ID, **Apr. 29,** blow up mills and destroy $250,000 worth of property.

The 1st Hague Peace Conference adjourns, **July 29;** the 26 nations agree to create the Hague Court.

Secretary of State John Hay sends a letter to countries with interests in China, **Sept. 6,** proclaiming an Open-Door Policy to make China an open international market.

Capt. Alfred Dreyfus is pardoned of treason by the French government, **Sept. 19,** after a new trial precipitated by Emile Zola's *"J'Accuse"* open letter in a Paris newspaper reveals Dreyfus was victim of an anti-Semitic plot.

The Boer War begins in southern Africa when Pres. Paul Kruger of the Boer Republic, **Oct. 12,** takes steps to block the British from acquiring the rich Transvaal.

Art. Paul Gauguin's *Two Tahitian Women,* Augustus Saint-Gaudens's *The Puritan,* Jean Edouard Vuillard's *Paysages et intérieurs.*

Drama. *Uncle Vanya* by Anton Chekhov, *Caesar and Cleopatra* by George Bernard Shaw.

Literature. *The Awakening* by Kate Chopin, *The Blue Hotel* by Stephen Crane, "A Message to Garcia" by Elbert Hubbard, *The Turn of the Screw* by Henry James, "The White Man's Burden" by Rudyard Kipling, *McTeague* by Frank Norris, *The Gentleman From Indiana* by Booth Tarkington, *The War of the Worlds* by H.G. Wells.

Music. *Enigma Variations* by Edward Elgar; the opera *Cinderella,* with music by Jules Massenet; sheet music to Scott Joplin's "Maple Leaf Rag" published.

Nonfiction. *The School and Society* by John Dewey, *The Philadelphia Negro* by W.E.B. Du Bois, *The Theory of the Leisure Class* by Thorstein Veblen.

Popular Songs. "Hello, Ma Baby" by Joseph E. Howard, lyrics by Ida Emerson; "My Wild Irish Rose" by Chauncey Olcott; "O Sole Mio!" by Edoardo di Capna, lyrics by Giovanni Capurro.

Science and Technology. German researchers Felix Hoffman and Hermann Dreser perfect aspirin; French chemists Marie and Pierre Curie isolate radium.

Miscellaneous. The boll weevil enters the U.S. from Mexico, devastating agriculture in cotton-growing states. Coca-Cola is bottled for the first time, by two Chattanooga, TN, lawyers. Wesson Oil is developed by David Wesson, a chemist at the Southern Oil Co.

1949 — 50 Years Ago

The UN arranges a cease-fire in Kashmir, **Jan. 1,** ending a war between India and Pakistan.

The U.S. Supreme Court upholds the Taft-Hartley Act, **Jan. 3,** ruling that states have the right to ban closed shops.

Congress raises the president's salary to $100,000, plus $50,000 tax-free for expenses, **Jan. 19.**

Pres. Harry S. Truman is inaugurated, **Jan. 20.**

Chiang Kai-shek resigns as president of China, **Jan. 21,** as his Nationalist forces lose ground in their long civil war with the Communists.

Israel and Egypt sign an armistice, **Feb. 24,** in a war that began in 1948; separate armistices are signed by Israel and other Arab nations throughout the year.

Air Force pilots flying in the B-50 Superfortress *Lucky Lady II,* **Mar. 2,** complete the first nonstop round-the-world flight in 94 hrs, 1 min, refueling in the air 4 times.

France recognizes the independence of Indochina's non-Communist government, **Mar. 8.**

Newfoundland joins the Dominion of Canada, **Mar. 31.**

The North Atlantic Treaty Organization (NATO) is authorized, **Apr. 4;** takes effect **Aug. 24.**

The Republic of Ireland is formally proclaimed, **Apr. 18,** but Britain reasserts its claims to Northern Ireland, **May 17.**

The Soviets officially lift the Berlin blockade, **May 12,** after 11 months.

The Federal Republic of Germany is officially established from the postwar occupation zones administered by the Western Allies, **May 23.**

The last U.S. combat troops are withdrawn from Korea, **June 29.**

Pres. Truman signs the National Security Act, **Aug. 10,** creating the Department of Defense from the War Department. Gen. Omar Bradley is named first chairman of the Joint Chiefs of Staff, **Aug. 11.**

Some 480,000 coal workers strike, **Sept. 19.** Pres. Truman invokes the Taft-Hartley Act, **Sept. 30,** but strikers refuse to obey the injunction. The strike is settled after UMW leaders are cited for contempt and then acquitted.

Pres. Truman announces, **Sept. 23,** that the Soviets have developed an atomic bomb.

Iva Toguri D'Aquino (Tokyo Rose) is found guilty of treason, **Sept. 29,** for making radio broadcasts for Japan during World War II; she receives a 6-year prison sentence.

The People's Republic of China is proclaimed under Mao Zedong, **Oct. 1.**

The German Democratic Republic is established, **Oct. 7,** under Soviet auspices.

Eleven leaders of the U.S. Communist Party are convicted, **Oct. 14,** of advocating a violent overthrow of the government.

Permanent United Nations headquarters in New York City dedicated **Oct. 24.**

Pres. Truman signs a measure, **Oct. 26,** raising the minimum wage from 40¢ to 75¢ an hour.

The Netherlands cedes sovereignty to Indonesia, **Dec. 27,** after four years of war.

Art. Marc Chagall's *Red Sun,* Raoul Dufy's *The Studio,* Pablo Picasso's *Woman With a Fish Hat;* architect Philip Johnson designs the Glass House in New Canaan, CT.

Drama. *Romulus the Great* by Friedrich Dürrenmatt, *Member of the Wedding* by Carson McCullers, *Death of a Salesman* by Arthur Miller.

Literature. *The Man With the Golden Arm* by Nelson Algren, *The Sheltering Sky* by Paul Bowles, *The Third Man* by Graham Greene, *Point of No Return* by John P. Marquand, *A Rage to Live* by John O'Hara, *1984* by George Orwell, *The Greatest Story Ever Told* by Fulton Oursler; Margaret Mitchell dies, **Aug. 16,** after being hit by a car.

Movies. *Adam's Rib* with Spencer Tracy, Katharine Hepburn, Judy Holliday; *All the King's Men* with Broderick Crawford, Mercedes McCambridge; *Sands of Iwo Jima* with John Wayne; *The Third Man* with Orson Welles, Joseph Cotten, Trevor Howard; *Twelve O'Clock High* with Gregory Peck, Dean Jagger; *White Heat* with James Cagney; Ingrid Bergman, involved in an affair with Roberto Rossellini, announces, **Aug. 5,** that she is ending her marriage and film career.

Music. *The Age of Anxiety* by Leonard Bernstein.

Musicals. *Gentlemen Prefer Blondes* with Carol Channing, music by Jule Styne, lyrics by Leo Rubin; *South Pacific* with Ezio Pinza, Mary Martin, music by Richard Rodgers, lyrics by Oscar Hammerstein II.

Nonfiction. *The Second Sex* by Simone de Beauvoir, *The Elementary Structures of Kinship* by Claude Lévi-Strauss, *King Solomon's Ring* by Konrad Lorenz, *A Guide to Confident Living* by Norman Vincent Peale, *Peace of Soul* by Fulton J. Sheen, *The Need for Roots* by Simone Weil.

Popular Songs. "Dear Hearts and Gentle People" by Sammy Fein, lyrics by Bob Hilliard; "Mona Lisa" by Jay Livingston and Ray Evans; "Rudolph, the Red-Nosed Reindeer" by Johnny Marks; "Scarlet Ribbons (for Her Hair)" by Evelyn Danzig, lyrics by Jack Segal; "Some Enchanted Evening" by Richard Rodgers, lyrics by Oscar Hammerstein II.

Science and Technology. The pituitary hormone ACTH is synthesized by researchers at Merck Laboratories. The antibiotic oxytetracycline is developed. Neomycin is isolated by Selman Waksman. The Framingham heart study begins in Mass., tracking subjects' long-term health.

Sports. Joe Louis retires, **Mar. 1** (but comes back in 1950), and Ezzard Charles becomes world heavyweight champion, defeating Jersey Joe Walcott in Chicago, **June 22.** The Zamboni machine is invented, to remake ice surfaces for hockey and skating.

Television. *The Goldbergs* becomes television's first situation comedy. The first Emmy awards are presented.

Miscellaneous. The German Volkswagen is introduced in the U.S. Silly Putty is introduced by advertising man Peter C.L. Hodgson of New Haven, CT. General Mills and Pillsbury unveil prepared cake mixes. Unicef sells its first Christmas cards.

1974 — 25 Years Ago

Secretary of State Henry Kissinger mediates a disengagement agreement in the Sinai between Egypt and Israel, **Jan. 17.**

Heiress Patricia Hearst is kidnapped in Berkeley, CA, by members of the Symbionese Liberation Army, **Feb. 5.** She joins the radical group, taking part in a San Francisco bank robbery, **Apr. 15.**

A 410-4 vote by the House of Representatives gives the Judiciary Committee, under Rep. Peter Rodino Jr., broad powers to pursue its impeachment inquiry against Pres. Richard Nixon, **Feb. 6.** Hearings open **May 9.**

The final Skylab space mission ends, **Feb. 8,** after its 3-man crew returns to earth.

Seven former Nixon associates, including H.R. Haldeman, John Ehrlichman, and John Mitchell, are indicted, **Mar. 1,** for conspiring to obstruct justice in the investigation of the Watergate break-in. The trial begins **Oct. 1.**

The Arab oil embargo against the U.S. is officially lifted, **Mar. 18.**

Mariner 10 takes the first close-up pictures of Mercury, **Mar. 29.**

French Pres. Georges Pompidou dies, **Apr. 2;** he is succeeded by conservative Valery Giscard d'Estaing.

Helmut Schmidt becomes chancellor of West Germany, **May 16,** succeeding Willy Brandt, who resigned **May 6** as a result of a spy scandal.

India sets off a nuclear device, **May 18.**

Mediated by Secretary of State Kissinger, Israel and Syria sign a truce on the Golan Heights, **May 31.**

Argentine Pres. Juan Perón dies, **July 1,** and is succeeded by his wife, Isabel.

John Ehrlichman and three White House "plumbers" are found guilty, **July 12,** of conspiracy to violate the rights of Pentagon Papers leaker Daniel Ellsberg's psychiatrist by breaking into his office in 1971.

Greek army officers stage a coup in Cyprus, **July 15,** prompting Turkey to invade the island, **July 20.** The Greek military junta collapses, **July 23.**

The U.S. Supreme Court rules, 8-0, that Pres. Nixon must turn over 64 White House tapes to special prosecutor Leon Jaworski, **July 24.**

The House Judiciary Committee begins televised impeachment hearings, **July 24,** and on **July 27-30,** votes 3 articles of impeachment against Pres. Nixon.

Former Nixon aide John Dean is sentenced, **Aug. 2,** to 3 years in prison after pleading guilty in Watergate cover-up.

Pres. Nixon announces his resignation, **Aug. 8,** and resigns on **Aug. 9,** succeeded by Vice Pres. Gerald Ford. Ford nominates Nelson Rockefeller to be vice president, **Aug. 20;** he is sworn in on **Dec. 19.** Ford grants Nixon an unconditional pardon for any federal crimes he committed while president, **Sept. 8.**

Ethiopian Emperor Haile Selassie is overthrown by the military, **Sept. 12.**

Pres. Ford offers amnesty to Vietnam draft evaders and deserters, **Sept. 16,** in exchange for public service.

The National Guard is mobilized in Boston, **Oct. 15,** in the wake of violence over court-ordered school busing.

Residents of Washington, DC, for the first time elect their own mayor and city council, **Nov. 5.**

Eight present and former members of the Ohio National Guard are acquitted in the 1970 deaths of four Kent State University students, **Nov. 8.**

Congress passes the Freedom of Information Act, **Nov. 21,** over Pres. Ford's veto.

Pres. Ford and Soviet leader Leonid Brezhnev conclude a treaty limiting strategic nuclear arms, **Nov. 23-24.**

Dance. Soviet ballet dancer Mikhail Baryshnikov defects to the West, **June 29.**

Drama. *Absurd Person Singular* by Alan Ayckbourn, *Equus* by Peter Shaffer, *Travesties* by Tom Stoppard.

Literature. *Jaws* by Peter Benchley, *Something Happened* by Joseph Heller, *Tinker, Tailor, Soldier, Spy* by John le Carré, *Centennial* by James Michener.

Movies. *Alice Doesn't Live Here Anymore* with Ellen Burstyn; *The Apprenticeship of Duddy Kravitz* with Richard Dreyfuss; *Blazing Saddles* with Cleavon Little, Gene Wilder; *Chinatown* with Jack Nicholson, Faye Dunaway; *The Godfather, Part II* with Al Pacino, Robert DeNiro; *The Great Gatsby* with Robert Redford, Mia Farrow.

Musicals. *Candide* with Lewis J. Stadlen, Mark Baker, music by Leonard Bernstein, lyrics by John Latouche, Richard Wilbur, Dorothy Parker, Stephen Sondheim; *Gypsy* with Angela Lansbury, music by Jule Styne, lyrics by Stephen Sondheim; *The Magic Show* with Doug Henning, music and lyrics by Stephen Schwartz.

Nonfiction. After publication of *The Gulag Archipelago,* Soviet authorities arrest Aleksandr Solzhenitsyn and deport him to the West; *All the President's Men* by Carl Bernstein and Bob Woodward, *Plain Speaking: An Oral Biography of Harry S Truman* by Merle Miller, *About Behaviorism* by B.F. Skinner, *Working* by Studs Terkel.

Popular Songs. "Annie's Song" and "Sunshine on My Shoulder" by John Denver; "I Honestly Love You" by Peter Allen, lyrics by Jeff Barry; "The Way We Were" by Marvin Hamlisch, lyrics by Alan and Marilyn Bergman; "(You're) Havin' My Baby" by Paul Anka.

Science and Technology. The National Cancer Institute reports the standard radical mastectomy may be too drastic in treating many breast cancer cases. The Heimlich maneuver is introduced as first aid for choking. Scientists report that gases from aerosol cans are damaging the ozone layer.

Sports. Girls are allowed to play Little League baseball. Hank Aaron breaks Babe Ruth's career home run record when he hits number 715 in Atlanta, **Apr. 8.** Frank Robinson becomes the first black major league manager when he signs with Cleveland, **Oct. 3.** Muhammad Ali regains the world heavyweight championship from George Foreman, **Oct. 30.**

Television. Situation comedies *All in the Family, Chico and the Man, The Jeffersons, M*A*S*H, Sanford and Son.*

Miscellaneous. A recession begins in the U.S. and Europe. Streaking becomes a fad, especially on college campuses. The ironclad *Monitor,* lost during the Civil War, is reported found off Hatteras, NC. *People* magazine begins publication.

Notable Quotes in 1998

"I have never had sexual relations with Monica Lewinsky. I've never had an affair with her."
Pres. Bill Clinton, in his deposition in the Paula Corbin Jones sexual misconduct lawsuit, Jan. 17, 1998.

"I am going to say this again: I did not have sexual relations with that woman, Miss Lewinsky. I never told anybody to lie, not a single time—never. These allegations are false. And I need to go back to work for the American people."
Pres. Bill Clinton, Jan. 26, in a speech at the White House.

"I'd give anything in the world not to have to admit what I've had to admit today."
Pres. Bill Clinton, during his videotaped grand-jury appearance, Aug. 17.

"In a deposition in January, I was asked questions about my relationship with Monica Lewinsky. While my answers were legally accurate, I did not volunteer information. Indeed I did have a relationship with Ms. Lewinsky that was not appropriate. In fact, it was wrong. It constituted a critical lapse in judgment and a personal failure on my part for which I am solely and completely responsible . . . I misled people, including my wife. I deeply regret that."
Pres. Bill Clinton in his Aug. 17 speech to the nation.

"Such behavior is not just inappropriate—it is immoral."
Sen. Joseph Lieberman (D, CT), speaking on the Senate floor about Clinton's conduct in the Lewinsky scandal, Sept. 3.

"I made a bad mistake. It was indefensible, and I'm sorry about it."
Pres. Clinton, apologizing explicitly for the first time, in an appearance with Irish Prime Minister Bertie Ahern, Sept. 4.

"The Office of the Independent Counsel . . . hereby submits substantial and credible information that President William Jefferson Clinton committed acts that may constitute grounds for an impeachment."
From independent counsel *Kenneth Starr*'s Sept. 9 report to the House of Representatives.

"This is personal, and not impeachable. The salacious allegations in this referral are simply intended to humiliate, embarrass and politically damage the president."
Clinton's private attorney *David Kendall*, after the release of independent counsel Kenneth Starr's report.

"I'm really sorry for everything that's happened. And I hate Linda Tripp."
Monica Lewinsky, during an appearance before a grand jury convened by Kenneth Starr.

"Do I know what's in this bill? Are you kidding? Only God knows what's in this conference report."
West Virginia *Sen. Robert Byrd*, on the $520 billion, 4,000-page omnibus spending bill passed by Congress in Oct. 1998.

"Let our actions today send this message loud and clear. There are no expendable American targets. There will be no sanctuary for terrorists. We will defend our people, our interests, and our values."
Pres. Bill Clinton, following the missile assaults in Afghanistan and Sudan after bombings of U.S. embassies in Kenya and Tanzania.

"It shows that the best way to resolve our problem is by spilling our sweat together and not our blood across the divide."
Irish Catholic leader *John Hume*, after the Northern Ireland peace agreement.

"Today is a day when Israel and our entire region are more secure."
Israeli Prime Min. Benjamin Netanyahu, after signing the Oct. Middle East peace agreement.

"We will never leave the peace process, and we will never go back to violence and confrontation."
PLO Chairman Yasir Arafat, after signing the Oct. Middle East peace agreement.

"I wish Pol Pot were still alive. I still want to know what happened, why Pol Pot killed so many people, why he killed my brothers. Yes, I would like to hear him say why he killed them."
Cambodian legal assistant *Oum Bun Thoeun*, after learning of the death of Pol Pot.

"They kicked one, and he was alive. They shot him again. When they kicked me, I didn't move."
A 42-year-old ethnic Albanian, reportedly the sole survivor of a Serbian massacre in Kosovo in which 13 villagers were killed.

"I am a terrorist and I am proud of it."
World Trade Center bomber *Ramzi Ahmed Yousef*, after being sentenced to life plus 240 years in prison.

"Today, we have evened the score with India."
Pakistani Prime Min. Nawaz Sharif, following his country's first nuclear tests, conducted in response to India's tests.

"I'm terribly sorry, but would you mind if my wife and I butted in? The thing is, I've got to go and see the queen at 6 o'clock."
British Prime Min. Tony Blair, to parents ahead of him on line for a parent-teacher meeting at his children's school.

"My hair does not deserve so much attention."
Russian Pres. Boris Yeltsin, responding online to an Irish woman who complimented his thick hair.

"Me."
Former Secretary of State Henry Kissinger, who was joking around when he was asked at *Time* magazine's 75th-anniversary party what man had changed history over the past 75 years.

"We want to expiate the sins of our ancestors. Guilty are those who committed this heinous crime, and those who have been justifying it for decades—all of us."
Russian Pres. Boris Yeltsin, at the funeral of Tsar Nicholas II, who was buried in 1998, 80 years after he and his family were murdered by Bolshevik zealots.

"I would like to say that [my family's] reaction to—to today's plea agreement is one of deep relief. We—we feel it is the appropriate, just and civilized resolution to this tragedy in light of Ted's diagnosed mental illness."
David Kaczynski, following the guilty plea made by his brother Theodore Kaczynski, the Unabomber, in return for life in prison rather than a sentence of death.

"I'm king of the world!"
Titanic director *James Cameron*, quoting a line from the movie after receiving the Academy Award for directing.

"Even if I did do this, it would have to have been because I loved her very much, right?"
O.J. Simpson, discussing the murder of his ex-wife, Nicole Brown, in an interview in *Esquire* magazine.

"It's the babies that are dead, and babies that did it."
Teacher *Christy Hall*, on the shooting deaths of 4 students and a teacher by 2 other students at a Jonesboro, AR, school.

"My reaction is that free speech not only lives, it rocks!"
Talk-show host *Oprah Winfrey*, following her victory in a defamation suit for disparaging comments about beef.

"I guess we still have some bugs to work out."
Microsoft chairman *Bill Gates*, whose computer system crashed while he was demonstrating the new Windows 98.

"I'll make this statement: he was in the protocol, and it's a great drug."
Elizabeth Dole, describing the anti-impotence medication Viagra, after her husband Bob Dole helped test the drug.

"I think the time is right."
Cal Ripken, after removing himself from the lineup, having played in 2,632 consecutive games.

"To all my family, my son, the Cubs, Sammy Sosa, it's unbelievable. Thank you, St. Louis."
Mark McGwire, after he hit his 62d home run of the season, breaking Roger Maris's record.

"I won't say anything about us being the greatest. But there hasn't been anybody better."
George Steinbrenner, after the Yankees swept the San Diego Padres for their 24th world championship, following an American League record season of 114 wins.

"I have lost my girlfriend, and it is very sad."
Former Beatle *Paul McCartney*, on the death of his wife, Linda.

Offbeat News Stories, 1998

Golden Age: Marie-Louise Febronie Meilleur, certified by the *Guinness Book of World Records* as the world's oldest person, died Apr. 16 in an Ontario nursing home at the age of 117. She was survived by 85 grandchildren, 80 great-grandchildren, 57 great-great-grandchildren, and 4 great-great-great-grandchildren. Felicie Young Cormier, who claimed to be 118 (but lacked the birth certificate to prove it), had died in Crowley, LA, just before midnight on Apr. 14. The mantle of "world's oldest" thus passed to Sarah Knauss of Allentown, PA, born Sept. 24, 1880. When told the news, the 117-year-old woman replied, "So what?"

Easy Payment Plan: In April, the Internal Revenue Service sent Lorie Marling of Columbus, OH, a bill for $270 billion in back taxes. The letter, which the IRS later admitted was a mistake, offered to let her pay the debt in three installments of only $90 billion each.

Bionic Grandma: Under the heading "Medical Extremes," the *Guinness Book of World Records* cited Norma Wickwire of Inverness, FL, for having had 8 of her 10 major joints replaced—both knees, both hips, both shoulders, an ankle, and an elbow. "It's a heck of a way to get famous," said the 76-year-old woman, who has rheumatoid arthritis and osteoporosis.

Better Wed Than Dead: When UN-sponsored weapons inspections resumed in Iraq in March, one of the first sites Scott Ritter and his UNSCOM team visited was a previously off-limits Special Security Organization facility, suddenly dark because of a mysterious "power failure." In each room the flashlight-wielding inspectors entered, the story was the same: empty shelves, a nearly bare desk, and at each desk a lone man with a mustache. What were the men doing there? We're marriage registrars, the Iraqi officials indicated, one by one. "Each desk had its piece of paper and its sharpened pencil and 5 empty files," an inspection team member later told the *Washington Post*. "It almost showed a sense of humor."

Unwelcome News: A spokesman for Cendant Corp. confirmed in October that its Welcome Wagon subsidiary would end a 70-year tradition of making personal deliveries of greeting baskets to new homeowners. Instead, newcomers will be mailed a bound directory of discount coupons. Welcome Wagon visits, which peaked in 1968 at about 1.5 million annually, had diminished to 580,000 in 1997.

A Great Idea That Didn't Hold Water: To rustle up some federal research dollars for his home state, Sen. Patrick Leahy in February slipped into an otherwise obscure bill a sentence that qualified Vermont's Lake Champlain as a sixth "Great Lake." When Leahy's creative geography became public knowledge, indignant senators and commentators ridiculed the change, noting that even Ontario, smallest of the Big Five, covers a surface area 17 times greater than that of Champlain. The abashed Leahy beat a retreat, sponsoring an amendment that abandoned Champlain's grandiose ambitions while preserving Vermont's eligibility for the additional research funds.

Special Delivery: Defying incredible odds, 3 sisters in Orem, UT, all gave birth the same day, Mar. 11, 1998. Although she wasn't due until Apr. 4, Karralee Morgan, 28, went first—she delivered a son at 7:18 AM. The 2d sister, Marrianne Asay, 27, gave birth to a son at 3:25 PM, and finally, Jennifer Hone, 24, the 3d sister, delivered a daughter at 8:58 PM.

Luck of the Draw: Results of the 1998 mayoral race in Estancia, NM, were dead even: each candidate had received 68 votes in this small town in central New Mexico. According to state rules, the 2 candidates had to choose a game of chance to break the tie, winner take all. Unable to agree on the game of chance, JoAnn Carlson, the challenger, and James Farrington, the incumbent, flipped a coin to decide whose preference would be played out—Carlson's roll of the dice or Farrington's 5-card draw. Carlson lost the coin toss, the card game, and the mayor's seat.

Miscellaneous Facts, 1998

—**Atomic Audit:** The total spent by the U.S. on nuclear weapons and weapons-related programs since 1940 is nearly $5.5 trillion (in constant 1996 dollars), according to a June 30 report by the Brookings Institution. The U.S. spent more on its nuclear arsenal during 1940-96 than on any other budget category except nonnuclear defense ($13.2 trillion) and Social Security ($7.9 trillion). According to an article published in March by the Natural Resources Defense Council, these states led the U.S. in numbers of nuclear weapons: New Mexico, 2,450; Georgia, 2,000; Washington, 1,685; Nevada, 1,350; and North Dakota, 1,140.

—**Bridge to the Past:** The Norwegian highway department is replacing an ugly pedestrian bridge near Oslo with a scaled-down version of an elliptical arch originally designed in 1502 by Leonardo da Vinci. Leonardo's visionary proposal, which was meant to cross the Golden Horn in Istanbul, was rejected by the Ottoman sultan.

—**Net Notes:** How big is the World Wide Web? In a July 5 article in the *New York Times*, estimates ranged from about 200 million pages to between 500 million and 1 billion pages, with Internet traffic up more than a hundredfold over the last 3 years. A report on the "emerging digital economy" issued in April by the U.S. Commerce Department projected that sales of goods over the Internet could surpass $300 billion by 2002. Relevant Knowledge, a market research firm, estimated in September that 5.9 million netizens downloaded independent counsel Kenneth Starr's report on the Clinton-Lewinsky scandal.

—**Titanic Achievements:** The bean counters in residence at boxofficeguru.com calculate that James Cameron's *Titanic* passed the $600 million box-office mark in the U.S. and Canada on Aug. 27, in its 252d day of release. The film also racked up about $1.2 billion in overseas revenues, for a worldwide total of $1.8 billion—almost double the previous high set by *Jurassic Park* in 1993.

—**Sex Surveys:** Analyzing the results of the General Social Survey, the February issue of *American Demographics* magazine reported that people who watch public television have more sex than those who watch prime-time dramas, jazz aficionados have more sex than rock and rap fans, liberals have more sex than moderates or conservatives, and people who smoke, drink, and own guns have more sex than those who don't. Among teens, sexual activity was down and condom use up, according to results of the federal Youth Risk Behavior Survey issued Sept. 17. The Allan Guttmacher Institute announced Oct. 14 that the teen pregnancy rate in the U.S. had fallen to a 23-year low.

—**Getting and Giving:** Released in late September, *Forbes* magazine's annual list of the 400 richest Americans was headed for the 5th consecutive year by Microsoft chief Bill Gates, with a fortune of $58.4 billion. Next on the list, which included a record 189 billionaires, were investment adviser Warren Buffett ($29.4 billion) and Microsoft co-founder Paul Allen ($22 billion). A $327 million contribution by James and Virginia Stowers, both cancer survivors, to establish a medical research institute in Kansas City, MO, topped *Slate* magazine's roster of 60 leading U.S. charitable donations during the 1st half of 1998.

—**Record Feats:** Swimming 6 to 8 hours a day, and resting in a 40-ft boat that accompanied him on his 3,716-mi journey, Ben Lecomte of France became the 1st person to swim across the Atlantic, July 16-Sept. 25. With a nonstop smooch of 28 hours, 35 minutes, and 23 seconds, Roberta and Mark Griswold of Allen Park, MI, won the Longest Kiss Competition, sponsored by Breath Savers in late March. Self-proclaimed "pushup king" Jeffrey Warrick of Buffalo, NY, set a new world mark June 20 by doing 46,200 pushups in 24 hours; 5 days later, on NBC's *Today* show, he shattered the standard for most pushups in an hour with an impressive total of 1,881.

UNITED STATES GOVERNMENT

EXECUTIVE BRANCH

PRESIDENT

Vice President

Executive Office of the President

White House Office
Office of the Vice President
Council of Economic Advisers
Council on Environmental Quality
National Security Council
Office of Administration
Office of Management and Budget
Office of National Drug Control Policy
Office of Policy Development
Office of Science and Technology Policy
Office of the U.S. Trade Representative

LEGISLATIVE BRANCH

CONGRESS

Senate House

Architect of the Capitol
U.S. Botanic Garden
General Accounting Office
Government Printing Office
Library of Congress
Congressional Budget Office

JUDICIAL BRANCH

Supreme Court of the United States

Courts of Appeals
District Courts
Territorial Courts
Court of International Trade
Court of Federal Claims
Court of Appeals for the Armed Forces
Tax Court
Court of Veterans Appeals
Administrative Office of the Courts
Federal Judicial Center
Sentencing Commission

The Clinton Administration

As of Oct. 31, 1998; mailing addresses are for Washington, DC.

Terms of office of the president and vice president: Jan. 20, 1997, to Jan. 20, 2001.

President — Bill Clinton receives an annual salary of $200,000 (taxable), and an annual expense allowance of $50,000 (nontaxable) for costs resulting from official duties. In addition, up to $100,000 a year may be spent on travel expenses and $19,000 on official entertainment (both nontaxable), available for allocation within the Executive Office of the President.

Vice President — Albert Gore Jr. receives an annual salary of $175,400, plus $10,000 for expenses, all taxable.

The Cabinet Department Heads

(Salary: $151,800 per year)

Secretary of State — Madeleine K. Albright
Secretary of the Treasury — Robert E. Rubin
Secretary of Defense — William S. Cohen
Attorney General — Janet Reno
Secretary of the Interior — Bruce Babbitt
Secretary of Agriculture — Dan Glickman
Secretary of Commerce — William M. Daley
Secretary of Labor — Alexis M. Herman
Secretary of Health and Human Services — Donna E. Shalala
Secretary of Housing and Urban Development — Andrew M. Cuomo
Secretary of Transportation — Rodney E. Slater
Secretary of Energy — Bill Richardson
Secretary of Education — Richard W. Riley
Secretary of Veterans Affairs — Togo D. West Jr.

The White House Staff

1600 Pennsylvania Ave. NW 20500

Chief of Staff to the President — John Podesta
Asst. to the President & Deputy Chief of Staff — vacant
Asst. to the President & Deputy Chief of Staff — Maria Echaveste
Senior Adviser on Policy & Strategy — Rahm Emanuel
Assistants to the President:
- **Counsel to the President** — Charles F. C. Ruff
- **Deputy Counsel to the President** — Bruce Lindsey
- **Special Counsel** — Greg Craig
- **Domestic Policy Council** — Bruce Reed
  - **Office of National AIDS Policy** — Sandy Thurman, dir.
- **Presidential Personnel** — Bob Nash
- **Press Secretary** — Joseph Lockhart
- **Legislative Affairs** — Lawrence Stein
- **Communications** — Ann Lewis/Sidney Blumenthal
- **National Economic Policy** — Gene Sperling
- **Intergovernmental Affairs** — Mickey Ibarra
- **National Security** — Samuel R. Berger
- **Staff Secretary** — Phil Caplan
- **Political Affairs** — Craig Smith
- **Public Liaison** — Minyon Moore
- **Management & Administration** — Virginia Apuzzo
- **Counselor to the President** — Doug Sosnik/Paul Begala
- **Cabinet Secretary** — Thurgood Marshall Jr.
- **Director of Presidential Scheduling** — Stephanie Streett
- **Director of Speechwriting** — Michael Waldman
- **Chief of Staff to the First Lady** — Melanne Verveer
- **Special Projects** — Todd Stern

Executive Agencies

Council of Economic Advisers — Janet Yellen, chair
Office of Administration — Ada Posey, dir.
Office of Science & Technology Policy — Neal F. Lane
Office of Nat. Drug Control Policy — Barry R. McCaffrey
Office of Management and Budget — Jacob J. Lew, dir.
U.S. Trade Representative — Charlene Barshefsky
Council on Environ. Quality — Kathleen McGinty, chair

Department of State

2201 C St. NW 20520

Secretary of State — Madeleine K. Albright
Deputy Secretary — Strobe Talbott
Chief of Staff — Elaine K. Shocas
U.S. Ambassador to the United Nations — A. Peter Burleigh, act.
Under Sec. for Political Affairs — Thomas R. Pickering
Under Sec. for Management — Bonnie R. Cohen
Under Sec. for Global Affairs — vacant
Under Sec. for Economic, Business, & Agricultural Affairs — Stuart Eizenstat
Under Sec. for Arms Control & International Security Affairs — John D. Holum
Policy Planning Director — vacant
Chief of Protocol — Mary Mel French
Inspector General — Jacqueline L. Williams-Bridgers
Legal Adviser — David R. Andrews
Director General of the Foreign Service & Director of Personnel — Edward W. Grehm Jr.
Assistant Secretaries for:
- **Administration** — Patrick F. Kennedy
- **African Affairs** — Susan E. Rice
- **Consular Affairs** — Mary A. Ryan
- **Democracy, Human Rights, & Labor** — John Shattuck
- **Diplomatic Security** — Patrick F. Kennedy, act.
- **East Asian & Pacific Affairs** — Stanley Roth
- **Economic & Business Affairs** — Alan Larson
- **European & Canadian Affairs** — Marc Grossman
- **Intelligence & Research** — Phyllis E. Oakley
- **Inter-American Affairs** — vacant
- **International Narcotics & Law** — vacant
- **International Organization Affairs** — Princeton Lyman
- **Legislative Affairs** — Barbara Larkin
- **Near Eastern Affairs** — Martin S. Indyk
- **Oceans, International Environmental, & Scientific Affairs** — Melinda Kimble
- **Politico-Military Affairs** — Eric D. Newson, act.
- **Population, Refugees, & Migration** — Julia V. Taft
- **Public Affairs** — James P. Rubin
- **South Asian Affairs** — Karl Inderfurth

Department of the Treasury

1500 Pennsylvania Ave. NW 20220

Secretary of the Treasury — Robert E. Rubin
Deputy Sec. of the Treasury — Lawrence H. Summers
Under Sec. for Domestic Finance — John Hawke
Under Sec. for International Affairs — David Lipton
Under Sec. for Enforcement — James Johnson
General Counsel — Edward Knight
Inspector General — vacant
Assistant Secretaries for:
- **Economic Policy** — David Wilcox
- **Enforcement** — James Johnson
- **Fiscal Affairs** — Donald Hammond, act.
- **International Affairs** — Tim Geithner
- **Legislative Affairs** — Linda Robertson
- **Public Affairs** — Howard Schloss
- **Tax Policy** — Donald Lubick
- **Management** — Nancy Killefer
- **Financial Institutions** — Richard Carnell

Treasurer of the U.S. — Mary Ellen Withrow
Bureaus:
- **Alcohol, Tobacco, & Firearms** — John W. Magaw, dir.
- **Comptroller of the Currency** — Julie L. Williams, act. comm.
- **Customs** — Raymond W. Kelly, comm.
- **Engraving & Printing** — Tom Ferguson, act. dir.
- **Federal Law Enforcement Training Center** — W. Ralph Basham, dir.
- **Financial Management Service** — Richard Gregg, comm.
- **Internal Revenue Service** — Charles Rossotti, comm.
- **Mint** — Philip N. Diehl, dir.
- **Public Debt** — Van Zeck, comm.
- **U.S. Secret Service** — Lewis C. Merletti, dir.
- **Office of Thrift Supervision** — Ellen S. Seidman

Department of Defense

The Pentagon 20301

Secretary of Defense — William S. Cohen
Deputy Secretary — John J. Hamre
Under Sec. for Acquis. and Technol. — Jacques S. Gansler
Under Sec. for Personnel & Readiness — Rudy de Leon
Under Sec. for Policy — Walter B. Slocombe
Assistant Secretaries for:
- **Command, Control, Communications, & Intelligence** — Arthur L. Money
- **Health Affairs** — Dr. Sue Bailey
- **International Security Policy** — Franklin C. Miller
- **Legislative Affairs** — Sandra Stuart
- **Program Analysis & Evaluation** — William J. Lynn III
- **Public Affairs** — Kenneth Bacon
- **Spec. Operations & Low Intensity Conflict**— H. Allen Holmes

Principal Dep. Asst. Sec. for Reserve Affairs — Charles L. Cragin
Comptroller — William J. Lynn III
General Counsel — Judith Miller
Operational Test & Evaluation — Phillip E. Coyle III
Chairman, Joint Chiefs of Staff — Gen. Henry Hugh Shelton
Secretary of the Army — Louis Caldera
Secretary of the Navy — John Dalton[1]
Secretary of the Air Force —F. Whitten Peters, act.

Department of Justice

Constitution Ave. & 10th St. NW 20530

Attorney General — Janet Reno
Deputy Attorney General — Eric H. Holder Jr.
Associate Attorney General — Raymond C. Fischer
Solicitor General — Seth Waxman
Office of Inspector General — Michael R. Bromwich
Assistants:
- **Antitrust Division** — Joel I. Klein
- **Civil Division** — Frank W. Hunger
- **Civil Rights Division** — Bill Lann Lee, act.
- **Criminal Division** — John C. Keeney, act.
- **Environ. & Nat. Resources Division** — Lois J. Schiffer
- **Justice Programs** — Laurie Robinson
- **Legal Counsel** — Dawn Johnsen, act.
- **Policy Development** — Eleanor D. Acheson
- **Legislative Affairs** — Tony Sutin, act.
- **Administration** — Stephen R. Colgate
- **Tax Division** — Loretta C. Argrett

Executive Secretariat — Anna Gatons
Office of Public Affairs — Bert Brandenburg
Office of Information & Privacy — Richard L. Huff/Daniel J. Metcalf
Community Oriented Policing Services — Joseph Brann, dir.
Federal Bureau of Investigation — Louis J. Freeh, dir.
Exec. Off. for Immigration Review — Tony Moscato, dir.
Bureau of Prisons — Kathleen M. Hawk Sawyer, dir.
Comm. Relations Service — Rose Ochi, dir.
Drug Enforcement Adm. — Tom Constantine
Office of Intelligence Policy & Review — Fran Fragos Townsend, counsel
Exec. Off. for National Security — Daniel Seikaly, dir.
Off. of Professional Responsibility — Richard M. Rogers, act.
Exec. Off. for U.S. Trustees — Joseph Patchan, dir.
Foreign Claims Comm. — Delissa Ridgway, comm.
Exec. Off. for U.S. Attorneys — Donna Bucella, dir.
Immigr. & Naturaliz. Service — Doris Meissner, comm.
Pardon Attorney — Roger Adams, act.
U.S. Parole Commission — Michael Gaines, chair
U.S. Marshals Service — Eduardo Gonzalez, dir.
U.S. Natl. Cen. Bureau of INTERPOL — John Imhoff, chief
Office of Intergovernmental Affairs — Nick Gess
Office of Tribal Justice — Thomas LeClaire
Violence Against Women Act — Bonnie Campbell

Department of the Interior

1849 C St. NW 20240

Secretary of the Interior — Bruce Babbitt
Deputy Secretary — vacant
Assistant Secretaries for:
- **Fish, Wildlife, & Parks** — Donald Barry
- **Indian Affairs** — Kevin Gover
- **Intergovernmental Affairs** — Grace Garcia, act.
- **Land & Minerals** — Robert Armstrong
- **Policy, Management, & Budget** — M. John Berry
- **Water & Science** — Patricia J. Beneke

Bureau of Land Management — Patrick Shea, dir.
Bureau of Reclamation — Eluid L. Martinez, comm.
Fish & Wildlife Service — Jamie Rappaport Clark, dir.
Geological Survey — Thomas Casadevall, act. dir.
Mineral Management Service — Cynthia Quarterman, dir.
National Park Service — Robert G. Stanton, dir.
Surf. Mining Reclam. & Enforcement — Kathy Karpan, dir.
Communications — Michael Gauldin, dir.
Off. of Congr. & Legisl. Affairs — David Alberswerth, act.
Solicitor — John D. Leshy
External Affairs — Jana Prewitt
Exec. Secretariat & Regulatory Affairs — Julie Faulkner

Department of Agriculture

1400 Independence Ave. SW 20250

Secretary of Agriculture — Dan Glickman
Deputy Secretary — Richard Rominger
Under Secretaries for:
- **Farm & Foreign Agric. Services** — Gus Schumacher Jr.
- **Food, Nutrition, & Consumer Services** — Shirley R. Watkins
- **Food Safety** — Catherine Woteki
- **Natural Resources & Environment** — Jim Lyons
- **Research, Education, & Economics** — Miley Gonzalez
- **Rural Development** — Jill Long Thompson

Assistant Secretaries for:
- **Administration** — Reba Pittman Evans, act.
- **Congressional Relations** — J. David Carlin
- **Marketing & Regulatory Programs** — Michael Dunn

General Counsel — Charlie Rawls
Inspector General — Roger C. Viadero
Chief Financial Officer — Sally Thompson
Chief Information Officer — Anne F. Thomson Reed
Chief Economist — Keith Collins
Communications/Press Secretary — Tom Amontree

Department of Commerce

14th St. between Constitution & Pennsylvania Ave. NW 20230

Secretary of Commerce — William M. Daley
Deputy Secretary — Robert Mallett
Chief of Staff — David Lane
General Counsel — Andrew Pincus

Assistant Secretaries:
Chief Financial Officer & Asst. Secretary for Administration — W. Scott Gould
Economic Development Adm. — Phillip Singerman
Export Admin. — R. Roger Majak
Export Enforcement — F. Amanda Debusk
Import Administration — Robert LaRussa
Legislative Affairs — Deborah Kilmer
Market Access & Compliance — Patrick Mulloy
Natl. Telecomm. Information Adm. — Clarence Irving Jr.
Oceans & Atmosphere — Terry Garcia
Patent & Trademark Office & Comm. — Bruce Lehman
Trade Development — Michael Copps
U.S. & Foreign Commercial Service — Awilda Marquez
Bureau of the Census — Kenneth Prewitt, dir.
Bureau of Economic Analysis — J. Steven Landerfeld, dir.
Under Sec. for Oceans & Atmosphere — D. James Baker
Under Sec. for Export Admin. — William Reinsch
Under Sec. for International Trade — David Aaron
Under Sec. for Econ. Affairs — Robert Shapiro
Under Sec. for Technology — Gary Bachula, act.
Natl. Technical Info. Service — Donald Johnson
Natl. Inst. for Standards & Tech. — Raymond Kammer
Minority Business Dev. Agency — Courtland Cox
Public Affairs — Mary Hanley
Press Secretary — vacant

Department of Labor

200 Constitution Ave. NW 20210

Secretary of Labor — Alexis M. Herman
Deputy Secretary — Kathryn Higgins
Chief of Staff — Lee Satterfield
Assistant Secretaries for:
Admin. & Management — Patricia W. Lattimore
Congressional & Intergov. Affairs — Geri Palast
Employment & Training — Ray Bramucci
Employment Standards — Bernard E. Anderson
Occupational Safety & Health — Charles Jeffress
Mine Safety & Health — Davitt McAteer
Pension & Welfare Benefits — E. Olena Berg
Policy — Rick McGahey
Public Affairs — Susan R. King
Veterans Employment & Training — Al Borrego
Solicitor of Labor — Marvin Kristov, act.
Bureau of International Affairs — Andrew Samet, act.
Women's Bureau — Dolores Crockett, act.
Inspector General — Charles C. Masten
Bureau of Labor Statistics — Katharine G. Abraham

Department of Health and Human Services

200 Independence Ave. SW 20201

Secretary of Health & Human Services — Donna E. Shalala
Deputy Secretary — Kevin L. Thurm
Chief of Staff — Mary Beth Donahue
Assistant Secretaries for:
Health — David Satcher
Legislation — Rich Tarplin
Management & Budget — John Callahan
Planning & Evaluation — Margaret Hamburg
Public Affairs — Melissa Skolfield
Aging — Jeanette Takamura
Children & Families — Olivia Golden, act.
General Counsel — Harriet Rabb
Inspector General — June Gibbs Brown
Surgeon General — David Satcher
Health Care Financing Adm. — Nancy Ann DeParle

Department of Housing and Urban Development

451 7th St. SW 20410

Sec. of Housing & Urban Development — Andrew M. Cuomo
Deputy Secretary — Saul Ramirez, act.
Assistant Secretaries for:
Administration — vacant
Community Planning & Development — Saul Ramirez
Fair Housing & Equal Opportunity — Eva Plaza
Housing & Federal Housing Commissioner — vacant
Cong. & Intergov. Relations — Halbert C. DeCell III
Policy Development & Research — vacant
Public Affairs — vacant
Public & Indian Housing — vacant
General Counsel — Gail Laster
Inspector General — Susan M. Gaffney
Chief Financial Officer — Richard F. Keevey
Government National Mortgage Assn. — vacant
Off. of Federal Housing Enterprise Oversight — Mark Kinsey, dir.

Department of Transportation

400 7th St. SW 20590

Secretary of Transportation — Rodney E. Slater
Deputy Secretary — Mortimer L. Downey
Assistant Secretaries for:
Administration — Melissa Allen
Budget & Programs — Jack Basso
Governmental Affairs — Steven O. Palmer
Aviation & International Affairs — Charles Hunnicutt
Transportation — Eugene Conti
Public Affairs — Steve Akey
U.S. Coast Guard Commandant — Adm. James M. Loy
Federal Aviation Admin. — Jane Garvey
Federal Highway Admin. — Kenneth Wykle
Federal Railroad Admin. — Jolene Molitoris
Maritime Admin. — Clyde Hart
Nat. Highway Traffic Safety Adm. — Ricardo Martinez
Federal Transit Admin. — Gordon J. Linton
Research & Special Programs Admin. — Kelley Coyner
St. Lawrence Seaway Devel. Corp. — David Sanders, act.

Department of Energy

1000 Independence Ave. SW 20585

Secretary of Energy — Bill Richardson
Deputy Secretary — vacant
Under Secretary — Ernest I. Moniz
Chief of Staff — Gary Falle
Deputy Chief of Staff for Intl. Policy — Rebecca Gaghen
Deputy Chief of Staff for Administration & Domestic Policy — LeeAnn Inadomi
General Counsel — Maryann Sullivan
Inspector General — John C. Layton
Assistant Secretaries for:
Congressional & Intergov. Affairs — John Angell
Energy Efficiency & Renewable Energy — Dan Reichen
Defense Programs — Victor Reis
Policy, Planning, & Prog. Evaluation — Robert Gee
Environmental Restoration & Waste Management — James M. Owendoff
Administration & Human Resource Management — Richard Farrell
Environment, Safety, & Health — vacant
Fossil Energy — Robert Kripwicz, act.
Nuclear Energy — Bill Magwood, dir.
Energy Information Adm. — Jay E. Hakes, adm.
Economic Impact & Diversity — Sarah Summerville, dir.
Hearings & Appeals — George Breznay, dir.
Energy Research — Martha Krebs, dir.
Civilian Radioactive Waste Management — Lake H. Barrett, act. dir.
Nonproliferation & National Security — Rose Gottemoller
Chief Financial Officer — Mike Telson
Energy Advisory Board — Skila Harris, dir.
Office of Public Affairs — Brooke Anderson, dir.

Department of Education

400 Maryland Ave., SW 20202

Secretary of Education — Richard W. Riley
Deputy Secretary — Marshall S. Smith, act.
Chief of Staff — Leslie T. Thornton
Inspector General — John P. Higgins, act.
General Counsel — Judith Winston
Assistant Secretaries for:
Adult & Vocational Education — Patricia McNeil
Civil Rights — Norma V. Cantu
Educational Research & Improvement — Kent McGuire
Elementary & Secondary Educ. — Gerald N. Tirozzi
Intergov. & Interagency Affairs — Mario Moreno
Legislative & Congressional Affairs — Scott Fleming
Postsecondary Education — David Longanecker
Special Educ. & Rehab. Services — Judith Heumann
Bilingual Educ. & Minor. Lang. Affairs — Delia Pompa, dir.
Rehab. Services Admin. — Frederic K. Schroeder, comm.
Education Statistics — Pascal Forgione, comm.

Department of Veterans Affairs

810 Vermont Ave. NW 20420

Secretary of Veterans Affairs — Togo D. West Jr.
Deputy — Hershel W. Gober
Assistant Secretaries for:
Congressional Affairs — Philip Riggin, act.
Management — Mark Catlett, act.
Human Resources & Adm. — Eugene Brickhouse
Policy & Planning — Dennis Duffy
Public & Intergovernmental Affairs — John Hanson, act.
Inspector General — Richard J. Griffith
Under Sec. for Benefits — Joseph Thompson
Under Sec. for Health — Kenneth W. Kizer, M.D.
National Cemetery System — Jerry W. Bowen, dir.
General Counsel — Leigh Bradley
Board of Veterans Appeals — Roger K. Bauer, act. chair
Board of Contract Appeals — Guy H. McMichael III, chair
Small & Disadvantaged Business Utilization — Scott S. Denniston, dir.
Veterans Service Organization Liaison — Allen F. Kent

(1) Richard J. Danzig was scheduled to replace John Dalton, Nov. 16, 1998.

Notable U.S. Government Agencies

Source: *The U.S. Government Manual*; National Archives and Records Administration; World Almanac research

All addresses are Washington, DC, unless otherwise noted; as of Oct. 31, 1998;
= confirmed by Senate but not installed; * = independent agency

Bureau of Alcohol, Tobacco, and Firearms — John W. Magaw, dir. (Dept. of Treas., 650 Mass. Ave NW, 20226).

Bureau of the Census — Kenneth Prewitt, dir. (Dept. of Commerce, 4700 Silver Hill Rd., Suitland, MD 20746).

Bureau of Economic Analysis — J. Steven Landerfeld, dir. (Dept. of Commerce, 1441 L St. NW, 20230).

Bureau of Indian Affairs — Kevin Gover, asst. sec. (Dept. of the Interior, 1849 C St. NW, 20240).

Bureau of Prisons — Kathleen M. Hawk Sawyer, dir. (Dept. of Justice, 320 First St. NW, 20534).

Centers for Disease Control & Prevention — Jeffrey P. Koplan, dir. (Dept. of HHS, 1600 Clifton Rd. NE, Mailstop D14, Atlanta, GA 30333).

***Central Intelligence Agency** — George J. Tenet, dir. (Wash., DC 20505).

***Commission on Civil Rights** — Mary Frances Berry, chair (624 9th St. NW, 20425).

***Commodity Futures Trading Commission** — Brooksley Born, chair (3 Lafayette Center, 1155 21st St. NW, 20581).

***Consumer Product Safety Commission** — Ann Brown, chair (East West Towers, 4330 East West Hwy., Bethesda, MD 20814).

***Environmental Protection Agency** — Carol M. Browner, adm. (401 M St. SW, 20460).

***Equal Employment Opportunity Commission** — Paul Igasaki, act. chair (1801 L St. NW, 20507).

***Export-Import Bank of the United States** — James A. Harmon, pres. and chair (811 Vermont Ave. NW, 20571).

***Farm Credit Administration** — Marsha P. Martin, chair, Farm Credit Administration Board (1501 Farm Credit Drive, McLean, VA 22102).

Federal Aviation Administration — Jane Garvey, adm. (Dept. of Trans., 800 Independence Ave. SW, 20591).

Federal Bureau of Investigation — Louis J. Freeh, dir. (Dept. of Justice, 935 Pennsylvania Ave. NW, 20535).

***Federal Communications Commission** — William E. Kennard, chair (1919 M St. NW, 20554).

***Federal Deposit Insurance Corporation** — Donna Tanoue, act. chair (550 17th St. NW, 20429).

***Federal Election Commission** — Scott Thomas, act. chair (999 E St. NW, 20463).

***Federal Emergency Management Agency** — James Lee Witt, dir. (500 C St. SW, 20472).

***Federal Energy Regulatory Commission** — James J. Hoecker, chair (888 1st St. NE, 20426).

Federal Highway Administration — Kenneth Wykle, adm. (Dept. of Trans., 400 7th St. SW, 20590).

***Federal Maritime Commission** — Harold J. Creel Jr., chair (800 N. Capitol St. NW, 20573).

***Federal Mine Safety & Health Review Commission** — Mary Lu Jordan, chair (1730 K St. NW, 20006).

***Federal Reserve System** — Alan Greenspan, chair, Board of Governors (20th St. & C St. NW, 20551).

***Federal Trade Commission** — Robert Pitofsky, chair (Pennsylvania Ave. at 6th St. NW, 20580).

Fish & Wildlife Service — Jamie Rappaport Clark, dir. (Dept. of the Interior, 1849 C St. NW, 20240).

Food and Drug Administration — Jane E. Henney #, comm. (Dept. of HHS, 5600 Fishers Ln., Rockville, MD 20857).

Forest Service — Mike Dombeck, chief (Dept. of Agriculture, 201 14th St. SW, 20250).

General Accounting Office — (cong. agency) David Michael Walker, comptroller gen. (441 G St. NW, 20548).

***General Services Administration** — David Barram, adm. (18th St. & F St. NW, 20405).

Government Printing Office — (cong. agency) Michael F. DiMario, public printer (732 N. Capitol St. NW, 20401).

Immigration & Naturalization Service — Doris Meissner, comm. (Dept. of Justice, 425 I St. NW, 20536).

***Inter-American Foundation** — Maria Otero, chair (901 N Stuart St., 10th floor, Arlington, VA 22203).

Internal Revenue Service — Charles Rossotti, comm. (Dept. of Treas., 1111 Constitution Ave. NW, 20224).

Library of Congress — (cong. agency) Dr. James H. Billington, Librarian of Congress (101 Indep. Ave. SE, 20540).

***National Aeronautics and Space Administration** — Daniel S. Goldin, adm. (300 E St. SW, 20546).

***National Archives & Records Administration** — John W. Carlin, archivist (8601 Adelphi Rd., College Park, MD 20740).

***National Endowment for the Arts** — William J. Ivey, chair (1100 Pennsylvania Ave. NW, 20506).

***National Endowment for the Humanities** — William Ferris, chair (1100 Pennsylvania Ave. NW, 20506).

National Institutes of Health — Harold E. Varmus, dir. (Dept. of HHS, 9000 Rockville Pike, Bethesda, MD 20892).

***National Labor Relations Board** — vacant (1099 14th St. NW, 20570).

National Oceanic and Atmospheric Administration — D. James Baker, undersec. (Dept. of Commerce, 14th & Constitution Ave. NW, 20230).

National Park Service — Robert G. Stanton, dir. (Dept. of the Interior, 1849 C St. NW, 20240).

***National Railroad Passenger Corp. (Amtrak)** — George Warrington, act. chair, Pres. & CEO (60 Mass. Ave. NE, 20002).

***National Science Foundation** — Aemon Kelly, chair, National Science Board (4201 Wilson Blvd., Arlington, VA 22230).

***National Transportation Safety Board** — Jim Hall, chair (490 L'Enfant Plaza SW, 20594).

***Nuclear Regulatory Commission** — Shirley Ann Jackson, chair (11555 Rockville Pike, Rockville, MD 20852).

Occupational Safety & Health Administration — Charles Jeffress, asst. sec. (Dept. of Labor, 200 Constitution Ave. NW, 20210).

***Occupational Safety & Health Review Commission** — Stuart E. Weisberg, chair (1120 20th St. NW, 9th Floor, 20036).

***Office of Government Ethics** — Stephen D. Potts, dir. (1201 New York Ave. NW, Suite 500, 20005).

***Office of Personnel Management** — Janice Lachance, dir. (1900 E St. NW, 20415-0001).

***Office of Special Counsel** — Elaine D. Kaplan, sp. counsel (1730 M St. NW, Suite 216, 20036).

***Peace Corps** — Mark Gearan, dir. (1111 20th St., NW, 20526).

***Postal Rate Commission** — Edward J. Gleiman, chair (1333 H St. NW, 20268).

***Securities and Exchange Commission** — Arthur Levitt, chair (450 5th St. NW, 20549).

***Selective Service System** — Gil Coronado, dir. (National Headquarters, 1515 Wilson Blvd., Arlington, VA 22209-2425).

***Small Business Administration** — Aida Alvarez, adm. (409 Third St. SW, 20416).

Smithsonian Institution — (quasi-official agency) I. Michael Hayman, sec. (1000 Jefferson Dr. SW, 20560).

***Social Security Administration** — Kenneth S. Apfel, comm. (6401 Security Blvd., Baltimore, MD 21235).

Surgeon General — David Satcher (Pub. Health Service, HHS, Parklawn Bldg., 5600 Fishers Ln., Rm. 18-66, Rockville, MD 20857).

***Tennessee Valley Authority** — Craven Crowell, chair, Board of Directors (400 W. Summit Hill Dr., Knoxville, TN 37902, and One Mass. Ave. NW, Suite 300, 20001).

***Trade and Development Agency** — J. Joseph Grandmaison, dir. (1621 N. Kent St., Suite 300, Arlington, VA 22209).

United States Coast Guard — Adm. James M. Loy, commandant (Dept. of Trans., 2100 2d St. SW, 20593).

United States Customs Service — Raymond W. Kelly, comm. (Dept. of Treas., 1300 Pennsylvania Ave. NW, 20229).

***United States International Trade Commission** — Lynn M. Bragg, chair (500 E St. SW, 20436).

United States Mint — Philip N. Diehl, dir. (Dept. of Treas., 633 3d St. NW, 20220).

***United States Postal Service** —William J. Henderson, Postmaster General (475 L'Enfant Plaza SW, 20260).

United States Secret Service — Lewis C. Merletti, dir. (Dept. of Treas., 1800 G St. NW, 20223).

CONGRESS

The One Hundred and Sixth Congress

With Preliminary 1998 Election Results

Source: Voter News Service; World Almanac research

Data subject to change; based on unofficial returns as of Nov. 5; does not include all absentee ballots

The 106th Congress convenes on Jan. 6, 1999.

The Senate

Rep., 55; Dem., 45; Total, 100. *Incumbent. Boldface denotes the 1998 election winner.

Terms are for 6 years and end Jan. 3 of the year preceding the senator's name in the following table. Annual salary, $136,700; President Pro Tempore, Majority Leader, and Minority Leader, $151,800. To be eligible for the Senate, one must be at least 30 years old, a U.S. citizen for at least 9 years, and a resident of the state from which chosen. Congress must meet annually on Jan. 3, unless it has, by law, appointed a different day.

The ZIP code of the Senate is 20510; the telephone number is 202-224-3121.

Senate officials in 1998 (105th Congress) were: President Pro Tempore, Strom Thurmond; Majority Leader, Trent Lott; Majority Whip, Don Nickles; Minority Leader, Tom Daschle; Minority Whip, Wendell Ford.

D-Democrat; R-Republican; ACP-A Connecticut Party; C-Conservative; IN-Independence; L-Liberal; RL-Right to Life

Term ends	Senator (Party)/Service from[1]	1998 Election
	Alabama	
2003	Jeff Sessions (R)/1/7/97	
2005	**Richard Shelby*** (R)/1/6/87	**805,337**
	Clayton Suddith (D)	471,408
	Alaska	
2003	Ted Stevens (R)/12/24/68	
2005	**Frank H. Murkowski*** (R)/1981	**141,116**
	Joseph A. "Joe" Sonneman (D)	36,944
	Arizona	
2001	Jon Kyl (R)/1/4/95	
2005	**John McCain*** (R)/1/6/87	**624,831**
	Ed Ranger (D)	251,608
	Arkansas	
2003	Tim Hutchinson (R)/1/7/97	
2005	**Blanche Lambert Lincoln** (D)/1/6/99	**386,822**
	Fay Boozman (R)	294,139
	California	
2001	Dianne Feinstein (D)/11/10/92	
2005	**Barbara Boxer*** (D)/1993	**3,910,981**
	Matt Fong (R)	3,154,036
	Colorado	
2003	Wayne Allard (R)/1/7/97	
2005	**Ben Nighthorse Campbell*** (R)/1993	**827,479**
	Dottie Lamm (D)	464,091
	Connecticut	
2001	Joe Lieberman (D,ACP)/1989	
2005	**Christopher J. Dodd*** (D)/1981	**605,583**
	Gary A. Franks (R)	300,339
	Delaware	
2001	William V. Roth, Jr. (R)/1/1/71	
2003	Joseph R. Biden, Jr. (D)/1973	
	Florida	
2001	Connie Mack (R)/1989	
2005	**Bob Graham*** (D)/1/6/87	**2,424,611**
	Charlie Crist (R)	1,451,245
	Georgia	
2003	Max Cleland (D)/1/7/97	
2005	**Paul Douglas Coverdell*** (R)/1993	**911,940**
	Michael J. Coles (D)	790,786
	Hawaii	
2001	Daniel K. Akaka (D)/4/28/90	
2005	**Daniel K. Inouye*** (D)/1963	**309,955**
	Crystal Young (R)	69,360
	Idaho	
2003	Larry E. Craig (R)/1991	
2005	**Mike Crapo** (R)/1/6/99	**255,600**
	Bill Mauk (D)	104,434
	Illinois	
2003	Richard J. Durbin (D)/1/7/97	
2005	**Peter G. Fitzgerald** (R)/1/6/99	**1,698,444**
	Carol Moseley-Braun* (D)/1993	1,567,114
	Indiana	
2001	Richard G. Lugar (R)/1977	
2005	**Evan Bayh** (D)/1/6/99	**1,006,224**
	Paul Helmke (R)	549,522
	Iowa	
2003	Tom Harkin (D)/1985	
2005	**Chuck Grassley*** (R)/1981	**640,518**
	David Osterberg (D)	292,101
	Kansas	
2003	Pat Roberts (R)/1/7/97	
2005	**Sam Brownback*** (R)/1/7/97	**470,022**
	Paul Feleciano, Jr. (D)	227,735
	Kentucky	
2003	Mitch McConnell (R)/1985	
2005	**Jim Bunning** (R)/1/6/99	**568,534**
	Scotty Baesler (D)	561,474
	Louisiana	
2003	Mary L. Landrieu (D)/1/7/97	
2005	**John B. Breaux*** (D)/1/6/87	**619,671**
	"Jim" Donelon (R)	306,237
	Maine	
2001	Olympia J. Snowe (R)/1/4/95	
2003	Susan M. Collins (R)/1/7/97	
	Maryland	
2001	Paul S. Sarbanes (D)/1977	
2005	**Barbara Ann Mikulski*** (D)/1/6/87	**1,034,834**
	Ross Z. Pierpont (R)	426,499
	Massachusetts	
2001	Edward M. Kennedy (D)/11/7/62	
2003	John F. Kerry (D)/1/2/85	
	Michigan	
2001	Spencer Abraham (R)/1/4/95	
2003	Carl Levin (D)/1979	
	Minnesota	
2001	Rod Grams (R)/1/4/95	
2003	Paul David Wellstone (D)/1991	
	Mississippi	
2001	Trent Lott (R)/1989	
2003	Thad Cochran (R)/12/27/78	
	Missouri	
2001	John Ashcroft (R)/1/4/95	
2005	**Christopher (Kit) Bond*** (R)/1/6/87	**830,581**
	Jeremiah W. (Jay) Nixon (D)	690,111

Term ends	Senator (Party)/Service from[1]	1998 Election
	Montana	
2001	Conrad Burns (R)/1989	
2003	Max Baucus (D)/12/15/78	
	Nebraska	
2001	Bob Kerrey (D)/1989	
2003	Chuck Hagel (R)/1/7/97	
	Nevada	
2001	Richard H. Bryan (D)/1989	
2005	**Harry Reid*** (D)/1/6/87	**208,579**
	John Ensign (R)	208,120
	New Hampshire	
2003	Robert Smith (R)/12/7/90	
2005	**Judd Gregg*** (R)/1993	**212,502**
	George Condodemetraky (D)	88,518
	New Jersey	
2001	Frank R. Lautenberg (D)/12/27/82	
2003	Robert G. Torricelli (D)/1/7/97	
	New Mexico	
2001	Jeff Bingaman (D)/1983	
2003	Pete V. Domenici (R)/1973	
	New York	
2001	Daniel Patrick Moynihan (D,L)/1977	
2005	**Charles E. Schumer** (D,IN,L)/1/6/99	**2,371,295**
	Alfonse D'Amato* (R,C,RL)/1981	1,956,795
	North Carolina	
2003	Jesse Helms (R)/1973	
2005	**John Edwards** (D)/1/6/99	**1,010,195**
	Lauch Faircloth* (R)/1993	926,917
	North Dakota	
2001	Kent Conrad (D)/1/6/87	
2005	**Byron L. Dorgan*** (D)/12/14/92	**134,293**
	Donna Nalewaja (R)	74,695
	Ohio	
2001	Mike Dewine (R)/1/4/95	
2005	**George V. Voinovich** (R)/1/6/99	**1,886,942**
	Mary O. Boyle (D)	1,456,518
	Oklahoma	
2003	James M. Inhofe (R)/11/21/94	
2005	**Don Nickles*** (R)/1981	**570,682**
	Don E. Carroll (D)	268,898
	Oregon	
2003	Gordon Smith (R)/1/7/97	
2005	**Ron Wyden*** (D)/2/6/96	**264,918**
	John Lim (R)	160,764
	Pennsylvania	
2001	Rick Santorum (R)/1/4/95	
2005	**Arlen Specter*** (R)/1981	**1,803,259**
	Bill Lloyd (D)	1,018,389
	Rhode Island	
2001	John H. Chafee (R)/12/29/76	
2003	John F. Reed (D)/1/7/97	
	South Carolina	
2003	Strom Thurmond (R)/11/7/56	
2005	**Ernest Hollings*** (D)/11/9/66	**553,362**
	Bob Inglis (R)	483,322
	South Dakota	
2003	Tim Johnson (D)/1/7/97	
2005	**Tom Daschle*** (D)/1/6/87	**162,880**
	Ron Schmidt (R)	95,438
	Tennessee	
2001	Bill Frist (R)/1/4/95	
2003	Fred Thompson (R)/12/9/94	
	Texas	
2001	Kay Bailey Hutchison (R)/6/5/93	
2003	Phil Gramm (R)/1985	
	Utah	
2001	Orrin G. Hatch (R)/1977	
2005	**Robert F. Bennett*** (R)/1993	**315,070**
	Scott Leckman (D)	162,481
	Vermont	
2001	Jim Jeffords (R)/1989	
2005	**Patrick Leahy*** (D)/1975	**148,264**
	Fred H. Tuttle (R)	46,583
	Virginia	
2001	Charles S. Robb (D)/1989	
2003	John W. Warner (R)/1/2/79	
	Washington	
2001	Slade Gorton (R)/1989	
2005	**Patty Murray*** (D)/1993	**807,505**
	Linda Smith (R)	576,674
	West Virginia	
2001	Robert C. Byrd (D)/1959	
2003	John D. Rockefeller IV (D)/1/15/85	
	Wisconsin	
2001	Herbert H. Kohl (D)/1989	
2005	**Russ Feingold*** (D)/1993	**888,620**
	Mark W. Neumann (R)	850,210
	Wyoming	
2001	Craig Thomas (R)/1/4/95	
2003	Michael B. Enzi (R)/1/7/97	

(1) Jan. 3, unless otherwise noted.

The House of Representatives

Rep., 223; Dem., 211 (including 1 Dem. leading but not decided); Ind., 1; Total, 435.
***Incumbent. Boldface denotes the 1998 election winner.**

Members' terms to Jan. 3, 2001. Annual salary, $136,700; Speaker of the House, $175,400; Majority Leader and Minority Leader, $151,800. To be eligible for membership, a person must be at least 25 years of age, a U.S. citizen for at least 7 years, and a resident of the state from which he or she is chosen. The ZIP code of the House is 20515; the telephone number is 202-225-3121.

House officials in 1998 (105th Congress) were: Speaker, Newt Gingrich; Majority Leader, Dick Armey; Majority Whip, Tom DeLay; Minority Leader, Richard A. Gephardt; Minority Whip, David E. Bonior.

D-Democrat; R-Republican; AI-American Independent; C-Conservative; GR-Green; I-Independent; IA- Independent American; IN-Independence; L-Liberal; LB-Libertarian; NL-Natural Law; RF-Reform; RL-Right to Life; TX-Taxpayers.

Dist.	Representative (Party)	1998 Election
	Alabama	
1.	**H. L. Sonny Callahan*** (R)	**Unopposed**
2.	**Terry Everett*** (R)	**129,863**
	Joe Fondren (D)	57,655
3.	**Bob Riley*** (R)	**101,490**
	Joe Turnham (D)	73,296
4.	**Robert Aderholt*** (R)	**106,277**
	Don Bevill (D)	82,045
5.	**Bud Cramer*** (D)	**134,696**
	Gil Aust (R)	58,507
6.	**Spencer Bachus*** (R)	**145,270**
	Donna Wesson Smalley (D)	57,448
7.	**Earl F. Hillard*** (D)	**Unopposed**
	Alaska	
	Don Young* (R)	**118,837**
	Jim Duncan (D)	65,906

Dist.	Representative (Party)	1998 Election

Arizona

Dist.	Representative (Party)	1998 Election
1.	**Matt Salmon*** (R)	**85,081**
	David Mendoza (D)	47,667
2.	**Ed Pastor*** (D)	**53,421**
	Ed Barron (R)	22,283
3.	**Bob Stump*** (R)	**124,275**
	Stuart Marc Starky (D)	61,697
4.	**John Shadegg*** (R)	**88,716**
	Eric Ehst (D)	43,820
5.	**Jim Kolbe*** (R)	**96,144**
	Tom Volgy (D)	83,992
6.	**J.D. Hayworth*** (R)	**96,063**
	Steve Owens (D)	81,962

Arkansas

Dist.	Representative (Party)	1998 Election
1.	**Marion Berry*** (D)	**Unopposed**
2.	**Vic Snyder*** (D)	**100,281**
	Phil Wyrick (R)	72,749
3.	**Asa Hutchinson*** (R)	**154,592**
	Ralph Forbes (RF)	36,850
4.	**Jay Dickey*** (R)	**92,194**
	Judy Smith (D)	68,139

California

Dist.	Representative (Party)	1998 Election
1.	**Mike Thompson** (D)	**110,099**
	Mark C. Luce (R)	58,104
2.	**Wally Herger*** (R)	**117,687**
	Roberts "Rob" Braden (D)	65,602
3.	**Doug Ose** (R)	**95,551**
	Sandie Dunn (D)	81,211
4.	**John T. Doolittle*** (R)	**137,333**
	David Shapiro (D)	76,273
5.	**Robert T. Matsui*** (D)	**123,067**
	Robert S. Dinsmore (R)	44,641
6.	**Lynn Woolsey*** (D)	**144,998**
	Ken McAuliffe (R)	63,481
7.	**George Miller*** (D)	**117,423**
	Norman H. Reece (R)	35,534
8.	**Nancy Pelosi*** (D)	**119,583**
	David J. Martz (R)	16,053
9.	**Barbara Lee*** (D)	**126,232**
	Claiborne "Clay" Sanders (R)	19,978
10.	**Ellen O. Tauscher*** (D)	**114,938**
	Charles Ball (R)	94,200
11.	**Richard W. Pombo*** (R)	**52,491**
	Robert L. Figueroa (D)	88,307
12.	**Tom Lantos*** (D)	**106,661**
	Robert H. Evans, Jr. (R)	30,094
13.	**Fortney Pete Stark*** (D)	**91,911**
	James R. Goetz (R)	34,496
14.	**Anna G. Eshoo*** (D)	**111,973**
	John C. "Chris" Haugen (R)	46,543
15.	**Tom Campbell*** (R)	**96,493**
	Dick Lane (D)	61,018
16.	**Zoe Lofgren*** (D)	**73,689**
	Horace Eugene Thayn (R)	23,737
17.	**Sam Farr*** (D)	**91,687**
	Bill McCampbell (R)	46,558
18.	**Gary A. Condit*** (D)	**104,094**
	Linda M. Degroat (LB)	15,824
19.	**George Radanovich*** (R)	**110,103**
	Jonathan Richter (LB)	28,226
20.	**Cal Dooley*** (D)	**50,637**
	Cliff Unruh (R)	32,596
21.	**Bill Thomas*** (R)	**107,913**
	John Evans (RF)	28,776
22.	**Lois Capps*** (D)	**85,548**
	Thomas J. Bordonaro, Jr. (R)	68,069
23.	**Elton W. Gallegly*** (R)	**79,420**
	Daniel "Dan" Gonzalez (D)	53,641
24.	**Brad Sherman*** (D)	**89,925**
	Randy Hoffman (R)	58,842
25.	**Howard "Buck" McKeon*** (R)	**101,019**
	Bruce R. Acker (LB)	34,571
26.	**Howard L. Berman*** (D)	**62,099**
	Juan Carlos Ros (LB)	5,973
27.	**James E. Rogan** (R)	**70,210**
	Barry A. Gordon (D)	65,413
28.	**David Dreier*** (R)	**81,314**
	Janice M. Nelson (D)	55,626
29.	**Henry A. Waxman*** (D)	**116,213**
	Mike Gottlieb (R)	34,871
30.	**Xavier Becerra*** (D)	**52,358**
	Patricia Parker (R)	11,677
31.	**Matthew G. Martinez*** (D)	**55,402**
	Frank C. Moreno (R)	17,621
32.	**Julian C. Dixon*** (D)	**100,291**
	Laurence Ardito (R)	12,881
33.	**Lucille Roybal-Allard*** (D)	**39,708**
	Wayne Miller (R)	5,736
34.	**Grace Flores Napolitano** (D)	**69,598**
	Ed Perez (R)	29,252
35.	**Maxine Waters*** (D)	**71,111**
	Gordon Michael Mego (AI)	8,344
36.	**Steven T. Kuykendall** (R)	**78,686**
	Janice Hahn (D)	75,434
37.	**Juanita Millender-McDonald*** (D)	**64,381**
	Saul E. Lankster (R)	11,203
38.	**Steve Horn*** (R)	**64,083**
	Peter Mathews (D)	54,012
39.	**Ed Royce*** (R)	**87,747**
	A. "Cecy" R. Groom (D)	47,692
40.	**Jerry Lewis*** (R)	**92,991**
	Robert "Bob" Conaway (D)	45,736
41.	**Gary G. Miller** (R)	**62,892**
	Eileen R. Ansari (D)	48,259
42.	**George E. Brown, Jr.*** (D)	**59,297**
	Elia Pirozzi (R)	43,091
43.	**Ken Calvert*** (R)	**74,226**
	Mike Rayburn (D)	51,017
44.	**Mary Bono*** (R)	**88,079**
	Ralph Waite (D)	52,872
45.	**Dana Rohrabacher*** (R)	**83,223**
	Patricia W. Neal (D)	53,601
46.	**Loretta Sanchez*** (D)	**40,542**
	Robert Kenneth "Bob" Dornan (R)	28,307
47.	**Christopher Cox*** (R)	**117,075**
	Christina Avalos (D)	51,297
48.	**Ron Packard*** (R)	**120,260**
	Sharon K. Miles (NL)	20,323
49.	**Brian P. Bilbray*** (R)	**76,566**
	Christine T. Kehoe (D)	72,510
50.	**Bob Filner*** (D)	**Unopposed**
51.	**Randy "Duke" Cunningham*** (R)	**106,086**
	Dan Kripke (D)	60,330
52.	**Duncan Hunter*** (R)	**100,424**
	Lynn Badler (LB)	19,027

Colorado

Dist.	Representative (Party)	1998 Election
1.	**Diana DeGette*** (D)	**116,628**
	Nancy McClanahan (R)	52,452
2.	**Mark Udall** (D)	**113,933**
	Bob Greenlee (R)	108,379
3.	**Scott McInnis*** (R)	**148,787**
	Reed Kelley (D)	69,948
4.	**Bob Schaffer*** (R)	**131,319**
	Susan Kirkpatrick (D)	89,974
5.	**Joel Hefley*** (R)	**155,779**
	Ken Alford (D)	55,609
6.	**Tom Tancredo** (R)	**111,292**
	Henry L. Strauss (D)	86,573

Connecticut

Dist.	Representative (Party)	1998 Election
1.	**John B. Larson** (D)	**85,236**
	Kevin O'Connor (R)	58,145
2.	**Sam Gejdenson*** (D)	**99,522**
	Gary M. Koval (R)	57,687
3.	**Rosa L. DeLauro*** (D)	**109,214**
	Martin T. Reust (R)	42,061
4.	**Christopher Shays*** (R)	**94,867**
	Jonathan Kantrowitz (D)	40,980
5.	**Jim Maloney*** (D)	**77,883**
	Mark Nielsen (R)	75,399
6.	**Nancy L. Johnson*** (R)	**97,821**
	Charlotte Koskoff (D)	63,087

Delaware

Dist.	Representative (Party)	1998 Election
	Michael N. Castle* (R)	**120,605**
	Dennis E. Williams (D)	57,847

Dist.	Representative (Party)	1998 Election
	Florida	
1.	**Joe Scarborough*** (R)	**Unopposed**
2.	**Allen Boyd*** (D)	**Unopposed**
3.	**Corrine Brown*** (D)	**66,362**
	Bill Randall (R)	53,074
4.	**Tillie K. Fowler*** (R)	**Unopposed**
5.	**Karen L. Thurman*** (D)	**131,995**
	Jack Gargan (RF)	67,133
6.	**Clifford (Cliff) B. Stearns*** (R)	**Unopposed**
7.	**John L. Mica*** (R)	**Unopposed**
8.	**Bill McCollum*** (R)	**104,146**
	Al Krulick (D)	54,187
9.	**Michael Bilirakis*** (R)	**Unopposed**
10.	**C. W. Bill Young*** (R)	**Unopposed**
11.	**Jim Davis*** (D)	**85,167**
	Joe Chillura (R)	46,107
12.	**Charles T. Canady*** (R)	**Unopposed**
13.	**Dan Miller*** (R)	**Unopposed**
14.	**Porter Goss*** (R)	**Unopposed**
15.	**Dave Weldon*** (R)	**129,232**
	David R. Golding (D)	75,639
16.	**Mark Foley*** (R)	**Unopposed**
17.	**Carrie P. Meek*** (D)	**Unopposed**
18.	**Ileana Ros-Lehtinen*** (R)	**Unopposed**
19.	**Robert Wexler*** (D)	**Unopposed**
20.	**Peter Deutsch*** (D)	**Unopposed**
21.	**Lincoln Diaz-Balart*** (R)	**84,017**
	Patrick Cusack (D)	28,378
22.	**Clay Shaw*** (R)	**Unopposed**
23.	**Alcee L. Hastings*** (D)	**Unopposed**
	Georgia	
1.	**Jack Kingston*** (R)	**Unopposed**
2.	**Sanford Dixon Bishop, Jr.*** (D)	**78,952**
	Joseph Francis McCormick, Jr. (R)	59,282
3.	**Michael A. (Mac) Collins*** (R)	**Unopposed**
4.	**Cynthia McKinney*** (D)	**100,485**
	Sunny J. Warren (R)	63,730
5.	**John Lewis*** (D)	**109,177**
	John H. Lewis, Sr. (R)	29,877
6.	**Newt Gingrich*** (R)	**162,722**
	Gary "Bats" Pelphrey (D)	67,819
7.	**Bob Barr*** (R)	**85,982**
	James F. "Jim" Williams (D)	69,293
8.	**Saxby Chambliss*** (R)	**87,810**
	Ronald L. Cain (D)	53,101
9.	**Nathan Deal*** (R)	**Unopposed**
10.	**Charlie Norwood*** (R)	**87,674**
	Marion Denise Spencer Freeman (D)	60,140
11.	**John Linder*** (R)	**119,888**
	Vincent Littman (D)	53,296
	Hawaii	
1.	**Neil Abercrombie*** (D)	**113,686**
	Gene Ward (R)	66,661
2.	**Patsy Takemoto Mink*** (D)	**143,114**
	Carol J. Douglass (R)	49,896
	Idaho	
1.	**Helen Chenoweth*** (R)	**108,911**
	Dan Williams (D)	88,707
2.	**Mike Simpson** (R)	**89,727**
	Richard H. Stallings (D)	76,102
	Illinois	
1.	**Bobby L. Rush*** (D)	**136,970**
	Marlene White Ahimaz (R)	17,704
2.	**Jesse L. Jackson, Jr.*** (D)	**142,608**
	Robert Gordon III (R)	15,611
3.	**William O. Lipinski*** (D)	**112,679**
	Robert Marshall (R)	43,301
4.	**Luis V. Gutierrez*** (D)	**51,803**
	John Birch (R)	10,120
5.	**Rod R. Blagojevich*** (D)	**91,399**
	Alan Spitz (R)	32,465
6.	**Henry J. Hyde*** (R)	**111,169**
	Thomas A. Cramer (D)	49,678
7.	**Danny K. Davis*** (D)	**125,798**
	Dorn E. Van Cleave III (LB)	9,582
8.	**Philip M. Crane*** (R)	**72,820**
	Mike Rothman (D)	34,782
9.	**Janice D. (Jan) Schakowsky** (D)	**104,809**
	Herbert Sohn (R)	32,771
10.	**John E. Porter*** (R)	**Unopposed**
11.	**Gerald C. Weller*** (R)	**99,778**
	Gary S. Mueller (D)	69,694
12.	**Jerry F. Costello*** (D)	**99,605**
	William Melvin Price (R)	65,409
13.	**Judy Biggert** (R)	**121,720**
	Susan W. Hynes (D)	77,699
14.	**J. Dennis Hastert*** (R)	**117,304**
	Robert A. Cozzi, Jr. (D)	50,844
15.	**Thomas W. Ewing*** (R)	**104,255**
	Laurel Lunt Prussing (D)	65,054
16.	**Donald Manzullo*** (R)	**Unopposed**
17.	**Lane A. Evans*** (D)	**100,128**
	Mark Baker (R)	94,072
18.	**Ray LaHood*** (R)	**Unopposed**
19.	**David D. Phelps** (D)	**123,249**
	Brent Winters (R)	90,185
20.	**John M. Shimkus*** (R)	**121,103**
	Rick Verticchio (D)	76,475
	Indiana	
1.	**Peter J. Visclosky*** (D)	**92,382**
	Michael Petyo (R)	33,486
2.	**David M. McIntosh*** (R)	**98,938**
	Sherman A. Boles (D)	62,052
3.	**Tim Roemer*** (D)	**84,427**
	Daniel A. Holtz (R)	60,776
4.	**Mark E. Souder*** (R)	**93,033**
	Mark J. Wehrle (D)	53,959
5.	**Steve Buyer*** (R)	**101,367**
	David Steele (D)	58,146
6.	**Dan Burton*** (R)	**133,235**
	Bob Kern (D)	31,185
7.	**Edward A. Pease*** (R)	**109,511**
	Samuel (Dutch) Hillenburg (D)	44,550
8.	**John N. Hostettler*** (R)	**91,265**
	Gail Riecken (D)	81,869
9.	**Baron Hill** (D)	**93,155**
	Jean Leising (R)	88,084
10.	**Julia M. Carson*** (D)	**65,951**
	Gary A. Hofmeister (R)	44,919
	Iowa	
1.	**Jim Leach*** (R)	**106,350**
	Bob Rush (D)	79,559
2.	**Jim Nussle*** (R)	**103,667**
	Bob Tully (D)	82,441
3.	**Leonard L. Boswell*** (D)	**107,534**
	Larry McKibben (R)	77,783
4.	**Greg Ganske*** (R)	**129,177**
	Jon Dvorak (D)	67,041
5.	**Tom Latham*** (R)	**Unopposed**
	Kansas	
1.	**Jerry Moran*** (R)	**151,399**
	Jim Phillips (D)	36,187
2.	**Jim Ryun*** (R)	**107,408**
	Jim Clark (D)	68,898
3.	**Dennis Moore** (D)	**102,299**
	Vince Snowbarger* (R)	92,801
4.	**Todd Tiahrt*** (R)	**94,092**
	Jim Lawing (D)	61,432
	Kentucky	
1.	**Edward Whitfield*** (R)	**95,184**
	Tom Barlow (D)	77,525
2.	**Ron Lewis*** (R)	**113,023**
	Bob Evans (D)	62,691
3.	**Anne Meagher Northup*** (R)	**100,690**
	Chris Gorman (D)	92,865
4.	**Ken Lucas** (D)	**93,458**
	Gex "Jay" Williams (R)	81,538
5.	**Harold "Hal" Rogers*** (R)	**140,979**
	Sidney Jane Bailey-Bamer (D)	39,400
6.	**Ernest Fletcher** (R)	**103,846**
	Ernie Scorsone (D)	90,023

Dist.	Representative (Party)	1998 Election
	Louisiana	
1.	**Robert L. "Bob" Livingston*** (R)	**Unopposed**
2.	**William J. Jefferson*** (D)	**102,056**
	Don-Terry Veal (D)	10,799
3.	**W.J. "Billy" Tauzin*** (R)	**Unopposed**
4.	**"Jim" McCrery*** (R)	**Unopposed**
5.	**John Cooksey*** (R)	**Unopposed**
6.	**Richard Baker*** (R)	**96,944**
	Marjorie McKeithen (D)	94,072
7.	**Chris John*** (D)	**Unopposed**

In Louisiana, all candidates of all parties ran against each other on Nov. 3, 1998, in an open primary, unless they were unopposed incumbents, in which case they were declared elected. Candidates who received more than 50% of the primary vote were also declared elected. All districts had candidates that were declared elected after the Nov. 3 election, and therefore a Dec. runoff was not needed.

Dist.	Representative (Party)	1998 Election
	Maine	
1.	**Thomas H. Allen*** (D)	**129,942**
	Ross J. Connelly (R)	77,601
2.	**John E. Baldacci*** (D)	**132,461**
	Johnathan Reisman (R)	42,244
	Maryland	
1.	**Wayne T. Gilchrest*** (R)	**130,087**
	Irving Pinder (D)	58,320
2.	**Robert L. Ehrlich Jr.*** (R)	**140,644**
	Kenneth T. Bosley (D)	62,709
3.	**Benjamin L. Cardin*** (D)	**134,941**
	Colin Felix Harby (R)	38,378
4.	**Albert R. Wynn*** (D)	**126,755**
	John B. Kimble (R)	20,619
5.	**Steny H. Hoyer*** (D)	**123,339**
	Robert B. Ostrom (R)	64,637
6.	**Roscoe Bartlett*** (R)	**122,434**
	Timothy D. McCown (D)	71,047
7.	**Elijah E. Cummings*** (D)	**112,546**
	Kenneth Kondner (R)	18,049
8.	**Constance A. Morella*** (R)	**127,833**
	Ralph G. Neas (D)	83,997
	Massachusetts	
1.	**John W. Olver*** (D)	**121,466**
	Gregory L. Morgan (R)	47,656
2.	**Richard E. Neal*** (D)	**Unopposed**
3.	**James P. McGovern*** (D)	**108,223**
	Matthew J. Amorello (R)	79,054
4.	**Barney Frank*** (D)	**Unopposed**
5.	**Martin T. Meehan*** (D)	**127,358**
	David E. Coleman (R)	52,705
6.	**John F. Tierney*** (D)	**117,095**
	Peter G. Torkildsen (R)	91,035
7.	**Edward J. Markey*** (D)	**137,032**
	Patricia H. Long (R)	56,901
8.	**Michael E. Capuano** (D)	**99,390**
	Philip Hyde III (R)	14,102
9.	**John Joseph Moakley*** (D)	**Unopposed**
10.	**William D. Delahunt*** (D)	**164,645**
	Eric V. Bleicken (R)	70,322
	Michigan	
1.	**Bart Stupak*** (D)	**130,121**
	Michelle A. McManus (R)	87,752
2.	**Peter Hoekstra*** (R)	**146,802**
	Bob Shrauger (D)	61,161
3.	**Vernon Ehlers*** (R)	**146,201**
	John Ferguson Jr. (D)	49,432
4.	**Dave Camp*** (R)	**154,052**
	Dan Marsh (LB)	11,423

Dist.	Representative (Party)	1998 Election
5.	**James A. Barcia*** (D)	**134,507**
	Donald W. Brewster (R)	51,061
6.	**Fred Upton*** (R)	**113,254**
	Clarence J. Annen (D)	45,345
7.	**Nick Smith*** (R)	**105,854**
	Jim Berryman (D)	72,990
8.	**Debbie Stabenow*** (D)	**125,167**
	Susan Munsell (R)	84,255
9.	**Dale E. Kildee*** (D)	**105,262**
	Tom McMillin (R)	78,797
10.	**David E. Bonior*** (D)	**107,861**
	Brian Palmer (R)	93,326
11.	**Joe Knollenberg*** (R)	**144,247**
	Travis Reeds (D)	76,097
12.	**Sander Levin*** (D)	**103,577**
	Leslie Touma (R)	78,177
13.	**Lynn Nancy Rivers*** (D)	**99,703**
	Tom Hickey (R)	68,041
14.	**John Conyers, Jr.*** (D)	**121,586**
	Vendella M. Collins (R)	15,461
15.	**Carolyn Cheeks Kilpatrick*** (D)	**106,582**
	Chrysanthea D. Boyd-Fields (R)	12,639
16.	**John D. Dingell*** (D)	**113,051**
	William Morse (R)	52,173
	Minnesota	
1.	**Gil Gutknecht*** (R)	**131,188**
	Tracy L. Beckman (D)	108,370
2.	**David Minge*** (D)	**148,312**
	Craig Duehring (R)	99,471
3.	**Jim Ramstad*** (R)	**202,698**
	Stan J. Leino (D)	66,196
4.	**Bruce F. Vento*** (D)	**127,575**
	Dennis Newinski (R)	94,507
5.	**Martin Olav Sabo*** (D)	**139,081**
	Frank Taylor (R)	58,045
6.	**Bill Luther*** (D)	**148,521**
	John Kline (R)	136,688
7.	**Collin C. Peterson*** (D)	**169,531**
	Aleta Edin (R)	66,489
8.	**James L. Oberstar*** (D)	**163,311**
	Jerry Shuster (R)	67,118
	Mississippi	
1.	**Roger F. Wicker*** (R)	**65,833**
	Rex N. Weathers (D)	29,912
2.	**Bennie G. Thompson*** (D)	**78,671**
	Will Chipman (LB)	31,999
3.	**Charles W. "Chip" Pickering, Jr.*** (R)	**84,164**
	C.T. Scarborough (LB)	15,292
4.	**Ronnie Shows** (D)	**71,133**
	Delbert Hosemann (R)	60,594
5.	**Gene Taylor*** (D)	**77,071**
	Randy McDonnell (R)	19,011
	Missouri	
1.	**William (Bill) Clay, Sr.*** (D)	**90,825**
	Richmond A. Soluade, Sr. (R)	30,634
2.	**James M. Talent*** (R)	**142,313**
	John Ross (D)	57,565
3.	**Richard A. Gephardt*** (D)	**98,281**
	William J. Federer (R)	74,003
4.	**Ike Skelton*** (D)	**128,156**
	Cecilia D. Noland (R)	50,994
5.	**Karen McCarthy*** (D)	**101,215**
	Penny D. Bennett (R)	47,558
6.	**Pat (Patsy Ann) Danner*** (D)	**136,776**
	Jeff Bailey (R)	51,679
7.	**Roy Blunt*** (R)	**129,746**
	Marc Perkel (D)	43,415
8.	**Jo Ann Emerson*** (R)	**104,275**
	Anthony J. (Tony) Heckemeyer (D)	59,423
9.	**Kenny Hulshof*** (R)	**117,195**
	Linda Vogt (D)	66,861
	Montana	
	Rick Hill* (R)	**172,326**
	Dusty Deschamps (D)	146,089

Nebraska

Dist.	Representative (Party)	1998 Election
1.	**Doug Bereuter*** (R)	**133,249**
	Don Eret (D)	47,799
2.	**Lee Terry** (R)	**104,548**
	Michael Scott (D)	54,599
3.	**Bill Barrett*** (R)	**148,907**
	Jerry Hickman (LB)	26,835

Nevada

Dist.	Representative (Party)	1998 Election
1.	**Shelley Berkley** (D)	**79,315**
	Don Chairez (R)	73,540
2.	**Jim Gibbons*** (R)	**201,468**
	Christopher Horne (IA)	20,725

New Hampshire

Dist.	Representative (Party)	1998 Election
1.	**John E. Sununu*** (R)	**104,077**
	Peter Flood (D)	51,617
2.	**Charles Bass*** (R)	**84,875**
	Mary Rauh (D)	72,274

New Jersey

Dist.	Representative (Party)	1998 Election
1.	**Robert E. Andrews*** (D)	**89,298**
	Ronald L. Richards (R)	27,468
2.	**Frank A. LoBiondo*** (R)	**92,998**
	Derek Hunsberger (D)	43,600
3.	**Jim Saxton*** (R)	**96,308**
	Steven J. Polansky (D)	54,626
4.	**Christopher H. Smith*** (R)	**91,698**
	Larry Schneider (D)	51,723
5.	**Marge Roukema*** (R)	**105,927**
	Mike Schneider (D)	55,161
6.	**Frank Pallone Jr.*** (D)	**77,722**
	Michael Ferguson (R)	55,011
7.	**Bob Franks*** (R)	**75,926**
	Maryanne S. Connelly (D)	64,337
8.	**Bill J. Pascrell Jr.*** (D)	**80,003**
	Mathew J. Kirnan (R)	46,069
9.	**Steven R. Rothman*** (D)	**90,452**
	Steve Lonegan (R)	47,576
10.	**Donald M. Payne*** (D)	**79,235**
	William Stanley Wnuck (R)	10,386
11.	**Rodney P. Frelinghuysen*** (R)	**100,924**
	John P. Scollo (D)	44,057
12.	**Rush Holt** (D)	**91,573**
	Mike Pappas* (R)	86,448
13.	**Robert Menendez*** (D)	**68,556**
	Theresa de Leon (R)	14,243

New Mexico

Dist.	Representative (Party)	1998 Election
1.	**Heather A. Wilson*** (R)	**66,164**
	Phillip J. Maloof (D)	61,250
2.	**Joe Skeen*** (R)	**84,774**
	E. Shirley Baca (D)	61,517
3.	**Tom Udall** (D)	**84,165**
	Bill Redmond* (R)	67,694

New York

Dist.	Representative (Party)	1998 Election
1.	**Michael P. Forbes*** (R,C,IN,RL)	**93,664**
	William G. Holst (D,I)	52,136
2.	**Rick A. Lazio*** (R,C)	**81,119**
	John C. Bace (D)	36,394
3.	**Peter T. King*** (R,C,RL)	**112,252**
	Kevin N. Langberg (D)	59,981
4.	**Carolyn McCarthy*** (D,IN)	**86,157**
	Gregory R. Becker (R,C,RL)	76,874
5.	**Gary L. Ackerman*** (D,IN,L)	**90,792**
	David C. Pinzon (R,C)	46,373
6.	**Gregory W. Meeks*** (D,IN,L)	**Unopposed**
7.	**Joseph Crowley*** (D)	**45,082**
	James J. Dillon (R)	18,167
8.	**Jerrold L. Nadler*** (D,L)	**100,670**
	Theodore Howard (R)	16,730
9.	**Anthony Weiner** (D,IN)	**63,774**
	Louis Telano (R)	23,065
10.	**Edolphus Towns*** (D,L)	**69,328**
	Ernestine M. Brown (R)	5,067
11.	**Major R. Owens*** (D,L)	**57,097**
	David Greene (R,C)	6,300
12.	**Nydia M. Velazquez*** (D)	**45,752**
	Rosemarie Markgraf (R)	6,705
13.	**Vito J. Fossella*** (R,C,RL)	**70,901**
	Eugene V. Prisco (D,L)	36,207
14.	**Carolyn B. Maloney*** (D,IN,L)	**101,848**
	Stephanie E. Kupferman (R)	30,426
15.	**Charles B. Rangel*** (D,L)	**82,973**
	David E. Cunningham (R)	5,116
16.	**Jose E. Serrano*** (D,L)	**64,509**
	Thomas W. Bayley, Jr. (R)	2,396
17.	**Eliot L. Engel*** (D,L)	**75,443**
	Peter Fiumefreddo (R,C,IN)	10,592
18.	**Nita M. Lowey*** (D)	**83,583**
	Marion M. Conner (RL)	2,952
19.	**Sue W. Kelly*** (R,C)	**98,512**
	Dick Collins (D)	52,503
20.	**Benjamin A. Gilman*** (R)	**90,752**
	Paul J. Feiner (D,IN,L)	61,524
21.	**Michael R. McNulty*** (D,C,IN)	**138,913**
	Lauren Ayers (R)	48,404
22.	**John E. Sweeney** (R,C,IN)	**100,257**
	Jean P. Bordewich (D)	76,029
23.	**Sherwood L. Boehlert*** (R)	**104,841**
	David Vickers (C,RL)	26,586
24.	**John M. McHugh*** (R,C)	**109,269**
	Neil P. Tallon (D)	28,698
25.	**James T. Walsh*** (R,C)	**114,938**
	Yvonne Rothenberg (D,L)	50,906
26.	**Maurice D. Hinchey*** (D,IN,L)	**102,908**
	Wm. H. Bud Walker (R,C)	52,050
27.	**Thomas M. Reynolds** (R,C)	**99,864**
	Bill Cook (D,IN,RL)	71,649
28.	**Louise M. Slaughter*** (D)	**113,742**
	Richard A. Kaplan (R,IN)	54,397
29.	**John J. La Falce*** (D,IN,L)	**93,217**
	Chris Collins (R,C)	66,632
30.	**Jack Quinn*** (R,C,IN)	**110,327**
	Crystal D. Peoples (D)	52,716
31.	**Amo Houghton*** (R,C)	**103,824**
	Caleb Rossiter (D)	38,112

North Carolina

Dist.	Representative (Party)	1998 Election
1.	**Eva M. Clayton*** (D)	**84,930**
	Ted Tyler (R)	50,178
2.	**Bob Etheridge*** (D)	**98,994**
	Dan Page (R)	72,112
3.	**Walter B. Jones*** (R)	**82,517**
	Jon Williams (D)	49,472
4.	**David Price*** (D)	**127,919**
	Tom Roberg (R)	92,685
5.	**Richard Burr*** (R)	**116,939**
	Mike Robinson (D)	54,736
6.	**Howard Coble*** (R)	**111,351**
	Jeffrey D. Bentley (LB)	14,237
7.	**Mike McIntyre*** (D)	**122,838**
	Paul Meadows (LB)	11,755
8.	**Robert C. "Robin" Hayes** (R)	**67,382**
	Mike Taylor (D)	63,765
9.	**Sue Myrick*** (R)	**108,800**
	Rory Blake (D)	46,955
10.	**T. Cass Ballenger*** (R)	**117,738**
	Deborah Garrett Eddins (LB)	19,822
11.	**Charles H. Taylor*** (R)	**111,292**
	David Young (D)	83,479
12.	**Mel Watt*** (D)	**81,650**
	John "Scott" Keadle (R)	61,482

North Dakota

Dist.	Representative (Party)	1998 Election
	Earl Pomeroy* (D)	**119,077**
	Kevin Cramer (R)	87,137

Ohio

Dist.	Representative (Party)	1998 Election
1.	**Steve Chabot*** (R)	**90,060**
	Roxanne Qualls (D)	79,016
2.	**Rob Portman*** (R)	**150,740**
	Charles W. Sanders (D)	48,141
3.	**Tony P. Hall*** (D)	**111,890**
	John S. Shondel (R)	49,594
4.	**Michael G. Oxley*** (R)	**109,948**
	Paul McClain (D)	62,537
5.	**Paul E. Gillmor*** (R)	**122,288**
	Susan Davenport Darrow (D)	61,056
6.	**Ted Strickland*** (D)	**101,231**
	Nancy P. Hollister (R)	76,949
7.	**Dave Hobson*** (R)	**118,729**
	Donald E. Minor, Jr. (D)	49,058
8.	**John A. Boehner*** (R)	**125,645**
	John W. Griffin (D)	51,980
9.	**Marcy Kaptur*** (D)	**128,844**
	Edward S. Emery (R)	30,117
10.	**Dennis J. Kucinich*** (D)	**107,852**
	Joe Slovenec (R)	53,767
11.	**Stephanie Tubbs Jones** (D)	**111,173**
	James D. Hereford (R)	18,733
12.	**John R. Kasich*** (R)	**162,300**
	Edward S. Brown (D)	81,551
13.	**Sherrod Brown*** (D)	**115,168**
	Grace L. Drake (R)	71,789
14.	**Thomas C. Sawyer*** (D)	**104,243**
	Tom Watkins (R)	62,027
15.	**Deborah Pryce*** (R)	**108,560**
	Adam Clay Miller (D)	47,684
16.	**Ralph Regula*** (R)	**114,770**
	Peter D. Ferguson (D)	64,631
17.	**James A. Traficant, Jr.*** (D)	**122,169**
	Paul H. Alberty (R)	57,125
18.	**Bob Ney*** (R)	**111,488**
	Robert L. Burch (D)	73,678
19.	**Steven C. LaTourette*** (R)	**124,388**
	Elizabeth Kelley (D)	62,993

Oklahoma

Dist.	Representative (Party)	1998 Election
1.	**Steve Largent*** (R)	**91,031**
	Howard Plowman (D)	56,309
2.	**Tom A. Coburn*** (R)	**85,581**
	Kent Pharaoh (D)	59,042
3.	**Wes Watkins*** (R)	**89,802**
	Walt Roberts (D)	55,163
4.	**J.C. Watts, Jr.*** (R)	**83,272**
	Ben Odom (D)	52,107
5.	**Ernest Istook*** (R)	**103,217**
	M. C. Smothermon (D)	48,182
6.	**Frank D. Lucas*** (R)	**85,261**
	Paul M. Barby (D)	43,555

Oregon

Dist.	Representative (Party)	1998 Election
1.	**David Wu**[1] (D)	**40,198**
	Molly Bordonaro (R)	34,516
2.	**Greg Walden** (R)	**72,339**
	Kevin M. Campbell (D)	42,555
3.	**Earl Blumenauer*** (D)	**48,749**
	Bruce Alexander Knight (LB)	6,063
4.	**Peter A. DeFazio*** (D)	**73,776**
	Steve J. Webb (R)	34,135
5.	**Darlene Hooley*** (D)	**42,497**
	Marylin Shannon (R)	30,425

Pennsylvania

Dist.	Representative (Party)	1998 Election
1.	**Robert A. Brady*** (D)	**75,552**
	William M. Harrison (R)	15,914
2.	**Chaka Fattah*** (D)	**97,417**
	Anne Marie Mulligan (R)	15,827
3.	**Robert A. Borski*** (D)	**66,419**
	Charles F. Dougherty (R)	44,363
4.	**Ron Klink*** (D)	**103,202**
	Mike Turzai (R)	58,323
5.	**John E. Peterson*** (R)	**99,341**
	William M. Belitskus (GR)	17,556
6.	**Tim Holden*** (D)	**84,568**
	John Meckley (R)	53,549
7.	**Curt Weldon*** (R)	**119,120**
	Martin J. D'Urso (D)	46,526
8.	**Jim Greenwood*** (R)	**93,740**
	Bill Tuthill (D)	48,279
9.	**Bud Shuster*** (R)	**Unopposed**
10.	**Don Sherwood** (R)	**84,025**
	Patrick Casey (D)	83,419
11.	**Paul E. Kanjorski*** (D)	**88,561**
	Stephen A. Urban (R)	43,849
12.	**John P. Murtha*** (D)	**100,040**
	Timothy E. Holloway (R)	46,181
13.	**Joseph M. Hoeffel** (D)	**94,272**
	Jon D. Fox* (R)	84,872
14.	**William J. Coyne*** (D)	**82,746**
	Bill Ravotti (R)	52,747
15.	**Pat Toomey** (R)	**81,348**
	Roy C. Afflerbach (D)	66,583
16.	**Joseph R. Pitts*** (R)	**95,801**
	Robert S. Yorczyk (D)	40,037
17.	**George W. Gekas*** (R)	**Unopposed**
18.	**Mike Doyle*** (D)	**97,643**
	Dick Walker (R)	46,764
19.	**Bill Goodling*** (R)	**96,268**
	Linda G. Ropp (D)	40,614
20.	**Frank Mascara*** (D)	**Unopposed**
21.	**Phil English*** (R)	**93,452**
	Larry Klemens (D)	54,866

Rhode Island

Dist.	Representative (Party)	1998 Election
1.	**Patrick J. Kennedy*** (D)	**90,505**
	Ronald G. Santa (R)	37,067
2.	**Robert A. Weygand*** (D)	**106,903**
	John O. Matson (R)	36,719

South Carolina

Dist.	Representative (Party)	1998 Election
1.	**Mark Sanford*** (R)	**114,746**
	Joe Innella (NL)	11,114
2.	**Floyd D. Spence*** (R)	**118,076**
	Jane Frederick (D)	82,439
3.	**Lindsey Graham*** (R)	**Unopposed**
4.	**Jim DeMint** (R)	**105,091**
	D. Glenn Reese (D)	73,186
5.	**John Spratt*** (D)	**93,882**
	Mike Burkhold (R)	65,805
6.	**James E. Clyburn*** (D)	**115,198**
	Gary McLeod (R)	41,179

South Dakota

Dist.	Representative (Party)	1998 Election
	John R. Thune* (R)	**194,170**
	Jeff Moser (D)	64,429

Tennessee

Dist.	Representative (Party)	1998 Election
1.	**William L. Jenkins*** (R)	**68,899**
	Kay C. White (D)	30,712
2.	**John J. Duncan*** (R)	**90,850**
	Robert O. Watson (I)	4,380
3.	**Zach Wamp*** (R)	**74,863**
	James M. Lewis, Jr. (D)	36,991
4.	**William V. Hilleary*** (R)	**62,901**
	Jerry W. Cooper (D)	42,663
5.	**Bob Clement*** (D)	**74,533**
	William M. Lancaster (I)	6,155
6.	**Bart Gordon*** (D)	**74,704**
	Walt Massey (R)	62,254
7.	**Ed Bryant*** (R)	**Unopposed**
8.	**John S. Tanner*** (D)	**Unopposed**
9.	**Harold E. Ford, Jr.*** (D)	**75,428**
	Claude Burdikoff (R)	18,078

Texas

Dist.	Representative (Party)	1998 Election
1.	**Max Sandlin*** (D)	**80,689**
	Dennis Boerner (R)	55,132
2.	**Jim Turner*** (D)	**81,824**
	Brian Babin (R)	57,181
3.	**Sam Johnson*** (R)	**103,391**
	Ken Ashby (LB)	9,815
4.	**Ralph M. Hall*** (D)	**82,985**
	Jim Lohmeyer (R)	58,944
5.	**Pete Sessions*** (R)	**58,628**
	Victor Morales (D)	45,950
6.	**Joe Barton*** (R)	**112,035**
	Ben B. Boothe (D)	39,700
7.	**Bill Archer*** (R)	**110,999**
	Drew Parks (LB)	7,889
8.	**Kevin Brady*** (R)	**123,359**
	Don L. Richards (LB)	11,580
9.	**Nick Lampson*** (D)	**86,051**
	Tom Cottar (R)	49,105
10.	**Lloyd Doggett*** (D)	**116,111**
	Vincent J. May (LB)	20,151
11.	**Chet Edwards*** (D)	**71,704**
	Vince Hanke (LB)	15,209
12.	**Kay Granger*** (R)	**66,737**
	Tom Hall (D)	39,084
13.	**Mac Thornberry*** (R)	**81,205**
	Mark Harmon (D)	37,047
14.	**Ron Paul*** (R)	**84,495**
	Loy Sneary (D)	67,984
15.	**Ruben Hinojosa*** (D)	**48,282**
	Tom Haughey (R)	33,018
16.	**Silvestre Reyes*** (D)	**67,477**
	Stu Nance (LB)	5,328
17.	**Charlie Stenholm*** (D)	**79,651**
	Rudy Izzard (R)	66,835
18.	**Sheila Jackson Lee*** (D)	**82,079**
	James Galvan (LB)	9,172
19.	**Larry Combest*** (R)	**108,249**
	Sidney Blankenship (D)	21,141
20.	**Charlie Gonzalez** (D)	**50,343**
	James Walker (R)	28,324
21.	**Lamar Smith*** (R)	**161,971**
	Jeffrey Charles Blunt (LB)	15,338
22.	**Tom DeLay*** (R)	**87,806**
	Hill Kemp (D)	45,381
23.	**Henry Bonilla*** (R)	**73,136**
	Charlie Urbina Jones (D)	40,242
24.	**Martin Frost*** (D)	**52,931**
	Shawn Terry (R)	37,358
25.	**Ken Bentsen*** (D)	**58,444**
	John M. Sanchez (R)	41,620
26.	**Dick Armey*** (R)	**113,095**
	Joe Turner (LB)	15,339
27.	**Solomon P. Ortiz*** (D)	**61,337**
	Erol A. Stone (R)	34,301
28.	**Ciro D. Rodriguez*** (D)	**71,844**
	Edward Elmer (LB)	7,503
29.	**Gene Green*** (D)	**44,276**
	Lea Sherman (I)	2,014
30.	**Eddie Bernice Johnson*** (D)	**46,291**
	Carrie Kelleher (R)	19,270

Utah

Dist.	Representative (Party)	1998 Election
1.	**James V. Hansen*** (R)	**109,370**
	Steve Beierlein (D)	49,186
2.	**Merrill Cook*** (R)	**93,367**
	Lily Eskelsen (D)	76,865
3.	**Chris Cannon*** (R)	**99,983**
	Will Christensen (IA)	20,555

Vermont

Dist.	Representative (Party)	1998 Election
	Bernie Sanders* (I)	**130,615**
	Mark Candon (R)	67,585

Virginia

Dist.	Representative (Party)	1998 Election
1.	**Herbert H. "Herb" Bateman*** (R)	**76,510**
	Bradford L. Phillips (I)	13,173
2.	**Owen B. Pickett*** (D)	**Unopposed**
3.	**Robert C. "Bobby" Scott*** (D)	**48,132**
	Robert S. "Bob" Barnett (I)	14,546
4.	**Norman Sisisky*** (D)	**Unopposed**
5.	**Virgil H. Goode, Jr.*** (D)	**Unopposed**
6.	**Robert W. "Bob" Goodlatte*** (R)	**89,593**
	David A. Bowers (D)	40,122
7.	**Thomas J. "Tom" Bliley, Jr.*** (R)	**77,047**
	Bradley E. Evans (I)	20,293
8.	**James P. Moran, Jr.*** (D)	**97,336**
	Demaris H. Miller (R)	48,064
9.	**Frederick C. "Rick" Boucher*** (D)	**87,115**
	J. A. "Joe" Barta (R)	55,956
10.	**Frank R. Wolf*** (R)	**103,635**
	Cornell W. Brooks (D)	36,476
11.	**Thomas M. Davis III*** (R)	**90,969**
	C. W. "Levi" Levy (I)	18,666

Washington

Dist.	Representative (Party)	1998 Election
1.	**Jay Inslee** (D)	**80,294**
	Rick White* (R)	68,187
2.	**Jack Metcalf*** (R)	**97,368**
	Grethe Cammermeyer (D)	79,700
3.	**Brian Baird** (D)	**100,868**
	Don Benton (R)	83,043
4.	**Doc Hastings*** (R)	**96,075**
	Gordon Allen Pross (D)	34,851
5.	**George Nethercutt*** (R)	**92,764**
	Brad Lyons (D)	62,336
6.	**Norm Dicks*** (D)	**106,620**
	Bob Lawrence (R)	49,057
7.	**Jim McDermott*** (D)	**118,511**
	Stan Lippmann (RF)	11,894
8.	**Jennifer Dunn*** (R)	**78,909**
	Heidi Behrens-Benedict (D)	56,925
9.	**Adam Smith*** (D)	**76,274**
	Ron Taber (R)	41,422

West Virginia

Dist.	Representative (Party)	1998 Election
1.	**Alan B. Mollohan*** (D)	**104,055**
	Richard Kerr (LB)	18,843
2.	**Bob Wise*** (D)	**98,397**
	Sally Anne Kay (R)	28,785
3.	**Nick Joe Rahall, II*** (D)	**77,941**
	Joe Whelan (LB)	12,040

Wisconsin

Dist.	Representative (Party)	1998 Election
1.	**Paul Ryan** (R)	**107,392**
	Lydia Carol Spottswood (D)	80,747
2.	**Tommy Baldwin** (D)	**117,014**
	Josephine W. Musser (R)	103,493
3.	**Ron Kind*** (D)	**128,379**
	Troy A. Brechler (R)	51,009
4.	**Jerry Kleczka*** (D)	**100,042**
	Tom Reynolds (R)	76,806
5.	**Tom Barrett*** (D)	**121,103**
	Jack Melvin (R)	33,503
6.	**Thomas E. Petri*** (R)	**143,638**
	Timothy J. Farness (TX)	11,244
7.	**David R. Obey*** (D)	**115,621**
	Scott West (R)	75,043
8.	**Mark Green** (R)	**112,311**
	Jay Johnson* (D)	93,538
9.	**F. James Sensenbrenner, Jr.*** (R)	**175,081**
	Jeffrey M. Gonyo (I)	16,390

Wyoming

Dist.	Representative (Party)	1998 Election
	Barbara Cubin* (R)	**100,657**
	Scott Farris (D)	67,398

The following members of Congress are nonvoting: Carlos A. Romero Barceló (D), resident commissioner, Puerto Rico; Eleanor Holmes Norton (D), District of Columbia; Robert Underwood (D), Guam; Eni F. H. Faleomavaega (D), American Samoa; Donna Christian Green (D), Virgin Islands.

(1) Leading as of Nov. 5, 1998.

Congressional Committees

Senate Standing Committees

(as of Oct. 1998)

Agriculture, Nutrition, and Forestry
Chairman: Richard G. Lugar, IN
Ranking Dem.: Tom Harkin, IA

Appropriations
Chairman: Ted Stevens, AK
Ranking Dem.: Robert C. Byrd, WV

Armed Services
Chairman: Strom Thurmond, SC
Ranking Dem.: Carl Levin, MI

Banking, Housing, and Urban Affairs
Chairman: Alfonse D'Amato, NY
Ranking Dem.: Paul S. Sarbanes, MD

Budget
Chairman: Pete V. Domenici, NM
Ranking Dem.: Frank R. Lautenberg, NJ

Commerce, Science, and Transportation
Chairman: John McCain, AZ
Ranking Dem.: Ernest Hollings, SC

Energy and Natural Resources
Chairman: Frank H. Murkowski, AK
Ranking Dem.: Dale Bumpers, AR

Environment and Public Works
Chairman: John H. Chafee, RI
Ranking Dem.: Max Baucus, MT

Finance
Chairman: William V. Roth, Jr., DE
Ranking Dem.: Daniel Patrick Moynihan, NY

Foreign Relations
Chairman: Jesse Helms, NC
Ranking Dem.: Joseph R. Biden, Jr., DE

Governmental Affairs
Chairman: Fred Thompson, TN
Ranking Dem.: John Glenn, OH

Indian Affairs
Chairman: Ben Nighthorse Campbell, CO
Ranking Dem.: Daniel K. Inouye, HI

Judiciary
Chairman: Orrin G. Hatch, UT
Ranking Dem.: Patrick Leahy, VT

Labor and Human Resources
Chairman: Jim Jeffords, VT
Ranking Dem.: Edward M. Kennedy, MA

Rules and Administration
Chairman: John W. Warner, VA
Ranking Dem.: Wendell H. Ford, KY

Small Business
Chairman: Christopher (Kit) Bond, MO
Ranking Dem.: John F. Kerry, MA

Veterans' Affairs
Chairman: Arlen Specter, PA
Ranking Dem.: John D. Rockefeller IV, WV

Senate Special Committee

(as of Oct. 1998)

Aging
Chairman: Charles Grassley, IA
Ranking Dem.: John B. Breaux, LA

Senate Select Committees

(as of Oct. 1998)

Ethics
Chairman: Robert Smith, NH
Ranking Dem.: Harry Reid, NV

Intelligence
Chairman: Richard Shelby, AL
V. Chairman: Bob Kerrey, NE

House Select Committee

(as of Oct. 1998)

Intelligence
Chairman: Porter Goss, FL
Ranking Dem.: Norm Dicks, WA

Joint Committees of Congress

(as of Oct. 1998)

Economic
Chairman: Rep. Jim Saxton, NJ
V. Chairman: Sen. Connie Mack, FL

Library
Chairman: Rep. Bill Thomas, CA
V. Chairman: Sen. Ted Stevens, AK

Printing
Chairman: Sen. John W. Warner, VA
V. Chairman: Rep. Bill Thomas, CA

Taxation
Chairman: Sen. William V. Roth, Jr., DE
V. Chairman: Rep. Bill Archer, TX

House Standing Committees

(as of Oct. 1998)

Agriculture
Chairman: Robert F. (Bob) Smith, OR
Ranking Dem.: Charlie Stenholm, TX

Appropriations
Chairman: Robert L. "Bob" Livingston, LA
Ranking Dem.: David R. Obey, WI

Banking and Financial Services
Chairman: Jim Leach, IA
Ranking Dem.: John J. La Falce, NY

Budget
Chairman: John R. Kasich, OH
Ranking Dem.: John Spratt, SC

Commerce
Chairman: Thomas J. "Tom" Bliley, Jr., VA
Ranking Dem.: John D. Dingell, MI

Education and the Workforce
Chairman: Bill Goodling, PA
Ranking Dem.: William (Bill) Clay, Sr., MO

Government Reform and Oversight
Chairman: Dan Burton, IN
Ranking Dem.: Henry A. Waxman, CA

House Oversight
Chairman: Bill Thomas, CA
Ranking Dem.: Sam Gejdenson, CT

International Relations
Chairman: Benjamin A. Gilman, NY
Ranking Dem.: Lee H. Hamilton, IN

Judiciary
Chairman: Henry J. Hyde, IL
Ranking Dem.: John Conyers, Jr., MI

National Security
Chairman: Floyd D. Spence, SC
Ranking Dem.: Ike Skelton, MO

Resources
Chairman: Don Young, AK
Ranking Dem.: George Miller, CA

Rules
Chairman: Gerald B. H. Solomon, NY
Ranking Dem.: John Joseph Moakley, MA

Science
Chairman: F. James Sensenbrenner, Jr., WI
Ranking Dem.: George E. Brown, Jr., CA

Small Business
Chairman: James M. Talent, MO
Ranking Dem.: Nydia M. Velazquez, NY

Standards of Official Conduct
Chairman: James V. Hansen, UT
Ranking Dem.: Howard L. Berman, CA

Transportation and Infrastructure
Chairman: Bud Shuster, PA
Ranking Dem.: James L. Oberstar, MN

Veterans' Affairs
Chairman: Bob Stump, AZ
Ranking Dem.: Lane A. Evans, IL

Ways and Means
Chairman: Bill Archer, TX
Ranking Dem.: Charles B. Rangel, NY

Speakers of the House of Representatives

(as of Oct. 1998)

Party designations: A, American; D, Democratic; DR, Democratic-Republican; F, Federalist; R, Republican; W, Whig

Name	Party	State	Tenure
Frederick Muhlenberg	F	PA	1789-1791
Jonathan Trumbull	F	CT	1791-1793
Frederick Muhlenberg	F	PA	1793-1795
Jonathan Dayton	F	NJ	1795-1799
Theodore Sedgwick	F	MA	1799-1801
Nathaniel Macon	DR	NC	1801-1807
Joseph B. Varnum	DR	MA	1807-1811
Henry Clay	DR	KY	1811-1814
Langdon Cheves	DR	SC	1814-1815
Henry Clay	DR	KY	1815-1820
John W. Taylor	DR	NY	1820-1821
Philip P. Barbour	DR	VA	1821-1823
Henry Clay	DR	KY	1823-1825
John W. Taylor	D	NY	1825-1827
Andrew Stevenson	D	VA	1827-1834
John Bell	D	TN	1834-1835
James K. Polk	D	TN	1835-1839
Robert M. T. Hunter	D	VA	1839-1841
John White	W	KY	1841-1843
John W. Jones	D	VA	1843-1845
John W. Davis	D	IN	1845-1847
Robert C. Winthrop	W	MA	1847-1849
Howell Cobb	D	GA	1849-1851
Linn Boyd	D	KY	1851-1855
Nathaniel P. Banks	A	MA	1856-1857
James L. Orr	D	SC	1857-1859
William Pennington	R	NJ	1860-1861
Galusha A. Grow	R	PA	1861-1863
Schuyler Colfax	R	IN	1863-1869
Theodore M. Pomeroy	R	NY	1869
James G. Blaine	R	ME	1869-1875
Michael C. Kerr	D	IN	1875-1876
Samuel J. Randall	D	PA	1876-1881
Joseph W. Keifer	R	OH	1881-1883
John G. Carlisle	D	KY	1883-1889
Thomas B. Reed	R	ME	1889-1891
Charles F. Crisp	D	GA	1891-1895
Thomas B. Reed	R	ME	1895-1899
David B. Henderson	R	IA	1899-1903
Joseph G. Cannon	R	IL	1903-1911
Champ Clark	D	MO	1911-1919
Frederick H. Gillett	R	MA	1919-1925
Nicholas Longworth	R	OH	1925-1931
John N. Garner	D	TX	1931-1933
Henry T. Rainey	D	IL	1933-1935
Joseph W. Byrns	D	TN	1935-1936
William B. Bankhead	D	AL	1936-1940
Sam Rayburn	D	TX	1940-1947
Joseph W. Martin Jr.	R	MA	1947-1949
Sam Rayburn	D	TX	1949-1953
Joseph W. Martin Jr.	R	MA	1953-1955
Sam Rayburn	D	TX	1955-1961
John W. McCormack	D	MA	1962-1971
Carl Albert	D	OK	1971-1977
Thomas P. O'Neill Jr.	D	MA	1977-1987
James Wright	D	TX	1987-1989
Thomas S. Foley	D	WA	1989-1995
Newt Gingrich	R	GA	1995-

Floor Leaders in the U.S. Senate Since the 1920s

Majority Leaders

Name	Party	State	Tenure
Charles Curtis[1]	R	KS	1925-1929
James E. Watson	R	IN	1929-1933
Joseph T. Robinson	D	AR	1933-1937
Alben W. Barkley	D	KY	1937-1947
Wallace H. White	R	ME	1947-1949
Scott W. Lucas	D	IL	1949-1951
Ernest W. McFarland	D	AZ	1951-1953
Robert A. Taft	R	OH	1953
William F. Knowland	R	CA	1953-1955
Lyndon B. Johnson	D	TX	1955-1961
Mike Mansfield	D	MT	1961-1977
Robert C. Byrd	D	WV	1977-1981
Howard H. Baker Jr.	R	TN	1981-1985
Robert J. Dole	R	KS	1985-1987
Robert C. Byrd	D	WV	1987-1989
George J. Mitchell	D	ME	1989-1995
Robert J. Dole	R	KS	1995-1996
Trent Lott	R	MS	1996-

Minority Leaders

Name	Party	State	Tenure
Oscar W. Underwood[2]	D	AL	1920-1923
Joseph T. Robinson	D	AR	1923-1933
Charles L. McNary	R	OR	1933-1944
Wallace H. White	R	ME	1944-1947
Alben W. Barkley	D	KY	1947-1949
Kenneth S. Wherry	R	NE	1949-1951
Henry Styles Bridges	R	NH	1951-1953
Lyndon B. Johnson	D	TX	1953-1955
William F. Knowland	R	CA	1955-1959
Everett M. Dirksen	R	IL	1959-1969
Hugh D. Scott	R	PA	1969-1977
Howard H. Baker Jr.	R	TN	1977-1981
Robert C. Byrd	D	WV	1981-1987
Robert J. Dole	R	KS	1987-1995
Thomas A. Daschle	D	SD	1995-

Note: Majority and Minority Leaders as of Oct. 1998. (1) First Republican to be designated floor leader. (2) First Democrat to be designated floor leader.

Political Divisions of the U.S. Senate and House of Representatives, 1901-98

Source: *1995-1996 Congressional Directory*; Senate Library; all figures reflect immediate post-election party breakdown

(reflects Nov. 3, 1998, preliminary election results)

		Senate					House of Representatives				
Congress	Years	No. of Sen.	Demo-crats	Repub-licans	Other parties	Vacant	No. of Rep.	Demo-crats	Repub-licans	Other parties	Vacant
57th	1901-03	90	29	56	3	2	357	153	198	5	1
58th	1903-05	90	32	58			386	178	207		1
59th	1905-07	90	32	58			386	136	250		
60th	1907-09	92	29	61		2	386	164	222		
61st	1909-11	92	32	59		1	391	172	219		
62d	1911-13	92	42	49		1	391	228	162	1	
63d	1913-15	96	51	44	1		435	290	127	18	
64th	1915-17	96	56	39	1		435	231	193	8	3
65th	1917-19	96	53	42	1		435	210[1]	216	9	
66th	1919-21	96	47	48	1		435	191	237	7	
67th	1921-23	96	37	59			435	132	300	1	2
68th	1923-25	96	43	51	2		435	207	225	3	
69th	1925-27	96	40	54	1	1	435	183	247	5	
70th	1927-29	96	47	48	1		435	195	237	3	

(continued)

Political Divisions of the U.S. Senate and House of Representatives, 1901-98 *(continued)*

		Senate					House of Representatives				
Congress	Years	No. of Sen.	Demo-crats	Repub-licans	Other parties	Vacant	No. of Rep.	Demo-crats	Repub-licans	Other parties	Vacant
71st	1929-31	96	39	56	1		435	163	267	1	4
72d	1931-33	96	47	48	1		435	216[2]	218	1	
73d	1933-35	96	59	36	1		435	313	117	5	
74th	1935-37	96	69	25	2		435	322	103	10	
75th	1937-39	96	75	17	4		435	333	89	13	
76th	1939-41	96	69	23	4		435	262	169	4	
77th	1941-43	96	66	28	2		435	267	162	6	
78th	1943-45	96	57	38	1		435	222	209	4	
79th	1945-47	96	57	38	1		435	243	190	2	
80th	1947-49	96	45	51			435	188	246	1	
81st	1949-51	96	54	42			435	263	171	1	
82d	1951-53	96	48	47	1		435	234	199	2	
83d	1953-55	96	46	48	2		435	213	221	1	
84th	1955-57	96	48	47	1		435	232	203		
85th	1957-59	96	49	47			435	234	201		
86th	1959-61	98	64	34			436[3]	283	153		
87th	1961-63	100	64	36			437[4]	262	175		
88th	1963-65	100	67	33			435	258	176		1
89th	1965-67	100	68	32			435	295	140		
90th	1967-69	100	64	36			435	248	187		
91st	1969-71	100	58	42			435	243	192		
92d	1971-73	100	54	44	2		435	255	180		
93d	1973-75	100	56	42	2		435	242	192	1	
94th	1975-77	100	60	37	2		435	291	144	1	
95th	1977-79	100	61	38	1		435	292	143		
96th	1979-81	100	58	41	1		435	277	158		
97th	1981-83	100	46	53	1		435	242	192	1	
98th	1983-85	100	46	54			435	269	166		
99th	1985-87	100	47	53			435	253	182		
100th	1987-89	100	55	45			435	258	177		
101st	1989-91	100	55	45			435	260	175		
102d	1991-93	100	56	44			435	267	167	1	
103d	1993-95	100	57	43			435	258	176	1	
104th	1995-97	100	48	52			435	204	230	1	
105th	1997-99	100	45	55			435	207	227	1	
106th	1999-2001	100	45	55			435	211[5]	223	1	

(1) Democrats organized House with help of other parties. (2) Democrats organized House due to Republican deaths. (3) Proclamation declaring Alaska a state issued Jan. 3, 1959. (4) Proclamation declaring Hawaii a state issued Aug. 21, 1959. (5) Includes 1 Democrat leading but not decided as of Nov. 5, 1998.

Congressional Bills Vetoed, 1789-1998

Source: Senate Library

	Regular vetoes	Pocket vetoes	Total vetoes	Vetoes overridden
Washington	2	—	2	—
John Adams	—	—	—	—
Jefferson	—	—	—	—
Madison	5	2	7	—
Monroe	1	—	1	—
John Q. Adams	—	—	—	—
Jackson	5	7	12	—
Van Buren	—	1	1	—
William Harrison	—	—	—	—
Tyler	6	4	10	1
Polk	2	1	3	—
Taylor	—	—	—	—
Fillmore	—	—	—	—
Pierce	9	—	9	5
Buchanan	4	3	7	—
Lincoln	2	4	6	—
Andrew Johnson	21	8	29	15
Grant	45	48	93	4
Hayes	12	1	13	1
Garfield	—	—	—	—
Arthur	4	8	12	1
Cleveland	304	110	414	2

	Regular vetoes	Pocket vetoes	Total vetoes	Vetoes overridden
Benjamin Harrison	19	25	44	1
Cleveland	42	128	170	5
McKinley	6	36	42	—
Theodore Roosevelt	42	40	82	1
Taft	30	9	39	1
Wilson	33	11	44	6
Harding	5	1	6	—
Coolidge	20	30	50	4
Hoover	21	16	37	3
Franklin Roosevelt	372	263	635	9
Truman	180	70	250	12
Eisenhower	73	108	181	2
Kennedy	12	9	21	—
Lyndon Johnson	16	14	30	—
Nixon	26	17	43	7
Ford	48	18	66	12
Carter	13	18	31	2
Reagan	39	39	78	9
Bush[1]	29	15	44	1
Clinton[2,3]	25	—	25	4
Total[1,3]	**1,473**	**1,064**	**2,537**	**108**

(1) Excluded from the figures are 2 additional bills, which Pres. Bush claimed to be vetoed but Congress considered enacted into law because the president failed to return them to Congress during a recess period. (2) As of Oct. 31, 1998. (3) Does not include line-item veto, which was ruled unconstitutional by the Supreme Court on June 25, 1998.

Librarians of Congress

Librarian	Served	Appointed by President
John J. Beckley	1802-1807	Jefferson
Patrick Magruder	1807-1815	Jefferson
George Watterston	1815-1829	Madison
John Silva Meehan	1829-1861	Jackson
John G. Stephenson	1861-1864	Lincoln
Ainsworth Rand Spofford	1864-1897	Lincoln
John Russell Young	1897-1899	McKinley
Herbert Putnam	1899-1939	McKinley
Archibald MacLeish	1939-1944	F. D. Roosevelt
Luther H. Evans	1945-1953	Truman
L. Quincy Mumford	1954-1974	Eisenhower
Daniel J. Boorstin	1975-1987	Ford
James H. Billington	1987-	Reagan

Judiciary of the U.S.

(data as of Oct. 1998)

Justices of the United States Supreme Court

The Supreme Court comprises the chief justice of the U.S. and 8 associate justices, all appointed by the president with advice and consent of the Senate. Salaries: chief justice, $175,400 annually; associate justice, $167,900 annually. The Supreme Court is at the U.S. Supreme Court Bldg., 1 First St. NE, Washington, DC 20543.

Members of the Supreme Court at the start of the 1998–99 term (Oct. 5, 1998): Chief justice: William H. Rehnquist; associate justices: Stephen G. Breyer, Ruth Bader Ginsburg, Anthony M. Kennedy, Sandra Day O'Connor, Antonin Scalia, David H. Souter, John Paul Stevens, Clarence Thomas.

Name,[1] apptd. from	Service Term	Service Yrs	Born	Died
John Jay, NY	1789-1795	5	1745	1829
John Rutledge, SC	1789-1791	1	1739	1800
William Cushing, MA	1789-1810	20	1732	1810
James Wilson, PA	1789-1798	8	1742	1798
John Blair, VA	1789-1796	6	1732	1800
James Iredell, NC	1790-1799	9	1751	1799
Thomas Johnson, MD	1791-1793	1	1732	1819
William Paterson, NJ	1793-1806	13	1745	1806
John Rutledge,[2] SC	1795	—	1739	1800
Samuel Chase, MD	1796-1811	15	1741	1811
Oliver Ellsworth, CT	1796-1800	4	1745	1807
Bushrod Washington, VA	1798-1829	31	1762	1829
Alfred Moore, NC	1799-1804	4	1755	1810
John Marshall, VA	1801-1835	34	1755	1835
William Johnson, SC	1804-1834	30	1771	1834
Henry B. Livingston, NY	1806-1823	16	1757	1823
Thomas Todd, KY	1807-1826	18	1765	1826
Joseph Story, MA	1811-1845	33	1779	1845
Gabriel Duval, MD	1811-1835	22	1752	1844
Smith Thompson, NY	1823-1843	20	1768	1843
Robert Trimble, KY	1826-1828	2	1777	1828
John McLean, OH	1829-1861	32	1785	1861
Henry Baldwin, PA	1830-1844	14	1780	1844
James M. Wayne, GA	1835-1867	32	1790	1867
Roger B. Taney, MD	1836-1864	28	1777	1864
Philip P. Barbour, VA	1836-1841	4	1783	1841
John Catron, TN	1837-1865	28	1786	1865
John McKinley, AL	1837-1852	15	1780	1852
Peter V. Daniel, VA	1841-1860	19	1784	1860
Samuel Nelson, NY	1845-1872	27	1792	1873
Levi Woodbury, NH	1845-1851	5	1789	1851
Robert C. Grier, PA	1846-1870	23	1794	1870
Benjamin R. Curtis, MA	1851-1857	6	1809	1874
John A. Campbell, AL	1853-1861	8	1811	1889
Nathan Clifford, ME	1858-1881	23	1803	1881
Noah H. Swayne, OH	1862-1881	18	1804	1884
Samuel F. Miller, IA	1862-1890	28	1816	1890
David Davis, IL	1862-1877	14	1815	1886
Stephen J. Field, CA	1863-1897	34	1816	1899
Salmon P. Chase, OH	1864-1873	8	1808	1873
William Strong, PA	1870-1880	10	1808	1895
Joseph P. Bradley, NJ	1870-1892	21	1813	1892
Ward Hunt, NY	1872-1882	9	1810	1886
Morrison R. Waite, OH	1874-1888	14	1816	1888
John M. Harlan, KY	1877-1911	34	1833	1911
William B. Woods, GA	1880-1887	6	1824	1887
Stanley Matthews, OH	1881-1889	7	1824	1889
Horace Gray, MA	1881-1902	20	1828	1902
Samuel Blatchford, NY	1882-1893	11	1820	1893
Lucius Q.C. Lamar, MS	1888-1893	5	1825	1893
Melville W. Fuller, IL	1888-1910	21	1833	1910
David J. Brewer, KS	1889-1910	20	1837	1910
Henry B. Brown, MI	1890-1906	15	1836	1913
George Shiras Jr, PA	1892-1903	10	1832	1924
Howell E. Jackson, TN	1893-1895	2	1832	1895
Edward D. White, LA	1894-1910	16	1845	1921
Rufus W. Peckham, NY	1895-1909	13	1838	1909
Joseph McKenna, CA	1898-1925	26	1843	1926
Oliver W. Holmes, MA	1902-1932	29	1841	1935
William R. Day, OH	1903-1922	19	1849	1923
William H. Moody, MA	1906-1910	3	1853	1917
Horace H. Lurton, TN	1909-1914	4	1844	1914
Charles E. Hughes, NY	1910-1916	5	1862	1948
Willis Van Devanter, WY	1910-1937	26	1859	1941
Joseph R. Lamar, GA	1910-1916	5	1857	1916
Edward D. White, LA	1910-1921	10	1845	1921
Mahlon Pitney, NJ	1912-1922	10	1858	1924
James C. McReynolds, TN	1914-1941	26	1862	1946
Louis D. Brandeis, MA	1916-1939	22	1856	1941
John H. Clarke, OH	1916-1922	5	1857	1945
William H. Taft, CT	1921-1930	8	1857	1930
George Sutherland, UT	1922-1938	15	1862	1942
Pierce Butler, MN	1922-1939	16	1866	1939
Edward T. Sanford, TN	1923-1930	7	1865	1930
Harlan F. Stone, NY	1925-1941	16	1872	1946
Charles E. Hughes, NY	1930-1941	11	1862	1948
Owen J. Roberts, PA	1930-1945	15	1875	1955
Benjamin N. Cardozo, NY	1932-1938	6	1870	1938
Hugo L. Black, AL	1937-1971	34	1886	1971
Stanley F. Reed, KY	1938-1957	19	1884	1980
Felix Frankfurter, MA	1939-1962	23	1882	1965
William O. Douglas, CT	1939-1975	36	1898	1980
Frank Murphy, MI	1940-1949	9	1890	1949
Harlan F. Stone, NY	1941-1946	5	1872	1946
James F. Byrnes, SC	1941-1942	1	1879	1972
Robert H. Jackson, NY	1941-1954	12	1892	1954
Wiley B. Rutledge, IA	1943-1949	6	1894	1949
Harold H. Burton, OH	1945-1958	13	1888	1964
Fred M. Vinson, KY	1946-1953	7	1890	1953
Tom C. Clark, TX	1949-1967	18	1899	1977
Sherman Minton, IN	1949-1956	7	1890	1965
Earl Warren, CA	1953-1969	16	1891	1974
John Marshall Harlan, NY	1955-1971	16	1899	1971
William J. Brennan Jr, NJ	1956-1990	33	1906	1997
Charles E. Whittaker, MO	1957-1962	5	1901	1973
Potter Stewart, OH	1958-1981	23	1915	1985
Byron R. White, CO	1962-1993	31	1917	
Arthur J. Goldberg, IL	1962-1965	3	1908	1990
Abe Fortas, TN	1965-1969	4	1910	1982
Thurgood Marshall, NY	1967-1991	24	1908	1993
Warren E. Burger, VA	1969-1986	17	1907	1995
Harry A. Blackmun, MN	1970-1994	24	1908	
Lewis F. Powell Jr, VA	1972-1987	15	1907	1998
William H. Rehnquist, AZ	1972-1986	14	1924	
John Paul Stevens, IL	1975-		1920	
Sandra Day O'Connor, AZ	1981-		1930	
William H. Rehnquist, AZ	1986-		1924	
Antonin Scalia, VA	1986-		1936	
Anthony M. Kennedy, CA	1988-		1936	
David H. Souter, NH	1990-		1939	
Clarence Thomas, VA	1991-		1948	
Ruth Bader Ginsburg, DC	1993-		1933	
Stephen Breyer, MA	1994-		1938	

(1) Chief justices in italics. (2) Rejected Dec. 15, 1795.

U.S. Courts of Appeals

(Salaries, $145,000. CJ means Chief Judge)

Federal Circuit — Haldane Robert Mayer, CJ; Giles S. Rich, Pauline Newman, Paul R. Michel, S. Jay Plager, Alan D. Lourie, Raymond C. Clevenger III, Randall R. Rader, Alvin A. Schall, William C. Bryson, Arthur J. Gajarsa; Clerk's Office, Washington, DC 20439.

District of Columbia — Harry T. Edwards, CJ; Patricia M. Wald, Laurence H. Silberman, Stephen F. Williams, Douglas Ginsburg, David B. Sentelle, Karen LeCraft Henderson, A. Raymond Randolph, Judith W. Rogers, David S. Tatel, Merrick B. Garland; Clerk's Office, Washington, DC 20001.

First Circuit (ME, MA, NH, RI, Puerto Rico) — Juan R. Torruella, CJ; Bruce M. Selya, Michael Boudin, Norman H. Stahl, Sandra Lynch; Clerk's Office, Boston, MA 02109.

Second Circuit (CT, NY, VT) — Ralph K. Winter, CJ; Wilfred Feinberg, James L. Oakes, Ellsworth Van Graafeiland, Thomas J. Meskill, Amalya L. Kearse, Jon O. Newman, Richard J. Cardamone, Roger J. Miner, John M. Walker Jr, Joseph M. McLaughlin, Dennis Jacobs, Pierre N. Leval, Guido Calabresi, José A. Cabranes, Fred I. Parker, Chester J. Straub, Rosemary S. Pooler, Robert D. Sack; Clerk's Office, New York, NY 10007.

Third Circuit (DE, NJ, PA, Virgin Islands) — Edward R. Becker, CJ; Dolores K. Sloviter, Walter K. Stapleton, Carol Los Mansmann, Morton I. Greenberg, Anthony J. Scirica, Richard L. Nygaard, Samuel A. Alito Jr, Jane R. Roth, Timothy K. Lewis, Theodore A. McKee, Marjorie O. Rendell; Clerk's Office, Philadelphia, PA 19106.

Fourth Circuit (MD, NC, SC, VA, WV) — J. Harvie Wilkinson III, CJ; H. Emory Widener Jr, K. K. Hall, Francis D. Murnaghan Jr, Sam J. Ervin III, William W. Wilkins Jr, Paul V. Niemeyer, Clyde H. Hamilton, J. Michael Luttig, Karen J. Williams, M. Blane Michael, Diana Gribbon Motz; Clerk's Office, Richmond, VA 23219.

Fifth Circuit (LA, MS, TX) — Henry A. Politz, CJ; Carolyn Dineen King, E. Grady Jolly, Patrick E. Higginbotham, W. Eugene Davis, Edith H. Jones, Jerry E. Smith, John M. Duhé Jr, Jacques L. Wiener Jr, Rhesa H. Barksdale, Emilio M. Garza, Harold R. DeMoss Jr, Fortunato P. Benavides, Carl E. Stewart, Robert M. Parker, James L. Dennis; Clerk's Office, New Orleans, LA 70130.

Sixth Circuit (KY, MI, OH, TN) — Boyce F. Martin Jr, CJ; Gilbert S. Merritt, Cornelia G. Kennedy, David A. Nelson, James L. Ryan, Danny J. Boggs, Alan E. Norris, Richard F. Suhrheinrich, Eugene E. Siler Jr, Alice M. Batchelder, Martha Craig Daughtrey, Karen Nelson Moore, R. Guy Cole, Eric L. Clay, Ronald Lee Gilman; Clerk's Office, Cincinnati, OH 45202.

Seventh Circuit (IL, IN, WI) — Richard A. Posner, CJ; Thomas E. Fairchild, Walter J. Cummings, Wilbur F. Pell Jr, William J. Bauer, Harlington Wood Jr, Richard D. Cudahy, Jesse E. Eschbach, John L. Coffey, Joel M. Flaum, Frank H. Easterbrook, Kenneth F. Ripple, Daniel A. Manion, Michael S. Kanne, Ilana D. Rovner, Diane P. Wood, Terence T. Evans; Clerk's Office, Chicago, IL 60604.

Eighth Circuit (AR, IA, MN, MO, NE, ND, SD) — Pasco M. Bowman, CJ; Theodore McMillian, Richard S. Arnold, George G. Fagg, Roger L. Wollman, C. Arlen Beam, James B. Loken, David R. Hansen, Morris S. Arnold, Diana E. Murphy, John D. Kelly; Clerk's Office, St. Louis, MO 63101.

Ninth Circuit (AK, AZ, CA, HI, ID, MT, NV, OR, WA, Guam, N. Mariana Islands) — Procter Hug Jr, CJ; James R. Browning, Melvin Brunetti, Ferdinand F. Fernandez, Betty B. Fletcher, Susan P. Graber, Michael Daly Hawkins, Andrew J. Kleinfeld, Alex Kozinski, M. Margaret McKeown, Thomas G. Nelson, Diarmuid F. O'Scannlain, Harry Pregerson, Stephen R. Reinhardt, Pamela Ann Rymer, Mary M. Schroeder, Barry G. Silverman, A. Wallace Tashima, Sidney R. Thomas, David R. Thompson, Stephen S. Trott, Kim M. Wardlaw; Clerk's Office, San Francisco, CA 94119.

Tenth Circuit (CO, KS, NM, OK, UT, WY) — Stephanie K. Seymour, CJ; John C. Porfilio, Stephen H. Anderson, Deanell R. Tacha, Bobby R. Baldock, Wade Brorby, David M. Ebel, Paul J. Kelly, Robert H. Henry, Mary Beck Briscoe, Carlos Lucero, Michael R. Murphy; Clerk's Office, Denver, CO 80257.

Eleventh Circuit (AL, FL, GA) — Joseph W. Hatchett, CJ; Gerald B. Tjoflat, R. Lanier Anderson III, J. L. Edmondson, Emmett R. Cox, Stanley F. Birch Jr, Joel F. Dubina, Susan H. Black, Ed Carnes, Rosemary Barkett, Frank M. Hull, Stanley Marcus; Clerk's Office, Atlanta GA 30303.

U.S. District Courts

(Salaries, $136,700. CJ means Chief Judge)

Alabama — **Northern:** Sam C. Pointer Jr, CJ; U. W. Clemon, Edwin L. Nelson, Sharon Lovelace Blackburn, C. Lynwood Smith Jr; Clerk's Office, Birmingham 35203. **Middle:** W. Harold Albritton, CJ; Myron H. Thompson, Ira DeMent; Clerk's Office, Montgomery 36101. **Southern:** Charles R. Butler Jr, CJ; A.T. Howard, R.W. Vollmer, W.B. Hand, T.V. Pittman; Clerk's Office, Mobile 36602.

Alaska — James K. Singleton, CJ; H. Russel Holland, John W. Sedwick; James M. Fitzgerald, James A. Von der Heydt; Clerk's Office, Anchorage 99513.

Arizona — Robert C. Broomfield, CJ; William D. Browning, Paul G. Rosenblatt, Roger G. Strand, Stephen M. McNamee, John M. Roll, Roslyn Silver, Frank R. Zappata, Alfredo Marquez, Raner C. Collins; Clerk's Office, Phoenix 85025.

Arkansas — **Eastern:** Susan Webber Wright, CJ; Stephen M. Reasoner; George Howard Jr, William R. Wilson Jr, James M. Moody; Clerk's Office, Little Rock 72201-3325. **Western:** Jimm Larry Hendren, CJ; H. Franklin Waters, Robert T. Dawson, Harry F. Barnes; Clerk's Office, Fort Smith 72902.

California — **Northern:** Marilyn H. Patel, CJ; Samuel Conti, Spencer Williams, William H. Orrick Jr, William A. Ingram, William W Schwarzer, Thelton E. Henderson, Charles A. Legge, D. Lowell Jensen, Fern M. Smith, Vaughn R. Walker, James Ware, Saundra Brown Armstrong, Ronald M. Whyte, Claudia Wilken, Maxine M. Chesney, Susan Illston, Charles R. Breyer, Martin J. Jenkins, Jeremy Fogel; Clerk's Office, San Francisco 94102. **Eastern:** William B. Shubb, CJ; Lawrence K. Karlton, CJ Emeritus; David F. Levi, Oliver W. Wanger, Garland E. Burrell, Anthony W. Ishii, Frank C. Damrell Jr; Clerk's Office, Sacramento 95814. **Central:** Terry J. Hatter Jr, CJ; Manuel L. Real, Consuelo B. Marshall, Alicemarie H. Stotler, William D. Keller, Stephen V. Wilson, J. Spencer Letts, Dickran M. Tevrizian, Ronald S. W. Lew, Gary L. Taylor, Lourdes G. Baird, Linda H. McLaughlin, Audrey B. Collins, Richard A. Paez, Robert J. Timlin, George H. King, Dean D. Pregerson, Christina A. Snyder, Carlos R. Moreno, Margaret M. Morrow, A. Howard Matz; Clerk's Office, Los Angeles 90012. **Southern:** Marilyn L. Huff, CJ; Judith N. Keep, Irma E. Gonzalez, Napoleon A. Jones Jr, Barry T. Moskowitz, Jeffrey T. Miller, Edward J. Schwartz, Howard B. Turrentine, Gordon Thompson Jr, Leland C. Nielsen, William B. Enright, John S. Rhoades, Rudi M. Brewster, Earl B. Gilliam; Clerk's Office, San Diego 92101.

Colorado — Richard P. Matsch, CJ; John L. Kane Jr, Lewis T. Babcock, Edward W. Nottingham, Daniel B. Sparr, Wiley Y. Daniel, Walker D. Miller; Clerk's Office, Denver 80294.

Connecticut —Alfred V. Covello, CJ; Robert N. Chatigny, Dominic J. Squatrito, Alvin W. Thompson, Janet Bond Arterton, Janet C. Hall, Christopher F. Droney; Clerk's Office, Bridgeport 06604, Hartford 06103, New Haven 06510.

Delaware — Joseph J. Farnan Jr, CJ; Sue L. Robinson, Roderick R. McKelvie; Clerk's Office, Wilmington 19801.

District of Columbia — Norma Holloway Johnson, CJ; John Garrett Penn, Thomas P. Jackson, Thomas F. Hogan, Stanley Sporkin, Royce C. Lamberth, Gladys Kessler, Paul L. Friedman, Ricardo M. Urbina, Emmet G. Sullivan, James Robertson, Colleen Kollar-Kotelly, Richard W. Roberts, Clerk's Office, Washington DC 20001.

Florida — **Northern:** C. Roger Vinson, CJ; Lacey A. Collier, Robert L. Hinkle, Stephen Mickle; Clerk's Office, Tallahassee 32301. **Middle:** Elizabeth A. Kovachevich, CJ; Wm. Terrell Hodges, George Kendall Sharp, Patricia C. Fawsett, Harvey E. Schlesinger, Ralph W. Nimmons Jr, Anne C. Conway, Steven D. Merryday, Susan C. Bucklew, Henry L. Adams Jr, Richard A. Lazzara; Clerk's Office, Orlando, 32801. **Southern:** Edward B. Davis, CJ; Lenore C. Nesbitt, Stanley Marcus, William J. Zloch, Kenneth L. Ryskamp, Federico A. Moreno, Shelby Highsmith, Donald L. Graham, K. Michael Moore, Ursula Ungaro-Benages, Wilkie D. Ferguson Jr, Daniel T. K. Hurley, Joan A. Lenard, Donald M. Middlebrooks, Alan S. Gold, William P. Dimitrouleas; Clerk's Office, Miami 33128.

Georgia — **Northern:** G. Ernest Tidwell, CJ; Harold L. Murphy, Orinda D. Evans, J. Owen Forrester, Jack T. Camp, Julie E. Carnes, Clarence Cooper, Willis B. Hunt Jr, Thomas W. Thrash, Jr, Richard W. Story; Clerk's Office, Atlanta 30303. **Middle:** Duross Fitzpatrick, CJ; J. Robert Elliott, W. Louis Sands, Hugh Lawson; Clerk's Office, Macon 31202. **Southern:** Dudley H. Bowen Jr, CJ; B. Avant Edenfield, William T. Moore Jr; Clerk's Office, Savannah 31412.

Hawaii — Alan C. Kay, CJ; David A. Ezra, Helen Gillmor, Susan Mollwey; Clerk's Office, Honolulu 96850.

Idaho — Edward J. Lodge, CJ; B. Lynn Winmill; Clerk's Office, Boise 83724.

Illinois — **Northern:** Marvin E. Aspen, CJ; Charles P. Kocoras, Charles R. Norgle Sr, James F. Holderman, Ann C. Williams, Harry D. Leinenweber, James B. Zagel, Suzanne B. Conlon, George M. Marovich, George W. Lindberg, Wayne R. Andersen, Philip G. Reinhard, Ruben Castillo, Blanche M. Manning, David H. Coar, Robert W. Gettleman, Elaine E. Bucklo, Joan B. Gottschall; Clerk's Office, Chicago 60604. **Central:** Michael M. Mihm, CJ; Joe Billy McDade, Michael P. McCuskey; Clerk's Office, Springfield 62701. **Southern:** J. Phil Gilbert, CJ; William D. Stiehl, Paul E. Riley, James L. Foreman, William L. Beatty, G. Patrick Murphy; Clerk's Office, East St. Louis 62202.

Indiana — **Northern:** William C. Lee, CJ; Allen Sharp, James T. Moody, Robert L. Miller Jr, Rudy Lozano; Clerk's Office, South Bend 46601. **Southern:** Sarah E. Barker, CJ; S. Hugh Dillin, Larry J. McKinney, John Daniel Tinder, David F. Hamilton, Richard L. Young; Clerk's Office, Indianapolis 46204.

Iowa — **Northern:** Michael J. Melloy, CJ; Mark W. Bennett; Clerk's Office, Cedar Rapids 52401. **Southern:** Charles R. Wolle, CJ; Ronald E. Longstaff, Robert W. Pratt; Clerk's Office, Des Moines 50309.

Kansas — G. Thomas Van Bebber, CJ; John W. Lungstrum, Monti L. Belot, Kathryn H. Vratil, J. Thomas Marten; Clerk's Office, Kansas City 66101.

Kentucky — **Eastern:** William Bertelsman, CJ; Henry R. Wilhoit Jr, Karl S. Forester, Joseph M. Hood, Jennifer B. Coffman; Clerk's Office, Lexington 40588-3074. **Western:** Charles R. Simpson III, CJ; John G. Heyburn II, Jennifer B. Coffman, Thomas B. Russell, Joseph P. McKinley Jr; Clerk's Office, Louisville 40202.

Louisiana — **Eastern:** Morley L. Sear, CJ; A. J. McNamara, Martin L. C. Feldman, Edith Brown Clement, Ginger Berrigan, Stanwood R. Duval Jr, Eldon E. Fallon, Sarah S. Vance, Mary Ann Viel Lemmo, G. Thomas Porteous Jr, Ivan L. R. Lemelle; Clerk's Office, New Orleans 70130. **Middle:** Frank J. Polozola, CJ; John V. Parker, Ralph E. Tyson; Clerk's Office, Baton Rouge 70801. **Western:** F. A. Little Jr, CJ; Rebecca F. Doherty, Richard T. Haik Sr, James T. Trimble Jr, Donald E. Walter, Tucker L. Melançon; Clerk's Office, Shreveport 71101.

Maine — D. Brock Hornby, CJ; Gene Carter, Morton A. Brody; Clerk's Office, Portland 04101.

Maryland — J. Frederick Motz, CJ; Frederic N. Smalkin, William M. Nickerson, Marvin J. Garbis, Benson Everett Legg, Catherine C. Blake, Andre M. Davis, Deborah K. Chasanow, Peter J. Messitte, Alexander Williams Jr; Clerk's Office, Baltimore 21201.

Massachusetts — Joseph L. Tauro, CJ; Robert E. Keeton, William G. Young, Mark L. Wolf, Douglas P. Woodlock, Edward F. Harrington, Nathaniel M. Gorton, Richard G. Stearns, Reginald C. Lindsay, Patti B. Saris, Nancy Gertner, George A. O'Toole, Rya W. Zobel, Michael A. Ponsor; Clerk's Office, Boston 02210.

Michigan — **Eastern:** Anna Diggs Taylor, CJ; Avern Cohn, Lawrence P. Zatkoff, Patrick J. Duggan, Bernard A. Friedman, Paul V. Gadola, Gerald E. Rosen, Robert H. Cleland, Nancy G. Edmunds, Denise Page-Hood, Paul D. Borman, John Corbett O'Meara, Arthur Tarnow; Victoria A. Roberts; George C. Steeh; Clerk's Office, Detroit 48226. **Western:** Richard A. Enslen, CJ; Robert H. Bell, David W. McKeague, Gordon J. Quist; Clerk's Office, Grand Rapids 49503.

Minnesota — Paul A. Magnuson, CJ; James M. Rosenbaum, David S. Doty, Richard H. Kyle, Michael J. Davis, John R. Tunheim, Ann D. Montgomery; Clerk's Office, St. Paul 55101.

Mississippi — **Northern:** Neal Biggers, CJ; Glen H. Davidson; Clerk's Office, Oxford 38655. **Southern:** Tom S. Lee, CJ; William H. Barbour Jr, Henry T. Wingate, Walter J. Gex III, Charles W. Pickering Sr, David Bramlette; Clerk's Office, Jackson 39201.

Missouri — **Eastern:** Jean C. Hamilton, CJ; Donald J. Stohr, Carol E. Jackson, Charles A. Shaw, Catherine D. Perry, E. Richard Webber, Rodney W. Sippel; Clerk's Office, St. Louis 63101. **Western:** D. Brook Bartlett, CJ; Dean Whipple, Fernando J. Gaitan Jr, Ortrie D. Smith, Gary A. Fenner, Nanette Laughrey; Clerk's Office, Kansas City 64106.

Montana — Jack D. Shanstrom, CJ; Charles C. Lovell, Donald W. Molloy; Clerk's Office, Billings 59101.

Nebraska — William G. Cambridge, CJ; Richard G. Kopf, Thomas M. Shanahan, Joseph F. Batillon; Clerk's Office, Omaha 68101.

Nevada — Howard D. McKibben, CJ; Philip M. Pro, David W. Hagen; Clerk's Office, Las Vegas 89101, Reno 89501.

New Hampshire —Paul J. Barbadoro, CJ; Joseph A. DiClerico, Steven J. McAuliffe; Clerk's Office, Concord 03301.

New Jersey — Anne E. Thompson, CJ; John W. Bissell, Maryanne Trump Barry, Joseph H. Rodriguez, Garrett E. Brown Jr, Alfred J. Lechner Jr, Nicholas H. Politan, Alfred M. Wolin, John C. Lifland, William G. Bassler, Mary L. Cooper, Joseph E. Irenas, Jerome B. Simandle, William H. Walls, Stephen M. Orlofsky, Joseph A. Greenaway Jr, Katharine S. Hayden; Clerk's Office, Newark 07101.

New Mexico — John E. Conway, CJ; James A. Parker, C. Leroy Hansen, Martha Vazquez, Bruce D. Black; Clerk's Office, Albuquerque 87103.

New York — **Northern:** Thomas J. McAvoy, CJ; Frederick J. Scullin Jr, Lawrence E. Kahn; Clerk's Office, Syracuse 13261-7367. **Eastern:** Charles P. Sifton, CJ; Thomas C. Platt Jr, Raymond J. Dearie, Edward R. Korman, Reena Raggi, Arthur D. Spatt, Carol Bagley Amon, Sterling Johnson Jr, Denis R. Hurley, David G. Trager, Joanna Seybert, Allyne R. Ross, John Gleeson, Nina Gershon, Fredric Block; Clerk's Office, Brooklyn 11201. **Southern:** Thomas P. Griesa, CJ; Charles L. Brieant, John E. Sprizzo, Lewis A. Kaplan, Michael B. Mukasey, Kimba Wood, Robert P. Patterson Jr, Lawrence McKenna, John S. Martin Jr, Loretta A. Preska, Sonia Sotomayer, Harold Baer Jr, Deborah A. Batts, Denny Chin, Denise L. Cote, John Koeltl, Allen G. Schwartz, Barrington D. Parker Jr, Shira A. Scheindlin, Sidney H. Stein, Jed S. Rakoff, Barbara S. Jones, Richard C. Casey; Clerk's Office New York City 10007. **Western:** David J. Larimer, CJ; Richard J.

Arcara, William M. Skretny, Charles J. Siragusa, John T. Curtin, John T. Elfvin, Michael A. Telesca; Clerk's Office, Buffalo 14202, Rochester 14614.

North Carolina — **Eastern:** Terrence W. Boyle, CJ; James C. Fox, Malcolm J. Howard; Clerk's Office, Raleigh 27611. **Middle:** Frank W. Bullock, CJ; N. Carlton Tilley Jr, William L. Osteen Sr, James A. Beaty Jr; Clerk's Office, Greensboro 27402. **Western:** Graham C. Mullen, CJ; Richard L. Voorhees, Lacy H. Thornburg; Clerk's Office, Asheville 28801, Charlotte 28202, Statesville 28687.

North Dakota — Rodney S. Webb, CJ; Patrick A. Conmy; Judge; Clerk's Office, Bismarck 58502.

Ohio — **Northern:** George W. White, CJ; Paul R. Matia, Lesley Brooks Wells, James G. Carr, Solomon Oliver Jr, David A. Katz, Kathleen McDonald O'Malley, Peter C. Economus, Donald C. Nugent, Patricia A. Gaughan, James S. Gwin, Dan Aaron Polster; Clerk's Office, Cleveland 44114. **Southern:** Walter Herbert Rice, CJ; John D. Holschuh, Herman J. Weber, James L. Graham, George C. Smith, S. Arthur Spiegel, Sandra S. Beckwith, Edmund A. Sargus Jr, Susan J. Dlott, Joseph P. Kinneary, Algenon L. Marbley; Clerk's Office, Columbus 43215.

Oklahoma — **Northern:** Terry C. Kern, CJ; Sven Erik Holmes, Michael Burrage; Clerk's Office, Tulsa 74103. **Eastern:** Michael Burrage CJ; Frank H. Seay; Clerk's Office, Muskogee 74401. **Western:** David L. Russell, CJ; Ralph G. Thompson, Wayne E. Alley, Robin J. Cauthron, Tim Leonard, Vicki Miles-LaGrange; Clerk's Office, Oklahoma City 73102.

Oregon — Michael R. Hogan, CJ; Garr M. King, Robert E. Jones, Ann L. Aiken, Ancer L. Haggerty; Clerk's Office, Portland 97204.

Pennsylvania — **Eastern:** Edward N. Cahn, CJ; Norma L. Shapiro, James T. Giles, Robert F. Kelly, Franklin S. Van Antwerpen, Robert S. Gawthrop III, Lowell A. Reed Jr, Jan E. Dubois, Herbert J. Hutton, Jay C. Waldman, Ronald L. Buckwalter, Stewart Dalzell, William H. Yohn Jr, Harvey Bartle III, John R. Padova, J. Curtis Joyner, Eduardo C. Robreno, Anita B. Brody, Bruce W. Kauffman; Clerk's Office, Philadelphia 19106. **Middle:** Sylvia H. Rambo, CJ; James F. McClure Jr, Thomas I. Vanaskie, A. Richard Caputo; Clerk's Office, Scranton 18501. **Western:** Donald E. Ziegler, CJ; William L. Standish, D. Brooks Smith, Donald J. Lee, Donetta W. Ambrose, Gary L. Lancaster, Robert J. Cindrich, Sean J. McLaughlin; Clerk's Office, Pittsburgh 15230.

Rhode Island — Ronald R. Lagueux, CJ; Ernest C. Torres, Mary M. Lisi; Clerk's Office, Providence 02903.

South Carolina — C. Weston Houck, CJ; G. Ross Anderson Jr, Joseph F. Anderson Jr, David C. Norton, Dennis W. Shedd, Henry M. Herlong Jr, William B. Traxler Jr, Cameron McGowan Currie, Patrick Michael Duffy; Clerk's Office, Columbia 29201.

South Dakota — Richard H. Battey, CJ; Lawrence L. Piersol, Charles B. Kornmann; Clerk's Office, Rapid City 57701.

Tennessee — **Eastern:** James H. Jarvis, CJ; Thomas G. Hull, R. Allan Edgar, R. Leon Jordan, Curtis L. Collier; Clerk's Office, Knoxville 37902. **Middle:** Robert L. Echols, CJ; Thomas A. Higgins, Todd J. Campbell; Clerk's Office, Nashville 37203. **Western:** Julia S. Gibbons, CJ; James D. Todd, Jerome Turner, John Phipps McCalla, Bernice B. Donald; Clerk's Office, Memphis 38103.

Texas — **Northern:** Jerry Buchmeyer, CJ; Mary Lou Robinson, A. Joe Fish, Robert B. Maloney, Sidney A. Fitzwater, Samuel R. Cummings, John H. McBryde, Jorge A. Solis, Terry Means, Joe Kendall, Sam A. Lindsay; Clerk's Office, Dallas 75242. **Southern:** George P. Kazen, CJ; Filemon B. Vela, Hayden W. Head Jr, Ricardo H. Hinojosa, Lynn N. Hughes, David Hittner, Kenneth M. Hoyt, Sim Lake, Melinda Harmon, John D. Rainey, Samuel B. Kent, Ewing Werlein Jr, Lee H. Rosenthal, Janis Graham Jack, Vanessa D. Gilmore, Nancy F. Atlas, Hilda G. Taglia; Clerk's Office, Houston 77002. **Eastern:** Richard A. Schell, CJ; Howell Cobb, Paul N. Brown, John Hannah Jr, David Folsom, Thad Heartfield, Joe J. Fisher; Clerk's Office, Tyler 75702. **Western:** Harry Lee Hudspeth, CJ; David Briones, Hipolito F. Garcia, Edward C. Prado, Fred Biery, Orlando L. Garcia, James R. Nowlin, Sam Sparks, Walter S. Smith Jr, W. Royal Furgeson; Clerk's Office, San Antonio 78206.

Utah —David Sam, CJ; Dee Benson, Tena Campbell, Dale A. Kimball, J. Thomas Greene, Bruce Jenkins, David K. Winder; Clerk's Office, Salt Lake City 84101.

Vermont — J. Garvan Murtha, CJ, William K. Sessions III; Clerk's Office, Burlington 05402.

Virginia — **Eastern:** Claude M. Hilton, CJ; James R. Spencer, Thomas S. Ellis III, Rebecca Beach Smith, Henry Coke Morgan Jr, Robert E. Payne, Raymond A. Jackson, Leonie M. Brinkema; Clerk's Office, Alexandria 22314. **Western:** Samuel G. Wilson, CJ; James C. Turk, James P. Jones, Norman K. Moon; Clerk's Office, Roanoke 24006.

Washington — **Eastern:** Wm. Fremming Nielsen, CJ; Fred Van Sickle, Robert H. Whaley, Edward F. Shea; Clerk's Office, Spokane 99210. **Western:** John C. Coughenour, CJ; Barbara Jacobs Rothstein, Robert J. Bryan, William L. Dwyer, Thomas S. Zilly, Franklin D. Burgess; Clerk's Office, Seattle 98104, Tacoma 98402.

West Virginia — **Northern:** Frederick P. Stamp Jr, CJ; Irene M. Keeley, W. Craig Broadwater; Clerk's Office, Wheeling 26003. **Southern:** Charles H. Haden II, CJ; John T. Copenhaver Jr, David A. Faber, Joseph R. Goodwin, Robert C. Chambers; Clerk's Office, Charleston 25329.

Wisconsin — **Eastern:** J. P. Stadtmueller, CJ; Rudolph T. Randa, Charles N. Clevert, Lynn S. Adelman; Clerk's Office, Milwaukee 53202. **Western:** John C. Shabaz; CJ; Barbara B. Crabb, Clerk's Office, Madison 53701.

Wyoming — Alan B. Johnson, CJ; Clarence A. Brimmer, William F. Downes; Clerk's Office, Cheyenne 82001.

U.S. Territorial District Courts

Guam — John S. Unpingco, CJ; Clerk's Office, Agana 96910.

Northern Mariana Islands — Alex R. Munson, CJ; Clerk's Office, Saipan MP 96950.

Puerto Rico — Carmen Consuelo Cerezo, CJ; Juan M. Perez-Gimenez, Hector M. Laffitte, Jose Antonio Fuste, Salvador E. Casellas, Daniel R. Dominguez; Clerk's Office, Hato Rex 00918.

Virgin Islands — Thomas K. Moore, CJ; Raymond L. Finch; Clerk's Office, St. Croix 00820.

U.S. Court of International Trade

New York, NY 10278-0001 (Salaries, $136,700)

Chief Judge — Gregory W. Carman.

Judges — Jane A. Restani, Thomas J. Aquilino Jr, Richard W. Goldberg, Donald C. Pogue, Evan J. Wallach, Judith M. Barzilay, Delissa A. Ridgway.

U.S. Court of Federal Claims

Washington, DC 20005 (Salaries, $136,700)

Chief Judge — Loren A. Smith.

Judges —John P. Wiese, Christine Odell Cook Miller, Marian Blank Horn, Eric G. Bruggink, Bohdan A. Futey, Roger B. Andewelt, James T. Turner, Robert H. Hodges, Diane Gilbert Weinstein.

U.S. Tax Court

Washington, DC 20217 (Salaries, $136,700)

Chief Judge — Mary Ann Cohen

Judges — Renato Beghe, Herbert L. Chabot, John O. Colvin, Joel Gerber, Julian I. Jacobs, Carolyn Miller Parr, Robert P. Ruwe, James S. Halpern, Carolyn P. Chiechi, David Laro, Stephen J. Swift, Thomas B. Wells, Laurence J. Whalen, Maurice B. Foley, Juan F. Vasquez, Joseph H. Gale, L. Paige Marvel, Michael B. Thornton.

U.S. Court of Veterans Appeals

Washington, D.C. 20004 (Salaries, $136,700)

Chief Judge — Frank Q. Nebeker.

Judges — Kenneth B. Kramer, John J. Farley 3d, Ronald M. Holdaway, Donald L. Ivers, Jonathan R. Steinberg, William P. Greene Jr.

STATE AND LOCAL GOVERNMENT

Mayors of Selected U.S. Cities

Reflects Nov. 3, 1998, elections (preliminary results)

D, Democrat; R, Republican; N-P, Non-Partisan; I, Independent; Prog. Coal., Progressive Coalition

City	Name	Next Election
Abilene, TX	Gary McCaleb, N-P	1999, May
Akron, OH	Donald L. Plusquellic, D	1999, Nov.
Alameda, CA	Ralph J. Appezzato, N-P	2002, Nov.
Albany, GA	Thomas Coleman, D	1999, Nov.
Albany, NY	Gerald D. Jennings, D	2001, Nov.
Albuquerque, NM	Jim Baca, D	2001, Oct.
Alexandria, LA	Edward G. Randolph Jr., D	2001, Oct.
Alexandria, VA	Kerry J. Donley, D	2000, May
Alhambra, CA	Julio Fuentes, N-P	(1)
Allentown, PA	William Heydt, R	2001, Nov.
Amarillo, TX	Kel Seliger, N-P	1999, May
Ames, IA	Ted Tedesco, N-P	2001, Nov.
Anaheim, CA	Tom Daly, N-P	2002, Nov.
Anchorage, AK	Rick Mystrom, R	2000, Apr.
Anderson, IN	J. Mark Lawler, D	1999, Nov.
Anderson, SC	Richard A. Shirley, N-P	2000, June
Ann Arbor, MI	Ingrid B. Sheldon, R	2000, Nov.
Annapolis, MD	Dean Johnson, R	2001, Nov.
Appleton, WI	Timothy M. Hanna, N-P	2000, Apr.
Arcadia, CA	Gary A. Kovacic, N-P	1999, Apr.
Arlington, MA	Charles Lyons, D	1999, Mar.
Arlington, TX	Elzie Odom, N-P	1999, May
Arlington Hts., IL	Arlene J. Mulder, N-P	2001, Apr.
Arvada, CO	Robert G. Frie, N-P	1999, Nov.
Asheville, NC	Leni Sitnick, N-P	2001, Nov.
Athens, GA	Doc Eldridge, D	2002, Nov.
Atlanta, GA	Bill Campbell, D	2001, Nov.
Atlantic City, NJ	James Whelan, N-P	2002, May
Augusta, GA	Larry Sconyers, N-P	1999, Nov.
Augusta, ME	William E. Dowling, NA	2000, Nov.
Aurora, CO	Paul E. Tauer, N-P	1999, Nov.
Aurora, IL	David L. Stover, N-P	2001, Apr.
Austin, TX	Kirk Watson, N-P	2000, May
Bakersfield, CA	Bob Price, N-P	2000, Mar.
Baldwin Park, CA	Bette Lowes, N-P	1999, Mar.
Baltimore, MD	Kurt Schmoke, D	1999, Nov.
Baton Rouge, LA	Tom E. McHugh, D	2000, Nov.
Battle Creek, MI	Ted Dearing, N-P	1999, Nov.
Bayonne, NJ	Joseph Doria, N-P	2002, May
Baytown, TX	Pete C. Alfaro, N-P	2001, May
Beaumont, TX	David W. Moore, N-P	2000, May
Belleville, IL	Mark Kern, N-P	2001, Apr.
Bellevue, WA	Mike Creighton, N-P	2000, Jan.
Bellflower, CA	Art Olivier, N-P	1999, Mar.
Bellingham, WA	Mark Asmundson, N-P	1999, Nov.
Berkeley, CA	Shirley Dean, N-P	1998, Dec.
Bethlehem, PA	Donald T. Cunningham, D	2001, Nov.
Beverly Hills, CA	Les Bronte, N-P	1999, Mar.
Billings, MT	Charles F. Tooley, N-P	2001, Nov.
Biloxi, MS	A. J. Holloway, R	2001, June
Binghamton, NY	Richard A. Bucci, R	2001, Nov.
Birmingham, AL	Richard Arrington Jr., D	1999, Oct.
Bismarck, ND	Bill Sorensen, R	2002, June
Bloomfield, NJ	John Bukowski, R	2001, Nov.
Bloomington, IL	Judy Markowitz, N-P	2001, Apr.
Bloomington, IN	John Fernandez, D	1999, Nov.
Bloomington, MN	Coral Houle, N-P	1999, Nov.
Boca Raton, FL	Carol G. Hanson, N-P	1999, Mar.
Boise, ID	Brent Coles, N-P	2001, Nov.
Bossier City, LA	George Dement, N-P	2001, Apr.
Boston, MA	Thomas M. Menino, D	2001, Nov.
Boulder, CO	Bob Greenlee, N-P	2001, Nov.
Bridgeport, CT	Joseph P. Ganim, D.	1999, Nov.
Bristol, CT	Frank N. Nicastro, D	1999, Nov.
Brockton, MA	John T. Yunits Jr., D	1999, Nov.
Broken Arrow, OK	Jim Reynolds, N-P	1999, Apr.
Brooklyn Park, MN	Grace Arbogast, N-P	2002, Nov.
Brownsville, TX	Henry Gonzalez, N-P	1999, May
Bryan, TX	Lonnie Stabler, N-P	1999, May
Buena Park, CA	Gerald N. Sigler, N-P	2000, Nov.
Buffalo, NY	Anthony M. Masiello, D	2001, Nov.
Burbank, CA	Dave Golonski, R	1999, May
Burlington, VT	Peter A.Clavelle, Prog. Coal.	1999, Mar.
Calumet City, IL	Gerome P. Genova, I	2001, Apr.
Camarillo, CA	Kevin Kildee, N-P	1999, Nov.
Cambridge, MA	Francis H. Duehay, D	2000, Jan.
Camden, NJ	Milton Milan, D	2001, May
Canton, OH	Richard D. Watkins, R	1999, Nov.
Cape Coral, FL	Roger G. Butler, N-P	2000, Nov.
Carlsbad, CA	Claude A. Lewis, N-P	2000, Nov.
Carson, CA	Peter D. Fajardo, N-P	1999, Mar.
Carson City, NV	Ray Masayko, N-P	2000, Nov.
Casper, WY	Ed Opeela, N-P	1999, Nov.

City	Name	Next Election
Cedar Rapids, IA	Lee R. Clancey, N-P	1999, Nov.
Champaign, IL	Dan McCollum, N-P	1999, Apr.
Chandler, AZ	Jay Tibshraeny, N-P	2000, Jan.
Charleston, SC	Joseph P. Riley Jr., D	1999, Nov.
Charleston, WV	G. Kemp Melton, D	1999, Apr.
Charlotte, NC	Patrick McCrory, R	1999, Nov.
Charlottesville, VA	Ray Griffin, D	2000, May
Chattanooga, TN	Jon Kinsey, N-P	2001, Mar.
Chesapeake, VA	William E. Ward, N-P	2000, May
Chester, PA	Aaron Wilson, R	1999, Nov.
Cheyenne, WY	Leo Pando, N-P	2000, Nov.
Chicago, IL	Richard M. Daley, D	1999, Apr.
Chicopee, MA	Richard J. Kos, N-P	1999, Nov.
Chino, CA	Eunice Ulloa, R	2000, Nov.
Chula Vista, CA	Shirley Horton, N-P	2002, Jun.
Cicero, IL	Betty Loren-Maltese, R	2001, Apr.
Cincinnati, OH	Roxanne Qualls, D	1999, Nov.
Clarksville, TN	Donald W. Trotter, N-P	2002, Nov.
Clearwater, FL	Rita Garvey, N-P	1999, Mar.
Cleveland, OH	Michael R. White, D	2001, Nov.
Cleveland Hts., OH	Edward J. Kelley, N-P	2000, Jan.
Clinton, IA	La Metta Wynn, N-P	1999, Nov.
Clifton, NJ	James Anzaldi, R	2002, May
Colorado Spgs., CO	Mary Lou Makepeace, R	1999, Apr.
Columbia, MO	Darwin Hindman, N-P	2001, Apr.
Columbia, SC	Robert D. Coble, N-P	2002, Apr.
Columbus, GA	Bobby Peters, D	2002, Nov.
Columbus, OH	Gregory S. Lashutka, R	1999, Nov.
Compton, CA	Omar Bradley, N-P	2001, June
Concord, CA	Mark Peterson, N-P	1998, Dec.
Concord, NH	William Veroneau, N-P	1999, Nov.
Coon Rapids, MN	Lonnie McCauley, N-P	2002, Nov.
Coral Gables, FL	Raul Valdes-Fauli, N-P	1999, Apr.
Coral Springs, FL	John Sommerer, N-P	2000, Mar.
Corona, CA	Darrell Talbert, N-P	1998, Dec.
Corpus Christi, TX	Loyd Neal, N-P	1999, Apr.
Costa Mesa, CA	(2)	2000, Nov.
Council Bluffs, IA	Tom Hanafan, N-P	2001, Nov.
Covington, KY	Denny Bowman, D	1999, Nov.
Cranston, RI	Michael A. Traficante, R	1998, Nov.
Cuyahoga Falls, OH	Donald L. Robart, R	2001, Nov.
Dallas, TX	Ronald Kirk, N-P	1999, June
Daly City, CA	(3)	2000, Nov.
Danbury, CT	Gene F. Eriquez, D	1999, Nov.
Danville, VA	Ruby B. Archie, N-P	2000, July
Davenport, IA	Phillip Yerington, N-P	1999, Nov.
Davis, CA	Julie Partansky, N-P	2000, Apr.
Dayton, OH	Michael R. Turner, N-P	2001, Nov.
Daytona Beach, FL	Baron H. Asher, N-P	1999, Oct.
Dearborn , MI	Michael Guido, N-P	2001, Nov.
Dearborn Hts., MI	Ruth A. Canfield, N-P	2001, Nov.
Decatur, IL	Terry M. Howley, N-P	1999, Apr.
Delray Beach, FL	Jay Alperin, N-P	2000, Mar.
Denton, TX	Jack Miller, N-P	2000, May
Denver, CO	Wellington E. Webb, N-P	1999, May
Des Moines, IA	Preston Daniels, N-P	1999, Nov.
Des Plaines, IL	Paul Jung, N-P	2001, Apr.
Detroit, MI	Dennis W. Archer, D	2001, Nov.
Dothan, AL	Chester L. Sowell III, N-P	2001, July
Dover, DE	James L. Hutchinson, N-P	2000, Apr.
Downey, CA	Garry McCaughan, N-P	(4)
Dubuque, IA	Terrance M. Duggan, N-P	2001, Nov.
Duluth, MN	Gary Doty, N-P	1999, Nov.
Durham, NC	Nicholas Tennyson, N-P	1999, Nov.
East Hartford, CT	Timothy Larson, D	1999, Nov.
East Lansing, MI	Mark S. Meadows, N-P	1999, Nov.
East Orange, NJ	Robert L. Bowser, D	2001, Nov.
Edison, NJ	George Spadoro, D	2002, Nov.
Edmond, OK	Robert Rudkin, N-P	1999, Apr.
El Cajon, CA	Joan Shoemaker, N-P	2000, Nov.[5]
Elgin, IL	Kevin Kelly, N-P	1999, Apr.
Elizabeth, NJ	J. C. Bollwage, D	2000, Nov.
Elkhart, IN	James P. Perron, D	1999, Nov.
El Monte, CA	Patricia Wallach, D	1999, Mar.
El Paso, TX	Carlos Ramirez, N-P	1999, May
Elyria, OH	Michael B. Keys, D	1999, Nov.
Enfield, CT	Mary Lou Strom, R	1999, Nov.
Enid, OK	Michael Cooper, N-P	1999, Apr.
Erie, PA	Joyce Savocchio, D	2001, Nov.
Escondido, CA	Lori Holt Pfieler, N-P	2000, Nov.
Euclid, OH	Paul Oyaski, D	1999, Nov.
Eugene, OR	James D. Torrey, N-P	2000, Nov.
Evanston, IL	Lorraine Morton, N-P	2001, Apr.

(continued)

City	Name	Next Election
Evansville, IN	Frank F. McDonald II, D.	1999, Nov.
Everett, WA	Edward D. Hansen, N-P.	2001, Nov.
Fairbanks, AK	James C. Hayes, N-P	2001, Oct.
Fairfield, CA	George Pettygrove, N-P.	2001, Nov.
Fairfield, CT	Kenneth A. Flatto, D	1999, Nov.
Fall River, MA	Edward Lambert Jr., D.	1999, Nov.
Fargo, ND	Bruce Furness, N-P.	2002, Apr.
Farmington Hills, MI	Aldo Vagnozzi, N-P	1999, Nov.
Fayetteville, NC	J. L. Dawkins, N-P.	1999, Nov.
Fitchburg, MA	Mary Whitney, N-P	1999, Nov.
Flagstaff, AZ	Christopher Bavasi, N-P	2000, Apr.
Flint, MI	Woodrow Stanley, D	1999, Nov.
Florissant, MO	James J. Eagan, N-P.	1999, Apr.
Fontana, CA	David Eshleman, D	2000, Nov.
Ft. Collins, CO	Ann Azari, N-P	1999, Apr.
Ft. Lauderdale, FL	Jim Naugle, N-P	2000, Mar.
Ft. Smith, AR	C. Raymond Baker, N-P	2002, Nov.
Ft. Wayne, IN	Paul Helmke, R.	1999, Nov.
Ft. Worth, TX	Kenneth L. Barr, N-P.	1999, May
Fountain Valley, CA	Laurann Cook, N-P	1998, Dec.
Frankfort, KY	William I. May Jr., N-P	2000, Nov.
Fremont, CA	Gus Morrison, N-P.	1999, Nov.
Fresno, CA	Jim Patterson, N-P	2000, Mar.
Fullerton, CA	Don Bankhead, N-P	2000, Nov.
Gadsden, AL	Steven A. Means, N-P	2002, Nov.
Gainesville, FL	Paula M. DeLaney, N-P.	2001, Nov
Galveston, TX	Roger Quiorga, N-P	2000, May
Gardena, CA	Donald L. Dear, N-P	1999, Mar.
Garden Grove, CA	Bruce Broadwater, N-P	2000, Nov.
Garland, TX	Jim Spence, N-P	2001, May
Gary, IN	Scott King, D	1999, Nov.
Gastonia, NC	Porter McAteer, N-P	1999, Nov.
Glendale, AZ	Elaine M. Scruggs, N-P	2000, May
Glendale, CA	Eileen Givens, N-P	1999, Apr.
Grand Forks, ND	Patricia A. Owens, N-P	2000, June
Grand Prairie, TX	Charles V. England, N-P	2000, May
Grand Rapids, MI	John H. Logie, N-P	1999, Nov.
Greeley, CO	LaVern C. Nelson, N-P	1999, Nov.
Green Bay, WI	Paul F. Jadin, N-P	1999, Apr.
Greensboro, NC	Carolyn S. Allen, N-P.	1999, Nov.
Greenville, SC	Knox H. White, R	1999, Nov.
Greenwich, CT	Tom R. Ragland, R	1999, Nov.
Groton, CT	Jane Dauphinais, N-P	1999, Nov.
Gulfport, MS	Bob Short, R.	2001, June
Hamden, CT	Barbara DeNicola, R	1999, Nov.
Hamilton, OH	Thomas Nye, N-P	1999, Nov.
Hammond, IN	Duane W. Dedelow Jr., R.	1999, Nov.
Hampton, VA	James L. Eason, N-P.	2000, May
Harrisburg, PA	Stephen R. Reed, D	2001, Nov.
Hartford, CT	Michael P. Peters, N-P	1999, Nov.
Haverhill, MA	James A. Rurak, D	1999, Nov.
Hawthorne, CA	Larry Guidi, N-P	1999, Nov.
Hayward, CA	Roberta Cooper, N-P.	2002, June
Helena, MT	Colleen McCarthy, N-P	2001, Nov.
Henderson, NV	James B. Gibson, N-P	2001, June
Hialeah, FL	Raul L. Martinez, R	2001, Nov.
High Point, NC	Rebecca R. Smothers, N-P	1999, Nov.
Hoboken, NJ	Anthony Russo, N-P	2001, May
Hollywood, FL	Mara Giulianti, N-P.	2000, Mar.
Holyoke, MA	Daniel Szostkiewicz, D	1999, Nov.
Honolulu, HI	Jeremy Harris, N-P	2000, Nov.
Houston, TX	Lee Brown, N-P	1999, Nov.
Huntington, WV	Jean Dean, R	2000, Nov.
Huntington Beach, CA	Shirley Dettloff, N-P.	1998, Dec.
Huntington Park, CA	Richard Loya, N-P.	[4]
Huntsville, AL	Loretta Spencer, N-P.	2000, Aug.
Idaho Falls, ID	Linda Milam, N-P.	2001, Nov.
Independence, MO	Rondell F. Stewart, N-P	2000, Apr.
Indianapolis, IN	Stephen Goldsmith, R	1999, Nov.
Inglewood, CA	Roosevelt F. Dorn, N-P	2002, Nov.
Iowa City, IA	Ernest W. Lehman, N-P	2000, Jan.
Irvine, CA	Christina Shea, N-P.	2000, Nov.
Irving, TX	Morris Parrish, N-P	1999, May
Irvington, NJ	Sara B. Bost, D	2002, May
Jackson, MS	Harvey Johnson, D	2001, June
Jacksonville, FL	John A. Delaney, R	1999, May
Janesville, WI	Steve Sheiffer, N-P	[6]
Jefferson City, MO	Duane Schreimann, D	1999, Apr.
Jersey City, NJ	Bret Schundler, R	2001, May
Johnson City, TN	Bob May, N-P	1999, Apr.
Joliet, IL	Arthur Schultz, N-P	1999, Apr.
Juneau, AK	Dennis Egan, D.	2000, Oct.
Kalamazoo, MI	Robert B. Jones, N-P.	1999, Nov.
Kansas City, KS	Carol S. Marinovich, N-P	2001, Sept.
Kansas City, MO	Emanuel Cleaver II, D	1999, Mar.
Kenner, LA	Louis J. Congemi, R	2002, Apr.
Kenosha, WI	John Antaramian, D.	2000, Apr.
Kettering, OH	Marilou W. Smith, N-P	2001, Nov.
Killeen, TX	Fred Latham, N-P.	2000, May
Knoxville, TN	Victor Ashe, R	1999, Nov.
Kokomo, IN	James Trobaugh, R	1999, Nov.
LaCrosse, WI	John D. Medinger, N-P	2001, Apr.
Lafayette, IN	Dave Heath, R	1999, Nov.
La Habra, CA	Dorothy Rush, N-P	1998, Dec.
Lake Charles, LA	Willie L. Mount, D	2001, May
Lakeland, FL	Ralph L. Fletcher, N-P	2000, Nov.
Lakewood, CA	Larry Van Nostran, N-P.	1999, Mar.
Lakewood, CO	Linda Morton, N-P	1999, Nov.
Lakewood, OH	Madeline Cain, D	1999, Nov.
La Mesa, CA	Arthur Madrid, N-P	2000, Nov.
La Mirada, CA	Hal Malkin, N-P	1999, Mar.
Lancaster, CA	Frank C. Roberts, N-P	2000, Apr.
Lancaster, PA	Charles W. Smithgall, R	2001, Nov.
Lansing, MI	David Hollister, N-P	2001, Nov.
Laredo, TX	Elizabeth G. "Betty" Flores, N-P	2002, May
Largo, FL	Thomas D. Feaster, N-P	2000, Mar
Las Cruces, NM	Ruben A. Smith, D	1999, Nov.
Las Vegas, NV	Jan Laverty Jones, D	1999, June
Lawrence, KS	Mike Wildgen, N-P	1999, Apr.
Lawrence, MA	Patricia Dowling, N-P.	2001, Nov.
Lawton, OK	Cecil Powell, D.	2001, Mar.
Lexington, KY	Pam Miller, N-P	1999, Jan.
Lima, OH	David J. Berger, N-P.	2002, Nov.
Lincoln, NE	Mike Johanns, R	1999, May
Little Rock, AR	Jim Dailey, N-P	2002, Nov.
Livermore, CA	Cathie Brown, N-P	1999, Nov.
Livonia, MI	Jack E. Kirksey, N-P.	1999, Nov.
Lodi, CA	Jack A. Sieglock, N-P	1999, Nov.
Long Beach, CA	Beverly O'Neill, N-P	2002, Apr.
Longmont, CO	Leona Stoecker, N-P	1999, Nov.
Longview, TX	David McWhorter, N-P.	1999, May
Lorain, OH	Joe Koziura, D	1999, Nov.
Los Angeles, CA	Richard Riordan, N-P	2001, June
Louisville, KY	David Armstrong, D	2002, Nov.
Lowell, MA	Eileen M. Donoghue, D.	2000, Jan.
Lubbock, TX	Windy Sitton, R	2000, Apr.
Lynchburg, VA	D.L. (Pete) Warren, N-P	2000, July
Lynn, MA	Patrick J. McManus, D	1999, Nov.
Lynwood, CA	Armando Rea, N-P.	1999, Nov.
Macon, GA	Jim Marshall, D	1999, Nov.
Madison, WI	Susan J.M. Bauman, N-P	1999, Apr.
Malden, MA	Richard Howard, D	1999, Nov.
Manchester, CT	Stephen T. Cassano, N-P	1999, Nov.
Manchester, NH	Raymond J. Wieczorek, R	1999, Nov.
Mansfield, OH	Lydia J. Reid, D	1999, Nov.
Marietta, GA	Ansley L. Meaders, D	1999, Nov.
McAllen, TX	Leo Montalvo, R.	2001, May
Medford, MA	Michael J. McGlynn, D	1999, Nov.
Medford, OR	Lindsay Berryman, N-P.	2002, Nov.
Melbourne, FL	John Buckley, N-P	2000, Nov.
Memphis, TN	Willie W. Herenton, D	1999, Oct.
Mentor, OH	Richard Hennig, N-P.	[6]
Merced, CA	MaryJo Knudsen, N-P.	1999, Nov.
Meriden, CT	Joseph Marinan Jr., N-P	1999, Nov.
Meridian, MS	John Robert Smith, R	2001, June
Mesa, AZ	Wayne Brown, N-P.	2000, Mar.
Mesquite, TX	Mike Anderson, N-P	1999, May
Miami, FL	Joe Carollo, N-P.	2001, Nov.
Miami Beach, FL	Otis T. Wallace, D	1999, Jan.
Midland, TX	Robert E. Burns, N-P	2001, May
Midwest City, OK	Eddie O. Reed, N-P	2002, Apr.
Milford, CT	Frederick L. Lisman, R	1999, Nov.
Milpitas, CA	Henry Manayan, N-P	2000, Nov.
Milwaukee, WI	John O. Norquist, D	2000, Apr.
Minneapolis, MN	Sharon Sayles Belton, D.	2001, Nov.
Minnetonka, MN	Karen J. Anderson, N-P	2001, Nov.
Mobile, AL	Michael C. Dow, R, I.	2001, Aug.
Modesto, CA	Richard A. Lang, N-P	1999, Nov.
Monroe, LA	Abe E. Pierce III, D.	2000, Mar.
Montclair, NJ	William N. Farlie Jr., N-P.	2000, May
Montebello, CA	Art Payan, N-P.	1999, Nov.
Monterey Park, CA	Francisco Alonso, N-P	1999, Mar.
Montgomery, AL	Emory Folmar, R	1999, Oct.
Montpelier, VT	William Fraser, N-P	[6]
Moreno Valley, CA	William H. Batey II, N-P	1998, Dec.
Mt. Prospect, IL	Gerald "Skip" Farley, N-P	1999, Apr.
Mt. Vernon, NY	Ernest D. Davis, D	1999, Nov.
Mountain View, CA	Ralph Faravelli, N-P	1999, Jan.
Muncie, IN	Dan Cannan, R	1999, Nov.
Muskogee, OK	James Bushnell, N-P	2000, Apr.
Napa, CA	Ed Henderson, N-P	1999, Mar.
Naperville, IL	George Pradel, N-P	1999, Apr.
Nashua, NH	Donald C. Davidson, N-P	1999, Nov.
Nashville, TN	Philip N. Bredesen, D	1999, Aug.

City	Name	Next Election
National City, CA	George H. Waters, R	2002, Nov.
Newark, NJ	Sharpe James, D	2002, May
New Bedford, MA	Frederick M. Kalisz Jr., N-P.	1999, Nov.
New Britain, CT	Lucian J. Pawlak, D	1999, Sept.
New Haven, CT	John DeStefano Jr., D	1999, Nov.
New Orleans, LA	Marc H. Morial, D	2002, Feb.
Newport Beach, CA	(7)	2000, Nov.
Newport News, VA	Joe S. Frank, N-P	2002, May
New Rochelle, NY	Timothy Idoni, D	1999, Nov.
Newton, MA	David B. Cohen, N-P	2001, Nov.
New York, NY	Rudolph Giuliani, R	2001, Nov.
Niagara Falls, NY	James Galie, D	1999, Nov.
Norfolk, VA	Paul D. Fraim, N-P	2000, May
Norman, OK	Dr. William Nation, N-P	1999, Apr.
North Charleston, SC	R. Keith Summey, R	1999, June
N. Little Rock, AR	Patrick Henry Hays, N-P	1999, Nov.
Norwalk, CA	Jesse M. Luera, N-P	1999, Apr.
Norwalk, CT	Frank J. Esposito, R	1999, Nov.
Novato, CA	(8)	1999, Nov.
Oakland, CA	Jerry Brown, N-P	2002, Nov.
Oak Park, IL	Barbara Furlong, N-P	2001, Apr.
Oceanside, CA	Dick Lyon, N-P	2000, Nov.
Odessa, TX	Mike Atkins, N-P	2000, May
Ogden, UT	Glenn J. Mecham, N-P	1999, Nov.
Oklahoma City, OK	Kirk Humphreys, N-P	2002, Apr.
Olympia, WA	Bob Jacobs, N-P	1999, Nov.
Omaha, NE	Hal Daub, R	2001, June
Ontario, CA	Gary C. Ovitt, N-P	2002, Nov.
Orange, CA	Joanne Coontz, N-P	2000, Nov.
Orlando, FL	Glenda Hood, N-P	2000, Sept.
Oshkosh, WI	Melanie Bloechl, N-P	2000, Apr.
Overland Park, KS	Ed Eilert, R	2001, Apr.
Owensboro, KY	Waymond Morris, N-P	1999, Nov.
Oxnard, CA	Manuel M. Lopez, N-P	2000, Nov.
Palm Springs, CA	William G. Kleindienst, N-P	1999, Nov.
Palo Alto, CA	Dick Rosenbaum, N-P	1999, Jan.
Parma, OH	Gerald M. Boldt, D	1999, Nov.
Pasadena, CA	Chris Holden, N-P	1999, May
Pasadena, TX	Johnny Isbell, N-P	2001, May
Passaic, NJ	Margie Semler, N-P	2001, May
Paterson, NJ	Martin G. Barnes, R	2002, May
Pawtucket, RI	James E. Doyle, D	1999, Nov.
Peabody, MA	Peter Torigian, D	1999, Nov.
Pembroke Pines, FL	Alex G. Fekete, N-P	2000, Mar.
Pensacola, FL	John R. Fogg, N-P	1999, June
Peoria, IL	Lowell G. Grieves, N-P	2001, Apr.
Philadelphia, PA	Edward Rendell, D	1999, Nov.
Phoenix, AZ	Skip Rimsza, N-P	1999, Oct.
Pico Rivera, CA	Garth G. Gardener, N-P	1999, Mar.
Pierre, SD	Gary Drewes, N-P	1999, Apr.
Pine Bluff, AR	Jerry Taylor, N-P	2000, Nov.
Pittsburgh, PA	Tom Murphy, D	2001, Nov.
Pittsfield, MA	Gerald S. Doyle, N-P	1999, Nov.
Plainfield, NJ	Albert McWilliams, N-P	2002, Nov.
Plano, TX	John Longstreet, N-P	2000, May
Plantation, FL	Frank Veltri, D	1999, Mar.
Pocatello, ID	Gregory R. Anderson, N-P	2001, Nov.
Pomona, CA	Eddie Cortez, N-P	1999, Apr.
Pompano Beach, FL	William F. Griffin, N-P	2000, Mar.
Pontiac, MI	Walter Moore, N-P	2001, Nov.
Port Arthur, TX	Oscar Ortiz, D	2001, May
Portland, ME	Thomas Kane, N-P	(4)
Portland, OR	Vera Katz, N-P	2000, Nov.
Portsmouth, VA	James W. Holley III, N-P	2000, May
Providence, RI	Vincent A. Cianci Jr., I	2002, Nov.
Provo, UT	Lewis K. Billings, N-P	2001, Nov.
Quincy, IL	Charles W. Scholz, D	2001, Apr.
Quincy, MA	James A. Sheets, D	1999, Nov.
Racine, WI	James M. Smith, N-P	1999, Apr.
Raleigh, NC	Tom Fetzer, N-P	1999, Oct.
Rancho Cucamonga, CA	William Alexander, N-P	2002, Nov.
Rapid City, SD	Jim Shaw, N-P	1999, May
Reading, PA	Paul Angstadt, R	1999, Nov.
Redding, CA	David Kehoe, N-P	1999, Apr.
Redondo Beach, CA	Gregory C. Hill, N-P	2001, Mar.
Redwood City, CA	Dianne Howard, N-P	1999, Dec.
Reno, NV	Jeff Griffin, N-P	1999, June
Rialto, CA	John Longville, N-P	2000, Nov.
Richardson, TX	Gary Slagel, N-P	1999, May
Richmond, CA	Rosemary M. Corbin, D	2001, Nov.
Richmond, VA	Timothy Kaine, N-P	2000, July
Riverside, CA	Ronald O. Loveridge, N-P	2001, Dec.
Roanoke, VA	David A. Bowers, D	2000, May
Rochester, MN	Charles J. Canfield, N-P	1999, Nov.
Rochester, NY	William A. Johnson Jr., D	1999, Nov.
Rochester Hills, MI	Kenneth D. Snell, N-P	1999, Nov.
Rock Hill, SC	Doug Echols, N-P	2001, Oct.
Rock Island, IL	Mark W. Schwiebert, N-P	2001, Apr.
Rockford, IL	Charles E. Box, D	2001, Apr.
Rockville, MD	Rose G. Krasnow, N-P	1999, Nov.
Rome, NY	Joseph A. Griffo, R	1999, Nov.
Rosemead, CA	Robert Bruesch, N-P	1999, Apr.
Roseville, MI	Gerald K. Alsip, N-P	2001, Nov.
Roswell, NM	Bill B. Owen, N-P	2002, Mar.
Royal Oak, MI	Dennis G. Cowan, N-P	1999, Nov.
Sacramento, CA	Joseph Serna Jr., N-P	2000, Nov.
Saginaw, MI	Reed Phillips, N-P	(6)
St. Charles, MO	Robert L. Moeller, N-P	1999, Apr.
St. Clair Shores, MI	Curtis L. Dumas, N-P	1999, Nov.
St. Cloud, MN	Larry Meyer, N-P	2001, Nov.
St. Joseph, MO	Larry R. Stobbs, N-P	2002, Apr.
St. Louis, MO	Clarence Harmon, D	2001, Apr.
St. Louis Park, MN	Gail Dorfman, N-P	1999, Nov.
St. Paul, MN	Norm Coleman, N-P	2001, Nov.
St. Petersburg, FL	David J. Fischer, N-P	2001, Mar.
Salem, OR	Michael Swaim, N-P	2000, Nov.
Salinas, CA	Anna Caballero, N-P	2000, Nov.
Salt Lake City, UT	Deedee Corradini, D	1999, Nov.
San Angelo, TX	Johnny Fender, N-P	1999, May
San Antonio, TX	Howard W. Peak, N-P	1999, May
San Bernardino, CA	Judith Valles, D	2001, Nov.
San Diego, CA	Susan Golding, R	2000, Nov.
Sandy City, UT	Thomas M. Dolan, N-P	2000, Nov.
San Francisco, CA	Willie L. Brown Jr., N-P	1999, Jan.
San Jose, CA	Ron Gonzales, D	2002, Nov.
San Leandro, CA	Shelia Young, N-P	2002, June
San Mateo, CA	Sue Lempert, N-P	1998, Dec.
San Rafael, CA	Albert J. Boro, N-P	1999, Nov.
Santa Ana, CA	Miguel Pulido, N-P	2000, Nov.
Santa Barbara, CA	Harriet Miller, N-P	2001, Nov.
Santa Clara, CA	Judy Nadler, N-P	2002, Nov.
Santa Clarita, CA	Jan Heidt, N-P	1998 Dec.
Santa Cruz, CA	(7)	2000, Nov.
Santa Fe, NM	Larry Delgado, N-P	2002, Mar.
Santa Maria, CA	(9)	2000, Nov.
Santa Monica, CA	(10)	2000, Nov.
Santa Rosa, CA	Sharon Wright, N-P	1998, Dec.
Sarasota, FL	Gene M. Pillot, N-P	1999, Mar.
Savannah, GA	Floyd Adams Jr., N-P	1999, Nov.
Schaumburg, IL	Al Larson, N-P	1999, Apr.
Schenectady, NY	Albert Jurczynski, R	1999, Nov.
Scottsdale, AZ	Sam Kathryn Campana, R	2002, Mar.
Scranton, PA	James P. Connors, R	2001, Nov.
Seattle, WA	Paul Schell, D	2001, Nov.
Sheboygan, WI	James R. Schramm, N-P	2001, Apr.
Shreveport, LA	Keith Hightower, D	2002, Nov.
Simi Valley, CA	Bill Davis, N-P	2000, Nov.
Sioux City, IA	Thomas Padgett, N-P	2002, Jan.
Sioux Falls, SD	Gary Hanson, N-P	1999, Jan.
Skokie, IL	Jacqueline B. Gorell, N-P	2001, Apr.
Somerville, MA	Michael E. Capuano, D	1999, Nov.
South Bend, IN	Stephen J. Luecke, D	1999, Nov.
South Gate, CA	Mary Ann Buckles, N-P	1999, Apr.
Southfield, MI	Donald F. Fracassi, R	2001, Nov.
Sparks, NV	Bruce H. Breslow, N-P	1999, June
Spartanburg, SC	James E. Talley, N-P	2001, Nov.
Spokane, WA	John Talbott, N-P	2001, Nov.
Springfield, IL	Karen Hasara, N-P	1999, Apr.
Springfield, MA	Michael J. Albano, D	1999, Nov.
Springfield, MO	Leland L. Gannaway, N-P	1999, Apr.
Springfield, OH	Warren R. Copeland, N-P	2000, Jan.
Stamford, CT	Dannel P. Malloy, D	2001, Nov.
Sterling Hts., MI	Richard J. Notte, N-P	1999, Nov.
Stockton, CA	Gary Podesto, N-P	2000, Nov.
Stratford, CT	Debbie Rose, N-P	1999, Nov.
Sunnyvale, CA	Jim Roberts, N-P	1999, Nov.
Suffolk, VA	Joe S. Frank, D	2002, July
Sunrise, FL	Steven B. Feren, N-P	2001, Mar.
Syracuse, NY	Roy A. Bernardi, R	2001, Nov.
Tacoma, WA	Brian Ebersole, N-P	1999, Nov.
Tallahassee, FL	Scott Maddox, N-P	2002, Nov.
Tampa, FL	Dick A. Greco, N-P	1999, Mar.
Taunton, MA	Robert Nunes, D	1999, Nov.
Taylor, MI	Gregory E. Pitoniak, D	2001, Nov.
Tempe, AZ	Neil G. Giuliano, N-P	2000, Apr.
Temple, TX	J. W. Perry, N-P	2000, May
Terre Haute, IN	James Jenkins, D	1999, Nov.
Thornton, CO	Margaret W. Carpenter, N-P	1999, Nov.
Thousand Oaks, CA	Robert O. Price, N-P	2000, Nov.
Titusville, FL	Larry Bartley, N-P	2000, Nov.
Toledo, OH	Carty Finkbeiner, N-P	2000, Nov.
Topeka, KS	Joan Wagnon, N-P	2001, Apr.
Torrance, CA	Dee Hardison, N-P	2002, Mar.
Trenton, NJ	Douglas H. Palmer, N-P	2002, May
Troy, MI	Jeanne M. Stine, N-P	2001, Apr.

(continued)

City	Name	Next Election
Troy, NY	Mark Pattison, D	2000, Jan.
Tucson, AZ	George Miller, D	1999, Nov.
Tulsa, OK	M. Susan Savage, D	2002, Mar.
Tuscaloosa, AL	Alvin DuPont, D	2001, Aug.
Tyler, TX	Kevin Eltife, N-P	2000, May
Union City, NJ	Raul "Rudy" Garcia, D	2000, May
Upland, CA	Robert R. Nolan, N-P	2000, Nov.
Utica, NY	Edward Hanna, I	1999, Nov.
Vacaville, CA	David A. Fleming, N-P	2002, Nov.
Vallejo, CA	Gloria Exlin, N-P	1999, Nov.
Vancouver, WA	Royce E. Pollard, N-P	1999, Nov.
Vineland, NJ	Anthony Campanella, R	2000, June
Virginia Beach, VA	Meyera E. Oberndorf, I	2000, May
Visalia, CA	Wally Gregory, N-P	1999, Nov.
Vista, CA	Gloria E. McClellan, R	2002, Nov.
Waco, TX	Michael D. Morrison, N-P	2000, May
Walnut Creek, CA	Gene Wolfe, N-P	1998, Dec.
Waltham, MA	William F. Stanley, D	1999, Nov.
Warren, MI	Mark Steenbergh, N-P	1999, Nov.
Warren, OH	Henry Angelo, D	1999, Nov.
Warwick, RI	Lincoln Chafee, R	2000, Nov.
Washington, DC	Anthony A. Williams, D	2002, Nov.
Waterbury, CT	Philip A. Giordano, R	1999, Nov.
Waterloo, IA	John R. Rooff III, R	1999, Nov.
Waukegan, IL	William F. Durkin, D	2001, Apr.
Waukesha, WI	Carol Lombardi, N-P	2002, Apr.
Wauwatosa, WI	Maricolette Walsh, N-P	2000, Apr.
W. Allis, WI	Jeannette Bell, N-P	2000, Mar.
W. Covina, CA	Richard Melendez, N-P	1999, Mar.
W. Hartford, CT	Robert Bouvier, R	1999, Nov.
W. Haven, CT	H. Richard Borer Jr., D	1999, Nov.
W. Palm Beach, FL	Nancy Graham, N-P	1999, Mar.
Westland, MI	Robert J. Thomas, D	2001, Nov.
Westminster, CA	Frank G. Fry, N-P	2000, Nov.
Westminster, CO	Nancy Heil, N-P	1999, Nov.
Wheaton, IL	C. James Carr, N-P	1999, Apr.
White Plains, NY	Joseph Delfino, R	2001, Nov.
Whittier, CA	Greg Nordbak, N-P	2000, Apr.
Wichita, KS	Bob Knight, N-P	1999, Apr.
Wichita Falls, TX	Kay Yeager, N-P	2000, May
Wilkes-Barre, PA	Thomas McGroarty, D	1999, Nov.
Wilmington, DE	James Sills, D	2000, Nov.
Wilmington, NC	Hamilton E. Hicks Jr., N-P	1999, Oct.
Winston-Salem, NC	Jack Cavanagh Jr., N-P	2001, Nov.
Woodbridge, NJ	James E. McGreevey, D	1999, Nov.
Woonsocket, RI	Susan D. Menard, N-P	1999, Nov.
Worcester, MA	Raymond V. Mariano, N-P	1999, Nov.
Wyandotte, MI	Lawrence S. Stec, N-P	2001, Apr.
Wyoming, MI	Douglas L. Hoekstra Jr., N-P	2001, Nov.
Yakima, WA	John Puccinelli, N-P	2000, Jan.
Yonkers, NY	John Spencer, R	1999, Nov.
York, PA	Charles Robertson, D	2001, Nov.
Youngstown, OH	George M. McKelvey, D	2001, Nov.
Yuma, AZ	Marilyn R. Young, N-P	2001, Nov.

NA = not available. (1) Position of mayor rotated among city council members every 9 mos. (2) Mayor to be appointed by city council Dec. 7, 1998. (3) Mayor to be appointed by city council late Nov. 1998. (4) Position of mayor rotated among city council members every 12 mos. (5) Incumbent listed; sought reelection Nov. 3, 1998; race undecided as of Nov. 5. (6) City manager; hired, not elected. (7) Mayor to be appointed by city council Nov. 24, 1998. (8) Mayor to be appointed by city council Nov. 10, 1998. (9) Race undecided as of Nov. 5, 1998. (10) Mayor to be appointed by city council Dec. 8, 1998.

Governors of States and Puerto Rico

Reflects Nov. 3, 1998, elections (preliminary results)

State	Capital, ZIP Code	Governor	Party	Term years	Term expires	Annual salary[1]
Alabama	Montgomery 36130	Don Siegelman	Dem.	4	Jan. 2003	$87,643
Alaska	Juneau 99811	Tony Knowles	Dem.	4	Dec. 2002	81,648
Arizona	Phoenix 85007	Jane Dee Hull	Rep.	4	Jan. 2003	75,000
Arkansas	Little Rock 72201	Mike Huckabee	Rep.	4	Jan. 2003	60,000
California	Sacramento 95814	Gray Davis	Dem.	4	Jan. 2003	131,000
Colorado	Denver 80203	Bill Owens	Rep.	4	Jan. 2003	70,000
Connecticut	Hartford 06106	John G. Rowland	Rep.	4	Jan. 2003	78,000
Delaware	Dover 19901	Thomas R. Carper	Dem.	4	Jan. 2001	107,000
Florida	Tallahassee 32399	Jeb Bush	Rep.	4	Jan. 2003	110,962
Georgia	Atlanta 30334	Roy E. Barnes	Dem.	4	Jan. 2003	115,939
Hawaii	Honolulu 96813	Ben Cayetano	Dem.	4	Dec. 2002	94,780
Idaho	Boise 83720	Dirk Kempthorne	Rep.	4	Jan. 2003	85,000
Illinois	Springfield 62706	George H. Ryan	Rep.	4	Jan. 2003	130,261
Indiana	Indianapolis 46204	Frank O'Bannon	Dem.	4	Jan. 2001	77,200
Iowa	Des Moines 50319	Tom Vilsack	Dem.	4	Jan. 2003	104,352
Kansas	Topeka 66612	Bill Graves	Rep.	4	Jan. 2003	85,225
Kentucky	Frankfort 40601	Paul Patton	Dem.	4	Dec. 1999	95,526
Louisiana	Baton Rouge 70804	M. J. "Mike" Foster Jr.	Rep.	4	Jan. 2000	95,000
Maine	Augusta 04333	Angus S. King Jr.	Ind.	4	Jan. 2003	70,000
Maryland	Annapolis 21401	Parris N. Glendening	Dem.	4	Jan. 2003	120,000
Massachusetts	Boston 02133	Paul Cellucci	Rep.	4	Jan. 2003	90,000
Michigan	Lansing 48909	John Engler	Rep.	4	Jan. 2003	127,300
Minnesota	St. Paul 55155	Jesse Ventura	RF[2]	4	Jan. 2003	114,506
Mississippi	Jackson 39205	Kirk Fordice	Rep.	4	Jan. 2000	83,160
Missouri	Jefferson City 65102	Mel Carnahan	Dem.	4	Jan. 2001	112,755
Montana	Helena 59620	Marc Racicot	Rep.	4	Jan. 2001	78,246
Nebraska	Lincoln 68509	Mike Johanns	Rep.	4	Jan. 2003	65,000
Nevada	Carson City 89710	Kenny Guinn	Rep.	4	Jan. 2003	90,000
New Hampshire	Concord 03301	Jeanne Shaheen	Dem.	2	Jan. 2001	90,547
New Jersey	Trenton 08625	Christine Todd Whitman	Rep.	4	Jan. 2002	85,000
New Mexico	Santa Fe 87503	Gary E. Johnson	Rep.	4	Jan. 2003	90,000
New York	Albany 12224	George E. Pataki	Rep.	4	Jan. 2003	130,000
North Carolina	Raleigh 27603	James B. Hunt Jr.	Dem.	4	Jan. 2001	107,132
North Dakota	Bismarck 58505	Edward T. Schafer	Rep.	4	Jan. 2001	75,372
Ohio	Columbus 43266	Bob Taft	Rep.	4	Jan. 2003	115,762
Oklahoma	Oklahoma City 73105	Frank Keating	Rep.	4	Jan. 2003	101,140
Oregon	Salem 97310	John Kitzhaber	Dem.	4	Jan. 2003	88,300
Pennsylvania	Harrisburg 17120	Tom Ridge	Rep.	4	Jan. 2003	105,035
Rhode Island	Providence 02903	Lincoln C. Almond	Rep.	4	Jan. 2003	69,900
South Carolina	Columbia 29211	Jim Hodges	Dem.	4	Jan. 2003	106,078
South Dakota	Pierre 57501	William J. Janklow	Rep.	4	Jan. 2003	82,271
Tennessee	Nashville 37243	Don Sundquist	Rep.	4	Jan. 2003	85,000
Texas	Austin 78711	George W. Bush	Rep.	4	Jan. 2003	115,345
Utah	Salt Lake City 84114	Michael O. Leavitt	Rep.	4	Jan. 2001	90,700
Vermont	Montpelier 05609	Howard Dean	Dem.	2	Jan. 2001	105,402
Virginia	Richmond 23219	James S. Gilmore III	Rep.	4	Jan. 2002	124,855
Washington	Olympia 98504	Gary Locke	Dem.	4	Jan. 2001	121,000
West Virginia	Charleston 25305	Cecil H. Underwood	Rep.	4	Jan. 2001	90,000
Wisconsin	Madison 53707	Tommy G. Thompson	Rep.	4	Jan. 2003	115,699
Wyoming	Cheyenne 82002	Jim Geringer	Rep.	4	Jan. 2003	95,000
Puerto Rico	San Juan 00936	Pedro J. Rossello	NPP[3]	4	Jan. 2001	70,000

(1) Salary in effect in 1998. (2) Reform Party. (3) New Progressive Party.

Races for Governor, 1998

Source: Voter News Service

(preliminary returns, subject to change, pending official results)

State	Democrat	Vote	Republican	Vote	Other	Vote
AL	**Don Siegelman**	**752,087**	Fob James, Jr.*	546,504		
AK	**Tony Knowles***	**95,952**	John Lindauer	32,342		
AZ	Paul Johnson	329,229	**Jane Dee Hull***	**556,269**		
AR	Bill Bristow	267,529	**Mike Huckabee***	**415,931**		
CA	**Gray Davis**	**4,305,746**	Dan Lungren	2,842,173		
CO	Gail Schoettler	639,214	**Bill Owens**	**646,997**		
CT	Barbara B. Kennelly	342,011	**John G. Rowland***	**607,672**		
FL	Buddy MacKay	1,765,921	**Jeb Bush**	**2,174,741**		
GA	**Roy E. Barnes**	**942,987**	Guy Millner	787,014		
HI	**Ben Cayetano***	**200,725**	Linda Lingle	195,229		
ID	Robert C. Huntley	107,616	**Dirk Kempthorne**	**250,805**		
IL	Glenn W. Poshard	1,561,144	**George H. Ryan**	**1,698,462**		
IA	**Tom Vilsack**	**497,834**	Jim Ross Lightfoot	442,625		
KS	Tom Sawyer	163,641	**Bill Graves***	**529,414**		
ME	Thomas J. Connolly	48,836	James B. Longley, Jr.	77,627	**Angus S. King Jr.*** (I)	**239,194**
MD	**Parris N. Glendening***	**826,609**	Ellen R. Sauerbrey	662,554		
MA	Scott Harshbarger	900,171	**Paul Cellucci***	**965,008**		
MI	Geoffrey Fieger	1,136,541	**John Engler***	**1,875,501**		
MN	Hubert H. "Skip" Humphrey III	581,497	Norm Coleman	713,410	**Jesse Ventura** (RF)	**768,356**
NE	Bill Hoppner	246,472	**Mike Johanns**	**288,673**		
NV	Jan Laverty Jones	182,238	**Kenny Guinn**	**223,798**		
NH	**Jeanne Shaheen***	**209,851**	Jay Lucas	101,475		
NM	Martin J. Chavez	206,855	**Gary E. Johnson***	**241,157**		
NY	Peter F. Vallone	1,442,925	**George E. Pataki***	**2,427,874**	Tom Golisano (IN)	350,491
OH	Lee Fisher	1,470,964	**Bob Taft**	**1,650,061**		
OK	Laura Boyd	357,552	**Frank Keating***	**505,498**		
OR	**John Kitzhaber***	**284,643**	Bill Sizemore	141,200		
PA	Ivan Itkin	929,198	**Tom Ridge***	**1,725,744**	Peg Luksik (CP)	312,230
RI	Myrth York	124,838	**Lincoln C. Almond***	**151,168**		
SC	**Jim Hodges**	**561,332**	David Beasley*	479,086		
SD	Bernie Hunhoff	85,417	**William J. Janklow***	**166,616**		
TN	John J. Hooker	287,241	**Don Sundquist***	**668,687**		
TX	Garry Mauro	1,157,411	**George W. Bush***	**2,569,131**		
VT	**Howard Dean***	**116,731**	Ruth Dwyer	86,624		
WI	Ed Garvey	678,998	**Tommy G. Thompson***	**1,048,897**		
WY	John P. Vinich	70,661	**Jim Geringer***	**97,299**		

* Denotes incumbent. **Boldface** denotes winner. (CP)=Constitutional Party, (I)=Independent, (IN)=Independence Party, (RF)=Reform Party

State Officials, Salaries, Party Membership

As of Oct. 1998; †=independent

Alabama

Governor — Fob James Jr., R, $87,643
Lt. Gov. — Don Siegelman, D, $12 per day, plus $50 per day expenses, plus $3,780 per mo expenses
Sec. of State — Jim Bennett, R, $61,779
Atty. Gen. — William Pryor, R, $115,695
Treasurer — Lucy Baxley, D, $61,779
Legislature: meets annually at Montgomery the 3d Tues. in Apr., 1st year of term of office; 1st Tues. in Feb., 2d and 3d yr; 2d Tues. in Jan., 4th yr. Members receive $10 per day salary, plus $50 per day expenses, plus $2,280 per mo expenses.
Senate — Dem., 21; Rep., 14. Total, 35
House — Dem., 69; Rep., 36. Total, 105

Alaska

Governor — Tony Knowles, D, $81,648
Lt. Gov. — Fran Ulmer, D, $76,188
Atty. General — Bruce Botelho, D, $86,808
Legislature: meets annually in Jan. at Juneau for 120 days with a 10-day extension possible upon 2/3 vote. First session in odd years. Members receive $24,120 annually, plus $161 per diem.
Senate — Dem., 8; Rep., 12. Total, 20
House — Dem., 17; Rep., 22; 1 other. Total, 40

Arizona

Governor — Jane Dee Hull, R, $75,000
Sec. of State — Betsey Bayless, R, $54,600
Atty. Gen. — Grant Woods, R, $76,400
Treasurer — Tony West, R, $54,600
Legislature: meets annually in Jan. at Phoenix. Each member receives an annual salary of $15,000.
Senate — Dem., 12; Rep., 18. Total, 30
House — Dem., 22; Rep., 38. Total, 60

Arkansas

Governor — Mike Huckabee, R, $60,000
Lt. Gov. — Winthrop P. Rockefeller, R, $29,000
Sec. of State — Sharon Priest, D, $37,500
Atty. Gen. — Winston Bryant, D, $50,000
Treasurer — Jimmie Lou Fisher, D, $37,500
Auditor — Gus Wingfield, D, $37,500
General Assembly: meets odd years in Jan. at Little Rock. Members receive $12,500 annually.
Senate — Dem., 28; Rep., 7. Total, 35
House — Dem., 85; Rep., 14; 1 vacant. Total, 100

California

Governor — Pete Wilson, R, $131,000
Lt. Gov. — Gray Davis, D, $98,280
Sec. of State — Bill Jones, R, $98,280
Controller — Kathleen Connell, D, $98,280
Atty. Gen. — Dan Lungren, R, $111,384
Legislature: meets at Sacramento on the 1st Mon. in Dec. of even-numbered years; each session lasts 2 years. Members receive $78,624 annually, plus $101 per diem.
Senate — Dem., 22; Rep., 16; 1 ind; 1 vacancy. Total, 40
Assembly — Dem., 43; Rep., 37. Total , 80

Colorado

Governor — Roy Romer, D, $70,000
Lt. Gov. — Gail Schoettler, D, $48,500
Sec. of State — Victoria (Vikki) Buckley, R, $48,500
Atty. Gen. — Gale Norton, R, $60,000
Treasurer — Bill Owens, R, $48,500
General Assembly: meets annually in Jan. at Denver. Members receive $17,500 annually.
Senate — Dem., 15; Rep., 20. Total, 35
House — Dem., 24; Rep., 41. Total, 65

(continued)

Connecticut

Governor — John G. Rowland, R, $78,000
Lt. Gov. — M. Jodi Rell, R, $55,000
Sec. of the State — Miles S. Rapoport, D, $50,000
Treasurer — Paul Sylvester, R, $50,000
Comptroller — Nancy S. Wyman, D, $50,000
Atty. Gen. — Richard Blumenthal, D, $60,000
General Assembly: meets annually odd years in Jan. and even years in Feb., at Hartford. Members receive $16,760 annually, plus $4,500 (senator), $3,500 (representative) per year for expenses.
Senate — Dem., 19; Rep., 17. Total, 36
House — Dem., 96; Rep., 55. Total, 151

Delaware

Governor — Thomas R. Carper, D, $107,000
Lt. Gov. — Ruth Ann Minner, D, $44,600
Sec. of State — Edward J. Freel, D, $89,900
Atty. Gen. — M. Jane Brady, R, $99,100
Treasurer — Janet C. Rzewnicki, R, $79,700
General Assembly: meets annually the 2d Tues. in Jan. and continues until June 30, at Dover. Members receive $28,300 annually, plus $5,500 expense allowance.
Senate — Dem., 13; Rep., 8. Total, 21
House — Dem., 14; Rep., 27. Total, 41

Florida

Governor — Lawton Chiles, D, $110,962
Lt. Gov. — Kenneth "Buddy" McKay, D, $106,290
Sec. of State — Sandra Mortham, R, $109,841
Comptroller — Robert R. Milligan, R, $109,841
Atty. Gen. — Robert Butterworth, D, $109,841
Treasurer — Bill Nelson, D, $109,841
Legislature: meets annually at Tallahassee. Members receive $26,388 annually, plus expense allowance.
Senate — Dem., 17; Rep., 23. Total, 40
House — Dem., 55; Rep., 64; 1 vacancy. Total, 120

Georgia

Governor — Zell Miller, D, $115,939
Lt. Gov. — Pierre Howard, D, $75,725
Sec. of State — Lewis Massey, D, $93,120
Atty. Gen. — Thurbert Baker, D, $106,300
General Assembly: meets annually in Atlanta. Members receive $11,348 annually ($75 per diem and $4,800 expense reimbursement).
Senate — Dem., 34; Rep., 22. Total, 56
House — Dem., 101; Rep., 79. Total, 180

Hawaii

Governor — Ben Cayetano, D, $94,780
Lt. Gov. — Mazie K. Hirono, D, $90,041
Atty. Gen. — Margery Bronster, D, $85,302
Comptroller — Raymond Sato, $85,302
Dir. of Budget & Finance — Earl Anzai, $85,302
Legislature: meets annually on 3d Wed. in Jan. at Honolulu. Members receive $32,000 annually, plus expenses.
Senate — Dem., 23; Rep., 2. Total, 25
House — Dem., 39; Rep., 12. Total, 51

Idaho

Governor — Philip E. Batt, R, $85,000
Lt. Gov. — C. L. "Butch" Otter, R, $22,500
Sec. of State — Pete T. Cenarrusa, R, $67,500
Treasurer — Lydia Justice Edwards, R, $67,500
Atty. Gen. — Alan Lance, R, $75,000
Legislature: meets annually the Mon. on or nearest Jan. 9 at Boise. Members receive $12,360 annually, plus $75 per day during session if required to maintain a 2d residence, $40 if no 2d residence; plus $50 per day when engaged in legislative business when legislature is not in session.
Senate — Dem., 5; Rep., 30. Total, 35
House — Dem., 11; Rep., 59. Total, 70

Illinois

Governor — Jim Edgar, R, $130,261
Lt. Gov. — Vacant
Sec. of State — George H. Ryan, R, $114,936
Comptroller — Loleta A. Didrickson, R, $99,611
Atty. Gen. — Jim Ryan, R, $114,936
Treasurer — Judy Baar Topinka, R, $99,611
General Assembly: meets annually in Jan. at Springfield. Members receive $49,807 annually.
Senate — Dem., 28; Rep., 31. Total, 59
House — Dem., 60; Rep., 58. Total, 118

Indiana

Governor — Frank O'Bannon, D, $77,200
Lt. Gov. — Joseph E. Kernan, D, $64,000
Sec. of State — Sue Anne Gilroy, R, $46,000
Atty. Gen. — Jeffrey A. Modesitt, D, $59,200
Treasurer — Joyce Brinkman, R, $46,000
Auditor — Morris Wooden, R, $46,000
General Assembly: meets annually in Jan. at Indianapolis. Members receive $11,600 annually, plus $105 per day while in session, $25 per day while not in session.
Senate — Dem., 19; Rep., 31. Total, 50
House — Dem., 50; Rep., 50. Total, 100

Iowa

Governor — Terry E. Branstad, R, $104,352
Lt. Gov. — Joy Corning, R, $73,046
Sec. of State — Paul D. Pate, R, $82,939
Atty. Gen. — Tom Miller, D, $99,379
Treasurer — Michael L. Fitzgerald, D, $82,939
Auditor — Richard D. Johnson, R, $82,939
Sec. of Agriculture — Dale M. Cochran, D, $82,939
General Assembly: meets annually in Jan. at Des Moines. Members receive $20,120 annually, plus expense allowance.
Senate — Dem., 22; Rep., 28. Total, 50
House — Dem., 46; Rep., 54. Total, 100

Kansas

Governor — Bill Graves, R, $85,225
Lt. Gov. — Gary Sherrer, R, $25,072
Sec. of State — Ron Thornburgh, R, $68,860
Atty. Gen. — Carla Stovall, R, $79,187
Treasurer — Clyde Graeber, R, $68,860
Legislature: meets annually in Jan. at Topeka. Members receive $72 per day salary, plus $80 per day expenses while in session, $600 per month while not in session.
Senate — Dem., 13; Rep., 27. Total, 40
House — Dem., 48; Rep., 77. Total, 125

Kentucky

Governor — Paul Patton, D, $95,526
Lt. Gov. — Steve Henry, D, $81,210
Sec. of State — John Y. Brown III, D, $81,210
Atty. Gen. —A. B. Chandler III, D, $81,210
Treasurer — John Kennedy Hamilton, D, $81,210
Auditor — Ed Hatchett, D, $81,210
General Assembly: meets even years in Jan. at Frankfort. Members receive $105 per day, plus $88 per day expenses during session and $1,003 per month for expenses for interim.
Senate — Dem., 20; Rep., 18. Total, 38
House — Dem., 65; Rep., 34; 1 vacancy. Total, 100

Louisiana

Governor — M. J. "Mike" Foster Jr., R, $95,000
Lt. Gov. — Kathleen Babineaux Blanco, D, $85,000
Sec. of State — W. Fox McKeithen, R, $85,000
Atty. Gen. — Richard Ieyoub, D, $85,000
Treasurer — Ken Duncan, D, $85,000
Legislature: meets in odd-numbered years at Baton Rouge starting last Mon. in Mar., for 60 legislative days of 85 calendar days; meets in even-numbered years on last Mon. in Apr. for 30 days of 45 calendar days. Members receive $16,800 annually, plus $101 per day expenses while in session.
Senate — Dem., 25; Rep., 14. Total, 39.
House — Dem., 78; Rep., 26, 1 vacancy. Total, 105.

Maine

Governor — Angus S. King Jr. †, $70,000
Sec. of State — Dan A. Gwadosky, D, $54,184
Atty. Gen. — Andrew Ketterer, D, $79,914
Treasurer — Dale McCormick, D, $54,184
State Auditor — Gail M. Chase, D, $63,813
Legislature: meets annually at Augusta first Wed. in Dec. and Wed. after first Tues. in Jan., in even numbered years. Members receive $10,500 for first regular session, $7,500 for 2d, plus expenses; presiding officers receive 50% more.
Senate — Dem., 19; Rep., 15; 1 ind. Total, 35
House — Dem., 81; Rep., 69; 1 ind. Total, 151

Maryland

Governor — Parris N. Glendening, D, $120,000
Lt. Gov. — Kathleen Kennedy Townsend, D, $100,000
Comptroller — Robert L. Swann, D, $100,000
Atty. Gen. — J. Joseph Curran Jr., D, $100,000
Sec. of State — John Willis, D, $70,000
Treasurer —Richard N. Dixon, D, $100,000
General Assembly: meets 90 consecutive days annually beginning on 2d Wed. in Jan. at Annapolis. Members receive $29,700 annually, plus expenses.
Senate — Dem., 32; Rep., 15. Total, 47
House — Dem., 100; Rep., 41. Total, 141

Massachusetts

Governor — Paul Cellucci, R, $90,000
Lt. Gov. — (vacancy)
Sec. of State — William Francis Galvin, D, $75,000
Atty. Gen. — L. Scott Harshbarger, D, $80,000

Treasurer — Joseph Malone, R, $60,000
Auditor — A. Joseph DeNucci, D, $75,000
General Court (legislature): meets Jan. biennially in Boston. Members receive $46,410 annually.
Senate — Dem., 33; Rep., 7. Total, 40
House — Dem., 130; Rep., 30. Total, 160

Michigan

Governor — John Engler, R, $127,300
Lt. Gov. — Connie B. Binsfeld, R, $93,978
Sec. of State — Candice S. Miller, R, $112,439
Atty. Gen. — Frank J. Kelley, D, $112,000
Treasurer — Douglas B. Roberts (appointed), $102,980
Legislature: meets annually in Jan. at Lansing. Members receive $53,192 annually.
Senate — Dem., 16; Rep., 21; 1 vacancy. Total, 38
House — Dem., 58; Rep., 52. Total, 110

Minnesota

(DFL means Democratic-Farmer-Labor Party)
Governor — Arne H. Carlson, R, $114,506
Lt. Gov. — Joanne E. Benson, R, $62,980
Sec. of State — Joan Anderson Growe, DFL, $62,980
Atty. Gen. — Hubert H. Humphrey 3d, DFL, $89,454
Treasurer — Michael McGrath, DFL, $62,980
Auditor — Judith H. Dutcher, R, $68,709
Legislature: meets for a total of 120 days within every 2 years, at St. Paul. Members receive $29,657 annually, plus expense allowance during session.
Senate — DFL, 42; R, 24; 1 ind. Total, 67
House — DFL, 70; R, 64. Total, 134

Mississippi

Governor — Kirk Fordice, R, $83,160
Lt. Gov. — Ronnie Musgrove, D, $40,800
Sec. of State — Eric Clark, D, $75,000
Atty. Gen. — Mike Moore, D, $90,800
Treasurer — Marshall Bennett, D, $75,000
Auditor — Phil Bryant, R, $75,000
Legislature: meets annually in Jan. at Jackson. Members receive $10,000 per regular session, plus travel allowance, and $1,500 per month when not in session.
Senate — Dem., 34; Rep., 18. Total, 52
House — Dem., 84; Rep., 34; 2 ind., 2 vacancies. Total, 122

Missouri

Governor — Mel Carnahan, D, $112,755
Lt. Gov. — Roger B. Wilson, D, $68,188
Sec. of State — Rebecca McDowell Cook, D, $90,471
Atty. Gen. — Jeremiah W. Nixon, D, $97,899
Treasurer — Bob Holden, D, $90,471
State Auditor — Margaret Kelly, R, $90,471
General Assembly: meets annually at Jefferson City beginning 1st Wed. after 1st Mon. in Jan. Members receive $29,082 annually.
Senate — Dem., 19; Rep., 15. Total, 34
House — Dem., 85; Rep., 76; 1 ind; 1 vacancy. Total, 163

Montana

Governor — Marc Racicot, R, $78,246
Lt. Gov. — Judy Martz, R, $53,407
Sec. of State — Mike Cooney, D, $58,658
Atty. Gen. — Joe Mazurek, D, $66,756
Legislative Assembly: meets odd years in Jan. at Helena. Members receive $58.50 per legislative day, plus $70 per day for expenses while in session.
Senate — Dem., 16; Rep., 34. Total, 50
House — Dem., 35; Rep., 65. Total, 100

Nebraska

Governor — Ben Nelson, D, $65,000
Lt. Gov. — Kim Robak, D, $47,000
Sec. of State — Scott Moore, R, $52,000
Atty. Gen. — Don Stenberg, R, $64,500
Treasurer — David Heineman, R, $49,500
Legislature: Unicameral body composed of 49 members who are elected on a nonpartisan ballot and are called senators; meets annually in Jan. at Lincoln. Members receive $12,000 annually, plus expenses.

Nevada

Governor — Robert Miller, D, $90,000
Lt. Gov. — Lonnie Hammargren, R, $20,000
Sec. of State — Dean Heller, R, $62,500
Comptroller — Darrel Daines, R, $62,500
Atty. Gen. — Frankie Sue Del Papa, D, $85,000
Treasurer — Robert Seale, R, $62,500
Legislature: meets at Carson City odd years starting on 3d Mon. in Jan. for 60 days. Members receive $130 per day salary, plus $66 per day expenses, while in session.
Senate — Dem., 9; Rep., 12. Total, 21
Assembly — Dem., 25; Rep., 17. Total, 42

New Hampshire

Governor — Jeanne Shaheen, D, $90,547
Sec. of State — William M. Gardner, D, $72,206
Atty. Gen. — Philip T. McLaughlin, D, $80,832
Treasurer — Georgie A. Thomas, R, $72,206
General Court (Legislature): meets every year in Jan. at Concord. Members receive $200, presiding officers $250, biannually.
Senate — Dem., 9; Rep., 15. Total, 24
House — Rep., 248; Dem., 142; 2 ind.; 8 lib. Total, 400

New Jersey

Governor — Christine Todd Whitman, R, $85,000
Sec. of State — Carol Cronheim (acting), R, $70,000
Atty. Gen. — Peter Verniero, R, $115,000
Treasurer — James A. DiEleuterio Jr, R, $115,000
Legislature: meets throughout the year at Trenton. Members receive $35,000 annually, except president of Senate and speaker of Assembly, who receive 1/3 more.
Senate — Dem., 16; Rep., 24. Total, 40
Assembly — Dem., 31; Rep., 49. Total, 80

New Mexico

Governor — Gary E. Johnson, R, $90,000
Lt. Gov. — Walter Bradley, R, $65,000
Sec. of State — Stephanie Gonzales, D, $65,000
Atty. Gen. — Tom Udall, D, $72,500
Treasurer — Michael A. Montoya, D, $65,000
Legislature: meets starting on the 3d Tues. in Jan. at Santa Fe; odd years for 60 days, even years for 30 days. Members receive $75 per day while in session.
Senate — Dem., 25; Rep., 17. Total, 42
House — Dem., 42; Rep., 28. Total, 70

New York

Governor — George E. Pataki, R, $130,000
Lt. Gov. — Elizabeth McCaughey-Ross, D, $110,000
Sec. of State — Alexander F. Treadwell, R, $90,832
Comptroller — H. Carl McCall, D, $110,000
Atty. Gen. — Dennis Vacco, R, $110,000
Legislature: meets annually in Jan. at Albany. Members receive $57,500 annually, plus $130 per day expenses.
Senate — Dem., 26; Rep., 35. Total, 61
Assembly — Dem., 97; Rep., 53. Total, 150

North Carolina

Governor — James B. Hunt Jr., D, $107,132
Lt. Gov. — Dennis Wicker, D, $94,552, plus expenses
Sec. of State — Elaine F. Marshall, D, $94,552
Atty. Gen. — Michael Easley, D, $94,552
Treasurer — Harlan E. Boyles, D, $94,552
General Assembly: meets odd years in Jan. at Raleigh. Members receive $13,951 annually and an expense allowance of $559 per month, plus subsistence and travel allowance while in session. Also meets in even years for a short session (about 6-8 weeks), usually in May.
Senate — Dem., 30; Rep., 20. Total, 50
House — Dem., 59; Rep., 61. Total, 120

North Dakota

Governor — Edward T. Schafer, R, $75,372
Lt. Gov. — Rosemarie Myrdal, R, $61,994
Sec. of State — Alvin A. Jaeger, R, $57,120
Atty. Gen. — Heidi Heitkamp, D, $64,464
Treasurer — Kathi Gilmore, D, $57,120
Legislative Assembly: meets odd years in Jan. at Bismarck. Members receive $250 per month salary, plus $111 per calendar day salary during session and $39 per day expenses plus any additional state or local taxes on lodging, with a limit of $650 per month.
Senate — Dem., 18; Rep., 29; 1 vacancy. Total, 48
House — Dem., 25; Rep., 69; 4 vacancies. Total, 98

Ohio

Governor — George V. Voinovich, R, $115,762
Lt. Gov. — Nancy P. Hollister, R, $59,862
Sec. of State — Bob Taft, R, $85,517
Atty. Gen. — Betty Montgomery, R, $85,517
Treasurer — J. Kenneth Blackwell, R, $85,517
Auditor — Jim Petro, R, $85,517
General Assembly: meets odd years at Columbus starting on 1st Mon. in Jan. Members receive $42,426 annually.
Senate — Dem., 12; Rep., 21. Total, 33
House — Dem., 39; Rep., 60. Total, 99

Oklahoma

Governor — Frank Keating, R, $101,140
Lt. Gov. — Mary Fallin, R, $75,530
Sec. of State — Tom Cole, R, $65,000

(continued)

Atty. Gen. — Drew Edmondson, D, $94,349
Treasurer — Robert Butkin, D, $82,004
Auditor— Clifton Scott, D, $82,004
Legislature: meets annually at noon the first Mon. in Feb. at Oklahoma City. In odd-numbered years, the session includes one day (1st Tuesday after 1st Monday) in Jan. Members receive $38,400 annually.
Senate — Dem., 33; Rep., 15. Total, 48
House — Dem., 65; Rep., 36. Total, 101

Oregon

Governor — John Kitzhaber, D, $88,300
Sec. of State — Phil Keisling, D, $67,900
Atty. Gen. — Hardy Myers, D, $72,800
Treasurer — Jim Hill, D, $67,900
Legislative Assembly: meets odd years in Jan. at Salem. Members receive $1,208 monthly, $86 expenses per day during session and when attending meetings during the interim, plus $400 expense account during interim.
Senate — Dem., 10; Rep., 20. Total, 30
House — Dem., 28; Rep., 31; 1 ind. Total, 60

Pennsylvania

Governor — Tom Ridge, R, $105,035
Lt. Gov. — Mark Schweiker, R, $83,027
Sec. of the Commonwealth — Yvette Kane, R, $72,024
Atty. Gen. — D. Michael Fisher, R, $104,000
Treasurer — Barbara Hafer, R, $104,000
General Assembly — convenes annually in Jan. at Harrisburg. Members receive $57,367 annually, plus expenses.
Senate — Dem., 20; Rep., 30. Total, 50.
House — Dem., 99; Rep., 104. Total, 203

Rhode Island

Governor — Lincoln C. Almond, R, $69,900
Lt. Gov. — Bernard A. Jackvony, R, $52,000
Sec. of State — James R. Langevin, D, $52,000
Atty. Gen. — Jeffrey B. Pine, R, $55,000
Treasurer — Nancy J. Mayer, R, $52,000
General Assembly: meets annually in Jan. at Providence. Members receive $10,000 annually.
Senate — Dem., 40; Rep., 10. Total, 50
House — Dem., 84; Rep., 16. Total, 100

South Carolina

Governor — David Beasley, R, $106,078
Lt. Gov. — Robert L. Peeler, R, $46,545
Sec. of State — Jim Miles, R, $92,007.
Comptroller Gen. — Earle E. Morris Jr., D, $92,007
Atty. Gen. — Charles M. Condon, R, $92,007
Treasurer — Richard Eckstrom, R, $92,007
General Assembly: meets annually in Jan. at Columbia. Members receive $10,400 annually, plus $88 per day for expenses.
Senate — Dem., 26; Rep., 20. Total, 46
House — Dem., 51; Rep., 72, 1 ind. Total, 124

South Dakota

Governor — William J. Janklow, R, $82,271
Lt. Gov. — Carole Hillard, R, $59,740
Sec. of State — Joyce Hazeltine, R, $55,900
Treasurer — Dick Butler, D, $55,900
Atty. Gen. — Mark Barnett, R, $69,876
Auditor — Vernon Larson, R, $55,900
Legislature: meets annually in Jan. at Pierre. Members receive $6,000 for 40-day session in odd-numbered years, and $6,000 for 35-day session in even-numbered years, plus $95 per legislative day.
Senate — Dem., 13; Rep., 22. Total, 35
House — Dem., 22; Rep., 48. Total, 70

Tennessee

Governor — Don Sundquist, R, $85,000
Lt. Gov. — John S. Wilder, D, $49,500
Sec. of State — Riley C. Darnell, D, $88,212
Comptroller — William Snodgrass, D, $88,212
Atty. Gen. — John Knox Walkup, D, $107,820
General Assembly: meets annually in Jan. at Nashville. Members receive $16,500 annual salary, plus $129 per day expenses while in session.
Senate — Dem., 18; Rep., 15. Total, 33
House — Dem., 61; Rep., 38. Total, 99

Texas

Governor — George W. Bush, R, $115,345
Lt. Gov. — Bob Bullock, D, $7,200
Sec. of State — Alberto R. Gonzales, R, $76,966
Comptroller — John Sharp, D, $92,217
Atty. Gen. — Dan Morales, D, $92,217
Railroad Commissioners — Carole Keeton Rylander, R, Chair; Barry Williamson, R; Charles R. Matthews, R; $92,217
Legislature: meets odd years in Jan. at Austin. Members receive $7,200 annually, plus $95 per day expenses while in session.
Senate — Dem., 17; Rep., 14. Total, 31
House — Dem., 82; Rep., 68. Total, 150

Utah

Governor — Michael O. Leavitt, R, $90,700
Lt. Gov. — Olene S. Walker, R, $70,500
Atty. Gen. — Jan Graham, D, $76,300
Auditor — Auston G. Johnson, R, $72,800
Treasurer — Edward T. Alter, R, $70,500
Legislature: convenes for 45 days on 3d Mon. in Jan. each year at Salt Lake City; Members receive $100 per day, plus $38 a day expenses.
Senate — Dem., 9; Rep., 20. Total, 29
House — Dem., 20; Rep., 55. Total, 75

Vermont

Governor — Howard Dean, D, $105,402
Lt. Gov. — Douglas A. Racine, D, $43,939
Sec. of State — Jim Milne, R, $66,325
Atty. Gen. — William H. Sorrell, D, $79,675
Treasurer — James Douglas, R, $66,325
Auditor — Edward Flanagan, D, $66,325
General Assembly: meets in Jan. at Montpelier (annual and biennial session). Members receive $536 per week while in session plus $105 per day for special session, plus expenses.
Senate — Dem., 17; Rep., 13. Total, 30
House — Dem., 90; Rep., 56; Prog. Coalition, 3; 1 ind. Total, 150

Virginia

Governor — James S. Gilmore III, R, $124,855
Lt. Gov. — John H. Hager, R, $36,321
Atty. Gen. — Mark L. Earley, R, $110,667
Sec. of the Commonwealth — Anne P. Petera, R, $112,969
Treasurer — Susan F. Dewey, R, $97,437
General Assembly: meets annually in Jan. at Richmond. Members receive $18,000 (senate), $17,640 (assembly) annually, plus expense and mileage allowances.
Senate — Dem., 19; Rep., 21. Total, 40
House — Dem., 50; Rep., 49; 1 ind. Total, 100

Washington

Governor — Gary Locke, D, $121,000
Lt. Gov. — Brad Owen, D, $62,700
Sec. of State — Ralph Munro, R, $69,000
Atty. Gen. — Christine Gregoire, D, $93,000
Treasurer — Mike Murphy, D, $84,100
Legislature: meets annually in Jan. at Olympia. Members receive $28,300 annually, plus $80 per diem while in session, and $80 per diem for attending meetings during interim.
Senate — Dem., 23; Rep., 26. Total, 49
House — Dem., 41; Rep., 57. Total, 98

West Virginia

Governor — Cecil H. Underwood, R, $90,000
Sec. of State — Ken Hechler, D, $65,000
Atty. Gen. — Darrell McGraw, D, $75,000
Treasurer — John D. Perdue, D, $65,000
Comm. of Agric. — Gus Douglass, D, $70,000
Auditor — Glen B. Gainer 3d, D, $70,000
Legislature: meets annually in Jan. at Charleston, except after gubernatorial elections, when the legislature meets in Feb. Members receive $15,000 annually.
Senate — Dem., 25; Rep., 9. Total, 34
House — Dem., 74; Rep., 26. Total, 100

Wisconsin

Governor — Tommy G. Thompson, R, $115,699
Lt. Gov. — Scott McCallum, R, $60,183
Sec. of State — Douglas La Follette, D, $54,610
Treasurer — Jack Voight, R, $54,610
Atty. Gen. — James E. Doyle, D, $112,274
Legislature: meets in Jan. at Madison. Members receive $41,809 annually, plus $75 per day expenses.
Senate — Dem., 15; Rep., 17; 1 vacancy. Total, 33
Assembly — Dem., 43; Rep., 52; 4 vacancies. Total, 99

Wyoming

Governor — Jim Geringer, R, $95,000
Sec. of State — Diana J. Ohman, R, $77,000
Atty. Gen. — William U. Hill, R, $80,000
Treasurer — Stan Smith, R, $77,000
Auditor — Dave Ferrari, R, $77,000
Legislature: meets odd years in Jan., even years in Feb., at Cheyenne. Members receive $125 per day while in session, plus $80 per day for expenses.
Senate — Dem., 9; Rep., 21. Total, 30.
House — Dem., 17; Rep., 43. Total, 60.

CABINETS OF THE U.S.

The U.S. Cabinet and Its Role

The heads of major executive departments of government constitute the Cabinet. This institution, not provided for in the U.S. Constitution, developed as an advisory body out of the desire of presidents to consult on policy matters. Aside from its advisory role, the Cabinet as a body has no function and wields no executive authority. The president may or may not consult it and is not bound by its advice. Most presidents also confer with numerous advisers outside the Cabinet. A group of regular informal advisers to the president has been known in American history as a "kitchen cabinet." The formal Cabinet (which may include other officials besides department heads, as designated by the president) meets at times set by the president. Members of Pres. Bill Clinton's Cabinet listed here are as of Oct. 7, 1998.

Secretaries of State

The Department of Foreign Affairs was created by act of Congress on July 27, 1789, and the name changed to Department of State on Sept. 15.

President	Secretary	Home	Apptd.
Washington	Thomas Jefferson	VA	1789
"	Edmund Randolph	VA	1794
"	Timothy Pickering	PA	1795
Adams, J.	Timothy Pickering	PA	1797
"	John Marshall	VA	1800
Jefferson	James Madison	VA	1801
Madison	Robert Smith	MD	1809
"	James Monroe	VA	1811
Monroe	John Quincy Adams	MA	1817
Adams, J.Q.	Henry Clay	KY	1825
Jackson	Martin Van Buren	NY	1829
"	Edward Livingston	LA	1831
"	Louis McLane	DE	1833
"	John Forsyth	GA	1834
Van Buren	John Forsyth	GA	1837
Harrison, W.H.	Daniel Webster	MA	1841
Tyler	Daniel Webster	MA	1841
"	Abel P. Upshur	VA	1843
"	John C. Calhoun	SC	1844
Polk	John C. Calhoun	SC	1845
"	James Buchanan	PA	1845
Taylor	James Buchanan	PA	1849
"	John M. Clayton	DE	1849
Fillmore	John M. Clayton	DE	1850
"	Daniel Webster	MA	1850
"	Edward Everett	MA	1852
Pierce	William L. Marcy	NY	1853
Buchanan	William L. Marcy	NY	1857
"	Lewis Cass	MI	1857
"	Jeremiah S. Black	PA	1860
Lincoln	Jeremiah S. Black	PA	1861
"	William H. Seward	NY	1861
Johnson, A.	William H. Seward	NY	1865
Grant	Elihu B. Washburne	IL	1869
"	Hamilton Fish	NY	1869
Hayes	Hamilton Fish	NY	1877
"	William M. Evarts	NY	1877
Garfield	William M. Evarts	NY	1881
"	James G. Blaine	ME	1881
Arthur	James G. Blaine	ME	1881
"	F.T. Frelinghuysen	NJ	1881
Cleveland	F.T. Frelinghuysen	NJ	1885
"	Thomas F. Bayard	DE	1885
Harrison, B.	Thomas F. Bayard	DE	1889
"	James G. Blaine	ME	1889
Harrison, B.	John W. Foster	IN	1892
Cleveland	Walter Q. Gresham	IN	1893
"	Richard Olney	MA	1895
McKinley	Richard Olney	MA	1897
"	John Sherman	OH	1897
"	William R. Day	OH	1898
"	John Hay	DC	1898
Roosevelt, T.	John Hay	DC	1901
"	Elihu Root	NY	1905
"	Robert Bacon	NY	1909
Taft	Robert Bacon	NY	1909
"	Philander C. Knox	PA	1909
Wilson	Philander C. Knox	PA	1913
"	William J. Bryan	NE	1913
"	Robert Lansing	NY	1915
"	Bainbridge Colby	NY	1920
Harding	Charles E. Hughes	NY	1921
Coolidge	Charles E. Hughes	NY	1923
"	Frank B. Kellogg	MN	1925
Hoover	Frank B. Kellogg	MN	1929
"	Henry L. Stimson	NY	1929
Roosevelt, F.D.	Cordell Hull	TN	1933
"	E.R. Stettinius Jr.	VA	1944
Truman	E.R. Stettinius Jr.	VA	1945
"	James F. Byrnes	SC	1945
"	George C. Marshall	PA	1947
"	Dean G. Acheson	CT	1949
Eisenhower	John Foster Dulles	NY	1953
"	Christian A. Herter	MA	1959
Kennedy	Dean Rusk	NY	1961
Johnson, L.B.	Dean Rusk	NY	1963
Nixon	William P. Rogers	NY	1969
"	Henry A. Kissinger	DC	1973
Ford	Henry A. Kissinger	DC	1974
Carter	Cyrus R. Vance	NY	1977
"	Edmund S. Muskie	ME	1980
Reagan	Alexander M. Haig Jr.	CT	1981
"	George P. Shultz	CA	1982
Bush	James A. Baker 3d	TX	1989
"	Lawrence S. Eagleburger	MI	1992
Clinton	Warren M. Christopher	CA	1993
"	Madeleine K. Albright	DC	1997

Secretaries of the Treasury

The Treasury Department was organized by act of Congress on Sept. 2, 1789.

President	Secretary	Home	Apptd.
Washington	Alexander Hamilton	NY	1789
"	Oliver Wolcott	CT	1795
Adams, J.	Oliver Wolcott	CT	1797
"	Samuel Dexter	MA	1801
Jefferson	Samuel Dexter	MA	1801
"	Albert Gallatin	PA	1801
Madison	Albert Gallatin	PA	1809
"	George W. Campbell	TN	1814
"	Alexander J. Dallas	PA	1814
"	William H. Crawford	GA	1816
Monroe	William H. Crawford	GA	1817
Adams, J.Q.	Richard Rush	PA	1825
Jackson	Samuel D. Ingham	PA	1829
"	Louis McLane	DE	1831
"	William J. Duane	PA	1833
"	Roger B. Taney	MD	1833
"	Levi Woodbury	NH	1834
Van Buren	Levi Woodbury	NH	1837
Harrison, W.H.	Thomas Ewing	OH	1841
Tyler	Thomas Ewing	OH	1841
"	Walter Forward	PA	1841
Tyler	John C. Spencer	NY	1843
"	George M. Bibb	KY	1844
Polk	Robert J. Walker	MS	1845
Taylor	William M. Meredith	PA	1849
Fillmore	Thomas Corwin	OH	1850
Pierce	James Guthrie	KY	1853
Buchanan	Howell Cobb	GA	1857
"	Phillip F. Thomas	MD	1860
"	John A. Dix	NY	1861
Lincoln	Salmon P. Chase	OH	1861
"	William P. Fessenden	ME	1864
"	Hugh McCulloch	IN	1865
Johnson, A.	Hugh McCulloch	IN	1865
Grant	George S. Boutwell	MA	1869
"	William A. Richardson	MA	1873
"	Benjamin H. Bristow	KY	1874
"	Lot M. Morrill	ME	1876
Hayes	John Sherman	OH	1877
Garfield	William Windom	MN	1881
Arthur	Charles J. Folger	NY	1881

(continued)

Secretaries of the Treasury (*continued*)

President	Secretary	Home	Apptd.
Arthur	Walter Q. Gresham	IN	1884
"	Hugh McCulloch	IN	1884
Cleveland	Daniel Manning	NY	1885
"	Charles S. Fairchild	NY	1887
Harrison, B.	William Windom	MN	1889
"	Charles Foster	OH	1891
Cleveland	John G. Carlisle	KY	1893
McKinley	Lyman J. Gage	IL	1897
Roosevelt, T.	Lyman J. Gage	IL	1901
"	Leslie M. Shaw	IA	1902
"	George B. Cortelyou	NY	1907
Taft	Franklin MacVeagh	IL	1909
Wilson	William G. McAdoo	NY	1913
"	Carter Glass	VA	1918
"	David F. Houston	MO	1920
Harding	Andrew W. Mellon	PA	1921
Coolidge	Andrew W. Mellon	PA	1923
Hoover	Andrew W. Mellon	PA	1929
"	Ogden L. Mills	NY	1932
Roosevelt, F.D.	William H. Woodin	NY	1933
"	Henry Morgenthau, Jr.	NY	1934
Truman	Fred M. Vinson	KY	1945
"	John W. Snyder	MO	1946
Eisenhower	George M. Humphrey	OH	1953
"	Robert B. Anderson	CT	1957
Kennedy	C. Douglas Dillon	NJ	1961
Johnson, L.B.	C. Douglas Dillon	NJ	1963
"	Henry H. Fowler	VA	1965
"	Joseph W. Barr	IN	1968
Nixon	David M. Kennedy	IL	1969
"	John B. Connally	TX	1971
"	George P. Shultz	IL	1972
"	William E. Simon	NJ	1974
Ford	William E. Simon	NJ	1974
Carter	W. Michael Blumenthal	MI	1977
"	G. William Miller	RI	1979
Reagan	Donald T. Regan	NY	1981
"	James A. Baker 3d	TX	1985
"	Nicholas F. Brady	NJ	1988
Bush	Nicholas F. Brady	NJ	1989
Clinton	Lloyd Bentsen	TX	1993
"	Robert E. Rubin	NY	1995

Secretaries of Defense

The Department of Defense, originally designated the National Military Establishment, was created Sept. 18, 1947. It is headed by the secretary of defense, a member of the president's Cabinet. The departments of the army, of the navy, and of the air force function within the Defense Department, and since 1947 their secretaries have not been members of the president's Cabinet.

President	Secretary	Home	Apptd.
Truman	James V. Forrestal	NY	1947
"	Louis A. Johnson	WV	1949
"	George C. Marshall	PA	1950
"	Robert A. Lovett	NY	1951
Eisenhower	Charles E. Wilson	MI	1953
"	Neil H. McElroy	OH	1957
"	Thomas S. Gates Jr.	PA	1959
Kennedy	Robert S. McNamara	MI	1961
Johnson, L.B.	Robert S. McNamara	MI	1963
"	Clark M. Clifford	MD	1968
Nixon	Melvin R. Laird	WI	1969
Nixon	Elliot L. Richardson	MA	1973
"	James R. Schlesinger	VA	1973
Ford	James R. Schlesinger	VA	1974
"	Donald H. Rumsfeld	IL	1975
Carter	Harold Brown	CA	1977
Reagan	Caspar W. Weinberger	CA	1981
"	Frank C. Carlucci	PA	1987
Bush	Richard B. Cheney	WY	1989
Clinton	Les Aspin	WI	1993
"	William J. Perry	CA	1994
"	William S. Cohen	ME	1997

Secretaries of War

The War Department (which included jurisdiction over the navy until 1798) was created by act of Congress on Aug. 7, 1789, and Gen. Henry Knox was commissioned secretary of war under that act on Sept. 12, 1789.

President	Secretary	Home	Apptd.
Washington	Henry Knox	MA	1789
"	Timothy Pickering	PA	1795
"	James McHenry	MD	1796
Adams, J.	James McHenry	MD	1797
"	Samuel Dexter	MA	1800
Jefferson	Henry Dearborn	MA	1801
Madison	William Eustis	MA	1809
"	John Armstrong	NY	1813
"	James Monroe	VA	1814
"	William H. Crawford	GA	1815
Monroe	John C. Calhoun	SC	1817
Adams, J.Q.	James Barbour	VA	1825
"	Peter B. Porter	NY	1828
Jackson	John H. Eaton	TN	1829
"	Lewis Cass	MI	1831
"	Benjamin F. Butler	NY	1837
Van Buren	Joel R. Poinsett	SC	1837
Harrison, W.H.	John Bell	TN	1841
Tyler	John Bell	TN	1841
"	John C. Spencer	NY	1841
"	James M. Porter	PA	1843
"	William Wilkins	PA	1844
Polk	William L. Marcy	NY	1845
Taylor	George W. Crawford	GA	1849
Fillmore	Charles M. Conrad	LA	1850
Pierce	Jefferson Davis	MS	1853
Buchanan	John B. Floyd	VA	1857
"	Joseph Holt	KY	1861
Lincoln	Simon Cameron	PA	1861
"	Edwin M. Stanton	PA	1862
Johnson, A.	Edwin M. Stanton	PA	1865
"	John M. Schofield	IL	1868
Grant	John A. Rawlins	IL	1869
"	William T. Sherman	OH	1869
"	William W. Belknap	IA	1869
"	Alphonso Taft	OH	1876
"	James D. Cameron	PA	1876
Hayes	George W. McCrary	IA	1877
"	Alexander Ramsey	MN	1879
Garfield	Robert T. Lincoln	IL	1881
Arthur	Robert T. Lincoln	IL	1881
Cleveland	William C. Endicott	MA	1885
Harrison, B.	Redfield Proctor	VT	1889
"	Stephen B. Elkins	WV	1891
Cleveland	Daniel S. Lamont	NY	1893
McKinley	Russel A. Alger	MI	1897
"	Elihu Root	NY	1899
Roosevelt, T.	Elihu Root	NY	1901
"	William H. Taft	OH	1904
"	Luke E. Wright	TN	1908
Taft	Jacob M. Dickinson	TN	1909
"	Henry L. Stimson	NY	1911
Wilson	Lindley M. Garrison	NJ	1913
"	Newton D. Baker	OH	1916
Harding	John W. Weeks	MA	1921
Coolidge	John W. Weeks	MA	1923
"	Dwight F. Davis	MO	1925
Hoover	James W. Good	IL	1929
"	Patrick J. Hurley	OK	1929
Roosevelt, F.D.	George H. Dern	UT	1933
"	Harry H. Woodring	KS	1937
"	Henry L. Stimson	NY	1940
Truman	Robert P. Patterson	NY	1945
"	Kenneth C. Royall[1]	NC	1947

(1) Last member of the Cabinet with this title. The War Department became the Department of the Army and became a branch of the Department of Defense in 1947.

Secretaries of the Navy

The Navy Department was created by act of Congress on Apr. 30, 1798.

President	Secretary	Home	Apptd.
Adams, J.	Benjamin Stoddert	MD	1798
Jefferson	Benjamin Stoddert	MD	1801
Jefferson	Robert Smith	MD	1801
Madison	Paul Hamilton	SC	1809
Madison	William Jones	PA	1813
"	Benjamin W. Crowninshield	MA	1814
Monroe	Benjamin W. Crowninshield	MA	1817
"	Smith Thompson	NY	1818
"	Samuel L. Southard	NJ	1823
Adams, J.Q.	Samuel L. Southard	NJ	1825
Jackson	John Branch	NC	1829
"	Levi Woodbury	NH	1831
"	Mahlon Dickerson	NJ	1834
Van Buren	Mahlon Dickerson	NJ	1837
"	James K. Paulding	NY	1838
Harrison, W.H.	George E. Badger	NC	1841
Tyler	George E. Badger	NC	1841
"	Abel P. Upshur	VA	1841
"	David Henshaw	MA	1843
"	Thomas W. Gilmer	VA	1844
"	John Y. Mason	VA	1844
Polk	George Bancroft	MA	1845
"	John Y. Mason	VA	1846
Taylor	William B. Preston	VA	1849
Fillmore	William A. Graham	NC	1850
	John P. Kennedy	MD	1852
Pierce	James C. Dobbin	NC	1853
Buchanan	Isaac Toucey	CT	1857
Lincoln	Gideon Welles	CT	1861
Johnson, A.	Gideon Welles	CT	1865
Grant	Adolph E. Borie	PA	1869
Grant	George M. Robeson	NJ	1869
Hayes	Richard W. Thompson	IN	1877
"	Nathan Goff Jr.	WV	1881
Garfield	William H. Hunt	LA	1881
Arthur	William E. Chandler	NH	1882
Cleveland	William C. Whitney	NY	1885
Harrison, B.	Benjamin F. Tracy	NY	1889
Cleveland	Hilary A. Herbert	AL	1893
McKinley	John D. Long	MA	1897
Roosevelt, T.	John D. Long	MA	1901
"	William H. Moody	MA	1902
"	Paul Morton	IL	1904
"	Charles J. Bonaparte	MD	1905
"	Victor H. Metcalf	CA	1906
"	Truman H. Newberry	MI	1908
Taft	George von L. Meyer	MA	1909
Wilson	Josephus Daniels	NC	1913
Harding	Edwin Denby	MI	1921
Coolidge	Edwin Denby	MI	1923
"	Curtis D. Wilbur	CA	1924
Hoover	Charles Francis Adams	MA	1929
Roosevelt, F.D.	Claude A. Swanson	VA	1933
"	Charles Edison	NJ	1940
"	Frank Knox	IL	1940
"	James V. Forrestal	NY	1944
Truman	James V. Forrestal[1]	NY	1945

(1) Last member of Cabinet with this title. The Navy Department became a branch of the Department of Defense when the latter was created on Sept. 18, 1947.

Attorneys General

The office of attorney general was established by act of Congress on Sept. 24, 1789. It officially reached Cabinet rank in Mar. 1792, when the first attorney general, Edmund Randolph, attended his initial Cabinet meeting. The Department of Justice, headed by the attorney general, was created June 22, 1870.

President	Attorney General	Home	Apptd.
Washington	Edmund Randolph	VA	1789
"	William Bradford	PA	1794
"	Charles Lee	VA	1795
Adams, J.	Charles Lee	VA	1797
Jefferson	Levi Lincoln	MA	1801
"	John Breckenridge	KY	1805
"	Caesar A. Rodney	DE	1807
Madison	Caesar A. Rodney	DE	1807
"	William Pinkney	MD	1811
"	Richard Rush	PA	1814
Monroe	Richard Rush	PA	1817
"	William Wirt	VA	1817
Adams, J.Q.	William Wirt	VA	1825
Jackson	John M. Berrien	GA	1829
"	Roger B. Taney	MD	1831
"	Benjamin F. Butler	NY	1833
Van Buren	Benjamin F. Butler	NY	1837
"	Felix Grundy	TN	1838
"	Henry D. Gilpin	PA	1840
Harrison, W.H.	John J. Crittenden	KY	1841
Tyler	John J. Crittenden	KY	1841
"	Hugh S. Legare	SC	1841
"	John Nelson	MD	1843
Polk	John Y. Mason	VA	1845
"	Nathan Clifford	ME	1846
"	Isaac Toucey	CT	1848
Taylor	Reverdy Johnson	MD	1849
Fillmore	John J. Crittenden	KY	1850
Pierce	Caleb Cushing	MA	1853
Buchanan	Jeremiah S. Black	PA	1857
"	Edwin M. Stanton	PA	1860
Lincoln	Edward Bates	MO	1861
"	James Speed	KY	1864
Johnson, A.	James Speed	KY	1865
"	Henry Stanbery	OH	1866
"	William M. Evarts	NY	1868
Grant	Ebenezer R. Hoar	MA	1869
"	Amos T. Akerman	GA	1870
"	George H. Williams	OR	1871
"	Edwards Pierrepont	NY	1875
"	Alphonso Taft	OH	1876
Hayes	Charles Devens	MA	1877
Garfield	Wayne MacVeagh	PA	1881
Arthur	Benjamin H. Brewster	PA	1882
Cleveland	Augustus Garland	AR	1885
Harrison, B.	William H. H. Miller	IN	1889
Cleveland	Richard Olney	MA	1893
"	Judson Harmon	OH	1895
McKinley	Joseph McKenna	CA	1897
"	John W. Griggs	NJ	1898
"	Philander C. Knox	PA	1901
Roosevelt, T.	Philander C. Knox	PA	1901
"	William H. Moody	MA	1904
"	Charles J. Bonaparte	MD	1906
Taft	George W. Wickersham	NY	1909
Wilson	J.C. McReynolds	TN	1913
"	Thomas W. Gregory	TX	1914
"	A. Mitchell Palmer	PA	1919
Harding	Harry M. Daugherty	OH	1921
Coolidge	Harry M. Daugherty	OH	1923
"	Harlan F. Stone	NY	1924
"	John G. Sargent	VT	1925
Hoover	William D. Mitchell	MN	1929
Roosevelt, F.D.	Homer S. Cummings	CT	1933
"	Frank Murphy	MI	1939
"	Robert H. Jackson	NY	1940
"	Francis Biddle	PA	1941
Truman	Thomas C. Clark	TX	1945
"	J. Howard McGrath	RI	1949
"	J.P. McGranery	PA	1952
Eisenhower	Herbert Brownell Jr.	NY	1953
"	William P. Rogers	MD	1957
Kennedy	Robert F. Kennedy	MA	1961
Johnson, L.B.	Robert F. Kennedy	MA	1963
"	N. de B. Katzenbach	IL	1964
"	Ramsey Clark	TX	1967
Nixon	John N. Mitchell	NY	1969
"	Richard G. Kleindienst	AZ	1972
"	Elliot L. Richardson	MA	1973
"	William B. Saxbe	OH	1974
Ford	William B. Saxbe	OH	1974
"	Edward H. Levi	IL	1975
Carter	Griffin B. Bell	GA	1977
"	Benjamin R. Civiletti	MD	1979
Reagan	William French Smith	CA	1981
"	Edwin Meese 3d	CA	1985
"	Richard Thornburgh	PA	1988
Bush	Richard Thornburgh	PA	1989
"	William P. Barr	NY	1991
Clinton	Janet Reno	FL	1993

Secretaries of the Interior

The Department of the Interior was created by act of Congress on Mar. 3, 1849.

President	Secretary	Home	Apptd.
Taylor	Thomas Ewing	OH	1849
Fillmore	Thomas M. T. McKennan	PA	1850
"	Alex H. H. Stuart	VA	1850
Pierce	Robert McClelland	MI	1853
Buchanan	Jacob Thompson	MS	1857
Lincoln	Caleb B. Smith	IN	1861
"	John P. Usher	IN	1863
Johnson, A.	John P. Usher	IN	1865
"	James Harlan	IA	1865
"	Orville H. Browning	IL	1866
Grant	Jacob D. Cox	OH	1869
"	Columbus Delano	OH	1870
"	Zachariah Chandler	MI	1875
Hayes	Carl Schurz	MO	1877
Garfield	Samuel J. Kirkwood	IA	1881
Arthur	Henry M. Teller	CO	1882
Cleveland	Lucius Q.C. Lamar	MS	1885
"	William F. Vilas	WI	1888
Harrison, B.	John W. Noble	MO	1889
Cleveland	Hoke Smith	GA	1893
"	David R. Francis	MO	1896
McKinley	Cornelius N. Bliss	NY	1897
"	Ethan A. Hitchcock	MO	1898
Roosevelt, T.	Ethan A. Hitchcock	MO	1901
"	James R. Garfield	OH	1907
Taft	Richard A. Ballinger	WA	1909
Taft	Walter L. Fisher	IL	1911
Wilson	Franklin K. Lane	CA	1913
"	John B. Payne	IL	1920
Harding	Albert B. Fall	NM	1921
"	Hubert Work	CO	1923
Coolidge	Hubert Work	CO	1923
"	Roy O. West	IL	1929
Hoover	Ray Lyman Wilbur	CA	1929
Roosevelt, F.D.	Harold L. Ickes	IL	1933
Truman	Harold L. Ickes	IL	1945
"	Julius A. Krug	WI	1946
"	Oscar L. Chapman	CO	1949
Eisenhower	Douglas McKay	OR	1953
"	Fred A. Seaton	NE	1956
Kennedy	Stewart L. Udall	AZ	1961
Johnson, L.B.	Stewart L. Udall	AZ	1963
Nixon	Walter J. Hickel	AK	1969
"	Rogers C.B. Morton	MD	1971
Ford	Rogers C.B. Morton	MD	1971
"	Stanley K. Hathaway	WY	1975
"	Thomas S. Kleppe	ND	1975
Carter	Cecil D. Andrus	ID	1977
Reagan	James G. Watt	CO	1981
"	William P. Clark	CA	1983
"	Donald P. Hodel	OR	1985
Bush	Manuel Lujan	NM	1989
Clinton	Bruce Babbitt	AZ	1993

Secretaries of Agriculture

The Department of Agriculture was created by act of Congress on May 15, 1862. On Feb. 8, 1889, its commissioner was renamed secretary of agriculture and became a member of the Cabinet.

President	Secretary	Home	Apptd.
Cleveland	Norman J. Colman	MO	1889
Harrison, B.	Jeremiah M. Rusk	WI	1889
Cleveland	J. Sterling Morton	NE	1893
McKinley	James Wilson	IA	1897
Roosevelt, T.	James Wilson	IA	1901
Taft	James Wilson	IA	1909
Wilson	David F. Houston	MO	1913
"	Edwin T. Meredith	IA	1920
Harding	Henry C. Wallace	IA	1921
Coolidge	Henry C. Wallace	IA	1923
"	Howard M. Gore	WV	1924
"	William M. Jardine	KS	1925
Hoover	Arthur M. Hyde	MO	1929
Roosevelt, F.D.	Henry A. Wallace	IA	1933
"	Claude R. Wickard	IN	1940
Truman	Clinton P. Anderson	NM	1945
Truman	Charles F. Brannan	CO	1948
Eisenhower	Ezra Taft Benson	UT	1953
Kennedy	Orville L. Freeman	MN	1961
Johnson, L.B.	Orville L. Freeman	MN	1963
Nixon	Clifford M. Hardin	IN	1969
"	Earl L. Butz	IN	1971
Ford	Earl L. Butz	IN	1974
"	John A. Knebel	VA	1976
Carter	Bob Bergland	MN	1977
Reagan	John R. Block	IL	1981
"	Richard E. Lyng	CA	1986
Bush	Clayton K. Yeutter	NE	1989
"	Edward Madigan	IL	1991
Clinton	Mike Espy	MS	1993
"	Dan Glickman	KS	1995

Secretaries of Commerce and Labor

The Department of Commerce and Labor, created by Congress on Feb. 14, 1903, was divided by Congress Mar. 4, 1913, into separate departments of Commerce and Labor. The secretary of each was made a Cabinet member.

Secretaries of Commerce and Labor

President	Secretary	Home	Apptd.
Roosevelt, T.	George B. Cortelyou	NY	1903
"	Victor H. Metcalf	CA	1904
"	Oscar S. Straus	NY	1906
Taft	Charles Nagel	MO	1909

Secretaries of Labor

President	Secretary	Home	Apptd.
Wilson	William B. Wilson	PA	1913
Harding	James J. Davis	PA	1921
Coolidge	James J. Davis	PA	1923
Hoover	James J. Davis	PA	1929
"	William N. Doak	VA	1930
Roosevelt, F.D.	Frances Perkins	NY	1933
Truman	L.B. Schwellenbach	WA	1945
"	Maurice J. Tobin	MA	1949
Eisenhower	Martin P. Durkin	IL	1953
"	James P. Mitchell	NJ	1953
Kennedy	Arthur J. Goldberg	IL	1961
"	W. Willard Wirtz	IL	1962
Johnson, L.B.	W. Willard Wirtz	IL	1963
Nixon	George P. Shultz	IL	1969
"	James D. Hodgson	CA	1970
"	Peter J. Brennan	NY	1973
Ford	Peter J. Brennan	NY	1974
"	John T. Dunlop	CA	1975
"	W.J. Usery Jr.	GA	1976
Carter	F. Ray Marshall	TX	1977
Reagan	Raymond J. Donovan	NJ	1981
"	William E. Brock	TN	1985
"	Ann D. McLaughlin	DC	1987
Bush	Elizabeth Hanford Dole	NC	1989
"	Lynn Martin	IL	1991
Clinton	Robert B. Reich	MA	1993
"	Alexis M. Herman	AL	1997

Secretaries of Commerce

President	Secretary	Home	Apptd.
Wilson	William C. Redfield	NY	1913
"	Joshua W. Alexander	MO	1919
Harding	Herbert C. Hoover	CA	1921
Coolidge	Herbert C. Hoover	CA	1923
"	William F. Whiting	MA	1928
Hoover	Robert P. Lamont	IL	1929

President	Secretary	Home	Apptd.
Hoover	Roy D. Chapin	MI	1932
Roosevelt, F.D.	Daniel C. Roper	SC	1933
"	Harry L. Hopkins	NY	1939
"	Jesse Jones	TX	1940
"	Henry A. Wallace	IA	1945
Truman	Henry A. Wallace	IA	1945
"	W. Averell Harriman	NY	1947
"	Charles Sawyer	OH	1948
Eisenhower	Sinclair Weeks	MA	1953
"	Lewis L. Strauss	NY	1958
"	Frederick H. Mueller	MI	1959
Kennedy	Luther H. Hodges	NC	1961
Johnson, L.B.	Luther H. Hodges	NC	1963
"	John T. Connor	NJ	1965
"	Alex B. Trowbridge	NJ	1967
"	Cyrus R. Smith	NY	1968
Nixon	Maurice H. Stans	MN	1969
"	Peter G. Peterson	IL	1972
"	Frederick B. Dent	SC	1973
Ford	Frederick B. Dent	SC	1974
"	Rogers C.B. Morton	MD	1975
"	Elliot L. Richardson	MA	1975
Carter	Juanita M. Kreps	NC	1977
"	Philip M. Klutznick	IL	1979
Reagan	Malcolm Baldrige	CT	1981
"	C. William Verity Jr.	OH	1987
Bush	Robert A. Mosbacher	TX	1989
"	Barbara H. Franklin	PA	1992
Clinton	Ronald H. Brown	DC	1993
"	Mickey Kantor	CA	1996
"	William M. Daley	IL	1997

Secretaries of Housing and Urban Development

The Department of Housing and Urban Development was created by act of Congress on Sept. 9, 1965.

President	Secretary	Home	Apptd.
Johnson, L.B.	Robert C. Weaver	WA	1966
"	Robert C. Wood	MA	1969
Nixon	George W. Romney	MI	1969
"	James T. Lynn	OH	1973
Ford	James T. Lynn	OH	1974
"	Carla Anderson Hills	CA	1975
Carter	Patricia Roberts Harris	DC	1977
"	Moon Landrieu	LA	1979
Reagan	Samuel R. Pierce Jr.	NY	1981
Bush	Jack F. Kemp	NY	1989
Clinton	Henry G. Cisneros	TX	1993
"	Andrew M. Cuomo	NY	1997

Secretaries of Transportation

The Department of Transportation was created by act of Congress on Oct. 15, 1966.

President	Secretary	Home	Apptd.
Johnson, L.B.	Alan S. Boyd	FL	1966
Nixon	John A. Volpe	MA	1969
"	Claude S. Brinegar	CA	1973
Ford	Claude S. Brinegar	CA	1974
"	William T. Coleman Jr.	PA	1975
Carter	Brock Adams	WA	1977
"	Neil E. Goldschmidt	OR	1979
Reagan	Andrew L. Lewis Jr.	PA	1981
"	Elizabeth Hanford Dole	NC	1983
"	James H. Burnley	NC	1987
Bush	Samuel K. Skinner	IL	1989
"	Andrew H. Card Jr.	MA	1992
Clinton	Federico F. Peña	CO	1993
"	Rodney E. Slater	AR	1997

Secretaries of Energy

The Department of Energy was created by federal law on Aug. 4, 1977.

President	Secretary	Home	Apptd.
Carter	James R. Schlesinger	VA	1977
"	Charles Duncan Jr.	WY	1979
Reagan	James B. Edwards	SC	1981
"	Donald P. Hodel	OR	1982
"	John S. Herrington	CA	1985
Bush	James D. Watkins	CA	1989
Clinton	Hazel R. O'Leary	MN	1993
"	Federico F. Peña	CO	1997
"	Bill Richardson	NM	1998

Secretaries of Health, Education, and Welfare

The Department of Health, Education, and Welfare was created by Congress on Apr. 11, 1953. On Sept. 27, 1979, it was divided by Congress into separate departments of Education and of Health and Human Services, with the secretary of each being a Cabinet member.

President	Secretary	Home	Apptd.
Eisenhower	Oveta Culp Hobby	TX	1953
"	Marion B. Folsom	NY	1955
"	Arthur S. Flemming	OH	1958
Kennedy	Abraham A. Ribicoff	CT	1961
"	Anthony J. Celebrezze	OH	1962
Johnson, L.B.	Anthony J. Celebrezze	OH	1963
"	John W. Gardner	NY	1965
"	Wilbur J. Cohen	MI	1968
Nixon	Robert H. Finch	CA	1969
"	Elliot L. Richardson	MA	1970
"	Caspar W. Weinberger	CA	1973
Ford	Caspar W. Weinberger	CA	1974
"	Forrest D. Mathews	AL	1975
Carter	Joseph A. Califano Jr.	DC	1977
"	Patricia Roberts Harris	DC	1979

Secretaries of Health and Human Services

President	Secretary	Home	Apptd.
Carter	Patricia Roberts Harris	DC	1979
Reagan	Richard S. Schweiker	PA	1981
"	Margaret M. Heckler	MA	1983
Reagan	Otis R. Bowen	IN	1985
Bush	Louis W. Sullivan	GA	1989
Clinton	Donna E. Shalala	WI	1993

Secretaries of Education

President	Secretary	Home	Apptd.
Carter	Shirley Hufstedler	CA	1979
Reagan	Terrel Bell	UT	1981
"	William J. Bennett	NY	1985
"	Lauro F. Cavazos	TX	1988
Bush	Lauro F. Cavazos	TX	1989
"	Lamar Alexander	TN	1991
Clinton	Richard W. Riley	SC	1993

Secretaries of Veterans Affairs

The Department of Veterans Affairs was created on Oct. 25, 1988, when Pres. Ronald Reagan signed a bill that made the Veterans Administration into a Cabinet department, effective Mar. 15, 1989.

President	Secretary	Home	Apptd.
Bush	Edward J. Derwinski	IL	1989
Clinton	Jesse Brown	IL	1993
Clinton	Togo D. West Jr.	NC	1998

ECONOMICS

U.S. Budget Receipts and Outlays, 1995-98

Source: Financial Management Service, U.S. Dept. of the Treasury

For the fiscal year 1998 the federal budget showed a surplus of $70.0 bil, just under 1% of the GDP. This was the first budget surplus since 1969, and the largest as a percentage of GDP since 1956. In dollar terms it was the largest federal surplus ever.

(in millions of dollars; many figures do not add to totals because of independent rounding or omitted subcategories, including some subcategories with negative values.)

Classification	Fiscal 1995[1]	Fiscal 1996[1]	Fiscal 1997[1]	Fiscal 1998[1]
NET RECEIPTS				
Individual income taxes	$590,243	$656,417	$737,466	$828,597
Corporation income taxes	157,004	171,824	182,294	188,677
Social insurance taxes and contributions:				
Federal old-age and survivors insurance	284,091	311,869	336,728	358,784
Federal disability insurance	66,989	55,623	55,261	57,016
Federal hospital insurance	96,025	104,998	110,710	119,863
Railroad retirement fund	3,942	3,872	4,051	4,353
Total employment taxes and contributions	451,046	476,362	506,750	540,016
Other insurance and retirement:				
Unemployment	28,878	28,584	28,202	27,484
Federal employees retirement	4,461	4,389	4,344	4,261
Non-federal employees	89	80	74	74
Total social insurance taxes and contributions	**484,474**	**509,415**	**539,371**	**571,835**
Excise taxes	57,484	54,015	56,926	57,669
Estate and gift taxes	14,763	17,189	19,845	24,076
Customs duties	19,300	18,671	17,927	18,297
Deposits of earnings by Federal Reserve Banks	23,378	20,477	19,636	24,540
All other miscellaneous receipts	4,847	4,755	25,127	32,270
Net Budget Receipts	**$1,351,495**	**$1,452,763**	**$1,578,955**	**$1,721,421**
NET OUTLAYS				
Legislative Branch	$2,621	$2,272	$2,362	$2,543
The Judiciary	2,903	3,061	3,259	3,463
Executive Office of the President:				
The White House Office	37	39	39	46
Office of Management and Budget	56	55	56	49
Total Executive Office	**213**	**202**	**219**	**213**
Funds appropriated to the President:				
International security assistance	4,952	4,254	4,403	4,951
Multilateral assistance	2,194	2,077	2,141	1,850
Agency for International Development	3,252	3,059	2,814	2,457
International Development Assistance	5,557	5,229	2,902	2,514
Total funds appropriated to the President	**11,164**	**9,716**	**10,128**	**9,000**
Agriculture Department:				
Food stamp program	25,554	25,359	22,857	20,141
Farm Service Agency	9,123	8,350	7,417	10,421
Forest Service	3,765	3,411	3,209	3,399
Total Agriculture Department	**56,667**	**54,338**	**52,549**	**53,950**
Commerce Department:				
Bureau of the Census	293	260	282	542
Total Commerce Department	**3,403**	**3,703**	**3,780**	**4,047**
Defense Department—Military:				
Military personnel	70,807	66,669	69,722	68,976
Operation and maintenance	90,882	88,629	92,465	92,883
Procurement	54,984	48,912	47,691	48,186
Research, development, test, evaluation	34,710	36,561	37,026	37,423
Military construction	6,826	6,684	6,188	6,046
Total Defense Department—Military	**259,565**	**253,258**	**258,330**	**256,136**
Defense Department—Civil	31,664	32,535	30,282	31,215
Education Department	31,321	29,900	30,014	30,492
Energy Department	17,618	16,199	14,470	14,444
Health and Human Services Department:				
Public Health Service	20,728	21,405	21,755	23,670
Health Care Financing Adm.	310,657	354,898	369,714	379,950
Food and Drug Administration	858	865	873	838
National Institutes of Health	10,883	10,217	11,199	12,501
Total Health and Human Services Dept.	**303,075**	**319,802**	**339,541**	**350,563**
Housing and Urban Development Department	29,045	25,512	27,525	30,224
Interior Department	7,390	6,720	6,722	7,234
Justice Department:				
Federal Bureau of Investigation	2,041	2,305	2,700	2,949
Drug Enforcement Agency	788	746	969	1,099
Immigration and Naturalization Service	1,805	2,246	2,770	3,593
Federal Prison System	2,748	3,013	2,939	2,682
Total Justice Department	**10,786**	**11,951**	**14,315**	**16,129**
Labor Department:				
Unemployment Trust Fund	25,205	26,146	24,299	23,408
Total Labor Department	**32,093**	**32,496**	**30,461**	**30,002**
State Department	5,347	4,955	5,245	4,585
Transportation Department:				
Federal Aviation Administration	9,206	8,925	8,815	9,242
Total Transportation Department	**38,776**	**38,776**	**39,835**	**39,468**
Treasury Department:				
Internal Revenue Service	25,617	28,595	31,386	33,153
Interest on the public debt	332,414	343,955	355,796	363,824
Total Treasury Department	**348,480**	**365,336**	**379,345**	**390,100**
Veterans Affairs Department	37,769	36,915	39,277	41,776
Environmental Protection Agency	6,349	6,046	6,167	6,300
General Services Administration	709	625	1,083	1,136

(continued)

Classification	Fiscal 1995[1]	Fiscal 1996[1]	Fiscal 1997[1]	Fiscal 1998[1]
National Aeronautics and Space Administration	$13,377	$13,882	$14,358	$14,206
Office of Personnel Management	41,279	42,872	45,404	46,307
Small Business Administration	678	872	334	–78
Social Security Administration	362,226	375,232	393,309	408,202
Other independent agencies:				
Corporation for Natl. and Community Service[2]	425	477	564	592
Corporation for Public Broadcasting	286	275	260	250
District of Columbia	714	712	717	818
Equal Employment Opportunity Commission	234	224	231	244
Export-Import Bank of the U.S.	–53	–560	–114	–208
Federal Communications Commission	935	978	1,001	1,769
Federal Deposit Insurance Corporation	–17,557	–8,732	–14,181	–4,122
Legal Services Corporation	429	282	282	285
National Archives & Records Adm.	219	199	198	210
National Foundation on the Arts and Humanities	355	285	230	207
National Labor Relations Board	174	166	175	177
National Science Foundation	2,847	3,012	3,131	3,188
Nuclear Regulatory Commission	28	57	51	38
Railroad Retirement Board	4,359	5,007	4,870	4,837
Securities and Exchange Commission	122	42	–20	–231
Smithsonian Institution	432	432	491	488
Tennessee Valley Authority	1,313	757	–337	–784
U.S. Information Agency	1,160	1,174	1,166	1,150
Total other independent agencies	–1,470	8,577	–2,489	11,639
Undistributed offsetting receipts	–137,635	–135,649	–154,970	–161,035
NET BUDGET OUTLAYS	**$1,515,412**	**$1,560,094**	**$1,600,911**	**$1,651,383**
Less net receipts	1,351,495	1,452,763	1,578,955	1,721,421
DEFICIT(–) OR SURPLUS (+)	**$–163,917**	**$–107,331**	**$–21,957**	**$+70,039**

(1) Fical year ends Sept. 30. (2) Formerly Action.

Summary of Receipts, Outlays, and Surpluses or Deficits, 1936-94

Source: Financial Management Service, U.S. Dept. of the Treasury

(millions of dollars)

Fiscal Year[1]	Receipts	Outlays	Surplus or Deficit (–)[2]
1936	$3,923	$8,228	$–4,304
1937	5,387	7,580	–2,193
1938	6,751	6,840	–89
1939	6,295	9,141	–2,846
1940	6,548	9,468	–2,920
1941	8,712	13,653	–4,941
1942	14,634	35,137	–20,503
1943	24,001	78,555	–54,554
1944	43,747	91,304	–47,557
1945	45,159	92,712	–47,553
1946	39,296	55,232	–15,936
1947	38,514	34,496	4,018
1948	41,560	29,764	11,796
1949	39,415	38,835	580
1950	39,443	42,562	–3,119
1951	51,616	45,514	6,102
1952	66,167	67,686	–1,519
1953	69,608	76,101	–6,493
1954	69,701	70,855	–1,154
1955	65,451	68,444	–2,993
1956	74,587	70,640	3,947
1957	79,990	76,578	3,412
1958	79,636	82,405	–2,769
1959	79,249	92,098	–12,849
1960	92,492	92,191	301
1961	94,388	97,723	–3,335
1962	99,676	106,821	–7,146
1963	106,560	111,316	–4,756
1964	112,613	118,528	–5,915
1965	116,817	118,228	–1,411
1966	130,835	134,532	–3,698
1967	$148,822	$157,464	$–8,643
1968	152,973	178,134	–25,161
1969	186,882	183,640	3,242
1970	192,807	195,649	–2,842
1971	187,139	210,172	–23,033
1972	207,309	230,681	–23,373
1973	230,799	245,707	–14,908
1974	263,224	269,359	–6,135
1975	279,090	332,332	–53,242
1976	298,060	371,779	–73,719
Transition quarter[3]	81,232	95,973	–14,741
1977	355,559	409,203	–53,644
1978	399,561	458,729	–59,168
1979	463,302	503,464	–40,162
1980	517,112	590,920	–73,808
1981	599,272	678,209	–78,936
1982	617,766	745,706	–127,940
1983	600,562	808,327	–207,764
1984	666,457	851,781	–185,324
1985	734,057	946,316	–212,260
1986	769,091	990,231	–221,140
1987	854,143	1,003,804	–149,661
1988	908,166	1,063,318	–155,151
1989	990,701	1,144,020	–153,319
1990	1,031,308	1,251,776	–220,469
1991	1,054,265	1,323,757	–269,492
1992	1,090,453	1,380,794	–290,340
1993	1,153,226	1,408,532	–255,306
1994	1,257,451	1,460,553	–203,102

(1) Fiscal years 1936 to 1976 end June 30; after 1976, fiscal years end Sept. 30. (2) May not equal difference between figures shown, because of rounding. (3) Transition quarter covers July 1, 1976-Sept. 30, 1976.

Budget Receipts and Outlays, 1789-1935

Source: U.S. Dept. of the Treasury; annual statements for years ending June 30 unless otherwise noted

(thousands of dollars)

Yearly Average	Receipts	Outlays
1789-1800[1]	$5,717	$5,776
1801-1810[2]	13,056	9,086
1811-1820[2]	21,032	23,943
1821-1830[2]	21,928	16,162
1831-1840[2]	30,461	24,495
1841-1850[2]	28,545	34,097
1851-1860	60,237	60,163
1861-1865	160,907	683,785
1866-1870	$447,301	$377,642
1871-1875	336,830	287,460
1876-1880	288,124	255,598
1881-1885	366,961	257,691
1886-1890	375,448	279,134
1891-1895	352,891	363,599
1896-1900	434,877	457,451
1901-1905	$559,481	$535,559
1906-1910	628,507	639,178
1911-1915	710,227	720,252
1916-1920	3,483,652	8,065,333
1921-1925	4,306,673	3,578,989
1926-1930	4,069,138	3,182,807
1931-1935	2,770,973	5,214,874

(1) Average for period March 4, 1789, to Dec. 31, 1800. (2) Years from 1801 to 1842 end Dec. 31; average for 1841-1850 is for the period Jan. 1, 1841, to June 30, 1850.

Public Debt of the U.S.

Source: Bureau of Public Debt, U.S. Dept. of the Treasury

Fiscal year	Debt (billions)	Debt per cap. (dollars)	Interest paid (billions)	% of federal outlays	Fiscal year	Debt (billions)	Debt per cap. (dollars)	Interest paid (billions)	% of federal outlays
1870	$2.4	$61.06	—	—	1980	$907.7	$3,985	$74.9	12.7
1880	2.0	41.60	—	—	1981	997.9	4,338	95.6	14.1
1890	1.1	17.80	—	—	1982	1,142.0	4,913	117.4	15.7
1900	1.2	16.60	—	—	1983	1,377.2	5,870	128.8	15.9
1910	1.1	12.41	—	—	1984	1,572.3	6,640	153.8	18.1
1920	24.2	228	—	—	1985	1,823.1	7,598	178.9	18.9
1930	16.1	131	—	—	1986	2,125.3	8,774	190.2	19.2
1940	43.0	325	$1.0	10.5	1987	2,350.3	9,615	195.4	19.5
1950	256.1	1,688	5.7	13.4	1988	2,602.3	10,534	214.1	20.1
1955	272.8	1,651	6.4	9.4	1989	2,857.4	11,545	240.9	21.0
1960	284.1	1,572	9.2	10.0	1990	3,233.3	13,000	264.8	21.1
1965	313.8	1,613	11.3	9.6	1991	3,665.3	14,436	285.5	21.6
1970	370.1	1,814	19.3	9.9	1992	4,064.6	15,846	292.3	21.2
1975	533.2	2,475	32.7	9.8	1993	4,411.5	17,105	292.5	20.8
1976	620.4	2,852	37.1	10.0	1994	4,692.8	18,025	296.3	20.3
1977	698.8	3,170	41.9	10.2	1995	4,974.0	18,930	332.4	22.0
1978	771.5	3,463	48.7	10.6	1996	5,224.8	19,805	344.0	22.0
1979	826.5	3,669	59.8	11.9	1997	5,413.1	20,026	355.8	22.2

Note: Through 1976 the fiscal year ended June 30. From 1977 on, the fiscal year ends Sept. 30.

Consumer Price Index

The Consumer Price Index (CPI) is a measure of the average change in prices over time of one or more kinds of basic consumer goods and services. From Jan. 1978, the Bureau of Labor Statistics began publishing CPIs for 2 population groups: (1) a CPI for all urban consumers (CPI-U), which covers about 80% of the total population; and (2) a CPI for urban wage earners and clerical workers (CPI-W), which covers about 32% of the total population. The CPI-U includes, in addition to wage earners and clerical workers, groups such as professional, managerial, and technical workers, the self-employed, short-term workers, the unemployed, retirees, and others not in the labor force.

The CPI is based on prices of food, clothing, shelter, and fuels; transportation fares; charges for doctors' and dentists' services; drug prices; and prices of other goods and services bought for day-to-day living. The index currently measures price changes from a designated reference period, 1982-84, which equals 100.0. Use of this reference period began in Jan. 1988.

U.S. Consumer Price Indexes, First Half 1998

Source: Bureau of Labor Statistics, U.S. Dept. of Labor

(Data are semiannual averages of monthly figures)

	CPI-U (all urban consumers)		CPI-W (urban wage-earners/clerical)	
(1982–84=100)	1st half 1998	% change 2d half 1997 to 1st half 1998	1st half 1998	% change 2d half 1997 to 1st half 1998
ALL ITEMS	**162.3**	**0.7**	**159.0**	**0.6**
Food, beverages	160.3	1.1	159.6	1.1
Housing	159.4	1.1	155.7	0.9
Apparel	133.4	0.8	131.8	0.2
Transportation	141.9	–1.4	140.8	–1.7
Medical care	240.2	1.9	239.5	1.8
Recreation	100.9	0.9	100.8	0.8
Other goods, services	234.1	2.8	231.5	3.1
Services	183.0	1.3	179.8	1.1
SPECIAL INDEXES				
All items less food	162.8	0.7	158.8	0.4
Commodities less food	132.1	–0.8	132.0	–0.9
Nondurables	146.6	0.0	146.2	–0.2
Energy	103.7	–6.9	102.9	–7.2
All items less energy	170.0	1.3	166.7	1.3

Consumer Price Indexes (CPI-U),[1] Annual Percent Change, 1986-97

Source: Bureau of Labor Statistics, U.S. Dept. of Labor

	1986	1987	1988	1989	1990	1991	1992	1993	1994	1995	1996	1997
ALL ITEMS	**1.9**	**3.6**	**4.1**	**4.8**	**5.4**	**4.2**	**3.0**	**3.0**	**2.6**	**2.8**	**3.0**	**2.3**
Food	3.2	4.1	4.1	5.8	5.8	2.9	1.2	2.2	2.4	2.8	3.3	2.6
Shelter	5.5	4.7	4.8	4.5	5.4	4.5	3.3	3.0	3.1	3.2	3.2	3.1
Rent, residential	5.8	4.1	3.8	3.9	5.6	6.1	2.5	2.3	2.5	2.5	2.7	2.9
Fuel and other utilities	–2.3	–1.1	–1.4	3.3	3.5	3.3	2.2	3.0	1.0	0.7	3.1	2.6
Apparel and upkeep	0.9	4.4	4.3	2.8	4.6	3.7	2.5	1.4	–0.2	–1.0	–0.2	0.9
Private transportation	–4.7	–3.0	3.3	4.9	5.2	2.6	2.2	2.3	3.1	3.7	2.7	0.7
New cars	4.2	3.6	2.0	2.0	1.8	3.8	2.5	2.4	3.4	2.2	1.7	0.2
Gasoline	–21.9	–4.0	0.9	9.5	14.1	–1.8	–0.2	–1.3	0.5	1.6	6.1	–0.1
Public transportation	5.9	3.5	1.8	5.0	10.1	4.4	1.7	10.3	3.0	2.3	3.4	2.6
Medical care	7.5	6.6	6.5	7.7	9.0	8.7	7.4	5.9	4.8	4.5	3.5	2.8
Entertainment	3.4	3.3	4.3	5.2	4.7	4.5	2.8	2.5	2.9	2.5	3.4	2.1
Commodities	–0.9	3.2	3.5	4.7	5.2	4.2	2.0	1.9	1.7	1.9	2.6	1.4

(1) The Consumer Price Index CPI-U measures the average change in prices of goods and services purchased by all urban consumers.

U.S. Consumer Price Indexes for Selected Items and Groups, 1970-97

Source: Bureau of Labor Statistics, U.S. Dept. of Labor

(1982-84 = 100, unless otherwise noted. Annual averages of monthly figures. For all urban consumers.)

	1970	1975	1980	1985	1990	1995	1996	1997
ALL ITEMS	**38.8**	**53.8**	**82.4**	**107.6**	**130.7**	**152.4**	**156.9**	**160.5**
Food and beverages	**40.1**	**60.2**	**86.7**	**105.6**	**132.1**	**148.9**	**153.7**	**157.7**
Food	39.2	59.8	86.8	105.6	132.4	148.4	153.3	157.3
Food at home	39.9	61.8	88.4	104.3	132.3	148.8	154.3	158.1
Cereals and bakery products	37.1	62.9	83.9	107.9	140.0	167.5	174.0	177.6
Meats, poultry, fish, and eggs	44.6	67.0	92.0	100.1	130.0	138.8	144.8	148.5
Dairy products	44.7	62.6	90.9	103.2	126.5	132.8	142.1	145.5
Fruits and vegetables	37.8	56.9	82.1	106.4	149.0	177.7	183.9	187.5
Sugar and sweets	30.5	65.3	90.5	105.8	124.7	137.5	143.7	147.8
Fats and oils	39.2	73.5	89.3	106.9	126.3	137.3	140.5	141.7
Nonalcoholic beverages	27.1	41.3	91.4	104.3	113.5	131.7	128.6	133.4
Other prepared foods	39.6	58.9	83.6	106.4	131.2	151.1	156.2	161.2
Food away from home	37.5	54.5	83.4	108.3	133.4	149.0	152.7	157.0
Alcoholic beverages	52.1	65.9	86.4	106.4	129.3	153.9	158.5	162.8
Housing	**36.4**	**50.7**	**81.1**	**107.7**	**128.5**	**148.5**	**152.8**	**156.8**
Shelter	35.5	48.8	81.0	109.8	140.0	165.7	171.0	176.3
Renters' costs[1]	46.5	58.0	80.9	111.8	146.7	174.3	180.2	186.4
Maintenance and repairs	35.8	54.1	82.4	106.5	122.2	135.0	139.0	143.7
Fuel and other utilities[1]	29.1	45.4	75.4	106.5	111.6	123.7	127.5	130.8
Energy services	31.8	50.0	75.8	106.9	117.4	119.2	122.1	125.1
Household furnishings and operation	46.8	63.4	86.3	103.8	113.3	123.0	124.7	125.4
House furnishings	55.5	69.8	88.5	101.7	106.7	111.2	111.3	110.6
Apparel and upkeep	**59.2**	**72.5**	**90.9**	**105.0**	**124.1**	**132.0**	**131.7**	**132.9**
Apparel commodities	63.3	76.7	92.9	104.0	122.0	127.0	128.2	129.1
Men's and boys'	62.2	75.5	89.4	105.0	120.4	126.2	127.7	130.1
Women's and girls'	71.8	85.5	96.0	104.9	122.6	126.9	124.7	126.1
Footwear	56.8	69.6	91.8	102.3	117.4	125.4	126.6	127.6
Transportation	**37.5**	**50.1**	**83.1**	**106.4**	**120.5**	**139.1**	**143.0**	**144.3**
Private	37.5	50.6	84.2	106.2	118.8	136.3	140.0	141.0
New cars	53.0	62.9	88.4	106.1	121.4	139.0	141.4	141.7
Used cars	31.2	43.8	62.3	113.7	117.6	156.5	157.0	151.1
Gasoline	27.9	45.1	97.5	98.6	101.0	99.8	105.9	105.8
Public	35.2	43.5	69.0	110.5	142.6	175.9	181.9	186.7
Medical care	**34.0**	**47.5**	**74.9**	**113.5**	**162.8**	**220.5**	**228.2**	**234.6**
Entertainment	**47.5**	**62.0**	**83.6**	**107.9**	**132.4**	**153.9**	**159.1**	**162.5**
Other goods and services	**40.9**	**53.9**	**75.2**	**114.5**	**159.0**	**206.9**	**215.4**	**224.8**
Tobacco products	43.1	54.7	72.0	116.7	181.5	225.7	232.8	243.7
Personal care	43.5	57.9	81.9	106.3	130.4	147.1	150.1	152.7
Toilet goods and personal care appliances	42.7	58.0	79.6	107.6	128.2	143.1	144.3	144.2
Personal care services	44.2	57.7	83.7	108.9	132.8	151.5	156.6	162.4
Personal and educational expenses	35.5	48.7	70.9	119.1	170.2	235.5	247.5	259.7

(1) Dec. 1982 = 100.

Consumer Price Indexes by Region and Selected Cities, 1997-98

Source: Bureau of Labor Statistics, U.S. Dept. of Labor

	CPI-U Indexes[1]			% change	CPI-W Indexes[2]			% change
(1982-84 = 100)	Avg. 1997	July 1998	Aug. 1998	Aug. 1997-Aug. 1998	Avg. 1997	July 1998	Aug. 1998	Aug. 1997-Aug. 1998
U.S. CITY AVERAGE	**156.9**	**163.2**	**163.4**	**1.6**	**154.1**	**159.8**	**160.0**	**1.4**
Northeast urban	**163.6**	**169.9**	**170.5**	**1.6**	**161.1**	**166.6**	**167.1**	**1.3**
Size A—More than 1,500,000	164.3	170.7	171.4	1.8	160.7	166.5	167.1	1.6
Size B/C—50,000 to 1,500,000	161.4	102.0	102.2	1.0	159.2	101.5	101.7	0.7
Midwest urban	**153.0**	**159.8**	**159.5**	**1.5**	**149.6**	**155.9**	**155.6**	**1.3**
Size A—More than 1,500,000	153.6	161.2	161.0	1.9	149.6	156.5	156.4	1.8
Size B/C—50,000 to 1,500,000	152.1	102.2	102.0	1.1	148.2	101.9	101.7	0.9
Size D—Nonmetro. (less than 50,000)	149.7	153.5	153.3	0.5	147.8	151.7	151.4	0.3
South urban	**153.6**	**159.3**	**159.5**	**1.5**	**152.2**	**157.2**	**157.5**	**1.3**
Size A—More than 1,500,000	152.7	158.5	158.9	1.9	150.9	156.1	156.3	1.5
Size B/C—50,000 to 1,500,000	156.3	102.4	102.5	1.1	152.5	101.9	102.1	1.0
Size D—Nonmetro. (less than 50,000)	152.6	160.0	160.2	2.4	153.1	160.4	160.6	2.3
West urban	**157.6**	**164.3**	**164.8**	**2.0**	**154.5**	**160.3**	**160.7**	**1.7**
Size A—More than 1,500,000	157.7	165.1	165.6	2.4	153.0	159.3	159.7	2.0
Size B/C—50,000 to 1,500,000	162.3	102.3	102.5	1.0	159.2	102.1	102.3	0.8
Selected areas								
Chicago–Gary–Kenosha, IL–IN–WI	157.4	166.5	165.4	1.8	152.4	160.6	159.6	1.9
L.A.–Riverside–Orange County, CA	157.5	162.1	162.6	1.8	152.1	155.9	156.1	1.4
New York, NY–Northern NJ–Long Island, NY–NJ–CT–PA	166.9	173.6	174.2	2.0	163.1	169.1	169.7	1.8
Boston–Brockton–Nashua, MA–NH–ME–CT		170.7	—	—	162.2	168.8	—	—
Cleveland–Akron, OH		159.9	—	—	152.6	152.1	—	—
Dallas–Fort Worth, TX	148.8	154.2	—	—	153.1	154.0	—	—
Washington–Baltimore, DC–MD–VA–WV	159.6	102.8	—	—	162.2	102.5	—	—
Atlanta, GA		—	161.9	—	144.3	—	159.1	—
Detroit–Ann Arbor–Flint, MI	152.5	—	160.5	2.3	151.8	—	155.1	2.3
Houston–Galveston–Brazoria, TX	142.7	—	147.4	1.4	148.7	—	146.1	0.8
Miami–Fort Lauderdale, FL	153.7	—	160.8	—	156.9	—	158.0	—
Philadelphia–Wilmington–Atlantic City, PA–DE–NJ–MD	—	—	168.6	1.1	148.9	—	167.9	1.2
San Francisco–Oakland–San Jose, CA	155.1	—	166.6	3.3	147.7	—	162.7	2.9
Seattle–Tacoma–Bremerton, WA	—	—	168.5	—	142.0	—	163.8	—

(1) For all urban consumers. (2) For urban wage-earners and clerical workers. — = not available.

Consumer Price Index, 1915-1998

Source: Bureau of Labor Statistics, U.S. Dept. of Labor

(1967 = 100. Annual averages of monthly figures, specified for all urban consumers.)

Prices as measured by the U.S. Consumer Price Index have risen steadily since World War II. What cost $1.00 in 1967 (the reference year) cost about 30 cents in 1915, 54 cents in 1945, and $4.86 by 1998.

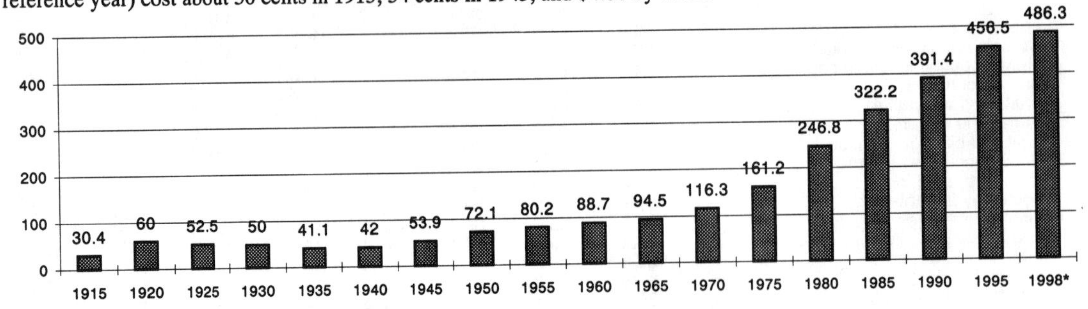

*Average for 1st half 1998.

Percentage Change in Consumer Prices in Selected Countries

Source: International Monetary Fund

(annual averages)

COUNTRY	1975-1980	1980-1985	1991-1992	1992-1993	1993-1994	1994-1995	1995-1996	1996-1997
Canada	8.7	7.4	1.5	1.8	0.2	2.2	1.6	1.6
France	10.5	9.6	2.4	2.1	1.7	1.8	2.0	1.2
Germany	4.1	3.9	4.0	4.1	3.0	1.8	1.5	1.8
Italy	16.3	13.7	5.1	4.5	4.0	5.2	4.0	2.0
Japan	6.5	2.7	1.7	1.3	0.7	–0.1	0.1	1.7
Spain	18.6	12.2	5.9	4.6	4.7	4.7	3.6	2.0
Sweden	10.5	9.0	2.3	4.6	2.2	2.5	0.5	0.5
Switzerland	2.3	4.3	4.1	3.3	0.8	1.8	0.8	0.5
United Kingdom	14.4	7.2	3.7	1.6	2.5	3.4	2.4	3.1
United States	8.9	5.5	3.0	3.0	2.6	2.8	3.0	2.3

Index of Leading Economic Indicators

Source: The Conference Board

The index of leading economic indicators is used to project the U.S. economy's performance. The index is made up of 10 measurements of economic activity that tend to change direction in advance of the overall economy. The index has predicted economic downturns from 8 to 20 months in advance and recoveries from 1 to 10 months in advance; however, it can be inconsistent, and has occasionally shown "false signals" of recessions.

Components

Average weekly hours of production workers in manufacturing
Average weekly initial claims for unemployment insurance, state programs
Manufacturers' new orders for consumer goods and materials, adjusted for inflation
Vendor performance (slower deliveries diffusion index)
Manufacturers' new orders, nondefense capital goods industries, adjusted for inflation
New private housing units authorized by local building permits
Stock prices, 500 common stocks
Money supply: M-2, adjusted for inflation
Interest rate spread, 10-yr Treasury bonds less federal funds
Consumer expectations (researched by Univ. of Michigan)

U.S. Gross Domestic Product, Gross National Product, Net National Product, National Income, and Personal Income

Source: Bureau of Economic Analysis, U.S. Dept. of Commerce

(billions of dollars)

	1960	1970	1980	1990	1996[R]	1997
GROSS DOMESTIC PRODUCT	—	—	—	$5,546.1	$7,661.6	$8,110.9
Gross national product	$515.3	$1,015.5	$2,732.0	5,567.8	7,674.0	8,102.9
Less: Consumption of fixed capital	46.4	88.8	303.8	602.7	832.0	871.8
Equals: Net national product	**468.9**	**926.6**	**2,428.1**	**4,965.1**	**6,842.0**	**7,231.1**
Less: Indirect business tax and nontax liability	45.3	94.0	213.3	444.0	606.4	627.2
Business transfer payments	2.0	4.1	12.1	26.8	33.8	35.1
Statistical discrepancy	–2.8	–1.1	4.9	7.8	–32.2	–55.8
Plus: Subsidies less current surplus of government enterprises	0.4	2.9	5.7	4.5	22.0	21.9
Equals: National income	**424.9**	**832.6**	**2,203.5**	**4,491.0**	**6,256.0**	**6,646.5**
Less: Corporate profits with inventory valuation and capital consumption adjustments	49.5	74.7	177.2	380.6	750.4	817.9
Net interest	11.3	41.2	200.9	463.7	418.6	432.0
Contributions for social insurance	21.9	62.2	216.5	503.1	688.0	727.0
Wage accruals less disbursements	0.0	0.0	0.0	0.1	9.3	3.7
Plus: Personal interest income	27.5	81.8	312.6	666.3	719.4	747.3
Personal dividend income	24.9	69.3	271.9	698.2	248.2	260.3
Government transfer payments to persons	12.9	22.2	52.9	144.4	1,041.5	1,083.3
Business transfer payments	2.0	4.1	12.1	21.3	26.4	27.2
Equals: PERSONAL INCOME	**409.4**	**831.8**	**2,258.5**	**4,673.8**	**6,425.2**	**6,784.0**

(R) Revised figures.

U.S. Gross Domestic Product

Source: Bureau of Economic Analysis, U.S. Dept. of Commerce

(billions of dollars)

	1997	First Quarter 1998[1]	Second Quarter 1998[1]
Gross domestic product	**$8,110.9**	**$8,384.2**	**$8,431.7**
Personal consumption expenditures	**5,493.7**	**5,676.5**	**5,771.0**
Durable goods	673.0	705.1	718.2
Nondurable goods	1,600.6	1,633.1	1,657.7
Services	3,220.1	3,338.2	3,395.2
Gross private domestic investment	**1,256.0**	**1,366.6**	**1,346.6**
Fixed investment	1,188.6	1,271.1	1,300.3
Nonresidential	860.7	921.3	938.7
Structures	240.2	245.0	243.7
Producers' durable equipment	620.5	676.3	695.1
Residential	327.9	349.8	361.6
Change in business inventories	67.4	95.5	46.3
Net exports of goods and services	**$-93.4**	**$-123.7**	**$-166.7**
Exports	965.4	973.3	948.6
Goods	688.3	694.5	666.8
Services	277.1	278.8	281.9
Imports	1,058.8	1,097.1	1,115.3
Goods	888.3	920.9	937.4
Services	170.4	176.2	177.9
Government consumption expenditures and gross investment	**1,454.6**	**1,464.9**	**1,480.7**
Federal	520.2	511.6	520.3
National defense	346.0	331.6	339.2
Nondefense	174.3	180.0	181.1
State and local	934.4	953.3	960.4

(1) Seasonally adjusted at annual rates.

Countries With Highest Gross Domestic Product and Per Capita GDP[1]

Source: Central Intelligence Agency, *The World Factbook 1997*; Bureau of Economic Analysis, U.S. Dept. of Commerce

Gross Domestic Product[2]

(billions of dollars; 1996 estimates unless otherwise noted)

1. United States	$7,661.6	21. Taiwan	$315.0
2. China	3,390.0[4]	22. Argentina	296.9
3. Japan	2,850.0	23. Pakistan	296.5
4. Germany	1,700.0	24. Poland	246.3
5. India	1,538.0	25. South Africa	227.0
6. France	1,220.0	26. Malaysia	214.7
7. United Kingdom	1,190.0[2]	27. Saudi Arabia	205.6
8. Italy	1,120.0	28. Belgium	204.8
9. Brazil	1,022.0	29. Colombia	201.4
10. Indonesia	779.7	30. Venezuela	197.0
11. Mexico	777.3	31. Philippines	194.2
12. Russia	767.0[5]	32. Sweden	184.3
13. Canada	721.0	33. Egypt	183.9
14. South Korea	647.2	34. Switzerland	161.3
15. Spain	593.0	35. Ukraine	161.1[5]
16. Thailand	455.7	36. Austria	157.6
17. Australia	430.5	37. Bangladesh	155.1
18. Turkey	379.1	38. Nigeria	143.5
19. Iran	343.5	39. Portugal	122.1
20. Netherlands	317.8	40. Chile	120.6

Per Capita Gross Domestic Product[3]

(dollars; 1996 estimates unless otherwise noted)

1. United States	$28,600	21. Austria	$19,700
2. Norway	26,200	22. Italy	19,600
3. Canada	25,000	23. Finland	19,000
3. Monaco	25,000	24. Bahamas	18,700[7]
5. Luxembourg	24,500[7]	25. New Zealand	18,500
6. U. Arab Emirates	23,800	26. Andorra	18,000[7]
7. Australia	23,600	27. San Marino	16,900[6]
8. Liechtenstein	23,000	28. Ireland	16,800
9. Denmark	22,700	29. Kuwait	16,700
9. Japan	22,700	30. Israel	16,400
11. Switzerland	22,600	31. Brunei	15,800[7]
12. Qatar	21,300	32. Spain	15,300
13. Singapore	21,200	33. Taiwan	14,700
14. France	20,900	34. South Korea	14,200
15. Sweden	20,800	35. Cyprus	13,700[8]
16. Netherlands	20,500	36. Trinidad & Tob.	13,500
17. United Kingdom	20,400	37. Bahrain	13,000
17. Germany	20,400	38. Malta	12,600
19. Belgium	20,300	39. Portugal	12,400
20. Iceland	19,800	40. Slovenia	12,300

(1) International data are from CIA's *The World Factbook;* U.S. data are supplied by the Bureau of Economic Analysis. International GDP estimates are derived from purchasing power parity calculations, which involve the use of intl. dollar price weights applied to the quantities of goods and services produced in a given economy. (2) The former British colony of Hong Kong (part of China from July 1, 1997) had a GDP of $163.6 billion in 1996. (3) These territories had large per capita GDPs: Bermuda (UK) $29,000, Hong Kong (then UK, now China) $26,000, Cayman Islands (UK) $23,800, Aruba (Neth.) $21,000, Guam (U.S.) $19,000, Faroe Islands (Den.) $16,300, Greenland (Den., 1995) $15,500, Macao (Port.) $13,600. (4) 1996 estimate as extrapolated from World Bank estimate with use of official Chinese growth figures for 1996; may overstate the GDP by as much as 25%. (5) 1996 estimate as extrapolated from World Bank estimate for 1994. (6) 1994 estimate. (7) 1995 estimate. (8) Does not include Turkish-held area.

Chapter 11

Chapter 11 refers to the provisions in the Federal Bankruptcy Code for court-supervised reorganization of debtor companies. A company files for Chapter 11 protection when it can no longer pay its creditors or when it expects future liabilities it cannot hope to pay, such as product liability damage awards. In 1991, the U.S. Supreme Court ruled that the provision of federal bankruptcy law that permits corporations to reorganize while continuing to operate was also available for use by individuals. The Bankruptcy Reform Act of 1994 further amended Chapter 11.

Process

1. Bankruptcy filing imposes an automatic stay.

- Creditors generally cannot file or continue suits for repayment.
- Debts are frozen and creditors generally must stop collection actions. This is called the "automatic stay."
- Debtor's day-to-day operations continue.
- Spending, borrowing, and asset sales outside of the debtor's normal course of business must be approved by the court.
- Secured creditors can ask the court for exemption from the automatic stay to undertake or continue to recover the collateral that secures their claim.

2. Unsecured creditors form a committee.

- The U.S. trustee appoints the committee, which ordinarily consists of the 7 largest unsecured creditors who are willing to serve on the panel.
- The U.S. trustee can appoint additional committees to represent other creditors and shareholders.
- The committee chooses representatives to deal with the debtor company.
- The committee and U.S. trustee oversee the debtor's business operations.
- Creditors and the U.S. trustee can ask the court to appoint an examiner to investigate possible fraud or mismanagement.
- Creditors and the U.S. trustee can ask the court to order the appointment of a case trustee to run the debtor company.
- If the court orders the appointment, the U.S. trustee selects the case trustee unless a party asks that creditors be allowed to elect the case trustee.

3. The committee, other creditors, and the debtor company negotiate a reorganization plan.

- Parties negotiate a plan for the reorganization of the debtor's business and repayment of frozen debts. This step can take months or years.
- Only the debtor can file a reorganization plan with the court for the first 120 days of the bankruptcy case. The court can extend the so-called "exclusivity" period and often does so.
- If the debtor does not file a plan during the exclusivity period, if the debtor's plan is not approved by the court, or if a trustee is appointed, any party can file a plan.

(continued)

Chapter 11 *(continued)*

- The proponent of the plan prepares a disclosure statement, which must be approved by the court at a separate hearing.

4. Creditors and shareholders vote on the plan.

- Only creditors and shareholders whose claims and interests are impaired or affected by the plan vote on it.
- A class of creditors accepts the plan if the plan is approved by creditors who hold more than half of the claims in the class by number and at least two-thirds of the claims by amount.
- A class of shareholders accepts the plan if the plan is approved by shareholders who hold at least two-thirds of the equity interest in the class by amount.

5. Judge considers the plan.

- The bankruptcy judge approves the plan if it complies with the Bankruptcy Code and all impaired classes approve.
- If at least one of the impaired classes approves the plan and it meets certain statutory tests, the judge can confirm the plan in a so-called "cramdown," even if not all impaired classes approve.

6. Reorganized company emerges.

- Generally, the debtor's debts are discharged.
- The debtor and creditors must comply with the confirmed plan.
- The automatic stay ends and a permanent injunction goes into effect against any effort to collect prepetition debts other than as provided in the plan.
- The reorganized debtor operates like a normal company.
- Only about 17% of the debtors who file Chapter 11 cases get their plans confirmed.

Expedited Procedure for Small Businesses

- The Bankruptcy Reform Act of 1994 included an expedited confirmation process to be used in Chapter 11 cases filed by small businesses.
- The debtor can elect to use the new process if it has less than $2 million in debts and its primary business is not owning or operating real estate.
- The court can order that a creditors' committee not be appointed.
- Unless the court orders otherwise, the debtor's exclusivity period for filing a plan is shortened to 100 days and all plans must be filed within 160 days.
- The court may conditionally approve the disclosure statement. This saves time by combining the court hearing on the disclosure statement with the hearing on confirmation of the plan.

State Finances
Revenue, Expenditures, Debt, and Taxes

Source: Census Bureau, U.S. Dept. of Commerce

(fiscal year 1996)

State	Revenue (millions)	Expenditures (millions)	Debt (millions)	Per capita[1] debt	Per capita[1] taxes	Per capita[1] expenditures
Alabama	$12,741	$12,127	$3,645	$853	$1,230	$2,838
Alaska	8,254	5,630	3,177	5,233	2,503	9,274
Arizona	12,594	11,898	2,936	663	1,447	2,687
Arkansas	8,653	7,050	2,142	853	1,478	2,809
California	123,342	113,361	45,859	1,439	1,811	3,556
Colorado	11,866	10,312	3,577	936	1,261	2,697
Connecticut	14,349	13,530	16,415	5,014	2,392	4,132
Delaware	3,619	3,248	4,279	5,901	2,329	4,480
Florida	41,680	36,454	15,515	1,077	1,368	2,532
Georgia	22,409	20,013	6,200	843	1,400	2,722
Hawaii	6,383	5,947	5,117	4,322	2,601	5,023
Idaho	4,384	3,501	1,454	1,223	1,562	2,945
Illinois	36,991	34,111	22,676	1,914	1,458	2,879
Indiana	16,550	15,368	6,117	1,047	1,444	2,631
Iowa	9,245	8,853	2,065	724	1,557	3,104
Kansas	7,864	7,276	1,161	452	1,547	2,829
Kentucky	13,788	11,842	7,030	1,810	1,671	3,049
Louisiana	14,296	14,030	7,452	1,713	1,128	3,225
Maine	4,267	4,240	3,160	2,542	1,526	3,411
Maryland	16,041	15,554	9,691	1,911	1,610	3,067
Massachusetts	25,197	24,950	29,295	4,809	2,045	4,095
Michigan	38,047	35,080	13,668	1,425	1,994	3,656
Minnesota	20,525	17,325	4,858	1,043	2,199	3,719
Mississippi	8,865	8,217	2,232	822	1,421	3,025
Missouri	17,051	12,841	7,128	1,330	1,345	2,396
Montana	3,476	3,136	2,244	2,553	1,429	3,568
Nebraska	4,999	4,490	1,402	849	1,434	2,718
Nevada	5,997	4,831	2,259	1,409	1,802	3,014
New Hampshire	3,561	3,240	5,833	5,020	720	2,788
New Jersey	35,857	32,315	25,602	3,205	1,801	4,045
New Mexico	8,129	6,740	2,147	1,253	1,787	3,935
New York	94,277	82,420	73,122	4,021	1,878	4,532
North Carolina	23,387	21,221	4,513	616	1,623	2,898
North Dakota	2,569	2,064	819	1,272	1,530	3,204
Ohio	43,823	35,517	12,628	1,130	1,401	3,179
Oklahoma	10,609	9,265	3,889	1,178	1,399	2,807
Oregon	15,432	11,858	6,086	1,900	1,378	3,701
Pennsylvania	42,796	38,699	15,046	1,248	1,518	3,210
Rhode Island	4,271	4,061	5,506	5,561	1,565	4,102
South Carolina	12,602	12,400	5,324	1,439	1,382	3,352
South Dakota	2,284	1,975	1,704	2,328	998	2,698
Tennessee	14,749	13,829	3,069	577	1,163	2,599
Texas	51,118	46,082	14,576	762	1,112	2,409
Utah	6,773	6,172	2,464	1,232	1,457	3,086
Vermont	2,146	2,061	1,718	2,917	1,428	3,499
Virginia	20,072	17,717	8,793	1,317	1,333	2,654
Washington	24,790	21,086	8,991	1,625	1,913	3,811
West Virginia	6,866	6,970	2,830	1,550	1,517	3,817
Wisconsin	25,072	16,990	9,127	1,769	1,995	3,293
Wyoming	2,348	2,062	799	1,661	1,301	4,287
UNITED STATES[2]	**967,005**	**859,959**	**447,339**	**1,690**	**1,583**	**3,248**

(1) Per capita amounts are based on population figures of the resident U.S. population (excluding the District of Columbia) as of July 1, 1996. (2) Totals in this line may not add because of rounding.

State and Local Government Receipts and Current Expenditures

Source: Bureau of Economic Analysis, U.S. Dept. of Commerce

(billions of dollars)

	1996[R]	1997	First Quarter 1998[1]
Receipts	**$1,045.2**	**$1,094.3**	**$1,123.3**
Personal tax and nontax receipts	203.5	219.9	230.4
Income taxes	151.9	164.3	172.3
Nontaxes	29.5	32.0	33.6
Other	22.1	23.6	24.5
Corporate profits tax accruals	33.1	36.0	35.1
Indirect business tax and nontax accruals	511.9	533.4	548.0
Sales taxes	252.0	261.5	268.4
Property taxes	202.7	209.1	213.9
Other	57.2	62.8	65.7
Contributions for social insurance	77.8	79.9	81.1
Federal grants-in-aid	218.9	225.0	228.7
Current expenditures	**922.6**	**960.1**	**983.0**
Consumption expenditures	724.7	758.8	776.7
Transfer payments to persons	293.5	304.1	312.6
Net interest paid	$–71.3	$–77.4	$–80.7
Interest paid	63.3	63.3	63.6
Less: Interest received by government	134.5	140.6	144.3
Less: Dividends received by government	13.7	14.8	15.7
Subsidies less current surplus of government enterprises	–10.7	–10.6	–9.9
Subsidies	0.4	0.4	0.4
Less: Current surplus of government enterprises	11.0	10.9	10.3
Less: Wage accruals less disbursements	0.0	0.0	0.0
Surplus or deficit (–), national income and product accounts	**122.6**	**134.1**	**140.2**

(R) Revised figures. (1) Seasonally adjusted at annual rates.

State and Local Government Current Expenditures and Gross Investment, by Function

Source: Bureau of Economic Analysis, U.S. Dept. Of Commerce

(millions of dollars)

	1996			1997		
	Total[1]	Current Expends.	Gross Invest-ment[2]	Total[1]	Current Expends.	Gross Invest-ment[2]
TOTAL	**$1,084,663**	**$922,571**	**$162,092**	**$1,135,758**	**$960,147**	**$175,611**
Central executive, legislative, and judicial activities	**66,708**	**63,465**	**3,243**	**71,725**	**68,150**	**3,575**
Administrative, legislative, and judicial activities	36,807	34,688	2,119	38,921	36,593	2,328
Tax collection and financial management	29,901	28,777	1,124	32,804	31,557	1,247
Civilian safety	**112,194**	**104,597**	**7,597**	**118,689**	**110,537**	**8,152**
Police	50,382	47,749	2,633	53,218	50,390	2,828
Fire	19,496	17,975	1,521	20,297	18,613	1,684
Correction	42,316	38,873	3,443	45,174	41,534	3,640
Education	**388,080**	**352,079**	**36,001**	**407,721**	**367,955**	**39,766**
Elementary and secondary	296,980	271,668	25,312	312,962	284,993	27,969
Higher	66,887	57,247	9,640	70,195	59,693	10,502
Libraries	5,454	4,836	618	5,747	5,104	643
Other	18,759	18,328	431	18,817	18,165	652
Health and hospitals	**27,652**	**22,237**	**5,415**	**27,450**	**21,827**	**5,623**
Health	25,476	23,649	1,827	26,408	24,406	2,002
Hospitals	2,176	–1,412	3,588	1,042	–2,579	3,621
Income support, social security, and welfare	**245,655**	**244,892**	**763**	**255,974**	**255,216**	**758**
Govt. employees retirement and disability	–2,387	–2,387	—	1,768	1,768	—
Workers' compensation and temporary disability insurance	9,811	9,811	—	10,021	10,021	—
Medical care	163,610	163,610	—	169,123	169,123	—
Welfare and social services	74,621	73,858	763	75,062	74,304	758
Veterans' benefits and services	**269**	**148**	**21**	**277**	**260**	**17**
Housing and community services	**28,640**	**4,282**	**24,358**	**30,877**	**5,525**	**25,352**
Housing, comm. dev., urban renewal	5,319	1,579	3,740	6,852	2,899	3,953
Water	5,770	–3,265	9,035	6,308	–3,428	9,736
Sewerage	10,423	455	9,968	10,612	597	10,015
Sanitation	7,128	5,513	1,615	7,105	5,457	1,648
Recreational and cultural activities	**16,648**	**12,234**	**4,414**	**17,142**	**12,388**	**4,754**
Energy	**–3,573**	**–7,518**	**3,945**	**–3,250**	**–7,688**	**4,438**
Gas utilities	–918	–1,224	306	–1,139	–1,404	265
Electric utilities	–2,655	–6,294	3,639	–2,111	–6,284	4,173
Agriculture	**4,504**	**4,247**	**257**	**4,643**	**4,379**	**264**
Natural resources	**11,481**	**9,066**	**2,415**	**11,897**	**9,331**	**2,566**
Transportation	**126,383**	**65,238**	**61,145**	**134,408**	**67,866**	**66,542**
Highways	100,371	52,453	47,918	106,923	54,610	52,313
Water	1,572	63	1,509	1,705	71	1,634
Air	2,459	–1,199	3,658	2,741	–1,268	4,009
Transit and railroad	21,981	13,921	8,060	23,039	14,453	8,586
Economic development, regulation, and services	**8,090**	**7,734**	**356**	**8,488**	**8,103**	**385**
Labor training and services	**5,484**	**5,360**	**124**	**5,474**	**5,345**	**129**
Commercial activities	**–12,572**	**–12,840**	**268**	**–13,919**	**–14,224**	**305**
Publicly owned liquor store systems	–624	–635	11	–648	–658	10
Govt.-administered lotteries, parimutuels	–12,239	–12,239	—	–13,527	–13,527	—
Other	291	34	257	256	–39	295
Net interest paid[2]	**–2,117**	**–2,117**	—	**–6,452**	**–6,452**	—
Other and unallocable	**61,137**	**49,367**	**11,770**	**64,614**	**51,629**	**12,985**

(1) Sum of current expenditures and gross investment. (2) Excludes interest received by social insurance funds, which is netted against expenditures for the appropriate functions.

Banks in the U.S.—Number, Deposits

Source: Federal Deposit Insurance Corp. (as of Dec. 31, 1997)

Comprises all FDIC-insured commercial and savings banks, including savings and loan institutions (S&Ls).

	TOTAL NUMBER OF BANKS					TOTAL DEPOSITS (millions of dollars)				
		Commercial banks[1]					Commercial banks[1]			
Year	ALL BANKS	Natl.	State	Non-members	All savings	ALL DEPOSITS	Natl.	State	Non-members	All savings
1935	**15,295**	5,386	1,001	7,735	1,173	**$ 45,102**[2]	$24,802	$13,653	$5,669	$978[2]
1940	**15,772**	5,144	1,342	6,956	2,330	**67,494**	35,787	20,642	7,040	4,025
1945	**15,969**	5,017	1,864	6,421	2,667	**151,524**	77,778	41,865	16,307	15,574
1950	**16,500**	4,958	1,912	6,576	3,054	**171,963**	84,941	41,602	19,726	25,694
1955	**17,001**	4,692	1,847	6,698	3,764	**235,211**	102,796	55,739	26,198	50,478
1960	**17,549**	4,530	1,641	6,955	4,423	**310,262**	120,242	65,487	34,369	90,164
1965	**18,384**	4,815	1,405	7,327	4,837	**467,633**	185,334	78,327	51,982	151,990
1970	**18,205**	4,621	1,147	7,743	4,694	**686,901**	285,436	101,512	95,566	204,367
1975	**18,792**	4,744	1,046	8,595	4,407	**1,157,648**	450,308	143,409	187,031	376,900
1980	**18,763**	4,425	997	9,013	4,328	**1,832,716**	656,752	191,183	344,311	640,470
1985	**18,033**	4,959	1,070	8,378	3,626	**3,140,827**	1,241,875	354,585	521,628	1,022,739
1990	**15,158**	3,979	1,009	7,355	2,815	**3,637,292**	1,558,915	397,797	693,438	987,142
1993	**13,220**	3,304	969	6,685	2,262	**3,528,487**	1,576,725	476,093	701,512	774,157
1994	**12,603**	3,075	976	6,400	2,152	**3,611,618**	1,630,171	533,261	711,006	737,180
1995	**11,970**	2,858	1,042	6,040	2,030	**3,769,477**	1,695,817	614,924	716,829	741,907
1996	**11,670**	2,763	1,024	5,902	1,981	**3,788,905**	1,795,110	567,809	698,497	727,489
1997	**9,143**	2,597	992	5,554	1,779	**3,421,696**	2,004,855	729,009	687,832	704,115

(1) "Nonmembers" are banks that are not members of the Federal Reserve System; "National" and "State" institutions are members. (2) Figures for 1935 do not include data for S&Ls (not available).

Largest U.S. Bank Holding Companies

Source: *American Banker* (as of Dec. 31, 1997)

Bank Holding Company	Assets (millions)
Chase Manhattan Corp., New York, NY	$365,521
Citicorp, New York, NY	310,897
NationsBank, Charlotte, NC	264,562
J.P. Morgan & Co., New York, NY	262,159
BankAmerica Corp., San Francisco, CA	260,159
First Union Corp., Charlotte, NC	157,274
Bankers Trust New York Corp., New York, NY	140,102
Bank One Corp., Columbus, OH	115,901
First Chicago NBD Corp	114,096
Wells Fargo Bank, San Francisco, CA	97,456
Norwest Corp., Minneapolis, MN	88,540
Fleet Financial Group Inc., Boston, MA	85,535
PNC Bank Corp., Pittsburgh, PA	75,120
KeyCorp., Cleveland, OH	73,699
U.S. Bancorp Inc., Minneapolis, MN	71,295
BankBoston Corp.	69,268
Wachovia Corp., Winston-Salem, NC	65,397
Bank of New York, NY	59,953
SunTrust Banks Inc., Atlanta, GA	57,983
Republic New York Corp., New York, NY	55,638
National City Corp., Cleveland, OH	54,686
CoreStates Financial Corp., Philadelphia, PA	48,461
Barnett Banks Inc., Jacksonville, FL	46,438
Mellon Bank Corp., Pittsburgh, PA	44,892
State Street Corp., Boston, MA	37,975

Bank Holding Company	Assets (millions)
Comerica Inc., Detroit, MI	$36,292
HSBC Americas Inc., Buffalo, NY	31,518
SouthTrust Corp., Birmingham, AL	30,906
Unionbancal Corp., San Francisco, CA	30,585
Summit Bancorp, Princeton, NJ	29,964
Mercantile Bancorp, Inc., St. Louis, MO	29,955
BB&T Corp., Winston-Salem, NC	29,178
Huntington Bancshares Inc., Columbus, OH	26,730
Northern Trust Corp., Chicago, IL	25,315
Crestar Financial Corp., Richmond, VA	24,900
LaSalle National Corp., Chicago, IL	24,876
Regions Financial Corp., Birmingham, AL	23,034
Harris Bankcorp, Chicago, IL	22,224
Fifth Third Bancorp, Cincinnati, OH	21,375
MBNA Corp., Wilmington, DE	21,305
First of America Bank Corp., Kalamazoo, MI	21,080
Firstar Corp., Milwaukee, WI	19,844
Marshall & Ilsley Corp., Milwaukee, WI	19,477
Popular Inc., San Juan, PR	19,300
AmSouth Bancorp, Birmingham, AL	18,622
Union Planters Corp., Memphis, TN	18,105
First Security Corp., Salt Lake City, UT	17,307
Citizens Financial Group, Inc., Providence, RI	16,791
Pacific Century Financial Corp., Honolulu, HI	14,996
First Empire State Corp., Buffalo, NY	14,003

U.S. Bank Failures

Source: Federal Deposit Insurance Corp.

Year	Closed or assisted	Year	Closed or assisted	Year	Closed or assisted	Year	Closed or assisted	Year	Closed or assisted
1934	61	1960	2	1971	6	1982	42	1990	169
1935	32	1961	9	1972	3	1983	48	1991	127
1936	72	1963	2	1973	6	1984	80	1992	122
1937	84	1964	8	1975	14	1985	120	1993	41
1938	81	1965	9	1976	17	1986	145	1994	13
1939	72	1966	8	1978	7	1987	203	1995	6
1940	48	1967	4	1979	10	1988	221	1996	5
1955	5	1969	9	1980	11	1989	207	1997	1
1959	3	1970	8	1981	10				

World's Largest Banking Companies[1]

Source: *American Banker* (Aug. 1998)

Banks	Assets (millions)
Bank of Tokyo-Mitsubishi Ltd., Tokyo, Japan	$691,920
Deutsche Bank, AG, Frankfurt, Germany	580,069
Sumitomo Bank Ltd., Osaka Japan	483,730
Credit Suisse Group, Zurich, Switzerland	473,830
HSBC Holdings, Plc., London, United Kingdom	471,038
Dai-Ichl Kangyo Bank Ltd., Tokyo, Japan	433,103
Sanwa Bank Ltd., Osaka, Japan	427,980
Credit Agricole Mutual, Paris, France	419,763
Fuji Bank Ltd., Tokyo, Japan	414,173
ABN-AMRO Bank, N.V., Amsterdam, Netherlands	412,772
Societe Generale, Paris, France	410,842
Sakura Bank Ltd., Tokyo, Japan	399,492
Union Bank of Switzerland, Zurich, Switzerland	395,087
Norin Chunkin Bank, Tokyo, Japan	392,554
BarclaysBank Plc., London, United Kingdom	385,950
Dresdner Bank, Frankfurt, Germany	371,371
Industrial Bank of Japan Ltd., Tokyo, Japan	369,954
Chase Manhattan Corp., New York, United States	365,521
Banque Nationale de Paris, France	339,648
Westdeutsche Landesbank Girozentrale, Düsseldorf, Ger.	335,816
Citicorp, New York, United States	310,897
ING Bank, Amsterdam, Netherlands	307,560
NatWest Group, London, United Kingdom	304,942
Swiss Bank Corporation, Basel, Switzerland	300,259
Commerzbank, Frankfurt, Germany	286,947
Mitsubishi Trust & Banking Corp., Tokyo, Japan	269,524
NationsBank Corp., Charlotte, N.C., United States	$264,562
Tokal Bank Ltd., Nagoya, Japan	262,424
JP Morgan & Co., Inc., New York, United States	262,159
BankAmerica Corp., San Francisco, United States	260,159
Lloyds TSB Group Inc., London, United Kingdom	260,043
Sumitomo Trust & Banking Co., Ltd., Osaka, Japan	254,190
Credit Lyonnais, Paris, France	250,150
Bayerische Vereinsbank AG, Munich, Germany	249,831
Abbey National Plc, London, United Kingdom	248,040
Compagnie Financiere de Paribas, Paris, France	245,061
Mitsui Trust & Banking Co., Ltd., Tokyo, Japan	241,916
Bayerische Landesbank Girozentrale, Munich, Ger.	241,714
Asahi Bank, Ltd., Tokyo, Japan	219,939
Halifax Plc, Leeds, United Kingdom	215,625
Rabobank Group, Utrecht, Netherlands	208,740
Deutsche Genossenschaftsbank, Frankfurt, Ger..	207,769
Bayerische Hypotheken-und Wechsel-Bank AG, Munich, Ger.	203,567
Dexia Belgium, Brussels, Belgium	202,959
Bankgesellschaft Berlin AG, Berlin, Germany	197,365
Long Term Credit Bank of Japan, Tokyo, Japan	188,497
Royal Bank of Canada, Toronto, Canada	171,219
Grupo Santander, Spain	170,927
Canadian Imperial Bank of Commerce, Toronto, Canada	166,472
Yasuda Trust & Banking Co., Ltd., Tokyo, Japan.	165,784

(1) Includes bank holding companies and commercial and savings banks. **Note:** Data for U.S. companies listed include assets not included in "Largest U.S. Commercial Banks" table.

Federal Deposit Insurance Corporation (FDIC)

The Federal Deposit Insurance Corporation (FDIC) is the independent deposit insurance agency created by Congress to maintain stability and public confidence in the nation's banking system. In its unique role as deposit insurer of banks and savings associations, and in cooperation with other federal and state regulatory agencies, the FDIC seeks to promote the safety and soundness of insured depository institutions in the U.S. financial system by identifying, monitoring, and addressing risks to the deposit insurance funds. The FDIC aims at promoting public understanding and sound public policies by providing financial and economic information and analyses. It seeks to minimize disruptive effects from the failure of banks and savings associations. It seeks to ensure fairness in the sale of financial products and the provision of financial services.

The FDIC's income consists of assessments on insured banks and income from investments; it receives no appropriations from Congress. The Corporation may borrow from the U.S. Treasury, not to exceed $30 billion outstanding, but the agency has made no such borrowings since it was organized in 1933. The FDIC's Bank Insurance Fund was $28.9 billion (unaudited) and the Savings Association Insurance Fund stood at $9.6 billion (unaudited), as of June 30, 1998.

Federal Reserve Board Discount Rate

The discount rate is the rate of interest set by the Federal Reserve that member banks are charged when borrowing money through the Federal Reserve System. Includes any changes through Oct. 1998.

Effective date	Rate
1980:	
Feb. 15	13
May 30	12
June 13	11
July 28	
Sept. 26	
Nov. 17	12
Dec. 5	10
1981:	11
May 5	14
Nov. 2	13
Dec. 4	12
1982:	
July 20	11½
Aug. 2	11
Aug. 16	10½
Aug. 27	10
Oct. 12	9½
Nov. 22	9
Dec. 15	8½
1984:	
April 9	9
Nov. 21	8½
Dec. 24	8
1985:	
May 20	7½
1986:	
March 7	7
April 21	6½
July 11	6
Aug. 21	5½
1987:	
Sept. 4	6
1988:	
Aug. 9	6½
1989:	
Feb. 24	7
1990:	
Dec. 18	6½
1991:	
Apr. 30	5½
Sept. 13	5
Nov. 6	4½
Dec. 20	3½
1992:	
July 3	3
1994:	
May 17	3½
Aug. 16	4
Nov. 15	4¾
1995:	
Feb. 1	5¼
1996:	
Jan. 31	5
1998:	
Oct. 15	4¾

Federal Reserve System

The Federal Reserve System is the central bank for the U.S. The system was established on Dec. 23, 1913, originally to give the country an elastic currency, to provide facilities for discounting commercial paper, and to improve the supervision of banking. Since then, the system's responsibilities have been broadened. Over the years, stability and growth of the economy, a high level of employment, stability in the purchasing power of the dollar, and reasonable balance in transactions with other countries have come to be recognized as primary objectives of governmental economic policy.

The Federal Reserve System consists of the Board of Governors, the 12 District Reserve Banks and their branch offices, and the Federal Open Market Committee. Several advisory councils help the board meet its varied responsibilities.

The hub of the system is the 7-member Board of Governors in Washington. The members of the board are appointed by the president and confirmed by the Senate, to serve 14-year terms. The president also appoints the chairman and vice chairman of the board from among the board members for 4-year terms that may be renewed. As of Oct. 1998 the board members were: Alan Greenspan, Chair; Alice M. Rivlin, Vice Chair; Edward W. Kelley Jr.; Roger W. Ferguson Jr.; Edward M. Gramlich; and Laurence H. Meyer; there was 1 vacancy.

The board is the policy-making body. In addition to those responsibilities, it supervises the budget and operations of the Reserve Banks, approves the appointments of their presidents, and appoints 3 of each District Bank's directors, including the chairman and vice chairman of each Reserve Bank's board.

(continued)

The 12 Reserve Banks and their branch offices serve as the decentralized portion of the system, carrying out day-to-day operations such as circulating currency and coin and providing fiscal agency functions and payments mechanism services. The District Banks are in Boston, New York, Philadelphia, Cleveland, Richmond, Atlanta, Chicago, St. Louis, Minneapolis, Kansas City, Dallas, and San Francisco.

The system's principal function is monetary policy, which it controls using 3 tools: reserve requirements, the discount rate, and open market operations. Uniform reserve requirements, set by the board, are applied to the transaction accounts and nonpersonal time deposits of all depository institutions. Responsibility for setting the discount rate (the interest rate at which depository institutions can borrow money from the Reserve Banks) is shared by the Board of Governors and the Reserve Banks. Changes in the discount rate are recommended by the individual boards of directors of the Reserve Banks and are subject to approval by the Board of Governors.

The most important tool of monetary policy is open market operations (the purchase and sale of government securities). Responsibility for influencing the cost and availability of money and credit through the purchase and sale of government securities lies with the Federal Open Market Committee (FOMC), which is composed of the 7 members of the Board of Governors, the president of the Federal Reserve Bank of New York, and 4 other Federal Reserve Bank presidents, who each serve one-year terms on a rotating basis. The committee bases its decisions on economic and financial developments and outlook, setting yearly growth objectives for key measures of money supply and credit. The decisions of the committee are carried out by the Domestic Trading Desk of the Federal Reserve Bank of New York.

The Federal Reserve Act prescribes a Federal Advisory Council, consisting of 1 member from each Federal Reserve District, who is elected annually by the Board of Directors of each of the 12 Federal Reserve Banks. The council meets with the Federal Reserve Board 4 times a year to discuss business and financial conditions and make advisory recommendations.

The Consumer Advisory Council is a statutory body, including both consumer and creditor representatives, which advises the Board of Governors on its implementation of consumer regulations and other consumer-related matters.

Following the passage of the Monetary Control Act of 1980, the Board of Governors established the Thrift Institutions Advisory Council to provide information and views on the special needs and problems of thrift institutions. The group is composed of representatives of mutual savings banks, savings and loan associations, and credit unions.

United States Mint

Source: United States Mint, U.S. Dept. of the Treasury

The United States Mint was created on Apr. 2, 1792, by an act of Congress, which established the U.S. national coinage system. Supervision of the mint was a function of the secretary of state, but in 1799 the mint became an independent agency reporting directly to the president. The mint was made a statutory bureau of the Treasury Department in 1873, with a director appointed by the president to oversee its operations.

The mint manufactures and ships all U.S. coins for circulation to Federal Reserve banks and branches, which issue coins to the public and business community through depository institutions. The mint also safeguards the Treasury Department's stored gold and silver and other monetary assets.

The composition of dimes, quarters, and half dollars, traditionally produced from silver, was changed by the Coinage Act of 1965, which mandated that these coins be minted from a cupronickel-clad alloy and reduced the silver content of the half dollar to 40%. In 1970, legislative action mandated that the half dollar and a dollar coin be minted from the same alloy.

The Eisenhower dollar was minted from 1971 through 1978, when legislation called for the minting of the smaller Susan B. Anthony dollar coin. The Anthony dollar, which was minted from 1979 through 1981, marked the first time that a woman, other than a mythical figure, appeared on a U.S. coin produced for general circulation.

Mint headquarters are in Washington, DC. Mint production facilities are in Philadelphia, Denver, San Francisco, and West Point, NY. In addition, the mint is responsible for the U.S. Bullion Depository at Fort Knox, KY.

Proof coin sets, silver proof coin sets, and uncirculated coin sets are available from the mint. The mint also produces ongoing series of national and historic medals in honor of significant persons, events, and sites.

Since 1982, the mint has produced the following congressionally authorized commemorative coins: 1982 George Washington half dollar; 1984 U.S. Olympic coins; 1986 U.S. Statue of Liberty coins; 1987 Bicentennial of the U.S. Constitution coins; 1989 U.S. Congressional coins; 1990 Eisenhower Centennial coin; 1991 United Services Organization 59th Anniversary coin; 1991 Korean War Memorial coin; 1991 Mount Rushmore Anniversary coins; 1992 U.S. Olympic coins; 1992 White House 200th Anniversary coin; 1992 Christopher Columbus Quincentenary coins; 1993 Bill of Rights coins; 1993 World War II 50th Anniversary coins; 1994 World Cup USA coins; Thomas Jefferson 250th Anniversary coin; U.S. Veterans coins (featuring the Prisoner of War coin, Vietnam Veterans Memorial coin, and Women in Military Service for America coin); Bicentennial of the U.S. Capitol Commemorative Silver Dollar; 1995 Civil War Battlefield coins; 1995/1996 U.S. Olympic Games of the Atlanta Centennial Games; 1997 U.S. Botanic Garden Silver Dollar; 1997 Franklin Delano Roosevelt Gold coin; 1997 Gold and Silver Jackie Robinson Commemorative coins; 1997 National Law Enforcement Memorial Silver Dollar; Black Revolutionary War Patriots Silver Dollar; Robert F. Kennedy Silver Dollar; and the National Law Enforcement Officers Memorial Silver Dollar.

The congressionally authorized American Eagle gold, platinum, and silver bullion coins are available through dealers worldwide. The gold and platinum eagles are sold in one-ounce, half-ounce, quarter-ounce, and one-tenth-ounce sizes. The American eagle silver bullion coin contains one troy ounce of .999 fine silver and is priced according to the daily market value of silver. These coins also are available in proof condition, separately priced.

The mint offers free public tours and operates sales centers at the U.S. mints in Denver and Philadelphia; it also operates a sales center at Union Station, in Washington, DC.

Further information is available from the U.S. Mint, Customer Service Center, 10003 Derekwood Ln., Lanham, MD 20706. Telephone: (202) 283-COIN. Website: http:/www.usmint.gov

Portraits on U.S. Treasury Bills, Bonds, Notes, and Savings Bonds

Denomination	Savings bonds	Treasury bills*	Treasury bonds*	Treasury notes*
$50	Washington		Jefferson	
75	Adams			
100	Jefferson		Jackson	
200	Madison			
500	Hamilton		Washington	
1,000	Franklin	H. McCulloch	Lincoln	Lincoln
5,000	Revere	J. G. Carlisle	Monroe	Monroe
10,000	J. Wilson	J. Sherman	Cleveland	Cleveland
50,000		C. Glass		
100,000		A. Gallatin	Grant	Grant
1,000,000		O. Wolcott	T. Roosevelt	T. Roosevelt
100,000,000				Madison
500,000,000				McKinley

*The U.S. Treasury discontinued issuing treasury bill, bond, and note certificates in 1986. Since then, all issues of marketable treasury securities have been available only in book-entry form, although some certificates remain in circulation.

Denominations of U.S. Currency

Since 1969 the largest denomination of U.S. currency that has been issued is the $100 bill. As larger-denomination bills reach the Federal Reserve Bank, they are removed from circulation. Because some discontinued currency is expected to be in the hands of holders for many years, the description of the various denominations below is continued.

Amt.	Portrait	Embellishment on back	Amt.	Portrait	Embellishment on back
$1	Washington	Great Seal of U.S.	$100	Franklin	Independence Hall
2	Jefferson	Signers of Declaration	500	McKinley	Ornate denominational marking
5	Lincoln	Lincoln Memorial	1,000	Cleveland	Ornate denominational marking
10	Hamilton	U.S. Treasury	5,000	Madison	Ornate denominational marking
20	Jackson	White House	10,000	Chase	Ornate denominational marking
50	Grant	U.S. Capitol	100,000*	W. Wilson	Ornate denominational marking

*For use only in transactions between Federal Reserve System and Treasury Department.

U.S. Currency and Coin

Source: Financial Management Service, U.S. Dept. of the Treasury (Mar. 31, 1998)

Amounts Outstanding and in Circulation

Currency	Total currency and coin	Total currency	Federal Reserve notes[1]	U.S. notes	Currency no longer issued
Amounts outstanding	$578,754,228,818	$553,616,700,920	$553,090,040,787	$270,822,616	$255,837,517
Less amounts held by:					
Treasury	262,467,444	9,038,219	8,827,757	20,739	189,723
Federal Reserve banks	103,512,965,883	102,995,156,948	102,995,153,338	—	3,610
Amounts in circulation	$474,978,795,491	$450,612,505,753	$450,086,059,692	$270,801,877	$255,644,184

Coins[2]	Total	Dollars[3]	Fractional coins
Amounts outstanding	$25,137,527,898	$2,024,703,898	$23,112,824,000
Less amounts held by:			
Treasury	253,429,225	46,161,259	207,267,966
Federal Reserve banks	517,808,935	58,910,442	458,898,493
Amounts in circulation	$24,366,289,738	$1,919,632,197	$22,446,657,541

Currency in Circulation by Denominations

Denomination	Total currency in circulation	Federal Reserve notes[1]	U.S. notes	Currency no longer issued
$1	$6,428,507,478	$6,281,226,920	$143,481	$147,137,077
$2	1,134,295,750	1,001,789,322	132,493,966	12,462
$5	7,446,247,295	7,304,074,560	110,362,210	31,810,525
$10	13,283,351,020	13,260,796,620	5,950	22,548,450
$20	82,716,154,960	82,696,050,520	3,380	20,101,060
$50	46,687,063,750	46,675,569,850	—	11,493,900
$100	292,600,123,900	292,550,339,900	27,792,800	21,991,200
$500	144,177,000	143,989,000	—	188,000
$1,000	167,389,000	167,183,000	—	206,000
$5,000	1,755,000	1,700,000	—	55,000
$10,000	3,440,000	3,340,000	—	100,000
Fractional parts	485	—	—	485
Partial notes[4]	115	—	90	25
TOTAL CURRENCY	**$450,612,505,753**	**$450,086,059,692**	**$270,801,877**	**$255,644,184**

Comparative Totals of Money in Circulation — Selected Dates

Date	Dollars (in millions)	Per capita[5]	Date	Dollars (in millions)	Per capita[5]	Date	Dollars (in millions)	Per capita[5]
Mar. 31, 1998	474,979.0	1,762.42	June 30, 1975	81,196.4	380.08	June 30, 1940	7,847.5	59.40
Mar. 31, 1997	444,534.0	1,664.58	June 30, 1970	54,351.0	265.39	June 30, 1935	5,567.1	43.75
Mar. 31, 1996	416,280.0	1,573.15	June 30, 1965	39,719.8	204.14	June 30, 1930	4,522.0	36.74
Mar. 31, 1995	401,610.0	1,531.39	June 30, 1960	32,064.6	177.47	June 30, 1925	4,815.2	41.56
Mar. 31, 1990	257,664.4	1,028.71	June 30, 1955	30,229.3	182.90	June 30, 1920	5,467.6	51.36
June 30, 1985	185,890.7	778.58	June 30, 1950	27,156.3	179.03	June 30, 1915	3,319.6	33.01
June 30, 1980	127,097.2	558.28	June 30, 1945	26,746.4	191.14	June 30, 1910	3,148.7	34.07

(1) Issued on or after July 1, 1929. (2) Excludes coin sold to collectors at premium prices. (3) Includes $481,781,898 in standard silver dollars. (4) Represents value of certain partial denominations not presented for redemption. (5) Based on Bureau of the Census estimates of population.

The requirement for a gold reserve against U.S. notes was repealed by Public Law 90-269, approved Mar. 18, 1968. Silver certificates issued on and after July 1, 1929, became redeemable from the general fund on June 24, 1968. The amount of security after those dates has been reduced accordingly.

New U.S. Currency Designs

On Mar. 25, 1996, the U.S. Treasury issued a redesigned $100 note incorporating many new and modified anticounterfeiting features. The note was the first of the U.S. currency series to be redesigned. A new $50 note was issued Oct. 27, 1997, and the new $20 bill was released into circulation Sept. 24, 1998. New $10 and $5 notes are expected to be issued simultaneously in 2000; a new $1 note with a more modest redesign will follow. Old notes are being removed from circulation as they are returned to the Federal Reserve.

The new $100 bill has: a larger portrait, moved off-center; a watermark (seen only when held up to the light) to the right of the portrait, depicting the same person; a security thread that glows red when exposed to ultraviolet light in a dark environment; color-shifting ink that changes from green to black when viewed at different angles, to appear in the numeral on the lower, front right-hand corner of the bill; microprinting in the numeral in the note's lower, front left-hand corner and on the portrait; and other features for security, machine authentication, and processing of the currency. The redesigned $20 and $50 bills incorporate the same features as the $100 bill, with the notable addition of a low-vision feature, a large (14-mm high, as compared to 7.8-mm on the old design), dark numeral on a light background on the back of the note. (The security thread in the $50 glows yellow; in the $20 it glows green.) The low-vision feature will appear on subsequent redesigned notes in the series. More new currency information is available on the U.S. Treasury's website: http:/www.ustreas.gov

MILLENNIUM FACT BOX

Parade of Quarters

Source: United States Mint, U.S. Dept. of the Treasury

Beginning in Jan. 1999, a series of five quarter dollars with new reverses will be issued each year through 2008, celebrating each of the 50 states. To make room on the reverse of the commemorative quarters for each state's design, certain design elements will be moved , thereby creating a new obverse design as well. The coins will be issued in the sequence the states became part of the Union (date each state entered the union is shown below).

1999	2000	2001	2002	2003
Delaware Dec. 7, 1787	Massachusetts Feb. 6, 1788	New York July 26, 1788	Tennessee June 1, 1796	Illinois Dec. 3, 1818
Pennsylvania Dec. 12, 1787	Maryland Apr. 28, 1788	North Carolina Nov. 21, 1789	Ohio Mar. 1, 1803	Alabama Dec. 14, 1819
New Jersey Dec. 18, 1787	South Carolina May 23, 1788	Rhode Island May 29, 1790	Louisiana Apr. 30, 1812	Maine Mar. 15, 1820
Georgia Jan. 2, 1788	New Hampshire June 21, 1788	Vermont Mar. 4, 1791	Indiana Dec. 11, 1816	Missouri Aug. 10, 1821
Connecticut Jan. 9, 1788	Virginia June 25, 1788	Kentucky June 1, 1792	Mississippi Dec. 10, 1817	Arkansas June 15, 1836
2004	**2005**	**2006**	**2007**	**2008**
Michigan Jan. 26, 1837	California Sept. 9, 1850	Nevada Oct. 31, 1864	Montana Nov. 8, 1889	Oklahoma Nov. 16, 1907
Florida Mar. 3, 1845	Minnesota May 11, 1858	Nebraska Mar. 1, 1867	Washington Nov. 11, 1889	New Mexico Jan. 6, 1912
Texas Dec. 29, 1845	Oregon Feb. 14, 1859	Colorado Aug. 1, 1876	Idaho July 3, 1890	Arizona Feb. 14, 1912
Iowa Dec. 28, 1846	Kansas Jan. 29, 1861	North Dakota Nov. 2, 1889	Wyoming July 10, 1890	Alaska Jan. 3, 1959
Wisconsin May 29, 1848	West Virginia June 20, 1863	South Dakota Nov. 2, 1889	Utah Jan. 4, 1896	Hawaii Aug. 21, 1959

Consumer Credit Outstanding, 1995-97

Source: Federal Reserve System

(billions of dollars)

Estimated amounts of credit outstanding as of end of year. Not seasonally adjusted.

	1995	1996	1997
Total	**$1,131.9**	**$1,214.9**	**$1,264.1**
Ratio to disposable personal income[1] (percent)	21.3%	23.7%	21.8%
By major holder			
Commercial banks	$507.8	$529.4	$512.6
Finance companies	152.6	152.4	160.0
Credit unions	131.9	144.1	152.4
Savings institutions	40.1	44.7	47.2
Nonfinancial business	85.1	77.7	78.9
Pools of securitized assets[2]	214.4	266.5	313.1
By major type of credit[3]			
Automobile	354.1	393.2	417.0
Commercial banks	$149.1	$154.0	$155.3
Finance companies	70.6	86.7	87.0
Pools of securitized assets[2]	44.4	52.4	65.0
Revolving	435.7	522.9	555.9
Commercial banks	210.3	228.6	219.8
Finance companies	53.5	32.5	38.6
Pools of securitized assets[2]	147.9	188.7	221.5
Other	342.2	298.8	291.3
Commercial banks	148.4	146.8	137.5
Finance companies	82.0	33.2	34.4
Nonfinancial business	31.5	32.8	34.0
Pools of securitized assets[2]	22.1	25.4	26.6

(1) Based on 4th quarter seasonally adjusted disposable personal income at annual rates as published by the U.S. Bureau of Economic Analysis. (2) Outstanding balances of pools upon which securities have been issued; these balances are no longer carried on the balance sheets of the loan originator. (3) Totals include estimates for certain holders for which only consumer credit totals are available.

Leading U.S. Businesses in 1997

Source: FORTUNE Magazine

(millions of dollars in revenues)

Aerospace

Boeing	$45,800
Lockheed Martin	28,069
United Technologies	24,713
AlliedSignal	14,472
Textron	10,544
Northrop Grumman	9,153
General Dynamics	4,062
B.F. Goodrich	3,471

Airlines

AMR	$18,570
UAL	17,378
Delta Air Lines	13,590
NWA	10,226
US Airways Group	8,514
Continental Airlines	7,213
Southwest Airlines	3,817
Trans World Airlines	3,328
America West Holdings	1,875
Alaska Air Group	1,739

Apparel

Nike	$9,187
VF	5,222
Reebok International	3,637
Liz Claiborne	2,413
Fruit of the Loom	2,140
Nine West Group	1,865
Kellwood	1,521
Warnaco Group	1,436
Jones Apparel Group	1,387

Beverages

Pepsico	$29,292
Coca-Cola	18,868
Coca-Cola Enterprises	11,278
Anheuser-Busch	11,066
Whitman	3,250
Adolph Coors	1,822

Building Materials, Glass

Owens-Illinois	$4,680
Owens-Corning	4,373
Corning	4,129
USG	2,874
Armstrong World Inds.	2,199
Johns Manville	1,648

Chemicals

E. I. du Pont de Nemours	$41,304
Dow Chemical	20,018
Occidental Petroleum	11,061
Monsanto	9,457
PPG Industries	7,379
Union Carbide	6,502
FMC	5,232
Sherwin-Williams	4,881
Praxair	4,735
Eastman Chemical	4,678

Commercial Banks

Citicorp	$34,697
Chase Manhattan Corp.	30,381
BankAmerica Corp.	23,585
Nationsbank Corp.	21,734
J.P. Morgan & Co.	17,701
First Union Corp.	14,329
Banc One Corp.	13,219
Bankers Trust N.Y. Corp.	12,176
First Chicago NBD Corp.	10,098
Norwest Corp.	9,660

Computer and Data Services

Electronic Data Systems	$15,236
Unisys	6,636
Computer Sciences	5,616
First Data	5,235
Automatic Data Proc.	4,112
Comdisco	2,819
Dun & Bradstreet	2,154
Micro Warehouse	2,126
Equifax	1,706
America Online	1,685

Computer Peripherals

Seagate Technology	$8,940
Quantum	5,319
Western Digital	4,178
EMC	2,938
Lexmark International	2,494
Imation	2,202
Storage Technology	2,145

Computer Software

Microsoft	$11,358
Oracle	5,684
Computer Assoc. Intl.	4,040

Computers, Office Equipment

IBM	$78,508
Hewlett-Packard	42,895
Compaq Computer	24,584
Xerox	18,166
Digital Equipment	13,047
Dell Computer	12,327
Sun Microsystems	8,598
Apple Computer	7,081
NCR	6,589
Gateway 2000	6,294

Diversified Financials

Travelers Group	$37,609
Fannie Mae	27,777
American Express	17,760
Fed. Home Loan Mortgage	14,399
Marsh & McLennan	6,009
AON	5,751
Household International	5,503

Electronics, Electrical Equip.

General Electric	$90,840
Motorola	29,794
Lucent Technologies	26,360
Raytheon	13,674
Emerson Electric	12,299
Rockwell International	11,759
Whirlpool	8,617
Eaton	7,563

Electronics, Semiconductors

Intel	$25,070
Texas Instruments	10,562
Applied Materials	4,074
National Semiconductor	2,507
Advanced Micro Devices	2,356

Entertainment

Walt Disney	$22,473
Viacom	13,505
Time Warner	13,294
CBS	9,632

Food

ConAgra	$24,002
Sara Lee	19,734
RJR Nabisco Holdings	17,057
Archer Daniels Midland	13,853
IBP	13,259
Best Foods	9,818
H. J. Heinz	9,357
Farmland Industries	9,148
Campbell Soup	7,964
Kellogg	6,830

Food and Drug Stores

Kroger	$26,567
Safeway	22,484
American Stores	19,139
Albertson's	14,690
Walgreen	13,363
Winn-Dixie Stores	13,219
CVS	13,086
Publix	11,224

Food Services

McDonald's	$11,409
ProSource	3,901
Darden Restaurants	3,172
Advantica	2,609
Viad	2,417
Wendy's International	2,037

Forest and Paper Products

International Paper	$20,096
Georgia-Pacific	13,094
Kimberly-Clark	12,547
Weyerhaeuser	11,210
Fort James	7,259
Champion International	5,736
Boise Cascade	5,493
Mead	5,077
Stone Container	4,849
Union Camp	4,477

Furniture

Leggett & Platt	$2,909
Furniture Brands Intl.	1,808
Herman Miller	1,496

General Merchandisers

Wal-Mart Stores	$119,299
Sears Roebuck	41,296
Kmart	32,183
J. C. Penney	30,546
Dayton Hudson	27,757
Federated Dept. Stores	15,668
May Department Stores	12,685

Health Care

Columbia/HCA Healthcare	$18,819
United Healthcare	11,794
Pacificare Health Systems	8,983
Tenet Healthcare	8,691
Humana	7,880
Foundation Health Systems	7,235
Medpartners	6,331
Wellpoint Health Networks	5,826

Hotels, Casinos, Resorts

Marriott International	$12,034
ITT	6,658
Hilton Hotels	5,316
Harrah's Entertainment	1,619
Mirage Resorts	1,419

Industrial and Farm Equip.

Caterpillar	$18,925
Deere	12,791
Dresser Industries	7,458
Ingersoll-Rand	7,103
Case	6,024
American Standard	6,008
Cummins Engine	5,625
Black & Decker	4,941
Dover	4,548

Insurance (Life and Health)

Prudential of America[1]	$37,073
TIAA-CREF[2]	29,348
Metropolitan Life[1]	24,374
Cigna (Stock)	20,038
New York Life (Mutual)	18,899
Aetna (Stock)	18,540
Northwestern Mut. Life (Mut.)	13,430

Insurance (Property and Casualty)

State Farm Ins. (Mutual)	$43,957
American Intl. Group (Stock)	30,520
Allstate (Stock)	24,949
Loews (Stock)	19,648
Hartford Fin'l. Svces. (Stock)	13,305
Nationwide Ins. Enterprise[1]	12,644

Mail, Pkg., Freight Delivery

United Parcel Svce.	$22,458
Fdx	11,520

Metal Products

Gillette	$10,062
Crown Cork & Seal	8,495
Fortune Brands	7,001
Tyco International	6,598
ITW	5,220
Masco	3,760

Metals

Alcoa	$13,482
Reynolds Metals	6,900
Inland Steel Industries	5,047
Bethlehem Steel	4,631
LTV	4,446
Nucor	4,184
Phelps Dodge	3,914
Allegheny Teledyne	3,745

Motor Vehicles and Parts

General Motors	$178,174
Ford Motor	153,627
Chrysler	61,147
Johnson Controls	11,387
TRW	10,831

Petroleum Refining

Exxon	$122,379
Mobil	59,978
Texaco	45,187
Chevron	36,376
Amoco	32,836
USX	21,057
Atlantic Richfield	19,272

Pharmaceuticals

Merck	$23,637
Johnson & Johnson	22,629
Bristol-Myers Squibb	16,701

(continued)

Pharmaceuticals (continued)

American Home Products	14,196
Pfizer	12,504
Abbott Laboratories	11,883
Eli Lilly	8,518
Warner-Lambert	8,180
Schering-Plough	6,778
Pharmacia & Upjohn	6,710

Publishing & Printing

R.R. Donnelley & Sons	$6,396
Gannett	4,729
McGraw-Hill	3,534
Times Mirror	3,319
Knight-Ridder	3,139
New York Times	2,866
Reader's Digest Assn.	2,839
Tribune	2,720
Dow Jones	2,573

Railroads

Union Pacific	$11,014
CSX	10,621
Burlington Northern Santa Fe	8,412
Norfolk Southern	5,165

Rubber and Plastic Prods.

Goodyear Tire	$13,155
Rubbermaid	2,400
Mark IV Industries	2,294
M.A. Hanna	2,200

Scientific, Photog., and Control Equip.

Minnesota Mining & Mfg.	$15,070
Eastman Kodak	14,713
Honeywell	8,028
Baxter International	6,138
Thermo Electron	3,558
Becton Dickinson	2,811
Medtronic	2,438

Securities

Merrill Lynch	$31,731
Morgan Stanley Dean Witter	27,132
Lehman Bros. Holdings	16,883
Paine Webber Group	6,657

Soaps, Cosmetics

Procter & Gamble	$35,764
Colgate-Palmolive	9,057
Avon Products	5,079
Estée Lauder	3,382
Clorox	2,533
Revlon	2,391

Specialty Retailers

Home Depot	$24,156
Costco	21,874
Toys "R" Us	11,038
Republic Industries	10,306
Lowe's	10,137
Limited	9,189
Best Buy	7,771
Circuit City Group	7,664
TJX	7,389

Telecommunications

AT&T	$53,261
Bell Atlantic	30,194
SBC Communications	24,856
GTE	23,260
BellSouth	20,561
MCI Communications	19,653
Ameritech	15,998
US West	15,352
Sprint	14,874

Temporary Help

Manpower	$7,259
Olsten	4,113
Kelly Services	3,853

Textiles

Shaw Industries	$3,576
Springs Industries	2,226
Burlington Industries	2,091
Mohawk Industries	1,901
Westpoint Stevens	1,820

Tobacco

Philip Morris	$56,114
Universal	4,113
Dimon	2,513

Toys, Sporting Goods

Mattel	$4,835
Hasbro	3,189

Transportation Equipment

Brunswick	$3,657
Trinity Industries	2,641
Harley-Davidson	1,763

Utilities, Gas and Electric

Duke Energy	$16,309
PG&E Corp.	15,400
Southern	12,611
Entergy	9,562
Edison International	9,235
Utilicorp United	8,926
Texas Utilities	7,946

Wholesalers

Ingram Micro	$16,582
Supervalu	16,552
Fleming	15,373
Sysco	14,455
McKesson	13,479

(1) Not a stock co., but reported financial data according to Generally Accepted Accounting Principles. (2) Not a mutual co., but reported financial data based on statutory accounting.

U.S. Corporations With Largest Revenues in 1997

Source: FORTUNE Magazine

(millions of dollars)

Company, headquarters	Revenues
General Motors, Detroit, MI	$178,174
Ford Motor, Dearborn, MI	153,627
Exxon, Irving, TX	122,379
Wal-Mart Stores, Bentonville, AR	119,299
General Electric, Fairfield, CT	90,840
IBM, Armonk, NY	78,508
Chrysler, Auburn Hills, MI	61,147
Mobil, Fairfax, VA	59,978
Philip Morris, New York, NY	56,114
AT&T, New York, NY	53,261
Boeing, Seattle, WA	$45,800
Texaco, White Plains, NY	45,187
State Farm Insurance Cos., Bloomington, IL	43,957
Hewlett-Packard, Palo Alto, CA	42,895
E. I. Du Pont de Nemours, Wilmington, DE	41,304
Sears Roebuck, Hoffman Estates, IL	41,296
Travelers Group, New York, NY	37,609
Prudential Insurance Co. of America, Newark, NJ	$37,073
Chevron, San Francisco, CA	36,376
Procter & Gamble, Cincinnati, OH	35,764
Citicorp, New York, NY	34,697
Amoco, Chicago, IL	32,836
Kmart, Troy, MI	32,183
Merrill Lynch, New York, NY	31,731
J.C. Penney, Plano, TX	30,546

Largest Corporate Mergers or Acquisitions in U.S.

Source: Securities Data Co.

(as of Oct. 1998; an * denotes an announced merger or acquisition not yet complete; year = year effective or announced)

Company	Acquirer	Dollars	Year
Citicorp	Travelers Group Inc.	$72.6 bil	1998
Ameritech Corp.*	SBC Communications Inc.	72.4 bil	1998
GTE Corp.*	Bell Atlantic Corp.	70.9 bil	1998
Tele-Communications*	AT&T Corp.	69.9 bil	1998
BankAmerica Corp.	NationsBank Corp.	61.6 bil	1998
Amoco Corp.*	British Petroleum Co. PLC	55.0 bil	1998
MCI Communications	WorldCom Inc.	43.4 bil	1998
Chrysler Corp.*	Daimler-Benz AG	40.5 bil	1998
Wells Fargo & Co.*	Norwest Corp.	34.4 bil	1998
US West Media Group	shareholders	31.7 bil	1998
NYNEX	Bell Atlantic	30.8 bil	1997
Electronic Data Sys.	shareholders	29.7 bil	1996
First Chicago NBD	BANC ONE Corp.	29.6 bil	1998
RJR Nabisco	Kohlberg Kravis Roberts	29.4 bil	1989
Associates First Capital	shareholders	26.6 bil	1998
Lucent Technologies	shareholders	24.1 bil	1996
Pacific Telesis Group	SBC Communications	22.4 bil	1997
General Re Corp.*	Berkshire Hathaway Inc.	22.3 bil	1998
Waste Management	USA Waste Services Inc.	20.0 bil	1998
Capital Cities/ABC	Walt Disney	18.3 bil	1996
SunAmerica Inc.*	American Int'l. Group.	18.1 bil	1998
CoreStates Financial	First Union Corp.	17.1 bil	1998
McCaw Cellular Communications	AT&T	16.7 bil	1994
McDonnell Douglas	Boeing	15.8 bil	1997
Warner Comm.	Time	15.1 bil	1990
MFS Communications	WorldCom	14.9 bil	1996
Barnett Banks	NationsBank Corp.	14.8 bil	1998
HF Ahmanson & Co.	Washington Mutual	14.7 bil	1998
HBO & Co.*	McKesson Corp.	13.8 bil	1998
Kraft	Philip Morris	13.7 bil	1988
ITT Corp.	Starwood Lodging	13.5 bil	1998
Gulf Oil	Standard Oil of CA	13.4 bil	1984
Fred Meyer*	Kroger Co.	13.0 bil	1998
Conrail	Investor group	12.8 bil	1997
HFS	CUC International	12.4 bil	1997
Central & South West*	American Electric Power	12.3 bil	1997
Squibb	Bristol-Myers	11.9 bil	1989
American Stores Co.*	Albertson's Inc.	11.8 bil	1998
Allstate	shareholders	11.8 bil	1995
Teleport Communications Group	AT&T	11.0 bil	1998
First Interstate Bancorp	Wells Fargo	10.9 bil	1996
Conoco*	shareholders	10.9 bil	1998
Morgan Stanley Grp.	Dean Witter Discover	10.6 bil	1997
Chase Manhattan	Chemical Banking	10.4 bil	1996
Getty Oil	Texaco	10.1 bil	1984
Continental Cablevision	US WEST Media Group	10.0 bil	1996
Contel	GTE	10.0 bil	1991
PanEnergy	Duke Power	10.0 bil	1997
IMS International	shareholders	9.7 bil	1998
Boatmen's Bancshares	NationsBank	9.7 bil	1997
Paramount	Viacom	9.6 bil	1994
American Cyanamid	American Home Products	9.6 bil	1994
Hughes Aircraft*	Raytheon	9.5 bil	1997
US West Media Grp.	shareholders	9.3 bil	1995

U.S. Corporate Profits by Industry[1]

Source: Bureau of Economic Analysis, U.S. Dept. of Commerce

(billions of dollars)

	1996[R]	1997	First quarter 1998[2]
CORPORATE PROFITS with inventory valuation and capital consumption adjustments	**$750.4**	**$817.3**	**$829.2**
DOMESTIC industries	**654.0**	**718.9**	**730.6**
Financial	105.5	124.7	131.3
Nonfinancial	548.5	594.2	599.3
REST OF THE WORLD	**96.4**	**99.0**	**98.6**
Receipts from rest of world	134.5	149.5	146.1
Less: Payments to rest of world	38.1	50.4	47.5
CORPORATE PROFITS with inventory valuation adjustment	**679.0**	**741.2**	**744.3**
DOMESTIC industries	**582.6**	**642.2**	**645.8**
Financial	110.7	130.0	136.3
Federal Reserve banks	21.8	23.3	24.5
Other	88.9	106.6	111.8
Nonfinancial	471.8	512.3	509.4
Manufacturing	195.6	214.4	197.1
Durable goods	97.2	107.3	100.8
Primary metal industries	5.4	5.6	6.3
Fabricated metal prods.	14.2	15.5	12.6
Industrial machinery, equip.	$26.1	$27.6	$23.2
Electronic, other electric equip.	20.1	24.8	21.9
Motor vehicles and equip.	2.4	3.8	6.2
Other	29.0	30.0	30.7
Nondurable goods	98.5	107.1	96.2
Food and kindred prods.	22.0	22.7	20.6
Chemicals and allied prods.	28.8	28.1	27.0
Petroleum and coal prods.	10.9	18.0	10.9
Other	36.7	38.3	37.8
Transportation and public utils.	92.7	88.4	91.7
Transportation	14.8	17.6	17.3
Communications	35.8	31.2	34.1
Electric, gas, sanitary srvcs.	42.1	39.7	40.3
Wholesale trade	37.9	49.8	51.5
Retail trade	51.8	61.2	67.4
Other	93.8	98.5	101.8
REST OF THE WORLD	**96.4**	**99.0**	**98.6**

(1) Figures are rounded; therefore, some totals may not add. (2) Seasonally adjusted at annual rates. (R) Revised figures.

Fastest-Growing U.S. Franchises in 1997[1]

Source: Entrepreneur Magazine, Jan. 1998

Company	Business	Minimum start-up cost[2]
McDonald's	hamburgers, chicken, salads	$363,600
Burger King Corp.	hamburgers, chicken, salads	320,000
Yogen Früz/Bresler's Ice Cream/ICBIY	frozen yogurt, ice cream	55,000
7-Eleven Convenience Stores	convenience stores	12,500
Jani-King	commercial cleaning	1,900
Subway	sandwiches, salads	50,200
Baskin-Robbins USA Co.	ice cream	47,300
Coverall Cleaning Concepts	commercial office cleaning	240
Arby's Inc.	roast beef sandwiches, subs, chicken	878,000
Taco Bell Corp.	Mexican fast food	191,400
Dunkin' Donuts	donuts, baked goods	70,300
Carlson Wagonlit Travel	travel agencies	45,500
Jazzercise Inc.	fitness centers	1,400
Blimpie Intl. Inc.	sandwiches, salads	85,300
Mail Boxes Etc.	postal/ business srvcs.	$79,000
Miracle Ear Hearing Systems	health-care products and services	57,000
Futurekids Inc.	children's computer learning centers	35,000
Papa John's Pizza	pizza	131,000
Holiday Inn Worldwide	hotels	varies
Choice Hotels International	hotels	varies
Proforce USA	commercial cleaning	780
GNC Franchising Inc.	vitamin/nutrition stores	75,000
Domino's Pizza	pizza	76,500
KFC	chicken	1,100,000
Churchs Chicken	chicken	189,800
Orion Food Systems Inc.	misc. fast food	varies
Great Clips Inc.	family hair salons	69,100
Re/Max Intl. Inc.	real estate services	20,000
Super 8 Motels Inc.	motels	218,000
Coldwell Banker Real Estate Corp.	residential real estate brokerage	8,500

(1) Based on the number of new franchise units added. (2) Not including franchise fee, which varies.

Largest U.S. Black-Owned Companies in 1997

Source: Black Enterprise Magazine

Company, Location (Business)	Sales (millions)
TLC Beatrice International Holdings, New York, NY (international food processor and distributor)	$2,230.0
Johnson Publishing Co., Chicago, IL (publishing, broadcasting, TV production, cosmetics, hair care)	325.7
Philadelphia Coca-Cola Bottling Co., Philadelphia, PA (soft drink bottling)	325.0
Pulsar Data Systems, Lanham, MD (computer systems integration and network design)	166.0
H. J. Russell & Co., Atlanta, GA (construction, property mgt., airport concessions, real estate development)	163.8
Uniworld Group, New York, NY (advertising, promotion, event mktg., direct response mktg.)	157.9
Granite Broadcasting Corp., New York, NY (network TV affiliates)	154.8
Convenience Corp. of America, W. Palm Beach, FL (convenience stores)	137.4
Burrell Communications Group, Chicago, IL (advertising, public relations, consumer promotion, direct response mktg.)	134.7
BET Holdings, Washington, DC (cable TV network, magazine publishing)	132.7
The Bing Group, Detroit, MI (steel processing; metal stamping distribution)	$129.5
Envirotest Systems Corp., Sunnyvale, CA (vehicle emissions testing)	124.5
The Anderson-Dubose Co., Solon, OH (food, paper products, and operating supplies distributor)	122.2
Stop Shop Save Food Markets, Baltimore, MD (supermarkets)	108.0
Sylvest Management Systems Corp., Lanham, MD (computer and network integration)	107.5
Midwest Stamping Co., Bowling Green, OH (automotive metal stamping and assemblies)	106.8
Mays Chemical Co., Indianapolis, IN (industrial chemicals distributor)	105.3
Barden Companies, Detroit, MI (radio broadcasting, real estate development, casino gaming)	93.2
Essence Communications, New York, NY (magazine publishing; catalog sales, entertainment)	92.8
Soft Sheen Products, Chicago, IL (hair care products manufacturer)	91.4

U.S. Capital Gains Tax

Source: U.S. Chamber of Commerce; as of Sept. 1998

The following shows how the maximum tax rate on net long-term capital gains for individuals has changed since 1960.

Year	Maximum rate (percentage)	Year	Maximum rate (percentage)	Year	Maximum rate (percentage)	Year	Maximum rate (percentage)	Year	Maximum rate (percentage)
1960	25.0	1971	32.5	1978	28.0	1987	28.0	1990	28.0[3]
1970	29.5	1972	35.0[1]	1981	20.0	1988	33.0[2]	1997	20.0[4]

(1) From 1972 to 1976, the interplay of minimum tax and maximum tax resulted in a marginal rate of 49.125%. (2) Statutory maximum of 28%, but "phase-out" notch increased marginal rate to 33%; interplay of all "phase-outs" could have increased the effective marginal rate to 49.5%. (3) The Budget Act of 1990 increased the statutory rate to 31% and capped the marginal rate at 28%; however, some taxpayers faced effective marginal rates of more than 34% because of the phase-out of personal exemptions and itemized deductions. (4) New rate is for those who, after July 28, 1997, sell capital assets held for more than 18 mos (12 mos for sales after Dec. 31, 1997). A 10% capital gains rate applies to individuals in the 15% income tax bracket. (Those who, after July 28, 1997, but before Jan. 1, 1998, sell capital assets held between 12 and 18 mos will be taxed at the old top rate of 28%. Those who sold capital assets after May 6, 1997, but before July 29, 1997, will be taxed at the 20% rate, so long as such assets were held for at least a year.) For capital assets purchased after 2000 and held for at least 5 years, a top rate of 18% applies (8% for those in the 15% income tax bracket).

1998 Federal Corporate Tax Rates

Taxable Income Amount	Tax Rate	Taxable Income Amount	Tax Rate
Not more than $50,000	15%	$335,001 to $10,000,000	34%
$50,001 to $75,000	25%	$10,000,001 to $15,000,000	35%
$75,001 to $100,000	34%	$15,000,001 to $18,333,333	38%
$100,001 to $335,000	39%	More than $18,333,333	35%

Personal service corporations (used by professional individuals such as attorneys and doctors) pay a flat rate of 35%.

Global Stock Markets

Source: The Conference Board; not seasonally adjusted

Stock price indexes (1990=100):	1996	1997	1998 Jan.	Feb.	Mar.	Apr.	May	June
United States	202.9	263.3	294.7	315.4	331.2	334.2	327.9	340.8
Japan	72.9	63.5	57.7	58.4	57.3	54.3	54.4	54.9
Germany	127.6	178.7	204.9	217.5	234.9	237.1	251.6	262.2
France	116.0	152.8	174.5	188.3	213.3	213.5	222.4	231.3
United Kingdom	175.8	206.6	234.3	247.9	257.0	257.6	258.9	253.4
Italy	98.0	134.3	184.0	194.3	239.3	220.9	236.1	222.1
Canada	154.0	188.8	195.8	207.3	220.9	224.0	221.9	215.3

Foreign Exchange Rates, 1970-97

Source: International Monetary Fund

(National currency units per dollar except as indicated; data are annual averages)

Year	Australia (dollar)	Austria (schilling)	Belgium (franc)	Canada (dollar)	Denmark (krone)	France (franc)	Germany[1] (deutsche mark)	Greece (drachma)
1970	1.1136	25.880	49.680	1.0103	7.489	5.5200	3.6480	30.00
1975	1.3077	17.443	36.799	1.0175	5.748	4.2876	2.4613	32.29
1980	1.1400	12.945	29.237	1.1693	5.634	4.2250	1.8175	42.62
1985	0.7003	20.690	59.378	1.3655	10.596	8.9852	2.9440	138.12
1990	0.7813	11.370	33.418	1.1668	6.189	5.4453	1.6157	158.51
1991	0.7791	11.676	34.148	1.1457	6.396	5.6421	1.6595	182.27
1992	0.7353	10.989	32.150	1.2087	6.036	5.2938	1.5617	190.62
1993	0.6801	11.632	34.597	1.2901	6.484	5.6632	1.6533	229.25
1994	0.7317	11.422	33.456	1.3656	6.361	5.5520	1.6228	242.60
1995	0.7415	10.081	29.480	1.3724	5.602	4.9915	1.4331	231.66
1996	0.7829	10.587	30.962	1.3635	5.799	5.1155	1.5048	240.71
1997	0.7441	12.204	35.774	1.3846	6.604	5.8367	1.7341	273.06

Year	India (rupee)	Ireland (pound)	Italy (lira)	Japan (yen)	Malaysia (ringgit)	Mexico (new peso)	Netherlands (guilder)	Norway (krone)
1970	7.576	2.3959	623	357.60	3.0900	—	3.5970	7.1400
1975	8.409	2.2216	653	296.78	2.4030	—	2.5293	5.2282
1980	7.887	2.0577	856	226.63	2.1767	—	1.9875	4.9381
1985	12.369	1.0656	1,909	238.54	2.4830	—	3.3214	8.5972
1990	17.504	1.6585	1,198	144.79	2.7049	2.8126	1.8209	6.2597
1991	22.742	1.6155	1,241	134.71	2.7501	3.0184	1.8697	6.4829
1992	25.918	1.7053	1,232	126.65	2.5474	3.0949	1.7585	6.2145
1993	30.493	1.4671	1,574	111.20	2.5741	3.1156	1.8573	7.0941
1994	31.374	1.4978	1,612	102.21	2.6243	3.3751	1.8200	7.0576
1995	32.427	1.6038	1,629	94.06	2.5044	6.4194	1.6057	6.3352
1996	35.433	1.6006	1,543	108.78	2.5159	7.6009	1.6859	6.4498
1997	36.313	1.5180	1,703	120.99	2.8132	7.9141	1.9513	7.0734

Year	Portugal (escudo)	Singapore (dollar)	South Korea (won)	Spain (peseta)	Sweden (krona)	Switzerland (franc)	Thailand (baht)	United Kingdom (pound)
1970	28.75	3.0800	310.57	69.72	5.1700	4.3160	21.000	2.3959
1975	25.51	2.3713	484.00	57.43	4.1530	2.5839	20.379	2.2216
1980	50.08	2.1412	607.43	71.76	4.2309	1.6772	20.476	2.3243
1985	170.39	2.2002	870.02	170.04	8.6039	2.4571	27.159	1.2963
1990	142.55	1.8125	707.76	101.93	5.9188	1.3892	25.585	1.7847
1991	144.48	1.7276	733.35	103.91	6.0475	1.4340	25.517	1.7694
1992	135.00	1.6290	780.65	102.38	5.8238	1.4062	25.400	1.7655
1993	160.80	1.6158	802.67	127.26	7.7834	1.4776	25.319	1.5020
1994	165.99	1.5274	803.45	133.96	7.7160	1.3677	25.150	1.5316
1995	151.11	1.4174	771.27	124.69	7.1333	1.1825	24.915	1.5785
1996	154.24	1.4100	804.45	126.66	6.7060	1.2360	25.343	1.5617
1997	175.31	1.4848	951.29	146.41	7.6349	1.4513	31.364	1.6377

(1) West Germany prior to 1991.

Foreign Direct Investment[1] in the U.S. by Selected Countries and Territories

Source: Bureau of Economic Analysis; U.S. Dept. of Commerce

(millions of dollars)

	1996	1997
ALL COUNTRIES[2]	**$630,045**	**$681,651**
Canada	**53,845**	**64,022**
Europe[2]	**410,425**	**425,220**
Austria	1,791	1,831
Belgium	3,979	6,771
Denmark	2,118	3,025
Finland	2,818	3,089
France	49,307	47,088
Germany	62,242	69,701
Ireland	9,776	10,514
Italy	2,699	3,318
Luxembourg	10,284	6,218
Netherlands	73,803	84,862
Norway	2,421	3,971
Spain	1,128	2,643
Sweden	9,470	13,147
Switzerland	35,101	38,574
United Kingdom	142,607	129,551
South and Central America[2]	**7,810**	**10,049**
Brazil	591	698

	1996	1997
Mexico	$1,078	$1,723
Panama	5,561	6,645
Other Western Hemisphere[2]	**16,817**	**25,652**
Bahamas	−1,859	1,986
Bermuda	921	3,423
Netherlands Antilles	9,124	7,701
UK islands, Caribbean[2]	8,368	11,954
Africa	**717**	**1,608**
Middle East[2]	**6,177**	**6,882**
Israel	1,960	2,292
Kuwait	2,572	2,881
Saudi Arabia	1,484	1,573
Asia and Pacific[2]	**134,255**	**148,218**
Australia	9,747	16,229
Hong Kong	947	1,757
Japan	118,116	123,514
Malaysia	445	465
Singapore	1,468	2,776
South Korea	394	−327
Taiwan	2,298	2,778

(1) The book value of foreign direct investors' equity in, and net outstanding loans to, their U.S. affiliates. A U.S. affiliate is a U.S. business enterprise in which a single foreign direct investor owns at least 10% of the voting securities or the equivalent. (2) Totals include countries or territories not shown.

U.S. Direct Investment[1] Abroad in Selected Countries and Territories

Source: Bureau of Economic Analysis, U.S. Dept. of Commerce

(millions of dollars)

	1990	1996	1997
ALL COUNTRIES[2]	**$424,086**	**$796,494**	**$860,723**
Canada	**67,033**	**91,587**	**99,859**
Europe[2]	**211,194**	**399,632**	**420,934**
Austria	889	2,902	2,621
Belgium	9,050	18,604	17,403
Denmark	1,597	2,171	2,576
Finland	551	1,033	1,338
France	18,874	34,000	34,615
Germany	27,259	44,259	43,931
Greece	288	506	638
Ireland	6,880	11,749	14,476
Italy	13,117	18,687	17,749
Luxembourg	1,390	6,377	9,796
Netherlands	22,658	44,667	64,648
Norway	3,815	6,103	6,262
Portugal	598	1,854	1,498
Spain	7,704	11,393	11,642
Sweden	1,600	7,629	7,299
Switzerland	25,199	35,751	35,203
Turkey	494	1,025	1,076
United Kingdom	68,224	142,560	138,765
Eastern Europe	NA	6,480	7,743
South America[2]	**23,760**	**52,153**	**67,112**
Argentina	2,956	8,060	9,766
Brazil	14,918	26,166	35,727
Chile	1,368	6,745	7,767
Colombia	1,728	3,468	3,727
Ecuador	387	855	1,175
Peru	410	2,075	2,595
Venezuela	1,490	3,592	5,176
Central America[2]	**17,719**	**38,905**	**48,881**
Costa Rica	NA	1,205	1,580
Guatemala	NA	217	357
Honduras	NA	145	183

	1990	1996	1997
Mexico	$9,398	$18,747	$25,395
Panama	7,409	18,256	20,958
Other Western Hemisphere[2]	**30,113**	**53,151**	**56,489**
Bahamas	3,309	2,021	1,515
Barbados	NA	865	801
Bermuda	21,737	33,783	33,092
Dominican Republic	NA	465	476
Jamaica	604	1,675	1,687
Netherlands Antilles	−2,229	3,594	5,393
Trinidad and Tobago	508	1,057	602
UK islands, Caribbean	4,800	9,008	12,143
Africa[2]	**4,861**	**7,568**	**10,253**
Egypt	1,465	1,647	1,570
Nigeria	161	978	1,465
South Africa	956	1,437	2,347
Middle East[2]	**3,973**	**8,743**	**8,959**
Israel	756	1,886	2,286
Saudi Arabia	1,981	3,098	3,079
United Arab Emirates	519	789	682
Asia and Pacific[2]	**61,869**	**140,402**	**142,704**
Australia	14,846	28,769	26,125
China	NA	2,883	5,013
Hong Kong	6,187	16,022	19,065
India	513	1,139	1,684
Indonesia	3,226	7,571	7,395
Japan	20,997	39,593	35,569
Malaysia	1,384	5,277	5,623
New Zealand	3,131	5,519	5,191
Philippines	1,629	3,349	3,403
Singapore	3,385	14,150	17,514
South Korea	2,178	5,510	6,528
Taiwan	2,014	4,509	4,944
Thailand	1,585	5,254	3,537

(1) The book value of U.S. direct investors' equity in, and net outstanding loans to, their foreign affiliates. A foreign affiliate is a foreign business enterprise in which a single U.S. investor owns at least 10% of the voting securities or the equivalent. (2) Total includes countries not shown. NA = not available.

U.S. Holdings of Foreign Stocks

Source: Bureau of Economic Analysis, U.S. Dept. Of Commerce

(billions of dollars)

	1995[R]	1996[R]	1997
Western Europe	$362.0	$468.8	$585.5
Of which: Switzerland	30.4	33.9	47.6
Netherlands	52.9	64.8	77.4
France	31.3	42.8	56.7
Germany	31.7	40.5	47.9
Sweden	23.6	34.2	36.6
United Kingdom	137.6	185.4	277.8
Spain	17.7	22.8	25.9

	1995[R]	1996[R]	1997
Canada	$46.9	$67.0	$79.0
Japan	128.5	126.4	120.4
Latin America	32.0	76.8	103.3
Of which: Mexico	18.8	22.1	26.1
Other countries and territories	129.7	137.8	113.1
Of which: Hong Kong	24.3	37.3	27.7
Australia	21.8	26.1	33.9
TOTAL HOLDINGS	**699.1**	**876.8**	**1,001.3**

(R) Revised figures.

U.S. International Transactions

Source: Bureau of Economic Analysis, U.S. Dept. of Commerce; revised as of July 1997

(millions of dollars)

	1965	1970	1975	1980	1985	1990	1995	1997
Exports of goods, services, and income[1]	**$42,722**	**$68,387**	**$157,936**	**$344,440**	**$382,749**	**$700,455**	**$991,490**	**$1,179,380**
Merchandise adjusted, excluding military[2]	26,461	42,469	107,088	224,250	215,915	389,307	575,871	679,325
Services	8,824	14,171	25,497	47,584	73,155	147,824	218,739	258,268
Income receipts on U.S. assets abroad	7,437	11,748	25,351	72,606	93,679	163,324	196,880	241,787
Imports of goods, services, and income	**–32,708**	**–59,901**	**–132,745**	**–333,774**	**–484,037**	**–757,758**	**–1,086,539**	**–1,294,904**
Merchandise adjusted, excluding military[2]	–21,510	–39,866	–98,185	–249,750	–338,088	–498,337	–749,431	–877,279
Services	–9,111	–14,520	–21,996	–41,491	–72,862	–120,019	–147,036	–170,520
Income payments on foreign assets in the U.S.	–2,088	–5,515	–12,564	–42,532	–73,087	–139,402	–190,072	–247,105
Unilateral transfers, net	**–4,583**	**–6,156**	**–7,075**	**–8,349**	**–22,700**	**–34,588**	**–34,046**	**–39,691**
U.S. assets abroad, net (increase/capital outflow [–])	**–5,716**	**–9,337**	**–39,703**	**–86,967**	**–39,889**	**–74,011**	**–307,207**	**–478,502**
U.S. official reserve assets, net	1,225	2,481	–849	–8,155	–3,858	–2,158	–9,742	–1,010
U.S. government assets, other than official reserve assets, net	–1,605	–1,589	–3,474	–5,162	–2,821	2,307	–549	174
U.S. private assets, net	–5,336	–10,229	–35,380	–73,651	–33,211	–74,160	–296,916	–477,666
Foreign assets in the U.S., net (increase/capital inflow [+])	**742**	**6,359**	**17,170**	**62,612**	**146,383**	**140,992**	**451,234**	**733,441**
Statistical discrepancy (sum of above items with sign reversed)	**–457**	**–219**	**4,417**	**20,886**	**17,494**	**24,911**	**–14,931**	**–99,724**
Memorandum:								
Balance on current account	5,431	2,331	18,116	2,317	–123,987	–91,892	–129,095	–155,215

(1) Excludes transfers of goods and services under U.S. military grant programs. (2) Excludes exports of goods under U.S. military agency sales contracts identified in Census export documents, excludes imports of goods under direct defense expenditures identified in Census import documents, and reflects various other adjustments.

Gold Reserves of Central Banks and Governments

Source: International Financial Statistics, IMF; million fine troy ounces

Year end	All countries[1]	United States	Belgium	Canada	France	Germany	Italy	Japan	Nether-lands	Switzer-land	United Kingdom
1975	1,018.71	274.71	42.17	21.95	100.93	117.61	82.48	21.11	54.33	83.20	21.03
1980	952.99	264.32	34.18	20.98	81.85	95.18	66.67	24.23	43.94	83.28	18.84
1985	949.39	262.65	34.18	20.11	81.85	95.18	66.67	24.33	43.94	83.28	19.03
1986	949.11	262.04	34.18	19.72	81.85	95.18	66.67	24.23	43.94	83.28	19.01
1987	944.49	262.38	33.63	18.52	81.85	95.18	66.67	24.23	43.94	83.28	19.01
1988	946.65	261.87	33.67	17.14	81.85	95.18	66.67	24.23	43.94	83.28	19.00
1989	941.04	261.93	30.23	16.10	81.85	95.18	66.67	24.23	43.94	83.28	18.99
1990	939.01	261.91	30.23	14.76	81.85	95.18	66.67	24.23	43.94	83.28	18.94
1991	938.01	261.91	30.23	12.96	81.85	95.18	66.67	24.23	43.94	83.28	18.89
1992	927.55	261.84	25.04	9.94	81.85	95.18	66.67	24.23	43.94	83.28	18.61
1993	922.02	261.79	25.04	6.05	81.85	95.18	66.67	24.23	35.05	83.28	18.45
1994	917.98	261.73	25.04	3.89	81.85	95.18	66.67	24.23	34.77	83.28	18.44
1995	908.79	261.70	20.54	3.41	81.85	95.18	66.67	24.23	34.77	83.28	18.43
1996	906.10	261.66	15.32	3.09	81.85	95.18	66.67	24.23	34.77	83.28	18.43
1997	890.57	261.64	15.32	3.09	81.89	95.18	66.67	24.23	27.07	83.28	18.42

(1) Covers IMF members with reported gold holdings. For countries not listed above, see International Financial Statistics.

U.S. National Income by Industry[1]

Source: Bureau of Economic Analysis, U.S. Dept. of Commerce

(billions of dollars)

	1960	1970	1980	1990	1995R	1996R	1997
National income without capital consumption adjustment	**$428.6**	**$835.1**	**$2,263.9**	**$4,513.6**	**$5,895.7**	**$6,212.7**	**$6,598.0**
Domestic industries	**425.1**	**827.8**	**2,216.3**	**4,492.0**	**5,878.1**	**6,200.3**	**6,606.0**
Private industries	**371.6**	**695.4**	**1,894.5**	**3,830.2**	**5,054.5**	**5,351.8**	**5,728.5**
Agriculture, forestry, fisheries	17.8	25.9	61.4	98.0	87.1	106.4	106.0
Mining	5.6	8.4	43.8	36.8	45.3	47.9	52.5
Construction	22.5	47.4	126.6	222.0	266.5	289.2	305.1
Manufacturing	125.3	215.6	532.1	859.5	1,065.2	1,085.9	1,151.0
Durable goods	73.4	127.7	313.7	483.1	603.3	617.9	659.4
Nondurable goods	52.0	87.9	218.4	376.3	461.8	468.0	491.6
Transportation, public utilities	35.8	64.4	177.3	326.3	442.8	464.7	480.9
Transportation	18.5	31.5	85.8	139.2	184.3	195.0	208.0
Communications	8.2	17.6	48.1	91.6	129.5	137.0	139.3
Electric, gas, sanitary services	9.1	86.8	43.4	95.5	129.0	132.7	133.6
Wholesale trade	25.0	47.5	143.3	261.7	325.1	350.9	384.2
Retail trade	41.3	79.9	189.4	392.3	481.1	509.6	543.2
Finance, insurance, real estate	51.3	96.4	279.5	684.2	1,021.6	1,089.2	1,192.0
Services	46.9	109.8	341.0	949.4	1,319.9	1,407.9	1,513.6
Government	**53.5**	**132.4**	**321.8**	**661.1**	**823.6**	**848.5**	**877.5**

(1) Figures may not add because of rounding. Total national income also includes income from outside the U.S. (R) Revised figures.

U.S. National Income by Type of Income[1]

Source: Bureau of Economic Analysis, U.S. Dept. of Commerce

(billions of dollars)

	1960	1970	1980	1990	1995[R]	1996[R]	1997
NATIONAL INCOME[2]	**$424.9**	**$832.6**	**$2,203.5**	**$4,491.0**	**$5,923.7**	**$6,256.0**	**$6,646.5**
Compensation of employees	**296.7**	**618.3**	**1,638.2**	**3,297.6**	**4,208.9**	**4,409.0**	**4,687.2**
Wages and salaries	272.8	551.5	1,372.0	2,745.0	3,441.9	3,640.4	3,893.6
Government	49.2	117.1	260.1	516.0	622.7	640.9	664.2
Other	223.7	434.3	1,111.8	2,229.0	2,819.2	2,999.5	3,229.4
Supplements to wages and salaries	23.8	66.8	266.3	552.5	767.0	768.6	793.7
Employer contrib. for social ins.	12.6	34.3	127.9	278.3	365.3	381.7	400.7
Other labor income	11.2	32.5	138.4	274.3	401.6	387.0	392.9
Proprietors' income with adjustments	**52.1**	**80.2**	**180.7**	**363.3**	**488.1**	**527.7**	**551.2**
Farm	11.6	14.7	20.5	41.9	22.4	38.9	35.5
Nonfarm	40.5	65.4	160.1	321.4	465.6	488.8	515.8
Rental income of persons, with capital consumption adjustment	**15.3**	**18.2**	**6.6**	**–14.2**	**133.7**	**150.2**	**158.2**
Corp. profits with inventory adjustment	**49.8**	**69.5**	**194.0**	**354.7**	**613.0**	**679.0**	**741.2**
Corp. profits before tax	49.9	76.0	237.1	365.7	635.6	680.2	734.4
Corp. profits tax liability	22.7	34.4	84.8	138.7	211.0	226.1	246.1
Corp. profits after tax	27.2	41.7	152.3	227.1	424.6	454.1	488.3
Dividends	12.9	22.5	54.7	153.5	205.3	261.9	275.1
Undistributed profits	14.3	19.2	97.6	73.6	219.3	192.3	213.2
Inventory valuation adjustment	–0.2	–6.6	–43.1	–11.0	–22.6	–1.2	6.9
Net interest	**11.3**	**41.2**	**200.9**	**463.7**	**420.6**	**418.6**	**432.0**

(1) Figures do not add, because of rounding and incomplete enumeration. (2) National income is the aggregate of labor and property earnings that arises in the production of goods and services. It is the sum of employee compensation, proprietors' income, rental income, adjusted corporate profits, and net interest. It measures the total factor costs of goods and services produced by the economy. Income is measured before deduction of taxes. Total national income figures include adjustments not itemized. (R) Revised.

Distribution of U.S. Total Personal Income[1]

Source: Bureau of Economic Analysis, U.S. Dept. of Commerce

(billions of dollars)

Year	Personal income	Personal taxes	Disposable personal income	Personal outlays	Personal Savings: Amount	Personal Savings: As pct. of disposable income
1960	$411.7	$48.7	$362.9	$339.6	$23.3	6.4%
1965	555.8	61.9	493.9	456.2	37.8	7.6
1970	836.1	109.0	727.1	666.1	61.0	8.4
1975	1,315.6	156.4	1,159.2	1,054.8	104.4	9.0
1980	2,285.7	312.4	1,973.3	1,811.5	161.8	8.2
1985	3,439.6	437.7	3,002.0	2,795.8	206.2	6.9
1990	4,791.6	624.8	4,166.8	3,958.1	208.7	5.0
1991	4,968.5	624.8	4,343.7	4,097.4	246.4	5.7
1992	5,264.2	650.5	4,613.7	4,341.0	272.6	5.9
1993	5,480.1	689.9	4,790.2	4,575.8	214.4	4.5
1994[R]	5,757.9	739.1	5,018.9	4,842.1	176.8	3.5
1995[R]	6,072.1	795.0	5,277.0	5,097.2	179.8	3.4
1996[R]	6,425.2	890.5	5,534.7	5,376.2	158.5	2.9
1997	6,784.0	989.0	5,795.1	5,674.1	121.0	2.1

(1) Figures may not add because of rounding. (R) Revised figures.

MILLENNIUM FACT BOX

Record One-Day Gains and Losses on the Dow Jones Industrial Average

Source: Dow Jones & Co., Inc.; as of Oct. 1998

GREATEST POINT GAINS

Rank	Date	Close	Net Chg	% Chg
1.	9/8/98	8,020.78	380.53	4.98
2.	10/28/97	7,498.32	337.17	4.71
3.	9/1/98	7,827.43	288.36	3.82
4.	9/2/97	7,879.78	257.36	3.38
5.	9/23/98	8,154.41	257.21	3.26
6.	11/3/97	7,674.39	232.31	3.12
7.	2/2/98	8,107.78	201.28	2.55
8.	12/1/97	8,013.11	189.98	2.43
9.	10/21/87	2,027.85	186.84	10.15
10.	9/11/98	7,795.50	179.96	2.36

GREATEST POINT LOSSES

Rank	Date	Close	Net Chg	% Chg
1.	10/27/97	7,161.15	−554.26	−7.18
2.	8/31/98	7,539.07	−512.61	−6.37
3.	10/19/87	1,738.74	−508.00	−22.61
4.	8/27/98	8,165.99	−357.36	−4.19
5.	8/4/98	8,487.31	−299.43	−3.41
6.	9/10/98	7,615.54	−249.48	−3.17
7.	8/15/97	7,694.66	−247.37	−3.11
8.	9/30/98	7,842.62	−237.90	−2.94
9.	1/9/98	7,580.42	−222.20	−2.85
10.	9/17/98	7,873.77	−216.01	−2.67

GREATEST % GAINS

Rank	Date	Close	Net Chg	% Chg
1.	10/6/31	99.34	12.86	14.87
2.	10/30/29	258.47	28.40	12.34
3.	9/21/32	75.16	7.67	11.36
4.	10/21/87	2,027.85	186.84	10.15
5.	8/3/32	58.22	5.06	9.52
6.	2/11/32	78.60	6.80	9.47
7.	11/14/29	217.28	18.59	9.36
8.	12/18/31	80.69	6.90	9.35
9.	2/13/32	85.82	7.22	9.19
10.	5/6/32	59.01	4.91	9.08

GREATEST % LOSSES

Rank	Date	Close	Net Chg	% Chg
1.	10/19/87	1,738.74	−508.00	−22.61
2.	10/28/29	260.54	−38.33	−12.82
3.	10/29/29	230.07	−30.57	−11.73
4.	11/6/29	232.13	−25.55	−9.92
5.	12/18/1899	58.27	−5.57	−8.72
6.	8/12/32	63.11	−5.79	−8.40
7.	3/14/07	76.23	−6.89	−8.29
8.	10/25/87	1,793.93	−156.83	−8.04
9.	7/21/33	88.71	−7.55	−7.84
10.	10/18/37	125.73	−10.57	−7.75

Dow Jones Industrial Average Since 1961

High		Year	Low		High		Year	Low	
Dec.13	734.91	**1961**	Jan. 3	610.25	Nov. 20	1000.17	**1980**	Apr. 21	759.13
Jan. 3	726.01	**1962**	June 26	535.76	Apr. 27	1024.05	**1981**	Sept. 25	824.01
Dec. 18	767.21	**1963**	Jan. 2	646.79	Dec. 27	1070.55	**1982**	Aug. 12	776.92
Nov. 18	891.71	**1964**	Jan. 2	766.08	Nov. 29	1287.20	**1983**	Jan. 3	1027.04
Dec. 31	969.26	**1965**	June 28	840.59	Jan. 6	1286.64	**1984**	July 24	1086.57
Feb. 9	995.15	**1966**	Oct. 7	744.32	Dec. 16	1553.10	**1985**	Jan. 4	1184.96
Sept. 25	943.08	**1967**	Jan. 3	786.41	Dec. 2	1955.57	**1986**	Jan. 22	1502.29
Dec. 3	985.21	**1968**	Mar. 21	825.13	Aug. 25	2722.42	**1987**	Oct. 19	1738.74
May 14	968.85	**1969**	Dec. 17	769.93	Oct. 21	2183.50	**1988**	Jan. 20	1879.14
Dec. 29	842.00	**1970**	May 6	631.16	Oct. 9	2791.41	**1989**	Jan. 3	2144.64
Apr. 28	950.82	**1971**	Nov. 23	797.97	July 16	2999.75	**1990**	Oct. 11	2365.10
Dec. 11	1036.27	**1972**	Jan. 26	889.15	Dec. 31	3168.83	**1991**	Jan. 9	2470.30
Jan. 11	1051.70	**1973**	Dec. 5	788.31	June 1	3413.21	**1992**	Oct. 9	3136.58
Mar. 13	891.66	**1974**	Dec. 6	577.60	Dec. 29	3794.33	**1993**	Jan. 20	3241.95
July 15	881.81	**1975**	Jan. 2	632.04	Jan. 31	3978.36	**1994**	Apr. 4	3593.35
Sept. 21	1014.79	**1976**	Jan. 2	858.71	Dec. 13	5216.47	**1995**	Jan. 30	3832.08
Jan. 3	999.75	**1977**	Nov. 2	800.85	Dec. 27	6560.91	**1996**	Jan. 10	5032.94
Sept. 8	907.74	**1978**	Feb. 28	742.12	Aug. 6	8259.31	**1997**	Apr. 11	6391.69
Oct. 5	897.61	**1979**	Nov. 7	796.67	July 17	9337.97	**1998***	Aug. 31	7539.07

*As of Oct.15.

Milestones of the Dow Jones Industrial Average

(as of Oct. 15, 1998)

First close over...		First close over...		First close over...	
100	Jan. 12, 1906	5,000	Nov. 21, 1995	8,400	Feb. 18, 1998
500	Mar. 12, 1956	5,500	Feb. 8, 1996	8,500	Feb. 27, 1998
1,000	Nov. 14, 1972	6,000	Oct. 14, 1996	8,600	Mar. 10, 1998
1,500	Dec. 11, 1985	6,500	Nov. 25, 1996	8,700	Mar. 16, 1998
2,000	Jan. 8, 1987	7,000	Feb. 13, 1997	8,800	Mar. 19, 1998
2,500	July 17, 1987	7,500	June 10, 1997	8,900	Mar. 20, 1998
3,000	April 17, 1991	8,000	July 16, 1997	9,000	Apr. 6, 1998
3,500	May 19, 1993	8,100	July 24, 1997	9,100	Apr. 14, 1998
4,000	Feb. 23, 1995	8,200	July 30, 1997	9,200	May 13, 1998
4,500	June 16, 1995	8,300	Feb. 12, 1998	9,300	July 16, 1998

Components of the Dow Jones Averages

(as of Oct. 1998)

Dow Jones Industrial Average

AlliedSignal
Aluminum Co. of America (Alcoa)
American Express
AT&T
Boeing
Caterpillar
Chevron
Coca-Cola
DuPont
Eastman Kodak
Exxon
General Electric
General Motors
Goodyear Tire & Rubber
Hewlett-Packard
IBM
International Paper
Johnson & Johnson
McDonald's
Merck
Minnesota Mining & Manufacturing
Morgan (J.P.)
Philip Morris
Procter & Gamble
Sears, Roebuck
Travelers Group
Union Carbide
United Technologies
Wal-Mart
Walt Disney

Dow Jones Transportation Average

Airborne Freight
Alaska Air Group
Alexander & Baldwin
AMR (American Airlines)
Burlington Northern Santa Fe
CNF Transportation
CSX
Delta Air Lines
FDX
GATX
Norfolk Southern
Roadway Express
Ryder System
Southwest Air Lines
UAL (United Air Lines)
Union Pacific
US Airways
USFreightways
XTRA
Yellow Corp.

Dow Jones Utility Average

American Electric Power
Columbia Energy Group
Consolidated Edison
Consolidated Natural Gas
Duke Energy
Edison International
Enron
Houston Industries
PECO
PG&E
Public Service Enterprise Group
Southern Co.
Texas Utilities
Unicom
Williams Cos.

Most Active Common Stocks in 1997

New York Exchange	Volume (millions of shares)
Compaq Computer Corp.	1,231.6
Philip Morris Cos., Inc.	1,107.8
AT&T Corp.	1,052.7
Micron Technology Inc.	1,003.3
PepsiCo, Inc.	879.8
IBM	875.7
General Electric Company	840.5
Coca-Cola Company	753.5
Wal-Mart Stores Inc.	736.7
Columbia/HCA Health Corporation	700.8
Telecomm Brasil Telebras	679.4
Merck and Company, Inc.	655.8
Seagate Technology, Inc.	645.8
Hewlett-Packard Company	643.4
Boeing Company	638.7

American Exchange	Volume (millions of shares)
Standard & Poor's Depositary Receipts	769.7
Viacom Inc. Class B	206.7
XCL Ltd.	172.8
Harken Energy Corp.	147.6
Trans World Airlines	138.1
Nabors Industries, Inc.	137.1
Hasbro, Inc.	131.6
Echo Bay Mines Ltd.	127.4
ITS Corporation	113.1
Grey Wolf	105.9
Tubos de Acero de Mexico	100.9
IVAX Corporation	95.4
Royal Oak Mines, Inc.	90.4
Pegasus Gold Inc.	75.0
Metromedia International Group, Inc.	62.3

NASDAQ	Volume (millions of shares)
Cisco Systems, Inc.	5,386.6
Ascend Communications, Inc.	3,892.0
Intel Corp.	3,887.9
Dell Computer Corp.	3,719.0
Tele-Communications, Inc.	2,456.3
3Com Corp.	2,200.4
Microsoft Corp.	2,097.9
Oracle Corp.	1,970.2
Applied Materials, Inc.	1,804.2
WorldCom, Inc.	1,784.8
FORE Systems, Inc.	1,519.5
Sun Microsystems, Inc.	1,490.3
PairGain Technologies, Inc.	1,474.6
MCI Communications Corp.	1,457.7
Altera Corp.	1,396.4

Average Yields of Long-Term Treasury, Corporate, and Municipal Bonds

Source: Office of Market Finance, U.S. Dept. of the Treasury

Period	Treasury 30-year bonds	New Aa corporate bonds[1]	New Aa municipal bonds[2]
1986			
June	7.57	9.39	7.75
Dec.	7.37	8.87	6.70
1987			
June	8.57	9.64	7.69
Dec.	9.12	10.22	7.83
1988			
June	9.00	10.08	7.67
Dec.	9.01	10.05	7.40
1989			
June	8.27	9.24	6.94
Dec.	7.90	9.23	6.76
1990			
June	8.46	9.69	6.98
Dec.	8.24	9.55	6.85
1991			
June	8.47	9.37	6.90
Dec.	7.70	8.55	6.43
1992			
June	7.84	8.45	6.32
Dec.	7.44	8.12	6.02
1993			
June	6.81	7.48	5.54
Dec.	6.25	7.22	5.27
1994			
June	7.40	8.16	5.96
Dec.	7.87	8.66	6.63
1995			
June	6.57	7.42	5.61
Dec.	6.06	7.02	5.46
1996			
June	7.06	8.00	5.82
Dec.	6.55	7.45	5.47
1997			
Jan.	6.83	7.62	5.53
Feb.	6.69	7.54	5.40
Mar.	6.93	7.85	5.59
Apr.	7.09	8.04	5.73
May	6.94	7.90	5.53
June	6.77	7.71	5.39
July	6.51	7.44	5.27
Aug.	6.58	7.30	5.27
Sept.	6.50	7.04	5.25
Oct.	6.33	6.90	5.26
Nov.	6.11	6.79	5.23
Dec.	5.99	6.68	5.07
1998			
Jan.	5.81	6.62	4.93
Feb.	5.89	6.66	4.96
Mar.	5.95	6.63	5.10

(1) Treasury series based on 3-week moving average of reoffering yields of new corporate bonds rated Aa by Moody's Investors Service with an original maturity of at least 20 years. (2) Index of new reoffering yields on 20-year general obligations rated Aa by Moody's Investors Service.

Performance of Mutual Funds by Type

Source: CDA/Wiesenberger, Rockville, MD, 800-232-2285

(data for period ending Aug. 31, 1998)

FUND TYPE	Fund objective	1-Yr Total return No.	1-Yr Total return Avg.	5-Yr Annual return No.	5-Yr Annual return Avg.
Stock	Natural resources	57	-38.39	30	-0.15
	Equity income	191	0.51	100	12.47
	Financial services	39	3.49	15	18.32
	Precious metals	43	-48.75	28	-15.72
	Growth and income	583	-0.66	296	13.56
	Health/biotechnology	38	-4.27	15	17.38
	Aggressive growth	166	-14.81	83	8.43
	Small capital gains	566	-18.61	197	8.95
	Real estate	72	-12.78	11	3.27
	S&P 500 Index	79	7.27	46	17.83
	Technology/comm.	74	-9.86	24	15.36
	Utilities	103	15.86	52	9.12
	Mid-capital gains	178	-10.35	60	10.41
	Domestic growth	1,143	-3.20	505	13.28
International stock	Emerging equity	158	-46.22	19	-7.84
	Global income	268	1.55	126	4.85
	Global equity	293	-4.15	110	9.59
	Non-U.S. equity	731	-12.46	231	4.23
	Emerging income	25	-34.33	4	3.05
Hybrid	Asset allocation-Domestic	240	2.89	80	10.62
	Asset allocation-Global	65	-2.75	16	6.13
	Balanced-domestic	330	2.33	151	10.28
	Balanced-global	28	1.01	4	6.25
Bond	Corporate-Investment grade	59	8.36	27	6.06
	Corporate high yield	207	1.25	96	7.95
	Convertible	45	-5.30	27	8.86
	U.S. Treasury	58	11.69	38	6.32
	U.S. Gov't./agency	268	9.55	162	5.59
	U.S. Gov't./ short & intermediate	219	7.75	130	5.13
	U.S. Gov't./long	24	12.61	18	6.27
	General Bond-short & intermediate	144	7.73	92	5.63
	General Bond-long	22	7.91	11	6.64
	General Bond-Investment grade	395	8.03	207	5.79
	General mortgage	91	6.78	64	5.36
	Loan participation	4	6.95	4	6.86
	Multi-sector	123	3.37	56	6.54
Municipal bond	National	428	7.42	267	5.35
	California	134	7.89	89	5.60
	New York	122	7.95	80	5.30
	Single state	1,210	7.80	741	5.35
	High yield	67	8.53	39	6.12
	Insured	131	7.83	84	5.42

Chicago Board of Trade, Contracts Traded 1988, 1997

	1988	1997	% change 1988-97
FUTURES GROUP			
Agricultural	37,544,203	48,864,241	30.2
Financial	77,309,257	140,391,980	81.6
Stock index	1,231,371	755,476	−38.6
Metals	674,031	44,590	−93.4
Total futures	**116,758,862**	**190,056,287**	**62.8**
OPTIONS GROUP			
Agricultural	5,578,491	13,159,368	135.9
Financial	20,692,839	39,311,358	90.0
Metals	8,303	68	−99.2
Stock index	—	156,132	—
PCS insurance	—	15,706	—
Total options	**26,279,633**	**52,642,632**	**100.3**
COMBINED FUTURES AND OPTIONS			
Agricultural	43,122,694	62,023,609	43.8
Financial	98,002,096	179,703,338	83.4
Stock index	1,231,371	911,608	−26.0
Metals	682,334	44,658	−93.5
Insurance	—	—	—
PCS insurance	—	15,706	—
GRAND TOTAL	**143,038,495**	**242,698,919**	**69.7**

Selected Personal Consumption Expenditures in the U.S., 1991-97

Source: Bureau of Economic Analysis, U.S. Dept. of Commerce

(billions of dollars)

	1991	1992	1993R	1994R	1995R	1996R	1997
Food & tobacco	**$693.8**	**$709.5**	**$733.4**	**$761.7**	**$783.8**	**$805.2**	**$832.3**
Food purchased for off-premise consumption	419.1	423.3	435.6	451.6	462.2	477.0	494.2
Purchased meals and beverages	223.1	228.6	243.0	254.3	264.1	268.8	277.2
Tobacco products	43.8	49.6	46.6	47.3	48.7	50.2	51.4
Clothing, accessories, jewelry	**265.7**	**283.5**	**298.1**	**312.7**	**323.4**	338.0	**353.3**
Shoes	31.9	33.6	34.4	36.0	36.8	38.5	39.8
Clothing and accessories less shoes	179.3	191.7	201.8	211.6	217.7	226.9	237.9
Jewelry and watches	31.4	33.2	35.6	37.7	39.3	41.4	43.1
Personal care	**59.1**	**63.1**	**65.1**	**68.4**	**71.9**	**75.0**	**79.4**
Toilet articles, preparations	39.4	41.4	43.1	45.3	47.2	49.7	52.6
Barber shops, beauty parlors, health clubs	19.7	21.8	22.0	23.0	24.7	25.3	26.8
Housing	**616.5**	**646.8**	**672.8**	**712.7**	**750.3**	**787.4**	**829.8**
Owner-occupied nonfarm dwellings—space rent	434.1	457.8	480.9	507.0	532.2	559.1	590.3
Tenant-occupied nonfarm dwellings—rent	155.8	160.5	162.1	174.0	184.6	193.2	203.2
Rental value of farm dwellings	5.2	5.3	5.5	5.8	5.9	6.1	6.3
Household operation	**448.4**	**470.6**	**504.1**	**535.0**	**562.8**	**592.8**	**620.7**
Furniture, including bedding	38.4	39.8	42.7	45.9	48.0	50.6	54.8
Kitchen and other household appliances	21.6	22.2	24.0	25.6	27.2	28.5	29.7
China, glassware, tableware, utensils	18.9	20.7	22.0	24.0	25.3	27.0	28.6
Other durable house furnishings	42.3	45.5	48.2	52.3	54.5	57.9	61.8
Semidurable house furnishings	21.6	23.2	25.0	27.2	28.9	30.7	32.8
Household utilities	145.4	148.6	160.3	163.8	168.5	176.6	178.5
Telephone, telegraph	63.5	70.3	74.5	82.6	90.2	97.1	104.2
Medical care	**668.7**	**733.2**	**785.5**	**826.1**	**871.6**	**912.4**	**957.3**
Drug preparations, sundries	70.9	75.0	78.1	81.6	85.7	91.1	98.1
Physicians	152.1	167.2	172.5	180.0	191.4	198.2	205.2
Dentists	34.7	38.5	40.8	43.9	47.6	49.5	52.6
Hospitals and nursing homes	293.4	320.0	341.1	357.0	375.9	389.8	408.1
Health insurance	37.3	42.7	53.6	55.0	53.6	57.4	58.0
Personal business	**318.9**	**341.7**	**357.4**	**370.4**	**389.1**	**416.2**	**459.1**
Brokerage charges, investment counseling	25.3	30.4	35.7	36.2	38.8	46.6	54.4
Bank service charges, trust services, safe deposit box	25.7	28.0	30.7	31.6	33.9	37.3	41.5
Legal services	42.9	46.5	47.9	48.8	49.1	53.0	55.9
Funeral, burial expenses	9.4	10.1	10.8	11.1	12.2	13.3	13.8
Transportation	**436.8**	**471.5**	**504.0**	**542.2**	**572.3**	**611.6**	**636.4**
User-operated transportation	401.4	435.7	465.5	502.6	530.1	567.3	588.3
New autos	75.3	82.1	86.4	91.2	87.1	85.8	86.2
Used autos	32.0	35.5	40.2	44.1	52.4	55.8	57.3
Repair, greasing, washing, parking, storage, rental, leasing	85.2	94.4	102.4	116.4	128.7	143.6	154.9
Gasoline and oil	103.9	106.6	107.6	109.4	114.4	124.5	126.5
Tolls	2.1	2.3	2.5	2.6	2.8	2.8	3.0
Insurance premiums less claims paid	22.6	25.5	26.8	27.5	29.4	31.5	34.4
Purchased local transportation	7.9	8.0	8.4	8.9	9.2	10.0	10.4
Mass transit systems	5.3	5.4	5.6	5.9	6.0	6.5	6.8
Taxicab	2.6	2.6	2.8	3.0	3.2	3.5	3.6
Purchased intercity transportation	27.5	27.9	30.1	30.7	33.0	34.3	37.7
Railway (excl. commutation)	0.8	0.8	0.8	0.7	0.8	0.8	0.8
Bus	1.1	1.1	1.0	1.1	1.3	1.1	1.2
Airline	23.0	23.3	25.4	25.8	27.7	28.5	31.5
Recreation	**292.0**	**310.8**	**340.2**	**370.2**	**402.5**	**432.3**	**462.9**
Books, maps	16.9	17.7	19.0	20.6	22.1	24.2	25.2
Magazines, newspapers, sheet music	21.9	21.6	22.7	24.5	25.5	27.6	29.1
Nondurable toys and sport supplies	32.8	34.2	36.6	39.7	42.2	45.1	47.8
Wheel goods, sports and photographic equipment, boats, pleasure aircraft	29.5	29.9	32.6	35.6	39.1	42.3	48.1
Video & audio prods., computers, musical instruments	57.3	61.2	68.1	78.5	85.2	92.0	96.5
Flowers, seeds, potted plants	11.3	12.3	12.7	13.4	13.9	14.8	15.9
Admissions to specified spectator amusements	15.7	16.6	18.1	19.0	20.2	21.9	23.3
Motion picture theaters	5.3	5.0	5.2	5.6	6.0	6.2	6.6
Legitimate theater, opera	6.0	6.8	7.8	8.2	8.7	9.3	10.0
Spectator sports	4.5	4.8	5.1	5.2	5.5	6.4	6.7
Clubs, fraternal organizations	9.6	10.3	11.2	11.8	12.7	13.0	13.8
Commercial participant amusements	23.8	27.2	31.5	36.2	41.5	44.7	49.1
Education and research	**86.1**	**93.1**	**98.5**	**104.7**	**112.2**	**119.7**	**129.4**
Higher education	48.0	52.0	55.5	59.0	62.2	65.7	69.6
Nursery, elementary, and secondary schools	18.0	19.3	20.1	21.4	22.8	23.5	25.7
Religious and welfare activities	**104.1**	**115.6**	**121.3**	**131.2**	**139.8**	**151.1**	**157.6**
TOTAL personal consumption expenditures	**$3,975.1**	**$4,219.8**	**$4,459.2**	**$4,717.0**	**$4,957.7**	**$5,215.7**	**$5,493.7**

R= revised figures.

Minerals

Source: U.S. Geological Survey, U.S. Dept. of the Interior; as of mid-1998

Aluminum: the second most abundant metallic element in the earth's crust. Bauxite is the main source of aluminum; convert to aluminum equivalent by multiplying by 0.232. Guinea and Australia have 49% of the world's reserves. Aluminum is used in the U.S. principally in transportation (34%), packaging (25%), and building (15%).

Chromium: about 2/3 of the world's production of chromite, the chief source of chromium, is in India, Kazakhstan, and South Africa. The chemical and metallurgical industries use about 90% of the chromite consumed in the world.

Cobalt: used in superalloys for jet engines, chemicals (paint driers, catalysts, magnetic coatings, and rechargable batteries), permanent magnets, and cemented carbides for cutting tools. Canada, Congo (formerly Zaire), Finland, Norway, Russia, and Zambia account for more than 90% of world cobalt (refinery) production. The U.S. uses about 1/3 of world consumption. Although its resources are relatively large, the U.S. has not produced cobalt since 1971; most U.S. resources are low-grade, and production from these deposits is not economically feasible.

Columbium (niobium): used mostly as an additive in steelmaking and in superalloys. Brazil and Canada are the world's leading columbium raw materials (feedstock) producers. There is no U.S. columbium mining industry.

Copper: main uses of copper in the U.S. are in building construction (42%), electrical and electronic products (25%), transportation (13%), industrial machinery and equipment (12%), and consumer and general products (8%). The leading producer is Chile, followed by the U.S., Canada, Australia, Indonesia, Russia, China, Peru, Poland, Zambia, and Mexico. Principal mining states are Arizona, Utah, and New Mexico.

Gold: used in the U.S. in jewelry and the arts (55%), electronics and other industries (42%), and dentistry (3%). South Africa has about half the world's resources; significant quantities are also present in the U.S., Australia, Canada, the former Soviet Union, and Brazil. Gold is mined in nearly all the Western U.S. states and in Alaska.

Iron ore: the source of primary iron for the world's iron and steel industries. Major iron ore producers include Australia, Brazil, China, and the former Soviet Union.

Lead: the U.S., Australia, China, Peru, and Canada are the world's largest producers of lead. Transportation accounts for the major end use in the U.S., with 89% used in batteries, bearings, casting metals, and solders. Other uses include emergency power supply batteries, construction sheeting, sporting ammunition, and power cable coverings. The U.S. produces and consumes about 25% of the world's lead metal, including primary and recycled material.

Manganese: essential to iron and steel production. The U.S., Japan, and Western Europe have exhausted nearly all of their economically minable manganese. South Africa and the former Soviet Union have over 75% of the world's reserves.

Nickel: vital to the stainless steel industry; used to make superalloys for the chemical and aerospace industries. Leading producers include Russia, Canada, Australia, New Caledonia, and Indonesia.

Platinum-Group Metals: the platinum group consists of 6 closely related metals: platinum, palladium, rhodium, ruthenium, iridium, and osmium. They commonly occur together in nature and are among the scarcest of the metallic elements. They are consumed in the U.S. by the following industries: automotive, electrical and electronic, chemical, and dental and medical. The automotive, chemical, and petroleum-refining industries use platinum-group metals mainly as catalysts. Russia and South Africa have most of the world's reserves.

Silver: used in the following U.S. industries: photography, electrical and electronic products, sterlingware, electroplated ware, and jewelry. Silver is mined in more than 60 countries. Nevada produces more than 40% of U.S. silver, Idaho 16%.

Tantalum: a refractory metal with unique electrical, chemical, and physical properties; used in the U.S. mostly to produce electronic components, mainly tantalum capacitors. Australia, Brazil, and Canada are the leading tantalum raw-material producers. There is no U.S. tantalum mining industry.

Titanium: Approximately 95% of consumption is in the form of titanium dioxide, a white pigment in paint, paper, and plastics. As a metal, titanium is used primarily in commercial and military aerospace. Major mining operations are in Australia, Canada, Norway, and South Africa. U.S. mine production is in Florida and Virginia.

Vanadium: used as an alloying element in steel and aerospace titanium alloys, as a catalyst in the production of maleic and phthalic anhydride, and in the production of sulfuric acid. China, South Africa, and Russia are the world's largest producers of vanadium-bearing ores and concentrates.

Zinc: used as a protective coating on steel, as diecastings, as an alloying metal with copper to make brass, and as a component of chemical compounds in rubber and paints. It is mined in 46 countries. China is the leading producer, followed by Canada, Australia, Peru, the U.S., and Mexico. In the U.S., mine production comes mostly from Alaska, Tennessee, New York, and Missouri.

World Mineral Reserve Base

Source: U.S. Geological Survey, U.S. Dept. of the Interior; as of mid-1998

Mineral	Reserve Base[1]	Mineral	Reserve Base[1]
Aluminum	28,000 mil metric tons[2]	Manganese	5,000 mil metric tons
Chromium	7,500 mil metric tons	Nickel	134 mil metric tons
Cobalt	9.0 mil metric tons	Platinum-Group Metals	78 mil kilograms
Columbium	4.2 mil metric tons	Silver	420,000 metric tons
Copper	630 mil metric tons	Tantalum	24,000 metric tons
Gold	72,000 metric tons[3]	Titanium	610 mil metric tons[5]
Iron ore	270,000 mil metric tons[4]	Vanadium	27 mil metric tons
Lead	120 mil metric tons	Zinc	430 mil metric tons

(1) Includes demonstrated reserves that are currently economic or marginally economic, plus some that are currently subeconomic. (2) Bauxite. (3) Excludes China and some other countries for which reliable data were not available. (4) Crude ore. (5) Titanium dioxide (TiO_2) content of ilmenite and rutile.

U.S. Nonfuel Mineral Production—10 Leading States in 1997

Source: U.S. Geological Survey, U.S. Dept. of the Interior

Rank/State	Value (millions)	Percent of U.S. total	Principal minerals
1. Arizona	$3,520	8.91	Copper, sand & gravel (construction), cement, molybdenum, lime
2. Nevada	3,030	7.69	Gold, copper, silver, sand & gravel (construction), diatomite
3. California	2,810	7.13	Cement, sand & gravel (construction), boron minerals, stone (crushed), gold
4. Georgia	1,770	4.49	Clays, stone (crushed), cement, sand & gravel (construction)
5. Utah	1,760	4.46	Copper, gold, molybdenum, magnesium metal, sand & gravel (construction)
6. Florida	1,740	4.42	Phosphate rock, stone (crushed), cement, sand & gravel (construction), titanium minerals
7. Texas	1,700	4.31	Cement, stone (crushed), sand & gravel (construction), magnesium metal, salt
8. Minnesota	1,600	4.06	Iron ore, sand & gravel (construction & industrial), stone (crushed & dimension)
9. Michigan	1,560	3.96	Cement, iron ore, sand & gravel (construction), magnesium compounds, stone (crushed)
10. Missouri	1,320	3.34	Stone (crushed), lead, cement, lime, zinc

U.S. Nonfuel Mineral Production

Source: U.S. Geological Survey, U.S. Dept. of the Interior

Production as measured by mine shipments, sales, or marketable production (including consumption by producers).

		1992	1993	1994	1995	1996	1997
Beryllium (metal equivalent)	metric tons	193	198	173	202	211	231
Copper (recoverable content of ores, etc.)	thousand metric tons	1,760	1,800	1,850	1,850	1,920	1,940
Gold (recoverable content of ores, etc.)	metric tons	330.2	331.0	326.2	317.0	321.0R	357.0
Iron ore, usable (includes byproduct material)	million metric tons	55.6	55.7	58.4	62.5	62.1	62.9
Lead (in concentrate)	thousand metric tons	397	355	363	386	426R	448
Magnesium metal (primary)	thousand metric tons	137	132	128	142	133	125
Molybdenum (content of ore and concentrate)	metric tons	49,725	36,803	46,810	58,000	56,000	58,900
Nickel (content of ore and concentrate)	metric tons	6,671	2,464	—	1,557	1,333	—
Silver (recoverable content of ores, etc.)	metric tons	1,800	1,640	1,480	1,560	1,570	2,150
Zinc (recoverable content of ores, etc.)	thousand metric tons	523	488	570	614	598R	605
Asbestos	thousand metric tons	16	14	10	W	10	7
Barite	thousand metric tons	326	315	583	543	662	692
Boron minerals	thousand metric tons	554	574	550	728	581	604
Bromine	million kilograms	171	177	195	218	227	247
Cement (portland, masonry, etc.)	thousand metric tons	69,585	73,807	77,948	76,906	79,266R	80,900E
Clays	thousand metric tons	40,237	40,700	42,000	43,100	43,100	41,500
Diatomite	thousand metric tons	625E	649	646	722	729	773
Feldspar	thousand metric tons	725	770	765	880	890	900E
Fluorspar	thousand metric tons	51	56	49	51	8	—
Garnet (industrial)	metric tons	54,100	51,500	41,100	39,900	46,200	53,600
Gemstones	million dollars	66.2	57.7	50.5	48.7	43.6	25.0
Gypsum	thousand metric tons	14,900	15,800	17,200	16,600	17,500	18,500
Helium (extracted from natural gas)	million cubic meters	92.0	99.3	112.0	101.0	103.0	106.0
Helium (Grade A sold)	million cubic meters	94.4	95.6	100.4	96.1	94.7	98.0
Iodine	thousand kilograms	1,995	1,935	1,630	1,220	1,270	1,320
Lime	thousand metric tons	16,199	16,932	17,393	18,530	19,225	19,678
Mica (scrap & flake)	thousand metric tons	85	88	110	108	97	114
Peat	thousand metric tons	599	616	574	648	549	660
Perlite (sold and used by producers)	thousand metric tons	541	569	644	700	684	706
Phosphate rock (marketable product)	thousand metric tons	46,965	35,494	41,115	43,500	45,400	43,300
Potash (K_2O equivalent)	thousand metric tons	1,705	1,506	1,400	1,480	1,390	1,400
Pumice and pumicite	thousand metric tons	481	469	490	529	612	577
Salt	thousand metric tons	34,784	38,200	39,700	40,800	42,900	35,900
Sand and gravel (construction)	thousand metric tons	834,000	869,000	891,000	907,000	914,000	961,000E
Sand and gravel (industrial)	thousand metric tons	25,195	26,220	27,300	28,200	27,800	28,700
Soda ash (sodium carbonate)	thousand metric tons	9,379	8,959	9,321	10,100	10,200	10,700
Sodium sulfate (natural)	thousand metric tons	337	322	298	327	306	318
Stone (crushed)	million metric tons	1,050	1,120	1,230	1,260	1,330	1,400E
Stone (dimension)	thousand metric tons	1,140	1,280	1,190	1,160	1,150	1,160E
Sulfur (in all forms)	thousand metric tons	10,663	10,959	11,500	11,800	12,000	12,000E
Talc	thousand metric tons	997	968	935	1,060	994	1,050
Vermiculite	thousand metric tons	190	190	177	171	W	W

(R) Revised figures. (E) Estimated. (W) Withheld to avoid disclosing company proprietary data. (—) No production.

U.S. Reliance on Foreign Supplies of Minerals

Source: U.S. Geological Survey, U.S. Dept. of the Interior

Mineral	Percent imported in 1997	Major sources (1993-1996)	Major uses
Arsenic	100%	China, Japan, Hong Kong, Germany	Wood preservatives, agric. chemicals, nonferrous alloys
Bauxite and alumina	100	Australia, Guinea, Jamaica, Brazil	Aluminum prod., abrasives, chemicals, refractories
Columbium	100	Brazil, Canada, Germany	Steelmaking, superalloys
Fluorspar	100	China, South Africa, Mexico	Hydrofluoric acid, aluminum fluoride, steelmaking
Graphite (natural)	100	Mexico, China, Canada, Madagascar, Brazil	Refractories, brake linings, lubricants, foundry dressings and molds
Manganese	100	South Africa, Gabon, Australia, France	Steelmaking, batteries, agricultural chemicals
Mica, sheet (natural)	100	India, Belgium, China, Brazil	Electronic and electrical equipment
Strontium (celestite)	100	Mexico	Television picture tubes, ferrite magnets, pyrotechnics
Thallium	100	Belgium, Mexico, Canada	Superconductor materials, electronics, alloys, glass
Thorium	100	France	Ceramics, alloys, welding electrodes
Yttrium	100	China, Japan	TV manuf., fluorescent lights, temperature sensors
Gemstones	99	Israel, Belgium, India	Jewelry, carvings, gem and mineral collections
Tin	85	Brazil, Bolivia, Indonesia, China	Cans and containers, electrical, construction, transportation
Tungsten	85	China, Russia, Germany, Bolivia	Cemented carbide parts, electronic components, steel
Platinum	84	South Africa, Russia, UK, Germany	Catalysts, jewelry
Tantalum	80	Australia, Thailand, Germany, Brazil	Electronic components
Cobalt	78	Norway, Zambia, Finland, Canada, Russia	Superalloys, cemented carbides, paint driers, magnetic alloys
Palladium	78	Russia, South Africa, UK, Belgium	Catalysts, jewelry
Chromium	76	South Africa, Turkey, Russia, Kazakhstan, Zimbabwe	Ferroalloys, chemicals, refractories
Potash	76	Canada, Russia, Belarus, Israel	Fertilizer, chemicals
Barite	72	China, India, Mexico, Morocco	Oil and gas well drilling fluids
Zinc	70	Canada, Mexico, Spain, Peru	Galvanizing, alloys
Iodine	65	Japan, Chile, Canada	Animal feed supplements, catalysts, inks, disinfectants
Stone (dimension)	64	Italy, India, Brazil, Canada	Construction
Peat	58	Canada	Horticulture, agriculture
Nickel	54	Canada, Norway, Russia, Australia	Stainless steel, other alloys

U.S. Copper, Lead, and Zinc Production, 1950-97

Source: U.S. Geological Survey, U.S. Dept. of the Interior

	Copper		Lead		Zinc	
Year	Quantity (metric tons)	Value ($1,000)	Quantity (metric tons)	Value ($1,000)	Quantity (metric tons)	Value ($1,000)
1950	827	379,122	390,839	113,078	565,516	167,000
1960	1,037	733,706	223,774	57,722	395,013	112,365
1970	1,560	1,984,484	518,698	178,609	484,560	163,650
1975	1,282	1,814,763	563,783	267,230	425,792	366,097
1980	1,181	2,666,931	550,366	515,189	317,103	261,671
1985	1,105	1,631,000	413,955	174,008	226,545	201,607
1990	1,586	4,310,000	483,704	490,750	515,355	847,485
1991	1,630	3,931,000	465,931	343,907	517,804	602,426
1992	1,760	4,179,000	397,076	307,337	523,430	673,800
1993	1,800	3,635,000	355,185	248,540	488,283	496,795
1994	1,850	4,430,000	363,000	298,000	570,000	619,000
1995	1,850	5,640,000	386,000	359,000	614,000	756,000
1996	1,920	4,610,000	426,000	459,000	598,000	674,000
1997	1,940	4,570,000	448,000	460,000	605,000	860,000

U.S. Pig Iron and Raw Steel Output, 1940-97

Source: American Iron and Steel Institute

(net tons)

Year	Total pig iron	Raw steel
1940	46,071,666	66,982,686
1945	53,223,169	79,701,648
1950	64,586,907	96,836,075
1955	76,857,417	117,036,085
1960	66,480,648	99,281,601
1965	88,184,901	131,461,601
1970	91,435,000	131,514,000
1975	79,923,000	116,642,000
1980	68,721,000	111,835,000
1985	50,446,000	88,259,000
1990	54,750,000	98,906,000
1991	48,637,000	87,896,000
1992	52,224,000	92,949,000
1993	53,082,000	97,877,000
1994	54,426,000	100,579,000
1995	56,097,000	104,930,000
1996	54,485,000	105,309,478
1997	54,679,000	108,561,182

Steel figures include only that portion of the capacity and production of steel for castings used by foundries operated by companies producing steel ingots.

World Gold Production, 1975-97

Source: U.S. Geological Survey, U.S. Dept. of the Interior

(troy ounces)

		Africa			North and South America				Other			
Year	World prod.	South Africa	Ghana	Congo (Zaire)	United States	Canada	Mexico	Colombia	Australia	China	Philip-pines	USSR[1]
1975	38,476,371	22,937,820	523,889	115,743	1,052,252	1,653,611	144,710	308,864	526,821	NA	502,577	NA
1980	39,197,315	21,669,468	353,000	96,452	969,782	1,627,477	195,991	510,439	547,591	NA	753,452	8,425,000
1985	49,283,691	21,565,230	299,363	257,206	2,427,232	2,815,118	265,693	1,142,385	1,881,491	1,950,000	1,062,997	8,700,000
1986	51,534,056	20,513,665	287,127	257,206	3,739,015	3,364,700	250,615	1,285,878	2,413,842	2,100,000	1,296,400	8,850,000
1987	53,033,614	19,176,500	327,598	385,809	4,947,040	3,724,000	256,822	853,600	3,558,954	2,300,000	1,048,081	8,850,000
1988	60,308,973	19,965,611	355,620	401,884	6,459,534	4,334,338	292,508	932,822	5,046,059	2,507,758	980,019	8,925,046
1989	65,335,998	19,530,290	429,470	340,798	8,543,449	5,127,850	276,914	948,640	6,544,702	2,893,567	964,265	9,773,826
1990	70,206,932	19,454,414	541,419	299,002	9,458,395	5,446,722	311,283	943,689	7,849,186	3,215,074	790,619	9,709,524
1991	70,422,599	19,326,133	845,918	282,927	9,454,311	5,676,278	326,073	1,120,260	7,530,283	3,858,089	833,219	8,359,193
1992	73,529,583	19,742,838	997,702	225,055	10,616,561	5,189,194	318,003	1,032,618	7,825,491	4,501,104	729,886	8,231,554
1993	73,300,000	19,907,772	1,250,000	280,000	10,642,314	4,916,781	356,873	883,149	7,947,535	5,144,119	508,818	8,228,179
1994	73,000,000	18,637,078	1,400,000	357,000	10,488,247	4,710,000	446,895	883,149	8,236,634	5,144,119	469,754	8,172,719
1995	72,300,000	16,800,000	1,710,000	322,000	10,200,000	4,890,000	652,000	680,000	8,150,000	4,500,000	873,000	4,250,000*
1996	73,900,000	16,000,000	1,580,000	264,000	10,300,000	5,350,000	787,000	710,000	9,310,000	4,660,000	1,020,000	3,950,000*
1997	77,500,000	15,500,000	1,670,000	257,000	11,480,000	5,440,000	836,000	605,000	10,000,000	5,630,000	1,090,000	3,700,000*

NA=not available. (1) USSR as constituted prior to Dec. 1991. (*) Russia only.

U.S. and World Silver Production, 1930-97

Source: U.S. Geological Survey, U.S. Dept. of the Interior

(metric tons)

Year[1]	United States	World
1930	1,578	7,736
1935	1,428	6,865
1940	2,164	8,565
1945	904	5,039
1950	1,347	6,323
1955	1,134	6,967
1960	1,120	7,505
1965	1,238	8,007
1970	1,400	9,670
1975	1,087	9,428
1980	1,006	10,556
1985	1,227	13,051
1989	2,008	16,041
1990	2,120	16,600
1991	1,860	15,600
1992	1,800	14,600
1993	1,640	14,300
1994	1,490	14,000
1995	1,560	15,100
1996	1,570	15,200
1997	2,150	16,400

(1) Largest production of silver in the United States was in 1915—2,332 metric tons.

Aluminum Summary, 1980-97

Source: U.S. Geological Survey, U.S. Dept. of the Interior

Item	Unit	1980	1985	1990	1992	1993	1994	1995	1996[4]	1997[4]
U.S. production	1,000 metric tons	6,231	5,262	6,441	6,798	6,639	6,385	6,563	6,860	7,290
Primary aluminum	1,000 metric tons	4,654	3,500	4,048	4,042	3,695	3,299	3,375	3,577	3,603
Secondary aluminum[1]	1,000 metric tons	1,577	1,762	2,393	2,756	2,944	3,086	3,188	3,310	3,690
Primary aluminum value	Billion dollars	7.8	3.8	6.6	5.1	4.3	5.2	6.4	5.6	6.1
Price (Primary alum.)[2]	Cents/lb.	76.1	48.8	74.0	57.5	53.3	71.2	85.9	71.3	77.1
Imports for consumption[3]	1,000 metric tons	647	1,420	1,514	1,725	2,544	3,382	2,975	2,810	3,080
Exports[3]	1,000 metric tons	1,346	908	1,659	1,453	1,207	1,365	1,610	1,500	1,570
World production	1,000 metric tons	15,383	15,398	19,299	19,500	19,800	19,200	19,700	20,800	21,400

(1) Recoverable metal content from purchased scrap, old and new. (2) Average prices for primary aluminum, quoted by *Metals Week.* (3) Crude and semicrude (incl. metal and alloys, plates, bars, etc., and scrap). (4) All data in metric tons, except primary production, have been rounded to 3 significant figures.

Economic and Financial Glossary

Source: Reviewed by William M. Gentry, Graduate School of Business, Columbia University

Annuity contract: An investment vehicle sold by insurance companies. Annuity buyers can elect to receive periodic payments for the rest of their lives. Annuities provide insurance against outliving one's wealth.

Arbitrage: A form of hedged investment meant to capture slight differences in the prices of 2 related securities—for example, buying gold in London and selling it at a higher price in New York.

Balanced budget: A budget is balanced when receipts equal expenditures. When receipts exceed expenditures, there is a **surplus;** when they fall short of expenditures, there is a **deficit.**

Balance of payments: The difference between all payments, for some categories of transactions, made to and from foreign countries over a set period of time. A *favorable* balance of payments exists when more payments are coming in than going out; an *unfavorable* balance of payments obtains when the reverse is true. Payments may include gold, the cost of merchandise and services, interest and dividend payments, money spent by travelers, and repayment of principal on loans.

Balance of trade (trade gap): The difference between exports and imports, in both actual funds and credit. A nation's balance of trade is *favorable* when exports exceed imports and *unfavorable* when the reverse is true.

Bear market: A market in which prices are falling.

Bearer bond: A bond issued in bearer form rather than being registered in a specific owner's name. Ownership is determined by possession.

Bond: A written promise, or IOU, by the issuer to repay a fixed amount of borrowed money on a specified date and generally to pay interest at regular intervals in the interim.

Bull market: A market in which prices are on the rise.

Capital gain (loss): An increase (decrease) in the market value of an asset over some period of time. For tax purposes, capital gains are typically calculated from when an asset is bought to when it is sold.

Commercial paper: An extremely short-term corporate IOU, generally due in 270 days or less.

Convertible bond: A corporate bond (see below) that may be converted into a stated number of shares of common stock. Its price tends to fluctuate along with fluctuations in the price of the stock and with changes in interest rates.

Consumer price index (CPI): A statistical measure of the change in the price of consumer goods.

Corporate bond: A bond issued by a corporation. The bond normally has a stated life and pays a fixed rate of interest. Considered safer than the common or preferred stock of the same company.

Cost of living: The cost of maintaining a standard of living measured in terms of purchased goods and services. Inflation typically measures changes in the cost of living.

Cost-of-living adjustments: Changes in promised payments, such as retirement benefits, to account for changes in the cost of living.

Credit crunch (liquidity crisis): A situation in which cash for lending is in short supply.

Debenture: An unsecured bond backed only by the general credit of the issuing corporation.

Deficit spending: Government spending in excess of revenues, generally financed with the sale of bonds. A deficit increases the government debt.

Deflation: A decrease in the level of prices.

Depression: A long period of economic decline when prices are low, unemployment is high, and there are many business failures.

Derivatives: Financial contracts, such as options, whose values are based on, or *derived* from, the price of an underlying financial asset or indicator such as a stock or an interest rate.

Devaluation: The official lowering of a nation's currency, decreasing its value in relation to foreign currencies.

Discount rate: The rate of interest set by the Federal Reserve that member banks are charged when borrowing money through the Federal Reserve System.

Disposable income: Income after taxes that is available to persons for spending and saving.

Diversification: Investing in more than one asset in order to reduce the riskiness of the overall asset portfolio. By holding more than one asset, losses on some assets may be offset by gains realized on other assets.

Dividend: Discretionary payment by a corporation to its shareholders, usually in the form of cash or stock shares.

Dow Jones Industrial Average: An index of stock market prices, based on the prices of 30 leading companies on the New York Stock Exchange.

Econometrics: The use of statistical methods to study economic and financial data.

Federal Deposit Insurance Corporation (FDIC): A U.S. government-sponsored corporation that insures accounts in national banks and other qualified institutions against bank failures.

Federal Reserve System: The entire banking system of the U.S., incorporating 12 Federal Reserve banks (one in each of 12 Federal Reserve districts), 24 Federal Reserve branch banks, all national banks, and state-chartered commercial banks and trust companies that have been admitted to its membership. The governors of the system greatly influence the nation's monetary and credit policies.

Full employment: The economy is said to be at full employment when everyone who wishes to work at the going wage-rate for his or her type of labor is employed, save only for the small amount of unemployment due to the time it takes to switch from one job to another.

Futures: A futures contract is an agreement to buy or sell a specific amount of a commodity or financial instrument at a particular price at a set date in the future. For example, futures based on a stock index (such as the Dow Jones Industrial Average) are bets on the future price of that group of stocks.

Golden parachute: Provisions in contracts of some high-level executives guaranteeing substantial severance benefits if they lose their position in a corporate takeover.

Government bond: A bond issued by the U.S. Treasury, considered a safe investment. Government bonds are divided into 2 categories—those that are not marketable and those that are. *Savings bonds* cannot be bought and sold once the original purchase is made. Marketable bonds fall into several categories. *Treasury bills* are short-term U.S. obligations, maturing in 3, 6, or 12 months. *Treasury notes* mature in up to 10 years. *Treasury bonds* mature in 10 to 30 years. *Indexed bonds* are adjusted for inflation.

Greenmail: A company buying back its own shares for more than the going market price to avoid a threatened hostile takeover.

Gross domestic product (GDP): The market value of all goods and services that have been bought for final use during a period of time. It became the official measure of the size of the U.S. economy in 1991, replacing *gross national product (GNP),* in use since 1941. GDP covers workers and capital employed within the nation's borders. GNP covers production by U.S. residents regardless of where it takes place. The switch aligned U.S. terminology with that of most other industrialized countries.

Hedge fund: A flexible investment fund for a limited number of large investors (the minimum investment is typically $1 million). Hedge funds use a variety of investment techniques, including those forbidden to mutual funds, such as short-selling and heavy leveraging.

Hedging: Taking 2 positions whose gains and losses will offset each other if prices change, in order to limit risk.

Individual retirement account (IRA): A self-funded tax-advantaged retirement plan that allows employed individuals to contribute up to a maximum yearly sum. With a *traditional* IRA, individuals contribute pre-tax earnings and defer income taxes until retirement. With a *Roth* IRA, individuals contribute after-tax earnings but do not pay taxes on future withdrawals (the interest is never taxed). *401(k) plans* are employer-sponsored plans similar to traditional IRAs, but having higher contribution limits.

Inflation: An increase in the level of prices.

Insider information: Important facts about the condition or plans of a corporation that have not been released to the general public.

Interest: The cost of borrowing money.

Investment bank: A financial institution that arranges the initial issuance of stocks and bonds and offers companies advice about acquisitions and divestitures.

Junk bonds: Bonds issued by companies with low credit ratings. They typically pay relatively high interest rates because of the fear of default.

Leading indicators: A series of 11 indicators from different segments of the economy used by the U.S. Commerce Department to predict when changes in the level of economic activity will occur.

Leverage: The extent to which a purchase was paid for with borrowed money. Amplifies the potential gain or loss for the purchaser.

Leveraged buyout (LBO): An acquisition of a company in which much of the purchase price is borrowed, with the debt to be repaid from future profits or by subsequently selling off company assets. A leveraged buyout is typically carried out by a small group of investors, often including incumbent management.

Liquid assets: Assets consisting of cash and/or items that are easily converted into cash.

Margin account: A brokerage account that allows a person to trade securities on credit. A **margin call** is a demand for more collateral on the account.

Money supply: The currency held by the public, plus checking accounts in commercial banks and savings institutions.

Mortgage-backed securities: Created when a bank, builder, or government agency gathers together a group of mortgages and then sells bonds to other institutions and the public. The investors receive their proportionate share of the interest payments on the loans as well as the principal payments. Usually, the mortgages in question are guaranteed by the government.

Municipal bond: Issued by governmental units such as states, cities, local taxing authorities, and other agencies. Interest is exempt from U.S.—and sometimes state and local—income tax. *Municipal bond unit investment trusts* offer a portfolio of many different municipal bonds chosen by professionals. The income is exempt from federal income taxes.

Mutual fund: A portfolio of professionally bought and managed financial assets in which you pool your money along with that of many other people. A share price is based on net asset value, or the value of all the investments owned by the funds, less any debt, and divided by the total number of shares. The major advantage, relative to investing individually in only a small number of stocks, is less risk—the holdings are spread out over many assets and if one or two do badly the remainder may shield you from the losses. *Bond funds* are mutual funds that deal in the bond market exclusively. *Money market mutual funds* buy in the so-called money market—institutions that need to borrow large sums of money for short terms. These funds often offer special checking account advantages.

National debt: The debt of the national government, as distinguished from the debts of political subdivisions of the nation and of private business and individuals.

National debt ceiling: Total borrowing limit set by Congress beyond which the U.S. national debt cannot rise. This limit is periodically raised by congressional vote.

Option: A type of contractual agreement between a buyer and a seller to buy or sell shares of a security. A **call** option contract gives the right to purchase shares of a specific stock at a stated price within a given period of time. A **put** option contract gives the buyer the right to sell shares of a specific stock at a stated price within a given period of time.

Per capita income: The total income of a group divided by the number of people in the group.

Prime interest rate: The rate charged by banks on short-term loans to large commercial customers with the highest credit rating.

Producer price index: A statistical measure of the change in the price of wholesale goods. It is reported for 3 different stages of the production chain: crude, intermediate, and finished goods.

Program trading: Trading techniques involving large numbers and large blocks of stocks, usually used in conjunction with computer programs. Techniques include *index arbitrage,* in which traders profit from price differences between stocks and futures contracts on stock indexes, and *portfolio insurance,* which is the use of stock-index futures to protect stock investors from potentially large losses when the market drops.

Public debt: The total of a nation's debts owed by state, local, and national government. Increases in this sum, reflected in public-sector deficits, indicate how much of the nation's spending is being financed by borrowing rather than by taxation.

Recession: A mild decrease in economic activity marked by a decline in real (inflation-adjusted) GDP, employment, and trade, usually lasting from 6 months to a year, and marked by widespread decline in many sectors of the economy.

Savings Association Insurance Fund (SAIF): Created in 1989 to insure accounts in savings and loan associations up to $100,000.

Seasonal adjustment: Statistical changes made to compensate for regular fluctuations in data that are so great they tend to distort the statistics and make comparisons meaningless. For instance, seasonal adjustments are made for a slowdown in housing construction in midwinter and for the rise in farm income in the fall after summer crops are harvested.

Short-selling: Borrowing shares of stock from a brokerage firm and selling them, hoping to buy the shares back at a lower price, return them, and realize a profit from the decline in prices.

Stagnation: Economic slowdown in which there is little growth in the GDP, capital investment, and real income.

Stock: *Common stocks* are shares of ownership in a corporation. For publicly held firms, the stock typically trades on an exchange, such as the New York Stock Exchange; for closely held firms, the founders and managers own most of the stock. There can be wide swings in the prices of this kind of stock. *Preferred stock* is a type of stock on which a fixed dividend must be paid before holders of common stock are issued their share of the issuing corporation's earnings. Preferred stock is less risky than common stock. *Convertible preferred stock* can be converted into the common stock of the company that issued the preferred. *Over-the-counter stock* is not traded on the major or regional exchanges, but rather through dealers from whom you buy directly. *Blue chip* stocks are so called because they have been leading stocks for a long time. *Growth* stocks are from companies that reinvest their earnings, rather than pay dividends, with the expectation of future stock price appreciation.

Supply-side economics: A school of thinking about economic policy holding that lowering income tax rates will inevitably lead to enhanced economic growth and general revitalization of the economy.

Takeover: Acquisition of one company by another company or group by sale or merger. A *friendly takeover* occurs when the acquired company's management is agreeable to the merger; when management is opposed to the merger, it is a *hostile* takeover.

Tender offer: A public offer to buy a company's stock; usually priced at a premium above the market.

Zero coupon bond: A corporate or government bond that is issued at a deep discount from the maturity value and pays no interest during the life of the bond. It is redeemable at face value.

AGRICULTURE

U.S. Farms—Number and Acreage by State, 1996 and 1997

Source: National Agricultural Statistics Service, U.S. Dept. of Agriculture

State	Farms (1,000) 1996	Farms (1,000) 1997	Acreage (mil) 1996	Acreage (mil) 1997	Acreage per farm 1996	Acreage per farm 1997
U.S.	**2,064**	**2,058**	**970**	**968**	**470**	**471**
Alabama	45.0	45.0	9.8	9.7	218	216
Alaska	0.5	0.5	0.9	0.9	1,804	1,804
Arizona	7.5	7.5	35.4	35.4	4,720	4,720
Arkansas	43.0	42.5	15.0	14.8	349	348
California	82.0	84.0	30.0	30.0	366	357
Colorado	24.5	24.5	32.5	32.5	1,327	1,327
Connecticut	3.8	3.9	0.4	0.4	100	97
Delaware	2.5	2.4	0.6	0.6	226	235
Florida	40.0	40.0	10.3	10.3	258	258
Georgia	43.0	43.0	11.8	11.8	274	274
Hawaii	4.6	4.6	1.6	1.6	346	346
Idaho	22.0	22.0	13.5	13.5	614	614
Illinois	76.0	76.0	28.1	28.0	370	368
Indiana	61.0	62.0	15.9	15.9	261	256
Iowa	98.0	98.0	33.2	33.2	339	339
Kansas	66.0	64.0	47.8	47.8	724	747
Kentucky	88.0	88.0	14.0	13.9	159	158
Louisiana	27.0	26.5	8.7	8.5	322	321
Maine	7.4	7.3	1.3	1.3	181	184
Maryland	13.7	13.0	2.1	2.1	153	162
Massachusetts	6.1	6.2	0.6	0.6	93	92
Michigan	53.0	51.0	10.6	10.5	200	206
Minnesota	87.0	87.0	29.8	29.8	343	343
Mississippi	44.0	43.0	12.6	12.5	286	291
Missouri	104.0	102.0	30.0	29.9	288	293
Montana	23.0	24.0	59.7	59.6	2,596	2,483
Nebraska	56.0	55.0	47.0	47.0	839	855
Nevada	2.5	2.5	8.8	8.8	3,520	3,520
New Hampshire	2.4	2.4	0.4	0.4	179	179
New Jersey	9.2	9.4	0.8	0.8	91	88
New Mexico	13.5	13.5	43.7	43.5	3,237	3,222
New York	36.0	36.0	7.7	7.7	214	214
N. Carolina	58.0	57.0	9.2	9.0	159	158
N. Dakota	31.0	30.5	40.3	40.2	1,300	1,318
Ohio	72.0	73.0	15.1	15.1	210	207
Oklahoma	72.0	73.0	34.0	34.0	472	466
Oregon	38.5	37.5	17.5	17.5	455	467
Pennsylvania	50.0	50.0	7.7	7.7	154	154
Rhode Island	0.7	0.7	0.06	0.06	90	90
S. Carolina	21.5	21.5	5.0	5.0	233	233
S. Dakota	32.5	32.5	44.0	44.0	1,354	1,354
Tennessee	80.0	80.0	11.8	11.8	148	148
Texas	205.0	205.0	129.0	129.0	629	629
Utah	13.4	13.4	11.0	11.0	821	821
Vermont	6.0	6.0	1.4	1.4	225	225
Virginia	47.0	47.0	8.6	8.5	183	181
Washington	36.0	36.0	15.7	15.7	436	436
W. Virginia	20.0	20.0	3.7	3.7	185	185
Wisconsin	79.0	79.0	16.8	16.8	213	213
Wyoming	9.1	9.1	34.6	34.6	3,802	3,802

MILLENNIUM FACT BOX

Farm Workers Become Less Common*

Source: U.S. Dept. of Agriculture, Economic Research Service

Of the approximately 2.9 mil workers in the U.S. in 1820, 71.8%, or about 2.1 mil, were employed in farm occupations. The percentage of U.S. workers in farm occupations had declined drastically by the turn of the century, and by 1994 only 2.5% of all U.S. workers were employed in farm occupations.

(percent of total U.S. workers in farm occupations)

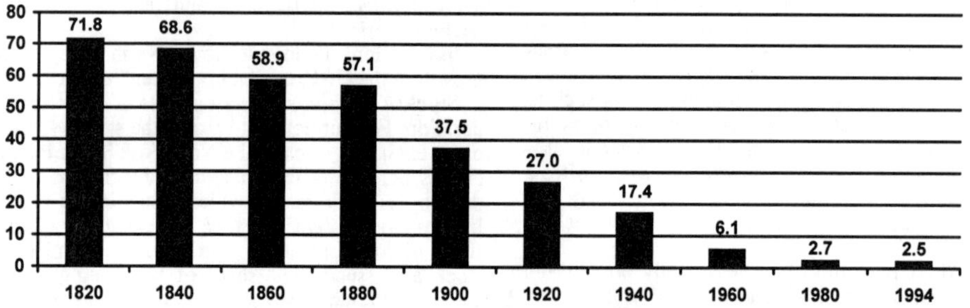

* Figures not compiled for years after 1994. Total workers for 1994 are employed workers age 15 and older; total workers for 1980 are members of the experienced civilian labor force ages 16 and older; total workers for 1900 to 1960 are members of the experienced civilian labor force 14 and older; total workers for 1820 to 1880 are gainfully employed workers 10 and older.

Livestock on Farms in the U.S., 1900-98

Source: National Agricultural Statistics Service, U.S. Dept. of Agriculture

(in thousands)

Year (On Jan. 1)	All cattle[1]	Milk cows	Sheep and lambs	Hogs and pigs[2]
1900	59,739	16,544	48,105	51,055
1910	58,993	19,450	50,239	48,072
1920	70,400	21,455	40,743	60,159
1930	61,003	23,032	51,565	55,705
1940	68,309	24,940	52,107	61,165
1950	77,963	23,853	29,826	58,937
1955	96,592	23,462	31,582	50,474
1960	96,236	19,527	33,170	59,026
1965	109,000	16,981	25,127	56,106
1970	112,369	12,091	20,423	57,046
1975	132,028	11,220	14,515	54,693
1980	111,242	10,758	12,699	67,318
1985	109,582	10,777	10,716	54,073
1990	95,816	10,015	11,358	53,788
1991	96,393	9,966	11,174	54,416
1992	97,556	9,728	10,797	57,649
1993	99,176	9,658	10,201	58,202
1994	100,988	9,528	9,742	57,904
1995	102,755	9,487	8,886	59,990
1996	103,487	9,416	8,461	57,150
1997*	101,460	9,309	7,937	58,263
1998[3]	99,501	9,191	7,616	61,600

* Figures revised by USDA NASS, Jan. 1998. (1) From 1966, includes milk cows and heifers that have calved. (2) 1900-95, as of Dec. 1 of preceding year; 1996-98 as of June 1 of same year. (3) Total estimated value on farms, as of Jan. 1, 1998 (Dec. 1, 1997 for hogs and pigs), was (avg. value per head in parentheses): cattle, $59,933,705,000 ($602); sheep and lambs, $776,311,000 ($102); hogs and pigs, $4,962,403,000 ($81).

U.S. Farms, 1940-97

Source: National Agricultural Statistics Service, U.S. Dept. of Agriculture

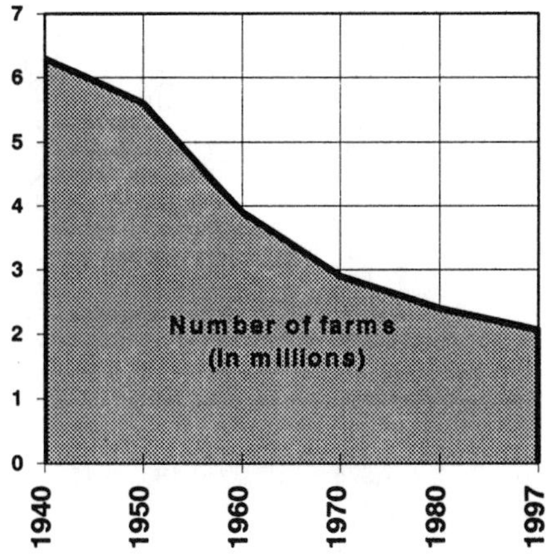

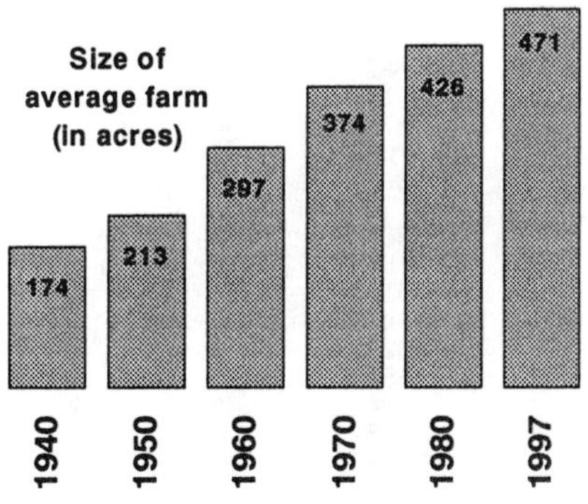

Eggs: U.S. Production, Price, and Value, 1996-97[1]

Source: National Agricultural Statistics Service, U.S. Dept. of Agriculture

STATE	Eggs produced[2] 1996 (mil)	Eggs produced[2] 1997 (mil)	Price per dozen[2] 1996 (cents)	Price per dozen[2] 1997 (cents)	Value of production 1996 (1,000 dollars)	Value of production 1997 (1,000 dollars)
AL	2,481	2,499	1.090	1.060	225,358	220,745
AR	3,433	3,215	1.050	1.030	300,388	275,954
CA	6,569	6,663	0.671	0.621	367,317	344,810
CO	827	855	0.756	0.719	52,101	51,229
CT	950	917	0.740	0.598	58,583	45,697
DE	147	112	1.190	1.150	14,578	10,733
FL	2,502	2,499	0.633	0.594	131,981	123,701
GA	4,584	4,867	0.911	0.885	348,002	358,941
HI	180	172	0.869	0.901	13,035	12,914
ID	258	236	0.700	0.700	15,050	13,767
IL	902	838	0.689	0.620	51,790	43,297
IN	5,663	5,652	0.678	0.637	319,960	300,027
IA	5,011	5,528	0.591	0.526	246,792	242,311
KS	315	322	0.574	0.566	15,068	15,188
KY	664	717	0.792	0.750	43,824	44,813
LA	477	460	0.964	0.908	38,319	34,807
ME	1,449	1,434	0.720	0.694	86,940	82,933
MD	938	882	0.796	0.732	62,221	53,802
MA	142	156	0.740	0.610	8,757	7,930
MI	1,318	1,327	0.623	0.560	68,426	61,927
MN	3,087	2,957	0.585	0.559	150,491	137,747
MS	1,523	1,547	1.210	1.130	153,569	145,676
MO	1,674	1,719	0.665	0.592	92,768	84,804
MT	108	88	0.660	0.570	5,940	4,180
NE	2,341	2,469	0.560	0.520	109,247	106,990
NH	42	46	0.810	0.830	2,835	3,182
NJ	475	463	0.728	0.623	28,817	24,037
NM	306	302	0.675	0.593	17,213	14,924
NY	1,042	931	0.771	0.666	66,949	51,671
NC	2,988	2,788	0.875	0.875	217,875	203,292
ND	55	50	0.585	0.530	2,681	2,208
OH	6,502	6,976	0.662	0.614	358,694	356,939
OK	916	842	0.876	0.893	66,868	62,659
OR	741	783	0.739	0.644	45,633	42,021
PA	5,640	5,788	0.628	0.653	295,160	314,964
RI	43	24	0.720	0.590	2,580	1,180
SC	1,224	1,228	0.854	0.768	87,108	78,592
SD	534	542	0.520	0.500	23,140	22,583
TN	257	255	0.913	0.930	19,553	19,763
TX	3,986	4,186	0.875	0.768	290,646	267,904
UT	464	436	0.566	0.576	21,885	20,928
VT	27	50	0.770	0.660	1,733	2,750
VA	888	862	0.953	0.901	70,522	64,722
WA	1,413	1,410	0.764	0.650	89,961	76,375
WV	227	245	1.190	1.210	22,511	24,704
WI	896	998	0.606	0.564	45,248	46,906
WY	2.4	3.5	0.750	0.630	150	184
Other[3]	69	61	0.670	0.610	3,864	3,111
U.S.[4]	**76,281**	**77,401**	**0.749**	**0.702**	**4,762,131**	**4,530,522**

(1) Estimates cover the 12-month period from Dec. 1 of the previous year through Nov. 30. (2) Average of all eggs sold by producers, including hatching eggs. (3) AK, AZ, and NV combined to avoid disclosure of individual operations; totals listed under "other." AK price estimates discontinued in 1995. (4) Total states may not equal U.S. total because of rounding.

U.S. Meat Production and Consumption, 1940-97

Source: Economic Research Service, U.S. Dept. of Agriculture

(in millions of pounds)

Year	Beef Production	Beef Consumption[2]	Veal Production	Veal Consumption[2]	Lamb and mutton Production	Lamb and mutton Consumption[2]	Pork Production	Pork Consumption[2]	All red meats[1] Production	All red meats[1] Consumption[2]	All Poultry Production	All Poultry Consumption[2]
1940	7,175	7,257	981	981	876	873	10,044	9,701	19,076	18,812	NA	NA
1950	9,534	9,529	1,230	1,206	597	596	10,714	10,390	22,075	21,721	3,174	3,097
1960	14,728	15,465	1,109	1,118	769	857	13,905	14,057	30,511	31,497	6,310	6,168
1970	21,684	23,451	588	613	551	669	14,699	14,957	37,522	39,689	10,193	9,981
1980	21,643	23,560	400	420	318	351	16,617	16,838	38,978	41,701	14,173	13,525
1990	22,743	24,031	327	325	363	397	15,354	16,031	38,787	40,784	23,468	22,151
1991	22,917	24,113	306	305	363	396	15,999	16,392	39,585	41,207	24,700	23,270
1992	23,086	24,261	310	312	348	388	17,233	17,461	40,977	42,422	26,201	24,394
1993	23,049	24,006	285	286	337	381	17,088	17,408	40,759	42,081	27,329	25,099
1994	24,386	25,125	293	291	308	345	17,696	17,811	42,683	43,571	29,113	25,754
1995	25,222	25,533	319	319	287	348	17,849	17,768	43,677	43,968	30,393	25,944
1996	25,525	25,863	378	378	268	334	17,117	16,795	43,288	43,370	32,015	26,760
1997	25,490	25,609	334	341	260	333	17,274	16,821	43,358	43,096	32,964	27,269

(1) Meats may not add to total because of rounding. (2) Consumption (also called total disappearance) is estimated as: production plus beginning stocks, plus imports, minus exports, minus ending stocks. NA = not available.

U.S. Government Agricultural Payments by State, 1997[1]

Source: Economic Research Service, U.S. Dept. of Agriculture

(in thousands of dollars)

State	Feed Grains[2]	Wheat[2]	Rice[2]	Cotton[2]	Wool Act[2]	Conservation[3]	Miscellaneous	Total
Alabama	$-318	$-3	$0	$-112	$0	$25,138	$41,081	$65,785
Alaska	0	0	0	0	0	990	500	1,490
Arizona	-140	-59	0	-933	-7	787	47,019	46,667
Arkansas	-1,502	-394	7	-505	0	12,912	264,339	274,857
California	-1,022	-147	-11	-1,217	6	13,200	209,727	220,536
Colorado	-8,687	-318	0	0	0	78,338	106,292	175,626
Connecticut	-77	0	0	0	0	162	1,299	1,384
Delaware	-571	-1	0	0	0	347	5,950	5,725
Florida	-106	-1	0	-11	0	5,967	13,198	19,047
Georgia	-892	-38	0	-249	0	27,866	82,520	109,207
Hawaii	0	0	0	0	0	163	391	554
Idaho	-301	-528	0	0	1	38,583	72,675	110,429
Illinois	-81,151	-135	0	0	0	62,071	571,701	552,486
Indiana	-44,556	-71	0	0	0	30,364	279,429	265,166
Iowa	-86,847	-1	0	0	0	148,216	651,533	712,901
Kansas	-29,526	-1,356	0	0	0	151,940	408,725	529,784
Kentucky	-7,354	-39	0	0	0	22,353	68,107	83,067
Louisiana	-824	-42	-27	-534	0	7,578	151,195	157,346
Maine	-66	0	0	0	0	2,170	2,093	4,197
Maryland	-1,962	-4	0	0	0	2,152	19,304	19,490
Massachusetts	-45	0	0	0	0	211	1,030	1,196
Michigan	-19,121	-90	0	0	1	20,854	119,642	121,287
Minnesota	-56,472	-540	0	0	-5	86,946	387,120	417,049
Mississippi	-629	-26	5	-520	0	35,562	135,469	169,861
Missouri	-15,484	-145	0	-72	0	104,659	189,108	278,066
Montana	-422	-571	0	0	1	101,164	130,745	230,918
Nebraska	-82,023	-282	0	0	0	69,287	467,616	454,598
Nevada	-1	-5	0	0	0	940	1,161	2,096
New Hampshire	-30	0	0	0	0	172	747	889
New Jersey	-537	0	0	0	0	226	3,940	3,629
New Mexico	-1,228	-35	0	-25	0	18,201	22,085	38,998
New York	-4,622	-13	0	0	0	4,601	39,667	39,633
North Carolina	-3,349	-28	0	-61	0	17,744	73,459	87,764
North Dakota	-5,178	-1,305	0	0	5	103,387	264,640	361,549
Ohio	-25,323	-146	0	0	0	25,899	185,998	186,429
Oklahoma	-1,622	-916	0	-66	0	49,644	158,561	205,601
Oregon	-103	-170	0	0	2	26,371	37,328	63,429
Pennsylvania	-2,910	-3	0	0	0	7,447	30,936	35,471
Rhode Island	-1	0	0	0	0	35	88	122
South Carolina	-1,325	-35	0	-80	0	12,242	32,242	43,044
South Dakota	-18,150	-262	0	0	0	70,459	216,067	268,113
Tennessee	-2,899	-53	3	-97	0	20,310	58,944	76,209
Texas	-23,460	-579	-30	-1,366	10	157,557	516,435	648,567
Utah	-154	-8	0	0	0	9,491	10,767	20,095
Vermont	-129	0	0	0	0	741	2,481	3,093
Virginia	-1,580	-21	0	-2	0	5,989	26,204	30,590
Washington	-373	-556	0	0	0	53,529	94,680	147,279
West Virginia	-183	0	0	0	0	2,425	3,433	5,675
Wisconsin	-26,168	-9	0	0	0	45,635	157,114	176,572
Wyoming	-302	-29	0	0	-3	10,241	12,481	22,387
UNITED STATES	**$-559,723**	**$-8,964**	**$-54**	**$-5,851**	**$14**	**$1,693,264**	**$6,377,266**	**$7,495,953**

(1) Includes both cash payments and payment-in-kind (PIK) for fiscal year. (2) Negatives indicate that the current year's Advanced Deficiency Payments were less than refunds from producers to government because advances paid in the previous year were too high. (3) Includes amount paid under agriculture and conservation programs (Conservation Reserve, Agriculture Conservation, Emergency Conservation, and Great Plains Program). Totals may not add because of rounding.

U.S. Federal Food Assistance Programs, 1988-97[1]

Source: Food and Nutrition Service, U.S. Dept. of Agriculture

(in millions of dollars)

Program	1988	1989	1990	1991	1992	1993	1994	1995	1996	1997
Food stamps[2]	$12,317	$12,932	$15,491	$18,769	$22,462	$23,653	$24,493	$24,621	$24,331	$21,477
Puerto Rico nutrition asst.[3]	879	908	937	963	1,002	1,040	1,079	1,131	1,143	1,174
Natl. school lunch[4]	3,730	3,769	3,834	4,224	4,564	4,750	5,016	5,160	5,355	5,554
School breakfast[5]	482	513	596	685	787	869	959	1,048	1,119	1,214
WIC[6]	1,798	1,911	2,122	2,301	2,597	2,825	3,169	3,440	3,695	3,844
Summer food service[7]	133	146	164	182	204	220	230	237	250	244
Child/adult care[7]	628	697	813	945	1,094	1,225	1,354	1,464	1,534	1,571
Special milk	19	18	19	20	20	19	18	17	17	17
Nutrition for the elderly[4]	146	146	142	144	151	153	152	148	145	145
Food distrib. to Indian reserv.[7]	62	65	66	65	62	63	65	65	70	71
Commodity supp. food prog.[7]	62	73	85	93	105	113	107	99	100	99
Food dist.—charitable inst.[8]	159	136	104	93	116	91	105	64	11	6
Emergency food assistance[9]	645	310	334	301	272	271	264	135	79	192
Other costs[10]	58	72	75	82	91	111	124	144	146	133
TOTAL[11]	**$21,118**	**$21,696**	**$24,781**	**$28,867**	**$33,527**	**$35,403**	**$37,135**	**$37,773**	**$37,995**	**$35,742**

(1) All data are for fiscal (not calendar) years. (2) Includes federal share of state administrative expenses and other federal costs. (3) Puerto Rico participated in the Food Stamp Program from FY 1975 until July 1982, when it initiated a separate grant program. (4) Includes cash payments and commodity costs (entitlement, bonus, and cash in lieu). (5) Excludes startup costs. (6) Includes the WIC Farmers Market Nutrition Program, program studies and special grants. (7) Includes commodity costs and administrative expenditures. (8) Includes summer camps. (9) Includes the Emergency Food Assistance Program (TEFAP) for all years, and the Soup Kitchens/Food Banks Program (1989-96). (10) Includes certain miscellaneous child nutrition costs. (11) Excludes Food Program Administration (federal) costs. Totals may not add because of rounding.

U.S. Farm Marketings by State, 1996-97

Source: Economic Research Service, U.S. Dept. of Agriculture

(in thousands of dollars)

	1996 FARM MARKETINGS			1997 FARM MARKETINGS		
State/Rank[1]	**Total**	**Crops**	**Livestock and products**	**Total**	**Crops**	**Livestock and products**
Alabama (26)	$3,173,595	$810,637	$2,362,958	$3,227,434	$796,157	$2,431,277
Alaska (50)	29,418	23,310	6,108	32,426	26,152	6,274
Arizona (31)	2,146,417	1,307,590	838,827	2,151,560	1,263,148	888,412
Arkansas (11)	5,886,786	2,530,163	3,356,623	5,862,203	2,446,386	3,415,817
California (1)	23,309,526	17,096,190	6,213,336	24,849,653	18,555,414	6,294,239
Colorado (17)	4,229,447	1,470,312	2,759,135	4,399,249	1,387,670	3,011,579
Connecticut (43)	489,113	252,413	236,700	496,459	278,719	217,740
Delaware (40)	757,036	183,580	573,456	747,653	174,181	573,472
Florida (9)	6,130,658	4,942,465	1,188,193	6,243,366	4,978,525	1,264,841
Georgia (10)	5,687,046	2,407,786	3,279,260	5,885,210	2,443,316	3,441,894
Hawaii (45)	482,589	416,594	65,995	482,599	414,602	67,997
Idaho (24)	3,409,945	2,080,687	1,329,258	3,315,014	1,926,430	1,388,584
Illinois (5)	9,049,998	6,988,895	2,061,103	9,276,040	7,339,362	1,936,678
Indiana (14)	5,558,099	3,663,444	1,894,655	5,506,236	3,610,023	1,896,213
Iowa (3)	12,852,687	7,395,907	5,456,780	12,840,692	7,310,947	5,529,745
Kansas (6)	7,869,209	3,298,882	4,570,327	9,001,475	3,984,532	5,016,943
Kentucky (21)	3,550,232	1,831,347	1,718,885	3,632,928	1,654,874	1,978,054
Louisiana (32)	2,342,068	1,654,858	687,210	2,139,969	1,480,538	659,431
Maine (44)	485,111	223,574	261,537	486,119	227,767	258,352
Maryland (36)	1,533,770	633,267	900,503	1,538,383	623,088	915,295
Massachusetts (41)	477,698	368,631	109,067	532,276	430,352	101,924
Michigan (22)	3,642,927	2,194,946	1,447,981	3,587,753	2,235,720	1,352,033
Minnesota (8)	8,808,931	4,640,508	4,168,423	8,155,006	4,100,778	4,054,228
Mississippi (23)	3,462,784	1,528,505	1,934,279	3,476,300	1,469,913	2,006,387
Missouri (13)	4,950,421	2,500,276	2,450,145	5,563,617	2,768,474	2,795,143
Montana (33)	2,027,226	1,230,299	796,927	2,063,342	1,071,848	991,494
Nebraska (4)	9,454,041	4,176,780	5,277,261	10,092,232	4,550,182	5,542,050
Nevada (47)	286,002	132,566	153,436	310,008	129,884	180,124
New Hampshire (48)	160,907	88,605	72,302	166,070	96,733	69,337
New Jersey (39)	800,958	605,395	195,563	776,311	596,189	180,122
New Mexico (34)	1,709,056	511,567	1,197,489	1,913,484	559,783	1,353,701
New York (28)	3,043,034	998,487	2,044,547	2,895,699	1,036,861	1,858,838
North Carolina (7)	7,831,309	3,403,986	4,427,323	8,302,454	3,608,816	4,693,638
North Dakota (25)	3,532,393	2,995,616	536,777	3,312,959	2,702,197	610,762
Ohio (16)	5,121,783	3,176,785	1,944,998	5,344,658	3,475,782	1,868,876
Oklahoma (18)	3,565,551	1,126,250	2,439,301	4,362,549	1,301,498	3,061,051
Oregon (27)	2,976,542	2,320,012	656,530	3,111,750	2,372,207	739,543
Pennsylvania (20)	4,142,509	1,277,932	2,864,577	4,127,690	1,338,876	2,788,814
Rhode Island (49)	82,867	71,573	11,294	82,849	73,616	9,233
South Carolina (35)	1,602,056	864,846	737,210	1,694,361	897,383	796,978
South Dakota (19)	3,683,512	2,050,747	1,632,765	4,237,050	2,417,031	1,820,019
Tennessee (30)	2,371,873	1,374,213	997,660	2,291,672	1,286,707	1,004,965
Texas (2)	13,053,234	5,295,205	7,758,029	13,460,835	5,276,900	8,183,935
Utah (37)	873,143	227,004	646,139	952,959	238,069	714,890
Vermont (42)	534,666	97,609	437,057	512,612	96,830	415,782
Virginia (29)	2,378,146	900,163	1,477,983	2,393,848	856,183	1,537,665
Washington (15)	5,680,980	4,016,590	1,664,390	5,382,015	3,778,247	1,603,768
West Virginia (46)	388,170	79,979	308,191	394,104	70,587	323,517
Wisconsin (12)	6,061,542	1,773,464	4,288,078	5,756,477	1,686,063	4,070,414
Wyoming (38)	661,979	184,338	477,641	844,675	198,796	645,879
UNITED STATES	**$202,338,990**	**$109,424,778**	**$92,914,212**	**$208,212,283**	**$111,644,336**	**$96,567,947**

(1) States ranked by 1997 total.

Value of U.S. Agricultural Exports and Imports, 1976-97[1]

Source: Economic Research Service, U.S. Dept. of Agriculture

(in billions of dollars, except percent)

Year	Trade balance	Agric. exports	Percentage of all exports	Agric. imports	Percentage of all imports
1976	$12.3	$22.7	20	$10.5	9
1977	10.6	24.0	20	13.4	9
1978	13.4	27.3	21	13.9	8
1979	15.8	32.0	19	16.2	8
1980	23.2	40.5	19	17.3	7
1981	26.4	43.8	19	17.3	7
1982	23.6	39.1	18	15.5	6
1983	18.5	34.8	18	16.3	7
1984	19.1	38.0	18	18.9	6
1985	11.5	31.2	15	19.7	6
1986	5.4	26.3	13	20.9	6
1987	$7.2	$27.9	12	$20.7	5
1988	14.3	35.3	12	21.0	5
1989	18.1	39.7	12	21.6	5
1990	17.7	40.4	11	22.7	5
1991	15.1	37.8	10	22.7	5
1992	18.2	42.6	10	24.5	5
1993	18.3	42.9	10	24.6	4
1994	17.4	44.0	9	26.6	4
1995	24.9	54.7	10	29.9	4
1996	27.3	59.9	10	32.6	4
1997	21.6	57.4	9	35.8	4

(1) Fiscal year (Oct.-Sept.).

Farm Business Real Estate Debt Outstanding, by Lender Groups,[1] 1960-96

Source: Economic Research Service, U.S. Dept. of Agriculture

(in thousands of dollars)

Dec. 31	Total farm real estate debt[2]	AMOUNTS HELD BY PRINCIPAL LENDER GROUPS				
		Farm Credit System[2]	Farm Services Agency[3]	Life insurance companies[4]	All operating banks	Other[5]
1960	$11,309,593	$2,222,301	$623,895	$2,651,587	$1,355,733	$4,456,068
1970	27,505,932	6,420,357	2,179,873	5,122,291	3,328,876	10,454,540
1980	89,692,429	33,224,684	7,435,059	11,997,922	7,765,058	29,269,705
1985	100,076,120	42,168,554	9,820,913	11,272,689	10,731,881	26,082,096
1986	90,407,602	35,592,540	9,713,096	10,377,063	11,942,258	22,782,645
1987	82,398,048	30,646,143	9,430,087	9,355,026	13,541,447	19,425,345
1988	77,832,498	28,445,452	8,979,749	9,039,395	14,433,688	16,934,218
1989	75,978,245	26,895,927	8,203,215	9,113,109	15,685,485	16,080,503
1990	74,731,876	25,924,490	7,639,490	9,703,958	16,288,128	15,175,805
1991	74,943,896	25,305,300	7,040,851	9,545,804	17,416,527	15,631,629
1992	75,421,266	25,407,547	6,394,446	8,765,021	18,756,852	16,095,415
1993	76,042,688	24,901,858	5,838,438	8,986,288	19,596,382	16,719,722
1994	77,679,834	24,596,715	5,465,063	9,025,132	21,079,145	17,513,779
1995	79,286,915	24,851,298	5,055,018	9,091,957	22,276,504	18,012,138
1996	81,929,727	25,819,377	4,718,980	9,493,434	23,353,554	18,544,385

(1) Exclude operator households. (2) Includes data for joint stock land banks and real estate loans by Agricultural Credit Assn. (3) Includes loans made directly by Farm Services Agency for farm ownership, soil and water loans to individuals, Native American tribe land acquisition, grazing associations, and half of economic emergency loans. Also includes loans for rural housing on farm tracts and labor housing. (4) American Council of Life Insurance. (5) Estimated by ERS, USDA. Includes Commodity Credit Corporation storage and drying facility loans.

Grain, Hay, Potato, Cotton, Soybean, Tobacco Production, by State, 1997

Source: National Agricultural Statistics Service, U.S. Dept. of Agriculture

1997 State	Barley (1,000 bu)	Corn, grain (1,000 bu)	Cotton (Upland) (1,000 b)	All hay (1,000 t)	Oats (1,000 bu)	Potatoes (1,000 cwt)	Soybeans (1,000 bu)	Tobacco (1,000 lb)	All wheat (1,000 bu)
Alabama	—	23,055	550.0	1,575	1,150	1,148	9,625	—	4,200
Alaska	—	—	—	—	—	—	—	—	—
Arizona	6,834	8,500	847.0	1,640	—	1,705	—	—	8,775
Arkansas	—	21,875	1,683.0	2,370	1,275	—	108,275	—	39,360
California	9,900	44,200	2,191.0	8,616	2,450	16,188	—	—	43,680
Colorado	10,080	150,380	—	4,388	1,904	28,037	—	—	94,700
Connecticut	—	NE	—	113	—	—	—	3,600	—
Delaware	3,115	15,840	—	48	—	966	6,351	—	5,329
Florida	—	6,400	119.1	598	—	8,181	988	19,053	585
Georgia	—	55,000	1,919.0	1,560	2,240	—	8,610	89,225	15,840
Hawaii	—	—	—	—	—	—	—	—	—
Idaho	60,040	6,200	—	5,148	1,500	135,430	—	—	114,060
Illinois	—	1,425,450	—	3,354	5,550	1,495	427,850	—	70,150
Indiana	—	719,550	—	2,333	2,100	1,323	237,600	18,690	38,280
Iowa	—	1,656,000	—	5,190	17,885	273	483,600	—	1,134
Kansas	320	386,100	8.7	6,840	5,120	—	88,800	—	506,000
Kentucky	1,050	120,510	—	5,590	—	—	44,160	498,328	28,620
Louisiana	—	57,330	986.0	832	—	—	39,150	—	4,255
Maine	—	NE	—	276	1,750	19,170	—	—	—
Maryland	4,000	37,350	—	474	660	952	14,700	12,000	14,620
Massachusetts	—	NE	—	168	—	675	—	2,077	—
Michigan	1,440	263,250	—	3,760	5,490	14,250	72,765	—	33,480
Minnesota	27,540	857,850	—	6,488	17,980	20,440	261,300	—	78,890
Mississippi	—	50,290	1,821.0	1,800	—	—	64,170	—	7,525
Missouri	—	332,920	565.0	7,194	1,674	1,479	177,025	7,035	57,200
Montana	63,600	1,890	—	5,480	3,850	3,328	—	—	185,630
Nebraska	408	1,151,700	—	6,505	4,550	9,204	141,450	—	70,300
Nevada	420	—	—	1,505	—	2,967	—	—	1,575
New Hampshire	—	NE	—	89	—	—	—	—	—
New Jersey	300	10,044	—	282	—	594	3,960	—	2,040
New Mexico	—	14,875	93.0	1,682	—	4,022	—	—	9,975
New York	—	75,400		3,384	7,700	8,408	—	—	7,560
North Carolina	1,400	77,430	930.0	1,178	1,700	3,420	38,570	731,419	34,840
North Dakota	101,250	59,895	—	4,130	18,000	21,525	34,510	—	267,695
Ohio	—	462,300	—	3,850	7,800	1,175	197,560	22,300	68,670
Oklahoma	336	26,600	183.0	5,052	2,070	—	9,600	—	178,200
Oregon	8,280	4,290	—	3,374	2,850	27,161	—	—	63,430
Pennsylvania	5,100	97,515	—	3,767	9,440	3,190	14,235	15,360	9,100
Rhode Island	—	NE	—	14	—	208	—	—	—
South Carolina	180	32,495	410.0	600	1,800	—	13,420	126,360	15,000
South Dakota	4,940	333,200	—	8,090	17,050	1,050	120,750	—	99,213
Tennessee	—	66,300	662.0	3,702	—	—	43,520	114,292	16,650
Texas	235	248,400	5,140.0	10,790	5,720	3,447	11,200	—	118,900
Utah	8,170	3,105	—	2,685	666	915	—	—	9,174
Vermont	—	NE	—	533	—	—	—	—	—
Virginia	5,525	30,225	137.2	2,251	—	1,463	11,270	117,576	17,000
Washington	37,240	18,050	—	3,270	1,360	88,060	—	—	168,080
West Virginia	—	3,515	—	1,056	200	—	—	3,060	486
Wisconsin	3,575	402,600	—	5,900	20,790	27,923	42,240	5,690	8,075
Wyoming	9,200	7,695	—	2,596	1,830	140	—	—	8,276
UNITED STATES	**374,478**	**9,365,574**	**18,245.0**	**152,120**	**176,104**	**459,912**	**2,727,254**	**1,786,065**	**2,526,552**

NE = Not estimated. bu = bushels, b = bales (480-lbs), t = tons, cwt = hundredweight.

Production of Principal U.S. Crops, 1988-97

Source: National Agricultural Statistics Service, U.S. Dept. of Agriculture

Year	Corn for grain (1,000 bu)	Oats (1,000 bu)	Barley (1,000 bu)	Sorghum for grain (1,000 bu)	All wheat (1,000 bu)	Rye (1,000 bu)	Flax-seed (1,000 bu)	Upland Cotton (1,000 b)	Cotton-seed (1,000 t)
1988	4,928,681	217,375	289,994	576,686	1,812,201	14,689	1,615	15,412.5	6,061.8
1989	7,531,953	373,587	404,203	615,420	2,036,618	13,647	1,215	12,196.6	4,677.4
1990	7,934,028	357,654	422,196	573,303	2,729,778	10,176	3,812	15,505.4	5,968.5
1991	7,474,765	243,851	464,326	584,860	1,980,139	9,734	6,200	17,614.3	6,925.5
1992	9,476,698	294,229	455,090	875,022	2,466,798	11,440	3,288	16,219.5	6,230.1
1993	6,336,470	206,770	398,041	534,172	2,396,440	10,340	3,480	16,134.6	6,343.2
1994	10,102,735	229,008	374,862	649,206	2,320,981	11,341	2,922	19,662.0	7,603.9
1995	7,373,876	162,027	359,562	460,373	2,182,591	10,064	2,211	17,532.2	6,848.7
1996[1]	9,293,435	155,273	395,751	802,974	2,285,133	9,016	1,602	18,413.5	7,143.5
1997[2]	9,365,574	176,104	374,478	653,106	2,526,552	8,912	2,171	18,245.0	6,934.6

Year	Tobacco (1,000 lb)	All hay (1,000 t)	Beans, dry edible (1,000 cwt)	Peas, dry edible (1,000 cwt)	Peanuts[3] (1,000 lb)	Soy-beans[4] (1,000 bu)	Potatoes (1,000 cwt)	Sweet potatoes (1,000 cwt)
1988	1,369,500	125,736	19,253	3,868	3,980,917	1,548,841	356,438	10,945
1989	1,367,188	144,706	23,729	3,883	3,989,995	1,923,666	370,444	11,358
1990	1,626,380	146,212	32,379	2,372	3,602,770	1,925,947	402,110	12,594
1991	1,664,372	152,073	33,765	3,715	4,926,570	1,986,539	417,622	11,203
1992	1,721,671	146,903	22,615	2,535	4,284,416	2,190,354	425,367	12,005
1993	1,613,319	146,799	21,913	3,292	3,392,415	1,870,958	428,693	11,053
1994	1,582,896	150,060	29,028	2,255	4,247,455	2,516,694	467,054	13,395
1995	1,268,538	154,166	30,812	4,765	4,247,455	2,176,814	443,606	12,906
1996[1]	1,517,334	149,457	27,960	2,671	3,661,205	2,382,364	498,633	13,456
1997[2]	1,786,065	152,120	29,156	5,816	3,537,050	2,727,254	459,912	13,025

Year	Rice (1,000 cwt)	Sugar-cane (1,000 t)	Sugar beets (1,000 t)	Pecans[5] (1,000 lb)	Apples (1,000 t)	Grapes (1,000 t)	Peaches (1,000 t)	Oranges[6] (1,000 bx)	Grape-fruit[6] (1,000 bx)
1988	159,897	29,904	24,810	308,200	4,560.0	6,033.7	1,311.1	200,250	68,700
1989	154,487	29,426	25,131	250,500	4,958.4	5,930.9	1,181.5	209,050	69,500
1990	156,088	28,136	27,513	205,000	4,828.4	5,659.9	1,121.1	184,415	49,300
1991	159,367	30,252	28,203	299,000	4,853.4	5,555.9	1,347.8	178,950	55,500
1992	179,658	30,363	29,143	166,000	5,284.3	6,052.1	1,336.0	209,610	55,265
1993	156,110	31,101	26,249	365,000	5,342.4	6,023.2	1,330.1	255,760	68,375
1994	197,779	30,929	31,853	199,000	5,667.8	5,870.6	1,253.3	240,450	65,100
1995	173,871	30,944	27,954	268,000	5,292.5	5,922.3	1,150.8	263,605	71,050
1996[1]	171,321	29,462	26,680	221,500	5,196.0	5,554.3	1,058.2	263,890	66,200
1997[2]	178,896	31,693	29,886	338,100	5,193.1	7,282.4	1,325.6	292,620	70,200

(1) Revised. (2) Preliminary. (3) Harvested for nuts. (4) Harvested for beans. (5) Utilized production only. (6) Crop year ending in year cited.

Principal U.S. Crops: Area Planted and Harvested, 1995-97

Source: National Agricultural Statistics Service, U.S. Dept. of Agriculture

(in thousand acres)

State	Area planted[1] 1995	1996	1997	Area harvested[1] 1995	1996	1997
AL	2,204	2,255	2,373	2,093	2,169	2,188
AZ	795	835	808	787	831	800
AR	8,435	8,680	8,345	8,198	8,535	8,206
CA	5,220	5,202	5,172	4,660	4,770	4,678
CO	6,104	6,456	6,479	5,748	5,511	6,100
CT	112	120	112	107	115	109
DE	507	500	509	499	492	494
FL	1,070	1,109	1,089	1,027	1,084	1,060
GA	4,237	4,336	4,419	3,864	3,990	4,062
HI	53	46	35	53	46	35
ID	4,483	4,507	4,493	4,306	4,383	4,336
IL	23,221	23,926	23,740	22,526	23,183	23,534
IN	11,942	12,648	12,964	11,785	12,395	12,786
IA	23,502	24,197	24,711	22,872	24,007	24,513
KS	22,428	24,171	23,497	21,363	20,899	22,850
KY	5,709	5,844	5,852	5,454	5,640	5,648
LA	3,857	4,035	4,040	3,786	3,994	3,963
ME	364	327	296	358	316	287
MD	1,548	1,575	1,556	1,463	1,521	1,500
MA	134	131	133	131	125	128
MI	6,790	7,023	7,032	6,647	6,774	6,893
MN	19,151	20,001	20,510	18,556	19,722	20,079
MS	4,850	4,880	4,770	4,739	4,790	4,696
MO	12,056	13,275	13,424	11,689	12,794	13,267
MT	9,697	10,774	10,423	9,245	10,342	9,939
NE	18,280	18,811	19,121	17,769	18,227	18,696
NV	516	525	520	512	522	517
NH	85	84	70	83	82	69
NJ	452	427	435	413	394	413
NM	1,282	1,318	1,290	869	933	1,137
NY	3,045	3,018	3,070	2,981	2,941	3,017
NC	4,639	4,757	4,916	4,351	4,525	4,671
ND	20,707	22,651	22,271	20,120	22,237	21,091
OH	10,025	10,173	10,726	9,883	10,011	10,528
OK	10,621	11,341	10,935	8,635	8,935	9,295
OR	2,389	2,454	2,390	2,260	2,359	2,293
PA	4,146	4,140	4,313	4,050	4,035	4,202
RI	11	11	10	11	11	10
SC	1,976	1,971	2,030	1,871	1,892	1,962
SD	14,334	16,910	17,535	13,947	16,235	16,545
TN	4,892	4,999	4,925	4,530	4,703	4,673
TX	22,600	24,343	23,389	17,870	18,162	19,979
UT	1,099	1,139	1,126	1,042	1,070	1,068
VT	387	345	365	379	326	358
VA	2,910	2,936	2,926	2,748	2,794	2,774
WA	4,144	4,461	4,369	4,011	4,378	4,236
WV	650	657	646	642	646	637
WI	8,194	8,161	8,012	7,792	7,849	7,677
WY	1,883	1,836	1,911	1,820	1,783	1,847
U.S.[2]	**318,237**	**334,371**	**334,139**	**301,032**	**313,518**	**319,894**

(1) Crops included in area planted are corn, sorghum, oats, barley, winter wheat, rye, durum wheat, other spring wheat, rice, soybeans, peanuts, sunflower, cotton, dry edible beans, potatoes, and sugar beets. Harvested acreage is used for all hay, tobacco, and sugarcane in computing total area planted. Includes double-cropped acres and unharvested small grains planted as cover crops. (2) State figures do not add to U.S. totals because of sunflower and sugar-beet unallocated acreage.

Average Prices Received by U.S. Farmers, 1940-97

Source: Natl. Agricultural Statistics Service, U.S. Dept. of Agriculture

Figures below represent dollars per 100 lb for hogs, beef cattle, veal calves, sheep, lamb, and milk (wholesale); dollars per head for milk cows; cents per lb for chickens, broilers, turkeys, and wool; cents per dozen for eggs; weighted calendar year prices for livestock and livestock products other than wool. For 1943-63, wool prices are weighted on marketing year basis. The marketing year was changed in 1964 from a calendar year to a Dec.-Nov. basis for hogs, chickens, broilers, and eggs.

Year	Hogs	Cattle (beef)	Calves (veal)	Sheep	Lambs	Milk cows	Milk	Chickens (excl. broilers)	Broilers	Turkeys	Eggs	Wool
1940	5.39	7.56	8.83	3.95	8.10	61	1.82	13.0	17.3	15.2	18.0	28.4
1950	18.00	23.30	26.30	11.60	25.10	198	3.89	22.2	27.4	32.8	36.3	62.1
1960	15.30	20.40	22.90	5.61	17.90	223	4.21	12.2	16.9	25.4	36.1	42.0
1970	22.70	27.10	34.50	7.51	26.40	332	5.71	9.1	13.6	22.6	39.1	35.4
1975	46.10	32.20	27.20	11.30	42.10	412	8.75	9.9	26.3	34.8	54.5	44.8
1980	38.00	62.40	76.80	21.30	63.60	1,190	13.05	11.0	27.7	41.3	56.3	88.1
1984	47.10	57.30	59.90	16.40	60.10	895	13.46	15.9	33.7	48.9	72.3	79.5
1985	44.00	53.70	62.10	23.90	67.70	860	12.76	14.8	30.1	49.1	57.1	63.3
1986	49.30	52.60	61.10	25.60	69.00	820	12.51	12.5	34.5	47.1	61.6	66.8
1987	51.20	61.10	78.50	29.50	77.60	920	12.54	11.0	28.7	34.8	54.9	91.7
1988	42.30	66.60	89.20	25.60	69.10	990	12.26	9.2	33.1	38.6	52.8	138.0
1989	42.50	69.50	90.80	24.40	66.10	1,030	13.56	14.9	36.6	40.9	68.9	124.0
1990	53.70	74.60	95.60	23.20	55.50	1,160	13.74	9.3	32.6	39.4	70.9	80.0
1991	49.10	72.70	98.00	19.70	52.20	1,100	12.27	7.1	30.8	38.4	67.8	55.0
1992	41.60	71.30	89.00	25.80	59.50	1,130	13.15	8.6	31.8	37.7	57.6	74.0
1993	45.20	72.60	91.20	28.60	64.40	1,160	12.84	10.0	34.0	39.0	63.4	51.0
1994	39.90	66.70	87.20	30.90	65.60	1,170	13.01	7.6	35.0	40.4	61.4	78.0
1995	40.50	61.80	73.10	28.00	78.20	1,130	12.78	6.5	34.4	41.6	62.4	104.0
1996[1]	51.90	58.70	58.40	29.90	82.20	1,090	14.75	6.6	38.1	43.3	74.9	70.0
1997[2]	52.90	63.10	78.90	37.90	90.30	1,100	13.36	7.7	37.7	39.9	70.2	84.0

Figures below represent cents per lb for cotton, apples, and peanuts; dollars per bushel for oats, wheat, corn, barley, and soybeans; dollars per 100 lb for rice, sorghum, and potatoes; dollars per ton for cottonseed and baled hay; weighted crop year prices. The marketing year is described as follows: apples, June-May; wheat, oats, barley, hay, and potatoes, July-June; cotton, rice, peanuts, and cottonseed, Aug.-July; soybeans, Sept.-Aug.; and corn and sorghum grain, Oct.-Sept.

Year	Corn	Wheat	Upland cotton*	Oats	Barley	Rice	Soybeans	Sorghum	Peanuts	Cottonseed	Hay	Potatoes	Apples
1940	0.62	0.67	9.8	0.30	0.39	1.80	0.89	0.87	3.7	21.70	9.78	0.85	NA
1950	1.52	2.00	39.9	0.79	1.19	5.09	2.47	1.88	10.9	86.60	21.10	1.50	NA
1960	1.00	1.74	30.1	0.60	0.84	4.55	2.13	1.49	10.0	42.50	21.70	2.00	2.7
1970	1.33	1.33	21.9	0.62	0.97	5.17	2.85	2.04	12.8	56.40	26.10	2.21	6.5
1975	2.54	3.55	51.1	1.45	2.42	8.35	4.92	4.21	19.0	97.00	52.10	4.48	8.8
1980	3.11	3.91	74.4	1.79	2.86	12.80	7.57	5.25	25.1	129.00	71.00	6.55	12.1
1984	2.63	3.39	58.7	1.67	2.29	8.04	5.84	4.15	27.9	99.50	72.70	5.69	15.5
1985	2.23	3.08	56.8	1.23	1.98	6.53	5.05	3.45	24.4	66.00	67.60	3.92	17.3
1986	1.50	2.42	51.5	1.21	1.61	3.75	4.78	2.45	29.2	80.00	59.70	5.03	19.1
1987	1.94	2.57	63.7	1.56	1.81	7.27	5.88	3.04	28.0	82.50	65.00	4.38	12.7
1988	2.54	3.72	55.6	2.61	2.80	6.83	7.42	4.05	28.0	118.00	85.20	6.02	17.4
1989	2.36	3.72	63.6	1.49	2.42	7.35	5.69	3.75	28.0	105.00	85.40	7.36	13.9
1990	2.28	2.61	67.1	1.14	2.14	6.68	5.74	3.79	34.7	121.00	80.60	6.08	20.9
1991	2.37	3.00	56.8	1.21	2.10	7.58	5.58	4.01	28.3	71.00	71.20	4.96	25.1
1992	2.07	3.24	53.7	1.32	2.04	5.89	5.56	3.38	30.0	97.50	74.30	5.52	19.5
1993	2.50	3.26	58.1	1.36	1.99	7.98	6.40	4.13	30.4	113.00	84.70	6.18	18.4
1994	2.26	3.45	72.0	1.22	2.03	6.78	5.48	3.80	28.9	101.00	86.70	5.58	18.6
1995	3.24	4.55	75.4	1.67	2.89	9.15	6.72	5.69	29.3	106.00	82.20	6.77	24.0
1996[1]	2.71	4.30	69.3	1.96	2.74	9.96	7.35	4.17	28.1	126.00	95.80	4.93	20.8
1997[2]	2.60	3.45	66.9	1.60	2.40	9.75	6.50	4.00	26.1	121.00	102.50	5.68	22.2

*Beginning in 1964, 480-lb net weight bales. NA = Not available. (1) Revised. (2) Preliminary.

Grain Storage Capacity at Principal U.S. Grain Centers, Aug. 1998

Source: Chicago Board of Trade Market Information Dept.

(in bushels)

	Capacity
Atlantic Coast	12,000,000
Great Lakes	
Toledo, OH	63,100,000
Duluth, MN	60,000,000
Chicago, IL	14,700,000
Buffalo, NY	15,200,000
Milwaukee, WI	NA
River Points	
Kansas City, MO	94,200,000
Minneapolis, MN	75,000,000
St. Joseph, MO	14,900,000
Atchison, KS	23,400,000
St. Louis, MO	9,100,000
Omaha-Council Bluffs, NE	6,800,000
Sioux City, IA	9,000,000

	Capacity
Southwest	
Texas High Plains	58,800,000
Fort Worth, TX	68,000,000
Enid, OK	NA
Gulf Points	
South Mississippi Region	45,000,000
Texas Gulf	38,800,000
Plains	
Topeka, KS	50,700,000
Salina, KS	44,100,000
Wichita, KS	34,300,000
Lincoln, NE	33,000,000
Hutchinson, KS	29,600,000
Hastings-Grand Island, NE	48,700,000
Pacific NW	
Puget Sound (incl. Portland)	32,100,000
California Ports	NA

NA= Not available.

Southwest/Texas High Plains — Amarillo, Lubbock, Hereford, Plainview, TX. **Atlantic Coast** — Albany, NY; Philadelphia, PA; Baltimore, MD; Norfolk, VA. **Gulf Points/South Mississippi Region** — New Orleans, Baton Rouge, Ama, Belle Chasse, LA; Mobile, AL. **Texas Gulf** — Houston, Galveston, Beaumont, Port Arthur, Corpus Christi, Brownsville, TX. **Pacific NW** — Seattle, Tacoma, WA; Portland, OR; Columbia River.

World Wheat, Rice, and Corn Production, 1997

Source: UN Food and Agriculture Organization

(in thousands of metric tons)

Country	Wheat	Rice[1]	Corn
Afghanistan	2,710	400*	360F
Argentina	14,300	1,208	15,540
Australia	18,554	1,352	371
Austria	1,290F	—	1,620F
Bangladesh	1,454	28,183	2
Belgium-Lux.	1,661	—	276
Brazil	2,450	9,334	34,611
Bulgaria	3,774*	9*	1,650*
Cambodia	—	3,415	65F
Canada	24,270	—	7,180
Chile	1,562	107	780
China	122,600	198,471F	105,395*
Colombia	50	1,802	1,008
Croatia	834	—	2,183
Cuba	—	300F	90*
Czech Rep.	3,640	—	285
Denmark	4,834F	—	—
Ecuador	24	1,053	598F
Egypt	5,849	5,585*	5,329*
Ethiopia	1,980F	—	3,300F
Finland	477	—	—
France	33,891	120	16,813
Germany	19,867	—	3,061
Greece	2,016	230F	2,045
Hungary	5,270	7F	6,811
India	68,710*	123,012*	9,800
Indonesia	—	49,254	9,325
Iran	10,045	2,562	1,000*
Iraq	1,063*	244*	121*
Ireland	704	—	—
Italy	6,901	1,395	9,778
Japan	573	12,531	—
Kazakhstan	8,955	255	111
Kenya	252	55	2,214
Korea, North	100	2,347	1,138
Korea, South	7	7,100	75
Laos	—	1,660	80F
Madagascar	5*	2,558	178
Malaysia	—	1,970*	48*
Mexico	3,645	490	18,463
Moldova	1,200*	—	1,692
Morocco	2,316	32	374
Myanmar	87*	17,673	286
Nepal	1,072	3,711	1,360*
Netherlands	1,146	—	95*
New Zealand	256F	—	200F
Nigeria	66	3,268	5,354
Pakistan	16,651	6,546	1,260F
Peru	126	1,460	823
Philippines	—	11,269	4,332
Poland	8,193	—	417
Portugal	305	164	825
Romania	7,156	11	12,680
Russia	44,258	328	2,675
Slovakia	1,886	—	819
South Africa	2,294	3F	8,657
Spain	4,630	735	4,440
Sri Lanka	—	2,610	33F
Sweden	2,057	—	—
Switzerland	584	—	210
Syria	3,031	—	303
Thailand	—	21,280	4,550F
Turkey	18,650	285	2,000
Turkmenistan	430F	55*	60F
Ukraine	17,377	86	5,376
United Kingdom	15,130*	—	—
United States	68,761	8,115	237,897
Uruguay	628F	1,026	162
Uzbekistan	1,700F	294*	220F
Venezuela	—	792	1,199
Vietnam	—	26,397F	1,500F
Yugoslavia	2,927*	—	6,869*
Zimbabwe	300*	—	2,192
World, total	**608,846**	**570,906**	**589,390**

* Unofficial figure. F=Food and Agriculture Organization (FAO) estimate. Where production is small or nonexistent, — is indicated. Because not all countries are reported on this table, country totals do not add to world totals. (1) Rice paddy.

Wheat, Rice, and Corn—Exports and Imports of 10 Leading Countries

Source: UN Food and Agriculture Organization

(in thousands of metric tons; ranked for 1996)

Leading exporters	EXPORTS[1] 1994	1995	1996
Wheat	**1994**	**1995**	**1996**
U.S.	30,571	32,420	31,150
Canada	21,378	16,960	16,520
Australia	12,730	7,818	14,568
France	12,650	16,310	14,550
Germany	5,524	3,682	4,200
United Kingdom	3,494	2,669	3,675
Argentina	5,172	6,913	3,532
Kazakhstan	1,060*	2,486	1,909
Romania	—	632	1,281
India	87	632	1,094*
Rice	**1994**	**1995**	**1996**
Thailand	4,859	6,198	5,454
U.S.	2,822	3,084	2,640
India	891	4,913	2,491
Pakistan	984	1,852	1,601
Vietnam	1,983	1,988	1,045*
Italy	620	524	608
Australia	585	542	567
China	1,630	236	357
Egypt	247	157	328
United Arab Emirates	160	276	276F
Corn	**1994**	**1995**	**1996**
U.S.	35,877	60,240	52,410
France	8,010	6,474	6,652
Argentina	4,154	6,001	6,425
Canada	381	444	513
Belgium-Lux.	489	443	377
Brazil	5	11	351
Germany	319	244	276
Yugoslavia, Fed Rep.	—	—	255
Zimbabwe	1,280	288	235
South Africa	3,760	1,508	220*

Leading importers	IMPORTS[1] 1994	1995	1996
Wheat	**1994**	**1995**	**1996**
China	8,281	12,602	9,194
Brazil	6,123	6,135	7,664
Italy	4,907	5,079	6,262
Japan	6,352	5,965	5,928
Egypt	6,597	5,070	5,121*
Indonesia	3,297	4,054	4,116
Iran	2,324	3,100*	3,874*
Netherlands	2,503	2,485	2,849
Belgium-Lux.	1,937	2,719	2,776
Morocco	1,191	2,549	2,240
Rice	**1994**	**1995**	**1996**
Indonesia	630	3,158	2,150
Philippines	2	263	867
Brazil	987	871	792
China	517	1,646	765
Saudi Arabia	434	605	721
Korea (North)	60	654	654F
Bangladesh	63	817	630
Malaysia	341	428	578
Senegal	348	441	541
Iran	482	1,300*	483
Corn	**1994**	**1995**	**1996**
Japan	15,930	16,580	16,004
Korea (South)	5,749	9,035	8,679
China	5,601	11,702	6,429
Mexico	2,747	2,687	5,843
Egypt	2,021	2,425	2,472*
Malaysia	1,969	2,383	2,227
Spain	2,339	2,912	2,031
Colombia	1,044	1,154	1,700
Belgium-Lux.	1,557	1,816	1,596
Netherlands	1,981	1,590	1,453

* Unofficial figure. F=Food and Agriculture Organization (FAO) estimate. Where production is small or nonexistent, — is indicated. (1) By marketing years.

World Commercial Catch of Fish, Crustaceans, and Mollusks,[1] by Major Fishing Areas, 1991-96[2]

Source: U.S. Dept. of Commerce, Natl. Oceanic and Atmospheric Admin., Natl. Marine Fisheries Service

(in thousands of metric tons; live weight)

Area	1991	1992	1993	1994	1995	1996
Marine						
Pacific Ocean	52,358	54,378	56,393	63,057	63,201	64,903
Atlantic Ocean	23,792	24,343	23,690	23,648	24,827	24,706
Indian Ocean	6,879	7,363	7,869	7,737	8,010	8,242
TOTAL	**83,029**	**86,084**	**87,952**	**94,442**	**96,038**	**97,851**
Inland Waters						
N. America	551	584	579	573	540	561
S. America	331	357	375	403	425	402
Europe	493	504	497	509	527	513
Former USSR	764	667	544	460	416	416
Asia	10,798	11,668	13,372	15,245	17,335	19,326
Africa	1,808	1,839	1,864	1,805	1,974	1,919
Oceania	23	25	23	21	23	22
TOTAL	**14,768**	**15,644**	**17,254**	**19,016**	**21,240**	**23,159**
GRAND TOTAL	**97,797**	**101,728**	**105,206**	**113,458**	**117,278**	**121,010**

(1) Does not include marine mammals and aquatic plants. (2) Revised back to 1992.

Commercial Catch of Fish, Crustaceans, Mollusks,[1] by Selected Country, 1990-96[2]

Source: U.S. Dept. of Commerce, Natl. Oceanic and Atmospheric Admin., Natl. Marine Fisheries Service

(in thousands of metric tons; live weight)

Country	1991	1992	1993	1994	1995	1996
China	13,125	16,579	19,708	23,834	28,418	31,937
Peru	6,888	7,508	9,008	12,005	8,943	9,522
Chile	6,006	6,502	6,035	7,839	7,591	6,911
Japan	9,301	8,502	8,081	7,398	6,787	6,793
United States[3]	5,487	5,604	5,940	5,926	5,638	5,394
India	4,045	4,233	4,546	4,738	4,906	5,260
Russia	7,047	5,611	4,461	3,781	4,374	4,729
Indonesia	3,352	3,439	3,685	3,917	4,145	4,402
Thailand	2,972	3,246	3,385	3,522	3,756	3,648
Norway	2,173	2,561	2,588	2,551	2,803	2,963

(1) Does not include marine mammals and aquatic plants. (2) Revised back to 1992. (3) Includes weight of clam, oyster, scallop, and other mollusk shells. This weight is not included in U.S. landings statistics shown elsewhere.

U.S. Commercial Landings of Fish and Shellfish, 1986-97[1]

Source: U.S. Dept. of Commerce, Natl. Oceanic and Atmospheric Admin., Natl. Marine Fisheries Service

Year	Landings for human food		Landings for industrial purposes[2]		TOTAL	
	mil lb	mil dollars	mil lb	mil dollars	mil lb	mil dollars
1986	3,393	$2,641	2,638	$122	6,031	$2,763
1987	3,946	2,979	2,950	136	6,896	3,115
1988	4,588	3,362	2,604	158	7,192	3,520
1989	6,204	3,111	2,259	127	8,463	3,238
1990	7,041	3,366	2,363	156	9,404	3,522
1991	7,031	3,169	2,453	139	9,484	3,308
1992	7,618	3,531	2,019	147	9,637	3,678
1993	8,214	3,317	2,253	154	10,467	3,471
1994	7,936	3,751	2,525	95	10,461	3,846
1995	7,667	3,625	2,121	145	9,788	3,770
1996	7,474	3,355	2,091	132	9,565	3,487
1997	7,248	3,304	2,598	163	9,846	3,467

Note: Data do not include landings outside the 50 states or products of aquaculture, except oysters and clams.
(1) Statistics on landings are shown in round weight for all items except univalve and bivalve mollusks such as clams, oysters, and scallops, which are shown in weight of meats (excluding the shell). All data are preliminary. (2) Processed into meal, oil, solubles, and shell products or used as bait or animal food.

U.S. Domestic Landings, by Regions, 1996-97[1]

Source: U.S. Dept. of Commerce, Natl. Oceanic and Atmospheric Admin., Natl. Marine Fisheries Service

Region	1996		1997	
	1,000 lb	1,000 dollars	1,000 lb	1,000 dollars
New England	641,821	$564,169	643,158	$574,854
Middle Atlantic	241,936	181,869	236,951	199,986
Chesapeake	728,830	158,736	688,142	169,319
South Atlantic	268,990	209,407	298,683	213,385
Gulf	1,496,875	680,304	1,790,310	758,682
Pacific Coast and Alaska	6,129,410	1,610,508	6,125,787	1,464,962
Great Lakes	25,156	17,432	26,185	16,724
Hawaii	31,870	64,288	36,568	68,693
TOTAL	**9,564,888**	**3,486,713**	**9,845,784**	**3,466,605**

(1) Landings reported in round (live) weight items except for univalve and bivalve mollusks (e.g., clams, oysters, scallops), which are reported in weight of meats (excluding shell). Landings for Mississippi River Drainage Area states not included (not available).

EMPLOYMENT

Employment and Unemployment in the U.S., 1940-97

Source: Bureau of Labor Statistics, U.S. Dept. of Labor

(civilian labor force, persons 16 years of age and older; annual averages; in thousands)

Year[1]	Employed	Unemployed	Unemployment rate	Year[1]	Employed	Unemployed	Unemployment rate
1940[2]	47,520	8,120	14.6%	1989	117,342	6,528	5.3%
1950	58,918	3,288	5.0	1990[3]	118,793	7,047	5.6
1960	65,778	3,852	5.5	1991	117,718	8,628	6.8
1970	78,678	4,093	4.9	1992	118,482	9,613	7.5
1980	99,303	7,637	7.1	1993	120,259	8,940	6.9
1985	107,150	8,312	7.2	1994[4]	123,060	7,996	6.1
1986	109,597	8,237	7.0	1995	124,900	7,404	5.6
1987	112,440	7,425	6.2	1996	126,708	7,236	5.4
1988	114,988	6,701	5.5	1997[5]	129,558	6,739	4.9

(1) **Early unemployment rates:** 1915, 9.7; 1916, 4.8; 1917, 4.8; 1918, 1.4; 1919, 2.3; 1920, 4.0; 1921, 11.9; 1922, 7.6; 1923, 3.2; 1924, 5.5; 1925, 4.0; 1926, 1.9; 1927, 4.1; 1928, 4.4; 1929, 3.2; 1930, 8.7; 1931, 15.9; 1932, 23.6; 1933, 24.9; 1934, 21.7; 1935, 20.1; 1936, 16.9; 1937, 14.3; 1938, 19.0; 1939, 17.2. (2) Persons 14 years of age and older. (3) Beginning in 1990, data incorporate 1990 census-based population controls, adjusted for the estimated undercount. (4) Beginning in 1994, not strictly comparable with prior years, because of a major redesign of the survey used. (5) 1997 not strictly comparable with 1994-96 because of revisions in population controls used in the household survey.

Unemployment Insurance Data, by State, 1997

Source: Employment and Training Admin., U.S. Dept. of Labor; state programs only

STATE	Monetarily eligible claimants	First payments	Final payments	Initial claims	Benefits paid	Average weekly benefit	Employers subject to state law
AL	159,551	134,862	29,872	318,540	$187,747,208	$144.67	86,953
AK	50,594	43,617	17,726	100,378	110,857,736	175.76	15,707
AZ	97,830	68,786	22,088	157,898	136,208,318	146.52	95,680
AR	131,325	93,074	30,374	209,645	173,946,699	198.24	58,141
CA	1,403,081	1,072,565	425,145	3,065,949	2,447,456,396	151.85	815,463
CO	94,732	63,696	24,879	120,591	161,522,054	212.73	118,319
CT	120,242	113,507	32,224	204,992	347,810,234	211.37	94,101
DE	25,040	20,962	7,957	37,237	64,287,059	193.70	23,085
FL	321,585	245,979	102,090	446,247	615,200,654	191.94	352,970
GA	260,830	180,316	47,480	317,802	268,707,852	162.47	170,022
HI	47,459	38,057	13,286	94,693	154,337,178	268.83	26,911
ID	53,963	45,225	13,055	110,274	89,869,635	187.20	35,582
IL	372,104	320,203	112,619	652,052	1,109,826,051	217.41	267,021
IN	166,997	121,128	36,113	259,463	208,781,046	185.90	122,949
IA	95,337	79,155	16,114	133,302	172,597,298	205.03	67,182
KS	65,966	49,393	14,516	103,664	101,705,111	204.41	64,666
KY	146,193	114,235	19,750	264,604	214,411,401	175.91	78,538
LA	95,080	68,628	20,223	166,664	139,397,940	132.61	89,752
ME	46,103	41,610	18,742	82,927	92,795,912	151.75	36,027
MD	158,620	107,224	34,765	219,947	308,626,566	195.93	123,356
MA	210,264	177,517	60,806	331,943	686,082,679	262.85	161,062
MI	463,199	348,054	99,050	690,461	873,134,424	221.75	207,656
MN	127,397	109,566	32,104	209,226	330,552,454	242.00	120,238
MS	82,134	61,281	17,015	171,000	109,544,462	142.24	50,615
MO	194,715	140,250	38,090	361,476	261,962,070	154.21	125,131
MT	34,728	26,735	8,938	55,375	54,162,849	166.09	28,949
NE	39,628	26,578	8,384	51,820	47,405,935	162.81	43,010
NV	83,867	63,824	19,342	128,108	171,508,521	203.88	38,672
NH	25,765	16,791	112	36,346	31,641,243	165.74	35,980
NJ	324,709	282,924	125,966	519,105	1,059,563,473	258.50	215,702
NM	38,559	29,851	9,961	59,479	69,668,865	158.00	40,347
NY	533,385	490,304	250,841	1,025,396	1,625,912,000	203.78	446,023
NC	322,178	201,307	35,862	700,794	346,356,620	198.27	157,623
ND	28,541	18,584	5,103	37,927	36,109,407	176.11	18,759
OH	315,134	253,881	56,221	555,459	662,961,134	207.99	228,524
OK	58,292	40,628	13,937	98,976	81,650,850	176.78	72,175
OR	161,065	137,048	40,194	340,397	339,105,667	198.14	96,048
PA	493,552	429,874	111,217	1,053,254	1,338,234,210	227.50	236,289
RI	52,636	49,077	17,555	113,489	149,937,011	223.63	30,918
SC	144,784	92,189	22,023	279,397	162,053,750	168.62	81,794
SD	11,634	8,992	922	19,365	15,494,979	155.68	21,255
TN	220,151	165,297	50,515	424,030	292,585,932	163.31	107,791
TX	607,200	345,121	216,046	707,565	893,781,194	195.87	373,350
UT	48,304	34,124	8,897	57,005	71,765,584	193.08	46,506
VT	24,885	21,081	3,605	40,691	45,636,242	173.52	19,918
VA	163,561	101,414	23,214	279,539	180,613,117	179.20	152,076
WA	268,752	197,549	59,581	512,209	662,693,516	239.82	171,151
WV	62,216	55,641	12,413	88,574	128,466,651	180.20	37,924
WI	255,698	210,504	40,698	468,858	442,374,001	188.47	117,994
WY	15,236	10,967	3,437	24,249	25,297,320	181.80	17,828
DC	25,706	21,026	11,743	31,812	68,691,852	233.48	24,022
PR	135,155	132,049	61,270	253,526	228,618,949	94.25	46,611
VI	3,397	2,388	1,138	2,590	5,723,897	187.86	NA
U.S.	**9,489,059**	**7,324,638**	**2,505,218**	**16,796,310**	**$18,605,383,208**	**$192.78**	**6,314,359**

NA=Not available.

Unemployment Rates, by Selected Country, 1975-98

Source: Bureau of Labor Statistics, U.S. Dept. of Labor; civilian labor force, seasonally adjusted; Oct. 1998

Time Period	U.S.	Australia	Canada	France	Germany[1]	Italy[2]	Japan	Sweden	UK
1975	8.5	4.9	6.9	4.2	3.4	3.4	1.9	1.6	4.6
1980	7.1	6.1	7.5	6.5	2.8	4.4	2.0	2.0	7.0
1981	7.6	5.8	7.6	7.6	4.0	4.9	2.2	2.5	10.5
1982	9.7	7.2	11.0	8.3	5.6	5.4	2.4	3.1	11.3
1983	9.6	10.0	11.9	8.6	6.9[3]	5.9	2.7	3.5	11.8
1984	7.5	9.0	11.3	10.0	7.1	5.9	2.8	3.1	11.7
1985	7.2	8.3	10.5	10.5	7.2	6.0	2.6	2.8	11.2
1986	7.0	8.1	9.6	10.6	6.6	7.5[3]	2.8	2.6	11.2
1987	6.2	8.1	8.9	10.8	6.3	7.9	2.9	2.2[3]	10.3
1988	5.5	7.2	7.8	10.3	6.3	7.9	2.5	1.9	8.6
1989	5.3	6.2	7.5	9.6	5.7	7.8	2.3	1.6	7.2
1990	5.6[3]	6.9	8.1	9.1	5.0	7.0	2.1	1.8	6.9
1991	6.8	9.6	10.4	9.6	4.3P	6.9[3]	2.1	3.1	8.8
1992	7.5	10.8	11.3	10.4[3]	4.6P	7.3P	2.2	5.6	10.1
1993	6.9	10.9	11.2	11.8	5.7P	10.2P[3]	2.5	9.3	10.5
1994	6.1[3]	9.7	10.4	12.3	6.5P	11.3P	2.9	9.6	9.7
1995	5.6	8.5	9.5	11.8	9.4[4]	12.0P	3.2	9.1	8.7
1996	5.4	8.6	9.7	12.5	10.4[4]	12.1P	3.4	9.9	8.2
1997	4.9	8.6	9.2	12.4P	11.4[4]	12.3P	3.4	9.8P	7.0
1st quarter	5.3	8.7	9.6	12.4	—	12.3	3.3	10.6	7.4
2d quarter	4.9	8.7	9.4	12.5	—	12.4	3.4	10.4	7.2
3d quarter	4.9	8.6	9.0	12.5	—	12.2	3.4	9.5	6.9
4th quarter	4.7	8.3	8.9	12.3	—	12.3	3.5	8.8	6.6
1998									
1st quarter	4.7	8.1	8.6	12.0	—	12.1	3.7	8.4	6.4
2d quarter	4.4	8.1	8.4	11.8	—	12.4	4.2	8.2	6.2

P=Preliminary. **Note:** For the sake of comparisons, U.S. unemployment rate concepts were applied to unemployment data for other countries. Quarterly and monthly figures for France were calculated by applying annual adjustment factors to current published data and are less precise indicators of unemployment under U.S. concepts than the annual figures. (1) Former West Germany only, except where indicated. (2) Quarterly rates are for first month of quarter. (3) As a result of revisions in survey methodology, there are breaks in the data series for the U.S. (1990, 1994), France (1992), Germany (1983), Italy (1986, 1991, 1993), and Sweden (1987); data prior to a survey change are not fully comparable to data after a survey change. (4) Figures are for unified Germany; not adjusted by BLS. Dashes (—) indicate unavailable data.

Employed Persons in the U.S., by Occupation and Sex, 1996-97

Source: Bureau of Labor Statistics, U.S. Dept. of Labor

(in thousands)

	TOTAL 16 years and older		MEN 16 years and older		WOMEN 16 years and older	
	1996	**1997**	**1996**	**1997**	**1996**	**1997**
TOTAL	**126,708**	**129,558**	**68,207**	**69,685**	**58,501**	**59,873**
Managerial and professional specialty	36,497	37,686	18,744	19,249	17,754	18,437
Executive, administrative, and managerial	17,746	18,440	9,979	10,271	7,767	9,170
Officials and administrators, public administration	716	694	384	372	332	322
Other executive, administrative, and managerial	12,656	13,143	7,703	7,951	4,953	5,191
Management-related occupations	4,374	4,604	1,892	1,948	2,481	2,655
Professional specialty	18,752	19,245	8,764	8,978	9,987	10,267
Engineers	1,960	2,036	1,793	1,841	167	195
Mathematical and computer scientists	1,345	1,494	933	1,040	412	454
Natural scientists	536	529	379	385	157	164
Health diagnosing occupations	960	1,027	715	769	245	259
Health assessment and treating occupations	2,812	2,886	403	391	2,409	2,495
Teachers, college and university	889	869	502	498	387	371
Teachers, except college and university	4,724	4,798	1,207	1,166	3,517	3,632
Lawyers and judges	911	925	647	678	264	247
Other professional specialty occupations	4,616	4,681	2,186	2,231	2,430	2,450
Technical, sales, and administrative support	37,683	36,309	13,489	13,760	24,194	24,549
Technicians and related support	3,926	4,214	1,865	2,028	2,061	2,186
Sales occupations	15,404	15,734	7,782	7,840	7,622	7,894
Administrative support, including clerical	18,353	18,361	3,842	3,892	14,511	14,469
Service occupations	17,177	17,537	6,967	7,122	10,210	10,416
Precision production, craft, and repair	13,587	14,124	12,368	12,868	1,219	1,256
Mechanics and repairers	4,521	4,675	4,335	4,494	185	181
Construction trades	5,108	5,378	4,981	5,251	127	127
Other precision production, craft, and repair	3,959	4,071	3,052	3,123	906	948
Operators, fabricators, and laborers	18,197	18,389	13,750	1,358	4,447	4,540
Machine operators, assemblers, and inspectors	7,874	7,962	4,902	4,962	2,972	3,000
Transportation and material moving occupations	5,302	5,389	4,799	4,872	504	518
Motor vehicle operators	4,025	4,089	3,575	3,629	450	461
Other transportation and material moving occupations	1,277	1,300	1,223	1,243	54	57
Handlers, equipment cleaners, helpers, and laborers	5,021	5,048	4,049	4,025	971	1,023
Construction laborers	809	811	778	773	31	37
Other handlers, equipment cleaners, etc.	4,212	2,307	3,272	1,794	940	514
Farming, forestry, and fishing	3,566	3,503	2,889	2,828	677	675

Note: Totals may not add because of independent rounding.

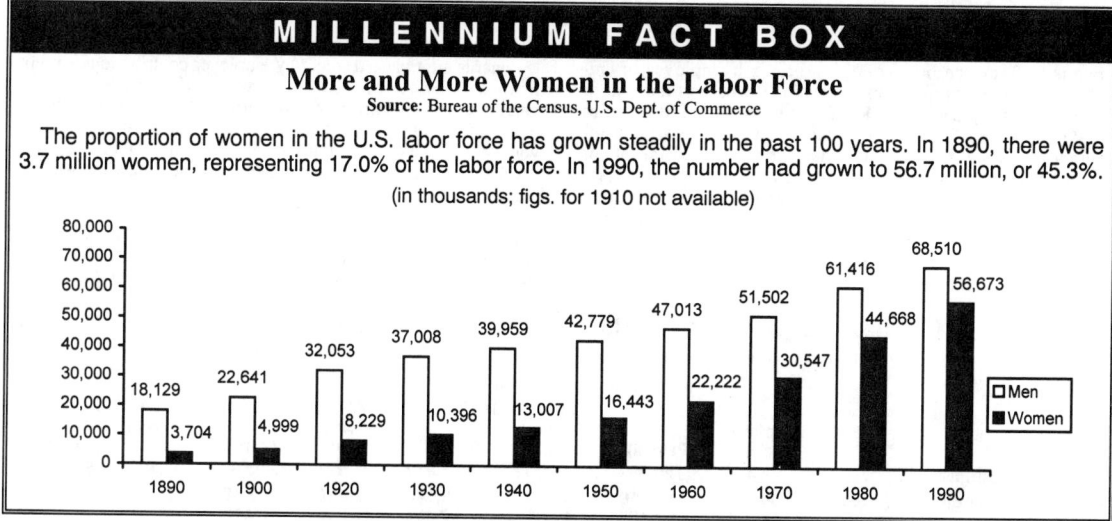

MILLENNIUM FACT BOX

More and More Women in the Labor Force

Source: Bureau of the Census, U.S. Dept. of Commerce

The proportion of women in the U.S. labor force has grown steadily in the past 100 years. In 1890, there were 3.7 million women, representing 17.0% of the labor force. In 1990, the number had grown to 56.7 million, or 45.3%.

(in thousands; figs. for 1910 not available)

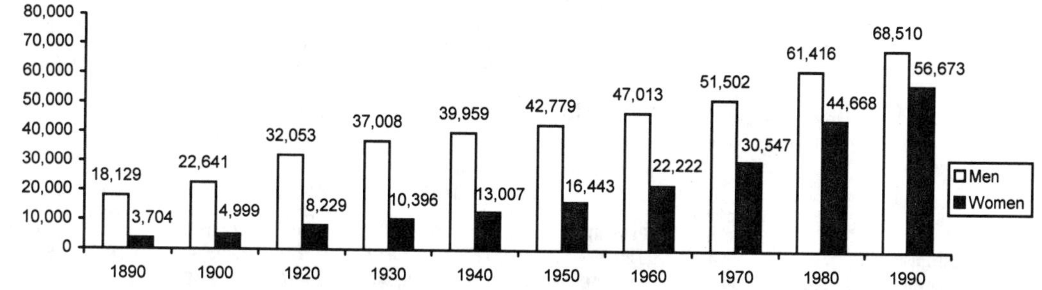

U.S. Unemployment Rates by Selected Characteristics, 1995-98

Source: Bureau of Labor Statistics, U.S. Dept. of Labor; seasonally adjusted, quarterly averages

	1995				1996				1997				1998	
	I	II	III	IV	I	II	III	IV	I	II	III	IV	I	II
TOTAL (all civilian workers)	5.5	5.6	5.7	5.6	5.6	5.4	5.3	5.3	5.3	4.9	4.9	4.7	4.7	4.4
Men, 20 years and older	4.7	4.9	4.9	4.8	4.9	4.7	4.5	4.4	4.5	4.1	4.1	4.0	3.8	3.6
Women, 20 years and older	4.9	5.0	5.0	4.8	4.9	4.8	4.7	4.8	4.7	4.4	4.3	4.0	4.3	4.0
Both sexes, 16 to 19 years	16.7	17.3	17.8	17.6	17.3	16.5	16.6	16.6	17.0	15.9	16.3	15.0	14.6	14.0
White	4.8	4.9	4.9	4.9	4.9	4.7	4.6	4.6	4.5	4.1	4.2	4.0	4.0	3.8
Black	10.2	10.4	11.0	9.9	10.6	10.3	10.5	10.6	10.9	10.2	9.6	9.7	9.4	8.7
Black and other	9.4	9.6	10.0	9.2	9.5	9.3	9.2	9.2	9.5	9.1	8.4	8.4	8.2	7.5
Hispanic origin	9.4	9.2	9.2	9.5	9.6	9.2	8.7	8.0	8.3	7.7	7.6	7.4	6.9	6.9
Married men, spouse present	3.2	3.4	3.4	3.2	3.1	3.0	3.0	3.0	2.8	2.7	2.6	2.5	2.5	2.3
Married women, spouse present	3.8	3.9	4.1	3.8	3.7	3.7	3.4	3.6	3.3	3.2	3.1	2.8	3.1	2.8
Women who maintain families	8.4	8.5	7.7	7.5	7.8	7.8	8.6	8.5	9.1	7.7	7.8	7.8	7.6	7.4
OCCUPATION														
Managerial and professional specialty	2.4	2.4	2.5	2.5	2.4	2.4	2.3	2.3	2.1	2.0	2.0	1.8	1.9	1.7
Technical, sales, and administrative support	4.4	4.6	4.4	4.3	4.5	4.4	4.5	4.6	4.3	4.1	4.1	3.9	4.1	3.8
Precision production, craft, and repair	5.7	6.1	6.4	5.9	5.7	5.4	5.4	5.5	5.0	4.7	4.8	4.8	4.4	4.1
Operators, fabricators, and laborers	7.9	8.3	8.5	8.2	8.3	8.0	7.6	7.7	8.1	7.3	7.6	7.1	6.4	6.5
Farming, forestry, and fishing	7.7	8.2	7.6	8.0	7.9	8.0	6.7	7.5	7.4	7.0	6.8	7.0	6.7	6.2
INDUSTRY														
Nonagricultural private wage and salary workers	5.6	5.8	5.9	5.8	5.7	5.6	5.4	5.4	5.3	5.0	5.0	4.8	4.7	4.5
Goods-producing industries	6.1	6.5	6.6	6.5	6.3	6.1	5.7	5.9	5.7	5.3	5.3	4.9	4.9	4.6
Mining	5.0	4.5	4.0	7.4	6.0	3.9	4.2	6.1	4.7	2.4	4.2	3.7	3.5	2.5
Construction	11.1	11.7	12.0	11.5	10.7	10.0	9.4	9.7	9.6	8.5	8.8	8.5	8.1	7.4
Manufacturing	4.6	5.0	5.1	5.0	5.0	4.9	4.6	4.7	4.4	4.3	4.2	3.7	3.8	3.7
Durable goods	4.1	4.4	4.5	4.5	4.8	4.6	4.1	4.5	4.0	3.5	3.4	3.1	3.3	3.1
Nondurable goods	5.3	5.9	5.9	5.7	5.3	5.3	5.3	5.1	5.1	5.4	5.2	4.7	4.6	4.5
Service-producing industries	5.4	5.5	5.6	5.5	5.5	5.4	5.3	5.2	5.2	4.9	4.8	4.7	4.6	4.5
Transportation and public utilities	4.7	4.4	4.4	4.3	4.0	4.3	4.1	4.0	4.1	3.1	3.6	3.2	3.4	3.2
Wholesale and retail trade	6.4	6.5	6.7	6.4	6.6	6.5	6.3	6.2	6.4	6.2	6.2	6.0	5.7	5.3
Finance, insurance, and real estate	3.3	3.5	3.2	3.0	2.6	2.6	2.8	3.0	3.2	3.0	3.0	2.7	2.6	2.1
Services	5.3	5.5	5.5	5.5	5.6	5.5	5.3	5.1	4.9	4.7	4.5	4.4	4.6	4.6
Government workers	3.0	3.0	2.9	2.8	2.8	3.0	2.9	2.9	2.9	2.5	2.6	2.3	2.5	2.1
Agricultural wage/salary workers	10.3	11.7	10.4	11.9	10.6	10.3	9.2	10.4	8.9	9.1	8.7	9.3	9.6	8.0

Note: Beginning in Jan. 1997, data reflect revised population controls used in the household survey. Beginning in Jan. 1998, data reflect new composite estimation procedures and revised population controls used in the household survey.

Unemployment Insurance

Source: Unemployment Insurance Service, U.S. Dept. of Labor

Unlike old-age and survivors insurance, which is entirely a federal program, unemployment insurance in the U.S. is a federal-state system that provides insured wage earners partial replacement for lost wages during a period of involuntary unemployment. The program protects most wage and salary workers. During fiscal year 1997, an estimated 118 million workers in commerce, industry, agriculture, and government were covered under the federal-state system.

Each state, as well as the District of Columbia, Puerto Rico, and the Virgin Islands, has its own law and operates its own program. The amount and duration of the weekly benefits are determined by state laws and are based on prior wages and length of employment. States are required to extend the duration of benefits when unemployment in the state rises to and remains above specified levels; costs of extended benefits are shared by the state and federal governments. *(continued)*

Unemployment Insurance *(continued)*

Under the Federal Unemployment Tax Act, the federal tax rate is 6.2% on the first $7,000 paid to each employee of employers with one or more employees in 20 weeks of the year or with a quarterly payroll of $1,500 or more. A credit of up to 5.4% is allowed for taxes paid under state unemployment insurance laws that meet certain criteria, for a net federal rate of 0.8%; subject employers also pay a state unemployment tax. Governmental agencies and certain nonprofit organizations are not subject to the federal tax; these employers reimburse states for benefits paid to former employees.

The secretary of labor certifies states for administrative grants to operate the program (under the Social Security Act) and for employer tax credit (under the Federal Unemployment Tax Act).

Benefits are financed solely by employer contributions, except in Alaska, New Jersey, and Pennsylvania, where employees also contribute. Benefits are paid through the states' public employment offices, at which unemployed workers must register for work and to which they must report regularly for referral to a possible job during the time when they are drawing weekly benefit payments.

During fiscal year 1997, $21.0 billion in benefits were paid under all unemployment insurance programs to 7.6 million beneficiaries. They received an average payment of $192.28 weekly for total unemployment, which lasted an average of 14.8 weeks.

Civilian Employment of the Federal Government, May 1998

Source: Statistical Analysis and Services Division, U.S. Office of Personnel Management

(payroll in thousands of dollars)

	ALL AREAS		UNITED STATES		WASH., D.C., MSA		OVERSEAS	
	Employment	Payroll	Employment	Payroll	Employment	Payroll	Employment	Payroll
TOTAL, all agencies[1]	**2,779,406**	**$9,720,389**	**2,676,003**	**$9,364,847**	**321,927**	**$1,425,408**	**103,403**	**$355,542**
Legislative Branch	**30,745**	**119,619**	**30,735**	**119,543**	**29,416**	**113,469**	**10**	**76**
Congress	17,215	62,455	17,215	62,455	17,215	62,455	—	—
U.S. Senate	6,412	23,221	6,412	23,221	6,412	23,221	—	—
House of Representatives	10,788	39,172	10,788	39,172	10,788	39,172	—	—
Architect of the Capitol	1,744	5,504	1,744	5,504	1,744	5,504	—	—
Congressional Budget Ofc	220	1,215	220	1,215	220	1,215	—	—
General Accounting Ofc	3,283	18,007	3,281	17,991	2,333	13,071	2	16
Government Printing Ofc.	3,443	12,718	3,443	12,718	3,105	11,705	—	—
Library of Congress	4,369	17,411	4,361	17,351	4,340	17,285	8	60
U.S. Tax Court	280	1,401	280	1,401	276	1,380	—	—
Judicial Branch	**31,092**	**125,605**	**30,723**	**124,265**	**1,716**	**8,916**	**369**	**1,340**
Supreme Court	383	1,962	383	1,962	383	1,962	—	—
U.S. Courts	30,709	123,643	30,340	122,303	1,333	6,954	369	1,340
Executive Branch	**2,717,569**	**9,475,165**	**2,614,545**	**9,121,039**	**290,795**	**1,303,023**	**103,024**	**354,126**
Exec Ofc of the President	1,605	8,128	1,596	8,068	1,596	8,068	9	60
White House Office	399	1,676	399	1,676	399	1,676	—	—
Ofc of Vice President	20	127	20	127	20	127	—	—
Ofc of Mgmt & Budget	502	2,833	502	2,833	502	2,833	—	—
Ofc of Administration	173	728	173	728	173	728	—	—
Council Economic Advisors	31	145	31	145	31	145	—	—
Ofc of Policy Development	28	157	28	157	28	157	—	—
National Security Council	42	210	42	210	42	210	—	—
Ofc of Natl Drug Control	114	635	114	635	114	635	—	—
Ofc of U.S. Trade Rep.	162	871	153	811	153	811	9	60
Executive Departments	1,650,197	5,949,332	1,566,903	5,664,752	214,414	969,527	83,294	284,580
State	24,618	109,703	8,710	39,114	7,499	32,542	15,908	70,589
Treasury	153,729	543,062	152,537	537,522	21,080	100,957	1,192	5,540
Defense, Total	726,690	2,529,162	669,099	2,350,625	66,703	269,563	57,591	178,537
Defense, Mil Funct Total	700,685	2,452,655	643,181	2,274,399	65,796	266,025	57,504	178,256
Defense, Civ Funct Total	26,005	76,507	25,918	76,226	907	3,538	87	281
Dept of the Army	242,775	747,164	218,511	670,939	19,926	50,485	24,264	76,225
Army, Mil Funct Total	216,771	670,658	192,594	594,714	19,019	46,947	24,177	75,944
Army, Civil Funct Total	26,004	76,506	25,917	76,225	907	3,538	87	281
Corps of Engineers	25,948	76,170	25,861	75,889	851	3,202	87	281
Dept of the Navy	198,774	896,034	188,905	862,254	26,818	136,287	9,869	33,780
Dept of the Air Force	167,477	485,268	159,917	468,320	5,492	13,979	7,560	16,948
Defense Log Agcy	43,622	146,589	42,466	142,999	2,981	12,048	1,156	3,590
Other Def Act (excl DLA)	74,042	254,107	59,300	206,113	11,486	56,764	14,742	47,994
Justice	120,104	489,018	117,721	479,099	21,063	105,840	2,383	9,919
Interior	71,803	264,091	71,470	262,964	7,731	35,726	333	1,127
Agriculture	100,161	319,022	98,859	315,578	11,373	48,134	1,302	3,444
Commerce	40,365	143,065	39,587	140,133	19,241	84,335	778	2,932
Labor	15,786	61,883	15,749	61,743	5,304	23,544	37	140
Health and Human Services	59,462	251,075	59,263	250,086	26,498	121,765	199	989
Housing & Urban Dev	9,852	44,947	9,777	44,619	2,839	14,708	75	328
Transportation	64,046	345,365	63,530	342,622	9,887	53,435	516	2,743
Energy	16,246	88,662	16,240	88,612	5,529	37,647	6	50
Education	4,801	20,200	4,799	20,189	3,343	14,411	2	11
Veterans Affairs	242,534	740,077	239,562	731,846	6,324	26,920	2,972	8,231
Independent Agencies	1,065,767	3,517,705	1,046,046	3,448,219	74,785	325,428	19,721	69,486
Bd of Gov, Fed Rsrv Sys.	1,675	8,805	1,675	8,805	1,675	8,805	—	—
Environmtl Protect Agcy	18,307	83,158	18,268	82,977	6,130	30,387	39	181
Equal Employ Opp Comm	2,586	10,631	2,586	10,631	674	3,068	—	—
Federal Communic Comm	2,027	9,918	2,025	9,905	1,677	8,472	2	13
Federal Deposit Ins Corp.	7,762	40,740	7,750	40,678	2,581	15,355	12	62
Fed Emergency Mgmt Agcy.	5,294	17,845	5,165	17,550	2,020	7,692	129	295
General Svcs Admin.	14,196	54,812	14,107	54,558	4,775	21,159	89	254
Natl Aero & Space Admin	18,985	93,694	18,962	93,566	4,062	20,976	23	128
Natl Fnd Arts & Humanities	330	1,533	330	1,533	330	1,533	—	—
Peace Corps	1,092	3,868	647	2,470	518	2,110	445	1398
Securities & Exchange Comm	2,810	13,364	2,810	13,364	1,780	8,479	—	—
Smithsonian Inst., Total	5,211	17,151	5,035	16,659	4,588	15,084	176	492
Social Security Admin	65,857	340,590	65,338	337,937	1,552	9,690	521	2,653
U.S. Postal Service	858,066	2,559,252	854,082	2,544,908	22,798	75,753	3,984	14,344

U.S. Occupational Illnesses, by Industry and Type of Illness, 1996

Source: Bureau of Labor Statistics, U.S. Dept. of Labor

(percent distribution)

Occupational illness	All private sector[1]	GOODS PRODUCING Agriculture[2]	Mining[3]	Construction	Manufacturing	SERVICE PRODUCING Trans. and pub. utilities	Wholesale	Retail	Finance[4]	Service
TOTAL [1,880,500 cases].	**100.0**	**100.0**	**100.0**	**100.0**	**100.0**	**100.0**	**100.0**	**100.0**	**100.0**	**100.0**
Nature of injury, illness:										
Sprains, strains	43.6	34.2	38.8	37.6	38.2	52.6	44.4	41.9	40.1	49.3
Bruises, contusions	9.3	9.5	10.4	7.1	8.9	10.0	9.9	11.3	7.1	8.7
Cuts, lacerations	7.1	9.9	9.0	10.3	8.3	3.4	5.8	9.9	6.2	4.6
Fractures	6.4	7.7	14.0	9.9	6.8	5.5	7.0	5.9	6.4	4.9
Carpal tunnel syndrome	1.6	0.5	—	0.7	2.7	0.7	1.0	1.4	3.8	1.5
Tendinitis	0.9	0.4	—	0.3	1.9	0.4	0.5	0.7	1.3	0.7
Heat burns	1.5	0.7	1.4	1.2	1.8	0.5	0.7	2.7	0.9	1.5
Chemical burns	0.6	0.3	0.7	0.4	0.9	0.4	0.7	0.6	0.6	0.5
Amputations	0.5	0.7	0.7	0.7	1.2	0.2	0.6	0.3	0.2	0.1
Multiple injuries	3.2	3.5	6.2	3.0	2.8	2.9	3.9	3.2	3.9	3.5
Source of injury, illness:										
Chemicals/chem. products	1.9	1.7	6.8	1.1	2.4	1.0	1.3	1.6	1.8	2.2
Containers	14.5	8.7	6.2	5.2	14.0	21.6	22.0	22.5	9.7	8.4
Furniture, fixtures	3.6	0.6	0.5	2.1	2.8	1.6	2.6	5.6	5.2	5.4
Machinery	6.6	6.7	14.3	6.2	11.2	3.1	6.6	6.5	5.4	3.5
Parts and materials	11.1	7.1	16.7	24.2	17.8	8.9	13.4	6.0	4.1	3.7
Worker motion or position	14.5	12.0	2.8	11.9	18.4	14.6	11.6	12.5	18.7	14.2
Floor, ground surface	16.2	16.7	14.7	18.0	10.5	17.8	13.4	18.8	26.7	18.5
Tools, instruments, equip.	6.1	10.2	8.0	10.5	6.3	3.7	4.1	6.4	4.5	5.3
Vehicles	8.0	9.5	10.0	5.7	4.8	16.7	13.7	7.2	5.9	6.8
Health care patient	4.6	—	—	—	—	0.6	—	—	1.0	18.9
Event or exposure:										
Contact with object/equip.	26.2	31.7	43.2	32.9	33.1	20.1	29.2	27.5	18.8	17.3
Struck by object	12.7	14.6	21.5	17.9	14.1	9.7	15.0	14.9	8.7	8.3
Struck against object	6.8	9.3	8.9	7.5	7.6	5.4	6.9	7.5	6.2	5.5
Caught in object	4.2	4.0	11.2	3.3	8.2	2.6	5.0	3.0	1.7	2.0
Fall to lower level	5.2	7.6	10.0	11.7	3.2	7.6	5.4	3.6	8.5	4.0
Fall to same level	11.7	9.3	7.6	8.0	8.1	10.7	8.0	16.2	18.9	14.8
Slips, trips (without fall)	3.2	2.7	0.9	2.9	2.6	3.7	2.6	3.4	3.0	3.7
Overexertion	28.0	19.1	26.0	23.0	26.0	30.4	31.3	26.1	19.0	32.9
Overexertion in lifting	16.6	10.9	10.1	13.2	14.4	17.2	20.2	18.5	12.4	18.5
Repetitive motion	3.9	1.3	0.5	1.6	7.9	1.8	2.3	3.0	8.4	2.9
Exposed to harmful substance	4.6	5.3	3.7	3.9	5.4	3.0	3.0	4.9	4.6	5.3
Transportation accidents	4.1	5.1	2.9	4.0	1.9	8.2	7.2	3.4	4.4	4.0
Fires, explosions	0.2	0.3	0.8	0.5	0.2	0.2	0.2	0.2	0.3	0.1
Assault, by person	1.0	0.2	—	0.1	0.1	0.3	0.1	1.0	1.3	2.9

Note: Dashes (—) indicate that data are not available or do not meet publication guidelines. Because of rounding and classifications not shown, percentages may not add to 100. All injuries and illnesses reported involved days away from work. (1) Private sector includes all industries except government, but excludes farms with fewer than 11 employees. (2) Agriculture includes forestry and fishing, but excludes farms with fewer than 11 employees. (3) Data conforming to OSHA definition for mining operators in coal, metal, and nonmetal mining and for employers in railroad transportation are provided to the Bureau of Labor Statistics by the Mine Safety and Health Administration, U.S. Dept. of Labor; and by the Federal Railroad Administration, U.S. Dept. of Transportation. Independent mining contractors are excluded from the coal, metal, and nonmetal industries. (4) Finance includes insurance and real estate.

Fatal Occupational Injuries, 1997

Source: Bureau of Labor Statistics, U.S. Dept. of Labor

	FATALITIES Number	Percentage
TRANSPORTATION INCIDENTS	**2,599**	**42**
Highway	1,387	22
Collision between vehicles	639	10
Vehicle struck stationary object	280	5
Noncollision	384	6
Nonhighway (farm, industrial premises)	377	6
Aircraft	261	4
Worker struck by a vehicle	367	6
Water vehicle	109	2
Railway	93	1
ASSAULTS AND VIOLENT ACTS	**1,103**	**18**
Homicide	856	14
Shooting	705	11
Stabbing	73	1
Self-inflicted injury	212	3
FALLS	**715**	**11**
Fall to lower level	652	10
Fall on same level	44	1

	FATALITIES Number	Percentage
CONTACT WITH OBJECTS AND EQUIPMENT	**1,034**	**17**
Struck by object	578	9
Struck by falling object	384	6
Struck by flying object	53	1
Caught in or compressed by equipment or objects	320	5
Caught in or crushed in collapsing materials	118	2
EXPOSURE TO HARMFUL SUBSTANCE OR ENVIRONMENTS	**550**	**9**
Contact with electric current	297	5
Contact with temperature extremes	40	1
Exposure to caustic, noxious, or allergenic substances	123	2
Oxygen deficiency	87	1
FIRES AND EXPLOSIONS	**196**	**3**
OTHER EVENTS OR EXPLOSIONS	**21**	**—**
TOTAL	**6,218**	**100**

Note: Totals for categories may include subcategories not shown separately. Percentages, based on incidence rate per total fatalities, may not add to totals because of rounding. Dashes (—) indicate less than 0.5% or unavailable data.
(1) Totals may include agencies not listed or may not add because of independent rounding.

U.S. Wage and Salary Workers Paid Hourly Rates, Second Quarter 1998

Source: Bureau of Labor Statistics, U.S. Dept. of Labor; unpublished tabulations from Current Population Survey

(in thousands)

SEX AND AGE	Total hourly workers	$5.15[1] or less	Less than $10.00	$10.00 or more
Total, 16 years and older	**71,348**	**4,547**	**39,605**	**31,743**
16 to 24 years	16,511	2,279	14,179	2,332
20 to 24 years	9,954	830	7,879	2,075
25 years and older	54,838	2,269	25,427	29,411
25 to 54 years	47,496	1,835	21,552	25,944
25 to 34 years	16,909	704	8,800	8,109
35 to 44 years	18,297	704	7,610	10,687
45 to 54 years	12,289	427	5,141	7,148
55 years and older	7,342	433	3,874	3,468
55 to 64 years	5,683	247	2,694	2,989
65 years and older	1,659	186	1,180	479
Men, 16 years and older	35,840	1,605	16,774	19,066
16 to 24 years	8,532	903	6,997	1,535
20 to 24 years	5,263	278	3,896	1,367
25 years and older	27,308	702	9,777	17,531
Women, 16 years and older	35,509	2,942	22,832	12,677
16 to 24 years	7,978	1,376	7,181	797
20 to 24 years	4,691	552	3,984	707
25 years and older	27,530	1,566	15,650	11,880
RACE AND HISPANIC ORIGIN				
White				
Total, 16 years and older	58,629	3,542	31,989	26,640
Men	29,795	1,245	13,668	16,127
Women	28,835	2,298	18,322	10,513
Black				
Total, 16 years and older	9,519	846	5,896	3,623
Men	4,405	305	2,374	2,031
Women	5,115	541	3,523	1,592
Hispanic origin				
Total, 16 years and older	9,026	551	6,284	2,742
Men	5,312	222	3,448	1,864
Women	3,714	330	2,837	877
FULL- AND PART-TIME STATUS				
Full-time workers				
Total, 16 years and older	53,997	1,863	25,876	28,621
Men	30,477	737	12,209	18,268
Women	23,520	1,126	13,666	9,854
Part-time workers				
Total, 16 years and older	17,188	2,674	13,645	3,543
Men	5,284	862	4,523	761
Women	11,904	1,811	9,122	2,782

Note: Data refer to the sole or principal job, exclude the self-employed, and are not seasonally adjusted. Totals may not add because of independent rounding or because all subcategories are not listed. Full- or part-time status on the principal job is not identifiable for some multiple jobholders. Data for "other races" are not presented, and Hispanics are included in both white and black population groups.The data are from unpublished work tables and should not be considered as if part of an official BLS news release. (1) $5.15 = minimum wage starting Sept. 1, 1997.

Federal Minimum Hourly Wage Rates Since 1950

Source: Bureau of Labor Statistics, U.S. Dept. of Labor

The Fair Labor Standards Act of 1938 and subsequent amendments provide for minimum wage-coverage applicable to nonprofessional workers in specified nonsupervisory employment categories.

EFFECTIVE DATE	NONFARM WORKERS: Under laws prior to 1966[1]	NONFARM WORKERS: Percent of avg. earnings[2]	NONFARM WORKERS: Under 1966 and later provis.[3]	FARM WORKERS[4]
Jan. 25, 1950	$0.75	54	NA	NA
Mar. 1, 1956	1.00	52	NA	NA
Sept. 3, 1961	1.15	50	NA	NA
Sept. 3, 1963	1.25	51	NA	NA
Feb. 1, 1967	1.40	50	$1.00	$1.00
Feb. 1, 1968	1.60	54	1.15	1.15
Feb. 1, 1969	(5)	(5)	1.30	1.30
Feb. 1, 1970	(5)	(5)	1.45	(5)
Feb. 1, 1971	(5)	(5)	1.60	(5)
May 1, 1974	2.00	46	1.90	1.60
Jan. 1, 1975	$2.10	45	$2.00	$1.80
Jan. 1, 1976	2.30	46	2.20	2.00
Jan. 1, 1977	(5)	(5)	2.30	2.20
Jan. 1, 1978	2.65	44	2.65	2.65
Jan. 1, 1979	2.90	45	2.90	2.90
Jan. 1, 1980	3.10	43	3.10	3.10
Jan. 1, 1981	3.35	42	3.35	3.35
Apr. 1, 1990	3.80[6]	35	3.80[6]	3.80[6]
Apr. 1, 1991	4.25[6]	38	4.25[6]	4.25[6]
Oct. 1, 1996	4.75[7]	37	4.75[7]	4.75[7]
Sept. 1, 1997	5.15	NA	5.15	5.15

NA = not applicable. (1) Applies to workers covered prior to 1961 Amendments and, after Sept. 1965, to workers covered by 1961 Amendments. Rates set by 1961 Amendments were: Sept. 1961, $1.00; Sept. 1964, $1.15; and Sept. 1965, $1.25. (2) Percent of gross average hourly earnings of production workers in manufacturing. (3) Applies to workers newly covered by Amendments of 1966, 1974, and 1977, and Title IX of Education Amendments of 1972. (4) Included in coverage as of 1966, 1974, and 1977 Amendments. (5) No change in rate. (6) Training wage for workers age 16-19 in first 6 months of first job: Apr. 1, 1990, $3.35; Apr. 1, 1991, $3.62. The training wage expired Mar. 31, 1993. (7) Under 1996 legislation, a subminimum training wage of $4.25 an hour was established for employees under 20 years of age during their first 90 consecutive calendar days of employment with an employer. For workers receiving gratuities, the minimum wage remained $2.13 per hour.

Hourly Compensation Costs, by Selected Country, 1975-96

Source: Bureau of Labor Statistics, U.S. Dept. of Labor

(in U.S. dollars, compensation for production workers in manufacturing)

Country/Territory	1975	1985	1990	1996
Australia	$5.62	$8.20	$13.07	$16.69
Austria	4.51	7.58	17.75	24.95
Belgium	6.41	8.97	19.17R	25.89
Canada	5.96	10.94	15.84R	16.66
Denmark	6.28	8.13	18.02R	24.24
Finland	4.61	8.16	21.03	23.56
France	4.52	7.52	15.98R	21.19
Germany[1]	6.35	9.60	22.03R	31.87
Greece	1.69	3.66	6.76R	9.63
Hong Kong[2]	0.76	1.73	3.20	5.14
Ireland	3.03	5.92	11.66R	13.85
Israel	2.25	4.06	8.55	10.99
Italy	4.67	7.63	17.45R	17.48
Japan	3.00	6.34	12.80	20.84
Korea, South	$0.32	$1.23	$3.71	$8.22
Luxembourg	6.50R	7.81R	16.74R	22.55
Mexico	1.47	1.59	1.58R	1.50
Netherlands	6.58	8.75	18.06R	23.14
New Zealand	3.21	4.47	8.33	11.03
Norway	6.77	10.37	21.47	25.03
Portugal	1.58	1.53	3.77	5.58
Singapore	0.84	2.47	3.78	8.32
Spain	2.53	4.66	11.38R	13.40
Sri Lanka	0.28	0.28	0.35	0.48
Sweden	7.18	9.66	20.93	24.56
Switzerland	6.09	9.66	20.86	28.34
Taiwan	0.40	1.50	3.93R	5.82
United Kingdom	3.37	6.27	12.70R	14.13
United States	6.36	13.01	14.91	17.70

(1) Data are for area covered by the former West Germany. (2) Now part of China. (R) Revised.

Top 15 U.S. Metropolitan Areas, by Average Annual Salary, 1996

Source: Bureau of Labor Statistics, U.S. Dept. of Labor

Rank	Metropolitan area	Average annual salary[1]
1.	New York, NY	$45,028
2.	San Jose, CA.	44,819
3.	San Francisco, CA	40,016
4.	Middlesex–Somerset–Hunterdon, NJ	39,631
5.	New Haven–Bridgeport–Stamford–Danbury–Waterbury, CT	39,488
6.	Newark NJ	38,886
7.	Trenton, NJ	37,598
8.	Bergen–Passaic, NJ	36,840
9.	Jersey City, NJ	$36,833
10.	Washington, D.C.-MD-VA-WV	36,383
11.	Detroit, MI	35,748
12.	Hartford, CT	34,819
13.	Kokomo, IN	34,779
14.	Oakland, CA	34,402
15.	Boston-Worcester-Lawrence-Lowell-Brockton, MA-NH	34,383

Note: Jacksonville, NC, recorded the **lowest average annual pay** among U.S. metropolitan areas in 1996—$17,534—followed by Yuma, AZ ($18,213), Myrtle Beach, SC ($18,551), McAllen–Edinburg–Mission, TX ($18,928), and Brownsville–Harlingen–San Benito, TX ($19,056). The average annual salary in the 5 bottom-ranked metropolitan areas averaged 37-42% below the nationwide metropolitan average of $30,250. (1) Data are preliminary and include workers covered by Unemployment Insurance and Unemployment Compensation for Federal Employees programs.

Average Hours and Earnings of U.S. Production Workers, 1968-97[1]

Source: Bureau of Labor Statistics, U.S. Dept. of Labor

(annual averages)

Year	Weekly hours	Hourly earnings	Weekly earnings
1968	37.8	$2.85	$107.73
1969	37.7	3.04	114.61
1970	37.1	3.23	119.83
1971	36.9	3.45	127.31
1972	37.0	3.70	136.90
1973	36.9	3.94	145.39
1974	36.5	4.24	154.76
1975	36.1	4.53	163.53
1976	36.1	4.86	175.45
1977	36.0	5.25	189.00
1978	35.8	5.69	203.70
1979	35.7	6.16	219.91
1980	35.3	6.66	235.10
1981	35.2	7.25	255.20
1982	34.8	7.68	267.26
1983	35.0	$8.02	$280.70
1984	35.2	8.32	292.86
1985	34.9	8.57	299.09
1986	34.8	8.76	304.85
1987	34.8	8.98	312.50
1988	34.7	9.28	322.02
1989	34.6	9.66	334.24
1990	34.5	10.01	345.35
1991	34.3	10.32	353.98
1992	34.4	10.57	363.61
1993	34.5	10.83	373.64
1994	34.7	11.12	385.86
1995	34.5	11.43	394.34
1996	34.4	11.81	406.26
1997P	34.6	12.26	424.20

P= preliminary figures. (1) Private-industry production workers in mining and manufacturing; construction workers; nonsupervisory workers in services, transportation, and public utilities; wholesale or retail trade; finance, insurance, or real estate.

Educational Attainment by Labor-Force Status and Occupation, Mar. 1997

Source: Bureau of the Census, U.S. Dept. of Commerce

Characteristics	Number of persons (1,000)	PERCENTAGE WITH: High school degree or more	Some college or more	Bachelor's degree or more
Civilian labor force, 25 years and older				
Employed	109,399	89.3	56.5	29.2
Not employed	5,035	74.4	36.9	13.3
Not in the labor force	55,437	68.3	32.9	14.1
Total, employed persons, 25-64 years old	**105,611**	**89.8**	**57.0**	**29.4**
Executive, admin., and managerial	16,688	97.3	76.3	47.8
Professional specialty occupations	17,514	99.3	99.3	75.5
Technicians and related support occupations	3,576	97.9	78.2	29.8
Sales occupations	11,670	93.7	61.0	29.6
Administrative support occupations, includ. clerical	14,961	96.1	53.8	15.7
Private household occupations	516	63.4	24.6	5.6
Other service occupations	11,783	80.9	36.9	9.4
Farming, forestry, and fishing	2,370	66.9	30.8	11.0
Precision products, craft, and repair	12,204	82.8	35.5	6.8
Machine operators, assemblers, and inspectors	6,703	74.5	22.5	4.1
Transportation and material moving	4,519	78.6	27.5	4.7
Handlers, equip. cleaners, helpers, and laborers	3,107	73.6	25.9	6.9

Median Weekly Earnings of Wage and Salary Workers in the U.S. by Age, Sex, and Union Affiliation, 1996-97

Source: Bureau of Labor Statistics, U.S. Dept. of Labor

	1996				1997			
SEX AND AGE	TOTAL	Members of unions[1]	Represented by unions[2]	Non-union	TOTAL	Members of unions[1]	Represented by unions[2]	Non-union
Total, 16 years and older	$490	$615	$610	$462	$503	$640	$632	$478
16 to 24 years	298	371	362	294	306	385	384	302
25 years and older	520	625	621	498	540	655	648	511
25 to 34 years	463	554	548	447	481	579	572	466
35 to 44 years	559	636	632	530	579	675	666	548
45 to 54 years	594	687	686	552	607	704	697	578
55 to 64 years	535	620	616	505	558	661	657	512
65 years and older	384	510	510	367	393	614	609	374
Men, 16 years and older	557	653	651	520	579	683	679	539
16 to 24 years	307	375	369	303	317	402	404	313
25 years and older	599	669	668	580	615	697	693	595
25 to 34 years	499	591	587	485	515	607	603	503
35 to 44 years	632	683	683	617	651	712	708	630
45 to 54 years	698	718	721	682	713	744	741	698
55 to 64 years	643	667	664	633	669	702	701	649
65 years and older	477	589	593	424	452	677	672	415
Women, 16 years and older	418	549	543	398	431	577	568	411
16 to 24 years	284	358	339	280	292	353	351	289
25 years and older	444	560	555	420	462	587	581	437
25 to 34 years	415	497	495	405	427	521	514	416
35 to 44 years	463	561	556	439	482	592	585	461
45 to 54 years	481	620	616	445	495	627	620	465
55 to 64 years	420	524	523	395	433	582	575	408
65 years and older	334	417	413	321	348	—	586	324

Note: Data refer to the sole or principal job of full-time workers. Excluded are self-employed workers whose businesses are incorporated, although they technically qualify as wage and salary workers. (1) Including members of an employee association similar to a union. (2) Including members of a labor union or employee association similar to a union, and others whose jobs are covered by a union or an employee-association contract. Dashes (—) indicate unavailable data.

Work Stoppages (Strikes and Lockouts) in the U.S., 1960-97

Source: Bureau of Labor Statistics, U.S. Dept. of Labor; involving 1,000 workers or more

Year	Number of stoppages[1]	Workers involved[1] (thousands)	Work days idle[1] (thousands)
1960	222	896	13,260
1965	268	999	15,140
1970	381	2,468	52,761
1971	298	2,516	35,538
1972	250	975	16,764
1973	317	1,400	16,260
1974	424	1,796	31,809
1975	235	965	17,563
1976	231	1,519	23,962
1977	298	1,212	21,258
1978	219	1,006	23,774
1979	235	1,021	20,409
1980	187	795	20,844
1981	145	729	16,908
1982	96	656	9,061
1983	81	909	17,461
1984	62	376	8,499
1985	54	324	7,079
1986	69	533	11,861
1987	46	174	4,481
1988	40	118	4,381
1989	51	452	16,996
1990	44	185	5,926
1991	40	392	4,584
1992	35	364	3,989
1993	35	182	3,981
1994	45	322	5,020
1995	31	192	5,771
1996	37	273	4,889[2]
1997	29	339	4,497

(1) Numbers cover stoppages that began in the year indicated. Days of idleness include all stoppages in effect. (2) Revised.

Work Stoppages Involving 5,000 Workers or More Beginning in 1997

Source: Bureau of Labor Statistics, U.S. Dept. of Labor

Employer, location, union	Began	Ended	Workers involved[1]	Estimated days idle in 1997[1]
Chrysler Corp., Interstate; Automobile Workers (UAW)	4/10	5/9	15,100[2]	306,800
Kaiser Permanente, Northern CA; California Nurses Assn.	4/16	4/16	17,000	17,000
Goodyear Tire and Rubber Co., Interstate; Steelworkers	4/20	5/8	12,000	168,000
General Motors Corp., Pontiac, MI; Automobile Workers (UAW)	4/23	7/19	5,900[2]	359,900
General Motors Corp., Delphi Packard Electric Division, Warren, OH; Electrical Workers (IUE)	5/13	5/14	8,000	16,000
Kaiser Permanente, Northern CA; California Nurses Assn.	7/17	7/18	10,500	21,000
General Motors Corp., MI; Automobile Workers (UAW)	7/23	7/27	14,100[3]	25,200
Shaw's Supermarkets, Inc., RI and southeast MA; Food and Commercial Workers	7/28	7/30	6,200	18,600
United Parcel Service, Interstate; Teamsters	8/4	8/21[4]	180,000	2,032,500
Kaiser Permanente, Northern CA; California Nurses Assn.	9/8	9/9	20,300	40,600
Kaiser Permanente, Northern CA; California Nurses Assn.	11/10	11/10	8,900	8,900

(1) Workers and days idle are rounded to the nearest 100. (2) Excludes workers in Canada and Mexico. (3) Excludes workers in Canada. (4) All workers went back to work on 8/19/97, with the exception of members of 2 locals in Chicago.

Labor Union Directory

Source: Bureau of Labor Statistics, U.S. Dept. of Labor; AFL-CIO; World Almanac research, as of Aug. 1998.

(*) Independent union; all others affiliated with AFL-CIO.

Actors and Artistes of America, Associated (AAAA), 165 W 46th St., Suite 500, New York, NY 10036; founded 1919; Theodore Bikel, Pres.; no individual members, 7 National Performing Arts Unions are affiliates; approx. 100,000 combined membership.

Actors' Equity Association, 165 W 46th St., New York, NY 10036; founded 1913; Ron Silver, Pres. (since 1991); 40,000 active members.

Air Line Pilots Association, 1625 Massachusetts Ave. NW, Washington, DC 20036; founded 1931; J. Randolph Babbitt, Pres. (since 1990); 50,000 members, 49 airlines.

Aluminum, Brick & Glass Workers International Union (ABGWIU), 3362 Hollenberg Drive, Bridgeton, MO 63044; founded 1953 (merged with Steelworkers, Jan. 20, 1997).

American Federation of Labor & Congress of Industrial Organizations (AFL-CIO), 815 16th St. NW, Washington, DC 20006; founded 1955; John J. Sweeney, Pres. (since 1995); 13 mil. members.

Automobile, Aerospace & Agricultural Implement Workers of America, International Union, United (UAW), 8000 E Jefferson Ave., Detroit, MI 48214; founded 1935; Stephen P. Yokich, Pres. (since 1995); 1.3 mil. members, 1,130 locals.

Bakery, Confectionery & Tobacco Workers International Union (BC&T), 10401 Connecticut Ave., Kensington, MD 20895; founded 1886; Frank Hurt, Pres. (since 1992); 125,000 members.

Boilermakers, Iron Shipbuilders, Blacksmiths, Forgers and Helpers, International Brotherhood of (IBBISB/BF&H), 753 State Ave., Suite 570, Kansas City, KS 66101; founded 1880; Charles W. Jones, Int'l Pres. (since 1983); 82,419 members, 368 locals.

Bricklayers and Allied Craftworkers, International Union of, 815 15th St. NW, Washington, DC 20005; founded 1865; John T. Joyce, Pres. (since 1979); 100,000 members, 300 locals.

Carpenters and Joiners of America, United Brotherhood of, 101 Constitution Ave. NW, Washington, DC 20001; founded 1881; Douglas J. McCarron, Gen. Pres. (since 1995); 500,000 members, 1,000 locals.

Chemical Workers Union, International (ICWU), 1655 W Market St., Akron, OH 44313; founded 1944 (merged with Food and Commercial Workers, July 1, 1996).

Clothing and Textile Workers Union, Amalgamated (ACTWU), 15 Union Square, New York, NY 10003; founded 1976 (merged with International Ladies' Garment Workers' to form Needletrades, Industrial, and Textile Employees, June 1995).

Communications Workers of America (CWA), 501 3d St. NW, Washington, DC 20001; founded 1938; Morton Bahr, Pres. (since 1985); 630,000 members, 1,400 locals.

Distillery, Wine & Allied Workers International Union (DWU), 66 Grand Ave., Englewood, NJ 07631; founded 1940 (merged with Food and Commercial Workers, Oct. 1, 1995).

***Education Association, National,** 1201 16th St. NW, Washington, DC 20036; founded 1857; Bob Chase, Pres. (since 1996); 2.4 mil. members, 13,500 affiliates.

Electrical Workers, International Brotherhood of (IBEW), 1125 15th St. NW, Washington, DC 20005; founded 1891; John J. Barry, Pres. (since 1986); 750,000 members, 1,090 locals.

Electronic, Electrical, Salaried, Machine and Furniture Workers, International Union of (IUE), 1126 16th St. NW, Washington, DC 20036; founded 1949; Edward L. Fire, Pres. (since 1997); 125,000 members, 400 locals.

Engineers, International Union of Operating (IUOE), 1125 17th St. NW, Washington, DC 20036; founded 1896; Frank Hanley, Pres.; 360,000 members, 175 locals.

Farm Workers of America, United (UFW), 29700 Woodford-Tehachapi Rd., PO Box 62, Keene, CA 93531; founded 1962; Arturo S. Rodríguez, Pres. (since 1993); 50,000 members.

***Federal Employees, National Federation of (NFFE),** 1016 16th St. NW, Suite 300, Washington, DC 20036; founded 1917; Albert Schmidt, Pres. (1998); 150,000 members, 350 locals.

Fire Fighters, International Association of, 1750 New York Ave. NW, Washington, DC 20006; founded 1918; Alfred K. Whitehead, Pres. (since 1988); 225,123 members, 2,508 locals.

Firemen and Oilers, National Conference of, 1100 Circle 75 Parkway NW, Suite 350, Atlanta, GA 30339; founded 1898; Jimmy L. Walker, Pres.; 26,000 members, 147 locals.

Flight Attendants, Association of, 1275 K St. NW, Washington, DC 20005; founded 1945; Patricia A. Friend, Intl Pres.; 43,000 members.

Food and Commercial Workers International Union, United (UFCW), 1775 K St. NW, Washington, DC 20006-1598; founded 1979 following merger; Douglas H. Dority, Pres. (since 1994); 1.4 mil. members, 997 locals.

Garment Workers of America, United (UGWA), 4207 Lebanon Rd., Hermitage, TN 37076; founded 1891 (merged with Food and Commercial Workers, Dec. 1, 1994).

Garment Workers' Union, International Ladies' (ILGWU), 1710 Broadway, New York, NY 10019; founded 1900 (merged with Amalgamated Clothing and Textile Workers to form Needletrades, Industrial, and Textile Employees, June 1995).

Glass, Molders, Pottery, Plastics & Allied Workers Intl. Union (GMP), 608 E Baltimore Pike, PO Box 607, Media, PA 19063; founded 1842; James Rankin, Pres. (since 1997); 65,000 members, 370 locals.

Government Employees, American Federation of (AFGE), 80 F St. NW, Washington, DC 20001; founded 1932; Bobby L. Harnage Sr., Pres.; 200,000 members, 1,100 locals.

Grain Millers, American Federation of (AFGM), 4949 Olson Memorial Hwy., Minneapolis, MN 55422; founded 1936; Larry R. Jackson, Pres. (since 1991); 21,000 members, 190 locals.

Graphic Communications International Union (GCIU), 1900 L St. NW, Washington, DC 20036; founded 1983; James J. Norton, Pres. (since 1985); 160,000 members, 330 locals.

Hotel Employees and Restaurant Employees International Union, 1219 28th St. NW, Washington, DC 20007; Edward T. Hanley, Gen. Pres. (since 1973); 400,000 members, 190 locals.

Iron Workers, International Association of Bridge, Structural, Ornamental and Reinforcing, 1750 New York Ave. NW, Suite 400, Washington, DC 20006; founded 1896; Jake West, Pres. (since 1989); 120,000 members, 242 locals.

Laborers' International Union of North America (LIUNA), 905 16th St. NW, Washington, DC 20006-1765; founded 1903; Arthur A. Coia, Pres. (since 1993); 750,000 members, 624 locals.

Leather Goods, Plastics Novelty, and Service Workers' Union, International, 265 W 14th St., Suite 711, New York, NY 10011; Andrew McKenzie, Gen. Pres. (since 1992); 5,500 members, 80 locals.

Letter Carriers, National Association of (NALC), 100 Indiana Ave. NW, Washington, DC 20001-2144; founded 1889; Vincent R. Sombrotto, Pres. (since 1978); 315,000 members, 2,909 locals.

Locomotive Engineers, Brotherhood of (BLE), The Standard Bldg. Mezzanine, 1370 Ontario St., Cleveland, OH 44113-1702; founded 1863; Clarence V. Monin, Pres. (since 1996); 55,000 members, 623 divisions.

Longshore & Warehouse Union, International (ILWU), 1188 Franklin St., San Francisco, CA 94109-6800; founded 1937; Brian T. McWilliams, Pres. (since 1994); 60,000 members, 74 locals.

Longshoremen's Association, International (ILA), 17 Battery Pl., Suite 1530, New York, NY 10004; John M. Bowers, Pres. (since 1987); 65,100 members, 345 locals.

Machinists and Aerospace Workers, International Association of (IAM), 9000 Machinists Pl., Upper Marlboro, MD 20772-2687; founded 1888; R. Thomas Buffenbarger, Pres. (since 1997); 731,780 members, 1,194 locals.

Maintenance of Way Employees, Brotherhood of (BMWE), 26555 Evergreen Rd., Suite 200, Southfield, MI 48076; founded 1887; M. A. "Mac" Fleming, Pres. (since 1990); 50,000 members, 790 locals.

Marine Engineer Beneficial Assn. (MEBA), 444 N Capitol St. NW, Suite 800, Washington, DC 20001; founded 1875; Alex Shandrowsky, Pres. (since 1996); 4,242 members, 25 locals.

Maritime Union, National (NMU), 1150 17th St., NW, Washington, DC 20036; Rene Lioeanjie, Pres. (since 1997); 50,000 members.

Mine Workers of America, United (UMWA), 900 15th St. NW, Washington, DC 20005; founded 1890; Cecil E. Roberts, Pres. (since 1995); 130,000 members, 600 locals.

Musicians of the United States and Canada, American Federation of (AF of M), 1501 Broadway, Suite 600, New York, NY 10036; founded 1896; Steve Young, Pres. (since 1995); 125,000 members, 324 locals.

Needletrades, Industrial, and Textile Employees, Union of (UNITE), 1710 Broadway, New York, NY 10019; founded 1995; Jay Mazur, Pres. (since 1995); 285,000 members, 1,138 locals.

Newspaper Guild-Communications Workers of America (CWA) The, 501 3d St. NW, Suite 250, Washington, DC 20001-2797; founded 1933; Linda Foley, Pres. (since 1995); 34,000 members, 90 locals.

***Nurses Association, American (ANA),** 600 Maryland Ave. SW, Suite 100-W, Washington, DC 20024-2571; founded 1897; Beverly L. Malone, Pres. (since 1996); 177,408 members, 53 constituent state & territorial assns.

Office and Professional Employees International Union (OPEIU), 265 W 14th St., Suite 610, New York, NY 10011; founded 1945 (AFL Charter); Michael Goodwin, Pres. (since 1994); 130,000 members, 200 locals.

Oil, Chemical and Atomic Workers International Union (OCAW), 255 Union Blvd., PO Box 281200, Lakewood, CO 80228-8200; Robert E. Wages, Pres. (since 1991); 87,000 members, 350 locals.

Painters and Allied Trades, International Brotherhood of (IBPAT), 1750 New York Ave. NW, Washington, DC 20006; founded 1887; A. L. "Mike" Monroe, Gen. Pres.; 130,000 members, 440 locals.

Paperworkers International Union, United (UPIU), 3340 Perimeter Hill Dr., PO Box 1475, Nashville, TN 37211; founded 1884; Boyd D. Young, Pres. (since 1996); 255,000 members, 1,300 locals.

***Plant Guard Workers of America, International Union, United (UPGWA),** 25510 Kelly Rd., Roseville, MI 48066; founded 1948; Gene McConville, Pres. (since 1990); 20,000 members, 180 locals.

Plasterers' and Cement Masons' International Association of the United States & Canada, Operative, 14405 Laurel Pl., Suite 300, Laurel, MD; 20707; founded 1864; John J. Dougherty, Pres.; 40,000 members, 115 locals.

Plumbing and Pipe Fitting Industry of the United States and Canada, United Association of Journeymen and Apprentices of the, 901 Massachusetts Ave. NW, PO Box 37800, Washington, DC 20001; founded 1889; Martin J. Maddaloni, Gen. Pres. (since 1997); 295,500 members, 354 locals.

***Police, National Fraternal Order of,** 1410 Donelson Pike, A-17, Nashville, TN 37217; Gilbert G. Gallegos, Natl. Pres. (since 1995); 270,000 members, 1,992 affiliates.

Police Associations, International Union of, 1421 Prince St., Suite 330, Alexandria, VA 22314; Sam A. Cabral, Pres. (since 1995); 50,000 members, 400 locals.

***Postal Supervisors, National Association of,** 1727 King St., Suite 400, Alexandria, VA 22314-2753; Vincent Palladino, Pres. (since 1992); 36,000 members, 400 locals.

Postal Workers Union, American (APWU), 1300 L St. NW, Washington, DC 20005; founded 1971; Moe Biller, Pres. (since 1980); 350,000 members, 1,850 locals.

Retail, Wholesale, and Department Store Union, 30 E 29th St., 4th Fl., New York, NY 10016; Lenore Miller, Pres.; 100,000 members, 157 locals.

Roofers, Waterproofers & Allied Workers, United Union of, 1660 L St. NW, Suite 800, Washington, DC 20036; founded 1906; Earl Kruse, Pres. (since 1985); 25,000 members, 110 locals.

Rubber, Cork, Linoleum and Plastic Workers of America, United (URW), 570 White Pond Dr., Akron, OH 44320-1156; founded 1935 (merged with Steelworkers, July 1, 1995).

***Rural Letter Carriers' Association, National,** 1630 Duke St., 4th Fl., Alexandria, VA 22314; founded 1903; Steven Smith, Pres. (since 1997); 96,000 members; 50 state org.

Seafarers International Union of North America (SIU), 5201 Auth Way and Britannia Way, Camp Springs, MD 20746; founded 1938; Michael Sacco, Pres. (since 1988); 85,000 members, 18 affiliates.

Service Employees International Union (SEIU), 1313 L St. NW, Washington, DC 20005; founded 1921; Andrew L. Stern, Pres. (since 1996); 1,111,078 members, 421 locals.

Sheet Metal Workers' International Association (SMWIA), 1750 New York Ave. NW, Washington, DC 20006; founded 1888; Arthur Moore, Pres. (since 1993); 150,000 members, 203 locals.

State, County, and Municipal Employees, American Federation of (AFSCME), 1625 L St. NW, Washington, DC 20036; Gerald W. McEntee, Pres. (since 1981); 1.3 mil. members, 3,617 locals.

Steelworkers of America, United (USWA), 5 Gateway Center, Pittsburgh, PA 15222; founded 1936; George F. Becker, Intl. Pres. (since 1994); 700,000 members, 2,600 locals.

Teachers, American Federation of (AFT), 555 New Jersey Ave. NW, Washington, DC 20001; founded 1916; Sandra Feldman, Pres. (since 1997); 984,000 members, 2,267 locals.

Teamsters, Chauffeurs, Warehousemen, and Helpers of America, International Brotherhood of (IBT), 25 Louisiana Ave. NW, Washington, DC 20001; founded 1903; Ronald R. Carey, Gen. Pres. (since 1992); 1.4 mil. members, 569 locals.

Television and Radio Artists, American Federation of, 260 Madison Ave., 7th fl., New York, NY 10016; founded 1937; Shelby Scott, Pres. (since 1993); 75,000 members, 35 locals.

Theatrical Stage Employees, Moving Picture Technicians, Artists and Allied Crafts of the United States and Canada, International Alliance of (IATSE), 1515 Broadway, Suite 601, New York, NY 10036; founded 1893; Thomas C. Short, Pres. (since 1994); 90,000 members, 555 locals.

Transit Union, Amalgamated (ATU), 5025 Wisconsin Ave. NW, 3rd Fl., Washington, DC 20016; founded 1892; James LaSala, Pres. (since 1986); 155,000 members, 275 locals.

Transportation-Communications International Union (TCU), 3 Research Place, Rockville, MD 20850; founded 1899; Robert A. Scardelletti, Pres. (since 1991); 100,000 members, 450 locals.

Transportation Union, United (UTU), 14600 Detroit Ave., Cleveland, OH 44107; founded 1969; Charles L. Little, Pres. (since 1995); 80,000 members, 680 locals.

Transport Workers Union of America, 80 West End Ave., 5th Fl., New York, NY 10023; founded 1934; Sonny Hall, Pres. (since 1993); 125,000 members, 92 locals.

***Treasury Employees Union, National (NTEU),** 901 E St. NW, Suite 600, Washington, DC 20004; founded 1938; Robert M. Tobias, Natl. Pres. (since 1983); 155,000 represented, 226 chapters.

United Textile Workers of America, Council of (CUTWA), 763 Walnut Knoll Lane, Cordova, TN 38018; founded 1901 (merged with Food and Commercial Workers, Nov. 1, 1995).

***University Professors, American Association of (AAUP),** 1012 14th St. NW, Suite 500, Washington, DC 20005; founded 1915; James T. Richardson, Pres.; 44,000 members, 850 chapters.

Utility Workers Union of America (UWUA), 815 16th St. NW, Washington, DC 20006; founded 1945; Donald Wightman, Pres. (since 1996); 50,000 members, 225 locals.

U.S. Union Membership, 1930-97

Source: Bureau of Labor Statistics, U.S. Dept. of Labor

Year	Labor force[1] (thousands)	Union members[2] (thousands)	Percentage of labor force
1930	29,424	3,401	11.6
1935	27,053	3,584	13.2
1940	32,376	8,717	26.9
1945	40,394	14,322	35.5
1950	45,222	14,267	31.5
1955	50,675	16,802	33.2
1960	54,234	17,049	31.4
1965	60,815	17,299	28.4
1970	70,920	19,381	27.3
1975	76,945	19,611	25.5
1980	90,564	19,843	21.9
1985	94,521	16,996	18.0
1986	96,903	16,975	17.5
1987	99,303	16,913	17.0
1988	101,407	17,002	16.8
1989	103,480	16,960	16.4
1990	103,905	16,740	16.1
1991	102,786	16,568	16.1
1992	103,688	16,390	15.8
1993	105,067	16,598	15.8
1994	107,989	16,748	15.5
1995	110,038	16,360	14.9
1996	111,960	16,269	14.5
1997	114,533	16,110	14.1

(1) Does not include agricultural employment; from 1985, does not include self-employed or unemployed persons. (2) From 1930 to 1980, includes dues-paying members of traditional trade unions, regardless of employment status; from 1985, includes members of employee associations that engage in collective bargaining with employers.

TAXES

Federal Income Tax

Source: George W. Smith III, CPA, Nationally Syndicated Tax Author and Columnist

Congress in 1998 was undecided on how to simplify the federal tax code. Congressional debate to achieve income tax reform coupled with a balanced budget most likely will continue well into the 21st century. With no radical restructuring in sight, many of the recently enacted tax laws will continue to have a major impact on taxpayers for years to come.

Highlights of New Legislation

One of the major pieces of tax legislation signed into law by Pres. Bill Clinton (Aug. 5, 1997) was the massive Taxpayer Relief Act, which provided the biggest tax reductions in almost 2 decades. On July 22, 1998, a 2d major bill, the Internal Revenue Service Restructuring and Reform Act, was signed; it overhauled the operations of the IRS. Together, these 2 bills added more than 1,000 amendments and 425 new sections to the already voluminous Tax Code. The following are some of the sweeping changes affecting individuals, families, and investors, as well as large and small businesses.

Innocent Spouse Relief. The IRS Reform Act provides a separate liability section for taxpayers who are divorced, legally separated, or living apart for at least 12 months. In effect, this section prevents a divorced or separated spouse from being held liable for the other spouse's taxes.

$400 Dependent Credit. The Taxpayer Relief Act provides for a $400 credit to be deducted from an individual's 1998 federal tax for each child under the age of 17 who can be taken as a dependent. Dependents must be either the taxpayer's son or daughter, a descendant of the son or daughter, a stepchild, or an eligible foster child. The credit increases to $500 per child starting in 1999.

Higher income taxpayers must reduce the allowable child credit by $50 for each $1,000 (or fraction thereof) by which modified adjusted gross income (AGI) exceeds $110,000 for a joint return, $75,000 for an unmarried individual, and $55,000 for married individuals filing separate returns.

Lower-income families with children may use the credit to offset Social Security taxes as well as income taxes.

Education Incentives. Many individuals will be able to take a new educational credit, up to a maximum of $1,500 per student, on their tax returns starting in 1998. The *Hope Scholarship Credit* is deducted from an individual's federal income taxes. This credit applies to qualified tuition and related expenses for the student's first 2 years of postsecondary education in a degree or certificate program at an eligible educational institution. The credit does not apply to room and board or cost of books, nor is the credit refundable.

Another new educational credit, the *Lifetime Learning Credit*, is available for taxpayers whose postsecondary education expenses are not eligible for the Hope credit. This credit is equal to 20% of qualified tuition and fees paid after June 30, 1998, for the taxpayer, spouse, or dependents. The maximum amount of the credit per taxpayer is $1,000 ($5,000 of expenses x 20%) for expenses paid in taxable years beginning before 2003, and $2,000 ($10,000 x 20%) thereafter. The credit is deducted from the individual's federal income tax.

The Lifetime Learning Credit is allowed only for years in which the Hope credit is not used. Also, it may not be taken in any year in which funds are withdrawn from an Educational IRA. Like the Hope credit, the Lifetime credit is nonrefundable.

The credit begins to phase out when modified adjusted gross income (AGI) exceeds $40,000 for singles and $80,000 on a joint return, with full phaseout at $50,000 for singles and $100,000 on joint returns.

Employer-Paid Tuition. Congress renewed this tax-free provision through May 31, 2000. Up to $5,250 for tuition, school fees, and related education expenses paid by an employer to employees under an educational assistance program are tax-free to employees. This is an annual election by the employer. Most graduate-level courses do not qualify for the exclusion.

Student Loan Interest. Starting in 1998, the Taxpayer Relief Act allows taxpayers to deduct interest paid on qualified higher education loans during the first 60 months. If interest payments were made before 1998, months in which those payments were required count against the 60-month time limit. These loans must have been for the taxpayer, spouse, or any dependents. However, an individual who is a dependent of another taxpayer may not deduct any interest he or she paid. Married individuals must file a joint return in order to claim the deduction. The deduction begins to phase out when adjusted gross income (AGI) on a joint return reaches $60,000, and is completely gone when it hits $75,000. For single individuals the amounts are $40,000 to $55,000.

The maximum deduction is $1,000 for 1998, $1,500 for 1999, $2,000 for the year 2000, and $2,500 thereafter. This is an "above-the-line" page 1, Form 1040, deduction that is allowed whether or not the taxpayer itemizes deductions.

Capital Gains. Under the Taxpayer Relief Act, the long-term capital gains tax rate for individual taxpayers was reduced to 20% from the previous 28% maximum for qualified investments held more than 18 months. For taxpayers in the 15% bracket, the maximum net capital gains rate is 10%. The IRS Reform Act reduced the time requirement to 12 months on qualified investments. Congress also made the effective date retroactive to Jan. 1, 1998.

Five-Year Rule. Congress also lowered the capital gains rate to 18% starting Jan. 1, 2001, if the taxpayer holds the investment more than 5 years; 8% if in the 15% tax bracket. Further, if the taxpayer is in a bracket higher than 15%, the 5-year holding period would apply only to investments acquired after Dec. 31, 2000. For individuals in the 15% tax bracket, the investment does not have to be acquired after the year 2000 in order to have the 5-year period begin.

Hobbies. Capital gains on collectibles such as art, antiques, jewelry, stamps, and coins are still taxed at a maximum 28%. Certain newly minted gold and silver coins issued by the federal government are eligible for the lower rates.

Real Estate. Gain attributable to depreciation that was deducted from real estate will be recaptured at a maximum 25% tax rate. The balance of the gain will be taxed at a maximum rate of 20%.

Sale of Homestead. Homeowners filing a 1998 joint income tax return may exclude up to $500,000 in gain from the sale of their principal residence. This election is reusable every 2 years. Homeowners who have resided in their home fewer than 2 years may prorate the exclusion based on the amount of time in the home.

For single taxpayers the excludable amount of gain is up to $250,000. Married couples who do not share a principal residence with their spouse but still continue to file a joint tax return also may claim the $250,000 exclusion for a qualifying sale or exchange of each spouse's principal residence.

The Taxpayer Relief Act repeals the previous 2-year reporting requirement for home gains and the one-time $125,000 exclusion for individuals age 55 or older.

IRA Changes. Starting in 1998, an individual is not disqualified from making a deductible IRA contribution because his or her spouse is an active participant in another plan (see Adjustments to Income below).

IRA distributions for qualifying first-time home-buying expenses of up to $10,000 can be withdrawn without an early withdrawal penalty. The taxpayer must pay income taxes on any amounts distributed.

Beginning in 1998, a trust or educational custodial account can be set up for paying qualified higher education expenses of the account holder. Annual contributions of up to $500 a year per child may be made until he or she reaches age 18. Earnings on the contributions can be distributed tax-free to the IRA beneficiary if used to pay for these education expenses. Contributions are limited depending on the creator's adjusted gross income (AGI), and they are nondeductible.

The Roth IRA. This plan starts in 1998. Although contributions paid into a Roth IRA are not deductible, distributions of funds, including investment earnings held in the account for 5 years or longer and paid on or after the day an individual attains age 59½, are tax-free at the time of withdrawal. There are limitations on the amount that can be paid into a Roth IRA depending on the taxpayer's adjusted gross income (AGI).

Also tax-free are any funds paid from the Roth IRA to an estate or beneficiary on or after an individual's death or to an individual who is disabled. Amounts up to $10,000 used for a first-time home purchase or to pay for "qualified higher education expenses" of the taxpayer, spouse, or any child or grandchild of the taxpayer or spouse are tax-free as well.

There is a one-time-only opportunity in 1998 for individuals to roll a traditional IRA into a Roth IRA if their adjusted gross income is less than $100,000. All income resulting from the rollover will be taxed equally over a 4-year period. If the individual dies during the 4-year period, any remaining income from the rollover must be included on the individual's final federal income tax return.

Individuals in 1998 can make an election to include the entire taxable portion in their gross income. This could benefit individuals who expect to be in a significantly lower tax bracket in 1998 than in the following 3 years.

There is no penalty on the rollover as long as the funds remain in the Roth IRA.

Retirement Distributions. The Taxpayer Relief Act repealed the 15% excise tax on excess distributions from qualified retirement plans, tax-sheltered annuities, and IRAs. The excise tax on excess retirement accumulations is also repealed. Prior legislation merely suspended the excise tax penalty.

Dependent's Standard Deduction. Congress increased the basic standard deduction in 1998 for dependents who can be claimed on another's return to the greater of $700 or the dependent's earned income plus $250, but not to exceed the basic standard deduction for nondependent individuals. The 1998 standard deduction for a dependent is $4,250.

Charitable Mileage. Congress increased the mileage deduction to 14 cents per mile for an individual who uses his or her automobile in volunteer work for qualified charities. This increase starts in 1998. However, the medical and moving mileage rates remain at 10 cents per mile.

Employee Meals. Meals provided on the premises for the convenience of the employer will not be taxable to the employee. The cost of the meals will be fully deductible by the employer if more than half of all employees receiving them are given the meals for the employer's convenience.

Home Office. Beginning in 1999, taxpayers will be able to claim deductions for an office in their home when they conduct administrative or management activities for their business, providing they do not perform substantial administrative activities at another fixed location.

Self-Employed Health Insurance. The Taxpayer Relief Act eventually will allow a 100%, page 1, Form 1040, deduction of health insurance for the self-employed. The deduction for 1998 and 1999 is 45% of the cost.

Employer's Tax Deposit. Beginning July 1, 1998, the minimum employer's federal tax deposit threshold is raised from $500 to $1,000.

Corporate AMT Tax. The corporate alternative minimum tax (AMT) is repealed starting in 1998 for small businesses, provided that a 3-year average of $5 mil or less annual gross receipts test is met. A corporation will continue to be exempt from AMT as long as its average gross receipts for the prior 3 years does not exceed $7.5 mil.

Penalties. Taxpayers will not have to pay a penalty for underpayment of estimated federal income tax unless the amount of the underpayment in 1998 is $1,000 or more. Starting in 1999, taxpayers with AGI over $150,000 can avoid an underpayment penalty by paying 105% of the preceding year's income tax liability.

Foreign Income. Starting in 1998, the Taxpayer Relief Act increased the foreign earned income exclusion to $72,000.

Estate and Gift Tax. Congress enacted annual increases in the estate and gift tax exemption starting in 1998 and lasting through 2006; it reaches $1 mil in 2006. For 1998, the exemption amount increased $25,000 to $625,000. Beginning in 1999, the $10,000-per-person annual exclusion for gifts will be indexed for inflation.

Confidentiality. The IRS Reform Act extends attorney-client confidentiality to certified public accountants and enrolled agents in connection with noncriminal tax proceedings before the IRS and courts.

Other Current Tax Regulations

Social Security Earnings Limits. Starting in 1998, individuals age 65-69 can, without reducing their Social Security benefits, earn up to $14,500. However, for each $3 of earned income above this amount, individuals lose $1 of benefits.

Age 62 to 64. The maximum amount individuals in this age group can earn in 1998 without losing any Social Security benefits is $9,120. Individuals will lose $1 of their Social Security benefits for every $2 of earned income exceeding $9,120.

Age 70 or Over. Individuals in this age group will not lose benefits regardless of the amount of their earnings.

$4,000 IRA Deduction. The maximum tax-deferred IRA retirement contribution for a married couple filing a joint return was increased to $4,000 per year, but not to exceed the total combined earned income if less than $4,000. Each spouse can contribute up to $2,000 annually even if a spouse had little or no income. There are exceptions.

Retirement Planning. Legislation in 1996 eliminated the 5-year averaging for lump sum distributions from qualified retirement plans beginning after 1999. However, prior rules that applied to individuals who attained age 50 before Jan. 1, 1986, remain in effect.

The definition now of a highly compensated employee is an individual who is a 5% or more owner, or an employee who earns more than $80,000 and is in the top 20% of all employees within the company ranked by compensation.

Age 70½ Plus. Any employee who works beyond age 70½ and is not a 5% or more owner of the business can continue to defer profit-sharing and pension retirement plan distributions (and any resulting income tax liability). The owner of an IRA, however, must begin receiving distributions from the IRA by Apr. 1 of the calendar year following the year in which he or she reaches age 70½ even if the individual is not retired.

Death Benefits. Qualified accelerated death benefits paid under a life insurance contract to terminally ill persons (certified as expected to die within 24 months) are now excludable from gross income. A similar exclusion applies to the sale or assignment of death benefits under a life insurance contract to another person. Accelerated death benefits paid to a chronically ill person under a long-term care rider are tax-free, up to $175 per day.

Adoption Credit. An adoption expense credit is available for up to $5,000 of qualified expenses for each eligible adopted person. The credit limit is per person, not per year, and increases to $6,000 for an eligible person with special needs. Adoption expenses paid for through a nondiscriminatory employee adoption-assistance program may be excluded from gross income. The adoption credit and exclusion begins to phase out when AGI is between $75,000 and $115,000.

Long-Term Care. Premiums for long-term care insurance contracts are a deductible medical expense up to annual limits based on age. Long-term care benefits received under a qualifying policy will be tax-free, subject to certain per diem restrictions.

Domestic Workers. The 1998 threshold dollar amount for paying Social Security and federal unemployment taxes on domestic employees, including nannies and housekeepers, has been increased to $1,100. Household workers under 18 are exempt unless working in a household is their principal occupation. Household employers must apply for an employer ID number and issue employee wage statements (Form W-2).

Medical Savings Accounts. MSAs are intended to meet costs not covered by a high-deductible health plan. MSAs may be offered only by employers who, on the average, had no more than 50 employees in either of the 2 preceding years and provided high-deductible health plans. Self-employed individuals may use MSAs to pay health care expenses.

The annual insurance deductible amount for an MSA to qualify must be between $1,500 and $2,250 for individuals and between $3,000 and $4,500 for families. The distributions from MSAs are tax-free if used for qualified medical expenses. Distributions not used for medical expenses are subject to regular income tax plus a 15% penalty. Penalty does not apply after age 65 or upon death or disability. Self-employed individuals can exclude from income any payments for injury or sickness under a self-insured plan similar to traditional insurance plans.

Damage Awards. Tax-free treatment for damage awards is limited to damages attributable to a physical injury or sickness, or to actual medical expenses.

Employment Tax Rates. The maximum wage base for withholding Social Security tax increased to $68,400 for 1998. The tax rate remains at 6.2%. The Medicare tax rate is 1.45%. There is no maximum wage base for Medicare. All wages are subject to the Medicare tax. Both employer and employee (each) pay these tax rates. Self-employed individuals pay both parts, 12.4% and 2.9%, for a total of 15.3% on net earnings.

Elective Withholding. Taxpayers receiving Social Security benefits (and certain other federal payments) may elect to have federal tax withheld at a rate of 7%, 15%, 28%, or 31%. States must permit elective federal withholding from unemployment compensation at 15%.

Business Equipment. The election to expense instead of depreciating the cost of certain business assets is called a "Section 179 Expense Election." The maximum amount deductible for 1998 is $18,500.

Business Mileage. The standard mileage tax rate deduction for business use of an auto was increased for 1998 to 32½ cents a mile. Starting in 1998, the rate also applies to leased cars used in business.

Corporate Eligibility. The maximum number of eligible shareholders of an S corporation was increased from 35 to 75. S corporations can now own 80% or more of a C corporation.

SIMPLE Retirement Plan. A simplified retirement plan titled Savings Incentive Match Plan for Employees (SIMPLE) is available for businesses with 100 or fewer employees, including self-employed individuals. It is generally easier to implement and more cost effective to administrate than a traditional 401(k). As in such plans, employees can defer up to $6,000 in compensation, deferring taxes on these amounts. A SIMPLE plan can operate either as an IRA or as a 401(k).

Electronic Payroll Taxes. The IRS has extended the deadline to Jan. 1, 1999, for businesses that had federal employment taxes of more than $50,000 for the calendar year 1995 to begin making all federal tax deposit payments electronically using the Electronic Federal Tax Payment System (EFTPS). Failure to do so will result in a 10% penalty for each deposit. For more information, call the IRS Customer Service at 1-800-945-8400 or 1-800-555-4477.

Postmark. The IRS must accept the postmark of couriers such as UPS and FedEx as proof of timely mailing.

More You Should Know About

Retirement. The maximum dollar amount on an individual's elective deferral of income to a 401(k) retirement plan was adjusted to $10,000 for 1998.

Federal law now provides that a state may not impose an income tax on any individual's retirement income if the person is no longer a resident of that state.

Children's Income. Parents may elect to include on their income tax return the unearned income of a dependent child under age 14 whose unearned income is more than $700 but less than $6,500. The income must consist solely of interest and dividends. Form 8814, *Parent's Election to Report Child's Interest and Dividends,* must be attached to the parents' tax return. This election is not available if estimated tax payments were made during the year in the child's name.

If a dependent child with taxable income cannot file an income tax return, the parent, guardian, or other legally responsible person must file a return for the child.

An individual may not claim a dependency exemption in 1998 for a child who qualifies as a full-time student and is over age 23 at the end of the year, unless the child's gross income is less than $2,700.

Education Expenses. Interest earned on U.S. Series EE bonds issued after 1989 may be exempt from federal income tax if the bonds are used to pay college tuition and fees for a taxpayer, spouse, or dependent. There is a phaseout rule if income is too high. Married taxpayers filing separately are not eligible.

Donations. Taxpayers deducting individual charitable contributions of $250 or more must obtain written substantiation from the charity. If the amount is more than $75, the charity must include a breakdown of the payment indicating how much was a (deductible) contribution and what (if any) was the (nondeductible) value of goods or services received.

Interest. Borrowers can generally deduct the points paid on their principal home mortgage loan providing they itemize deductions on Schedule A. The buyer can also deduct "seller-paid points" on purchase of a principal residence.

Interest paid on investments is deductible on Form 1040, Schedule A, but only up to the amount of net investment income. Capital gains income can be included as investment income when figuring the limitation. However, the taxpayer will have to reduce the amount of net long-term capital gain eligible for capital gains treatment in order to offset the additional investment interest deduction.

Intangible Write-offs. Congress now allows patents, trademarks, and certain other intangible assets to be amortized over a 15-year period. The cost of goodwill and customer/patient lists are included in this 15-year write-off period.

Business Expenses. The deduction for qualified business meals and entertainment expenses is limited to 50% of their cost. A receipt is required for business meals, entertainment, and transportation costs above $75. Adequate records must be kept substantiating the time, place, date, and business purpose of the expense.

Expenses paid for business assignments away from home in a single location that last for more than one year are no longer considered temporary nor deductible. Travel expenses paid for other individuals (including a spouse) traveling with the taxpayer on a business trip are not deductible unless the individual (1) is an employee, (2) has a bona fide business purpose for the travel, and (3) would otherwise be allowed to deduct the travel expense.

Dues paid to business, social, athletic, luncheon, sporting, and country clubs, including airport and hotel clubs, are not deductible, but dues paid to the Chamber of Commerce and business Economic Clubs remain deductible.

Empowerment Zones. A 20% employment tax credit is available to most employers for qualified wages paid to each full- or part-time employee who is a resident of one of 11 federal empowerment zones (distressed areas designated for economic revitalization by the U.S. government).

The 20% credit is deducted from the employer's federal income tax liability for the first $15,000 of wages paid per employee up to a credit of $3,000 per employee. The full 20% credit has been extended through 2001. To qualify, an employee must perform substantially all employment services within the zone and in the employer's trade or business.

Tax Estimates. 1999 federal estimated tax payment due dates for individuals are: 1st quarter, Apr. 15, 1999; 2d quarter, June 15; 3d quarter, Sept. 15; the 4th and final quarterly payment is due Jan. 17, 2000. *Caution:* The safe-harbor rules for individuals paying their 1999 quarterly estimated tax with adjusted gross income over $150,000 requires that they pay

105% of their prior year income tax to be penalty proof. Different filing dates may apply for state estimated taxes.

Owe Tax? If taxpayers cannot pay any balance owed on their individual federal income tax by Apr. 15, 1999, they may apply for monthly installment payments by attaching Form 9465, *Installment Agreement Request,* to the tax return. Penalty and interest will continue to accrue on any balance owed. There is a $43 IRS fee if the request is approved.

Tax Electronic Refunds. Taxpayers may have their refund deposited electronically directly into their checking or savings account. According to the IRS, qualifying refunds to taxpayers filing their returns electronically are issued within 21 days.

IRS Services. Federal tax forms, tax legislation, relevant court decisions, and other information and resources are available from the IRS via the following:

World Wide Web: http://www.irs.ustreas.gov
FTP: ftp://ftp.irs.ustreas.gov
IRIS at FedWorld: (703) 321-8020
Fax: (703) 368-9694
Forms/Publications: 1-800-829-3676

The IRS provides videotaped instructions both in English and in Spanish available at participating libraries. Many instructions, publications, and forms are now printed in Spanish; for more information, call 1-800-TAX-FORM and ask for free IRS Publication 1SP, *Derechos del Contribuyents.*

Hearing Impaired. The IRS telephone service for hearing-impaired persons is available for taxpayers who have access to TDD equipment. The toll-free number is 1-800-829-4059.

Who Must File a Tax Return?

Most U.S. citizens and resident aliens will have to file a 1998 income tax return if the person's gross income for the year is at least as much as shown in the following table:

Filing Status	**1998 Gross Inome**
Single	
• Under 65	$ 6,950
• 65 or older	8,000
Married filing jointly	
• Both spouses under 65	12,500
• One spouse 65 or older	13,350
• Both spouses 65 or older	14,200
Married filing separately	2,700
Head of Household	
• Under 65	8,950
• 65 or older	10,000
Qualifying widow(er)	
• Under 65	9,800
• 65 or older	10,650

A tax return must be filed if:

- Taxpayer had net earnings of $400 or more from self-employment for the year.
- Taxpayer received advance earned income credit payments during the year from an employer or is entitled to receive a refundable earned income credit.
- Taxpayer paid estimated income tax payments during 1998 or expects an income tax refund.
- Taxpayer has losses to be carried back or forward.
- Additional taxes are owed for:
  —Social Security tax on unreported tips.
  —Alternative minimum tax.
  —Recapture of investment credit.
  —Tax attributable to qualified retirement distributions (including IRAs), annuities, and modified endowment contracts.

When to File

U.S. individual income tax returns for 1998 are required to be filed with the IRS no later than Thurs., Apr. 15, 1999. An individual who cannot file on time should file Form 4868, *Application for Automatic Extension of Time to File U.S. Individual Income Tax Return.* This form gives the taxpayer an automatic 4-month extension of time to file, until Mon., Aug. 16, 1999. However, this is not an extension of time to pay the tax. The taxpayer will owe interest and may be charged a penalty on any federal income tax owed and not paid to the IRS by Apr. 15, 1999.

Which Tax Return to File?

Most U.S. citizens can use one of the following basic income tax forms: 1040EZ, 1040A, or 1040. Forms 1040EZ and 1040A are shorter and simpler than Form 1040.

You may be able to use the shortest of the 3 forms, Form 1040EZ, if:

- You are single or married filing jointly and do not claim any dependents.
- You are not 65 or older or blind.
- You have income only from wages, salaries, tips, taxable scholarships or fellowships, unemployment compensation, or Alaska Permanent Fund dividends, and do not have over $400 of taxable interest income.
- Your taxable income is less than $50,000.
- You do not itemize deductions, claim any adjustments to income, or have tax credits other than the earned income credit.
- You did not receive any advance earned income credit payments.
- You did not make any estimated tax payments.

Or, you may be able to use Form 1040A if:

- You have income from wages, salaries, tips, taxable scholarships or fellowships, interest, and dividends.
- You have income from IRA distributions, pensions, annuities, unemployment compensation, and taxable Social Security or railroad retirement benefits.
- Your taxable income is less than $50,000.
- You do not itemize deductions.
- You claim a deduction for qualified IRA contributions.
- You claim a credit for child and dependent care expenses, credit for the elderly or the disabled, the earned income credit, or the adoption credit.
- You report employment taxes on wages paid to household employees on Schedule H.
- You take the education exclusion for interest income earned from Series EE U.S. Savings Bonds.
- You received advance earned income credit payments.
- You owe alternative minimum tax.
- You have made estimated tax payments.
- You filed for an extension of time to file.

You will have to file Form 1040 if any of these apply:

- Your taxable income is $50,000 or more.
- You plan to itemize deductions.
- You receive any nontaxable dividends or capital gain distributions.
- You have foreign bank accounts and/or foreign trusts.
- You have taxable refunds of state or local income taxes.
- You have business, farm, or rental income or losses.
- You sold or exchanged capital assets or business property.
- You have miscellaneous income such as alimony not allowed on Form 1040EZ or 1040A.
- You have additional adjustments to income, like payments for alimony or moving expenses.
- You are allowed a foreign tax credit or certain other credits to which you are entitled.
- You have other taxes to pay such as self-employment tax or Social Security tax on tips.
- You have losses that are to be carried back or forward.
- You are required to file additional forms such as **Form 2106**, Employee Business Expenses; **Form 2555**, Foreign Earned Income; **Form 3903**, Moving Expenses; **Form 4972**, Tax on Lump-Sum Distributions.

1998 Individual Income Tax Rates

Single

Tax Rate	Taxable Income
15%	$0 to $25,350
28%	$25,351 to $61,400
31%	$61,401 to $128,100
36%	$128,101 to $278,450
39.6%	More than $278,450

Married Filing Jointly or Qualifying Widow(er)

Tax Rate	Taxable Income
15%	$0 to $42,350
28%	$42,351 to $102,300
31%	$102,301 to $155,950
36%	$155,951 to $278,450
39.6%	More than $278,450

Married Filing Separately

Tax Rate	Taxable Income
15%	$0 to $21,175
28%	$21,176 to $51,150
31%	$51,151 to $77,975
36%	$77,976 to $139,225
39.6%	More than $139,225

Head of Household

Tax Rate	Taxable Income
15%	$0 to $33,950
28%	$33,951 to $87,700
31%	$87,701 to $142,000
36%	$142,001 to $278,450
39.6%	More than $278,450

Estates and Trusts

Tax Rate	Taxable Income
15%	$0 to $1,700
28%	$1,701 to $4,000
31%	$4,001 to $6,100
36%	$6,101 to $8,350
39.6%	More than $8,350

The AMT Tax. The alternative minimum tax (AMT) rate for noncorporate taxpayers is 26% for alternative minimum taxable income less the exemption amount up to $175,000 ($87,500 for married individuals filing separately). Above that dollar level, a 28% rate applies.

Dependent Exemptions

The deductible exemption amount for each individual taxpayer or dependent for 1998 has been increased to $2,700. Each year since 1990 the IRS has adjusted the exemption amount for inflation.

Exemption Phaseout. The deduction for each exemption is reduced by 2% for each $2,500 ($1,250 for married filing separately) or fraction thereof by which adjusted gross income for 1998 exceeds the following amounts:

Married filing jointly	$186,800
Qualifying widow(er)	$186,800
Head of household	$155,650
Single	$124,500
Married filing separately	$93,400

The exemption amount is fully phased out when adjusted gross income is more than $122,500 ($61,250 for married filing separately) over the above threshold amount

Standard Deduction

The standard deduction is a flat amount that is subtracted from the adjusted gross income (AGI) of taxpayers who do not itemize deductions. The amount depends on filing status and is adjusted annually for inflation.

1998 Basic Standard Deduction

Single	$4,250
Married filing jointly or qualifying widow(er)	$7,100
Married filing separately	$3,550
Head of household	$6,250

These figures are not applicable if an individual can be claimed as a dependent on another person's tax return.

Caution: Taxpayers with itemized deductions totaling more than the above amounts usually should itemize deductions.

An individual claimed as a dependent on another person's income tax return generally may claim on his or her own tax return only the larger of $700 or the individual's earned income, plus $250, not to exceed $4,250. Earned income includes wages, salaries, commissions, and tips. It also includes net profit from self-employment received as compensation for personal services rendered. Any part of a scholarship or fellowship grant that must be included in gross income also is considered earned income.

Taxpayers in certain categories may claim an additional standard deduction.

1998 Additional Standard Deduction

Single or head of household, age 65 or older OR blind	$1,050
Single or head of household, age 65 or older AND blind	$2,100
Married filing jointly or qualifying widow(er), age 65 or older OR blind (per person)	$850
Married filing jointly or qualifying widow(er), age 65 or older AND blind (per person)	$1,700
Married filing separately, age 65 or older OR blind	$850
Married filing separately, age 65 or older AND blind	$1,700

Persons who claim a deduction because of blindness must attach a doctor's statement to their income tax return.

Tax Tip: For tax purposes, an individual is considered 65 years of age beginning on the day preceding his or her 65th birthday. Therefore, a taxpayer whose 65th birthday falls on Jan. 1, 1999, is entitled to take the additional standard deduction on his or her tax return for 1998.

Adjustments to Income

The Changing IRA Rules. Taxpayers may contribute to their IRAs even if they are covered by an employer-sponsored qualified retirement plan. However, the amount that can be deducted on their income tax return depends on total income.

Married taxpayers filing jointly in 1998 with adjusted gross income (AGI) of $50,000 or less may take the maximum IRA deduction allowed, regardless of whether either spouse is an active participant in a qualified retirement plan. Single taxpayers in a qualified plan may deduct up to the maximum IRA contribution, provided their AGI is $30,000 or less. Above these amounts, the IRA deduction begins to phase out over the next $10,000 of AGI if a taxpayer is an active participant in a qualified retirement plan.

No longer will an individual be considered an active participant in an employer-sponsored plan merely because the individual's spouse is an active participant for any part of a plan year. The maximum deductible IRA contribution for an individual who is not an active participant, but whose spouse is, will now be phased out at a new and higher AGI dollar level between $150,000 and $160,000. This provision begins in 1998.

A taxpayer not covered by a qualified employer retirement plan may deduct an IRA contribution up to the lesser of $2,000 or the amount of earned income, regardless of total income.

IRA distributions used to pay medical expenses in excess of 7.5% of AGI are exempt from the 10% penalty for early withdrawal. In addition, the penalty will not apply to distributions taken early by certain unemployed, formerly unemployed, or self-employed individuals to pay for health insurance.

Moving Expenses. Taxpayers who change jobs or are transferred during the year usually can deduct part of their moving expenses. These expenses include travel and the cost of moving household goods to their new home. The cost of meals is no longer deductible. The standard mileage rate remains at 10 cents per mile plus parking and tolls.

The new job must be at least 50 miles farther from the former home than the old job. Employees must work full time for at least 39 weeks during the first 12 months after they arrive in the general area of their new job. Taxpayers no longer have to itemize deductions to deduct moving expenses. These expenses are now an adjustment to income, reported on page 1, Form 1040. Moves within the U.S. are reported on Form 3903, *Moving Expenses.*

Itemized Deductions

If the total amount of itemized deductions is more than the standard deduction, taxpayers generally should itemize deductions. The following examples are but a few of the deductions that may be reported on Schedule A, Form 1040.

• Most mortgage interest paid on a taxpayer's primary residence and on taxpayer's 2d home is fully deductible. There are limitations, however.

• Interest paid on home equity loans is deductible, but only on the first $100,000 of equity debt.

• Investment interest expense is deductible only to the extent of net investment income. Any investment interest expense not deducted is carried over to future years.

• State and local income taxes, real estate taxes, and personal property taxes are fully deductible. Sales taxes are no longer deductible.

• Only the total amount of medical expenses that exceeds 7.5% of the taxpayer's adjusted gross income is deductible. Cosmetic surgery for congenital abnormality, personal injury resulting from an accident or trauma, or a disfiguring disease is allowed as a medical deduction.

• Casualty and theft losses are deductible subject to the $100 limitation rule for each occurrence. Only the excess amount over 10% of AGI is deductible.

• Miscellaneous items, such as union and professional dues, tax preparation fees, safe-deposit box rental expense, and employee business expenses are deductible insofar as they exceed 2% of AGI.

• Amounts spent for tools and supplies used at work are deductible if they wear out within 1 year from the date of purchase. Tools expected to last more than a year will have to be depreciated. These expenses are subject to the 2% rule.

• Armed forces reservists can deduct the unreimbursed cost of their uniforms if regulations restrict the individual from wearing them except while on duty as a reservist.

• Unreimbursed employee business expenses including travel, automobile, telephone, and gifts are deductible on Schedule A as miscellaneous itemized deductions. Only 50% of the cost of customer meals and entertainment is deductible. All these expenses are subject to the 2% rule.

• Individuals can deduct gambling losses, including the cost of lottery tickets, on Schedule A, but only up to the amount of their gambling winnings reported on Page 1, Form 1040.

Many itemized deductions otherwise allowed are further reduced by the smaller of these two figures: 3% of a taxpayer's AGI in excess of the 1998 threshold amount of $124,500 ($62,250 for married taxpayers filing separately) OR 80% of the amount of these itemized deductions otherwise allowable for the year. This provision does not apply to medical expenses, investment interest expense, casualty losses, or gambling losses to the extent of gambling winnings.

1998 Earned Income Credit

Lower-income workers who have dependent children and maintain a household may be eligible for a refundable earned income credit. The credit is based on earned income such as wages, commissions, and tips.

The maximum earned income credit for an individual with one qualifying child is $2,271. However, the credit is phased out as earned income increases, disappearing once adjusted gross income reaches $26,473. For an individual with 2 or more qualifying children, the maximum credit is $3,756. It is fully phased out once AGI reaches $30,095.

The credit has been extended to include persons who do not have a qualifying child. For those individuals the maximum credit is $341. To qualify: (1) earned income and adjusted gross income (AGI) must be less than $10,030, (2) an individual or spouse must be at least 25 years old and less than 65 years old, and (3) an individual cannot be claimed as a dependent on another person's return.

The IRS will help individuals filing for the credit if they need assistance. Many people may qualify for the credit even if they are not otherwise required to file a return. However, a tax return must be filed to receive the refund.

The Welfare Reform Act added several more restrictions to the earned income credit: (1) The credit cannot be taken by individuals who are not authorized to be employed in the U.S. (2) Individuals must include their own Social Security number and, if married, their spouse's Social Security number on the return claiming the credit. (3) The individual's "disqualified" income cannot exceed $2,300. Disqualified income includes interest, dividends and, if greater than zero, net rent, royalty income, and capital-gains net income.

Taxable Social Security Benefits

Up to 50% of Social Security benefits may be taxable income if the person's total income is:

• over $25,000 but less than $34,000 for single, head of household, qualifying widow(er), or married and filing separately, *and the spouses lived apart for all of the year.*

• over $32,000 but less than $44,000 for married individuals filing jointly.

For people with incomes exceeding these maximum amounts, 85% of Social Security benefits become taxable. Below these amounts, 50% is taxable income. If the taxpayer is married, filing separately, and lived with a spouse at any time during the year, the amounts are reduced to zero.

Most Social Security benefits will not be taxable if this is the only income received during 1998.

IRS Tax Audit

The IRS received about 118 mil individual income tax returns in 1998; only about 1 out of every 100 will be audited. The IRS is very good at selecting returns that will yield additional taxes. Nevertheless, if your return is selected, it does not necessarily mean you will incur additional tax liability.

If you do not agree with the tax examiner's report, you can meet with the examiner's supervisor to discuss your case further. If you still do not agree, you have the right to appeal the findings through a separate Appeals Office. You can also appeal to the U.S. Tax Court.

Your Rights as a Taxpayer

Under the *Taxpayer Bill of Rights 1,* the IRS must explain, in easy-to-understand language, any actions it proposes to take against a taxpayer and modify some of its audit and collection procedures.

Congress also enacted the *Taxpayer Bill of Rights 2.* This legislation created an Office of the Taxpayer Advocate within the IRS, with authority to order IRS personnel to issue refund checks and meet deadlines for resolving disputes. The legislation also requires the agency to pay a taxpayer's legal fees if the latter wins the case and the IRS cannot show it was "substantially justified" in pursuing it.

The recently passed IRS Restructuring and Reform Act created even more changes with the IRS, including a 9-member independent oversight board to watch over the IRS management. The Reform Act also shifts the burden of proof to the IRS under certain circumstances in disputes dealing with income, estate, and gift taxes and establishes formal procedures designed to ensure due process when the IRS seeks to collect taxes by levy, including seizure.

Individuals can learn more about their rights by obtaining IRS Publication 1, *Your Rights as a Taxpayer;* call 1-800-TAX-FORM for a free copy.

State Government Individual Income Taxes

Source: Reproduced with permission from *CCH State Tax Guide*, published and copyrighted by CCH Inc., 2700 Lake Cook Road, Riverwoods, IL 60015

Below are basic state tax rates on taxable income, for 1998 unless otherwise indicated. Alaska, Florida, Nevada, South Dakota, Texas, Washington, and Wyoming did not have state income taxes and are thus not listed. For further details, see notes which follow.

Alabama
1st $1,000 .... 2%
Next $5,000 .... 4%
Over $6,000 .... 5%

Arizona*
1st $20,000 ...... 2.88%
Next $30,000 ...... 3.24%
Next $50,000 ...... 3.82%
Next $200,000 ..... 4.74%
$300,001 and over ... 5.1%

Arkansas
1st $2,999 .... 1%
Next $3,000 .... 2.5%
Next $3,000 .... 3.5%
Next $6,000 .... 4.5%
Next $10,000 ...... 6%
$25,000 or over...... 7%

California*
$0 to $10,262 .... 1%
$10,263 to $24,322 ... 2%
$24,323 to $38,386 ... 4%
$38,387 to $53,288 ... 6%
$53,289 to $67,346 ... 8%
$67,347 and over 9.3%

Colorado
5% of federal taxable income

Connecticut
1st $15,000 ...... 3%
Over $15,000 ...... 4.5%

Delaware
$2,000 to $5,000..... 2.6%
Next $5,000 .... 4.3%
Next $10,000 ...... 5.2%
Next $5,000 .... 5.6%
Next $35,000 ...... 5.95%
Over $60,000 ...... 6.4%

District of Columbia
1st $10,000 ...... 6%
2d $10,000 ...... 8%
Over $20,000 ...... 9.5%

Georgia
1st $1,000 .... 1%
Next $2,000 .... 2%
Next $2,000 .... 3%
Next $2,000 .... 4%
Next $3,000 .... 5%
Over $10,000 ...... 6%

Hawaii
1st $3,000 .... 2%
Next $2,000 .... 4%
Next $2,000 .... 6%
Next $4,000 .... 7.25%
Next $10,000 ...... 8%
Next $10,000 ...... 8.75%
Next $10,000 ...... 9.5%
Over $41,000 ..... 10%

Idaho*
1st $1,000 .... 2%
2d $1,000 .... 4%
3d $1,000 .... 4.5%
4th $1,000 .... 5.5%
5th $1,000 .... 6.5%
Next $2,500 .... 7.5%
Next $12,500 ...... 7.8%
Over $20,000 ...... 8.2%

Illinois
3% of taxable net income

Indiana
3.4% of adj. gross income

Iowa
$0 to $1,136 .... 0.36%
$1,137 to $2,272 ..... 0.72%
$2,273 to $4,544 ..... 2.43%
$4,545 to $10,224 .... 4.5%
$10,225 to $17,040 ... 6.12%
$17,041 to $22,720 ... 6.48%
$22,721 to $34,080 ... 6.8%
$34,081 to $51,120 ... 7.92%
Over $51,120 .... 8.98%

Kansas
1st $30,000 ...... 3.5%
Next $30,000 ...... 6.25%
Over $60,000 ...... 6.45%

Kentucky
1st $3,000 .... 2%
Next $1,000 .... 3%
Next $1,000 .... 4%
Next $3,000 .... 5%
Over $8,000 .... 6%

Louisiana*
1st $10,000 ...... 2%
Next $40,000 ...... 4%
Over $50,000 ...... 6%

Maine
Less than $4,150..... 2%
$4,150 to $8,249 ..... 4.5%
$8,250 to $16,499 .... 7%
$16,500 or more 8.5%

Maryland
1st $1,000 .... 2%
2d $1,000 .... 3%
3d $1,000 .... 4%
Over $3,000 .... 4.875%

Massachusetts
Interest, dividends, cap. gains............ 12%
5 classes of cap. gain income 0-5%
All other income...... 5.95%

Michigan
4.4% of taxable income

Minnesota
$0 to $24,800 .... 6%
$24,801 to $98,540 ... 8%
Over $98,540 .... 8.5%

Mississippi
1st $5,000 .... 3%
Next $5,000 .... 4%
Over $10,000 ...... 5%

Missouri
1st $1,000 .... 1.5%
2d $1,000 .... 2%
3rd $1,000 .... 2.5%
4th $1,000 .... 3%
5th $1,000 .... 3.5%
6th $1,000 .... 4%
7th $1,000 4.5%
8th $1,000 5%
9th $1,000 5.5%
Over $9,000 6%

Montana
$0 to $1,999 .... 2%
$2,000 to $3,899 ..... 3% less $20
$3,900 to $7,899 ..... 4% less $59
$7,900 to $11,799 .... 5% less $138
$11,800 to $15,799 ... 6% less $256
$15,800 to $19,699 ... 7% less $414
$19,700 to $27,599 ... 8% less $611
$27,600 to $39,399 ... 9% less $887
$39,400 to $68,999 .. 10% less $1,281
$69,000 and over.... 11% less $1,971

Nebraska
1st $4,000......... 2.51%
Next $26,000....... 3.49%
Next $16,750....... 5.01%
Over $46,750....... 6.68%

New Hampshire
5% of interest and dividends

New Jersey
1st $20,000....... 1.4%
Next $30,000....... 1.75%
Next $20,000....... 2.45%
Next $10,000....... 3.5%
Next $70,000....... 5.525%
Over $150,000...... 6.37%

New Mexico*
Not over $8,000...... 1.7%
$8,001 to $16,000 .... 3.2%
$16,001 to $24,000 ... 4.7%
$24,001 to $40,000 ... 6%
$40,001 to $64,000 ... 7.1%
$64,001 to $100,000 .. 7.9%
Over $100,000....... 8.2%

New York
1st $16,000....... 4%
Next $6,000........ 4.5%
Next $4,000........ 5.25%
Next $14,000....... 5.9%
Over $40,000....... 6.85%

North Carolina
Up to $21,250....... 6%
Next $78,750....... 7%
Over $100,000...... 7.75%

North Dakota
1st $3,000......... 2.67%
Next $2,000......... 4%
Next $3,000......... 5.33%
Next $7,000......... 6.67%
Next $10,000........ 8%
Next $10,000....... 9.33%
Next $15,000..... 10.67%
Over $50,000..... 12%

Ohio
1st $5,000....... 0.673%
Next $5,000....... 1.347%
Next $5,000....... 2.694%
Next $5,000....... 3.368%
Next $20,000...... 4.040%
Next $40,000...... 4.715%
Next $20,000...... 5.388%
Next $100,000..... 6.255%
Over $200,000..... 6.799%

Oklahoma
1st $2,000....... 0.5%
Next $3,000....... 1%
Next $2,500....... 2%
Next $2,300....... 3%
Next $2,400....... 4%
Next $2,800....... 5%
Next $6,000....... 6%
Remainder......... 7%

Oregon
1st $2,250....... 5%
Next $3,450....... 7%
Over $5,700....... 9%

Pennsylvania 2.8%

Rhode Island
27.5% of federal liability

South Carolina
1st $2,310....... 2.5%
Next $2,310....... 3%
Next $2,310....... 4%
Next $2,310....... 5%
Next $2,310....... 6%
$11,551 and over 7%

Tennessee
6% of interest and dividends

Utah
1st $1,500....... 2.3%
Next $1,500....... 3.3%
Next $1,500....... 4.2%
Next $1,500....... 5.2%
Next $1,500....... 6%
Over $7,500....... 7%

Vermont
25% of federal income tax

Virginia
1st $3,000....... 2%
Next $2,000....... 3%
Next $12,000...... 5%
Over $17,000...... 5.75%

West Virginia
1st $10,000...... 3%
Next $15,000...... 4%
Next $15,000...... 4.5%
Next $20,000...... 6%
Over $60,000...... 6.5%

Wisconsin*
$0 to $10,000....... 4.77%
$10,001 to $20,000... 6.37%
$20,001 and over 6.77%

* = Community property state in which, in general, one-half of the community income is taxable to each spouse.

Alabama: Rates shown are for married persons filing jointly. Single persons, heads of families, married persons filing separately, and estates or trusts are taxed at 2% of the first $500 of taxable income, 4% on the next $2,500, and 5% on the rest.
Arizona: Effective Jan. 1, 1998, for married persons filing jointly and heads of households, the rates are as shown. Effective Jan. 1, 1998, for single taxpayers, rates range from 2.88% of the first $10,000 of taxable income to 5.1% of taxable income over $150,000.
California: Rates shown are the 1998 inflation-adjusted rates for residents who are joint taxpayers or surviving spouses with dependents. For single taxpayers, married persons filing separately, and fiduciaries, rates range from 1% on the first $5,131 of taxable income to 9.3% on taxable income over $33,673. For unmarried heads of households, rates range from 1% on the first $10,264 of taxable income to 9.3% on taxable income over $45,833. A 7% alternative minimum tax is imposed.
Colorado: Alternative minimum tax imposed. Qualified taxpayers may pay alternative tax of 0.5% of gross receipts from sales.
Connecticut: Rates shown are for married individuals filing jointly or persons filing as a surviving spouse. For: (1) unmarried individuals and married individuals filing separately, rates are 3% on the first $7,500 of Conn. taxable income and $225 plus 4.5% of the excess over $7,500; (2) for heads of households, rates are 3% of the first $12,000 of taxable income and $360 plus 4.5% of the excess over $12,000; and (3) for trusts or estates, rates are 4.5% of taxable income. For tax years beginning in 1999, and thereafter, rates are: (1) for

unmarried individuals and married individuals filing separately, 3% on Conn. taxable income of up to $10,000 and $300 plus 4.5% of taxable income in excess of $10,000; (2) for heads of households, 3% for taxable income of up to $16,000 and $480 plus 4.5% of taxable income in excess of $16,000; (3) for married individuals filing jointly or persons filing as a surviving spouse, 3% on taxable income of up to $20,000 and $600 plus 4.5% of taxable income over $20,000. The Commissioner of Revenue services issued new withholding tables effective July 1, 1998. Resident estates and trusts are subject to the 4.5% income tax rate on all of their income. Additional state minimum tax imposed on resident individuals, trusts, and estates is equal to the amount by which the Conn. minimum tax exceeds the Conn. basic income tax [the lesser of (a) 19% of adjusted federal tentative minimum tax, or (b) 5% of adjusted federal alternative minimum taxable income]. Separate provisions apply for non- and part-year resident individuals, trusts, and estates.

District of Columbia: The tax on unincorporated business is 9.975%. Minimum tax, $100.

Georgia: Rates shown are for married persons filing jointly and heads of households. Single persons pay at rates ranging from 1% on taxable net income not over $750 to 6% on taxable net income over $7,000. Married persons filing separately pay at rates ranging from 1% on taxable net income not over $500 to 6% on taxable net income over $5,000.

Hawaii: Rates shown are for taxpayers filing jointly and surviving spouses. For heads of households, rates range from 2% of taxable income up to $3,000 to 10% of taxable income of $41,000 and over. For unmarried individuals (other than a surviving spouse or head of household), married individuals filing separately, and estates and trusts, the rates range from 2% of taxable income up to $1,500 to 10% of taxable income over $20,500.

Idaho: Each person (joint returns deemed one person) filing return pays additional $10.

Illinois: Additional personal property replacement tax of 1.5% of net income is imposed on partnerships, trusts, and S corporations.

Iowa: An alternative minimum tax is imposed equal to 75% of the maximum state individual income tax rate for the tax year of the state alternative minimum taxable income.

Kansas: Rates shown are for married individuals filing joint returns. For tax year 1998, for single individuals and married individuals filing separate returns, the rate is 3.5% of the first $15,000 of Kansas taxable income. (This rate will remain unchanged for 1999). The rate for these individuals with taxable income that is more than $15,000 but less than $30,001 is $525 plus 6.75% of the excess over $15,000. The rate for these individuals with taxable income that is more than $30,000 is $1,537.50 plus 7.75% of the excess over $30,000. For tax year 1999, for single individuals and married individuals filing separate returns with taxable income that is more than $15,000 but less than $30,001, the rate is $525 plus 6.25% of the excess over $15,000. The rate for these individuals with taxable income that is more than $30,000 is $1,462.50 plus 7.45% of the excess over $30,000.

Louisiana: These are the maximum tax rates for individuals. For joint returns, the tax is determined as if net income and personal exemption credits were reduced by one-half. Actual tax is determined from tax tables.

Maine: Rates shown are 1998 rates for single individuals and married persons filing separately. For unmarried or legally separated individuals who qualify as heads of household, tax rates range from 2% if taxable income is less than $6,200 to 8.5% if taxable income is $24,750 or more. For married individuals filing jointly and widows or widowers permitted to file a joint federal return, tax rates range from 2% if taxable income is less than $8,250 to 8.5% if taxable income is $33,000 or more. Additional state minimum tax is imposed equal to the amount by which the state minimum tax (27% of adjusted federal tentative minimum tax) exceeds Maine income tax liability, other than withholding tax liability.

Maryland: For a tax year beginning after 1998 but before 2000, income over $3,000 will be taxed at a rate of 4.85%. For a tax year beginning after 1999 but before 2001, income over $3,000 will be taxed at a rate of 4.85%.

Michigan: Persons with business activity in Michigan are also subject to a single business tax on an adjusted tax base.

Minnesota: Rates shown are 1998 amounts for married individuals filing jointly and surviving spouses. For single individuals, the tax is 6% on the first $16,960 of taxable income, 8% on income over $16,960 but not over $55,730, and 8.5% on income over $55,730; for married individuals filing separately, tax is 6% on the first $12,400 of income, 8% on income over $12,400 but not over $49,270, and 8.5% on income over $49,270; for unmarried heads of households, tax is 6% on the first $20,890 of taxable income, 8% on income over $20,890 but not over $83,930, and 8.5% on income over $83,930. A 7% alternative minimum tax is imposed.

Montana: Rates shown are 1998 amounts, as indexed for inflation. Minimum tax, $1.

Nebraska: Rates shown are for married couples filing jointly and qualified surviving spouses. Rates for married couples filing separately range from 2.51% of the first $2,000 to 6.68% of taxable income over $23,375. Rates for heads of households range from 2.51% of the first $3,800 to 6.68% of taxable income over $35,000. Rates for single individuals range from 2.51% of the first $2,400 to 6.68% of taxable income over $26,500. Rates for estates range from 2.51% of the first $500 to 6.68% for taxable income over $15,150.

New Jersey: Rates shown are for married persons filing jointly, heads of households, and surviving spouses. Rates for married persons filing separately, unmarried individuals, and estates and trusts range from 1.4% of the first $20,000 of taxable income to 6.37% of taxable income over $75,000.

New Mexico: Rates shown are for married persons filing jointly and surviving spouses. For married persons filing separately, rates range from 1.7% on the first $4,000 of taxable income to 8.2% on taxable income over $50,000. For heads of households, rates range from 1.7% on the first $7,000 of taxable income to 8.2% on taxable income over $83,000. For single individuals, estates, and trusts, rates range from 1.7% of the first $5,500 of taxable income to 8.2% of taxable income over $65,000. Qualified taxpayers may pay alternative tax of 0.75% of gross receipts from New Mexico sales.

New York: Rates shown are for married individuals filing jointly and surviving spouses. Separate schedules are set out for heads of households (ranging from 4% on the first $11,000 of taxable income to 6.85% on taxable income over $30,000) and for unmarried individuals, married individuals filing separately, and estates and trusts (ranging from 4% of the first $8,000 of taxable income to 6.85% of taxable income over $20,000). In addition, individuals, estates, and trusts are subject to a 6% tax on minimum taxable income. A tax table benefit recapture supplemental tax is imposed on some individuals.

North Carolina: Rates shown are for married persons filing jointly. For heads of households rates are 6% on the first $17,000, 7% of next $63,000, 7.75% of excess over $80,000. For unmarried individuals (other than surviving spouses and heads of households), the rate is 6% of first $12,750, 7% of next $47,250, 7.75% of excess over $60,000. For married filing separately the rate is 6% of first $10,625, 7% of next $39,375, 7.75% of excess over $50,000.

North Dakota: Individuals, estates, and trusts are allowed an optional method of computing the tax. The optional tax is 14% of the taxpayer's adjusted federal income tax liability for the tax year.

Ohio: Rates shown are for 1998. The rates reflect the 9.339% tax cut for the 1998 tax year.

Oklahoma: Rates shown are for heads of households, married persons filing jointly, and a surviving spouse not deducting federal income taxes. Single persons, married persons filing separately, and estates and trusts not deducting federal income taxes pay at rates ranging from 0.5% on the first $1,000 of taxable income to 7% on taxable income over $10,000. Optional rates (ranging from 0.5% to 10%) are enacted for taxpayers who deduct federal income taxes.

Oregon: Rates shown are 1997 amounts for single or married filing separately. Rates for joint filers, heads of households, and qualifying widow(er)s are 5% of the first $4,500, 7% for $4,501 to $11,400, and 9% over $11,400.

Rhode Island: This is the 1998 rate. For 1999, the rate is 26.5% of federal liability.

Utah: Rates shown are for married persons filing jointly and heads of households. Married taxpayers filing separately, single taxpayers, and estates and trusts pay at rates ranging from 2.35% on taxable income not over $750 to 7% on taxable income over $3,750. Rates for single taxpayers, estates and trusts, and married couples filing separately range from 2.3% of the first $750 of taxable income to 7% of taxable income over $3,750.

West Virginia: A minimum tax is also imposed, equal to the excess by which an amount equal to 25% of any federal minimum tax or alternative minimum tax for the tax year exceeds the total tax due for the tax year.

Wisconsin: Rates shown are for married persons filing jointly. Rates for married persons filing separately range from 4.77% of the first $5,000 of taxable income to 6.77% of taxable income over $10,000. The rates for fiduciaries and single individuals range from 4.77% of the first $7,500 of taxable income to 6.77% of taxable income over $15,000. Alternative minimum tax is imposed. For tax years beginning on or after Jan. 1, 1998, a temporary recycling surcharge is imposed on individuals, estates, partnerships, trusts, and exempt trusts, except those entities engaged only in farming, at the rate of the greater of $25 or 0.2173% of net business income. The maximum surcharge is $9,800. An individual, estate, trust, exempt trust, or partnership engaged in farming is subject to a surcharge of $25.

ENERGY

U.S. Energy Summary, 1997

Source: Energy Information Administration, U.S. Dept. of Energy, *Annual Energy Review 1997*

Energy consumption in the U.S. in 1997 grew by less than 1%, for the lowest year-to-year growth in 6 years, although reaching an all-time high of over 94 quadrillion British thermal units (Btu), according to preliminary data. Weather was the major cause of the slow growth, as a warm winter and very cool summer resulted in lower-than-expected energy consumption. The increase that occurred resulted from a rise in the consumption of petroleum and coal; use of nuclear electric power declined by 6.7%, while consumption of renewable energy fell by 2.3%. Petroleum consumption increased by 0.27 million barrels per day to 18.58 million barrels per day. Consumption of coal reached an all-time high of 1.03 billion short tons in 1997, up 2.1% from the 1996 level. The energy intensity of the economy, measured in terms of energy consumption per dollar of gross domestic product, fell from 1996, continuing a long-term trend. About 13,000 Btu of energy were consumed for each 1992 dollar in 1997, compared with about 19,000 Btu in the early 1970s.

U.S. total energy production in 1997 held steady at the 1996 record level of 72.3 quadrillion Btu. Increases in the production of coal, natural gas, and conventional hydroelectric power were offset by decreases in the production of nuclear electric power, biofuels, and crude oil. Coal production increased 2.3% to a record level of 1.09 billion short tons, while generation of conventional hydroelectric power increased by 3.6% to an all-time high of 360 billion kilowatt hours. Crude oil (including lease condensate) production continued to drop, to 13.6 quadrillion Btu, its lowest level in 43 years.

U.S. net imports of energy increased to an all-time high of 20.4 quadrillion Btu in 1997, an increase of 5.9% from the 1996 level. Most of the increase was accounted for by petroleum net imports, which increased by 5.0% to a record level of 19.1 quadrillion Btu. U.S. net imports of petroleum totaled 8.9 million barrels per day in 1997. Members of OPEC supplied 4.46 million barrels per day, or half the total. Although coal remained the primary U.S. energy export, coal exports fell 7.7% to 83.5 million short tons in 1997.

U.S. Energy Overview, 1960-97

Source: Energy Information Administration, U.S. Dept. of Energy, *Annual Energy Review 1997*

(in quadrillion Btu)

Activity and energy source	1960	1965	1970	1975	1980	1985	1990[1]	1995	1996	1997P
Production	**41.49**	**49.34**	**62.07**	**59.86**	**64.76**	**64.87**	**70.76R**	**71.04R**	**72.32R**	**72.32**
Fossil fuels	39.87	47.23	59.19	54.73	59.01	57.54	58.56	57.41	58.20R	58.75
Coal	10.82	13.06	14.61	14.99	18.60	19.33	22.46	21.98	22.65R	23.17
Natural gas (dry)	12.66	15.78	21.67	19.64	19.91	16.98	18.36	19.10	19.30R	19.47
Crude oil[2]	14.93	16.52	20.40	17.73	18.25	18.99	15.57	13.89	13.72R	13.57
Natural gas plant liquids	1.46	1.88	2.51	2.37	2.25	2.24	2.17	2.44	2.53	2.54
Nuclear electric power	0.01	0.04	0.24	1.90	2.74	4.15	6.16	7.18	7.17	6.69
Hydroelectric pumped storage[3]	(4)	(4)	(4)	(4)	(4)	(4)	–0.04	–0.03	–0.03	–0.04
Renewable energy	1.61	2.07	2.65	3.23	3.01	3.18	6.07R	6.48R	6.98R	6.93
Conventional hydroelectric power[5]	1.61	2.06	2.63	3.15	2.90	2.97	3.01	3.21	3.59	3.72
Geothermal energy	(*)	(*)	0.01	0.07	0.11	0.20	0.33R	0.32R	0.34	0.37
Biofuels[6]	(*)	(*)	(*)	(*)	(*)	0.01	2.63	2.85R	2.94R	2.72
Solar energy	0	0	0	0	0	0	0.07	0.07	0.08	0.08
Wind energy	0	0	0	0	0	(*)	0.02	0.03	0.04	0.04
Imports	**4.23**	**5.92**	**8.39**	**14.11**	**15.97**	**12.10**	**18.99**	**22.48**	**23.97R**	**24.96**
Coal	0.01	(*)	(*)	0.02	0.03	0.05	0.07	0.18	0.18	0.19
Natural gas	0.16	0.47	0.85	0.98	1.01	0.95	1.55	2.90	3.00R	3.04
All crude oil and petroleum pdcts.[7]	4.00	5.40	7.47	12.95	14.66	10.61	17.12	18.86	20.27R	21.22
Other[8]	0.06	0.04	0.07	0.16	0.28	0.49	0.26	0.54	0.52R	0.52
Exports	**1.48**	**1.85**	**2.66**	**2.36**	**3.72**	**4.23**	**4.91**	**4.58**	**4.71R**	**4.57**
Coal	1.02	1.38	1.94	1.76	2.42	2.44	2.77	2.32	2.37	2.19
Natural gas	0.01	0.03	0.07	0.07	0.05	0.06	0.09	0.16	0.16R	0.16
All crude oil and petroleum pdcts.[7]	0.48	0.39	0.55	0.44	1.16	1.66	1.82	1.99	2.06	2.10
Other[8]	0.02	0.06	0.11	0.08	0.09	0.08	0.23	0.11	0.12R	0.13
Adjustments[9]	**–0.43**	**–0.72**	**–1.37**	**–1.07**	**–1.05**	**1.24**	**–0.75R**	**1.93R**	**2.29R**	**1.50**
Consumption[10]	**43.80**	**52.68**	**66.43**	**70.55**	**75.96**	**73.98**	**84.09R**	**90.86R**	**93.87**	**94.21**
Fossil fuels	42.14	50.58	63.52	65.35	69.98	66.22	71.95R	76.94	79.43R	80.36
Coal	9.84	11.58	12.26	12.66	15.42	17.48	19.10	20.09R	21.01R	22.59
Coal coke net imports	–0.01	–0.02	–0.06	0.01	–0.04	–0.01	(*)	0.03	(*)	0.02
Natural gas[11]	12.39	15.77	21.79	19.95	20.39	17.83	19.30	22.16	22.56R	22.56
Petroleum[12]	19.92	23.25	29.52	32.73	34.20	30.92	33.55	34.66	35.86R	36.31
Nuclear electric power	0.01	0.04	0.24	1.90	2.74	4.15	6.16	7.18	7.17	6.69
Hydroelectric pumped storage[3]	(4)	(4)	(4)	(4)	(4)	(4)	–0.04	–0.03	–0.03	–0.04
Renewable energy	1.66	2.06	2.67	3.29	3.23	3.61	6.17R	6.76R	7.31R	7.14
Conventional hydroelectric power[5,13]	1.66	2.06	2.65	3.22	3.12	3.40	3.10	3.47	3.91	3.94
Geothermal energy[14]	(*)	(*)	0.01	0.07	0.11	0.20	0.35R	0.34R	0.35	0.37
Biofuels[6]	(*)	(*)	(*)	(*)	(*)	0.01	2.63	2.85R	2.94R	2.72
Solar energy	0	0	0	0	0	0	0.07	0.07	0.07	0.08
Wind energy	0	0	0	0	0	(*)	0.02	0.03	0.04	0.04

(1) Starting in 1990, expanded coverage of nonelectric utility use of renewable energy resulted in an increase in total energy production and consumption figures. (2) Includes lease condensate. (3) Total pumped storage facility production minus energy used for pumping. (4) Before 1990, pumped storage is included in conventional hydroelectric power. (5) Starting in 1990, pumped storage is removed and expanded coverage of industrial use of hydroelectric power is included. (6) These include wood, wood waste, peat, wood liquors, railroad ties, pitch, wood sludge, municipal solid waste, agricultural waste, straw, tires, landfill gases, fish oils, and/or other waste. (7) Includes imports of crude oil for the Strategic Petroleum Reserve, which began in 1977. (8) Coal coke and small amts. of electricity transmitted across U.S. borders with Canada and Mexico. (9) A balancing item. Includes stock changes, losses, gains, miscellaneous blending components, and unaccounted-for supply. (10) Starting in 1990, "Consumption" includes the part of net imports of electricity derived from nonrenewable energy sources. (11) Includes supplemental gaseous fuels. (12) Petroleum products supplied, including natural gas plant liquids and crude oil burned as fuel. (13) Starting in 1990, includes only the part of net imports of electricity derived from hydroelectric power. (14) Includes electricity imports from Mexico derived from geothermal energy. R=revised data. P=preliminary data. (*)=Less than 0.005 quadrillion Btu. **Note:** Totals may not equal sum of components as a result of independent rounding.

World Energy Consumption and Production Trends

Source: Energy Information Administration, U.S. Dept. of Energy, International Energy Database, July 1998

The world's consumption of primary energy—petroleum, natural gas, coal, net hydroelectric, nuclear, geothermal, solar, wind electric power, and biofuels (primarily for the United States)—increased from 366 quadrillion Btu (British thermal units) in 1995 to 376 quadrillion Btu in 1996. The 29 countries of the Organization for Economic Cooperation and Development (OECD), which includes some of the world's largest economies (the United States, Japan, and Germany), continued to dominate global energy use. OECD nations accounted for more than 58% of the world's primary energy consumption in 1996. World production of primary energy increased from 365 quadrillion Btu in 1995 to 375 quadrillion Btu in 1996. World production of petroleum in 1996 was almost 70 million barrels per day, or 146 quadrillion Btu; petroleum remained the most heavily used source of energy.

In 1996, 3 countries—the United States, Russia, and China—were the world's leading producers (40%) and consumers (42%) of energy. Russia and the United States alone supplied 30% of the world total. The U.S. alone accounted for 25% of the world's total energy consumption. The U.S. consumed 30% more energy than it produced—an imbalance of 21.6 quadrillion Btu.

World's Major Producers of Primary Energy, 1996

Source: Energy Information Administration, International Energy Database; quadrillion Btu

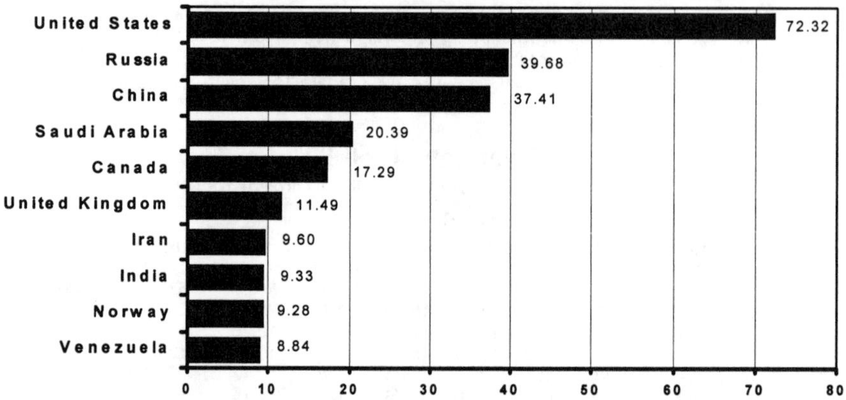

World's Major Consumers of Primary Energy, 1996

Source: Energy Information Administration, International Energy Database; quadrillion Btu

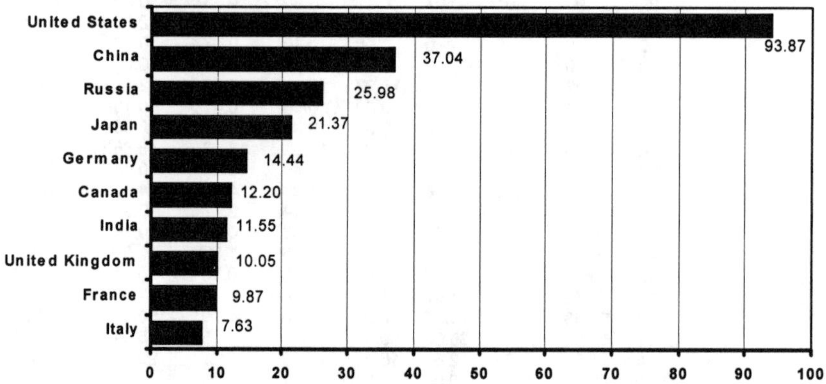

U.S. Petroleum Trade, 1974-97

Source: Energy Information Administration, U.S. Dept. of Energy, *Monthly Energy Review,* June 1998

(in thousands of barrels per day; average for the year)

Year	Imports from Persian Gulf[1]	Total imports	Total exports	Net imports[2]	Petroleum products supplied	Year	Imports from Persian Gulf[1]	Total imports	Total exports	Net imports[2]	Petroleum products supplied
1974	1,039	6,112	221	5,892	16,653	1986	912	6,224	785	5,439	16,281
1975	1,165	6,056	209	5,846	16,322	1987	1,077	6,678	764	5,914	16,665
1976	1,840	7,313	223	7,090	17,461	1988	1,541	7,402	815	6,587	17,283
1977	2,448	8,807	243	8,565	18,431	1989	1,861	8,061	859	7,202	17,325
1978	2,219	8,363	362	8,002	18,847	1990	1,966	8,018	857	7,161	16,988
1979	2,069	8,456	471	7,985	18,513	1991	1,845	7,627	1,001	6,626	16,714
1980	1,519	6,909	544	6,365	17,056	1992	1,778	7,888	950	6,938	17,033
1981	1,219	5,996	595	5,401	16,058	1993	1,782	8,620	1,003	7,618	17,237
1982	696	5,113	815	4,298	15,296	1994	1,728	8,996	942	8,054	17,718
1983	442	5,051	739	4,312	15,231	1995	1,573	8,835	949	7,886	17,725
1984	506	5,437	722	4,715	15,726	1996	1,604	9,399	981	8,419	18,234
1985	311	5,067	781	4,286	15,726	1997	1,755	10,162	1,003	9,158	18,620

(1) Bahrain, Iran, Iraq, Kuwait, Qatar, Saudi Arabia, and the United Arab Emirates. (2) Net imports are total imports minus total exports. **Notes:** Beginning in Oct. 1977, imports for the Strategic Petroleum Reserves are included. U.S. geographic coverage includes the 50 states and the District of Columbia. U.S. exports include shipments to U.S. territories, and imports include receipts from U.S. territories. Figures in this table may not add, because of independent rounding.

Appliance Use in U.S. Households, 1980-97

Source: Energy Information Administration, U.S. Dept. of Energy, *Annual Energy Review 1997*

(percentage of households)

Appliance	1980	1982	1984	1987	1990	1993	1997	Change 1980-97
Total households (millions)	82	84	86	90	94	97	101	+20
Type of appliances								
Electric appliances								
Television set (color)	82	85	88	93	96	98	99	+17
Clothes washer	74	72	74	76	76	77	77	+3
Range (stove-top burner)	54	53	54	57	58	61	60	+6
Oven, regular or microwave	59	59	63	79	88	91	91	+32
Oven, microwave	14	21	34	61	79	84	83	+69
Clothes dryer	47	45	46	51	53	57	55	+8
Dishwasher	37	36	38	43	45	45	50	+13
Dehumidifier	9	9	9	10	12	9	NA	NA
Swimming-pool pump[2]	3	3	NA	NA	5	5	5	+2
Gas appliances[3]								
Range (stove-top or burner)	46	47	45	43	42	38	39	-7
Oven	42	42	42	41	41	36	37	-5
Clothes dryer	14	15	16	15	16	15	16	+2
Outdoor gas grill	9	11	13	20	26	29	NA	NA
Refrigerators[4]								
One	86	86	88	86	84	85	85	-1
Two or more	14	13	12	14	15	15	15	+1
Air conditioning								
Central[5]	27	28	30	36	39	44	47	+20
Individual room units[5]	30	30	30	30	29	25	25	-5
Portable kerosene heaters	(1)	3	6	6	5	2	2	+2

(1) Less than 0.5%. (2) All reported swimming pools were assumed to have an electric pump for filtering and circulating the water, except for 1993, when a filtering system was made explicit. (3) Includes natural gas or liquefied petroleum gases. (4) Fewer than 0.5% of the households did not have a refrigerator. (5) Households with both central and individual room units are counted only under "Central." NA= not available. **Note:** Percentages may not add because of independent rounding.

Energy Consumption, Total and Per Capita, by State, 1995

Source: Energy Information Administration, U.S. Dept. of Energy, State Energy Data Report 1995 (released Dec. 1997)

Total Consumption

Rank	State	Trillion Btu	Rank	State	Trillion Btu
1.	Texas	10,511.5	28.	Arizona	1,058.9
2.	California	7,577.0	29.	Mississippi	1,058.8
3.	Ohio	4,038.0	30.	Oregon	1,046.2
4.	New York	3,913.4	31.	Kansas	1,040.6
5.	Pennsylvania	3,885.7	32.	Arkansas	997.9
6.	Louisiana	3,813.6	33.	West Virginia	818.9
7.	Illinois	3,804.3	34.	Connecticut	786.3
8.	Florida	3,518.6	35.	Alaska	686.3
9.	Michigan	3,157.0	36.	Utah	638.4
10.	Indiana	2,592.1	37.	Nebraska	580.3
11.	New Jersey	2,542.9	38.	New Mexico	575.0
12.	Georgia	2,512.1	39.	Nevada	537.2
13.	North Carolina	2,328.1	40.	Maine	513.3
14.	Washington	2,158.6	41.	Idaho	456.2
15.	Virginia	2,056.0	42.	Wyoming	405.2
16.	Tennessee	1,975.2	43.	Montana	378.9
17.	Alabama	1,933.3	44.	North Dakota	350.1
18.	Kentucky	1,770.4	45.	New Hampshire	284.5
19.	Wisconsin	1,749.1	46.	Delaware	264.0
20.	Missouri	1,662.8	47.	Hawaii	254.8
21.	Minnesota	1,622.1	48.	South Dakota	235.8
22.	Massachusetts	1,493.8	49.	Rhode Island	235.1
23.	South Carolina	1,400.7	50.	District of Columbia	177.8
24.	Oklahoma	1,359.6	51.	Vermont	149.9
25.	Maryland	1,311.9		**Total U.S.**	**90,547.4**
26.	Colorado	1,075.2			
27.	Iowa	1,067.3			

Consumption per Capita

Rank	State	Million Btu	Rank	State	Million Btu
1.	Alaska	1,139.1	28.	New Mexico	340.3
2.	Louisiana	879.1	29.	Oregon	332.9
3.	Wyoming	845.6	30.	Michigan	331.0
4.	Texas	559.1	31.	Utah	326.0
5.	North Dakota	545.8	32.	North Carolina	323.2
6.	Kentucky	459.0	32.	South Dakota	323.2
7.	Alabama	455.3	34.	Illinois	322.7
8.	West Virginia	448.7	35.	Pennsylvania	322.2
9.	Indiana	447.2	36.	District of Columbia	320.7
10.	Montana	435.4	37.	New Jersey	319.9
11.	Oklahoma	415.2	38.	Missouri	312.6
12.	Maine	414.4	39.	Virginia	310.8
13.	Kansas	405.9	40.	Colorado	286.9
14.	Arkansas	401.6	41.	Maryland	260.4
15.	Washington	396.2	42.	Vermont	256.3
16.	Mississippi	392.7	43.	Florida	248.1
17.	Idaho	391.2	44.	New Hampshire	247.8
18.	South Carolina	382.0	45.	Massachusetts	246.1
19.	Tennessee	376.5	46.	Arizona	246.0
20.	Iowa	375.4	47.	Connecticut	240.4
21.	Delaware	368.1	48.	California	240.0
22.	Ohio	362.7	49.	Rhode Island	237.0
23.	Nebraska	354.0	50.	Hawaii	216.1
24.	Minnesota	351.5	51.	New York	215.1
25.	Nevada	350.3		**Total U.S.**	**344.4**
26.	Georgia	348.5			
27.	Wisconsin	341.5			

Gasoline Retail Prices, U.S. City Average, 1974-98

Source: Energy Information Administration, U.S. Dept. of Energy, *Monthly Energy Review,* June 1998

(cents per gallon, including taxes)

Average	Leaded regular	Unleaded regular	Unleaded premium	All types[1]	Average	Leaded regular	Unleaded regular	Unleaded premium	All types[1]
1974	53.2	NA	NA	NA	1987	89.7	94.8	109.3	95.7
1975	56.7	NA	NA	NA	1988	89.9	94.6	110.7	96.3
1976	59.0	61.4	NA	NA	1989	99.8	102.1	119.7	106.0
1977	62.2	65.6	NA	NA	1990	114.9	116.4	134.9	121.7
1978	62.6	67.0	NA	65.2	1991	NA	114.0	132.1	119.6
1979	85.7	90.3	NA	88.2	1992	NA	112.7	131.6	119.0
1980	119.1	124.5	NA	122.1	1993	NA	110.8	130.2	117.3
1981[2]	131.1	137.8	147.0[3]	135.3	1994	NA	111.2	130.5	117.4
1982	122.2	129.6	141.5	128.1	1995	NA	114.7	133.6	120.5
1983	115.7	124.1	138.3	122.5	1996	NA	123.1	141.3	128.8
1984	112.9	121.2	136.6	119.8	1997	NA	123.4	141.6	129.1
1985	111.5	120.2	134.0	119.6	1998 (Jan-June)	NA	108.2	126.8	113.7
1986	85.7	92.7	108.5	93.1					

(1) Also includes types of motor gasoline not shown separately. (2) In Sept. 1981, the Bureau of Labor Statistics changed the weights used in the calculation of average motor gasoline prices. Starting in Sept. 1981, gasohol is included in the average for all types, and unleaded premium is weighted more heavily. (3) Based on Sept. through Dec. data only. **Note:** Geographic coverage for 1974-77 is 56 urban areas; for 1978 and later, 85 urban areas. NA = not available.

World Crude Oil and Natural Gas Reserves, Jan. 1, 1997

Sources: Energy Information Administration, U.S. Dept. of Energy, *Annual Energy Review 1997; Oil and Gas Journal (OGJ)*, Dec. 1996; *World Oil (WO)*, Aug. 1997

Region and country	Crude oil (billion barrels)		Natural gas (trillion cubic feet)	
	OGJ	*WO*	*OGJ*	*WO*
North America	**75.7**	**76.0**	**302.3**	**298.5**
Canada	4.9	5.5	68.1	68.1
Mexico	48.8	48.5	67.7	63.9
United States	22.0	22.0	166.5	166.5
Central and South America	**79.1**	**91.2**	**208.5**	**213.9**
Argentina	2.4	2.6	21.9	24.3
Bolivia	0.1	0.1	4.5	4.4
Brazil	4.8	7.0	5.4	8.3
Colombia	2.8	3.4	8.3	8.0
Ecuador	2.1	3.3	3.7	3.4
Peru	0.8	0.7	7.0	7.0
Trinidad and Tobago	0.6	0.6	12.4	12.1
Venezuela	64.9	72.6	141.6	143.0
Other	0.0	0.7	0.0	*
Western Europe	**18.5**	**34.8**	**167.9**	**242.3**
Denmark	1.0	0.9	3.9	3.7
Germany	0.4	0.4	11.6	12.1
Italy	0.7	0.7	10.5	9.8
Netherlands	0.1	0.1	64.1	62.3
Norway	11.2	26.9	47.7	123.3
United Kingdom	4.5	5.0	24.7	26.8
Other	0.0	0.1	0.0	0.4
Eastern Europe and Former USSR	**59.0**	**185.1**	**2,000.4**	**1,953.6**
Hungary	0.1	0.1	3.3	3.1
Romania	1.6	1.0	14.0	4.5
Former USSR	57.0	183.8	1,977.0	1,939.3
Other[1]	0.0	*	0.0	1.2
Middle East	**676.4**	**635.7**	**1,617.1**	**1,675.0**
Bahrain	0.2	0.1	5.2	5.0
Iran	93.0	90.5	741.6	812.2
Iraq	112.0	112.0	118.0	118.5
Kuwait	96.5	94.7	52.9	52.7
Oman	5.1	3.6	30.0	21.1
Qatar	3.7	3.9	250.0	244.8
Saudi Arabia	261.5	261.8	189.1	191.5
Syria	2.5	2.4	8.3	8.2
United Arab Emirates	97.8	63.5	204.9	203.6
Yemen	4.0	3.1	16.9	17.0
Other	0.0	*	0.0	0.2
Africa	**67.6**	**76.2**	**328.6**	**344.6**
Algeria	9.2	13.0	130.3	138.9
Angola	5.4	3.6	1.7	1.7
Cameroon	0.4	0.1	3.9	3.9
Congo Republic	1.5	1.6	3.2	4.3
Egypt	3.7	3.7	20.4	20.4
Libya	29.5	29.5	46.3	46.3
Nigeria	15.5	20.8	104.7	109.7
Tunisia	0.3	0.3	2.4	2.7
Other	0.0	2.1	0.0	15.2
Far East and Oceania	**42.3**	**60.8**	**321.8**	**448.7**
Australia	1.8	3.7	19.4	83.5
Brunei	1.4	1.1	14.1	13.5
China	24.0	34.1	41.4	39.6
India	4.3	5.0	24.2	19.5
Indonesia	5.0	9.2	72.3	135.9
Malaysia	4.0	5.2	80.2	79.1
New Zealand	0.1	0.1	2.4	2.2
Pakistan	0.2	0.2	22.0	18.3
Papua New Guinea	0.3	0.3	1.5	8.6
Thailand	0.3	0.3	7.1	7.1
Other	0.0	0.6	0.0	20.2
World	**1,018.5**	**1,160.1**	**4,946.7**	**5,176.6**

(1) Albania, Bulgaria, Czech Republic, Poland, and Slovakia. * Value less than 50 mil bbl of crude oil or less than 50 bil cu ft natural gas. **Notes:** Data for Kuwait and Saudi Arabia include one-half of the reserves in the Neutral Zone between Kuwait and Saudi Arabia. All reserve figures except those for the former USSR and natural gas reserves in Canada are proved reserves recoverable with present technology and prices. Former USSR figures are "explored reserves," which include proved, probable, and some partially possible. The Canadian natural gas figures include proved and some probable. Totals may not equal sum of components as a result of independent rounding.

Nuclear Electricity Generation by Selected Country, Mar. 1998

Source: Energy Information Administration, U.S. Dept. of Energy, *Monthly Energy Review*, June 1998

(billion kilowatt-hours; E = estimate)

Argentina	0.7	France	34.7[E]	Lithuania	1.3	Sweden	7.3
Belgium	3.7	Germany	14.0	Mexico	0.9	Switzerland	2.4
Brazil	0.4	Hungary	1.1	Netherlands	0.4	Taiwan	3.4
Bulgaria	2.2	India	1.0[E]	Russia	11.1	Ukraine	7.2
Canada	7.2	Japan	27.3	South Africa	1.4	United Kingdom	10.1[E]
Finland	2.0	Korea, South	6.7	Spain	4.6	United States	55.6[E]

Nations Most Reliant on Nuclear Energy, 1997

Source: International Atomic Energy Agency, May 1998

(Nuclear electricity generation as % of total)

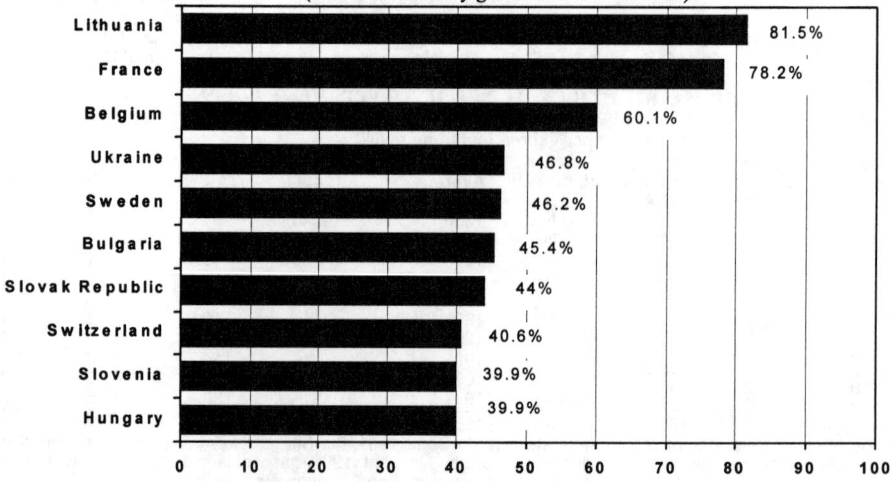

World Nuclear Power Summary

Source: International Atomic Energy Agency, May 1998

Country	Reactors in operation: No. of units	Reactors in operation: Total MW(e)	Reactors under construction: No. of units	Reactors under construction: Total MW(e)	Nuclear electricity supplied in 1997: TW(e).h[1]	Nuclear electricity supplied in 1997: % of total	Total operating experience to Dec. 31, 1997: Years	Total operating experience to Dec. 31, 1997: Months
Argentina	2	935	1	692	7.45	11.40	38	7
Armenia	1	376	—	—	1.43	25.67	30	4
Belgium	7	5,712	—	—	45.10	60.05	149	7
Brazil	1	626	1	1,245	3.16	1.09	15	9
Bulgaria	6	3,538	—	—	16.44	45.38	95	1
Canada	16	11,994	—	—	77.86	14.16	390	7
China	3	2,167	4	3,090	11.35	0.79	14	5
Czech Republic	4	1,648	2	1,824	12.49	19.34	46	8
Finland	4	2,455	—	—	20.00	30.40	75	4
France	59	62,853	1	1,450	376.00	78.17	993	1
Germany	20	22,282	—	—	161.40	31.76	550	7
Hungary	4	1,729	—	—	13.97	39.88	50	2
India	10	1,695	4	808	8.72	2.32	149	1
Iran	—	—	2	2,111	—	—	—	—
Japan	54	43,850	1	796	318.10	35.22	810	2
Kazakhstan	1	70	—	—	0.30	0.58	24	6
Korea, South	12	9,770	6	5,120	73.19	34.08	123	7
Lithuania	2	2,370	—	—	10.85	81.47	24	6
Mexico	2	1,308	—	—	10.46	6.48	11	11
Netherlands	1	449	—	—	2.30	2.77	53	—
Pakistan	1	125	1	300	0.37	0.65	26	3
Romania	1	650	1	650	5.40	9.67	1	6
Russia	29	19,843	4	3,375	99.68	13.63	584	6
Slovakia	4	1,632	4	1,552	10.80	43.99	69	5
Slovenia	1	632	—	—	4.79	39.91	16	3
South Africa	2	1,842	—	—	12.63	6.51	26	3
Spain	9	7,320	—	—	53.10	29.34	165	2
Sweden	12	10,040	—	—	67.00	46.24	243	2
Switzerland	5	3,079	—	—	23.97	40.57	113	10
Taiwan	6	4,884	—	—	34.85	26.35	98	1
Ukraine	16	13,765	4	3,800	74.61	46.84	206	1
United Kingdom	35	12,968	—	—	89.30	27.45	1,133	4
United States	107	99,188	—	—	629.42	20.14	2,246	11
Total	**437**	**351,795**	**36**	**26,813**	**2,276.49**	**—**	**8,577**	**8**

(1) 1 terawatt-hour [TW(e).h] = 10^6 megawatt-hour [MW(e).h]. For an average power plant, 1 TW(e).h = 0.39 megatonnes of coal equivalent (input) and 0.23 megatonnes of oil equivalent (input). **Note:** In 1997, no reactors were shut down.

U.S. Nuclear Reactor Units and Power Plant Operations

Source: Energy Information Administration, U.S. Dept. of Energy, *Monthly Energy Review,* June 1998

Year	Number of reactor units: Licensed for operation: Operable	Licensed for operation: In startup	Construction permits: Granted	Construction permits: Pending	On order	Announced	Total	Total design capacity (million KWs)	Nuclear-based electricity generation (million net KW-hours)	Nuclear portion of domestic electricity generation (percent)
1977	65	2	78	49	13	2	209	203	250,883	11.8
1978	70	0	88	32	5	0	195	191	276,403	12.5
1979	68	0	90	24	3	0	185	180	255,155	11.4
1980	70	1	82	12	3	0	168	162	251,116	11.0
1981	74	0	76	11	2	0	163	157	272,674	11.9
1982	77	2	60	3	2	0	144	134	282,773	12.6
1983	80	3	53	0	2	0	138	129	293,677	12.7
1984	86	6	38	0	2	0	132	123	327,634	13.6
1985	95	3	30	0	2	0	130	121	383,691	15.5
1986	100	7	19	0	2	0	128	119	414,038	16.6
1987	107	4	14	0	2	0	127	119	455,270	17.7
1988	108	3	12	0	0	0	123	115	526,973	19.5
1989	110	1	10	0	0	0	121	113	529,355	19.0
1990	111	0	8	0	0	0	119	111	576,862	20.5
1991	111	0	8	0	0	0	119	111	612,565	21.7
1992	109	0	8	0	0	0	117	111	618,776	22.1
1993	109	0	7	0	0	0	116	110	610,291	21.2
1994	109	0	7	0	0	0	116	110	640,440	22.0
1995	109	1	6	0	0	0	116	110	673,402	22.5
1996	110	0	6	0	0	0	116	110	674,729	21.9
1997	107	0	3	0	0	0	110	102	628,644	20.1

ENVIRONMENT

Greenhouse Effect and Global Warming

Source: U.S. Environmental Protection Agency

The Earth naturally absorbs incoming solar radiation and emits thermal radiation back into space. Some of the thermal radiation is trapped by certain so-called greenhouse gases in the atmosphere, which increases warming of the Earth's surface and atmosphere. In recent years, carbon dioxide (CO_2), a naturally occurring greenhouse gas, has been building up in the atmosphere as the result of human activities such as the burning of fossil fuels (coal, oil, and natural gas) and deforestation. Water vapor, methane (CH_4), nitrous oxide (N_2O), and ozone (O_3) are also naturally occurring greenhouse gases. Greenhouse gases that are mostly human-made include chlorofluorocarbons (CFCs), hydrochlorofluorocarbons (HCFCs), hydrofluorocarbons (HFCs), perfluorocarbons (PFCs), and sulfur hexafluoride (SF_6). Several nongreenhouse gases (carbon monoxide [CO], oxides of nitrogen [NO_x], and nonmethane volatile organic compounds [NMVOCs]) contribute indirectly to the greenhouse effect by producing greenhouse gases during chemical transformations or by influencing the atmospheric lifetimes of greenhouse gases.

Since 1800, atmospheric concentrations of CO_2, CH_4, and N_2O have increased by 30%, 145%, and 15%, respectively. This increasing buildup is believed by many scientists to be the major cause of higher than normal average global temperatures in the 1990s; 1997 was the hottest year on record (global average temp. 62.45°F), and the 4 next-hottest years on record were also in the 1990s. Over the past century, the Earth's average temperature has risen by approximately 1°F, and some scientists believe that it could rise by 2° to 6°F over the next century. This global warming could speed the melting of the polar ice caps, inundate coastal lowlands, and cause major changes in crop production and natural habitat. The United States is the world's leading producer of greenhouse gases, followed by the former Soviet republics, China, Japan, Germany, and India.

In Dec. 1997, a United Nations summit on global warming was held in Kyoto, Japan. Delegates from over 150 nations attended and adopted an international treaty to set some limits on emissions of CO_2, CH_4, N_2O, HFCs, PFCs, and SF_6. The accord, known as the Kyoto Protocol, called for an overall reduction in emissions of 5.2% below 1990 levels by the year 2012, significantly below the 15% reduction proposed by the European Union. Under the accord, the 15 EU nations agreed to reductions of 8%, the U.S. to 7%, and Japan to 6%. Developing nations were permitted to limit their emissions voluntarily. The accord allowed high-emissions nations to meet their targets by purchasing pollution rights from nations that have exceeded their goal, although the mechanism for buying and selling such emissions permits was not worked out. No penalties for noncompliance were specified.

U.S. Greenhouse Gas Emissions From Human Activities, 1990-95

Source: U.S. Environmental Protection Agency

GAS AND SOURCE	1990	1991	1992	1993	1994	1995
Carbon dioxide (CO_2)	**1,228**	**1,213**	**1,235**	**1,268**	**1,291**	**1,305**
Fossil fuel combustion	1,336	1,320	1,340	1,370	1,391	1,403
Industrial processes and other	17	16	17	18	19	19
Total	1,353	1,336	1,357	1,388	1,410	1,422
Forests[1,2]	*(125)*	*(123)*	*(122)*	*(120)*	*(119)*	*(117)*
Methane (CH_4)	**170**	**172**	**173**	**171**	**176**	**177**
Landfills	56	58	58	60	62	64
Agriculture	50	51	52	52	54	55
Coal mining	24	23	22	20	21	20
Oil and natural gas systems	33	33	34	33	33	33
Other	6	7	7	6	6	6
Nitrous oxide (N_2O)	**36**	**37**	**37**	**38**	**39**	**40**
Agriculture	17	17	17	18	18	18
Fossil fuel consumption	11	11	12	12	12	12
Industrial processes	8	8	8	8	9	9
Hydrofluorocarbons (HFCs)[3]	**12**	**12**	**13**	**14**	**17**	**21**
Perfluorocarbons (PFCs)[3]	**5**	**5**	**5**	**5**	**7**	**8**
Sulfur hexafluoride (SF_6)[3]	**7**	**7**	**8**	**8**	**8**	**8**
TOTAL U.S. EMISSIONS	**1,583**	**1,570**	**1,592**	**1,624**	**1,657**	**1,676**
NET U.S. EMISSIONS[4]	**1,458**	**1,447**	**1,470**	**1,504**	**1,538**	**1,559**

Note: Emissions are given in millions of metric tons of carbon equivalent (MMTCE), a measurement used by the Intergovernmental Panel on Climate Change (IPCC) to compare greenhouse gases. Totals may not equal the sum of the individual source categories due to rounding. (1) Carbon dioxide absorbed by forests. (2) These estimates for the conterminous U.S. for 1990-91 and 1993-95 are interpolated from forest inventories in 1987 and 1992, and projections through 2040. The methodology reflects long-term averages rather than specific events in any given year. (3) These gases have extremely high global warming potential, and PFCs and SF_6 have long atmospheric lifetimes. (4) Total emissions minus carbon dixoide absorbed by forests.

Net U.S. Greenhouse Gas Emissions, 1995

Source: U.S. Environmental Protection Agency

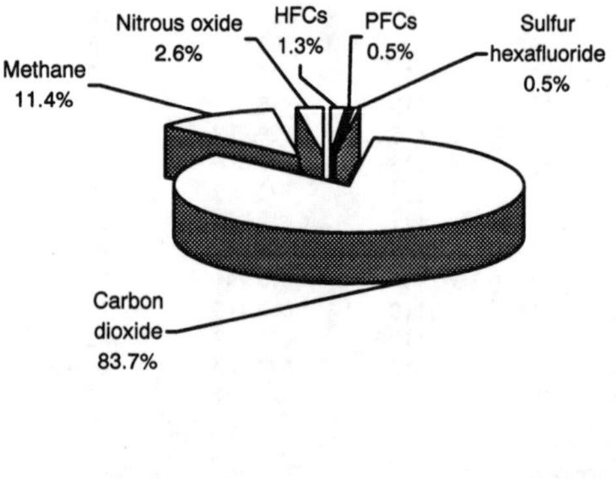

World Carbon Dioxide Emissions from Fossil Fuel Combustion, 1996

Source: Energy Information Administration, 1998

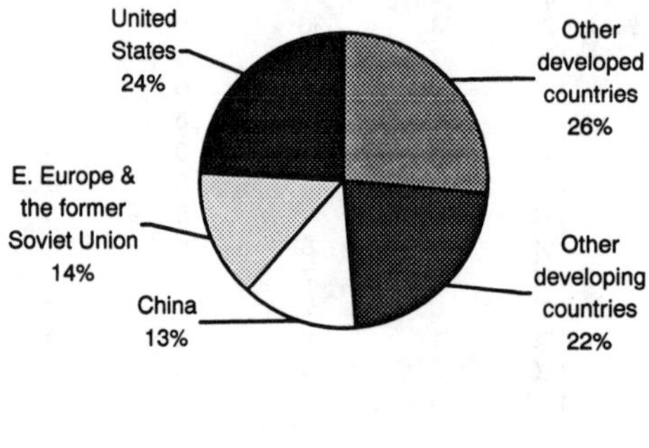

Toxics Release Inventory, 1995-96

Source: U.S. Environmental Protection Agency

Reported industrial releases of toxic chemicals into the environment in the U.S. by major manufacturing facilities (excluding power plants and mining facilities) decreased 3.8% from the 1995 figure and 45.6% from the figure for 1988, the baseline year. Totals below may not add because of rounding.

Pollutant releases	1996 mil lb	1995 mil lb
Air releases	1,452	1,567
Surface water releases	173	160
Underground injection	204	240
On-site land releases	309	283
TOTAL	**2,139**	**2,250**
Pollutant transfers		
To recycling	2,151	2,238
To energy recovery	477	517
To treatment	290	287
To publicly owned treatment works	236	245
Other transfers	3	2
TOTAL	**3,157**	**3,290**

Top industries, total releases	1996 mil lb	1995 mil lb
Chemicals	785	844
Primary metals	565	524
Paper	228	238
Plastics	116	127
Transportation equipment	111	121
Top carcinogens, air/water/land releases		
Dichloromethane	54	57
Styrene	42	42
Trichloroethylene	21	25
Formaldehyde	21	19
Acetaldehyde	13	14
Chloroform	10	11

Top 10 States, Total Releases, 1995-96

Source: U.S. Environmental Protection Agency

State	1996 mil lb	1995 mil lb
Texas	267	302
Louisiana	185	177
Ohio	145	152
Pennsylvania	122	127
Indiana	109	109
Illinois	108	116
Tennessee	104	111
Alabama	103	115
Michigan	90	97
North Carolina	85	91

Emissions of Principal Air Pollutants in the U.S., 1987-1996

Source: U.S. Environmental Protection Agency, Office of Air Quality Planning and Standards

(in thousand short tons; estimated)

Source	1987	1988	1989	1990	1991	1992	1993	1994	1995	1996
Carbon monoxide[1]	108,879	117,169	104,447	96,535	98,461	95,123	95,291	99,677	89,721	88,822
Lead	7.7	7.1	5.5	5.0	4.2	3.8	3.9	4.0	3.9	3.9
Nitrogen oxides[2]	22,806	24,526	24,057	23,792	23,772	24,137	24,482	24,892	23,935	23,393
Volatile organic compounds[2]	23,194	24,167	22,383	20,985	21,100	20,695	20,895	21,546	20,586	19,086
Particulate matter[3]	3,504	3,721	3,678	3,436	3,358	3,413	3,318	3,305	3,293	3,288
Sulfur dioxide	22,308	22,767	22,907	23,136	22,496	22,240	21,879	21,262	18,552	19,113
TOTAL[4]	**180,699**	**192,357**	**177,478**	**167,889**	**169,191**	**165,612**	**165,869**	**170,686**	**156,091**	**153,706**

(1) The observed increase in carbon monoxide emissions between 1993 and 1994 is attributed to 2 sources: transportation emissions (up 2%) and wildfire emissions (up 160%). (2) Ozone, a major air pollutant and the primary constituent of smog, is not emitted directly to the air but is formed by sunlight acting on emissions of nitrogen oxides and volatile organic compounds. (3) Does not include natural sources. (4) Totals are rounded, as are components of totals.

Carbon Monoxide Emission Estimates, 1987-96

Source: U.S. Environmental Protection Agency, Office of Air Quality Planning and Standards; in thousand short tons

Source	1987	1988	1989	1990	1991	1992	1993	1994	1995	1996
Fuel combustion	6,967	7,379	7,449	5,510	5,856	6,155	5,586	5,519	5,934	5,962
Industrial processes	6,851	7,034	7,013	5,852	5,740	5,683	5,898	5,839	5,790	5,817
Transportation	86,209	86,861	81,832	73,965	78,114	76,233	76,794	78,706	70,947	69,946
Miscellaneous	8,852	15,895	8,153	11,208	8,751	7,052	7,013	9,614	7,050	7,099
TOTAL[1]	**108,879**	**117,169**	**104,447**	**96,535**	**98,461**	**95,123**	**95,291**	**99,677**	**89,721**	**88,822**

(1) Totals may not add because of rounding.

Lead Emission Estimates, 1987-96

Source: U.S. Environmental Protection Agency, Office of Air Quality Planning and Standards; in short tons

Source	1987	1988	1989	1990	1991	1992	1993	1994	1995	1996
Fuel combustion	510	511	505	500	495	491	495	494	487	493
Industrial processes	3,004	3,090	3,161	3,278	3,081	2,734	2,869	3,005	2,892	2,812
Transportation	4,167	3,452	1,802	1,197	592	584	547	544	564	564
Miscellaneous	0	0	0	0	0	0	0	0	0	0
TOTAL[1]	**7,681**	**7,053**	**5,468**	**4,975**	**4,168**	**3,808**	**3,911**	**4,043**	**3,943**	**3,869**

(1) Totals may not add because of rounding.

Nitrogen Oxides Emission Estimates, 1987-96

Source: U.S. Environmental Protection Agency, Office of Air Quality Planning and Standards; in thousand short tons

Source	1987	1988	1989	1990	1991	1992	1993	1994	1995	1996
Fuel combustion	10,014	10,472	10,537	10,895	10,779	10,928	11,111	11,015	10,827	10,494
Industrial processes	841	860	852	892	816	857	861	878	873	880
Transportation	11,598	12,467	12,374	11,633	11,891	12,098	12,285	12,616	11,998	11,781
Miscellaneous	352	727	293	371	286	254	225	383	237	239
TOTAL[1]	**22,806**	**24,526**	**24,057**	**23,792**	**23,772**	**24,137**	**24,482**	**24,892**	**23,935**	**23,393**

(1) Totals may not add because of rounding.

Air Quality of Selected U.S. Metropolitan Areas[1], 1987-96

Source: U.S. Environmental Protection Agency, Office of Air Quality Planning and Standards

Metropolitan statistical area	1987	1988	1989	1990	1991	1992	1993	1994	1995	1996
Atlanta, GA	27	21	3	17	6	5	17	4	19	6
Bakersfield, CA	67	87	76	60	65	32	56	47	49	56
Baltimore, MD	28	43	9	12	20	5	14	17	14	3
Boston, MA–NH	5	15	4	1	4	1	3	1	1	0
Chicago, IL	17	23	4	3	8	7	1	8	4	3
Dallas, TX	10	14	7	8	1	3	5	1	13	2
Denver, CO	37	19	11	9	7	7	3	2	2	1
Detroit, MI	9	17	10	3	8	1	2	8	11	3
El Paso, TX	32	16	33	27	13	17	10	10	4	9
Fresno, CA	49	29	47	29	33	27	28	11	19	31
Hartford, CT	20	27	11	7	14	9	9	10	9	1
Houston, TX	67	61	41	59	42	30	26	29	54	28
Las Vegas, NV–AZ	7	31	46	22	12	5	8	12	7	3
Los Angeles–Long Beach, CA	201	239	226	180	184	185	146	136	103	88
Miami, FL	4	5	4	1	2	0	0	0	0	1
Minneapolis–St. Paul, MN–WI	14	3	7	3	2	1	0	5	3	1
New Haven–Meriden, CT	20	16	7	10	22	3	11	8	8	2
New York, NY	44	46	18	18	22	4	6	8	8	4
Orange County, CA	58	63	66	47	40	43	25	14	6	6
Philadelphia, PA–NJ	35	35	19	14	25	3	21	6	14	5
Phoenix–Mesa, AZ	42	27	30	9	4	10	7	9	13	5
Pittsburgh, PA	10	20	9	8	4	1	3	2	7	0
Riverside–San Bernardino, CA	171	180	178	144	144	156	142	124	113	94
Sacramento, CA	52	72	57	41	46	21	11	11	16	12
St. Louis, MO–IL	17	20	13	8	6	3	6	11	14	4
Salt Lake City–Ogden, UT	7	11	15	2	19	10	3	10	1	3
San Diego, CA	61	84	91	61	40	37	17	16	14	4
San Francisco, CA	1	2	1	0	0	0	0	0	1	0
Seattle–Bellevue–Everett, WA	14	20	8	5	2	1	0	0	0	0
Ventura, CA	54	83	59	36	49	25	16	24	30	25
Washington, DC–MD–VA–WV	26	37	8	5	16	2	13	7	8	2

(1) Data indicate the number of days metropolitan statistical areas failed to meet acceptable air-quality standards at trend sites (Pollutant Standards Index rating over 100).

Hazardous Waste Sites in the U.S., 1998

Source: U.S. Environmental Protection Agency, *National Priorities List,* Mar. 1998

	Final		Proposed		
State	Gen	Fed	Gen	Fed	Total
Alabama	9	3	1	0	13
Alaska	1	6	0	0	7
Arizona	7	3	0	0	10
Arkansas	11	0	0	0	11
California	68	23	3	0	94
Colorado	12	3	2	0	17
Connecticut	13	1	0	0	14
Delaware	16	1	0	0	17
District of Columbia	0	0	0	1	1
Florida	47	6	2	0	55
Georgia	13	2	2	0	17
Hawaii	1	3	0	0	4
Idaho	5	2	2	0	9
Illinois	34	4	3	0	41
Indiana	29	0	1	0	30
Iowa	15	1	1	0	17
Kansas	9	1	0	1	11
Kentucky	15	1	0	0	16
Louisiana	12	1	3	0	16
Maine	9	3	0	0	12
Maryland	10	5	0	1	16
Massachusetts	22	8	1	0	31
Michigan	72	0	1	1	74
Minnesota	26	2	0	0	28
Mississippi	1	0	2	0	3
Missouri	19	3	0	0	22
Montana	8	0	1	0	9
Nebraska	9	1	0	0	10
Nevada	1	0	0	0	1
New Hampshire	17	1	0	0	18
New Jersey	102	6	2	0	110
New Mexico	8	1	1	0	10
New York	75	4	1	0	80
North Carolina	21	2	0	0	23
North Dakota	0	0	0	0	0
Ohio	30	3	2	2	37
Oklahoma	9	1	1	0	11
Oregon	8	2	1	0	11
Pennsylvania	91	6	3	0	100
Rhode Island	10	2	0	0	12
South Carolina	24	2	0	0	26
South Dakota	1	1	0	0	2
Tennessee	10	3	1	1	15
Texas	22	4	4	0	30
Utah	8	4	4	0	16
Vermont	8	0	0	0	8
Virginia	18	7	0	1	26
Washington	33	14	0	0	47
West Virginia	4	2	1	0	7
Wisconsin	39	0	0	0	39
Wyoming	2	1	0	0	3
American Samoa	0	0	0	0	0
Guam	1	1	0	0	2
Puerto Rico	9	1	0	0	10
Virgin Islands	2	0	0	0	2
TOTALS	**1,046**	**151**	**46**	**8**	**1,251**

Note: Gen = general superfund sites; Fed = federal facility sites.

Watersheds in the U.S.

Source: U.S. Environmental Protection Agency

A watershed is a water drainage area, or land areas bounded by ridges that catch rain and snow and drain to rivers, lakes, and groundwater within the drainage area. In its first comprehensive assessment of watersheds in the continental U.S., released in Oct. 1997, the Environmental Protection Agency (EPA) concluded that 16% of the 2,111 watersheds had good water quality, 36% had moderate water quality, and 21% had more serious problems; there was insufficient information to fully characterize the remaining 27%. The data indicate that polluted runoff from urban and rural areas is a major contributor to water quality problems, threatening water quality even in currently healthy watersheds.

The EPA categorized the watersheds by combining nationally available data from 15 individual databases, from both public and private sources, into a single Index of Watershed Indicators. The indicators include 7 used to assess watershed conditions (quality) and 8 used to assess vulnerability to degradation from pollution. You can find information about your own watershed on the Internet by going to the following website: http://www.epa.gov/surf/index2.html

U.S. List of Endangered and Threatened Species

Source: Fish and Wildlife Service, U.S. Dept. of Interior; as of Aug. 31, 1998

Group	ENDANGERED		THREATENED		Total listed species	Species with recovery plans
	U.S. only	Foreign only	U.S. only	Foreign only		
Mammals	59	251	8	16	334	44
Birds	75	178	15	6	274	75
Reptiles	14	64	21	14	114	29
Amphibians	9	8	7	1	25	11
Fishes	68	11	40	0	118	86
Snails	15	1	7	0	23	19
Clams	61	2	8	0	71	45
Crustaceans	16	0	3	0	19	7
Insects	28	4	9	0	41	22
Arachnids	5	0	0	0	5	4
Animals, subtotal	**350**	**519**	**118**	**37**	**1,024**	**342**
Flowering plants	529	1	115	0	645	411
Conifers	2	0	1	2	5	1
Ferns and others	26	0	2	0	28	26
Plants, subtotal	**557**	**1**	**118**	**2**	**678**	**438**
Grand total	**907**	**520**	**236**	**39**	**1,702**[1]	**780**[2]

(1) When separate populations of a species are listed as endangered and as threatened, those species are tallied twice. Those species are the argali, bull trout, chimpanzee, chinook salmon, gray wolf, green sea turtle, leopard, olive ridley sea turtle, piping plover, roseate tern, saltwater crocodile, steelhead, and Steller sea lion. (2) There are 494 approved recovery plans. Some recovery plans cover more than one species, and a few species have separate plans covering different parts of their ranges. Recovery plans are drawn up only for listed species that occur in the U.S.

Some Endangered Animal Species

Source: Fish and Wildlife Service, U.S. Dept. of the Interior

Common name	Scientific name	Range
Armadillo, giant	Pridontes maximus	Venezuela, Guyana to Argentina
Bat, gray	Myotis grisescens	Central, southeastern U.S.
Bear, brown	Ursus arctos arctos	Italy
Bison, wood	Bison bison athabascae	Canada, northwestern U.S.
Bobcat	Felis rufus escuinapae	Central Mexico
Camel, Bactrian	Camelus bactrianus	Mongolia, China
Caribou, woodland	Rangifer tarandus caribou	U.S., Canada
Cheetah	Acinonyx jubatus	Africa to India
Chimpanzee, pygmy	Pan paniscus	Congo (formerly Zaire)
Chinchilla	Chinchilla brevicaudata boliviana	Bolivia
Condor, California	Gymnogyps californianus	U.S. (AZ, CA, OR), Mexico (Baja California)
Cougar, eastern	Felis concolor couguar	Eastern N America
Crane, hooded	Grus monacha	Japan, Russia
Crane, whooping	Grus americana	Canada, Mexico, U.S. (Rocky Mts. to Carolinas)
Crocodile, American	Crocodylus acutus	U.S. (FL), Mexico, Caribbean Sea, Central and S America
Deer, Columbian white-tailed	Odocoileus virginianus leucurus	U.S. (OR, WA)
Dolphin, Chinese river	Lipotes vexillifer	China
Elephant, Asian	Elephas maximus	S central and southeastern Asia
Falcon, American peregrine	Falco peregrinus anatum	U.S. (AK), Canada to Mexico
Fox, northern swift	Vulpes velox hebes	U.S., Canada
Gorilla	Gorilla gorilla	Central and W Africa
Hawk, Hawaiian	Buteo solitarius	U.S. (HI)
Hyena, brown	Hyaena brunnea	Southern Africa
Kangaroo, Tasmanian forester	Macropus giganteus tasmaniensis	Australia (Tasmania)
Leopard	Panthera pardus	Africa and Asia
Lion, Asiatic	Panthera leo persica	Turkey to India
Manatee, West Indian	Trichechus manatus	Southeastern U.S., Caribbean Sea, S America
Monkey, spider	Ateles geoffroyi frontatus	Costa Rica, Nicaragua
Ocelot	Felis pardalis	U.S. (AZ, TX) to Central and S America
Orangutan	Pongo pygmaeus	Borneo, Sumatra
Ostrich, West African	Struthio camelus spatzi	W Sahara
Otter, marine	Lutra felina	Peru south to Straits of Magellan
Panda, giant	Ailuropoda melanoleuca	China
Panther, Florida	Felis concolor coryi	U.S. (LA, AR east to SC, FL)
Parakeet, golden	Aratinga guarouba	Brazil
Parrot, imperial	Amazona imperialis	West Indies (Dominica)
Penguin, Galapagos	Spheniscus mendiculus	Ecuador (Galapagos Islands)
Python, Indian	Python molurus molurus	Sri Lanka, India
Rhinoceros, black	Diceros bicornis	Sub-Saharan Africa
Rhinoceros, northern white	Ceratotherium simum cottoni	Congo (formerly Zaire), Sudan, Uganda, Central African Republic
Salamander, Chinese giant	Andrias davidianus davidianus	Western China
Squirrel, Carolina northern flying	Glaucomys sabrinus coloratus	U.S. (NC, TN)
Stork, oriental white	Ciconia ciconia boyciana	China, Japan, Korea, Russia
Tiger	Panthera tigris	Asia
Tortoise, Galapagos	Geochelone elephantopus	Ecuador (Galapagos Islands)
Turtle, leatherback sea	Dermochelys coriacea	Tropical, temperate, and subpolar seas
Turtle, Plymouth red-bellied	Pseudemys rubriventris bangsi	U.S. (MA)
Whale, gray	Eschrichtius robustus	N Pacific Ocean
Whale, humpback	Megaptera novaeangliae	Oceania
Wolf, red	Canis rufus	Southeastern U.S. to central TX
Woodpecker, ivory-billed	Campephilus principalis	S central and southeastern U.S., Cuba
Yak, wild	Bos grunniens mutus	China (Tibet), India
Zebra, mountain	Equus zebra zebra	South Africa

Classification

Source: *Funk & Wagnalls New Encyclopedia*

In biology, classification is the identification, naming, and grouping of organisms into a formal system. The 2 fields that are most directly concerned with classification are taxonomy and systematics. Although the 2 disciplines overlap considerably, taxonomy is more concerned with nomenclature (naming) and with constructing hierarchical systems, and systematics with uncovering evolutionary relationships. Two kingdoms of living forms, Plantae and Animalia, have been recognized since Aristotle established the first taxonomy in the 4th century BC. In addition, there are the following 3 kingdoms: Protista (one-celled organisms), Monera (bacteria and blue-green algae; also known as the kingdom Procaryotae), and Fungi. The 7 basic categories of classification (from most general to most specific) are: kingdom, phylum (or division), class, order, family, genus, and species. Below are 2 examples:

ZOOLOGICAL HIERARCHY

Kingdom	Phylum	Class	Order	Family	Genus	Species Name	Common name
Animalia	Chordata	Mammalia	Primates	Hominidae	Homo	Homo sapiens	Human

BOTANICAL HIERARCHY

Kingdom	Division*	Class	Order	Family	Genus	Species Name	Common name
Plantae	Magnoliophyta	Magnoliopsida	Magnoliales	Magnoliaceae	Magnolia	M. virginiana	Sweet Bay

* In botany, the division is generally used in place of the phylum.

Gestation, Longevity, and Incubation of Animals

Information reviewed and updated by Ronald M. Nowak, ed. *Walker's Mammals of the World* (5th ed., Johns Hopkins University Press, 1991). Average longevity figures supplied by Ronald T. Reuther. These apply to animals in captivity; the potential life span of animals is rarely attained in nature. Figures on gestation and incubation are averages based on estimates by leading authorities.

ANIMAL	Gestation (days)	Average longevity (years)	Maximum longevity (yr-mo)
Ass	365	12	47
Baboon	187	20	45
Bear: Black	219	18	36-10
Grizzly	225	25	50
Polar	240	20	38
Beaver	105	5	50
Bison	285	15	40
Camel (Bactrian)	406	12	50
Cat (domestic)	63	12	28
Chimpanzee	230	20	53
Chipmunk	31	6	8
Cow	284	15	30
Deer (white-tailed)	201	8	20
Dog (domestic)	61	12	20
Elephant (African)	660	35	70
Elephant (Asian)	645	40	77
Elk	250	15	26-8
Fox (red)	52	7	14
Giraffe	425	10	33-7
Goat (domestic)	151	8	18
Gorilla	258	20	54
Guinea pig	68	4	8
Hippopotamus	238	41	54-4
Horse	330	20	50
Kangaroo (gray)	36	7	24
Leopard	98	12	23
Lion	100	15	30
Monkey (rhesus)	166	15	37
Moose	240	12	27
Mouse (meadow)	21	3	4
Mouse (dom. white)	19	3	6
Opossum (American)	13	1	5
Pig (domestic)	112	10	27
Puma	90	12	20
Rabbit (domestic)	31	5	13
Rhinoceros (black)	450	15	45
Rhinoceros (white)	480	20	50
Sea lion (California)	350	12	30
Sheep (domestic)	154	12	20
Squirrel (gray)	44	10	23-6
Tiger	105	16	26-3
Wolf (maned)	63	5	13
Zebra (Grant's)	365	15	50

Incubation time (days)

ANIMAL	Days
Chicken	21
Duck	30
Goose	30
Pigeon	18
Turkey	26

Speeds of Animals

Source: *Natural History* magazine. Copyright © The American Museum of Natural History, 1974

ANIMAL	mph
Cheetah	70
Pronghorn antelope	61
Wildebeest	50
Lion	50
Thomson's gazelle	50
Quarterhorse	47.5
Elk	45
Cape hunting dog	45
Coyote	43
Gray fox	42
Hyena	40
Zebra	40
Mongolian wild ass	40
Greyhound	39.35
Whippet	35.50
Rabbit (domestic)	35
Mule deer	35
Jackal	35
Reindeer	32
Giraffe	32
White-tailed deer	30
Wart hog	30
Grizzly bear	30
Cat (domestic)	30
Human	27.89
Elephant	25
Black mamba snake	20
Six-lined race runner	18
Wild turkey	15
Squirrel	12
Pig (domestic)	11
Chicken	9
Spider (Tegenaria atrica)	1.17
Giant tortoise	0.17
Three-toed sloth	0.15
Garden snail	0.03

Most of these measurements are for maximum speeds over approximate quarter-mile distances. Exceptions are the lion and elephant, whose speeds were clocked in the act of charging; the whippet, which was timed over a 200-yd course; the cheetah, timed over a 100-yd distance; the human, timed for a 15-yd segment of a 100-yd run (of 13.6 sec); and the black mamba, six-lined race runner, spider, giant tortoise, three-toed sloth, and garden snail, which were measured over various small distances.

Major Venomous Animals

Snakes

Asian pit viper — from 2 ft to 5 ft long; throughout Asia; reactions and mortality vary, but most bites cause tissue damage, and mortality is generally low.

Australian brown snake — 4 ft to 7 ft long; very slow onset of cardiac or respiratory distress; moderate mortality, but because death can be sudden and unexpected, it is the most dangerous of the Australian snakes; antivenom.

Barba Amarilla or fer-de-lance — up to 7 ft long; from tropical Mexico to Brazil; severe tissue damage common; moderate mortality; antivenom.

Black mamba — up to 14 ft long, fast-moving; S and C Africa; rapid onset of dizziness, difficulty breathing, erratic heartbeat; mortality high, nears 100% without antivenom.

Boomslang — less than 6 ft long; in African savannahs; rapid onset of nausea and dizziness, often followed by slight recovery and then sudden death from internal hemorrhaging; bites rare, mortality high; antivenom.

Bushmaster — up to 12 ft long; wet tropical forests of C and S America; few bites occur, but mortality rate is high.

Common or Asian cobra — 4 ft to 8 ft long; throughout southern Asia; considerable tissue damage, sometimes paralysis; mortality probably not more than 10%; antivenom.

Copperhead — less than 4 ft long; from New England to Texas; pain and swelling; very seldom fatal; antivenom seldom needed.

Coral snake — 2 ft to 5 ft long; in Americas south of Canada; bite may be painless; slow onset of paralysis, impaired breathing; mortalities rare, but high without antivenom and mechanical respiration.

Cottonmouth water moccasin — up to 5 ft long; wetlands of southern U.S. from Virginia to Texas. Rapid onset of severe pain, swelling; mortality low, but tissue destruction can be extensive; antivenom.

Death adder — less than 3 ft long; Australia; rapid onset of faintness, cardiac and respiratory distress; at least 50% mortality without antivenom.

Desert horned viper — in dry areas of Africa and western Asia; swelling and tissue damage; low mortality; antivenom.

European viper — 1 ft to 3 ft long; bleeding and tissue damage; mortality low; antivenom.

Gaboon viper — more than 6 ft long; fat; 2-in. fangs; south of the Sahara; massive tissue damage, internal bleeding; few recorded bites.

King cobra — up to 16 ft long; throughout southern Asia; rapid swelling, dizziness, loss of consciousness, difficulty breathing, erratic heartbeat; mortality varies sharply with amount of venom involved, but most bites involve nonfatal amounts; antivenom.

Krait — up to 5 ft long; in SE Asia; rapid onset of sleepiness; numbness; as much as 50% mortality even with use of antivenom.

Puff adder — up to 5 ft long; fat; south of the Sahara and throughout the Middle East; rapid large swelling, great pain, dizziness; moderate mortality, often from internal bleeding; antivenom.

Rattlesnake — 2 ft to 6 ft long; throughout W Hemisphere; rapid onset of severe pain, swelling; mortality low, but amputation of affected digits is sometimes necessary; antivenom. Mojave rattler may produce temporary paralysis.

Ringhals, or spitting, cobra — 5 ft to 7 ft long; southern Africa; squirts venom through holes in front of fangs as a defense; venom is severely irritating, can cause blindness.

Russell's viper or tic-polonga — more than 5 ft long; throughout Asia; internal bleeding; bite reports common; moderate mortality rate; antivenom.

Saw-scaled or carpet viper — as much as 2 ft long; in dry areas from India to Africa; severe bleeding, fever; high mortality, causes more human fatalities than any other snake; antivenom.

Sea snakes — throughout Pacific, Indian oceans except NE Pacific; almost painless bite, variety of muscle pain, paralysis; mortality rate low, many bites not envenomed; some antivenoms.

Sharp-nosed pit viper or one hundred pace snake — up to 5 ft long; in S Vietnam, Taiwan, and China; the most toxic of Asian pit vipers; very rapid onset of swelling and tissue damage, internal bleeding; moderate mortality; antivenom.

Taipan — up to 11 ft long; in Australia and New Guinea; rapid paralysis with severe breathing difficulty; mortality nears 100% without antivenom.

Tiger snake — 2 ft to 6 ft long; S Australia; pain, numbness, mental disturbances with rapid onset of paralysis; may be the most deadly of all land snakes, although antivenom is quite effective.

Yellow or Cape cobra — 7 ft long; in S Africa; most toxic venom of any cobra; rapid onset of swelling, breathing and cardiac difficulties; mortality is high without treatment; antivenom.

Note: Not all bites by venomous snakes are actually envenomed. Any animal bite, however, carries the danger of tetanus, and anyone suffering a venomous snake bite should seek medical attention. Antivenoms do not cure; they are only an aid in the treatment of bites. Mortality rates above are for envenomed bites; low mortality, c. 2% or less; moderate, 2%-5%; high, 5%-15%.

Lizards

Gila monster — as much as 24 in. long, with heavy body and tail; in high desert in SW U.S. and N Mexico; immediate severe pain and transient low blood pressure; no recent mortality.

Mexican beaded lizard — similar to Gila monster, Mexican west coast; reaction and mortality rate similar to Gila monster.

Insects

Ants, bees, wasps, hornets, etc. Global distribution. Usual reaction is piercing pain in area of sting. Not directly fatal, except in cases of massive multiple stings. However, many people suffer allergic reactions — swelling and rashes — and a few may die within minutes from severe sensitivity to the venom (anaphylactic shock).

Spiders, Scorpions

Atrax spider — also known as funnel whip spider; several varieties, often large; in Australia; slow onset of breathing, circulation difficulties; low mortality; antivenom.

Black widow — small, round-bodied with red hourglass marking; the widow and its relatives are found in tropical and temperate zones; severe musculoskeletal pain, weakness, breathing difficulty, convulsions; may be more serious in small children; low mortality; antivenom. The **redback** spider of Australia has the hourglass marking on its back, rather than on its front, but is otherwise identical to the black widow.

Brown recluse, or fiddleback, spider — small, oblong body; throughout U.S.; pain with later ulceration at place of bite; in severe cases fever, nausea, and stomach cramps; ulceration may last months; very low mortality.

Scorpion — crablike body with stinger in tail, various sizes, many varieties throughout tropical and subtropical areas; various symptoms may include severe pain spreading from the wound, numbness, severe agitation, cramps; severe reaction may include respiratory failure; low mortality, usually in children; antivenoms.

Tarantula — large, hairy spider found around the world; the American tarantula, and probably all other tarantulas, are harmless to humans, though their bite may cause some pain and swelling.

Sea Life

Cone-shell — mollusk in small, beautiful shell; in the S Pacific and Indian oceans; shoots barbs into victims; paralysis; low mortality.

Octopus — global distribution, usually in warm waters; all varieties produce venom, but only a few can cause death; rapid onset of paralysis with breathing difficulty.

Portuguese man-of-war — jellyfishlike, with tentacles up to 70 ft long; in most warm water areas; immediate severe pain; not directly fatal, though shock may cause death in rare cases.

Sea wasp — jellyfish, with tentacles up to 30 ft long, in the S Pacific; very rapid onset of circulatory problems; high mortality because of speed of toxic reaction; antivenom.

Stingray — several varieties of differing sizes; found in tropical and temperate seas and some fresh water; severe pain, rapid onset of nausea, vomiting, breathing difficulties; wound area may ulcerate, gangrene may appear; seldom fatal.

Stonefish — brownish fish that lies motionless as a rock on bottom in shallow water; throughout S Pacific and Indian oceans; extraordinary pain, rapid paralysis; low mortality; antivenom available, amount determined by number of puncture wounds; warm water relieves pain.

Major U.S. Public Zoological Parks

Source: *World Almanac* questionnaire, 1998; budget and attendance in millions

Zoo	Budget	Attendance	Acres	Species	Some major attractions
Albuquerque (NM) Biological Park	$8.8	1.0	240	483	Polar Bear Exhibit, Shark Tank, Great Apes, Mexican Wolves *for further information: (505) 764-6200.*
Arizona-Sonora Desert Museum (Tucson, AZ)	5.0	0.6	20	317	Desert Grasslands, Hummingbird Aviary, Pollination Gardens *for further information: (520) 883-2702.*
Audubon Zoo (New Orleans)	11.0	0.9	58	400	White alligators, Louisiana Swamp, Reptile Encounter *for further information: (800) 774-7394.*
Baltimore Zoo	8.1	0.6	180	295	Children's zoo, Chimpanzee Forest, African Watering Hole *for further information: (410) 366-LION.*
Bronx Zoo (N.Y.C.)	34.5	2.0	265	607	Jungle World, Baboon Reserve, Himalayan Highlands Habitat *for further information: (718) 367-1010.*
Brookfield Zoo (Chicago area)	41.0	2.0	216	400	Living Coast, The Swamp, Habitat Africa!, 7 Seas Panorama *for further information: (708) 485-0263.*
Buffalo (NY) Zoological Gardens	4.6	0.4	23.5	175	Children's Zoo, Gorilla Troop, World of Wildlife Center *for further information: (716) 837-3900.*
Cincinnati Zoo and Botanical Garden	15.7	1.3	70	712	Jungle Trails, Wings of the World, Reptile House *for further information: (800) 94-HIPPO.*
Cleveland Metroparks Zoo	8.0	1.3	165	599	Wolf Wilderness, African Savannah, Monkey Island *for further information: (216) 661-6500.*
Columbus Zoo (Powell, OH)	12.0	1.3	90	650	African Forest, prairie dog habitat, migratory songbird aviary *for further information: (800) MONKEYS.*
Dallas Zoo	8.0	0.6	85	350	Wilds of Africa, Chimpanzee Forest, Gorilla Exhibit *for further information: (214) 670-5656.*
Denver Zoo	13.0	1.5	80	672	Tropical Discovery, Primate Panorama, Northern Shores *for further information: (303) 376-4800.*
Detroit Zoological Park	11.4	1.4	125	271	Penguinarium, Great Apes of Harambee, Interpretive Gallery *for further information: (248) 398-0900.*
Houston Zoological Gardens	13.0	1.4	55	700	Tropical bird house, Mystery of the Vanishing Amphibians *for further information: (713) 284-1300.*
Lincoln Park Zoological Gardens (Chicago)	17.0	3.0	35	289	Great Ape house, Farm-in-the-Zoo, Kovler Lion House *for further information: (312) 742-2000.*
Los Angeles Zoo	17.2	1.3	80	350	Tiger Falls, Great ape families, Walk through aviary *for further information: (323) 644-4200.*
Louisville (KY) Zoo	8.1	0.7	133	413	Islands Village, walk-through Bird Trail, African Panorama *for further information: (502) 459-2181.*
Memphis (TN) Zoo	7.3	0.7	70+	400	Cat Country, Animals of the Night, Primate Canyon *for further information: (901) 276-WILD.*
Miami Metrozoo	7.1	0.5	300	185	white tiger, koalas, Komodo dragons, Asian River Life *for further information: (305) 251-0401.*
Milwaukee County Zoo	15.9	1.4	194	350	Jurassic Park/Lost World, Train, Zoomobile, Carousel *for further information: (414) 771-3040.*
Minnesota Zoo (Apple Valley)	16.0	1.2	500	403	Discovery Bay, Tropics Trail, World of Birds Show, Zoolab *for further information: (800) 366-7811.*
National Zoo (Washington, DC)	24.0	3.0	163	500	Amazonia, Panda Exhibit, Komodo Dragons *for further information: (202) 673-4666.*
Oklahoma City Zoological Park & Botanical Garden	8.3	0.8	110	2,600	Aquaticus, Cat Forest, Lion Overlook, Great EscApe *for further information: (405) 424-3344.*
Omaha's Henry Doorly Zoo	6.2	1.2	130	630	Indoor rain forest, cat complex, aquarium, 3D IMAX theater *for further information: (402) 733-8401.*
Oregon Zoo (Portland)	24.6	1.1	64	232	African Rain Forest and Savannah, Alaska Tundra *for further information: (503) 226-1561.*
Philadelphia Zoo	16.0	1.2	42	400	white lions, blue-eyed lemurs, giant river otter *for further information: (215) 243-1100.*
Phoenix (AZ) Zoo	14.0	1.2	125	363	Arizona Trail, Forest of Uco, Africa Trail, Tropics Trail *for further information: (602) 273-1341.*
Point Defiance Zoo & Aquarium (Tacoma, WA)	6.9	0.5	29	290	Rocky Shores, Pacific walrus and sea otters, Arctic Tundra *for further information: (253) 591-5337.*
Riverbanks Zoological Park (Columbia, SC)	5.5	0.9	170	497	Aquarium Reptile Complex, Botanical Garden, Coral Reef *for further information: (803) 779-8717.*
St. Louis Zoo	31.1	2.5	91	713	Big Cat Country, Jungle of the Apes, Children's Zoo *for further information: (314) 781-0900.*
San Diego Wild Animal Park	NA	1.5	2,200	400	Heart of Africa walking safari, Wgasa Bush Line Monorail *for further information: (619) 234-3153.*
San Diego Zoo	NA	3.5	100	800	Giant Pandas, Polar Bear Plunge, Hippo Beach, Skyfari *for further information: (619) 234-3153.*
San Francisco Zoo	13.2	0.9	75	281	Gorilla World, Koala Crossing, rainbow lorikeet exhibit *for further information: (415) 753-7080.*
Toledo (OH) Zoological Gardens	12.4	0.8	62	633	Hippoquarium, aquarium, aviary, Primate Forest *for further information: (419) 385-5721.*
Tulsa (OK) Zoo and Living Museum	3.2	0.7	70	400	African Savanna, Chimpanzee Connection, Elephant Encounter *for further information: (918) 669-6600.*
Woodland Park Zoo (Seattle)	13.9	1.0	92	280	Tropical Rain Forest, Elephant Forest, African Savanna *for further information: (206) 684-4800.*
Zoo Atlanta	10.0	0.8	39	210	Gorillas of the Ford African Rain Forest, Masai Mara *for further information: (404) 624-5600.*

Note: NA = Not available.

Major Canadian Public Zoological Parks

Source: *World Almanac* questionnaire, 1998; budget in millions of dollars (Canadian), attendance in millions

Zoo	Budget	Attendance	Acres	Species	Major attractions
Assiniboine Park Zoo (Winnipeg)	$2.6	0.5	50	350	Kinsmen Discovery Centre, Tropical House, Monkey House *for further information: (204) 986-6921.*
Calgary	13.0	0.9	100	273	Canadian Wilds, Prehistoric Park, Northern Forests *for further information: (800) 588-9993.*
Granby Zoo (Quebec)	5.0	0.4	70	225	AFRIKA Pavilion, AMAZOO water park, Ile du Fort Magik *for further information: (877) GRANBYZOO.*
Toronto Zoo	23.1	1.2	710	477	African Savanna, White Lion, Komodo Dragons *for further information: (416) 392-5929.*

Top 50 American Kennel Club Registrations

Source: American Kennel Club, New York, NY; covers (new) dogs registered during calendar year shown

Breed	Rank 1997	Number registered 1997	Rank 1996	Number registered 1996
Labrador Retriever	1	158,366	1	149,505
Rottweiler	2	75,489	2	89,867
German Shepherd Dog	3	75,177	3	79,076
Golden Retriever	4	70,158	4	68,993
Poodle	5	54,773	6	56,803
Beagle	6	54,470	5	56,946
Dachshund	7	51,904	7	48,426
Cocker Spaniel	8	41,439	8	45,305
Yorkshire Terrier	9	41,283	9	40,216
Pomeranian	10	39,357	10	39,712
Shih Tzu	11	39,075	11	38,055
Chihuahua	12	38,926	12	36,562
Boxer	13	38,047	13	36,398
Miniature Schnauzer	14	32,351	16	31,834
Shetland Sheepdog	15	32,086	14	33,577
Siberian Husky	16	24,432	17	25,557
Dalmatian	17	22,726	15	32,972
Miniature Pinscher	18	22,297	18	20,355
Pug	19	20,082	19	18,398
Boston Terrier	20	18,185	21	17,816
Maltese	21	17,428	23	16,902
Doberman Pinscher	22	17,385	20	17,919
Basset Hound	23	17,152	22	17,032
Germ. Shorthaired Pointer	24	14,380	24	15,024
English Springer Spaniel	25	13,796	25	14,715
Bulldog	26	13,673	27	13,468
Pekingese	27	12,871	28	13,157
Bichon Frise	28	12,587	30	12,199
Great Dane	29	11,878	32	12,052
Collie	30	11,724	29	12,542
Lhasa Apso	31	11,223	33	11,903
Chinese Shar-Pei	32	10,772	31	12,178
Brittany	33	10,710	34	11,539
Akita	34	10,124	35	11,161
Chow Chow	35	9,536	26	13,587
W. Highland White Terrier	36	8,805	36	8,171
Pembroke Welsh Corgi	37	8,281	38	7,452
Saint Bernard	38	7,849	37	7,519
Weimaraner	39	7,701	39	7,314
Australian Shepherd	40	6,140	40	6,026
Mastiff	41	5,270	43	4,807
Chesapeake Bay Retriever	42	5,204	42	5,540
Scottish Terrier	43	5,151	41	5,578
Great Pyrenees	44	4,709	45	4,521
Cairn Terrier	45	4,423	46	4,256
Alaskan Malamute	46	4,409	44	4,616
Airedale Terrier	47	3,225	48	3,316
Samoyed	48	3,199	47	3,678
Newfoundland	49	3,075	50	2,984
Vizsla	50	2,992	54	2,738

Cat Breeds

Source: The Cat Fanciers' Association, Manasquan, NJ

Only a small percentage of house cats in the U.S. are pedigreed or registered with one of the official registering bodies, the largest of which is the Cat Fanciers' Assn., Inc., sponsor of 650 clubs. The Cat Fanciers' Assn. recognized 36 breeds as of Dec. 31, 1997 (in order of registration totals): Persian, Maine Coon, Siamese, Abyssinian, Exotic, Oriental, Scottish Fold, American Shorthair, Birman, Burmese, Tonkinese, Ocicat, Cornish Rex, Devon Rex, Russian Blue, British Shorthair, Norwegian Forest Cat, Manx, Somali, Ragdoll, Colorpoint Shorthair, Egyptian Mau, Japanese Bobtail, American Curl, Chartreux, Balinese, Turkish Angora, Singapura, Selkirk Rex, Javanese, Bombay, Korat, American Wirehair, Turkish Van, European Burmese, and Havana Brown.

Trees of the U.S.

Source: American Forests, Washington, DC, 1998

Approximately 825 native and naturalized species of trees are grown in the U.S. The oldest living tree is believed to be a bristlecone pine tree in California named Methuselah, estimated to be 4,700 years old. The world's largest known living tree, the General Sherman giant sequoia in California, weighs more than 6,167 tons—as much as 41 blue whales or 740 elephants.

American Forests recognizes and lists the "National Champion" (largest known, by total mass) of each U.S. tree species. Anyone can nominate candidates for the 1998-99 *National Register of Big Trees*; for information, write to American Forests, PO Box 2000, Washington, DC 20013, or check their website: http://www.amfor.org

Listed here, in alphabetical order, are ten National Champion trees selected by American Forests as worthy of note.

Selected National Champion Trees

Tree Type	Girth at 4.5 ft. (in.)	Height (ft.)	Crown Spread (ft.)	Total Points	Location
American Beech[1]	279	115	138	429	Harwood, MD
Black Willow	400	76	92	499	Grand Traverse County, MI
Coast Douglas-Fir	438	329	60	782	Coos County, OR
Coast Redwood[2]	867	313	101	1,205	Prairie Creek Redwoods State Park, CA
Giant Sequoia	998	275	107	1,300	Sequoia National Park, CA
Loblolly Pine	188	148	83	357	Warren, AR
Pinyon Pine	213	69	52	295	Cuba, NM
Sugar Maple	274	65	54	353	Kitzmiller, MD
Sugar Pine	442	232	29	681	Dorrington, CA
White Oak	382	96	119	508	Wye Mills State Park, MD

(1) Replaces American Elm, which was damaged by fire. (2) Remeasurement in 1997.

ARTS AND MEDIA

Some Notable Movies, Sept. 1997-Aug. 1998

MOVIE	STARS	DIRECTOR
Afterglow	Julie Christie, Nick Nolte, Lara Flynn Boyle	Alan Rudolph
Amistad	Morgan Freeman, Anthony Hopkins, Djimon Hounsou, Matthew McConaughey	Steven Spielberg
Apostle, The	Robert Duvall, Farrah Fawcett, Billy Bob Thornton, June Carter Cash, Miranda Richardson	Robert Duvall
Armageddon	Bruce Willis, Billy Bob Thornton, Liv Tyler, Ben Affleck, Will Patton	Michael Bay
As Good As It Gets	Jack Nicholson, Helen Hunt, Greg Kinnear	James L. Brooks
Boogie Nights	Mark Wahlberg, Julianne Moore, Burt Reynolds	Paul Thomas Anderson
Bulworth	Warren Beatty, Halle Berry, Don Cheadle, Oliver Platt, Paul Sorvino	Warren Beatty
Deconstructing Harry	Woody Allen, Kirstie Alley, Hazelle Goodman, Elisabeth Shue	Woody Allen
Deep Impact	Robert Duvall, Téa Leoni, Elijah Wood	Mimi Leder
Dr. Dolittle	Eddie Murphy, Ossie Davis, Oliver Platt	Betty Thomas
Ever After	Drew Barrymore, Anjelica Huston, Dougray Scott, Jeanne Moreau	Andy Tennant
Flubber	Robin Williams, Marcia Gay Harden, Christopher McDonald	Les Mayfield
Full Monty, The	Robert Carlyle, Tom Wilkinson, Mark Addy	Peter Cattaneo
Godzilla	Matthew Broderick, Jean Reno	Roland Emmerich
Good Will Hunting	Robin Williams, Matt Damon, Ben Affleck, Minnie Driver, Stellan Skarsgård	Gus Van Sant
Great Expectations	Ethan Hawke, Gwyneth Paltrow, Anne Bancroft, Robert DeNiro	Alfonso Cuaron
Horse Whisperer, The	Robert Redford, Kristin Scott Thomas	Robert Redford
How Stella Got Her Groove Back	Angela Bassett, Taye Diggs, Whoopi Goldberg	Kevin Rodney Sullivan
Jackie Brown	Pam Grier, Samuel L. Jackson, Robert Forster, Bridget Fonda, Michael Keaton, Robert DeNiro	Quentin Tarantino
L.A. Confidential	Kevin Spacey, Russell Crowe, Guy Pearce, James Cromwell, Kim Basinger	Curtis Hanson
Lethal Weapon 4	Mel Gibson, Danny Glover, Joe Pesci, Rene Russo, Chris Rock	Richard Donner
Lost in Space	Gary Oldman, William Hurt	Stephen Hopkins
Man in the Iron Mask, The	Leonardo DiCaprio, Jeremy Irons, John Malkovich, Gerard Depardieu, Gabriel Byrne	Randall Wallace
Mask of Zorro, The	Antonio Banderas, Anthony Hopkins, Catherine Zeta-Jones	Martin Campbell
Mercury Rising	Bruce Willis, Alec Baldwin	Harold Becker
MouseHunt	Nathan Lane, Lee Evans, Maury Chaykin, Christopher Walken	Gore Verbinski
Mrs. Brown	Judi Dench, Billy Connolly	John Madden
Mulan	Eddie Murphy, Pat Morita, Harvey Fierstein, Ming-Na Wen, June Foray, Lea Salonga, Donny Osmond	Barry Cook, Tony Bancroft
Negotiator, The	Samuel L. Jackson, Kevin Spacey	F. Gary Gray
Out of Sight	George Clooney, Jennifer Lopez	Steven Soderbergh
Perfect Murder, A	Michael Douglas, Gwyneth Paltrow, Viggo Mortensen	Andrew Davis
Parent Trap, The	Dennis Quaid, Natasha Richardson, Lindsay Lohan	Nancy Meyers
Primary Colors	John Travolta, Emma Thompson, Billy Bob Thornton, Adrian Lester	Mike Nichols
Saving Private Ryan	Tom Hanks, Edward Burns, Matt Damon, Tom Sizemore	Steven Spielberg
Scream 2	Neve Campbell, Courtney Cox, David Arquette, Jada Pinkett, Sarah Michelle Gellar, Jamie Kennedy	Wes Craven
Six Days, Seven Nights	Harrison Ford, Anne Heche	Ivan Reitman
Snake Eyes	Nicholas Cage, Gary Sinise	Brian DePalma
Sphere	Dustin Hoffman, Sharon Stone, Samuel L. Jackson	Barry Levinson
Sweet Hereafter, The	Ian Holm, Sarah Polley	Atom Egoyan
There's Something About Mary	Cameron Diaz, Matt Dillon, Ben Stiller	Bobby & Peter Farrelly
Titanic	Leonardo DiCaprio, Kate Winslet, Kathy Bates, Gloria Stuart	James Cameron
Tomorrow Never Dies	Pierce Brosnan, Jonathan Pryce, Michelle Yeoh, Teri Hatcher	Roger Spottiswoode
Truman Show, The	Jim Carrey, Ed Harris, Harry Shearer	Peter Weir
Twilight	Paul Newman, Susan Sarandon, Gene Hackman	Robert Benton
Ulee's Gold	Peter Fonda, Patricia Richardson, Christine Dunford, Tom Wood II	Victor Nunez
U.S. Marshals	Tommy Lee Jones, Wesley Snipes, Robert Downey Jr.	Stuart Baird
Wag the Dog	Dustin Hoffman, Robert DeNiro, Anne Heche, Denis Leary	Barry Levinson
Why Do Fools Fall in Love	Halle Berry, Vivica A. Fox, Lela Rochon, Larenz Tate	Gregory Nava
Wings of the Dove, The	Helena Bonham Carter, Linus Roache, Alison Elliott	Iain Softley
X-Files, The	David Duchovny, Gillian Anderson	Rob Bowman

Top 50 Movies, 1997

Source: *Variety*, Jan. 26-Feb. 1, 1998; box-office grosses in the U.S. and Canada during calendar year 1997

Rank/Title	Title	Gross (millions)
1.	Men in Black	$250.0
2.	The Lost World: Jurassic Park	229.1
3.	Liar Liar	181.4
4.	Air Force One	171.9
5.	Star Wars (reissue)	138.3
6.	My Best Friend's Wedding	126.7
7.	Titanic	112.6
8.	Face/Off	112.3
9.	Batman & Robin	107.3
10.	George of the Jungle	105.2
11.	Con Air	101.1
12.	Contact	100.9
13.	Hercules	90.1
14.	Jerry Maguire	88.3
15.	Scream	78.6
16.	Flubber	77.2
17.	Conspiracy Theory	76.1
18.	Scream 2	75.6
19.	Tomorrow Never Dies	$73.3
20.	I Know What You Did Last Summer	70.3
21.	The Empire Strikes Back (reissue)	67.6
22.	Dante's Peak	67.2
23.	Anaconda	65.9
24.	The Fifth Element	63.8
25.	In & Out	63.1
26.	The Saint	61.4
27.	Michael	60.2
28.	Jungle 2 Jungle	59.9
29.	Kiss the Girls	59.7
30.	Devil's Advocate	59.0
31.	Spawn	54.9
32.	The English Patient	54.8
33.	Starship Troopers	54.2
34.	Austin Powers: International Man of Mystery	53.9
35.	The Jackal	$52.6
36.	Anastasia	50.2
37.	Breakdown	50.2
38.	Absolute Power	50.1
39.	Evita	49.6
40.	Volcano	49.3
41.	Speed 2: Cruise Control	48.6
42.	The Game	48.3
43.	G.I. Jane	48.2
44.	Alien Resurrection	45.5
45.	Return of the Jedi (reissue)	45.5
46.	Cop Land	44.9
47.	Bean	44.9
48.	Nothing to Lose	44.5
49.	John Grisham's The Rainmaker	43.6
50.	Soul Food	43.2

All-Time Top 50 American Movies Through 1997

Source: *Variety* magazine

Rank	Title/Date	Gross[1] (millions)
1.	Star Wars (1977)	$461.0
2.	Titanic (1997)	427.0
3.	E.T.: The Extra-Terrestrial (1982)	399.8
4.	Jurassic Park (1993)	357.1
5.	Forrest Gump (1994)	329.7
6.	The Lion King (1994)	312.9
7.	Return of the Jedi (1983)	309.2
8.	Independence Day (1996)	306.2
9.	The Empire Strikes Back (1980)	290.3
10.	Home Alone (1990)	285.8
11.	Jaws (1975)	260.0
12.	Batman (1989)	251.2
13.	Men in Black (1997)	250.0
14.	Raiders of the Lost Ark (1981)	242.4
15.	Twister (1996)	241.7
16.	Ghostbusters (1984)	238.6
17.	Beverly Hills Cop (1984)	234.8
18.	The Lost World: Jurassic Park (1997)	$229.1
19.	Mrs. Doubtfire (1993)	219.2
20.	Ghost (1990)	217.6
21.	Aladdin (1992)	217.4
22.	Back to the Future (1985)	208.2
23.	Terminator 2 (1991)	204.8
24.	Indiana Jones and the Last Crusade (1989)	197.2
25.	Gone with the Wind (1939)	191.9
26.	Toy Story (1995)	191.8
27.	Dances With Wolves (1990)	184.2
28.	Batman Forever (1995)	184.0
29.	The Fugitive (1993)	183.9
30.	Liar Liar (1997)	179.5
31.	Mission: Impossible (1996)	181.0
32.	Indiana Jones and the Temple of Doom (1984)	179.9
33.	Pretty Woman (1990)	178.4
34.	Tootsie (1982)	$177.2
35.	Top Gun (1986)	176.8
36.	Snow White and the Seven Dwarfs (1937)	175.3
37.	Crocodile Dundee (1986)	174.8
38.	Home Alone 2 (1992)	173.6
39.	Rain Man (1988)	172.8
40.	Air Force One (1997)	172.4
41.	Apollo 13 (1995)	172.1
42.	Three Men and a Baby (1987)	167.8
43.	Robin Hood: Prince of Thieves (1991)	165.5
44.	The Exorcist (1973)	165.0
45.	Batman Returns (1992)	162.8
46.	The Sound of Music (1965)	160.5
47.	The Firm (1993)	158.3
48.	Fatal Attraction (1987)	156.6
49.	The Sting (1973)	156.0
50.	Close Encounters of the Third Kind (1977)	155.7

(1) Gross is in absolute dollars based on box office sales in the U.S. and Canada. Ticket prices favor recent films, but older films have the advantage of reissues.

MILLENNIUM FACT BOX

100 Best American Movies of All Time

Source: American Film Institute

This much-debated list was compiled in 1998 by the American Film Institute, on the basis of ballots sent to 1,500 figures in the film world, including screenwriters, directors, and critics, as well as to President Bill Clinton and Vice President Al Gore. Those judging were asked to select from a pool of 400 titles picked by the institute. Criteria for judging included historical significance, critical recognition and awards, and popularity as measured by box office, syndication, video sales, and video rental revenues.

The year when each film was first released is in parentheses.

1. Citizen Kane (1941)
2. Casablanca (1942)
3. The Godfather (1972)
4. Gone With the Wind (1939)
5. Lawrence of Arabia (1962)
6. The Wizard of Oz (1939)
7. The Graduate (1967)
8. On the Waterfront (1954)
9. Schindler's List (1993)
10. Singin' in the Rain (1952)
11. It's a Wonderful Life (1946)
12. Sunset Boulevard (1950)
13. The Bridge on the River Kwai (1957)
14. Some Like It Hot (1959)
15. Star Wars (1977)
16. All About Eve (1950)
17. The African Queen (1951)
18. Psycho (1960)
19. Chinatown (1974)
20. One Flew Over the Cuckoo's Nest (1975)
21. The Grapes of Wrath (1940)
22. 2001: A Space Odyssey (1968)
23. The Maltese Falcon (1941)
24. Raging Bull (1980)
25. E.T.: The Extra-Terrestrial (1982)
26. Dr. Strangelove (1964)
27. Bonnie and Clyde (1967)
28. Apocalypse Now (1979)
29. Mr. Smith Goes to Washington (1939)
30. Treasure of the Sierra Madre (1948)
31. Annie Hall (1977)
32. The Godfather Part II (1974)
33. High Noon (1952)
34. To Kill a Mockingbird (1962)
35. It Happened One Night (1934)
36. Midnight Cowboy (1969)
37. The Best Years of Our Lives (1946)
38. Double Indemnity (1944)
39. Doctor Zhivago (1965)
40. North by Northwest (1959)
41. West Side Story (1961)
42. Rear Window (1954)
43. King Kong (1933)
44. The Birth of a Nation (1915)
45. A Streetcar Named Desire (1951)
46. A Clockwork Orange (1971)
47. Taxi Driver (1976)
48. Jaws (1975)
49. Snow White and the Seven Dwarfs (1937)
50. Butch Cassidy and the Sundance Kid (1969)
51. The Philadelphia Story (1940)
52. From Here to Eternity (1953)
53. Amadeus (1984)
54. All Quiet on the Western Front (1930)
55. The Sound of Music (1965)
56. M*A*S*H (1970)
57. The Third Man (1949)
58. Fantasia (1940)
59. Rebel Without a Cause (1955)
60. Raiders of the Lost Ark (1981)
61. Vertigo (1958)
62. Tootsie (1982)
63. Stagecoach (1939)
64. Close Encounters of the Third Kind (1977)
65. The Silence of the Lambs (1991)
66. Network (1976)
67. The Manchurian Candidate (1962)
68. An American in Paris (1951)
69. Shane (1953)
70. The French Connection (1971)
71. Forrest Gump (1994)
72. Ben-Hur (1959)
73. Wuthering Heights (1939)
74. The Gold Rush (1925)
75. Dances With Wolves (1990)
76. City Lights (1931)
77. American Graffiti (1973)
78. Rocky (1976)
79. The Deer Hunter (1978)
80. The Wild Bunch (1969)
81. Modern Times (1936)
82. Giant (1956)
83. Platoon (1986)
84. Fargo (1996)
85. Duck Soup (1933)
86. Mutiny on the Bounty (1935)
87. Frankenstein (1931)
88. Easy Rider (1969)
89. Patton (1970)
90. The Jazz Singer (1927)
91. My Fair Lady (1964)
92. A Place in the Sun (1951)
93. The Apartment (1960)
94. Goodfellas (1990)
95. Pulp Fiction (1994)
96. The Searchers (1956)
97. Bringing Up Baby (1938)
98. Unforgiven (1992)
99. Guess Who's Coming to Dinner (1967)
100. Yankee Doodle Dandy (1942)

Most Popular Movie Videos

Source: Alexander & Associates/Video Flash, New York, NY

Top 10 Rentals, 1997

1. The Rock
2. Jerry Maguire
3. Independence Day
4. The Nutty Professor
5. Scream
6. Liar Liar
7. Ransom
8. Phenomenon
9. A Time to Kill
10. Men in Black

All Time Top 10 Rentals[1]

1. Top Gun
2. Pretty Woman
3. Home Alone
4. The Little Mermaid
5. Ghost
6. Beauty and the Beast
7. Terminator 2: Judgment Day
8. Forrest Gump
9. Lion King
10. Dances With Wolves

Top 10 Sales, 1997

1. Independence Day
2. Bambi
3. The Hunchback of Notre Dame
4. Space Jam
5. 101 Dalmatians (live)
6. Jerry Maguire
7. Sleeping Beauty
8. Toy Story
9. Men in Black
10. The Lost World: Jurassic Park

All Time Top 10 Sales[2]

1. The Lion King
2. Aladdin
3. Cinderella
4. Beauty and the Beast
5. Snow White and the Seven Dwarfs
6. Forrest Gump
7. Toy Story
8. 101 Dalmatians (animated)
9. Jurassic Park
10. Pocahontas

(1) Rented Mar. 1, 1987-Dec. 30, 1997. (2) Sold Feb. 16, 1988-Dec. 30, 1997.

National Film Registry, 1989-97

Source: National Film Registry, Library of Congress

"Culturally, historically, or esthetically significant" films placed on the National Film Registry, Library of Congress. Films selected in 1997 are indicated by an * after the year of release.

Adam's Rib (1949)
The Adventures of Robin Hood (1938)
The African Queen (1951)
All About Eve (1950)
All That Heaven Allows (1955)
All Quiet on the Western Front (1930)
An American in Paris (1951)
American Graffiti (1973)
A Movie (1958)
Annie Hall (1977)
The Apartment (1960)
The Awful Truth (1937)
Badlands (1973)
The Band Wagon (1953)
The Bank Dick (1940)
The Battle of San Pietro (1945)
Ben-Hur (1926)*
The Best Years of Our Lives (1946)
Big Business (1929)
The Big Parade (1925)
The Big Sleep (1946)*
The Birth of a Nation (1915)
The Black Pirate (1926)
Blacksmith Scene (1893)
Blade Runner (1982)
The Blood of Jesus (1941)
Bonnie and Clyde (1967)
The Bridge on the River Kwai (1957)*
Bringing Up Baby (1938)
Broken Blossoms (1919)
Cabaret (1972)
Carmen Jones (1954)
Casablanca (1942)
Castro Street (1966)
Cat People (1942)
Chan Is Missing (1982)
The Cheat (1915)
Chinatown (1974)
Chulas Fronteras (1976)
Citizen Kane (1941)
City Lights (1931)
The Conversation (1974)
The Cool World (1963)
Cops (1922)*
A Corner in Wheat (1909)
The Crowd (1928)
Czechoslovakia 1968 (1968)*
David Holzman's Diary (1968)
The Day the Earth Stood Still (1951)
The Deer Hunter (1978)
Destry Rides Again (1939)
Detour (1946)
Dodsworth (1936)
Dog Star Man (1964)
Double Indemnity (1944)
Dr. Strangelove (or, How I Learned to Stop Worrying and Love the Bomb) (1964)
Duck Soup (1933)
Eaux D'Artifice (1953)
El Norte (1983)
E.T.: The Extra-Terrestrial (1982)
The Exploits of Elaine (1914)
Fantasia (1940)
Fatty's Tintype Tangle (1915)
Flash Gordon serial (1936)
Footlight Parade (1933)
Force of Evil (1948)
The Forgotten Frontier (1931)
The Four Horsemen of the Apocalypse (1921)
Frankenstein (1931)
Frank Film (1973)
Freaks (1932)
The Freshman (1925)
Fury (1936)
The General (1927)
Gerald McBoing Boing (1951)
Gertie the Dinosaur (1914)
Gigi (1958)
The Godfather (1972)
The Godfather, Part II (1974)
The Gold Rush (1925)
Gone With the Wind (1939)
The Graduate (1967)
The Grapes of Wrath (1940)
Grass (1925)*
The Great Dictator (1940)*
The Great Train Robbery (1903)
Greed (1924)
Harlan County, U.S.A. (1976)
Harold and Maude (1972)*
The Heiress (1949)
Hell's Hinges (1916)
High Noon (1952)
High School (1968)
Hindenburg Disaster Newsreel Footage (1937)*
His Girl Friday (1940)
Hospital (1970)
The Hospital (1971)
How Green Was My Valley (1941)
How the West Was Won (1962)*
The Hustler (1961)*
I Am a Fugitive From a Chain Gang (1932)
Intolerance (1916)
Invasion of the Body Snatchers (1956)
It Happened One Night (1934)
It's a Wonderful Life (1946)
The Italian (1915)
Jammin' the Blues (1944)
The Jazz Singer (1927)
Killer of Sheep (1977)
King Kong (1933)
Knute Rockne, All American (1940)*
The Lady Eve (1941)
Lassie Come Home (1943)
The Last of the Mohicans (1920)
Lawrence of Arabia (1962)
The Learning Tree (1969)
Letter From an Unknown Woman (1948)
The Life and Death of 9413—A Hollywood Extra (1928)*
Life and Times of Rosie the Riveter (1980)
The Little Fugitive (1953)*
Louisiana Story (1948)
Love Me Tonight (1932)
Magical Maestro (1952)
The Magnificent Ambersons (1942)
The Maltese Falcon (1941)
The Manchurian Candidate (1962)
Manhattan (1921)
March of Time: Inside Nazi Germany—1938 (1938)
Marty (1955)
M*A*S*H (1970)
Mean Streets (1973)*
Meet Me in St. Louis (1944)
Meshes of the Afternoon (1943)
Midnight Cowboy (1969)
Mildred Pierce (1945)
Modern Times (1936)
Morocco (1930)
Motion Painting No. 1 (1947)*
Mr. Smith Goes to Washington (1939)
The Music Box (1932)*
My Darling Clementine (1946)
The Naked Spur (1953)*
Nanook of the North (1922)
Nashville (1975)
A Night at the Opera (1935)
The Night of the Hunter (1955)
Ninotchka (1939)
North by Northwest (1959)
Nothing but a Man (1964)
One Flew Over the Cuckoo's Nest (1975)
On the Waterfront (1954)
The Outlaw Josey Wales (1976)
Out of the Past (1947)
Paths of Glory (1957)
The Philadelphia Story (1940)
Pinocchio (1940)
A Place in the Sun (1951)
Point of Order (1964)
The Poor Little Rich Girl (1917)
Primary (1960)
The Prisoner of Zenda (1937)
The Producers (1968)
Psycho (1960)
Pull My Daisy (1959)
Raging Bull (1980)
Rear Window (1954)*
Rebel Without a Cause (1955)
Red River (1948)
Republic Steel Strike Riots Newsreel Footage (1937)*
Return of the Secaucus 7 (1980)*
Ride the High Country (1962)
Rip Van Winkle (1896)
The River (1937)
Road to Morocco (1942)
Safety Last (1923)
Salesman (1969)
Salt of the Earth (1954)
Scarface (1932)
The Searchers (1956)
Seventh Heaven (1927)
Shadow of a Doubt (1943)
Shadows (1959)
Shane (1953)
She Done Him Wrong (1933)
Sherlock, Jr. (1924)
Shock Corridor (1963)
Show Boat (1936)
Singin' in the Rain (1952)
Snow White (1933)
Snow White and the Seven Dwarfs (1937)
Some Like It Hot (1959)
Stagecoach (1939)
Star Wars (1977)
Sullivan's Travels (1941)
Sunrise (1927)
Sunset Boulevard (1950)
Sweet Smell of Success (1957)
Tabu (1933)
Taxi Driver (1976)
Tevye (1939)
The Thief of Bagdad (1924)
The Thin Man (1934)*

To Be or Not To Be (1942)
To Fly (1976)
To Kill a Mockingbird (1962)
Topaz (1943-45)
Top Hat (1935)
Touch of Evil (1958)
The Treasure of the Sierra Madre (1948)
Trouble in Paradise (1932)
Tulips Shall Grow (1942)*
2001: A Space Odyssey (1968)
Verbena Tragica (1939)
Vertigo (1958)
West Side Story (1961)*
What's Opera, Doc? (1957)
Where Are My Children? (1916)
The Wind (1928)
Wings (1927)*
Within Our Gates (1920)
The Wizard of Oz (1939)
A Woman Under the Influence (1974)
Woodstock (1970)
Yankee Doodle Dandy (1942)
Zapruder Film (1963)

Record Long-Run Broadway Plays[1]

Source: The League of American Theatres and Producers, Inc., New York, NY

Title	Performances	Title	Performances	Title	Performances
*Cats	6,533	Magic Show	1,920	Mame	1,508
A Chorus Line	6,137	Gemini	1,819	Grease (revival)	1,505
Oh! Calcutta! (revival)	5,962	Deathtrap	1,793	Same Time, Next Year	1,453
*Les Miserables	4,615	Harvey	1,775	Arsenic and Old Lace	1,444
*The Phantom of the Opera	4,318	Dancin'	1,774	The Sound of Music (original)	1,443
42nd Street	3,485	La Cage aux Folles	1,761	How to Succeed in Business Without Really Trying (original)	1,417
Grease (original)	3,388	Hair	1,750	Me and My Girl	1,409
Fiddler on the Roof	3,242	*Beauty and the Beast	1,720	Hellzapoppin	1,404
Life With Father	3,224	The Wiz	1,672	The Music Man	1,375
Tobacco Road	3,182	Born Yesterday	1,642	Smokey Joe's Café	1,357
*Miss Saigon	2,980	Crazy for You	1,638	Funny Girl	1,348
Hello Dolly	2,844	Ain't Misbehavin'	1,604	Mummenchanz	1,326
My Fair Lady	2,717	The Best Little Whorehouse in Texas	1,584	Oh! Calcutta! (original)	1,314
Annie	2,377	Mary, Mary	1,572	Brighton Beach Memoirs	1,299
Man of La Mancha	2,329	Evita	1,567	Angel Street	1,295
Abie's Irish Rose	2,327	The Voice of the Turtle	1,557	Lightnin'	1,291
Oklahoma!	2,212	Barefoot in the Park	1,530		
Pippin	1,944	Dreamgirls	1,521		
South Pacific	1,925				

(1) Number of performances through May 31, 1998. * Still running May 31, 1998.

Broadway Season Statistics, 1959-98

Source: The League of American Theatres and Producers, Inc., New York, NY

Season	Gross (mil $)	Attendance (mil)	Playing Weeks	New Productions
1959-1960	46	7.9	1,156	58
1960-1961	44	7.7	1,210	48
1961-1962	44	6.8	1,166	53
1962-1963	44	7.4	1,134	54
1963-1964	40	6.8	1,107	63
1964-1965	50	8.2	1,250	67
1965-1966	54	9.6	1,295	68
1966-1967	55	9.3	1,269	69
1967-1968	59	9.5	1,259	74
1968-1969	58	8.6	1,209	67
1969-1970	53	7.1	1,047	62
1970-1971	55	7.4	1,107	49
1971-1972	52	6.5	1,157	55
1972-1973	45	5.4	889	55
1973-1974	46	5.7	907	43
1974-1975	57	6.6	1,101	54
1975-1976	71	7.3	1,136	55
1976-1977	93	8.8	1,349	54
1977-1978	114	9.6	1,433	42
1978-1979	134	9.6	1,542	50
1979-1980	146	9.6	1,540	61
1980-1981	197	11.0	1,544	60
1981-1982	223	10.1	1,455	48
1982-1983	209	8.4	1,258	50
1983-1984	227	7.9	1,097	36
1984-1985	208	7.3	1,075	33
1985-1986	190	6.5	1,045	33
1986-1987	206	7.0	1,038	41
1987-1988	252	8.1	1,116	32
1988-1989	265	8.0	1,097	30
1989-1990	282	8.0	1,061	35
1990-1991	267	7.3	970	28
1991-1992	293	7.4	903	37
1992-1993	328	7.9	1,019	33
1993-1994	356	8.1	1,061	37
1994-1995	406	9.0	1,118	29
1995-1996	436	9.5	1,146	38
1996-1997	499	10.6	1,347	37
1997-1998	558	11.5	1,442	33

Some Notable Broadway Theater Openings, 1997-98 Season

A View From the Bridge. Revival of Arthur Miller's 1965 drama. Directed by Michael Mayer. With Anthony LaPaglia, Caren Browning, and Brittany Murphy.

Art. A comedy about 3 friends and their differing opinions about a piece of artwork purchased by one of them. By Yasmina Reza, translated by Christopher Hampton. Directed by Matthew Warchus. With Alan Alda, Victor Garber, and Alfred Molina.

The Beauty Queen of Leenane. A drama about a manipulative mother and her lonely, middle-aged daughter in Ireland. By Martin McDonagh. Directed by Garry Hynes. With Marie Mullen, Anna Manahan, Brian F. O'Byrne, and Tom Murphy.

Cabaret. A revival of the 1966 Kander and Ebb musical production set in Germany at the start of the Third Reich. Book by Joe Masteroff. Directed by Sam Mendes. With Natasha Richardson, Alan Cummings, Ron Rifkin, and Mary Louise Wilson.

The Diary of Anne Frank. Adaptation by Wendy Kesselman. Directed by James Lapine. With Natalie Portman, Georger Hearn, Linda Lavin, Harris Yulin, Austin Pendleton, Sophie Hayden, Missy Yager, and Jonathan Kaplan.

The Lion King. Adapted from 1994 Walt Disney film about a lion cub destined to be king. Book adapted by Roger Allers and Irene Mecchi. Music and lyrics by Elton John and Tim Rice. Directed by Julie Taymor. With John Vickery, Samuel E. Wright, Max Casella, Geoff Hoyle, Tsidii Le Loka, and Tom Robbins.

Ragtime: The Musical. Based on E.L. Doctorow's novel about 3 families in turn-of-the-century America. Book by Terrence McNally. Music by Stephen Flaherty. Lyrics by Lynn Ahrens. Directed by Frank Galati. With Brian Stokes Mitchell, Peter Friedman, Marin Mazzie, Audra McDonald, Mark Jacoby, and Judy Kaye.

The Scarlet Pimpernel. Musical based on novels by Baroness Orczy; set during the French Revolution. Book and lyrics by Nan Knighton. Music by Frank Wildhorn. Directed by Peter Hunt. With Christine Andreas, Terrence Mann, and Douglas Sills.

The Sound of Music. Revival of the 1959 musical set in Austria on the eve of WW II about a naval captain, his 7 children, and their governess. Book by Howard Lindsay and Russel Crouse. Music by Richard Rodgers. Lyrics by Oscar Hammerstein II. Directed by Susan H. Schulman. With Rebecca Luker and Michael Siberry.

Some Notable Nonprofit Professional Theater Companies in the U.S.

Source: Theatre Communications Group, Inc.

Theater Company	City	State
Actors Theatre of Louisville	Louisville	KY
Alabama Shakespeare Festival	Montgomery	AL
Alley Theater	Houston	TX
Alliance Theatre Company	Atlanta	GA
American Conservatory Theatre	San Francisco	CA
American Repertory Theatre	Cambridge	MA
Arena Stage	Washington	DC
Berkeley Repertory Theatre	Berkeley	CA
Center Stage	Baltimore	MD
Children's Theatre Company, The	Minneapolis	MN
Cincinnati Playhouse in the Park	Cincinnati	OH
Cleveland Play House, The	Cleveland	OH
Denver Center Theatre Company	Denver	CO
Goodman Theatre	Chicago	IL
Guthrie Theater, The	Minneapolis	MN
Hartford Stage Company	Hartford	CT
Huntington Theatre Company	Boston	MA
Lincoln Center Theater	New York	NY
Manhattan Theatre Club	New York	NY
Mark Taper Forum	Los Angeles	CA
McCarter Theatre	New Brunswick	NJ
Milwaukee Repertory Theater	Milwaukee	WI
Oregon Shakespeare Festival	Ashland	OR
People's Light and Theatre Company	Malvern	PA
Pittsburgh Public Theater	Pittsburgh	PA
Roundabout Theatre Company	New York	NY
Seattle Repertory Theatre	Seattle	WA
Shakespeare Theatre	Washington	DC
South Coast Repertory	Costa Mesa	CA
Steppenwolf Theatre Company	Chicago	IL
TheatreWorks/USA	New York	NY

U.S. Symphony Orchestras[1]

Source: American Symphony Orchestra League, 1156 Fifteenth St. NW, Suite 800, Washington, DC 20005; data as of July 1998

Symphony Orchestra[2]	Music Director[3]
Alabama Symphony (AL)	Mark Gibson
American (NY)	Leon Botstein
Atlanta (GA)	Yoel Levi
Austin (TX)	Peter Bay
Baltimore (MD)	David Zinman
Boston (MA)	Seiji Ozawa
Brooklyn Philharmonic (NY)	Robert Spano
Buffalo Philharmonic (NY)	Maximiano Valdes
Charlotte (NC)	Peter McCoppin
Chicago (IL)	Daniel Barenboim
Cincinnati (OH)	Jesus Lopez-Cobos
Cleveland (OH)	Christoph von Dohnányi
Colorado (Denver)	Marin Alsop
Colorado Springs (CO)	Yaacov Bergman
Columbus (OH)	Alessandro Siciliani
Dallas (TX)	Andrew Litton
Dayton Philharmonic (OH)	Neal Gittleman
Detroit (MI)	Neeme Jarvi
Florida Orchestra (Tampa)	Jahja Ling
Florida Philharmonic (Ft. Lauderdale)	James Judd
Florida Symphonic Pops (Boca Raton)	Crafton Beck
Fort Wayne Philharmonic (IN)	Edvard Tchivzhel
Fort Worth (TX)	John Giordano
Grand Rapids (MI)	Catherine Comet
Grant Park (Chicago, IL)	—
Hartford (CT)	Michael Lankester
Houston (TX)	Christoph Eschenbach
Indianapolis (IN)	Raymond Leppard
Jacksonville (FL)	Roger Nierenberg
Kansas City (MO)	William McGlaughlin
Knoxville (TN)	Kirk Trevor
Long Beach (CA)	JoAnn Falletta
Los Angeles Chamber Orch. (CA)	Jeffrey Kahane
Los Angeles Philharmonic (CA)	Esa-Pekka Salonen
Louisiana Philharmonic (New Orleans)	Klauspeter Seibel
Louisville Orchestra (KY)	Max Bragado-Darman
Memphis (TN)	Alan Balter
Milwaukee (WI)	Andreas Delfs
Minnesota (Minneapolis)	Eiji Oue
Naples Philharmonic (FL)	Christopher Seaman
Nashville Symphony (TN)	Kenneth S. Schermerhorn
National (Washington, DC)	Leonard Slatkin
New Haven (CT)	Michael Palmer
New Jersey (Newark)	Zdenek Macal
New Mexico (Albuquerque)	David Lockington
New World Symphony (Miami Beach, FL)	Michael Tilson Thomas
New York Philharmonic (NYC)	Kurt Masur
New York Pops (NY)	Skitch Henderson
North Carolina Symphony (Raleigh)	Gerhardt Zimmermann
Oklahoma City Philharmonic (OK)	Joel A. Levine
Omaha Symphony (NE)	Victor Yampolsky
Oregon Symphony (Portland)	James DePreist
Pacific Symphony (Santa Ana, CA)	Carl St. Clair
Philadelphia (PA)	Wolfgang Sawallisch
Philharmonia Baroque (CA)	Nicholas McGegan
Phoenix (AZ)	Hermann Michael
Pittsburgh (PA)	Mariss Jansons
Portland (ME)	Toshiyuki Shimada
Richmond Symphony (VA)	George Manahan
Rochester Philharmonic Orch. (NY)	Christopher Seaman
St. Louis (MO)	Hans Vonk
St. Paul Chamber Orch. (MN)	Hugh Wolff
San Antonio (TX)	Christopher Wilkins
San Francisco (CA)	Michael Tilson Thomas
San Jose (CA)	Leonid Grin
Savannah (GA)	Philip B. Greenberg
Seattle (WA)	Gerard Schwarz
Spokane (WA)	Fabio Mechetti
Syracuse (NY)	Fabio Mechetti
Tucson (AZ)	George Hanson
Tulsa Philharmonic (OK)	Kenneth Jean
Utah (Salt Lake City)	Keith Lockhart
Virginia Symphony (Norfolk)	JoAnn Falletta
West Virginia (Charleston)	Thomas Conlin

(1) Includes only orchestras with annual expenses $2 mil or greater. (2) Orchestra name = place name + Symphony Orchestra, unless otherwise indicated. (3) General title; listed is highest-ranking member of conducting personnel. — indicates vacancy.

U.S. Opera Companies With Budgets of $1 Million or More

Source: OPERA America, 1156 15th Street NW, Washington, DC 20005-1704; July 1998

Academy of Vocal Arts (Phila., PA); K. James McDowell, dir.
American Musical Theatre of San Jose (CA); Dianna Shuster, art. dir.
American Opera Music Theater Co. (New York, NY); Diana Corto, art. dir.
Arizona Opera (Tucson); David Speers, gen. dir.
Aspen Opera Theater Center (CO); Robert Harth, pres./ceo
Atlanta Opera (GA); Alfred Kennedy, exec. dir.
Austin Lyric Opera (TX); Joseph McClain, gen. dir.
Baltimore Opera Company (MD); Michael Harrison, gen. dir.
Boston Lyric Opera Company (MA); Janice Mancini Del Sesto, gen. dir.
Brooklyn Academy of Music (NY); Harvey Lichtenstein, pres./exec. prod.
Central City Opera (Denver, CO); Pelham Pearce, mng. dir.
Chicago Opera Theater (IL); Mark Tiarks, gen. dir.
Cincinnati Opera (OH); Patricia K. Beggs, mng. dir.
Civic Light Opera (Pittsburgh, PA); Charles Gray, exec. dir.
Cleveland Opera (OH); David Bamberger, gen. dir.
Connecticut Opera (Hartford); George D. Osborne, gen. dir.
Dallas Opera (TX); Plato Karayanis, gen. dir.
Dayton Opera (OH); Ardith Hamilton, mng. dir.
Florentine Opera Company (Milwaukee, WI); Dennis Hanthorn, gen. dir.
Florida Grand Opera (Miami, FL); Robert Heuer, gen. dir./ceo
Fort Worth Opera (TX); William Walker, gen. dir.
Glimmerglass Opera (Cooperstown, NY); Esther Nelson, gen. dir.
Goodspeed Opera House (East Haddam, CT); Michael Price, exec. dir.
Hawaii Opera Theatre (Honolulu, HI); Henry G. Akina, gen./art. dir.
Houston Grand Opera (TX); David Gockley, gen. dir.
Indianapolis Opera Company (IN); John C. Pickett, exec. dir.
Kentucky Opera (Louisville); Deborah S. Sandler, gen. dir.
L.A. Opera (CA); Peter Hemmings, gen. dir.

Lyric Opera of Kansas City (MO); Evan R. Luskin, gen. dir.
Lyric Opera of Chicago (IL); William Mason, gen. dir.
Metro Lyric Opera (Allenhurst, NJ); Era Tognoli, gen./art. dir.
Metropolitan Opera (New York, NY); Joseph Volpe, gen. mgr.
Michigan Opera Theatre (Detroit); David DiChiera, gen. dir.
Minnesota Opera (Minneapolis); Kevin Smith, gen. dir.
New York City Opera (NY); Paul Kellogg, gen. dir.
New Jersey State Opera (Newark); Alfredo Silipigni, art. dir.
New Orleans Opera Association (LA); Robert Tannenbaum, gen. dir.
Ohio Light Opera (Wooster); James Stuart, art. dir.
Opera Carolina (Charlotte, NC); James W. Wright, pres./gen. dir.
Opera Colorado (Denver, CO); Stephen Seifert, exec. dir.
Opera/Columbus (Columbus, OH); William F. Russell, gen. dir.
Opera Company of Boston, Inc. (MA); Sarah Caldwell, art. dir.
Opera Company of Phil. (PA); Robert B. Driver, gen. dir.
Opera Delaware (Wilmington); Leland P. Kimball III, gen. dir.
Opera Festival of New Jersey (Princeton); Deborah S. Sandler, gen. dir.
Opera Grand Rapids (MI); Robert Lyall, gen. dir.
Opera Memphis (TN); Michael Ching, gen./art. dir.
Opera Omaha (NE); Jane Hill, exec. dir.
Opera Pacific (Santa Ana, CA); Martin Hubbard, exec. dir.
Opera San Jose (CA); Irene Dalis, gen. dir.
Opera Theatre of St. Louis (MO); Charles MacKay, gen. dir.
Orlando Opera (FL); Robert Swedberg, gen. dir.
Palm Beach Opera (FL); Herbert P. Benn, gen. dir.
Pittsburgh Opera (PA); Mark Weinstein, exec. dir.
Portland Opera (OR); Robert Bailey, gen. dir.
San Diego Opera (CA); Ian D. Campbell, gen. dir.
San Francisco Opera (CA); Lotfi Mansouri, gen. dir.
San Bernardino Civic Light Opera Association (CA); Keith Stava, gen. mgr.
San Diego Civic Light Opera Association, Inc. (CA); Cinda Lucas, bd. dirs.
Santa Barbara Civic Light Opera (CA); Paul Iannaccone, exec. prod.
Santa Fe Opera (NM); John Crosby, gen. dir.
Sarasota Opera (FL); Deane Allyn, exec. dir.
Seattle Opera (WA); Speight Jenkins, gen. dir.
Skylight Opera Theatre (Milwaukee, WI); Joan Lounsbery, mng. dir.
Tulsa Opera (OK); Carol I. Crawford, gen./art. dir.
Utah Festival Opera Company (Logan); Michael Ballam, gen. dir.
Utah Opera (Salt Lake City); Anne Ewers, gen. dir.
Virginia Opera (Norfolk); Peter Mark, gen./art. dir.
Washington Opera (DC); Patricia Mossel, exec. dir.
West Virginia Symphony Orchestra (Charleston); Paul A. Helfrich, exec. dir.

Some Notable U.S. Dance Companies

Source: DanceUSA

Organization	City	State
African-American Dance Ensemble	Durham	NC
Alabama Ballet	Birmingham	AL
Alvin Ailey American Dance Theater	New York	NY
American Ballet Theatre	New York	NY
American Repertory Ballet Company	New Brunswick	NJ
The Atlanta Ballet, Inc.	Atlanta	GA
Ballet Arizona	Phoenix	AZ
Ballet Austin	Austin	TX
Ballet Concierto de Puerto Rico	Santurce	PR
Ballet Hispanico of New York	New York	NY
Ballet Internationale, Inc.	Indianapolis	IN
Ballet Memphis	Memphis	TN
Ballet Omaha	Omaha	NE
Ballet West	Salt Lake City	UT
BalletMet Columbus	Columbus	OH
Betty Salamun's DANCECIRCUS	Milwaukee	WI
Bill T. Jones/Arnie Zane Dance Company	New York	NY
Boston Ballet	Boston	MA
Caribbean Dance Company of the Virgin Islands	St. Croix	USVI
Carolina Ballet	Raleigh	NC
Carolyn Dorfman Dance Company	Union	NJ
Charleston Ballet Theatre	Charleston	SC
Chen & Dancers	New York	NY
Cincinnati Ballet	Cincinnati	OH
Collage Dance Theatre	Los Angeles	CA
Contemporary Dance/Fort Worth	Forth Worth	TX
Dallas Black Dance Theatre	Dallas	TX
Dance Alloy	Pittsburgh	PA
Dance Theatre of Harlem	New York	NY
DanceBrazil	New York	NY
David Gordon/Pick Up Co.	New York	NY
Dayton Ballet	Dayton	OH
Dayton Contemporary Dance Co.	Dayton	OH
Demetrius Klein Dance Company	Lake Worth	FL
Denishawn Repertory Dancers	New York	NY
Diavolo Dance Theater	Santa Monica	CA
Donald Byrd/The Group	Brooklyn	NY
Doug Varone & Dancers/DOVA, Inc.	New York	NY
EIKO & KOMA	New York	NY
Elisa Monte Dance Company	New York	NY
Flamenco Vivo Carlota Santana	New York	NY
Fort Worth Dallas Ballet	Forth Worth	TX
Garth Fagan Dance	Rochester	NY
Hartford Ballet	Hartford	CT
Houston Ballet Foundation	Houston	TX
Hubbard Street Dance Chicago	Chicago	IL
James Sewell Ballet	Minneapolis	MN
Jazz Tap Ensemble	Los Angeles	CA
Joe Goode Performance Group	San Francisco	CA
The Joffrey Ballet of Chicago	Chicago	IL
June Watanabe in Company	San Rafael	CA
Karen Bamonte Dance Works	Philadelphia	PA
Kim Robards Dance	Denver	CO
Ko-Thi Dance Company	Milwaukee	WI
Lar Lubovitch Dance Company	New York	NY
Laura Dean Musicians and Dancers	Bahama	NC
Lily Cai Chinese Dance Company	San Francisco	CA
Limón Dance Company	New York	NY
LINES Contemporary Ballet	San Francisco	CA
Liz Lerman Dance Exchange	Takoma Park	MD
Louisville Ballet	Louisville	KY
Lucinda Childs Dance Company	New York	NY
Malashock Dance & Company	San Diego	CA
Margaret Jenkins Dance Company	San Francisco	CA
Maria Benitez Teatro Flamenco	Santa Fe	NM
Mark Morris Dance Group	New York	NY
Merce Cunningham Dance Company	New York	NY
Meredith Monk/The House Foundation	New York	NY
Milwaukee Ballet	Milwaukee	WI
Montgomery Ballet	Montgomery	AL
Muntu Dance Theatre	Chicago	IL
Nai-Ni Chen Dance Company	Fort Lee	NJ
Nashville Ballet	Nashville	TN
New York City Ballet	New York	NY
North Carolina Dance Theatre	Charlotte	NC
Ohio Ballet	Akron	OH
Oregon Ballet Theatre	Portland	OR
Pacific Northwest Ballet	Seattle	WA
The Parsons Dance Company	New York	NY
Pat Graney Company	Seattle	WA
Paul Taylor Dance Foundation	New York	NY
Paula Josa-Jones/Performance Works	Chilmark	MA
Pittsburgh Ballet Theatre	Pittsburgh	PA
Rhythm In Shoes	Dayton	OH
Richmond Ballet	Richmond	VA
River North Dance Company	Chicago	IL
San Francisco Ballet	San Francisco	CA
San Jose Cleveland Ballet	San Jose	CA
The Solomons Company/Dance	New York	NY
State Ballet of Missouri	Kansas City	MO
Stephen Petronio Dance Company	New York	NY
Stuart Pimsler Dance & Theater	Columbus	OH
Tennessee Children's Dance Ensemble	Knoxville	TN
Trinity Irish Dance Company	Chicago	IL
Trisha Brown Company	New York	NY
Tulsa Ballet Theatre	Tulsa	OK
The Washington Ballet	Washington	DC

Some Notable Museums

This unofficial list of the largest museums in the U.S. by budget was compiled with the assistance of the American Association of Museums, a national association representing the concerns of the museum community. Association members also include zoos, aquariums, arboretums, botanical gardens, and planetariums, but these are not included in *The World Almanac* listing. See also U.S. and Canadian Public Zoological Parks in the Environment chapter.

Museum	City	State
American Museum of Natural History	New York	NY
Amon Carter Museum of Western Art	Ft. Worth	TX
The Art Institute of Chicago	Chicago	IL
Autry Museum of Western Heritage	Los Angeles	CA
Brooklyn Museum of Art	Brooklyn	NY
Busch-Reisinger Museum	Cambridge	MA
California Academy of Science	San Francisco	CA
Carnegie Museums of Pittsburgh	Pittsburgh	PA
Chicago Historical Society	Chicago	IL
Children's Museum of Indianapolis	Indianapolis	IN
Cincinnati Art Museum	Cincinnati	OH
Cincinnati Museum Center	Cincinnati	OH
Cleveland Museum of Art	Cleveland	OH
Colonial Williamsburg	Williamsburg	VA
Corning Museum of Glass	Corning	NY
Dallas Museum of Art	Dallas	TX
Denver Art Museum	Denver	CO
Denver Museum of Natural History	Denver	CO
Detroit Institute of Arts	Detroit	MI
Exploratorium	San Francisco	CA
The Field Museum of Natural History	Chicago	IL
Fine Arts Museum of San Francisco	San Francisco	CA
Franklin Institute	Philadelphia	PA
The Frick Collection	New York	NY
Harvard University Art Museum	Cambridge	MA
Henry F. Dupont Winterthur Museum	Winterthur	DE
Henry Ford Museum/Greenfield Village	Dearborn	MI
High Museum of Art	Atlanta	GA
Houston Museum of Natural Science	Houston	TX
Jamestown-Yorktown Foundation	Williamsburg	VA
Jewish Museum	New York	NY
L.A. County Museum of Art	Los Angeles	CA
Liberty Science Center, Liberty State Park	Jersey City	NJ
Maryland Academy of Sciences	Baltimore	MD
Maryland Science Center	Baltimore	MD
Metropolitan Museum of Art	New York	NY
Milwaukee Public Museum	Milwaukee	WI
Minneapolis Institute of Art	Minneapolis	MN
Museum of African American History	Detroit	MI
Museum of Contemporary Art	Los Angeles	CA
Museum of Fine Arts	Boston	MA
Museum of Fine Arts	Houston	TX
Museum of Modern Art	New York	NY
Museum of New Mexico	Santa Fe	NM
Museum of Science	Boston	MA
The Museum of Television & Radio	Beverly Hills	CA
Mystic Seaport Museum	Mystic	CT
National Air & Space Museum	Washington	DC
National Baseball Hall of Fame and Museum, Inc.	Cooperstown	NY
National Gallery of Art	Washington	DC
National Museum of American History-Smithsonian Inst.	Washington	DC
National Museum of Natural History	Washington	DC
Nelson-Atkins Museum of Art	Kansas City	MO
New York Historical Society	New York	NY
New York State Museum	Albany	NY
The Newseum	Arlington	VA
Ohio Historical Society	Columbus	OH
Peabody Essex Museum	Salem	MA
Pennsylvania Historical & Museum Commission	Harrisburg	PA
Philadelphia Museum of Art	Philadelphia	PA
Public Museum of Grand Rapids	Grand Rapids	MI
Rock & Roll Hall of Fame and Museum Inc.	Cleveland	OH
San Diego Museum of Art	San Diego	CA
San Francisco Museum of Modern Art	San Francisco	CA
Science Museum of Minnesota	Saint Paul	MN
Scottsdale Museum of Contemp. Art	Scottsdale	AZ
St. Louis Science Center	St. Louis	MO
Toledo Museum of Art	Toledo	OH
U.S. Holocaust Memorial Museum	Washington	DC
Univ. of Pennsylvania Museum, University of Pennsylvania	Philadelphia	PA
Virginia Museum of Fine Arts	Richmond	VA
Wadsworth Atheneum	Hartford	CT
Walker Art Center	Minneapolis	MN
Whitney Museum of American Art	New York	NY

100 Best-Selling U.S. Magazines

Source: Audit Bureau of Circulations, Schaumburg, IL

General magazines, exclusive of groups and comics; also excluding magazines that failed to file reports to ABC by press time. Based on total average paid circulation during the 6 months ending Dec. 31, 1997.

Magazine	Circulation
1. NRTA/AARP Bulletin	20,415,981
2. Modern Maturity	20,390,755
3. Reader's Digest	15,038,708
4. TV Guide	13,103,187
5. National Geographic Magazine	9,012,074
6. Better Homes and Gardens	7,605,187
7. Family Circle	5,107,477
8. Good Housekeeping	4,739,592
9. Ladies' Home Journal	4,590,155
10. Woman's Day	4,461,023
11. McCall's	4,216,145
12. Time	4,155,806
13. People Weekly	3,608,111
14. Prevention	3,310,278
15. Sports Illustrated	3,223,810
16. Newsweek	3,177,407
17. Playboy	3,169,697
18. Redbook	2,889,466
19. Home & Away	2,759,565
20. The American Legion Magazine	2,734,318
21. Cosmopolitan	2,701,916
22. Seventeen	2,567,613
23. Southern Living	2,474,463
24. Martha Stewart Living	2,339,799
25. National Enquirer	2,324,678
26. U.S. News & World Report	2,224,003
27. YM	2,221,937
28. Glamour	2,115,642
29. Smithsonian	2,065,432
30. Star	1,948,247
31. V.F.W. Magazine	1,935,807
32. Money	1,935,402
33. 'Teen	1,842,186
34. Ebony	1,819,431
35. Field & Stream	1,751,772
36. Parents	1,745,292
37. Country Living	1,697,742
38. Life	1,568,565
39. Popular Science	1,558,655
40. Golf Digest	1,529,671
41. Men's Health	1,511,345
42. Woman's World	1,505,637
43. Sunset	1,471,825
44. Popular Mechanics	1,425,692
45. First for Women	1,408,419
46. Cooking Light	1,387,037
47. Outdoor Life	1,377,139
48. American Rifleman	1,341,176
49. Golf Magazine	1,339,970
50. Entertainment Weekly	1,315,550
51. Boys' Life	1,310,841
52. Scholastic Parent & Child	1,277,007
53. Consumers Digest	1,260,139
54. Rolling Stone	1,250,129
55. Discover	1,215,198
56. New Woman	1,177,730
57. Car and Driver	1,176,665
58. PC Magazine	1,176,351
59. Mademoiselle	1,169,766
60. Endless Vacation	1,134,896
61. Vogue	1,126,193
62. PC World	1,124,589
63. Parenting Magazine	1,118,069
64. Soap Opera Digest	1,107,276
65. Self	1,102,858
66. Us	1,100,074
67. Vanity Fair	1,096,168
68. Country Home	1,087,613
69. Scouting	1,085,386
70. The Family Handyman	1,074,413
71. Kiplinger's Personal Finance Magazine	1,069,054
72. Motor Trend	1,068,200
73. Bon Appetit	1,067,312

Magazine	Circulation
74. American Homestyle & Gardening	1,067,108
75. Weight Watchers Magazine	1,063,978
76. AAA Going Places	1,061,301
77. Home	1,048,015
78. Health	1,045,339
79. In Style	1,044,595
80. Sesame Street Magazine	1,029,596
81. Michigan Living	1,015,337
82. Travel & Leisure	1,008,844
83. PC/Computing	1,008,615
84. Essence	1,000,273
85. Shape	970,832
86. Family Fun	968,048
87. Globe	961,390
88. Elle	948,014
89. The American Hunter	944,612
90. Today's Homeowner	927,998
91. Victoria	926,729
92. American Health for Women	926,430
93. Jet	923,414
94. Penthouse	922,832
95. Fitness	912,646
96. Country America	903,304
97. Business Week	901,891
98. Gourmet	880,681
99. House Beautiful	877,584
100. Nation's Business	857,569

MILLENNIUM FACT BOX

100 Best Novels of the Century

This much debated list of 100 best novels, restricted to those written in English, was drawn up in 1998 by the editorial board of Modern Library, a division of Random House.

1. *Ulysses*, James Joyce
2. *The Great Gatsby*, F. Scott Fitzgerald
3. *A Portrait of the Artist as a Young Man*, James Joyce
4. *Lolita*, Vladimir Nabokov
5. *Brave New World*, Aldous Huxley
6. *The Sound and the Fury*, William Faulkner
7. *Catch-22*, Joseph Heller
8. *Darkness at Noon*, Arthur Koestler
9. *Sons and Lovers*, D. H. Lawrence
10. *The Grapes of Wrath*, John Steinbeck
11. *Under the Volcano*, Malcolm Lowry
12. *The Way of All Flesh*, Samuel Butler
13. *1984*, George Orwell
14. *I, Claudius*, Robert Graves
15. *To the Lighthouse*, Virginia Woolf
16. *An American Tragedy*, Theodore Dreiser
17. *The Heart Is a Lonely Hunter*, Carson McCullers
18. *Slaughterhouse Five*, Kurt Vonnegut
19. *Invisible Man*, Ralph Ellison
20. *Native Son*, Richard Wright
21. *Henderson the Rain King*, Saul Bellow
22. *Appointment in Samarra*, John O'Hara
23. *U.S.A.* (trilogy), John Dos Passos
24. *Winesburg, Ohio*, Sherwood Anderson
25. *A Passage to India*, E. M. Forster
26. *The Wings of the Dove*, Henry James
27. *The Ambassadors*, Henry James
28. *Tender Is the Night*, F. Scott Fitzgerald
29. *The Studs Lonigan Trilogy*, James T. Farrell
30. *The Good Soldier*, Ford Madox Ford
31. *Animal Farm*, George Orwell
32. *The Golden Bowl*, Henry James
33. *Sister Carrie*, Theodore Dreiser
34. *A Handful of Dust*, Evelyn Waugh
35. *As I Lay Dying*, William Faulkner
36. *All the King's Men*, Robert Penn Warren
37. *The Bridge of San Luis Rey*, Thornton Wilder
38. *Howards End*, E. M. Forster
39. *Go Tell It on the Mountain*, James Baldwin
40. *The Heart of the Matter*, Graham Greene
41. *Lord of the Flies*, William Golding
42. *Deliverance*, James Dickey
43. *A Dance to the Music of Time* (series), Anthony Powell
44. *Point Counter Point*, Aldous Huxley
45. *The Sun Also Rises*, Ernest Hemingway
46. *The Secret Agent*, Joseph Conrad
47. *Nostromo*, Joseph Conrad
48. *The Rainbow*, D. H. Lawrence
49. *Women in Love*, D. H. Lawrence
50. *Tropic of Cancer*, Henry Miller
51. *The Naked and the Dead*, Norman Mailer
52. *Portnoy's Complaint*, Philip Roth
53. *Pale Fire*, Vladimir Nabokov
54. *Light in August*, William Faulkner
55. *On the Road*, Jack Kerouac
56. *The Maltese Falcon*, Dashiell Hammett
57. *Parade's End*, Ford Madox Ford
58. *The Age of Innocence*, Edith Wharton
59. *Zuleika Dobson*, Max Beerbohm
60. *The Moviegoer*, Walker Percy
61. *Death Comes to the Archbishop*, Willa Cather
62. *From Here to Eternity*, James Jones
63. *The Wapshot Chronicles*, John Cheever
64. *The Catcher in the Rye*, J. D. Salinger
65. *A Clockwork Orange*, Anthony Burgess
66. *Of Human Bondage*, W. Somerset Maugham
67. *Heart of Darkness*, Joseph Conrad
68. *Main Street*, Sinclair Lewis
69. *The House of Mirth*, Edith Wharton
70. *The Alexandria Quartet*, Lawrence Durrell
71. *A High Wind in Jamaica*, Richard Hughes
72. *A House for Mr. Biswas*, V. S. Naipaul
73. *The Day of the Locust*, Nathaniel West
74. *A Farewell to Arms*, Ernest Hemingway
75. *Scoop*, Evelyn Waugh
76. *The Prime of Miss Jean Brodie*, Muriel Spark
77. *Finnegans Wake*, James Joyce
78. *Kim*, Rudyard Kipling
79. *A Room With a View*, E. M. Forster
80. *Brideshead Revisited*, Evelyn Waugh
81. *The Adventures of Augie March*, Saul Bellow
82. *Angle of Repose*, Wallace Stegner
83. *A Bend in the River*, V. S. Naipaul
84. *The Death of the Heart*, Elizabeth Bowen
85. *Lord Jim*, Joseph Conrad
86. *Ragtime*, E. L. Doctorow
87. *The Old Wives' Tale*, Arnold Bennett
88. *The Call of the Wild*, Jack London
89. *Loving*, Henry Green
90. *Midnight's Children*, Salman Rushdie
91. *Tobacco Road*, Erskine Caldwell
92. *Ironweed*, William Kennedy
93. *The Magus*, John Fowles
94. *Wide Sargasso Sea*, Jean Rhys
95. *Under the Net*, Iris Murdoch
96. *Sophie's Choice*, William Styron
97. *The Sheltering Sky*, Paul Bowles
98. *The Postman Always Rings Twice*, James M. Cain
99. *The Ginger Man*, J. P. Donleavy
100. *The Magnificent Ambersons*, Booth Tarkington

Some Notable New Books, 1997

Source: List published by American Library Association, Chicago, IL, 1998, for books published in 1997

Fiction

¡Yo!, Julia Alvarez
Alias Grace, Margaret Atwood
The Jade Peony, Wayson Choy
Reading in the Dark, Seamus Deane
Cold Mountain, Charles Frazier
The Agüero Sisters, Cristina Garcia
The Wind-Up Bird Chronicle, Haruki Murakami
The Wishbones, Tom Perrotta
News of the Spirit, Lee Smith
The Far Euphrates, Aryeh Lev Stollman
Blu's Hanging, Lois-Ann Yamanaka

Poetry

Primate Behavior, Sarah Lindsay
What Are Big Girls Made of?, Marge Piercy
The Bounty, Derek Walcott

Nonfiction

T. Rex and the Crater of Doom, Walter Alvarez
All Over but the Shoutin', Rick Bragg
Blood Rites: Origins and History of the Passions of War, Barbara Ehrenreich
A People's Tragedy: A History of the Russian Revolution, Orlando Figes
Next of Kin: What Chimpanzees Have Taught Me About Who We Are, Roger Fouts and Stephen Tukel Mills
Ornament and Silence: Essays on Women's Lives, Kennedy Fraser
The Perfect Storm: A True Story of Men Against the Sea, Sebastian Junger
Into Thin Air: A Personal Account of the Mt. Everest Disaster, Jon Krakauer
American Scripture: Making the Declaration of Independence, Pauline Maier
Bad Land: An American Romance, Jonathan Raban
Utopia Parkway: The Life and Work of Joseph Cornell, Deborah Solomon
The River at the Center of the World: A Journey Up the Yangtze and Back in Chinese Time, Simon Winchester

Some Notable New Books for Children and Young Adults, 1997

Source: List published by American Library Association, Chicago, IL, 1998, for books published in 1997

All Ages

Hoops, Robert Burleigh
Noah's Ark, Heinz Janisch
Harlem, Walter Dean Myers
Echoes of the Elders: The Stories and Paintings of Chief Lelooska, ed. Christine Normandin
The Beauty of the Beast: Poems From the Animal Kingdom, ed. Jack Prelutsky
Mysterious Thelonious, Chris Raschka
In Daddy's Arms I Am Tall: African Americans Celebrating Fathers, Javaka Steptoe

Younger Readers

My Life With the Wave, Catherine Cowan
The Hunterman and the Crocodile: A West African Folktale, Baba Wagué Diakité
Gabriella's Song, Candace Fleming
Mr. Semolina-Semolinus: A Greek Folktale, Anthony L. Manna and Christodoula Mitakidou
Little Oh, Laura Krauss Melmed
To Market, to Market, Anne Miranda
Rumpelstiltskin's Daughter, Diane Stanley
The Gardener, Sarah Stewart
There Was an Old Lady Who Swallowed a Fly, Simms Taback
Mailing May, Michael O. Tunnell
Ginger, Charlotte Voake

Middle Grade Readers

Lou Gehrig: The Luckiest Man, David A. Adler
The Paper Dragon, Marguerite W. Davol
Sun & Spoon, Kevin Henkes
Marven of the Great North Woods, Kathryn Lasky
Nim and the War Effort, Milly Lee
Ella Enchanted, Gail Carson Levine*
Passage to Freedom: The Sugihara Story, Ken Mochizuki
An Extraordinary Life: The Story of a Monarch Butterfly, Laurence Pringle
Lily's Crossing, Patricia Reilly
The Sea King's Daughter: A Russian Legend, Aaron Shepard
The Bone Man: A Native American Modoc Tale, Laura Simms
Sky Pioneer: A Photobiography of Amelia Earhart, Corinne Szabo
Leon's Story, Leon Walter Tillage*
A Drop of Water, Walter Wick
Rapunzel, Paul O. Zelinsky

Junior High School Age-Readers

The Iron Ring, Lloyd Alexander*
The Tulip Touch, Anne Fine
Charles A. Lindbergh: A Human Hero, James Cross Giblin*
Out of the Dust, Karen Hesse*
The Robber and Me, Josef Holub
Red Scarf Girl: A Memoir of the Cultural Revolution, Ji Li Jiang*
Stones in Water, Donna Jo Napoli*
Habibi, Naomi Shihab Nye*
Wringer, Jerry Spinelli

Young Adult (Teenage)—Nonfiction

Just People and Other Poems for Young Readers & Pen/Pen/Poem: A Young Writer's Way to Begin, Kathi Appelt
Growing Up in Coal Country, Susan Campbell Bartoletti
The Seamstress, Sara Tuvel Bernstein
I Have Lived a Thousand Years: Growing Up in the Holocaust, Livia Bitton-Jackson
Poetry After Lunch: Poems to Read Aloud, Joyce Armstrong Carroll and Edward E. Wilson
The Company We Keep: America's Endangered Species, Douglas Chadwick and Joel Sartore
Bound Feet & Western Dress, Pang-Mei Natasha Chang
Venus to the Hoop, Sara Corbett
The Triumphant Spirit: Portraits & Stories of Holocaust Survivors...Their Messages of Hope & Compassion, Nick Del Cazo and others
Jack London: A Biography, Daniel Dyer
Joycelyn Elders, M.D.: From Sharecropper's Daughter to Surgeon General of the United States of America, Joycelyn Elders and David Chanoff
Encyclopedia of the Cat, Bruce Fogle
Planet Hunters: The Search for Other Worlds, Dennis B. Fradin
Jump Ball: A Basketball Season in Poems, Mel Glenn
The Taking of Room 114, Mel Glenn
The Human Mind Explained: An Owner's Guide to the Mysteries of the Mind, Susan Greenfield
Into Thin Air: A Personal Account of the Mt. Everest Disaster, Jon Krakauer
In a Sacred Manner I Live: Native American Wisdom, Neil Philip
Flight of Passage, Buck Rinker
Over the Top of the World: Explorer Will Steger's Trek Across the Arctic, Will Steger and Jon Bowermaster
Imaginary Animals, Charles Sullivan
Little X: Growing Up in the Nation of Islam, Sonsyrea Tate

Young Adult (Teenage)—Fiction

Joy School, Elizabeth Berg
Tangerine, Edward Bloor
Bone Dance, Martha Brooks
Bull Catcher, Alden R. Carter
What Girls Learn, Karen Cook
What Child Is This? A Christmas Story, Caroline B. Cooney
Tenderness, Robert Cormier
Chasing Redbird, Sharon Creech
Blood and Chocolate, Annette Curtis
Trader, Charles De Lint
Painting the Black, Carl Deuker
The Window, Michael Dorris
Forged by Fire, Sharon M. Draper
Seedfolks, Paul Fleischman
Shade's Children, Nix Garth
No Easy Answers: Short Stories About Teenagers Making Tough Choices, Donald R. Gallo
Sons of Liberty, Adele Griffin
Leaving Fishers, Margaret Peterson Haddix
Flyers, Daniel Hayes
Bug Park, James P. Hogan
The Watcher, James Howe
Cloudy in the West, Elmer Kelton
Song in the Silence, Elizabeth Kerner
The Woman in the Wall, Patrice Kindl
Kingship, Trudy Krisher
Someone to Love, Francess Lantz
Necessary Roughness, Marie G. Lee
The Luckiest Girl in the World, Steven Levenkron
Secret Diary of Anne Boleyn, Robin Maxwell
Working Days: Short Stories About Teenagers at Work, Anne Mazer
When She Was Good, Norma Fox Mazer
Swallowing Stones, Joyce McDonald
Rose Daughter, Robin McKinley
Inside the Walls of Troy, Clemence McLaren
Jubilee Journey, Carolyn Meyer
Outrageously Alice, Phyllis Reynolds Naylor
Dancing on the Edge, Han Nolan
Peeling the Onion, Wendy Orr
The War in Georgia, Jerrie Oughton
The Schernoff Discoveries, Gary Paulsen
The Queen's Man, Sharon Kay Penman
The Subtle Knife, Philip Pullman
The Starlite Drive-In, Marjorie Reynolds
Acquaintance With Darkness, Ann Rinaldi
Leaving Home, Hazel Rochman and Darlene Z. McCampbell
Stranded in Harmony, Barbara Shoup
The Dark Side of Nowhere, Neal Shusterman
Virtual War, Gloria Skurzynski
Buried Onions, Gary Soto
Doing Time: Notes From the Undergrad, Rob Thomas
Whistle Me Home, Barbara Wersba
The True Colors of Caitlynne Jackson, Carol Lynch Williams
Breakaway, Paul Yee

*Also recommended for older readers.

Best-Selling Books, 1997

Source: *Publishers Weekly*, Apr. 7, 1998

Rankings are based on copies "shipped and billed" in 1997, minus returns through Feb. 24, 1998.

Hardcover Fiction

1. *The Partner*, John Grisham
2. *Cold Mountain*, Charles Frazier
3. *The Ghost*, Danielle Steel
4. *The Ranch*, Danielle Steel
5. *Special Delivery*, Danielle Steel
6. *Unnatural Exposure*, Patricia Cornwell
7. *The Best Laid Plans*, Sidney Sheldon
8. *Pretend You Don't See Her*, Mary Higgins Clark
9. *Cat & Mouse*, James Patterson
10. *Hornet's Nest*, Patricia Cornwell
11. *The Letter*, Richard Paul Evans
12. *Flood Tide*, Clive Cussler
13. *Violin*, Anne Rice
14. *The Matarese Countdown*, Robert Ludlum
15. *Plum Island*, Nelson DeMille

Hardcover Nonfiction

1. *Angela's Ashes*, Frank McCourt
2. *Simple Abundance*, Sarah Ban Breathnach
3. *Midnight in the Garden of Good and Evil*, John Berendt
4. *The Royals*, Kitty Kelley
5. *Joy of Cooking*, Irma S. Rombauer, Marion Rombauer Becker, and Ethan Becker
6. *Diana: Her True Story*, Andrew Morton
7. *Into Thin Air*, Jon Krakauer
8. *Conversations With God, Book 1*, Neale Donald Walsch
9. *Men Are From Mars*, John Gray
10. *Eight Weeks to Optimum Health*, Andrew Weil
11. *Just As I Am*, Billy Graham
12. *The Man Who Listens to Horses*, Monty Roberts
13. *The Millionaire Next Door*, Thomas J. Stanley and William D. Danko

14. *The Perfect Storm*, Sebastian Junger
15. *Kids Are Punny*, Rosie O'Donnell

Trade Paperback

1. *Don't Sweat the Small Stuff and It's All Small Stuff*, Richard Carlson
2. *Chicken Soup for the Woman's Soul*, Jack Canfield, Mark Victor Hansen, et al.
3. *She's Come Undone*, Wally Lamb
4. *Chicken Soup for the Mother's Soul*, Jack Canfield, Mark Victor Hansen, et al.
5. *Wizard and Glass*, Stephen King
6. *Stones From the River*, Ursula Hegi
7. *Prescription for Nutritional Healing*, James F. & Phyllis A. Balch
8. *Windows 95 for Dummies, 2nd ed.*, Andy Rathbone
9. *Chicken Soup for the Christian Soul*, Jack Canfield, Mark Victor Hansen, et al.
10. *Songs in Ordinary Time*, Mary McGarry Morris
11. *A 4th Course of Chicken Soup for the Soul*, Jack Canfield, Mark Victor Hansen, et al.
12. *Rapture of Canaan*, Sheri Reynolds
13. *Heart of a Woman*, Maya Angelou
14. *Petals on the River*, Kathleen E. Woodiwiss
15. *Undaunted Courage*, Stephen E. Ambrose

Mass-Market Paperback

1. *The Runaway Jury*, John Grisham
2. *Five Days in Paris*, Danielle Steel
3. *Malice*, Danielle Steel
4. *Silent Honor*, Danielle Steel
5. *Executive Orders*, Tom Clancy
6. *Moonlight Becomes You*, Mary Higgins Clark
7. *Desperation*, Stephen King
8. *My Gal Sunday*, Mary Higgins Clark
9. *Airframe*, Michael Crichton
10. *Cause of Death*, Patricia Cornwell
11. *The Deep End of the Ocean*, Jacquelyn Mitchard
12. *Ticktock*, Dean Koontz
13. *The Regulators*, Richard Bachman
14. *The Lost World*, Michael Crichton
15. *The Hornet's Nest*, Patricia Cornwell

Almanacs, Atlases, and Annuals

1. *The World Almanac and Book of Facts 1998*, ed. Robert Famighetti
2. *Ernst and Young Tax Guide 1997*
3. *The World Almanac and Book of Facts 1997*, ed. Robert Famighetti
4. *The Old Farmer's Almanac, 1998*, ed. Judson D. Hale
5. *Birnbaum's Walt Disney World 1998*, Birnbaum Travel Guides

Leading U.S. Daily Newspapers, 1997

Source: 1998 Editor & Publisher International Yearbook

(Circulation as of Sept. 30, 1997; m = morning, e = evening)

As of Feb. 1, 1998, the number of U.S. daily newspapers had declined to 1,509, a net loss of 11 since Feb. 1, 1997. Average daily circulation for the 6 months ending Sept. 30, 1997, was 56,727,902, down 255,388 from the same period in 1996, the smallest decrease since 1989. For the first time in 78 years of records, morning circulation newspapers headed the list of ceased daily publication, with 11 of the 14 losses. Sunday editions increased by 13, to 903, during 1997. Average Sunday circulation for the 6 months ending Sept. 30, 1997, fell 311,351, to 60,486,463. An emerging trend is for papers to combine resources to produce joint Sunday editions; these grew from 9 editions involving 19 papers in 1995 to 14 involving 34 in 1997.

Newspaper		Circulation
1. New York (NY) *Wall Street Journal*	(m)	1,774,880
2. Arlington (VA) *USA Today*	(m)	1,629,665
3. New York (NY) *Times*	(m)	1,074,741
4. Los Angeles (CA) *Times*	(m)	1,050,176
5. Washington (DC) *Post*	(m)	775,894
6. New York (NY) *Daily News*	(m)	721,256
7. Chicago (IL) *Tribune*	(m)	653,554
8. Long Island (NY) *Newsday*	(m)	568,914
9. Houston (TX) *Chronicle*	(m)	549,101
10. Chicago (IL) *Sun-Times*	(m)	484,379
11. San Francisco (CA) *Chronicle*	(m)	484,218
12. Dallas (TX) *Morning News*	(m)	481,032
13. Boston (MA) *Globe*	(m)	476,966
14. Phoenix (AZ) *Arizona Republic*	(m)	437,118
15. New York (NY) *Post*	(m)	436,226
16. Philadelphia (PA) *Inquirer*	(m)	428,233
17. Newark (NJ) *Star-Ledger*	(m)	406,010
18. Minneapolis (MN) *Star Tribune*	(m)	387,412
19. Detroit (MI) *Free Press*	(m)	384,624
20. Cleveland (OH) *Plain Dealer*	(m)	383,586
21. San Diego (CA) *Union-Tribune*	(all day)	375,598
22. Miami (FL) *Herald*	(m)	356,803
23. Orange County (CA) *Registers*	(m)	356,520
24. Portland (OR) *Oregonian*	(all day)	342,454
25. St. Petersburg (FL) *Times*	(m)	342,189
26. Denver (CO) *Post*	(m)	337,372
27. St. Louis (MO) *Post-Dispatch*	(m)	313,594
28. Baltimore (MD) *Sun*	(m)	312,826
29. Denver (CO) *Rocky Mountain News*	(m)	302,953
30. Atlanta (GA) *Constitution* .	(m)	296,669
31. San Jose (CA) *Mercury News*	(m)	290,811
32. Milwaukee (WI) *Journal Sentinel*	(m)	288,173
33. Sacramento (CA) *Bee*	(m)	281,471
34. Boston (MA) *Herald*	(m)	277,106
35. Kansas City (MO) *Star*	(m)	276,349
36. Buffalo (NY) *News* .	(all day)	262,085
37. New Orleans (LA) *Times-Picayune*	(m)	260,552
38. Orlando (FL) *Sentinel*	(all day)	258,037
39. Fort Lauderdale (FL) *Sun-Sentinel*	(m)	257,118
40. Detroit (MI) News	(e)	246,638
41. Columbus (OH) *Dispatch*	(m)	246,095
42. Pittsburgh (PA) *Post-Gazette*	(m)	243,024
43. Tampa (FL) *Tribune*	(m)	240,990
44. Charlotte (NC) *Observer*	(m)	239,016
45. Los Angeles (CA) *Investors Business Daily*	(m)	234,596
46. Fort Worth (TX) *Star-Telegram*	(m)	229,701
47. Louisville (KY) *Courier-Journal*	(m)	228,185
48. Seattle (WA) Times	(e)	227,162
49. Omaha (NE) *World-Herald*	(all day)	225,761
50. Indianapolis (IN) *Star*	(m)	224,372
51. San Antonio (TX) *Express-News*	(m)	216,232
52. Hartford (CT) *Courant*	(m)	210,800
53. Richmond (VA) *Times-Dispatch*	(m)	209,690
54. Oklahoma City (OK) *Daily Oklahoman*	(m)	204,376
55. Los Angeles (CA) *Daily News*	(m)	201,669
56. Norfolk (VA) *Virginian-Pilot*	(m)	200,696
57. St. Paul (MN) *Pioneer Press*	(m)	200,275
58. Seattle (WA) *Post-Intelligencer*	(m)	197,921
59. Cincinnati (OH) *Enquirer*	(m)	194,328
60. Austin (TX) *American-Statesman*	(m)	178,643
61. Rochester (NY) *Democrat and Chronicle*	(m)	176,762
62. Jacksonville (FL) *Times-Union*	(m)	176,346
63. Philadelphia (PA) *Daily News*	(m)	175,290
64. Memphis (TN) *Commercial Appeal*	(m)	174,938
65. West Palm Beach (FL) *Palm Beach Post*	(m)	174,171
66. Little Rock (AR) *Democrat-Gazette*	(m)	170,766
67. Providence (RI) *Journal*	(m)	170,292
68. Des Moines (IA) *Registers*	(m)	164,912
69. Riverside (CA) *Press-Enterprise*	(m)	162,551
70. Tulsa (OK) *World*	(m)	162,186
71. Dayton (OH) *Daily News*	(m)	159,072
72. Las Vegas (NV) *Review-Journal*	(m)	158,441
73. Neptune (NJ) *Asbury Park Press*	(all day)	156,821
74. Raleigh (NC) *News & Observer*	(m)	153,408
75. Fresno (CA) *Bee*	(m)	152,718
76. Birmingham (AL) *News*	(m)	150,346
77. Nashville (TN) *Tennessean*	(m)	146,914
78. Bergen County (NJ) *Record*	(m)	146,089
79. Toledo (OH) *Blade*	(m)	145,800
80. Akron (OH) *Beacon Journal*	(m)	145,055
81. Grand Rapids (MI) Press	(e)	138,907
82. Arlington Heights (IL) *Daily Herald*	(m)	132,090
83. Salt Lake City (UT) *Tribune*	(m)	129,836
84. Allentown (PA) *Morning Call*	(m)	128,581
85. Tacoma (WA) *News Tribune*	(m)	128,498
86. Wilmington (DE) *News Journal*	(all day)	123,869
87. Columbia (SC) *State*	(m)	121,699
88. San Francisco (CA) *Examiner*	(e)	120,856
89. Spokane (WA) *Spokesman-Review*	(m)	116,391
90. Knoxville (TN) *News-Sentinel*	(m)	115,264
91. Albuquerque (NM) *Journal*	(m)	113,694
92. Lexington (KY) *Herald-Leader*	(m)	112,139
93. Atlanta (GA) *Journal*	(e)	108,876
94. Worcester (MA) *Telegram & Gazette*	(m)	108,769
95. Charleston (SC) *Post & Courier*	(m)	108,637
96. Sarasota (FL) *Herald-Tribune*	(m)	108,271
97. Los Angeles (CA) *La Opinion*	(m)	106,790
98. Jackson (MS) *Clarion-Ledger*	(m)	104,375
99. Long Beach (CA) *Press-Telegram*	(m)	104,078
100. Honolulu (HI) *Advertiser*	(m)	102,236

Leading Canadian Daily Newspapers, 1997

Source: *1998 Editor & Publisher International Yearbook*

(Circulation as of Sept. 30, 1997; m = morning)

For the year ending Feb. 1, 1998, Canadian dailies increased by 2, to 108. Daily and Sunday circulation increased for the first time since 1992, with daily circulation growing by 44,952, to 4,747,608, in the 6 months ending Sept. 30, 1997. During the same period, Sunday circulation increased by 131,332, to 3,163,147.

Newspaper		Circulation
Toronto (ON) *Star*	(m)	465,212
Toronto (ON) *Globe and Mail*	(m)	307,990
Montreal (QC) *Le Journal*	(m)	258,912
Toronto (ON) *Sun*	(m)	230,830
Vancouver (BC) *Sun*	(m)	177,475
Montreal (QC) *La Presse*	(m)	159,399
Vancouver (BC) *Province*	(m)	154,092
Montreal (QC) *Gazette*	(m)	140,650
Edmonton (AB) *Journal*	(m)	139,704
Ottawa (ON) *Citizens*	(m)	136,762

U.S. Commercial Radio Stations, by Format, 1992-98

Source: M Street Corporation, Nashville, TN © 1998; counts are for Aug. of each year

Stations, by primary format	1992	1993	1994	1995	1996	1997	1998
Country	2,552	2,612	2,642	2,608	2,558	2,502	2,393
Adult Contemporary (AC)	1,963	1,895	1,784	1,661	1,592	1,521	1,562
News, Talk, Business, Sports	648	841	1,028	1,165	1,262	1,313	1,356
Religion (Teaching and Music)	837	915	926	970	996	1,054	1,075
Rock (Album, Modern, Classic)	592	643	721	808	868	942	782
Oldies and Classic Hits	731	734	714	718	725	753	975
Spanish and Ethnic	385	421	470	492	515	549	565
Adult Standards	412	421	435	469	474	536	563
Urban, Black, Urban AC	313	321	328	342	348	358	347
Top-40	578	441	358	324	314	351	379
Easy Listening	171	116	106	6285	5791	4787	40
Variety	72	68	63	63	65	51	51
Jazz	52	45	43	8158	8854	9050	90
Classical, Fine Arts	48	45	44	39	41	46	42
Pre-Teen	3	13	19	26	30	35	32
Comedy	0	0	1	0	0	0	0
Off Air	352	345	369	323	298	162	114
Changing formats/not available	15	14	6	9	6	3	14
TOTAL STATIONS	**9,724**	**9,890**	**10,057**	**10,160**	**10,237**	**10,313**	**10,380**

Top-Grossing North American Concert Tours, 1985-97

Source: Pollstar, Fresno, CA

Artist (Year)	Total gross[1]	Cities/ Shows
1. The Rolling Stones (1994)	$121.2	43/60
2. Pink Floyd (1994)	103.5	39/59
3. The Rolling Stones (1989)	98.0	33/60
4. The Rolling Stones (1997)	89.3	26/33
5. U2 (1997)	79.9	37/46
6. The Eagles (1994)	79.4	32/54
7. The New Kids on the Block (1990)	74.1	122/152
8. U2 (1992)	67.0	61/73
9. The Eagles (1995)	63.3	46/58
10. Barbra Streisand (1994)	58.9	6/22
11. The Grateful Dead (1994)	$52.4	29/84
12. Elton John/Billy Joel (1994)	47.7	14/21
13. The Grateful Dead (1993)	45.6	29/81
14. Kiss (1996)	43.6	75/92
15. Boyz II Men (1995)	43.2	133/134
16. Billy Joel (1990)	43.0	53/95
17. The Who (1989)	41.7	27/39
18. Bruce Springsteen & the E St. Band (1985)	39.1	21/40
19. R.E.M. (1995)	38.7	63/81
20. Paul McCartney (1990)	37.9	21/32

(1) In mils. Not adjusted for inflation.

Sales of Recorded Music and Music Videos, by Genre and Format, 1993-97

Source: Recording Industry Assn. of America, Washington, DC

Breakdown is by percentage of all recorded music sold.

GENRE	1993	1994	1995	1996	1997
Rock	30.2	35.1	33.5	32.6	32.5
Country	18.7	16.3	16.7	14.7	14.4
R&B	10.6	9.6	11.3	12.1	11.2
Pop	11.9	10.3	10.1	9.3	10.1
Rap	9.2	7.9	6.7	8.9	9.4
Gospel	3.2	3.3	3.1	4.3	4.5
Classical	3.3	3.7	2.9	3.4	2.8
Jazz	3.1	3.0	3.0	3.3	2.8
Oldies	1.0	0.8	1.0	0.8	0.8
Soundtracks	0.7	1.0	0.9	0.8	1.2
New Age	1.0	1.0	0.7	0.7	0.8
Children's	0.4	0.4	0.5	0.7	0.9
Other	4.6	5.3	7.0	5.2	5.7

FORMAT	1993	1994	1995	1996	1997
Compact disc (CD)	51.1	58.4	65.0	68.4	70.2
Cassette	38.0	32.1	25.1	19.3	18.2
LP	0.3	0.8	0.5	0.6	0.7
Singles (all types)	9.2	7.4	7.5	9.3	9.3
Music video	1.3	0.8	0.9	1.0	0.6

Note: Totals may not equal 100% because of "Don't know/no answer" responses to survey.

Sales of Recorded Music and Music Videos, by Units Shipped and Value, 1989-97

Source: Recording Industry Assn. of America, Washington, DC

(in millions, net after returns)

FORMAT	1989	1990	1991	1992	1993	1994	1995	1996	1997	% change 1996-97
Compact disc (CD)										
Units shipped	207.2	286.5	333.3	407.5	495.4	662.1	722.9	778.9	753.1	–3.3
Dollar value	2,587.5	3,451.6	4,337.7	5,326.5	6,511.4	8,464.5	9,377.4	9,934.7	9,915.1	–0.2
CD single										
Units shipped	–0.1	1.1	5.7	7.3	7.8	9.3	21.5	43.2	66.7	54.4
Dollar value	–0.7	6.0	35.1	45.1	45.8	56.1	110.9	184.1	272.7	48.1
Cassette										
Units shipped	446.2	442.2	360.1	366.4	339.5	345.4	272.6	225.3	172.6	–23.4
Dollar value	3,345.8	3,472.4	3,019.6	3,116.3	2,915.8	2,976.4	2,303.6	1,905.3	1,522.7	–20.1
Cassette single										
Units shipped	76.2	87.4	69.0	84.6	85.6	81.1	70.7	59.9	42.2	–29.5
Dollar value	194.6	257.9	230.4	298.8	298.5	274.9	236.3	189.3	133.5	–29.5
LP/EP										
Units shipped	34.6	11.7	4.8	2.3	1.2	1.9	2.2	2.9	2.7	–6.9
Dollar value	220.3	86.5	29.4	13.5	10.6	17.8	25.1	36.8	33.3	–9.5
Vinyl single										
Units shipped	36.6	27.6	22.0	19.8	15.1	11.7	10.2	10.1	7.5	–25.7
Dollar value	116.4	94.4	63.9	66.4	51.2	47.2	46.7	47.5	35.6	–25.1
Music video										
Units shipped	6.1	9.2	6.1	7.6	11.0	11.2	12.6	16.9	18.6	10.1
Dollar value	115.4	172.3	118.1	157.4	213.3	231.1	220.3	236.1	323.9	37.2
TOTAL UNITS	**806.7**	**865.7**	**801.0**	**895.5**	**955.6**	**1,122.7**	**1,112.7**	**1,137.2**	**1,063.4**	**–6.5**
TOTAL VALUE	**6,579.4**	**7,541.1**	**7,834.2**	**9,024.0**	**10,046.6**	**12,068.0**	**12,320.3**	**12,533.8**	**12,236.8**	**–2.4**

NA = Not applicable. (1) Cassette singles were introduced in the second half of the year. The figure here represents 6-month sales. (2) Total includes discontinued configurations not itemized in the table.

Multi-Platinum and Platinum Awards for Recorded Music and Music Videos, 1997

Source: Recording Industry Assn. of America, Washington, DC

To achieve platinum status, an album must reach a minimum sale of 1 mil units in LPs, tapes, and CDs, with a manufacturer's dollar volume of at least $2 mil based on one-third of the suggested retail list price for each record, tape, or CD sold. To achieve multi-platinum status, an album must reach a minimum sale of at least 2 mil units in LPs, tapes, and CDs, with a manufacturer's dollar volume of at least $4 mil based on one-third of the list price.

Singles must sell 1 mil units to achieve a platinum award and 2 mil to achieve a multi-platinum award. EP singles count as 2 units. Double-CD sets count as 2 units. Music videos (long form) must sell 100,000 units to qualify for a platinum award and must sell more than 200,000 units for a multi-platinum award. Video singles, which must have a maximum running time of 15 minutes and no more than 2 songs per title, must sell 50,000 units to qualify for a platinum award and at least 100,000 units to qualify for a multi-platinum award.

Awards listed were for albums and singles released in 1997 and for music videos released at any time. No multi-platinum or platinum video singles were awarded in 1997.

Albums, Multi-Platinum

(numbers in parentheses = millions sold)

Aqua, *Aquarium* (2)
Erykah Badu, *Baduizm* (2)
Mary J. Blige, *Share My World* (2)
Bone Thugs 'n Harmony, *The Art of War* (3)
Boyz II Men, *Evolution* (2)
Garth Brooks, *Sevens* (5)
Mariah Carey, *Butterfly* (2)
Chumbawamba, *Tubthumper* (2)
Fleetwood Mac, *The Dance* (2)
Hanson, *Middle of Nowhere* (4)
Mase, *Harlem World* (2)
Tim McGraw, *Everywhere* (2)
Metallica, *Reload* (2)
Notorious B.I.G., *Life After Death* (6)
Prodigy, *The Fat of the Land* (2)
Puff Daddy and the Family, *No Way Out* (4)
LeAnn Rimes, *You Light Up My Life—Inspirational Songs* (3)
LeAnn Rimes, *The Early Years* (2)
Soundtrack, *Gang Related* (2)
Soundtrack, *Men in Black* (2)
Spice Girls, *Spice* (5)
George Strait, *Carryin' Your Love With Me* (2)
Barbra Streisand, *Higher Ground* (3)
Tru, *Tru 2 Da Game* (2)
2 Pac, *R U Still Down? (Remember Me)* (4)
Shania Twain, *Come On Over* (2)
Wu-Tang Clan, *Wu-Tang Forever* (4)
Trisha Yearwood, *Songbook—A Collection* (2)

Albums, Platinum

Aerosmith, *Nine Lives*
Backstreet Boys, *Backstreet Boys*
Brooks and Dunn, *Greatest Hits*
Meredith Brooks, *Blurring the Edges*
Busta Rhymes, *When Disaster Strikes*
Missy Elliott, *Supa Dupa Fly*
En Vogue, *EV3*
God's Property, *From Kirk Franklin's Nu Nation*
Hanson, *Snowed In*
Enrique Iglesias, *Vivir*
Janet Jackson, *The Velvet Rope*
Jamiroquai, *Travelling Without Moving*
Wyclef Jean (Fugee Allstars), *The Carnival*
Kenny G, *Greatest Hits*
Led Zeppelin, *BBC Sessions*
Live, *Secret Samhadi*
LSG, *LSG*
Master P, *Ghetto D*
Dave Matthews Band, *Live at Redrocks*
Sara McLachlan, *Surfacing*
Mighty Mighty Bosstones, *Let's Face It*
Oasis, *Be Here Now*
Offspring, *Ixnay on the Hombre*
The Rolling Stones, *Bridges to Babalon*
Rome, *Rome*
Savage Garden, *Savage Garden*
Scarface, *The Untouchable*
Selena, *Selena (Soundtrack)*
Smash Mouth, *Fush Yu Mang*
Will Smith, *Big Willie Style*
Soundtrack, *Howard Stern—Private Parts*
Soundtrack, *Batman and Robin*
Soundtrack, *Soul Food*
Sugar Ray, *Floored*
Third Eye Blind, *Third Eye Blind*
311, *Transistor*
U2, *Pop*
Usher, *My Way*
Various, *Pure Moods*

Singles, Multi-Platinum

(numbers in parentheses = millions sold)

Elton John, *Candle in the Wind/Something About the Way You Look Tonight* (11)
Puff Daddy, *Can't Nobody Hold Me Down* (2)
Puff Daddy and Faith Evans, *I'll Be Missing You* (3)
LeAnn Rimes, *How Do I Live* (2)

(continued)

Singles, Platinum

Az Yet, *Hard To Say I'm Sorry*
Backstreet Boys, *Quit Playing Games (With My Heart)*
Bone Thugs 'n Harmony, *Look Into My Eyes*
Boyz II Men, *4 Seasons of Loneliness*
Mariah Carey, *Honey*
Changing Faces, *G.H.E.T.T.O.U.T.*
Hanson, *Mmmbop*
LSG, *My Body*
Tim McGraw, *It's Your Love*
Monica, *For You I Will*
Mark Morrison, *Return of the Mack*
Notorious B.I.G., *Hypnotize*
Notorious B.I.G., *Mo Money Mo Problems*
112, *Cupid*
Puff Daddy and the Family, *Been Around the World*
Rome, *I Belong To You*
Somethin' For the People, *My Love Is the Shhh!*
Usher, *You Make Me Wanna...*

Music Videos, Multi-Platinum

(numbers in parentheses = millions sold)

Michael Flatley, *Lord of the Dance* (8)
Hanson, *Hanson* (4)
Various, *I'm Bout It* (2)

Music Videos, Platinum

Big Idea Productions, *Larry Boy and the Fib From Outer Space*
Alanis Morissette, *Jagged Little Pill—Live*

Top-Selling Video Games, 1997

Source: The NPD TRSTS Video Game Tracking Service, The NPD Group, Inc., Port Washington, NY; ranked by units sold

	Title
1.	Nintendo 64 Mario Kart 64
2.	Nintendo 64 Star Fox 64 with Rumble Pak
3.	Nintendo 64 Super Mario 64 3
4.	Ninendo 64 Diddy Kong Racing
5.	Nintendo 64 GoldenEye 007
6.	Sony Playstation Final Fantasy VII
7.	Sony Playstation NFL Gameday '98
8.	Nintendo 64 Star Wars: Shadows of the Empire
9.	Sony Playstation Madden NFL '98
10.	Sony Playstation Crash Bandicoot
11.	Nintendo 64 Turok: Dinosaur Hunter
12.	Sony Playstation NBA Live '98
13.	Nintendo 64 Cruisin' USA
14.	Sony Playstation Tomb Raider 2
15.	Sony Playstation Crash Bandicoot 2

U.S. Television Set Owners

Source: Nielsen Media Research; Dec. 31, 1997

Of the 98.0 million homes (98% of U.S. households) that owned at least one TV set in 1997:

99% had color televisions
34% had 2 TV sets
40% had 3 or more TV sets
84% had a VCR
67% received basic cable
35% received premium cable

Some Television Addresses, Phone Numbers, Internet Sites

BROADCAST

ABC–American Broadcasting Co.
77 W 66th St.
New York, NY 10023 (212) 456-7777
Website: http://www.abc.com

CBS–Columbia Broadcasting System
51 W 52nd St.
New York, NY 10019 (212) 975-4321
Website: http://www.cbs.com

NBC–National Broadcasting Co.
30 Rockefeller Plaza
New York, NY 10112 (212) 664-4444
Website: http://www.nbc.com

Fox Television
205 E 67th St.
New York, NY 10021 (212) 452-5555
Website: http://www.fox.com

PBS–Public Broadcasting Service
1320 Braddock Place
Alexandria, VA 22314 (703) 739-5000
Website: http://www.pbs.org

CABLE

A&E–Arts & Entertainment Network
235 E 45th St.
New York, NY 10017 (212) 210-1400
Website: http://www.aetv.com

AMC–American Movie Classics
Rainbow Media Holdings, Inc.
150 Crossways Park W
Woodbury, NY 11797 (516) 396-3000
Website: http://www.amctv.com

BET–Black Entertainment Television
1 BET Plaza, 1900 W Place, NE
Washington, DC 20018 (202) 608-2000
Website: http://www.msbet.com

CNBC–Consumer News and Business Channel
2200 Fletcher Ave.
Fort Lee, NJ 07024 (201) 585-2622
Website: http://www.cnbc.com

CNN–Cable News Network
One CNN Center, Box 105366
Atlanta, GA 30348-5366 (404) 827-1500
Website: http://www.cnn.com

C-SPAN–Cable-Satellite Public Affairs Network
400 N Capitol St. NW, Suite 650
Washington, DC 20001 (202) 737-3220
Website: http://www.c-span.org

DIS–The Disney Channel
3800 W Alameda Ave.
Burbank, CA 91505 (818) 569-7500
Website: http://www.disneychannel.com

ESPN–ESPN, Inc.
ESPN Plaza, 935 Middle St.
Bristol, CT 06010 (860) 585-2000
Website: http://espn.com

LIF–Lifetime
309 W 49th St.
New York, NY 10019 (212) 424-7000
Website: http://www.lifetimetv.com

MSNBC
1 MSNBC Plaza
Secaucus, NJ 07094 (201) 583-5000
Website: http://www.msnbc.com

MTV–Music Television
MTV Networks, Inc.
1515 Broadway
New York, NY 10036 (212) 258-8000
Website: http://www.mtv.com

NICK–Nickelodeon/Nick at Nite
MTV Networks, Inc.
1515 Broadway
New York, NY 10036 (212) 258-8000
Websites: http://www.nick.com
http://www.nick-at-nite.com

TBS–Turner Broadcasting System
Turner Entertainment Group
One CNN Center, Box 105366
Atlanta, GA 30348-5366
(404) 827-1700
Website: http://www.turner.com

TDC–The Discovery Channel
Discovery Communications
7700 Wisconsin Ave., Suite 700
Bethesda, MD 20814 (301) 986-0444
Website: http://www.discovery.com

USA–USA Network
USA Networks
1230 Ave. of the Americas
New York, NY 10020 (212) 408-9100
Website: http://www.usanetwork.com

Number of Cable TV Systems, 1975-98

Source: *Television and Cable Factbook*, Warren Publishing, Inc., Washington, DC; estimates as of Jan. 1

Year	Systems	Year	Systems	Year	Systems	Year	Systems
1975	3,506	1981	4,375	1987	7,900	1993	11,108
1976	3,681	1982	4,825	1988	8,500	1994	11,214
1977	3,832	1983	5,600	1989	9,050	1995	11,215
1978	3,875	1984	6,200	1990	9,575	1996	11,220
1979	4,150	1985	6,600	1991	10,704	1997	10,943
1980	4,225	1986	7,500	1992	11,073	1998	10,845

Top 20 Cable Video Networks, 1998

Source: *Cable Television Developments,* Natl. Cable Television Assn., Jan.-Apr. 1998; ranked by number of subscribers

Rank	Network[1]	Affiliates	Subscribers (mil)
1.	The Discovery Channel (1985)	NA	73.5
2.	ESPN (1979)	27,600[1]	73.0
	TBS (1976)	11,668	73.0
4.	TNT (Turner Network Television) (1988)	10,657	72.4
5.	C-SPAN (1979)	6,191	71.4
	TNN (The Nashville Network) (1983)	NA	71.4
7.	CNN (1980)	11,528	71.0
	The Weather Channel (1982)	7,000	71.0
9.	USA Network (1980)	12,500[2]	69.7
10.	LIFETIME Television (1984)	8,300	69.5
11.	Headline News (1982)	6,917	68.0
12.	AMC (American Movie Classics) (1984)	NA	67.0
13.	Arts & Entertainment Network (1984)	12,000[3]	66.9
	The Family Channel (1977)	13,352	66.9
15.	MTV: Music Television (1981)	9,176	66.7
16.	Nickelodeon (1979)	11,788	66.0
	Nick at Nite (1985)	11,711	66.0
18.	CNBC (1989)	5,822[1]	64.0
	The Learning Channel (1980)	NA	64.0
20.	QVC Network (1986)	6,427[4]	63.0

NA = Not available. **Note:** Data include noncable affiliates. (1) Date in parentheses is year service began. (2) Includes SMATV. (3) U.S. and Canada. (4) Data as of Oct. 1997.

U.S. Households With Cable Television, 1977-97

Source: Nielsen Media Research

Year	Basic cable subscribers	As % of households with TVs
1977	12,168,450	16.6
1978	13,391,910	17.9
1979	14,814,380	19.4
1980	17,671,490	22.6
1981	23,219,200	28.3
1982	29,340,570	35.0
1983	34,113,790	40.5
1984	37,290,870	43.7
1985	39,872,520	46.2
1986	42,237,140	48.1
1987	44,970,880	50.5
1988	48,636,520	53.8
1989	52,564,470	57.1
1990	54,871,330	59.0
1991	55,786,390	60.6
1992	57,211,600	61.5
1993	58,834,440	62.5
1994	60,483,600	63.4
1995	62,956,470	65.7
1996	64,654,160	66.7
1997	65,929,420	67.3

Average Television Viewing Time, May 1998

Source: Nielsen Media Research (hours: minutes per week)

Group	Age	Mon.-Fri. 10 AM-4:30 PM	Mon.-Fri. 4:30 PM-7:30 PM	Mon.-Sun. 8-11 PM	Sat. 7 AM-1 PM	Mon.-Fri. 11:30 PM-1 AM
Women	18+	5:06	3:39	8:56	0:42	1:27
	18-24	4:10	2:29	5:49	0:40	1:17
	25-54	4:10	2:56	8:20	0:29	1:26
	55+	7:15	5:29	11:16	0:39	1:33
Men	18+	3:09	2:47	8:10	0:46	1:23
	18-24	2:44	1:57	5:14	0:35	1:16
	25-54	2:34	2:18	7:55	0:26	1:27
	55+	4:43	4:20	10:13	0:37	1:19
Teens	12-17	1:46	2:51	6:02	0:38	0:46
Children	2-5	5:34	2:49	4:13	0:39	0:26
	6-11	1:47	2:40	4:48	1:05	0:29
TOTAL		**3:48**	**3:07**	**7:43**	**0:42**	**1:13**

TV Viewing Shares, Broadcast Years 1988-1997[1]

Source: *Cable TV Facts,* Cable Advertising Bureau, New York, NY

All Television Households[2]

	'88	'89	'90	'91	'92	'93	'94	'95	'96	'97
Network Affiliates	61	58	55	53	54	53	52	48	46	43
Indep. TV Stations[3]	20	20	20	21	20	21	21	22	21	20
Public TV Stations	4	3	3	3	3	4	4	3	3	3
Basic Cable	15	17	21	24	24	25	26	30	33	36
Pay Cable	7	7	6	6	6	5	5	6	6	13

All Cable Households[2]

	'88	'89	'90	'91	'92	'93	'94	'95	'96	'97
Network Affiliates	52	49	46	46	47	46	44	41	40	38
Indep. TV Stations[3]	17	16	16	17	16	17	17	17	17	17
Public TV Stations	3	3	3	2	3	3	3	3	3	3
Basic Cable	25	28	32	35	35	36	37	42	43	46
Pay Cable	11	11	10	9	8	8	8	8	8	8

Pay Cable Households[2]

	'88	'89	'90	'91	'92	'93	'94	'95	'96	'97
Network Affiliates	48	45	43	41	43	42	42	38	36	35
Indep. TV Stations[3]	17	16	16	16	16	16	17	17	18	17
Public TV Stations	3	2	2	2	2	2	3	2	3	2
Basic Cable	24	27	30	34	33	35	36	41	43	46
Pay Cable	18	18	18	17	17	16	15	15	14	13

(1) Broadcast year (season) ends in May of the year shown, began the previous Sept. (2) Share figures refer to percentage of the viewing audience for all television viewing, 24 hours/day. As a result of multiset use and rounding of numbers, share figures add to more than 100. (3) Independent shares include those for Fox.

Favorite Syndicated Programs, 1997-98

Source: Nielsen Media Research, Sept. 1, 1997-May 20, 1998

Average audience percentages, or ratings, are estimates of the percentage of TV-owning households watching a program.

Rank	Program	Avg. audience (%)
1.	Wheel of Fortune (Mon.-Fri.)	11.6
2.	Jeopardy (Mon.-Fri.)	9.8
3.	Wheel of Fortune (Mon.)	8.7
4.	Wheel of Fortune (Wed.)	8.5
5.	Home Improvement (Mon.-Fri.)	8.0
5.	Star Wars (Special Edition)	8.0
7.	Jeopardy (Wed.)	7.8
7.	Portfolio XV	7.8
9.	Seinfeld (Mon.-Sat.)	7.4
10.	Jeopardy (Mon.)	7.3
10.	Oprah Winfrey Show (Mon.-Fri.)	7.3
12.	WCW Wrestling	7.1
13.	Jeopardy (Fri.)	7.0
13.	X-Files (various weeks)	7.0
15.	Jeopardy (Mon.)	6.9
16.	Oprah Winfrey Show (Wed.)	6.6
17.	Buena Vista I	6.5
17.	ESPN NFL Regular Season	6.5
17.	Oprah Winfrey Show (Mon.)	6.5
20.	MMN Home Team Baseball	6.2

TV Parental Guidelines

On Dec. 19, 1996, representatives of the television industry announced the creation of TV Parental Guidelines, a rating system intended to give parents advance information about the content of programs. The guidelines, modeled after the Motion Picture Ratings System and developed by a broad spectrum of industry representatives, began to appear on broadcast and cable television programs in Jan. 1997. On July 10, 1997, most of the television industry, after negotiations with advocacy groups, agreed to add the labels D, L, S, and V to the existing ratings. The added labels, which went into effect by Oct. 1, provide more specific information about the degree of violence, coarse language, and sexually suggestive content. Some of the networks that did not add the labels Oct. 1 began to add their own parental advisories to shows.

There are two categories of ratings, one for children's programs and one for programs not specifically designed for children. The ratings are as follows:

The following categories apply to programs designed solely for children:

TV Y **All Children.** *This program is designed to be appropriate for all children.* Whether animated or live action, the themes and elements in this program are specifically designed for a very young audience, including children ages 2-6. This program is not expected to frighten younger children.

TV Y7 **Directed to Older Children.** *This program is designed for children age 7 and above.* It may be more appropriate for children who have acquired the developmental skills needed to distinguish between make-believe and reality. Themes and elements in this program may include mild fantasy or comedic violence, or may frighten children under the age of 7. Therefore, parents may wish to consider the suitability of this program for their very young children. Programs containing fantasy violence that may be more intense or more combative than other programs in this category are designated as **TV-Y7-FV.**

The following categories apply to programs designed for the entire audience:

TV G **General Audience.** *Most parents would find this program suitable for all ages.* Although this rating does not signify a program designed specifically for children, most parents may let younger children watch this program unattended. It contains little or no violence, no strong language, and little or no sexual dialogue or situations.

TV PG **Parental Guidance Suggested.** *This program contains material that parents may find unsuitable for younger children.* Many parents may want to watch it with their younger children. The theme itself may call for parental guidance and/or the program contains one or more of the following: moderate violence (V), some sexual situations (S), infrequent coarse language (L), or some suggestive dialogue (D).

TV 14 **Parents Strongly Cautioned.** *This program contains some material that many parents would find unsuitable for children under 14 years of age.* Parents are strongly urged to exercise greater care in monitoring this program and are cautioned against letting children under the age of 14 watch unattended. This program contains one or more of the following: intense violence (V), intense sexual situations (S), strong coarse language (L), or intensely suggestive dialogue (D).

TV MA **Mature Audience Only.** *This program is specifically designed to be viewed by adults and therefore may be unsuitable for children under 17.* This program contains one or more of the following: graphic violence (V), explicit sexual activity (S), or crude, indecent language (L).

When a program is broadcast, the appropriate icon should appear in the upper left corner of the picture frame for the first 15 seconds. If the program is longer than 1 hour, the icon should be repeated at the beginning of the 2d hour. Guidelines are also displayed in TV listings in a number of newspapers and magazines.

Favorite Prime-Time Television Programs, 1997-98

Source: Nielsen Media Research

Data are for regularly scheduled network programs (Sept. 1, 1997–May 20, 1998); ranked by average audience percentage. Average audience percentages, or ratings, are estimates of the percentage of all TV-owning households that are watching a particular program. Audience share percentages are estimates of the percentage of those watching TV that are tuned into a particular program.

Rank	Program	Average audience	Audience share
1.	Seinfeld	22.0	33
2.	E.R.	20.7	34
3.	Veronica's Closet	16.8	26
4.	Friends	16.4	27
5.	NFL Monday Night Football	15.0	26
6.	Touched by an Angel	14.4	22
7.	60 Minutes	13.9	24
8.	Union Square	13.6	21
9.	CBS Sunday Night Movie	13.3	21
10.	Frasier	12.0	18
	Home Improvement	12.0	18
	Just Shoot Me	12.0	19
13.	Dateline NBC-Tuesday	11.5	20
	NFL Monday Showcase	11.5	18
15.	Dateline NBC-Monday	11.4	19
16.	Drew Carey Show	11.1	17
	Fox NFL Sunday-Post	11.1	18
18.	20/20	10.9	20
19.	NYPD Blue	10.8	18
	Primetime Live	10.8	18
	X-Files	10.8	16
22.	Fox NFL Sunday-Post Game	10.7	18
23.	Law and Order	10.2	17
24.	20/20-Monday	10.0	15
25.	Diagnosis Murder	9.8	15
	King of the Hill	9.8	15
27.	Mad About You	9.7	16
28.	Cosby	9.5	15
	Dateline NBC-Friday	9.5	17
	Dharma & Greg	9.5	15
	NBC Sunday Night Movie	9.5	15
32.	Hiller and Diller	9.3	15
	Simpsons	9.3	15
	Walker, Texas Ranger	9.3	17
35.	Dateline NBC, 8 P.M. Sunday	9.2	15
	Everybody Loves Raymond	9.2	14
37.	Soul Man	9.1	14
38.	Lateline	9.0	14
39.	Chicago Hope	8.9	15
	JAG	8.9	14
	Promised Land	8.9	14
42.	Ellen	8.8	14
	Two Guys, a Girl & a Pizza Place	8.8	14
44.	ABC Sunday Night Movie	8.5	13
	3rd Rock From the Sun	8.5	13
	20/20-Thursday	8.5	14
47.	Caroline in the City	8.4	13
	CBS Tuesday Night Movie	8.4	14
	Spin City	8.4	14
50.	Beverly Hills, 90210	8.3	14
	Cybill	8.3	13
	Kids Say the Darndest Things	8.3	16
	The Nanny	8.3	14

All-Time Top Television Programs

Source: Nielsen Media Research, Jan. 1961-May 17, 1998

Estimates exclude unsponsored or joint network telecasts or programs under 30 minutes long. Ranked by rating (percentage of TV-owning households tuned in to the program).

Rank	Program	Telecast date	Network	Rating (%)	Avg. audience (in thousands)
1.	M*A*S*H (last episode)	2/28/83	CBS	60.2	50,150
2.	Dallas (Who Shot J.R.?)	11/21/80	CBS	53.3	41,470
3.	Roots-Pt. 8	1/30/77	ABC	51.1	36,380
4.	Super Bowl XVI	1/24/82	CBS	49.1	40,020
5.	Super Bowl XVII	1/30/83	NBC	48.6	40,480
6.	XVII Winter Olympics - 2d Wed.	2/23/94	CBS	48.5	45,690
7.	Super Bowl XX	1/26/86	NBC	48.3	41,490
8.	Gone With the Wind-Pt. 1	11/7/76	NBC	47.7	33,960
9.	Gone With the Wind-Pt. 2	11/8/76	NBC	47.4	33,750
10.	Super Bowl XII	1/15/78	CBS	47.2	34,410
11.	Super Bowl XIII	1/21/79	NBC	47.1	35,090
12.	Bob Hope Christmas Show	1/15/70	NBC	46.6	27,260
13.	Super Bowl XVIII	1/22/84	CBS	46.4	38,800
	Super Bowl XIX	1/20/85	ABC	46.4	39,390
15.	Super Bowl XIV	1/20/80	CBS	46.3	35,330
16	Super Bowl XXX	1/28/96	NBC	46.0	44,150
	ABC Theater (The Day After)	11/20/83	ABC	46.0	38,550
18.	Roots-Pt. 6	1/28/77	ABC	45.9	32,680
	The Fugitive	8/29/67	ABC	45.9	25,700
20.	Super Bowl XXI	1/25/87	CBS	45.8	40,030
21.	Roots-Pt. 5	1/27/77	ABC	45.7	32,540
22.	Super Bowl XXVIII	1/30/94	NBC	45.5	42,860
	Cheers (last episode)	5/20/93	NBC	45.5	42,360
24.	Ed Sullivan	2/9/64	CBS	45.3	23,240
25.	Super Bowl XXVII	1/31/93	NBC	45.1	41,990
26.	Bob Hope Christmas Show	1/14/71	NBC	45.0	27,050
27.	Roots-Pt. 3	1/25/77	ABC	44.8	31,900
28.	Super Bowl XXXII	1/25/98	NBC	44.5	43,630
29.	Super Bowl XI	1/9/77	NBC	44.4	31,610
	Super Bowl XV	1/25/81	NBC	44.4	34,540
31.	Super Bowl VI	1/16/72	CBS	44.2	27,450
32.	XVII Winter Olympics - 2d Fri.	2/25/94	CBS	44.1	41,540
	Roots-Pt. 2	1/24/77	ABC	44.1	31,400
34.	Beverly Hillbillies	1/8/64	CBS	44.0	22,570
35.	Roots-Pt. 4	1/26/77	ABC	43.8	31,190
	Ed Sullivan	2/16/64	CBS	43.8	22,445
37.	Super Bowl XXIII	1/22/89	NBC	43.5	39,320
38.	Academy Awards	4/7/70	ABC	43.4	25,390
39.	Super Bowl XXXI	1/26/97	FOX	43.3	42,000
40.	Thorn Birds-Pt. 3	3/29/83	ABC	43.2	35,990
41.	Thorn Birds-Pt. 4	3/30/83	ABC	43.1	35,900
42.	CBS NFC Championship	1/10/82	CBS	42.9	34,960
43.	Beverly Hillbillies	1/15/64	CBS	42.8	21,960
44.	Super Bowl VII	1/14/73	NBC	42.7	27,670
45.	Thorn Birds-Pt. 2	3/28/83	ABC	42.5	35,400

Top-Rated TV Shows of Each Season, 1950-51 to 1997-98

Source: Nielsen Media Research; regular series programs, Sept.-May season

Season	Program	Rating[1]	TV-owning households (in thousands)
1950-51	Texaco Star Theatre	61.6	10,320
1951-52	Godfrey's Talent Scouts	53.8	15,300
1952-53	I Love Lucy	67.3	20,400
1953-54	I Love Lucy	58.8	26,000
1954-55	I Love Lucy	49.3	30,700
1955-56	$64,000 Question	47.5	34,900
1956-57	I Love Lucy	43.7	38,900
1957-58	Gunsmoke	43.1	41,920
1958-59	Gunsmoke	39.6	43,950
1959-60	Gunsmoke	40.3	45,750
1960-61	Gunsmoke	37.3	47,200
1961-62	Wagon Train	32.1	48,555
1962-63	Beverly Hillbillies	36.0	50,300
1963-64	Beverly Hillbillies	39.1	51,600
1964-65	Bonanza	36.3	52,700
1965-66	Bonanza	31.8	53,850
1966-67	Bonanza	29.1	55,130
1967-68	Andy Griffith	27.6	56,670
1968-69	Rowan & Martin Laugh-In	31.8	58,250
1969-70	Rowan & Martin Laugh-In	26.3	58,500
1970-71	Marcus Welby, MD	29.6	60,100
1971-72	All in the Family	34.0	62,100
1972-73	All in the Family	33.3	64,800
1973-74	All in the Family	31.2	66,200
1974-75	All in the Family	30.2	68,500
1975-76	All in the Family	30.1	69,600
1976-77	Happy Days	31.5	71,200
1977-78	Laverne & Shirley	31.6	72,900
1978-79	Laverne & Shirley	30.5	74,500
1979-80	60 Minutes	28.2	76,300
1980-81	Dallas	31.2	79,900
1981-82	Dallas	28.4	81,500
1982-83	60 Minutes	25.5	83,300
1983-84	Dallas	25.7	83,800
1984-85	Dynasty	25.0	84,900
1985-86	Cosby Show	33.8	85,900
1986-87	Cosby Show	34.9	87,400
1987-88	Cosby Show	27.8	88,600
1988-89	Roseanne	25.5	90,400
1989-90	Roseanne	23.4	92,100
1990-91	Cheers	21.6	93,100
1991-92	60 Minutes	21.7	92,100
1992-93	60 Minutes	21.6	93,100
1993-94	Home Improvement	21.9	94,200
1994-95	Seinfeld	20.5	95,400
1995-96	E.R.	22.0	95,900
1996-97	E.R.	21.2	97,000
1997-98	Seinfeld	22.0	98,000

(1) Rating is percent of TV-owning households tuned in to the program. Data prior to 1988-89 exclude Alaska and Hawaii.

100 Leading U.S. Advertisers, 1997

Source: Competitive Media Reporting and Publishers Information Bureau, New York, © copyright 1998

(in thousands of dollars)

Rank	Advertiser	Ad spending
1.	General Motors	$2,226,933.5
2.	Procter & Gamble	1,703,053.3
3.	Philip Morris	1,319,015.9
4.	Chrysler	1,311,789.2
5.	Ford	973,127.7
6.	Pepsico	797,405.4
7.	Time Warner	779,108.1
8.	Walt Disney	746,296.9
9.	Johnson & Johnson	738,702.4
10.	Sears Roebuck & Co.	734,145.5
11.	Diageo PLC	685,044.9
12.	Unilever PLC	618,975.9
13.	News Corp.	613,822.9
14.	Ford Motor Co.*	609,455.1
15.	Toyota Motor	592,327.2
16.	McDonalds	580,802.4
17.	Federated Dept. Stores	532,544.6
18.	General Motors*	512,113.0
19.	Sony	493,344.4
20.	AT&T	475,857.0
21.	General Motors*	469,032.1
22.	MCI Communications	455,381.6
23.	Nissan Motor Co.	452,708.8
24.	National Amusements	450,607.2
25.	May Department Stores	445,958.0
26.	Honda Motor Co.	436,509.2
27.	Circuit City Stores	433,078.5
28.	General Mills	416,864.6
29.	Kellogg Co.	403,559.5
30.	Bristol-Myers Squibb Co.	398,325.1
31.	Ford Motor Co.*	372,322.6
32.	Warner-Lambert	371,569.4
33.	JC Penney	362,472.1
34.	Dayton Hudson	333,961.1
35.	American Home Products	$333,720.1
36.	Chrysler Corp.*	330,535.9
37.	L'Oreal	325,359.6
38.	U.S. Government	323,917.4
39.	Coca-Cola	316,290.0
40.	American Express	314,591.0
41.	Seagram	311,293.5
42.	Mars	310,611.3
43.	Toyota Motor Co.*	302,622.9
44.	RJR Nabisco Holdings	295,048.2
45.	Sprint	290,513.6
46.	K-Mart	268,936.4
47.	IBM	265,729.2
48.	Valassis Communications	264,701.8
49.	Anheuser-Busch	264,201.5
50.	SmithKline Beecham	261,801.4
51.	Campbell Soup	250,776.5
52.	Mattel	245,631.9
53.	Visa Intl.	242,028.9
54.	Nestlé	236,111.1
55.	Mazda	232,165.7
56.	Novartis Agricultural	227,090.5
57.	Philips Electronics	226,106.7
58.	Nike	211,232.2
59.	Bell Atlantic	210,324.8
60.	Clorox	203,001.2
61.	Nissan Motor Co.*	202,918.0
62.	Glaxo Wellcome	200,750.2
63.	Pfizer	197,733.2
64.	Hasbro	194,836.8
65.	SBC Communications	194,481.7
66.	Microsoft	193,162.8
67.	Chrysler Corp. dealer assn.	191,295.5
68.	Home Depot	$189,493.5
69.	Tandy	186,325.8
70.	Bayer Group	183,116.0
71.	Toyota*	180,880.4
72.	SC Johnson & Sons	177,859.2
73.	Hershey Foods	177,654.5
74.	Quaker Oats	177,004.3
75.	Montgomery Ward	174,071.1
76.	Wendy's Intl.	173,063.4
77.	Wal-Mart Stores	172,655.0
78.	Ralston Purina	169,689.8
79.	Best Buy	169,249.7
80.	Gillette	167,749.6
81.	Merck & Co.	158,526.9
82.	Volkswagen AG	157,769.2
83.	MacAndrews and Forbes Holdings	155,885.0
84.	Dillard Department Stores	154,545.3
85.	Honda Motor Co.*	151,827.9
86.	Morgan Stanley Dean Witter OSCVR & Co.	148,012.8
87.	Colgate-Palmolive Co.	141,610.6
88.	Cadbury Schweppes	139,861.6
89.	Adolph Coors	139,617.2
90.	Schering-Plough	139,428.9
91.	Wm. Wrigley Jr. Co.	139,334.7
92.	Sara Lee	138,847.2
93.	Darden Restaurants	138,459.4
94.	BellSouth	135,097.6
95.	Mitsubishi	131,159.0
96.	Prudential Insurance	128,972.3
97.	Eastman Kodak	128,778.2
98.	HFS	128,418.2
99.	Kimberly-Clark	125,751.1
100.	Dominos Pizza	122,628.9

* local dealers

U.S. Ad Spending by Selected Categories, 1997

Source: Competitive Media Reporting and Publishers Information Bureau, New York, © copyright 1998

(in thousands of dollars, Jan.-Dec. 1997)

Category	Total ad spending	Magazine	Sunday magazines	Local newspaper	Network TV	Spot TV	Syndicated TV	Cable TV	Netwo radic
Automotive	$12,873,404.6	$1,777,129.8	$45,319.6	$4,120,547.2	$2,315,505.3	$3,431,897.7	$135,322.5	$567,867.1	$69,0C
Retail	10,860,715.2	403,821.6	88,639.2	5,482,469.3	994,792.9	2,775,426.1	99,626.6	339,601.4	102,5ç
Business, cons. services	9,031,819.8	1,014,614.8	54,901.2	2,455,826.4	1,371,275.9	1,980,770.9	215,539.9	722,916.0	128,64
Entertainment	5,889,334.3	82,581.0	3,440.6	740,420.4	1,962,970.3	2,072,369.9	277,403.6	410,998.6	10,81
Food	4,194,030.0	684,020.1	55,863.0	24,761.4	1,403,905.7	906,726.6	385,103.0	526,170.9	68,30
Drugs & remedies ..	3,981,337.1	814,166.4	122,917.6	221,529.6	1,354,513.0	557,145.4	292,713.1	412,245.0	104,27
Toiletries/cosmet...	3,684,209.6	1,120,349.5	19,119.3	5,860.9	1,479,120.8	262,733.3	315,211.5	409,275.0	40,06
Travel & hotels ...	2,836,365.8	564,956.3	44,098.5	1,161,440.7	182,080.1	291,624.1	9,509.5	205,384.8	35,77
Computers, office equip.	2,332,557.7	1,085,979.0	7,938.6	173,814.2	403,900.8	129,543.1	17,691.9	176,096.7	27,53
Direct response cos.	1,879,960.9	1,089,644.2	364,128.4	155,470.1	32,104.8	28,849.9	11,555.1	85,876.8	33,57
Candy, snacks, & soft drinks	1,796,549.7	132,095.0	7,043.8	5,266.0	794,759.8	280,474.9	219,999.7	241,631.3	62,74
Ins. & real estate ..	1,738,816.8	196,347.2	11,187.9	652,541.7	206,897.4	343,945.6	9,608.7	102,421.0	19,97
Publishing & media	1,629,514.8	406,427.9	15,534.8	300,943.6	65,105.0	312,666.5	23,130.2	199,696.7	80,36
Apparel, footwear ..	1,400,887.3	755,796.8	34,038.7	8,083.8	325,981.3	57,958.2	40,030.0	143,057.9	2,36
Sporting goods, toys.	1,202,692.4	240,305.0	220.0	10,953.3	333,260.6	189,533.4	126,389.7	285,774.7	2,58
Electronic equip. ...	968,500.2	244,368.6	32,367.3	31,456.3	232,517.3	124,106.9	61,041.8	221,996.6	7,77
Household equip. ..	924,795.2	184,593.6	17,523.7	10,824.3	340,648.5	120,252.1	75,860.4	139,604.0	24,96
Beer & wine	835,518.7	61,193.7	2,468.5	8,822.2	439,354.6	134,506.2	11,064.6	106,706.5	6,94
Soaps & cleansers	712,949.8	143,994.3	5,027.7	985.1	271,829.8	94,797.1	74,583.9	110,837.2	6,71
Jewelry, optical ...	643,723.2	296,596.8	15,059.3	16,397.8	185,568.3	27,841.8	27,523.4	53,479.8	4,66
Cigarettes	596,235.1	307,464.2	8,386.5	5,629.3	73,619.9	1,842.8	17,901.3	16,251.9	5,77
Miscellaneous	569,256.6	219,105.4	724.8	12,939.8	—	310.5	—	—	
Building materials	521,491.5	175,346.7	8,848.4	31,061.0	80,561.4	92,320.9	10,081.9	105,182.0	4,62
Pets & pet foods ..	391,813.9	92,334.8	6,313.5	10,143.1	125,691.4	67,781.0	27,271.0	53,488.5	1,67
Gasoline, lubricants	382,990.7	27,426.3	509.0	9,105.9	87,210.2	119,860.3	10,304.2	55,698.6	7,70
Hshld. furnishings .	297,788.4	185,977.0	13,778.3	11,008.1	29,650.1	22,238.7	5,647.1	24,846.3	75
Horticulture, farming	285,431.7	23,215.0	24,329.2	57,175.9	32,970.8	64,368.3	11,938.7	32,385.1	1,12
Liquor	266,406.6	208,734.3	6,296.5	6,390.3	—	434.3	—	2,765.8	
Freight, industrial ..	178,767.1	44,880.2	26.5	6,871.7	68,651.3	15,696.9	196.6	16,685.8	2,18
Industrial materials.	137,431.7	54,404.6	4.9	7,235.1	30,277.0	13,841.2	2,739.6	11,441.8	2,03
Bus. propositions	80,871.4	44,160.2	333.6	12,097.5	—	3,310.7	—	355.1	
Airplanes (not travel)	38,211.1	15,895.5	13.9	7,449.2	103.2	4,382.4	—	683.3	
Misc. not classified .	28,116.9	3,131.6	221.3	11,995.2	313.5	5,029.5	—	491.8	5
Not classified	1,954.5	—	—	—	—	—	—	—	
TOTAL	**73,214,448.2**	**12,701,056.6**	**1,016,644.4**	**15,777,516.4**	**15,225,141.0**	**14,534,589.2**	**2,514,989.5**	**5,781,916.0**	**865,64**

1998 IN PICTURES

AP/WIDE WORLD PHOTOS/CNN

It was a year of turmoil for Pres. Bill Clinton, as he battled for political survival amid an ongoing investigation of alleged wrongdoing by independent counsel Kenneth Starr. On Aug. 17 he testified before a grand jury convened by Starr and addressed the American people on TV (above); he admitted that, despite earlier denials, he had engaged in a relationship with former White House intern Monica Lewinsky that was "not appropriate." On Oct. 8 the U.S. House, voting largely along party lines, approved an inquiry into possible impeachment.

National Scene

AP/WIDE WORLD PHOTOS

CNN/SYGMA

The televised picture above right shows Pres. Bill Clinton and Monica Lewinsky during a November 1996 ceremony outside the White House. In 1998 their relationship was a focus of investigation by independent counsel Kenneth Starr—shown (left) leaving the White House after Clinton testified on the matter to a grand jury by closed-circuit TV, Aug. 17. The Starr report, with vanloads of other documents, was delivered to Congress Sept. 9 (below left) and was soon made public, as were other materials, including Clinton's taped grand jury testimony. Below right, House Judiciary Committee Chairman Henry Hyde (R, IL) receives the Starr report, which alleged possible impeachable offenses by Clinton, including perjury and obstruction of justice.

AP/WIDE WORLD PHOTOS

ROBERT VISSER/SYGMA

AP/WIDE WORLD PHOTOS

AP/WIDE WORLD PHOTOS

Bombs exploded outside U.S. embassies in Nairobi, Kenya, and Dar-es-Salaam, Tanzania, on Aug. 7, killing over 200 people, including 12 Americans. Here, rescuers in Nairobi carry a woman out of the rubble. On Aug. 20 the U.S. launched cruise missiles against targets in Sudan and Afghanistan allegedly tied to terrorism. The U.S. linked the bombings to exiled Saudi millionaire Osama bin Laden (inset).

On July 24 a gunman burst into the Capitol, killing two Capitol police officers in a corridor shootout; the suspect and a tourist were wounded. Below, the slain officers, Jacob Chestnut and John Gibson, lie in honor at a ceremony in the Rotunda attended by the president and members of Congress.

AP/WIDE WORLD PHOTOS

AP/WIDE WORLD PHOTOS/NASA

Astronaut Andrew Thomas (left) and Russian cosmonauts Pavel Vinogradov (top) and Anatoly Solovyev bid good-bye just before their docking module hatch closed, Jan. 28, and they entered the *Mir* space station. Thomas began a 4-month stay on *Mir*, the last by an American.

Viagra, a drug that treats male impotence, went on the market in April; in the first 3 months, doctors wrote 4 million Viagra prescriptions, generating over $400 million for the manufacturer, Pfizer Inc.

© EVAN AGOSTINI/GAMMA-LIAISON

LEIGH DAUGHTRIDGE/SIPA PRESS

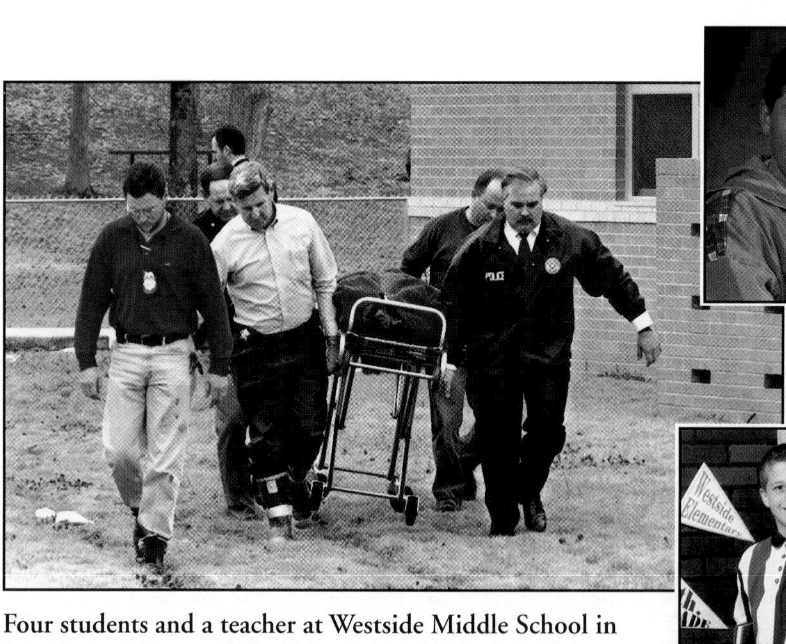

BISHOP'S PHOTOGRAPHY/SYGMA

RODNEY FREEDOM/JONESBORO SUN/SYGMA

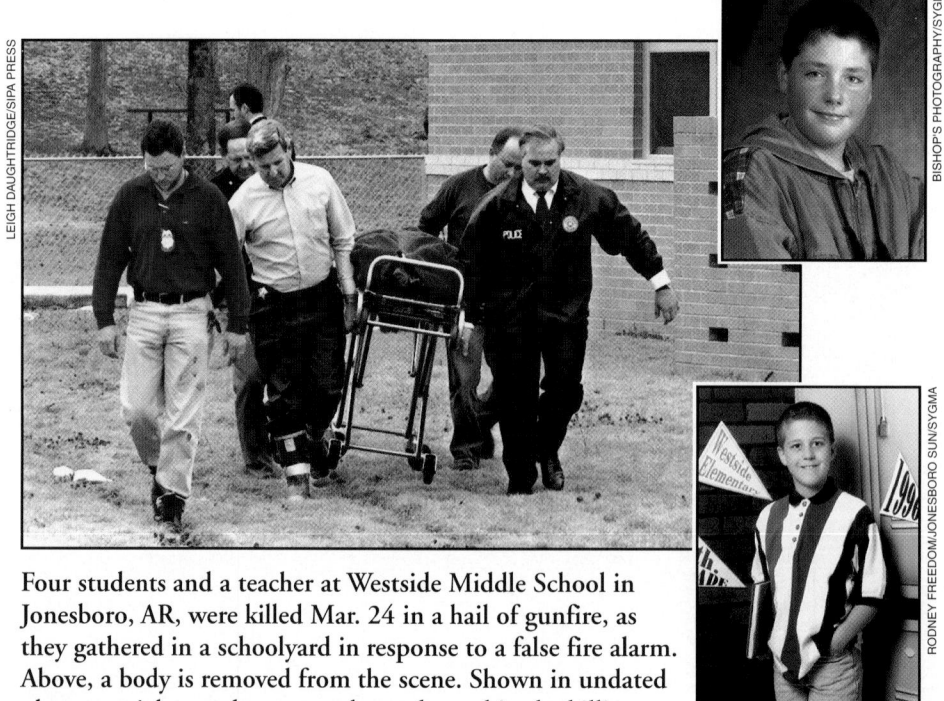

Four students and a teacher at Westside Middle School in Jonesboro, AR, were killed Mar. 24 in a hail of gunfire, as they gathered in a schoolyard in response to a false fire alarm. Above, a body is removed from the scene. Shown in undated photos at right are the two students charged in the killings: Mitchell Johnson, 13 (above), and Andrew Golden, 11.

ELECTION '98

RICK MAIMAN/SYGMA

AP/WIDE WORLD PHOTOS

Among races that attracted national attention, incumbent Sen. Alfonse D'Amato (R, NY), above left, faced a challenge from Rep. Chuck Schumer (above, right), who had beaten former vice-presidential candidate Geraldine Ferraro in the Democratic primary. In California (at right), Lt. Gov. Gray Davis (D; left) and Attorney Gen. Dan Lungren (R) vied for the governorship. In Texas (below), incumbent Gov. George Bush (R) campaigned for a second term.

AP/WIDE WORLD PHOTOS

BOB DAEMMRICH/SYGMA

PEOPLE

AP/WIDE WORLD PHOTOS

Kenny McCaughey, left, gives his son Kenny a kiss, as Bobbi McCaughey holds their daughter Natalie, at a groundbreaking ceremony for their much-needed new house, May 20 in Carlisle, IA. The couple became parents of septuplets Nov. 19, 1997.

Talk show host Oprah Winfrey exults after an Amarillo, TX, jury ruled in her favor Feb. 26. Winfrey was sued by cattle ranchers for allegedly defaming the beef industry by raising scares about mad cow disease.

AP/WIDE WORLD PHOTOS

DORAL CHENOWETH III/COLUMBUS DISPATCH/SYGMA

John Jarrell, outside his northeast Columbus, OH, home, July 30, enjoys some good news. He was one of the "Lucky 13" workers at an Automation Tooling Systems plant who split a Powerball lottery jackpot worth $296 million.

Comic actor Phil Hartman and his wife, Brynn, shown here in 1992, were found dead, May 28, at their Encino, CA, home. The former *Saturday Night Live* star was apparently shot by his wife in a murder-suicide.

AP/WIDE WORLD PHOTOS

Former Sen. Barry Goldwater was laid to rest in funeral services, June 3, at Arizona State University. Admired widely by friend and foe alike, the 1964 Republican presidential candidate (inset) died May 29 at the age of 89.

AP/WIDE WORLD PHOTOS

HULTON-DEUTSCH COLL./CORBIS

SIPA PRESS

The Spice Girls perform in New York City's Madison Square Garden, July 1, during a U.S. tour that delighted their young fans. From left to right: Melanie Chisholm (Sporty Spice), Victoria Adams (Posh Spice), Melanie Brown (Scary Spice), and Emma Bunton (Baby Spice). Not shown is Geri Halliwell (Ginger Spice), who dropped out of the group in May.

Roy Rogers, the straight-shooting singing cowboy star of the 40s and 50s, died July 6 at the age of 86. He is shown here with his wife, Dale Evans, and his trusty horse, Trigger, in a 1952 photo.

AP/WIDE WORLD PHOTOS

DISASTERS

AP/WIDE WORLD PHOTOS

Firefighter Mike Pultorak battles a wildfire on Route 92, southwest of Daytona Beach, FL, on June 25. More than 150,000 acres of land burned in the state's worst outbreak of wildfires since 1932.

Frances Nafziger (below, left) and her granddaughter Lynette Gabrielson sift through the remains of Frances's bedroom amid the devastation of Spencer, SD. The small town was flattened May 30 by a tornado that killed 6 and injured 150.

AP/WIDE WORLD PHOTOS

AP/WIDE WORLD PHOTOS

Relatives of victims killed in the Sept. 2 crash of Swissair Flight 111 join in a prayer service 3 days later at the coastal village of Peggy's Cove, Nova Scotia. All 229 aboard died when the plane crashed in the Atlantic about 5 miles offshore.

Photos continue on page 809.

NATIONAL DEFENSE

Data as of Oct. 15, 1998.

Chief Commanding Officers of the U.S. Military

Chairman, Joint Chiefs of Staff
Gen. Henry Hugh Shelton

Vice Chairman
Gen. Joseph W. Ralston

The Joint Chiefs of Staff consists of the Chairman and Vice Chairman of the Joint Chiefs of Staff; the Chief of Staff, U.S. Army; the Chief of Naval Operations; the Chief of Staff, U.S. Air Force; and the Commandant of the Marine Corps.

Army

Chief of Staff	**Date of Rank**
Reimer, Dennis J.	June 21, 1991
Other Generals	
Bramlett, David A.	Sept. 1, 1996
Clark , Wesley K.	June 21, 1996
Crouch, William W.	Jan. 1, 1995
Hartzog, William W.	Dec. 1, 1994
Schoomaker, Peter J.	Oct. 24, 1997
Shelton, Henry H.	Mar. 1, 1996
Shinseki, Eric K.	Aug. 5, 1997
Tilelli, John H., Jr.	July 19, 1994
Wilson, Johnnie E.	May 1, 1996

Air Force

Chief of Staff	
Ryan, Michael E.	Apr. 4, 1996
Other Generals	
Babbitt, George T., Jr.	June 1, 1997
Eberhart, Ralph E.	Aug. 1, 1997
Estes, Howell M., III	Oct. 1, 1996
Gamble, Patrick K.	Oct. 1, 1998
Gordon, John A.	Oct. 31, 1997
Hawley, Richard E.	Aug. 1, 1995
Jumper, John P.	Nov. 17, 1997
Myers, Richard B.	Sept. 1, 1997
Newton, Lloyd W.	Apr. 1, 1997
Ralston, Joseph W.	July 1, 1995
Robertson, Charles T. , J	Sept. 1, 1998

Navy

Chief of Naval Operations	**Date of Rank**
Adm. Jay L. Johnson (aviator)	Apr. 1, 1996
Other Admirals	
Bowman, Frank L. (submariner)	Oct. 1, 1996
Clemins, Archie R. (submariner)	Jan. 1, 1997
Gehman, Harold W., Jr. (surface warfare)	Oct. 1, 1996
Lopez, Thomas J. (surface warfare)	July 31, 1996
Mies, Richard W. (submariner)	Aug. 1, 1998
Piling, Donald L. (surface warfare)	Oct. 30, 1997
Prueher, Joseph W. (aviator)	June 1, 1995
Reason, J. Paul (surface warfare)	Feb. 1, 1997

Marine Corps

Commandant of the Marine Corps (CMC)	
Gen. Charles C. Krulak	July 1, 1995
Other Generals	
Dake, Terrence R.	Sept. 5, 1998
Wilhelm, Charles E.	Sept. 25, 1997
Zinn, Anthony C.	Aug. 8, 1997

Coast Guard

Commandant, with rank of Admiral	
James M. Loy	May 29, 1998
Vice Commandant, with rank of Vice Admiral	
James C. Card	May 23, 1997

Unified Defense Commands Commanders in Chief

U.S. European Command, Stuttgart-Vaihingen, Germany — Gen. Wesley K. Clark (USA) (concurrently NATO Supreme Allied Commander, Europe)

U.S. Pacific Command, Honolulu, HI — Adm. Joseph W. Prueher (USN)

U.S. Atlantic Command, Norfolk, VA — Adm. Harold W. Gehman, Jr. (USN) (concurrently NATO Supreme Allied Commander, Atlantic)

U.S. Special Operations Command, MacDill AFB, Florida — Gen. Peter J. Schoomaker (USA)

U.S. Transportation Command, Scott AFB, Illinois — Gen. Charles T. Robertson Jr. (USAF)

U.S. Central Command, MacDill AFB, Florida — Gen. Anthony C. Zinni (USMC)

U.S. Southern Command, Quarry Heights, Panama — Lt. Gen. Charles E. Wilhelm (USMC)

U.S. Space Command, Peterson AFB, Colorado — Gen. Richard B. Myers (USAF)

U.S. Strategic Command, Offutt AFB, Nebraska — Adm. Richard W. Mies (USN)

North Atlantic Treaty Organization International Commands

Supreme Allied Commander, Europe (SACEUR) — Gen. Wesley K. Clark (USA)

Deputy Supreme Allied Commander, Europe (DSACEUR) — Gen. Sir Jeremy MacKenzie (UKA)

Supreme Allied Commander, Atlantic — Adm. Harold W. Gehman, Jr. (USN)

Commander in Chief, Allied Forces Southern Europe — Adm. James O. Ellis (USN)

Commander in Chief, Allied Forces Central Europe — Gen. Joachim Spiering (GEA)

Commander in Chief, Allied Forces Northwestern Europe — Air Chief Marshal Sir John Cheshire (RAF)

Chairman, NATO Military Committee — Gen. Klaus Naumann (GEA)

Principal U.S. Military Training Centers

Army

Name, PO address	ZIP	Nearest city
Aberdeen Proving Ground, MD	21005	Aberdeen
Carlisle Barracks, PA	17013	Carlisle
Fort Benning, GA	31905	Columbus
Fort Bliss, TX	79916	El Paso
Fort Bragg, NC	28307	Fayetteville
Fort Gordon, GA	30905	Augusta
Fort Huachuca, AZ	85613	Sierra Vista
Fort Jackson, SC	29207	Columbia
Fort Knox, KY	40121	Louisville
Fort Leavenworth, KS	66027	Leavenworth
Fort Lee, VA	23801	Petersburg
Fort McClellan, AL	36205	Anniston
Fort Rucker, AL	36362	Dothan
Fort Sill, OK	73503	Lawton
Fort Leonard Wood, MO	65473	Rolla
Joint Readiness Training Center, Ft. Polk, LA	71459	Leesville
National Training Center, Ft. Irwin, CA	92311	Barstow, CA
The Judge Advocate General School, VA	22901	Charlottesville

Navy

Name	ZIP	Nearest city	Name	ZIP	Nearest city
Naval Education & Training Ctr.	32508	Pensacola, FL	Naval Education & Training Ctr.	02841	Newport, RI
Naval Air Training Center	78419	Corpus Christi, TX	Naval Post Graduate School. .	93943	Monterey, CA
Training Command, Atlantic Fleet	23511	Norfolk, VA	Naval Submarine School	06349	Groton, CT
Training Command, Pacific Fleet	92143	San Diego, CA	Naval Training Ctr., Great Lakes	60088	N. Chicago, IL
Naval Aviation Schools Command	32508	Pensacola, FL	Naval War College	02841	Newport, RI

Marine Corps

Name, PO address	ZIP	Nearest city	Name, PO address	ZIP	Nearest city
MCB Camp Lejeune, NC.....	28542	Jacksonville	MCAS Cherry Point, NC.....	28533	Havelock
MCB Camp Pendleton, CA ...	92055	Oceanside	MCAS Miramar, CA	92145	San Diego
MCB Kaneohe Bay, HI	96863	Kailua	MCAS New River, NC.......	28545	Jacksonville
MCAGCC Twentynine Palms, CA	92278	Palm Springs	MCAS Beaufort, SC	29904	Beaufort
MCCDC Quantico, VA.......	22134	Quantico	MCAS Yuma, AZ	85369	Yuma
MCRD Parris Island, SC	29905	Beaufort	MCMWTC Bridgeport, CA....	93517	Bridgeport
MCRD San Diego, CA.......	92140	San Diego			

MCB = Marine Corps Base. MCCDC = Marine Corps Combat Development Command. MCAS = Marine Corps Air Station. MCRD = Marine Corps Recruit Depot. MCAGCC = Marine Corps Air-Ground Combat Center. MCMWTC = Marine Corps Mountain Warfare Training Center.

Air Force

Name, PO address	ZIP	Nearest city	Name, PO address	ZIP	Nearest city
Goodfellow AFB, TX	76908	San Angelo	Maxwell AFB, AL...........	36112	Montgomery
Keesler AFB, MS............	39534	Biloxi	Sheppard AFB, TX..........	76311	Wichita Falls
Lackland AFB, TX...........	78236	San Antonio			

All are Air Education and Training Command Bases.

Personal Salutes and Honors, U.S.

The U.S. national salute, 21 guns, is also the salute to a national flag. U.S. independence is commemorated by the salute to the Union—one gun for each state—fired at noon July 4, at all military posts provided with suitable artillery.

A 21-gun salute on arrival and departure, with 4 ruffles and flourishes, is rendered to the president of the United States, to an ex-president, and to a president-elect. The national anthem or "Hail to the Chief," as appropriate, is played for the president, and the national anthem for the others. A 21-gun salute on arrival and departure, with 4 ruffles and flourishes, also is rendered to the sovereign or chief of state of a foreign country or a member of a reigning royal family; the national anthem of his or her country is played. The music is considered an inseparable part of the salute and immediately follows the ruffles and flourishes without pause. For the Honors March, generals receive the "General's March," admirals receive the "Admiral's March," and all others receive the 32-bar medley of "The Stars and Stripes Forever."

GRADE, TITLE, OR OFFICE	Salute (in guns) Arriving	Leaving	Ruffles and flourishes	Music
Vice president of United States........................	19		4	Hail, Columbia
Speaker of the House...............................	19		4	Honors March
U.S. or foreign ambassador	19		4	Nat. anthem of official
Premier or prime minister............................	19		4	Nat. anthem of official
Secretary of Defense, Army, Navy, or Air Force	19	19	4	Honors March
Other cabinet members, Senate president pro tempore, governor, or chief justice of U.S.....................	19		4	Honors March
Chairman, Joint Chiefs of Staff........................	19	19	4	
Army chief of staff, chief of naval operations, Air Force chief of staff, Marine commandant	19	19	4	Honors March
General of the Army, general of the Air Force, fleet admiral...	19	19	4	
Generals, admirals.................................	17	17	4	
Assistant secretaries of Defense, Army, Navy, or Air Force ...	17	17	4	Honors March
Chair of a committee of Congress.....................	17		4	Honors March

Other salutes (on arrival only) include: 15 guns, with 3 ruffles and flourishes, for U.S. envoys or ministers and foreign envoys or ministers accredited to the U.S.; 15 guns, for a lieutenant general or vice admiral; 13 guns, with 2 ruffles and flourishes, for a major general or rear admiral (upper half) and for U.S. ministers resident and ministers resident accredited to the U.S.; 11 guns, with 1 ruffle and flourish, for a brigadier general or rear admiral (lower half) and for U.S. charges d'affaires and like officials accredited to the U.S.; 11 guns, no ruffles and flourishes, for consuls general accredited to the U.S.

Military Units, U.S. Army and Air Force

Army Units. Squad: In infantry usually 10 enlisted personnel under a staff sergeant. **Platoon:** In infantry 4 squads under a lieutenant. **Company:** Headquarters section and 3 platoons under a captain. (Company-size unit in the artillery is a battery; in the cavalry, a troop.) **Battalion:** Hdqts. and 4 or more companies under a lieutenant colonel. (Battalion-size unit in the cavalry is a squadron.) **Brigade:** Hdqts. and 3 or more battalions under a colonel. **Division:** Hdqts. and 3 brigades with artillery, combat support, and combat service support units under a major general. **Army Corps:** Two or more divisions with corps troops under a lieutenant general. **Field Army:** Hdqts. and 2 or more corps with field Army troops under a general.

Air Force Units. Flight: Numerically designated flights are the lowest level unit in the Air Force. They are used primarily where there is a need for small mission elements to be incorporated into an organized unit. **Squadron:** A squadron is the basic unit in the Air Force. It is used to designate the mission units in operational commands. **Group:** The group is a flexible unit composed of 2 or more squadrons whose functions may be operational, support, or administrative in nature

The Federal Service Academies

U.S. Military Academy, West Point, NY. Founded 1802. Awards BS degree and Army commission for a 5-year service obligation. For admissions information, write Admissions Office, Bldg. 606, USMA, West Point, NY 10996.

U.S. Naval Academy, Annapolis, MD. Founded 1845. Awards BS degree and Navy or Marine Corps commission for a 5-year service obligation. For admissions information, write Dean of Admissions, Naval Academy, Annapolis, MD 21402.

U.S. Air Force Academy, Colorado Springs, CO. Founded 1954. Awards BS degree and Air Force commission for a 6-year service obligation. For admissions information, write Registrar, U.S. Air Force Academy, CO 80840-5025.

U.S. Coast Guard Academy, New London, CT. Founded 1876. Awards BS degree and Coast Guard commission for a 5-year service obligation. For admissions information, write Director of Admissions, Coast Guard Academy, New London, CT 06320.

U.S. Merchant Marine Academy, Kings Point, NY. Founded 1943. Awards BS degree, a license as a deck, engineer, or dual officer, and a U.S. Naval Reserve commission. Service obligations vary according to options taken by the graduate. For admissions information, write Admission Office, U.S. Merchant Marine Academy, Kings Point, NY 11024.

U.S. Army, Navy, Air Force, Marine Corps, and Coast Guard Insignia

Source: Dept. of the Army, Dept. of the Navy, Dept. of the Air Force, U.S. Dept. of Defense

Army

General of the Armies — Gen. John J. Pershing, the only person to have held this rank, in life, was authorized to prescribe his own insignia, but never wore in excess of four stars. The rank originally was established posthumously by Congress for George Washington in 1799, and he was promoted to the rank by joint resolution of Congress, approved by Pres. Gerald Ford, Oct. 19, 1976.

General of the Army — Five silver stars fastened together in a circle and the coat of arms of the United States in gold color metal with shield and crest enameled.

General	Four silver stars
Lieutenant General	Three silver stars
Major General	Two silver stars
Brigadier General	One silver star
Colonel	Silver eagle
Lieutenant Colonel	Silver oak leaf
Major	Gold oak leaf
Captain	Two silver bars
First Lieutenant	One silver bar
Second Lieutenant	One gold bar

Warrant Officers

Grade Five — Silver bar with 4 enamel silver squares
Grade Four — Silver bar with 4 enamel black squares
Grade Three — Silver bar with 3 enamel black squares
Grade Two — Silver bar with 2 enamel black squares
Grade One — Silver bar with 1 enamel black squares

Noncommissioned Officers

Sergeant Major of the Army (E-9) — Three chevrons above 3 arcs, with an American Eagle centered on the chevrons, flanked by 2 stars—one star on each side of the eagle. Also wears distinctive red and white shield collar insignia.

Command Sergeant Major (E-9) — Three chevrons above 3 arcs with a 5-pointed star with a wreath around the star between the chevrons and arcs.

Sergeant Major (E-9) — Three chevrons above 3 arcs with a 5-pointed star between the chevrons and arcs.

First Sergeant (E-8) — Three chevrons above 3 arcs with a lozenge between the chevrons and arcs.

Master Sergeant (E-8) — Three chevrons above 3 arcs.
Sergeant First Class (E-7) — Three chevrons above 2 arcs.
Staff Sergeant (E-6) — Three chevrons above 1 arc.
Sergeant (E-5) — Three chevrons.
Corporal (E-4) — Two chevrons.

Specialists

Specialist (E-4) — Eagle device only.

Other enlisted

Private First Class (E-3) — One chevron above one arc.
Private (E-2) — One chevron.
Private (E-1) — None.

Air Force

Insignia for Air Force officers are identical to those of the Army. Insignia for enlisted personnel are worn on both sleeves and consist of a star and an appropriate number of rockers. Chevrons appear above 5 rockers for the top 3 noncommissioned officer ranks, as follows (in ascending order): Master Sergeant, 1 chevron; Senior Master Sergeant, 2 chevrons; and Chief Master Sergeant, 3 chevrons. The insignia of the Chief Master Sergeant of the Air Force has 3 chevrons and a wreath around the star design.

Navy

The following are worn on the lower sleeves of the Service Dress Blue uniform. They are of gold embroidery.

Rank	Insignia
Fleet Admiral*	1 two inch with 4 one-half inch
Admiral	1 two inch with 3 one-half inch
Vice Admiral	1 two inch with 2 one-half inch
Rear Admiral (upper half)	1 two inch with 1 one-half inch
Rear Admiral (lower half)	1 two inch
Captain	4 one-half inch
Commander	3 one-half inch
Lieutenant Commander	2 one-half inch with 1 one-quarter inch between
Lieutenant	2 one-half inch
Lieutenant (j.g.)	1 one-half inch with one-quarter inch above
Ensign	1 one-half inch

Warrant Officer-W-4 — ½" stripe with 1 break
Warrant Officer W-3 — ½" stripe with 2 breaks, 2" apart
Warrant Officer W-2 — ½" stripe with 3 breaks, 2" apart
Warrant Officer W-1 — ¼" stripe with 3 breaks, 2" apart

Enlisted personnel (noncommissioned petty officers)—A rating badge worn on the upper left sleeve, consisting of a spread eagle, appropriate number of chevrons, and centered specialty mark.

*The rank of Fleet Admiral is reserved for wartime use only.

Marine Corps

Marine Corps' distinctive cap and collar ornament is the Marine Corps Emblem—a combination of the American eagle, a globe, and an anchor. Marine Corps and Army officer insignia are similar. Marine Corps enlisted insignia, although basically similar to Army's, feature crossed rifles beneath the chevrons. Marine Corps enlisted rank insignia are as follows:

Sergeant Major of the Marine Corps (E-9) — Same as Sergeant Major (below) but with Marine Corps emblem in the center with a 5-pointed star on both sides of the emblem.

Sergeant Major (E-9) — Three chevrons above 4 rockers with a 5-pointed star in the center.

Master Gunnery Sergeant (E-9) — Three chevrons above 4 rockers with a bursting bomb insignia in the center.

First Sergeant (E-8) — Three chevrons above 3 rockers with a diamond in the middle.

Master Sergeant (E-8) — Three chevrons above 3 rockers with crossed rifles in the middle.

Gunnery Sergeant (E-7) — Three chevrons above 2 rockers with crossed rifles in the middle.

Staff Sergeant (E-6) —Three chevrons above 1 rocker with crossed rifles in the middle.

Sergeant (E-5) — Three chevrons above crossed rifles.
Corporal (E-4) — Two chevrons above crossed rifles.
Lance Corporal (E-3) — One chevron above crossed rifles.
Private First Class (E-2) — One chevron.
Private (E-1) — None.

Coast Guard

Coast Guard insignia follow Navy custom, with certain minor changes such as the officer cap insignia. The Coast Guard shield is worn on both sleeves of officers and on the right sleeve of all enlisted personnel.

U.S. Army Personnel on Active Duty[1]

Source: Department of the Army, U.S. Dept. of Defense

Date[2]	Total strength	Commissioned officers			Warrant officers		Enlisted personnel		
		Total	Male	Female[3]	Male[4]	Female	Total	Male	Female
1940	267,767	17,563	16,624	939	763	—	249,441	249,441	—
1942	3,074,184	203,137	190,662	12,475	3,285	—	2,867,762	2,867,762	—
1943	6,993,102	557,657	521,435	36,222	21,919	0	6,413,526	6,358,200	55,325
1944	7,992,868	740,077	692,351	47,726	36,893	10	7,215,888	7,144,601	71,287
1945	8,266,373	835,403	772,511	62,892	56,216	44	7,374,710	7,283,930	90,780
1946	1,889,690	257,300	240,643	16,657	9,826	18	1,622,546	1,605,847	16,699
1950	591,487	67,784	63,375	4,409	4,760	22	518,921	512,370	6,551
1955	1,107,606	111,347	106,173	5,174	10,552	48	985,659	977,943	7,716
1960	871,348	91,056	86,832	4,224	10,141	39	770,112	761,833	8,279
1965	967,049	101,812	98,029	3,783	10,285	23	854,929	846,409	8,520
1970	1,319,735	143,704	138,469	5,235	23,005	13	1,153,013	1,141,537	11,476
1975	781,316	89,756	85,184	4,572	13,214	22	678,324	640,621	37,703
1980 (Sept. 30)	772,661	85,339	77,843	7,496	13,265	113	673,944	612,593	61,351
1985 (Sept. 30)	776,244	94,103	83,563	10,540	15,296	288	666,557	598,639	67,918
1990 (Mar. 31)	746,220	91,330	79,520	11,810	15,177	470	639,713	567,015	72,698
1993 (Mar. 31)	590,324	76,714	66,336	10,378	12,359	441	500,810	443,942	56,868
1994	553,627	74,956	64,281	10,675	12,448	535	465,688	405,664	60,024
1995	521,036	72,646	62,250	10,396	12,053	599	435,807	377,832	57,975
1996 (May 31)	493,330	68,850	58,875	9,975	11,456	660	408,511	351,669	56,842
1997 (May 31)	487,297	67,986	58,270	9,716	11,021	719	403,072	342,817	60,255
1998	491,707	67,048	56,650	10,398	10,989	661	402,000	345,149	56,851

(1) Represents strength of the active Army, including Philippine Scouts, retired Regular Army personnel on extended active duty, and National Guard and Reserve personnel on extended active duty; excludes U.S. Military Academy cadets, contract surgeons, and National Guard and Reserve personnel not on extended active duty. (2) June 30, unless otherwise noted; data for 1940 to 1946 include personnel in the Army Air Forces and its predecessors (Air Service and Air Corps). (3) Includes women doctors, dentists, and Medical Service Corps officers for 1946 and subsequent years, women in the Army Nurse Corps for all years, and the Women's Army Corps and Women's Medical Specialists Corps (dietitians, physical therapists, and occupational specialists) for 1943 and subsequent years. (4) Act of Congress approved Apr. 27, 1926, directed the appointment as warrant officers of field clerks still in active service. Includes flight officers as follows: 1943, 5,700; 1944, 13,615; 1945, 31,117; 1946, 2,580.

U.S. Navy Personnel on Active Duty

Date	Officers	Nurses	Enlisted	Officer Candidates	Total
1940 (June)	13,162	442	144,824	2,569	160,997
1945 (June)	320,293	11,086	2,988,207	61,231	3,380,817
1950 (June)	42,687	1,964	331,860	5,037	381,538
1960 (June)	67,456	2,103	544,040	4,385	617,984
1970 (June)	78,488	2,273	605,899	6,000	692,660
1980 (June)[1]	63,100	—	464,100	—	527,200
1990 (Sept.)	74,429	—	530,133	—	604,562
1991 (Oct.)	70,824	—	494,923	—	565,747
1992 (Mar.)	71,826	—	500,459	—	572,285
1993 (Mar.)	66,787	—	445,409	—	512,196
1994 (Apr.)	64,430	—	418,378	—	482,808
1995 (May)	61,075	—	402,626	—	463,701
1996 (June)	60,013	—	376,595	—	436,608
1997 (June)	57,341	—	340,616	—	397,957
1998 (Sept.)	55,007	—	326,196	—	381,203

(1) Starting in 1980, "Nurses" are included with "Officers," and "Officer Candidates" are included with "Enlisted."

U.S. Marine Corps Personnel on Active Duty

(midyear personnel figures)

Year	Officers	Enlisted	Total	Year	Officers	Enlisted	Total	Year	Officers	Enlisted	Total
1940	1,800	26,545	28,345	1980	18,198	170,271	188,469	1994	18,430	159,949	178,379
1945	37,067	437,613	474,680	1990	19,958	176,694	196,652	1995	18,017	153,929	171,946
1950	7,254	67,025	74,279	1991	19,753	174,287	194,040	1996	18,146	154,141	172,287
1960	16,203	154,418	170,621	1992	19,132	165,397	184,529	1997	18,089	154,240	172,329
1970	24,941	234,796	259,737	1993	18,878	161,205	180,083	1998	17,984	154,648	172,632

U.S. Air Force Personnel on Active Duty

(as of May 1)

Year[1]	Strength	Year[1]	Strength	Year[1]	Strength	Year[1]	Strength
1907	3	1942	764,415	1970	791,078	1993	444,351
1918	195,023	1943	2,197,114	1980	557,969	1994	426,327
1920	9,050	1944	2,372,292	1986	608,200	1995	400,051
1930	13,531	1945	2,282,259	1990	535,233	1996	389,400
1940	51,165	1950	411,277	1991	510,432	1997	378,681
1941	152,125	1960	814,213	1992	470,315	1998	363,479

(1) Prior to 1947, data are for U.S. Army Air Corps and Air Service of the Signal Corps.

U.S. Coast Guard Personnel on Active Duty

(midyear personnel figures)

Year	Total	Officers	Cadets	Enlisted	Year	Total	Officers	Cadets	Enlisted
1970	37,689	5,512	653	31,524	1989	37,453	6,614	867	29,972
1975	36,788	5,630	1,177	29,981	1990	37,308	6,475	820	29,860
1980	39,381	6,463	877	32,041	1991	38,280	7,095	900	30,285
1981	39,760	6,519	981	32,260	1992	39,185	7,348	919	30,918
1983	39,708	6,535	811	32,362	1993	38,832	7,724	691	30,417
1984	38,705	6,790	759	31,156	1994	37,284	7,401	881	29,002
1985	38,595	6,775	733	31,087	1995	36,731	7,489	841	28,401
1986	37,284	6,577	754	29,953	1996	35,229	7,270	830	27,129
1987	38,576	6,644	859	31,073	1997	34,717	7,079	868	26,770
1988	37,723	6,530	887	30,306	1998	34,890	7,140	805	26,945

Chairmen of the Joint Chiefs of Staff

Gen. of the Army Omar N. Bradley, USA	8/16/49–8/14/53
Adm. Arthur W. Radford, USN	8/15/53–8/14/57
Gen. Nathan F. Twining, USAF	8/15/57 – 9/30/60
Gen. Lyman L. Lemnitzer, USA	10/1/60 – 10/30/62
Gen. Maxwell D. Taylor, USA	10/1/62 – 7/3/64
Gen. Earle G. Wheeler, USA	7/3/64 – 7/2/70
Adm. Thomas H. Moorer, USN	7/3/70 – 6/30/74
Gen. George S. Brown, USAF	7/1/74 – 6/20/78
Gen. David C. Jones, USAF	6/21/78 – 6/18/82
Gen. John W. Vessey Jr., USA	6/18/82 – 9/30/85
Adm. William J. Crowe, Jr., USN	10/1/85 – 9/30/89
Gen. Colin L. Powell, USA	10/1/89 – 9/30/93
Gen. John M. Shalikashvili, USA	10/1/93 – 9/30/97
Gen. Henry H. Shelton, USA	10/1/97–

Women in the U.S. Armed Forces

Source: U.S. Dept. of Defense

Women in the Army, Navy, Air Force, Marines, and Coast Guard are fully integrated with male personnel. Expansion of military women's programs began in the Department of Defense in fiscal year 1973.

Admission of women to the service academies began in the fall of 1976.

Under rules instituted in 1993, women were allowed to fly combat aircraft and serve aboard warships. Women remained restricted from service in ground combat units.

Between Apr. 1993 and July 1994, almost 260,000 positions in the armed forces were opened to women. In July 1994, 80.2% of all jobs and 92% of all career fields in the military had been opened to women. As of June 30, 1998, women made up 13.9% of the armed forces.

Women Active Duty Troops in 1998

Service	% Women
Army	14.8
Navy	13.0
Marines	5.8
Air Force	18.0
Coast Guard	9.8

Women on Active Duty, All Services*: 1973-97

Year	% Women	Year	% Women
1973	2.5	1987	10.2
1975	4.6	1993	11.6
1981	8.9	1998	13.9

*Not including the Coast Guard, which is a part of the Dept. of Transportation.

African American Service in U.S. Wars

American Revolution. About 5,000 African Americans served in the Continental Army, mostly in integrated units, some in all-black combat units.

Civil War. Some 200,000 African Americans served in the Union Army; 38,000 were killed, and 22 won the Medal of Honor (the nation's highest award).

World War I. About 367,000 African Americans served in the armed forces, 100,000 in France.

World War II. Over 1 mil African Americans served in the armed forces; all-black fighter and bomber AAF units and infantry divisions gave distinguished service. (By 1954, the armed forces were completely desegregated.)

Korean War. Approximately 3,100 African Americans lost their lives in combat.

Vietnam War. 274,937 African Americans served in the armed forces (1965-74); 5,681 were killed in combat.

Persian Gulf War. About 104,000 African Americans served in the Kuwaiti theater—20% of all U.S. troops, compared with 8.7% of all troops for World War II and 9.8% for Vietnam.

Defense Contracts

Source: U.S. Dept. of Defense

(in thousands of dollars)

The 50 companies (including their subsidiaries) or organizations receiving the largest dollar volume of prime contract awards from the U.S. Department of Defense during fiscal year 1997.

Lockheed Martin	$11,637,526	Foundation Health Systems	$655,884	Logicon	$336,602
Boeing	9,644,855	Avondale Industries	622,329	Sverdrup	328,222
Northrop Grumman	3,475,752	Humana	621,449	FMC	325,176
General Dynamics	3,012,018	United Defense LP	610,986	The Renco Group	313,805
Raytheon	2,863,236	Tracor	554,663	Motorola	310,840
General Motors	2,829,943	AlliedSignal	547,030	Mitre	304,358
United Technologies	1,810,297	Exxon	538,621	Aerospace	297,682
General Electric	1,677,067	DynCorp	534,754	OHM	293,795
Litton Industries	1,602,659	Texas Instruments	528,904	Shell Oil	293,291
Textron	1,445,066	Standard Missile	471,932	Halliburton	290,497
Science Applications Intl.	1,094,560	Rockwell International	453,764	Federal Express	289,324
GTE	889,899	BDM International	380,523	Nassco Holdings	287,783
ITT Industries	781,999	Alliant Techsystems	378,035	Johnson Controls	284,011
TRW	789,618	U.S. Dept. of Energy	375,543	Chevron	278,096
CBS	777,325	MIT	368,290	Stewart & Stevenson Svcs.	267,650
Newport News Shipbuilding	719,991	Electronic Data Systems	358,777	Bechtel Group	266,508
Computer Sciences	704,328	Longbow LLC	338,015		

For Further Information on the U.S. Armed Forces

Army — Office of the Chief of Public Affairs, Attention: Public Communications Division—CR, Army 1500 Wash., DC 20310-1500. **Website:** http://www.army.mil

Navy — Chief of Information, 1200 Navy Pentagon, Wash., DC 20350-1200. **Website:** http://www.navy.mil

Air Force — Office of Public Affairs, 1690 Air Force, Pentagon, Wash., DC 20330-1690. **Website:** http://www.af.mil

Marine Corps — Commandant of the Marine Corps (Code PA), Headquarters, U.S. Marine Corps, Wash. DC 20380-1775. **Website:** http://www.usmc.mil

Coast Guard — Commandant (G-CP), U.S. Coast Guard, 2100 Second St. SW, Wash., DC 20593-0001. **Website:** http://www.uscg.mil

Additional information on all the U.S. Armed Forces branches, as well as many other related organizations, can be accessed through DefenseLINK, the official Internet site of the Dept. of Defense: http://www.defenselink.mil

U.S. Veteran Population

Source: U.S. Dept. of Veterans Affairs; as of July 1998

(in thousands)

TOTAL VETERANS IN CIVILIAN LIFE[1]	**25,188**
Total wartime veterans[2]	**19,300**
Total Persian Gulf War	2,048
Persian Gulf War with service in Vietnam era	300
Persian Gulf War with no prior wartime service	1,748
Total Vietnam era	8,166
Vietnam era with service in Korean conflict	476
Vietnam era with no prior wartime service	7,690
Total Korean conflict	4,179
Korean conflict with service in WWII	641
Korean conflict with no prior wartime service	3,538
World War II	6,319
World War I	5
Total peacetime veterans	**5,888**
Total post-Vietnam era	3,018
Service between Korean conflict and Vietnam era only	2,732
Other peacetime	137

Note: Details may not add to total shown due to rounding. (1) There are an indeterminate number of Mexican Border period veterans, 18 of whom were receiving benefits in July 1997. (2) The category "wartime veterans" equals the sum of veterans from each listed war with no prior wartime service. The data refer only to veterans living in the U.S. and Puerto Rico; data on veterans living elsewhere are not available.

Veterans Compensation and Pension Case Payments

Source: 1900-1980: Dept. of Veterans Affairs; 1990-1997: Natl. Center for Veteran Analysis and Statistics

Fiscal year	Living veteran cases	Deceased veteran cases	Total cases	Total expenditures (dollars)	Fiscal year	Living veteran cases	Deceased veteran cases	Total cases	Total expenditures (dollars)
1900	752,510	241,019	993,529	$138,462,130	1970	3,127,338	1,487,176	4,614,514	$5,253,839,611
1910	602,622	318,461	921,083	159,974,056	1980	3,195,395	1,450,785	4,646,180	11,046,637,368
1920	419,627	349,916	769,543	316,418,030	1990	2,746,329	837,596	3,583,925	14,674,411,000
1930	542,610	298,223	840,833	418,432,809	1994	2,658,704	683,200	3,341,904	17,188,447,000
1940	610,122	239,176	849,298	429,138,465	1995	2,668,576	661,679	3,330,255	17,765,045,000
1950	2,368,238	658,123	3,026,361	2,009,462,298	1996	2,671,026	637,232	3,308,258	17,055,809,000
1960	3,008,935	950,802	3,959,737	3,314,761,383	1997	2,666,785	613,976	3,280,761	19,284,287,000

Active Duty U.S. Military Personnel Strengths, Worldwide

Source: U.S. Dept. of Defense

(as of Mar. 31, 1998)

U.S. Territories & Special Locations	
U.S., 48 contiguous states	965,097
Alaska	16,393
Hawaii	34,772
Guam	4,235
Johnston Atoll	262
Puerto Rico	2,122
Transients	29,193
Afloat	103,747
TOTAL[1]	**1,155,826**
Europe	
Belgium	1,689
Bosnia and Herzegovina	7,181
Croatia	550
Germany	65,641
Greece	454
Greenland	130
Hungary	1,219
Iceland	1,716
Italy	11,398
Macedonia, F.Y.R. of	367
Netherlands	712
Norway	166
Portugal	1,053
Spain	2,268
Turkey	2,690
United Kingdom	11,349
Afloat	3,979
TOTAL[1]	**112,880**
Former Soviet Republics	
Afloat	2,128
TOTAL[1]	**2,224**
East Asia & Pacific	
Australia	638
Japan	41,171
Korea, South	36,639
Singapore	170
Thailand	245
Afloat	14,623
TOTAL[1]	**93,707**
North Africa, Middle East & South Asia	
Bahrain	951
Diego Garcia	619
Egypt	1,053
Kuwait	1,207
Saudi Arabia	1,632
Afloat	15,501
TOTAL[1]	**21,262**
Other Western Hemisphere	
Belize	171
Canada	164
Cuba (Guantánamo)	1,431
Haiti	485
Honduras	774
Panama	4,609
Venezuela	138
Afloat	4,103
TOTAL[1]	**12,279**
TOTAL WORLDWIDE[2]	**1,408,370**

(1) Countries and areas with fewer than 100 assigned U.S. military members not listed; regional totals include personnel stationed in those countries and areas not shown. (2) Total worldwide also includes U.S. military personnel stationed in Sub-Saharan Africa (320), as well as undistributed personnel (9,872 total—7,421 ashore, 2,451 afloat).

The Medal of Honor

The Medal of Honor is the highest military award for bravery that can be given to any individual in the United States. The first Army Medals were awarded on Mar. 25, 1863, and the first Navy Medals went to sailors and Marines on Apr. 3, 1863.

On Dec. 21, 1861, Pres. Abraham Lincoln signed into law a bill to create the Navy Medal of Honor. Lincoln later (July 14, 1862) approved a resolution providing for the presentation of Medals of Honor to enlisted men of the Army and Voluntary Forces, making it a law. The law was amended on March 3, 1863 to extend its provisions to include officers as well as enlisted men.

The Medal of Honor is awarded in the name of Congress to a person who, while a member of the armed forces, distinguishes himself or herself conspicuously by gallantry and intrepidity at the risk of life above and beyond the call of duty while engaged in an action against any enemy of the United States; while engaged in military operations involving conflict with an opposing foreign force; or while serving with friendly foreign forces engaged in an armed conflict against an opposing armed force in which the United States is not a belligerent party. The deed performed must have been one of personal bravery or self-sacrifice so conspicuous as to clearly distinguish the individual above his or her comrades and must have involved risk of life. Incontestable proof of the performance of service is required, and each recommendation for award of this decoration is considered on the standard of extraordinary merit.

Prior to World War I, the 2,625 Army Medal of Honor awards up to that time were reviewed to determine which past awards met new stringent criteria. The Army removed 911 names from the list, most of them former members of a volunteer infantry group during the Civil War who had been induced to extend their enlistments when they were promised the medal. However, in 1977 a medal was restored to Dr. Mary Walker, and in 1989 medals were restored to Buffalo Bill Cody and 7 other Indian scouts.

Since that review, Medals of Honor have been awarded in the following numbers:

World War I	124	Korean War	131
Peacetime (1920-40)	18	Vietnam War	240
World War II	441	Somalia	2

The figure for World War II includes 7 African-American soldiers who were awarded Medals of Honor (6 of them posthumously) in Jan. 1997. Previously, no black soldier had received the medal for World War II service; an Army inquiry begun in 1993 concluded that the prevailing political climate and Army practices of the time had prevented proper recognition of heroism on the part of black soldiers in that war.

Nations With Largest Armed Forces, by Active-Duty Troop Strength, 1997

Source: *The Military Balance, 1997-98* (International Institute for Strategic Studies, published by Oxford University Press, UK)

	Troop strength				Navy			
	Active troops (thousands)	Reserve troops (thousands)	Defense expend. ($ bil)[1]	Tanks (MBT) (army only)	Cruisers/ Frigates/ Destroyers	Sub-marines	Combat aircraft FGA (air force only)	Combat aircraft fighters (air force only)
1. CHINA	2,840.0	1,200+	38.0	8,500	36F/18D	61	400+	2,748 est.
2. UNITED STATES	1,447.6	1,711.7	267.1[2]	7,836	30C/44F/57D**	95	52 tactic. ftr. sqn	
3. RUSSIA	1,240.0	20,000	71.0	15,500	22C/18F/19D**	128	725	415
4. India*	1,145.0	528.4	10.4	3,314	18F/6D**	17	17 sqn	20 sqn
5. N. Korea	1,055.0	4,700.0	5.4	3,000	3F	26	525 total FGA/ftr.	
6. S. Korea	672.0	4,500.0	15.5	2,130	33F/7D	6	255	130
7. Turkey	639.0	378.7	7.0	4,205	16F/5D	15	11 sqn	7 sqn
8. Pakistan*	587.0	513.0	3.7	2,120#	8F/3D	9	123	242
9. Iran	518.0	350.0	3.4	1,390	3F/1D	3	150	114
10. Vietnam	492.0	3-4,000	1.0	1,315	7F	—	71	124
11. Indonesia	461.0	400.0	4.7	355#	17F	2	54	12
12. Egypt	450.0	254.0	2.7	3,700	8F/1D	8	135	338
13. Myanmar	429.0	NA	2.0	130	—	—	24	36
14. Iraq	387.5	650.0	1.3	2,700	2F	—	130	180
15. Ukraine	387.4	1,000.0	1.3	4,063	4 total	3	200	424
16. FRANCE	380.8	292.5	47.2	768#	1C/35F/4D**	14	7 sqn	5 sqn
17. Taiwan	376.0	1,657.5	13.6	719	18F/18D	4	344 total FGA/ftr.	
18. Germany	347.1	315.0	39.2	3,248	12F/3D	16	8 sqn	8 sqn
19. Italy	325.2	484.0	23.8	1,325	1C/26F/4D**	8	8 sqn	7 sqn
20. Syria	320.0	500.0	1.6	4,600	4F	3	154	310
21. Brazil	314.7	1,115.0	10.6	287#	18F/3D**	6	78	16
22. Thailand	266.0	200.0	4.3	277#	14F**	—	47	41
23. Poland	241.8	406.0	3.1	1,729	1F/1D	3	109	231
24. Japan	235.6	46.7	44.5	1,110	48F/10D	16	70	228
25. Romania	227.0	427.0	0.7	1,255	6F/1D	1	88	203
26. UNITED KINGDOM	213.8	378.4	33.5	541	23F/12D**	15	11 sqn	6 sqn
27. Spain	197.5	431.9	8.6	776	17F**	8	3 sqn	9 sqn
28. Morocco	196.3	150.0	1.6	524	1F	—	47	15
29. Israel	175.0	430.0	9.6	4,300	—	3	412 total FGA/ftr.	
30. Mexico	175.0	300.0	3.1	—	4F/3D	—	—	10

Nations with known strategic nuclear capability in all capital letters. *India and Pakistan tested nuclear devices in 1998. MBT=main battle tank. FGA=fighter, ground attack; Sqn= squadron (12-24 aircraft). #=light tanks only. **Denotes navies with aircraft carriers, as follows: U.S. 12, UK 3, France 2, India 1, Italy 1, Russian 1, Brazil 1, Spain 1, Thailand 1. (1) 1996 figures unless otherwise noted. (2) 1997. NA = not available.

Directors of the Central Intelligence Agency

In 1942, Pres. Franklin D. Roosevelt established the Office of Strategic Services (OSS); it was disbanded in 1945. In 1946, Pres. Harry Truman established the Central Intelligence Group (CIG) to operate under the National Intelligence Authority (NIA). A 1997 law replaced the NIA with the National Security Council and the CIG with the Central Intelligence Agency.

Director	Served	Appointed by President	Director	Served	Appointed by President
Adm. Sidney W. Souers	1946	Truman	William E. Colby	1973-1976	Nixon
Gen. Hoyt S. Vandenberg	1946-1947	Truman	George Bush	1976-1977	Ford
Adm. Roscoe H. Hillenkoetter	1947-1950	Truman	Adm. Stansfield Turner	1977-1981	Carter
Gen. Walter Bedell Smith	1950-1953	Truman	William J. Casey	1981-1987	Reagan
Allen W. Dulles	1953-1961	Eisenhower	William H. Webster	1987-1991	Reagan
John A. McCone	1961-1965	Kennedy	Robert M. Gates	1991-1993	Bush
Adm. William F. Raborn Jr.	1965-1966	Johnson	R. James Woolsey	1993-1995	Clinton
Richard Helms	1966-1973	Johnson	John M. Deutch	1995-1997	Clinton
James R. Schlesinger	1973	Nixon	George J. Tenet	1997-	Clinton

Nuclear Arms Treaties and Negotiations: A Historical Overview

Aug. 5, 1963—Limited Test Ban Treaty signed in Moscow by U.S., USSR, and Britain; prohibited testing of nuclear weapons in space, above ground, and under water.

Jan. 27, 1967—Outer Space Treaty banned the introduction of nuclear weapons and other weapons of mass destruction into orbit around the earth, their installation on the moon or other celestial body, or their station in space.

July 1, 1968—Nuclear Nonproliferation Treaty, with U.S., USSR, and Great Britain as major signers, limited spread of nuclear material for military purposes by agreement not to assist nonnuclear nations in getting or making nuclear weapons. Extended indefinitely, May 11, 1995.

May 26, 1972—Strategic Arms Limitation Treaty (SALT I) signed in Moscow by U.S. and USSR. This short-term agreement imposed a 5-year freeze on both testing and deployment of intercontinental ballistic missiles (ICBMs) as well as submarine-launched ballistic missiles (SLBMs). In the area of defensive nuclear weapons, the separate **ABM Treaty** limited antiballistic missiles to 2 sites of 100 antiballistic missile launchers in each country (amended in 1974 to one site in each country). ABM Treaty amended Sept. 1997 to allow flexibility in development of shorter-range nuclear weapons.

July 3, 1974—ABM Treaty Revision (protocol on antiballistic missile systems) and **Threshold Test Ban Treaty** on limiting underground testing of nuclear weapons to 150 kilotons were signed by U.S. and USSR in Moscow.

Sept. 1977—U.S. and USSR agreed to continue to abide by SALT I, despite its expiration date.

June 18, 1979—SALT II signed in Vienna by the U.S. and USSR, constrained offensive nuclear weapons, limiting each side to 2,400 missile launchers and heavy bombers; ceiling to apply until Jan. 1, 1985. Treaty also set a subceiling of 1,320 ICBMs and SLBMs with multiple warheads on each side. SALT II never reached the Senate floor for ratification because Pres. Jimmy Carter withdrew support following Dec. 1979 Soviet invasion of Afghanistan.

Dec. 8, 1987—Intermediate-Range Nuclear Forces (INF) Treaty signed in Washington, D.C., by USSR leader Mikhail Gorbachev and U.S. Pres. Ronald Reagan, eliminating all U.S. and Soviet intermediate- and shorter-range nuclear missiles from Europe and Asia. Ratified, with conditions, by U.S. Senate on May 27, 1988; by USSR on June 1, 1988. Entered into force June 1, 1988.

July 31, 1991—Strategic Arms Reduction Treaty (START I) signed in Moscow by USSR and U.S. to reduce strategic offensive arms by about 30% in 3 phases over 7 years. START I was the first treaty to mandate reductions by the superpowers. Treaty was approved by U.S. Senate Oct. 1, 1992. With the Soviet Union breakup in Dec. 1991, 4 former Soviet republics became independent nations with strategic nuclear weapons—Russia, Ukraine, Kazakhstan, and Belarus. The last 3 agreed in principle in 1992 to transfer their nuclear weapons to Russia and ratify START I. The Russian Supreme Soviet voted to ratify, Nov. 4, 1992, but Russia decided not to provide instruments of ratification until the other 3 republics ratified START I and acceded to the Nuclear Nonproliferation Treaty (NPT) as nonnuclear nations. By late 1994, all 3 nations had done so, and NPT entered into force on Dec. 5, 1994. In Dec. 1996, Belarus was the last of the 3 to give up its nuclear weapons.

Jan. 3, 1993—START II signed in Moscow by U.S. and Russia. Potentially the broadest disarmament pact in history, it called for both sides to reduce their long-range nuclear arsenals to about one-third of their then-current levels within a decade and disable and dismantle launching systems. The U.S. ratified START II on Jan. 26, 1996. On Sept. 26, 1997, the U.S. and Russia signed an agreement that would delay the dismantling of launching systems under START II to the end of 2007 (they would still be disabled by 2003). The accord was expected to facilitate Russian ratification of START II. Russia and the U.S. also agreed in writing to work toward further strategic arms cuts in a 3d round of START negotiations.

Sept. 24, 1996—Comprehensive Test Ban Treaty (CTBT) signed by U.S. and Russia. The CTBT bans all nuclear weapon tests and other nuclear explosions. It is intended to help prevent the nuclear powers from developing more advanced weapons, while limiting the ability of other states to acquire such devices. As of Sept. 15, 1998, the CTBT had been signed by 150 nations, including China, Russia, the U.S., the U.K, and France. It had been ratified by 21, including France and the U.K.

Monthly Military Pay Scale[1]

Source: U.S. Dept. of Defense; effective Jan. 1, 1998

	Years of Service						
Rank/Grade	**2**	**4**	**8**	**12**	**16**	**20**	**26**
General—0-10 (2)	$7,832.40	$7,832.40	$8,133.00	$8,583.60	$9,197.70	$9,813.60	$10,424.70
Lt. General—0-9	6,881.40	7,028.10	7,206.60	7,506.60	8,133.00	8,583.60	9,197.70
Major General—0-8	6,255.90	6,404.10	6,881.40	7,206.60	7,506.60	8,133.00	8,333.70
Brig. General—0-7	5,389.80	5,389.80	5,631.60	5,958.00	6,881.40	7,354.80	7,354.80
Colonel—0-6	4,109.40	4,379.10	4,379.10	4,379.10	5,243.70	5,631.60	6,461.70
Lt. Colonel—0-5	3,512.70	3,755.70	3,755.70	4,077.60	4,676.70	5,094.60	5,272.50
Major—0-4	3,070.80	3,275.40	3,483.30	3,930.30	4,290.30	4,407.90	4,407.90
Captain—0-3	2,619.90	3,099.00	3,363.60	3,721.20	3,812.40	3,812.40	3,812.40
1st Lt.—0-2	2,231.70	2,771.40	2,828.70	2,828.70	2,828.70	2,828.70	2,828.70
2d Lt.—0-1	1,846.50	2,231.70	2,231.70	2,231.70	2,231.70	2,231.70	2,231.70
Chief Warrant—W-4	2,561.70	2,619.90	2,859.90	3,188.10	3,453.60	3,660.30	4,077.60
Warrant Officer—W-1	1,815.30	1,967.10	2,144.40	2,323.50	2,501.70	2,681.10	2,681.10
Sgt. Major—E-9 (3)	(3)	(3)	(3)	2,839.80	2,970.90	3,096.00	3,576.00
Master Sgt.—E-8	0.00	0.00	2,328.90	2,458.80	2,589.60	2,713.50	3,193.50
Sgt. 1st class—E-7	1,755.60	1,884.30	2,010.60	2,139.60	2,299.80	2,394.30	2,873.10
Staff Sgt.—E-6	1,524.90	1,655.70	1,779.90	1,940.10	2,065.80	2,097.00	2,097.00
Sergeant—E-5	1,336.20	1,462.20	1,621.80	1,748.10	1,779.90	1,779.90	1,779.90
Corporal—E-4	1,209.30	1,379.10	1,433.70	1,433.70	1,433.70	1,433.70	1,433.70
Pvt. 1st class—E-3	1,137.90	1,230.30	1,230.30	1,230.30	1,230.30	1,230.30	1,230.30
Private—E-2	1,038.30	1,038.30	1,038.30	1,038.30	1,038.30	1,038.30	1,038.30
Recruit—E-1	926.10	926.10	926.10	926.10	926.10	926.10	926.10

(1) The basic pay shown in this table is without a cap. The actual amount of pay received is limited to $9,225.00 per month. (2) While serving as Chairman or Vice Chairman of the Joint Chiefs of Staff, Chief of Staff of the Army or Air Force, Chief of Naval Operations, Commandant of the Marine Corps or Coast Guard, the amount of basic pay is $11,502.60, regardless of years of service; however, the amount received is limited to $9,225.00 per month. (3) While serving as Sergeant Major of the Army, Master Chief Petty Officer of the Navy or Coast Guard, Chief Master Sergeant of the Air Force, or Sergeant Major of the Marine Corps, basic pay is $4,346.40 per month.

Casualties in Principal Wars of the U.S.

Source: U.S. Dept. of Defense, U.S. Coast Guard

Data prior to World War I are based on incomplete records in many cases. Casualty data are confined to dead and wounded personnel and, therefore, exclude personnel captured or missing in action who were subsequently returned to military control. Dash (—) indicates information is not available. Off. = officers.

War	Branch of service	Number serving	CASUALTIES Battle deaths	Other deaths	Wounds not mortal[7]	Total
Revolutionary War	**Total**	**—**	**4,435**	**—**	**6,188**	**—**
1775-83	Army	184,000	4,044	—	6,004	—
	Navy	to	342	—	114	—
	Marines	250,000	49	—	70	—
War of 1812	**Total**	**286,730** [8]	**2,260**	**—**	**4,505**	**6,765**
1812-15	Army	—	1,950	—	4,000	5,950
	Navy	—	265	—	439	704
	Marines	—	45	—	66	111
Mexican War	**Total**	**78,789** [8]	**1,733**	**11,550**	**4,152**	**17,435**
1846-48	Army	—	1,721	11,550	4,102	17,373
	Navy	—	1	—	3	4
	Marines	—	11	—	47	58
	Coast Guard[12]	71 off.	—	—	—	—
Civil War	**Total**	**2,213,582** [8]	**140,415**	**224,097**	**281,881**	**646,392**
Union forces	Army	2,128,948	138,154	221,374	280,040	639,568
1861-65	Navy	—	2,112	2,411	1,710	6,233
	Marines	84,415	148	312	131	591
Confederate forces	**Total**	**—**	**74,524**	**59,297**	**—**	**133,821**
(estimate)[1]	Army	600,000	—	—	—	—
1863-66	Navy	to	—	—	—	—
	Marines	1,500,000	—	—	—	—
	Coast Guard[12]	219 off.	1	—	—	—
Spanish-American	**Total**	**307,420**	**385**	**2,061**	**1,662**	**4,108**
War	Army[3]	280,564	369	2,061	1,594	4,024
1898	Navy	22,875	10	0	47	57
	Marines	3,321	6	0	21	27
	Coast Guard[12]	660	0	—	—	—
World War I	**Total**	**4,743,826**	**53,513**	**63,195**	**204,002**	**320,710**
April 6, 1917-	Army[4]	4,057,101	50,510	55,868	193,663	300,041
Nov. 11, 1918	Navy	599,051	431	6,856	819	8,106
	Marines	78,839	2,461	390	9,520	12,371
	Coast Guard	8,835	111	81	—	192
World War II	**Total**	**16,353,659**	**292,131**	**115,185**	**671,846**	**1,079,162**
Dec. 7, 1941-	Army[5]	11,260,000	234,874	83,400	565,861	884,135
Dec. 31, 1946[2]	Navy[6]	4,183,466	36,950	25,664	37,778	100,392
	Marines	669,100	19,733	4,778	68,207	91,718
	Coast Guard	241,093	574	1,343	—	1,917
Korean War[9]	**Total**	**5,764,143**	**33,667**	**3,249**	**103,284**	**140,200**
June 25, 1950-	Army	2,834,000	27,709	2,452	77,596	107,757
July 27, 1953	Navy	1,177,000	493	160	1,576	2,226
	Marines	424,000	4,267	339	23,744	28,353
	Air Force	1,285,000	1,198	298	368	1,864
	Coast Guard	44,143	—	—	—	—
Vietnam War[10]	**Total**	**8,752,000**	**47,393**	**10,800**	**153,363**	**211,556**
Aug. 4, 1964-	Army	4,368,000	30,929	7,272	96,802	135,003
Jan. 27, 1973	Navy	1,842,000	1,631	931	4,178	6,740
	Marines	794,000	13,085	1,753	51,392	66,230
	Air Force	1,740,000	1,741	842	931	3,514
	Coast Guard	8,000	7	2	60	69
Persian Gulf War	**Total**	**467,939** [11]	**148**	**151**	**467**	**766**
1991	Army	246,682	98	105	—	—
	Navy	98,852	6	14	—	—
	Marines	71,254	24	26	—	—
	Air Force	50,751	20	6	—	—
	Coast Guard	400	—	—	—	—

(1) Authoritative statistics for the Confederate forces are not available. An estimated 26,000-31,000 Confederate personnel died in Union prisons.
(2) Data are for Dec. 1, 1941, through Dec. 31, 1946, when hostilities were officially terminated by Presidential Proclamation; few battle deaths or wounds not mortal were incurred after Japanese acceptance of Allied peace terms on Aug. 14, 1945. Numbers serving Dec. 1, 1941-Aug. 31, 1945, were: Total—14,903,213; Army—10,420,000; Navy—3,883,520; Marine Corps—599,693.
(3) Number serving covers the period April 21-Aug. 13, 1898, while dead and wounded data are for the period May 1-Aug. 31, 1898. Active hostilities ceased on Aug. 13, 1898, but ratifications of the treaty of peace were not exchanged between the United States and Spain until April 11, 1899.
(4) Includes Army Air Forces battle deaths and wounds not mortal, as well as casualties suffered by American forces in northern Russia to Aug. 25, 1919, and in Siberia to April 1, 1920. Other deaths covered the period April 1, 1917-Dec. 31, 1918.
(5) Includes Army Air Forces.
(6) Battle deaths and wounds not mortal include casualties incurred in Oct. 1941 due to hostile action.
(7) Marine Corps data for World War II, the Spanish-American War, and prior wars represent the number of individuals wounded, whereas all other data in this column represent the total number (incidence) of wounds.
(8) As reported by the Commissioner of Pensions in his Annual Report for Fiscal Year 1903.
(9) As a result of an ongoing Dept. of Defense review of available Korean War casualty record information, updates to previously reported figures for battle deaths and other deaths are reflected in this table.
(10) Number serving covers the period Aug. 4, 1964-Jan. 27, 1973 (date of ceasefire). Includes casualties incurred in Mayaguez Incident. Wounds not mortal exclude 150,332 persons not requiring hospital care.
(11) Estimated, because deployment figures changed continually.
(12) Actually the U.S. Revenue Cutter Services, predecessor to the U.S. Coast Guard.

AEROSPACE

Memorable Moments in Human Spaceflight

Sources: National Aeronautics and Space Administration; Congressional Research Service; World Almanac research

Note: U.S. space missions are in **boldface**. Other missions were sponsored by the Soviet Union or, later, the Commonwealth of Independent States. All dates are Eastern standard time. EVA = extravehicular activity. ASTP = Apollo-Soyuz Test Project. Number of total flights by each crew member is given in parentheses when flight listed is not the first.

Dates	Mission[1]	Crew (no. of flights)	Duration (hr:min)	Remarks
4/12/61	Vostok 1	Yuri A. Gagarin	1:48	1st human orbital flight
5/5/61	**Mercury-Redstone 3**	**Alan B. Shepard Jr.**	**0:15**	**1st American in space**
7/21/61	**Mercury-Redstone 4**	**Virgil I. Grissom**	**0:15**	**Spacecraft sank, Grissom rescued**
8/6/61-8/7/61	Vostok 2	Gherman S. Titov	25:18	1st spaceflight of more than 24 hrs
2/20/62	**Mercury-Atlas 6**	**John H. Glenn Jr.**	**4:55**	**1st American in orbit; 3 orbits**
5/24/62	**Mercury-Atlas 7**	**M. Scott Carpenter**	**4:56**	**Manual retrofire error caused 250-mi landing overshoot**
8/11/62-8/15/62	Vostok 3	Andrian G. Nikolayev	94:22	Vostok 3 and 4 made 1st group flight
8/12/62-8/15/62	Vostok 4	Pavel R. Popovich	70:57	On 1st orbit it came within 3 mi of Vostok 3
10/3/62	**Mercury-Atlas 8**	**Walter M. Schirra Jr.**	**9:13**	**Landed 5 mi from target**
5/15/63-5/16/63	**Mercury-Atlas 9**	**L. Gordon Cooper**	**34:19**	**1st U.S. evaluation of effects of one day in space on a person; 22 orbits**
6/14/63-6/19/63	Vostok 5	Valery F. Bykovsky	119:06	Vostok 5 and 6 made 2d group flight
6/16/63-6/19/63	Vostok 6	Valentina V. Tereshkova	70:50	1st woman in space; passes within 3 mi of Vostok 5
10/12/64-10/13/64	Voskhod 1	Vladimir M. Komarov, Konstantin P. Feoktistov, Boris B. Yegorov	24:17	1st 3-person orbital flight; 1st without space suits
3/18/65-3/19/65	Voskhod 2	Pavel I. Belyayev, Aleksei A. Leonov	26:02	Leonov made 1st "space walk" (10 min)
3/23/65	**Gemini-Titan 3**	**Grissom (2), John W. Young**	**4:53**	**1st piloted spacecraft to change its orbital path**
6/3/65-6/7/65	**Gemini-Titan 4**	**James A. McDivitt, Edward H. White 2d**	**97:56**	**White was 1st American to "walk in space" (36 min)**
8/21/65-8/29/65	**Gemini-Titan 5**	**Cooper (2), Charles Conrad Jr.**	**190:55**	**Longest-duration human flight to date**
12/15/65-12/16/65	**Gemini-Titan 6A**	**Schirra (2), Thomas P. Stafford**	**25:51**	**Completed 1st U.S. space rendezvous, with Gemini 7**
12/4/65-12/18/65	**Gemini-Titan 7**	**Frank Borman, James A. Lovell**	**330:35**	**Longest-duration Gemini flight**
3/16/66	**Gemini-Titan 8**	**Neil A. Armstrong, David R. Scott**	**10:41**	**1st docking of one space vehicle with another; mission aborted, control malfunction; 1st Pacific landing**
6/3/66-6/6/66	**Gemini-Titan 9A**	**Stafford (2), Eugene A. Cernan**	**72:21**	**Performed rendezvous maneuvers, including simulation of lunar module rendezvous**
7/18/66-7/21/66	**Gemini-Titan 10**	**Young (2), Michael Collins**	**70:47**	**1st use of Agena target vehicle's propulsion systems; 1st orbital docking**
9/12/66-9/15/66	**Gemini-Titan 11**	**Conrad (2), Richard F. Gordon Jr.**	**71:17**	**1st tethered flight; highest Earth-orbit altitude (850 mi)**
11/11/66-11/15/66	**Gemini-Titan 12**	**Lovell (2), Edwin W. "Buzz" Aldrin Jr.**	**94:34**	**Final Gemini mission; 5½ hr EVA**
4/23/67-4/24/67	Soyuz 1	Komarov (2)	26:40	Crashed on reentry, killing Komarov
10/11/68-10/22/68	**Apollo-Saturn 7**	**Schirra (3), Donn F. Eisele, R. Walter Cunningham**	**260:09**	**1st piloted flight of Apollo spacecraft command-service module only; live TV footage of crew**
12/21/68-12/27/68	**Apollo-Saturn 8**	**Borman (2), Lovell (3), William A. Anders**	**147:00**	**1st lunar orbit and piloted lunar return reentry (command-service module only); views of lunar surface televised to Earth**
1/14/69-1/17/69	Soyuz 4	Vladimir A. Shatalov	71:21	Docked with Soyuz 5
1/15/69-1/18/69	Soyuz 5	Boris V. Volyanov, Aleksei S. Yeliseyev, Yevgeny V. Khrunov	72:54	Docked with 4; Yeliseyev and Khrunov transferred to Soyuz 4 via a spacewalk
3/3/69-3/13/69	**Apollo-Saturn 9**	**McDivitt (2), D. Scott (2), Russell L. Schweickart**	**241:00**	**1st piloted flight of lunar module**
5/18/69-5/26/69	**Apollo-Saturn 10**	**Stafford (3), Young (3), Cernan (2)**	**192:03**	**1st lunar module orbit of Moon, 50,000 ft from Moon surface**

Dates	Mission[1]	Crew (no. of flights)	Duration (hr:min)	Remarks
7/16/69-7/24/69	**Apollo-Saturn 11**	**Armstrong (2), Collins (2), Aldrin (2)**	**195:18**	**1st lunar landing made by Armstrong and Aldrin (7/20); collected 48.5 lb of soil, rock samples; lunar stay time 21:36:21**
10/11/69-10/16/69	Soyuz 6	Georgi S. Shonin, Valery N. Kubasov	118:43	1st welding of metals in space
10/12/69-10/17/69	Soyuz 7	Anatoly V. Flipchenko, Vladislav N. Volkov, Viktor V. Gorbatko	118:40	Space lab construction test made; Soyuz 6, 7, and 8: 1st time 3 spacecraft, 7 crew members orbited the Earth at once
10/13/69[2]	Soyuz 8	Shatalov (2), Yeliseyev (2)	118:51	Part of space lab construction team
11/14/69-11/24/69	**Apollo-Saturn 12**	**Conrad (3), Richard F. Gordon Jr. (2), Alan L. Bean**	**244:36**	**Conrad and Bean made 2d Moon landing (11/18); collected 74.7 lb of samples, lunar stay time 31:31**
4/11/70-4/17/70	**Apollo-Saturn 13**	**Lovell (4), Fred W. Haise Jr., John L. Swigart Jr.**	**142:54**	**Aborted after service module oxygen tank ruptured; crew returned safely using lunar module**
6/1/70-6/19/70	Soyuz 9	Nikolayev (2), Vitaliy I. Sevastyanov	424:59	Longest human spaceflight to date
1/31/71-2/9/71	**Apollo-Saturn 14**	**A. Shepard (2), Stuart A. Roosa, Edgar D. Mitchell**	**216:01**	**Shepard and Mitchell made 3d Moon landing (2/3); collected 96 lb of lunar samples; lunar stay 33:31**
4/19/71[2]	Salyut 1[3]	(Occupied by Soyuz 11 crew)		1st space station
4/22/71[2]	Soyuz 10	Shatalov (3), Yeliseyev (3), Nikolay N. Rukavishnikov	47:46	1st successful docking with a space station; failed to enter space station
6/6/71-6/30/71	Soyuz 11	Georgi T. Dobrovolskiy, V. Volkov (2), Viktor I. Patsayev	570:22	Docked and entered Salyut 1 space station; orbited in Salyut 1 for 23 days, crew died during reentry from loss of pressurization
7/26/71-8/7/71	**Apollo-Saturn 15**	**D. Scott (3), James B. Irwin, Alfred M. Worden**	**295:12**	**Scott and Irwin made 4th Moon landing (7/30); 1st lunar rover use; 1st deep space walk; 170 lb of samples; 66:55 stay**
4/16/72-4/27/72	**Apollo-Saturn 16**	**Young (4), Charles M. Duke Jr., Thomas K. Mattingly 2d**	**265:51**	**Young and Duke made 5th Moon landing (4/20); colleced 213 lb of lunar samples; lunar stay 71:2**
12/7/72-12/19/72	**Apollo-Saturn 17**	**Cernan (3), Ronald E. Evans, Harrison H. Schmitt**	**301:51**	**Cernan and Schmitt made 6th lunar landing (12/11); collected 243 lb of samples; record lunar stay of more than 75 hr**
5/14/73[2]	**Skylab 1[4]**	**(Occupied by Skylab 2, 3, and 4 crews)**		**1st U.S. space station**
5/25/73-6/22/73	**Skylab 2**	**Conrad (4), Joseph P. Kerwin, Paul J. Weitz**	**672:49**	**1st Amer. piloted orbiting space station; crew repaired damage caused during boost**
7/28/73-9/25/73	**Skylab 3**	**Bean (2), Owen K. Garriott, Jack R. Lousma**	**1,427:09**	**Crew systems and operational tests; exceeded pre-mission plans for scientific activities; 13 hrs EVA 13:44**
11/16/73-2/8/74	**Skylab 4**	**Gerald P. Carr, Edward G. Gibson, William Pogue**	**2,017:15**	**Final Skylab mission**
7/15/75-7/21/75	Soyuz 19 (ASTP)	Leonov (2), Kubasov (2)	143:31	U.S.-USSR joint flight; crews linked up in space (7/17), conducted experiments, shared meals, and held a joint news conference
7/15/75-7/24/75	**Apollo (ASTP)**	**Vance Brand, Stafford (4), Donald K. Slayton**	**217:28**	**Joint flight with Soyuz 19**
12/10/77[2]	Soyuz 26	Yuri V. Romanenko, Georgiy M. Grechko (2)	2,314:00	1st multiple docking to a space station (Soyuz 26 and 27 docked at Salyut 6)
1/10/78[2]	Soyuz 27	Vladimir A. Dzhanibekov	142:59	*See Soyuz 26*
3/2/78[2]	Soyuz 28	Aleksei A. Gubarev (2), Vladimir Remek	190:16	1st international crew launch; Remek was 1st Czech in space
4/12/81-4/14/81	**Columbia (STS-1)**	**Young (5), Robert L. Crippen**	**54:21**	**1st space shuttle to fly into Earth's orbit**
11/12/81-11/14/81	**Columbia (STS-2)**	**Joe H. Engle, Richard H. Truly**	**54:13**	**1st scientific payload; 1st reuse of space shuttle**
11/11/82-11/16/82	**Columbia (STS-5)**	**Brand (2), Robert Overmyer, William Lenoir, Joseph Allen**	**122:14**	**1st 4-person crew**
6/18/83-6/24/83	**Challenger (STS-7)**	**Crippen (2), Frederick Hauck, Sally K. Ride, John M. Fabian, Norman Thagard**	**146:24**	**Ride was 1st U.S. woman in space; 1st 5-person crew**
6/27/83[2]	Soyuz T-9	Vladimir A. Lyakhov (2), Aleksandr Pavlovich Aleksandrov	3,585:46	Docked at Salyut 7; 1st construction in space
8/30/83-9/5/83	**Challenger (STS-8)**	**Truly (2), Daniel Brandenstein, William Thornton, Guion Bluford, Dale Gardner**	**145:09**	**Bluford was 1st U.S. black in space**
11/28/83-12/8/83	**Columbia (STS-9)**	**Young (6), Brewster Shaw Jr., Robert Parker, Garriott (2), Byron Lichtenberg, Ulf Merbold**	**247:47**	**1st 6-person crew; 1st Spacelab mission**
2/3/84-2/11/84	**Challenger (41-B)**	**Brand (3), Robert Gibson, Ronald McNair, Bruce McCandless, Robert Stewart**	**191:16**	**1st untethered EVA**

Dates	Mission[1]	Crew (no. of flights)	Duration (hr:min)	Remarks
2/8/84-4/11/84	Soyuz T-10B	Leonid Kizim, Vladimir Solovyov, Oleg Atkov	1,510:43	Docked with Salyut 7; crew set space duration record of 237 days
4/3/84-10/2/84	Soyuz T-11	Yury Malyshev (2), Gennady Strekalov (3), Rakesh Sharma	4,365:48	Docked with Salyut 7; Sharma 1st Indian in space
4/6/84-4/13/84	**Challenger (41-C)**	**Crippen (3), Francis R. Scobee, George D. Nelson, Terry J. Hart, James D. van Hoften**	**167:40**	**1st in-orbit satellite repair**
7/17/84[2]	Soyuz T-12	Dzhanibekov (4), Svetlana Y. Savitskaya (2), Igor P. Volk	283:14	Docked at Salyut 7; Savitskaya was 1st woman to perform EVA
8/30/84-9/5/84	**Discovery (41-D)**	**Henry W. Hartsfield (2), Michael L. Coats, Richard M. Mullane, Steven A. Hawley, Judith A. Resnik, Charles D. Walker**	**144:56**	**1st flight of U.S. nonastronaut (Walker)**
10/5/84-10/13/84	**Challenger (41-G)**	**Crippen (4), Jon A. McBride, Kathryn D. Sullivan, Ride (2), Marc Garneau, David C. Leestma, Paul D. Scully-Power**	**197:24**	**1st 7-person crew**
11/8/84-11/16/84	**Discovery (51-A)**	**Hauck (2); David M. Walker, Dr. Anna L. Fisher, J. Allen (2), D. Gardner (2)**	**191:45**	**1st satellite retrieval/repair**
4/12/85-4/19/85	**Discovery (51-D)**	**Karol J. Bobko, Donald E. Williams, Jake Garn, Walker (2), Jeffrey A. Hoffman, S. David Griggs, M. Rhea Seddon**	**167:55**	**Garn was 1st Senator in space**
6/17/85-6/24/85	**Discovery (51-G)**	**Brandenstein (2), John O. Creighton, Shannon W. Lucid, Steven R. Nagel, Fabian (2), Prince Sultan Salman al-Saud, Patrick Baudry**	**169:39**	**Launched 3 satellites; Salman al-Saud was 1st Arab in space; Baudry was 1st French person on U.S. mission**
10/3/85-10/7/85	**Atlantis (51-J)**	**Bobko (3), Ronald J. Grabe, David C. Hilmers, Stewart (2), William A. Pailes**	**97:47**	**1st Atlantis flight**
10/30/85-11/6/85	**Challenger (61-A)**	**Hartsfield (3), Nagel (2), Buchli (2), Bluford (2), Bonnie J. Dunbar, Wubbo J. Ockels, Richard Furrer, Ernst Messerschmid**	**168:45**	**1st 8-person crew; 1st German Spacelab mission**
11/26/85-12/3/85	**Atlantis (61-B)**	**Shaw (2), Bryan D. O'Connor, Sherwood C. Spring, Mary L. Cleave, Jerry L. Ross, C. Walker (3), Rodolfo Neri**	**165:05**	**Space structures assembly test; Neri was 1st Mexican in space**
1/12/86-1/18/86	**Columbia (61-C)**	**R. Gibson (2), Charles F. Bolden Jr., Hawley (2), G. Nelson (2), Franklin R. Chang-Diaz, Robert J. Cenker, Bill Nelson**	**146:04**	**B. Nelson was 1st U.S. Representative in space; material and astronomy experiments conducted**
1/28/86	**Challenger (51-L)**	**Scobee (2), Michael J. Smith, Resnik (2), Ellison S. Onizuka (2), Ronald E. McNair, Gregory B. Jarvis, Christa McAuliffe**	**—**	**Exploded 73 sec after liftoff; all were killed**
2/20/86[2]	Mir[3]	—	—	Space station with 6 docking ports launched
3/13/86[2]	Soyuz T-15	Kizim (3), Solovyov (2)	3,000:01	Ferry between stations; docked at *Mir*
2/5/87-12/29/87	Soyuz TM-2	Romanenko (3), Aleksandr I. Laveikin	7,835:38	Romanenko set endurance record, since broken
7/22/87-12/29/87	Soyuz TM-3	Aleksandr Viktorenko, Aleksandr Pavlovich Aleksandrov (2), Mohammed Faris	3,847:16	Docked with *Mir*; Faris 1st Syrian in space
12/21/87-12/21/88	Soyuz TM-4	V. Titov (2), Muso Manarov, Anatoly Levchenko	8,782:39	Docked with *Mir*
6/7/88-6/17/88	Soyuz TM-5	Viktor Savinykh (3), Anatoly Solovyev, Aleksandr Panayotov Aleksandrov	236:13	Docked with *Mir*; Aleksandrov 1st Bulgarian in space
9/29/88-10/3/88	**Discovery (STS-26)**	**Hauck (3), Richard O. Covey (2), Hilmers (2), G. Nelson (2), John M. Lounge (2)**	**97:00**	**Redesigned shuttle makes 1st flight**
5/4/89-5/8/89	**Atlantis (STS-30)**	**D. Walker (2), Grabe (2), Thagard (2), Cleave (2), Mark C. Lee**	**96:56**	**Launched Venus orbiter *Magellan***
10/18/89-10/23/89	**Atlantis (STS-34)**	**Williams (2), Michael J. McCulley, Lucid (2), Chang-Diaz (2), Ellen S. Baker**	**119:39**	**Launched Jupiter probe and orbiter *Galileo***
4/24/90-4/29/90	**Discovery (STS-31)**	**McCandless (2), Sullivan (2), Loren J. Shriver (2), Bolden (2), Hawley (3)**	**121:16**	**Launched Hubble Space Telescope**
10/6/90-10/10/90	**Discovery (STS-41)**	**Richard N. Richards (2), Robert D. Cabana, Bruce E. Melnick, William M. Shepherd (2), Thomas D. Akers**	**98:10**	**Launched *Ulysses* spacecraft to investigate interstellar space and the Sun**
4/5/91-4/11/91	**Atlantis (STS-37)**	**Nagel (3), Kenneth D. Cameron, Linda Godwin, Ross (3), Jay Apt**	**144:32**	**Launched Gamma Ray Observatory to measure celestial gamma rays**
5/18/91-10/10/91	Soyuz TM-12	Anatoly Artsebarskiy, Sergei Krikalev (2) (to *Mir*), Helen Sharman	3,471:22	Docked with *Mir;* Sharman 1st from United Kingdom in space
3/17/92-3/25/92	Soyuz TM-14	Viktorenko (3) (to *Mir*), Alexandr Kaleri (to *Mir*), Klaus-Dietrich Flade, Aleksandr Volkov (3) (from *Mir*), Krikalev (2) (from *Mir*)	3,495:11	First human CIS space mission; docked with *Mir* 3/19; Viktorenko and Kaleri to *Mir*, Volkov and Krikalev from *Mir;* Krikalev was in space 313 days
5/7/92-5/16/92	**Endeavour (STS-49)**	**Brandenstein (4), Kevin C. Chilton, Melnick (2), Pierre J. Thuot (2), Richard J. Hieb (2), Kathryn Thornton (2), Akers (2)**	**213:30**	**1st 3-person EVA; satellite recovery and redeployment**
9/12/92-9/21/92	**Endeavour (STS-47)**	**R. Gibson (4), Curtis L. Brown Jr., Lee (2), Apt (2), N. Jan Davis, Mae Carol Jemison, Mamoru Mohri**	**190:30**	**Jemison was 1st black woman in space; Lee and Davis were 1st married couple to travel together in space; 1st Japanese Spacelab**

Dates	Mission[1]	Crew (no. of flights)	Duration (hr:min)	Remarks
10/22/92-11/1/92	**Columbia (STS-52)**	**James D. Wetherbee (2), Michael A. Baker (2), Shepherd (3), Tamara E. Jernigan (2), Charles L. Veach (2), Steven G. MacLean**	**236:57**	**Studied influence of gravity on basic fluid and solidification processes**
4/8/93-4/17/93	**Discovery (STS-56)**	**Cameron (2), Stephen S. Oswald (2), C. Michael Foale (2), Ellen Ochoa, Kenneth D. Cockrell**	**222:08**	**2d atmospheric mission; Ochoa was 1st Hispanic woman in space**
6/21/93-7/1/93	**Endeavour (STS-57)**	**Grabe (4), Brian J. Duffy (2), G. David Low (3), Nancy J. Sherlock, Peter J. K. Wisoff, Janice E. Voss**	**239:46**	**Carried Spacelab commercial payload module**
10/18/93-11/1/93	**Columbia (STS-58)**	**John E. Blaha (4), Richard A. Searfoss, Lucid (4), David A. Wolf, William A. McArthur, Martin J. Fettman**	**336:29**	**Studied effects of microgravity**
12/2/93-12/13/93	**Endeavour (STS-61)**	**Covey (3), Kenneth D. Bowersox (2), Claude Nicollier (2), Story Musgrave (5), Akers (3), K. Thornton (3), Hoffman (4)**	**259:58**	**Hubble Space Telescope repaired; Akers set new U.S. EVA duration record (29 hr, 40 min)**
2/3/94-2/11/94	**Discovery (STS-60)**	**Bolden (3), Kenneth S. Reightier Jr. (2), Davis, (2), Chang-Diaz (3), Ronald M. Sega, Krikalev (3)**	**199:10**	**Krikalev was 1st Russian on U.S. shuttle**
4/9/94-4/20/94	**Endeavour (STS-59)**	**Sidney M. Gutierrez (2), Chilton (2), Apt (3), Michael R. Clifford (2), Godwin (2), Thomas D. Jones**	**269:50**	**Gathered data about the Earth and the effects humans have on its carbon, water, and energy cycles**
7/1/94-11/4/94	Soyuz TM-19	Yuri I. Malenchenko, Talgat A. Musabayev, Merbold (2) (from *Mir*)	3,022:53	Docked with *Mir*; Merbold from *Mir*
9/9/94-9/20/94	**Discovery (STS-64)**	**Richards (4), L. Blaine Hammond Jr. (2), Jerry M. Linenger, Susan J. Helms (2), Carl J. Meade (3), Lee (3)**	**262:50**	**Performed atmospheric research; 1st untethered EVA in over 10 years**
2/3/95-2/11/95	**Discovery (STS-63)**	**Wetherbee (3), Eileen M. Collins, Bernard A. Harris (2), Foale (3), Voss (2), V. Titov (4)**	**198:29**	***Discovery* and Russian space station rendezvous**
3/2/95-3/18/95	**Endeavour (STS-67)**	**Oswald (3), William G. Gregory, Samuel T. Durrance (2), Ronald Parise (2), Wendy B. Lawrence, Jernigan (3), John M. Grunsfeld**	**399:09**	**Shuttle data made available on the Internet; astronomy research conducted**
3/14/95-3/22/95	Soyuz TM-21	Thagard (2), Vladimir Dezhurov, Strekalov (5)	2,688[5]	Docked with *Mir* 3/16/95; Thagard was 1st Amer. on the Russ. spacecraft; Valery Polyakov returned to Earth, 3/22/95, after record stay in space (439 days)
6/27/95-7/7/95	**Atlantis (STS-71)**	**R. Gibson (5), Charles J. Precourt (2), E. Baker (3), Gregory J. Harbaugh (3), Dunbar (4), Solovyev (4) (to *Mir*), Nikolai M. Budarin (to *Mir*), Thagard (5) (from *Mir*), Strekalov (from *Mir*), Dezhurov (from *Mir*)**	**269:47**	**1st *Mir* docking; exchanged crew members with *Mir*; Thagard, with his stay on *Mir*, had spent 115 days in space**
10/20/95-11/5/95	**Columbia (STS-73)**	**Bowersox (3), Kent Rominger, K. Thornton (4), Catherine Coleman, Michael Lopez-Alegria, Fred Leslie, Albert Sacco**	**381:52**	**Most ever first-time space flyers; near-weightlessness experiments conducted in microgravity laboratory**
11/8/95-11/20/95	**Atlantis (STS-74)**	**Cameron (3), James D. Halsell Jr. (2), Chris Hadfield, Ross (5), McArthur (2)**	**196:30**	**2d *Mir* docking (11/15-11/18); erected a 15-ft permanent docking tunnel to *Mir* for future use by U.S. orbiters**
1/11/96-1/20/96	**Endeavour (STS-72)**	**Duffy (3), Brent W. Jett Jr., Winston E. Scott, Leroy Chiao (2), Daniel T. Barry, Koichi Wakata**	**214:01**	**Released NASA space probe; retrieved Japanese satellite; 13 hrs EVA**
2/22/96-3/9/96	**Columbia (STS-75)**	**Andrew M. Allen (3), Scott J. Horowitz, Chang-Diaz (5), Umberto Guidoni, Hoffman (5), Maurizio Cheli, Nicollier (3)**	**377:40**	**Lost an Italian satellite when its tether was severed; microgravity experiments performed; singe marks found on 2 O-rings**
3/22/96-3/31/96	**Atlantis (STS-76)**	**Chilton (3), Searfoss (2), Sega (2), Clifford (3) Godwin (3), Lucid (5) (to *Mir*)**	**221:15**	**3d *Mir* docking (5 days); Lucid to *Mir*; 2-person EVA**
6/20/96-7/7/96	**Columbia (STS-78)**	**Terence T. Henricks (4), Kevin R. Kregel (2), Helms (3), Richard M. Linnehan, Charles E. Brady, Jean-Jacques Favier, Robert Brent Thirsk**	**405:48**	**Studied weightlessness with the Life/Microgravity Spacelab on board**
9/16/96-9/26/96	**Atlantis (STS-79)**	**Apt (4), Terry Wilcutt (2), William Readdy (3), Akers (4), Carl E. Walz (3), Lucid (5) (from *Mir*), Blaha (5) (to *Mir*)**	**243:19**	**Docked with *Mir* 9/18/96; exchanged crew members, including Lucid, who set U.S. and women's individual duration in space record (188 days)**
11/19/96-12/7/96	**Columbia (STS-80)**	**Cockrell (3), Rominger (2), Jernigan (4), Jones (3), Musgrave (6)**	**423:53**	**Longest-duration shuttle flight; Musgrave was oldest person to fly in space; 2 science satellites deployed and retrieved**
1/12/97-1/22/97	**Atlantis (STS-81)**	**M. Baker (4), Jett (2), Wisoff (3), Grunsfeld (2), Marsha Ivins (4), Linenger (2) (to *Mir*), Blaha (5) (from *Mir*)**	**243:30**	**Docked with *Mir* 1/14-1/19/97; Linenger to *Mir*, Blaha from *Mir*, spent 128 days in space**

Dates	Mission[1]	Crew (no. of flights)	Duration (hr:min)	Remarks
2/11/97-2/21/97	**Discovery (STS-82)**	**Bowersox (4), Horowitz (2), Joe Tanner (2), Hawley (4), Harbaugh (4), Lee (4), Steve Smith (2)**	**238:47**	**Increased capabilities of Hubble Space Telescope; 5 EVAs used to service it**
5/15/97-5/24/97	**Atlantis (STS-84)**	**Precourt (3), E. Collins (2), Jean-François Clervoy (2), Carlos Noriega, Ed Lu, Elena Kondakova, Foale (4) (to *Mir*), Linenger (2) (from *Mir*)**	**221:20**	**Docked with *Mir* 5/16-5/21/97; Foale to *Mir*; Linenger from *Mir*, 132 days in space, 2d longest time for an American; stay on *Mir* marked by troubles incl. fire 2/23**
7/1/97-7/17/97	**Columbia (STS-94)**	**Halsell (4), Susan L. Still (2), Janice Voss (4), Donald A. Thomas (4), Michael Gernhardt (3), Roger Crouch (2), Greg Linteris (2)**	**376:46**	**Reflight of Microgravity Science Laboratory-1 mission (STS-83) that was aborted 4/8/97 because of problem with fuel cell**
8/5/97-2/19/98	Soyuz TM-26	Solovyev (5), Pavel Vinogradov	4,743:35	Docked with *Mir* 8/7/97; repaired damaged space station
8/7/97-8/19/97	**Discovery (STS-85)**	**Brown (4), Rominger (3), Davis (3), Robert L. Curbeam Jr., Stephen K. Robinson, Bjarni V. Tryggvason**	**284:27**	**Deployed and retrieved satellite designed to study Earth's middle atmosphere; demonstrated robotic arm**
9/25/97-10/6/97	**Atlantis (STS-86)**	**Wetherbee (4), Michael J. Bloomfield, V. Titov (4), Scott Parazynski (2), Jean-Loup Chrétien (3), Lawrence (2), Wolf (2) (to *Mir*), Foale (4) (from *Mir*)**	**236:24**	**Docked with *Mir* 9/27-10/3/97; delivered new computer to *Mir*; Wolf to *Mir*; Foale from *Mir*; stay on *Mir* marked by collision with cargo ship 6/25, worst such collision ever**
1/22/98-1/31/98	**Endeavour (STS-89)**	**Wilcutt (3), Joe F. Edwards Jr., Dunbar (5), Michael P. Anderson, James F. Reilly II, Salizhan Sharipov, Andrew Thomas (2) (to *Mir*), Wolf (2) (from *Mir*)**	**211:48**	**Docked with *Mir* 1/24-1/29/98; delivered water and cargo; Thomas to *Mir*; Wolf from *Mir*, 128 days in space**
1/29/98-8/25/98	Soyuz TM-27	Musabayev (2), Budarin (2), Leopold Eyharts	4,923:36	Docked with *Mir* 1/31/98
4/17/98-5/3/98	**Columbia (STS-90)**	**Searfoss (3), Scott D. Altman, Linnehan (2), Dafydd Rhys Williams, Kathryn P. Hire, Jay C. Buckey, James A. Pawelczyk**	**381:50**	**Studied effects of microgravity on the nervous systems of the crew and over 2,000 live animals; 1st surgery in space on animals meant to survive.**
6/2/98-6/12/98	**Discovery (STS-91)**	**Precourt (4), Dominic L. Gorie, Lawrence (3), Chang-Diaz (6), Janet L. Kavandi, Valery Ryumin (4), A. Thomas (2) (from *Mir*)**	**235:53**	**Final docking mission with *Mir*; Thomas from *Mir*, 141 days in space**

Note: As of Sept. 1998, there have been 91 space shuttle flights, 66 since the 1986 *Challenger* explosion. Active shuttles include the *Columbia* (25 flights), the *Discovery* (24), the *Atlantis* (20), and the *Endeavour* (12). (The *Challenger* completed 9 missions.)

Four Soviets died in spaceflights: Komarov was killed on Soyuz 1 (1967) when the parachute lines tangled during descent; the 3-person Soyuz 11 crew (1971) was asphyxiated. Seven Americans died in the *Challenger* explosion, and 3 astronauts—Virgil I. Grissom, Edward H. White, and Roger B. Chaffee—died in the Jan. 27, 1967, Apollo 1 fire on the ground at Cape Kennedy, FL.

(1) For space shuttle flights, mission name is in parentheses following the name of the orbiter. (2) Launch date. (3) Space stations, such as the *Salyuts* and *Mir*, have been used to house crews since 1971. (4) Skylab 1 deteriorated and fell from orbit without burning up upon entering the atmosphere. Pieces fell on Australia and the Indian Ocean; no one was injured. (5) Approximate crew duration for Thagard's stay. Crew did not return together.

Individuals Who Have Flown in Space, 1961-98

Source: Congressional Research Service; World Almanac research; as of Sept. 30, 1998

Country	No. of individs.	Country	No. of individs.	Country	No. of individs.	Country	No. of individs.
United States	254	Canada	8	India	1	Romania	1
Russia/CIS	93	Cuba	1	Italy	3	Saudi Arabia	1
Afghanistan	1	Czechoslovakia	1	Japan	5	Switzerland	1
Austria	1	France	8	Mexico	1	Syria	1
Belgium	1	Germany	10	Mongolia	1	United Kingdom	1
Bulgaria	2	Hungary	1	Netherlands	1	Vietnam	1
				Poland	1	**TOTAL**	**400**

Note: All individuals flew on either a Russian/CIS-sponsored mission or on a U.S.-sponsored mission. All cosmonauts who were citizens of the USSR at the time of launch are included under "Russia/CIS." "Germany" includes former E and W Germany.

Summary of Worldwide Successful Announced Payloads, 1957-97

Source: National Aeronautics and Space Administration

(A payload is something carried into space by a rocket.)

Year	Total[1]	Russia[2]	United States	Japan	European Space Agency	China	France	India	United Kingdom	Germany	Canada
1957-59	24	6	18	—	—	—	—	—	—	—	—
1960-69	1,035	399	614	—	2	—	4	—	1	—	—
1970-79	1,366	1,028	247	18	5	8	14	1	6	3	4
1980-89	1,431	1,132	191	26	14	16	5	9	4	7	5
1990	159	96	31	7	1	5	2	1	5	1	0
1991	157	101	30	2	4	1	6	1	2	1	2
1992	128	77	27	3	1	2	3	2	0	1	1
1993	104	59	29	1	2	1	2	1	0	0	0
1994	109	64	27	4	1	5	0	2	0	2	0
1995	87	45	24	2	2	1	3	1	0	1	1
1996	69	23	32	1	10	2	0	1	0	0	0
1997	85	27	37	2	12	6	0	1	0	0	0
TOTAL	**4,754**	**3,057**	**1,307**	**66**	**54**	**47**	**39**	**20**	**18**	**16**	**13**

(1) Includes launches sponsored by countries not shown. (2) Figures for 1957-91 are for the Soviet Union; 1992-96 figures are for the Commonwealth of Independent States.

Notable U.S. Planetary Science Missions

Source: National Aeronautics and Space Administration

Spacecraft	Launch date (Coordinated Universal Time)	Mission	Remarks
Mariner 2	Aug. 27, 1962	Venus	Passed within 22,000 mi of Venus 12/14/62; contact lost 1/3/63 at 54 million mi
Ranger 7	July 28, 1964	Moon	Yielded over 4,000 photos of lunar surface
Mariner 4	Nov. 28, 1964	Mars	Passed behind Mars 7/14/65; took 22 photos from 6,000 mi
Ranger 8	Feb. 17, 1965	Moon	Yielded over 7,000 photos of lunar surface
Surveyor 3	Apr. 17, 1967	Moon	Scooped and tested lunar soil
Mariner 5	June 14, 1967	Venus	In solar orbit; closest Venus fly-by 10/19/67
Mariner 6	Feb. 24, 1969	Mars	Came within 2,000 mi of Mars 7/31/69; collected data, photos
Mariner 7	Mar. 27, 1969	Mars	Came within 2,000 mi of Mars 8/5/69
Mariner 9	May 30, 1971	Mars	First craft to orbit Mars 11/13/71; sent back over 7,000 photos
Pioneer 10	Mar. 2, 1972	Jupiter	Passed Jupiter 12/4/73; exited the planetary system 6/13/83; transmission ended 3/31/97 at 6.39 billion mi
Pioneer 11	Apr. 5, 1973	Jupiter, Saturn	Passed Jupiter 12/3/74; Saturn 9/1/79; discovered an additional ring and 2 moons around Saturn; operating in outer solar system; transmission ended 9/95
Mariner 10	Nov. 3, 1973	Venus, Mercury	Passed Venus 2/5/74; arrived Mercury 3/29/74. 1st time gravity of 1 planet (Venus) used to whip spacecraft toward another (Mercury)
Viking 1	Aug. 20, 1975	Mars	Landed on Mars 7/20/76; did scientific research, sent photos; functioned 6½ years
Viking 2	Sept. 9, 1975	Mars	Landed on Mars 9/3/76; functioned 3½ years
Voyager 1	Sept. 5, 1977	Jupiter, Saturn	Encountered Jupiter 3/5/79, provided evidence of Jupiter ring; passed near Saturn 11/12/80
Voyager 2	Aug. 20, 1977	Jupiter, Saturn, Uranus, Neptune	Encountered Jupiter 7/9/79; Saturn 8/25/81; Uranus 1/24/86; Neptune 8/25/89
Pioneer Venus 1	May 20, 1978	Venus	Entered Venus orbit 12/4/78; spent 14 years studying planet; ceased operating 10/19/92
Pioneer Venus 2	Aug. 8, 1978	Venus	Encountered Venus 12/9/78; probes impacted on surface
Magellan	May 4, 1989	Venus	Orbit and map Venus; monitored geological activity on surface; ceased operating 10/12/94
Galileo	Oct. 18, 1989	Jupiter	Used Earth's gravity to propel it toward Jupiter; encountered Venus Feb. 1990; encountered Jupiter 12/7/95; released probe to Jovian surface; encountered moons Ganymede, Europa, Io, and Callisto
Mars Observer	Sept. 25, 1992	Mars	Communication was lost 8/21/93
Near Earth Asteroid Rendezvous (NEAR)	Feb. 17, 1996	The asteroid Eros	Expected rendezvous with Eros, early 1999; to orbit and study the asteroid for about 1 year
Mars Global Surveyor	Nov. 7, 1996	Mars	Began orbiting Mars 9/11/97; began 2-year mapping survey of entire Martian surface; discovered magnetism on planet; observed Martian moon Phobos
Mars Pathfinder	Dec. 4, 1996	Mars	Landed on Mars 7/4/97; rover Sojourner made measurements of the Martian climate and soil composition, sending thousands of surface images; ceased operating 9/27/97
Cassini	Oct. 15, 1997	Saturn	Scheduled to reach Saturn in 2004; to study planet's atmosphere, rings, and moons; probe will land on moon Titan
Lunar Prospector	Jan. 6, 1998	Moon	1-year mission to map abundance of 10 elements on Moon's surface; began sending back data 1/6/98; discovered water-ice at both Lunar poles 3/5/98

Notable Proposed U.S. Space Missions

Source: National Aeronautics and Space Administration; as of Oct. 15, 1998

Planned Launch date	Mission	Purpose
Oct. 1998	Spartan 201	Study of the Sun
Dec. 1998	Mars Climate Orbiter	Imaging of Mars atmosphere
Jan. 1999	Mars Polar Lander	Search for near-surface ice and records of cyclic climate change
Feb. 1999	Stardust	Gather dust samples from comet Wild-2 and return samples to Earth
Mar. 1999	Wide-Field Infrared Explorer	4-month survey to detect galaxies with high rates of star formation
2000	High Energy Transient Explorer II	Study of gamma ray bursts
Dec. 2001	Space InfraRed Telescope Facility	High-sensitivity observations of celestial sources

Note: All spacecraft to be launched by expendable rockets, except Spartan 201, which was scheduled to be launched with space shuttle *Discovery* in Oct. 1998.

Traffic at World Airports, 1997

Source: Airports Council International-North America

Airport	Passenger Arrivals and Departures
London, UK (Heathrow)	57,974,931
Tokyo/Haneda, Japan (Tokyo Intl.)	49,302,268
Frankfurt, Germany (Rhein/Main)	40,262,691
Seoul, South Korea (Kimpo Intl.)	36,757,280
Paris, France (Charles De Gaulle)	35,293,661
Amsterdam, Netherlands (Schiphol)	31,569,977
Hong Kong, China (Hong Kong Intl.)	29,020,369
London, UK (Gatwick)	26,961,453
Toronto, Ontario (Lester B. Pearson Intl.)	26,082,713
Tokyo, Japan (Narita)	25,667,577
Singapore (Changi)	25,174,344
Bangkok, Thailand (Bangkok Intl.)	25,142,879
Paris, France (Orly)	25,059,211
Rome, Italy (Fiumicino)	25,001,038
Madrid, Spain (Barajas)	23,601,727
Sydney, Australia (Kingsford Smith)	20,621,826
Zurich, Switzerland (Zurich)	18,291,882
Munich, Germany (Munich)	17,894,704
Mexico City, Mexico (Mexico City)	17,833,094
Beijing, China (Beijing Capital Intl.)	16,907,954
Copenhagen, Denmark (Copenhagen)	16,837,115
Palma de Mallorca, Spain (Palma de Mallorca)	16,557,622
Manchester, UK (Manchester)	16,167,915
Kuala Lumpur, Malaysia (Subang-Kuala Lumpur Intl.)	16,020,704
Taipei, Taiwan (Chiang Kai-shek)	15,993,293

Note: Excludes U.S. airports. Includes only airports participating in the Airports Council International Annual Airport Traffic Statistics collection.

Traffic at U.S. Airports, 1997

Source: Airports Council International-North America

Airport	Passenger Arrivals and Departures	Airport	Passenger Arrivals and Departures
Chicago (O'Hare–ORD)	70,294,601	Phoenix (Sky Harbor Intl.–PHX)	30,536,061
Atlanta (Hartsfield Intl.–ATL)	68,205,769	Las Vegas (McCarran Intl.–LAS)	30,305,553
Dallas/Ft. Worth (DFW)	60,488,713	Minneapolis/St. Paul (MSP)	29,070,480
Los Angeles (LAX)	60,142,588	Houston (IAH)	28,701,092
San Francisco (SFO)	40,499,947	St. Louis (Lambert St. Louis Intl.–STL)	27,657,026
Denver (DEN)	34,972,936	Orlando (MCO)	27,305,249
Miami (MIA)	34,533,268	Boston (Logan Intl.–BOS)	25,457,752
Detroit (DTW)	31,520,656	Seattle-Tacoma (SEA)	24,678,614
New York (J. F. Kennedy Intl.–JFK)	31,228,956	Honolulu (HNL)	24,044,293
Newark (EWR)	30,866,374	Charlotte (CLT)	22,797,594

U.S. Scheduled Airline Traffic, 1995-97

Source: Air Transport Association of America

Passenger traffic	1995	1996	1997
Revenue passengers enplaned (000)	**547,800**	**581,200**	**598,900**
Revenue passenger miles (000)	540,656,000	578,663,000	605,434,000
Available seat miles (000)	807,078,000	835,071,000	860,564,000
Revenue passenger load factor (%)	67.0	69.3	70.4
Cargo traffic	**16,921,000**	**17,775,000**	**20,513,000**
Revenue freight and express (ton miles)	14,578,000	15,301,000	17,959,000
Revenue U.S. Mail (ton miles)	2,343,000	2,454,000	2,554,000
Financial			
Passenger revenue ($000)	$69,594,000	$75,286,000	$79,469,000
Net profit ($000)	$2,314,000	$2,804,000	$5,195,000
Employees	**546,987**	**564,425**	**586,509**

Leading U.S. Passenger Airlines, 1997

Source: Air Transport Association of America

(in thousands)

Airline	Passengers	Airline	Passengers	Airline	Passengers
Delta	103,133	Alaska	12,245	Horizon Air	3,686
United	84,203	Simmons	6,045	American Trans Air	3,157
American	81,083	Reno	5,308	Continental Micronesia	2,579
US Airways	58,659	Aloha	5,191	Trans States	2,386
Southwest	55,946	Hawaiian	4,938	Mesa	2,077
Northwest	54,650	Continental Express	4,890	Air Wisconsin	1,943
Continental	38,756	AirTran	3,905	Carnival	1,829
TWA	23,370	Atlantic Southeast	3,775	Western Pacific	1,753
America West	18,294				

Airline On-Time Arrivals, 1995-98

Source: Office of General Counsel, U.S. Dept. of Transportation

(percent of arrivals within 15 min. of scheduled time, for leading airlines)

Airline	2d quarter 1998	1st quarter 1998 (rank)	1997 (rank)	1996 (rank)	1995 (rank)
1. Southwest	82.5	77.0 (3)	81.9 (1)	81.8 (1)	82.3 (1)
2. American	81.0	79.6 (2)	79.1 (4)	72.2 (6)	77.5 (7)
3. Delta	77.3	75.0 (4)	74.1 (10)	71.2 (7)	76.2 (9)
4. US Airways	75.8	81.5 (1)	80.1 (3)	75.7 (4)	79.8 (3)
5. Alaska	75.2	70.7 (9)	74.9 (8)	68.6 (9)	76.7 (8)
6. Continental	73.8	72.0 (7)	78.2 (5)	76.6 (2)[1]	79.5 (4)
7. TWA	72.8	73.9 (5)	80.2 (2)	68.5 (10)	74.3 (10)
8. America West	71.5	67.9 (10)	77.5 (6)	70.8 (8)	77.6 (6)
9. United	70.7	71.6 (8)	75.9 (7)	73.8 (5)	77.7 (5)
10. Northwest	67.2	73.6 (6)	74.7 (9)	76.6 (3)[1]	80.7 (2)
Average for all 10 airlines	**75.7**	**75.4**	**77.7**	**74.5**	**78.7**

Note: All domestic scheduled-service passenger flights, including those with mechanical delays, are included. A canceled flight is counted as a delay. The on-time performance database tracks only these 10 leading airlines, which account for more than 90% of domestic operating revenues. (1) When figures are carried out to several decimal places, Continental had the better on-time performance of these two carriers.

U.S. Airline Safety, Scheduled Commercial Carriers, 1981-97

Source: Air Transport Association of America

	Departures (millions)	Fatal accidents	Fatalities	Fatal accidents per 100,000 departures		Departures (millions)	Fatal accidents	Fatalities	Fatal accidents per 100,000 departures
1981	5.2	4	4	0.077	1990	6.9	6	39	0.087
1982[1]	5.0	4	234	0.060	1991	6.8	4	62	0.059
1983	5.0	4	15	0.079	1992	7.1	4	33	0.057
1984	5.4	1	4	0.018	1993	7.2	1	1	0.014
1985	5.8	4	197	0.069	1994	7.5	4	239	0.053
1986[1]	6.4	2	5	0.016	1995	8.1	2	166	0.025
1987[1]	6.6	4	231	0.046	1996	8.2	3	342	0.036
1988[1]	6.7	3	285	0.030	1997	8.2	3	3	0.037
1989	6.6	8	131	0.121					

(1) Sabotage-caused accidents are included in the number of fatal accidents and fatalities, but not in the calculation of accident rates.

Aircraft Operating Statistics, 1997

Source: Air Transport Association of America; figures are averages for most commonly used models

	No. of seats	Speed airborne (mph)	Flight length (mi)	Fuel (gal per hr)	Operating cost per hr
B747-100	447	520	2,661	3,638	$6,447
B747-400	396	538	4,988	3,410	6,859
B747-200/300	374	525	3,489	3,663	7,300
B747-F	0	496	2,191	3,810	7,497
L-1011-100/200	310	495	1,206	2,428	3,720
B-777	292	521	2,927	2,117	4,241
DC-10-10	289	500	1,540	2,287	5,281
DC-10-40	285	504	1,921	2,651	4,746
DC-10-30	265	520	2,554	2,667	6,078
MD-11	253	524	3,123	2,462	6,406
A300-600	249	473	1,228	1,678	5,237
L-1011-500	223	517	2,222	2,376	3,829
B767-300ER	214	495	2,217	1,602	3,558
B757-200	186	465	1,198	1,050	2,675
B767-200ER	181	488	2,184	1,409	3,348
MD-90	150	435	764	808	$1,636
B727-200	150	437	720	1,287	2,504
B727-F	0	434	529	1,284	4,993
A320-100/200	148	460	1,153	820	2,177
B737-400	144	414	692	792	2,124
MD-80	141	432	790	933	2,087
B737-300	131	417	601	776	1,918
DC-9-50	122	374	342	915	1,923
B737-100/200	113	389	460	824	1,904
B737-500	110	420	636	747	1,743
DC-9-40	109	388	496	839	1,500
DC-9-30	101	385	474	810	1,988
F-100	97	383	497	646	2,002
DC-9-10	71	381	422	743	1,409

National Aviation Hall of Fame

The National Aviation Hall of Fame at Dayton, OH, is dedicated to honoring the outstanding pioneers of air and space.

Allen, William M.
Andrews, Frank M.
Armstrong, Harry G.
Armstrong, Neil A.
Arnold, Henry H. "Hap"
Atwood, John Leland
Balchen, Bernt
Baldwin, Thomas S.
Beachey, Lincoln
Beech, Olive A.
Beech, Walter H.
Bell, Alexander Graham
Bell, Lawrence D.
Bellanca, Giuseppe Mario
Bendix, Vincent T.
Boeing, William E.
Bong, Richard I.
Borman, Frank
Boyd, Albert
Bradley, Mark E.
Brown, George "Scratchley"
Brukner, Clayton John
Byrd, Richard E.
Cessna, Clyde V.
Chamberlin, Clarence D.
Chanute, Octave
Chennault, Claire L.
Cochran (Odlum), Jacqueline
Collins, Michael
Combs, Harry B.
Conrad Jr., Charles
Crawford, Frederick C.
Crossfield, A. Scott
Cunningham, Alfred A.
Curtiss, Glenn H.
Dargue, Herbert Arthur
Davis Jr., Benjamin O.
DeSeversky, Alexander P.
Doolittle, James H.
Douglas, Donald W.
Draper, Charles S.
Eaker, Ira C.
Earhart (Putnam), Amelia
Eielson, C. Benjamin
Ellyson, Theodore G.
Ely, Eugene B.
Everest, Frank K.
Fairchild, Sherman M.
Fleet, Reuben H.
Fokker, Anthony H.G.
Ford, Henry
Foss, Joseph
Foulois, Benjamin D.
Frye, Jack
Gabreski, Francis S.
Gentile, Dominic "Don"
Gilruth, Robert R.
Glenn Jr., John H.
Goddard, George W.
Goddard, Robert H.
Godfrey, Arthur
Goldwater, Barry M.
Grissom, Virgil I.
Gross, Robert E.
Grumman, Leroy R.
Guggenheim, Harry F.
Haughton, Daniel J.
Hegenberger, Albert F.
Heinemann, Edward H.
Hoover, Robert A.
Hughes, Howard R.
Ingalls, David S.
James Jr., Daniel "Chappie"
Jeppesen, Elrey B.
Johnson, Clarence L.
Johnston, Alvin M. "Tex"
Jones, Thomas V.
Kenney, George C.
Kettering, Charles F.
Kindelberger, James H.
Kittinger Jr., Joseph William
Knabenshue, A. Roy
Knight, William J.
Lahm, Frank P.
Langley, Samuel P.
Lear Sr., William P.
LeMay, Curtis E.
LeVier, Anthony W.
Lindbergh, Anne M.
Lindbergh, Charles A.
Link, Edwin A.
Lockheed, Allan H.
Loening, Grover
Lovell Jr., James A.
Lufbery, Raoul
Luke Jr., Frank
Macready, Carl B.
Macready, John A.
Martin, Glenn L.
McCampbell, David
McDonnell, James S.
Meyer, John C.
Mitchell, William "Billy"
Mitscher, Marc A.
Montgomery, John J.
Moorer, Thomas H.
Moss, Sanford A.
Neumann, Gerhard
Nichols, Ruth R.
Norden, Carl L.
Northrop, John K.
Pangborn, Clyde Edward
Patterson, William A.
Piper Sr., William T.
Pitcairn, Harold Frederick
Post, Wiley H.
Read, Albert C.
Reeve, Robert C.
Rentschler, Frederick B.
Richardson, Holden C.
Rickenbacker, Edward V.
Rodgers, Calbraith P.
Rogers, Will
Rushworth, Robert A.
Rutan, Elbert "Burt" L.
Ryan, T. Claude
Schirra, Walter M.
Schriever, Bernard A.
Selfridge, Thomas E.
Shepard Jr., Alan B.
Sikorsky, Igor I.
Six, Robert F.
Slayton, Donald K. "Deke"
Smith, C.R.
Spaatz, Carl A.
Sperry Sr., Elmer A.
Sperry Sr., Lawrence B.
Stafford, Thomas Patten
Stanley, Robert M.
Stapp, John P.
Stearman, Lloyd C.
Taylor, Charles E.
Thomas, Lowell
Tibbets Jr., Paul W.
Towers, John H.
Trippe, Juan T.
Turner, Roscoe
Twining, Nathan F.
Vandenberg, Hoyt
von Braun, Wernher
von Karman, Theodore
von Ohain, Hans P.
Vought, Chance M.
Wade, Leigh
Walden, Henry W.
Wells, Edward
Williams, Sam
Wilson, Thornton A.
Woolman, Collett Everman "C.E."
Wright, Orville
Wright, Wilbur
Yeager, Charles E.
Young, John W.

Some Notable Aviation Firsts[1]

1903 — On Dec. 17, near Kitty Hawk, NC, brothers Wilbur and Orville Wright made the first human-carrying, powered flight. Each made 2 flights; the longest, about 852 ft, lasted 59 sec.

1907 — U.S. airplane manufacturing company formed by Glenn H. Curtiss.

1908 — First airplane passenger, Lt. Frank P. Lahm, rode with Wilbur Wright in a brief (6 min, 24 sec) flight.

1911 — The first transportation of mail by airplane officially approved by the U.S. Postal Service began on Sept. 23. It lasted one week. In 1918, limited scheduled air mail service began. By 1921, scheduled transcontinental airmail service began between New York City and San Francisco.

1914 — The first scheduled passenger airline service began. It operated between St. Petersburg and Tampa, FL.

1919 — The first airline food, a basket lunch, was served as part of a commercial airline service.

1930 — Ellen Church became the first flight attendant.

1939 — On Aug. 27, the German Heinkel He 178 made the first successful flight powered by a jet engine.

1947 — Mach 1, the sound barrier, was broken by Amer. Charles E. ("Chuck") Yeager in a Bell X-1 rocket-powered aircraft.

1947 — Largest airplane ever flown, Howard Hughes's "Spruce Goose," flew 1 mi at an altitude of 80 ft.

1953 — Jacqueline Cochran became the first woman to fly faster than sound.

1960 — Convair B-58, the first supersonic bomber, was introduced.

1968 — The supersonic speed of Mach 2 was accomplished for the first time, in a Tupolev Tu-144. The plane had an approximate maximum speed of 1,200 mph.

1970 — The Tupolev Tu-144, during commercial transport, exceeded Mach 2. It reached about 1,335 mph at 53,475 ft.

1976 — The Concorde began the first scheduled supersonic commercial service.

(1) Excludes notable around-the-world and international trips.

Some Notable Around-the-World and Intercontinental Trips

	From/To	Miles	Time	Date
Nellie Bly	New York/New York		72d 06h 11m	1889
George Francis Train	New York/New York		67d 12h 03m	1890
Charles Fitzmorris	Chicago/Chicago		60d 13h 29m	1901
J. W. Willis Sayre	Seattle/Seattle		54d 09h 42m	1903
J. Alcock-A.W. Brown [1]	Newfoundland/Ireland	1,960	16h 12m	June 14-15, 1919
Two U.S. Army airplanes	Seattle/Seattle	26,103	35d 01h 11m	1924
Richard E. Byrd, Floyd Bennett [2]	Spitsbergen (Nor.)/N. Pole	1,545	15h 30m	May 9, 1926
Amundsen-Ellsworth-Nobile Polar Expedition (in a dirigible)	Spitsbergen (Nor.)/over N. Pole to Teller, Alaska		80h	May 11-14,1926
E.S. Evans and L. Wells (*New York World*)	New York/New York	18,410 [3]	28d 14h 36m 05s	June 16-July 14, 1926
Charles Lindbergh [4]	New York/Paris	3,610	33h 29m 30s	May 20-21, 1927
Amelia Earhart, W. Stultz, L. Gordon	Newfoundland/Wales		20h 40m	June 17-18, 1928
Graf Zeppelin	Friedrichshafen, Ger./Lakehurst, NJ	6,630	4d 15h 46m	Oct. 11-15, 1928
Graf Zeppelin	Friedrichshafen, Ger./Lakehurst, NJ	21,700	20d 04h	Aug. 14-Sept. 4, 1929
Wiley Post and Harold Gatty (Monoplane Winnie Mae)	New York/New York	15,474	8d 15h 51m	July 1, 1931
C. Pangborn-H. Herndon Jr. [5]	Misawa, Japan/Wenatchee, Wash.	4,458	41h 34m	Oct. 3-5, 1931
Amelia Earhart [6]	Newfoundland/Ireland	2,026	14h 56m	May 20-21, 1932
Wiley Post (Monoplane Winnie Mae) [7]	New York/New York	15,596	115h 36m 30s	July 15-22, 1933
Hindenburg Zeppelin	Lakehurst, NJ/Frankfort, Ger.		42h 53m	Aug. 9-11, 1936
H. R. Ekins (Scripps-Howard Newspapers in race) (Zeppelin Hindenburg to Germany, airplanes from Frankfurt)	Lakehurst, NJ/Lakehurst, NJ	25,654	18d 11h 14m 33s	Oct. 19, 1936
Howard Hughes and 4 assistants	New York/New York	14,824	3d 19h 08m 10s	July 10-13, 1938
Douglas Corrigan	New York/Dublin		28h 13m	July 17-18, 1938
Mrs. Clara Adams (Pan American Clipper)	Port Washington, NY/ Newark, NJ		16d 19h 04m	June 28-July 15, 1939
Globester, U.S. Air Transport Command	Washington, DC/Washington, DC	23,279	149h 44m	Oct. 4, 1945
Capt. William P. Odom (A-26 Reynolds Bombshell)	New York/New York	20,000	78h 55m 12s	Apr. 12-16, 1947
America, Pan American 4-engine Lockheed Constellation [8]	New York/New York	22,219	101h 32m	June 17-30, 1947
Col. Edward Eagan	New York/New York	20,559	147h 15m	Dec. 13, 1948
USAF B-50 Lucky Lady II (Capt. James Gallagher) [9]	Ft. Worth, TX/Ft. Worth, TX	23,452	94h 01m	Mar. 2, 1949
Col. D. Schilling, USAF [10]	England/Limestone, ME.	3,300	10h 01m	Sept. 22, 1950
C.F. Blair Jr.	Norway/Alaska	3,300	10h 29m	May 29, 1951
Two U.S. S-55	Massachusetts/Scotland	3,410	42h 30m	July 15-31, 1952
Canberra Bomber [11]	N. Ireland/Newfoundland	2073	04h 34m	Aug. 26, 1952
	Newfoundland/N. Ireland	2073	03h 25m	Aug. 26, 1952
Three USAF B-52 Stratofortresses [12]	Merced, CA/CA	24,325	45h 19m	Jan. 15-18, 1957
Max Conrad	Chicago/Rome	5,000	34h 03m	Mar. 5-6, 1959
USSR TU-114 [13]	Moscow/New York	5,092	11h 06m	June 28, 1959
Boeing 707-320	New York/Moscow	c.5,090	08h 54m	July 23, 1959
Peter Gluckmann (solo)	San Francisco/San Francisco	22,800	29d	Aug. 22-Sept. 20, 1959
Sue Snyder	Chicago/Chicago	21,219	62h 59m	June 22-24, 1960
Max Conrad (solo)	Miami/Miami	25,946	8d 18h 35m 57s	Feb. 28-Mar. 8, 1961
Sam Miller & Louis Fodor	New York/New York		46h 28m	Aug. 3-4, 1963
Robert & Joan Wallick	Manila/Manila	23,129	5d 06h 17m 10s	June 2-7, 1966
Arthur Godfrey, Richard Merrill Fred Austin, Karl Keller	New York/New York	23,333	86h 9m 01s	June 4-7, 1966
Trevor K. Brougham	Darwin, Australia/Darwin	24,800	5d 05h 57m	Aug. 5-10, 1972
Walter H. Mullikin, Albert Frink, Lyman Watt, Frank Cassaniti, Edward Shields	New York/New York	23,137	1d 22h 50s	May 1-3, 1976
Arnold Palmer	Denver/Denver	22,985	57h 7m 12s	May 17-19, 1976
Boeing 747 [14]	San Francisco/San Francisco	26,382	57h 25m 42s	Oct. 28-31, 1977
Richard Rutan & Jeana Yeager [15]	Edwards AFB, CA	24,986	09d 03m 44s	Dec. 14-23, 1986
Concorde	New York/New York	1,114 mph	31h 27m 49s	Aug. 15-16, 1995
Col. Douglas L. Raaberg and crew, B1 bomber [16]	Dyess AFB, Abilene, TX/Dyess AFB	6,250	36h 13m 36s	June 3, 1995
Linda Finch [17]	Oakland, CA/Oakland, CA	26,000	73d	Mar. 17-May 28, 1997
Steve Fossett	Argentina/Coral Sea (off Australia)	15,200	8d 13h 58m	Aug. 7-16, 1998

(1) Nonstop transatlantic flight. (2) Claim of reaching N. Pole in dispute; if claim is untrue, then Amundsen-Ellsworth-Nobile were the first to fly over N. Pole. (3) Includes mileage by train and auto, 4,110; by plane, 6,300; by steamship, 8,000. (4) Solo transatlantic flight in the Ryan monoplane "Spirit of St. Louis." (5) Nonstop transpacific flight. (6) First woman's transoceanic solo flight. (7) First to fly solo around N circumference of the world and first to fly twice around the world. (8) Inception of regular commercial global air service. (9) First nonstop round-the-world flight, refueled 4 times in flight. (10) Nonstop jet transatlantic flight. (11) Transatlantic round trip on same day. (12) First nonstop global flight by jet planes; refueled in flight by KC-97 aerial tankers; average speed approx. 525 mph. (13) Nonstop between Moscow and New York. (14) Speed record around the world over both Earth's poles. (15) Circled Earth nonstop without refueling. (16) Refueled in flight 6 times. Tested B-1B bomber by bombing 3 prearranged target sites on 3 continents. (17) Followed the intended around-the-world flight route (1937) of Amelia Earhart.

METEOROLOGY

National Weather Service Watches and Warnings

Source: National Weather Service, NOAA, U.S. Dept. of Commerce; *Glossary of Meteorology,* American Meteorological Society

National Weather Service forecasters issue a *Severe Thunderstorm* or *Tornado Watch* for a specific area when a severe convective storm that usually covers a relatively small geographic area or moves in a narrow path is sufficiently intense to threaten life and/or property. Examples include thunderstorms with large hail, damaging winds, and/or tornadoes. Excessive localized convective rains are not classified as severe storms but are often the product of severe local storms. Such rainfall may result in phenomena that threaten life and property, such as flash floods. Although cloud-to-ground lightning is not a criterion for severe local storms, it is acknowledged to be a leading cause of storm deaths and injuries.

A *Watch* alerts people that threatening weather is likely. Under a Watch, they should remain alert for approaching storms, activate a plan for action, and monitor ongoing events closely. A *Warning* means that severe weather is occurring or has been indicated by radar; immediate action should be taken by people in the storm's path.

Severe Thunderstorm—a thunderstorm that produces a tornado, winds of at least 50 knots (58 mph), and/or hail at least 3/4 inch in diameter. A thunderstorm with winds of at least 35 knots (40 mph) and/or hail at least 1/2 inch in diameter is defined as approaching severe. A *Severe Thunderstorm Watch* is issued for a specific area where such storms are most likely to develop. A *Severe Thunderstorm Warning* indicates that a severe thunderstorm has been sighted or indicated by radar.

Tornado—a violent rotating column of air (winds over 200 mph), usually pendant to a cumulonimbus cloud, with circulation reaching the ground. A tornado nearly always starts as a funnel cloud and may be accompanied by a loud roaring noise. On a local scale, it is the most destructive of all atmospheric phenomena. Tornado paths have varied in length from a few feet to more than 100 miles (avg. 5 mi); in diameter from a few feet to more than a mile (avg. 220 yd); average forward speed, 30 mph.

Cyclone—an atmospheric circulation of winds rotating counterclockwise in the northern hemisphere and clockwise in the southern hemisphere. Tornadoes, hurricanes, and the lows shown on weather maps are all examples of cyclones of various size and intensity. Cyclones are usually accompanied by precipitation or stormy weather.

Subtropical Storm—an atmospheric circulation of one-minute sustained surface winds, 34 knots (39 mph) or more. Depending on its characteristics and intensity, it can develop into a tropical storm or a hurricane.

Tropical Storm—an atmospheric circulation of one-minute sustained surface winds within a range of 34 to 63 knots (39 to 73 mph). A *Tropical Storm Watch* is an announcement that a tropical storm or tropical storm conditions may pose a threat to coastal areas generally within 36 hours. A *Tropical Storm Warning* is an announcement that tropical storm conditions pose a threat along a specified segment of coastline within 24 hours.

Hurricane—a severe cyclone originating over tropical ocean waters and having one-minute sustained surface winds 64 knots (73 mph) or higher. (West of the international date line, in the western Pacific, such storms are known as *typhoons.*) The area of hurricane-force winds forms a circle or an oval, sometimes as wide as 300 mi in diameter. In the lower latitudes, hurricanes usually move west or northwest at 10 to 15 mph. When the center approaches 25° to 30° North Latitude, the direction of motion often changes to northeast, with increased forward speed.

Blizzard—a severe weather condition characterized by strong winds bearing a great amount of snow. The National Weather Service specifies winds of 35 mph or higher and sufficient falling and/or blowing snow to frequently reduce visibility to less than 1/4 mi. for at least 3 hours.

Flood—Flooding takes many forms. *River Flooding:* This natural process occurs when rains, sometimes coupled with melting snow, fill river basins with too much water too quickly; torrential rains from decaying hurricanes or tropical systems can also be a major cause of river flooding. *Coastal Flooding:* Winds from tropical storms and hurricanes or intense offshore low pressure systems can drive ocean water inland and cause significant flooding. Coastal floods can also be produced by sea waves called *tsunamis,* sometimes referred to as tidal waves; these waves are produced by earthquakes or volcanic activity. *Flash Flooding:* Usually due to copious amounts of rain falling in a short time, flash flooding typically occurs within 6 hours of the rain event. Flash floods account for the majority of flood deaths in the U.S. *Urban Flooding:* Urbanization significantly increases runoff over what would occur on natural terrain, making flash flooding in these areas extremely dangerous. Streets can become swift-moving rivers, and basements can become death traps as they fill with water. *Ice Jam Flooding:* Ice can accumulate at natural or artificial obstructions and stop the flow of water. As the water flow is stopped, water builds up and flooding can occur upstream. If the jam suddenly gives way, the gush of ice and water can cause serious downstream flash flooding.

Flash Flood or Flood Watch: Flash flooding or flooding is possible within a designated area.

Flash Flood or Flood Warning: Flash flooding or flooding has been reported or is imminent; all necessary precautions should be taken immediately.

Urban and Small Stream Advisory: Small streams, streets, and low-lying areas such as railroad underpasses and urban storm drains are flooding.

National Weather Service Marine Warnings and Advisories

Small Craft Advisory alerts mariners to sustained (exceeding 2 hours) weather and/or sea conditions, either present or forecast, potentially hazardous to small boats. Although "small craft" is not defined, hazardous conditions generally include winds of 18 to 33 knots and/or dangerous wave conditions. It is the responsibility of the mariner, based on experience and on the location and size or type of boat, to determine whether conditions are hazardous to the boat. Upon receiving word of a Small Craft Advisory, the mariner should immediately obtain the latest marine forecast to determine the reason for the advisory.

Gale Warning indicates that winds within the range 34 to 47 knots, not directly associated with a tropical storm, are forecast for the area.

Tropical Storm Warning indicates that winds within the range of 34 to 63 knots are forecast in a specified coastal area to occur within 24 hours or less. Issued only for winds of tropical weather systems.

Storm Warning indicates that winds 48 knots or above, not directly associated with a tropical storm, are forecast for the area.

Hurricane Warning indicates that winds 64 knots or greater are forecast for the area within 24 hours. Issued only for winds produced by tropical weather systems.

Special Marine Warning indicates potentially hazardous weather conditions, usually of short duration (2 hours or less) and producing wind speeds of 34 knots or more, not adequately covered by existing marine warnings.

Primary sources of dissemination are commercial radio, TV, U.S. Coast Guard radio stations, and NOAA VHF-FM broadcasts. These NOAA broadcasts on 162.40 to 162.55 MHz can usually be received 20-40 mi from the transmitting antenna site, depending on terrain and quality of the receiver used. Where transmitting antennas are on high ground, the range may be somewhat greater, reaching 60 mi or more.

Monthly Normal Temperatures, Precipitation

Source: National Climatic Data Center, NESDIS, NOAA, U.S. Dept. of Commerce

The temperatures given here are based on records for the 30-year period 1961-90. For stations that did not have continuous records from the same site for the entire 30 years, the means have been adjusted to the record at the present site.

Figures are for airport stations unless otherwise indicated. * = city station. T = temperature in Fahrenheit; P = precipitation in inches; L = less than 0.05 inch.

	Jan.		Feb.		Mar.		Apr.		May		June		July		Aug.		Sept.		Oct.		Nov.		Dec.	
Station	**T**	**P**	**T**	**P**	**T**	**P**	**T**	**P**	**T**	**P**	**T**	**P**	**T**	**P**	**T**	**P**	**T**	**P**	**T**	**P**	**T**	**P**	**T**	**P**
Albany, NY	21	2.4	24	2.3	34	2.9	46	3.0	58	3.4	67	3.6	72	3.2	70	3.5	61	3.0	50	2.8	40	3.2	27	2.9
Albuquerque, NM	34	0.4	40	0.5	47	0.5	55	0.5	64	0.5	74	0.6	79	1.4	76	1.6	69	1.0	57	0.9	44	0.4	35	0.5
Anchorage, AK	15	0.8	19	0.8	26	0.7	36	0.7	47	0.7	54	1.1	58	1.7	56	2.4	48	2.7	35	2.0	21	1.1	16	1.1
Asheville, NC	36	3.3	39	3.9	47	4.6	55	3.4	63	4.4	69	4.2	73	4.5	72	4.7	66	3.9	56	3.6	48	3.6	40	3.5
Atlanta, GA	41	4.8	45	4.8	54	5.8	62	4.3	69	4.3	76	3.6	79	5.0	78	3.7	73	3.4	62	3.1	53	3.9	45	4.3
Atlantic City, NJ	31	3.5	33	3.1	42	3.6	50	3.6	60	3.3	69	2.6	75	3.8	73	4.1	66	2.9	55	2.8	46	3.6	36	3.3
Baltimore, MD	32	3.1	35	3.1	44	3.4	53	3.1	63	3.7	73	3.7	77	3.7	76	3.9	69	3.4	57	3.0	47	3.3	37	3.4
Barrow, AK	–13	0.2	–18	0.2	–15	0.2	–2	0.2	19	0.2	34	0.3	39	0.9	38	1.0	31	0.6	14	0.5	–2	0.3	–11	0.2
Birmingham, AL	42	5.1	46	4.7	54	6.2	62	5.0	69	4.9	76	3.7	80	5.3	79	3.6	73	3.9	63	2.8	53	4.3	45	5.1
Bismarck, ND	9	0.5	16	0.4	28	0.8	43	1.7	55	2.2	64	2.7	71	2.1	68	1.7	57	1.5	46	0.9	29	0.5	14	0.5
Boise, ID	29	1.5	36	1.2	43	1.3	49	1.2	58	1.1	67	1.8	74	0.4	73	0.4	63	0.8	52	0.8	40	1.5	30	1.4
Boston, MA	29	3.6	30	3.6	39	3.7	48	3.6	58	3.3	68	3.1	74	2.8	72	3.2	65	3.1	55	3.3	45	4.2	34	4.0
Buffalo, NY	24	2.7	25	2.3	34	2.7	45	2.9	57	3.1	66	3.6	71	3.1	69	4.2	62	3.5	51	3.1	41	3.8	29	3.7
Burlington, VT	16	1.8	18	1.6	31	2.2	44	2.8	56	3.1	65	3.5	71	3.7	68	4.1	59	3.3	48	2.9	37	3.1	23	2.4
Caribou, ME	9	2.4	12	1.9	25	2.4	38	2.5	51	3.1	61	2.9	66	4.0	63	4.1	54	3.5	43	3.1	31	3.6	15	3.2
Charleston, SC	48	3.5	51	3.3	58	4.3	65	2.7	73	4.0	78	6.4	82	6.8	81	7.2	76	4.7	67	2.9	58	2.5	51	3.2
Chicago, IL	21	1.5	25	1.4	37	2.7	49	3.6	59	3.3	69	3.8	73	3.7	72	4.2	64	3.8	53	2.4	40	2.9	27	2.5
Cleveland, OH	25	2.0	27	2.2	37	2.9	48	3.1	58	3.5	68	3.7	72	3.5	70	3.4	64	3.4	53	2.5	43	3.2	31	3.1
Columbus, OH	26	2.2	30	2.2	41	3.3	51	3.2	61	3.9	69	4.0	73	4.3	72	3.7	66	3.0	54	2.2	43	3.2	32	2.9
Dallas-Ft. Worth, TX	43	1.8	48	2.2	57	2.8	66	3.5	73	4.9	81	3.0	85	2.3	85	2.2	77	3.4	67	3.5	56	2.3	47	1.8
Denver, CO	30	0.5	33	0.6	39	1.3	48	1.7	57	2.4	67	1.8	74	1.9	71	1.5	62	1.2	51	1.0	39	0.9	31	0.6
Des Moines, IA	19	1.0	25	1.1	37	2.3	51	3.4	62	3.7	72	4.5	77	3.8	74	4.2	65	3.5	54	2.6	39	1.8	24	1.3
Detroit, MI	23	1.8	25	1.7	36	2.6	47	3.0	58	2.9	68	3.6	72	3.2	71	3.4	63	2.9	51	2.1	40	2.7	28	2.8
Dodge City, KS	30	0.5	35	0.6	43	1.6	55	2.0	64	3.0	74	3.1	80	3.2	78	2.7	69	1.9	57	1.3	43	0.8	32	0.6
Duluth, MN	7	1.2	12	0.8	24	1.9	39	2.3	51	3.0	60	3.8	66	3.6	64	4.0	54	3.8	44	2.5	28	1.8	13	1.2
Fairbanks, AK	–10	0.5	–4	0.4	11	0.4	31	0.3	49	0.6	60	1.4	63	1.9	57	2.0	46	1.0	25	0.9	3	0.8	–7	0.9
Fresno, CA	46	2.0	51	1.8	55	1.9	61	1.0	69	0.3	77	0.1	82	L	80	L	75	0.2	65	0.5	54	1.4	45	1.4
Galveston, TX*	53	3.3	55	2.3	62	2.2	69	2.4	76	3.6	81	4.4	83	4.0	84	4.5	80	5.9	73	2.8	64	3.4	56	3.5
Grand Junction, CO	25	0.6	34	0.5	43	0.9	52	0.7	62	0.9	72	0.5	79	0.6	76	0.8	67	0.8	55	1.0	40	0.7	29	0.6
Grand Rapids, MI	22	1.8	24	1.4	34	2.6	46	3.4	58	3.1	67	3.7	72	3.2	70	3.6	61	4.2	50	2.8	38	3.3	27	2.9
Hartford, CT	25	3.4	28	3.2	38	3.6	49	3.9	60	4.1	69	3.8	74	3.2	72	3.7	63	3.8	52	3.6	42	4.0	30	3.9
Helena, MT	20	0.6	26	0.4	34	0.7	43	1.0	53	1.8	62	1.9	69	1.1	67	1.3	55	1.2	45	0.6	32	0.5	21	0.6
Honolulu, HI	73	3.6	73	2.2	74	2.2	76	1.5	78	1.1	79	0.5	81	0.6	81	0.4	81	0.8	80	2.3	77	3.0	74	3.8
Houston, TX	50	3.2	54	3.3	61	2.7	68	4.2	75	4.7	80	4.0	83	3.3	82	3.7	78	4.9	70	3.7	61	3.4	54	3.7
Huron, SD	13	0.4	19	0.8	32	1.2	46	2.0	58	2.7	68	3.3	74	2.3	72	2.0	61	1.4	49	1.4	32	0.7	18	0.5
Indianapolis, IN	26	2.3	30	2.5	41	3.8	52	3.7	63	4.0	72	3.5	75	4.5	73	3.6	67	2.9	55	2.6	43	3.2	31	3.3
Jackson, MS	44	5.2	48	4.7	57	5.8	65	5.6	72	5.1	79	3.2	82	4.5	81	3.8	76	3.6	65	3.3	56	4.8	48	5.9
Jacksonville, FL	52	3.3	55	3.9	61	3.7	67	2.8	73	3.6	79	5.7	82	5.6	81	7.9	78	7.0	70	2.9	62	2.1	55	2.7
Juneau, AK	24	4.5	28	3.7	33	3.3	40	2.8	47	3.4	53	3.1	56	4.2	55	5.3	49	6.7	42	7.8	32	4.9	27	4.4
Kansas City, MO	26	1.1	31	1.1	43	2.5	55	3.1	64	5.0	73	4.7	79	4.4	76	4.0	68	4.9	57	3.3	43	1.9	30	1.6
Knoxville, TN	36	4.2	40	4.1	49	5.1	58	3.7	65	4.1	73	4.0	77	4.7	76	3.1	70	3.1	58	2.8	49	3.8	40	4.5
Lander, WY	20	0.5	25	0.6	34	1.2	43	2.1	53	2.3	63	1.5	71	0.8	69	0.5	58	1.1	47	1.1	31	0.8	21	0.6
Lexington, KY	31	2.9	35	3.2	45	4.4	55	3.9	64	4.5	72	3.7	76	5.0	75	3.9	68	3.2	57	2.6	46	3.4	36	4.0
Little Rock, AR	39	3.9	44	4.4	53	5.3	62	6.2	70	7.0	78	7.8	82	8.2	81	8.1	74	7.4	63	6.3	52	5.2	43	4.3
Los Angeles, CA*	58	2.9	60	3.1	61	2.6	63	1.0	66	0.2	70	L	74	L	75	0.1	74	0.5	70	0.3	63	2.0	58	2.0
Louisville, KY	32	2.9	36	3.3	46	4.7	56	4.2	65	4.6	73	3.5	77	4.5	76	3.5	70	3.2	58	2.7	47	3.7	37	3.6
Marquette, MI*	12	2.2	14	1.7	24	2.8	37	2.6	50	3.0	59	3.5	65	2.9	63	3.4	54	4.1	44	3.6	30	2.9	17	2.6
Memphis, TN	40	3.7	44	4.4	53	5.4	63	5.5	71	5.0	79	3.6	83	3.8	81	3.4	74	3.5	63	3.0	53	5.1	44	5.7
Miami, FL	67	2.0	69	2.1	72	2.4	75	2.9	79	6.2	81	9.3	83	5.7	83	7.6	82	7.6	78	5.6	74	2.7	69	1.8
Milwaukee, WI	19	1.6	23	1.5	33	2.7	44	3.5	55	2.8	65	3.2	71	3.5	69	3.5	62	3.4	50	2.4	38	2.5	24	2.3
Minneapolis, MN	12	1.0	18	0.9	31	1.9	46	2.4	59	3.4	68	4.1	74	3.5	71	3.6	61	2.7	49	2.2	33	1.6	18	1.1
Mobile, AL	50	4.8	53	5.5	61	6.4	68	4.5	75	5.7	80	5.0	82	6.9	82	7.0	78	5.9	68	2.9	60	4.1	53	5.3
Moline, IL	20	1.5	25	1.2	37	3.0	50	3.9	61	4.3	71	4.3	75	5.0	73	4.2	65	4.0	53	2.9	40	2.5	25	2.2
Nashville, TN	36	3.6	40	3.8	50	4.9	59	4.4	68	4.9	76	3.6	79	4.0	78	3.5	72	3.5	60	2.6	50	4.1	41	4.6
Newark, NJ	31	3.4	33	3.0	42	3.9	52	3.8	63	4.1	73	3.2	78	4.5	76	3.9	69	3.7	58	3.1	47	3.9	36	3.5
New Orleans, LA	51	5.1	54	6.0	62	4.9	69	4.5	75	4.6	80	5.8	82	6.1	82	6.2	78	5.5	69	3.1	61	4.4	55	5.8
New York, NY*	32	3.4	34	3.3	42	4.1	53	4.2	63	4.4	72	3.7	77	4.4	76	4.0	68	3.9	58	3.6	48	4.5	37	3.9
Norfolk, VA	39	3.8	41	3.5	49	3.7	57	3.1	66	3.8	74	3.8	78	5.1	77	4.8	72	3.9	61	3.2	53	2.9	44	3.2
Oklahoma City, OK	36	1.1	41	1.6	50	2.7	60	2.8	68	5.2	77	4.3	82	2.6	81	2.6	73	3.8	62	3.2	50	2.0	39	1.4
Omaha, NE	21	0.7	27	0.8	39	2.0	52	2.7	62	4.5	72	3.9	77	3.5	74	3.2	65	3.7	53	2.3	39	1.5	25	1.0
Philadelphia, PA	30	3.2	33	2.8	42	3.5	52	3.6	63	3.8	72	3.7	77	4.3	76	3.8	68	3.4	56	2.6	46	3.3	36	3.4
Phoenix, AZ	54	0.7	58	0.7	62	0.9	70	0.2	79	0.1	88	0.1	94	0.8	92	1.0	86	0.9	75	0.7	62	0.7	54	1.0
Pittsburgh, PA	26	2.5	29	2.4	39	3.4	50	3.2	60	3.6	68	3.7	72	3.8	71	3.2	64	3.0	52	2.4	42	2.9	32	2.9
Portland, ME	21	3.5	23	3.3	33	3.7	43	4.1	53	3.6	62	3.4	69	3.1	67	2.9	59	3.1	49	3.9	39	5.2	27	4.6
Portland, OR	40	5.4	44	3.9	47	3.6	51	2.4	57	2.1	64	1.5	68	0.6	69	1.1	63	1.8	55	2.7	46	5.3	40	6.1
Providence, RI	28	4.1	30	3.7	37	4.3	47	4.0	57	3.5	67	2.8	73	3.0	71	4.0	64	3.5	54	3.8	44	4.2	33	4.5
Raleigh, NC	39	3.6	42	3.4	50	3.7	59	2.9	67	3.7	74	3.7	78	4.4	77	4.4	71	3.3	60	2.7	51	2.9	43	3.1
Rapid City, SD	22	0.4	27	0.5	34	1.0	45	1.9	55	2.7	65	3.1	72	2.0	71	1.7	60	1.2	49	1.1	35	0.6	24	0.5
Reno, NV	33	1.1	38	1.0	43	0.7	49	0.4	57	0.7	65	0.5	72	0.3	70	0.3	60	0.4	51	0.4	40	0.9	33	1.0
Richmond, VA	37	3.2	39	3.2	48	3.6	57	3.0	66	3.8	74	3.6	78	5.0	77	4.4	70	3.3	59	3.5	50	3.2	40	3.3
St. Louis, MO	29	1.8	34	2.1	45	3.6	57	3.5	66	4.0	75	3.7	80	3.9	78	2.9	70	3.1	58	2.7	46	3.3	34	3.0
Salt Lake City, UT	28	1.1	34	1.2	42	1.9	50	2.1	59	1.8	69	0.9	78	0.8	76	0.9	65	1.3	53	1.4	41	1.3	30	1.4
San Antonio, TX	49	1.7	54	1.8	62	1.5	69	2.5	76	4.2	82	3.8	85	2.2	85	2.5	79	3.4	70	3.2	60	2.6	52	1.5
San Diego, CA	57	1.8	59	1.5	60	1.8	62	0.8	64	0.2	67	0.1	71	L	73	0.1	71	0.2	68	0.4	62	1.5	57	1.6
San Francisco, CA	49	4.4	52	3.2	53	3.1	56	1.4	58	0.2	62	0.1	63	L	64	0.1	65	0.2	61	1.2	55	2.9	49	3.1
San Juan, PR	77	2.8	77	2.1	78	2.3	79	3.8	81	5.9	82	4.0	83	4.4	83	5.3	82	5.3	82	5.7	80	5.9	78	4.7
Sault Ste. Marie, MI*	13	2.4	14	1.7	24	2.3	38	2.4	51	2.7	58	3.1	64	2.7	63	3.6	55	3.7	45	3.2	33	3.5	19	2.9
Savannah, GA	49	3.6	52	3.2	59	3.8	66	3.0	74	4.1	79	5.7	82	6.4	81	7.4	77	4.5	67	2.4	59	2.2	52	3.0
Scottsbluff, NE	25	0.5	30	0.5	36	1.1	47	1.6	56	2.8	67	2.6	74	2.1	72	1.1	61	1.1	50	0.8	36	0.6	26	0.6
Seattle, WA	41	5.4	44	4.0	47	3.8	50	2.5	56	1.8	61	1.6	65	0.9	66	1.2	61	1.9	54	3.3	46	5.7	42	6.0
Spokane, WA	27	2.0	33	1.5	39	1.5	46	1.2	54	1.4	62	1.3	69	0.7	68	0.7	59	0.7	47	1.0	35	2.2	28	2.4
Springfield, MO	31	1.8	36	2.2	46	3.9	56	4.2	65	4.4	73	5.1	78	2.9	77	3.5	69	4.6	58	3.6	46	3.8	35	3.2
Syracuse, NY	22	2.3	24	2.2	34	2.8	46	3.3	57	3.3	65	3.8	70	3.8	68	3.5	62	3.8	51	3.2	41	3.7	28	3.2
Tampa, FL	60	2.0	62	3.1	67	3.0	71	1.2	77	3.1	81	5.5	82	6.6	82	7.6	81	6.0	75	2.0	68	1.8	62	2.2
Washington, DC	31	2.7	34	2.8	43	3.2	53	3.1	62	4.0	71	3.9	76	3.5	74	3.9	67	3.4	55	3.2	45	3.3	35	3.2
Wilmington, DE	31	3.0	33	2.9	43	3.4	52	3.4	63	3.8	72	3.6	76	4.2	75	3.4	68	3.4	56	2.9	46	3.3	36	3.5

Normal High and Low Temperatures, Precipitation

Source: National Climatic Data Center, NESDIS, NOAA, U.S. Dept. of Commerce

The normal temperatures given here are based on records for the 30-year period 1961-90. The extreme temperatures (through 1990) are listed for the stations shown and may not agree with the state records shown on page 223.

Figures are for airport stations unless otherwise indicated. * = city station. Temperatures are Fahrenheit.

State	Station	Normal temperature January Max.	January Min.	July Max.	July Min.	Extreme temperature Highest	Extreme temperature Lowest	Normal annual precipitation (inches)
Alabama	Mobile	60	40	91	73	104	3	63.96
Alaska	Anchorage	21	8	65	52	85	–34	15.91
Alaska	Barrow	–7	–19	45	34	79	–56	4.49
Arizona	Phoenix	66	41	106	81	122	17	7.66
Arkansas	Little Rock	49	29	92	72	112	–5	72.10
California	Los Angeles*	68	49	84	65	112	28	14.77
California	San Diego	66	49	76	66	111	29	9.9
California	San Francisco	56	42	72	54	106	20	19.70
Colorado	Denver	43	16	88	59	104	–30	15.40
Connecticut	Hartford	33	16	85	62	102	–26	44.14
Delaware	Wilmington	39	22	86	67	102	–14	40.84
District of Columbia	Washington–National	42	27	89	71	104	–5	38.63
Florida	Jacksonville	64	41	91	72	105	7	51.32
Florida	Miami	75	59	89	76	98	30	55.91
Georgia	Atlanta	50	32	88	70	105	–8	50.77
Georgia	Savannah	60	38	91	72	105	3	49.22
Hawaii	Honolulu	80	66	88	74	94	53	22.02
Idaho	Boise	36	22	90	58	111	–25	12.11
Illinois	Chicago	29	13	84	63	104	–27	35.82
Illinois	Moline	28	11	86	65	106	-27	39.08
Indiana	Indianapolis	34	17	86	65	104	–23	39.94
Iowa	Des Moines	28	11	87	67	108	–24	33.12
Kentucky	Lexington	39	22	86	66	103	–21	44.55
Kentucky	Louisville	40	23	87	67	105	–20	44.39
Louisiana	New Orleans	61	42	91	73	102	11	61.88
Maine	Caribou	19	–2	77	55	96	–41	36.60
Maine	Portland	30	11	79	58	103	–39	44.34
Maryland	Baltimore	40	23	87	67	105	–7	40.76
Massachusetts	Boston	36	22	82	65	102	–12	41.51
Michigan	Detroit	30	16	83	61	104	–21	32.62
Michigan	Sault Ste. Marie*	21	5	76	51	98	–36	34.23
Minnesota	Duluth	16	–2	77	55	97	–39	30.00
Minnesota	Minneapolis-St. Paul	21	3	84	63	105	–34	28.32
Mississippi	Jackson	56	33	92	71	106	2	55.37
Missouri	Kansas City	35	17	89	68	109	–23	37.62
Missouri	St. Louis	38	21	89	70	107	–18	37.51
Montana	Helena	30	10	85	53	105	–42	11.60
Nebraska	Omaha	31	11	88	66	114	–23	29.86
Nebraska	Scottsbluff	38	12	90	59	109	–42	15.27
Nevada	Reno	45	21	92	51	105	–16	7.53
New Jersey	Atlantic City	40	21	85	65	106	–11	40.29
New Mexico	Albuquerque	47	22	93	64	105	–17	8.88
New York	Albany	30	11	84	60	100	–28	36.17
New York	Buffalo	30	17	80	62	99	–20	38.58
New York	New York–La Guardia	37	26	84	69	107	–3	42.12
North Carolina	Asheville	47	25	83	62	100	–16	47.59
North Carolina	Raleigh	49	29	88	68	105	–9	41.43
North Dakota	Bismarck	20	–2	84	56	109	–44	15.47
Ohio	Cleveland	32	18	82	61	104	–19	36.63
Ohio	Columbus	34	19	84	63	102	–19	38.09
Oregon	Portland	45	34	80	57	107	–3	36.30
Pennsylvania	Philadelphia	38	23	86	67	104	–7	41.41
Pennsylvania	Pittsburgh	34	19	83	62	103	–18	36.85
Rhode Island	Providence	37	19	82	63	104	–13	45.53
South Carolina	Charleston	58	38	90	73	104	6	51.53
South Dakota	Huron	24	2	87	62	112	–39	20.08
South Dakota	Rapid City	34	11	86	58	110	–30	16.64
Tennessee	Memphis	49	31	92	73	108	–13	52.10
Tennessee	Nashville	46	27	90	69	107	–17	47.30
Texas	Galveston*	58	47	87	79	101	8	42.28
Texas	Houston	61	40	93	72	107	7	46.07
Utah	Salt Lake City	36	19	92	64	107	–30	16.18
Vermont	Burlington	25	8	81	60	101	–30	34.47
Virginia	Norfolk	47	31	86	70	104	–3	44.64
Virginia	Richmond	46	26	88	68	105	–12	43.16
Washington	Seattle-Tacoma	45	35	75	55	99	0	37.19
Washington	Spokane	33	21	83	54	108	–25	16.49
Wisconsin	Milwaukee	26	12	80	62	103	–26	32.93
Wyoming	Lander	31	8	86	56	101	–37	13.01

Mean Annual Snowfall (inches) based on record through 1990: Boston, MA, 42; Sault Ste. Marie, MI, 113; Albany, NY, 65.2; Burlington, VT, 78.6; Lander, WY, 66; Juneau, AK, 105.8.

Wettest Spot: Mount Waialeale, HI, on the island of Kauai, is the rainiest place in the United States and in the world, according to the National Geographic Society; it has an average annual rainfall of 460 inches.

Below are the official temperature extremes through mid-1998. There are many unofficial claims. To qualify as official meteorological data, readings must be taken on approved instruments in a sheltered and ventilated location.

Highest Temperature: A temperature of 136° F observed at Azizia (Al Aziziyah), near Tripoli, Libya, on Sept. 13, 1922, is generally accepted as the world's highest temperature recorded under standard conditions.

The record high in the United States was 134° F in Death Valley, CA, July 10, 1913.

Lowest Temperature: A record low temperature of –129° F was recorded at the Soviet Antarctica station of Vostok on July 21, 1983.

The record low in the United States was –80° F at Prospect Creek, AK, Jan. 23, 1971.

The lowest official temperature on the North American continent was recorded at –81° F in Feb. 1947, at an airport in the Yukon called Snag.

Annual Climatological Data

Source: National Climatic Data Center, NESDIS, NOAA, U.S. Dept. of Commerce

1997		Temperature °F				Precipitation[1]						Fastest[2] wind		No. of days			
									Sleet or snow								
Station	Elev. (ft)	Highest	Date	Lowest	Date	Total (in.)	Greatest in 24 hours	Date	Total (in.)	Greatest in 24 hours	Date	MPH	Date	Clear*	Cloudy*	Prec. .01 in. or more	Snow, sleet 1 in. or more
Albany, NY	275	96	7/15	–8	1/19	34.72	2.02	3/31	78.0	14.6	3/31	46	3/6	69	185	143	22
Albuquerque, NM	5,311	98	7/2	3	1/15	12.36	1.41	9/20-21	18.7	3.5	12/20	51	12/22	167	87	81	6
Anchorage, AK	114	80	6/28	–21	1/6	19.48	2.82	8/21-22	53.8	4.6	12/28	39	3/16	61	239	113	20
Asheville, NC	2,140	91	8/17	6	1/17	49.38	4.36	6/26-27	10.2	1.9	12/31	38	4/17	99	153	129	5
Atlanta, GA	1,010	95	9/20	15	1/17	51.68	3.38	9/24-25	—	—	—	38	8/18	110	149	128	0
Atlantic City, NJ	64	98	7/15	2	1/19	55.34	13.50	8/20-21	—	—	—	—	—	94	160	119	—
Baltimore, MD	148	101	8/16	1	1/19	38.34	2.75	8/20	15.2	5.8	2/08	41	3/6	105	152	117	5
Barrow, AK	31	61	8/10	–41	1/6	5.14	0.49	8/3-4	42.5	2.9	9/29-30	41	3/12	66	187	79	14
Birmingham, AL	620	97	9/20	12	1/17	55.49	2.46	7/22	1.7	1.6	12/29	—	—	99	155	128	1
Bismarck, ND	1,647	99	8/24	–31	1/17	14.90	1.96	4/5	66.3	15.2	4/5	49	4/6	93	165	90	15
Boise, ID	2,838	101	8/7	8	1/13	11.09	0.82	4/23	4.3	2.7	1/25	40	6/11	120	155	79	1
Boston, MA	15	95	7/17	0	1/19	30.39	1.64	11/8-9	—	—	—	48	11/1	98	164	—	—
Buffalo, NY	705	87	7/14	–5	1/19	41.08	2.05	9/28-29	100.7	12.1	1/10	54	2/27	54	208	191	26
Burlington, VT	332	91	8/10	–17	1/19	30.62	1.46	7/8-9	103.6	—	—	38	1/22	58	206	165	30
Caribou, ME	624	88	7/26	–32	1/19	35.37	1.71	6/13-14	163.0	18.1	3/6	38	12/3	59	206	150	35
Charleston, SC	40	97	7/4	23	1/18	62.57	4.91	6/6	—	—	—	44	6/27	102	155	124	—
Chicago, IL	658	97	7/26	–9	1/17	31.71	3.78	2/20-21	—	—	—	43	10/26	84	176	124	—
Cleveland, OH	777	92	6/25	–4	1/19	35.36	2.73	9/19-20	46.8	5.6	12/6	45	2/27	66	202	167	14
Columbus, OH	813	94	7/27	–1	1/17	38.16	2.14	8/16-17	—	—	—	47	7/2	72	190	128	—
Dallas-Ft. Worth, TX	551	101	7/29	17	1/29	45.00	3.53	12/20-21	—	—	—	45	6/22	135	133	85	—
Denver, CO	5,282	98	7/18	–14	1/12	19.57	3.06	7/29-30	—	—	—	52	3/27	115	120	101	—
Des Moines, IA	938	96	7/25	–13	1/28	28.53	1.96	10/12-13	—	—	—	47	6/21	105	164	96	—
Detroit, MI	637	95	7/14	–6	1/19	32.42	2.11	9/9-10	—	—	—	51	2/27	75	185	142	—
Duluth, MN	1,428	86	8/2	–26	1/26	20.98	2.65	6/24	93.9	13.3	1/4	37	4/29	77	187	113	26
Fairbanks, AK	436	88	6/30	–51	1/7	6.74	0.82	6/8-9	56.4	4.9	10/21-22	30	5/29	70	210	89	21
Fresno, CA	328	108	8/7	26	12/27	7.68	1.02	11/25-26	—	—	—	29	3/30	194	98	42	—
Grand Rapids, MI	793	94	7/14	–7	1/19	29.62	3.05	2/20-21	92.2	7.1	1/9	52	4/6	64	205	146	33
Hartford, CT	169	93	8/16	–1	1/19	37.75	1.66	11/1	—	—	—	43	3/6	82	175	128	—
Helena, MT	3,828	94	8/3	–33	1/12	10.57	1.08	5/24-25	—	—	—	46	9/15	82	179	95	—
Honolulu, HI	7	94	9/2	57	1/23	19.99	3.17	1/3-4	0.0	0.0	—	32	1/3	90	94	105	0
Houston, TX	96	99	8/21	20	2/20	60.22	4.28	3/12	0.0	0.0	—	37	4/11	90	161	121	0
Huron, SD	1,281	98	7/16	–22	1/17	24.21	1.74	10/12-13	—	—	—	57	4/6	104	154	93	—
Indianapolis, IN	795	99	7/27	–12	1/12	32.89	2.50	2/26-27	24.3	7.4	1/9	47	4/6	88	179	120	8
Jackson, MS	291	97	7/28	15	1/18	58.94	6.49	6/10	4.8	4.8	12/14	43	4/4	110	108	116	1
Jacksonville, FL	26	98	7/4	23	1/19	57.27	3.73	8/1	T	T	4/23	43	4/23	94	144	130	0
Kansas City, MO	979	98	7/27	–14	1/28	33.07	1.87	4/10-11	29.8	5.0	1/27	43	6/28	120	149	105	12
Knoxville, TN	979	96	8/16	7	1/11	50.13	2.53	9/23-24	—	—	—	41	7/4	97	162	148	2
Lander, WY	5,557	97	7/16	–12	1/12	14.65	1.36	5/25-26	—	—	—	55	10/30	114	129	83	—
Lexington, KY	966	96	7/27	0	1/12	59.13	5.56	3/1	—	—	—	43	1/05	89	174	136	—
Little Rock, AR	257	100	7/28	12	1/17	49.76	3.02	9/23	4.7	4.7	2/13	—	—	119	147	108	1
Los Angeles, CA	97	97	10/16	39	12/27	12.03	1.51	12/6	—	—	—	—	—	147	103	27	0
Louisville, KY	477	98	7/26	1	1/11	49.71	7.22	3/1	7.2	1.3	1/9	40	3/25	93	171	121	3
Marquette, MI	1,415	90	6/24	–17	1/17	32.89	1.90	1/4-5	259.0	28.0	3/13-14	—	—	—	—	162	53
Memphis, TN	258	99	7/28	8	1/11	71.88	3.25	9/23	4.5	3.6	1/10	—	—	118	151	113	1
Miami, FL	7	94	8/7	37	1/19	70.61	5.89	6/9	0.0	0.0	—	38	5/28	74	115	158	0
Milwaukee, WI	679	92	7/16	–8	1/17	32.75	4.23	6/21	51.9	5.5	1/24	48	4/6	90	175	116	16
Minn.-St. Paul, MN	834	94	6/23	–18	1/28	34.43	3.71	7/17	—	—	—	37	5/5	95	169	130	—
Mobile, AL	211	97	9/21	21	1/18	80.14	10.07	7/19	—	—	—	36	7/19	102	147	139	—
Moline, IL	592	98	7/26	–15	1/28	34.92	2.27	9/16	—	—	—	57	8/3	101	164	139	—
Nashville, TN	590	99	7/27	5	1/11	54.95	4.20	11/30	—	—	—	38	1/4	102	156	123	—
Newark, NJ	7	101	7/15	3	1/19	42.35	4.64	7/24-25	17.9	3.5	3/3	47	7/18	93	160	123	8
New Orleans, LA	4	95	9/22	27	1/17	51.68	3.68	11/28-29	—	—	—	40	8/20	101	146	136	—
New York, NY	132	97	7/15	4	1/19	43.93	4.39	7/24-25	9.9	3.5	1/11	34	12/29	107	132	130	4
Norfolk, VA	24	98	7/4	14	1/19	37.48	2.73	7/23-24	—	—	—	36	7/24	106	153	112	—
Oklahoma City, OK	1,285	98	9/18	6	1/28	33.09	1.84	10/11-12	—	—	—	45	2/21	139	130	80	—
Philadelphia, PA	5	98	8/16	6	1/19	32.52	1.54	8/20-21	13.1	3.3	2/8-9	41	8/17	93	160	121	5
Phoenix, AZ	1,109	114	7/15	33	12/26	4.67	0.76	1/13-14	0.0	0.0	—	37	7/9	211	70	37	0
Pittsburgh, PA	1,137	91	7/27	–1	1/19	34.54	2.90	5/24-25	—	—	—	41	7/18	59	203	149	—
Portland, ME	43	91	8/16	–6	1/19	37.49	2.76	4/18-19	—	—	—	41	11/1	101	165	120	—
Portland, OR	21	94	7/4	26	1/15	43.81	1.76	1/17	—	—	—	39	3/30	68	222	167	—
Providence, RI	51	96	7/17	0	1/19	37.97	2.01	11/8-9	—	—	—	46	3/6	98	164	125	—
Raleigh, NC	416	99	8/17	12	1/19	40.81	4.27	7/23-24	0.8	0.4	1/11	45	2/21	111	149	113	0
Rapid City, SD	3,162	98	7/15	–16	1/12	23.83	3.19	4/5	—	—	—	61	4/5	111	139	95	—
Reno, NV	4,404	102	8/6	–2	1/14	7.75	1.09	1/1-2	—	—	—	45	1/25	158	114	53	—
Richmond, VA	164	99	7/15	4	1/19	34.13	2.36	7/22-23	—	—	—	41	5/15	100	160	107	—
St. Louis, MO	535	99	7/26	–3	1/12	31.23	2.19	2/26-27	24.8	6.6	1/9	44	4/30	101	164	104	8
Salt Lake City, UT	4,221	100	7/15	8	12/26	16.93	1.12	5/24-25	47.0	5.4	1/23	40	8/10	125	139	100	18
San Antonio, TX	788	102	8/17	22	12/13	33.92	3.37	6/21-22	—	—	—	46	5/27	105	141	100	—
San Diego, CA	13	92	9/24	39	12/27	7.00	1.08	1/12-13	—	—	—	34	12/11	146	102	32	—
San Francisco, CA	8	93	5/17	33	1/14	20.39	2.29	11/25-26	—	—	—	44	4/8	160	105	68	—
San Juan, PR	13	94	9/10	67	1/31	—	1.58	1/21-22	0.0	0.0	—	—	—	73	89	187	0
Sault Ste. Marie, MI	718	88	7/14	–26	1/18	27.86	1.86	6/23-24	—	—	—	34	4/6	66	209	157	—
Savannah, GA	46	99	7/4	22	1/19	55.70	3.98	7/30-31	—	—	—	45	7/17	104	152	125	—
Scottsbluff, NE	3,943	102	7/16	–10	1/13	20.35	2.41	5/24-25	—	—	—	55	4/5	115	138	82	—
Seattle, WA	400	88	8/12	21	1/14	43.26	2.32	3/18-19	—	—	—	41	3/30	71	201	171	—
Spokane, WA	2,356	99	8/3	6	1/27	17.45	1.41	4/19-20	—	—	—	46	4/20	86	191	111	—
Springfield, MO	1,278	97	8/4	–10	1/12	38.48	2.27	2/20-21	17.8	5.5	1/8	34	3/24	115	155	119	6
Syracuse, NY	410	94	7/15	–8	1/19	32.62	1.53	12/29-30	152.3	18.8	12/29-30	46	2/22	63	205	187	45
Tampa, FL	19	96	6/21	31	1/19	67.71	8.45	9/26-27	T	T	4/26	44	4/23	101	121	107	0
Washington, DC	10	105	8/17	11	1/19	33.82	2.72	5/25-26	6.4	3.2	2/8	43	7/28	96	164	109	2
Wilmington, DE	74	99	7/15	6	1/19	28.02	2.31	8/20	—	—	—	41	3/6	97	164	116	—

*To get partly cloudy days, deduct the total of clear and cloudy days from 365 (1 yr). (T) Trace. (—) Data not available or incomplete. (1) Where one date is shown, it is the starting date of the storm (which may have lasted more than one day). (2) Sustained for at least 2 minutes, not peak gust.

Record Temperatures by State Through 1996

Source: National Climatic Data Center, NESDIS, NOAA, U.S. Dept. of Commerce

State	Lowest °F	Highest °F	Latest date	Station	Approx. elevation in feet
Alabama	-27		Jan. 30, 1966	New Market	760
		112	Sept. 5, 1925	Centerville	345
Alaska	-80		Jan. 23, 1971	Prospect Creek	1,100
		100	June 27, 1915	Fort Yukon	420*
Arizona	-40		Jan. 7, 1971	Hawley Lake	8,180
		128	June 29, 1994[1]	Lake Havasu City	505
Arkansas	-29		Feb. 13, 1905	Pond	1,250
		120	Aug. 10, 1936	Ozark	396
California	-45		Jan. 20, 1937	Boca	5,532
		134	July 10, 1913	Greenland Ranch	-178
Colorado	-61		Feb. 1, 1985	Maybell	5,920
		118	July 11, 1888	Bennett	5,484
Connecticut	-32		Feb. 16, 1943	Falls Village	585
		106	July 15, 1995	Danbury	450
Delaware	-17		Jan. 17, 1893	Millsboro	20
		110	July 21, 1930	Millsboro	20
Florida	-2		Feb. 13, 1899	Tallahassee	193
		109	June 29, 1931	Monticello	207
Georgia	-17		Jan. 27, 1940	CCC Camp F-16	1,000*
		112	July 24, 1952	Louisville	132
Hawaii	12		May 17, 1979	Mauna Kea Obs. 111.2	13,770
		100	Apr. 27, 1931	Pahala	850
Idaho	-60		Jan. 18, 1943	Island Park Dam	6,285
		118	July 28, 1934	Orofino	1,027
Illinois	-35		Feb. 3, 1996[1]	Mount Carroll	817
		117	July 14, 1954	East St. Louis	410
Indiana	-36		Jan. 19, 1994	New Whiteland	785
		116	July 14, 1936	Collegeville	672
Iowa	-47		Feb. 3, 1996[1]	Elkader	770
		118	July 20, 1934	Keokuk	614
Kansas	-40		Feb. 13, 1905	Lebanon	1,812
		121	July 24, 1936[1]	Alton (near)	1,651
Kentucky	-37		Jan. 19, 1994	Shelbyville	730
		114	July 28, 1930	Greensburg	581
Louisiana	-16		Feb. 13, 1899	Minden	194
		114	Aug. 10, 1936	Plain Dealing	268
Maine	-48		Jan. 19, 1925	Van Buren	510
		105	July 10, 1911[1]	North Bridgton	450
Maryland	-40		Jan. 13, 1912	Oakland	2,461
		109	July 10, 1936[1]	Cumberland; Frederick	623; 325
Massachusetts	-35		Jan. 12, 1981	Chester	640
		107	Aug. 2, 1975	Chester; New Bedford	640; 120
Michigan	-51		Feb. 9, 1934	Vanderbilt	785
		112	July 13, 1936	Mio	963
Minnesota	-60		Feb. 2, 1996	Tower	1,430
		114	July 6, 1936[1]	Moorhead	904
Mississippi	-19		Jan. 30, 1966	Corinth	420
		115	July 29, 1930	Holly Springs	600
Missouri	-40		Feb. 13, 1905	Warsaw	700
		118	July 14, 1954[1]	Warsaw; Union	700; 560
Montana	-70		Jan. 20, 1954	Rogers Pass	5,470
		117	July 5, 1937	Medicine Lake	1,950
Nebraska	-47		Feb. 12, 1899	Camp Clarke	3,700
		118	July 24, 1936[1]	Minden	2,169
Nevada	-50		Jan. 8, 1937	San Jacinto	5,200
		125	June 29, 1994[1]	Laughlin	605
New Hampshire	-46		Jan. 28 1925	Pittsburg	1,575
		106	July 4, 1911	Nashua	125
New Jersey	-34		Jan. 5, 1904	River Vale	70
		110	July 10, 1936	Runyon	18
New Mexico	-50		Feb. 1, 1951	Gavilan	7,350
		122	June 27, 1994	Waste Isolat. Pilot Plt.	3,418
New York	-52		Feb. 18, 1979[1]	Old Forge	1,720
		108	July 22, 1926	Troy	35
North Carolina	-34		Jan. 21, 1985	Mt. Mitchell	6,525
		110	Aug. 21, 1983	Fayetteville	213
North Dakota	-60		Feb. 15, 1936	Parshall	1,929
		121	July 6, 1936	Steele	1,857
Ohio	-39		Feb. 10, 1899	Milligan	800
		113	July 21, 1934[1]	Gallipolis (near)	673
Oklahoma	-27		Jan. 18, 1930	Watts	958
		120	June 27, 1994[1]	Tipton	1,350
Oregon	-54		Feb. 10, 1933[1]	Seneca	4,700
		119	Aug. 10, 1898	Pendleton	1,074
Pennsylvania	-42		Jan. 5, 1904	Smethport	1,500
		111	July 10, 1936[1]	Phoenixville	100
Rhode Island	-25		Feb. 5, 1996	Greene	425
		104	Aug. 2, 1975	Providence	51
South Carolina	-19		Jan. 21, 1985	Caesars Head	3,115
		111	June 28, 1954[1]	Camden	170
South Dakota	-58		Feb. 17, 1936	McIntosh	2,277
		120	July 5, 1936	Gannvalley	1,750
Tennessee	-32		Dec. 30, 1917	Mountain City	2,471
		113	Aug. 9, 1930[1]	Perryville	377

State	Lowest °F	Highest °F	Latest date	Station	Approx. elevation in feet
Texas	−23		Feb. 8, 1933 [1]	Seminole	3,275
		120	*Aug. 12, 1936*	*Seymour*	*1,291*
Utah	−69		Feb. 1, 1985	Peter's Sink	8,092
		117	*Jul. 5, 1985*	*Saint George*	*2,880*
Vermont	−50		Dec. 30, 1933	Bloomfield	915
		105	*July 4, 1911*	*Vernon*	*310*
Virginia	−30		Jan. 22, 1985	Mountain Lake Bio. Station	3,870
		110	*July 15, 1954*	*Balcony Falls*	*725*
Washington	−48		Dec. 30, 1968	Mazama; Winthrop	2,120; 1,755
		118	*Aug. 5, 1961* [1]	*Ice Harbor Dam*	*475*
West Virginia	−37		Dec. 30, 1917	Lewisburg	2,200
		112	*July 10, 1936* [1]	*Martinsburg*	*435*
Wisconsin	−54		Jan. 24, 1922	Danbury	908
		114	*July 13, 1936*	*Wisconsin Dells*	*900*
Wyoming	−66		Feb. 9, 1933	Riverside R.S.	6,650
		114	*July 12, 1900*	*Basin*	*3,500*

* Estimated. (1) Also on earlier dates at the same or other places.

World Temperature and Precipitation

Source: World Meteorological Organization

Average daily maximum and minimum temperatures and annual precipitation are based on records for the 30-year period 1961-90. The length of record of extreme temperatures includes all available years of data for a given location and is usually for a longer period; record temperatures may have been measured at a different location within the city. Surface elevations are supplied by the WMO and may differ from city elevation figures in other sections of *The World Almanac*. NA = not available.

Station	Surface elevation (feet)	Temperature °F: Average Daily, January Max.	January Min.	July Max.	July Min.	Extreme Max.	Extreme Min.	Average annual precipitation (inches)
Algiers, Algeria	82	61.7	42.6	87.1	65.3	NA	NA	27.0
Athens, Greece	49	56.1	44.6	88.9	73.0	NA	NA	14.6
Auckland, New Zealand	20	74.8	61.2	58.5	46.4	NA	NA	49.4
Bangkok, Thailand	66	89.6	69.8	90.9	77.0	104	51	59.0
Berlin, Germany	190	35.2	26.8	73.6	55.2	107	−4	23.3
Bogotá, Colombia	8,357	67.3	41.7	64.6	45.5	75	21	32.4
Bombay (Mumbai), India	36	85.3	66.7	86.2	77.5	110	46	85.4
Bucharest, Romania	298	34.7	22.1	83.8	60.1	105	−18	23.4
Budapest, Hungary	456	34.2	24.8	79.7	59.7	103	−10	20.3
Buenos Aires, Argentina	82	85.8	67.3	59.7	45.7	104	22	45.2
Cairo, Egypt	243	65.8	48.2	93.9	71.1	118	34	1.0
Cape Town, South Africa	138	79.0	60.3	63.3	44.6	105	28	20.5
Caracas, Venezuela	2,739	79.9	60.8	81.3	66.0	96	45	36.1
Casablanca, Morocco	203	62.8	47.1	77.7	66.7	NA	NA	16.8
Copenhagen, Denmark	16	35.6	28.4	68.9	55.0	NA	NA	NA
Damascus, Syria	2,004	54.3	32.9	97.2	61.9	NA	NA	5.6
Dublin, Ireland	279	45.7	36.5	66.0	52.5	86	8	28.8
Geneva, Switzerland	1,364	38.3	27.9	76.3	53.2	101	−3	35.6
Havana, Cuba	164	78.4	65.5	88.3	74.8	NA	NA	46.9
Hong Kong, China	203	65.5	56.5	88.7	79.9	97	32	87.2
Istanbul, Turkey	108	47.8	37.2	82.8	65.3	105	7	27.4
Jerusalem, Israel	2,483	53.4	39.4	83.8	63.0	107	26	23.2
Lagos, Nigeria	125	90.0	72.3	82.8	72.1	NA	NA	59.3
Lima, Peru	43	79.0	66.9	66.4	59.4	NA	NA	0.2
London, England	203	44.1	32.7	71.1	52.3	99	2	29.7
Manila, Philippines	79	85.8	74.8	89.1	76.8	NA	NA	49.6
Mexico City, Mexico	7,570	70.3	43.7	73.8	53.2	NA	NA	33.4
Montreal, Canada	118	21.6	5.2	79.2	59.7	100	−36	37.0
Nairobi, Kenya	5,897	77.9	50.9	71.6	48.6	NA	NA	41.9
Paris, France	213	42.8	33.6	75.2	55.2	105	−1	25.6
Prague, Czech Republic	1,197	32.7	22.5	73.9	53.2	98	−16	20.7
Reykjavik, Iceland	200	35.4	26.6	55.9	46.9	76	−3	31.5
Rome, Italy	79	53.8	35.4	88.2	62.1	NA	NA	33.0
San Salvador, El Salvador	2,037	86.5	61.3	86.2	66.4	105	45	68.3
São Paulo, Brazil	2,598	81.1	65.7	71.2	53.1	NA	NA	57.4
Shanghai, China	23	45.9	32.9	88.9	76.6	104	10	43.8
Singapore	52	85.8	73.6	87.4	75.6	NA	NA	84.6
Stockholm, Sweden	171	30.7	23.0	71.4	56.1	97	−26	21.2
Sydney, Australia	10	79.5	65.5	62.4	43.9	114	32	46.4
Tehran, Iran	3,906	45.0	30.0	98.2	75.2	109	−5	9.1
Tokyo, Japan	118	49.1	34.2	83.8	72.1	NA	NA	55.4
Toronto, Canada	567	27.5	12.0	80.2	57.6	105	−26	30.8

Hurricane and Tornado Classifications

Source: National Weather Service, NOAA, U.S. Dept. of Commerce

The Saffir-Simpson Hurricane Scale is a 1-5 rating based on a hurricane's intensity. The scale is used to give an estimate of the potential property damage and flooding expected along the coast from a hurricane landfall. Wind speed is the determining factor in the scale. The Fujita (or F) Scale, created by T. Theodore Fujita, is used to classify tornadoes. The F Scale uses rating numbers from 0 to 5, based on the amount and type of wind damage.

Saffir-Simpson Scale (Hurricanes)

Category	Wind Speed	Severity	Storm Surge[1]
1	74-95 MPH	Weak	4-5 feet
2	96-110 MPH	Moderate	6-8 feet
3	111-130 MPH	Strong	9-12 feet
4	131-155 MPH	Very Strong	13-18 feet
5	> 155 MPH	Devastating	> 18 feet

(1) Above normal tides.

Fujita Scale (Tornadoes)

Rank	Wind Speed	Damage	Strength
F-0	40-72 MPH	Light	Weak
F-1	73-112 MPH	Moderate	Weak
F-2	113-157 MPH	Considerable	Strong
F-3	158-206 MPH	Severe	Strong
F-4	207-260 MPH	Devastating	Violent
F-5	> 261 MPH	Incredible	Violent

Hurricane Names in 1999

Source: National Weather Service, NOAA, U.S. Dept. of Commerce

Names assigned to Atlantic hurricanes, 1999 — Arlene, Bret, Cindy, Dennis, Emily, Floyd, Gert, Harvey, Irene, Jose, Katrina, Lenny, Maria, Nate, Ophelia, Philippe, Rita, Stan, Tammy, Vince, Wilma.

Names assigned to Eastern Pacific hurricanes, 1999 — Adrian, Beatriz, Calvin, Dora, Eugene, Fernanda, Greg, Hilary, Irwin, Jova, Kenneth, Lidia, Max, Norma, Otis, Pilar, Ramon, Selma, Todd, Veronica, Wiley, Xina, York, Zelda.

Tides and Their Causes

Source: U.S. Dept. of Commerce, Natl. Oceanic & Atmospheric Admin. (NOAA), Natl. Ocean Service (NOS)

The tides are a natural phenomenon involving the alternating rise and fall in the large fluid bodies of the earth caused by the combined gravitational attraction of the sun and moon. The combination of these two variable influences produces the complex recurrent cycle of the tides. Tides may occur in both oceans and seas, to a limited extent in large lakes, in the atmosphere, and, to a very minute degree, in the earth itself. The length of time between succeeding tides varies as the result of many factors.

The tide-generating force represents the difference between (1) the centrifugal force produced by the revolution of the earth around the common center-of-gravity of the earth-moon system and (2) the gravitational attraction of the moon acting upon the earth's overlying waters. Since, on the average, the moon is only 238,856 miles from the earth compared with the sun's much greater distance of 92,980,000 miles, this closer distance outranks the much smaller mass of the moon compared with that of the sun, and the moon's tide-raising force is, accordingly, 2.5 times that of the sun.

The effect of the tide-generating forces of the moon and sun acting tangentially to the earth's surface (the so-called "tractive force") tends to cause a maximum accumulation of the waters of the oceans at two diametrically opposite positions on the surface of the earth and to withdraw compensating amounts of water from all points 90° degrees removed from the positions of these tidal bulges. As the earth rotates beneath the maxima and minima of these tide-generating forces, a sequence of two high tides, separated by two low tides, ideally is produced each day (semidiurnal tide).

Twice in each lunar month, when the sun, moon, and earth are directly aligned, with the moon between the earth and the sun (at new moon) or on the opposite side of the earth from the sun (at full moon), the sun and the moon exert their gravitational force in a mutual or additive fashion. The highest high tides and lowest low tides are produced at these times. These are called *spring* tides. At two positions 90° degrees in between, the gravitational forces of the moon and sun—imposed at right angles—tend to counteract each other to the greatest extent, and the range between high and low tides is reduced. These are called *neap* tides. This semi-monthly variation between the spring and neap tides is called the *phase inequality.*

The inclination to the equator of the moon's monthly orbit and the inclination of the sun to the equator during the earth's yearly orbit produce a difference in the height of succeeding high tides and in the extent of depression of succeeding low tides that is known as the *diurnal inequality.* In most cases, this produces a so-called *mixed tide.* In extreme cases, these phenomena may result in only one high tide and one low tide each (*diurnal tide*). There are other monthly and yearly variations in the tide because of the elliptical shape of the orbits themselves.

The datum for Charting and Predictions is Mean Lower Low Water (MLLW). This became effective Jan. 1989 according to the convention of 1980, which prescribed that data on all United States coastlines would be the same; namely, Mean Higher High Water (MHHW), Mean High Water (MHW), Mean Tide Level (MTL), Mean Sea Level (MSL), Mean Low Water (MLW), Mean Lower Low Water (MLLW). Diurnal range of tide is the difference in height between MHHW and MLLW. Mean range of tide is the difference in height between MHW and MLW.

The actual range of tide in the open ocean is less than in the shoreline regions. However, as the ocean tide approaches shoal waters and its effects are augmented, the tidal range may be greatly increased. In Nova Scotia along the narrow channel of the Bay of Fundy, the range of tides, or difference between high and low waters, may reach 43-1/2 feet or more (under spring tide conditions) as a result of resonant amplification.

At New Orleans, the periodic rise and fall of the diurnal tide is affected by the seasonal stages of the Mississippi River, being about 10 inches at low stage and zero at high. The Canadian Tide Tables for 1972 gave a maximum range of nearly 50 feet at Leaf Basin, Ungava Bay, Quebec.

In every case, actual high or low tide can vary considerably from the average, as a result of weather conditions such as strong winds, abrupt barometric pressure changes, or prolonged periods of extreme high or low pressure.

The Average Rise and Fall of Tides[1]

Places	Ft.	In.	Places	Ft.	In.	Places	Ft.	In.
Baltimore, MD	1	8	Hampton Roads, VA	2	10	St. John's, Nfld.	2	7[2]
Boston, MA	10	4	Key West, FL	1	10	St. Petersburg, FL	2	3
Charleston, SC	5	10	Mobile, AL	1	6	San Diego, CA	5	9
Cristobal, Panama	1	1	New London, CT	3	1	Sandy Hook, NJ	5	2
Eastport, ME	19	4	Newport, RI	3	11	San Francisco, CA	5	10
Ft. Pulaski, GA	7	6	New York, NY	5	1	Seattle, WA	11	4
Galveston, TX	1	5	Philadelphia, PA	6	9	Vancouver, B.C.	10	6
Halifax, N.S.	4	5[2]	Portland, ME	9	11	Washington, DC	3	2

(1) Diurnal range. (2) Mean range.

Speed of Winds in the U.S.

Source: National Climatic Data Center, NESDIS, NOAA, U.S. Dept. of Commerce

Miles per hour — average high through 1997. Wind velocities in true values.

Station	Avg.	High	Station	Avg.	High	Station	Avg.	High
Albuquerque, NM	8.9	52	Helena, MT	7.7	73	Mt. Washington, NH	35.4	231
Anchorage, AK	7.1	75	Honolulu, HI	11.3	46	New Orleans, LA	8.1	69
Atlanta, GA	9.1	60	Houston, TX	7.8	51	New York, NY(b)	9.3	40
Baltimore, MD	9.0	80	Indianapolis, IN	9.6	47	Omaha, NE	10.5	58
Bismarck, ND	10.2	54	Jacksonville, FL	7.9	46	Philadelphia, PA	9.5	73
Boston, MA	12.5	54	Kansas City, MO	10.7	48	Phoenix, AZ	6.2	43
Buffalo, NY	11.9	91	Las Vegas, NV	9.3	53	Pittsburgh, PA	9.1	58
Cape Hatteras, NC	11.0	60	Lexington, KY	9.1	46	Portland, OR	7.9	88
Casper, WY	12.8	81	Little Rock, AR	7.8	65	Rochester, NY	9.7	59
Chicago, IL	10.4	58	Los Angeles, CA	6.2	49	St. Louis, MO	9.7	52
Cleveland, OH	10.5	53	Louisville, KY	8.3	46	Salt Lake City, UT	8.8	71
Dallas-Ft. Worth, TX	10.7	73	Memphis, TN	8.8	51	San Diego, CA	7.0	56
Denver, CO	8.6	46	Miami, FL	9.2	(a)86	San Francisco, CA	8.7	47
Des Moines, IA	10.7	76	Milwaukee, WI	11.5	54	Seattle, WA	9.0	66
Detroit, MI	10.3	51	Minn.-St. Paul, MN	10.5	51	Spokane, WA	8.9	59
Hartford, CT	8.4	46	Mobile, AL	8.9	63	Washington, DC	9.4	46

(a) Highest velocity ever recorded in Miami area was 132 mph, at former station in Miami Beach in Sept. 1926. (b) Data for Central Park; Battery Place data through 1960, avg. 14.5, high 113.

El Niño

Source: National Weather Service, NOAA

El Niño is a naturally occurring climate phenomenon characterized by warmer-than-normal ocean temperatures in the equatorial eastern Pacific and along the tropical western coasts of Central and South America. The term *El Niño*, Spanish for "the Christ Child," was originally used by Ecuadorian and Peruvian fishermen to refer to a warm ocean current typically appearing around Christmastime and lasting for several months. Fish are less abundant during these warm intervals, so fishermen often take a break to repair equipment and spend time with their families. In some years, however, the water remains especially warm into May or even June. Over the years, the term has come to be reserved for those exceptionally strong, warm intervals that not only disrupt fishermen's lives but also bring heavy rains.

The first known record of El Niño is attributed to Francisco Pizzaro, a Spaniard who in 1525 described unusual desert rainfall in northern Peru and its El Niño association. El Niño episodes occur generally every 2 to 6 years and typically last 12 to 18 months. Recent El Niño episodes include 1972-73, 1977-78, 1982-83, 1986-87, 1991-92, and 1997-98.

The intensity of El Niño events varies—some are strong, such as the 1982-83 and 1997-98 events; others are considerably weaker, based on intensity and area encompassed by the abnormally warm ocean temperatures. The eastward extent of the warmer than normal water varies from episode to episode. Both of these characteristics affect the patterns of temperature and precipitation variations associated with El Niño in the U.S. and elsewhere.

The 1997-98 El Niño, one of the most powerful climate events of the century, strongly impacted global weather patterns. The extremely warm temperatures in the equatorial Pacific, combined with shifts in trade winds across the tropics, contributed to wildfires in Indonesia; significant crop loss in Argentina and New Zealand; devastating floods in Chile, Peru, southern Brazil, and northern Argentina; mudslides in California; and record rains in the southeastern U.S.

El Niño has a significant influence on weather and climate patterns around the globe, and its impacts are most clearly seen in the wintertime. During El Niño years, winter temperatures in the continental U.S. tend to be warmer than normal in the northern and west coast states and cooler than normal in the Southeast. Conditions tend to be wetter than normal over central and southern California and the southwest U.S. and across much of the southern third of the contiguous 48 states, particularly along the Gulf Coast, and drier than normal over the northern portions of the Rocky Mountains and in the Ohio valley region. Globally, El Niño brings wetter than normal conditions to Peru and Chile and drier than normal conditions to Australia and Indonesia. It should be noted that El Niño is only one of a number of factors influencing seasonal variations of climate.

The opposite of El Niño is La Niña, with colder than normal sea surface temperatures in the tropical Pacific. La Niña typically brings wetter than normal conditions to the Pacific Northwest and warmer than normal temperatures to much of the southern U.S. during winter months.

El Niño and La Niña episodes are detected and monitored by observing systems, including satellites, moored buoys, and drifting buoys released by volunteer ships crossing the Pacific Ocean. Highly sophisticated numerical computer models of the global ocean and atmosphere use data from the observing systems to predict the onset and evolution of El Niño and its associated impacts. Numerous other models at research institutions worldwide also use the data from the observing systems to increase the understanding of El Niño and improve forecasting techniques.

Wind Chill Table

Source: National Weather Service, NOAA, U.S. Dept. of Commerce

Temperature and wind combine to cause heat loss from body surfaces. The following table shows that, for example, a temperature of 20 degrees Fahrenheit, plus a wind of 20 miles per hour, causes a body heat loss equal to that in minus 10 degrees temperature with no wind. In other words, a 20-mph wind makes 20 degrees feel like minus 10.

The top line of figures shows temperatures in degrees Fahrenheit. The column at far left shows wind speeds up to 45 mph. (Wind speeds greater than 45 mph have little additional chilling effect.)

MPH	35	30	25	20	15	10	5	0	–5	–10	–15	–20	–25	–30	–35	–40	–45
5	33	27	21	16	12	7	0	–5	–10	–15	–21	–26	–31	–36	–42	–47	–52
10	22	16	10	3	–3	–9	–15	–22	–27	–34	–40	–46	–52	–58	–64	–71	–77
15	16	9	2	–5	–11	–18	–25	–31	–38	–45	–51	–58	–65	–72	–78	–85	–92
20	12	4	–3	–10	–17	–24	–31	–39	–46	–53	–60	–67	–74	–81	–88	–95	–103
25	8	1	–7	–15	–22	–29	–36	–44	–51	–59	–66	–74	–81	–88	–96	–103	–110
30	6	–2	–10	–18	–25	–33	–41	–49	–56	–64	–71	–79	–86	–93	–101	–109	–116
35	4	–4	–12	–20	–27	–35	–43	–52	–58	–67	–74	–82	–89	–97	–105	–113	–120
40	3	–5	–13	–21	–29	–37	–45	–53	–60	–69	–76	–84	–92	–100	–107	–115	–123
45	2	–6	–14	–22	–30	–38	–46	–54	–62	–70	–78	–85	–93	–102	–109	–117	–125

Heat Index

The heat index is a measure of the contribution high humidity makes, in combination with abnormally high temperatures, to reducing the body's ability to cool itself. For example, the index shows that an air temperature of 100 degrees Fahrenheit with a relative humidity of 50% has the same effect on the human body as a temperature of 120 degrees. Sunstroke and heat exhaustion are likely when the heat index reaches 105. This index is a measure of what hot weather "feels like" to the average person for various temperatures and relative humidities.

	Air Temperature*										
	70	75	80	85	90	95	100	105	110	115	120
Relative Humidity	Apparent Temperature*										
0%	64	69	73	78	83	87	91	95	99	103	107
10%	65	70	75	80	85	90	95	100	105	111	116
20%	66	72	77	82	87	93	99	105	112	120	130
30%	67	73	78	84	90	96	104	113	123	135	148
40%	68	74	79	86	93	101	110	123	137	151	
50%	69	75	81	88	96	107	120	135	150		
60%	70	76	82	90	100	114	132	149			
70%	70	77	85	93	106	124	144				
80%	71	78	86	97	113	136					
90%	71	79	88	102	122						
100%	72	80	91	108							

*Degrees Fahrenheit

Ultraviolet (UV) Index Forecast

Source: National Weather Service, NOAA, U.S. Dept. of Commerce

The National Weather Service (NWS), Environmental Protection Agency (EPA), and Centers for Disease Control and Prevention (CDC) developed and began offering a UV index on June 28, 1994, in response to increasing incidence of skin cancer, cataracts, and other effects from exposure to the sun's harmful rays. The UV Index is now a regular element of NWS atmospheric forecasts.

UV Index number and forecast. The UV Index number, ranging from 0 to 10+, is an indication of the amount of UV radiation reaching the earth's surface over the one-hour period around noon. The lower the number, the less the radiation. The UV Index forecast is produced for 58 cities by the NWS Climate Prediction Center. The index number is based on several factors: latitude, day of year, time of day, total atmospheric ozone, elevation, and predicted cloud conditions. The index is valid for a radius of about 30 miles around a listed city; however, adjustments should be made for a number of factors.

Ozone. Ozone is measured by a NOAA polar orbiting satellite. The more ozone, the lower the UV radiation at the surface.

Cloudiness. Increased cloudiness lowers the Index number.

Reflectivity. Reflective surfaces intensify UV exposure. As an example, grass reflects 2.5% to 3% of UV radiation reaching the surface; sand, 20% to 30%; snow and ice, 80% to 90%; water, up to 100% (depending on reflection angle).

Elevation. At higher elevations, UV radiation travels a shorter distance to reach the surface so there is less atmosphere to absorb the rays. For every 4,000 ft. one travels above sea level, the UV Index increases by 1 unit. Snow and lack of pollutants intensify UV exposure at higher altitudes.

Latitude. The closer to the equator, the higher the UV radiation level.

Accuracy. After gathering data from 20 UV sensors (during June-Oct. 1994), the NWS determined that 32% of UV Index forecasts for that period were correct, 76% were within ±1 UV Index unit, and about 90% were within ±2 units. Unpredictable cloudiness, haze, and pollution contribute to forecast error.

SPF number. The UV Index is not linked in any way to the SPF number on suntan lotions and sunscreens. For an explanation of the SPF factor, contact the product's manufacturer or the Food and Drug Administration.

Further information. For precautions to take after learning the UV Index number, call the U.S. EPA hotline (800-296-1996) or your doctor. For questions on scientific aspects, call the NWS at 301-713-0622.

Global Measured Extremes of Temperature and Precipitation

Source: National Climatic Data Center; based on records through Dec. 1997

Highest Temperature Extremes

Continent	Highest Temp. (deg F)	Place	Elevation (Feet)	Date
Africa	136°	Azizia, Libya	367	Sept. 13, 1922
North America	134	Death Valley, CA (Greenland Ranch)	178	July 10, 1913
Asia	129	Tirat Tsvi, Israel	722	June 21, 1942
Australia	128	Cloncurry, Queensland	622	Jan. 16, 1889
Europe	122	Seville, Spain	26	Aug. 4, 1881
South America	120	Rivadavia, Argentina	676	Dec. 11, 1905
Oceania	108	Tuguegarao, Philippines	72	Apr. 29, 1912
Antarctica	59	Vanda Station, Scott Coast	49	Jan. 5, 1974

Lowest Temperature Extremes

Continent	Lowest Temp. (deg F)	Place	Elevation (Feet)	Date
Antarctica	−129.0°	Vostok	11,220	July 21, 1983
Asia	−90.0	Oimekon, Russia	2,625	Feb. 6, 1933
Asia	−90.0	Verkhoyansk, Russia	350	Feb. 7, 1892
Greenland	−87.0	Northice	7,687	Jan. 9, 1954
North America	−81.4	Snag, Yukon, Canada	2,120	Feb. 3, 1947
Europe	−67.0	Ust'Shchugor, Russia	279	Jan.*
South America	−27.0	Sarmiento, Argentina	879	June 1, 1907
Africa	−11.0	Ifrane, Morocco	5,364	Feb. 11, 1935
Australia	−9.4	Charlotte Pass, NSW	5,758	June 29, 1994
Oceania	14.0	Haleakala Summit, Maui, HI	9,750	Jan. 2, 1961

*Exact day and year unknown, lowest in 15-year period.

Highest Average Annual Precipitation Extremes

Continent	Highest Avg. (Inches)	Place	Elevation (Feet)	Years of Record
South America	523.6(1,2)	Lloro, Colombia	520(3)	29
Asia	467.4(1)	Mawsynram, India	4,597	38
Oceania	460.0(1)	Mt. Waialeale, Kauai, HI	5,148	30
Africa	405.0	Debundscha, Cameroon	30	32
South America	354.0(2)	Quibdo, Colombia	120	16
Australia	340.0	Bellenden Ker, Queensland	5,102	9
North America	256.0	Henderson Lake, British Columbia	12	14
Europe	183.0	Crkvica, Bosnia-Herzegovina	3,337	22

(1) The value given is continent's highest and possibly the world's depending on measurement practices, procedures, and period of record variations. (2) The official greatest average annual precipitation for South America is 354 inches at Quibdo, Colombia. The 523.6 inches average at Lloro, Colombia (14 miles SE and at a higher elevation than Quibdo) is an estimated amount. (3) Approximate elevation.

Lowest Average Annual Precipitation Extremes

Continent	Lowest Avg. (Inches)	Place	Elevation (Feet)	Years of Record
South America	0.03	Arica, Chile	95	59
Africa	<0.1	Wadi Halfa, Sudan	410	39
Antarctica	0.8(1)	Amundsen-Scott South Pole Station	9,186	10
North America	1.2	Batagues, Mexico	16	14
Asia	1.8	Aden, Yemen	22	50
Australia	4.05	Mulka (Troudaninna), South Australia	160(2)	42
Europe	6.4	Astrakhan, Russia	45	25
Oceania	8.93	Puako, Hawaii, HI	5	13

(1) The value given is the average amount of solid snow accumulating in one year as indicated by snow markers. The liquid content of the snow is undetermined. (2) Approximate elevation.

DISASTERS

As of Oct. 1998. Listings are selective and generally do not include disasters with relatively low fatalities.

Some Notable Shipwrecks Since 1854

(Figures indicate estimated lives lost. Does not include military disasters.)

1854, Mar.—City of Glasgow; Brit. steamer missing in N Atlantic; 480.

1854, Sept. 27—Arctic; U.S. (Collins Line) steamer sunk in collision with French steamer *Vesta* near Cape Race; 285-351.

1856, Jan. 23—Pacific; U.S. (Collins Line) steamer missing in N Atlantic; 186-286.

1858, Sept. 23—Austria; German steamer destroyed by fire in N Atlantic; 471.

1863, Apr. 27—Anglo-Saxon; Brit. steamer wrecked at Cape Race; 238.

1865, Apr. 27—Sultana; Mississippi River steamer blew up near Memphis, TN; 1,450.

1869, Oct. 27—Stonewall; steamer burned on Mississippi River below Cairo, IL; 200.

1870, Jan. 25—City of Boston; Brit. (Inman Line) steamer vanished between New York and Liverpool; 177.

1870, Oct. 19—Cambria; Brit. steamer wrecked off N Ireland; 196.

1872, Nov. 7—Mary Celeste; U.S. half-brig sailed from New York for Genoa; found abandoned in Atlantic 4 weeks later; crew never heard from; loss of life unknown.

1873, Jan. 22—Northfleet; Brit. steamer foundered off Dungeness, England; 300.

1873, Apr. 1—Atlantic; Brit. (White Star) steamer wrecked off Nova Scotia; 585.

1873, Nov. 23—Ville du Havre; French steamer sank after collision with Brit. sailing ship *Loch Earn*; 226.

1875, May 7—Schiller; German steamer wrecked off Scilly Isles; 312.

1875, Nov. 4—Pacific; U.S. steamer sank after collision off Cape Flattery; 236.

1878, Sept. 3—Princess Alice; Brit. steamer sank after collision in Thames River; 700.

1878, Dec. 18—Byzantin; French steamer sank after collision in Dardanelles; 210.

1881, May 24—Victoria; steamer capsized in Thames River, Canada; 200.

1883, Jan. 19—Cimbria; German steamer sank in collision with Brit. steamer *Sultan* in North Sea; 389.

1887, Nov. 15—Wah Yeung; Brit. steamer burned at sea; 400.

1890, Feb. 17—Duburg; Brit. steamer wrecked, China Sea; 400.

1890, Sept. 19—Ertogrul; Turkish frigate foundered off Japan; 540.

1891, Mar. 17—Utopia; Brit. steamer sank in collision with Brit. ironclad *Anson* off Gibraltar; 562.

1895, Jan. 30—Elbe; German steamer sank in collision with Brit. steamer *Craithie* in North Sea; 332.

1895, Mar. 11—Reina Regenta; Spanish cruiser foundered near Gibraltar; 400.

1898, Feb. 15—Maine; U.S. battleship blown up in Havana Harbor; 260.

1898, July 4—La Bourgogne; French steamer sank in collision with Brit. sailing ship *Cromartyshire* off Nova Scotia; 549.

1898, Nov. 26—Portland; U.S. steamer wrecked off Cape Cod; 157.

1904, June 15—General Slocum; excursion steamer burned in East River, New York City; 1,030.

1904, June 28—Norge; Danish steamer wrecked on Rockall Island, Scotland; 620.

1906, Aug. 4—Sirio; Italian steamer wrecked off Cape Palos, Spain; 350.

1908, Mar. 23—Matsu Maru; Japanese steamer sank in collision near Hakodate, Japan; 300.

1909, Aug. 1—Waratah; Brit. steamer, Sydney to London, vanished; 300.

1910, Feb. 9—General Chanzy; French steamer wrecked off Minorca, Spain; 200.

1911, Sept. 25—Liberté; French battleship exploded at Toulon; 285.

1912, Mar. 5—Principe de Asturias; Spanish steamer wrecked off Spain; 500.

1912, Apr. 14-15—Titanic; Brit. (White Star) steamer hit iceberg in N Atlantic; 1,503.

1912, Sept. 28—Kichemaru; Japanese steamer sank off Japanese coast; 1,000.

1914, May 29—Empress of Ireland; Brit. (Canadian Pacific) steamer sunk in collision with Norwegian collier in St. Lawrence River; 1,014.

1915, May 7—Lusitania; Brit. (Cunard Line) steamer torpedoed and sunk by German submarine off Ireland; 1,198.

1915, July 24—Eastland; excursion steamer capsized in Chicago River; 812.

1916, Feb. 26—Provence; French cruiser sank in Mediterranean; 3,100.

1916, Mar. 3—Principe de Asturias; Spanish steamer wrecked near Santos, Brazil; 558.

1916, Aug. 29—Hsin Yu; Chinese steamer sank off Chinese coast; 1,000.

1917, Dec. 6—Mont Blanc, Imo; French ammunition ship and Belgian steamer collided in Halifax Harbor; 1,600.

1918, Apr. 25—Kiang-Kwan; Chinese steamer sank in collision off Hankow; 500.

1918, July 12—Kawachi; Japanese battleship blew up in Tokayama Bay; 500.

1918, Oct. 25—Princess Sophia; Canadian steamer sank off Alaskan coast; 398.

1919, Jan. 17—Chaonia; French steamer lost in Straits of Messina, Italy; 460.

1919, Sept. 9—Valbanera; Spanish steamer lost off Florida coast; 500.

1921, Mar. 18—Hong Kong; steamer wrecked in South China Sea; 1,000.

1922, Aug. 26—Niitaka; Japanese cruiser sank in storm off Kamchatka, USSR; 300.

1924, June 12—USS Mississippi; U.S. battleship; explosions in gun turret, off San Pedro, CA; 48.

1927, Oct. 25—Principessa Mafalda; Italian steamer blew up, sank off Porto Seguro, Brazil; 314.

1928, Nov. 12—Vestris; Brit. steamer sank off Virginia; 113.

1934, Sept. 8—Morro Castle; U.S. steamer, Havana to New York, burned off Asbury Park, NJ; 134.

1939, May 23—Squalus; U.S. submarine sank off Portsmouth, NH; 26.

1939, June 1—Thetis; Brit. submarine sank in Liverpool Bay; 99.

1942, Feb. 18—Truxtun and Pollux; U.S. destroyer and cargo ship ran aground, sank off Newfoundland; 204.

1942, Oct. 2—Curacao; Brit. cruiser sank after collision with liner Queen Mary; 338.

1944, Dec. 17-18—3 U.S. Third Fleet destroyers sank during typhoon in Philippine Sea; 790.

1947, Jan. 19—Himera; Greek steamer hit a mine off Athens; 392.

1947, Apr. 16—Grandcamp; French freighter exploded in Texas City, TX, harbor, starting fires; 510.

1948, Nov.—Chinese army evacuation ship exploded and sank off S Manchuria; 6,000.

1948, Dec. 3—Kiangya; Chinese refugee ship wrecked in explosion S of Shanghai; 1,100+.

1949, Sept. 17—Noronic; Canadian Great Lakes Cruiser burned at Toronto dock; 130.

1952, Apr. 26—Hobson and Wasp; U.S. destroyer and aircraft carrier collided in Atlantic; 176.

1954, May 26—Pennington; sank off Rhode Island coast; 103.

1954, Sept. 26—Toya Maru; Japanese ferry sank in Tsugaru Strait, Japan; 1,172.

1956, July 26—Andrea Doria and **Stockholm;** Italian liner and Swedish liner collided off Nantucket; 51.

1957, July 14—Eshghabad; Soviet ship ran aground in Caspian Sea; 270.

1960, Dec. 19—Constellation; U.S. aircraft carrier caught fire in Brooklyn Navy Yard, NY; 49.

1961, July 8—Save; Portuguese ship ran aground off Mozambique; 259.

1962, Apr. 8—Dara; Brit. liner exploded in Persian Gulf; 236.

1963, Apr. 10—Thresher; U.S. Navy atomic submarine sank in N Atlantic; 129.

1964, Feb. 10—Voyager and **Melbourne;** Australian destroyer *Voyager* sank after collision with Australian aircraft carrier *Melbourne* off New South Wales; 82.

1965, Nov. 13—Yarmouth Castle; Panamanian registered cruise ship burned and sank off Nassau; 89.

1967, July 29—Forrestal; U.S. aircraft carrier caught fire off N Vietnam; 134.

1968, Jan. 25—Dakar; Israeli submarine vanished in Mediterranean Sea; 69.

1968, late May—Scorpion; U.S. nuclear submarine sank in Atlantic near Azores; 99 (located Oct. 31).

1969, June 2—Evans; U.S. destroyer cut in half by Australian carrier *Melbourne*, S China Sea; 74.

1970, Mar. 4—Eurydice; French submarine sank in Mediterranean near Toulon; 57.

1970, Dec. 15—Namyong-Ho; South Korean ferry sank in Korea Strait; 308.

1974, May 1—Motor launch capsized off Bangladesh; 250.

1974, Sept. 26—Soviet destroyer sank in Black Sea; 200+.

1975, Nov. 10—Edmund Fitzgerald; U.S. cargo ship sank during storm on Lake Superior; 29.

1976, Oct. 20—George Prince and **Frosta;** ferryboat and Norwegian tanker collided on Mississippi R. at Luling, LA; 77.

1976, Dec. 25—Patria; Egyptian liner caught fire and sank in the Red Sea; 100.

1979, Aug. 14—23 yachts competing in Fastnet yacht race sank or abandoned during storm in S Irish Sea; 18.

1981, Jan. 27—Tamponas II; Indonesian passenger ship caught fire and sank in Java Sea; 580.

1981, May 26—Nimitz; U.S. Marine combat jet crashed on deck of U.S. aircraft carrier; 14.

1983, Feb. 12—Marine Electric; coal freighter sank during storm off Chincoteague, VA; 33.

1983, May 25—10th of Ramadan; Nile steamer caught fire and sank in Lake Nasser; 357.

1986, Apr. 20—ferry sinks near Barisal, Bangladesh; 262.

1986, Aug. 31—Soviet passenger ship *Admiral Nakhimov* and Soviet freighter *Pyotr Vasev* collided in Black Sea; 398.

1987, Mar. 6—British ferry capsized off Zeebrugge, Belgium; 189.

1987, Dec. 20—Philippine ferry *Dona Paz* and oil tanker *Victor* collided in Tablas Strait; 4,341.

1988, Aug. 6—Indian ferry capsized on Ganges R.; 400+.

1989, Apr. 19—USS Iowa; explosion in gun turret; 47.

1989, Aug. 20—Brit. barge *Bowbelle* struck Brit. pleasure cruiser *Marchioness* on Thames R. in central London; 56.

1989, Sept. 10—Romanian pleasure boat and Bulgarian barge collided on Danube R.; 161.

1991, Apr. 10—Auto ferry and oil tanker collided outside Livorno Harbor, Italy; 140.

1991, Dec. 14—Salem Express; ferry rammed coral reef near Safaga, Egypt; 462.

1993, Feb. 17—Neptune; ferry capsized off Port-au-Prince, Haiti; 500+.

1993, Oct. 10—West Sea Ferry; capsized in Yellow Sea near W South Korea during storm; 285.

1994, Sept. 28—Estonia; ferry sank in Baltic Sea when water entered through bow door; 1,049.

1996, May 21—Bukoba; ferry sank in Lake Victoria (Africa); 500.

1997, Feb. 20—Tamil refugee boat sank off Sri Lanka; 165.

1997, Mar. 28—Albanian refugee boat sank in Adriatic Sea after being rammed by Italian navy warship *Sibilla*; 83.

1997, Sept. 8—Pride of la Gonâve; Haitian ferry sank off Montrouis, Haiti; 200+.

1998, Apr. 4—Nigeria; passenger boat capsized off coast near Ibaka beach; 280.

1998, Sept. 2—Congo; 2 passenger boats capsized on Lake Kivu, near Bukavu; 200+.

1998, Sept. 18—Philippines; passenger ferry sank south of Manila; 97.

Some Notable Aircraft Disasters Since 1937

Date	Aircraft	Site of accident	Deaths
1937, May 6	German zeppelin Hindenburg	Burned at mooring, Lakehurst, NJ	36*
1944, Aug. 23	U.S. Air Force B-24 Liberator bomber	Hit school, Freckleton, England	61*
1945, July 28	U.S. Army B-25	Hit Empire State Building, New York, NY	14*
1952, Dec. 20	U.S. Air Force C-124	Fell, burned, Moses Lake, WA	87
1953, Mar. 3	Canadian Pacific Comet Jet	Karachi, Pakistan	11[1]
1953, June 18	U.S. Air Force C-124	Crashed, burned near Tokyo	129
1955, Oct. 6	United Airlines DC-4	Crashed in Medicine Bow Peak, WY	66
1955, Nov. 1	United Airlines DC-6B	Exploded, crashed near Longmont, CO	44[2]
1956, June 20	Venezuelan Super-Constellation	Crashed in Atlantic off Asbury Park, NJ	74
1956, June 30	TWA Super-Const., United DC-7	Collided over Grand Canyon, AZ	128
1960, Dec. 16	United DC-8 jet, TWA Super-Const.	Collided over New York City	134[3]
1962, Mar. 16	Flying Tiger Super-Constellation	Vanished in W Pacific	107
1962, June 3	Air France Boeing 707 jet	Crashed on takeoff from Paris	130
1962, June 22	Air France Boeing 707 jet	Crashed in storm, Guadeloupe, W.I.	113
1963, June 3	Chartered Northwest Airlines DC-7	Crashed in Pacific off British Columbia	101
1963, Nov. 29	Trans-Canada Airlines DC-8F	Crashed after takeoff from Montreal	118
1965, May 20	Pakistani Boeing 720-B	Crashed at Cairo, Egypt, airport	121
1966, Jan. 24	Air India Boeing 707 jetliner	Crashed on Mont Blanc, France-Italy	117
1966, Feb. 4	All-Nippon Boeing 727	Plunged into Tokyo Bay	133
1966, Mar. 5	BOAC Boeing 707 jetliner	Crashed on Mount Fuji, Japan	124
1966, Dec. 24	U.S. military-chartered CL-44	Crashed into village in South Vietnam	129*
1967, Apr. 20	Swiss Britannia turboprop	Crashed at Nicosia, Cyprus	126
1967, July 19	Piedmont Boeing 727, Cessna 310	Collided in air, Hendersonville, NC	82
1968, Apr. 20	S. African Airways Boeing 707	Crashed on takeoff, Windhoek, South-West Africa	122
1968, May 3	Braniff International Electra	Crashed in storm near Dawson, TX	85
1969, Mar. 16	Venezuelan DC-9	Crashed after takeoff from Maracaibo, Venezuela	155[4]
1969, Dec. 8	Olympic Airways DC-6B	Crashed near Athens in storm	93
1970, Feb. 15	Dominican DC-9	Crashed into sea on takeoff from Santo Domingo	102
1970, July 3	British chartered jetliner	Crashed near Barcelona, Spain	112
1970, July 5	Air Canada DC-8	Crashed near Toronto International Airport	108
1970, Aug. 9	Peruvian turbojet	Crashed after takeoff from Cuzco, Peru	101*
1970, Nov. 14	Southern Airways DC-9	Crashed in mountains near Huntington, WV	75[5]
1971, July 30	All-Nippon Boeing 727 and Japanese Air Force F-86	Collided over Morioka, Japan	162[6]
1971, Sept. 4	Alaska Airlines Boeing 727	Crashed into mountain near Juneau, AK	111
1972, Aug. 14	East German Ilyushin-62	Crashed on takeoff, East Berlin	156
1972, Oct. 13	Aeroflot Ilyushin-62	Crashed near Moscow	176
1972, Dec. 3	Chartered Spanish airliner	Crashed on takeoff, Canary Islands	155
1972, Dec. 29	Eastern Airlines Lockheed Tristar	Crashed on approach to Miami Intl. Airport	101
1973, Jan. 22	Chartered Boeing 707	Burst into flames during landing, Kano Airport, Nigeria	176
1973, Feb. 21	Libyan jetliner	Shot down by Israeli fighter planes over Sinai	108
1973, Apr. 10	British Vanguard turboprop	Crashed during snowstorm at Basel, Switzerland	104
1973, June 3	Soviet Supersonic TU-144	Crashed near Goussainville, France	14[7]
1973, July 11	Brazilian Boeing 707	Crashed on approach to Orly Airport, Paris	122
1973, July 31	Delta Airlines jetliner	Crashed, landing in fog at Logan Airport, Boston	89
1973, Dec. 23	French Caravelle jet	Crashed in Morocco	106
1974, Mar. 3	Turkish DC-10 jet	Crashed at Ermenonville near Paris	346
1974, Apr. 23	Pan American 707 jet	Crashed in Bali, Indonesia	107
1974, Dec. 1	TWA-727	Crashed in storm, Upperville, VA	92
1974, Dec. 4	Dutch-chartered DC-8	Crashed in storm near Colombo, Sri Lanka	191
1975, Apr. 4	Air Force Galaxy C-5A	Crashed near Saigon, S Viet., after takeoff (carrying orphans)	172
1975, June 24	Eastern Airlines 727 jet	Crashed in storm, JFK Airport, NY	113
1975, Aug. 3	Chartered 707	Hit mountainside, Agadir, Morocco	188
1976, Sept. 10	British Airways Trident, Yugoslav DC-9	Collided near Zagreb, Yugoslavia	176
1976, Sept. 19	Turkish 727	Hit mountain, S Turkey	155
1976, Oct. 13	Bolivian 707 cargo jet	Crashed in Santa Cruz, Bolivia	100[8]
1977, Mar. 27	KLM 747, Pan American 747	Collided on runway, Tenerife, Canary Islands	582[9]
1977, Nov. 19	TAP Boeing 727	Crashed on Madeira	130
1977, Dec. 4	Malaysian Boeing 737	Hijacked, then exploded in mid-air over Straits of Johore	100
1977, Dec. 13	U.S. DC-3	Crashed after takeoff at Evansville, IN	29[10]

(*continued*)

Some Notable Aircraft Disasters Since 1937 (*continued*)

Date	Aircraft	Site of accident	Deaths
1978, Jan. 1	Air India 747	Exploded, crashed into sea off Bombay	213
1978, Sept. 25	Boeing 727, Cessna 172	Collided in air, San Diego, CA	150
1978, Nov. 15	Chartered DC-8	Crashed near Colombo, Sri Lanka	183
1979, May 25	American Airlines DC-10	Crashed after takeoff at O'Hare Intl. Airport, Chicago	275[11]
1979, Aug. 17	Two Soviet Aeroflot jetliners	Collided over Ukraine	173
1979, Nov. 26	Pakistani Boeing 707	Crashed near Jidda, Saudi Arabia	156
1979, Nov. 28	New Zealand DC-10	Crashed into mountain in Antarctica	257
1980, Mar. 14	Polish Ilyushin 62	Crashed making emergency landing, Warsaw	87[12]
1980, Aug. 19	Saudi Arabian Tristar	Burned after emergency landing, Riyadh	301
1981, Dec. 1	Yugoslavian DC-9	Crashed into mountain in Corsica	178
1982, Jan. 13	Air Florida Boeing 737	Crashed into Potomac R. after takeoff	78
1982, July 9	Pan Am Boeing 727	Crashed after takeoff in Kenner, LA	153[13]
1983, Sept. 1	S. Korean Boeing 747	Shot down after violating Soviet airspace	269
1983, Nov. 27	Colombian Boeing 747	Crashed near Barajas Airport, Madrid	183
1985, Feb. 19	Spanish Boeing 727	Crashed into Mt. Oiz, Spain	148
1985, June 23	Air-India Boeing 747	Crashed into Atlantic Ocean S of Ireland	329
1985, Aug. 2	Delta Air Lines L-1011	Crashed at Dallas-Ft. Worth Intl. Airport	137
1985, Aug. 12	Japan Air Lines Boeing 747	Crashed into Mt. Ogura, Japan	520[14]
1985, Dec. 12	Arrow Air DC-8	Crashed after takeoff in Gander, Newfoundland	256[15]
1986, Mar. 31	Mexican Boeing 727	Crashed NW of Mexico City	166
1986, Aug. 31	Aeromexico DC-9	Collided with Piper PA-28 over Cerritos, CA	82[16]
1987, May 9	Polish Ilyushin 62M	Crashed after takeoff in Warsaw, Poland	183
1987, Aug. 16	Northwest Airlines MD-82	Crashed after takeoff in Romulus, MI	156
1987, Nov. 28	S. African Boeing 747	Crashed into Indian Ocean near Mauritius	159
1987, Nov. 29	S. Korean Boeing 707	Exploded over Thai-Burmese border	155
1988, Mar. 17	Colombian Boeing 707	Crashed into mountainside near Venezuela border	137
1988, July 3	Iranian A300 Airbus	Shot down by U.S. Navy warship *Vincennes* over Persian Gulf	290
1988, Dec. 21	Pan Am Boeing 747	Exploded and crashed in Lockerbie, Scotland	270[17]
1989, Feb. 8	U.S. Boeing 707	Crashed into mountain in Azores Islands off Portugual	144
1989, June 7	Suriname DC-8	Crashed near Paramaribo Airport, Suriname	168
1989, July 19	United Airlines DC-10	Crashed while landing in Sioux City, IA	111
1989, Sept. 19	French DC-10	Exploded in air over Niger	171
1991, May 26	Lauda-Air Boeing 767-300	Exploded over rural Thailand	223
1991, July 11	Nigerian DC-8	Crashed while landing at Jidda, Saudi Arabia	261
1991, Oct. 5	Indonesian military transport	Crashed after takeoff from Jakarta	137*
1992, July 31	Thai Airbus A-300-310	Crashed into mountain S. of Kathmandu, Nepal	113
1992, Oct. 4	El Al Boeing 747-200F	Crashed into 2 apartment bldgs., Amsterdam, Netherlands	120*
1994, Jan. 3	Aeroflot TU-154	Crashed and exploded after takeoff in Irkhutsk, Russia	125[18]
1994, Apr. 26	China Airlines Airbus A-300-600R	Crashed at Japan's Nagoya Airport	264
1994, June 16	China Northwest Airlines TU-154	Crashed 10 min. after takeoff	160
1994, Sept. 8	USAir Boeing 737-300	Crashed in Aliquippa, PA, near Pittsburgh Intl. Airport	132
1994, Oct. 31	American Eagle ATR-72-210	Crashed in field near Roselawn, IN	68
1995, Aug. 11	Aviateca Boeing 737	Crashed into Chichontepec volcano, El Salvador	65
1995, Dec. 20	American Airlines Boeing 757	Crashed into mountain 50 mi N of Cali, Colombia	160
1996, Jan. 8	Antonova 32 cargo jet	Crashed into central market, Kinshasa, Zaire	350+*
1996, Feb. 6	Turkish Boeing 757	Crashed into Atlantic Ocean, off Dominican Republic	189
1996, Apr. 25	T-43, a military version of a Boeing 737	Crashed into mountain near Dubrovnik, Croatia	35[19]
1996, May 11	ValuJet DC-9	Crashed into the Florida Everglades after takeoff	110
1996, July 17	Trans World Airlines Boeing 747	Exploded and crashed in Atlantic Ocean, off Long Isl., NY	230
1996, Aug. 29	Vnukovo TU-154	Crashed into mountain on Arctic island of Spitsbergen	141
1996, Oct. 2	Aeroperu Boeing 757	Crashed in Pacific after takeoff from Lima, Peru	70
1996, Oct. 31	Brazilian TAM Fokker-100	Crashed into houses in São Paulo, Brazil	98[20]
1996, Nov. 7	Nigerian Boeing 727	Crashed into a lagoon 40 mi SE of Lagos, Nigeria	143
1996, Nov. 12	Saudi Arabian Boeing 747, Kazakh Ilyushin-76 cargo plane	Collided in midair near New Delhi, India	349[21]
1996, Nov. 23	Ethiopian Boeing 767	Hijacked, then crashed in Indian Ocean off the Comoros	127
1997, Jan. 9	Comair Embraer 120	Crashed on approach into Detroit Metro. Airport	29
1997, Feb. 4	2 Sikorsky CH-53 transport helicopters	Collided in midair over northern Galilee, Israel	73
1997, May 8	China Southern Airlines Boeing 737	Crashed on approach into Shenzhen's Huangtian Airport	35
1997, July 11	Cubana de Aviación Antonov-24	Crashed into the Caribbean off SE Cuba	44
1997, Aug. 6	Korean Air Boeing 747-300	Crashed into jungle on Guam on approach into airport	228
1997, Sept. 3	Vietnamese Airlines Tupolev TU-134	Crashed on approach into Phnom Penh airport	64
1997, Sept. 14	U.S. C-141 cargo plane, German TU-154	Collided in midair off SW Africa	33
1997, Sept. 26	Indonesian Airbus A-300	Crashed near Medan, Indonesia, airport	234
1997, Oct. 10	Austral Airlines DC-9-32	Crashed and exploded near Neuvo Berlin, Uruguay	74
1997, Dec. 6	Russian AN-124 transport cargo plane	Crashed into apartment complex near Irkutsk, Siberia	67*
1997, Dec. 15	Chartered TU-154 from Tajikistan	Crashed in desert near Sharja, U.A.E., airport	85
1997, Dec. 17	Chartered Yakovlev-42 from Ukraine	Crashed in mountains near Katerini, Greece	70
1997, Dec. 19	SilkAir Boeing 737-300	Crashed in Musi River, Sumatra, Indonesia	104
1998, Jan. 14	Afghan cargo plane	Crashed into mountain, SW Pakistan	50+
1998, Feb. 2	Cebu Pacific Air DC-9-32	Crashed into mountain near Cagayan de Oro, Philippines	104
1998, Feb. 16	China Airlines Airbus 300-622R	Crashed on approach to airport, Taipei, Taiwan	203[22]
1998, Apr. 20	Air France Boeing 727-200	Crashed into mountain after takeoff from Bogotá, Colombia	53
1998, Sept. 2	Swissair MD-11	Crashed into Atlantic Ocean off Halifax, Nova Scotia	229
1998, Sept. 25	Pauknair BAE146	Crashed into hillside in Morocco	38
1998, Oct. 11	Congo Air Lines Boeing 727	Shot down by rebels in Kindu, Congo	40

*Including those on ground and in buildings. (1) First fatal crash of commercial jet plane. (2) Caused by bomb planted by John G. Graham in insurance plot to kill his mother, a passenger. (3) Incl. all 128 aboard planes and 6 on ground. (4) Killed 84 on the plane and 71 on the ground. (5) Incl. 43 Marshall Univ. football players and coaches. (6) Airliner-fighter crash; pilot of fighter parachuted to safety, was arrested for negligence. (7) First supersonic plane crash; killed 6 crewmen and 8 on ground; there were no passengers. (8) Crew of 3 killed; 97, mostly children, killed on the ground. (9) World's worst airline disaster. (10) Incl. Univ. of Evansville basketball team. (11) Incl. 2 on the ground. Highest death toll in U.S. aviation history. (12) Incl. 22 members of U.S. boxing team. (13) Incl. 8 on the ground. (14) Worst single-plane disaster. (15) Incl. 248 members of U.S. 101st Airborne Division. (16) Incl. 15 on the ground. (17) Incl. 11 on the ground. (18) Incl. 1 on the ground. (19) Incl. U.S. Sec. of Commerce Ronald Brown. (20) Incl. 2 on the ground. (21) World's worst midair collision. (22) Incl. 6 on the ground.

Some Notable Railroad Disasters

Date	Location	Deaths
1876, Dec. 29	Ashtabula, OH	92
1880, Aug. 11	Mays Landing, NJ	40
1887, Aug. 10	Chatsworth, IL	81
1888, Oct. 10	Mud Run, PA	55
1891, June 14	Nr. Basel, Switzerland	100
1896, July 30	Atlantic City, NJ	60
1903, Dec. 23	Laurel Run, PA	53
1904, Aug. 7	Eden, CO	96
1904, Sept. 24	New Market, TN	56
1906, Mar. 16	Florence, CO	35
1906, Oct. 28	Atlantic City, NJ	40
1906, Dec. 30	Washington, DC	53
1907, Jan. 2	Volland, KS	33
1907, Jan. 19	Fowler, IN	29
1907, Feb. 16	New York, NY	22
1907, Feb. 23	Colton, CA	26
1907, May 11	Lompoc, CA	36
1907, July 20	Salem, MI	33
1908, Sept. 25	Young's Point, MT	21
1909, Jan. 15	Dotsero, CO	21
1910, Mar. 1	Wellington, WA	96
1910, Mar. 21	Green Mountain, IA	55
1911, Aug. 25	Manchester, NY	29
1912, July 4	East Corning, NY	39
1912, July 5	Ligonier, PA	23
1914, Aug. 5	Tipton Ford, MO	43
1914, Sept. 15	Lebanon, MO	28
1915, May 22	Nr. Gretna, Scotland	227
1916, Mar. 29	Amherst, OH	27
1917, Sept. 28	Kellyville, OK	23
1917, Dec. 12	Modane, France	543[1]
1917, Dec. 20	Shepherdsville, KY	46
1918, June 22	Ivanhoe, IN	68
1918, July 9	Nashville, TN	101
1918, Nov. 1	Brooklyn, NY	97
1919, Jan. 12	South Byron, NY	22
1919, Dec. 20	Onawa, ME	23
1921, Feb. 27	Porter, IN	37
1921, Dec. 5	Woodmont, PA	27
1922, Aug. 5	Sulphur Spring, MO	34
1922, Dec. 13	Humble, TX	22
1923, Sept. 27	Lockett, WY	31
1925, June 16	Hackettstown, NJ	50
1925, Oct. 27	Victoria, MS	21
1926, Sept. 5	Waco, CO	30
1937, July 16	Nr. Patna, India	107
1938, June 19	Saugus, MT	47
1939, Aug. 12	Harney, NV	24
1939, Dec. 22	Near Magdeburg, Germany	132
1939, Dec. 22	Near Friedrichshafen, Germany	99
1940, Apr. 19	Little Falls, NY	31
1940, July 31	Cuyahoga Falls, OH	43
1943, Aug. 29	Wayland, NY	27
1943, Sept. 6	Frankford Junction, Philadelphia, PA	79
1943, Dec. 16	Between Rennert and Buie, NC	72
1944, Jan. 16	Leon Prov., Spain	500
1944, Mar. 2	Salerno, Italy	521
1944, July 6	High Bluff, TN	35
1944, Aug. 4	Near Stockton, GA	47
1944, Sept. 14	Dewey, IN	29
1944, Dec. 31	Bagley, UT	50
1945, Aug. 9	Michigan, ND	34
1946, Mar. 20	Aracaju, Mexico	185
1946, Apr. 25	Naperville, IL	45
1947, Feb. 18	Gallitzin, PA	24
1949, Oct. 22	Nr. Dwor, Poland	200+
1950, Feb. 17	Rockville Centre, NY	31
1950, Sept. 11	Coshocton, OH	33
1950, Nov. 22	Richmond Hill, NY	79
1951, Feb. 6	Woodbridge, NJ	84
1952, Mar. 4	Nr. Rio de Janeiro, Brazil	119
1952, July 9	Rzepin, Poland	160
1952, Oct. 8	Harrow, England	112
1953, Mar. 27	Conneaut, OH	21
1955, Apr. 3	Guadalajara, Mexico	300
1956, Jan. 22	Los Angeles, CA	30
1957, Sept. 1	Kendal, Jamaica	178
1957, Sept. 29	Montgomery, W Pakistan	250
1957, Dec. 4	London, England	90
1958, May 8	Rio de Janeiro, Brazil	128
1958, Sept. 15	Elizabethport, NJ	48
1960, Nov. 14	Pardubice, Czech.	110
1962, Jan. 8	Woerden, Netherlands	91
1962, May 3	Tokyo, Japan	163
1964, July 26	Porto, Portugal	94
1970, Feb. 1	Buenos Aires, Argentina	236
1972, June 16	Vierzy, France	107
1972, July 21	Seville, Spain	76
1972, Oct. 6	Saltillo, Mexico	208
1972, Oct. 30	Chicago, IL	45
1974, Aug. 30	Zagreb, Yugoslavia	153
1975, Feb. 28	London subway train	41
1977, Jan. 18	Granville, Australia	83
1981, June 6	Bihar, India	500+
1982, Jan. 27	El Asnam, Algeria	130
1982, July 11	Tepic, Mexico	120
1983, Feb. 19	Empalme, Mexico	100
1988, Dec. 12	London, England	115
1989, Jan. 15	Maizdi Khan, Bangladesh	110+
1990, Jan. 4	Sindh Prov., Pakistan	210+
1991, May 14	Shigaraki, Japan	42
1993, Sept. 22	Big Bayou Conot, AL	47
1994, Mar. 8	Nr. Durban, South Africa	63
1994, Sept. 22	Tolunda, Angola	300
1995, Aug. 20	Firozabad, India	300+
1997, Mar. 3	Punjab State, Pakistan	125
1997, Mar. 31	Huarte Arakil, Spain	21
1997, Apr. 29	Rongjiawan Station, Hunan, China	58
1997, May 4	Rwanda	100+
1997, Sept. 14	Central India	77
1998, June 3	Eschede, Germany	102
1998, Feb. 19	Yaounde, Cameroon	100+

(1) World's worst train wreck; passenger train derailed.

Principal U.S. Mine Disasters Since 1900

Source: Bureau of Mines, U.S. Dept. of the Interior; Mine Safety and Health Admin., U.S. Dept. of Labor

(All are bituminous-coal mines unless otherwise noted.)

Date	Location	Deaths
1900, May 1	Scofield, UT	200
1902, May 19	Coal Creek, TN	184
1902, July 10	Johnstown, PA	112
1903, June 30	Hanna, WY	169
1904, Jan. 25	Cheswick, PA	179
1905, Feb. 26	Virginia City, AL	112
1907, Jan. 29	Stuart, WV	84
1907, Dec. 6	Monongah, WV	361
1907, Dec. 19	Jacobs Creek, PA	239
1908, Nov. 28	Marianna, PA	154
1909, Nov. 13	Cherry, IL	259
1910, Jan. 31	Primero, CO	75
1910, May 5	Palos, AL	90
1910, Nov.8	Delagua, CO	79
1911, Apr. 8	Littleton, AL	128
1911, Dec. 9	Briceville, TN	84
1912, Mar. 26	Jed, WV	83
1913, Apr. 23	Finleyville, PA	96
1913, Oct. 22	Dawson, NM	263
1914, Apr. 28	Eccles, WV	181
1915, Mar. 2	Layland, WV	112
1917, Apr. 27	Hastings, CO	121
1917, June 8	Butte, MT[1]	163
1919, June 5	Wilkes-Barre, PA[2]	92
1922, Nov. 6	Spangler, PA	77
1922, Nov. 22	Dolomite, AL	90
1923, Feb. 8	Dawson, NM	120
1923, Aug. 14	Kemmerer, WY	99
1924, Mar. 8	Castle Gate, UT	171
1924, Apr. 28	Benwood, WV	119
1926, Jan. 13	Wilburton, OK	91
1927, Apr. 30	Everettville, WV	97
1928, May 19	Mather, PA	195
1930, Nov. 5	Millfield, OH	82
1940, Jan. 10	Bartley, WV	91
1947, Mar. 25	Centralia, IL	111
1951, Dec. 21	West Frankfort, IL	119
1968, Nov. 20	Farmington, WV	78
1970, Dec. 30	Hyden, KY	38
1972, May 2	Kellogg, ID[1]	91
1976, Mar. 9	Oven Fork, KY	15
1981, Apr. 15	Redstone, CO	15
1981, Dec. 8	Whitwell, TN	13
1984, Dec. 19	Huntington, UT	27
1989, Sept. 13	Sturgis, KY	10

Note: World's worst mine disaster killed 1,549 workers in Honkeiko Colliery in Manchuria, Apr. 25, 1942. (1) Metal mine. (2) Anthracite mine.

Some Notable U.S. Tornadoes Since 1925

Date	Location	Deaths
1925, Mar. 18	MO, IL, IN	689
1927, Apr. 12	Rock Springs, TX	74
1927, May 9	AR, Poplar Bluff, MO	92
1927, Sept. 29	St. Louis, MO	90
1930, May 6	Hill, Navarro, Ellis Co., TX	41
1932, Mar. 21	AL (series of tornadoes)	268
1936, Apr. 5	MS, GA	455
1936, Apr. 6	Gainesville, GA	203
1938, Sept. 29	Charleston, SC	32
1942, Mar. 16	Central to NE Mississippi	75
1942, Apr. 27	Rogers and Mayes Co., OK	52
1944, June 23	OH, PA, WV, MD	150
1945, Apr. 12	OK-AR	102
1947, Apr. 9	TX, OK, KS	169
1948, Mar. 19	Bunker Hill and Gillespie, IL	33
1949, Jan. 3	LA and AR	58
1952, Mar. 21	AR, MO, TN (series)	208
1953, May 11	Waco, TX	114
1953, June 8	MI, OH	142
1953, June 9	Worcester and vicinity, MA	90
1953, Dec. 5	Vicksburg, MS	38
1955, May 25	KS, MO, OK, TX	115
1957, May 20	KS, MO	48
1958, June, 4	NW Wisconsin	30
1959, Feb. 10	St. Louis, MO	21
1960, May 5, 6	Southeastern OK, AR	30
1965, Apr. 11	IN, IL, OH, MI, WI	271
1966, Mar. 3	Jackson, MS	57
1966, Mar. 3	MS, AL	61
1967, Apr. 21	IL, MI	33
1968, May 15	Midwest	71
1969, Jan. 23	MS	32
1971, Feb. 21	Mississippi delta	110
1973, May 26-27	South, Midwest (series)	47
1974, Apr. 3-4	AL, GA, TN, KY, OH	315
1977, Apr. 4	AL, MS, GA	22
1979, Apr. 10	TX, OK	60
1984, Mar. 28	NC, SC	57
1985, May 31	NY, PA, OH, Ont. (series)	75
1987, May 22	Saragosa, TX	29
1989, Nov. 15	Huntsville, AL	18
1990, Aug. 28	Northern IL	25
1991, Apr. 26	KS, OK	23
1992, Nov. 21-23	South, Midwest	26
1994, Mar. 27-28	AL, TN, GA, NC, SC (series)	52
1995, May 6-7	Southern OK, northern TX	23
1997, Mar. 1	Central AR	26
1997, May 27	Jarrell, TX	27
1998, Feb. 22-23	Central FL	42
1998, Mar. 20	Northeast GA	12
1998, Mar. 24	Eastern India	145
1998, Apr. 8	AL, GA, MS	39
1998, Apr. 16	AK, KY, TN	10
1998, May 30	Spencer, SD	6

Some Notable Hurricanes, Typhoons, Blizzards, Other Storms

H.—hurricane; T.—typhoon

Date	Location	Deaths
1888, Mar. 11-14	Blizzard, eastern U.S.	400
1900, Aug.-Sept.	H., Galveston, TX	6,000
1906, Sept. 19-24	H., LA, MS	350
1906, Sept. 18	Typhoon, Hong Kong	10,000
1915, Sept. 29	H., LA	500
1926, Sept. 11-22	H., FL, AL	243
1926, Oct. 20	H., Cuba	600
1928, Sept. 6-20	H., southern FL	1,836
1930, Sept. 3	H., Dominican Republic	2,000
1935, Aug. 29-Sept. 10	H., Caribbean, southeastern U.S.	400+
1938, Sept. 21	H., Long Island, NY; New England	600
1940, Nov. 11-12	Blizzard, NE, Midwest U.S.	144
1942, Oct. 15-16	H., Bengal, India	40,000
1944, Sept. 9-16	H., NC to New England	46
1947, Dec. 26	Blizzard, NYC, N Atlantic states	55
1952, Oct. 22	Typhoon, Philippines	440
1954, Aug. 30	H. *Carol*, northeastern U.S.	68
1954, Oct. 5-18	H. *Hazel*, E Canada, U.S.; Haiti	347
1955, Aug. 12-13	H. *Connie*, NC, SC, VA, MD	43
1955, Aug. 7-21	H. *Diane*, eastern U.S.	400
1955, Sept. 19	H. *Hilda*, Mexico	200
1955, Sept. 22-28	H. *Janet*, Caribbean	500
1956, Feb. 1-29	Blizzard, W Europe	1,000
1957, June 25-30	H. *Audrey*, TX to AL	390
1958, Feb. 15-16	Blizzard, northeastern U.S.	171
1959, Sept. 17-19	T. *Sarah*, Japan, S. Korea	2,000
1959, Sept. 26-27	T. *Vera*, Honshu, Japan	4,466
1960, Sept. 4-12	H. *Donna*, Caribbean, E U.S.	148
1961, Sept. 11-14	H. *Carla*, TX	46
1961, Oct. 31	H. *Hattie*, Br. Honduras	400
1963, May 28-29	Windstorm, Bangladesh	22,000
1963, Oct. 4-8	H. *Flora*, Caribbean	6,000
1964, Oct. 4-7	H. *Hilda*, LA, MS, GA	38
1964, June 30	T. *Winnie*, N Philippines	107
1964, Sept. 5	T. *Ruby*, Hong Kong and China	735
1965, May 11-12	Windstorm, Bangladesh	17,000
1965, June 1-2	Windstorm, Bangladesh	30,000
1965, Sept. 7-12	H. *Betsy*, FL, MS, LA	74
1965, Dec. 15	Windstorm, Bangladesh	10,000
1966, June 4-10	H. *Alma*, Honduras, SE U.S.	51
1966, Sept. 24-30	H. *Inez*, Carib., FL, Mexico	293
1967, July 9	T. *Billie*, SW Japan	347
1967, Sept. 5-23	H. *Beulah*, Carib., Mex., TX	54
1967, Dec. 12-20	Blizzard, Southwest U.S.	51
1968, Nov. 18-28	T. *Nina*, Philippines	63
1969, Aug. 17-18	H. *Camille*, MS, LA	256
1970, July 30-Aug. 5	H. *Celia*, Cuba, FL, TX	31
1970, Aug. 20-21	H. *Dorothy*, Martinique	42
1970, Sept. 15	T. *Georgia*, Philippines	300
1970, Oct. 14	T. *Sening*, Philippines	583
1970, Oct. 15	T. *Titang*, Philippines	526
1970, Nov. 13	Cyclone, Bangladesh	300,000
1971, Aug. 1	T. *Rose*, Hong Kong	130
1972, June 19-29	H. *Agnes*, FL to NY	118
1972, Dec. 3	T. *Theresa*, Philippines	169
1973, June-Aug.	Monsoon rains, India	1,217
1974, June 11	Storm Dinah, Luzon Isl., Phil.	71
1974, July 11	T. *Gilda*, Japan, S. Korea	108
1974, Sept. 19-20	H. *Fifi*, Honduras	2,000
1974, Dec. 25	Cyclone leveled Darwin, Austral.	50
1975, Sept. 13-27	H. *Eloise*, Caribbean, NE U.S.	71
1976, May 20	T. *Olga*, floods, Philippines	215
1977, July 25, 31	T. *Thelma*, T. *Vera*, Taiwan	39
1978, Oct. 27	T. *Rita*, Philippines	c. 400
1979, Aug. 30-Sept. 7	H. *David*, Caribbean, E U.S.	1,100
1980, Aug. 4-11	H. *Allen*, Caribbean, TX	272
1981, Nov. 25	T. *Irma*, Luzon Isl., Phil.	176
1983, June	Monsoon, India	900
1983, Aug. 18	H. *Alicia*, southern TX	17
1984, Sept. 2	T. *Ike*, S Philippines	1,363
1985, May 25	Cyclone, Bangladesh	10,000
1985, Oct. 26-Nov. 6	H. *Juan*, SE U.S.	97
1987, Nov. 25	T. *Nina*, Philippines	650
1988, Sept. 10-17	H. *Gilbert*, Caribbean, Gulf of Mexico	260
1989, Sept. 16-22	H. *Hugo*, Caribbean, SE U.S.	504
1990, May 6-11	Cyclones, SE India	450
1991, Apr. 30	Cyclone, Bangladesh	139,000
1991, Nov. 5	Tropical storm, Philippines	7,000+
1992, Aug. 24-26	H. *Andrew*, southern FL, LA	14
1993, Mar. 13-14	Blizzard, eastern U.S.	200
1993, June	Monsoon, Bangladesh	2,000
1994, Nov. 8-18	Storm Gordon, Caribbean, FL	830
1995, Sept. 4-6	H. *Luis*, Caribbean	14
1995, Sept. 13-22	H. *Marilyn*, Virgin Isls., Carib.	13
1995, Oct. 2-4	H. *Opal*, S Mexico, FL, AL	59
1995, Nov. 2-3	T. *Angela*, Philippines	600+
1996, Jan. 7-8	Blizzard, northeastern U.S.	100
1996, July 8-13	H. *Bertha*, Carib., eastern U.S.	15
1996, Aug. 22	Blizzard, Himalayas, N India	239
1996, Aug. 29-Sept. 6	H. *Fran*, Carib., NC, VA, WV	28
1996, Sept. 9-10	H. *Hortense*, Caribbean	24
1996, Sept. 9	T. *Sally*, S China	114
1996, Nov. 6	Cyclone, Andhra Pradesh, India	1,000+
1996, Nov. 24-25	Ice storms, TX to MO	26
1996, Dec. 25	Tropical storm, E Malaysia	100+
1997, May 19	Cyclone, Bangladesh	108
1997, May 26	Rain storm, Philippines	29
1997, July 2	Storms, southeastern MI	16
1997, Aug. 18	Typhoon, Taiwan	24
1997, Sept. 27	Cyclone, S Bangladesh	c. 35
1997, Oct. 8-10	H. *Pauline*, SW Mexico	230
1997, Oct. 13	Cyclone, Tongi, Bangladesh	15+
1998, Feb. 4-6	Blizzard, KY, WV	10+
1998, June 9	Cyclone, Gujarat, India	1,320
1998, Aug.	Monsoon, Bangladesh	326
1998, Sept. 21-23	H. *Georges*, Caribbean, FL Keys, U.S. Gulf Coast	600+

Some Notable Floods, Tidal Waves

Date	Location	Deaths
1228	Holland	100,000
1642	China	300,000
1883, Aug. 27	Indonesia	36,000
1887	Huang He River, China	900,000
1889, May 31	Johnstown, PA	2,209
1900, Sept. 8	Galveston, TX	5,000
1903, June 15	Heppner, OR	325
1911	Chang Jiang River, China	100,000
1913, Mar. 25-27	OH, IN	732
1915, Aug. 17	Galveston, TX	275
1928, Mar. 13	Dam collapse, Saugus, CA	450
1928, Sept. 13	Lake Okeechobee, FL	2,000
1931, Aug.	Huang He River, China	3,700,000
1937, Jan. 22	OH, MS Valleys	250
1939	N China	200,000
1946, Apr. 1	HI, AK	159
1947, Sept. 20	Honshu Island, Japan	1,900
1951, Aug.	Manchuria	1,800
1953, Jan. 31	W Europe	2,000
1954, Aug. 17	Farahzad, Iran	2,000
1955, Oct. 7-12	India, Pakistan	1,700
1959, Nov. 1	W Mexico	2,000
1959, Dec. 2	Frejus, France	412
1960, Oct. 10	Bangladesh	6,000
1960, Oct. 31	Bangladesh	4,000
1962, Feb. 17	North Sea coast, Germany	343
1962, Sept. 27	Barcelona, Spain	445
1963, Oct. 9	Dam collapse, Vaiont, Italy	1,800
1966, Nov. 3-4	Florence, Venice, Italy	113
1967, Jan. 18-24	E Brazil	894
1967, Mar. 19	Rio de Janeiro, Brazil	436
1967, Nov. 26	Lisbon, Portugal	464
1968, Aug. 7-14	Gujarat State, India	1,000
1968, Oct. 7	NE India	780
1969, Jan. 18-26	Southern CA	100
1969, Mar. 17	Mundau Valley, Alagoas, Brazil	218
1969, Aug. 20-22	Western VA	189
1969, Sept. 15	South Korea	250
1969, Oct. 1-8	Tunisia	500
1970, May 20	Central Romania	160
1970, July 22	Himalayas, India	500
1971, Feb. 26	Rio de Janeiro, Brazil	130
1972, Feb. 26	Buffalo Creek, WV	118
1972, June 9	Rapid City, SD	236
1972, Aug. 7	Luzon Isl., Philippines	454
1972, Aug. 19-31	Pakistan	1,500
1974, Mar. 29	Tubaro, Brazil	1,000
1974, Aug. 12	Monty-Long, Bangladesh	2,500
1976, June 5	Teton Dam collapse, ID	11
1976, July 31	Big Thompson Canyon, CO	139
1976, Nov. 17	East Java, Indonesia	136
1977, July 19-20	Johnstown, PA	68
1977, Nov. 6	Toccoa, GA	39
1978, June-Sept.	N India	1,200
1979, Jan.-Feb.	Brazil	204
1979, July 17	Lomblem Isl., Indonesia	539
1979, Aug. 11	Morvi, India	15,000
1980, Feb. 13-22	Southern CA, AZ	26
1981, Apr.	N China	550
1981, July	Sichuan, Hubei Prov., China	1,300
1982, Jan. 23	Nr. Lima, Peru	600
1982, May 12	Guangdong, China	430
1982, Sept. 17-21	El Salvador, Guatemala	1,300+
1984, Aug-Sept.	South Korea	200+
1985, July 19	Dam collapse, N Italy	361
1987, Aug.-Sept.	N Bangladesh	1,000+
1988, Sept.	N India	1,000+
1990, June 14	Shadyside, OH	23
1991, Dec. 18-26	TX	18
1992, Feb. 9-15	Southern CA	13
1993, July-Aug.	Midwest	48
1994, July	GA, AL	32
1995, Jan. 30-Feb. 9	NW Europe	40
1995, Mar. 8-15	CA	15
1995, July	Hunan Province, China	1,200
1995, Aug. 19	SW Morocco	136
1995, Dec. 25	KwaZulu Natal, South Africa	166
1996, Jan.	Northeastern U.S.	15+
1996, Feb. 17	Biak Isl., Indonesia	105
1996, April	Afghanistan	100+
1996, June-July	S China	315
1996, Aug. 7	Pyrenees Mts., Spain	71
1996, Dec.-1997, Jan.	Northwestern U.S.	29
1997, Feb.-Mar.	Bolivia	16
1997, Mar.	Ohio R. Valley	35
1997, July	Poland, Czech Republic	98
1997, Oct.	Israel, Egypt, Jordan	19
1997, Nov.	Spanish-Portuguese border	31+
1997, Nov.	Bardera, Somalia	1,300+
1998, Jan.	Kenya	86
1998, Feb.	California to Tijuana, Mexico	30+
1998, Mar.	SW Pakistan	300+
1998, July-Aug.	China	3,000+
1998, July-Sept.	Bangladesh	850
1998, July 17	Papua New Guinea	3,000
1998, Aug. 24	S Texas, Mexico	16

Some Major Earthquakes

Source: Global Volcanism Network, Smithsonian Institution; U.S. Geological Survey, Dept. of the Interior; World Almanac research

Magnitude of earthquakes (Mag.) is measured on the Richter scale; each higher number represents a tenfold increase in energy. Adopted in 1935, the scale is applied to earthquakes here as far back as reliable seismograms are available.

Date	Location	Deaths	Mag.
526, May 20	Antioch, Syria	250,000	NA
856	Corinth, Greece	45,000	"
1057	Chihli, China	25,000	"
1169, Feb. 11	Near Mt. Etna, Sicily	15,000[1]	"
1268	Cilicia, Asia Minor	60,000	"
1290, Sept. 27	Chihli, China	100,000	"
1293, May 20	Kamakura, Japan	30,000	"
1531, Jan. 26	Lisbon, Portugal	30,000	"
1556, Jan. 24	Shaanxi, China	830,000	"
1667, Nov.	Shemaka, Caucasia	80,000	"
1693, Jan. 11	Catania, Italy	60,000	"
1730, Dec. 30	Hokkaido, Japan	137,000	"
1737, Oct. 11	India, Calcutta	300,000	"
1755, June 7	N Persia	40,000	"
1755, Nov. 1	Lisbon, Portugal	60,000	8.75*
1783, Feb. 4	Calabria, Italy	30,000	NA
1797, Feb. 4	Quito, Ecuador	41,000	"
1811-12	New Madrid, MO (series)	NA	8.7*
1822, Sept. 5	Asia Minor, Aleppo	22,000	NA
1828, Dec. 28	Echigo, Japan	30,000	"
1868, Aug. 13-15	Peru, Ecuador	40,000	"
1875, May 16	Venezuela, Colombia	16,000	"
1886, Aug. 31	Charleston, SC	60	6.6
1896, June 15	Japan, sea wave	27,120	NA
1905, Apr. 4	Kangra, India	19,000	8.6
1906, Apr. 18-19	San Francisco, CA	503[2]	8.3
1906, Aug. 17	Valparaiso, Chile	20,000	8.6
1907, Oct. 21	Central Asia	12,000	8.1
1908, Dec. 28	Messina, Italy	83,000	7.5
1915, Jan. 13	Avezzano, Italy	29,980	7.5
1918, Oct. 11	Mona Passage, P.R.	116	7.5
1920, Dec. 16	Gansu, China	200,000	8.6
1923, Sept. 1	Yokohama, Japan	143,000	8.3
1925, Mar. 16	Yunnan, China	5,000	7.1
1927, May 22	Nan-Shan, China	200,000	8.3
1932, Dec. 25	Gansu, China	70,000	7.6
1933, Mar. 2	Japan	2,990	8.9
1933, Mar. 10	Long Beach, CA	115	6.2
1934, Jan. 15	India, Bihar-Nepal	10,700	8.4
1935, May 30	Quetta, India	50,000	7.5
1939, Jan. 25	Chillan, Chile	28,000	8.3
1939, Dec. 26	Erzincan, Turkey	30,000	8.0
1946, Dec. 20	Honshu, Japan	1,330	8.4
1948, June 28	Fukui, Japan	5,390	7.3
1949, Aug. 5	Pelileo, Ecuador	6,000	6.8
1950, Aug. 15	Assam, India	1,530	8.7
1953, Mar. 18	NW Turkey	1,200	7.2
1956, June 10-17	N Afghanistan	2,000	7.7
1957, July 2	N Iran	1,200	7.4
1957, Dec. 13	W Iran	1,130	7.3
1960, Feb. 29	Agadir, Morocco	12,000	5.9
1960, May 21-30	S Chile	5,000	9.5
1962, Sept. 1	NW Iran	12,230	7.3
1963, July 26	Skopje, Yugoslavia	1,100	6.0
1964, Mar. 27	Alaska	131	9.2
1966, Aug. 19	E Turkey	2,520	7.1
1968, Aug. 31	NE Iran	12,000	7.3
1970, Jan. 4	Yunnan Prov., China	10,000	7.5
1970, Mar. 28	W Turkey	1,100	7.3
1970, May 31	N Peru	66,000	7.8

(continued)

Some Major Earthquakes *(continued)*

Date	Location	Deaths	Mag.
1971, Feb. 9	San Fernando Val., CA. .	65	6.6
1972, Apr. 10	S Iran	5,054	7.1
1972, Dec. 23	Managua, Nicaragua . . .	5,000	6.2
1974, Dec. 28	Pakistan (9 towns)	5,200	6.3
1975, Sept. 6	Turkey (Lice, etc.)	2,300	6.7
1976, Feb. 4	Guatemala	23,000	7.5
1976, May 6	NE Italy.	1,000	6.5
1976, June 25	Irian Jaya, New Guinea	422	7.1
1976, July 27	Tangshan, China.	255,000	8.0
1976, Aug. 16	Mindanao, Philippines. . .	8,000	7.8
1976, Nov. 24	NW Iran-USSR border . .	5,000	7.3
1977, Mar. 4	Romania.	1,500	7.2
1977, Aug. 19	Indonesia	200	8.0
1977, Nov. 23	NW Argentina.	100	8.2
1978, Sept. 16	NE Iran.	15,000	7.8
1979, Sept. 12	Indonesia	100	8.1
1979, Dec. 12	Colombia, Ecuador	800	7.9
1980, Oct. 10	NW Algeria	3,500	7.7
1980, Nov. 23	S Italy.	3,000	7.2
1981, June 11	S Iran	3,000	6.9
1981, July 28	S Iran	1,500	7.3
1982, Dec. 13	W Arabian Peninsula . . .	2,800	6.0
1983, May 26	N Honshu, Japan.	81	7.7
1983, Oct. 30	E Turkey.	1,342	6.9
1985, Mar. 3	Chile.	146	7.8
1985, Sept. 19	Michoacan, Mexico	9,500	8.1
1986, Oct. 10	El Salvador	1,000+	5.5
1987, Mar. 6	Colombia-Ecuador.	4,000+	7.0
1988, Aug. 20	India-Nepal border.	1,450	6.6
1988, Nov. 6	China-Burma border. . . .	1,000	7.3
1988, Dec. 7	Soviet Armenia	55,000	7.0
1989, Oct. 17	San Francisco Bay area. .	62	7.1
1990, May 30	N Peru	115	6.3
1990, June 20	W Iran.	40,000+	7.7
1990, July 16	Luzon, Philippines.	1,621	7.8
1991, Feb. 1	Pakistan, Afgh. border. .	1,200	6.8
1991, Oct. 19	N India.	2,000	7.0
1992, Mar. 13, 15	E Turkey	4,000	6.2/6.0
1992, June 28	S California	1	7.5/6.6
1992, Dec. 12	Flores Isl., Indonesia. . .	2,500	7.5
1993, July 12	off Hokkaido, Japan . . .	200+	7.7
1993, Sept. 29	Maharashtra, S India. . .	9,748[3]	6.3
1994, Jan. 17	Northridge, CA	61	6.8
1994, Feb. 15	S Sumatra, Indon.	215	7.0
1994, June 6	Cauca, SW Colombia . .	1,000	6.8
1994, Aug. 19	N Algeria	164	6.0
1995, Jan. 16	Kobe, Japan.	5,502	6.9
1995, May 27	Sakhalin Isl., Russia . . .	1,989	7.5
1995, Oct. 1	SW Turkey.	73	6.0
1995, Oct. 9	W coast, Mexico	c. 40+	7.6
1996, Feb. 3	SW China.	200+	7.0
1996, Feb. 17	Irian Jaya, Indonesia. . .	53	7.5
1997, Feb. 4	Turkmen.-Iran border . .	79	6.9
1997, Feb. 27	W Pakistan.	100+	7.3
1997, Feb. 28	NW Iran	1000+	6.1
1997, May 10	N Iran	1,560	7.5
1997, May 21	Madhya Pradesh, India .	40+	6.1
1997, July 9	NE Venezuela.	82	6.9
1997, Sept. 26	Central Italy	11	5.5/5.7
1997, Sept. 28	Sulawesi, Indonesia. . . .	17+	5.9
1997, Oct. 15	Illapel, Chile	8	6.8
1997, Nov. 21	Chittagong, Bangladesh.	7+	6.1
1998, Jan. 10	Zhangbei, China	50	6.2
1998, Feb. 4, 8	Takhar province, NE Afghanistan.	2,323	6.1
1998, May 22	Central Bolivia.	105	6.5
1998, May 30	NE Afghanistan.	4,700+	6.9
1998, July 9	Azores Islands, Portugal	10	5.8

(*) estimated from earthquake intensity. NA=not available. (1) Once thought to have been a volcanic eruption; evidence indicates a destructive earthquake and tsunami occurred on this date. (2) With subsequent fires, death toll rose to 700. (3) Official death toll released by Indian government. Other sources reported estimates of 30,000 deaths.

Other Recent Earthquakes

Source: Global Volcanism Network, Smithsonian Institution; dates are Greenwich Mean Time

Date	Location	Magnitude
1996, July 15	Guerrero, Mexico	6.5
July 21	Sulawesi Island, Indonesia	6.9
Aug. 2	Solomon Islands	7.1
Aug. 5	SE of Fiji Islands	6.5
Aug. 5	Tonga.	6.7
Sept. 5	NE of Easter Island	7.1
Sept. 5	SE of Taiwan.	6.6
Oct. 9	Cyprus	6.8
Oct. 13	Solomon Islands	7.0
Oct. 18	S Japan	6.6
Nov. 6	Bonin Islands.	6.6
Nov. 19	E Kashmir	6.8
Dec. 2	E of Kyushu, Japan	6.7
1997, Jan. 11	SW Mexico	7.1
Mar. 11	Mindanao, Philippines	6.8
Apr. 21	SW Pacific, between Santa Cruz Islands and Vanuatu. . . .	7.5
Apr. 22	Trinidad and Tobago.	6.7
May 3	Kermadec Islands, N.Z.	6.9
July 16	Central Chile	6.5
Aug. 29	Papua New Guinea.	6.8
Sept. 20	Kermadec Islands, N.Z.	7.2
Oct. 14	Fiji Islands	7.7
Nov. 25	Sulawesi, Indonesia	7.1
Dec. 5	E coast of Kamchatka, Russia . .	7.9
1998, Mar. 25	Balleny Islands	8.2
Apr. 1	Sumatra, Indonesia.	7.0
Apr. 27	Irian Jaya, Indonesia.	7.4
May 3	Ryukyu Island, SE of Taiwan . . .	7.4
June 1	Kamchatka, Russia.	6.5

Some Notable Fires Since 1835

(See also Some Notable Explosions Since 1910.)

Date	Location	Deaths
1835, Dec. 16	New York, NY, 500 bldgs. destroyed	—
1845, May	Canton, China, theater	1,670
1871, Oct. 8	Chicago, $196 million loss; 17,000 bldgs. destroyed	250
1871, Oct. 8	Peshtigo, WI, forest fire.	1,182
1872, Nov. 9	Boston, 800 bldgs. destroyed	—
1876, Dec. 5	Brooklyn, NY, theater	295
1877, June 20	St. John, New Brunswick	100
1881, Dec. 8	Ring Theater, Vienna	850
1887, May 25	Opera Comique, Paris	200
1887, Sept. 4	Exeter, England, theater	200
1894, Sept. 1	MN, forest fire	413
1897, May 4	Paris, charity bazaar.	150
1900, June 30	Hoboken, NJ, docks	326
1902, Sept. 20	Birmingham, AL, church	115
1903, Dec. 30	Iroquois Theater, Chicago.	602
1908, Jan. 13	Rhoads Theater, Boyertown, PA . .	170
1908, Mar. 4	Collinwood, OH, school.	176
1911, Mar. 25	Triangle Shirtwaist factory, NY, NY	146
1913, Oct. 14	Mid Glamorgan, Wales, colliery . . .	439
1918, Apr. 13	Norman, OK, state hospital	38
1918, Oct. 12	Cloquet, MN, forest fire.	400
1919, June 20	Mayagüez Theater, San Juan, P.R.	150
1923, May 17	Camden, SC, school	76
1924, Dec. 24	Babb's Switch, OK, school.	35
1929, May 15	Cleveland, OH, clinic	125
1930, Apr. 21	Columbus, OH, penitentiary	320
1931, July 24	Pittsburgh, PA, home for aged	48
1934, Dec. 11	Hotel Kerns, Lansing, MI	34
1938, May 16	Atlanta, GA, Terminal Hotel	35
1940, Apr. 23	Natchez, MS, dance hall	198
1942, Nov. 28	Cocoanut Grove, Boston	491
1942, Dec. 12	St. John's, Nfld., hostel	100
1943, Sept. 7	Gulf Hotel, Houston, TX.	55
1944, July 6	Ringling Circus, Hartford, CT	168
1946, June 5	LaSalle Hotel, Chicago	61
1946, Dec. 7	Winecoff Hotel, Atlanta	119
1946, Dec. 12	NY, NY, ice plant, tenement	37
1949, Apr. 5	Effingham, IL, hospital.	77
1950, Jan. 7	Davenport, IA, Mercy Hospital	41
1953, Mar. 29	Largo, FL, nursing home	35
1953, Apr. 16	Chicago, metalworking plant	35
1957, Feb. 17	Warrenton, MO, home for aged . . .	72
1958, Mar. 19	New York, NY, loft building.	24
1958, Dec. 1	Chicago, parochial school	95
1958, Dec. 16	Bogotá, Colombia, store	83

Date	Location	Deaths
1959, June 23	Stalheim, Norway, resort hotel	34
1960, Mar. 12	Pusan, Korea, chemical plant	68
1960, July 14	Guatemala City, mental hospital	225
1960, Nov. 13	Amude, Syria, movie theater	152
1961, Jan. 6	Thomas Hotel, San Francisco	20
1961, Dec. 8	Hartford, CT, hospital	16
1961, Dec. 17	Niteroi, Brazil, circus	323
1963, May 4	Diourbel, Senegal, theater	64
1963, Nov. 18	Surfside Hotel, Atlantic City, NJ	25
1963, Nov. 23	Fitchville, OH, rest home	63
1963, Dec. 29	Roosevelt Hotel, Jacksonville, FL	22
1964, May 8	Manila, apartment bldg.	30
1964, Dec. 18	Fountaintown, IN, nursing home	20
1965, Mar. 1	LaSalle, Quebec, apartment	28
1965, Aug. 11-16	Watts riot fires, CA	30+
1966, Mar. 11	Numata, Japan, 2 ski resorts	31
1966, Aug. 13	Melbourne, Australia, hotel	29
1966, Sept. 12	Anchorage, AK, hotel	14
1966, Oct. 17	New York, NY, bldg. (firefighters)	12
1966, Dec. 7	Erzurum, Turkey, barracks	68
1967, Feb. 7	Montgomery, AL, restaurant	25
1967, May 22	Brussels, Belgium, store	322
1967, July 16	Jay, FL, state prison	37
1968, Feb. 26	Shrewsbury, England, hospital	22
1968, May 11	Vijayawada, India, wedding hall	58
1968, Nov. 18	Glasgow, Scotland, factory	24
1969, Dec. 2	Notre Dame, Can., nursing home	54
1970, Jan. 9	Marietta, OH, nursing home	27
1970, Mar. 20	Seattle, WA, hotel	19
1970, Nov. 1	Grenoble, France, dance hall	145
1970, Dec. 20	Tucson, AZ, hotel	28
1971, Mar. 6	Burghoezli, Switzerland, psychiatric clinic	28
1971, Apr., 20	Bangkok, Thailand, hotel	24
1971, Dec., 25	Seoul, South Korea, hotel	162
1972, May 13	Osaka, Japan, nightclub	116
1972, July 5	Sherborne, England, hospital	30
1973, Feb. 6	Paris, France, school	21
1973, June 24	New Orleans, LA, bar	32
1973, Nov. 6	Fukui, Japan, train	28
1973, Nov. 29	Kumamoto, Japan, dept. store	107
1973, Dec. 2	Seoul, South Korea, theater	50
1974, Feb. 1	São Paulo, Brazil, bank building	189
1974, June 30	Port Chester, NY, discotheque	24
1974, Nov. 3	Seoul, S. Korea, hotel, disco	88
1975, Dec. 12	Mina, Saudi Arabia, tent city	138
1976, Oct. 24	Bronx, NY, social club	25
1977, Feb. 25	Moscow, Russia, Rossiya hotel	45
1977, May 28	Southgate, KY, nightclub	164
1977, June 9	Abidjan, Ivory Coast, nightclub	41
1977, June 26	Columbia, TN, jail	42
1977, Nov. 14	Manila, Philippines, hotel	47
1978, Jan. 28	Kansas City, Coates House Hotel	16
1978, Aug. 19	Abadan, Iran, movie theater	425+
1979, July 14	Saragossa, Spain, hotel	80
1979, Dec. 31	Chapais, Quebec, social club	42
1980, May 20	Kingston, Jamaica, nursing home	157
1980, Nov. 21	MGM Grand Hotel, Las Vegas	84
1980, Dec. 4	Stouffer Inn, Harrison, NY	26
1981, Jan. 9	Keansburg, NJ, boarding home	30
1981, Feb. 10	Las Vegas Hilton	8
1981, Feb. 14	Dublin, Ireland, discotheque	44
1982, Sept. 4	Los Angeles, apartment house	24
1982, Nov. 8	Biloxi, MS, county jail	29
1983, Feb. 13	Turin, Italy, movie theater	64
1983, Dec. 17	Madrid, Spain, discotheque	83
1984, May 11	Great Adventure Amusement Pk., NJ	8
1985, Apr. 21	Tabaco, Phil., movie theater	44
1985, Apr. 26	Buenos Aires, Argentina, hospital	79
1985, May 11	Bradford, England, soccer stadium	53
1986, Dec. 31	Puerto Rico, Dupont Plaza Hotel	96
1987, May 6-June 2	N China, forest fire	193
1987, Nov. 17	London, England, subway	30
1988, Mar. 20	Lashio, Burma, 2,000 buildings	134
1990, Mar. 25	Bronx, NY, social club	87
1991, Mar. 3	Addis Ababa, Ethiopia, munitions dump	260+
1991, Sept. 3	Hamlet, NC, processing plant	25
1991, Oct. 20-21	Oakland, Berkeley, CA, wildfire	24
1993, Apr. 19	Waco, TX, cult compound	72
1994, May 10	Bangkok, Thailand, toy factory	213
1994, July 4-10	Glenwood Springs, CO (firefighters)	14
1994, Dec. 10	Karamay, China, theater	300
1994, Nov. 2	Durunka, Egypt, burning fuel flood	500
1995, Oct. 28	Baku, Azerbaijan, subway train	300
1995, Dec. 23	Mandi Dabwali, India, school	500+
1996, Mar. 19	Quezon City, Philippines, nightclub	150+
1996, Mar. 28	Bogor, Indonesia, shopping mall	78
1996, Apr. 11	Düsseldorf, Germany, airport	16
1996, Oct. 22	Caracas, Venezuela, jail	25
1996, Nov. 20	Hong Kong, building	39
1997, Feb. 23	Baripada, India, worship site	164
1997, Apr. 15	Mina, Saudi Arabia, encampment	343
1997, June 7	Thanjavur, India, temple	60+
1997, June 13	New Delhi, India, movie theater	60
1997, July 11	Pattaya, Thailand, hotel	90
1997, Sept. 29	Home for retarded children, near Colina, Chile	30
1998, Mar. 26	School dorm., Mazeras, India	22

Some Notable Explosions Since 1910

(See also Principal U.S. Mine Disasters Since 1910.)

Date	Location	Deaths
1910, Oct. 1	Los Angeles Times Bldg.	21
1913, Mar. 7	Dynamite, Baltimore harbor	55
1915, Sept. 27	Gasoline tank car, Ardmore, OK	47
1917, Apr. 10	Munitions plant, Eddystone, PA	133
1917, Dec. 6	Halifax Harbor, Canada	1,654
1918, May 18	Chemical plant, Oakdale, PA	193
1918, July 2	Explosives, Split Rock, NY	50
1918, Oct. 4	Shell plant, Morgan Station, NJ	64
1919, May 22	Food plant, Cedar Rapids, IA	44
1920, Sept. 16	Wall Street, NY, NY, bomb	30
1921, Sept. 21	Chem. storage facility, Oppau, Ger.	561
1924, Jan. 3	Food plant, Pekin, IL	42
1927, May 18	Bath school, Lansing, MI	38
1928, April 13	Dance hall, West Plains, MO	40
1937, Mar. 18	New London, TX, school	311
1940, Sept. 12	Hercules Powder, Kenvil, NJ	55
1942, June 5	Ordnance plant, Elwood, IL	49
1944, Apr. 14	Bombay, India, harbor	700
1944, July 17	Port Chicago, CA, pier	322
1944, Oct. 21	Liquid gas tank, Cleveland	135
1947, Apr. 16	Texas City, TX, pier	576
1948, July 28	Farben works, Ludwigshafen, Ger.	184
1950, May 19	Munitions barges, S. Amboy, NJ	30
1956, Aug. 7	Dynamite trucks, Cali, Colombia	1,100
1958, Apr. 18	Sunken munitions ship, Okinawa, Japan	40
1958, May 22	Nike missiles, Leonardo, NJ	10
1959, Apr. 10	World War II bomb, Philippines	38
1959, June 28	Rail tank cars, Meldrin, GA	25
1959, Aug. 7	Dynamite truck, Roseburg, OR	13
1959, Nov. 2	Jamuri Bazar, India, explosives	46
1959, Dec. 13	2 apt. bldgs., Dortmund, Ger.	26
1960, Mar. 4	Belgian munitions ship, Havana, Cuba	100
1960, Oct. 25	Gas, Windsor, Ont., store	11
1962, Jan. 16	Gas pipeline, Edson, Alberta	8
1962, Oct. 3	Telephone Co. office, NY, NY	23
1963, Jan. 2	Packing plant, Terre Haute, IN	16
1963, Mar. 9	Dynamite plant, S. Africa	45
1963, Aug. 13	Explosives dump, Gauhaiti, India	32
1963, Oct. 31	State Fair Coliseum, Indianapolis, IN	73
1964, July 23	Bone, Algeria, harbor munitions	100
1965, Mar. 4	Gas pipeline, Natchitoches, LA	17
1965, Aug. 9	Missile silo, Searcy, AR	53
1965, Oct. 21	Bridge, Tila Bund, Pakistan	80
1965, Oct. 30	Cartagena, Colombia	48
1965, Nov. 24	Armory, Keokuk, IA	20
1966, Oct. 13	Chemical plant, La Salle, Quebec	11
1967, Feb. 17	Chemical plant, Hawthorne, NJ	11
1967, Dec. 25	Apartment bldg., Moscow, USSR	20
1968, Apr. 6	Sports store, Richmond, IN	43
1970, Apr. 8	Subway construction, Osaka, Japan	73
1971, June 24	Tunnel, Sylmar, CA	17
1971, June 28	School, fireworks, Puebla, Mexico	13
1971, Oct. 21	Shopping center, Glasgow, Scotland	20
1973, Feb., 10	Liquid gas tank, Staten Island, NY	40
1975, Dec. 27	Coal mine, Chasnala, India	431
1976, Apr. 13	Lapua, Finland, munitions works	40
1977, Nov. 11	Freight train, Iri, South Korea	57
1977, Dec. 22	Grain elevator, Westwego, LA	35
1978, Feb. 24	Derailed tank car, Waverly, TN	12
1978, July 11	Propylene tank truck, Spanish coastal campsite	150
1980, Oct. 23	School, Ortuella, Spain	64
1982, Apr. 25	Antiques exhibition, Todi, Italy	33

(continued)

Some Notable Explosions Since 1910 *(continued)*

Date	Location	Deaths
1982, Nov. 2	Salang Tunnel, Afghanistan	1,000-3,000
1984, Feb. 25	Oil pipeline, Cubatao, Brazil	508
1984, June 21	Naval supply depot, Severomorsk, USSR	200+
1984, Nov. 19	Gas storage area, NE Mexico City	334
1984, Dec. 3	Chemical plant, Bhopal, India	3,849
1984, Dec. 5	Coal mine, Taipei, Taiwan	94
1985, June 25	Fireworks factory, Hallett, OK	21
1988, Apr. 10	Pakistani army ammunitions dump nr. Rawalpindi and Islamabad	100
1988, May 5	Shell Oil Company, Norco, LA	7
1988, July 6	Oil rig, North Sea	167
1989, June 3	Gas pipeline, between Ufa, Asha, USSR	650+
1992, Mar. 3	Coal mine, Kozlu, Turkey	270+
1992, Apr. 22	Sewer, Guadalajara, Mexico	190
1992, May 9	Coal mine, Plymouth, Nova Scotia	26
1993, Feb. 26	World Trade Center, NY, NY	6
1994, July 18	Jewish community center, Buenos Aires, Argentina	100
1995, Apr. 19	Fed'l. office building, Oklahoma City	168[1]
1995, Apr. 29	Subway construction, South Korea	110
1995, Nov. 13	Military facility, Riyadh, Saudi Arabia	7
1996, Jan. 31	Bank, Colombo, Sri Lanka	53
1996, Feb. 25	Jerusalem and Ashkelon, Israel	27
1996, Mar. 3-4	Jerusalem and Tel Aviv, Israel	33
1996, June 25	U.S. military housing complex, near Dhahran, Saudi Arabia	19
1996, July 24	Train, Colombo, Sri Lanka	54
1996, Nov. 10	Cemetery, Moscow, Russia	13
1996, Nov. 16	Russian military apartment, Dagestan region, Russia	68
1996, Nov. 21	Building, San Juan, Puerto Rico	29
1996, Nov. 27	Coal mine, Shanxi province, China	91+
1996, Dec. 2	Train, Haryana, India	12
1996, Dec. 30	Train, Assam, India	59+
1997, Jan. 7	Shopping district, Algiers, Algeria	13
1997, Jan. 18	Near courthouse, Lahore, Pakistan	25
1997, Mar. 19	Ammunition depot, Jalalabad, Afghanistan	16
1997, July 8	Train, Punjab, India	36
1997, July 9	Military airfield, S Romania	16
1997, July 30	Market, Jerusalem	15
1997, Nov. 19	Car, Hyderabad, India	23
1997, Dec. 2	Coal mine, Novokuznetsk, Siberia	68
1997, Dec. 6	Trains, southern India	10+
1998, Jan. 17	Coal mine, Sokobanja, Serbia	29
1998, Feb. 14	Oil tankers (2), Yaounde, Cameroon	120
1998, Feb. 14	17 bombs, Coimbatore, India	50
1998, Feb. 23	Train, near El Affroune, Algiers	18
1998, Mar. 5	Bus, Colombo, Sri Lanka	32
1998, Mar. 9	Train, Lahore, Pakistan	10
1998, Apr. 4	Coal mine, Donetsk, Ukraine	63
1998, Aug. 7	Bomb, U.S. Embassy, Nairobi, Kenya	213
	Bomb, U.S. Embassy, Dar-es-Salaam, Tanzania	11
1998, Aug. 15	Car bomb, Omagh, Ireland	29
1998, Aug. 16	Coal mine, Luhansk, Ukraine	24
1998, Aug. 31	Marketplace in Algiers	17
1998, Sept. 8	Two buses, Sao Paulo, Brazil	59
1998, Oct. 17	Oil pipeline, Jesse, Nigeria	700+

(1) Includes a rescue worker who died during the rescue effort.

Notable Nuclear Accidents

Oct. 7, 1957 — A fire in the Windscale plutonium production reactor N of Liverpool, England, released radioactive material. In 1983, the British government said that 39 people had probably died of cancer as a result.

1957 — A chemical explosion in Kasli, USSR (now in Russia), in tanks containing nuclear waste, spread radioactive material and forced a major evacuation.

Jan. 3, 1961 — An experimental reactor at a federal installation near Idaho Falls, ID, killed 3 workers—the only deaths in U.S. reactor operations. Radiation was contained.

Oct. 5, 1966 — A sodium cooling system malfunction caused a partial core meltdown at the Enrico Fermi demonstration breeder reactor, near Detroit, MI. Radiation contained.

Jan. 21, 1969 — A coolant malfunction from an experimental underground reactor at Lucens Vad, Switzerland released a large amount of radiation into a cavern, which was then sealed.

Mar. 22, 1975 — A fire at the Brown's Ferry reactor in Decatur, AL, burned out electrical controls, lowering the cooling water to dangerous levels.

Mar. 28, 1979 — The worst commercial nuclear accident in the U.S. occurred as equipment failures and human mistakes led to a loss of coolant and a partial core meltdown at the Three Mile Island reactor in Middletown, PA.

Feb. 11, 1981 — Eight workers were contaminated when over 100,000 gallons of radioactive coolant leaked into the containment building of TVA's Sequoyah 1 plant in Tennessee.

Apr. 25, 1981 — Some 100 workers were exposed to radiation during repairs of a nuclear plant at Tsuruga, Japan.

Jan. 6, 1986 — A cylinder of nuclear material burst after being improperly heated at a Kerr-McGee plant at Gore, OK. One worker died; 100 were hospitalized.

Apr. 26, 1986 — In the worst accident in the history of the nuclear power industry, fires and explosions resulting from an unauthorized experiment at the Chernobyl nuclear power plant near Kiev, USSR (now in Ukraine), left at least 31 dead in the immediate aftermath and spread radioactive material over much of Europe. An estimated 135,000 people were evacuated from areas around Chernobyl, some of which were uninhabitable for years. As a result of the radiation released into the atmosphere, tens of thousands of excess cancer deaths (as well as increased rates of birth defects) were expected in succeeding decades.

Record Oil Spills

The number of tons can be multiplied by 7 to estimate roughly the number of barrels spilled; the exact number of barrels in a ton varies with the type of oil. Each barrel contains 42 gallons.

Name, place	Date	Cause	Tons
Ixtoc I oil well, S Gulf of Mexico	June 3, 1979	Blowout	600,000
Nowruz oil field, Persian Gulf	Feb. 1983	Blowout	600,000 (est.)
Atlantic Empress & *Aegean Captain*, off Trinidad and Tobago	July 19, 1979	Collision	300,000
Castillo de Bellver, off Cape Town, South Africa	Aug. 6, 1983	Fire	250,000
Amoco Cadiz, near Portsall, France	Mar. 16, 1978	Grounding	223,000
Torrey Canyon, off Land's End, England	Mar. 18, 1967	Grounding	119,000
Sea Star, Gulf of Oman	Dec. 19, 1972	Collision	115,000
Urquiola, La Coruna, Spain	May 12, 1976	Grounding	100,000
Hawaiian Patriot, N Pacific	Feb. 25, 1977	Fire	99,000
Othello, Tralhavet Bay, Sweden	Mar. 20, 1970	Collision	60,000-100,000

Other Notable Oil Spills

Name, place	Date	Cause	Gallons
Persian Gulf	began Jan. 23, 1991	Spillage by Iraq	130,000,000[1]
Braer, off Shetland Islands	Jan. 5, 1993	Grounding	26,000,000
Aegean Sea, off N Spain	Dec. 3, 1992	Unknown	21,500,000
Sea Empress, off SW Wales	Feb. 15, 1996	Grounding	18,000,000
World Glory, off South Africa	June 13, 1968	Hull failure	13,524,000
Exxon Valdez, Prince William Sound, AK	Mar. 24, 1989	Grounding	10,080,000
Keo, off MA	Nov. 5, 1969	Hull failure	8,820,000
Storage tank, Sewaren, NJ	Nov. 4, 1969	Tank rupture	8,400,000
Ekofisk oil field, North Sea	Apr. 22, 1977	Well blowout	8,200,000
Argo Merchant, Nantucket, MA	Dec. 15, 1976	Grounding	7,700,000

Name, place	Date	Cause	Gallons
Pipeline, West Delta, LA	Oct. 15, 1967	Dragging anchor	6,720,000
Tanker off Japan	Nov. 30, 1971	Ship broke in half	6,258,000
Usinsk, Russian Arctic	Aug. 12, 1994	Pipeline rupture	4,300,000
Storage tank, Monongahela River	Jan. 2, 1988	Tank rupture	3,800,000 (est.)[2]

(1) Est. by Saudi Arabia. Some estimates as low as 25 mil gal. (2) Other estimates are as high as 84.6 mil gal.

Historic Assassinations Since 1865

1865—Apr. 14. U.S. Pres. Abraham Lincoln shot by John Wilkes Booth in Washington, DC; died Apr. 15.

1881—Mar. 13. Alexander II, of Russia.—July 2. U.S. Pres. James A. Garfield shot by Charles J. Guiteau, Washington, DC; died Sept. 19.

1894—June 24. Pres. Sadi Carnot of France, by Italian anarchist, Sante Caserio, in Lyon.

1898—Sept. 10. Empress Elizabeth of Austria, stabbed by Italian anarchist Luigi Luccheni.

1900—July 29. Umberto I, king of Italy.

1901—Sept. 6. U.S. Pres. William McKinley in Buffalo, NY; died Sept. 14. Leon Czolgosz executed for the crime.

1908—Feb. 1. King Carlos I of Portugal and his son Luis Felipe, in Lisbon.

1913—Feb. 23. Mex. Pres. Francisco I. Madero and Vice Pres. Jose Pino Suarez.—Mar. 18. George, king of Greece.

1914—June 28. Archduke Francis Ferdinand of Austria-Hungary and his wife in Sarajevo, Bosnia (later part of Bosnia and Herzegovina), by Gavrilo Princip.

1916—Dec. 30. Grigori Rasputin, politically powerful Russian monk.

1918—July 12. Grand Duke Michael of Russia, at Perm.—July 16. Nicholas II, abdicated as czar of Russia; his wife, the Czarina Alexandra; their son, Czarevitch Alexis; their daughters, Grand Duchesses Olga, Tatiana, Marie, Anastasia; and 4 members of their household, executed by Bolsheviks at Ekaterinburg.

1920—May 20. Mexican Pres. Gen. Venustiano Carranza in Tlaxcalantongo.

1922—Aug. 22. Michael Collins, Irish revolutionary.—Dec. 16. Polish Pres.Gabriel Narutowicz in Warsaw.

1923—July 20. Gen. Francisco "Pancho" Villa, ex-rebel leader, in Parral, Mexico.

1928—July 17. Gen. Alvaro Obregon, president-elect of Mexico, in San Angel, Mexico.

1932—May 6. Pres. Paul Doumer of France shot by Russian émigré, Pavel Gorgulov, in Paris.

1934—July 25. In Vienna, Austrian Chancellor Engelbert Dollfuss by Nazis.

1935—Sept. 8. U.S. Sen. Huey P. Long shot in Baton Rouge, LA, by Dr. Carl Austin Weiss, who was slain by Long's bodyguards; Long died Sept. 10.

1940—Aug. 20. Leon Trotsky (Lev Bronstein), 63, exiled Russian war minister, near Mexico City, by Ramon Mercador del Rio, a Spaniard.

1948—Jan. 30. Mohandas K. Gandhi, 78, shot in New Delhi, India, by Nathuram Vinayak Godse.—Sept. 17. Count Folke Bernadotte, UN mediator for Palestine, by Jewish extremists in Jerusalem.

1951—July 20. King Abdullah ibn Hussein of Jordan.—Oct. 16. Prime Min. Liaquat Ali Khan of Pakistan shot in Rawalpindi.

1956—Sept. 21. Pres. Anastasio Somoza of Nicaragua, shot in Leon; died Sept. 29.

1957—July 26. Pres. Carlos Castillo Armas of Guatemala, in Guatemala City by one of his own guards.

1958—July 14. King Faisal of Iraq; his uncle, Crown Prince Abdullah; and July 15, Prem. Nuri as-Said, by rebels in Baghdad.

1959—Sept. 25. Prime Min. Solomon Bandaranaike of Ceylon, by Buddhist monk in Colombo.

1961—Jan. 17. Ex-Prem. Patrice Lumumba of the Congo, in Katanga Province.—May 30. Dominican dictator Rafael Leonidas Trujillo Molina, near Ciudad Trujillo.

1963—June 12. Medgar W. Evers, NAACP's Mississippi field secretary, by Byron De Law Beckwith in Jackson, MS.—Nov. 2. Pres. Ngo Dinh Diem of South Vietnam and his brother, Ngo Dinh Nhu, in a military coup.—Nov. 22. U.S. Pres. John F. Kennedy shot in Dallas, TX; accused gunman Lee Harvey Oswald was murdered by Jack Ruby while awaiting trial.

1965—Jan. 21. Iranian Prem. Hassan Ali Mansour in Tehran; 4 executed.—Feb. 21. Malcolm X, black nationalist, shot in New York City.

1966—Sept. 6. Prime Min. Hendrik F. Verwoerd of South Africa stabbed to death in parliament at Cape Town.

1968—Apr. 4. Rev. Dr. Martin Luther King Jr. fatally shot in Memphis, TN; James Earl Ray convicted of crime.—June 5. Sen. Robert F. Kennedy (D, NY) shot in Los Angeles; Sirhan Sirhan, convicted of crime.

1971—Nov. 28. Prime Min. Wasfi Tal of Jordan, in Cairo, by Palestinian guerrillas.

1973—Mar. 2. U.S. Amb. Cleo A. Noel Jr., U.S. Charge d'Affaires George C. Moore, and Belgian Charge d'Affaires Guy Eid killed by Palestinian guerrillas in Khartoum, Sudan.

1974—Aug. 19. U.S. Amb. to Cyprus, Rodger P. Davies, killed by sniper's bullet in Nicosia.

1975—Feb. 11. Pres. Richard Ratsimandrava, of Madagascar, shot in Tananarive.—Mar. 25. King Faisal of Saudi Arabia shot by nephew Prince Musad Abdel Aziz, in royal palace, Riyadh.—Aug. 15. Bangladesh Pres. Sheik Mujibur Rahman killed in coup.

1976—Feb. 13. Nigerian head of state, Gen. Murtala Ramat Mohammed, by self-styled "young revolutionaries."

1977—Mar. 16. Kamal Jumblat, Lebanese Druse chieftain, shot near Beirut.—Mar. 18. Congo Pres. Marien Ngouabi shot in Brazzaville.

1978—July 9. Former Iraqi Prem. Abdul Razak Al-Naif shot in London.

1979—Feb. 14. U.S. Amb. Adolph Dubs shot by Afghan Muslim extremists in Kabul.—Aug. 27. Lord Mountbatten, World War II hero, and 2 others killed when a bomb exploded on his fishing boat off the coast of Co. Sligo, Ire. IRA claimed responsibility.—Oct. 26. South Korean Pres. Park Chung Hee and 6 bodyguards fatally shot by Kim Jae Kyu, head of South Korean CIA, and 5 aides in Seoul.

1980—Apr. 12. Liberian Pres. William R. Tolbert slain in military coup.—Sept. 17. Former Nicaraguan Pres. Anastasio Somoza Debayle shot in Paraguay.

1981—Oct. 6. Egyptian Pres. Anwar al-Sadat shot by commandos while reviewing military parade in Cairo.

1982—Sept. 14. Lebanese Pres.-elect Bashir Gemayel killed by bomb in east Beirut.

1983—Aug. 21. Philippine opposition leader Benigno Aquino Jr. shot by gunman at Manila International Airport.

1984—Oct. 31. Indian Prime Min. Indira Gandhi shot and killed by 2 Sikh bodyguards, in New Delhi.

1986—Feb. 28. Swedish Prem. Olof Palme shot by gunman on Stockholm street.

1987—June 1. Lebanese Prem. Rashid Karami killed when bomb exploded aboard a helicopter.

1988—Apr. 16. PLO military chief Khalil Wazir (Abu Jihad) gunned down by Israeli commandos in Tunisia.

1989—Aug. 18. Colombian presidential candidate Luis Carlos Galan killed by Medellín cartel drug traffickers at campaign rally in Bogotá.—Nov. 22. Lebanese Pres. Rene Moawad killed when bomb exploded next to his motorcade.

1990—Mar. 22. Presidential candidate Bernando Jamamillo Ossa shot by gunman at an airport in Bogotá.

1991—May 21. Rajiv Gandhi, former prime min. of India, killed by bomb during election rally in Madras.

1992—June 29. Mohammed Boudiaf, pres. of Algeria, shot by gunman in Annaba.

1993—May 1. Ranasinghe Premadasa, pres. of Sri Lanka, killed by bomb in Colombo.

1994—Mar. 23. Luis Donaldo Colosio, Mexican presidential candidate, shot by gunman Mario Aburto Martinez. —Apr. 6. Burundian Pres. Cyprien Ntaryamira and Rwandan Pres. Juvenal Habyarimana killed, with 8 others, when their plane was apparently shot down.

1995—Nov. 4. Yitzhak Rabin, prime min. of Israel, shot by gunman Yigal Amir at peace rally in Tel Aviv.

1996—Oct. 2. Andrei Lukanov, former Bulgarian prime minister, shot outside his home by an unidentified gunman.

1998—Feb. 6. Claude Erigmac, prefect of Corsica, shot in the back while walking to a concert, by two unidentified gunmen.

Assassination Attempts

1912—Oct. 14. Former U.S. Pres. Theodore Roosevelt shot and wounded by demented man in Milwaukee, WI.

1933—Feb. 15. In Miami, FL, Joseph Zangara, anarchist, shot at Pres.-elect Franklin D. Roosevelt, but a woman seized his arm, and the bullet fatally wounded Mayor Anton J. Cermak, of Chicago, who died Mar. 6. Zangara was electrocuted on Mar. 20, 1933.

1944—July 20. Adolf Hitler was injured when a bomb, planted by a German officer, exploded in Hitler's headquarters. One aide was killed and 12 were injured in the explosion.

1950—Nov. 1. In an attempt to assassinate Pres. Harry Truman, 2 members of a Puerto Rican nationalist movement—Griselio Torresola and Oscar Collazo—tried to shoot their way into Blair House. Torresola was killed, and a White House policeman, Pvt. Leslie Coffelt, was fatally shot.

1970—Nov. 27. Pope Paul VI unharmed by knife-wielding assailant who attempted to attack him in Manila airport.

1972—May 15. Alabama Gov. George Wallace shot in Laurel, MD, by Arthur Bremer; seriously crippled.

1975—Sept. 5. Pres. Gerald R. Ford unharmed when a Secret Service agent grabbed a pistol aimed at him by Lynette (Squeaky) Fromme, a Charles Manson follower, in Sacramento.—Sept. 22. Pres. Ford again unharmed when Sara Jane Moore fired a revolver at him.

1980—May 29. Civil rights leader Vernon E. Jordan Jr. shot and wounded in Ft. Wayne, IN.

1981—Jan. 16. Irish political activist Bernadette Devlin McAliskey and her husband shot and seriously wounded by 3 members of a Protestant paramilitary group in Co. Tyrone, Ire.—Mar. 30. Pres. Ronald Reagan, along with Press Sec. James Brady, Secret Service agent Timothy J. McCarthy, and Washington, DC, policeman Thomas Delahanty shot and seriously wounded by John W. Hinckley Jr. in Washington, DC.—May 13. Pope John Paul II and 2 bystanders shot and wounded by Mehmet Ali Agca, an escaped Turkish murderer, in St. Peter's Square, Rome.

1982—May 12. Pope John Paul II unharmed after guards overpowered a man with a knife, in Fatima, Portugal.

1984—Oct. 12. British Prime Min. Margaret Thatcher narrowly escaped injury when a bomb, said to have been planted by the IRA, exploded at the Grand Hotel in Brighton, England, during a Conservative Party conference. Four died, including a member of Parliament.

1986—Sept. 7. Chilean Pres. Gen. Augusto Pinochet Ugarte escaped unharmed when his motorcade was attacked by rebels using rockets, bazookas, grenades, and rifles.

1994—Oct. 29. Pres. Bill Clinton unharmed when Francisco Duran, later convicted of attempted assassination, shot at a tourist resembling Clinton outside the White House.

1995—June 26. Egyptian Pres. Hosni Mubarak unharmed when gunmen fired on his motorcade in Addis Ababa, Ethiopia. Four died, including 2 Ethiopian police officers.

1997—Feb. 12. Colombian Pres. Ernesto Samper Pizano unharmed when a bomb exploded on a runway in Barranquilla as his plane was preparing to land.—Apr. 30. Tajik Pres. Imamali Rakhmanov injured when a grenade was thrown at him. 2 others were killed.

1998—Feb. 9. Georgian Pres. Eduard A. Shevardnadze unharmed when gunmen fired on his motorcade in Tbilisi, Georgia. Three died, including 2 bodyguards and 1 assailant.

Notable U.S. Kidnappings Since 1924

Robert Franks, 13, in Chicago, **May 22, 1924,** by 2 youths, Richard Loeb and Nathan Leopold, who killed boy. Demand for $10,000 ignored. Loeb died in prison; Leopold paroled 1958.

Charles A. Lindbergh Jr., 20 mos. old, in Hopewell, NJ, **Mar. 1, 1932;** found dead **May 12.** Ransom of $50,000 paid to man identified as Bruno Richard Hauptmann, 35, paroled German convict who entered U.S. illegally. Hauptmann was convicted after spectacular trial at Flemington, and electrocuted in Trenton, NJ, prison, **Apr. 3, 1936.**

William A. Hamm Jr., 39, in St. Paul, **June 15, 1933.** $100,000 paid. Alvin Karpis given life, paroled in 1969.

Charles F. Urschel, in Oklahoma City, **July 22, 1933.** Released **July 31** after $200,000 paid. George "Machine Gun" Kelly and 5 others sentenced to life.

Brooke L. Hart, 22, in San Jose, CA. Thomas Thurmond and John Holmes arrested after demanding $40,000 ransom. When Hart's body was found in San Francisco Bay, **Nov. 26, 1933,** a mob attacked the jail in San Jose and lynched the 2 kidnappers.

George Weyerhaeuser, 9, in Tacoma, WA, **May 24, 1935.** Returned home **June 1** after $200,000 paid. Kidnappers given 20 to 60 years.

Charles Mattson, 10, in Tacoma, WA, **Dec. 27, 1936.** Found dead **Jan. 11, 1937.** Kidnapper asked $28,000, but failed to contact for delivery.

Arthur Fried, in White Plains, NY, **Dec. 4, 1937.** Body not found. Two kidnappers executed.

Robert C. Greenlease, 6, taken from Kansas City, MO, school **Sept. 28, 1953,** and held for $600,000. His body was found Oct. 7. Bonnie Brown Heady and Carl A. Hall pleaded guilty and were executed.

Peter Weinberger, 32 days old, Westbury, NY, **July 4, 1956,** for $2,000 ransom, not paid. Child found dead. Angelo John LaMarca, 31, convicted, executed.

Lee Crary, 8, in Everett, WA, **Sept. 22, 1957;** $10,000 ransom, not paid. He escaped after 3 days, led police to George E. Collins, who was convicted.

Frank Sinatra Jr., 19, from hotel room in Lake Tahoe, CA, **Dec. 8, 1963.** Released **Dec. 11** after his father paid $240,000 ransom. Three men sentenced to prison.

Barbara Jane Mackle, 20, abducted **Dec. 17, 1968,** from Atlanta, GA, motel; found unharmed 3 days later, buried in a coffin-like box 18 inches underground, after her father had paid $500,000 ransom; Gary Steven Krist sentenced to life, Ruth Eisenmann-Schier to 7 years.

Mrs. Roy Fuchs, 35, and 3 children held hostage 2 hours, **May 14, 1969,** in Long Island, NY, released after her husband, a bank manager, paid kidnappers $129,000 in bank funds; 4 men arrested, ransom recovered.

Virginia Piper, 49, abducted **July 27, 1972,** from her home in suburban Minneapolis; found unharmed near Duluth 2 days later after her husband paid $1 million ransom.

Patricia "Patty" Hearst, 19, taken from her Berkeley, CA, apartment **Feb. 4, 1974.** "Symbionese Liberation Army" captors demanded her father, publisher Randolph Hearst, give millions to the area's poor. Implicated in a San Francisco bank holdup, **Apr. 15.** the FBI, **Sept. 18, 1975,** captured her and others; they were indicted on various charges. Patricia Hearst convicted of bank robbery, **Mar. 20, 1976;** released from prison under executive clemency, **Feb. 1, 1979.** In 1978, William and Emily Harris were sentenced to 10 years to life for the kidnapping; both were paroled in 1983.

J. Reginald Murphy, 40, an editor of *Atlanta* (GA) *Constitution,* kidnapped **Feb. 20, 1974;** freed **Feb. 22** after newspaper paid $700,000 ransom. William A. H. Williams arrested; most of the money recovered.

E. B. Reville, Hepzibah, GA, banker, and wife, Jean, kidnapped **Sept. 30, 1974.** Ransom of $30,000 paid. He was found alive; Jean Reville was found dead **Oct. 2.**

Jack Teich, Kings Point, NY, steel executive, seized **Nov. 12, 1974;** released **Nov. 19** after payment of $750,000.

Adam Walsh, 6, abducted from a Hollywood, FL, department store, **July 27, 1981.** Although his severed head was found 2 weeks later at Vero Beach, FL, his body was never recovered. John Walsh, Adam's father, became active in raising awareness about missing children.

Sidney J. Reso, oil company executive, seized **Apr. 29, 1992;** died **May 3;** Arthur D. Seale and wife, Irene, arrested **June 19.** Arthur Seale pleaded guilty, sentenced to life in prison; Irene Seale sentenced to 20-year prison term.

Polly Klaas, 12, Petaluma, CA, abducted at knife point, **Oct. 1, 1993,** during a slumber party at her home. Police arrested Richard Allen Davis on **Nov. 30;** he led them to her body, found **Dec. 4** in wooded area of Cloverdale, CA. Davis was found guilty **June 18, 1996,** and was sentenced to death **Sept. 26.**

Marshall I. Wais, 79, owner of 2 San Francisco steel companies, kidnapped **Nov. 19, 1996,** from his San Francisco home. Released unharmed the same day after $500,000 ransom paid; Thomas William Taylor and Michael K. Robinson arrested the same day.

EDUCATION

Historical Overview of U.S. Public Elementary and Secondary Schools

Source: National Center for Education Statistics, U.S. Dept. of Education

	1969-70	1979-80	1989-90	1990-91	1991-92	1992-93	1993-94	1994-95	1995-96
Pupils and teachers (thousands)									
Total U.S. population	201,385	224,567	246,819	249,440	252,137	255,028	257,783	260,292	262,761
Population 5-17 years of age	52,386	48,041	44,947	45,312	45,918	46,662	47,419	48,110	48,911
Percentage 5-17 years of age	26	21.4	18.2	18.2	18.2	18.3	18.4	18.5	18.6
Enrollment (thousands)									
Elementary and secondary	45,550	41,651	40,543	41,217	42,047	42,816	43,465	44,111	44,840
Kindergarten & grades 1-8	32,513	28,034	29,152	29,878	30,506	31,081	31,504	31,898	32,341
Grades 9-12	13,037	13,616	11,390	11,338	11,541	11,735	11,961	12,213	12,500
Percentage pop. 5-17 enrolled	87	86.7	90.2	91.0	91.6	91.8	91.7	91.7	91.7
Percentage in high schools	28.6	32.7	28.1	27.5	27.4	27.4	27.5	27.7	27.9
High school graduates (thousands)	2,589	2,748	2,320	2,235	2,212	2,233	2,221	2,274	2,281
Average school term (in days)	178.9	178.5	*	179.8	*	*	*	*	*
Total instructional staff (thousands)	2,286	2,406	2,986	3,051	3,104	3,140	3,209	3,281	3,352
Teachers, librarians, and other nonsupervisory instructional staff (thousands)	2,195	2,300	2,860	2,924	2,975	3,017	3,088	3,161	3,231
Revenue & expenditures (millions)									
Total revenue	$40,267	$96,881	$208,548	$223,341	$234,486	$247,626	$260,142	$273,149	$287,703
Total expenditures	40,683	95,962	212,770	229,430	241,567	252,935	265,285	279,000	293,611
Current elem. and secondary	34,218	86,984	188,229	202,038	211,216	220,948	231,543	243,878	255,080
Capital outlay	4,659	6,506	17,781	19,771	20,797	22,172	23,747	24,456	27,548
Other	636	598	2,983	3,296	4,392	4,379	4,682	5,149	4,725
Interest on school debt	1,171	1,874	3,776	4,325	5,162	5,437	5,335	5,518	6,259
Salaries and pupil cost									
Avg. annual salary of instruct. staff[1]	$9,047	$16,715	$32,638	$34,401	$35,550	$36,454	$37,383	$38,441	$39,451
Expenditure per capita total pop.	202	427	862	920	958	992	1,029	1,072	1,117
Current expenditure per pupil ADA[2]	816	2,272	4,980	5,258	5,421	5,584	5,767	5,989	6,146

Note: Because of rounding, details may not add to totals. * = Data not collected. (1) Includes supervisors, principals, teachers, and nonsupervisory instructional staff. (2) ADA means average daily attendance in elementary and secondary schools.

Programs for the Disabled, 1988-97[1]

Source: Office of Special Education and Rehabilitative Services, U.S. Dept. of Education

(Number of children up to 21 years old served annually in educational programs for the disabled; in thousands.)

Type of Disability	1988-89	1989-90	1990-91	1991-92	1992-93	1993-94	1994-95	1995-96	1996-97
All disabilities	4,527	4,641	4,762	4,949	5,176	5,365	5,539	5,745	5,920
Learning disabilities	1,970	2,050	2,130	2,234	2,351	2,408	2,489	2,579	2,651
Speech impairments	967	973	985	997	994	1,014	1,015	1,022	1,045
Mental retardation	564	548	534	538	518	536	555	570	579
Serious emotional disturbance	376	381	390	399	400	414	427	438	446
Hearing impairments	56	57	58	60	60	64	64	67	68
Orthopedic impairments	47	48	49	51	52	56	60	63	66
Other health impairments	43	52	55	58	65	82	106	133	160
Visual impairments	23	22	23	24	23	24	24	25	25
Multiple disabilities	85	86	96	97	102	108	88	93	98
Deafness/blindness	2	2	1	1	1	1	1	1	1
Autism and other	*	*	*	5	19	24	30	38	45
Preschool disabilities[2]	394	422	441	484	590	634	680	717	737

Note: Counts are based on reports from the 50 states and the District of Columbia. Details may not add to totals because of rounding. * = Data not collected. (1) Includes students served under Chapter I and Individuals With Disabilities Education Act (IDEA). (2) Includes preschool children 3-5 years and 0-5 years served under Chapter I and IDEA, respectively.

Technology in U.S. Public Schools, 1995-98

Source: Quality Education Data, Inc., Denver, CO

Technology	Number of schools				Percentage of schools			
	1995	1996	1997	1998	1995	1996	1997	1998
Schools with modems[1]	**30,768**	**37,889**	**40,876**	**61,930**	**36.6**	**44.8**	**47.7**	**71.0**
Elementary[2]	16,010	20,250	22,234	35,066	31.1	39.2	42.6	66.4
Junior high[3]	5,652	6,929	7,417	10,996	41.1	50.0	52.7	76.3
Senior high[4]	8,790	10,277	10,781	14,540	52.1	60.7	62.6	82.7
Schools with networks[1]	**24,604**	**29,875**	**32,299**	**49,178**	**29.2**	**35.3**	**37.7**	**56.4**
Elementary[2]	11,693	14,868	16,441	26,422	22.7	28.8	31.5	50.0
Junior high[3]	4,599	5,590	6,035	9,003	33.5	40.3	42.8	62.5
Senior high[4]	8,159	9,166	9,565	12,853	48.3	54.2	55.5	73.1
Schools with CD-ROMs[1]	**34,480**	**43,499**	**46,388**	**64,200**	**41.0**	**51.5**	**54.1**	**73.6**
Elementary[2]	18,343	24,353	26,377	37,908	35.6	47.1	50.5	71.7
Junior high[3]	6,510	7,952	8,410	11,023	47.4	57.3	59.7	76.5
Senior high[4]	9,327	10,756	11,140	13,985	55.3	63.5	64.6	79.5
Schools with Internet access[1]	**NA**	**14,211**	**35,762**	**60,224**	**NA**	**16.8**	**41.7**	**69.1**
Elementary[2]	NA	7,608	21,026	34,195	NA	14.7	40.3	64.7
Junior high[3]	NA	2,707	5,752	10,888	NA	19.5	40.8	75.5
Senior high[4]	NA	3,736	8,984	13,829	NA	22.1	52.1	78.6

NA=Not applicable. (1) Includes schools for special and adult education, not shown separately. (2) Includes preschool and schools with grade spans of K-3, K-5, K-6, K-8, and K-12. (3) Includes schools with grade spans of 4-8, 7-8, and 7-9. (4) Includes vocational technical and alternative high schools and schools with grade spans of 7-12, 9-12, and 10-12.

Students per Computer in U.S. Public Schools

Source: *QED's Technology in Public Schools, 16th Edition*

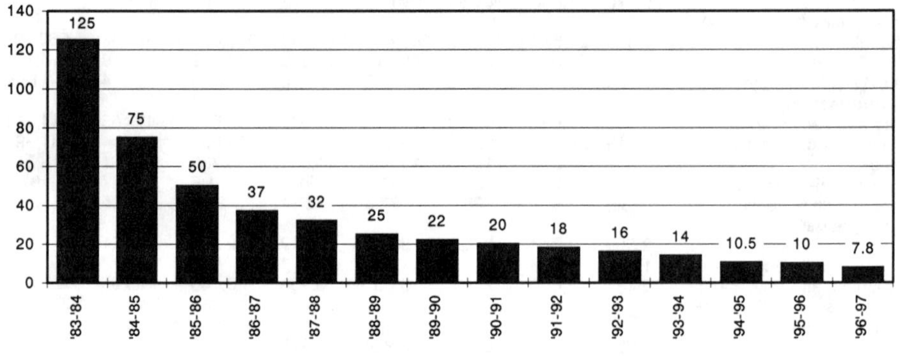

Enrollment and Teachers in Public Schools, Fall 1996*

Source: National Center for Education Statistics, U.S. Dept. of Education; National Education Association

	Local school districts	Classroom teachers	Total enrollment	Pupils per teacher	Teacher's avg. pay[1]	Instr. aides	Expend. per pupil
U.S.	**14,883**	**2,666,034**	**45,592,213**	**17.1**	**$39,385**	**518,649**	**$6,146**
Alabama	127	45,040	748,156	16.6	32,818	7,146	4,716
Alaska	56	7,418	129,919	17.5	51,738	1,649	9,012
Arizona	227	40,521	799,250	19.7	33,850	10,157	4,860
Arkansas	314	26,680	457,349	17.1	30,578	3,837	4,710
California	1,006	248,857	5,687,901	22.9	43,725	57,896	5,108
Colorado	176	36,398	673,438	18.5	37,052	6,532	5,521
Connecticut	166	36,551	527,129	14.4	50,730	7,506	8,817
Delaware	19	6,642	110,549	16.6	42,439	898	7,267
District of Columbia	1	5,288	78,648	14.9	46,350	499	9,565
Florida	67	120,471	2,242,212	18.6	34,475	26,814	5,894
Georgia	181	79,091	1,346,761	17.0	37,378	16,386	5,377
Hawaii	1	10,576	187,653	17.7	38,377	916	6,051
Idaho	112	13,078	245,252	18.8	32,775	2,153	4,465
Illinois	916	116,274	1,973,040	17.0	43,873	24,006	6,128
Indiana	295	56,708	983,415	17.3	39,682	16,070	6,040
Iowa	390	32,593	502,941	15.4	34,040	6,421	5,772
Kansas	304	30,875	466,293	15.1	36,811	5,003	5,971
Kentucky	176	39,331	656,089	16.7	34,525	7,982	5,545
Louisiana	66	47,334	793,296	16.6	29,650	10,002	4,988
Maine	285	15,551	213,593	13.7	34,349	4,028	6,546
Maryland	24	47,943	818,583	17.1	41,739	6,989	7,382
Massachusetts	353	64,574	933,898	14.5	43,930	13,868	7,613
Michigan	633	88,051	1,684,386	19.1	49,277	18,556	7,166
Minnesota	419	48,245	847,204	17.6	39,106	11,255	6,162
Mississippi	153	29,293	503,967	17.2	29,547	8,615	4,250
Missouri	536	59,436	900,042	15.1	33,975	7,752	5,626
Montana	481	10,268	164,627	16.0	30,617	2,003	5,847
Nebraska	680	20,174	291,967	14.5	32,668	3,629	6,083
Nevada	17	14,805	282,131	19.1	37,093	1,615	5,320
New Hampshire	178	12,692	198,308	15.6	36,640	3,852	5,958
New Jersey	608	88,903	1,208,179	13.6	50,442	14,925	9,955
New Mexico	89	19,971	332,632	16.7	30,152	4,723	4,587
New York	719	185,104	2,843,131	15.4	49,034	29,467	9,549
North Carolina	119	75,239	1,210,108	16.1	33,315	23,537	5,090
North Dakota	243	7,892	120,123	15.2	28,230	1,572	4,979
Ohio	661	108,602	1,844,389	17.0	38,977	10,567	6,266
Oklahoma	551	39,491	620,695	15.7	30,606	7,379	4,881
Oregon	248	26,757	537,854	20.1	42,150	6,546	6,615
Pennsylvania	501	106,432	1,804,256	17.0	47,650	16,180	7,492
Rhode Island	36	10,656	151,324	14.2	44,300	1,594	7,936
South Carolina	95	41,463	653,011	15.7	33,608	7,945	5,096
South Dakota	177	9,625	143,331	14.9	27,341	2,450	4,780
Tennessee	140	54,790	905,089	16.5	35,340	10,570	4,548
Texas	1,044	247,650	3,828,975	15.5	33,648	42,686	5,473
Utah	40	19,734	481,812	24.4	32,950	5,004	3,867
Vermont	284	7,751	106,341	13.7	36,299	3,105	6,837
Virginia	141	74,523	1,096,093	14.7	36,654	12,056	5,433
Washington	296	48,307	974,504	20.2	38,788	9,333	6,044
West Virginia	55	20,888	304,052	14.6	33,398	2,943	6,325
Wisconsin	428	54,769	879,259	16.1	39,899	10,608	7,094
Wyoming	49	6,729	99,058	14.7	32,022	1,424	6,243

*Full-time elementary and secondary day schools only. (1) 1997-98; National Education Association estimate.

Mathematics, Reading, and Science Achievement of U.S. Students

Source: National Assessment of Educational Progress, National Center for Education Statistics, U.S. Dept. of Education

Percent of students who scored at or above proficient level in national tests. NA = not administered.

	Grade 4				Grade 8		
	Mathematics		Reading		Mathematics		Science
State[1]	1992	1996	1992	1994	1992	1996	1996
AL	43	48	20	23	39	45	18
AK	NA	65	NA	NA	NA	68	31
AZ	53	57	21	24	55	57	23
AR	47	54	23	24	44	52	22
CA	46	46	19	18	50	51	20
CO	61	67	25	28	64	67	32
CT	67	75	34	38	64	70	36
DE	55	54	24	23	52	55	21
DC	23	20	NA	NA	22	20	5
FL	52	55	21	23	49	54	21
GA	53	53	25	26	48	51	21
HI	52	53	17	19	46	51	15
IN	60	72	30	33	60	68	30
IA	72	74	36	35	76	78	36
KY	51	60	23	26	51	56	23
LA	39	44	15	15	37	38	13
ME	75	75	36	41	72	77	41
MD	55	59	24	26	54	57	25
MA	68	71	36	36	63	68	37
MI	61	68	NA	NA	58	67	32
MN	71	76	31	33	74	75	37
MS	36	42	14	18	33	36	12
MO	62	66	30	31	62	64	28
MT	NA	71	NA	35	NA	75	41
NE	67	70	31	34	70	76	35
NV	NA	57	38	36	NA	NA	NA
NJ	68	68	35	33	NA	NA	NA
NM	50	51	23	21	48	51	19
NY	57	64	27	27	57	61	27
NC	50	64	25	30	47	56	24
ND	72	75	35	38	78	77	41
OR	NA	65	NA	NA	NA	67	32
PA	65	68	32	30	NA	NA	NA
RI	54	61	28	32	56	60	26
SC	48	48	22	20	48	48	17
TN	47	58	23	27	47	53	22
TX	56	69	24	26	53	59	23
UT	66	69	30	30	67	70	32
VT	NA	67	NA	NA	NA	72	34
VA	59	62	31	26	57	58	27
WA	NA	67	NA	27	NA	67	27
WV	52	63	25	26	47	54	21
WI	71	74	33	35	71	75	39
WY	69	64	33	32	67	68	34
U.S. AVG.	**57**	**62**	**27**	**28**	**56**	**61**	**27**

(1) Only participating states are included.

Revenues[1] for Public Elementary and Secondary Schools, by State, 1997-98

Source: National Education Association; estimated; in thousands

		Federal		State		Local and intermediate	
State	Total	Amount	%	Amount	%	Amount	%
U.S.	$314,187,289	$21,337,815	6.8	$155,321,093	49.4	$137,528,381	43.8
Alabama	4,030,356	379,707	9.4	2,601,160	64.5	1,049,489	26.0
Alaska	1,183,024 *	148,479 *	12.6 *	751,882 *	63.6 *	282,663 *	23.9 *
Arizona	4,388,915 *	344,440 *	7.8 *	2,108,912 *	48.1 *	1,935,563 *	44.1 *
Arkansas	2,322,451	193,028	8.3	1,535,550	66.1	593,873	25.6
California	35,054,650 *	3,108,332 *	8.9 *	19,920,649 *	56.8 *	12,025,669 *	34.3 *
Colorado	4,183,998 *	235,150 *	5.6 *	1,860,095 *	44.5 *	2,088,753 *	49.9 *
Connecticut	5,112,950	235,980	4.6	2,064,560	40.4	2,812,410	55.0
Delaware	966,422	68,906	7.1	650,099	67.3	247,417	25.6
District of Columbia	452,084 *	67,102 *	14.8 *		0	384,982 *	85.2 *
Florida	14,583,108	1,058,483	7.3	7,067,649	48.5	6,456,976	44.3
Georgia	8,579,628	563,428	6.6	4,485,220	52.3	3,530,980	41.2
Hawaii	1,364,412	101,842	7.5	1,231,799	90.3	30,771	2.3
Idaho	1,344,671 *	87,524 *	6.5 *	870,387 *	64.7 *	386,760 *	28.8 *
Illinois	13,649,628 *	954,160 *	7.0 *	3,651,254 *	26.7 *	9,044,214 *	66.3 *
Indiana	7,006,752 *	346,390 *	4.9 *	3,758,925 *	53.6 *	2,901,437 *	41.4 *
Iowa	3,189,269	117,484	3.7	1,726,779	54.1	1,345,006	42.2
Kansas	3,090,829	165,692	5.4	1,814,830	58.7	1,110,307	35.9
Kentucky	3,881,816 *	290,277 *	7.5 *	2,562,918 *	66.0 *	1,028,621 *	26.5 *
Louisiana	4,251,305 *	510,950 *	12.0 *	2,117,148 *	49.8 *	1,623,207 *	38.2 *
Maine	1,520,325	95,181	6.3	698,005	45.9	727,139	47.8
Maryland	6,267,608	358,393	5.7	2,524,148	40.3	3,385,067	54.0
Massachusetts	7,533,212 *	385,065 *	5.1 *	2,719,766 *	36.1 *	4,428,381 *	58.8 *
Michigan	13,579,423 *	896,321 *	6.6 *	11,102,410 *	81.8 *	1,580,692 *	11.6 *
Minnesota	6,504,296 *	252,395 *	3.9 *	3,725,754 *	57.3 *	2,526,147 *	38.8 *
Mississippi	2,502,975 *	325,505	13.0 *	1,422,642 *	56.8 *	754,828 *	30.2 *
Missouri	5,841,090 *	344,710 *	5.9 *	2,336,931 *	40.0 *	3,159,449 *	54.1 *
Montana	989,202	97,500	9.9	481,142	48.6	410,560	41.5
Nebraska	1,688,662 *	65,586 *	3.9 *	627,379 *	37.2 *	995,697*	59.0 *
Nevada	1,754,717	74,068	4.2	550,787	31.4	1,129,862	64.4
New Hampshire	1,365,391 *	42,742 *	3.1 *	83,529 *	6.1 *	1,239,120 *	90.8 *
New Jersey	12,555,896 *	390,079 *	3.1 *	4,737,699 *	37.7 *	7,428,118 *	59.2 *
New Mexico	2,328,142	204,965	8.8	1,638,853	70.4	484,324	20.8
New York	27,690,556	1,807,000	6.5	11,165,000	40.3	14,718,556	53.2
North Carolina	7,127,549	506,055 *	7.1	4,689,505	65.8	1,931,989	27.1
North Dakota	668,941	77,790	11.6	279,109	41.7	312,042	46.6
Ohio	12,694,407	857,850	6.8	5,495,244	43.3	6,341,313	50.0
Oklahoma	3,119,028 *	302,007 *	9.7 *	1,950,627 *	62.5 *	866,394 *	27.8 *
Oregon	3,525,000	250,000	7.1	2,175,000	61.7	1,100,000	31.2
Pennsylvania	15,327,396 *	843,587 *	5.5 *	6,315,350 *	41.2 *	8,168,459*	53.3 *
Rhode Island	1,271,975	66,103	5.2	538,797	42.4	667,075	52.4
South Carolina	4,156,500	312,000	7.5	2,176,100	52.4	1,668,400	40.1
South Dakota	787,412 *	73,441 *	9.3 *	249,994 *	31.7 *	463,977 *	58.9 *
Tennessee	4,491,405 *	355,640 *	7.9 *	2,314,163 *	51.5 *	1,821,602 *	40.6 *
Texas	23,920,057	1,832,912	7.7	10,282,362	43.0	11,804,783	49.4
Utah	2,248,932	141,412	6.3	1,408,832	62.6	698,688	31.1
Vermont	814,567 *	39,447 *	4.8 *	228,020 *	28.0 *	547,100 *	67.2 *
Virginia	6,661,612	361,680	5.4	2,468,859	37.1	3,831,073	57.5 *
Washington	6,722,916	465,411	6.9	4,588,341	68.2	1,669,164	24.8
West Virginia	2,176,238	186,962	8.6	1,367,620	62.8	621,656	28.6
Wisconsin	7,054,119	304,000	4.3	3,881,491	55.0	2,868,628	40.7
Wyoming	661,472	44,654	6.8	317,818	48.0	299,000	45.2

* Indicates NEA estimate. (1) Included as revenue receipts are all appropriations from general funds of federal, state, county, and local governments; receipts from taxes levied for school purposes; income from permanent school funds and endowments; and income from leases of school lands and miscellaneous sources (interest on bank deposits, tuition, gifts, school lunch charges, etc.).

Public High School Graduation Rates, 1995-96

Source: National Center for Education Statistics, U.S. Dept. of Education

	Grad. rate (%)[1]	Rank
U.S.	**68.1**	
Alabama	57.8	46T
Alaska	64.7	38
Arizona	58.4	43T
Arkansas	74.9	19T
California	65.3	37
Colorado	71.9	27
Connecticut	73.5	23
Delaware	65.8	35
District of Columbia	53.2	51
Florida	57.8	46T
Georgia	55.0	49
Hawaii	74.8	21
Idaho	79.6	11
Illinois	80.0	10
Indiana	70.1	31
Iowa	85.3	4T
Kansas	75.8	16T
Kentucky	68.1	33
Louisiana	57.9	45
Maine	72.4	25
Maryland	73.9	22
Massachusetts	75.8	16T
Michigan	69.6	32
Minnesota	85.3	4T
Mississippi	56.8	48
Missouri	71.2	29
Montana	82.8	8
Nebraska	82.9	6T
Nevada	65.4	36
New Hampshire	74.9	19T
New Jersey	82.9	6T
New Mexico	63.4	39T
New York	62.0	42
North Carolina	62.4	41
North Dakota	89.0	2
Ohio	70.6	30
Oklahoma	73.0	24
Oregon	66.6	34
Pennsylvania	76.3	14
Rhode Island	71.4	28
South Carolina	54.4	50
South Dakota	86.6	3
Tennessee	63.4	39T
Texas	58.4	43T
Utah	78.4	12
Vermont	89.9	1
Virginia	75.5	18
Washington	72.2	26
West Virginia	76.1	15
Wisconsin	80.4	9
Wyoming	77.8	13

T=Tied in rank with one or more states. **Note:** Data exclude ungraded pupils and have not been adjusted for interstate migration. (1) Graduates as percentage of fall 1992 9th-grade enrollment.

MILLENNIUM FACT BOX

High School Graduation Becomes More Common

During the early 20th century, the percentage of high school graduates among 17-year-olds increased dramatically; it reached around 70% in recent decades.

School year	Total graduates	Graduates per 100 17-year-olds
1899-1900	95,000	6.4
1909-10	156,000	8.8
1919-20	311,000	16.8
1929-30	667,000	29.0
1939-40	1,221,000	50.8
1949-50	1,200,000	59.0
1959-60	1,858,000	69.5
1969-70	2,889,000	76.9
1979-80	3,043,000	71.4
1989-90	2,587,000	74.2

Institutions of Higher Education–Charges, 1969-70 to 1998-99

Source: National Center for Education Statistics, U.S. Dept. of Education; The College Board

Figures for 1969-70 are average charges for full-time resident degree-credit students; figures for later years are average charges per full-time equivalent student. Room and board are based on full-time students. These figures are enrollment-weighted, according to the number of full-time-equivalent undergraduates, and thus vary from averages given elsewhere.

	TUITION AND FEES			BOARD RATES (7-day basis)[1]			DORMITORY CHARGES		
	All institutions	2-yr	4-yr	All institutions	2-yr	4-yr	All institutions	2-yr	4-yr
Public (in-state)									
1969-70	$323	$178	$427	$511	$465	$540	$369	$308	$395
1979-80	583	355	840	867	894	898	715	572	749
1989-90	1,356	756	2,035	1,635	1,581	1,728	1,513	962	1,561
1990-91	1,454	824	2,159	1,691	1,594	1,767	1,612	1,050	1,658
1991-92	1,624	937	2,410	1,780	1,612	1,852	1,731	1,074	1,789
1992-93	1,782	1,025	2,349	1,841	1,668	1,854	1,756	1,106	1,816
1993-94	1,942	1,125	2,537	1,880	1,681	1,895	1,873	1,190	1,934
1994-95	2,057	1,192	2,681	1,949	1,712	1,967	1,959	1,232	2,023
1995-96[2]	NA	1,330	2,811	NA	—[3]	3,932[4]	NA	—[4]	—[4]
1996-97[2]	NA	1,465	2,975	NA	—[3]	4,167[4]	NA	—[4]	—[4]
1997-98[2]	NA	1,567	3,111	NA	—[3]	4,358[4]	NA	—[4]	—[4]
1998-99[2]	NA	1,633	3,243	NA	—[3]	4,530[4]	NA	—[4]	—[4]
Private									
1969-70	1,533	1,034	1,809	561	546	608	436	413	503
1979-80	3,130	2,062	3,811	955	924	1,078	827	769	999
1989-90	8,147	5,196	10,348	1,948	1,811	2,339	1,923	1,663	2,411
1990-91	8,772	5,570	11,379	2,074	1,989	2,470	2,063	1,744	2,654
1991-92	9,434	5,752	12,192	2,252	2,090	2,727	2,221	1,789	2,860
1992-93	9,942	6,059	10,294	2,344	1,875	2,354	2,348	1,970	2,362
1993-94	10,572	6,370	10,952	2,434	1,970	2,445	2,490	2,067	2,506
1994-95	11,111	6,914	11,481	2,509	2,023	2,520	2,587	2,233	2,601
1995-96[2]	NA	6,339	12,216	NA	4,063[4]	5,166[4]	NA	—[4]	—[4]
1996-97[2]	NA	6,613	12,994	NA	4,346[4]	5,363[4]	NA	—[4]	—[4]
1997-98[2]	NA	7,079	13,785	NA	4,442[4]	5,575[4]	NA	—[4]	—[4]
1998-99[2]	NA	7,333	14,508	NA	4,666[4]	5,765[4]	NA	—[4]	—[4]

(1) Data for 1989-90 through 1993-94 reflect 20 meals per week rather than 7 days per week. (2) 1995-96 through 1998-99 figures supplied by the College Board; earlier figures from National Center for Educational Statistics. (3) Sample too small to provide meaningful information. (4) Board and dormitory figures for 1995-96 through 1998-99 are combined. NA = not available.

Top 20 Colleges and Universities in Endowment Assets[1]

Source: National Association of College and University Business Officers (NACUBO)

College/University	Endowment assets[2]	College/University	Endowment assets[2]
1. Harvard University	$10,919,670	11. Washington University	$2,798,221
2. University of Texas	6,709,945	12. University of Pennsylvania	2,535,312
3. Yale University	5,742,000	13. Rice University	2,321,757
4. Princeton University	4,940,900	14. Cornell University	2,125,070
5. Stanford University	4,473,825	15. University of Chicago	2,031,131
6. Emory University	4,273,543	16. University of Michigan	1,988,835
7. University of California	3,133,252	17. Northwestern University	1,798,900
8. Massachusetts Institute of Technology	3,045,756	18. University of Notre Dame	1,467,808
9. Columbia University	3,038,907	19. Vanderbilt University	1,339,788
10. Texas A&M University	2,951,463	20. Dartmouth College	1,277,753

Note: Figures are for market value of endowment assets, excluding pledges a'nd working capital. (1) As of June 30, 1997. (2) In thousands.

U.S. Higher Education Trends: Bachelor's Degrees Conferred

Source: National Center for Education Statistics, U.S. Dept. of Education

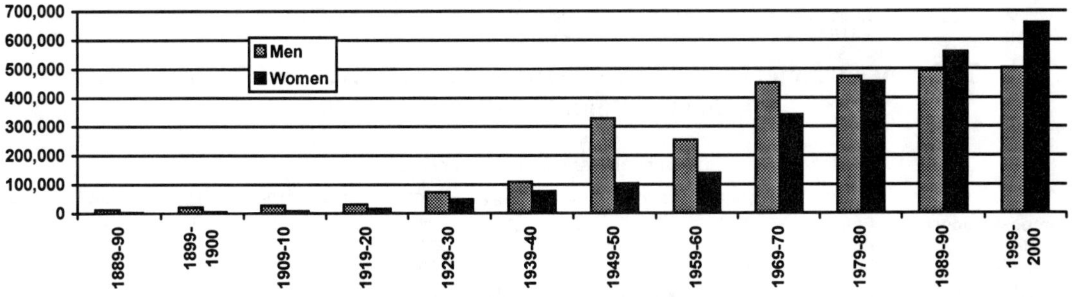

Figures for 1999-2000 are projected.

Financial Aid for College and Other Postsecondary Education

Reviewed by National Assoc. of Student Financial Aid Administrators

The cost of postsecondary education in the U.S. has increased greatly, but financial aid, which may be in the form of grants (no repayment needed), loans, and/or work-study programs, is widely available. Most aid is limited to family financial need as determined by standard formulas. Students interested in receiving aid are advised to apply, without making prior assumptions. Financial aid personnel at each school can provide information about programs available to students, steps to apply for them, and deadlines, all of which may vary.

First-time applicants for federal aid must file a Free Application for Federal Student Aid (FAFSA), generally as soon as possible after Jan. 1 for the academic year starting the following September. Figures provided must agree with federal income tax forms filed for the previous year. Other possible sources of aid include state governments, employers and unions, civic organizations, and the institutions themselves. There are also special federal programs that pay for postsecondary education in return for service: AmeriCorps (phone: 1-800-942-2677; website: http://www.cns.gov/americorps.html) and ROTC (phone: 1-800-USA-ROTC). Additional forms and certain fees may be required if a student is to be considered for institutional aid. Aid must be reapplied for annually.

A federal formula, based on information provided on the FAFSA, takes into account such factors as family after-tax income in the preceding calendar year, parental assets and length of time to retirement, and unusual expenses (such as very high medical expenses). The resulting Expected Family Contribution, or EFC (which is divided among the family members in college), is subtracted from the total cost of attendance for each person (including room and board or allowance for living costs) to determine financial need, and thus the maximum federal aid for which the family may be eligible. (Some institutions use a separate formula for needs-based institutional aid.) Some schools guarantee to meet full financial need of each admitted student; others try to do so but may fall short, depending on availability of funds. Outside scholarships (even if non-needs-based) are taken into account in determining need.

The aid package offered by each school may include one or more of the following resources: Federal Pell Grants, for those with relatively great financial need; Federal Supplementary Educational Opportunity Grants, for those with greatest financial need; grants from the school; federal work-study or other work programs; low-interest Perkins loans; and subsidized and unsubsidized Stafford loans. Unsubsidized Stafford loans are available without need, as are all PLUS loans to parents. Loans have varying requirements. Repayment of Perkins and Stafford loans does not begin until after graduation; deferments are available under certain circumstances. For PLUS loans, parents must pass a credit check and begin repayment of both principal and interest while the student is still in school. Legislation passed by Congress in 1998 reduced interest rates on student loans and increased maximum Pell Grants.

Certain federal income tax credits—dollar for dollar reductions of the amount of tax due—are available to families who meet income and other requirements; see the chapter on Taxes.

Rules for financial aid are complex and changeable. *The Student Guide*, a comprehensive resource on financial aid from the U.S. Dept. of Education, can be found at the website http://www.ed.gov/prog_info/SFA/StudentGuide

Further information and FAFSA forms are available from the school or from the Federal Student Aid Information Center, PO Box 84, Washington, DC 20044; phone: 1-800-4-FED-AID, Mon.-Fri., 8 AM - 8 PM Eastern Time. The Information Center also has a free booklet called *The EFC Formula Book*. FAFSA forms can be obtained online at http://www.fafsa.ed.gov

Salaries of College Professors, 1997-98

Source: American Association of University Professors

	MEN Type of institution			WOMEN Type of institution		
Teaching level	Public	Private/ Independent	Church-related	Public	Private/ Independent	Church-related
Doctoral level						
Professor	$76,172	$96,322	$81,755	$68,749	$87,220	$75,611
Associate	55,057	63,210	58,469	51,521	59,183	55,396
Assistant	46,541	54,862	48,619	43,386	50,229	45,665
Master's level						
Professor	62,405	68,384	65,733	59,751	63,224	59,479
Associate	50,340	52,227	51,396	48,206	48,858	47,847
Assistant	41,608	41,901	41,712	39,838	40,494	39,216
General 4-year						
Professor	57,085	65,693	51,212	54,300	61,652	48,346
Associate	47,191	49,055	42,228	45,550	47,298	40,785
Assistant	39,487	40,203	35,430	38,117	39,322	34,663
2-year						
Professor	54,441	45,401	33,728	50,672	40,661	34,566
Associate	45,965	40,382	32,624	43,017	34,059	31,392
Assistant	39,616	34,272	27,141	37,638	32,871	27,943

ACT (formerly American College Testing) Mean Scores and Characteristics of College-Bound Students, 1989-98

Source: ACT, Inc.

(for school year ending in year shown)

	UNIT[1]	1989[2]	1990[2]	1991[2]	1992[2]	1993[2]	1994[2]	1995[2]	1996[2]	1997[2]	1998[2]
Composite Scores	**Points**	**20.6**	**20.6**	**20.6**	**20.6**	**20.7**	**20.8**	**20.8**	**20.9**	**21.0**	**21.0**
Male	Points	19.3	21.0	20.9	20.9	21.0	20.9	21.0	21.0	21.1	21.2
Female	Points	18.0	20.3	20.4	20.5	20.5	20.7	20.7	20.8	20.8	20.9
English Score	**Points**	**18.4**	**20.5**	**20.3**	**20.2**	**20.3**	**20.3**	**20.2**	**20.3**	**20.3**	**20.4**
Male	Points	17.8	20.1	19.8	19.8	19.8	19.8	19.8	19.8	19.9	19.9
Female	Points	18.9	20.9	20.7	20.6	20.6	20.7	20.6	20.7	20.7	20.8
Math Score	**Points**	**17.1**	**19.9**	**20.0**	**20.0**	**20.1**	**20.2**	**20.2**	**20.2**	**20.6**	**20.8**
Male	Points	18.3	20.7	20.6	20.7	20.8	20.8	20.9	20.9	21.3	21.5
Female	Points	16.1	19.3	19.4	19.5	19.6	19.6	19.7	19.7	20.1	20.2
Participants											
Total Number	**1,000**	**855**	**817**	**796**	**832**	**875**	**892**	**945**	**925**	**959**	**995**
Male	Percent	46	46	45	45	45	45	44	44	44	43
White	Percent	80	79	79	79	79	79	80	79	74	76
Black	Percent	9	9	9	9	9	9	9	9	10	11
Composite Scores											
27 or above	Percent	14	12	11	12	12	13	13	13	14	14
18 or below	Percent	32	35	35	35	35	34	34	34	33	33

(1) Minimum point score, 1; maximum score, 36. Test scores and characteristics of college-bound students are based on the performance of all ACT-tested students who graduated in the spring of a given school year and who took the ACT Assessment during junior or senior year of high school. (2) Beginning with the Oct. 1989 test (1990 scores), an entirely new ACT Assessment was introduced. The Enhanced ACT Assessment increases the emphasis on rhetorical skills in the measurement of writing proficiency, increases the number of advanced math items, and includes a new reading test that features inferential and reasoning skills and a test designed to measure science reasoning. The Enhanced ACT also provides subscores in English, mathematics, and reading. The composite scores for 1989 have been converted to provide a basis of comparison; all 1990-98 scores are for the Enhanced ACT. It is not possible to compare directly these data and data from earlier years.

ACT Average Composite Scores by State, 1997-98

Source: ACT, Inc.

State	Avg. Composite Score	% Grads Taking ACT[1]	State	Avg. Composite Score	% Grads Taking ACT[1]	State	Avg. Composite Score	% Grads Taking ACT[1]	State	Avg. Composite Score	% Grads Taking ACT[1]
AL	20.1	64	IL	21.4	69	MT	21.9	56	RI	22.2	2
AK	21.3	37	IN	21.4	20	NE	21.8	71	SC	19.0	14
AZ	21.4	29	IA	22.1	65	NV	21.4	43	SD	21.4	70
AR	20.4	68	KS	21.7	74	NH	22.5	4	TN	19.8	77
CA	21.2	12	KY	20.2	67	NJ	20.7	4	TX	20.3	32
CO	21.6	63	LA	19.5	76	NM	20.1	65	UT	21.6	68
CT	21.8	3	ME	22.0	4	NY	22.0	15	VT	22.0	7
DE	21.3	4	MD	20.9	10	NC	19.4	12	VA	20.7	6
DC	17.6	10	MA	21.6	5	ND	21.4	78	WA	22.6	18
FL	20.8	39	MI	21.3	68	OH	21.4	60	WV	20.1	60
GA	20.2	16	MN	22.2	63	OK	20.5	69	WI	22.3	66
HI	21.6	18	MS	18.7	81	OR	22.7	12	WY	21.4	65
ID	21.5	63	MO	21.5	66	PA	21.4	7	**U.S.**	**21.0**	**37**

(1) Based on number of high school graduates in 1998, as projected by the Western Interstate Commission for Higher Education, and number of students in the class of 1998 who took the ACT.

SAT Mean Verbal and Math Scores of College-Bound Seniors, 1988-98

Source: The College Board

(recentered scale; for school year ending in year shown)

	Unit	1988	1989	1990	1991	1992	1993	1994	1995	1996	1997	1998
Verbal Scores	**Points**	**505**	**504**	**500**	**499**	**500**	**500**	**499**	**504**	**505**	**505**	**505**
Male	Points	512	510	505	503	504	504	501	505	507	507	509
Female	Points	499	498	496	495	496	497	497	502	503	503	502
Math Scores	**Points**	**501**	**502**	**501**	**500**	**501**	**503**	**504**	**506**	**508**	**511**	**512**
Male	Points	521	523	521	520	521	524	523	525	527	530	531
Female	Points	483	482	483	482	484	484	487	490	492	494	496

Note: In 1995, the College Board recentered the scoring scale for the SAT by reestablishing the original mean score of 500 on the 200-800 scale. For 1988-95, individual student scores were converted to the recentered score, and then the mean was recomputed. For 1996-98, most students received scores on the recentered scale. (Any score on the original scale was converted to the recentered score prior to computing the mean.)

SAT Mean Scores by State, 1988 and 1995-98

Source: The College Board

(recentered scale; for school year ending in year shown)

	1988		1995		1996		1997		1998		% Grads. Taking
	Verbal	Math	Verbal	Math	Verbal	Math	Verbal	Math	Verbal	Math	SAT[1]
Alabama	554	540	565	555	565	558	561	555	562	558	8
Alaska	518	501	521	513	521	513	520	517	521	520	52
Arizona	531	523	524	520	525	521	523	522	525	528	32
Arkansas	554	536	556	542	566	550	567	558	568	555	6
California	500	508	492	509	495	511	496	514	497	516	47
Colorado	537	532	538	538	536	538	536	539	537	542	31
Connecticut	513	498	507	502	507	504	509	507	510	509	80
Delaware	510	493	505	494	508	495	505	498	501	493	70
District of Columbia	479	461	485	471	489	473	490	475	488	476	83
Florida	499	495	497	496	498	496	499	499	500	501	52
Georgia	480	473	483	477	484	477	486	481	486	482	64
Hawaii	484	505	483	507	485	510	483	512	483	513	55
Idaho	543	523	544	532	543	536	544	539	545	544	16
Illinois	540	540	563	574	564	575	562	578	564	581	13
Indiana	490	486	492	494	494	494	494	497	497	500	59
Iowa	587	588	589	595	590	600	589	601	593	601	5
Kansas	568	557	576	571	579	571	578	575	582	585	9
Kentucky	551	535	552	542	549	544	548	546	547	550	13
Louisiana	551	533	560	552	559	550	560	553	562	558	8
Maine	508	493	504	497	504	498	507	504	504	501	68
Maryland	509	501	506	503	507	504	507	507	506	508	65
Massachusetts	508	499	505	502	507	504	508	508	508	508	77
Michigan	532	533	559	565	557	565	557	566	558	569	11
Minnesota	546	549	580	591	582	593	582	592	585	598	9
Mississippi	557	539	572	557	569	557	567	551	562	549	4
Missouri	547	539	569	566	570	569	567	568	570	573	8
Montana	547	547	549	553	546	547	545	548	543	546	24
Nebraska	562	561	568	570	567	568	562	564	565	571	8
Nevada	517	510	511	508	508	507	508	509	510	513	33
New Hampshire	523	511	520	515	520	514	521	518	523	520	74
New Jersey	500	495	496	503	498	505	497	508	497	508	79
New Mexico	553	543	559	549	554	548	554	545	554	551	12
New York	497	495	495	498	497	499	495	502	495	503	76
North Carolina	478	470	488	482	490	486	490	488	490	492	62
North Dakota	572	569	587	602	596	599	588	595	590	599	5
Ohio	529	521	536	535	536	535	535	536	536	540	24
Oklahoma	558	542	565	553	566	557	568	560	568	564	8
Oregon	517	507	525	522	523	521	525	524	528	528	53
Pennsylvania	502	489	496	489	498	492	498	495	497	495	71
Rhode Island	508	496	502	490	501	491	499	493	501	495	72
South Carolina	477	468	478	473	480	474	479	474	478	473	61
South Dakota	585	573	579	576	574	566	574	570	584	581	5
Tennessee	560	543	571	560	563	552	564	556	564	557	13
Texas	494	490	495	501	495	500	494	501	494	501	51
Utah	572	553	585	576	583	575	576	570	572	570	4
Vermont	514	499	506	499	506	500	508	502	508	504	71
Virginia	507	498	504	494	507	496	506	497	507	499	66
Washington	525	517	519	517	519	519	523	523	524	526	53
West Virginia	528	519	525	509	526	506	524	508	525	513	18
Wisconsin	549	551	574	585	577	586	579	590	581	594	7
Wyoming	550	545	551	544	544	544	543	543	548	546	10
National Average	**505**	**501**	**504**	**506**	**505**	**508**	**505**	**511**	**505**	**512**	**43**

Note: In 1995, the College Board recentered the scoring scale for the SAT by reestablishing the original mean score of 500 on the 200-800 scale. The College Board states that comparing states or ranking them on the basis of SAT scores alone is invalid, and the College Board discourages doing so. (1) Based on number of high school graduates in 1998, as projected by the Western Interstate Commission for Higher Education, and number of students in the class of 1998 who took the SAT.

Top 50 Public Libraries in the U.S. and Canada

Source: Public Library Data Service, Statistical Report 1998, Public Library Association

Ranked at end of the 1997 fiscal year by population served.

Population served	Library name and location	No. of branches[1]	No. of holdings	Circulation	Annual acquisition expenditures
3,681,708	Los Angeles Public Library (CA)	66	5,743,103	10,964,844	$8,068,394
3,370,340	Los Angeles Public Library, County of (CA)	85	7,425,092	14,913,713	5,120,104
3,070,302	New York Public Library, The Branch Libraries (NY)	85	11,445,971	11,581,151	NA
2,783,726	Chicago Public Library (IL)	79	8,100,000	8,305,158	11,000,000
2,300,664	Brooklyn Public Library (NY)	59	6,630,186	10,201,587	7,253,790
1,951,000	Queens Borough Public Library (NY)	62	9,237,300	15,550,132	9,016,244
1,822,989	Houston Public Library (TX)	36	5,187,973	5,855,908	5,771,405
1,709,909	Miami-Dade Public Library System (FL)	30	3,357,879	9,561,834	3,979,546
1,585,577	Free Library of Philadelphia (PA)	52	7,891,532	6,503,585	7,051,719
1,423,729	Broward County Library System (FL)	32	2,044,766	6,914,151	4,566,267
1,336,449	Carnegie Library of Pittsburgh (PA)	19	6,582,144	3,014,520	1,607,079
1,310,500	San Antonio Public Library (TX)	18	1,754,291	3,740,166	2,466,348
1,218,700	San Diego Public Library (CA)	33	2,670,375	6,573,161	2,268,106
1,217,345	Phoenix Public Library (AZ)	12	1,811,933	6,191,053	3,011,189
1,140,590	Sacramento Public Library (CA)	22	1,424,871	3,593,687	2,438,285
1,108,229	Hawaii State Public Library System (HI)	49	3,077,276	7,568,174	1,651,606
1,090,600	Riverside City and County Public Library (CA)	27	1,788,065	3,650,781	441,426
1,087,393	King County Library System (WA)	40	3,677,923	13,265,885	5,046,366
1,047,350	Dallas Public Library (TX)	22	2,932,589	4,010,243	2,296,464
1,027,974	Detroit Public Library (MI)	25	2,804,428	1,654,320	2,703,970
1,016,376	Montréal, Bibliothèque de (Quebec)	24	2,476,605	5,502,638	2,021,538
1,003,464	Providence Public Library (RI)	9	1,189,815	757,376	718,700
975,000	San Bernardino County Library (CA)	27	1,098,000	2,983,900	876,000
968,532	Buffalo & Erie County Public Library (NY)	52	3,414,367	8,997,924	3,336,217
946,340	San Diego County Library (CA)	32	1,045,816	2,855,166	841,146
932,000	Fairfax County Public Library (VA)	19	2,666,615	9,468,607	3,544,952
910,855	Tampa-Hillsborough County Public Library (FL)	19	245,654	3,780,330	3,069,155
873,458	Memphis & Shelby County Public Libraries (TN)	22	1,818,285	3,708,563	1,833,620
868,000	San Jose Public Library System (CA)	17	1,371,952	6,034,303	2,924,515
857,616	Cincinnati & Hamilton County, Public Library of (OH)	41	8,582,637	12,502,014	6,467,686
843,000	St. Louis County Library (MO)	17	3,023,237	8,893,755	4,094,032
828,000	Montgomery County Dept. of Public Libraries (MD)	22	2,583,225	9,610,259	4,611,910
799,375	Tucson-Pima Library (AZ)	18	1,178,845	5,066,618	2,027,180
790,498	Calgary Public Library (Alberta)	14	2,305,733	10,804,376	2,778,924
780,694	Atlanta-Fulton Public Library (GA)	32	2,155,559	2,446,131	2,577,371
779,900	Contra Costa County Library (Pleasant Hill, CA)	22	1,254,784	3,658,228	1,410,442
779,534	Jacksonville Public Libraries (FL)	17	2,721,642	3,673,812	2,160,327
778,100	San Francisco Public Library (CA)	26	2,393,837	5,547,488	2,798,731
773,810	Prince George's County Memorial Library System (MD)	18	1,966,729	4,303,986	2,340,912
770,684	Indianapolis-Marion County Public Library (IN)	21	1,748,839	8,779,536	5,512,894
744,506	Orange County Library System (FL)	11	1,456,179	4,577,306	2,212,033
743,640	Columbus Metropolitan Library (OH)	20	2,433,636	11,811,189	6,142,432
717,500	Enoch Pratt Free Library (Baltimore, MD)	28	2,477,468	1,140,090	2,683,175
717,400	Macomb County Library (MI)	0	135,259	204,171	311,038
713,968	Rochester Public Library (NY)	10	1,051,452	1,638,291	1,065,132
711,658	Hennepin County Library (MN)	25	2,043,594	10,600,661	4,082,851
699,506	Baltimore County Public Library (MD)	15	1,777,905	10,680,044	3,769,547
664,937	Louisville Free Public Library (KY)	15	1,075,558	3,137,926	2,394,006
649,181	Palm Beach County Library System (FL)	14	1,037,282	4,620,560	3,560,249
637,049	Toronto Public Library (Ontario)	33	2,087,863	8,534,293	2,285,211

(1) Main branch not included. NA= not available.

Number of Public Libraries and Operating Income, by State

Source: Public Libraries Survey, National Center for Education Statistics, U.S. Dept. of Education

(data for fiscal year 1995 unless otherwise indicated; operating income in thousands)

State	No. of libraries[1]	Operating income[2]	State	No. of libraries[1]	Operating income[2]	State	No. of libraries[1]	Operating income[2]
Alabama	273	$49,601	Kentucky	188	$49,525	Ohio	684	$445,990
Alaska	102	19,080	Louisiana	322	67,552	Oklahoma	192	38,904
Arizona	159	78,420	Maine	273	20,735[3]	Oregon	201	72,302
Arkansas	196	25,328	Maryland	187	130,273	Pennsylvania	640	174,935[3]
California	1,030	610,849	Massachusetts	491	146,064	Rhode Island	74	23,882
Colorado	235	98,194	Michigan	659	195,329[3]	South Carolina	180	49,000
Connecticut	244	103,310	Minnesota	361	110,235	South Dakota	134	11,632
Delaware	30	10,816	Mississippi	243	25,479	Tennessee	284	57,020
District of Columbia	27	21,069	Missouri	346	102,432	Texas	753	198,802[3]
Florida	428	259,944	Montana	110	12,824	Utah	96	36,077
Georgia	366	102,960	Nebraska	283	27,440	Vermont	204	9,459[3]
Hawaii	49	22,942	Nevada	78	28,312	Virginia	308	137,800
Idaho	141	17,161	New Hampshire	238	23,451	Washington	309	161,427
Illinois	772	370,126	New Jersey	455	249,755	West Virginia	174	19,536
Indiana	427	168,992	New Mexico	92	20,361	Wisconsin	451	119,083
Iowa	554	51,603	New York	1,067	642,425	Wyoming	74	11,848
Kansas	372	53,805	North Carolina	352	103,220			
			North Dakota	86	6,762	**U.S. Total**	**15,994**	**$5,594,069**

(1) Includes central libraries and branches. (2) Some totals may be underestimated because of nonresponse. (3) These libraries reported data for fiscal year 1993 or 1994.

American Colleges and Universities

General Information for the 1997–98 Academic Year

Source: Peterson's, Copyright 1998

These listings include only accredited undergraduate degree-granting institutions in the United States and the U.S. territories that have a total institutional enrollment of 1,000 or more. Four-year colleges (those that award a bachelor's degree as their highest undergraduate degree) are listed first, followed by two-year colleges (those that award an associate as their highest or primary undergraduate degree). Individual institutions are alphabetized by full title except for "The" (for example, The University of Iowa is alphabetized under U, not under T or I). Data reported only for institutions that provided updated information on Peterson's Annual Survey of Undergraduate Institutions for the 1997–98 academic year.

All institutions are coeducational except those where the ZIP code is followed directly by: (1)–men only, (2)–primarily men, (3)–women only, (4)–primarily women.

Year is that of founding.

The Tuition & Fees column shows the annual tuition and required fees for full-time students, or the tuition and standard fees per credit hour (cr. hr.). Where tuition costs vary according to residence, the figure is given for the most local resident and is coded: (A)–area residents, (S)–state residents; all other figures apply to all students regardless of residence. Where annual expenses are expressed as a lump sum (including full-time tuition, mandatory fees, and room and board), the figure is coded: (C)–comprehensive fee. Room & Board is the average cost for one academic year. For both Tuition & Fees and Room & Board, figure listed is for the latest year available.

Control: 1–independent (nonprofit), 2–independent-religious, 3–proprietary (profit-making), 4–federal, 5–state, 6–commonweath (Puerto Rico), 7–territory (U.S. territories), 8–county, 9–district, 10–city, 11–state and local, 12–state-related. Degree means the highest degree offered (B–bachelor's, M–master's, F–first professional, D–doctorate).

Enrollment is the total number of matriculated undergraduate and (if applicable) graduate students.

Faculty is the total number of faculty members teaching undergraduate courses and (if applicable) graduate courses.

NA indicates that data are not available or not applicable.

Four-Year Colleges

Name, address	Year	Tuition & Fees	Room & Board	Control, Degree	Enrollment	Faculty
Abilene Christian U, Abilene, TX 79699-9100	1906	$9,180	$3,810	2-D	4,507	286
Acad of Art Coll, San Francisco, CA 94105-3410	1929	$14,910	NA	3-M	4,976	493
Adams State Coll, Alamosa, CO 81102	1921	$1,958 (S)	$4,424	5-M	2,331	151
Adelphi U, Garden City, NY 11530	1896	$14,720	$6,600	1-D	5,594	580
Adrian Coll, Adrian, MI 49221-2575	1859	$12,830	$4,120	2-B	1,000	92
Alabama Ag & Mech U, Normal, AL 35762-1357	1875	$2,168 (S)	$2,678	5-D	5,094	347
Alabama State U, Montgomery, AL 36101-0271	1867	$2,030 (S)	$3,300	5-M	5,273	324
Albany State U, Albany, GA 31705-2717	1903	$2,124 (S)	$3,225	5-M	3,226	173
Albertus Magnus Coll, New Haven, CT 06511-1189	1925	$17,262	$7,636	2-M	1,549	68
Albion Coll, Albion, MI 49224-1831	1835	$16,806	$4,980	2-B	1,500	117
Albright Coll, Reading, PA 19612-5234	1856	$18,310	$5,450	2-B	1,388	113
Alcorn State U, Lorman, MS 39096-9402	1871	$2,429 (S)	$2,324	5-M	2,847	207
Alfred U, Alfred, NY 14802-1205	1836	$8,602 (S)	$6,406	1-D	2,329	200
Allegheny Coll, Meadville, PA 16335	1815	$19,360	$4,720	2-B	1,890	199
Allegheny U of the Health Sciences, Philadelphia, PA 19102-1192	1848	$9,660	NA	1-D	3,283	1,446
Allentown Coll of St. Francis de Sales, Center Valley, PA 18034-9568	1964	$11,750	$5,470	2-M	2,236	108
Alma Coll, Alma, MI 48801-1599	1886	$13,823	$5,052	2-B	1,407	143
Alvernia Coll, Reading, PA 19607-1799	1958	$11,320	$5,200	2-B	1,214	136
Alverno Coll, Milwaukee, WI 53234-3922 (3)	1887	$9,722	$3,890	2-M	2,072	191
Amber U, Garland, TX 75041-5595	1971	$4,025	NA	2-M	1,561	65
American InterContinental U, Atlanta, GA 30326-1019	1977	$10,300	NA	3-M	1,016	66
American Intl Coll, Springfield, MA 01109-3189	1885	$11,244	$5,692	1-D	1,889	122
American Military U, Manassas Park, VA 20111	1991	$4,835	NA	3-M	1,115	130
American U, Washington, DC 20016-8001	1893	$18,555	$7,250	2-D	10,710	1,002
Amherst Coll, Amherst, MA 01002	1821	$23,027	$6,080	1-B	1,642	204
Anderson Coll, Anderson, SC 29621-4035	1911	$9,475	$4,145	2-B	1,012	86
Anderson U, Anderson, IN 46012-3495	1917	$13,360	$4,330	2-D	2,165	204
Andrews U, Berrien Springs, MI 49104	1874	$11,577	$3,510	2-D	3,152	318
Angelo State U, San Angelo, TX 76909	1928	$2,242 (S)	$3,908	5-M	6,234	266
Anna Maria Coll, Paxton, MA 01612	1946	$12,240	$5,256	2-M	1,668	84
Appalachian State U, Boone, NC 28608	1899	$1,840 (S)	$3,008	5-D	12,108	828
Aquinas Coll, Grand Rapids, MI 49506-1799	1886	$12,950	$4,324	2-M	2,458	187
Arizona State U, Tempe, AZ 85287	1885	$2,059 (S)	$4,500	5-D	44,255	1,972
Arizona State U West, Phoenix, AZ 85069-7100	1984	$2,059 (S)	NA	5-M	4,807	279
Arkansas State U, State University, AR 72467	1909	$2,280 (S)	$2,840	5-D	10,012	513
Arkansas Tech U, Russellville, AR 72801-2222	1909	$2,126 (S)	$2,676	5-M	4,238	285
Armstrong Atlantic State U, Savannah, GA 31419-1997	1935	$1,836 (S)	$4,116	5-M	5,696	380
Art Ctr Coll of Design, Pasadena, CA 91103-1999	1930	$17,180	NA	1-M	1,433	385
Asbury Coll, Wilmore, KY 40390-1198	1890	$12,020	$3,390	2-B	1,258	118
Ashland U, Ashland, OH 44805-3702	1878	$13,601	$5,116	2-F	5,737	213
Assumption Coll, Worcester, MA 01615-0005	1904	$15,595	$6,400	2-M	2,592	221
Athens State Coll, Athens, AL 35611-1902	1822	$1,845 (S)	NA	5-B	2,671	135
Auburn U, Auburn University, AL 36849-0001	1856	$2,610 (S)	NA	5-D	21,505	1,262
Auburn U Montgomery, Montgomery, AL 36124-4023	1967	$2,289 (S)	NA	5-D	5,526	359
Audrey Cohen Coll, New York, NY 10013-1919	1964	$8,860	NA	1-M	1,116	94
Augsburg Coll, Minneapolis, MN 55454-1351	1869	$14,616	$5,134	2-M	2,817	325
Augustana Coll, Rock Island, IL 61201-2296	1860	$15,300	$4,689	2-B	2,277	191
Augustana Coll, Sioux Falls, SD 57197	1860	$13,112	$3,903	2-M	1,691	161
Augusta State U, Augusta, GA 30904-2200	1925	$1,926 (S)	NA	5-M	5,479	274
Aurora U, Aurora, IL 60506-4892	1893	$11,310	$4,320	1-M	2,121	251
Austin Coll, Sherman, TX 75090-4440	1849	$14,205	$5,393	2-M	1,202	98
Austin Peay State U, Clarksville, TN 37044-0001	1927	$2,280 (S)	$3,260	5-M	7,803	492
Averett Coll, Danville, VA 24541-3692	1859	$12,500	$4,200	2-M	2,361	302
Avila Coll, Kansas City, MO 64145-1698	1916	$10,860	$4,400	2-M	1,246	138

Name, address	Year	Tuition & Fees	Room & Board	Control, Degree	Enroll-ment	Faculty
Azusa Pacific U, Azusa, CA 91702-7000	1899	$13,947	$4,482	2-D	5,069	501
Babson Coll, Babson Park, MA 02157-0310	1919	$20,365	$8,100	1-M	3,336	204
Baker Coll of Flint, Flint, MI 48507-5508	1911	$6,300	NA	1-B	3,934	156
Baker Coll of Mount Clemens, Clinton Township, MI 48035-4701	1990	$5,850	NA	1-B	1,261	64
Baker Coll of Muskegon, Muskegon, MI 49442-3497	1888	$6,480	NA	1-B	2,234	113
Baker Coll of Owosso, Owosso, MI 48867-4400	1984	$5,850	NA	1-B	1,850	109
Baldwin-Wallace Coll, Berea, OH 44017-2088	1845	$13,275	$4,881	2-M	4,539	548
Ball State U, Muncie, IN 47306-1099	1918	$3,414 (S)	$4,120	5-D	19,419	1,086
Bard Coll, Annandale-on-Hudson, NY 12504	1860	$22,220	$6,812	1-D	1,201	160
Barnard Coll, New York, NY 10027-6598 (3)	1889	$20,976	$8,736	1-B	2,313	285
Barry U, Miami Shores, FL 33161-6695	1940	$13,550	$5,850	2-D	6,899	552
Barton Coll, Wilson, NC 27893	1902	$10,150	$3,778	2-B	1,303	80
Baruch Coll of the City U of New York, New York, NY 10010-5585	1919	$3,330 (S)	NA	11-D	15,071	770
Bates Coll, Lewiston, ME 04240-6028	1855	$28,650 (C)	NA	1-B	1,611	176
Bayamón Central U, Bayamón, PR 00960-1725	1970	$4,025	NA	2-M	2,961	199
Bayamón Technological U Coll, Bayamón, PR 00959-1919	1971	$1,090 (S)	NA	6-B	5,826	247
Baylor U, Waco, TX 76798	1845	$10,266	$4,566	2-D	12,472	655
Beaver Coll, Glenside, PA 19038-3295	1853	$15,840	$6,520	2-M	2,705	290
Belhaven Coll, Jackson, MS 39202-1789	1883	$9,370	$3,380	2-M	1,317	80
Bellarmine Coll, Louisville, KY 40205-0671	1950	$10,970	$3,580	2-M	2,678	184
Bellevue U, Bellevue, NE 68005-3098	1965	$3,650	NA	1-M	2,928	93
Belmont U, Nashville, TN 37212-3757	1951	$10,300	$3,890	2-M	2,986	371
Beloit Coll, Beloit, WI 53511-5596	1846	$19,050	$4,140	1-B	1,292	134
Bemidji State U, Bemidji, MN 56601-2699	1919	$3,118 (S)	$3,084	5-M	4,650	201
Benedict Coll, Columbia, SC 29204	1870	$7,502	$3,982	2-B	2,208	142
Benedictine U, Lisle, IL 60532-0900	1887	$12,330	$4,610	2-D	2,709	245
Bentley Coll, Waltham, MA 02154-4705	1917	$16,495	$6,755	1-M	5,946	356
Berea Coll, Berea, KY 40404	1855	$195	$3,330	1-B	1,464	140
Berklee Coll of Music, Boston, MA 02215-3693	1945	$15,100	$7,890	1-B	2,933	359
Berry Coll, Mount Berry, GA 30149-0159	1902	$10,210	$4,536	1-M	2,070	126
Bethel Coll, Mishawaka, IN 46545-5591	1947	$11,500	$3,700	2-M	1,526	134
Bethel Coll, St. Paul, MN 55112-6999	1871	$13,840	$4,950	2-M	2,612	228
Bethune-Cookman Coll, Daytona Beach, FL 32114-3099	1904	$8,047	$4,984	2-B	2,523	214
Biola U, La Mirada, CA 90639-0001	1908	$14,286	$4,902	2-D	3,257	269
Birmingham-Southern Coll, Birmingham, AL 35254	1856	$13,960	$5,200	2-M	1,531	133
Black Hills State U, Spearfish, SD 57799-9502	1883	$2,878 (S)	$2,614	5-M	3,445	105
Bloomfield Coll, Bloomfield, NJ 07003-9981	1868	$9,650	$4,850	2-B	1,997	215
Bloomsburg U of Pennsylvania, Bloomsburg, PA 17815-1905	1839	$4,278 (S)	$3,368	5-M	7,499	395
Bluefield State Coll, Bluefield, WV 24701-2198	1895	$2,044 (S)	NA	5-B	2,513	157
Bluffton Coll, Bluffton, OH 45817-1196	1899	$12,375	$5,121	2-M	1,053	89
Boise State U, Boise, ID 83725-0399	1932	$2,294 (S)	$3,264	5-D	15,433	860
Boricua Coll, New York, NY 10032-1560	1974	$6,300	NA	1-M	1,190	116
Boston Coll, Chestnut Hill, MA 02167-9991	1863	$20,292	$7,770	2-D	13,640	1,117
Boston U, Boston, MA 02215	1839	$23,148	$7,870	1-D	29,387	3,013
Bowdoin Coll, Brunswick, ME 04011-2546	1794	$22,905	$6,115	1-B	1,605	163
Bowie State U, Bowie, MD 20715	1865	$3,357 (S)	$4,253	5-M	5,167	251
Bowling Green State U, Bowling Green, OH 43403	1910	$4,422 (S)	$4,626	5-D	17,328	866
Bradley U, Peoria, IL 61625-0002	1897	$12,690	$4,690	1-M	5,861	475
Brandeis U, Waltham, MA 02254-9110	1948	$22,851	$6,970	1-D	4,276	498
Brenau U, Gainesville, GA 30501-3697 (4)	1878	$10,740	$6,610	1-M	2,366	211
Brewton-Parker Coll, Mt. Vernon, GA 30445-0197	1904	$5,760	$2,670	2-B	1,652	183
Briar Cliff Coll, Sioux City, IA 51104-2100	1930	$11,880	$4,180	2-B	1,011	71
Bridgewater Coll, Bridgewater, VA 22812-1599	1880	$13,270	$5,970	2-B	1,066	91
Bridgewater State Coll, Bridgewater, MA 02325-0001	1840	$3,324 (S)	$4,343	5-M	8,926	492
Brigham Young U, Provo, UT 84602-1001	1875	$2,630	$4,130	2-D	32,161	1,828
Brigham Young U–Hawaii Campus, Laie, Oahu, HI 96762-1294	1955	$2,665	$4,900	2-B	2,294	149
Brooklyn Coll of the City U of New York, Brooklyn, NY 11210-2889	1930	$3,413 (S)	NA	11-M	15,007	980
Brown U, Providence, RI 02912	1764	$23,124	$6,776	1-D	7,579	721
Bryant Coll, Smithfield, RI 02917-1284	1863	$14,800	$6,700	1-M	3,266	191
Bryn Mawr Coll, Bryn Mawr, PA 19010-2899 (3)	1885	$21,430	$7,500	1-D	1,826	221
Bucknell U, Lewisburg, PA 17837	1846	$21,210	$5,200	1-M	3,543	280
Buena Vista U, Storm Lake, IA 50588	1891	$14,848	$4,375	2-M	2,693	100
Butler U, Indianapolis, IN 46208-3485	1855	$15,690	$5,430	1-M	3,911	403
Cabrini Coll, Radnor, PA 19087-3698	1957	$13,200	$6,830	2-M	2,056	198
Caldwell Coll, Caldwell, NJ 07006-6195	1939	$10,800	$5,300	2-M	1,827	144
California Baptist Coll, Riverside, CA 92504-3206	1950	$8,236	$4,594	2-M	2,009	178
California Coll of Arts & Crafts, San Francisco, CA 94107	1907	$15,052	$4,894	1-M	1,073	239
California Inst of Technology, Pasadena, CA 91125-0001	1891	$18,816	$5,700	1-D	1,925	353
California Inst of the Arts, Valencia, CA 91355-2340	1961	$18,185	NA	1-M	1,140	279
California Lutheran U, Thousand Oaks, CA 91360-2787	1959	$15,415	$5,985	2-M	2,590	209
California Polytechnic State U, San Luis Obispo, San Luis Obispo, CA 93407	1901	$2,231 (S)	$5,553	5-M	16,735	951
California State Polytechnic U, Pomona, Pomona, CA 91768-2557	1938	$1,923 (S)	$5,300	5-M	17,246	972
California State U, Bakersfield, Bakersfield, CA 93311-1099	1970	$1,965 (S)	$4,185	5-M	5,717	315
California State U, Chico, Chico, CA 95929-0722	1887	$2,075 (S)	$5,129	5-M	14,247	890
California State U, Dominguez Hills, Carson, CA 90747-0001	1960	$1,821 (S)	NA	5-M	12,378	724
California State U, Fresno, Fresno, CA 93740	1911	$1,806 (S)	$5,610	5-D	18,113	1,099
California State U, Fullerton, Fullerton, CA 92834-9480	1957	$1,947 (S)	NA	5-M	24,906	1,457
California State U, Hayward, Hayward, CA 94542-3000	1957	$1,827 (S)	NA	5-M	12,863	695
California State U, Long Beach, Long Beach, CA 90840-0119	1949	$1,846 (S)	$5,200	5-M	27,809	1,470
California State U, Los Angeles, Los Angeles, CA 90032-8530	1947	$1,757 (S)	NA	5-M	19,160	1,123
California State U, Northridge, Northridge, CA 91330	1958	$1,980 (S)	NA	5-M	27,653	1,480
California State U, Sacramento, Sacramento, CA 95819-6048	1947	$1,982 (S)	$5,100	5-M	23,481	1,336
California State U, San Bernardino, San Bernardino, CA 92407-2397	1965	$1,896 (S)	$4,174	5-M	13,280	571
California State U, San Marcos, San Marcos, CA 92096	1990	$1,720 (S)	NA	5-M	4,678	323
California State U, Stanislaus, Turlock, CA 95382	1957	$1,915 (S)	$5,461	5-M	6,213	345
California U of Pennsylvania, California, PA 15419-1394	1852	$4,475 (S)	$4,106	5-M	5,783	332
Calvin Coll, Grand Rapids, MI 49546-4388	1876	$12,250	$4,340	2-M	4,071	317

Name, address	Year	Tuition & Fees	Room & Board	Control, Degree	Enroll-ment	Faculty
Cameron U, Lawton, OK 73505-6377	1908	$2,180 (S)	$2,600	5-M	5,147	382
Campbellsville U, Campbellsville, KY 42718-2799	1906	$7,302	$3,440	2-M	1,521	117
Campbell U, Buies Creek, NC 27506	1887	$10,003	$3,610	2-D	3,359	349
Canisius Coll, Buffalo, NY 14208-1098	1870	$13,882	$5,950	2-M	4,490	393
Capital U, Columbus, OH 43209-2394	1830	$14,760	$4,200	2-F	3,988	397
Cardinal Stritch U, Milwaukee, WI 53217-3985	1937	$10,130	$4,280	2-M	5,316	572
Carleton Coll, Northfield, MN 55057-4001	1866	$21,885	$4,440	1-B	1,880	197
Carlow Coll, Pittsburgh, PA 15213-3165 (4)	1929	$11,708	$4,692	2-M	2,377	206
Carnegie Mellon U, Pittsburgh, PA 15213-3891	1900	$20,375	$6,225	1-D	7,912	810
Carroll Coll, Helena, MT 59625-0002	1909	$11,490	$4,540	2-B	1,206	107
Carroll Coll, Waukesha, WI 53186-5593	1846	$14,420	$4,440	2-M	2,521	189
Carson-Newman Coll, Jefferson City, TN 37760	1851	$10,610	$3,830	2-M	2,308	193
Carthage Coll, Kenosha, WI 53140-1994	1847	$15,365	$4,415	2-M	2,104	124
Case Western Reserve U, Cleveland, OH 44106	1826	$17,940	$5,050	1-D	9,908	1,949
Castleton State Coll, Castleton, VT 05735	1787	$4,506 (S)	$5,086	5-M	1,840	169
Catawba Coll, Salisbury, NC 28144-2488	1851	$11,352	$4,500	2-M	1,307	96
The Catholic U of America, Washington, DC 20064	1887	$17,110	$7,036	2-D	5,616	648
Cedar Crest Coll, Allentown, PA 18104-6196 (3)	1867	$15,820	$5,745	2-B	1,675	147
Cedarville Coll, Cedarville, OH 45314-0601	1887	$9,312	$4,716	2-B	2,559	173
Central Bible Coll, Springfield, MO 65803-1096	1922	$4,750	$3,250	2-B	1,014	63
Central Coll, Pella, IA 50219-1999	1853	$12,802	$4,350	2-B	1,120	127
Central Connecticut State U, New Britain, CT 06050-4010	1849	$3,614 (S)	$5,300	5-M	11,625	768
Central Methodist Coll, Fayette, MO 65248-1198	1854	$10,710	$4,150	2-M	1,292	90
Central Michigan U, Mount Pleasant, MI 48859	1892	$3,546 (S)	$4,320	5-D	24,747	859
Central Missouri State U, Warrensburg, MO 64093	1871	$2,640 (S)	$4,080	5-M	10,320	498
Central State U, Wilberforce, OH 45384	1887	$3,318 (S)	$4,695	5-M	1,051	121
Central Washington U, Ellensburg, WA 98926	1891	$2,826 (S)	$4,269	5-M	8,438	417
Centre Coll, Danville, KY 40422-1394	1819	$14,600	$4,800	1-B	1,001	101
Chadron State Coll, Chadron, NE 69337	1911	$2,148 (S)	$3,060	5-M	2,931	163
Chaminade U of Honolulu, Honolulu, HI 96816-1578	1955	$10,900	$5,200	2-M	2,613	205
Chapman U, Orange, CA 92866	1861	$18,750	$6,806	2-F	3,806	371
Charleston Southern U, Charleston, SC 29423-8087	1964	$9,248	$3,562	2-M	2,481	133
Chestnut Hill Coll, Philadelphia, PA 19118-2693 (3)	1924	$14,265	$6,200	2-D	1,429	151
Cheyney U of Pennsylvania, Cheyney, PA 19319	1837	$4,023 (S)	$4,528	5-M	1,430	114
Christian Brothers U, Memphis, TN 38104-5581	1871	$11,930	$3,730	2-M	1,869	162
Christopher Newport U, Newport News, VA 23606-2998	1960	$3,466 (S)	$4,650	5-M	4,878	306
The Citadel, The Military Coll of South Carolina, Charleston, SC 29409	1842	$3,499 (S)	$3,950	5-M	3,766	199
City Coll of the City U of New York, New York, NY 10031-6977	1847	$3,309 (S)	NA	11-D	12,061	981
City U, Bellevue, WA 98004-6442	1973	$6,000	NA	1-M	11,162	1,369
Claflin Coll, Orangeburg, SC 29115	1869	$5,580	$3,044	2-B	1,005	79
Clarion U of Pennsylvania, Clarion, PA 16214	1867	$4,419 (S)	$3,330	5-M	5,948	376
Clarke Coll, Dubuque, IA 52001-3198	1843	$12,439	$4,555	2-M	1,160	122
Clarkson U, Potsdam, NY 13699	1896	$18,593	$6,510	1-D	2,745	183
Clark U, Worcester, MA 01610-1477	1887	$20,940	$4,250	1-D	3,083	260
Clayton Coll & State U, Morrow, GA 30260-0285	1969	$2,168 (S)	NA	5-B	4,713	239
Clemson U, Clemson, SC 29634	1889	$3,392 (S)	$3,888	5-D	16,396	1,339
Cleveland State U, Cleveland, OH 44115-2440	1964	$3,528 (S)	$4,410	5-D	15,655	850
Clinch Valley Coll of the U of Virginia, Wise, VA 24293	1954	$3,348 (S)	$4,284	5-B	1,515	97
Coastal Carolina U, Conway, SC 29528-6054	1954	$3,100 (S)	$4,640	5-M	4,408	268
Coe Coll, Cedar Rapids, IA 52402-5070	1851	$16,320	$4,570	2-M	1,318	122
Colby Coll, Waterville, ME 04901-8840	1813	$29,190 (C)	NA	1-B	1,753	157
Coleman Coll, La Mesa, CA 91942-1532	1963	$9,000	NA	1-M	1,071	68
Colgate U, Hamilton, NY 13346-1386	1819	$22,770	$6,110	1-M	2,847	258
Coll Misericordia, Dallas, PA 18612-1098	1924	$13,830	$6,150	2-M	1,697	158
Coll of Aeronautics, Flushing, NY 11371 (2)	1932	$7,600	NA	1-B	1,102	57
Coll of Charleston, Charleston, SC 29424-0002	1770	$3,290 (S)	$3,850	5-B	9,252	663
Coll of Mount St. Joseph, Cincinnati, OH 45233-1670	1920	$11,950	$5,050	2-M	2,213	225
Coll of Mount Saint Vincent, Riverdale, NY 10471-1093	1911	$13,580	$6,430	1-M	1,597	146
The Coll of New Jersey, Ewing, NJ 08628	1855	$4,843 (S)	$5,996	5-M	6,780	624
Coll of New Rochelle, New Rochelle, NY 10805-2308 (4)	1904	$11,100	$5,700	1-M	7,065	219
Coll of Notre Dame, Belmont, CA 94002-1997	1851	$14,976	$6,500	2-M	1,782	194
Coll of Notre Dame of Maryland, Baltimore, MD 21210-2476 (3)	1873	$14,086	$6,130	2-M	3,100	90
Coll of Our Lady of the Elms, Chicopee, MA 01013-2839	1928	$12,950	$5,000	2-M	1,098	101
Coll of Saint Benedict, Saint Joseph, MN 56374 (3)	1887	$14,758	$4,706	2-B	1,980	163
Coll of St. Catherine, St. Paul, MN 55105-1789 (3)	1905	$14,258	$4,230	2-M	2,897	191
Coll of Saint Elizabeth, Morristown, NJ 07960-6989 (4)	1899	$13,060	$5,950	2-M	1,791	167
Coll of Saint Mary, Omaha, NE 68124-2377 (3)	1923	$11,814	$4,290	2-B	1,001	148
The Coll of Saint Rose, Albany, NY 12203-1419	1920	$11,719	$5,966	1-M	3,973	284
Coll of St. Scholastica, Duluth, MN 55811-4199	1912	$13,995	$3,957	2-M	2,030	170
Coll of Santa Fe, Santa Fe, NM 87505-7634	1947	$13,240	$4,724	1-M	1,417	204
Coll of Staten Island of the City U of New York, Staten Island, NY 10314-6600	1955	$3,326 (S)	NA	11-M	12,040	854
Coll of the Holy Cross, Worcester, MA 01610-2395	1843	$21,080	$7,100	2-B	2,730	261
Coll of the Ozarks, Point Lookout, MO 65726	1906	$150	$2,200	2-B	1,563	110
The Coll of West Virginia, Beckley, WV 25802-2830	1933	$3,600	$3,960	1-B	1,981	142
Coll of William & Mary, Williamsburg, VA 23187-8795	1693	$5,032 (S)	$4,586	5-D	7,572	587
The Coll of Wooster, Wooster, OH 44691	1866	$19,300	$5,070	2-B	1,714	144
Colorado Christian U, Lakewood, CO 80226-7499	1914	$10,010	$4,560	2-M	1,910	236
The Colorado Coll, Colorado Springs, CO 80903-3294	1874	$19,980	$5,100	1-M	2,041	187
The Colorado Inst of Art, Denver, CO 80203-2903	1952	$10,260	$5,490	3-B	1,694	130
Colorado School of Mines, Golden, CO 80401-1887	1874	$5,069 (S)	$4,730	5-D	3,199	290
Colorado State U, Fort Collins, CO 80523-0015	1870	$3,083 (S)	$5,050	5-D	22,344	939
Colorado Tech U, Colorado Springs, CO 80907-3896	1965	$6,838	NA	3-D	1,793	92
Columbia Coll, Chicago, IL 60605-1997	1890	$8,618	NA	1-M	8,473	1,148
Columbia Coll, Columbia, MO 65216-0002	1851	$9,244	$4,144	2-M	7,435	85
Columbia Coll, Columbia, SC 29203-5998 (3)	1854	$12,150	$4,300	2-M	1,368	90
Columbia Coll, New York, NY 10027	1754	$22,650	$7,344	1-B	3,763	527
Columbia Union Coll, Takoma Park, MD 20912-7794	1904	$11,790	$4,150	2-B	1,212	43

Name, address	Year	Tuition & Fees	Room & Board	Control, Degree	Enroll-ment	Faculty
Columbia U, School of Engineering & Applied Sci, New York, NY 10027	1864	$22,650	$7,344	1-D	1,178	95
Columbus Coll of Art & Design, Columbus, OH 43215-1758	1879	$11,880	$5,800	1-B	1,547	152
Columbus State U, Columbus, GA 31907-5645	1958	$2,463 (S)	$3,825	5-M	5,405	339
Concord Coll, Athens, WV 24712-1000	1872	$2,310 (S)	$3,708	5-B	2,780	151
Concordia Coll, Moorhead, MN 56562	1891	$12,655	$3,645	2-B	2,931	270
Concordia Coll, Seward, NE 68434-1599	1894	$11,310	$3,786	2-M	1,191	114
Concordia U, Irvine, CA 92612-3299	1972	$14,550	$5,380	2-M	1,063	104
Concordia U, River Forest, IL 60305-1499	1864	$11,987	$5,024	2-M	1,860	193
Concordia U at St. Paul, St. Paul, MN 55104-5494	1893	$11,980	$4,500	2-M	1,347	117
Connecticut Coll, New London, CT 06320-4196	1911	$28,475 (C)	NA	1-M	1,857	174
Converse Coll, Spartanburg, SC 29302-0006 (3)	1889	$14,445	$4,080	1-M	1,474	83
Coppin State Coll, Baltimore, MD 21216-3698	1900	$3,624 (S)	$4,884	5-M	3,540	202
Cornell Coll, Mount Vernon, IA 52314-1098	1853	$17,840	$4,850	2-B	1,079	133
Cornell U, Ithaca, NY 14853-0001	1865	$9,374 (S)	$7,110	1-D	18,428	1,526
Cornerstone Coll, Grand Rapids, MI 49505-5897	1941	$10,026	$4,392	2-B	1,160	106
Creighton U, Omaha, NE 68178-0001	1878	$12,756	$4,940	2-D	6,292	835
Cumberland Coll, Williamsburg, KY 40769-1372	1889	$8,430	$3,776	2-M	1,698	91
Cumberland U, Lebanon, TN 37087-3554	1842	$8,190	$3,400	1-M	1,150	91
Curry Coll, Milton, MA 02186-9984	1879	$15,700	$5,815	1-M	1,909	210
Daemen Coll, Amherst, NY 14226-3592	1947	$10,980	$5,500	1-M	1,914	167
Dakota State U, Madison, SD 57042-1799	1881	$3,027 (S)	$2,694	5-B	1,333	78
Dallas Baptist U, Dallas, TX 75211-9299	1965	$7,800	$3,422	2-M	3,493	230
Daniel Webster Coll, Nashua, NH 03063-1300	1965	$13,845	$5,662	1-B	1,072	77
Dartmouth Coll, Hanover, NH 03755	1769	$23,012	$6,495	1-D	5,407	487
Davenport Coll of Business, Grand Rapids, MI 49503	1866	$8,508	NA	1-B	2,381	136
Davenport Coll of Business, Lansing Campus, Lansing, MI 48933	1979	$8,418	NA	1-B	1,153	105
David Lipscomb U, Nashville, TN 37204-3951	1891	$8,470	$3,910	2-M	2,546	194
David N. Myers Coll, Cleveland, OH 44115-1096	1848	$7,800	NA	1-B	1,145	85
Davidson Coll, Davidson, NC 28036-1719	1837	$20,595	$5,918	2-B	1,623	155
Delaware State U, Dover, DE 19901-2277	1891	$2,970 (S)	$4,862	5-M	3,320	174
Delaware Valley Coll, Doylestown, PA 18901-2697	1896	$14,929	$5,655	1-B	2,089	129
Delta State U, Cleveland, MS 38733-0001	1925	$2,354 (S)	$2,400	5-D	4,012	292
Denison U, Granville, OH 43023	1831	$20,250	$5,370	1-B	2,025	166
DePaul U, Chicago, IL 60604-2287	1898	$13,490	$5,841	2-D	17,804	1,354
DePauw U, Greencastle, IN 46135-1772	1837	$17,050	$5,616	2-B	2,334	217
Detroit Coll of Business, Dearborn, MI 48126-3799	1962	$6,264	NA	1-M	3,343	276
Detroit Coll of Business–Flint, Flint, MI 48504-1700	1974	$4,644	NA	1-B	1,015	120
Detroit Coll of Business, Warren Campus, Warren, MI 48092-5209	1962	$6,264	NA	1-B	2,095	147
DeVry Inst of Technology, Addison, IL 60101-6106	1982	$7,308	NA	3-B	3,712	121
DeVry Inst of Technology, Chicago, IL 60618-5994	1931	$7,308	NA	3-B	3,492	171
DeVry Inst of Technology, Columbus, OH 43209-2705	1952	$7,308	NA	3-B	2,883	98
DeVry Inst of Technology, Decatur, GA 30030-2198	1969	$7,308	NA	3-B	2,889	157
DeVry Inst of Technology, Irving, TX 75063-2440	1969	$7,308	NA	3-B	2,640	148
DeVry Inst of Technology, Kansas City, MO 64131-3698	1931	$7,308	NA	3-B	2,414	92
DeVry Inst of Technology, Long Beach, CA 90806	1984	$7,308	NA	3-B	1,814	91
DeVry Inst of Technology, Phoenix, AZ 85021-2995	1967	$7,308	NA	3-B	3,252	118
DeVry Inst of Technology, Pomona, CA 91768-2642	1983	$7,308	NA	3-B	3,307	142
Dickinson Coll, Carlisle, PA 17013-2896	1773	$21,600	$5,840	1-B	1,842	186
Dickinson State U, Dickinson, ND 58601-4896	1918	$2,131 (S)	$2,618	5-B	1,736	108
Doane Coll, Crete, NE 68333-2430	1872	$11,450	$3,450	2-M	1,809	104
Dominican Coll of San Rafael, San Rafael, CA 94901-2298	1890	$15,424	$6,968	1-M	1,465	185
Dominican U, River Forest, IL 60305-1099	1901	$13,700	$4,880	2-M	1,800	180
Dordt Coll, Sioux Center, IA 51250-1697	1955	$11,450	$3,030	2-M	1,301	95
Dowling Coll, Oakdale, NY 11769-1999	1955	$12,630	NA	1-M	3,489	424
Drake U, Des Moines, IA 50311-4516	1881	$15,200	$4,970	1-D	5,184	269
Drew U, Madison, NJ 07940-1493	1867	$21,396	$6,114	2-D	2,305	255
Drexel U, Philadelphia, PA 19104-2875	1891	$15,048	$7,266	1-D	10,455	832
Drury Coll, Springfield, MO 65802-3791	1873	$10,060	$3,856	1-M	1,683	122
Duke U, Durham, NC 27708-0586	1838	$22,173	$6,853	2-D	11,581	2,100
Duquesne U, Pittsburgh, PA 15282-0001	1878	$14,066	$5,978	2-D	9,500	672
D'Youville Coll, Buffalo, NY 14201-1084	1908	$10,040	$4,760	1-M	1,832	161
Earlham Coll, Richmond, IN 47374-4095	1847	$18,618	$4,544	2-B	1,025	132
East Carolina U, Greenville, NC 27858-4353	1907	$1,848 (S)	$3,680	5-D	18,271	1,351
East Central U, Ada, OK 74820-6899	1909	$1,812 (S)	$2,066	5-M	4,087	225
Eastern Coll, St. Davids, PA 19087-3696	1952	$13,200	$5,654	2-M	2,496	230
Eastern Connecticut State U, Willimantic, CT 06226-2295	1889	$3,838 (S)	$5,048	5-M	4,632	310
Eastern Illinois U, Charleston, IL 61920-3099	1895	$3,112 (S)	$3,919	5-M	11,777	670
Eastern Kentucky U, Richmond, KY 40475-3101	1906	$2,060 (S)	$3,240	5-M	15,424	966
Eastern Mennonite U, Harrisonburg, VA 22802-2462	1917	$12,600	$4,700	2-F	1,225	129
Eastern Michigan U, Ypsilanti, MI 48197	1849	$3,529 (S)	$4,528	5-D	22,730	1,202
Eastern Nazarene Coll, Quincy, MA 02170-2999	1918	$11,440	$3,975	2-M	1,508	67
Eastern New Mexico U, Portales, NM 88130	1934	$1,716 (S)	$2,942	5-M	3,495	226
Eastern Oregon U, La Grande, OR 97850-2899	1929	$3,231	$4,165	5-M	1,945	103
Eastern Washington U, Cheney, WA 99004-2431	1882	$2,622 (S)	$4,294	5-M	7,537	349
East Stroudsburg U of Pennsylvania, East Stroudsburg, PA 18301	1893	$4,322 (S)	$3,720	5-M	5,687	271
East Tennessee State U, Johnson City, TN 37614-0734	1911	$2,100 (S)	$2,520	5-D	11,596	935
East Texas Baptist U, Marshall, TX 75670-1498	1912	$6,750	$3,098	2-M	1,292	103
Eckerd Coll, St. Petersburg, FL 33711	1958	$17,130	$4,660	2-B	1,443	124
Edgewood Coll, Madison, WI 53711-1998	1927	$10,280	$4,380	2-M	1,957	170
Edinboro U of Pennsylvania, Edinboro, PA 16444	1857	$4,193 (S)	$3,674	5-M	7,083	414
Elizabeth City State U, Elizabeth City, NC 27909-7806	1891	$1,720 (S)	$3,232	5-B	2,000	149
Elizabethtown Coll, Elizabethtown, PA 17022-2298	1899	$16,930	$4,900	2-B	1,703	164
Elmhurst Coll, Elmhurst, IL 60126-3296	1871	$11,900	$5,000	2-B	2,842	177
Elmira Coll, Elmira, NY 14901	1855	$20,276	$6,690	1-M	1,958	74
Elon Coll, Elon College, NC 27244	1889	$11,542	$4,170	2-M	3,685	260
Embry-Riddle Aeronautical U, Prescott, AZ 86301-3720	1978	$9,920	$4,950	1-B	1,512	83
Embry-Riddle Aeronautical U, Daytona Beach, FL 32114-3900	1926	$9,890	$4,600	1-M	4,586	226

Name, address	Year	Tuition & Fees	Room & Board	Control, Degree	Enroll-ment	Faculty
Embry-Riddle Aeronautical U, Extended Campus, Daytona Beach, FL 32114	1970	$1,590	NA	1-M	6,623	2,200
Emerson Coll, Boston, MA 02116-1511	1880	$17,826	$8,250	1-D	3,885	285
Emmanuel Coll, Boston, MA 02115 (3)	1919	$14,550	$6,785	2-M	1,552	108
Emory U, Atlanta, GA 30322-1100	1836	$21,120	$6,800	2-D	11,109	2,486
Emporia State U, Emporia, KS 66801-5087	1863	$1,982 (S)	$3,560	5-D	5,320	310
Endicott Coll, Beverly, MA 01915-2096	1939	$13,508	$7,160	1-M	1,270	161
Evangel Coll, Springfield, MO 65802-2191	1955	$8,850	$3,550	2-B	1,616	122
The Evergreen State Coll, Olympia, WA 98505	1967	$2,742 (S)	$4,530	5-M	4,084	173
Fairfield U, Fairfield, CT 06430-5195	1942	$18,310	$7,024	2-M	5,179	384
Fairleigh Dickinson U, Florham-Madison Campus, Madison, NJ 07940	1942	$14,122	$6,040	1-M	3,400	240
Fairmont State Coll, Fairmont, WV 26554	1865	$2,040 (S)	$3,600	5-B	6,623	457
Fashion Inst of Technology, New York, NY 10001-5992	1944	$2,710 (S)	$5,425	11-M	11,696	841
Faulkner U, Montgomery, AL 36109-3398	1942	$6,980	$3,700	2-F	2,420	131
Felician Coll, Lodi, NJ 07644-2198	1942	$10,012	$5,400	2-M	1,160	97
Ferris State U, Big Rapids, MI 49307-2742	1884	$3,908 (S)	$4,792	5-F	9,468	494
Finch U of Health Scis/The Chicago Medical School, North Chicago, IL 60064	1912	$11,342	NA	1-D	1,428	354
Fitchburg State Coll, Fitchburg, MA 01420-2697	1894	$3,346 (S)	$4,410	5-M	5,847	305
Flagler Coll, St. Augustine, FL 32085-1027	1968	$5,950	$3,680	1-B	1,655	137
Florida Ag & Mech U, Tallahassee, FL 32307	1887	$2,105 (S)	$3,198	5-D	10,991	727
Florida Atlantic U, Boca Raton, FL 33431-0991	1961	$2,022 (S)	$4,680	5-D	18,823	1,169
Florida Inst of Technology, Melbourne, FL 32901-6975	1958	$15,550	$4,640	1-D	4,135	408
Florida Intl U, Miami, FL 33199	1965	$2,035 (S)	$7,378	5-D	30,012	1,241
Florida State U, Tallahassee, FL 32306	1857	$1,988 (S)	$4,570	5-D	30,401	1,455
Fontbonne Coll, St. Louis, MO 63105-3098	1917	$10,150	$4,400	2-F	2,054	175
Fordham U, New York, NY 10458	1841	$17,014	$7,810	2-D	13,668	1,183
Fort Hays State U, Hays, KS 67601-4099	1902	$1,992 (S)	$3,400	5-M	5,616	302
Fort Lewis Coll, Durango, CO 81301-3999	1911	$2,084 (S)	$4,236	5-B	4,440	250
Fort Valley State U, Fort Valley, GA 31030-3298	1895	$2,157 (S)	$3,075	5-F	2,804	152
Framingham State Coll, Framingham, MA 01701-9101	1839	$3,150 (S)	$3,944	5-M	5,315	288
Franciscan U of Steubenville, Steubenville, OH 43952-6701	1946	$11,370	$4,730	2-M	1,997	137
Francis Marion U, Florence, SC 29501-0547	1970	$3,390 (S)	$3,310	5-M	3,554	195
Franklin & Marshall Coll, Lancaster, PA 17604-3003	1787	$22,664	$4,906	1-B	1,843	172
Franklin Pierce Coll, Rindge, NH 03461-0060	1962	$16,170	$5,050	1-M	3,265	130
Franklin U, Columbus, OH 43215-5399	1902	$5,314	NA	1-M	4,092	229
Freed-Hardeman U, Henderson, TN 38340-2399	1869	$7,524	$3,760	2-M	1,600	105
Fresno Pacific U, Fresno, CA 93702-4709	1944	$11,936	$4,100	2-M	1,546	169
Friends U, Wichita, KS 67213	1898	$9,975	$3,250	1-M	2,729	188
Frostburg State U, Frostburg, MD 21532-1099	1898	$3,544 (S)	$4,786	5-M	5,199	334
Furman U, Greenville, SC 29613	1826	$16,419	$4,449	1-M	2,840	200
Gallaudet U, Washington, DC 20002-3625	1864	$6,283	$6,709	1-D	1,697	297
Gannon U, Erie, PA 16541	1925	$12,994	$4,860	2-M	3,227	261
Gardner-Webb U, Boiling Springs, NC 28017	1905	$9,620	$4,630	2-M	2,932	174
Geneva Coll, Beaver Falls, PA 15010-3599	1848	$11,534	$4,750	2-M	1,956	122
George Fox U, Newberg, OR 97132-2697	1891	$15,520	$4,920	2-D	2,235	170
George Mason U, Fairfax, VA 22030-4444	1957	$4,296 (S)	$5,120	5-D	23,826	1,489
Georgetown Coll, Georgetown, KY 40324-1696	1829	$10,190	$4,180	2-M	1,626	137
Georgetown U, Washington, DC 20057	1789	$21,405	$8,091	2-D	12,532	1,683
The George Washington U, Washington, DC 20052	1821	$21,360	$7,325	1-D	19,356	2,214
Georgia Coll & State U, Milledgeville, GA 31061	1889	$2,064 (S)	$4,203	5-M	5,512	346
Georgian Court Coll, Lakewood, NJ 08701-2697 (4)	1908	$11,116	$4,750	2-M	2,350	194
Georgia Southern U, Statesboro, GA 30460-8126	1906	$2,256 (S)	$3,465	5-D	13,963	935
Georgia Southwestern State U, Americus, GA 31709-4693	1906	$2,145 (S)	$3,222	5-M	2,414	153
Georgia State U, Atlanta, GA 30303-3083	1913	$2,673 (S)	NA	5-D	24,276	1,437
Gettysburg Coll, Gettysburg, PA 17325-1411	1832	$22,430	$5,038	1-B	2,111	221
Glenville State Coll, Glenville, WV 26351-1200	1872	$1,956 (S)	$3,480	5-B	2,288	172
Golden Gate U, San Francisco, CA 94105-2968	1853	$8,472	NA	1-D	5,646	523
Goldey-Beacom Coll, Wilmington, DE 19808-1999	1886	$7,200	NA	1-M	1,650	73
Gonzaga U, Spokane, WA 99258	1887	$15,487	$5,170	2-D	3,950	283
Gordon Coll, Wenham, MA 01984-1899	1889	$15,760	$4,950	2-M	1,375	110
Goshen Coll, Goshen, IN 46526-4794	1894	$11,450	$4,000	2-B	1,016	112
Goucher Coll, Baltimore, MD 21204-2794	1885	$18,525	$6,925	1-M	1,382	154
Governors State U, University Park, IL 60466	1969	$2,278 (S)	NA	5-M	6,200	282
Grand Canyon U, Phoenix, AZ 85017-3030	1949	$8,946	$3,740	2-M	2,245	196
Grand Valley State U, Allendale, MI 49401-9403	1960	$3,408 (S)	$4,640	5-M	15,676	818
Grand View Coll, Des Moines, IA 50316-1599	1896	$11,410	$3,775	2-B	1,433	135
Grantham Coll of Engineering, Slidell, LA 70460-6815	1951	$3,800	NA	3-B	2,300	13
Greensboro Coll, Greensboro, NC 27401-1875	1838	$9,990	$4,700	2-B	1,051	101
Grinnell Coll, Grinnell, IA 50112-0805	1846	$17,568	$5,152	1-B	1,363	164
Grove City Coll, Grove City, PA 16127-2104	1876	$6,576	$3,816	2-M	2,292	145
Guilford Coll, Greensboro, NC 27410-4173	1837	$14,750	$5,270	2-B	1,402	123
Gustavus Adolphus Coll, St. Peter, MN 56082-1498	1862	$16,120	$4,010	2-B	2,418	222
Gwynedd-Mercy Coll, Gwynedd Valley, PA 19437-0901	1948	$12,280	$5,800	2-M	1,706	181
Hamline U, St. Paul, MN 55104-1284	1854	$14,850	$4,799	2-D	3,071	324
Hampshire Coll, Amherst, MA 01002	1965	$23,780	$6,225	1-B	1,152	92
Hampton U, Hampton, VA 23668	1868	$9,596	$4,150	1-D	5,704	378
Hannibal-LaGrange Coll, Hannibal, MO 63401-1940	1858	$7,590	$2,780	2-B	1,086	85
Hanover Coll, Hanover, IN 47243-0108	1827	$10,085	$4,275	2-B	1,092	106
Harding U, Searcy, AR 72149-0001	1924	$7,712	$3,986	2-M	3,754	262
Hardin-Simmons U, Abilene, TX 79698-0001	1891	$8,130	$3,240	2-F	2,312	169
Hartwick Coll, Oneonta, NY 13820-4020	1797	$22,235	$5,850	1-B	1,494	141
Harvard U, Cambridge, MA 02138	1636	$22,802	$7,278	1-D	17,425	1,746
Hastings Coll, Hastings, NE 68902-0269	1882	$11,368	$3,758	2-M	1,059	101
Haverford Coll, Haverford, PA 19041-1392	1833	$21,740	$7,720	1-B	1,147	109
Hawaii Pacific U, Honolulu, HI 96813-2785	1965	$7,500	$7,800	1-M	8,390	552
Heidelberg Coll, Tiffin, OH 44883-2462	1850	$16,260	$5,135	2-M	1,480	107
Henderson State U, Arkadelphia, AR 71999-0001	1890	$2,166 (S)	$2,856	5-M	3,773	220
Hendrix Coll, Conway, AR 72032-3080	1876	$10,408	$4,000	2-B	1,034	96

Name, address	Year	Tuition & Fees	Room & Board	Control, Degree	Enroll-ment	Faculty
Heritage Coll, Toppenish, WA 98948-9599	1982	$6,450	NA	1-M	1,152	168
High Point U, High Point, NC 27262-3598	1924	$10,420	$5,300	2-M	2,743	196
Hillsdale Coll, Hillsdale, MI 49242-1298	1844	$12,680	$5,430	1-B	1,197	117
Hiram Coll, Hiram, OH 44234-0067	1850	$16,514	$5,092	2-B	1,151	94
Hobart & William Smith Colls, Geneva, NY 14456-3397	1822	$22,380	$6,564	1-B	1,843	172
Hofstra U, Hempstead, NY 11549	1935	$13,544	$6,730	1-D	12,439	1,104
Hollins U, Roanoke, VA 24020-1688 (3)	1842	$15,320	$5,975	1-M	1,099	90
Holy Family Coll, Philadelphia, PA 19114-2094	1954	$10,620	NA	2-M	2,587	239
Hood Coll, Frederick, MD 21701-8575 (4)	1893	$16,418	$6,592	2-M	1,856	86
Hope Coll, Holland, MI 49422-9000	1866	$14,878	$4,534	2-B	2,911	275
Hope Intl U, Fullerton, CA 92831-3138	1928	$9,190	$3,619	2-M	1,022	128
Houghton Coll, Houghton, NY 14744	1883	$12,765	$4,238	2-B	1,411	135
Houston Baptist U, Houston, TX 77074-3298	1960	$8,535	$2,974	2-M	2,286	138
Howard Payne U, Brownwood, TX 76801-2715	1889	$7,620	$3,630	2-B	1,489	123
Howard U, Washington, DC 20059-0002	1867	$8,985	$4,162	1-D	10,438	1,808
Humboldt State U, Arcata, CA 95521-8299	1913	$1,926 (S)	$5,194	5-M	7,492	519
Hunter Coll of the City U of New York, New York, NY 10021-5085	1870	$3,329 (S)	NA	11-M	19,689	1,299
Husson Coll, Bangor, ME 04401-2999	1898	$8,800	$4,740	1-M	1,263	95
Idaho State U, Pocatello, ID 83209	1901	$1,726 (S)	$3,580	5-D	11,886	725
Illinois Inst of Technology, Chicago, IL 60616-3793	1890	$16,460	$4,940	1-D	6,100	535
Illinois State U, Normal, IL 61790-2200	1857	$4,004 (S)	$3,975	5-D	20,331	996
Illinois Wesleyan U, Bloomington, IL 61702-2900	1850	$18,376	$4,824	1-B	2,021	165
Immaculata Coll, Immaculata, PA 19345-0500 (4)	1920	$12,115	$5,856	2-D	2,312	183
Indiana Inst of Technology, Fort Wayne, IN 46803-1297	1930	$11,500	$4,430	1-B	1,400	53
Indiana State U, Terre Haute, IN 47809-1401	1865	$3,196 (S)	$4,143	5-D	10,784	706
Indiana U Bloomington, Bloomington, IN 47405	1820	$3,929 (S)	$4,900	5-D	34,937	1,635
Indiana U East, Richmond, IN 47374-1289	1971	$2,849 (S)	NA	5-B	2,309	187
Indiana U Kokomo, Kokomo, IN 46904-9003	1945	$2,890 (S)	NA	5-M	2,927	181
Indiana U Northwest, Gary, IN 46408-1197	1959	$2,895 (S)	NA	5-M	5,256	354
Indiana U of Pennsylvania, Indiana, PA 15705-1087	1875	$4,204 (S)	$3,408	5-D	13,736	824
Indiana U–Purdue U Fort Wayne, Fort Wayne, IN 46805-1499	1917	$3,321 (S)	NA	5-M	10,749	737
Indiana U South Bend, South Bend, IN 46634-7111	1922	$2,985 (S)	NA	5-M	7,169	540
Indiana U Southeast, New Albany, IN 47150-6405	1941	$2,847 (S)	NA	5-M	5,520	384
Indiana Wesleyan U, Marion, IN 46953-4999	1920	$11,204	$4,310	2-M	6,057	138
Inter American U of Puerto Rico, Arecibo Campus, Arecibo, PR 00614	1957	$2,620	NA	1-M	4,115	238
Inter American U of Puerto Rico, Bayamón Campus, Bayamón, PR 00957	NA	$2,800	NA	1-B	5,154	258
Inter American U of Puerto Rico, San Germán Campus, San Germán, PR 00683-5008	1912	$3,354	NA	1-M	6,022	329
Iona Coll, New Rochelle, NY 10801-1890	1940	$13,420	$7,720	1-M	4,897	344
Iowa State U of Science & Technology, Ames, IA 50011	1858	$2,766 (S)	$3,647	5-D	25,384	1,561
Ithaca Coll, Ithaca, NY 14850-7020	1892	$16,900	$7,340	1-M	5,897	513
Jackson State U, Jackson, MS 39217	1877	$2,380 (S)	$3,296	5-D	6,333	382
Jacksonville State U, Jacksonville, AL 36265-9982	1883	$2,060 (S)	$2,980	5-M	7,619	350
Jacksonville U, Jacksonville, FL 32211-3394	1934	$13,900	$4,900	1-M	2,157	230
James Madison U, Harrisonburg, VA 22807	1908	$4,148 (S)	$4,846	5-D	14,115	880
Jamestown Coll, Jamestown, ND 58405	1883	$8,770	$3,180	2-B	1,072	76
New Jersey City U, Jersey City, NJ 07305-1957	1927	$3,828 (S)	$5,000	5-M	8,503	245
John Brown U, Siloam Springs, AR 72761-2121	1919	$9,802	$4,478	2-M	1,403	96
John Carroll U, University Heights, OH 44118-4581	1886	$14,620	$5,804	2-M	4,391	392
John Jay Coll of Criminal Justice, the City U of New York, New York, NY 10019-1093	1964	$3,309 (S)	NA	11-M	11,963	689
Johns Hopkins U, Baltimore, MD 21218-2699	1876	$21,675	$7,355	1-D	5,022	413
Johnson & Wales U, North Miami, FL 33181	1992	$15,855	NA	1-B	1,054	46
Johnson & Wales U, Providence, RI 02903-3703	1914	$12,807	$5,550	1-D	8,124	332
Johnson & Wales U, Charleston, SC 29403	1984	$13,689	NA	1-B	1,325	49
Johnson C. Smith U, Charlotte, NC 28216	1867	$8,469	$3,328	1-B	1,357	88
Johnson State Coll, Johnson, VT 05656-9405	1828	$4,641 (S)	$5,086	5-M	1,622	127
Juniata Coll, Huntingdon, PA 16652-2119	1876	$17,580	$5,205	1-B	1,204	99
Kalamazoo Coll, Kalamazoo, MI 49006-3295	1833	$17,976	$5,565	1-B	1,241	102
Kansas State U, Manhattan, KS 66506	1863	$2,467 (S)	$3,640	5-D	20,306	1,389
Kean U, Union, NJ 07083	1855	$3,669 (S)	NA	5-M	11,537	883
Kennesaw State U, Kennesaw, GA 30144-5591	1963	$2,013 (S)	NA	5-M	13,108	573
Kent State U, Kent, OH 44242-0001	1910	$4,460 (S)	$4,152	5-D	20,743	1,340
Kentucky State U, Frankfort, KY 40601	1886	$2,050 (S)	$3,190	12-M	2,288	157
Kenyon Coll, Gambier, OH 43022-9623	1824	$22,850	$3,990	1-B	1,551	145
Kettering U, Flint, MI 48504-4898	1919	$14,232	$3,863	1-M	3,239	156
King's Coll, Wilkes-Barre, PA 18711-0801	1946	$14,000	$6,120	2-M	2,222	168
Knox Coll, Galesburg, IL 61401	1837	$19,074	$5,076	1-B	1,195	115
Kutztown U of Pennsylvania, Kutztown, PA 19530	1866	$4,219 (S)	$3,650	5-M	7,920	443
Lafayette Coll, Easton, PA 18042-1798	1826	$21,202	$6,560	2-B	2,185	232
Lake Forest Coll, Lake Forest, IL 60045-2399	1857	$19,560	$4,550	1-M	1,190	118
Lake Superior State U, Sault Sainte Marie, MI 49783-1699	1946	$3,642 (S)	$4,646	5-M	3,369	191
Lamar U, Beaumont, TX 77710	1923	$1,868 (S)	$3,200	5-D	9,677	554
Lambuth U, Jackson, TN 38301	1843	$6,194	$3,950	2-B	1,012	82
La Roche Coll, Pittsburgh, PA 15237-5898	1963	$10,400	$5,408	2-M	1,568	151
La Salle U, Philadelphia, PA 19141-1199	1863	$14,850	$6,170	2-M	5,452	298
La Sierra U, Riverside, CA 92515	1922	$14,025	$4,065	2-D	1,466	113
Lawrence Technological U, Southfield, MI 48075-1058	1932	$9,340	NA	1-M	3,645	328
Lawrence U, Appleton, WI 54912-0599	1847	$19,620	$4,575	1-B	1,179	171
Lebanon Valley Coll, Annville, PA 17003-0501	1866	$15,980	$5,110	2-M	1,856	183
Lee U, Cleveland, TN 37320-3450	1918	$5,638	$3,680	2-M	2,870	178
Lehigh U, Bethlehem, PA 18015-3094	1865	$21,350	$6,220	1-D	6,316	470
Lehman Coll of the City U of New York, Bronx, NY 10468-1589	1931	$3,320 (S)	NA	11-M	9,386	694
Le Moyne Coll, Syracuse, NY 13214-1399	1946	$13,450	$5,680	2-M	3,131	227
Lenoir-Rhyne Coll, Hickory, NC 28601	1891	$12,386	$4,500	2-M	1,616	137
Lesley Coll, Cambridge, MA 02138-2790 (3)	1909	$14,606	$6,700	1-D	6,128	876
LeTourneau U, Longview, TX 75607-7001	1946	$10,744	$4,770	2-M	2,204	143

Name, address	Year	Tuition & Fees	Room & Board	Control, Degree	Enroll-ment	Faculty
Lewis & Clark Coll, Portland, OR 97219-7899	1867	$18,530	$5,770	1-F	3,023	283
Lewis-Clark State Coll, Lewiston, ID 83501-2698	1893	$1,868 (S)	$3,400	5-B	2,981	303
Lewis U, Romeoville, IL 60446	1932	$13,024	$5,500	2-M	3,977	274
Liberty U, Lynchburg, VA 24502	1971	$7,680	$4,800	2-D	6,646	269
Lincoln Memorial U, Harrogate, TN 37752-1901	1897	$8,000	$3,500	1-M	1,811	116
Lincoln U, Jefferson City, MO 65102	1866	$2,076 (S)	$3,276	5-M	3,041	202
Lincoln U, Lincoln University, PA 19352	1854	$4,180 (S)	$4,440	12-M	2,020	178
Lindenwood U, St. Charles, MO 63301-1695	1827	$10,150	$5,000	2-M	4,788	278
Lindsey Wilson Coll, Columbia, KY 42728-1298	1903	$8,760	$4,400	2-M	1,425	60
Linfield Coll, McMinnville, OR 97128-6894	1849	$16,960	$5,180	2-B	2,709	126
Lock Haven U of Pennsylvania, Lock Haven, PA 17745-2390	1870	$4,062 (S)	$3,880	5-M	3,538	211
Loma Linda U, Loma Linda, CA 92350	1905	$10,530	NA	2-D	3,400	1,162
Long Island U, Brooklyn Campus, Brooklyn, NY 11201-8423	1926	$14,496	$5,500	1-D	8,052	902
Long Island U, C.W. Post Campus, Brookville, NY 11548-1300	1954	$14,530	$6,025	1-D	8,171	1,076
Long Island U, Southampton Coll, Southampton, NY 11968-9822	1963	$14,600	$6,850	1-M	1,563	111
Longwood Coll, Farmville, VA 23909-1800	1839	$4,416 (S)	$4,280	5-M	3,352	212
Loras Coll, Dubuque, IA 52004-0178	1839	$13,750	$5,005	2-M	1,776	136
Louisiana State U & Ag & Mech Coll, Baton Rouge, LA 70803	1860	$2,711 (S)	$3,772	5-D	28,066	1,316
Louisiana State U in Shreveport, Shreveport, LA 71115-2399	1965	$2,230 (S)	$6,095	5-M	4,259	206
Louisiana Tech U, Ruston, LA 71272	1894	$2,567 (S)	$2,805	5-D	9,500	438
Loyola Coll, Baltimore, MD 21210-2699	1852	$16,560	$7,240	2-D	6,241	452
Loyola Marymount U, Los Angeles, CA 90045-8350	1911	$16,495	$6,736	2-F	6,721	518
Loyola U Chicago, Chicago, IL 60611-2196	1870	$16,054	$6,380	2-D	13,604	961
Loyola U New Orleans, New Orleans, LA 70118-6195	1912	$13,354	$5,830	2-F	5,079	390
Luther Coll, Decorah, IA 52101-1045	1861	$15,630	$3,700	2-B	2,400	224
Lycoming Coll, Williamsport, PA 17701-5192	1812	$16,160	$4,770	2-B	1,465	107
Lynchburg Coll, Lynchburg, VA 24501-3199	1903	$16,415	$4,400	2-M	1,972	165
Lyndon State Coll, Lyndonville, VT 05851	1911	$4,516 (S)	$5,086	5-M	1,229	108
Lynn U, Boca Raton, FL 33431-5598	1962	$17,200	$6,250	1-D	1,782	168
Macalester Coll, St. Paul, MN 55105-1899	1874	$18,758	$5,430	2-B	1,774	205
Madonna U, Livonia, MI 48150-1173	1947	$6,040	$4,334	2-M	3,905	289
Maharishi U of Mgmt, Fairfield, IA 52557	1971	$14,670	$4,960	1-D	1,422	96
Malone Coll, Canton, OH 44709-3897	1892	$11,280	$4,600	2-M	2,242	171
Manchester Coll, North Manchester, IN 46962-1225	1889	$12,660	$4,550	2-M	1,067	96
Manhattan Coll, Riverdale, NY 10471	1853	$14,555	$7,250	2-M	3,076	244
Manhattanville Coll, Purchase, NY 10577-2132	1841	$17,300	$8,000	1-M	1,925	214
Mankato State U, Mankato, MN 56002-8400	1868	$2,983 (S)	$2,965	5-M	12,507	574
Mansfield U of Pennsylvania, Mansfield, PA 16933	1857	$4,404 (S)	$3,704	5-M	2,907	202
Marian Coll, Indianapolis, IN 46222-1997	1851	$13,406	$4,644	2-B	1,418	134
Marian Coll of Fond du Lac, Fond du Lac, WI 54935-4699	1936	$11,370	$4,188	2-M	2,276	140
Marietta Coll, Marietta, OH 45750-4000	1835	$16,150	$4,586	1-M	1,290	109
Marist Coll, Poughkeepsie, NY 12601-1387	1929	$13,098	$6,772	1-M	4,618	388
Marquette U, Milwaukee, WI 53201-1881	1881	$15,384	$5,530	2-D	10,610	1,035
Marshall U, Huntington, WV 25755-2020	1837	$2,184 (S)	$4,420	5-D	13,388	881
Mars Hill Coll, Mars Hill, NC 28754	1856	$8,900	$3,800	2-B	1,244	123
Mary Baldwin Coll, Staunton, VA 24401 (4)	1842	$14,415	$7,000	2-M	1,547	126
Marygrove Coll, Detroit, MI 48221-2599	1905	$9,056	NA	2-M	3,603	60
Maryland Inst, Coll of Art, Baltimore, MD 21217-4192	1826	$16,760	$5,200	1-M	1,143	178
Marymount Manhattan Coll, New York, NY 10021-4597	1936	$12,290	NA	1-B	2,140	156
Marymount U, Arlington, VA 22207-4299	1950	$12,770	$5,810	2-M	3,512	357
Maryville U of Saint Louis, St. Louis, MO 63141-7299	1872	$10,910	$5,000	1-M	3,055	264
Mary Washington Coll, Fredericksburg, VA 22401-5358	1908	$3,556 (S)	$5,080	5-M	3,840	240
Marywood U, Scranton, PA 18509-1598	1915	$14,003	$5,700	2-D	2,948	247
Massachusetts Coll of Art, Boston, MA 02115-5882	1873	$3,964 (S)	$6,348	5-M	2,289	159
Massachusetts Coll of Liberal Arts, North Adams, MA 01247-4100	1894	$3,437 (S)	$4,840	5-M	1,679	136
Massachusetts Coll of Pharmacy & Allied Health Scis, Boston, MA 02115-5896	1823	$14,508	$7,500	1-D	1,666	195
Massachusetts Inst of Technology, Cambridge, MA 02139-4307	1861	$23,100	$5,610	1-D	9,880	925
The Master's Coll & Seminary, Santa Clarita, CA 91321-1200	1927	$12,180	$4,798	2-M	1,198	131
McKendree Coll, Lebanon, IL 62254-1299	1828	$10,400	$4,600	2-B	1,848	152
McMurry U, Abilene, TX 79697	1923	$9,075	$3,760	2-B	1,410	129
McNeese State U, Lake Charles, LA 70609-2495	1939	$2,012 (S)	$2,310	5-M	8,117	300
Medical Coll of Georgia, Augusta, GA 30912-1003	1828	$2,526 (S)	NA	5-D	2,020	761
Mercer U, Macon, GA 31207-0003	1833	$14,656	$4,882	2-D	6,801	339
Mercer U, Cecil B. Day Campus, Atlanta, GA 30341-4155	1968	$9,300	NA	2-F	2,001	48
Mercy Coll, Dobbs Ferry, NY 10522-1189	1951	$7,600	$6,600	1-M	7,364	665
Mercyhurst Coll, Erie, PA 16546	1926	$12,750	$4,884	2-M	2,689	190
Meredith Coll, Raleigh, NC 27607-5298 (3)	1891	$8,490	$3,750	2-M	2,552	247
Merrimack Coll, North Andover, MA 01845-5800	1947	$14,530	$7,200	2-M	2,732	168
Mesa State Coll, Grand Junction, CO 81502-2647	1925	$1,986 (S)	$4,538	5-M	4,703	294
Messiah Coll, Grantham, PA 17027	1909	$12,990	$5,500	2-B	2,616	224
Methodist Coll, Fayetteville, NC 28311-1420	1956	$11,900	$4,580	2-B	1,720	134
Metro State Coll of Denver, Denver, CO 80217-3362	1963	$1,976 (S)	NA	5-B	17,343	976
Miami U, Oxford, OH 45056	1809	$5,512 (S)	$4,810	12-D	16,328	1,290
Michigan State U, East Lansing, MI 48824-1020	1855	$4,789 (S)	$4,052	5-D	42,603	3,426
Michigan Technological U, Houghton, MI 49931-1295	1885	$4,062 (S)	$4,420	5-D	6,302	406
MidAmerica Nazarene U, Olathe, KS 66062-1899	1966	$10,022	$4,810	2-M	1,400	121
Middlebury Coll, Middlebury, VT 05753-6002	1800	$29,340 (C)	NA	1-D	2,176	227
Middle Tennessee State U, Murfreesboro, TN 37132	1911	$2,196 (S)	$3,343	5-D	18,366	930
Midland Lutheran Coll, Fremont, NE 68025-4200	1883	$12,250	$3,450	2-B	1,033	70
Midway Coll, Midway, KY 40347-1120 (3)	1847	$8,160	$4,500	2-B	1,021	50
Midwestern State U, Wichita Falls, TX 76308-2096	1922	$2,091 (S)	$3,633	5-M	5,770	262
Millersville U of Pennsylvania, Millersville, PA 17551-0302	1855	$4,400 (S)	$4,510	5-M	7,564	440
Millikin U, Decatur, IL 62522-2084	1901	$14,079	$5,070	2-B	1,997	231
Millsaps Coll, Jackson, MS 39210-0001	1890	$13,612	$5,701	2-M	1,362	106
Mills Coll, Oakland, CA 94613-1000 (3)	1852	$16,522	$6,800	1-D	1,115	161
Milwaukee School of Engineering, Milwaukee, WI 53202-3109	1903	$14,325	$3,855	1-M	3,029	228
Mississippi Coll, Clinton, MS 39058	1826	$8,364	$3,630	2-F	3,532	247

Name, address	Year	Tuition & Fees	Room & Board	Control, Degree	Enroll-ment	Faculty
Mississippi State U, Mississippi State, MS 39762	1878	$2,731 (S)	$4,100	5-D	15,628	823
Mississippi U for Women, Columbus, MS 39701-9998 (4)	1884	$2,284 (S)	$2,557	5-M	3,309	198
Mississippi Valley State U, Itta Bena, MS 38941-1400	1946	$2,353 (S)	$2,350	5-M	2,234	160
Missouri Baptist Coll, St. Louis, MO 63141-8698	1964	$8,820	$4,230	2-B	2,395	105
Missouri Southern State Coll, Joplin, MO 64801-1595	1937	$2,384 (S)	$3,240	5-B	5,485	283
Missouri Valley Coll, Marshall, MO 65340-3197	1889	$10,500	$5,000	2-B	1,404	68
Missouri Western State Coll, St. Joseph, MO 64507-2294	1915	$2,534 (S)	$3,302	5-B	5,124	315
Molloy Coll, Rockville Centre, NY 11571-5002	1955	$10,400	NA	1-M	2,297	284
Monmouth Coll, Monmouth, IL 61462-1998	1853	$14,630	$4,410	2-B	1,044	96
Monmouth U, West Long Branch, NJ 07764-1898	1933	$14,442	$6,793	1-M	5,311	398
Montana State U–Billings, Billings, MT 59101-9984	1927	$2,517 (S)	$3,620	5-M	4,277	273
Montana State U–Bozeman, Bozeman, MT 59717	1893	$2,677 (S)	$4,025	5-D	11,603	641
Montana State U–Northern, Havre, MT 59501-7751	1929	$2,504 (S)	$3,650	5-M	1,704	118
Montana Tech of The U of Montana, Butte, MT 59701-8997	1895	$2,542 (S)	$3,568	5-M	1,786	122
Montclair State U, Upper Montclair, NJ 07043-1624	1908	$3,694 (S)	$5,546	5-M	12,808	774
Montreat Coll, Montreat, NC 28757-1267	1916	$10,042	$3,940	2-M	1,021	51
Moody Bible Inst, Chicago, IL 60610-3284	1886	$830	$4,480	2-M	1,404	144
Moorhead State U, Moorhead, MN 56563-0002	1885	$2,908 (S)	$3,256	5-M	6,466	340
Moravian Coll, Bethlehem, PA 18018-6650	1742	$17,276	$5,580	2-M	1,830	144
Morehead State U, Morehead, KY 40351	1922	$2,150 (S)	$3,200	5-M	8,200	458
Morehouse Coll, Atlanta, GA 30314 (1)	1867	$9,724	$6,214	1-B	3,000	248
Morgan State U, Baltimore, MD 21251	1867	$3,412 (S)	$5,090	5-D	6,299	340
Morningside Coll, Sioux City, IA 51106-1751	1894	$12,306	$4,390	2-M	1,166	118
Morris Brown Coll, Atlanta, GA 30314-4140	1881	$8,210	$4,750	2-B	2,093	158
Mount Aloysius Coll, Cresson, PA 16630-1900	1939	$9,520	$4,580	2-B	1,399	125
Mount Holyoke Coll, South Hadley, MA 01075-1414 (3)	1837	$22,340	$6,525	1-B	1,860	214
Mount Mary Coll, Milwaukee, WI 53222-4597 (3)	1913	$10,740	$3,784	2-M	1,309	158
Mount Mercy Coll, Cedar Rapids, IA 52402-4797	1928	$11,860	$3,945	2-B	1,200	106
Mount Olive Coll, Mount Olive, NC 28365	1951	$8,700	$3,750	2-B	1,381	85
Mount Saint Mary Coll, Newburgh, NY 12550-3494	1960	$10,200	$5,250	1-M	2,077	167
Mount St. Mary's Coll, Los Angeles, CA 90049-1597 (4)	1925	$15,216	$5,338	2-M	1,984	234
Mount Saint Mary's Coll & Seminary, Emmitsburg, MD 21727-7799	1808	$15,650	$6,450	2-F	1,798	149
Mount Senario Coll, Ladysmith, WI 54848-2128	1962	$9,500	$3,400	1-B	1,140	66
Mount Union Coll, Alliance, OH 44601-3993	1846	$14,290	$3,870	2-B	1,935	126
Muhlenberg Coll, Allentown, PA 18104-5586	1848	$18,660	$5,025	2-B	2,370	206
Murray State U, Murray, KY 42071-0009	1922	$2,300 (S)	$3,560	5-M	8,811	384
Muskingum Coll, New Concord, OH 43762	1837	$10,785	$4,500	2-M	1,431	115
The Natl Coll of Chiropractic, Lombard, IL 60148-4583	1906	$10,504	NA	1-F	1,012	95
Natl U, La Jolla, CA 92037-1011	1971	$6,975	NA	1-M	13,397	1,500
Nazareth Coll of Rochester, Rochester, NY 14618-3790	1924	$12,985	$5,985	1-M	2,782	173
Nebraska Wesleyan U, Lincoln, NE 68504-2796	1887	$11,220	$3,614	2-B	1,709	169
Neumann Coll, Aston, PA 19014-1298	1965	$12,940	$6,300	2-M	1,239	133
New Hampshire Coll, Manchester, NH 03106-1045	1932	$13,570	$5,980	1-D	5,765	201
New Jersey Inst of Technology, Newark, NJ 07102-1982	1881	$5,466 (S)	$6,382	5-D	8,133	591
New Mexico Highlands U, Las Vegas, NM 87701	1893	$1,662 (S)	$2,706	5-M	2,544	169
New Mexico Inst of Mining & Technology, Socorro, NM 87801	1889	$2,073 (S)	$3,530	5-D	1,419	117
New Mexico State U, Las Cruces, NM 88003-8001	1888	$2,196 (S)	$3,390	5-D	15,067	670
New School Bachelor of Arts, New School for Social Research, New York, NY 10011-8603	1919	$13,420	NA	1-D	7,179	618
New York Inst of Technology, Old Westbury, NY 11568-8000	1955	$10,630	$6,280	1-F	8,982	734
New York U, New York, NY 10012-1019	1831	$21,730	$8,170	1-D	36,684	4,722
Niagara U, Niagara University, NY 14109	1856	$12,890	$5,658	1-M	3,079	265
Nicholls State U, Thibodaux, LA 70310	1948	$2,507 (S)	$2,720	5-M	7,173	310
Nichols Coll, Dudley, MA 01571	1815	$11,325	$6,400	1-M	1,542	76
Norfolk State U, Norfolk, VA 23504-3907	1935	$3,000 (S)	$4,166	5-D	7,659	545
North Carolina Ag & Tech State U, Greensboro, NC 27411	1891	$1,622 (S)	$3,850	5-D	7,468	519
North Carolina Central U, Durham, NC 27707-3129	1910	$1,944 (S)	$3,384	5-F	5,664	376
North Carolina State U, Raleigh, NC 27695	1887	$2,200 (S)	$3,910	5-D	22,199	1,593
North Carolina Wesleyan Coll, Rocky Mount, NC 27804-8677	1956	$8,144	$4,952	2-B	1,582	65
North Central Coll, Naperville, IL 60566-7063	1861	$13,845	$5,070	2-M	2,709	205
North Dakota State U, Fargo, ND 58105	1890	$2,566 (S)	$3,135	5-D	9,408	530
Northeastern Illinois U, Chicago, IL 60625-4699	1961	$2,470 (S)	NA	5-M	10,224	475
Northeastern State U, Tahlequah, OK 74464-2399	1846	$1,740 (S)	$2,610	5-D	8,503	449
Northeastern U, Boston, MA 02115-5096	1898	$16,511	$8,265	1-D	24,325	2,172
Northeast Louisiana U, Monroe, LA 71209-0001	1931	$1,952 (S)	NA	5-D	10,942	588
Northern Arizona U, Flagstaff, AZ 86011	1899	$2,080 (S)	$3,500	5-D	19,618	935
Northern Illinois U, De Kalb, IL 60115-2854	1895	$3,837 (S)	$4,000	5-D	22,082	1,203
Northern Kentucky U, Highland Heights, KY 41099	1968	$2,120 (S)	$3,439	5-F	11,763	750
Northern Michigan U, Marquette, MI 49855-5301	1899	$2,986 (S)	$4,340	5-M	7,787	354
Northern State U, Aberdeen, SD 57401-7198	1901	$2,535 (S)	$2,750	5-M	2,646	135
North Georgia Coll & State U, Dahlonega, GA 30597-1001	1873	$2,052 (S)	$3,219	5-M	3,344	196
North Greenville Coll, Tigerville, SC 29688-1892	1892	$7,400	$4,280	2-B	1,038	100
North Park U, Chicago, IL 60625-4895	1891	$14,690	$4,820	2-D	2,004	86
Northwestern Coll, Orange City, IA 51041-1996	1882	$11,300	$3,300	2-B	1,177	105
Northwestern Coll, St. Paul, MN 55113-1598	1902	$13,920	$4,176	2-B	1,664	177
Northwestern Oklahoma State U, Alva, OK 73717	1897	$1,802 (S)	$2,316	5-M	1,871	108
Northwestern State U of Louisiana, Natchitoches, LA 71497	1884	$2,177 (S)	$2,416	5-D	8,873	316
Northwestern U, Evanston, IL 60208	1851	$22,458	$6,675	1-D	15,487	2,649
Northwest Missouri State U, Maryville, MO 64468-6001	1905	$2,813 (S)	$3,890	5-M	6,280	259
Northwest Nazarene Coll, Nampa, ID 83686-5897	1913	$12,456	$3,519	2-M	1,774	96
Northwood U, Midland, MI 48640-2398	1959	$10,889	$4,878	1-M	2,903	59
Norwich U, Northfield, VT 05663	1819	$14,950	$5,717	1-M	2,791	179
Notre Dame Coll, Manchester, NH 03104-2299	1950	$12,396	$5,560	2-M	1,255	99
Nova Southeastern U, Fort Lauderdale, FL 33314-7721	1964	$10,570	$5,797	1-D	15,782	1,262
Nyack Coll, Nyack, NY 10960-3698	1882	$11,100	$4,860	2-M	1,433	55
Oakland U, Rochester, MI 48309-4401	1957	$3,734 (S)	$4,250	5-D	14,379	666
Oberlin Coll, Oberlin, OH 44074-1090	1833	$22,438	$6,358	1-B	2,904	339

Name, address	Year	Tuition & Fees	Room & Board	Control, Degree	Enroll-ment	Faculty
Occidental Coll, Los Angeles, CA 90041-3392	1887	$19,957	$5,890	1-M	1,580	188
Oglethorpe U, Atlanta, GA 30319-2797	1835	$15,920	$4,990	1-M	1,230	123
Ohio Dominican Coll, Columbus, OH 43219-2099	1911	$9,350	$4,720	2-B	1,883	110
Ohio Northern U, Ada, OH 45810-1599	1871	$19,815	$4,875	2-F	2,927	240
The Ohio State U, Columbus, OH 43210	1870	$3,660 (S)	$5,094	5-D	48,278	4,151
Ohio U, Athens, OH 45701-2979	1804	$4,275 (S)	$4,698	5-D	19,564	1,186
Ohio U–Zanesville, Zanesville, OH 43701-2695	1946	$3,117 (S)	NA	5-M	1,222	70
Ohio Wesleyan U, Delaware, OH 43015	1842	$20,040	$6,370	2-B	1,893	172
Oklahoma Baptist U, Shawnee, OK 74801-2558	1910	$8,336	$3,250	2-M	2,211	174
Oklahoma City U, Oklahoma City, OK 73106-1402	1904	$8,512	$3,990	2-F	4,323	355
Oklahoma Panhandle State U, Goodwell, OK 73939-0430	1909	$1,510 (S)	$2,170	5-B	1,234	73
Oklahoma State U, Stillwater, OK 74078	1890	$2,357 (S)	$4,344	5-D	19,350	1,173
Old Dominion U, Norfolk, VA 23529	1930	$3,976 (S)	$4,866	5-D	18,557	942
Olivet Nazarene U, Kankakee, IL 60901-0592	1907	$10,838	$4,560	2-M	2,285	145
Oral Roberts U, Tulsa, OK 74171-0001	1963	$10,460	$4,728	2-D	3,966	223
Oregon Inst of Technology, Klamath Falls, OR 97601-8801	1947	$3,309 (S)	$3,910	5-M	2,462	156
Oregon State U, Corvallis, OR 97331	1868	$3,540 (S)	$5,064	5-D	14,490	2,204
Otterbein Coll, Westerville, OH 43081	1847	$14,997	$4,750	2-M	2,697	160
Ouachita Baptist U, Arkadelphia, AR 71998-0001	1886	$8,090	$3,040	2-B	1,619	150
Our Lady of Holy Cross Coll, New Orleans, LA 70131-7399	1916	$5,580	NA	2-M	1,300	108
Our Lady of the Lake U of San Antonio, San Antonio, TX 78207-4689	1895	$10,872	$4,206	2-D	3,666	236
Pace U, New York, NY 10038	1906	$13,820	$6,100	1-D	13,317	1,266
Pacific Lutheran U, Tacoma, WA 98447	1890	$15,680	$4,890	2-M	3,555	315
Pacific U, Forest Grove, OR 97116-1797	1849	$16,695	$4,564	1-D	1,854	204
Palm Beach Atlantic Coll, West Palm Beach, FL 33416-4708	1968	$9,900	$4,638	2-M	1,932	152
Palmer Coll of Chiropractic, Davenport, IA 52803-5287	1897	$14,520	NA	1-D	1,818	129
Park Coll, Parkville, MO 64152-4358	1875	$4,410	$4,430	2-M	8,395	96
Parsons School of Design, New School for Social Research, New York, NY 10011-8878	1896	$18,540	$8,555	1-M	2,011	403
Pennsylvania State U Abington Coll, Abington, PA 19001-3918	1950	$5,682 (S)	NA	12-B	3,218	181
Pennsylvania State U Altoona Coll, Altoona, PA 16601-3760	1929	$5,682 (S)	$4,640	12-B	3,727	208
Pennsylvania State U at Erie, The Behrend Coll, Erie, PA 16563	1948	$5,832 (S)	$4,640	12-M	3,327	212
Pennsylvania State U Berks Campus of the Berks–Lehigh Valley Coll, Reading, PA 19610-6009	1924	$5,682 (S)	$4,640	12-B	1,817	109
Pennsylvania State U Harrisburg Campus of the Capital Coll, Middletown, PA 17057-4898	1966	$5,832 (S)	$4,640	12-D	3,466	213
Pennsylvania State U U Park Campus, University Park, PA 16802	1855	$5,832 (S)	$4,640	12-D	40,538	2,190
Pepperdine U, Malibu, CA 90263-0001	1937	$20,210	$6,980	2-D	7,804	310
Peru State Coll, Peru, NE 68421	1867	$2,085 (S)	$3,060	5-M	1,807	98
Pfeiffer U, Misenheimer, NC 28109-0960	1885	$9,816	$4,000	2-M	1,814	52
Philadelphia Coll of Bible, Langhorne, PA 19047-2990	1913	$9,520	$4,890	2-M	1,280	126
Philadelphia Coll of Textiles & Sci, Philadelphia, PA 19144-5497	1884	$13,466	$6,080	1-M	3,308	366
Piedmont Coll, Demorest, GA 30535-0010	1897	$8,200	$3,930	2-M	1,587	127
Pittsburg State U, Pittsburg, KS 66762-5880	1903	$2,016 (S)	$3,396	5-M	6,355	313
Plattsburgh State U of New York, Plattsburgh, NY 12901-2681	1889	$3,845 (S)	$4,476	5-M	5,920	361
Plymouth State Coll of the U System of New Hampshire, Plymouth, NH 03264	1871	$4,342 (S)	$4,564	5-M	4,228	295
Point Loma Nazarene U, San Diego, CA 92106-2899	1902	$12,464	$5,220	2-M	2,358	251
Point Park Coll, Pittsburgh, PA 15222-1984	1960	$11,406	$5,174	1-M	2,270	211
Polytechnic U, Brooklyn Campus, Brooklyn, NY 11201-2990	1854	$19,150	$4,240	1-D	2,333	293
Polytechnic U of Puerto Rico, Hato Rey, PR 00919	1966	$4,560	NA	1-M	4,622	249
Pomona Coll, Claremont, CA 91711	1887	$20,680	$8,180	1-B	1,421	156
Pontifical Catholic U of Puerto Rico, Ponce, PR 00731-6382	1948	$3,910	$2,660	2-F	7,514	654
Portland State U, Portland, OR 97207-0751	1946	$3,180 (S)	$5,850	5-D	16,997	746
Prairie View A&M U, Prairie View, TX 77446-0188	1878	$2,364 (S)	$3,953	5-M	6,004	354
Pratt Inst, Brooklyn, NY 11205-3899	1887	$17,151	$7,153	1-M	3,640	502
Presbyterian Coll, Clinton, SC 29325	1880	$14,806	$4,216	2-B	1,116	119
Princeton U, Princeton, NJ 08544-1019	1746	$23,820	$6,711	1-D	6,605	886
Providence Coll, Providence, RI 02918	1917	$16,655	$6,919	2-M	5,507	391
Purchase Coll, State U of New York, Purchase, NY 10577-1400	1967	$3,879 (S)	$5,264	5-M	3,297	252
Purdue U, West Lafayette, IN 47907	1869	$3,368 (S)	$4,800	5-D	35,715	2,233
Purdue U Calumet, Hammond, IN 46323-2094	1951	$3,088 (S)	NA	5-M	9,974	457
Purdue U North Central, Westville, IN 46391-9528	1967	$2,979 (S)	NA	5-M	3,369	235
Queens Coll, Charlotte, NC 28274-0002	1857	$9,410	$5,830	2-M	1,652	108
Queens Coll of the City U of New York, Flushing, NY 11367-1597	1937	$3,393 (S)	NA	11-M	16,381	1,095
Quincy U, Quincy, IL 62301-2699	1860	$12,410	$4,420	2-M	1,149	96
Quinnipiac Coll, Hamden, CT 06518-1904	1929	$14,880	$7,190	1-F	5,571	390
Radford U, Radford, VA 24142	1910	$3,180 (S)	$4,416	5-M	8,534	468
Ramapo Coll of New Jersey, Mahwah, NJ 07430-1680	1969	$4,206 (S)	$5,734	5-M	4,821	293
Randolph-Macon Coll, Ashland, VA 23005-5505	1830	$16,240	$4,175	2-B	1,093	155
Reed Coll, Portland, OR 97202-8199	1909	$22,340	$6,200	1-M	1,338	121
Regis Coll, Weston, MA 02193-1571 (3)	1927	$15,250	$6,900	2-M	1,336	146
Reinhardt Coll, Waleska, GA 30183-0128	1883	$6,210	$4,263	2-B	1,071	49
Rensselaer Polytechnic Inst, Troy, NY 12180-3590	1824	$20,604	$6,786	1-D	6,356	342
Rhode Island Coll, Providence, RI 02908-1924	1854	$3,076 (S)	$5,200	5-M	8,622	640
Rhode Island School of Design, Providence, RI 02903-2784	1877	$19,670	$6,390	1-F	2,001	315
Rhodes Coll, Memphis, TN 38112-1690	1848	$17,518	$5,110	2-M	1,432	150
Rice U, Houston, TX 77005	1912	$14,306	$6,200	1-D	4,209	594
The Richard Stockton Coll of New Jersey, Pomona, NJ 08240-9988	1969	$3,776 (S)	$4,760	5-M	6,205	338
Rider U, Lawrenceville, NJ 08648-3001	1865	$15,410	$6,270	1-M	5,078	403
Rivier Coll, Nashua, NH 03060-5086	1933	$13,190	$5,525	2-M	2,886	219
Roanoke Coll, Salem, VA 24153-3794	1842	$16,410	$5,250	2-B	1,698	163
Robert Morris Coll, Chicago, IL 60601-2592	1913	$10,500	NA	1-B	3,581	246
Robert Morris Coll, Moon Township, PA 15108-1189	1921	$8,339	$4,934	1-M	4,846	296
Roberts Wesleyan Coll, Rochester, NY 14624-1997	1866	$12,400	$4,260	2-M	1,414	131
Rochester Inst of Technology, Rochester, NY 14623-5604	1829	$16,359	$6,417	1-D	12,352	1,081
Rockford Coll, Rockford, IL 61108-2393	1847	$14,750	$4,800	1-M	1,264	132
Rockhurst Coll, Kansas City, MO 64110-2561	1910	$11,790	$4,760	2-M	2,792	192

Name, address	Year	Tuition & Fees	Room & Board	Control, Degree	Enroll-ment	Faculty
Roger Williams U, Bristol, RI 02809	1956	$15,840	$7,080	1-F	3,805	232
Rollins Coll, Winter Park, FL 32789-4499	1885	$20,010	$6,340	1-M	2,166	255
Roosevelt U, Chicago, IL 60605-1394	1945	$11,030	$5,500	1-D	6,605	530
Rose-Hulman Inst of Technology, Terre Haute, IN 47803-3920	1874	$18,105	$5,300	1-M	1,757	130
Rowan U, Glassboro, NJ 08028-1701	1923	$4,241 (S)	$5,326	5-D	9,367	360
Russell Sage Coll, Troy, NY 12180-4115 (3)	1916	$14,230	$5,760	1-B	1,021	140
Rutgers, The State U of New Jersey, Camden Coll of Arts & Scis, Camden, NJ 08102	1927	$5,190 (S)	$5,314	5-B	2,188	171
Rutgers, The State U of New Jersey, Coll of Engineering, Piscataway, NJ 08854-8058	1864	$5,836 (S)	$5,314	5-B	2,206	136
Rutgers, The State U of New Jersey, Cook Coll, New Brunswick, NJ 08903	1921	$5,817 (S)	$5,314	5-B	3,284	94
Rutgers, The State U of New Jersey, Douglass Coll, New Brunswick, NJ 08901-1414 (3)	1918	$5,349 (S)	$5,314	5-B	3,014	926
Rutgers, The State U of New Jersey, Livingston Coll, Piscataway, NJ 08854	1969	$5,382 (S)	$5,314	5-B	3,160	926
Rutgers, The State U of New Jersey, Newark Coll of Arts & Scis, Newark, NJ 07102-1896	1946	$5,151 (S)	$5,314	5-B	3,621	347
Rutgers, The State U of New Jersey, Rutgers Coll, New Brunswick, NJ 08901	1766	$5,386 (S)	$5,314	5-B	10,680	926
Rutgers, The State U of New Jersey, U Coll–Newark, Newark, NJ 07102	1934	$138/cr. hr. (S)	NA	5-B	1,790	347
Rutgers, The State U of New Jersey, U Coll–New Brunswick, New Brunswick, NJ 08903	1934	$138/cr. hr. (S)	NA	5-B	2,846	926
Sacred Heart U, Fairfield, CT 06432-1000	1963	$13,475	$6,570	2-M	5,900	349
Saginaw Valley State U, University Center, MI 48710	1963	$3,448 (S)	$4,375	5-M	7,493	466
St. Ambrose U, Davenport, IA 52803-2898	1882	$12,850	$4,810	2-M	2,776	210
Saint Anselm Coll, Manchester, NH 03102-1310	1889	$16,670	$6,160	2-B	2,007	163
Saint Augustine's Coll, Raleigh, NC 27610-2298	1867	$6,560	$4,088	2-B	1,639	119
St. Bonaventure U, St. Bonaventure, NY 14778-2284	1858	$13,100	$5,378	2-M	2,822	173
St. Cloud State U, St. Cloud, MN 56301-4498	1869	$3,082 (S)	$3,066	5-D	13,946	627
St. Edward's U, Austin, TX 78704-6489	1885	$10,730	$4,700	2-M	3,101	190
St. Francis Coll, Brooklyn Heights, NY 11201-4398	1884	$7,680	$3,150	2-B	2,136	157
Saint Francis Coll, Loretto, PA 15940-0600	1847	$14,342	$6,250	2-M	1,904	174
St. John Fisher Coll, Rochester, NY 14618-3597	1948	$12,500	$5,700	2-M	1,964	164
Saint John's U, Collegeville, MN 56321 (1)	1857	$14,758	$4,574	2-F	1,823	172
St. John's U, Jamaica, NY 11439	1870	$12,230	NA	2-D	18,523	1,088
Saint Joseph Coll, West Hartford, CT 06117-2700 (4)	1932	$14,490	$5,725	2-M	1,938	84
Saint Joseph's Coll, Standish, ME 04084-5263	1912	$11,710	$5,530	2-M	5,040	96
St. Joseph's Coll, New York, Brooklyn, NY 11205-3688	1916	$8,326	NA	1-B	1,292	134
St. Joseph's Coll, Suffolk Campus, Patchogue, NY 11772-2399	1916	$8,917	NA	1-M	2,781	216
Saint Joseph's U, Philadelphia, PA 19131-1395	1851	$16,165	$6,972	2-M	7,027	430
St. Lawrence U, Canton, NY 13617-1455	1856	$21,435	$6,340	1-M	2,021	181
Saint Leo Coll, Saint Leo, FL 33574-2008	1889	$10,996	$5,240	2-M	1,675	125
Saint Louis U, St. Louis, MO 63103-2097	1818	$15,050	$5,290	2-D	14,229	2,681
Saint Martin's Coll, Lacey, WA 98503-7500	1895	$13,120	$4,590	2-M	1,653	68
Saint Mary's Coll, Notre Dame, IN 46556 (3)	1844	$15,652	$5,197	2-B	1,347	176
Saint Mary's Coll of California, Moraga, CA 94575	1863	$15,998	$7,119	2-M	4,238	162
St. Mary's Coll of Maryland, St. Mary's City, MD 20686	1840	$6,875 (S)	$5,645	5-B	1,682	162
Saint Mary's U of Minnesota, Winona, MN 55987-1399	1912	$12,495	$4,120	2-D	5,134	303
St. Mary's U of San Antonio, San Antonio, TX 78228-8507	1852	$10,608	$4,768	2-D	4,203	306
Saint Michael's Coll, Colchester, VT 05439	1904	$15,900	$7,000	2-M	2,729	212
St. Norbert Coll, De Pere, WI 54115-2099	1898	$14,434	$5,120	2-M	2,000	170
St. Olaf Coll, Northfield, MN 55057-1098	1874	$16,500	$4,020	2-B	2,975	366
Saint Peter's Coll, Jersey City, NJ 07306-5997	1872	$14,366	$5,060	2-M	3,698	360
St. Thomas Aquinas Coll, Sparkill, NY 10976	1952	$10,700	$6,700	1-M	2,215	150
St. Thomas U, Miami, FL 33054-6459	1961	$11,840	$4,000	2-F	2,203	132
Saint Vincent Coll, Latrobe, PA 15650	1846	$13,461	$4,642	2-B	1,238	109
Saint Xavier U, Chicago, IL 60655-3105	1847	$12,560	$5,184	2-M	3,719	261
Salem Coll, Winston-Salem, NC 27108-0548 (4)	1772	$12,415	$7,320	2-M	1,002	84
Salisbury State U, Salisbury, MD 21801-6837	1925	$3,842 (S)	$5,140	5-M	6,022	342
Salve Regina U, Newport, RI 02840-4192	1934	$16,300	$7,250	2-D	2,168	195
Samford U, Birmingham, AL 35229-0002	1841	$9,432	$4,396	2-D	4,485	399
Sam Houston State U, Huntsville, TX 77341	1879	$1,586 (S)	$3,290	5-D	12,712	524
San Diego State U, San Diego, CA 92182	1897	$1,854 (S)	$6,730	5-D	29,898	2,264
San Francisco State U, San Francisco, CA 94132-1722	1899	$1,982 (S)	$5,935	5-M	27,420	1,557
San Jose State U, San Jose, CA 95192-0001	1857	$2,017 (S)	$5,306	5-M	26,897	1,644
Santa Clara U, Santa Clara, CA 95053-0001	1851	$16,635	$7,026	2-D	7,946	569
Sarah Lawrence Coll, Bronxville, NY 10708	1926	$23,076	$7,219	1-M	1,388	238
Savannah Coll of Art & Design, Savannah, GA 31402-3146	1978	$13,500	$6,375	1-M	3,464	195
Savannah State U, Savannah, GA 31404	1890	$2,226 (S)	$3,495	5-M	2,745	155
School of the Art Inst of Chicago, Chicago, IL 60603-3103	1866	$17,160	NA	1-M	2,228	419
School of the Museum of Fine Arts, Boston, MA 02115	1876	$15,890	NA	1-M	1,133	142
School of Visual Arts, New York, NY 10010-3994	1947	$13,890	NA	3-M	5,195	749
Seattle Pacific U, Seattle, WA 98119-1997	1891	$14,541	$5,574	2-D	3,321	208
Seattle U, Seattle, WA 98122	1891	$14,805	$5,199	2-D	5,739	389
Seton Hall U, South Orange, NJ 07079-2697	1856	$13,600	$7,020	2-D	10,114	733
Seton Hill Coll, Greensburg, PA 15601 (4)	1883	$12,640	$4,730	2-M	1,078	93
Shawnee State U, Portsmouth, OH 45662-4344	1986	$3,063 (S)	$4,500	5-B	3,223	239
Shaw U, Raleigh, NC 27601-2399	1865	$6,304	$4,052	2-B	2,327	276
Shenandoah U, Winchester, VA 22601-5195	1875	$14,400	$5,050	2-D	1,927	249
Shepherd Coll, Shepherdstown, WV 25443-3210	1871	$2,228 (S)	$4,139	5-B	4,025	290
Shippensburg U of Pennsylvania, Shippensburg, PA 17257-2299	1871	$4,344 (S)	$3,722	5-M	6,674	363
Shorter Coll, Rome, GA 30165-4298	1873	$8,260	$4,250	2-B	1,639	98
Siena Coll, Loudonville, NY 12211-1462	1937	$12,710	$5,635	2-M	3,011	241
Siena Heights U, Adrian, MI 49221-1796	1919	$10,700	$4,330	2-M	1,287	110
Silver Lake Coll, Manitowoc, WI 54220-9319	1869	$9,986	$4,226	2-M	1,050	135
Simmons Coll, Boston, MA 02115 (3)	1899	$18,564	$7,228	1-D	3,494	371
Simpson Coll & Graduate School, Redding, CA 96003-8606	1921	$9,110	$3,900	2-M	1,248	91
Simpson Coll, Indianola, IA 50125-1297	1860	$13,095	$4,290	2-B	1,958	109
Skidmore Coll, Saratoga Springs, NY 12866-1632	1903	$21,988	$6,354	1-M	2,603	185

Name, address	Year	Tuition & Fees	Room & Board	Control, Degree	Enroll-ment	Faculty
Slippery Rock U of Pennsylvania, Slippery Rock, PA 16057	1889	$4,302 (S)	$3,590	5-D	7,038	402
Smith Coll, Northampton, MA 01063 (3)	1871	$21,512	$7,250	1-D	3,199	276
Sonoma State U, Rohnert Park, CA 94928-3609	1960	$2,130 (S)	$5,769	5-M	7,050	474
South Carolina State U, Orangeburg, SC 29117-0001	1896	$2,974 (S)	$2,836	5-D	4,657	229
South Dakota School of Mines & Technology, Rapid City, SD 57701	1885	$3,378 (S)	$2,910	5-D	2,210	145
South Dakota State U, Brookings, SD 57007	1881	$2,912 (S)	$2,482	5-D	8,867	539
Southeastern Coll of the Assemblies of God, Lakeland, FL 33801-6099	1935	$4,999	$3,274	2-B	1,069	87
Southeastern Louisiana U, Hammond, LA 70402	1925	$2,155 (S)	$2,400	5-M	15,241	645
Southeastern Oklahoma State U, Durant, OK 74701-0609	1909	$1,879 (S)	$2,619	5-M	3,946	206
Southeast Missouri State U, Cape Girardeau, MO 63701-4799	1873	$3,000 (S)	$6,920	5-M	8,231	378
Southern Adventist U, Collegedale, TN 37315-0370	1892	$9,736	$3,628	2-M	1,695	98
Southern Arkansas U–Magnolia, Magnolia, AR 71753	1909	$1,896 (S)	$2,530	5-M	2,676	154
Southern California Coll, Costa Mesa, CA 92626-6597	1920	$11,848	$4,860	2-M	1,312	167
Southern Connecticut State U, New Haven, CT 06515-1355	1893	$3,568 (S)	$5,366	5-M	11,395	754
Southern Illinois U at Carbondale, Carbondale, IL 62901-6806	1869	$3,420 (S)	$3,649	5-D	21,908	1,057
Southern Illinois U at Edwardsville, Edwardsville, IL 62026-0001	1957	$2,276 (S)	$4,066	5-F	11,207	771
Southern Methodist U, Dallas, TX 75275	1911	$16,790	$6,454	2-D	9,708	678
Southern Oregon U, Ashland, OR 97520	1926	$3,204 (S)	$4,380	5-M	5,426	219
Southern Polytechnic State U, Marietta, GA 30060-2896	1948	$1,998 (S)	$3,450	5-M	3,918	202
Southern U & Ag & Mech Coll, Baton Rouge, LA 70813	1880	$2,068 (S)	$3,270	5-D	9,815	539
Southern Utah U, Cedar City, UT 84720-2498	1897	$1,854 (S)	$2,502	5-M	5,852	217
Southern Wesleyan U, Central, SC 29630-1020	1906	$10,180	$3,540	2-M	1,337	46
Southwest Baptist U, Bolivar, MO 65613-2597	1878	$8,347	$2,580	2-M	3,593	180
Southwestern Adventist U, Keene, TX 76059	1894	$8,500	$4,084	2-M	1,106	80
Southwestern Assemblies of God U, Waxahachie, TX 75165-2397	1927	$5,350	$3,946	2-M	1,490	70
Southwestern Oklahoma State U, Weatherford, OK 73096-3098	1901	$1,798 (S)	$2,320	5-M	4,478	240
Southwestern U, Georgetown, TX 78626	1840	$14,000	$5,270	2-B	1,215	138
Southwest Missouri State U, Springfield, MO 65804-0094	1905	$3,214 (S)	$3,594	5-M	16,468	836
Southwest State U, Marshall, MN 56258-1598	1963	$3,056 (S)	$2,957	5-M	3,123	130
Southwest Texas State U, San Marcos, TX 78666	1899	$2,214 (S)	$3,901	5-D	20,652	943
Spalding U, Louisville, KY 40203-2188	1814	$10,396	$2,990	2-D	1,563	180
Spelman Coll, Atlanta, GA 30314-4399 (3)	1881	$10,095	$6,370	1-B	1,937	209
Spring Arbor Coll, Spring Arbor, MI 49283-9799	1873	$10,686	$4,190	2-M	2,242	103
Springfield Coll, Springfield, MA 01109-3797	1885	$14,825	$5,018	1-D	2,490	232
Spring Hill Coll, Mobile, AL 36608-1791	1830	$13,860	$4,980	2-M	1,745	90
Stanford U, Stanford, CA 94305-9991	1891	$21,389	$7,560	1-D	16,496	1,534
State U of New York at Albany, Albany, NY 12222-0001	1844	$4,173 (S)	$5,241	5-D	16,051	835
State U of New York at Binghamton, Binghamton, NY 13902-6000	1946	$4,110 (S)	$5,114	5-D	12,156	838
State U of New York at Buffalo, Buffalo, NY 14260	1846	$4,340 (S)	$5,604	5-D	23,429	1,484
State U of New York at Farmingdale, Farmingdale, NY 11735	1912	$3,950 (S)	$5,686	5-B	5,508	324
State U of New York at New Paltz, New Paltz, NY 12561-2499	1828	$3,885 (S)	$5,020	5-M	7,641	534
State U of New York at Oswego, Oswego, NY 13126	1861	$3,945 (S)	$5,728	5-M	7,802	391
State U of New York at Stony Brook, Stony Brook, NY 11794	1957	$3,932 (S)	$5,758	5-D	17,831	1,682
State U of New York Coll at Brockport, Brockport, NY 14420-2997	1867	$3,940 (S)	$4,960	5-M	8,492	479
State U of New York Coll at Buffalo, Buffalo, NY 14222-1095	1867	$3,791 (S)	$4,560	5-M	10,821	703
State U of New York Coll at Cortland, Cortland, NY 13045	1868	$3,974 (S)	$5,300	5-M	6,306	432
State U of New York Coll at Fredonia, Fredonia, NY 14063	1826	$4,075 (S)	$4,650	5-M	4,593	333
State U of New York Coll at Geneseo, Geneseo, NY 14454-1401	1871	$4,016 (S)	$4,700	5-M	5,560	348
State U of New York Coll at Old Westbury, Old Westbury, NY 11568	1965	$3,731 (S)	$5,903	5-B	3,647	228
State U of New York Coll at Oneonta, Oneonta, NY 13820-4015	1889	$3,908 (S)	$5,456	5-M	5,406	337
State U of New York Coll at Potsdam, Potsdam, NY 13676	1816	$3,899 (S)	$4,900	5-M	4,038	288
State U of New York Coll of Environmental Sci & Forestry, Syracuse, NY 13210	1911	$3,413 (S)	$7,360	5-D	1,632	141
State U of New York Empire State Coll, Saratoga Springs, NY 12866	1971	$3,545 (S)	NA	5-M	7,542	329
State U of New York Inst of Technology at Utica/Rome, Utica, NY 13504-3050	1966	$3,939 (S)	$5,880	5-M	2,498	162
State U of West Georgia, Carrollton, GA 30118	1933	$2,088 (S)	$3,399	5-M	8,422	384
Stephen F. Austin State U, Nacogdoches, TX 75962	1923	$1,513 (S)	$3,682	5-D	12,041	680
Stetson U, DeLand, FL 32720-3781	1883	$15,765	$4,655	1-F	2,857	227
Stevens Inst of Technology, Hoboken, NJ 07030	1870	$19,360	$6,724	1-D	3,248	201
Stonehill Coll, Easton, MA 02357	1948	$15,730	$7,350	2-B	2,715	189
Strayer U, Washington, DC 20005-2603	1892	$8,100	NA	3-M	9,419	364
Suffolk U, Boston, MA 02108-2770	1906	$12,920	$8,350	1-D	6,290	619
Sullivan Coll, Louisville, KY 40205	1864	$8,904	NA	3-M	2,481	88
Susquehanna U, Selinsgrove, PA 17870-1001	1858	$18,350	$5,230	2-B	1,725	161
Swarthmore Coll, Swarthmore, PA 19081-1397	1864	$22,000	$7,500	1-B	1,370	179
Syracuse U, Syracuse, NY 13244-0003	1870	$18,056	$7,760	1-D	14,557	1,377
Taylor U, Upland, IN 46989-1001	1846	$13,484	$4,410	2-B	1,884	137
Teikyo Post U, Waterbury, CT 06723-2540	1890	$12,260	$5,600	1-B	1,334	24
Temple U, Philadelphia, PA 19122-6096	1884	$6,150 (S)	$5,772	12-D	27,670	2,480
Tennessee State U, Nashville, TN 37209-1561	1912	$3,069 (S)	$3,060	5-D	8,625	369
Tennessee Technological U, Cookeville, TN 38505	1915	$2,116 (S)	$3,180	5-D	8,263	460
Texas A&M U, College Station, TX 77843	1876	$2,777 (S)	$4,276	5-D	41,461	2,299
Texas A&M U at Galveston, Galveston, TX 77553-1675	1962	$2,834 (S)	$3,653	5-B	1,111	89
Texas A&M U–Commerce, Commerce, TX 75429-3011	1889	$2,288 (S)	$3,816	5-D	7,693	382
Texas A&M U–Corpus Christi, Corpus Christi, TX 78412-5503	1947	$1,954 (S)	NA	5-D	6,024	405
Texas A&M U–Kingsville, Kingsville, TX 78363	1925	$2,180 (S)	$3,484	5-D	6,050	342
Texas A&M U–Texarkana, Texarkana, TX 75505-5518	1971	$1,586 (S)	NA	5-M	1,046	49
Texas Christian U, Fort Worth, TX 76129-0002	1873	$11,090	$3,860	2-D	7,273	505
Texas Lutheran U, Seguin, TX 78155-5999	1891	$10,370	$3,772	2-B	1,344	98
Texas Southern U, Houston, TX 77004-4584	1947	$2,064 (S)	$4,000	5-D	7,282	524
Texas Tech U, Lubbock, TX 79409	1923	$2,607 (S)	$4,290	5-D	25,022	1,024
Texas Wesleyan U, Fort Worth, TX 76105-1536	1890	$7,950	$3,700	2-F	3,136	238
Texas Woman's U, Denton, TX 76204 (4)	1901	$1,980 (S)	$3,360	5-D	9,378	750
Thiel Coll, Greenville, PA 16125-2181	1866	$13,390	$5,220	2-B	1,012	107
Thomas More Coll, Crestview Hills, KY 41017-3495	1921	$11,250	$4,500	2-M	1,402	174
Tiffin U, Tiffin, OH 44883-2161	1888	$9,210	$4,400	1-M	1,277	80
Toccoa Falls Coll, Toccoa Falls, GA 30598-1000	1907	$7,525	$3,708	2-M	1,032	76

Name, address	Year	Tuition & Fees	Room & Board	Control, Degree	Enroll-ment	Faculty
Towson U, Towson, MD 21252-0001	1866	$4,120 (S)	$5,044	5-M	15,524	1,034
Transylvania U, Lexington, KY 40508-1797	1780	$13,260	$4,990	2-B	1,027	90
Trevecca Nazarene U, Nashville, TN 37210-2834	1901	$9,090	$4,038	2-M	1,516	115
Trinity Coll, Hartford, CT 06106-3100	1823	$22,470	$6,320	1-M	2,215	306
Trinity Coll, Washington, DC 20017-1094 (3)	1897	$12,490	$3,530	2-M	1,489	136
Trinity Intl U, Deerfield, IL 60015-1284	1897	$12,630	$4,630	2-D	2,571	161
Trinity U, San Antonio, TX 78212-7200	1869	$14,724	$5,970	2-M	2,560	281
Tri-State U, Angola, IN 46703-1764	1884	$11,900	$4,850	1-B	1,116	86
Troy State U Dothan, Dothan, AL 36304-0368	1961	$2,229 (S)	NA	5-M	2,102	133
Troy State U Montgomery, Montgomery, AL 36103-4419	1957	$2,085 (S)	NA	5-M	3,349	190
Truman State U, Kirksville, MO 63501-4221	1867	$3,274 (S)	$3,992	5-M	6,421	399
Tufts U, Medford, MA 02155	1852	$22,811	$6,804	1-D	8,742	1,018
Tulane U, New Orleans, LA 70118-5669	1834	$22,066	$6,600	1-D	10,921	758
Tusculum Coll, Greeneville, TN 37743-9997	1794	$11,800	$3,900	2-M	1,526	163
Tuskegee U, Tuskegee, AL 36088	1881	$8,662	$4,104	1-F	3,023	306
Union Coll, Barbourville, KY 40906-1499	1879	$9,340	$3,120	2-M	1,016	77
Union Coll, Schenectady, NY 12308-2311	1795	$22,135	$6,330	1-M	2,425	208
The Union Inst, Cincinnati, OH 45206-1925	1969	$7,296	NA	1-D	2,036	109
Union U, Jackson, TN 38305-3697	1823	$8,180	$3,005	2-M	1,953	159
United States Air Force Acad, USAF Academy, CO 80840-5025	1954	$0 (C)	NA	4-B	4,096	558
United States Intl U, San Diego, CA 92131-1799	1952	$11,745	$4,800	1-D	1,331	111
United States Military Acad, West Point, NY 10996	1802	$0 (C)	NA	4-B	4,087	591
United States Naval Acad, Annapolis, MD 21402-5000	1845	$0 (C)	NA	4-B	3,994	600
The U of Akron, Akron, OH 44325-0001	1870	$3,660 (S)	$4,490	5-D	23,538	1,771
The U of Alabama, Tuscaloosa, AL 35487	1831	$2,594 (S)	$3,610	5-D	18,324	1,021
The U of Alabama at Birmingham, Birmingham, AL 35294	1969	$2,850 (S)	NA	5-D	14,933	1,737
The U of Alabama in Huntsville, Huntsville, AL 35899	1950	$2,832 (S)	$3,700	5-D	6,464	447
U of Alaska Anchorage, Anchorage, AK 99508-8060	1954	$2,466 (S)	$6,591	5-M	14,765	982
U of Alaska Fairbanks, Fairbanks, AK 99775-7480	1917	$2,410 (S)	$3,690	5-D	7,686	717
The U of Arizona, Tucson, AZ 85721	1885	$2,058 (S)	$4,930	5-D	33,737	1,551
U of Arkansas, Fayetteville, AR 72701-1201	1871	$2,661 (S)	$3,867	5-D	14,322	906
U of Arkansas at Little Rock, Little Rock, AR 72204-1099	1927	$3,026 (S)	NA	5-D	10,959	801
U of Baltimore, Baltimore, MD 21201-5779	1925	$3,804 (S)	NA	5-F	4,609	262
U of Bridgeport, Bridgeport, CT 06601	1927	$13,644	$6,810	1-D	2,427	266
U of California, Davis, Davis, CA 95616	1905	$4,332 (S)	$6,050	5-D	24,551	1,602
U of California, Los Angeles, Los Angeles, CA 90095	1919	$4,050 (S)	$6,490	5-D	35,558	3,276
U of California, Riverside, Riverside, CA 92521-0102	1954	$4,126 (S)	$6,209	5-D	9,850	451
U of California, San Diego, La Jolla, CA 92093-5003	1959	$4,200 (S)	$6,682	5-D	18,667	1,427
U of California, Santa Barbara, Santa Barbara, CA 93106	1909	$4,098 (S)	$6,407	5-D	18,940	901
U of California, Santa Cruz, Santa Cruz, CA 95064	1965	$4,181 (S)	$6,690	5-D	10,638	593
U of Central Arkansas, Conway, AR 72035-0001	1907	$2,692 (S)	$2,920	5-D	8,938	504
U of Central Oklahoma, Edmond, OK 73034-5209	1890	$1,806 (S)	$2,481	5-M	13,928	701
U of Central Texas, Killeen, TX 76540-1416	1973	$3,224	$4,652	1-M	1,117	56
U of Chicago, Chicago, IL 60637-1513	1891	$22,476	$7,604	1-D	11,849	1,840
U of Cincinnati, Cincinnati, OH 45221	1819	$4,359 (S)	$5,643	5-D	28,161	1,257
U of Colorado at Boulder, Boulder, CO 80309	1876	$2,939 (S)	$4,566	5-D	25,109	1,522
U of Colorado at Colorado Springs, Colorado Springs, CO 80933-7150	1965	$2,520 (S)	$4,790	5-D	6,440	447
U of Colorado at Denver, Denver, CO 80217-3364	1912	$2,204 (S)	NA	5-D	13,092	668
U of Connecticut, Storrs, CT 06269	1881	$5,096 (S)	$5,462	5-D	18,205	1,071
U of Dallas, Irving, TX 75062-4799	1955	$12,144	$4,920	2-D	2,897	211
U of Dayton, Dayton, OH 45469-1611	1850	$14,670	$4,670	2-D	10,208	772
U of Delaware, Newark, DE 19716	1743	$4,574 (S)	$4,770	12-D	18,230	1,016
U of Denver, Denver, CO 80208	1864	$17,886	$5,743	1-D	8,667	423
U of Detroit Mercy, Detroit, MI 48219-0900	1877	$12,986	$5,080	2-D	6,929	589
U of Evansville, Evansville, IN 47722-0002	1854	$13,880	$4,900	2-M	3,023	193
The U of Findlay, Findlay, OH 45840-3653	1882	$13,878	$5,360	2-M	4,017	289
U of Florida, Gainesville, FL 32611	1853	$1,930 (S)	$4,610	5-D	41,713	1,633
U of Georgia, Athens, GA 30602	1785	$2,838 (S)	$4,323	5-D	29,693	3,075
U of Great Falls, Great Falls, MT 59405	1932	$8,100	$3,520	2-M	1,164	98
U of Hartford, West Hartford, CT 06117-1599	1877	$17,320	$7,200	1-D	7,089	737
U of Hawaii at Hilo, Hilo, HI 96720-4091	1970	$2,186 (S)	$4,810	5-B	2,462	281
U of Hawaii at Manoa, Honolulu, HI 96822	1907	$2,950 (S)	$4,740	5-D	17,356	1,413
U of Houston, Houston, TX 77204-2163	1927	$1,993 (S)	$4,405	5-D	31,602	898
U of Houston–Clear Lake, Houston, TX 77058-1098	1974	$2,106 (S)	NA	5-M	6,947	411
U of Houston–Downtown, Houston, TX 77002-1001	1974	$2,046 (S)	NA	5-B	8,194	377
U of Houston–Victoria, Victoria, TX 77901-4450	1973	$1,776 (S)	NA	5-M	1,491	84
U of Idaho, Moscow, ID 83844-4140	1889	$1,942 (S)	$3,824	5-D	11,027	625
U of Illinois at Chicago, Chicago, IL 60607-7128	1946	$3,898 (S)	$5,526	5-D	24,578	2,711
U of Illinois at Springfield, Springfield, IL 62794-9243	1969	$2,789 (S)	NA	5-M	4,463	246
U of Illinois at Urbana–Champaign, Urbana, IL 61801	1867	$4,120 (S)	$5,078	5-D	36,019	1,896
U of Indianapolis, Indianapolis, IN 46227-3697	1902	$12,990	$4,550	2-D	3,829	321
The U of Iowa, Iowa City, IA 52242	1847	$2,760 (S)	$4,046	5-D	28,409	1,712
U of Kansas, Lawrence, KS 66045	1866	$2,385 (S)	$3,736	5-D	27,567	1,975
U of Kentucky, Lexington, KY 40506-0032	1865	$2,736 (S)	$3,388	5-D	23,540	2,237
U of Louisville, Louisville, KY 40292-0001	1798	$2,630 (S)	$4,982	5-D	20,283	1,798
U of Maine, Orono, ME 04469	1865	$4,344 (S)	$4,906	5-D	8,917	634
U of Maine at Augusta, Augusta, ME 04330-9410	1965	$3,255 (S)	NA	5-B	5,248	207
U of Maine at Farmington, Farmington, ME 04938-1990	1863	$3,520 (S)	$4,406	5-B	2,337	149
U of Maine at Presque Isle, Presque Isle, ME 04769-2888	1903	$3,210 (S)	$3,918	5-B	1,413	93
U of Mary, Bismarck, ND 58504-9652	1959	$8,055	$3,150	2-M	2,148	155
U of Mary Hardin-Baylor, Belton, TX 76513	1845	$6,944	$3,250	2-M	2,313	194
U of Maryland, Baltimore County, Baltimore, MD 21250-5398	1966	$4,570 (S)	$4,998	5-D	9,863	755
U of Maryland, Coll Park, College Park, MD 20742-5045	1856	$4,460 (S)	$5,667	5-D	32,711	1,955
U of Maryland Eastern Shore, Princess Anne, MD 21853-1299	1886	$3,240 (S)	$4,330	5-D	3,204	280
U of Maryland U Coll, College Park, MD 20742-1600	1947	$5,490 (S)	NA	5-M	13,786	658
U of Massachusetts Amherst, Amherst, MA 01003-0001	1863	$5,572 (S)	$4,520	5-D	24,884	1,314
U of Massachusetts Boston, Boston, MA 02125-3393	1964	$4,297 (S)	NA	5-D	12,828	818

Name, address	Year	Tuition & Fees	Room & Board	Control, Degree	Enroll-ment	Faculty
U of Massachusetts Dartmouth, North Dartmouth, MA 02747-2300	1895	$1,744 (S)	$4,828	5-D	6,366	427
U of Massachusetts Lowell, Lowell, MA 01854-2881	1894	$4,422 (S)	$4,580	5-D	12,322	602
The U of Memphis, Memphis, TN 38152	1912	$2,412 (S)	$3,500	5-D	19,851	1,205
U of Miami, Coral Gables, FL 33124	1925	$19,512	$7,352	1-D	13,651	2,351
U of Michigan, Ann Arbor, MI 48109	1817	$5,710 (S)	$5,342	5-D	36,995	3,624
U of Michigan–Dearborn, Dearborn, MI 48128-1491	1959	$4,850 (S)	NA	5-M	8,179	411
U of Michigan–Flint, Flint, MI 48502-2186	1956	$3,559 (S)	NA	5-M	6,488	242
U of Minnesota, Crookston, Crookston, MN 56716-5001	1966	$4,568 (S)	$3,687	5-B	2,219	85
U of Minnesota, Duluth, Duluth, MN 55812-2496	1947	$4,316 (S)	$3,912	5-M	9,653	510
U of Minnesota, Morris, Morris, MN 56267	1959	$4,554 (S)	$3,714	5-B	1,947	120
U of Minnesota, Twin Cities Campus, Minneapolis, MN 55455-0213	1851	$4,450 (S)	$4,311	5-D	45,410	2,722
U of Mississippi, University, MS 38677-9702	1844	$2,631 (S)	$3,186	5-D	11,179	522
U of Mississippi Medical Ctr, Jackson, MS 39216-4505	1955	$2,106 (S)	NA	5-D	1,366	644
U of Missouri–Columbia, Columbia, MO 65211	1839	$4,280 (S)	$4,290	5-D	22,552	1,644
U of Missouri–Kansas City, Kansas City, MO 64110-2499	1929	$4,278 (S)	$4,270	5-D	10,445	726
U of Missouri–Rolla, Rolla, MO 65409-0910	1870	$4,194 (S)	$4,220	5-D	4,976	383
U of Missouri–St. Louis, St. Louis, MO 63121-4499	1963	$4,396 (S)	$4,845	5-D	15,576	1,040
U of Mobile, Mobile, AL 36663-0220	1961	$7,260	$4,080	2-M	2,117	151
The U of Montana–Missoula, Missoula, MT 59812-0002	1893	$2,630 (S)	$3,917	5-D	12,124	590
U of Montevallo, Montevallo, AL 35115	1896	$3,180 (S)	$3,116	5-M	3,125	202
U of Nebraska at Kearney, Kearney, NE 68849-0001	1903	$2,269 (S)	$3,034	5-M	7,133	430
U of Nebraska at Omaha, Omaha, NE 68182	1908	$2,356 (S)	NA	5-D	13,710	772
U of Nebraska–Lincoln, Lincoln, NE 68588	1869	$2,829 (S)	$3,700	5-D	22,827	1,519
U of Nebraska Medical Ctr, Omaha, NE 68198-0001	1869	$2,732 (S)	NA	5-D	2,618	709
U of Nevada, Las Vegas, Las Vegas, NV 89154-9900	1957	$1,642 (S)	$5,300	5-D	19,249	1,090
U of Nevada, Reno, Reno, NV 89557	1874	$2,109 (S)	$5,095	5-D	12,442	668
U of New England, Biddeford, ME 04005-9526	1953	$14,085	$5,820	1-F	2,478	179
U of New Hampshire, Durham, NH 03824	1866	$5,889 (S)	$4,524	5-D	13,960	883
U of New Haven, West Haven, CT 06516-1916	1920	$13,100	$5,700	1-D	4,976	546
U of New Mexico, Albuquerque, NM 87131-2039	1889	$2,165 (S)	$4,119	5-D	23,956	2,006
U of New Orleans, New Orleans, LA 70148	1958	$2,512 (S)	$3,150	5-D	15,833	692
U of North Alabama, Florence, AL 35632-0001	1830	$2,184 (S)	$3,260	5-M	5,575	272
U of North Carolina at Asheville, Asheville, NC 28804-3299	1927	$1,834 (S)	$3,826	5-M	3,179	270
The U of North Carolina at Chapel Hill, Chapel Hill, NC 27599	1789	$2,165 (S)	$4,760	5-D	24,231	2,640
U of North Carolina at Charlotte, Charlotte, NC 28223-0001	1946	$1,718 (S)	$3,446	5-D	16,511	931
U of North Carolina at Greensboro, Greensboro, NC 27412-0001	1891	$2,021 (S)	$3,661	5-D	12,308	767
U of North Carolina at Pembroke, Pembroke, NC 28372-1510	1887	$1,510 (S)	$2,910	5-M	3,034	207
U of North Carolina at Wilmington, Wilmington, NC 28403-3201	1947	$1,796 (S)	$4,260	5-M	9,176	527
U of North Dakota, Grand Forks, ND 58202	1883	$2,946 (S)	$3,117	5-D	10,363	731
U of Northern Colorado, Greeley, CO 80639	1890	$2,578 (S)	$4,420	5-D	11,860	576
U of Northern Iowa, Cedar Falls, IA 50614	1876	$2,752 (S)	$3,452	5-D	13,503	820
U of North Florida, Jacksonville, FL 32224-2645	1965	$2,006 (S)	$3,492	5-D	11,389	660
U of North Texas, Denton, TX 76203-6737	1890	$2,187 (S)	$3,842	5-D	25,013	979
U of Notre Dame, Notre Dame, IN 46556	1842	$19,947	$5,060	2-D	10,275	944
U of Oklahoma, Norman, OK 73019-0390	1890	$2,311 (S)	$3,800	5-D	25,975	2,021
U of Oregon, Eugene, OR 97403	1872	$3,408 (S)	$4,646	5-D	17,530	1,168
U of Osteopathic Medicine & Health Scis, Des Moines, IA 50312-4104	1898	$12,070	NA	1-F	1,155	108
U of Pennsylvania, Philadelphia, PA 19104	1740	$22,250	$7,430	1-D	21,643	3,632
U of Phoenix, Phoenix, AZ 85072-2069	1976	$5,352	NA	3-M	41,467	4,621
U of Pittsburgh, Pittsburgh, PA 15260	1787	$6,164 (S)	$5,414	12-D	25,461	3,394
U of Pittsburgh at Greensburg, Greensburg, PA 15601-5860	1963	$6,074 (S)	$4,280	12-B	1,501	90
U of Pittsburgh at Johnstown, Johnstown, PA 15904-2990	1927	$6,154 (S)	$4,720	12-B	3,096	188
U of Portland, Portland, OR 97203-5798	1901	$15,520	$4,710	2-M	2,606	251
U of Puerto Rico, Aguadilla Regional Coll, Aguadilla, PR 00604-0160	1972	$1,638 (S)	NA	6-B	3,312	133
U of Puerto Rico at Arecibo, Arecibo, PR 00613	1967	$1,559 (S)	NA	6-B	4,665	251
U of Puerto Rico at Ponce, Ponce, PR 00732-7186	1970	$1,090 (S)	NA	6-B	4,345	186
U of Puerto Rico, Cayey U Coll, Cayey, PR 00737	1967	$970 (S)	NA	6-B	3,944	246
U of Puerto Rico, Humacao U Coll, Humacao, PR 00791	1962	$1,020 (S)	NA	6-B	4,320	283
U of Puerto Rico, Medical Scis Campus, San Juan, PR 00936-5067	1950	$1,200 (S)	NA	6-D	2,795	759
U of Puget Sound, Tacoma, WA 98416-0005	1888	$18,940	$4,920	1-M	3,011	293
U of Redlands, Redlands, CA 92373-0999	1907	$18,545	$7,096	1-M	1,490	639
U of Rhode Island, Kingston, RI 02881	1892	$4,592 (S)	$5,764	5-D	13,437	626
U of Richmond, University of Richmond, VA 23173	1830	$17,570	$4,143	1-F	4,425	515
U of Rio Grande, Rio Grande, OH 45674	1876	$3,589 (A)	$4,605	1-M	2,000	111
U of Rochester, Rochester, NY 14627-0001	1850	$21,020	$7,185	1-D	8,451	1,331
U of St. Francis, Joliet, IL 60435-6188	1920	$11,950	$4,740	2-M	4,333	139
U of Saint Francis, Fort Wayne, IN 46808-3994	1890	$10,710	$4,270	2-M	1,005	102
U of St. Thomas, St. Paul, MN 55105-1096	1885	$14,660	$4,769	2-D	10,436	723
U of St. Thomas, Houston, TX 77006-4696	1947	$10,550	$4,690	2-D	2,506	205
U of San Diego, San Diego, CA 92110-2492	1949	$15,780	$6,970	2-D	6,694	525
U of San Francisco, San Francisco, CA 94117-1080	1855	$15,950	$7,260	2-D	7,975	770
U of Science & Arts of Oklahoma, Chickasha, OK 73018-0001	1908	$1,368 (S)	$2,670	5-B	1,393	85
U of Scranton, Scranton, PA 18510-4622	1888	$15,880	$7,011	2-M	4,816	383
U of South Carolina, Columbia, SC 29208	1801	$3,534 (S)	$3,830	5-D	25,447	1,449
U of South Carolina–Aiken, Aiken, SC 29801-6309	1961	$3,014 (S)	$3,576	5-M	3,004	231
U of South Carolina Spartanburg, Spartanburg, SC 29303-4932	1967	$3,014 (S)	$3,200	5-M	3,549	214
U of South Dakota, Vermillion, SD 57069-2390	1862	$3,012 (S)	$2,912	5-D	7,392	356
U of Southern California, Los Angeles, CA 90089	1880	$20,480	$6,748	1-D	28,342	3,508
U of Southern Colorado, Pueblo, CO 81001-4901	1933	$2,191 (S)	$4,508	5-M	5,066	222
U of Southern Indiana, Evansville, IN 47712-3590	1965	$2,705 (S)	NA	5-M	8,300	443
U of Southern Maine, Portland, ME 04104-9300	1878	$3,938 (S)	$4,646	5-F	10,236	582
U of Southern Mississippi, Hattiesburg, MS 39406-5167	1910	$2,590 (S)	$2,565	5-D	14,599	706
U of South Florida, Tampa, FL 33620-9951	1956	$2,086 (S)	$4,596	5-D	34,036	1,652
U of Southwestern Louisiana, Lafayette, LA 70503	1898	$1,947 (S)	$2,592	5-D	17,020	642
The U of Tampa, Tampa, FL 33606-1490	1931	$14,652	$4,780	1-M	2,896	220
U of Tennessee at Chattanooga, Chattanooga, TN 37403-2598	1886	$2,200 (S)	NA	5-M	8,528	580
The U of Tennessee at Martin, Martin, TN 38238-1000	1927	$2,240 (S)	$3,104	5-M	5,997	260

Name, address	Year	Tuition & Fees	Room & Board	Control, Degree	Enroll-ment	Faculty
U of Tennessee, Knoxville, Knoxville, TN 37996	1794	$2,576 (S)	$3,802	5-D	25,397	1,453
The U of Texas at Arlington, Arlington, TX 76019-0407	1895	$2,088 (S)	NA	5-D	19,286	972
The U of Texas at Austin, Austin, TX 78712	1883	$2,866 (S)	$3,901	5-D	48,857	2,517
The U of Texas at Dallas, Richardson, TX 75083-0688	1969	$2,414 (S)	NA	5-D	9,330	448
The U of Texas at El Paso, El Paso, TX 79968-0001	1913	$2,266 (S)	NA	5-D	15,176	795
The U of Texas at San Antonio, San Antonio, TX 78249-0617	1969	$2,744 (S)	NA	5-D	17,494	867
The U of Texas at Tyler, Tyler, TX 75799-0001	1971	$2,084 (S)	$6,029	5-M	3,393	219
The U of Texas–Houston Health Science Ctr, Houston, TX 77225-0036	1972	$2,455 (S)	NA	5-D	3,089	1,046
The U of Texas Medical Branch at Galveston, Galveston, TX 77555	1891	$1,674 (S)	NA	5-D	2,127	1,334
U of the Arts, Philadelphia, PA 19102-4944	1870	$15,070	NA	1-M	1,624	357
U of the District of Columbia, Washington, DC 20008-1175	1976	$2,360 (S)	NA	9-M	4,754	615
U of the Incarnate Word, San Antonio, TX 78209-6397	1881	$10,840	$4,627	2-M	3,312	308
U of the Pacific, Stockton, CA 95211-0197	1851	$19,365	$5,770	1-D	5,585	592
U of the Sacred Heart, San Juan, PR 00914-0383	1935	$4,095	NA	2-M	4,915	368
U of the Scis in Philadelphia, Philadelphia, PA 19104-4495	1821	$13,290	$5,985	1-D	2,135	205
U of the South, Sewanee, TN 37383-1000	1857	$17,730	$4,660	2-D	1,355	158
U of the Virgin Islands, Charlotte Amalie, St. Thomas, VI 00802-9990	1962	$2,676 (S)	$5,466	7-M	2,610	240
U of Toledo, Toledo, OH 43606-3398	1872	$3,952 (S)	$4,194	5-D	20,307	1,346
U of Tulsa, Tulsa, OK 74104-3189	1894	$12,930	$4,410	2-D	4,171	408
U of Utah, Salt Lake City, UT 84112	1850	$2,601 (S)	$4,620	5-D	25,883	1,456
U of Vermont, Burlington, VT 05405-0160	1791	$7,550 (S)	$5,272	5-D	10,368	1,024
U of Virginia, Charlottesville, VA 22903	1819	$4,786 (S)	$4,279	5-D	21,942	1,866
U of Washington, Seattle, WA 98195	1861	$3,366 (S)	$4,671	5-D	35,367	3,892
The U of West Alabama, Livingston, AL 35470	1835	$2,568 (S)	$3,003	5-M	2,068	122
U of West Florida, Pensacola, FL 32514-5750	1963	$1,985 (S)	NA	5-D	8,038	209
U of Wisconsin–Eau Claire, Eau Claire, WI 54702-4004	1916	$2,872 (S)	$2,986	5-M	10,484	522
U of Wisconsin–Green Bay, Green Bay, WI 54311-7001	1968	$2,738 (S)	NA	5-M	5,419	289
U of Wisconsin–La Crosse, La Crosse, WI 54601-3742	1909	$2,859 (S)	$3,060	5-M	9,086	469
U of Wisconsin–Madison, Madison, WI 53706-1380	1848	$3,242 (S)	$4,880	5-D	40,196	2,545
U of Wisconsin–Milwaukee, Milwaukee, WI 53201-0413	1956	$3,327 (S)	NA	5-D	21,525	1,381
U of Wisconsin–Oshkosh, Oshkosh, WI 54901-8602	1871	$2,609 (S)	$2,658	5-M	10,960	538
U of Wisconsin–Parkside, Kenosha, WI 53141-2000	1968	$2,705 (S)	$4,000	5-M	4,696	275
U of Wisconsin–River Falls, River Falls, WI 54022-5001	1874	$2,750 (S)	$3,036	5-M	5,441	318
U of Wisconsin–Stevens Point, Stevens Point, WI 54481-3897	1894	$2,790 (S)	$3,188	5-M	8,446	435
U of Wisconsin–Stout, Menomonie, WI 54751	1891	$2,619 (S)	$3,062	5-M	7,418	413
U of Wisconsin–Superior, Superior, WI 54880-2873	1893	$2,652 (S)	$3,200	5-M	2,574	160
U of Wisconsin–Whitewater, Whitewater, WI 53190-1790	1868	$2,772 (S)	$2,812	5-M	10,563	471
U of Wyoming, Laramie, WY 82071	1886	$2,330 (S)	$4,278	5-D	11,094	683
Upper Iowa U, Fayette, IA 52142-1857	1857	$9,750	$3,770	1-M	4,109	182
Ursinus Coll, Collegeville, PA 19426-1000	1869	$17,380	$5,690	2-B	1,194	141
Ursuline Coll, Pepper Pike, OH 44124-4398 (4)	1871	$12,128	$4,460	2-M	1,233	133
Utah State U, Logan, UT 84322	1888	$2,175 (S)	$3,510	5-D	21,234	787
Utica Coll of Syracuse U, Utica, NY 13502-4892	1946	$14,912	$5,650	1-B	2,018	172
Valdosta State U, Valdosta, GA 31698	1906	$1,974 (S)	$3,465	5-D	9,779	472
Valparaiso U, Valparaiso, IN 46383-6493	1859	$15,060	$3,930	2-F	3,603	356
Vanderbilt U, Nashville, TN 37240-1001	1873	$21,478	$7,430	1-D	10,210	2,126
Vassar Coll, Poughkeepsie, NY 12604	1861	$22,090	$6,470	1-M	2,361	258
Villa Julie Coll, Stevenson, MD 21153	1952	$9,240	NA	1-M	1,951	165
Villanova U, Villanova, PA 19085-1699	1842	$19,133	$7,400	2-D	10,019	750
Virginia Commonwealth U, Richmond, VA 23284-9005	1838	$4,111 (S)	$4,540	5-D	22,702	2,523
Virginia Military Inst, Lexington, VA 24450	1839	$6,380 (S)	$3,695	5-B	1,282	134
Virginia Polytechnic Inst & State U, Blacksburg, VA 24061	1872	$4,147 (S)	$3,420	5-D	27,208	1,574
Virginia State U, Petersburg, VA 23806-2096	1882	$3,307 (S)	$4,910	5-M	4,200	275
Virginia Union U, Richmond, VA 23220-1170	1865	$8,980	$3,950	2-D	1,700	104
Virginia Wesleyan Coll, Norfolk, VA 23502-5599	1961	$13,400	$5,550	2-B	1,436	107
Viterbo Coll, La Crosse, WI 54601-4797	1890	$11,150	$4,250	2-M	2,622	227
Wagner Coll, Staten Island, NY 10301	1883	$16,000	$6,000	1-M	2,036	172
Wake Forest U, Winston-Salem, NC 27109	1834	$19,450	$5,450	1-D	6,124	1,708
Walla Walla Coll, College Place, WA 99324-1198	1892	$12,693	$3,380	2-M	1,653	191
Walsh Coll of Accountancy & Business Administration, Troy, MI 48007	1922	$4,758	NA	1-M	3,335	127
Walsh U, North Canton, OH 44720-3396	1958	$10,680	$4,990	2-M	1,492	122
Wartburg Coll, Waverly, IA 50677-1003	1852	$13,610	$4,010	2-B	1,528	130
Washburn U of Topeka, Topeka, KS 66621	1865	$3,150 (S)	$3,300	10-F	6,281	430
Washington & Jefferson Coll, Washington, PA 15301-4801	1781	$18,000	$4,350	1-B	1,218	111
Washington & Lee U, Lexington, VA 24450-0303	1749	$16,195	$5,620	1-F	2,052	194
Washington Coll, Chestertown, MD 21620-1197	1782	$18,250	$5,740	1-M	1,152	103
Washington State U, Pullman, WA 99164-1610	1890	$3,270 (S)	$4,426	5-D	20,243	1,253
Washington U in St. Louis, St. Louis, MO 63130-4899	1853	$22,422	$6,922	1-D	11,606	2,452
Wayland Baptist U, Plainview, TX 79072-6998	1908	$6,200	$3,314	2-M	4,190	302
Waynesburg Coll, Waynesburg, PA 15370-1222	1849	$10,550	$4,260	2-M	1,290	95
Wayne State Coll, Wayne, NE 68787	1910	$2,140 (S)	$2,860	5-M	3,839	228
Wayne State U, Detroit, MI 48202	1868	$3,399 (S)	NA	5-D	30,729	2,826
Weber State U, Ogden, UT 84408-1001	1889	$1,935 (S)	$3,810	5-M	14,613	465
Webster U, St. Louis, MO 63119-3194	1915	$10,910	$5,030	1-D	11,756	662
Wellesley Coll, Wellesley, MA 02181 (3)	1870	$21,660	$6,670	1-B	2,283	333
Wentworth Inst of Technology, Boston, MA 02115-5998	1904	$11,500	$6,200	1-B	3,094	164
Wesleyan U, Middletown, CT 06459-0260	1831	$22,980	$6,210	1-D	3,335	344
Wesley Coll, Dover, DE 19901	1873	$11,709	$5,019	2-M	1,249	88
West Chester U of Pennsylvania, West Chester, PA 19383	1871	$4,162 (S)	$4,376	5-M	11,430	717
Western Illinois U, Macomb, IL 61455-1390	1899	$3,037 (S)	$3,838	5-M	12,200	644
Western Intl U, Phoenix, AZ 85021-2718	1978	$5,280	NA	3-M	1,436	100
Western Kentucky U, Bowling Green, KY 42101-3576	1906	$2,140 (S)	$2,700	5-M	14,543	827
Western Maryland Coll, Westminster, MD 21157-4390	1867	$17,730	$5,350	1-M	2,785	213
Western Michigan U, Kalamazoo, MI 49008	1903	$3,655 (S)	$4,398	5-D	26,132	1,219
Western Montana Coll of The U of Montana, Dillon, MT 59725-3598	1893	$2,036 (S)	$3,632	5-B	1,122	75
Western New England Coll, Springfield, MA 01119-2654	1919	$11,448	$6,120	1-F	4,738	314
Western New Mexico U, Silver City, NM 88062-0680	1893	$855 (S)	$2,786	5-M	2,580	145

Name, address	Year	Tuition & Fees	Room & Board	Control, Degree	Enroll-ment	Faculty
Western Oregon U, Monmouth, OR 97361	1856	$3,153 (S)	$4,128	5-M	4,088	261
Western State Coll of Colorado, Gunnison, CO 81231	1901	$2,152 (S)	$4,790	5-B	2,517	143
Western Washington U, Bellingham, WA 98225-5996	1893	$2,772 (S)	$4,635	5-M	11,476	564
Westfield State Coll, Westfield, MA 01086	1838	$3,094 (S)	$4,441	5-M	4,937	333
West Liberty State Coll, West Liberty, WV 26074	1837	$2,200 (S)	$3,200	5-B	2,397	138
Westminster Coll, New Wilmington, PA 16172-0001	1852	$15,430	$4,315	2-M	1,571	122
Westminster Coll of Salt Lake City, Salt Lake City, UT 84105-3697	1875	$11,246	$4,358	1-M	2,126	214
Westmont Coll, Santa Barbara, CA 93108-1099	1937	$17,998	$6,048	2-B	1,263	122
West Texas A&M U, Canyon, TX 79016-0001	1909	$1,744 (S)	$2,969	5-M	6,489	359
West Virginia State Coll, Institute, WV 25112-1000	1891	$2,184 (S)	$3,450	5-B	4,603	253
West Virginia U, Morgantown, WV 26506	1867	$2,336 (S)	$4,832	5-D	22,238	1,575
West Virginia U Inst of Technology, Montgomery, WV 25136	1895	$2,370 (S)	$3,858	5-M	2,554	199
West Virginia Wesleyan Coll, Buckhannon, WV 26201	1890	$16,750	$4,100	2-M	1,686	148
Wheaton Coll, Wheaton, IL 60187-5593	1860	$13,780	$4,740	2-D	2,725	286
Wheaton Coll, Norton, MA 02766	1834	$20,820	$6,470	1-B	1,443	135
Wheeling Jesuit U, Wheeling, WV 26003-6295	1954	$14,200	$4,980	2-M	1,556	102
Wheelock Coll, Boston, MA 02215 (4)	1888	$15,520	$6,000	1-M	1,308	170
Whitman Coll, Walla Walla, WA 99362	1859	$19,756	$5,640	1-B	1,375	177
Whittier Coll, Whittier, CA 90608-0634	1887	$18,634	$6,232	1-F	2,104	128
Whitworth Coll, Spokane, WA 99251-0001	1890	$15,593	$5,300	2-M	2,043	102
Wichita State U, Wichita, KS 67260	1895	$2,489 (S)	$3,760	5-D	14,061	758
Widener U, Chester, PA 19013-5792	1821	$14,380	$6,200	1-D	7,305	441
Wilkes U, Wilkes-Barre, PA 18766-0002	1933	$15,091	$6,564	1-F	2,834	225
Willamette U, Salem, OR 97301-3931	1842	$20,290	$5,280	2-F	2,502	237
William Jewell Coll, Liberty, MO 64068-1843	1849	$11,850	$3,560	2-B	1,153	163
William Paterson U of New Jersey, Wayne, NJ 07470-8420	1855	$3,786 (S)	$5,100	5-M	8,941	326
Williams Coll, Williamstown, MA 01267	1793	$22,990	$6,300	1-M	2,069	262
William Woods U, Fulton, MO 65251-1098	1870	$12,300	$5,000	2-M	1,279	83
Wilmington Coll, New Castle, DE 19720-6491	1967	$5,750	NA	1-D	4,155	480
Wilmington Coll, Wilmington, OH 45177	1870	$12,500	$4,590	2-B	1,033	108
Wingate U, Wingate, NC 28174	1896	$11,690	$4,100	2-M	1,230	105
Winona State U, Winona, MN 55987-5838	1858	$3,019 (S)	$3,150	5-M	6,739	350
Winston-Salem State U, Winston-Salem, NC 27110-0003	1892	$1,574 (S)	$3,757	5-B	2,865	235
Winthrop U, Rock Hill, SC 29733	1886	$3,938 (S)	$3,764	5-M	5,574	428
Wittenberg U, Springfield, OH 45501-0720	1845	$19,140	$4,860	2-B	2,088	166
Wofford Coll, Spartanburg, SC 29303-3663	1854	$15,390	$4,410	2-B	1,074	85
Woodbury U, Burbank, CA 91510	1884	$15,170	$5,685	1-M	1,049	181
Worcester Polytechnic Inst, Worcester, MA 01609-2280	1865	$18,910	$6,240	1-D	3,776	294
Worcester State Coll, Worcester, MA 01602-2597	1874	$2,615 (S)	$4,140	5-M	5,505	247
Wright State U, Dayton, OH 45435	1964	$3,708 (S)	$4,500	5-D	15,343	950
Xavier U, Cincinnati, OH 45207-2111	1831	$14,520	$5,900	2-D	6,504	530
Xavier U of Louisiana, New Orleans, LA 70125-1098	1925	$8,215	$4,700	2-F	3,506	252
Yale U, New Haven, CT 06520	1701	$23,100	$6,850	1-D	11,059	2,986
Yeshiva U, New York, NY 10033-3201	1886	$14,590	$4,590	1-D	5,329	1,092
York Coll of Pennsylvania, York, PA 17405-7199	1787	$6,100	$4,390	1-M	5,117	419
York Coll of the City U of New York, Jamaica, NY 11451-0001	1967	$3,292 (S)	NA	11-B	6,030	405
Youngstown State U, Youngstown, OH 44555-0002	1908	$3,558 (S)	$4,350	5-D	12,324	784

Two-Year Colleges

Unless otherwise indicated, the highest undergraduate degree offered by two-year colleges is the associate degree. Figures for Room & Board are given where applicable.

Name, address	Year	Tuition & Fees	Room & Board	Control, Degree	Enroll-ment	Faculty
Abraham Baldwin Ag Coll, Tifton, GA 31794-2601	1933	$1,490 (S)	$3,000	5	2,631	118
Adirondack Comm Coll, Queensbury, NY 12804	1960	$2,268 (S)		11	3,379	244
Aiken Tech Coll, Aiken, SC 29802-0696	1972	$1,018 (S)		11	2,463	101
Aims Comm Coll, Greeley, CO 80632-0069	1967	$1,329 (A)		9	6,579	370
Alabama Southern Comm Coll, Monroeville, AL 36460	1965	$1,792 (S)		5	1,800	107
Alamance Comm Coll, Graham, NC 27253-8000	1959	$591 (S)		5	3,129	240
Albuquerque Tech Voc Inst, Albuquerque, NM 87106-4096	1965	$741 (S)		5	16,069	862
Alexandria Tech Coll, Alexandria, MN 56308-3707	1961	$2,355 (S)		5	1,812	89
Allan Hancock Coll, Santa Maria, CA 93454-6399	1920	$390 (S)		11	8,658	503
Allegany Coll of Maryland, Cumberland, MD 21502-2596	1961	$2,465 (A)		11	2,688	214
Allen County Comm Coll, Iola, KS 66749-1607	1923	$1,504 (S)	$2,900	11	1,701	140
Alpena Comm Coll, Alpena, MI 49707-1495	1952	$1,790 (A)		11	2,125	89
Alvin Comm Coll, Alvin, TX 77511-4898	1949	$742 (A)		11	2,765	141
Amarillo Coll, Amarillo, TX 79178-0001	1929	$510 (A)		11	7,292	424
American River Coll, Sacramento, CA 95841-4286	1955	$390 (S)		9	21,373	790
Angelina Coll, Lufkin, TX 75902-1768	1968	$657 (A)	$2,550	11	3,942	201
Anne Arundel Comm Coll, Arnold, MD 21012-1895	1961	$1,873 (A)		11	11,852	570
Anoka-Ramsey Comm Coll, Coon Rapids, MN 55433-3470	1965	$2,338 (S)		5	4,567	170
Anson Comm Coll, Polkton, NC 28135-0126	1962	$581 (S)		5	1,187	102
Antelope Valley Coll, Lancaster, CA 93536-5426	1929	$390 (S)		11	9,578	400
Arapahoe Comm Coll, Littleton, CO 80160-9002	1965	$1,784 (S)		5	7,459	298
Arizona Western Coll, Yuma, AZ 85366-0929	1962	$840 (S)	$3,250	11	6,198	268
Arkansas State U–Beebe Branch, Beebe, AR 72012-1000	1927	$1,128 (S)	$2,180	5	2,854	120
The Art Inst of Atlanta, Atlanta, GA 30326-1018	1949	$9,984		3-B	1,559	100
The Art Inst of Dallas, Dallas, TX 75231-9959	1978	$10,800		3	1,200	84
The Art Inst of Fort Lauderdale, Fort Lauderdale, FL 33316-3000	1968	$9,945		3-B	2,300	150
The Art Inst of Houston, Houston, TX 77056-4115	1978	$10,890		3	1,437	78
The Art Inst of Philadelphia, Philadelphia, PA 19103-5198	1966	$10,827		3	2,200	120
The Art Inst of Pittsburgh, Pittsburgh, PA 15222-3269	1921	$10,305	$5,925	3	2,581	107
The Art Inst of Seattle, Seattle, WA 98121-1642	1982	$10,260		3	2,720	200
Asheville-Buncombe Tech Comm Coll, Asheville, NC 28801-4897	1959	$586 (S)		5	4,062	435
Asnuntuck Comm-Tech Coll, Enfield, CT 06082-3800	1972	$1,814 (S)		5	2,080	106

Name, address	Year	Tuition & Fees	Room & Board	Control, Degree	Enroll-ment	Faculty
Athens Area Tech Inst, Athens, GA 30601-1500	1958	$849 (S)		5	1,653	100
Atlanta Metro Coll, Atlanta, GA 30310-4498	1974	$1,300 (S)		5	2,016	73
Atlantic Comm Coll, Mays Landing, NJ 08330-2699	1966	$2,070 (A)		8	5,505	310
Augusta Tech Inst, Augusta, GA 30906	1961	$822 (S)		5	2,712	189
Austin Comm Coll, Austin, TX 78752-4390	1972	$1,110 (A)		9	26,000	1,406
Bainbridge Coll, Bainbridge, GA 31717	1972	$1,256 (S)		5	1,090	57
Bakersfield Coll, Bakersfield, CA 93305-1299	1913	$392 (S)		11	12,685	496
Baltimore City Comm Coll, Baltimore, MD 21215-7893	1947	$2,050 (S)		5	5,926	248
Barstow Coll, Barstow, CA 92311-6699	1959	$390 (S)		11	3,700	128
Barton County Comm Coll, Great Bend, KS 67530-9283	1969	$1,408 (S)	$2,650	11	6,465	292
Bay de Noc Comm Coll, Escanaba, MI 49829-2511	1963	$1,754 (A)		8	2,206	143
Beaufort County Comm Coll, Washington, NC 27889-1069	1967	$578 (S)		5	1,256	110
Belleville Area Coll, Belleville, IL 62221-5899	1946	$1,044 (A)		9	13,417	801
Bellevue Comm Coll, Bellevue, WA 98007-6484	1966	$1,446 (S)		5	10,171	572
Belmont Tech Coll, St. Clairsville, OH 43950-9735	1971	$2,223 (S)		5	1,636	101
Bergen Comm Coll, Paramus, NJ 07652-1595	1965	$2,555 (A)		8	11,298	657
Berkeley Coll, West Paterson, NJ 07424-3353	1931	$11,835	$7,485	3	1,980	122
Berkeley Coll, New York, NY 10017-4604	1945	$11,835		3	1,252	89
Berkshire Comm Coll, Pittsfield, MA 01201-5786	1960	$2,112 (S)		5	2,328	180
Bessemer State Tech Coll, Bessemer, AL 35021-0308	1966	$1,560 (S)		5	1,465	100
Bevill State Comm Coll, Sumiton, AL 35148	1969	$1,275 (S)		5	3,678	63
Big Bend Comm Coll, Moses Lake, WA 98837-3299	1962	$1,515 (S)	$3,700	5	1,920	154
Bishop State Comm Coll, Mobile, AL 36603-5898	1965	$1,437 (S)		5	3,733	249
Bismarck State Coll, Bismarck, ND 58506-5587	1939	$1,809 (S)	$2,405	5	2,481	117
Black Hawk Coll, Moline, IL 61265-5899	1946	$1,696 (A)		11	5,960	534
Blackhawk Tech Coll, Janesville, WI 53547-5009	1968	$1,798 (S)		9	3,047	293
Black River Tech Coll, Pocahontas, AR 72455	1972	$1,178 (A)		5	1,156	70
Blinn Coll, Brenham, TX 77833-4049	1883	$1,030 (A)	$2,947	11	10,205	410
Blue Mountain Comm Coll, Pendleton, OR 97801-1000	1962	$1,602 (S)		11	1,600	256
Blue Ridge Comm Coll, Flat Rock, NC 28731-9624	1969	$590 (S)		11	1,433	207
Blue Ridge Comm Coll, Weyers Cave, VA 24486-0080	1965	$1,475 (S)		5	2,824	141
Borough of Manhattan Comm Coll of the City U of New York, New York, NY 10007-1079	1963	$2,590 (S)		11	16,186	1,058
Bossier Parish Comm Coll, Bossier City, LA 71111-5801	1967	$1,110 (S)		5	4,108	158
Bowling Green State U–Firelands Coll, Huron, OH 44839-9791	1968	$3,258 (S)		5	1,294	75
Brazosport Coll, Lake Jackson, TX 77566-3199	1948	$386 (A)		11	3,561	181
Brevard Comm Coll, Cocoa, FL 32922-6597	1960	$936 (S)		5	14,344	1,335
Briarcliffe Coll, Bethpage, NY 11714	1966	$8,320		3	1,178	87
Bristol Comm Coll, Fall River, MA 02720-7395	1965	$2,340 (S)		5	5,149	244
Bronx Comm Coll of the City U of New York, Bronx, NY 10453	1959	$2,610 (S)		11	7,653	390
Brookdale Comm Coll, Lincroft, NJ 07738-1597	1967	$2,046 (A)		8	11,591	558
Brooks Coll, Long Beach, CA 90804-3291	1971	$9,210	$5,080	3	1,100	57
Broome Comm Coll, Binghamton, NY 13902-1017	1946	$2,391 (S)		11	5,422	335
Broward Comm Coll, Fort Lauderdale, FL 33301-2298	1960	$1,170 (S)		5	25,007	775
Brown Inst, Mendota Heights, MN 55120	1946	$8,550		3	1,822	96
Bucks County Comm Coll, Newtown, PA 18940-1525	1964	$2,130 (A)		8	9,047	452
Bunker Hill Comm Coll, Boston, MA 02129	1973	$2,294 (S)		5	5,886	126
Butler County Comm Coll, El Dorado, KS 67042-3280	1927	$1,318 (S)	$3,300	11	7,246	573
Butler County Comm Coll, Butler, PA 16003-1203	1965	$1,650 (A)		8	3,096	220
Cabrillo Coll, Aptos, CA 95003-3194	1959	$420 (S)		9	13,147	552
Caldwell Comm Coll & Tech Inst, Hudson, NC 28638-2397	1964	$578 (S)		5	2,854	331
Calhoun Comm Coll, Decatur, AL 35609-2216	1965	$1,350 (S)		5	7,249	340
Camden County Coll, Blackwood, NJ 08012-0200	1967	$1,920 (A)		11	11,935	627
Cape Cod Comm Coll, West Barnstable, MA 02668-1599	1961	$2,453 (S)		5	3,209	258
Cape Fear Comm Coll, Wilmington, NC 28401-3993	1959	$581 (S)		5	4,155	211
Capital Comm Tech Coll, Hartford, CT 06105-2354	1946	$1,814 (S)		5	2,886	180
Carl Albert State Coll, Poteau, OK 74953-5208	1934	$1,260 (S)	$2,503	5	2,169	160
Carl Sandburg Coll, Galesburg, IL 61401-9576	1967	$1,792 (A)		11	2,635	208
Carroll Comm Coll, Westminster, MD 21157	1993	$2,271 (A)		11	2,362	191
Carroll Tech Inst, Carrollton, GA 30117	1968	$1,473 (S)		5	1,832	101
Carteret Comm Coll, Morehead City, NC 28557-2989	1963	$587 (S)		5	1,333	93
Casper Coll, Casper, WY 82601-4699	1945	$1,090 (S)	$2,550	9	3,945	185
Catawba Valley Comm Coll, Hickory, NC 28602-9699	1960	$616 (S)		11	3,202	250
Catonsville Comm Coll, Catonsville, MD 21228-5381	1957	$2,056 (A)		8	8,850	509
Cayuga County Comm Coll, Auburn, NY 13021-3099	1953	$2,618 (S)		11	2,820	181
Cecil Comm Coll, North East, MD 21901-1999	1968	$1,920 (A)		8	1,334	172
Cedar Valley Coll, Lancaster, TX 75134-3799	1977	$530 (A)		5	2,646	120
Central Alabama Comm Coll, Alexander City, AL 35011-0699	1965	$1,437 (S)		5	1,859	140
Central Arizona Coll, Coolidge, AZ 85228-9779	1961	$794 (S)	$3,280	8	3,556	440
Central Carolina Comm Coll, Sanford, NC 27330-9000	1962	$587 (S)		11	3,056	192
Central Carolina Tech Coll, Sumter, SC 29150-2499	1963	$848 (A)		5	2,356	144
Central Comm Coll–Grand Island Campus, Grand Island, NE 68802	1976	$1,320 (S)		11	2,794	112
Central Comm Coll–Hastings Campus, Hastings, NE 68902-1024	1966	$1,325 (S)	$2,400	11	2,320	114
Central Comm Coll–Platte Campus, Columbus, NE 68602-1027	1968	$1,325 (S)	$2,400	11	1,983	84
Central Florida Comm Coll, Ocala, FL 34478-1388	1957	$1,312 (S)		11	5,965	212
Centralia Coll, Centralia, WA 98531-4099	1925	$1,416 (S)		5	3,400	121
Central Lakes Coll, Brainerd, MN 56401-3904	1938	$2,209 (S)		5	3,176	140
Central Maine Tech Coll, Auburn, ME 04210-6498	1964	$2,340 (S)	$3,500	5	1,060	77
Central Ohio Tech Coll, Newark, OH 43055-1767	1971	$2,484 (S)		5	1,568	149
Central Oregon Comm Coll, Bend, OR 97701-5998	1949	$1,802 (A)	$4,675	9	3,545	184
Central Piedmont Comm Coll, Charlotte, NC 28235-5009	1963	$560 (S)		11	14,175	1,235
Central Texas Coll, Killeen, TX 76540-1800	1967	$672 (S)	$2,742	11	17,769	328
Central Virginia Comm Coll, Lynchburg, VA 24502-2498	1966	$1,477 (S)		5	4,024	171
Central Wyoming Coll, Riverton, WY 82501-2273	1966	$1,290 (S)	$2,618	11	1,675	140
Century Comm & Tech Coll, White Bear Lake, MN 55110	1970	$2,172 (S)		5	6,786	322
Cerro Coso Comm Coll, Ridgecrest, CA 93555-9571	1973	$390 (S)		5	5,402	286
Chabot Coll, Hayward, CA 94545-5001	1961	$390 (S)		5	13,222	933
Chaffey Coll, Rancho Cucamonga, CA 91737-3002	1883	$410 (S)		9	14,000	540

Name, address	Year	Tuition & Fees	Room & Board	Control, Degree	Enroll-ment	Faculty
Champlain Coll, Burlington, VT 05402-0670	1878	$9,785	$6,880	1-B	2,249	171
Chandler-Gilbert Comm Coll, Chandler, AZ 85225-2479	1985	$1,120 (A)		11	3,910	195
Charles County Comm Coll, La Plata, MD 20646-0910	1958	$2,418 (A)		11	6,055	338
Charles Stewart Mott Comm Coll, Flint, MI 48503-2089	1923	$1,836 (A)		9	9,040	420
Chattahoochee Tech Inst, Marietta, GA 30060	1961	$906 (S)		5	2,066	76
Chattahoochee Valley State Comm Coll, Phenix City, AL 36869-7928	1974	$1,425 (S)		5	1,858	97
Chattanooga State Tech Comm Coll, Chattanooga, TN 37406-1018	1965	$1,147 (S)		5	8,434	626
Chemeketa Comm Coll, Salem, OR 97309-7070	1955	$1,530 (S)		11	8,687	685
Chesapeake Coll, Wye Mills, MD 21679-0008	1965	$2,117 (A)		11	2,026	141
Chesterfield-Marlboro Tech Coll, Cheraw, SC 29520-1007	1967	$1,000 (A)		11	1,062	66
Chipola Jr Coll, Marianna, FL 32446-3065	1947	$1,290 (S)	$1,950	5	2,350	142
Chippewa Valley Tech Coll, Eau Claire, WI 54701-6120	1912	$1,710 (S)		9	3,756	400
Cincinnati State Tech & Comm Coll, Cincinnati, OH 45223-2690	1966	$3,218 (S)		5	5,664	505
Cisco Jr Coll, Cisco, TX 76437-9321	1940	$920 (A)	$2,350	11	2,592	98
Citrus Coll, Glendora, CA 91741-1899	1915	$414 (S)		11	10,784	392
City Coll of San Francisco, San Francisco, CA 94112-1821	1935	$410 (S)		11	90,000	1,117
City Colls of Chicago, Harold Washington Coll, Chicago, IL 60601	1962	$1,475 (A)		11	8,531	221
City Colls of Chicago, Harry S Truman Coll, Chicago, IL 60640-5616	1956	$1,400 (A)		11	4,256	160
City Colls of Chicago, Kennedy-King Coll, Chicago, IL 60621-3733	1935	$1,400 (A)		11	8,073	106
City Colls of Chicago, Malcolm X Coll, Chicago, IL 60612-3145	1911	$1,400 (A)		11	3,263	93
City Colls of Chicago, Olive-Harvey Coll, Chicago, IL 60628-1645	1970	$1,400 (A)		11	3,631	133
City Colls of Chicago, Richard J. Daley Coll, Chicago, IL 60652-1242	1960	$1,475 (A)		11	10,067	140
City Colls of Chicago, Wilbur Wright Coll, Chicago, IL 60634-1591	1934	$1,475 (A)		11	6,416	218
Clackamas Comm Coll, Oregon City, OR 97045-7998	1966	$1,296 (S)		9	6,263	519
Clark Coll, Vancouver, WA 98663-3598	1933	$1,568 (S)		5	10,885	320
Clark State Comm Coll, Springfield, OH 45501-0570	1962	$2,430 (S)		5	2,507	161
Clatsop Comm Coll, Astoria, OR 97103-3698	1958	$1,665 (S)		8	1,205	165
Cleveland Comm Coll, Shelby, NC 28152	1965	$588 (S)		5	1,918	91
Cleveland Inst of Electronics, Cleveland, OH 44114-3636	1934	$1,335		3	5,534	10
Cleveland State Comm Coll, Cleveland, TN 37320-3570	1967	$1,162 (S)		5	3,484	203
Clinton Comm Coll, Plattsburgh, NY 12901-9573	1969	$2,446 (S)		11	1,650	179
Clovis Comm Coll, Clovis, NM 88101-8381	1971	$548 (A)		5	3,841	180
Coahoma Comm Coll, Clarksdale, MS 38614-9799	1949	$885 (S)	$2,288	11	1,141	85
Coastal Bend Coll, Beeville, TX 78102-2197	1965	$520 (A)	$2,375	8	2,888	140
Coastal Carolina Comm Coll, Jacksonville, NC 28546-6877	1964	$756 (S)		11	3,365	195
Coastal Georgia Comm Coll, Brunswick, GA 31520-3644	1961	$1,316 (S)		5	1,875	79
Coastline Comm Coll, Fountain Valley, CA 92708-2597	1976	$402 (S)		11	11,665	350
Cochise Coll, Douglas, AZ 85607-9724	1962	$810 (S)	$3,006	11	1,343	88
Cochise Coll, Sierra Vista, AZ 85635-2317	1977	$810 (S)		11	3,026	253
Coconino Comm Coll, Flagstaff, AZ 86003	1991	$880 (S)		5	2,985	205
Coffeyville Comm Coll, Coffeyville, KS 67337-5063	1923	$1,280 (S)	$2,800	11	1,967	65
Colby Comm Coll, Colby, KS 67701-4099	1964	$1,152 (S)	$3,264	11	2,117	63
Coll of Alameda, Alameda, CA 94501-2109	1970	$394 (S)		11	4,681	166
Coll of DuPage, Glen Ellyn, IL 60137-6599	1967	$1,440 (A)		11	33,490	1,622
Coll of Eastern Utah, Price, UT 84501-2699	1937	$1,312 (S)	$2,790	5	3,564	124
Coll of Lake County, Grayslake, IL 60030-1198	1967	$1,530 (A)		9	13,577	777
Coll of St. Catherine–Minneapolis, Minneapolis, MN 55454-1494	1964	$10,500		2-M	1,132	116
Coll of San Mateo, San Mateo, CA 94402-3784	1922	$410 (S)		11	11,681	476
Coll of Southern Idaho, Twin Falls, ID 83303-1238	1964	$1,150 (A)	$3,380	11	4,737	270
Coll of The Albemarle, Elizabeth City, NC 27906-2327	1960	$588 (S)		5	2,061	118
Coll of the Canyons, Santa Clarita, CA 91355-1899	1969	$322 (S)		11	7,600	351
Coll of the Desert, Palm Desert, CA 92260-9305	1959	$418 (S)		11	10,125	320
Coll of the Mainland, Texas City, TX 77591-2499	1967	$439 (A)		11	3,546	180
Coll of the Redwoods, Eureka, CA 95501-9300	1964	$410 (S)	$4,971	11	6,927	376
Coll of the Siskiyous, Weed, CA 96094-2899	1957	$410 (S)	$4,072	11	3,071	206
Collin County Comm Coll District, McKinney, TX 75070-2906	1985	$724 (A)		11	10,784	604
Colorado Mountain Coll, Alpine Campus, Steamboat Springs, CO 80487	1965	$1,270 (A)	$4,700	9	1,283	132
Colorado Northwestern Comm Coll, Rangely, CO 81648-3598	1962	$470 (A)	$3,870	9	2,060	191
Columbia Basin Coll, Pasco, WA 99301-3397	1955	$1,635 (S)		5	6,845	350
Columbia-Greene Comm Coll, Hudson, NY 12534-0327	1969	$2,358 (S)		11	1,542	114
Columbia State Comm Coll, Columbia, TN 38402-1315	1966	$1,156 (S)		5	4,165	248
Columbus State Comm Coll, Columbus, OH 43216-1609	1963	$2,124 (S)		5	16,340	911
Comm Coll of Allegheny County, Pittsburgh, PA 15233-1894	1966	$2,201 (A)		8	17,154	3,436
Comm Coll of Aurora, Aurora, CO 80011-9036	1983	$1,746 (S)		5	4,300	255
Comm Coll of Beaver County, Monaca, PA 15061-2588	1966	$2,080 (A)		5	2,164	149
Comm Coll of Denver, Denver, CO 80217-3363	1970	$1,956 (S)		5	6,112	596
Comm Coll of Rhode Island, Warwick, RI 02886-1807	1964	$1,746 (S)		5	15,220	661
Comm Coll of Southern Nevada, North Las Vegas, NV 89030-4296	1971	$1,185 (S)		5	24,728	1,123
Comm Coll of the Air Force, Maxwell Air Force Base, AL 36112-6613	1972	$0 (C)		4	395,434	5,928
Comm Coll of Vermont, Waterbury, VT 05676-0120	1970	$3,204 (S)		5	4,493	518
Connors State Coll, Warner, OK 74469-9700	1908	$1,223 (S)	$1,874	5	2,028	137
Corning Comm Coll, Corning, NY 14830-3297	1956	$2,666 (S)		11	5,100	189
Cosumnes River Coll, Sacramento, CA 95823-5799	1970	$390 (S)		9	14,000	425
County Coll of Morris, Randolph, NJ 07869-2086	1966	$2,387 (A)		8	8,248	631
Cowley County Comm Coll & Voc-Tech School, Arkansas City, KS 67005-1147	1922	$1,240 (S)	$2,470	11	3,886	184
Crafton Hills Coll, Yucaipa, CA 92399-1799	1972	$358 (S)		11	5,200	184
Craven Comm Coll, New Bern, NC 28562-4984	1965	$588 (S)		5	2,265	202
Crowder Coll, Neosho, MO 64850-9160	1963	$1,440 (A)	$3,000	11	1,738	184
Cuesta Coll, San Luis Obispo, CA 93403-8106	1964	$412 (S)		9	8,656	361
The Culinary Inst of America, Hyde Park, NY 12538-1499	1946	$13,990		1-B	2,067	120
Cuyahoga Comm Coll, Eastern Campus, Highland Hills, OH 44122	1971	$1,871 (A)		11	4,673	201
Cuyahoga Comm Coll, Metro Campus, Cleveland, OH 44115-3123	1963	$1,871 (A)		11	5,589	320
Cuyahoga Comm Coll, Western Campus, Parma, OH 44130-5199	1966	$1,871 (A)		11	10,810	580
Cypress Coll, Cypress, CA 90630-5897	1966	$390 (S)		11	14,048	425
Dabney S. Lancaster Comm Coll, Clifton Forge, VA 24422	1964	$1,646 (S)		5	1,647	160
Dalton Coll, Dalton, GA 30720-3797	1963	$1,218 (S)		5	3,053	120

Name, address	Year	Tuition & Fees	Room & Board	Control, Degree	Enroll-ment	Faculty
Danville Area Comm Coll, Danville, IL 61832-5199	1946	$1,240 (A)		11	2,860	134
Danville Comm Coll, Danville, VA 24541-4088	1967	$1,535 (S)		5	3,888	149
Darton Coll, Albany, GA 31707-3098	1965	$1,330 (S)		5	2,559	146
Davidson County Comm Coll, Lexington, NC 27293-1287	1958	$579 (S)		11	2,103	346
Dean Coll, Franklin, MA 02038-1994	1865	$13,275	$6,300	1	1,309	70
De Anza Coll, Cupertino, CA 95014-5793	1967	$474 (S)		11	24,088	939
DeKalb Tech Inst, Clarkston, GA 30021-2397	1961	$1,152 (S)		5	2,721	443
Delaware County Comm Coll, Media, PA 19063-1094	1967	$2,070 (A)		11	9,040	519
Delaware Tech & Comm Coll, Jack F. Owens Campus, Georgetown, DE 19947	1967	$1,386 (S)		5	3,221	200
Delaware Tech & Comm Coll, Stanton/Wilmington Campus, Newark, DE 19713	1968	$1,386 (S)		5	6,794	463
Delaware Tech & Comm Coll, Terry Campus, Dover, DE 19904	1972	$1,386 (S)		5	1,994	159
Delgado Comm Coll, New Orleans, LA 70119-4399	1921	$1,256 (S)		5	14,111	794
Del Mar Coll, Corpus Christi, TX 78404-3897	1935	$877 (A)		11	10,424	535
Delta Coll, University Center, MI 48710	1961	$1,776 (A)		9	10,007	515
Denmark Tech Coll, Denmark, SC 29042-0327	1948	$1,080 (S)	$2,862	5	1,102	44
DeVry Inst, North Brunswick, NJ 08902-3362	1969	$7,308		3	3,157	120
Diné Coll, Tsaile, AZ 86556	1968	$620	$2,940	4	1,732	152
Dixie Coll, St. George, UT 84770-3876	1911	$1,372 (S)	$2,757	5	5,140	200
Dodge City Comm Coll, Dodge City, KS 67801-2399	1935	$1,342 (S)	$3,240	11	4,580	163
Doña Ana Branch Comm Coll, Las Cruces, NM 88003-8001	1973	$768 (A)	$3,229	11	4,196	265
Dundalk Comm Coll, Baltimore, MD 21222-4694	1970	$1,882 (A)		8	2,800	162
Dunwoody Inst, Minneapolis, MN 55403	1914	$6,000		1	1,176	75
Durham Tech Comm Coll, Durham, NC 27703-5023	1961	$584 (S)		5	4,712	423
Dutchess Comm Coll, Poughkeepsie, NY 12601-1595	1957	$2,395 (S)		11	6,120	410
Dyersburg State Comm Coll, Dyersburg, TN 38024	1969	$1,152 (S)		5	2,349	153
East Central Coll, Union, MO 63084-0529	1968	$1,392 (A)		9	3,239	181
East Central Comm Coll, Decatur, MS 39327-0129	1928	$1,000 (S)	$1,830	11	1,991	123
Eastern Arizona Coll, Thatcher, AZ 85552-0769	1888	$652 (S)	$3,250	11	4,917	232
Eastern Maine Tech Coll, Bangor, ME 04401-4206	1966	$2,664 (S)	$3,600	5	1,248	133
Eastern New Mexico U–Roswell, Roswell, NM 88202-6000	1958	$678 (A)		5	2,836	150
Eastern Oklahoma State Coll, Wilburton, OK 74578-4999	1908	$1,288 (S)	$1,920	5	2,217	54
Eastern Wyoming Coll, Torrington, WY 82240-1699	1948	$1,450 (S)	$2,600	11	1,463	189
Eastfield Coll, Mesquite, TX 75150-2099	1970	$530 (A)		11	7,936	91
East Georgia Coll, Swainsboro, GA 30401-2699	1973	$1,232 (S)		5	1,043	41
East Mississippi Comm Coll, Scooba, MS 39358-0158	1927	$1,040 (S)	$1,850	11	1,923	85
ECPI Coll of Technology, Hampton, VA 23462	1966	$6,210		3	1,959	25
ECPI Coll of Technology, Virginia Beach, VA 23462	1966	$6,210		3	1,959	127
Edgecombe Comm Coll, Tarboro, NC 27886-9399	1968	$581 (S)		11	1,902	150
Edison Comm Coll, Fort Myers, FL 33906-6210	1962	$1,250 (S)		11	9,324	724
Edmonds Comm Coll, Lynnwood, WA 98036-5999	1967	$1,401 (S)	$4,020	11	8,072	439
Education America–Tampa Tech Inst Campus, Tampa, FL 33612	1948	$8,100		3-B	1,272	48
Elaine P. Nunez Comm Coll, Chalmette, LA 70043-1249	1992	$1,110 (S)		5	2,107	113
El Camino Coll, Torrance, CA 90506-0001	1947	$410 (S)		5	23,283	533
Elgin Comm Coll, Elgin, IL 60123-7193	1949	$1,290 (A)		11	9,181	459
El Paso Comm Coll, El Paso, TX 79998-0500	1969	$990 (S)		8	19,845	1,254
Enterprise State Jr Coll, Enterprise, AL 36331-1300	1965	$1,487 (S)		5	1,705	125
Essex County Coll, Newark, NJ 07102-1798	1966	$2,186 (A)		8	8,130	270
Eugenio María de Hostos Comm Coll of the City U of New York, Bronx, NY 10451	1968	$2,550 (S)		11	4,177	429
Everett Comm Coll, Everett, WA 98201-1327	1941	$1,481 (S)		5	6,709	290
Fairleigh Dickinson U, Edward Williams Coll, Hackensack, NJ 07601	1964	$13,776	$6,040	1	1,580	51
Fashion Inst of Design & Merchandising, Los Angeles Campus, Los Angeles, CA 90015-1421	1969	$13,100		3	1,743	125
Fayetteville Tech Comm Coll, Fayetteville, NC 28303-0236	1961	$569 (S)		5	6,885	851
Feather River Comm Coll District, Quincy, CA 95971	1968	$412 (S)		11	1,200	95
Fergus Falls Comm Coll, Fergus Falls, MN 56537-1009	1960	$2,331 (S)	$4,218	5	1,488	78
Finger Lakes Comm Coll, Canandaigua, NY 14424-8395	1965	$2,504 (S)		11	4,092	234
Fiorello H. LaGuardia Comm Coll of the City U of New York, Long Island City, NY 11101-3071	1970	$2,610 (A)		11	10,925	653
Fisher Coll, Boston, MA 02116-1500	1903	$12,300	$6,600	1	2,538	36
Flathead Valley Comm Coll, Kalispell, MT 59901-2622	1967	$1,626 (A)		11	1,730	111
Florence-Darlington Tech Coll, Florence, SC 29501-0548	1963	$1,120 (A)		5	3,241	209
Florida Comm Coll at Jacksonville, Jacksonville, FL 32202-4030	1963	$1,245 (S)		5	18,482	1,493
Florida Keys Comm Coll, Key West, FL 33040-4397	1965	$1,274 (S)		5	1,973	94
Florida Natl Coll, Hialeah, FL 33012	1982	$4,000		3	1,104	70
Floyd Coll, Rome, GA 30162-1864	1970	$1,864 (S)		5	2,747	66
Foothill Coll, Los Altos Hills, CA 94022-4599	1958	$488 (S)		11	15,292	524
Forsyth Tech Comm Coll, Winston-Salem, NC 27103-5197	1964	$574 (S)		5	4,334	535
Fort Scott Comm Coll, Fort Scott, KS 66701	1919	$1,260 (S)	$2,700	11	1,579	64
Fox Valley Tech Coll, Appleton, WI 54913-2277	1967	$2,118 (S)		11	6,974	1,241
Frank Phillips Coll, Borger, TX 79008-5118	1948	$780 (A)	$2,186	11	1,101	96
Frederick Comm Coll, Frederick, MD 21702-2097	1957	$2,330 (A)		11	4,100	272
Fresno City Coll, Fresno, CA 93741-0002	1910	$412 (S)		9	17,921	832
Front Range Comm Coll, Westminster, CO 80030-2105	1968	$1,580 (S)		5	10,382	696
Fullerton Coll, Fullerton, CA 92832-2095	1913	$410 (S)		11	18,823	678
Fulton-Montgomery Comm Coll, Johnstown, NY 12095-3790	1964	$2,484 (S)		11	1,774	94
Gadsden State Comm Coll, Gadsden, AL 35902-0227	1985	$1,437 (S)	$2,250	5	5,198	288
Gainesville Coll, Gainesville, GA 30503-1358	1964	$1,221 (S)		5	2,868	111
Galveston Coll, Galveston, TX 77550-7496	1967	$744 (S)		11	2,189	105
Garden City Comm Coll, Garden City, KS 67846-6399	1919	$1,216 (S)	$3,050	8	2,717	148
Garland County Comm Coll, Hot Springs, AR 71913	1973	$908 (A)		11	1,940	103
Gaston Coll, Dallas, NC 28034-1499	1963	$593 (S)		11	3,598	370
Gateway Comm Coll, Phoenix, AZ 85034-1795	1968	$1,120 (A)		11	6,406	300
Gateway Tech Coll, Kenosha, WI 53144-1690	1911	$1,782 (S)		11	8,147	488
Gavilan Coll, Gilroy, CA 95020-9599	1919	$332 (S)		11	4,615	164
Genesee Comm Coll, Batavia, NY 14020-9704	1966	$2,790 (S)		11	4,019	219

Name, address	Year	Tuition & Fees	Room & Board	Control, Degree	Enroll-ment	Faculty
George Corley Wallace State Comm Coll, Selma, AL 36702-1049	1966	$1,451 (S)		5	1,823	78
George C. Wallace State Comm Coll, Dothan, AL 36303-9234	1949	$1,464 (S)		5	3,500	180
Georgia Perimeter Coll, Decatur, GA 30034-3897	1964	$1,522 (S)		5	15,468	1,050
Germanna Comm Coll, Locust Grove, VA 22508-2102	1970	$1,490 (S)		5	3,500	135
Glendale Comm Coll, Glendale, AZ 85302-3090	1965	$1,098 (A)		11	17,069	740
Glendale Comm Coll, Glendale, CA 91208-2894	1927	$436 (S)		11	13,871	807
Glen Oaks Comm Coll, Centreville, MI 49032-9719	1965	$1,590 (A)		11	1,442	96
Gloucester County Coll, Sewell, NJ 08080	1967	$2,015 (A)		8	4,695	215
Gogebic Comm Coll, Ironwood, MI 49938	1932	$1,431 (A)		11	1,278	91
Golden West Coll, Huntington Beach, CA 92647-2748	1966	$426 (S)		11	11,787	420
Gordon Coll, Barnesville, GA 30204-1762	1852	$1,300 (S)	$2,534	5	2,348	99
Grand Rapids Comm Coll, Grand Rapids, MI 49503-3201	1914	$1,614 (A)		9	13,098	511
Grays Harbor Coll, Aberdeen, WA 98520-7599	1930	$1,493 (S)		5	2,708	201
Grayson County Coll, Denison, TX 75020-8299	1964	$960 (A)	$2,200	11	2,873	176
Great Lakes Coll, Midland, MI 48642	1907	$5,933		1	1,359	124
Greenfield Comm Coll, Greenfield, MA 01301-9739	1962	$2,387 (S)		5	2,159	152
Green River Comm Coll, Auburn, WA 98092-3699	1965	$1,658 (S)		5	7,174	411
Greenville Tech Coll, Greenville, SC 29606-5616	1962	$1,080 (A)		5	8,906	539
Grossmont Coll, El Cajon, CA 92020-1799	1961	$410 (S)		11	15,920	653
Guilford Tech Comm Coll, Jamestown, NC 27282-0309	1958	$560 (S)		11	6,611	385
Gulf Coast Comm Coll, Panama City, FL 32401-1058	1957	$1,259 (S)		5	5,953	315
Hagerstown Comm Coll, Hagerstown, MD 21742-6590	1946	$2,430 (A)		8	3,022	203
Halifax Comm Coll, Weldon, NC 27890-0809	1967	$572 (S)		11	1,334	68
Harford Comm Coll, Bel Air, MD 21015-1698	1957	$2,004 (A)		11	4,510	452
Harrisburg Area Comm Coll, Harrisburg, PA 17110-2999	1964	$1,973 (A)		11	10,521	587
Harry M. Ayers State Tech Coll, Anniston, AL 36202-1647	1966	$1,200 (S)		5	1,080	39
Hartnell Coll, Salinas, CA 93901-1697	1920	$398 (S)		9	7,400	363
Hawkeye Comm Coll, Waterloo, IA 50704-8015	1967	$2,175 (S)		11	3,944	218
Haywood Comm Coll, Clyde, NC 28721-9453	1964	$578 (S)		11	1,540	118
Heald Coll, Schools of Business & Technology, Hayward, CA 94545	1863	$6,300		1	1,070	75
Heald Coll, Schools of Business & Technology, San Francisco, CA 94103	1863	$6,660		1	11,000	37
Heartland Comm Coll, Bloomington, IL 61701	1990	$1,140 (A)		9	3,343	191
Henry Ford Comm Coll, Dearborn, MI 48128-1495	1938	$1,710 (A)		9	13,000	994
Herkimer County Comm Coll, Herkimer, NY 13350	1966	$2,430 (S)		11	2,542	143
Hesser Coll, Manchester, NH 03103-7245	1900	$8,220	$4,260	3-B	2,660	99
Hibbing Comm Coll, Hibbing, MN 55746-3300	1916	$2,271 (S)		5	1,042	100
Highland Comm Coll, Freeport, IL 61032-9341	1962	$1,373 (A)		11	2,612	169
Highland Comm Coll, Highland, KS 66035	1858	$1,519 (S)	$2,668	11	2,522	195
Highline Comm Coll, Des Moines, WA 98198-9800	1961	$1,515 (S)		5	9,289	223
High-Tech Inst, Phoenix, AZ 85014-4901	NA	$9,325		3	1,622	72
Hill Coll of the Hill Jr Coll District, Hillsboro, TX 76645-0619	1923	$810 (A)	$2,660	9	2,695	155
Hillsborough Comm Coll, Tampa, FL 33631-3127	1968	$1,245 (S)		5	17,964	757
Hinds Comm Coll, Raymond, MS 39154-9799	1917	$1,070 (S)		11	11,680	890
Hocking Coll, Nelsonville, OH 45764-9588	1968	$2,157 (S)	$3,800	5	4,974	242
Holmes Comm Coll, Goodman, MS 39079-0369	1928	$1,054 (S)	$1,570	11	2,645	125
Holyoke Comm Coll, Holyoke, MA 01040-1099	1946	$2,476 (S)		5	5,322	235
Housatonic Comm-Tech Coll, Bridgeport, CT 06604-4704	1965	$1,814 (S)		5	3,291	177
Houston Comm Coll System, Houston, TX 77270-7849	1971	$900 (A)		11	38,463	2,387
Howard Coll, Big Spring, TX 79720-3702	1945	$748 (A)	$2,604	11	2,058	161
Howard Comm Coll, Columbia, MD 21044-3197	1966	$2,607 (A)		11	5,081	318
Hudson County Comm Coll, Jersey City, NJ 07306	1974	$2,918 (A)		11	4,161	237
Hudson Valley Comm Coll, Troy, NY 12180-6096	1953	$2,465 (S)		11	9,581	511
Hutchinson Comm Coll & Area Voc School, Hutchinson, KS 67501	1928	$1,312 (S)	$2,590	11	3,618	264
Illinois Central Coll, East Peoria, IL 61635-0001	1967	$1,344 (A)		11	12,341	658
Illinois Eastern Comm Colls, Frontier Comm Coll, Fairfield, IL 62837	1976	$1,056 (A)		11	1,893	177
Illinois Eastern Comm Colls, Lincoln Trail Coll, Robinson, IL 62454	1969	$1,056 (A)		11	1,339	79
Illinois Eastern Comm Colls, Olney Central Coll, Olney, IL 62450	1962	$1,146 (A)		11	1,427	85
Illinois Eastern Comm Colls, Wabash Valley Coll, Mount Carmel, IL 62863	1960	$1,056 (A)		11	2,675	90
Imperial Valley Coll, Imperial, CA 92251-0158	1922	$312 (S)		11	8,058	310
Independence Comm Coll, Independence, KS 67301-0708	1925	$1,332 (S)	$2,836	5	1,418	153
Indiana Business Coll, Indianapolis, IN 46204-1108	1902	$5,985		3	2,000	70
Indian Hills Comm Coll, Ottumwa, IA 52501-1398	1966	$1,650 (S)	$1,950	11	3,495	139
Indian River Comm Coll, Fort Pierce, FL 34981-5596	1960	$1,260 (S)		5	10,966	869
Instituto Comercial de Puerto Rico Jr Coll, San Juan, PR 00919-0304	1946	$3,172		3	2,831	92
Inver Hills Comm Coll, Inver Grove Heights, MN 55076-3224	1969	$2,168 (S)		5	4,793	220
Iowa Lakes Comm Coll, Estherville, IA 51334-2295	1967	$2,210 (S)	$2,410	11	2,429	107
Iowa Western Comm Coll, Council Bluffs, IA 51502	1966	$2,160 (S)	$3,000	9	3,951	218
Isothermal Comm Coll, Spindale, NC 28160-0804	1965	$588 (S)		5	1,673	92
Itasca Comm Coll, Grand Rapids, MN 55744	1922	$2,422 (S)		5	1,120	68
Itawamba Comm Coll, Fulton, MS 38843	1947	$900 (S)	$1,740	11	3,500	102
ITT Tech Inst, Indianapolis, IN 46268-1119	1966	$10,482		3-M	1,000	42
Ivy Tech State Coll–Central Indiana, Indianapolis, IN 46206-1763	1963	$1,937 (S)		5	4,942	326
Ivy Tech State Coll–Columbus, Columbus, IN 47203-1868	1963	$1,937 (S)		5	2,890	200
Ivy Tech State Coll–Eastcentral, Muncie, IN 47302-9448	1968	$1,937 (S)		5	2,351	249
Ivy Tech State Coll–Kokomo, Kokomo, IN 46903-1373	1968	$1,937 (S)		5	1,410	141
Ivy Tech State Coll–Lafayette, Lafayette, IN 47905-5266	1968	$1,937 (S)		5	2,486	146
Ivy Tech State Coll–Northcentral, South Bend, IN 46619-3837	1968	$1,937 (S)		5	2,732	226
Ivy Tech State Coll–Northeast, Fort Wayne, IN 46805-1430	1969	$1,937 (S)		5	3,144	280
Ivy Tech State Coll–Northwest, Gary, IN 46409-1499	1963	$1,937 (S)		5	2,921	221
Ivy Tech State Coll–Southcentral, Sellersburg, IN 47172-1829	1968	$1,937 (S)		5	1,669	128
Ivy Tech State Coll–Southwest, Evansville, IN 47710-3398	1963	$1,937 (S)		5	2,476	235
Ivy Tech State Coll–Wabash Valley, Terre Haute, IN 47802	1966	$1,937 (S)		5	2,351	167
Ivy Tech State Coll–Whitewater, Richmond, IN 47374-1220	1963	$1,937 (S)		5	1,126	112
Jackson Comm Coll, Jackson, MI 49201-8399	1928	$1,613 (A)		8	7,224	435
Jackson State Comm Coll, Jackson, TN 38301-3797	1967	$1,218 (S)		5	3,633	215
James H. Faulkner State Comm Coll, Bay Minette, AL 36507	1965	$1,680 (S)	$2,325	5	2,922	153
James Sprunt Comm Coll, Kenansville, NC 28349-0398	1964	$600 (S)		5	1,068	84
Jamestown Comm Coll, Jamestown, NY 14701-1999	1950	$2,830 (S)		11	3,500	263

Name, address	Year	Tuition & Fees	Room & Board	Control, Degree	Enroll-ment	Faculty
Jefferson Coll, Hillsboro, MO 63050-2441	1963	$1,408 (A)		11	3,963	197
Jefferson Comm Coll, Watertown, NY 13601	1961	$2,494 (S)		11	3,279	204
Jefferson Comm Coll, Steubenville, OH 43952-3598	1966	$1,770 (A)		11	1,434	114
Jefferson Davis Comm Coll, Brewton, AL 36427	1965	$1,446 (S)		5	1,600	66
Jefferson State Comm Coll, Birmingham, AL 35215-3098	1965	$1,395 (S)		5	5,235	286
John A. Logan Coll, Carterville, IL 62918-9900	1967	$1,080 (A)		11	5,130	246
John M. Patterson State Tech Coll, Montgomery, AL 36116-2699	1962	$1,584 (S)		5	1,113	63
Johnson County Comm Coll, Overland Park, KS 66210-1299	1967	$1,472 (S)		11	15,271	686
Johnston Comm Coll, Smithfield, NC 27577-2350	1969	$588 (S)		5	2,407	257
John Tyler Comm Coll, Chester, VA 23831	1967	$1,480 (S)		5	4,930	233
Joliet Jr Coll, Joliet, IL 60431-8938	1901	$1,380 (A)		11	10,647	507
Jones County Jr Coll, Ellisville, MS 39437-3901	1928	$792 (S)	$1,800	11	4,296	175
J. Sargeant Reynolds Comm Coll, Richmond, VA 23285-5622	1972	$1,457 (S)		5	9,610	469
Kalamazoo Valley Comm Coll, Kalamazoo, MI 49003-4070	1966	$1,271 (A)		11	8,655	377
Kankakee Comm Coll, Kankakee, IL 60901-0888	1966	$1,216 (A)		11	3,419	143
Kansas City Kansas Comm Coll, Kansas City, KS 66112-3003	1923	$1,140 (S)		11	5,452	349
Kaskaskia Coll, Centralia, IL 62801-7878	1966	$1,280 (A)		11	2,687	189
Kellogg Comm Coll, Battle Creek, MI 49017-3397	1956	$1,470 (A)		11	4,673	305
Kent State U, Trumbull Campus, Warren, OH 44483-1998	1954	$3,056 (S)		5	2,179	139
Kent State U, Tuscarawas Campus, New Philadelphia, OH 44663-9403	1962	$3,056 (S)		5	1,482	116
Kilgore Coll, Kilgore, TX 75662-3299	1935	$832 (A)	$2,600	11	4,206	212
Kingsborough Comm Coll of the City U of New York, Brooklyn, NY 11235	1963	$2,600 (S)		11	15,516	792
Kingwood Coll, Kingwood, TX 77339-3801	1984	$864 (A)		11	3,895	244
Kirkwood Comm Coll, Cedar Rapids, IA 52406-2068	1966	$1,767 (S)		11	11,164	582
Kirtland Comm Coll, Roscommon, MI 48653-9699	1966	$1,580 (A)		9	1,357	95
Kishwaukee Coll, Malta, IL 60150	1967	$1,400 (A)		11	3,146	198
Labette Comm Coll, Parsons, KS 67357-4299	1923	$1,209 (S)	$2,200	11	2,981	234
Lackawanna Jr Coll, Scranton, PA 18509	1894	$7,310		1	1,051	46
Lake City Comm Coll, Lake City, FL 32025	1962	$1,140 (S)	$3,409	5	2,355	209
Lake Land Coll, Mattoon, IL 61938-9366	1966	$1,424 (A)		11	5,182	304
Lakeland Comm Coll, Kirtland, OH 44094-5198	1967	$1,963 (A)		11	8,145	631
Lake Michigan Coll, Benton Harbor, MI 49022-1899	1946	$1,530 (A)		9	3,203	240
Lakeshore Tech Coll, Cleveland, WI 53015-1414	1967	$1,734 (S)		11	2,518	300
Lake-Sumter Comm Coll, Leesburg, FL 34788-8751	1962	$1,236 (S)		11	2,539	117
Lake Tahoe Comm Coll, South Lake Tahoe, CA 96150-4524	1975	$417 (S)		11	3,400	177
Lake Washington Tech Coll, Kirkland, WA 98034-8506	1949	$1,401		9	4,855	307
Lamar Comm Coll, Lamar, CO 81052-3999	1937	$2,062 (S)	$4,040	5	1,113	51
Lamar U–Orange, Orange, TX 77630-5899	1969	$1,818 (S)		5	1,562	80
Lamar U–Port Arthur, Port Arthur, TX 77641-0310	1909	$1,770 (S)		5	2,362	133
Lane Comm Coll, Eugene, OR 97405-0640	1964	$1,640 (S)		11	8,857	503
Laney Coll, Oakland, CA 94607-4893	1953	$394 (S)		11	11,213	315
Lansing Comm Coll, Lansing, MI 48901-7210	1957	$1,207 (A)		11	15,690	919
Laramie County Comm Coll, Cheyenne, WY 82007-3299	1968	$1,070 (S)	$3,360	8	4,148	255
Laredo Comm Coll, Laredo, TX 78040-4395	1946	$700 (A)		11	7,446	359
Lawson State Comm Coll, Birmingham, AL 35221-1798	1965	$1,404 (S)		5	1,589	105
Lee Coll, Baytown, TX 77522-0818	1934	$422 (A)		9	6,010	358
Lehigh Carbon Comm Coll, Schnecksville, PA 18078-2598	1967	$2,130 (A)		11	3,908	246
Lewis & Clark Comm Coll, Godfrey, IL 62035-2466	1970	$1,368 (A)		9	5,421	345
Lima Tech Coll, Lima, OH 45804-3597	1971	$2,368 (S)		5	2,470	167
Lincoln Land Comm Coll, Springfield, IL 62794-9256	1967	$1,356 (A)		9	6,160	400
Linn-Benton Comm Coll, Albany, OR 97321	1966	$1,620 (S)		11	5,605	474
Long Beach City Coll, Long Beach, CA 90808-1780	1927	$410 (S)		5	25,100	777
Longview Comm Coll, Lee's Summit, MO 64081-2105	1969	$1,457 (A)		11	7,905	282
Lorain County Comm Coll, Elyria, OH 44035	1963	$2,291 (A)		11	7,020	360
Lord Fairfax Comm Coll, Middletown, VA 22645-0047	1969	$1,446 (S)		5	3,414	161
Los Angeles City Coll, Los Angeles, CA 90029-3590	1929	$390 (S)		9	15,000	625
Los Angeles Harbor Coll, Wilmington, CA 90744-2397	1949	$407 (S)		11	7,895	251
Los Angeles Mission Coll, Sylmar, CA 91342-3244	1974	$384 (S)		11	6,569	115
Los Angeles Pierce Coll, Woodland Hills, CA 91371-0001	1947	$436 (S)		11	14,502	510
Los Angeles Valley Coll, Van Nuys, CA 91401-4096	1949	$412 (S)		11	15,655	482
Los Medanos Coll, Pittsburg, CA 94565-5197	1974	$312 (S)		9	7,183	244
Louisiana State U at Alexandria, Alexandria, LA 71302-9121	1960	$1,132 (S)		5	2,409	89
Louisiana State U at Eunice, Eunice, LA 70535-1129	1967	$1,056 (S)		5	2,572	120
Lower Columbia Coll, Longview, WA 98632-0310	1934	$1,464 (S)		5	4,022	160
Luzerne County Comm Coll, Nanticoke, PA 18634-9804	1966	$1,800 (A)		8	6,134	427
Macomb Comm Coll, Warren, MI 48093-3896	1954	$1,628 (A)		9	23,236	793
Macon State Coll, Macon, GA 31206	1968	$1,268 (S)		5-B	3,602	164
Macon Tech Inst, Macon, GA 31206-3628	1966	$816 (S)		5	2,424	138
Madison Area Tech Coll, Madison, WI 53704-2599	1911	$1,934 (S)		9	13,030	1,881
Manatee Comm Coll, Bradenton, FL 34206-7046	1957	$1,207 (S)		5	7,263	279
Maple Woods Comm Coll, Kansas City, MO 64156-1299	1969	$1,457 (A)		11	4,680	184
Marion Tech Coll, Marion, OH 43302-5694	1971	$2,421 (S)		12	1,750	105
Marshalltown Comm Coll, Marshalltown, IA 50158-4760	1927	$1,856 (S)		9	1,300	107
Massachusetts Bay Comm Coll, Wellesley Hills, MA 02181-5359	1961	$2,250 (S)		5	4,418	263
McDowell Tech Comm Coll, Marion, NC 28752-9724	1964	$577 (S)		5	1,070	58
McLennan Comm Coll, Waco, TX 76708-1499	1965	$1,140 (A)		8	5,493	284
Merced Coll, Merced, CA 95348-2898	1962	$412 (S)		11	7,273	421
Mercer County Comm Coll, Trenton, NJ 08690-1004	1966	$2,130 (A)		11	8,117	361
Meridian Comm Coll, Meridian, MS 39307	1937	$1,000 (S)	$2,120	11	3,007	255
Merritt Coll, Oakland, CA 94619-3196	1953	$364 (S)		11	5,278	201
Mesabi Range Comm & Tech Coll, Virginia, MN 55792-3448	1918	$2,347 (S)		5	1,421	71
Mesa Comm Coll, Mesa, AZ 85202-4866	1965	$972 (A)		11	23,536	852
Metro Comm Coll, Omaha, NE 68103-0777	1974	$1,238 (S)		11	11,213	568
Miami-Dade Comm Coll, Miami, FL 33132-2296	1960	$1,344 (S)		11	48,449	2,070
Miami U–Hamilton Campus, Hamilton, OH 45011-3399	1968	$3,118 (S)		5-B	2,670	170
Miami U–Middletown Campus, Middletown, OH 45042-3497	1966	$3,118 (S)		5-B	2,423	165
Middle Georgia Coll, Cochran, GA 31014-1599	1884	$1,550 (S)	$3,200	5	2,035	229
Middlesex Comm Coll, Bedford, MA 01730-1655	1970	$2,114 (A)		5	6,125	377

Name, address	Year	Tuition & Fees	Room & Board	Control, Degree	Enroll-ment	Faculty
Middlesex Comm–Tech Coll, Middletown, CT 06457-4889	1966	$1,814 (S)		5	2,237	120
Middlesex County Coll, Edison, NJ 08818-3050	1964	$2,578 (A)		8	11,000	552
Midland Coll, Midland, TX 79705-6399	1969	$900 (A)		11	4,000	194
Midlands Tech Coll, Columbia, SC 29202-2408	1974	$1,100 (A)		11	9,468	661
Mid-Plains Comm Coll, North Platte, NE 69101-9491	1965	$1,302 (S)		9	1,934	133
Mid-South Comm Coll, West Memphis, AR 72301	1993	$822 (A)		5	1,317	81
Mid-State Tech Coll, Wisconsin Rapids, WI 54494-5599	1917	$1,821 (S)		11	2,661	90
Mineral Area Coll, Park Hills, MO 63601-1000	1922	$1,178 (A)		9	2,567	157
Minneapolis Comm & Tech Coll, Minneapolis, MN 55403-1779	1965	$2,206 (S)		5	6,225	363
Mission Coll, Santa Clara, CA 95054-1897	1977	$392 (S)		11	8,594	376
Mississippi County Comm Coll, Blytheville, AR 72316-1109	1975	$874 (A)		5	2,181	76
Mississippi Delta Comm Coll, Moorhead, MS 38761-0668	1926	$920 (S)	$1,450	9	2,477	130
Mississippi Gulf Coast Comm Coll, Perkinston, MS 39573-0047	1911	$890 (S)	$1,706	9	9,982	753
Mitchell Comm Coll, Statesville, NC 28677-5293	1852	$584 (S)		5	1,525	85
Moberly Area Comm Coll, Moberly, MO 65270-1304	1927	$1,115 (A)		11	2,043	146
Modesto Jr Coll, Modesto, CA 95350-5800	1921	$334 (S)		11	16,940	509
Mohave Comm Coll, Kingman, AZ 86401	1971	$720 (S)		5	5,600	349
Monroe Coll, Bronx, NY 10468-5407	1933	$9,140		3-B	2,737	110
Monroe Comm Coll, Rochester, NY 14623-5780	1961	$2,654 (S)		11	13,628	1,236
Monroe County Comm Coll, Monroe, MI 48161-9047	1964	$1,144 (A)		8	3,575	201
Montana State U Coll of Technology–Great Falls, Great Falls, MT 59405	1969	$2,064 (S)		5	1,027	108
Montcalm Comm Coll, Sidney, MI 48885-0300	1965	$1,629 (A)		11	2,185	153
Monterey Peninsula Coll, Monterey, CA 93940-4799	1947	$430 (S)		5	15,475	388
Montgomery Coll, Conroe, TX 77384	NA	$830 (A)		11	3,860	179
Montgomery Coll–Germantown Campus, Germantown, MD 20876	1975	$2,402 (A)		11	3,475	186
Montgomery Coll–Rockville Campus, Rockville, MD 20850-1196	1965	$2,402 (A)		11	12,397	648
Montgomery Coll–Takoma Park Campus, Takoma Park, MD 20912	1946	$2,402 (A)		11	4,167	227
Montgomery County Comm Coll, Blue Bell, PA 19422-0796	1964	$2,220 (A)		8	8,766	696
Moorpark Coll, Moorpark, CA 93021-1695	1967	$442 (S)		8	11,883	450
Moraine Park Tech Coll, Fond du Lac, WI 54936-1940	1967	$1,814 (S)		11	6,851	405
Moraine Valley Comm Coll, Palos Hills, IL 60465-0937	1967	$1,457 (A)		11	13,347	546
Morgan Comm Coll, Fort Morgan, CO 80701-4399	1967	$1,792 (S)		5	1,200	153
Morton Coll, Cicero, IL 60804-4398	1924	$1,488 (A)		11	4,644	214
Motlow State Comm Coll, Tullahoma, TN 37388-8100	1969	$1,210 (S)		5	3,389	229
Mountain Empire Comm Coll, Big Stone Gap, VA 24219-0700	1972	$1,575 (S)		5	2,946	150
Mountain View Coll, Dallas, TX 75211-6599	1970	$530 (A)		11	5,340	264
Mount Ida Coll, Newton Centre, MA 02159-3310	1899	$12,562	$8,534	1-B	1,563	222
Mt. San Antonio Coll, Walnut, CA 91789-1399	1946	$332 (S)		9	24,003	789
Mt. San Jacinto Coll, San Jacinto, CA 92583-2399	1963	$408 (S)		11	6,472	215
Mount Wachusett Comm Coll, Gardner, MA 01440-1000	1963	$2,910 (S)		5	2,806	214
Murray State Coll, Tishomingo, OK 73460-3130	1908	$1,446 (S)	$2,218	5	1,715	73
Muskingum Area Tech Coll, Zanesville, OH 43701-2694	1969	$2,910 (S)		11	2,184	104
Napa Valley Coll, Napa, CA 94558-6236	1942	$290 (S)		11	6,638	304
Nash Comm Coll, Rocky Mount, NC 27804-0488	1967	$588 (S)		5	1,743	106
Nashville State Tech Inst, Nashville, TN 37209-4515	1970	$1,202 (S)		5	6,901	294
Nassau Comm Coll, Garden City, NY 11530-6793	1959	$2,210 (S)		11	20,881	1,523
Naugatuck Valley Comm–Tech Coll, Waterbury, CT 06708-3000	1992	$1,814 (S)		5	4,889	299
Navarro Coll, Corsicana, TX 75110-4899	1946	$979 (A)	$2,852	11	3,467	175
Neosho County Comm Coll, Chanute, KS 66720-2699	1936	$1,271 (S)	$2,800	11	1,500	96
Newbury Coll, Brookline, MA 02146-5750	1962	$12,330	$6,980	1-B	4,773	101
New England Coll of Finance, Boston, MA 02111-2671	1909	$6,040		1-B	1,554	360
New England Inst of Technology, Warwick, RI 02886-2244	1940	$10,350		1-B	2,375	208
New England Inst of Technology & Florida Culinary Inst, West Palm Beach, FL 33407-2384	1983	$6,900		3	1,196	68
New Hampshire Comm Tech Coll, Manchester/Stratham, Manchester, NH 03102-8528	1945	$3,164 (S)		5	3,241	200
New Hampshire Comm Tech Coll, Nashua/Claremont, Nashua, NH 03063	1967	$3,164 (S)		5	1,158	118
New Hampshire Tech Inst, Concord, NH 03301-7412	1964	$3,388 (S)	$4,348	5	2,477	126
New Mexico Jr Coll, Hobbs, NM 88240-9123	1965	$332 (A)	$3,200	11	2,763	129
New Mexico State U–Alamogordo, Alamogordo, NM 88311-0477	1958	$768 (A)		5	2,009	134
New Mexico State U–Carlsbad, Carlsbad, NM 88220-3509	1950	$744 (A)		5	1,383	64
New River Comm Coll, Dublin, VA 24084-1127	1969	$1,501 (S)		5	3,501	189
New York City Tech Coll of the City U of New York, Brooklyn, NY 11201	1946	$3,289 (S)		11-B	11,126	655
Niagara County Comm Coll, Sanborn, NY 14132-9460	1962	$2,610 (S)		11	4,847	336
Nicolet Area Tech Coll, Rhinelander, WI 54501-0518	1968	$2,338 (S)		11	1,384	84
Normandale Comm Coll, Bloomington, MN 55431-4399	1968	$2,228 (S)		5	7,292	230
Northampton County Area Comm Coll, Bethlehem, PA 18020-7599	1967	$2,190 (A)	$4,410	11	5,433	475
North Arkansas Coll, Harrison, AR 72601	1974	$936 (A)		11	2,209	128
North Central Michigan Coll, Petoskey, MI 49770-8717	1958	$1,515 (A)	$4,482	8	2,011	146
North Central Missouri Coll, Trenton, MO 64683-1824	1925	$1,425 (A)	$2,900	9	1,244	77
North Central Tech Coll, Mansfield, OH 44901-0698	1961	$2,668 (S)		5	2,619	182
Northcentral Tech Coll, Wausau, WI 54401-1880	1912	$1,933 (S)		9	3,622	228
North Central Texas Coll, Gainesville, TX 76240-4699	1924	$600 (A)	$2,130	8	4,243	195
North Country Comm Coll, Saranac Lake, NY 12983-0089	1967	$2,360 (S)		11	1,104	119
Northeast Comm Coll, Norfolk, NE 68702-0469	1973	$1,344 (S)		11	4,440	213
Northeastern Jr Coll, Sterling, CO 80751-2344	1941	$1,876 (S)	$4,440	5	2,038	75
Northeast Iowa Comm Coll, Peosta Campus, Peosta, IA 52068-9776	1970	$2,328 (S)		11	1,700	66
Northeast State Tech Comm Coll, Blountville, TN 37617-0246	1966	$1,150 (S)		5	3,800	224
Northeast Texas Comm Coll, Mount Pleasant, TX 75456-1307	1985	$950 (A)	$2,400	11	2,027	114
Northern Essex Comm Coll, Haverhill, MA 01830	1960	$1,992 (S)		5	5,767	404
Northern New Mexico Comm Coll, Española, NM 87532	1909	$538 (S)	$2,480	5	2,134	160
Northern Virginia Comm Coll, Annandale, VA 22003-3796	1965	$1,441 (S)		5	36,338	1,347
North Harris Coll, Houston, TX 77073	1972	$830 (A)		11	9,726	196
North Hennepin Comm Coll, Minneapolis, MN 55445-2231	1966	$2,496 (S)		5	5,106	200
North Idaho Coll, Coeur d'Alene, ID 83814-2199	1933	$1,128 (A)		11	3,631	270
North Iowa Area Comm Coll, Mason City, IA 50401-7299	1918	$1,975 (S)	$3,032	11	2,849	107
North Lake Coll, Irving, TX 75038-3899	1977	$530 (A)		8	6,233	342
Northland Comm & Tech Coll, Thief River Falls, MN 56701	1965	$2,522 (S)		5	1,828	111

Name, address	Year	Tuition & Fees	Room & Board	Control, Degree	Enroll-ment	Faculty
Northland Pioneer Coll, Holbrook, AZ 86025-0610	1974	$720 (S)		11	4,191	275
North Seattle Comm Coll, Seattle, WA 98103-3599	1970	$1,497 (S)		5	8,313	393
North Shore Comm Coll, Danvers, MA 01923-4093	1965	$2,404 (S)		5	5,131	335
NorthWest Arkansas Comm Coll, Bentonville, AR 72712	1989	$912 (A)		11	3,239	201
Northwest Coll, Powell, WY 82435-1898	1946	$1,326 (S)	$2,932	11	1,739	181
Northwestern Business Coll, Chicago, IL 60630-2298	1902	$7,500		3	1,225	41
Northwestern Coll, Lima, OH 45805-1498	1920	$6,804		1	1,808	58
Northwestern Connecticut Comm-Tech Coll, Winsted, CT 06098-1798	1965	$1,814 (S)		5	1,792	94
Northwestern Michigan Coll, Traverse City, MI 49686-3061	1951	$1,767 (A)	$4,190	11	3,872	93
Northwest Mississippi Comm Coll, Senatobia, MS 38668-1701	1927	$1,000 (S)	$1,760	11	4,850	200
Northwest-Shoals Comm Coll, Muscle Shoals, AL 35662	1961	$1,485 (S)	$2,637	5	3,635	205
Northwest State Comm Coll, Archbold, OH 43502-9542	1968	$2,346 (S)		5	2,253	136
Northwest Tech Coll, Bemidji, MN 56601	1993	$2,053 (S)		5	5,000	400
Norwalk Comm-Tech Coll, Norwalk, CT 06854-1655	1961	$1,814 (S)		5	5,247	347
Oakland Comm Coll, Bloomfield Hills, MI 48304-2266	1964	$1,496 (A)		11	24,223	788
Oakton Comm Coll, Des Plaines, IL 60016-1268	1969	$1,193 (A)		9	10,007	557
Ocean County Coll, Toms River, NJ 08754-2001	1964	$2,164 (A)		8	7,458	349
Odessa Coll, Odessa, TX 79764-7127	1946	$856 (A)	$1,949	11	5,051	208
Ohio U–Southern Campus, Ironton, OH 45638-2214	1956	$2,865 (S)		5-B	2,554	125
Okaloosa-Walton Comm Coll, Niceville, FL 32578-1295	1963	$1,080 (S)		11	9,324	274
Oklahoma City Comm Coll, Oklahoma City, OK 73159-4419	1969	$1,308 (S)		5	9,923	363
Oklahoma State U, Oklahoma City, Oklahoma City, OK 73107-6120	1961	$1,667 (S)		5	4,065	223
Oklahoma State U, Okmulgee, Okmulgee, OK 74447-3901	1946	$2,273 (S)	$2,568	5	2,320	138
Olympic Coll, Bremerton, WA 98337-1699	1946	$1,503 (S)		5	5,463	358
Onondaga Comm Coll, Syracuse, NY 13215	1962	$2,626 (A)		11	6,000	477
Orangeburg-Calhoun Tech Coll, Orangeburg, SC 29118-8299	1968	$1,008 (A)		11	1,823	141
Orange Coast Coll, Costa Mesa, CA 92628-5005	1947	$352 (S)		11	22,383	799
Orange County Comm Coll, Middletown, NY 10940-6437	1950	$2,285 (S)		11	5,714	449
Otero Jr Coll, La Junta, CO 81050-3415	1941	$1,446 (S)	$3,450	5	1,086	53
Owensboro Comm Coll, Owensboro, KY 42303-1899	1986	$1,100 (S)		5	2,300	131
Owens Comm Coll, Findlay, OH 45840	1983	$1,916 (S)		5	1,689	155
Owens Comm Coll, Toledo, OH 43699-1947	1966	$1,916 (S)		5	11,872	664
Oxnard Coll, Oxnard, CA 93033-6699	1975	$410 (S)		5	6,278	288
Ozarks Tech Comm Coll, Springfield, MO 65801	1990	$1,364 (A)		9	5,129	150
Palm Beach Comm Coll, Lake Worth, FL 33461-4796	1933	$1,245 (S)		5	16,294	749
Palomar Coll, San Marcos, CA 92069-1487	1946	$412 (S)		11	25,156	1,227
Panola Coll, Carthage, TX 75633-2397	1947	$796 (A)	$2,764	11	1,717	104
Paradise Valley Comm Coll, Phoenix, AZ 85032-1200	1985	$1,120 (A)		11	6,012	246
Paris Jr Coll, Paris, TX 75460-6298	1924	$974 (A)	$3,070	11	2,912	117
Parkland Coll, Champaign, IL 61821-1899	1967	$1,410 (A)		9	7,848	460
Pasadena City Coll, Pasadena, CA 91106-2041	1924	$412 (S)		11	23,006	824
Pasco-Hernando Comm Coll, Dade City, FL 33523-7599	1972	$1,266 (S)		5	6,435	262
Passaic County Comm Coll, Paterson, NJ 07505-1179	1968	$2,460 (S)		8	3,713	276
Patrick Henry Comm Coll, Martinsville, VA 24115-5311	1962	$1,410 (S)		5	2,440	141
Paul D. Camp Comm Coll, Franklin, VA 23851-0737	1971	$1,430 (S)		5	1,550	59
Pearl River Comm Coll, Poplarville, MS 39470	1909	$980 (S)	$1,706	11	2,720	167
Peirce Coll, Philadelphia, PA 19102-4603	1865	$7,112		1-B	2,343	123
Pellissippi State Tech Comm Coll, Knoxville, TN 37933-0990	1974	$1,172 (S)		5	8,170	412
Pennsylvania Coll of Technology, Williamsport, PA 17701-5778	1965	$6,540 (S)	$3,950	12-B	5,017	376
Pennsylvania State U Delaware County Campus of the Commonwealth Coll, Media, PA 19063-5596	1966	$5,654 (S)		12-B	1,546	99
Pennsylvania State U DuBois Campus of the Commonwealth Coll, DuBois, PA 15801-3199	1935	$5,654 (S)		12	1,071	78
Pennsylvania State U Hazleton Campus of the Commonwealth Coll, Hazleton, PA 18201-1291	1934	$5,654 (S)	$4,640	12	1,280	83
Pennsylvania State U Mont Alto Campus of the Commonwealth Coll, Mont Alto, PA 17237-9703	1929	$5,654 (S)	$4,640	12	1,140	77
Pennsylvania State U Shenango Campus of the Commonwealth Coll, Sharon, PA 16146-1537	1965	$5,654 (S)		12	1,017	89
Pennsylvania State U Worthington Scranton Campus of the Commonwealth Coll, Dunmore, PA 18512-1699	1923	$5,654 (S)		12	1,516	102
Pennsylvania State U York Campus of the Commonwealth Coll, York, PA 17403-3298	1926	$5,654 (S)		12	2,027	123
Penn Valley Comm Coll, Kansas City, MO 64111	1969	$1,457 (A)		11	3,949	206
Pensacola Jr Coll, Pensacola, FL 32504-8998	1948	$1,304 (S)		5	10,363	819
Phillips Comm Coll of the U of Arkansas, Helena, AR 72342-0785	1965	$888 (A)		11	2,287	70
Phoenix Coll, Phoenix, AZ 85013-4234	1920	$1,098 (A)		11	10,900	540
Piedmont Comm Coll, Roxboro, NC 27573-1197	1970	$587 (S)		5	1,390	95
Piedmont Tech Coll, Greenwood, SC 29648-1467	1966	$1,590 (S)		5	3,415	225
Piedmont Virginia Comm Coll, Charlottesville, VA 22902-7589	1972	$1,572 (S)		5	4,079	262
Pierce Coll, Lakewood, WA 98498-1999	1967	$1,650 (S)		5	5,628	579
Pikes Peak Comm Coll, Colorado Springs, CO 80906-5498	1968	$1,740 (S)		5	8,804	498
Pitt Comm Coll, Greenville, NC 27835-7007	1961	$587 (S)		11	4,670	327
Pittsburgh Tech Inst, Pittsburgh, PA 15222-2560	1946	$13,080		3	1,120	77
Polk Comm Coll, Winter Haven, FL 33881-4299	1964	$1,256 (S)		5	5,489	240
Porterville Coll, Porterville, CA 93257-6058	1927	$430 (S)		5	2,836	140
Portland Comm Coll, Portland, OR 97280-0990	1961	$1,665 (S)		11	38,245	1,215
Potomac State Coll of West Virginia U, Keyser, WV 26726-2698	1901	$1,926 (S)	$3,954	5	1,209	83
Prairie State Coll, Chicago Heights, IL 60411-8226	1958	$1,680 (A)		11	5,559	323
Pratt Comm Coll & Area Voc School, Pratt, KS 67124-8317	1938	$1,280 (S)	$2,720	9	1,421	54
Prince George's Comm Coll, Largo, MD 20774-2199	1958	$2,830 (A)		8	11,962	574
Pueblo Comm Coll, Pueblo, CO 81004-1499	1933	$1,791 (S)		5	4,381	310
Pulaski Tech Coll, North Little Rock, AR 72118	1945	$1,056 (S)		5	2,462	145
Queensborough Comm Coll of the City U of New York, Bayside, NY 11364	1958	$2,602 (S)		11	10,299	701
Quincy Coll, Quincy, MA 02169-4522	1958	$2,580		10	4,706	69
Quinebaug Valley Comm-Tech Coll, Danielson, CT 06239-1440	1971	$1,814 (S)		5	1,220	81
Quinsigamond Comm Coll, Worcester, MA 01606-2092	1963	$2,250 (S)		5	4,936	371
Randolph Comm Coll, Asheboro, NC 27204-1009	1962	$582 (S)		5	1,442	73

Name, address	Year	Tuition & Fees	Room & Board	Control, Degree	Enroll-ment	Faculty
Ranken Tech Coll, St. Louis, MO 63113	1907	$6,300		1	1,529	93
Rappahannock Comm Coll, Glenns, VA 23149-2616	1970	$1,461 (S)		12	2,263	141
Raritan Valley Comm Coll, Somerville, NJ 08876-1265	1965	$2,100 (A)		8	5,496	289
Reading Area Comm Coll, Reading, PA 19603-1706	1971	$2,040 (A)		8	2,857	249
Redlands Comm Coll, El Reno, OK 73036	1938	$1,416 (S)		5	1,857	133
Red Rocks Comm Coll, Lakewood, CO 80228-1255	1969	$1,842 (S)		5	7,957	276
Red Wing/Winona Tech Coll, Winona, MN 55987	1992	$2,206 (S)		5	1,514	84
Reedley Coll, Reedley, CA 93654-2099	1926	$390 (S)		11	7,804	221
Rend Lake Coll, Ina, IL 62846-9801	1967	$1,152 (A)		5	3,857	180
Renton Tech Coll, Renton, WA 98056	1942	$1,710		5	7,428	421
Richard Bland Coll of the Coll of William & Mary, Petersburg, VA 23805	1961	$2,040 (S)		5	1,192	49
Richland Comm Coll, Decatur, IL 62521-8513	1971	$1,295 (A)		9	3,388	215
Richmond Comm Coll, Hamlet, NC 28345-1189	1964	$584 (S)		5	1,138	100
Ricks Coll, Rexburg, ID 83460-4107	1888	$1,950	$2,040	2	8,277	402
Ridgewater Coll, Willmar, MN 56201-1097	1961	$2,330 (S)		5	3,625	244
Rio Hondo Coll, Whittier, CA 90601-1699	1960	$454 (S)		11	15,000	710
Rio Salado Coll, Tempe, AZ 85281-6950	1978	$1,120 (A)		11	8,898	494
Riverland Comm Coll, Austin, MN 55912	1940	$2,287 (S)		5	2,615	152
Riverside Comm Coll, Riverside, CA 92506-1293	1916	$430 (S)		11	22,515	550
Roane State Comm Coll, Harriman, TN 37748-5011	1971	$1,066 (S)		5	5,587	337
Robeson Comm Coll, Lumberton, NC 28359-1420	1965	$588 (S)		5	1,596	114
Rochester Comm & Tech Coll, Rochester, MN 55904-4999	1915	$2,206 (S)		5	4,241	225
Rockland Comm Coll, Suffern, NY 10901-3699	1959	$2,400 (S)		11	6,442	586
Rock Valley Coll, Rockford, IL 61114-5699	1964	$1,390 (A)		9	8,433	260
Rogers U, Claremore, OK 74017-3252	1909	$1,349 (S)	$2,452	5	3,389	270
Rogue Comm Coll, Grants Pass, OR 97527-9298	1970	$1,620 (S)		11	3,484	459
Rose State Coll, Midwest City, OK 73110-2799	1968	$1,008 (S)		11	7,424	412
Rowan-Cabarrus Comm Coll, Salisbury, NC 28145-1595	1963	$589 (S)		5	3,676	229
Sacramento City Coll, Sacramento, CA 95822-1386	1916	$312 (S)		11	16,583	726
Saint Augustine Coll, Chicago, IL 60640-3501	1980	$6,420		1-B	1,135	129
Saint Charles County Comm Coll, St. Peters, MO 63376-0975	1986	$1,440 (A)		5	5,068	253
St. Clair County Comm Coll, Port Huron, MI 48061-5015	1923	$1,885 (A)		11	4,004	258
St. Cloud Tech Coll, St. Cloud, MN 56303-1240	1948	$2,158 (S)		5	2,363	121
St. Louis Comm Coll at Florissant Valley, St. Louis, MO 63135-1499	1963	$1,344 (A)		9	7,365	350
St. Paul Tech Coll, St. Paul, MN 55102-1800	1922	$2,161 (S)		12	3,400	565
St. Petersburg Jr Coll, St. Petersburg, FL 33731-3489	1927	$1,660 (S)		11	17,575	899
St. Philip's Coll, San Antonio, TX 78203-2098	1898	$878 (A)		9	7,577	427
Salem Comm Coll, Carneys Point, NJ 08069-2799	1972	$1,780 (A)		8	1,124	74
Salt Lake Comm Coll, Salt Lake City, UT 84130-0808	1948	$1,542 (S)		5	23,590	1,242
Sampson Comm Coll, Clinton, NC 28329-0318	1965	$591 (S)		11	1,054	102
Sandhills Comm Coll, Pinehurst, NC 28374-8299	1963	$588 (S)		11	2,386	148
San Diego City Coll, San Diego, CA 92101-4787	1914	$390 (S)		11	13,085	250
San Diego Mesa Coll, San Diego, CA 92111-4998	1964	$412 (S)		11	21,663	676
San Diego Miramar Coll, San Diego, CA 92126-2999	1969	$395 (S)		11	9,100	231
San Jacinto Coll–North Campus, Houston, TX 77049-4599	1974	$644 (A)		11	3,727	229
San Jacinto Coll–South Campus, Houston, TX 77089-6099	1979	$684 (A)		11	4,608	215
San Joaquin Delta Coll, Stockton, CA 95207-6370	1935	$390 (S)		9	16,406	572
San Juan Coll, Farmington, NM 87402-4699	1958	$360 (S)		8	3,807	252
Santa Ana Coll, Santa Ana, CA 92706-3398	1915	$425 (S)		5	24,706	1,799
Santa Barbara City Coll, Santa Barbara, CA 93109-2394	1908	$407 (S)		11	12,343	578
Santa Fe Comm Coll, Gainesville, FL 32606-6200	1966	$1,494 (S)		11	12,524	625
Santa Fe Comm Coll, Santa Fe, NM 87505	1983	$506 (A)		11	3,497	275
Santa Monica Coll, Santa Monica, CA 90405-1628	1929	$446 (S)		11	23,158	987
Santa Rosa Jr Coll, Santa Rosa, CA 95401-4395	1918	$332 (S)		11	28,180	1,153
Schenectady County Comm Coll, Schenectady, NY 12305-2294	1968	$2,455 (S)		11	3,578	181
Schoolcraft Coll, Livonia, MI 48152-2696	1961	$1,640 (A)		9	9,420	421
Scott Comm Coll, Bettendorf, IA 52722-6804	1966	$1,755 (S)		11	6,088	235
Scottsdale Comm Coll, Scottsdale, AZ 85250-2699	1969	$1,120 (A)		11	9,418	455
Seattle Central Comm Coll, Seattle, WA 98122-2400	1966	$1,527 (S)		5	10,303	388
Seminole Comm Coll, Sanford, FL 32773-6199	1966	$1,328 (S)		11	8,312	502
Seminole State Coll, Seminole, OK 74818-0351	1931	$1,335 (S)	$2,200	5	1,633	77
Seward County Comm Coll, Liberal, KS 67905-1137	1969	$1,408 (S)	$3,100	11	2,325	214
Shasta Coll, Redding, CA 96049-6006	1948	$321 (S)	$3,176	11	10,591	397
Shawnee Comm Coll, Ullin, IL 62992-9725	1967	$1,216 (A)		11	1,961	200
Shelby State Comm Coll, Memphis, TN 38174-0568	1970	$1,152 (S)		5	5,058	342
Sheridan Coll, Sheridan, WY 82801-1500	1948	$1,296 (S)	$3,040	11	2,706	222
Shoreline Comm Coll, Seattle, WA 98133-5696	1964	$1,449 (S)		5	8,539	333
Sierra Coll, Rocklin, CA 95677-3397	1936	$410 (S)	$4,230	5	15,920	518
Sinclair Comm Coll, Dayton, OH 45402-1460	1887	$1,457 (A)		11	17,239	913
Skagit Valley Coll, Mount Vernon, WA 98273-5899	1926	$1,458 (S)		5	6,182	344
Skyline Coll, San Bruno, CA 94066-1698	1969	$334 (S)		11	8,598	268
Snead State Comm Coll, Boaz, AL 35957-0734	1898	$1,380 (S)	$1,650	5	1,663	84
Snow Coll, Ephraim, UT 84627-1203	1888	$1,254 (S)	$2,550	5	2,743	126
Solano Comm Coll, Suisun City, CA 94585-3197	1945	$407 (S)		11	10,231	374
South Arkansas Comm Coll, El Dorado, AR 71731-7010	1975	$922 (A)		5	1,189	63
Southeast Arkansas Tech Coll, Pine Bluff, AR 71603	1991	$910 (S)		5	1,468	89
Southeast Comm Coll, Lincoln Campus, Lincoln, NE 68520-1299	1973	$1,356 (S)		9	5,032	565
Southeast Comm Coll, Milford Campus, Milford, NE 68405-9397	1941	$1,626 (S)	$2,145	9	1,016	89
Southeastern Baptist Theological Seminary, Wake Forest, NC 27588	1950	$4,020		2-D	1,326	53
Southeastern Comm Coll, Whiteville, NC 28472-0151	1964	$581 (S)		5	1,610	145
Southeastern Comm Coll, North Campus, West Burlington, IA 52655	1968	$1,740 (S)	$2,990	11	2,594	94
Southeastern Illinois Coll, Harrisburg, IL 62946-4925	1960	$1,056 (A)		5	3,477	184
Southeast Tech Inst, Sioux Falls, SD 57107-9910	1968	$2,374		5	2,091	113
Southern Maine Tech Coll, South Portland, ME 04106	1946	$2,585 (S)	$5,200	5	2,430	148
Southern State Comm Coll, Hillsboro, OH 45133-9487	1975	$2,619 (S)		5	1,600	88
Southern Union State Comm Coll, Wadley, AL 36276	1922	$1,437 (S)	$2,250	5	4,500	217
South Florida Comm Coll, Avon Park, FL 33825-9356	1965	$1,260 (S)		5	2,333	213
South Georgia Coll, Douglas, GA 31533-5098	1906	$1,312 (S)	$2,490	5	1,148	54

Name, address	Year	Tuition & Fees	Room & Board	Control, Degree	Enroll-ment	Faculty
South Mountain Comm Coll, Phoenix, AZ 85040	1979	$898 (A)		11	2,462	184
South Plains Coll, Levelland, TX 79336-6595	1958	$786 (A)	$2,400	11	6,291	353
South Puget Sound Comm Coll, Olympia, WA 98512-6292	1970	$1,615 (S)		5	4,355	247
South Seattle Comm Coll, Seattle, WA 98106-1499	1970	$1,482 (S)		5	6,582	194
Southside Virginia Comm Coll, Alberta, VA 23821-9719	1970	$1,547 (S)		5	3,621	182
South Suburban Coll, South Holland, IL 60473-1270	1927	$1,332 (A)		11	9,136	384
Southwestern Coll, Chula Vista, CA 91910-7299	1961	$435 (S)		11	16,139	661
Southwestern Comm Coll, Creston, IA 50801	1966	$2,046 (S)	$2,760	5	1,142	75
Southwestern Comm Coll, Sylva, NC 28779	1964	$577 (S)		5	1,616	160
Southwestern Michigan Coll, Dowagiac, MI 49047-9793	1964	$1,674 (A)		11	2,802	197
Southwestern Oregon Comm Coll, Coos Bay, OR 97420-2912	1961	$1,734	$4,905	11	2,861	243
Southwest Mississippi Comm Coll, Summit, MS 39666	1918	$850 (S)	$1,700	11	1,647	89
Southwest Missouri State U–West Plains, West Plains, MO 65775	1963	$2,130 (S)	$3,700	5	1,320	74
Southwest Texas Jr Coll, Uvalde, TX 78801-6297	1946	$702 (A)	$2,120	11	3,452	166
Southwest Virginia Comm Coll, Richlands, VA 24641	1968	$1,430 (S)		5	4,055	235
Southwest Wisconsin Tech Coll, Fennimore, WI 53809-9778	1967	$1,799 (S)		11	1,896	101
Spokane Comm Coll, Spokane, WA 99217-5399	1963	$1,452 (S)		5	6,294	367
Spokane Falls Comm Coll, Spokane, WA 99224-5288	1967	$1,401 (S)		5	8,842	346
Spoon River Coll, Canton, IL 61520-9801	1959	$1,536 (A)		5	1,950	189
Springfield Tech Comm Coll, Springfield, MA 01105-1296	1967	$2,510 (S)		5	6,283	333
Stanly Comm Coll, Albemarle, NC 28001-7458	1971	$588 (S)		5	1,483	76
Stark State Coll of Technology, Canton, OH 44720-7299	1970	$3,114 (S)		11	4,413	210
State Tech Inst at Memphis, Memphis, TN 38134-7693	1967	$1,156 (S)		5	9,049	761
State U of New York Coll of Agriculture & Technology at Cobleskill, Cobleskill, NY 12043	1916	$3,771 (S)	$5,540	5-B	2,186	145
State U of New York Coll of Agriculture & Technology at Morrisville, Morrisville, NY 13408	1908	$3,765 (S)	$5,588	5-B	2,767	171
State U of New York Coll of Technology at Alfred, Alfred, NY 14802	1908	$3,757 (S)	$5,056	5-B	2,888	176
State U of New York Coll of Technology at Canton, Canton, NY 13617	1906	$3,500 (S)	$5,300	5	2,103	107
State U of New York Coll of Technology at Delhi, Delhi, NY 13753	1913	$3,687 (S)	$5,420	5-B	1,893	141
Suffolk County Comm Coll–Ammerman Campus, Selden, NY 11784	1962	$2,408 (S)		11	11,371	782
Suffolk County Comm Coll–Eastern Campus, Riverhead, NY 11901	1977	$2,408 (S)		11	2,158	216
Suffolk County Comm Coll–Western Campus, Brentwood, NY 11717	1974	$2,408 (S)		11	5,685	349
Sullivan County Comm Coll, Loch Sheldrake, NY 12759	1962	$2,656 (S)		11	1,696	106
Surry Comm Coll, Dobson, NC 27017-0304	1965	$623 (S)		5	2,692	98
Sussex County Comm Coll, Newton, NJ 07860	1981	$2,310 (A)		11	2,294	188
Tacoma Comm Coll, Tacoma, WA 98466	1965	$1,521 (S)		5	5,413	299
Taft Coll, Taft, CA 93268-2317	1922	$420 (S)	$2,720	11	1,054	66
Tallahassee Comm Coll, Tallahassee, FL 32304-2895	1966	$1,205 (S)		11	10,533	383
Tarrant County Jr Coll, Fort Worth, TX 76102-6599	1967	$884 (A)		8	25,856	1,153
Tech Career Insts, New York, NY 10001-2705	1909	$6,245		3	3,594	192
Tech Coll of the Lowcountry, Beaufort, SC 29901-1288	1972	$1,000 (S)		5	1,853	69
Temple Coll, Temple, TX 76504-7435	1926	$930 (A)	$2,830	9	2,897	125
Texarkana Coll, Texarkana, TX 75599-0001	1927	$690 (A)		11	4,303	196
Texas State Tech Coll, Sweetwater, TX 79556-4108	1970	$1,620 (S)	$4,300	5	1,000	139
Texas State Tech Coll–Harlingen, Harlingen, TX 78550-3697	1967	$1,293 (S)	$2,820	5	3,190	167
Texas State Tech Coll–Waco/Marshall Campus, Waco, TX 76705	1965	$2,031 (S)		5	4,280	331
Thomas Tech Inst, Thomasville, GA 31792	1963	$846 (S)		5	1,076	45
Three Rivers Comm Coll, Poplar Bluff, MO 63901-2393	1966	$1,054 (A)		11	2,300	67
Three Rivers Comm-Tech Coll, Norwich, CT 06360	1963	$1,814 (S)		5	3,573	187
Tidewater Comm Coll, Portsmouth, VA 23703	1968	$1,696 (S)		5	17,907	760
Tomball Coll, Tomball, TX 77375-4036	1988	$830 (A)		11	4,240	230
Tompkins Cortland Comm Coll, Dryden, NY 13053-9533	1968	$2,708 (S)		11	2,554	196
Treasure Valley Comm Coll, Ontario, OR 97914-3423	1962	$1,680 (S)	$3,261	11	3,700	113
Tri-County Comm Coll, Murphy, NC 28906-7919	1964	$581 (S)		5	1,047	55
Tri-County Tech Coll, Pendleton, SC 29670-0587	1962	$1,000 (A)		5	3,363	251
Trident Tech Coll, Charleston, SC 29423-8067	1964	$1,064 (A)		11	8,730	523
Trinidad State Jr Coll, Trinidad, CO 81082-2396	1925	$1,962 (S)	$3,282	5	2,449	175
Trinity Valley Comm Coll, Athens, TX 75751-2765	1946	$608 (A)	$2,766	11	4,382	224
Triton Coll, River Grove, IL 60171-9983	1964	$1,518 (A)		5	17,576	712
Truckee Meadows Comm Coll, Reno, NV 89512-3901	1971	$948 (S)		5	9,133	511
Truett-McConnell Coll, Cleveland, GA 30528-9799	1946	$5,550	$2,925	2	2,027	155
Tulsa Comm Coll, Tulsa, OK 74135-6198	1968	$1,140 (S)		5	26,000	1,200
Tunxis Comm Tech Coll, Farmington, CT 06032-3026	1969	$1,814 (S)		5	3,335	175
Tyler Jr Coll, Tyler, TX 75711-9020	1926	$826 (A)	$2,400	11	8,224	364
UAB Walker Coll, Jasper, AL 35501-4967	1938	$2,213 (S)	$2,145	5	1,002	51
Ulster County Comm Coll, Stone Ridge, NY 12484	1961	$2,596 (S)		11	2,513	164
Umpqua Comm Coll, Roseburg, OR 97470-0226	1964	$1,610 (S)		11	1,701	148
Union County Coll, Cranford, NJ 07016-1528	1933	$2,579 (A)		11	9,235	391
The U of Akron–Wayne Coll, Orrville, OH 44667-9192	1972	$3,443 (S)		5	1,385	113
U of Alaska Anchorage, Kenai Peninsula Coll, Soldotna, AK 99669	1964	$2,229 (S)		5	1,688	107
U of Alaska Anchorage, Matanuska-Susitna Coll, Palmer, AK 99645	1958	$1,772 (S)		5	1,182	111
U of Alaska Southeast, Sitka Campus, Sitka, AK 99835-9418	1962	$1,896 (S)		5	1,290	104
U of Arkansas Comm Coll at Hope, Hope, AR 71801-0140	1966	$860 (A)		5	1,251	76
U of Hawaii–Hawaii Comm Coll, Hilo, HI 96720-4091	1954	$1,034 (S)	$3,813	5	2,170	149
U of Hawaii–Honolulu Comm Coll, Honolulu, HI 96817-4598	1920	$956 (S)		5	3,970	185
U of Hawaii–Kauai Comm Coll, Lihue, HI 96766-9591	1965	$946 (S)		5	1,123	77
U of Hawaii–Leeward Comm Coll, Pearl City, HI 96782-3393	1968	$999 (S)		5	6,000	243
U of Hawaii–Maui Comm Coll, Kahului, HI 96732	1967	$1,002 (S)		5	2,744	148
U of Kentucky, Ashland Comm Coll, Ashland, KY 41101-3683	1937	$1,100 (S)		5	2,271	143
U of Kentucky, Elizabethtown Comm Coll, Elizabethtown, KY 42701	1964	$1,100 (S)		5	3,595	181
U of Kentucky, Hazard Comm Coll, Hazard, KY 41701-2403	1968	$1,100 (S)		5	2,212	156
U of Kentucky, Hopkinsville Comm Coll, Hopkinsville, KY 42241-2100	1965	$1,100 (S)		5	2,752	158
U of Kentucky, Lexington Comm Coll, Lexington, KY 40506-0235	1965	$2,036 (S)		5	5,550	301
U of Kentucky, Madisonville Comm Coll, Madisonville, KY 42431-9185	1968	$1,100 (S)		5	2,412	167
U of Kentucky, Maysville Comm Coll, Maysville, KY 41056	1967	$1,100 (S)		5	1,409	111
U of Kentucky, Paducah Comm Coll, Paducah, KY 42002-7380	1932	$1,100 (S)		5	2,794	143
U of Kentucky, Prestonsburg Comm Coll, Prestonsburg, KY 41653	1964	$1,100 (S)		5	2,573	129

Name, address	Year	Tuition & Fees	Room & Board	Control, Degree	Enroll-ment	Faculty
U of Kentucky, Somerset Comm Coll, Somerset, KY 42501-2973	1965	$1,140 (S)		5	2,558	153
U of Kentucky, Southeast Comm Coll, Cumberland, KY 40823-1099	1960	$1,140 (S)		5	2,112	150
U of New Mexico–Gallup, Gallup, NM 87301-5603	1968	$720 (S)		5-B	2,612	159
U of New Mexico–Los Alamos Branch, Los Alamos, NM 87544-2233	1980	$752 (S)		5	1,000	96
U of New Mexico–Valencia Campus, Los Lunas, NM 87031-7633	1981	$720 (S)		5	1,507	93
U of North Dakota–Lake Region, Devils Lake, ND 58301-1598	1941	$1,878 (S)	$2,612	5	1,084	54
U of Puerto Rico, Colegio Regional de la Montaña, Utuado, PR 00641	1979	$1,486 (S)		6-B	1,330	76
U of South Carolina at Beaufort, Beaufort, SC 29902-4601	1959	$1,988 (S)		5	1,039	80
U of South Carolina at Lancaster, Lancaster, SC 29721-0889	1959	$1,988 (S)		5	1,064	52
U of South Carolina at Sumter, Sumter, SC 29150-2498	1966	$1,988 (S)		5	1,368	72
U of Wisconsin–Fox Valley, Menasha, WI 54952-8002	1933	$2,081 (S)		5	1,239	58
U of Wisconsin–Waukesha, Waukesha, WI 53188-2799	1966	$2,098 (S)		5	1,635	77
Utah Valley State Coll, Orem, UT 84058-0001	1941	$1,519 (S)		5-B	15,994	607
Valencia Comm Coll, Orlando, FL 32802-3028	1967	$1,275 (S)		5	24,470	976
Vance-Granville Comm Coll, Henderson, NC 27536-0917	1969	$588 (S)		5	2,638	284
Ventura Coll, Ventura, CA 93003-3899	1925	$412 (S)		11	11,695	574
Vernon Regional Jr Coll, Vernon, TX 76384-4092	1972	$801 (A)	$2,100	11	1,750	98
Victoria Coll, Victoria, TX 77901-4494	1925	$784 (A)		8	3,822	120
Victor Valley Coll, Victorville, CA 92392-5849	1961	$308 (S)		5	10,218	325
Vincennes U, Vincennes, IN 47591-5202	1801	$2,541 (S)	$4,194	5	5,788	383
Virginia Highlands Comm Coll, Abingdon, VA 24212-0828	1967	$1,525 (S)		5	3,227	129
Virginia Western Comm Coll, Roanoke, VA 24038	1966	$1,434 (S)		5	7,661	290
Vista Comm Coll, Berkeley, CA 94704-5102	1974	$360 (S)		11	4,000	146
Volunteer State Comm Coll, Gallatin, TN 37066-3188	1970	$1,146 (S)		5	6,835	404
Wake Tech Comm Coll, Raleigh, NC 27603-5696	1958	$568 (S)		11	7,080	546
Walker Tech Inst, Rock Springs, GA 30739	1966	$816		5	1,178	59
Wallace State Comm Coll, Hanceville, AL 35077-2000	1966	$1,170 (S)		5	4,865	330
Walla Walla Comm Coll, Walla Walla, WA 99362-9267	1967	$1,545 (S)		5	5,343	416
Washington State Comm Coll, Marietta, OH 45750-9225	1971	$2,565 (S)		5	2,019	132
Washtenaw Comm Coll, Ann Arbor, MI 48106	1965	$1,726 (A)		11	10,488	595
Wayne Comm Coll, Goldsboro, NC 27533-8002	1957	$588 (S)		11	2,619	157
Wayne County Comm Coll, Detroit, MI 48226-3010	1967	$1,770 (A)		11	9,413	400
Weatherford Coll, Weatherford, TX 76086-5699	1869	$858 (A)	$2,599	11	2,579	146
Wenatchee Valley Coll, Wenatchee, WA 98801-1799	1939	$1,461 (S)	$3,780	11	3,074	203
Westark Comm Coll, Fort Smith, AR 72913-3649	1928	$884 (A)		11	5,721	240
Westchester Comm Coll, Valhalla, NY 10595-1698	1946	$2,583 (S)		11	10,858	791
Western Iowa Tech Comm Coll, Sioux City, IA 51102-5199	1966	$2,040 (S)		5	3,539	238
Western Nebraska Comm Coll, Scottsbluff, NE 69361	1921	$1,020 (S)	$2,720	11	2,008	242
Western Nevada Comm Coll, Carson City, NV 89703-7316	1971	$1,095 (S)		5	4,965	437
Western Oklahoma State Coll, Altus, OK 73521-1397	1926	$1,196 (S)		5	1,624	93
Western Texas Coll, Snyder, TX 79549-9502	1969	$907 (A)	$2,200	11	1,180	55
Western Wisconsin Tech Coll, La Crosse, WI 54602-0908	1911	$1,843 (S)		9	4,568	184
Western Wyoming Comm Coll, Rock Springs, WY 82902-0428	1959	$1,098 (S)	$2,610	11	2,749	232
Westmoreland County Comm Coll, Youngwood, PA 15697	1970	$1,440 (A)		8	5,770	390
West Shore Comm Coll, Scottville, MI 49454-9716	1967	$1,234 (A)		9	1,376	81
West Virginia Northern Comm Coll, Wheeling, WV 26003-3699	1972	$1,438 (S)		5	2,592	166
Whatcom Comm Coll, Bellingham, WA 98226-8003	1970	$1,440 (S)		5	3,742	178
Wilkes Comm Coll, Wilkesboro, NC 28697	1965	$588 (S)		5	1,798	173
William Rainey Harper Coll, Palatine, IL 60067-7398	1965	$1,438 (A)		11	13,215	1,018
Wilson Tech Comm Coll, Wilson, NC 27893-3310	1958	$581 (S)		5	1,295	93
Wisconsin Indianhead Tech Coll, New Richmond Campus, New Richmond, WI 54017-1738	1972	$1,824 (S)		9	2,881	65
Wisconsin Indianhead Tech Coll, Rice Lake Campus, Rice Lake, WI 54868	1941	$1,824 (S)		9	2,390	79
Wisconsin Indianhead Tech Coll, Superior Campus, Superior, WI 54880-5207	1912	$1,926 (S)		9	1,905	76
Wytheville Comm Coll, Wytheville, VA 24382-3308	1967	$1,445 (S)		5	2,331	142
Yakima Valley Comm Coll, Yakima, WA 98907-2520	1928	$1,431 (S)	$4,500	5	3,946	292
Yavapai Coll, Prescott, AZ 86301-3297	1966	$744 (S)	$3,240	11	4,834	487
York Tech Coll, Rock Hill, SC 29730-3395	1961	$948 (A)		5	3,476	230

College Freshman Attitudes, 1997

Source: *The American Freshman: National Norms for Fall 1997*

According to the 32d annual survey of college freshmen conducted by the American Council on Education and UCLA, record numbers of students beginning college in 1997 expected to earn master's degrees (39.4%) and PhDs (15.3%). The percent who expected to have a B average or better rose to an all-time high of 49.7%, compared to a low of 32.7% in 1972. At the same time, freshmen reported spending less time studying or doing homework than ever before—an average of only 3.8 hours per week in 1997, compared to 4.9 hours in 1987. The percentage of freshmen who "overslept and missed class or appointment" rose to an all-time high of 34.5%.

The percentage of students describing themselves politically as "middle of the road" rose to 54.8% in 1997 from 52.7% in 1996, while those identifying themselves as "conservative" or "far right" fell to 20.8% from 22.7%. The percent of students who considered themselves "liberal" or "far left" was virtually unchanged at 24.4%. A record low of 26.7% felt that "keeping up-to-date with political affairs" is an important or essential goal, down from a high of 57.8% in 1966. The proportion of freshman committed to "influencing social values" fell to 37.6%, down from a high of 43.3% in 1992.

Support for keeping abortion legal fell for the fifth year in a row, to 53.5%, from a high of 64.9% in 1990. While 33.9% of freshmen believed that "it is important to have laws prohibiting homosexual relationships," 49.8% agreed that "same sex couples should have the right to legal marital status." A desire for "helping promote racial understanding" dropped to 31.8%, compared to a high of 42.0% in 1992. The proportion of students who believed "becoming involved in programs to clean up the environment" is important or essential declined to 19.4% in 1997, down from 33.6% in 1992.

The percentage of freshmen who reported frequent or occasional beer drinking continued to decline, from an all-time high of 75.2% in 1981 to 52.7% in 1997. The percentage who reported frequently smoking cigarettes was the highest in 30 years, at 16.1%, almost double the percentage cited in 1987 (8.9%). The view that "marijuana should be legalized" has grown in the 1990s—reaching 35.2% in 1997 from a record low of 16.7% in 1989.

ASSOCIATIONS AND SOCIETIES

Source: World Almanac questionnaire

Selected list, by first key word in each title. Founding year in parentheses; last figure after ZIP code = membership as reported by organization. Information, especially website addresses, subject to change. For other organizations, see also Directory of Sports Organizations, under Sports; Where to Get Help directory, under Health; Labor Union Directory, under Employment; lists of religious groups' headquarters (for U.S. and for Canada), under Religious Information; international organizations, under Nations of the World.

Aaron Burr Accord (1985), P.O. Box 4644, Seattle, WA 98104; 357.

Aaron Burr Assn. (1946), 4520 King Edward Ct., Annandale, VA 22003; 220.

Abortion Federation, Natl. (1977), 1755 Massachusetts Ave. NW, Ste. 600, Wash., DC 20036; 400; http://www.prochoice.org

Accountants, American Institute of Certified Public (1887), 1211 Ave. of the Americas, New York, NY 10036; 330,000; http://www.aicpa.org

Accountants, Natl. Assn. of Enrolled Federal Tax (1960), P.O. Box 59-009, Chicago, IL 60659.

Accountants for Cooperatives, Natl. Soc. of (1936), 6320 Augusta Dr., Ste. 800, Springfield, VA 22150; 2,000.

Acoustical Society of America (1929), 500 Sunnyside Blvd., Woodbury, NY 11797; 6,800; http://asa.aip.org/index.html

Actuaries, Society of (1949), 475 N. Martingale Rd., Ste. 800, Schaumburg, IL 60173; 16,500; http://www.soa.org

Advertisers, Assn. of Natl. (1910), 708 Third Ave., New York, NY 10017; 225 cos.; http://www.ana.net

Advertising Agencies, American Assn. of (1917), 405 Lexington Ave., New York, NY 10174; 600 agencies; http://www.commercepark.com/AAAA

Aeronautic Assn., Natl. (1904), 1815 N. Fort Myer Dr., Arlington, VA 22209; 6,000; http://www.naa.ycg.org

Aerospace Industries Assn. of America (1919), 1250 Eye St. NW, Wash., DC 20005; 50 cos.

African Violet Soc. of America (1946), 2375 North, Beaumont, TX 77702; 12,000; http://avsa.org

Afro-American Life and History, Assn. for the Study of (1915), 1407 14th St. NW, Wash., DC 20005; 1,400.

AFS Intl. Intercultural Programs (1947), 220 E. 42d St., New York, NY 10017; 475,000.

Agricultural Economics Assn., American (1910), 1110 Buckeye Ave., Ames, IA 50010; 3,516; http://www.aaea.org

Agricultural Engineers, American Soc. of (ASAE) (1907), 2950 Niles Rd., St. Joseph, MI 49085; 8,000; http://www.asae.org

Agricultural History Society (1919), 1800 M St. NW, Rm. 2103, Wash., DC 20036; 1,400.

Agronomy, American Society of (1907), 677 S. Segoe Rd., Madison, WI 53711; 12,000; http://www.agronomy.org

Aircraft Owners and Pilots Assn. (1939), 421 Aviation Way, Frederick, MD 21701; 340,000; http://www.aopa.org

Air Force Assn. (1946), 1501 Lee Hwy., Arlington, VA 22209; 176,000; http://www.afa.org

Air Force Gunners Assn. (1986), 453 Plaza Circle, Bossier City, LA 71111; 1,700.

Air & Waste Management Assn. (1907), One Gateway Center, 3d Fl., Pittsburgh, PA 15222; 16,000; http://www.awma.org

Al-Anon Family Groups, Inc. (1951), 1600 Corporate Landing Pkwy., Virginia Beach, VA 23454; 600,000; http://www.al-anon.alateen.org

Alcoholics Anonymous (1935), P.O. Box 459, Grand Central Station, New York, NY 10163; 2 mil+; http://www.alcoholics-anonymous.org

Alcoholism and Drug Dependence, Inc., Natl. Council on (1944), 12 W. 21st St., New York, NY 10010; http://www.ncadd.org

Alcohol Problems, American Council on (1895), 3426 Bridgeland Dr., Bridgeton, MO 63044; 36 state affiliates.

Alexander Graham Bell Assn. for the Deaf (1890), 3417 Volta Pl. NW, Wash., DC 20007; 5,000; http://www.agbell.org

Allergy, Asthma, and Immunology, American Academy of (1943), 611 E. Wells St., Milwaukee, WI 53202; 5,000; http://www.aaaai.org

Alpha Delta Kappa (1947), 1615 West 92d St., Kansas City, MO 64114; 56,000; http://www.alphadeltakappa.org

Alpine Club, American (1902), 710 Tenth St., Ste. 100, Golden, CO 80401; 3,750; http://www.AmericanAlpineClub.org

Alzheimer's Assn. (1980), 919 Michigan Ave., Chicago, IL 60611; http://www.alz.org

Amateur Radio Union, Intl. (IARU) (1925), P.O. Box 31095, Newington, CT 06131; 146 org.; http://www.iaru.org

American Bar Association, 750 N. Lake Shore Dr., Chicago, IL 60611; http://www.abanet.org

American Indian Affairs, Inc., Assn. on (1922), P.O. Box 268, Sisseton, SD 57262; 25,000.

American Indians, Natl. Congress of (1944), 2010 Massachusetts Ave. NW, Wash., DC 20036; 3,000; http://www.ncai.org

American Legion (1919), P.O. Box 1055, Indianapolis, IN 46206; 2.9 mil.; http://www.legion.org

American Legion Auxiliary (1921), 777 N. Meridian St., 3rd Floor, Indianapolis, IN 46204; 960,000; http://www.legion-aux.org

Americares Foundation (1982), 161 Cherry St., New Canaan, CT 06840; http://www.americares.org

Amnesty Intl. USA (1961), 322 8th Ave., New York, NY 10001; http://www.amnesty.usa.org

Amputation Foundation, Inc., Natl. (1919), 38-40 Church St., Malverne, NY 11565; 2,000.

AMVETS (American Veterans) (1947); **AMVETS Natl. Auxiliary** (1946), 4647 Forbes Blvd., Lanham, MD 20706; 250,000; http://www.amvets.org

Amusement Parks and Attractions, Intl. Assn. of (1918), 1448 Duke St., Alexandria, VA 22314; 5,000; http://www.iaapa.org

Animals, American Society for Prevention of Cruelty to (ASPCA) (1866), 424 E. 92d St., New York, NY 10128; 299,000; http://www.aspca.org

Animal Protection Institute (1968), 2831 Fruitridge Rd., Sacramento, CA 95820; 75,000; http://www.api4animals.org

Animal Welfare Institute (1951), P.O. Box 3650, Wash., DC 20007; 5,271; http://www.animalwelfare.com

Anthropological Assn., American (1902), 4350 N. Fairfax Dr., Ste. 640, Arlington, VA 22203; 10,000; http://www.ameranthassn.org

Antiquarian Society, American (1812), 185 Salisbury St., Worcester, MA 01609; 655.

Appalachian Mountain Club (1876), 5 Joy St., Boston, MA 02178; 76,000; http://www.outdoors.org

Appalachian Trail Conference (1925), Washington & Jackson Sts., Harpers Ferry, WV 25425; 23,000; http://www.atconf.org

Appraisers, American Society of (1936), 555 Herndon Pkwy., Ste. 125, Herndon, VA 22070; 6,500; http://www.appraisers.org

Arab Americans, Natl. Assn. of (1972), 1212 New York Ave. NW, Wash., DC 20005; http://www.naaa.net/index.html

Arbitration Assn., American (1926), 140 W. 51st St., New York, NY 10020; 10,000; http://www.adr.org

Arc, The (1950), 500 E. Border St., Ste. 300, Arlington, TX 76010; 140,000; http://www.thearc.org

Archaeological Institute of America (1879), 656 Beacon St., Boston, MA 02215; 10,000; http://www.archaeological.org

Archery Assn. of the U.S., Inc., Natl. (1879), One Olympic Plaza, Colorado Springs, CO 80909; 6,000; http://www.USArchery.org

Architects, American Institute of (1857), 1735 New York Ave. NW, Wash., DC 20006; 55,000; http://www.aia.org

Architectural Historians, Society of (1940), 1365 North Astor St., Chicago, IL 60610; 3,500; http://www.sah.org

Armed Forces Communications and Electronics Assn. (1946), 4400 Fair Lakes Ct., Fairfax, VA 22033; 40,000.

Army, Assn. of the United States (1950), 2425 Wilson Blvd., Arlington, VA 22201; 117,000; http://www.ausa.org

Arthritis Foundation (1948), 1330 W. Peachtree St., Atlanta, GA 30309; 400,000; http://www.arthritis.org

Arts, American Council for the (1960), One E. 53d St., New York, NY 10022; 1,500; http://www.artsusa.org

Arts, American Federation of (1909), 41 E. 65th St., New York, NY 10021; 520+ museums/inst

Arts, Americans for the (1996), 1000 Vermont Ave., 12th Fl., Wash., DC 20005; 2,500; http://www.artsusa.org

Arts and Letters, American Academy of (1898), 633 W. 155 St., New York, NY 10032; 250.

Arts and Letters, Natl. Society of (1944), 4227 46th St., NW, Wash., DC 20016; 1,600; http://www.arts-nsal.org

Arts and Sciences, American Academy of (1780), Norton's Woods, 136 Irving St., Cambridge, MA 02138; 633; http://www.amacad.org

Associated Press (1848), 50 Rockefeller Plaza, New York, NY 10020; 1,550 newspapers, 6,000 U.S. broadcast stations, 8,500 intl. subscribers; http://www.ap.org

Association Executives, American Society of (1925), 1575 Eye St. NW, Wash., DC 20005; 23,400; http://www.asaenet.org

Astrologers, Inc., American Federation of (1938), P.O. Box 22040, Tempe, AZ 85285; 4 mil+; http://www.astrologers.com

Astronautical Society, American (1954), 6352 Rolling Mill Pl. #102, Springfield, VA 22152; 1,400; http://www.astronautical.org
Astronomical Society, American (1899), 2000 Florida Ave. NW, Ste. 400, Wash., DC 20009; 6,375; http://www.aas.org
Ataxia Foundation, Natl. (1957), 2600 Fernbrook Ln., Ste. 119, Minneapolis, MN 55447; 9,304; http://www.ataxia.org
Atheists, Inc., American (1964), P.O. Box 140195, Austin, TX 78714; 2,400; http://www.atheists.org
Amateur Radio Union, Intl. (1925), P.O. Box 310905, Newington, CT 06131; 146 orgs.; http://www.iaru.org
Auctioneers Assn., Natl. (1949), 8880 Ballentine, Overland Park, KS 66214; 5,578; http://www.auctioneers.org
Audubon Society, Natl. (1905), 700 Broadway, New York, NY 10003; 550,000; http://www.audubon.org
Authors Guild, The (1912), 330 W. 42d St., 29th Floor, New York, NY 10036; 7,200; http://www.authorsguild.org
Authors League of America (1912), 330 W. 42nd St., 29th Floor, New York, NY 10036; 15,000.
Authors Registry, The (1995), 330 W. 42d St., 29th Fl., New York, NY 10036; representing approx. 50,000 authors http://www.webcom.com/registry
Autism Society of America (1965), 7910 Woodmont Ave., Ste. 650, Bethesda, MD 20814; 23,000; http://www.autism-society.org
Autograph Collectors Club, Universal (1965), P.O. Box 6181, Wash., DC 20044; 1,850; http://www.uacc.org
Automobile Assn., American (1902), 1000 AAA Dr., Heathrow, FL 32746; 40 mil; http://www.aaa.com
Automobile Club of America, Antique (1935), 501 W. Governor Rd., Hershey, PA 17033; 53,000; http://www.aaca.org/frame.htm
Automobile Dealers Assn., Natl. (1917), 8400 Westpark Dr., McLean, VA 22102; 19,500; http://www.nadanet.com
Automobile License Plate Collectors Assn. (1954), P.O. Box 7, Horner, WV 26372; 2,500; http://www.alpca.org
Automotive Hall of Fame (1936), 21400 Oakwood Blvd., Dearborn, MI 48124; 700 visiting members.

Badminton Assn., U.S. (1936), One Olympic Plaza, Colorado Springs, CO 80909; 2,500+.
Baker Street Irregulars (1934), P.O. Box 2189, Easton, MD 21601; 300.
Bald-Headed Men of America (1972), 102 Bald Dr., Morehead City, NC 28557; approx. 36,000.
Ball Players of America, Assn. of Prof. (1924), 12062 Valley View St., Ste. 211, Garden Grove, CA 92845; 10,000.
Bankers Assn., American (1875), 1120 Connecticut Ave. NW, Wash., DC 20036; http://www.aba.com
Bankers Assn. of America, Independent (1930), One Thomas Circle NW, Ste. 950, Wash., DC 20005; 5,800 banks; http://www.ibaa.org
Bar Assn., Federal (1920), 1815 H St. NW, Ste. 408, Wash., DC 20006; 15,000; http://www.access.digex.net/~fedbar
Barber Shop Quartet Singing in America, Inc., Soc. for the Preservation & Encouragement of (1938), 6315 Third Ave., Kenosha, WI 53141; 33,000; http://www.spebsqsa.org
Baseball Congress, American Amateur (1935), 118 Redfield Plaza, Marshall, MI 49068; 14,500 teams; http://www.voyager.net/aabc
Baseball Congress, Natl. (1931), 300 S. Sycamore, Wichita, KS 67213; 7,500; http://www.wichitawranglers.com
Baseball Players of America, Assn. of Prof. (1924), 12062 Valley View St., Ste. 211, Garden Grove, CA 92845; 16,000+.
Baseball Research, Inc., Society for American (1970), P.O. Box 93183, Cleveland, OH 44101; 7,000; http://www.sabr.org
Battleship Assn., American (1964), P.O. Box 711247, San Diego, CA 92171; 2,210.
Beer Can Collectors of America (1970), 747 Merus Ct., Fenton, MO 63026; 4,000; http://www.bcca.com/index.html
Beta Gamma Sigma, Inc. (1913), 11701 Borman Dr., Ste. 320, St. Louis, MO 63146; 400,000; http://www.betagammasigma.org
Beta Sigma Phi (1931), 1800 W. 91st Pl., Kansas City, MO 64114; 200,000; http://www.dmr1.com/bsp
Better Business Bureaus, Council of (1970), 4200 Wilson Blvd., Ste. 800, Arlington, VA 22203; 138 bureaus; http://www.council.bbb.org
Bible Society, American (1816), 1865 Broadway, New York, NY 10023; 280,000; http://www.americanbible.org
Biblical Literature, Society of (1880), 1201 Clairmont Ave., Ste. 300, Decatur, GA 30033; 6,000+.
Bibliographical Society of America (1904), P.O. Box 1537, Lenox Hill Station, New York, NY 10021; 1,500; http://www.cla.sc.edu/Engl/BSA
Big Brothers/Big Sisters of America (1902), 230 N. 13th St., Philadelphia, PA 19107; 494 agencies; http://bbbsa.org
Biochemistry and Molecular Biology, American Society for (1906), 9650 Rockville Pike, Bethesda, MD 20814; 10,000; http://www.faseb.org/asbmb
Biological Sciences, American Institute of (1947), 730 11th St. NW, Wash., DC 20001; 5,000; http://www.aibs.org/core/index.html
Biology, Society for Integrative and Comparative (1890), 401 N. Michigan Ave. Chicago, IL 60611; 2,200.
Black History Honors & Awards, Contemporary & (1990), 6514 Georgia Rd., Birmingham, AL 35212; 152.
Blind, American Council of the (1961), 1155 15th St. NW, Ste. 720, Wash., DC 20005; 45,000; http://www.acb.org
Blind, Natl. Federation of the (1940), 1800 Johnson St., Baltimore, MD 21230; 60,000; http://www.nfb.org
Blinded Veterans Assn. (1945), 477 H St. NW, Wash., DC 20001; 7,900.
Blindness America, Prevent (1908), 500 E. Remington Rd., Schaumburg, IL 60173; http://www.preventblindness.org
Blueberry Council, North American (1965), 4995 Golden Foothill Pkwy., Ste. 2, El Dorado Hills, CA 95762; http://www.webcom.com/bberry
B'nai B'rith Intl. (1853), 1640 Rhode Island Ave. NW, Wash., DC 20036; 150,000; http://www.bnaibrith.org
Boat Owners Assn. of the U.S. (1966), 880 S. Pickett St., Alexandria, VA 22304; 500,000.
Bookplate Collectors and Designers, American Soc. of (1922), 605 N. Stoneman Ave., #F, Alhambra, CA 91801; 200.
Booksellers Assn., American (1900), 828 S. Broadway, Tarrytown, NY 10591; 8,000; http://www.bookweb.org/aba
Boy Scouts of America (1910), 1325 Walnut Hill Lane, Irving, TX 75015; 5.6 mil; http://www.bsa.scouting.org
Boys & Girls Clubs of America (1906), 1230 W. Peachtree St. NW, Atlanta, GA 30309; 2.85 mil; http://www.bgca.org
Bread for the World, Inc. (1974), 1100 Wayne Ave., Ste. 1000, Silver Spring, MD 20910; 44,000; http://www.bread.org
Bridge League, American Contract (1937), 2990 Airways Blvd., Memphis, TN 38116; 170,000; http://www.acbl.org
Brith Sholom (1905), 3939 Conshohocken Ave., Philadelphia, PA 19131; 6,000.
Broadcasters, Natl. Assn. of (1922-23), 1771 N St. NW, Wash., DC 20036; http://www.nab.org
Burroughs Bibliophiles, The (1960), 454 Elaine Dr., Pittsburgh, PA 15236; 812.
Business Clubs, Inc., Natl. American (AMBUCS) (1922), 3315 N. Main St., High Point, NC 27265; 5,574; http://www.ambucs.com
Business Communicators, Intl. Assn. of (1970), One Hallidie Plaza, Ste. 600, San Francisco, CA 94102; 12,500; http://www.iabc.com/homepage.htm
Business Education Assn., Natl. (1946), 1914 Association Dr., Reston, VA 20191; 12,000; http://www.nbea.org/nbea.html
Business Women's Assn., American (1949), 9100 Ward Pkwy., P.O. Box 8728, Kansas City, MO 64114; 80,000; http://www.abwahq.org
Button Society, Natl. (1938), 2733 Juno Pl., Akron, OH 44333; 4,600+.
Byron Society of America, The (1971), c/o Prof. Charles E. Robinson, Dept. of English, Univ. of Delaware, Newark, DE 19716; 400.

Camp Fire Boys & Girls (1910), 4601 Madison, Kansas City, MO 64112; 700,000; http://www.campfire.org
Camping Assn., American (1910), 5000 State Rd. 67 N., Martinsville, IN 46131; 5,400; http://www.aca-camps.org
Cancer Society, American (1913), 1599 Clifton Rd. NE, Atlanta, GA 30329; http://www.cancer.org/frames.html
Cartoonists Society, Natl. (1946), Columbus Circle Station, P.O. Box 20267, New York, NY 10023; 500+; http:www.unitedmedia.com/ncs/ncs.html
Cat Fanciers' Assn. (1906), 1805 Atlantic Ave., Manasquan, NJ 08736; 650 clubs; http://www.cfainc.org
Catholic Bishops, U.S. Natl. Conference of (1917), 3211 4th St. NE, Wash., DC 20017; 402 members, 350 staff.
Catholic Church Extension Society (1905), 35 E. Wacker Dr., #400, Chicago, IL 60601; 90,000.
Catholic Daughters of the Americas (1903), 10 W. 71st St., New York, NY 10023; 117,815.
Catholic Educational Assn., Natl. (1904), 1077 30th St. NW, Ste. 100, Wash., DC 20007; 26,000; http://www.ncea.org
Catholic Historical Soc., American (1884), 263 S. Fourth St., P.O. Box 84, Philadelphia, PA 19105; 750.
Catholic Library Association (1921), 100 North St., Ste. 224, Pittsfield, MA 01201; 1,000; http://www.cathla.org
Catholic Rural Life Conference, Natl. (1923), 4625 Beaver Ave., Des Moines, IA 50310; 4,000+.
Catholic War Veterans, USA, Inc. (1935), 441 N. Lee St., Alexandria, VA 22314; 25,000.
Cemetery Assn., American (1887), 1895 Preston White Dr., #220, Reston, VA 22091; 2,200.

Ceramic Society, American (1898), 735 Ceramic Place, Westerville, OH 43081; 10,000; http://www.acers.org
Cereal Chemists, American Assn. of (1915), 3340 Pilot Knob Rd., St. Paul, MN 55121; 4,000; http://www.scisoc.org/aacc
Cerebral Palsy Assns., Inc., United (1949), 1660 L St. NW, Ste. 700, Wash., DC 20036; 150; http://www.ucpa.org
Chamber of Commerce of the U.S.A. (1912), 1615 H St. NW, Wash., DC 20062; 215,000.
Chamber Music Players, Inc., Amateur (1947), 1123 Broadway, New York, NY 10010; 4,300.
Chartered Life Underwriters, American Soc. of (1927), 270 Bryn Mawr Ave., Bryn Mawr, PA 19010; 30,000.
Checker Federation, American (1948), P.O. Drawer 365, Petal, MS 39465; 1,000.
Chemical Engineers, American Inst. of (1908), 345 E. 47th St., New York, NY 10017; 60,000; http://www.che.ufl.edu.aiche
Chemical Manufacturers Assn. (1872), 1300 Wilson Blvd., Arlington, VA 22209; 191 cos.; http://www.cmahq.com
Chemical Society, American (1876), 1155 16th St. NW, Wash., DC 20036; 151,000; http://www.acs.org
Chess Federation, U.S. (1949), 186 Rt. 9W, New Windsor, NY 12553; 84,327; http://www.uschess.org/uscf
Chess League of America, Correspondence (1897), P.O. Box 59625, Schaumburg, IL 60159; 1,000.
Chiefs of Police, Intl. Assn. of (1893), 515 N. Washington St., Alexandria, VA 22314; 16,000+; http://www.theiacp.org
Childhood Education Intl., Assn. for (1892), 17904 Georgia Avenue, Suite 215, Olney, MD 20832; 10,000; http://www.udel.edu/bateman/acei
Children's Aid Society (1853), 105 E. 22d St., New York, NY 10010; 1,207.
Children's Book Council (1945), 568 Broadway, Ste. 404, New York, NY 10012; 80 publishing houses; http://www.cbcbooks.org.
Child Welfare League of America (1920), 440 First St. NW, Ste. 310, Wash., DC 20001; 900+ agencies; http://www.cwla.org
Chiropractic Assn., American (1963), 1701 Clarendon Blvd., Arlington, VA 22209; 19,000; http://www.amerchiro.org/aca
Chris-Craft Antique Boat Club, Inc. (1973), 217 S. Adams St., Tallahassee, FL 32301; 2,700; http://www.chris-craft.org
Christian Endeavor Union, World's (1895), 1221 E. Broad St., Columbus, OH 43205; 3 mil.
Christian Laity Counseling Board, Inc. (1970), 5901 Plainfield Dr., Charlotte, NC 28215; 52.5 mil.
Christians and Jews, Natl. Conference of (1927), 71 Fifth Ave., Ste. 1100, New York, NY 10003.
Church Women United (1941), 475 Riverside Dr., Ste. 500, New York, NY 10115; http://www.churchwomen.org
Cincinnati, Society of the (1783), 2118 Massachusetts Ave. NW, Wash., DC 20008; 3,300.
Cities, Natl. League of (1924), 1301 Pennsylvania Ave. NW, Wash., DC 20004; 1,450 cities; http://www.cais.com/nlc
Civic League, Natl. (1894), 1445 Market St., Ste. 300, Denver, CO 80202; 921; http://www.ncl.org/ncl
Civil Air Patrol (1941), HQ CAP-USAF, Maxwell AFB, AL 36112; 63,000; http://www.cap.af.mil
Civil Engineers, American Society of (1852), 345 E. 47th St., New York, NY 10017; 104,000; http://www.asce.org
Civil Liberties Union, American (ACLU) (1920), 132 W. 43d St., New York, NY 10036; 250,000; http://www.aclu.org
Civitan International, Inc. (1917), One Civitan Pl., Birmingham, AL 35213; 60,000; http://www.civitan.org
Clean Energy Research Institute (1974), Univ. of Miami, Coral Gables, FL, 33124; 500.
CLU & ChFC, American Soc. of (1928), 270 S. Bryn Mawr Ave., Bryn Mawr, PA 19010; 33,000; http://www.asclu.org
Coal Assn., Natl. (1917), 1130 17th St. NW, Wash., DC 20036; 150 corporate members.
Coaster Enthusiasts, American (1978), P.O. Box 8226, Chicago, IL 60680; 4,700+.
Coast Guard Combat Veterans Assn. (1985), 17728 Striley Dr., Ashton, MD 20861; 1,800.
Codependents Anonymous (1986), 5150 N. 16th St., Phoenix, AZ 85016; http://www.ourcoda.org
Collectors Association Inc., American (1939), P.O. Box 39106, Minneapolis, MN 55439; 3,586; http://www.collector.com
College Admission Counseling, Natl. Assn. for (1937), 1631 Prince St., Alexandria, VA 22314; 6,300; http://www.nacac.com
College Board, The (1900), 45 Columbus Ave., New York, NY 10023; 2,900 institutions; http://www.collegeboard.org
College English Assn. (1934), English Dept., Winthrop Univ., Rock Hill, SC 29733; 1,200.
College Music Society (1958), 202 W. Spruce St., Missoula, MT 59802; 6,300; http://www.music.org
Colleges and Employers, Natl. Assn. of (1956), 62 Highland Ave., Bethlehem, PA 18017; 3,375; http://www.jobweb.org
Colleges and Universities, Assn. of American (1915), 1818 R St. NW, Wash., DC 20009; 680 institutions; http://www.aacu-edu.org
Collegiate Schools of Business, American Assembly of (1916), 600 Emerson Rd. Ste. 300, St. Louis, MO 63141; 850 inst.
Colonial Dames XVII Century, Natl. Society of (1915), 1300 New Hampshire Ave. NW, Wash., DC 20036; 14,000.
Commerce, U.S. Junior Chamber of (1915), 4 W. 21st St., Tulsa, OK 74114; 200,000.
Commercial Collectors Assn., Int'l. (1971), 4040 W. 70th St., Minneapolis, MN 55435; 360.
Commercial Law League of America (1895), 150 N. Michigan Ave., Ste. 600, Chicago, IL 60601; 4,600; http://www.clla.org
Commercial Travelers of America, The Order of United (1888), 632 N. Park St., Columbus, OH 43215; 170,000.
Common Cause (1970), 1250 Connecticut Ave., NW, Wash., DC 20036; http://www.commoncause.org
Communication Assn., National (1914), 5105 Backlick Rd., Bldg. E, Annandale, VA 22003; 7,000; http://www.natcom.org
Community Cultural Center Assn., American (1980), 149 Cannongate III, Nashua, NH 03063; http://pw1.netcom.com/~mjanz/index.html
Community Colleges, American Assn. of (1920), One Dupont Circle NW, Ste. 410, Wash., DC 20036; 1,113 inst; http://www.aacc.nche.edu
Composers, Authors & Publishers, American Soc. of (ASCAP) (1914), One Lincoln Plaza, New York, NY 10023; 24,000; http://www.ascap.com
Composers/USA, Natl. Assn. of (1932), Box 49256, Barrington Station, Los Angeles, CA 90049; 700; http://user1thebook.cpm/nacusa
Computing Machinery, Assn. for (1947), 1515 Broadway, 17th Fl., New York, NY 10036; 85,000.
Computing Professionals, Inst. for Certification of (1973), 2200 E. Devon Ave., Ste. 247, Des Plaines, IL 60018; 50,000+.
Concerned Women for America (1979), 370 L'Enfant Promenade SW, Ste. 800, Wash., DC 20024; 500,000; http://www.cwfa.org
Concrete Institute, American (1904), 22400 W. Seven Mile Rd., Detroit, MI 48219; 20,000; http://www.aci-int.org
Congress of Racial Equality (CORE) (1942), 30 Cooper Square, 9th Fl., New York, NY 10003; http://www.core-online.org
Conscientious Objectors, Central Committee for (1948), 1515 Cherry St., Philadelphia, PA 19102; http://www.libertynet.org/ccco
Constantian Society, The (1970), 840 Old Washington Rd., McMurray, PA 15317; 595.
Construction Industry Manufacturers Assn. (1911), 111 E. Wisconsin Ave., Ste. 1000, Milwaukee, WI 53202; 410 cos.; http://www.cimanet.com
Construction Specifications Institute (1948), 601 Madison St., Alexandria, VA 22314; 17,000; http://www.csinet.org
Consumer Credit Assn., Intl. (1912), 243 N. Lindbergh Blvd., St. Louis, MO 63141; 20,000.
Consumer Federation of America (1968), 1424 16th St. NW, Ste. 604, Wash., DC 20036; 250 organizations; http://www.stateandlocal.org
Consumer Interests, American Council on (ACCI) (1953), 240 Stanley Hall, Univ. of Missouri, Columbia, MO 65211; 1,200; http://riker.ps.missouri.edu/DH/ACCI/
Consumer Protection Institute (1970), 5901 Plainfield Dr., Charlotte, NC 28215.
Consumers Union of the U.S. (1936), 101 Truman Ave., Yonkers, NY 10703; 405,990; http://www.consumersunion.org
Contractors of America, General (1919), 1957 E St. NW, Wash., DC 20006; 32,000.
Co-op America (1982), 1612 K St. NW, Ste. 600, Wash., DC 20006; 48,000 individuals, 2,000 businesses; http://www.coopamerica.org
Cooperative Business Assn., Natl. (1916), 1401 New York Ave. NW, Ste. 1100, Wash., DC 20005; 540; http://www.cooperative.org
Cooperative League of the U.S.A. (1916), 1401 New York Ave. NW, Ste. 1100, Wash., DC 20005; 285 co-ops.
Correctional Assn., American (1870), 4380 Forbes Blvd., Lanham, MD 20706; 20,000+.
Correctional Officers, Intl. Assn. of (1977), 8600 Glenarden Pkwy., Glenarden, MD 20706.
Cosmetology Assn., Natl. (1921), 3510 Olive St., St. Louis, MO 63103; 32,000; http://www.nca-now.com
Cotton Council of America, Natl. (1938), 1918 N. Pkwy., Memphis, TN 38112; http://www.cotton.org
Counseling Assn., American (1952), 5999 Stevenson Ave., Alexandria, VA 22304; 55,000; http://www.counseling.org

Count Dracula Society (1962), 334 W. 54th St., Los Angeles, CA 90037; 500.
Country Music Assn. (1958), One Music Circle S, Nashville, TN 37203; 6,588; http://www.countrymusic.org
Crafts & Creative Industries, Assn. of (ACCI) (1976), 1100-H Brandywine Blvd., P.O. Box 2188, Zanesville, OH 43702; 6,000.
Creative Children and Adults, Natl. Assn. for (1974), 8080 Springvalley Dr., Cincinnati, OH 45236; 6,000.
Credit Assn., Intl. (1912), 243 N. Lindbergh Blvd., St. Louis, MO 63141; 4,950; http://www.ica-credit.org
Credit Union Natl. Assn. & Affiliates (1934), 5710 Mineral Point Rd., Madison, WI 53705; 51 credit union leagues.
Cribbage Congress, American (1979), P.O. Box 10486, Napa, CA 94581; 6,800; http://www.cribbage.org
Crime and Delinquency, Natl. Council on (1907), 685 Market St., Ste. 620, San Francisco, CA 94105; 500 members; http://www.nccd.com
Criminology, American Society of (1941), 1314 Kinnear Rd., Ste. 212, Columbus, OH 43212; 2,600; http://www.asc41.com
Crop Protection Assn., American (1933), 1156 15th St. NW, Ste. 900, Wash., DC 20005; 80 cos.; http://www.acpa.org
Crop Science Society of America (1955), 677 S. Segoe Rd., Madison, WI 53711; 4,450; http://www.crops.org
Cryogenic Soc. of America, Inc. (1964), 1033 South Blvd., Ste. 13, Oak Park, IL 60302; 550; http://www.csa.fnal.gov
Customs Brokers and Forwarders Assn. of America, Natl. (1897), 1200 18th St. NW, #901, Wash., DC 20036; 700 cos.; http://ncbfaa.org
Cystic Fibrosis Foundation (1955), 6931 Arlington Rd., Bethesda, MD 20814; http://www.cff.org
Dairy Council, Natl. (1915), 6300 N. River Rd., Rosemont, IL 60018.
Dairy and Food Industries Supply Assn. (1917), 6245 Executive Blvd., Rockville, MD 20852; 800 cos.
Dairy Goat Assn., American (1904), 209 W. Main St., Spindale, NC 28160; 13,000.
Dark-Sky Association, Intl. (1987), 3225 N. First Ave., Tucson, AZ 85719; 2,300; http://www.darksky.org
Daughters of the American Revolution, Natl. Society (1890), 1776 D St. NW, Wash., DC 20006; 178,000; http://www.dar.org
Daughters of the British Empire, Natl. Society (1909), 800 Carrington Dr., Raleigh, NC 27615; 5,000; http://www.mindspring.com/~dbesociety
Daughters of the Confederacy, United (1894), 328 North Blvd., Richmond, VA 23220; 24,000.
Deaf, Natl. Assn. of the (1880), 814 Thayer Ave., Silver Spring, MD 20910; 5,500; http://www.nad.org
Defense Preparedness Assn., American (1919), 2101 Wilson Blvd., Ste. 400, Arlington, VA 22201; 28,000.
Delta Kappa Gamma Society Intl. (1929), 416 W. 12th St., Austin, TX 78701; 165,000.
Delta Mu Delta (1913), P.O. Box 46935, St. Louis, MO 63146; 90,000; http://home.earthlink.net/~deltamudelta
Democratic Natl. Committee (1848), 430 S. Capitol St. SE, Wash., DC 20003; 432 elected members; http://www.democrats.org/index.html
DeMolay International (1919), 10200 N. Executive Hills Blvd., Kansas City, MO 64153; 30,000; http://www.demolay.org
Dental Assn., American (1859), 211 E. Chicago Ave., Chicago, IL 60611; 140,000; http://www.ada.org
Descendants of Washington's Army at Valley Forge, Society of (1976), P.O. Box 915, Valley Forge, PA 19482; 982.
Desert Protective Council (1954), P.O. Box 2312, Valley Center, CA 92082; 400+.
Destroyer Escort Sailors Assn., Inc. (1975), P.O. Box 805, Vienna, VA 22183; 11,000.
Diabetes Assn., American (1940), 1660 Duke St., Alexandria, VA 22314; 300,000; http://www.diabetes.org/custom.asp
Diabetes Institute, American (1970), 5901 Plainfield Dr., Charlotte, NC 28215.
Dialect Society, American (1889), c/o Allan Metcalf, English Dept., MacMurray College, Jacksonville, IL 62650; 550; http://www.dfjp.com/ads/
Digital Printing & Imaging Assn. (1992), 10015 Main St., Fairfax, VA 22031; 800 firms; http://www.dpia.org
Directors Guild of America (1936), 7920 Sunset Blvd., Los Angeles, CA 90046; 9,700; http://dga.org/dga/index.html
Disabled American Veterans (1920), 3725 Alexandria Pike, Cold Spring, KY 41076; 1,077,276; http://www.dav.org
Disabled Sports USA (1967), 451 Hungerford Dr., Ste. 100, Rockville, MD 20850; 60,000+; http://www.dsusa.org/~dsusa/dsusa.html
Dogs on Stamps Study Unit (1979), 202A Newport Rd., Cranbury, NJ 08512; 400.
Dozenal Society of America (1944), Math Dept., Nassau Community College, Garden City, NY 11530; 144.
Ducks Unlimited (1937), One Waterfowl Way, Memphis, TN 38120; 620,000; http://www.ducks.org
Eaglehunters Intl. (1994), P.O. Box 1539, Hernando, FL 34442; 800.
Eagles, Fraternal Order of (1898), 12660 W. Capitol Dr., Brookfield, WI 53055; 1.1 mil.
Easter Seals (1919), 230 W. Monroe, Ste. 1800, Chicago, IL 60606; 105 affiliates; http://www.easter-seals.org
Eastern Star, General Grand Chapter, Order of the (1876), 1618 New Hampshire Ave. NW, Wash., DC 20009; 1.5 mil.
Economic Assn., American (1885), 2014 Broadway, Ste. 305, Nashville, TN 37203; 20,000.
Edsel Club, Intl. (1969), 3240 Sitter Ley Road NW, Canal Winchester, OH 43110; 1,052.
Education, American Council on (1918), One Dupont Circle NW, #800, Wash., DC 20036; 1,800; http://www.acenet.edu
Education, Council for Advancement & Support of (1974), 11 Dupont Circle NW, Wash., DC 20036; 2,950 schools.
Education, Natl. Assn. for Family and Community (1936), 5963 Jefferson St., Bington, KY 41005; 45,000.
Educational Research Assn., American (1916), 1230 17th St. NW, Wash., DC 20036; 23,000; http://www.aera.net
Education of Young Children, Natl. Assn. for the (1926), 1509 16th St. NW, Wash., DC 20036; 95,000.
Educators for World Peace, Intl. Assn. of (1969), P.O. Box 3282, Mastin Lake Station, Huntsville, AL 35810; 25,500.
Egalitarian Communities, Federation of (1976), HC-3, Box 3370-WABF, Tecumseh, MO 65760; 200; http://www.crl.com/~eastwind/fec.html
8th Air Force Historical Society (1975), P.O. Box 7215, St. Paul, MN 55107; 18,000.
88th Infantry Division Assn., Inc. (1948), P.O. Box 925, Havertown, PA 19083; 5,477.
84th Infantry Div. Railsplitters Society, Inc. (1945), P.O. Box 827, Sioux Falls, SD 57101; 2,900.
82d Airborne Division Assn., Inc. (1946), NFCS, P.O. Box 9308, Fayetteville, NC 28311; 23,000+.
Electrical and Electronics Engineers, Institute of (1884), 345 E. 47th St., New York, NY 10017; 320,000; http://www.ieee.org
Electrical Manufacturers Assn., Natl. (1926), 2101 L St. NW, Wash., DC 20037; 560 cos.; http://www.nema.org
Electrochemical Society, Inc. (1902), 10 S. Main St., Pennington, NJ 08534; 7,000; http://www.electrochem.org
Electronic Industries Assn. (1924), 2001 Pennsylvania Ave., Wash., DC 20006; 1,058 cos.
Electronics Technicians, Intl. Society of Certified (1970), 2708 W. Berry, Ft. Worth, TX 76109; 2,000.
Electroplaters and Surface Finishers Society, American (1908), 12644 Research Pkwy., Orlando, FL 32826; 7,200; http://www.aesf.org
Elks, U.S.A., Benevolent and Protective Order of (1868), 2750 N. Lakeview Ave., Chicago, IL 60614; 1.2 mil.; http://www.elks.org/elksmag
Energy Engineers, Assn. of (1977), 4025 Pleasantdale Rd., Ste. 420, Atlanta, GA 30340; 8,000; http://www.aeecenter.org
Engineering, Natl. Academy of (1964), 2101 Constitution Ave. NW, Wash., DC 20418; 1,893.
Engineering in Agricultural, Food, and Biological Systems, Society for (1907), 2950 Niles Rd., St. Joseph, MI 49085; 8,000.
Engineers, Natl. Society of Professional (1934), 1420 King St., Alexandria, VA 22314; 54,000; http://www.nspe.org
English, U.S. (1983), 1747 Pennsylvania Ave. NW, Ste. 1100, Wash., DC 20006; approx. 1 mil.
English-Speaking Union of the U.S. (1920), 16 E. 69th St., New York, NY 10021; 18,000.
Entomological Society of America (1889), 9301 Annapolis Rd., Lanham, MD 20706; 6,500; http://www.entsoc.org
Environmental Health Assn., Natl. (1937), 720 S. Colorado Blvd., Ste. 970 South, Denver, CO 80222; 5,100; http://www.neha.org
Environmental Medicine, American Academy of (1965), P.O. Box CN 1001-8001, New Hope, PA 18938; 550; http://www.aaem.com
Esperanto League for North America Inc. (1954), P.O. Box 1129, El Cerrito, CA 94530; 900+; http://www.esperanto-usa.org
Evangelism Crusades Inc., Intl. (1959), 14617 Victory Blvd., Van Nuys, CA 91411; 125.
Exchange Club, Natl. (1911), 3050 Central Ave., Toledo, OH 43606; 33,000; http://www.nationalexchangeclub.com
Experimental Aircraft Assn. (1953), P.O. Box 3086, Oshkosh, WI 54903; 170,000; http://www.eaa.org
Exploration Geophysicists, Society of (1930), P.O. Box 702740, Tulsa, OK 74170; 14,500.

Fairs & Expositions, Intl. Assn. of (1919), P.O. Box 985, Springfield, MO 65809; 2,500.
Family Campers and RVers (1949), 4804 Transit Rd., Bldg. 2, Depew, NY 14043; 56,000 families.
Family Physicians, American Academy of (1947), 8880 Ward Pkwy., Kansas City, MO 64114; 85,000; http://www.aafp.org
Family Relations, Natl. Council on (1938), 3989 Central Ave. NE, Ste. 550, Minneapolis, MN 55421; 4,000; http://www.ncfr.com
Family Service America (1911), 11700 W. Lake Park Dr., Milwaukee, WI 53224; 250 agencies.
Farm Bureau Federation, American (1919), 225 Touhy Ave., Park Ridge, IL 60068; 4 mil; http://www.fb.com
Farmers of America Org., Natl. Future (1928), 5632 Mt. Vernon Memorial Hwy., Alexandria, VA 22309; 294,000 families; http://www.ffa.org
Farmers Union, Natl. (1902), 11900 E. Cornell Ave., Aurora, CO 80014; 300,000; http://www.nfu.org
Fat Acceptance, Inc., Natl. Assn. to Advance (NAAFA) (1969), P.O. Box 188620, Sacramento, CA 95818; 5,000; http://www.naafa.org
Fellowship of Reconciliation (1914), 521 N. Broadway, Nyack, NY 10960; 35,000; http://www.nonviolence.org/~nvweb/for
Feminists for Life of America (1972), 733 15th St. NW, Ste. 1100, Wash., DC 20005; 5,000; http://www.serve.com/fem4life
Financial Analysts Federation (1945), 5 Boar's Head Lane, Charlottesville, VA 22903; 22,700.
Financial Executives Institute (1938), 10 Madison Ave., P.O. Box 1938, Morristown, NJ 07962; 14,000; http://www.fei.org
Financial Women Intl. (1976), 200 North Glebe Rd., Ste. 820, Arlington, VA 22203; 6,500; http://www.fwi.org
Financiers, Inc., Intl. Society of (1979), P.O. Box 18508, Asheville, NC 28814; 350; http://www.insofin.com
Fire Chiefs, Intl. Assn. of (1873), 4025 Fair Ridge Dr., Fairfax, VA 22033; 12,000; http://www.iafc.org
Fire Protection Assn., Natl. (1896), One Batterymarch Park, Quincy, MA 02269; 68,000; http://www.nfpa.org
Fire Protection Engineers, Soc. of (1950), 7315 Wisconsin Ave., Ste. 1225W, Bethesda, MD 20814; 4,600; http://www.sfpe.org
First Amendment Studies, Inc., Institute for (1984), P.O. Box 589, Great Barrington, MA 01230; 10,000; http://www.ifas.org
Fisheries Soc., American (1870), 5410 Grosvenor Lane, Ste. 110, Bethesda, MD 20814; 8,500; http://www.fisheries.org
Fleet Reserve Assn. (1924), 125 N. West St., Alexandria, VA 22314; 158,000.
Fly Fishers, Fed. of (1965), 502 S. 19th, Ste. 1, Bozeman, MT 59715; 11,000.
Flying Disc Federation, World (1985), Gnejsvägen 24, 85357, Sundsvall, Sweden; 15,000.
Food Technologists, Institute of (1939), 221 N. LaSalle, Ste. 300, Chicago, IL 60601; 28,000; http://www.ift.org
Footwear Industries of America (1869), 1420 K St. NW, Ste. 600, Wash., DC 20005; 200; http://www.fia.org
Foreign Student Affairs, Natl. Assn. for (1948), 1875 Connecticut Ave., Ste. 1000, Wash., DC 20009; 6,800.
Foreign Study, American Institute for (1964), 102 Greenwich Ave., Greenwich, CT 06830; 300,000; http://www.aifs.com
Foreign Trade Council, Inc., Natl. (1914), 1625 K St. NW, Wash., DC 20006; 580 cos.; http://www.usaengage.org
Forensic Sciences, American Academy of (1948), P.O. Box 669, Colorado Springs, CO 80901; 5,000; http://www.aafs.org
Foresters, Society of American (1900), 5400 Grosvenor La., Bethesda, MD 20814; 18,800; http://www.safnet.org
Forest History Society (1946), 701 Wm. Vickers Ave., Durham, NC 27701; 1,500; http://www.lib.duke.edu/forest
Forest & Paper Assn., American (1993), 1111 19th St. NW, Wash., DC 20036; 400 cos.; http://www.afandpa.org
Forest Products Society (1947), 2801 Marshall Ct., Madison, WI 53705; 2,500.
Forestry Assn., American (1875), 1516 P St. NW, Wash., DC 20005; 150,000.
Forests, American (1875), 910 17th St. NW, Ste. 600, Wash., DC 20006; 25,000; http://www.amfor.org
Fortean Organization, Intl. (1965), P.O. Box N, College Park, MD 20740; 800-1,000.
Foundrymen's Society, American (1896), 505 State St., Des Plaines, IL 60016; 13,000; http://www.afsinc.org
4-H Clubs (1914), 1400 Independence Ave., U.S. Dept of Agriculture, Wash., DC 20250; 5.5 mil.
458th Service Squadron Assn. (1991), 2114 W 29th St., Erie, PA 16508; 135.
Frederick A. Cook Society, (1940), P.O. Box 11421, Pittsburgh, PA 15238; 178.
Freedom From Religion Foundation (1978), P.O. Box 750, Madison, WI 53701; 3,500.
Freedom of Information Center (1958), 127 Neff Annex, Univ. of Missouri, Columbia, MO 65211; http://www.missouri.edu/foiwww
Freedoms Foundation at Valley Forge (1949), 1601 Valley Forge Rd., Valley Forge, PA 19482.
Freemansonry, Supreme Council Ancient and Accepted Scottish Rite of, Northern Masonic Jurisdiction (1813), PO Box 519, 33 Marrett Rd., Lexington, MA 02173; 322,995; **Southern Jurisdiction** (1801), P.O. Box 3467, 1733 16th St. NW, Wash., DC 20009; 478,747; http://www.freemasonry.org
Free Men, Natl. Coalition of (1977), P.O. Box 129, Manhasset, NY 11030; http://www.ncfm.org
French Institute/Alliance Française (1898), 22 E. 60th St., New York, NY 10022; 7,500; http://www.fiaf.org
Friendship and Good Will, Intl. Soc. of (1978), 412 Cherry Hills Dr., Bakersfield, CA 93309; 4,168.
Frozen Food Institute, American (1942), 2000 Corporate Ridge, Ste. 1000, McLean, VA 22102; 575; http://www.affi.com
Funeral & Memorial Societies of America (1963), P.O. Box 10, Hinesburg, VT 05461; 500,000; http://www.funerals.org/famsa

Galactic Society Intl. (1986), Box 326, Rock Hill, SC 29731; 300.
Gamblers Anonymous (1957), P.O. Box 17173, Los Angeles, CA 90017; http://www.gamblersanonymous.org
Garden Club of America (1913), 598 Madison Ave., New York, NY 10022; 15,000; http://www.gcamerica.org
Garden Clubs, Natl. Council of State (1929), 4401 Magnolia Ave., St. Louis, MO 63110; 308,623.
Gardeners of America Inc., The (1932), 5560 Merle Hay Rd., Johnston, IA 50131; 7,400.
Gas Appliance Manufacturers Assn. (1935), 1901 N. Moore St., Ste. 1100, Arlington, VA 22209; 260 cos.; http://www.gamanet.org
Gas Assn., American (1918), 1515 Wilson Blvd., Arlington, VA 22209; 229 cos.; 3,000; http://www.aga.com
Gay and Lesbian Task Force, Natl. (1973), 2320 17th St. NW, Wash., DC 20009; 35,000.
Genealogical Society, Natl. (1903), 4527 17th St. NW, Arlington, VA 22207; 15,000.
Genetic Association, American (1905), P.O. Box 257, Buckeystown, MD 21717.
Geographers, Assn. of American (1904), 1710 16th St. NW, Wash., DC 20009; 7,100; http://www.aag.org
Geographic Education, Natl. Council for (1915), 16A Leonard Hall, IUP, Indiana, PA 15705; 2,500; http://www.ncge.org
Geographic Society, Natl. (1888), 1145 17th St. NW, Wash., DC 20036; 9.7 mil; http://www.nationalgeographic.com
Geographical Society, The American (1851), 120 Wall St., Ste. 100, New York, NY 10005; 1,500.
Geological Society of America (1888), 3300 Penrose Pl., P.O. Box 9140, Boulder, CO 80301; 15,358; http://www.geosociety.org
Geriatrics Society, American (1942), 770 Lexington Ave., Ste. 300, New York, NY 10021; 6,500.
Gideons Intl. (1899), 2900 Lebanon Rd., Nashville, TN 37214; 131,000; http://www.gideons.org
Gifted Children, Natl. Assn. for (1954), 1707 L St. NW, Ste. 550, Wash., DC 20036; 8,000; http://www.nagc.org
Girl Scouts of the U.S.A. (1912), 420 5th Ave., New York, NY 10018; 3.5 mil; http://www.gsusa.org
Girls Incorporated (1945), 30 E. 33d St., New York, NY 10016; http://www.girlsinc.org
Glenn Miller Birthplace Society (1976), 107 East Main St., P.O. Box 61, Clarinda, IA 51632; 1,500.
Gold Star Mothers, Inc., American (1928), 2128 Leroy Place NW, Wash., DC 20008; under 2,000.
Golf Assn., U.S. (1894), Golf House, P.O. Box 708, Far Hills, NJ 07931; 8,631 clubs.
Gospel Music Assn. (1964), 1205 Division St., Nashville, TN 37203; 5,500; http://www.gospelmusic.org
Government Finance Officers Assn. (1906), 180 N. Michigan Ave., Ste. 800, Chicago, IL 60601; 13,600; http://www.financenet.gov/gfoa.htm
Governors' Assn., Natl. (1908), Hall of the States, 444 N. Capitol #267, Wash., DC 20001; 55 govs.; http://www.nga.org
Graduate Schools, Council of (1960), One Dupont Circle NW, #430 Wash., DC 20036; 415 institutions; http://www.cgsnet.org
Grandmother Clubs of America, Inc., Natl. Federation of (1938), 27 E. Monroe St., Rm. 519, Chicago, IL 60603; 4,200.
Graphic Arts, American Institute of (1914), 164 5th Ave., New York, NY 10010; 9,000; http://www.aiga.org

Gray Panthers (1970), P.O. Box 21477, Wash., DC 20009; 50,000.
Great Council of the U.S., Improved Order of Red Men (1847), 4521 Speight Ave., Waco, TX 76711; 26,000; http://www.members.xoom.com/redmen
Green Mountain Club (1910), Rt. 100, RR1, Box 650, Waterbury Ctr., VT 05677; 7,500; http://www.greenmountainclub.org
Grocers Assn., Nat'l. (1982), 1825 Samuel Morse Dr., Reston, VA 22190; 2,500.
Grocery Manufacturers of America (1908), 1010 Wisconsin Ave., Ste. 800, Wash., DC 20007; 140 cos.; http://www.gmabrands.com
Ground Water Assn., Natl. (1948), 601 Dempsey Rd., Westerville, OH 43081; 17,000; http://www.ngwa.org
Group Against Smokers' Pollution, Inc. (GASP) (1971), P.O. Box 632, College Park, MD 20741; 10,000+.
Guide Dog Foundation for the Blind, Inc. (1946), 371 E. Jericho Tpk., Smithtown, NY 11787; 120,000; http://www.guidedog.org
Gyro Intl. (1912), 1096 Mentor Ave., Painesville, OH 44077; 4,600.

Hadassah, the Women's Zionist Organization of America (1912), 50 W. 58th St., New York, NY 10019; 385,000; http://www.hadassah.org
Hairdressers and Cosmetologists Assn., Natl. (1921), 3510 Olive St., St. Louis, MO 63103; 50,406.
Handball Assn., U.S. (1951), 2333 N. Tucson Blvd., Tucson, AZ 85716; 8,200; http://www.ushandball.org
Handicapped, Federation of the (1935), 211 W. 14th St., New York, NY 10011; 650.
Health Council, Natl. (1920), 1730 M St. NW, Ste. 500, Wash., DC 20036.
Health Info. Management Assn., American (1928), 919 N. Michigan Ave., Chicago, IL 60611; 38,000; http://www.ahima.org
Healthcare Strategy and Market Development of the American Hospital Assn., Soc. for (1996), One N. Franklin, Chicago, IL 60606; 5,000.
Hearing Society, Intl. (1951), 20361 Middlebelt Rd., Livonia, MI 48152; 3,000.
Hearing and Speech Action, Natl. Assn. for (1910), 10801 Rockville Pike, Rockville, MD 20852.
Heart Assn., American (1924), 7272 Greenville Ave., Dallas, TX 75231; http://www.americanheart.org
Heating, Refrigerating & Air-Conditioning Engineers, Inc., American Soc. of (1894), 1791 Tullie Cir. NE, Atlanta, GA 30329; 50,000; http://www.ashrae.org
Hebrew Immigrant Aid Society (HIAS) (1880), 333 7th Ave., New York, NY 10001.
Helicopter Assn. Intl. (1948), 1635 Prince St., Alexandria, VA 22314; 3,000.
Helicopter Society, American (1943), 217 N. Washington St., Alexandria, VA 22314; 6,140; http://www.vtol.org
Hemispheric Affairs, Council on (1975), 1444 I St., NW, Ste. 211, Wash., DC 20005; 1,900; http://www.coha.org
Hibernians in America, Ancient Order of (1836), 1301 S.W. 26th Ave., Ft. Lauderdale, FL 33312; 200,000; http://www.aoh.com
Highpointers Club (1987), P.O. Box 70, Arcadia, MO 63621; 1,425; http://www.cris.com/~Mfedor/statehps/statehipointer.shtml
High School Assns., Natl. Federation of State (1920), P.O. Box 20626, Kansas City, MO 64195; 51 state assns.
High School Band Directors Hall of Fame, Natl. (1985), 519 N. Halifax Ave., Daytona Beach, FL 32118; approx. 3,000; http://www.bocanet.com/band/default.htm
High Twelve International. (1921), 15456 Ivanhoe Dr., Visalia, CA 93292; 20,000.
Hiking Society, American (1976), P.O. Box 20160, Wash., DC 20041; 5,500; http://www.orca.org/ahs
Historians, Organization of American (1907), 112 N. Bryan St., Bloomington, IN 47408; 12,000; http://www.indiana.edu/~oah
Historic Preservation, Natl. Trust for (1949), 1785 Massachusetts Ave. NW, Wash., DC 20036; 250,000.
Historical Assn., American (1884), 400 A St. SE, Wash., DC 20003; 16,000; http://www.chnm.gmu.edu/aha
Historical Review, Institute for (1978), P.O. Box 2739, Newport Beach, CA 92659; http://www.ihr.org
Historical Society, United States (1971), 1st and Main Sts., Richmond, VA 23219; 250,000.
Hockey, U.S.A. (1936), 1775 Bob Johnson Dr., Colorado Springs, CO 80906; 540,000; http://usahockey.org.
Home Builders, Natl. Assn. of (1942), 1201 15th St. NW, Wash., DC 20005; 157,000; http://www.nahb.com
Home Economics Assn., American (1909), 1555 King St., Alexandria, VA 22314; 20,000.
Homeless, Natl. Coalition for the (1984), 1612 K St. NW, Wash., DC 20006; 1,388; http://neh.ari.net
Homemakers of America, Future (1945), 1910 Association Dr., Reston, VA 22091; 281,000+; http://www.fhahero.org
Honor Society, Natl. (1921), 1904 Association Dr., Reston, VA 22091; 21,000.
Horatio Alger Soc. (1965), P.O. Box 70361, Richmond, VA 23255; 235; http://www.ihot.com/~has
Horse Council, American (1969), 1700 K St. NW, #300, Wash., DC 20006; 2,000 members, 191 org.
Horse Protection Assn., American (1966), 1000 29th St. NW, Ste. T-100, Wash., DC 20007; 8,000.
Hospital Assn., American (1899), 1 N. Franklin, Chicago, IL 60606; 5,100 hospitals; http://www.aha.org
Hostelling Intl., American Youth Hostels (1934), 733 15th Street NW, Ste. 840, Wash., DC 20005; 118,000; http://www.hiayh.org
Hotel & Motel Assn., American (1910), 1201 New York Ave. NW, Wash., DC 20005; 10,000+; http://www.ahma.com
Hot Rod Assn., Natl. (1951), 2035 Financial Way, Glendora, CA 91741; 85,000; http://www.nhraonline.com
Huguenot Society, Natl. (1951), 3917 Heritage Hills Dr. #104, Bloomington, MN 55437; 5,000; http://huguenot.netnation.com.
Humane Society of the U.S. (1954), 2100 L St. NW, Wash., DC 20037; 650,000; http://www.hsus.org
Human Resource Management, Society for (1948), 1800 Duke St., Alexandria, VA 22314; 100,000; http://www.shrm.org
Husbandry, Natl. Grange of the Order of Patrons of (1867), 1616 H St. NW, Wash., DC 20006; 28,000.
Hybrid & Alternative Vehicle Society (1994), 3301 N. Belaire Dr., Altadena, CA 91001; 5,000.
Hydrogen Energy, Intl. Assn. for (1975), P.O. Box 248266, Coral Gables, FL 33124; 2,500.

***Idaho* Assn., U.S.S.** (1957), P.O. Box 11247, San Diego, CA 92171; 520.
Identification, Intl. Assn. for (1915), P.O. Box 2423, Alameda, CA 94501; 4,100.
Illuminating Engineering Society of N. America (1906), 120 Wall St., 17th Fl., New York, NY 10005; 10,000; http://www.iesna.org
Illustrators, Inc., Society of (1901), 128 E. 63d St., New York, NY 10021; 950; http://www.societyillustrators.org
Immigration Reform, Federation for American (1979), 1666 Connecticut Ave. NW, #400, Wash., DC; 70,000
Impotence Inst. of America (1983), 2020 Pennsylvania Ave. NW, Ste. 292, Wash., DC 20006.
Indoor Sports Club, Inc., The (1930), 16 Liberty St., Larkspur, CA 94939; 400.
Industrial and Applied Mathematics, Society for (1952), 3600 Univ. City Science Ctr., Philadelphia, PA 19104; 9,000; http://www.iam.org
Industrial Designers Society of America (1965), 1142-E Walker Rd., Great Falls, VA 22066; 2,350; http://www.idsa.org
Industrial Engineers, Institute of (1948), 25 Technology Park, Norcross, GA 30092; 25,000; http://www.iienet.org
Industrial Health Foundation (1935), 34 Penn Circle W, Pittsburgh, PA 15206; 170 cos.
Industrial Security, American Soc. for (1955), 1625 Prince St., Alexandria, VA 22313; 30,000; http://www.asisonline.org
Information and Image Management, Assn. for (1943), 1100 Wayne Ave., Ste. 1100, Silver Spring, MD 20910; 11,000.
Information Industry Assn. (1968), 1625 Massachusetts Ave. NW, Ste. 700, Wash., DC 20036; 550 cos.
Insurance Assn., American (1964), 1130 Connecticut Ave. NW, Ste. 1000, Wash., DC 20036; 250+ cos.; http://www.aiadc.org
Intellectual Property Owners (1972), 1255 23d St. NW, Ste. 850, Wash., DC 20037; 450; http://www.ipo.org
Intelligence Officers, Assn. of Former (1975), 6723 Whittier Ave., Ste. 303A, McLean, VA 22101; 2,700.
Intercollegiate Athletics, Natl. Assn. of (1937), 6120 S. Yale Ave., Ste. 1450, Tulsa, OK 74136; 352 schools; http://www.naia.org
Interconnecting & Packaging Electronic Circuits, The Institute for (1957), 2215 Sanders Rd., Northbrook, IL 60062; 2,400 cos.; http://www.ipc.org
Interior Designers, American Society of (1975), 608 Massachusetts Ave. NE, Wash., DC 20002; 30,500; http://www.asid.org
Intl. Colleges and Universities, Assn. of (1973), 1301 S. Noland Rd., Independence, MO 64055; 8,729 ind., 26 inst.
Intl. Education, Institute of (1919), 809 United Nations Plaza, New York, NY 10017; 650 U.S. colleges and universities; http://www.iie.org

Intl. Educational Exchange, Council on (1947), 205 E. 42d St., New York, NY 10017; 240 organizations; http://www.ciee.org
Intl. Educators, Assn. of (NAFSA) (1948), 1875 Connecticut Ave., Ste. 1000, Wash., DC 20009; 7,500; http://www.nafsa.org
Intl. Law, American Society of (1906), 2223 Massachusetts Ave. NW, Wash., DC 20008; 4,200; http://www.asil.org
Inventors, American Assn. of (1891), 2020 Pennsylvania Ave. NW, Wash., DC 20006; 5,727.
Investigative Pathology, Inc., American Soc. for (1900), 9650 Rockville Pike, Bethesda, MD 20814; 1,800; http://www.asip.uthscsa.edu
Investment Clubs, Natl. Assn. of (1951), 1515 E. Eleven Mile Rd., Royal Oak, MI 48067; 140,000.
Investment Management and Research, Assn. for (1990), 5 Boar's Head La., Charlottesville, VA 22901; 29,000.
Investors Corp., Natl. Assn. of (1951), 711 W. Thirteen Mile Rd., Madison Heights, MI 48701; 640,000; http://www.better-investing.org
Irish American Cultural Inst. (1962), 1 Lackawanna Pl., Morristown, NJ 07960; 5,000; http://www.irishaci.com
Irish Historical Society, American (1897), 991 5th Ave., New York, NY 10028; 850; http://www.aihs.org
Iron and Steel Engineers, Assn. of (1907), Three Gateway Center, Ste. 1900, Pittsburgh, PA 15222; 11,650; http://www.aise.org
Iron and Steel Institute, American (1855), 1101 17th St. NW, Ste. 1300, Wash., DC 20036; 1,100; http://www.steel.org
Islamic Relations, Council on American- (1994), 1050 17th St. NW, Ste. 490, Wash., DC 20036.
Italian Historical Society of America (1949), 111 Columbia Heights, Brooklyn, NY 11201.

Jail Assn., American (1981), 2053 Day Rd., Ste. 100, Hagerstown, MD 21740; 4,600; http://www.corrections.com/aja
Jane Austen Society of North America (1979), 254 E. 68th St., #21D, New York, NY 10021; 3,700; http://www.jasna.org
Japanese American Citizens League (1929), 1765 Sutter St., San Francisco, CA 94115; 23,900; http://www.jacl.org
Jewish Book Council (1946), 15 E. 26th St., New York, NY 10010.
Jewish Committee, American (1906), 165 E. 56th St., New York, NY 10022; 50,000; http://www.ajc.org
Jewish Community Centers Assn. (1917), 15 E. 26th St., New York, NY 10010.
Jewish Congress, American (1918), 15 E. 84th St., New York, NY 10028; 50,000; http://www.ajcongress.org/rght_col.htm
Jewish Federations, Council of (1932), 730 Broadway, New York, NY 10003; 200 agencies.
Jewish Historical Society, American (1892), 2 Thornton Rd., Waltham, MA 02154; 3,500; http://www.ajhs.org
Jewish War Veterans of the U.S.A. (1896), 1811 R St. NW, Wash., DC 20009; 100,000; http://www.penfed.org/jwv/home.htm
Jewish Women, Natl. Council of (1893), 53 W. 23d St., 6th Fl., New York, NY 10010; 90,000; http://www.ncjw.org
Job's Daughters, Intl. Order of (1920), 233 W. 6th St., Papillion, NE 68046; 21,000.
John Birch Society (1958), 770 Westhill Blvd, P.O. Box 8040, Appleton, WI 54913; nearly 100,000; http://www.jbs.org
Joint Action in Community Service (JACS), 5225 Wisconsin Ave. NW, Ste. 404, Wash., DC 20015.
Joseph Diseases Foundation, Inc., Intl. (1997), 4047 First St., Ste. 107, Livermore, CA 94550; 3,578.
Journalists, Society of Professional (1909), P.O. Box 77, Greencastle, IN 46135; 13,500; http://spj.org/spjheme.htm
Journalists and Authors, American Society of (1948), 1501 Broadway, Ste. 302, New York, NY 10036; 1,055; http://www.asja.org
Judaism, American Council for (1943), P.O. Box 9009, Alexandria, VA 22304.
Judicature Society, American (1913), 180 N. Michigan Ave., Ste. 600, Chicago, IL 60601; 10,000; http://www.ajs.org
Jugglers Assn., Intl. (1947), P.O. Box 218, Montague, MA 01351; 3,500, http://www.juggle.org
Junior Achievement (1919), One Education Way, Colorado Springs, CO 80906; 300,000; http://www.ja.org/index.asp
Junior Auxiliaries, Natl. Assn. of (1941), P.O. Box 1873, Greenville, MS 38701; 11,700; http://www.tecinfo.com/~nanajet
Junior College Athletic Assn., Natl. (1938), P.O. Box 7305, Colorado Springs, CO 80933; 530; http://www.njcaa.org
Junior Leagues, Assn. of (1921), 660 First Ave., New York, NY 10016; 195,000.

Kappa Delta Epsilon (1933), 2561 Rocky Ridge Road, Birmingham, AL 35243; about 35,000.
Kidney Fund, The American (1971), 6110 Executive Blvd., Ste. 1010, Rockville, MD 20852; http://www.arbon.com/kidney
Kiwanis International (1915), 3636 Woodview Trace, Indianapolis, IN 46268; 310,000; http://www.kiwanis.org
Knights of Columbus (1882), One Columbus Plaza, New Haven, CT 06510; 1,560,633.
Knights of Pythias (1864), 1495 Hancock St., Quincy, MA 02169; http://www.pythias.org
Krishna Consciousness, Intl. Soc. for (ISKON) (1966), 3764 Watseka Ave., Los Angeles, CA 92109; 300 temples.

La Leche League Intl. (1956), 1400 N. Meacham Rd., Schaumburg, IL 60173; 50,000+; http://www.lalecheleague.org
Lady Bird Johnson Wildflower Center (1982), 4801 La Crosse Ave., Austin, TX 78739; 22,000; http://www.wildflower.org
Lambs Inc., The (1874), 3 W. 51st St., New York, NY 10019; 200.
Landscape Architects, American Society of (1899), 636 Eye St., NW, Wash., DC 20001; 12,000; http://www.asla.org
Language Teachers Assns., Natl. Federation of Modern (1916), Gannon Univ., Erie, PA 16541; 7,200.
Law Libraries, American Assn. of (1906), 53 W. Jackson Blvd., #940, Chicago, IL 60604; 5,000; http://lawlib.wuacc.edu/aallnet/aallnet.html
Learned Societies, American Council of (1919), 228 E. 45th St., New York, NY 10017; 56 societies; http://www.acls.org
Lefthanders Intl. (1974), P.O. Box 8249, Topeka, KS 66608; 50,000.
Legal Administrators, Assn. of (1971), 175 E. Hawthorn Pkwy., Ste. 325, Vernon Hills, IL 60061; 8,055; http://www.alanet.org
Legal Secretaries, Natl. Assn. of (1929), 314 E 3rd St., Ste. 210, Tulsa, OK 74120; http://www.nals.org
Legion of Valor of the U.S.A. (1890), 92 Oak Leaf Lane, Chapel Hill, NC 27516; 753.
Leif Ericson Society (1962), 128 Asbury Ave., Ste. 103, Evanston, IL 60202; 1,100.
Leprosy Missions, Inc., American (1906), One Alm Way, Greenville, SC 29601; http://www.leprosy.org
Leukemia Society of America (1949), 600 Third Ave., New York, NY 10016; approx. 1 mil volunteers; http://www.leukemia.org
Lewis and Clark Trail Heritage Foundation, Inc. (1968), P.O. Box 3434, Great Falls, MT 59403; 2,200; discovery@lewisandclark.org
Lewis Carroll Society of North America (1974), 18 Fitzharding Pl., Owings Mill, MD 21117; 350; http://www.lewiscarroll.org/carroll.html
Libertarian Party (1971), 2600 Virginia Ave. NW, Ste. 100, Wash., DC 20037; 186,000; http://www.lp.org
Liberty Lobby (1955), 300 Independence Ave. SE, Wash., DC 20003; 95,000; http://www.spotlight.org
Libraries Assn., Special (1909), 1700 18th St. NW, Wash., DC 20009; 15,000; http://www.sla.org
Library Assn., American (1876), 50 E. Huron St., Chicago, IL 60611; 57,000; http://www.ala.org
Life Insurance, American Council of (1976), 1001 Pennsylvania Ave. NW, Wash., DC 20004; 532 firms.
Lighter-Than-Air Society (1952), 1436 Triplett Blvd., Akron, OH 44306; 900.
Linguistic Society of America (1924), 1325 18th St. NW, Ste. 211, Wash., DC 20036; 6,500; http://www.lsadc.org
Lions Clubs Intl. (1917), 300 22d St., Oak Brook, IL 60523; 1,400,000; http://www.lionsclubs.org
Literacy Volunteers of America, Inc. (1962), 635 James St., Syracuse, NY 13203; 111,319; http://www.literacyvolunteers.org
Little League Baseball, Inc. (1939), P.O. Box 3485, Williamsport, PA 17701; 3 mil; http://www.littleleague.org
Little People of America (1961), 27 Sunrise Lane, Ransom Canyon, TX 79366; 6,500; http://www.-bfs.ucsd.edu/dwarfism/lpa.htm
Logistics Engineers, International Soc. of (1966), 8100 Professional Place, Ste. 211, New Carrollton, MD 20785; 5,200; http://www.sole.org
London Club (1975), Rt. 1, Lecompton, KS 66050; 100+.
Lung Assn., American (1904), 1740 Broadway, New York, NY 10019; http://www.lungusa.org
Lutheran Education Assn. (1942), 7400 Augusta St., River Forest, IL 60305; 3,800.
Magazine Publishers of America (1919), 319 Third Ave., New York, NY 10022; 360 cos.

Magicians, Intl. Brotherhood of (1922), 11137C S. Towne Sq., St. Louis, MO 63123; 14,000; http://www.magician.org
Magicians, Society of American (1902), P.O. Box 510260, St. Louis, MO 63151; 5,500; http://www.uelectric.com/sam
Management Accountants, Institute of (1919), 10 Paragon Dr., Montvale, NJ 07645; 80,000; http://www.rutgers.edu/Accounting/raw/ima/ima.htm
Management Assn. Intl., American (1923), 1601 Broadway, New York, NY 10019; 70,000+; http://www.amanet.org
Management Consulting Firms, Assn. of (1929), 521 5th Ave., 35th Fl., New York, NY 10175; 50 firms.
Management Education, The Intl. Association for (1916), 600 Emerson Rd., Ste. 300, St. Louis, MO 63141; 900 organizations; http://www.aacsb.edu
Manufacturing Engineers, Soc. of (1932), One SME Dr., Dearborn, MI 48121; 70,000; http://www.sme.org
Manufacturers, Natl. Assn. of (1895), 1331 Pennsylvania Ave. NW, Ste. 1500 N. Tower, Wash., DC 20004; 14,000 cos.; http://www.nam.org
Manufacturers' Agents Natl. Assn. (1947), 23016 Mill Creek Rd., Laguna Hills, CA 92653; 7,000; http://www.MANAonline.org
March of Dimes (1938), 1275 Mamaroneck Ave., White Plains, NY 10605; http://www.modimes.org
Marine Corps League (1937), P.O. Box 3070, Merrifield, VA 22116; 42,000; http://www.mcleague.org
Market Technicians Association (1973), One World Trade Center, Ste. 4447, New York, NY 10048; 900; http://www.mta-usa.org
Marketing Assn., American (1937), 250 S. Wacker Dr., Chicago, IL 60606; 41,000; http://www.ama.org
Masonic Relief Assn. of U.S. and Canada (1889), 3827 Canal St., New Orleans, LA 70119.
Masons, Royal Arch, General Grand Chapter (1797), P.O. Box 489, Danville, KY 40423; 220,000.
Material & Process Engineering, Soc. for the Advancement of (1944), 1161 Parkview Dr., Covina, CA 91724; 6,000; http://www.et.byu.edu/~sampe
Mathematical Society, American (1888), 201 Charles St., Providence, RI 02904; 28,000; http://www.ams.org
Mathematical Statistics, Institute of (1935), 3401 Investment Blvd., Ste. 7, Hayward, CA 94545; 3,800; http://www.mstat.org
Mayflower Descendants, General Society of (1897), 4 Winslow St., P.O. Box 3297, Plymouth, MA 02361; 30,000+.
Mayors, U.S. Conference of (1932), 1620 Eye St. NW, Wash., DC 20006.
Mechanical Engineers, American Soc. of (1881), 345 E. 47th St., New York, NY 10017; 120,000; http://www.asme.org
Medical Assn., Aerospace (1929), 320 S. Henry St., Alexandria, VA 22314; 3,600; http://www.asma.org
Medical Assn., American (1847), 515 N. State St., Chicago, IL 60610; 300,000; http://www.ama-assn.org
Medical Assn., Natl. (1895), 1012 Tenth St. NW, Wash., DC 20001; 22,000.
Medical Library Assn. (1898), 6 N. Michigan Ave., Ste. 300, Chicago, IL 60602; 3,800 people, 1,200 instits; http://www.mlanet.org
Medical Record Assn., American (1928), 919 N. Michigan Ave., Chicago, IL 60611; 31,000.
Medieval Academy of America (1925), 1430 Massachusetts Ave., Ste. 313, Cambridge, MA 02138; 4,500; http://www.georgetown.edu/medievalacademy
Mended Hearts (1951), 7320 Greenville Ave., Dallas, TX 75231; 20,000; http://www.mendedhearts.org
Mensa, Ltd., American (1960), 1229 Corporate Dr. W, Arlington, TX 76006; 45,000; http://www.us.mensa.org
Mental Health Assn., Natl. (1909), 1021 Prince St., Alexandria, VA 22314; 325 affiliates.
Mental Health Program Directors, Natl. Assn. of State (1959), 66 Canal Ctr. Plaza, Ste. 302, Alexandria, VA 22314; 55.
Mentally Ill, Natl. Alliance for the (1980), 200 North Glebe Rd., Arlington, VA 22203; 140,000; http://www.nami.org
Merchant Marine Veterans of World War II, U.S. (1989), P.O. Box 629, San Pedro, CA 90733; 3,456; http://www.lanevictoryship.com
Merrill's Marauders Assn. (1947), 11244 N. 33d St., Phoenix, AZ 85028; 1,756.
Metallurgy Institute Intl., American Powder (1959), 105 College Rd. East, Princeton, NJ 08540; 2,800.
Metal Powder Industries Federation (1944), 105 College Rd. E, Princeton, NJ 08540; 275 cos.; http://www.mpif.org
Metals Intl. (ASM), American Society for (1913), 9639 Kinsman Rd., Materials Park, OH 44073; 43,000; http://www.asm-intl.org
Meteorological Society, American (1919), 45 Beacon St., Boston, MA 02108; 11,000.
Metric Assn., Inc., U.S. (1916), 10245 Andasol Ave., Northridge, CA 91235; 1,200.
Microbiology, American Society for (1899), 1325 Massachusetts Ave. NW, Wash., DC 20005; 43,000; http://www.asmusa.org
Mideast Educational & Training Services, American (1951), 1730 M St. NW, Ste. 1100, Wash., DC 20036; 190 inst.
Military Order of the Loyal Legion of the U.S. (1865), 1805 Pine St., Philadelphia, PA 19103; 900; http://suvcw.org/mollus.htm
Military Order of the Purple Heart of the USA (1958), 5413-B Backlick Rd., Springfield, VA 22151; 32,000; http://www.purpleheart.org
Military Order of the World Wars (1920), 435 N. Lee St., Alexandria, VA 22314; 13,000.
Military Surgeons of the U.S., Assn. of (1898), 9320 Old Georgetown Rd., Bethesda, MD 20814; 11,000; http://www.amsus.org
Mining Association, Natl. (1995), 1130 17th St. NW, Washington DC 20036; 340; http://www.nma.org
Mining Engineers, Society of (1871), 8307 Shaffer Pkwy., Littleton, CO 80127; 23,058.
Mining, Metallurgy and Exploration, Inc., Society for (1871), P.O. Box 625002, Littleton, CO 80162; 16,141; http://www.smenet.org
Mining, Metallurgical and Petroleum Engineers, American Institute of (1871), 345 E. 47th St., 14th Fl., New York, NY 10017; 100,000; http://www.idis.com/aime
Missing and Exploited Children, Natl. Center for (1984), 2101 Wilson Blvd., Ste. 550, Arlington, VA 22201; http://www.missingkids.com
Model A Ford Club of America, Inc. (1957), 250 S Cypress St., La Habra, CA 90631; 15,500; http://www.mafca.com
Model Railroad Assn., Natl. (1935), 4121 Cromwell Rd., Chattanooga, TN 37421; 24,500; http://www.mcs.net/~weyand/nmra
Modern Language Assn. of America (1883), 10 Astor Pl., New York, NY 10003; 32,000; http://www.mla.org
Moose Intl., Inc. (1988), Mooseheart, IL 60539; 1.8 mil.
Mothers, Inc.®, American (1935), 301 Park Ave., New York, NY 10022; 6,000; http://www.americanmothers.org
Mothers of Twins Clubs, Natl. Organization of (1960), P.O. Box 23188, Albuquerque, NM 87192; 14,000.
Motion Picture Arts & Sciences, Academy of (1927), 8949 Wilshire Blvd., Beverly Hills, CA 90211; 5,900; http://www.ampas.org
Motion Picture & Television Engineers, Soc. of (1916), 595 W. Hartsdale Ave., White Plains, NY 10607; http://www.smpte.org
Motorcyclist Assn., American (1924), 33 Collegeview Rd., Westerville, OH 43081; 225,000; http://www.ama-cycle.org
Motor Fire Apparatus in America, Soc. for the Preservation & Appreciation of Antique (1958), P.O. Box 2005, Syracuse, NY 13220; 3,000.
Multiple Sclerosis Society, Natl. (1946), 733 Third Ave., New York, NY 10017; 518,567; http://www.nmss.org
Muscular Dystrophy Assn., Inc. (1950), 3300 E. Sunrise Dr., Tucson, AZ 85718; http://www.mdausa.org
Museums, American Assn. of (1906), 1575 Eye St. NW, Ste. 400, Wash., DC 20005; 16,000; http://www.aam-us.org
Music Center, American (1939), 30 W. 26th St., New York, NY 10010; 2,500; http://www.amc.net
Music Educators Natl. Conference (1907), 1806 Robert Fulton Dr., Reston, VA 22091; 65,000+.
Music Scholarship Assn., American (1956), 1030 Carew Tower, Cincinnati, OH 45202; 1,000; http://www.amsa_wpc.org
Music Teachers Natl. Assn. (1876), 441 Vine St., Ste. 505, Cincinnati, OH 45202; 24,000; http://www.mtna.org
Musicological Society, Inc., American (1934), 201 S. 34th St., Philadelphia, PA 19104; 3,500; http://www.musdra.ucdavis.edu/AMS/AMS.html
Muzzle Loading Rifle Assn., Natl. (1933), P.O. Box 67, Friendship, IN 47021; 23,000; http://www.nmlra.org
Myasthenia Gravis Foundation of America (1952), 222 S. Riverside Plaza, Ste. 1540, Chicago, IL 60606; 30,000; http://www.med.unc.edu/mgfa
Mystery Writers of America (1945), 17 E. 47th St., 6th Fl., New York, NY 10017; 2,600; http://www.bookwire.com/mwa

NA'AMAT USA (1925), 200 Madison Ave., New York, NY 10016; 50,000, U.S.; 900,000 worldwide; http://www.namatusa.org
Name Society, American (1951), Dept. of Modern Languages, Box G-1224, Baruch College, 17 Lexington Ave., New York, NY 10010; 400.
Narcotics Anonymous (1953), 19737 Nordhoff Pl., Chatsworth, CA 91311; 450,000; http://www.wsoinc.com

Natl. Assn. for the Advancement of Colored People (NAACP) (1909), 4805 Mt. Hope Dr., Baltimore, MD 21215; http://www.naacp.org
National Guard Assn. of the U.S. (1878), One Massachusetts Ave. NW, Wash., DC 20001; 56,000; http://www.ngaus.org
National Party for America (1996), 10799 Sherman Grove Ave., # 18, Sunland, CA; 91040; 5,200.
National Press Club (1908), 529 14th St. NW, Wash., DC 20045; 4,800; http://npc.press.org
Nature Conservancy, The (1951), 1815 N. Lynn St., Arlington, VA 22209; 900,000; http://www.tnc.org
Naturists, Inc., The (1976), 454 N. Main St., Oshkosh, WI 54901; 25,000; http://www.naturist.com
Nautical Archaeology, Institute of (1972), P.O. Drawer HG, College Station, TX 77841; 1,150; http://nautarch.tamu.edu/ina/inamain.htm.
Naval Architects & Marine Engineers, Society of (1893), 601 Pavonia Ave., Ste. 400, Jersey City, NJ 07306; 10,000.
Naval Engineers, American Soc. of (1888), 1452 Duke St., Alexandria, VA 22314; 5,600; http://www.jhuapl.edu/ASNE
Naval Institute, U.S. (1873), 118 Maryland Ave., Annapolis, MD 21402; http://www.usni.org
Naval Reserve Assn. (1954), 1619 King St., Alexandria, VA 22314; 23,000; http://www.navy-reserve.org/nra
Navigation, The Institute of (1945), 1800 Diagonal Rd., Ste. 480, Alexandria, VA 22314; 3,000; http://www.ion.org
Navy League of the U.S. (1902), 2300 Wilson Blvd., Arlington, VA 22201; 71,308.
Needlework Guild of America, Inc (NGA, Inc.) (1885), 1007-B Street Rd., Southampton, PA 18966; 100,000.
Negro College Fund, United (1944), 8260 Willow Oaks Corporate Dr., Fairfax, VA; 41 institutions; http://www.uncf.org
Neurofibromatosis Foundation, Natl. (1978), 95 Pine St., 16th Fl., New York, NY 10005; 40,000; http://www.nf.org
Newspaper Assn. of America (NAA) (1992), 1921 Gallows Rd., #4, Vienna, VA 22182; 1,800; http://www.naa.org
Newspaper Marketing Assn., Intl. (1930), 11600 Sunrise Valley Dr., Reston, VA 22071; 1,532; http://www.inma.org
Newswomen's Club of New York, Inc. (1922), 15 Gramercy Park S., New York, NY 10011; 230.
Ninety-Nines (Intl. Organization of Women Pilots) (1929), Box 965, Will Rogers Airport, Oklahoma City, OK 73159; 6,400; http://www.ninety-nines.org
Nobel Center, American (1946), 45 Southport Woods Dr., Southport, CT 06490; 1,000.
Non-Commissioned Officers Assn. (1960), 10635 IH 35 North, San Antonio, TX 78233; 160,000; http://www.ncoausa.org
Northern Cross Society (1986), Rt. One, Big Springs, KS 66050; 100+.
Notaries, American Society of (1965), P.O. Box 5707, Tallahassee, FL 32314; 20,000; http://www.notaries.com
Nuclear Society, American (1954), 555 N. Kensington Ave., La Grange Park, IL 60525; 16,000; http://www.ans.org
Nude Recreation, American Assn. for (1931), 1703 N. Main St., Kissimmee, FL 34744; 45,000; http://www.aanr.com
Numismatic Assn., American (1891), 818 N. Cascade Ave., Colorado Springs, CO 80903; 30,000; http://www.money.org
Numismatic Society, The American (1858), Broadway at 155th St., New York, NY 10032; http://www.amnumsoc2.org
Nursing, Natl. League for (1952), 350 Hudson St., New York, NY 10014; 16,000; http://www.nln.org
Nutritional Sciences, American Society for (1928), 9650 Rockville Pike, Bethesda, MD 20814; 3,400; http://www.arvo.org/asns

Odd Fellows, Independent Order of (1819), 422 Trade St., Winston-Salem, NC 27101; 450,000.
Old Crows, Assn. of (1964), 1000 N. Payne St., Alexandria, VA 22314; 25,000; http://www.aochq.org
Opthalmology, American Academy of (1979), 655 Beach St., San Francisco, CA 94109; 21,000; http://www.eyenet.org
Optical Society of America (1917), 2010 Massachusetts Ave. NW, Wash., DC 20036; 11,000; http://www.osa.org
Optimist Intl. (1919), 4494 Lindell Blvd., St. Louis, MO 63108; 149,000; http://www.optimist.org
Optometric Assn., American (1898), 243 N. Lindbergh Blvd., St. Louis, MO 63141; 31,000; http://www.aoanet.org
Organists, American Guild of (1896), 475 Riverside Dr., Ste. 1260, New York, NY 10115; 20,200; http://www.agohq.org
Oriental Society, American (1842), Univ. of Michigan, Hatcher Graduate Library, 110D, Ann Arbor, MI 48109; 1,350; http://umich.edu/~aos
ORT Federation, American (Org. for Rehabilitation Through Training) (1924), 817 Broadway, 10th Fl., New York, NY 10003; 20,000.
Ornithologists' Union, American (1883), c/o Division of Birds, MRC-116, Smithsonian Institution, Wash., DC 20560; 4,500; http://www.pica.wru.umt.edu/AOU/AOU.html
Osteopathic Assn., American (1897), 142 E. Ontario, Chicago, IL 60611; 28,974; http://www.am-osteo-assn.org
Ostomy Assn., Inc., United (1962), 19772 MacArthur Blvd., Ste. 200, Irvine, CA 92612, 30,000; http://www.uoa.org
Outlaw and Lawman History, Inc., Natl. Assn. for (NOLA) (1974), 1201 Holly Ct., Harker Heights, TX 76548; approx. 450.
Overeaters Anonymous (1960) 6075 Zenith Ct., NE, Rio Rancho, NM 87124; approx. 100,000; http://www.overeatersanonymous.org

Paralyzed Veterans of America (1947), 801 18th St. NW, Wash., DC 20006; 18,000; http://www.pva.org
Parametric Analysts, Intl. Soc. of (1978), P.O. Box 6402, Chesterfield, MO 63006; 300+.
Parapsychology Institute of America (1971), P.O. Box 5442, Babylon, NY 11707; 1,100.
Parents Without Partners (1957), 401 N. Michigan Ave., Chicago, IL 60611; 70,000; http://www. parentswithoutpartners.org
Parkinson's Disease Foundation, Inc. (1957), 710 W. 168th St., New York, NY 10032; 95,000.
Parliamentarians, Natl. Assn. of (1930), 213 S. Main St., Independence, MO 64050; 4,292; http://www.parliamentarians.org
Pasta Assn., Natl. (1904), 2101 Wilson Blvd., Ste. 920, Arlington, VA 22201; 74 cos.; http://www.ilovepasta.org
Pathologists, American Assn. (1976), 9650 Rockville Pike, Bethesda, MD 20814; 2,000.
Pathologists, American Society of Clinical (1922), 2100 W. Harrison St., Chicago, IL 60612; 79,000; http://www.ascp.org
Patton Society (1970), 3116 Thorn St., San Diego, CA 92104; 250; http://members.aol.com/PattonsGHQ/homeghq.html.
Pearl Harbor History Associates, Inc. (1985), P.O. Box 1007, Stratford, CT 06614; 300.
PEN American Center, Inc. (1922), 568 Broadway, Rm. 401, New York, NY 10012; 2,800; http://www.pen.org
Pen Friends, Intl. (1967), P.O. Box 290065, Brooklyn, NY 11229; 300,000; http://www.global-homebiz.com/ipf.html
Pension Plan, Committee for a Natl. (1979), P.O. Box 27851, Las Vegas, NV 89126; 350.
Pen Women, Natl. League of American (1897), 1300 17th St. NW, Wash., DC 20036; 4,010.
P.E.O. (Philanthropic Educational Organization) Sisterhood (1869), 3700 Grand Ave., Des Moines, IA 50312; 242,000.
People for the Ethical Treatment of Animals (PETA) (1980), 501 Front St., Norfolk, VA 23510; 600,000; http://www.peta-online.org
Performance Improvement, Intl. Society for (1962), 1300 L St. NW, #1250, Wash., DC 20005; 6,000; http://www.ispi.org/nav.htm
Personnel Administration, American Society for (1948), 606 N. Washington St., Alexandria, VA 22314; 40,000.
Petroleum Equipment Inst. (1951), 6514 E. 69 St., Tulsa, OK 74133; 1,755 cos.; http://www.peinet.org
Petroleum Geologists, American Assn. of (1917), P.O. Box 979, 1444 S. Boulder, Tulsa, OK 74101; http://www.geobyte.com
Petroleum Institute, American (1919), 1220 L St. NW, Wash., DC 20005; 400 companies; http://www.api.org
Pharmaceutical Assn., American (1852), 2215 Constitution Ave. NW, Wash., DC 20037; 50,000; http://www.aphanet.org
Phi Beta Kappa (1776), 1811 Q St. NW, Wash., DC 20009; approx. 500,000; http://www.pbk.org
Phi Delta Kappa (1906), 408 N. Union, P.O. Box 789, Bloomington, IN 47402; 172,000; http://www.gammatheta.com
Philatelic Golf Society (1987), P.O. Box 2183, Norfolk, VA 23501; 240.
Philatelic Society, American (1886), 100 Oakwood Ave., P.O. Box 8000, State College, PA 16803; 56,500; http://www.west.net/~stamps1/aps.html
Philological Assn., American (1869), Dept. of Classics, College of the Holy Cross, Worcester, MA 01610; 3,300.
Philosophical Assn., American (1900), Univ. of Delaware, Newark, DE 19716; 10,000; http://www.udel.edu/apa
Philosophical Enquiry, Intl. Soc. For (1974), 5409 Pipers Gap Dr., Memphis, TN 38134; 700+.
Philosophical Society, American (1743), 104 S. 5th St., Philadelphia, PA 19106; 690.
Photogrammetry and Remote Sensing, American Society for (1934), 5410 Grosvenor Ln., Ste. 210, Bethesda, MD 20814; 7,880; http://www.asprs.org/asprs
Photographers of America, Inc., Professional (1880), 229 Peachtree Street, NE, Atlanta, GA 30303; 14,000; http://www.ppa-world.org
Photographic Society of America (1934), 3000 United Founders Blvd., Ste. 103, Oklahoma City, OK 73112; 7,000; http://www.psa-photo.org
Physical Therapy Assn., American (1921), 1111 N. Fairfax St., Alexandria, VA 22314; 70,000; http://www.apta.org

Physically Handicapped, Inc., Natl. Assn. of the (1958), NAPH Business Office, Scarlet Oaks, 440 Lafayette Ave., #GA4, Cincinnati, OH 45220; approx. 600.
Physics, American Inst. of (1931), One Physics Ellipse, College Park, MD 20740; 100,000; http://www.aip.org
Physiological Society, American (1887), 9650 Rockville Pike, Bethesda, MD 20814; 8,300; http://www.faseb.org/aps
Phytopathological Society, American (1908), 3340 Pilot Knob Rd., St. Paul, MN 55121; 5,000; http://www.scisoc.org
Pilgrim Society (1820), 75 Court St., Plymouth, MA 02360; 900.
Pilot Intl. & Pilot Intl. Foundation (1921, 1975), P.O. Box 4844, 244 College St., Macon, GA 31208; 26,000.
Pi Mu Epsilon National Honorary Mathematics Society (1914), 100 Grant St., De Pere, WI 54115; 110,000; http://www.snc.edu/pme/
Planetary Society (1979), 65 N. Catalina Ave., Pasadena, CA 91106; 100,000.
Planned Parenthood Federation of America, Inc. (1916), 810 Seventh Ave., New York, NY 10019; http://www.plannedparenthood.org
Plastic Modelers Society, Intl. (1963), P.O. Box 6138, Warner Robins, GA 31095; 4,750.
Plastics Engineers, Society of (1942), 14 Fairfield Dr., Brookfield, CT 06804; 37,000; http://www.4spe.org
Plastics Industry, Inc., Society of the (1937), 1801 K Street, NW, Ste. 600K, Wash., DC 20006; 2,000+ companies; http://www.socplas.org
Platform Assn., Intl. (1830), Box 250, Winnetka, IL 60093; 5,000; http://www.internationalplatform.com
Poetry Day Committee, Natl. (1947), 1110 N. Venetian Dr., Miami, FL 33139; 17,500.
Poetry Society of America (1910), 15 Gramercy Park, New York, NY 10003; 2,500; http://www.bookwire.com/psa/psa.html
Poets, The Academy of American (1934), 584 Broadway, Ste. 1208, New York, NY 10012; 6,800; http://www.poets.org
Police Assn., Intl. (1950 in UK, 1962 in U.S.), P.O. Box 613-1822, South Miami, FL 33243; 276,000+; http://www.ipa-usa.org
Polish Army Veterans Assn. of America (1921), 155 Noble St., Brooklyn, NY 11222; 3,500.
Polish Cultural Society of America, Inc. (1940), P.O. Box 31, Wall St., New York, NY 10005; 103,981.
Political Items Collectors, American (1945), P.O. Box 340339, San Antonio, TX 78234; 3,300; http://www.collectors.org/apic/ari/apic.html
Political Science, Academy of (1880), 475 Riverside Dr., Ste. 1,274, New York, NY 10115; 6,489.
Political Science Assn., American (1903), 1527 New Hampshire Ave. NW, Wash., DC 20036; 16,200; http://www.apsanet.org
Political Science Assn., Southern (1928), Dept. of Political Science, University of Mississippi, University, MS 38677; 1200; http://www.olemiss.edu/orgs/spsa
Political & Social Science, American Academy of (1889), 3937 Chestnut St., Philadelphia, PA 19104; 3,200.
Polo Assn., U.S. (1890), 4059 Iron Works Parkway, Ste. 1, Lexington, KY 40511; over 3,000; http://www.uspolo.org
Population Assn. of America (1931), 721 Ellsworth Dr., Ste. 303, Silver Spring, MD 20910; 3,000.
Portuguese-American Federation, Inc., The (1974), P.O. Box 694, Bristol, RI 02809; 234.
Portuguese Continental Union of the U.S.A. (1925), 899 Boylston St., Boston, MA 02115; 6,297; http://members.aol.com/UPCEUA
Postmasters of the U.S., Natl. Assn. of (1898), 8 Herbert St., Arlington, VA 22305; 43,000.
Postmasters, Natl. League of (1904), 1023 N. Royal St., Alexandria, VA 22314; 28,000.
Poultry Science Assn. (1908), 1111 N. Dunlap Ave. Savoy, IL 61874; 2,100; http://www.psa.uiuc.edu
Power Boat Assn., American (1903), P.O. Box 377, Eastpointe, MI 48021; 6,000.
Precancel Collectors, Inc., Natl. Assn. of (1950), 84 W National Dr., Newark, OH 43055; 7,700+.
Press and Radio Club (1948), 29 Bradley Dr., Montgomery, AL 36109; 772.
Printing Industries of America, Inc. (1887), 100 Dangerfield Rd., Alexandria, VA 22314; 14,000; http://www.printing.org
Prisoners of War, American Ex- (1942), 3201 E. Pioneer Pkwy., #40, Arlington, TX 76010; 31,000.
Procrastinators Club of America (1956), P.O. Box 712, Bryn Athyn, PA 19009; 14,500+.
Production and Inventory Control Soc., American (1957), 500 W. Annandale Rd., Falls Church, VA 22046; 69,114.
Protection of Old Fishes, Soc. for the (1967), School of Fisheries, 357980, Univ. of Washington, Seattle, WA 98195; 200.
Psoriasis Foundation, Natl. (1968), 6600 SW 92d Ave., Ste. 300, Portland, OR 97223; 40,000; http://www.psoriasis.org
Psychiatric Assn., American (1844), 1400 K St. NW, Wash., DC 20005; 40,453; http://www.psych.org
Psychical Research, American Society for (1885), 5 W. 73d St., New York, NY 10023; approx 5,000; aspr@aspr.com
Psychoanalytic Assn., American (1911), 309 E. 49th St., New York, NY 10017; 3,000; http://apsa.org
Psychological Assn., American (1892), 750 1st St. NE, Wash., DC 20002; 142,000; http://www.apa.org
Psychological Assn. for Psychoanalysis, Inc., Natl. (1948), 150 W. 13th St., New York, NY 10011; 362; http://www.npap.org
PTA (Natl. Congress of Parents and Teachers) (1897), 330 N. Wabash Ave., Ste. 2100, Chicago, IL 60611; 6.5 mil; http://www.pta.org
Public Administration, American Soc. for (1939), 1120 G St. NW, Wash., DC 20005; 11,000+; http://www.aspanet.org
Public Health Assn., World Fed. of (1967), 1015 15th St. NW, Wash., DC 20005; 48 natl. assn.
Public Relations Soc. of America, Inc. (1947), 33 Irving Pl., 3d Fl., New York, NY 10003; 17,383; http://www.prsa.org
Publishers, Assn. of American (1970), 71 5th Ave., New York, NY 10003; 180 cos.; http://www.publishers.org
Pulp and Paper Industries, Technical Assn. of the (TAPPI) (1915), 15 Technology Pkwy. S, Norcross, GA 30092; 34,000; http://www.tappi.org
Puppeteers of America (1936), 5 Cricklewood Path, Pasadena, CA 91107; 2,400; http://www.puppeteers.org
Puzzle Buffs Intl. (1979), 1772 State Rd., Cuyahoga Falls, OH 44223; 65,000; http://www.puzzlebuffs.com

Quality Control, American Society for (ASQC) (1946), 611 E. Wisconsin Ave., Milwaukee, WI 53201; 140,000; http://www.asqc.org
Quota International, Inc. (1919), 1420 21st St. NW, Wash., DC 20036; 11,000+; http://www.quota.org

Rabbis, Central Conference of American (1889), 355 Lexington Ave., New York, NY 10017; 1,800; http://ccarnet.orghttp://ccarnet.org
Racquetball Assn., American Amateur (1968), 815 N. Weber, Colorado Springs, CO.
Racquetball Assn., U.S. (1968), 1685 W. Vintah, Colorado Springs, CO 80904; 25,000; http://www.racquetball.org
Radio Relay League, American (1914), 225 Main St., Newington, CT 06111; 172,000; http://www.arrl.org
Radio and Television Society Foundation, Intl. (1962), 420 Lexington Ave., Ste. 1714, New York, NY 10170; 1,100.
Railway Historical Society, Natl. (1935), P.O. Box 58547, Philadelphia, PA 19102; 14,402; http://www.rrhistorical.com/nrhs
Railway Progress Institute (1908), 700 N. Fairfax St., Ste. 601, Alexandria, VA 22314; 96 cos.; http://www.rpi.org
Range Management, Society for (1948), 1839 York St., Denver, CO 80206; 5,000; http://www.srm.org
Reading Assn., Intl. (1956), 800 Barksdale Rd., P.O. Box 8139, Newark, DE 19714; 95,000; http://www.reading.org
Real Estate Institute, Intl. (1972), 8383 E. Evans Rd., Scottsdale, AZ 85260; 2,846.
Rebekah Assemblies, Intl. Assn. of (1922), 422 Trade St., Winston-Salem, NC 27101; 127,026.
Records Managers & Administrators, Assn. of (1976), 4200 Somerset Dr., Ste. 215, Prairie Village, KS 66208; 9,600; http://www.arma.org/hq
Recreation and Park Assn., Natl. (1965), 2775 S. Quincy St., Ste. 300, Arlington, VA 22206; 23,533; http://www.nrpa.org
Recycling Coalition, Natl. (1979), 1727 King St., Ste. 105, Alexandria, VA 22514; 3,500.
Red Cross, American (1881), 8111 Gatehouse Rd., Falls Church, VA 22042; 1.44 mil volunteers; http://www.redcross.org
Rehabilitation Assn., Natl. (1925), 633 S. Washington St., Alexandria, VA 22314; approx. 11,000; http://www.nationalrehaborg
Religion, American Academy of (1964), 1703 Clifton Rd. NE, Ste. G-5, Atlanta, GA 30329; 8,000; http://www.aar-site.org
Renaissance Society of America (1954), 24 W. 12th St., 3d Fl., New York, NY 10011; 3,700; http://www.r-s-a.org
Republican National Committee (1856), 310 1st St. SE, Wash., DC 20003; http://www.rnc.org
Reserve Officers Assn. of the U.S. (1922), One Constitution Ave. NE, Wash., DC 20003; 95,000.
Restaurant Assn., Natl. (1919), 1200 17th St. NW, Wash., DC 20036; 33,000; http://www.restaurant.org
Retail Federation, Natl. (1918), 95 Pine St., NW, Ste. 1000, Wash., DC 20004; 50,000; http://www.nrf.com
Retired Credit Union People, Natl. Assn. for (1978), P.O. Box 391, 5910 Mineral Pt. Rd., Madison, WI 53705; 81,180.

Retired Federal Employees, Natl. Assn. of (1921), 1533 New Hampshire Ave. NW, Wash., DC 20036; 500,000.
Retired Officers Assn. (1929), 201 N. Washington St., Alexandria, VA 22314; 396,000; http://www.troa.org
Retired Persons, American Assn. of (1958), 601 E St. NW, Wash., DC 20049; 32 mil.; http://www.aarp.org
Retired Teachers Assn., Natl. (1947), 1909 K St. NW, Wash., DC 20049; 540,000.
Revolver Assn., U.S. (1904), 49 River Street, Quincy, MA 02169; 1,366.
Reye's Syndrome Foundation, Natl. (1974), 426 N. Lewis, P.O. Box 829, Bryan, OH 43506; 5,000; http://www.bright.net/~reyessyn
Richard III Society (1969), P.O. Box 13786, New Orleans, LA 70185; 700; http://www.r3.org
Rifle Assn., Natl. (1871), 11250 Waples Mill Rd., Fairfax, VA 22030; approx 3 mil; http://www.nra.org
Road & Transportation Builders Assn., American (1902), The ARTBA Building, 1010 Massachusetts Ave. NW, Wash., DC 20001; 4,000; http://www.artba-hg.org
Roller Skating, U.S.A. (1937), 4730 South St., P.O. Box 6579, Lincoln, NE 68506; 30,000; http://www.usacrs.com
Rose Society, American (1892), P.O. Box 30,000, Shreveport, LA 71130; 23,000; http://www.ars.org
Rotary Intl. (1905), 1560 Sherman Ave., Evanston, IL 60201; 1,203,726; http://www.rotary.org
Running and Fitness Assn., American (1968), 4405 East West Highway, Ste. 405, Bethesda, MD 20814; approx. 16,500; http://www.arfa.org
Ruritan Natl., Inc. (1928), P.O. Box 487, Dublin, VA 24084; 35,000.

Safety Council, Natl. (1913), 1121 Spring Lake Dr., Itasca, IL 60143; 18,000; http://www.nsc.org
Safety Engineers, American Soc. of (1911), 1800 E. Oakton St., Des Plaines, IL 60018; 32,000; http://www.asse.org
Safety and Fairness Everywhere, Nat'l. Organization Taunting (NOT-SAFE) (1982), P.O. Box 5743-WA, Montecito, CA 93108; 1,471.
St. Paul, Natl. Guild of (1937), 601 Hill 'n Dale, Lexington, KY 40503; 13,652.
Salespersons, Natl. Assn. of Professional (1970), P.O. Box 76461, Atlanta, GA 30358; 35,000.
Salt Institute (1914), 700 N. Fairfax St., Ste. 600, Alexandria, VA, 22314; 8 cos, 27 assoc; http://www.saltinstitute.org
Sand Castle Builders, Intl. Society of (1988), 172 N. Pershing Ave., Akron, OH 44313; 200.
Save-the-Redwoods League (1918), 114 Sansome St., Ste. 605, San Francisco, CA 94104; 50,000; http://www.savetheredwoods.org
School Administrators, American Assn. of (1865), 1801 N. Moore St., Arlington, VA 22209; 16,409; http://www.aasa.org
School Boards Assn., Natl. (1940), 1680 Duke St., Alexandria, VA 22314; http://www.nsba.org
School Counselor Assn., American (1952), 801 N. Fairfax St., Alexandria, VA 22314; approx. 11,000; http://www.schoolcounselor.org
Schools of Art, Natl. Assn. of (1944), 11250 Roger Bacon Dr., Reston, VA 22090; 553 institutions.
Science, American Assn. for the Advancement of (1848), 1200 New York Ave. NW, Wash., DC 20005; 144,000; http://www.aaas.org
Science Fiction Society, World (1939), P.O. Box 1270, Kendall Sq. Sta., Cambridge, MA 02142; 5,000.
Science Service (1922), 1719 N St. NW, Wash., DC 20036; 200,000; http://www.sciserv.org
Sciences, Natl. Academy of (1863), 2101 Constitution Ave. NW, Wash., DC 20418; 4,000+; http://www.nas.edu
Science Teachers Assn., Natl. (1944), 1840 Wilson Blvd., Arlington, VA 22201; 53,000; http://www.nsta.org
Science Writers, Natl. Assn. of (1934), P.O. Box 294, Greenlawn, NY 11740; 1,801; http://www.nasw.org
Scrabble® Assn., Natl. (1980), P.O. Box 700, 120 Front St., Greenport, NY 11944; 10,000+; http://www.scrabble.com
Screen Actors Guild (1933), 5757 Wilshire Blvd., Los Angeles, CA 90036; 90,000; http://www.sag.com
Screenprinting & Graphic Imaging Assn., The Intl. (1948), 10015 Main St., Fairfax, VA 22031; 3,400 cos.; http://www.sgia.org
Screen Printing Technical Foundation (1985), 10015 Main St., Fairfax, VA 22031; 3,300.
Sculpture Soc., Natl. (1893), 1177 Ave. of the Americas, New York, NY 10036; 270.
Seamen's Service, United (1942), One World Trade Center, Ste. 2161, New York, NY 10048.
2d Air Division Assn. (1947), 06-410 Delaire Landing Rd., Philadelphia, PA 19114; 7,852.
Secondary School Principals, Natl. Assn. of (1916), 1904 Association Dr., Reston, VA 20191; 41,000; http://www.nassp.org
Secretaries Intl.®, Professional/The Assn. for Office Professionals™ (1942), 10502 N.W. Ambassador Dr., Kansas City, MO 64152; 27,000; http://www.psi.org
Secular Humanism, Council for (1980), P.O. Box 664, Amherst, NY 14226; 4,000; http://www.secularhumanism.org
Securities Industry Assn. (1972), 120 Broadway, New York, NY 10271; 715 firms.
Separation of Church & State, Americans United for (1947), 1816 Jefferson Place NW, Wash., DC 20036; 50,000; http://www.au.org
Sertoma International (1912), 1912 E. Meyer Blvd., Kansas City, MO 64132; 24,992; http://www.sertoma.org
Sexuality Information & Education Council of the U.S. (SIECUS) (1964), 130 W. 42d St., Ste. 350, New York, NY 10036; http://www.siecus.org
Sharkhunters (1983), P.O. Box 1539, Hernando, FL 34442; 5,500; http://www.thegrid.net/sharkhunters
Shipbuilders Council of America (1921), 901 Washington St., Ste. 204, Alexandria, VA 22314; 50 organizations; http://www.shipbuilders.org
Ships in Bottles Assn. of America (1983), P.O. Box 180550, Coronado, CA 92178; 250.
Shrine of North America, The (1872), 2900 N. Rocky Point Dr., Tampa, FL 33607; approx 600,000; http://shrinershq.org
Sierra Club (1892), 85 2d St., 2d Fl., San Francisco, CA 94105; 550,000; http://www.sierraclub.org
Sigma Beta Delta (1994), P.O. Box 46935, St. Louis, MO 63146; 9,000; http://www.sigmabetadelta.org
Skeet Shooting Assn., Natl. (1946), P.O. Box 680007, San Antonio, TX 78268; 15,800; http://nssa-nsca.com/nssa/index.html
Ski Team Foundation, U.S. (1964), 1500 Kearns Blvd., Park City, UT 84060; 60,000.
Small Business United, Natl. (1937), 1156 15th St. NW, Ste. 1100, Wash., DC 20005; 65,000+; http://www.nsbu.org
Social Sciences, Natl. Institute of (1865), 1192 Park Ave., 15B, New York, NY 10128; 315.
Social Work Education, Council on (1952), 1600 Duke St., Alexandria, VA 22314; 4,000; http://www.cswe.org
Sociological Assn., American (1905), 1722 N St. NW, Wash., DC 20036; 13,000; http://www.asanet.org
Softball Assn. of America, Amateur (1933), 2801 N.E. 50th St., Oklahoma City, OK 73111; 4.5 mil; http://www.softball.org
Soft Drink Assn., Natl. (1921), 1101 16th St. NW, Wash., DC 20036; 1,700; http://www.nsda.org
Soil Science Society of America (1936), 677 S. Segoe Rd., Madison, WI 53711; 5,800; http://www.soils.org
Soil & Water Conservation Society of America (1949), 7515 N.E. Ankeny Rd., Ankeny, IA 50021; 10,000.
Soldiers', Sailors', Marines' and Airmen's Club (1919), 283 Lexington Avenue, New York, NY 10016; 2,000; http://www.ssmacluborg
Songwriters Guild of America (1933), 1500 Harbor Blvd., Weehawken, NJ 07087; 5,000+; http://www.gibson.com/fog/sga/new/body.htm
Sons of the American Legion (1932), Box 1055, Indianapolis, IN 46206; 161,376.
Sons of the American Revolution, Natl. Society of (1889), 1000 S. Fourth St., Louisville, KY 40203; 27,000; http://www.sar.org
Sons of Confederate Veterans (1896), 740 Mooresville Pike, Columbia, TN 38401; 26,000; http://www.scv.org
Sons of the Desert (1965), P.O. Box 8341, Universal City, CA 91608; 5,000-10,000.
Sons of Italy in America, Order of (1905), 219 E St. NE, Wash. DC 20002; 500,000; http://www.osia.org
Sons of Norway (1895), 1455 W. Lake St., Minneapolis, MN 55408; 68,925; http://www.sofn.com
Sons of the Republic of Texas, The (1934), 1717 8th St., Bay City, TX 77414; 4,000; http://www.tgn.net/~srttexas
Soroptimist Intl. of the Americas (1921), Two Penn Center Plaza, Ste. 1000, Philadelphia, PA 19102; 50,000; http://www.soroptimist.org
Southern Christian Leadership Conference (1957), 334 Auburn Ave. NE, Atlanta, GA 30303; 1 mil.
Space Education Assn., U.S. (1973), 231 School Lane, Rheems, PA 17570; 1,000.
Space Society, Natl. (1974), 600 Pennsylvania Ave SE, Ste. 201, Wash., DC 20003; 25,000; http://www.nss.org
Speech-Language-Hearing Assn., American (1925), 10801 Rockville Pike, Rockville, MD 20852; 93,000; http://www.asha.org
Speedskating Union of the U.S., Amateur (1927), 1033 Shady Lane, Glen Ellyn, IL 60137; 3,000.
Speleological Society, Natl. (1941), 2813 Cave Ave., Huntsville, AL 35810; 11,642; http://www.caves.org

Spiritual Awareness and Holistic Principles of Body, Mind and Spirit, Inc., Assn. for (1986), P.O. Box 41, Clifton Hill, MO 65244; 5,500.
Sports Car Club of America (1944), 9033 E. Eastern Pl., Englewood, CO 80112; 50,000+; http://www.scca.org
Sportscasters Assn., The American (1980), 5 Beekman St., New York, NY 10038; 500.
State & Local History, American Assn. for (1944), 530 Church St., Ste. 600, Nashville, TN 37219; 5,000; http://www.aaslh.org
State Governments, Council of (1933), P.O. Box 11910, Lexington, KY 40517; 50 states, 4 territories; http://www.csg.org
Statistical Assn., American (1839), 1429 Duke St., Alexandria, VA 22314; 18,000; http://www.amstat.org
Steamship Historical Society of America, Inc. (1935), 300 Ray Dr., Ste. 4, Providence, RI 02906; 3,500; http://www.sshsa.org
Steel Construction, American Institute of (1921), 1 E. Wacker Dr., Ste. 3100, Chicago, IL 60601; 2,770; http://www.aisc.org
Stock Exchange, American (1911), 86 Trinity Pl., New York, NY 10006; 871; http://www.amex.com, cgi-bin/WebObjects/AmexWeb
Stock Exchange, New York (1792), 11 Wall St., New York, NY 10005; http://www.nyse.com
Stock Exchange, Philadelphia (1790), 1900 Market St., Philadelphia, PA 19103; 504; http://www.phlx.com
Student Councils, Natl. Assn. of (1931), 1904 Association Dr., Reston, VA 22091; 9,000 schools.
Stuttering Project, Natl. (1977), 5100 E. LaPalma Ave., #208, Anaheim Hills, CA 92807; 2,800; http://www.nspstutter.org
Submarine Veterans of WWII, U.S.(1955), 317 N. Palm Ave., Frostproof, FL 33843; 8,250.
SIDs Alliance (1987), 1314 Bedford Ave., Ste. 210, Baltimore, MD 21208; http://www.sidsalliance.org
Surgeons, American College of (1913), 633 N. Saint Clair St., Chicago, IL 60611; 56,000; http://www.face.org
Symphony Orchestra League, American (1942), 1156 Fifteenth St. NW, Ste. 800, Wash., DC 20005; 840.

Table Tennis Assn., U.S. (1933), One Olympic Plaza, Colorado Springs, CO 80909; 8,500; http://www.usatt.org
Tailhook Assn. (1956), 9696 Business Park Ave., P.O. Box 26700, San Diego, CA 92131; 11,800.
Tall Buildings and Urban Habitat, Council on (1969), Lehigh Univ., 11 E. Packer Ave., Bethlehem, PA 18015; 1,700; http://www.lehigh.edu/ctbuh/
Tau Beta Pi Association (1885), P.O. Box 2697, Knoxville, TN 37901; 375,000; http://www.tbp.org
Tax Administrators, Federation of (1937), 444 N. Capitol St. NW, Ste. 348, Wash., DC 20001; http://www.taxadmin.org
Tax Foundation, Inc. (1937), 1250 H St. NW, Ste. 750, Wash., DC 20005; 50 U.S. states; http://www.taxfoundation.org
Taxpayers Union, Natl. (1969), 108 N. Alfred St., Alexandria, VA 22314; 300,000; http://www.ntu.org
Tea Assn. of the U.S.A., Inc. (1899), 420 Lexington Ave., New York, NY 10170; 120 corps.
Teachers of English, Natl. Council of (1911), 1111 W. Kenyon Rd., Urbana, IL 61801; 68,000; http://www.ncte.org
Teachers of English to Speakers of Other Languages (1966), 1600 Cameron St., Ste. 300, Alexandria, VA 22314; 17,432; http://www.tesol.edu
Teachers of French, American Assn. of (1927), Mailcode 4510, Southern Illinois University, Carbondale, IL 62901; 9,550; http://aatf.utsa.edu
Teachers of German, Inc., American Assn. of (AATG) (1926), 112 Haddontowne Ct. #104, Cherry Hill, NJ 08034; 7,000; http://www.aatg.org
Teachers of Mathematics, Natl. Council of (1920), 1906 Association Dr., Reston, VA 22091; 120,000; http://www.nctm.org
Teachers of Singing, Natl. Assn. of (1944), 2800 Univ. Blvd. N., J.U. Sta., Jacksonville, FL 32211; 5,574; http://www.nats.org
Teachers of Spanish & Portuguese, American Assn. of (1917), 8 Frasier Hall, Univ. of Northern Colorado, Greeley, CO 80939; 13,000.
Technology Honor Society, American (ATHS) (1995), 1904 Association Dr., Reston, VA 20191; 125 chapts; http://www.technology.org
Telephone Pioneer Assn., Independent (1920), 1401 H Street NW, Ste. 600, Wash., DC 20005.
Television Arts & Sciences, Natl. Academy of (1947), 111 W. 57th St., Ste. 1020, New York, NY 10019; 12,000; http://www.emmyonline.org
Testing & Materials, American Society for (1898), 100 Barr Harbor Dr., West Conshohocken, PA 19428; 35,000; http://www.astm.org
Tetra Society of North America (1992), Box 27, Ste. A-304, Plaza of Nations, 770 Pacific Blvd. S., Vancouver, BC V6B 5E7; 500; http://orcn.ahs.uwo.ca/TETRA
Textile Manufacturers Institute, American (1949), 1130 Connecticut Ave. NW, Ste 1200, Wash., DC 20036; 114 cos.; http://www.atmi.org
Theodore Roosevelt Assn. (1920), P.O. Box 719, Oyster Bay, NY 11771; 1,600.
Theological Library Assn., American (1947), 820 Church St., Ste. 300, Evanston, IL 60201; 188 libraries; http://www.atla.com
Theological Schools in the U.S. and Canada, The Assn. of (1918), 10 Summit Park Dr., Pittsburgh, PA 15275; 229; http://www.ats.edu
Theosophical Society in America, The (1875), P.O. Box 270, St., Wheaton, IL 60189; 4,000; http://www.theosophical.org
Therapy Dogs International, Inc. (1976), 88 Bartley Rd., Flanders, NJ 07836; 5,000+; http://www.tdi-dog.org
Thoreau Society, Inc. (1941), 44 Baker Farm, Lincoln, MA 01773; 1,500.
Thoroughbred Racing Assns. (1942), 420 Fair Hill Dr., Ste. 1, Elkton, MD 21921; 41 racing associations; http://www.traofna.com
Tin Can Sailors (1976), P.O. Box 100, Somerset, MA 02726; 18,000; http://www.destroyers.org
Titanic Historical Society, Inc. (1963), 208 Main St., P.O. Box 51053, Indian Orchard, MA 01151; 5,110; http://www.titanic1.org
Toastmasters Intl. (1924), 23182 Arroyo Vista, Rancho Santa Margarite, CA 92688; 170,000; http://www.toastmasters.org
Topical Assn., American (1949), P.O. Box 65749, Tucson, AZ 85728; approx. 7,000.
Toy Manufacturers of America (1916), 200 Fifth Ave., New York, NY 10010; 265; http://www.toy~tma.com
Totally Useless Skills, Institute of (1987), P.O. Box 181, Temple, NH 03084; 757+.
Trade Assn., Intl. (1990), 8383 E. Evans Rd., Scottsdale, AZ 85260; 1,000.
Trademark Assn., Intl. (1878), 1133 Avenue of the Americas, New York, NY 10036; 3,500; http://www.inta.org
Trail Assn., North Country (1980), 49 Monroe Center NW, Ste. 200B, Grand Rapids, MI 49503; 750; http://people.delphi.com/wesboyd/ncnst.htm
Training in Communication, Intl. (1938), 2519 Woodland Dr., Anaheim, CA 92801; 15,000
Transit Assn., American Public (1974), 1201 New York Ave. NW, Wash., DC 20005; 1,100 organizations; http://www.apta.com
Translators Assn., American (1959), 1800 Diagonal Rd., Ste. 220, Alexandria, VA 22314; 6,500; http://www.atanet.org
Transportation Engineers, Inst. of (1930), 525 School St. SW, Ste. 410, Wash., DC 20024; 12,800; http://www.ite.org
Trapshooting Assn. of America, Amateur (1923), 601 W. National Rd., Vandalia, OH 45377; 84,342; http://www.shootata.com
Travel Agents, American Society of (1931), 1101 King St., Ste. 200, Alexandria, VA 22314; 28,500; http://www.astanet.com
Travelers Protective Assn. of America (1890), 3755 Lindell Blvd., St. Louis, MO 63108; 137,979.
Treasury Management Assn. (1979), 7315 Wisconsin Ave., Ste. 600W, Bethesda, MD 20814; 10,000; http://www.tma-net.org
Trilateral Commission (1973), 345 E. 46th St., New York, NY 10017; 365; http://www.trilateral.org
Truck Historical Soc., American (1972), 300 Office Park Dr., Ste. 120, Birmingham, AL 35223; 19,800; http://www.aths.org
Trucking Assns., American (1933), 2200 Mill Rd., Alexandria, VA 22314; 4,000 cos.; http://www.truckline.com
T. S. Eliot Society (1980), 5007 Waterman Blvd., St. Louis, MO 63108; 175.
Tuberous Sclerosis Assn., Natl. (1974), 8181 Professional Place, Ste. 110, Landover, MD 20785; 4,000; http://www.ntsa.org

UFO Society of America (1997), 10799 Sherman Grove Ave, #18, Sunland, CA 91040; 520.
UFOs, Natl. Investigation Committee on (1967) P.O. Box 73, Van Nuys, CA 91408; 1,000.
UNICEF, U.S. Committee for (1947), 333 E. 38th St., New York, NY 10016; http://www.unicefusa.org
Underwriters, Natl. Assn. of Life (1890), 1922 F St. NW, Wash., DC 20006; 143,000.
Underwriters (CPCU), Soc. of Chartered Property and Casualty (1944), Kahler Hall, 720 Providence Rd., Malvern, PA 19355; 28,000.
Uniformed Services, Natl. Assn. for (1968), 5535 Hempstead Way, Springfield, VA 22151; 160,000; http://www.naus.org

United Nations Assn. of the U.S.A. (1923, as League of Nations Assn.; 1945), 801 2nd Ave., New York, NY 10017; 25,000; http://www.unausa.org
United Press Intl. (1907), 1400 Eye St. NW, Wash., DC 20005; http://www.upi.com/homepage.html
United Order True Sisters, Inc., (1846), 100 State St., Albany, NY 12207; 3,000.
United Way of America (1932), 701 N. Fairfax St., Alexandria, VA 22314; 1,353; http://www.unitedway.org
Universities, Assn. of American (1900), 1200 New York Ave., NW, Ste. 550, Wash., DC 20005; 62 institutions; http://www.tulane.edu/~aau
University Continuing Education Assn., (1915), One Dupont Circle, Ste. 615, Wash., DC 20036; 420 institutions; http://www.nucea.edu
University Foundation, Intl. (1973), 1301 S. Noland Rd., Independence, MO 64055; 62,311.
University Women, American Assn. of (1881), 1111 16th St. NW, Wash., DC 20036; 150,000; http://www.aauw.org
Urban League, Natl. (1910), 500 E. 62d St., New York, NY 10020; http://www.nul.org
USENIX Association (1975), 2560 Ninth Street, Ste. 215, Berkeley, CA 94710; 7,024; http://www.usenix.org
USO, Inc. (United Service Organizations) (1941), Washington Navy Yard, 901 M St. SE, Bldg. 198, Wash., DC 20374; http://www.uso.org
USS *Forrestal* CVA/CV/AVT-59 Assn., Inc. (1991), 300 Cassady Ave., Virginia Beach, VA 23452; 1,409; http://www.erols.com/routts/cv59.htm
Utility Commissioners, Natl. Assn. of Regulatory (NARUC) (1889), 1100 Pennsylvania Ave. NW, Ste. 603, Wash., DC 20004; 100 agencies; http://www.naruc.org

Vampire Research Center (1972), P.O. Box 5442, Babylon, NY 11707; 700.
Variety Clubs Intl. (1928), 350 5th Ave., Ste. 1119, New York, NY 10018; 15,000.
Ventriloquists, North American Assn. of (1944), P.O. Box 420, Littleton, CO 80160; 1,756.
Veterans of Foreign Wars of the U.S. (1899), 406 W. 34th St., Kansas City, MO 64111; http:/www.vfw.org
Veterans of Foreign Wars of the U.S, Ladies Auxiliary to the (1914), 406 W. 34th St., Kansas City, MO 64111; 744,818; http://www.ladiesauvfw.com
Veterans of Underage Military Service (1991), 100 Village Lane, Philadelphia, PA 19154; 1,138.
Veterans of the Vietnam War, Inc. (1980), 760 Jumper Rd., Wilkes-Barre, PA 18702; 15,000; http://www.vvnw.org/vvnw/
Veterans of World War I of the USA, Inc. (1958), P.O. Box 8027, Alexandria, VA 22306; 7,900.
Veterinary Medical Assn., American (1863), 1931 N. Meacham Rd., Schaumburg, IL 60173; 59,263; http://www.avma.org
Victorian Society in America (1966), 219 S. Sixth St., Philadelphia, PA 19106; http://www.libertynet.org/vicsoc
Viewers for Quality Television, Inc. (1987), P.O. Box 195, Fairfax Station, VA 22039; 3,000; http://www.vqt.com
Virgil Fox Society (1977), 88 Chestnut St., Brooklyn, NY 11208; 400.
Volleyball, U.S.A. (1928), 3595 E. Fountain Blvd., Ste. I-2, Colorado Springs, CO 80910; 110,000.

War Mothers, American (1925), 2615 Woodley Pl. NW, Wash., DC 20008; approx. 1,000.
Watch & Clock Collectors, Natl. Assn. of (1943), 514 Poplar St., Columbia, PA 17512; 35,000+; http://www.nawcc.org
Watercolor Society, American (1866), 47 5th Ave., New York, NY 10003; 500+; http://www.watercolor-online.com/aws
Water Environment Federation (1928), 601 Wythe St., Alexandria, VA 22314; 40,000; http://www.wef.org
Water Pollution Control Administration, Assn. of State and Interstate (1961), 750 First St. NE, Ste. 910, Wash., DC 20002; 85.
Water Pollution Control Federation (1928), 601 Wythe St., Alexandria, VA 22314; 32,000.
Water Ski Assn., American (1939), 799 Overlook Dr. SE, Winter Haven, FL 33830; 30,000.
Water Works Assn., American (1881), 6666 W. Quincy Ave., Denver, CO 80235; 55,000; http://www.awwa.org
Welding Society, American (1919), 550 N.W. LeJeune Rd., Miami, FL 33126; 47,500; http://www.amweld.org
Wheelchair Sports, USA (1956), 3595 E. Fountain Blvd., Ste. L-1, Colorado Springs, CO 80910; 4,600.
Widows, Society of Military (1968), 5535 Hempstead Way, Springfield, VA 22151; 2,000.
Wilderness Institute, Natl. (1989), P.O. Box 25766, Wash., DC 20007; http://www.nwi.org/
Wildlife, Defenders of (1947), 1244 19th St. NW, Wash., DC 20036; 80,000; http://www.defenders.org
Wildlife Federation, Natl. (1936), 1400 16th St. NW, Wash., DC 20036; 4.7 mil; http://www.nwf.org
Wildlife Management Institute (1911), 1101 14th St. NW, Ste. 801, Wash., DC 20005; 250; http://www.wildlifemgt.org/wmi
William Penn Assn. (1886), 709 Brighton Rd., Pittsburgh, PA 15233; 90,000.
Wireless Pioneers, The Society of (1968), P.O. Box 86, Geyserville, CA 95441; 1,500; http://web.mountain.net/~carto/sowp001.htm
Wizard of Oz Club, Inc., The Intl. (1957), P.O. Box 10117, Berkeley, CA 94709; 2,000; http://www.ozclub.org/~iwoc/
Women, Natl. Organization for (NOW) (1966), 1000 16th St. NW, Ste. 700, Wash., DC 20036; 250,000; http://www.now.org
Women Artists Inc., Natl. Assn. of (1889), 41 Union Sq. W, #906, New York, NY 10003; 850.
Women in Communications, Association for (1909 as Theta Sigma Phi), 1244 Ritchie Hwy., Ste. 6, Arnold, MD 21012; 7,500; http://www.womcom.org
Women Engineers, Society of (1950), 120 Wall St., 11th Fl., New York, NY 10005; 16,500; http://www.swe.org
Women in Radio and TV, Inc., American (1950), 1650 Tyson's Blvd., Ste. 200, McLean, VA 22102; 1,500.
Women of the U.S., Inc., Natl. Council of (1888), 777 UN Plaza, 7th Fl., New York, NY 10017; 500 members, 33 affiliate org.
Women Strike for Peace (1961), 110 Maryland Ave. NE, Ste. 102, Wash., DC 20002; 5,000.
Women Voters of the U.S., League of (1920), 1730 M St. NW, Wash., DC 20036; 100,000; http://www.lwv.org
Women World War Veterans (1919), 237 Madison Ave., New York, NY 10016; 35,000.
Women's Army Corps Veterans Assn. (1984), P.O. Box 5577, Ft. McClellan, AL 36205; 4,000.
Women's Christian Temperance Union, Natl. (1874), 1730 Chicago Ave., Evanston, IL 60201; 12,594.
Women's Clubs, General Federation of (1890), 1734 N St. NW, Wash., DC, 20036; 300,000 U.S; http://www.gfwc.org
Women's Clubs, Natl. Fed. of Business & Prof. (1919), 2012 Massachusetts Ave. NW, Wash., DC 20036; 70,000.
Women's Intl. League for Peace & Freedom (1915), 1213 Race St., Philadelphia, PA 19107; 8,000.
Women's Legal Defense Fund (1971), 1875 Connecticut Ave. NW, Ste. 710, Wash., DC 20009; 2,500.
Woodmen of America, Modern (1883), 1701 1st Ave., Rock Island, IL 61201; 375,000; http://www.modern-woodmen.org
Woodmen of the World Life Insurance Soc. (1890), 1700 Farnam St., Omaha, NE 68102; 850,000.
Workmen's Circle (1900), 45 E. 33d St., New York, NY 10016; 35,000.
World Council of Churches, U.S. Conference for the (1948), 475 Riverside Drive, New York, NY 10115; 317 denominations.
World Federalist Assn. (1975), 418 7th St. SE, Wash., DC 20003; 9,000; http://www.wfa.org
World Future Society (1966), 7910 Woodmont Ave., Ste. 450, Bethesda, MD 20814; 30,000; http://www.wfs.org/wfs
World Learning Inc. (1932), Kipling Rd., P.O. Box 676, Brattleboro, VT 05153; 2,500; http://www.worldlearning.org
World Wildlife Fund (1961), 1250 24th St. NW, Wash., DC 20037; 1.25 mil; http://www.worldwildlife.org
World's Fair Collectors Soc., Inc. (1968), P.O. Box 20806, Sarasota, FL 34276; 550; http://members.aol.com/bbqprod/wfcs.html
Writers Guild of America, West (1933), 7000 W. Third St., Los Angeles, CA 90048; 8,500; http://www.wga.org

Yachting Assn., Southern California (1921), 5855 Naples Plaza, Ste. 211, Long Beach, CA 90803; 90 clubs & orgs., 21,500 families; http://www.scya.org
YMCA (Young Men's Christian Assns.) of the U.S.A. (1864 in IL, 1883 in NY,), 101 N. Wacker Dr., Chicago, IL 60606; 16 mil.; http://www.ymca.net
Young America's Foundation (1969), 110 Elden St., Herndon, VA 22170.
Young Women's Christian Assn. of the U.S.A. (1906), Empire State Bldg., Suite 301, 350 Fifth Ave., New York, NY 10018; http://www.ywca.org

Zero Population Growth (1968), 1400 16th St. NW, Ste. 320, Wash., DC 20036; 55,000+; http://www.zpg.org
Zionist Organization of America (1897), 4 E. 34th St., New York, NY 10016; 110,000; http://www.zoa.org
Zoo and Aquarium Assn., American (1924), 7970-D Old Georgetown Rd., Bethesda, MD 20814; 182 zoos & aquariums, 7,000 individuals; http://www.aza.org

ASTRONOMY AND CALENDAR

Edited by Dr. Lee T. Shapiro, Planetarium Director
Morehead Planetarium, University of North Carolina at Chapel Hill

Celestial Events Summary, 1999

A series of lunar occultations of both Neptune and Uranus begins in Apr., while in Oct. an ongoing series of lunar occultations of Regulus comes to an end. A good year for meteor showers, the Moon is a day or so before waxing quarter phase for the Lyrids near Apr. 21-22, just past new phase for the Perseids near Aug. 11-12, just past waxing quarter phase for the Leonids near Nov. 16-17, and a few days before waxing quarter for the Geminids near Dec. 13-14. Meteor showers are generally better viewed after midnight with the Geminids an annual exception, good most of the night. Try to view the Leonids in 1999, and catch a possible meteor storm.

At the start of the year Jupiter and Saturn are high in the evening sky, with Mars the only noticeable planet in the morning sky. In late Feb., Venus joins Jupiter and Saturn for interesting groupings. Jupiter and Saturn, close together throughout the year, disappear from the evening sky in Mar., reappearing in the morning sky in May, staying up longer each night until late Oct. when both planets are visible all night long. Venus stays bright in the early evening sky from early in the year until late July, then shows up in the early morning sky from Sept. through the end of the year. Mars rises about the middle of the night at the beginning of the year, rising early until late Apr. when it is up all night long. Mars stays visible in the night sky throughout the year, though by year's end it is low in the SW sky. Mercury as always switches back and forth between the morning and evening sky, never truly easily visible at any time. The best time for Mercury in 1999 is around the end of Nov. On Nov. 15, late in the afternoon, Mercury transits the Sun, as last occurred in 1993. Transits, like solar eclipses, involve the Sun, and one must be very careful to not look directly at the Sun because of danger of eye damage.

Most months there are pretty views of Venus (2d-brightest object in the night sky) with a crescent Moon (either waxing or waning). On Feb. 18 look for the Moon, Venus, and Jupiter low in the West about 1/2 hr after sunset. Near the end of Jan. watch for Venus, Jupiter, and Saturn lined up in the evening sky. Although progress is not always steady, Jupiter is slowly catching up with Saturn all year; however, it does not achieve conjunction until mid-2000.

Astronomical Positions Defined

Two celestial bodies are in **conjunction** when they are due N and S of each other, either in **Right Ascension** (with respect to the N celestial pole) or in **Celestial Longitude** (with respect to the N ecliptic pole). If the bodies are seen near each other, they will rise and set at nearly the same time. For the inner planets—Mercury and Venus—**inferior conjunction** occurs when the planets pass between Earth and the Sun, while **superior conjunction** occurs when either Mercury or Venus is on the far side of the Sun. They are in **opposition** when their Right Ascensions differ by exactly 12 hours, or when their Celestial Longitudes differ by 180°. One of the 2 objects in opposition will rise while the other is setting. **Quadrature** refers to the arrangement where the coordinates of 2 bodies differ by exactly 90°. These terms may refer to the relative positions of any 2 bodies as seen from Earth, but one of the bodies is so frequently the Sun that mention of the Sun is omitted in this case; otherwise, both bodies are named. When objects are in conjunction, the alignment is not perfect, and one is usually passing above or below the other. The geocentric angular separation between the Sun and an object is termed **elongation**. Elongation is limited only for Mercury and Venus; the greatest elongation for each of these bodies is noted in the appropriate table and is approximately the time for longest observation. The term **perihelion** means point in an orbit that is nearest to the Sun, and **aphelion**, the point farthest from Earth. The term **perigee** means point in an orbit that is nearest Earth, **apogee** point that is farthest from Earth. An **occultation** of a planet or a star is an **eclipse** of it by some other body, usually the Moon.

Celestial Events Highlights, 1999

(Coordinated Universal Time, or UTC—the standard time of the prime meridian)

January

Mercury, very low in the SE at sunrise, moves closer to the Sun and unsightable.

Venus, close to the Sun at the beginning of the month, becomes clearly visible after sunset by end of the month. Look for it paired beneath waxing crescent Moon on the 19th, half an hour after sunset; enters Capricornus on the 4th and Aquarius on the 26th.

Mars is in the S before sunrise; watch for the grouping with the Moon and Spica on the 8th and 9th.

Jupiter, in the S at dusk at start of month, is low in the WSW by month's end, entering Pisces on the 15th.

Saturn is in the S at dusk; by the end of the month sits in the WSW highest of a triple stack of planets with Venus lowest and Jupiter in between.

Moon passes Regulus on the 5th, Mars on the 9th, Venus on the 19th, Jupiter on the 21st, Saturn on the 24th, and occults Aldebaran on the 27th.

Jan. 1—Pluto already in Ophiuchus stays there all year; Neptune and Uranus, already in Capricornus, stay there all year.

Jan. 2—Mercury at aphelion.

Jan. 3—Earth at perihelion, 91.4 mil mi from the Sun.

Jan. 4—Venus enters Capricornus.

Jan. 5—Venus 1.7° S of Neptune; Moon 0.2° N of star Regulus in Leo.

Jan. 8—Mars 4° N of star Spica in Virgo.

Jan. 9—Moon 3° N of Mars.

Jan. 13—Venus 0.9° S of Uranus.

Jan. 15—Jupiter enters Pisces.

Jan. 19—Moon 2° N of Venus.

Jan. 20—Sun enters Capricornus

Jan. 21—Moon 1.8° S of Jupiter.

Jan. 22—Neptune in conjunction with the Sun.

Jan. 24—Moon 2° S of Saturn.

Jan. 26—Venus enters Aquarius.

Jan. 27—Moon 0.5° N of star Aldebaran in Taurus occults Aldebaran (visible in N America).

Jan. 31—Penumbral lunar eclipse, hardly noticeable; see details under Eclipses.

February

Mercury, still close to the Sun, at superior conjunction on the 4th, begins to emerge from the Sun's glare by the end of the month in the early evening sky.

Venus, brilliant but low in the W, enters Pisces on the 17th, makes a pretty triple with the thin waxing crescent Moon and Jupiter on the 18th, and passes through Cetus on the 27th and 28th.

Mars, still the only prominent planet in the morning sky, is seen in the S at dawn, entering Libra on the 15th.

Jupiter getting lower in the evening sky makes a very close pair with Venus on the 23d.

Saturn getting lower in the sky in the early evening, is getting closer to Venus and Jupiter. On the 19th and the 20th see a double-double with Saturn/Moon and Jupiter/Venus pairs in the W.

Moon occults Regulus on the 2d, passes Mars on the 7th, Neptune on the 14th, produces an annular solar eclipse on the 16th, then passes Venus and Jupiter on the 18th and Saturn on the 20th.

Feb. 2—Moon 0.3° N of Regulus occults Regulus (visible in N America); Uranus in conjunction with Sun.

Feb. 4—Mercury in superior conjunction, passing beyond the Sun.

Feb. 7—Moon 3° N of Mars.

Feb. 14—Moon 1.5° N of Neptune.

Feb. 15—Mars enters Libra; Mercury at perihelion.

Feb. 16—Annular solar eclipse; see details under eclipses. Sun enters Aquarius.

Feb. 17—Venus enters Pisces.

Feb. 18—Moon 1.8° S of Venus and 2° S of Jupiter.

Feb. 20—Moon 3° S of Saturn.

Feb. 23—Moon 0.4° N of Aldebaran occults Aldebaran; Venus 0.1° N of Jupiter.

Feb. 27—Venus enters Cetus.

Feb. 28—Venus enters Pisces.

March

Mercury low in the W after sunset, begins retrograde motion on the 9th and retreats back into the Sun's glare by mid-month, passing inferior conjunction on the 19th.

Venus, getting lower in the W, still bright, enters Aries on the 17th, and triples with thin waxing crescent Moon and Saturn on the 20th.

Mars, up for a good part of the night, is getting lower in SW at dawn, begins retrograde motion on the 18th.

Jupiter disappears early in Mar. into glare of the setting Sun, entering Cetus on the 14th, Pisces on the 24th.

Saturn gets lower in the W in the early evening sky, enters Aries on the 30th.

Moon passes Mars on the 7th, Neptune on the 13th, Uranus on the 14th, Jupiter on the 18th, Venus and Saturn on the 20th, and occults Aldebaran on the 22d.

Mar. 1—Moon 0.2° N of Regulus occults Regulus.

Mar. 3—Mercury at greatest eastern elongation of 18° (E of Sun and setting after Sun).

Mar. 7—Moon 3° N of Mars.

Mar. 9—Mercury stationary, begins retrograde motion.

Mar. 12—Sun enters Pisces.

Mar. 13—Moon 1.4° N of Neptune.

Mar. 14—Moon 1.3° N of Uranus; Jupiter enters Cetus.

Mar. 15—Pluto stationary, begins retrograde motion.

Mar. 17—Venus enters Aries.

Mar. 18—Mars stationary, begins retrograde motion; Moon 3° S of Jupiter.

Mar. 19—Mercury at inferior conjunction passing between Earth and Sun.

Mar. 20—Moon 5° S of Venus and 3° S of Saturn; Venus 3° N of Saturn; Vernal Equinox at 8:46 PM EST (1:46 UTC, Mar. 21), spring begins in the northern hemisphere, autumn in the southern hemisphere.

Mar. 22—Moon 0.6° N of Aldebaran occults Aldebaran (visible in N America); Venus at aphelion.

Mar. 24—Jupiter enters Pisces.

Mar. 28—Moon 0.3° N of Regulus occults Regulus.

Mar. 30—Saturn enters Aries and stays there for the rest of the year; Mercury at aphelion.

April

Mercury, very low in the E before sunrise, resumes direct motion on the 1st.

Venus, very low in the W after sunset, enters Taurus on the 8th, pairs with the Moon on the 18th, and passes Aldebaran on the 21st.

Mars, up all night now, enters Virgo on the 16th and is at opposition on the 24th.

Jupiter, still lost in the glare of the Sun, begins to emerge into the morning sky near the end of the month.

Saturn is lost in the glare of the Sun and is in conjunction with the Sun on the 27th.

Moon passes Mars on the 3d, occults Neptune on the 10th, Uranus on the 11th, and Mercury on the 14th, passes Venus on the 18th, occults Aldebaran on the 19th and Regulus on the 24th, and passes Mars again on the 29th.

Apr. 1—Jupiter in conjunction with Sun; Mercury stationary, resumes direct motion.

Apr. 3—Moon 3° N of Mars.

Apr. 8—Venus enters Taurus.

Apr. 10—Moon 1.1° N of Neptune occults Neptune.

Apr. 11—Moon 1.0° N of Uranus occults Uranus.

Apr. 14—Moon 1.1° S of Mercury occults Mercury.

Apr. 16—Mercury at greatest western elongation of 28° (W of Sun and rising before Sun); Mars enters Virgo.

Apr. 18—Moon 7° S of Venus.

Apr. 19—Moon 0.7° N of Aldebaran occults Aldebaran (visible in N America); Sun enters Aries.

Apr. 21—Venus 7° N of Aldebaran.

Apr. 24—Mars at opposition; Moon 0.5° N of Regulus occults Regulus (visible in N America).

Apr. 27—Saturn in conjunction with Sun.

Apr. 29—Moon 4° N of Mars.

May

Mercury, very low in the E, is paired with Jupiter on the 1st and disappears in the glare of the Sun by mid-month, with superior conjunction on the 25th.

Venus, very low in the WNW after sunset, enters Gemini on the 8th and passes Pollux on the 30th.

Mars, now setting a couple of hours before sunrise, is closest to Earth on the 1st.

Jupiter, low in the E at dusk, is appearing higher in sky.

Saturn emerges from the glow of the Sun in the E as the month ends.

Moon occults Neptune on the 7th and Uranus on the 8th, passes Jupiter on the 13th, occults Aldebaran on the 16th, passes Venus on the 18th, occults Regulus on the 22d, and passes Mars on the 26th.

May 1—Mercury 1.7° S of Jupiter; Mars closest to Earth at 53.8 mil mi.

May 7—Neptune stationary, begins retrograde; Moon 0.9° N of Neptune occults Neptune (visible in N America).

May 8—Moon 0.7° N of Uranus occults Uranus (visible in N America); Venus enters Gemini.

May 13—Moon 4° S of Jupiter; Mercury 0.7° N of Saturn; Mercury at perihelion.

May 15—Sun enters Taurus.

May 16—Moon 0.9° N of Aldebaran occults Aldebaran (visible in N America).

May 18—Moon 6° S of Venus.

May 22—Moon 0.7° N of Regulus occults Regulus (visible in N America); Uranus stationary, begins retrograde.

May 25—Mercury at superior conjunction.

May 26—Moon 5° N of Mars.

May 30—Venus 4° S of star Pollux in Gemini.

May 31—Pluto at opposition.

June

Mercury returns to the evening sky in the WNW early in the evening and passes Pollux on the 21st.

Venus, low in the W after sunset, enters Cancer on the 3d and Leo on the 25th.

Mars, in the S at dusk, sets about the middle of the night, resumes direct motion on the 5th.

Jupiter, prominent in the morning sky, rises a couple of hours before sunrise; look for a triple with thin waning crescent Moon and Saturn on the 10th.

Saturn, not far from Jupiter in the morning sky, but lower and dimmer.

Moon occults Neptune on the 3d and Uranus on the 4th, passes Jupiter on the 10th, Saturn on the 11th, Mercury on the 15th, and Venus on the 17th, occults Regulus on the 18th, and passes Mars on the 22d.

June 3—Moon 0.7° N of Neptune occults Neptune; Venus enters Cancer.

June 4—Moon 0.5° N of Uranus occults Uranus.

June 5—Mars stationary, resumes direct motion.

June 10—Moon 4° S of Jupiter.

June 11—Moon 3° S of Saturn; Venus at greatest eastern elongation of 45°.

June 15—Moon 4° S of Mercury.

June 17—Moon 2° S of Venus.

June 18—Moon 1.0° N of Regulus occults Regulus.

June 21—Mercury 5° S of Pollux; Northern Solstice at 19:49 UTC (3:49 PM EDT), summer begins in the northern hemisphere, winter in the southern hemisphere.

June 22—Sun enters Gemini; Moon 6° N of Mars.

June 25—Venus enters Leo.

June 26—Mercury at aphelion.

June 28—Mercury at greatest eastern elongation of 26°.

July

Mercury leaves the evening sky back towards the Sun beginning retrograde on the 12th and passing inferior conjunction on the 26th.

Venus, at its brightest, still visible at dusk, passes Regulus on the 13th and begins retrograde on the 27th as it enters Sextans.

Mars low in the SW at dusk, sets about the middle of the night, enters Libra on the 25th.

Jupiter rises about midnight, high in the E at dawn, enters Aries on the 1st; look for a triple with crescent Moon and Saturn on the 8th.

Saturn rises about midnight, high in the E at dawn.

Moon occults Neptune on the 1st, Uranus on the 2d, passes Jupiter on the 7th, Saturn on the 8th, occults Aldebaran on the 10th, passes Mercury on the 14th, Mars on the 20th, occults Neptune again on the 28th the same night of a partial lunar eclipse, and occults Uranus on the 29th.

July 1—Jupiter enters Aries; Moon 0.6° N of Neptune occults Neptune.

July 2—Moon 0.4° N of Uranus occults Uranus.

July 6—Earth at aphelion, 94.5 mil mi from the Sun.

July 7—Moon 4° S of Jupiter.

July 8—Moon 3° S of Saturn.

July 10—Moon 0.8° N of Aldebaran occults Aldebaran (visible in N America).

July 12—Mercury stationary, begins retrograde.

July 13—Venus 1.5° S of Regulus.

July 14—Moon 3° N of Mercury.

July 15—Moon 1.1° N of Regulus occults Regulus; Venus at perihelion.

July 20—Moon 7° N of Mars.

July 21—Sun enters Cancer.

July 25—Mars enters Libra.

July 26—Neptune at opposition; Mercury at inferior conjunction.

July 27—Venus stationary, enters Sextans, and begins retrograde.

July 28—Moon 0.6° N of Neptune occults Neptune (visible in N America). Partial lunar eclipse; see details under eclipses.

July 29—Moon 0.5° N of Uranus occults Uranus (visible in N America).

August

Mercury resumes direct motion on the 5th, visible very low in the ENE about 1 hour before sunrise and passes Venus on the 26th.

Venus closest to Earth on the 20th, enters Hydra on the 21st, enters Leo on the 29th, by the end of the month very low in the E during dawn.

Mars very low in the SW at dusk.

Jupiter, drawing closer to Saturn, rises a few hours after sunset, begins retrograde on the 25th.

Saturn also rises a few hours after sunset, begins retrograde on the 30th.

Moon passes Saturn on the 5th, occults Aldebaran on the 6th and Mercury on the 10th, passes Mars on the 18th, occults Neptune on the 24th and Uranus on the 25th, and passes Jupiter on the 31st.

Aug. 4—Moon 4° S of Jupiter.

Aug. 5—Moon 3° S of Saturn; Mercury stationary, resumes direct motion.

Aug. 6—Moon 0.8° N of Aldebaran occults Aldebaran (visible in N America).

Aug. 7—Uranus at opposition.

Aug. 9—Mercury at perihelion.

Aug. 10—Moon 1.2° N of Mercury occults Mercury (visible in N America); Venus 8° S of Regulus.

Aug. 11—Sun enters Leo.

Aug. 14—Mercury at greatest western elongation of 19°.

Aug. 18—Moon 7° N of Mars.

Aug. 20—Venus at inferior conjunction, closest to Earth at 26.8 mil mi.

Aug. 21—Venus enters Hydra; Pluto stationary, resumes direct motion.

Aug. 24—Moon 0.7° N of Neptune occults Neptune.

Aug. 25—Jupiter stationary, begins retrograde; Moon 0.6° N of Uranus occults Uranus.

Aug. 26—Mercury 10° N of Venus.

Aug. 29—Venus enters Leo.

Aug. 30—Saturn stationary, begins retrograde.

Aug. 31—Moon 4° S of Jupiter.

September

Mercury passes superior conjunction on the 8th to begin to emerge from the glare of the Sun very low in the WSW during early dusk by the end of the month, passing Spica on the 30th.

Venus now visible in the early morning low in the E and again at its brightest, enters Cancer on the 1st, resumes direct motion on the 9th, and enters Leo on the 18th.

Mars hanging around in the early evening sky low in the SW, enters Scorpius on the 2d, enters Ophiuchus on the 15th, yet passes Antares (its "rival") on the 17th.

Jupiter, rising an hour or so after sunset, is up most of the night.

Saturn also rises an hour or so after sunset and is up most of the night.

Moon passes Venus on the 7th and Mars on the 16th, occults Neptune on the 20th and Uranus on the 21st, passes Jupiter on the 27th and Saturn on the 28th, and occults Aldebaran on the 30th.

Sept. 1—Moon 3° S of Saturn; Venus enters Cancer.

Sept. 2—Mars enters Scorpius; Moon 0.8° N of Aldebaran occults Aldebaran.

Sept. 7—Moon 8° N of Venus.

Sept. 8—Mercury in superior conjunction; Moon 1.1° N of Regulus occults Regulus.

Sept. 9—Venus stationary, resumes direct motion.

Sept. 11—Moon 0.9° S of minor planet Vesta occults Vesta.

Sept. 15—Mars enters Ophiuchus.

Sept. 16—Moon 7° N of Mars.

Sept. 17—Sun enters Virgo; Mars 3° N of Antares in Scorpius.

Sept. 18—Venus enters Leo.

Sept. 20—Moon 0.7° N of Neptune occults Neptune (visible in N America).

Sept. 21—Moon 0.6° N of Uranus occults Uranus.

Sept. 22—Mercury at aphelion.

Sept. 23—Autumnal Equinox at 11:31 UTC (7:31 AM EDT), autumn begins in the northern hemisphere, spring begins in the southern hemisphere.

Sept. 27—Moon 4° S of Jupiter.

Sept. 28—Moon 3° S of Saturn.

Sept. 30—Moon 1.0° N of Aldebaran occults Aldebaran (visible in N America); Mercury 1.7° N of Spica.

October

Mercury is very low in the SW in early dusk.

Venus is low in the E before dawn.

Mars getting lower in the WSW at dusk, enters Sagittarius on the 11th.

Jupiter, up all night, enters Pisces on the 13th and is at opposition on the 23d.

Saturn is up all night, follows Jupiter across the sky.

Moon passes Venus on the 5th, Mercury on the 11th, and Mars on the 15th, occults Neptune on the 18th and Uranus on the 19th, passes Jupiter on the 24th and Saturn on the 25th.

Oct. 5—Moon 5° N of Venus; Moon 1.2° N of Regulus occults Regulus.

Oct. 8—Venus 3° S of Regulus.

Oct. 11—Mars enters Sagittarius; Moon 7° N of Mercury.

Oct. 13—Jupiter enters Pisces; Neptune stationary, resumes direct motion.

Oct. 15—Moon 5° N of Mars.

Oct. 18—Moon 0.5° N of Neptune occults Neptune.

Oct. 19—Moon 0.4° N of Uranus occults Uranus (visible in N America).

Oct. 23—Uranus stationary; Jupiter at opposition.

Oct. 24—Moon 4° S of Jupiter; Mercury at greatest eastern elongation of 24°.

Oct. 27—Moon 1.2° N of Aldebaran occults Aldebaran.

Oct. 31—Sun enters Libra; Venus at greatest western elongation of 46°.

November

Mercury moves back into the glare of the Sun early in the month, begins retrograde on the 5th, passes inferior conjunction on the 15th, resumes direct motion on the 25th, and visible low in the ESE at dawn at month's end.

Venus, prominent in the ESE before dawn, enters Virgo on the 3d and passes Spica on the 29th.

Mars, still visible in the SW at dusk, enters Capricornus on the 25th.

Jupiter, up most of the night, is the brightest object except for the Moon most of the night sky until Venus rises as Jupiter sets a couple of hours before sunrise.

Saturn, also up most of the night, still near Jupiter, sets a couple of hours before sunrise.

Moon passes Venus on the 3d, Mars on the 13th, occults Neptune on the 14th, Uranus on the 15th, passes Jupiter on the 20th, and Saturn on the 22d.

Nov 2—Venus at aphelion; Mars at aphelion.

Nov. 3—Moon 3° N of Venus; Venus enters Virgo.

Nov. 5—Mercury stationary, begins retrograde; Mercury at perihelion.

Nov. 6—Saturn at opposition.

Nov. 13—Moon 3° N of Mars.

Nov. 14—Moon 0.2° N of Neptune occults Neptune.

Nov. 15—Moon 0.1° N of Uranus occults Uranus; Mercury at inferior conjunction transits Sun.

Nov. 20—Moon 4° N of Jupiter.

Nov. 22—Moon 3° N of Saturn.

Nov. 23—Sun enters Scorpius; Moon 1.3° N of Aldebaran occults Aldebaran.

Nov. 25—Mars enters Capricornus; Mercury stationary, resumes direct motion.

Nov. 28—Mars 1.7° S of Neptune.

Nov. 29—Venus 4° N of Spica.

Nov. 30—Sun enters Ophiuchus.

December

Mercury returns to sky during dawn, with greatest W elongation on the 3d, passing Antares on the 17th.

Venus getting lower in the SE in the early morning.

Mars, low in the SW early in the evening, enters Aquarius on the 31st.

Jupiter, high in the SE at the end of dusk, resumes direct motion on the 21st.

Saturn, high in the ESE at the end of dusk, sets about 5 hours before sunrise.

Moon passes Venus on the 3d, Mercury on the 6th, occults Neptune on the 11th, Mars and Uranus on the 12th, passes Jupiter on the 18th, and Saturn on the 19th.

Dec. 3—Pluto in conjunction with Sun; Mercury at greatest western elongation of 20°; Moon 3° N of Venus.

Dec. 5—Moon 0.4° N of Vesta occults Vesta.

Dec. 6—Moon 3° N of Mercury.

Dec. 11—Moon 0.07° S of Neptune occults Neptune.

Dec. 12—Moon 0.6° N of Mars occults Mars (visible in N America); Moon 0.2° S of Uranus occults Uranus; Venus enters Libra.

Dec. 14—Mars 0.7° S of Uranus.

Dec. 17—Mercury 5° N of Antares.

Dec. 18—Sun enters Sagittarius; Moon 4° S of Jupiter.

Dec. 19—Moon 3° S of Saturn; Mercury at aphelion.

Dec. 21—Jupiter stationary, resumes direct motion; Moon 1.3° N of Aldebaran occults Aldebaran.

Dec. 22—Southern Solstice at 7:44 UTC (2:44 AM EST), winter begins in the northern hemisphere, summer begins in the southern hemisphere.

Dec. 31—Mars enters Aquarius.

Meteor Showers

When a chunk of material, ice or rock, plunges into Earth's atmosphere and burns up in a fiery display, the event is a **meteor.** While the chunk of material is still in space, it is a **meteoroid.** If a portion of the material survives passage through the atmosphere and reaches the ground, the remnant on the ground is a **meteorite.**

Meteors come from 2 basic sources. Sporadic meteors, which occur throughout the year, seem to originate from the asteroid belt. Other meteors, which come in groups and seem to occur at the same time each year, are called meteor showers and seem to originate as leftover material from comets. As a comet orbits the Sun and the Sun slowly boils away some of the comet's material, the comet leaves a trail of tiny particles dispersed along the comet's path. If Earth's orbit and this path intersect, then once a year, as Earth reaches that point in its orbit, there will be a **meteor shower.**

Meteor showers vary in strength, but usually the 3 best meteor showers of the year are the Perseids around Aug. 12, the Orionids around Oct. 21, and the Geminids around Dec. 13. The showers feature meteors at the rate of about 60 per hour. Best observing conditions occur with the absence of moonlight, usually when the Moon's phase is between waning crescent and waxing 1st quarter. Meteor showers are also usually better after the middle of the night.

After 2 spectacular comets in 2 years—Comet Hyakutake in 1996 and Comet Hale-Bopp in 1997—there is the possibility of a spectacular Leonid meteor storm in 1999. For most meteor showers the cometary debris is relatively uniformly scattered along the comet's orbit. However, in the case of the Leonid meteor shower, which occurs every year around Nov. 17-18, the cometary debris, from Comet Temple-Tuttle, seems to be bunched up in one stretch. That means that most years when Earth crosses the orbit of this comet, the meteor shower produced is relatively weak. However, approximately every 33 years Earth encounters the bunched-up debris. Sometimes the storm is a disappointment, as it was in 1899 and 1933; at other times it is a roaring success, as in 1833 and 1866. In 1966 observers on the W coast of the U.S. were treated to an awesome display of meteors in the early morning as the rate peaked at 150,000 meteors per hour. In 1999 the Moon will be 1 day past Waxing Quarter, and the peak outburst is expected to last about 3 hours. However, predictions are varied both as to good locations (Europe or Eastern U.S.) and as to number of meteors (a few to 5,000 per hour). Interested observers in N America should start observing about 1.5 hours after sunset from a location free of lights and trees.

Rising and Setting of Planets, 1999

Coordinated Universal Time (0 designates midnight)

Venus, 1999

Date	20° N Latitude		30° N Latitude		40° N Latitude		50° N Latitude		60° N Lattude	
	Rise	Set	Rise	Set	Rise	Set	Rise	Set	Rise	Set
	h m	h m	h m	h m	h m	h m	h m	h m	h m	h m
Jan.1	7 42	18 39	8 02	18 19	8 27	17 54	9 03	17 19	10 04	16 17
11	7 50	18 57	8 08	18 39	8 29	18 18	9 00	17 48	9 49	16 58
21	7 56	19 13	8 09	18 59	8 27	18 42	8 50	18 19	9 28	17 42
31	7 58	19 29	8 08	19 19	8 20	19 07	8 36	18 51	9 02	18 25
Feb. 10	7 57	19 43	8 03	19 37	8 10	19 31	8 19	19 22	8 33	19 08
20	7 56	19 56	7 57	19 55	7 58	19 54	8 00	19 52	8 03	19 50
Mar.2	7 53	20 09	7 50	20 12	7 46	20 16	7 41	20 22	7 32	20 31
12	7 51	20 22	7 43	20 29	7 34	20 39	7 21	20 53	7 01	21 13
22	7 50	20 35	7 38	20 47	7 23	21 02	7 03	21 23	6 30	21 57
Apr.1	7 50	20 49	7 34	21 05	7 14	21 25	6 46	21 54	6 00	22 41
11	7 53	21 03	7 33	21 23	7 09	21 48	6 34	22 23	5 33	23 25
21	7 58	21 18	7 36	21 40	7 07	22 09	6 26	22 50	5 11	0 03
May1	8 06	21 31	7 41	21 56	7 10	22 27	6 25	23 12	4 57	0 38
11	8 15	21 43	7 50	22 07	7 18	22 39	6 32	23 26	4 59	0 58
21	8 25	21 50	8 01	22 14	7 30	22 45	6 45	23 30	5 17	0 58
31	8 34	21 53	8 12	22 16	7 43	22 44	7 02	23 25	5 46	0 42
June 10	8 41	21 51	8 21	22 11	7 56	22 36	7 20	23 11	6 18	0 15
20	8 44	21 44	8 27	22 00	8 06	22 21	7 37	22 50	6 47	23 38
30	8 41	21 30	8 28	21 43	8 11	22 00	7 48	22 23	7 10	23 00
July 10	8 32	21 10	8 22	21 20	8 09	21 32	7 52	21 49	7 24	22 16
20	8 13	20 40	8 06	20 47	7 57	20 56	7 44	21 08	7 25	21 27
30	7 41	20 00	7 36	20 05	7 30	20 11	7 21	20 20	7 07	20 33
Aug. 9	6 53	19 07	6 49	19 11	6 44	19 16	6 37	19 23	6 27	19 33
19	5 51	18 07	5 47	18 11	5 42	18 16	5 34	18 23	5 23	18 35
29	4 47	17 08	4 42	17 14	4 35	17 21	4 25	17 30	4 10	17 46
Sept. 8	3 55	16 22	3 48	16 29	3 39	16 38	3 26	16 51	3 07	17 10
18	3 19	15 50	3 10	15 58	3 00	16 09	2 46	16 23	2 23	16 45
28	2 56	15 29	2 48	15 38	2 37	15 49	2 22	16 03	1 59	16 26
Oct. 8	2 45	15 16	2 37	15 24	2 27	15 34	2 14	15 47	1 52	16 08
18	2 41	15 07	2 34	15 13	2 26	15 21	2 15	15 32	1 58	15 49
28	2 41	15 00	2 37	15 04	2 32	15 10	2 24	15 17	2 13	15 28
Nov. 7	2 45	14 55	2 44	14 56	2 42	14 58	2 39	15 01	2 34	15 05
17	2 52	14 51	2 53	14 49	2 55	14 47	2 57	14 45	3 01	14 41
27	3 00	14 48	3 05	14 43	3 11	14 37	3 19	14 29	3 31	14 17
Dec. 7	3 10	14 46	3 19	14 38	3 29	14 28	3 42	14 14	4 03	13 52
17	3 22	14 47	3 34	14 35	3 48	14 21	4 08	14 01	4 38	13 30
27	3 35	14 50	3 50	14 35	4 09	14 17	4 34	13 51	5 14	13 10

Mars, 1999

Date	20° N Latitude		30° N Latitude		40° N Latitude		50° N Latitude		60° N Latitude	
	Rise	Set	Rise	Set	Rise	Set	Rise	Set	Rise	Set
	h m	h m	h m	h m	h m	h m	h m	h m	h m	h m
Jan. 1	0 35	12 23	0 40	12 19	0 45	12 13	0 52	12 06	1 03	11 55
11	0 17	11 59	0 23	11 53	0 30	11 46	0 40	11 36	0 54	11 21
21	23 54	11 34	0 04	11 27	0 13	11 18	0 25	11 06	0 43	10 47
31	23 33	11 09	23 41	11 00	23 52	10 50	0 08	10 35	0 30	10 13
Feb.10	23 09	10 41	23 18	10 32	23 30	10 20	23 46	10 04	0 13	9 39
20	22 42	10 12	22 53	10 02	23 05	9 49	23 23	9 31	23 50	9 04
Mar. 2	22 12	9 40	22 23	9 29	22 37	9 16	22 55	8 57	23 24	8 28
12	21 38	9 05	21 49	8 54	22 04	8 40	22 23	8 21	22 53	7 51
22	20 59	8 26	21 11	8 15	21 25	8 01	21 44	7 41	22 14	7 11
Apr. 1	20 15	7 43	20 26	7 32	20 40	7 18	20 59	6 59	21 28	6 29
11	19 25	6 55	19 36	6 44	19 49	6 31	20 07	6 13	20 35	5 45
21	18 31	6 04	18 41	5 54	18 54	5 41	19 10	5 24	19 36	4 58
May 1	17 36	5 11	17 45	5 02	17 56	4 50	18 12	4 35	18 36	4 11
11	16 42	4 19	16 50	4 11	17 01	4 00	17 15	3 46	17 37	3 24
21	15 52	3 31	16 00	3 22	16 10	3 12	16 24	2 59	16 44	2 38
31	15 08	2 46	15 16	2 38	15 26	2 28	15 39	2 15	16 00	1 54
June 10	14 29	2 06	14 38	1 58	14 48	1 47	15 02	1 34	15 24	1 12
20	13 56	1 30	14 05	1 21	14 16	1 10	14 31	0 55	14 55	0 32
30	13 27	0 58	13 37	0 48	13 50	0 36	14 07	0 19	14 33	23 49
July 10	13 02	0 29	13 14	0 18	13 28	0 04	13 47	23 42	14 17	23 12
20	12 41	0 03	12 54	23 47	13 09	23 32	13 31	23 10	14 05	22 36
30	12 22	23 37	12 37	23 22	12 54	23 04	13 19	22 40	13 58	22 01
Aug. 9	12 06	23 15	12 22	22 59	12 42	22 39	13 09	22 12	13 54	21 27
19	11 52	22 56	12 09	22 38	12 31	22 16	13 02	21 46	13 52	20 55
29	11 39	22 39	11 59	22 20	12 22	21 56	12 56	21 22	13 53	20 25
Sept. 8	11 29	22 23	11 49	22 03	12 15	21 37	12 51	21 01	13 55	19 57
18	11 19	22 10	11 41	21 48	12 08	21 21	12 47	20 42	13 56	19 33
28	11 11	21 59	11 33	21 36	12 02	21 08	12 43	20 27	13 57	19 13
Oct. 8	11 03	21 49	11 26	21 26	11 55	20 57	12 37	20 15	13 55	18 57
18	10 55	21 41	11 19	21 18	11 48	20 49	12 30	20 06	13 48	18 48
28	10 47	21 35	11 10	21 12	11 39	20 43	12 21	20 02	13 37	18 46
Nov. 7	10 39	21 29	11 01	21 07	11 29	20 39	12 09	20 00	13 20	18 49
17	10 30	21 24	10 51	21 04	11 17	20 37	11 54	20 01	12 59	18 56
27	10 20	21 20	10 40	21 01	11 04	20 37	11 37	20 03	12 34	19 06
Dec. 7	10 09	21 15	10 27	20 58	10 48	20 37	11 18	20 07	12 07	19 18
17	9 57	21 11	10 12	20 56	10 31	20 37	10 56	20 12	11 38	19 31
27	9 44	21 06	9 57	20 53	10 12	20 38	10 33	20 17	11 07	19 44

Jupiter, 1999

Date	20° N Latitude Rise h m	Set h m	30° N Latitude Rise h m	Set h m	40° N Latitude Rise h m	Set h m	50° N Latitude Rise h m	Set h m	60° N Latitude Rise h m	Set h m
Jan. 1	10 54	22 45	10 57	22 41	11 01	22 37	11 07	22 31	11 15	22 23
11	10 19	22 12	10 22	22 09	10 26	22 06	10 30	22 01	10 37	21 54
21	9 45	21 40	9 48	21 38	9 50	21 35	9 54	21 32	9 59	21 27
31	9 12	21 09	9 14	21 08	9 16	21 06	9 18	21 03	9 22	21 00
Feb. 10	8 39	20 39	8 40	20 38	8 41	20 37	8 42	20 36	8 44	20 34
20	8 07	20 09	8 07	20 09	8 07	20 09	8 07	20 09	8 07	20 09
Mar. 2	7 34	19 39	7 34	19 40	7 33	19 41	7 31	19 42	7 29	19 45
12	7 02	19 10	7 01	19 11	6 59	19 13	6 56	19 16	6 52	19 20
22	6 30	18 41	6 28	18 43	6 25	18 46	6 21	18 50	6 15	18 56
Apr. 1	5 58	18 12	5 55	18 15	5 51	18 19	5 46	18 24	5 38	18 33
11	5 27	17 43	5 23	17 47	5 18	17 51	5 11	17 58	5 01	18 09
21	4 55	17 13	4 50	17 18	4 44	17 24	4 36	17 32	4 24	17 45
May 1	4 23	16 44	4 17	16 50	4 11	16 56	4 01	17 06	3 47	17 20
11	3 51	16 15	3 45	16 21	3 37	16 29	3 26	16 39	3 10	16 56
21	3 19	15 45	3 12	15 52	3 03	16 00	2 51	16 12	2 33	16 31
31	2 46	15 14	2 38	15 22	2 29	15 31	2 16	15 44	1 56	16 05
June 10	2 13	14 44	2 05	14 52	1 55	15 02	1 41	15 16	1 19	15 38
20	1 40	14 12	1 31	14 21	1 20	14 32	1 05	14 47	0 42	15 10
30	1 06	13 40	0 57	13 49	0 45	14 01	0 29	14 16	0 05	14 41
July 10	0 31	13 07	0 22	13 16	0 10	13 28	23 50	13 45	23 24	14 11
20	23 53	12 33	23 43	12 43	23 30	12 55	23 13	13 12	22 46	13 39
30	23 16	11 57	23 06	12 08	22 53	12 20	22 36	12 38	22 08	13 06
Aug. 9	22 39	11 21	22 29	11 31	22 16	11 44	21 58	12 02	21 30	12 31
19	22 01	10 43	21 51	10 54	21 38	11 07	21 20	11 25	20 51	11 53
29	21 22	10 04	21 12	10 14	20 59	10 27	20 41	10 45	20 12	11 14
Sept. 8	20 42	9 23	20 31	9 34	20 19	9 47	20 01	10 04	19 33	10 32
18	20 00	8 41	19 50	8 51	19 38	9 04	19 20	9 21	18 53	9 49
28	19 18	7 58	19 08	8 08	18 56	8 20	18 39	8 37	18 13	9 03
Oct. 8	18 35	7 14	18 26	7 23	18 14	7 35	17 58	7 51	17 32	8 17
18	17 52	6 29	17 42	6 38	17 31	6 49	17 16	7 05	16 51	7 29
28	17 08	5 44	16 59	5 52	16 48	6 03	16 34	6 18	16 10	6 41
Nov. 7	16 24	4 59	16 16	5 07	16 06	5 17	15 52	5 31	15 29	5 54
17	15 41	4 14	15 33	4 22	15 23	4 32	15 10	4 46	14 49	5 07
27	14 59	3 31	14 51	3 39	14 41	3 48	14 28	4 01	14 08	4 22
Dec. 7	14 17	2 49	14 10	2 57	14 00	3 06	13 48	3 19	13 28	3 39
17	13 37	2 09	13 29	2 16	13 20	2 25	13 07	2 38	12 48	2 58
27	12 58	1 29	12 50	1 37	12 41	1 46	12 28	1 59	12 08	2 19

Saturn, 1999

Date	20° N Latitude Rise h m	Set h m	30° N Latitude Rise h m	Set h m	40° N Latitude Rise h m	Set h m	50° N Latitude Rise h m	Set h m	60° N Latitude Rise h m	Set h m
Jan. 1	12 46	1 16	12 39	1 23	12 30	1 32	12 18	1 44	12 00	2 03
11	12 07	0 37	12 00	0 45	11 51	0 53	11 39	1 05	11 20	1 24
21	11 29	23 56	11 21	0 07	11 12	0 16	11 00	0 28	10 41	0 47
31	10 51	23 19	10 43	23 26	10 34	23 35	10 21	23 48	10 02	0 11
Feb. 10	10 14	22 42	10 06	22 50	9 56	22 59	9 43	23 13	9 23	23 33
20	9 37	22 06	9 29	22 14	9 19	22 24	9 05	22 38	8 44	22 59
Mar. 2	9 00	21 31	8 52	21 39	8 42	21 50	8 28	22 04	8 05	22 26
12	8 24	20 56	8 16	21 05	8 05	21 16	7 50	21 30	7 27	21 53
22	7 49	20 22	7 40	20 31	7 28	20 42	7 13	20 57	6 49	21 21
Apr. 1	7 13	19 47	7 04	19 57	6 52	20 09	6 36	20 25	6 11	20 50
11	6 38	19 13	6 28	19 23	6 16	19 35	5 59	19 52	5 33	20 19
21	6 03	18 40	5 53	18 50	5 40	19 02	5 23	19 20	4 55	19 47
May 1	5 28	18 06	5 17	18 16	5 04	18 30	4 46	18 48	4 17	19 16
11	4 53	17 32	4 42	17 43	4 28	17 57	4 09	18 15	3 40	18 45
21	4 17	16 58	4 06	17 09	3 52	17 23	3 33	17 43	3 02	18 14
31	3 42	16 24	3 31	16 36	3 16	16 50	2 56	17 10	2 25	17 42
June 10	3 07	15 50	2 55	16 02	2 40	16 16	2 20	16 37	1 47	17 10
20	2 31	15 15	2 19	15 27	2 04	15 42	1 43	16 03	1 10	16 37
30	1 55	14 40	1 43	14 52	1 28	15 08	1 06	15 29	0 32	16 04
July 10	1 19	14 04	1 07	14 17	0 51	14 33	0 29	14 55	23 50	15 30
20	0 43	13 28	0 30	13 41	0 14	13 57	23 48	14 19	23 13	14 55
30	0 05	12 52	23 49	13 05	23 33	13 21	23 10	13 43	22 34	14 19
Aug. 9	23 24	12 14	23 11	12 27	22 55	12 43	22 32	13 06	21 56	13 42
19	22 46	11 36	22 33	11 49	22 16	12 05	21 54	12 28	21 18	13 04
29	22 07	10 57	21 54	11 10	21 38	11 26	21 15	11 49	20 39	12 25
Sept. 8	21 27	10 18	21 14	10 30	20 58	10 47	20 36	11 09	20 00	11 45
18	20 47	9 37	20 34	9 50	20 18	10 06	19 56	10 28	19 20	11 04
28	20 06	8 56	19 54	9 09	19 38	9 25	19 16	9 47	18 41	10 22
Oct. 8	19 25	8 14	19 13	8 27	18 57	8 42	18 35	9 04	18 01	9 39
18	18 44	7 32	18 31	7 44	18 16	8 00	17 55	8 21	17 20	8 55
28	18 02	6 49	17 49	7 01	17 34	7 17	17 13	7 37	16 40	8 11
Nov. 7	17 20	6 06	17 08	6 18	16 53	6 33	16 32	6 54	15 59	7 27
17	16 37	5 24	16 26	5 35	16 11	5 50	15 51	6 10	15 19	6 42
27	15 55	4 41	15 44	4 53	15 30	5 07	15 10	5 27	14 38	5 58
Dec. 7	15 14	3 59	15 02	4 10	14 48	4 24	14 29	4 44	13 58	5 15
17	14 33	3 17	14 21	3 28	14 07	3 43	13 48	4 02	13 17	4 33
27	13 52	2 36	13 41	2 47	13 27	3 01	13 08	3 21	12 37	3 51

Star Tables

These tables include stars of visual magnitude 2.4 and brighter (the lower the number, the brighter the star). Stars of variable magnitude are designated by v. Coordinates are for mid-1999. If no parallax figures are given, the trigonometric parallax figure is smaller than the margin for error, and the distance given is obtained by indirect methods. Greek letters in the star names indicate perceived degree of relative brightness within the constellation, alpha being the brightest.

To find the time when the star is on the meridian, subtract Right Ascension of Mean Sun (from sidereal timetable, page 292) from the star's Right Ascension, first adding 24h to the latter if necessary. Mark this result PM if less than 12h, but if greater than 12, subtract 12h and mark the remainder AM.

	Star	Magnitude	Parallax "	Light yrs	Right ascen. h m	Declination ° '
α	Andromedae (Alpheratz)	2.06	0.02	90	0 08.4	+29 05
β	Cassiopeiae (Caph)	2.27v	0.07	45	0 09.2	+59 08
α	Phoenicia (Ankaa)	2.39	0.04	93	0 26.2	–42 18
α	Cassiopeiae (Schedar)	2.23	0.01	150	0 40.5	+56 32
β	Ceti (Deneb Kaitos)	2.04	0.06	57	0 43.5	–17 59
β	Andromedae (Mirach)	2.06	0.04	76	1 09.7	+35 37
α	Eridani (Achernar)	0.46	0.02	118	1 37.7	–57 14
γ	Andromedae (Almaak)	2.26		260	2 03.8	+42 19
α	Arietis (Hamal)	2.00	0.04	76	2 07.1	+23 27
o	Ceti (Mira)	2.00	0.01	103	2 19.2	–2 59
α	Ursae Minoris (Polaris)	2.02v		680	2 30.6	+89 15
β	Persei (Algol)	2.12v	0.03	105	3 08.1	+40 57
α	Persei (Mirfak)	1.80	0.03	150	3 24.3	+49 51
α	Tauri (Aldebaran)	0.85v	0.05	68	4 35.9	+16 30
β	Orionis (Rigel)	0.12v		900	5 14.5	– 8 12
α	Aurigae (Capella)	0.08v	0.07	45	5 16.6	+46 00
γ	Orionis (Bellatrix)	1.64	0.03	470	5 25.1	+ 6 21
β	Tauri (Elnath)	1.65	0.02	300	5 26.2	+28 36
δ	Orionis (Mintaka)	2.23v		1500	5 31.9	– 0 18
ε	Orionis (Alnilam)	1.70		1600	5 36.2	– 1 12
ζ	Orionis (Alnitak)	2.05	0.02	1600	5 40.6	– 1 56
κ	Orionis (Saiph)	2.06	0.01	2100	5 47.7	– 9 40
α	Orionis (Betelgeuse)	0.50v		520	5 55.1	+ 7 24
β	Aurigae (Menkalinan)	1.90v	0.04	88	5 59.4	+44 57
β	Canis Majoris (Mirzam)	1.98	0.01	750	6 22.6	–17 57
α	Carinae (Canopus)	–0.72	0.02	98	6 23.9	–52 42
γ	Geminorum (Alhena)	1.93	0.03	105	6 37.6	+16 24
α	Canis Majoris (Sirius)	–1.46	0.38	8.7	6 45.1	–16 43
ε	Canis Majoris (Adhara)	1.50		680	6 58.6	–28 58
δ	Canis Majoris (Wezen)	1.86		2100	7 08.3	–26 24
α	Geminorum (Castor)	1.99	0.07	45	7 34.5	+31 53
α	Canis Minoris (Procyon)	0.38	0.29	11.3	7 39.2	+ 5 14
β	Geminorum (Pollux)	1.14	0.09	35	7 45.2	+28 02
ζ	Puppis (Naos)	2.25		2400	8 03.5	–40 00
γ	Velorum (Al Suhail)	1.82		520	8 09.5	–47 20
ε	Carinae (Avior)	1.86		340	8 22.5	–59 31
δ	Velorum	1.96	0.04	76	8 44.7	–54 42
λ	Velorum (Suhail)	2.21	0.02	750	9 08.0	–43 26
β	Carinae (Miaplacidus)	1.68	0.04	86	9 13.2	–69 43
ι	Carinae (Tureis)	2.25		750	9 17.0	–59 17
α	Hydrae (Alphard)	1.98	0.02	94	9 27.5	– 8 39
α	Leonis (Regulus)	1.35	0.04	84	10 08.3	+11 58
β	Ursae Majoris (Merak)	2.37	0.04	78	11 01.8	+56 23
α	Ursae Majoris (Dubhe)	1.79	0.03	105	11 03.7	+61 46
β	Leonis (Denebola)	2.14	0.08	43	11 49.0	+14 35
α	Crucis (Acrux)	1.58		370	12 26.6	–63 06
γ	Crucis (Gacrux)	1.63		220	12 31.1	–57 07
γ	Centauri	2.17		160	12 41.6	–48 58
β	Crucis (Becrux)	1.25v		490	12 47.7	–59 41
ε	Ursae Majoris (Alioth)	1.77v	0.01	68	12 54.0	+55 58
ζ	Ursae Majoris (Mizar)	2.27	0.04	88	13 23.9	+54 56
α	Virginis (Spica)	0.97v	0.02	220	13 25.2	–11 09
ε	Centauri	2.30v		570	13 39.9	–53 28
η	Ursae Majoris (Alkaid)	1.86		210	13 47.5	+49 19
β	Centauri (Hadar)	0.61v	0.02	490	14 03.8	–60 22
η	Centauri (Menkent)	2.06	0.06	55	14 06.7	–36 22
α	Bootis (Arcturus)	–0.04	0.09	36	14 15.6	+19 11
ε	Centauri	2.31v		390	14 35.5	–42 09
α	Centauri (Rigel Kentaurus)	–0.01	0.75	4.3	14 39.6	–60 50
α	Lupi	2.30v		430	14 41.9	–47 23
ε	Bootis (Izar)	2.40	0.01	103	14 44.9	+27 04
β	Ursae Minoris (Kochab)	2.08	0.03	105	14 50.7	+74 10
α	Coronae Borealis (Gemma)	2.23v	0.04	76	15 34.7	+26 43
δ	Scorpii (Dschubba)	2.32		590	16 00.3	–22 37
α	Scorpii (Antares)	0.96v	0.02	520	16 29.4	–26 26
α	Trianguli Australis (Atria)	1.92	0.02	82	16 48.6	–69 02
ε	Scorpii	2.29	0.05	66	16 50.1	–34 17
λ	Scorpii (Shaula)	1.63v		310	17 33.6	–37 06
α	Ophiuchi (Rasalhague)	2.08	0.06	58	17 34.9	+12 34
θ	Scorpii	1.87	0.02	650	17 37.3	–43 00
γ	Draconis (Eltanin)	2.23	0.02	108	17 56.6	+51 30
ε	Sagittarii (Kaus Australis)	1.85	0.02	124	18 24.1	–34 23
α	Lyrae (Vega)	0.03	0.12	26.5	18 36.9	+38 47
o	Sagittarii (Nunki)	2.02		300	18 55.2	–26 18
α	Aquilae (Altair)	0.77	0.20	16.5	19 50.8	+ 8 52
γ	Cygni (Sadr)	2.20		750	20 22.2	+40 15
α	Pavonis (Peacock)	1.94		310	20 25.6	–56 44
α	Cygni (Deneb)	1.25		1600	20 41.4	+45 17
ε	Pegasi (Enif)	2.39		780	21 44.2	+ 9 52
α	Gruis (Al Nair)	1.74	0.05	64	22 08.2	–46 58
β	Gruis	2.11v		280	22 42.6	–46 53
α	Piscis Austrinis (Fomalhaut)	1.16	0.14	22.6	22 57.6	–29 37

Morning and Evening Stars, 1999

(Coordinated Universal Time)

	Morning	Evening
Jan.	Mercury Mars Neptune from Jan. 22 Pluto	Venus Mars Jupiter Saturn Uranus Neptune to Jan. 22
Feb.	Mercury to Feb. 4 Mars Uranus from Feb. 2 Neptune Pluto	Mercury from Feb. 4 Venus Jupiter Saturn Uranus to Feb. 2
Mar.	Mercury from Mar. 19 Mars Uranus Neptune Pluto	Mercury to Mar. 19 Venus Jupiter Saturn
Apr.	Mercury Mars to Apr. 24 Jupiter from Apr. 1 Saturn from Apr. 27 Uranus Neptune Pluto	Venus Mars from Apr. 24 Jupiter to Apr. 1 Saturn to Apr. 27
May	Mercury to May 25 Jupiter Saturn Uranus Neptune Pluto to May 30	Mercury from May 25 Venus Mars Pluto from May 31
June	Jupiter Saturn Uranus Neptune	Mercury Venus Mars Pluto
July	Mercury from July 26 Jupiter Saturn Uranus Neptune to July 26	Mercury to July 26 Venus Mars Neptune from July 26 Pluto

(continued)

Morning and Evening Stars, 1999 *(continued)*

	Morning	Evening
Aug.	Mercury Venus from Aug. 20 Jupiter Saturn Uranus to Aug. 7	Venus to Aug. 20 Mars Uranus from Aug. 7 Neptune Pluto
Sept.	Mercury to Sept. 8 Venus Jupiter Saturn	Mercury from Sept. 8 Mars Uranus Neptune Pluto
Oct.	Venus Jupiter to Oct. 23 Saturn	Mercury Mars Jupiter from Oct. 23 Uranus Neptune Pluto
Nov.	Mercury from Nov. 15 Venus Saturn to Nov. 6	Mercury to Nov. 15 Mars Jupiter Saturn from Nov. 6 Uranus Neptune Pluto
Dec.	Mercury Venus Pluto from Dec. 3	Mars Jupiter Saturn Uranus Neptune Pluto to Dec. 2

Greenwich Sidereal Time for 0^h UTC (Coordinated Universal Time), 1999

(Add 12 hours to obtain Right Ascension of Mean Sun)

Date	d	h	m	Date	d	h	m	Date	d	h	m
Jan.	1	6	40.8	May	1	14	33.9	Sept.	8	23	06.5
	11	7	20.3		11	15	13.4		18	23	45.9
	21	7	59.7		21	15	52.8		28	0	25.3
	31	8	39.1		31	16	32.2	Oct.	8	1	04.8
Feb.	10	9	18.6	June	10	17	11.6		18	1	44.2
	20	9	58.0		20	17	51.1		28	2	23.6
Mar.	2	10	37.4		30	18	30.5	Nov.	7	3	03.0
	12	11	16.8	July	10	19	09.9		17	3	42.5
	22	11	56.2		20	19	49.3		27	4	21.9
Apr.	1	12	35.7		30	20	28.8	Dec.	7	5	01.3
	11	13	15.1	Aug.	9	21	08.2		17	5	40.7
	21	13	54.5		19	21	47.6		27	6	20.2
					29	22	27.0				

Astronomical Constants; Speed of Light

The following were adopted as part of the International Astronomical Union System of Astronomical Constants (1976): **Speed of light**, 299,792.458 km per sec., or about 186,282 statute mi per sec.; **solar parallax**, 8″.794148; **Astronomical Unit**, 149,597,870 km, or 92,955,807 mi; **constant of nutation**, 9″.2025; and **constant of aberration**, 20″.49552.

The Zodiac

The Sun's apparent yearly path among the stars is known as the ecliptic. The zone, 18° wide, 9° on each side of the **ecliptic**, is known as the **zodiac**. Inside this zone are the apparent paths of the Sun, Moon, Earth, and the other planets. Only Pluto regularly strays outside this band on the celestial sphere. The zodiac is used both astrologically and astronomically. Though the two had a common beginning, they are no longer the same.

Beginning at the point on the ecliptic that marks the position of the Sun at the vernal equinox and proceeding eastward, the astrological zodiac is divided into 12 signs of approximately 30° each, shown below. These signs are named from the 12 constellations of the zodiac with which the signs coincided in the time of the astronomer Hipparchus, about 2,000 years ago. Owing to the precession of the equinoxes, that is to say, to the retrograde motion of the equinoxes along the ecliptic, each sign in the zodiac has, in the course of 2,000 years, moved backward about 30° into the constellation W of it; the sign Aries is now in the constellation Pisces, for example, and so on. The vernal equinox will move from Pisces into Aquarius about the middle of the 26th century.

The astronomical constellations of the zodiac, unlike the astrological signs, are not equal in size. The ecliptic actually moves through parts of 13, not 12, astronomical constellations, the 13th being Ophiuchus. Also, the constellation of the scorpion is called Scorpius, while the sign is called Scorpio. Because of the width of the zodiac, it actually cuts through parts of 26 different constellations, not just 12.

The signs of the zodiac, with their Latin and English names, are shown in the next column.

Spring	1.	♈	Aries	The Ram
	2.	♉	Taurus	The Bull
	3.	♊	Gemini	The Twins
Summer	4.	♋	Cancer	The Crab
	5.	♌	Leo	The Lion
	6.	♍	Virgo	The Virgin
Autumn	7.	♎	Libra	The Balance
	8.	♏	Scorpio	The Scorpion
	9.	♐	Sagittarius	The Archer
Winter	10.	♑	Capricorn	The Goat
	11.	♒	Aquarius	The Water Bearer
	12.	♓	Pisces	The Fishes

Although the ecliptic does not pass through the constellation of Cetus, it comes so close that on Mar. 28, 1999, the disk of the Sun will clip a corner of Cetus. The constellations of the zodiac with the approximate dates that the Sun is in each constellation in 1999, are as follows:

Jan. 1 - Jan. 20	Sagittarius
Jan. 20 - Feb. 16	Capricornus
Feb. 16 - Mar. 12	Aquarius
Mar. 12 - Apr. 19	Pisces
Apr. 19 - May 15	Aries
May 15 - June 22	Taurus
June 22 - July 21	Gemini
July 21 - Aug. 11	Cancer
Aug. 11 - Sept. 17	Leo
Sept. 17 - Oct. 31	Virgo
Oct. 31 - Nov. 23	Libra
Nov. 23 - Nov. 30	Scorpius
Nov. 30 - Dec. 18	Ophiuchus
Dec. 18 - Dec. 31	Sagittarius

Constellations

Culturally, constellations are imagined patterns among the stars that, in some cases, have been recognized through millennia of tradition. In the early days of astronomy, knowledge of the constellations was necessary in order to function as an astronomer. For today's astronomers, constellations are simply areas on the entire sky in which interesting objects await observation and interpretation.

Because Western culture has prevailed in establishing modern science, equally viable and interesting constellations and celestial traditions of other cultures (of Asia or Africa, for example) are not well-known outside their regions of origin. Even the patterns with which we are most familiar today have undergone considerable change over the centuries, because the Western heritage embraces teachings of cultures disparate in time as well as place.

Today, 88 constellations are formally recognized. Although many of these have their origins in ancient days, some are "modern," contrived out of unclaimed stars by astronomers a few centuries ago. Unclaimed stars were those too faint or inconveniently placed to be included in the more prominent constellations.

When astronomers began to travel to S Africa in the 16th and 17th cent., they found a sky that itself was unknown to them and showed numerous brilliant stars. Thus, we find constellations in the southern hemisphere that depict technological marvels of the time, as well as some arguably traditional forms, such as the "fly."

Many of the commonly recognized constellations had their origins in ancient Asia Minor—Syria, Babylonia, etc. These were adopted by the Greeks and Romans, who translated their names and stories into their own languages, modifying some details in the process. After the declines of these cultures, most such knowledge entered oral tradition or remained hidden in monastic libraries. Beginning in the 8th cent., the Muslim explosion spread through the Mediterranean world. Wherever possible, everything was translated into Arabic to be taught in the universities the Muslims established all over their new-found world.

In the 13th cent., Alphonsus XX of Spain, an avid student of astronomy, succeeded in having Ptolemy's *Almagest,* as its Arabian title was known, translated into Latin. It thus became widely available to European scholars. In the process, the constellation names were translated, but the star names were retained in their Arabic forms. Transliterating Arabic into the Roman alphabet has never been an exact art, so many of the star names we use today only seem Arabic to those who are not scholars.

Names of stars often indicated what parts of the traditional figures they represented: Deneb, the tail of the swan; Betelgeuse, the armpit of the giant. Thus, the names were an indication of the position in the sky of a particular star, provided one recognized the traditional form of the mythic figure.

Usage of Latin names for the constellations couples often inconceivable creatures, represented in unimaginable configurations, with names that often seem unintelligible. Avoiding traditional names, astronomers may designate the brighter stars in a constellation with Greek letters, usually in order of brightness. Thus, the "alpha star" is often the brightest star of that constellation. The "of" implies possession, so the genitive (possessive) form of the constellation name is used, as in Alpha Orionis, the first star of Orion (Betelgeuse). Astronomers usually use a 3-letter form for the constellation name, as indicated here.

Until the 1920s, astronomers used curved boundaries for the constellation areas. As these were rather arbitrary at best, the International Astronomical Union adopted new constellation boundaries that ran due north-south and east-west, filling the sky much as the contiguous states fill up the area of the "lower 48" United States.

Within these boundaries, and occasionally crossing them, popular "asterisms" are recognized: the so-called Big Dipper is a small part of the constellation Ursa Major, the big bear; the Sickle is the traditional head and mane of Leo, the lion; one of the horntips of Taurus, the bull, properly belongs to Auriga, the charioteer; the northeast star of the Great Square of Pegasus is Alpha Andromedae.

It is unlikely that further change will occur in the realm of the celestial constellations.

Name	Genitive	Abbrev.	Meaning
Andromeda	Andromedae	And	Chained Maiden
Antlia	Antliae	Ant	Air Pump
Apus	Apodis	Aps	Bird of Paradise
Aquarius	Aquarii	Aqr	Water Bearer
Aquila	Aquilae	Aql	Eagle
Ara	Arae	Ara	Altar
Aries	Arietis	Ari	Ram
Auriga	Aurigae	Aur	Charioteer
Boötes	Boötis	Boo	Herdsmen
Caelum	Caeli	Cae	Chisel
Camelopardalus	Camelopardalis	Cam	Giraffe
Cancer	Cancri	Cnc	Crab
Canes Venatici	Canum Venaticorum	CVn	Hunting Dogs
Canis Major	Canis Majoris	CMa	Great Dog
Canis Minor	Canis Minoris	CMi	Little Dog
Capricornus	Capricorni	Cap	Sea-goat
Carina	Carinae	Car	Keel
Cassiopeia	Cassiopeiae	Cas	Queen
Centaurus	Centauri	Cen	Centaur
Cepheus	Cephei	Cep	King
Cetus	Ceti	Cet	Whale
Chamaeleon	Chamaeleontis	Cha	Chameleon
Circinus	Circini	Cir	Compasses (art)
Columba	Columbae	Col	Dove
Coma Berenices	Comae Berenices	Com	Berenice's Hair
Corona Australis	Coronae Australis	CrA	Southern Crown
Corona Borealis	Coronae Borealis	CrB	Northern Crown
Corvus	Corvi	Crv	Crow
Crater	Crateris	Crt	Cup
Crux	Crucis	Cru	Cross (southern)
Cygnus	Cygni	Cyg	Swan
Delphinus	Delphini	Del	Dolphin
Dorado	Doradus	Dor	Goldfish
Draco	Draconis	Dra	Dragon
Equuleus	Equulei	Equ	Little Horse
Eridanus	Eridani	Eri	River
Fornax	Fornacis	For	Furnace
Gemini	Geminorum	Gem	Twins
Grus	Gruis	Gru	Crane (bird)
Hercules	Herculis	Her	Hercules
Horologium	Horologii	Hor	Clock
Hydra	Hydrae	Hya	Water Snake (female)
Hydrus	Hydri	Hyi	Water Snake (male)
Indus	Indi	Ind	Indian
Lacerta	Lacertae	Lac	Lizard
Leo	Leonis	Leo	Lion
Leo Minor	Leonis Minoris	LMi	Little Lion
Lepus	Leporis	Lep	Hare
Libra	Librae	Lib	Balance
Lupus	Lupi	Lup	Wolf
Lynx	Lyncis	Lyn	Lynx
Lyra	Lyrae	Lyr	Lyre
Mensa	Mensae	Men	Table Mountain
Microscopium	Microscopii	Mic	Microscope
Monoceros	Monocerotis	Mon	Unicorn
Musca	Muscae	Mus	Fly
Norma	Normae	Nor	Square (rule)
Octans	Octantis	Oct	Octant
Ophiuchus	Ophiuchi	Oph	Serpent Bearer
Orion	Orionis	Ori	Hunter
Pavo	Pavonis	Pav	Peacock
Pegasus	Pegasi	Peg	Flying Horse
Perseus	Persei	Per	Hero
Phoenix	Phoenicis	Phe	Phoenix
Pictor	Pictoris	Pic	Painter
Pisces	Piscium	Psc	Fishes
Piscis Austrinius	Piscis Austrini	PsA	Southern Fish
Puppis	Puppis	Pup	Stern (deck)
Pyxis	Pyxidis	Pyx	Compass (sea)
Reticulum	Reticuli	Ret	Reticle
Sagitta	Sagittae	Sge	Arrow
Sagittarius	Sagittarii	Sgr	Archer
Scorpius	Scorpii	Sco	Scorpion
Sculptor	Sculptoris	Scl	Sculptor
Scutum	Scuti	Sct	Shield
Serpens	Serpentis	Ser	Serpent
Sextans	Sextantis	Sex	Sextant
Taurus	Tauri	Tau	Bull
Telescopium	Telescopii	Tel	Telescope
Triangulum	Trianguli	Tri	Triangle
Triangulum Australe	Trianguli Australis	TrA	Southern Triangle
Tucana	Tucanae	Tuc	Toucan
Ursa Major	Ursae Majoris	UMa	Great Bear
Ursa Minor	Ursae Minoris	UMi	Little Bear
Vela	Velorum	Vel	Sail
Virgo	Virginis	Vir	Maiden
Volans	Volantis	Vol	Flying Fish
Vulpecula	Vulpeculae	Vul	Fox

Aurora Borealis and Aurora Australis

The Aurora Borealis, also called the Northern Lights, is a broad display of rather faint light in the northern skies at night. The Aurora Australis, a similar phenomenon, appears at the same time in southern skies. The aurora appears in a wide variety of forms. Sometimes it is seen as a quiet glow, almost foglike in character; sometimes as vertical streamers in which there may be considerable motion; sometimes as a series of luminous expanding arcs. There are many colors, with white, yellow, and red predominating.

The auroras are most vivid and most frequently seen at about 20 degrees from the magnetic poles, along the northern coast of the N American continent and the eastern part of the northern coast of Europe. The Aurora Borealis has been seen as far S as Key West, and the Aurora Australis has been seen as far N as Australia and New Zealand. Such occurrences are rare, however.

The Sun produces a stream of charged particles, called the solar wind. These particles, mainly electrons and protons, approach Earth at speeds on the order of 300 mi per second. Some of these particles are trapped by Earth's magnetic field, forming the Van Allen belts—two donut shaped radiation bands around Earth. Excess amounts of these charged particles, often produced by solar flares, follow Earth's magnetic lines of force toward Earth's magnetic poles. High in the atmosphere, collisions between solar and terrestrial atoms result in the glow in the upper atmosphere called the aurora. The glow may be vivid where the lines of magnetic force converge near the magnetic poles.

The auroral displays appear at heights ranging from 50 to about 600 mi and have given us a means of estimating the extent of Earth's atmosphere.

The auroras are often accompanied by magnetic storms whose forces, also guided by the lines of force of Earth's magnetic field, disrupt electrical communication. Since the Sun is now entering the next solar cycle, the increase in sunspots is expected to have an effect on both aurora and electrical communication.

Eclipses, 1999

(in Coordinated Universal Time, standard time of the prime meridian)

There are 4 eclipses in 1999, 1 total eclipse of the Sun, 1 annular eclipse of the Sun, 1 partial eclipse of the Moon, and 1 penumbral eclipse of the Moon. Penumbral eclipses of the Moon are not very noticeable. There is also a transit of the Sun by Mercury, which last occurred in Nov. 1993 and will not occur again until May 2003.

I. Penumbral eclipse of the Moon, Jan. 31

Penumbral eclipses of the Moon are not very noticeable, since direct sunlight still reaches all portions of the daytime side of the Moon. Unlike partial or total Lunar eclipses, there is no distinct shadow (the umbra) observable on the Moon. The beginning of the eclipse will be visible in part of Antarctica, the Arctic Ocean, Australia, New Zealand, most of Asia, the western S Pacific Ocean, most of the N Pacific Ocean, and western N America. The end of the eclipse will be visible in most of Africa, Europe, Asia, Australia, Antarctica, the Arctic Ocean, and the Indian Ocean.

Circumstances of the Eclipse

Event	Date	h	m
Penumbral eclipse begins	Jan. 31	14	4
Middle of eclipse	31	16	18
Penumbral eclipse ends	31	18	30

II. Annular eclipse of the Sun, Feb. 16

The path of the annular eclipse is in the southern hemisphere, starting S of Africa across the southern Indian Ocean, crossing Australia, and ending in the Coral Sea.

Circumstances of the Eclipse

Event	Date	h	m
Partial eclipse begins	Feb. 16	3	52
Annular eclipse begins	16	4	57
Central eclipse at midday	16	6	20
Annular eclipse ends	16	8	10
Partial eclipse ends	16	9	15

III. Partial eclipse of the Moon, July 28

The penumbral phases, like a penumbral eclipse, are not very noticeable. The beginning of the partial eclipse is visible in Australia, New Zealand, the Pacific Ocean, N America (except NE part), Central America, western S America, and most of Antarctica. The end of the partial eclipse is visible in Australia, New Zealand, the E Indian Ocean, the S Pacific Ocean (except the extreme E part), the N Pacific Ocean, and extreme western N America.

Circumstances of the Eclipse

Event	Date	h	m
Penumbral eclipse begins	July 28	8	56
Partial eclipse begins	28	10	22
Middle of eclipse	28	11	34
Partial eclipse ends	28	12	46
Penumbral eclipse ends	28	14	11

Magnitude of the eclipse: 0.402

IV. Total eclipse of the Sun, Aug. 11

The path of totality begins off N America, crosses the N Atlantic Ocean, crosses Europe from SW England, France, S Belgium, Luxembourg, S Germany, Austria, Hungary, Romania, the Black Sea, and Turkey, then over N Iraq, S Pakistan, and India.

Circumstances of the Eclipse

Event	Date	h	m
Partial eclipse begins	Aug. 11	8	26
Total eclipse begins	11	9	30
Central eclipse at midday	11	10	51
Total eclipse ends	11	12	36
Partial eclipse ends	11	13	40

V. Transit of Mercury, Nov. 15

The complete transit will be visible in NE Australia, most of the North Island of New Zealand, extreme eastern Asia, the N Pacific Ocean, the northern S Pacific Ocean, N America (except the NE), and western S America.

Circumstances of the Transit

Event	Date	h	m
Transit begins	Nov. 15	21	15
Middle of transit	15	21	41
Transit ends	15	22	7

Total Solar Eclipses, 1955-2015

Total solar eclipses actually take place nearly as often as total lunar eclipses; they occur at a rate of about 3 every 4 years, while total lunar eclipses come at a rate of about 5 every 6 years. However, total lunar eclipses are visible over at least half of the Earth, while total solar eclipses can be seen only along a very narrow path up to a few hundred miles wide and a few thousand miles long. Observing a total solar eclipse is thus a rarity for most people. Unlike lunar eclipses, solar eclipses can be dangerous to observe. This is not because the Sun emits more potent rays during a solar eclipse than at other times, but because the Sun is always dangerous to observe directly and people are particularly likely to stare at it during a solar eclipse.

Date	Duration[1] m	s	Width (mi)	Path of Totality
1955, June 20	7	7	157	SE Asia, Philippines, Pacific Ocean
1956, June 8	4	44	266	S Pacific Ocean
1958, Oct. 12	5	10	129	Pacific Ocean, Chile, Argentina
1959, Oct. 2	3	1	75	New England, Atlantic Ocean, Africa
1961, Feb. 15	2	45	160	Europe, Soviet Union
1962, Feb. 5	4	8	91	Borneo, New Guinea, Pacific Ocean
1963, July 20	1	39	63	Pacific Ocean, Alaska, Canada, Maine
1965, May 30	5	15	123	New Zealand, Pacific Ocean
1966, Nov. 12	1	57	52	Pacific Ocean, S America, Atlantic Ocean
1968, Sept. 22	0	39	64	Soviet Union, China
1970, Mar. 7	3	27	95	Pacific Ocean, Mexico, Eastern U.S., Canada
1972, July 10	2	35	109	Siberia, Alaska, Canada
1973, June 30	7	3	159	Atlantic Ocean, Central Africa, Indian Ocean
1974, June 20	5	8	214	Indian Ocean, Australia
1976, Oct. 23	4	46	123	Africa, Indian Ocean, Australia
1977, Oct. 12	2	37	61	Pacific Ocean, Colombia, Venezuela
1979, Feb. 26	2	49	185	NW U.S., Canada, Greenland
1980, Feb. 16	4	8	92	Africa, Indian Ocean, India, Burma, China
1981, July 31	2	2	67	Soviet Union, Pacific Ocean
1983, June 11	5	10	123	Indian Ocean, Indonesia, New Guinea
1984, Nov. 22	1	59	53	New Guinea, Pacific Ocean
1985, Nov. 12	1	58	430	Antarctica
1986, Oct. 3h	0	1	1	N Atlantic Ocean
1987, Mar. 29h	0	7	3	S Atlantic Ocean, Africa
1988, Mar. 18	3	46	104	Sumatra, Borneo, Philippines, Pacific Ocean
1990, July 22	2	32	125	Finland, Soviet Union, Aleutian Islands
1991, July 11	6	53	160	Hawaii, Mexico, Central America, Colombia, Brazil
1992, June 30	5	20	182	S Atlantic Ocean
1994, Nov. 3	4	23	117	Peru, Bolivia, Paraguay, Brazil
1995, Oct. 24	2	9	48	Iran, India, SE Asia
1997, Mar. 9	2	50	221	Mongolia, Siberia
1998, Feb. 26	4	8	94	Galapagos Islands, Panama, Colombia, Venezuela
1999, Aug. 11	2	22	69	Europe, Middle East, India
2001, June 21	4	56	125	Atlantic Ocean, Africa, Madagascar
2002, Dec. 4	2	4	54	S Africa, Indian Ocean, Australia
2003, Nov. 23	1	57	338	Antarctica
2005, Apr. 8h	0	42	17	Pacific Ocean, NW S America
2006, Mar. 29	4	7	118	Atlantic Ocean, Africa, Asia
2008, Aug. 1	2	27	157	Arctic Ocean, Asia
2009, July 22	6	39	160	Asia, Pacific Ocean
2010, July 11	5	20	164	Pacific Ocean, southern S America
2012, Nov. 13	4	2	112	N Australia, Pacific Ocean
2013, Nov. 3h	1	40	36	Atlantic Ocean, Africa
2015, Mar. 20	2	47	304	N Atlantic Ocean, Arctic Ocean

h = indicates annular-total hybrid eclipse. (1) Duration refers to length of time at optimal viewing area.

Eclipses in the 21st Century

During the 21st century Halley's Comet will return (2061-62), and there will be 8 total solar eclipses that are visible somewhere in the continental United States. The first comes after a long gap; the last one to be seen was on Feb. 26, 1979, in the northwestern U.S.

Date	Path of Totality
Aug. 21, 2017	Oregon to South Carolina
Apr. 8, 2024	Mexico to Texas and up through Maine
Aug. 23, 2044	Montana to North Dakota
Aug. 12, 2045	N California to Florida
Mar. 30, 2052	Florida to Georgia
May 11, 2078	Louisiana to North Carolina
May 1, 2079	New Jersey to the lower edge of New England
Sept. 14, 2099	North Dakota to Virginia

Beginnings of the Universe

One of the dominating astronomical discoveries of the 20th century was the realization that the galaxies of the universe all seem to be moving away from us. It turned out that they are moving away not just from us but from one another—that is, the universe seems to be expanding. Hence, scientists conclude that the universe must once, very long ago, have been extremely compact and dense. Although there are alternatives to this theory and still many questions unresolved, much of the observational evidence currently available supports the idea that the universe we know began its existence between 8 and 20 bil years ago as an explosion of a super-dense, super-small concentration of matter.

This explosion of matter giving birth to the universe is called the **Big Bang**. On the subatomic level, according to this theory, there were vast changes of energy and matter and the way physical laws operated during the first 5 minutes. After those minutes the percentages of the basic matter of the universe—hydrogen, helium, and lithium—were set. Everything was so compact and so hot that radiation dominated the early universe and there were no stable, un-ionized atoms. At first, the universe was opaque, in the sense that any energy emitted was quickly absorbed and then re-emitted by free electrons. As the universe expanded, the density and the temperature continued to drop. A few hundred thousand years after the initial Big Bang, the temperature had dropped far enough that electrons and nuclei could combine to form stable atoms as the universe became transparent. Once that had occurred the radiation, which had been trapped, was free to escape.

In the 1940s, George Gamov and others predicted that astronomers should be able to see remnants of this escaped radiation. Astronomers continued to refine the theories and were preparing to build equipment to search for this background radiation when physicists Arno Penzias and Robert Wilson of the Bell Telephone Laboratories in NJ inadvertently beat them to the punch (the 2 were later awarded a Nobel Prize). Despite the Big Bang's success at predicting the existence of **cosmic background radiation**, there are still many unresolved questions, and astronomers are still working on modifications of the theory.

The Solar System

The planets of the solar system, in order of mean distance from the Sun, are Mercury, Venus, Earth, Mars, Jupiter, Saturn, Uranus, Neptune, and Pluto (Pluto sometimes nearer than Neptune). Both Uranus and Neptune are visible through good binoculars, but Pluto is so distant and so small that only large telescopes or long-exposure photographs can make it visible.

Because Mercury and Venus are nearer to the Sun than is Earth, their motions about the Sun are seen from Earth as wide swings first to one side of the Sun then to the other, though both planets are passing continuously around the Sun in almost circular orbits. When their passage takes them either between Earth and the Sun or beyond the Sun as seen from Earth, they are invisible to us. Because of geometry of the planetary orbits, Mercury and Venus require much less time to pass between Earth and the Sun than around the far side of the Sun; so their periods of visibility and invisibility are unequal.

The planets that lie farther from the Sun than does Earth may be seen for longer periods and are invisible only when so located in our sky that they rise and set at about the same time as the Sun—and thus become overwhelmed by the Sun's great brilliance. Although several of the giant planets seem to emit their own energy, they are observed from Earth as a result of sunlight reflecting from their surfaces or cloud layers. Mercury and Venus, because they are between Earth and the Sun, show phases very much as the Moon does. The planets farther from the Sun are always seen as full, although Mars does occasionally present a slightly gibbous phase—like the Moon when not quite full.

The planets appear to move rapidly among the stars because of being closer. The stars are also in motion, some of them at tremendous speeds, but they are so far away that their motion does not change their apparent positions in the heavens sufficiently to be perceived. The nearest star is about 7,000 times farther away than the most distant planet in our solar system.

Planets and the Sun, by Selected Characteristics

Sun and Planets	Semi-Diameter: at unit distance ′ ″	at mean least distance ′ ″	in mi mean s.d.	Volume[1]	Mass[1]	Density[1]	Sidereal period d	h	m	s	Gravity at surface[1]	Reflecting power Pct°	Daytime surface temp. °F
Sun	959.62	—	432,449	1,299,370	332,946	0.26	24	16	48		27.90	—	+10,000
Mercury	3.37	5.5	1,516	0.056	0.0553	0.98	58	15	36		0.38	0.11	725
Venus	8.34	30.1	3,761	0.8570	0.8151	0.94	243	R			0.91	0.65	870
Earth	—	—	3,959	1.000	1.000	1.00		23	56	4.2	1.00	0.37	68
Moon	2.40	932.4	1,080	0.0203	0.0123	0.61	27	7	44		0.17	0.12	212
Mars	4.69	8.95	2,106	0.1506	0.1075	0.71		24	37	22	0.38	0.15	–76
Jupiter	98.35	23.4	43,441	1,321	317.83	0.24		9	55	30	2.36	0.52	–160
Saturn	82.83	9.7	36,184	764	95.16	0.12		10	30	0	0.92	0.47	–218
Uranus	35.4	1.9	15,759	63	14.54	0.24		17	14	R	0.89	0.51	–323
Neptune	33.4	1.2	15,301	58	17.15	0.30		16	7		1.12	0.41	–330
Pluto	1.9	0.05	707	0.006	0.0021	0.37	6	9	18	R	0.07	0.3	–369

(1) Earth = 1. R = Retrograde rotation.

Planet Superlatives

Largest, most massive, planet	Jupiter	Smallest, least massive planet	Pluto
Fastest orbiting planet	Mercury	Slowest orbiting planet	Pluto
Most eccentric orbit	Pluto	Most circular orbit	Venus
Longest (synodic) day	Mercury	Shortest (synodic) day	Jupiter
Coldest planet	Pluto	Hottest planet	Venus
Most moons	Saturn (18)	No moons	Mercury, Venus
Planet with largest moon	Jupiter	Planet with moon with most eccentric orbit	Neptune
Greatest average density	Earth	Lowest average density	Saturn
Tallest mountain	Mars	Deepest oceans	Jupiter

The Planets: Motion, Distance, and Brightness

Planet	Mean daily motion ″	Orbital velocity mi per sec.	Sidereal revolution days	Synodic revolution days	Distance from Sun in millions of mi Max.	Min.	Distance from Earth in millions of mi Max.	Min.	Light at[1] perihelion	aphelion
Mercury	14,732	29.75	88.0	115.9	43.4	28.6	138	48	10.57	4.59
Venus	5,768	21.76	224.7	583.9	67.7	66.8	162	24	1.94	1.89
Earth	3,548	18.51	365.3	—	94.5	91.4	—	—	1.03	0.97
Mars	1,886	14.99	687.0	779.9	154.8	128.4	249	34	0.524	0.361
Jupiter	299	8.12	4,332.6	398.9	507.0	460.2	602	366	0.0408	0.0336
Saturn	120	5.99	10,759.2	378.1	936.0	837.4	1,030	743	0.0123	0.0099
Uranus	42	4.23	30,685.4	369.7	1,867.0	1,699.0	1,962	1,604	0.0030	0.0025
Neptune	21	3.38	60,189.0	367.5	2,818.0	2,770.0	2,912	2,676	0.00113	0.00109
Pluto	14	2.95	90,465.0	366.7	4,586.0	2,762.0	4,681	2,668	0.00113	0.00041

(1) Light at perihelion and aphelion is solar illumination in units of mean illumination at Earth.

Planets of the Solar System

Note: AU = astronomical unit (92.96 mil mi, mean distance of Earth from the Sun); d = 1 Earth synodic (solar) day (24 hrs); synodic day = rotation period of a planet measured with respect to the Sun (the "true" day, i.e. the time from midday to midday, or from sunrise to sunrise); sidereal day = the rotation period of a planet with respect to the stars

Mercury

Distance from Sun	
Perihelion	28.6 mil mi
Semi-major axis	0.387 AU
Aphelion	43.4 mil mi
Period of revolution around Sun	87.97 d
Orbital eccentricity	0.2056
Orbital inclination	7.005°
Synodic day (midday to midday)	175.97 d
Sidereal day	58.65 d
Rotational inclination	~0.1°
Mass (Earth = 1)	0.0553
Mean radius	1,516 mi
Mean density (Earth = 1)	0.98
Natural satellites	0
Average surface temperature	333° F

Mercury, the nearest planet to the Sun, is the 2d-smallest of the 9 known planets. Its diameter is 3,032 mi; its mean distance from the Sun is 36,000,000 mi.

Mercury moves with great speed in its journey about the Sun, averaging about 30 mi a second to complete its circuit in about 88 Earth days. Mercury rotates upon its axis over a period of nearly 59 days, thus exposing all its surface periodically to the Sun. Because its orbital period is only about 50% longer than its sidereal rotation, the solar (synodic) day on Mercury, or the time from one sunrise to the next, is about 176 days, twice as long as a Mercurian year. It is believed that the surface passing before the Sun may reach a temperature of about 840° F, while the temperature on the nighttime side may fall as low as –300° F. Although Mercury is the closest planet to the Sun, it has by far the largest range of temperature change from day to night.

Uncertainty about conditions on Mercury and its motion arises from its short angular distance from the Sun as seen from Earth. Mercury is too much in line with the Sun to be observed against a dark sky, but is always seen during either morning or evening twilight.

Mariner 10 passed Mercury 3 times in 1974 and 1975. Less than half of the surface was photographed, revealing a degree of cratering similar to that of the Moon. A very thin atmosphere of hydrogen and helium may be made up of gases of the solar wind temporarily concentrated by the presence of Mercury. The discovery of a weak but permanent magnetic field was a surprise to scientists. It has been held that both a fluid core and rapid rotation are necessary for the generation of a planetary magnetic field. Mercury may demonstrate the contrary; the field may reveal something about the history of Mercury. In 1992, radar mapping of Mercury with radio telescopes on Earth revealed evidence of possible water ice near its north and south poles.

Venus

Distance from Sun	
Perihelion	66.8 mil mi
Semi-major axis	0.723 AU
Aphelion	67.7 mil mi
Period of revolution around Sun	224.70 d
Orbital eccentricity	0.0068
Orbital inclination	3.395°
Synodic day (midday to midday)	116.75 d (retrograde)
Sidereal day	243.02 d (retrograde)
Rotational inclination	177.3°
Mass (Earth = 1)	0.8151
Mean radius	3,761 mi
Mean density (Earth = 1)	0.943
Natural satellites	0
Average surface temperature	870° F

Venus, slightly smaller than Earth, moves about the Sun at a mean distance of 67,000,000 mi in 225 Earth days. Its synodical revolution—its return to the same relationship with Earth and the Sun, which is a result of the combination of its own motion with that of Earth—is 584 days. As a result, every 19 months Venus is nearer to Earth than any other planet in the solar system. The planet is covered with a dense, white, cloudy atmosphere that conceals whatever is below it. This same cloud reflects sunlight efficiently so that when Venus is favorably situated, it is the 3d-brightest object in the sky, exceeded only by the Sun and the Moon.

Spectral analysis of sunlight reflected from Venus's cloud tops has shown features that can best be explained by identifying material of the clouds as sulfuric acid. In 1956, radio astronomers at the Naval Research Laboratories in Washington, DC, found a temperature for Venus of about 600° F. Subsequent work and data from the *Mariner 2* space probe in 1962 confirmed a high temperature. *Mariner 2* was unable to detect the existence of a magnetic field even as weak as 1/100,000 of Earth's magnetic field.

In 1967, a Soviet space probe, *Venera 4*, and the American *Mariner 5* arrived at Venus within a few hours of each other. *Venera 4* was designed to allow an instrument package to land gently on the surface via parachute. It ceased to transmit information in about 75 minutes when its temperature reading went above 500° F, when it was still about 20 mi above the surface. *Mariner 5* went around the night side of Venus at a distance of about 6,000 mi. Its radio signals passed to Earth through Venus's atmosphere twice (once on the night side and once on the day side). The results were startling. Venus's atmosphere is nearly all carbon dioxide (96.5%), with 3.5% nitrogen and trace amounts of sulfur dioxide, argon, water, carbon dioxide, helium, and neon. It exerts a pressure at the planet's surface of as much as 90 times Earth's normal sea-level pressure of one atmosphere. Because Earth and Venus are about the same size and were presumably formed at the same time by the same general process and from the same mixture of chemical elements, one is faced with the question: Which is the planet with the unusual history—Earth or Venus? Recent measurements indicate that Venus has a surface temperature of almost 900° F as a result of an extreme greenhouse effect. Because of the thick atmosphere, the temperature is essentially the same both day and night.

Radar astronomers using powerful transmitters as well as sensitive receivers and computers succeeded in determining the rotation period of Venus. It turns out to be 243 days clockwise—in other words, contrary to the spin of the other planets and to its own motion around the Sun. If it were exactly 243.16 days, Venus would present the same face toward Earth at every inferior conjunction. This rate and sense of rotation allows a solar day (sunrise to sunrise) on Venus of 116.8 Earth days. Any part of Venus will receive sunlight on its clouds for more than 58 days and then return to darkness for 58 days.

Mariner 10 passed Venus before traveling on to Mercury in 1974. The carbon dioxide molecule found in such abundance in the atmosphere is rather opaque to certain ultraviolet wavelengths, enabling sensitive television cameras to photograph the Venusian cloud cover. Photos radioed to Earth showed a spiral pattern in the clouds from the equator to the poles.

In 1978, two U.S. *Pioneer* probes arrived at Venus. One went into orbit around Venus; the other split into 5 separate probes targeted for widely spaced entry points to sample different conditions. The probes confirmed expected high surface temperatures and high winds aloft. Winds of about 200 mi per hour there may account for the transfer of heat into the night side despite the low rotation speed of the planet. However, surface winds were light at the time. The probes detected 4 layers of clouds and more light on the surface than expected solely from sunlight. This light allowed Soviet scientists to obtain, in 1975 and later in 1982, 4 photos of rocks on the surface. Sulfur seems to play a large role in the chemistry of Venus, and reactions involving sulfur may be responsible for the glow. To learn more about the weather and atmospheric circulation on Venus, the orbiter took daily photos of the daylight-side cloud cover. It confirmed the cloud pattern and its circulation shown by *Mariner 10*. The orbiter's radar produced maps of the entire planet showing large craters, continent size highlands, and extensive dry lowlands.

The Venus orbiter *Magellan* was launched in 1989. It was equipped to observe Venus by a side-scanning radar system, together with one to gather data on the variations in elevations directly beneath the craft. *Magellan* mapped all but a small fraction of the planet. The side-looking radar illuminated the surface and its features with radio waves and recorded the strength and distance of the returning echoes. Computer processing produced a view of the landscape as if it had been seen through a clear atmosphere from above, near sunset, with a visibility better than about 500 feet on Venus. Information on vertical relief had a resolution of about 30 feet.

Craters more than 20 mi wide are believed to have been caused by impacting bodies. Theia Mons, a huge shield volcano, has a diameter of over 500 mi and a height of over 3 mi. (Compare this to the largest Hawaiian volcano, which is only about 125 mi in diameter, but with a height of nearly 5.5 mi from the ocean floor.) Many lava flows have been seen, and some old craters and plains seem to be filled with lava.

Most of the surface is believed to be younger than 1 bil to 500 mil years old. Modifications of previously existing surface features have been caused by weathering and by tectonic actions such as faulting. Tectonic actions on Venus are distinctly different from such actions on Earth. The intense heat at the surface can prevent surface materials from cooling to the same brittle condition as on Earth. No activity on Venus seems to be similar to Earth's moving tectonic plates, but local stretching and compressing may produce rift valleys and higher plains and mountains. Although there is no weathering due to water, the action of winds is in evidence. Extensive sand dunes have been seen, and windblown deposits indicate stable wind patterns for very long periods of time. Although there are deep regions, somewhat similar to Earth's ocean basins, there is no water to fill them. The orbit of *Magellan* was adjusted to a nearly circular shape about 300 mi from the planet's surface in 1993. In this mode, variation in *Magellan*'s orbital speed revealed information on irregularities in the gravitational field, presumably due to details in the internal structure of the planet. Although *Magellan* ceased operating in 1994, its data about the topography of Venus's surface will keep teams of analysts and theoreticians busy for years.

Mars

Distance from Sun	
Perihelion	128.4 mil mi
Semi-major axis	1.524 AU
Aphelion	154.8 mil mi
Period of revolution around Sun	686.98 d (1.88 y)
Orbital eccentricity	0.0934
Orbital inclination	1.85°
Synodic day (midday to midday)	24h 41m 58s
Sidereal day	24h 37m 22s
Rotational inclination	25.19°
Mass (Earth = 1)	0.1075
Mean radius	2,106 mi
Mean density (Earth = 1)	0.713
Natural satellites	2
Average surface temperature	−76° F

Mars is the first planet beyond Earth, away from the Sun. Mars's diameter is about 4,213 mi. Although Mars's orbit is nearly circular, it is somewhat more eccentric than the orbits of many of the other planets, and Mars is more than 25 mil mi farther from the Sun in some parts of its year than it is in others. Mars takes 687 Earth days to make one circuit of the Sun, traveling at about 15 mi a second. The planet rotates upon its axis in almost the same period of time as Earth—24 hours and 37 minutes. Mars's mean distance from the Sun is 141 mil mi, so its temperature would be lower than that on Earth even if its atmosphere were not so thin. *Mariner 4*, in 1965, reported that atmospheric pressure on Mars is between 1% and 2% of Earth's atmospheric pressure. As is the case with Venus, the thin atmosphere appears to be composed largely of carbon dioxide. The planet is exposed to an influx of cosmic radiation about 100 times as intense as that on Earth.

Deductions from years of telescopic observation indicate that about 5/8 of the surface of Mars is a desert of reddish rock, sand, and soil. The rest is covered by irregular patches that appear generally green, in hues that change through the year. These were formerly held to be some sort of primitive vegetation, but the findings of *Mariner 4* of a complete lack of water and oxygen showed that such growth is not possible.

Mars's axis of rotation is inclined from a vertical to the plane of its orbit about the Sun by about 25°, and therefore Mars has seasons as does Earth. White caps form about the poles of Mars, growing in the winter and shrinking in the summer. These polar caps are now believed to be both water ice and carbon dioxide ice. It is the carbon dioxide that is seen to come and go with the seasons. The water ice is apparently in many layers with dust between them, indicating climatic cycles.

The photographs sent back by *Mariner 4* showed faint, ill-defined, broad, dark markings, the nature of which could not be positively determined. *Mariners 6* and *7* in 1969 sent back many photographs of higher quality showing cratering similar to the earlier views, but also other types of terrain. Some regions seemed featureless over large areas; others were chaotic, showing high relief without apparent organization into mountain chains or craters. *Mariner 9*, the first spacecraft to orbit Mars (1971), transmitted more than 10,000 photographs covering 100% of the surface. Although these photos and other data show that Mars resembles no other planet we know, there are features clearly of volcanic origin. One of these is Olympus Mons, apparently a shield volcano whose caldera is more than 50 mi wide and whose outer slopes are more than 300 mi in diameter; it stands 15 mi above the surrounding plain—the tallest known mountain in the solar system. Some features may have been produced by cracking (faulting) of the surface and the sliding of one region over or past another. Many craters seem to have been produced by impacting bodies that may have come from the nearby asteroid belt. Features near the S pole may have been produced by glaciers no longer present. Valles Marineris, a huge series of interrelated canyons, stretches more than 3,000 mi.

Although the Russians landed a probe on the Martian surface in 1971, it transmitted for only 90 seconds. In 1976, the U.S. landed 2 *Viking* spacecraft on the Martian surface. The landers had devices aboard to perform chemical analyses of the soil in search of evidence of life; results were inconclusive. The 2 *Viking* orbiters returned the best pictures up to then of Martian topographic features. Scientists believe many of these features can be explained only if Mars once had large quantities of flowing water.

In 1996, 2 more U.S. spacecraft—the Mars *Pathfinder* and the Mars *Global Surveyor*—were launched towards Mars. On July 4, 1997, using a unique array of balloons, *Pathfinder* bounced to a safe landing on Mars. It actually bounded about 40 feet high after striking the ground at 40 mph and bounced 15 more times before coming to a halt. Preliminary geological results from the *Pathfinder* indicate that in its beginning stages Mars melted to a sufficient extent to separate into dense and lighter layers. It also appears that there was an era when the planet had large amounts of flooding waters on its surface. The *Surveyor*, which went into orbit around Mars on Sept. 11, 1997, has already reported the presence of a very weak magnetic field that may have been stronger in the distant past. *Surveyor* has taken a new picture of the "face" on Mars, showing the supposed facial features were just an artifact of the angle of sunlight and the lower resolution. While *Surveyor* went through prolonged atmospheric braking maneuvers during 1997 and 1998, it also studied Phobos and found evidence that the surface of this Martian moon may be covered by a fine powder at least 3 ft thick.

Mars's position in its orbit and its speed around that orbit in relation to Earth's position and speed bring the planet fairly close to Earth on occasions about 2 years apart and then move Mars and Earth too far apart for favorable observation. Every 15-17 years, the close approaches are especially favorable for observation.

Mars has 2 satellites, discovered in 1877 by Asaph Hall. The outer satellite, Deimos, revolves around the planet in about 31 hours. The inner satellite, Phobos, whips around Mars in a little more than 7 hours, making 3 trips around the planet each Martian day. Since it orbits Mars faster than the planet rotates, Phobos rises in the W and sets in the E, opposite to what other bodies appear to do in the Martian sky. *Mariner* and *Viking* photos show these satellites to be irregularly shaped and pitted with numerous craters. Phobos also exhibits a system of linear grooves, each about 1/3 mi across and roughly parallel. Phobos measures about 8 by 12 mi and Deimos about 5 by 7.5 mi.

Of the tens of thousands of meteorites found on Earth, approximately a dozen of them may have originated on Mars. In 1996, a NASA research team concluded that a meteorite found in 1984 on an Antarctic ice field not only might be a rock blasted from the surface of Mars but also might contain evidence that life existed on Mars more than 3.5 bil years ago. The meteorite has been age-dated to about 4.5 bil years. The scientists theorize that 3.5 bil years ago, Mars may have been warmer and wetter, and microscopic life may have formed and left evidence in the rock, including possible fossilized microscopic organisms. Then, 16 mil years ago, it is believed that a huge asteroid or comet struck Mars, blasting material, including this rock, into space. The rock may have entered Earth's atmosphere about 13,000 years ago, landing in Antarctica. The evidence is intriguing, but not conclusive, and even if the above conclusions are correct they indicate the presence only of microscopic life, at a time far in the past.

Jupiter

Distance from Sun	
Perihelion	460.2 mil mi
Semi-major axis	5.203 AU
Aphelion	507.0 mil mi
Period of revolution around Sun	11.86 y
Orbital eccentricity	0.0485
Orbital inclination	1.305°
Synodic day (midday to midday)	9h 55m 33s
Sidereal day	9h 55m 30s
Rotational inclination	3.12°
Mass (Earth = 1)	317.8
Mean radius	43,441 mi
Mean density (Earth = 1)	0.24
Natural satellites	16
Average temperature*	–160° F

*i.e., temperature where atmosphere pressure equals 1 Earth atmosphere.

Jupiter is the largest of the planets. Its equatorial diameter is nearly 89,000 mi, 11 times the diameter of Earth. Its polar diameter is about 6,000 mi shorter. This noticeable oblateness is a result of the liquidity of the planet and its extremely rapid rate of rotation; a day is less than 10 Earth hours long. For a planet this size, this rotational speed is amazing. A point on Jupiter's equator moves at a speed of 22,000 mi per hour, as compared with 1,000 mi for a point on Earth's equator. Jupiter is at an average distance of 480 mil mi from the Sun and takes almost 12 Earth years to make one complete circuit of the Sun.

The major chemical constituents of Jupiter's atmosphere are molecular hydrogen (H_2) and helium (He). Minor constituents include methane (CH_4), ammonia (NH_3), ethane (C_2H_6), and water (H_2O). The temperature at the tops of clouds may be about –280° F. The clouds are probably ammonia ice crystals, becoming ammonia droplets lower down. There may be a space before water ice crystals show up as clouds; in turn, these become water droplets near the bottom of the entire cloud layer. The total atmosphere may be only a few hundred mi in depth, pulled down by the surface gravity (2.36 times Earth's gravity) to a relatively thin layer. The gases become denser with depth, until they may turn into a slush or slurry. There is no sharp interface between the gaseous atmosphere and the hydrogen ocean that accounts for most of Jupiter's volume. *Pioneer 10* and *11*, passing Jupiter in 1973 and 1974, provided evidence for considering Jupiter almost entirely liquid hydrogen. Long before a rocky core about the size of Earth is reached, scientists believe hydrogen mixed with helium becomes a liquid metal at very high temperature and pressure. Jupiter's cloudy atmosphere is a fairly good reflector of sunlight and makes it appear far brighter than any stars.

Jupiter's magnetic field is by far the strongest of any planet. Electrical activity caused by this field is so strong that it discharges billions of watts into Earth's magnetic field daily. At lower layers, under enormous pressure, the liquid hydrogen takes on the properties of a metal. It is likely that this liquid metallic hydrogen is the source for both Jupiter's persistent radio noise and its improbably strong magnetic field.

Fourteen of Jupiter's 16 known satellites were found through Earth-based observations. Four of the moons are large and bright, rivaling Earth's Moon and Mercury in diameter, and may be seen through binoculars. They move rapidly around Jupiter, and it is easy to observe their change of position from night to night. The other satellites are much smaller, in all but one instance much farther from Jupiter, and cannot be seen except through powerful telescopes. The 4 outermost satellites revolve around Jupiter clockwise as seen from the north, contrary to the motions of most satellites in the solar system and to the direction of revolution of planets around the Sun. These moons may be captured asteroids. Jupiter's mass is more than twice the mass of all the other planets put together.

Photographs from *Pioneer 10* and *11* were far surpassed by those of *Voyager 1* and *2*, both of which rendezvoused with Jupiter in 1979. The Great Red Spot exhibited internal counterclockwise rotation. Much turbulence was seen in adjacent material passing N or S of it. The satellites Amalthea, Io, Europa, Ganymede, and Callisto were photographed, some in great detail. Each is individual and unique, with no similarities to other known planets or satellites. Io has active volcanoes that probably have ejected material into a doughnut-shaped ring enveloping its orbit about Jupiter. This is not to be confused with the thin, flat disklike ring closer to Jupiter's surface.

During July 16-22, 1994, 21 large fragments of Comet Shoemaker-Levy 9 collided with Jupiter in a dramatic barrage. Moving at 134,000 mph, stretched out like a 21-car freight train, the fragments impacted one after another against Jupiter. Massive plumes of gas erupted from the impact sites, forming brilliant fireballs and leaving dark blotches and smears behind. One of the largest chunks, labeled the G fragment, impacted with the force of 6 mil megatons of TNT, 100,000 times the power of the largest nuclear bomb ever detonated. It produced a plume 1,200-1,600 mi high and 5,000 mi wide and left a dark discoloration larger than Earth.

The *Galileo* spacecraft went into orbit around Jupiter and released an atmospheric probe into the Jovian atmosphere in Dec. 1995. The probe, traveling at a speed of over 100,000 mph, survived deceleration forces of 230 times Earth's gravity as it plunged inward, relaying information about Jupiter's atmosphere for 57.6 minutes. Initial findings revealed a relatively dry atmosphere for the planet, with the upper atmosphere being warmer and denser than expected. The probe gave evidence of wind speeds of more than 400 mph and a relative absence of lightning. Further study indicated that the cloud structure may not be typical for Jupiter as a whole. During 1998-9, *Galileo* continued an extended mission to study Europa, Callisto, and Io. Already that mission has revealed an atmosphere of hydrogen and carbon dioxide on Callisto and discovered volcanic ice flows and ice rafts on the surface of Europa that indicate the possibility of liquid beneath that moon's surface.

Saturn

Distance from Sun	
Perihelion	837.4 mil mi
Semi-major axis	9.539 AU
Aphelion	936.0 mil mi
Period of revolution around Sun	29.46 y
Orbital eccentricity	0.0532
Orbital inclination	2.485° 29′ 7″
Synodic day (midday to midday)	10h 30m 2s
Sidereal day	10h 30m 0s
Rotational Inclination	26.73°
Mass (Earth = 1)	95.16
Mean radius	36,184 mi
Mean density (Earth = 1)	0.124
Natural satellites	18
Average temperature*	–220° F

*i.e., temperature where atmosphere pressure equals 1 Earth atmosphere.

Saturn, last of the planets visible to the unaided eye, is almost twice as far from the Sun as Jupiter, almost 900 mil mi. It is 2d in size to Jupiter, but its mass is much smaller. Saturn's specific gravity is less than that of water. Its diameter is almost 75,000 mi at the equator; its rotational speed spins it completely around in a little more than 10 hours, and its atmosphere is much like that of Jupiter, except that its temperature at the top of its cloud layer is at least 100° F lower. At about 300° F below zero, the ammonia would be frozen out of Saturn's clouds. The theoretical construction of Saturn resembles that of Jupiter; it likely has a small dense center surrounded by a layer of liquid and a deep atmosphere.

Until *Pioneer 11* passed Saturn in 1979, only 10 satellites of the planet were known from ground-based observations. *Pioneer 11* discovered 2 more, and the other 6 were found in the *Voyager 1* and *2* flybys, which also yielded more information about Saturn's icy satellites. In 1995, astronomers using the Hubble Space Telescope detected evidence for previously unknown moons of Saturn, but these results have not been confirmed.

Saturn's ring system begins about 7,000 mi above the visible disk of Saturn, lying above its equator and extending about 35,000 mi into space. The diameter of the ring system visible from Earth is about 170,000 mi; the rings are estimated to be no thicker than 10 mi. In 1973, radar observation showed the ring particles to be large chunks of material averaging a meter on a side.

Voyager 1 and *2* observations showed the rings to be considerably more complex than had been believed. To the untrained eye, the *Voyager* photographs could be mistaken for pictures of a colorful phonograph record. In Oct. 1997, the *Cassini* spacecraft was launched. It is scheduled to reach Saturn in 2004 to study this planet, its rings, and its satellites.

Uranus

Distance from Sun	
Perihelion	1,699 mil mi
Semi-major axis	19.179 AU
Aphelion	1,867 mil mi
Period of revolution around Sun	84.01 y
Orbital eccentricity	0.0472
Orbital inclination	0.773°
Synodic day (midday to midday)	17h 14m 23s (retrograde)
Sidereal day	17h 14m 24s (retrograde)
Rotational inclination	97.86°
Mass (Earth = 1)	14.5
Mean radius	15,759 mi
Mean density (Earth = 1)	0.239
Natural satellites	17
Average temperature*	–320° F

*i.e., temperature where atmosphere pressure equals 1 Earth atmosphere.

Voyager 2, after passing Saturn in 1981, headed for a rendezvous with Uranus, culminating in a flyby in 1986.

Uranus, discovered by Sir William Herschel on Mar. 13, 1781, lies 1.8 bil mi from the Sun, taking 84 years to make its circuit around our star. Uranus has a diameter of about 32,000 mi and spins once in some 17.4 hours, according to flyby magnetic data. One of the most fascinating features of Uranus is how far over it is tipped. Its N pole lies 98° from being directly up and down to its orbit plane. Thus, its seasons are extreme. When the Sun rises at the N pole, it stays up for 42 Earth years; then it sets, and the N pole is in darkness (and winter) for 42 Earth years.

Uranus has 17 moons (2 most recently having been sighted in late 1997, but not fully confirmed), which have orbits lying in the plane of the planet's equator. In that plane there is also a complex of rings, 9 of which were discovered in 1978. Invisible from Earth, the 9 original rings were found by observers watching Uranus pass before a star. As they waited, they saw their photoelectric equipment register several short eclipses of the star; then the planet occulted the star as expected. After the star came out from behind Uranus, the star winked out several more times. Subsequent observations and analyses indicated the 9 narrow, nearly opaque rings circling Uranus. Evidence from the *Voyager 2* flyby has shown the ring particles to be predominantly a yard or so in diameter.

In addition to photos of the 10 new, very small satellites, *Voyager 2* returned detailed photos of the 5 large satellites. As in the case of other satellites newly observed in the

Voyager program, these bodies proved to be entirely different from one another and from any others. Miranda has grooved markings, reminiscent of Jupiter's Ganymede, but often arranged in a chevron pattern. Ariel shows rifts and channels. Umbriel is extremely dark, prompting some observers to regard its surface as among the oldest in the system. Titania has rifts and fractures, but not the evidence of flow found on Ariel. Oberon's main feature is its surface saturated with craters, unrelieved by other formations.

Uranus is likely to have a rocky core, surrounded by a thick, icy mantle or perhaps a liquid mantle of water, methane, and ammonia, on top of which is a slushy layer of hydrogen and helium that gradually becomes an atmosphere. In addition to its rotational tilt, Uranus's magnetic field axis is tipped an incredible 58.6° from its rotational axis and is displaced about 1/3 of its radius away from the planet's center.

Neptune

Distance from Sun	
Perihelion	2,770 mil mi
Semi-major axis	30.057 AU
Aphelion	2,818 mil mi
Period of revolution around Sun	164.79 y
Orbital eccentricity	0.0086
Orbital inclination	1.768°
Synodic day (midday to midday)	16h 6m 37s
Sidereal day	16h 6m 36s
Rotational inclination	29.56°
Mass (Earth = 1)	17.15
Mean radius	15,301 mi
Mean density (Earth = 1)	0.297
Natural satellites	8
Average temperature*	–330° F

*i.e., temperature where atmosphere pressure equals 1 Earth atmosphere.

Neptune, the most distant planet from the Sun at the start of 1999, lies at an average distance of 2.8 bil mi. It was the last planet visited in *Voyager 2*'s epic 12-year trek (1977-89) from Earth.

As with the other giant planets, Neptune may have no solid surface, or exact diameter. However, a mean value of 30,600 mi may be assigned to a diameter between atmosphere levels where the pressure is about the same as sea level on Earth. Without a solid surface it is challenging to determine a "true" rotation rate for a giant planet. Astronomers use a determination of the rotation rate of the planet's magnet field to indicate the internal rotation rate, which in the case of Neptune is 16.1 hours. Neptune orbits the Sun in 164.8 years in a nearly circular orbit. Neptune was discovered in 1846; not until 2010 will it have completed one full trip around the Sun since its discovery.

Voyager 2, which passed 3,000 mi from Neptune's N pole, found a magnetic field that is considerably asymmetric to the planet's structure, similar to, but not so extreme as, that found at Uranus.

Neptune's atmosphere was seen to be quite blue, with quickly changing white clouds often suspended high above an apparent surface. There is a Great Dark Spot, reminiscent of the Great Red Spot of Jupiter. Observations with the Hubble Space Telescope have shown that the Great Dark Spot originally seen by *Voyager* has apparently dissipated, but a new dark spot has since appeared. Atmospheric constituents are mostly hydrocarbon compounds. Although lightning and auroras have been found on other giant planets, only the aurora phenomenon has been seen on Neptune.

Six new satellites were definitively discerned around Neptune by *Voyager 2*. Five of these satellites orbit Neptune in a half day or less. Of the 8 satellites of Neptune in all, the largest, Triton, is in a retrograde orbit, suggesting that it was captured rather than being coeval with Neptune. Triton's large size, sufficient to raise significant tides on the planet, may one day, billions of years from now, cause Triton to come close enough to Neptune for it to be torn apart. Nereid was found in 1949 and has the highest orbital eccentricity (0.75) of any moon. Its long looping orbit suggests that it, too, was captured. Each of the satellites that has been photographed by the 2 *Voyagers* in the planetary encounters has been different from any of the other satellites, and certainly different from any of the planets. Only about half of Triton has been observed, but its terrain shows cratering and a strange regional feature described as resembling the skin of a cantaloupe. Triton has a tenuous atmosphere of nitrogen with a trace of hydrocarbons and evidence of active geysers injecting material into it. At –390° F, the wintertime parts of Triton are the coldest regions yet found in the solar system.

Voyager 2 also confirmed the existence of at least 3 rings composed of very fine particles. There may be some clumpiness in the rings' structure. It is not known whether Neptune's satellites influence the formation or maintenance of the rings.

As with the other giant planets, Neptune is emitting more energy than it receives from the Sun. *Voyager* found the excess to be 2.7 times the solar contribution. Cooling from internal heat sources and from the heat of formation of the planets is thought to be responsible.

Pluto

Distance from Sun	
Perihelion	2,762 mil mi
Semi-major axis	39.529 AU
Aphelion	4,586 mil mi
Period of revolution around Sun	247.69 y
Orbital eccentricity	0.2482
Orbital inclination	17.121°
Synodic day (midday to midday)	6d 9h 18m (retrograde)
Sidereal day	6d 9h 18m (retrograde)
Rotational inclination	122.46°
Mass (Earth = 1)	0.0021
Mean radius	707 mi
Mean density (Earth = 1)	0.371
Natural satellites	1
Average surface temperature	–370° F

Although Pluto on the average stays about 3.6 bil mi from the Sun, its orbit is so eccentric that its minimum distance of 2.76 bil mi is less than the distance of Neptune at the start of 1999. At this time, Pluto reclaims from Neptune the title of most distant planet. At its mean distance, Pluto takes 247.7 years to circumnavigate the Sun, a 3/2 resonance with Neptune. Until recently, this was about all that was known of Pluto.

About a century ago, a hypothetical planet was believed to lie beyond Neptune and Uranus because neither planet followed paths predicted by astronomers when all known gravitational influences were considered. In little more than a guess, a mass of 1 Earth was assigned to the mysterious body, and mathematical searches were begun. Amid some controversy abou the validity of the predictive process, Pluto was discovered nearly where it had been predicted to lie, by Clyde Tombaugh at the Lowell Observatory in Flagstaff, AZ, in 1930.

At the U.S. Naval Observatory, also in Flagstaff, in 1978, James Christy obtained a photograph of Pluto that was distinctly elongated. Repeated observations of this shape and its variation were convincing evidence of the discovery of a satellite of Pluto, now named Charon. Subsequent observations show it to be 730 mi across, more than 12,000 mi from Pluto, and taking 6.4 days to move around Pluto. In this same length of time, Pluto and Charon both rotate once around their individual axes. The Pluto-Charon system thus appears to rotate as virtually a rigid body. Gravitational laws allow these interactions to give the mass of Pluto as 0.0021 of Earth. This mass, together with a new diameter for Pluto of 1,413 mi, make the density about twice that of water. Theorists predict that Pluto has a rocky core, surrounded by a thick mantle of ice.

It is now clear that Pluto, the body found by Tombaugh, could not have influenced Neptune and Uranus to go astray. Although a 10th planet might be out there somewhere, theorists no longer believe that there are unexplained perturbations in the orbit of Uranus or Neptune that might be caused by it. Astronomers have discovered more than 2 dozen asteroid-size objects, somewhat beyond Pluto, in a region called the Kuiper Belt, where some comets are believed to originate.

Because the rotational axis of the system is tipped from the reference plane of the solar system by about 98.3°, there is only a short interval every half solar period when Pluto and Charon alternately eclipse each other. Both worlds are approximately spherical, but they are otherwise different. Pluto is red; Charon gray. Charon's surface is identified as water ice; Pluto's surface is frozen methane. Large regions on Pluto are dark, others light; Pluto has spots and, perhaps, polar caps. Although extremely cold, Pluto appears to possess a thin nitrogen-methane atmosphere, at least while it is closer to the Sun. When Pluto occulted a star, the star's light faded in such a way as to have passed through a haze layer lying above the planet's surface, indicating an inversion of temperatures—110 K above and 50 K below—suggesting Pluto has primitive weather.

MILLENNIUM FACT BOX

Seeing New Objects Beyond Pluto

As we end this century, advances in technology are enabling astronomers to begin to detect planet- and asteroid-like objects beyond the orbit of Pluto. These discoveries can be expected to increase significantly as we enter the new millennium. The objects come in 2 categories: Kuiper Belt Objects relatively nearby beyond the orbit of Pluto and extra-solar planets existing outside our solar system.

In 1951, astronomer Gerard Kuiper suggested that there is a remnant of the original nebula that formed our solar system in the region extending from about the orbit of Pluto out to 50 AU from the Sun. This region would be a source for most of the short-period comets like Comet Halley. In 1992, the first such object was found; since then more than 4 dozen such objects have been found. Compared to Pluto's orbital period of 247.69 years, their orbital periods range from about 210 to 750 years. The diameters of these objects range from 60 to 240 mi, relative to Pluto's 1,400 mi. Although much smaller than Pluto, they may be comparable to Pluto in composition and origin. Systematic searches for more of these objects continue.

As of mid-1998 there was observational evidence for the existence of planets in 10 star systems beyond our solar system, as well as for planets orbiting 2 pulsars. Most of these suspected planets are found by the effect their mass has on the motion of the star they orbit. The masses of these planets range from about 0.5 to 10 times Jupiter's mass, except for the planets found around the pulsars, which may be only a few times the mass of the Earth. Although most of the evidence is indirect, in May 1998, astronomers working with the Hubble Space Telescope reported the first image of what may be a planet ejected from a newly forming binary star system. The closest such planet, with about 1.6 Jupiter's mass, was found circling a faint red dwarf star called Gliese 876, only about 15 light-years from our Sun.

The Sun

The Sun, the controlling body of Earth's solar system, is a star often described as average. Yet, the Sun's mass and luminosity are greater than that of 80% of the stars in Earth's galaxy. On the other hand, most of the stars that can be easily seen on any clear night are bigger and brighter than the Sun. It is the Sun's proximity to Earth that makes it appear tremendously large and bright. The Sun is 400,000 times as bright as the full moon and gives Earth 6 mil times as much light as do all the other stars put together. A series of nuclear fusion reactions where hydrogen nuclei are converted to helium nuclei produces the heat and light that make life possible on Earth.

The Sun has a diameter of 864,000 mi and, on average, is 92,956,000 mi from Earth. It is 1.41 times as dense as water. The light of the Sun reaches Earth in 499 seconds, or in slightly more than 8 minutes. The average solar surface temperature has been measured at a value of 5,800 K, or about 10,000° F. The interior temperature of the Sun is theorized to be about 27,000,000° F.

When Sunlight is analyzed with a spectroscope, it is found to consist of a continuous spectrum composed of all the colors of the rainbow in order, crossed by many dark lines. The dark "absorption lines" are produced by gaseous materials in the outer layers of the Sun. More than 60 of the natural terrestrial elements have been identified in the Sun, all in gaseous form because of the Sun's intense heat.

Spheres and Corona

The radiating surface of the Sun is called the **photosphere**; just above it is the **chromosphere.** The chromosphere is visible to the naked eye only at total solar eclipses, appearing then to be a pinkish-violet layer with occasional great prominences projecting above its general level. With proper instruments, the chromosphere can be seen or photographed whenever the Sun is visible without waiting for a total eclipse. Above the chromosphere is the **corona,** also visible to the naked eye only at times of total eclipse. Instruments also permit the brighter portions of the corona to be studied whenever conditions are favorable. The pearly light of the corona surges mil of mi from the Sun. Iron, nickel, and calcium are believed to be principal contributors to the composition of the corona, all in a state of extreme attenuation and high ionization that indicates temperatures nearly 2 mil degrees Fahrenheit.

Sunspots

There is an intimate connection between Sunspots and the corona. At times of low Sunspot activity, the fine streamers of the corona are longer above the Sun's equator than over the polar regions of the Sun; during periods of high Sunspot activity, the corona extends fairly evenly outward from all regions of the Sun, but to a much greater distance in space. Sunspots are dark, irregularly shaped regions whose diameters may reach lengths of tens of thousands of mi. The average life of a Sunspot group is from 2 to 3 weeks, but some Sunspot groups have lasted for more than a year by being carried repeatedly around as the Sun rotated upon its axis.

The record for the duration of a Sunspot is 18 months. Sunspots reach a low point, on average, every 11.3 years, with a peak of activity occurring irregularly between 2 successive minima. We are past the beginning of the next sunspot cycle, which is expected to be stronger than average. The SOHO spacecraft completed a 2-year mission in 1998, detecting the presence of "rivers" of plasma beneath the photosphere of the Sun and discovering a magnetic "carpet" in the photosphere that seems to account for a substantial portion of the energy used to heat the corona.

The Moon

Distance from Earth	
Perigee	225,745 mi
Semi-major axis	238,856 mi
Apogee	251,978 mi
Period of revolution	27.322 d
Synodic orbital period (period of phases)	29.53 d
Orbital eccentricity	0.0549
Orbital inclination	5.145°
Sidereal day (rotation period)	27.322 d
Rotational inclination	6.68°
Mass (Earth = 1)	0.0123
Mean radius	1,080 mi
Mean density (Earth = 1)	0.6051
Average surface temperature	–10° F

The Moon completes a circuit around Earth in a period whose mean or average duration is 27 days, 7 hours, 43.2 minutes. This is the Moon's **sidereal period**. Because of the motion of the Moon in common with Earth around the Sun, the mean duration of the lunar month—the period from one New Moon to the next New Moon—is 29 days, 12 hours, 44.05 minutes. This is the Moon's **synodic period**.

The mean distance of the Moon from Earth is 238,856 mi. Because the orbit of the Moon about Earth is not circular but elliptical, however, the maximum distance from Earth that the Moon may reach is 251,967 mi and the least distance is 225,745 mi. (All distances are from the center of one body to the center of the other.)

The Moon rotates on its axis in a period of time that is exactly equal to its sidereal revolution about Earth: 27.322 days. Thus the backside or farside of the Moon always faces away from Earth. This does not mean that the backside is always dark, since the Sun is the main source of light in the Solar System. The farside of the Moon gets just as much direct sunlight as the nearside. At New Moon phase, the farside of the Moon is fully lit. With its long day and night, the daytime temperature can reach 260° F, while the coldest nighttime temperature may reach –280° F. This day-to-night temperature change is exceeded only by that on Mercury.

The Moon's revolution about Earth is irregular because of its elliptical orbit. The Moon's rotation, however, is regular, and this, together with the irregular revolution, produces what is called "libration in longitude," which permits the observer on Earth to see first farther around the E side and then farther around the W side of the Moon. The Moon's variation N or S of the ecliptic permits one to see farther over first one pole and then the other of the Moon; this is called "libration in latitude." These two libration effects permit observers on Earth to see a total of about 60% of the Moon's surface over a period of time.

The hidden side of the Moon was first photographed in 1959 by the Soviet space vehicle *Lunik III*. The moon's farside does appear noticeably different from the nearside, in that the farside has practically none of the large lava plains, called maria, so prominent on the nearside of the Moon.

Although the Apollo missions indicated that the Moon lacked any water, in 1996, the U.S. *Clementine* spacecraft may have detected ice in a deep crater near the Moon's south pole. In 1998, NASA's *Lunar Prospector* spacecraft detected further evidence for the existence of perhaps as much as 6 bil tons of water-ice at the Moon's N and S poles.

Tides on Earth are caused mainly by the Moon, because of its proximity to Earth. The ratio of the tide-raising power of the Moon to that of the Sun is 11 to 5.

Harvest Moon and Hunter's Moon

The Harvest Moon, the full Moon nearest the autumnal equinox, ushers in a period of several successive days when the Moon rises soon after sunset. This phenomenon gives farmers in temperate latitudes extra hours of light in which to harvest their crops before frost and winter come. The 1999 Harvest Moon falls on Sept. 25 UTC. Harvest Moon in the southern hemisphere temperate latitudes falls on Mar. 31.

The next full Moon after Harvest Moon is called the Hunter's Moon; it is accompanied by a similar but less marked phenomenon. In 1999, the Hunter's Moon occurs on Oct. 24, northern hemisphere; Apr. 30, southern hemisphere.

Moon's Perigee and Apogee, 1999

(Coordinated Universal Time, standard time of the prime meridian)

Perigee

Date	Hour	Date	Hour
Jan. 26	21	Aug. 8	00
Feb. 20	15	Sept. 2	18
Mar. 20	00	Sept. 28	17
Apr. 17	5	Oct. 26	13
May 15	15	Nov. 23	22
June 13	1	Dec. 22	11
July 11	6		

Apogee

Date	Hour	Date	Hour
Jan. 11	12	July 23	6
Feb. 8	9	Aug. 19	23
Mar. 8	5	Sept. 16	19
Apr. 4	22	Oct. 14	14
May 2	6	Nov. 11	6
May 29	8	Dec. 8	11
June 25	16		

Moon Phases, 1999

(Coordinated Universal Time, standard time of the prime meridian)

New Moon				Waxing Quarter				Full Moon				Waning Quarter			
Month	d	h	m	Month	d	h	m	Month	d	h	m	Month	d	h	m
Jan.	17	15	46	Jan.	24	19	15	Jan.	2	2	49	Jan.	9	14	22
Feb.	16	6	39	Feb.	23	2	43	Jan.	31	16	6	Feb.	8	11	58
Mar.	17	18	48	Mar.	24	10	18	Mar.	2	6	58	Mar.	10	8	40
Apr.	16	4	22	Apr.	22	19	1	Mar.	31	22	49	Apr.	9	2	51
May	15	12	5	May	22	5	34	Apr.	30	14	55	May	8	17	28
June	13	19	3	June	20	18	13	May	30	6	40	June	7	4	20
July	13	2	24	July	20	9	00	June	28	21	37	July	6	11	57
Aug.	11	11	8	Aug.	19	1	47	July	28	11	25	Aug.	4	17	27
Sept.	9	22	2	Sept.	17	20	6	Aug.	26	23	48	Sept.	2	22	17
Oct.	9	11	34	Oct.	17	15	00	Sept.	25	10	15	Oct.	2	4	2
Nov.	8	3	53	Nov.	16	9	3	Oct.	24	21	2	Oct.	31	12	4
Dec.	7	22	32	Dec.	16	0	50	Nov.	23	7	4	Nov.	29	23	18
								Dec.	22	17	31	Dec.	29	14	4

Earth: Size, Computation of Time, Seasons

Distance from the Sun	
Perihelion	91.4 mil mi
Semi-major axis	1.00002 AU
Aphelion	94.5 mil mi
Period of revolution	365.3d
Orbital eccentricity	0.0167
Orbital inclination	0.0°
Sidereal day (Rotation period)	23h 56m 4.2s
Synodic day (midday to midday)	24h 0m 0s
Rotational inclination	23.45°
Mass (Earth = 1)	1.00
Mean radius	3,959 mi
Mean density (Earth = 1)	1.00
Natural satellites	1
Average surface temperature	45° F

Size and Dimensions

Earth is the 5th-largest planet and the 3d from the Sun. Its mass is 6 sextillion, 590 quintillion short tons. Using the parameters of an ellipsoid adopted by the International Astronomical Union in 1964 and recognized by the International Union of Geodesy and Geophysics in 1967, the length of the equator is 24,901.55 mi, the length of a meridian is 24,859.82 mi, the equatorial diameter is 7,926.41 mi, and the area of this reference ellipsoid is approximately 196,938,800 sq mi.

Earth is considered a solid, rigid mass with a dense core of magnetic, probably metallic material with a radius of about 2,200 mi. The outer 2/3 part of the core is probably liquid. Around the core is a thick shell or mantle of dense rock. A section of the mantle, the asthenosphere, is somewhat plasticlike and under slow steady pressure can flow like a liquid. The mantle, in turn, is covered by a thin crust forming the solid granite and basalt base of the continents and ocean basins. Over broad areas of Earth's surface, the crust has a thin cover of sedimentary rock such as sandstone, shale, and limestone formed by weathering of Earth's surface and deposition of sands, clays, and plant and animal remains.

The temperature in Earth increases about 1° F with every 100 to 200 feet in depth, in the upper 100 km of Earth, and the temperature near the core is believed to be near the melting point of the core materials under the conditions at that depth. The heat of Earth is believed to be derived from radioactivity in the rocks, pressures developed within Earth, and the original heat of formation.

Atmosphere of Earth

Earth's atmosphere is a blanket composed of nitrogen, oxygen, and argon, in amounts of about 77%, 21%, and 1% by volume. Also present in minute quantities are carbon dioxide, hydrogen, neon, helium, krypton, and xenon. Water vapor displaces other gases and varies from nearly zero to about 4% by volume. The atmosphere rests on Earth's surface with the weight equivalent to a layer of water 34 ft deep. For about 300,000 ft upward, the gases remain in the proportions stated. Gravity holds the gases to Earth. The weight of the air compresses it at the bottom so that the greatest density is at Earth's surface. Pressure, as well as density, decreases as height increases because the weight pressing upon any layer is always less than that pressing upon the layers below.

The temperature of the air drops with increased height until the **tropopause** is reached. Altitude of the tropopause may vary from 25,000 to 60,000 ft. The atmosphere below the tropopause is the **troposphere,** which contains 90% of the air and the tallest mountains. This is also where most weather phenomena occur. The atmosphere for about 20 mi above the tropopause is the **stratosphere,** where the temperature generally increases with height except at high latitudes in winter. The stratophere also contains ozone, which prevents ultraviolet rays from reaching Earth's surface. The height of the **ozone** layer varies from approximately 12 to 21 mi above Earth. Traces exist as low as 6 mi and as high as 35 mi. A temperature maximum near the 30-mi level is called the **stratopause.**

Above this boundary is the **mesosphere,** where the temperature decreases with height to a minimum, the **mesopause,** at a height of 50 mi. Extending above the mesosphere to the outer fringes of the atmosphere is the **thermosphere,** a region where temperature increases with height to a value measured in thousands of degrees Fahrenheit. The lower portion of this region, extending from 50 to about 400 mi in altitude, is characterized by a high ion density and is thus called the **ionosphere.** Most meteors are in the lower thermosphere or the mesophere at the time they are observed. The outer region is called the **exosphere;** this is the region where gas molecules traveling at high speed may escape into outer space, above 600 mi.

Longitude, Latitude

Position on the globe is measured by means of meridians and parallels. Meridians, which are imaginary lines drawn around Earth through the poles, determine **longitude.** The meridian running through Greenwich, England, is the **prime meridian of longitude,** and all others are either E or west. Parallels, which are imaginary circles parallel with the equator, determine **latitude.** The length of a degree of longitude varies as the cosine of the latitude. At the equator a degree of longitude is 69.171 statute mi; this is gradually reduced toward the poles. Value of a longitude degree at the poles is zero.

Latitude is reckoned by the number of degrees N or S of the equator, an imaginary circle on Earth's surface everywhere equidistant between the two poles. According to the International Astronomical Union ellipsoid of 1964, the length of a degree of latitude is 68.708 statute mi at the equator and varies slightly N and S because of the oblate form of the globe; at the poles it is 69.403 statute mi.

Definitions of Time

Earth rotates on its axis and follows an elliptical orbit around the Sun. The rotation makes the Sun appear to move across the sky from E to W. This rotation determines day and night, and the complete rotation, in relation to the Sun, is called the **apparent** or **true solar day.** A sundial thus measures **apparent solar time.** This length of time varies, but an average determines the **mean solar day** of 24 hours.

The mean solar day and **mean solar time** are in universal use for civil purposes. Mean solar time may be obtained from apparent solar time by correcting observations of the Sun for the **equation of time.** Mean solar time may be as much as 16 minutes behind or 14 minutes ahead of apparent solar time.

Sidereal time is the measure of time defined by the diurnal motion of the vernal equinox and is determined from observation of the meridian transits of stars. One complete rotation of Earth relative to the equinox is called the **sidereal day.** The **mean sidereal day** is 23 hours, 56 minutes, 4.091 seconds of mean solar time.

The interval required for Earth to make one absolute revolution around the Sun is a **sidereal year;** it consisted of 365 days, 6 hours, 9 minutes, and 9.5 seconds of mean solar time (approximately 24 hours per day) in 1900 and has been increasing at the rate of 0.0001 second annually.

The **tropical year,** upon which our calendar is based, is the interval between 2 consecutive returns of the Sun to the vernal equinox. The tropical year consisted of 365 days, 5 hours, 48 minutes, and 46 seconds in 1900. It has been decreasing at the rate of 0.530 second per century. The **calendar year** begins at 12 o'clock midnight precisely, local clock time, on the night of Dec. 31-Jan. 1. The day and the calendar month also begin at midnight by the clock.

On Jan. 1, 1972, the Bureau International des Poids et Mesures in Paris introduced International Atomic Time (TAI) as the most precisely determined time scale for astronomical usage. The fundamental unit of TAI in the international system of units is the second, defined as the duration of 9,192,631,770 periods of the radiation corresponding to the transition between 2 hyperfine levels of the ground state of the cesium 133 atom. Coordinated Universal Time (UTC), which serves as the basis for civil timekeeping and is the standard time of the prime meridian, is officially defined by a formula which relates UTC to mean sidereal time in Greenwich, England. (UTC has replaced GMT as the basis for standard time for the world.)

The Zones and Seasons

The 5 zones of Earth's surface are the Torrid, lying between the Tropics of Cancer and Capricorn; the N Temperate, between Cancer and the Arctic Circle; the S Temperate, between Capricorn and the Antarctic Circle; and the 2 Frigid Zones, between the Polar Circles and the Poles.

The inclination or tilt of Earth's axis, 23° 27′ away from a perpendicular to the Earth's orbit of the Sun, determines the seasons. These are commonly marked in the N Temperate Zone, where spring begins at the vernal equinox, summer at the summer solstice, autumn at the autumnal equinox, and winter at the winter solstice.

In the S Temperate Zone, the seasons are reversed. Spring begins at the autumnal equinox, summer at the winter solstice, etc.

The points at which the Sun crosses the equator are the equinoxes, when day and night are most nearly equal. The points at which the Sun is at a maximum distance from the equator are the solstices. Days and nights are then most unequal. However, at the equator, day and night are equal throughout the year.

In June, the North Pole is tilted 23° 27′ toward the Sun, and the days in the northern hemisphere are longer than the nights, while the days in the southern hemisphere are shorter than the nights. In Dec., the North Pole is tilted 23° 27′ away from the Sun, and the situation is reversed.

The Seasons in 1999

In 1999 the 4 seasons will begin in the northern hemisphere as shown. (Add one hour to Eastern Standard Time for Atlantic Time; subtract one hour for Central, 2 for Mountain, 3 for Pacific, 4 for Alaska, 5 for Hawaii-Aleutian. Also shown is Coordinated Universal Time.)

Seasons	Date	UTC	EST
Vernal Equinox (spring)	Mar. 21	1:46	20:46*
Northern Solstice (summer)	June 21	19:49	14:49
Autumnal Equinox (autumn)	Sept. 23	11:31	6:31
Southern Solstice (winter)	Dec. 22	7:44	2:44

*previous day

Poles of Earth

The geographic (rotation) poles, or points where Earth's axis of rotation cuts the surface, are not absolutely fixed in the body of Earth. The pole of rotation describes an irregular curve about its mean position.

Two periods have been detected in this motion: (1) an annual period due to seasonal changes in barometric pressure, to load of ice and snow on the surface, and to other phenomena of seasonal character; (2) a period of about 14 months due to the shape and constitution of Earth.

In addition, there are small but as yet unpredictable irregularities. The whole motion is so small that the actual pole at any time remains within a circle of 30 or 40 feet in radius centered at the mean position of the pole.

The pole of rotation for the time being is of course the pole having a latitude of 90° and an indeterminate longitude.

Magnetic Poles

The **north magnetic pole** of Earth is that region where the magnetic force is vertically downward, and the **south magnetic pole** is that region where the magnetic force is vertically upward. A compass placed at the magnetic poles experiences no directive force in azimuth.

There are slow changes in the distribution of Earth's magnetic field. This slow temporal change is referred to as the Secular change of the main magnetic field. The position of the magnetic poles shifts due to the Secular. The center of the area designated as the north magnetic pole was estimated to be in about latitude 70.5° N and longitude 96° W in 1905; from recent nearby measurements and studies of the secular changes, the position in 1970 was estimated as latitude 76.2° N and longitude 101° W. Improved data account for at least part of the change.

The position of the south magnetic pole in 1912 was near 71° S and longitude 150° E. In 1970 it was estimated at latitude 66° S and longitude 139.1° E.

The direction of the horizontal components of the magnetic field at any point is known as magnetic N at that point, and the angle by which it deviates E or W of true N is known as the magnetic declination or, in the mariner's terminology, the **variation of the compass.**

A compass without error points in the direction of magnetic north. (In general, this is not the direction of the magnetic north pole.) If one follows the direction indicated by the N end of the compass, he or she will travel along a rather irregular curve that eventually reaches the north magnetic pole (though not usually by a great-circle route). However, the action of the compass should not be thought of as due to any influence of the distant pole, but simply as an indication of the distribution of Earth's magnetism at the place of observation.

Rotation of Earth

The speed of rotation of Earth about its axis has been found to be slightly variable. The variations may be classified as:

(A) **Secular.** Tidal friction acts as a brake on the rotation and causes a slow secular increase in the length of the day, about 1 millisecond per century.

(B) **Irregular.** The speed of rotation may increase for a number of years, about 5 to 10, and then start decreasing. The maximum difference from the mean in the length of the day during a century is about 5 milliseconds. The accumulated difference in time has amounted to approximately 44 seconds since 1900. The cause is probably motion in the interior of Earth.

(C) **Periodic.** Seasonal variations exist with periods of 1 year and 6 months. The cumulative effect is such that each year, Earth is late about 30 milliseconds near June 1 and is ahead about 30 milliseconds near Oct. 1. The maximum seasonal variation in the length of the day is about 0.5 millisecond. It is believed that the principal cause of the annual variation is the seasonal change in the wind patterns of the northern and southern hemispheres. The semiannual variation is due chiefly to tidal action of the Sun, which distorts the shape of Earth slightly.

The secular and irregular variations were discovered by comparing time based on the rotation of Earth with time based on the orbital motion of the Moon about Earth and of the planets about the Sun. The periodic variation was determined largely with the aid of quartz-crystal clocks The introduction of the cesium-beam atomic clock in 1955 made it possible to determine in greater detail than before the nature of the irregular and periodic variations.

Chronological Eras

Era	Year	Begins in 1999
Byzantine	7508	Sept. 14
Jewish	5760	Sept. 10[1]
Roman (Ab Urbe Condita)	2752	Jan. 14
Nabonassar (Babylonian)	2748	Apr. 24
Japanese	2659	Jan. 1
Grecian (Seleucidae)	2311	Sept. 14 or Oct. 14
Diocletian	1716	Sept. 12
Indian (Saka)	1921	Mar. 22
Islamic/Muslim (Hijra)	1420	Apr. 16[1]

(1) Year begins at sunset.

Chronological Cycles, 1999

Dominical Letter	C	Golden Number (Lunar Cycle)	V	Roman Indiction	7
Epact	13	Solar Cycle	20	Julian Period (year of)	6712

Twilight

Twilight is that evening period of waning light from the time of sunset to dark, often termed dusk. Morning twilight, a time of increasing light, is called **dawn**. The source of this light is the Sun shining on the atmosphere above the observer. Twilight is a time of very slowly changing sky illumination with no abrupt variations. Nevertheless, there are 3 commonly accepted divisions in this smooth continuum defined by the distance the Sun lies below the astronomical horizon: civil twilight, nautical twilight, and astronomical twilight. The **astronomical horizon** is that great circle lying 90° from the zenith, the point directly over the observer's head. Twilight ends in the evening or begins in the morning at a particular time. Nominally, evening events are repeated in reverse order in the morning. **Civil twilight** is the time from the moment of sunset, when the Sun's apparent upper edge is just at the horizon, until the center of the Sun is 6° directly below the horizon. In many states, this is the time in the evening when automobile headlights must be turned on, not to see better, but to be seen by other drivers. After this time, a newspaper becomes increasingly difficult to read in the absence of artificial light. **Nautical twilight** ends when the Sun's center is 12° below the horizon. By this time in the evening, the bright stars used by navigators have appeared, and the horizon may still be seen. After this time, the horizon is more difficult to perceive, preventing navigators from sighting stars. **Astronomical twilight** ends in the evening when the Sun is 18° below the horizon and the sky is dark enough, at least away from the Sun's location, to allow astronomical work to proceed. Sunlight, however, is still shining on the higher levels of the atmosphere from the observer's zenith to the horizon toward the Sun. Although not named as a period of twilight, when the Sun is 24° below the horizon, no part of the observer's atmosphere, even toward the Sun, receives any sunlight. In the tropics, the Sun moves nearly vertically, accomplishing its 6°, 12°, or 18° depression very quickly. In the polar regions, the Sun's diurnal motion may actually be nearly along the horizon, prolonging the twilight period or even not permitting darkness to fall at all. In mid-latitudes, civil twilight may last about a half hour; nautical, an hour; and astronomers can go to work in about 90 minutes. The twilight tables given in *The World Almanac* are for the beginning of morning twilight and the end of evening astronomical twilight, and are presented for reference only. Although the instant of the Sun's horizontal depression may be calculated precisely, the phenomena associated with the event are sufficiently imprecise that the table is not recalculated each year.

Astronomical Twilight—Meridian of Greenwich

Date	20° Morn.	20° Even.	30° Morn.	30° Even.	40° Morn.	40° Even.	50° Morn.	50° Even.	60° Morn.	60° Even.
	h m	h m	h m	h m	h m	h m	h m	h m	h m	h m
Jan. 1	5 17	**6 51**	5 31	**6 37**	5 45	**6 23**	6 00	**6 08**	6 18	**5 49**
11	5 20	**6 56**	5 33	**6 44**	5 45	**6 31**	5 58	**6 18**	6 14	**6 03**
21	5 21	**7 02**	5 32	**6 51**	5 42	**6 41**	5 53	**6 30**	6 04	**6 19**
Feb. 1	5 20	**7 08**	5 28	**6 59**	5 36	**6 52**	5 42	**6 46**	5 47	**6 41**
11	5 17	**7 12**	5 23	**7 06**	5 27	**7 03**	5 29	**7 01**	5 27	**7 03**
21	5 12	**7 16**	5 14	**7 13**	5 15	**7 13**	5 12	**7 17**	5 02	**7 26**
Mar. 1	5 07	**7 18**	5 07	**7 19**	5 04	**7 22**	4 56	**7 30**	4 40	**7 47**
11	4 59	**7 22**	4 55	**7 25**	4 48	**7 33**	4 35	**7 47**	4 08	**8 14**
21	4 50	**7 25**	4 43	**7 32**	4 31	**7 44**	4 11	**8 05**	3 33	**8 44**
Apr. 1	4 40	**7 28**	4 29	**7 40**	4 11	**7 57**	3 43	**8 26**	2 47	**9 24**
11	4 30	**7 32**	4 15	**7 47**	3 53	**8 10**	3 16	**8 48**	1 56	**10 11**
21	4 21	**7 36**	4 02	**7 56**	3 35	**8 24**	2 48	**9 12**		
May 1	4 13	**7 42**	3 50	**8 04**	3 17	**8 38**	2 17	**9 39**		
11	4 06	**7 47**	3 40	**8 14**	3 00	**8 53**	1 45	**10 10**		
21	4 01	**7 53**	3 31	**8 22**	2 46	**9 08**	1 10	**10 47**		
June 1	3 57	**7 59**	3 25	**8 31**	2 35	**9 22**				
11	3 56	**8 03**	3 22	**8 37**	2 29	**9 31**				
21	3 57	**8 06**	3 23	**8 41**	2 28	**9 36**				
July 1	4 00	**8 07**	3 26	**8 41**	2 32	**9 35**				
11	4 05	**8 06**	3 32	**8 38**	2 42	**9 28**				
21	4 10	**8 03**	3 40	**8 32**	2 54	**9 18**	1 12	**10 57**		
Aug. 1	4 16	**7 56**	3 49	**8 23**	3 09	**9 02**	1 53	**10 17**		
11	4 21	**7 49**	3 58	**8 12**	3 24	**8 45**	2 23	**9 45**		
21	4 25	**7 41**	4 06	**7 59**	3 38	**8 27**	2 50	**9 15**		
Sept. 1	4 29	**7 30**	4 14	**7 45**	3 52	**8 07**	3 15	**8 43**	1 55	**10 01**
11	4 33	**7 20**	4 21	**7 31**	4 04	**7 48**	3 36	**8 16**	2 39	**9 11**
21	4 35	**7 10**	4 28	**7 18**	4 15	**7 30**	3 54	**7 50**	3 14	**8 30**
Oct. 1	4 38	**7 01**	4 34	**7 05**	4 26	**7 12**	4 12	**7 26**	3 44	**7 54**
11	4 40	**6 53**	4 40	**6 53**	4 36	**6 56**	4 28	**7 04**	4 10	**7 22**
21	4 43	**6 46**	4 46	**6 43**	4 46	**6 42**	4 43	**6 45**	4 34	**6 53**
Nov. 1	4 47	**6 40**	4 53	**6 34**	4 57	**6 29**	5 00	**6 26**	4 59	**6 27**
11	4 51	**6 37**	5 00	**6 28**	5 07	**6 20**	5 14	**6 13**	5 20	**6 07**
21	4 55	**6 36**	5 07	**6 25**	5 17	**6 14**	5 28	**6 04**	5 39	**5 52**
Dec. 1	5 01	**6 37**	5 14	**6 24**	5 26	**6 12**	5 40	**5 58**	5 55	**5 42**
11	5 06	**6 40**	5 20	**6 26**	5 34	**6 12**	5 49	**5 57**	6 08	**5 38**
21	5 12	**6 45**	5 26	**6 30**	5 41	**6 16**	5 56	**6 00**	6 16	**5 41**
31	5 16	**6 50**	5 30	**6 36**	5 44	**6 22**	6 00	**6 07**	6 18	**5 48**

Calculation of Rise Times

The Daily Calendar pages contain rise and set times for the Sun and Moon for the Greenwich Meridian at N latitudes 20°, 30°, 40°, 50°, and 60°. From day to day, the values for the Sun at any particular latitude do not change very much. This means that whatever time the Sun rises or sets at the 0° meridian, it will rise or set at the same time at the Standard Time meridian of your time zone. Standard Time meridians occur every 15° of longitude (15° E and W, 30° E and W, etc.) The corrections necessary to observe that event from your location will be to account for your distance from the Standard Time meridian and for your latitude. Thus, if your latitude is about 45°, sunrise on Jan. 1, 1999, is roughly halfway between 7:22 and 7:29 am on the Standard Time meridian for your time zone. If you are 7.5° west of your Standard Time meridian, sunrise will be about 1/2 hour later than this; if 7.5° east, about 1/2 hour earlier.

The Moon, however, moves its own diameter, about one-half degree, in an hour, or about 13.2° in one complete turn of Earth—one day. Most of this is eastward against the background stars of the sky, but some is also N or S movement. All this motion considerably affects the times of rise or set, as you can see from the adjacent entries in the table. Thus, it is necessary to take your longitude into account in addition to your latitude. If you have no need for total accuracy, simply note that the time will be between the 4 values (see example below) you find surrounding your location and the dates of interest.

The process of finding more accurate corrections is called interpolation. In the example, linear interpolation involving simple differences is used. In extreme cases, higher order interpolation should be used. If such cases are important to you, it is suggested that you plot the times, draw smooth curves through the plots, and interpolate by eye between the relevant curves. Some people find this exercise fun.

Let's find the times of the moonrise for the May Full Moon and sunset the same day at Norfolk, VA.

First, where is Norfolk, VA? Find Norfolk's latitude and longitude in the "Latitude, Longitude, and Altitude of U.S. and Canadian Cities" table found in the World Exploration and Geography section of The World Almanac. You must also know the time zone in which the city is located, which you can estimate from the "International Time Zones" map in the map section of *The World Almanac*.

I. Norfolk, VA: 36° 50′ 48′′ N
76° 17′ 8′′ W

IA. Convert these values to decimals:
48/60 = 0.8
50 + 0.8 = 50.8
50.8/60 = 0.85
36 + 0.85 = 36.85 N
8/60 = 0.13
17 + 0.13 = 17.13
17.13/60 = 0.29
76 + 0.29 = 76.29 W

IB. Fraction Norfolk lies between 30° and 40°:
36.85 – 30 = 6.85; 6.85/10 = 0.685

IC. Fraction world must turn between Greenwich and Norfolk:
76.29/360 = 0.212

ID. Norfolk is in the Eastern Standard Time zone and the EST meridian is 75°, thus 76.29 is 76.29 – 75 = 1.29° W of the Eastern Standard Meridian. In 24 hours, there are 24 × 60 = 1,440 minutes; 1,440/360 = 4 minutes for every degree around Earth. So events happen 4 x 1.29 = 5.2 minutes later in Norfolk than at the 75° meridian. (If the location is E of the Standard Meridian, events happen earlier.)

IE. The values IB and IC are interpolates for Norfolk; ID is the time correction from local to Standard time for Norfolk. These values need never be calculated again for Norfolk.

IIA. To find the time of moonrise we start from the table of Moon Phases, 1999, we see that May's Full Moon occurs on May 30. We need the Greenwich times for moonrise at latitudes 30° and 40°, and for May 30 and 31, the day of the Full Moon and the next day. These values are found in the Astronomy Daily Calendar 1999: we then compute the difference between the two latitudes.

	30°	Diff.	40°
May 30	19:08	0:21	19:29
May 31	20:00	0:23	20:23

IIB. We want IB and the May 30 time difference:
0.685 x 21 = 14.4
Add this to the May 30, 30° rise time:
19:08 + 14.4 = 19:22.4
And for May 31:
0.685 x 23 = 15.8
Add this to the May 31, 30° rise time:
20:00 + 15.8 = 20:15.8
These 2 times are for the latitude of Norfolk, but for the Greenwich meridian.

IIC. To get the time for Norfolk meridian, take the difference between these 2 times just determined,
20:15.8 – 19:22.4 = 53.4 minutes,
and find what fraction of this 24-hour change took place while Earth turned between Greenwich and Norfolk, 0.212 (See IC)
53.4 x 0.212 = 11.3 minutes after 19:22.4
Thus 19:22.4 + 11.3 = 19:33.7 is the time the Full Moon will rise in the local time of Norfolk.

IID. But this happens 5.2 minutes (See ID) later by EST clock time at Norfolk, thus
19:33.7 + 5.2 = 19:38.9 EST
But this is late spring, and daylight time is in effect;
19:39 + 1:00 = 20:39 EDT is the rise time for the Full Moon at Norfolk the evening of May 30, 1999.

IIIA. To find the time of sunset we need the Greenwich times for sunset at latitudes 30° and 40°. These values are found in the Astronomy Daily Calendar 1999: we then compute the difference between the two latitudes.

	30°	Diff.	40°
May 30	18:55	0:26	19:21

IIIB. We want IB and the May 30 time difference:
0.685 x 26 = 17.8
Add this to the May 30, 30° set time:
18:55 + 17.8 = 19:12.8
This is the local time for the latitude of Norfolk.

IIIC. But this happens 5.2 minutes (See ID) later by EST clock time at Norfolk, thus
19:12.8 + 5.2 = 19:18 EST
But this is summer, and daylight time is in effect;
19:18 + 1:00 = 20:18 EDT is sunset at Norfolk on May 30, 1999.

January 1999

1st Month **31 days**

Coordinated Universal Time (Greenwich Mean Time)

NOTE: For each day, numbers on first line indicate Sun. Numbers on second line indicate *Moon.* Degrees are North Latitude.

Moon Phases: FM = full moon; LQ = last quarter; NM = new moon; FQ = first quarter. Sun's distance is in Astronomical Units.

CAUTION: Must be converted to local time. For instructions see "Calculation of Rise Times."

Day of month, of week, *of year*	Sun on Meridian *Moon Phase* h m s	Sun's Declination ° ′ *Distance*	20° Rise Sun *Moon* h m	20° Set Sun *Moon* h m	30° Rise Sun *Moon* h m	30° Set Sun *Moon* h m	40° Rise Sun *Moon* h m	40° Set Sun *Moon* h m	50° Rise Sun *Moon* h m	50° Set Sun *Moon* h m	60° Rise Sun *Moon* h m	60° Set Sun *Moon* h m
1 FR	12 03 23	–23 03	6 35	17 32	6 56	17 11	7 22	16 45	7 59	16 08	9 02	15 05
1		*.9833*	*17 10*	*5 40*	*16 52*	*5 58*	*16 29*	*6 20*	*15 58*	*6 52*	*15 05*	*7 44*
2 SA	12 03 52	–22 58	6 35	17 32	6 56	17 12	7 22	16 46	7 58	16 09	9 02	15 06
2	*2 49 FM*	*.9832*	*18 10*	*6 41*	*17 52*	*6 59*	*17 30*	*7 21*	*16 59*	*7 53*	*16 07*	*8 46*
3 SU	12 04 19	–22 53	6 36	17 33	6 56	17 13	7 22	16 47	7 58	16 10	9 01	15 08
3		*.9832*	*19 10*	*7 37*	*18 54*	*7 54*	*18 34*	*8 15*	*18 06*	*8 44*	*17 20*	*9 32*
4 MO	12 04 47	–22 47	6 36	17 34	6 56	17 13	7 22	16 48	7 58	16 12	9 01	15 09
4		*.9832*	*20 08*	*8 29*	*19 55*	*8 43*	*19 38*	*9 02*	*19 15*	*9 26*	*18 38*	*10 06*
5 TU	12 05 14	–22 41	6 36	17 34	6 57	17 14	7 22	16 49	7 58	16 13	9 00	15 11
5		*.9832*	*21 04*	*9 16*	*20 54*	*9 27*	*20 42*	*9 42*	*20 24*	*10 01*	*19 57*	*10 31*
6 WE	12 05 40	–22 34	6 36	17 35	6 57	17 15	7 22	16 49	7 58	16 14	8 59	15 13
6		*.9833*	*21 57*	*9 59*	*21 51*	*10 07*	*21 43*	*10 17*	*21 32*	*10 30*	*21 15*	*10 51*
7 TH	12 06 06	–22 27	6 37	17 36	6 57	17 16	7 22	16 50	7 57	16 15	8 58	15 14
7		*.9833*	*22 48*	*10 38*	*22 46*	*10 43*	*22 42*	*10 48*	*22 37*	*10 56*	*22 30*	*11 07*
8 FR	12 06 32	–22 20	6 37	17 36	6 57	17 16	7 22	16 51	7 57	16 16	8 57	15 16
8		*.9833*	*23 38*	*11 16*	*23 39*	*11 17*	*23 40*	*11 18*	*23 41*	*11 19*	*23 44*	*11 22*
9 SA	12 06 57	–22 12	6 37	17 37	6 57	17 17	7 22	16 52	7 57	16 18	8 56	15 18
9	*14 22 LQ*	*.9833*	*none*	*11 52*	*none*	*11 50*	*none*	*11 47*	*none*	*11 42*	*none*	*11 36*
10 SU	12 07 22	–22 03	6 37	17 38	6 57	17 18	7 22	16 53	7 56	16 19	8 55	15 20
10		*.9834*	*0 26*	*12 29*	*0 31*	*12 23*	*0 37*	*12 15*	*0 44*	*12 05*	*0 56*	*11 50*
11 MO	12 07 46	–21 54	6 37	17 38	6 57	17 19	7 21	16 54	7 56	16 20	8 54	15 22
11		*.9834*	*1 15*	*13 06*	*1 23*	*12 57*	*1 33*	*12 45*	*1 46*	*12 30*	*2 07*	*12 05*
12 TU	12 08 10	–21 45	6 38	17 39	6 57	17 20	7 21	16 55	7 55	16 22	8 53	15 24
12		*.9834*	*2 04*	*13 45*	*2 15*	*13 33*	*2 29*	*13 18*	*2 48*	*12 57*	*3 18*	*12 24*
13 WE	12 08 33	–21 35	6 38	17 40	6 57	17 20	7 21	16 56	7 54	16 23	8 51	15 26
13		*.9835*	*2 53*	*14 27*	*3 07*	*14 12*	*3 25*	*13 53*	*3 49*	*13 28*	*4 28*	*12 46*
14 TH	12 08 55	–21 25	6 38	17 40	6 57	17 21	7 21	16 58	7 54	16 24	8 50	15 29
14		*.9835*	*3 44*	*15 11*	*4 00*	*14 54*	*4 21*	*14 33*	*4 49*	*14 04*	*5 36*	*13 16*
15 FR	12 09 17	–21 14	6 38	17 41	6 57	17 22	7 20	16 59	7 53	16 26	8 48	15 31
15		*.9836*	*4 35*	*15 59*	*4 53*	*15 41*	*5 15*	*15 18*	*5 47*	*14 47*	*6 39*	*13 54*
16 SA	12 09 38	–21 04	6 38	17 42	6 57	17 23	7 20	17 00	7 52	16 27	8 47	15 33
16		*.9837*	*5 27*	*16 50*	*5 45*	*16 32*	*6 08*	*16 09*	*6 40*	*15 37*	*7 34*	*14 43*
17 SU	12 09 58	–20 52	6 38	17 42	6 56	17 24	7 19	17 01	7 51	16 29	8 45	15 35
17	*15 46 NM*	*.9837*	*6 18*	*17 44*	*6 35*	*17 27*	*6 58*	*17 05*	*7 28*	*16 35*	*8 20*	*15 45*
18 MO	12 10 18	–20 40	6 38	17 43	6 56	17 25	7 19	17 02	7 51	16 30	8 43	15 38
18		*.9838*	*7 07*	*18 39*	*7 23*	*18 24*	*7 43*	*18 05*	*8 11*	*17 39*	*8 56*	*16 56*
19 TU	12 10 37	–20 28	6 38	17 44	6 56	17 26	7 18	17 03	7 50	16 32	8 42	15 40
19		*.9839*	*7 55*	*19 36*	*8 08*	*19 24*	*8 25*	*19 09*	*8 48*	*18 48*	*9 24*	*18 14*
20 WE	12 10 55	–20 16	6 38	17 44	6 56	17 26	7 18	17 04	7 49	16 34	8 40	15 42
20		*.9839*	*8 41*	*20 33*	*8 51*	*20 24*	*9 04*	*20 14*	*9 21*	*19 59*	*9 47*	*19 36*
21 TH	12 11 12	–20 03	6 38	17 45	6 55	17 27	7 17	17 05	7 48	16 35	8 38	15 45
21		*.9840*	*9 25*	*21 30*	*9 31*	*21 26*	*9 39*	*21 20*	*9 50*	*21 12*	*10 06*	*21 00*
22 FR	12 11 29	–19 49	6 38	17 45	6 55	17 28	7 17	17 07	7 47	16 37	8 36	15 47
22		*.9841*	*10 08*	*22 27*	*10 10*	*22 27*	*10 13*	*22 27*	*10 17*	*22 26*	*10 23*	*22 25*
23 SA	12 11 45	–19 36	6 38	17 46	6 55	17 29	7 16	17 08	7 46	16 38	8 34	15 50
23		*.9842*	*10 51*	*23 25*	*10 49*	*23 29*	*10 47*	*23 34*	*10 44*	*23 41*	*10 40*	*23 51*
24 SU	12 12 00	–19 22	6 37	17 47	6 54	17 30	7 15	17 09	7 45	16 40	8 32	15 52
24	*19 15 FQ*	*.9843*	*11 35*	*none*	*11 29*	*none*	*11 22*	*none*	*11 12*	*none*	*10 57*	*none*
25 MO	12 12 14	–19 07	6 37	17 47	6 54	17 31	7 15	17 10	7 43	16 42	8 30	15 55
25		*.9844*	*12 21*	*0 24*	*12 11*	*0 32*	*11 59*	*0 42*	*11 42*	*0 56*	*11 17*	*1 18*
26 TU	12 12 28	–18 53	6 37	17 48	6 54	17 32	7 14	17 11	7 42	16 43	8 28	15 57
26		*.9845*	*13 10*	*1 24*	*12 56*	*1 36*	*12 40*	*1 51*	*12 17*	*2 11*	*11 41*	*2 44*
27 WE	12 12 40	–18 38	6 37	17 49	6 53	17 32	7 13	17 12	7 41	16 45	8 26	16 00
27		*.9846*	*14 02*	*2 25*	*13 45*	*2 40*	*13 25*	*2 59*	*12 58*	*3 25*	*12 13*	*4 08*
28 TH	12 12 52	–18 22	6 37	17 49	6 53	17 33	7 12	17 14	7 40	16 47	8 24	16 03
28		*.9847*	*14 57*	*3 26*	*14 39*	*3 43*	*14 17*	*4 05*	*13 46*	*4 35*	*12 54*	*5 25*
29 FR	12 13 03	–18 06	6 36	17 50	6 52	17 34	7 12	17 15	7 38	16 48	8 22	16 05
29		*.9848*	*15 55*	*4 26*	*15 36*	*4 44*	*15 14*	*5 07*	*14 42*	*5 38*	*13 49*	*6 32*
30 SA	12 13 13	–17 50	6 36	17 50	6 52	17 35	7 11	17 16	7 37	16 50	8 20	16 08
30		*.9849*	*16 54*	*5 23*	*16 36*	*5 41*	*16 15*	*6 03*	*15 45*	*6 33*	*14 56*	*7 24*
31 SU	12 13 23	–17 34	6 36	17 51	6 51	17 36	7 10	17 17	7 36	16 52	8 17	16 10
31	*16 06 FM*	*.9851*	*17 52*	*6 16*	*17 37*	*6 32*	*17 19*	*6 52*	*16 53*	*7 19*	*16 11*	*8 03*

February 1999

2d Month **28 days**

Coordinated Universal Time (Greenwich Mean Time)

NOTE: For each day, numbers on first line indicate Sun. Numbers on second line indicate *Moon*. Degrees are North Latitude.

Moon Phases: FM = full moon; LQ = last quarter; NM = new moon; FQ = first quarter. Sun's distance is in Astronomical Units.

CAUTION: Must be converted to local time. For instructions see "Calculation of Rise Times."

Day of month, of week, *of year*	Sun on Meridian *Moon Phase* h m s	Sun's Declination ° ′ *Distance*	20° Rise Sun *Moon* h m	20° Set Sun *Moon* h m	30° Rise Sun *Moon* h m	30° Set Sun *Moon* h m	40° Rise Sun *Moon* h m	40° Set Sun *Moon* h m	50° Rise Sun *Moon* h m	50° Set Sun *Moon* h m	60° Rise Sun *Moon* h m	60° Set Sun *Moon* h m
1 MO	12 13 31	–17 17	6 36	17 52	6 51	17 37	7 09	17 18	7 34	16 53	8 15	16 13
32		*.9852*	*18 49*	*7 05*	*18 38*	*7 19*	*18 23*	*7 35*	*18 03*	*7 57*	*17 30*	*8 32*
2 TU	12 13 39	–17 00	6 35	17 52	6 50	17 38	7 08	17 20	7 33	16 55	8 13	16 16
33		*.9853*	*19 44*	*7 51*	*19 36*	*8 01*	*19 26*	*8 13*	*19 12*	*8 29*	*18 50*	*8 55*
3 WE	12 13 46	–16 43	6 35	17 53	6 49	17 38	7 07	17 21	7 31	16 57	8 10	16 18
34		*.9855*	*20 37*	*8 32*	*20 33*	*8 39*	*20 27*	*8 46*	*20 19*	*8 57*	*20 07*	*9 13*
4 TH	12 13 52	–16 25	6 35	17 53	6 49	17 39	7 06	17 22	7 30	16 59	8 08	16 21
35		*.9856*	*21 28*	*9 11*	*21 27*	*9 14*	*21 26*	*9 17*	*21 25*	*9 22*	*21 23*	*9 28*
5 FR	12 13 57	–16 07	6 34	17 54	6 48	17 40	7 05	17 23	7 28	17 00	8 05	16 23
36		*.9858*	*22 18*	*9 49*	*22 21*	*9 48*	*22 24*	*9 47*	*22 29*	*9 45*	*22 37*	*9 42*
6 SA	12 14 02	–15 49	6 34	17 54	6 47	17 41	7 04	17 25	7 27	17 02	8 03	16 26
37		*.9860*	*23 07*	*10 26*	*23 13*	*10 21*	*23 21*	*10 16*	*23 32*	*10 08*	*23 49*	*9 56*
7 SU	12 14 06	–15 31	6 33	17 55	6 47	17 42	7 03	17 26	7 25	17 04	8 00	16 29
38		*.9861*	*23 56*	*11 03*	*none*	*10 55*	*none*	*10 45*	*none*	*10 32*	*none*	*10 11*
8 MO	12 14 08	–15 12	6 33	17 56	6 46	17 43	7 02	17 27	7 24	17 05	7 58	16 31
39	*11 58 LQ*	*.9863*	*none*	*11 41*	*0 05*	*11 30*	*0 17*	*11 16*	*0 34*	*10 58*	*1 01*	*10 29*
9 TU	12 14 11	–14 53	6 33	17 56	6 45	17 43	7 01	17 28	7 22	17 07	7 55	16 34
40		*.9865*	*0 45*	*12 21*	*0 58*	*12 07*	*1 13*	*11 50*	*1 35*	*11 27*	*2 11*	*10 49*
10 WE	12 14 12	–14 34	6 32	17 57	6 44	17 44	7 00	17 29	7 20	17 09	7 53	16 37
41		*.9867*	*1 35*	*13 04*	*1 50*	*12 48*	*2 09*	*12 28*	*2 36*	*12 00*	*3 19*	*11 15*
11 TH	12 14 13	–14 14	6 32	17 57	6 44	17 45	6 58	17 30	7 19	17 11	7 50	16 39
42		*.9868*	*2 25*	*13 50*	*2 42*	*13 32*	*3 04*	*13 10*	*3 34*	*12 40*	*4 24*	*11 49*
12 FR	12 14 13	–13 55	6 31	17 58	6 43	17 46	6 57	17 32	7 17	17 12	7 47	16 42
43		*.9870*	*3 16*	*14 39*	*3 34*	*14 21*	*3 57*	*13 58*	*4 29*	*13 26*	*5 23*	*12 33*
13 SA	12 14 12	–13 35	6 31	17 58	6 42	17 47	6 56	17 33	7 15	17 14	7 45	16 45
44		*.9872*	*4 07*	*15 32*	*4 25*	*15 14*	*4 48*	*14 52*	*5 20*	*14 21*	*6 13*	*13 28*
14 SU	12 14 10	–13 15	6 30	17 59	6 41	17 48	6 55	17 34	7 13	17 16	7 42	16 47
45		*.9874*	*4 58*	*16 27*	*5 15*	*16 11*	*5 36*	*15 51*	*6 05*	*15 23*	*6 53*	*14 36*
15 MO	12 14 08	–12 54	6 29	17 59	6 40	17 48	6 54	17 35	7 11	17 18	7 39	16 50
46		*.9876*	*5 47*	*17 24*	*6 02*	*17 11*	*6 20*	*16 54*	*6 45*	*16 30*	*7 25*	*15 52*
16 TU	12 14 05	–12 34	6 29	17 59	6 39	17 49	6 52	17 36	7 10	17 19	7 37	16 53
47	*6 39 NM*	*.9878*	*6 34*	*18 22*	*6 46*	*18 12*	*7 00*	*18 00*	*7 20*	*17 42*	*7 51*	*17 15*
17 WE	12 14 01	–12 13	6 28	18 00	6 39	17 50	6 51	17 38	7 08	17 21	7 34	16 55
48		*.9880*	*7 20*	*19 21*	*7 28*	*19 15*	*7 38*	*19 07*	*7 51*	*18 57*	*8 12*	*18 41*
18 TH	12 13 57	–11 52	6 28	18 00	6 38	17 51	6 50	17 39	7 06	17 23	7 31	16 58
49		*.9882*	*8 05*	*20 20*	*8 09*	*20 18*	*8 14*	*20 16*	*8 20*	*20 13*	*8 30*	*20 08*
19 FR	12 13 52	–11 31	6 27	18 01	6 37	17 51	6 48	17 40	7 04	17 24	7 28	17 00
50		*.9884*	*8 49*	*21 19*	*8 49*	*21 22*	*8 48*	*21 25*	*8 48*	*21 29*	*8 47*	*21 36*
20 SA	12 13 46	–11 09	6 26	18 01	6 36	17 52	6 47	17 41	7 02	17 26	7 26	17 03
51		*.9886*	*9 34*	*22 19*	*9 29*	*22 26*	*9 23*	*22 34*	*9 16*	*22 46*	*9 05*	*23 04*
21 SU	12 13 39	–10 48	6 26	18 02	6 35	17 53	6 46	17 42	7 00	17 28	7 23	17 06
52		*.9888*	*10 20*	*23 19*	*10 11*	*23 30*	*10 00*	*23 43*	*9 46*	*none*	*9 24*	*none*
22 MO	12 13 32	–10 26	6 25	18 02	6 34	17 54	6 44	17 43	6 58	17 30	7 20	17 08
53		*.9890*	*11 07*	*none*	*10 55*	*none*	*10 40*	*none*	*10 19*	*0 02*	*9 46*	*0 31*
23 TU	12 13 24	–10 04	6 25	18 03	6 33	17 54	6 43	17 44	6 56	17 31	7 17	17 11
54	*2 43 FQ*	*.9892*	*11 58*	*0 19*	*11 42*	*0 33*	*11 23*	*0 51*	*10 57*	*1 16*	*10 15*	*1 56*
24 WE	12 13 16	–9 42	6 24	18 03	6 32	17 55	6 41	17 46	6 54	17 33	7 14	17 13
55		*.9895*	*12 51*	*1 19*	*12 34*	*1 36*	*12 12*	*1 57*	*11 42*	*2 26*	*10 52*	*3 15*
25 TH	12 13 07	–9 20	6 23	18 03	6 31	17 56	6 40	17 47	6 52	17 35	7 11	17 16
56		*.9897*	*13 47*	*2 18*	*13 29*	*2 36*	*13 06*	*2 59*	*12 34*	*3 31*	*11 41*	*4 23*
26 FR	12 12 57	–8 58	6 22	18 04	6 30	17 57	6 39	17 48	6 50	17 36	7 09	17 18
57		*.9899*	*14 44*	*3 15*	*14 26*	*3 33*	*14 04*	*3 56*	*13 33*	*4 27*	*12 42*	*5 19*
27 SA	12 12 47	–8 36	6 22	18 04	6 29	17 57	6 37	17 49	6 48	17 38	7 06	17 21
58		*.9901*	*15 41*	*4 08*	*15 25*	*4 25*	*15 06*	*4 46*	*14 38*	*5 15*	*13 53*	*6 02*
28 SU	12 12 36	–8 13	6 21	18 05	6 28	17 58	6 36	17 50	6 46	17 40	7 03	17 24
59		*.9904*	*16 38*	*4 58*	*16 25*	*5 13*	*16 08*	*5 30*	*15 46*	*5 55*	*15 09*	*6 34*

March 1999

3d Month **31 days**

Coordinated Universal Time (Greenwich Mean Time)

NOTE: For each day, numbers on first line indicate Sun. Numbers on second line indicate *Moon*. Degrees are North Latitude.

Moon Phases: FM = full moon; LQ = last quarter; NM = new moon; FQ = first quarter. Sun's distance is in Astronomical Units.

CAUTION: Must be converted to local time. For instructions see "Calculation of Rise Times."

Day of month, of week, *of year*	Sun on Meridian *Moon Phase* h m s	Sun's Declination ° ′ *Distance*	20° Rise Sun *Moon* h m	20° Set Sun *Moon* h m	30° Rise Sun *Moon* h m	30° Set Sun *Moon* h m	40° Rise Sun *Moon* h m	40° Set Sun *Moon* h m	50° Rise Sun *Moon* h m	50° Set Sun *Moon* h m	60° Rise Sun *Moon* h m	60° Set Sun *Moon* h m
1 MO	12 12 24	–7 50	6 20	18 05	6 27	17 59	6 34	17 51	6 44	17 41	7 00	17 26
60		*.9906*	*17 33*	*5 44*	*17 23*	*5 55*	*17 11*	*6 09*	*16 54*	*6 28*	*16 28*	*6 58*
2 TU	12 12 13	–7 28	6 19	18 05	6 25	17 59	6 33	17 52	6 42	17 43	6 57	17 29
61	*6 58 FM*	*.9908*	*18 27*	*6 27*	*18 20*	*6 35*	*18 13*	*6 44*	*18 02*	*6 57*	*17 46*	*7 17*
3 WE	12 12 00	–7 05	6 19	18 06	6 24	18 00	6 31	17 53	6 40	17 45	6 54	17 31
62		*.9911*	*19 18*	*7 07*	*19 16*	*7 11*	*19 13*	*7 16*	*19 09*	*7 23*	*19 03*	*7 34*
4 TH	12 11 48	–6 42	6 18	18 06	6 23	18 01	6 30	17 55	6 38	17 46	6 51	17 34
63		*.9913*	*20 09*	*7 45*	*20 10*	*7 45*	*20 12*	*7 46*	*20 14*	*7 47*	*20 18*	*7 48*
5 FR	12 11 34	–6 19	6 17	18 06	6 22	18 01	6 28	17 56	6 36	17 48	6 48	17 36
64		*.9916*	*20 58*	*8 22*	*21 03*	*8 19*	*21 10*	*8 15*	*21 18*	*8 10*	*21 31*	*8 02*
6 SA	12 11 21	–5 55	6 16	18 07	6 21	18 02	6 27	17 57	6 34	17 50	6 45	17 39
65		*.9918*	*21 47*	*8 59*	*21 56*	*8 53*	*22 06*	*8 45*	*22 21*	*8 34*	*22 44*	*8 17*
7 SU	12 11 06	–5 32	6 16	18 07	6 20	18 03	6 25	17 58	6 32	17 51	6 42	17 41
66		*.9921*	*22 37*	*9 37*	*22 48*	*9 27*	*23 03*	*9 15*	*23 23*	*8 59*	*23 55*	*8 33*
8 MO	12 10 52	–5 09	6 15	18 07	6 19	18 03	6 24	17 59	6 30	17 53	6 39	17 44
67		*.9924*	*23 26*	*10 17*	*23 40*	*10 04*	*23 58*	*9 48*	*none*	*9 26*	*none*	*8 52*
9 TU	12 10 37	–4 46	6 14	18 08	6 18	18 04	6 22	18 00	6 28	17 54	6 36	17 46
68		*.9926*	*none*	*10 58*	*none*	*10 43*	*none*	*10 24*	*0 23*	*9 57*	*1 04*	*9 15*
10 WE	12 10 22	–4 22	6 13	18 08	6 16	18 05	6 20	18 01	6 26	17 56	6 33	17 49
69	*8 40 LQ*	*.9929*	*0 16*	*11 42*	*0 33*	*11 25*	*0 53*	*11 03*	*1 22*	*10 34*	*2 10*	*9 45*
11 TH	12 10 06	–3 59	6 12	18 08	6 15	18 05	6 19	18 02	6 23	17 58	6 30	17 51
70		*.9932*	*1 06*	*12 29*	*1 24*	*12 11*	*1 47*	*11 48*	*2 18*	*11 17*	*3 11*	*10 23*
12 FR	12 09 51	–3 35	6 11	18 09	6 14	18 06	6 17	18 03	6 21	17 59	6 27	17 54
71		*.9934*	*1 57*	*13 19*	*2 15*	*13 01*	*2 38*	*12 39*	*3 10*	*12 07*	*4 04*	*11 13*
13 SA	12 09 35	–3 11	6 11	18 09	6 13	18 07	6 16	18 04	6 19	18 01	6 24	17 56
72		*.9937*	*2 46*	*14 13*	*3 04*	*13 56*	*3 26*	*13 34*	*3 57*	*13 04*	*4 48*	*12 14*
14 SU	12 09 18	–2 48	6 10	18 09	6 12	18 07	6 14	18 05	6 17	18 02	6 21	17 59
73		*.9940*	*3 35*	*15 08*	*3 51*	*14 53*	*4 11*	*14 35*	*4 39*	*14 09*	*5 23*	*13 26*
15 MO	12 09 02	–2 24	6 09	18 09	6 11	18 08	6 12	18 06	6 15	18 04	6 18	18 01
74		*.9943*	*4 23*	*16 06*	*4 37*	*15 54*	*4 53*	*15 39*	*5 16*	*15 19*	*5 51*	*14 46*
16 TU	12 08 45	–2 00	6 08	18 10	6 09	18 09	6 11	18 07	6 13	18 06	6 15	18 03
75		*.9945*	*5 10*	*17 05*	*5 20*	*16 57*	*5 32*	*16 47*	*5 49*	*16 33*	*6 14*	*16 11*
17 WE	12 08 28	–1 37	6 07	18 10	6 08	18 09	6 09	18 08	6 11	18 07	6 12	18 06
76	*18 48 NM*	*.9948*	*5 56*	*18 05*	*6 02*	*18 01*	*6 09*	*17 56*	*6 19*	*17 50*	*6 34*	*17 40*
18 TH	12 08 11	–1 13	6 06	18 10	6 07	18 10	6 08	18 09	6 08	18 09	6 09	18 08
77		*.9951*	*6 41*	*19 05*	*6 43*	*19 06*	*6 45*	*19 07*	*6 47*	*19 08*	*6 51*	*19 10*
19 FR	12 07 53	–0 49	6 05	18 11	6 06	18 10	6 06	18 10	6 06	18 11	6 06	18 11
78		*.9954*	*7 27*	*20 07*	*7 24*	*20 12*	*7 21*	*20 19*	*7 16*	*20 28*	*7 09*	*20 41*
20 SA	12 07 36	–0 25	6 05	18 11	6 05	18 11	6 04	18 11	6 04	18 12	6 03	18 13
79		*.9956*	*8 14*	*21 09*	*8 07*	*21 19*	*7 58*	*21 30*	*7 46*	*21 47*	*7 28*	*22 12*
21 SU	12 07 18	–0 02	6 04	18 11	6 03	18 12	6 03	18 12	6 02	18 14	6 00	18 16
80		*.9959*	*9 03*	*22 11*	*8 51*	*22 25*	*8 37*	*22 41*	*8 19*	*23 04*	*7 50*	*23 41*
22 MO	12 07 00	+0 22	6 03	18 11	6 02	18 12	6 01	18 14	6 00	18 15	5 57	18 18
81		*.9962*	*9 54*	*23 13*	*9 39*	*23 30*	*9 21*	*23 50*	*8 56*	*none*	*8 16*	*none*
23 TU	12 06 42	+0 46	6 02	18 12	6 01	18 13	6 00	18 15	5 58	18 17	5 54	18 21
82		*.9965*	*10 47*	*none*	*10 30*	*none*	*10 09*	*none*	*9 39*	*0 18*	*8 51*	*1 04*
24 WE	12 06 24	+1 09	6 01	18 12	6 00	18 14	5 58	18 16	5 55	18 18	5 51	18 23
83	*10 18 FQ*	*.9967*	*11 42*	*0 14*	*11 24*	*0 32*	*11 01*	*0 54*	*10 30*	*1 25*	*9 37*	*2 18*
25 TH	12 06 06	+1 33	6 00	18 12	5 59	18 14	5 56	18 17	5 53	18 20	5 48	18 26
84		*.9970*	*12 39*	*1 11*	*12 21*	*1 30*	*11 58*	*1 53*	*11 27*	*2 24*	*10 34*	*3 18*
26 FR	12 05 48	+1 57	5 59	18 13	5 57	18 15	5 55	18 18	5 51	18 22	5 45	18 28
85		*.9973*	*13 36*	*2 05*	*13 19*	*2 23*	*12 59*	*2 44*	*12 30*	*3 14*	*11 42*	*4 04*
27 SA	12 05 30	+2 20	5 58	18 13	5 56	18 15	5 53	18 19	5 49	18 23	5 42	18 30
86		*.9976*	*14 32*	*2 56*	*14 18*	*3 11*	*14 00*	*3 30*	*13 36*	*3 56*	*12 56*	*4 38*
28 SU	12 05 12	+2 44	5 58	18 13	5 55	18 16	5 51	18 20	5 47	18 25	5 39	18 33
87		*.9978*	*15 27*	*3 42*	*15 16*	*3 54*	*15 02*	*4 10*	*14 43*	*4 31*	*14 13*	*5 04*
29 MO	12 04 53	+3 07	5 57	18 13	5 54	18 17	5 50	18 21	5 44	18 26	5 36	18 35
88		*.9981*	*16 20*	*4 24*	*16 12*	*4 34*	*16 03*	*4 45*	*15 50*	*5 00*	*15 30*	*5 24*
30 TU	12 04 35	+3 30	5 56	18 14	5 52	18 17	5 48	18 22	5 42	18 28	5 33	18 38
89		*.9984*	*17 12*	*5 05*	*17 08*	*5 10*	*17 03*	*5 17*	*16 56*	*5 26*	*16 47*	*5 40*
31 WE	12 04 17	+3 54	5 55	18 14	5 51	18 18	5 47	18 23	5 40	18 29	5 30	18 40
90	*22 49 FM*	*.9987*	*18 02*	*5 43*	*18 02*	*5 45*	*18 02*	*5 47*	*18 02*	*5 50*	*18 02*	*5 55*

April 1999

4th Month **30 days**

Coordinated Universal Time (Greenwich Mean Time)

NOTE: For each day, numbers on first line indicate Sun. Numbers on second line indicate *Moon.*
Degrees are North Latitude.

Moon Phases: FM = full moon; LQ = last quarter; NM = new moon; FQ = first quarter.
Sun's distance is in Astronomical Units.

CAUTION: Must be converted to local time. For instructions see "Calculation of Rise Times."

Day of month, of week, *of year*	Sun on Meridian *Moon Phase* h m s	Sun's Declination ° ′ *Distance*	20° Rise Sun *Moon* h m	20° Set Sun *Moon* h m	30° Rise Sun *Moon* h m	30° Set Sun *Moon* h m	40° Rise Sun *Moon* h m	40° Set Sun *Moon* h m	50° Rise Sun *Moon* h m	50° Set Sun *Moon* h m	60° Rise Sun *Moon* h m	60° Set Sun *Moon* h m
1 TH	12 03 59	+4 17	5 54	18 14	5 50	18 18	5 45	18 24	5 38	18 31	5 27	18 43
91		*.9990*	*18 52*	*6 20*	*18 55*	*6 18*	*19 00*	*6 16*	*19 06*	*6 13*	*19 16*	*6 09*
2 FR	12 03 41	+4 40	5 53	18 14	5 49	18 19	5 43	18 25	5 36	18 33	5 24	18 45
92		*.9993*	*19 41*	*6 57*	*19 48*	*6 52*	*19 57*	*6 45*	*20 10*	*6 36*	*20 29*	*6 23*
3 SA	12 03 24	+5 03	5 52	18 15	5 48	18 20	5 42	18 26	5 34	18 34	5 21	18 47
93		*.9996*	*20 30*	*7 35*	*20 41*	*7 26*	*20 54*	*7 15*	*21 12*	*7 00*	*21 41*	*6 38*
4 SU	12 03 06	+5 26	5 52	18 15	5 46	18 20	5 40	18 27	5 31	18 36	5 18	18 50
94		*.9999*	*21 20*	*8 13*	*21 33*	*8 01*	*21 50*	*7 47*	*22 13*	*7 27*	*22 51*	*6 55*
5 MO	12 02 48	+5 49	5 51	18 15	5 45	18 21	5 39	18 28	5 29	18 37	5 15	18 52
95		*1.0001*	*22 09*	*8 54*	*22 25*	*8 39*	*22 45*	*8 21*	*23 13*	*7 56*	*23 59*	*7 16*
6 TU	12 02 31	+6 12	5 50	18 15	5 44	18 21	5 37	18 29	5 27	18 39	5 12	18 55
96		*1.0004*	*22 59*	*9 37*	*23 17*	*9 20*	*23 39*	*8 59*	*none*	*8 30*	*none*	*7 43*
7 WE	12 02 14	+6 35	5 49	18 16	5 43	18 22	5 35	18 30	5 25	18 40	5 09	18 57
97		*1.0007*	*23 49*	*10 22*	*none*	*10 04*	*none*	*9 41*	*0 10*	*9 10*	*1 02*	*8 17*
8 TH	12 01 57	+6 57	5 48	18 16	5 42	18 23	5 34	18 31	5 23	18 42	5 06	19 00
98		*1.0010*	*none*	*11 10*	*0 07*	*10 52*	*0 30*	*10 29*	*1 03*	*9 56*	*1 57*	*9 01*
9 FR	12 01 41	+7 20	5 47	18 16	5 41	18 23	5 32	18 32	5 21	18 44	5 03	19 02
99	*2 51 LQ*	*1.0013*	*0 38*	*12 01*	*0 56*	*11 43*	*1 19*	*11 21*	*1 51*	*10 50*	*2 44*	*9 57*
10 SA	12 01 24	+7 42	5 46	18 17	5 39	18 24	5 31	18 33	5 19	18 45	5 00	19 05
100		*1.0016*	*1 26*	*12 55*	*1 43*	*12 38*	*2 04*	*12 18*	*2 34*	*11 50*	*3 22*	*11 03*
11 SU	12 01 08	+8 04	5 46	18 17	5 38	18 24	5 29	18 34	5 17	18 47	4 57	19 07
101		*1.0019*	*2 14*	*13 50*	*2 28*	*13 36*	*2 47*	*13 20*	*3 12*	*12 56*	*3 52*	*12 18*
12 MO	12 00 53	+8 26	5 45	18 17	5 37	18 25	5 28	18 35	5 15	18 48	4 54	19 09
102		*1.0022*	*3 00*	*14 47*	*3 11*	*14 37*	*3 26*	*14 24*	*3 46*	*14 07*	*4 16*	*13 39*
13 TU	12 00 38	+8 48	5 44	18 17	5 36	18 26	5 26	18 36	5 12	18 50	4 51	19 12
103		*1.0025*	*3 45*	*15 46*	*3 53*	*15 40*	*4 03*	*15 32*	*4 16*	*15 22*	*4 37*	*15 05*
14 WE	12 00 22	+9 10	5 43	18 18	5 35	18 26	5 25	18 37	5 10	18 51	4 48	19 14
104		*1.0028*	*4 30*	*16 46*	*4 34*	*16 44*	*4 39*	*16 42*	*4 45*	*16 39*	*4 55*	*16 35*
15 TH	12 00 08	+9 32	5 42	18 18	5 34	18 27	5 23	18 38	5 08	18 53	4 45	19 17
105		*1.0030*	*5 16*	*17 48*	*5 15*	*17 51*	*5 14*	*17 54*	*5 13*	*17 59*	*5 12*	*18 07*
16 FR	11 59 53	+9 53	5 42	18 18	5 33	18 27	5 22	18 39	5 06	18 55	4 42	19 19
106	*4 22 NM*	*1.0033*	*6 02*	*18 51*	*5 57*	*18 59*	*5 51*	*19 08*	*5 42*	*19 21*	*5 30*	*19 41*
17 SA	11 59 39	+10 14	5 41	18 19	5 32	18 28	5 20	18 40	5 04	18 56	4 39	19 22
107		*1.0036*	*6 51*	*19 55*	*6 42*	*20 07*	*6 30*	*20 22*	*6 14*	*20 42*	*5 50*	*21 14*
18 SU	11 59 26	+10 35	5 40	18 19	5 31	18 29	5 19	18 41	5 02	18 58	4 36	19 24
108		*1.0039*	*7 43*	*21 00*	*7 29*	*21 15*	*7 13*	*21 34*	*6 50*	*22 01*	*6 15*	*22 44*
19 MO	11 59 12	+10 56	5 39	18 19	5 30	18 29	5 17	18 42	5 00	18 59	4 33	19 27
109		*1.0042*	*8 37*	*22 04*	*8 21*	*22 21*	*8 00*	*22 43*	*7 32*	*23 14*	*6 47*	*none*
20 TU	11 59 00	+11 17	5 39	18 20	5 28	18 30	5 16	18 43	4 58	19 01	4 30	19 29
110		*1.0044*	*9 34*	*23 04*	*9 16*	*23 23*	*8 53*	*23 46*	*8 22*	*none*	*7 29*	*0 06*
21 WE	11 58 47	+11 38	5 38	18 20	5 27	18 31	5 14	18 44	4 56	19 02	4 28	19 32
111		*1.0047*	*10 32*	*none*	*10 14*	*none*	*9 51*	*none*	*9 18*	*0 19*	*8 24*	*1 13*
22 TH	11 58 35	+11 58	5 37	18 20	5 26	18 31	5 13	18 45	4 54	19 04	4 25	19 34
112	*19 01 FQ*	*1.0050*	*11 31*	*0 01*	*11 13*	*0 19*	*10 51*	*0 42*	*10 21*	*1 13*	*9 30*	*2 05*
23 FR	11 58 24	+12 18	5 36	18 21	5 25	18 32	5 11	18 46	4 52	19 06	4 22	19 37
113		*1.0052*	*12 28*	*0 54*	*12 12*	*1 10*	*11 53*	*1 30*	*11 27*	*1 58*	*10 44*	*2 43*
24 SA	11 58 12	+12 39	5 36	18 21	5 24	18 33	5 10	18 47	4 50	19 07	4 19	19 39
114		*1.0055*	*13 23*	*1 41*	*13 11*	*1 55*	*12 56*	*2 12*	*12 35*	*2 35*	*12 01*	*3 11*
25 SU	11 58 02	+12 58	5 35	18 21	5 23	18 33	5 09	18 48	4 48	19 09	4 16	19 42
115		*1.0058*	*14 16*	*2 25*	*14 08*	*2 35*	*13 57*	*2 48*	*13 42*	*3 05*	*13 18*	*3 32*
26 MO	11 57 52	+13 18	5 34	18 22	5 22	18 34	5 07	18 49	4 47	19 10	4 13	19 44
116		*1.0060*	*15 08*	*3 05*	*15 03*	*3 12*	*14 57*	*3 21*	*14 48*	*3 32*	*14 35*	*3 49*
27 TU	11 57 42	+13 37	5 34	18 22	5 21	18 34	5 06	18 50	4 45	19 12	4 10	19 47
117		*1.0063*	*15 58*	*3 44*	*15 57*	*3 47*	*15 55*	*3 51*	*15 53*	*3 56*	*15 50*	*4 04*
28 WE	11 57 32	+13 56	5 33	18 22	5 20	18 35	5 05	18 51	4 43	19 13	4 08	19 49
118		*1.0065*	*16 48*	*4 21*	*16 50*	*4 20*	*16 53*	*4 19*	*16 57*	*4 19*	*17 03*	*4 17*
29 TH	11 57 24	+14 15	5 32	18 23	5 20	18 36	5 03	18 52	4 41	19 15	4 05	19 52
119		*1.0068*	*17 37*	*4 57*	*17 43*	*4 53*	*17 50*	*4 48*	*18 01*	*4 41*	*18 17*	*4 31*
30 FR	11 57 16	+14 34	5 32	18 23	5 19	18 36	5 02	18 53	4 39	19 16	4 02	19 54
120	*14 55 FM*	*1.0071*	*18 26*	*5 34*	*18 35*	*5 26*	*18 47*	*5 17*	*19 03*	*5 04*	*19 29*	*4 45*

May 1999

5th Month **31 days**

Coordinated Universal Time (Greenwich Mean Time)

NOTE: For each day, numbers on first line indicate Sun. Numbers on second line indicate *Moon*. Degrees are North Latitude.

Moon Phases: FM = full moon; LQ = last quarter; NM = new moon; FQ = first quarter. Sun's distance is in Astronomical Units.

CAUTION: Must be converted to local time. For instructions see "Calculation of Rise Times."

Day of month, of week, *of year*	Sun on Meridian *Moon Phase* h m s	Sun's Declination ° ′ *Distance*	20° Rise Sun *Moon* h m	20° Set Sun *Moon* h m	30° Rise Sun *Moon* h m	30° Set Sun *Moon* h m	40° Rise Sun *Moon* h m	40° Set Sun *Moon* h m	50° Rise Sun *Moon* h m	50° Set Sun *Moon* h m	60° Rise Sun *Moon* h m	60° Set Sun *Moon* h m
1 SA	11 57 08	+14 52	5 31	18 23	5 18	18 37	5 01	18 54	4 37	19 18	3 59	19 57
121		*1.0073*	*19 15*	*6 12*	*19 28*	*6 01*	*19 44*	*5 48*	*20 05*	*5 29*	*20 41*	*5 01*
2 SU	11 57 01	+15 11	5 31	18 24	5 17	18 38	5 00	18 55	4 36	19 19	3 57	19 59
122		*1.0076*	*20 05*	*6 52*	*20 20*	*6 38*	*20 39*	*6 21*	*21 06*	*5 57*	*21 50*	*5 20*
3 MO	11 56 54	+15 29	5 30	18 24	5 16	18 38	4 58	18 56	4 34	19 21	3 54	20 02
123		*1.0078*	*20 55*	*7 34*	*21 12*	*7 18*	*21 34*	*6 57*	*22 04*	*6 29*	*22 55*	*5 44*
4 TU	11 56 48	+15 46	5 29	18 24	5 15	18 39	4 57	18 57	4 32	19 22	3 51	20 04
124		*1.0081*	*21 44*	*8 18*	*22 03*	*8 00*	*22 26*	*7 38*	*22 59*	*7 07*	*23 54*	*6 15*
5 WE	11 56 42	+16 04	5 29	18 25	5 14	18 40	4 56	18 58	4 30	19 24	3 49	20 06
125		*1.0083*	*22 33*	*9 05*	*22 52*	*8 47*	*23 16*	*8 23*	*23 48*	*7 50*	*none*	*6 55*
6 TH	11 56 37	+16 21	5 28	18 25	5 13	18 40	4 55	18 59	4 29	19 25	3 46	20 09
126		*1.0086*	*23 21*	*9 55*	*23 39*	*9 36*	*none*	*9 13*	*none*	*8 41*	*0 44*	*7 46*
7 FR	11 56 33	+16 38	5 28	18 26	5 13	18 41	4 54	19 00	4 27	19 27	3 43	20 11
127		*1.0088*	*none*	*10 46*	*none*	*10 29*	*0 02*	*10 08*	*0 33*	*9 37*	*1 24*	*8 47*
8 SA	11 56 29	+16 54	5 27	18 26	5 12	18 42	4 53	19 01	4 25	19 28	3 41	20 14
128	*17 28 LQ*	*1.0091*	*0 08*	*11 40*	*0 24*	*11 25*	*0 44*	*11 06*	*1 11*	*10 40*	*1 56*	*9 57*
9 SU	11 56 26	+17 11	5 27	18 26	5 11	18 42	4 51	19 02	4 24	19 30	3 38	20 16
129		*1.0093*	*0 53*	*12 34*	*1 07*	*12 23*	*1 23*	*12 08*	*1 46*	*11 47*	*2 21*	*11 14*
10 MO	11 56 24	+17 27	5 26	18 27	5 10	18 43	4 50	19 03	4 22	19 31	3 36	20 19
130		*1.0096*	*1 37*	*13 31*	*1 47*	*13 22*	*2 00*	*13 12*	*2 16*	*12 58*	*2 42*	*12 36*
11 TU	11 56 22	+17 42	5 26	18 27	5 10	18 43	4 49	19 04	4 21	19 33	3 33	20 21
131		*1.0098*	*2 21*	*14 28*	*2 27*	*14 24*	*2 34*	*14 19*	*2 44*	*14 13*	*3 00*	*14 02*
12 WE	11 56 20	+17 58	5 25	18 27	5 09	18 44	4 48	19 05	4 19	19 34	3 31	20 24
132		*1.0100*	*3 05*	*15 28*	*3 07*	*15 28*	*3 09*	*15 29*	*3 12*	*15 30*	*3 16*	*15 31*
13 TH	11 56 19	+18 13	5 25	18 28	5 08	18 45	4 47	19 06	4 18	19 36	3 28	20 26
133		*1.0103*	*3 50*	*16 29*	*3 47*	*16 35*	*3 44*	*16 41*	*3 39*	*16 50*	*3 33*	*17 03*
14 FR	11 56 19	+18 28	5 25	18 28	5 08	18 45	4 46	19 07	4 16	19 37	3 26	20 28
134		*1.0105*	*4 37*	*17 33*	*4 30*	*17 43*	*4 21*	*17 55*	*4 09*	*18 11*	*3 51*	*18 37*
15 SA	11 56 19	+18 42	5 24	18 29	5 07	18 46	4 45	19 08	4 15	19 39	3 24	20 31
135	*12 05 NM*	*1.0107*	*5 27*	*18 39*	*5 16*	*18 52*	*5 02*	*19 09*	*4 42*	*19 33*	*4 13*	*20 11*
16 SU	11 56 20	+18 57	5 24	18 29	5 06	18 47	4 44	19 09	4 14	19 40	3 21	20 33
136		*1.0109*	*6 21*	*19 45*	*6 06*	*20 02*	*5 47*	*20 23*	*5 21*	*20 52*	*4 40*	*21 41*
17 MO	11 56 22	+19 11	5 23	18 30	5 06	18 47	4 44	19 10	4 12	19 41	3 19	20 35
137		*1.0111*	*7 18*	*20 49*	*7 01*	*21 08*	*6 39*	*21 31*	*6 08*	*22 04*	*5 18*	*22 58*
18 TU	11 56 24	+19 24	5 23	18 30	5 05	18 48	4 43	19 11	4 11	19 43	3 17	20 38
138		*1.0113*	*8 18*	*21 51*	*7 59*	*22 09*	*7 36*	*22 33*	*7 03*	*23 05*	*6 08*	*24 00*
19 WE	11 56 26	+19 37	5 23	18 30	5 05	18 49	4 42	19 12	4 10	19 44	3 14	20 40
139		*1.0115*	*9 19*	*22 47*	*9 01*	*23 04*	*8 38*	*23 26*	*8 06*	*23 56*	*7 12*	*none*
20 TH	11 56 29	+19 50	5 22	18 31	5 04	18 49	4 41	19 13	4 08	19 46	3 12	20 42
140		*1.0117*	*10 19*	*23 38*	*10 02*	*23 53*	*9 42*	*none*	*9 13*	*none*	*8 26*	*0 45*
21 FR	11 56 33	+20 03	5 22	18 31	5 04	18 50	4 40	19 13	4 07	19 47	3 10	20 44
141		*1.0119*	*11 17*	*none*	*11 03*	*none*	*10 46*	*0 11*	*10 23*	*0 36*	*9 45*	*1 17*
22 SA	11 56 37	+20 15	5 22	18 32	5 03	18 50	4 39	19 14	4 06	19 48	3 08	20 47
142	*5 34 FQ*	*1.0121*	*12 12*	*0 24*	*12 02*	*0 36*	*11 49*	*0 50*	*11 32*	*1 10*	*11 04*	*1 40*
23 SU	11 56 42	+20 27	5 22	18 32	5 03	18 51	4 39	19 15	4 05	19 49	3 06	20 49
143		*1.0123*	*13 05*	*1 06*	*12 58*	*1 14*	*12 50*	*1 24*	*12 39*	*1 38*	*12 22*	*1 59*
24 MO	11 56 47	+20 38	5 21	18 32	5 02	18 52	4 38	19 16	4 04	19 51	3 04	20 51
144		*1.0125*	*13 55*	*1 45*	*13 53*	*1 50*	*13 49*	*1 55*	*13 45*	*2 02*	*13 38*	*2 14*
25 TU	11 56 52	+20 50	5 21	18 33	5 02	18 52	4 37	19 17	4 03	19 52	3 02	20 53
145		*1.0127*	*14 45*	*2 22*	*14 46*	*2 23*	*14 47*	*2 24*	*14 49*	*2 25*	*14 52*	*2 27*
26 WE	11 56 58	+21 00	5 21	18 33	5 01	18 53	4 37	19 18	4 02	19 53	3 00	20 55
146		*1.0129*	*15 34*	*2 59*	*15 39*	*2 56*	*15 44*	*2 52*	*15 53*	*2 47*	*16 05*	*2 40*
27 TH	11 57 05	+21 11	5 21	18 34	5 01	18 53	4 36	19 18	4 01	19 54	2 58	20 57
147		*1.0130*	*16 22*	*3 35*	*16 31*	*3 29*	*16 41*	*3 21*	*16 56*	*3 10*	*17 18*	*2 53*
28 FR	11 57 12	+21 21	5 21	18 34	5 01	18 54	4 36	19 19	4 00	19 55	2 57	20 59
148		*1.0132*	*17 12*	*4 12*	*17 23*	*4 02*	*17 38*	*3 50*	*17 58*	*3 34*	*18 30*	*3 08*
29 SA	11 57 19	+21 31	5 20	18 34	5 00	18 55	4 35	19 20	3 59	19 57	2 55	21 01
149		*1.0134*	*18 01*	*4 51*	*18 16*	*4 38*	*18 34*	*4 22*	*18 59*	*4 00*	*19 40*	*3 26*
30 SU	11 57 27	+21 40	5 20	18 35	5 00	18 55	4 34	19 21	3 58	19 58	2 53	21 03
150	*6 40 FM*	*1.0135*	*18 51*	*5 32*	*19 08*	*5 17*	*19 29*	*4 57*	*19 59*	*4 31*	*20 48*	*3 47*
31 MO	11 57 36	+21 49	5 20	18 35	5 00	18 56	4 34	19 22	3 57	19 59	2 52	21 05
151		*1.0137*	*19 41*	*6 16*	*20 00*	*5 58*	*20 23*	*5 36*	*20 55*	*5 06*	*21 50*	*4 16*

6th Month

June 1999

30 days

Coordinated Universal Time (Greenwich Mean Time)

NOTE: For each day, numbers on first line indicate Sun. Numbers on second line indicate *Moon.* Degrees are North Latitude.

Moon Phases: FM = full moon; LQ = last quarter; NM = new moon; FQ = first quarter. Sun's distance is in Astronomical Units.

CAUTION: Must be converted to local time. For instructions see "Calculation of Rise Times."

Day of month, of week, *of year*	Sun on Meridian *Moon Phase* h m s	Sun's Declination ° ′ *Distance*	20° Rise Sun *Moon* h m	20° Set Sun *Moon* h m	30° Rise Sun *Moon* h m	30° Set Sun *Moon* h m	40° Rise Sun *Moon* h m	40° Set Sun *Moon* h m	50° Rise Sun *Moon* h m	50° Set Sun *Moon* h m	60° Rise Sun *Moon* h m	60° Set Sun *Moon* h m
1 TU	11 57 44	+21 58	5 20	18 36	5 00	18 56	4 34	19 22	3 56	20 00	2 50	21 07
152		*1.0139*	*20 31*	*7 02*	*20 50*	*6 44*	*21 13*	*6 20*	*21 47*	*5 47*	*22 43*	*4 52*
2 WE	11 57 54	+22 06	5 20	18 36	4 59	18 57	4 33	19 23	3 56	20 01	2 49	21 08
153		*1.0140*	*21 19*	*7 51*	*21 38*	*7 32*	*22 01*	*7 09*	*22 33*	*6 35*	*23 27*	*5 39*
3 TH	11 58 03	+22 14	5 20	18 36	4 59	18 57	4 33	19 24	3 55	20 02	2 47	21 10
154		*1.0142*	*22 06*	*8 42*	*22 23*	*8 24*	*22 44*	*8 02*	*23 13*	*7 30*	*none*	*6 37*
4 FR	11 58 13	+22 21	5 20	18 37	4 59	18 58	4 32	19 24	3 54	20 03	2 46	21 12
155		*1.0143*	*22 51*	*9 34*	*23 06*	*9 18*	*23 24*	*8 58*	*23 49*	*8 30*	*0 01*	*7 44*
5 SA	11 58 23	+22 28	5 20	18 37	4 59	18 58	4 32	19 25	3 54	20 04	2 45	21 13
156		*1.0145*	*23 35*	*10 28*	*23 46*	*10 15*	*none*	*9 58*	*none*	*9 35*	*0 28*	*8 58*
6 SU	11 58 34	+22 35	5 20	18 37	4 59	18 59	4 32	19 26	3 53	20 05	2 43	21 15
157		*1.0146*	*none*	*11 22*	*none*	*11 12*	*0 00*	*11 00*	*0 20*	*10 43*	*0 49*	*10 17*
7 MO	11 58 45	+22 41	5 20	18 38	4 58	18 59	4 31	19 26	3 53	20 05	2 42	21 16
158	*4 20 LQ*	*1.0148*	*0 17*	*12 18*	*0 25*	*12 12*	*0 35*	*12 04*	*0 48*	*11 54*	*1 07*	*11 39*
8 TU	11 58 56	+22 47	5 20	18 38	4 58	19 00	4 31	19 27	3 52	20 06	2 41	21 17
159		*1.0149*	*1 00*	*13 14*	*1 03*	*13 13*	*1 08*	*13 11*	*1 14*	*13 08*	*1 23*	*13 03*
9 WE	11 59 08	+22 52	5 20	18 39	4 58	19 00	4 31	19 27	3 52	20 07	2 40	21 19
160		*1.0150*	*1 42*	*14 13*	*1 42*	*14 16*	*1 41*	*14 19*	*1 40*	*14 24*	*1 39*	*14 31*
10 TH	11 59 20	+22 57	5 20	18 39	4 58	19 00	4 31	19 28	3 51	20 08	2 40	21 20
161		*1.0151*	*2 27*	*15 13*	*2 22*	*15 21*	*2 15*	*15 30*	*2 07*	*15 42*	*1 55*	*16 02*
11 FR	11 59 32	+23 02	5 20	18 39	4 58	19 01	4 31	19 28	3 51	20 08	2 39	21 21
162		*1.0153*	*3 14*	*16 17*	*3 04*	*16 28*	*2 53*	*16 43*	*2 38*	*17 03*	*2 14*	*17 35*
12 SA	11 59 44	+23 06	5 20	18 39	4 58	19 01	4 31	19 29	3 51	20 09	2 38	21 22
163		*1.0154*	*4 05*	*17 22*	*3 51*	*17 37*	*3 35*	*17 56*	*3 12*	*18 23*	*2 37*	*19 07*
13 SU	11 59 57	+23 10	5 20	18 40	4 58	19 02	4 31	19 29	3 51	20 10	2 37	21 23
164	*19 03 NM*	*1.0155*	*5 00*	*18 28*	*4 43*	*18 46*	*4 23*	*19 08*	*3 54*	*19 40*	*3 08*	*20 32*
14 MO	12 00 09	+23 14	5 20	18 40	4 58	19 02	4 31	19 30	3 50	20 10	2 37	21 24
165		*1.0156*	*5 59*	*19 32*	*5 40*	*19 51*	*5 17*	*20 15*	*4 45*	*20 48*	*3 51*	*21 44*
15 TU	12 00 22	+23 17	5 20	18 40	4 58	19 02	4 31	19 30	3 50	20 11	2 36	21 25
166		*1.0157*	*7 01*	*20 33*	*6 42*	*20 51*	*6 18*	*21 14*	*5 45*	*21 46*	*4 49*	*22 38*
16 WE	12 00 35	+23 19	5 21	18 41	4 59	19 03	4 31	19 31	3 50	20 11	2 36	21 25
167		*1.0158*	*8 03*	*21 28*	*7 45*	*21 44*	*7 23*	*22 04*	*6 52*	*22 32*	*6 00*	*23 17*
17 TH	12 00 48	+23 21	5 21	18 41	4 59	19 03	4 31	19 31	3 50	20 12	2 36	21 26
168		*1.0159*	*9 04*	*22 18*	*8 48*	*22 31*	*8 29*	*22 48*	*8 03*	*23 10*	*7 20*	*23 45*
18 FR	12 01 01	+23 23	5 21	18 41	4 59	19 03	4 31	19 31	3 50	20 12	2 36	21 27
169		*1.0160*	*10 02*	*23 03*	*9 50*	*23 13*	*9 35*	*23 25*	*9 15*	*23 41*	*8 43*	*none*
19 SA	12 01 14	+23 25	5 21	18 41	4 59	19 04	4 31	19 32	3 50	20 12	2 36	21 27
170		*1.0160*	*10 57*	*23 44*	*10 49*	*23 50*	*10 39*	*23 57*	*10 25*	*none*	*10 04*	*0 06*
20 SU	12 01 27	+23 26	5 21	18 42	4 59	19 04	4 31	19 32	3 50	20 13	2 36	21 27
171	*18 13 FQ*	*1.0161*	*11 50*	*none*	*11 46*	*none*	*11 40*	*none*	*11 33*	*0 07*	*11 22*	*0 23*
21 MO	12 01 40	+23 26	5 21	18 42	4 59	19 04	4 31	19 32	3 51	20 13	2 36	21 28
172		*1.0162*	*12 40*	*0 22*	*12 40*	*0 25*	*12 40*	*0 27*	*12 39*	*0 31*	*12 38*	*0 37*
22 TU	12 01 54	+23 26	5 22	18 42	5 00	19 04	4 31	19 32	3 51	20 13	2 36	21 28
173		*1.0162*	*13 30*	*0 59*	*13 33*	*0 58*	*13 38*	*0 56*	*13 43*	*0 54*	*13 52*	*0 50*
23 WE	12 02 06	+23 26	5 22	18 42	5 00	19 04	4 32	19 33	3 51	20 13	2 36	21 28
174		*1.0163*	*14 19*	*1 36*	*14 26*	*1 31*	*14 35*	*1 24*	*14 47*	*1 16*	*15 06*	*1 03*
24 TH	12 02 19	+23 25	5 22	18 43	5 00	19 05	4 32	19 33	3 51	20 13	2 37	21 28
175		*1.0163*	*15 08*	*2 13*	*15 18*	*2 04*	*15 31*	*1 53*	*15 49*	*1 39*	*16 18*	*1 17*
25 FR	12 02 32	+23 24	5 22	18 43	5 00	19 05	4 32	19 33	3 52	20 13	2 37	21 28
176		*1.0164*	*15 57*	*2 51*	*16 11*	*2 39*	*16 28*	*2 24*	*16 51*	*2 04*	*17 29*	*1 33*
26 SA	12 02 45	+23 23	5 23	18 43	5 01	19 05	4 33	19 33	3 52	20 13	2 38	21 28
177		*1.0164*	*16 47*	*3 31*	*17 03*	*3 16*	*17 23*	*2 58*	*17 51*	*2 33*	*18 38*	*1 53*
27 SU	12 02 57	+23 21	5 23	18 43	5 01	19 05	4 33	19 33	3 53	20 13	2 38	21 27
178		*1.0165*	*17 37*	*4 14*	*17 55*	*3 57*	*18 18*	*3 36*	*18 49*	*3 06*	*19 43*	*2 18*
28 MO	12 03 10	+23 18	5 23	18 43	5 01	19 05	4 33	19 33	3 53	20 13	2 39	21 27
179	*21 37 FM*	*1.0165*	*18 27*	*4 59*	*18 46*	*4 41*	*19 10*	*4 18*	*19 43*	*3 45*	*20 40*	*2 51*
29 TU	12 03 22	+23 16	5 23	18 43	5 02	19 05	4 34	19 33	3 54	20 13	2 40	21 26
180		*1.0165*	*19 17*	*5 48*	*19 35*	*5 29*	*19 59*	*5 05*	*20 32*	*4 31*	*21 27*	*3 35*
30 WE	12 03 34	+23 12	5 24	18 43	5 02	19 05	4 34	19 33	3 54	20 13	2 41	21 26
181		*1.0166*	*20 05*	*6 38*	*20 22*	*6 20*	*20 44*	*5 57*	*21 15*	*5 24*	*22 05*	*4 29*

July 1999

7th Month **31 days**

Coordinated Universal Time (Greenwich Mean Time)

NOTE: For each day, numbers on first line indicate Sun. Numbers on second line indicate *Moon*.
Degrees are North Latitude.

Moon Phases: FM = full moon; LQ = last quarter; NM = new moon; FQ = first quarter.
Sun's distance is in Astronomical Units.

CAUTION: Must be converted to local time. For instructions see "Calculation of Rise Times."

Day of month, of week, *of year*	Sun on Meridian *Moon Phase* h m s	Sun's Declination ° ′ *Distance*	20° Rise Sun *Moon* h m	20° Set Sun *Moon* h m	30° Rise Sun *Moon* h m	30° Set Sun *Moon* h m	40° Rise Sun *Moon* h m	40° Set Sun *Moon* h m	50° Rise Sun *Moon* h m	50° Set Sun *Moon* h m	60° Rise Sun *Moon* h m	60° Set Sun *Moon* h m
1 TH	12 03 45	+23 09	5 24	18 43	5 02	19 05	4 35	19 33	3 55	20 13	2 42	21 25
182		*1.0166*	*20 51*	*7 31*	*21 06*	*7 14*	*21 25*	*6 53*	*21 52*	*6 23*	*22 34*	*5 34*
2 FR	12 03 57	+23 05	5 24	18 43	5 03	19 05	4 35	19 33	3 55	20 12	2 43	21 24
183		*1.0166*	*21 35*	*8 24*	*21 47*	*8 10*	*22 03*	*7 52*	*22 24*	*7 27*	*22 57*	*6 46*
3 SA	12 04 08	+23 01	5 25	18 44	5 03	19 05	4 36	19 32	3 56	20 12	2 44	21 24
184		*1.0166*	*22 17*	*9 18*	*22 27*	*9 07*	*22 38*	*8 53*	*22 53*	*8 34*	*23 16*	*8 04*
4 SU	12 04 19	+22 56	5 25	18 44	5 03	19 05	4 36	19 32	3 57	20 12	2 45	21 23
185		*1.0166*	*22 59*	*10 13*	*23 04*	*10 05*	*23 11*	*9 56*	*23 19*	*9 44*	*23 32*	*9 24*
5 MO	12 04 29	+22 51	5 25	18 44	5 04	19 05	4 37	19 32	3 57	20 11	2 46	21 22
186		*1.0167*	*23 40*	*11 08*	*23 41*	*11 05*	*23 43*	*11 01*	*23 44*	*10 55*	*23 47*	*10 47*
6 TU	12 04 40	+22 45	5 26	18 44	5 04	19 05	4 37	19 32	3 58	20 11	2 48	21 21
187	*11 57 LQ*	*1.0167*	*none*	*12 04*	*none*	*12 05*	*none*	*12 06*	*none*	*12 08*	*none*	*12 11*
7 WE	12 04 50	+22 39	5 26	18 44	5 05	19 05	4 38	19 32	3 59	20 10	2 49	21 20
188		*1.0167*	*0 23*	*13 02*	*0 19*	*13 07*	*0 15*	*13 14*	*0 10*	*13 23*	*0 02*	*13 38*
8 TH	12 04 59	+22 33	5 26	18 43	5 05	19 05	4 38	19 31	4 00	20 09	2 51	21 18
189		*1.0167*	*1 07*	*14 02*	*0 59*	*14 12*	*0 50*	*14 24*	*0 38*	*14 40*	*0 19*	*15 07*
9 FR	12 05 08	+22 26	5 27	18 43	5 06	19 04	4 39	19 31	4 01	20 09	2 52	21 17
190		*1.0167*	*1 54*	*15 04*	*1 43*	*15 18*	*1 28*	*15 35*	*1 09*	*15 58*	*0 39*	*16 37*
10 SA	12 05 17	+22 19	5 27	18 43	5 06	19 04	4 40	19 30	4 02	20 08	2 54	21 16
191		*1.0166*	*2 46*	*16 08*	*2 30*	*16 25*	*2 12*	*16 46*	*1 46*	*17 15*	*1 05*	*18 04*
11 SU	12 05 26	+22 11	5 27	18 43	5 07	19 04	4 40	19 30	4 03	20 08	2 55	21 14
192		*1.0166*	*3 41*	*17 12*	*3 24*	*17 31*	*3 02*	*17 54*	*2 31*	*18 27*	*1 41*	*19 22*
12 MO	12 05 34	+22 03	5 28	18 43	5 07	19 04	4 41	19 30	4 04	20 07	2 57	21 13
193		*1.0166*	*4 41*	*18 14*	*4 22*	*18 33*	*3 58*	*18 57*	*3 25*	*19 30*	*2 30*	*20 25*
13 TU	12 05 41	+21 55	5 28	18 43	5 08	19 03	4 42	19 29	4 05	20 06	2 59	21 11
194	*2 24 NM*	*1.0166*	*5 43*	*19 13*	*5 25*	*19 30*	*5 01*	*19 52*	*4 29*	*20 22*	*3 34*	*21 12*
14 WE	12 05 48	+21 47	5 29	18 43	5 08	19 03	4 43	19 29	4 06	20 05	3 01	21 10
195		*1.0165*	*6 45*	*20 06*	*6 29*	*20 21*	*6 08*	*20 40*	*5 39*	*21 05*	*4 51*	*21 46*
15 TH	12 05 55	+21 38	5 29	18 43	5 09	19 03	4 43	19 28	4 07	20 04	3 03	21 08
196		*1.0165*	*7 46*	*20 55*	*7 33*	*21 06*	*7 16*	*21 20*	*6 52*	*21 40*	*6 14*	*22 10*
16 FR	12 06 01	+21 28	5 29	18 43	5 09	19 02	4 44	19 27	4 08	20 03	3 05	21 06
197		*1.0164*	*8 44*	*21 39*	*8 34*	*21 46*	*8 22*	*21 56*	*8 05*	*22 09*	*7 38*	*22 29*
17 SA	12 06 06	+21 18	5 30	18 42	5 10	19 02	4 45	19 27	4 09	20 02	3 07	21 04
198		*1.0164*	*9 40*	*22 19*	*9 33*	*22 23*	*9 26*	*22 28*	*9 16*	*22 34*	*9 00*	*22 44*
18 SU	12 06 11	+21 08	5 30	18 42	5 10	19 02	4 46	19 26	4 10	20 01	3 09	21 02
199		*1.0163*	*10 32*	*22 57*	*10 30*	*22 58*	*10 28*	*22 58*	*10 24*	*22 58*	*10 19*	*22 58*
19 MO	12 06 16	+20 58	5 30	18 42	5 11	19 01	4 46	19 26	4 12	20 00	3 11	21 00
200		*1.0162*	*11 23*	*23 35*	*11 25*	*23 31*	*11 27*	*23 26*	*11 30*	*23 20*	*11 35*	*23 11*
20 TU	12 06 20	+20 47	5 31	18 42	5 12	19 01	4 47	19 25	4 13	19 59	3 13	20 59
201	*9 00 FQ*	*1.0162*	*12 13*	*none*	*12 18*	*none*	*12 25*	*23 55*	*12 35*	*23 43*	*12 50*	*23 25*
21 WE	12 06 23	+20 36	5 31	18 41	5 12	19 00	4 48	19 24	4 14	19 58	3 15	20 56
202		*1.0161*	*13 02*	*0 12*	*13 11*	*0 04*	*13 23*	*none*	*13 38*	*none*	*14 03*	*23 40*
22 TH	12 06 26	+20 24	5 32	18 41	5 13	19 00	4 49	19 23	4 15	19 57	3 17	20 54
203		*1.0160*	*13 51*	*0 49*	*14 04*	*0 39*	*14 19*	*0 26*	*14 41*	*0 08*	*15 15*	*23 58*
23 FR	12 06 28	+20 12	5 32	18 41	5 13	18 59	4 50	19 23	4 16	19 56	3 19	20 52
204		*1.0159*	*14 41*	*1 29*	*14 56*	*1 15*	*15 15*	*0 58*	*15 42*	*0 35*	*16 25*	*none*
24 SA	12 06 29	+20 00	5 32	18 40	5 14	18 59	4 51	19 22	4 18	19 54	3 21	20 50
205		*1.0158*	*15 31*	*2 10*	*15 49*	*1 54*	*16 10*	*1 34*	*16 41*	*1 06*	*17 32*	*0 21*
25 SU	12 06 30	+19 48	5 33	18 40	5 14	18 58	4 52	19 21	4 19	19 53	3 23	20 48
206		*1.0157*	*16 22*	*2 55*	*16 40*	*2 37*	*17 04*	*2 14*	*17 36*	*1 43*	*18 32*	*0 51*
26 MO	12 06 30	+19 35	5 33	18 40	5 15	18 58	4 52	19 20	4 20	19 52	3 26	20 46
207		*1.0156*	*17 11*	*3 42*	*17 30*	*3 23*	*17 54*	*3 00*	*18 27*	*2 27*	*19 24*	*1 30*
27 TU	12 06 30	+19 22	5 33	18 39	5 16	18 57	4 53	19 19	4 22	19 50	3 28	20 43
208		*1.0155*	*18 00*	*4 32*	*18 19*	*4 14*	*18 41*	*3 50*	*19 13*	*3 17*	*20 06*	*2 21*
28 WE	12 06 29	+19 08	5 34	18 39	5 16	18 56	4 54	19 18	4 23	19 49	3 30	20 41
209	*11 25 FM*	*1.0154*	*18 48*	*5 25*	*19 04*	*5 07*	*19 24*	*4 45*	*19 52*	*4 14*	*20 38*	*3 23*
29 TH	12 06 28	+18 54	5 34	18 39	5 17	18 56	4 55	19 17	4 24	19 48	3 32	20 39
210		*1.0153*	*19 33*	*6 19*	*19 47*	*6 03*	*20 04*	*5 44*	*20 27*	*5 18*	*21 03*	*4 34*
30 FR	12 06 26	+18 40	5 35	18 38	5 17	18 55	4 56	19 16	4 26	19 46	3 35	20 36
211		*1.0152*	*20 17*	*7 13*	*20 27*	*7 01*	*20 40*	*6 46*	*20 57*	*6 25*	*21 24*	*5 51*
31 SA	12 06 23	+18 26	5 35	18 38	5 18	18 54	4 57	19 15	4 27	19 45	3 37	20 34
212		*1.0151*	*20 59*	*8 08*	*21 06*	*8 00*	*21 14*	*7 49*	*21 24*	*7 34*	*21 41*	*7 11*

August 1999

8th Month **31 days**

Coordinated Universal Time (Greenwich Mean Time)

NOTE: For each day, numbers on first line indicate Sun. Numbers on second line indicate *Moon*. Degrees are North Latitude.

Moon Phases: FM = full moon; LQ = last quarter; NM = new moon; FQ = first quarter.
Sun's distance is in Astronomical Units.

CAUTION: Must be converted to local time. For instructions see "Calculation of Rise Times."

Day of month, of week, *of year*	Sun on Meridian *Moon Phase* h m s	Sun's Decli-nation ° ′ *Distance*	20° Rise Sun *Moon* h m	20° Set Sun *Moon* h m	30° Rise Sun *Moon* h m	30° Set Sun *Moon* h m	40° Rise Sun *Moon* h m	40° Set Sun *Moon* h m	50° Rise Sun *Moon* h m	50° Set Sun *Moon* h m	60° Rise Sun *Moon* h m	60° Set Sun *Moon* h m
1 SU	12 06 20	+18 11	5 35	18 37	5 19	18 54	4 58	19 14	4 29	19 43	3 39	20 32
213		*1.0150*	*21 41*	*9 04*	*21 43*	*8 59*	*21 46*	*8 54*	*21 50*	*8 46*	*21 56*	*8 34*
2 MO	12 06 16	+17 56	5 36	18 37	5 19	18 53	4 59	19 13	4 30	19 42	3 42	20 29
214		*1.0149*	*22 22*	*10 00*	*22 21*	*9 59*	*22 18*	*9 59*	*22 15*	*9 59*	*22 11*	*9 58*
3 TU	12 06 11	+17 40	5 36	18 36	5 20	18 52	5 00	19 12	4 31	19 40	3 44	20 27
215		*1.0148*	*23 05*	*10 56*	*22 59*	*11 00*	*22 52*	*11 06*	*22 42*	*11 12*	*22 27*	*11 23*
4 WE	12 06 06	+17 25	5 36	18 36	5 20	18 51	5 01	19 11	4 33	19 38	3 47	20 24
216	*17 27 LQ*	*1.0146*	*23 50*	*11 55*	*23 40*	*12 03*	*23 28*	*12 13*	*23 11*	*12 27*	*22 45*	*12 50*
5 TH	12 06 01	+17 09	5 37	18 35	5 21	18 51	5 02	19 10	4 34	19 37	3 49	20 21
217		*1.0145*	*none*	*12 54*	*none*	*13 07*	*none*	*13 22*	*23 45*	*13 43*	*23 08*	*14 17*
6 FR	12 05 54	+16 53	5 37	18 35	5 22	18 50	5 02	19 09	4 36	19 35	3 51	20 19
218		*1.0144*	*0 39*	*13 56*	*0 25*	*14 11*	*0 08*	*14 31*	*none*	*14 58*	*23 38*	*15 43*
7 SA	12 05 48	+16 36	5 37	18 34	5 22	18 49	5 03	19 08	4 37	19 34	3 54	20 16
219		*1.0142*	*1 31*	*14 58*	*1 14*	*15 16*	*0 53*	*15 38*	*0 25*	*16 10*	*none*	*17 03*
8 SU	12 05 40	+16 20	5 38	18 33	5 23	18 48	5 04	19 06	4 39	19 32	3 56	20 14
220		*1.0141*	*2 27*	*15 59*	*2 09*	*16 18*	*1 46*	*16 42*	*1 13*	*17 15*	*0 19*	*18 11*
9 MO	12 05 32	+16 03	5 38	18 33	5 23	18 47	5 05	19 05	4 40	19 30	3 58	20 11
221		*1.0139*	*3 27*	*16 58*	*3 08*	*17 17*	*2 44*	*17 39*	*2 11*	*18 11*	*1 15*	*19 04*
10 TU	12 05 24	+15 45	5 38	18 32	5 24	18 46	5 06	19 04	4 41	19 28	4 01	20 08
222		*1.0138*	*4 28*	*17 53*	*4 10*	*18 10*	*3 48*	*18 30*	*3 17*	*18 58*	*2 26*	*19 43*
11 WE	12 05 15	+15 28	5 39	18 32	5 25	18 45	5 07	19 03	4 43	19 27	4 03	20 05
223	*11 08 NM*	*1.0136*	*5 29*	*18 44*	*5 14*	*18 57*	*4 55*	*19 14*	*4 29*	*19 36*	*3 46*	*20 11*
12 TH	12 05 05	+15 10	5 39	18 31	5 25	18 44	5 08	19 01	4 44	19 25	4 06	20 03
224		*1.0134*	*6 29*	*19 30*	*6 17*	*19 40*	*6 02*	*19 52*	*5 42*	*20 08*	*5 10*	*20 32*
13 FR	12 04 55	+14 52	5 39	18 30	5 26	18 44	5 09	19 00	4 46	19 23	4 08	20 00
225		*1.0133*	*7 26*	*20 13*	*7 18*	*20 18*	*7 08*	*20 26*	*6 55*	*20 35*	*6 34*	*20 49*
14 SA	12 04 44	+14 34	5 40	18 30	5 26	18 43	5 10	18 59	4 47	19 21	4 11	19 57
226		*1.0131*	*8 21*	*20 53*	*8 17*	*20 54*	*8 12*	*20 57*	*8 05*	*21 00*	*7 55*	*21 04*
15 SU	12 04 33	+14 15	5 40	18 29	5 27	18 42	5 11	18 57	4 49	19 19	4 13	19 54
227		*1.0129*	*9 13*	*21 31*	*9 13*	*21 29*	*9 13*	*21 26*	*9 14*	*21 23*	*9 14*	*21 18*
16 MO	12 04 21	+13 57	5 40	18 28	5 28	18 41	5 12	18 56	4 50	19 17	4 15	19 52
228		*1.0127*	*10 04*	*22 08*	*10 08*	*22 03*	*10 13*	*21 55*	*10 20*	*21 46*	*10 31*	*21 31*
17 TU	12 04 08	+13 38	5 40	18 28	5 28	18 40	5 13	18 55	4 52	19 15	4 18	19 49
229		*1.0125*	*10 54*	*22 46*	*11 02*	*22 37*	*11 12*	*22 25*	*11 25*	*22 10*	*11 45*	*21 46*
18 WE	12 03 55	+13 19	5 41	18 27	5 29	18 39	5 14	18 53	4 53	19 14	4 20	19 46
230		*1.0123*	*11 44*	*23 25*	*11 55*	*23 13*	*12 09*	*22 57*	*12 28*	*22 36*	*12 59*	*22 03*
19 TH	12 03 42	+12 59	5 41	18 26	5 29	18 38	5 15	18 52	4 55	19 12	4 23	19 43
231	*1 47 FQ*	*1.0121*	*12 34*	*none*	*12 48*	*23 51*	*13 05*	*23 32*	*13 30*	*23 06*	*14 10*	*22 24*
20 FR	12 03 28	+12 40	5 41	18 25	5 30	18 37	5 16	18 50	4 56	19 10	4 25	19 40
232		*1.0119*	*13 24*	*0 06*	*13 40*	*none*	*14 01*	*none*	*14 30*	*23 40*	*15 18*	*22 51*
21 SA	12 03 14	+12 20	5 42	18 25	5 31	18 35	5 17	18 49	4 58	19 08	4 27	19 37
233		*1.0117*	*14 14*	*0 49*	*14 32*	*0 32*	*14 55*	*0 10*	*15 27*	*none*	*16 21*	*23 26*
22 SU	12 02 58	+12 00	5 42	18 24	5 31	18 34	5 18	18 48	4 59	19 06	4 30	19 34
234		*1.0115*	*15 04*	*1 35*	*15 23*	*1 16*	*15 46*	*0 53*	*16 20*	*0 20*	*17 16*	*none*
23 MO	12 02 43	+11 40	5 42	18 23	5 32	18 33	5 19	18 46	5 01	19 04	4 32	19 32
235		*1.0113*	*15 53*	*2 24*	*16 12*	*2 05*	*16 35*	*1 41*	*17 07*	*1 08*	*18 02*	*0 11*
24 TU	12 02 27	+11 20	5 42	18 22	5 32	18 32	5 20	18 45	5 02	19 02	4 35	19 29
236		*1.0111*	*16 41*	*3 15*	*16 58*	*2 57*	*17 20*	*2 35*	*17 49*	*2 03*	*18 38*	*1 09*
25 WE	12 02 11	+10 59	5 43	18 22	5 33	18 31	5 21	18 43	5 04	19 00	4 37	19 26
237		*1.0109*	*17 28*	*4 09*	*17 43*	*3 53*	*18 01*	*3 32*	*18 26*	*3 04*	*19 06*	*2 17*
26 TH	12 01 54	+10 39	5 43	18 21	5 33	18 30	5 22	18 42	5 05	18 58	4 39	19 23
238	*23 48 FM*	*1.0107*	*18 13*	*5 04*	*18 24*	*4 51*	*18 39*	*4 34*	*18 58*	*4 10*	*19 29*	*3 32*
27 FR	12 01 37	+10 18	5 43	18 20	5 34	18 29	5 22	18 40	5 07	18 56	4 42	19 20
239		*1.0104*	*18 56*	*6 00*	*19 04*	*5 50*	*19 14*	*5 38*	*19 27*	*5 20*	*19 47*	*4 53*
28 SA	12 01 20	+9 57	5 43	18 19	5 34	18 28	5 23	18 39	5 08	18 53	4 44	19 17
240		*1.0102*	*19 39*	*6 57*	*19 43*	*6 51*	*19 47*	*6 43*	*19 54*	*6 33*	*20 03*	*6 17*
29 SU	12 01 02	+9 36	5 44	18 18	5 35	18 27	5 24	18 37	5 10	18 51	4 47	19 14
241		*1.0100*	*20 21*	*7 53*	*20 21*	*7 52*	*20 20*	*7 50*	*20 19*	*7 47*	*20 18*	*7 42*
30 MO	12 00 44	+9 14	5 44	18 17	5 36	18 25	5 25	18 35	5 11	18 49	4 49	19 11
242		*1.0098*	*21 04*	*8 51*	*21 00*	*8 54*	*20 54*	*8 57*	*20 46*	*9 02*	*20 34*	*9 09*
31 TU	12 00 25	+8 53	5 44	18 17	5 36	18 24	5 26	18 34	5 13	18 47	4 51	19 08
243		*1.0095*	*21 49*	*9 49*	*21 40*	*9 57*	*21 29*	*10 05*	*21 14*	*10 17*	*20 51*	*10 36*

September 1999

9th Month **30 days**

Coordinated Universal Time (Greenwich Mean Time)

NOTE: For each day, numbers on first line indicate Sun. Numbers on second line indicate *Moon.* Degrees are North Latitude.

Moon Phases: FM = full moon; LQ = last quarter; NM = new moon; FQ = first quarter. Sun's distance is in Astronomical Units.

CAUTION: Must be converted to local time. For instructions see "Calculation of Rise Times."

Day of month, of week, *of year*	Sun on Meridian *Moon Phase* h m s	Sun's Decli-nation ° ′ *Distance*	20° Rise Sun *Moon* h m	20° Set Sun *Moon* h m	30° Rise Sun *Moon* h m	30° Set Sun *Moon* h m	40° Rise Sun *Moon* h m	40° Set Sun *Moon* h m	50° Rise Sun *Moon* h m	50° Set Sun *Moon* h m	60° Rise Sun *Moon* h m	60° Set Sun *Moon* h m
1 WE	12 00 06	+8 31	5 44	18 16	5 37	18 23	5 27	18 32	5 14	18 45	4 54	19 05
244		*1.0093*	*22 36*	*10 49*	*22 23*	*11 00*	*22 08*	*11 14*	*21 46*	*11 33*	*21 12*	*12 04*
2 TH	11 59 47	+8 10	5 44	18 15	5 37	18 22	5 28	18 31	5 16	18 43	4 56	19 02
245	*22 17 LQ*	*1.0091*	*23 27*	*11 50*	*23 11*	*12 04*	*22 51*	*12 23*	*22 24*	*12 49*	*21 40*	*13 30*
3 FR	11 59 28	+7 48	5 45	18 14	5 38	18 21	5 29	18 29	5 17	18 41	4 58	18 59
246		*1.0088*	*none*	*12 51*	*none*	*13 08*	*23 40*	*13 30*	*23 09*	*14 00*	*22 16*	*14 51*
4 SA	11 59 08	+7 26	5 45	18 13	5 38	18 20	5 30	18 28	5 19	18 39	5 01	18 56
247		*1.0086*	*0 21*	*13 51*	*0 03*	*14 10*	*none*	*14 34*	*none*	*15 07*	*23 06*	*16 02*
5 SU	11 58 48	+7 04	5 45	18 12	5 39	18 18	5 31	18 26	5 20	18 37	5 03	18 53
248		*1.0084*	*1 18*	*14 49*	*0 59*	*15 08*	*0 35*	*15 32*	*0 02*	*16 04*	*none*	*16 59*
6 MO	11 58 28	+6 41	5 45	18 11	5 39	18 17	5 32	18 24	5 22	18 34	5 05	18 50
249		*1.0081*	*2 17*	*15 45*	*1 59*	*16 02*	*1 36*	*16 23*	*1 04*	*16 53*	*0 10*	*17 42*
7 TU	11 58 08	+6 19	5 46	18 10	5 40	18 16	5 33	18 23	5 23	18 32	5 08	18 47
250		*1.0079*	*3 17*	*16 36*	*3 00*	*16 50*	*2 40*	*17 08*	*2 12*	*17 33*	*1 25*	*18 13*
8 WE	11 57 48	+5 57	5 46	18 10	5 40	18 15	5 34	18 21	5 25	18 30	5 10	18 44
251		*1.0076*	*4 16*	*17 23*	*4 02*	*17 34*	*3 46*	*17 48*	*3 23*	*18 07*	*2 46*	*18 36*
9 TH	11 57 27	+5 34	5 46	18 09	5 41	18 13	5 35	18 20	5 26	18 28	5 12	18 41
252	*22 02 NM*	*1.0074*	*5 13*	*18 06*	*5 04*	*18 14*	*4 52*	*18 23*	*4 35*	*18 35*	*4 09*	*18 54*
10 FR	11 57 06	+5 11	5 46	18 08	5 42	18 12	5 36	18 18	5 28	18 26	5 15	18 38
253		*1.0071*	*6 09*	*18 47*	*6 03*	*18 51*	*5 56*	*18 55*	*5 46*	*19 01*	*5 32*	*19 09*
11 SA	11 56 45	+4 49	5 46	18 07	5 42	18 11	5 37	18 16	5 29	18 23	5 17	18 35
254		*1.0069*	*7 02*	*19 26*	*7 00*	*19 26*	*6 59*	*19 25*	*6 56*	*19 24*	*6 52*	*19 23*
12 SU	11 56 24	+4 26	5 47	18 06	5 43	18 10	5 38	18 15	5 31	18 21	5 20	18 32
255		*1.0066*	*7 54*	*20 04*	*7 56*	*20 00*	*8 00*	*19 55*	*8 04*	*19 47*	*8 10*	*19 37*
13 MO	11 56 03	+4 03	5 47	18 05	5 43	18 09	5 38	18 13	5 32	18 19	5 22	18 29
256		*1.0063*	*8 45*	*20 42*	*8 51*	*20 34*	*8 59*	*20 24*	*9 10*	*20 11*	*9 26*	*19 51*
14 TU	11 55 42	+3 40	5 47	18 04	5 44	18 07	5 39	18 11	5 34	18 17	5 24	18 26
257		*1.0061*	*9 35*	*21 21*	*9 45*	*21 09*	*9 57*	*20 55*	*10 14*	*20 36*	*10 41*	*20 07*
15 WE	11 55 21	+3 17	5 47	18 03	5 44	18 06	5 40	18 10	5 35	18 15	5 27	18 23
258		*1.0058*	*10 25*	*22 01*	*10 38*	*21 47*	*10 55*	*21 29*	*11 17*	*21 05*	*11 54*	*20 26*
16 TH	11 54 59	+2 54	5 47	18 02	5 45	18 05	5 41	18 08	5 36	18 13	5 29	18 20
259		*1.0055*	*11 15*	*22 43*	*11 31*	*22 26*	*11 51*	*22 05*	*12 18*	*21 37*	*13 04*	*20 50*
17 FR	11 54 38	+2 31	5 48	18 01	5 45	18 04	5 42	18 06	5 38	18 10	5 31	18 17
260	*20 06 FQ*	*1.0052*	*12 05*	*23 28*	*12 23*	*23 09*	*12 45*	*22 46*	*13 17*	*22 14*	*14 09*	*21 21*
18 SA	11 54 17	+2 08	5 48	18 00	5 46	18 02	5 43	18 05	5 39	18 08	5 34	18 14
261		*1.0050*	*12 55*	*none*	*13 14*	*23 56*	*13 38*	*23 32*	*14 11*	*22 58*	*15 08*	*22 02*
19 SU	11 53 55	+1 44	5 48	17 59	5 46	18 01	5 44	18 03	5 41	18 06	5 36	18 11
262		*1.0047*	*13 44*	*0 15*	*14 03*	*none*	*14 27*	*none*	*15 00*	*23 50*	*15 57*	*22 54*
20 MO	11 53 34	+1 21	5 48	17 59	5 47	18 00	5 45	18 01	5 42	18 04	5 38	18 07
263		*1.0044*	*14 32*	*1 05*	*14 50*	*0 46*	*15 13*	*0 23*	*15 44*	*none*	*16 36*	*23 57*
21 TU	11 53 12	+0 58	5 48	17 58	5 47	17 59	5 46	18 00	5 44	18 01	5 41	18 04
264		*1.0041*	*15 19*	*1 57*	*15 35*	*1 40*	*15 55*	*1 18*	*16 23*	*0 48*	*17 07*	*none*
22 WE	11 52 51	+0 35	5 49	17 57	5 48	17 57	5 47	17 58	5 45	17 59	5 43	18 01
265		*1.0038*	*16 05*	*2 51*	*16 18*	*2 36*	*16 34*	*2 18*	*16 57*	*1 52*	*17 32*	*1 09*
23 TH	11 52 30	+0 11	5 49	17 56	5 49	17 56	5 48	17 56	5 47	17 57	5 45	17 58
266		*1.0035*	*16 49*	*3 47*	*16 59*	*3 35*	*17 11*	*3 21*	*17 27*	*3 00*	*17 51*	*2 28*
24 FR	11 52 09	−0 12	5 49	17 55	5 49	17 55	5 49	17 55	5 48	17 55	5 48	17 55
267		*1.0033*	*17 33*	*4 44*	*17 38*	*4 36*	*17 45*	*4 26*	*17 54*	*4 13*	*18 08*	*3 52*
25 SA	11 51 48	−0 35	5 49	17 54	5 50	17 54	5 50	17 53	5 50	17 53	5 50	17 52
268	*10 51 FM*	*1.0030*	*18 16*	*5 41*	*18 17*	*5 38*	*18 19*	*5 33*	*18 21*	*5 27*	*18 24*	*5 18*
26 SU	11 51 27	−0 59	5 50	17 53	5 50	17 52	5 51	17 51	5 52	17 50	5 52	17 49
269		*1.0027*	*19 00*	*6 40*	*18 56*	*6 41*	*18 52*	*6 42*	*18 47*	*6 44*	*18 39*	*6 46*
27 MO	11 51 07	−1 22	5 50	17 52	5 51	17 51	5 52	17 50	5 53	17 48	5 55	17 46
270		*1.0024*	*19 45*	*7 40*	*19 37*	*7 45*	*19 28*	*7 52*	*19 15*	*8 02*	*18 56*	*8 16*
28 TU	11 50 46	−1 46	5 50	17 51	5 51	17 50	5 53	17 48	5 55	17 46	5 57	17 43
271		*1.0021*	*20 32*	*8 41*	*20 21*	*8 51*	*20 06*	*9 03*	*19 47*	*9 20*	*19 16*	*9 47*
29 WE	11 50 26	−2 09	5 50	17 50	5 52	17 49	5 54	17 47	5 56	17 44	5 59	17 40
272		*1.0019*	*21 23*	*9 43*	*21 07*	*9 57*	*20 49*	*10 14*	*20 23*	*10 38*	*19 41*	*11 17*
30 TH	11 50 06	−2 32	5 50	17 49	5 52	17 47	5 55	17 45	5 58	17 42	6 02	17 37
273		*1.0016*	*22 16*	*10 45*	*21 59*	*11 02*	*21 36*	*11 23*	*21 06*	*11 53*	*20 15*	*12 42*

October 1999

10th Month **31 days**

Coordinated Universal Time (Greenwich Mean Time)

NOTE: For each day, numbers on first line indicate Sun. Numbers on second line indicate *Moon*. Degrees are North Latitude.

Moon Phases: FM = full moon; LQ = last quarter; NM = new moon; FQ = first quarter. Sun's distance is in Astronomical Units.

CAUTION: Must be converted to local time. For instructions see "Calculation of Rise Times."

Day of month, of week, *of year*	Sun on Meridian *Moon Phase* h m s	Sun's Declination ° ′ *Distance*	20° Rise Sun *Moon* h m	20° Set Sun *Moon* h m	30° Rise Sun *Moon* h m	30° Set Sun *Moon* h m	40° Rise Sun *Moon* h m	40° Set Sun *Moon* h m	50° Rise Sun *Moon* h m	50° Set Sun *Moon* h m	60° Rise Sun *Moon* h m	60° Set Sun *Moon* h m
1 FR	11 49 47	–2 56	5 51	17 49	5 53	17 46	5 56	17 43	5 59	17 40	6 04	17 34
274		*1.0013*	*23 13*	*11 46*	*22 54*	*12 05*	*22 30*	*12 28*	*21 57*	*13 01*	*21 00*	*13 57*
2 SA	11 49 27	–3 19	5 51	17 48	5 54	17 45	5 57	17 42	6 01	17 37	6 07	17 31
275	*4 02 LQ*	*1.0010*	*none*	*12 45*	*23 52*	*13 04*	*23 29*	*13 28*	*22 56*	*14 02*	*22 00*	*14 58*
3 SU	11 49 08	–3 42	5 51	17 47	5 54	17 44	5 58	17 40	6 02	17 35	6 09	17 28
276		*1.0007*	*0 11*	*13 41*	*none*	*13 59*	*none*	*14 21*	*none*	*14 52*	*23 11*	*15 44*
4 MO	11 48 50	–4 05	5 51	17 46	5 55	17 42	5 59	17 38	6 04	17 33	6 11	17 25
277		*1.0005*	*1 10*	*14 32*	*0 53*	*14 48*	*0 31*	*15 07*	*0 01*	*15 34*	*none*	*16 17*
5 TU	11 48 32	–4 28	5 52	17 45	5 55	17 41	6 00	17 37	6 05	17 31	6 14	17 22
278		*1.0002*	*2 08*	*15 19*	*1 54*	*15 32*	*1 36*	*15 48*	*1 11*	*16 09*	*0 30*	*16 42*
6 WE	11 48 14	–4 51	5 52	17 44	5 56	17 40	6 01	17 35	6 07	17 29	6 16	17 19
279		*.9999*	*3 05*	*16 03*	*2 54*	*16 12*	*2 40*	*16 23*	*2 21*	*16 38*	*1 51*	*17 01*
7 TH	11 47 56	–5 15	5 52	17 43	5 57	17 39	6 02	17 34	6 08	17 27	6 19	17 16
280		*.9996*	*4 00*	*16 44*	*3 53*	*16 49*	*3 44*	*16 55*	*3 32*	*17 04*	*3 13*	*17 16*
8 FR	11 47 39	–5 38	5 53	17 43	5 57	17 38	6 03	17 32	6 10	17 25	6 21	17 13
281		*.9993*	*4 54*	*17 23*	*4 50*	*17 24*	*4 47*	*17 25*	*4 41*	*17 27*	*4 33*	*17 30*
9 SA	11 47 23	–6 00	5 53	17 42	5 58	17 37	6 04	17 30	6 11	17 22	6 23	17 10
282	*11 34 NM*	*.9990*	*5 46*	*18 01*	*5 47*	*17 58*	*5 48*	*17 55*	*5 49*	*17 50*	*5 52*	*17 43*
10 SU	11 47 06	–6 23	5 53	17 41	5 58	17 35	6 05	17 29	6 13	17 20	6 26	17 07
283		*.9987*	*6 37*	*18 39*	*6 42*	*18 32*	*6 48*	*18 24*	*6 56*	*18 13*	*7 09*	*17 56*
11 MO	11 46 51	–6 46	5 53	17 40	5 59	17 34	6 06	17 27	6 15	17 18	6 28	17 04
284		*.9985*	*7 27*	*19 17*	*7 36*	*19 07*	*7 47*	*18 54*	*8 01*	*18 37*	*8 24*	*18 11*
12 TU	11 46 35	–7 09	5 54	17 39	6 00	17 33	6 07	17 26	6 16	17 16	6 31	17 01
285		*.9982*	*8 18*	*19 56*	*8 30*	*19 43*	*8 45*	*19 27*	*9 05*	*19 04*	*9 39*	*18 28*
13 WE	11 46 21	–7 31	5 54	17 38	6 00	17 32	6 08	17 24	6 18	17 14	6 33	16 58
286		*.9979*	*9 08*	*20 38*	*9 23*	*20 22*	*9 42*	*20 02*	*10 08*	*19 34*	*10 50*	*18 50*
14 TH	11 46 06	–7 54	5 54	17 38	6 01	17 31	6 09	17 23	6 19	17 12	6 36	16 55
287		*.9976*	*9 58*	*21 21*	*10 15*	*21 03*	*10 37*	*20 41*	*11 07*	*20 10*	*11 58*	*19 18*
15 FR	11 45 53	–8 16	5 55	17 37	6 02	17 30	6 10	17 21	6 21	17 10	6 38	16 53
288		*.9973*	*10 48*	*22 07*	*11 07*	*21 48*	*11 30*	*21 24*	*12 03*	*20 51*	*13 00*	*19 54*
16 SA	11 45 39	–8 38	5 55	17 36	6 02	17 29	6 11	17 20	6 23	17 08	6 41	16 50
289		*.9970*	*11 37*	*22 56*	*11 56*	*22 36*	*12 20*	*22 12*	*12 54*	*21 38*	*13 52*	*20 40*
17 SU	11 45 27	–9 00	5 55	17 35	6 03	17 28	6 12	17 18	6 24	17 06	6 43	16 47
290	*15 00 FQ*	*.9967*	*12 25*	*23 46*	*12 44*	*23 28*	*13 07*	*23 05*	*13 40*	*22 33*	*14 35*	*21 38*
18 MO	11 45 15	–9 22	5 56	17 35	6 03	17 27	6 13	17 17	6 26	17 04	6 45	16 44
291		*.9964*	*13 11*	*none*	*13 29*	*none*	*13 50*	*none*	*14 20*	*23 33*	*15 09*	*22 46*
19 TU	11 45 03	–9 44	5 56	17 34	6 04	17 26	6 14	17 15	6 27	17 02	6 48	16 41
292		*.9961*	*13 57*	*0 39*	*14 11*	*0 22*	*14 30*	*0 02*	*14 55*	*none*	*15 35*	*none*
20 WE	11 44 52	–10 06	5 56	17 33	6 05	17 25	6 15	17 14	6 29	17 00	6 50	16 38
293		*.9959*	*14 40*	*1 32*	*14 52*	*1 19*	*15 06*	*1 02*	*15 26*	*0 39*	*15 56*	*0 01*
21 TH	11 44 42	–10 27	5 57	17 32	6 05	17 24	6 16	17 13	6 31	16 58	6 53	16 35
294		*.9956*	*15 24*	*2 28*	*15 31*	*2 18*	*15 41*	*2 06*	*15 53*	*1 49*	*16 13*	*1 22*
22 FR	11 44 32	–10 49	5 57	17 32	6 06	17 23	6 17	17 11	6 32	16 56	6 55	16 33
295		*.9953*	*16 06*	*3 24*	*16 10*	*3 19*	*16 14*	*3 11*	*16 20*	*3 02*	*16 29*	*2 46*
23 SA	11 44 24	–11 10	5 57	17 31	6 07	17 22	6 18	17 10	6 34	16 54	6 58	16 30
296		*.9950*	*16 50*	*4 23*	*16 49*	*4 21*	*16 48*	*4 20*	*16 46*	*4 17*	*16 44*	*4 14*
24 SU	11 44 15	–11 31	5 58	17 30	6 08	17 21	6 19	17 08	6 36	16 52	7 00	16 27
297	*21 02 FM*	*.9947*	*17 35*	*5 22*	*17 29*	*5 26*	*17 22*	*5 30*	*17 13*	*5 36*	*17 00*	*5 44*
25 MO	11 44 08	–11 52	5 58	17 30	6 08	17 20	6 21	17 07	6 37	16 50	7 03	16 24
298		*.9945*	*18 22*	*6 24*	*18 12*	*6 32*	*18 00*	*6 42*	*17 43*	*6 56*	*17 18*	*7 17*
26 TU	11 44 01	–12 13	5 59	17 29	6 09	17 19	6 22	17 06	6 39	16 48	7 06	16 21
299		*.9942*	*19 13*	*7 28*	*18 59*	*7 40*	*18 42*	*7 56*	*18 18*	*8 17*	*17 41*	*8 51*
27 WE	11 43 55	–12 33	5 59	17 29	6 10	17 18	6 23	17 04	6 40	16 47	7 08	16 19
300		*.9939*	*20 08*	*8 32*	*19 50*	*8 49*	*19 29*	*9 09*	*18 59*	*9 37*	*18 11*	*10 23*
28 TH	11 43 49	–12 53	5 59	17 28	6 10	17 17	6 24	17 03	6 42	16 45	7 11	16 16
301		*.9936*	*21 05*	*9 37*	*20 46*	*9 55*	*20 22*	*10 18*	*19 49*	*10 51*	*18 53*	*11 46*
29 FR	11 43 45	–13 14	6 00	17 27	6 11	17 16	6 25	17 02	6 44	16 43	7 13	16 13
302		*.9934*	*22 05*	*10 39*	*21 45*	*10 58*	*21 21*	*11 23*	*20 47*	*11 57*	*19 49*	*12 55*
30 SA	11 43 41	–13 33	6 00	17 27	6 12	17 15	6 26	17 01	6 45	16 41	7 16	16 11
303		*.9931*	*23 05*	*11 37*	*22 47*	*11 56*	*22 24*	*12 19*	*21 52*	*12 52*	*20 59*	*13 47*
31 SU	11 43 38	–13 53	6 01	17 26	6 13	17 14	6 27	16 59	6 47	16 39	7 18	16 08
304	*12 04 LQ*	*.9929*	*none*	*12 30*	*23 48*	*12 47*	*23 29*	*13 08*	*23 01*	*13 37*	*22 17*	*14 24*

November 1999

11th Month **30 days**

Coordinated Universal Time (Greenwich Mean Time)

NOTE: For each day, numbers on first line indicate Sun. Numbers on second line indicate *Moon.*
Degrees are North Latitude.

Moon Phases: FM = full moon; LQ = last quarter; NM = new moon; FQ = first quarter.
Sun's distance is in Astronomical Units.

CAUTION: Must be converted to local time. For instructions see "Calculation of Rise Times."

Day of month, of week, *of year*	Sun on Meridian *Moon Phase* h m s	Sun's Declination ° ′ *Distance*	20° Rise Sun *Moon* h m	20° Set Sun *Moon* h m	30° Rise Sun *Moon* h m	30° Set Sun *Moon* h m	40° Rise Sun *Moon* h m	40° Set Sun *Moon* h m	50° Rise Sun *Moon* h m	50° Set Sun *Moon* h m	60° Rise Sun *Moon* h m	60° Set Sun *Moon* h m
1 MO	11 43 36	–14 13	6 01	17 26	6 13	17 13	6 28	16 58	6 49	16 38	7 21	16 05
305		*.9926*	*0 04*	*13 19*	*none*	*13 33*	*none*	*13 50*	*none*	*14 13*	*23 38*	*14 50*
2 TU	11 43 34	–14 32	6 02	17 25	6 14	17 13	6 30	16 57	6 50	16 36	7 23	16 03
306		*.9924*	*1 01*	*14 03*	*0 49*	*14 14*	*0 33*	*14 26*	*0 12*	*14 43*	*none*	*15 10*
3 WE	11 43 34	–14 51	6 02	17 25	6 15	17 12	6 31	16 56	6 52	16 34	7 26	16 00
307		*.9921*	*1 56*	*14 44*	*1 47*	*14 51*	*1 37*	*14 59*	*1 22*	*15 09*	*0 59*	*15 26*
4 TH	11 43 34	–15 10	6 03	17 24	6 16	17 11	6 32	16 55	6 54	16 33	7 29	15 58
308		*.9919*	*2 49*	*15 23*	*2 45*	*15 26*	*2 39*	*15 29*	*2 31*	*15 33*	*2 19*	*15 39*
5 FR	11 43 35	–15 28	6 03	17 24	6 17	17 10	6 33	16 54	6 55	16 31	7 31	15 55
309		*.9916*	*3 41*	*16 01*	*3 40*	*15 59*	*3 40*	*15 58*	*3 39*	*15 55*	*3 37*	*15 52*
6 SA	11 43 37	–15 47	6 04	17 23	6 17	17 10	6 34	16 53	6 57	16 30	7 34	15 53
310		*.9914*	*4 32*	*16 38*	*4 35*	*16 33*	*4 39*	*16 26*	*4 45*	*16 17*	*4 54*	*16 04*
7 SU	11 43 40	–16 05	6 04	17 23	6 18	17 09	6 35	16 52	6 59	16 28	7 36	15 50
311		*.9911*	*5 22*	*17 15*	*5 29*	*17 06*	*5 38*	*16 55*	*5 50*	*16 41*	*6 10*	*16 18*
8 MO	11 43 43	–16 22	6 05	17 23	6 19	17 08	6 36	16 51	7 00	16 26	7 39	15 48
312	*3 53 NM*	*.9909*	*6 12*	*17 54*	*6 23*	*17 42*	*6 36*	*17 27*	*6 55*	*17 06*	*7 25*	*16 33*
9 TU	11 43 48	–16 40	6 05	17 22	6 20	17 08	6 38	16 50	7 02	16 25	7 41	15 45
313		*.9906*	*7 02*	*18 35*	*7 16*	*18 19*	*7 34*	*18 00*	*7 58*	*17 34*	*8 38*	*16 52*
10 WE	11 43 53	–16 57	6 06	17 22	6 21	17 07	6 39	16 49	7 04	16 23	7 44	15 43
314		*.9904*	*7 53*	*19 17*	*8 09*	*19 00*	*8 30*	*18 38*	*8 59*	*18 07*	*9 48*	*17 17*
11 TH	11 43 59	–17 14	6 06	17 22	6 21	17 06	6 40	16 48	7 05	16 22	7 47	15 41
315		*.9902*	*8 43*	*20 02*	*9 01*	*19 43*	*9 24*	*19 19*	*9 57*	*18 46*	*10 53*	*17 50*
12 FR	11 44 06	–17 31	6 07	17 21	6 22	17 06	6 41	16 47	7 07	16 21	7 49	15 38
316		*.9899*	*9 32*	*20 50*	*9 51*	*20 30*	*10 16*	*20 06*	*10 50*	*19 31*	*11 49*	*18 32*
13 SA	11 44 14	–17 47	6 07	17 21	6 23	17 05	6 42	16 46	7 09	16 19	7 52	15 36
317		*.9897*	*10 20*	*21 39*	*10 39*	*21 20*	*11 04*	*20 56*	*11 38*	*20 22*	*12 36*	*19 25*
14 SU	11 44 23	–18 03	6 08	17 21	6 24	17 05	6 43	16 45	7 10	16 18	7 54	15 34
318		*.9895*	*11 07*	*22 30*	*11 25*	*22 12*	*11 48*	*21 50*	*12 19*	*21 20*	*13 12*	*20 28*
15 MO	11 44 32	–18 19	6 09	17 20	6 25	17 04	6 45	16 44	7 12	16 17	7 57	15 32
319		*.9892*	*11 51*	*23 22*	*12 08*	*23 07*	*12 28*	*22 48*	*12 55*	*22 22*	*13 40*	*21 39*
16 TU	11 44 42	–18 34	6 09	17 20	6 25	17 04	6 46	16 43	7 14	16 15	7 59	15 29
320	*9 03 FQ*	*.9890*	*12 35*	*none*	*12 48*	*none*	*13 04*	*23 49*	*13 26*	*23 28*	*14 02*	*22 56*
17 WE	11 44 54	–18 49	6 10	17 20	6 26	17 03	6 47	16 43	7 15	16 14	8 02	15 27
321		*.9888*	*13 17*	*0 15*	*13 26*	*0 03*	*13 38*	*none*	*13 54*	*none*	*14 20*	*none*
18 TH	11 45 06	–19 04	6 10	17 20	6 27	17 03	6 48	16 42	7 17	16 13	8 04	15 25
322		*.9886*	*13 58*	*1 09*	*14 04*	*1 01*	*14 11*	*0 52*	*14 20*	*0 38*	*14 35*	*0 17*
19 FR	11 45 18	–19 18	6 11	17 20	6 28	17 02	6 49	16 41	7 18	16 12	8 07	15 23
323		*.9883*	*14 40*	*2 05*	*14 41*	*2 01*	*14 43*	*1 57*	*14 45*	*1 50*	*14 49*	*1 41*
20 SA	11 45 32	–19 32	6 11	17 19	6 29	17 02	6 50	16 41	7 20	16 11	8 09	15 21
324		*.9881*	*15 23*	*3 03*	*15 20*	*3 04*	*15 16*	*3 05*	*15 11*	*3 06*	*15 04*	*3 08*
21 SU	11 45 46	–19 46	6 12	17 19	6 30	17 02	6 51	16 40	7 21	16 10	8 11	15 19
325		*.9879*	*16 08*	*4 03*	*16 01*	*4 08*	*15 51*	*4 15*	*15 39*	*4 24*	*15 20*	*4 39*
22 MO	11 46 01	–19 59	6 13	17 19	6 30	17 01	6 52	16 39	7 23	16 09	8 14	15 18
326		*.9877*	*16 58*	*5 05*	*16 46*	*5 16*	*16 31*	*5 28*	*16 11*	*5 46*	*15 40*	*6 13*
23 TU	11 46 17	–20 12	6 13	17 19	6 31	17 01	6 54	16 39	7 25	16 08	8 16	15 16
327	*7 04 FM*	*.9875*	*17 51*	*6 11*	*17 35*	*6 25*	*17 16*	*6 43*	*16 49*	*7 08*	*16 06*	*7 48*
24 WE	11 46 34	–20 24	6 14	17 19	6 32	17 01	6 55	16 38	7 26	16 07	8 19	15 14
328		*.9873*	*18 49*	*7 17*	*18 30*	*7 35*	*18 07*	*7 57*	*17 35*	*8 28*	*16 42*	*9 19*
25 TH	11 46 52	–20 37	6 15	17 19	6 33	17 01	6 56	16 38	7 28	16 06	8 21	15 12
329		*.9871*	*19 50*	*8 23*	*19 30*	*8 42*	*19 06*	*9 07*	*18 31*	*9 41*	*17 32*	*10 39*
26 FR	11 47 10	–20 48	6 15	17 19	6 34	17 00	6 57	16 37	7 29	16 05	8 23	15 11
330		*.9869*	*20 53*	*9 26*	*20 34*	*9 45*	*20 10*	*10 10*	*19 36*	*10 44*	*18 39*	*11 42*
27 SA	11 47 29	–21 00	6 16	17 19	6 35	17 00	6 58	16 37	7 30	16 04	8 25	15 09
331		*.9868*	*21 55*	*10 24*	*21 38*	*10 42*	*21 16*	*11 04*	*20 47*	*11 35*	*19 57*	*12 26*
28 SU	11 47 49	–21 11	6 16	17 19	6 35	17 00	6 59	16 36	7 32	16 03	8 28	15 08
332		*.9866*	*22 54*	*11 16*	*22 41*	*11 31*	*22 23*	*11 50*	*22 00*	*12 16*	*21 21*	*12 57*
29 MO	11 48 09	–21 21	6 17	17 19	6 36	17 00	7 00	16 36	7 33	16 03	8 30	15 06
333	*23 18 LQ*	*.9864*	*23 51*	*12 03*	*23 41*	*12 14*	*23 29*	*12 29*	*23 12*	*12 48*	*22 45*	*13 19*
30 TU	11 48 30	–21 32	6 18	17 19	6 37	17 00	7 01	16 36	7 35	16 02	8 32	15 05
334		*.9863*	*none*	*12 45*	*none*	*12 53*	*none*	*13 03*	*none*	*13 16*	*none*	*13 36*

December 1999

12th Month **31 days**

Coordinated Universal Time (Greenwich Mean Time)

NOTE: For each day, numbers on first line indicate Sun. Numbers on second line indicate *Moon*. Degrees are North Latitude.

Moon Phases: FM = full moon; LQ = last quarter; NM = new moon; FQ = first quarter. Sun's distance is in Astronomical Units.

CAUTION: Must be converted to local time. For instructions see "Calculation of Rise Times."

Day of month, of week, *of year*	Sun on Meridian *Moon Phase* h m s	Sun's Declination ° ′ *Distance*	20° Rise Sun *Moon* h m	20° Set Sun *Moon* h m	30° Rise Sun *Moon* h m	30° Set Sun *Moon* h m	40° Rise Sun *Moon* h m	40° Set Sun *Moon* h m	50° Rise Sun *Moon* h m	50° Set Sun *Moon* h m	60° Rise Sun *Moon* h m	60° Set Sun *Moon* h m
1 WE	11 48 52	–21 42	6 18	17 19	6 38	17 00	7 02	16 35	7 36	16 01	8 34	15 03
335		*.9861*	*0 46*	*13 25*	*0 40*	*13 29*	*0 32*	*13 34*	*0 22*	*13 40*	*0 06*	*13 50*
2 TH	11 49 15	–21 51	6 19	17 19	6 39	17 00	7 03	16 35	7 37	16 01	8 36	15 02
336		*.9860*	*1 38*	*14 02*	*1 36*	*14 02*	*1 33*	*14 02*	*1 30*	*14 02*	*1 25*	*14 02*
3 FR	11 49 38	–22 00	6 20	17 20	6 39	17 00	7 04	16 35	7 39	16 00	8 38	15 01
337		*.9858*	*2 29*	*14 39*	*2 31*	*14 35*	*2 33*	*14 30*	*2 37*	*14 24*	*2 42*	*14 14*
4 SA	11 50 02	–22 09	6 20	17 20	6 40	17 00	7 05	16 35	7 40	16 00	8 40	15 00
338		*.9857*	*3 18*	*15 16*	*3 24*	*15 08*	*3 32*	*14 59*	*3 42*	*14 46*	*3 58*	*14 27*
5 SU	11 50 26	–22 17	6 21	17 20	6 41	17 00	7 06	16 35	7 41	15 59	8 42	14 59
339		*.9855*	*4 08*	*15 54*	*4 18*	*15 43*	*4 30*	*15 29*	*4 46*	*15 10*	*5 13*	*14 41*
6 MO	11 50 52	–22 24	6 21	17 20	6 42	17 00	7 07	16 35	7 42	15 59	8 43	14 58
340		*.9854*	*4 58*	*16 33*	*5 11*	*16 19*	*5 27*	*16 01*	*5 50*	*15 37*	*6 26*	*14 58*
7 TU	11 51 17	–22 32	6 22	17 20	6 42	17 00	7 08	16 35	7 44	15 59	8 45	14 57
341	*22 32 NM*	*.9852*	*5 48*	*17 15*	*6 04*	*16 58*	*6 24*	*16 37*	*6 52*	*16 08*	*7 38*	*15 20*
8 WE	11 51 43	–22 38	6 23	17 21	6 43	17 00	7 09	16 35	7 45	15 59	8 47	14 56
342		*.9851*	*6 38*	*17 59*	*6 57*	*17 41*	*7 19*	*17 17*	*7 51*	*16 44*	*8 45*	*15 49*
9 TH	11 52 10	–22 45	6 23	17 21	6 44	17 00	7 10	16 35	7 46	15 58	8 49	14 56
343		*.9850*	*7 28*	*18 46*	*7 48*	*18 26*	*8 12*	*18 02*	*8 46*	*17 27*	*9 45*	*16 28*
10 FR	11 52 37	–22 51	6 24	17 21	6 45	17 01	7 10	16 35	7 47	15 58	8 50	14 55
344		*.9848*	*8 17*	*19 35*	*8 37*	*19 15*	*9 01*	*18 51*	*9 36*	*18 16*	*10 36*	*17 17*
11 SA	11 53 04	–22 56	6 25	17 22	6 45	17 01	7 11	16 35	7 48	15 58	8 52	14 54
345		*.9847*	*9 04*	*20 25*	*9 23*	*20 07*	*9 47*	*19 44*	*10 20*	*19 12*	*11 16*	*18 17*
12 SU	11 53 32	–23 01	6 25	17 22	6 46	17 01	7 12	16 35	7 49	15 58	8 53	14 54
346		*.9846*	*9 50*	*21 16*	*10 07*	*21 00*	*10 28*	*20 40*	*10 57*	*20 12*	*11 46*	*19 25*
13 MO	11 54 00	–23 06	6 26	17 22	6 47	17 01	7 13	16 35	7 50	15 58	8 54	14 54
347		*.9845*	*10 33*	*22 08*	*10 47*	*21 55*	*11 05*	*21 39*	*11 30*	*21 16*	*12 09*	*20 39*
14 TU	11 54 28	–23 10	6 26	17 23	6 47	17 02	7 14	16 35	7 51	15 58	8 55	14 53
348		*.9844*	*11 14*	*23 01*	*11 25*	*22 51*	*11 39*	*22 39*	*11 58*	*22 23*	*12 28*	*21 56*
15 WE	11 54 57	–23 14	6 27	17 23	6 48	17 02	7 14	16 36	7 52	15 58	8 57	14 53
349		*.9843*	*11 54*	*23 54*	*12 02*	*23 49*	*12 11*	*23 41*	*12 24*	*23 32*	*12 43*	*23 17*
16 TH	11 55 26	–23 17	6 27	17 23	6 49	17 02	7 15	16 36	7 52	15 58	8 58	14 53
350	*0 50 FQ*	*.9842*	*12 34*	*none*	*12 38*	*none*	*12 42*	*none*	*12 48*	*none*	*12 57*	*none*
17 FR	11 55 55	–23 20	6 28	17 24	6 49	17 03	7 16	16 36	7 53	15 59	8 59	14 53
351		*.9841*	*13 15*	*0 49*	*13 14*	*0 47*	*13 13*	*0 46*	*13 12*	*0 43*	*13 10*	*0 39*
18 SA	11 56 24	–23 22	6 29	17 24	6 50	17 03	7 16	16 36	7 54	15 59	9 00	14 53
352		*.9840*	*13 58*	*1 45*	*13 52*	*1 48*	*13 46*	*1 52*	*13 37*	*1 57*	*13 25*	*2 05*
19 SU	11 56 54	–23 24	6 29	17 25	6 50	17 03	7 17	16 37	7 54	15 59	9 00	14 53
353		*.9839*	*14 43*	*2 45*	*14 33*	*2 52*	*14 22*	*3 02*	*14 06*	*3 15*	*13 41*	*3 35*
20 MO	11 57 24	–23 25	6 30	17 25	6 51	17 04	7 17	16 37	7 55	16 00	9 01	14 54
354		*.9838*	*15 33*	*3 47*	*15 19*	*3 59*	*15 02*	*4 14*	*14 39*	*4 35*	*14 03*	*5 08*
21 TU	11 57 53	–23 26	6 30	17 26	6 51	17 04	7 18	16 38	7 56	16 00	9 02	14 54
355		*.9837*	*16 28*	*4 52*	*16 11*	*5 08*	*15 49*	*5 28*	*15 20*	*5 55*	*14 32*	*6 41*
22 WE	11 58 23	–23 26	6 31	17 26	6 52	17 05	7 19	16 38	7 56	16 01	9 02	14 55
356	*17 31 FM*	*.9836*	*17 28*	*5 58*	*17 08*	*6 17*	*16 44*	*6 40*	*16 11*	*7 13*	*15 14*	*8 09*
23 TH	11 58 53	–23 26	6 31	17 27	6 52	17 05	7 19	16 39	7 57	16 01	9 03	14 55
357		*.9836*	*18 31*	*7 04*	*18 11*	*7 24*	*17 47*	*7 49*	*17 12*	*8 24*	*16 13*	*9 23*
24 FR	11 59 23	–23 26	6 32	17 27	6 53	17 06	7 19	16 39	7 57	16 02	9 03	14 56
358		*.9835*	*19 36*	*8 07*	*19 18*	*8 26*	*18 55*	*8 50*	*18 22*	*9 23*	*17 28*	*10 19*
25 SA	11 59 52	–23 25	6 32	17 28	6 53	17 06	7 20	16 40	7 57	16 02	9 03	14 57
359		*.9835*	*20 39*	*9 04*	*20 24*	*9 21*	*20 04*	*9 42*	*19 37*	*10 10*	*18 53*	*10 57*
26 SU	12 00 22	–23 23	6 33	17 28	6 54	17 07	7 20	16 41	7 58	16 03	9 03	14 57
360		*.9834*	*21 40*	*9 55*	*21 28*	*10 09*	*21 13*	*10 25*	*20 53*	*10 48*	*20 21*	*11 24*
27 MO	12 00 52	–23 21	6 33	17 29	6 54	17 08	7 21	16 41	7 58	16 04	9 04	14 58
361		*.9834*	*22 38*	*10 41*	*22 30*	*10 51*	*22 20*	*11 03*	*22 07*	*11 19*	*21 46*	*11 43*
28 TU	12 01 21	–23 19	6 33	17 29	6 55	17 08	7 21	16 42	7 58	16 05	9 04	14 59
362		*.9834*	*23 32*	*11 23*	*23 28*	*11 29*	*23 24*	*11 36*	*23 18*	*11 45*	*23 09*	*11 59*
29 WE	12 01 50	–23 16	6 34	17 30	6 55	17 09	7 21	16 43	7 58	16 05	9 03	15 00
363	*14 04 LQ*	*.9833*	*none*	*12 03*	*none*	*12 04*	*none*	*12 06*	*none*	*12 08*	*none*	*12 12*
30 TH	12 02 19	–23 12	6 34	17 31	6 55	17 10	7 21	16 43	7 58	16 06	9 03	15 02
364		*.9833*	*0 24*	*12 40*	*0 25*	*12 38*	*0 25*	*12 34*	*0 26*	*12 30*	*0 28*	*12 24*
31 FR	12 02 48	–23 09	6 35	17 31	6 55	17 10	7 22	16 44	7 59	16 07	9 03	15 03
365		*.9833*	*1 15*	*13 17*	*1 19*	*13 11*	*1 25*	*13 03*	*1 33*	*12 52*	*1 45*	*12 36*

Perpetual Calendar

The number shown for each year indicates which Gregorian calendar to use. For 1583-1802, see "Gregorian Calendar" on page 322. For 1803-20, use numbers for 1983-2000, respectively. For Julian Calendar, see "Julian Calendar" on page 322.

1821 2	1847 6	1873 4	1899 1	1925 5	1951 2	1977 7	2003 4	2029 2	2055 6
1822 3	1848 . . . 14	1874 5	1900 2	1926 6	1952 . . . 10	1978 1	2004 . . . 12	2030 3	2056 . . . 14
1823 4	1849 2	1875 6	1901 3	1927 7	1953 5	1979 2	2005 7	2031 4	2057 2
1824 . . . 12	1850 3	1876 . . . 14	1902 4	1928 8	1954 6	1980 . . . 10	2006 1	2032 . . . 12	2058 3
1825 7	1851 4	1877 2	1903 5	1929 3	1955 7	1981 5	2007 2	2033 7	2059 4
1826 1	1852 . . . 12	1878 3	1904 . . . 13	1930 4	1956 8	1982 6	2008 . . . 10	2034 1	2060 . . . 12
1827 2	1853 7	1879 4	1905 1	1931 5	1957 3	1983 7	2009 5	2035 2	2061 7
1828 . . . 10	1854 1	1880 . . . 12	1906 2	1932 . . . 13	1958 4	1984 8	2010 6	2036 . . . 10	2062 1
1829 5	1855 2	1881 7	1907 3	1933 1	1959 5	1985 3	2011 7	2037 5	2063 2
1830 6	1856 . . . 10	1882 1	1908 . . . 11	1934 2	1960 . . . 13	1986 4	2012 8	2038 6	2064 . . . 10
1831 7	1857 5	1883 2	1909 6	1935 3	1961 1	1987 5	2013 3	2039 7	2065 5
1832 8	1858 6	1884 . . . 10	1910 7	1936 . . . 11	1962 2	1988 . . . 13	2014 4	2040 8	2066 6
1833 3	1859 7	1885 5	1911 1	1937 6	1963 3	1989 1	2015 5	2041 3	2067 7
1834 4	1860 8	1886 6	1912 9	1938 7	1964 . . . 11	1990 2	2016 . . . 13	2042 4	2068 8
1835 5	1861 3	1887 7	1913 4	1939 1	1965 6	1991 3	2017 1	2043 5	2069 3
1836 . . . 13	1862 4	1888 8	1914 5	1940 9	1966 7	1992 . . . 11	2018 2	2044 . . . 13	2070 4
1837 1	1863 5	1889 3	1915 6	1941 4	1967 1	1993 6	2019 3	2045 1	2071 5
1838 2	1864 . . . 13	1890 4	1916 . . . 14	1942 5	1968 9	1994 7	2020 . . . 11	2046 2	2072 . . . 13
1839 3	1865 1	1891 5	1917 2	1943 6	1969 4	1995 1	2021 6	2047 3	2073 1
1840 . . . 11	1866 2	1892 . . . 13	1918 3	1944 . . . 14	1970 5	1996 9	2022 7	2048 . . . 11	2074 2
1841 6	1867 3	1893 1	1919 4	1945 2	1971 6	1997 4	2023 1	2049 6	2075 3
1842 7	1868 . . . 11	1894 2	1920 . . . 12	1946 3	1972 . . . 14	1998 5	2024 9	2050 7	2076 . . . 11
1843 1	1869 6	1895 3	1921 7	1947 4	1973 2	1999 6	2025 4	2051 1	2077 6
1844 9	1870 7	1896 . . . 11	1922 1	1948 . . . 12	1974 3	2000 . . . 14	2026 5	2052 9	2078 7
1845 4	1871 1	1897 6	1923 2	1949 7	1975 4	2001 2	2027 6	2053 4	2079 1
1846 5	1872 9	1898 7	1924 . . . 10	1950 1	1976 . . . 12	2002 3	2028 . . . 14	2054 5	2080 9

1

JANUARY

S	M	T	W	T	F	S
1	2	3	4	5	6	7
8	9	10	11	12	13	14
15	16	17	18	19	20	21
22	23	24	25	26	27	28
29	30	31				

FEBRUARY

S	M	T	W	T	F	S
			1	2	3	4
5	6	7	8	9	10	11
12	13	14	15	16	17	18
19	20	21	22	23	24	25
26	27	28				

MARCH

S	M	T	W	T	F	S
			1	2	3	4
5	6	7	8	9	10	11
12	13	14	15	16	17	18
19	20	21	22	23	24	25
26	27	28	29	30	31	

APRIL

S	M	T	W	T	F	S
						1
2	3	4	5	6	7	8
9	10	11	12	13	14	15
16	17	18	19	20	21	22
23	24	25	26	27	28	29
30						

MAY

S	M	T	W	T	F	S
	1	2	3	4	5	6
7	8	9	10	11	12	13
14	15	16	17	18	19	20
21	22	23	24	25	26	27
28	29	30	31			

JUNE

S	M	T	W	T	F	S
				1	2	3
4	5	6	7	8	9	10
11	12	13	14	15	16	17
18	19	20	21	22	23	24
25	26	27	28	29	30	

JULY

S	M	T	W	T	F	S
						1
2	3	4	5	6	7	8
9	10	11	12	13	14	15
16	17	18	19	20	21	22
23	24	25	26	27	28	29
30	31					

AUGUST

S	M	T	W	T	F	S
		1	2	3	4	5
6	7	8	9	10	11	12
13	14	15	16	17	18	19
20	21	22	23	24	25	26
27	28	29	30	31		

SEPTEMBER

S	M	T	W	T	F	S
					1	2
3	4	5	6	7	8	9
10	11	12	13	14	15	16
17	18	19	20	21	22	23
24	25	26	27	28	29	30

OCTOBER

S	M	T	W	T	F	S
1	2	3	4	5	6	7
8	9	10	11	12	13	14
15	16	17	18	19	20	21
22	23	24	25	26	27	28
29	30	31				

NOVEMBER

S	M	T	W	T	F	S
			1	2	3	4
5	6	7	8	9	10	11
12	13	14	15	16	17	18
19	20	21	22	23	24	25
26	27	28	29	30		

DECEMBER

S	M	T	W	T	F	S
					1	2
3	4	5	6	7	8	9
10	11	12	13	14	15	16
17	18	19	20	21	22	23
24	25	26	27	28	29	30
31						

2 — 2001

JANUARY

S	M	T	W	T	F	S
	1	2	3	4	5	6
7	8	9	10	11	12	13
14	15	16	17	18	19	20
21	22	23	24	25	26	27
28	29	30	31			

FEBRUARY

S	M	T	W	T	F	S
				1	2	3
4	5	6	7	8	9	10
11	12	13	14	15	16	17
18	19	20	21	22	23	24
25	26	27	28			

MARCH

S	M	T	W	T	F	S
				1	2	3
4	5	6	7	8	9	10
11	12	13	14	15	16	17
18	19	20	21	22	23	24
25	26	27	28	29	30	31

APRIL

S	M	T	W	T	F	S
1	2	3	4	5	6	7
8	9	10	11	12	13	14
15	16	17	18	19	20	21
22	23	24	25	26	27	28
29	30					

MAY

S	M	T	W	T	F	S
		1	2	3	4	5
6	7	8	9	10	11	12
13	14	15	16	17	18	19
20	21	22	23	24	25	26
27	28	29	30	31		

JUNE

S	M	T	W	T	F	S
					1	2
3	4	5	6	7	8	9
10	11	12	13	14	15	16
17	18	19	20	21	22	23
24	25	26	27	28	29	30

JULY

S	M	T	W	T	F	S
1	2	3	4	5	6	7
8	9	10	11	12	13	14
15	16	17	18	19	20	21
22	23	24	25	26	27	28
29	30	31				

AUGUST

S	M	T	W	T	F	S
			1	2	3	4
5	6	7	8	9	10	11
12	13	14	15	16	17	18
19	20	21	22	23	24	25
26	27	28	29	30	31	

SEPTEMBER

S	M	T	W	T	F	S
						1
2	3	4	5	6	7	8
9	10	11	12	13	14	15
16	17	18	19	20	21	22
23	24	25	26	27	28	29
30						

OCTOBER

S	M	T	W	T	F	S
	1	2	3	4	5	6
7	8	9	10	11	12	13
14	15	16	17	18	19	20
21	22	23	24	25	26	27
28	29	30	31			

NOVEMBER

S	M	T	W	T	F	S
				1	2	3
4	5	6	7	8	9	10
11	12	13	14	15	16	17
18	19	20	21	22	23	24
25	26	27	28	29	30	

DECEMBER

S	M	T	W	T	F	S
						1
2	3	4	5	6	7	8
9	10	11	12	13	14	15
16	17	18	19	20	21	22
23	24	25	26	27	28	29
30	31					

3

JANUARY

S	M	T	W	T	F	S
		1	2	3	4	5
6	7	8	9	10	11	12
13	14	15	16	17	18	19
20	21	22	23	24	25	26
27	28	29	30	31		

FEBRUARY

S	M	T	W	T	F	S
					1	2
3	4	5	6	7	8	9
10	11	12	13	14	15	16
17	18	19	20	21	22	23
24	25	26	27	28		

MARCH

S	M	T	W	T	F	S
					1	2
3	4	5	6	7	8	9
10	11	12	13	14	15	16
17	18	19	20	21	22	23
24	25	26	27	28	29	30
31						

APRIL

S	M	T	W	T	F	S
	1	2	3	4	5	6
7	8	9	10	11	12	13
14	15	16	17	18	19	20
21	22	23	24	25	26	27
28	29	30				

MAY

S	M	T	W	T	F	S
			1	2	3	4
5	6	7	8	9	10	11
12	13	14	15	16	17	18
19	20	21	22	23	24	25
26	27	28	29	30	31	

JUNE

S	M	T	W	T	F	S
						1
2	3	4	5	6	7	8
9	10	11	12	13	14	15
16	17	18	19	20	21	22
23	24	25	26	27	28	29
30						

JULY

S	M	T	W	T	F	S
	1	2	3	4	5	6
7	8	9	10	11	12	13
14	15	16	17	18	19	20
21	22	23	24	25	26	27
28	29	30	31			

AUGUST

S	M	T	W	T	F	S
				1	2	3
4	5	6	7	8	9	10
11	12	13	14	15	16	17
18	19	20	21	22	23	24
25	26	27	28	29	30	31

SEPTEMBER

S	M	T	W	T	F	S
1	2	3	4	5	6	7
8	9	10	11	12	13	14
15	16	17	18	19	20	21
22	23	24	25	26	27	28
29	30					

OCTOBER

S	M	T	W	T	F	S
		1	2	3	4	5
6	7	8	9	10	11	12
13	14	15	16	17	18	19
20	21	22	23	24	25	26
27	28	29	30	31		

NOVEMBER

S	M	T	W	T	F	S
					1	2
3	4	5	6	7	8	9
10	11	12	13	14	15	16
17	18	19	20	21	22	23
24	25	26	27	28	29	30

DECEMBER

S	M	T	W	T	F	S
1	2	3	4	5	6	7
8	9	10	11	12	13	14
15	16	17	18	19	20	21
22	23	24	25	26	27	28
29	30	31				

4

JANUARY

S	M	T	W	T	F	S
			1	2	3	4
5	6	7	8	9	10	11
12	13	14	15	16	17	18
19	20	21	22	23	24	25
26	27	28	29	30	31	

FEBRUARY

S	M	T	W	T	F	S
						1
2	3	4	5	6	7	8
9	10	11	12	13	14	15
16	17	18	19	20	21	22
23	24	25	26	27	28	

MARCH

S	M	T	W	T	F	S
						1
2	3	4	5	6	7	8
9	10	11	12	13	14	15
16	17	18	19	20	21	22
23	24	25	26	27	28	29
30	31					

APRIL

S	M	T	W	T	F	S
		1	2	3	4	5
6	7	8	9	10	11	12
13	14	15	16	17	18	19
20	21	22	23	24	25	26
27	28	29	30			

MAY

S	M	T	W	T	F	S
				1	2	3
4	5	6	7	8	9	10
11	12	13	14	15	16	17
18	19	20	21	22	23	24
25	26	27	28	29	30	31

JUNE

S	M	T	W	T	F	S
1	2	3	4	5	6	7
8	9	10	11	12	13	14
15	16	17	18	19	20	21
22	23	24	25	26	27	28
29	30					

JULY

S	M	T	W	T	F	S
		1	2	3	4	5
6	7	8	9	10	11	12
13	14	15	16	17	18	19
20	21	22	23	24	25	26
27	28	29	30	31		

AUGUST

S	M	T	W	T	F	S
					1	2
3	4	5	6	7	8	9
10	11	12	13	14	15	16
17	18	19	20	21	22	23
24	25	26	27	28	29	30
31						

SEPTEMBER

S	M	T	W	T	F	S
	1	2	3	4	5	6
7	8	9	10	11	12	13
14	15	16	17	18	19	20
21	22	23	24	25	26	27
28	29	30				

OCTOBER

S	M	T	W	T	F	S
			1	2	3	4
5	6	7	8	9	10	11
12	13	14	15	16	17	18
19	20	21	22	23	24	25
26	27	28	29	30	31	

NOVEMBER

S	M	T	W	T	F	S
						1
2	3	4	5	6	7	8
9	10	11	12	13	14	15
16	17	18	19	20	21	22
23	24	25	26	27	28	29
30						

DECEMBER

S	M	T	W	T	F	S
	1	2	3	4	5	6
7	8	9	10	11	12	13
14	15	16	17	18	19	20
21	22	23	24	25	26	27
28	29	30	31			

5 — 1998

JANUARY

S	M	T	W	T	F	S
				1	2	3
4	5	6	7	8	9	10
11	12	13	14	15	16	17
18	19	20	21	22	23	24
25	26	27	28	29	30	31

FEBRUARY

S	M	T	W	T	F	S
1	2	3	4	5	6	7
8	9	10	11	12	13	14
15	16	17	18	19	20	21
22	23	24	25	26	27	28

MARCH

S	M	T	W	T	F	S
1	2	3	4	5	6	7
8	9	10	11	12	13	14
15	16	17	18	19	20	21
22	23	24	25	26	27	28
29	30	31				

APRIL

S	M	T	W	T	F	S
			1	2	3	4
5	6	7	8	9	10	11
12	13	14	15	16	17	18
19	20	21	22	23	24	25
26	27	28	29	30		

MAY

S	M	T	W	T	F	S
					1	2
3	4	5	6	7	8	9
10	11	12	13	14	15	16
17	18	19	20	21	22	23
24	25	26	27	28	29	30
31						

JUNE

S	M	T	W	T	F	S
	1	2	3	4	5	6
7	8	9	10	11	12	13
14	15	16	17	18	19	20
21	22	23	24	25	26	27
28	29	30				

JULY

S	M	T	W	T	F	S
			1	2	3	4
5	6	7	8	9	10	11
12	13	14	15	16	17	18
19	20	21	22	23	24	25
26	27	28	29	30	31	

AUGUST

S	M	T	W	T	F	S
						1
2	3	4	5	6	7	8
9	10	11	12	13	14	15
16	17	18	19	20	21	22
23	24	25	26	27	28	29
30	31					

SEPTEMBER

S	M	T	W	T	F	S
		1	2	3	4	5
6	7	8	9	10	11	12
13	14	15	16	17	18	19
20	21	22	23	24	25	26
27	28	29	30			

OCTOBER

S	M	T	W	T	F	S
				1	2	3
4	5	6	7	8	9	10
11	12	13	14	15	16	17
18	19	20	21	22	23	24
25	26	27	28	29	30	31

NOVEMBER

S	M	T	W	T	F	S
1	2	3	4	5	6	7
8	9	10	11	12	13	14
15	16	17	18	19	20	21
22	23	24	25	26	27	28
29	30					

DECEMBER

S	M	T	W	T	F	S
		1	2	3	4	5
6	7	8	9	10	11	12
13	14	15	16	17	18	19
20	21	22	23	24	25	26
27	28	29	30	31		

6 — 1999

JANUARY

S	M	T	W	T	F	S
					1	2
3	4	5	6	7	8	9
10	11	12	13	14	15	16
17	18	19	20	21	22	23
24	25	26	27	28	29	30
31						

FEBRUARY

S	M	T	W	T	F	S
	1	2	3	4	5	6
7	8	9	10	11	12	13
14	15	16	17	18	19	20
21	22	23	24	25	26	27
28						

MARCH

S	M	T	W	T	F	S
	1	2	3	4	5	6
7	8	9	10	11	12	13
14	15	16	17	18	19	20
21	22	23	24	25	26	27
28	29	30	31			

APRIL

S	M	T	W	T	F	S
				1	2	3
4	5	6	7	8	9	10
11	12	13	14	15	16	17
18	19	20	21	22	23	24
25	26	27	28	29	30	

MAY

S	M	T	W	T	F	S
						1
2	3	4	5	6	7	8
9	10	11	12	13	14	15
16	17	18	19	20	21	22
23	24	25	26	27	28	29
30	31					

JUNE

S	M	T	W	T	F	S
		1	2	3	4	5
6	7	8	9	10	11	12
13	14	15	16	17	18	19
20	21	22	23	24	25	26
27	28	29	30			

JULY

S	M	T	W	T	F	S
				1	2	3
4	5	6	7	8	9	10
11	12	13	14	15	16	17
18	19	20	21	22	23	24
25	26	27	28	29	30	31

AUGUST

S	M	T	W	T	F	S
1	2	3	4	5	6	7
8	9	10	11	12	13	14
15	16	17	18	19	20	21
22	23	24	25	26	27	28
29	30	31				

SEPTEMBER

S	M	T	W	T	F	S
			1	2	3	4
5	6	7	8	9	10	11
12	13	14	15	16	17	18
19	20	21	22	23	24	25
26	27	28	29	30		

OCTOBER

S	M	T	W	T	F	S
					1	2
3	4	5	6	7	8	9
10	11	12	13	14	15	16
17	18	19	20	21	22	23
24	25	26	27	28	29	30
31						

NOVEMBER

S	M	T	W	T	F	S
	1	2	3	4	5	6
7	8	9	10	11	12	13
14	15	16	17	18	19	20
21	22	23	24	25	26	27
28	29	30				

DECEMBER

S	M	T	W	T	F	S
			1	2	3	4
5	6	7	8	9	10	11
12	13	14	15	16	17	18
19	20	21	22	23	24	25
26	27	28	29	30	31	

7

JANUARY

S	M	T	W	T	F	S
						1
2	3	4	5	6	7	8
9	10	11	12	13	14	15
16	17	18	19	20	21	22
23	24	25	26	27	28	29
30	31					

FEBRUARY

S	M	T	W	T	F	S
		1	2	3	4	5
6	7	8	9	10	11	12
13	14	15	16	17	18	19
20	21	22	23	24	25	26
27	28					

MARCH

S	M	T	W	T	F	S
		1	2	3	4	5
6	7	8	9	10	11	12
13	14	15	16	17	18	19
20	21	22	23	24	25	26
27	28	29	30	31		

APRIL

S	M	T	W	T	F	S
					1	2
3	4	5	6	7	8	9
10	11	12	13	14	15	16
17	18	19	20	21	22	23
24	25	26	27	28	29	30

MAY

S	M	T	W	T	F	S
1	2	3	4	5	6	7
8	9	10	11	12	13	14
15	16	17	18	19	20	21
22	23	24	25	26	27	28
29	30	31				

JUNE

S	M	T	W	T	F	S
			1	2	3	4
5	6	7	8	9	10	11
12	13	14	15	16	17	18
19	20	21	22	23	24	25
26	27	28	29	30		

JULY

S	M	T	W	T	F	S
					1	2
3	4	5	6	7	8	9
10	11	12	13	14	15	16
17	18	19	20	21	22	23
24	25	26	27	28	29	30
31						

AUGUST

S	M	T	W	T	F	S
	1	2	3	4	5	6
7	8	9	10	11	12	13
14	15	16	17	18	19	20
21	22	23	24	25	26	27
28	29	30	31			

SEPTEMBER

S	M	T	W	T	F	S
				1	2	3
4	5	6	7	8	9	10
11	12	13	14	15	16	17
18	19	20	21	22	23	24
25	26	27	28	29	30	

OCTOBER

S	M	T	W	T	F	S
						1
2	3	4	5	6	7	8
9	10	11	12	13	14	15
16	17	18	19	20	21	22
23	24	25	26	27	28	29
30	31					

NOVEMBER

S	M	T	W	T	F	S
		1	2	3	4	5
6	7	8	9	10	11	12
13	14	15	16	17	18	19
20	21	22	23	24	25	26
27	28	29	30			

DECEMBER

S	M	T	W	T	F	S
				1	2	3
4	5	6	7	8	9	10
11	12	13	14	15	16	17
18	19	20	21	22	23	24
25	26	27	28	29	30	31

8

JANUARY

S	M	T	W	T	F	S
1	2	3	4	5	6	7
8	9	10	11	12	13	14
15	16	17	18	19	20	21
22	23	24	25	26	27	28
29	30	31				

FEBRUARY

S	M	T	W	T	F	S
			1	2	3	4
5	6	7	8	9	10	11
12	13	14	15	16	17	18
19	20	21	22	23	24	25
26	27	28	29			

MARCH

S	M	T	W	T	F	S
				1	2	3
4	5	6	7	8	9	10
11	12	13	14	15	16	17
18	19	20	21	22	23	24
25	26	27	28	29	30	31

APRIL

S	M	T	W	T	F	S
1	2	3	4	5	6	7
8	9	10	11	12	13	14
15	16	17	18	19	20	21
22	23	24	25	26	27	28
29	30					

MAY

S	M	T	W	T	F	S
		1	2	3	4	5
6	7	8	9	10	11	12
13	14	15	16	17	18	19
20	21	22	23	24	25	26
27	28	29	30	31		

JUNE

S	M	T	W	T	F	S
					1	2
3	4	5	6	7	8	9
10	11	12	13	14	15	16
17	18	19	20	21	22	23
24	25	26	27	28	29	30

JULY

S	M	T	W	T	F	S
1	2	3	4	5	6	7
8	9	10	11	12	13	14
15	16	17	18	19	20	21
22	23	24	25	26	27	28
29	30	31				

AUGUST

S	M	T	W	T	F	S
			1	2	3	4
5	6	7	8	9	10	11
12	13	14	15	16	17	18
19	20	21	22	23	24	25
26	27	28	29	30	31	

SEPTEMBER

S	M	T	W	T	F	S
						1
2	3	4	5	6	7	8
9	10	11	12	13	14	15
16	17	18	19	20	21	22
23	24	25	26	27	28	29
30						

OCTOBER

S	M	T	W	T	F	S
	1	2	3	4	5	6
7	8	9	10	11	12	13
14	15	16	17	18	19	20
21	22	23	24	25	26	27
28	29	30	31			

NOVEMBER

S	M	T	W	T	F	S
				1	2	3
4	5	6	7	8	9	10
11	12	13	14	15	16	17
18	19	20	21	22	23	24
25	26	27	28	29	30	

DECEMBER

S	M	T	W	T	F	S
						1
2	3	4	5	6	7	8
9	10	11	12	13	14	15
16	17	18	19	20	21	22
23	24	25	26	27	28	29
30	31					

9

JANUARY

S	M	T	W	T	F	S
	1	2	3	4	5	6
7	8	9	10	11	12	13
14	15	16	17	18	19	20
21	22	23	24	25	26	27
28	29	30	31			

FEBRUARY

S	M	T	W	T	F	S
				1	2	3
4	5	6	7	8	9	10
11	12	13	14	15	16	17
18	19	20	21	22	23	24
25	26	27	28	29		

MARCH

S	M	T	W	T	F	S
					1	2
3	4	5	6	7	8	9
10	11	12	13	14	15	16
17	18	19	20	21	22	23
24	25	26	27	28	29	30
31						

APRIL

S	M	T	W	T	F	S
	1	2	3	4	5	6
7	8	9	10	11	12	13
14	15	16	17	18	19	20
21	22	23	24	25	26	27
28	29	30				

MAY

S	M	T	W	T	F	S
			1	2	3	4
5	6	7	8	9	10	11
12	13	14	15	16	17	18
19	20	21	22	23	24	25
26	27	28	29	30	31	

JUNE

S	M	T	W	T	F	S
						1
2	3	4	5	6	7	8
9	10	11	12	13	14	15
16	17	18	19	20	21	22
23	24	25	26	27	28	29
30						

JULY

S	M	T	W	T	F	S
	1	2	3	4	5	6
7	8	9	10	11	12	13
14	15	16	17	18	19	20
21	22	23	24	25	26	27
28	29	30	31			

AUGUST

S	M	T	W	T	F	S
				1	2	3
4	5	6	7	8	9	10
11	12	13	14	15	16	17
18	19	20	21	22	23	24
25	26	27	28	29	30	31

SEPTEMBER

S	M	T	W	T	F	S
1	2	3	4	5	6	7
8	9	10	11	12	13	14
15	16	17	18	19	20	21
22	23	24	25	26	27	28
29	30					

OCTOBER

S	M	T	W	T	F	S
		1	2	3	4	5
6	7	8	9	10	11	12
13	14	15	16	17	18	19
20	21	22	23	24	25	26
27	28	29	30	31		

NOVEMBER

S	M	T	W	T	F	S
					1	2
3	4	5	6	7	8	9
10	11	12	13	14	15	16
17	18	19	20	21	22	23
24	25	26	27	28	29	30

DECEMBER

S	M	T	W	T	F	S
1	2	3	4	5	6	7
8	9	10	11	12	13	14
15	16	17	18	19	20	21
22	23	24	25	26	27	28
29	30	31				

10

JANUARY

S	M	T	W	T	F	S
		1	2	3	4	5
6	7	8	9	10	11	12
13	14	15	16	17	18	19
20	21	22	23	24	25	26
27	28	29	30	31		

FEBRUARY

S	M	T	W	T	F	S
					1	2
3	4	5	6	7	8	9
10	11	12	13	14	15	16
17	18	19	20	21	22	23
24	25	26	27	28	29	

MARCH

S	M	T	W	T	F	S
						1
2	3	4	5	6	7	8
9	10	11	12	13	14	15
16	17	18	19	20	21	22
23	24	25	26	27	28	29
30	31					

APRIL

S	M	T	W	T	F	S
		1	2	3	4	5
6	7	8	9	10	11	12
13	14	15	16	17	18	19
20	21	22	23	24	25	26
27	28	29	30			

MAY

S	M	T	W	T	F	S
				1	2	3
4	5	6	7	8	9	10
11	12	13	14	15	16	17
18	19	20	21	22	23	24
25	26	27	28	29	30	31

JUNE

S	M	T	W	T	F	S
1	2	3	4	5	6	7
8	9	10	11	12	13	14
15	16	17	18	19	20	21
22	23	24	25	26	27	28
29	30					

JULY

S	M	T	W	T	F	S
		1	2	3	4	5
6	7	8	9	10	11	12
13	14	15	16	17	18	19
20	21	22	23	24	25	26
27	28	29	30	31		

AUGUST

S	M	T	W	T	F	S
					1	2
3	4	5	6	7	8	9
10	11	12	13	14	15	16
17	18	19	20	21	22	23
24	25	26	27	28	29	30
31						

SEPTEMBER

S	M	T	W	T	F	S
	1	2	3	4	5	6
7	8	9	10	11	12	13
14	15	16	17	18	19	20
21	22	23	24	25	26	27
28	29	30				

OCTOBER

S	M	T	W	T	F	S
			1	2	3	4
5	6	7	8	9	10	11
12	13	14	15	16	17	18
19	20	21	22	23	24	25
26	27	28	29	30	31	

NOVEMBER

S	M	T	W	T	F	S
						1
2	3	4	5	6	7	8
9	10	11	12	13	14	15
16	17	18	19	20	21	22
23	24	25	26	27	28	29
30						

DECEMBER

S	M	T	W	T	F	S
	1	2	3	4	5	6
7	8	9	10	11	12	13
14	15	16	17	18	19	20
21	22	23	24	25	26	27
28	29	30	31			

11

JANUARY

S	M	T	W	T	F	S
			1	2	3	4
5	6	7	8	9	10	11
12	13	14	15	16	17	18
19	20	21	22	23	24	25
26	27	28	29	30	31	

FEBRUARY

S	M	T	W	T	F	S
						1
2	3	4	5	6	7	8
9	10	11	12	13	14	15
16	17	18	19	20	21	22
23	24	25	26	27	28	29

MARCH

S	M	T	W	T	F	S
1	2	3	4	5	6	7
8	9	10	11	12	13	14
15	16	17	18	19	20	21
22	23	24	25	26	27	28
29	30	31				

APRIL

S	M	T	W	T	F	S
			1	2	3	4
5	6	7	8	9	10	11
12	13	14	15	16	17	18
19	20	21	22	23	24	25
26	27	28	29	30		

MAY

S	M	T	W	T	F	S
					1	2
3	4	5	6	7	8	9
10	11	12	13	14	15	16
17	18	19	20	21	22	23
24	25	26	27	28	29	30
31						

JUNE

S	M	T	W	T	F	S
	1	2	3	4	5	6
7	8	9	10	11	12	13
14	15	16	17	18	19	20
21	22	23	24	25	26	27
28	29	30				

JULY

S	M	T	W	T	F	S
			1	2	3	4
5	6	7	8	9	10	11
12	13	14	15	16	17	18
19	20	21	22	23	24	25
26	27	28	29	30	31	

AUGUST

S	M	T	W	T	F	S
						1
2	3	4	5	6	7	8
9	10	11	12	13	14	15
16	17	18	19	20	21	22
23	24	25	26	27	28	29
30	31					

SEPTEMBER

S	M	T	W	T	F	S
		1	2	3	4	5
6	7	8	9	10	11	12
13	14	15	16	17	18	19
20	21	22	23	24	25	26
27	28	29	30			

OCTOBER

S	M	T	W	T	F	S
				1	2	3
4	5	6	7	8	9	10
11	12	13	14	15	16	17
18	19	20	21	22	23	24
25	26	27	28	29	30	31

NOVEMBER

S	M	T	W	T	F	S
1	2	3	4	5	6	7
8	9	10	11	12	13	14
15	16	17	18	19	20	21
22	23	24	25	26	27	28
29	30					

DECEMBER

S	M	T	W	T	F	S
		1	2	3	4	5
6	7	8	9	10	11	12
13	14	15	16	17	18	19
20	21	22	23	24	25	26
27	28	29	30	31		

12

JANUARY

S	M	T	W	T	F	S
				1	2	3
4	5	6	7	8	9	10
11	12	13	14	15	16	17
18	19	20	21	22	23	24
25	26	27	28	29	30	31

FEBRUARY

S	M	T	W	T	F	S
1	2	3	4	5	6	7
8	9	10	11	12	13	14
15	16	17	18	19	20	21
22	23	24	25	26	27	28
29						

MARCH

S	M	T	W	T	F	S
	1	2	3	4	5	6
7	8	9	10	11	12	13
14	15	16	17	18	19	20
21	22	23	24	25	26	27
28	29	30	31			

APRIL

S	M	T	W	T	F	S
				1	2	3
4	5	6	7	8	9	10
11	12	13	14	15	16	17
18	19	20	21	22	23	24
25	26	27	28	29	30	

MAY

S	M	T	W	T	F	S
						1
2	3	4	5	6	7	8
9	10	11	12	13	14	15
16	17	18	19	20	21	22
23	24	25	26	27	28	29
30	31					

JUNE

S	M	T	W	T	F	S
		1	2	3	4	5
6	7	8	9	10	11	12
13	14	15	16	17	18	19
20	21	22	23	24	25	26
27	28	29	30			

JULY

S	M	T	W	T	F	S
				1	2	3
4	5	6	7	8	9	10
11	12	13	14	15	16	17
18	19	20	21	22	23	24
25	26	27	28	29	30	31

AUGUST

S	M	T	W	T	F	S
1	2	3	4	5	6	7
8	9	10	11	12	13	14
15	16	17	18	19	20	21
22	23	24	25	26	27	28
29	30	31				

SEPTEMBER

S	M	T	W	T	F	S
			1	2	3	4
5	6	7	8	9	10	11
12	13	14	15	16	17	18
19	20	21	22	23	24	25
26	27	28	29	30		

OCTOBER

S	M	T	W	T	F	S
					1	2
3	4	5	6	7	8	9
10	11	12	13	14	15	16
17	18	19	20	21	22	23
24	25	26	27	28	29	30
31						

NOVEMBER

S	M	T	W	T	F	S
	1	2	3	4	5	6
7	8	9	10	11	12	13
14	15	16	17	18	19	20
21	22	23	24	25	26	27
28	29	30				

DECEMBER

S	M	T	W	T	F	S
			1	2	3	4
5	6	7	8	9	10	11
12	13	14	15	16	17	18
19	20	21	22	23	24	25
26	27	28	29	30	31	

13

JANUARY

S	M	T	W	T	F	S
					1	2
3	4	5	6	7	8	9
10	11	12	13	14	15	16
17	18	19	20	21	22	23
24	25	26	27	28	29	30
31						

FEBRUARY

S	M	T	W	T	F	S
	1	2	3	4	5	6
7	8	9	10	11	12	13
14	15	16	17	18	19	20
21	22	23	24	25	26	27
28	29					

MARCH

S	M	T	W	T	F	S
		1	2	3	4	5
6	7	8	9	10	11	12
13	14	15	16	17	18	19
20	21	22	23	24	25	26
27	28	29	30	31		

APRIL

S	M	T	W	T	F	S
					1	2
3	4	5	6	7	8	9
10	11	12	13	14	15	16
17	18	19	20	21	22	23
24	25	26	27	28	29	30

MAY

S	M	T	W	T	F	S
1	2	3	4	5	6	7
8	9	10	11	12	13	14
15	16	17	18	19	20	21
22	23	24	25	26	27	28
29	30	31				

JUNE

S	M	T	W	T	F	S
			1	2	3	4
5	6	7	8	9	10	11
12	13	14	15	16	17	18
19	20	21	22	23	24	25
26	27	28	29	30		

JULY

S	M	T	W	T	F	S
					1	2
3	4	5	6	7	8	9
10	11	12	13	14	15	16
17	18	19	20	21	22	23
24	25	26	27	28	29	30
31						

AUGUST

S	M	T	W	T	F	S
	1	2	3	4	5	6
7	8	9	10	11	12	13
14	15	16	17	18	19	20
21	22	23	24	25	26	27
28	29	30	31			

SEPTEMBER

S	M	T	W	T	F	S
				1	2	3
4	5	6	7	8	9	10
11	12	13	14	15	16	17
18	19	20	21	22	23	24
25	26	27	28	29	30	

OCTOBER

S	M	T	W	T	F	S
						1
2	3	4	5	6	7	8
9	10	11	12	13	14	15
16	17	18	19	20	21	22
23	24	25	26	27	28	29
30	31					

NOVEMBER

S	M	T	W	T	F	S
		1	2	3	4	5
6	7	8	9	10	11	12
13	14	15	16	17	18	19
20	21	22	23	24	25	26
27	28	29	30			

DECEMBER

S	M	T	W	T	F	S
				1	2	3
4	5	6	7	8	9	10
11	12	13	14	15	16	17
18	19	20	21	22	23	24
25	26	27	28	29	30	31

14

2000

JANUARY

S	M	T	W	T	F	S
						1
2	3	4	5	6	7	8
9	10	11	12	13	14	15
16	17	18	19	20	21	22
23	24	25	26	27	28	29
30	31					

FEBRUARY

S	M	T	W	T	F	S
		1	2	3	4	5
6	7	8	9	10	11	12
13	14	15	16	17	18	19
20	21	22	23	24	25	26
27	28	29				

MARCH

S	M	T	W	T	F	S
			1	2	3	4
5	6	7	8	9	10	11
12	13	14	15	16	17	18
19	20	21	22	23	24	25
26	27	28	29	30	31	

APRIL

S	M	T	W	T	F	S
						1
2	3	4	5	6	7	8
9	10	11	12	13	14	15
16	17	18	19	20	21	22
23	24	25	26	27	28	29
30						

MAY

S	M	T	W	T	F	S
	1	2	3	4	5	6
7	8	9	10	11	12	13
14	15	16	17	18	19	20
21	22	23	24	25	26	27
28	29	30	31			

JUNE

S	M	T	W	T	F	S
				1	2	3
4	5	6	7	8	9	10
11	12	13	14	15	16	17
18	19	20	21	22	23	24
25	26	27	28	29	30	

JULY

S	M	T	W	T	F	S
						1
2	3	4	5	6	7	8
9	10	11	12	13	14	15
16	17	18	19	20	21	22
23	24	25	26	27	28	29
30	31					

AUGUST

S	M	T	W	T	F	S
		1	2	3	4	5
6	7	8	9	10	11	12
13	14	15	16	17	18	19
20	21	22	23	24	25	26
27	28	29	30	31		

SEPTEMBER

S	M	T	W	T	F	S
					1	2
3	4	5	6	7	8	9
10	11	12	13	14	15	16
17	18	19	20	21	22	23
24	25	26	27	28	29	30

OCTOBER

S	M	T	W	T	F	S
1	2	3	4	5	6	7
8	9	10	11	12	13	14
15	16	17	18	19	20	21
22	23	24	25	26	27	28
29	30	31				

NOVEMBER

S	M	T	W	T	F	S
			1	2	3	4
5	6	7	8	9	10	11
12	13	14	15	16	17	18
19	20	21	22	23	24	25
26	27	28	29	30		

DECEMBER

S	M	T	W	T	F	S
					1	2
3	4	5	6	7	8	9
10	11	12	13	14	15	16
17	18	19	20	21	22	23
24	25	26	27	28	29	30
31						

Julian and Gregorian Calendars; Leap Year; Century

Calendars based on the movements of the sun and moon have been used since ancient times, but none has been perfect. The **Julian calendar**, under which Western nations measured time until AD 1582, was authorized by Julius Caesar in 46 BC, the year 709 of Rome. His expert was a Greek, Sosigenes. The Julian calendar, on the assumption that the length of the true year was 365 1/4 days, gave every 4th year 366 days. St. Bede the Venerable, an Anglo-Saxon monk, announced in AD 730 that the 365 1/4-day Julian year was 11 min, 14 sec too long, a cumulative error of about a day every 128 years, but nothing was done about this for more than 800 years.

By 1582 the accumulated error was estimated to amount to 10 days. In that year Pope Gregory XIII decreed that the day following Oct. 4, 1582, should be called Oct. 15, thus dropping 10 days and initiating what became known as the **Gregorian calendar**.

However, with common years 365 days and a 366-day leap year every 4th year, the error in the length of the year would have recurred at the rate of a little more than 3 days every 400 years. Therefore, 3 of every 4 centesimal years (years ending in 00) were made common years, not leap years. Thus, 1600 was a leap year; 1700, 1800, and 1900 were not, but 2000 will be. **Leap years** are those years divisible by 4, except centesimal years, which are common unless divisible by 400.

The Gregorian calendar was adopted at once by France, Italy, Spain, Portugal, and Luxembourg. Within 2 years most German Catholic states, Belgium, and parts of Switzerland and the Netherlands were brought under the new calendar, and Hungary followed in 1587. The rest of the Netherlands, along with Denmark and the German Protestant states, made the change in 1699-1700. (German Protestants retained the Julian calendar's reckoning of the movable feast of Easter until 1776.)

The British government imposed the Gregorian calendar on all its possessions, including the American colonies, in 1752, decreeing that the day following Sept. 2, 1752, should be called Sept. 14, a loss of 11 days. All dates preceding were marked OS, for Old Style. In addition, New Year's Day was moved to Jan. 1 from Mar. 25 (e.g., under the old reckoning, Mar. 24, 1700, had been followed by Mar. 25, 1701). George Washington's birthdate, which was Feb. 11, 1731, OS, became Feb. 22, 1732, NS (New Style). In 1753 Sweden also went Gregorian, but it retained the Julian calendar's rules for Easter until 1844.

In 1793 the French revolutionary government adopted a calendar of 12 months of 30 days with 5 extra days in September of each common year and a 6th every 4th year. Napoleon reinstated the Gregorian calendar in 1806.

The Gregorian system later spread to non-European regions, first in the European colonies and then in independent countries, replacing traditional calendars at least for official purposes. Japan in 1873, Egypt in 1875, China in 1912, and Turkey in 1925 made the change, usually in conjunction with political upheaval. In China, the republican government began reckoning years from its 1911 founding. After 1949, the Communists adopted the Common, or Christian Era, year count, even for the traditional lunar calendar.

In 1918 the Soviet Union decreed that the day after Jan. 31, 1918, OS, would be Feb. 14, 1918, NS. Greece changed over in 1923. For the first time in history, all major cultures now have one calendar. (The Russian Orthodox Church, however, has retained the Julian calendar, as have various Middle Eastern Christian sects.)

To convert from the Julian to the Gregorian calendar, add 10 days to dates Oct. 5, 1582, through Feb. 28, 1700; after that date add 11 days through Feb. 28, 1800; 12 days through Feb. 28, 1900; and 13 days through Feb. 28, 2100.

A **century** consists of 100 consecutive years. The 1st century AD may be said to have run from the years 1 through 100. The 20th century by this reckoning would consist of the years 1901 through 2000 and would technically end Dec. 31, 2000, as would the millennium. The 21st century would thus technically begin Jan. 1, 2001.

Julian Calendar

To find which of the 14 calendars printed on pages 320-21 applies to any year, starting Jan. 1, under the Julian system, find the century for the desired year in the 3 leftmost columns below. Read across and find the year in the 4 top rows. Then read down. The number in the intersection is the calendar designation for that year.

Year (last 2 figures of desired year)

				01	**02**	**03**	**04**	**05**	**06**	**07**	**08**	**09**	**10**	**11**	**12**	**13**	**14**	**15**	**16**	**17**	**18**	**19**	**20**	**21**	**22**	**23**	**24**	**25**	**26**	**27**	**28**
				29	**30**	**31**	**32**	**33**	**34**	**35**	**36**	**37**	**38**	**39**	**40**	**41**	**42**	**43**	**44**	**45**	**46**	**47**	**48**	**49**	**50**	**51**	**52**	**53**	**54**	**55**	**56**
				57	**58**	**59**	**60**	**61**	**62**	**63**	**64**	**65**	**66**	**67**	**68**	**69**	**70**	**71**	**72**	**73**	**74**	**75**	**76**	**77**	**78**	**79**	**80**	**81**	**82**	**83**	**84**
Century			**00**	**85**	**86**	**87**	**88**	**89**	**90**	**91**	**92**	**93**	**94**	**95**	**96**	**97**	**98**	**99**													
0	**700**	**1400**	12	7	1	2	10	5	6	7	8	3	4	5	13	1	2	3	11	6	7	1	9	4	5	6	14	2	3	4	12
100	**800**	**1500**	11	6	7	1	9	4	5	6	14	2	3	4	12	7	1	2	10	5	6	7	8	3	4	5	13	1	2	3	11
200	**900**	**1600**	10	5	6	7	8	3	4	5	13	1	2	3	11	6	7	1	9	4	5	6	14	2	3	4	12	7	1	2	10
300	**1000**	**1700**	9	4	5	6	14	2	3	4	12	7	1	2	10	5	6	7	8	3	4	5	13	1	2	3	11	6	7	1	9
400	**1100**	**1800**	8	3	4	5	13	1	2	3	11	6	7	1	9	4	5	6	14	2	3	4	12	7	1	2	10	5	6	7	8
500	**1200**	**1900**	14	2	3	4	12	7	1	2	10	5	6	7	8	3	4	5	13	1	2	3	11	6	7	1	9	4	5	6	14
600	**1300**	**2000**	13	1	2	3	11	6	7	1	9	4	5	6	14	2	3	4	12	7	1	2	10	5	6	7	8	3	4	5	13

Gregorian Calendar

Choose the desired year from the table below or from page 320 (for years 1803 to 2080). The number after each year designates which calendar to use for that year, as shown on pages 320-21. (The Gregorian calendar was inaugurated Oct. 15, 1582. From that date to Dec. 31, 1582, use calendar 6.)

1583-1802

1583	7	1603	4	1623	1	1643	5	1663	2	1683	6	1703	2	1723	6	1743	3	1763	7	1783	4
1584	8	1604	12	1624	9	1644	13	1664	10	1684	14	1704	10	1724	14	1744	11	1764	8	1784	12
1585	3	1605	7	1625	4	1645	1	1665	5	1685	2	1705	5	1725	2	1745	6	1765	3	1785	7
1586	4	1606	1	1626	5	1646	2	1666	6	1686	3	1706	6	1726	3	1746	7	1766	4	1786	1
1587	5	1607	2	1627	6	1647	3	1667	7	1687	4	1707	7	1727	4	1747	1	1767	5	1787	2
1588	13	1608	10	1628	14	1648	11	1668	8	1688	12	1708	8	1728	12	1748	9	1768	13	1788	10
1589	1	1609	5	1629	2	1649	6	1669	3	1689	7	1709	3	1729	7	1749	4	1769	1	1789	5
1590	2	1610	6	1630	3	1650	7	1670	4	1690	1	1710	4	1730	1	1750	5	1770	2	1790	6
1591	3	1611	7	1631	4	1651	1	1671	5	1691	2	1711	5	1731	2	1751	6	1771	3	1791	7
1592	11	1612	8	1632	12	1652	9	1672	13	1692	10	1712	13	1732	10	1752	14	1772	11	1792	8
1593	6	1613	3	1633	7	1653	4	1673	1	1693	5	1713	1	1733	5	1753	2	1773	6	1793	3
1594	7	1614	4	1634	1	1654	5	1674	2	1694	6	1714	2	1734	6	1754	3	1774	7	1794	4
1595	1	1615	5	1635	2	1655	6	1675	3	1695	7	1715	3	1735	7	1755	4	1775	1	1795	5
1596	9	1616	13	1636	10	1656	14	1676	11	1696	8	1716	11	1736	8	1756	12	1776	9	1796	13
1597	4	1617	1	1637	5	1657	2	1677	6	1697	3	1717	6	1737	3	1757	7	1777	4	1797	1
1598	5	1618	2	1638	6	1658	3	1678	7	1698	4	1718	7	1738	4	1758	1	1778	5	1798	2
1599	6	1619	3	1639	7	1659	4	1679	1	1699	5	1719	1	1739	5	1759	2	1779	6	1799	3
1600	14	1620	11	1640	8	1660	12	1680	9	1700	6	1720	9	1740	13	1760	10	1780	14	1800	4
1601	2	1621	6	1641	3	1661	7	1681	4	1701	7	1721	4	1741	1	1761	5	1781	2	1801	5
1602	3	1622	7	1642	4	1662	1	1682	5	1702	1	1722	5	1742	2	1762	6	1782	3	1802	6

The Julian Period

How many days have you lived? To determine this, multiply your age by 365, add the number of days since your last birthday, and account for all leap years. Chances are your calculations will go wrong somewhere. Astronomers, however, find it convenient to express dates and time intervals in days rather than in years, months, and days. This is done by placing events within the Julian period.

The Julian period was devised in 1582 by the French classical scholar Joseph Scaliger (1540-1609) and named after his father, Julius Caesar Scaliger, not after the Julian calendar. Scaliger began Julian Day (JD) #1 at noon, Jan. 1, 4713 BC, the most recent time that 3 major chronological cycles began on the same day: 1) the 28-year solar cycle, after which dates in the Julian calendar (e.g., Feb. 11) return to the same days of the week (e.g., Monday); (2) the 19-year lunar cycle, after which the phases of the moon return to the same dates of the year; and (3) the 15-year indiction cycle, used in ancient Rome to regulate taxes. It will take 7,980 years to complete the period, the product of 28, 19, and 15.

Noon of Dec. 31, 1998, marks the beginning of JD 2,451,179; that many days will have passed since the start of the Julian period. The JD at noon of any date in 1999 may be found by adding to this figure the day of the year for that date, which can be obtained from the left half of the "How Far Apart Are Two Dates" chart.

How Far Apart Are Two Dates?

This table covers a period of 2 years. To use, find the **boldface number** for each date and subtract the smaller from the larger. Example—for days from Feb. 10, 1998, to Dec. 15, 1999, subtract 41 from 714; the result is 673. For leap year, such as 2000, one day must be added; thus Feb. 10, 1999, and Dec. 15, 2000, are 674 days apart.

First Year

Date	Jan.	Feb.	Mar.	April	May	June	July	Aug.	Sept.	Oct.	Nov.	Dec.
1	**1**	**32**	**60**	**91**	**121**	**152**	**182**	**213**	**244**	**274**	**305**	**335**
2	**2**	**33**	**61**	**92**	**122**	**153**	**183**	**214**	**245**	**275**	**306**	**336**
3	**3**	**34**	**62**	**93**	**123**	**154**	**184**	**215**	**246**	**276**	**307**	**337**
4	**4**	**35**	**63**	**94**	**124**	**155**	**185**	**216**	**247**	**277**	**308**	**338**
5	**5**	**36**	**64**	**95**	**125**	**156**	**186**	**217**	**248**	**278**	**309**	**339**
6	**6**	**37**	**65**	**96**	**126**	**157**	**187**	**218**	**249**	**279**	**310**	**340**
7	**7**	**38**	**66**	**97**	**127**	**158**	**188**	**219**	**250**	**280**	**311**	**341**
8	**8**	**39**	**67**	**98**	**128**	**159**	**189**	**220**	**251**	**281**	**312**	**342**
9	**9**	**40**	**68**	**99**	**129**	**160**	**190**	**221**	**252**	**282**	**313**	**343**
10	**10**	**41**	**69**	**100**	**130**	**161**	**191**	**222**	**253**	**283**	**314**	**344**
11	**11**	**42**	**70**	**101**	**131**	**162**	**192**	**223**	**254**	**284**	**315**	**345**
12	**12**	**43**	**71**	**102**	**132**	**163**	**193**	**224**	**255**	**285**	**316**	**346**
13	**13**	**44**	**72**	**103**	**133**	**164**	**194**	**225**	**256**	**286**	**317**	**347**
14	**14**	**45**	**73**	**104**	**134**	**165**	**195**	**226**	**257**	**287**	**318**	**348**
15	**15**	**46**	**74**	**105**	**135**	**166**	**196**	**227**	**258**	**288**	**319**	**349**
16	**16**	**47**	**75**	**106**	**136**	**167**	**197**	**228**	**259**	**289**	**320**	**350**
17	**17**	**48**	**76**	**107**	**137**	**168**	**198**	**229**	**260**	**290**	**321**	**351**
18	**18**	**49**	**77**	**108**	**138**	**169**	**199**	**230**	**261**	**291**	**322**	**352**
19	**19**	**50**	**78**	**109**	**139**	**170**	**200**	**231**	**262**	**292**	**323**	**353**
20	**20**	**51**	**79**	**110**	**140**	**171**	**201**	**232**	**263**	**293**	**324**	**354**
21	**21**	**52**	**80**	**111**	**141**	**172**	**202**	**233**	**264**	**294**	**325**	**355**
22	**22**	**53**	**81**	**112**	**142**	**173**	**203**	**234**	**265**	**295**	**326**	**356**
23	**23**	**54**	**82**	**113**	**143**	**174**	**204**	**235**	**266**	**296**	**327**	**357**
24	**24**	**55**	**83**	**114**	**144**	**175**	**205**	**236**	**267**	**297**	**328**	**358**
25	**25**	**56**	**84**	**115**	**145**	**176**	**206**	**237**	**268**	**298**	**329**	**359**
26	**26**	**57**	**85**	**116**	**146**	**177**	**207**	**238**	**269**	**299**	**330**	**360**
27	**27**	**58**	**86**	**117**	**147**	**178**	**208**	**239**	**270**	**300**	**331**	**361**
28	**28**	**59**	**87**	**118**	**148**	**179**	**209**	**240**	**271**	**301**	**332**	**362**
29	**29**	—	**88**	**119**	**149**	**180**	**210**	**241**	**272**	**302**	**333**	**363**
30	**30**	—	**89**	**120**	**150**	**181**	**211**	**242**	**273**	**303**	**334**	**364**
31	**31**	—	**90**	—	**151**	—	**212**	**243**	—	**304**	—	**365**

Second Year

Date	Jan.	Feb.	Mar.	April	May	June	July	Aug.	Sept.	Oct.	Nov.	Dec.
1	**366**	**397**	**425**	**456**	**486**	**517**	**547**	**578**	**609**	**639**	**670**	**700**
2	**367**	**398**	**426**	**457**	**487**	**518**	**548**	**579**	**610**	**640**	**671**	**701**
3	**368**	**399**	**427**	**458**	**488**	**519**	**549**	**580**	**611**	**641**	**672**	**702**
4	**369**	**400**	**428**	**459**	**489**	**520**	**550**	**581**	**612**	**642**	**673**	**703**
5	**370**	**401**	**429**	**460**	**490**	**521**	**551**	**582**	**613**	**643**	**674**	**704**
6	**371**	**402**	**430**	**461**	**491**	**522**	**552**	**583**	**614**	**644**	**675**	**705**
7	**372**	**403**	**431**	**462**	**492**	**523**	**553**	**584**	**615**	**645**	**676**	**706**
8	**373**	**404**	**432**	**463**	**493**	**524**	**554**	**585**	**616**	**646**	**677**	**707**
9	**374**	**405**	**433**	**464**	**494**	**525**	**555**	**586**	**617**	**647**	**678**	**708**
10	**375**	**406**	**434**	**465**	**495**	**526**	**556**	**587**	**618**	**648**	**679**	**709**
11	**376**	**407**	**435**	**466**	**496**	**527**	**557**	**588**	**619**	**649**	**680**	**710**
12	**377**	**408**	**436**	**467**	**497**	**528**	**558**	**589**	**620**	**650**	**681**	**711**
13	**378**	**409**	**437**	**468**	**498**	**529**	**559**	**590**	**621**	**651**	**682**	**712**
14	**379**	**410**	**438**	**469**	**499**	**530**	**560**	**591**	**622**	**652**	**683**	**713**
15	**380**	**411**	**439**	**470**	**500**	**531**	**561**	**592**	**623**	**653**	**684**	**714**
16	**381**	**412**	**440**	**471**	**501**	**532**	**562**	**593**	**624**	**654**	**685**	**715**
17	**382**	**413**	**441**	**472**	**502**	**533**	**563**	**594**	**625**	**655**	**686**	**716**
18	**383**	**414**	**442**	**473**	**503**	**534**	**564**	**595**	**626**	**656**	**687**	**717**
19	**384**	**415**	**443**	**474**	**504**	**535**	**565**	**596**	**627**	**657**	**688**	**718**
20	**385**	**416**	**444**	**475**	**505**	**536**	**566**	**597**	**628**	**658**	**689**	**719**
21	**386**	**417**	**445**	**476**	**506**	**537**	**567**	**598**	**629**	**659**	**690**	**720**
22	**387**	**418**	**446**	**477**	**507**	**538**	**568**	**599**	**630**	**660**	**691**	**721**
23	**388**	**419**	**447**	**478**	**508**	**539**	**569**	**600**	**631**	**661**	**692**	**722**
24	**389**	**420**	**448**	**479**	**509**	**540**	**570**	**601**	**632**	**662**	**693**	**723**
25	**390**	**421**	**449**	**480**	**510**	**541**	**571**	**602**	**633**	**663**	**694**	**724**
26	**391**	**422**	**450**	**481**	**511**	**542**	**572**	**603**	**634**	**664**	**695**	**725**
27	**392**	**423**	**451**	**482**	**512**	**543**	**573**	**604**	**635**	**665**	**696**	**726**
28	**393**	**424**	**452**	**483**	**513**	**544**	**574**	**605**	**636**	**666**	**697**	**727**
29	**394**	—	**453**	**484**	**514**	**545**	**575**	**606**	**637**	**667**	**698**	**728**
30	**395**	—	**454**	**485**	**515**	**546**	**576**	**607**	**638**	**668**	**699**	**729**
31	**396**	—	**455**	—	**516**	—	**577**	**608**	—	**669**	—	**730**

Chinese Calendar, Asian Festivals

Source: Chinese Information and Culture Center, New York, NY

The Chinese calendar (like the Islamic calendar; see Religious Information section) is a lunar calendar. It is divided into 12 months of 29 or 30 days (compensating for the lunar month's mean duration of 29 days, 12 hr, 44.05 min). This calendar is synchronized with the solar year by the addition of extra months at fixed intervals.

The Chinese calendar runs on a 60-year cycle. The cycles 1876-1935 and 1936-95, with the years grouped under their 12 animal designations, are printed below, along with the first 24 years of the current cycle. It began in 1996 and will last until 2055. The year 1999 (Lunar Year 4697) is found in the 4th column, under Hare (Rabbit), and is known as a Year of the Hare (or Rabbit). Readers can find the animal name for the year of their birth, marriage, etc., in the same chart. (Note: The first 3-7 weeks of each Western year belong to the previous Chinese year and animal designation.)

Both the Western (Gregorian) and traditional lunar calendars are used publicly in China and in North and South Korea, and 2 New Year's celebrations are held. In Taiwan, in overseas Chinese communities, and in Vietnam, the lunar calendar is used only to set the dates for traditional festivals, with the Gregorian system in general use.

The 4-day Chinese New Year, Hsin Nien, the 3-day Vietnamese New Year festival, Tet, and the 3-to-4-day Korean festival, Suhl, begin at the 2d new moon after the winter solstice. The new moon in the Far East, which is west of the International Date Line, may be one day later than the new moon in the U.S. The festivals may start, therefore, anywhere between Jan. 21 and Feb. 19 of the Gregorian calendar. Feb. 16 marks the start of the new Chinese year in 1999.

Rat	Ox	Tiger	Hare (Rabbit)	Dragon	Snake	Horse	Sheep (Goat)	Monkey	Rooster	Dog	Pig
1876	1877	1878	1879	1880	1881	1882	1883	1884	1885	1886	1887
1888	1889	1890	1891	1892	1893	1894	1895	1896	1897	1898	1899
1900	1901	1902	1903	1904	1905	1906	1907	1908	1909	1910	1911
1912	1913	1914	1915	1916	1917	1918	1919	1920	1921	1922	1923
1924	1925	1926	1927	1928	1929	1930	1931	1932	1933	1934	1935
1936	1937	1938	1939	1940	1941	1942	1943	1944	1945	1946	1947
1948	1949	1950	1951	1952	1953	1954	1955	1956	1957	1958	1959
1960	1961	1962	1963	1964	1965	1966	1967	1968	1969	1970	1971
1972	1973	1974	1975	1976	1977	1978	1979	1980	1981	1982	1983
1984	1985	1986	1987	1988	1989	1990	1991	1992	1993	1994	1995
1996	1997	1998	1999	2000	2001	2002	2003	2004	2005	2006	2007
2008	2009	2010	2011	2012	2013	2014	2015	2016	2017	2018	2019

Standard Time, Daylight Saving Time, and Others

Source: National Imagery and Mapping Agency; U.S. Dept. of Transportation

Standard Time

Standard Time is reckoned from the Prime Meridian of Longitude in Greenwich, England. The world is divided into 24 zones, each 15° of arc, or one hour in time apart. The Greenwich meridian (0°) extends through the center of the initial zone, and the zones to the east are numbered from 1 to 12, with the prefix "minus" indicating the number of hours to be subtracted to obtain Greenwich Time. Each zone extends 7.5° on either side of its central meridian.

Westward zones are similarly numbered, but prefixed "plus," showing the number of hours that must be added to get Greenwich Time. Although these zones apply generally to sea areas, the Standard Time maintained in many countries does not coincide with zone time. A graphical representation of the zones is shown on the Standard Time Zone Chart of the World published by the National Imagery and Mapping Agency. This chart is available from the National Ocean Service (NOS), Distribution Division, N/ACC3, Riverdale, MD 20737-1199; telephone: (800) 638-8972.

The U.S. and possessions are divided into 10 Standard Time zones. Each zone is approximately 15° of longitude in width. All places in each zone use, instead of their own local time, the time counted from the transit of the "mean sun" across the Standard Time meridian that passes near the middle of that zone. These time zones are designated as Atlantic, Eastern, Central, Mountain, Pacific, Alaska, Hawaii-Aleutian, Samoa, Wake Island, and Guam; the time in these zones is reckoned from the 60th, 75th, 90th, 105th, 120th, 135th, 150th, and 165th meridians west of Greenwich and the 165th and 150th meridians east of Greenwich. The time zone line wanders to conform to local geographical regions. The time in the various zones in the U.S. and U.S. territories west of Greenwich is earlier than Greenwich Time by 4, 5, 6, 7, 8, 9, 10, and 11 hours, respectively. However, Wake Island and Guam cross the International Date Line and are 12 and 10 hours later than Greenwich Time, respectively.

24-Hour Time

Twenty-four-hour time is widely used in scientific work throughout the world. In the U.S. it is used also in operations of the armed forces. In Europe it is frequently used by the transportation networks in preference to the 12-hour AM and PM system. With the 24-hour system the day begins at midnight, and times are designated 0000 through 2359.

International Date Line

The Date Line, approximately coinciding with the 180th meridian, separates the calendar dates. The date must be advanced one day when crossing in a westerly direction and set back one day when crossing in an easterly direction. The Date Line frequently deviates from the 180th meridian because of decisions made by individual nations affected. The line is deflected eastward through the Bering Strait and westward of the Aleutians to prevent separating these areas by date. The line is deflected eastward of the Tonga and New Zealand Islands in the South Pacific for the same reason. More recently it was deflected much farther eastward to include all of Kiribati. The line is established by international custom; there is no international authority prescribing its exact course.

Daylight Saving Time

Daylight Saving Time is achieved by advancing the clock one hour. Daylight Saving Time in the U.S. begins each year at 2 AM on the first Sunday in Apr. and ends at 2 AM on the last Sunday in Oct.

Daylight Saving Time was first observed in the U.S. during World War I, and then again during World War II. In the intervening years, some states and communities observed Daylight Saving Time, using whatever beginning and ending dates they chose. In 1966, Congress passed the Uniform Time Act, which provided that any state or territory that chooses to observe Daylight Saving Time must begin and end on the federal dates. Any state could, by law, exempt itself; a 1972 amendment to the act authorized states split by time zones to observe Daylight Saving Time in one time zone and standard time in the other time zone. Currently, Arizona, Hawaii, the eastern time zone portion of Indiana, Puerto Rico, the U.S. Virgin Islands, and American Samoa do not observe Daylight Saving Time.

Congress and the secretary of transportation both have authority to change time zone boundaries. Since 1966 there have been a number of changes to U.S. time zone boundaries. In addition, efforts to conserve energy have prompted various changes in the times that Daylight Saving Time is observed.

International Usage

Adjusting clock time so as to gain the added daylight on summer evenings is common throughout the world.

Canada, which extends over 6 time zones, generally observes Daylight Saving Time from the first Sunday of Apr. until the last Sunday of Oct. Saskatchewan remains on standard time all year. Communities elsewhere in Canada also may exempt themselves from Daylight Saving Time. Mexico, which occupies 3 time zones, observes Daylight Saving Time during the same period as most of Canada.

Member nations of the European Union (EU) observe a "summer-time period," the EU's version of Daylight Saving Time, from the last Sunday of March until the last Sunday in Oct.

Russia, which extends over 11 time zones, maintains its Standard Time 1 hour fast for its zone designation. Additionally, it proclaims Daylight Saving Time from the last Sunday in March until the 4th Sunday in Oct.

China, which extends across 5 time zones, has decreed that the entire country be placed on Greenwich Time plus 8 hours. Daylight Saving Time is not observed. Japan, which lies within one time zone, also does not modify its legal time during the summer months.

Many countries in the Southern Hemisphere maintain Daylight Saving Time, generally from Oct. to Mar.; however, most countries near the equator do not deviate from Standard Time.

See also the "International Time Zones" map on page 500.

Standard Time Differences—World Cities

The time indicated in the table is fixed by law and is called the legal time or, more generally, Standard Time. Use of Daylight Saving Time varies widely. * Indicates morning of the following day. At 12:00 noon, Eastern Standard Time, the Standard Time (in 24-hour time) in selected cities is as follows:

Addis Ababa	20 00	Casablanca	17 00	Madrid	18 00	Sarajevo	18 00
Amsterdam	18 00	Copenhagen	18 00	Manila	1 00*	Seoul	2 00*
Athens	19 00	Dhaka	23 00	Mecca	20 00	Shanghai	1 00*
Auckland	5 00*	Dublin	17 00	Melbourne	3 00*	Singapore	1 00*
Baghdad	20 00	Geneva	18 00	Montevideo	14 00	Stockholm	18 00
Bangkok	0 00*	Helsinki	19 00	Moscow	20 00	Sydney	3 00*
Beijing	1 00*	Ho Chi Minh City	0 00*	Munich	18 00	Taipei	1 00*
Belfast	17 00	Hong Kong	1 00*	Nagasaki	2 00*	Tashkent	22 00
Berlin	18 00	Istanbul	19 00	Nairobi	20 00	Tehran	20 30
Bogotá	12 00	Jakarta	0 00*	New Delhi	22 30	Tel Aviv	19 00
Bombay (Mumbai)	22 30	Jerusalem	19 00	Oslo	18 00	Tokyo	2 00*
Brussels	18 00	Johannesburg	19 00	Paris	18 00	Vladivostok	3 00*
Bucharest	19 00	Karachi	22 00	Prague	18 00	Vienna	18 00
Budapest	18 00	Kathmandu	22 45	Quito	12 00	Warsaw	18 00
Buenos Aires	14 00	Kiev	19 00	Rio de Janeiro	14 00	Wellington	5 00*
Cairo	19 00	Lagos	18 00	Rome	18 00	Yangon (Rangoon)	23 30
Calcutta	22 30	Lima	12 00	St. Petersburg	20 00	Yokohama	2 00*
Cape Town	19 00	Lisbon	17 00	Santiago	13 00	Zurich	18 00
Caracas	13 00	London	17 00				

Standard Time Differences—North American Cities

At 12:00 noon, Eastern Standard Time, the Standard Time in North American cities is as follows:

Akron, OH	12 00 Noon	Galveston, TX	11 00 AM	Philadelphia, PA	12 00 Noon
Albuquerque, NM	10 00 AM	Grand Rapids, MI	12 00 Noon	*Phoenix, AZ	10 00 AM
Atlanta, GA	12 00 Noon	Halifax, NS	1 00 PM	Pierre, SD	11 00 AM
Austin, TX	11 00 AM	Hartford, CT	12 00 Noon	Pittsburgh, PA	12 00 Noon
Baltimore, MD	12 00 Noon	Havana, Cuba	12 00 Noon	Portland, ME	12 00 Noon
Birmingham, AL	11 00 AM	Helena, MT	10 00 AM	Portland, OR	9 00 AM
Bismarck, ND	11 00 AM	*Honolulu, HI	7 00 AM	Providence, RI	12 00 Noon
Boise, ID	10 00 AM	Houston, TX	11 00 AM	Quebec, Que.	12 00 Noon
Boston, MA	12 00 Noon	*Indianapolis, IN	12 00 Noon	*Regina, Sask.	11 00 AM
Buffalo, NY	12 00 Noon	Jacksonville, FL	12 00 Noon	Reno, NV	9 00 AM
Butte, MT	10 00 AM	Juneau, AK	8 00 AM	Richmond, VA	12 00 Noon
Calgary, Alta.	10 00 AM	Kansas City, MO	11 00 AM	Rochester, NY	12 00 Noon
Charleston, SC	12 00 Noon	*Kingston, Jamaica	12 00 Noon	Sacramento, CA	9 00 AM
Charleston, WV	12 00 Noon	Knoxville, TN	12 00 Noon	St. John's, Nfld.	1 30 PM
Charlotte, NC	12 00 Noon	Lexington, KY	12 00 Noon	St. Louis, MO	11 00 AM
Charlottetown, PEI.	1 00 PM	Lincoln, NE	11 00 AM	St. Paul, MN	11 00 AM
Chattanooga, TN	12 00 Noon	Little Rock, AR	11 00 AM	Salt Lake City, UT	10 00 AM
Cheyenne, WY	10 00 AM	Los Angeles, CA	9 00 AM	San Antonio, TX	11 00 AM
Chicago, IL	11 00 AM	Louisville, KY	12 00 Noon	San Diego, CA	9 00 AM
Cleveland, OH	12 00 Noon	*Mexico City, Mexico	11 00 AM	San Francisco, CA	9 00 AM
Colorado Spr., CO	10 00 AM	Memphis, TN	11 00 AM	*San Juan, PR	1 00 PM
Columbus, OH	12 00 Noon	Miami, FL	12 00 Noon	Santa Fe, NM	10 00 AM
Dallas, TX	11 00 AM	Milwaukee, WI	11 00 AM	Savannah, GA	12 00 Noon
*Dawson, Yuk.	9 00 AM	Minneapolis, MN	11 00 AM	Seattle, WA	9 00 AM
Dayton, OH	12 00 Noon	Mobile, AL	11 00 AM	Shreveport, LA	11 00 AM
Denver, CO	10 00 AM	Montreal, Que	12 00 Noon	Sioux Falls, SD	11 00 AM
Des Moines, IA	11 00 AM	Nashville, TN	11 00 AM	Spokane, WA	9 00 AM
Detroit, MI	12 00 Noon	Nassau, Bahamas	12 00 Noon	Tampa, FL	12 00 Noon
Duluth, MN	11 00 AM	New Haven, CT	12 00 Noon	Toledo, OH	12 00 Noon
Edmonton, Alta.	10 00 AM	New Orleans, LA	11 00 AM	Topeka, KS	11 00 AM
El Paso, TX	10 00 AM	New York, NY	12 00 Noon	Toronto, Ont.	12 00 Noon
Erie, PA	12 00 Noon	Nome, AK	8 00 AM	*Tucson, AZ	10 00 AM
Evansville, IN	11 00 AM	Norfolk, VA	12 00 Noon	Tulsa, OK	11 00 AM
Fairbanks, AK	8 00 AM	Oklahoma City, OK	11 00 AM	Vancouver, BC	9 00 AM
Flint, MI	12 00 Noon	Omaha, NE	11 00 AM	Washington, DC	12 00 Noon
*Fort Wayne, IN	12 00 Noon	Ottawa, Ont.	12 00 Noon	Wichita, KS	11 00 AM
Fort Worth, TX	11 00 AM	*Panama City, Panama	12 00 Noon	Wilmington, DE	12 00 Noon
Frankfort, KY	12 00 Noon	Peoria, IL	11 00 AM	Winnipeg, Man.	11 00 AM

Note: This same table can be used for Daylight Saving Time when it is in effect, but allowance must be made for cities that do not observe it; they are marked with an asterisk. Daylight Saving Time is one hour later than Standard Time.

U.S. Legal or Public Holidays, 1999

Technically, the U.S. observes no national holidays; each state has jurisdiction over its holidays, which are designated by legislative enactment or executive proclamation. The president and the U.S. Congress can legally designate holidays only for the District of Columbia and for federal employees. In practice, however, most states observe the federal legal public holidays. Federal legal public holidays are New Year's Day, Martin Luther King Jr.'s Birthday, Washington's Birthday (often called Presidents' Day), Memorial Day, Independence Day, Labor Day, Columbus Day, Veterans Day, Thanksgiving, and Christmas.

Chief Legal or Public Holidays

When a holiday falls on a Saturday or a Sunday, it is usually observed on the preceding Friday or the following Monday. For some holidays, government and business closing practices vary. In most states, the office of the secretary of state can provide details for holiday closings.

The following will be legal or public holidays in most states in 1999:

Jan. 1 (Fri.) — New Year's Day
Jan. 18 (3d Mon. in Jan.) — Martin Luther King Jr.'s Birthday
Feb. 12 (Fri.) — Lincoln's Birthday
Feb. 15 (3d Mon. in Feb.) — Washington's Birthday, or Presidents' Day, or Washington-Lincoln Day
May 31 (last Mon. in May) — Memorial Day, or Decoration Day
July 4 (Sun.) — Independence Day
Sept. 6 (1st Mon. in Sept.) — Labor Day
Nov. 11 (Thurs.) — Veterans Day
Nov. 25 (4th Thurs. in Nov.) — Thanksgiving
Dec. 25 (Sat.) — Christmas Day

In some states these will also be holidays in 1999:

Apr. 2 (Fri.) — Good Friday (In some states, observed for half or part of day.)
Oct. 11 (2d Mon. in Oct.) — Columbus Day, or Discoverers' Day, or Pioneers' Day
Nov. 2 (1st Tues. after 1st Mon. in Nov.) — Election Day

Selected International Holidays, 1999

Jan. 25 — Australia Day obsvd., Australia
Feb. 5 — Constitution Day, Mexico
Feb. 13-16 — Carnival, Brazil
Mar. 8 — Commonwealth Day, Canada, Great Britain
Mar. 17 — St. Patrick's Day, Ireland
Mar. 21 — Benito Juarez's Birthday, Mexico
Apr. 8 — Buddha's Birthday, Korea, Japan
Apr. 23 — National Sovereignty Day, Turkey
May 5 — Cinco de Mayo (Battle of Puebla Day), Mexico
May 17 — Constitution Day, Norway
May 24 — Victoria Day, Canada
June 18 — Dragon Boat Festival, China
June 23 — Midsummer Eve, Baltics, Scandinavia
July 1 — Canada Day, Canada
July 14 — Bastille Day, France
Aug. 30 — St. Rose of Lima, Peru
Sept. 6 — Labor Day, Canada
Sept. 16 — Independence Day, Mexico
Sept. 19 — St. Gennaro, Italy
Oct. 3 — German Unification Day, Germany
Oct. 12 — Día de la Raza, Mexico
Oct. 11 — Thanksgiving Day, Canada
Nov. 1-2 — Day of the Dead, Mexico
Nov. 5 — Guy Fawkes Day, Great Britain
Nov. 11 — Remembrance Day, Canada
Dec. 12 — Jamhuri Day, Kenya; Guadalupe Day, Mexico
Dec. 26 — Boxing Day, Australia, Canada, Great Britain, New Zealand

NOTED PERSONALITIES

Widely Known Americans of the Present

Political leaders, journalists, and other widely known living persons. This list excludes many in categories listed elsewhere in Noted Personalities, such as Writers of the Present and Entertainment Personalities, or in the Sports section.

Roger Ailes, b 5/15/40 (Warren, OH), TV exec.
Madeleine K. Albright, b 5/15/37 (Prague, Czech.), sec. of state.
Lamar Alexander, b 7/3/40 (Maryville, TN), former TN gov., presid. candidate.
Stephen E. Ambrose, b 1/10/36 (Decatur, IL), historian.
Walter H. Annenberg, b 3/13/08 (Milwaukee, WI), publisher, philanthropist.
Roone Arledge, b 7/8/31 (Forest Hills, NY), TV exec.
Richard K. Armey, b 7/7/40 (Cando, ND), House majority leader.
Neil Armstrong, b 8/5/30 (Wapakoneta, OH), former astronaut.
Bruce Babbitt, b 6/27/38 (Los Angeles), interior sec.
F. Lee Bailey, b 6/10/33 (Waltham, MA), attorney.
Russell Baker, b 8/14/25 (Loudoun Co., VA), columnist.
Dave Barry, b 7/3/47 (Armonk, NY), humorist.
Marion Barry, b 3/6/36 (Itta Bena, MS), Wash., DC, mayor.
William J. Bennett, b 7/31/43 (Brooklyn, NY), author, former education sec.
Lloyd Bentsen, b 2/11/21 (Mission, TX), former senator, treasury sec., vice-presid. nominee.
Samuel "Sandy" Berger, b 10/28/45 (Sharon, CT), national security adviser.
Joseph R. Biden Jr., b 11/20/42 (Scranton, PA), senator.
James H. Billington, b 6/1/29 (Bryn Mawr, PA), librarian of Congress.
Harry A. Blackmun, b 11/12/08 (Nashville, IL), former Sup. Ct. justice.
Julian Bond, b 1/14/40 (Nashville, TN), civil rights leader.
David Bonior, b 6/6/45 (Detroit), House minority whip.
Daniel Boorstin, b 10/1/14 (Atlanta), historian, former librarian of Congress.
Erskine Bowles, b 6/28/38 (Monterey, CA), White House chief of staff.
Barbara Boxer, b 11/11/40 (Brooklyn, NY), senator.
Bill Bradley, b 7/28/43 (Crystal City, MO), former senator, pro basketball player.
Ed Bradley, b 6/22/41 (Philadelphia), TV journalist.
James Brady, b 9/17/44 (Grand Rapids, MI), former presidential press sec., gun control advocate.
Jimmy Breslin, b 10/17/30 (Jamaica, NY), columnist, author.
Stephen Breyer, b 8/15/38 (San Francisco), Sup. Ct. justice.
David Brinkley, b 7/10/20 (Wilmington, NC), TV journalist.
David Broder, b 9/11/29 (Chicago Heights, IL), journalist.
Tom Brokaw, b 2/6/40 (Webster, SD), TV journalist.
Joyce Brothers, b 9/20/28 (NY City), psychologist.
Edmund G. ("Jerry") Brown, Jr., b 4/7/38 (San Francisco), Oakland mayor, former CA gov.
Willie Brown, b 3/20/34 (Mineola, TX), San Francisco mayor.
Carol M. Browner, b 12/16/55, (Miami, FL), EPA head.
Pat Buchanan, b 11/2/38 (Wash., DC), journalist, former presid. candidate.
Art Buchwald, b 10/20/25 (Mt. Vernon, NY), humorist.
William F. Buckley Jr., b 11/24/25 (NY City), columnist, author.
Warren Buffett, b 8/30/30 (Omaha, NE), investor.
Dan Burton, b 6/21/38 (Indianapolis), U.S. representative.
Barbara Bush, b 6/8/25 (Rye, NY), former first lady.
George Bush, b 6/12/24 (Milton, MA), former president.
George W. Bush, b 7/6/46 (New Haven, CT), TX gov.
Robert Byrd, b 11/20/17 (N. Wilkesboro, NC), senator, former majority leader.
Ron Carey, b 3/22/36 (NY City), former labor leader.
Jimmy Carter, b 10/1/24 (Plains, GA), former president.
Rosalynn Carter, b 8/18/27 (Plains, GA), former first lady.
James Carville Jr., b 10/25/44 (Fort Benning, GA), political consultant.
Steve Case, b 8/21/58 (Honolulu, HI), America Online exec.
Julia Child, b 8/15/12 (Pasadena, CA), TV chef, author.
Noam Chomsky, b 12/7/28 (Philadelphia), linguist, political activist.
Connie Chung, b 8/20/46 (Wash., DC), TV journalist.
Liz Claiborne, b 3/31/29 (Brussels, Belg.), fashion designer.
Bill Clinton, b 8/19/46 (Hope, AR), U.S. president.
Chelsea Clinton, b 2/27/80 (Little Rock, AR), daughter of Pres. Clinton and Hillary Rodham Clinton.
Hillary Rodham Clinton, b 10/26/47 (Chicago), first lady.
Johnnie L. Cochran Jr., b 10/2/37 (Shreveport, LA), attorney.
William Cohen, b 8/28/40 (Bangor, ME), defense sec.
Joan Ganz Cooney, b 10/30/29 (Phoenix, AZ), children's TV producer.
Bob Costas, b 3/22/52 (NY City), TV journalist.
Katie Couric, b 1/7/57 (Wash., DC), TV journalist.
Walter Cronkite, b 11/4/16 (St. Joseph, MO), TV journalist.
Andrew Cuomo, b 12/6/57 (NY City), HUD sec.
Mario Cuomo, b 6/15/32 (Queens, NY), former NY gov.
Richard M. Daley, b 4/24/42 (Chicago), Chicago mayor.
William M. Daley, b 8/9/48 (Chicago), commerce sec.
Alfonse M. D'Amato, b 8/1/37 (Brooklyn, NY), senator.
Thomas Daschle, b 12/9/47 (Aberdeen, SD), Senate minority leader.
Tom D. DeLay, b 4/8/47 (Laredo, TX), House majority whip.
Alan Dershowitz, b 9/1/38 (Brooklyn, NY), attorney.
Barry Diller, b 2/2/42 (San Francisco), TV exec.
Christopher Dodd, b 5/27/44 (Willimantic, CT), senator.
Elizabeth Dole, b 7/29/36 (Salisbury, NC), Red Cross leader, former transportation sec., labor sec.
Robert Dole, b 7/22/23 (Russell, KS), former Senate majority leader, presid. nominee.
Pete Domenici, b 5/7/32 (Albuquerque, NM), senator.
Sam Donaldson, b 3/11/34 (El Paso, TX), TV journalist.
Elizabeth Drew, b 11/16/35 (Cincinnati), journalist.
Michael S. Dukakis, b 11/3/33 (Boston), former MA gov., presid. nominee.
Roger Ebert, b 6/18/42 (Urbana, IL), film critic.
Marian Wright Edelman, b 6/6/39 (Bennettsville, SC), children's rights advocate.
Michael Eisner, b 3/7/42 (NY City), Disney Co. exec.
John Engler, b 10/12/48 (Mount Pleasant, ME), MI gov.
James Fallows, b 8/2/49 (Philadelphia), journalist.
Jerry Falwell, b 8/11/33 (Lynchburg, VA), TV evangelist, religious educator.
Louis Farrakhan, b 5/11/33 (NY City), Nation of Islam leader.
Dianne Feinstein, b 6/22/33 (San Francisco), senator.
Geraldine Ferraro, b 8/26/35 (Newburgh, NY), former U.S. representative, vice-presid. nominee.
Larry Flynt, b 11/1/42 (Magoffin Co., KY), publisher.
Shelby Foote, b 11/17/16 (Greenville, MS), historian.
Malcolm "Steve" Forbes Jr., b 7/18/47 (Morristown, NJ), publisher, former presid. candidate.
Betty Ford, b 4/8/18 (Chicago), former first lady.
Gerald R. Ford, b 7/14/13 (Omaha, NE), former president.
John Hope Franklin, b 1/2/15 (Rentisville, OK), historian.
Louis Freeh, b 1/6/50 (Jersey City, NJ), FBI director.
Betty Friedan, b 2/4/21 (Peoria, IL), author, feminist.
Milton Friedman, b 7/31/12 (Brooklyn, NY), economist.
John Kenneth Galbraith, b 10/15/08 (Iona Station, Ont.), economist.
Bill Gates, b 10/28/55 (Seattle), Microsoft exec.
Henry Louis Gates Jr., b 9/16/50 (Keyser, WV), scholar.
David Geffen, b 2/21/43 (Brooklyn, NY), entertainment exec.
Richard Gephardt, b 1/31/41 (St. Louis, MO), House minority leader.
Louis Gerstner, b 3/1/42 (Mineola, NY), IBM exec.
Newt Gingrich, b 6/17/43 (Harrisburg, PA), House speaker.
Ruth Bader Ginsburg, b 3/15/33 (Bklyn., NY), Sup. Ct. justice.
Rudolph Giuliani, b 5/28/44 (NY City), NY City mayor.
John Glenn, b 7/18/21 (Cambridge, OH), senator, astronaut.
Dan Glickman, b 11/24/44 (Wichita, KS), agriculture sec.
Ellen Goodman, b 4/11/41 (Newton, MA), columnist.
Doris Kearns Goodwin, b 1/4/43 (Rockville Centre, NY), historian, TV commentator.
Berry Gordy, b 11/28/29 (Detroit), Motown founder.
Al Gore Jr., b 3/31/48 (Wash., DC), U.S. vice president.
Tipper Gore, b 8/19/48 (Wash., DC), wife of vice president.
Stephen Jay Gould, b 9/10/41 (NY City), biologist, author.
Billy Graham, b 11/7/18 (Charlotte, NC), evangelist.
Katharine Graham, b 6/16/17 (NY City), newspaper publisher, author.
Phil Gramm, b 7/8/42 (Ft. Benning, GA), senator, former presid. contender.
Jeff Greenfield, b 6/10/43 (NY City), TV journalist.
Alan Greenspan, b 3/6/26 (NY City), Fed chairman.
Andrew Grove, b 9/2/36 (Budapest, Hungary), Intel exec.
Bryant Gumbel, b 9/29/48 (New Orleans), TV journalist.
David Halberstam, b 4/10/34 (NY City), journalist, author.
Pete Hamill, b 6/24/35 (Brooklyn, NY), journalist, author.
Paul Harvey, b 9/4/18 (Tulsa, OK), radio journalist.
Orrin Hatch, b 3/22/34 (Homestead Park, PA), senator.
Hugh Hefner, b 4/9/26 (Chicago), publisher.
Jesse Helms, b 10/18/21 (Monroe, NC), senator.
Leona Helmsley, b c1920 (NY City), real estate exec.
Heloise, b 4/15/51 (Waco, TX), advice columnist.
Alexis Herman, b 7/16/47 (Mobile, AL), labor sec.
Anita Hill, b 7/10/56 (Morris, OK), legal scholar, complainant against Clarence Thomas.
H. Wayne Huizenga, b 12/29/39 (Evergreen Park, IL), entrepreneur, sports exec.
Kay Bailey Hutchison, b 7/22/43 (Galveston, TX), senator.
Henry J. Hyde, b 4/18/24 (Chicago), U.S. representative, Judiciary Committee chairman.

Lee Iacocca, b 10/15/24 (Allentown, PA), former auto exec.
Carl Icahn, b 1936 (Queens, NY), financier.
Patricia Ireland, b 10/19/45 (Oak Park, IL), feminist leader.
Molly Ivins, b 1944 (Texas), columnist.
Rev. Jesse Jackson, b 10/8/41 (Greenville, SC), civil rights leader, former presid. contender.
Steve Jobs, b 2/24/55 (California), Apple Computer exec.
Lady Bird Johnson, b 12/22/12 (Karnack, TX), former first lady.
Vernon E. Jordan Jr., b 8/15/35 (Atlanta), attorney, former civil rights leader.
John R. Kasich, b 5/13/52 (McKees Rocks, PA), U.S. representative.
Donna Karan, b 10/2/48 (Forest Hills, NY), fashion designer.
Jeffrey Katzenberg, b 1950 (NY City), entertainment exec.
Jack Kemp, b 7/13/35 (Los Angeles), former vice-presid. nominee, HUD sec., pro football quarterback.
Anthony Kennedy, b 7/23/36 (Sacramento, CA), Sup. Ct. justice.
Caroline Kennedy Schlossberg, b 11/27/57 (Boston), author, daughter of Pres. Kennedy.
Edward M. Kennedy, b 2/22/32 (Brookline, MA), senator.
John F. Kennedy Jr., b 11/25/60 (Wash., DC), magazine editor, son of Pres. Kennedy.
Jack Kevorkian, b 5/26/28 (Pontiac, MI), physican, assisted-suicide activist.
Coretta Scott King, b 4/27/27 (Marion, AL), civil rights leader, widow of Martin Luther King Jr.
Larry King, b 11/19/34 (Brooklyn, NY), TV journalist.
Michael Kinsley, b 3/9/51 (Detroit), journalist, editor.
Jeane J. Kirkpatrick, b 11/19/26 (Duncan, OK), political scientist, former ambassador to UN.
Henry Kissinger, b 5/27/23 (Fuerth, Germany), former sec. of state, national security adviser, Nobel Peace Prize winner.
Calvin Klein, b 11/19/42 (NY City), fashion designer.
Joe Klein, b 9/7/46 (New York), journalist, author.
Philip H. Knight, b 2/24/38 (Oregon), CEO of Nike.
Edward I. Koch, b 12/12/24 (NY City), former NY City mayor.
C. Everett Koop, b 10/14/16 (Brooklyn, NY), former surgeon general.
Ted Koppel, b 2/8/40 (Lancashire, England), TV journalist.
Brian Lamb, b 10/9/41 (Lafayette, IN), cable TV exec., journalist.
Ann Landers, b 7/4/18 (Sioux City, IA), advice columnist.
Estee Lauder, b 9/1/08 (NY City), founder, cosmetics and fragrance firm.
Matt Lauer, b 1957 (NY City), TV journalist.
Ralph Lauren, b 10/14/39 (Bronx, NY), fashion designer.
Norman Lear, b 7/27/22 (New Haven, CT), TV producer, political activist.
Jim Lehrer, b 5/19/34 (Wichita, KS), TV journalist, author.
Monica Lewinsky, b 7/23/73 (San Francisco), former White House intern, key figure in White House scandal.
Rush Limbaugh, b 1/12/51 (Cape Girardeau, MO), radio talk-show host.
Anne Morrow Lindbergh, b 1906 (Englewood, NJ), author, former aviator, widow of Charles A. Lindbergh.
Gary Locke, b 1/21/50 (Seattle), WA gov.
Frank Lorenzo, b 5/19/40 (NY City), airline exec.
Trent Lott, b 10/9/41 (Grenada, MS), Senate majority leader.
Shannon Lucid, b 1/14/43 (Shanghai, China), astronaut.
Richard G. Lugar, b 4/4/32 (Indianapolis), senator.
Janet Maslin, b 8/12/49 (NY City), film critic.
Mary Matalin, b 8/19/53 (Chicago), political commentator.
John McCain III, b 8/29/36 (Panama Canal Zone), senator.
Michael McCurry, b 10/27/54 (Charleston, SC), former White House press sec.
George McGovern, b 7/19/22 (Avon, SD), former senator, presid. candidate.
John McLaughlin, b 3/29/27 (Providence, RI), TV journalist.
Robert S. McNamara, b 6/9/16 (San Francisco), former defense sec., World Bank head, author.
Kweisi Mfume, b 10/24/48 (Baltimore), civil rights leader, former U.S. representative.
Kate Millett, b 9/14/34 (St. Paul, MN), author, feminist.
George Mitchell, b 8/20/33, (Waterville, ME), former Senate majority leader, Northern Ireland peace negotiator.
Walter Mondale, b 1/5/28 (Ceylon, MN), former senator, presid. nominee.
Marc Morial, b 1/3/58 (New Orleans), New Orleans mayor.
Carol Moseley-Braun, b 8/16/47 (Chicago), senator.
Bill Moyers, b 6/5/34 (Hugo, OK), TV journalist, author.
Daniel P. Moynihan, b 3/16/27 (Tulsa, OK), senator, author.
Rupert Murdoch, b 3/11/31 (Melbourne, Aust.), media exec.
Ralph Nader, b 2/27/34 (Winsted, CT), consumer advocate.
Don Nickles, b 12/6/48 (Ponca City, OK), senator.
Oliver North, b 10/7/43 (San Antonio, TX), radio talk-show host, former National Security Council aide.
Eleanor Holmes Norton, b 6/13/37 (Wash., DC), U.S. House delegate.
Robert Novak, b 2/26/31 (Joliet, IL), journalist.
Sam Nunn, b 9/8/38 (Perry, GA), former senator.
Sandra Day O'Connor, b 3/26/30 (El Paso, TX), Sup. Ct. justice.
Michael Ovitz, b 12/4/46 (Encino, CA), entertainment exec.
Camille Paglia, b 1947 (Endicott, NY), scholar, author.
Leon F. Panetta, b 6/28/38 (Monterey, CA), former White House chief of staff, U.S. representative.
Rosa Parks, b 2/4/13 (Tuskegee, AL), civil rights activist.
George Pataki, b 6/24/45 (Peekskill, NY), NY gov.
Jane Pauley, b 10/31/50 (Indianapolis), TV journalist.
H. Ross Perot, b 6/27/30 (Texarkana, TX), entrepreneur, former presid. nominee.
George Plimpton, b 3/18/27 (NY City), author, editor.
Norman Podhoretz, b 1/16/30 (NY City), author, editor.
Alvin F. Poussaint, b 5/15/34 (NY City), child psychiatrist.
Colin Powell, b 4/5/37 (NY City), former Joint Chiefs of Staff chairman, national security adviser.
Dan Quayle, b 2/4/47 (Indianapolis), former U.S. vice president, senator.
Anna Quindlen, b 7/8/53 (Philadelphia), author, columnist.
Dan Rather, b 10/31/31 (Wharton, TX), TV journalist.
Nancy Reagan, b 7/6/23 (NY City), former first lady.
Ronald Reagan, b 2/6/11 (Tampico, IL), former president.
Sumner Redstone, b 5/27/23 (Boston), media exec.
Ralph Reed, b 6/24/61 (Portsmouth, VA), political adviser.
William Rehnquist, b 10/1/24 (Milwaukee), Sup. Ct. chief justice.
Robert B. Reich, b 6/24/46 (Scranton, PA), economist, former labor sec.
Janet Reno, b 7/21/38 (Miami, FL), attorney general.
Ann Richards, b 9/3/33 (Waco, TX), former TX gov.
Bill Richardson, b 11/15/47 (Pasadena, CA), energy sec., former UN ambassador, congressman.
Sally K. Ride, b 5/26/51 (Encino, CA), former astronaut.
Richard Riley, b 1/2/33 (Greenville, SC), education sec.
Richard Riordan, b 1930 (Flushing, NY), Los Angeles mayor.
Cokie Roberts, b 12/27/43 (New Orleans), TV journalist.
Oral Roberts, b 1/24/18 (nr. Ada, OK), TV evangelist, educator.
Pat Robertson, b 3/22/30 (Lexington, VA), religious broadcasting exec, former presid. candidate.
David Rockefeller, b 6/12/15 (NY City), banker.
John D. "Jay" Rockefeller 4th, b 6/18/37 (NY City), senator, former WV gov.
Laurance S. Rockefeller, b 5/26/10 (NY City), philanthropist.
Roy Romer, b 10/31/38 (Garden City, KS), CO gov., Democratic National Committee chairman.
Andy Rooney, b 1/14/19 (Albany, NY), TV commentator.
Robert Rubin, b 8/29/38 (NY City), treasury sec.
Louis Rukeyser, b 1/30/33 (NY City), TV journalist, financial analyst.
Tim Russert, b 5/7/50 (Buffalo, NY), TV journalist.
William Safire, b 12/17/29 (NY City), columnist.
Paul Samuelson, b 5/15/15 (Gary, IN), economist.
Diane Sawyer, b 12/22/45 (Glasgow, KY), TV journalist.
Antonin Scalia, b 3/11/36 (Trenton, NJ), Sup. Ct. justice.
Arthur Schlesinger Jr., b 10/15/17 (Columbus, OH), historian.
Kurt L. Schmoke, b 12/1/49 (Baltimore), Baltimore mayor.
Phyllis Schlafly, b 8/15/24 (St. Louis, MO) political activist.
Daniel Schorr, b 8/31/16 (NY City), TV journalist.
Patricia Schroeder, b 7/30/40 (Portland, OR), former senator.
Robert Schuller, b 9/16/26 (Alton, IA), TV evangelist.
H. Norman Schwarzkopf, b 8/22/34 (Trenton, NJ), former military leader.
Glenn T. Seaborg, b 4/19/12 (Ishpeming, MI), chemist.
Allan H. ("Bud") Selig, b 7/30/34 (Milwaukee), baseball commissioner.
Donna E. Shalala, b 2/14/41 (Cleveland), sec. of health and human services.
Bernard Shaw, b 1940 (Chicago), TV journalist.
Henry Hugh Shelton, b 1/2/42 (Speed, NC), chairman of Joint Chiefs of Staff.
Maria Shriver, b 11/6/55 (Chicago), TV journalist.
George P. Shultz, b 12/13/20 (NY City), former sec. of state, other cabinet posts.
O. J. Simpson, b 7/9/47 (San Francisco), former football star, murder defendant.
Gene Siskel, b 1/26/46 (Chicago), film critic.
Rodney Slater, b 2/23/55 (Tutwyler, MS), transportation sec.
Liz Smith, b 2/2/23 (Ft. Worth, TX), gossip columnist.
David H. Souter, b 9/17/39 (Melrose, MA), Sup. Ct. justice.
George Soros, b 8/12/30 (Budapest, Hungary), financier, philanthropist.
Arlen Specter, b 2/12/30 (Wichita, KS), senator.
Kenneth Starr, b 7/21/46 (Vernon, TX), independent counsel.
Shelby Steele, b 1/1/46 (Chicago), scholar, critic.
George Steinbrenner, b 7/4/30 (Rocky River, OH), NY Yankees owner.
Gloria Steinem, b 3/25/34 (Toledo, OH), author, feminist.
George Stephanopoulos, b 2/10/61 (Fall River, MA), TV journalist, former presid. adviser.
David J. Stern, b 9/22/42 (NY City), basketball comm.
John Paul Stevens, b 4/20/20 (Chicago), Sup. Ct. justice.

Martha Stewart, b 8/3/41 (Nutley, NJ), homemaking adviser, entrepreneur.
John J. Sweeney, b 5/5/34 (NY City), labor leader.
Arthur Ochs Sulzberger Jr., b 9/22/51 (Mt. Kisco, NY), newspaper publisher.
John H. Sununu, b 7/2/39 (Havana, Cuba), political commentator, former White House chief of staff.
Paul Tagliabue, b 11/24/40 (Jersey City, NJ), football comm.
George Tenet, b 1/5/53 (Queens, NY), CIA director.
Clarence Thomas, b 6/23/48 (Savannah, GA), Sup. Ct. justice.
Helen Thomas, b 8/4/20 (Winchester, KY), journalist.
R. David Thomas, b 7/2/32 (Atlantic City, NJ), Wendy's founder.
Fred Thompson, b 8/19/42 (Sheffield, AL), senator.
Hunter S. Thompson, b 7/18/37 (Louisville, KY), journalist, author.
Tommy G. Thompson, b 11/19/41 (Elroy, WI), WI gov.
J. Strom Thurmond, b 12/5/02 (Edgefield, SC), senator.
Laurence Tisch, b 3/15/23 (NY City), entertainment exec.
Margaret Truman, b 2/17/24 (Independence, MO), author, daughter of Pres. Truman.
Donald Trump, b 1946 (NY City), real estate exec.
Ted Turner, b 11/19/38 (Cincinnati), TV exec, philanthropist.
Peter Ueberroth, b 9/2/37 (Chicago), sports & travel exec.
Jack Valenti, b 9/5/21 (Houston, TX), movie industry exec.
Abigail Van Buren, b 7/4/18 (Sioux City, IA), advice columnist.
George Voinovitch, b 7/13/31, (Cleveland), OH gov.
Mike Wallace, b 5/9/18 (Brookline, MA), TV journalist.
Barbara Walters, b 9/25/31 (Boston), TV journalist.
J. C. Watts, b 11/18/57 (Eufaula, OK), U.S. representative.
Andrew Weil, b 6/8/42 (Philadelphia), health adviser.
Caspar Weinberger, b 8/18/17 (San Francisco), business exec, former defense sec., other cabinet posts.
Jann Wenner, b 1/7/46 (NY City), publisher.
Cornel West, b 6/2/53 (Tulsa, OK), scholar, critic.
Christine Todd Whitman, b 9/26/46 (New York), NJ gov.
Elie Wiesel, b 9/30/28 (Sighet, Romania), scholar, author, Nobel Peace Prize winner.
L. Douglas Wilder, b 1/17/31 (Richmond, VA), former VA gov.
George Will, b 5/4/41 (Champaign, IL), journalist, author.
Jody Williams, b 10/9/50 (Brattleboro, VT), anti-landmine activist, Nobel Peace Prize winner.
Pete Wilson, b 8/23/33 (Lake Forest, IL), CA gov.
William Julius Wilson, b 12/20/35 (Derry Twp., PA), sociologist, author.
Bob Woodward, b 3/26/43 (Geneva, IL), journalist, author.

Noted African-Americans of the Past

See also other categories.

Ralph David Abernathy, 1926-90, organizer, 1957, pres., 1968, Southern Christian Leadership Conference.
Crispus Attucks, c1723-70, leader of group of colonists that clashed with British soldiers in 1770 Boston Massacre.
Benjamin Banneker, 1731-1806, inventor, astronomer, mathematician, gazetteer.
James P. Beckwourth, 1798-c1867, western fur trader, scout; Beckwourth Pass in N California named for him.
Mary McCleod Bethune, 1875-1955, adviser to FDR and Truman; founder, pres., Bethune-Cookman College.
Henry Blair, 19th cent., pioneer inventor; obtained patents for a corn-planter, 1834, and cotton-planter, 1836.
Edward Bouchet, 1852-1918, first black to earn a PhD at a U.S. university (Yale, 1876); first elected to Phi Beta Kappa.
Tom Bradley, 1917-98, first African-American mayor of Los Angeles.
Sterling A. Brown, 1901-89, poet, literature professor; helped establish African-American literary criticism.
William Wells Brown, 1815-84, novelist, dramatist; first African American to publish a novel.
Ralph Bunche, 1904-71, first black to win the Nobel Peace Prize, 1950; undersecretary of the UN, 1950.
George Washington Carver, 1864-1943, botanist, chemist, and educator; revolutionized the economy of the South.
Charles Waddell Chesnutt, 1858-1932, author known primarily for his short stories, including *The Conjure Woman.*
Eldridge Cleaver, 1935-98, revolutionary social critic; former "minister of information" for Black Panthers; *Soul on Ice.*
James Cleveland, 1931-91, composer, musician, singer; first black gospel artist to appear in Carnegie Hall.
Countee Cullen, 1903-46, poet, played a prominent role in the Harlem Renaissance of the 1920s; *The Black Christ.*
Benjamin O. Davis Sr., 1877-1970, first African-American general, 1940, in U.S. Army.
William L. Dawson, 1886-1970, Illinois congressman, first black chairman of a major U.S. House committee.
Aaron Douglas, 1900-79, painter; "father of black American art."
Frederick Douglass, 1817-95, author, editor, orator, diplomat; edited abolitionist weekly *The North Star.*
St. Clair Drake, 1911-90, black studies pioneer, *Black Metropolis* (1945, with Horace R. Cayton).
Charles Richard Drew, 1904-50, physician, pioneered in development of blood banks; director of American Red Cross blood donor project in WW2.
William Edward Burghardt (W.E.B.) Du Bois, 1868-1963, historian, sociologist; a founder of the NAACP, 1909.
Paul Laurence Dunbar, 1872-1906, poet, novelist; won fame with *Lyrics of Lowly Life,* 1896.
Jean Baptiste Point du Sable, c1750-1818, pioneer trader and first settler of Chicago, 1779.
Henry O. Flipper, 1856-1940, first African-American to graduate, 1877, from West Point.
Marcus Garvey, 1887-1940, founded Universal Negro Improvement Assn., 1911.
Ewart Guinier, 1911-90, trade unionist; first chairman of Harvard Univ.'s Dept. of African American Studies.
Prince Hall, 1735-1807, activist; founded black Freemasonry; served in American Revolutionary war.
Jupiter Hammon, c1720-1800, poet; first African-American to have his works published, 1761.
Lorraine Hansberry, 1930-65, playwright; won New York Drama Critics Circle Award, 1959; *A Raisin in the Sun.*
William H. Hastie, 1904-76, first black federal judge, appointed 1937; governor of Virgin Islands, 1946-49.
Matthew A. Henson, 1866-1955, member of Peary's 1909 expedition to the North Pole; placed U.S. flag at the pole.
Chester Himes, 1909-84, novelist; *Cotton Comes to Harlem.*
William A. Hinton, 1883-1959, physician, developed tests for syphilis; first black prof., 1949, at Harvard Med. School.
Charles Hamilton Houston, 1895-1950, lawyer, Howard University instructor, champion of minority rights,
Langston Hughes, 1902-67, poet, lyric writer, author; a major influence in the Harlem Renaissance of the 1920s.
Daniel James Jr., 1920-78, first black 4-star general, 1975; commander, North American Air Defense Command.
Henry Johnson, 1897-1929, first American decorated by France in WW1 with the Croix de Guerre.
James Weldon Johnson, 1871-1938, poet, novelist, diplomat; lyricist for *Lift Every Voice and Sing.*
Barbara Jordan, 1936-96, congresswoman, orator, educator; first black woman to win a seat in the Texas senate, 1966.
Ernest Everett Just, 1883-1941, marine biologist; studied egg development; author, *Biology of Cell Surfaces,* 1941.
Rev. Martin Luther King Jr., 1929-68, civil rights leader; led 1956 Montgomery, AL, boycott; founder, pres., Southern Christian Leadership Conference, 1957; Nobel laureate (1964); assassinated.
Lewis H. Latimer, 1848-1928, associate of Edison; supervised installation of first electric street lighting in NYC.
Mickey Leland, 1944-89, U.S. representative from Texas, 1978 until death; chairman of Congressional Black Caucus.
Henry Lewis, 1932-1996, (U.S.) conductor; first black conductor and musical director of major American orchestra.
Malcolm X (Little), 1925-65, Black Muslim, black nationalist leader; promoted black pride; assassinated.
Thurgood Marshall, 1908-93, first black U.S. solicitor general, 1965; first black justice of U.S. Sup. Ct., 1967-91.
Jan Matzeliger, 1852-89, invented lasting machine, patented 1883, which revolutionized the shoe industry.
Benjamin Mays, 1895-1984, educator, civil rights leader; headed Morehouse College, 1940-67.
Ronald McNair, 1950-86, physicist, astronaut; killed in *Challenger* explosion.
Dorie Miller, 1919-43, Navy hero of Pearl Harbor attack.
Willard Motley, 1912-65, novelist; *Knock on Any Door.*
Elijah Muhammad, 1897-1975, founded Black Muslims, 1931.
Pedro Alonzo Niño, navigator of Columbus's Niña, 1492.
Frederick D. Patterson, 1901-88, founder of United Negro College Fund, 1944.
Harold R. Perry, 1916-91, first black American Roman Catholic bishop in the 20th cent.
Adam Clayton Powell Jr., 1908-72, early civil rights leader, congressman, 1945-69.
Joseph H. Rainey, 1832-87, first black elected to U.S. House, 1869, from South Carolina.
A. Philip Randolph, 1889-1979, organized Brotherhood of Sleeping Car Porters, 1925; an organizer of 1941 and 1963 March on Washington movements.
Hiram R. Revels, 1822-1901, first African-American U.S. senator, elected in Mississippi, served 1870-71.
Norbert Rillieux, 1806-94; invented a vacuum pan evaporator, 1846, revolutionizing sugar-refining industry.

Paul Robeson, 1898-1976, actor, singer, civil rights activist; graduated first in class at Rutgers, 1918.
Jackie Robinson, 1919-72, first African-American baseball player to play in the major leagues, 1947, and be inducted into the Baseball Hall of Fame, 1962.
Bayard Rustin, 1910-87, an organizer of the 1963 March on Washington; exec. director, A. Philip Randolph Institute.
Peter Salem, at the Battle of Bunker Hill, June 17, 1775, shot and killed British commander Maj. John Pitcairn.
Carl Stokes, 1927-1996, first black mayor of a major American city (Cleveland), 1967-72.
Willard Townsend, 1895-1957, organized the United Transport Service Employees (redcaps), 1935.
Sojourner Truth, 1797-1883, born Isabella Baumfree; preacher, abolitionist; worked for black educational opportunity.
Harriet Tubman, 1823-1913, Underground Railroad conductor, nurse and spy for Union Army in the Civil War.
Nat Turner, 1800-31, led most significant of more than 200 slave revolts in U.S., in Southampton, VA; hanged.
Booker T. Washington, 1856-1915, founder, 1881, and first pres. of Tuskegee Institute; author, *Up From Slavery.*
Harold Washington, 1922-87, first black mayor of Chicago.
Robert C. Weaver, 1907-97, first African-Amerian appointed to cabinet; secretary of HUD.
Phillis Wheatley, c1753-84, poet; 2d American woman and first black woman to be published, 1770.
Walter White, 1893-1955, exec. sec., NAACP, 1931-55.
Roy Wilkins, 1901-81, exec. director, NAACP, 1955-77.
Daniel Hale Williams, 1858-1931, surgeon; performed one of first two open-heart operations, 1893.
Granville T. Woods, 1856-1910, invented third-rail system now used in subways, and automatic air brake.
Carter G. Woodson, 1875-1950, historian; founded Assn. for the Study of Negro Life and History.
Frank Yerby, 1916-91, first best-selling African-American novelist; *The Foxes of Harrow.*
Coleman A. Young, 1918-97, first African-American mayor of Detroit, 1974-93.

Selected Architects and Some of Their Achievements

Max Abramovitz, b 1908, Avery Fisher Hall, NYC; U.S. Steel Bldg. (now USX Towers), Pittsburgh, PA.
Henry Bacon, 1866-1924, Lincoln Memorial, Wash., DC.
Pietro Belluschi, 1899-1994, Juilliard School, Lincoln Center, Pan Am, now MetLife, Bldg. (with Walter Gropius), NYC.
Marcel Breuer, 1902-81, Whitney Museum of American Art (with Hamilton Smith), NYC.
Charles Bulfinch, 1763-1844, State House, Boston; Capitol (part), Wash., DC.
Gordon Bunshaft, 1909-90, Lever House, Park Ave, NYC; Hirshhorn Museum, Wash., DC.
Daniel H. Burnham, 1846-1912, Union Station, Wash. DC; Flatiron Bldg., NYC.
Irwin Chanin, 1892-1988, theaters, skyscrapers, NYC.
Lucio Costa, 1902-98, master plan for city of Brasilia, with Oscar Niemeyer.
Ralph Adams Cram, 1863-1942, Cath. of St. John the Divine, NYC; U.S. Military Acad. (part), West Point, NY.
R. Buckminster Fuller, 1895-1983, U.S. Pavilion (geodesic domes), Expo 67, Montreal.
Frank O. Gehry, b 1929, Hollywood Bowl Shell (phase I), Los Angeles, CA.
Cass Gilbert, 1859-1934, Custom House, Woolworth Bldg., NYC; Supreme Court Bldg., Wash., DC.
Bertram G. Goodhue, 1869-1924, Capitol, Lincoln, NE; St. Thomas's Church, St. Bartholomew's Church, NYC.
Walter Gropius, 1883-1969, Pan Am Bldg. (now MetLife Bldg.) (with Pietro Belluschi), NYC.
Lawrence Halprin, b 1916, Ghirardelli Sq., San Francisco; Nicollet Mall, Minneapolis; FDR Memorial, Wash., DC.
Peter Harrison, 1716-75, Touro Synagogue, Redwood Library, Newport, RI.
Wallace K. Harrison, 1895-1981, Metropolitan Opera House, Lincoln Center, NYC.
Thomas Hastings, 1860-1929, NY Public Library (with John Carrère), Frick Mansion, NYC.
James Hoban, 1762-1831, White House, Wash., DC.
Raymond Hood, 1881-1934, Rockefeller Center (part), Daily News, NYC; Tribune, Chicago, IL.
Richard M. Hunt, 1827-95, Metropolitan Museum (part), NYC; National Observatory, Wash., DC.
William Le Baron Jenney, 1832-1907, Home Insurance (demolished 1931), Chicago, IL.
Philip C. Johnson, b 1906, AT&T headquarters (now 550 Madison Ave.), NYC; Transco Tower, Houston, TX.
Albert Kahn, 1869-1942, General Motors Bldg., Detroit, MI.
Louis Kahn, 1901-74, Salk Laboratory, La Jolla, CA; Yale Art Gallery, New Haven, CT.
Christopher Grant LaFarge, 1862-1938, Roman Catholic Chapel, West Point, NY.
Benjamin H. Latrobe, 1764-1820, Capitol (part), Wash., DC; State Capitol Bldg., Richmond, VA.
Le Corbusier, (Charles-Edouard Jeanneret), 1887-1965, Salvation Army Hostel and Swiss Dormitory, both Paris; master plan for cities of Algiers and Buenos Aires.
William Lescaze, 1896-1969, Philadelphia Savings Fund Society; Borg-Warner Bldg., Chicago.
Maya Lin, b 1959, Vietnam Veterans Memorial, Wash., DC.
Charles Rennie Mackintosh, 1868-1928, Glasgow School of Art; Hill House, Helensburgh.
Bernard R. Maybeck, 1862-1957, Hearst Hall, Univ. of CA, Berkeley; First Church of Christ Scientist, Berkeley, CA.
Charles F. McKim, 1847-1909, Public Library, Boston; Columbia Univ. (part), NYC.
Charles M. McKim, b 1920, KUHT-TV Transmitter Bldg., Lutheran Church of the Redeemer, Houston, TX.
Richard Meier, b 1934, Getty Center Museum, Los Angeles, CA; High Museum of Art, Atlanta, GA.
Ludwig Mies van der Rohe, 1886-1969, Seagram Bldg., (with Philip C. Johnson), NYC; National Gallery, Berlin.
Robert Mills, 1781-1855, Washington Monument, Wash., DC.
Charles Moore, 1925-93, Sea Ranch, near San Francisco; Piazza d'Italia, New Orleans, LA.
Richard J. Neutra, 1892-1970, Mathematics Park, Princeton, NJ; Orange Co. Courthouse, Santa Ana, CA.
Oscar Niemeyer, b 1907, government buildings, Brasilia Palace Hotel, all Brasilia.
Gyo Obata, b 1923, Natl. Air & Space Museum, Smithsonian Inst., Wash., DC; Dallas-Ft. Worth Airport.
Frederick L. Olmsted, 1822-1903, Central Park, NYC; Fairmount Park, Philadelphia, PA.
I(eoh) M(ing) Pei, b 1917, East Wing, Natl. Gallery of Art, Wash., DC; Pyramid, The Louvre, Paris; Rock & Roll Hall of Fame and Museum, Cleveland, OH.
Cesar Pelli, b 1926, World Financial Center, Carnegie Hall Tower, NYC; Petronas Twin Towers, Malaysia.
William Pereira, 1909-85, Cape Canaveral; Transamerica Bldg., San Francisco, CA.
John Russell Pope, 1874-1937, National Gallery, Wash., DC.
John Portman, b 1924, Peachtree Center, Atlanta, GA.
George Browne Post, 1837-1913, NY Stock Exchange; Capitol, Madison, WI.
James Renwick Jr., 1818-95, Grace Church, St. Patrick's Cath., NYC.; Corcoran (now Renwick) Gallery, Wash., DC.
Henry H. Richardson, 1838-86, Trinity Church, Boston, MA.
Kevin Roche, b 1922, Oakland Museum, Oakland, CA; Fine Arts Center, University of Massachusetts, Amherst.
James Gamble Rogers, 1867-1947, Columbia-Presbyterian Medical Center, NYC; Northwestern Univ., Evanston, IL.
John Wellborn Root, 1887-1963, Palmolive Bldg., Chicago; Hotel Statler, Wash., DC.
Paul Rudolph, b 1918, Jewitt Art Center, Wellesley Colllege, MA; Art & Architecture Bldg., Yale Univ., New Haven, CT.
Eero Saarinen, 1910-61, Gateway to the West Arch, St. Louis, MO; Trans World Flight Center, NYC.
Louis Skidmore, 1897-1962, Atomic Energy Commission town site, Oak Ridge, TN; Terrace Plaza Hotel, Cincinnati, OH.
Clarence S. Stein, 1882-1975, Temple Emanu-El, NYC.
Edward Durell Stone, 1902-78, U.S. Embassy, New Delhi, India; (H. Hartford) Gallery of Modern Art, NYC.
Louis H. Sullivan, 1856-1924, Auditorium Bldg., Chicago, IL.
Richard Upjohn, 1802-78, Trinity Church, NYC.
Max O. Urbahn, 1912-95, Vehicle Assembly Bldg., Cape Canaveral, FL.
Ralph T. Walker, 1889-1973, NY Telephone Bldg. (now NYNEX); IBM Research Lab, Poughkeepsie, NY.
Roland A. Wank, 1898-1970, Cincinnati Union Terminal, OH; head architect (1933-44), Tennessee Valley Authority.
Stanford White, 1853-1906, Washington Arch in Washington Square Park, first Madison Square Garden, NYC.
Frank Lloyd Wright, 1867-1959, Imperial Hotel, Tokyo; Guggenheim Museum, NYC; Marin County Civic Center, San Francisco; Kaufmann "Fallingwater" house, Bear Run, PA.
William Wurster, 1895-1973, Ghirardelli Sq., San Francisco; Cowell College, UC, Berkeley, CA.
Minoru Yamasaki, 1912-86, World Trade Center, NYC.

Noted Artists, Photographers, and Sculptors of the Past

Artists are painters unless otherwise indicated.

Berenice Abbott, 1898-1991, (U.S.) photographer. Documentary of New York City, *Changing New York* (1939).
Ansel Easton Adams, 1902-84, (U.S.) photographer. Landscapes of the American Southwest.
Washington Allston, 1779-1843, (U.S.) landscapist. *Belshazzar's Feast.*
Albrecht Altdorfer, 1480-1538, (Ger.) landscapist.
Andrea del Sarto, 1486-1530, (It.) frescoes. *Madonna of the Harpies.*
Fra Angelico, c1400-55, (It.) Renaissance muralist. *Madonna of the Linen Drapers' Guild.*
Diane Arbus, 1923-71, (U.S.) photographer. Disturbing images.
Alexsandr Archipenko, 1887-1964, (U.S.) sculptor. *Boxing Match, Medranos.*
Eugène Atget, 1856-1927, (Fr.) photographer. Parisian life.
John James Audubon, 1785-1851, (U.S.) *Birds of America.*
Hans Baldung-Grien, 1484-1545, (Ger.) *Todentanz.*
Ernst Barlach, 1870-1938, (Ger.) Expressionist sculptor. *Man Drawing a Sword.*
Frederic-Auguste Bartholdi, 1834-1904, (Fr.) *Liberty Enlightening the World, Lion of Belfort.*
Fra Bartolommeo, 1472-1517, (It.) *Vision of St. Bernard.*
Aubrey Beardsley, 1872-98, (Br.) illustrator. *Salome, Lysistrata, Morte d'Arthur, Volpone.*
Max Beckmann, 1884-1950, (Ger.) Expressionist. *The Descent From the Cross.*
Gentile Bellini, 1426-1507, (It.) Renaissance. *Procession in St. Mark's Square.*
Giovanni Bellini, 1428-1516, (It.) *St. Francis in Ecstasy.*
Jacopo Bellini, 1400-70, (It.) *Crucifixion.*
George Wesley Bellows, 1882-1925, (U.S.) sports artist, portraitist, landscapist. *Stag at Sharkey's, Edith Clavell.*
Thomas Hart Benton, 1889-1975, (U.S.) American regionalist. *Threshing Wheat, Arts of the West.*
Gianlorenzo Bernini, 1598-1680, (It.) Baroque sculpture. *The Assumption.*
Albert Bierstadt, 1830-1902, (U.S.) landscapist. *The Rocky Mountains, Mount Corcoran.*
George Caleb Bingham, 1811-79, (U.S.) *Fur Traders Descending the Missouri.*
William Blake, 1752-1827, (Br.) engraver. *Book of Job, Songs of Innocence, Songs of Experience.*
Rosa Bonheur, 1822-99, (Fr.) *The Horse Fair.*
Pierre Bonnard, 1867-1947, (Fr.) Intimist. *The Breakfast Room, Girl in a Straw Hat.*
Gutzon Borglum, 1871-1941, (U.S.) sculptor. Mt. Rushmore Memorial.
Hieronymus Bosch, 1450-1516, (Flem.) religious allegories. *The Crowning With Thorns.*
Sandro Botticelli, 1444-1510, (It.) Renaissance. *Birth of Venus, Adoration of the Magi, Guiliano de'Medici.*
Margaret Bourke-White, 1906-71, (U.S.) photographer, photojournalist. WW2, USSR, rural South during the Depression.
Mathew Brady, c1823-96, (U.S.) photographer. Official photographer of the Civil War.
Constantin Brancusi, 1876-1957, (Romanian-Fr.) Nonobjective sculptor. *Flying Turtle, The Kiss.*
Georges Braque, 1882-1963, (Fr.) Cubist. *Violin and Palette.*
Pieter Bruegel the Elder, c1525-69, (Flem.) *The Peasant Dance, Hunters in the Snow, Magpie on the Gallows.*
Pieter Bruegel the Younger, 1564-1638, (Flem.) *Village Fair, The Crucifixion.*
Edward Burne-Jones, 1833-98, (Br.) Pre-Raphaelite artist-craftsman. *The Mirror of Venus.*
Alexander Calder, 1898-1976, (U.S.) sculptor. *Lobster Trap and Fish Tail.*
Julia Cameron, 1815-79, (Br.) photographer. Considered one of the most important portraitists of the 19th cent.
Robert Capa (Andrei Friedmann), 1913-54, (Hung.-U.S.) photographer. War photojournalist; invasion of Normandy.
Michelangelo Merisi da Caravaggio, 1573-1610, (It.) Baroque. *The Supper at Emmaus.*
Emily Carr, 1871-1945, (Can.) landscapist. *Blunden Harbour, Big Raven, Rushing Sea of Undergrowth.*
Carlo Carrà, 1881-1966, (It.) Metaphysical school. *Lot's Daughters, The Enchanted Room.*
Mary Cassatt, 1844-1926, (U.S.) Impressionist. *The Cup of Tea, Woman Bathing, The Boating Party.*
George Catlin, 1796-1872, (U.S.) American Indian life. *Gallery of Indians, Buffalo Dance.*
Benvenuto Cellini, 1500-71, (It.) Mannerist sculptor, goldsmith. *Perseus and Medusa, Salt Cellar of Francis I.*
Paul Cézanne, 1839-1906, (Fr.) *Card Players, Mont-Sainte-Victoire With Large Pine Trees.*
Marc Chagall, 1887-1985, (Russ.) Jewish life and folklore. *I and the Village, The Praying Jew.*
Jean Simeon Chardin, 1699-1779, (Fr.) still lifes. *The Kiss, The Grace.*
Frederick Church, 1826-1900, (U.S.) Hudson River school. *Niagara, Andes of Ecuador.*
Giovanni Cimabue, 1240-1302, (It.) Byzantine mosaicist. *Madonna Enthroned With St. Francis.*
Claude Lorrain (Claude Gellé), 1600-82, (Fr.) ideal-landscapist. *The Enchanted Castle.*
Thomas Cole, 1801-48, (U.S.) Hudson River school. *The Ox-Bow, In the Catskills.*
John Constable, 1776-1837, (Br.) landscapist. *Salisbury Cathedral From the Bishop's Grounds.*
John Singleton Copley, 1738-1815, (U.S.) portraitist. *Samuel Adams, Watson and the Shark.*
Lovis Corinth, 1858-1925, (Ger.) Expressionist. *Apocalypse.*
Jean-Baptiste-Camille Corot, 1796-1875, (Fr.) landscapist. *Souvenir de Mortefontaine, Pastorale.*
Correggio, 1494-1534, (It.) Renaissance muralist. *Mystic Marriages of St. Catherine.*
Gustave Courbet, 1819-77, (Fr.) Realist. *The Artist's Studio.*
Lucas Cranach the Elder, 1472-1553, (Ger.) Protestant Reformation portraitist. *Luther.*
Imogen Cunningham, 1883-1976, (U.S.) photographer, portraitist. Plant photography.
Nathaniel Currier, 1813-88, and **James M. Ives,** 1824-95, (both U.S.) lithographers. *A Midnight Race on the Mississippi, American Forest Scene—Maple Sugaring.*
John Steuart Curry, 1897-1946, (U.S.) Americana, murals. *Baptism in Kansas.*
Salvador Dalí, 1904-89, (Sp.) Surrealist. *Persistence of Memory, The Crucifixion.*
Honoré Daumier, 1808-79, (Fr.) caricaturist. *The Third-Class Carriage.*
Jacques-Louis David, 1748-1825, (Fr.) Neoclassicist. *The Oath of the Horatii.*
Arthur Davies, 1862-1928, (U.S.) Romantic landscapist. *Unicorns, Leda and the Dioscuri.*
Willem de Kooning, 1904-1997, (Dutch-U.S.) abstract expressionist. *Excavation, Woman I, Door to the River.*
Edgar Degas, 1834-1917, (Fr.) *The Ballet Class.*
Eugène Delacroix, 1798-1863, (Fr.) Romantic. *Massacre at Chios, Liberty Leading the People.*
Paul Delaroche, 1797-1856, (Fr.) historical themes. *Children of Edward IV.*
Luca Della Robbia, 1400-82, (It.) Renaissance terracotta artist. *Cantoria* (singing gallery), Florence cathedral.
Donatello, 1386-1466, (It.) Renaissance sculptor. *David, Gattamelata.*
Jean Dubuffet, 1902-85, (Fr.) painter, sculptor, printmaker. *Group of Four Trees.*
Marcel Duchamp, 1887-1968, (Fr.) Dada artist. *Nude Descending a Staircase, No. 2.*
Raoul Dufy, 1877-1953, (Fr.) Fauvist. *Chateau and Horses.*
Asher Brown Durand, 1796-1886, (U.S.) Hudson River school. *Kindred Spirits.*
Albrecht Dürer, 1471-1528, (Ger.) Renaissance painter, engraver, woodcuts. *St. Jerome in His Study, Melencolia I.*
Anthony van Dyck, 1599-1641, (Flem.) Baroque portraitist. *Portrait of Charles I Hunting.*
Thomas Eakins, 1844-1916, (U.S.) Realist. *The Gross Clinic.*
Alfred Eisenstaedt, 1898-1995, (Ger.-U.S.) photographer, photojournalist. Famous for V-J Day, Aug. 14, 1945, photograph of sailor and nurse in Times Square, NYC.
Peter Henry Emerson, 1856-1936, (Br.) photographer. Promoted photography as an independent art form.
Jacob Epstein, 1880-1959, (Br.) religious and allegorical sculptor. *Genesis, Ecce Homo.*
Jan van Eyck, c1390-1441, (Flem.) naturalistic panels. *Adoration of the Lamb.*
Roger Fenton, 1819-68, (Br.) photographer. Crimean War.
Anselm Feuerbach, 1829-80, (Ger.) Romantic Classicist. *Judgment of Paris, Iphigenia.*
John Bernard Flannagan, 1895-1942, (U.S.) animal sculptor. *Triumph of the Egg.*
Jean-Honoré Fragonard, 1732-1806, (Fr.) Rococo. *The Swing.*
Daniel Chester French, 1850-1931, (U.S.) *The Minute Man of Concord;* seated *Lincoln,* Lincoln Memorial, Wash., DC.
Caspar David Friedrich, 1774-1840, (Ger.) Romantic landscapes. *Man and Woman Gazing at the Moon.*
Thomas Gainsborough, 1727-88, (Br.) portraitist. *The Blue Boy, The Watering Place, Orpin the Parish Clerk.*
Alexander Gardner, 1821-82, (U.S.) photographer. Civil War; railroad construction; Great Plains Indians.
Paul Gauguin, 1848-1903, (Fr.) Post-impressionist. *The Tahitians, Spirit of the Dead Watching.*
Lorenzo Ghiberti, 1378-1455, (It.) Renaissance sculptor. Gates of Paradise baptistery doors, Florence.

Alberto Giacometti, 1901-66, (Swiss) attenuated sculptures of solitary figures. *Man Pointing.*
Giorgione, c1477-1510, (It.) Renaissance. *The Tempest.*
Giotto di Bondone, 1267-1337, (It.) Renaissance. *Presentation of Christ in the Temple.*
François Girardon, 1628-1715, (Fr.) Baroque sculptor of classical themes. *Apollo Tended by the Nymphs.*
Vincent van Gogh, 1853-90, (Dutch) *The Starry Night, L'Arlesienne, Bedroom at Arles, Self-Portrait.*
Arshile Gorky, 1905-48, (U.S.) Surrealist. *The Liver Is the Cock's Comb.*
Francisco de Goya y Lucientes, 1746-1828, (Sp.) *The Naked Maja, The Disasters of War* (etchings).
El Greco, 1541-1614, (Sp.) *View of Toledo, Assumption of the Virgin.*
Horatio Greenough, 1805-52, (U.S.) Neo-classical sculptor.
Matthias Grünewald, 1480-1528, (Ger.) mystical religious themes. *The Resurrection.*
Frans Hals, c1580-1666, (Dutch) portraitist. *Laughing Cavalier, Gypsy Girl.*
Austin Hansen, 1910-96, (U.S.) photographer. Harlem, NY, life.
Childe Hassam, 1859-1935, (U.S.) Impressionist. *Southwest Wind, July 14 Rue Daunon.*
Edward Hicks, 1780-1849, (U.S.) folk painter. *The Peaceable Kingdom.*
Lewis Wickes Hine, 1874-1940, (U.S.) photographer. Studies of immigrants, children in industry.
Hans Hofmann, 1880-1966, (U.S.) early abstract Expressionist. *Spring, The Gate.*
William Hogarth, 1697-1764, (Br.) caricaturist. *The Rake's Pro ress.*
Katsushika Hokusai, 1760-1849, (Jpn.) printmaker. *Crabs.*
Hans Holbein the Elder, 1460-1524, (Ger.) late Gothic. *Presentation of Christ in the Temple.*
Hans Holbein the Younger, 1497-1543, (Ger.) portraitist. *Henry VIII, The French Ambassadors.*
Winslow Homer, 1836-1910, (U.S.) naturalist painter, marine themes. *Marine Coast, High Cliff.*
Edward Hopper, 1882-1967, (U.S.) realistic urban scenes. *Nighthawks, House by the Railroad.*
Jean-Auguste-Dominique Ingres, 1780-1867, (Fr.) Classicist. *Valpincon Bather.*
George Inness, 1825-94, (U.S.) luminous landscapist. *Delaware Water Gap.*
William Henry Jackson, 1843-1942, (U.S.) photographer. American West, building of Union Pacific Railroad.
Donald Judd, 1928-94, (U.S.) sculptor, major Minimalist.
Frida Kahlo, 1907-54, (Mex.) painter; *Self-Portrait With Monkey.*
Vasily Kandinsky, 1866-1944, (Russ.) Abstractionist. *Capricious Forms, Improvisation 38 (second version).*
Paul Klee, 1879-1940, (Swiss) Abstractionist. *Twittering Machine, Pastoral, Death and Fire.*
Gustav Klimt, 1862-1918, (Austrian) cofounder of Vienna Secession Movement, *The Kiss.*
Oscar Kokoschka, 1886-1980, (Austrian) Expressionist. *View of Prague, Harbor of Marseilles.*
Kathe Kollwitz, 1867-1945, (Ger.) printmaker, social justice themes. *The Peasant War.*
Gaston Lachaise, 1882-1935, (U.S.) figurative sculptor. *Standing Woman.*
John La Farge, 1835-1910, (U.S.) muralist. *Red and White Peonies, The Ascension.*
Sir Edwin (Henry) Landseer, 1802-73, (Br.) painter, sculptor. *Shoeing, Rout of Comus.*
Dorothea Lange, 1895-1965, (U.S.), photographer. Depression photographs, migrant farm workers.
Fernand Léger, 1881-1955, (Fr.) machine art. *The Cyclists.*
Leonardo da Vinci, 1452-1519, (It.) *Mona Lisa, Last Supper, The Annunciation.*
Emanuel Leutze, 1816-68, (U.S.) historical themes. *Washington Crossing the Delaware.*
Roy Lichtenstein, 1923-97, (U.S.) pop artist.
Jacques Lipchitz, 1891-1973, (Fr.) Cubist sculptor. *Harpist.*
Filippino Lippi, 1457-1504, (It.) Renaissance.
Fra Filippo Lippi, 1406-69, (It.) Renaissance. *Coronation of the Virgin, Madonna and Child With Angels.*
Morris Louis, 1912-62, (U.S.) abstract Expressionist. *Signa, Stripes, Alpha-Phi.*
Aristide Maillol, 1861-1944, (Fr.) sculptor. *L'Harmonie.*
Édouard Manet, 1832-83, (Fr.) forerunner of Impressionism. *Luncheon on the Grass, Olympia.*
Andrea Mantegna, 1431-1506, (It.) Renaissance frescoes. *Triumph of Caesar.*
Franz Marc, 1880-1916, (Ger.) Expressionist. *Blue Horses.*
John Marin, 1870-1953, (U.S.) Expressionist seascapes. *Maine Island.*
Reginald Marsh, 1898-1954, (U.S.) satirical artist. *Tattoo and Haircut.*
Masaccio, 1401-28, (It.) Renaissance. *The Tribute Money.*
Henri Matisse, 1869-1954, (Fr.) Fauvist. *Woman With the Hat.*
Michelangelo Buonarroti, 1475-1564, (It.) *Pietà, David, Moses, The Last Judgment,* Sistine Chapel ceiling.
Jean-Francois Millet, 1814-75, (Fr.) painter of peasant subjects. *The Gleaners, The Man With a Hoe.*
Joan Miró, 1893-1983, (Sp.) Exuberant colors, playful images. Catalan landscape, *Dutch Interior.*
Amedeo Modigliani, 1884-1920, (It.) *Reclining Nude.*
Piet Mondrian, 1872-1944, (Dutch) Abstractionist. *Composition With Red, Yellow and Blue.*
Claude Monet, 1840-1926, (Fr.) Impressionist. *The Bridge at Argenteuil, Haystacks.*
Henry Moore, 1898-1986, (Br.) sculptor of large-scale, abstract works. *Reclining Figure* (several).
Gustave Moreau, 1826-98, (Fr.) Symbolist. *The Apparition, Dance of Salome.*
James Wilson Morrice, 1865-1924, (Can.) landscapist. *The Ferry, Quebec, Venice, Looking Over the Lagoon.*
William Morris, 1834-1896, (Br.) decorative artist, leader of the Arts and Crafts movement.
Grandma Moses, 1860-1961, (U.S.) folk painter. *Out for the Christmas Trees, Thanksgiving Turkey.*
Edvard Munch, 1863-1944, (Nor.) Expressionist. *The Cry.*
Bartolome Murillo, 1618-82, (Sp.) Baroque religious artist. *Vision of St. Anthony, The Two Trinities.*
Eadweard Muybridge, 1830-1904, (Br.-U.S.) photographer. Studies of motion, *Animal Locomotion.*
Nadar (Gaspar-Félix Tournachon), 1820-1910, (Fr.) photographer, caricaturist, portraitist. Invented photo-essay.
Barnett Newman, 1905-70, (U.S.) abstract Expressionist. *Stations of the Cross.*
Isamu Noguchi, 1904-88, (U.S.) abstract sculptor, designer. *Kouros, BirdC(MU),* sculptural gardens.
Georgia O'Keeffe, 1887-1986, (U.S.) Southwest motifs. *Cow's Skull: Red, White, and Blue, The Shelton With Sunspots.*
José Clemente Orozco, 1883-1949, (Mex.) frescoes. *House of Tears, Pre-Columbian Golden Age.*
Timothy H. O'Sullivan, 1840-82, (U.S.) Civil War photographer.
Charles Willson Peale, 1741-1827, (U.S.) Amer. Revolutionary portraitist. *The Staircase Group,* U.S. presidents.
Rembrandt Peale, 1778-1860, (U.S.) portraitist. Thomas Jefferson.
Pietro Perugino, 1446-1523, (It.) Renaissance. *Delivery of the Keys to St. Peter.*
Pablo Picasso, 1881-1973, (Sp.) painter, sculptor. *Guernica; Dove; Head of a Woman; Head of a Bull, Metamorphosis.*
Piero della Francesca, c1415-92, (It.) Renaissance. *Duke of Urbino, Flagellation of Christ.*
Camille Pissarro, 1830-1903, (Fr.) Impressionist. *Boulevard des Italiens, Morning, Sunlight; Bather in the Woods.*
Jackson Pollock, 1912-56, (U.S.) abstract Expressionist. *Autumn Rhythm.*
Nicolas Poussin, 1594-1665, (Fr.) Baroque pictorial classicism. *St. John on Patmos.*
Maurice B. Prendergast, c1860-1924, (U.S.) Post-impressionist water colorist. *Umbrellas in the Rain.*
Pierre-Paul Prud'hon, 1758-1823, (Fr.) Romanticist. *Crime Pursued by Vengeance and Justice.*
Pierre Cecile Puvis de Chavannes, 1824-98, (Fr.) muralist. *The Poor Fisherman.*
Raphael Sanzio, 1483-1520, (It.) Renaissance. *Disputa, School of Athens, Sistine Madonna.*
Man Ray, 1890-1976, (U.S.) Dada artist. *Observing Time, The Lovers, Marquis de Sade.*
Odilon Redon, 1840-1916, (Fr.) Symbolist painter, lithographer. *In the Dream, Vase of Flowers.*
Rembrandt van Rijn, 1606-69, (Dutch) *The Bridal Couple, The Night Watch.*
Frederic Remington, 1861-1909, (U.S.) painter, sculptor. Portrayer of the American West, *Bronco Buster.*
Pierre-Auguste Renoir, 1841-1919, (Fr.) Impressionist. *The Luncheon of the Boating Party, Dance in the Country.*
Joshua Reynolds, 1723-92, (Br.) portraitist. *Mrs. Siddons As the Tragic Muse.*
Diego Rivera, 1886-1957, (Mex.) frescoes. *The Fecund Earth.*
Henry Peach Robinson, 1830-1901 (Br.) photographer. A leader of "high art" photography.
Norman Rockwell, 1894-1978, (U.S.) painter, illustrator. *Saturday Evening Post* covers.
Auguste Rodin, 1840-1917, (Fr.) sculptor. *The Thinker.*
Mark Rothko, 1903-70, (U.S.) abstract Expressionist. *Light, Earth and Blue.*
Georges Rouault, 1871-1958, (Fr.) Expressionist. *Three Judges.*
Henri Rousseau, 1844-1910, (Fr.) primitive exotic themes. *The Snake Charmer.*
Theodore Rousseau, 1812-67, (Swiss-Fr.) landscapist. *Under the Birches, Evening.*
Peter Paul Rubens, 1577-1640, (Flem.) Baroque. *Mystic Marriage of St. Catherine.*
Jacob van Ruisdael, c1628-82, (Dutch) landscapist. *Jewish Cemetery.*
Charles M. Russell, 1866-1926, (U.S.) Western life.

Salomon van Ruysdael, c1600-70, (Dutch) landscapist. *River with Ferry-Boat.*
Albert Pinkham Ryder, 1847-1917, (U.S.) seascapes and allegories. *Toilers of the Sea.*
Augustus Saint-Gaudens, 1848-1907, (U.S.) memorial statues. *Farragut, Mrs. Henry Adams (Grief).*
Andrea Sansovino, 1460-1529, (It.) Renaissance sculptor. *Baptism of Christ.*
Jacopo Sansovino, 1486-1570, (It.) Renaissance sculptor. *St. John the Baptist.*
John Singer Sargent, 1856-1925, (U.S.) Edwardian society portraitist. The Wyndham Sisters, Madam X.
Georges Seurat, 1859-91, (Fr.) Pointillist. *Sunday Afternoon on the Island of La Grande Jatte.*
Gino Severini, 1883-1966, (It.) Futurist and Cubist. *Dynamic Hieroglyph of the Bal Tabarin.*
Ben Shahn, 1898-1969, (U.S.) social and political themes. Sacco and Vanzetti series, *Seurat's Lunch, Handball.*
Charles Sheeler, 1883-1965, (U.S.) abstractionist.
David Alfaro Siqueiros, 1896-1974, (Mex.) political muralist. *March of Humanity.*
David Smith, 1906-65, (U.S.) welded metal sculpture. *Hudson River Landscape, Zig, Cubi* series.
Edward Steichen, 1879-1973, (U.S.) photographer. Credited with transforming photography into an art form.
Alfred Stieglitz, 1864-1946, (U.S.) photographer, editor; helped create acceptance of photography as art.
Paul Strand, 1890-1976, (U.S.) photographer. People, nature, landscapes.
Gilbert Stuart, 1755-1828, (U.S.) portraitist. George Washington, Thomas Jefferson, James Madison.
Thomas Sully, 1783-1872, (U.S.) portraitist. *Col. Thomas Handasyd Perkins, The Passage of the Delaware.*
William Henry Fox Talbot, 1800-77, (Br.) photographer. *Pencil of Nature,* early photographically illustrated book.
George Tames, 1919-94, (U.S.) photographer. Chronicled presidents, political leaders.
Yves Tanguy, 1900-55, (Fr.) Surrealist. *Rose of the Four Winds, Mama, Papa Is Wounded!*
Giovanni Battista Tiepolo, 1696-1770, (It.) Rococo frescoes. *The Crucifixion.*
Jacopo Tintoretto, 1518-94, (It.) Mannerist. *The Last Supper.*
Titian, c1485-1576, (It.) Renaissance. *Venus and the Lute Player, The Bacchanal.*
Jose Rey Toledo, 1916-94, (U.S.) Native American artist. Captured the essence of tribal dances on canvas.
Henri de Toulouse-Lautrec, 1864-1901, (Fr.) *At the Moulin Rouge.*
John Trumbull, 1756-1843, (U.S.) historical themes. *The Declaration of Independence.*
J(oseph) M(allord) W(illiam) Turner, 1775-1851, (Br.) Romantic landscapist. *Snow Storm.*
Paolo Uccello, 1397-1475, (It.) Gothic-Renaissance. *The Rout of San Romano.*
Maurice Utrillo, 1883-1955, (Fr.) Impressionist. *Sacre-Coeur de Montmartre.*
John Vanderlyn, 1775-1852, (U.S.) Neo-classicist. *Ariadne Asleep on the Island of Naxos.*
Diego Velázquez, 1599-1660, (Sp.) Baroque. *Las Meninas, Portrait of Juan de Pareja.*
Jan Vermeer, 1632-75, (Dutch) interior genre subjects. *Young Woman With a Water Jug.*
Paolo Veronese, 1528-88, (It.) devotional themes, vastly peopled canvases. *The Temptation of St. Anthony.*
Andrea del Verrocchio, 1435-88, (It.) Florentine sculptor. *Colleoni.*
Maurice de Vlaminck, 1876-1958, (Fr.) Fauvist landscapist.
Andy Warhol, 1928-87, (U.S.) Pop Art. *Campbell's Soup Cans, Marilyn Diptych.*
Antoine Watteau, 1684-1721, (Fr.) Rococo painter of "scenes of gallantry." *The Embarkation for Cythera.*
George Frederic Watts, 1817-1904, (Br.) painter and sculptor of grandiose allegorical themes. *Hope.*
Benjamin West, 1738-1820, (U.S.) realistic historical themes. *Death of General Wolfe.*
Edward Weston, 1886-1958, (U.S.) photographer. Landscapes of American West.
James Abbott McNeill Whistler, 1834-1903, (U.S.) *Arrangement in Grey and Black, No. 1: The Artist's Mother.*
Archibald M. Willard, 1836-1918, (U.S.) *The Spirit of '76.*
Grant Wood, 1891-1942, (U.S.) Midwestern regionalist. *American Gothic, Daughters of Revolution.*
Ossip Zadkine, 1890-1967, (Russ.) School of Paris sculptor. *The Destroyed City, Musicians, Christ.*

Noted Business Leaders, Industrialists, and Philanthropists of the Past

Elizabeth Arden (F. N. Graham), 1884-1966, (U.S.) Canadian-born founder of cosmetics empire.
Philip D. Armour, 1832-1901, (U.S.) industrialist; streamlined meatpacking.
John Jacob Astor, 1763-1848, (U.S.) German-born fur trader, banker, real estate magnate; at death, richest in U.S.
Francis W. Ayer, 1848-1923, (U.S.) ad industry pioneer.
August Belmont, 1816-90, (U.S.) German-born financier.
James B. (Diamond Jim) Brady, 1856-1917, (U.S.) financier, philanthropist, legendary bon vivant.
Adolphus Busch, 1839-1913, (U.S.) German-born businessman; established brewery empire.
Asa Candler, 1851-1929, (U.S.) founded Coca-Cola Co.
Andrew Carnegie, 1835-1919, (U.S.) Scottish-born industrialist; philanthropist; founded Carnegie Steel Co.
Tom Carvel, 1908-89, (Gr.-U.S.) founded ice cream chain.
William Colgate, 1783-1857, (Br.-U.S.) Br.-born businessman, philanthropist; founded soap-making empire.
Jay Cooke, 1821-1905, (U.S.) financier; sold $1 billion in Union bonds during Civil War.
Peter Cooper, 1791-1883, (U.S.) industrialist, inventor, philanthropist; founded Cooper Union (1859).
Ezra Cornell, 1807-74, (U.S.) businessman, philanthropist; headed Western Union, established university.
Erastus Corning, 1794-1872, (U.S.) financier; headed N.Y. Central.
Charles Crocker, 1822-88, (U.S.) railroad builder, financier.
Samuel Cunard, 1787-1865, (Can.) pioneered trans-Atlantic steam navigation.
Marcus Daly, 1841-1900, (U.S.) Irish-born copper magnate.
W. Edwards Deming, 1900-93, (U.S.) quality-control expert who revolutionized Japanese manufacturing.
Walt Disney, 1901-66, (U.S.) pioneer in cinema animation; built entertainment empire.
Herbert H. Dow, 1866-1930, (U.S.) founder of chemical co.
James Duke, 1856-1925, (U.S.) founded American Tobacco, Duke Univ.
Eleuthere I. du Pont, 1771-1834, (Fr.-U.S.) gunpowder manufacturer; founded one of the largest business empires.
Thomas C. Durant, 1820-85, (U.S.) railroad official, financier.
William C. Durant, 1861-1947, (U.S.) industrialist; formed General Motors.
George Eastman, 1854-1932, (U.S.) inventor; manufacturer of photographic equipment.
Marshall Field, 1834-1906, (U.S.) merchant; founded Chicago's largest department store.
Harvey Firestone, 1868-1938, (U.S.) founded tire company.
Avery Fisher, 1906-94, (U.S.) industrialist, philanthropist, founded Fisher electronics.
Henry M. Flagler, 1830-1913, (U.S.) financier; helped form Standard Oil; developed Florida as resort state.
Malcolm Forbes, 1919-90, (U.S.) magazine publisher.
Henry Ford, 1863-1947, (U.S.) auto maker; developed first popular low-priced car.
Henry Ford 2d, 1917-87, (U.S.) headed auto company founded by grandfather.
Henry C. Frick, 1849-1919, (U.S.) steel and coke magnate who had a prominent role in the development of U.S. Steel.
Jakob Fugger (Jakob the Rich), 1459-1525, (Ger.) headed leading banking, trading house, in 16th-cent. Europe.
Alfred C. Fuller, 1885-1973, (U.S.) Canadian-born businessman; founded brush company.
Elbert H. Gary, 1846-1927, (U.S.) one of the organizers of U.S. Steel; chairman of the board of directors, 1903-27.
Jean Paul Getty, 1892-1976, (U.S.) founded oil empire.
Amadeo P. Giannini, 1870-1949, (U.S.) founded Bank of America.
Stephen Girard, 1750-1831, (U.S.) French-born financier, philanthropist; richest man in U.S. at his death.
Jay Gould, 1836-92, (U.S.) railroad magnate, financier.
Hetty Green, 1834-1916, (U.S.) financier, the "witch of Wall St."; richest woman in U.S. in her day.
William Gregg, 1800-67, (U.S.) launched textile industry in S.
Meyer Guggenheim, 1828-1905, (U.S.) Swiss-born merchant, philanthropist; built merchandising, mining empires.
Armand Hammer, 1898-1990, (U.S.) headed Occidental Petroleum; promoted U.S.-Soviet ties.
Edward H. Harriman, 1848-1909, (U.S.) railroad financier, administrator; headed Union Pacific.
Henry J. Heinz, 1844-1919, (U.S.) founded food empire.
James J. Hill, 1838-1916, (U.S.) Canadian-born railroad magnate, financier; founded Great Northern Railway.
Conrad N. Hilton, 1888-1979, (U.S.) hotel chain founder.
Howard Hughes, 1905-76, (U.S.) industrialist, aviator, movie maker.
H. L. Hunt, 1889-1974, (U.S.) oil magnate.
Collis P. Huntington, 1821-1900, (U.S.) railroad magnate.
Henry E. Huntington, 1850-1927, (U.S.) railroad builder, philanthropist.
Walter L. Jacobs, 1898-1985, (U.S.) founder of the first rental car agency, which later became Hertz.
Howard Johnson, 1896-1972, (U.S.) founded restaurants.
Henry J. Kaiser, 1882-1967, (U.S.) industrialist; built empire in steel, aluminum.

Minor C. Keith, 1848-1929, (U.S.) railroad magnate; founded United Fruit Co.
Will K. Kellogg, 1860-1951, (U.S.) businessman, philanthropist; founded breakfast food co.
Richard King, 1825-85, (U.S.) cattleman; founded half-million-acre King Ranch in Texas.
William S. Knudsen, 1879-1948, (U.S.) Danish-born auto industry executive.
Samuel H. Kress, 1863-1955, (U.S.) businessman, art collector, philanthropist; founded "dime store" chain.
Ray A. Kroc, 1902-84, (U.S.) founded fast-food chain, McDonald's Corporation.
Alfred Krupp, 1812-87, (Ger.) armaments magnate.
William Levitt, 1907-94, (U.S.) industrialist, "suburb maker".
Thomas Lipton, 1850-1931, (Scot.) merchant, tea empire.
James McGill, 1744-1813, (Scot.-Can.) founded university.
Andrew W. Mellon, 1855-1937, (U.S.) financier, industrialist; benefactor of National Gallery of Art.
Charles E. Merrill, 1885-1956, (U.S.) financier; developed firm of Merrill Lynch.
John Pierpont Morgan, 1837-1913, (U.S.) most powerful figure in finance and industry at the turn of the cent.
Malcolm Muir, 1885-1979, (U.S.) created *Business Week* magazine; headed *Newsweek,* 1937-61.
Samuel Newhouse, 1895-1979, (U.S.) publishing and broadcasting magnate; built communications empire.
Aristotle Onassis, 1906-75, (Gr.) shipping magnate.
William S. Paley, 1901-90, (U.S.) built CBS communic. empire.
George Peabody, 1795-1869, (U.S.) merchant, financier, philanthropist.
James C. Penney, 1875-1971, (U.S.) businessman; developed department store chain.
William C. Procter, 1862-1934, (U.S.) headed soap company.
John D. Rockefeller, 1839-1937, (U.S.) industrialist; established Standard Oil.
John D. Rockefeller Jr., 1874-1960, (U.S.) philanthropist; established foundation; provided land for United Nations.
Meyer A. Rothschild, 1743-1812, (Ger.) founded international banking house.
Thomas Fortune Ryan, 1851-1928, (U.S.) financier; a founder of American Tobacco.
David Sarnoff, 1891-1971, (U.S.) broadcasting pioneer; established first radio network, NBC.
Richard Sears, 1863-1914, (U.S.) founded mail-order co.
Werner von Siemens, 1816-92, (Ger.) industrialist; inventor.
Alfred P. Sloan, 1875-1966, (U.S.) industrialist, philanthropist; headed General Motors.
A. Leland Stanford, 1824-93, (U.S.) railroad official, philanthropist; founded university.
Nathan Straus, 1848-1931, (U.S.) German-born merchant, philanthropist; headed Macy's.
Levi Strauss, c1829-1902, (U.S.) pants manufacturer.
Clement Studebaker, 1831-1901, (U.S.) wagon, carriage (maker).
Gustavus Swift, 1839-1903, (U.S.) pioneer meatpacker.
Gerard Swope, 1872-1957, (U.S.) industrialist, economist; headed General Electric.
James Walter Thompson, 1847-1928, (U.S.) ad executive.
Alice Tully, 1902-93, (U.S.) philanthropist, arts patron.
Theodore N. Vail, 1845-1920, (U.S.) organized Bell Telephone system; headed AT&T.
Cornelius Vanderbilt, 1794-1877, (U.S.) financier; established steamship, railroad empires.
Henry Villard, 1835-1900, (U.S.) German-born railroad executive, financier.
George Westinghouse, 1846-1914, (U.S) inventor, manufacturer; organized Westinghouse Electric Co., 1886.
Charles R. Walgreen, 1873-1939, (U.S.) founded drugstore chain.
DeWitt Wallace, 1889-1981, (U.S.) and **Lila Wallace,** 1889-1984, (U.S.) cofounders of *Reader's Digest* magazine.
Sam Walton, 1918-92, (U.S.) founder of Wal-Mart stores.
John Wanamaker, 1838-1922, (U.S.) pioneered department-store merchandising.
Aaron Montgomery Ward, 1843-1913, (U.S.) established first mail-order firm.
Thomas J. Watson, 1874-1956, (U.S.) IBM head, 1914-56.
John Hay Whitney, 1905-82, (U.S.) publisher, sportsman, philanthropist.
Charles E. Wilson, 1890-1961, (U.S.) auto industry exec., public official.
Frank W. Woolworth, 1852-1919, (U.S.) created 5 & 10 chain.
William Wrigley Jr., 1861-1932, (U.S.) founded chewing gum co.

Noted American Cartoonists

Reviewed by Lucy Shelton Caswell, Professor and Curator, Cartoon Research Library, Ohio State University

Scott Adams, b 1957, Dilbert.
Charles Addams, 1912-88, macabre cartoons.
Brad Anderson, b 1924, Marmaduke.
Sergio Aragones, b 1937, *MAD Magazine.*
Peter Arno, 1904-68, *The New Yorker.*
Tex Avery, 1908-80, animator, Bugs Bunny, Porky Pig.
George Baker, 1915-75, The Sad Sack.
Carl Barks, b 1901, Donald Duck comic books.
C. C. Beck, 1910-89, Captain Marvel.
Jim Berry, b 1932, Berry's World.
Herb Block (Herblock), b 1909, political cartoonist.
George Booth, b 1926, *The New Yorker.*
Berkeley Breathed, b 1957, Bloom County.
Dik Browne, 1917-89, Hi & Lois, Hagar the Horrible.
Marjorie Buell, 1904-93, Little Lulu.
Ernie Bushmiller, 1905-82, Nancy.
Milton Caniff, 1907-88, Terry & the Pirates, Steve Canyon.
Al Capp, 1909-79, Li'l Abner.
Roz Chast, b 1954, *The New Yorker.*
Paul Conrad, 1924, political cartoonist.
Roy Crane, 1901-77, Captain Easy, Buz Sawyer.
Robert Crumb, b 1943, underground cartoonist.
Shamus Culhane, 1908-96, animator.
Jay N. Darling (Ding), 1876-1962, political cartoonist.
Jack Davis, b 1926, *MAD Magazine.*
Jim Davis, b 1945, Garfield.
Billy DeBeck, 1890-1942, Barney Google.
Rudolph Dirks, 1877-1968, The Katzenjammer Kids.
Walt Disney, 1901-66, produced animated cartoons, created Mickey Mouse, Donald Duck.
Steve Ditko, b 1927, Spider-Man.
Mort Drucker, b 1929, *MAD Magazine.*
Will Eisner, b 1917, The Spirit.
Jules Feiffer, b 1929, political cartoonist.
Bud Fisher, 1884-1954, Mutt & Jeff.
Ham Fisher, 1900-55, Joe Palooka.
Max Fleischer, 1883-1972, Betty Boop.
Hal Foster, 1892-1982, Tarzan, Prince Valiant.
Fontaine Fox, 1884-1964, Toonerville Folks.
Isadore "Friz" Freleng, 1905-95, animator, Yosemite Sam, Porky Pig, Sylvester and Tweety Bird.
Rube Goldberg, 1883-1970, Boob McNutt.
Chester Gould, 1900-85, Dick Tracy.
Harold Gray, 1894-1968, Little Orphan Annie.
Matt Groening, b 1954, Life in Hell, The Simpsons.
Cathy Guisewite, b 1950, Cathy.
Bill Hanna, b 1910, & **Joe Barbera,** b 1911, animators, Tom & Jerry, Yogi Bear, Flintstones.
Johnny Hart, b 1931, BC, Wizard of Id.
Oliver Harrington, 1912-95, Bootsie.
Alfred Harvey, 1913-94, created Casper the Friendly Ghost.
Jimmy Hatlo, 1898-1963, Little Iodine.
John Held Jr., 1889-1958, Jazz Age.
George Herriman, 1881-1944, Krazy Kat.
Harry Hershfield, 1885-1974, Abie the Agent.
Al Hirschfeld, b 1903, *N.Y. Times* theater caricaturist.
Burne Hogarth, 1911-96, Tarzan.
Helen Hokinson, 1900-49, *The New Yorker.*
Nicole Hollander, b 1939, Sylvia.
Lynn Johnston, b 1947, For Better or For Worse.
Chuck Jones, b 1912, animator, Bugs Bunny, Porky Pig.
Mike Judge, b. 1962, Beavis and Butt-head, King of the Hill.
Bob Kane, b 1916, Batman.
Bil Keane, b 1922, The Family Circus.
Walt Kelly, 1913-73, Pogo.
Hank Ketcham, b 1920, Dennis the Menace.
Ted Key, b 1912, Hazel.
Frank King, 1883-1969, Gasoline Alley.
Jack Kirby, 1917-94, Fantastic Four, The Incredible Hulk.
Rollin Kirby, 1875-1952, political cartoonist.
B(ernard) Kliban, 1935-91, cat books.
Edward Koren, b 1935, *The New Yorker.*
Harvey Kurtzman, 1921-93, *MAD Magazine.*
Walter Lantz, 1900-94, Woody Woodpecker.
Gary Larson, b 1950, The Far Side.
Mell Lazarus, b 1929, Momma, Miss Peach.
Stan Lee, b 1922, Marvel Comics.
David Levine, b 1926, *N.Y. Review of Books* caricatures.
Doug Marlette, b 1949, political cartoonist, Kudzu.
Don Martin, b 1931, *MAD Magazine.*
Bill Mauldin, b 1921, political cartoonist.
Jeff MacNelly, b 1947, political cartoonist, Shoe.
Winsor McCay, 1872-1934, Little Nemo.
John T. McCutcheon, 1870-1949, political cartoonist.
George McManus, 1884-1954, Bringing Up Father.
Dale Messick, b 1906, Brenda Starr.
Norman Mingo, 1896-1980, Alfred E. Neuman.
Bob Montana, 1920-75, Archie.
Dick Moores, 1909-86, Gasoline Alley.
Willard Mullin, 1902-78, sports cartoonist; Dodgers "Bum," Mets "Kid."
Russell Myers, b 1938, Broom Hilda.

Thomas Nast, 1840-1902, political cartoonist; Republican elephant.
Pat Oliphant, b 1935, political cartoonist.
Frederick Burr Opper, 1857-1937, Happy Hooligan.
Richard Outcault, 1863-1928, Yellow Kid, Buster Brown.
Mike Peters, b 1943, cartoonist, Mother Goose & Grimm.
George Price, 1901-95, *The New Yorker.*
Antonio Prohias, 1921(?)-98, Spy vs. Spy.
Alex Raymond, 1909-56, Flash Gordon, Jungle Jim.
Forrest (Bud) Sagendorf, 1915-94, Popeye.
Art Sansom, 1920-91, The Born Loser.
Charles Schulz, b 1922, Peanuts.
Elzie C. Segar, 1894-1938, Popeye.
Joe Shuster, 1914-92, & **Jerry Siegel**, 1914-96, Superman.
Sidney Smith, 1887-1935, The Gumps.
Otto Soglow, 1900-75, Little King, Canyon Kiddies.
Art Spiegelman, b 1948, Raw, Maus.
William Steig, b 1907, *The New Yorker.*
Paul Szep, b 1941, political cartoonist.
James Swinnerton, 1875-1974, Little Jimmy.
Paul Terry, 1887-1971, animator of Mighty Mouse.
Bob Thaves, b 1924, Frank and Ernest.
James Thurber, 1894-61, *The New Yorker.*
Garry Trudeau, b 1948, Doonesbury.
Mort Walker, b 1923, Beetle Bailey.
Bill Watterson, b 1958, Calvin and Hobbes.
Russ Westover, 1887-1966, Tillie the Toiler.
Signe Wilkinson, b 1950, political cartoonist.
Frank Willard, 1893-1958, Moon Mullins.
J. R. Williams, 1888-1957, The Willets Family, Out Our Way.
Gahan Wilson, b 1930, *The New Yorker.*
Tom Wilson, b 1931, Ziggy.
Art Young, 1866-1943, political cartoonist.
Chic Young, 1901-73, Blondie.

Noted Economists, Educators, Historians, and Social Scientists of the Past

For Psychologists see Scientists of the Past.

Brooks Adams, 1848-1927, (U.S.) historian, political theoretician; *The Law of Civilization and Decay.*
Henry Adams, 1838-1918, (U.S.) historian; *History of the United States of America, The Education of Henry Adams.*
Francis Bacon, 1561-1626, (Eng.) philosopher, essayist, and statesman; championed observation and induction.
George Bancroft, 1800-91, (U.S.) historian; wrote 10-volume *History of the United States.*
Jack Barbash, 1911-94, (U.S.) labor economist who helped create the AFL-CIO.
Henry Barnard, 1811-1900, (U.S.) public school reformer.
Charles A. Beard, 1874-1948, (U.S.) historian; *The Economic Basis of Politics.*
Bede (the Venerable), c673-735, (Br.) scholar, *historian; Ecclesiastical History of the English People.*
Ruth Benedict, 1887-1948, (U.S.) anthropologist; studied Indian tribes of the Southwest.
Sir Isaiah Berlin, 1909-97, (Br.) philosopher, historian; *The Age of Enlightenment.*
Louis Blanc, 1811-82, (Fr.) Socialist leader and historian.
Sarah G. Blanding, 1899-1985, (U.S.) head of Vassar College, 1946-64.
Leonard Bloomfield, 1887-1949, (U.S.) linguist; *Language.*
Franz Boas, 1858-1942, (U.S.) German-born anthropologist; studied American Indians.
Van Wyck Brooks, 1886-1963, (U.S.) historian; critic of New England culture, especially literature.
Edmund Burke, 1729-97, (Ir.) British parliamentarian and political philosopher; Reflections on the Revolution in France.
Nicholas Murray Butler, 1862-1947, (U.S.) educator; headed Columbia Univ., 1902-45; Nobel Peace Prize, 1931.
Joseph Campbell, 1904-87, (U.S.) author, editor, teacher; wrote books on mythology, folklore.
Thomas Carlyle, 1795-1881, (Sc.) historian, critic; *Sartor Resartus, Past and Present, The French Revolution.*
Edward Channing, 1856-1931, (U.S.) historian; wrote 6-volume *History of the United States.*
Henry Steele Commager, 1902-98, (U.S.) hisorian, educator; wrote *The Growth of the American Republic.*
John R. Commons, 1862-1945, (U.S.) economist, labor historian; *Legal Foundations of Capitalism.*
Benedetto Croce, 1866-1952, (It.) philosopher, statesman, and historian; *Philosophy of the Spirit.*
Bernard A. De Voto, 1897-1955, (U.S.) historian; wrote trilogy on American West; edited Mark Twain manuscripts.
Melvil Dewey, 1851-1931, (U.S.) devised decimal system of library-book classification.
Emile Durkheim, 1858-1917, (Fr.) a founder of modern sociology; *The Rules of Sociological Method.*
Friedrich Engels, 1820-95, (Ger.) political writer; with Marx wrote the *Communist Manifesto.*
Irving Fisher, 1867-1947, (U.S.) economist; contributed to the development of modern monetary theory.
John Fiske, 1842-1901, (U.S.) historian and lecturer; popularized Darwinian theory of evolution.
Charles Fourier, 1772-1837, (Fr.) utopian socialist.
Giovanni Gentile, 1875-1944, (It.) philosopher, educator; reformed Italian educational system.
Sir James George Frazer, 1854-1941, (Br.) anthropologist; studied myth in religion; *The Golden Bough.*
Henry George, 1839-97, (U.S.) economist, reformer; led single-tax movement.
Edward Gibbon, 1737-94, (Br.) historian; *The History of the Decline and Fall of the Roman Empire.*
Francesco Guicciardini, 1483-1540, (It.) historian; *Storia d'Italia,* principal historical work of the 16th cent.
Thomas Hobbes, 1588-1679, (Eng.) philosopher, political theorist; *Leviathan.*
Richard Hofstadter, 1916-70, (U.S.) historian; *The Age of Reform.*
John Holt, 1924-85, (U.S.) educator and author.
John Maynard Keynes, 1883-1946, (Br.) economist; principal advocate of deficit spending.
Russell Kirk, 1918-94, (U.S.), social philosopher; *The Conservative Mind.*
Alfred L. Kroeber, 1876-1960, (U.S.) cultural anthropologist; studied Indians of North and South America.
Christopher Lasch, 1932-94, (U.S.) social critic, historian; *The Culture of Narcissism.*
James L. Laughlin, 1850-1933, (U.S.) economist; helped establish Federal Reserve System.
Lucien Lévy-Bruhl, 1857-1939, (Fr.) philosopher; studied the psychology of primitive societies; *Primitive Mentality.*
John Locke, 1632-1704, (Eng.) philosopher and political theorist; *Two Treatises of Government.*
Thomas B. Macaulay, 1800-59, (Br.) historian, statesman.
Niccolò Machiavelli, 1469-1527, (It.) writer, statesman. *The Prince.*
Bronislaw Malinowski, 1884-1942, (Pol.) considered the father of social anthropology.
Thomas R. Malthus, 1766-1834, (Br.) economist; famed for *Essay on the Principle of Population.*
Horace Mann, 1796-1859, (U.S.) pioneered modern public school system.
Karl Mannheim, 1893-1947, (Hung.) sociologist, historian; *Ideology and Utopia.*
Karl Marx, 1818-83, (Ger.) political philosopher, proponent of Communism; *Communist Manifesto, Das Kapital.*
Giuseppe Mazzini, 1805-72, (It.) political philosopher.
William H. McGuffey, 1800-73, (U.S.) whose *Reader* was a mainstay of 19th-cent. U.S. public education.
George H. Mead, 1863-1931, (U.S.) philosopher, social psychologist.
Margaret Mead, 1901-78, (U.S.) cultural anthropologist; popularized field, *Coming of Age in Samoa.*
Alexander Meiklejohn, 1872-1964, (U.S.) Br.-born educator; championed academic freedom and experimental curricula.
James Mill, 1773-1836, (Sc.) philosopher, historian, economist; a proponent of utilitarianism.
Perry G. Miller, 1905-63, (U.S.) historian; interpreted 17th-cent. New England.
Theodor Mommsen, 1817-1903, (Ger.) historian; *The History of Rome.*
Charles-Louis Montesquieu, 1689-1755, (Fr.) social philosopher; *The Spirit of Laws.*
Maria Montessori, 1870-1952, (It.) educator, physician; originated Montessori method of student self-motivation.
Samuel Eliot Morison, 1887-1976, (U.S.) historian; chronicled voyages of early explorers.
Lewis Mumford, 1895-1990, (U.S.) sociologist, critic; *The Culture of Cities.*
Gunnar Myrdal, 1898-1987, (Swed.) economist, social scientist; *Asian Drama: An Inquiry Into the Poverty of Nations.*
Joseph Needham, 1900-95, (Br.) scientific historian; *Science and Civilization in China.*
Allan Nevins, 1890-1971, (U.S.) historian, biographer; *The Ordeal of the Union.*
José Ortega y Gasset, 1883-1955, (Sp.) philosopher; advocated control by elite, *The Revolt of the Masses.*
Robert Owen, 1771-1858, (Br.) political philosopher, reformer; pioneer in cooperative movement.
Thomas (Tom) Paine, 1737-1809, (U.S.) political theorist, writer. *Common Sense.*
Vilfredo Pareto, 1848-1923, (It.) economist, sociologist.
Francis Parkman, 1823-93, (U.S.) historian; *France and England in North America.*
Elizabeth P. Peabody, 1804-94, (U.S.) education pioneer; founded 1st kindergarten in U.S., 1860.
William Prescott, 1796-1859, (U.S.) early American historian; *The Conquest of Peru.*
Pierre Joseph Proudhon, 1809-65, (Fr.) social theorist; the father of anarchism, *The Philosophy of Property.*

François Quesnay, 1694-1774, (Fr.) economic theorist.
David Ricardo, 1772-1823, (Br.) economic theorist; advocated free international trade.
Jean-Jacques Rousseau, 1712-78, (Fr.) social philosopher; the father of romantic sensibility; *Confessions.*
Edward Sapir, 1884-1939, (Ger.-U.S.) anthropologist; studied ethnology and linguistics of U.S. Indian groups.
Ferdinand de Saussure, 1857-1913, (Swiss) a founder of modern linguistics.
Hjalmar Schacht, 1877-1970, (Ger.) economist.
Joseph Schumpeter, 1883-1950, (Czech.-U.S.) economist, sociologist.
Elizabeth Seton, 1774-1821, (U.S.) nun; est. parochial school education in U.S.; first native-born American saint.
George Simmel, 1858-1918, (Ger.) sociologist, philosopher; helped establish German sociology.
Adam Smith, 1723-90, (Br.) economist; advocated laissez-faire economy and free trade, *The Wealth of Nations.*
Jared Sparks, 1789-1866, (U.S.) historian, educator, editor; *The Library of American Biography.*
Oswald Spengler, 1880-1936, (Ger.) philosopher and historian; *The Decline of the West.*
William G. Sumner, 1840-1910, (U.S.) social scientist, economist; laissez-faire economy, Social Darwinism.
Hippolyte Taine, 1828-93, (Fr.) historian; basis of naturalistic school; *The Origins of Contemporary France.*
A(lan) J(ohn) P(ercivale) Taylor, 1906-89, (Br.) historian; *The Origins of the Second World War.*
Nikolaas Tinbergen, 1907-88, (Dutch-Br.) ethologist; pioneer in study of animal behavior.
Alexis de Tocqueville, 1805-59, (Fr.) political scientist, historian; *Democracy in America.*
Francis E. Townsend, 1867-1960, (U.S.) led old-age pension movement, 1933.
Arnold Toynbee, 1889-1975, (Br.) historian; *A Study of History,* sweeping analysis of hist. of civilizations.
George Trevelyan, 1838-1928, (Br.) historian, statesman; favored "literary" over "scientific" history; *History of England.*
Barbara Tuchman, 1912-89, (U.S.) author of popular history books, *The Guns of August, The March of Folly.*
Frederick J. Turner, 1861-1932, (U.S.) historian, educator; *The Frontier in American History.*
Thorstein B. Veblen, 1857-1929, (U.S.) economist, social philosopher; *The Theory of the Leisure Class.*
Giovanni Vico, 1668-1744, (It.) historian, philosopher; regarded by many as first modern historian; *New Science.*
Izaak Walton, 1593-1683, (Eng.) wrote biographies; political-philosophical study of fishing, *The Compleat Angler.*
Sidney J., 1859-1947, and **Beatrice,** 1858-1943, **Webb,** (Br.) leading figures in Fabian Society and Labor Party.
Max Weber, 1864-1920, (Ger.) sociologist; *The Protestant Ethic and the Spirit of Capitalism.*
Emma Hart Willard, 1787-1870, (U.S.) pioneered higher education for women

Noted American Journalists of the Past

Reviewed by Dean Mills, Dean, Missouri School of Journalism

See also Business Leaders; Cartoonists; Writers of the Past.

Franklin P. Adams (F.P.A.), 1881-1960, humorist; wrote column "The Conning Tower."
Joseph W. Alsop, 1910-89, and **Stewart Alsop,** 1914-74, Washington-based political analysts, columnists.
Brooks Atkinson, 1894-1984, theater critic.
James Gordon Bennett, 1795-1872, editor and publisher; founded *New York Herald.*
James Gordon Bennett, 1841-1918, succeeded father, financed expeditions, founded afternoon paper.
Elias Boudinot, d 1839, founding editor of first Native American newspaper in U.S., *Cherokee Phoenix* (1828-34).
Margaret Bourke-White, 1904-71, photojournalist.
Arthur Brisbane, 1864-1936, editor; helped introduce "yellow jounalism" with sensational, simply written articles.
Heywood Broun, 1888-1939, author, columnist; founded American Newspaper Guild.
Herb Caen, 1916-97, longtime columnist for *San Francisco Chronicle* and *Examiner.*
John Campbell, 1653-1728, published *Boston News-Letter,* first continuing newspaper in the American colonies.
Jimmy Cannon, 1909-73, syndicated sports columnist.
John Chancellor, 1927-96, TV journalist; anchored *NBC Nightly News.*
Harry Chandler, 1864-1944, *Los Angeles Times* publisher, 1917-41; made it a dominant force.
Marquis Childs, 1903-90, reporter and columnist for *St. Louis Post-Dispatch* and United Feature syndicate.
Elizabeth Cochrane (Nellie Bly), pioneer woman journalist, investig. reporter, noted for series on trip around the world.
Charles Collingwood, 1917-85, CBS news correspondent, foreign affairs reporter, documentary host.
Howard Cosell, 1920-95, TV and radio sportscaster.
Gardner Cowles, 1861-1946, publisher; founder of Cowles newspaper chain.
Cyrus Curtis, 1850-1933, publisher of *Saturday Evening Post, Ladies Home Journal, Country Gentleman.*
Charles Anderson Dana, 1819-97, editor, publisher; made *New York Sun* famous for its news reporting.
Elmer (Holmes) Davis, 1890-1958, *New York Times* editorial writer; radio commentator.
Richard Harding Davis, 1864-1916, war correspondent, travel writer, fiction writer.
Benjamin Day, 1810-89, published *New York Sun* beginning in 1833, introducing penny press to the U.S.
Frederick Douglass, 1817-95, ex-slave, social reformer, newspaper editor.
Finley Peter Dunne, 1867-1936, humorist, social critic, wrote "Mr. Dooley" columns.
Mary Baker Eddy, 1821-1910, founded Christian Science movement and *Christian Science Monitor.*
Marshall Field III, 1893-1956, retail magnate, *Chicago Sun* founder.
Doris Fleeson, 1901-70, war correspondent, columnist.
James Franklin, 1697-1735, printer, pioneer journalist, publisher of *New England Courant* and *Rhode Island Gazette.*
Fred W. Friendly, 1915-98, radio, TV reporter, announcer, producer, executive, collaborator with Edward R. Murrow.
Margaret Fuller, 1810-50, social reformer, transcendentalist, critic and foreign correspondent for *New York Tribune.*
Frank E. Gannett, 1876-1957, founded newspaper chain.
William Lloyd Garrison, 1805-79, abolitionist; publisher of *The Liberator.*
Elizabeth Meriwether Gilmer (Dorothy Dix), 1861-1951, reporter, pioneer of the advice column genre.
Edwin Lawrence Godkin, 1831-1902, founder of *The Nation,* editor of *New York Evening Post.*
Sheilah Graham, 1904-89, Hollywood gossip columnist.
Horace Greeley, 1811-72, editor and politician; founded *New York Tribune.*
Gilbert Hovey Grosvenor, 1875-1966, longtime editor of *National Geographic* magazine.
John Gunther, 1901-70, *Chicago Daily News* foreign correspondent, author.
Sarah Josepha Buell Hale, 1788-1879, writer, first female magazine editor; edited *Ladies' Magazine* (later *Godey's Lady's Book).*
Benjamin Harris, 1673-1716, publisher (1690) of *Publick Occurrences,* first newspaper in the American colonies, suppressed after one issue.
William Randolph Hearst, 1863-1951, founder of Hearst newspaper chain and one of the pioneer yellow journalists.
Gabriel Heatter, 1890-1972, radio commentator.
John Hersey, 1914-98, foreign correspondent for *Time, Life,* and *The New Yorker*; author.
Marguerite Higgins, 1920-66, reporter, war correspondent.
Hedda Hopper, 1885-1966, Hollywood gossip columnist.
Roy Howard, 1883-1964, editor, executive, Scripps-Howard papers and United Press (later United Press International).
Chet (Chester Robert) Huntley, 1911-74, co-anchor of NBC's *Huntley-Brinkley Report.*
Ralph Ingersoll, 1900-85, editor, *Fortune, Time, Life* exec.
H. V. (Hans von) Kaltenborn, 1878-1965, radio commentator, reporter.
Murray Kempton, 1917-97, reporter, columnist for magazines and newspapers, including *New York Post.*
John S. Knight, 1894-1981, editor, publisher; founded Knight newspaper group, which merged into Knight-Ridder.
Joseph Kraft, 1942-86, foreign policy columnist.
Arthur Krock, 1886-1974, *New York Times* political writer, Washington bureau chief.
Charles Kuralt, 1934-97, TV anchor and host of CBS "On the Road" feature stories about life in the U.S.
David Lawrence, 1888-1973, reporter, columnist, publisher; founded *U.S. News & World Report.*
Frank Leslie, 1821-80, engraver and publisher of newspapers and magazines, notably *Leslie's Illustrated Newspaper.*
A(bbott) J(oseph) Liebling, 1904-63, foreign correspondent, critic, principally with *The New Yorker.*
Walter Lippmann, 1889-1974, political analyst, social critic, columnist, author.
Peter Lisagor, 1915-76, Washington bureau chief, *Chicago Daily News;* broadcast commentator.
David Ross Locke, 1833-88, humorist, satirist under pseudonym P.V. Nasby; owned *Toledo (Ohio) Blade.*
Elijah Parish Lovejoy, 1802-37, abolitionist editor in St. Louis and in Alton, IL; killed by proslavery mob.

Clare Booth Luce, 1903-87, war correspondent for *Life;* diplomat, playwright.
Henry R. Luce, 1898-1967, founded *Time, Fortune, Life, Sports Illustrated.*
C(harles) K(enny) McClatchy, 1858-1936 founder of McClatchy newspaper chain.
Samuel McClure, 1857-1949, founder (1893) of *McClure's Magazine,* famous for its investigative reporting.
Anne O'Hare McCormick, 1889-1954, foreign correspondent, first woman member of *New York Times* editorial board.
Robert R. McCormick, 1880-1955, editor, publisher, executive of *Chicago Tribune* and *New York Daily News.*
Dwight Macdonald, 1906-1982, reporter, social critic for *The New Yorker, The Nation, Esquire.*
Ralph McGill, 1893-1969, crusading editor and publisher of *Atlanta Constitution.*
O(scar) O(dd) McIntyre, 1884-1938, feature writer, syndicated columnist concentrating on everyday life in New York City.
Don Marquis, 1878-1937, humor columnist for *New York Sun* and *New York Tribune;* wrote "Archy and Mehitobel" stories.
Robert Maynard, 1937-97, first African-American editor and then owner of major U.S. paper, the *Oakland Tribune.*
Joseph Medill, 1823-99, longtime editor of *Chicago Tribune.*
H(enry) L(ouis) Mencken, 1880-1956, reporter, editor, columnist with *Baltimore Sun* papers; anti-establishment viewpoint.
Edwin Meredith, 1876-1928, founder of magazine company.
Frank A. Munsey, 1854-1925, owner, editor, and publisher of newspapers and magazines, including *Munsey's Magazine.*
Edward R. Murrow, 1908-65, broadcast reporter, executive; reported from Britain in WW2; hosted *See It Now, Person to Person.*
William Rockhill Nelson, 1841-1915, cofounder, editor, and publisher, *Kansas City Star.*
Adolph S. Ochs, 1858-1935, publisher; built *New York Times* into a leading newspaper.
Louella Parsons, 1881-1972, Hollywood gossip columnist.
Alicia Patterson, 1906-63, reporter, editor, and cofounder of *Newsday.*
Drew (Andrew Russell) Pearson, 1879-1969, investigative reporter and columnist.
(James) Westbrook Pegler, 1894-1969, reporter, columnist.
Shirley Povich, 1905-98, sports columnist.
Joseph Pulitzer, 1847-1911, *New York World* publisher; founded Columbia Journalism School, established Pulitzer Prizes.
Joseph Pulitzer II, 1885-1955, longtime *St. Louis Post-Dispatch* editor, publisher; built it into major paper.
Ernie (Ernest Taylor) Pyle, 1900-45, reporter, war correspondent; killed in WW2.
Henry Raymond, 1820-69, cofounder, editor, *New York Times*; made it model of objective journalism.
Harry Reasoner, 1923-91, TV reporter, anchor.
John Reed, 1887-1920, reporter, foreign correspondent famous for coverage of Bolshevik Revolution.
Whitelaw Reid, 1837-1912, longtime editor, *New York Tribune.*
James Reston, 1909-95 *New York Times* political reporter, columnist.
Frank Reynolds, 1923-83, TV reporter, anchor.
(Henry) Grantland Rice, 1880-1954, sportswriter.
Jacob Riis, 1849-1914, reporter, photographer; exposed slum conditions in *How the Other Half Lives.*
Max Robinson, 1939-88, TV journalist, first African-American to anchor network news, 1978.
Harold Ross, 1892-1951, founder, editor, The *New Yorker.*
Mike Royko, 1932-97, columnist for *Chicago Sun-Times* and *Chicago Tribune.*
(Alfred) Damon Runyon, 1884-1946, sportswriter, columnist; stories collected in *Guys and Dolls.*
John B. Russwurm, 1799-1851, cofounded (1827) nation's first black newspaper, *Freedom's Journal,* in NYC.
Adela Rogers St. Johns, 1894-1988, reporter, sportswriter for Hearst newspapers.
Harrison Salisbury, 1908-93, reporter, foreign correspondent; a Soviet specialist.
E(dward) W(yllis) Scripps, 1854-1926, founded first large U.S. newspaper chain, pioneered syndication.
Eric Sevareid, 1912-92, war correspondent, radio newscaster, TV commentator.
William L. Shirer, 1904-93, broadcaster, foreign correspondent; wrote *The Rise and Fall of the Third Reich.*
Red (Walter) Smith, 1905-82, sportswriter.
Edgar P. Snow, 1905-71, correspondent, expert on Chinese Communist movement.
Lawrence Spivak, 1900-94, co-creator, moderator, producer of *Meet the Press.*
(Joseph) Lincoln Steffens, 1866-1936, muckraking journalist.
I(sidor) F(einstein) Stone, 1907-89, one-man editor of *I.F. Stone's Weekly.*
Arthur Hays Sulzberger, 1891-1968, longtime publisher of *New York Times.*
C(yrus) L(eo) Sulzberger, 1912-93, *New York Times* foreign correspondent and columnist.
David Susskind, 1920-87, TV producer, public affairs talk-show host (*Open End*).
John Cameron Swayze, 1906-95, newscaster, anchor of *Camel News Caravan.*
Herbert Bayard Swope, 1882-1958, war correspondent and editor of *New York World.*
Ida Tarbell, 1857-1944, muckraking journalist.
Isaiah Thomas, 1750-1831, printer, publisher, cofounder of revolutionary journal, *Massachusetts Spy.*
Lowell Thomas, 1892-1981, radio newscaster, world traveler.
Dorothy Thompson, 1894-1961, foreign correspondent, columnist, radio commentator.
Ida Bell Wells-Barnett, 1862-1931, African-American reporter, editor, anti-lynching crusader.
William Allen White, 1868-1944, editor, publisher; made *Emporia* (KS) *Gazette* known worldwide.
Walter Winchell, 1897-1972, reporter, columnist, broadcaster of celebrity news.
John Peter Zenger, 1697-1746, printer and journalist; acquitted in precedent-setting libel suit (1735).

Notable Military and Naval Leaders of the Past

Reviewed by Alan C. Aimone, USMA Library

Creighton Abrams, 1914-74, (U.S.) commanded forces in Vietnam, 1968-72.
Alexander the Great, 356-323 B.C., (Maced.) conquered Persia and much of the world known to Europeans.
Harold Alexander, 1891-1969, (Br.) led Allied invasion of Italy, 1943, WW2.
Ethan Allen, 1738-89, (U.S.) headed Green Mountain Boys; captured Ft. Ticonderoga, 1775, Amer. Rev.
Edmund Allenby, 1861-1936, (Br.) in Boer War, WW1; led Egyptian expeditionary force, 1917-18.
Benedict Arnold, 1741-1801, (U.S.) victorious at Saratoga; tried to betray West Point to British, Amer. Rev.
Henry "Hap" Arnold, 1886-1950, (U.S.) commanded Army Air Force in WW2.
John Barry, 1745-1803, (U.S.) won numerous sea battles during Amer. Rev.
Belisarius, c505-565, (Byzant.) won remarkable victories for Byzantine Emperor Justinian I.
Pierre Beauregard, 1818-93, (U.S.) Confed. general, ordered bombardment of Ft. Sumter that began Civil War.
Gebhard von Blücher, 1742-1819, (Ger.) helped defeat Napoleon at Waterloo.
Napoleon Bonaparte, 1769-1821, (Fr.) defeated Russia and Austria at Austerlitz, 1805; invaded Russia, 1812; defeated at Waterloo, 1815.
Edward Braddock, 1695-1755, (Br.) commanded forces in French and Indian War.
Omar N. Bradley, 1893-1981, (U.S.) headed U.S. ground troops in Normandy invasion, 1944, WW2.
John Burgoyne, 1722-92, (Br.) defeated at Saratoga, Amer. Rev.
Julius Caesar, 100-44 BC (Rom.) general and politician; conquered N Gaul; overthrew Roman Republic.
Claire Lee Chennault, 1893-1958, (U.S.) headed Flying Tigers in WW2.
Mark W. Clark, 1896-1984, (U.S.) helped plan N African invasion in WW2; commander of UN forces, Korean War.
Karl von Clausewitz, 1780-1831, (Pruss.) military theorist.
Lucius D. Clay, 1897-1978, (U.S.) led Berlin airlift, 1948-49.
Henry Clinton, 1738-95, (Br.) commander of forces in Amer. Rev., 1778-81.
Cochise, c1815-74, (Nat. Am.) chief of Chiricahua band of Apache Indians in Southwest.
Charles Cornwallis, 1738-1805, (Br.) victorious at Brandywine, 1777; surrendered at Yorktown, Amer. Rev.
Hernan Cortes, 1485-1547, (Sp.) led Spanish conquistadors in the defeat of the Aztec empire, 1519-28.
Crazy Horse, 1849-77, (Nat. Am.) Sioux war chief victorious at battle of Little Big Horn.
George Armstrong Custer, 1839-76, (U.S.) U.S. army officer defeated and killed at battle of Little Big Horn.
Moshe Dayan, 1915-81, (Isr.) directed campaigns in the 1967, 1973 Arab-Israeli wars.
Stephen Decatur, 1779-1820, (U.S.) naval hero of Barbary wars, War of 1812.
Anton Denikin, 1872-1947, (Russ.) led White forces in Russian civil war.
George Dewey, 1837-1917, (U.S.) destroyed Spanish fleet at Manila, 1898, Span.-Amer. War.
Karl Doenitz, 1891-1980, (Ger.) submarine com. in chief and naval commander, WW2.
Hugh C. Dowding, 1883-1970, (Br.) headed RAF, 1936-40, WW2.

Jubal Early, 1816-94, (U.S.) Confed. general, led raid on Washington, 1864, Civil War.
Dwight D. Eisenhower, 1890-1969, (U.S.) commanded Allied forces in Europe, WW2.
David Farragut, 1801-70, (U.S.) Union admiral, captured New Orleans, Mobile Bay, Civil War.
Ferdinand Foch, 1851-1929, (Fr.) headed victorious Allied armies, 1918, WW1.
Nathan Bedford Forrest, 1821-77, (U.S.) Confed. general, led raids against Union supply lines, Civil War.
Frederick the Great, 1712-86, (Pruss.) led Prussia in Seven Years War.
Horatio Gates, 1728-1806, (U.S.) commanded army at Saratoga, Amer. Rev.
Genghis Khan, 1162-1227, (Mongol) unified Mongol tribes and subjugated much of Asia, 1206-21.
Geronimo, 1829-1909, (Nat. Am.) leader of Chiricahua band of Apache Indians.
Charles G. Gordon, 1833-85, (Br.) led forces in China, Crimean War; killed at Khartoum.
Ulysses S. Grant, 1822-85, (U.S.) headed Union army, Civil War, 1864-65; forced Lee's surrender, 1865.
Nathanael Greene, 1742-86, (U.S.) defeated British in Southern campaign, 1780-81.
Heinz Guderian, 1888-1953, (Ger.) tank theorist, led panzer forces in Poland, France, Russia, WW2.
Che (Ernesto) Guevara, 1928-67, (Arg.) guerrilla leader; prominent in Cuban revolution; killed in Bolivia.
Gustavus Adolphus, 1594-1632, (Swed.) King; military tactician reformer; led forces in Thirty Years' War.
Douglas Haig, 1861-1928, (Br.) led British armies in France, 1915-18, WW1.
William F. Halsey, 1882-1959, (U.S.) defeated Japanese fleet at Leyte Gulf, 1944, WW2.
Hannibal, 247-183 B.C., (Carthag.) invaded Rome, crossing Alps, in Second Punic War, 218-201 B.C.
Sir Arthur Travers Harris, 1895-1984, (Br.) led Britain's WW2 bomber command.
Richard Howe, 1726-99, (Br.) commanded navy in Amer. Rev., 1776-78; June 1 victory against French, 1794.
William Howe, 1729-1814, (Br.) commanded forces in Amer. Rev., 1776-78.
Isaac Hull, 1773-1843, (U.S.) sunk British frigate Guerriere, War of 1812.
Thomas (Stonewall) Jackson, 1824-63, (U.S.) Confed. general, led Shenandoah Valley campaign, Civil War.
Joseph Joffre, 1852-1931, (Fr.) headed Allied armies, won Battle of the Marne, 1914, WW1.
Chief Joseph, c1840-1904, (Nat. Am.) chief of the Nez Percé, led his tribe across 3 states seeking refuge in Canada; surrendered about 30 mi from Canadian border.
John Paul Jones, 1747-92, (U.S.) commanded Bonhomme Richard in victory over Serapis, Amer. Rev., 1779.
Stephen Kearny, 1794-1848, (U.S.) headed Army of the West in Mexican War.
Albert Kesselring, 1885-1960 (Ger.) field marshall who led the defense of Italy in WW2.
Ernest J. King, 1878-1956, (U.S.) key WW2 naval strategist.
Horatio H. Kitchener, 1850-1916, (Br.) led forces in Boer War; victorious at Khartoum; organized army in WW1.
Henry Knox, 1750-1806, (U.S.) general in Amer. Rev.; first sec. of war under U.S. Constitution.
Lavrenti Kornilov, 1870-1918, (Russ.) commander-in-chief, 1917; led counter-revolutionary march on Petrograd.
Thaddeus Kosciusko, 1746-1817, (Pol.) aided Amer. Rev.
Walter Krueger, 1881-1967, (U.S.) led Sixth Army in WW2 in Southwest Pacific.
Mikhail Kutuzov, 1745-1813, (Russ.) fought French at Borodino, Napoleonic Wars, 1812; abandoned Moscow; forced French retreat.
Marquis de Lafayette, 1757-1834, (Fr.) aided Amer. Rev.
T(homas) E. Lawrence (of Arabia), 1888-1935, (Br.) organized revolt of Arabs against Turks in WW1.
Henry (Light-Horse Harry) Lee, 1756-1818, (U.S.) cavalry officer in Amer. Rev.
Robert E. Lee, 1807-70, (U.S.) Confed. general defeated at Gettysburg, Civil War; surrendered to Grant, 1865.
Curtis May, 1906-90, (U.S.) Air Force commander in WW2, Korean War, and Vietnam War.
Lyman Lemnitzer, 1899-1988, (U.S.) WW2 hero, later general, chairman of Joint Chiefs of Staff.
James Longstreet, 1821-1904, (U.S.) aided Lee at Gettysburg, Civil War.
Maurice, Count of Nassau, 1567-1625, (Dutch) military innovator; led forces in Thirty Years' War.
Douglas MacArthur, 1880-1964, (U.S.) commanded forces in SW Pacific in WW2; headed occupation forces in Japan, 1945-51; UN commander in Korean War.
Erich von Manstein, 1887-1973, (Ger.) served in WW1 and WW2, planned invasion of France (1940), convicted of war crimes.
Carl Gustaf Mannerheim, 1867-1951, (Finn.) army officer and pres. of Finland 1944-46.
Francis Marion, 1733-95, (U.S.) led guerrilla actions in South Carolina during Amer. Rev.
Duke of Marlborough, 1650-1722, (Br.) led forces against Louis XIV in War of the Spanish Succession.
George C. Marshall, 1880-1959, (U.S.) chief of staff in WW2; authored Marshall Plan.
George B. McClellan, 1826-85, (U.S.) Union general, commanded Army of the Potomac, 1861-62, Civil War.
George Meade, 1815-72, (U.S.) commanded Union forces at Gettysburg, Civil War.
Billy Mitchell, 1879-1936, (U.S.) WW1 air-power advocate; court-martialed for insubordination, later vindicated.
Helmuth von Moltke, 1800-91, (Ger.) victorious in Austro-Prussian, Franco-Prussian wars.
Louis de Montcalm, 1712-59, (Fr.) headed troops in Canada, French and Indian War; defeated at Quebec, 1759.
Bernard Law Montgomery, 1887-1976, (Br.) stopped German offensive at Alamein, 1942, WW2; helped plan Normandy.
Daniel Morgan, 1736-1802, (U.S.) victorious at Cowpens, 1781, Amer. Rev.
Louis Mountbatten, 1900-79, (Br.) Supreme Allied Commander of SE Asia, 1943-46, WW2.
Joachim Murat, 1767-1815, (Fr.) led cavalry at Marengo, Austerlitz, and Jena, Napoleonic Wars.
Horatio Nelson, 1758-1805, (Br.) naval commander, destroyed French fleet at Trafalgar.
Michel Ney, 1769-1815, (Fr.) commanded forces in Switz., Aust., Russ., Napoleonic Wars; defeated at Waterloo.
Chester Nimitz, 1885-1966, (U.S.) commander of naval forces in Pacific in WW2.
George S. Patton, 1885-1945, (U.S.) led assault on Sicily, 1943, Third Army invasion of Europe, WW2.
Oliver Perry, 1785-1819, (U.S.) won Battle of Lake Erie in War of 1812.
John Pershing, 1860-1948, (U.S.) commanded Mexican border campaign, 1916, Amer. Expeditionary Force, WW1.
Henri Philippe Pétain, 1856-1951, (Fr.) defended Verdun, 1916; headed Vichy government in WW2.
George E. Pickett, 1825-75, (U.S.) Confed. general famed for "charge" at Gettysburg, Civil War.
Charles Portal, 1893-1971, (Br.) chief of staff, Royal Air Force, 1940-45, led in Battle of Britain.
Hyman Rickover, 1900-86, (U.S.) father of nuclear navy.
Matthew Bunker Ridgway, 1895-1993, (U.S.) commanded Allied ground forces in Korean War.
Erwin Rommel, 1891-1944, (Ger.) headed Afrika Korps, WW2.
Gerd von Rundstedt, 1875-1953, (Ger.) supreme commander in West, 1942-45, WW2.
Aleksandr Samsonov, 1859-1914, (Russ.) led invasion of E Prussia, WW1, defeated at Tannenberg, 1914.
Winfield Scott, 1786-1866, (U.S.) hero of War of 1812; headed forces in Mexican War, took Mexico City.
Philip Sheridan, 1831-88, (U.S.) Union cavalry officer, headed Army of the Shenandoah, 1864-65, Civil War.
William T. Sherman, 1820-91, (U.S.) Union general, sacked Atlanta during "march to the sea," 1864, Civil War.
Carl Spaatz, 1891-1974, (U.S.) directed strategic bombing against Germany, later Japan, in WW2.
Raymond Spruance, 1886-1969, (U.S.) victorious at Midway Island, 1942, WW2.
Joseph W. Stilwell, 1883-1946, (U.S.) headed forces in the China, Burma, India theater in WW2.
J.E.B. Stuart, 1833-64, (U.S.) Confed. cavalry commander, Civil War.
Aleksandr Suvorov, 1729-1800, (Rus.) victorious commander of Allied Russian and Austrian armies against Ottoman Turks in Russo-Turkish War.
George H. Thomas, 1816-70, (U.S.) saved Union army at Chattanooga, 1863; won at Nashville, 1864, Civil War.
Semyon Timoshenko, 1895-1970, (USSR) defended Moscow, Stalingrad, WW2; led winter offensive, 1942-43.
Alfred von Tirpitz, 1849-1930, (Ger.) responsible for submarine blockade in WW1.
Sebastien Le Prestre de Vauban, 1633-1707, (Fr.) innovative military engineer and theorist.
Jonathan M. Wainwright, 1883-1953, (U.S.) forced to surrender on Corregidor, 1942, WW2.
George Washington, 1732-99, (U.S.) led Continental army, 1775-83, Amer. Rev.
Archibald Wavell, 1883-1950, (Br.) commanded forces in N and E Africa, and SE Asia in WW2.
Anthony Wayne, 1745-96, (U.S.) captured Stony Point, 1779, Amer. Rev.
Duke of Wellington, 1769-1852, (Br.) defeated Napoleon at Waterloo, 1815.
James Wolfe, 1727-59, (Br.) captured Quebec from French, 1759, French and Indian War.
Isoroku Yamamoto, 1884-1943, (Jpn.) com. in chief of Japanese fleet and naval planner before and during WW2.
Georgi Zhukov, 1895-1974, (Russ.) defended Moscow, 1941, led assault on Berlin, 1945, WW2.

Noted Philosophers and Religious Figures of the Past

For other Greeks and Romans, see Historical Figures chapter.

Lyman Abbott, 1835-1922, (U.S.) clergyman, reformer; advocate of Christian Socialism.
Pierre Abelard, 1079-1142, (Fr.) philosopher, theologian, teacher; used dialectic method to support Christian beliefs.
Felix Adler, 1851-1933, (U.S.) German-born founder of the Ethical Culture Society.
(St.) Anselm, c1033-1109, (It.) philosopher-theologian, church leader; "ontological argument" for God's existence.
(St.) Thomas Aquinas, 1225-74, (It.) preeminent medieval philosopher-theologian; *Summa Theologica.*
Aristotle, 384-322 BC, (Gr.) pioneering wide-ranging philosopher, logician, ethician, naturalist.
(St.) Augustine, 354-430, (N Africa) philosopher, theologian, bishop; *Confessions, City of God, On the Trinity.*
J. L. Austin, 1911-60, (Br.) ordinary-language philosopher.
Averroes (Ibn Rushd), 1126-98, (Sp.) Islamic philosopher, physician.
Avicenna (Ibn Sina), 980-1037, (Iran.) Islamic philosopher, scientist.
A(lfred) J(ules) Ayer, 1910-89, (Br.) philosopher; logical positivist; *Language, Truth, and Logic.*
Roger Bacon, c1214-94, (Eng.) philosopher and scientist.
Bahaullah (Mirza Husayn Ali), 1817-92, (Pers.) founder of Bahá'í faith.
Karl Barth, 1886-1968, (Swiss) theologian; a leading force in 20th-cent. Protestantism.
Thomas à Becket, 1118-70, (Eng.) archbishop of Canterbury; opposed Henry II; murdered by King's men.
(St.) Benedict, c480-547, (It.) founded the Benedictines.
Jeremy Bentham, 1748-1832, (Br.) philosopher, reformer; enunciated utilitarianism.
Henri Bergson, 1859-1941, (Fr.) philosopher of evolution.
George Berkeley, 1685-1753, (Ir.) idealist philosopher, churchman.
John Biddle, 1615-62, (Eng.) founder of English Unitarianism.
Jakob Boehme, 1575-1624, (Ger.) theosophist and mystic.
Dietrich Bonhoeffer, 1906-1945 (Ger.) Lutheran theologian, pastor; executed as opponent of Nazis.
William Brewster, 1567-1644, (Eng.) headed Pilgrims.
Emil Brunner, 1889-1966, (Swiss) Protestant theologian.
Giordano Bruno, 1548-1600, (It.) philosopher, pantheist.
Martin Buber, 1878-1965, (Ger.) Jewish philosopher, theologian; *I and Thou.*
Buddha (Siddhartha Gautama), c563-c483 BC, (Indian) philosopher; founded Buddhism.
John Calvin, 1509-64, (Fr.) theologian; a key figure in the Protestant Reformation.
Rudolph Carnap, 1891-1970, (U.S.) German-born analytic philosopher; a founder of logical positivism.
William Ellery Channing, 1780-1842, (U.S.) clergyman; early spokesman for Unitarianism.
Auguste Comte, 1798-1857, (Fr.) philosopher; originated positivism.
Confucius, 551-479 BC, (Chin.) founder of Confucianism.
John Cotton, 1584-1652, (Eng.) Puritan theologian.
Thomas Cranmer, 1489-1556, (Eng.) churchman; wrote much of *Book of Common Prayer.*
René Descartes, 1596-1650, (Fr.) philosopher, mathematician; "father of modern philosophy." *Discourse on Method, Meditations on First Philosophy.*
John Dewey, 1859-1952, (U.S.) philosopher, educator; instrumentalist theory of knowledge; helped inaugurate progressive education movement.
Denis Diderot, 1713-84, (Fr.) philosopher, encyclopedist.
John Duns Scotus, c1266-1308, (Sc.) Franciscan philosopher and theologian.
Mary Baker Eddy, 1821-1910, (U.S.) founder of Christian Science; *Science and Health.*
Jonathan Edwards, 1703-58, (U.S.) preacher, theologian.
(Desiderius) Erasmus, c1466-1536, (Dutch) Renaissance humanist; *On the Freedom of the Will.*
Johann Fichte, 1762-1814, (Ger.) idealist philosopher.
Michel Foucault, 1926-84, (Fr.) structuralist philosopher, historian.
George Fox, 1624-91, (Br.) founder of Society of Friends.
(St.) Francis of Assisi, 1182-1226, (It.) founded Franciscans.
al-Ghazali, 1058-1111, Islamic philosopher.
Georg W. F. Hegel, 1770-1831, (Ger.) idealist philosopher; *Phenomenology of Mind.*
Martin Heidegger, 1889-1976, (Ger.) existentialist philosopher; affected many fields; *Being and Time.*
Johann G. Herder, 1744-1803, (Ger.) philosopher, cultural historian; a founder of German Romanticism.
Thomas Hobbes, 1588-1679, (Eng.) philosopher, political theorist; *Leviathan.*
David Hume, 1711-76, (Sc.) leading empiricist philosopher; *Enquiry Concerning Human Understanding.*
Jan Hus, 1369-1415, (Czech.) religious reformer.
Edmund Husserl, 1859-1938, (Ger.) philosopher; founded the phenomenological movement.
Thomas Huxley, 1825-95, (Br.) philosopher, educator.
William Inge, 1860-1954, (Br.) theologian; explored mystic aspects of Christianity.
William James, 1842-1910, (U.S.) philosopher, psychologist; pragmatist; studied religious experience.
Karl Jaspers, 1883-1969, (Ger.) existentialist philosopher.
Joan of Arc, 1412-1431, (Fr.) national heroine and a patron saint of France; key figure in the Hundred Years' War.
Immanuel Kant, 1724-1804, (Ger.) philosopher; founder of modern critical philosophy; *Critique of Pure Reason.*
Thomas à Kempis, c1380-1471, (Ger.) monk, devotional writer; *Imitation of Christ.* attributed to him.
Soren Kierkegaard, 1813-55, (Dan.) religious philosopher; pre-existentialist; *Either/Or, The Sickness Unto Death.*
John Knox, 1505-72, (Sc.) leader of the Protestant Reformation in Scotland.
Lao-Tzu, 604-531 BC, (Chin.) philosopher; considered the founder of the Taoist religion.
Gottfried von Leibniz, 1646-1716, (Ger.) rationalistic philosopher, logician, mathematician.
John Locke, 1632-1704, (Eng.) political theorist, empiricist philosopher; *Essay Concerning Human Understanding.*
(St.) Ignatius Loyola, 1491-1556, (Sp.) founder of the Jesuits.
Martin Luther, 1483-1546, (Ger.) leader of the Protestant Reformation, founded Lutheran church.
Jean-Francois Lyotard, 1924-98, (Fr.) postmodern philosopher, lecturer; *The Post-Modern Condition.*
Maimonides, 1135-1204, (Sp.) major Jewish philosopher.
Gabriel Marcel, 1889-1973, (Fr.) Roman Catholic existentialist philosopher, dramatist, and critic,
Jacques Maritain, 1882-1973, (Fr.) Neo-Thomist philosopher.
Cotton Mather, 1663-1728, (U.S.) defender of orthodox Puritanism; founded Yale, 1701.
Philipp Melanchthon, 1497-1560, (Ger.) theologian, humanist; an important voice in the Reformation.
Maurice Merleau-Ponty, 1908-61, (Fr.) existentialist philosopher; *Phenomenology of Perception.*
Thomas Merton, 1915-68, (U.S.) Trappist monk, spiritual writer; *The Seven Storey Mountain.*
John Stuart Mill, 1806-73, (Br.) philosopher, economist; libertarian political theorist; *Utilitarianism.*
Muhammad, c570-632, (Arab) the prophet of Islam.
Dwight Moody, 1837-99, (U.S.) evangelist.
G(eorge) E(dward) Moore, 1873-1958, (Br.) philosopher; *Principia Ethica,* "A Defense of Common Sense."
Elijah Muhammad, 1897-1975, (U.S.) leader of the Black Muslim sect.
Heinrich Muhlenberg, 1711-87, (Ger.) organized the Lutheran Church in America.
John H. Newman, 1801-90, (Br.) Roman Catholic convert, cardinal; led Oxford Movement; *Apologia pro Vita Sua.*
Reinhold Niebuhr, 1892-1971, (U.S.) Protestant theologian.
Friedrich Nietzsche, 1844-1900, (Ger.) philosopher; *The Birth of Tragedy, Beyond Good and Evil, Thus Spake Zarathustra.*
Blaise Pascal, 1623-62, (Fr.) philosopher, mathematician; Pensées.
(St.) Patrick, c389-c461, (Br.) brought Christianity to Ireland.
(St.) Paul, ?-c67, a key proponent of Christianity; his epistles are first Christian theological writing.
Norman Vincent Peale, 1898-1993, (U.S.) religious leader, author; *The Power of Positive Thinking.*
C(harles) S. Peirce, 1839-1914, (U.S.) philosopher, logician; originated concept of pragmatism, 1878.
Plato, c428-347 BC, (Gr.) philosopher; wrote classic Socratic dialogues; argued for universal truths and independent reality of ideas or forms; *Republic.*
Plotinus, 205-70, (Rom.) a founder of neo-Platonism; *Enneads.*
Josiah Royce, 1855-1916, (U.S.) idealist philosopher.
Bertrand Russell, 1872-1970, (Br.) philosopher, logician; one of the founders of modern logic; a prolific popular writer.
Charles T. Russell, 1852-1916, (U.S.) founder of Jehovah's Witnesses.
Gilbert Ryle, 1900-76, (Br.) analytic philosopher; *The Concept of Mind.*
George Santayana, 1863-1952, (U.S.) philosopher, writer, critic; *The Sense of Beauty, The Realms of Being.*
Jean-Paul Sartre, 1905-80, (Fr.) philosopher, novelist, playwright. *Nausea, No Exit, Being and Nothingness.*
Friedrich von Schelling, 1775-1854, (Ger.) philosopher of romantic movement.

Friedrich Schleiermacher, 1768-1834, (Ger.) theologian; a founder of modern Protestant theology.
Arthur Schopenhauer, 1788-1860, (Ger.) philosopher; *The World as Will and Idea.*
Albert Schweitzer, 1875-1965, (Ger.) theologian, social philosopher, medical missionary.
Joseph Smith, 1805-44, (U.S.) founded Latter-day Saints (Mormon) movement, 1830.
Socrates, 469-399 BC, (Gr.) influential philosopher immortalized by Plato.
Herbert Spencer, 1820-1903, (Br.) philosopher of evolution.
Baruch de Spinoza, 1632-77, (Dutch) rationalist philosopher; *Ethics.*
Billy Sunday, 1862-1935, (U.S.) evangelist.
Pierre Teilhard de Chardin, 1881-1955, (Fr.) Jesuit priest, paleontologist, philosopher-theologian; *The Divine Milieu.*
Daisetz Teitaro Suzuki, 1870-1966, (Jpn.) Buddhist scholar.
(St.) Theresa of Lisieux, 1873-97, (Fr.) Carmelite nun revered for everyday sanctity; *The Story of a Soul.*
Emanuel Swedenborg, 1688-1772, (Swed.) philosopher, mystic.
Paul Tillich, 1886-1965, (U.S.) German-born philosopher and theologian; brought depth psychology to Protestantism.
John Wesley, 1703-91, (Br.) theologian, evangelist; founded Methodism.
Alfred North Whitehead, 1861-1947, (Br.) philosopher, mathematician; *Process and Reality.*
William of Occam, c1285-c1349 (Eng.) medieval scholastic philosopher; nominalist.
Roger Williams, c1603-83, (U.S.) clergyman; championed religious freedom and separation of church and state.
Ludwig Wittgenstein, 1889-1951, (Austrian) philosopher; major influence on contemporary language philosophy; *Tractatus Logico-Philosophicus, Philosophical Investigations.*
John Wycliffe, 1320-84, (Eng.) theologian, reformer.
(St.) Francis Xavier, 1506-52, (Sp.) Jesuit missionary, "Apostle of the Indies."
Brigham Young, 1801-77, (U.S.) Mormon leader after Smith's assassination; colonized Utah.
Huldrych Zwingli, 1484-1531, (Swiss) theologian; led Swiss Protestant Reformation.

Noted Political Leaders of the Past

(Modern royalty, U.S. presidents, vice presidents, Supreme Court justices, signers of Decl. of Indep. listed elsewhere.)

Abu Bakr, 573-634, Muslim leader, first caliph, chosen successor to Muhammad.
Dean Acheson, 1893-1971, (U.S.) sec. of state; architect of cold war foreign policy.
Samuel Adams, 1722-1803, (U.S.) patriot, Boston Tea Party firebrand.
Konrad Adenauer, 1876-1967, (Ger.) West German chancellor.
Emilio Aguinaldo, 1869-1964, (Philip.) revolutionary; fought against Spain and the U.S.
Akbar, 1542-1605, greatest Mogul emperor of India.
Salvador Allende Gossens, 1908-1973, (Chilean) Marxist pres. 1970-73; ousted and died in coup.
Herbert H. Asquith, 1852-1928, (Br.) liberal prime min.; instituted major social reform.
Atahualpa, ?-1533, Inca (ruling chief) of Peru.
Kemal Ataturk, 1881-1938, (Turk.) founded modern Turkey.
Clement Attlee, 1883-1967, (Br.) Labour party leader, prime min.; enacted natl. health, nationalized many industries.
Stephen F. Austin, 1793-1836, (U.S.) led Texas colonization.
Mikhail Bakunin, 1814-76, (Russ.) revolutionary; leading exponent of anarchism.
Arthur J. Balfour, 1848-1930, (Br.) foreign sec. under Lloyd George; issued Balfour Declaration backing Zionism.
Bernard M. Baruch, 1870-1965, (U.S.) financier, govt. adviser.
Fulgencio Batista y Zaldívar, 1901-73, (Cub.) Cuban pres. (1940-44, 1952-59) and dictator, overthrown by Castro.
Lord Beaverbrook, 1879-1964, (Br.) financier, statesman, newspaper owner.
Menachem Begin, 1913-92, (Isr.) Israeli prime min., shared 1978 Nobel Peace Prize.
Eduard Benes, 1884-1948, (Czech.) pres. during interwar and post-WW2 eras.
David Ben-Gurion, 1886-1973, (Isr.) first prime min. of Israel, 1948-53, 1955-63.
Thomas Hart Benton, 1782-1858, (U.S.) Missouri senator; championed agrarian interests and westward expansion.
Aneurin Bevan, 1897-1960, (Br.) Labour party leader.
Ernest Bevin, 1881-1951, (Br.) Labour party leader, foreign minister; helped lay foundation for NATO.
Otto von Bismarck, 1815-98, (Ger.) statesman known as the Iron Chancellor; uniter of Germany, 1870.
James G. Blaine, 1830-93, (U.S.) Republican politician, diplomat; influential in launching Pan-American movement.
Léon Blum, 1872-1950, (Fr.) socialist leader, writer; headed first Popular Front government.
Simón Bolívar, 1783-1830, (Venez.) S. Amer. Revolutionary who liberated much of the continent from Spanish rule.
William E. Borah, 1865-1940, (U.S.) isolationist senator; helped block U.S. membership in League of Nations.
Cesare Borgia, 1476-1507, (It.) soldier, politician; an outstanding figure of the Italian Renaissance.
Willy Brandt, 1913-92, (Ger.) statesman, chancellor of West Germany, 1969-74; promoted East/West peace, *Ostpolitik.*
Leonid Brezhnev, 1906-82, (USSR) Soviet leader, 1964-82.
William J. Brennan Jr., 1906-97, (U.S.) associate justice of U.S. Sup. Ct. (1956-90); a leading liberal force.
Aristide Briand, 1862-1932, (Fr.) foreign min.; chief architect of Locarno Pact and anti-war Kellogg-Briand Pact.
William Jennings Bryan, 1860-1925, (U.S.) Democratic, populist leader, orator; 3 times lost race for presidency.
William C. Bullitt, 1891-1967, (U.S.) diplomat; first ambassador to USSR, ambassador to France.
Ralph Bunche, 1904-71, (U.S.) a founder and key diplomat of United Nations for more than 20 years.
John C. Calhoun, 1782-1850, (U.S.) political leader; champion of states' rights and a symbol of the Old South.
Robert Castlereagh, 1769-1822, (Br.) foreign sec.; guided Grand Alliance against Napoleon.
Camillo Benso Cavour, 1810-61, (It.) statesman; largely responsible for uniting Italy under the House of Savoy.
Nicolae Ceausescu, 1918-89, (Roman.) Communist leader, head of state 1967-89.
Austen Chamberlain, 1863-1937, (Br.) statesman; won the Nobel Peace Prize, helped finalize Locarno Treaties, both 1925.
Neville Chamberlain, 1869-1940, (Br.) Conservative prime min. whose appeasement of Hitler led to Munich Pact.
Chiang Kai-shek, 1887-1975, (Chin.) Nationalist Chinese pres. whose government was driven from mainland to Taiwan.
Winston Churchill, 1874-1965, (Br.) prime min., soldier, author; guided Britain through WW2.
Galeazzo Ciano, 1903-44, (It.) fascist foreign minister; helped create Rome-Berlin Axis, executed by Mussolini.
Henry Clay, 1777-1852, (U.S.) "The Great Compromiser," one of the most influential pre-Civil War political leaders.
Georges Clemenceau, 1841-1929, (Fr.) twice prem., Wilson's antagonist at Paris Peace Conference after WW1.
DeWitt Clinton, 1769-1828, (U.S.) political leader; responsible for promoting idea of the Erie Canal.
Robert Clive, 1725-74, (Br.) first administrator of Bengal; laid foundation for British Empire in India.
Jean Baptiste Colbert, 1619-83, (Fr.) statesman; influential under Louis XIV, created the French navy.
Oliver Cromwell, 1599-1658, (Br.) Lord Protector of England, led parliamentary forces during Civil War.
Curzon of Kedleston, 1859-1925, (Br.) viceroy of India, foreign sec.; major force in post-WW1 world.
Édouard Daladier, 1884-1970, (Fr.) radical socialist politician, arrested by Vichy, interned by Germans until 1945.
Georges Danton, 1759-94, (Fr.) leading French Rev. figure.
Jefferson Davis, 1808-89, (U.S.) pres. of the Confederacy.
Charles G. Dawes, 1865-1951, (U.S.) statesman, banker; advanced plan to stabilize post-WW1 German finances.
Alcide De Gasperi, 1881-1954, (It.) prime min.; founder of Christian Democratic party.
Charles De Gaulle, 1890-1970, (Fr.) general, statesman; first pres. of the Fifth Republic.
Deng Xiaoping, 1904-97, (Chin.) "paramount leader" of China; backed economic modernization.
Eamon De Valera, 1882-1975, (Ir.-U.S.) statesman; led fight for Irish independence.
Thomas E. Dewey, 1902-71, (U.S.) New York governor; twice loser in try for presidency.
Ngo Dinh Diem, 1901-63, (Viet.) South Vietnamese pres.; assassinated in government takeover.
Everett M. Dirksen, 1896-1969, (U.S.) Senate Republican minority leader, orator.
Benjamin Disraeli, 1804-81, (Br.) prime min.; considered founder of modern Conservative party.
Engelbert Dollfuss, 1892-1934, (Austrian) chancellor; assassinated by Austrian Nazis.
Andrea Doria, 1466-1560, (It.) Genoese admiral, statesman; called "Father of Peace" and "Liberator of Genoa."
Stephen A. Douglas, 1813-61, (U.S.) Democratic leader, orator; opposed Lincoln for the presidency.
Alexander Dubcek, 1921-92, (Czech.) statesman whose attempted liberalization was crushed, 1968.
John Foster Dulles, 1888-1959, (U.S.) sec. of state under Eisenhower, cold war policy-maker.

Friedrich Ebert, 1871-1925, (Ger.) Social Democratic movement leader; 1st pres. of Weimar Republic, 1919-25.
Sir Anthony Eden, 1897-1977, (Br.) foreign sec., prime min. during Suez invasion of 1956.
Ludwig Erhard, 1897-1977, (Ger.) economist, West German chancellor; led nation's economic rise after WW2.
Hamilton Fish, 1808-93, (U.S.) sec. of state, successfully mediated disputes with Great Britain, Latin America.
James V. Forrestal, 1892-1949, (U.S.) sec. of navy, first sec. of defense.
Francisco Franco, 1892-1975, (Sp.) leader of rebel forces during Spanish Civil War and dictator of Spain.
Benjamin Franklin, 1706-90, (U.S.) printer, publisher, author, inventor, scientist, diplomat.
Louis de Frontenac, 1620-98, (Fr.) governor of New France (Canada); encouraged explorations, fought Iroquois.
J. William Fulbright, 1905-95, (U.S.) U.S. senator; leading figure in U.S. foreign policy during cold war years.
Hugh Gaitskell, 1906-63, (Br.) Labour party leader; major force in reversing its stand for unilateral disarmament.
Albert Gallatin, 1761-1849, (U.S.) sec. of treasury; instrumental in negotiating end of War of 1812.
Léon Gambetta, 1838-82, (Fr.) statesman, politician; one of the founders of the Third Republic.
Indira Gandhi, 1917-84, (In.) daughter of Jawaharlal Nehru, prime min. of India, 1966-77, 1980-84; assassinated.
Mohandas K. Gandhi, 1869-1948, (In.) political leader, ascetic; led movement against British rule; assassinated.
Giuseppe Garibaldi, 1807-82, (It.) patriot, soldier; a leader in the Risorgimento, Italian unification movement.
William E. Gladstone, 1809-98, (Br.) prime min. 4 times; dominant force of Liberal party from 1868 to 1894.
Paul Joseph Goebbels, 1897-1945, (Ger.) Nazi propagandist, master of mass psychology.
Barry Goldwater, 1909-98 (U.S.) conservative U.S. senator and 1964 Republican presid. nominee.
Klement Gottwald, 1896-1953, (Czech.) Communist leader; ushered Communism into his country.
Alexander Hamilton, 1755-1804, (U.S.) first treasury sec.; champion of strong central government.
Dag Hammarskjold, 1905-61, (Swed.) statesman; UN sec.-general.
John Hay, 1838-1905, (U.S.) sec. of state; primarily associated with Open Door Policy toward China.
Patrick Henry, 1736-99, (U.S.) major revolutionary figure, remarkable orator.
Édouard Herriot, 1872-1957, (Fr.) Radical Socialist leader; twice prem., pres. of National Assembly.
Theodor Herzl, 1860-1904, (Hung.) founded modern Zionism.
Heinrich Himmler, 1900-45, (Ger.) head of Nazi SS and Gestapo.
Paul von Hindenburg, 1847-1934, (Ger.) field marshal, WW1; 2d pres. of Weimar Republic, 1925-34.
Adolf Hitler, 1889-1945, (Ger.) dictator; built Nazism, launched WW2, presided over the Holocaust.
Ho Chi Minh, 1890-1969, (Viet.) N Vietnamese pres., Vietnamese Communist leader.
Harry L. Hopkins, 1890-1946, (U.S.) New Deal administrator; closest adviser to FDR during WW2.
Edward M. House, 1858-1938, (U.S.) diplomat; confidential adviser to Woodrow Wilson.
Samuel Houston, 1793-1863, (U.S.) leader of struggle to win control of Texas from Mexico.
Cordell Hull, 1871-1955, (U.S.) sec. of state, 1933-44; initiated reciprocal trade to lower tariffs, helped organize UN.
Hubert H. Humphrey, 1911-78, (U.S.) Minnesota Democrat; senator; vice pres., pres. candidate.
Jinnah, Muhammad Ali, 1876-1948, (Pak.) founder, first governor-general of Pakistan.
Benito Juarez, 1806-72, (Mex.) rallied his country against foreign threats, sought to create democratic, federal republic.
Constantine Karamanlis, 1907-98, (Gr.) Greek prime min. (1955-63, 1974-80); restored democracy; later president.
Frank B. Kellogg, 1856-1937, (U.S.) sec. of state; negotiated Kellogg-Briand Pact to outlaw war.
Robert F. Kennedy, 1925-68, (U.S.) attorney general, senator; assassinated while seeking presid. nomination.
Aleksandr Kerensky, 1881-1970, (Russ.) headed provisional government after Feb. 1917 revolution.
Ayatollah Ruhollah Khomeini, 1900-89, (Iranian), religious-political leader, spearheaded overthrow of shah, 1979.
Nikita Khrushchev, 1894-1971, (USSR) prem., first sec. of Communist party; initiated de-Stalinization.
Kim Il Sung, 1912-94, (Korean) N Korean dictator, 1948-94.
Lajos Kossuth, 1802-94, (Hung.) principal figure in 1848 Hungarian revolution.
Pyotr Kropotkin, 1842-1921, (Russ.) anarchist; championed the peasants but opposed Bolshevism.
Kublai Khan, c1215-94, Mongol emperor; founder of Yüan dynasty in China.
Béla Kun, 1886-c1939, (Hung.) member of 3d Communist Internat.; tried to foment worldwide revolution.
Robert M. LaFollette, 1855-1925, (U.S.) Wisconsin public official; leader of progressive movement.
Fiorello La Guardia, 1882-1947, (U.S.) colorful New York City reform mayor.
Pierre Laval, 1883-1945, (Fr.) politician, Vichy foreign min.; executed for treason.
Andrew Bonar Law, 1858-1923, (Br.) Conservative party politician; led opposition to Irish home rule.
Vladimir Ilyich Lenin (Ulyanov), 1870-1924, (Russ.) revolutionary; founder of Bolshevism, Soviet leader 1917-24.
Ferdinand de Lesseps, 1805-94, (Fr.) diplomat, engineer; conceived idea of Suez Canal.
Rene Levesque, 1922-87, (Can.) prem. of Quebec, 1976-85; led unsuccessful fight to separate from Canada.
Maxim Litvinov, 1876-1951, (Pol.-Russ.) revolutionary, commissar of foreign affairs; favored cooperation with West.
Liu Shaoqi, c1898-1974, (Chin.) Communist leader; fell from grace during Cultural Revolution.
David Lloyd George, 1863-1945, (Br.) Liberal party prime min.; laid foundations for modern welfare state.
Henry Cabot Lodge, 1850-1924, (U.S.) Republican senator; led opposition to participation in League of Nations.
Huey P. Long, 1893-1935, (U.S.) Louisiana political demagogue, governor; assassinated.
Rosa Luxemburg, 1871-1919, (Ger.) revolutionary; leader of the German Social Democratic party and Spartacus party.
J. Ramsay MacDonald, 1866-1937, (Br.) first Labour party prime min. of Great Britain.
Harold Macmillan, 1895-1986, (Br.) prime min. of Great Britain, 1957-63.
Joseph R. McCarthy, 1908-57, (U.S.) senator, extremist in searching out alleged Communists and pro-Communists.
Makarios III, 1913-77, (Cypriot) Greek Orthodox archbishop; first pres. of Cyprus.
Mao Zedong, 1893-1976, (Chin.) chief Chinese Marxist theorist, revolutionary, political leader; led Chinese revolution establishing his nation as Communist state.
Jean Paul Marat, 1743-93, (Fr.) revolutionary, politician; identified with radical Jacobins; assassinated.
José Martí, 1853-95, (Cub.) patriot, poet; leader of Cuban struggle for independence.
Jan Masaryk, 1886-1948, (Czech.) foreign min.; died by mysterious alleged suicide following Communist coup.
Thomas G. Masaryk, 1850-1937, (Czech.) statesman, philosopher; first pres. of Czechoslovak Republic.
Jules Mazarin, 1602-61, (Fr.) cardinal, statesman; prime min. under Louis XIII and queen regent Anne of Austria.
Giusseppe Mazzini, 1805-72, (It.), reformer dedicated to Risorgimento movement for renewal of Italy.
Tom Mboya, 1930-69, (Kenyan) political leader; instrumental in securing independence for Kenya.
Cosimo I de' Medici, 1519-74, (It.) Duke of Florence, grand duke of Tuscany.
Lorenzo de' Medici, the Magnificent, 1449-92, (It.) merchant prince; a towering figure in Italian Renaissance.
Catherine de Médicis, 1519-89, (Fr.) queen consort of Henry II, regent of France; influential in Catholic-Huguenot wars.
Golda Meir, 1898-1978, (Isr.) a founder of the state of Israel and prime min., 1969-74.
Klemens W. N. L. Metternich, 1773-1859, (Austrian) statesman; arbiter of post-Napoleonic Europe.
François Mitterrand, 1916-96, (Fr.) pres. of France, 1981-95.
Mobutu Sese Seko, 1930-97, (Zaire) longtime ruler of Zaire (now Congo) (1965-97); exiled after 1997 rebellion.
Guy Mollet, 1905-75, (Fr.) social politician, resistance leader.
Henry Morgenthau Jr., 1891-1967, (U.S.) sec. of treasury; fund-raiser for New Deal and U.S. WW2 activities.
Gouverneur Morris, 1752-1816, (U.S.) statesman, diplomat; financial expert who helped plan decimal coinage system.
Benito Mussolini, 1883-1945, (It.) dictator and leader of the Italian fascist state; assassinated.
Imre Nagy, c1896-1958, (Hung.) Communist prem.; assassinated after Soviets crushed 1956 uprising.
Gamal Abdel Nasser, 1918-70, (Egypt.) leader of Arab unification, 2d Egyptian pres.
Jawaharlal Nehru, 1889-1964, (In.) prime min.; guided India through its early years of independence.
Kwame Nkrumah, 1909-72, (Ghan.) 1st prime min., 1957-60, and pres., 1960-66, of Ghana.
Frederick North, 1732-92, (Br.) prime min.; his inept policies led to loss of American colonies.
Daniel O'Connell, 1775-1847, (Ir.) political leader; known as The Liberator.
Omar, c581-644, Muslim leader; 2d caliph, led Islam to become an imperial power.

Thomas P. (Tip) O'Neill Jr., 1912-94, (U.S.) U.S. congressman, Speaker of the House, 1977-86.

Ignace Paderewski, 1860-1941, (Pol.) statesman, pianist; composer, briefly prime min., an ardent patriot.

Viscount Palmerston, 1784-1865, (Br.) Whig-Liberal prime min., foreign minister; embodied British nationalism.

Andreas George Papandreou, 1919-1996, (Gk.) leftist politician, served 2 times as prem., (1981-89, 1993-96).

Georgios Papandreou, 1888-1968, (Gk.) Republican politician; served 3 times as prime min.

Franz von Papen, 1879-1969, (Ger.) politician; played major role in overthrow of Weimar Republic and rise of Hitler.

Charles Stewart Parnell, 1846-1891, (Ir.) nationalist leader; "uncrowned king of Ireland."

Lester Pearson, 1897-1972, (Can.) diplomat, Liberal party leader, prime min.

Robert Peel, 1788-1850, (Br.) reformist prime min., founder of Conservative party.

Eva (Evita) Perón, 1919-52 (Arg.) highly influential 2d wife of Juan Perón.

Juan Perón, 1895-1974, (Arg.) dynamic pres. of Argentina (1946-55 and 1973-74).

Joseph Pilsudski, 1867-1935, (Pol.) statesman; instrumental in reestablishing Polish state in the 20th cent.

Charles Pinckney, 1757-1824, (U.S.) founding father; his Pinckney plan was largely incorporated into constitution.

Christian Pineau, 1905-95, (Fr.) leader of French Resistance during WW2; French foreign minister, 1956-58.

William Pitt, the Elder, 1708-78, (Br.) statesman; the "Great Commoner," transformed Britain into imperial power.

William Pitt, the Younger, 1759-1806, (Br.) prime min. during French Revolutionary wars.

Georgi Plekhanov, 1857-1918, (Russ.) revolutionary, social philosopher; called "father of Russian Marxism."

Raymond Poincaré, 1860-1934, (Fr.) 9th pres. of the Republic; advocated harsh punishment of Germany after WW1.

Pol Pot, 1925-98, (Camb.) leader of Khmer Rouge; ruled Cambodia, 1975-79; responsible for mass deaths.

Georges Pompidou, 1911-74, (Fr.) Gaullist political leader; pres. 1969-74.

Grigori Potemkin, 1739-91, (Russ.) field marshal; favorite of Catherine II.

Lewis F. Powell Jr., 1907-98, (U.S.) Sup. Ct. Justice.

Yitzhak Rabin, 1922-95, (Isr.) military, political leader; prime min. of Israel, 1974-77, 1992-95; assassinated.

Edmund Randolph, 1753-1813, (U.S.) attorney; prominent in drafting, ratification of constitution.

John Randolph, 1773-1833, (U.S.) Southern planter; strong advocate of states' rights.

Jeannette Rankin, 1880-1973, (U.S.) pacifist; first woman member of U.S. Congress.

Walter Rathenau, 1867-1922, (Ger.) industrialist, statesman.

Sam Rayburn, 1882-1961, (U.S.) Democratic leader; representative for 47 years, House Speaker for 17.

Paul Reynaud, 1878-1966, (Fr.) statesman; prem. in 1940 at the time of France's defeat by Germany.

Syngman Rhee, 1875-1965, (Korean) first pres. of S Korea.

Cecil Rhodes, 1853-1902, (Br.) imperialist, industrial magnate; established Rhodes scholarships in his will.

Cardinal de Richelieu, 1585-1642, (Fr.) statesman, known as "red eminence;" chief minister to Louis XIII.

Maximilien Robespierre, 1758-94, (Fr.) leading figure in French Revolution and Reign of Terror.

Nelson Rockefeller, 1908-79, (U.S.) Republican governor of NY, 1959-73; U.S. vice pres., 1974-77.

George W. Romney, 1907-95, (U.S.) auto exec.; 3-term Republican governor of Michigan.

Eleanor Roosevelt, 1884-1962, (U.S.) influential First Lady, humanitarian, UN diplomat.

Elihu Root, 1845-1937, (U.S.) lawyer, statesman, diplomat; leading Republican supporter of the League of Nations.

Dean Rusk, 1909-95, (U.S.) statesman; sec. of state, 1961-69, during Vietnam War.

John Russell, 1792-1878, (Br.) Liberal prime min. during the Irish potato famine.

Anwar al-Sadat, 1918-81, (Egypt.) pres., 1970-1981, promoted peace with Israel; Nobel laureate; assassinated.

António de Salazar, 1889-1970, (Port.) longtime dictator.

José de San Martin, 1778-1850, S Amer. revolutionary; protector of Peru.

Eisaku Sato, 1901-75, (Jpn.) prime min.; presided over Japan's post-WW2 emergence as major world power.

Abdul Aziz Ibn Saud, c1880-1953, king of Saudi Arabi, 1932-53.

Philipp Scheidemann, 1865-1939, (Ger.) Social Democratic leader; first chancellor of the German republic.

Robert Schuman, 1886-1963, (Fr.) statesman; founded European Coal and Steel Community.

Carl Schurz, 1829-1906, (U.S.) German-American political leader, journalist, orator, dedicated reformer.

Kurt Schuschnigg, 1897-1977, (Austrian) chancellor; unsuccessful in stopping his country's annexation by Germany.

William H. Seward, 1801-72, (U.S.) anti-slavery activist; as U.S. sec. of state purchased Alaska.

Carlo Sforza, 1872-1952, (It.) foreign min., anti-fascist.

Sitting Bull, c1831-90, (Nat. Am.) Sioux leader in Battle of Little Bighorn over George A. Custer, 1876.

Alfred E. Smith, 1873-1944, (U.S.) New York Democratic governor; first Roman Catholic to run for presidency.

Margaret Chase Smith, 1897-1995, (U.S.) congresswoman, senator; 1st woman elected to both houses of Congress.

Jan C. Smuts, 1870-1950, (S. African) statesman, philosopher, soldier, prime min.

Paul Henri Spaak, 1899-1972, (Belg.) statesman, socialist leader.

Joseph Stalin, 1879-1953, (USSR) Soviet dictator, 1924-53; instituted forced collectivization, massive purges, and labor camps, causing millions of deaths.

Edwin M. Stanton, 1814-69, (U.S.) sec. of war, 1862-68, during the Civil War.

Edward R. Stettinius Jr., 1900-49, (U.S.) industrialist, sec. of state who coordinated aid to WW2 allies.

Adlai E. Stevenson, 1900-65, (U.S.) Democratic leader, diplomat, Illinois governor, presidential candidate.

Henry L. Stimson, 1867-1950, (U.S.) statesman; served in 5 administrations, foreign policy adviser in 30s and 40s.

Gustav Stresemann, 1878-1929, (Ger.) chancellor, foreign minister; strove to regain friendship for post-WW1 Germany.

Sukarno, 1901-70, (Indon.) dictatorial first pres. of the Indonesian republic.

Sun Yat-sen, 1866-1925, (Chin.) revolutionary; leader of Kuomintang, regarded as the father of modern China.

Robert A. Taft, 1889-1953, (U.S.) conservative Senate leader, called "Mr. Republican."

Charles de Talleyrand, 1754-1838, (Fr.) statesman, diplomat; the major force of the Congress of Vienna of 1814-15.

U Thant, 1909-74 (Bur.) statesman, UN sec.-general.

Norman M. Thomas, 1884-1968, (U.S.) social reformer; 6 times Socialist party presidential candidate.

Josip Broz Tito, 1892-1980, (Yug.) pres. of Yugoslavia from 1953, WW2 guerrilla chief, postwar rival of Stalin.

Palmiro Togliatti, 1893-1964, (It.) major leader of Italian Communist party.

Hideki Tojo, 1885-1948, (Jpn.) statesman, soldier; prime min. during most of WW2.

François Toussaint L'Ouverture, c1744-1803, (Haitian) patriot, martyr; thwarted French colonial aims.

Leon Trotsky, 1879-1940, (Russ.) revolutionary, founded Red Army, expelled from party in conflict with Stalin; assassinated.

Rafael L. Trujillo Molina, 1891-1961, (Dom.) dictator of Dominican Republic, 1930-61; assassinated.

Moise K. Tshombe, 1919-69, (Cong.) pres. of secessionist Katanga, prem. of Congo.

William M. Tweed, 1823-78, (U.S.) politician; absolute leader of Tammany Hall, NYC's Democratic political machine.

Walter Ulbricht, 1893-1973, (Ger.) Communist leader of German Democratic Republic.

Arthur H. Vandenberg, 1884-1951, (U.S.) senator; proponent of anti-Communist bipartisan foreign policy after WW2.

Eleutherios Venizelos, 1864-1936, (Gk.) most prominent Greek statesman in early 20th cent.; expanded territory.

Hendrik F. Verwoerd, 1901-66, (S. African) prime min.; rigorously applied apartheid policy despite protest.

George Wallace, 1919-98, (U.S.) former segregationist governor of Alabama and presid. candidate.

Robert Walpole, 1676-1745, (Br.) statesman; generally considered Britain's first prime min.

Daniel Webster, 1782-1852, (U.S.) orator, politician; advocate of business interests during Jacksonian agrarianism.

Chaim Weizmann, 1874-1952, (Russ.-Isr.) Zionist leader, scientist; first Israeli pres.

Wendell L. Willkie, 1892-1944, (U.S.) Republican who tried to unseat FDR when he ran for his 3d term.

Harold Wilson, 1916-95, (Br.) Labour party leader; prime min., 1964-70, 1974-76.

Emiliano Zapata, c1879-1919, (Mex.) revolutionary; major influence on modern Mexico.

Todor Zhivkov, 1911-98, (Bulg.) Communist ruler of Bulgaria from 1954 until ousted in a 1989 coup.

Zhou Enlai, 1898-1976, (Chin.) diplomat, prime min.; a leading figure of the Chinese Communist party.

Noted Scientists of the Past

Revised by Peter Barker, Prof. & Chair, Dept. of the Hist. of Science, Univ. of Oklahoma

For pre-modern scientists see also Philosophers and Religious Figures of the Past and Historical Figures chapter.

Albertus Magnus, c1200-1280, (Ger.) theologian, philosopher; helped found medieval study of natural science.

Alhazen (Ibn al-Haytham), c965-ca.1040, mathematician, astronomer; optical theorist.

Andre-Marie Ampère, 1775-1836, (Fr.) mathematician, chemist; founder of electrodynamics.

John V. Atanasoff, 1903-95, (U.S.) physicist; co-inventor of Atanasoff-Berry Computer (1939-41), regarded in law as the original "automatic electronic digital computer".

Amedeo Avogadro, 1776-1856, (It.) chemist, physicist; proposed that equal volumes of gas contain equal numbers of molecules, permitting determination of molecular weights.

John Bardeen, 1908-91, (U.S.) only double Nobel laureate in physics (transistor-1956, superconductivity-1972).

A. H. Becquerel, 1852-1908, (Fr.) physicist; discovered radioactivity in uranium (1896).

Alexander Graham Bell, 1847-1922, (U.S.) inventor; first to patent and commercially exploit the telephone (1876).

Daniel Bernoulli, 1700-82, (Swiss) mathematician; developed fluid dynamics and kinetic theory of gases.

Clifford Berry, 1918-1963, (U.S.) collaborated with Atanasoff on the ABC computer (1939-41).

Jöns Jakob Berzelius, 1779-1848, (Swed.) chemist; developed modern chemical symbols and formulas, discovered selenium and thorium.

Henry Bessemer, 1813-98, (Br.) engineer; invented Bessemer steel-making process.

Bruno Betteleheim, 1903-90, (Austrian-U.S.) psychoanalyst specializing in autistic and other disturbed children; *Uses of Enchantment* (1976).

Louis Blériot, 1872-1936, (Fr.) engineer; monoplane pioneer, first Channel flight (1909).

Franz Boas, 1858-1942, (Ger.-U.S.) founded modern anthropology; studied Pacific Coast tribes.

Niels Bohr, 1885-1962, (Dan.) atomic and nuclear physicist; founded quantum mechanics.

Max Born, 1882-1970, (Ger.) atomic and nuclear physicist; helped develop quantum mechanics.

Satyendranath Bose, 1894-1974, (In.) physicist; forerunner of modern quantum theory for integral-spin particles.

Louis de Broglie, 1892-1987, (Fr.) physicist; proposed quantum wave-particle duality.

Robert Bunsen, 1811-99, (Ger.) chemist; pioneered spectroscopic analysis, discovering rubidium and caesium.

Luther Burbank, 1849-1926, (U.S.) naturalist; developed plant breeding into a modern science.

Vannevar Bush, 1890-1974, (U.S.) electrical engineer; developed differential analyzer, an early analogue computer; directed WWII Office of Scientific Research and Development.

Marvin Camras, 1916-95, (U.S.) inventor, electrical engineer; invented magnetic tape recording.

Alexis Carrel, 1873-1944, (Fr.) surgeon, biologist; developed methods of suturing blood vessels and transplanting organs.

Rachel Carson, 1907-64, (U.S.) marine biologist, author; spurred concern for environment with *Silent Spring* (1962).

George Washington Carver, c1864-1943, (U.S.) agricultural scientist, nutritionist; improved and pioneered new uses for peanuts and sweet potatoes.

James Chadwick, 1891-1974, (Br.) physicist; discovered the neutron (1932); led British Manhattan Project group in U.S. (1943-45).

Daryl Chapin, 1906-95, (U.S.) physicist; with Calvin Fuller and Gerald Pearson of the solar energy cell (1954).

Albert Claude, 1898-1983, (Belg.-U.S.) a founder of modern cell biology; determined role of mitochondria.

Nicolaus Copernicus, 1473-1543, (Pol.) first modern astronomer to propose sun as center of the planets' motions.

Jacques Yves Cousteau, 1910-1997, (Fr.) oceanographer; co-inventor, with E. Gagnan, of the Aqualung (1943).

Seymour Cray, 1925-96, (U.S.) computer industry pioneer; developed supercomputers.

Marie, 1867-1934 (Pol.-Fr.) and **Pierre Curie**, 1859-1906, (Fr.) physical chemists; pioneer investigators of radioactivity, discovered radium and polonium (1898).

Gottlieb Daimler, 1834-1900, (Ger.) engineer, inventor; pioneer automobile manufacturer.

John Dalton, 1766-1844, (Br.) chemist, physicist; formulated atomic theory, made first table of atomic weights.

Charles Darwin, 1809-82, (Br.) naturalist; established theory of organic evolution; *Origin of Species* (1859).

Lee De Forest, 1873-1961, (U.S.) inventor of triode, pioneer in wireless telegraphy, sound pictures, television.

Max Delbruck, 1906-81, (Ger.-U.S.) founded molecular biology.

Rudolf Diesel, 1858-1913, (Ger.) mechanical engineer; patented Diesel engine (1892).

Theodosius Dobzhansky, 1900-75, (Russ.-U.S.) biologist; reconciled genetics and natural selection contributing to "modern synthesis" in evolution.

Christian Doppler, 1803-53, (Austrian) physicist; showed change in wave frequency caused by motion of source, now known as Doppler effect.

J. Presper Eckert Jr., 1919-95, (U.S.) co-inventor, with Mauchly, of the ENIAC computer (1943-45).

Thomas A. Edison, 1847-1931, (U.S.) inventor; held more than 1,000 patents, including incandescent electric lamp.

Paul Ehrlich, 1854-1915, (Ger.) medical researcher in immunology and bacteriology; pioneered antitoxin production.

Albert Einstein, 1879-1955, (Ger.-U.S.) theoretical physicist; founded relativity theory, replacing Newton's theories of space, time, and gravity. Proved E=mc2 (1905).

John F. Enders, 1897-1985, (U.S.) virologist, helped discover vaccines against polio, measles, mumps and chicken pox.

Erik Erikson, 1902-94, (U.S.) psychoanalyst, author; theory of developmental stages of life, *Childhood and Society* (1950).

Leonhard Euler, 1707-83, (Swiss) mathematician, physicist; pioneer of calculus, revived ideas of Fermat.

Gabriel Fahrenheit, 1686-1736, (Ger.) physicist; improved thermometers and introduced Fahrenheit temperature scale.

Michael Faraday, 1791-1867, (Br.) chemist, physicist; discovered electrical induction and invented dynamo (1831).

Philo T. Farnsworth, 1906-71, (U.S.) inventor; built first television system (San Francisco), 1928).

Pierre de Fermat, 1601-65, (Fr.) mathematician; founded modern theory of numbers.

Enrico Fermi, 1901-54, (It.-U.S.) nuclear physicist; demonstrated first controlled chain reaction (Chicago, 1942).

Richard Feynman, 1918-88, (U.S.) theoretical physicist, author; founder of Quantum Electrodynamics (QED).

Alexander Fleming, 1881-1955, (Br.) bacteriologist; discovered penicillin (1928).

Jean B. J. Fourier, 1768-1830, (fr.) introduced method of analysis in math and physics now known as Fourier Series.

Sigmund Freud, 1856-1939, (Austrian) psychiatrist; founder of psychoanalysis. *Interpretation of Dreams* (1901).

Galileo Galilei, 1564-1642, (It.) physicist; used telescope to vindicate Copernicus, founded modern science of motion.

Luigi Galvani, 1737-98, (It.) physiologist; studied electricity in living organisms.

Carl Friedrich Gauss, 1777-1855, (Ger.) math. physicist; completed program of Fermat and Euler in number theory.

Joseph Gay-Lussac, 1778-1850, (Fr.) chemist, physicist; investigated behavior of gases, law of combining volumes, discovered boron.

Josiah W. Gibbs, 1839-1903, (U.S.) theoretical physicist, chemist; founded chemical thermodynamics.

Robert H. Goddard, 1882-1945, (U.S.) physicist; invented liquid fuel rocket (1926).

George W. Goethals, 1858-1928, (U.S.) chief engineer who completed Panama Canal (1907-14).

William C. Gorgas, 1854-1920, (U.S.) physician; pioneer in prevention of yellow fever and malaria.

Ernest Haeckel, 1834-1919, (Ger.) zoologist, evolutionist; early Darwinist, introduced modern concept of "ecology."

Otto Hahn, 1879-1968, (Ger.) chemist; with Meitner discovered nuclear fission (1938).

Edmund Halley, 1656-1742, (Br.) astronomer; predicted return of 1682 comet ("Halley's Comet") in 1759.

William Harvey, 1578-1657, (Br.) physician, anatomist; discovered circulation of the blood (1628).

Werner Heisenberg, 1901-76, (Ger.) physicist; developed matrix mechanics and uncertainty principle (1927).

Hermann von Helmholtz, 1821-94, (Ger.) physicist, physiologist; formulated principle of conservation of energy.

William Herschel, 1738-1822, (Ger.-Br.) astronomer; discovered Uranus (1781).

Heinrich Hertz, 1857-94, (Ger.) physicist; discovered radio waves and photo-electric effect (1886-7).

David Hilbert, 1862-1943, (Ger.) mathematician; contributed to algebra, calculus and foundational studies (formalism).

Edwin P. Hubble, 1889-1953, (U.S.) astronomer; discovered observational evidence of expanding universe.

Alexander von Humboldt, 1769-1859, (Ger.) naturalist, author; explored S America, created ecology.

Edward Jenner, 1749-1823, (Br.) physician; pioneered vaccination, introduced term "virus."

James Joule, 1818-89, (Br.) physicist; found relation between heat and mechanical energy (conservation of energy).

Carl Jung, 1875-1961, (Swiss) psychiatrist; founder of analytical psychology.

Sister Elizabeth Kenny, 1886-1952, (Austral.) nurse; developed treatment for polio.
Johannes Kepler, 1571-1630, (Ger.) astronomer; discovered laws of planetary motion.
Al-Khawarizmi, early 9th cent., (Arab.), mathematician; regarded as founder of algebra.
Robert Koch, 1843-1910 (Ger.) bacteriologist; isolated bacterial causes of tuberculosis and other diseases.
Georges Köhler, 1946-95, (Ger.) immunologist; co-inventor, with Cesar Milstein, of monoclonal antibody technique.
Jacques Lacan, 1901-81, (Fr.) controversial influential psychoanalyst.
Joseph Lagrange, 1736-1813, (Fr.) geometer, astronomer; showed that gravity of earth and moon cancels creating stable points in space around them.
Jean B. Lamarck, 1744-1829, (Fr.) naturalist; forerunner of Darwin in evolutionary theory.
Pierre Simon de Laplace, 1749-1827, (Fr.) astronomer, physicist; proposed nebular origin for solar system.
Antoine Lavoisier, 1743-94, (Fr.) a founder of mod. chemistry.
Ernest O. Lawrence, 1901-58, (U.S.) physicist; invented the cyclotron.
Jerome Lejeune, 1927-94, (Fr.) geneticist; discovered chromosomal cause of Down syndrome (1959).
Louis 1903-72, and **Mary Leakey**, 1913-96, (Br.) early hominid paleoanthropologists; discovered remains in Africa.
Anton van Leeuwenhoek, 1632-1723, (Dutch) founder of microscopy.
Kurt Lewin, 1890-1947, (Ger.-U.S.) social psychologist; studied human motivation and group dynamics.
Justus von Liebig, 1803-73, (Ger.) founded quantitative organic chemistry.
Joseph Lister, 1827-1912, (Br.) physician; pioneered antiseptic surgery.
Konrad Lorenz, 1903-89, (Austrian) ethologist; pioneer in study of animal behavior.
Percival Lowell, 1855-1916, (U.S.) astronomer; predicted the existence of Pluto.
Louis, 1864-1948, and **Auguste Lumière**, 1862-1954, (Fr.) invented cinematograph and made first motion picture (1895).
Guglielmo Marconi, 1874-1937, (It.) physicist; developed wireless telegraphy.
John W. Mauchly, 1907-80, (U.S.) co-inventor, with Eckert, of computer ENIAC (1943-45).
James Clerk Maxwell, 1831-79, (Br.) physicist; unified electricity and magnetism; electromagnetic theory of light.
Maria Goeppert Mayer, 1906-72, (Ger.-U.S.) physicist; developed shell model of atomic nuclei.
Barbara McClintock, 1902-92, (U.S.) geneticist; showed that some genetic elements are mobile.
Lise Meitner, 1878-1968, (Austrian) co-discoverer, with Hahn, of nuclear fission (1938).
Gregor J. Mendel, 1822-84, (Austrian) botanist, monk; his experiments became the foundation of modern genetics.
Dmitri Mendeleyev, 1834-1907, (Russ.) chemist; established Periodic Table of the Elements.
Franz Mesmer, 1734-1815, (Ger.) physician; introduced hypnotherapy.
Albert A. Michelson, 1852-1931, (U.S.) physicist; invented interferometer.
Robert A. Millikan, 1868-1953, (U.S.) physicist; measured electronic charge.
Thomas Hunt Morgan, 1866-1945, (U.S.) geneticist, embryologist; established role of chromosomes in heredity.
Isaac Newton, 1642-1727, (Br.) natural philosopher; discovered law of gravitation, laws of motion; with G.W. Liebniz, founded calculus.
Robert N. Noyce, 1927-90, (U.S.) inventor of the microchip.
J. Robert Oppenheimer, 1904-67, (U.S.) physicist; scientific director of Manhattan project.
Wilhelm Ostwald, 1853-1932, (Ger.) chemist, philosopher; main founder of modern physical chemistry.
Louis Pasteur, 1822-95, (Fr.) chemist; showed that germs cause disease and fermentation, originated pasteurization.
Linus C. Pauling, 1901-94, (U.S.) chemist; studied chemical bonds; campaigned for nuclear disarmament.
Jean Piaget, 1896-1980, (Swiss) psychologist; four-stage theory of intellectual development in children.
Max Planck, 1858-1947, (Ger.) physicist; introduced quantum hypothesis (1900).
Roy J. Plunkett, 1910-94, (U.S.) chemist; created Teflon.
Walter S. Reed, 1851-1902, (U.S.) army physician; proved mosquitoes transmit yellow fever.
Bernhard Riemann, 1826-66, (Ger.) mathematician; developed non-Euclidean geometry used by Einstein.
Wilhelm Roentgen, 1845-1923, (Ger.) physicist; discovered X-rays (1895).
Carl Rogers, 1902-87, (U.S.) psychotherapist, author; originated nondirective therapy.
Ernest Rutherford, 1871-1937, (Br.) physicist; pioneer investigator of radioactivity, identified the atomic nucleus (1911).
Albert B. Sabin, 1906-93, (Russ.-U.S.), developed oral polio live-virus vaccine.
Carl Sagan, 1934-96, (U.S.) astronomer, author.
Jonas Salk, 1914-95, (U.S.) developed first successful polio vaccine, widely used in U.S. after 1955.
Giovanni Schiaparelli, 1835-1910, (It.) astronomer; reported canals on Mars.
Erwin Schrödinger, 1887-1961, (Austrian) physicist; developed wave equation for quantum systems.
Harlow Shapley, 1885-1972, (U.S.) astronomer; mapped galactic clusters and position of Sun in our own galaxy.
B(urrhus) F(rederick) Skinner, 1904-89, (U.S.) psychologist; leading advocate of behaviorism.
Roger W. Sperry, 1913-94, (U.S.) neuorobiologist; established different functions of right and left sides of brain.
Benjamin Spock, 1903-98, (U.S.) pediatrician, pre-eminent child care expert; *Common Sense Book of Baby and Child Care.*
Charles P. Steinmetz, 1865-1923, (Ger.-U.S.) electrical engineer; developed basic ideas on alternating current.
Leo Szilard, 1898-1964, (Hung.-U.S.) physicist; helped start Manhattan project, later opposed nuclear weapons.
Nikola Tesla, 1856-1943, (Serb.-U.S.) invented many electrical devices including a.c. dynamos, transformers and motors.
William Thomson (Lord Kelvin), 1824-1907, (Br.) physicist; instrumental in success of first transatlantic telegraph cable (1865); proposed Kelvin absolute temperature scale.
Alan Turing, 1912-54, (Br.) mathematician; helped develop basis for computers.
Rudolf Virchow, 1821-1902, (Ger.) pathologist; pioneered the modern theory that diseases affect the body through cells.
Alessandro Volta, 1745-1827, (It.) physicist; pioneer in electricity.
Werner von Braun, 1912-77, (Ger.-U.S.) developed rockets for warfare and space exploration.
John Von Neumann, 1903-57, (Hung.-U.S.) mathematician; originated game theory; basic design for modern computers.
Alfred Russell Wallace, 1823-1913, (Br.) naturalist; proposed concept of evolution independently of Darwin.
John B. Watson, 1878-1958, (U.S.) psychologist; a founder of behaviorism.
James E. Watt, 1736-1819, (Br.) mechanical engineer, inventor; invented modern steam engine (1765).
Alfred L. Wegener, 1880-1930, (Ger.) meteorologist, geophysicist; postulated continental drift.
Norbert Wiener, 1894-1964, (U.S.) mathematician; founder of cybernetics.
Sewall Wright, 1889-1988, (U.S.) evolutionary theorist; helped found population genetics.
Wilhelm Wundt, 1832-1920, (Ger.) founder of experimental psychology.
Ferdinand von Zeppelin, 1838-1917, (Ger.) soldier, aeronaut, airship designer.

Noted Social Reformers, Activists, and Humanitarians of the Past

Jane Addams, 1860-1935, (U.S.) cofounder of Hull House; won Nobel Peace Prize, 1931.
Susan B. Anthony, 1820-1906, (U.S.) a leader in temperance, anti-slavery, and woman suffrage movements.
Thomas Barnardo, 1845-1905, (Br.) social reformer; pioneered in care of destitute children.
Clara Barton, 1821-1912, (U.S.) organized Amer. Red Cross.
Henry Ward Beecher, 1813-87, (U.S.) clergyman, abolitionist.
Amelia Bloomer, 1818-94, (U.S.) suffragette, social reformer.
William Booth, 1829-1912, (Br.) founded Salvation Army.
John Brown, 1800-59, (U.S.) abolitionist who led murder of 5 pro-slavery men, was hanged.
Frances Xavier (Mother) Cabrini, 1850-1917, (It.-U.S.) Italian-born nun; founded charitable institutions; first American canonized as a saint, 1946.
Carrie Chapman Catt, 1859-1947, (U.S.) suffragette.
Cesar Chavez, 1927-93, (U.S.) labor leader; helped establish United Farm Workers of America.
Clarence Darrow, 1857-1938, (U.S.) lawyer; defender of "underdog," opponent of capital punishment.
Dorothy Day, 1897-1980, (U.S.) founder of Catholic Worker movement.
Eugene V. Debs, 1855-1926, (U.S.) labor leader; led Pullman strike, 1894; 4-time Socialist presidential candidate.
Dorothea Dix, 1802-87, (U.S.) crusader for the mentally ill.
Thomas Dooley, 1927-61, (U.S.) "jungle doctor," noted for efforts to supply medical aid to developing countries.
Marjory Stoneman Douglas, 1890-1998, (U.S.) writer and environmentalist; campaigned to save Florida Everglades.
William Lloyd Garrison, 1805-79, (U.S.) abolitionist.

Emma Goldman, 1869-1940, (Russ.-U.S.) published anarchist *Mother Earth,* birth-control advocate.
Samuel Gompers, 1850-1924, (U.S.) labor leader.
Michael Harrington, 1928-89, (U.S.) exposed poverty in affluent U.S. in *The Other America,* 1963.
Sidney Hillman, 1887-1946, (U.S.) labor leader; helped organize CIO.
Samuel G. Howe, 1801-76, (U.S.) social reformer; changed public attitudes toward the handicapped.
Helen Keller, 1880-1968, (U.S.) crusader for better treatment for the handicapped; deaf and blind herself.
Maggie Kuhn, 1905-95, (U.S.) founded Gray Panthers, 1970.
William Kunstler, 1919-95, (U.S.) civil liberties attorney.
John L. Lewis, 1880-1969, (U.S.) labor leader; headed United Mine Workers, 1920-60.
Karl Menninger, 1893-1990, (U.S.) with brother William founded Menninger Clinic and Menninger Foundation.
Lucretia Mott, 1793-1880, (U.S.) reformer, pioneer feminist.
Philip Murray, 1886-1952, (U.S.) Scottish-born labor leader.
Florence Nightingale, 1820-1910, (Br.) founder of modern nursing.
Emmeline Pankhurst, 1858-1928, (Br.) woman suffragist.
Walter Reuther, 1907-70, (U.S.) labor leader; headed UAW.
Jacob Riis, 1849-1914, (U.S.) crusader for urban reforms.
Margaret Sanger, 1883-1966, (U.S.) social reformer; pioneered the birth-control movement.
Earl of Shaftesbury (A. A. Cooper), 1801-85, (Br.) social reformer.
Elizabeth Cady Stanton, 1815-1902, (U.S.) woman suffrage pioneer.
Lucy Stone, 1818-93, (U.S.) feminist, abolitionist.
Mother Teresa of Calcutta, 1910-97, (Alban.) nun; founded order to care for sick and dying poor; won 1979 Nobel Peace Prize.
Philip Vera Cruz, 1905-94, (Filipino-U.S.) helped to found the United Farm Workers Union.
William Wilberforce, 1759-1833, (Br.) social reformer; prominent in struggle to abolish the slave trade.
Frances E. Willard, 1839-98, (U.S.) temperance, women's rights leader.
Mary Wollstonecraft, 1759-97, (Br.) wrote *Vindication of the Rights of Women.*

Notable Writers of the Present

Name (Birthplace)	Birthdate
Chinua Achebe (Ogidi, Nigeria)	11/16/30
Alice Adams (Fredericksburg, VA)	8/14/26
Edward Albee (Wash., DC)	3/12/28
Jorge Amado (Bahia, Brazil)	8/1/12
Martin Amis (Oxford, Eng.)	8/25/49
Maya Angelou (St. Louis, MO)	4/4/28
Oscar Arias Sanchez (Heredia, Costa Rica)	9/13/41
John Ashbery (Rochester, NY)	1927
Margaret Atwood (Ottawa, Ont.)	11/18/39
Louis Auchincloss (Lawrence, NY)	9/27/17
John Barth (Cambridge, MD)	5/27/30
Ann Beattie (Wash., DC)	9/7/47
Saul Bellow (Lachine, Que.)	7/10/15
Peter Benchley (NYC)	5/8/40
Thomas Berger (Cincinnati, OH)	7/20/24
Judy Blume (Elizabeth, NJ)	2/12/38
Ray Bradbury (Waukegan, IL)	8/22/20
Barbara Taylor Bradford (Leeds, Eng.)	5/10/33
Gwendolyn Brooks (Topeka, KS)	6/7/17
Hortense Calisher (NYC)	12/20/11
Tom Clancy (Baltimore, MD)	1947
Mary Higgins Clark (NYC)	12/24/31
Beverly Cleary (McMinnville, OR)	4/12/16
Evan S. Connell (Kansas City, MO)	8/17/24
Pat Conroy (Atlanta, GA)	10/26/45
Robin Cook (NYC)	5/4/40
Harry Crews (Alma, GA)	6/6/35
Michael Crichton (Chicago, IL)	10/23/42
Janet Dailey (Storm Lake, IA)	5/21/44
Joan Didion (Sacramento, CA)	12/5/34
E. L. Doctorow (NYC)	1/6/31
Takako Doi (Hyogo, Jap.)	11/30/28
Rita Dove (Akron, OH)	8/28/52
John Gregory Dunne (Hartford, CT)	5/25/32
James Ellroy (Los Angeles)	3/4/48
Louise Erdrich (Little Falls, MN)	7/6/54
Laura Esquivel (Mexico City, Mexico)	1950
Howard Fast (NYC)	11/11/14
Horton Foote (Wharton, TX)	3/14/16
Frederick Forsyth (Ashford, Eng.)	1938
Paula Fox (NYC)	4/22/23
Marilyn French (NYC)	11/21/29
Brian Friel (Omagh, Ire.)	11/9/29
Carlos Fuentes (Mexico City, Mex.)	11/11/28
William Gaddis (NYC)	1922
Gabriel Garcia Marquez (Aracata, Colombia)	3/6/28
Frank Gilroy (NYC)	10/13/25
Gail Godwin (Birmingham, AL)	6/18/37
William Goldman (Chicago, IL)	8/12/31
Nadine Gordimer (Springs, S. Africa)	11/20/23
Mary Gordon (Long Island, NY)	12/8/49
Sue Grafton (Louisville, KY)	4/24/40
Günter Grass (Danzig, Ger.)	10/16/27
Shirley Ann Grau (New Orleans, LA)	7/8/29
John Grisham (Jonesboro, AR)	2/8/55
John Guare (NYC)	2/5/38
Arthur Hailey (Luton, Eng.)	4/5/20
Robert Hass (San Francisco, CA)	1941
Vaclav Havel (Prague, Czech.)	10/5/36
Joseph Heller (Brooklyn, NY)	5/1/23
Mark Helprin (NYC)	6/28/47
S. E. Hinton (Tulsa, OK)	1948
Ted Hughes (Mytholmroyd, Eng.)	8/17/30
John Irving (Exeter, NH)	3/2/42
John Jakes (Chicago, IL)	3/31/32
P. D. James (Oxford, Eng.)	8/3/20
Erica Jong (NYC)	3/26/42
Garrison Keillor (Anoka, MN)	8/7/42
Thomas Keneally (Sydney, Austral.)	10/7/35
William Kennedy (Albany, NY)	1/16/28
Stephen King (Portland, ME)	9/21/47
Barbara Kingsolver (Annapolis, MD)	4/8/55
Maxine Hong Kingston (Stockton, CA)	10/27/40
Galway Kinnell (Providence, RI)	2/1/27
John Knowles (Fairmont, WV)	9/16/26
Kenneth Koch (Cincinnati, OH)	2/27/25
Dean Koontz (Everett, PA)	7/9/45
Judith Krantz (NYC)	1/9/28
Maxine Kumin (Philadelphia, PA)	6/6/25
John Le Carré (Poole, Eng.)	10/19/31
Ursula LeGuin (Berkeley, CA)	10/21/29
Madeleine L'Engle (NYC)	11/29/18
Elmore Leonard (New Orleans, LA)	10/11/25
Doris Lessing (Kermanshah, Persia)	10/22/19
Ira Levin (NYC)	8/27/29
Robert Ludlum (NYC)	5/25/27
Alison Lurie (Chicago, IL)	9/3/26
Nagib Mahfuz (Cairo, Egypt)	12/11/11
Norman Mailer (Long Branch, NJ)	1/31/23
David Mamet (Chicago, IL)	11/30/47
Bobbie Ann Mason (nr. Mayfield, KY)	5/1/40
Cormac McCarthy (Providence, RI)	7/20/33
Frank McCourt (Brooklyn, NY)	1930
Colleen McCullough (Wellington, N.S.W.)	6/1/37
Thomas McGuane (Wyandotte, MI)	12/11/39
Larry McMurtry (Wichita Falls, TX)	6/3/36
Arthur Miller (NYC)	10/17/15
Toni Morrison (Lorain, OH)	2/18/31
Walter Mosley (Los Angeles, CA)	1952
Alice Munro (Wingham, Ont.)	7/10/31
Iris Murdoch (Dublin, Ire.)	7/15/19
V. S. Naipaul (Port-of-Spain, Trin.)	8/17/32
Joyce Carol Oates (Lockport, NY)	6/16/38
Tim O'Brien (Austin, MN)	10/1/46
Cynthia Ozick (NYC)	4/17/28
Grace Paley (NYC)	12/11/22
Marge Piercy (Detroit, MI)	3/31/36
Robert Pinsky (Long Branch, NJ)	10/20/40
Harold Pinter (London, Eng.)	10/10/30
Chaim Potok (NYC)	2/17/29
Reynolds Price (Macon, NC)	2/1/33
E. Annie Proulx (Norwich, CT)	8/22/35
Mario Puzo (NYC)	10/15/20
Thomas Pynchon (Glen Cove, NY)	5/8/37
David Rabe (Dubuque, IA)	3/10/40
Ishmael Reed (Chattanooga, TN)	2/22/38
Ruth Rendell (England)	2/17/30
Anne Rice (New Orleans, LA)	10/14/41
Adrienne Rich (Baltimore, MD)	5/16/29
Philip Roth (Newark, NJ)	3/19/33
Salman Rushdie (Bombay, India)	6/19/47
J. D. Salinger (NYC)	1/1/19
Maurice Sendak (NYC)	6/10/28
Sidney Sheldon (Chicago, IL)	2/11/17
Sam Shepard (Ft. Sheridan, IL)	11/5/43
Carol Shields (Oak Park, IL)	6/2/35
Shel Silverstein (Chicago, IL)	1932
Neil Simon (NYC)	7/4/27
Jane Smiley (Los Angeles, CA)	9/26/49
Aleksandr Solzhenitsyn (Kislovodsk, Russia)	12/11/18
Susan Sontag (NYC)	1/28/33

Name (Birthplace)	Birthdate
Wole Soyinka (Abeokuta, Nigeria)	7/13/34
Mickey Spillane (Brooklyn, NY)	3/9/18
Danielle Steel (NYC)	8/14/47
Richard Stern (NYC)	2/25/28
Mary Stewart (Sunderland, Eng.)	9/17/16
Tom Stoppard (Zlin, Czech.)	7/13/37
William Styron (Newport News, VA)	6/11/25
Amy Tan (Oakland, CA)	2/19/52
Paul Theroux (Medford, MA)	4/10/41
Scott F. Turow (Chicago, IL)	4/12/49
Anne Tyler (Minneapolis, MN)	10/25/41
John Updike (Shillington, PA)	3/18/32
Leon Uris (Baltimore, MD)	8/3/24
Gore Vidal (West Point, NY)	10/3/25
Paula Vogel (Wash. DC)	11/16/51
Kurt Vonnegut Jr. (Indianapolis, IN)	11/11/22
Alice Walker (Eatonton, GA)	2/9/44
Robert James Waller (Rockford, IA)	8/1/39
Joseph Wambaugh (East Pittsburgh, PA)	1/22/37
Wendy Wasserstein (NYC)	10/10/50
Eudora Welty (Jackson, MS)	4/13/09
August Wilson (Pittsburgh, PA)	4/27/45
Lanford Wilson (Lebanon, MO)	4/13/37
Tom Wolfe (Richmond, VA)	3/2/31
Tobias Wolff (Birmingham, AL)	6/19/45
Herman Wouk (NYC)	5/27/15

Poets Laureate

There is no record of the origin of the office of Poet Laureate of England. Henry III (1216-72) reportedly had a Versificator Regis, or King's Poet, paid 100 shillings a year. Other poets said to have filled the role include Geoffrey Chaucer (d 1400), Edmund Spenser (d 1599), Ben Jonson (d 1637), and Sir William d'Avenant (d 1668).

The first official English poet laureate was John Dryden, appointed 1668, for life (as is customary). Thomas Shadwell was named in 1689; Nahum Tate, 1692; Nicholas Rowe, 1715; Rev. Laurence Eusden, 1718; Colley Cibber, 1730; William Whitehead, 1757; Rev. Thomas Warton, 1785; Henry James Pye, 1790; Robert Southey, 1813; William Wordsworth, 1843; Alfred, Lord Tennyson, 1850; Alfred Austin, 1896; Robert Bridges, 1913; John Masefield, 1930; C. Day Lewis, 1968; Sir John Betjeman, 1972; Ted Hughes, 1984.

In the U.S., the appointment is made by the Librarian of Congress and is not for life. Robert Penn Warren was the first, in 1986, followed by Richard Wilbur, 1987, Howard Nemerov, 1988; Mark Strand, 1990; Joseph Brodsky, 1991; Mona Van Duyn, 1992; Rita Dove, 1993; Robert Hass, 1995; Robert Pinsky, 1997.

Noted Writers of the Past

See also Greeks and Romans in Historical Figures chapter; Journalists.

James Agee, 1909-55, (U.S.) novelist. *A Death in the Family.*
Conrad Aiken, 1889-1973, (U.S.) poet, critic. *Ushant.*
Louisa May Alcott, 1832-88, (U.S.) novelist. *Little Women.*
Sholom Aleichem, 1859-1916, (Russ.) Yiddish writer. *Tevye's Daughter, Adventures of Mottel, The Old Country.*
Vicente Aleixandre, 1898-1984, (Sp.) poet. *La destrucción o el amor, Dialogolos del conocimiento.*
Horatio Alger, 1832-1899, (U.S.) "rags-to-riches" books.
Kingsley Amis, 1922-95, (Br.) novelist, critic. *Lucky Jim.*
Hans Christian Andersen, 1805-75, (Dan.) author of fairy tales. *The Princess and the Pea, The Ugly Duckling.*
Maxwell Anderson, 1888-1959, (U.S.) playwright. *What Price Glory?, High Tor, Winterset, Key Largo.*
Sherwood Anderson, 1876-1941, (U.S.) short-story writer. "Death in the Woods"; *Winesburg, Ohio* (collection).
Matthew Arnold, 1822-88, (Br.) poet, critic. "Thrysis," "Dover Beach," "The Gypsy Scholar," "Culture and Anarchy."
Isaac Asimov, 1920-92, (U.S.) science-fiction writer. *I Robot.*
W(ystan) H(ugh) Auden, 1907-73, (Br.) poet, playwright, literary critic. "The Age of Anxiety."
Jane Austen, 1775-1817, (Br.) novelist. *Pride and Prejudice, Sense and Sensibility, Emma, Mansfield Park.*
Isaac Babel, 1894-1941, (Russ.) short-story writer, playwright. *Odessa Tales, Red Cavalry.*
James Baldwin, 1924-87, author, playwright. *The Fire Next Time, Blues for Mister Charlie, Just Above My Head.*
Honoré de Balzac, 1799-1850, (Fr.) novelist. *Le Père Goriot, Cousine Bette, Eugénie Grandet.*
James M. Barrie, 1860-1937, (Br.) playwright, novelist. *Peter Pan, Dear Brutus, What Every Woman Knows.*
Charles Baudelaire, 1821-67, (Fr.) poet. *Les Fleurs du Mal.*
L(yman) Frank Baum, 1856-1919, (U.S.) writer. *Wizard of Oz* series.
Simone de Beauvoir, 1908-86, (Fr.) novelist, essayist. *The Second Sex, Memoirs of a Dutiful Daughter.*
Samuel Beckett, 1906-89, (Ir.) novelist, playwright. *Waiting for Godot, Endgame* (plays); *Murphy, Watt, Molloy* (novels).
Brendan Behan, 1923-64, (Ir.) playwright. *The Quare Fellow, The Hostage, Borstal Boy.*
Robert Benchley, 1889-1945, (U.S.) humorist.
Stephen Vincent Benét, 1898-1943, (U.S.) poet, novelist. *John Brown's Body.*
John Berryman, 1914-72, (U.S.) poet. *Homage to Mistress Bradstreet.*
Ambrose Bierce, 1842-1914, (U.S.) short-story writer, journalist. *In the Midst of Life, The Devil's Dictionary.*
Elizabeth Bishop, 1911-79, (U.S.) poet. *North and South—A Cold Spring.*
William Blake, 1757-1827, (Br.) poet, artist. *Songs of Innocence, Songs of Experience, The Marriage of Heaven and Hell.*
Giovanni Boccaccio, 1313-75, (It.) poet. *Decameron.*
Heinrich Böll, 1917-85, (Ger.) novelist, short-story writer. *Group Portrait With Lady.*
Jorge Luis Borges, 1900-86, (Arg.) short-story writer, poet, essayist. *Labyrinths.*
James Boswell, 1740-95, (Sc.) biographer. *The Life of Samuel Johnson.*
Pierre Boulle, (1913-94), (Fr.) novelist. *The Bridge Over the River Kwai, Planet of the Apes.*
Anne Bradstreet, c1612-72, (U.S.) poet. *The Tenth Muse Lately Sprung Up in America.*
Bertolt Brecht, 1898-1956, (Ger.) dramatist, poet. *The Threepenny Opera, Mother Courage and Her Children.*
Charlotte Brontë, 1816-55, (Br.) novelist. *Jane Eyre.*
Emily Brontë, 1818-48, (Br.) novelist. *Wuthering Heights.*
Elizabeth Barrett Browning, 1806-61, (Br.) poet. *Sonnets From the Portuguese, Aurora Leigh.*
Joseph Brodsky, 1940-96, (Russ.-U.S.) poet. *A Part of Speech, Less Than One, To Urania.*
Robert Browning, 1812-89, (Br.) poet. "My Last Duchess," "Fra Lippo Lippi," *The Ring and The Book.*
Pearl S. Buck, 1892-1973, (U.S.) novelist. *The Good Earth.*
Mikhail Bulgakov, 1891-1940, (Russ.) novelist, playwright. *The Heart of a Dog, The Master and Margarita.*
John Bunyan, 1628-88, (Br.) writer. *Pilgrim's Progress.*
Anthony Burgess, 1917-93, (Br.) author. *A Clockwork Orange.*
Frances Hodgson Burnett, 1849-1924, (Br.-U.S.) novelist. *The Secret Garden.*
Robert Burns, 1759-96, (Sc.) poet. "Flow Gently, Sweet Afton," "My Heart's in the Highlands," "Auld Lang Syne."
Edgar Rice Burroughs, 1875-1950, (U.S.) novelist. *Tarzan of the Apes.*
William S. Burroughs, 1914-97, (U.S.) novelist. *Naked Lunch.*
George Gordon, Lord Byron, 1788-1824, (Br.) poet. *Don Juan, Childe Harold, Manfred, Cain.*
Italo Calvino, 1923-85, (It.) novelist, short-story writer. *If on a Winter's Night a Traveler.*
Albert Camus, 1913-60, (Fr.) writer. *The Stranger, The Fall.*
Karel Capek, 1890-1938, (Czech.) playwright, novelist, essayist. *R.U.R. (Rossum's Universal Robots).*
Truman Capote, 1924-84, (U.S.) author. *Other Voices, Other Rooms, Breakfast at Tiffany's, In Cold Blood.*
Lewis Carroll (Charles Dodgson), 1832-98, (Br.) writer, mathematician. *Alice's Adventures in Wonderland.*
Giacomo Casanova, 1725-98, (It.) adventurer, memoirist.
Willa Cather, 1873-1947, (U.S.) novelist. *O Pioneers!, My Ántonia, Death Comes for the Archbishop.*
Miguel de Cervantes Saavedra, 1547-1616, (Sp.) novelist, dramatist, poet. *Don Quixote.*
Raymond Chandler, 1888-1959, (U.S.) writer of detective fiction. Philip Marlowe series.
Geoffrey Chaucer, c1340-1400, (Br.) poet. *The Canterbury Tales, Troilus and Criseyde.*
John Cheever, 1912-82, (U.S.) novelist, short-story writer. *The Wapshot Scandal,* "The Country Husband."
Anton Chekhov, 1860-1904, (Russ.) short-story writer, dramatist. *Uncle Vanya, The Cherry Orchard, The Three Sisters.*
G(ilbert) K(eith) Chesterton, 1874-1936, (Br.) critic, novelist, relig. apologist. Father Brown series of mysteries.
Kate Chopin, 1851-1904, (U.S.) writer. *The Awakening.*
Agatha Christie, 1890-1976, (Br.) mystery writer; created Miss Marple, Hercule Poirot; *And Then There Were None, Murder on the Orient Express, Murder of Roger Ackroyd.*
James Clavell, 1925-94, (Br.-U.S.) novelist. *Shogun, King Rat.*
Jean Cocteau, 1889-1963, (Fr.) writer, visual artist, filmmaker. *The Beauty and the Beast, Les Enfants Terribles.*
Samuel Taylor Coleridge, 1772-1834, (Br.) poet, critic. "Kubla Khan," "The Rime of the Ancient Mariner."

(Sidonie) Colette, 1873-1954, (Fr.) novelist. *Claudine, Gigi.*
Wilkie Collins, 1824-89, (Br.) Novelist. *The Moonstone.*
Joseph Conrad, 1857-1924, (Br.) novelist. *Lord Jim, Heart of Darkness, The Nigger of the Narcissus, Nostromo.*
James Fenimore Cooper, 1789-1851, (U.S.) novelist. *Leatherstocking Tales, The Last of the Mohicans.*
Pierre Corneille, 1606-84, (Fr.) dramatist. *Medeé, Le Cid.*
Hart Crane, 1899-1932, (U.S.) poet. "The Bridge."
Stephen Crane, 1871-1900, (U.S.) novelist, short-story writer. *The Red Badge of Courage,* "The Open Boat."
E. E. Cummings, 1894-1962, (U.S.) poet. *Tulips and Chimneys.*
Roald Dahl, 1916-90, (Br.-U.S.) writer. *Charlie and the Chocolate Factory, James and the Giant Peach.*
Gabriele D'Annunzio, 1863-1938, (It.) poet, novelist, dramatist. *The Child of Pleasure, The Intruder, The Victim.*
Dante Alighieri, 1265-1321, (It.) poet. *The Divine Comedy.*
Robertson Davies, 1913-95, (Can.) novelist, playwright, essayist. Salterton Trilogy, Deptford Trilogy, Cornish Trilogy.
Daniel Defoe, 1660-1731, (Br.) writer. *Robinson Crusoe, Moll Flanders, Journal of the Plague Year.*
Peter De Vries, 1910-93, (U.S.) journalist, writer. *The Tunnel of Love, Let Me Count the Ways.*
Charles Dickens, 1812-70, (Br.) novelist. *David Copperfield, Oliver Twist, Great Expectations, A Tale of Two Cities.*
James Dickey, 1923-1997, (U.S.) poet, novelist. *Deliverance.*
Emily Dickinson, 1830-86, (U.S.) lyric poet. "Because I could not stop for Death . . .", "Success is counted sweetest . . ."
Isak Dinesen (Karen Blixen), 1885-1962, (Dan.) author. *Out of Africa, Seven Gothic Tales, Winter's Tales.*
John Donne, 1573-1631, (Br.) poet, divine. *Songs and Sonnets.*
José Donoso, 1924-96, (Chil.) surreal novelist and short-story writer. *The Obscene Bird of Night.*
John Dos Passos, 1896-1970, (U.S.) novelist. *U.S.A.*
Fyodor Dostoyevsky, 1821-81, (Russ.) novelist. *Crime and Punishment, The Brothers Karamazov, The Possessed.*
Arthur Conan Doyle, 1859-1930, (Br.) novelist. Sherlock Holmes mystery stories.
Theodore Dreiser, 1871-1945, (U.S.) novelist. *An American Tragedy, Sister Carrie.*
John Dryden, 1631-1700, (Br.) poet, dramatist, critic. *All for Love, Mac Flecknoe, Absalom and Achitophel.*
Alexandre Dumas, 1802-70, (Fr.) novelist, dramatist. *The Three Musketeers, The Count of Monte Cristo.*
Alexandre Dumas (fils), 1824-95, (Fr.) dramatist, novelist. *La Dame aux Camélias, Le Demi-Monde.*
Ilya G. Ehrenburg, 1891-1967, (Russ.) writer. *The Thaw.*
George Eliot (Mary Ann Evans or Marian Evans), 1819-80, (Br.) novelist. *Silas Marner, Middlemarch.*
T(homas) S(tearns) Eliot, 1888-1965, (Br.) poet, critic. *The Waste Land,* "The Love Song of J. Alfred Prufrock."
Stanley Elkin, 1930-95, (U.S.) novelist, short story writer. *A Modern Comedy, George Mills, Searches and Seizures.*
Ralph Ellison, 1914-94, (U.S.), writer. *Invisible Man.*
Ralph Waldo Emerson, 1803-82, (U.S.) poet, essayist. "Brahma," "Nature," "The Over-Soul," "Self-Reliance."
James T. Farrell, 1904-79, (U.S.) novelist. *Studs Lonigan.*
William Faulkner, 1897-1962, (U.S.) novelist. *Sanctuary, Light in August, The Sound and the Fury, Absalom, Absalom!*
Edna Ferber, 1887-1968, (U.S.) novelist, short-story writer, playwright. *So Big, Cimarron, Show Boat.*
Henry Fielding, 1707-54, (Br.) novelist. *Tom Jones.*
F(rancis) Scott Fitzgerald, 1896-1940, (U.S.) short-story writer, novelist. *The Great Gatsby, Tender Is the Night.*
Gustave Flaubert, 1821-80, (Fr.) novelist. *Madame Bovary.*
Ian Fleming, 1908-64, (Br.) novelist; James Bond spy thrillers.
Ford Madox Ford, 1873-1939, (Br.) novelist, critic, poet. *The Good Soldier.*
C(ecil) S(cott) Forester, 1899-1966, (Br.) writer. Horatio Hornblower books.
E(dward) M(organ) Forster, 1879-1970, (Br.) novelist. *A Passage to India, Howards End.*
Anatole France, 1844-1924, (Fr.) writer. *Penguin Island, My Friend's Book, The Crime of Sylvestre Bonnard.*
Robert Frost, 1874-1963, (U.S.) poet. "Birches," "Fire and Ice," "Stopping by Woods on a Snowy Evening."
John Galsworthy, 1867-1933, (Br.) novelist, dramatist. *The Forsyte Saga.*
Erle Stanley Gardner, 1889-1970, (U.S.) mystery writer; created Perry Mason.
Jean Genet, 1911-86, (Fr.) playwright, novelist. *The Maids.*
Kahlil Gibran, 1883-1931, (Lebanese-U.S.) mystical novelist, essayist, poet. *The Prophet.*
André Gide, 1869-1951, (Fr.) writer. *The Immoralist, The Pastoral Symphony, Strait Is the Gate.*
Allen Ginsberg, 1926-1997, (U.S.) Beat poet. "Howl," "Kaddish," "The Fall of America: Poems of These States."
Jean Giraudoux, 1882-1944, (Fr.) novelist, dramatist. *Electra, The Madwoman of Chaillot, Ondine, Tiger at the Gate.*
Johann Wolfgang von Goethe, 1749-1832, (Ger.) poet, dramatist, novelist. *Faust, Sorrows of Young Werther.*
Nikolai Gogol, 1809-52, (Russ.) short-story writer, dramatist, novelist. *Dead Souls, The Inspector General.*
William Golding, 1911-93, (Br.) novelist. *Lord of the Flies.*
Oliver Goldsmith, 1728-74, (Br.-Ir.) dramatist, novelist. *The Vicar of Wakefield, She Stoops to Conquer.*
Maxim Gorky, 1868-1936, (Russ.) dramatist, novelist. *The Lower Depths.*
Robert Graves, 1895-1985, (Br.) poet, classical scholar, novelist. *I, Claudius; The White Goddess.*
Thomas Gray, 1716-71, (Br.) poet. "Elegy Written in a Country Churchyard," "The Progress of Poesy."
Julien Green, 1900-98, (U.S.-Fr.) expatriate American, became major French novelist. *Moira, Each Man in His Darkness.*
Graham Greene, 1904-91, (Br.) novelist. *The Power and the Glory, The Heart of the Matter, The Ministry of Fear.*
Zane Grey, 1872-1939, (U.S.) writer of western stories.
Jakob Grimm, 1785-1863, (Ger.) philologist, folklorist; with brother **Wilhelm,** 1786-1859, collected *Grimm's Fairy Tales.*
Alex Haley, 1921-92, (U.S.) author. *Roots.*
Dashiell Hammett, 1894-1961, (U.S.) detective-story writer; created Sam Spade. *The Maltese Falcon, The Thin Man.*
Knute Hamsun, 1859-1952 (Nor.) novelist. *Hunger.*
Thomas Hardy, 1840-1928, (Br.) novelist, poet. *The Return of the Native, Tess of the D'Urbervilles, Jude the Obscure.*
Joel Chandler Harris, 1848-1908, (U.S.) short-story writer. Uncle Remus series.
Moss Hart, 1904-61, (U.S.) playwright. *Once in a Lifetime, You Can't Take It With You, The Man Who Came to Dinner.*
Bret Harte, 1836-1902, (U.S.) short-story writer, poet. *The Luck of Roaring Camp.*
Jaroslav Hasek, 1883-1923, (Czech.) writer, playwright. *The Good Soldier Schweik.*
John Hawkes, 1925-98, (U.S.) experimental fiction writer. *The Goose on the Grave, Blood Oranges.*
Nathaniel Hawthorne, 1804-64, (U.S.) novelist, short-story writer. *The Scarlet Letter,* "Young Goodman Brown."
Heinrich Heine, 1797-1856, (Ger.) poet. *Book of Songs.*
Lillian Hellman, 1905-84, (U.S.) playwright, author of memoirs. *The Little Foxes, An Unfinished Woman, Pentimento.*
Ernest Hemingway, 1899-1961, (U.S.) novelist, short-story writer. *A Farewell to Arms, For Whom the Bell Tolls.*
O. Henry (W. S. Porter), 1862-1910, (U.S.) short-story writer. "The Gift of the Magi."
George Herbert, 1593-1633, (Br.) poet. "The Altar," "Easter Wings."
Zbigniew Herbert, 1924-98, (Pol.) poet. "Apollo and Marsyas."
Robert Herrick, 1591-1674, (Br.) poet. "To the Virgins to Make Much of Time."
James Herriot (James Alfred Wight), 1916-95, (Br.) novelist, veterinarian. *All Creatures Great and Small.*
John Hersey, 1914-93, (U.S.) novelist, journalist. *Hiroshima, A Bell for Adano.*
Hermann Hesse, 1877-1962, (Ger.) novelist, poet. *Death and the Lover, Steppenwolf, Siddhartha.*
James Hilton, 1900-54, (Br.) novelist. *Lost Horizon.*
Oliver Wendell Holmes, 1809-94, (U.S.) poet, novelist. *The Autocrat of the Breakfast-Table.*
Gerard Manley Hopkins, 1844-89, (Br.) poet. "Pied Beauty."
A(lfred) E. Housman, 1859-1936, (Br.) poet. *A Shropshire Lad.*
William Dean Howells, 1837-1920, (U.S.) novelist, critic. *The Rise of Silas Lapham.*
Langston Hughes, 1902-67, (U.S.) poet, playwright. *The Weary Blues, One-Way Ticket, Shakespeare in Harlem.*
Victor Hugo, 1802-85, (Fr.) poet, dramatist, novelist. *Notre Dame de Paris, Les Misérables.*
Zora Neale Hurston, 1903-60, (U.S.) novelist, folklorist. *Their Eyes Were Watching God, Mules and Men.*
Aldous Huxley, 1894-1963, (Br.) writer. *Brave New World.*
Henrik Ibsen, 1828-1906, (Nor.) dramatist, poet. *A Doll's House, Ghosts, The Wild Duck, Hedda Gabler.*
William Inge, 1913-73, (U.S.) playwright. *Picnic; Come Back, Little Sheba; Bus Stop.*
Eugene Ionesco, 1910-94, (Fr.) surrealist dramatist. *The Bald Soprano, The Chairs.*
Washington Irving, 1783-1859, (U.S.) writer. "Rip Van Winkle," "The Legend of Sleepy Hollow."
Christopher Isherwood, 1904-1986, (Br.) novelist, playwright. *The Berlin Stories.*
Shirley Jackson, 1919-65, (U.S.) writer. "The Lottery."
Henry James, 1843-1916, (U.S.) novelist, short-story writer, critic. *The Portrait of a Lady, The Ambassadors, Daisy Miller.*
Robinson Jeffers, 1887-1962, (U.S.) poet, dramatist. *Tamar and Other Poems, Medea.*
Samuel Johnson, 1709-84, (Br.) author, scholar, critic. *Dictionary of the English Language, Vanity of Human Wishes.*
Ben Jonson, 1572-1637, (Br.) dramatist, poet. *Volpone.*

James Joyce, 1882-1941, (Ir.) writer. *Ulysses, Dubliners, A Portrait of the Artist as a Young Man, Finnegans Wake.*
Ernst Junger, 1895-1998, (Ger.) novelist, essayist. *The Peace, On the Marble Cliff.*
Franz Kafka, 1883-1924, (Ger.) novelist, short-story writer. *The Trial, Amerika, The Castle, The Metamorphosis.*
George S. Kaufman, 1889-1961, (U.S.) playwright. *The Man Who Came to Dinner, You Can't Take It With You, Stage Door.*
Nikos Kazantzakis, 1883-1957, (Gk.) novelist. *Zorba the Greek, A Greek Passion.*
Alfred Kazin, 1915-98 (U.S.) author, critic, teacher. *On Native Grounds.*
John Keats, 1795-1821, (Br.) poet. "Ode on a Grecian Urn," "Ode to a Nightingale," "La Belle Dame Sans Merci."
Jack Kerouac, 1922-1969, (U.S.), author, Beat poet. *On the Road, The Dharma Bums,* "Mexico City Blues."
Joyce Kilmer, 1886-1918, (U.S.) poet. "Trees."
Rudyard Kipling, 1865-1936, (Br.) author, poet. "The White Man's Burden," "Gunga Din," *The Jungle Book.*
Jean de la Fontaine, 1621-95, (Fr.) poet. *Fables choisies.*
Pär Lagerkvist, 1891-1974, (Swed.) poet, dramatist, novelist. *Barabbas, The Sybil.*
Selma Lagerlöf, 1858-1940, (Swed.) novelist. *Jerusalem, The Ring of the Lowenskolds.*
Alphonse de Lamartine, 1790-1869, (Fr.) poet, novelist, statesman. *Méditations poétiques.*
Charles Lamb, 1775-1834, (Br.) essayist. *Specimens of English Dramatic Poets, Essays of Elia.*
Giuseppe di Lampedusa, 1896-1957, (It.) novelist. *The Leopard.*
William Langland, c1332-1400, (Eng.) poet. *Piers Plowman.*
Ring Lardner, 1885-1933, (U.S.) short-story writer, humorist.
Louis L'Amour, 1908-88, (U.S.) western author, screenwriter. *Hondo, The Cherokee Trail.*
D(avid) H(erbert) Lawrence, 1885-1930, (Br.) novelist. *Sons and Lovers, Women in Love, Lady Chatterley's Lover.*
Halldor Laxness, 1902-98, (Icelandic) novelist. *Iceland's Bell.*
Mikhail Lermontov, 1814-41, (Russ.) novelist, poet. "Demon," *Hero of Our Time.*
Alain-René Lesage, 1668-1747, (Fr.) novelist. *Gil Blas de Santillane.*
Gotthold Lessing, 1729-81, (Ger.) dramatist, philosopher, critic. *Miss Sara Sampson, Minna von Barnhelm.*
C(live) S(taples) Lewis, 1898-1963, (Br.) critic, novelist, religious writer. *Allegory of Love; The Lion, the Witch and the Wardrobe, Out of the Silent Planet.*
Sinclair Lewis, 1885-1951, (U.S.) novelist. *Babbitt, Main Street, Arrowsmith, Dodsworth.*
Vachel Lindsay, 1879-1931, (U.S.) poet. *General William Booth Enters Into Heaven, The Congo.*
Hugh Lofting, 1886-1947, (Br.) writer. Dr. Doolittle series.
Jack London, 1876-1916, (U.S.) novelist, journalist. *Call of the Wild, The Sea-Wolf, White Fang.*
Henry Wadsworth Longfellow, 1807-82, (U.S.) poet. *Evangeline, The Song of Hiawatha.*
Amy Lowell, 1874-1925, (U.S.) poet, critic. "Lilacs."
James Russell Lowell, 1819-91, (U.S.) poet, editor. *Poems, The Biglow Papers.*
Robert Lowell, 1917-77, (U.S.) poet. "Lord Weary's Castle."
Archibald MacLeish, 1892-1982, (U.S.) poet. *Conquistador.*
Bernard Malamud, 1914-86, (U.S.) short-story writer, novelist. "The Magic Barrel," *The Assistant, The Fixer.*
Stéphane Mallarmé, 1842-98, (Fr.) poet. *Poésies.*
Sir Thomas Malory, ?-1471, (Br.) writer. *Morte d'Arthur.*
Andre Malraux, 1901-76, (Fr.) novelist. *Man's Fate.*
Osip Mandelstam, 1891-1938, (Russ.) poet. *Stone, Tristia.*
Thomas Mann, 1875-1955, (Ger.) novelist, essayist. *Buddenbrooks, The Magic Mountain,* "Death in Venice."
Katherine Mansfield, 1888-1923, (Br.) short-story writer. "Bliss."
Christopher Marlowe, 1564-93, (Br.) dramatist, poet. *Tamburlaine the Great,* Dr. *Faustus, The Jew of Malta.*
Andrew Marvell, 1621-78, (Br.) poet. "To His Coy Mistress."
John Masefield, 1878-1967, (Br.) poet. "Sea Fever," "Cargoes," *Salt Water Ballads.*
Edgar Lee Masters, 1869-1950, (U.S.) poet, biographer. *Spoon River Anthology.*
W(illiam) Somerset Maugham, 1874-1965, (Br.) author. *Of Human* Bondage, *The Moon and Sixpence.*
Guy de Maupassant, 1850-93, (Fr.) novelist, short-story writer. "A Life," "Bel-Ami," "The Necklace."
François Mauriac, 1885-1970, (Fr.) novelist, dramatist. *Viper's Tangle, The Kiss to the Leper.*
Vladimir Mayakovsky, 1893-1930, (Russ.) poet, dramatist. *The Cloud in Trousers.*
Mary McCarthy, 1912-89, (U.S.) critic, novelist, memoirist. *Memories of a Catholic Girlhood.*
Carson McCullers, 1917-67, (U.S.) novelist. *The Heart Is a Lonely Hunter, Member of the Wedding.*
Herman Melville, 1819-91, (U.S.) novelist, poet. *Moby-Dick, Typee, Billy Budd, Omoo.*
George Meredith, 1828-1909, (Br.) novelist, poet. *The Ordeal of Richard Feverel, The Egoist.*
Prosper Mérimée, 1803-70, (Fr.) author. *Carmen.*
James Merrill, 1926-95, (U.S.) poet. *Divine Comedies.*
James Michener, 1907-97, (U.S.) novelist. *Tales of the South Pacific.*
Edna St. Vincent Millay, 1892-1950, (U.S.) poet. *The Harp Weaver and Other Poems, A Few Figs From Thistles.*
Henry Miller, 1891-1980, (U.S.) erotic novelist. *Tropic of Cancer.*
A(lan) A(lexander) Milne, 1882-1956, (Br.) author. *Winnie-the-Pooh.*
John Milton, 1608-74, (Br.) poet, writer. *Paradise Lost, Comus, Lycidas, Areopagitica.*
Mishima Yukio (Hiraoka Kimitake), 1925-70, (Jpn.) writer. *Confessions of a Mask.*
Gabriela Mistral, 1889-1957, (Chil.) poet. *Sonnets of Death.*
Margaret Mitchell, 1900-49, (U.S.) novelist. *Gone With the Wind.*
Jean Baptiste Molière, 1622-73, (Fr.) dramatist. *Le Tartuffe, Le Misanthrope, Le Bourgeois Gentilhomme.*
Ferenc Molnár, 1878-1952, (Hung.) dramatist, novelist. *Liliom, The Guardsman, The Swan.*
Michel de Montaigne, 1533-92, (Fr.) essayist. *Essais.*
Eugenio Montale, 1896-1981, (It.) poet.
Clement C. Moore, 1779-1863, (U.S.) poet, educator. "A Visit From Saint Nicholas."
Marianne Moore, 1887-1972, (U.S.) poet.
Alberto Moravia, 1907-90, (It.) novelist, short-story writer. *The Time of Indifference.*
Sir Thomas More, 1478-1535, (Br.) writer, statesman, saint. *Utopia.*
Wright Morris, 1910-98 (U.S.) novelist. *My Uncle Dudley.*
Murasaki Shikibu, c978-1026, (Jpn.) novelist. *The Tale of Genji.*
Alfred de Musset, 1810-57, (Fr.) poet, dramatist. *La Confession d'un Enfant du Siècle.*
Vladimir Nabokov, 1899-1977, (Russ.-U.S.) novelist. *Lolita.*
Ogden Nash, 1902-71, (U.S.) poet of light verse.
Pablo Neruda, 1904-73, (Chil.) poet. *Twenty Love Poems and One Song of Despair, Toward the Splendid City.*
Sean O'Casey, 1884-1964, (Ir.) dramatist. *Juno and the Paycock, The Plough and the Stars.*
Frank O'Connor (Michael Donovan), 1903-66, (Ir.) short-story writer. "Guests of a Nation."
Flannery O'Connor, 1925-64, (U.S.) novelist, short-story writer. *Wise Blood,* "A Good Man Is Hard to Find."
Clifford Odets, 1906-63, (U.S.) playwright. *Waiting for Lefty, Awake and Sing, Golden Boy, The Country Girl.*
John O'Hara, 1905-70, (U.S.) novelist, short-story writer. *From the Terrace, Appointment in Samarra, Pal Joey.*
Omar Khayyam, c1028-1122, (Per.) poet. *Rubaiyat.*
Eugene O'Neill, 1888-1953, (U.S.) playwright. *Emperor Jones, Anna Christie, Long Day's Journey Into Night.*
George Orwell, 1903-50, (Br.) novelist, essayist. *Animal Farm, Nineteen Eighty-Four.*
John Osborne, 1929-95, (Br.) dramatist, novelist. *Look Back in Anger, The Entertainer.*
Wilfred Owen, 1893-1918 (Br.) poet. "Dulce et Decorum Est."
Dorothy Parker, 1893-1967, (U.S.) poet, short-story writer. *Enough Rope, Laments for the Living.*
Boris Pasternak, 1890-1960, (Russ.) poet, novelist. *Doctor Zhivago.*
Octavio Paz, 1914-98, (Mex.) poet, essayist. *The Labyrinth of Solitude, They Shall Not Pass!, The Sun Stone.*
Samuel Pepys, 1633-1703, (Br.) public official, diarist.
S(idney) J(oseph) Perelman, 1904-79, (U.S.) humorist. *The Road to Miltown, Under the Spreading Atrophy.*
Charles Perrault, 1628-1703, (Fr.) writer. *Tales From Mother Goose* (*Sleeping Beauty, Cinderella*).
Petrarch (Francesco Petrarca), 1304-74, (It.) poet. *Africa, Trionfi, Canzoniere.*
Luigi Pirandello, 1867-1936, (It.) novelist, dramatist. *Six Characters in Search of an Author.*
Sylvia Plath, 1932-63, (U.S.) author, poet. *The Bell Jar.*
Edgar Allan Poe, 1809-49, (U.S.) poet, short-story writer, critic. "Annabel Lee," "The Raven," "The Purloined Letter."
Alexander Pope, 1688-1744, (Br.) poet. *The Rape of the Lock, The Dunciad, An Essay on Man.*
Katherine Anne Porter, 1890-1980, (U.S.) novelist, short-story writer. *Ship of Fools.*
Ezra Pound, 1885-1972, (U.S.) poet. *Cantos.*
J(ohn) B. Priestley, 1894-1984, (Br.) novelist, dramatist. *The Good Companions.*
Marcel Proust, 1871-1922, (Fr.) novelist. *Remembrance of Things Past.*
Aleksandr Pushkin, 1799-1837, (Russ.) poet, novelist. *Boris Godunov, Eugene Onegin, The Bronze Horseman.*
François Rabelais, 1495-1553, (Fr.) writer. *Gargantua.*
Jean Racine, 1639-99, (Fr.) dramatist. *Andromaque, Phèdre, Bérénice, Britannicus.*
Ayn Rand, 1905-82, (Russ.-U.S.) novelist, moral theorist. *The Fountainhead, Atlas Shrugged.*
Erich Maria Remarque, 1898-1970, (Ger.-U.S.) novelist. *All Quiet on the Western Front.*

Samuel Richardson, 1689-1761, (Br.) novelist. *Pamela; or Virtue Rewarded.*
Rainer Maria Rilke, 1875-1926, (Ger.) poet. *Life and Songs, Duino Elegies, Poems From the Book of Hours.*
Arthur Rimbaud, 1854-91, (Fr.) poet. *A Season in Hell.*
Edwin Arlington Robinson, 1869-1935, (U.S.) poet. "Richard Cory," "Miniver Cheevy," *Merlin.*
Theodore Roethke, 1908-63, (U.S.) poet. *Open House, The Waking, The Far Field.*
Romain Rolland, 1866-1944, (Fr.) novelist, biographer. *Jean-Christophe.*
Pierre de Ronsard, 1524-85, (Fr.) poet. *Sonnets pour Hélène, La Franciade.*
Christina Rossetti, 1830-94, (Br.) poet. "When I Am Dead, My Dearest."
Dante Gabriel Rossetti, 1828-82, (Br.) poet, painter. "The Blessed Damozel."
Edmond Rostand, 1868-1918, (Fr.) poet, dramatist. *Cyrano de Bergerac.*
Damon Runyon, 1880-1946, (U.S.) short-story writer, journalist. *Guys and Dolls, Blue Plate Special.*
John Ruskin, 1819-1900, (Br.) critic, social theorist. *Modern Painters, The Seven Lamps of Architecture.*
Antoine de Saint-Exupéry, 1900-44, (Fr.) writer. *Wind, Sand and Stars, The Little Prince.*
Saki, or H(ector) H(ugh) Munro, 1870-1916, (Br.) writer. *The Chronicles of Clovis.*
George Sand (Amandine Lucie Aurore Dupin), 1804-76, (Fr.) novelist. *Indiana, Consuelo.*
Carl Sandburg, 1878-1967, (U.S.) poet. *The People, Yes; Chicago Poems, Smoke and Steel, Harvest Poems.*
William Saroyan, 1908-81, (U.S.) playwright, novelist. *The Time of Your Life, The Human Comedy.*
May Sarton, 1914-95, (Belg.-U.S.) poet, novelist. *Encounter in April, Anger.*
Dorothy L. Sayers, 1893-1957, (Br.) mystery writer; created Lord Peter Wimsey.
Richard Scarry, 1920-94, (U.S.) author of children's books. *Richard Scarry's Best Story Book Ever.*
Friedrich von Schiller, 1759-1805, (Ger.) dramatist, poet, historian. *Don Carlos, Maria Stuart, Wilhelm Tell.*
Sir Walter Scott, 1771-1832, (Sc.) novelist, poet. *Ivanhoe.*
Jaroslav Seifert, 1902-86, (Czech.) poet.
Dr. Seuss (Theodor Seuss Geisel), 1904-91, (U.S.) children's book author and illustrator. *The Cat in the Hat.*
William Shakespeare, 1564-1616, (Br.) dramatist, poet. *Romeo and Juliet, Hamlet, King Lear, Julius Caesar,* sonnets.
George Bernard Shaw, 1856-1950, (Ir.-Br.) playwright, critic. *St. Joan, Pygmalion, Major Barbara, Man and Superman.*
Mary Wollstonecraft Shelley, 1797-1851, (Br.) novelist, feminist. *Frankenstein. The Last Man.*
Percy Bysshe Shelley, 1792-1822, (Br.) poet. *Prometheus Unbound, Adonais,* "Ode to the West Wind," "To a Skylark."
Richard B. Sheridan, 1751-1816, (Br.) dramatist. *The Rivals, School for Scandal.*
Robert Sherwood, 1896-1955, (U.S.) playwright, biographer. *The Petrified Forest, Idiot's Delight, Abe Lincoln in Illinois.*
Mikhail Sholokhov, 1906-84, (Russ.) writer. *The Silent Don.*
Upton Sinclair, 1878-1968, (U.S.) novelist. *The Jungle.*
Isaac Bashevis Singer, 1904-91, (Pol.-U.S.) novelist, short-story writer, in Yiddish. *The Magician of Lubin.*
C(harles) P(ercy) Snow, 1905-80, (Br.) novelist, scientist. *Strangers and Brothers, Corridors of Power.*
Stephen Spender, 1909-95, (Br.) poet, critic, novelist. *Twenty Poems,* "Elegy for Margaret."
Edmund Spenser, 1552-99, (Br.) poet. *The Faerie Queen.*
Johanna Spyri, 1827-1901, (Swiss) children's author. *Heidi.*
Christina Stead, 1903-83, (Austral.) novelist, short-story writer. *The Man Who Loved Children.*
Richard Steele, 1672-1729, (Br.) essayist, playwright, began the *Tatler* and *Spectator. The Conscious Lovers.*
Gertrude Stein, 1874-1946, (U.S.) writer. *Three Lives.*
John Steinbeck, 1902-68, (U.S.) novelist. *The Grapes of Wrath, Of Mice and Men, The Winter of Our Discontent.*
Stendhal (Marie Henri Beyle), 1783-1842, (Fr.) novelist. *The Red and the Black, The Charterhouse of Parma.*
Laurence Sterne, 1713-68, (Br.) novelist. *Tristram Shandy.*
Wallace Stevens, 1879-1955, (U.S.) poet. *Harmonium, The Man With the Blue Guitar, Notes Toward a Supreme Fiction.*
Robert Louis Stevenson, 1850-94, (Br.) novelist, poet, essayist. *Treasure Island, A Child's Garden of Verses.*
Bram Stoker, 1845-1910, (Br.) writer. *Dracula.*
Rex Stout, 1886-1975, (U.S.) mystery writer; created Nero Wolfe.
Harriet Beecher Stowe, 1811-96, (U.S.) novelist. *Uncle Tom's Cabin.*
Lytton Strachey, 1880-1932, (Br.) biographer, critic. *Eminent Victorians. Queen Victoria, Elizabeth and Essex.*
August Strindberg, 1849-1912, (Swed.) dramatist, novelist. *The Father, Miss Julie, The Creditors.*
Jonathan Swift, 1667-1745, (Br.) satirist, poet. *Gulliver's Travels,* "A Modest Proposal."
Algernon C. Swinburne, 1837-1909, (Br.) writer. *Atalanta in Calydon.*
John M. Synge, 1871-1909, (Ir.) poet, dramatist. *Riders to the Sea, The Playboy of the Western World.*
Rabindranath Tagore, 1861-1941, (In.) author, poet. *Sadhana, The Realization of Life, Gitanjali.*
Booth Tarkington, 1869-1946, (U.S.) novelist. *Seventeen.*
Peter Taylor, 1917-94, (U.S.) novelist. *A Summons to Memphis.*
Sara Teasdale, 1884-1933, (U.S.) poet. *Helen of Troy and Other Poems, Rivers to the Sea, Flame and Shadow.*
Alfred, Lord Tennyson, 1809-92, (Br.) poet. *Idylls of the King, In Memoriam,* "The Charge of the Light Brigade."
William Makepeace Thackeray, 1811-63, (Br.) novelist. *Vanity Fair, Henry Esmond, Pendennis.*
Dylan Thomas, 1914-53, (Welsh) poet. *Under Milk Wood, A Child's Christmas in Wales.*
Henry David Thoreau, 1817-62, (U.S.) writer, philosopher, naturalist. *Walden,* "Civil Disobedience."
James Thurber, 1894-1961, (U.S.) humorist, cartoonist. "The Secret Life of Walter Mitty," *My Life and Hard Times.*
J(ohn) R(onald) R(euel) Tolkien, 1892-1973, (Br.) writer. *The Hobbit, Lord of the Rings* trilogy.
Leo Tolstoy, 1828-1910, (Russ.) novelist, short-story writer. *War and Peace, Anna Karenina,* "The Death of Ivan Ilyich."
Anthony Trollope, 1815-82, (Br.) novelist. *The Warden, Barchester Towers,* the Palliser novels.
Ivan Turgenev, 1818-83, (Russ.) novelist, short-story writer. *Fathers and Sons, First Love, A Month in the Country.*
Amos Tutuola, 1920-97, (Nigerian) novelist. *The Palm-Wine Drinkard, My Life in the Bush of Ghosts.*
Mark Twain (Samuel Clemens), 1835-1910, (U.S.) novelist, humorist. *The Adventures of Huckleberry Finn, Tom Sawyer; Life on the Mississippi.*
Sigrid Undset, 1881-1949, (Nor.) novelist, poet. *Kristin Lavransdatter.*
Paul Valéry, 1871-1945, (Fr.) poet, critic. *La Jeune Parque, The Graveyard by the Sea.*
Jules Verne, 1828-1905, (Fr.) novelist. *Twenty Thousand Leagues Under the Sea.*
François Villon, 1431-63?, (Fr.) poet. *The Lays, The Grand Testament.*
Voltaire (F.M. Arouet), 1694-1778, (Fr.) writer of "philosophical romances"; philosopher, historian; *Candide.*
Robert Penn Warren, 1905-89, (U.S.) novelist, poet, critic. *All the King's Men.*
Evelyn Waugh, 1903-66, (Br.) novelist. *The Loved One, Brideshead Revisited, A Handful of Dust.*
H(erbert) G(eorge) Wells, 1866-1946, (Br.) novelist. *The Time Machine, The Invisible Man, The War of the Worlds.*
Rebecca West, 1893-1983, (Br.) novelist, critic, journalist. *Black Lamb and Grey Falcon.*
Edith Wharton, 1862-1937, (U.S.) novelist. *The Age of Innocence, The House of Mirth, Ethan Frome.*
E(lwyn) B(rooks) White, 1899-1985, (U.S.) essayist, novelist. *Here Is New York, Charlotte's Web, Stuart Little.*
Patrick White, 1912-90, (Austral.) novelist. *The Tree of Man.*
T(erence) H(anbury) White, 1906-64, (Br.) author. *The Once and Future King, A Book of Beasts.*
Walt Whitman, 1819-92, (U.S.) poet. *Leaves of Grass.*
John Greenleaf Whittier, 1807-92, (U.S.) poet, journalist. *Snow-Bound.*
Oscar Wilde, 1854-1900, (Ir.) novelist, playwright. *The Picture of Dorian Gray, The Importance of Being Earnest.*
Laura Ingalls Wilder, 1867-1957, (U.S.) novelist. Little House on the Prairie series of children's books.
Thornton Wilder, 1897-1975, (U.S.) playwright. *Our Town, The Skin of Our Teeth, The Matchmaker.*
Tennessee Williams, 1911-83, (U.S.) playwright. *A Streetcar Named Desire, Cat on a Hot Tin Roof, The Glass Menagerie.*
William Carlos Williams, 1883-1963, (U.S.) poet, physician. *Tempers, Al Que Quiere! Paterson,* "This Is Just to Say."
Edmund Wilson, 1895-1972, (U.S.) critic, novelist. *Axel's Castle, To the Finland Station.*
P(elham) G(renville) Wodehouse, 1881-1975, (Br.-U.S.) humorist. The "Jeeves" novels, *Anything Goes.*
Thomas Wolfe, 1900-38, (U.S.) novelist. *Look Homeward, Angel; You Can't Go Home Again, Of Time and the River.*
Virginia Woolf, 1882-1941, (Br.) novelist, essayist. *Mrs. Dalloway, To the Lighthouse, A Room of One's Own.*
William Wordsworth, 1770-1850, (Br.) poet. "Tintern Abbey," "Ode: Intimations of Immortality," *The Prelude.*
Richard Wright, 1908-60, novelist, short-story writer. *Native Son, Black Boy, Uncle Tom's Children.*
William Butler Yeats, 1865-1939, (Ir.) poet, playwright. "The Second Coming," *The Wild Swans at Coole.*
Émile Zola, 1840-1902, (Fr.) novelist. *Nana, Thérèsè Raquin.*

Notable Figures of the Past in Dance

Source: Reviewed by Gary Parks, Reviews editor, *Dance* magazine

Alvin Ailey, 1931-89, (U.S.) modern dancer, choreographer; melded modern dance and Afro-Caribbean techniques.
Frederick Ashton, 1904-88, (Br.) ballet choreographer; director of Great Britain's Royal Ballet, 1963-70.
Fred Astaire, 1899-1987, (U.S.) dancer, actor; teamed with dancer/actress **Ginger Rogers** (1911-95) in movie musicals.
George Balanchine, 1904-83, (Russ.-U.S.) ballet choreographer, teacher; most influential exponent of the neoclassical style; founded, with Lincoln Kirstein, School of American Ballet and New York City Ballet.
Carlo Blasis, 1803-78, (It.) ballet dancer, choreographer, writer; his teaching methods are standards of classical dance.
August Bournonville, 1805-79, (Dan.) ballet dancer, choreographer, teacher; developed a distinctly Danish style known for its exuberance and lightness.
Gisella Caccialanza, 1914-97, (U.S.) ballerina, charter member of Balanchine's American Ballet.
Enrico Cecchetti, 1850-1928, (It.) ballet dancer, leading dancer of Russia's Imperial Ballet; his technique is basis for Britain's Imperial Society of Teachers of Dancing.
Gower Champion, 1921-80, (U.S.) dancer, choreographer, director; with his wife **Marge,** b 1923, (U.S.) choreographed and danced in Broadway musicals and films.
John Cranko, 1927-73, (S. African) choreographer; created narrative ballets based on literary works.
Agnes de Mille, 1909-93, (U.S.) ballerina, choreographer; known for using American themes, she choreographed the ballet *Rodeo* and the musical *Oklahoma.*
Sergei Diaghilev, 1872-1929, (Russ.) impresario; founded Les Ballet Russes; saw ballet as an art unifying dance, drama, music, and decor.
Alexandra Danilova, 1903-97, (Russ.) ballerina; noted teacher at the School of American Ballet.
Isadora Duncan, 1877-1927, (U.S.) expressive dancer who united free movement with serious music; one of the founders of modern dance.
Fanny Elssler, 1810-84, (Austrian) ballerina of the Romantic period; known for dramatic skill and sensual style.
Michel Fokine, 1880-1942, (Russ.) ballet dancer, choreographer, teacher; rejected strict classicism in favor of dramatically expressive style.
Margot Fonteyn, 1919-91, (Br.) prima ballerina, Royal Ballet of Great Britain; famed performance partner of Rudolf Nureyev.
Bob Fosse, 1927-87, (U.S.) jazz dancer, choreographer, director; Broadway musicals and film.
Serge Golovine, 1924-98, (Fr.) ballet dancer with Grand Ballet du Marquis de Cuevas; choreographer.
Martha Graham, 1893-1991, (U.S.) modern dancer, choreographer; created and codified her own dramatic technique.
Martha Hill, 1901-95, (U.S.) educator; leading figure in modern dance; founded American Dance Festival.
Doris Humphrey, 1895-1958, (U.S.) modern dancer, choreographer, writer, teacher; known for her intellect and choreographic range.
Robert Joffrey, 1930-88, (U.S.) ballet dancer, choreographer; cofounded with **Gerald Arpino,** b 1928, (U.S.), the Joffrey Ballet.
Kurt Jooss, 1901-79, (Ger.) choreographer, teacher; created expressionist works using modern and classical techniques.
Tamara Karsavina, 1885-1978, (Russ.) prima ballerina of Russia's Imperial Ballet and Diaghilev's Ballets Russes; partner of Nijinsky.
Nora Kaye, 1920-87, (U.S.) ballerina with Metropolitan Opera Ballet and Ballet Theater (now American Ballet Theatre).
Lincoln Kirstein, 1907-96 (U.S.) brought ballet as an art form to U.S.; founded, with George Balanchine, School of American Ballet and New York City Ballet.
Serge Lifar, 1905-86, (Russ.-Fr.) prem. danseur, choreographer; director of dance at Paris Opera, 1930-45, 1947-58.
José Limón, 1908-72, (Mex.-U.S.) modern dancer, choreographer, teacher; developed technique based on Humphrey.
Catherine Littlefield, 1908-51, (U.S.) ballerina, choreographer, teacher; pioneer of American ballet.
Léonide Massine, 1896-1979, (Russ.-U.S.) ballet dancer, choreographer; created "symphonic ballet" using concert music previously thought unsuitable for dance.
Kenneth MacMillan, 1929-92, (Br.) ballet dancer, choreographer; director of Royal Ballet of Great Britain 1970-77.
Vaslav Nijinsky, 1890-50, (Russ.) prem. danseur, choreographer; leading member of Diaghilev's Ballets Russes; his ballets were revolutionary for their time.
Alwin Nikolais, 1910-93, (U.S.) modern choreographer; created dance theater utilizing mixed media effects.
Jean-George Noverre, 1727-1810, (Fr.) ballet choreographer, teacher, writer; his theories on dramatic ballet remain influential; called the "Shakespeare of the dance."
Rudolf Nureyev, 1938-93, (Russ.) prem. danseur, choreographer; leading male dancer of his generation; director of dance at Paris Opera, 1983-89.
Ruth Page, 1903-91, (U.S.) ballerina, choreographer; danced and directed ballet at Chicago Lyric Opera.
Anna Pavlova, 1881-1931, (Russ.) prima ballerina; toured all over the world with her own company to great acclaim.
Marius Petipa, 1818-1910, (Fr.) ballet dancer, choreographer; as ballet master of the Imperial Ballet, he established Russian classicism as leading style of late 19th cent.
Pearl Primus, 1919-95, (Trinidad-U.S.) modern dancer, choreographer, scholar; combined African, Caribbean, and African-American styles.
Jerome Robbins, 1918-98, (U.S.) choreographer, director, dancer; *The King and I, West Side Story, Fiddler on the Roof.*
Bill (Bojangles) Robinson, 1878-1949, (U.S.) tap dancer; called the King of Tapology, he attained fame on stage and screen rare for an African-American of his era.
Ruth St. Denis, 1877-1968, (U.S.) interpretive dancer, choreographer, teacher; touring widely, she influenced many early modern dancers.
Ted Shawn, 1891-1972, (U.S.) modern dancer, choreographer; teamed with Ruth St. Denis to form Denishawn dance company and school.
Marie Taglioni, 1804-84, (It.) ballerina, teacher; in title role of *La Sylphide* established image of the ethereal ballerina.
Antony Tudor, 1908-87, (Br.) choreographer, teacher; exponent of the "psychological ballet."
Galina Ulanova, 1910-98, (Rus.) revered ballerina with Bolshoi Ballet.
Mary Wigman, 1886-1973, (Ger.) modern dancer, choreographer, teacher; influential in European expressionist dance.
Agrippina Vaganova, 1879-1951, (Russ.) ballet teacher, director; codified Soviet ballet technique that developed virtuosity.

Composers of Classical and Avant Garde Music

Carl Philipp Emanuel Bach, 1714-88, (Ger.) Cantatas, passions, numerous keyboard and instrumental works.
Johann Christian Bach, 1735-82, (Ger.) Concertos, operas, sonatas.
Johann Sebastian Bach, 1685-1750, (Ger.) St. Matthew Passion, The Well-Tempered Clavier.
Samuel Barber, 1910-81, (U.S.) Adagio for Strings, Vanessa.
Béla Bartók, 1881-1945, (Hung.) Concerto for Orchestra, The Miraculous Mandarin.
Amy Beach (Mrs. H. H. A. Beach), 1867-1944, (U.S.) The Year's at the Spring, Fireflies, The Chambered Nautilus.
Ludwig van Beethoven, 1770-1827, (Ger.) Concertos (Emperor), sonatas (Moonlight, Pathetique), 9 symphonies.
Vincenzo Bellini, 1801-35, (It.) I Puritani, La Sonnambula, Norma.
Alban Berg, 1885-1935, (Austrian) Wozzeck, Lulu.
Hector Berlioz, 1803-69, (Fr.) Damnation of Faust, Symphonie Fantastique, Requiem.
Leonard Bernstein, 1918-90, (U.S.) Chichester Psalms, Jeremiah Symphony, Mass.
Georges Bizet, 1838-75, (Fr.) Carmen, Pearl Fishers.
Ernest Bloch, 1880-1959, (Swiss-U.S.) Macbeth (opera), Schelomo, Voice in the Wilderness.
Luigi Boccherini, 1743-1805, (It.) Chamber music and guitar pieces.
Alexander Borodin, 1833-87, (Russ.) Prince Igor, In the Steppes of Central Asia, Polovtzian Dances.
Pierre Boulez, b 1925, (Fr.) LeVisage nuptial, Edats/Multiple, Domaines.
Johannes Brahms, 1833-97, (Ger.) Liebeslieder Waltzes, Acad. Festival Overture, chamber music, 4 symphonies.
Benjamin Britten, 1913-76, (Br.) Peter Grimes, Turn of the Screw, A Ceremony of Carols, War Requiem.
Anton Bruckner, 1824-96, (Austrian) 9 symphonies.
Dietrich Buxtehude, 1637-1707, (Dan.) Organ works, vocal music.
William Byrd, 1543-1623, (Br.) Masses, motets.
John Cage, 1912-92, (U.S.) Winter Music, Fontana Mix.
Emmanuel Chabrier, 1841-94, (Fr.) Le Roi Malgré Lui, Espana.
Gustave Charpentier, 1860-1956, (Fr.) Louise.
Frédéric Chopin, 1810-49, (Pol.) Mazurkas, waltzes, etudes, nocturnes, polonaises, sonatas.
Aaron Copland, 1900-90, (U.S.) Appalachian Spring, Fanfare for the Common Man, Lincoln Portrait.
Claude Debussy, 1862-1918, (Fr.) Pelleas et Melisande, La Mer, Prelude to the Afternoon of a Faun.
Gaetano Donizetti, 1797-1848, (It.) Elixir of Love, Lucia di Lammermoor, Daughter of the Regiment.
Paul Dukas, 1865-1935, (Fr.) Sorcerer's Apprentice.

Antonin Dvorak, 1841-1904, (Czech.) Songs My Mother Taught Me, Symphony in E Minor (From the New World).
Edward Elgar, 1857-1934, (Br.) Enigma Variations, Pomp and Circumstance.
Manuel de Falla, 1876-1946, (Sp.) El Amor Brujo, La Vida Breve, The Three-Cornered Hat.
Gabriel Faurè, 1845-1924, (Fr.) Requiem, Elègie for Cello and Piano.
Cesar Franck, 1822-90, (Belg.) Symphony in D minor, Violin Sonata.
George Gershwin, 1898-1937, (U.S.) Rhapsody in Blue, An American in Paris, Porgy and Bess.
Philip Glass, b 1937, (U.S.) Einstein on the Beach, The Voyage.
Mikhail Glinka, 1804-57, (Russ.) A Life for the Tsar, Ruslan and Ludmilla.
Christoph W. Gluck, 1714-87, (Ger.) Alceste, Iphigènie en Tauride.
Charles Gounod, 1818-93, (Fr.) Faust, Romeo and Juliet.
Edvard Grieg, 1843-1907, (Nor.) Peer Gynt Suite, Concerto in A minor for piano.
George Frideric Handel, 1685-1759, (Ger.-Br.) Messiah, Water Music.
Howard Hanson, 1896-1981, (U.S.) Symphonies No. 1 (Nordic) and No. 2 (Romantic).
Roy Harris, 1898-1979, (U.S.) Symphonies.
(Franz) Joseph Haydn, 1732-1809, (Austrian) Symphonies (Clock, London, Toy), chamber music, oratorios.
Paul Hindemith, 1895-1963, (U.S.) Mathis der Maler.
Gustav Holst, 1874-1934, (Br.) The Planets.
Arthur Honegger, 1892-1955, (Fr.) Judith, Le Roi David, Pacific 231.
Alan Hovhaness, b 1911, (U.S.) Symphonies, Magnificat.
Engelbert Humperdinck, 1854-1921, (Ger.) Hansel and Gretel.
Charles Ives, 1874-1954, (U.S.) Concord Sonata, symphonies.
Aram Khachaturian, 1903-78, (Russ.) Ballets, piano pieces, Sabre Dance.
Zoltán Kodaly, 1882-1967, (Hung.) Háry János, Psalmus Hungaricus.
Fritz Kreisler, 1875-1962, (Austrian) Caprice Viennois, Tambourin Chinois.
Edouard Lalo, 1823-92, (Fr.) Symphonie Espagnole.
Ruggero Leoncavallo, 1857-1919, (It.) Pagliacci.
Franz Liszt, 1811-86, (Hung.) 20 Hungarian rhapsodies, symphonic poems.
Edward MacDowell, 1861-1908, (U.S.) To a Wild Rose.
Gustav Mahler, 1860-1911, (Austrian) Das Lied von der Erde; 9 complete symphonies.
Pietro Mascagni, 1863-1945, (It.) Cavalleria Rusticana.
Jules Massenet, 1842-1912, (Fr.) Manon, Le Cid, Thaïs.
Felix Mendelssohn, 1809-47, (Ger.) A Midsummer Night's Dream, Songs Without Words, violin concerto.
Gian-Carlo Menotti, b 1911, (It.-U.S.) The Medium, The Consul, Amahl and the Night Visitors.
Claudio Monteverdi, 1567-1643, (It.) Opera, masses, madrigals.
Modest Moussorgsky, 1839-81, (Russ.) Boris Godunov, Pictures at an Exhibition.
Wolfgang Amadeus Mozart, 1756-91, (Austrian) Chamber music, concertos, operas (Magic Flute, Marriage of Figaro), 41 symphonies.
Jacques Offenbach, 1819-80, (Fr.) Tales of Hoffmann.
Carl Orff, 1895-1982, (Ger.) Carmina Burana.
Johann Pachelbel, 1653-1706, (Ger.) Canon and Gigue in D major.
Ignacy Paderewski, 1860-1941, (Pol.) Minuet in G.
Niccolò Paganini, 1782-1840, (It.) Caprices for violin solo.
Giovanni Palestrina, c1525-94, (It.) Masses, madrigals.
Krzystof Pendercki, b 1933, (Pol.) Psalmus, Polymorphia, De natura sonoris.
Francis Poulenc, 1899-1963, (Fr.) Dialogues des Carmèlites.
Mel Powell, 1923-98, (U.S.) *Duplicates: A Concerto for Two Pianos and Orchestra, Cantilena Concertante.*
Sergei Prokofiev, 1891-1953, (Russ.) Classical Symphony, Love for Three Oranges, Peter and the Wolf.
Giacomo Puccini, 1858-1924, (It.) La Boheme, Manon Lescaut, Tosca, Madama Butterfly.
Henry Purcell, 1659-95, (Eng.) Dido and Aeneas.
Sergei Rachmaninoff, 1873-1943, (Russ.) Concertos, preludes (Prelude in C sharp minor), symphonies.
Maurice Ravel, 1875-1937, (Fr.) Bolèro, Daphnis et Chloè, Piano Concerto in D for Left Hand Alone.
Nikolai Rimsky-Korsakov, 1844-1908, (Russ.) Golden Cockerel, Scheherazade, Flight of the Bumblebee.
Gioacchino Rossini, 1792-1868, (It.) Barber of Seville, Othello, William Tell.
Camille Saint-Saëns, 1835-1921, (Fr.) Carnival of Animals (The Swan), Samson and Delilah, Danse Macabre.
Alessandro Scarlatti, 1660-1725, (It.) Cantatas, oratorios, operas.
Domenico Scarlatti, 1685-1757, (It.) Harpsichord works.
Alfred Schnittke, 1934-98 (Sov.-Ger.) *Life With an Idiot.*
Arnold Schoenberg, 1874-1951, (Austrian) Pelleas and Melisande, Pierrot Lunaire, Verklärte Nacht.
Franz Schubert, 1797-1828, (Austrian) Chamber music (Trout Quintet), lieder, symphonies (Unfinished).
Robert Schumann, 1810-56, (Ger.) Die Frauenliebe und Leben, Träumerei.
Dimitri Shostakovich, 1906-75, (Russ.) Symphonies, Lady Macbeth of the District Mzensk.
Jean Sibelius, 1865-1957, (Finn.) Finlandia.
Bedrich Smetana, 1824-84, (Czech.) The Bartered Bride.
Karlheinz Stockhausen, b 1928, (Ger.) KontraPunkte, Kontakte for Electronic Instruments.
Richard Strauss, 1864-1949, (Ger.) Salome, Elektra, Der Rosenkavalier, Thus Spake Zarathustra.
Igor Stravinsky, 1882-1971, (Russ.) Noah and the Flood, The Rake's Progress, The Rite of Spring.
Toru Takemitsu, 1930-96, (Jpn.) Requiem for Strings, Dorian Horizon.
Peter I. Tchaikovsky, 1840-93, (Russ.) Nutcracker, Swan Lake, The Sleeping Beauty.
Virgil Thomson, 1896-1989, (U.S.) Opera, film music, Four Saints in Three Acts.
Dmitri Tiomkin, 1894-1979, (Russ.-U.S.) film scores, including *High Noon.*
Sir Michael Tippet, 1905-98, (Br.) *A Child of Our Time, The Midsummer Marriage, The Knot Garden.*
Ralph Vaughan Williams, 1872-1958, (Eng.) Fantasiz on a Theme by Thomas Tallis, symphonies, vocal music.
Giuseppe Verdi, 1813-1901, (It.) Aida, Rigoletto, Don Carlo, Il Trovatore, La Traviata, Falstaff, Macbeth.
Heitor Villa-Lobos, 1887-1959, (Brazil) Bachianas Brasileiras.
Antonio Vivaldi, 1678-1741, (It.) Concerto grossos (The Four Seasons).
Richard Wagner, 1813-83, (Ger.) Rienzi, Tannhäuser, Lohengrin, Tristan und Isolde.
Carl Maria von Weber, 1786-1826, (Ger.) Der Freischutz.

Composers of Operettas, Musicals, and Popular Music

Richard Adler, b 1921, (U.S.) *Pajama Game; Damn Yankees.*
Milton Ager, 1893-1979, (U.S.) I Wonder What's Become of Sally; Hard Hearted Hannah; Ain't She Sweet?
Arthur Altman, 1910-94, (U.S.) *All or Nothing at All.*
Leroy Anderson, 1908-75, (U.S.) Sleigh Ride, Blue Tango, Syncopated Clock.
Paul Anka, b 1941, (Can.) My Way; *Tonight Show* theme.
Harold Arlen, 1905-86, (U.S.) Stormy Weather; Over the Rainbow; Blues in the Night; That Old Black Magic.
Burt Bacharach, b 1928, (U.S.) Raindrops Keep Fallin' on My Head; Walk on By; What the World Needs Now Is Love.
Ernest Ball, 1878-1927, (U.S.) Mother Machree; When Irish Eyes Are Smiling.
Irving Berlin, 1888-1989, (U.S.) *Annie Get Your Gun; Call Me Madam;* God Bless America; White Christmas.
Leonard Bernstein, 1918-90, (U.S.) *On the Town; Wonderful Town; Candide; West Side Story.*
Eubie Blake, 1883-1983, (U.S.) *Shuffle Along;* I'm Just Wild About Harry.
Jerry Bock, b 1928, (U.S.) *Mr. Wonderful; Fiorello; Fiddler on the Roof; The Rothschilds.*
Carrie Jacobs Bond, 1862-1946, (U.S.) I Love You Truly.
Nacio Herb Brown, 1896-1964, (U.S.) Singing in the Rain; You Were Meant for Me; All I Do Is Dream of You.
Hoagy Carmichael, 1899-1981, (U.S.) Stardust; Georgia on My Mind; Old Buttermilk Sky.
George M. Cohan, 1878-1942, (U.S.) Give My Regards to Broadway; You're a Grand Old Flag; Over There.
Cy Coleman, b 1929, (U.S.) *Sweet Charity;* Witchcraft.
John Frederick Coots, 1897-?, (U.S.) Santa Claus Is Coming to Town; You Go to My Head; For All We Know.
Noel Coward, 1899-1973, (Br.) *Bitter Sweet;* Mad Dogs and Englishmen; Mad About the Boy.
Neil Diamond, b 1941, (U.S.) I'm a Believer; Sweet Caroline.
Walter Donaldson, 1893-1947, (U.S.) My Buddy; Carolina in the Morning; Makin' Whoopee.
Vernon Duke, 1903-69, (U.S.) April in Paris.
Bob Dylan, b 1941, (U.S.) Blowin' in the Wind.
Gus Edwards, 1879-1945, (U.S.) School Days; By the Light of the Silvery Moon; In My Merry Oldsmobile.
Sherman Edwards, 1919-81, (U.S.) See You in September; Wonderful! Wonderful!
Duke Ellington, 1899-1974, (U.S.) Sophisticated Lady; Satin Doll; It Don't Mean a Thing; Solitude.
Sammy Fain, 1902-89, (U.S.) I'll Be Seeing You; Love Is a Many-Splendored Thing.
Fred Fisher, 1875-1942, (U.S.) Peg O' My Heart; Chicago.
Stephen Collins Foster, 1826-64, (U.S.) My Old Kentucky Home; Old Folks at Home.
Rudolf Friml, 1879-1972, (Czech-U.S.) *The Firefly; Rose Marie; Vagabond King; Bird of Paradise.*
John Gay, 1685-1732, (Br.) *The Beggar's Opera.*
George Gershwin, 1898-1937, (U.S.) Someone to Watch Over Me; I've Got a Crush on You; Embraceable You.
Morton Gould, 1913-96, (U.S.) Fall River Suite, Holocaust Suite, Spirituals for Orchestra, Stringmusic.

Ferde Grofe, 1892-1972, (U.S.) Grand Canyon Suite.
Marvin Hamlisch, b 1944, (U.S.) The Way We Were; Nobody Does It Better; *A Chorus Line.*
Ray Henderson, 1896-1970, (U.S.) *George White's Scandals;* That Old Gang of Mine; Five Foot Two, Eyes of Blue.
Victor Herbert, 1859-1924, (Ir.-U.S.) *Mlle. Modiste; Babes in Toyland; The Red Mill; Naughty Marietta; Sweethearts.*
Jerry Herman, b 1933, (U.S.) *Hello Dolly; Mame.*
Brian Holland, b 1941, **Lamont Dozier,** b 1941, **Eddie Holland,** b 1939, (all U.S.) Heat Wave; Stop! In the Name of Love; Baby, I Need Your Loving.
Antonio Carlos Jobim, 1927-94, (Brazil) *The Girl From Ipanema; Desafinado; One Note Samba.*
Billy (William Martin) Joel, b 1949, (U.S.) *Just the Way You Are; Honesty;* Piano Man.
Scott Joplin, 1868-1917, (U.S.) Maple Leaf Rag; *Treemonisha.*
John Kander, b 1927, (U.S.) *Cabaret; Chicago; Funny Lady.*
Jerome Kern, 1885-1945, (U.S.) *Sally; Sunny; Show Boat.*
Carole King, b 1942, (U.S.) Will You Love Me Tomorrow?; Natural Woman; One Fine Day; Up on the Roof.
Burton Lane, 1912-1997, (U.S.) *Finian's Rainbow.*
Franz Lehar, 1870-1948, (Hung.) *Merry Widow.*
Jerry Leiber, & **Mike Stoller,** both b 1933, (both U.S.) Hound Dog; Searchin'; Yakety Yak; Love Me Tender.
Mitch Leigh, b 1928, (U.S.) *Man of La Mancha.*
John Lennon, 1940-80, & **Paul McCartney,** b 1942, (both Br.) I Want to Hold Your Hand; She Loves You.
Andrew Lloyd Webber, b 1948, (Br.) *Jesus Christ Superstar; Evita; Cats; The Phantom of the Opera.*
Frank Loesser, 1910-69, (U.S.) *Guys and Dolls; Where's Charley?; The Most Happy Fella; How to Succeed ....*
Frederick Loewe, 1901-88, (Austrian-U.S.) *Brigadoon; Paint Your Wagon; My Fair Lady; Camelot.*
Henry Mancini, 1924-94, (U.S.) Moon River; Days of Wine and Roses; Pink Panther Theme.
Barry Mann, b 1939, & **Cynthia Weil,** b 1937, (both U.S.) You've Lost That Loving Feeling.
Jimmy McHugh, 1894-1969, (U.S.) Don't Blame Me; I'm in the Mood for Love; I Feel a Song Coming On.
Alan Menken, b 1950, (U.S.) *Little Shop of Horrors.*
Joseph Meyer, 1894-1987, (U.S.) If You Knew Susie; California, Here I Come; Crazy Rhythm.
Chauncey Olcott, 1858-1932, (U.S.) Mother Machree.
Jerome "Doc" Pomus, 1925-91, (U.S.) Save the Last Dance for Me; A Teenager in Love.
Cole Porter, 1893-1964, (U.S.) *Anything Goes; Kiss Me Kate; Can Can; Silk Stockings.*
Smokey Robinson, b 1940, (U.S.) Shop Around; My Guy; My Girl; Get Ready.
Richard Rodgers, 1902-79, (U.S.) *Oklahoma!; Carousel; South Pacific; The King and I; The Sound of Music.*
Sigmund Romberg, 1887-1951, (Hung.) *Maytime; The Student Prince; Desert Song; Blossom Time.*
Harold Rome, 1908-93, (U.S.) *Pins and Needles; Call Me Mister; Wish You Were Here; Fanny; Destry Rides Again.*
Vincent Rose, b 1880-1944, (U.S.) Avalon; Whispering; Blueberry Hill.
Harry Ruby, 1895-1974, (U.S.) Three Little Words; Who's Sorry Now?
Arthur Schwartz, 1900-84, (U.S.) *The Band Wagon;* Dancing in the Dark; By Myself; That's Entertainment.
Neil Sedaka, b 1939, (U.S.) Breaking Up Is Hard to Do.
Paul Simon, b 1942, (U.S.) Sounds of Silence; I Am a Rock; Mrs. Robinson; Bridge Over Troubled Waters.
Stephen Sondheim, b 1930, (U.S.) *A Little Night Music; Company; Sweeney Todd; Sunday in the Park With George.*
John Philip Sousa, 1854-1932, (U.S.) *El Capitan;* Stars and Stripes Forever.
Oskar Straus, 1870-1954, (Austrian) *Chocolate Soldier.*
Johann Strauss, 1825-99, (Austrian) *Gypsy Baron; Die Fledermaus;* waltzes: Blue Danube; Artist's Life.
Charles Strouse, b 1928, (U.S.) *Bye Bye, Birdie; Annie.*
Jule Styne, 1905-94, (Br.-U.S.) *Gentlemen Prefer Blondes; Bells Are Ringing; Gypsy; Funny Girl.*
Arthur S. Sullivan, 1842-1900, (Br.) *H.M.S. Pinafore; Pirates of Penzance; The Mikado.*
Deems Taylor, 1885-1966, (U.S.) *Peter Ibbetson.*
Harry Tobias, 1905-94, (U.S.) *I'll Keep the Lovelight Burning.*
Egbert van Alstyne, 1882-1951, (U.S.) In the Shade of the Old Apple Tree; Memories; Pretty Baby.
Jimmy Van Heusen, 1913-90, (U.S.) Moonlight Becomes You; Swinging on a Star; All the Way; Love and Marriage.
Albert von Tilzer, 1878-1956, (U.S.) I'll Be With You in Apple Blossom Time; Take Me Out to the Ball Game.
Harry von Tilzer, 1872-1946, (U.S.) Only a Bird in a Gilded Cage; On a Sunday Afternoon.
Fats Waller, 1904-43, (U.S.) Honeysuckle Rose; Ain't Misbehavin'.
Harry Warren, 1893-1981, (U.S.) You're My Everything; We're in the Money; I Only Have Eyes for You.
Jimmy Webb, b 1946, (U.S.) Up, Up and Away; By the Time I Get to Phoenix; Didn't We?; Wichita Lineman.
Kurt Weill, 1900-50, (Ger.-U.S.) *Threepenny Opera; Lady in the Dark; Knickerbocker Holiday; One Touch of Venus.*
Percy Wenrich, 1887-1952, (U.S.) When You Wore a Tulip; Moonlight Bay; Put On Your Old Gray Bonnet.
Richard A. Whiting, 1891-1938, (U.S.) Till We Meet Again; Sleepytime Gal; Beyond the Blue Horizon; My Ideal.
John Williams, b 1932, (U.S.) *Jaws; E.T.; Star Wars* series; *Raiders of the Lost Ark* series.
Meredith Willson, 1902-84, (U.S.) *The Music Man.*
Stevie Wonder, b 1950, (U.S.) You Are the Sunshine of My Life; Signed, Sealed, Delivered, I'm Yours.
Vincent Youmans, 1898-1946, (U.S.) *Two Little Girls in Blue; Wildflower; No, No, Nanette; Hit the Deck; Rainbow; Smiles.*

Lyricists

Howard Ashman, 1950-91, (U.S.) Little Shop of Horrors; The Little Mermaid.
Johnny Burke, 1908-84, (U.S.) Misty; Imagination.
Irving Caesar, 1895-1996, (U.S.) Swanee; Tea for Two; Just a Gigolo.
Sammy Cahn, 1913-93, (U.S.) High Hopes; Love and Marriage; The Second Time Around; It's Magic.
Leonard Cohen, b 1934, (Can.) Suzanne; Stranger Song.
Betty Comden, b 1919, (U.S.) and **Adolph Green,** b 1915, (U.S.) The Party's Over; Just in Time; New York, New York.
Hal David, b 1921, (U.S.) What the World Needs Now Is Love.
Buddy De Sylva, 1895-1950, (U.S.) When Day Is Done; Look for the Silver Lining; April Showers.
Howard Dietz, 1896-1983, (U.S.) Dancing in the Dark; You and the Night and the Music; That's Entertainment.
Al Dubin, 1891-1945, (U.S.) Tiptoe Through the Tulips; Anniversary Waltz; Lullaby of Broadway.
Fred Ebb, b 1936, (U.S.) Cabaret; Zorba; Woman of the Year.
Dorothy Fields, 1905-74, (U.S.) On the Sunny Side of the Street; Don't Blame Me; The Way You Look Tonight.
Ira Gershwin, 1896-1983, (U.S.) The Man I Love; Fascinating Rhythm; S'Wonderful; Embraceable You.
William S. Gilbert, 1836-1911, (Br.) The Mikado; H.M.S. Pinafore; Pirates of Penzance.
Gerry Goffin, b 1939, (U.S.) Will You Love Me Tomorrow; Take Good Care of My Baby; Up on the Roof.
Mack Gordon, 1905-59, (Pol.-U.S.) You'll Never Know; The More I See You; Chattanooga Choo-Choo.
Oscar Hammerstein II, 1895-1960, (U.S.) Ol' Man River; Oklahoma; Carousel.
E. Y. (Yip) Harburg, 1898-1981, (U.S.) Brother, Can You Spare a Dime; April in Paris; Over the Rainbow.
Lorenz Hart, 1895-1943, (U.S.) Isn't It Romantic; Blue Moon; Lover; Manhattan; My Funny Valentine.
DuBose Heyward, 1885-1940, (U.S.) Summertime.
Gus Kahn, 1886-1941, (U.S.) Memories; Ain't We Got Fun.
Alan J. Lerner, 1918-86, (U.S.) Brigadoon; My Fair Lady; Camelot; Gigi; On a Clear Day You Can See Forever.
Johnny Mercer, 1909-76, (U.S.) Blues in the Night; Come Rain or Come Shine; Laura; That Old Black Magic.
Bob Merrill, 1921-98, (U.S.) People; Doggie in the Window.
Jack Norworth, 1879-1959, (U.S.) Take Me Out to the Ball Game; Shine On Harvest Moon.
Mitchell Parish, 1901-93, (U.S.) Stairway to the Stars; Stardust.
Andy Razaf, 1895-1973, (U.S.) Honeysuckle Rose; Ain't Misbehavin'; S'posin'.
Leo Robin, 1900-84, (U.S.) Thanks for the Memory; Hooray for Love; Diamonds Are a Girl's Best Friend.
Paul Francis Webster, 1907-84, (U.S.) Secret Love; The Shadow of Your Smile; Love Is a Many-Splendored Thing.
Jack Yellen, 1892-1991, (U.S.) Down by the O-Hi-O; Ain't She Sweet; Happy Days Are Here Again.

Notable Opera Singers of the Past

Frances Alda, 1883-1952, (NZ) soprano
Paul Althouse, 1889-1954, (U.S.) tenor
Pasquale Amato, 1878-1942, (It.) baritone
Marian Anderson, 1902-93, (U.S.) contralto
Jussi Björling, 1911-60, (Swed.) tenor
Lucrezia Bori, 1887-1960, (It.) soprano
Maria Callas, 1923-77, (U.S.) soprano
Emma Calvé, 1858-1942, (Fr.) soprano
Enrico Caruso, 1873-1921, (It.) tenor
Feodor Chaliapin, 1873-1938, (Russ.) bass
Boris Christoff, 1914-93, (Bulg.) bass
Richard Crooks, 1900-72, (U.S.) tenor
Giuseppe De Luca, 1876-1950, (It.) baritone
Edouard De Reszke, 1853-1917, (Pol.) bass
Jean De Reszke, 1850-1925, (Pol.) tenor
Emmy Destinn, 1878-1930, (Czech.) soprano

(continued)

Todd Duncan, 1903-98, (U.S.) baritone
Emma Eames, 1865-1952, (U.S.) soprano
Geraldine Farrar, 1882-1967, (U.S.) soprano
Kirsten Flagstad, 1895-1962, (Nor.) soprano
Olive Fremstad, 1871-1951, (Swed.-U.S.) soprano
Amelita Galli-Curci, 1882-1963, (It.) soprano
Mary Garden, 1874-1967, (Br.) soprano
Beniamino Gigli, 1890-1957, (It.) tenor
Tito Gobbi, 1913-84, (It.) baritone
Frieda Hempel, 1885-1955, (Ger.) soprano
Maria Jeritza, 1887-1982, (Czech.) soprano
Alexander Kipnis, 1891-1978, (Russ.-U.S.) bass
Lilli Lehmann, 1848-1929, (Ger.) soprano
Lotte Lehmann, 1888-1976, (Ger.-U.S.) soprano
Jenny Lind, 1820-87, (Swed.) soprano
John McCormack, 1884-1945, (Ir.) tenor
Blanche Marchesi, 1863-1940, (Fr.) soprano
Nellie Melba, 1861-1931, (Austral.) soprano.
Lauritz Melchior, 1890-1973, (Dan.) tenor
Zinka Milanov, 1906-89, (Yugo.) soprano
Lillian Nordica, 1857-1914, (U.S.) soprano
Adelina Patti, 1843-1919, (It.) soprano
Peter Pears, 1910-86, (Eng.) tenor
Jan Peerce, 1904-84, (U.S.) tenor
Ezio Pinza, 1892-1957, (It.) bass
Lily Pons, 1898-1976, (Fr.) soprano
Rosa Ponselle, 1897-1981, (U.S.) soprano
Hermann Prey, 1929-98, (Ger.) baritone.
Marcella Sembrich, 1858-1935, (Pol.) soprano
Eleanor Steber, 1916-90, (U.S.) soprano
Ferrucio Tagliavini, 1913-95, (It.) tenor
Luisa Tetrazzini, 1871-1940, (It.) soprano
Lawrence Tibbett, 1896-1960, (U.S.) baritone
Richard Tucker, 1913-75, (U.S.) tenor
Pauline Viardot, 1821-1910, (Fr.) mezzo-soprano
Leonard Warren, 1911-60, (U.S.) baritone

Notable Blues and Jazz Artists of the Past

Julian "Cannonball" Adderley, 1928-75, alto sax
Louis "Satchmo" Armstrong, 1900-71, trumpet, singer; "scat" vocals
Mildred Bailey, 1907-51, blues singer
Chet Baker, 1929-88, trumpet
Count Basie, 1904-84, orchestra leader, piano
Sidney Bechet, 1897-1959, early innovator, soprano sax
Bix Beiderbecke, 1903-31, cornet, piano, composer
Tommy Benford, 1906-94, drummer
Bunny Berigan, 1909-42, trumpet, singer
Barney Bigard, 1906-80, clarinet
Ed Blackwell, 1929-92, drummer
Jimmy Blanton, 1921-42, bass
Charles "Buddy" Bolden, 1868-1931, cornet; formed first jazz band.
Big Bill Broonzy, 1893-1958, blues singer, guitar
Clifford Brown, 1930-56, trumpet
Don Byas, 1912-72, tenor sax
Cab Calloway, 1907-94, band leader
Harry Carney, 1910-74, baritone sax
Betty Carter, 1930-98, jazz singer
Sidney Catlett, 1910-51, drums
Doc Cheatham, 1905-97, trumpet
Don Cherry, 1937-95, lyrical jazz trumpet
Charlie Christian, 1919-42, guitar
Kenny Clarke, 1914-85, modern drums
Buck Clayton, 1911-91, trumpet, arranger
James Cleveland, 1931-91, gospel singer
Al Cohn, 1925-88, tenor sax, composer
Cozy Cole, 1909-81, drums
Johnny Coles, 1926-96, trumpet
John Coltrane, 1926-67, tenor sax innovator
Eddie Condon, 1904-73, guitar, band leader; Dixieland
Tadd Dameron, 1917-65, piano, composer
Eddie "Lockjaw" Davis, 1921-86, tenor sax
Miles Davis, 1926-91, trumpet; pioneer of cool jazz
Wild Bill Davison, 1906-89, cornet, early Chicago jazz
Paul Desmond, 1924-77, alto sax
Vic Dickenson, 1906-84, trombone, composer
Willy Dixon, 1915-92, songwriter, blues, "You Shook Me"
Warren "Baby" Dodds, 1898-1959, Dixieland drummer
Johnny Dodds, 1892-1940, clarinet
Jimmy Dorsey, 1904-57, clarinet, alto sax; band leader
Tommy Dorsey, 1905-56, trombone; band leader
Roy Eldridge, 1911-89, trumpet, drums, singer
Duke Ellington, 1899-1974, piano, band leader, composer
Bill Evans, 1929-80, piano
Gil Evans, 1912-88, composer, arranger, piano
Tal Farlow, 1921-98, jazz guitarist
Ella Fitzgerald, 1918-1996, jazz vocalist, "first lady of song"
"Red" Garland, 1923-84, piano
Erroll Garner, 1921-77, piano, composer, "Misty"
Stan Getz, 1927-91, tenor sax
Dizzy Gillespie, 1917-93, trumpet, composer; bop developer
Benny Goodman, 1909-86, clarinet; band, combo leader
Dexter Gordon, 1923-90, tenor sax, bop-derived style
Bobby Hackett, 1915-76, trumpet, cornet
W. C. Handy, 1873-1958, composer, "St. Louis Blues"
Coleman Hawkins, 1904-69, tenor sax, "Body and Soul"
Fletcher Henderson, 1898-1952, orchestra leader, arranger
Woody Herman, 1913-87, clarinet, alto sax, band leader
Jay C. Higginbotham, 1906-73, trombone
Earl "Fatha" Hines, 1905-83, piano, songwriter
Johnny Hodges, 1906-70, alto sax
Billie Holiday, 1915-59, blues singer, "Strange Fruit"
John Lee Hooker, b. 1917, blues singer and guitarist
Sam "Lightnin" Hopkins, 1912-82, blues singer, guitarist
Howlin' Wolf, 1910-1976, blues singer, harmonica, guitar
Mahalia Jackson, 1911-72, gospel singer
Blind Lemon Jefferson, 1897-1930, blues singer, guitar
Little Willie John, 1937-68, singer, songwriter
Bunk Johnson, 1879-1949, cornet, trumpet
James P. Johnson, 1891-1955, piano, composer
Robert Johnson, 1912-38, blues songwriter, singer, guitarist
Jo Jones, 1911-85, drums
Philly Joe Jones, 1923-85, drums
Thad Jones, 1923-86, trumpet, cornet
Scott Joplin, 1868-1917, ragtime composer
Louis Jordan, 1908-75, singer, alto sax
Stan Kenton, 1912-79, orchestra leader, composer, piano
Albert King, 1923-92, blues guitarist
Gene Krupa, 1909-73, drums, band and combo leader
Scott LaFaro, 1936-61, bass
Huddie Ledbetter (Leadbelly), 1888-1949, blues singer, guitar
Mel Lewis, 1929-90, drummer, orchestra leader
Jimmie Lunceford, 1902-47, band leader, sax
Jimmy McPartland, 1907-91, trumpet
Carmen McRae, 1920-94, jazz singer
Glenn Miller, 1904-44, trombone, dance band leader
Charles Mingus, 1922-79, bass, composer, combo leader
Thelonious Monk, 1920-82, piano, composer, combo leader; bop developer
Wes Montgomery, 1925-68, guitar
"Jelly Roll" Morton, 1885-1941, composer, piano, singer
Bennie Moten, 1894-1935, piano
Gerry Mulligan, 1927-96, baritone sax, songwriter, "cool school"
Turk Murphy, 1915-87, trombone, band leader
Theodore "Fats" Navarro, 1923-50, trumpet
Red Nichols, 1905-65, cornet, combo leader
King Oliver, 1885-1938, cornet, band leader; Louis Armstrong
Sy Oliver, 1910-88, Swing Era arranger, composer, conductor
Kid Ory, 1886-1973, trombone, "Muskrat Ramble"
Charlie "Bird" Parker, 1920-55, alto sax, noted jazz improviser
Joe Pass, 1929-94, guitarist
Art Pepper, 1925-82, alto sax
Oscar Pettiford, 1922-60, a leading bop-era bassist
Bud Powell, 1924-66, piano; modern jazz pioneer
Louis Prima, 1911-78, singer, band leader.
Don Pullen, 1942-95, piano; percussive pianist
Sun Ra, 1915?-93, bandleader, pianist, composer
Gertrude "Ma" Rainey, 1886-1939, blues singer
Don Redman, 1900-64, composer, arranger
Django Reinhardt, 1910-53, guitar; influenced Amer. jazz
Buddy Rich, 1917-87, drums, band leader
Red Rodney, 1928-94, trumpeter
Frank Rosollino, 1926-78, trombone
Jimmy Rowles, 1918-96, jazz composer, accompanist
Jimmy Rushing, 1903-72, blues singer
Pee Wee Russell, 1906-69, clarinet
Zoot Sims, 1925-85, tenor, alto sax, clarinet
Zutty Singleton, 1898-1975, Dixieland drummer
Bessie Smith, 1894-1937, blues singer
Clarence "Pinetop" Smith, 1904-29, piano, singer; pioneer of boogie woogie
Willie "The Lion" Smith, 1897-1973, stride style pianist
Muggsy Spanier, 1906-67, cornet, band leader
Billy Strayhorn, 1915-67, composer, piano
Sonny Stitt, 1924-82, alto, tenor sax
Art Tatum, 1910-56, piano; technical virtuoso
Art Taylor, 1929-95, jazz drummer, bandleader
Jack Teagarden, 1905-64, trombone, singer
Dave Tough, 1908-48, drums
Lennie Tristano, 1919-78, piano, composer
Joe Turner, 1911-85, blues singer
Sarah Vaughan, 1924-90, singer
Joe Venuti, 1904-78, first great jazz violinist
T-Bone Walker, 1910-75, guitarist; electric blues guitar
Thomas "Fats" Waller, 1904-43, piano, singer, composer
Dinah Washington, 1924-63, singer
Ethel Waters, 1896-1977, jazz and blues singer
Muddy Waters, 1915-83, blues singer, songwriter
Johnny Watson, 1935-96, rhythm and blues guitarist
Chick Webb, 1902-39, band leader, drums
Ben Webster, 1909-73, tenor sax

Junior Wells, 1934-98, blues singer, harmonica
Paul Whiteman, 1890-1967, jazz orchestra leader
Charles "Cootie" Williams, 1908-85, trumpet, band leader
Mary Lou Williams, 1914-81, piano, composer
Teddy Wilson, 1912-86, piano, composer
Kai Winding, 1922-83, trombone, composer
Jimmy Yancey, 1894-1951, piano
Lester "Pres" Young, 1909-59, tenor sax, composer

Noted Country Music Artists of the Past

Roy Acuff, 1903-92, guitarist, singer, songwriter; "Wabash Cannon Ball"
Boudleaux Bryant, 1920-87, songwriter, singer; "Hey Joe"
Carter Family (original members, **"Mother" Maybelle** 1909-78; **Alvin,** 1891-1960, **Sara**, 1898-1979) "Wildwood Flower"
Patsy Cline, 1932-63, singer; "Crazy"
Vernon Dalhart, 1883-1948, singer; "The Death of Floyd Collins"
John Denver, 1943-97, singer, songwriter; "Rocky Mountain High"
Jimmy Driftwood, 1907-98, singer, songwriter; "The Battle of New Orleans"
Lester Flatt, 1914-79, singer, guitarist; "Foggy Mountain Breakdown"
Red Foley, 1910-68, singer; "Blues in My Heart"
Tennessee Ernie Ford, 1919-91, singer, songwriter; "Shotgun Boogie"
Lefty Frizzell, 1928-75, singer, guitarist; "Long Black Veil"
Woody Guthrie, 1912-67, singer, songwriter; "This Land Is Your Land"
Kendall L. Hayes, 1936-95, song writer; "Walk On By"
Uncle Dave Macon, 1870-1952, singer, banjo player and comedian
J. D. Miller, 1923-96, songwriter; "Honky-Tonk Angels"
Roger Miller, 1936-92, singer, songwriter; "King of the Road"
Bill Monroe, 1911-96, singer, songwriter, and mandolin player, "father of Bluegrass music"; "Mule Skinner Blues"
Minnie Pearl, 1912-96, comedienne, Grand Ole Opry star
Jim Reeves, 1924-64, singer, songwriter; "Four Walls"
Charlie Rich (Silver Fox), 1932-95, singer, songwriter; "The Most Beautiful Girl"
Tex Ritter, 1907-74, singer, songwriter; "Jingle, Jangle, Jingle"
Marty Robbins, 1925-82, singer, songwriter; "A White Sport Coat and a Pink Carnation"
Jimmie Rodgers, 1897-1933, singer, songwriter; "T for Texas"
Fred Rose, 1898-1954, songwriter, singer, musician, "Blue Eyes Cryin' in the Rain"
Original Sons of the Pioneers, Leonard Slye (Roy Rogers), 1911-98, Bob Nolan, 1908-80, singers, songwriters, "Tumbling Tumbleweed"; Tim Spencer, 1905-74, singer, songwriter, "Careless Kisses"; Hugh Farr, 1903-80, Karl Farr, 1909-61, Lloyd Perryman, 1917-77, singers
Merle Travis, 1917-83, singer, guitarist, songwriter; "16 Tons"
Ernest Tubb, 1914-84, singer, songwriter and guitarist; "The Yellow Rose of Texas"
Conway Twitty, 1933-93, singer, songwriter; "Hello Darlin' "
Dottie West, 1932-91, singer, songwriter; "Here Comes My Baby"
Hank Williams Sr., 1923-53, singer, songwriter; "Your Cheatin' Heart"
Bob Wills, 1905-75, singer, bandleader, songwriter; "San Antonio Rose"

Noted Rock and Roll, Rhythm and Blues, and Rap Artists

AC/DC: "Back in Black"
Bryan Adams: "Cuts Like a Knife"
Aerosmith: "Sweet Emotion"
***The Allman Brothers Band (1995):** "Ramblin' Man"
***The Animals (1994):** "House of the Rising Sun"
Paul Anka: "Lonely Boy"
Fiona Apple: "Criminal"
The Association: "Cherish"
Frankie Avalon: "Venus"
Backstreet Boys: "Everybody"
Erykah Badu: "On and On"
***La Vern Baker (1991):** "I Cried a Tear"
***Hank Ballard[1] and the Midnighters (1990):** "Work With Me, Annie"
***The Band (1994):** "The Weight"
***The Beach Boys (1988):** "Good Vibrations"
Beastie Boys: "(You Gotta) Fight for Your Right (to Party)"
***The Beatles (1988):** *Sgt. Pepper's Lonely Hearts Club Band*
Beck: "Loser"
***The Bee Gees (1997):** "Stayin' Alive"
Pat Benatar: "Hit Me With Your Best Shot"
***Chuck Berry (1986):** "Johnny B. Goode"
The Big Bopper: "Chantilly Lace"
Bjork: "Human Behavior"
Black Sabbath: "Paranoid"
***Bobby "Blue" Bland (1992):** "Turn On Your Love Light"
Mary J. Blige: *My Life*
Blind Faith: "Can't Find My Way Home"
Blondie: "Heart of Glass"
Blood, Sweat, and Tears: "Spinning Wheel"
Gary "U.S." Bonds: "Quarter to Three"
Bon Jovi: "Livin' on a Prayer"
***Booker T. and the Mgs (1992):** "Green Onions"
Earl Bostic: "Flamingo"
***David Bowie (1996):** "Space Oddity"
Boyz II Men: "I'll Make Love to You"
Toni Braxton: "Un-Break My Heart"
***James Brown (1986):** "Papa's Got a Brand New Bag"
***Ruth Brown (1993):** "Lucky Lips"
Jackson Browne: "Doctor My Eyes"
***Buffalo Springfield (1997):** "For What It's Worth"
Jimmy Buffet: "Margaritaville"
Bush: "Glycerine"
***The Byrds (1991):** "Turn! Turn! Turn!"
Mariah Carey: "Vision of Love"
The Cars: "Shake It Up"
***Johnny Cash (1992):** "I Walk the Line"
***Ray Charles (1986):** "Georgia on My Mind"
Cheap Trick: "Surrender"
Chubby Checker: "The Twist"
Chicago: "Saturday in the Park"
Eric Clapton: "Layla"
The Clash: "Rock the Casbah"
***The Coasters (1987):** "Yakety Yak"
***Eddie Cochran (1987):** "Summertime Blues"
Joe Cocker: "With a Little Help From My Friends"
Phil Collins: "Against All Odds"
***Sam Cooke (1986):** "You Send Me"
Coolio: "Gangsta's Paradise"
Alice Cooper: "School's Out"
Elvis Costello: "Alison"
***Cream (1993):** "Sunshine of Your Love"
***Creedence Clearwater Revival (1993):** "Proud Mary"
***Crosby, Stills, and Nash (1997):** "Suite: Judy Blue Eyes"
Sheryl Crow: "All I Want to Do"
The Cure: "Boys Don't Cry"
The Crystals: "Da Doo Ron Ron"
Cypress Hill: "Insane in the Brain"
Danny and the Juniors: "At the Hop"
***Bobby Darin (1990):** "Splish Splash"
Spencer Davis Group: "Gimme Some Lovin' "
Deep Purple: "Smoke on the Water"
Def Leppard: "Photograph"
Depeche Mode: "Strange Love"
***Bo Diddley (1987):** "Who Do You Love?"
***Dion[1] and the Belmonts (1989):** "A Teenager in Love"
Celine Dion: "Because You Loved Me"
Dire Straits: "Money for Nothing"
***Fats Domino (1986):** "Blueberry Hill"
Donovan: "Mellow Yellow"
The Doobie Brothers: "What a Fool Believes"
***The Doors (1993):** "Light My Fire"
***The Drifters (1988):** "Save the Last Dance for Me"
Duran Duran: "Hungry Like the Wolf"
***Bob Dylan (1988):** "Like a Rolling Stone"
***The Eagles (1998):** "Hotel California"
Earth, Wind, and Fire: "Shining Star"
***Duane Eddy (1994):** "Rebel-Rouser"
Emerson, Lake, and Palmer: "Lucky Man"
En Vogue: "Hold On"
The Eurythmics: "Sweet Dreams (Are Made of This)"
***The Everly Brothers (1986):** "Wake Up, Little Susie"
The Five Satins: "In the Still of the Night"
***Fleetwood Mac (1998):** *Rumours*
***The Four Seasons (1990):** "Sherry"
***The Four Tops (1990):** "I Can't Help Myself (Sugar Pie, Honey Bunch)"
***Aretha Franklin (1987):** "Respect"
Peter Gabriel: "Shock the Monkey"
Marvin Gaye (1987): "I Heard It Through the Grapevine"
Genesis: "No Reply at All"
Grand Funk Railroad: "We're an American Band"
Grand Master Flash and the Furious Five: "The Message"
***The Grateful Dead (1994):** "Uncle John's Band"
***Al Green (1995):** "Let's Stay Together"
Greenday: "Time of Your Life"
Guns N' Roses: "Sweet Child o' Mine"
***Bill Haley[1] and His Comets (1987):** "Rock Around the Clock"
Hall and Oates: "Kiss on My List"
Hanson: "MMMBop"
Heart: "Barracuda"
***Jimi Hendrix (1992):** "Purple Haze"
Herman's Hermits: "Mrs. Brown, You've Got a Lovely Daughter"
***Buddy Holly[1] and the Crickets (1986):** "That'll Be the Day"
***John Lee Hooker (1991):** "Boogie Chillun"
Hootie and the Blowfish: *Cracked Rear* View
Whitney Houston: "I Will Always Love You"
***The Impressions (1991):** "For Your Precious Love"
INXS: "Need You Tonight"
***The Isley Brothers (1992):** "It's Your Thing"

***The Jackson Five (1997):** "ABC"
Janet Jackson: *Rhythm Nation*
Michael Jackson: *Thriller*
***Etta James (1993):** "Tell Mama"
Tommy James & The Shondells: "Crimson and Clover"
Jay and the Americans: "This Magic Moment"
***Jefferson Airplane (1996):** "White Rabbit"
Jethro Tull: *Aqualung*
Jewel: "You Were Meant for Me"
Joan Jett: "I Love Rock 'n' Roll"
Billy Joel: "Piano Man"
***Elton John (1994):** "Candle in the Wind"
***Little Willie John (1996):** "Sleep"
***Janis Joplin (1995):** "Me and Bobby McGee"
K.C. and the Sunshine Band: "Get Down Tonight"
***B.B. King (1987):** "The Thrill Is Gone"
Carole King: *Tapestry*
***The Kinks (1990):** "You Really Got Me"
Kiss: "Rock 'n' Roll All Night"
***Gladys Knight and the Pips (1996):** "Midnight Train to Georgia"
***Led Zeppelin (1995):** "Stairway to Heaven"
Brenda Lee: "I'm Sorry"
***John Lennon (1994):** "Imagine"
***Jerry Lee Lewis (1986):** "Whole Lotta Shakin' Going On"
Little Anthony and the Imperials: "Tears on My Pillow"
***Little Richard (1986):** "Tutti Frutti"
L. L. Cool J: "Mama Said Knock You Out"
The Lovin' Spoonful: "Summer in the City"
***Frankie Lymon and the Teenagers (1993):** "Why Do Fools Fall in Love?"
Lynyrd Skynyrd: "Free Bird"
Madonna: "Material Girl"
***The Mamas and the Papas (1998):** "Monday, Monday"
Marilyn Manson: "Beautiful People"
***Bob Marley (1994):** *Exodus*
***Martha and the Vandellas (1995):** "Dancin' in the Streets"
The Marvelettes: "Please, Mr. Postman"
Dave Matthews Band: "Don't Drink the Water"
Paul McCartney: "Band on the Run"
Don McLean: "American Pie"
***Clyde McPhatter (1987):** "A Lover's Question"
Meat Loaf: "Paradise by the Dashboard Light"
John (Cougar) Mellencamp: "Jack and Diane"
Men at Work: "Who Can It Be Now?"
Metallica: "Enter Sandman"
George Michael: "Faith"
***Joni Mitchell (1997):** "Big Yellow Taxi"
The Monkees: "I'm a Believer"
Moody Blues: "Nights in White Satin"
Alanis Morissette: "Ironic"
***Van Morrison (1993):** "Brown-Eyed Girl"
***Ricky Nelson (1987):** "Hello, Mary Lou"
Nine Inch Nails: "Closer"
Nirvana: *Nevermind*
The Notorious B.I.G.: "Mo Money Mo Problems"
Oasis: "Wonderwall"
***Roy Orbison (1987):** "Oh, Pretty Woman"
Ozzy Osbourne: "Crazy Train"
***Parliament/Funkadelic (1997):** "One Nation Under a Groove"
Pearl Jam: "Jeremy"
***Carl Perkins (1987):** "Blue Suede Shoes"
Peter, Paul, and Mary: "Leavin' on a Jet Plane"
Tom Petty and the Heartbreakers: "Refugee"
***Wilson Pickett (1991):** "Land of 1,000 Dances"
***Pink Floyd (1996):** *The Wall*
***The Platters (1990):** "The Great Pretender"
The Police: "Every Breath You Take"
Poco: "Crazy Love"
Iggy Pop: "Lust for Life"
***Elvis Presley (1986):** "Love Me Tender"
The Pretenders: "Brass in Pocket"
***Lloyd Price (1998):** "Stagger Lee"
Prince (The Artist): "Purple Rain"
Procol Harum: "A Whiter Shade of Pale"
Public Enemy: "Fight the Power"
Puff Daddy and the Family: *No Way Out*
Queen: "Bohemian Rhapsody"
The Ramones: "I Wanna Be Sedated"
***Otis Redding (1989):** "(Sittin' on) the Dock of the Bay"
Red Hot Chili Peppers: "Under the Bridge"
***Jimmy Reed (1991):** "Ain't That Loving You, Baby?"
Lou Reed: "Walk on the Wild Side"
R.E.M.: "Losing My Religion"
The Righteous Brothers: "You've Lost That Lovin' Feelin' "
Johnny Rivers: "Poor Side of Town"
***Smokey Robinson[1] and the Miracles (1987):** "Shop Around"
***The Rolling Stones (1989):** "Satisfaction"
The Ronettes: "Be My Baby"
Linda Ronstadt: "You're No Good"
Run-D.M.C.: "Raisin' Hell"
Salt-N-Pepa: "Shoop"
***Sam and Dave (1992):** "Soul Man"
***Santana (1998):** "Black Magic Woman"
Seal: "Kiss From a Rose"
Neil Sedaka: "Breaking Up Is Hard to Do"
The Sex Pistols: "Anarchy in the U.K."
Tupac Shakur: "How Do U Want It"
Del Shannon: "Runaway"
***The Shirelles (1996):** "Soldier Boy"
Carly Simon: "You're So Vain"
Paul Simon: "50 Ways to Leave Your Lover"
***Simon and Garfunkel (1990):** "Bridge Over Troubled Water"
***Sly and the Family Stone (1993):** "Everyday People"
Smashing Pumpkins: "Today"
Patti Smith: "Because the Night"
Sonic Youth: "Bull in the Heather"
Soundgarden: "Black Hole Sun"
Spice Girls: "Wannabe"
Bruce Springsteen: "Born to Run"
Squeeze: "Tempted"
Steely Dan: "Rikki Don't Lose That Number"
Steppenwolf: "Born to Be Wild"
***Rod Stewart (1994):** "Maggie Mae"
Sting: "If You Love Somebody, Set Them Free"
The Sugar Hill Gang: "Rapper's Delight"
Donna Summer: "Bad Girls"
***The Supremes (1988):** "Stop! In the Name of Love"
Talking Heads: "Once in a Lifetime"
James Taylor: "You've Got a Friend"
***The Temptations (1989):** "My Girl"
Three Dog Night: "Joy to the World"
TLC: "Waterfalls"
T. Rex: "Bang a Gong (Get It On)"
***Big Joe Turner (1987):** "Shake, Rattle & Roll"
***Ike and Tina Turner (1991):** "Proud Mary"
***Tina Turner (1991):** "What's Love Got to Do With It?"
The Turtles: "Happy Together"
U2: "With or Without You"
Usher: "You Make Me Wanna"
Ritchie Valens: "La Bamba"
Van Halen: "Running With the Devil"
Stevie Ray Vaughan: "Crossfire"
***The Velvet Underground (1996):** "Sweet Jane"
***Gene Vincent[1] (1998):** "Be-Bop-A-Lula"
Tom Waits: "Downtown Train"
The Wallflowers: "One Headlight"
Dionne Warwick: "I Say a Little Prayer"
***Muddy Waters (1987):** "I Can't Be Satisfied"
Mary Wells: "My Guy"
***The Who (1990):** *Tommy*
***Jackie Wilson (1987):** "That's Why"
***Stevie Wonder (1989):** "You Are the Sunshine of My Life"
Wu-Tang Clan: "Protect Ya Neck"
***The Yardbirds (1992):** "For Your Love"
Yes: "Roundabout"
***Neil Young (1995):** "Down by the River"
***The Young Rascals/The Rascals (1997):** "Good Lovin' "
***Frank Zappa[1]/Mothers of Invention (1995):** *Sheik Yerbouti*
ZZ Top: "Legs"

*Inducted into Rock and Roll Hall of Fame as a performer between 1986 and 1998; year of induction in parentheses. (1) Only individual performer is a member of the Rock and Roll Hall of Fame. *Italics* = album; quotation marks = single.

Entertainers of the Present

actors, musicians, dancers, singers, producers, directors, radio-TV performers

Name	Birthplace	Birthdate
Abbado, Claudio	Milan, Italy	6/26/33
Abdul, Paula	San Fernando, CA.	6/19/62
Abraham, F. Murray	Pittsburgh, PA.	10/24/39
Adams, Bryan	Kingston, Ontario.	11/5/59
Adams, Don	New York, NY	4/19/26
Adams, Edie	Kingston, PA.	4/16/29
Adams, Joey	New York, NY	1/6/11
Adams, Mason	New York, NY	2/26/19
Adjani, Isabelle	Paris, France	6/27/55
Affleck, Ben	Berkeley, CA.	8/15/72
Agar, John	Chicago, IL	1/31/21
Agutter, Jenny	London, England	12/20/52
Aiello, Danny	New York, NY	6/20/33
Aimee, Anouk	Paris, France	4/27/34
Albanese, Licia	Bari, Italy	7/22/13
Alberghetti, Anna Maria	Pesaro, Italy	5/15/36
Albert, Eddie	Rock Island, IL	4/22/08
Albert, Marv	New York, NY	6/12/43
Alda, Alan	New York, NY	1/28/36
Alexander, Jane	Boston, MA	10/28/39
Alexander, Jason	Newark, NJ	9/23/59

Name	Birthplace	Birthdate
Allen, Debbie	Houston, TX	1/16/50
Allen, Joan	Rochelle, IL	8/20/56
Allen, Karen	Carrollton, IL	10/5/51
Allen, Steve	New York, NY	12/26/21
Allen, Tim	Denver, CO	6/13/53
Allen, Woody	Brooklyn, NY	12/1/35
Alley, Kirstie	Wichita, KS	1/12/51
Allman, Gregg	Nashville, TN	12/7/47
Allyson, June	New York, NY	10/7/17
Alonso, Maria Conchita	Cienfuegos, Cuba	6/29/57
Alpert, Herb	Los Angeles, CA	3/31/35
Altman, Robert	Kansas City, MO	2/20/25
Ames, Ed	Boston, MA	7/9/27
Amos, John	Newark, NJ	12/27/42
Amos, Tori	North Carolina	8/22/64
Anderson, Gillian	Chicago, IL	8/9/68
Anderson, Harry	Newport, RI	10/14/49
Anderson, Ian	Dunfermline, Scotland	8/10/47
Anderson, Kevin	Illinois	1/13/60
Anderson, Loni	St. Paul, MN	8/5/46
Anderson, Lynn	Grand Forks, ND	9/26/47
Anderson, Melissa Sue	Berkeley, CA	9/26/62
Anderson, Richard	Long Branch, NJ	8/8/26
Anderson, Richard Dean	Minneapolis, MN	1/23/50
Andersson, Bibi	Stockholm, Sweden	11/11/35
Andress, Ursula	Bern, Switzerland	3/19/36
Andrews, Anthony	London, England	1/12/48
Andrews, Julie	Walton, England	10/1/35
Andrews, Patty	Minneapolis, MN	2/16/20
Aniston, Jennifer	Sherman Oaks, CA	2/11/69
Anka, Paul	Ottawa, Ontario	7/30/41
Ann-Margret	Stockholm, Sweden	4/28/41
Antonioni, Michelangelo	Ferrara, Italy	9/29/12
Apple, Fiona	New York, NY	9/13/77
Applegate, Christina	Los Angeles, CA	11/25/72
Archer, Anne	Los Angeles, CA	8/25/47
Arkin, Adam	Brooklyn, NY	8/19/56
Arkin, Alan	New York, NY	3/26/34
Arnaz, Desi, Jr.	Los Angeles, CA	1/19/53
Arnaz, Lucie	Los Angeles, CA	7/17/51
Arness, James	Minneapolis, MN	5/26/23
Arnold, Eddy	Henderson, TN	5/15/18
Arnold, Tom	Ottumwa, IA	3/6/59
Arquette, Patricia	New York, NY	4/8/68
Arquette, Rosanna	New York, NY	8/10/59
Arroyo, Martina	New York, NY	2/2/37
Arthur, Beatrice	New York, NY	5/13/23
Ashley, Elizabeth	Ocala, FL	8/30/41
Asner, Ed	Kansas City, MO	11/15/29
Assante, Armand	New York, NY	10/4/49
Astin, John	Baltimore, MD	3/30/30
Atkins, Chet	Luttrell, TN	6/20/24
Atkinson, Rowan	Newcastle-Upon-Tyne, Eng.	1/6/55
Attenborough, Richard	Cambridge, England	8/29/23
Auberjonois, Rene	New York, NY	6/1/40
Aumont, Jean-Pierre	Paris, France	1/5/09
Austin, Patti	New York, NY	8/10/48
Autry, Alan	Shreveport, LA	7/31/52
Avalon, Frankie	Philadelphia, PA	9/18/39
Ax, Emmanuel	Lvov, Ukraine	6/8/49
Axton, Hoyt	Duncan, OK	3/25/38
Aykroyd, Dan	Ottawa, Ontario	7/1/52
Azaria, Hank	Forest Hills, NY	4/25/64
Aznavour, Charles	Paris, France	5/22/24
Babyface	Indianapolis, IN	4/10/59
Bacall, Lauren	New York, NY	9/16/24
Bacon, Kevin	Philadelphia, PA	7/8/58
Baez, Joan	Staten Island, NY	1/9/41
Bain, Conrad	Lethbridge, Alberta	2/4/23
Baio, Scott	Brooklyn, NY	9/22/61
Baker, Anita	Toledo, OH	1/26/58
Baker, Carroll	Johnstown, PA	5/28/31
Baker, Diane	Hollywood, CA	2/25/38
Baker, Joe Don	Groesbeck, TX	2/12/36
Baker, Kathy	Midland, TX	6/8/50
Bakula, Scott	St. Louis, MO	10/9/55
Baldwin, Alec	Massapequa, NY	4/3/58
Baldwin, Daniel	Massapequa, NY	10/5/60
Baldwin, Stephen	Massapequa, NY	5/12/66
Baldwin, William	Massapequa, NY	2/21/63
Ballard, Kaye	Cleveland, OH	11/20/26
Bancroft, Anne	New York, NY	9/17/31
Banderas, Antonio	Málaga, Spain	8/10/60
Banks, Tyra	Los Angeles, CA	12/4/73
Bannon, Jack	Los Angeles, CA	6/14/40
Baranski, Christine	Buffalo, NY	5/2/52
Barbeau, Adrienne	Sacramento, CA	6/11/45
Bardot, Brigitte	Paris, France	9/28/34
Barker, Bob	Darrington, WA	12/12/23
Barkin, Ellen	New York, NY	4/16/55
Barrie, Barbara	Chicago, IL	5/23/31
Barry, Gene	New York, NY	6/14/19
Barty, Billy	Millsboro, PA	10/25/24
Barrymore, Drew	Los Angeles, CA	2/22/75
Bartoli, Cecilia	Rome, Italy	6/4/66
Baryshnikov, Mikhail	Riga, Latvia	1/28/48
Basinger, Kim	Athens, GA	12/8/53
Bassett, Angela	New York, NY	8/16/58
Bassey, Shirley	Cardiff, Wales	1/8/37
Bateman, Jason	Rye, NY	1/14/69
Bateman, Justine	Rye, NY	2/19/66
Bates, Alan	Allestree, England	2/17/34
Bates, Kathy	Memphis, TN	6/28/48
Battle, Kathleen	Portsmouth, OH	8/13/48
Baxter, Meredith	Los Angeles, CA	6/21/47
Bean, Orson	Burlington, VT	7/22/28
Beatty, Ned	Louisville, KY	7/6/37
Beatty, Warren	Richmond, VA	3/30/37
Beck (Hansen)	Los Angeles, CA	7/8/70
Beck, Jeff	Surrey, England	6/24/44
Beck, John	Chicago, IL	1/28/43
Bedelia, Bonnie	New York, NY	3/25/48
Begley, Ed, Jr.	Los Angeles, CA	9/16/49
Belafonte, Harry	New York, NY	3/1/27
Bel Geddes, Barbara	New York, NY	10/31/22
Belmondo, Jean-Paul	Neuilly-sur-Seine, France	4/9/33
Belushi, Jim	Chicago, IL	6/15/54
Belzer, Richard	Bridgeport, CT	8/4/44
Benatar, Pat	Brooklyn, NY	1/10/53
Benedict, Dirk	Helena, MT	3/1/45
Bening, Annette	Topeka, KS	5/29/58
Benjamin, Richard	New York, NY	5/22/38
Bennett, Tony	New York, NY	8/3/26
Benson, George	Pittsburgh, PA	3/22/43
Benson, Robby	Dallas, TX	1/21/56
Berenger, Tom	Chicago, IL	5/31/50
Bergen, Candice	Beverly Hills, CA	5/9/46
Bergen, Polly	Knoxville, TN	7/14/30
Bergman, Ingmar	Uppsala, Sweden	7/14/18
Berle, Milton	New York, NY	7/12/08
Berlinger, Warren	Brooklyn, NY	8/31/37
Berman, Lazar	Leningrad, Russia	2/26/30
Berman, Shelley	Chicago, IL	2/3/26
Bernard, Crystal	Dallas, TX	9/30/64
Bernhard, Sandra	Flint, MI	6/6/55
Bernsen, Corbin	N. Hollywood, CA	9/7/54
Berry, Chuck	St. Louis, MO	10/18/26
Berry, Halle	Cleveland, OH	8/14/68
Berry, Ken	Moline, IL	11/3/33
Bertinelli, Valerie	Wilmington, DE	4/23/60
Bertolucci, Bernardo	Parma, Italy	3/16/41
Bialik, Mayim	San Diego, CA	12/12/75
Bikel, Theodore	Vienna, Austria	5/2/24
Billingsley, Barbara	Los Angeles, CA	12/22/22
Binoche, Juliette	Paris, France	4/9/64
Birney, David	Washington, DC	4/23/39
Bishop, Joey	Bronx, NY	2/3/18
Bisset, Jacqueline	Weybridge, England	9/13/44
Bissett, Josie	Seattle, WA	10/5/69
Björk (Gudmundsdottir)	Rheinberg, Iceland	10/21/66
Black, Clint	Katy, TX	2/4/62
Black, Karen	Park Ridge, IL	7/1/42
Blades, Ruben	Panama City, Panama	7/16/48
Blair, Linda	St. Louis, MO	1/22/59
Blake, Robert	Nutley, NJ	9/18/33
Bledsoe, Tempestt	Chicago, IL	8/1/73
Bloom, Claire	London, England	2/15/31
Blyth, Ann	Mt. Kisco, NY	8/16/28
Bochco, Steven	New York, NY	12/16/43
Bogarde, Dirk	London, England	3/28/20
Bogdanovich, Peter	Kingston, NY	7/30/39
Bogosian, Eric	Boston, MA	4/24/53
Bologna, Joseph	Brooklyn, NY	12/30/38
Bolton, Michael	New Haven, CT	2/26/53
Bonet, Lisa	San Francisco, CA	11/16/67
Bonham Carter, Helena	London, England	5/23/66
Bon Jovi, Jon	Sayreville, NJ	3/2/62
Bono (Vox)	Dublin, Ireland	5/10/60
Boone, Debby	Hackensack, NJ	9/22/56
Boone, Pat	Jacksonville, FL	6/1/34
Boreanaz, David	Buffalo, NY	5/16/71

Name	Birthplace	Birthdate
Borge, Victor	Copenhagen, Denmark	1/3/09
Borgnine, Ernest	Hamden, CT	1/24/17
Bosson, Barbara	Charleroi, PA	11/1/39
Bosco, Philip	Jersey City, NJ	9/26/30
Bosley, Tom	Chicago, IL	10/1/27
Bostwick, Barry	San Mateo, CA	2/24/45
Bottoms, Timothy	Santa Barbara, CA	8/30/51
Bowie, David	London, England	1/8/47
Boxleitner, Bruce	Elgin, IL	5/12/50
Boy George	London, England	6/14/61
Boyle, Peter	Philadelphia, PA	10/18/33
Bracco, Lorraine	Brooklyn, NY	10/2/55
Bracken, Eddie	New York, NY	2/7/20
Branagh, Kenneth	Belfast, N. Ireland	12/10/60
Brando, Marlon	Omaha, NE	4/3/24
Brandy (Norwood)	McComb, MS	2/11/79
Braugher, Andre	Chicago, Il	7/1/62
Braxton, Toni	Severn, MD	10/7/68
Brennan, Eileen	Los Angeles, CA	9/3/35
Brenner, David	Philadelphia, PA	2/4/45
Brewer, Teresa	Toledo, OH	5/7/31
Bridges, Beau	Hollywood, CA	12/9/41
Bridges, Jeff	Los Angeles, CA	12/4/49
Brimley, Wilford	Salt Lake City, UT	9/27/34
Brinkley, Christie	Malibu, CA	2/2/54
Broderick, Matthew	New York, NY	3/21/62
Brolin, James	Los Angeles, CA	7/18/40
Bronson, Charles	Ehrenfeld, PA	11/3/22
Brooks, Albert	Beverly Hills, CA	7/22/47
Brooks, Foster	Louisville, KY	5/11/12
Brooks, Garth	Tulsa, OK	2/7/62
Brooks, James L	Brooklyn, NY	5/9/40
Brooks, Mel	New York, NY	6/28/26
Brosnan, Pierce	Co. Meath, Ireland	5/16/53
Brown, Blair	Washington, DC	1948
Brown, Bobby	Boston, MA	2/5/69
Brown, Bryan	Sydney, Australia	6/23/47
Brown, James	Pulaski, TN (?)	6/17/28 (?)
Brown, Les	Reinerton, PA	3/14/12
Browne, Jackson	Heidelberg, Germany	10/9/48
Browne, Roscoe Lee	Woodbury, NJ	5/2/25
Brubeck, Dave	Concord, CA	12/6/20
Bryson, Peabo	Greenville, SC	4/13/51
Buckley, Betty	Ft. Worth, TX	7/3/47
Buffett, Jimmy	Pascagoula, MS	12/25/46
Bujold, Genevieve	Montreal, Quebec	7/1/42
Bullock, Sandra	Arlington, VA	7/26/67
Bumbry, Grace	St. Louis, MO	1/4/37
Burghoff, Gary	Bristol, CT	5/24/40
Burke, Delta	Orlando, FL	7/30/56
Burnett, Carol	San Antonio, TX	4/26/33
Burns, Edward	New York, NY	1/29/68
Burrows, Darren E.	Winfield, KS	9/12/66
Burstyn, Ellen	Detroit, MI	12/7/32
Burton, LeVar	Landstuhl, W Germany	2/16/57
Burton, Tim	Burbank, CA	8/25/58
Buscemi, Steve	Brooklyn, NY	12/13/57
Busey, Gary	Goose Creek, TX	6/29/44
Busfield, Timothy	Lansing, MI	6/12/57
Butler, Brett	Montgomery, AL	1/30/58
Buttons, Red	New York, NY	2/5/19
Buzzi, Ruth	Westerly, RI	7/24/36
Byrne, David	Dumbarton, Scotland	5/14/52
Byrne, Gabriel	Dublin, Ireland	5/12/50
Caan, James	New York, NY	3/26/39
Caballe, Montserrat	Barcelona, Spain	4/12/33
Caesar, Sid	Yonkers, NY	9/8/22
Cage, Nicolas	Long Beach, CA	1/7/64
Cain, Dean	Mt. Clemens, MI	7/31/66
Caine, Michael	London, England	3/14/33
Caldwell, Sarah	Maryville, MO	3/6/24
Caldwell, Zoe	Melbourne, Australia	9/14/33
Calhoun, Rory	Los Angeles, CA	8/8/23
Cameron, James	Kapuskasiny, Ontario	8/16/54
Cameron, Kirk	Panorama City, CA	10/12/70
Camp, Hamilton	London, England	10/30/34
Campanella, Joseph	New York, NY	11/21/27
Campbell, Bruce	Royal Oak, MI	6/22/58
Campbell, Glen	Billstown, AR	4/22/36
Campbell, Naomi	London, England	5/22/70
Campbell, Neve	Toronto, Ontario	10/3/73
Campion, Jane	Wellington, New Zealand	1955
Cannell, Stephen J.	Los Angeles, CA	2/5/42
Cannon, Dyan	Tacoma, WA	1/4/37
Capshaw, Kate	Ft. Worth, TX	11/3/53
Cardinale, Claudia	Tunis, Tunisia	4/15/39
Carey, Drew	Cleveland, OH	5/23/58
Carey, Mariah	Huntington, NY	3/27/70
Cariou, Len	Winnipeg, Canada	9/30/39
Carlin, George	New York, NY	5/12/37
Carlisle Hart, Kitty	New Orleans, LA	9/3/15
Carmen, Eric	Cleveland, OH	8/11/49
Carney, Art	Mt. Vernon, NY	11/4/18
Carpenter, John	Carthage, NY	1/16/48
Carpenter, Mary Chapin	Princeton, NJ	2/21/58
Caron, Leslie	Boulogne, France	7/1/31
Carr, Vikki	El Paso, TX	7/19/41
Carradine, David	Hollywood, CA	10/8/36
Carradine, Keith	San Mateo, CA	8/8/49
Carreras, Jose	Barcelona, Spain	12/5/46
Carrere, Tia	Honolulu, HI	1/2/66
Carrey, Jim	Toronto, Ontario	1/17/62
Carroll, Diahann	Bronx, NY	7/17/35
Carroll, Pat	Shreveport, LA	5/5/27
Carson, Johnny	Corning, IA	10/23/25
Carson, Lisa Nicole	Brooklyn, NY	7/12/69
Carter, Benny	New York, NY	8/8/07
Carter, Dixie	McLemoresville, TN	5/25/39
Carter, Jack	New York, NY	6/24/23
Carter, June	Maces Spring, VA	6/23/29
Carter, Lynda	Phoenix, AZ	7/24/51
Carter, Nell	Birmingham, AL	9/13/48
Carter, Ron	Royal Oak Twp, MI	5/4/37
Cartwright, Nancy	Ohio	1959
Caruso, David	Forest Hills, NY	1/17/56
Carvey, Dana	Missoula, MT	4/2/55
Casadesus, Gaby	Marseilles, France	8/9/01
Cash, Johnny	Kingsland, AR	2/26/32
Cash, Rosanne	Memphis, TN	5/24/55
Cass, Peggy	Boston, MA	5/21/24
Cassidy, David	New York, NY	4/12/50
Castellaneta, Dan	Chicago, IL	1958
Cates, Phoebe	New York, NY	7/16/63
Cathbert, Lacey	Purvis, MS	9/30/82
Cavett, Dick	Gibbon, NE	11/19/36
Chamberlain, Richard	Beverly Hills, CA	3/31/35
Chan, Jackie	Hong Kong	4/7/54
Channing, Carol	Seattle, WA	1/31/23
Channing, Stockard	New York, NY	2/13/44
Chaplin, Geraldine	Santa Monica, CA	7/31/44
Chapman, Tracy	Cleveland, OH	3/30/64
Charisse, Cyd	Amarillo, TX	3/8/21
Charles, Ray	Albany, GA	9/23/30
Charo	Murcia, Spain	1/15/51
Chase, Chevy	New York, NY	10/8/43
Cheadle, Don	Kansas City, MO	11/29/64
Checker, Chubby	Philadelphia, PA	10/3/41
Cher	El Centro, CA	5/20/46
Chiklis, Michael	Lowell, MA	8/30/63
Chong, Rae Dawn	Vancouver, Canada	2/28/62
Chong, Thomas	Edmonton, Alberta	5/24/38
Chow Yun-Fat	Hong Kong	5/18/55
Christensen, Helena	Copenhagen, Denmark	12/25/68
Christie, Julie	Assam, India	4/14/40
Christopher, William	Evanston, IL	10/20/32
Church, Thomas Haden	El Paso, TX	6/17/61
Clapton, Eric	Surrey, England	3/30/45
Clark, Dick	Mt. Vernon, NY	11/30/29
Clark, Petula	Ewell, Surrey, England	11/15/32
Clark, Roy	Meherrin, VA	4/15/33
Clay, Andrew Dice	Brooklyn, NY	9/29/58
Clayburgh, Jill	New York, NY	4/30/44
Cleese, John	Weston-Super-Mare, Eng.	10/27/39
Cliburn, Van	Shreveport, LA	7/12/34
Clooney, George	Lexington, KY	5/6/61
Clooney, Rosemary	Maysville, KY	5/23/28
Close, Glenn	Greenwich, CT	3/19/47
Coburn, James	Laurel, NE	8/31/28
Coca, Imogene	Philadelphia, PA	11/18/08
Coen, Ethan	St. Louis Park, MN	9/21/57
Coen, Joel	St. Louis Park, MN	11/29/54
Cole, Gary	Park Ridge, IL	9/20/57
Cole, Natalie	Los Angeles, CA	2/6/50
Cole, Olivia	Memphis, TN	11/26/42
Coleman, Dabney	Austin, TX	1/3/32
Coleman, Gary	Zion, IL	2/8/68
Coleman, Ornette	Fort Worth, TX	3/9/30
Collins, Joan	London, England	5/23/33
Collins, Judy	Seattle, WA	5/1/39
Collins, Pauline	Exmouth, England	9/3/40
Collins, Phil	London, England	1/30/51

Name	Birthplace	Birthdate
Combs, Sean "Puffy"	Harlem, NY	11/9/69
Comden, Betty	Brooklyn, NY	5/3/19
Como, Perry	Canonsburg, PA	5/18/12
Connery, Sean	Edinburgh, Scotland	8/25/30
Connick, Harry, Jr.	New Orleans, LA	9/11/67
Conniff, Ray	Attleboro, MA	11/6/16
Connors, Mike	Fresno, CA	8/15/25
Conrad, Robert	Chicago, IL	3/1/35
Constantine, Michael	Reading, PA	5/22/27
Conti, Tom	Paisley, Scotland	11/22/41
Conway, Tim	Willoughby, OH	12/15/33
Cook, Barbara	Atlanta, GA	10/25/27
Cooke, Alistair	Manchester, England	11/20/08
Coolidge, Rita	Nashville, TN	5/1/45
Coolio	Los Angeles, CA	8/1/63
Cooper, Alice	Detroit, MI	2/4/48
Cooper, Jackie	Los Angeles, CA	9/15/21
Copperfield, David	Metuchen, NJ	9/16/56
Coppola, Francis Ford	Detroit, MI	4/7/39
Corbin, Barry	Lamesa, TX	10/16/40
Corby, Ellen	Racine, WI	6/3/13
Cord, Alex	New York, NY	8/3/31
Corea, Chick	Chelsea, MA	6/12/41
Corelli, Franco	Ancona, Italy	4/8/23
Corey, Jeff	New York, NY	8/10/14
Corley, Pat	Dallas, TX	6/1/30
Cosby, Bill	Philadelphia, PA	7/12/37
Costas, Bob	New York, NY	3/22/52
Costello, Elvis	London, England	8/25/54
Costner, Kevin	Compton, CA	1/18/55
Courtenay, Tom	Hull, England	2/25/37
Cox, Courteney	Birmingham, AL	6/15/64
Coyote, Peter	New York, NY	10/10/42
Cox, Ronny	Cloudcroft, NM	8/23/38
Crain, Jeanne	Barstow, CA	5/25/25
Crawford, Cindy	DeKalb, IL	2/20/66
Crawford, Michael	Salisbury, England	1/19/42
Crenna, Richard	Los Angeles, CA	11/30/26
Crespin, Regine	Marseilles, France	2/23/26
Cronyn, Hume	London, Ontario	7/18/11
Crosby, David	Los Angeles, CA	8/14/41
Cross, Ben	London, England	12/16/47
Crouse, Lindsay	New York, NY	5/12/48
Crow, Sheryl	Kennett, MO	2/11/62
Crowe, Cameron	Palm Springs, CA	7/13/57
Crowe, Russell	New Zealand	4/7/64
Crowell, Rodney	Houston, TX	8/17/50
Cruise, Tom	Syracuse, NY	7/3/62
Crystal, Billy	Long Beach, NY	3/14/47
Culkin, Macaulay	New York, NY	8/26/80
Cullum, John	Knoxville, TN	3/2/30
Culp, Robert	Oakland, CA	8/16/30
Cummings, Constance	Seattle, WA	5/15/10
Curry, Tim	Cheshire, England	4/19/46
Curtin, Jane	Cambridge, MA	9/6/47
Curtis, Jamie Lee	Los Angeles, CA	11/22/58
Curtis, Keene	Salt Lake City, UT	2/15/23
Curtis, Tony	New York, NY	6/3/25
Cusack, Joan	Evanston, IL	10/11/62
Cusack, John	Evanston, IL	6/28/66
Cyrus, Billy Ray	Flatwoods, KY	8/25/61
Dafoe, Willem	Appleton, WI	7/22/55
Dahl, Arlene	Minneapolis, MN	8/11/28
Dale, Jim	Rothwell, England	8/15/35
Dalton, Abby	Las Vegas, NV	8/15/32
Dalton, Timothy	Colwyn Bay, Wales	3/21/44
Daltrey, Roger	London, England	3/1/44
Daly, Timothy	Suffern, NY	3/1/58
Daly, Tyne	Madison, WI	2/21/47
Damon, Matt	Cambridge, MA	10/8/70
Damone, Vic	Brooklyn, NY	6/12/28
Danes, Claire	New York, NY	4/12/79
D'Angelo, Beverly	Columbus, OH	11/15/54
Dangerfield, Rodney	Babylon, NY	11/22/21
Daniels, Charlie	Wilmington, NC	10/28/36
Daniels, Jeff	Georgia	2/19/55
Daniels, William	Brooklyn, NY	3/31/27
Danner, Blythe	Philadelphia, PA	2/3/44
Danson, Ted	San Diego, CA	12/29/47
Danza, Tony	New York, NY	4/21/50
Darby, Kim	Hollywood, CA	7/8/48
David, Larry	Brooklyn, NY	1947
Davidson, John	Pittsburgh, PA	12/13/41
Davis, Ann B.	Schenectady, NY	5/5/26
Davis, Clifton	Chicago, IL	10/4/45

Name	Birthplace	Birthdate
Davis, Geena	Wareham, MA	1/21/57
Davis, Judy	Perth, Australia	1955
Davis, Mac	Lubbock, TX	1/21/42
Davis, Ossie	Cogdell, GA	12/18/17
Dawber, Pam	Farmington Hills, MI	10/18/51
Dawson, Richard	Hampshire, England	11/20/32
Day, Doris	Cincinnati, OH	4/3/24
Day, Laraine	Roosevelt, UT	10/13/20
Day-Lewis, Daniel	London, England	4/29/57
Dean, Jimmy	Plainview, TX	8/10/28
Dearie, Blossom	E. Durham, NY	4/28/26
De Camp, Rosemary	Prescott, AZ	11/14/10
DeCarlo, Yvonne	Vancouver, BC	9/1/22
Dee, Frances	Los Angeles, CA	11/26/07
Dee, Ruby	Cleveland, OH	10/27/23
Dee, Sandra	Bayonne, NJ	4/23/42
DeFranco, Buddy	Camden, NJ	2/17/23
DeGeneres, Ellen	Metairie, LA	1/26/58
DeHaven, Gloria	Los Angeles, CA	7/23/25
De Havilland, Olivia	Tokyo, Japan	7/1/16
Delaney, Kim	Philadelphia, PA	11/29/64
Delany, Dana	New York, NY	3/11/56
DeLaurentis, Dino	Torre Annunziata, Italy	8/8/19
Delon, Alain	Sceaux, France	11/8/35
DeLuise, Dom	Brooklyn, NY	8/1/33
Demme, Jonathan	Rockville Centre, NY	2/22/44
DeMornay, Rebecca	Santa Rosa, CA	11/29/61
Dench, Judi	York, England	12/9/34
Deneuve, Catherine	Paris, France	10/22/43
De Niro, Robert	New York, NY	8/17/43
Dennehy, Brian	Bridgeport, CT	7/9/38
Denver, Bob	New Rochelle, NY	1/9/35
DePalma, Brian	Newark, NJ	9/11/40
Depardieu, Gerard	Chateauroux, France	12/27/48
Depp, Johnny	Owensboro, KY	6/9/63
Derek, Bo	Long Beach, CA	11/20/56
Dern, Bruce	Chicago, IL	6/4/36
Dern, Laura	Santa Monica, CA	2/1/67
Devane, William	Albany, NY	9/5/37
DeVito, Danny	Neptune, NJ	11/17/44
DeWitt, Joyce	Wheeling, WV	4/23/49
Dey, Susan	Pekin, IL	12/10/52
Diamond, Neil	Brooklyn, NY	1/24/41
Diaz, Cameron	San Diego, CA	8/30/72
DiCaprio, Leonardo	Los Angeles, CA	11/11/74
Dick, Andy	Charleston, SC	12/21/66
Dickinson, Angie	Kulm, ND	9/30/31
Diddley, Bo	McComb, MS	12/20/28
Diller, Phyllis	Lima, OH	7/17/17
Dillman, Bradford	San Francisco, CA	4/14/30
Dion, Celine	Charlemagne, Quebec	3/30/68
Dillon, Matt	New Rochelle, NY	2/18/64
Dobson, Kevin	New York, NY	3/18/44
Doherty, Shannen	Memphis, TN	4/21/71
Dolenz, Mickey	Los Angeles, CA	3/8/45
Domingo, Placido	Madrid, Spain	1/21/41
Domino, Fats	New Orleans, LA	2/26/28
Donahue, Phil	Cleveland, OH	12/21/35
Donahue, Troy	New York, NY	1/27/36
D'Onofrio, Vincent	Brooklyn, NY	6/30/59
Dorn, Michael	Luling, TX	12/5/52
Dotrice, Roy	Guernsey, England	5/26/23
Douglas, Kirk	Amsterdam, NY	12/9/16
Douglas, Michael	New Brunswick, NJ	9/25/44
Down, Lesley-Ann	London, England	3/17/54
Downey, Robert, Jr.	New York, NY	4/4/65
Downs, Hugh	Akron, OH	2/14/21
Drescher, Fran	Queens, NY	9/30/57
Drew, Ellen	Kansas City, MO	11/23/15
Dreyfuss, Richard	Brooklyn, NY	10/29/47
Driver, Minnie	London, England	1/31/71
Dryer, Fred	Hawthorne, CA	7/6/46
Duchovny, David	New York, NY	8/7/60
Duffy, Julia	Minneapolis, MN	6/27/51
Duffy, Patrick	Townsend, MT	3/17/49
Dukakis, Olympia	Lowell, MA	6/20/31
Duke, Patty	New York, NY	12/14/46
Dukes, David	San Francisco, CA	6/6/45
Dullea, Keir	Cleveland, OH	5/30/36
Dunaway, Faye	Bascom, FL	1/14/41
Duncan, Sandy	Henderson, TX	2/20/46
Dunham, Katherine	Joliet, IL	6/22/10
Dunne, Griffin	New York, NY	6/8/55
Dunst, Kirsten	New Jersey	4/30/82
Durbin, Deanna	Winnipeg, Manitoba	12/4/21
Durning, Charles	Highland Falls, NY	2/28/23

Name	Birthplace	Birthdate
Dussault, Nancy	Pensacola, FL	6/30/36
Dutton, Charles S.	Baltimore, MD	1/30/51
Duvall, Robert	San Diego, CA	1/5/31
Duvall, Shelley	Houston, TX	7/7/49
Dylan, Bob	Duluth, MN	5/24/41
Dysart, Richard	Augusta, ME	3/30/29
Easton, Sheena	Bellshill, Scotland	4/27/59
Eastwood, Clint	San Francisco, CA	5/31/30
Ebert, Roger	Urbana, IL	6/18/42
Ebsen, Buddy	Belleville, IL	4/2/08
Eden, Barbara	Tucson, AZ	8/23/34
Edwards, Anthony	Santa Barbara, CA	7/19/63
Edwards, Blake	Tulsa, OK	7/26/22
Edwards, Ralph	Merino, CO	6/13/13
Eichhorn, Lisa	Reading, PA	2/4/52
Eikenberry, Jill	New Haven, CT	1/21/47
Ekberg, Anita	Malmo, Sweden	9/29/31
Ekland, Britt	Stockholm, Sweden	10/6/42
Elam, Jack	Miami, AZ	11/13/16
Elfman, Jenna	Los Angeles, CA	9/30/71
Elizondo, Hector	New York, NY	12/22/36
Elliott, Bob	Boston, MA	3/26/23
Elliott, Chris	New York, NY	1960
Elliott, Sam	Sacramento, CA	8/9/44
Elvira	Manhattan, KS	9/17/51
Enberg, Dick	Auburn Hills, MI	1/5/35
Englund, Robert	Hollywood, CA	6/6/48
Enya	Gweedore, Ireland	5/17/61
Ephron, Nora	New York, NY	5/19/41
Estefan, Gloria	Havana, Cuba	9/1/57
Estevez, Emilio	New York, NY	5/12/62
Estrada, Erik	New York, NY	3/16/49
Etheridge, Melissa	Leavenworth, KS	5/29/61
Evans, Dale	Uvalde, TX	10/31/12
Evans, Linda	Hartford, CT	11/18/42
Evans, Robert	New York, NY	6/29/30
Everett, Chad	South Bend, IN	6/11/36
Everett, Rupert	Norfolk, England	5/29/59
Everly, Don	Brownie, KY	2/1/37
Everly, Phil	Chicago, IL	1/19/39
Evigan, Greg	South Amboy, NJ	10/14/53
Fabares, Shelley	Santa Monica, CA	1/19/42
Fabian (Forte)	Philadelphia, PA	2/6/43
Fabio	Milan, Italy	3/15/61
Fabray, Nanette	San Diego, CA	10/27/20
Fairbanks, Douglas, Jr.	New York, NY	12/9/09
Fairchild, Morgan	Dallas, TX	2/3/50
Falana, Lola	Philadelphia, PA	9/11/46
Falk, Peter	New York, NY	9/16/27
Farentino, James	Brooklyn, NY	2/24/38
Fargo, Donna	Mt. Airy, NC	11/10/45
Farina, Dennis	Chicago, IL	2/29/44
Farr, Jamie	Toledo, OH	7/1/34
Farrell, Eileen	Willimantic, CT	2/13/20
Farrell, Mike	St. Paul, MN	2/6/39
Farrow, Mia	Los Angeles, CA	2/9/45
Faustino, David	California	3/3/74
Fawcett, Farrah	Corpus Christi, TX	2/2/47
Feinstein, Michael	Columbus, OH	9/7/56
Feldon, Barbara	Pittsburgh, PA	3/12/41
Feliciano, Jose	Lares, Puerto Rico	9/10/45
Fell, Norman	Philadelphia, PA	3/24/24
Feldshuh, Tovah	New York, NY	12/27/53
Fenn, Sherilyn	Detroit, MI	2/1/65
Ferrell, Conchata	Charleston, WV	3/28/43
Ferrer, Mel	Elberon, NJ	8/25/17
Fiedler, John	Platteville, WI	2/3/25
Field, Sally	Pasadena, CA	11/6/46
Fiennes, Ralph	Suffolk, England	12/22/62
Finney, Albert	Salford, England	5/9/36
Fiorentino, Linda	Philadelphia, PA	3/9/60
Firth, Colin	Grayshott, England	9/10/60
Firth, Peter	Yorkshire, England	10/27/53
Fischer-Dieskau, Dietrich	Berlin, Germany	5/28/25
Fishburne, Laurence	Augusta, GA	7/30/61
Fisher, Carrie	Beverly Hills, CA	10/21/56
Fisher, Eddie	Philadelphia, PA	8/10/28
Fitzgerald, Geraldine	Dublin, Ireland	11/24/13
Flack, Roberta	Black Mountain, NC	2/10/39
Flanagan, Fionnula	Dublin, Ireland	12/10/41
Fleming, Rhonda	Hollywood, CA	8/10/23
Fletcher, Louise	Birmingham, AL	7/22/34
Flockhart, Calista	Freeport, IL	11/11/64
Foch, Nina	Leyden, Netherlands	4/20/24
Fogelberg, Dan	Peoria, IL	8/13/51

Name	Birthplace	Birthdate
Fogerty, John	Berkeley, CA	5/28/45
Foley, Dave	Toronto, Ontario	1/4/63
Fonda, Bridget	Los Angeles, CA	1/27/64
Fonda, Jane	New York, NY	12/21/37
Fonda, Peter	New York, NY	2/23/40
Fontaine, Joan	Tokyo, Japan	10/22/17
Ford, Faith	Alexandria, LA	9/14/64
Ford, Glenn	Quebec, Canada	5/1/16
Ford, Harrison	Chicago, IL	7/13/42
Forman, Milos	Caslav, Czechoslovakia	2/18/32
Forsythe, John	Penns Grove, NJ	1/29/18
Foster, Jodie	New York, NY	11/19/62
Fox, James	London, England	5/19/39
Fox, Matthew	Crowheart, WY	1967
Fox, Michael J.	Edmonton, Alberta	6/9/61
Fox, Vivica A.	Indianapolis, IN	7/30/64
Foxworth, Robert	Houston, TX	11/1/41
Foxworthy, Jeff	Atlanta, GA	9/6/57
Frampton, Peter	Kent, England	4/22/50
Franciosa, Anthony	New York, NY	10/25/28
Francis, Anne	Ossining, NY	9/16/30
Francis, Arlene	Boston, MA	10/20/08
Francis, Connie	Newark, NJ	12/12/38
Franken, Al	New York, NY	5/21/51
Frankenheimer, John	Malba, NY	2/19/30
Franklin, Aretha	Memphis, TN	3/25/42
Franklin, Bonnie	Santa Monica, CA	1/6/44
Franz, Dennis	Maywood, IL	10/28/44
Fraser, Brendan	Indianapolis, IN	12/3/67
Freeman, Al, Jr.	San Antonio, TX	3/21/34
Freeman, Mona	Baltimore, MD	6/9/26
Freeman, Morgan	Memphis, TN	6/1/37
Fricker, Brenda	Dublin, Ireland	2/17/45
Friedkin, William	Chicago, IL	8/29/39
Frost, David	Tenterden, England	4/7/39
Fuentes, Daisy	Havana, Cuba	11/17/66
Funicello, Annette	Utica, NY	10/22/42
Funt, Allen	New York, NY	9/16/14
Gabor, Zsa Zsa	Budapest, Hungary	2/6/17
Gabriel, John	Niagara Falls, NY	5/25/31
Gabriel, Peter	London, England	2/13/50
Galway, James	Belfast, Ireland	12/8/39
Garagiola, Joe	St. Louis, MO	2/12/26
Garcia, Andy	Havana, Cuba	4/12/56
Garofalo, Janeane	New Jersey	9/28/64
Garfunkel, Art	New York, NY	11/5/41
Garland, Beverly	Santa Cruz, CA	10/17/26
Garner, James	Norman, OK	4/7/28
Garr, Teri	Lakewood, OH	12/11/45
Garrett, Betty	St. Joseph, MO	5/23/19
Garth, Jennie	Champaign, IL	4/3/72
Gatlin, Larry	Seminole, TX	5/2/48
Gayle, Crystal	Paintsville, KY	1/9/51
Gaynor, Mitzi	Chicago, IL	9/4/30
Gazzara, Ben	New York, NY	8/28/30
Geary, Anthony	Coalville, UT	5/29/47
Geary, Cynthia	Jackson, MS	3/21/66
Gedda, Nicolai	Stockholm, Sweden	7/11/25
Gellar, Sarah Michelle	New York, NY	4/14/77
Gere, Richard	Philadelphia, PA	8/31/49
Getty, Estelle	New York, NY	7/25/24
Ghostley, Alice	Eve, MO	8/14/26
Giannini, Giancarlo	Spezia, Italy	8/1/42
Gibb, Barry	Isle of Man, England	9/1/46
Gibb, Maurice	Manchester, England	12/22/49
Gibb, Robin	Manchester, England	12/22/49
Gibbons, Leeza	South Carolina	3/26/57
Gibbs, Marla	Chicago, IL	6/14/31
Gibson, Deborah	New York, NY	8/31/70
Gibson, Henry	Germantown, PA	9/21/35
Gibson, Mel	Peekskill, NY	1/3/56
Gibson, Thomas	Charleston, SC	7/3/62
Gielgud, John	London, England	4/14/04
Gifford, Frank	Santa Monica, CA	8/16/30
Gifford, Kathie Lee	Paris, France	8/16/53
Gilbert, Sara	Santa Monica, CA	1/29/75
Gilbert, Melissa	Los Angeles, CA	5/8/64
Gilberto, Astrud	Salvador, Brazil	3/30/40
Gill, Vince	Norman, OK	4/12/57
Gillette, Anita	Baltimore, MD	8/16/38
Gilley, Mickey	Natchez, MS	3/9/36
Gilpin, Peri	Waco, TX	5/27/63
Ginty, Robert	New York, NY	11/14/48
Givens, Robin	New York, NY	11/27/64
Glaser, Paul Michael	Cambridge, MA	3/25/42

Name	Birthplace	Birthdate
Glenn, Scott	Pittsburgh, PA	1/26/42
Gless, Sharon	Los Angeles, CA	5/31/43
Glover, Crispin	New York, NY	9/20/64
Glover, Danny	San Francisco, CA	7/22/47
Glover, Savion	Newark, NJ	1973
Godard, Jean Luc	Paris, France	12/3/30
Goldberg, Whoopi	New York, NY	11/13/49
Goldblum, Jeff	Pittsburgh, PA	10/22/52
Goldthwait, Bobcat	Syracuse, NY	5/1/62
Goldwyn, Tony	Los Angeles, CA	5/20/60
Gooding, Cuba, Jr.	Bronx, NY	1/2/68
Goodman, John	St. Louis, MO	6/20/52
Gordon-Levitt, Joseph	Los Angeles, CA	2/17/81
Gorme, Eydie	Bronx, NY	8/16/32
Gorshin, Frank	Pittsburgh, PA	4/5/34
Gossett, Louis, Jr.	Brooklyn, NY	5/27/36
Gould, Elliott	Brooklyn, NY	8/29/38
Gould, Harold	Schenectady, NY	12/10/23
Goulet, Robert	Lawrence, MA	11/26/33
Gowdy, Curt	Green River, WY	7/31/19
Graham, Heather	Milwaukee, WI	1/29/70
Graham, Virginia	Chicago, IL	7/4/12
Grammer, Kelsey	St. Thomas, Virgin Isl.	2/20/55
Granger, Farley	San Jose, CA	7/1/25
Grant, Amy	Augusta, GA	12/25/60
Grant, Hugh	London, England	9/9/60
Grant, Lee	New York, NY	10/31/29
Graves, Peter	Minneapolis, MN	3/18/26
Gray, Linda	Santa Monica, CA	9/12/40
Gray, Spaulding	Barrington, RI	6/5/41
Grayson, Kathryn	Winston-Salem, NC	2/9/22
Greco, Jose	Abruzzi, Italy	12/23/18
Green, Adolph	New York, NY	12/2/15
Green, Al	Forrest City, AR	4/13/46
Greene, Shecky	Chicago, IL	4/8/26
Greenwood, Bruce	Quebec, Canada	8/12/56
Greer, Jane	Washington, DC	9/9/24
Gregory, Cynthia	Los Angeles, CA	7/8/46
Gregory, Dick	St. Louis, MO	10/12/32
Gregory, James	Bronx, NY	12/23/11
Grey, Jennifer	New York, NY	3/22/60
Grey, Joel	Cleveland, OH	4/11/32
Grier, David Alan	Detroit, MI	6/30/55
Grier, Pam	Winston-Salem, NC	5/26/49
Griffin, Merv	San Mateo, CA	7/6/25
Griffith, Andy	Mount Airy, NC	6/1/26
Griffith, Melanie	New York, NY	8/9/57
Grimes, Tammy	Lynn, MA	1/30/34
Grizzard, George	Roanoke Rapids, NC	4/1/28
Grodin, Charles	Pittsburgh, PA	4/21/35
Grosbard, Ulu	Antwerp, Belgium	1/19/29
Gross, Michael	Chicago, IL	6/21/47
Guest, Christopher	New York, NY	2/5/48
Guillaume, Robert	St. Louis, MO	11/30/37
Guinness, Alec	London, England	4/2/14
Gumbel, Greg	New Orleans, LA	5/3/46
Guthrie, Arlo	New York, NY	7/10/47
Guttenberg, Steve	New York, NY	8/24/58
Guy, Buddy	Lettsworth, LA	7/30/36
Guy, Jasmine	Boston, MA	3/10/64
Hackett, Buddy	Brooklyn, NY	8/31/24
Hackman, Gene	San Bernardino, CA	1/30/30
Hagen, Uta	Gottingen, Germany	6/12/19
Haggard, Merle	Bakersfield, CA	4/6/37
Hagman, Larry	Weatherford, TX	9/21/31
Haid, Charles	San Francisco, CA	6/2/44
Haines, Connie	Savannah, GA	1/20/22
Hale, Barbara	DeKalb, IL	4/18/22
Hall, Arsenio	Cleveland, OH	2/12/55
Hall, Daryl	Pottstown, PA	10/11/48
Hall, Deidre	Milwaukee, WI	10/31/48
Hall, Huntz	New York, NY	8/15/19
Hall, Monty	Winnipeg, Manitoba	8/25/25
Hall, Tom T.	Olive Hill, KY	5/25/36
Hamill, Mark	Oakland, CA	9/25/51
Hamilton, George	Memphis, TN	8/12/39
Hamilton, Linda	Salisbury, MD	9/26/56
Hamlin, Harry	Pasadena, CA	10/30/51
Hammer	Oakland, CA	3/29/63
Hampton, Lionel	Birmingham, AL	4/12/13
Hancock, Herbie	Chicago, IL	4/12/40
Hanks, Tom	Oakland, CA	7/9/56
Hannah, Daryl	Chicago, IL	12/3/60
Hanson, Curtis	Los Angeles, CA	3/24/45
Hanson, Isaac	Tulsa, OK	11/17/80

Name	Birthplace	Birthdate
Hanson, Taylor	Tulsa, OK	4/14/83
Hanson, Zac	Tulsa, OK	10/22/85
Hardison, Kadeem	New York, NY	7/24/66
Harewood, Dorian	Dayton, OH	8/6/51
Harmon, Mark	Burbank, CA	9/2/51
Harper, Jessica	Chicago, IL	10/10/49
Harper, Tess	Mammoth Springs, AR	8/15/50
Harper, Valerie	Suffern, NY	8/22/40
Harrelson, Woody	Midland, TX	7/23/61
Harrington, Pat	New York, NY	8/13/29
Harris, Barbara	Evanston, IL	7/25/35
Harris, Ed	Englewood, NJ	11/28/50
Harris, Emmylou	Birmingham, AL	4/2/47
Harris, Julie	Grosse Pte. Park, MI	12/2/25
Harris, Neil Patrick	Albuquerque, NM	6/15/73
Harris, Richard	Co. Limerick, Ireland	10/1/33
Harris, Rosemary	Ashby, England	9/19/30
Harrison, George	Liverpool, England	2/25/43
Harrison, Gregory	Avalon, CA	5/31/50
Harry, Deborah	Miami, FL	7/1/45
Hart, Mary	Madison, SD	11/8/51
Hart, Melissa Joan	Sayville, NY	4/18/76
Hartley, Hal	Lindenhurst, NY	11/3/59
Hartley, Mariette	New York, NY	6/21/40
Hartman, David	Pawtucket, RI	5/19/35
Hartman, Lisa	Houston, TX	6/1/56
Hasselhoff, David	Baltimore, MD	7/17/52
Hatcher, Teri	Sunnyvale, CA	12/8/64
Hauer, Rutger	Breukelen, Netherlands	1/23/44
Haver, June	Rock Island, IL	6/10/26
Havoc, June	Seattle, WA	11/8/16
Hawke, Ethan	Austin, TX	11/6/70
Hawn, Goldie	Washington, DC	11/21/45
Hayden, Melissa	Toronto, Ontario	4/25/23
Hayek, Salma	Coatzacoalcos, Mexico	9/2/68
Hayes, Isaac	Covington, TN	8/20/42
Hays, Robert	Bethesda, MD	7/24/47
Heard, John	Washington, DC	3/7/45
Hearn, George	Memphis, TN	1935
Heche, Anne	Aurora, OH	5/25/69
Heckart, Eileen	Columbus, OH	3/29/19
Hedren, Tippi	New Ulm, MN	1/19/35
Helfgott, David	Melbourne, Australia	5/19/47
Helmond, Katherine	Galveston, TX	7/5/34
Hemingway, Mariel	Mill Valley, CA	11/21/61
Hemmings, David	Guildford, England	11/18/41
Hemsley, Sherman	Philadelphia, PA	2/1/38
Henderson, Florence	Dale, IN	2/14/34
Henderson, Skitch	Halstad, MN	1/27/18
Henley, Don	Gilmer, TX	7/22/47
Henner, Marilu	Chicago, IL	4/6/52
Henning, Doug	Ft. Garry, Manitoba	5/3/47
Henry, Buck	New York, NY	12/9/30
Hepburn, Katharine	Hartford, CT	5/12/07
Herman, Pee-Wee	Peekskill, NY	8/27/52
Herrmann, Edward	Washington, DC	7/21/43
Hershey, Barbara	Los Angeles, CA	2/5/48
Hesseman, Howard	Lebanon, OR	2/27/40
Heston, Charlton	Evanston, IL	10/4/24
Hewett, Christopher	Sussex, England	4/5/22
Hewitt, Jennifer Love	Waco, TX	2/21/79
Hickson, Joan	England	8/5/06
Hildegarde	Adell, WI	2/1/06
Hill, Arthur	Melfort, Sask.	8/1/22
Hill, Steven	Seattle, WA	2/24/22
Hill, George Roy	Minneapolis, MN	12/20/22
Hiller, Wendy	Stockport, England	8/15/12
Hillerman, John	Denison, TX	12/30/32
Hines, Gregory	New York, NY	2/14/46
Hines, Roy	Boston, MA	3/13/26
Hines, Jerome	Hollywood, CA	11/8/21
Hingle, Pat	Miami, FL	7/19/24
Hirsch, Judd	New York, NY	3/15/35
Hirt, Al	New Orleans, LA	11/7/22
Ho, Don	Kakaako, Oahu, HI	8/13/30
Hoffman, Dustin	Los Angeles, CA	8/8/37
Hogan, Paul	New South Wales, Australia	10/8/39
Holbrook, Hal	Cleveland, OH	2/17/25
Holder, Geoffrey	Trinidad	8/1/30
Holliday, Polly	Jasper, AL	8/2/37
Holliman, Earl	Delhi, LA	9/11/28
Holly, Lauren	Bristol, PA	10/28/63
Holm, Celeste	New York, NY	4/29/19
Hooker, John Lee	Clarksdale, MS	8/22/17
Hooks, Jan	Decatur, GA	4/23/57
Hope, Bob	London, England	5/29/03

Name	Birthplace	Birthdate
Hopkins, Anthony	Port Talbot, South Wales	12/31/37
Hopkins, Bo	Greenville, SC	2/2/42
Hopkins, Telma	Louisville, KY	10/28/48
Hopper, Dennis	Dodge City, KS	5/17/36
Horne, Lena	Brooklyn, NY	6/30/17
Horne, Marilyn	Bradford, PA	1/16/34
Hornsby, Bruce	Williamsburg, VA	11/23/54
Horsley, Lee	Muleshoe, TX	5/15/55
Hoskins, Bob	Suffolk, England	10/26/42
Houston, Whitney	E Orange, NJ	8/9/63
Howard, Ken	El Centro, CA	3/28/44
Howard, Ron	Duncan, OK	3/1/54
Howell, C. Thomas	Los Angeles, CA	12/7/66
Howes, Sally Ann	London, England	7/20/30
Hughes, Barnard	Bedford Hills, NY	7/16/15
Hulce, Tom	Whitewater, WI	12/6/53
Humperdinck, Engelbert	Madras, India	5/3/36
Hunt, Helen	Los Angeles, CA	6/15/63
Hunt, Linda	Morristown, NJ	4/2/45
Hunter, Holly	Conyers, GA	3/20/58
Hunter, Kim	Detroit, MI	11/12/22
Hunter, Tab	New York, NY	7/11/31
Hurley, Elizabeth	Hampshire, England	6/10/65
Hurt, John	Chesterfield, England	1/22/40
Hurt, Mary Beth	Marshalltown, IA	9/26/46
Hurt, William	Washington, DC	3/20/50
Hussey, Ruth	Providence, RI	10/30/14
Huston, Anjelica	Santa Monica, CA	7/8/51
Hutton, Betty	Battle Creek, MI	2/26/21
Hutton, Lauren	Charleston, SC	11/17/44
Hutton, Timothy	Malibu, CA	8/16/60
Hyman, Earle	Rocky Mount, NC	10/11/26
Ian, Janis	New York, NY	4/7/51
Ice-T	Newark, NJ	2/16/58
Idle, Eric	Durham, England	3/29/43
Idol, Billy	London, England	11/30/55
Iman	Mogadishu, Somalia	7/25/55
Iglesias, Julio	Madrid, Spain	9/23/43
Imus, Don	Riverside, CA	7/23/40
Ireland, Kathy	Santa Barbara, CA	3/8/63
Ingram, James	Akron, OH	2/16/56
Irons, Jeremy	Cowes, England	9/19/48
Irving, Amy	Palo Alto, CA	9/10/53
Irving, George S.	Springfield, MA	11/1/22
Ivey, Judith	El Paso, TX	9/4/51
Ivory, James	Berkeley, CA	6/7/28
Jackee	Winston-Salem, NC	8/14/56
Jackson, Anne	Allegheny, PA	9/3/25
Jackson, Glenda	Liverpool, England	5/9/36
Jackson, Janet	Gary, IN	5/16/66
Jackson, Jermaine	Gary, IN	12/11/54
Jackson, La Toya	Gary, IN	5/29/56
Jackson, Kate	Birmingham, AL	10/29/48
Jackson, Michael	Gary, IN	8/29/58
Jackson, Milt	Detroit, MI	1/1/22
Jackson, Samuel L.	Chattanooga, TN	12/21/48
Jacobi, Derek	London, England	10/22/38
Jagger, Mick	Dartford, England	7/26/43
James, Etta	Los Angeles, CA	1938
Janis, Conrad	New York, NY	2/11/28
Jardine, Al	Lima, OH	9/3/42
Jarmusch, Jim	Akron, OH	1/22/53
Jarreau, Al	Milwaukee, WI	3/12/40
Jarrette, Keith	Allentown, PA	5/8/45
Jeffreys, Anne	Goldsboro, NC	1/26/23
Jennings, Waylon	Littlefield, TX	6/15/37
Jeter, Michael	Lawrenceburg, TN	8/20/52
Jett, Joan	Philadelphia, PA	9/22/60
Jewel (Kilcher)	Homer, AK	5/3/74
Jewison, Norman	Toronto, Ontario	7/21/26
Jillian, Ann	Cambridge, MA	1/29/50
Joel, Billy	Bronx, NY	5/9/49
John, Elton	Middlesex, England	3/25/47
Johns, Glynis	Durban, S Africa	10/5/23
Johnson, Arte	Benton Harbor, MI	1/20/29
Johnson, Beverly	Buffalo, NY	10/13/52
Johnson, Don	Flatt Creek, MO	12/15/49
Johnson, J. J.	Indianapolis, IN	1/22/24
Johnson, Van	Newport, RI	8/25/16
Johnston, Bruce	Chicago, IL	6/24/44
Johnston, Kristen	Washington, DC	9/20/67
Jones, Charlie	Ft. Smith, AR	11/9/30
Jones, Davy	Manchester, England	12/30/45
Jones, Dean	Morgan City, AL	1/25/35
Jones, Elvin	Pontiac, MI	9/9/27

Name	Birthplace	Birthdate
Jones, George	Saratoga, TX	9/12/31
Jones, Grace	Spanishtown, Jamaica	5/19/52
Jones, Henry	Philadelphia, PA	8/1/12
Jones, Jack	Hollywood, CA	1/14/38
Jones, James Earl	Tate Co., MS	1/17/31
Jones, Jennifer	Tulsa, OK	3/2/19
Jones, Quincy	Chicago, IL	3/14/33
Jones, Shirley	Smithton, PA	3/31/34
Jones, Tom	Pontypridd, Wales	6/7/40
Jones, Tommy Lee	San Saba, TX	9/15/46
Jourdan, Louis	Marseilles, France	6/19/19
Jovovich, Milla	Kiev, Ukraine	12/19/75
Judd, Ashley	Los Angeles, CA	4/19/68
Judd, Naomi	Ashland, KY	1/11/46
Judd, Wynonna	Ashland, KY	5/3/64
Jump, Gordon	Dayton, OH	4/1/32
Kahn, Madeline	Boston, MA	9/29/42
Kanaly, Steve	Burbank, CA	3/14/46
Kane, Carol	Cleveland, OH	6/18/52
Karlen, John	New York, NY	5/28/33
Karn, Richard	Seattle, WA	2/17/56
Karras, Alex	Gary, IN	7/15/35
Kasem, Casey	Detroit, MI	4/27/33
Kavner, Julie	Los Angeles, CA	9/7/51
Kazan, Elia	Istanbul, Turkey	9/7/09
Kazan, Lainie	New York, NY	5/15/42
Keach, Stacy	Savannah, GA	6/2/41
Keaton, Diane	Santa Ana, CA	1/5/46
Keaton, Michael	Pittsburgh, PA	9/9/51
Keel, Howard	Gillespie, IL	4/13/17
Keeshan, Bob	Lynbrook, NY	6/27/27
Keitel, Harvey	Brooklyn, NY	5/13/39
Keith, David	Knoxville, TN	5/8/54
Keith, Penelope	Sutton, Surrey, Eng.	4/2/40
Kellerman, Sally	Long Beach, CA	6/2/37
Kelley, DeForest	Atlanta, GA	1/20/20
Kennedy, George	New York, NY	2/18/25
Kennedy, Jayne	Washington, DC	11/27/51
Kenny G	Seattle, WA	6/5/56
Kent, Allegra	Los Angeles, CA	8/11/37
Kercheval, Ken	Wolcottville, IN	7/15/35
Kerns, Joanna	San Francisco, CA	2/12/53
Kerr, Deborah	Helensburgh, Scotland	9/30/21
Kessel, Barney	Muskogee, OK	10/17/23
Khan, Chaka	Great Lakes, IL	3/23/53
Kidder, Margot	Yellowknife, N.W.T.	10/17/48
Kidman, Nicole	Honolulu, HI	6/20/67
Kiley, Richard	Chicago, IL	3/31/22
Kilmer, Val	Los Angeles, CA	12/31/59
Kimbrough, Charles	St. Paul, MN	5/23/36
King, Alan	Brooklyn, NY	12/26/27
King, B. B.	Itta Bena, MS	9/16/25
King, Carole	Brooklyn, NY	2/9/42
King, Larry	Brooklyn, NY	11/19/33
King, Perry	Alliance, OH	4/30/48
Kingsley, Ben	Yorkshire, England	12/31/43
Kinnear, Greg	Logansport, IN	6/17/63
Kinski, Nastassja	Berlin, W. Germany	1/24/60
Kirby, Bruno	New York, NY	4/28/49
Kirby, Durward	Covington, KY	8/24/12
Kirkland, Gelsey	Bethlehem, PA	12/29/53
Kitt, Eartha	North, SC	1/17/27
Klein, Robert	New York, NY	2/8/42
Klemperer, Werner	Cologne, Germany	3/22/19
Kline, Kevin	St. Louis, MO	10/24/47
Klugman, Jack	Philadelphia, PA	4/27/22
Knight, Gladys	Atlanta, GA	5/28/44
Knight, Shirley	Goessel, KS	7/5/36
Knight, Wayne	Cartersville, GA	8/7/55
Knotts, Don	Morgantown, WV	7/21/24
Konitz, Lee	Chicago, IL	10/13/27
Kopell, Bernie	New York, NY	6/21/33
Korman, Harvey	Chicago, IL	2/15/27
Kotto, Yaphet	New York, NY	11/15/37
Kramer, Stanley	New York, NY	9/29/13
Kristofferson, Kris	Brownsville, TX	6/22/36
Kubrick, Stanley	Bronx, NY	7/26/28
Kudrow, Lisa	Encino, CA	5/30/63
Kurtz, Swoosie	Omaha, NE	9/6/44
LaBelle, Patti	Philadelphia, PA	5/24/44
Ladd, Cheryl	Huron, SD	7/12/51
Ladd, Diane	Meridian, MS	11/29/32
Lahti, Christine	Detroit, MI	4/5/50
Laine, Cleo	Middlesex, England	10/28/27
Laine, Frankie	Chicago, IL	3/30/13

Name	Birthplace	Birthdate
Lake, Ricki	New York, NY	9/21/68
Lamarr, Hedy	Vienna, Austria	11/9/13
Lamas, Lorenzo	Santa Monica, CA	1/20/58
Lambert, Christopher	New York, NY	3/29/57
Landau, Martin	New York, NY	6/20/34
Landis, John	Chicago, IL	8/3/50
Lane, Diane	New York, NY	1/22/63
Lane, Nathan	Jersey City, NJ	2/3/56
lang, k.d.	Consort, Alberta	11/2/61
Lang, Stephen	New York, NY	7/11/52
Lange, Hope	Redding Ridge, CT	11/28/31
Lange, Jessica	Cloquet, MN	4/20/49
Langella, Frank	Bayonne, NJ	1/1/40
Langford, Frances	Lakeland, FL	4/4/13
Lansbury, Angela	London, England	10/16/25
LaPaglia, Anthony	Adelaide, Australia	1/31/59
Laredo, Ruth	Detroit, MI	11/20/37
Larroquette, John	New Orleans, LA	11/25/47
LaSalle, Eriq	Hartford, CT	6/23/63
Lauper, Cyndi	New York, NY	6/20/53
Laurie, Piper	Detroit, MI	1/22/32
Lavin, Linda	Portland, ME	10/15/37
Lawless, Lucy	Mount Albert, New Zealand	3/28/68
Lawrence, Carol	Melrose Park, IL	9/5/34
Lawrence, Joey	Montgomery, PA	4/20/76
Lawrence, Martin	Frankfurt, Germany	4/16/65
Lawrence, Steve	Brooklyn, NY	7/8/35
Lawrence, Vicki	Inglewood, CA	3/26/49
Leach, Robin	London, England	8/29/41
Leachman, Cloris	Des Moines, IA	4/4/26
Lear, Norman	New Haven, CT	7/27/22
Learned, Michael	Washington, DC	4/9/39
LeBlanc, Matt	Newton, MA	5/25/68
LeBon, Simon	Bushey, England	10/27/58
Lee, Ang	Taiwan	10/23/54
Lee, Brenda	Atlanta, GA	12/11/44
Lee, Christopher	London, England	5/27/22
Lee, Michele	Los Angeles, CA	6/24/42
Lee, Pamela Anderson	Comox, Canada	7/1/67
Lee, Peggy	Jamestown, ND	5/26/20
Lee, Spike	Atlanta, GA	3/20/57
Leeves, Jane	London, England	4/18/62
Legrand, Michel	Paris, France	2/24/32
Leguizamo, John	Bogota, Colombia	7/22/65
Leibman, Ron	New York, NY	10/11/37
Leigh, Janet	Merced, CA	7/6/27
Leigh, Jennifer Jason	Los Angeles, CA	2/5/62
Leighton, Laura	Iowa City, IA	3/14/69
Lemmon, Jack	Boston, MA	2/8/25
Lennox, Annie	Aberdeen, Scotland	12/25/54
Leno, Jay	New Rochelle, NY	4/28/50
Leonard, Robert Sean	Westwood, NJ	2/28/69
Leoni, Tea	New York, NY	2/25/66
Leslie, Joan	Detroit, MI	1/26/25
Leto, Jared	Bossier City, LA	12/26/71
Letterman, David	Indianapolis, IN	4/12/47
Levine, James	Cincinnati, OH	6/23/43
Levinson, Barry	Baltimore, MD	6/2/32
Lewis, Al	New York, NY	4/30/10
Lewis, Huey	New York, NY	7/5/51
Lewis, Jerry	Newark, NJ	3/16/26
Lewis, Jerry Lee	Ferriday, LA	9/29/35
Lewis, John	La Grange, IL	5/30/20
Lewis, Juliette	San Fernando Valley, CA	6/21/73
Lewis, Richard	New York, NY	6/29/47
Light, Judith	Trenton, NJ	2/9/50
Lightfoot, Gordon	Orillia, Ontario	11/17/38
Linden, Hal	New York, NY	3/20/31
Linkletter, Art	Saskatchewan, Canada	7/17/12
Linn-Baker, Mark	St. Louis, MO	6/17/53
Liotta, Ray	Newark, NJ	12/18/55
Lithgow, John	Rochester, NY	10/19/45
Little, Rich	Ottawa, Ontario	11/26/38
Little Richard	Macon, GA	12/5/32
L. L. Cool J	New York, NY	1/14/68
Lloyd, Christopher	Stamford, CT	10/22/38
Lloyd, Emily	England	9/29/70
Lloyd Webber, Andrew	London, England	3/22/48
Locke, Sondra	Shelbyville, TN	5/28/47
Lockhart, June	New York, NY	6/25/25
Locklear, Heather	Los Angeles, CA	9/25/61
Loggia, Robert	New York, NY	1/3/30
Loggins, Kenny	Everett, WA	1/17/47
Lollobrigida, Gina	Subiaco, Italy	7/4/27
Lom, Herbert	Prague, Czechoslovakia	1/9/17

Name	Birthplace	Birthdate
Long, Shelley	Ft. Wayne, IN	8/23/49
Lopez, Jennifer	Bronx, NY	1970
Loren, Sophia	Rome, Italy	9/20/34
Loring, Gloria	New York, NY	12/10/46
Loudon, Dorothy	Boston, MA	9/17/33
Louis-Dreyfus, Julia	New York, NY	1/13/61
Love, Courtney	San Francisco, CA	7/9/64
Love, Mike	Los Angeles, CA	3/15/41
Lovett, Lyle	Klein, TX	11/1/57
Lovitz, Jon	Tarzana, CA	7/21/57
Loveless, Patty	Pikeville, KY	1/4/57
Lowe, Rob	Charlottesville, VA	3/17/64
Lucas, George	Modesto, CA	5/14/44
Lucci, Susan	Scarsdale, NY	12/23/48
Luckinbill, Laurence	Ft. Smith, AR	11/21/34
Ludwig, Christa	Berlin, Germany	3/16/28
Lumet, Sidney	Philadelphia, PA	6/25/24
LuPone, Patti	Northport, NY	4/21/49
Lynch, David	Missoula, MT	1/20/46
Lynley, Carol	New York, NY	2/13/42
Lynn, Loretta	Butcher Hollow, KY	4/14/35
Ma, Yo Yo	Paris, France	10/7/55
Maazel, Lorin	Paris, France	3/6/30
MacArthur, James	Los Angeles, CA	12/8/37
MacCorkindale, Simon	Cambridge, England	2/12/52
MacDowell, Andie	Gaffney, SC	4/21/58
MacGraw, Ali	Pound Ridge, NY	4/1/38
MacLachlan, Kyle	Yakima, WA	2/22/59
MacLaine, Shirley	Richmond, VA	4/24/34
MacLeod, Gavin	Mt. Kisco, NY	2/28/30
MacNee, Patrick	London, England	2/6/22
MacNeil, Cornell	Minneapolis, MN	9/24/22
MacNicol, Peter	Dallas, TX	4/10/54
MacPherson, Elle	Sydney, Australia	3/29/64
Macchio, Ralph	Long Island, NY	11/4/62
Macy, Bill	Revere, MA	5/18/22
Macy, William H.	Miami, FL	3/13/50
Madden, John	Austin, MN	4/10/36
Madigan, Amy	Chicago, IL	9/11/51
Madonna (Ciccone)	Bay City, MI	8/16/58
Maher, Bill	Rivervale, NJ	1/20/56
Mahoney, John	Manchester, England	6/20/40
Majors, Lee	Wyandotte, MI	4/23/40
Malden, Karl	Chicago, IL	3/22/13
Malick, Wendie	Buffalo, NY	12/13/50
Malkovich, John	Christopher, IL	12/9/53
Malone, Dorothy	Chicago, IL	1/30/25
Manchester, Melissa	Bronx, NY	2/15/51
Mandel, Howie	Toronto, Ontario	11/29/55
Mandrell, Barbara	Houston, TX	12/25/48
Mangione, Chuck	Rochester, NY	11/29/40
Manilow, Barry	New York, NY	6/17/46
Mann, Herbie	New York, NY	4/16/30
Manoff, Dinah	New York, NY	1/25/58
Manson, Marilyn	Canton, OH	1/5/69
Mantegna, Joe	Chicago, IL	11/13/47
Marceau, Marcel	Strasbourg, France	3/22/23
Marchand, Nancy	Buffalo, NY	6/19/28
Margulies, Julianna	Spring Valley, NY	6/8/66
Marin, Cheech	Los Angeles, CA	7/13/46
Marinaro, Ed	New York, NY	3/31/50
Markova, Alicia	London, England	12/1/10
Marriner, Neville	Lincoln, England	4/15/24
Marsalis, Branford	New Orleans, LA	8/26/60
Marsalis, Wynton	New Orleans, LA	10/18/61
Marsh, Jean	London, England	7/1/34
Marshall, Garry	New York, NY	11/13/34
Marshall, Penny	New York, NY	10/15/43
Marshall, Peter	Huntington, WV	3/30/27
Martin, Dick	Detroit, MI	1/30/23
Martin, Steve	Waco, TX	4/14/45
Martin, Tony	San Francisco, CA	12/25/13
Martins, Peter	Copenhagen, Denmark	10/27/46
Mason, Jackie	Sheboygan, WI	6/9/31
Mason, Marsha	St. Louis, MO	4/3/42
Masterson, Mary Stuart	Los Angeles, CA	6/28/66
Mastrantonio, Mary Elizabeth	Lombard, IL	11/17/58
Masur, Kurt	Brieg, Germany	7/18/27
Masur, Richard	New York, NY	11/20/48
Mathers, Jerry	Sioux City, IA	6/2/48
Matheson, Tim	Glendale, CA	12/31/47
Mathis, Johnny	San Francisco, CA	9/30/35
Matlin, Marlee	Morton Grove, IL	8/24/65
Matthau, Walter	New York, NY	10/1/20

Name	Birthplace	Birthdate
Mature, Victor	Louisville, KY	1/29/16
May, Elaine	Philadelphia, PA	4/21/32
Mayfield, Curtis	Chicago, IL	6/3/42
Mayo, Virginia	St. Louis, MO	11/30/20
Mazursky, Paul	Brooklyn, NY	4/25/30
McArdle, Andrea	Philadelphia, PA	11/5/63
McBride, Patricia	Teaneck, NJ	8/23/42
McCallum, David	Glasgow, Scotland	9/19/33
McCambridge, Mercedes	Joliet, IL	3/17/18
McCarthy, Andrew	Westfield, NJ	11/29/62
McCarthy, Jenny	Chicago, IL	11/1/72
McCarthy, Kevin	Seattle, WA	2/15/14
McCartney, Paul	Liverpool, England	6/18/42
McCarver, Tim	Memphis, TN	10/16/41
McClanahan, Rue	Healdton, OK	2/21/36
McConaughey, Matthew	Uvalde, Texas	11/4/69
McCoo, Marilyn	Jersey City, NJ	9/30/43
McCormack, Mary	Plainsfield, NJ	4/8/69
McDermott, Dylan	Waterbury, CT	10/26/62
McDonnell, Mary	Wilkes-Barre, PA	1952
McDormand, Frances	Illinois	6/23/57
McDowell, Malcolm	Leeds, England	6/13/43
McEntire, Reba	McAlester, OK	3/28/55
McFerrin, Bobby	New York, NY	3/11/50
McGavin, Darren	Spokane, WA	5/7/22
McGillis, Kelly	Newport Beach, CA	7/9/57
McGoohan, Patrick	New York, NY	3/19/28
McGovern, Elizabeth	Evanston, IL	7/18/61
McGovern, Maureen	Youngstown, OH	7/27/49
McGregor, Ewan	Crieff, Scotland	3/31/71
McGuire, Al	New York, NY	9/7/31
McGuire, Dorothy	Omaha, NE	6/14/19
McKean, Michael	New York, NY	10/17/47
McKechnie, Donna	Pontiac, MI	11/16/42
McKellen, Ian	Burnley, England	5/25/39
McMahon, Ed	Detroit, MI	3/6/23
McNichol, Kristy	Los Angeles, CA	9/11/62
McPartland, Marian	Stough, England	3/20/20
McRaney, Gerald	Collins, MS	8/19/48
Meadows, Jayne	Wu Chang, China	9/27/20
Meara, Anne	New York, NY	9/20/29
Meat Loaf	Dallas, TX	9/27/47
Mehta, Zubin	Bombay, India	4/29/36
Mellencamp, John	Seymour, IN	10/7/51
Mendes, Sergio	Niteroi, Brazil	2/11/41
Menuhin, Yehudi	New York, NY	4/22/16
Mercer, Marian	Akron, OH	11/26/35
Merchant, Natalie	Jamestown, NY	10/26/63
Merrick, David	St. Louis, MO	11/27/12
Merrill, Dina	New York, NY	12/9/25
Merrill, Robert	Brooklyn, NY	6/4/19
Metcalf, Laurie	Carbondale, IL	6/16/55
Michael, George	Watford, England	6/26/63
Michaels, Al	New York, NY	11/12/44
Michaels, Lorne	Toronto, Canada	11/17/44
Midler, Bette	Paterson, NJ	12/1/45
Midori	Osaka, Japan	10/25/71
Milano, Alyssa	New York, NY	12/19/72
Miles, Sarah	Ingatestone, England	12/31/41
Miles, Vera	near Boise City, OK	8/23/29
Miller, Ann	Houston, TX	4/12/19
Miller, Dennis	Pittsburgh, PA	11/3/53
Miller, Mitch	Rochester, NY	7/4/11
Miller, Penelope Ann	Los Angeles, CA	1/13/64
Mills, Donna	Chicago, IL	12/11/42
Mills, John	Suffolk, England	2/22/08
Milner, Martin	Detroit, MI	12/28/27
Milnes, Sherrill	Downers Grove, IL	1/10/35
Milsap, Ronnie	Robinsville, NC	1/16/44
Minghella, Anthony	Isle of Wight, England	1/6/54
Minnelli, Liza	Los Angeles, CA	3/12/46
Mirren, Helen	London, England	7/2/46
Mitchell, Joni	McLeod, Alberta	11/7/43
Mr. T	Chicago, IL	5/21/52
Modine, Matthew	Loma Linda, CA	3/22/59
Moffat, Donald	Plymouth, England	12/26/30
Moffo, Anna	Wayne, PA	6/27/27
Molinaro, Al	Kenosha, WI	6/24/19
Moll, Richard	Pasadena, CA	1/13/43
Montalban, Ricardo	Mexico City, Mexico	11/25/20
Moody, Ron	London, England	1/8/24
Moore, Clayton	Chicago, IL	9/14/14
Moore, Demi	Roswell, NM	11/11/62
Moore, Dudley	London, England	4/19/35
Moore, Julianne	Boston, MA	12/30/60
Moore, Mary Tyler	Brooklyn, NY	12/29/36

Name	Birthplace	Birthdate
Moore, Melba	New York, NY	10/29/45
Moore, Roger	London, England	10/14/27
Moore, Terry	Los Angeles, CA	1/1/29
Moranis, Rick	Toronto, Ontario	4/18/53
Moreau, Jeanne	Paris, France	1/23/28
Moreno, Rita	Humacao, PR	12/11/31
Morgan, Harry	Detroit, MI	4/10/15
Moriarty, Michael	Detroit, MI	4/5/41
Morissette, Alanis	Ottawa, Ontario	6/1/74
Morita, Pat	Isleton, CA	6/28/32
Morris, Howard	New York, NY	9/4/25
Morrison, Van	Belfast, N. Ireland	8/31/45
Morrissey	Manchester, England	5/22/59
Morrow, Rob	New Rochelle, NY	9/21/62
Morse, Robert	Newton, MA	5/18/31
Morton, Joe	New York, NY	10/18/47
Moses, William	Los Angeles, CA	11/17/59
Moss, Kate	London, England	1/16/74
Muldaur, Diana	New York, NY	8/19/38
Mulgrew, Kate	Dubuque, IA	4/29/55
Mull, Martin	Chicago, IL	8/18/43
Mueller-Stahl, Armin	Tilsit, E. Prussia	12/17/20
Mulligan, Richard	New York, NY	11/13/32
Mulroney, Dermot	Alexandria, VA	10/31/63
Munsel, Patrice	Spokane, WA	5/14/25
Murphy, Ben	Jonesboro, AR	3/6/42
Murphy, Eddie	Brooklyn, NY	4/3/61
Murphy, Michael	Los Angeles, CA	5/5/38
Murray, Anne	Springhill, Nova Scotia	6/20/45
Murray, Bill	Evanston, IL	9/21/50
Murray, Don	Hollywood, CA	7/31/29
Musburger, Brent	Portland, OR	5/26/39
Muti, Riccardo	Naples, Italy	7/28/41
Myers, Mike	Toronto, Ontario	5/23/63
Nabors, Jim	Sylacauga, AL	6/12/33
Nash, Graham	Blackpool, England	2/2/42
Naughton, James	Middletown, CT	7/6/46
Neal, Patricia	Packard, KY	1/20/26
Nealon, Kevin	Bridgeport, CT	11/18/53
Neeson, Liam	Ballymena, N. Ireland	6/7/52
Neill, Sam	Ulster, N. Ireland	9/14/47
Nelligan, Kate	London, Ontario	3/16/51
Nelson, Craig T.	Spokane, WA	4/4/46
Nelson, Ed	New Orleans, LA	12/21/28
Nelson, Judd	Portland, ME	11/28/59
Nelson, Tracy	Santa Monica, CA	10/25/63
Nelson, Willie	Abbott, TX	4/30/33
Nero, Peter	New York, NY	5/22/34
Nesmith, Mike	Dallas, TX	12/30/42
Neuwirth, Bebe	Princeton, NJ	12/31/58
Neville, Aaron	New Orleans, LA	1/24/41
Newhart, Bob	Oak Park, IL	9/5/29
Newley, Anthony	Hackney, England	9/24/31
Newman, Paul	Cleveland, OH	1/26/25
Newman, Randy	Los Angeles, CA	11/28/43
Newton, Wayne	Norfolk, VA	4/3/42
Newton-John, Olivia	Cambridge, England	9/26/47
Nicholas, Denise	Detroit, MI	7/12/44
Nicholas, Fayard	Philadelphia, PA	10/20/14
Nicholas, Harold	Philadelphia, PA	3/27/24
Nichols, Mike	Berlin, Germany	11/6/31
Nicholson, Jack	Neptune, NJ	4/28/37
Nicks, Stevie	Phoenix, AZ	5/26/48
Nielsen, Leslie	Regina, Sask.	2/11/26
Nilsson, Birgit	Karup, Sweden	5/17/18
Nimoy, Leonard	Boston, MA	3/26/31
Nolte, Nick	Omaha, NE	2/8/40
Noone, Peter	Manchester, England	11/5/47
Norman, Jessye	Augusta, GA	9/15/45
Norris, Chuck	Ryan, OK	3/10/40
North, Sheree	Los Angeles, CA	1/17/33
Norton, Edward	Columbia, MD	1969
Noth, Christopher	Madison, WI	11/13/57
Novak, Kim	Chicago, IL	2/13/33
Nuyen, France	Marseille, France	7/31/39
Oates, John	New York, NY	4/7/48
O'Brian, Hugh	Rochester, NY	4/19/25
O'Brien, Conan	Brookline, MA	4/18/63
O'Brien, Margaret	San Diego, CA	1/15/37
Ocean, Billy	Fyzabad, Trinidad	1/21/50
O'Connor, Carroll	New York, NY	8/2/24
O'Connor, Donald	Chicago, IL	8/28/25
O'Connor, Sinead	Dublin, Ireland	12/8/66
Odetta	Birmingham, AL	12/31/30

Name	Birthplace	Birthdate
O'Donnell, Chris	Winnetka, IL	6/26/70
O'Donnell, Rosie	Commack, NY	3/21/62
O'Hara, Maureen	Dublin, Ireland	8/17/20
O'Herlihy, Dan	Wexford, Ireland	5/1/19
Oldman, Gary	London, England	3/21/58
Olin, Ken	Chicago, IL	7/30/54
Olin, Lena	Stockholm, Sweden	3/22/55
Olmos, Edward James	E. Los Angeles, CA	2/24/47
Olsen, Ashley	California	6/13/86
Olsen, Mary-Kate	California	6/13/86
Olsen, Merlin	Logan, UT	9/15/40
O'Neal, Ryan	Los Angeles, CA	4/20/41
O'Neal, Tatum	Los Angeles, CA	11/5/63
O'Neill, Ed	Youngstown, OH	4/12/46
Ontkean, Michael	Vancouver, B.C.	1/24/46
Orbach, Jerry	New York, NY	10/20/35
Orlando, Tony	New York, NY	4/3/44
Ormond, Julia	Epsom, England	1/4/65
Osbourne, Ozzy	Birmingham, England	12/3/48
O'Shea, Milo	Dublin, Ireland	6/2/26
Oslin, K.T.	Crosset, AR	1942
Osmond, Donny	Ogden, UT	12/9/57
Osmond, Marie	Ogden, UT	10/13/59
O'Toole, Annette	Houston, TX	4/1/53
O'Toole, Peter	Connemara, Ireland	8/2/32
Owens, Buck	Sherman, TX	8/12/29
Oz, Frank	Herford, England	5/25/44
Ozawa, Seiji	Shenyang, China	9/1/35
Paar, Jack	Canton, OH	5/1/18
Pacino, Al	New York, NY	4/25/40
Packer, Billy	Wellsville, NY	2/25/40
Page, Betty	Kingsport, TN	4/22/23
Page, Jimmy	Heston, England	1/9/44
Page, Patti	Claremore, OK	11/8/27
Paget, Debra	Denver, CO	8/19/33
Paige, Janis	Tacoma, WA	9/16/22
Palance, Jack	Lattimer, PA	2/18/20
Palin, Michael	Sheffield, England	5/5/43
Palmer, Betsy	East Chicago, IN	11/1/29
Palmer, Geoffrey	London, England	6/4/27
Palmer, Robert	Bately, England	1/19/49
Palminteri, Chazz	Bronx, NY	5/15/51
Paltrow, Gwyneth	Los Angeles, CA	9/28/73
Papas, Irene	Chiliomedion, Greece	3/9/26
Paquin, Anna	Wellington, New Zealand	6/24/82
Parker, Alan	London, England	2/14/44
Parker, Eleanor	Cedarville, OH	6/26/22
Parker, Fess	Ft. Worth, TX	8/16/25
Parker, Jameson	Baltimore, MD	11/18/47
Parker, Jean	Deer Lodge, MT	8/11/12
Parker, Mary-Louise	Fort Jackson, SC	8/2/64
Parker, Sarah Jessica	Nelsonville, OH	3/25/65
Parsons, Estelle	Lynn, MA	11/20/27
Parton, Dolly	Sevierville, TN	1/19/46
Patinkin, Mandy	Chicago, IL	11/30/52
Patric, Jason	Queens, NY	6/17/66
Pavarotti, Luciano	Modena, Italy	10/12/35
Paxton, Bill	Fort Worth, TX	5/17/55
Paycheck, Johnny	Greenfield, OH	5/31/41
Peck, Gregory	La Jolla, CA	4/5/16
Pendergrass, Teddy	Philadelphia, PA	3/26/50
Penn, Arthur	Philadelphia, PA	9/27/22
Penn, Robin Wright	Dallas, TX	4/8/66
Penn, Sean	Burbank, CA	8/17/60
Penny, Joe	London, England	9/14/56
Perez, Rosie	Brooklyn, NY	9/6/64
Perkins, Elizabeth	New York, NY	11/18/60
Perlman, Itzhak	Tel Aviv, Israel	8/31/45
Perlman, Rhea	Brooklyn, NY	3/31/48
Perlman, Ron	New York, NY	4/13/50
Perrine, Valerie	Galveston, TX	9/3/43
Perry, Luke	Fredericktown, OH	10/11/66
Perry, Mathew	Williamstown, MA	8/19/69
Persoff, Nehemiah	Jerusalem, Israel	8/14/20
Pesci, Joe	Newark, NJ	2/9/43
Peters, Bernadette	New York, NY	2/28/48
Peters, Brock	New York, NY	7/2/27
Peters, Roberta	New York, NY	5/4/30
Peterson, Oscar	Montreal, Quebec	8/15/25
Petty, Tom	Gainesville, FL	10/20/53
Pfeiffer, Michelle	Santa Ana, CA	4/29/57
Philbin, Regis	New York, NY	8/25/34
Phillips, Lou Diamond	Philippines	2/17/62
Phillips, Mackenzie	Alexandria, VA	11/10/59
Phillips, Michelle	Long Beach, CA	6/4/44

Name	Birthplace	Birthdate
Phoenix, Joaquin	Puerto Rico	10/28/74
Pickett, Wilson	Prattville, AL	3/18/41
Pierce, David Hyde	Albany, NY	4/3/59
Pinchot, Bronson	New York, NY	5/20/59
Pinkett Smith, Jada	Baltimore, MD	8/18/71
Pirner, David	Green Bay, WI	4/16/64
Piscopo, Joe	Passaic, NJ	6/17/51
Pitt, Brad	Shawnee, OK	12/18/64
Plant, Robert	W. Bromwich, England	8/20/48
Pleshette, Suzanne	New York, NY	1/31/37
Plowright, Joan	Brigg, England	10/28/29
Plummer, Amanda	New York, NY	3/23/57
Plummer, Christopher	Toronto, Ontario	12/13/27
Poitier, Sidney	Miami, FL	2/20/27
Polanski, Roman	Paris, France	8/18/33
Pollack, Sydney	Lafayette, IN	7/1/34
Ponti, Carlo	Milan, Italy	12/11/13
Pop, Iggy	Ann Arbor, MI	4/21/47
Portman, Natalie	Jerusalem, Israel	6/9/81
Posey, Parker	Baltimore, MD	11/8/64
Post, Markie	Palo Alto, CA	11/4/50
Poston, Tom	Columbus, OH	10/17/27
Potts, Annie	Nashville, TN	10/28/52
Povich, Maury	Washington, DC	1/17/39
Powell, Jane	Portland, OR	4/1/28
Powers, Stefanie	Hollywood, CA	11/2/42
Prentiss, Paula	San Antonio, TX	3/4/39
Presley, Priscilla	New York, NY	5/24/46
Preston, Billy	Houston, TX	9/9/46
Previn, Andre	Berlin, Germany	4/6/29
Price, Leontyne	Laurel, MS	2/10/27
Price, Ray	Perryville, TX	1/12/26
Pride, Charley	Sledge, MS	3/18/39
Priestley, Jason	Vancouver, British Columbia	8/28/69
Prince (The Artist)	Minneapolis, MN	6/7/58
Principal, Victoria	Fukuoka, Japan	1/3/50
Prosky, Robert	Philadelphia, PA	12/13/30
Pryce, Jonathan	Wales	6/1/47
Pryor, Richard	Peoria, IL	12/1/40
Puente, Tito	New York, NY	4/20/23
Pulliam, Keshia Knight	Newark, NJ	4/9/79
Pullman, Bill	Hornell, NY	12/17/54
Purcell, Sarah	Richmond, IN	10/8/48
Quaid, Dennis	Houston, TX	4/9/54
Quaid, Randy	Houston, TX	10/1/50
Queen Latifah	East Orange, NJ	3/18/70
Quinn, Aidan	Chicago, IL	3/8/59
Quinn, Anthony	Chihuahua, Mexico	4/21/15
Quinn, Martha	Albany, NY	5/11/59
Rachins, Alan	Cambridge, MA	10/10/47
Rae, Charlotte	Milwaukee, WI	4/22/26
Raffi	Cairo, Italy	7/8/48
Rainer, Luise	Vienna, Austria	1/12/10
Raitt, Bonnie	Burbank, CA	11/8/49
Ramey, Samuel	Colby, KS	3/28/42
Ramone, Dee Dee	Berlin, Germany	9/18/52
Ramone, Joey	Forest Hills, NY	5/19/51
Ramone, Johnny	Long Island, NY	10/8/51
Ramone, Tommy	Budapest, Hungary	1/29/52
Rampal, Jean-Pierre	Marseilles, France	1/7/22
Randall, Tony	Tulsa, OK	2/26/20
Randolph, John	New York, NY	6/1/15
Randolph, Joyce	Detroit, MI	10/21/25
Raphael, Sally Jessy	Easton, PA	2/25/43
Rashad, Phylicia	Houston, TX	6/17/48
Ratzenberger, John	Bridgeport, CT	4/6/47
Rawls, Lou	Chicago, IL	12/1/36
Reagan, Ronald	Tampico, IL	2/6/11
Reddy, Helen	Melbourne, Australia	10/25/41
Redford, Robert	Santa Monica, CA	8/18/37
Redgrave, Lynn	London, England	3/8/43
Redgrave, Vanessa	London, England	1/30/37
Reed, Jerry	Atlanta, GA	3/20/37
Reed, Lou	Long Island, NY	3/2/43
Reed, Oliver	London, England	2/13/38
Reed, Rex	Ft. Worth, TX	10/2/38
Reese, Della	Detroit, MI	7/6/31
Reeve, Christopher	New York, NY	9/25/52
Reeves, Keanu	Beirut, Lebanon	9/2/64
Regalbuto, Joe	New York, NY	8/24/49
Reid, Tim	Norfolk, VA	12/19/44
Reilly, Charles Nelson	New York, NY	1/13/31
Reiner, Carl	Bronx, NY	3/20/22
Reiner, Rob	Bronx, NY	3/6/45
Reinhold, Judge	Wilmington, DE	5/21/56

Name	Birthplace	Birthdate
Reinking, Ann	Seattle, WA	11/10/50
Reiser, Paul	New York, NY	3/30/57
Reitman, Ivan	Czechoslovakia	10/27/46
Resnik, Regina	New York, NY	8/30/24
Reynolds, Burt	Waycross, GA	2/11/36
Reynolds, Debbie	El Paso, TX	4/1/32
Reznor, Trent	Mercer, PA	5/17/65
Rhames, Ving	New York, NY	5/12/61
Ricci, Christina	Santa Monica, CA	2/12/80
Richards, Keith	Kent, England	12/18/43
Richards, Michael	Culver City, CA	7/21/49
Richardson, Ian	Edinburgh, Scotland	4/7/34
Richardson, Miranda	Lancashire, England	3/3/58
Richardson, Natasha	London, England	5/11/63
Richardson, Patricia	Bethesda, MD	2/23/51
Richie, Lionel	Tuskegee, AL	6/20/50
Rickles, Don	New York, NY	5/8/26
Rickman, Alan	Hammersmith, England	2/21/46
Riegert, Peter	New York, NY	4/11/47
Rigg, Diana	Doncaster, England	7/20/38
Rimes, LeAnn	Jackson, MS	8/28/82
Ringwald, Molly	Roseville, CA	2/18/68
Ritter, John	Burbank, CA	9/17/48
Rivera, Chita	Washington, DC	1/23/33
Rivera, Geraldo	New York, NY	7/4/43
Rivers, Joan	Brooklyn, NY	6/8/37
Roach, Max	Elizabeth City, NC	1/10/24
Robards, Jason, Jr.	Chicago, IL	7/26/22
Robbins, Tim	W. Covina, CA	10/16/58
Roberts, Doris	St. Louis, MO	11/4/29
Roberts, Eric	Biloxi, MS	4/18/56
Roberts, Julia	Smyrna, GA	10/28/67
Roberts, Pernell	Waycross, GA	5/18/30
Roberts, Tony	New York, NY	10/22/39
Robertson, Cliff	La Jolla, CA	9/9/25
Robertson, Dale	Harrah, OK	7/14/23
Robinson, Smokey	Detroit, MI	2/19/40
Roche, Eugene	Boston, MA	9/22/28
Rock, Chris	South Carolina	2/7/66
Rodgers, Jimmy	Camas, WA	9/18/33
Rodriquez, Johnny	Sabinal, TX	12/10/51
Rogers, Fred	Latrobe, PA	3/20/28
Rogers, Kenny	Houston, TX	8/21/38
Rogers, Mimi	Coral Gables, FL	1/27/56
Rogers, Wayne	Birmingham, AL	4/7/33
Rolle, Esther	Pompano Beach, FL	11/8/33
Rollins, Sonny	New York, NY	9/7/29
Romano, Ray	New York, NY	12/21/57
Ronstadt, Linda	Tucson, AZ	7/15/46
Rooney, Mickey	Brooklyn, NY	9/23/20
Rose, Axl	Lafayette, IN	2/6/62
Rose Marie	New York, NY	8/15/25
Roseanne	Salt Lake City, UT	11/3/52
Ross, Diana	Detroit, MI	3/26/44
Ross, Katharine	Hollywood, CA	1/29/42
Ross, Marion	Albert Lea, MN	10/25/28
Rossellini, Isabella	Rome, Italy	6/18/52
Rostropovich, Mstislav	Baku, Azerbaijan	3/12/27
Roth, David Lee	Bloomington, IN	10/10/54
Roth, Tim	London, England	5/14/61
Rotten, Johnny	England	1/31/56
Rourke, Mickey	Schenectady, NY	7/16/53
Routledge, Patricia	Berkenhead, England	2/17/29
Rowlands, Gena	Cambria, WI	6/19/34
Rudner, Rita	Coconut Grove, FL	9/17/56
Ruehl, Mercedes	Queens, NY	2/28/48
Rush, Barbara	Denver, CO	1/4/30
Rush, Geoffrey	Toowoomba, Australia	1951
Russell, Jane	Bemidji, MN	6/21/21
Russell, Ken	Southampton, England	7/3/27
Russell, Kurt	Springfield, MA	3/17/51
Russell, Mark	Buffalo, NY	8/23/32
Russell, Leon	Lawton, OK	4/2/41
Russell, Nipsey	Atlanta, GA	10/13/24
Russell, Theresa	San Diego, CA	3/20/57
Russo, Rene	Burbank, CA	2/17/54
Rutherford, Ann	Toronto, Ontario	11/2/20
Ruttan, Susan	Oregon City, OR	9/16/50
Ryan, Meg	Fairfield, CT	11/19/61
Ryan, Roz	Detroit, MI	7/7/51
Rydell, Bobby	Philadelphia, PA	4/26/42
Ryder, Winona	Winona, MN	10/29/71
Sabato, Antonio, Jr.	Italy	2/29/72
Sade	Ibadan, Nigeria	1/16/59
Sagal, Katie	Los Angeles, CA	1956
Saget, Bob	Philadelphia, PA	5/17/56
Sahl, Mort	Montreal, Quebec	5/11/27
Saint, Eva Marie	Newark, NJ	7/4/24
St. James, Susan	Los Angeles, CA	8/14/46
St. John, Jill	Los Angeles, CA	8/19/40
Sajak, Pat	Chicago, IL	10/26/47
Saks, Gene	New York, NY	11/8/21
Sales, Soupy	Franklinton, NC	1/8/26
Samms, Emma	London, England	8/28/60
Sandler, Adam	Brooklyn, NY	9/9/66
Sands, Julian	Yorkshire, England	1/15/58
Sanford, Isabel	New York, NY	8/29/17
San Giacomo, Laura	Hoboken, NJ	11/14/62
Sarandon, Susan	New York, NY	10/4/46
Sarnoff, Dorothy	New York, NY	5/25/17
Sartain, Gailard	Tulsa, OK	9/18/46
Savage, Ben	Chicago, IL	9/13/80
Savage, Fred	Highland Park, IL	7/9/76
Saxon, John	Brooklyn, NY	8/5/35
Sayles, John	Schenectady, NY	9/28/50
Scaggs, Boz	Dallas, TX	6/8/44
Scales, Prunella	Surrey, England	1933
Scalia, Jack	Brooklyn, NY	11/10/51
Schallert, William	Los Angeles, CA	7/6/22
Scheider, Roy	Orange, NJ	11/10/32
Schell, Maria	Vienna, Austria	1/15/26
Schell, Maximilian	Vienna, Austria	12/8/30
Schenkel, Chris	Bippus, IN	8/21/23
Schiffer, Claudia	Rheinbach, Germany	8/25/70
Schneider, John	Mt. Kisco, NY	4/8/54
Schneider, Rob	San Francisco, CA	10/31/64
Schroder, Rick	Staten Island, NY	4/3/70
Schwarzenegger, Arnold	Graz, Austria	7/30/47
Schwarzkopf, Elisabeth	Jarotschin, Poland	12/9/15
Schwimmer, David	Queens, NY	11/12/67
Sciorra, Annabella	New York, NY	3/24/64
Scofield, Paul	Hurst, Pierpont, England	1/21/22
Scolari, Peter	New Rochelle, IL	9/12/54
Scorsese, Martin	New York, NY	11/17/42
Scott, George C.	Wise, VA	10/18/27
Scott, Lizabeth	Scranton, PA	9/29/22
Scott, Martha	Jamesport, MO	9/22/14
Scott Thomas, Kristin	Cornwall, England	1960
Scotto, Renata	Savona, Italy	2/24/35
Scully, Vin	New York, NY	11/29/27
Seagal, Steven	Lansing, MI	4/10/51
Secor, Kyle	Tacoma, WA	5/31/60
Sedaka, Neil	New York, NY	3/13/39
Seeger, Pete	New York, NY	5/3/19
Segal, George	Great Neck, NY	2/13/34
Seidelman, Susan	Philadelphia, PA	12/11/52
Seinfeld, Jerry	New York, NY	4/29/55
Sellecca, Connie	New York, NY	5/25/55
Selleck, Tom	Detroit, MI	1/29/45
Severinsen, Doc	Arlington, OR	7/7/27
Sewell, Rufus	London, England	10/29/67
Seymour, Jane	Middlesex, England	2/15/51
Shackelford, Ted	Oklahoma City, OK	6/23/46
Shaffer, Paul	Thunder Bay, Ontario	11/28/49
Shandling, Garry	Chicago, IL	11/29/49
Shankar, Ravi	Benares, India	4/7/20
Sharif, Omar	Alexandria, Egypt	4/10/32
Shatner, William	Montreal, Quebec	3/22/31
Shaughnessy, Charles	London, England	2/9/55
Shaver, Helen	St. Thomas, Ontario	2/24/51
Shaw, Artie	New York, NY	5/23/10
Shea, John	N. Conway, NH	4/14/49
Shearer, Harry	Los Angeles, CA	12/23/43
Shearer, Moira	Scotland	1/17/26
Shearing, George	London, England	8/13/19
Sheedy, Ally	New York, NY	6/12/62
Sheen, Charlie	Los Angeles, CA	9/3/65
Sheen, Martin	Dayton, OH	8/3/40
Shelley, Carole	London, England	8/16/39
Shepard, Sam	Ft. Sheridan, IL	11/5/43
Shepherd, Cybill	Memphis, TN	2/18/49
Sheridan, Nicollette	Northington, England	11/21/63
Shields, Brooke	New York, NY	5/31/65
Shire, Talia	New York, NY	4/25/46
Short, Bobby	Danville, IL	9/15/24
Short, Martin	Hamilton, Ontario	3/26/50
Show, Grant	Detroit, MI	4/27/62
Shue, Andrew	South Orange, NJ	2/20/67
Shue, Elisabeth	Wilmington, DE	6/10/63
Shull, Richard B.	Evanston, IL	2/24/29
Sidney, Sylvia	New York, NY	8/8/10

Name	Birthplace	Birthdate
Siepi, Cesare	Milan, Italy	2/10/23
Sikking, James B.	Los Angeles, CA.	3/5/34
Sills, Beverly	Brooklyn, NY	5/25/29
Silver, Ron.	New York, NY.	7/2/46
Silverman, Jonathan.	Los Angeles, CA.	8/5/66
Silverstone, Alicia.	San Francisco, CA	10/4/76
Simmons, Gene	Haifa, Israel	8/25/49
Simmons, Jean	London, England	1/31/29
Simmons, Richard	New Orleans, LA	7/12/48
Simon, Carly	New York, NY.	6/25/45
Simon, Paul.	Newark, NJ	10/13/41
Simone, Nina.	Tyron, NC	2/21/33
Sinatra, Nancy	Jersey City, NJ	6/8/40
Sinbad	Benton Harbor, MI	11/10/56
Sinise, Gary.	Blue Island, IL	3/7/55
Singleton, John	Los Angeles, CA.	1/6/68
Siskel, Gene	Chicago, IL.	1/26/46
Skerritt, Tom	Detroit, MI	8/25/33
Slater, Christian	New York, NY.	8/19/69
Slater, Helen	Massapequa, NY	12/14/63
Slezak, Erika	Hollywood, CA	8/5/46
Slick, Grace.	Chicago, IL.	10/30/39
Smirnoff, Yakov	Odessa, Russia	1/24/51
Smith, Allison.	New York, NY.	12/9/69
Smith, Jaclyn.	Houston, TX.	10/26/47
Smith, Keely	Norfolk, VA.	3/9/35
Smith, Maggie	Ilford, England	12/28/34
Smith, Will.	Philadelphia, PA.	9/25/68
Smits, Jimmy.	New York, NY.	7/9/55
Smothers, Dick	New York, NY.	11/20/39
Smothers, Tom	New York, NY.	2/2/37
Snipes, Wesley	Orlando, FL	7/31/63
Snow, Hank.	Nova Scotia, Canada	5/9/14
Solti, Georg	Budapest, Hungary	10/21/12
Somers, Suzanne	San Bruno, CA.	10/16/46
Sommer, Elke	Berlin, Germany	11/5/41
Sorbo, Kevin	Mound, MN	9/24/58
Sorvino, Mira	Tenafly, NJ.	9/28/70
Sorvino, Paul	Brooklyn, NY	2/17/54
Sothern, Ann	Valley City, ND	1/22/09
Soul, David	Chicago, IL.	8/28/43
Spacek, Sissy	Quitman, TX.	12/25/49
Spacey, Kevin	S. Orange, NJ	7/26/59
Spade, David.	Birmingham, MI	7/22/65
Spader, James	Boston, MA	2/7/60
Spano, Joe	San Francisco, CA	7/7/46
Spector, Phil	Bronx, NY	12/25/40
Spelling, Aaron	Dallas, TX	4/22/28
Spelling, Tori	Los Angeles, CA.	5/16/73
Spielberg, Steven.	Cincinnati, OH	12/18/47
Springfield, Dusty.	London, England	4/16/39
Springfield, Rick.	Sydney, Australia	8/23/49
Springsteen, Bruce.	Freehold, NJ	9/23/49
Stack, Robert.	Los Angeles, CA.	1/13/19
Stafford, Jo	Coalinga, CA	11/12/18
Stahl, Richard	Detroit, MI	1/4/32
Stallone, Sylvester	New York, NY.	7/6/46
Stamos, John	Cypress, CA.	8/19/63
Stamp, Terence	Stepney, England	7/22/39
Stang, Arnold.	New York, NY.	9/28/25
Stanley, Kim	Tularosa, NM	2/11/25
Stanton, Harry Dean.	West Irvine, KY.	7/14/26
Stapleton, Jean	New York, NY.	1/19/23
Stapleton, Maureen	Troy, NY	6/21/25
Starr, Ringo	Liverpool, England	7/7/40
Steenburgen, Mary.	Newport, AR.	2/8/53
Steiger, Rod	W. Hampton, NY.	4/14/25
Stein, Ben	Washington, DC	11/25/44
Stephens, James	Mt. Kisco, NY.	5/18/51
Stern, Daniel	Stamford, CT	5/28/57
Stern, Howard	New York, NY.	1/12/54
Stern, Isaac.	Kreminiecz, Russia	7/21/20
Sternhagen, Frances	Washington, DC	1/13/30
Stevens, Andrew	Memphis, TN	6/10/55
Stevens, Cat	London, England	7/21/48
Stevens, Connie	Brooklyn, NY	8/8/38
Stevens, Rise	New York, NY.	6/11/13
Stevens, Stella.	Yazoo City, MS.	10/1/36
Stevenson, Parker	Philadelphia, PA.	6/4/52
Stewart, French	Albuquerque, NM	2/20/64
Stewart, Jon	Lawrence, NJ	1963
Stewart, Patrick	Mirfield, England.	7/13/40
Stewart, Rod	London, England	1/10/45
Stiers, David Ogden	Peoria, IL.	10/31/42
Stiller, Ben.	New York, NY.	11/30/65
Stiller, Jerry	New York, NY.	6/8/29
Stills, Stephen.	Dallas, TX.	1/3/45
Sting	Newcastle, England	10/2/51
Stipe, Michael.	Decatur, GA	1/4/60
Stockwell, Dean	Hollywood, CA.	3/5/36
Stoltz, Eric	American Samoa.	9/30/61
Stone, Dee Wallace.	Kansas City, KS	12/14/48
Stone, Oliver.	New York, NY	9/15/46
Stone, Sharon.	Meadville, PA	3/10/58
Stookey, Paul	Baltimore, MD	12/30/37
Storch, Larry.	New York, NY	1/8/23
Storm, Gale	Bloomington, TX	4/5/22
Stowe, Madeleine	Los Angeles, CA	8/18/58
Straight, Beatrice	Old Westbury, NY	8/2/18
Strait, George	Pearsall, TX	5/18/52
Strasser, Robin.	New York, NY	5/7/45
Stratas, Teresa	Toronto, Ontario	5/26/38
Strauss, Peter.	New York, NY	2/20/47
Streep, Meryl	Summit, NJ.	6/22/49
Streisand, Barbra	Brooklyn, NY.	4/24/42
Stringfield, Sherry	Colorado Springs, CO	6/24/67
Stritch, Elaine	Detroit, MI	2/2/26
Struthers, Sally	Portland, OR	7/28/48
Stuart, Gloria	Santa Monica, CA	7/4/10
Stuarti, Enzo.	Rome, Italy	3/3/25
Sullivan, Susan	New York, NY	11/18/44
Sumac, Yma.	Ichocan, Peru	9/10/27
Summer, Donna	Boston, MA.	12/31/48
Sutherland, Donald	St. John, New Brunswick	7/17/34
Sutherland, Joan.	Sydney, Australia.	11/7/26
Sutherland, Kiefer	London, England	12/20/66
Swayze, Patrick	Houston, TX	8/18/54
Swit, Loretta	Passaic, NJ.	11/4/37
Takei, George.	Los Angeles, CA	4/20/39
Tallchief, Maria	Fairfax, OK	1/24/25
Tarantino, Quentin	Knoxville, TN.	3/27/63
Taylor, Billy.	Greenville, SC.	7/24/21
Taylor, Buck	Hollywood, CA.	5/13/38
Taylor, Elizabeth	London, England	2/27/32
Taylor, James.	Boston, MA.	3/12/48
Taylor, Rip	Washington, DC	1/13/30
Taylor, Rod.	Sydney, Australia.	1/11/29
Taymor, Julie	Newton, MA	12/15/52
Te Kanawa, Kiri	Gisborne, New Zealand	3/6/44
Tebaldi, Renata	Pesaro, Italy	2/1/22
Temple Black, Shirley	Santa Monica, CA	4/23/28
Tennant, Victoria.	London, England	9/30/50
Tennille, Toni	Montgomery, AL	5/8/43
Tesh, John	Garden City, NY	7/9/52
Tharp, Twyla.	Portland, IN.	7/1/41
Thicke, Alan	Kirkland Lake, Ontario	3/1/47
Thiessen, Tiffani-Amber.	Long Beach, CA	1/23/74
Thomas, Jay.	New Orleans, LA	7/12/48
Thomas, Jonathan Taylor	Bethlehem, PA	9/8/81
Thomas, Marlo	Detroit, MI.	11/21/43
Thomas, Michael Tilson	Hollywood, CA.	12/21/44
Thomas, Philip Michael	Columbus, OH.	5/26/49
Thomas, Richard.	New York, NY	6/13/51
Thompson, Emma.	London, England	4/15/59
Thompson, Jack	Sydney, Australia.	8/31/40
Thompson, Lea.	Rochester, MN	5/31/61
Thompson, Sada.	Des Moines, IA	9/27/29
Thorne-Smith, Courtney.	San Francisco, CA.	11/8/68
Thornton, Billy Bob	Hot Springs, AR.	8/4/55
Thurman, Uma	Boston, MA.	4/29/70
Tiegs, Cheryl	Minnesota.	9/25/47
Tillis, Mel	Tampa, FL	8/8/32
Tilly, Jennifer	Los Angeles, CA	9/6/61
Tilly, Meg	Texada, B.C.	2/14/60
Todd, Richard.	Dublin, Ireland	6/11/19
Tomei, Marisa.	New York, NY	12/4/64
Tomlin, Lily.	Detroit, MI	9/1/39
Tomlinson, David	Scotland	5/7/17
Torme, Mel.	Chicago, IL	9/13/25
Tork, Peter	Washington, DC	2/13/44
Torn, Rip	Temple, TX.	2/6/31
Townsend, Robert.	Chicago, IL	2/6/57
Townshend, Peter.	Chiswick, England	5/19/45
Travanti, Daniel J.	Kenosha, WI	3/7/40
Travers, Mary	Louisville, KY.	11/9/36
Travis, Nancy	New York, NY	9/21/61
Travis, Randy	Marshville, NC.	5/4/59
Travolta, John.	Englewood, NJ	2/18/54
Trebek, Alex.	Sudbury, Ontario	7/22/40
Trevor, Claire	New York, NY	3/8/09
Tritt, Travis.	Marietta, GA	2/9/63

Name	Birthplace	Birthdate
Tucker, Michael	Baltimore, MD	2/6/44
Tucker, Tanya	Seminole, TX	10/10/58
Tune, Tommy	Wichita Falls, TX	2/28/39
Turlington, Christy	San Francisco, CA	1/2/69
Turner, Janine	Lincoln, NE	12/6/62
Turner, Kathleen	Springfield, MO	6/19/54
Turner, Tina	Brownsville, TN	11/26/39
Turturro, John	Brooklyn, NY	2/28/57
Twiggy	London, England	9/19/46
Tyler, Liv	Portland, ME	7/1/77
Tyler, Steven	Boston, MA	3/26/48
Tyson, Cicely	New York, NY	12/19/33
Uecker, Bob	Milwaukee, WI	1/26/35
Uggams, Leslie	New York, NY	5/25/43
Ullman, Tracey	Slough, England	12/30/59
Ullmann, Liv	Tokyo, Japan	12/16/38
Ulrich, Skeet	North Carolina	1/20/70
Underwood, Blair	Tacoma, WA	8/25/64
Urich, Robert	Toronto, Ohio	12/19/47
Ustinov, Peter	London, England	4/16/21
Vaccaro, Brenda	Brooklyn, NY	11/18/39
Vale, Jerry	New York, NY	7/8/31
Valente, Caterina	Paris, France	1/14/31
Valli, Frankie	Newark, NJ	5/3/37
Van Ark, Joan	New York, NY	6/16/43
Vance, Courtney B.	Detroit, MI	3/12/60
Vandross, Luther	New York, NY	4/20/51
Van Damme, Jean-Claude	Brussels, Belgium	10/18/60
Van Der Beek, James	Chesire, CT	4/8/77
Van Doren, Mamie	Rowena, SD	2/6/36
Van Dyke, Dick	West Plains, MO	12/13/25
Van Dyke, Jerry	Danville, IL	7/27/31
Van Halen, Eddie	Nijmegen, Netherlands	1/26/57
Van Patten, Dick	New York, NY	12/9/28
Van Peebles, Mario	Mexico	1/15/57
Van Sant, Gus	Louisville, KY	7/24/52
Vaughn, Robert	New York, NY	11/22/32
Vaughn, Vince	Minneapolis, MN	1970
Vedder, Eddie	Evanston, IL	12/23/65
Verdon, Gwen	Los Angeles, CA	1/13/25
Vereen, Ben	Miami, FL	10/10/46
Verrett, Shirley	New Orleans, LA	5/31/31
Vickers, Jon	Prince Albert, Sask.	10/26/26
Vincent, Jan-Michael	Denver, CO	7/15/44
Vinson, Helen	Beaumont, TX	9/17/07
Vinton, Bobby	Canonsburg, PA	4/16/35
Vitale, Dick	East Rutherford, NJ	6/9/40
Voight, Jon	Yonkers, NY	12/29/38
Von Stade, Frederica	Somerville, NJ	6/1/45
Von Sydow, Max	Lund, Sweden	4/10/29
Wagner, Jack	Washington, MO	10/3/59
Wagner, Lindsay	Los Angeles, CA	6/22/49
Wagner, Robert	Detroit, MI	2/10/30
Wahl, Ken	Chicago, IL	2/14/56
Wahlberg, Mark	Dorchester, MA	6/5/71
Wain, Bea	Bronx, NY	4/30/17
Waite, Ralph	White Plains, NY	6/22/29
Waits, Tom	Pomona, CA	12/7/49
Walden, Robert	New York, NY	9/25/43
Walken, Christopher	New York, NY	3/31/43
Wallace, Marcia	Creston, IA	11/1/42
Wallach, Eli	Brooklyn, NY	12/7/15
Walston, Ray	Laurel, MS	11/2/24
Walter, Jessica	New York, NY	1/31/44
Ward, Fred	San Diego, CA	1943
Ward, Sela	Meridian, MS	8/11/56
Ward, Simon	London, England	10/19/41
Warden, Jack	Newark, NJ	9/18/20
Warfield, Marsha	Chicago, IL	3/5/54
Warner, Malcolm-Jamal	Jersey City, NJ	8/18/70
Warren, Lesley Ann	New York, NY	8/16/46
Warrick, Ruth	St. Joseph, MO	6/29/16
Warwick, Dionne	East Orange, NJ	12/12/41
Washington, Denzel	Mt. Vernon, NY	12/28/54
Waters, John	Baltimore, MD	4/22/46
Waters, Roger	Great Bookham, England	9/9/44
Waterston, Sam	Cambridge, MA	11/15/40
Watts, Andre	Nuremberg, Germany	6/20/46
Wayans, Damon	New York, NY	9/4/60
Wayans, Keenen Ivory	New York, NY	6/8/58
Waxman, Al	Toronto, Ontario	3/2/35
Weathers, Carl	New Orleans, LA	1/14/48
Weaver, Dennis	Joplin, MO	6/4/24
Weaver, Fritz	Pittsburgh, PA	1/19/26
Weaver, Sigourney	New York, NY	10/8/49
Weir, Peter	Sydney, Australia	8/8/44
Weitz, Bruce	Norwalk, CT	5/27/43
Welch, Raquel	Chicago, IL	9/5/40
Weld, Tuesday	New York, NY	8/27/43
Wells, Kitty	Nashville, TN	8/30/19
Wendt, George	Chicago, IL	10/17/48
West, Adam	Walla Walla, WA	9/19/29
Wettig, Patricia	Cincinnati, OH	12/4/51
Whalley-Kilmer, Joanne	Manchester, England	8/25/64
Wheaton, Wil	Burbank, CA	7/29/72
Whitaker, Forest	Longview, TX	7/15/61
White, Barry	Galveston, TX	9/12/44
White, Betty	Oak Park, IL	1/17/22
White, Jaleel	Los Angeles, CA	11/27/76
White, Vanna	N Myrtle Beach, SC	2/18/57
Whiting, Margaret	Detroit, MI	7/22/24
Whitman, Stuart	San Francisco, CA	2/1/26
Whitmore, James	White Plains, NY	10/1/21
Widmark, Richard	Sunrise, MN	12/26/14
Wiest, Dianne	Kansas City, MO	3/28/48
Wilder, Billy	Vienna, Austria	6/22/06
Wilder, Gene	Milwaukee, WI	6/11/35
Williams, Andy	Wall Lake, IA	12/3/30
Williams, Barry	Santa Monica, CA	9/30/54
Williams, Billy Dee	New York, NY	4/6/37
Williams, Cindy	Van Nuys, CA	8/22/47
Williams, Esther	Los Angeles, CA	8/8/23
Williams, Hal	Columbus, OH	12/14/38
Williams, Hank, Jr.	Shreveport, LA	5/26/49
Williams, JoBeth	Houston, TX	1949
Williams, Montel	Baltimore, MD	7/3/56
Williams, Paul	Omaha, NE	9/19/40
Williams, Robin	Chicago, IL	7/21/52
Williams, Treat	Rowayton, CT	12/1/51
Williams, Vanessa	New York, NY	3/18/63
Williamson, Nicol	Hamilton, Scotland	9/14/38
Willis, Bruce	W. Germany	3/19/55
Wilson, Brian	Hawthorne, CA	6/20/42
Wilson, Demond	Valdosta, GA	10/13/46
Wilson, Elizabeth	Grand Rapids, MI	4/4/25
Wilson, Flip	Jersey City, NJ	12/8/33
Wilson, Nancy	Chillicothe, OH	2/20/37
Windom, William	New York, NY	9/28/23
Winfield, Paul	Los Angeles, CA	5/22/41
Winfrey, Oprah	Kosciusko, MS	1/29/54
Winger, Debra	Cleveland, OH	5/16/55
Winkler, Henry	New York, NY	10/30/45
Winningham, Mare	Phoenix, AZ	5/6/59
Winslet, Kate	Reading, England	10/5/75
Winter, Johnny	Beaumont,TX	2/23/44
Winters, Jonathan	Dayton, OH	11/11/25
Winters, Shelley	St. Louis, MO	8/18/22
Winwood, Steve	Birmingham, England	5/12/48
Wiseman, Joseph	Montreal, Quebec	5/15/18
Withers, Jane	Atlanta, GA	4/12/26
Witherspoon, Reese	Nashville, TN	4/22/76
Witt, Alicia	Worcester, MA	8/21/75
Wolf, Scott	Boston, MA	6/4/68
Wonder, Stevie	Saginaw, MI	5/13/50
Wong, Faye	Beijing, China	8/8/69
Woo, John	Guangzhau, China	5/1/46
Wood, Elijah	Cedar Rapids, IA	1/28/81
Woodard, Alfre	Tulsa, OK	11/2/53
Woods, James	Vernal, NJ	4/18/47
Woodward, Edward	Croyden, England	6/1/30
Woodward, Joanne	Thomasville, GA	2/27/30
Wopat, Tom	Lodi, WI	9/9/50
Worth, Irene	Nebraska	6/23/16
Wray, Fay	Alberta, Canada	9/10/07
Wright, Martha	Seattle, WA	3/23/26
Wright, Max	Detroit, MI	8/2/43
Wright, Steven	New York, NY	12/6/55
Wright, Teresa	New York, NY	10/27/18
Wyatt, Jane	Campgaw, NJ	8/10/11
Wyle, Noah	Hollywood, CA	6/4/71
Wyman, Bill	London, England	10/24/36
Wyman, Jane	St. Joseph, MO	1/4/14
Yankovic, Weird Al	Los Angeles, CA	10/23/59
Yanni	Kalamata, Greece	11/4/54
Yarborough, Glenn	Milwaukee, WI	1/12/30
Yarrow, Peter	New York, NY	5/31/38
Yearwood, Trisha	Monticello, GA	9/19/64
Yoakam, Dwight	Pikesville, KY	10/23/56

Name	Birthplace	Birthdate
York, Michael	Fulmer, England	3/27/42
York, Susannah	London, England	1/9/42
Young, Alan	Northumberland, England	11/19/19
Young, Burt	New York, NY	4/30/40
Young, Loretta	Salt Lake City, UT	1/6/13
Young, Neil	Toronto, Ontario	11/12/45
Young, Sean	Louisville, KY	11/20/59
Zane, Billy	Chicago, IL	2/24/66
Zeffirelli, Franco	Florence, Italy	2/12/23
Zellweger, Renee	Katy, TX	1969
Zemeckis, Robert	Chicago, IL	5/14/51
Zerbe, Anthony	Long Beach, CA	5/20/36
Zimbalist, Efrem, Jr.	New York, NY	11/30/23
Zimbalist, Stephanie	Encino, CA	10/8/56
Zimmer, Kim	Grand Rapids, MI	2/2/55
Zukerman, Pinchas	Tel Aviv, Israel	7/16/48
Zuniga, Daphne	San Francisco, CA	10/28/62

Entertainment Personalities of the Past

See also other lists.

Name	Born	Died
Abbott, Bud	**1895**	**1974**
Abbott, George	**1887**	**1995**
Acuff, Roy	**1903**	**1992**
Adams, Maude	**1872**	**1953**
Adler, Jacob P.	**1855**	**1926**
Adler, Luther	**1903**	**1984**
Adoree, Renee	**1898**	**1933**
Aherne, Brian	**1902**	**1986**
Ailey, Alvin	**1931**	**1989**
Akins, Claude	**1918**	**1994**
Albertson, Frank	**1909**	**1964**
Albertson, Jack	**1907**	**1981**
Allen, Fred	**1894**	**1956**
Allen, Gracie	**1906**	**1964**
Allen, Mel	**1913**	**1996**
Allgood, Sara	**1883**	**1950**
Ameche, Don	**1908**	**1993**
Ames, Leon	**1903**	**1993**
Amsterdam, Morey	**1914**	**1996**
Anderson, Judith	**1897**	**1992**
Anderson, Marian	**1902**	**1993**
Andrews, Dana	**1909**	**1992**
Andrews, Laverne	**1913**	**1967**
Andrews, Maxine	**1918**	**1995**
Anita Louise	**1915**	**1970**
Arbuckle, Fatty (Roscoe)	**1887**	**1933**
Arden, Eve	**1908**	**1990**
Arlen, Richard	**1900**	**1976**
Arliss, George	**1868**	**1946**
Armetta, Henry	**1888**	**1945**
Amsterdam, Morey	**1909?**	**1996**
Armstrong, Louis	**1900**	**1971**
Arnaz, Desi	**1917**	**1986**
Arnold, Edward	**1890**	**1956**
Arquette, Cliff	**1905**	**1974**
Arthur, Jean	**1900**	**1991**
Ashcroft, Peggy	**1907**	**1991**
Astaire, Fred	**1899**	**1987**
Astor, Mary	**1906**	**1987**
Atwill, Lionel	**1885**	**1946**
Auer, Mischa	**1905**	**1967**
Austin, Gene	**1900**	**1972**
Autry, Gene	**1907**	**1998**
Ayres, Lew	**1908**	**1996**
Backus, Jim	**1913**	**1989**
Bailey, Pearl	**1918**	**1990**
Bainter, Fay	**1892**	**1968**
Baker, Josephine	**1906**	**1975**
Balanchine, George	**1904**	**1983**
Ball, Lucille	**1911**	**1989**
Balsam, Martin	**1919**	**1996**
Bancroft, George	**1882**	**1956**
Bankhead, Tallulah	**1903**	**1968**
Banks, Leslie	**1890**	**1952**
Bara, Theda	**1890**	**1955**
Barnes, Binnie	**1903**	**1998**
Barnum, Phineas T.	**1810**	**1891**
Barrymore, Ethel	**1879**	**1959**
Barrymore, John	**1882**	**1942**
Barrymore, Lionel	**1878**	**1954**
Barrymore, Maurice	**1848**	**1905**
Barthelmess, Richard	**1897**	**1963**
Bartholomew, Freddie	**1924**	**1992**
Bartok, Eva	**1926**	**1998**
Basehart, Richard	**1914**	**1984**
Basie, Count	**1904**	**1984**
Baxter, Anne	**1923**	**1985**
Baxter, Warner	**1889**	**1951**
Beatty, Clyde	**1904**	**1965**
Beaubrun, Theodore	**1918**	**1998**
Beaumont, Hugh	**1909**	**1982**
Beavers, Louise	**1902**	**1962**
Beery, Noah, Sr.	**1884**	**1946**
Beery, Noah, Jr.	**1913**	**1994**
Beery, Wallace	**1889**	**1949**
Begley, Ed	**1901**	**1970**
Bellamy, Ralph	**1904**	**1991**
Belushi, John	**1949**	**1982**
Benaderet, Bea	**1906**	**1968**
Bendix, William	**1906**	**1964**
Bennett, Constance	**1904**	**1965**
Bennett, Joan	**1910**	**1990**
Bennett, Michael	**1943**	**1987**
Benny, Jack	**1894**	**1974**
Benzell, Mimi	**1924**	**1970**
Beradino, John	**1917**	**1996**
Berg, Gertrude	**1899**	**1966**
Bergen, Edgar	**1903**	**1978**
Bergman, Ingrid	**1915**	**1982**
Berkeley, Busby	**1895**	**1976**
Bernardi, Herschel	**1923**	**1986**
Bernhardt, Sarah	**1844**	**1923**
Bernie, Ben	**1893**	**1943**
Bessell, Ted	**1939**	**1996**
Bickford, Charles	**1889**	**1967**
Bissell, Whit	**1909**	**1996**
Bixby, Bill	**1934**	**1993**
Bjoerling, Jussi	**1911**	**1960**
Blackmer, Sidney	**1895**	**1973**
Blake, Amanda	**1931**	**1989**
Blaine, Vivian	**1921**	**1995**
Blanc, Mel	**1908**	**1989**
Blocker, Dan	**1928**	**1972**
Blondell, Joan	**1909**	**1979**
Blore, Eric	**1888**	**1959**
Blue, Ben	**1901**	**1975**
Bogart, Humphrey	**1899**	**1957**
Boland, Mary	**1880**	**1965**
Boles, John	**1895**	**1969**
Bolger, Ray	**1904**	**1987**
Bond, Ward	**1903**	**1960**
Bondi, Beulah	**1892**	**1981**
Bono, Sonny	**1935**	**1998**
Boone, Richard	**1917**	**1981**
Booth, Edwin	**1833**	**1893**
Booth, Junius Brutus	**1796**	**1852**
Booth, Shirley	**1898**	**1992**
Bow, Clara	**1905**	**1965**
Bowes, Maj. Edward	**1874**	**1946**
Boyd, Stephen	**1928**	**1977**
Boyd, William	**1898**	**1972**
Boyer, Charles	**1899**	**1978**
Brady, Alice	**1893**	**1939**
Brand, Neville	**1921**	**1992**
Brazzi, Rossano	**1916**	**1994**
Brennan, Walter	**1894**	**1974**
Brent, George	**1904**	**1979**
Brett, Jeremy	**1935**	**1995**
Brice, Fanny	**1891**	**1951**
Bridges, Lloyd	**1913**	**1998**
Broderick, Helen	**1891**	**1959**
Brown, Joe E.	**1892**	**1973**
Bruce, Lenny	**1926**	**1966**
Bruce, Nigel	**1895**	**1953**
Bruce, Virginia	**1910**	**1982**
Brynner, Yul	**1915**	**1985**
Buchanan, Edgar	**1903**	**1979**
Buñuel, Luis	**1900**	**1983**
Buono, Victor	**1938**	**1982**
Burke, Billie	**1885**	**1970**
Burnette, Smiley	**1911**	**1967**
Burns, George	**1896**	**1996**
Burr, Raymond	**1917**	**1993**
Burton, Richard	**1925**	**1984**
Busch, Mae	**1897**	**1946**
Bushman, Francis X.	**1883**	**1966**
Butterworth, Charles	**1896**	**1946**
Byington, Spring	**1893**	**1971**
Cabot, Bruce	**1904**	**1972**
Cabot, Sebastian	**1918**	**1977**
Cagney, James	**1899**	**1986**
Calhern, Louis	**1895**	**1956**
Callas, Maria	**1923**	**1977**
Calloway, Cab	**1907**	**1994**
Cambridge, Godfrey	**1933**	**1976**
Campbell, Mrs. Patrick	**1865**	**1940**
Candy, John	**1950**	**1994**
Cantor, Eddie	**1892**	**1964**
Capra, Frank	**1897**	**1991**
Carey, Harry	**1878**	**1947**
Carey, Macdonald	**1913**	**1994**
Carné, Marcel	**1906**	**1996**
Carpenter, Karen	**1950**	**1983**
Carradine, John	**1906**	**1988**
Carrillo, Leo	**1880**	**1961**
Carroll, Leo G.	**1892**	**1972**
Carroll, Madeleine	**1906**	**1987**
Carroll, Nancy	**1905**	**1965**
Carson, Jack	**1910**	**1963**
Caruso, Enrico	**1873**	**1921**
Casals, Pablo	**1876**	**1973**
Cassavetes, John	**1929**	**1989**
Castle, Irene	**1893**	**1969**
Castle, Vernon	**1887**	**1918**
Caulfield, Joan	**1922**	**1991**
Chaliapin, Feodor	**1873**	**1938**
Champion, Gower	**1919**	**1980**
Chandler, Jeff	**1918**	**1961**
Chaney, Lon	**1883**	**1930**
Chaney, Lon, Jr.	**1905**	**1973**
Chapin, Harry	**1942**	**1981**
Chaplin, Charles	**1889**	**1977**
Chatterton, Ruth	**1893**	**1961**
Cherrill, Virginia	**1908**	**1996**
Chevalier, Maurice	**1888**	**1972**
Clair, René	**1898**	**1981**
Clark, Bobby	**1888**	**1960**
Clark, Fred	**1914**	**1968**
Clift, Montgomery	**1920**	**1966**
Cline, Patsy	**1932**	**1963**
Clyde, Andy	**1892**	**1967**
Cobain, Kurt	**1967**	**1994**
Cobb, Lee J.	**1911**	**1976**
Coburn, Charles	**1877**	**1961**
Cohan, George M.	**1878**	**1942**
Cohen, Myron	**1902**	**1986**
Colbert, Claudette	**1903**	**1996**
Cole, Nat "King"	**1919**	**1965**
Collins, Ray	**1890**	**1965**
Colman, Ronald	**1891**	**1958**
Columbo, Russ	**1908**	**1934**
Connors, Chuck	**1921**	**1992**
Conrad, Charles J.	**1909**	**1998**
Conrad, William	**1920**	**1994**
Conried, Hans	**1917**	**1982**
Conte, Richard	**1911**	**1975**
Convy, Bert	**1933**	**1991**
Conway, Tom	**1904**	**1967**
Coogan, Jackie	**1914**	**1984**
Cook, Elisha	**1904**	**1995**
Cooke, Sam	**1935**	**1964**
Cooper, Gary	**1901**	**1961**
Cooper, Gladys	**1888**	**1971**
Cooper, Melville	**1896**	**1973**
Cornell, Katherine	**1893**	**1974**
Correll, Charles ("Andy")	**1890**	**1972**
Costello, Dolores	**1905**	**1979**

Name	Born	Died
Costello, Lou	1906	1959
Cotten, Joseph	1905	1994
Coward, Noel	1899	1973
Cox, Wally	1924	1973
Crabbe, Buster	1908	1983
Crane, Bob	1928	1978
Crawford, Broderick	1911	1986
Crawford, Joan	1904	1977
Crews, Laura Hope	1880	1942
Crisp, Donald	1880	1974
Croce, Jim	1942	1973
Crosby, Bing	1904	1977
Crothers, Scatman	1910	1986
Cugat, Xavier	1900	1990
Cukor, George	1899	1983
Cullen, Bill	1920	1990
Cummings, Robert	1908	1990
Currie, Finlay	1878	1968
Cushing, Peter	1913	1994
Dailey, Dan	1914	1978
Dandridge, Dorothy	1923	1965
Daniell, Henry	1894	1963
Daniels, Bebe	1901	1971
Darin, Bobby	1936	1973
Darnell, Linda	1921	1965
Darwell, Jane	1879	1967
Da Silva, Howard	1909	1986
Davenport, Harry	1866	1949
Davies, Marion	1897	1961
Davis, Bette	1908	1989
Davis, Joan	1907	1961
Davis, Sammy Jr.	1925	1990
Dean, James	1931	1955
Defore, Don	1917	1993
Dekker, Albert	1905	1968
Del Rio, Dolores	1908	1983
Demarest, William	1892	1983
DeMille, Agnes	1905	1993
DeMille, Cecil B.	1881	1959
Denison, Michael	1915	1998
Dennis, Sandy	1937	1992
Denny, Reginald	1891	1967
Denver, John	1943	1997
Derek, John	1926	1998
DeSica, Vittorio	1901	1974
Devine, Andy	1905	1977
Dewhurst, Colleen	1924	1991
De Wilde, Brandon	1942	1972
De Wolfe, Billy	1907	1974
Diamond, Selma	1920	1985
Dietrich, Marlene	1901	1992
Digges, Dudley	1879	1947
Disney, Walt	1901	1966
Dix, Richard	1894	1949
Donat, Robert	1905	1958
Donlevy, Brian	1889	1972
Douglas, Melvyn	1901	1981
Douglas, Paul	1907	1959
Dove, Billie	1900	1998
Draper, Ruth	1889	1956
Dresser, Louise	1881	1965
Dressler, Marie	1869	1934
Drew, Mrs. John	1820	1897
Dru, Joanne	1923	1996
Duchin, Eddy	1909	1951
Duff, Howard	1917	1990
Dumbrille, Douglass	1890	1974
Dumont, Margaret	1889	1965
Duncan, Isadora	1878	1927
Dunn, James	1905	1967
Dunne, Irene	1898	1990
Dunnock, Mildred	1904	1991
Durante, Jimmy	1893	1980
Duryea, Dan	1907	1968
Duse, Eleanora	1858	1924
Eagels, Jeanne	1894	1929
Eckstine, Billy	1914	1993
Eddy, Nelson	1901	1967
Edelman, Herb	1933	1996
Edwards, Cliff	1897	1971
Edwards, Gus	1879	1945
Edwards, Vince	1928	1996
Egan, Richard	1923	1987
Ellington, Duke	1899	1974

Name	Born	Died
Elliot, Cass	1941	1974
Elman, Mischa	1891	1967
Errol, Leon	1881	1951
Evans, Edith	1888	1976
Evans, Maurice	1901	1989
Ewell, Tom	1909	1994
Fairbanks, Douglas	1883	1939
Farley, Chris	1964	1997
Farmer, Frances	1914	1970
Farnum, Dustin	1870	1929
Farnum, William	1876	1953
Farrar, Geraldine	1882	1967
Farrell, Charles	1901	1990
Farrell, Glenda	1904	1971
Fassbinder, Rainer Werner	1946	1982
Fay, Frank	1897	1961
Faye, Alice	1912	1998
Fazenda, Louise	1895	1962
Feld, Fritz	1900	1993
Feldman, Marty	1933	1982
Fellini, Federico	1920	1993
Fenneman, George	1919	1997
Ferrer, Jose	1912	1992
Fetchit, Stepin	1898	1985
Fiedler, Arthur	1894	1979
Field, Betty	1918	1973
Fields, Gracie	1898	1979
Fields, W.C.	1879	1946
Fields, Totie	1931	1978
Finch, Peter	1916	1977
Fine, Larry	1902	1975
Firkusny, Rudolf	1912	1994
Fiske, Minnie Maddern	1865	1932
Fitzgerald, Barry	1888	1961
Flagstad, Kirsten	1895	1962
Fleming, Eric	1925	1966
Flippen, Jay C.	1900	1971
Flynn, Errol	1909	1959
Flynn, Joe	1925	1974
Foley, Red	1910	1968
Fonda, Henry	1905	1982
Fontaine, Frank	1920	1978
Fontanne, Lynn	1887	1983
Fonteyn, Margot	1919	1991
Ford, John	1895	1973
Ford, Paul	1901	1976
Ford, Tennessee Ernie	1919	1991
Ford, Wallace	1899	1966
Fosse, Bob	1927	1987
Foster, Phil	1914	1985
Foster, Preston	1901	1970
Fowley, Douglas V.	1911	1998
Foxx, Redd	1922	1991
Foy, Eddie	1857	1928
Franchi, Sergio	1933?	1990
Francis, Kay	1903	1968
Franciscus, James	1934	1991
Frann, Mary	1943	1998
Frawley, William	1893	1966
Friganza, Trixie	1870	1955
Frisco, Joe	1890	1958
Froman, Jane	1907	1980
Furness, Betty	1916	1994
Gabin, Jean	1904	1976
Gable, Clark	1901	1960
Gabor, Eva	1920	1995
Garbo, Greta	1905	1990
Garcia, Jerry	1942	1995
Gardenia, Vincent	1922	1992
Gardner, Ava	1922	1990
Garfield, John	1913	1952
Garland, Judy	1922	1969
Garson, Greer	1908	1996
Gaye, Marvin	1939	1984
Gaynor, Janet	1906	1984
Geer, Will	1902	1978
George, Gladys	1900	1954
Gibb, Andy	1958	1988
Gibson, Hoot	1892	1962
Gilbert, Billy	1894	1971
Gilbert, John	1895	1936
Gilford, Jack	1907	1990
Gillette, William	1855	1937
Gingold, Hermione	1897	1987

Name	Born	Died
Gish, Dorothy	1898	1968
Gish, Lillian	1893	1993
Gleason, Jackie	1916	1987
Gleason, James	1886	1959
Gluck, Alma	1884	1938
Gobel, George	1919	1991
Goddard, Paulette	1905	1990
Godfrey, Arthur	1903	1983
Godunov, Alexander	1949	1995
Goldwyn, Samuel	1882	1974
Gomez, Thomas	1905	1971
Goodman, Benny	1909	1986
Gorcey, Leo	1915	1969
Gordon, Gale	1906	1995
Gordon, Ruth	1896	1985
Gosden, Freeman ("Amos")	1899	1982
Gottschalk, Ferdinand	1869	1944
Gottschalk, Louis	1829	1869
Gould, Glenn	1932	1982
Gould, Morton	1913	1996
Grable, Betty	1916	1973
Graham, Martha	1894	1991
Grahame, Gloria	1925	1981
Granger, Stewart	1913	1993
Grant, Cary	1904	1986
Granville, Bonita	1923	1988
Greene, Lorne	1915	1987
Greenstreet, Sydney	1879	1954
Griffith, David Wark	1874	1948
Griffith, Hugh	1912	1980
Guardino, Harry	1925	1995
Guthrie, Woody	1912	1967
Gwenn, Edmund	1875	1959
Gwynne, Fred	1926	1993
Hale, Alan	1892	1950
Hale, Alan, Jr.	1918	1990
Haley, Bill	1925	1981
Haley, Jack	1899	1979
Hamilton, Margaret	1902	1985
Hammerstein, Oscar	1847	1919
Hardwicke, Cedric	1893	1964
Hardy, Oliver	1892	1957
Harlow, Jean	1911	1937
Harris, Phil	1904	1995
Harrison, Rex	1908	1990
Hart, William S.	1870	1946
Hartman, Phil	1948	1998
Harvey, Laurence	1928	1973
Hawkins, Jack	1910	1973
Hayakawa, Sessue	1890	1973
Hayden, Sterling	1916	1986
Hayes, Gabby	1885	1969
Hayes, Helen	1900	1993
Hayes, Peter Lind	1915	1998
Hayward, Leland	1902	1971
Hayward, Louis	1909	1985
Hayward, Susan	1917	1975
Hayworth, Rita	1918	1987
Healy, Ted	1896	1937
Heflin, Van	1910	1971
Heifetz, Jascha	1901	1987
Held, Anna	1873	1918
Hemingway, Margaux	1955	1996
Hendrix, Jimi	1942	1970
Henie, Sonja	1912	1969
Henreid, Paul	1908	1992
Henson, Jim	1936	1990
Hepburn, Audrey	1929	1993
Hersholt, Jean	1886	1956
Hickey, William	1928	1997
Hill, Benny	1925	1992
Hitchcock, Alfred	1899	1980
Hodiak, John	1914	1955
Holden, Fay	1894	1973
Holden, William	1918	1981
Holliday, Judy	1922	1965
Holloway, Sterling	1905	1992
Holly, Buddy	1936	1959
Holt, Jack	1888	1951
Holt, Tim	1918	1973
Homolka, Oscar	1898	1978
Hoon, Shannon	1967	1995
Hopkins, Miriam	1902	1972
Hopper, DeWolf	1858	1935
Hopper, William	1915	1970

Name	Born	Died
Horowitz, Vladimir	**1904**	**1989**
Horton, Edward Everett	**1886**	**1970**
Houdini, Harry	**1874**	**1926**
Houseman, John	**1902**	**1988**
Howard, Curly	**1903**	**1952**
Howard, Eugene	**1881**	**1965**
Howard, Joe	**1867**	**1961**
Howard, Leslie	**1890**	**1943**
Howard, Moe	**1897**	**1975**
Howard, Shemp	**1895**	**1955**
Howard, Tom	**1885**	**1955**
Howard, Trevor	**1916**	**1988**
Howard, Willie	**1885**	**1949**
Hudson, Rock	**1925**	**1985**
Hughes, Mary Beth	**1919**	**1995**
Hull, Henry	**1890**	**1977**
Hull, Josephine	**1886**	**1957**
Humphrey, Doris	**1895**	**1958**
Hunter, Jeffrey	**1925**	**1969**
Hunter, Ross	**1921**	**1996**
Husing, Ted	**1901**	**1962**
Huston, John	**1906**	**1987**
Huston, Walter	**1884**	**1950**
Hutchence, Michael	**1960**	**1997**
Hutton, Jim	**1934**	**1979**
Hutton, Robert	**1920**	**1994**
Ingram, Rex	**1895**	**1969**
Iturbi, Jose	**1895**	**1980**
Ireland, Jill	**1936**	**1990**
Ireland, John	**1915**	**1992**
Irving, Henry	**1838**	**1905**
Ives, Burl	**1909**	**1995**
Jackson, Joe	**1875**	**1942**
Jackson, Mahalia	**1911**	**1972**
Jaeckel, Richard	**1926**	**1997**
Jaffe, Sam	**1891**	**1984**
Jagger, Dean	**1903**	**1991**
James, Dennis	**1917**	**1997**
James, Harry	**1916**	**1983**
Janis, Elsie	**1889**	**1956**
Jannings, Emil	**1886**	**1950**
Janssen, David	**1930**	**1980**
Jenkins, Allen	**1900**	**1974**
Jessel, George	**1898**	**1981**
Johnson, Ben	**1918**	**1996**
Johnson, Chic	**1892**	**1962**
Jolson, Al	**1886**	**1950**
Jones, Brian	**1942**	**1969**
Jones, Buck	**1889**	**1942**
Jones, Carolyn	**1933**	**1983**
Jones, Spike	**1911**	**1965**
Joplin, Janis	**1943**	**1970**
Jory, Victor	**1902**	**1982**
Joslyn, Allyn	**1905**	**1981**
Julia, Raul	**1940**	**1994**
Kane, Helen	**1910**	**1966**
Karloff, Boris	**1887**	**1969**
Karns, Roscoe	**1893**	**1970**
Kaufman, Andy	**1949**	**1984**
Kaye, Danny	**1913**	**1987**
Kaye, Stubby	**1918**	**1997**
Kean, Charles	**1811**	**1868**
Kean, Mrs. Charles	**1806**	**1880**
Kean, Edmund	**1787**	**1833**
Keaton, Buster	**1895**	**1966**
Keeler, Ruby	**1910**	**1993**
Keith, Brian	**1921**	**1997**
Kellaway, Cecil	**1894**	**1973**
Kelly, Emmett	**1898**	**1979**
Kelly, Gene	**1912**	**1996**
Kelly, Grace	**1929**	**1982**
Kelly, Patsy	**1910**	**1981**
Kelton, Pert	**1907**	**1968**
Kendall, Kay	**1926**	**1959**
Kennedy, Arthur	**1914**	**1990**
Kennedy, Edgar	**1890**	**1948**
Kibbee, Guy	**1886**	**1956**
Kilbride, Percy	**1888**	**1964**
Knight, Ted	**1923**	**1986**
Kostelanetz, Andre	**1901**	**1980**
Kovacs, Ernie	**1919**	**1962**
Kruger, Otto	**1885**	**1974**
Kulp, Nancy	**1921**	**1991**
Kurosawa, Akira	**1910**	**1998**
Ladd, Alan	**1913**	**1964**
Lahr, Bert	**1895**	**1967**
Lake, Arthur	**1905**	**1987**
Lake, Veronica	**1919**	**1973**
Lamas, Fernando	**1915**	**1982**
Lamour, Dorothy	**1914**	**1996**
Lancaster, Burt	**1913**	**1994**
Lanchester, Elsa	**1902**	**1986**
Lane, Pricilla	**1917**	**1995**
Landis, Carole	**1919**	**1948**
Landis, Jessie Royce	**1904**	**1972**
Landon, Michael	**1936**	**1991**
Lang, Fritz	**1890**	**1976**
Langdon, Harry	**1884**	**1944**
Langtry, Lillie	**1853**	**1929**
Lanza, Mario	**1921**	**1959**
Larson, Nicolette	**1952**	**1998**
LaRue, Lash (Alfred)	**1917**	**1996**
Lauder, Harry	**1870**	**1950**
Laughton, Charles	**1899**	**1962**
Laurel, Stan	**1890**	**1965**
Lawford, Peter	**1923**	**1984**
Lawrence, Gertrude	**1898**	**1952**
Lean, David	**1908**	**1991**
Lee, Bernard	**1908**	**1981**
Lee, Bruce	**1940**	**1973**
Lee, Canada	**1907**	**1952**
Lee, Gypsy Rose	**1914**	**1970**
Leeds, Phil	**1916**	**1998**
LeGallienne, Eva	**1899**	**1991**
Lehmann, Lotte	**1888**	**1976**
Leigh, Vivien	**1913**	**1967**
Leighton, Margaret	**1922**	**1976**
Lennon, John	**1940**	**1980**
Lenya, Lotte	**1898**	**1981**
Leonard, Eddie	**1870**	**1941**
Leonard, Sheldon	**1907**	**1997**
LeRoy, Mervyn	**1900**	**1987**
Levant, Oscar	**1906**	**1972**
Levene, Sam	**1905**	**1980**
Levenson, Sam	**1911**	**1980**
Lewis, Joe E.	**1902**	**1971**
Lewis, Shari	**1934**	**1998**
Lewis, Ted	**1892**	**1971**
Liberace	**1919**	**1987**
Lind, Jenny	**1820**	**1887**
Lindfors, Viveca	**1920**	**1995**
Lindley, Audra	**1918**	**1997**
Lillie, Beatrice	**1894**	**1989**
Lloyd, Harold	**1893**	**1971**
Lloyd, Marie	**1870**	**1922**
Lockhart, Gene	**1891**	**1957**
Logan, Ella	**1913**	**1969**
Lombard, Carole	**1909**	**1942**
Lombardo, Guy	**1902**	**1977**
Long, Richard	**1927**	**1974**
Lopez, Vincent	**1895**	**1975**
Lord, Jack	**1920?**	**1998**
Lorne, Marion	**1888**	**1968**
Lorre, Peter	**1904**	**1964**
Lovejoy, Frank	**1912**	**1962**
Lowe, Edmund	**1890**	**1971**
Loy, Myrna	**1905**	**1993**
Lubitsch, Ernst	**1892**	**1947**
Lugosi, Bela	**1882**	**1956**
Lukas, Paul	**1894**	**1971**
Lunt, Alfred	**1892**	**1977**
Lupino, Ida	**1918**	**1995**
Lynde, Paul	**1926**	**1982**
Lynn, Diana	**1926**	**1971**
MacDonald, Jeanette	**1903**	**1965**
Mack, Ted	**1904**	**1976**
MacLane, Barton	**1902**	**1969**
MacMurray, Fred	**1908**	**1991**
MacRae, Gordon	**1921**	**1986**
Macready, George	**1909**	**1973**
Madison, Guy	**1922**	**1996**
Magnani, Anna	**1908**	**1973**
Maher, Joseph	**1933**	**1998**
Mancini, Henry	**1924**	**1994**
Main, Marjorie	**1890**	**1975**
Malle, Louis	**1932**	**1995**
Mansfield, Jayne	**1932**	**1967**
Mantovani, Annunzio	**1905**	**1980**
March, Fredric	**1897**	**1975**
March, Hal	**1920**	**1970**
Marley, Bob	**1945**	**1981**
Marshall, Brenda	**1915**	**1992**
Marshall, E.G.	**1910**	**1998**
Marshall, Herbert	**1890**	**1966**
Martin, Dean	**1917**	**1995**
Martin, Mary	**1913**	**1990**
Martin, Ross	**1920**	**1981**
Marvin, Lee	**1924**	**1987**
Marx, Arthur (Harpo)	**1888**	**1964**
Marx, Herbert (Zeppo)	**1901**	**1979**
Marx, Julius (Groucho)	**1890**	**1977**
Marx, Leonard (Chico)	**1886**	**1961**
Marx, Milton (Gummo)	**1893**	**1977**
Mason, James	**1909**	**1984**
Massey, Daniel	**1933**	**1998**
Massey, Raymond	**1896**	**1983**
Mastroianni, Marcello	**1924**	**1996**
Maxwell, Marilyn	**1921**	**1972**
Mayer, Louis B.	**1885**	**1957**
Maynard, Ken	**1895**	**1973**
Mazurki, Mike	**1909**	**1990**
McCartney, Linda	**1941**	**1998**
McClure, Doug	**1935**	**1995**
McCormack, John	**1884**	**1945**
McCrea, Joel	**1905**	**1990**
McDaniel, Hattie	**1895**	**1952**
McDowall, Roddy	**1928**	**1998**
McFarland, George "Spanky"	**1928**	**1993**
McHugh, Frank	**1899**	**1981**
McIntire, John	**1907**	**1991**
McLaglen, Victor	**1883**	**1959**
McMahon, Horace	**1907**	**1971**
McNeill, Don	**1907**	**1979**
McQueen, Butterfly	**1911**	**1995**
McQueen, Steve	**1930**	**1980**
Meadows, Audrey	**1924**	**1996**
Medford, Kay	**1920**	**1980**
Meek, Donald	**1880**	**1946**
Melba, Nellie	**1861**	**1931**
Melchior, Lauritz	**1890**	**1973**
Menjou, Adolphe	**1890**	**1963**
Menken, Helen	**1902**	**1966**
Mercouri, Melina	**1925**	**1994**
Mercury, Freddie	**1946**	**1991**
Meredith, Burgess	**1909**	**1997**
Merman, Ethel	**1908**	**1984**
Merritt, Theresa	**1924**	**1998**
Mifune, Toshiro	**1920**	**1997**
Milland, Ray	**1905**	**1986**
Miller, Glenn	**1904**	**1944**
Miller, Marilyn	**1898**	**1936**
Mills, Harry	**1913**	**1982**
Minnevitch, Borrah	**1903**	**1955**
Mineo, Sal	**1939**	**1976**
Miranda, Carmen	**1913**	**1955**
Mitchell, Cameron	**1918**	**1994**
Mitchell, Thomas	**1892**	**1962**
Mitchum, Robert	**1917**	**1997**
Mix, Tom	**1880**	**1940**
Monica, Corbett	**1930**	**1998**
Monroe, Marilyn	**1926**	**1962**
Monroe, Vaughn	**1911**	**1973**
Montand, Yves	**1921**	**1991**
Montez, Maria	**1917**	**1951**
Montgomery, Elizabeth	**1933**	**1995**
Montgomery, Robert	**1904**	**1981**
Moore, Colleen	**1900**	**1988**
Moore, Grace	**1901**	**1947**
Moore, Garry	**1914**	**1993**
Moore, Victor	**1876**	**1962**
Moorehead, Agnes	**1906**	**1974**
Morgan, Dennis	**1910**	**1994**
Morgan, Frank	**1890**	**1949**
Morgan, Helen	**1900**	**1941**
Morgan, Henry	**1915**	**1994**
Morley, Robert	**1908**	**1992**
Morris, Chester	**1901**	**1970**
Morris, Greg	**1934**	**1996**
Morris, Wayne	**1914**	**1959**
Morrison, Jim	**1943**	**1971**
Morrow, Vic	**1932**	**1982**
Mostel, Zero	**1915**	**1977**

Name	Born	Died
Mowbray, Alan	1897	1969
Mulhare, Edward	1923	1997
Mulligan, Gerry	1927	1996
Muni, Paul	1895	1967
Munshin, Jules	1915	1970
Murphy, Audie	1924	1971
Murphy, George	1902	1992
Murray, Mae	1885	1965
Nagel, Conrad	1896	1970
Naish, J. Carroll	1900	1973
Naldi, Nita	1898	1961
Nance, Jack	1943	1997
Natwick, Mildred	1908	1994
Negri, Pola	1897	1987
Nelson, Harriet (Hilliard)	1914	1994
Nelson, Ozzie	1906	1975
Nelson, Rick	1940	1985
Nesbit, Evelyn	1885	1967
Nijinsky, Vaslav	1890	1950
Nilsson, Anna Q.	1893	1974
Niven, David	1909	1983
Nolan, Jeanette	1911	1998
Nolan, Lloyd	1902	1985
Norman, Maidie	1913	1998
Normand, Mabel	1894	1930
Notorious B.I.G.	1972	1997
Novarro, Ramon	1899	1968
Nureyev, Rudolf	1938	1993
Oakie, Jack	1903	1978
Oakley, Annie	1860	1926
Oates, Warren	1928	1982
Oberon, Merle	1911	1979
O'Brien, Edmond	1915	1985
O'Brien, Pat	1899	1983
O'Connell, Arthur	1908	1981
O'Connell, Helen	1921	1993
O'Connor, Una	1880	1959
O'Keefe, Dennis	1908	1968
Oland, Warner	1880	1938
Olcott, Chauncey	1860	1932
Oliver, Edna May	1883	1942
Olivier, Laurence	1907	1989
Olsen, Ole	1892	1963
O'Neal, Patrick	1927	1994
O'Neill, James	1849	1920
Orbison, Roy	1936	1988
Ormandy, Eugene	1899	1985
O'Sullivan, Maureen	1911	1998
Ouspenskaya, Maria	1876	1949
Owen, Reginald	1887	1972
Paderewski, Ignace	1860	1941
Page, Geraldine	1924	1987
Pallette, Eugene	1889	1954
Palmer, Lilli	1914	1986
Pangborn, Franklin	1894	1958
Parks, Bert	1914	1992
Parks, Larry	1914	1975
Pasternack, Josef A.	1881	1940
Pastor, Tony (Vaudevillian)	1837	1908
Pastor, Tony (Bandleader)	1907	1969
Patti, Adelina	1843	1919
Patti, Carlotta	1840	1889
Patrick, Gail	1911	1980
Pavlova, Anna	1885	1931
Payne, John	1912	1989
Pearl, Minnie	1912	1996
Peerce, Jan	1904	1984
Pendleton, Nat	1899	1967
Penner, Joe	1905	1941
Peppard, George	1928	1994
Perkins, Anthony	1932	1992
Perkins, Carl	1932	1998
Peters, Susan	1921	1952
Phoenix, River	1970	1993
Piaf, Edith	1915	1963
Pickford, Mary	1893	1979
Pidgeon, Walter	1897	1984
Pinza, Ezio	1892	1957
Pitts, Zasu	1898	1963
Pleasance, Donald	1919	1995
Pons, Lily	1904	1976
Ponselle, Rosa	1897	1981
Powell, Dick	1904	1963
Powell, Eleanor	1912	1982
Powell, William	1892	1984
Power, Tyrone	1913	1958
Preminger, Otto	1905	1986
Presley, Elvis	1935	1977
Preston, Robert	1918	1987
Price, Vincent	1911	1993
Prima, Louis	1911	1978
Prinze, Freddie	1954	1977
Prowse, Juliet	1936	1996
Pyle, Denver	1920	1997
Quayle, Anthony	1913	1989
Questel, Mae	1908	1998
Rabb, Ellis	1930	1998
Rabbit, Eddie	1941	1998
Radner, Gilda	1946	1989
Raft, George	1895	1980
Rains, Claude	1890	1967
Ralston, Esther	1902	1994
Rathbone, Basil	1892	1967
Ratoff, Gregory	1897	1960
Ray, Aldo	1926	1991
Ray, Johnnie	1927	1990
Raye, Martha	1916	1994
Raymond, Gene	1908	1998
Redding, Otis	1941	1967
Redgrave, Michael	1908	1985
Reed, Donna	1921	1986
Reed, Robert	1932	1992
Reeves, George	1914	1959
Reilly, Hugh	1916	1998
Reinhardt, Max	1873	1943
Remick, Lee	1935	1991
Renaldo, Duncan	1904	1980
Rennie, Michael	1909	1971
Renoir, Jean	1894	1979
Rettig, Tommy	1941	1996
Reynolds, Marjorie	1923	1997
Rich, Charlie	1932	1995
Richardson, Ralph	1902	1983
Riddle, Nelson	1921	1985
Ritchard, Cyril	1898	1977
Ritter, Tex	1907	1974
Ritter, Thelma	1905	1969
Ritz, Al	1901	1965
Ritz, Harry	1906	1986
Ritz, Jimmy	1903	1985
Robbins, Jerome	1918	1998
Robbins, Marty	1925	1982
Robeson, Paul	1898	1976
Robinson, Bill	1878	1949
Robinson, Edward G.	1893	1973
Rochester (E. Anderson)	1905	1977
Roddenberry, Gene	1921	1991
Rodgers, Jimmie	1897	1933
Rogers, Ginger	1911	1995
Rogers, Roy	1911	1998
Rogers, Will	1879	1935
Roland, Gilbert	1905	1994
Rollins, Howard	1950	1996
Romero, Cesar	1907	1994
Rooney, Pat	1880	1962
Rose, Billy	1899	1966
Rossellini, Roberto	1906	1977
Rowan, Dan	1922	1987
Rubinstein, Artur	1887	1982
Ruggles, Charles	1886	1970
Russell, Bob	1908	1998
Russell, Gail	1924	1961
Russell, Lillian	1861	1922
Russell, Rosalind	1911	1976
Rutherford, Margaret	1892	1972
Ryan, Irene	1903	1973
Ryan, Robert	1909	1973
Sargent, Dick	1933	1994
St. Denis, Ruth	1877	1968
Sakall, S.Z.	1884	1955
Sale (Chic), Charles	1885	1936
Sanders, George	1906	1972
Sanders, Steve	1952	1998
Savalas, Telly	1924	1994
Schildkraut, Joseph	1895	1964
Schipa, Tito	1889	1965
Schnabel, Artur	1882	1951
Scott, Hazel	1920	1981
Scott, Randolph	1898	1987
Scott, Zachary	1914	1965
Scott-Siddons, Mrs.	1843	1896
Seberg, Jean	1938	1979
Seeley, Blossom	1892	1974
Segovia, Andres	1893	1987
Selena	1971	1995
Sellers, Peter	1925	1980
Selznick, David O.	1902	1965
Sennett, Mack	1884	1960
Serling, Rod	1924	1975
Shakur, Tupac	1971	1996
Shaw, Robert	1927	1978
Shawn, Ted	1891	1972
Shean, Al	1868	1949
Shearer, Norma	1902	1983
Sheridan, Ann	1915	1967
Shore, Dinah	1917	1994
Shubert, Lee	1875	1953
Siddons, Mrs. Sarah	1755	1831
Signoret, Simone	1921	1985
Silvers, Phil	1912	1985
Sim, Alastair	1900	1976
Sinatra, Frank	1915	1998
Sinclair, Madge	1938	1995
Sitka, Emil	1914	1998
Sjostrom, Victor	1879	1960
Skelton, Red	1913	1997
Skinner, Otis	1858	1942
Smith, Buffalo Bob	1917	1998
Smith, C. Aubrey	1863	1948
Smith, Kate	1907	1986
Sondergaard, Gale	1899	1985
Sousa, John Philip	1854	1932
Sparks, Ned	1884	1957
Stander, Lionel	1908	1994
Stanwyck, Barbara	1907	1990
Stevens, Inger	1934	1970
Stevenson, McLean	1929	1996
Stewart, James	1908	1997
Stickney, Dorothy	1896	1998
Stokowski, Leopold	1882	1977
Stone, Lewis	1879	1953
Stone, Milburn	1904	1980
Sturges, Preston	1898	1959
Sullavan, Margaret	1911	1960
Sullivan, Barry	1912	1994
Sullivan, Ed	1902	1974
Sullivan, Francis L.	1903	1956
Summerville, Slim	1892	1946
Swanson, Gloria	1899	1983
Swarthout, Gladys	1904	1969
Switzer, Carl "Alfalfa"	1926	1959
Talbot, Lyle	1904	1996
Talmadge, Norma	1893	1957
Tamiroff, Akim	1899	1972
Tandy, Jessica	1909	1994
Tanguay, Eva	1878	1947
Tati, Jacques	1908	1982
Taylor, Deems	1885	1966
Taylor, Dub	1907	1994
Taylor, Estelle	1899	1958
Taylor, Laurette	1887	1946
Taylor, Robert	1911	1969
Terry, Ellen	1847	1928
Thalberg, Irving	1899	1936
Thomas, Danny	1912	1991
Thomas, John Charles	1892	1960
Thorndike, Sybil	1882	1976
Tibbett, Lawrence	1896	1960
Tierney, Gene	1920	1991
Tiny Tim	1932?	1996
Tippett, Sir Michael	1905	1998
Todd, Michael	1909	1958
Tone, Franchot	1903	1968
Toscanini, Arturo	1867	1957
Tracy, Lee	1898	1968
Tracy, Spencer	1900	1967
Traubel, Helen	1903	1972
Treacher, Arthur	1894	1975
Tree, Herbert Beerbohm	1853	1917
Truex, Ernest	1890	1973
Truffaut, Francois	1932	1984

Name	Born	Died
Tucker, Forrest	1919	1986
Tucker, Richard	1913	1975
Tucker, Sophie	1884	1966
Turner, Lana	1920	1995
Turpin, Ben	1874	1940
Twelvetrees, Helen	1908	1959
Twitty, Conway	1933	1993
Valens, Ritchie	1941	1959
Valentino, Rudolph	1895	1926
Vallee, Rudy	1901	1986
Vance, Vivian	1912	1979
Van Fleet, Jo	1922	1996
Vaughan, Sarah	1924	1990
Veidt, Conrad	1893	1943
Velez, Lupe	1908	1944
Vera-Ellen	1926	1981
Vincent, Gene	1935	1971
Vicious, Sid	1958	1979
Von Stroheim, Erich	1885	1957
Von Zell, Harry	1906	1981
Walker, Junior	1942	1995
Walker, Nancy	1922	1992
Walker, Robert	1914	1951
Walsh, J. T.	1943	1998
Walsh, Raoul	1887	1980
Walter, Bruno	1876	1962
Ward, Helen	1916	1998
Warner, H. B.	1876	1958
Washington, Dinah	1924	1963
Waters, Ethel	1896	1977
Wayne, David	1914	1995
Wayne, John	1907	1979
Webb, Clifton	1891	1966
Webb, Jack	1920	1982
Weems, Ted	1901	1963
Weissmuller, Johnny	1904	1984
Welk, Lawrence	1903	1992
Welles, Orson	1915	1985
Wellman, William	1896	1975
West, Mae	1892	1980
Weston, Jack	1924	1996
Wheeler, Bert	1895	1968
White, Jesse	1919	1997
White, Pearl	1889	1938
Whiteman, Paul	1891	1967
Whitty, May	1865	1948
Wickes, Mary	1910	1995
Wilde, Cornel	1918	1989
Wilding, Michael	1912	1979
Williams, Bert	1877	1922
Williams, Guy	1924	1989
Williams, Hank Sr.	1923	1953
Williams, Wendy O.	1950	1998
Wills, Bob	1905	1975
Wills, Chill	1903	1978
Wilson, Carl	1946	1998
Wilson, Dennis	1944	1983
Wilson, Marie	1917	1972
Winninger, Charles	1884	1969
Withers, Grant	1904	1959
Wong, Anna May	1907	1961
Wood, Natalie	1938	1981
Wood, Peggy	1892	1978
Woolley, Monty	1888	1963
Wyler, William	1902	1981
Wynette, Tammy	1942	1998
Wynn, Ed	1886	1966
Wynn, Keenan	1916	1986
York, Dick	1929	1992
Young, Clara Kimball	1890	1960
Young, Gig	1913	1978
Young, Robert	1907	1998
Young, Roland	1887	1953
Youngman, Henny	1906	1998
Zanuck, Darryl F.	1902	1979
Zappa, Frank	1940	1993
Zinneman, Fred	1907	1997
Ziegfeld, Florenz	1869	1932
Zukor, Adolph	1873	1976

Original Names of Selected Entertainers

EDIE ADAMS: Elizabeth Edith Enke
EDDIE ALBERT: Edward Albert Heimberger
ALAN ALDA: Alphonso D'Abruzzo
JASON ALEXANDER: Jay Greenspan
FRED ALLEN: John Sullivan
WOODY ALLEN: Allen Konigsberg
JUNE ALLYSON: Ella Geisman
JULIE ANDREWS: Julia Wells
EVE ARDEN: Eunice Quedens
BEATRICE ARTHUR: Bernice Frankel
JEAN ARTHUR: Gladys Greene
FRED ASTAIRE: Frederick Austerlitz
ALAN AUTRY: Carlos Brown
BABYFACE: Kenneth Edmonds
LAUREN BACALL: Betty Joan Perske
ERYKAH BADU: Erica Wright
ANNE BANCROFT: Anna Maria Italiano
GENE BARRY: Eugene Klass
ORSON BEAN: Dallas Burrows
PAT BENATAR: Patricia Andrejewski
ROBBY BENSON: Robert Segal
TONY BENNETT: Anthony Benedetto
BUSBY BERKELEY: William Berkeley Enos
IRVING BERLIN: Israel Baline
JACK BENNY: Benjamin Kubelsky
JOEY BISHOP: Joseph Gottlieb
BONO (VOX): Paul Hewson
VICTOR BORGE: Borge Rosenbaum
DAVID BOWIE: David Robert Jones
BOY GEORGE: George Alan O'Dowd
FANNY BRICE: Fanny Borach
CHARLES BRONSON: Charles Buchinski
ALBERT BROOKS: Albert Einstein
MEL BROOKS: Melvin Kaminsky
GEORGE BURNS: Nathan Birnbaum
ELLEN BURSTYN: Edna Gilhooley
RICHARD BURTON: Richard Jenkins
RED BUTTONS: Aaron Chwatt
NICOLAS CAGE: Nicholas Coppola
MICHAEL CAINE: Maurice Micklewhite
MARIA CALLAS: Maria Kalogeropoulos
VIKKI CARR: Florencia Casillas
DIAHANN CARROLL: Carol Diahann Johnson
CYD CHARISSE: Tula Finklea
RAY CHARLES: Ray Charles Robinson
CHUBBY CHECKER: Ernest Evans
CHER: Cherilyn Sarkisian
PATSY CLINE: Virginia Patterson Hensley
LEE J. COBB: Leo Jacoby
CLAUDETTE COLBERT: Lily Chauchoin
MICHAEL CONNORS: Kreker Ohanian
ALICE COOPER: Vincent Furnier
DAVID COPPERFIELD: David Kotkin
HOWARD COSELL: Howard Cohen
ELVIS COSTELLO: Declan McManus
LOU COSTELLO: Louis Cristillo
PETER COYOTE: Peter Cohon
JOAN CRAWFORD: Lucille Le Sueur
MICHAEL CRAWFORD: Michael Dumble-Smith
TOM CRUISE: Thomas Mapother IV
TONY CURTIS: Bernard Schwartz
VIC DAMONE: Vito Farinola
RODNEY DANGERFIELD: Jacob Cohen
BOBBY DARIN: Walden Robert Cassotto
DORIS DAY: Doris von Kappelhoff
JAMES DEAN: James Byron
YVONNE DE CARLO: Peggy Middleton
SANDRA DEE: Alexandra Zuck
JOHN DENVER: Henry John Deutschendorf Jr.
BO DEREK: Mary Cathleen Collins
JOHN DEREK: Derek Harris
DANNY DEVITO: Daniel Michaeli
ANGIE DICKINSON: Angeline Brown
BO DIDDLEY: Elias Bates
PHYLLIS DILLER: Phyllis Driver
DIANA DORS: Diana Fluck
KIRK DOUGLAS: Issur Danielovitch
MELVYN DOUGLAS: Melvyn Hesselberg
BOB DYLAN: Robert Zimmerman
SHEENA EASTON: Sheena Shirley Orr
BARBARA EDEN: Barbara Huffman
ELVIRA: Cassandra Peterson
RON ELY: Ronald Pierce
ENYA: Eithne Ni Bhraonian
DALE EVANS: Frances Smith
CHAD EVERETT: Raymond Cramton
TOM EWELL: S. Yewell Tompkins
DOUGLAS FAIRBANKS: Douglas Ullman
MORGAN FAIRCHILD: Patsy McClenny
JAMIE FARR: Jameel Farah
ALICE FAYE: Alice Jeanne Leppert
STEPIN FETCHIT: Lincoln Perry
W.C. FIELDS: William Claude Dukenfield
BARRY FITZGERALD: William Shields
JOAN FONTAINE: Joan de Havilland
JOHN FORD: Sean O'Fearna
JOHN FORSYTHE: John Freund
JODIE FOSTER: Alicia Christian Foster
REDD FOXX: John Sanford
ANTHONY FRANCIOSA: Anthony Papaleo
ARLENE FRANCIS: Arlene Kazanjian
CONNIE FRANCIS: Concetta Franconero
GRETA GARBO: Greta Gustafsson
VINCENT GARDENIA: Vincent Scognamiglio
JOHN GARFIELD: Julius Garfinkle
JUDY GARLAND: Frances Gumm
JAMES GARNER: James Bumgarner
CRYSTAL GAYLE: Brenda Gayle Webb
KATHIE LEE GIFFORD: Kathie Epstein
PAULETTE GODDARD: Marion Levy
WHOOPI GOLDBERG: Caryn Johnson
EYDIE GORME: Edith Gormezano
STEWART GRANGER: James Stewart
CARY GRANT: Archibald Leach
LEE GRANT: Lyova Rosenthal
JOEL GREY: Joe Katz
ROBERT GUILLAUME: Robert Williams
BUDDY HACKETT: Leonard Hacker
HAMMER: Stanley Kirk Burrell
JEAN HARLOW: Harlean Carpentier
REX HARRISON: Reginald Carey
LAURENCE HARVEY: Larushka Skikne
HELEN HAYES: Helen Brown
SUSAN HAYWARD: Edythe Marriner
RITA HAYWORTH: Margarita Cansino
PEE-WEE HERMAN: Paul Reubenfeld
BARBARA HERSHEY: Barbara Herzstein
WILLIAM HOLDEN: William Beedle
BILLIE HOLIDAY: Eleanora Fagan
JUDY HOLLIDAY: Judith Tuvim
HARRY HOUDINI: Ehrich Weiss
CURLY, MOE, SHEMP HOWARD: Horwitz
LESLIE HOWARD: Leslie Stainer
ROCK HUDSON: Roy Scherer Jr. (later Fitzgerald)
ENGELBERT HUMPERDINCK: Arnold Dorsey
KIM HUNTER: Janet Cole
MARY BETH HURT: Mary Supinger
BETTY HUTTON: Betty Thornberg
ICE-T: Tracy Morrow
BILLY IDOL: William Broad
DAVID JANSSEN: David Meyer
ANN JILLIAN: Anne Nauseda
ELTON JOHN: Reginald Dwight
DON JOHNSON: Donald Wayne
AL JOLSON: Asa Yoelson
JENNIFER JONES: Phylis Isley
TOM JONES: Thomas Woodward
LOUIS JOURDAN: Louis Gendre
WYNONNA JUDD: Christina Ciminella
BORIS KARLOFF: William Henry Pratt
DANNY KAYE: David Kaminsky
DIANE KEATON: Diane Hall
MICHAEL KEATON: Michael Douglas
HOWARD KEEL: Harold Leek
CHAKA KHAN: Yvette Stevens
CAROLE KING: Carole Klein
LARRY KING: Larry Zeigler
BEN KINGSLEY: Krishna Banji
NASTASSJA KINSKI: Nastassja Nakszynski
TED KNIGHT: Tadeus Wladyslaw Konopka
CHERYL LADD: Cheryl Stoppelmoor
VERONICA LAKE: Constance Ockleman

HEDY LAMARR: Hedwig Kiesler
DOROTHY LAMOUR: Mary Leta Dorothy Slaton
MICHAEL LANDON: Eugene Orowitz
MARIO LANZA: Alfredo Cocozza
QUEEN LATIFAH: Dana Owens
STAN LAUREL: Arthur Jefferson
STEVE LAWRENCE: Sidney Leibowitz
BRENDA LEE: Brenda Mae Tarpley
BRUCE LEE: Lee Yuen Kam
GYPSY ROSE LEE: Rose Louise Hovick
MICHELLE LEE: Michelle Dusiak
PEGGY LEE: Norma Egstrom
JANET LEIGH: Jeanette Morrison
VIVIEN LEIGH: Vivian Hartley
HUEY LEWIS: Hugh Cregg
JERRY LEWIS: Joseph Levitch
HAL LINDEN: Harold Lipshitz
CAROLE LOMBARD: Jane Peters
JACK LORD: John Joseph Ryan
SOPHIA LOREN: Sophia Scicolone
PETER LORRE: Laszio Lowenstein
MYRNA LOY: Myrna Williams
BELA LUGOSI: Bela Ferenc Blasko
MOMS MABLEY: Loretta Mary Aitken
SHIRLEY MACLAINE: Shirley Beaty
ELLE MACPHERSON: Eleanor Gow
MADONNA: Madonna Louise Ciccone
LEE MAJORS: Harvey Lee Yeary 2d
KARL MALDEN: Malden Sekulovich
BARRY MANILOW: Barry Alan Pincus
JAYNE MANSFIELD: Vera Jane Palmer
MARILYN MANSON: Brian Warner
FREDRIC MARCH: Frederick Bickel
PETER MARSHALL: Pierre LaCock
WALTER MATTHAU: Walter Matuschanskayasky
DEAN MARTIN: Dino Crocetti
MEAT LOAF: Marvin Lee Aday
FREDDIE MERCURY: Frederick Bulsara
ETHEL MERMAN: Ethel Zimmerman
GEORGE MICHAEL: Georgios Panayiotou
RAY MILLAND: Reginald Truscott-Jones
ANN MILLER: Lucille Collier
JONI MITCHELL: Roberta Joan Anderson
MARILYN MONROE: Norma Jean Mortenson (later Baker)
YVES MONTAND: Ivo Livi
RON MOODY: Ronald Moodnick
DEMI MOORE: Demetria Guynes
GARRY MOORE: Thomas Garrison Morfit
RITA MORENO: Rosita Alverio
HARRY MORGAN: Harry Bratsburg
MR. T: Lawrence Tero
PAUL MUNI: Muni Weisenfreund
MIKE NICHOLS: Michael Igor Peschowsky
CHUCK NORRIS: Carlos Ray
NOTORIOUS B.I.G.: Christopher Wallace
HUGH O'BRIAN: Hugh Krampke
MAUREEN O'HARA: Maureen Fitzsimons
PATTI PAGE: Clara Ann Fowler
JACK PALANCE: Walter Palanuik
BERT PARKS: Bert Jacobson
MINNIE PEARL: Sarah Ophelia Cannon
BERNADETTE PETERS: Bernadette Lazzaro
EDITH PIAF: Edith Gassion
SLIM PICKENS: Louis Lindley
MARY PICKFORD: Gladys Smith
STEFANIE POWERS: Stefania Federkiewicz
PAULA PRENTISS: Paula Ragusa
ROBERT PRESTON: Robert Preston Meservey
PRINCE (THE ARTIST): Prince Rogers Nelson
DEE DEE RAMONE: Douglas Colvin
JOEY RAMONE: Jeffrey Hyman
JOHNNY RAMONE: John Cummings
TOMMY RAMONE: Tom Erdelyi
TONY RANDALL: Leonard Rosenberg
JOHNNIE RAY: John Alvin
MARTHA RAYE: Margaret O'Reed
DONNA REED: Donna Belle Mullenger
DELLA REESE: Delloreese Patricia Early
JOAN RIVERS: Joan Sandra Molinsky
EDWARD G. ROBINSON: Emmanuel Goldenberg
GINGER ROGERS: Virginia McMath
ROY ROGERS: Leonard Franklin Slye
MICKEY ROONEY: Joe Yule Jr.
JOHNNY ROTTEN: John Lydon
LILLIAN RUSSELL: Helen Leonard
MEG RYAN: Margaret Hyra
WINONA RYDER: Winona Horowitz
SOUPY SALES: Milton Hines
SUSAN SARANDON: Susan Tomaling
RANDOLPH SCOTT: George Randolph Crane
JANE SEYMOUR: Joyce Frankenberg
OMAR SHARIF: Michael Shalhoub
CHARLIE SHEEN: Carlos Irwin Estevez
MARTIN SHEEN: Ramon Estevez
BEVERLY SILLS: Belle Silverman
TALIA SHIRE: Talia Coppola
PHIL SILVERS: Philip Silversmith
SINBAD: David Atkins
"BUFFALO BOB" SMITH: Robert Schmidt
SUZANNE SOMERS: Suzanne Mahoney
ANN SOTHERN: Harriette Lake
ROBERT STACK: Robert Modini
BARBARA STANWYCK: Ruby Stevens
JEAN STAPLETON: Jeanne Murray
RINGO STARR: Richard Starkey
CONNIE STEVENS: Concetta Ingolia
STING: Gordon Sumner
DONNA SUMMER: La Donna Gaines
RIP TAYLOR: Charles Elmer Jr.
ROBERT TAYLOR: Spangler Brugh
DANNY THOMAS: Muzyad Yakhoob, later Amos Jacobs
TINY TIM: Herbert Khaury
RIP TORN: Elmore Rual Torn Jr.
RANDY TRAVIS: Randy Traywick
SOPHIE TUCKER: Sophia Kalish
TINA TURNER: Annie Mae Bullock
TWIGGY: Leslie Hornby
CONWAY TWITTY: Harold Lloyd Jenkins
RUDOLPH VALENTINO: Rudolpho D'Antonguolla
FRANKIE VALLI: Frank Castelluccio
GENE VINCENT: Vincent Eugene Craddock
SID VICIOUS: John Simon Ritchie
DAVID WAYNE: Wayne McMeekan
JOHN WAYNE: Marion Morrison
CLIFTON WEBB: Webb Hollenbeck
RAQUEL WELCH: Raquel Tejada
GENE WILDER: Jerome Silberman
SHELLEY WINTERS: Shirley Schrift
STEVIE WONDER: Stevland Morris
NATALIE WOOD: Natasha Gurdin
JANE WYMAN: Sarah Jane Fulks
GIG YOUNG: Byron Barr

Selected Royal Families of Europe

Name (Birthplace)	Birthdate
BELGIUM	
King Albert II (Brussels)	6/6/34
Queen Paola (Calabria, Italy)	9/11/37
Prince Philippe (Brussels)	4/15/60
Princess Astrid (Brussels)	6/5/62
Prince Laurent (Brussels)	10/19/63
UNITED KINGDOM	
Queen Elizabeth, Queen Mother (London)	8/4/00
Queen Elizabeth II (London)	4/21/26
Prince Philip (Corfu, Greece)	6/10/21
Prince Charles (London)	11/14/48
Prince William (London)	6/21/82
Prince Henry, or Harry (London)	9/15/84
Princess Anne (London)	8/15/50
Prince Andrew (London)	2/19/60
Princess Beatrice (London)	8/8/88
Princess Eugenie (London)	3/23/90
Prince Edward (London)	3/10/64
Princess Margaret (Glamis, Scotland)	8/21/30
DENMARK	
Queen Margrethe II (Copenhagen)	4/16/40
Prince Henrik (France)	6/11/34
Prince Frederik (Copenhagen)	5/26/68
Prince Joachim (Copenhagen)	6/7/69
Princess Alexandra (Hong Kong)	6/30/64
LIECHTENSTEIN	
Prince Hans-Adam II (Liechtenstein)	2/14/45
Princess Marie (Prague)	4/14/40
Crown Prince Alois (Liechtenstein)	6/11/68
Prince Maximilian (Liechtenstein)	5/16/69
Prince Constantin (Liechtenstein)	3/15/72
Princess Tatjana (Liechtenstein)	4/10/73
LUXEMBOURG	
Grand Duke Jean (Berg Castle, Luxembourg)	1/5/21
Grand Duchess Joséphine-Charlotte (Belgium)	10/11/27
Princess Marie-Astrid (Luxembourg)	2/17/54
Prince Henri (Luxembourg)	4/16/55
Prince Jean (Luxembourg)	5/15/57
Princess Margaretha (Luxembourg)	5/15/57
Prince Guillaume (Luxembourg)	5/1/63
MONACO	
Prince Rainier III (Monaco)	5/31/23
Prince Albert (Monte Carlo)	3/14/58
Princess Caroline (Monte Carlo)	1/23/57
Princess Stephanie (Monaco-Ville, Monaco)	2/1/65
NETHERLANDS	
Queen Beatrix (Baarn, Netherlands)	1/31/38
Prince Claus (Dotzingen, Germany)	6/9/26
Prince Willem-Alexander (Utrecht, Netherlands)	4/27/67
Prince Johan Friso (Utrecht, Netherlands)	9/25/68
Prince Constantijn (Utrecht, Netherlands)	10/11/69
NORWAY	
King Harald V (Skaugum, Norway)	2/21/37
Queen Sonja (Oslo)	7/4/37
Princess Märtha Louise (Oslo)	9/22/71
Crown Prince Haakon (Oslo)	7/20/73
SPAIN	
King Juan Carlos I (Rome, Italy)	1/5/38
Queen Sofía (Psychiko, Greece)	11/2/38
Princess Elena (Madrid)	12/20/63
Princess Cristina (Madrid)	6/13/65
Crown Prince Felipe (Madrid)	1/30/68
SWEDEN	
King Carl XVI Gustav (Stockholm)	4/30/46
Queen Silvia (Germany)	12/23/43
Crown Princess Victoria (Stockholm)	7/14/77
Prince Carl Philip (Stockholm)	5/13/79
Princess Madeleine (Stockholm)	6/10/82

UNITED STATES POPULATION

A Profile of America's Diversity—The View From the Census Bureau, 1998

by
James F. Holmes
Acting Director, Bureau of the Census
U.S. Department of Commerce

The United States—its people, economy, and landscape—is renowned for its remarkable diversity. This diversity is borne out by data the Census Bureau collects. Here are some examples:

Racial and Ethnic Composition

On Aug. 1, 1998, there were an estimated 270 million people living in the United States; on Census Day, Apr. 1, 1990, the nation's population was 249 mil. Of the 1998 population, an estimated 223 mil (83%) were White, 34 mil (13%) were Black, or African American; the American Indian and Alaska Native population was about 2 mil (1%); and Asians and Pacific Islanders numbered some 10 mil (4%). An estimated 30 mil (11%) were of Hispanic origin (persons of Hispanic origin may be of any race).

Age Structure

On Aug. 1, 1998, an estimated 70 mil Americans (26%) were under 18 years old. At the other end of the spectrum, 34 mil (13%) were 65 or older. At the farthest tip were about 62,000 centenarians (people who are 100 or older). This figure is a 68% increase from 1990 (37,000). The median age—with half of all Americans above and half below—was 35 years, the oldest it has ever been.

Income Spectrum

The nation's families had a median income of $44,568 in 1997. While 12% of all families had incomes of $100,000 and over, 10% were below the federal government's official poverty line—$16,400 for a family of 4.

Marriage and Families

In 1997, 6 in 10 adults ages 18 and older were married. However, Americans are marrying later than ever. The median age for first marriages, rising since the mid-1950s, reached an all-time high in 1996—24.8 years for women and 27.1 years for men. In all, 1 in 4 American adults have never been married. Yet the fastest-growing marital-status category is currently divorced persons, who comprise 10% of adults, up from 3% in 1970.

Of the 101 mil households in 1997, 70% were made up of families (2 or more related persons), 25% consisted of persons living alone, and 5% were 2 or more nonrelated people. Many households in the last category consisted of unmarried couples of opposite sexes. Married couples made up three-fourths of all families.

About half of the nation's 70 mil families included children. As of 1997, 68% of children lived with 2 parents, down from 85% in 1970. Nearly 30% lived with only 1 parent—85% of these with their mother.

Nearly 6 out of 10 women ages 15-44 in 1995 were mothers. Among the 35 mil mothers of childbearing ages, 11 mil had 1 child while 3 mil had 4 or more children.

Education

While 18% of Americans ages 25 and older lacked a high school diploma in 1997, 24% had a bachelor's degree or higher and 8% had a graduate degree.

The Foreign-Born Population

In 1997, an estimated 26 mil persons, or nearly 1 in every 10 residents of the United States, were foreign born, the highest level since 1930. Almost one-third of these foreign-born residents were naturalized citizens and nearly two-thirds had come to the United States since 1980. Five states had a larger percentage of foreign born than the United States as a whole: California (25%), New York (20%), Florida (16%), New Jersey (15%), and Texas (11%).

More than one-fourth of these immigrants—7 mil—were born in Mexico. Other leading immigrant homelands included the Philippines (1.1 mil), China and Hong Kong (1.1 mil), Cuba (913,000), Vietnam (770,000), and India (748,000).

Languages Spoken

As of 1990, the latest date for which statistics are available, 32 mil Americans spoke a language other than English at home, including 17 mil Spanish-speakers, nearly 2 mil who spoke French, and more than 1 mil each who spoke German, Chinese, or Italian.

Population Growth

Some parts of the nation are growing much faster than others. The fastest-growing states, metropolitan areas, cities, and counties are concentrated in the South and West. The states whose population rose the fastest between 1996 and 1997 were Nevada (4.7%), Arizona (2.7%), and Georgia and Utah (both 2.1%). Meanwhile, Las Vegas, NV–AZ, was the most rapidly growing metropolitan area from 1990 to 1996, with a 41% population increase, followed by Laredo, TX (33%), and McAllen-Edinburg-Mission, TX (29%).

The story for cities was much the same. Among those with more than 100,000 people in 1996, the fastest growing from 1990 to 1996 were Henderson, NV (88%), Chandler, AZ (59%), and Pembroke Pines, FL (54%). Among cities with 1 mil or more people, Phoenix, San Antonio, and Houston each gained more than 100,000 people during this period. Douglas County, CO, led all counties of 10,000 or more people during the 1996-97 period; its population climbed 13%. Maricopa County, AZ, however, experienced the largest numerical gain among counties, adding 83,000 people in a single year.

The Year 2050

According to Census Bureau projections, the U.S. population on July 1, 2050, will have risen to about 394 mil (193 mil male), with a median age of 38. While the White percentage is expected to decline through the middle of the next century, the percentage of all other racial and ethnic groups is expected to grow, with Hispanics showing the largest increase. For 2050, about 295 mil, or 75%, of the population is projected to be White, 61 mil (15%) Black or African American, 34 mil (9%) Asian or Pacific Islander, and 4 mil (1%) American Indian or Alaska Native. About 97 mil people (24%) are projected to be of Hispanic origin.

Persons With Disabilities

During the Oct. 1994-Jan. 1995 period, 54 mil Americans (1 in 5) reported some level of disability, and 26 mil of them (1 in 10) described their disability as severe.

Housing

The homes Americans live in are as varied as the population. Among the 98 mil housing units occupied year-round in 1995, 20% were built before 1940 and 24% during the 1980s or 1990s. Mobile homes or trailers comprised 6% of the housing units; single-family homes, 68%; and apartments in buildings with 20 or more units, 7%. Nearly two-thirds of all homes occupied year-round were owned by occupants.

International Trade

America's diversity also includes its list of leading trading partners. These include Canada ($53 bil in combined imports and exports during the first 2 months of 1998), Japan ($29 bil), Mexico ($27 bil), China ($12 bil), United Kingdom ($12 bil), Germany ($11 bil), Taiwan ($8 bil), France ($6 bil), South Korea ($6 bil), and Singapore ($5 bil).

State and Local Taxes

Reflecting diverse economies and histories, state and local governments rely on different kinds of tax revenues. For example, property taxes in 1995 generated 64% of all New

Hampshire's state and local tax revenues, at least 40% of all tax revenues in 7 other states (Maine, Montana, New Jersey, Rhode Island, South Dakota, Vermont, and Wyoming), but less than 15% of the revenues in 4 states (Alabama, Arkansas, Delaware, and New Mexico). Other significant tax revenue sources in 1995 included general sales taxes (more than 40% of the revenues for 4 states: Louisiana, New Mexico, Tennessee, and Washington), individual income taxes (more than 33% in 3 states: Massachusetts, Maryland, and Oregon), and severance taxes on the extraction of natural resources (43% in Alaska and 21% in Wyoming). While some states relied heavily on general sales and individual income taxes, others did not use them at all; 4 states levied no general sales tax (Delaware, Montana, New Hampshire, and Oregon) and 7 states had no individual income tax (Alaska, Florida, Nevada, South Dakota, Texas, Washington, and Wyoming).

State and Local Employees

State and local governments employ more than 1 out of every 8 U.S. workers, performing a variety of jobs. For example, 53% of all state and local employees worked in education services in 1995. More than 60% of the public employees in 4 states (Kentucky, Montana, Utah, and Vermont) worked in education, while in 2 states (Alaska and New York) and the District of Columbia, fewer than 45% did so. Similarly, the use of full- versus part-time public employees differed, in part because of labor market differences. In 1995, more than one-third of all state and local employees in 12 states (topped by North Dakota at 49% and Connecticut at 41%) worked part time.

Businesses and Workers

As of 1995, more than 100.3 mil persons worked for the nearly 5.4 mil employer businesses in the United States. The majority of these businesses (more than 4.8 mil, or nearly 90% of all businesses) employed fewer than 20 employees. These smaller businesses had estimated receipts of $2.7 tril—about 17% of the nation's total of $15.8 tril in receipts.

Los Angeles County, CA, had a net gain of 102,700 employees between 1994 and 1995, the most of any county in the country. Harris County, TX, was 2d with a gain of 89,400 employees, while Maricopa County, AZ, which added 76,100 employees, was 3d. The median growth in employment by county was 3.8%.

Milestones on the Road to Census 2000

Census Bureau officials took several steps in 1998 in an effort to make the rapidly approaching Census 2000 "simpler, less costly, and more accurate" than the 1990 census.

In March, the Census Bureau kicked off its Census 2000 Dress Rehearsal, the final dry run for Census 2000, by mailing out and hand delivering questionnaires at 3 sites around the United States. Procedures that were demonstrated included development of an address list, printing and mailing of questionnaires, marketing and promotion, and data collection, processing, and tabulation.

The sites chosen represented different types of challenges that Census 2000 will encounter. Sacramento, CA, represented urban conditions. An 11-county area surrounding Columbia, SC, provided an opportunity to demonstrate procedures in rural and suburban areas. Menominee County, WI, which includes the Menominee Indian Reservation, demonstrated special procedures planned for American Indian reservations.

As directed by Congress and the Clinton Administration, the Dress Rehearsal followed a dual track. In Sacramento and Menominee counties, in a departure from previous censuses, sampling and estimation were used to complete the job of counting. This meant that in every census tract, or neighborhood, where at least 90%, but fewer than 100%, of households responded, the Census Bureau sent an interviewer to a sample of the remaining addresses. However, sampling and estimation were not used in South Carolina. Instead, the Census Bureau employed enhanced components of a contingency option based exclusively on traditional data-collection methods.

Because Sacramento is highly urban and South Carolina is more rural, results of those 2 demonstrations will not be comparable. But they provide information that the Census Bureau can use to pursue either option in 2000.

As of Oct. 1998, however, it was not determined whether and to what extent the sampling method could be used in Census 2000. A federal district court in Washington, DC, in a suit brought by U.S. House Republicans, ruled Aug. 24 that use of sampling for data to be used in apportioning House seats would violate federal law. A similar ruling was handed down Sept. 24 by a federal district court in Virginia. The Clinton Administration appealed, and the Supreme Court agreed to hear the case. Another possible obstacle was opposition among Republicans to funding the use of sampling.

Dress Rehearsal respondents received a copy of 1 of the 2 proposed new census forms, which should take less time to fill out than those used in 1990. The short form (which went to the majority of respondents) contains only 7 questions—the fewest since 1820, when U.S. marshals took the census on horseback. The long form contains 52 questions, 5 fewer than in 1990. These questions were submitted to Congress in Mar. 1998.

The subjects for the census, announced in 1997, cover everything from age, sex, race, Hispanic origin, and household relationship to whether the person owns or rents (short-form subjects) to citizenship, ancestry, language spoken at home, plumbing and kitchen facilities, home heating fuel, and vehicles available, among other topics (long-form subjects). The Census 2000 questionnaire includes only one new subject, grandparents as caregivers, mandated by a 1996 law.

Because 5 1990 census questions (children ever born, year last worked, source of water, sewage disposal, and condominium status) were not explicitly mandated or required by federal law, the Census Bureau recommended that they not be included on the Census 2000 form.

The new questionnaires, featuring larger type, with instructions printed on the questionnaire itself, rather than in a separate guide as in 1990, are intended to be easier to read and understand than the forms used in the last census.

In late 1997, the Census Bureau awarded its Census 2000 advertising contract to Young & Rubicam, Inc., and a consortium of 4 partner agencies that specialize in reaching particular ethnic audiences. The goal of the advertising campaign is to increase initial mail returns of census questionnaires from the general public, targeted audiences, and historically undercounted populations. The 1990 census relied solely on pro bono public service advertising, which failed to reach large segments of the population.

The Census Bureau selected Scholastic Inc. to conduct a nationwide "Census in the Schools" project. This project, part of the bureau's strategy to encourage mail response, will communicate the importance of the census to school children via free educational materials provided to teachers.

In another development, Lockheed-Martin Mission Systems will integrate commercially available sorters, scanners, and processors in a system called Data Capture System 2000 (DCS 2000). In this system, the scanners will take electronic photos of the completed census forms; these images will be processed by software capable of recognizing a variety of hand-written responses—made by either pen or pencil—as alphabetic or numeric characters. The resulting data will be transmitted electronically to Census Bureau headquarters for statistical processing and analysis. More than 120 million questionnaires will flow through the DCS 2000 systems at 4 data capture centers around the country. With the use of DCS 2000 it is expected that census forms will be processed 20 times faster than they were in 1990.

Racial and Ethnic Classifications

In Oct. 1997, the Office of Management and Budget (OMB) announced revised standards for classifying federal data on race and ethnicity. The standards have 5 categories for data on race: American Indian and Alaska Native, Asian, Black or African American, Native Hawaiian and Other Pacific Islander, and White. There are 2 categories for data on ethnicity: Hispanic or Latino, and Not Hispanic or Latino. (Persons of Hispanic or Latino origin may be of any race.)

The Census Bureau's question on race is shown below as it will appear on the Census 2000 questionnaire. Although it lists more categories than identified in the standards, the categories fit into those in the standards, except "some other race."

What is this person's race?

__ White
__ Black, African American or Negro
__ American Indian or Alaska Native (includes space to write in tribe)
__ Asian Indian
__ Chinese
__ Filipino
__ Other Asian (includes space for write-ins)
__ Some Other Race (includes space for write-ins)*
__ Japanese
__ Korean
__ Vietnamese
__ Native Hawaiian
__ Guamanian or Chamorro
__ Samoan
__ Other Pacific Islander (includes space for write-ins)

The OMB standards permit respondents to report more than 1 race, so the instructions for the question say, "Mark [x] one or more ..." In the winter of 1998-99, the OMB expects to announce guidelines for tabulating the responses to the race question, particularly in those cases where respondents report 2 or more races.

The Hispanic origin question on the Census 2000 questionnaire is shown below:

Is this person Spanish/Hispanic/Latino?

__ No, not Spanish/Hispanic/Latino
__ Yes, Mexican, Mexican American, Chicano
__ Yes, other Spanish/Hispanic/Latino (includes space for write-ins)
__ Yes, Puerto Rican
__ Yes, Cuban

* The Census Bureau obtained an exemption from the OMB to include a "some other race" category.

Race and Hispanic Origin for the U.S., 1990 and 1980

Source: Bureau of the Census, U.S. Dept. of Commerce

	1990 Census		1980 Census		% change
Race	**Number**	**Percent**	**Number**	**Percent**	**1980-90**
All persons	**248,709,873[1]**	**100.0**	**226,545,805**	**100.0**	**9.8**
White	199,686,070	80.3	188,371,622	83.1	6.0
Black	29,986,060	12.1	26,495,025	11.7	13.2
American Indian, Eskimo, or Aleut	1,959,234	0.8	1,420,400	0.6	37.9
American Indian	1,878,285	0.8	1,364,033	0.6	37.7
Eskimo	57,152	0.0	42,162	0.0	35.6
Aleut	23,797	0.0	14,205	0.0	67.5
Asian-Pacific Islander	7,273,662	2.9	3,500,439[2]	1.5	107.8
Chinese	1,645,472	0.7	806,040	0.4	104.1
Filipino	1,406,770	0.6	774,652	0.3	81.6
Japanese	847,562	0.3	700,974	0.3	20.9
Asian Indian	815,447	0.3	361,531	0.2	125.6
Korean	798,849	0.3	354,593	0.2	125.3
Vietnamese	614,547	0.2	261,729	0.1	134.8
Hawaiian	211,014	0.1	166,814	0.1	26.5
Samoan	62,964	0.0	41,948	0.0	50.1
Guamanian	49,345	0.0	32,158	0.0	53.4
Other Asian-Pacific Islander	821,692	0.3	NA	NA	NA
Other race	9,804,847	3.9	6,758,319	3.0	45.1
Persons of Hispanic origin[3]	**22,354,059**	**9.0**	**14,608,673**	**6.4**	**53.0**
Mexican	13,495,938	5.4	8,740,439	3.9	54.4
Puerto Rican	2,727,754	1.1	2,013,945	0.9	35.4
Cuban	1,043,932	0.4	803,226	0.4	30.0
Other Hispanic	5,086,435	2.0	3,051,063	1.3	66.7

NA=Not available. (1) The race data are based on the U.S. population as tabulated in the 1990 census. Figures do not reflect corrections to the 1990 population census; the corrected 1990 U.S. population is 248,765,170. (2) The 1980 count of 3,500,439 Asian-Pacific Islanders, based on 100% tabulations, includes only the 9 Asian-Pacific Islander groups listed separately in the 1980 race item. A figure of 3,726,440, from sample tabulations, is more comparable to the 1990 count since it includes those groups. (3) May be of any race.

Estimated Population of American Colonies, 1630-1780

Source: Bureau of the Census, U.S. Dept. of Commerce; in thousands

Colony	1780	1770	1750	1740	1720	1700	1690	1670	1650	1630
TOTAL	**2,780.4**	**2,148.1**	**1,170.8**	**905.6**	**466.2**	**250.9**	**210.4**	**111.9**	**50.4**	**4.6**
Maine (counties)[1]	49.1	31.3	...	...	...	...	...	...	1.0	0.4
New Hampshire[2]	87.8	62.4	27.5	23.3	9.4	5.0	4.2	1.8	1.3	0.5
Vermont[3]	47.6	10.0	...	...	...	...	...	...	...	...
Plymouth and Massachusetts[1,2,4]	268.6	235.3	188.0	151.6	91.0	55.9	56.9	35.3	15.6	0.9
Rhode Island[2]	52.9	58.2	33.2	25.3	11.7	5.9	4.2	2.2	0.8	...
Connecticut[2]	206.7	183.9	111.3	89.6	58.8	26.0	21.6	12.6	4.1	...
New York[2]	210.5	162.9	76.7	63.7	36.9	19.1	13.9	5.8	4.1	0.4
New Jersey[2]	139.6	117.4	71.4	51.4	29.8	14.0	8.0	1.0	...	...
Pennsylvania[2]	327.3	240.1	119.7	85.6	31.0	18.0	11.4	...	...	...
Delaware[2]	45.4	35.5	28.7	19.9	5.4	2.5	1.5	0.7	0.2	...
Maryland[2]	245.5	202.6	141.1	116.1	66.1	29.6	24.0	13.2	4.5	...
Virginia[2]	538.0	447.0	231.0	180.4	87.8	58.6	53.0	35.3	18.7	2.5
North Carolina[2]	270.1	197.2	73.0	51.8	21.3	10.7	7.6	3.8	...	...
South Carolina[2]	180.0	124.2	64.0	45.0	17.0	5.7	3.9	0.2	...	...
Georgia[2]	56.1	23.4	5.2	2.0	...	...	...	...	...	...
Kentucky[5]	45.0	15.7	...	...	...	...	...	...	...	...
Tennessee[6]	10.0	1.0	...	...	...	...	...	...	...	...

(1) For 1660-1750, Maine counties are included with Massachusetts. Maine was part of Massachusetts until it became a separate state in 1820. (2) One of the original 13 states. (3) Admitted to statehood in 1791. (4) Plymouth became a part of the Province of Massachusetts in 1691. (5) Admitted to statehood in 1792. (6) Admitted to statehood in 1796.

U.S. Population by Official

STATE	1790[1]	1800[1]	1810[1]	1820	1830	1840	1850	1860	1870	1880	1890
AL	....	1	9	127,901	309,527	590,756	771,623	964,201	996,992	1,262,505	1,513,401
AK	....	....	....	....	....	....	....	....	....	33,426	32,052
AZ	....	....	....	....	....	....	....	....	9,658	40,440	88,243
AR	....	....	1	14,273	30,388	97,574	209,897	435,450	484,471	802,525	1,128,211
CA	....	....	....	....	....	....	92,597	379,994	560,247	864,694	1,213,398
CO	....	....	....	....	....	....	....	34,277	39,864	194,327	413,249
CT	238	251	262	275,248	297,675	309,978	370,792	460,147	537,454	622,700	746,258
DE	59	64	73	72,749	76,748	78,085	91,532	112,216	125,015	146,608	168,493
DC	....	8	16	23,336	30,261	33,745	51,687	75,080	131,700	177,624	230,392
FL	....	....	....	....	34,730	54,477	87,445	140,424	187,748	269,493	391,422
GA	83	163	252	340,989	516,823	691,392	906,185	1,057,286	1,184,109	1,542,180	1,837,353
HI	....	....	....	....	....	....	....	....	....	....	....
ID	....	....	....	....	....	....	....	....	14,999	32,610	88,548
IL	....	....	12	55,211	157,445	476,183	851,470	1,711,951	2,539,891	3,077,871	3,826,352
IN	....	6	25	147,178	343,031	685,866	988,416	1,350,428	1,680,637	1,978,301	2,192,404
IA	....	....	....	....	....	43,112	192,214	674,913	1,194,020	1,624,615	1,912,297
KS	....	....	....	....	....	....	....	107,206	364,399	996,096	1,428,108
KY	74	221	407	564,317	687,917	779,828	982,405	1,155,684	1,321,011	1,648,690	1,858,635
LA	....	....	77	153,407	215,739	352,411	517,762	708,002	726,915	939,946	1,118,588
ME	97	152	229	298,335	399,455	501,793	583,169	628,279	626,915	648,936	661,086
MD	320	342	381	407,350	447,040	470,019	583,034	687,049	780,894	934,943	1,042,390
MA	379	423	472	523,287	610,408	737,699	994,514	1,231,066	1,457,351	1,783,085	2,238,947
MI	....	....	5	8,896	31,639	212,267	397,654	749,113	1,184,059	1,636,937	2,093,890
MN	....	....	....	....	....	....	6,077	172,023	439,706	780,773	1,310,283
MS	....	8	31	75,448	136,621	375,651	606,526	791,305	827,922	1,131,597	1,289,600
MO	....	....	20	66,586	140,455	383,702	682,044	1,182,012	1,721,295	2,168,380	2,679,185
MT	....	....	....	....	....	....	....	....	20,595	39,159	142,924
NE	....	....	....	....	....	....	....	28,841	122,993	452,402	1,062,656
NV	....	....	....	....	....	....	....	6,857	42,491	62,266	47,355
NH	142	184	214	244,161	269,328	284,574	317,976	326,073	318,300	346,991	376,530
NJ	184	211	246	277,575	320,823	373,306	489,555	672,035	906,096	1,131,116	1,444,933
NM	....	....	....	....	....	....	61,547	93,516	91,874	119,565	160,282
NY	340	589	959	1,372,812	1,918,608	2,428,921	3,097,394	3,880,735	4,382,759	5,082,871	6,003,174
NC	394	478	556	638,829	737,987	753,419	869,039	992,622	1,071,361	1,399,750	1,617,949
ND	....	....	....	....	....	....	....	....	2,405[2]	36,909	190,983
OH	....	45	231	581,434	937,903	1,519,467	1,980,329	2,339,511	2,665,260	3,198,062	3,672,329
OK	....	....	....	....	....	....	....	....	....	....	258,657
OR	....	....	....	....	....	....	12,093	52,465	90,923	174,768	317,704
PA	434	602	810	1,049,458	1,348,233	1,724,033	2,311,786	2,906,215	3,521,951	4,282,891	5,258,113
RI	69	69	77	83,059	97,199	108,830	147,545	174,620	217,353	276,531	345,506
SC	249	346	415	502,741	581,185	594,398	668,507	703,708	705,606	995,577	1,151,149
SD	....	....	....	....	....	....	....	4,837[2]	11,776[2]	98,268	348,600
TN	36	106	262	422,823	681,904	829,210	1,002,717	1,109,801	1,258,520	1,542,359	1,767,518
TX	....	....	....	....	....	....	212,592	604,215	818,579	1,591,749	2,235,527
UT	....	....	....	....	....	....	11,380	40,273	86,786	143,963	210,779
VT	85	154	218	235,981	280,652	291,948	314,120	315,098	330,551	332,286	332,422
VA	692	808	878	938,261	1,044,054	1,025,227	1,119,348	1,219,630	1,225,163	1,512,565	1,655,980
WA	....	....	....	....	....	....	1,201	11,594	23,955	75,116	357,232
WV	56	79	105	136,808	176,924	224,537	302,313	376,688	442,014	618,457	762,794
WI	....	....	....	....	....	30,945	305,391	775,881	1,054,670	1,315,497	1,693,330
WY	....	....	....	....	....	....	....	....	9,118	20,789	62,555
U.S.	**3,929**	**5,308**	**7,240**	**9,638,453**	**12,866,020[3]**	**17,068,953[3]**	**23,191,876**	**31,443,321**	**38,558,371**	**50,189,209**	**62,979,766**

Note: Where possible, population shown is that of the 1990 area of the state. Members of the Armed Forces overseas or other U.S. nationals abroad are not included. Totals have been revised to include corrections of initial tabulated counts.
(1) Totals for 1790, 1800, and 1810 are in thousands. (2) 1860 figure is for Dakota Territory; 1870 figures are for parts of Dakota Territory. (3) U.S. total includes persons (5,318 in 1830 and 6,100 in 1840) on public ships in the service of the U.S. not credited to any region, division, or state.

Congressional Apportionment

Source: Bureau of the Census, U.S. Dept. of Commerce

	1990	1980		1990	1980		1990	1980		1990	1980		1990	1980
AL	7	7	ID	2	2	MN	8	8	ND	1	1	UT	3	3
AK	1	1	IL	20	22	MS	5	5	OH	19	21	VT	1	1
AZ	6	5	IN	10	10	MO	9	9	OK	6	6	VA	11	10
AR	4	4	IA	5	6	MT	1	2	OR	5	5	WA	9	8
CA	52	45	KS	4	5	NE	3	3	PA	21	23	WV	3	4
CO	6	6	KY	6	7	NV	2	2	RI	2	2	WI	9	9
CT	6	6	LA	7	8	NH	2	2	SC	6	6	WY	1	1
DE	1	1	ME	2	2	NJ	13	14	SD	1	1			
FL	23	19	MD	8	8	NM	3	3	TN	9	9	**TOTALS**	**435**	**435**
GA	11	10	MA	10	11	NY	31	34	TX	30	27			
HI	2	2	MI	16	18	NC	12	11						

The Constitution, in Article 1, Section 2, provided for a census of the population every 10 years to establish a basis for apportionment of representatives among the states. This apportionment largely determines the number of electoral votes allotted to each state.

The number of representatives of each state in Congress is determined by the state's population, but each state is entitled to one representative regardless of population. A congressional apportionment has been made after each decennial census except that of 1920.

Under provisions of a law that became effective Nov. 15, 1941, representatives are apportioned by the method of equal proportions. In the application of this method, the apportionment is made so that the average population per representative has the least possible variation between one state and any other. The first House of Representatives, in 1789, had 65 members, as provided by the Constitution. As the population grew, the number of representatives was increased, but the total membership has been fixed at 435 since the apportionment based on the 1910 census.

Census, 1790-1990

1900	1910	1920	1930	1940	1950	1960	1970	1980	1990
1,828,697	2,138,093	2,348,174	2,646,248	2,832,961	3,061,743	3,266,740	3,444,354	3,894,025	4,221,826
63,592	64,356	55,036	59,278	72,524	128,643	226,167	302,583	401,851	550,043
122,931	204,354	334,162	435,573	499,261	749,587	1,302,161	1,775,399	2,716,546	3,665,339
1,311,564	1,574,449	1,752,204	1,854,482	1,949,387	1,909,511	1,786,272	1,923,322	2,286,357	2,350,624
1,485,053	2,377,549	3,426,861	5,677,251	6,907,387	10,586,223	15,717,204	19,971,069	23,667,764	29,785,857
539,700	799,024	939,629	1,035,791	1,123,296	1,325,089	1,753,947	2,209,596	2,889,735	3,294,473
908,420	1,114,756	1,380,631	1,606,903	1,709,242	2,007,280	2,535,234	3,032,217	3,107,564	3,287,116
184,735	202,322	223,003	238,380	266,505	318,085	446,292	548,104	594,338	666,168
278,718	331,069	437,571	486,869	663,091	802,178	763,956	756,668	638,432	606,900
528,542	752,619	968,470	1,468,211	1,897,414	2,771,305	4,951,560	6,791,418	9,746,961	12,938,071
2,216,331	2,609,121	2,895,832	2,908,506	3,123,723	3,444,578	3,943,116	4,587,930	5,462,982	6,478,149
154,001	191,874	255,881	368,300	422,770	499,794	632,772	769,913	964,691	1,108,229
161,772	325,594	431,866	445,032	524,873	588,637	667,191	713,015	944,127	1,006,734
4,821,550	5,638,591	6,485,280	7,630,654	7,897,241	8,712,176	10,081,158	11,110,285	11,427,409	11,430,602
2,516,462	2,700,876	2,930,390	3,238,503	3,427,796	3,934,224	4,662,498	5,195,392	5,490,214	5,544,156
2,231,853	2,224,771	2,404,021	2,470,939	2,538,268	2,621,073	2,757,537	2,825,368	2,913,808	2,776,831
1,470,495	1,690,949	1,769,257	1,880,999	1,801,028	1,905,299	2,178,611	2,249,071	2,364,236	2,477,588
2,147,174	2,289,905	2,416,630	2,614,589	2,845,627	2,944,806	3,038,156	3,220,711	3,660,324	3,686,892
1,381,625	1,656,388	1,798,509	2,101,593	2,363,880	2,683,516	3,257,022	3,644,637	4,206,116	4,220,164
694,466	742,371	768,014	797,423	847,226	913,774	969,265	993,722	1,125,043	1,227,928
1,188,044	1,295,346	1,449,661	1,631,526	1,821,244	2,343,001	3,100,689	3,923,897	4,216,933	4,780,753
2,805,346	3,366,416	3,852,356	4,249,614	4,316,721	4,690,514	5,148,578	5,689,170	5,737,093	6,016,425
2,420,982	2,810,173	3,668,412	4,842,325	5,256,106	6,371,766	7,823,194	8,881,826	9,262,044	9,295,287
1,751,394	2,075,708	2,387,125	2,563,953	2,792,300	2,982,483	3,413,864	3,806,103	4,075,970	4,375,665
1,551,270	1,797,114	1,790,618	2,009,821	2,183,796	2,178,914	2,178,141	2,216,994	2,520,770	2,575,475
3,106,665	3,293,335	3,404,055	3,629,367	3,784,664	3,954,653	4,319,813	4,677,623	4,916,766	5,116,901
243,329	376,053	548,889	537,606	559,456	591,024	674,767	694,409	786,690	799,065
1,066,300	1,192,214	1,296,372	1,377,963	1,315,834	1,325,510	1,411,330	1,485,333	1,569,825	1,578,417
42,335	81,875	77,407	91,058	110,247	160,083	285,278	488,738	800,508	1,201,675
411,588	430,572	443,083	465,293	491,524	533,242	606,921	737,681	920,610	1,109,252
1,883,669	2,537,167	3,155,900	4,041,334	4,160,165	4,835,329	6,066,782	7,171,112	7,365,011	7,747,750
195,310	327,301	360,350	423,317	531,818	681,187	951,023	1,017,055	1,303,302	1,515,069
7,268,894	9,113,614	10,385,227	12,588,066	13,479,142	14,830,192	16,782,304	18,241,391	17,558,165	17,990,778
1,893,810	2,206,287	2,559,123	3,170,276	3,571,623	4,061,929	4,556,155	5,084,411	5,880,095	6,632,448
319,146	577,056	646,872	680,845	641,935	619,636	632,446	617,792	652,717	638,800
4,157,545	4,767,121	5,759,394	6,646,697	6,907,612	7,946,627	9,706,397	10,657,423	10,797,603	10,847,115
790,391	1,657,155	2,028,283	2,396,040	2,336,434	2,233,351	2,328,284	2,559,463	3,025,487	3,145,576
413,536	672,765	783,389	953,786	1,089,684	1,521,341	1,768,687	2,091,533	2,633,156	2,842,337
6,302,115	7,665,111	8,720,017	9,631,350	9,900,180	10,498,012	11,319,366	11,800,766	11,864,720	11,882,842
428,556	542,610	604,397	687,497	713,346	791,896	859,488	949,723	947,154	1,003,464
1,340,316	1,515,400	1,683,724	1,738,765	1,899,804	2,117,027	2,382,594	2,590,713	3,120,729	3,486,310
401,570	583,888	636,547	692,849	642,961	652,740	680,514	666,257	690,768	696,004
2,020,616	2,184,789	2,337,885	2,616,556	2,915,841	3,291,718	3,567,089	3,926,018	4,591,023	4,877,203
3,048,710	3,896,542	4,663,228	5,824,715	6,414,824	7,711,194	9,579,677	11,198,655	14,225,513	16,986,335
276,749	373,351	449,396	507,847	550,310	688,862	890,627	1,059,273	1,461,037	1,722,850
343,641	355,956	352,428	359,611	359,231	377,747	389,881	444,732	511,456	562,758
1,854,184	2,061,612	2,309,187	2,421,851	2,677,773	3,318,680	3,966,949	4,651,448	5,346,797	6,189,197
518,103	1,141,990	1,356,621	1,563,396	1,736,191	2,378,963	2,853,214	3,413,244	4,132,353	4,866,669
958,800	1,221,119	1,463,701	1,729,205	1,901,974	2,005,552	1,860,421	1,744,237	1,950,186	1,793,477
2,069,042	2,333,860	2,632,067	2,939,006	3,137,587	3,434,575	3,951,777	4,417,821	4,705,642	4,891,769
92,531	145,965	194,402	225,565	250,742	290,529	330,066	332,416	469,557	453,589
76,212,168	**92,228,496**	**106,021,537**	**123,202,624**	**132,164,569**	**151,325,798**	**179,323,175**	**203,302,031**	**226,542,203**	**248,765,170**

U.S. Center of Population, 1790-1990

Source: Bureau of the Census, U.S. Dept. of Commerce

The U.S. Center of Population is considered here as the center of population gravity, or that point upon which the U.S. would balance if it were a rigid plane without weight and the population distributed thereon, with each individual assumed to have equal weight and to exert an influence on a central point proportional to his or her distance from that point. The 1990 center is 818.6 miles from the 1790 center of population and is 39.5 miles SW of the 1980 center.

Year	N Lat °	′	″	W Long °	′	″	Approximate location
1790	39	16	30	76	11	12	23 miles east of Baltimore, MD
1800	39	16	6	76	56	30	18 miles west of Baltimore, MD
1810	39	11	30	77	37	12	40 miles northwest by west of Washington, DC (in VA)
1820	39	5	42	78	33	0	16 miles east of Moorefield, WV[1]
1830	38	57	54	79	16	54	19 miles west-southwest of Moorefield, WV[1]
1840	39	2	0	80	18	0	16 miles south of Clarksburg, WV[1]
1850	38	59	0	81	19	0	23 miles southeast of Parkersburg, WV[1]
1860	39	0	24	82	48	48	20 miles south by east of Chillicothe, OH
1870	39	12	0	83	35	42	48 miles east by north of Cincinnati, OH
1880	39	4	8	84	39	40	8 miles west by south of Cincinnati, OH (in KY)
1890	39	11	56	85	32	53	20 miles east of Columbus, IN
1900	39	9	36	85	48	54	6 miles southeast of Columbus, IN
1910	39	10	12	86	32	20	In the city of Bloomington, IN
1920	39	10	21	86	43	15	8 miles south-southeast of Spencer, Owen Co., IN
1930	39	3	45	87	8	6	3 miles northeast of Linton, Greene Co., IN
1940	38	56	54	87	22	35	2 miles southeast by east of Carlisle, Haddon township, Sullivan Co., IN
1950 (inc. Alaska & Hawaii)	38	48	15	88	22	8	3 miles northeast of Louisville, Clay Co., IL
1960	38	35	58	89	12	35	6½ miles northwest of Centralia, Clinton Co., IL
1970	38	27	47	89	42	22	5 miles east southeast of Mascoutah, St. Clair Co., IL
1980	38	8	13	90	34	26	¼ mile west of De Soto, Jefferson Co., MO
1990	37	52	20	91	12	55	9.7 miles northwest of Steelville, MO

(1) West Virginia was set off from Virginia on Dec. 31, 1862, and was admitted as a state on June 20, 1863.

U.S. Area and Population: 1790-1990

Source: Bureau of the Census, U.S. Dept. of Commerce

Census date	AREA (sq mi) Gross	Land	Water	POPULATION Number	per sq mi of land	Increase over preceding census Number	%
1990 (Apr. 1)	3,787,319[1]	3,536,278	251,041[1]	248,765,170	70.3	22,222,967	9.8
1980 (Apr. 1)	3,618,770	3,539,289	79,481	226,542,203	64.0	23,240,172	11.4
1970 (Apr. 1)	3,618,770	3,536,855	81,915	203,302,031	57.5	23,978,856	13.4
1960 (Apr. 1)	3,618,770	3,540,911	77,859	179,323,175	50.6	27,997,377	18.5
1950 (Apr. 1)	3,618,770	3,552,206	66,564	151,325,798	42.6	19,161,229	14.5
1940 (Apr. 1)	3,618,770	3,554,608	64,162	132,164,569	37.2	8,961,945	7.3
1930 (Apr. 1)	3,618,770	3,551,608	67,162	123,202,624	34.7	17,181,087	16.2
1920 (Jan. 1)	3,618,770	3,546,931	71,839	106,021,537	29.9	13,793,041	15.0
1910 (Apr. 15)	3,618,770	3,547,045	71,725	92,228,496	26.0	16,016,328	21.0
1900 (June 1)	3,618,770	3,547,314	71,456	76,212,168	21.5	13,232,402	21.0
1890 (June 1)	3,612,299	3,540,705	71,594	62,979,766	17.8	12,790,557	25.5
1880 (June 1)	3,612,299	3,540,705	71,594	50,189,209	14.2	11,630,838	30.2
1870 (June 1)	3,612,299	3,540,705	71,594	38,558,371	10.9	7,115,050	22.6
1860 (June 1)	3,021,295	2,969,640	51,655	31,443,321	10.6	8,251,445	35.6
1850 (June 1)	2,991,655	2,940,042	51,613	23,191,876	7.9	6,122,423	35.9
1840 (June 1)	1,792,552	1,749,462	43,090	17,068,953[2]	9.8	4,203,433	32.7
1830 (June 1)	1,792,552	1,749,462	43,090	12,866,020[2]	7.4	3,227,567	33.5
1820 (June 1)	1,792,552	1,749,462	43,090	9,638,453	5.5	2,398,572	33.1
1810 (Aug. 6)	1,722,685	1,681,828	40,857	7,239,881	4.3	1,931,398	36.4
1800 (Aug. 4)	891,364	864,746	26,618	5,308,483	6.1	1,379,269	35.1
1790 (Aug. 2)	891,364	864,746	26,618	3,929,214	4.5	—	—

(1) Includes inland, coastal, Great Lakes, and territorial water. Data for prior years cover inland water only. (2) U.S. total includes persons (5,318 in 1830 and 6,100 in 1840) on public ships in the service of the U.S. not credited to any region, division, or state.

Note: Percent changes are computed on the basis of change in population since the preceding census date, so the period covered therefore is not always exactly 10 years.

Population density figures given for various years represent the area within the boundaries of the U.S. that was under the jurisdiction on the date in question, including in some cases considerable areas not organized or settled and not actually covered by the census. In 1870, for example, Alaska was not covered by the census.

Population figures shown here may reflect corrections made to the initial tabulated census counts.

Population, by Sex, Race, Residence, and Median Age, 1790-1998

Source: Bureau of the Census, U.S. Dept. of Commerce

(in thousands, except as indicated)

Date	SEX Male	Female	RACE White	Black Number	Black Percent	Other	RESIDENCE Urban	Rural	MEDIAN AGE (years) All races	White	Black
Conterminous U.S.[1]											
1790 (Aug. 2)	NA	NA	3,172	757	19.3	NA	202	3,728	NA	NA	NA
1810 (Aug. 6)	NA	NA	5,862	1,378	19.0	NA	525	6,714	NA	16.0	NA
1820 (Aug. 7)	4,897	4,742	7,867	1,772	18.4	NA	693	8,945	16.7	16.6	17.2
1840 (June 1)	8,689	8,381	14,196	2,874	16.8	NA	1,845	15,224	17.8	17.9	17.6
1860 (June 1)	16,085	15,358	26,923	4,442	14.1	79	6,217	25,227	19.4	19.7	17.5
1870 (June 1)	19,494	19,065	33,589	4,880	12.7	89	9,902	28,656	20.2	20.4	18.5
1880 (June 1)	25,519	24,637	43,403	6,581	13.1	172	14,130	36,026	20.9	21.4	18.0
1890 (June 1)	32,237	30,711	55,101	7,489	11.9	358	22,106	40,841	22.0	22.5	17.8
1900 (June 1)	38,816	37,178	66,809	8,834	11.6	351	30,160	45,835	22.9	23.4	19.4
1920 (Jan. 1)	53,900	51,810	94,821	10,463	9.9	427	54,158	51,553	25.3	25.5	22.3
1930 (Apr. 1)	62,137	60,638	110,287	11,891	9.7	597	68,955	53,820	26.5	26.9	23.5
1940 (Apr. 1)	66,062	65,608	118,215	12,866	9.8	589	74,424	57,246	29.0	29.5	25.3
United States											
1950 (Apr. 1)	74,833	75,864	135,150	15,045	9.9	1,131	96,467	54,230	30.2	30.7	26.2
1960 (Apr. 1)	88,331	90,992	158,832	18,872	10.5	1,620	125,269	54,054	29.5	30.3	23.5
1970 (Apr. 1)[2]	98,912	104,300	177,749	22,580	11.1	2,883	149,647	53,565	28.1	28.9	22.4
1980 (Apr. 1)[3]	110,053	116,493	194,713	26,683	11.8	5,150	167,051	59,495	30.0	30.9	24.9
1985 (July 1, est.)	115,730	122,194	202,031	28,569	12.0	7,324	NA	NA	31.4	32.3	26.6
1990 (Apr. 1)[4]	121,239	127,470	199,686	29,986	12.1	9,233	187,053	61,656	32.9	34.4	28.1
1991 (July 1, est.)	122,984	129,122	210,979	31,107	12.3	10,020	NA	NA	33.1	34.1	28.1
1992 (July 1, est.)	124,506	130,496	212,885	31,670	12.4	10,446	NA	NA	33.4	34.4	28.5
1993 (July 1, est.)	125,938	131,858	214,760	32,168	12.5	10,867	NA	NA	33.7	34.7	28.7
1994 (July 1, est.)	127,216	133,076	216,413	32,653	12.5	11,227	NA	NA	34.0	35.0	29.0
1995 (July 1, est.)	128,569	134,321	218,149	33,095	12.6	11,646	NA	NA	34.3	35.3	29.2
1996 (July 1, est.)	129,746	135,434	219,686	33,514	12.6	11,979	NA	NA	34.6	35.7	29.5
1997 (July 1, est.)	131,018	136,618	221,334	33,947	12.7	12,355	NA	NA	34.9	36.0	29.7
1998 (July1, est.)	132,263	137,766	222,932	34,370	12.7	12,727	NA	NA	35.3	36.3	29.9

NA=Not available. **Note:** Urban and rural definitions may change from census to census. The figures in this table have been adjusted to be consistent with the 1990 urban and rural definitions. (1) Excludes Alaska and Hawaii. (2) The revised 1970 resident population count is 203,302,031, which incorporates changes due to errors found after tabulations were completed. The race and sex data shown here reflect the official 1970 census count; the residence data come from the tabulated count. (3) The race data shown for Apr. 1, 1980, have been modified. (4) The data shown are based on the U.S. population as tabulated in the 1990 census. Figures do not reflect corrections to the 1990 population. The corrected 1990 U.S. population is 248,765,170.

Immigrants Admitted, by Top 30 Metropolitan Areas of Intended Residence, 1996

Source: Immigration and Naturalization Service, U.S. Dept. of Justice

(fiscal year 1996)

Metropolitan Statistical Area	Number	Percentage
New York, NY	133,168	14.5
Los Angeles–Long Beach, CA	64,285	7.0
Miami, FL	41,527	4.5
Chicago, IL	39,989	4.4
Washington, DC–MD–VA	34,327	3.7
Houston, TX	21,387	2.3
Boston–Lawrence–Lowell–Brockton, MA	18,726	2.0
San Diego, CA	18,226	2.0
San Francisco, CA	18,171	2.0
Newark, NJ	17,939	2.0
Orange County, CA	17,580	1.9
Dallas, TX	15,915	1.7
Oakland, CA	15,759	1.7
Bergen–Passaic, NJ	15,682	1.7
San Jose, CA	13,854	1.5
Philadelphia, PA–NJ	13,034	1.4
Detroit, MI	11,929	1.3
Jersey City, NJ	11,399	1.2
Nassau–Suffolk, NY	10,594	1.2
Seattle–Bellevue–Everett, WA	10,429	1.1
Riverside–San Bernardino, CA	10,314	1.1
Fort Lauderdale, FL	10,290	1.1
Atlanta, GA	9,870	1.1
Middlesex–Somerset–Hunterdon, NJ	9,286	1.0
El Paso, TX	8,701	0.9
Minneapolis–St. Paul, MN–WI	7,615	0.8
Sacramento, CA	6,953	0.8
West Palm Beach–Boca Raton, FL	6,553	0.7
Honolulu, HI	6,553	0.7
Fort Worth–Arlington, TX	6,274	0.7
TOTAL immigrants admitted to U.S.	**915,900**	**100.0**

Immigrants Admitted, by State of Intended Residence, 1996

Source: Immigration and Naturalization Service, U.S. Dept. of Justice

(fiscal year 1996)

State	Number of immigrants	State	Number of immigrants	State	Number of immigrants	State	Number of immigrants
AL	1,782	KS	4,303	NY	154,095	WV	583
AK	1,280	KY	2,019	NC	7,011	WI	3,607
AZ	8,900	LA	4,092	ND	606	WY	280
AR	1,494	ME	1,028	OH	10,237		
CA	201,529	MD	20,732	OK	3,511		
CO	8,895	MA	23,085	OR	7,554	Other:	
CT	10,874	MI	17,253	PA	16,938	Guam	2,820
DE	1,377	MN	8,977	RI	3,098	N Mariana Isls.	176
DC	3,784	MS	1,073	SC	2,151	Puerto Rico	8,560
FL	79,461	MO	5,690	SD	519	Virgin Isls.	1,384
GA	12,608	MT	449	TN	4,343	Armed Service Posts	109
HI	8,436	NE	2,150	TX	83,385	Other or unknown	10
ID	1,825	NV	5,874	UT	4,250	**TOTAL**	**915,900**
IL	42,517	NH	1,512	VT	654		
IN	4,692	NJ	63,303	VA	21,375		
IA	3,037	NM	5,780	WA	18,833		

U.S. Foreign-Born Population, 1997

Source: Bureau of the Census, U.S. Dept. of Commerce

Percentage of U.S. Population That Is Foreign-Born, 1900-97

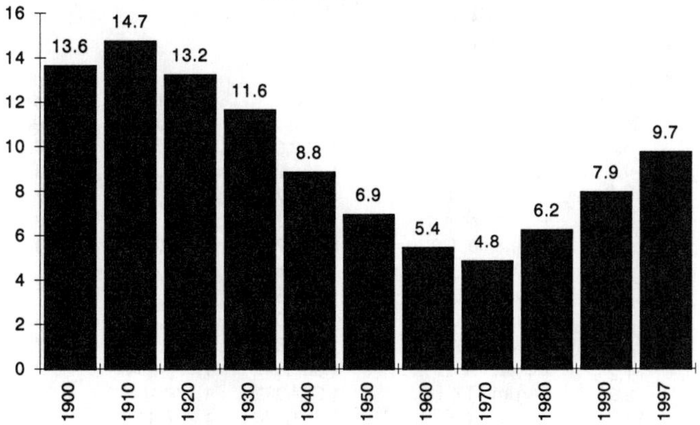

Highest-Ranking Countries of Birth of U.S. Foreign-Born Population, 1997

Country	Number (in thousands)
Mexico	7,017
Philippines	1,132
China (incl. Hong Kong)	1,107
Cuba	913
Vietnam	770
India	748
Dominican Republic	632
El Salvador	607
Great Britain	606
Korea	591
All countries	**25,779**

Population by State, 1990-97

Source: Bureau of the Census, U.S. Dept. of Commerce

Rank	State	1997 population	1990 population	Percentage change 1990-97
1.	CA	32,268,301	29,785,857	8.3
2.	TX	19,439,337	16,986,335	14.4
3.	NY	18,137,226	17,990,778	0.8
4.	FL	14,653,945	12,938,071	13.3
5.	PA	12,019,661	11,882,842	1.2
6.	IL	11,895,849	11,430,602	4.1
7.	OH	11,186,331	10,847,115	3.1
8.	MI	9,773,892	9,295,287	5.1
9.	NJ	8,052,849	7,747,750	3.9
10.	GA	7,486,242	6,478,149	15.6
11.	NC	7,425,183	6,632,448	12.0
12.	VA	6,733,996	6,189,197	8.8
13.	MA	6,117,520	6,016,425	1.7
14.	IN	5,864,108	5,544,156	5.8
15.	WA	5,610,362	4,866,669	15.3
16.	MO	5,402,058	5,116,901	5.6
17.	TN	5,368,198	4,877,203	10.1
18.	WI	5,169,677	4,891,769	5.7
19.	MD	5,094,289	4,780,753	6.6
20.	MN	4,685,549	4,375,665	7.1
21.	AZ	4,554,966	3,665,339	24.3
22.	LA	4,351,769	4,220,164	3.1
23.	AL	4,319,154	4,221,826	2.3
24.	KY	3,908,124	3,686,892	6.0
25.	CO	3,892,644	3,294,473	18.2
26.	SC	3,760,181	3,486,310	7.9
27.	OK	3,317,091	3,145,576	5.5
28.	CT	3,269,858	3,287,116	–0.5
29.	OR	3,243,487	2,842,337	14.1
30.	IA	2,852,423	2,776,831	2.7
31.	MS	2,730,501	2,575,475	6.0
32.	KS	2,594,840	2,477,588	4.7
33.	AR	2,522,819	2,350,624	7.3
34.	UT	2,059,148	1,722,850	19.5
35.	WV	1,815,787	1,793,477	1.2
36.	NM	1,729,751	1,515,069	14.2
37.	NV	1,676,809	1,201,675	39.5
38.	NE	1,656,870	1,578,417	5.0
39.	ME	1,242,051	1,227,928	1.2
40.	ID	1,210,232	1,006,734	20.2
41.	HI	1,186,602	1,108,229	7.1
42.	NH	1,172,709	1,109,252	5.7
43.	RI	987,429	1,003,464	–1.6
44.	MT	878,810	799,065	10.0
45.	SD	737,973	696,004	6.0
46.	DE	731,581	666,168	9.8
47.	ND	640,883	638,800	0.3
48.	AK	609,311	550,043	10.8
49.	VT	588,978	562,758	4.7
50.	DC	528,964	606,900	–12.8
51.	WY	479,743	453,589	5.8
	U.S.	**267,636,061**	**248,765,170**	**7.6**

Note: Population figures for 1990 include corrections to the original tabulated population.

Density of Population by State, 1920-90

Source: Bureau of the Census, U.S. Dept. of Commerce

(per square mile, land area only)

State	1920	1960	1980	1990
AL	45.8	64.2	76.6	79.6
AK*	0.1	0.4	0.7	1.0
AZ	2.9	11.5	23.9	32.3
AR	33.4	34.2	43.9	45.1
CA	22.0	100.4	151.4	190.8
CO	9.1	16.9	27.9	31.8
CT	286.4	520.6	637.8	678.4
DE	113.5	225.2	307.6	340.8
DC	7,292.9	12,523.9	10,132.3	9,882.8
FL	17.7	91.5	180.0	239.6
GA	49.3	67.8	94.1	111.9
HI*	39.9	98.5	150.1	172.5
ID	5.2	8.1	11.5	12.2
IL	115.7	180.4	205.3	205.6
IN	81.3	128.8	152.8	154.6
IA	43.2	49.2	52.1	49.7
KS	21.6	26.6	28.9	30.3
KY	60.1	76.2	92.3	92.8
LA	39.6	72.2	94.5	96.9
ME	25.7	31.3	36.3	39.8
MD	145.8	313.5	428.7	489.2
MA	479.2	657.3	733.3	767.6
MI	63.8	137.7	162.6	163.6
MN	29.5	43.1	51.2	55.0
MS	38.6	46.0	53.4	54.9
MO	49.5	62.6	71.3	74.3
MT	3.8	4.6	5.4	5.5
NE	16.9	18.4	20.5	20.5
NV	0.7	2.6	7.3	10.9
NH	49.1	67.2	102.4	123.7
NJ	420.0	805.5	986.2	1,042.0
NM	2.9	7.8	10.7	12.5
NY	217.9	350.6	370.6	381.0
NC	52.5	93.2	120.4	136.1
ND	9.2	9.1	9.4	9.3
OH	141.4	236.6	263.3	264.9
OK	29.2	33.8	44.1	45.8
OR	8.2	18.4	27.4	29.6
PA	194.5	251.4	264.3	265.1
RI	566.4	819.3	897.8	960.3
SC	55.2	78.7	103.4	115.8
SD	8.3	9.0	9.1	9.2
TN	56.1	86.2	111.6	118.3
TX	17.8	36.4	54.3	64.9
UT	5.5	10.8	17.8	21.0
VT	38.6	42.0	55.2	60.8
VA	57.4	99.6	134.7	156.3
WA	20.3	42.8	62.1	73.1
WV	60.9	77.2	80.8	74.5
WI	47.6	72.6	86.5	90.1
WY	2.0	3.4	4.9	4.7
U.S.	**29.9***	**50.6**	**64.0**	**70.3**

(*) For purposes of comparison, Alaska and Hawaii are included in above tabulation for 1920, even though not states then.

25 Largest Counties, by Population, 1990-97

Source: Bureau of the Census, U.S. Dept of Commerce

County	1997 population	1990 population	Percentage change, 1990-97
Los Angeles, CA	9,145,219	8,863,052	3.2
Cook, IL	5,076,786	5,105,044	–0.6
Harris, TX	3,158,095	2,818,101	12.1
San Diego, CA	2,722,650	2,498,016	9.0
Maricopa, AZ	2,696,198	2,122,101	27.1
Orange, CA	2,674,091	2,410,668	10.9
Kings, NY	2,240,384	2,300,664	–2.6
Wayne, MI	2,127,087	2,111,687	0.7
Miami-Dade, FL	2,044,600	1,937,194	5.5
Dallas, TX	2,023,140	1,852,810	9.2
Queens, NY	1,975,676	1,951,598	1.2
King, WA	1,632,852	1,507,305	8.3
San Bernardino, CA	1,615,817	1,418,380	13.9
Santa Clara, CA	1,609,037	1,497,577	7.4
New York, NY	1,536,220	1,487,536	3.3
Broward, FL	1,470,758	1,255,531	17.1
Philadelphia, PA	1,451,372	1,585,577	–8.5
Riverside, CA	1,447,791	1,170,413	23.7
Middlesex, MA	1,417,868	1,398,468	1.4
Cuyahoga, OH	1,386,803	1,412,140	–1.8
Alameda, CA	1,371,067	1,304,346	5.1
Suffolk, NY	1,362,616	1,321,768	3.1
Bexar, TX	1,332,547	1,185,394	12.4
Tarrant, TX	1,327,332	1,170,103	13.4
Nassau, NY	1,303,686	1,287,444	1.3

Note: The following are the **smallest counties**, by 1997 population: Yellowstone National Park, MT (39); Kalawao County, HI (81); Loving County, TX (106); King County, TX (348); Kenedy County, TX (427); Arthur County, NE (428); Petroleum County, MT (518); McPherson County, NE (556); San Juan County, CO (557); and Blaine County, NE (638).

Metropolitan Areas, 1990-96

Source: Bureau of the Census, U.S. Dept. of Commerce

(CMSAs and MSAs of more than 600,000 persons listed by 1996 population estimates)

Metropolitan statistical areas (MSAs) are defined for federal statistical use by the Office of Management and Budget (OMB), with technical assistance from the Bureau of the Census. Most individual metropolitan areas with populations over 1 million may, under specified circumstances, be subdivided into component Primary Metropolitan Statistical Areas (PMSAs), in which case the area as a whole is designated a Consolidated Metropolitan Statistical Area (CMSA).

Effective June 30, 1996, the Office of Management and Budget designated 258 MSAs, 76 PMSAs, and 19 CMSAs for the U.S. and Puerto Rico, based on standards published in the Federal Register on March 30, 1990, as applied to 1990 census data.

CMSAs and MSAs	Population 1990	Population 1996	Percentage change 1990-96
New York-Northern New Jersey-Long Island, NY-NJ-CT-PA CMSA	19,549,649	19,938,492	2.0
Los Angeles-Riverside-Orange County, CA CMSA	14,531,529	15,495,155	6.6
Chicago-Gary-Kenosha, IL-IN-WI CMSA	8,239,820	8,599,774	4.4
Washington-Baltimore, DC-MD-VA-WV CMSA	6,726,395	7,164,519	6.5
San Francisco-Oakland-San Jose, CA CMSA	6,249,881	6,605,428	5.7
Philadelphia-Wilmington-Atlantic City, PA-NJ-DE-MD CMSA	5,893,019	5,973,463	1.4
Boston-Worcester-Lawrence, MA-NH-ME-CT CMSA	5,455,403	5,563,475	2.0
Detroit-Ann Arbor-Flint, MI CMSA	5,187,171	5,284,171	1.9
Dallas–Fort Worth, TX CMSA	4,037,282	4,574,561	13.3
Houston–Galveston–Brazoria, TX CMSA	3,731,029	4,253,428	14.0
Atlanta, GA	2,959,500	3,541,230	19.7
Miami-Fort Lauderdale, FL CMSA	3,192,725	3,514,403	10.1
Seattle–Tacoma–Bremerton, WA CMSA	2,970,300	3,320,829	11.8
Cleveland-Akron, OH CMSA	2,859,644	2,913,430	1.9
Minneapolis–St. Paul, MN-WI	2,538,776	2,765,116	8.9
Phoenix-Mesa, AZ	2,238,498	2,746,703	22.7
San Diego, CA	2,498,016	2,655,463	6.3
St. Louis, MO-IL	2,492,348	2,548,238	2.2
Pittsburgh, PA	2,394,811	2,379,411	–0.6
Denver–Boulder–Greeley, CO CMSA	1,980,140	2,277,401	15.0
Tampa–St. Petersburg–Clearwater, FL	2,067,959	2,199,231	6.3
Portland–Salem, OR–WA CMSA	1,793,476	2,078,357	15.9
Cincinnati–Hamilton, OH–KY–IN, CMSA	1,817,569	1,920,931	5.7
Kansas City, MO-KS	1,582,874	1,690,343	6.8
Milwaukee–Racine, WI CMSA	1,607,183	1,642,658	2.2
Sacramento–Yolo, CA . CMSA	1,481,220	1,632,133	10.2
Norfolk–Virginia Beach–Newport News, VA–NC	1,444,710	1,540,252	6.6
Indianapolis, IN	1,380,491	1,492,297	8.1
San Antonio, TX	1,324,749	1,490,111	12.5
Columbus, OH	1,345,450	1,447,646	7.6
Orlando, FL	1,224,844	1,417,291	15.7
Charlotte-Gastonia-Rock Hill, NC-SC	1,162,140	1,321,068	13.7
New Orleans, LA	1,285,262	1,312,890	2.1
Salt Lake City-Ogden, UT	1,072,227	1,217,842	13.6
Las Vegas, NV-AZ	852,646	1,201,073	40.9
Buffalo-Niagara Falls, NY	1,189,340	1,175,240	–1.2
Hartford, CT	1,157,585	1,144,574	–1.1
Greensboro–Winston-Salem–High Point, NC	1,050,304	1,141,238	8.7
Providence-Fall River-Warwick, RI-MA	1,134,350	1,124,044	–0.9
Nashville, TN	985,026	1,117,178	13.4
Rochester, NY	1,062,470	1,088,037	2.4
Memphis, TN–AR–MS	1,007,306	1,078,151	7.0
Austin-San Marcos, TX	846,227	1,041,330	23.1
Oklahoma City, OK	958,839	1,026,657	7.1
Raleigh-Durham-Chapel Hill, NC	858,485	1,025,253	19.4
Grand Rapids-Muskegon-Holland, MI	937,891	1,015,099	8.2
Jacksonville, FL	906,727	1,008,633	11.2
West Palm Beach-Boca Raton, FL	863,503	992,840	15.0
Louisville, KY-IN	949,012	991,765	4.5
Dayton-Springfield, OH	951,270	950,661	–0.1
Richmond–Petersburg, VA	865,640	935,174	8.0
Greenville-Spartanburg-Anderson, SC	830,539	896,679	8.0
Birmingham, AL	839,942	894,702	6.5
Albany-Schenectady-Troy, NY	861,623	878,527	2.0
Honolulu, HI	836,231	871,766	4.2
Fresno, CA	755,580	861,753	14.1
Tucson, AZ	666,957	767,873	15.1
Tulsa, OK	708,954	756,493	6.7
Syracuse, NY	742,237	745,691	0.5
El Paso, TX	591,610	684,446	15.7
Omaha, NE–IA	639,580	681,698	6.6
Albuquerque, NM	589,131	670,092	13.7
Knoxville, TN	585,960	649,277	10.8
Scranton–Wilkes-Barre–Hazleton, PA	638,524	628,073	–1.6
Bakersfield, CA	544,981	622,729	14.3
Harrisburg-Lebanon-Carlisle, PA	587,986	614,755	4.6
Allentown-Bethlehem-Easton, PA	595,081	614,304	3.2
Toledo, OH	614,128	611,417	–0.4

Final 1990 census figures showed that the nation in that year had 40 metropolitan areas of at least 1 mil population, including 5 that had reached that size since 1980. The 40 areas had 132.9 mil people, or 53.4% of the U.S. population, in 1990. It is estimated that since the 1990 census, the populations of 7 additional metropolitan areas (Las Vegas, NV–AZ; Nashville, TN; Austin–San Marcos, TX; Oklahoma City, OK; Raleigh–Durham–Chapel Hill, NC; Grand Rapids–Muskegon–Holland, MI; and Jacksonville, FL) have increased to more than 1 mil. By 1996, 56.1% of the population lived in metropolitan areas that had a total of at least 1 mil inhabitants.

Some 211.8 mil people resided in metropolitan areas in 1996, an increase of more than 13.6 mil (6.9%) since 1990. The population outside metropolitan areas totaled 53.5 mil in 1996, up 3.0 mil (5.8%) from 1990. The metropolitan population in 1996 was 79.8% of the U.S. total, compared with 79.7% in 1990 and 76.2% in 1980.

Population of 100 Largest U.S. Cities, 1850-1996

Source: Bureau of the Census, U.S. Dept. of Commerce (100 most populous cities ranked by July 1, 1996, population estimates)

Rank	City	1996	1990	1980	1970	1950	1900	1850
1.	New York, NY	7,380,906	7,322,564	7,071,639	7,895,563	7,891,957	3,437,202	696,115
2.	Los Angeles, CA	3,553,638	3,485,557	2,968,528	2,811,801	1,970,358	102,479	1,610
3.	Chicago, IL	2,721,547	2,783,726	3,005,072	3,369,357	3,620,962	1,698,575	29,963
4.	Houston, TX	1,744,058	1,637,859	1,595,138	1,233,535	596,163	44,633	2,396
5.	Philadelphia, PA	1,478,002	1,585,577	1,688,210	1,949,996	2,071,605	1,293,697	121,376
6.	San Diego, CA	1,171,121	1,110,623	875,538	697,471	334,387	17,700	...
7.	Phoenix, AZ	1,159,014	984,310	789,704	584,303	106,818	5,544	...
8.	San Antonio, TX	1,067,816	959,295	785,940	654,153	408,442	53,321	3,488
9.	Dallas, TX	1,053,292	1,007,618	904,599	844,401	434,462	42,638	...
10.	Detroit, MI	1,000,272	1,027,974	1,203,368	1,514,063	1,849,568	285,704	21,019
11.	San Jose, CA	838,744	782,224	629,400	459,913	95,280	21,500	...
12.	Indianapolis, IN[1]	746,737	731,278	700,807	736,856	427,173	169,164	8,091
13.	San Francisco, CA	735,315	723,959	678,974	715,674	775,357	342,782	34,776
14.	Jacksonville, FL[1]	679,792	635,230	540,920	504,265	204,517	28,429	1,045
15.	Baltimore, MD	675,401	736,014	786,741	905,787	949,708	508,957	169,054
16.	Columbus, OH	657,053	632,945	565,021	540,025	375,901	125,560	17,882
17.	El Paso, TX	599,865	515,342	425,259	322,261	130,485	15,906	...
18.	Memphis, TN	596,725	618,652	646,174	623,988	396,000	102,320	8,841
19.	Milwaukee, WI	590,503	628,088	636,297	717,372	637,392	285,315	20,061
20.	Boston, MA	558,394	574,283	562,994	641,071	801,444	560,892	136,881
21.	Washington, DC	543,213	606,900	638,432	756,668	802,178	278,718	40,001
22.	Austin, TX	541,278	472,020	345,890	253,539	132,459	22,258	629
23.	Seattle, WA	524,704	516,259	493,846	530,831	467,591	80,671	...
24.	Nashville, TN[1]	511,263	488,366	455,651	426,029	174,307	80,865	10,165
25.	Cleveland, OH	498,246	505,616	573,822	750,879	914,808	381,768	17,034
26.	Denver, CO	497,840	467,610	492,686	514,678	415,786	133,859	...
27.	Portland, OR	480,824	463,634	368,148	379,967	373,628	90,426	...
28.	Fort Worth, TX	479,716	447,619	385,164	393,455	278,778	26,688	...
29.	New Orleans, LA	476,625	496,938	557,927	593,471	570,445	287,104	116,375
30.	Oklahoma City, OK	469,852	444,724	404,014	368,164	243,504	10,037	...
31.	Tucson, AZ	449,002	411,480	330,537	262,933	45,454	7,531	...
32.	Charlotte, NC	441,297	419,539	315,474	241,420	134,042	18,091	1,065
33.	Kansas City, MO	441,259	434,829	448,028	507,330	456,622	163,752	...
34.	Virginia Beach, VA	430,385	393,089	262,199	172,106	5,390	...	...
35.	Honolulu, HI[2]	423,475	377,059	365,048	324,871	248,034	39,306	...
36.	Long Beach, CA	421,904	429,321	361,498	358,879	250,767	2,252	...
37.	Albuquerque, NM	419,681	384,915	332,920	244,501	96,815	6,238	...
38.	Atlanta, GA	401,907	393,929	425,022	495,039	331,314	89,872	2,572
39.	Fresno, CA	396,011	354,091	217,491	165,655	91,669	12,470	...
40.	Tulsa, OK	378,491	367,302	360,919	330,350	182,740	1,390	...
41.	Las Vegas, NV	376,906	258,204	164,674	125,787	24,624	...	...
42.	Sacramento, CA	376,243	369,365	275,741	257,105	137,572	29,282	6,820
43.	Oakland, CA	367,230	372,242	339,337	361,561	384,575	66,960	...
44.	Miami, FL	365,127	358,648	346,681	334,859	249,276	1,681	...
45.	Omaha, NE	364,253	342,862	313,939	346,929	251,117	102,555	...
46.	Minneapolis, MN	358,785	368,383	370,951	434,400	521,718	202,718	...
47.	St. Louis, MO	351,565	396,685	452,801	622,236	856,796	575,238	77,860
48.	Pittsburgh, PA	350,363	369,879	423,959	520,089	676,806	321,616	46,601
49.	Cincinnati, OH	345,818	364,114	385,409	453,514	503,998	325,902	115,435
50.	Colorado Springs, CO	345,127	280,430	215,105	135,517	45,472	21,085	...
51.	Mesa, AZ	344,764	289,199	152,404	63,049	16,790	722	...
52.	Wichita, KS	320,395	304,017	279,838	276,554	168,279	24,671	...
53.	Toledo, OH	317,606	332,943	354,635	383,062	303,616	131,822	3,829
54.	Buffalo, NY	310,548	328,175	357,870	462,768	580,132	352,387	42,261
55.	Santa Ana, CA	302,419	293,827	204,023	155,710	45,533	4,933	...
56.	Arlington, TX	294,816	261,717	160,113	90,229	7,692	1,079	...
57.	Anaheim, CA	288,945	266,406	219,494	166,408	14,556	1,456	...
58.	Tampa, FL	285,206	280,015	271,577	277,714	124,681	15,839	...
59.	Corpus Christi, TX	280,260	257,453	232,134	204,525	108,287	4,703	...
60.	Newark, NJ	268,510	275,221	329,248	381,930	438,776	246,070	38,894
61.	Louisville, KY	260,689	269,555	298,694	361,706	369,129	204,731	43,194
62.	St. Paul, MN	259,606	272,235	270,230	309,866	311,349	163,065	1,112
63.	Birmingham, AL	258,543	265,347	284,413	300,910	326,037	38,415	...
64.	Riverside, CA	255,069	226,546	170,591	140,089	46,764	7,973	...
65.	Aurora, CO	252,341	222,103	158,588	74,974	11,421	202	...
66.	Anchorage, AK	250,505	226,338	174,431	48,081	11,254	...	...
67.	Raleigh, NC	243,835	212,092	150,255	122,830	65,679	13,643	4,518
68.	Lexington, KY	239,942	225,366	204,165	108,137	55,534	26,369	8,159
69.	St. Petersburg, FL	235,988	240,318	238,647	216,159	96,738	1,575	...
70.	Norfolk, VA	233,430	261,250	266,979	307,951	213,513	46,624	14,326
71.	Stockton, CA	232,660	210,943	148,283	109,963	70,853	17,506	...
72.	Jersey City, NJ	229,039	228,517	223,532	260,350	299,017	206,433	6,856
73.	Rochester, NY	221,594	230,356	241,741	295,011	332,488	162,608	36,403
74.	Akron, OH	216,882	223,019	237,177	275,425	274,605	42,728	3,266
75.	Baton Rouge, LA	215,882	219,531	220,394	165,921	125,629	11,269	3,905
76.	Lincoln, NE	209,192	191,972	171,932	149,518	98,884	40,169	...
77.	Bakersfield, CA	205,508	176,264	105,611	69,515	34,784	4,836	...
78.	Hialeah, FL	204,684	188,008	145,254	102,452	19,676	...	...
79.	Mobile, AL	202,581	196,263	200,452	190,026	129,009	38,469	20,515
80.	Richmond, VA	198,267	202,798	219,214	249,332	230,310	85,050	27,570
81.	Madison, WI	197,630	190,766	170,616	171,809	96,056	19,164	1,525
82.	Montgomery, AL	196,363	190,350	177,857	133,386	106,525	30,346	8,728
83.	Greensboro, NC	195,426	183,894	155,642	144,076	74,389	10,035	...
84.	Lubbock, TX	193,565	186,206	174,361	149,101	71,747	...	...
85.	Des Moines, IA	193,422	193,189	191,003	201,404	177,965	62,139	...
86.	Jackson, MS	192,923	202,062	202,895	153,968	98,271	7,816	1,881

Rank	City	1996	1990	1980	1970	1950	1900	1850
87.	Chesapeake, VA	192,342	151,982	114,486	89,580	...	...	...
88.	Plano, TX	192,280	127,885	72,331	17,872	2,126	1,304	...
89.	Shreveport, LA	191,558	198,525	206,989	182,064	127,206	16,013	1,728
90.	Huntington Beach, CA	190,751	181,519	170,505	115,960	5,237	...	...
91.	Yonkers, NY	190,316	188,082	195,351	204,297	152,798	47,931	...
92.	Garland, TX	190,055	180,635	138,857	81,437	10,571	819	...
93.	Grand Rapids, MI	188,242	189,126	181,843	197,649	176,515	87,565	2,686
94.	Fremont, CA	187,800	173,339	131,945	100,869	...	...	...
95.	Spokane, WA	186,562	177,165	171,300	170,516	161,721	36,848	...
96.	Fort Wayne, IN	184,783	191,839	172,391	178,269	133,607	45,115	4,282
97.	Glendale, CA	184,321	180,038	139,060	133,000	96,000	...	...
98.	San Bernardino, CA	183,474	170,036	118,794	104,251	63,058	6,150	...
99.	Columbus, GA[1]	182,828	178,683	169,441	155,028	79,611	17,614	9,621
100.	Glendale, AZ	182,219	147,864	96,988	36,228	8,179	...	...

Note: The Apr. 1, 1990, census counts include subsequent revisions and take account of subsequent and geographic changes. (1) Indianapolis, IN; Jacksonville, FL; Nashville-Davidson, TN; and Columbus, GA, are parts of consolidated city-county governments. Populations of other incorporated places in the county have been excluded from the population totals shown here. For years that predate the establishment of a consolidated city-county government, city population is shown. (2) Locations in Hawaii are called "census designated places (CDPs)." Although these areas are not incorporated, they are recognized for census purposes as large urban places. Honolulu CDP is coextensive with Honolulu Judicial District within the city and county of Honolulu.

Projections of Total Population, by Age, 1995-2050

Source: Bureau of the Census, U.S. Dept. of Commerce

Age	1995		2000		2010		2050	
	Population[1]	Percentage distribution	Population[1]	Percentage distribution	Population[1]	Percentage distribution	Population[1]	Percentage distribution
Total	262,820	100.0	274,634	100.0	297,716	100.0	393,931	100.0
Under 5 years	19,591	7.5	18,987	6.9	20,012	6.7	27,106	6.9
5-13 years	34,378	13.1	36,043	13.1	35,605	12.0	47,804	12.1
14-17 years	14,773	5.6	15,752	5.7	16,894	5.7	21,207	5.4
18-24 years	24,926	9.5	26,258	9.6	30,138	10.1	36,333	9.2
25-34 years	40,863	15.5	37,233	13.6	38,292	12.9	49,365	12.5
35-44 years	42,514	16.2	44,659	16.3	38,521	12.9	47,393	12.0
45-54 years	31,092	11.8	37,030	13.5	43,564	14.6	43,494	11.0
55-64 years	21,139	8.0	23,961	8.7	35,283	11.9	42,368	10.8
65 years and over	33,543	12.8	34,709	12.6	39,408	13.2	78,859	20.0
85 years and over	3,634	1.4	4,259	1.6	5,671	1.9	18,223	4.6
100 years and over	54	0.0	72	0.0	131	0.0	834	0.2

Note: All figures shown are for July 1 of the given year, exclude Armed Forces overseas, and are middle series population projections. For the series shown, different assumptions were made regarding fertility rates (lifetime births per woman), life expectancy, and immigration in the coming decades. Assumptions were based on July 1 estimates of U.S. population consistent with the 1990 decennial census, as enumerated. Yearly net immigration was assumed to be 820,000. Percentage distribution may not equal 100, because of overlapping categories shown and rounding. (1) In thousands.

U.S. Population, by Age, Sex, and Household, 1990

Source: Bureau of the Census, U.S. Dept. of Commerce; 1990 Census

Total population	**248,709,873[1]**
AGE	
Under 5 years	18,354,443
5 to 17 years	45,249,989
18 to 20 years	11,726,868
21 to 24 years	15,010,898
25 to 44 years	80,754,835
45 to 54 years	25,223,086
55 to 59 years	10,531,756
60 to 64 years	10,616,167
65 to 74 years	18,106,558
75 to 84 years	10,055,108
85 years and over	3,080,165
Median age	32.9
Under 18 years	63,604,432
Percentage of total population	25.6
65 years and over	31,241,831
Percentage of total population	12.6
SEX	
Male	121,239,418
Female	127,470,455
HOUSEHOLDS BY TYPES	
TOTAL HOUSEHOLDS	**91,947,410**
Family households (families)	64,517,947
Married-couple families	50,708,322
Percentage of total households	55.1
Other family, male householder	3,143,582
Other family, female householder	10,666,043
Nonfamily households	27,429,463
Percentage of total households	29.8
Householder living alone	22,580,420
Householder 65 years and over	8,824,845
Persons living in households	242,012,129
Persons per household	2.63
Persons living in group quarters	6,697,744
Institutionalized persons	3,334,018
Other persons in group quarters	3,363,726

(1) Data shown are based on the U.S. population as tabulated in the 1990 census, and do not reflect corrections to the 1990 population. The corrected 1990 U.S. population is 248,765,170.

MILLENNIUM FACT BOX

Shrinking U.S. Households, 1850-1997

Source: Bureau of the Census, U.S. Dept. of Commerce

As the size of American families decreased, the number of persons per household declined during the late 19th century and most of the 20th century, reaching a low by around 1990, then remaining relatively stable.

Year	Persons per household	Year	Persons per household	Year	Persons per household
1850	5.55	1910	4.54	1970	3.14
1860	5.28	1920	4.34	1975	2.94
1870	5.09	1930	4.11	1980	2.76
1880	5.04	1940	3.67	1985	2.69
1890	4.93	1950	3.37	1990	2.63
1900	4.76	1960	3.35	1997	2.64

U.S. Households, by Type, 1960-97

Source: Bureau of the Census, U.S. Dept. of Commerce

Year	Total U.S. households[1]	Married-couple households[1]	Unmarried-couple households[1]	Year	Total U.S. households[1]	Married-couple households[1]	Unmarried-couple households[1]
1960 . . .	52,799	39,254	439	1988	91,124	51,675	2,588
1970 . . .	63,401	44,728	523	1989	92,830	52,100	2,764
1980 . . .	80,776	49,112	1,589	1990	93,347	52,317	2,856
1981 . . .	82,368	49,294	1,808	1991	94,312	52,147	3,039
1982 . . .	83,527	49,630	1,863	1992	95,669	52,457	3,308
1983 . . .	83,918	49,908	1,891	1993	96,426	53,090	3,510
1984 . . .	85,407	50,090	1,988	1994	97,107	53,171	3,661
1985 . . .	86,789	50,350	1,983	1995	98,990	53,858	3,668
1986 . . .	88,458	50,933	2,220	1996	99,627	53,567	3,958
1987 . . .	89,479	51,537	2,334	1997	101,018	53,604	4,130

(1) Numbers in thousands.

Living Arrangements of Children, 1970-97

Source: Bureau of the Census, U.S. Dept. of Commerce

(as of Mar.; excludes persons under 18 years of age who maintained households or resided in group quarters)

		Percentage of children who live with—								
			MOTHER ONLY							
Race, Hispanic origin, and year	Number (1,000)	BOTH PARENTS	Total	Divorced	Married Spouse absent	Single[1]	Widowed	FATHER ONLY	NEITHER PARENT
White									
1970	58,790	90	8	3	3	Z	2	1	2
1980	52,242	83	14	7	4	1	2	2	2
1990	51,390	79	16	8	4	3	1	3	2
1995	55,315	76	18	8	5	4	1	3	3
1996	55,709	75	18	8	5	5	1	4	3
1997	55,868	75	18	8	4	5	1	4	3
Black									
1970	9,422	59	30	5	16	4	4	2	10
1980	9,375	42	44	11	16	13	4	2	12
1990	10,018	38	51	10	12	27	2	4	8
1995	11,301	33	52	11	11	29	2	4	11
1996	11,434	33	53	9	11	31	2	4	9
1997	11,369	35	52	9	11	31	1	5	8
Hispanic[2]									
1970	4,006[3]	78	NA	NA	NA	NA	NA	NA	NA
1980	5,459	75	20	6	8	4	2	2	4
1990	7,174	67	27	7	10	8	2	3	3
1995	9,842	63	28	8	9	10	1	4	4
1996	10,251	62	29	7	9	11	1	4	5
1997	10,525	64	27	7	7	12	1	4	5

NA = Not available. Z = Less than 0.5%. (1) Never married. (2) Hispanic persons may be of any race. (3) All persons under 18 years old.

Primary Child Care Arrangements for Preschoolers[1], 1977-94

Source: Bureau of the Census, U.S. Dept. of Commerce

	% Fall 1994	% Fall 1993	% Fall 1991	% Fall 1990	% Fall 1988	% Fall 1987	% Fall 1986	% Winter 1985	% Fall 1977[2]
Care in child's home	33.0	30.7	35.7	29.7	28.2	29.9	28.7	31.0	33.9
By father	18.5	15.9	20.0	16.5	15.1	15.3	14.5	15.7	14.4
By grandparent	5.9	6.5	7.2	5.2	5.7	5.1	5.2	5.7	NA
By other relative	3.5	3.3	3.2	2.9	2.2	3.3	3.4	3.7	12.6[3]
By nonrelative	5.1	5.0	5.4	5.0	5.3	6.2	5.5	5.9	7.0
Care in another home	31.3	32.1	31.0	35.1	36.8	35.6	40.7	37.0	40.7
By grandparent	10.4	10.0	8.6	9.1	8.2	8.7	10.2	10.2	NA
By other relative	5.5	5.5	4.5	5.9	5.0	4.6	6.5	4.5	18.3
By nonrelative	15.4	16.6	17.9	20.1	23.6	22.3	24.0	22.3	22.4
Organized child care facilities . .	29.4	30.1	23.0	27.5	25.8	24.4	22.4	23.1	13.0
Day/group care center	21.6	18.3	15.8	20.6	16.6	16.1	14.9	14.0	NA
Nursery school/preschool	7.8	11.6	7.3	6.9	9.2	8.3	7.5	9.1	NA
School-based activity	0.2	0.2	0.5	0.1	0.2	NA	NA	NA	NA
Child cares for self	0	0	0	0.1	0.1	0.3	0	0	0.4
Mother cares for child at work[4] .	5.5	6.2	8.7	6.4	7.6	8.9	7.4	8.1	11.4
Other arrangements[5]	0.9	0.9	1.1	1.1	1.3	1.0	0.8	0.8	0.6

NA = Not available. (1) For families with employed mothers. (2) Only for 2 youngest children under 5 yrs. of age. (3) Includes grandparents. (4) Includes mothers working for pay at home or away from home. (5) Includes children in kindergarten/grade school.

Poverty Level by Family Size, 1995-97

Source: Bureau of the Census, U.S. Dept. of Commerce

	1995	1996	1997		1995	1996	1997
1 person	$7,763	$7,995	$8,183	3 persons	$12,158	$12,516	$12,802
Under 65 years	7,929	8,163	8,350	4 persons	15,569	16,036	16,400
65 years and over	7,309	7,525	7,698	5 persons	18,408	18,952	19,380
2 persons	9,933	10,233	10,473	6 persons	20,804	21,389	21,886
Householder under 65 years . .	10,259	10,564	10,805	7 persons	23,552	24,268	24,802
				8 persons	26,237	27,091	27,593
Householder 65 years and over	9,219	9,491	9,712	9 persons or more	31,280	31,971	32,566

Poverty Rate

Source: Bureau of the Census, U.S. Dept. of Commerce

The poverty rate is the proportion of the population whose income falls below the government's official poverty level, which is adjusted each year for inflation. The national poverty rate was 13.3% in 1997, a decrease from the 1996 rate of 13.7%. Children remained overrepresented among the poor, with a poverty rate of 19.9%. The elderly were slightly underrepresented.

Poverty by Family Status, Sex, and Race, 1986-97

Source: Bureau of the Census, U.S. Dept. of Commerce

(numbers in thousands)

	1997		1996		1995		1990		1986	
	No.	%[1]	No.	%[1]	No.	%[1]	No.	%[1]	No.	%[1]
TOTAL POOR	**35,574**	**13.3**	**36,529**	**13.7**	**36,425**	**13.8**	**33,585**	**13.5**	**32,370**	**13.6**
In families	**26,217**	**11.6**	**27,376**	**12.2**	**27,501**	**12.3**	**25,232**	**12.0**	**24,754**	**12.0**
Head of household	7,324	10.3	7,708	11.0	7,532	10.8	7,098	10.7	7,023	10.9
Related children	13,422	19.2	13,764	19.8	13,999	20.2	12,715	19.9	12,257	19.8
Unrelated individuals	**8,687**	**20.8**	**8,452**	**20.8**	**8,247**	**20.9**	**7,446**	**20.7**	**6,846**	**21.6**
In families, female householder, no husband present	**13,494**	**35.1**	**13,796**	**35.8**	**14,205**	**36.5**	**12,578**	**37.2**	**11,944**	**38.3**
Head of household	3,995	31.6	4,167	32.6	4,057	32.4	3,768	33.4	3,613	34.6
Related children	7,928	49.0	7,990	49.3	8,364	50.3	7,363	53.4	6,943	54.4
Unrelated female individuals	**5,240**	**24.0**	**5,145**	**24.2**	**4,865**	**23.5**	**4,589**	**24.0**	**4,311**	**25.1**
All other families	**12,723**	**6.8**	**13,580**	**7.3**	**13,296**	**7.2**	**12,654**	**7.1**	**12,811**	**7.3**
Head of household	3,329	5.7	3,541	6.2	3,475	6.1	3,330	6.0	3,410	6.3
Related children	5,494	10.2	5,774	10.9	5,635	10.7	5,352	10.7	5,313	10.8
Unrelated male individuals	**3,447**	**17.4**	**3,308**	**17.0**	**3,382**	**18.0**	**2,857**	**16.9**	**2,536**	**17.5**
TOTAL WHITE POOR	**24,396**	**11.0**	**24,650**	**11.2**	**24,423**	**11.2**	**22,326**	**10.7**	**22,183**	**11.0**
In families	**17,258**	**9.3**	**17,621**	**9.6**	**17,593**	**9.6**	**15,916**	**9.0**	**16,393**	**9.4**
Head of household	4,990	8.4	5,059	8.6	4,994	8.5	4,622	8.1	4,811	8.6
Related children	8,441	15.4	8,488	15.5	8,474	15.5	7,696	15.1	7,714	15.3
Female householder, no spouse present	**2,305**	**27.7**	**2,276**	**27.3**	**2,200**	**26.6**	**2,010**	**26.8**	**2,041**	**28.2**
Unrelated individuals	**6,593**	**18.9**	**6,463**	**18.9**	**6,336**	**19.0**	**5,739**	**18.6**	**5,198**	**19.2**
TOTAL BLACK POOR	**9,116**	**26.5**	**9,694**	**28.4**	**9,872**	**29.3**	**9,837**	**31.9**	**8,983**	**31.1**
In families	**7,386**	**25.5**	**7,993**	**27.6**	**8,189**	**28.5**	**8,160**	**31.0**	**7,410**	**29.7**
Head of household	1,985	23.6	2,206	26.1	2,127	26.4	2,193	29.3	1,987	28.0
Related children	4,116	36.8	4,411	39.5	4,644	41.5	4,412	44.2	4,039	42.7
Female householder, no spouse present	**1,563**	**39.8**	**1,724**	**43.7**	**1,701**	**45.1**	**1,648**	**48.1**	**1,488**	**50.1**
Unrelated individuals	**1,645**	**31.0**	**1,606**	**32.2**	**1,551**	**32.6**	**1,491**	**35.1**	**1,431**	**38.5**

(1) Percentage of total U.S. population in each category who fell below poverty level and are enumerated here. For example, of all persons in families in 1997, 11.6%, or 26,217,000, were poor.

Persons Below Poverty Level, 1960-97

Source: Bureau of the Census, U.S. Dept. of Commerce

	Number below poverty level (in millions)				Percentage below poverty level				Avg. income cutoffs for family of 4 at poverty level[3]
Year	All races[1]	White	Black	Hispanic origin[2]	All races[1]	White	Black	Hispanic origin[2]	
1960	39.9	28.3	NA	NA	22.2	17.8	NA	NA	$3,022
1970	25.4	17.5	7.5	NA	12.6	9.9	33.5	NA	3,968
1980	29.3	19.7	8.6	3.5	13.0	10.2	32.5	25.7	8,414
1990	33.6	22.3	9.8	6.0	13.5	10.7	31.9	28.1	13,359
1991	35.7	23.7	10.2	6.3	14.2	11.3	32.7	28.7	13,924
1992	38.0	25.3	10.8	7.6	14.8	11.9	33.4	29.6	14,335
1993	39.3	26.2	10.9	8.1	15.1	12.2	33.1	30.6	14,763
1994	38.1	25.4	10.2	8.4	14.5	11.7	30.6	30.7	15,141
1995	36.4	24.4	9.9	8.6	13.8	11.2	29.3	30.3	15,569
1996	36.5	24.7	9.7	8.7	13.7	11.2	28.4	29.4	16,036
1997	35.6	24.4	9.1	8.3	13.3	11.0	26.5	27.1	16,400

NA = Not available. **Note:** Because of a change in the definition of poverty, data prior to 1980 are not directly comparable to data since 1980. (1) Includes other races not shown separately. (2) Persons of Hispanic origin may be of any race. (3) Figures for 1960-80 represent only nonfarm families.

Persons in Poverty, by State, 1996-97

Source: Bureau of the Census, U.S. Dept. of Commerce

State	1997 Percentage	1996 Percentage	State	1997 Percentage	1996 Percentage	State	1997 Percentage	1996 Percentage	State	1997 Percentage	1996 Percentage
AL	14.8	17.0	IL	11.6	12.3	MT	16.3	16.1	RI	11.9	10.8
AK	8.5	7.6	IN	8.2	8.6	NE	10.0	9.9	SC	13.1	16.5
AZ	18.8	18.3	IA	9.6	10.9	NV	9.6	9.6	SD	14.1	13.1
AR	18.4	16.0	KS	10.4	11.0	NH	7.7	5.8	TN	15.1	15.7
CA	16.8	16.8	KY	16.4	15.9	NJ	9.2	8.5	TX	16.7	17.0
CO	9.4	9.7	LA	18.4	20.1	NM	23.4	25.4	UT	8.3	8.0
CT	10.1	10.7	ME	10.7	11.2	NY	16.6	16.6	VT	10.9	11.4
DE	9.1	9.5	MD	9.3	10.2	NC	11.8	12.4	VA	12.5	11.2
DC	23.0	23.2	MA	11.2	10.5	ND	12.3	11.5	WA	10.5	12.2
FL	14.3	15.2	MI	10.7	11.7	OH	11.8	12.1	WV	17.5	17.6
GA	14.7	13.5	MN	9.7	9.5	OK	15.2	16.9	WI	8.5	8.7
HI	13.0	11.2	MS	18.6	22.0	OR	11.7	11.5	WY	12.7	12.0
ID	13.3	13.2	MO	10.6	9.5	PA	11.4	11.9			

Block Grants for Temporary Assistance for Needy Families, Fiscal Year 1997

Source: Admin. for Children and Families, Off. of Planning, Research, and Evaluation, U.S Dept. of Health and Human Services

State	Total assistance payments[1]	Average monthly caseload	Average monthly recipients	Average monthly children[2]	Average monthly payment per Family	Average monthly payment per Person
Alabama	$98,853	34,619	85,750	68,950	$237.95	$96.07
Alaska	66,717	12,023	35,371	23,011	462.43	157.18
Arizona	278,137	54,743	147,376	104,822	423.40	157.27
Arkansas	55,698	20,896	53,188	39,160	222.13	87.27
California	5,786,102	815,913	2,403,513	1,701,254	590.96	200.61
Colorado	127,145	29,816	79,591	60,042	355.36	133.12
Connecticut	427,437	55,799	154,345	103,802	638.36	230.78
Delaware	49,833	9,761	22,076	15,061	425.47	188.11
District of Columbia	127,506	24,119	66,272	47,070	440.54	160.33
Florida	752,521	171,271	451,318	338,758	366.14	138.95
Georgia	450,592	107,031	282,050	216,191	350.83	133.13
Guam	11,020	2,309	7,753	5,669	397.78	118.45
Hawaii	119,242	22,728	71,094	46,391	437.20	139.77
Idaho	12,648	6,445	16,090	13,536	163.53	65.50
Illinois	726,922	198,923	580,324	413,878	304.52	104.38
Indiana	191,141	45,778	122,354	86,478	347.95	130.18
Iowa	157,482	28,883	78,283	53,022	454.36	167.64
Kansas	164,083	20,176	53,695	40,042	677.71	254.65
Kentucky	224,542	65,088	157,807	111,460	287.48	118.57
Louisiana	145,158	56,614	187,459	138,030	213.67	64.53
Maine	106,837	18,470	49,397	32,361	482.04	180.24
Maryland	306,489	59,320	163,089	116,798	430.56	155.61
Massachusetts	652,402	77,989	207,138	136,055	697.11	262.47
Michigan	1,081,030	151,653	448,795	312,061	594.03	200.73
Minnesota	247,056	53,340	156,872	108,454	385.98	131.24
Mississippi	90,128	38,513	102,447	81,298	195.02	73.31
Missouri	311,013	71,774	196,937	144,752	361.10	131.60
Montana	48,738	9,126	26,855	18,313	445.05	151.24
Nebraska	63,482	13,586	36,859	25,424	389.39	143.52
Nevada	62,463	11,918	29,492	22,666	436.77	176.50
New Hampshire	68,923	7,915	19,735	13,664	725.69	291.04
New Jersey	482,524	100,317	250,767	173,826	400.83	160.35
New Mexico	140,618	26,954	81,450	56,892	434.76	143.87
New York	3,629,880	384,377	1,048,257	703,653	786.96	288.56
North Carolina	393,391	99,178	243,237	171,439	330.54	134.78
North Dakota	20,177	4,195	11,398	8,072	400.81	147.53
Ohio	895,747	184,830	493,554	358,311	403.86	151.24
Oklahoma	146,849	30,648	81,879	60,639	399.29	149.46
Oregon	230,628	24,307	62,485	45,219	790.67	307.58
Pennsylvania	851,704	163,563	460,607	324,843	433.93	154.09
Puerto Rico	45,053	47,726	143,770	98,983	78.67	26.11
Rhode Island	132,106	19,822	54,521	36,710	555.40	201.92
South Carolina	123,505	34,214	89,761	69,383	300.82	114.66
South Dakota	26,209	5,105	13,439	10,476	427.83	162.51
Tennessee	231,730	70,589	184,499	136,867	273.57	104.67
Texas	633,376	208,974	573,880	426,649	252.57	91.97
Utah	89,522	12,303	33,867	23,557	606.39	220.28
Vermont	63,883	8,293	23,024	14,589	641.95	231.21
Virgin Islands	2,948	1,278	4,528	3,402	192.17	54.25
Virginia	207,907	53,599	129,934	95,939	323.24	133.34
Washington	575,759	92,837	254,039	169,140	516.82	188.87
West Virginia	107,324	33,340	81,893	54,578	268.26	109.21
Wisconsin	344,185	41,648	119,916	93,592	688.69	239.19
Wyoming	14,651	2,749	7,320	5,899	444.17	166.78
U.S. TOTAL	**22,401,017**	**3,947,381**	**10,941,347**	**7,781,132**	**472.91**	**170.61**

Note: Under 1996 legislation, the Aid to Families With Dependent Children (AFDC) program was converted to a state block-grant program (Temporary Assistance to Needy Families [TANF]). Conversion dates varied from state to state, starting from Sept. 30, 1996. As of July 1, 1997, all states were operating under the new program. (1) Total assistance payments given in thousands. U.S. total equals $18,668,773 AFDC plus $3,723,244 TANF. The AFDC portion included federal, state, and local payments for AFDC-Basic, AFDC-Unemployed Parent, Job Opportunity and Basic Skills (JOBS), Home Repair programs, and payments to Indian tribes. The TANF portion represents the federal block-grant and state "maintenance of effort" expenditures; it includes administrative costs and other expenditures which were separately accounted under AFDC. (2) Because of changes in reporting requirements, no data on number of children are available after June 30, 1997. The figure shown is the average for the first 9 months of the fiscal year.

Median Income, by Sex, Race, Age, and Education, 1996-97

Source: Bureau of the Census, U.S. Dept. of Commerce

	1997	1996		1997	1996
MALE	**$35,248**	**$33,538**	**FEMALE**	**$26,029**	**$24,935**
Race			**Race**		
White	36,118	34,741	White	26,470	25,358
Black	26,897	27,136	Black	22,764	21,990
Hispanic origin[1]	21,799	21,265	Hispanic origin[1]	19,676	19,272
Age			**Age**		
Under 65 years	35,126	33,321	Under 65 years	25,978	24,899
65 and over	45,648	42,836	65 and over	30,358	27,070
Educational attainment			**Educational attainment**		
Less than 9th grade	19,291	17,962	Less than 9th grade	14,161	14,414
9th-12th grade (no diploma)	24,726	22,717	9th-12th grade (no diploma)	16,697	16,953
High school graduate	31,215	30,709	High school graduate	22,067	21,175
Some college, no degree	35,945	34,845	Some college, no degree	26,335	25,167
Associate degree	38,022	37,131	Associate degree	28,812	28,083
Bachelor's degree or more	53,450	51,436	Bachelor's degree or more	38,038	36,461

Note: Includes only full-time, year-round workers, 15 years old and over as of Mar. of the following year. (1) May be of any race.

U.S. Places of 5,000 or More Population—With ZIP and Area Codes

Source: U.S. Bureau of the Census, Dept. of Commerce; Bellcore; Lockheed Martin

The following is a list of places of 5,000 or more inhabitants recognized by the Bureau of the Census, U.S. Dept. of Commerce, based on 1996 population estimates. Also given are 1990 census populations. This list includes **places that are incorporated** under the laws of their respective states as cities, boroughs, towns, and villages, with the following exceptions: boroughs in Alaska and towns in the 6 New England states (Connecticut, Maine, Massachusetts, New Hampshire, Rhode Island, and Vermont), New York, and Wisconsin.

Places that the Census Bureau designates as **"census designated places" (CDPs)** are also included. These communities, marked (c), are statistically compatible with incorporated communities because of their population density. CDP boundaries can change from one census to another. Hawaii is the only state that has no incorporated places recognized by the Census Bureau; all places shown for Hawaii are CDPs.

This list also includes, in *italics*, **minor civil divisions (MCDs)** for the following states: Connecticut, Maine, Massachusetts, New Hampshire, Rhode Island, and Vermont. MCDs are not incorporated under the laws of the state and not recognized by the Census Bureau as CDPs, but are often the primary political or administrative divisions of a county. These areas may also serve as general-purpose local governments.

1996 estimates are not available for CDPs.

An **asterisk** (*) denotes that the ZIP code given is for general delivery; named streets and/or post office boxes within the community may differ. Consult the local postmaster for the correct ZIP code for specific addresses within the community.

Area codes, given in parentheses, refer only to home and business telephone numbers. Some regions have two area codes intermixed; these are known as overlays. States where this occurs are noted. When 2 area codes are listed for one place, consult local operators for assistance. For a listing in numerical order of all area codes in the U.S., Canada, and the Caribbean, see Consumer Information.

For some places listed, no area code and/or ZIP code is available.

Alabama

ZIP	Place		1996	1990
35005	Adamsville	(205)	5,065	5,161
35007	Alabaster	(205)	20,211	14,619
*35950	Albertville	(256)	16,508	14,507
*35010	Alexander City	(256)	15,635	14,917
36420	Andalusia	(334)	9,081	9,269
*36201	Anniston	(256)	25,774	26,638
35016	Arab	(256)	7,350	6,321
*35611	Athens	(256)	19,112	16,901
*36502	Atmore	(334)	7,979	8,046
35954	Attalla	(256)	6,865	6,859
*36830	Auburn	(334)	37,664	33,830
36507	Bay Minette	(334)	7,804	7,168
*35020	Bessemer	(205)	31,234	33,581
*35203	Birmingham	(205)	258,543	265,347
*35957	Boaz	(256)	7,640	6,928
*36426	Brewton	(334)	5,952	5,885
35220	Center Point(c)	(205)	—	22,658
36671	Chickasaw	(334)	6,433	6,649
*35045	Clanton	(205)	8,429	7,669
*35055	Cullman	(256)	18,195	13,367
36322	Daleville	(334)	5,352	5,117
36526	Daphne	(334)	14,972	11,291
*35601	Decatur	(256)	53,797	49,917
36732	Demopolis	(334)	7,623	7,512
*36302	Dothan	(334)	55,944	54,143
*36330	Enterprise	(334)	21,253	20,119
*36027	Eufaula	(334)	13,371	13,220
35064	Fairfield	(205)	11,490	12,200
*36532	Fairhope	(334)	12,045	9,189
*35630	Florence	(256)	38,999	36,426
*36535	Foley	(334)	6,433	4,937
35214	Forestdale(c)	(205)	—	10,395
*35967	Fort Payne	(256)	12,480	11,838
36362	Fort Rucker(c)	(334)	—	7,593
35068	Fultondale	(205)	6,538	6,400
*35901	Gadsden	(256)	41,493	42,523
35071	Gardendale	(205)	9,568	9,251
35905	Glencoe	(256)	5,024	4,687
36037	Greenville	(334)	7,589	7,847
35976	Guntersville	(256)	7,935	7,038
35570	Hamilton	(205)	6,221	6,171
35640	Hartselle	(256)	12,001	11,114
35080	Helena	(205)	8,410	4,303
35259	Homewood	(205)	23,156	23,644
*35244	Hoover	(205)	55,464	40,000
35023	Hueytown	(205)	15,122	15,280
*35801	Huntsville	(256)	170,424	159,880
35210	Irondale	(205)	9,214	9,458
36545	Jackson	(334)	6,117	5,819
36265	Jacksonville	(256)	9,526	10,283
*35501	Jasper	(205)	13,940	13,553
36863	Lanett	(334)	8,772	8,985
35094	Leeds	(205)	10,480	10,009
*35758	Madison	(256)	23,620	14,792
35228	Midfield	(205)	5,301	5,559
36054	Millbrook	(334)	8,925	6,046
*36601	Mobile	(334)	202,581	196,263
*36460	Monroeville	(334)	7,017	6,993
*36104	Montgomery	(334)	196,363	190,350
35004	Moody	(205)	6,285	4,921
35253	Mountain Brook	(205)	18,992	19,810
*35661	Muscle Shoals	(256)	10,487	9,611
*35476	Northport	(205)	20,024	17,297
35121	Oneonta	(205)	5,168	4,844
*36801	Opelika	(334)	24,041	22,122
36467	Opp	(334)	6,920	6,985
36203	Oxford	(256)	10,408	9,537
*36360	Ozark	(334)	12,745	13,030
35124	Pelham	(205)	13,082	9,421
*35125	Pell City	(205)	9,491	7,945
*36867	Phenix City	(334)	28,000	25,311
36272	Piedmont	(256)	5,214	5,347
35126	Pinson-Clay-Chalkville(c)	(205)	—	10,987
35127	Pleasant Grove	(205)	8,905	8,458
*36066	Prattville	(334)	24,269	19,816
36610	Prichard	(334)	32,887	34,320
35906	Rainbow City	(256)	8,492	7,667
36274	Roanoke	(334)	6,233	6,362
*35653	Russellville	(256)	8,343	7,812
36201	Saks(c)	(256)	—	11,138
36571	Saraland	(334)	12,714	11,760
36572	Satsuma	(334)	5,934	5,194
*35768	Scottsboro	(256)	14,133	13,786
*36701	Selma	(334)	22,745	23,755
35660	Sheffield	(256)	10,216	10,380
35901	Southside	(256)	6,622	5,580
*35150	Sylacauga	(256)	12,576	12,520
*35160	Talladega	(256)	18,246	18,175
36078	Tallassee	(334)	5,272	5,112
35217	Tarrant	(205)	7,554	8,046
*36582	Theodore(c)	(334)	—	6,509
36619	Tillman's Corner(c)	(334)	—	17,988
*36081	Troy	(334)	13,497	13,051
35173	Trussville	(205)	10,796	8,283
*35401	Tuscaloosa	(205)	82,379	77,759
35674	Tuscumbia	(256)	8,253	8,413
36083	Tuskegee	(334)	11,504	12,257
*36854	Valley	(334)	9,283	9,556
35266	Vestavia Hills	(205)	20,384	19,550
*36092	Wetumpka	(334)	5,868	4,670

Alaska (907)

ZIP	Place	1996	1990
*99501	Anchorage	250,505	226,338
99559	Bethel	5,952	4,674
*99708	College(c)	—	11,249
99702	Eielson AFB(c)	—	5,251
*99701	Fairbanks	32,960	30,843
*99801	Juneau	29,756	26,751
99611	Kenai	7,706	6,327
*99901	Ketchikan	8,274	8,263
*99615	Kodiak	7,677	6,365
99639	Ninilchik(c)	—	10,523
99835	Sitka	8,510	8,588
*99654	Wasilla	5,350	4,028

Arizona

ZIP	Place		1996	1990
*85220	Apache Junction	(602)	19,338	18,092
85323	Avondale	(602)	24,157	17,595
85603	Bisbee	(520)	6,515	6,288
85326	Buckeye	(602)	5,151	4,436
*86430	Bullhead City	(520)	27,410	21,951
86322	Camp Verde	(520)	7,552	6,243
*85222	Casa Grande	(520)	21,314	19,076
*85225	Chandler	(602)	142,918	89,862
86503	Chinle(c)	(520)	—	5,059
86323	Chino Valley	(520)	6,588	4,837
85228	Coolidge	(520)	7,166	6,934
86326	Cottonwood	(520)	6,937	5,918
86326	Cottonwood-Verde Village(c)	(520)	—	7,037
*85607	Douglas	(520)	15,015	13,908
85335	El Mirage	(602)	5,712	5,001
85231	Eloy	(520)	7,642	7,211
*86004	Flagstaff	(520)	55,094	45,857

ZIP	Place		1996	1990
85232	Florence	(520)	12,939	7,321
85726	Flowing Wells(c)	(520)	—	14,013
.....	Fortuna Foothills(c)	(520)	—	7,737
*85268	Fountain Hills	(602)	15,414	10,030
*85299	Gilbert	(602)	64,326	29,149
*85302	Glendale	(602)	182,219	147,864
*85501	Globe	(520)	6,683	6,062
85338	Goodyear	(602)	10,614	6,258
*85622	Green Valley(c)	(520)	—	13,231
85283	Guadalupe	(602)	5,344	5,458
86025	Holbrook	(520)	5,398	4,686
*86401	Kingman	(520)	17,270	13,208
*86403	Lake Havasu City	(520)	39,503	24,363
85653	Marana	(520)	5,711	2,565
*85201	Mesa	(602)	344,764	289,199
*86440	Mohave Valley(c)	(520)	—	6,962
.....	New Kingman-Butler(c)	(520)	—	11,627
*85621	Nogales	(520)	22,087	19,489
85737	Oro Valley	(520)	17,379	8,627
86040	Page	(520)	7,653	6,598
85253	Paradise Valley	(602)	14,077	11,773
*85541	Payson	(520)	10,978	8,377
*85345	Peoria	(602)	76,045	50,675
*85026	Phoenix	(602)	1,159,014	984,310
*86301	Prescott	(520)	32,841	26,592
*86301	Prescott Valley	(520)	16,919	8,904
*85546	Safford	(520)	8,828	7,359
85349	San Luis	(520)	9,539	4,212
*85251	Scottsdale	(602)	179,012	130,075
*86336	Sedona	(520)	9,109	7,720
*85901	Show Low	(520)	6,330	5,020
*85635	Sierra Vista	(520)	37,434	32,983
85635	Sierra Vista Southeast(c)	(520)	—	9,237
85350	Somerton	(520)	6,271	5,293
85713	South Tucson	(520)	5,924	5,171
*85351	Sun City(c)	(602)	—	38,126
*85351	Sun City West(c)	(602)	—	15,997
85248	Sun Lakes(c)	(602)	—	6,578
*85374	Surprise	(602)	10,340	7,122
*85285	Tempe	(602)	162,701	141,993
86045	Tuba City(c)	(520)	—	7,323
*85726	Tucson	(520)	449,002	411,480
*85390	Wickenburg	(520)	5,312	4,515
86047	Winslow	(520)	10,420	9,279
*85364	Yuma	(520)	60,519	56,966

Arkansas

ZIP	Place		1996	1990
71923	Arkadelphia	(870)	10,472	10,014
*72501	Batesville	(870)	9,632	9,187
72012	Beebe	(501)	5,242	4,455
*72714	Bella Vista(c)	(501)	—	9,083
*72015	Benton	(501)	22,036	18,177
72712	Bentonville	(501)	16,984	11,257
*72315	Blytheville	(870)	18,743	22,523
72022	Bryant	(501)	8,286	5,940
72023	Cabot	(501)	12,956	8,319
*71701	Camden	(870)	13,525	14,701
72830	Clarksville	(501)	6,887	5,833
*72032	Conway	(501)	35,827	26,481
71635	Crossett	(870)	6,239	6,282
71639	Dumas	(870)	5,194	5,520
*71730	El Dorado	(870)	22,419	23,146
*72701	Fayetteville	(501)	52,360	42,247
*72335	Forrest City	(870)	13,224	13,364
*72901	Fort Smith	(501)	75,776	72,798
72936	Greenwood	(501)	5,654	3,984
*72601	Harrison	(870)	11,537	9,936
72543	Heber Springs	(501)	6,453	5,628
72342	Helena	(870)	7,111	7,491
*71801	Hope	(870)	9,772	9,768
*71901	Hot Springs	(501)	36,255	32,462
*71901	Hot Springs Village(c)	(501)	—	6,361
*72076	Jacksonville	(501)	29,191	29,101
*72401	Jonesboro	(870)	52,656	46,535
*72201	Little Rock	(501)	175,752	175,727
*71753	Magnolia	(870)	10,941	11,151
72104	Malvern	(501)	9,627	9,236
72360	Marianna	(870)	5,473	6,033
72364	Marion	(870)	5,703	4,405
72113	Maumelle	(501)	7,962	6,714
71953	Mena	(501)	6,007	5,475
*71655	Monticello	(870)	8,379	8,119
72110	Morrilton	(501)	6,565	6,551
*72653	Mountain Home	(870)	11,236	9,027
72112	Newport	(870)	7,112	7,459
*72114	North Little Rock	(501)	60,468	61,829
72370	Osceola	(870)	8,265	9,165
*72450	Paragould	(870)	21,082	18,540
*71601	Pine Bluff	(870)	54,165	57,140
72455	Pocahontas	(870)	6,524	6,151
*72756	Rogers	(501)	35,355	24,692
*72801	Russellville	(501)	24,796	21,260
*72143	Searcy	(501)	17,157	15,180
72120	Sherwood	(501)	20,902	18,890
72761	Siloam Springs	(501)	10,055	8,151
*72764	Springdale	(501)	38,572	29,945
72160	Stuttgart	(870)	9,981	10,420
71854	Texarkana	(870)	22,918	22,631
72472	Trumann	(870)	6,468	6,346
*72956	Van Buren	(501)	18,601	14,979
71671	Warren	(870)	6,145	6,455
72390	West Helena	(870)	9,701	10,137
*72301	West Memphis	(870)	26,894	28,259
72396	Wynne	(870)	8,476	8,817

California

Area code (424) overlays area code (310). See introductory note.
Area code (661) goes into effect on Feb. 13, 1999. Before then use (805).
Area code (858) goes into effect on June 12, 1999. Before then use (619).

ZIP	Place		1996	1990
94301	Adelanto	(760)	14,554	6,815
*91376	Agoura Hills	(818)	20,718	20,385
*94501	Alameda	(510)	76,042	73,979
94507	Alamo(c)	(925)	—	12,277
94706	Albany	(510)	16,390	16,327
*91802	Alhambra	(323)/(626)	83,644	82,087
92656	Aliso Viejo(c)	(949)	—	7,612
90249	Alondra Park(c)	(310)	—	12,215
*91901	Alpine(c) (San Diego)	(619)	—	9,695
*91003	Altadena(c)	(626)	—	42,658
95945	Alta Sierra(c)	(530)	—	5,709
94589	American Canyon	(707)	7,880	7,734
*92803	Anaheim	(714)	288,945	266,406
96007	Anderson	(530)	8,748	8,299
*94509	Antioch	(925)	76,293	62,195
*92307	Apple Valley	(760)	54,865	46,079
*95003	Aptos(c)	(831)	—	9,061
*91006	Arcadia	(626)	50,483	48,284
*95521	Arcata	(707)	16,261	15,211
95825	Arden-Arcade(c)	(916)	—	92,040
*93420	Arroyo Grande	(805)	14,914	14,432
*90701	Artesia	(562)	15,758	15,464
93203	Arvin	(661)	10,726	9,286
94577	Ashland(c)	(510)	—	16,590
*93422	Atascadero	(805)	24,263	23,138
94027	Atherton	(650)	7,577	7,163
95301	Atwater	(209)	23,638	22,282
*95603	Auburn	(530)	12,129	10,653
95201	August(c)	(209)	—	6,376
93204	Avenal	(559)	11,835	9,770
91746	Avocado Heights(c)	(626)	—	14,232
91702	Azusa	(626)	42,124	41,203
*93302	Bakersfield	(661)	205,508	176,264
91706	Baldwin Park	(626)	71,414	69,330
92220	Banning	(909)	25,543	20,572
*92312	Barstow	(760)	23,196	21,472
94565	Bay Point(c)	(925)	—	17,453
93402	Baywood-Los Osos(c)	(805)	—	14,377
95903	Beale AFB(c)	(530)	—	6,912
92223	Beaumont	(909)	10,610	9,685
90201	Bell	(323)	35,077	34,365
*90706	Bellflower	(323)	63,220	61,815
90202	Bell Gardens	(213)/(323)/(562)	44,101	42,315
94002	Belmont	(650)	25,562	24,165
94510	Benicia	(707)	25,800	24,437
95005	Ben Lomond(c)	(831)	—	7,884
*94704	Berkeley	(510)	103,243	102,724
*90210	Beverly Hills	(213)/(310)/(323)	32,367	31,971
92315	Big Bear Lake	(909)	5,757	5,351
94506	Black Hawk(c)	(925)	—	6,199
92316	Bloomington(c)	(909)	—	15,116
*92225	Blythe	(760)	12,982	10,835
93637	Bonadella Ranchos-Madera Ranchos(c)	(559)	—	5,705
*91902	Bonita(c)	(619)	—	12,542
92021	Bostonia(c)	(619)	—	13,670
95006	Boulder Creek(c)	(831)	—	6,725
95416	Boyes Hot Springs(c)	(707)	—	5,973
92227	Brawley	(760)	22,954	18,923
*92822	Brea	(562)/(714)	34,790	32,873
94513	Brentwood	(925)	13,212	7,563
*90622	Buena Park	(714)	71,999	68,784
*91510	Burbank	(818)	96,579	93,649
*94010	Burlingame	(650)	27,716	26,666
*91372	Calabasas	(818)	17,407	16,577
*92231	Calexico	(760)	25,988	18,633
*93504	California City	(661)	9,275	5,955
92320	Calimesa	(909)	8,188	6,654
92233	Calipatria	(760)	7,330	2,701
*93010	Camarillo	(805)	57,090	52,297
93428	Cambria(c)	(805)	—	5,382
95682	Cameron Park(c)	(530)	—	11,897
*95008	Campbell	(408)	38,380	36,088
92055	Camp Pendleton North(c)	(949)	—	10,373
92055	Camp Pendleton South(c)	(949)	—	11,299
92587	Canyon Lake	(909)	12,068	9,991
95010	Capitola	(831)	10,377	10,171
*92008	Carlsbad	(760)	69,069	63,292
*95608	Carmichael(c)	(916)	—	48,702
*93013	Carpinteria	(805)	14,103	13,747
*90745	Carson	(310)	86,516	83,995
92077	Casa de Oro-Mt. Helix(c)	(619)	—	30,727
*94544	Castro Valley(c)	(510)	—	48,619
*92235	Cathedral City	(760)	36,327	30,085
95307	Ceres	(209)	31,146	26,413
90703	Cerritos	(562)	53,645	53,244

ZIP	Place	1996	1990
91724	Charter Oak(c) (626)	—	8,858
94541	Cherryland(c) (510)	—	11,088
92223	Cherry Valley(c) (909)	—	5,945
*95926	Chico (530)	45,965	39,970
*91708	Chino (909)	64,723	59,682
91709	Chino Hills (909)	42,071	37,868
93610	Chowchilla (559)	6,740	5,930
*91910	Chula Vista (619)	151,963	135,160
91702	Citrus(c) (626)	—	9,481
*95621	Citrus Heights(c) (916)	—	107,439
91711	Claremont (909)	33,507	32,610
94517	Clayton (925)	8,169	7,317
95422	Clearlake (707)	12,001	11,804
95425	Cloverdale (707)	5,505	4,924
*93612	Clovis (559)	63,246	50,323
92236	Coachella (760)	21,767	16,896
93210	Coalinga (559)	9,542	8,212
92324	Colton (909)	43,309	40,273
95932	Colusa (530)	5,408	4,934
90022	Commerce (323)/(562)	12,574	12,135
*90221	Compton (310)	91,700	90,454
*94520	Concord (925)	114,850	111,308
93212	Corcoran (559)	14,127	13,360
96021	Corning (530)	6,196	5,870
*91718	Corona (909)	100,208	75,943
*92199	Coronado (619)	25,701	26,540
*94925	Corte Madera (415)	8,195	8,272
*92628	Costa Mesa (714)/(949)	100,938	96,357
94931	Cotati (707)	6,251	5,714
94556	Country Club(c) (209)	—	9,325
*91722	Covina (626)	44,290	43,332
95531	Crescent City (707)	6,866	6,343
92325	Crestline(c) (909)	—	8,594
90201	Cudahy (323)	23,355	22,817
*90230	Culver City (230)/(310)/(323)	39,292	38,793
*95014	Cupertino (408)	42,831	39,967
90630	Cypress (714)	47,032	42,655
*94015	Daly City (415)/(650)	97,649	92,088
92629	Dana Point (949)	33,875	31,896
*94526	Danville (925)	38,395	31,306
*95616	Davis (530)	52,321	46,322
90250	Del Aire(c) (310)	—	8,040
*93215	Delano (661)	32,098	22,762
92014	Del Mar (858)	5,270	4,860
93953	Del Monte Forest(c) (831)	—	5,069
*92240	Desert Hot Springs (760)	14,819	11,668
91765	Diamond Bar (909)	54,138	53,672
93618	Dinuba (559)	14,562	12,743
94514	Discovery Bay(c) (925)	—	5,351
95620	Dixon (707)	13,047	10,417
*90241	Downey (562)	93,073	91,444
*91009	Duarte (626)	21,318	20,716
94568	Dublin (925)	25,231	23,229
93219	Earlimart(c) (661)	—	5,881
90220	East Compton(c) (310)	—	7,967
.....	East Foothills(c)	—	14,898
92343	East Hemet(c) (909)	—	17,611
90638	East La Mirada(c) (562)	—	9,367
90022	East Los Angeles(c) (323)/(562)	—	126,379
94303	East Palo Alto (650)	24,523	23,451
91117	East Pasadena(c)	—	5,910
93257	East Porterville(c) (559)	—	5,790
.....	East San Gabriel(c) (626)	—	12,736
93523	Edwards AFB(c) (661)	—	7,423
*92020	El Cajon (619)	92,057	88,918
*92244	El Centro (760)	37,369	31,405
94530	El Cerrito (510)	23,567	22,869
95762	El Dorado Hills(c) (916)	—	6,395
*95624	Elk Grove(c) (916)	—	17,483
*91734	El Monte (626)	110,026	106,162
*93446	El Paso de Robles (805)	20,187	18,583
93030	El Rio(c) (805)	—	6,419
90245	El Segundo (310)	15,607	15,223
*94802	El Sobrante(c) (510)	—	9,852
92630	El Toro(c) (949)	—	62,685
92709	El Toro Station(c) (949)	—	6,869
*94612	Emeryville (510)	6,356	5,740
*92024	Encinitas (760)	57,873	55,406
95320	Escalon (209)	5,280	4,437
*92025	Escondido (760)	116,184	108,648
*95501	Eureka (707)	26,202	27,025
93221	Exeter (559)	8,282	7,276
*94930	Fairfax (415)	6,824	6,931
94533	Fairfield (707)	85,610	78,650
95628	Fair Oaks(c) (Sacramento) (916)	—	26,867
96052	Fairview(c) (Trinity) (530)	—	9,045
*92028	Fallbrook(c) (760)	—	22,095
93223	Farmersville (559)	7,381	6,235
95018	Felton(c) (831)	—	5,350
*93015	Fillmore (805)	12,808	11,992
93622	Firebaugh (209)	5,589	4,429
90001	Florence-Graham(c) (323)	—	57,147
95828	Florin(c) (916)	—	24,330
*95630	Folsom (916)	41,103	29,802
*92334	Fontana (909)	104,124	87,535
95841	Foothill Farms(c) (916)	—	17,135
95437	Fort Bragg (707)	6,112	6,078
95540	Fortuna (707)	9,416	8,788
94404	Foster City (650)	29,698	28,176
*92728	Fountain Valley (714)	55,790	53,691
95019	Freedom(c) (831)	—	8,361
*94537	Fremont (510)	187,800	173,339
*93706	Fresno (559)	396,011	354,091
*92834	Fullerton (714)	120,188	114,144
95632	Galt (209)	15,647	8,889
*90247	Gardena (310)	53,104	51,481
95205	Garden Acres(c) (209)	—	8,547
*92842	Garden Grove (714)	149,208	142,965
92394	George AFB(c) (760)	—	5,085
*95020	Gilroy (408)	34,396	31,487
92509	Glen Avon(c) (909)	—	12,663
*91209	Glendale (323)/(626)/(818)	184,321	180,038
*91741	Glendora (626)	51,500	47,832
93561	Golden Hills(c)	—	5,423
93926	Gonzales (831)	5,451	4,660
92313	Grand Terrace (909)	12,132	10,946
*95945	Grass Valley (530)	9,566	9,048
93308	Greenacres(c) (661)	—	7,379
93927	Greenfield (Monterey) (831)	9,313	7,464
93433	Grover Beach (805)	11,744	11,602
93434	Guadalupe (805)	5,714	5,479
91745	Hacienda Heights(c) (626)	—	52,354
94019	Half Moon Bay (650)	10,389	8,886
*93230	Hanford (559)	36,213	30,463
90716	Hawaiian Gardens (323)	13,621	13,639
*90250	Hawthorne (213)/(310)/(323)	72,942	71,349
*94544	Hayward (510)	121,631	114,705
95448	Healdsburg (707)	9,674	9,469
*92546	Hemet (909)	51,350	36,366
94547	Hercules (510)	19,366	16,829
90254	Hermosa Beach (310)	18,522	18,219
*92340	Hesperia (760)	60,635	50,418
92346	Highland (909)	40,477	34,439
94010	Hillsborough (650)	11,307	10,667
*95023	Hollister (831)	25,070	19,318
92250	Holtville (760)	5,731	4,820
91720	Home Gardens(c) (909)	—	7,780
*92647	Huntington Beach (714)	190,751	181,519
90255	Huntington Park (323)	57,251	56,129
93234	Huron (559)	5,604	4,766
92251	Imperial (760)	6,731	4,113
*91932	Imperial Beach (619)	28,045	26,512
*92201	Indio (760)	43,741	36,850
*90301	Inglewood (213)/(310)/(323)	111,040	109,602
.....	Interlaken(c)	—	6,404
95640	Ione (209)	6,849	6,516
*92619	Irvine (714)/(949)	127,873	110,330
93117	Isla Vista(c) (805)	—	20,395
94914	Kentfield(c) (415)	—	6,030
93630	Kerman (559)	6,810	5,448
93930	King City (831)	8,547	7,634
93631	Kingsburg (559)	8,422	7,245
*91011	La Canada Flintridge (818)	19,738	19,378
*91224	La Crescenta-Montrose(c) (818)	—	16,968
90045	Ladera Heights(c) (310)	—	6,316
94549	Lafayette (925)	26,073	23,366
.....	Laguna(c)	—	9,828
*92652	Laguna Beach (949)	24,641	23,170
*92654	Laguna Hills (949)	29,414	22,719
*92607	Laguna Niguel (949)	51,701	44,723
*90631	La Habra (562)/(949)	53,704	51,263
90631	La Habra Heights (562)	6,429	6,226
92352	Lake Arrowhead(c) (909)	—	6,539
*92531	Lake Elsinore (909)	25,950	19,733
92630	Lake Forest (714)	73,117	56,065
92530	Lakeland Village(c) (909)	—	5,159
93535	Lake Los Angeles(c) (661)	—	7,977
92040	Lakeside(c) (619)	—	39,412
*90714	Lakewood (562)	75,462	73,553
*91941	La Mesa (619)	54,844	52,911
*90638	La Mirada (562)/(714)	43,871	40,452
93241	Lamont(c) (661)	—	11,517
*93539	Lancaster (661)	115,675	97,300
90623	La Palma (562)/(714)	16,092	15,392
*91747	La Puente (626)	38,462	36,955
92253	La Quinta (909)	17,987	11,215
95401	La Riviera(c) (916)	—	10,986
95403	Larkfield-Wikiup(c) (707)	—	6,779
*94939	Larkspur (415)	11,330	11,068
95330	Lathrop (209)	8,616	6,841
91750	La Verne (909)	31,996	30,843
*90260	Lawndale (310)	28,527	27,331
*91945	Lemon Grove (619)	25,297	23,984
93245	Lemoore (559)	16,394	13,622
90304	Lennox(c) (310)	—	22,757
95648	Lincoln (916)	8,788	7,248
95901	Linda(c) (530)	—	13,033
93247	Lindsay (559)	8,740	8,338
95062	Live Oak(c) (Santa Cruz) (831)	—	15,212
95953	Live Oak (Sutter) (530)	5,119	4,320
*94550	Livermore (925)	64,647	56,741
95334	Livingston (209)	10,015	7,317
*95240	Lodi (209)	54,585	51,874
92354	Loma Linda (909)	22,318	18,470
90717	Lomita (213)	19,803	19,442
*93436	Lompoc (805)	40,925	37,649
*90801	Long Beach (310)/(562)	421,904	429,321
95650	Loomis (916)	6,348	5,705
*90720	Los Alamitos (562)/(562)/(949)	12,492	11,788
*94022	Los Altos (650)	27,710	26,599

ZIP	Place		1996	1990
94022	Los Altos Hills	(650)	7,985	7,514
*90086	Los Angeles (213)/(310)/(323)/(818)		3,553,638	3,485,557
93635	Los Banos	(209)	19,009	14,519
*95030	Los Gatos	(408)	28,859	27,357
91709	Los Serranos(c)	(909)	—	7,099
94903	Lucas Valley-Marinwood(c)	(415)	—	5,982
90262	Lynwood (213)/(310)/(323)		62,916	61,945
93250	Mc Farland	(661)	7,133	7,005
95521	McKinleyville(c)	(707)	—	10,749
*93638	Madera	(559)	35,648	29,283
93637	Madera Acres(c)	(559)	—	5,245
95954	Magalia(c)	(530)	—	8,987
*90265	Malibu	(310)	12,349	11,730
*90266	Manhattan Beach	(310)	33,234	32,063
*95336	Manteca	(209)	45,500	40,773
92518	March AFB(c)	(909)	—	5,523
93933	Marina	(831)	23,645	26,512
*90291	Marina Del Rey(c)	(310)	—	7,431
94553	Martinez	(925)	33,459	31,810
95901	Marysville	(530)	12,141	12,324
90270	Maywood	(323)	28,200	27,893
93640	Mendota	(559)	7,317	6,821
*94025	Menlo Park	(650)	29,497	28,403
92359	Mentone(c)	(909)	—	5,675
*95340	Merced	(209)	58,099	56,155
94030	Millbrae	(650)	21,241	20,414
*94941	Mill Valley	(415)	12,928	13,029
*95035	Milpitas	(408)	58,626	50,690
91752	Mira Loma(c)	(909)	—	15,786
93641	Mira Monte(c)	(805)	—	7,744
*92690	Mission Viejo	(949)	84,689	72,820
*95350	Modesto	(209)	178,559	164,746
*91017	Monrovia	(626)	37,265	35,733
91763	Montclair	(909)	30,044	28,434
90640	Montebello	(323)	60,281	59,564
*93940	Monterey	(831)	27,722	31,954
*91754	Monterey Park (323)/(626)/(818)		61,912	60,738
*93021	Moorpark	(805)	28,843	25,494
*94556	Moraga	(925)	17,693	15,987
*92552	Moreno Valley	(909)	140,932	118,779
*95037	Morgan Hill	(408)	28,752	23,928
*93442	Morro Bay	(805)	9,955	9,664
*94041	Mountain View	(650)	70,619	67,365
*92564	Murrieta	(909)	23,033	18,557
92405	Muscoy(c)	(714)	—	7,541
*94558	Napa	(707)	65,030	61,865
*91950	National City	(619)	51,071	54,249
92363	Needles	(760)	6,431	5,191
94560	Newark	(510)	39,940	37,861
95360	Newman	(209)	5,691	4,158
*92658	Newport Beach	(949)	69,658	66,643
93444	Nipomo(c)	(805)	—	7,109
91760	Norco	(909)	25,576	23,302
95603	North Auburn(c)	(530)	—	10,301
94025	North Fair Oaks(c)	(650)	—	13,912
95660	North Highlands(c)	(916)	—	42,105
*90650	Norwalk	(562)	100,209	94,279
*94947	Novato	(415)	48,117	47,585
95361	Oakdale	(209)	14,646	11,978
*94617	Oakland	(510)	367,230	372,242
94561	Oakley(c)	(925)	—	18,374
93445	Oceano(c)	(805)	—	6,169
*92054	Oceanside	(760)	145,941	128,090
93308	Oildale(c)	(661)	—	26,553
*93023	Ojai	(805)	7,872	7,613
95961	Olivehurst(c)	(530)	—	9,738
*91761	Ontario	(909)	144,854	133,179
95060	Opal Cliffs(c)	(831)	—	5,940
*92863	Orange	(714)	119,890	110,658
93646	Orange Cove	(559)	7,177	5,604
95662	Orangevale(c)	(916)	—	26,266
94563	Orinda	(925)	18,578	16,642
95963	Orland	(530)	5,520	5,052
93647	Orosi(c)	(559)	—	5,486
*95965	Oroville	(530)	12,124	11,885
95965	Oroville East(c)	(530)	—	8,462
*93030	Oxnard	(805)	151,009	142,560
94044	Pacifica	(650)	40,023	37,670
93950	Pacific Grove	(831)	15,339	16,117
95968	Palermo(c)	(530)	—	5,260
*93590	Palmdale	(661)	106,540	70,262
*92260	Palm Desert	(760)	27,916	23,252
.....	Palm Desert Country(c)		—	5,626
*92262	Palm Springs	(760)	43,347	40,144
*94303	Palo Alto	(650)	58,304	55,900
90274	Palos Verdes Estates	(310)	13,721	13,512
*95969	Paradise	(530)	25,630	25,401
90723	Paramount	(562)	50,793	47,669
95823	Parkway-So. Sacramento(c)	(916)	—	31,903
93648	Parlier	(559)	9,887	7,938
*91109	Pasadena (323)/(626)/(818)		134,116	131,586
	Paso Robles. *See El Paso de Robles*			
95363	Patterson	(209)	9,593	8,626
92509	Pedley(c)		—	8,869
*92572	Perris	(909)	31,515	21,500
*94952	Petaluma	(707)	48,455	43,166
*90660	Pico Rivera	(562)	59,968	59,177
94620	Piedmont	(510)	10,536	10,602
94564	Pinole	(510)	18,900	17,460
*93449	Pismo Beach	(805)	8,127	7,669

ZIP	Place		1996	1990
94565	Pittsburg	(925)	50,813	47,607
*92871	Placentia	(714)	44,811	41,259
95667	Placerville	(530)	9,349	8,286
94523	Pleasant Hill	(925)	32,141	31,583
*94566	Pleasanton	(925)	57,275	50,570
*91769	Pomona	(909)	134,706	131,700
*93257	Porterville	(559)	34,518	29,521
*93041	Port Hueneme	(805)	20,193	20,322
*92064	Poway	(858)	47,274	43,396
93907	Prunedale(c)	(831)	—	7,393
*93551	Quartz Hill(c)	(661)	—	9,626
92065	Ramona(c)	(760)	—	13,040
*95670	Rancho Cordova(c)	(916)	—	48,731
*91729	Rancho Cucamonga	(909)	116,613	101,409
92270	Rancho Mirage	(760)	10,894	9,778
90275	Rancho Palos Verdes	(310)	42,340	41,667
91941	Rancho San Diego(c)	(619)	—	6,977
92688	Rancho Santa Margarita(c)	(949)	—	11,390
96080	Red Bluff	(530)	13,290	12,363
*96049	Redding	(530)	76,616	66,462
*92373	Redlands	(909)	66,693	62,667
*90277	Redondo Beach	(310)	62,367	60,167
*94063	Redwood City	(650)	71,140	66,072
93654	Reedley	(559)	18,451	15,791
*92377	Rialto	(909)	82,320	72,395
*94802	Richmond	(510)	91,018	86,019
*93556	Ridgecrest	(760)	30,627	28,295
95003	Rio Del Mar(c)	(831)	—	8,919
95673	Rio Linda(c)	(916)	—	9,481
95366	Ripon	(209)	8,736	7,455
95367	Riverbank	(209)	13,629	8,591
*92502	Riverside	(909)	255,069	226,546
*95677	Rocklin	(916)	27,214	18,806
94572	Rodeo(c)	(510)	—	7,589
*94928	Rohnert Park	(707)	39,477	36,326
90274	Rolling Hills Estates	(310)	7,955	7,789
93560	Rosamond(c)	(661)	—	7,430
95401	Roseland(c)	(707)	—	8,779
91770	Rosemead	(626)	52,700	51,638
95826	Rosemont(c)	(916)		22,851
*95678	Roseville	(916)	62,649	44,685
90720	Rossmoor(c)	(714)	—	9,893
91748	Rowland Heights(c)	(818)	—	42,647
92519	Rubidoux(c)	(909)	—	24,367
*95814	Sacramento	(916)	376,243	369,365
94574	Saint Helena	(707)	5,414	4,990
*93907	Salinas	(831)	111,757	108,777
*94960	San Anselmo	(415)	11,525	11,735
*92401	San Bernardino	(909)	183,474	170,036
94066	San Bruno	(650)	40,274	38,961
*93001	San Buenaventura (Ventura)	(805)	97,205	92,557
94070	San Carlos	(650)	27,675	26,382
*92674	San Clemente	(949)	45,415	41,100
*92138	San Diego (619)/(858)		1,171,121	1,110,623
92065	San Diego Country Estates(c)	(760)	—	6,874
91773	San Dimas	(909)	33,691	32,398
*91341	San Fernando	(818)	22,904	22,580
*94142	San Francisco	(415)	735,315	723,959
*91778	San Gabriel	(626)	37,697	37,120
93657	Sanger	(559)	18,248	16,839
*92581	San Jacinto	(909)	23,683	17,614
*95113	San Jose	(408)	838,744	782,224
*92690	San Juan Capistrano	(949)	29,029	26,183
*94577	San Leandro	(510)	69,976	68,223
94580	San Lorenzo(c)	(510)	—	19,987
*93401	San Luis Obispo	(805)	42,433	41,958
*92069	San Marcos	(760)	47,265	38,974
*91118	San Marino	(626)	12,949	12,959
*94402	San Mateo	(650)	90,161	85,619
94806	San Pablo	(510)	26,128	25,158
*94915	San Rafael	(415)	50,439	48,410
94583	San Ramon	(925)	39,868	35,303
*92702	Santa Ana (714)/(949)		302,419	293,827
*93102	Santa Barbara	(805)	86,154	85,571
*95050	Santa Clara	(408)	98,726	93,613
*91380	Santa Clarita	(661)	125,153	120,050
*95060	Santa Cruz	(831)	51,155	49,711
90670	Santa Fe Springs	(562)	15,238	15,520
*93454	Santa Maria	(805)	67,012	61,552
*90401	Santa Monica	(310)	88,471	86,905
*93060	Santa Paula	(805)	26,469	25,062
*95402	Santa Rosa	(707)	121,879	113,261
*92071	Santee	(619)	55,934	52,902
*95070	Saratoga	(408)	29,471	28,061
*94965	Sausalito	(415)	7,036	7,152
*95066	Scotts Valley	(831)	9,456	8,667
90740	Seal Beach	(714)	25,828	25,098
93955	Seaside	(831)	31,406	38,826
*95472	Sebastopol	(707)	7,331	7,008
93662	Selma	(559)	17,083	14,757
93263	Shafter	(661)	10,770	9,404
*96019	Shasta Lake	(916)	9,364	8,821
*91025	Sierra Madre	(626)	10,877	10,762
90806	Signal Hill	(562)	8,671	8,371
*93065	Simi Valley	(805)	106,974	100,218
92075	Solana Beach	(858)	13,399	12,956
93960	Soledad	(831)	9,550	13,426
95476	Sonoma	(707)	8,737	8,168
95073	Soquel(c)	(831)	—	9,188
91733	South El Monte	(626)	21,142	20,850

ZIP	Place	1996	1990
90280	South Gate. . . . . (323)/(562)	88,125	86,284
*96151	South Lake Tahoe . . . . (530)	23,301	21,586
95965	South Oroville(c) . . . . (530)	—	7,463
*91030	South Pasadena . . . (213)/(323)/(626)/(818)	24,091	23,936
*94080	South San Francisco . . . . . (650)	57,357	54,312
91770	South San Gabriel(c) . . . . . (626)	—	7,700
91744	South San Jose Hills(c) . . . (626)	—	17,814
90605	South Whittier(c) . . . . (562)	—	49,514
95991	South Yuba(c). . . . . (530)	—	8,816
*91977	Spring Valley(c) . . . . (619)	—	55,331
94309	Stanford(c). . . . . (650)	—	18,097
90680	Stanton . . . . (714)	32,614	30,491
*95208	Stockton . . . . (209)	232,660	210,943
94585	Suisun City. . . . . (707)	26,402	22,704
*92586	Sun City(c). . . . . (714)	—	14,930
*94086	Sunnyvale . . . . (408)	125,156	117,324
96130	Susanville . . . . (530)	13,089	12,130
93268	Taft. . . . . (661)	6,455	5,902
94941	Tamalpais-Homestead Valley(c) . . . . (415)	—	9,601
*93581	Tehachapi . . . . (661)	6,602	6,182
*92589	Temecula. . . . . (909)	39,315	27,099
91780	Temple City . . . . (626)	31,721	31,153
95965	Thermalito(c) . . . . (530)	—	5,646
*91359	Thousand Oaks. . . . . (805)	113,368	104,381
94920	Tiburon . . . . (415)	8,005	7,554
*90503	Torrance . . . . (310)	136,183	133,107
*95376	Tracy . . . . (209)	44,776	33,558
*96161	Truckee. . . . . (916)	9,994	8,848
*93274	Tulare . . . . (559)	39,927	33,249
*95380	Turlock . . . . (209)	48,994	42,224
*92781	Tustin . . . . (714)/(949)	62,222	50,689
92705	Tustin Foothills(c) . . . . (714)	—	24,358
*92277	Twentynine Palms . . . . (760)	14,157	11,821
92278	Twentynine Palms Base(c) . (760)	—	10,606
95060	Twin Lakes(c). . . . . (831)	—	5,379
95482	Ukiah . . . . (707)	14,687	14,632
94587	Union City . . . . (510)	58,294	53,762
*91785	Upland . . . . (909)	67,095	63,374
*95687	Vacaville . . . . (707)	81,355	71,476
91744	Valinda(c) . . . . (626)	—	18,735
*94590	Vallejo. . . . . (707)	109,593	109,199
92343	Valle Vista(c) . . . . (909)	—	8,751
93437	Vandenberg AFB(c). . . . . . (805)	—	9,846
93436	Vandenberg Village(c) . . . . (805)	—	5,971
	Ventura. *See San Buenaventura*		
*92393	Victorville. . . . . (760)	67,089	50,103
90043	View Park-Windsor Hills(c) . (310)	—	11,769
92667	Villa Park. . . . . (714)	6,646	6,299
.....	Vincent(c)	—	13,713
*93277	Visalia. . . . . (559)	87,787	75,659
*92083	Vista. . . . . (760)	78,494	71,861
*91788	Walnut. . . . . (909)	30,848	29,105
*94596	Walnut Creek . . . . (925)	62,786	60,569
90255	Walnut Park(c) . . . . (213)	—	14,722
93280	Wasco. . . . . (661)	18,307	12,412
95386	Waterford. . . . . (209)	6,703	4,771
*95076	Watsonville . . . . (831)	32,752	31,099
90044	West Athens(c) . . . . (310)	—	8,859
90502	West Carson(c). . . . . (323)	—	20,143
90247	West Compton(c) . . . . (310)	—	5,451
*91790	West Covina. . . . . (626)	101,526	96,226
90069	West Hollywood . . . . (310)/(323)	36,501	36,118
*91359	Westlake Village . . . . (805)	7,780	7,455
*92684	Westminster. . . . . (714)	82,425	78,293
90047	Westmont(c). . . . . (323)	—	31,044
91746	West Puente Valley(c) . . . . (626)	—	20,254
*95691	West Sacramento . . . . (916)	29,704	28,898
*90606	West Whittier-Los Nietos(c). (562)	—	24,164
*90605	Whittier . . . . (562)	78,740	77,671
92595	Wildomar(c) . . . . (909)	—	10,411
90222	Willowbrook(c) . . . . (323)	—	32,772
95988	Willows . . . . (530)	6,218	5,988
95492	Windsor. . . . . (707)	13,228	12,002
95694	Winters . . . . (707)	5,146	4,639
95388	Winton(c) . . . . (209)	—	7,559
92502	Woodcrest(c) . . . . (909)	—	7,796
93286	Woodlake. . . . . (559)	6,587	5,678
*95695	Woodland . . . . (530)	42,229	40,230
94062	Woodside. . . . . (650)	5,417	5,034
*92885	Yorba Linda . . . . (714)	58,124	52,422
96097	Yreka . . . . (530)	6,934	6,948
*95991	Yuba City. . . . . (530)	32,433	27,385
92399	Yucaipa. . . . . (909)	36,074	32,819
*92286	Yucca Valley . . . . (760)	18,723	16,539

Colorado

Area code (720) overlays area code (303). See introductory note.

ZIP	Place	1996	1990
*80840	Air Force Academy(c) . . . . (719)	—	9,062
81101	Alamosa . . . . (719)	7,739	7,579
80401	Applewood(c) . . . . (303)	—	11,069
*80004	Arvada . . . . (303)	96,340	89,261
*81611	Aspen . . . . (970)	5,245	5,049
*80017	Aurora. . . . . (303)	252,341	222,103
80908	Black Forest(c) . . . . (719)	—	8,143
*80302	Boulder . . . . (303)	90,928	85,127
80601	Brighton. . . . . (303)	16,116	14,203
*80020	Broomfield . . . . (303)	31,743	24,638
*81212	Canon City. . . . . (719)	14,804	12,687
80104	Castle Rock . . . . (303)	12,868	8,710
80120	Castlewood(c) . . . . (303)	—	24,392
80110	Cherry Hills Village . . . . . . (303)	6,332	5,245
81220	Cimarron Hills(c). . . . . (719)	—	11,160
81520	Clifton(c) . . . . (970)	—	12,671
*80903	Colorado Springs . . . . (719)	345,127	280,430
80120	Columbine(c) . . . . (303)	—	23,969
*80022	Commerce City . . . . (303)	17,540	16,466
81321	Cortez. . . . . (970)	8,781	7,284
*81625	Craig. . . . . (970)	8,504	8,091
*80202	Denver . . . . (303)	497,840	467,610
80022	Derby(c) . . . . (303)	—	6,043
*81301	Durango . . . . (970)	13,923	12,439
*80110	Englewood. . . . . (303)	31,575	29,396
80620	Evans . . . . (970)	7,160	5,876
*80439	Evergreen(c) . . . . (303)	—	7,582
80221	Federal Heights . . . . (303)	10,572	9,342
80913	Fort Carson(c) . . . . (719)	—	11,309
*80525	Fort Collins . . . . (970)	104,196	87,491
80621	Fort Lupton . . . . (970)	5,697	5,159
80701	Fort Morgan . . . . (970)	10,102	9,068
80817	Fountain . . . . (719)	11,823	10,754
81504	Fruitvale(c). . . . . (303)	—	5,222
81522	Gateway(c) . . . . (970)	—	7,510
*81601	Glenwood Springs. . . . . . . (970)	7,625	6,561
*80401	Golden . . . . (303)	15,021	13,127
*81501	Grand Junction . . . . (970)	34,540	32,893
*80631	Greeley . . . . (970)	68,593	60,454
*80111	Greenwood Village . . . . . . (303)	12,749	7,589
80501	Gunbarrel(c). . . . . (303)	—	9,388
*81230	Gunnison. . . . . (970)	5,129	4,636
80126	Highlands Ranch(c) . . . . . . (303)	—	10,181
80127	Ken Caryl(c) . . . . (303)	—	24,391
80026	Lafayette . . . . (303)	18,784	14,708
81050	La Junta . . . . (719)	7,998	7,678
*80226	Lakewood . . . . (303)	134,999	126,475
81052	Lamar. . . . . (719)	8,473	8,343
*80126	Littleton . . . . (303)	39,504	33,711
*80501	Longmont . . . . (303)	58,318	51,976
80027	Louisville . . . . (303)	17,780	12,363
*80538	Loveland . . . . (970)	44,923	37,357
*81401	Montrose . . . . (970)	11,003	8,854
80233	Northglenn . . . . (303)	29,214	27,195
80649	Orchard Mesa(c). . . . . (303)	—	5,977
*80134	Parker. . . . . (303)	11,802	5,450
*81003	Pueblo . . . . (719)	99,406	98,640
81503	Redlands(c) . . . . (970)	—	9,355
81650	Rifle . . . . (970)	5,411	4,858
81201	Salida . . . . (719)	5,029	4,737
80911	Security-Widefield(c) . . . . . (719)	—	23,822
80110	Sheridan . . . . (303)	5,492	4,976
80221	Sherrelwood(c) . . . . (303)	—	16,636
80122	Southglenn(c) . . . . (303)	—	43,087
*80477	Steamboat Springs . . . . . . (970)	6,768	6,695
80751	Sterling . . . . (970)	10,535	10,362
80906	Stratmoor(c). . . . . (719)	—	5,854
80229	Thornton . . . . (303)	67,217	55,031
81082	Trinidad . . . . (719)	8,831	8,580
80229	Welby(c) . . . . (303)	—	10,218
80030	Westminster. . . . . (303)	93,115	74,619
80221	Westminster East(c) . . . . . (303)	—	5,197
*80033	Wheat Ridge . . . . (303)	29,922	29,419
80550	Windsor. . . . . (970)	6,818	5,062
*80863	Woodland Park. . . . . (719)	6,179	4,610

Connecticut

See introductory note.

ZIP	Place	1996	1990
06401	Ansonia. . . . . (203)	17,865	18,403
06001	*Avon*. . . . . (860)	13,833	13,937
06403	*Beacon Falls* . . . . (203)	5,150	5,083
06037	*Berlin* . . . . (860)	17,197	16,787
06801	*Bethel*. . . . . (203)	17,767	17,541
06002	*Bloomfield* . . . . (860)	19,155	19,483
06405	*Branford* . . . . (203)	27,323	27,603
*06602	Bridgeport . . . . (203)	137,990	141,686
*06010	Bristol . . . . (860)	59,619	60,640
06804	*Brookfield* . . . . (203)	14,482	14,113
06234	*Brooklyn* . . . . (860)	6,906	6,681
06013	*Burlington* . . . . (860)	7,686	7,026
06019	*Canton* . . . . (860)	8,104	8,268
06040	Central Manchester(c) . . . . (860)	—	30,934
06410	*Cheshire* . . . . (203)	26,067	25,684
06413	*Clinton* . . . . (860)	13,022	12,767
06415	*Colchester*. . . . . (860)	12,620	10,980
06340	Conning Towers-Nautilus Park(c) . . . . (860)	—	10,013
06238	*Coventry* . . . . (860)	10,845	10,063
06416	*Cromwell*. . . . . (860)	12,447	12,286
*06810	Danbury . . . . (203)	65,506	65,585
06820	*Darien*. . . . . (203)	18,135	18,196
06418	Derby . . . . (203)	11,960	12,199
06422	*Durham*. . . . . (860)	6,346	5,732
06423	*East Haddam* . . . . (860)	7,304	6,676

ZIP	Place		1996	1990
06424	*East Hampton*	(860)	10,930	10,428
*06101	*East Hartford*	(860)	48,083	50,452
06512	*East Haven*	(203)	26,646	26,144
06333	*East Lyme*	(860)	16,026	15,340
06088	*East Windsor*	(860)	9,969	10,081
06612	*Easton*	(203)	6,577	6,303
06029	*Ellington*	(860)	11,521	11,197
*06082	*Enfield*	(860)	43,479	45,532
06426	*Essex*	(860)	6,095	5,904
*06430	*Fairfield*	(203)	53,522	53,418
*06032	*Farmington*	(860)	20,942	20,608
06033	Glastonbury Center(c)	(860)	—	7,082
06033	*Glastonbury*	(860)	28,500	27,901
06035	*Granby*	(860)	9,476	9,369
*06830	*Greenwich*	(203)	58,374	58,441
06351	*Griswold*	(860)	10,581	10,384
*06340	*Groton*	(860)	42,539	45,144
06340	Groton Town	(860)	9,657	9,837
06437	*Guilford*	(203)	19,986	19,848
06438	*Haddam*	(860)	7,111	6,769
*06514	*Hamden*	(203)	53,332	52,434
*06101	Hartford	(860)	133,086	139,739
06791	*Harwinton*	(860)	5,331	5,228
06082	Hazardville(c)	(860)	—	5,179
06248	*Hebron*	(860)	7,744	7,079
06037	Kensington(c)	(860)	—	8,306
06239	*Killingly*	(860)	16,052	15,889
06419	*Killingworth*	(860)	5,418	4,814
06249	*Lebanon*	(860)	6,337	6,041
06339	*Ledyard*	(860)	14,708	14,913
06759	*Litchfield*	(860)	8,593	8,365
06443	*Madison*	(203)	16,007	15,485
*06040	*Manchester*	(860)	51,666	51,618
06250	*Mansfield*	(860)	18,958	21,103
06447	*Marlborough*	(860)	5,667	5,535
*06450	Meriden	(203)	57,189	59,479
06762	*Middlebury*	(203)	6,017	6,145
06457	Middletown	(860)	43,243	42,762
06460	Milford	(203)	48,009	48,168
06468	*Monroe*	(203)	17,993	16,896
06353	*Montville*	(860)	16,990	16,673
06770	Naugatuck	(203)	30,319	30,625
*06050	New Britain	(860)	71,512	75,491
06840	*New Canaan*	(203)	17,931	17,864
06812	*New Fairfield*	(203)	13,381	12,911
06057	*New Hartford*	(860)	6,059	5,769
*06511	New Haven	(203)	124,665	130,474
*06101	*Newington*	(860)	28,379	29,208
06320	New London	(860)	25,038	28,540
06776	*New Milford*	(860)	25,236	23,629
06470	*Newtown*	(203)	22,516	20,779
06471	*North Branford*	(203)	13,757	12,996
06473	*North Haven*	(203)	22,088	22,247
*06856	Norwalk	(203)	77,977	78,331
06360	Norwich	(860)	35,869	37,391
06779	Oakville(c)	(860)	—	8,741
06371	*Old Lyme*	(860)	6,513	6,535
06475	*Old Saybrook*	(860)	9,673	9,552
06477	*Orange*	(203)	12,477	12,830
06478	*Oxford*	(203)	9,047	8,685
06379	Pawcatuck(c)	(860)	—	5,289
06374	*Plainfield*	(860)	14,482	14,363
06062	*Plainville*	(860)	16,910	17,392
06782	*Plymouth*	(860)	12,017	11,822
06480	*Portland*	(860)	8,772	8,418
06365	*Preston*	(860)	5,070	5,006
06712	*Prospect*	(203)	8,137	7,775
06260	Putnam(c)	(860)	—	6,835
06260	*Putnam*	(860)	8,930	9,031
06896	*Redding*	(203)	8,068	7,927
06877	Ridgefield Center(c)	(203)	—	6,363
06877	*Ridgefield*	(203)	21,679	20,919
06067	*Rocky Hill*	(860)	16,509	16,554
06483	*Seymour*	(203)	14,193	14,288
06484	Shelton	(203)	37,180	35,418
06082	Sherwood Manor(c)	(860)	—	6,357
06070	*Simsbury*	(860)	21,782	22,023
06071	*Somers*	(860)	9,358	9,108
06488	*Southbury*	(203)	16,370	15,818
06489	*Southington*	(860)	38,391	38,518
06074	*South Windsor*	(860)	22,500	22,090
06082	Southwood Acres(c)	(860)	—	8,963
06075	*Stafford*	(860)	11,497	11,091
*06904	Stamford	(203)	110,056	108,056
06378	*Stonington*	(860)	16,806	16,919
06268	Storrs(c)	(860)	—	12,198
06497	*Stratford*	(203)	49,096	49,389
06078	*Suffield*	(860)	11,216	11,427
06786	Terryville(c)	(860)	—	5,426
06787	*Thomaston*	(860)	7,273	6,947
06277	*Thompson*	(860)	8,975	8,668
06082	Thompsonville(c)	(860)	—	8,458
06084	*Tolland*	(860)	11,994	11,001
06790	Torrington	(860)	34,529	33,687
06611	*Trumbull*	(203)	33,291	32,016
06066	*Vernon*	(860)	29,414	29,841
06492	*Wallingford*	(203)	40,798	40,822
*06702	Waterbury	(203)	106,412	108,961
06385	*Waterford*	(860)	17,971	17,930
06795	*Watertown*	(860)	21,470	20,456
*06101	*West Hartford*	(860)	56,795	60,110
06516	West Haven	(203)	52,153	54,021
06498	*Westbrook*	(860)	5,524	5,414
06883	*Weston*	(203)	8,780	8,648
*06880	*Westport*	(203)	24,185	24,410
*06129	*Wethersfield*	(860)	25,179	25,651
06226	Willimantic(c)	(860)	—	14,746
06279	*Willington*	(860)	6,117	5,979
06897	*Wilton*	(203)	16,329	15,989
06094	*Winchester*	(860)	11,440	11,524
06280	*Windham*	(860)	21,598	22,039
06095	*Windsor*	(860)	27,663	27,817
06096	*Windsor Locks*	(860)	12,076	12,358
06098	Winsted(c)	(860)	—	8,254
06716	*Wolcott*	(203)	14,145	13,700
06525	*Woodbridge*	(203)	8,051	7,924
06798	*Woodbury*	(203)	8,508	8,131
06281	*Woodstock*	(860)	6,496	6,008

Delaware (302)

ZIP	Place	1996	1990
19713	Brookside(c)	—	15,307
19703	Claymont(c)	—	9,800
*19901	Dover	30,414	27,630
19809	Edgemoor(c)	—	5,853
19805	Elsmere	5,787	5,935
19963	Milford	6,557	6,032
*19711	Newark	27,870	26,463
19800	Pike Creek(c)	—	10,163
19973	Seaford	6,400	5,689
19977	Smyrna	5,502	5,231
19804	Stanton(c)	—	5,028
19803	Talleyville(c)	—	6,346
*19805	Wilmington	72,256	71,529
19720	Wilmington Manor(c)	—	8,568

District of Columbia (202)

ZIP	Place	1996	1990
*20090	Washington	543,213	606,900

Florida

Area code (786) overlays area code (305). See introductory note.

ZIP	Place		1996	1990
*32615	Alachua	(904)	5,274	4,547
*32714	Altamonte Springs	(407)	38,379	35,167
.....	Andover(c)		—	6,251
33572	Apollo Beach(c)	(813)	—	6,025
*32712	Apopka	(407)	18,380	13,611
*34266	Arcadia	(941)	6,390	6,488
32233	Atlantic Beach	(904)	12,821	11,636
33823	Auburndale	(941)	9,466	8,846
*33160	Aventura(c)	(305)	—	14,914
33825	Avon Park	(941)	8,101	8,078
32857	Azalea Park(c)	(407)	—	8,926
*33830	Bartow	(941)	15,003	14,716
.....	Bay Hill(c)		—	5,346
34667	Bayonet Point(c)	(727)	—	21,860
33505	Bayshore Gardens(c)	(941)	—	17,062
33589	Beacon Square(c)	(727)	—	6,265
34233	Bee Ridge(c)	(941)	—	6,406
32073	Bellair-Meadowbrook Terrace(c)	(904)	—	15,606
33430	Belle Glade	(561)	16,656	16,177
*34420	Belleview(c)	(352)	—	19,386
*34464	Beverly Hills(c)	(352)	—	6,163
*33509	Bloomingdale(c)	(813)	—	13,912
.....	Boca Del Mar(c)		—	17,754
*33431	Boca Raton	(561)	68,507	61,486
*34135	Bonita Springs(c)	(941)	—	13,600
*33436	Boynton Beach	(561)	50,742	46,284
*34206	Bradenton	(941)	47,219	43,769
*33509	Brandon(c)	(813)	—	57,985
32503	Brent(c)	(850)	—	21,624
33317	Broadview Park(c)	(954)	—	6,109
33313	Broadview-Pompano Park(c)	(954)	—	5,230
*34601	Brooksville	(352)	8,072	7,589
33311	Browardale(c)	(954)	—	6,257
33142	Brownsville(c)	(305)	—	15,607
34743	Buena Ventura Lakes(c)		—	14,148
32404	Callaway	(850)	13,060	12,253
32920	Cape Canaveral	(407)	8,377	8,014
*33909	Cape Coral	(941)	88,053	74,991
33055	Carol City(c)	(305)	—	53,331
*33688	Carrollwood(c)	(813)	—	7,195

ZIP	Place	1996	1990
*33601	Carrollwood Village(c) (813)	—	15,051
*32707	Casselberry (407)	24,487	20,736
33401	Century Village(c) (305)	—	8,363
*33758	Clearwater (727)	100,132	98,669
*34711	Clermont (352)	7,073	6,910
33440	Clewiston (941)	6,645	6,085
*32922	Cocoa (407)	18,279	17,722
*32931	Cocoa Beach (407)	12,635	12,123
32922	Cocoa West(c) (407)	—	6,160
*33063	Coconut Creek (954)	34,041	27,269
33064	Collier Manor-Cresthaven(c) (954)	—	7,322
33801	Combee Settlement(c) (941)	—	5,463
32809	Conway(c) (407)	—	13,159
33328	Cooper City (954)	28,637	21,335
33114	Coral Gables (305)	39,916	40,091
*33060	Coral Springs (954)	105,275	78,864
33157	Coral Terrace(c) (305)	—	23,255
*32536	Crestview (850)	11,649	9,886
33803	Crystal Lake(c) (941)	—	5,300
33157	Cutler(c) (305)	—	16,201
33157	Cutler Ridge(c) (305)	—	21,268
33884	Cypress Gardens(c) (941)	—	9,188
33919	Cypress Lake(c) (941)	—	10,491
*33525	Dade City (352)	5,867	5,633
33004	Dania (954)	14,456	13,183
33329	Davie (954)	58,501	47,143
*32114	Daytona Beach (904)	65,203	61,991
32713	De Bary(c) (407)	—	7,176
*33441	Deerfield Beach (954)	50,123	46,997
*32433	DeFuniak Springs (850)	5,467	5,200
*32720	De Land (904)	18,607	16,622
*33444	Delray Beach (561)	50,720	47,184
33617	Del Rio(c) (813)	—	8,248
*32738	Deltona(c) (407)	—	50,828
*32541	Destin (850)	10,555	8,090
.....	Doctor Phillips(c) (407)	—	7,963
*34698	Dunedin (727)	34,797	34,427
33610	East Lake-Orient Park(c) (813)	—	6,171
33940	East Naples(c) (941)	—	22,951
*32132	Edgewater (904)	17,445	15,351
32542	Eglin AFB(c) (850)	—	8,347
33614	Egypt Lake(c) (813)	—	14,580
34680	Elfers(c) (727)	—	12,356
*34223	Englewood(c) (941)	—	15,025
32534	Ensley(c) (850)	—	16,362
*32726	Eustis (352)	14,422	12,856
32804	Fairview Shores(c) (305)	—	13,192
*32034	Fernandina Beach (904)	9,941	8,765
32730	Fern Park(c) (407)	—	8,294
32514	Ferry Pass(c) (850)	—	26,301
33034	Florida City (305)	6,820	5,978
32960	Florida Ridge(c) (561)	—	12,218
32714	Forest City(c) (407)	—	10,638
.....	Forest Island Park(c)	—	5,988
*33310	Fort Lauderdale (954)	151,805	149,238
33841	Fort Meade (941)	5,246	5,151
*33902	Fort Myers (941)	45,917	44,947
*33931	Fort Myers Beach(c) (941)	—	9,284
*33922	Fort Myers Shores(c) (941)	—	5,460
*34981	Fort Pierce (561)	36,876	36,830
33452	Fort Pierce North(c) (561)	—	5,833
34982	Fort Pierce South(c) (561)	—	5,320
*32548	Fort Walton Beach (850)	21,933	21,407
*32043	Fruit Cove(c) (904)	—	5,904
34230	Fruitville(c) (941)	—	9,808
*32602	Gainesville (352)	87,295	85,075
33801	Gibsonia(c) (941)	—	5,168
33534	Gibsonton(c) (813)	—	7,706
32960	Gifford(c) (561)	—	6,278
33138	Gladeview(c) (954)	—	15,637
33143	Glenvar Heights(c) (305)	—	14,823
34116	Golden Gate(c) (941)	—	14,148
33055	Golden Glades(c) (305)	—	25,474
32733	Goldenrod(c) (407)	—	12,362
32560	Gonzalez(c) (850)	—	7,669
33170	Goulds(c) (305)	—	7,284
.....	Greater Northdale(c)	—	16,318
33454	Greenacres (561)	27,315	18,683
32043	Green Cove Springs (904)	5,156	4,497
*32561	Gulf Breeze (850)	5,894	5,530
33581	Gulf Gate Estates(c) (941)	—	11,622
33737	Gulfport (727)	11,539	11,709
*33844	Haines City (941)	12,352	11,683
*33009	Hallandale (305)/(954)	31,163	30,997
.....	Hammocks(c)	—	10,897
.....	Hamptons at Boca Raton(c)	—	11,686
*33010	Hialeah (305)	204,684	188,008
33016	Hialeah Gardens (305)	14,301	7,727
.....	Highpoint(c)	—	13,818
*33455	Hobe Sound(c) (561)	—	11,507
*34689	Holiday(c) (727)	—	19,360
32125	Holly Hill (904)	11,512	11,141
*33022	Hollywood (954)	127,894	121,720
*33030	Homestead (305)	23,005	26,694
33039	Homestead AFB(c) (305)	—	5,153
34447	Homosassa Springs(c) (352)	—	6,271
*34674	Hudson(c) (727)	—	7,344
*34142	Immokalee(c) (941)	—	14,120
32937	Indian Harbour Beach (407)	7,530	6,933
*34450	Inverness (352)	6,786	5,797
33880	Inwood(c) (941)	—	6,824
.....	Iona(c) (941)	—	9,565
33162	Ives Estates(c) (305)	—	13,531
*32203	Jacksonville (904)	679,792	635,230
*32250	Jacksonville Beach (904)	19,906	17,839
33880	Jan Phyl Village(c) (941)	—	5,308
33568	Jasmine Estates(c) (727)	—	17,136
*34957	Jensen Beach(c) (561)	—	9,884
*33458	Jupiter (561)	27,586	24,907
33183	Kendale Lakes(c) (305)	—	48,524
33256	Kendall(c) (305)	—	87,271
.....	Kendall Lakes West(c) (305)	—	6,038
33149	Key Biscayne (305)	9,896	8,854
33037	Key Largo(c) (305)	—	11,336
*33040	Key West (305)	25,339	24,832
*33573	Kings Point(c) (305)	—	12,422
*34744	Kissimmee (407)	36,510	30,337
*32159	Lady Lake (352)	12,315	8,071
*32055	Lake City (904)	10,469	9,626
*33804	Lakeland (941)	73,157	70,576
33801	Lakeland Highlands(c) (941)	—	9,972
32569	Lake Lorraine(c) (850)	—	6,779
33054	Lake Lucerne(c) (305)	—	9,478
33612	Lake Magdalene(c) (813)	—	15,973
*32746	Lake Mary (407)	7,988	5,929
33403	Lake Park (561)	6,735	6,704
.....	Lakes by the Bay(c)	—	5,615
32073	Lakeside(c) (904)	—	29,137
*33853	Lake Wales (941)	9,930	9,670
34951	Lakewood Park(c) (561)	—	7,211
*33461	Lake Worth (561)	28,491	28,564
34639	Land O'Lakes(c) (813)	—	7,892
33465	Lantana (561)	8,470	8,392
*33770	Largo (727)	65,793	65,910
33313	Lauderdale Lakes (954)	28,143	27,341
33313	Lauderhill (954)	50,522	49,015
34272	Laurel(c) (941)	—	8,245
33714	Lealman(c) (727)	—	21,748
*34748	Leesburg (352)	16,416	14,783
*33936	Lehigh Acres(c) (941)	—	13,611
33033	Leisure City(c) (305)	—	19,379
33074	Lighthouse Point (954)	10,639	10,378
33177	Lindgren Acres(c) (305)	—	22,290
*32060	Live Oak (904)	6,890	6,332
32860	Lockhart(c) (407)	—	11,636
34228	Longboat Key (941)	6,251	5,937
*32750	Longwood (407)	13,707	13,316
*33549	Lutz(c) (813)	—	10,552
32444	Lynn Haven (850)	11,722	9,298
.....	McGregor(c)	—	6,504
*32751	Maitland (407)	8,834	8,932
33550	Mango(c) (813)	—	8,700
33050	Marathon(c) (305)	—	8,857
*33937	Marco(c) (941)	—	9,493
33093	Margate (954)	50,575	42,985
*32446	Marianna (850)	6,172	6,292
*32901	Melbourne (407)	67,631	60,034
32666	Melrose Park(c) (954)	—	6,477
33561	Memphis(c) (941)	—	6,760
*32953	Merritt Island(c) (407)	—	32,886
*33101	Miami (305)	365,127	358,648
*33152	Miami Beach (305)	94,540	92,639
33023	Miami Gardens-Utopia-Carver(c) (954)	—	7,448
33014	Miami Lakes(c) (305)	—	12,750
33153	Miami Shores (305)	9,835	10,084
33166	Miami Springs (305)	13,149	13,268
32976	Micco(c) (561)	—	8,757
*32068	Middleburg(c) (904)	—	6,223
*32570	Milton (850)	7,635	7,216
32754	Mims(c) (407)	—	9,412
33023	Miramar (954)	50,956	40,663
*32757	Mount Dora (352)	8,766	7,316
32526	Myrtle Grove(c) (850)	—	17,402
*34102	Naples (941)	19,777	19,505
34102	Naples Park(c) (941)	—	8,002
33092	Naranja(c) (305)	—	5,790
32266	Neptune Beach (904)	7,086	6,816
*34653	New Port Richey (727)	14,797	14,044
33552	New Port Richey East(c) (727)	—	9,683
*32168	New Smyrna Beach (904)	17,995	16,549
*32578	Niceville (850)	11,955	10,509
33269	Norland(c) (305)	—	22,109
33308	North Andrews Gardens(c) (954)	—	9,002
33141	North Bay Village (305)	5,333	5,383
33918	North Fort Myers(c) (941)	—	30,027
33068	North Lauderdale (954)	28,277	26,473
33261	North Miami (305)	50,757	50,001
33160	North Miami Beach (305)	34,841	35,361
33940	North Naples(c) (941)	—	13,422
33408	North Palm Beach (561)	11,748	11,538
34287	North Port (941)	15,233	11,973
34234	North Sarasota(c) (941)	—	6,702
33307	Oakland Park (305)	28,135	26,326
33860	Oak Ridge(c) (407)	—	15,388
*34478	Ocala (352)	44,975	42,045
32548	Ocean City(c) (850)	—	5,422
32761	Ocoee (407)	18,942	12,778
33163	Ojus(c) (305)	—	15,519
34677	Oldsmar (813)	8,884	8,361

ZIP	Place		1996	1990
33265	Olympia Heights(c)	(305)	—	37,792
*33054	Opa-Locka	(305)	15,081	15,283
33054	Opa-Locka North(c)	(305)	—	6,568
*32763	Orange City	(904)	5,967	5,347
*32073	Orange Park	(904)	9,861	9,488
*32802	Orlando	(407)	173,902	164,674
32861	Orlo Vista(c)	(407)	—	5,990
*32174	Ormond Beach	(904)	32,266	29,721
32074	Ormond By-The-Sea(c)	(904)	—	8,157
*32765	Oviedo	(407)	20,073	11,114
32571	Pace(c)	(850)	—	6,277
.....	Page Park-Pine Manor(c)		—	5,116
33476	Pahokee	(561)	6,993	6,822
*32177	Palatka	(904)	10,857	10,447
*32909	Palm Bay	(407)	74,982	62,543
33480	Palm Beach	(561)	9,637	9,814
33403	Palm Beach Gardens	(561)	32,425	24,139
*32136	Palm Coast(c)	(904)	—	14,287
*34221	Palmetto	(941)	10,052	9,268
33157	Palmetto Estates(c)	(305)	—	12,293
*34683	Palm Harbor(c)	(727)	—	50,256
*33601	Palm River-Clair Mel(c)	(813)	—	13,691
33460	Palm Springs	(561)	9,761	9,763
33012	Palm Springs North(c)	(305)	—	5,300
32082	Palm Valley(c)	(904)	—	9,960
*32401	Panama City	(850)	35,986	34,396
32407	Panama City Beach	(850)	5,214	4,051
33060	Parkland	(954)	10,799	3,773
33029	Pembroke Pines	(954)	101,439	65,566
*32502	Pensacola	(850)	59,162	59,198
33257	Perrine(c)	(305)	—	15,576
*32347	Perry	(850)	7,340	7,151
32859	Pine Castle(c)	(407)	—	8,276
32858	Pine Hills(c)	(407)	—	35,322
.....	Pine Island Ridge(c)	(954)	—	5,244
*33781	Pinellas Park	(727)	43,980	43,571
33168	Pinewood(c)	(305)	—	15,518
33318	Plantation	(954)	78,674	66,814
*33566	Plant City	(813)	25,919	22,754
*33060	Pompano Beach	(954)	74,583	72,411
33064	Pompano Beach Highlands(c)	(954)	—	17,915
*33952	Port Charlotte(c)	(941)	—	41,535
32129	Port Orange	(904)	41,387	35,399
32927	Port St. John(c)	(407)	—	8,933
*34985	Port St. Lucie	(561)	75,532	55,761
34992	Port Salerno(c)	(561)	—	7,786
33032	Princeton(c)	(305)	—	7,073
*33950	Punta Gorda	(941)	12,552	10,637
*32351	Quincy	(850)	7,698	7,452
33156	Richmond Heights(c)	(305)	—	8,583
33312	Riverland(c)	(954)	—	5,376
33569	Riverview(c)	(813)	—	6,478
33419	Riviera Beach	(561)	28,627	27,646
*32955	Rockledge	(407)	18,899	16,023
33411	Royal Palm Beach	(561)	17,896	15,532
33570	Ruskin(c)	(813)	—	6,046
34695	Safety Harbor	(727)	15,924	15,120
*32084	Saint Augustine	(904)	12,167	11,695
*34769	Saint Cloud	(407)	14,489	12,684
*33733	Saint Petersburg	(727)	235,988	240,318
33736	Saint Petersburg Beach	(727)	9,756	9,200
33912	San Carlos Park(c)	(941)	—	11,785
33432	Sandalfoot Cove(c)	(305)	—	14,214
*32771	Sanford	(407)	35,559	32,387
33957	Sanibel	(941)	5,584	5,468
*34230	Sarasota	(941)	50,891	50,897
33577	Sarasota Springs(c)	(941)	—	16,088
32937	Satellite Beach	(407)	10,093	9,889
33055	Scott Lake(c)	(305)	—	14,588
*32958	Sebastian	(561)	13,014	10,248
*33870	Sebring	(941)	8,849	8,841
*33584	Seffner(c)	(813)	—	5,371
*33770	Seminole	(813)	9,715	9,251
*34242	Siesta Key(c)	(941)	—	7,772
34472	Silver Springs Shores(c)	(352)	—	6,421
32809	Sky Lake(c)	(407)	—	6,202
32703	South Apopka(c)	(407)	—	6,360
33493	South Bay	(561)	5,043	3,558
33505	South Bradenton(c)	(941)	—	20,398
32121	South Daytona	(904)	13,231	12,488
34277	Southgate(c)	(941)	—	7,324
34233	South Gate Ridge(c)	(941)	—	5,924
33243	South Miami	(305)	10,454	10,404
33157	South Miami Heights(c)	(305)	—	30,030
33707	South Pasadena	(727)	5,576	5,644
32937	South Patrick Shores(c)	(407)	—	10,249
34230	South Sarasota(c)	(941)	—	5,298
33595	South Venice(c)	(941)	—	11,951
32401	Springfield	(904)	9,312	8,719
*34601	Spring Hill(c)	(352)	—	31,117
32091	Starke	(904)	5,181	5,226
*34994	Stuart	(561)	12,537	11,936
*33573	Sun City Center(c)	(813)	—	8,326
33160	Sunny Isles(c)	(305)	—	11,772
*33322	Sunrise	(954)	77,592	65,683
33283	Sunset(c)	(305)	—	15,810
33144	Sweetwater	(305)	13,925	13,909
*32301	Tallahassee	(850)	136,812	124,773
33320	Tamarac	(954)	51,081	44,822
33144	Tamiami(c)	(305)	—	33,845

ZIP	Place		1996	1990
*33602	Tampa	(813)	285,206	280,015
*34689	Tarpon Springs	(727)	18,660	17,874
32778	Tavares	(352)	8,261	7,383
*33601	Temple Terrace	(813)	17,796	16,444
*32780	Titusville	(407)	41,543	39,394
32601	Town 'n' Country(c)	(813)	—	60,946
33740	Treasure Island	(727)	7,061	7,266
32867	Union Park(c)	(407)	—	6,890
33620	University West(c)	(813)	—	23,760
32401	Upper Grand Lagoon(c)	(850)	—	7,855
32580	Valparaiso	(850)	6,646	6,316
*34285	Venice	(941)	17,707	17,052
33595	Venice Gardens(c)	(941)	—	7,701
*32960	Vero Beach	(561)	16,458	17,350
32960	Vero Beach South(c)	(561)	—	16,973
.....	Villages of Oriole(c)	(561)	—	5,698
33901	Villas(c)	(941)	—	9,898
32507	Warrington(c)	(850)	—	16,040
33314	Washington Park(c)	(954)	—	6,930
32703	Wekiva Springs(c)	(407)	—	23,026
33414	Wellington(c)	(561)	—	20,670
33155	Westchester(c)	(305)	—	29,883
.....	Westgate-Belvedere Homes(c)		—	6,880
33138	West Little River(c)	(305)	—	33,575
32912	West Melbourne	(407)	9,144	8,398
33144	West Miami	(305)	5,621	5,727
*33406	West Palm Beach	(561)	79,305	67,764
.....	West Park(c)		—	10,347
32505	West Pensacola(c)	(850)	—	22,107
33168	Westview(c)	(305)	—	9,668
33165	Westwood Lakes(c)	(305)	—	11,522
.....	Whiskey Creek(c)		—	5,061
33305	Wilton Manors	(954)	12,091	11,804
33803	Winston(c)	(813)	—	9,118
*34787	Winter Garden	(407)	11,312	9,863
*33880	Winter Haven	(941)	25,484	24,725
*32789	Winter Park	(407)	23,247	24,260
*32707	Winter Springs	(407)	26,820	22,151
32547	Wright(c)	(904)	—	18,945
*32097	Yulee(c)	(904)	—	6,915
*33540	Zephyrhills	(813)	8,991	8,220

Georgia

Area code (678) overlays area code (770). See introductory note.

ZIP	Place		1996	1990
*30101	Acworth	(770)	6,927	4,519
31620	Adel	(912)	5,141	5,093
*31706	Albany	(912)	78,591	78,804
*30004	Alpharetta	(770)	20,477	13,002
31709	Americus	(912)	16,606	16,516
*30603	Athens[1]	(706)	89,405	45,734
*30301	Atlanta	(404)	401,907	393,929
30011	Auburn	(770)	5,108	3,139
*30903	Augusta	(706)	41,783	44,639
*31717	Bainbridge	(912)	10,898	10,803
30032	Belvedere Park(c)	(404)	—	18,089
31723	Blakely	(912)	5,754	5,595
*31520	Brunswick	(912)	15,525	16,433
*30518	Buford	(404)	9,880	8,771
31728	Cairo	(912)	9,312	9,035
*30701	Calhoun	(706)	7,948	7,135
31730	Camilla	(912)	5,303	5,124
30032	Candler-McAfee(c)	(404)	—	29,491
*30114	Canton	(770)	7,880	4,817
*30117	Carrollton	(770)	16,538	16,029
*30120	Cartersville	(770)	12,988	12,037
30125	Cedartown	(770)	7,733	7,978
30366	Chamblee	(404)	7,693	7,668
30021	Clarkston	(404)	5,859	5,385
30337	College Park	(404)	20,300	20,645
*31908	Columbus	(706)	182,828	178,683
30288	Conley(c)	(404)	—	5,528
*30013	Conyers	(404)	7,551	7,380
*31015	Cordele	(912)	10,763	10,836
.....	Country Club Estates(c)		—	7,500
*30014	Covington	(770)	9,906	9,860
*30720	Dalton	(706)	23,057	22,218
31742	Dawson	(912)	5,625	5,295
*30030	Decatur (DeKalb)	(404)	17,805	17,304
31520	Dock Junction(c)	(912)	—	7,094
30362	Doraville	(404)	8,299	7,626
*31533	Douglas	(912)	10,981	10,464
*30134	Douglasville	(404)	14,564	11,635
30333	Druid Hills(c)	(404)	—	12,174
*31021	Dublin	(912)	17,393	16,312
30096	Duluth	(404)	15,015	9,029
30356	Dunwoody(c)	(404)	—	26,302
31023	Eastman	(912)	5,025	5,241
30364	East Point	(404)	34,155	34,595
31024	Eatonton	(706)	6,900	6,479
30809	Evans(c)	(706)	—	13,713
30060	Fair Oaks(c)	(404)	—	6,996
30535	Fairview(c)	(706)	—	6,444
*30214	Fayetteville	(404)	8,531	5,827
31750	Fitzgerald	(912)	9,049	8,901
*30297	Forest Park	(404)	17,060	16,958
31905	Fort Benning South(c)	(706)	—	14,617
30905	Fort Gordon(c)	(706)	—	9,140
30742	Fort Oglethorpe	(706)	6,260	5,880

ZIP	Place		1996	1990
*31313	Fort Stewart(c)	(912)	—	13,774
31030	Fort Valley	(912)	8,191	8,198
30605	Gaines School(c)	(706)	—	11,354
*30501	Gainesville	(770)	19,069	17,885
31418	Garden City	(912)	7,591	7,410
31754	Georgetown(c)	(912)	—	5,554
30316	Gresham Park(c)	(404)	—	9,000
*30223	Griffin	(770)	21,506	21,347
30354	Hapeville	(404)	5,354	5,483
*31313	Hinesville	(912)	26,359	21,596
*31545	Jesup	(912)	9,471	8,958
*30144	Kennesaw	(404)	12,818	8,936
31548	Kingsland	(912)	9,830	5,411
30728	La Fayette	(706)	6,707	6,655
*30240	La Grange	(706)	25,452	25,574
30741	Lakeview(c)	(706)	—	5,237
*30045	Lawrenceville	(404)	19,232	17,250
*30047	Lilburn	(404)	11,134	9,301
30122	Lithia Springs(c)	(404)	—	11,403
30126	Mableton(c)	(404)	—	25,725
*31201	Macon	(912)	113,352	107,365
*30060	Marietta	(404)	50,937	44,129
30917	Martinez(c)	(706)	—	33,731
31061	Milledgeville	(912)	17,982	17,727
*30655	Monroe	(770)	13,982	9,759
*30260	Morrow	(404)	5,162	5,168
*31768	Moultrie	(912)	15,444	14,865
30087	Mountain Park(c)	(404)	—	11,025
31639	Nashville	(912)	5,200	4,782
*30263	Newnan	(770)	13,355	12,497
*30071	Norcross	(404)	6,360	5,947
30319	North Atlanta(c)	(404)	—	27,812
30033	North Decatur(c)	(404)	—	13,936
30033	North Druid Hills(c)	(404)	—	14,170
30032	Panthersville(c)	(404)	—	9,874
30269	Peachtree City	(404)	28,156	19,027
31069	Perry	(912)	9,657	9,452
31322	Pooler	(912)	5,174	4,649
30127	Powder Springs	(404)	10,092	6,862
31643	Quitman	(912)	5,150	5,292
30074	Redan(c)	(404)	—	24,376
31324	Richmond Hill	(912)	5,858	2,934
*30274	Riverdale	(404)	10,020	9,455
*30161	Rome	(706)	28,800	30,326
*30077	Roswell	(404)	55,462	47,986
31558	Saint Marys	(912)	12,446	8,204
31522	Saint Simons Island(c)	(912)	—	12,026
31082	Sandersville	(912)	6,616	6,290
30358	Sandy Springs(c)	(404)	—	67,842
*31402	Savannah	(912)	136,262	137,812
30079	Scottdale(c)	(404)	—	8,636
*30080	Smyrna	(404)	34,855	32,453
*30078	Snellville	(404)	15,418	12,084
30901	South Augusta(c)	(706)	—	55,998
*30458	Statesboro	(912)	21,309	20,770
30281	Stockbridge	(404)	5,251	3,359
*30086	Stone Mountain	(404)	7,053	6,494
30518	Sugar Hill	(404)	7,783	4,557
30747	Summerville	(706)	5,222	5,025
30401	Swainsboro	(912)	7,196	7,361
31791	Sylvester	(912)	6,395	6,023
30286	Thomaston	(706)	9,062	9,127
*31792	Thomasville	(912)	17,565	17,554
30824	Thomson	(706)	6,723	6,862
*31794	Tifton	(912)	14,205	14,215
*30577	Toccoa	(706)	8,780	8,720
*30084	Tucker(c)	(404)	—	25,781
30291	Union City	(404)	10,358	9,347
*31603	Valdosta	(912)	41,816	40,038
*30474	Vidalia	(912)	11,697	11,118
30180	Villa Rica	(770)	6,921	6,542
30339	Vinings(c)	(404)	—	7,417
*31088	Warner Robins	(912)	45,559	43,861
*31501	Waycross	(912)	15,821	16,410
30830	Waynesboro	(706)	5,549	5,669
30901	West Augusta(c)	(706)	—	27,637
31410	Wilmington Island(c)	(912)	—	11,230
30680	Winder	(770)	8,441	7,373
*30188	Woodstock	(770)	5,730	4,361

(1) Athens merged with Clarke County in 1991. The 1996 population is for all of Clarke County except for Winterville and Bogart, which are part of the county but are also separate incorporated places.

Hawaii (808)

See introductory note.

ZIP	Place	1996	1990
96701	Aiea(c)	—	8,906
96818	Aliamanu(c)	—	8,835
96706	Ewa Beach(c)	—	14,315
.....	Halawa(c)	—	13,408
96744	Heeia(c)	—	5,010
96853	Hickam Housing(c)	—	6,553
*96720	Hilo(c)	—	37,808
*96820	Honolulu(c)	423,475	377,059
*96732	Kahului(c)	—	16,889
96734	Kailua(c)	—	9,126
96863	Kailua(c)	—	36,818
96744	Kaneohe(c)	—	35,448
.....	Kaneohe Station(c)	—	11,662
96746	Kapaa(c)	—	8,149
96753	Kihei(c)	—	11,107
*96761	Lahaina(c)	—	9,073
96762	Laie(c)	—	5,577
96766	Lihue(c)	—	5,536
96792	Maili(c)	—	6,059
96792	Makaha(c)	—	7,990
96706	Makakilo(c)	—	9,828
96768	Makawao(c)	—	5,405
96789	Mililani Town(c)	—	29,359
96792	Nanakuli(c)	—	9,575
96782	Pearl City(c)	—	30,993
96788	Pukalani(c)	—	5,879
96786	Schofield Barracks(c)	—	19,597
.....	Village Park(c)	—	7,407
96786	Wahiawa(c)	—	17,386
96792	Waianae(c)	—	8,758
96793	Wailuku(c)	—	10,688
.....	Waimalu(c)	—	29,967
96796	Waimea(c)	—	5,972
96797	Waipahu(c)	—	31,435
96797	Waipio(c)	—	11,812
96786	Waipio Acres(c)	—	5,304

Idaho (208)

ZIP	Place	1996	1990
83401	Ammon	5,849	5,002
83221	Blackfoot	10,406	9,646
*83707	Boise City	152,737	126,685
83318	Burley	9,498	8,702
*83605	Caldwell	21,089	18,400
83202	Chubbuck	8,876	7,794
*83814	Coeur d'Alene	31,076	24,561
83616	Eagle	6,577	3,327
83617	Emmett	5,242	4,601
83714	Garden City	8,714	6,369
83333	Hailey	5,423	3,575
83835	Hayden	7,951	4,888
*83402	Idaho Falls	48,079	43,973
83338	Jerome	7,292	6,529
83501	Lewiston	30,271	28,082
*83642	Meridian	20,627	9,596
83843	Moscow	20,101	18,398
83647	Mountain Home	8,988	7,913
83648	Mountain Home AFB(c)	—	5,936
*83651	Nampa	37,558	28,365
83661	Payette	6,647	5,672
*83201	Pocatello	51,344	46,117
*83854	Post Falls	14,303	7,349
83440	Rexburg	14,204	14,298
83350	Rupert	5,669	5,455
83864	Sandpoint	6,748	5,203
*83301	Twin Falls	31,989	27,634
83672	Weiser	5,167	4,571

Illinois

Area code (224) overlays area code (847). See introductory note.

ZIP	Place		1996	1990
60101	Addison	(630)	33,580	32,053
60102	Algonquin	(847)	18,019	11,693
60803	Alsip	(708)	19,171	18,227
62002	Alton	(618)	31,562	33,064
60002	Antioch	(847)	7,398	6,105
*60005	Arlington Heights	(847)	76,740	75,463
*60505	Aurora	(630)	116,405	99,672
*60010	Barrington	(847)	9,885	9,538
60103	Bartlett	(630)	32,943	19,395
61607	Bartonville	(309)	6,487	6,555
60510	Batavia	(630)	21,591	17,076
60085	Beach Park	(847)	10,167	9,492
62618	Beardstown	(217)	5,089	5,270
*62220	Belleville	(618)	41,608	42,806
60104	Bellwood	(708)	20,122	20,241
61008	Belvidere	(815)	18,712	15,962
60106	Bensenville	(630)	18,023	17,767
62812	Benton	(618)	7,299	7,216
60163	Berkeley	(708)	5,034	5,137
60402	Berwyn	(708)	43,735	45,426
62010	Bethalto	(618)	9,750	9,507
60108	Bloomingdale	(630)	19,363	16,614
*61701	Bloomington	(309)	57,365	51,889
60406	Blue Island	(708)	20,661	21,203
*60440	Bolingbrook	(630)	51,312	40,843
60538	Boulder Hill(c)	(630)	—	8,894
60914	Bourbonnais	(815)	15,262	13,929
60915	Bradley	(815)	12,368	10,954
60455	Bridgeview	(708)	15,194	14,402
60153	Broadview	(708)	8,362	8,538
60513	Brookfield	(708)	18,396	18,876
60089	Buffalo Grove	(847)	41,169	36,417
60459	Burbank	(708)	27,714	27,600
60521	Burr Ridge	(630)	9,159	7,684
62206	Cahokia	(618)	16,803	17,550
60409	Calumet City	(708)	37,242	37,840
60643	Calumet Park	(708)	8,455	8,418
61520	Canton	(309)	13,957	13,959

ZIP	Place		1996	1990
*62901	Carbondale	(618)	26,676	27,033
62626	Carlinville	(217)	5,686	5,416
62821	Carmi	(618)	5,659	5,735
*60188	Carol Stream	(630)	36,779	31,759
60110	Carpentersville	(847)	24,629	23,049
60013	Cary	(847)	13,813	10,043
62801	Centralia	(618)	13,981	14,274
62206	Centreville	(618)	7,272	7,489
*61821	Champaign	(217)	64,002	63,502
60410	Channahon	(815)	6,340	4,266
61920	Charleston	(217)	20,186	20,398
62629	Chatham	(217)	7,611	6,074
62233	Chester	(618)	7,970	8,204
*60607	Chicago	(312)/(773)	2,721,547	2,783,726
*60411	Chicago Heights	(708)	31,899	32,966
60415	Chicago Ridge	(708)	14,018	13,643
61523	Chillicothe	(309)	6,084	5,959
60804	Cicero	(708)	70,915	67,436
60514	Clarendon Hills	(630)	7,206	6,994
61727	Clinton	(217)	7,407	7,437
62234	Collinsville	(618)	23,057	22,424
62236	Columbia	(618)	6,429	5,524
60478	Country Club Hills	(708)	16,120	15,431
60525	Countryside	(708)	6,049	5,961
60435	Crest Hill	(815)	12,190	10,999
60445	Crestwood	(708)	11,519	10,823
60417	Crete	(708)	7,765	6,773
61610	Creve Coeur	(309)	5,920	5,938
*60014	Crystal Lake	(815)	32,180	24,696
*61832	Danville	(217)	32,163	33,828
60561	Darien	(630)	23,037	20,556
*62525	Decatur	(217)	81,369	83,900
60015	Deerfield	(847)	18,294	17,327
60115	De Kalb	(815)	35,554	35,076
*60018	Des Plaines	(847)	54,836	53,414
61021	Dixon	(815)	15,482	15,134
60419	Dolton	(708)	24,102	23,956
*60515	Downers Grove	(630)	50,089	46,845
62832	Du Quoin	(618)	6,517	6,697
62024	East Alton	(618)	6,779	7,063
61244	East Moline	(309)	20,214	20,147
61611	East Peoria	(309)	22,201	21,378
*62201	East St. Louis	(618)	38,595	40,944
62025	Edwardsville	(618)	16,403	14,582
62401	Effingham	(217)	12,577	11,927
*60120	Elgin	(847)	86,034	77,010
*60007	Elk Grove Village	(847)	34,470	33,429
60126	Elmhurst	(630)	43,290	42,029
60707	Elmwood Park	(708)	22,760	23,206
*60201	Evanston	(847)	71,593	73,233
60805	Evergreen Park	(708)	20,584	20,874
62837	Fairfield	(618)	5,094	5,442
62208	Fairview Heights	(618)	14,701	14,768
60422	Flossmoor	(708)	9,045	8,651
60130	Forest Park	(708)	14,483	14,918
60020	Fox Lake	(847)	8,287	7,478
60423	Frankfort	(815)	9,607	7,180
.....	Frankfort Square(c)	(815)	—	6,227
60131	Franklin Park	(847)	18,125	18,485
61032	Freeport	(815)	26,173	25,840
60030	Gages Lake(c)	(847)	—	8,349
*61401	Galesburg	(309)	33,162	33,530
61254	Geneseo	(309)	6,258	5,990
60134	Geneva	(630)	16,943	12,625
62034	Glen Carbon	(618)	9,555	7,774
60022	Glencoe	(847)	8,435	8,499
60139	Glendale Heights	(630)	30,321	27,915
*60137	Glen Ellyn	(630)	25,759	24,919
60025	Glenview	(847)	39,159	38,436
60425	Glenwood	(708)	9,151	9,289
62035	Godfrey	(618)	16,610	15,671
.....	Goodings Grove(c)	(815)	—	14,054
62040	Granite City	(618)	31,449	32,766
60030	Grayslake	(847)	14,370	7,388
62246	Greenville	(618)	6,706	5,108
60031	Gurnee	(847)	22,489	13,715
60103	Hanover Park	(630)	35,599	32,918
62946	Harrisburg	(618)	9,594	9,318
60033	Harvard	(815)	6,857	5,975
60426	Harvey	(708)	29,097	29,771
60656	Harwood Heights	(708)	7,955	7,680
60047	Hawthorn Woods	(847)	5,498	4,423
60429	Hazel Crest	(708)	13,715	13,334
62948	Herrin	(618)	11,162	10,857
60457	Hickory Hills	(708)	14,053	13,021
62249	Highland	(618)	8,021	7,546
60035	Highland Park	(847)	30,998	30,575
60040	Highwood	(847)	5,094	5,331
60162	Hillside	(708)	7,595	7,672
*60521	Hinsdale	(630)	16,353	16,029
*60195	Hoffman Estates	(847)	48,708	46,363
60430	Homewood	(708)	19,279	19,278
60942	Hoopeston	(217)	5,549	5,871
60067	Inverness	(847)	6,739	6,516
60042	Island Lake	(847)	7,,464	4,449
60143	Itasca	(630)	8,144	6,947
*62650	Jacksonville	(217)	18,890	19,327
62052	Jerseyville	(618)	7,539	7,382
*60436	Joliet	(815)	86,749	77,217
60458	Justice	(708)	11,439	11,137
60901	Kankakee	(815)	27,217	27,541
61443	Kewanee	(309)	12,684	12,969
60525	La Grange	(708)	15,104	15,362
60526	La Grange Park	(708)	12,597	12,861
60044	Lake Bluff	(847)	5,589	5,486
60045	Lake Forest	(847)	18,296	17,836
60102	Lake in the Hills	(847)	16,889	5,900
60047	Lake Zurich	(847)	16,786	14,927
60438	Lansing	(708)	28,664	28,131
61301	La Salle	(815)	9,615	9,717
60439	Lemont	(630)	9,571	7,359
*60048	Libertyville	(847)	19,772	19,174
62656	Lincoln	(217)	15,257	15,418
60069	Lincolnshire	(847)	5,914	4,928
60645	Lincolnwood	(847)	11,342	11,365
60046	Lindenhurst	(847)	9,225	8,044
60532	Lisle	(630)	20,524	19,584
62056	Litchfield	(217)	6,731	6,883
60441	Lockport	(815)	12,173	9,401
60148	Lombard	(630)	41,806	39,408
60047	Long Grove	(847)	6,058	4,747
*61130	Loves Park	(815)	17,341	15,457
60411	Lynwood	(708)	7,518	6,535
60534	Lyons (Cook)	(708)	9,788	9,828
*60050	McHenry	(815)	19,144	16,343
61115	Machesney Park	(815)	19,014	19,033
61455	Macomb	(309)	18,069	19,952
60152	Marengo	(815)	5,299	4,768
62959	Marion	(618)	15,619	14,545
60426	Markham (Cook)	(708)	13,025	13,136
62258	Mascoutah	(618)	5,672	5,511
60443	Matteson	(708)	12,071	11,378
61938	Mattoon	(217)	18,267	18,441
60153	Maywood	(708)	26,185	27,139
*60160	Melrose Park	(708)	20,597	20,859
61342	Mendota	(815)	7,201	7,017
62960	Metropolis	(618)	6,822	6,734
60445	Midlothian	(708)	14,961	14,372
61264	Milan	(309)	5,794	5,753
60448	Mokena	(708)	12,011	6,128
*61265	Moline	(309)	42,757	43,080
61462	Monmouth	(309)	9,447	9,489
60538	Montgomery	(630)	5,173	4,487
60450	Morris	(815)	11,172	10,274
61550	Morton	(309)	14,894	13,799
60053	Morton Grove	(847)	22,258	22,373
62863	Mount Carmel	(618)	7,948	8,287
60056	Mount Prospect	(847)	54,040	53,168
62864	Mount Vernon	(618)	18,522	17,082
60060	Mundelein	(847)	27,034	21,224
62966	Murphysboro	(618)	9,094	9,176
*60540	Naperville	(630)	107,001	85,806
60451	New Lenox	(815)	13,088	9,698
60714	Niles	(847)	29,081	28,375
61761	Normal	(309)	42,655	40,023
60634	Norridge	(708)	14,444	14,459
60542	North Aurora	(630)	7,925	6,010
*60062	Northbrook	(708)	32,943	32,572
60064	North Chicago	(847)	31,665	34,978
60093	Northfield	(847)	5,271	4,777
60164	Northlake	(708)	11,953	12,505
60546	North Riverside	(708)	6,106	6,180
60521	Oak Brook	(630)	9,346	9,087
60452	Oak Forest	(708)	27,461	26,202
*60303	Oak Lawn	(708)	57,696	56,182
*60303	Oak Park	(708)	51,585	53,648
62269	O'Fallon	(618)	18,600	16,064
62450	Olney	(618)	8,796	8,873
60477	Orland Hills	(708)	6,232	5,510
*60462	Orland Park	(708)	45,657	35,720
60543	Oswego	(630)	8,297	3,949
61350	Ottawa	(815)	17,974	17,574
*60067	Palatine	(847)	44,460	41,554
60463	Palos Heights	(708)	12,194	11,478
60465	Palos Hills	(708)	18,654	17,803
62557	Pana	(217)	5,729	5,796
61944	Paris	(217)	9,207	9,016
60085	Park City	(847)	5,408	4,677
60466	Park Forest	(708)	24,513	24,656
60068	Park Ridge	(847)	37,039	37,075
61554	Pekin	(309)	32,433	32,254
*61601	Peoria	(309)	112,306	113,513
61603	Peoria Heights	(309)	6,732	6,930
61354	Peru	(815)	9,387	9,302
60544	Plainfield	(815)	7,340	4,557
60545	Plano	(630)	5,563	5,104
61764	Pontiac	(815)	12,070	11,428
61356	Princeton	(815)	6,953	7,197
60070	Prospect Heights	(847)	15,280	15,236
*62301	Quincy	(217)	40,545	39,682
61866	Rantoul	(217)	13,728	17,212
60471	Richton Park	(708)	11,323	10,523
60827	Riverdale	(708)	13,375	13,671
60305	River Forest	(708)	11,444	11,669
60171	River Grove	(708)	9,767	9,961
60546	Riverside	(708)	8,438	8,774
60472	Robbins	(708)	7,291	7,498
62454	Robinson	(618)	6,504	6,740
61068	Rochelle	(815)	9,364	8,769

ZIP	Place		1996	1990
61071	Rock Falls	(815)	9,449	9,669
*61125	Rockford	(815)	143,531	141,787
*61201	Rock Island	(309)	39,679	40,630
60008	Rolling Meadows	(847)	22,560	22,591
60446	Romeoville	(815)	15,496	14,101
60172	Roselle	(630)	23,044	20,819
60073	Round Lake Beach	(847)	22,211	16,406
*60174	Saint Charles	(630)	25,696	22,620
62881	Salem	(618)	7,463	7,470
60548	Sandwich	(815)	5,995	5,607
60411	Sauk Village	(708)	9,918	9,926
*60194	Schaumburg	(847)	74,294	68,586
60176	Schiller Park	(847)	11,043	11,189
62225	Scott AFB(c)	(618)	—	7,245
60436	Shorewood	(815)	7,451	6,264
61282	Silvis	(309)	6,867	6,926
*60077	Skokie	(847)	58,635	59,432
60177	South Elgin	(847)	12,635	7,474
60473	South Holland	(708)	21,747	22,105
*62703	Springfield	(217)	112,921	105,417
61362	Spring Valley	(815)	5,044	5,246
60475	Steger	(708)	9,642	9,329
61081	Sterling	(815)	14,811	15,142
60402	Stickney	(708)	5,676	5,678
60107	Streamwood	(630)	34,258	31,197
61364	Streator	(815)	13,941	14,121
60501	Summit	(708)	9,733	9,971
62221	Swansea	(618)	8,936	8,201
60178	Sycamore	(815)	10,938	9,896
62568	Taylorville	(217)	11,270	11,133
60477	Tinley Park	(708)	43,310	37,115
62294	Troy	(618)	7,054	6,019
60466	University Park	(708)	6,340	6,204
*61801	Urbana	(217)	33,179	36,383
62471	Vandalia	(618)	6,169	6,114
60061	Vernon Hills	(847)	17,792	15,319
60181	Villa Park	(630)	22,563	22,279
60555	Warrenville	(630)	12,276	11,389
61571	Washington	(309)	10,635	10,136
62204	Washington Park	(618)	7,063	7,431
62298	Waterloo	(618)	5,911	5,030
60970	Watseka	(815)	5,522	5,424
60084	Wauconda	(847)	8,461	6,294
*60085	Waukegan	(847)	74,166	69,481
60154	Westchester	(708)	17,596	17,301
*60185	West Chicago	(630)	16,892	14,808
60558	Western Springs	(708)	11,844	11,956
62896	West Frankfort	(618)	8,402	8,526
60559	Westmont	(630)	22,366	21,402
61604	West Peoria	(309)	5,510	5,309
*60187	Wheaton	(630)	54,173	51,441
60090	Wheeling	(847)	30,216	29,911
60514	Willowbrook	(630)	9,134	8,701
60091	Wilmette	(847)	26,036	26,694
60481	Wilmington	(815)	5,270	4,743
60190	Winfield	(630)	8,107	7,096
60093	Winnetka	(847)	11,940	12,210
60096	Winthrop Harbor	(847)	7,005	6,240
60097	Wonder Lake(c)	(815)	—	6,664
60191	Wood Dale	(630)	13,371	12,394
60517	Woodridge	(630)	28,854	26,359
62095	Wood River	(618)	11,097	11,490
60098	Woodstock	(815)	16,883	14,368
60482	Worth	(708)	11,220	11,208
60560	Yorkville	(630)	5,265	3,894
60099	Zion	(847)	22,111	19,783

Indiana

ZIP	Place		1996	1990
46001	Alexandria	(765)	5,769	5,709
*46011	Anderson	(765)	59,131	59,518
46703	Angola	(219)	8,248	5,851
46706	Auburn	(219)	10,533	9,386
47006	Batesville	(812)	5,330	4,720
47421	Bedford	(812)	14,667	13,817
46107	Beech Grove	(317)	13,239	13,383
*47408	Bloomington	(812)	66,479	62,015
46714	Bluffton	(219)	9,423	9,104
47601	Boonville	(812)	6,605	6,686
47834	Brazil	(812)	8,034	7,640
46112	Brownsburg	(317)	9,960	7,628
*46032	Carmel	(317)	36,837	25,380
46303	Cedar Lake	(219)	9,088	8,885
47111	Charlestown	(812)	6,022	5,889
46304	Chesterton	(219)	9,962	9,118
47129	Clarksville (Clark Co.)	(812)	19,749	19,838
46725	Columbia City	(219)	6,408	5,700
*47201	Columbus	(812)	32,963	33,948
47331	Connersville	(765)	15,493	15,550
47933	Crawfordsville	(765)	14,219	13,584
46307	Crown Point	(219)	19,007	17,728
46229	Cumberland	(317)	5,012	4,557
46733	Decatur	(219)	8,965	8,642
46514	Dunlap(c)	(219)	—	5,705
46311	Dyer	(219)	12,675	10,923
46312	East Chicago	(219)	31,761	33,892
*46515	Elkhart	(219)	44,224	44,661
46036	Elwood	(765)	9,119	9,494
*47708	Evansville	(812)	123,456	126,272
46038	Fishers	(317)	20,665	7,189
*46802	Fort Wayne	(219)	184,783	191,839
46041	Frankfort	(765)	15,231	14,754
46131	Franklin	(317)	16,356	12,932
46738	Garrett	(219)	5,220	5,349
*46401	Gary	(219)	110,975	116,646
46933	Gas City	(765)	5,758	6,296
*46526	Goshen	(219)	24,930	23,794
46530	Granger(c)	(219)	—	20,241
46135	Greencastle	(765)	9,366	8,984
46140	Greenfield	(317)	13,003	11,657
47240	Greensburg	(812)	10,128	9,286
*46142	Greenwood	(317)	30,600	26,507
46319	Griffith	(219)	18,085	17,914
*46320	Hammond	(219)	80,081	84,236
47348	Hartford City	(765)	6,951	6,960
46322	Highland	(219)	23,569	23,696
46342	Hobart	(219)	24,463	24,440
47542	Huntingburg	(812)	5,247	5,236
46750	Huntington	(219)	15,820	16,389
*46206	Indianapolis	(317)	746,737	731,278
*47546	Jasper	(812)	10,995	10,030
*47130	Jeffersonville	(812)	25,787	24,016
46755	Kendallville	(219)	8,754	7,773
*46902	Kokomo	(765)	45,785	44,996
*47901	Lafayette	(765)	44,344	44,622
.....	Lakes of the Four Seasons(c)	(219)	—	6,556
46405	Lake Station	(219)	13,983	13,899
*46350	La Porte	(219)	20,696	21,507
46226	Lawrence	(317)	32,642	26,849
46052	Lebanon	(765)	13,200	12,059
47441	Linton	(812)	5,951	5,814
46947	Logansport	(219)	16,254	16,865
46356	Lowell	(219)	7,162	6,430
47250	Madison	(812)	12,408	12,006
*46952	Marion	(765)	29,964	32,607
46151	Martinsville	(765)	12,155	11,677
*46401	Merrillville	(219)	30,577	27,257
*46360	Michigan City	(219)	32,979	33,822
*46544	Mishawaka	(219)	45,045	42,635
47960	Monticello	(219)	5,506	5,237
46158	Mooresville	(317)	7,553	5,541
47620	Mount Vernon	(812)	6,765	7,217
*47302	Muncie	(765)	69,058	71,170
46321	Munster	(219)	20,438	19,949
46550	Nappanee	(219)	5,812	5,474
*47150	New Albany	(812)	38,224	36,322
47362	New Castle	(765)	17,293	17,753
46774	New Haven	(219)	10,148	10,659
*46060	Noblesville	(317)	23,960	17,655
46962	North Manchester	(219)	6,341	6,383
47265	North Vernon	(812)	8,655	5,129
47130	Oak Park(c)	(812)	—	5,630
46970	Peru	(765)	11,146	12,843
46168	Plainfield	(317)	17,235	14,953
46563	Plymouth	(219)	9,779	8,291
46368	Portage	(219)	32,419	29,062
47371	Portland	(219)	6,075	6,483
47670	Princeton	(812)	7,273	8,127
47978	Rensselaer	(219)	5,250	5,045
*47374	Richmond	(765)	37,312	38,705
46975	Rochester	(219)	6,421	5,969
46173	Rushville	(765)	5,236	5,533
46373	Saint John	(219)	7,682	4,921
47167	Salem	(812)	6,164	5,619
46375	Schererville	(219)	23,322	20,155
47170	Scottsburg	(812)	5,708	5,334
47172	Sellersburg	(812)	6,028	5,914
47274	Seymour	(812)	16,535	15,605
46176	Shelbyville	(765)	16,429	15,347
*46624	South Bend	(219)	102,100	105,511
46383	South Haven(c)	(219)	—	6,112
46224	Speedway	(317)	12,582	13,092
47586	Tell City	(812)	8,007	8,088
*47808	Terre Haute	(812)	54,585	57,475
*46383	Valparaiso	(219)	25,804	24,414
47591	Vincennes	(812)	19,312	19,867
46992	Wabash	(219)	11,394	12,127
*46580	Warsaw	(219)	10,738	10,968
47501	Washington	(812)	10,992	10,864
46074	Westfield	(317)	7,426	3,304
*47901	West Lafayette	(765)	27,177	26,144
46391	Westville	(219)	5,549	5,255
47394	Winchester	(765)	5,130	5,095
46077	Zionsville	(317)	6,257	5,385

Iowa

ZIP	Place		1996	1990
50511	Algona	(515)	5,851	6,015
50009	Altoona	(515)	8,864	7,242
*50010	Ames	(515)	47,698	47,198
52205	Anamosa	(319)	5,578	5,100
50021	Ankeny	(515)	23,484	18,482
50022	Atlantic	(712)	7,229	7,432
52722	Bettendorf	(319)	31,015	28,139
*50036	Boone	(515)	12,741	12,392
52601	Burlington	(319)	26,853	27,208
51401	Carroll	(712)	10,093	9,579

ZIP	Place		1996	1990
50613	Cedar Falls	(319)	34,884	34,298
*52401	Cedar Rapids	(319)	113,482	108,772
52544	Centerville	(515)	5,515	5,936
50616	Charles City	(515)	7,617	7,878
51012	Cherokee	(712)	5,663	6,026
51632	Clarinda	(712)	5,066	5,104
50428	Clear Lake	(515)	8,298	8,183
*52732	Clinton	(319)	28,323	29,201
50325	Clive	(515)	10,419	7,446
52241	Coralville	(319)	11,789	10,347
*51501	Council Bluffs	(712)	55,569	54,315
50801	Creston	(515)	7,698	7,911
*52802	Davenport	(319)	97,010	95,333
52101	Decorah	(319)	8,360	8,063
51442	Denison	(712)	6,525	6,604
*50318	Des Moines	(515)	193,422	193,189
*52001	Dubuque	(319)	57,312	57,538
51334	Estherville	(712)	6,479	6,720
52556	Fairfield	(515)	10,020	9,768
50501	Fort Dodge	(515)	24,755	25,894
52627	Fort Madison	(319)	11,613	11,618
51534	Glenwood	(712)	5,129	4,960
50112	Grinnell	(515)	8,808	8,902
*51537	Harlan	(712)	5,148	5,148
52233	Hiawatha	(319)	5,843	4,986
50644	Independence	(319)	5,881	5,972
50125	Indianola	(515)	12,574	11,340
*52240	Iowa City	(319)	60,923	59,735
50126	Iowa Falls	(515)	5,251	5,435
50131	Johnston	(515)	6,196	4,702
52632	Keokuk	(319)	12,315	12,451
50138	Knoxville	(515)	8,312	8,232
51031	Le Mars	(712)	8,846	8,454
52057	Manchester	(319)	5,398	5,137
52060	Maquoketa	(319)	6,086	6,130
52302	Marion	(319)	22,896	20,422
50158	Marshalltown	(515)	25,321	25,178
*50401	Mason City	(515)	28,972	29,040
52641	Mount Pleasant	(319)	8,223	7,959
52761	Muscatine	(319)	23,096	22,881
50201	Nevada	(515)	6,052	6,009
50208	Newton	(515)	15,116	14,799
50211	Norwalk	(515)	6,592	5,726
50662	Oelwein	(319)	6,395	6,493
51041	Orange City	(712)	5,375	4,940
52577	Oskaloosa	(515)	10,594	10,600
52501	Ottumwa	(515)	24,187	24,488
50219	Pella	(515)	9,642	9,270
50220	Perry	(515)	7,269	6,652
*51566	Red Oak	(712)	6,244	6,264
51601	Shenandoah	(712)	5,516	5,572
51250	Sioux Center	(712)	5,599	5,074
*51101	Sioux City	(712)	83,791	80,505
51301	Spencer	(712)	11,194	11,066
50588	Storm Lake	(712)	8,880	8,769
*50318	Urbandale	(515)	26,902	23,775
52349	Vinton	(319)	5,387	5,103
52353	Washington	(319)	7,270	7,074
*50701	Waterloo	(319)	65,022	66,467
50677	Waverly	(319)	8,650	8,539
50595	Webster City	(515)	7,832	7,894
*50265	West Des Moines	(515)	40,380	31,702
50311	Windsor Heights	(515)	5,036	5,190

Kansas

ZIP	Place		1996	1990
67410	Abilene	(785)	6,520	6,242
67002	Andover	(316)	5,203	4,204
67005	Arkansas City	(316)	12,694	12,762
66002	Atchison	(913)	10,000	10,656
67010	Augusta	(316)	8,641	7,848
66952	Bel Aire	(316)	5,019	3,695
66012	Bonner Springs	(913)	6,541	6,413
66720	Chanute	(316)	9,248	9,488
67337	Coffeyville	(316)	12,242	12,917
67701	Colby	(785)	5,522	5,510
66901	Concordia	(785)	5,706	6,152
67037	Derby	(316)	17,496	14,691
67801	Dodge City	(316)	22,430	21,129
67042	El Dorado	(316)	12,809	11,495
66801	Emporia	(316)	24,866	25,512
66442	Fort Riley North(c)	(785)	—	12,848
66701	Fort Scott	(316)	8,324	8,362
67846	Garden City	(316)	25,366	24,097
66030	Gardner	(913)	5,601	4,277
67530	Great Bend	(316)	14,718	15,427
67601	Hays	(785)	17,991	17,814
67060	Haysville	(316)	8,683	8,364
*67501	Hutchinson	(316)	39,015	39,308
67301	Independence	(316)	9,623	10,030
66749	Iola	(316)	6,241	6,351
66441	Junction City	(785)	17,659	20,642
*66102	Kansas City	(913)	142,654	151,521
66043	Lansing	(913)	7,996	7,120
*66044	Lawrence	(785)	71,887	65,608
66048	Leavenworth	(913)	39,431	38,495
66209	Leawood	(913)	24,786	19,693
66214	Lenexa	(913)	37,462	34,110
*67901	Liberal	(316)	17,551	16,573
67460	McPherson	(316)	12,746	12,422
*66502	Manhattan	(785)	42,117	43,081
66202	Merriam	(913)	12,160	11,819
66203	Mission	(913)	9,535	9,504
67114	Newton	(316)	16,604	16,700
*66061	Olathe	(913)	78,666	63,402
66067	Ottawa	(785)	11,495	10,667
66204	Overland Park	(913)	131,053	111,790
67219	Park City	(316)	5,426	5,081
67357	Parsons	(316)	11,316	11,919
66762	Pittsburg	(316)	18,073	17,789
66208	Prairie Village	(913)	23,545	23,186
67124	Pratt	(316)	6,598	6,687
66205	Roeland Park	(913)	7,703	7,706
*67401	Salina	(785)	44,176	42,299
66203	Shawnee	(913)	43,006	37,962
*66601	Topeka	(785)	119,658	119,883
67880	Ulysses	(316)	5,947	5,474
67152	Wellington	(316)	8,539	8,517
*67202	Wichita	(316)	320,395	304,017
67156	Winfield	(316)	11,804	11,931

Kentucky

ZIP	Place		1996	1990
41001	Alexandria	(606)	7,158	5,592
*41101	Ashland	(606)	22,918	23,622
40004	Bardstown	(502)	7,594	6,712
41073	Bellevue	(606)	6,338	6,997
40403	Berea	(606)	10,007	9,129
*42101	Bowling Green	(502)	44,208	41,688
40261	Buechel(c)	(502)	—	7,081
41005	Burlington(c)	(606)	—	6,070
*42718	Campbellsville	(502)	10,666	9,592
*40701	Corbin	(606)	8,025	7,644
*41011	Covington	(606)	40,971	43,646
41031	Cynthiana	(606)	6,399	6,497
*40422	Danville	(606)	16,059	14,454
41074	Dayton	(606)	5,954	6,576
40243	Douglass Hills	(502)	5,195	5,431
41017	Edgewood	(606)	8,502	8,143
*42701	Elizabethtown	(502)	19,434	18,167
41018	Elsmere	(606)	7,737	6,847
41018	Erlanger	(606)	16,717	15,979
40118	Fairdale(c)	(502)	—	6,563
40291	Fern Creek(c)	(502)	—	16,406
41139	Flatwoods	(606)	7,964	7,799
*41042	Florence	(606)	19,726	18,586
42223	Fort Campbell North(c)	(502)	—	18,861
40121	Fort Knox(c)	(502)	—	21,495
41017	Fort Mitchell	(606)	7,156	7,438
41075	Fort Thomas	(606)	15,300	16,032
41011	Fort Wright	(606)	6,670	6,404
*40601	Frankfort	(502)	26,695	26,535
*42134	Franklin	(502)	7,240	7,607
40324	Georgetown	(502)	13,614	11,414
*42141	Glasgow	(502)	13,739	12,777
40330	Harrodsburg	(606)	7,768	7,335
*41701	Hazard	(606)	5,540	5,416
42420	Henderson	(502)	26,456	25,945
41076	Highland Heights	(606)	6,208	4,223
40228	Highview(c)	(502)	—	14,814
40229	Hillview	(502)	5,815	6,119
*42240	Hopkinsville	(502)	28,317	29,818
41051	Independence	(606)	12,567	10,444
*40299	Jeffersontown	(502)	25,596	23,223
40031	La Grange	(502)	5,040	3,853
40342	Lawrenceburg	(502)	7,593	5,911
40033	Lebanon	(502)	5,744	5,695
*42754	Leitchfield	(502)	5,308	4,965
*40507	Lexington	(606)	239,942	225,366
*40741	London	(606)	6,797	5,757
*40232	Louisville	(502)	260,689	269,555
40252	Lyndon	(502)	7,675	8,037
42431	Madisonville	(502)	19,059	18,693
42066	Mayfield	(502)	10,343	9,935
41056	Maysville	(606)	8,417	8,113
40965	Middlesboro	(606)	10,858	11,328
40253	Middletown	(502)	5,298	5,016
42633	Monticello	(606)	5,630	5,357
40351	Morehead	(606)	8,730	8,357
40353	Mount Sterling	(606)	5,332	5,362
40047	Mount Washington	(502)	7,051	5,256
42071	Murray	(502)	15,316	14,442
40218	Newburg(c)	(502)	—	21,647
*41071	Newport	(606)	16,957	18,871
*40356	Nicholasville	(606)	16,603	13,603
40259	Okolona(c)	(502)	—	18,902
*42301	Owensboro	(502)	54,350	53,577
*42003	Paducah	(502)	26,601	27,256
*40361	Paris	(606)	8,788	8,730
*41501	Pikeville	(606)	6,376	6,324
40268	Pleasure Ridge Park(c)	(502)	—	25,131
42445	Princeton	(502)	6,929	6,940
*40160	Radcliff	(502)	19,411	19,778
*40475	Richmond	(606)	26,227	21,183
42276	Russellville	(502)	7,851	7,454
40216	Saint Dennis(c)	(502)	—	10,326
40206	Saint Matthews	(502)	16,562	15,691
*40066	Shelbyville	(502)	6,954	6,155

ZIP	Place		1996	1990
40256	Shively	(502)	14,899	15,535
*42501	Somerset	(606)	12,236	10,735
41015	Taylor Mill	(606)	6,942	5,530
40272	Valley Station(c)	(502)	—	22,840
40383	Versailles	(606)	6,882	7,269
41016	Villa Hills	(606)	7,432	7,370
41101	Westwoods(c)	(606)	—	5,300
40769	Williamsburg	(606)	5,960	5,493
*40391	Winchester	(606)	16,021	15,799

Louisiana

ZIP	Place		1996	1990
*70510	Abbeville	(318)	11,460	11,769
*71301	Alexandria	(318)	46,051	49,049
70032	Arabi(c)	(504)	—	8,787
70094	Avondale(c)	(504)	—	5,813
*70714	Baker	(225)	13,223	13,087
*71220	Bastrop	(318)	13,767	13,916
*70821	Baton Rouge	(225)	215,882	219,531
70360	Bayou Cane(c)	(504)	—	15,876
70037	Belle Chasse(c)	(504)	—	8,512
*70427	Bogalusa	(504)	13,877	14,280
*71111	Bossier City	(318)	55,686	52,721
70517	Breaux Bridge	(318)	6,837	6,694
70094	Bridge City(c)	(504)	—	8,327
70811	Brownfields(c)	(225)	—	5,229
71291	Brownsville-Bawcomville(c)	(318)	—	7,397
70520	Carencro	(318)	5,921	5,518
*70043	Chalmette(c)	(504)	—	31,860
71291	Claiborne(c)	(318)	—	8,300
*70433	Covington	(504)	8,576	7,691
*70526	Crowley	(318)	13,809	13,983
70345	Cut Off(c)	(504)	—	5,325
*70726	Denham Springs	(225)	9,106	8,381
70634	De Ridder	(318)	11,103	10,475
70047	Destrehan(c)	(504)	—	8,031
70346	Donaldsonville	(225)	9,060	7,949
70072	Estelle(c)	(504)	—	14,091
70535	Eunice	(318)	11,182	11,162
71459	Fort Polk South(c)	(318)	—	10,911
70538	Franklin	(318)	8,761	9,004
70820	Gardere(c)	(225)	—	7,209
*70737	Gonzales	(225)	8,294	7,208
71245	Grambling	(318)	5,641	5,713
*70053	Gretna	(504)	16,862	17,208
*70401	Hammond	(504)	16,689	15,871
70123	Harahan	(504)	9,941	9,927
*70058	Harvey(c)	(504)	—	21,222
*70360	Houma	(504)	30,148	30,495
70544	Jeanerette	(318)	6,262	6,205
70502	Jefferson(c)	(504)	—	14,521
70546	Jennings	(318)	11,487	11,305
*70062	Kenner	(504)	72,345	72,033
70445	Lacombe(c)	(504)	—	6,523
*70501	Lafayette	(318)	104,899	101,852
*70601	Lake Charles	(318)	71,445	70,580
*70068	La Place(c)	(504)	—	24,194
70373	Larose(c)	(504)	—	5,772
*71446	Leesville	(318)	5,898	7,638
*70471	Mandeville	(504)	8,677	7,474
71052	Mansfield	(318)	5,223	5,389
71351	Marksville	(318)	5,442	5,526
*70072	Marrero(c)	(504)	—	36,671
70075	Meraux(c)	(504)	—	8,849
70812	Merrydale(c)	(318)	—	10,395
*70009	Metairie(c)	(504)	—	149,428
*71055	Minden	(318)	13,480	13,661
*71201	Monroe	(318)	54,588	54,909
*70380	Morgan City	(504)	13,996	14,531
70612	Moss Bluff(c)	(318)	—	8,039
*71457	Natchitoches	(318)	17,269	16,609
*70560	New Iberia	(318)	32,513	31,828
*70140	New Orleans	(504)	476,625	496,938
70760	New Roads	(225)	5,283	5,303
71463	Oakdale	(318)	7,951	6,837
70808	Oak Hills Place(c)	(225)	—	5,479
*70570	Opelousas	(318)	19,117	19,091
70392	Patterson	(504)	5,273	5,166
*71360	Pineville	(318)	14,315	15,308
*70764	Plaquemine	(225)	6,557	7,101
70454	Ponchatoula	(504)	5,694	5,425
70767	Port Allen	(225)	6,180	6,277
70601	Prien(c)	(318)	—	6,448
70394	Raceland(c)	(504)	—	5,564
70578	Rayne	(318)	8,561	8,502
71037	Red Chute(c)	(318)	—	5,431
70084	Reserve(c)	(504)	—	8,847
70123	River Ridge(c)	(504)	—	14,800
*71270	Ruston	(318)	19,853	20,071
70582	Saint Martinville	(318)	7,323	7,226
70087	Saint Rose(c)	(504)	—	6,259
70583	Scott	(318)	5,484	4,912
70817	Shenandoah(c)		—	13,429
*71102	Shreveport	(318)	191,558	198,525
*70458	Slidell	(504)	25,846	24,124
71075	Springhill	(318)	5,590	5,668
*70663	Sulphur	(318)	20,883	20,125
*71282	Tallulah	(318)	9,004	8,526
70056	Terrytown(c)	(504)	—	23,787
*70301	Thibodaux	(504)	14,015	14,125
70053	Timberlane(c)	(504)	—	12,614
70809	Village Saint George(c)	(225)	—	6,242
70586	Ville Platte	(318)	8,980	9,037
70092	Violet(c)	(504)	—	8,574
70094	Waggaman(c)	(504)	—	9,405
70669	Westlake	(318)	5,039	5,007
*71291	West Monroe	(318)	14,073	14,096
*70094	Westwego	(504)	11,172	11,218
71483	Winnfield	(318)	6,205	6,138
71295	Winnsboro	(318)	5,596	5,755
70791	Zachary	(225)	10,189	9,036

Maine (207)

See introductory note.

ZIP	Place	1996	1990
*04210	Auburn	22,997	24,309
*04330	Augusta	20,441	21,325
*04401	Bangor	31,649	33,181
04530	Bath	10,026	9,799
04915	Belfast	6,474	6,355
03901	*Berwick*	6,226	5,995
*04005	Biddeford	20,788	20,710
04412	Brewer	8,684	9,021
04011	Brunswick Center(c)	—	14,683
04011	*Brunswick*	20,827	20,906
04093	*Buxton*	7,039	6494
04843	*Camden*	5,096	5,060
04107	*Cape Elizabeth*	8,994	8,854
04736	Caribou	8,251	9,415
04021	*Cumberland*	6,384	5,836
03903	*Eliot*	5,518	5,329
04605	Ellsworth	6,292	5,975
04937	*Fairfield*	6,717	6,718
04105	*Falmouth*	8,280	7,610
04938	*Farmington*	7,883	7,436
04032	*Freeport*	7,303	6,905
04345	Gardiner	6,469	6,746
04038	*Gorham*	12,906	11,856
04039	*Gray*	6,466	5,904
04444	*Hampden*	6,128	5,974
04079	*Harpswell*	5,065	5,012
04730	Houlton Center(c)	—	5,627
04730	*Houlton*	5,893	6,613
04239	*Jay*	5,487	5,080
04043	*Kennebunk*	8,787	8,004
03904	Kittery Center(c)	—	5,151
03904	*Kittery*	9,156	9,372
*04240	Lewiston	36,830	39,757
04750	*Limestone*	8,170	9,922
04457	*Lincoln*	5,407	5,587
04250	*Lisbon*	9,342	9,457
04751	Loring AFB(c)	—	7,829
04462	Millinocket Center(c)	—	6,922
04462	*Millinocket*	6,518	6,956
04963	*Oakland*	5,373	5,595
04064	Old Orchard Beach Center(c)	—	7,789
04064	*Old Orchard Beach*	7,712	7,789
04468	Old Town	8,003	8,317
04473	Orono Center(c)	—	9,789
04473	*Orono*	9,119	10,573
*04101	Portland	63,123	64,157
04769	Presque Isle	9,213	10,550
04841	Rockland	7,905	7,972
04276	Rumford Compact(c)		5,419
04276	*Rumford*	6,880	7,078
04072	Saco	15,681	15,181
04073	Sanford Center(c)	—	10,296
04073	*Sanford*	20,801	20,463
*04074	*Scarborough*	14,075	12,518
04976	Skowhegan Center(c)	—	6,990
04976	*Skowhegan*	9,790	8,725
03908	*South Berwick*	6,112	5,877
*04101	South Portland	22,985	23,163
04084	*Standish*	8,397	7,678
04086	*Topsham*	8,950	8,746
04572	*Waldoboro*	5,248	4,601
04087	*Waterboro*	5,289	4,510
*04901	Waterville	16,400	17,173
04090	*Wells*	8,148	7,778
*04092	Westbrook	16,459	16,121
04062	*Windham*	13,975	13,020
04901	Winslow Center(c)	—	5,436
04901	*Winslow*	7,962	7,997
04364	*Winthrop*	6,015	5968
04096	*Yarmouth*	8,080	7,862
03909	*York*	10,162	9,818

Maryland

Area code (240) overlays area code (301). Area code (443) overlays area code (410). See introductory note.

ZIP	Place		1996	1990
21001	Aberdeen	(410)	13,090	13,087
21005	Aberdeen Proving Ground(c)	(410)	—	5,267
20783	Adelphi(c)	(301)	—	13,524
20762	Andrews AFB(c)	(410)	—	10,228

ZIP	Place		1996	1990
*21401	Annapolis	(410)	33,234	33,195
21227	Arbutus(c)	(410)	—	19,750
21012	Arnold(c)	(410)	—	20,261
20916	Aspen Hill(c)	(301)	—	45,494
21220	Ballenger Creek(c)	(410)	—	5,546
*21203	Baltimore	(410)	675,401	736,014
*21014	Bel Air	(410)	9,439	8,942
21050	Bel Air North(c)	(410)	—	14,880
21014	Bel Air South(c)	(410)	—	26,421
*20705	Beltsville(c)	(301)	—	14,476
*20814	Bethesda(c)	(301)	—	62,936
20710	Bladensburg	(301)	8,577	8,064
*20715	Bowie	(301)	40,181	37,642
21220	Bowleys Quarters(c)	(410)	—	5,595
21225	Brooklyn Park(c)	(410)	—	10,987
21716	Brunswick	(301)	6,071	5,117
20866	Burtonsville(c)	(410)	—	5,853
20818	Cabin John(c)	(301)	—	5,341
20619	California(c)	(410)	—	7,626
20705	Calverton(c)	(301)	—	12,046
21613	Cambridge	(410)	10,969	11,514
20748	Camp Springs(c)	(301)	—	16,392
21401	Cape St. Clair(c)	(410)	—	7,878
21234	Carney(c)	(410)	—	25,578
21228	Catonsville(c)	(410)	—	35,233
20657	Chesapeake Ranch Estates(c)	(301)	—	5,423
20784	Cheverly	(301)	6,393	6,023
*20825	Chevy Chase(c)	(301)	—	8,559
20783	Chillum(c)	(301)	—	31,309
20735	Clinton(c)	(301)	—	19,987
20904	Cloverly(c)	(301)	—	7,904
*21030	Cockeysville(c)	(410)	—	18,668
20914	Colesville(c)	(301)	—	18,819
*20740	College Park	(301)	24,987	23,714
*21045	Columbia(c)	(410)/(301)	—	75,883
20743	Coral Hills(c)	(410)	—	11,032
21114	Crofton(c)	(410)	—	12,781
*21502	Cumberland	(301)	22,341	23,712
20872	Damascus(c)	(301)	—	9,817
*20747	District Heights	(301)	7,153	6,711
21222	Dundalk(c)	(410)	—	65,800
21601	Easton	(410)	10,195	9,372
20737	East Riverdale(c)	(301)	—	14,187
21219	Edgemere(c)	(410)	—	9,226
21040	Edgewood(c)	(410)	—	23,903
21784	Eldersburg(c)	(410)	—	9,720
21227	Elkridge(c)	(410)	—	12,953
*21921	Elkton	(410)	10,308	9,073
*21043	Ellicott City(c)	(410)	—	41,396
21221	Essex(c)	(410)	—	40,872
20904	Fairland(c)	(301)	—	19,828
21047	Fallston(c)	(410)	—	5,730
21061	Ferndale(c)	(410)	—	16,355
20747	Forestville(c)	(301)	—	16,731
20755	Fort Meade(c)	(301)	—	12,509
*20749	Fort Washington(c)	(301)	—	24,032
*21701	Frederick	(301)	46,227	40,186
20744	Friendly(c)	(301)	—	9,028
21532	Frostburg	(301)	7,777	8,069
*20877	Gaithersburg	(301)	45,361	39,676
21055	Garrison(c)	(410)	—	5,045
*20874	Germantown(c)	(301)	—	41,145
20706	Glenarden	(301)	5,361	5,025
*21061	Glen Burnie(c)	(410)	—	37,305
20769	Glenn Dale(c)	(301)	—	9,689
20772	Greater Upper Marlboro(c)		—	11,528
*20770	Greenbelt	(301)	21,840	20,561
21122	Green Haven(c)	(410)	—	14,416
21771	Green Valley(c)	(301)	—	9,424
*21740	Hagerstown	(301)	34,633	35,306
21740	Halfway(c)	(301)	—	8,873
21078	Havre de Grace	(410)	10,092	8,952
20903	Hillandale(c)	(301)	—	10,318
20748	Hillcrest Heights(c)	(301)	—	17,136
*20780	Hyattsville	(301)	14,674	13,864
20794	Jessup(c)	(410)	—	6,537
21085	Joppatowne(c)	(410)	—	11,084
20785	Kentland(c)	(301)	—	7,967
20772	Kettering(c)	(301)	—	9,901
21122	Lake Shore(c)	(410)	—	13,269
20785	Landover(c)	(301)	—	5,052
20787	Langley Park(c)	(301)	—	17,474
20706	Lanham-Seabrook(c)	(301)	—	16,792
21227	Lansdowne-Baltimore Highlands(c)		—	15,509
20646	La Plata	(301)	6,504	5,841
20772	Largo(c)	(301)	—	9,475
*20707	Laurel	(301)	18,718	19,086
20653	Lexington Park(c)	(410)	—	9,943
21090	Linthicum(c)	(410)	—	7,547
21207	Lochearn(c)	(410)	—	25,240
21037	Londontowne(c)	(410)	—	6,992
21784	Long Meadow(c)	(410)	—	5,594
*21093	Lutherville-Timonium(c)	(410)	—	16,442
20748	Marlow Heights(c)	(301)	—	5,885
20772	Marlton(c)	(301)	—	5,523
20707	Maryland City(c)	(301)	—	6,813
21093	Mays Chapel(c)	(410)	—	10,132
21220	Middle River(c)	(410)	—	24,616
21207	Milford Mill(c)	(410)	—	22,547
20717	Mitchellville(c)	(301)	—	12,593
20879	Montgomery Village(c)	(301)	—	32,315
21771	Mount Airy	(301)/(410)	5,085	3,730
20712	Mount Rainier	(301)	8,408	7,954
21402	Naval Academy(c)	(410)	—	5,420
20784	New Carrollton	(301)	12,811	12,002
20815	North Bethesda(c)	(301)	—	29,656
20895	North Kensington(c)	(301)	—	8,607
20707	North Laurel(c)	(301)	—	15,008
20878	North Potomac(c)	(301)	—	18,456
*21842	Ocean City	(410)	6,766	5,146
21113	Odenton(c)	(410)	—	12,833
*20832	Olney(c)	(301)	—	23,019
21206	Overlea(c)	(410)	—	12,137
21117	Owings Mills(c)	(410)	—	9,474
*20750	Oxon Hill-Glassmanor(c)	(301)	—	35,794
20785	Palmer Park(c)	(301)	—	7,019
21234	Parkville(c)	(410)	—	31,617
21401	Parole(c)	(410)	—	10,054
*21122	Pasadena(c)	(410)	—	10,012
21128	Perry Hall(c)	(410)	—	22,723
21208	Pikesville(c)	(410)	—	24,815
*20850	Potomac(c)	(301)	—	45,634
21227	Pumphrey(c)	(410)	—	5,483
21133	Randallstown(c)	(301)	—	26,277
.....	Redland(c)	(301)	—	16,145
21136	Reisterstown(c)	(410)	—	19,314
*20737	Riverdale	(301)	5,120	4,843
21122	Riviera Beach(c)	(410)	—	11,376
*20850	Rockville	(301)	46,019	44,830
20772	Rosaryville(c)	(301)	—	8,976
21237	Rosedale(c)	(410)	—	18,703
.....	Rossmoor(c)		—	6,182
21221	Rossville(c)	(410)	—	9,492
20602	Saint Charles(c)	(301)	—	28,717
*21801	Salisbury	(410)	21,160	20,592
20763	Savage-Guilford(c)	(410)	—	9,669
20743	Seat Pleasant	(301)	5,694	5,359
21144	Severn(c)	(410)	—	24,499
21146	Severna Park(c)	(410)	—	25,879
*20907	Silver Spring(c)	(301)	—	76,046
21061	South Gate(c)	(410)	—	27,564
20895	South Kensington(c)	(301)	—	8,777
20707	South Laurel(c)	(301)	—	18,591
*20752	Suitland-Silver Hills(c)	(301)	—	35,111
*20913	Takoma Park	(301)	17,792	16,724
*20748	Temple Hills(c)	(301)	—	6,865
*21202	Towson(c)	(410)	—	49,445
*20602	Waldorf(c)	(301)	—	15,058
20743	Walker Mill(c)	(301)	—	10,920
21793	Walkersville	(301)	5,019	4,145
*21157	Westminster	(410)	15,073	13,060
20902	Wheaton-Glenmont(c)	(301)	—	53,720
21162	White Marsh(c)	(410)	—	8,183
20903	White Oak(c)	(301)	—	18,671
21207	Woodlawn(c) (Baltimore)	(410)	—	32,907
21284	Woodlawn(c) (Prince George's)	(410)	—	5,329

Massachusetts

See introductory note.

ZIP	Place		1996	1990
02351	*Abington*	(781)	14,683	13,817
01720	*Acton*	(978)	18,851	17,872
02743	*Acushnet*	(508)	9,843	9,554
01220	Adams Center(c)	(413)	—	6,356
01220	*Adams*	(413)	8,945	9,445
01001	Agawam	(413)	26,721	27,323
01913	Amesbury Center(c)	(978)	—	12,109
01913	*Amesbury*	(978)	15,784	14,997
*01002	Amherst Center(c)	(413)	—	17,824
*01002	*Amherst*	(413)	35,468	35,228
01810	Andover(c)	(978)	—	8,242
01810	*Andover*	(978)	30,891	29,151
02174	*Arlington*	(781)	43,656	44,630
01430	*Ashburnham*	(978)	5,471	5,433
01721	*Ashland*	(508)	12,940	12,066
01331	Athol Center(c)	(978)	—	8,732
01331	*Athol*	(978)	11,158	11,451
02703	Attleboro	(508)	39,070	38,383
01501	*Auburn*	(508)	15,002	15,005
01432	*Ayer*	(978)	7,378	6,871
02630	Barnstable	(508)	43,699	40,949
01730	*Bedford*	(781)	13,676	12,996
01007	*Belchertown*	(413)	11,756	10,579
02019	*Bellingham*	(508)	15,544	14,877
02178	*Belmont*	(781)	24,044	24,720
02779	*Berkley*	(508)	5,236	4,237
01915	Beverly	(978)	38,596	38,195
*01821	*Billerica*	(978)	38,861	37,609
01504	*Blackstone*	(508)	8,270	8,023
*02205	Boston	(617)	558,394	574,283
02532	*Bourne*	(508)	17,529	16,064
01921	*Boxford*	(978)	8,550	6,266
*02205	*Braintree*	(781)	34,708	33,836
02631	*Brewster*	(508)	9,261	8,440
02324	*Bridgewater*	(508)	23,692	21,249
*02403	Brockton	(508)	92,324	92,788

ZIP	Place		1996	1990
02146	*Brookline*	(617)	54,137	54,718
01803	*Burlington*	(781)	23,493	23,302
*02139	Cambridge	(617)	93,707	95,802
02021	*Canton*	(781)	20,314	18,530
02330	*Carver*	(508)	11,289	10,590
*02632	Centerville(c)	(508)	—	9,190
01507	*Charlton*	(508)	10,073	9,576
02633	*Chatham*	(508)	6,930	6,579
01824	*Chelmsford*	(978)	33,484	32,383
02150	Chelsea	(617)	27,608	28,710
*01020	Chicopee	(413)	54,532	56,632
01510	*Clinton*	(978)	13,071	13,222
01778	Cochituate(c)	(508)	—	6,046
02025	*Cohasset*	(781)	7,070	7,075
01742	*Concord*	(978)	17,792	17,076
*01226	*Dalton*	(413)	6,965	7,155
01923	*Danvers*	(978)	24,467	24,174
02714	*Dartmouth*	(508)	28,100	27,244
*02026	*Dedham*	(781)	23,741	23,782
02638	*Dennis*	(508)	14,423	13,864
02715	*Dighton*	(508)	5,871	5,631
01516	*Douglas*	(508)	6,145	5,438
01826	*Dracut*	(978)	27,769	25,594
01571	*Dudley*	(508)	9,676	9,540
*02332	*Duxbury*	(781)	15,007	13,895
02333	*East Bridgewater*	(508)	12,133	11,104
02536	East Falmouth(c)	(508)	—	5,577
01027	*Easthampton*	(413)	15,744	15,537
01028	*East Longmeadow*	(413)	13,890	13,367
02334	*Easton*	(508)	20,970	19,807
02149	Everett	(617)	35,006	35,701
02719	*Fairhaven*	(508)	15,975	16,132
*02722	Fall River	(508)	90,865	92,703
*02540	*Falmouth*	(508)	30,451	27,960
01420	Fitchburg	(978)	39,843	41,194
01433	Fort Devens(c)	(978)	—	8,973
02035	*Foxborough*	(508)	16,011	14,637
*01701	*Framingham*	(508)	64,536	64,989
02038	Franklin Center(c)	(508)	—	9,965
02038	Franklin	(508)	26,664	22,095
02702	*Freetown*	(508)	8,733	8,522
01440	Gardner	(978)	20,155	20,125
01833	*Georgetown*	(978)	7,054	6,384
*01930	Gloucester	(978)	29,267	28,716
01519	*Grafton*	(508)	13,286	13,035
01033	*Granby*	(413)	5,850	5,565
01230	*Great Barrington*	(413)	7,656	7,725
*01301	Greenfield Center(c)	(413)	—	14,016
01302	*Greenfield*	(413)	18,580	18,666
01450	*Groton*	(978)	8,789	7,511
01834	*Groveland*	(978)	5,610	5,214
02338	*Halifax*	(781)	6,844	6,526
01936	*Hamilton*	(978)	7,487	7,280
02339	*Hanover*	(781)	12,891	11,912
02341	*Hanson*	(781)	9,512	9,028
01451	*Harvard*	(978)	11,590	12,329
02645	*Harwich*	(508)	11,328	10,275
*01830	Haverhill	(978)	53,952	51,418
02043	*Hingham*	(781)	20,265	19,821
02343	*Holbrook*	(781)	11,092	11,041
01520	*Holden*	(508)	14,960	14,628
01746	*Holliston*	(508)	13,381	12,926
*01040	Holyoke	(413)	41,461	43,704
01747	*Hopedale*	(508)	5,621	5,666
01748	*Hopkinton*	(508)	10,805	9,191
01749	Hudson Center(c)	(978)	—	14,267
01749	*Hudson*	(978)	17,695	17,233
02045	*Hull*	(781)	10,472	10,466
02601	Hyannis(c)	(508)	—	14,120
01938	*Ipswich*	(978)	12,352	11,873
02364	*Kingston*	(781)	10,447	9,045
02347	*Lakeville*	(508)	8,596	7,785
01523	*Lancaster*	(978)	6,542	6,661
*01842	Lawrence	(978)	68,807	70,207
01238	*Lee*	(413)	5,743	5,849
01524	*Leicester*	(508)	10,327	10,191
01240	*Lenox*	(413)	5,022	5,069
01453	Leominster	(978)	39,263	38,145
02173	*Lexington*	(781)	29,484	28,974
01773	*Lincoln*	(781)	7,899	7,666
01460	*Littleton*	(978)	7,695	7,051
*01028	*Longmeadow*	(413)	14,864	15,467
*01853	Lowell	(978)	100,973	103,439
01056	*Ludlow*	(413)	18,786	18,820
01462	*Lunenburg*	(978)	9,285	9,117
*01901	Lynn	(781)	80,563	81,245
01940	*Lynnfield*	(781)	11,232	11,049
02148	Malden	(781)	52,749	53,884
01944	*Manchester-by-the-Sea* (formerly Manchester)	(978)	5,357	5,286
02048	*Mansfield*	(508)	18,806	16,568
01945	*Marblehead*	(781)	19,973	19,971
01752	Marlborough	(508)	32,974	31,813
02050	*Marshfield*	(781)	22,911	21,531
02648	Marstons Mills(c)	(508)	—	8,017
02649	*Mashpee*	(508)	8,935	7,884
02739	*Mattapoisett*	(508)	6,190	5,850
01754	*Maynard*	(978)	10,412	10,325
02052	*Medfield*	(508)	11,467	10,531
*02155	Medford	(781)	56,190	57,407
02053	*Medway*	(508)	11,391	9,931
02176	Melrose	(781)	27,426	28,150
01860	*Merrimac*	(978)	5,670	5,166
01844	Methuen	(978)	41,029	39,990
02346	Middleborough Center(c)	(508)	—	6,837
02346	*Middleborough*	(508)	19,200	17,867
01949	*Middleton*	(978)	5,624	4,921
01757	Milford Center(c)	(508)	—	23,339
01757	*Milford*	(508)	25,194	25,355
01527	*Millbury*	(508)	12,329	12,228
02054	*Millis*	(508)	7,965	7,613
02186	*Milton*	(617)	25,794	25,725
01057	*Monson*	(413)	7,949	7,776
01351	*Montague*	(413)	8,383	8,316
*02584	*Nantucket*	(508)	7,267	6,012
01760	*Natick*	(508)	31,310	30,510
*02205	*Needham*	(781)	27,828	27,557
*02740	New Bedford	(508)	96,903	99,922
01951	*Newbury*	(978)	5,985	5,623
01950	Newburyport	(978)	16,558	16,317
*02205	Newton	(617)	80,238	82,585
02056	*Norfolk*	(508)	10,389	9,259
01247	North Adams	(413)	15,847	16,797
01059	North Amherst(c)	(413)	—	6,239
*01060	Northampton	(413)	28,838	29,289
01845	*North Andover*	(978)	24,283	22,792
*02760	*North Attleborough*	(508)	25,550	25,038
01532	*Northborough*	(508)	12,801	11,929
01534	*Northbridge*	(508)	13,693	13,371
01864	*North Reading*	(978)	12,919	12,002
02766	*Norton*	(508)	15,659	14,265
02061	*Norwell*	(781)	9,652	9,279
02062	*Norwood*	(781)	28,899	28,700
01364	*Orange*	(978)	7,523	7,312
02653	*Orleans*	(508)	6,185	5,838
01540	Oxford Center(c)	(508)	—	5,969
01540	*Oxford*	(508)	13,034	12,588
01069	*Palmer*	(413)	11,907	12,054
*01960	Peabody	(978)	48,365	47,264
02359	*Pembroke*	(781)	16,010	14,544
01463	*Pepperell*	(978)	10,606	10,098
01866	Pinehurst(c)	(978)	—	6,614
*01201	Pittsfield	(413)	46,315	48,622
02762	*Plainville*	(508)	7,238	6,871
*02360	Plymouth Center(c)	(508)	—	7,258
*02360	*Plymouth*	(508)	48,329	45,608
*02205	Quincy	(617)	85,532	84,985
02368	*Randolph*	(781)	30,554	30,093
02767	*Raynham*	(508)	10,513	9,867
01867	*Reading*	(781)	22,956	22,539
02769	*Rehoboth*	(508)	9,354	8,656
02151	Revere	(781)	41,761	42,786
02370	*Rockland*	(781)	17,236	16,123
01966	*Rockport*	(978)	7,580	7,482
01969	*Rowley*	(978)	5,196	4,452
01543	*Rutland*	(508)	5,186	4,936
*01970	Salem	(978)	38,008	38,091
01952	*Salisbury*	(978)	7,093	6,882
02563	*Sandwich*	(508)	17,916	15,489
01906	*Saugus*	(781)	26,223	25,549
02066	*Scituate*	(781)	17,242	16,786
02771	*Seekonk*	(508)	13,269	13,046
02067	*Sharon*	(781)	16,684	15,517
01464	*Shirley*	(978)	7,463	6,118
01545	*Shrewsbury*	(508)	26,771	24,146
*02722	*Somerset*	(508)	17,719	17,655
*02205	Somerville	(617)	74,356	76,210
01002	South Amherst(c)	(413)	—	5,053
01772	*Southborough*	(508)	7,388	6,628
01550	Southbridge Center(c)	(508)	—	13,631
01550	*Southbridge*	(508)	17,447	17,816
01075	*South Hadley*	(413)	17,047	16,685
01077	*Southwick*	(413)	8,005	7,667
02664	South Yarmouth(c)	(508)	—	10,358
01562	Spencer Center(c)	(508)	—	6,306
01562	*Spencer*	(508)	12,091	11,645
*01101	Springfield	(413)	149,948	156,983
01564	*Sterling*	(978)	6,858	6,481
02180	*Stoneham*	(781)	22,131	22,203
02072	*Stoughton*	(781)	27,481	26,777
01775	*Stow*	(978)	5,731	5,328
01566	*Sturbridge*	(508)	7,911	7,775
01776	*Sudbury*	(978)	15,130	14,358
01590	*Sutton*	(508)	7,340	6,824
01907	*Swampscott*	(781)	13,676	13,650
02777	*Swansea*	(508)	15,533	15,411
02780	Taunton	(508)	51,937	49,832
01468	*Templeton*	(978)	6,991	6,438
01876	*Tewksbury*	(978)	28,644	27,266
01983	*Topsfield*	(978)	6,098	5,754
01469	*Townsend*	(978)	8,997	8,496
01879	*Tyngsborough*	(978)	9,800	8,642
01568	*Upton*	(508)	5,339	4,677
01569	*Uxbridge*	(508)	11,027	10,415
01880	*Wakefield*	(781)	24,756	24,825
02081	*Walpole*	(508)	22,251	20,223
*02205	Waltham	(781)	57,214	57,878
01082	Ware Center(c)	(413)	—	6,533
01082	*Ware*	(413)	9,817	9,808
02571	*Wareham*	(508)	19,545	19,232

ZIP	Place		1996	1990
*02205	Watertown	(781)	32,490	33,284
01778	*Wayland*	(508)	12,041	11,874
01570	Webster Center(c)	(508)	—	11,849
01570	*Webster*	(508)	16,089	16,196
02181	*Wellesley*	(781)	26,809	26,615
01581	*Westborough*	(508)	15,005	14,133
01583	*West Boylston*	(508)	6,625	6,611
02379	*West Bridgewater*	(508)	6,647	6,389
01742	West Concord(c)	(978)	—	5,761
*01085	Westfield	(413)	37,539	38,372
01886	*Westford*	(978)	18,642	16,392
01473	*Westminster*	(978)	6,562	6,191
02193	*Weston*	(781)	10,448	10,200
02790	*Westport*	(508)	13,993	13,852
*01089	*West Springfield*	(413)	26,192	27,537
02090	*Westwood*	(781)	12,935	12,557
02673	West Yarmouth(c)	(508)	—	5,409
*02205	*Weymouth*	(781)	54,847	54,063
01588	Whitinsville(c)	(508)	—	5,639
02382	*Whitman*	(781)	13,743	13,240
01095	*Wilbraham*	(413)	12,425	12,635
01267	*Williamstown*	(413)	8,041	8,220
01887	*Wilmington*	(978)	19,874	17,651
01475	*Winchendon*	(978)	8,931	8,805
01890	*Winchester*	(781)	20,318	20,267
02152	*Winthrop*	(617)	17,305	18,127
*01801	Woburn	(781)	36,628	35,943
*01613	Worcester	(508)	166,350	169,759
02093	*Wrentham*	(508)	10,049	9,006
02675	*Yarmouth*	(508)	22,335	21,174

Michigan

ZIP	Place		1996	1990
49221	Adrian	(517)	22,262	22,097
49224	Albion	(517)	9,884	10,066
49401	Allendale(c)	(616)	—	6,950
48101	Allen Park	(313)	31,423	31,092
48801	Alma	(517)	9,265	9,034
49707	Alpena	(517)	11,589	11,354
*48106	Ann Arbor	(734)	108,758	109,608
*48321	Auburn Hills	(248)	19,315	17,076
*49016	Battle Creek	(616)	53,430	53,516
*48707	Bay City	(517)	36,548	38,936
48505	Beecher(c)	(517)	—	14,465
48809	Belding	(616)	6,097	5,969
*49022	Benton Harbor	(616)	11,824	12,818
49022	Benton Heights(c)	(616)	—	5,465
48072	Berkley	(248)	16,766	16,960
48025	Beverly Hills	(248)	10,452	10,610
49307	Big Rapids	(616)	10,471	12,603
*48012	Birmingham	(248)	19,794	19,997
48301	Bloomfield(c)	(810)	—	42,137
48722	Bridgeport(c)	(517)	—	8,569
*48116	Brighton	(810)	6,418	5,686
48601	Buena Vista(c)		—	8,196
*48501	Burton	(810)	27,357	27,437
49601	Cadillac	(616)	10,498	10,104
*48185	Canton(c)	(734)	—	57,047
48724	Carrollton(c)	(517)	—	6,521
48015	Center Line	(810)	8,456	9,026
48813	Charlotte	(517)	8,002	8,083
49721	Cheboygan	(616)	5,216	4,997
48017	Clawson	(248)	13,759	13,874
*48046	Clinton(c)	(517)	—	85,866
49036	Coldwater	(517)	9,568	9,607
49321	Comstock Park(c)	(616)	—	6,530
49508	Cutlerville(c)	(616)	—	11,228
48423	Davison	(810)	5,615	5,693
*48120	Dearborn	(313)	91,418	89,286
*48127	Dearborn Heights	(313)	61,504	60,838
*48231	Detroit	(313)	1,000,272	1,027,974
49047	Dowagiac	(616)	6,101	6,418
49506	East Grand Rapids	(616)	10,564	10,807
*48826	East Lansing	(517)	48,192	50,677
48021	Eastpointe	(810)	32,803	35,283
49001	Eastwood(c)	(616)	—	6,340
48229	Ecorse	(313)	12,272	12,180
49829	Escanaba	(906)	13,556	13,659
49022	Fair Plain(c)	(616)	—	8,051
*48333	Farmington	(248)	10,071	10,170
48333	Farmington Hills	(248)	79,918	74,614
48430	Fenton	(810)	9,705	8,434
48220	Ferndale	(248)	24,485	25,084
48134	Flat Rock	(734)	7,697	7,290
*48501	Flint	(810)	134,881	140,925
48433	Flushing	(810)	8,422	8,542
49506	Forest Hills(c)	(616)	—	16,690
48026	Fraser	(810)	14,471	13,899
*48135	Garden City	(734)	32,336	31,846
48439	Grand Blanc	(810)	8,160	7,760
49417	Grand Haven	(616)	12,142	11,951
48837	Grand Ledge	(517)	7,770	7,562
*49501	Grand Rapids	(616)	188,242	189,126
*49418	Grandville	(616)	16,473	15,624
48838	Greenville	(616)	8,385	8,101
48138	Grosse Ile(c)	(734)	—	9,781
*48231	Grosse Pointe	(313)	5,695	5,681
48230	Grosse Pointe Farms	(313)	10,183	10,092
48230	Grosse Pointe Park	(313)	12,869	12,857

ZIP	Place		1996	1990
48230	Grosse Pointe Woods	(313)	17,828	17,715
48212	Hamtramck	(313)	18,262	18,372
48225	Harper Woods	(313)	14,955	14,903
48625	Harrison(c)	(517)	—	24,685
48840	Haslett(c)	(517)	—	10,230
49058	Hastings	(616)	6,349	6,549
48030	Hazel Park	(248)	19,734	20,051
48203	Highland Park	(313)	19,788	20,121
49242	Hillsdale	(517)	8,252	8,175
*49423	Holland	(616)	33,247	30,745
48442	Holly	(248)	6,024	5,595
48842	Holt(c)	(517)	—	11,744
49931	Houghton	(906)	7,426	7,498
*48844	Howell	(517)	9,348	8,147
49426	Hudsonville	(616)	6,757	6,170
48070	Huntington Woods	(248)	6,305	6,419
48141	Inkster	(313)/(734)	30,992	30,772
48846	Ionia	(616)	6,512	5,990
49801	Iron Mountain	(906)	8,530	8,525
49938	Ironwood	(906)	6,573	6,849
49849	Ishpeming	(906)	5,420	7,200
*49204	Jackson	(517)	35,899	37,425
*49428	Jenison(c)	(616)	—	17,882
*49001	Kalamazoo	(616)	77,460	80,277
49518	Kentwood	(616)	41,816	37,826
49802	Kingsford	(906)	5,520	5,480
49843	K.I. Sawyer AFB(c)	(906)	—	6,577
48144	Lambertville(c)	(734)	—	7,860
*48901	Lansing	(517)	127,916	127,321
48446	Lapeer	(810)	8,122	7,759
48146	Lincoln Park	(313)	42,167	41,832
*48150	Livonia	(734)	105,099	100,850
49431	Ludington	(616)	9,012	8,507
48071	Madison Heights	(248)	32,566	32,196
49660	Manistee	(616)	6,393	6,734
49855	Marquette	(906)	17,016	21,977
49068	Marshall	(616)	7,251	6,941
48040	Marysville	(810)	9,476	8,515
48854	Mason	(517)	7,374	6,768
48122	Melvindale	(313)	11,246	11,216
49858	Menominee	(906)	8,856	9,398
*48640	Midland	(517)	39,849	38,053
*48381	Milford	(248)	6,344	5,500
*48161	Monroe	(734)	22,563	22,902
*48046	Mount Clemens	(810)	17,170	18,405
*48804	Mount Pleasant	(517)	23,092	23,299
*49440	Muskegon	(616)	39,518	39,809
49444	Muskegon Heights	(616)	12,564	13,176
*48047	New Baltimore	(810)	5,901	5,798
49120	Niles	(616)	11,813	12,458
49505	Northview(c)	(616)	—	13,712
48167	Northville	(248)	6,497	6,226
49441	Norton Shores	(616)	22,710	21,755
*48376	Novi	(248)	43,634	32,998
48237	Oak Park	(248)	29,972	30,468
*48805	Okemos(c)	(517)	—	20,216
48867	Owosso	(517)	15,861	16,322
49770	Petoskey	(616)	7,241	6,056
48170	Plymouth	(734)	9,670	9,560
48170	Plymouth Township(c)	(734)	—	23,646
*48342	Pontiac	(248)	70,471	71,136
*49081	Portage	(616)	43,317	41,042
*48061	Port Huron	(810)	32,873	33,694
*48231	Redford(c)	(313)	—	54,387
48218	River Rouge	(313)	11,091	11,314
48192	Riverview	(734)	14,250	13,894
*48308	Rochester	(248)	7,452	7,130
48306	Rochester Hills	(248)	67,408	61,766
48174	Romulus	(313)/(734)	23,636	22,897
48066	Roseville	(810)	51,275	51,412
*48068	Royal Oak	(248)	64,942	65,410
*48605	Saginaw	(517)	65,014	69,512
48604	Saginaw Township North(c)	(517)	—	23,018
48603	Saginaw Township South(c)	(517)	—	13,987
48079	Saint Clair	(810)	5,492	5,116
*48080	Saint Clair Shores	(313)	64,065	68,107
48879	Saint Johns	(517)	7,555	7,392
49085	Saint Joseph	(616)	8,766	9,214
48176	Saline	(734)	7,193	6,663
49783	Sault Sainte Marie	(906)	15,300	14,689
49455	Shelby(c)	(616)	—	48,655
48609	Shields(c)	(517)	—	6,634
*48037	Southfield	(248)	76,184	75,727
48195	Southgate	(734)	31,438	30,771
49090	South Haven	(616)	5,429	5,563
48178	South Lyon	(248)	8,057	6,479
48161	South Monroe(c)	(734)	—	5,266
49015	Springfield	(248)	5,654	5,582
*48311	Sterling Heights	(810)	118,698	117,810
49091	Sturgis	(616)	10,387	10,130
48180	Taylor	(313)/(734)	71,939	70,811
49286	Tecumseh	(517)	8,032	7,462
48182	Temperance(c)	(734)	—	6,542
49093	Three Rivers	(616)	7,308	7,464
*49684	Traverse City	(616)	15,082	15,155
48183	Trenton	(734)	21,474	20,586
*48099	Troy	(248)	79,120	72,884
49504	Walker	(616)	18,971	17,279
*48390	Walled Lake	(248)	6,672	6,278
*48090	Warren	(810)	138,078	144,864

ZIP	Place		1996	1990
*48329	Waterford(c)	(248)	—	66,692
48917	Waverly(c)	(517)	—	15,614
48184	Wayne	(734)	20,661	19,899
*48325	West Bloomfield(c)	(248)	—	54,843
*48185	Westland	(313)/(734)	90,798	84,724
49019	Westwood(c)	(616)	—	8,957
48393	Wixom	(248)	10,498	8,550
48183	Woodhaven	(734)	12,828	11,631
48753	Wurtsmith AFB(c)	(517)	—	5,080
48192	Wyandotte	(734)	31,803	30,938
49509	Wyoming	(616)	66,571	63,891
*48197	Ypsilanti	(734)	23,045	24,846
49464	Zeeland	(616)	5,816	5,417

Minnesota

ZIP	Place		1996	1990
56007	Albert Lea	(507)	17,823	18,310
56308	Alexandria	(320)	8,295	8,029
55304	Andover	(612)	22,387	15,216
*55303	Anoka	(612)	17,780	17,192
55124	Apple Valley	(612)	42,949	34,598
55112	Arden Hills	(651)	9,482	9,199
55912	Austin	(507)	21,604	21,926
56425	Baxter	(218)	5,026	3,695
*56601	Bemidji	(218)	12,249	11,165
55449	Blaine	(612)/(651)	43,241	38,975
*55420	Bloomington	(612)	86,664	86,335
56401	Brainerd	(218)	13,285	12,353
55429	Brooklyn Center	(612)	28,132	28,887
55443	Brooklyn Park	(612)	61,335	56,381
55313	Buffalo	(612)	8,584	7,302
*55337	Burnsville	(612)/(651)	57,087	51,288
55008	Cambridge	(612)	5,386	5,094
55316	Champlin	(612)	20,654	16,849
55317	Chanhassen	(612)	17,045	11,736
55318	Chaska	(612)	14,700	11,339
55719	Chisholm	(218)	5,058	5,290
55014	Circle Pines	(612)	5,021	4,704
55720	Cloquet	(218)	10,946	10,885
55421	Columbia Heights	(612)	18,368	18,910
55433	Coon Rapids	(612)	62,790	52,978
55340	Corcoran	(612)	5,766	5,199
55016	Cottage Grove	(651)	29,486	22,935
56716	Crookston	(218)	7,943	8,119
55428	Crystal	(612)	23,292	23,788
55327	Dayton	(612)	5,027	4,443
*56501	Detroit Lakes	(218)	7,287	7,141
*55806	Duluth	(218)	83,699	85,493
55121	Eagan	(612)/(651)	57,294	47,409
55005	East Bethel	(612)	9,626	8,050
56721	East Grand Forks	(218)	8,827	8,658
*55344	Eden Prairie	(612)	47,630	39,311
55424	Edina	(612)	46,336	46,075
55330	Elk River	(612)	14,892	11,143
56031	Fairmont	(507)	11,098	11,265
55113	Falcon Heights	(651)	5,284	5,380
55021	Faribault	(507)	18,313	17,085
55024	Farmington	(612)/(651)	8,571	5,940
*56537	Fergus Falls	(218)	13,362	12,362
55025	Forest Lake	(651)	6,435	5,833
55432	Fridley	(612)	27886	28,335
55427	Golden Valley	(612)	20,560	20,971
*55744	Grand Rapids	(218)	8,162	7,976
*55304	Ham Lake	(612)	10,955	8,924
55033	Hastings	(651)	16,823	15,478
55810	Hermantown	(218)	7,679	6,761
*55746	Hibbing	(218)	17,600	18,046
*55343	Hopkins	(612)	16,262	16,529
55038	Hugo	(651)	5,562	4,417
55350	Hutchinson	(320)	12,268	11,459
56649	International Falls	(218)	8,000	8,301
*55075	Inver Grove Heights	(651)	26,962	22,477
55042	Lake Elmo	(651)	6,444	5,900
55044	Lakeville	(612)	36,843	24,854
55014	Lino Lakes	(651)	13,493	8,807
55355	Litchfield	(320)	6,052	6,041
55117	Little Canada	(651)	9,424	8,971
56345	Little Falls	(320)	7,521	7,371
55115	Mahtomedi	(651)	6,806	5,633
*56001	Mankato	(507)	31,271	31,459
55311	Maple Grove	(612)	45,142	38,736
55109	Maplewood	(651)	33,983	30,954
56258	Marshall	(507)	12,233	12,023
55118	Mendota Heights	(651)	11,193	9,388
*55440	Minneapolis	(612)	358,785	368,383
55345	Minnetonka	(612)	50,219	48,370
56265	Montevideo	(320)	5,377	5,499
*55362	Monticello	(612)	6,422	5,045
*56560	Moorhead	(218)	33,343	32,295
56267	Morris	(320)	5,412	5,613
55364	Mound	(612)	9,684	9,634
55112	Mounds View	(651)	12,769	12,541
55112	New Brighton	(651)	22,664	22,207
54427	New Hope	(612)	21,439	21,853
56073	New Ulm	(507)	13,438	13,132
55057	Northfield	(507)	15,819	14,684
56001	North Mankato	(507)	11,671	10,662
55109	North Saint Paul	(651)	12,568	12,376
55128	Oakdale	(651)	25,184	18,377
.....	Oak Grove	(612)	6,534	5,488
55323	Orono	(612)	7,447	7,285
.....	Otsego	(612)	6,030	5,219
55060	Owatonna	(507)	20,330	19,386
55421	Plymouth	(612)	60,103	50,889
55372	Prior Lake	(612)	13,714	11,482
55303	Ramsey	(612)	16,738	12,408
55066	Red Wing	(651)	15,688	15,134
55423	Richfield	(612)	34,387	35,710
55422	Robbinsdale	(612)	14,167	14,396
*55901	Rochester	(507)	75,638	70,729
55068	Rosemount	(612)/(651)	12,242	8,622
55113	Roseville	(651)	34,183	33,485
55418	Saint Anthony	(651)	7,831	7,727
*56301	Saint Cloud	(320)	50,801	48,812
55426	Saint Louis Park	(612)	42,828	43,787
*55101	Saint Paul	(651)	259,606	272,235
55071	Saint Paul Park	(651)	5,076	4,965
56082	Saint Peter	(507)	9,850	9,481
56377	Sartell	(320)	7,398	5,409
56379	Sauk Rapids	(320)	9,236	7,823
56378	Savage	(612)	15,373	9,906
55379	Shakopee	(612)	14,537	11,739
55126	Shoreview	(651)	25,981	24,587
55331	Shorewood	(612)	6,926	5,913
55075	South Saint Paul	(651)	19,787	20,197
55432	Spring Lake Park	(612)	6,860	6,532
*55082	Stillwater	(651)	15,585	13,882
56701	Thief River Falls	(218)	8,253	8,010
55127	Vadnais Heights	(651)	12,926	11,041
*55792	Virginia	(218)	8,988	9,410
56387	Waite Park	(320)	5,791	5,020
56093	Waseca	(507)	8,187	8,385
55118	West Saint Paul	(651)	19,070	19,248
55110	White Bear Lake	(651)	25,613	24,622
56201	Willmar	(320)	18,837	17,531
55987	Winona	(507)	24,788	25,435
55125	Woodbury	(651)	35,783	20,075
56187	Worthington	(507)	10,321	9,977

Mississippi

ZIP	Place		1996	1990
39730	Aberdeen	(601)	6,935	6,837
38821	Amory	(601)	7,154	7,093
38606	Batesville	(601)	7,046	6,403
*39520	Bay Saint Louis	(228)	9,433	8,063
*39530	Biloxi	(228)	48,414	46,319
38829	Booneville	(601)	8,304	7,955
*39042	Brandon	(601)	13,444	11,089
39601	Brookhaven	(601)	10,616	10,243
39046	Canton	(601)	10,328	10,062
38614	Clarksdale	(601)	19,381	19,717
*38732	Cleveland	(601)	15,161	15,384
*39056	Clinton	(601)	21,992	21,847
39429	Columbia	(601)	6,914	6,815
*39701	Columbus	(601)	22,724	23,799
38834	Corinth	(601)	12,264	11,820
39059	Crystal Springs	(601)	5,807	5,643
39532	D'Iberville	(228)	7,868	6,566
39074	Forest	(601)	5,363	5,062
39553	Gautier	(228)	11,030	10,088
*38701	Greenville	(601)	42,933	45,226
*38930	Greenwood	(601)	18,117	18,906
*38901	Grenada	(601)	11,155	10,864
39564	Gulf Hills(c)	(228)	—	5,004
*39501	Gulfport	(228)	64,829	64,045
*39401	Hattiesburg	(601)	47,803	45,325
*38635	Holly Springs	(601)	7,306	7,261
38637	Horn Lake	(601)	13,042	9,069
38751	Indianola	(601)	11,832	11,809
*39205	Jackson	(601)	192,923	202,062
39090	Kosciusko	(601)	6,863	6,986
*39440	Laurel	(601)	18,586	18,827
38756	Leland	(601)	6,084	6,366
39560	Long Beach	(228)	16,756	15,804
39339	Louisville	(601)	7,113	7,165
*39648	McComb	(601)	11,957	11,797
*39110	Madison	(601)	11,703	7,471
*39302	Meridian	(601)	40,835	41,036
*39563	Moss Point	(228)	18,356	17,837
*39120	Natchez	(601)	18,732	19,460
38652	New Albany	(601)	7,044	6,775
*39564	Ocean Springs	(228)	16,439	15,221
38654	Olive Branch	(601)	8,474	3,567
39567	Orange Grove(c)	(228)	—	15,676
38655	Oxford	(601)	11,714	10,026
*39567	Pascagoula	(228)	27,026	25,899
39571	Pass Christian	(228)	5,957	5,557
39288	Pearl	(601)	21,175	19,588
39465	Petal	(601)	8,684	7,883
39350	Philadelphia	(601)	7,523	6,758
39466	Picayune	(601)	11,733	10,633
38863	Pontotoc	(601)	5,068	4,570
39218	Richland	(601)	5,383	4,014
*39157	Ridgeland	(601)	15,579	11,714
38663	Ripley	(601)	5,574	5,371
39533	Saint Martin(c)	(228)	—	6,349
38671	Southaven	(601)	20,778	17,949
*39759	Starkville	(601)	19,907	18,458

ZIP	Place		1996	1990
*38801	Tupelo	(601)	35,194	30,685
*39180	Vicksburg	(601)	27,056	26,886
39576	Waveland	(228)	6,571	5,369
39367	Waynesboro	(601)	5,301	5,143
.....	West Hattiesburg(c)	(601)	—	5,450
39773	West Point	(601)	8,881	8,489
38967	Winona	(601)	5,796	5,965
39194	Yazoo City	(601)	11,898	12,427

Missouri

ZIP	Place		1996	1990
63123	Affton(c)	(314)	—	21,106
63010	Arnold	(314)	20,473	18,828
65605	Aurora	(417)	6,791	6,459
*63011	Ballwin	(314)	20,853	21,406
63137	Bellefontaine Neighbors	(314)	10,352	10,918
64012	Belton	(816)	20,862	18,145
63134	Berkeley	(314)	10,636	12,250
63031	Black Jack	(314)	6,295	6,131
*64015	Blue Springs	(816)	44,667	40,103
65613	Bolivar	(417)	8,119	6,845
65233	Boonville	(660)	7,597	7,095
*65616	Branson	(417)	5,039	3,706
63144	Brentwood	(314)	7,704	8,150
63045	Bridgeton	(314)	16,502	17,732
64429	Cameron	(816)	7,672	6,782
*63701	Cape Girardeau	(573)	35,464	34,475
64834	Carl Junction	(417)	5,080	4,123
64836	Carthage	(417)	11,381	10,747
63830	Caruthersville	(573)	7,096	7,389
*63017	Chesterfield	(314)	45,490	42,325
64601	Chillicothe	(660)	8,472	8,799
63105	Clayton	(314)	13,513	13,926
64735	Clinton	(660)	9,226	8,703
*65201	Columbia	(573)	76,756	69,133
63128	Concord(c)	(314)	—	19,859
63126	Crestwood	(314)	12,114	11,229
63141	Creve Coeur	(314)	12,093	12,289
63020	De Soto	(314)	6,009	5,993
63131	Des Peres	(314)	8,011	8,395
63841	Dexter	(573)	7,640	7,506
63011	Ellisville	(314)	7,841	7,183
63025	Eureka	(314)	5,250	4,683
64024	Excelsior Springs	(816)	11,293	10,373
63640	Farmington	(573)	13,210	11,596
63135	Ferguson	(314)	21,126	22,290
63028	Festus	(314)	8,353	8,105
*63033	Florissant	(314)	50,491	51,038
65473	Fort Leonard Wood(c)	(573)	—	15,863
65251	Fulton	(573)	10,785	10,033
64118	Gladstone	(816)	27,819	26,243
65254	Glasgow Village(c)	(573)	—	5,199
63122	Glendale	(314)	5,629	5,945
64030	Grandview	(816)	24,040	24,973
63401	Hannibal	(573)	17,870	18,004
64701	Harrisonville	(816)	8,450	7,696
63042	Hazelwood	(314)	14,754	15,512
*64050	Independence	(816)	114,980	112,301
63755	Jackson	(573)	10,893	9,256
*65101	Jefferson City	(573)	36,143	35,517
63136	Jennings	(314)	15,162	15,841
*64801	Joplin	(417)	43,698	40,866
*64108	Kansas City	(816)	441,259	434,829
63857	Kennett	(573)	10,788	10,941
63501	Kirksville	(660)	17,107	17,152
63122	Kirkwood	(314)	27,465	28,318
63124	Ladue (St. Louis Co.)	(314)	8,400	8,795
63367	Lake Saint Louis	(314)	8,833	7,536
65536	Lebanon	(417)	11,166	9,983
*64063	Lee's Summit	(816)	61,861	46,418
63125	Lemay(c)	(314)	—	18,005
*64068	Liberty	(816)	24,270	20,459
63552	Macon	(660)	5,399	5,571
63011	Manchester	(314)	6,929	6,447
63143	Maplewood	(314)	9,334	9,962
65340	Marshall	(660)	12,283	12,711
65706	Marshfield	(417)	5,219	4,374
63043	Maryland Heights	(314)	24,094	25,440
64468	Maryville	(816)	10,159	10,663
63129	Mehlville(c)	(314)	—	27,557
65265	Mexico	(573)	11,170	11,290
65270	Moberly	(660)	12,131	12,839
65708	Monett	(417)	7,312	6,529
63026	Murphy(c)	(314)	—	9,342
64850	Neosho	(417)	9,399	9,254
64772	Nevada	(417)	8,228	8,597
65714	Nixa	(417)	9,483	4,893
63129	Oakville(c)	(314)	—	31,750
63366	O'Fallon	(314)	29,564	17,427
63132	Olivette	(314)	7,168	7,573
63114	Overland	(314)	16,936	17,987
65721	Ozark	(417)	6,962	4,401
63601	Park Hills	(573)	8,164	7,866
63775	Perryville	(573)	7,439	6,933
*63901	Poplar Bluff	(573)	17,043	16,841
64083	Raymore	(816)	8,257	5,592
64133	Raytown	(816)	29,429	30,601
65738	Republic	(417)	6,651	6,290
64085	Richmond	(816)	5,766	5,738
63117	Richmond Heights	(314)	9,803	10,448
*65401	Rolla	(573)	15,579	14,090
63074	Saint Ann	(314)	13,714	14,449
*63301	Saint Charles	(314)	56,525	50,634
63114	Saint John	(314)	7,045	7,502
*64501	Saint Joseph	(816)	70,208	71,852
*63166	Saint Louis	(314)	351,565	396,685
63376	Saint Peters	(314)	48,493	40,660
63126	Sappington(c)	(314)	—	10,917
*65301	Sedalia	(660)	20,348	19,800
63119	Shrewsbury	(314)	6,288	6,416
63801	Sikeston	(573)	17,874	17,641
63138	Spanish Lake(c)	(314)	—	20,322
*65801	Springfield	(417)	143,407	140,494
63080	Sullivan	(573)	6,153	5,661
63127	Sunset Hills	(314)	5,314	4,915
63006	Town and Country	(314)	10,921	10,944
64683	Trenton	(660)	5,849	6,129
63084	Union	(314)	6,222	6,048
63130	University City	(314)	38,086	40,087
63088	Valley Park	(314)	5,797	4,165
64093	Warrensburg	(660)	17,076	15,244
63090	Washington	(314)	12,210	11,367
64870	Webb City	(417)	8,488	7,449
63119	Webster Groves	(314)	21,890	22,992
63385	Wentzville	(314)	5,063	4,640
65775	West Plains	(417)	10,748	9,214

Montana (406)

ZIP	Place	1996	1990
59711	Anaconda	10,093	10,356
*59101	Billings	91,195	81,125
*59715	Bozeman	28,522	22,660
*59701	Butte	34,051	33,336
*59401	Great Falls	57,758	55,125
59501	Havre	10,232	10,201
*59601	Helena	27,982	24,609
.....	Helena Valley West Central(c)	—	6,327
*59901	Kalispell	15,678	11,917
59044	Laurel	6,125	5,686
59457	Lewistown	6,380	6,097
59047	Livingston	7,509	6,701
59402	Malmstrom AFB(c)	—	5,938
59301	Miles City	8,882	8,461
*59801	Missoula	51,204	42,918
59801	Orchard Homes(c)	—	10,317
59937	Whitefish	5,793	4,368

Nebraska

ZIP	Place		1996	1990
69301	Alliance	(308)	9,702	9,765
68310	Beatrice	(402)	12,464	12,352
*68108	Bellevue	(402)	42,807	39,240
*68008	Blair	(402)	7,558	6,860
69337	Chadron	(308)	5,806	5,588
68108	Chalco(c)	(402)	—	7,337
*68601	Columbus	(402)	20,848	19,480
68333	Crete	(402)	5,093	4,841
*68025	Fremont	(402)	24,223	23,680
69341	Gering	(308)	7,876	7,946
*68802	Grand Island	(308)	41,177	39,487
*68901	Hastings	(402)	22,008	22,837
68949	Holdrege	(308)	5,912	5,671
*68847	Kearney	(308)	27,314	24,396
68128	La Vista	(402)	11,596	9,840
68850	Lexington	(308)	10,075	6,600
*68501	Lincoln	(402)	209,192	191,972
69001	McCook	(308)	7,926	8,112
68410	Nebraska City	(402)	6,766	6,547
*68701	Norfolk	(402)	23,423	21,476
*69101	North Platte	(308)	23,369	22,605
68113	Offutt AFB West(c)	(402)	—	10,883
69153	Ogallala	(308)	5,072	5,095
*68108	Omaha	(402)	364,253	342,862
*68108	Papillion	(402)	14,516	10,378
68048	Plattsmouth	(402)	6,863	6,415
68127	Ralston	(402)	6,251	6,236
*69361	Scottsbluff	(308)	14,400	13,711
68434	Seward	(402)	6,093	5,641
69162	Sidney	(308)	6,128	5,959
68776	South Sioux City	(402)	11,166	9,677
68787	Wayne	(402)	5,337	5,142
68467	York	(402)	8,146	7,940

Nevada

Area code (775) goes into effect on Dec. 12, 1998. Before then use (702).

ZIP	Place		1996	1990
*89005	Boulder City	(702)	14,249	12,567
*89701	Carson City	(775)	47,237	40,443
89112	East Las Vegas(c)	(702)	—	11,087
*89801	Elko	(775)	19,371	14,836
.....	Enterprise(c)		—	6,412
*89406	Fallon	(775)	7,940	6,430
89408	Fernley(c)	(775)	—	5,164
89410	Gardnerville Ranchos(c)	(775)	—	7,455
*89015	Henderson	(702)	122,339	64,948
*89450	Incline Village-Crystal Bay(c)	(775)	—	7,119

ZIP	Place		1996	1990
*89125	Las Vegas	(702)	376,906	258,204
*89024	Mesquite	(702)	6,200	1,871
89191	Nellis AFB(c)	(702)	—	8,377
*89030	North Las Vegas	(702)	78,659	47,849
*89041	Pahrump(c)	(775)	—	7,424
89109	Paradise(c)	(775)	—	124,682
*89501	Reno	(775)	155,499	133,850
*89431	Sparks	(775)	59,496	53,367
*89801	Spring Creek(c)	(702)	—	5,866
.....	Spring Valley(c)	(702)	—	51,726
89110	Sunrise Manor(c)	(702)	—	95,362
89433	Sun Valley(c)	(775)	—	11,391
89101	Winchester(c)	(702)	—	23,365
*89445	Winnemucca	(775)	8,004	6,102

New Hampshire (603)

See introductory note.

ZIP	Place	1996	1990
03031	*Amherst*	9,773	9,068
03811	*Atkinson*	6,275	5,188
03825	*Barrington*	6,811	6,164
03110	*Bedford*	14,593	12,563
03220	*Belmont*	6,129	5,796
03570	Berlin	10,669	11,824
03304	*Bow*	6,213	5,500
03743	Claremont	13,970	13,902
*03301	Concord	37,021	36,006
03818	*Conway*	8,643	7,940
03038	Derry Compact(c)	—	20,446
03038	*Derry*	31,452	29,603
*03820	Dover	25,766	25,042
03824	Durham Compact(c)	—	9,236
03824	*Durham*	10,844	11,818
03042	*Epping*	5,656	5,162
03833	Exeter Compact(c)	—	9,556
03833	*Exeter*	13,213	12,481
03835	*Farmington*	5,876	5,739
03235	Franklin	8,367	8,304
03246	*Gilford*	6,045	5,867
03045	*Goffstown*	15,548	14,621
03841	*Hampstead*	7,486	6,732
*03842	Hampton Compact(c)	—	7,989
*03842	*Hampton*	12,781	12,278
03755	Hanover Compact(c)	—	6,538
03755	*Hanover*	9,844	9,212
03049	*Hollis*	6,550	5,705
03106	*Hooksett*	9,511	9,002
03051	*Hudson*	21,344	19,530
03452	*Jaffrey*	5,330	5,361
03431	Keene	22,325	22,430
03848	*Kingston*	5,893	5,591
*03246	Laconia	16,264	15,743
*03766	Lebanon	12,571	12,183
03052	*Litchfield*	6,666	5,516
03561	*Littleton*	6,036	5,827
03053	Londonderry Compact(c)	—	10,114
03053	*Londonderry*	21,567	19,781
*03103	Manchester	100,967	99,332
03253	*Meredith*	5,019	4,837
03054	*Merrimack*	23,547	22,156
03055	Milford Compact(c)	—	8,015
03055	*Milford*	12,549	11,795
*03060	Nashua	81,094	79,662
03857	*Newmarket*	7,400	7,157
03773	*Newport*	6,192	6,110
03076	*Pelham*	10,600	9,408
03275	*Pembroke*	6,589	6,561
03458	*Peterborough*	5,555	5,239
03865	*Plaistow*	7,685	7,316
03264	*Plymouth*	5,959	5,811
*03801	Portsmouth	25,034	25,925
03077	*Raymond*	9,537	8,713
*03867	Rochester	27,704	26,630
03079	*Salem*	27,195	25,746
03874	*Seabrook*	6,749	6,503
03878	Somersworth	11,515	11,249
03885	*Stratham*	5,648	4,955
03275	Suncook(c)	—	5,214
03446	*Swanzey*	6,596	6,236
03281	*Weare*	7,000	6,193
03087	*Windham*	9,713	9,000
03894	*Wolfeboro*	5,193	4,807

New Jersey

See introductory note.

ZIP	Place		1996	1990
08201	Absecon	(609)	7,709	7,298
07401	Allendale	(201)	6,397	5,900
07712	Asbury Park	(732)	17,125	16,799
*08401	Atlantic City	(609)	38,361	37,986
08106	Audubon	(609)	8,995	9,205
07001	Avenel(c)	(732)	—	15,504
08007	Barrington	(609)	7,277	6,792
07002	Bayonne	(201)	60,499	61,464
08722	Beachwood	(732)	9,923	9,324
07109	Belleville(c)	(973)	—	34,213
*08031	Bellmawr	(609)	12,399	12,603

ZIP	Place		1996	1990
07719	Belmar	(732)	5,916	5,877
07621	Bergenfield	(201)	24,625	24,458
07922	Berkeley Heights Twp.(c)	(908)	—	11,980
08009	Berlin	(609)	5,943	5,672
07924	Bernardsville	(908)	6,928	6,597
08012	Blackwood(c)	(609)	—	5,120
07003	Bloomfield(c)	(973)	—	45,061
07403	Bloomingdale	(973)	7,565	7,530
07603	Bogota	(201)	7,925	7,824
07005	Boonton	(973)	8,502	8,343
08805	Bound Brook	(732)	9,617	9,487
*08723	Brick Twp.(c)	(732)	—	66,473
08302	Bridgeton	(609)	18,493	18,942
08807	Bridgewater Twp.(c)	(732)/(908)	—	32,509
08203	Brigantine	(609)	11,556	11,354
08015	Browns Mills(c)	(609)	—	11,429
07828	Budd Lake(c)	(973)	—	7,272
08016	Burlington	(609)	9,639	9,835
07405	Butler	(973)	7,721	7,392
*07006	Caldwell(c)	(973)	—	7,549
*08101	Camden	(609)	84,844	87,492
07072	Carlstadt	(201)	5,599	5,510
08069	Carney's Point Twp. (c)	(609)	—	8,443
07008	Carteret	(732)	19,086	19,025
07009	Cedar Grove Twp.(c)(Essex)	(973)	—	12,053
07928	Chatham	(973)	7,953	8,007
*08034	Cherry Hill Twp.(c)	(609)	—	69,319
08077	Cinnaminson Twp.(c)	(609)	—	14,583
07066	Clark Twp.(c)	(732)/(908)	—	14,629
08312	Clayton	(609)	6,827	6,155
08021	Clementon	(609)	5,477	5,601
07010	Cliffside Park	(201)	20,917	20,393
*07015	Clifton	(973)	71,305	71,984
07624	Closter	(201)	8,366	8,094
08108	Collingswood	(609)	14,820	15,289
07067	Colonia(c)	(732)	—	18,238
07016	Cranford Twp.(c)	(908)	—	22,633
07626	Cresskill	(201)	7,795	7,558
08759	Crestwood Village(c)	(732)	—	8,030
*07801	Dover	(973)	15,312	15,115
07628	Dumont	(201)	17,504	17,187
08812	Dunellen	(732)	6,594	6,528
08816	East Brunswick Twp.(c)	(732)	—	43,548
07936	East Hanover Twp.(c)	(973)	—	9,926
*07019	East Orange	(973)	70,534	73,552
07073	East Rutherford	(201)/(973)	8,045	7,902
07724	Eatontown	(732)	13,976	13,800
07020	Edgewater	(201)	5,218	5,001
08010	Edgewater Park Twp.(c)	(609)	—	8,388
*08818	Edison Twp.(c)	(732)/(908)	—	88,680
*07207	Elizabeth	(908)	110,149	110,002
07407	Elmwood Park	(201)	18,128	17,623
07630	Emerson	(201)	7,082	6,930
07631	Englewood	(201)	25,148	24,850
07632	Englewood Cliffs	(201)	5,776	5,634
08618	Ewing Twp.(c)	(609)	—	34,185
07004	Fairfield(c)	(973)	—	7,615
07704	Fair Haven	(732)	5,456	5,270
07410	Fair Lawn	(201)/(973)	30,876	30,548
07022	Fairview (Bergen)	(201)	11,138	10,733
07023	Fanwood	(908)	7,108	7,115
08518	Florence-Roebling(c)	(609)	—	8,564
07932	Florham Park	(973)	8,986	8,521
08863	Fords(c)	(732)	—	14,392
08640	Fort Dix(c)	(609)	—	10,205
07024	Fort Lee	(201)	33,118	31,997
07416	Franklin	(973)	5,262	4,977
07417	Franklin Lakes	(201)	10,270	9,873
*08873	Franklin Twp. (Somerset)(c)	(732)/(908)	—	42,780
07728	Freehold	(732)	10,869	10,742
07026	Garfield	(201)	27,054	26,727
08753	Gilford Park(c)	(732)	—	8,668
08028	Glassboro	(609)	17,463	15,614
08029	Glendora(c)	(609)	—	5,201
07028	Glen Ridge	(973)	6,722	7,076
07452	Glen Rock	(201)	11,060	10,883
08030	Gloucester City	(609)	12,302	12,649
07093	Guttenberg	(201)	8,266	8,268
*07602	Hackensack	(201)	37,467	37,049
07840	Hackettstown	(908)	8,586	8,120
08033	Haddonfield	(609)	11,332	11,633
08035	Haddon Heights	(609)	7,640	7,860
*07510	Haledon	(973)	6,893	6,951
*08609	Hamilton Twp. (Mercer)(c)	(609)	—	86,553
08037	Hammonton	(609)	12,433	12,208
07981	Hanover Twp.(c)	(973)	—	11,538
07029	Harrison	(973)	13,248	13,425
07604	Hasbrouck Heights	(201)	11,618	11,488
*07510	Hawthorne	(973)	17,082	17,084
07730	Hazlet Twp.(c)	(732)	—	21,976
08904	Highland Park (Middlesex)	(732)	13,287	13,279
07642	Hillsdale	(201)	10,024	9,750
07205	Hillside Twp.(c)	(908)/(973)	—	21,044
07030	Hoboken	(201)	33,136	33,397
08753	Holiday City-Berkeley(c)	(732)	—	14,293
.....	Holiday City South(c)	(732)	—	5,452
07843	Hopatcong	(973)	16,275	15,586
08525	Hopewell Twp. (Mercer)(c)	(609)	—	11,590
07111	Irvington(c)	(973)	—	59,774

ZIP	Place	1996	1990
08830	Iselin(c) (732)	—	16,141
08527	Jackson Twp.(c) (732)	—	33,283
08831	Jamesburg (732)	5,605	5,294
*07303	Jersey City (201)	229,039	228,517
07734	Keansburg (732)	11,195	11,069
07032	Kearny (201)/(973)	35,112	34,874
08824	Kendall Park(c) (908)	—	7,127
07033	Kenilworth (908)	7,613	7,574
07735	Keyport (732)	7,716	7,586
07405	Kinnelon (973)	8,944	8,470
07871	Lake Mohawk(c) (973)	—	8,930
08701	Lakewood(c) (732)	—	26,095
08879	Laurence Harbor(c) (732)	—	6,361
08648	Lawrenceville(c) (609)	—	6,446
*08733	Leisure Village West-Pine Lake Park(c) (732)	—	10,139
07605	Leonia (201)	8,449	8,365
07035	Lincoln Park (973)	11,201	10,978
07738	Lincroft(c) (732)	—	6,193
07036	Linden (732)/(908)	36,857	36,701
08021	Lindenwold (609)	18,328	18,734
08221	Linwood (609)	7,083	6,866
07424	Little Falls Twp.(c) (973)	—	11,294
07643	Little Ferry (201)	10,108	9,989
07739	Little Silver (732)	6,047	5,721
07039	Livingston Twp.(c) (973)	—	26,609
07644	Lodi (201)/(973)	22,736	22,355
07740	Long Branch (732)	28,918	28,658
*07946	Long Hill Twp.(c) (973)	—	7,826
07071	Lyndhurst Twp.(c) (201)	—	18,262
08641	McGuire AFB(c) (609)	—	7,580
07940	Madison (973)	15,727	15,850
08859	Madison Park(c) (732)	—	7,490
*07430	Mahwah Twp.(c) (201)	—	17,905
08736	Manasquan (732)	5,503	5,369
08835	Manville (908)	10,754	10,567
08052	Maple Shade Twp.(c) (609)	—	19,211
07040	Maplewood Twp.(c) (973)	—	21,756
08402	Margate City (609)	8,554	8,431
07746	Marlboro Twp.(c) (732)	—	27,974
08053	Marlton(c) (609)	—	10,228
07747	Matawan (732)	9,446	9,239
07607	Maywood (201)	9,634	9,536
08619	Mercerville-Hamilton Sq.(c) (609)	—	26,873
08840	Metuchen (732)	12,901	12,804
08846	Middlesex (732)	13,181	13,055
07748	Middletown Twp.(c) (732)	—	68,183
07432	Midland Park (201)	7,144	7,047
07041	Millburn Twp.(c) (973)	—	18,630
08850	Milltown (Middlesex) (732)	7,032	6,968
08332	Millville (609)	26,366	25,992
08094	Monroe Twp. (Gloucester)(c) (609)	—	26,703
*07042	Montclair(c) (973)	—	37,729
07645	Montvale (201)	7,092	6,946
07045	Montville Twp.(c) (973)	—	15,600
08057	Moorestown-Lenola(c) (609)	—	13,242
07950	Morris Plains (973)	5,279	5,219
*07960	Morristown (973)	16,357	16,189
07092	Mountainside (908)	6,655	6,657
08060	Mount Holly Twp.(c) (609)	—	10,639
08087	Mystic Island(c) (609)	—	7,400
07753	Neptune City (732)	5,062	4,997
*07753	Neptune Twp.(c) (732)	—	28,148
*07102	Newark (973)	268,510	275,221
*08901	New Brunswick (732)	41,534	41,711
07646	New Milford (201)	16,293	15,990
07974	New Providence (908)	11,793	11,439
07860	Newton (973)	7,917	7,521
07031	North Arlington (201)	14,002	13,790
07047	North Bergen Twp.(c) (201)	—	48,414
08902	North Brunswick Twp.(c) (732)	—	31,287
07006	North Caldwell (973)	6,583	6,706
08225	Northfield (609)	7,430	7,305
07508	North Haledon (973)	7,985	7,987
07060	North Plainfield (908)	18,947	18,820
07648	Norwood (201)	5,691	4,858
07110	Nutley(c) (973)	—	27,099
07436	Oakland (201)	12,253	11,997
*08758	Ocean Twp. (Ocean)(c) (609)/(732)	—	5,416
*08050	Ocean Acres(c) (609)	—	5,587
08226	Ocean City (609)	15,661	15,512
07757	Oceanport (732)	6,207	6,146
08857	Old Bridge(c) (732)	—	22,151
08857	Old Bridge Twp.(c) (732)	—	56,493
07675	Old Tappan (201)	5,006	4,254
07649	Oradell (201)	8,115	8,024
*07051	Orange(c) (973)	—	29,925
07650	Palisades Park (201)	14,810	14,536
08065	Palmyra (609)	6,950	7,056
*07652	Paramus (201)	25,552	25,004
07656	Park Ridge (201)	8,314	8,102
07054	Parsippany-Troy Hills Twp.(c) (973)	—	48,478
07055	Passaic (973)	57,039	58,041
*07510	Paterson (973)	150,270	140,891
08066	Paulsboro (609)	6,407	6,577
08110	Pennsauken Twp.(c) (609)	—	34,738
08069	Penns Grove (609)	5,164	5,228
08070	Pennsville Center(c) (609)	—	12,218
07440	Pequannock Twp.(c) (973)	—	12,844
*08861	Perth Amboy (732)	42,262	41,967
08865	Phillipsburg (908)	15,707	15,757
08021	Pine Hill (609)	10,472	9,854
*08854	Piscataway Twp.(c) (732)/(908)	—	47,089
08071	Pitman (609)	9,170	9,365
*07061	Plainfield (908)	46,254	46,577
08232	Pleasantville (609)	16,591	16,027
08742	Point Pleasant (732)	19,050	18,177
08742	Point Pleasant Beach (732)	5,302	5,112
07442	Pompton Lakes (973)	10,450	10,539
*08540	Princeton (609)	11,869	12,016
07065	Rahway (732)	25,228	25,325
08057	Ramblewood(c) (609)	—	6,181
07446	Ramsey (201)	14,343	13,228
07869	Randolph Twp.(c) (973)	—	19,974
08869	Raritan (908)	6,115	5,798
07701	Red Bank (732)	10,777	10,636
07657	Ridgefield (201)	10,114	9,996
07660	Ridgefield Park (201)	12,554	12,454
*07451	Ridgewood (201)/(973)	24,432	24,152
07456	Ringwood (973)	12,578	12,623
07661	River Edge (201)	10,764	10,603
08075	Riverside Twp.(c) (609)	—	7,974
07675	River Vale(c) (201)	—	9,410
07726	Robertsville(c) (732)	—	9,841
07662	Rochelle Park Twp.(c) (201)	—	5,587
07866	Rockaway (973)	6,435	6,243
07068	Roseland (973)	5,220	4,847
07203	Roselle (908)	20,205	20,314
07204	Roselle Park (908)	12,731	12,805
07760	Rumson (732)	6,821	6,701
08078	Runnemede (609)	8,930	9,042
07070	Rutherford (201)	18,000	17,790
07663	Saddle Brook Twp.(c) (201)/(973)	—	13,296
08079	Salem (609)	6,847	6,883
08872	Sayreville (732)	37,352	34,998
07076	Scotch Plains Twp.(c) (732)/(908)	—	21,150
*07094	Secaucus (201)	13,823	14,061
08753	Silverton(c) (732)	—	9,175
08083	Somerdale (609)	5,510	5,440
*08873	Somerset(c) (732)	—	22,070
08244	Somers Point (609)	11,217	11,216
08876	Somerville (908)	11,705	11,632
08879	South Amboy (732)	7,860	7,851
07079	South Orange Twp.(c) (973)	—	16,390
07080	South Plainfield (732)/(908)	20,682	20,489
08882	South River (732)	13,921	13,692
07871	Sparta Twp.(c) (973)	—	15,157
08884	Spotswood (732)	8,174	7,983
07081	Springfield Twp.(c) (908)/(973)	—	13,420
07762	Spring Lake Heights (732)	5,414	5,341
08084	Stratford (609)	7,476	7,614
07747	Strathmore(c) (732)	—	7,060
07876	Succasunna-Kenvil(c) (201)	—	11,781
*07901	Summit (908)	19,612	19,757
07666	Teaneck Twp.(c) (201)	—	37,825
07670	Tenafly (201)	13,480	13,326
07724	Tinton Falls (732)	15,079	12,361
*08753	Toms River(c) (732)	—	7,524
*07510	Totowa (973)	10,247	10,177
*08650	Trenton (609)	85,437	88,675
08520	Twin Rivers(c) (609)	—	7,715
07083	Union Twp. (Union)(c) (908)	—	50,024
07735	Union Beach (732)	6,405	6,156
07087	Union City (201)	57,126	58,012
07458	Upper Saddle River (201)	7,526	7,198
08406	Ventnor City (609)	10,954	11,005
07044	Verona(c) (973)	—	13,597
08251	Villas(c) (609)	—	8,136
*08360	Vineland (609)	—	54,780
07463	Waldwick (201)	10,023	9,757
07057	Wallington (201)/(973)	11,025	10,828
07465	Wanaque (201)/(973)	9,772	9,711
07882	Washington (908)	6,499	6,474
07675	Washington Twp.(Bergen)(c) (201)	—	9,245
07060	Watchung (908)	5,280	5,110
*07470	Wayne Twp.(c) (973)	—	47,025
07087	Weehawken Twp.(c) (201)	—	12,385
07007	West Caldwell(c) (973)	—	10,422
*07091	Westfield (732)/(908)	29,125	28,870
07728	West Freehold(c) (732)	—	11,166
07764	West Long Branch (732)	7,949	7,690
07480	West Milford Twp.(c) (973)	—	25,430
07093	West New York (201)	37,695	38,125
07052	West Orange(c) (973)	—	39,103
07424	West Paterson (973)	10,929	10,982
07675	Westwood (201)	10,644	10,446
07885	Wharton (973)	5,518	5,405
08610	White Horse(c) (609)	—	9,397
07886	White Meadow Lake(c) (973)	—	8,002
08094	Williamstown(c) (609)	—	10,891
08046	Willingboro Twp.(c) (609)	—	36,291
08095	Winslow Twp.(c) (609)	—	30,087
07095	Woodbridge(c) (732)	—	17,434
07095	Woodbridge Twp.(c) (732)	—	93,092
08096	Woodbury (609)	10,610	10,904
07675	Woodcliff Lake (201)	5,676	5,303
07075	Wood-Ridge (201)/(973)	7,607	7,506
07481	Wyckoff Twp.(c) (201)	—	15,372
08620	Yardville-Groveville(c) (609)	—	9,248
07726	Yorketown(c) (609)	—	6,313

New Mexico (505)

ZIP	Place	1996	1990
*88310	Alamogordo	29,036	27,596
*87101	Albuquerque	419,681	384,915
88021	Anthony(c)	—	5,160
*88210	Artesia	11,197	10,610
87410	Aztec	5,842	5,480
87002	Belen	7,838	6,547
87004	Bernalillo	7,450	5,960
87413	Bloomfield	5,830	5,214
87068	Bosque Farms	5,234	3,791
*88220	Carlsbad	26,535	24,952
*88101	Clovis	34,663	30,954
87048	Corrales	5,845	5,453
*88030	Deming	14,155	11,422
*87532	Espanola	9,008	8,389
*87401	Farmington	37,936	33,997
*87301	Gallup	20,591	19,157
87020	Grants	8,286	8,626
*88240	Hobbs	27,986	29,121
88330	Holloman AFB(c)	—	5,891
*88001	Las Cruces	74,779	62,360
87701	Las Vegas	16,437	14,753
87544	Los Alamos(c)	—	11,455
87031	Los Lunas	7,218	6,013
87107	Los Ranchos de Albuquerque	5,163	5,075
88260	Lovington	9,914	9,322
87107	North Valley(c)	—	12,507
87114	Paradise Hills(c)	—	5,513
88130	Portales	11,356	10,690
87740	Raton	7,766	7,372
*87124	Rio Rancho	46,565	32,512
*88201	Roswell	47,559	44,260
*88345	Ruidoso	5,714	4,600
87115	Sandia(c)	—	6,742
*87501	Santa Fe	66,522	56,537
87420	Shiprock(c)	—	7,687
*88061	Silver City	12,007	10,683
87801	Socorro	8,650	8,159
87105	South Valley(c)	—	35,701
88063	Sunland Park	9,265	8,179
87571	Taos	5,270	4,413
87901	Truth or Consequences	6,644	6,221
88401	Tucumcari	6,138	6,827
87544	White Rock(c)	—	6,192
87327	Zuni Pueblo(c)	—	5,857

New York

See introductory note.

ZIP	Place		1996	1990
10901	Airmont	(914)	7,709	7,674
*12201	Albany	(518)	103,564	100,031
11507	Albertson(c)	(516)	—	5,166
14411	Albion	(716)	6,935	5,863
14226	Amherst	(716)	112,431	111,711
*11701	Amityville	(516)	9,143	9,286
12010	Amsterdam	(518)	19,843	20,714
12603	Arlington(c)	(914)	—	11,948
*13021	Auburn	(315)	29,774	31,258
11702	Babylon	(516)	12,056	12,249
11510	Baldwin(c)	(516)	—	22,719
11510	Baldwin Harbor(c)	(516)	—	7,899
13027	Baldwinsville	(315)	6,651	6,591
12020	Ballston Spa	(518)	5,512	5,194
*14020	Batavia	(716)	16,095	16,310
14810	Bath	(607)	5,695	5,801
11705	Bayport(c)	(516)	—	7,702
11706	Bay Shore(c)	(516)	—	21,279
11709	Bayville	(516)	7,287	7,193
11751	Baywood(c)	(516)	—	7,351
12508	Beacon	(914)	13,275	13,243
11710	Bellmore(c)	(516)	—	16,438
11714	Bethpage(c)	(516)	—	15,761
*13902	Binghamton	(607)	48,294	53,008
11716	Bohemia(c)	(516)	—	9,556
11717	Brentwood(c)	(516)	—	45,218
10510	Briarcliff Manor	(914)	7,371	7,070
14610	Brighton (c)	(716)	—	34,455
14420	Brockport	(716)	8,209	8,749
10708	Bronxville	(914)	5,993	6,028
*14205	Buffalo	(716)	310,548	328,175
*14424	Canandaigua	(716)	10,736	10,725
13617	Canton	(315)	6,076	6,379
11514	Carle Place(c)	(516)	—	5,107
11516	Cedarhurst	(516)	5,715	5,716
11720	Centereach(c)	(516)	—	26,720
11934	Center Moriches(c)	(516)	—	5,987
11721	Centerport(Suffolk)(c)	(516)	—	5,333
11722	Central Islip(c)	(516)	—	26,028
*14225	Cheektowaga(c)	(716)	—	84,387
10977	Chestnut Ridge	(914)	7,919	7,517
13037	Chittenango	(315)	5,141	4,734
12065	CliftonPark	(518)	32,689	30,117
12047	Cohoes	(518)	15,215	16,825
12205	Colonie	(518)	7,996	8,019
11725	Commack(c)	(516)	—	36,124
10920	Congers(c)	(914)	—	8,003
11726	Copiague(c)	(516)	—	20,769
11727	Coram(c)	(516)	—	30,111
14830	Corning	(607)	11,356	11,938
13045	Cortland	(607)	18,733	19,801
*10520	Croton-on-Hudson	(914)	7,134	7,018
11729	Deer Park(c)	(516)	—	28,840
12054	Delmar(c)	(518)	—	8,360
14043	Depew	(716)	17,164	17,673
13214	DeWitt(c)	(315)	—	8,244
11746	Dix Hills(c)	(516)	—	25,849
10522	Dobbs Ferry	(914)	10,074	9,940
14048	Dunkirk	(716)	13,354	13,989
14052	East Aurora	(716)	6,429	6,647
10709	Eastchester(c)	(914)	—	18,537
12302	East Glenville(c)	(518)	—	6,518
11576	East Hills	(516)	6,781	6,746
11730	East Islip(c)	(516)	—	14,325
11758	East Massapequa(c)	(516)	—	19,550
11554	East Meadow(c)	(516)	—	36,909
11731	East Northport(c)	(516)	—	20,411
11772	East Patchogue(c)	(516)	—	20,195
14445	East Rochester	(716)	6,681	6,932
11518	East Rockaway	(516)	10,214	10,152
11786	East Shoreham(c)	(516)	—	5,461
*14901	Elmira	(607)	32,009	33,724
11003	Elmont(c)	(516)	—	28,612
11731	Elwood(c)	(516)	—	10,916
*13760	Endicott	(607)	12 399	13,531
13762	Endwell(c)	(607)	—	12,602
13219	Fairmount(c)	(315)	—	12,266
14450	Fairport	(716)	5,824	5,943
11735	Farmingdale	(516)	8,113	8,022
11738	Farmingville(c)	(516)	—	14,842
*11001	Floral Park	(516)	15,966	15,947
13603	Fort Drum(c)	(315)	—	11,578
11768	Fort Salonga(c)	(516)	—	9,176
11010	Franklin Square(Nassau)(c)	(516)	—	28,205
14063	Fredonia	(716)	10,222	10,436
11520	Freeport	(516)	40,164	39,894
13069	Fulton	(315)	12,536	12,929
*11530	Garden City	(516)	21,721	21,675
11040	Garden City Park(c)	(516)	—	7,437
14624	Gates-North Gates(c)	(716)	—	14,995
14454	Geneseo	(716)	7,323	7,187
14456	Geneva	(315)	13,890	14,143
11542	Glen Cove	(516)	24,716	24,149
12801	Glens Falls	(518)	14,772	15,023
12801	Glens Falls North(c)	(518)	—	7,978
12078	Gloversville	(518)	15,946	16,656
10924	Goshen	(914)	5,250	5,255
13642	Gouverneur	(315)	5,297	4,604
*11022	Great Neck	(516)	8,845	8,745
11020	Great Neck Plaza	(516)	5,921	5,897
14616	Greece(c)	(716)	—	15,632
11740	Greenlawn(c)	(516)	—	13,208
*10583	Greenville(Westchester)(c)	(914)	—	9,528
14075	Hamburg	(716)	10,026	10,442
11946	Hampton Bays(c)	(516)	—	7,893
10528	Harrison	(914)	23,658	23,308
10530	Hartsdale(c)	(914)	—	9,587
10706	Hastings-on-Hudson	(914)	8,021	8,000
*11788	Hauppauge(c)	(516)	—	19,750
10927	Haverstraw	(914)	9,390	9,438
*11551	Hempstead	(516)	46,609	45,982
13350	Herkimer	(315)	7,622	7,945
11557	Hewlett(c)	(516)	—	6,620
*11802	Hicksville(c)	(516)	—	40,174
10977	Hillcrest(c)	(914)	—	6,447
14468	Hilton	(716)	5,575	5,216
11741	Holbrook(c)	(516)	—	25,273
11742	Holtsville(c)	(516)	—	14,972
14843	Hornell	(607)	9,380	9,877
*14845	Horseheads	(607)	6,695	6,802
12534	Hudson	(518)	7,995	8,034
12839	Hudson Falls	(518)	7,457	7,651
11743	Huntington(c)	(516)	—	18,243
11746	Huntington Station(c)	(516)	—	28,247
13357	Ilion	(315)	8,467	8,888
11096	Inwood(c)	(516)	—	7,767
14617	Irondequoit(c)	(716)	—	52,322
10533	Irvington	(914)	6,426	6,348
11751	Islip(c)	(516)	—	18,924
11752	Islip Terrace(c)	(516)	—	5,530
*14850	Ithaca	(607)	28,507	29,541
*14702	Jamestown	(716)	33,154	34,681
10535	Jefferson Valley-Yorktown(c)	(914)	—	14,118
11753	Jericho(Nassau)(c)	(516)	—	13,141
13790	Johnson City	(607)	15,389	16,578
12095	Johnstown	(518)	8,768	9,058
14217	Kenmore	(716)	16,450	17,180
11754	Kings Park(c)	(516)	—	17,773
12401	Kingston	(914)	22,195	23,095
10950	Kiryas Joel	(914)	8,717	7,437
14218	Lackawanna	(716)	19,780	20,585
10512	Lake Carmel(c)	(914)	—	8,489
11755	Lake Grove	(516)	9,680	9,612
11779	Lake Ronkonkoma(c)	(516)	—	18,997
11552	Lakeview(c)	(516)	—	5,476
14086	Lancaster	(716)	11,406	11,940
10538	Larchmont	(914)	6,159	6,181
12110	Latham(c)	(518)	—	10,131
11559	Lawrence	(516)	6,542	6,513

ZIP	Place		1996	1990
11756	Levittown(c)	(516)	—	53,286
11757	Lindenhurst	(516)	26,499	26,879
13365	Little Falls	(315)	5,536	5,829
*14094	Lockport	(716)	23,300	24,426
11561	Long Beach	(516)	34,335	33,510
12211	Loudonville(c)	(518)	—	10,822
11563	Lynbrook	(516)	19,443	19,208
10541	Mahopac(c)	(914)	—	7,755
12953	Malone	(518)	7,509	6,777
11565	Malverne	(516)	9,076	9,054
10543	Mamaroneck	(914)	17,436	17,325
11030	Manhasset(c)	(516)	—	7,718
11050	Manorhaven	(516)	5,768	5,672
11949	Manorville(c)	(516)	—	6,198
11758	Massapequa(c)	(516)	—	22,018
11762	Massapequa Park	(516)	18,177	18,044
13662	Massena	(315)	11,471	11,716
11950	Mastic(c)	(516)	—	13,778
11951	Mastic Beach(c)	(516)	—	10,293
13211	Mattydale(c)	(315)	—	6,418
12118	Mechanicville	(518)	5,212	5,249
11763	Medford(c)	(516)	—	21,274
14103	Medina	(716)	6,810	6,686
11747	Melville(c)	(516)	—	12,586
11566	Merrick(c)	(516)	—	23,042
11953	Middle Island(c)	(516)	—	7,848
*10940	Middletown	(914)	24,192	24,160
11764	Miller Place(c)	(516)	—	9,315
11501	Mineola	(516)	19,054	19,005
10950	Monroe	(914)	7,664	6,672
10952	Monsey(c)	(914)	—	13,986
12701	Monticello	(914)	6,571	6,597
10970	Mount Ivy(c)	(914)	—	6,013
10549	Mount Kisco	(914)	9,182	9,108
11766	Mount Sinai(c)	(516)	—	8,023
*10551	Mount Vernon	(914)	67,112	67,153
12590	Myers Corner(c)	(914)	—	5,599
10954	Nanuet(c)	(914)	—	14,065
11767	Nesconset(c)	(516)	—	10,712
14513	Newark	(315)	9,822	9,849
*12550	Newburgh	(914)	26,248	26,454
11590	New Cassel(c)	(516)	—	10,257
10956	New City(c)	(914)	—	33,673
*11040	New Hyde Park	(516)	9,817	9,728
12561	New Paltz	(914)	5,257	5,470
*10802	New Rochelle	(914)	67,369	67,265
*12550	New Windsor Center(c)	(914)	—	8,898
*10001	New York	(212)/(718)	7,380,906	7,322,564
*14302	Niagara Falls	(716)	58,357	61,840
11701	North Amityville(c)	(516)	—	13,849
11703	North Babylon(c)	(516)	—	18,081
11706	North Bay Shore(c)	(516)	—	12,799
11710	North Bellmore(c)	(516)	—	19,707
11713	North Bellport(c)	(516)	—	8,182
11757	North Lindenhurst(c)	(516)	—	10,563
11758	North Massapequa(c)	(516)	—	19,365
11566	North Merrick(c)	(516)	—	12,113
11040	North New Hyde Park(c)	(516)	—	14,359
11772	North Patchogue(c)	(516)	—	7,374
11768	Northport	(516)	7,447	7,572
13212	North Syracuse	(315)	7,134	7,363
10591	North Tarrytown	(914)	8,146	8,152
14120	North Tonawanda	(716)	33,773	34,989
11580	North Valley Stream(c)	(516)	—	14,574
11793	North Wantagh(c)	(516)	—	12,276
13815	Norwich	(607)	7,327	7,613
10960	Nyack	(914)	6,688	6,558
11769	Oakdale(c)	(516)	—	7,875
11572	Oceanside(c)	(516)	—	32,423
13669	Ogdensburg	(315)	12,993	13,521
11804	Old Bethpage(c)	(516)	—	5,610
14760	Olean	(716)	16,494	16,946
13421	Oneida	(315)	10,958	10,850
13820	Oneonta	(607)	13,398	13,954
12550	Orange Lake(c)	(914)	—	5,196
10562	Ossining	(914)	22,788	22,582
13126	Oswego	(315)	18,522	19,195
11771	Oyster Bay(c)	(516)	—	6,687
11772	Patchogue	(516)	11,008	11,060
10965	Pearl River(c)	(914)	—	15,314
10566	Peekskill	(914)	20,805	19,536
10803	Pelham	(914)	6,375	6,413
10803	Pelham Manor	(914)	5,428	5,443
11714	Plainedge(c)	(516)	—	8,739
11803	Plainview(c)	(516)	—	26,207
*12901	Plattsburgh	(518)	19,043	21,255
12903	Plattsburgh AFB(c)	(518)	—	5,483
10570	Pleasantville	(914)	6,761	6,592
10573	Port Chester	(914)	24,859	24,728
11777	Port Jefferson	(516)	7,569	7,455
11776	Port Jefferson Station(c)	(516)	—	7,232
12771	Port Jervis	(914)	8,935	9,060
11050	Port Washington(c)	(516)	—	15,387
13676	Potsdam	(315)	9,617	10,251
*12601	Poughkeepsie	(914)	27,808	28,844
12144	Rensselaer	(518)	7,986	8,255
11961	Ridge(c)	(516)	—	11,734
11901	Riverhead(c)	(516)	—	8,814
*14692	Rochester	(716)	221,594	230,356
*11571	Rockville Centre	(516)	24,787	24,727
11778	Rocky Point(c)	(516)	—	8,596
12205	Roessleville(c)	(518)	—	10,753
*13440	Rome	(315)	40,979	44,350
11779	Ronkonkoma(c)	(516)	—	20,391
11575	Roosevelt(c)	(516)	—	15,030
11577	Roslyn Heights(c)	(516)	—	6,405
12303	Rotterdam(c)	(518)	—	21,228
10580	Rye	(914)	15,189	14,936
10573	Rye Brook	(914)	8,453	7,765
11780	Saint James(c)	(516)	—	12,703
14779	Salamanca	(716)	6,327	6,566
13454	Salisbury(c)	(315)	—	12,226
12983	Saranac Lake	(518)	5,258	5,377
12866	Saratoga Springs	(518)	25,118	25,001
11782	Sayville(c)	(516)	—	16,550
10583	Scarsdale	(914)	16,936	16,987
*12301	Schenectady	(518)	62,893	65,566
10940	Scotchtown(c)	(914)	—	8,765
12302	Scotia	(518)	7,505	7,359
11579	Sea Cliff	(516)	5,053	5,054
11783	Seaford(c)	(516)	—	15,597
11507	Searingtown(c)	(516)	—	5,020
11784	Selden(c)	(516)	—	20,608
13148	Seneca Falls	(315)	6,851	7,370
11733	Setauket-East Setauket(c)	(516)	—	13,634
11967	Shirley(Suffolk)(c)	(516)	—	22,936
11787	Smithtown(c)	(516)	—	25,638
13209	Solvay	(315)	6,455	6,717
11789	Sound Beach(c)	(516)	—	9,102
11735	South Farmingdale(c)	(516)	—	15,377
14850	South Hill(c)	(607)	—	5,423
11746	South Huntington(c)	(516)	—	9,624
14094	South Lockport(c)	(716)	—	7,112
11971	Southold(c)	(516)	—	5,192
14904	Southport(c)	(607)	—	7,753
11581	South Valley Stream(c)	(516)	—	5,328
10977	Spring Valley	(914)	22,291	21,802
*11790	Stony Brook(c)	(516)	—	13,726
10980	Stony Point(c) (Rockland)	(914)	—	10,587
10901	Suffern	(914)	11,059	11,055
11791	Syosset(c)	(516)	—	18,967
*13220	Syracuse	(315)	155,865	163,860
10983	Tappan(c)	(914)	—	6,867
10591	Tarrytown	(914)	10,756	10,739
11776	Terryville(c)	(516)	—	10,275
10984	Thiells(c)	(914)	—	5,204
10594	Thornwood(c)	(914)	—	7,025
*14150	Tonawanda	(716)	16,410	17,284
*14150	Tonawanda(c)	(716)	—	65,284
*12180	Troy	(518)	52,518	54,269
10707	Tuckahoe	(914)	6,424	6,302
11553	Uniondale(c)	(516)	—	20,328
*13504	Utica	(315)	61,368	68,637
10989	Valley Cottage(c)	(914)	—	9,007
*11582	Valley Stream	(516)	34,091	33,946
11792	Wading River(c)	(516)	—	5,317
12586	Walden	(914)	6,247	5,836
11793	Wantagh(c)	(516)	—	18,567
10990	Warwick	(914)	6,083	5,984
10992	Washingtonville	(914)	5,618	4,906
*13601	Watertown	(315)	28,700	29,429
12189	Watervliet	(518)	9,837	11,061
14580	Webster	(716)	5,340	5,464
14895	Wellsville	(716)	5,121	5,241
*11704	West Babylon(c)	(516)	—	42,410
11590	Westbury (Nassau)	(516)	13,176	13,060
14905	West Elmira(c)	(607)	—	5,218
12801	West Glens Falls(c)	(518)	—	5,964
10993	West Haverstraw	(914)	10,045	9,183
11552	West Hempstead(c)	(516)	—	17,689
11743	West Hills(c)	(516)	—	5,849
11795	West Islip(c)	(516)	—	28,419
12203	Westmere(c)	(518)	—	6,750
*10996	West Point(c)	(914)	—	8,024
14224	West Seneca(c)	(716)	—	47,866
13219	Westvale(c)	(315)	—	5,952
11798	Wheatley Heights(c)	(516)	—	5,027
*10602	White Plains	(914)	49,653	48,718
14231	Williamsville	(716)	5,311	5,583
11596	Williston Park	(516)	7,513	7,516
11797	Woodbury(c)	(516)	—	8,008
11598	Woodmere(c)	(516)	—	15,578
11798	Wyandach(c)	(516)	—	8,950
*10702	Yonkers	(914)	190,316	188,082
10598	Yorktown Heights(c)	(914)	—	7,690

North Carolina

ZIP	Place		1996	1990
*28001	Albemarle	(704)	14,547	14,940
27502	Apex	(919)	7,340	4,789
27263	Archdale	(336)	7,007	6,975
*27203	Asheboro	(336)	16,897	16,362
*28801	Asheville	(704)	64,067	63,379
28012	Belmont	(704)	8,503	8,434
28711	Black Mountain	(704)	7,572	7,156
28607	Boone	(704)	13,583	12,949
28712	Brevard	(704)	5,455	5,388
*27215	Burlington	(336)	40,402	39,498
*28547	Camp Lejeune(c)	(910)	—	36,716

ZIP	Place		1996	1990
27510	Carrboro	(919)	13,832	12,134
*27511	Cary	(919)	75,676	44,397
*27514	Chapel Hill	(919)	44,244	38,711
*28204	Charlotte	(704)	441,297	419,539
27520	Clayton	(919)	5,918	4,756
27012	Clemmons	(336)	6,681	6,020
*28328	Clinton	(910)	8,536	8,385
*28025	Concord	(704)	32,944	29,591
28613	Conover	(704)	5,995	5,465
*28334	Dunn	(910)	9,611	9,258
*27701	Durham	(919)	149,799	138,894
*27288	Eden	(336)	14,932	15,238
27932	Edenton	(252)	5,234	5,268
*27909	Elizabeth City	(252)	16,660	16,087
*28302	Fayetteville	(910)	79,631	75,850
28043	Forest City	(704)	7,434	7,475
28307	Fort Bragg(c)	(910)	—	34,744
27526	Fuquay-Varina	(919)	6,525	4,447
27529	Garner	(919)	17,004	14,716
*28052	Gastonia	(704)	56,575	54,725
*27530	Goldsboro	(919)	40,801	40,709
27253	Graham	(336)	11,337	10,368
*27420	Greensboro	(336)	195,426	183,894
*27834	Greenville	(252)	54,602	46,305
28540	Half Moon(c)	(910)	—	6,306
28345	Hamlet	(910)	6,349	6,722
28532	Havelock	(252)	20,437	20,300
27536	Henderson	(252)	15,100	15,655
*28739	Hendersonville	(704)	7,394	7,284
*28603	Hickory	(704)	30,523	28,474
*27260	High Point	(336)	74,417	69,428
27278	Hillsborough	(919)	6,468	4,263
28348	Hope Mills	(910)	9,273	8,272
*28540	Jacksonville	(910)	69,889	78,031
*28081	Kannapolis	(704)	35,631	31,592
*27284	Kernersville	(336)	13,362	11,860
28086	Kings Mountain	(704)	9,241	8,763
*28502	Kinston	(252)	25,072	25,295
*28352	Laurinburg	(910)	11,609	11,643
28645	Lenoir	(704)	16,373	16,337
27023	Lewisville	(336)	7,188	6,433
*27292	Lexington	(336)	16,239	16,581
*28092	Lincolnton	(704)	9,748	6,955
28461	Long Beach	(910)	5,450	3,816
*28358	Lumberton	(910)	19,129	18,733
28403	Masonboro(c)	(910)	—	7,010
*28105	Matthews	(704)	14,710	13,651
27302	Mebane	(919)	5,674	4,754
28227	Mint Hill	(704)	12,202	12,623
*28110	Monroe	(704)	19,827	18,623
28115	Mooresville	(704)	11,171	9,317
28557	Morehead City	(252)	6,567	6,046
*28655	Morganton	(704)	14,927	15,085
27030	Mount Airy	(336)	7,343	7,156
28120	Mount Holly	(704)	7,300	7,710
28365	Mount Olive	(919)	5,370	4,582
*28562	New Bern	(252)	21,464	20,728
27604	New Hope (Wake)(c)	(704)	—	5,694
28540	New River Station(c)	(910)	—	9,732
28658	Newton	(704)	10,886	11,134
27565	Oxford	(919)	7,698	7,965
*28374	Pinehurst	(910)	6,919	5,357
28399	Piney Green(c)	(910)	—	8,999
*27611	Raleigh	(919)	243,835	212,092
*27320	Reidsville	(336)	14,072	14,085
27870	Roanoke Rapids	(252)	15,978	15,722
*28379	Rockingham	(910)	9,082	9,399
*27801	Rocky Mount	(252)	52,635	49,438
27573	Roxboro	(336)	7,497	7,332
28601	Saint Stephens(c)	(704)	—	8,734
*28144	Salisbury	(704)	23,181	23,626
*27330	Sanford	(919)	21,153	18,887
28403	Seagate(c)	(910)	—	5,444
27576	Selma	(919)	5,939	4,600
*28150	Shelby	(704)	15,593	15,460
.....	Smith Creek(c)	(910)	—	7,461
27577	Smithfield	(919)	7,947	7,540
*28387	Southern Pines	(910)	10,168	9,213
28052	South Gastonia(c)	(704)	—	5,487
28390	Spring Lake	(910)	7,760	7,524
*28677	Statesville	(704)	20,509	20,647
27886	Tarboro	(252)	10,469	11,037
*27360	Thomasville	(336)	17,483	15,915
27370	Trinity(c)	(336)	—	5,469
*27587	Wake Forest	(919)	7,909	5,832
27889	Washington	(252)	9,298	9,160
28786	Waynesville	(704)	7,656	7,282
28472	Whiteville	(910)	5,297	5,340
27892	Williamston	(252)	5,800	5,870
*28402	Wilmington	(910)	62,192	55,530
*27893	Wilson	(252)	39,931	38,400
*27102	Winston-Salem	(336)	153,541	150,958

North Dakota (701)

ZIP	Place	1996	1990
*58501	Bismarck	53,514	49,272
58301	Devils Lake	7,672	7,782
*58601	Dickinson	16,094	16,097
*58102	Fargo	83,778	74,084
58237	Grafton	5,480	4,884
*58201	Grand Forks	50,675	49,417
*58201	Grand Forks AFB(c)	—	9,343
*58401	Jamestown	14,983	15,571
58554	Mandan	15,648	15,177
*58701	Minot	35,926	34,544
*58701	Minot AFB(c)	—	9,095
58072	Valley City	6,927	7,163
*58075	Wahpeton	9,039	8,751
58078	West Fargo	13,566	12,287
*58801	Williston	12,718	13,136

Ohio

ZIP	Place		1996	1990
45810	Ada	(419)	5,484	5,428
*44309	Akron	(330)	216,882	223,019
44601	Alliance	(330)	22,846	23,376
44001	Amherst	(440)	11,311	10,332
44805	Ashland	(419)	21,502	20,079
*44004	Ashtabula	(440)	21,315	21,633
45701	Athens	(740)	21,094	21,265
44202	Aurora	(330)	11,584	9,192
44515	Austintown(c)	(330)	—	32,371
44011	Avon	(440)	8,896	7,337
44012	Avon Lake	(440)	16,794	15,066
44203	Barberton	(330)	27,249	27,623
44140	Bay Village	(440)	16,401	17,000
44122	Beachwood	(216)	11,291	10,644
45434	Beavercreek	(937)	31,054	33,626
44146	Bedford	(216)/(440)	14,138	14,822
44146	Bedford Heights	(216)/(440)	11,790	12,131
43906	Bellaire	(740)	5,751	6,028
45305	Bellbrook	(937)	7,750	6,511
43311	Bellefontaine	(937)	12,295	12,126
44811	Bellevue	(419)	8,128	8,157
45714	Belpre	(740)	6,998	6,796
44017	Berea	(440)	18,909	19,051
43209	Bexley	(614)	12,691	13,088
43004	Blacklick Estates(c)	(614)	—	10,080
45242	Blue Ash	(513)	12,568	11,923
44513	Boardman(c)	(330)	—	38,596
43402	Bowling Green	(419)	28,307	28,303
44141	Brecksville	(440)	12,654	11,818
45211	Bridgetown North(c)	(513)	—	11,748
44147	Broadview Heights	(440)	13,923	12,219
44144	Brooklyn	(216)	11,251	11,706
44142	Brook Park	(216)/(440)	22,646	22,865
44212	Brunswick	(330)	31,641	28,218
43506	Bryan	(419)	8,658	8,348
44820	Bucyrus	(419)	13,134	13,496
43725	Cambridge	(740)	11,514	11,748
44405	Campbell	(330)	9,594	10,038
44406	Canfield	(330)	5,576	5,409
*44711	Canton	(330)	81,079	84,161
45005	Carlisle	(937)	5,058	4,872
45822	Celina	(419)	10,453	9,923
45459	Centerville (Montgomery)	(937)	22,456	21,082
45211	Cheviot	(513)	9,137	9,616
45601	Chillicothe	(740)	21,954	21,923
*45202	Cincinnati	(513)	345,818	364,114
43113	Circleville	(740)	12,088	11,666
*44101	Cleveland	(216)	498,246	505,616
44118	Cleveland Heights	(216)	54,293	54,052
43410	Clyde	(419)	6,113	6,087
44408	Columbiana	(330)	5,315	4,961
*43216	Columbus	(614)	657,053	632,945
44030	Conneaut	(440)	12,967	13,241
44410	Cortland	(330)	5,698	5,652
43812	Coshocton	(740)	12,247	12,193
45238	Covedale(c)	(513)	—	6,669
*44222	Cuyahoga Falls	(330)	49,278	48,950
*45401	Dayton	(937)	172,947	182,005
45236	Deer Park	(513)	5,835	6,181
43512	Defiance	(419)	16,718	16,787
43015	Delaware	(740)	20,267	19,966
45833	Delphos	(419)	6,908	7,093
45247	Dent(c)	(513)	—	6,416
44622	Dover (Tuscarawas)	(330)	11,879	11,329
45427	Drexel(c)	(937)	—	5,143
45663	Dry Run(c)	(614)	—	5,389
*43016	Dublin	(614)/(740)	23,891	16,366
44112	East Cleveland	(216)	31,141	33,096
44095	Eastlake	(440)	20,756	21,161
43920	East Liverpool	(330)	13,449	13,654
44413	East Palestine	(330)	5,191	5,168
45320	Eaton	(937)	7,532	7,396
44004	Edgewood(c)	(440)	—	5,189
*44035	Elyria	(440)	56,729	56,746
45322	Englewood	(937)	11,752	11,402
*44101	Euclid	(216)	52,472	54,875
45324	Fairborn	(937)	30,529	31,300
*45011	Fairfield	(513)	42,163	39,709

ZIP	Place		1996	1990
44313	Fairlawn	(330)	6,049	5,779
44126	Fairview Park	(440)	17,311	18,028
*45839	Findlay	(419)	36,900	35,703
45224	Finneytown(c)	(513)	—	13,096
45405	Forest Park	(513)	19,775	18,621
45230	Forestville(c)	(513)	—	9,185
45426	Fort McKinley(c)	(937)	—	9,740
44830	Fostoria	(419)	14,626	14,971
45005	Franklin	(513)	11,158	11,026
43420	Fremont	(419)	17,019	17,619
43230	Gahanna	(614)	31,338	23,898
44833	Galion	(419)	11,533	11,859
44125	Garfield Heights	(216)	30,207	31,739
44041	Geneva	(440)	6,470	6,597
44420	Girard	(330)	11,085	11,304
43212	Grandview Heights	(614)	6,637	7,010
44232	Green	(330)	21,653	19,179
45123	Greenfield	(937)	5,572	5,172
45331	Greenville	(937)	12,917	12,863
45239	Groesbeck(c)	(513)	—	6,684
43123	Grove City	(614)	23,902	19,661
*45011	Hamilton	(513)	61,833	61,436
45030	Harrison	(513)	7,404	7,520
43056	Heath	(740)	7,633	7,231
44134	Highland Heights	(440)	7,329	6,249
43026	Hilliard	(614)/(740)	18,324	11,794
45133	Hillsboro	(937)	6,884	6,235
44484	Howland Center(c)	(330)	—	6,732
44425	Hubbard	(330)	7,914	8,248
45424	Huber Heights	(937)	38,939	38,696
43081	Huber Ridge(c)	(614)	—	5,255
44236	Hudson Village	(330)	20,403	17,128
44839	Huron	(419)	7,381	7,067
44131	Independence (Cuyahoga)	(216)/(440)	6,728	6,500
45638	Ironton	(740)	12,871	12,751
45640	Jackson	(740)	6,333	6,167
*44240	Kent	(330)	27,072	28,835
43326	Kenton	(419)	8,382	8,356
43606	Kenwood(c)	(513)	—	7,469
45429	Kettering	(937)	58,204	60,569
44094	Kirtland	(440)	6,500	5,881
44107	Lakewood	(216)	55,731	59,718
43130	Lancaster	(740)	35,442	34,507
45039	Landen(c)	(513)	—	9,263
45036	Lebanon (Warren)	(513)	12,515	10,461
*45802	Lima	(419)	42,913	45,553
43228	Lincoln Village(c)	(614)	—	9,958
43138	Logan	(740)	7,488	6,725
43140	London	(614)/(740)	8,122	7,807
*44052	Lorain	(440)	69,800	71,245
44641	Louisville	(330)	8,240	8,087
45140	Loveland	(513)	11,776	10,122
44124	Lyndhurst	(216)/(440)	15,288	15,982
44056	Macedonia	(330)	8,685	7,509
.....	Mack South(c)		—	5,767
45243	Madeira	(513)	8,915	9,141
*44901	Mansfield	(419)	50,906	50,627
44137	Maple Heights	(216)	25,971	27,089
45750	Marietta	(740)	15,092	15,026
*43302	Marion	(740)	33,291	34,075
43935	Martins Ferry	(740)	7,643	8,003
43040	Marysville	(937)	12,232	10,362
45040	Mason	(513)	15,174	11,450
*44646	Massillon	(330)	30,671	30,969
43537	Maumee	(419)	15,157	15,561
44124	Mayfield Heights	(440)	19,149	19,847
*44256	Medina	(330)	22,019	19,231
*44060	Mentor	(440)	50,251	47,491
44060	Mentor-on-the-Lake	(216)	7,917	8,271
*45343	Miamisburg	(937)	18,308	17,834
44130	Middleburg Heights	(216)/(440)	14,744	14,702
*45042	Middletown	(513)	48,023	46,022
45150	Milford	(513)	5,839	5,660
45050	Monroe	(513)	5,079	4,490
45242	Montgomery	(513)	9,723	9,733
45439	Moraine	(937)	6,758	5,989
45231	Mount Healthy	(513)	7,205	7,580
43050	Mount Vernon	(740)	14,058	14,550
44262	Munroe Falls	(330)	5,485	5,359
43545	Napoleon	(419)	9,122	8,884
*43055	Newark	(740)	48,856	44,396
45344	New Carlisle	(937)	5,733	6,049
43764	New Lexington	(740)	5,422	5,117
44663	New Philadelphia	(330)	16,467	15,698
44446	Niles	(330)	21,110	21,128
45239	Northbrook(c)	(513)	—	11,471
44720	North Canton	(330)	15,736	14,904
45239	North College Hill	(513)	10,597	11,002
45251	Northgate(c)	(513)	—	7,864
44057	North Madison(c)	(440)	—	8,699
44070	North Olmsted	(440)	34,562	34,204
45502	Northridge(c) (Clark)	(937)	—	5,939
45414	Northridge(c) (Montgomery)	(937)	—	9,448
44039	North Ridgeville	(440)	23,070	21,564
44133	North Royalton	(440)	27,272	23,197
45322	Northview(c)	(937)	—	10,337
43619	Northwood	(419)	5,918	5,506
44203	Norton	(330)	11,541	11,477
44857	Norwalk	(419)	15,778	14,731
45212	Norwood	(513)	22,197	23,674
44146	Oakwood (Cuyahoga)	(440)	8,387	8,957
44074	Oberlin	(440)	7,931	8,191
44138	Olmsted Falls	(440)	7,013	6,741
*43601	Oregon	(419)	18,677	18,334
44667	Orrville	(330)	7,853	7,955
45431	Overlook-Page Manor(c)	(937)	—	13,242
45056	Oxford	(513)	18,700	18,937
44077	Painesville	(440)	15,660	15,769
44129	Parma	(216)/(440)	85,006	87,876
44130	Parma Heights	(216)/(440)	20,865	21,448
44124	Pepper Pike	(216)/(440)	6,171	6,185
44646	Perry Heights(c)	(330)	—	9,055
*43551	Perrysburg	(419)	13,234	12,551
43147	Pickerington	(614)/(740)	8,696	5,668
45356	Piqua	(937)	20,049	20,612
44319	Portage Lakes(c)	(330)	—	13,373
43452	Port Clinton	(419)	6,787	7,106
45662	Portsmouth	(740)	22,625	22,676
44266	Ravenna	(330)	11,829	12,069
45215	Reading	(513)	11,727	12,038
43068	Reynoldsburg	(614)/(740)	29,081	25,748
44143	Richmond Heights	(216)/(440)	9,691	9,611
44270	Rittman	(330)	6,590	6,147
44116	Rocky River	(440)	19,799	20,410
43460	Rossford	(419)	5,537	5,861
43950	Saint Clairsville	(740)	5,262	5,136
45885	Saint Marys	(419)	8,592	8,441
44460	Salem	(330)	12,188	12,233
*44870	Sandusky	(419)	29,008	29,764
44870	Sandusky South(c)	(419)	—	6,336
44131	Seven Hills	(216)/(440)	12,256	12,339
44120	Shaker Heights	(216)	29,206	30,955
45241	Sharonville	(513)	13,953	13,121
44054	Sheffield Lake	(440)	9,922	9,825
44875	Shelby	(419)	9,416	9,610
44878	Shiloh(c)	(419)	—	11,607
45365	Sidney	(937)	19,114	18,710
45236	Silverton	(513)	5,646	5,859
44139	Solon	(440)	20,171	18,548
44121	South Euclid	(216)	22,781	23,866
45066	Springboro	(513)	9,731	6,574
45246	Springdale	(513)	10,411	10,621
*45501	Springfield	(937)	67,460	70,487
43952	Steubenville	(740)	20,966	22,125
44224	Stow	(330)	30,864	27,998
44241	Streetsboro	(330)	10,905	9,932
44136	Strongsville	(440)	41,260	35,308
44471	Struthers	(330)	11,611	12,284
43560	Sylvania	(419)	16,568	17,489
44278	Tallmadge	(330)	15,767	14,870
45243	The Village of Indian Hill	(513)	5,567	5,383
44883	Tiffin	(419)	18,252	18,604
45371	Tipp City	(937)	6,365	6,483
*43601	Toledo	(419)	317,606	332,943
43964	Toronto	(740)	5,871	6,127
45067	Trenton	(513)	7,054	6,189
45426	Trotwood	(937)	8,619	8,816
45373	Troy	(937)	21,080	19,478
44087	Twinsburg	(330)	14,093	9,606
44683	Uhrichsville	(740)	5,644	5,604
45322	Union	(937)	5,430	5,531
44122	University Heights	(216)	13,946	14,787
43221	Upper Arlington	(614)	32,854	34,128
43351	Upper Sandusky	(419)	5,982	5,906
43078	Urbana	(937)	11,605	11,353
45377	Vandalia	(937)	14,155	13,872
45891	Van Wert	(419)	10,773	10,922
44089	Vermilion	(440)	11,434	11,127
*44281	Wadsworth	(330)	16,642	15,718
45895	Wapakoneta	(419)	9,414	9,214
*44481	Warren	(330)	48,347	50,793
44122	Warrensville Heights	(216)	15,218	15,884
43160	Washington	(740)	13,471	13,080
43567	Wauseon	(419)	6,712	6,322
45692	Wellston	(740)	6,280	6,049
45449	West Carrollton City	(937)	14,072	14,403
*43081	Westerville	(614)	33,701	30,269
44145	Westlake	(440)	30,037	27,018
45694	Wheelersburg(c)	(740)	—	5,113
43213	Whitehall	(614)	19,875	20,572
45239	White Oak(c)	(513)	—	12,430
44092	Wickliffe	(440)	14,112	14,558
44890	Willard	(419)	6,493	6,210
*44094	Willoughby	(440)	21,734	20,510
44094	Willoughby Hills	(440)	8,816	8,427
44095	Willowick	(440)	14,697	15,269
45177	Wilmington	(937)	11,765	11,199
45459	Woodbourne-Hyde Park(c)	(937)	—	7,837
44691	Wooster	(330)	23,591	22,427
43085	Worthington	(614)	14,540	14,869
45433	Wright-Patterson AFB(c)	(937)	—	8,579
45215	Wyoming	(513)	7,648	8,128
45385	Xenia	(937)	24,624	24,836
*44501	Youngstown	(330)	87,405	95,732
*43701	Zanesville	(740)	27,355	26,778

Oklahoma

ZIP	Place		1996	1990
*74820	Ada	(405)	15,630	15,820
*73521	Altus	(405)	22,598	21,910
73717	Alva	(405)	5,106	5,495
73005	Anadarko	(405)	6,588	6,586
*73401	Ardmore	(405)	23,484	23,079
*74003	Bartlesville	(918)	33,733	34,256
73008	Bethany	(405)	20,400	20,075
74008	Bixby	(918)	10,770	9,502
74631	Blackwell	(405)	7,282	7,538
*74012	Broken Arrow	(918)	69,175	58,043
*73018	Chickasha	(405)	15,977	14,988
73020	Choctaw	(405)	9,589	8,545
*74017	Claremore	(918)	17,982	13,280
73601	Clinton	(405)	8,895	9,298
74429	Coweta	(918)	6,514	6,159
74023	Cushing	(918)	7,186	7,218
73115	Del City	(405)	23,990	23,928
*73533	Duncan	(405)	22,057	21,732
*74701	Durant	(405)	13,075	12,929
*73034	Edmond	(405)	63,475	52,310
*73644	Elk City	(405)	10,977	10,428
73036	El Reno	(405)	16,025	15,414
*73701	Enid	(405)	45,724	45,309
73503	Fort Sill(c)	(405)	—	12,107
74033	Glenpool	(918)	7,533	6,688
*74344	Grove	(918)	5,161	4,020
73044	Guthrie	(405)	10,538	10,518
73942	Guymon	(405)	8,354	7,803
74437	Henryetta	(918)	5,968	5,872
74743	Hugo	(405)	6,008	5,978
74745	Idabel	(405)	7,310	6,957
74037	Jenks	(918)	8,654	7,493
*73501	Lawton	(405)	82,582	80,561
*74501	McAlester	(918)	17,566	16,739
*74354	Miami	(918)	12,594	13,142
73140	Midwest City	(405)	54,252	52,267
73153	Moore	(405)	44,472	40,318
*74401	Muskogee	(918)	37,891	37,708
73064	Mustang	(405)	12,036	10,434
73065	Newcastle	(405)	5,134	4,214
*73069	Norman	(405)	90,228	80,071
*73125	Oklahoma City	(405)	469,852	444,724
74447	Okmulgee	(918)	13,561	13,441
74055	Owasso	(918)	13,430	11,151
73075	Pauls Valley	(405)	5,966	6,150
73077	Perry	(405)	5,055	4,978
*74601	Ponca City	(405)	26,182	26,359
74953	Poteau	(918)	7,700	7,210
74361	Pryor Creek	(918)	8,921	8,327
73080	Purcell	(405)	5,111	4,784
74955	Sallisaw	(918)	7,673	7,122
74063	Sand Springs	(918)	16,770	15,346
*74066	Sapulpa	(918)	19,357	18,074
*74868	Seminole	(405)	6,830	7,071
*74801	Shawnee	(405)	26,833	26,017
74070	Skiatook	(918)	5,197	4,910
*74074	Stillwater	(405)	38,487	36,676
*74464	Tahlequah	(918)	11,742	10,398
74873	Tecumseh	(405)	5,914	5,750
73156	The Village	(405)	10,463	10,353
*74103	Tulsa	(918)	378,491	367,302
74301	Vinita	(918)	5,745	5,804
*74467	Wagoner	(918)	7,309	6,894
73123	Warr Acres	(405)	9,429	9,288
73096	Weatherford	(405)	9,799	10,124
*73801	Woodward	(405)	12,144	12,340
*73099	Yukon	(405)	22,921	20,935

Oregon

ZIP	Place		1996	1990
97321	Albany	(541)	37,919	33,523
97006	Aloha(c)	(503)	—	34,284
97601	Altamont(c)	(541)	—	18,591
97520	Ashland	(541)	17,678	16,252
97103	Astoria	(503)	9,844	10,069
97814	Baker City	(541)	9,693	9,140
*97005	Beaverton	(503)	63,224	53,307
*97701	Bend	(541)	31,733	23,740
97415	Brookings	(541)	5,001	4,400
97013	Canby	(503)	11,278	8,990
97225	Cedar Hills(c)	(503)	—	9,294
97291	Cedar Mill(c)	(503)	—	9,697
97502	Central Point	(541)	9,740	7,512
97058	City of the Dalles	(541)	11,317	11,021
97420	Coos Bay	(541)	15,448	15,076
97113	Cornelius	(503)	7,421	6,148
*97333	Corvallis	(541)	47,518	44,757
97424	Cottage Grove	(541)	7,607	7,403
97338	Dallas	(503)	11,573	9,422
*97440	Eugene	(541)	123,718	112,733
97439	Florence	(541)	6,214	5,171
97116	Forest Grove	(503)	14,685	13,559
97301	Four Corners(c)	(503)	—	12,156
97223	Garden Home-Whitford(c)	(503)	—	6,652
97027	Gladstone	(503)	11,715	10,152
*97526	Grants Pass	(541)	20,894	17,503
97470	Green(c)	(541)	—	5,076
*97030	Gresham	(503)	81,583	68,249
97303	Hayesville(c)	(503)	—	14,318
97230	Hazelwood(c)	(503)	—	11,480
97838	Hermiston	(541)	11,160	10,047
*97123	Hillsboro	(503)	52,479	37,598
97031	Hood River	(541)	5,213	4,632
97351	Independence	(503)	5,095	4,425
97222	Jennings Lodge(c)	(503)	—	6,530
97303	Keizer	(503)	27,642	21,884
*97601	Klamath Falls	(541)	18,580	17,737
97850	La Grande	(541)	12,228	11,766
*97034	Lake Oswego	(503)	34,661	30,576
97355	Lebanon	(541)	12,268	10,950
97367	Lincoln City	(541)	6,889	5,903
97128	McMinnville	(503)	23,136	17,894
*97501	Medford	(541)	56,067	47,021
97862	Milton-Freewater	(541)	5,886	5,533
97269	Milwaukie	(503)	20,024	18,670
97361	Monmouth	(503)	7,371	6,288
97132	Newberg	(503)	15,785	13,086
97365	Newport	(541)	9,786	8,437
97459	North Bend	(541)	9,927	9,614
97477	North Springfield(c)	(541)	—	5,451
97268	Oak Grove(c)	(503)	—	12,576
.....	Oak Hills(c)		—	6,450
.....	Oatfield(c)		—	15,348
97914	Ontario	(541)	10,638	9,394
97045	Oregon City	(503)	18,822	14,698
97801	Pendleton	(541)	15,893	15,142
*97208	Portland	(503)	480,824	463,634
97236	Powellhurst-Centennial(c)	(503)	—	28,756
97754	Prineville	(541)	5,954	5,355
97225	Raleigh Hills(c)	(503)	—	6,066
97756	Redmond	(541)	10,618	7,165
97404	River Road(c)	(541)	—	9,443
.....	Rockcreek(c)		—	8,282
97470	Roseburg	(541)	19,213	18,389
97470	Roseburg North(c)	(541)	—	6,831
97051	Saint Helens	(503)	8,429	7,535
*97301	Salem	(503)	122,566	107,793
97401	Santa Clara(c)	(541)	—	12,834
97138	Seaside	(503)	5,591	5,359
97140	Sherwood	(503)	5,945	3,093
97381	Silverton	(503)	6,473	5,635
*97477	Springfield	(541)	49,430	44,664
97383	Stayton	(503)	6,037	5,011
97479	Sutherlin	(541)	5,603	5,020
97386	Sweet Home	(541)	7,320	6,850
97281	Tigard	(503)	35,651	29,435
97060	Troutdale	(503)	12,318	7,852
97062	Tualatin	(503)	20,063	14,664
97225	West Haven-Sylvan(c)	(503)	—	6,009
97068	West Linn	(503)	20,141	16,389
97225	West Slope(c)	(503)	—	7,959
97503	White City(c)	(541)	—	5,891
97070	Wilsonville	(503)	11,644	7,510
97071	Woodburn	(503)	15,780	13,404

Pennsylvania

Area code (267) overlays area code (215).
Area code (484) overlays area code (610).
Area code (570) goes into effect on Dec. 5, 1998. Before then use (717).

ZIP	Place		1996	1990
15001	Aliquippa	(724)	12,769	13,374
*18105	Allentown (Lehigh)	(610)	102,211	105,301
*16603	Altoona	(814)	50,101	51,881
19002	Ambler	(215)/(610)	6,514	6,609
15003	Ambridge	(724)	7,787	8,133
18403	Archbald	(570)	6,417	6,291
19003	Ardmore(c)	(610)	—	12,646
15068	Arnold	(724)	5,855	6,113
19407	Audubon(c)	(610)	—	6,328
15202	Avalon	(412)	5,450	5,784
15234	Baldwin	(412)	21,004	21,923
18013	Bangor	(610)	5,201	5,383
15010	Beaver Falls	(724)	10,223	10,687
16823	Bellefonte	(814)	6,231	6,358
15202	Bellevue	(412)	8,589	9,126
18603	Berwick	(570)	10,626	10,976
15102	Bethel Park	(412)	33,661	33,823
*18016	Bethlehem	(610)	70,245	71,427
18447	Blakely	(570)	6,877	7,222
17815	Bloomsburg	(570)	12,349	12,439
19422	Blue Bell(c)	(215)/(610)	—	6,091
19061	Boothwyn(c)	(610)	—	5,069
16701	Bradford	(814)	10,577	9,625
15227	Brentwood	(412)	10,236	10,823
15017	Bridgeville	(412)	5,278	5,445
19007	Bristol	(215)	10,198	10,405
19015	Brookhaven	(610)	8,422	8,570
19008	Broomall(c)	(610)	—	10,930
*16001	Butler	(724)	15,179	15,714
15419	California	(724)	5,368	5,748
*17011	Camp Hill	(717)	7,554	7,831
15317	Canonsburg	(724)	8,822	9,200
18407	Carbondale	(570)	9,953	10,664
17013	Carlisle	(717)	18,039	18,419
15106	Carnegie	(412)	8,769	9,278

ZIP	Place	1996	1990
15108	Carnot-Moon(c) (412)	—	10,187
15234	Castle Shannon (412)	8,722	9,135
18032	Catasauqua (610)	6,447	6,662
17201	Chambersburg (717)	17,202	16,647
*19013	Chester (610)	40,660	41,856
19013	Chester Twp.(c) (610)	—	5,399
15025	Clairton (412)	9,055	9,656
16214	Clarion (814)	6,484	6,457
18411	Clarks Summit (570)	5,247	5,433
16830	Clearfield (814)	6,496	6,633
19018	Clifton Heights (610)	6,946	7,111
19320	Coatesville (610)	10,827	11,038
19426	Collegeville (610)	5,030	4,227
19023	Collingdale (610)	8,933	9,175
17109	Colonial Park(c) (Dauphin) (717)	—	13,777
17512	Columbia (717)	10,587	10,701
15425	Connellsville (724)	8,795	9,229
19428	Conshohocken (215)/(610)	8,195	8,064
15108	Coraopolis (412)	6,411	6,747
16407	Corry (814)	7,012	7,216
15205	Crafton (412)	6,761	7,188
19021	Croydon(c) (215)	—	9,967
19023	Darby (610)	10,870	11,140
19036	Darby Twp.(c) (610)	—	10,955
19333	Devon-Berwyn(c) (610)	—	5,019
18519	Dickson City (570)	5,964	6,276
15033	Donora (724)	5,648	5,928
15216	Dormont (412)	9,151	9,772
19335	Downingtown (610)	7,841	7,749
18901	Doylestown (215)	8,431	8,575
19026	Drexel Hill(c) (610)	—	29,744
15801	Du Bois (814)	8,117	8,286
18512	Dunmore (570)	14,647	15,403
15110	Duquesne (412)	7,907	8,525
19401	East Norriton(c) (215)/(610)	—	13,324
*18042	Easton (610)	25,782	26,276
18301	East Stroudsburg (570)	9,775	8,781
17402	East York(c) (717)	—	8,487
15005	Economy (724)	9,774	9,305
16412	Edinboro (814)	6,983	7,736
18704	Edwardsville (570)	5,099	5,399
17022	Elizabethtown (717)	10,677	9,952
16117	Ellwood City (724)	8,514	8,894
18049	Emmaus (610)	11,544	11,157
17025	Enola(c) (717)	—	5,961
17522	Ephrata (717)	12,954	12,133
*16501	Erie (814)	105,270	108,718
18643	Exeter (570)	6,043	5,691
19030	Fairless Hills(c) (215)	—	9,026
16121	Farrell (724)	6,585	6,835
19053	Feasterville-Trevose(c) (215)	—	6,696
16063	Fernway(c) (724)	—	9,072
19032	Folcroft (610)	7,412	7,506
19033	Folsom(c) (610)	—	8,173
15221	Forest Hills (412)	7,023	7,335
15238	Fox Chapel (412)	5,406	5,319
17931	Frackville (570)	6,064	4,700
16323	Franklin (814)	7,036	7,329
15143	Franklin Park (412)	11,213	10,109
18052	Fullerton(c) (610)	—	13,127
17325	Gettysburg (717)	8,735	7,025
15045	Glassport (412)	5,263	5,582
19036	Glenolden (610)	7,203	7,260
19038	Glenside(c) (215)	—	8,704
15601	Greensburg (724)	15,941	16,318
16125	Greenville (724)	6,395	6,734
16127	Grove City (412)	8,195	8,240
15101	Hampton Twp.(c) (Allegheny) (412)	—	15,568
17331	Hanover (717)	14,355	14,399
19438	Harleysville(c) (215)/(610)	—	7,405
*17105	Harrisburg (717)	50,886	52,376
15065	Harrison Twp.(c) (Allegheny) (412)	—	11,763
19040	Hatboro (215)	7,326	7,382
18201	Hazleton (570)	23,293	24,730
18055	Hellertown (610)	5,566	5,662
16148	Hermitage (724)	16,119	15,260
17033	Hershey(c) (717)	—	11,860
16648	Hollidaysburg (814)	5,443	5,624
16001	Homeacre-Lyndora(c) (724)	—	7,511
18431	Honesdale (717)	5,229	4,972
19044	Horsham(c) (215)	—	15,051
16652	Huntingdon (814)	6,992	6,843
15701	Indiana (724)	14,739	15,174
15644	Jeannette (724)	10,716	11,221
15344	Jefferson (412)	9,740	9,533
18229	Jim Thorpe (570)	5,121	5,048
*15907	Johnstown (814)	26,149	28,124
15108	Kennedy Twp.(c) (412)	—	7,152
19348	Kennett Square (610)	5,199	5,218
19406	King of Prussia(c) (215)/(610)	—	18,406
18704	Kingston (570)	13,574	14,507
19443	Kulpsville(c) (215)	—	5,183
*17604	Lancaster (717)	53,597	55,551
19446	Lansdale (215)	16,015	16,362
19050	Lansdowne (610)	11,408	11,712
15650	Latrobe (724)	9,299	9,265
17540	Leacock-Leola-Bareville(c) (717)	—	5,685
*17042	Lebanon (717)	23,791	24,800
18235	Lehighton (610)	5,784	5,914
*19055	Levittown(c) (215)	—	55,362
17837	Lewisburg (570)	5,647	5,785
17044	Lewistown (Mifflin) (717)	8,903	9,341
17112	Linglestown(c) (717)	—	5,862
19353	Lionville-Marchwood(c) (610)	—	6,468
17543	Lititz (717)	8,533	8,280
17745	Lock Haven (570)	9,074	9,230
17011	Lower Allen(c) (717)	—	6,329
15068	Lower Burrell (724)	12,370	12,251
15237	McCandless Twp.(c) (412)	—	28,781
*15134	McKeesport (412)	23,343	26,016
15136	McKees Rocks (412)	7,235	7,691
17948	Mahanoy City (570)	5,083	5,209
19002	Maple Glen(c) (215)	—	5,881
16335	Meadville (814)	14,106	14,318
17055	Mechanicsburg (717)	9,238	9,452
*19063	Media (610)	5,832	5,957
17057	Middletown (Dauphin) (717)	9,141	9,254
18017	Middletown (c) (Northampton) (610)	—	6,866
17551	Millersville (717)	7,958	8,099
17847	Milton (570)	6,492	6,746
17954	Minersville (570)	6,145	4,877
15061	Monaca (724)	6,580	6,739
15062	Monessen (724)	9,362	9,901
18936	Montgomeryville(c) (215)	—	9,114
18507	Moosic (570)	5,380	5,397
19067	Morrisville (Bucks) (215)	9,530	9,765
17851	Mount Carmel (570)	6,759	7,196
17552	Mount Joy (717)	6,517	6,398
15228	Mount Lebanon(c) (412)	—	34,414
15120	Munhall (412)	12,401	13,158
15146	Municipality of Monroeville (412)	28,591	29,169
15668	Municipality of Murrysville (724)	19,098	17,240
18634	Nanticoke (570)	11,505	12,267
18064	Nazareth (610)	5,529	5,713
19086	Nether Providence Twp.(c) (610)	—	12,730
15066	New Brighton (724)	6,581	6,854
*16108	New Castle (724)	26,845	28,334
17070	New Cumberland (717)	7,434	7,665
15068	New Kensington (724)	15,233	15,894
*19401	Norristown (610)	30,037	30,754
18067	Northampton (610)	9,025	8,717
15104	North Braddock (412)	6,711	7,036
15137	North Versailles(c) (412)	—	13,294
16421	Northwest Harborcreek(c) (814)	—	7,485
19074	Norwood (Delaware) (610)	6,157	6,162
15139	Oakmont (Allegheny) (412)	6,760	6,961
15238	O'Hara(c) (412)	—	9,096
16301	Oil City (814)	11,484	11,949
18518	Old Forge (570)	8,788	8,834
19075	Oreland(c) (215)	—	5,695
18071	Palmerton (610)	5,289	5,394
17078	Palmyra (717)	6,572	6,910
19301	Paoli(c) (610)	—	5,277
16801	Park Forest Village(c) (814)	—	6,703
17331	Parkville(c) (717)	—	5,009
15235	Penn Hills(c) (412)	—	57,632
19151	Penn Wynne(c) (215)	—	5,807
18944	Perkasie (215)	8,072	7,878
*19104	Philadelphia (215)	1,478,002	1,585,577
19460	Phoenixville (610)	15,327	15,066
*15233	Pittsburgh (412)	350,363	369,879
*18640	Pittston (570)	8,949	9,389
15236	Pleasant Hills (412)	8,485	8,884
15239	Plum (412)	26,530	25,609
18651	Plymouth (570)	6,665	7,134
19462	Plymouth Meeting(c) (215)/(610)	—	6,241
*19464	Pottstown (610)	21,614	21,831
17901	Pottsville (570)	15,857	16,603
17109	Progress(c) (717)	—	9,654
19076	Prospect Park (610)	6,674	6,764
15767	Punxsutawney (814)	6,811	6,782
18951	Quakertown (215)	8,975	8,982
19087	Radnor Twp.(c) (610)	—	27,676
*19612	Reading (610)	75,723	78,380
17356	Red Lion (717)	8,070	6,130
18954	Richboro(c) (215)	—	5,141
19078	Ridley Park (610)	7,456	7,592
15136	Robinson (Allegheny)(c) (412)	—	10,830
15237	Ross Twp.(c) (412)	—	35,102
15857	Saint Marys (814)	14,001	14,020
19464	Sanatoga(c) (610)	—	3,723
18840	Sayre (570)	5,610	5,791
17972	Schuylkill Haven (570)	5,493	5,610
15106	Scott Twp.(c) (412)	—	20,413
*18505	Scranton (570)	77,189	81,805
17870	Selinsgrove (570)	5,433	5,384
15116	Shaler Twp.(c) (412)	—	33,694
17872	Shamokin (570)	8,549	9,184
16146	Sharon (724)	16,766	17,533
19079	Sharon Hill (610)	5,658	5,771
17976	Shenandoah (570)	6,071	6,221
17404	Shiloh(c) (717)	—	5,315
17257	Shippensburg (717)	6,199	5,331
15501	Somerset (814)	6,337	6,454
18964	Souderton (215)	6,258	5,957
15129	South Park Twp.(c) (814)	—	14,292
17701	South Williamsport (570)	6,338	6,496
19064	Springfield (c) (Delaware) (610)	—	25,326
*16804	State College (814)	39,400	38,981

ZIP	Place		1996	1990
15136	Stowe Twp.(c)	(412)	—	9,202
18360	Stroudsburg	(570)	5,779	5,312
16323	Sugarcreek	(814)	5,464	5,532
17801	Sunbury	(570)	10,867	11,591
19081	Swarthmore	(610)	6,053	6,157
15218	Swissvale	(412)	10,018	10,637
18704	Swoyersville	(570)	5,394	5,630
18252	Tamaqua	(570)	7,525	7,943
15084	Tarentum	(724)	5,323	5,674
18517	Taylor	(570)	6,699	6,941
16354	Titusville	(814)	6,493	6,434
19401	Trooper(c)	(610)	—	7,370
15145	Turtle Creek	(412)	6,226	6,556
16686	Tyrone	(814)	5,688	5,743
15401	Uniontown (Fayette)	(724)	11,438	12,034
19063	Upper Providence Twp.(c)	(610)	—	9,477
15241	Upper Saint Clair(c)	(412)	—	19,023
15690	Vandergrift	(724)	5,618	5,904
19013	Village Green-Green Ridge(c)	(610)	—	9,026
16365	Warren	(814)	10,347	11,122
15301	Washington	(724)	15,184	15,864
17268	Waynesboro	(717)	9,874	9,578
15370	Waynesburg	(724)	5,409	4,270
17315	Weigelstown(c)	(717)	—	8,665
*19380	West Chester	(610)	17,958	18,041
19380	West Goshen(c)	(610)	—	8,948
*15122	West Mifflin	(412)	22,679	23,644
15905	Westmont	(814)	5,519	5,789
19401	West Norriton(c)	(610)	—	15,209
18643	West Pittston	(570)	5,297	5,590
15229	West View	(412)	7,362	7,734
15227	Whitehall (Allegheny)	(412)	13,968	14,451
15131	White Oak	(412)	8,410	8,761
*18703	Wilkes-Barre	(570)	44,407	47,523
15221	Wilkinsburg	(412)	19,719	21,080
15145	Wilkins Twp.(c)	(412)	—	7,487
*17701	Williamsport	(570)	30,537	31,933
19090	Willow Grove(c) (Montgomery)	(610)	—	16,325
17584	Willow Street(c)	(717)	—	5,817
15025	Wilson	(412)	7,679	7,830
19094	Woodlyn(c)	(610)	—	10,151
19038	Wyndmoor(c)	(215)	—	5,682
19610	Wyomissing	(610)	7,590	7,332
19050	Yeadon	(610)	11,692	11,980
*17405	York	(717)	40,779	42,192

Rhode Island (401)

See introductory note.

ZIP	Place	1996	1990
02806	*Barrington*	15,841	15,849
02809	*Bristol*	21,958	21,625
02830	*Burrillville*	16,102	16,230
02863	Central Falls	16,620	17,637
02813	*Charlestown*	6,995	6,478
02816	*Coventry*	32,221	31,083
*02904	Cranston	74,324	76,060
02864	*Cumberland*	29,274	29,038
02864	Cumberland Hill(c)	—	6,379
02818	*East Greenwich*	12,135	11,865
02914	East Providence	48,389	50,380
02822	*Exeter*	6,052	5,461
02814	*Glocester*	9,277	9,227
02828	Greenville(c)	—	8,303
02833	*Hopkinton*	7,620	6,873
02919	*Johnston*	26,551	26,542
02881	Kingston(c)	—	6,504
02865	*Lincoln*	18,760	18,045
02842	*Middletown*	19,184	19,460
02882	*Narragansett*	15,706	15,004
02840	Newport	24,295	28,227
02843	Newport East(c)	—	11,080
02852	*North Kingstown*	25,594	23,786
02908	*North Providence*	31,194	32,090
02896	*North Smithfield*	10,619	10,497
02859	Pascoag(c)	—	5,011
*02860	Pawtucket	69,068	72,644
02871	*Portsmouth*	16,725	16,857
*02904	Providence	152,558	160,728
02812	*Richmond*	6,484	5,351
02857	*Scituate*	10,000	9,796
02917	*Smithfield*	18,946	19,163
02879	*South Kingstown*	26,014	24,612
02878	Tiverton(c)	—	7,259
02878	*Tiverton*	14,192	14,312
02864	Valley Falls(c)	—	11,175
*02879	Wakefield-Peacedale(c)	—	7,134
02885	*Warren*	11,414	11,385
*02886	Warwick	84,514	85,427
02891	*Westerly*	22,773	21,605
02891	Westerly Center(c)	—	16,477
02893	*West Warwick*	29,120	29,268
02895	Woonsocket	41,817	43,877

South Carolina

ZIP	Place		1996	1990
29620	Abbeville	(864)	5,350	5,778
*29801	Aiken	(803)	22,834	20,386
*29621	Anderson	(864)	26,429	26,385
29812	Barnwell	(803)	5,394	5,255
.....	Batesburg-Leesville	(803)	6,189	6,107
*29902	Beaufort	(843)	9,897	9,576
29627	Belton	(864)	5,498	4,646
29841	Belvedere(c)	(803)	—	6,133
29512	Bennettsville	(843)	9,415	10,095
29611	Berea(c)	(864)	—	13,535
29115	Brookdale(c)	(803)	—	5,339
29902	Burton(c)	(843)	—	6,917
29020	Camden	(803)	6,330	6,696
29033	Cayce	(803)	11,900	10,807
*29402	Charleston	(843)	71,052	79,925
29520	Cheraw	(843)	5,150	5,553
29706	Chester	(803)	6,955	7,158
*29631	Clemson	(864)	12,174	11,145
29325	Clinton	(864)	9,432	9,603
*29201	Columbia	(803)	112,773	110,734
*29526	Conway	(843)	10,115	9,819
*29532	Darlington	(843)	9,124	7,310
29204	Dentsville(c)	(803)	—	11,839
29536	Dillon	(843)	6,724	6,829
*29640	Easley	(864)	16,880	15,179
*29501	Florence	(843)	30,168	29,913
29206	Forest Acres	(803)	7,124	7,181
*29715	Fort Mill	(803)	5,428	4,930
*29341	Gaffney	(864)	13,275	13,149
29605	Gantt(c)	(864)	—	13,891
29576	Garden City(c)	(843)	—	6,305
*29442	Georgetown	(843)	9,424	9,517
29445	Goose Creek	(843)	25,943	24,692
*29602	Greenville	(864)	57,064	58,256
*29646	Greenwood	(864)	19,642	20,807
*29650	Greer	(864)	11,464	10,322
29406	Hanahan	(843)	12,973	13,176
*29550	Hartsville	(843)	8,292	8,372
*29928	Hilton Head Island	(843)	29,088	23,694
29621	Homeland Park(c)	(864)	—	6,569
29063	Irmo	(803)	11,063	11,277
29456	Ladson(c)	(843)	—	13,540
29560	Lake City	(843)	7,096	7,153
*29720	Lancaster	(803)	8,669	8,914
29360	Laurens	(864)	9,468	9,694
*29072	Lexington	(803)	6,180	4,046
29571	Marion	(843)	7,566	7,658
29662	Mauldin	(864)	13,682	11,662
29461	Moncks Corner	(843)	5,815	5,599
*29464	Mount Pleasant	(843)	34,262	30,108
29574	Mullins	(843)	5,640	5,910
*29577	Myrtle Beach	(803)	25,456	24,848
29108	Newberry	(803)	10,156	10,543
*29841	North Augusta	(803)	16,397	15,684
29405	North Charleston	(843)	59,923	70,304
*29582	North Myrtle Beach	(843)	9,216	8,731
29565	Oak Grove(c)	(803)	—	7,173
*29115	Orangeburg	(803)	12,869	13,772
.....	Parker(c)		—	11,072
29905	Parris Island(c)	(843)	—	7,172
29072	Red Bank(c)	(803)	—	5,950
29020	Red Hill(c)	(843)	—	6,112
*29730	Rock Hill	(803)	44,061	41,610
29417	Saint Andrews(c)	(843)	—	25,692
29609	Sans Souci(c)	(864)	—	7,612
*29678	Seneca	(864)	8,133	7,726
29210	Seven Oaks(c)	(803)	—	15,722
*29681	Simpsonville	(864)	11,647	11,744
29577	Socastee(c)	(843)	—	10,426
*29306	Spartanburg	(864)	42,136	43,479
*29483	Summerville	(843)	24,395	22,519
*29150	Sumter	(803)	38,565	40,977
29687	Taylors(c)	(864)	—	19,619
29379	Union	(864)	9,756	9,840
29607	Wade Hampton(c)	(864)	—	20,014
29488	Walterboro	(843)	5,461	5,595
29611	Welcome(c)	(864)	—	6,560
*29169	West Columbia	(803)	10,994	10,974
29206	Woodfield(c)	(803)	—	8,862
29745	York	(803)	6,563	6,709

South Dakota (605)

ZIP	Place	1996	1990
*57401	Aberdeen	25,088	24,995
57006	Brookings	17,413	16,270
57706	Ellsworth AFB(c)	—	7,017
57350	Huron	12,428	12,448
57042	Madison	6,223	6,257
57301	Mitchell	14,191	13,798
57501	Pierre	13,422	12,906
*57701	Rapid City	57,642	54,523
57701	Rapid Valley(c)	—	5,968
*57101	Sioux Falls	113,223	100,836
57754	Spearfish	8,340	6,966
57069	Vermillion	10,521	10,034
57201	Watertown	19,619	17,632
57078	Yankton	13,969	12,703

Tennessee

ZIP	Place		1996	1990
37701	Alcoa	(423)	7,137	6,400
*37303	Athens	(423)	13,340	12,054
38184	Bartlett	(901)	35,735	26,989
37660	Bloomingdale(c)	(423)	—	10,953
38008	Bolivar	(901)	6,114	5,969
*37027	Brentwood	(615)	22,076	16,392
*37621	Bristol	(423)	23,275	23,421
38012	Brownsville	(901)	10,140	10,017
*37401	Chattanooga	(423)	150,425	152,393
37642	Church Hill	(423)	5,901	5,208
*37040	Clarksville	(615)	94,879	75,542
*37311	Cleveland	(423)	33,503	32,236
*37716	Clinton	(423)	9,320	8,972
37315	Collegedale	(423)	5,730	5,048
38017	Collierville	(901)	24,665	14,501
37663	Colonial Heights(c)	(423)	—	6,716
*38401	Columbia	(615)	32,043	28,583
*38501	Cookeville	(615)	25,224	21,744
38019	Covington	(901)	8,090	7,487
*38555	Crossville	(615)	9,036	6,930
37321	Dayton	(423)	6,271	5,671
*37055	Dickson	(615)	11,506	10,487
*38024	Dyersburg	(901)	18,658	16,317
37801	Eagleton Village(c)	(423)	—	5,169
37411	East Brainerd(c)	(423)	—	11,594
37412	East Ridge	(423)	20,482	21,101
*37643	Elizabethton	(423)	13,289	13,087
37650	Erwin	(423)	5,061	5,015
37062	Fairview	(615)	5,377	4,210
37922	Farragut	(423)	16,223	12,802
37334	Fayetteville	(615)	7,211	7,158
*37064	Franklin	(615)	25,648	20,098
37066	Gallatin	(615)	21,413	18,794
*38138	Germantown	(901)	31,772	33,016
*37072	Goodlettsville	(615)	12,770	11,219
*37743	Greeneville	(423)	13,780	13,532
37215	Green Hills(c)	(615)	—	6,763
38040	Halls(c)	(901)	—	6,450
37748	Harriman	(423)	7,070	7,119
37341	Harrison(c)	(423)	—	7,191
38340	Henderson	(901)	5,363	4,760
*37075	Hendersonville	(615)	37,261	32,188
38343	Humboldt	(901)	9,672	9,651
*38301	Jackson	(901)	50,406	49,115
37760	Jefferson City	(423)	7,339	5,875
*37601	Johnson City	(423)	55,542	50,354
*37662	Kingsport	(423)	41,335	40,457
*37950	Knoxville	(423)	167,535	169,761
37766	La Follette	(423)	7,488	7,192
37086	La Vergne	(615)	13,562	7,499
38464	Lawrenceburg	(615)	11,109	10,397
*37087	Lebanon	(615)	16,375	15,208
*37771	Lenoir City	(423)	8,890	6,147
37091	Lewisburg	(615)	10,975	9,879
38351	Lexington	(901)	6,448	5,810
37352	Lynchburg	(615)	5,241	4,721
38201	McKenzie	(901)	5,363	5,168
*37110	McMinnville	(423)	12,060	11,194
*37355	Manchester	(615)	8,482	7,709
38237	Martin	(901)	8,783	8,588
*37804	Maryville	(423)	23,042	19,208
*38101	Memphis	(901)	596,725	618,652
37343	Middle Valley(c)	(423)	—	12,255
38358	Milan	(901)	7,569	7,512
*38053	Millington	(901)	18,142	17,866
*37813	Morristown	(423)	21,906	21,316
*37122	Mount Juliet	(615)	7,430	5,389
*37130	Murfreesboro	(615)	53,966	44,922
*37202	Nashville	(615)	511,263	488,366
*37821	Newport	(423)	7,911	7,123
*37830	Oak Ridge	(423)	27,742	27,310
38242	Paris	(901)	9,626	9,332
37148	Portland	(615)	6,743	5,539
37849	Powell(c)	(423)	—	7,534
38478	Pulaski	(615)	8,667	7,916
37415	Red Bank	(423)	11,842	12,320
38063	Ripley	(901)	6,572	6,634
37854	Rockwood	(423)	5,435	5,348
38372	Savannah	(901)	6,705	6,547
*37862	Sevierville	(423)	9,742	7,178
37865	Seymour(c)	(423)	—	7,026
*37160	Shelbyville	(615)	15,766	14,049
37377	Signal Mountain	(423)	7,013	7,034
37167	Smyrna	(615)	20,708	14,717
*37379	Soddy-Daisy	(423)	8,884	8,240
37311	South Cleveland(c)	(423)	—	5,372
37172	Springfield	(615)	12,486	11,227
37874	Sweetwater	(423)	5,302	5,066
37388	Tullahoma	(423)	18,835	16,761
*38261	Union City	(901)	10,256	10,513
37188	White House	(615)	5,002	2,987
37398	Winchester	(615)	6,515	6,305

Texas

ZIP	Place		1996	1990
*79604	Abilene	(915)	108,476	106,707
75001	Addison	(972)	11,288	8,783
78516	Alamo	(956)	10,486	8,210
78209	Alamo Heights	(210)	6,882	6,502
77039	Aldine(c)	(281)	—	11,133
*78332	Alice	(512)	20,599	19,788
*75002	Allen	(972)	31,177	19,315
*79830	Alpine	(915)	6,077	5,622
*77511	Alvin	(281)	20,579	19,220
*79105	Amarillo	(806)	169,588	157,571
78750	Anderson Mill(c)		—	9,468
79714	Andrews	(915)	10,435	10,678
*77515	Angleton	(409)	20,200	17,140
*78336	Aransas Pass	(512)	7,893	7,180
*76004	Arlington	(817)	294,816	261,717
75751	Athens	(903)	11,588	10,982
75551	Atlanta	(972)	5,777	6,118
*78767	Austin	(512)	541,278	472,020
*76020	Azle	(817)	9,991	8,868
77518	Bacliff(c)	(409)	—	5,549
75180	Balch Springs	(972)	18,392	17,406
*77414	Bay City	(409)	18,705	18,170
*77520	Baytown	(281)	68,156	63,843
*77707	Beaumont	(409)	111,224	114,323
*76021	Bedford	(817)	49,431	43,762
*78102	Beeville	(512)	13,686	13,547
*77401	Bellaire	(713)	14,988	13,844
76715	Bellmead	(254)	8,953	8,336
76513	Belton	(254)	14,800	12,463
76126	Benbrook	(817)	21,139	19,564
*79720	Big Spring	(915)	23,248	23,093
*78006	Boerne	(830)	5,778	4,361
75418	Bonham	(903)	7,347	6,688
*79007	Borger	(806)	14,775	15,675
76230	Bowie	(940)	5,305	4,990
76825	Brady	(915)	5,862	5,946
76424	Breckenridge	(254)	5,853	5,665
*77833	Brenham	(409)	13,440	11,952
77611	Bridge City	(409)	8,229	8,010
79316	Brownfield	(806)	9,145	9,560
*78520	Brownsville	(956)	132,091	107,027
*76801	Brownwood	(915)	19,255	18,387
78717	Brushy Creek(c)	(903)	—	5,833
*77801	Bryan	(409)	58,247	55,002
76354	Burkburnett	(940)	10,740	10,145
*76028	Burleson	(817)	19,336	16,113
76520	Cameron	(254)	5,859	5,635
79015	Canyon	(806)	13,031	11,365
78130	Canyon Lake(c)	(830)	—	9,975
78834	Carrizo Springs	(830)	5,856	5,745
*75006	Carrolton	(972)	96,757	82,169
75633	Carthage	(903)	6,852	6,496
*75104	Cedar Hill	(972)	25,555	19,988
*78613	Cedar Park	(512)	10,727	5,161
77530	Channelview(c)	(281)	—	25,564
79201	Childress	(940)	5,404	5,055
*76031	Cleburne	(817)	23,904	22,205
*77327	Cleveland	(281)	7,437	7,124
77015	Cloverleaf(c)	(281)	—	18,230
77531	Clute	(409)	9,770	9,467
76834	Coleman	(915)	5,408	5,410
*77840	College Station	(409)	58,757	52,443
76034	Colleyville	(817)	18,704	12,724
79512	Colorado City	(915)	5,811	4,749
*75428	Commerce	(903)	7,071	6,825
*77301	Conroe	(409)	33,748	27,675
78109	Converse	(512)	10,911	8,887
75019	Coppell	(972)	26,545	16,881
76522	Copperas Cove	(254)	30,311	24,079
76205	Corinth	(940)	5,934	3,944
*78469	Corpus Christi	(512)	280,260	257,453
*75110	Corsicana	(903)	23,320	22,911
75835	Crockett	(409)	7,102	7,024
76036	Crowley	(817)	7,422	6,974
78839	Crystal City	(830)	8,400	8,263
77954	Cuero	(512)	6,500	6,700
79022	Dalhart	(806)	6,945	6,246
*75221	Dallas	(214)/(972)	1,053,292	1,007,618
77535	Dayton	(409)	6,197	5,042
77536	Deer Park	(281)	30,220	27,424
*78840	Del Rio	(830)	34,495	30,705
*75020	Denison	(903)	22,136	21,505
*76201	Denton	(940)	73,483	66,270
*75115	De Soto	(972)	34,993	30,544
75941	Diboll	(409)	5,220	4,341
77539	Dickinson	(281)	12,594	11,692
78537	Donna	(956)	14,832	12,652
79029	Dumas	(806)	13,814	12,871
*75138	Duncanville	(972)	36,008	35,008
76135	Eagle Mountain(c)	(817)	—	5,847
*78852	Eagle Pass	(830)	27,554	20,651
*78539	Edinburg	(956)	37,742	31,091
77957	Edna	(512)	6,081	5,343
77437	El Campo	(409)	10,654	10,511
78621	Elgin	(512)	5,813	4,846
*79910	El Paso	(915)	599,865	515,342
78543	Elsa	(956)	6,250	5,242
*75119	Ennis	(972)	15,375	13,869
*76039	Euless	(817)	41,627	38,149
76140	Everman	(817)	5,866	5,672
79838	Fabens(c)	(915)	—	5,599
78355	Falfurrias	(512)	5,994	5,788
75381	Farmers Branch	(972)	25,382	24,250

ZIP	Place	1996	1990
.....	First Colony(c)	—	18,327
78114	Floresville (830)	6,560	5,247
*75067	Flower Mound (972)	36,340	15,527
76119	Forest Hill (817)	11,873	11,482
75126	Forney (972)	5,260	4,070
79906	Fort Bliss(c) (915)	—	13,915
76544	Fort Hood(c) (254)	—	35,580
79735	Fort Stockton (915)	8,752	8,524
*76161	Fort Worth (817)	479,716	447,619
78624	Fredericksburg (830)	8,428	6,934
*77541	Freeport (409)	11,680	11,389
*77546	Friendswood (281)	28,218	22,814
*75034	Frisco (972)	17,412	6,138
*76240	Gainesville (940)	14,729	14,256
77547	Galena Park (713)	10,457	10,033
*77550	Galveston (409)	60,048	59,067
*75040	Garland (972)	190,055	180,635
76528	Gatesville (254)	12,130	11,492
*78626	Georgetown (512)	22,393	14,842
75644	Gilmer (903)	5,509	4,824
75647	Gladewater (903)	6,487	6,027
75115	Glenn Heights (972)	5,140	4,564
78629	Gonzales (830)	6,696	6,527
76450	Graham (940)	8,620	8,986
*76048	Granbury (817)	5,152	4,045
*75051	Grand Prairie (972)	109,231	99,606
*76051	Grapevine (817)	37,500	29,198
*75401	Greenville (903)	23,882	23,071
77619	Groves (409)	16,728	16,744
76117	Haltom City (817)	35,541	32,856
76543	Harker Heights (254)	17,131	12,932
*78550	Harlingen (956)	56,893	48,746
*75652	Henderson (903)	11,246	11,139
79045	Hereford (806)	15,092	14,745
76643	Hewitt (254)	10,557	8,983
78557	Hidalgo (956)	5,424	3,292
75205	Highland Park (972)	8,971	8,739
77562	Highlands(c) (281)	—	6,632
75067	Highland Village (972)	11,326	7,027
76645	Hillsboro (254)	7,846	7,072
77563	Hitchcock (409)	6,235	5,868
78861	Hondo (830)	8,043	6,018
*77052	Houston (281)/(713)	1,744,058	1,637,859
*77338	Humble (281)	13,152	12,060
*77340	Huntsville (409)	29,060	27,925
*76053	Hurst (817)	36,506	33,574
78362	Ingleside (512)	8,982	5,696
76367	Iowa Park (940)	6,339	6,072
*75015	Irving (972)	176,993	155,037
77029	Jacinto City (713)	9,761	9,343
75766	Jacksonville (972)	12,810	12,765
75951	Jasper (409)	7,773	7,160
77040	Jersey Village (713)	5,535	4,826
78729	Jollyville(c) (512)	—	15,206
*77449	Katy (281)	9,955	8,004
75142	Kaufman (972)	6,306	5,251
*76248	Keller (817)	20,231	13,683
79745	Kermit (915)	6,421	6,875
*78028	Kerrville (830)	19,986	17,384
*75662	Kilgore (903)	11,472	11,066
*76540	Killeen (254)	78,022	63,535
*78363	Kingsville (512)	25,375	25,276
77325	Kingwood(c) (281)	—	37,397
78219	Kirby (210)	8,851	8,326
78236	Lackland AFB(c) (210)	—	9,352
77566	Lake Jackson (409)	25,774	22,771
78734	Lakeway (512)	5,355	4,044
77568	La Marque (409)	14,631	14,120
79331	Lamesa (806)	10,421	10,809
76550	Lampasas (512)	7,948	6,382
*75146	Lancaster (972)	23,352	22,117
*77571	La Porte (281)	31,949	27,923
*78041	Laredo (956)	164,899	122,899
*77573	League City (281)	40,631	30,159
*78641	Leander (512)	6,456	3,398
78268	Leon Valley (210)	10,296	9,581
*79336	Levelland (806)	13,690	13,986
*75067	Lewisville (972)	61,517	46,521
77575	Liberty (281)	8,196	7,690
79339	Littlefield (806)	6,368	6,489
78233	Live Oak (210)	10,864	10,023
77351	Livingston (409)	6,931	5,019
78644	Lockhart (512)	10,657	9,205
*75606	Longview (903)	74,572	70,311
*79408	Lubbock (806)	193,565	186,206
*75901	Lufkin (409)	33,089	30,206
78648	Luling (830)	5,151	4,661
77657	Lumberton (409)	7,919	6,640
*78501	McAllen (956)	103,352	84,021
*75070	McKinney (972)	32,462	21,283
76063	Mansfield (817)	20,804	15,615
*78654	Marble Falls (512)	5,229	4,007
76661	Marlin (254)	6,304	6,386
*75670	Marshall (903)	24,147	23,682
78368	Mathis (512)	5,795	5,423
77477	Meadows (281)	6,141	4,606
78570	Mercedes (956)	14,393	12,694
*75149	Mesquite (972)	111,947	101,484
76667	Mexia (254)	6,572	6,933
*79701	Midland (915)	97,162	89,443
76065	Midlothian (972)	6,429	5,040
*76067	Mineral Wells (940)	14,862	14,935
*78572	Mission (956)	37,777	28,653
.....	Mission Bend(c)	—	24,945
*77489	Missouri City (281)	55,958	36,176
79756	Monahans (915)	7,086	8,101
*75455	Mount Pleasant (903)	12,867	12,291
*75961	Nacogdoches (409)	31,188	30,872
77868	Navasota (409)	7,586	6,296
77627	Nederland (409)	16,867	16,192
75570	New Boston (903)	5,349	5,057
*78130	New Braunfels (830)	33,906	27,334
*76161	North Richland Hills (817)	53,214	45,895
*79761	Odessa (915)	90,883	89,699
*77630	Orange (409)	18,953	19,370
*75801	Palestine (903)	19,117	18,042
*79065	Pampa (806)	19,066	19,959
*75460	Paris (903)	25,101	24,799
*77501	Pasadena (281)/(713)	131,620	119,604
*77581	Pearland (281)	26,854	18,927
78061	Pearsall (830)	7,490	6,924
78721	Pecan Grove(c)	—	9,502
79772	Pecos (915)	11,222	12,069
79070	Perryton (806)	7,374	7,619
*78660	Pflugerville (512)	8,168	4,444
78577	Pharr (956)	40,425	32,921
*79072	Plainview (806)	22,656	21,698
*75074	Plano (972)	192,280	127,885
78064	Pleasanton (830)	8,969	7,678
*77640	Port Arthur (409)	57,701	58,551
78578	Port Isabel (956)	5,062	4,467
78374	Portland (512)	13,584	12,224
77979	Port Lavaca (512)	11,946	10,886
77651	Port Neches (409)	13,321	12,908
78580	Raymondville (956)	9,639	8,880
76028	Rendon(c) (817)	—	7,658
*75080	Richardson (972)	81,133	74,840
76118	Richland Hills (817)	8,367	7,978
*77469	Richmond (281)	13,231	10,042
78582	Rio Grande City (956)	14,501	10,725
76114	River Oaks (817)	6,776	6,580
76701	Robinson (254)	7,903	7,111
78380	Robstown (512)	13,349	12,849
76567	Rockdale (512)	5,424	5,235
*78382	Rockport (512)	6,463	5,355
75087	Rockwall (972)	13,783	10,486
78584	Roma (956)	10,780	8,059
77471	Rosenberg (281)	26,442	20,183
*78681	Round Rock (512)	52,479	30,923
*75088	Rowlett (972)	35,746	23,260
75048	Sachse (972)	7,074	5,346
76179	Saginaw (817)	10,321	8,551
*76902	San Angelo (915)	88,098	84,462
*78265	San Antonio (210)	1,067,816	959,295
78586	San Benito (956)	23,047	20,125
78384	San Diego (512)	5,002	4,983
78589	San Juan (956)	16,454	12,561
*78666	San Marcos (512)	34,994	28,738
*77510	Santa Fe (281)	9,487	8,429
78154	Schertz (210)	13,696	10,597
77586	Seabrook (281)	8,648	6,685
75159	Seagoville (972)	9,863	8,969
77474	Sealy (409)	5,313	4,541
*78155	Seguin (830)	20,863	18,692
79360	Seminole (915)	6,627	6,342
*75090	Sherman (903)	33,155	31,584
77656	Silsbee (409)	6,785	6,368
78387	Sinton (512)	6,827	5,549
79364	Slaton (806)	6,156	6,078
*79549	Snyder (915)	11,662	12,195
79910	Socorro (915)	25,409	22,995
77587	South Houston (713)	15,064	14,207
76092	Southlake (817)	13,541	7,082
*77373	Spring(c) (281)	—	33,111
*77477	Stafford (281)	12,543	8,395
76401	Stephenville (254)	14,902	13,502
*77478	Sugar Land (281)	47,810	33,712
*75482	Sulphur Springs (903)	14,802	14,062
79556	Sweetwater (915)	11,763	11,967
76574	Taylor (512)	14,336	11,472
*76501	Temple (254)	51,394	46,150
*75160	Terrell (972)	14,060	12,490
*75501	Texarkana (903)	32,462	32,294
*77590	Texas City (409)	42,368	40,822
75056	The Colony (972)	25,453	22,113
77387	The Woodlands(c) (281)	—	29,205
*77375	Tomball (281)	7,237	6,370
.....	Town West(c)	—	6,166
79088	Tulia (806)	5,081	4,703
*75702	Tyler (903)	82,185	75,450
*78148	Universal City (512)	14,965	13,057
76308	University Park (972)	22,568	22,259
*78801	Uvalde (830)	16,119	14,729
*76384	Vernon (940)	11,345	12,001
*77901	Victoria (512)	61,059	55,076
*77662	Vidor (409)	11,021	10,935
*76702	Waco (254)	108,412	103,590
75501	Wake Village (903)	5,393	4,761
76148	Watauga (817)	22,639	20,009
*75165	Waxahachie (972)	20,324	17,984

ZIP	Place	Area code	1996	1990
*76086	Weatherford	(817)	17,382	14,804
77598	Webster	(281)	5,040	4,678
78728	Wells Branch(c)		—	7,094
*78596	Weslaco	(956)	26,975	22,739
79764	West Odessa(c)	(915)	—	16,568
77005	West University Place	(713)	13,810	12,920
77488	Wharton	(409)	9,308	9,011
75693	White Oak	(903)	5,741	5,136
76108	White Settlement	(817)	15,924	15,472
*76307	Wichita Falls	(940)	100,138	96,259
78239	Windcrest	(210)	5,684	5,331
76712	Woodway	(254)	9,844	8,695
75098	Wylie	(972)	10,894	8,716
77995	Yoakum	(512)	5,568	5,611
78076	Zapata(c)	(956)	—	7,119

Utah

ZIP	Place	Area code	1996	1990
84004	Alpine	(801)	5,161	3,492
84003	American Fork	(801)	19,451	15,722
*84010	Bountiful	(801)	39,595	37,544
84302	Brigham City	(435)	16,398	15,644
84109	Canyon Rim(c)	(801)	—	10,527
*84720	Cedar City	(435)	17,811	13,443
84014	Centerville	(801)	14,382	11,500
*84015	Clearfield	(801)	22,153	21,435
84015	Clinton	(801)	9,386	7,945
84121	Cottonwood Heights(c)	(801)	—	28,766
84121	Cottonwood West(c)	(801)	—	17,476
84020	Draper	(801)	12,478	7,143
84109	East Millcreek(c)	(801)	—	21,184
84025	Farmington	(801)	10,462	9,049
84032	Heber	(801)	5,299	4,782
84003	Highland	(801)	5,939	5,007
84117	Holladay-Cottonwood(c)	(801)	—	14,095
84737	Hurricane	(435)	5,821	3,915
84319	Hyrum	(435)	5,429	4,829
84037	Kaysville	(801)	17,781	13,961
84118	Kearns(c)	(801)	—	28,374
*84041	Layton	(801)	50,906	41,784
84043	Lehi	(801)	13,810	8,475
84042	Lindon	(801)	5,941	3,818
.....	Little Cottonwood Creek Valley(c)	(801)	—	5,042
*84321	Logan	(435)	39,276	32,771
84044	Magna(c)	(801)	—	17,829
84047	Midvale	(801)	11,867	11,886
84109	Millcreek(c)	(801)	—	32,230
84117	Mount Olympus(c)	(801)	—	7,413
84157	Murray	(801)	33,089	31,274
84341	North Logan	(435)	5,737	3,775
84404	North Ogden	(801)	13,731	11,593
84054	North Salt Lake	(801)	7,396	6,464
*84401	Ogden	(801)	65,720	63,943
.....	Oquirrh(c)	(801)	—	7,593
*84057	Orem	(801)	79,736	67,561
*84060	Park City	(801)	6,117	4,468
84651	Payson	(801)	11,139	9,510
84062	Pleasant Grove	(801)	19,357	13,476
84501	Price	(435)	8,711	8,712
*84601	Provo	(801)	99,606	86,835
84701	Richfield	(435)	6,057	5,593
84403	Riverdale	(801)	6,868	6,419
84065	Riverton	(801)	17,924	11,261
84067	Roy	(801)	28,517	24,595
*84770	Saint George	(435)	42,763	28,572
*84101	Salt Lake City	(801)	172,575	159,928
*84070	Sandy	(801)	94,593	75,240
84335	Smithfield	(435)	6,320	5,566
84095	South Jordan	(801)	23,518	12,215
84403	South Ogden	(801)	14,272	12,105
84165	South Salt Lake	(801)	10,166	10,129
84660	Spanish Fork	(801)	14,854	11,272
84663	Springville	(801)	15,855	13,950
84015	Sunset	(801)	5,067	5,128
84075	Syracuse	(801)	5,706	4,658
84107	Taylorsville-Bennion(c)	(801)	—	52,351
84074	Tooele	(435)	14,728	13,887
84047	Union(c)	(801)	—	13,684
*84078	Vernal	(435)	7,105	6,640
84780	Washington	(435)	6,121	4,198
84403	Washington Terrace	(801)	8,701	8,189
*84084	West Jordan	(801)	57,600	42,915
84015	West Point	(801)	5,481	4,258
*84119	West Valley City	(801)	99,136	86,969
84070	White City(c)	(801)	—	6,506
84087	Woods Cross	(801)	5,577	5,384

Vermont (802)

See introductory note.

ZIP	Place	1996	1990
05641	Barre	9,206	9,482
05641	*Barre*	7,758	7,411
05201	*Bennington*	16,328	16,451
05201	Bennington(c)	—	9,532
*05301	Brattleboro Center(c)	—	8,612
*05301	*Brattleboro*	12,136	12,241
*05401	Burlington	39,004	39,127
*05446	*Colchester*	16,092	14,731
05451	*Essex*	17,531	16,498
*05452	Essex Junction	8,546	8,396
05047	Hartford(c)	—	9,404
05849	*Lyndon*	5,572	5,371
*05753	*Middlebury*	8,248	8,034
05468	*Milton*	9,493	8,404
*05602	Montpelier	7,856	8,247
05661	*Morristown*	5,246	4,733
05663	*Northfield*	5,933	5,610
05101	*Rockingham*	5,391	5,484
*05701	Rutland	17,605	18,230
05478	Saint Albans	7,370	7,339
05478	*Saint Albans*	5,376	4,606
05819	*Saint Johnsbury*	7,523	7,608
05482	*Shelburne*	6,700	5,871
*05401	South Burlington	13,860	12,809
05156	*Springfield*	9,375	9,579
05488	*Swanton*	6,114	5,636
05495	*Williston*	6,602	4,887
05404	Winooski	6,651	6,649

Virginia

ZIP	Place	Area code	1996	1990
*24210	Abingdon	(540)	7,687	7,003
*22306	Alexandria	(703)	117,586	111,182
22003	Annandale(c)	(540)	—	50,975
22554	Aquia Harbour(c)	(703)	—	6,308
*22210	Arlington(c)	(703)	175,334	170,897
23005	Ashland	(804)	5,843	5,864
22041	Bailey's Crossroads(c)	(703)	—	19,507
24523	Bedford	(540)	6,530	6,177
22306	Belle Haven(c)	(757)	—	6,427
23234	Bellwood(c)	(804)	—	6,178
23234	Bensley(c)	(804)	—	5,093
*24060	Blacksburg	(540)	34,294	34,590
24605	Bluefield	(540)	5,004	5,363
23235	Bon Air(c)	(804)	—	16,413
*24203	Bristol	(540)	17,957	18,426
24416	Buena Vista	(540)	6,368	6,406
.....	Bull Run(c)	(540)	—	5,525
*22150	Burke(c)	(703)	—	57,734
24018	Cave Spring(c)	(540)	—	24,053
*20120	Centreville(c)	(703)	—	26,585
*20151	Chantilly(c)	(703)	—	29,337
*22906	Charlottesville	(804)	40,767	40,475
*23320	Chesapeake	(757)	192,342	151,982
*23831	Chester(c)	(804)	—	14,986
*24073	Christiansburg	(540)	15,687	15,004
24078	Collinsville(c)	(540)	—	7,280
23834	Colonial Heights	(804)	17,154	16,064
22901	Commonwealth(c)	(804)	—	5,538
.....	Countryside(c)		—	8,349
24426	Covington	(540)	6,781	7,198
22701	Culpeper	(540)	8,627	8,581
22193	Dale City(c)	(540)	—	47,170
*24541	Danville	(804)	53,472	53,056
23228	Dumbarton(c)	(804)	—	8,526
22027	Dunn Loring(c)	(703)	—	6,509
23222	East Highland Park(c)	(804)	—	11,850
23847	Emporia	(804)	5,831	5,479
23803	Ettrick(c)	(804)	—	5,290
*22030	Fairfax	(703)	20,990	19,894
*22046	Falls Church	(703)	9,781	9,522
23901	Farmville	(804)	6,823	6,505
24551	Forest(c)	(804)	—	5,624
22060	Fort Belvoir(c)	(703)	—	8,590
22308	Fort Hunt(c)	(703)	—	12,989
23801	Fort Lee(c)	(804)	—	6,895
22310	Franconia(c)	(703)	—	19,882
23851	Franklin	(757)	8,586	7,864
*22404	Fredericksburg	(540)	22,586	19,027
22630	Front Royal	(540)	13,094	11,880
24333	Galax	(540)	6,649	6,699
*23060	Glen Allen(c)	(804)	—	9,010
23062	Gloucester Point(c)	(804)	—	8,509
22066	Great Falls(c)	(703)	—	6,945
22306	Groveton(c)	(703)	—	19,997
*23670	Hampton	(757)	138,757	133,811
*22801	Harrisonburg	(540)	33,446	30,707
*20170	Herndon	(703)	19,156	16,139
23075	Highland Springs(c)	(804)	—	13,823
24019	Hollins(c)	(540)	—	13,305
23860	Hopewell	(804)	22,566	23,101
22303	Huntington(c)	(703)	—	7,489
22306	Hybla Valley(c)	(703)	—	15,491
22043	Idylwood(c)	(703)	—	14,710
22042	Jefferson(c)	(703)	—	25,782
22041	Lake Barcroft(c)	(703)	—	8,686
22191	Lake Ridge(c)	(540)	—	23,862
23228	Lakeside(c)	(804)	—	12,081
23060	Laurel(c)	(804)	—	13,011
*20175	Leesburg	(703)	21,270	16,202
24450	Lexington	(540)	7,164	6,959
22312	Lincolnia(c)	(703)	—	13,041
*22079	Lorton(c)	(703)	—	15,385
*24506	Lynchburg	(804)	67,250	66,049
*22101	McLean(c)	(703)	—	38,168
24572	Madison Heights(c)	(804)	—	11,700

ZIP	Place	1996	1990
*20110	Manassas (703)	33,200	27,957
20113	Manassas Park (703)	7,541	6,734
22030	Mantua(c) (703)	—	6,804
24354	Marion (540)	6,334	6,630
*24112	Martinsville (540)	15,850	16,162
*23111	Mechanicsville(c) (804)	—	22,027
*22116	Merrifield(c) (703)	—	8,399
.....	Montclair(c)	—	11,399
23231	Montrose(c) (804)	—	6,405
22121	Mount Vernon(c) (703)	—	27,485
22122	Newington(c) (703)	—	17,965
*23607	Newport News (757)	176,122	171,439
*23501	Norfolk (757)	233,430	261,250
22151	North Springfield(c) (703)	—	8,996
22124	Oakton(c) (703)	—	24,610
*23804	Petersburg (804)	38,234	37,027
22043	Pimmit Hills(c) (703)	—	6,019
23662	Poquoson (757)	11,922	11,005
*23707	Portsmouth (757)	101,308	103,910
24301	Pulaski (540)	9,431	9,985
22134	Quantico Station(c) (703)	—	7,425
*24141	Radford (540)	16,145	15,940
*20190	Reston(c) (703)	—	48,556
*23219	Richmond (804)	198,267	202,798
22901	Rio(c) (804)	—	5,133
*24022	Roanoke (540)	95,548	96,509
24281	Rose Hill(c) (540)	—	12,675
24153	Salem (540)	24,159	23,797
22044	Seven Corners(c) (703)	—	7,280
*23430	Smithfield (757)	5,522	4,686
24592	South Boston (804)	6,919	6,997
*22150	Springfield(c) (703)	—	23,706
*24402	Staunton (540)	24,800	24,461
*20164	Sterling(c) (703)	—	20,512
24477	Stuarts Draft(c) (540)	—	5,087
23162	Sudley(c) (540)	—	7,321
*23434	Suffolk (757)	58,901	52,143
22170	Sugarland Run(c) (703)	—	9,357
24502	Timberlake(c) (804)	—	10,314
23229	Tuckahoe(c) (804)	—	42,629
22101	Tysons Corner(c) (703)	—	13,124
22901	University Heights(c) (804)	—	6,900
*22180	Vienna (703)	14,612	14,852
24179	Vinton (540)	7,210	7,643
*23458	Virginia Beach (757)	430,385	393,089
*20186	Warrenton (540)	5,405	4,882
22980	Waynesboro (540)	18,928	18,549
22110	West Gate(c) (703)	—	6,565
22152	West Springfield(c) (703)	—	28,126
*23185	Williamsburg (757)	12,922	11,409
*22601	Winchester (540)	23,649	21,947
24592	Wolf Trap(c) (703)	—	13,133
*22191	Woodbridge(c) (540)	—	26,401
24382	Wytheville (540)	8,145	8,036
22110	Yorkshire(c) (703)	—	5,699

Washington

ZIP	Place	1996	1990
98520	Aberdeen (360)	16,598	16,565
98036	Alderwood Manor-Bothell North(c) (425)	—	22,945
98221	Anacortes (360)	13,903	11,451
98223	Arlington (360)	5,672	4,037
98335	Artondale(c) (253)	—	7,141
*98002	Auburn (253)	36,393	33,650
98604	Battle Ground (360)	5,048	3,758
*98009	Bellevue (425)	92,267	86,872
*98225	Bellingham (360)	61,043	52,179
98390	Bonney Lake (360)	9,308	7,494
*98011	Bothell (425)	14,922	12,345
*98337	Bremerton (360)	41,580	38,142
98036	Brier (425)	6,358	5,633
98178	Bryn Mawr-Skyway(c) (206)	—	12,514
98166	Burien (206)	26,882	27,507
98233	Burlington (360)	5,782	4,349
98607	Camas (360)	9,381	6,762
98055	Cascade-Fairwood(c) (425)	—	30,107
98684	Cascade Park East(c) (425)	—	6,996
98684	Cascade Park West(c) (425)	—	6,656
98531	Centralia (360)	13,281	12,101
98532	Chehalis (360)	7,053	6,527
99004	Cheney (509)	8,015	7,723
99403	Clarkston (509)	7,407	6,753
99324	College Place (509)	7,208	6,308
99114	Colville (509)	5,273	4,360
99218	Country Homes(c) (509)	—	5,126
98042	Covington-Sawyer-Wilderness(c)	—	24,321
98198	Des Moines (206)	17,811	17,283
99213	Dishman(c) (509)	—	9,671
.....	East Hill-Meridian(c)	—	42,696
98366	East Port Orchard(c) (360)	—	5,409
98056	East Renton Highlands(c) (425)	—	13,218
98801	East Wenatchee Bench(c) (509)	—	12,539
.....	Edgewood-North Hill(c)	—	9,120
*98020	Edmonds (425)	32,001	30,743
98387	Elk Plain(c)	—	12,197
98926	Ellensburg (509)	14,009	12,360
.....	Ellsworth North(c)	—	5,796
98022	Enumclaw (360)	9,500	7,227
98823	Ephrata (509)	6,304	5,349
99210	Esperance(c) (509)	—	11,236
*98201	Everett (425)	81,028	70,937
98411	Evergreen(c)	—	11,249
99218	Fairwood(c) (509)	—	5,807
*98002	Federal Way (253)	68,088	67,535
98248	Ferndale (360)	7,102	5,398
98466	Fircrest (253)	5,311	5,258
98597	Five Corners(c)	—	6,776
98433	Fort Lewis(c) (253)	—	22,224
98930	Grandview (509)	8,131	7,169
.....	Harbour Pointe(c)	—	9,107
98660	Hazel Dell North(c) (360)	—	6,924
98665	Hazel Dell South(c) (360)	—	5,796
98550	Hoquiam (360)	9,073	8,972
98011	Inglewood-Finn Hill(c) (425)	—	29,132
98027	Issaquah (425)	9,664	7,786
98626	Kelso (360)	12,226	11,767
98028	Kenmore(c) (425)	—	8,917
*99336	Kennewick (509)	51,184	42,148
*98031	Kent (253)/(425)	42,700	37,960
98033	Kingsgate(c) (425)	—	14,259
*98033	Kirkland (425)	43,778	40,059
98509	Lacey (360)	27,381	19,279
98155	Lake Forest North(c) (206)	—	8,002
98002	Lakeland North(c) (253)	—	14,402
98002	Lakeland South(c) (253)	—	9,027
98036	Lake Serene-North Lynnwood(c) (425)	—	14,290
98665	Lake Shore(c) (360)	—	6,268
98258	Lake Stevens (425)	5,101	3,435
98259	Lakewood(c) (253)	—	58,412
.....	Lea Hill(c)	—	6,876
98632	Longview (360)	33,767	31,499
98264	Lynden (360)	7,943	5,709
*98046	Lynnwood (425)	31,342	28,637
98012	Martha Lake(c) (425)	—	10,155
*98270	Marysville (360)	16,740	12,248
98040	Mercer Island (206)	21,277	20,816
98444	Midland(c) (253)	—	5,587
98082	Mill Creek (425)	8,686	7,180
98354	Milton (253)	5,632	4,995
98661	Minnehaha(c) (360)	—	9,661
98272	Monroe (360)	6,548	4,275
98837	Moses Lake (509)	13,984	11,235
98043	Mountlake Terrace (425)	20,119	19,320
*98273	Mount Vernon (360)	22,059	17,647
98275	Mukilteo (425)	13,501	11,575
98006	Newport Hills(c) (425)	—	14,736
98166	Normandy Park (206)	6,846	6,794
98155	North City-Ridgecrest(c) (206)	—	13,832
.....	North Creek-Canyon Park(c)	—	23,236
98166	North Hill(c) (206)	—	5,706
98270	North Marysville(c) (425)	—	18,711
98277	Oak Harbor (360)	19,356	17,176
*98501	Olympia (360)	39,006	33,729
99214	Opportunity(c) (509)	—	22,326
98662	Orchards North(c) (360)	—	6,479
98662	Orchards South(c) (360)	—	12,956
99344	Othello (509)	5,334	4,638
99027	Otis Orchards-East Farms(c) (360)	—	5,811
98047	Pacific (253)	5,843	4,622
.....	Paine Field-Lake Stickney(c)	—	18,670
98444	Parkland(c) (253)	—	20,882
98366	Parkwood(c) (360)	—	6,853
*99301	Pasco (509)	23,910	20,337
98027	Pine Lake(c) (425)	—	13,940
*98362	Port Angeles (360)	18,674	17,710
*98366	Port Orchard (360)	6,266	4,984
98368	Port Townsend (360)	8,727	7,001
98370	Poulsbo (360)	5,986	4,848
98390	Prairie Ridge(c)	—	8,278
*99163	Pullman (509)	24,643	23,478
*98371	Puyallup (253)	28,303	23,878
*98052	Redmond (425)	42,127	35,800
*98058	Renton (425)	45,155	41,688
99352	Richland (509)	37,445	32,315
98160	Richmond Beach-Innis Arden(c) (206)	—	7,242
98113	Richmond Highlands(c) (206)	—	26,037
98188	Riverton-Boulevard Park(c) (206)	—	15,337
.....	Sahalee(c)	—	13,951
98686	Salmon Creek(c) (360)	—	11,989
*98148	Seatac (206)	22,723	22,760
*98101	Seattle (206)/(425)	524,704	516,259
98284	Sedro Woolley (360)	7,506	6,333
98942	Selah (509)	6,200	5,113
98584	Shelton (360)	8,459	7,241
98155	Sheridan Beach(c) (206)	—	6,518
*98383	Silverdale(c) (360)	—	7,660
98201	Silver Lake-Fircrest(c) (360)	—	24,474
*98290	Snohomish (360)	8,337	6,499
98373	South Hill(c)	—	12,963
98387	Spanaway(c) (253)	—	15,001
*99210	Spokane (509)	186,562	177,165
98388	Steilacoom (253)	6,079	5,728
*98371	Summit(c) (253)	—	6,312
98390	Sumner (253)	7,908	7,535

ZIP	Place		1996	1990
98944	Sunnyside	(509)	12,434	11,238
*98402	Tacoma	(253)	179,114	176,664
98501	Tanglewilde-Thompson Place(c)	(360)	—	6,061
98948	Toppenish	(509)	8,019	7,419
98138	Tukwila	(206)	14,556	14,506
98501	Tumwater	(360)	11,520	9,976
98464	University Place(c)	(253)	—	27,701
*98661	Vancouver	(360)	59,982	54,651
98662	Vancouver Mall(c)	(360)	—	6,938
99037	Veradale(c)	(509)	—	7,836
99362	Walla Walla	(509)	28,529	26,482
.....	Waller(c)		—	6,415
98671	Washougal	(360)	5,599	4,764
*98801	Wenatchee	(509)	23,837	21,746
.....	West Lake Sammamish(c)		—	6,087
98258	West Lake Stevens(c)	(425)	—	12,453
99301	West Pasco(c)	(509)	—	7,312
99353	West Richland	(509)	6,170	3,962
99181	West Valley(c)		—	6,594
98166	White Center-Shorewood(c)	(206)	—	20,531
98072	Woodinville	(425)	8,660	7,628
98032	Woodmont Beach(c)	(253)	—	7,493
*98903	Yakima	(509)	65,110	58,427

West Virginia (304)

ZIP	Place	1996	1990
*25801	Beckley	18,353	18,274
24701	Bluefield	12,300	12,756
26330	Bridgeport	7,403	6,837
26201	Buckhannon	6,083	5,909
*25301	Charleston	56,098	57,287
*26301	Clarksburg	17,410	17,970
25301	Cross Lanes(c)	—	10,878
25064	Dunbar	8,525	8,697
26241	Elkins	7,699	7,494
*26554	Fairmont	19,731	20,210
26354	Grafton	5,527	5,524
*25704	Huntington	53,941	54,844
25526	Hurricane	5,320	4,461
26726	Keyser	5,545	5,870
*25401	Martinsburg	14,541	14,073
*26505	Morgantown	26,919	25,879
26041	Moundsville	10,161	10,753
26155	New Martinsville	6,585	6,705
25143	Nitro	6,737	6,851
25901	Oak Hill	6,934	6,812
*26101	Parkersburg	32,766	33,862
.....	Pea Ridge(c)	—	6,535
25550	Point Pleasant	5,066	4,996
24740	Princeton	6,814	7,043
25177	Saint Albans	12,055	12,241
25303	South Charleston	13,409	13,645
25569	Teays Valley(c)	—	8,436
26105	Vienna	11,248	10,862
26062	Weirton	21,731	22,124
26003	Wheeling	33,311	34,882

Wisconsin

See introductory note.

ZIP	Place		1996	1990
54301	Allouez	(920)	14,780	14,431
54720	Altoona	(715)	6,583	5,889
54409	Antigo	(715)	8,584	8,284
*59411	Appleton	(920)	65,862	65,695
54806	Ashland	(715)	8,771	8,695
54304	Ashwaubenon	(920)	17,529	16,376
53913	Baraboo	(608)	9,620	9,203
53916	Beaver Dam	(920)	14,414	14,196
54311	Bellevue Town(c)	(920)	—	7,541
*53511	Beloit	(608)	35,836	35,571
54923	Berlin	(920)	5,423	5,371
*53045	Brookfield	(414)	37,729	35,184
53209	Brown Deer	(414)	12,177	12,236
53105	Burlington	(414)	9,623	8,851
53012	Cedarburg	(414)	10,392	10,086
54729	Chippewa Falls	(715)	12,784	12,749
53110	Cudahy	(414)	18,123	18,659
53532	De Forest	(608)	6,262	4,882
53018	Delafield	(414)	6,026	5,347
53115	Delavan	(414)	7,104	6,073
54115	De Pere	(920)	19,116	16,594
*54703	Eau Claire	(715)	58,872	56,806
53121	Elkhorn	(414)	6,368	5,337
53122	Elm Grove	(414)	5,964	6,261
53714	Fitchburg	(608)	17,954	15,648
*54935	Fond du Lac	(920)	39,658	37,755
53538	Fort Atkinson	(920)	10,633	10,213
53217	Fox Point	(414)	6,846	7,238
53132	Franklin	(414)	25,867	21,855
53022	Germantown	(414)	16,907	13,658
53209	Glendale	(414)	13,646	14,088
53024	Grafton	(414)	9,660	9,340
*54303	Green Bay	(920)	102,076	96,466
53129	Greendale	(414)	14,828	15,128
53220	Greenfield	(414)	34,409	33,403
53130	Hales Corners	(414)	7,428	7,623
53027	Hartford	(414)	9,020	8,188
53029	Hartland	(414)	7,845	6,906
54303	Howard	(920)	12,907	9,874
54016	Hudson	(715)	7,392	6,378
*53545	Janesville	(608)	58,960	52,210
53549	Jefferson	(920)	6,515	6,078
54130	Kaukauna	(920)	12,182	11,982
*53140	Kenosha	(414)	86,888	80,426
54136	Kimberly	(414)	5,766	5,406
*54601	La Crosse	(608)	50,212	51,140
53147	Lake Geneva	(414)	6,570	5,979
54140	Little Chute	(920)	10,049	9,207
53558	McFarland	(608)	5,724	5,232
*53714	Madison	(608)	197,630	190,766
*54220	Manitowoc	(920)	33,388	32,521
54143	Marinette	(715)	11,979	11,843
54449	Marshfield	(715)	19,953	19,293
54952	Menasha	(920)	15,567	14,711
*53051	Menomonee Falls	(414)	30,395	26,840
54751	Menomonie	(715)	14,514	13,547
53097	Mequon	(414)	21,988	18,885
54452	Merrill	(715)	10,359	9,860
53562	Middleton	(608)	14,369	13,785
*53201	Milwaukee	(414)	590,503	628,088
53716	Monona	(608)	8,329	8,637
53566	Monroe	(608)	10,675	10,241
53149	Mukwonago	(414)	5,859	4,495
53150	Muskego	(414)	20,634	16,813
*54956	Neenah	(920)	23,936	23,219
*53151	New Berlin	(414)	36,215	33,592
54961	New London	(920)	7,115	6,658
54017	New Richmond	(715)	5,724	5,106
53154	Oak Creek	(414)	25,203	19,513
53066	Oconomowoc	(414)	11,484	10,993
54650	Onalaska	(608)	13,546	11,414
53575	Oregon	(608)	6,220	4,519
*54901	Oshkosh	(920)	57,957	55,006
53072	Pewaukee	(414)	6,823	5,287
53818	Platteville	(608)	9,919	9,862
53158	Pleasant Prairie	(414)	13,787	12,037
54467	Plover	(715)	10,109	8,176
53073	Plymouth	(920)	7,441	6,769
53901	Portage	(608)	9,319	8,640
53074	Port Washington	(414)	10,613	9,338
53821	Prairie du Chien	(608)	5,705	5,657
*53401	Racine	(414)	82,572	84,298
53959	Reedsburg	(608)	6,698	5,834
54501	Rhinelander	(715)	7,801	7,382
54868	Rice Lake	(715)	8,280	7,998
53581	Richland Center	(608)	4,965	5,018
54971	Ripon	(920)	7,340	7,241
54022	River Falls	(715)	11,535	10,610
53207	Saint Francis	(414)	9,094	9,245
54166	Shawano	(715)	7,689	7,598
*53081	Sheboygan	(920)	49,987	49,587
53085	Sheboygan Falls	(920)	6,194	5,823
53211	Shorewood	(414)	12,997	14,116
53172	South Milwaukee	(414)	20,609	20,958
54656	Sparta	(608)	8,248	7,788
54481	Stevens Point	(715)	22,774	23,002
53589	Stoughton	(608)	10,621	8,786
54235	Sturgeon Bay	(920)	9,348	9,176
53590	Sun Prairie	(608)	17,825	15,352
54880	Superior	(715)	27,396	27,134
53089	Sussex	(414)	8,137	5,039
54660	Tomah	(608)	8,061	7,572
54241	Two Rivers	(920)	13,088	13,030
53593	Verona	(608)	5,993	5,374
*53094	Watertown	(920)	20,563	19,142
*53186	Waukesha	(414)	60,197	56,894
53597	Waunakee	(608)	7,717	5,897
54981	Waupaca	(715)	5,683	4,946
53963	Waupun	(920)	9,839	8,844
*54403	Wausau	(715)	36,809	37,060
53213	Wauwatosa	(414)	46,759	49,366
53214	West Allis	(414)	60,550	63,221
*53095	West Bend	(414)	28,218	24,470
54476	Weston(c)	(715)	—	9,714
53217	Whitefish Bay	(414)	13,253	14,272
53190	Whitewater	(414)	13,236	12,636
*54494	Wisconsin Rapids	(715)	18,438	18,245

Wyoming (307)

ZIP	Place	1996	1990
*82609	Casper	48,800	46,765
*82009	Cheyenne	53,729	50,008
82414	Cody	8,721	7,897
82633	Douglas	5,432	5,076
*82930	Evanston	11,514	10,904
*82716	Gillette	19,202	17,545
82935	Green River	13,289	12,711
*83001	Jackson	5,614	4,708
82520	Lander	7,372	7,023
*82072	Laramie	26,583	26,687
82435	Powell	5,680	5,292
82301	Rawlins	8,947	9,380
82501	Riverton	10,050	9,202
*82901	Rock Springs	19,742	19,050
82801	Sheridan	14,730	13,904
82240	Torrington	5,950	5,651
82401	Worland	5,937	5,742

Populations and Areas of Counties and States

Source: U.S. Bureau of the Census, Dept. of Commerce; World Almanac research

State population figures below are estimates for July 1, 1997. For counties, July 1, 1997, population estimates and Apr. 1, 1990, decennial census figures are given. County areas may not add to total state areas because of rounding.

Alabama

(67 counties, 50,750 sq mi land; pop. 4,319,154)

County	County seat or courthouse	1997 Pop.	1990 Pop.	Land area sq mi
Autauga	Prattville	41,306	34,222	596
Baldwin	Bay Minette	128,842	98,280	1,597
Barbour	Clayton	26,782	25,417	885
Bibb	Centreville	18,588	16,576	622
Blount	Oneonta	45,081	39,248	646
Bullock	Union Springs	11,270	11,042	625
Butler	Greenville	21,692	21,892	777
Calhoun	Anniston	117,092	116,032	609
Chambers	Lafayette	36,825	36,876	597
Cherokee	Centre	21,590	19,543	553
Chilton	Clanton	36,349	32,458	694
Choctaw	Butler	15,894	16,018	914
Clarke	Grove Hill	28,489	27,240	1,239
Clay	Ashland	13,832	13,252	605
Cleburne	Heflin	14,092	12,730	560
Coffee	Elba	41,980	40,240	679
Colbert	Tuscumbia	53,047	51,666	595
Conecuh	Evergreen	14,083	14,054	851
Coosa	Rockford	11,554	11,063	653
Covington	Andalusia	37,362	36,478	1,035
Crenshaw	Luverne	13,645	13,635	610
Cullman	Cullman	74,241	67,613	739
Dale	Ozark	49,107	49,633	561
Dallas	Selma	47,133	48,130	981
De Kalb	Fort Payne	57,752	54,651	778
Elmore	Wetumpka	60,272	49,210	622
Escambia	Brewton	36,487	35,518	948
Etowah	Gadsden	104,313	99,840	535
Fayette	Fayette	18,176	17,962	628
Franklin	Russellville	29,613	27,814	636
Geneva	Geneva	24,828	23,647	576
Greene	Eutaw	9,902	10,153	646
Hale	Greensboro	16,390	15,498	644
Henry	Abbeville	15,636	15,374	562
Houston	Dothan	85,163	81,331	580
Jackson	Scottsboro	50,751	47,796	1,079
Jefferson	Birmingham	658,664	651,520	1,113
Lamar	Vernon	15,759	15,715	605
Lauderdale	Florence	84,241	79,661	670
Lawrence	Moulton	33,386	31,513	693
Lee	Opelika	98,501	87,146	609
Limestone	Athens	60,700	54,135	568
Lowndes	Hayneville	12,881	12,658	718
Macon	Tuskegee	23,314	24,928	611
Madison	Huntsville	272,293	238,912	805
Marengo	Linden	23,503	23,084	977
Marion	Hamilton	30,813	29,830	742
Marshall	Guntersville	78,893	70,832	567
Mobile	Mobile	398,276	378,643	1,233
Monroe	Monroeville	24,186	23,968	1,026
Montgomery	Montgomery	217,597	209,085	790
Morgan	Decatur	108,304	100,043	582
Perry	Marion	12,642	12,759	720
Pickens	Carrollton	20,964	20,699	882
Pike	Troy	28,604	27,595	671
Randolph	Wedowee	19,923	19,881	581
Russell	Phenix City	50,719	46,860	641
Saint Clair	Ashville & Pell City	60,838	49,811	634
Shelby	Columbiana	135,446	99,363	795
Sumter	Livingston	15,998	16,174	905
Talladega	Talladega	76,846	74,109	740
Tallapoosa	Dadeville	40,148	38,826	718
Tuscaloosa	Tuscaloosa	160,760	150,522	1,325
Walker	Jasper	70,733	67,670	795
Washington	Chatom	17,613	16,694	1,081
Wilcox	Camden	13,537	13,568	889
Winston	Double Springs	23,913	22,053	615

Alaska

(27 divisions, 570,374 sq mi land; pop. 609,311)

Census Division	1997 Pop.	1990 Pop.	Land area sq mi
Aleutians East Borough	2,322	2,464	6,985
Aleutians West Census Area	4,693	9,478	4,402
Anchorage Borough	251,047	226,338	1,698
Bethel Census Area	15,813	13,656	41,087
Bristol Bay Borough	1,340	1,410	519
Denali Borough	2,013	1,764	12,719
Dillingham Census Area	4,456	4,012	18,467
Fairbanks North Star Borough	84,301	77,720	7,362
Haines Borough	2,181	2,117	2,357
Juneau Borough	30,003	26,751	2,594
Kenai Peninsula Borough	47,561	40,802	16,079
Ketchikan Gateway Borough	13,809	13,828	1,220
Kodiak Island Borough	14,866	13,309	6,463
Lake and Peninsula Borough	1,776	1,668	23,632
Matanuska-Susitna Borough	54,400	39,683	24,694
Nome Census Area	8,897	8,288	23,013
North Slope Borough	7,191	5,979	87,861
Northwest Arctic Borough	6,625	6,113	35,863
Prince of Wales-Outer Ketchikan Census Area	7,157	6,278	7,325
Sitka Borough	8,478	8,588	2,882
Skagway-Hoonah-Angoon Census Area	3,792	3,680	8,012
Southeast Fairbanks Census Area	5,563	5,913	25,110
Valdez-Cordova Census Area	10,399	9,952	36,945
Wade Hampton Census Area	6,779	5,791	17,124
Wrangell-Petersburg Census Area	6,962	7,042	5,809
Yakutat Borough	833	705	4,865
Yukon-Koyukuk Census Area	6,054	6,714	145,287

Arizona

(15 counties, 113,642 sq mi land; pop. 4,554,966)

County	County seat or courthouse	1997 Pop.	1990 Pop.	Land area sq mi
Apache	Saint Johns	69,538	61,591	11,206
Cochise	Bisbee	112,248	97,624	6,170
Coconino	Flagstaff	113,719	96,591	18,619
Gila	Globe	48,377	40,216	4,768
Graham	Safford	31,097	26,554	4,630
Greenlee	Clifton	9,396	8,008	1,847
La Paz	Parker	14,917	13,844	4,500
Maricopa	Phoenix	2,696,198	2,122,101	9,204
Mohave	Kingman	128,884	93,497	13,312
Navajo	Holbrook	94,917	77,674	9,954
Pima	Tucson	780,150	666,957	9,187
Pinal	Florence	143,341	116,397	5,370
Santa Cruz	Nogales	37,870	29,676	1,238
Yavapai	Prescott	144,298	107,714	8,124
Yuma	Yuma	130,016	106,895	5,514

Arkansas

(75 counties, 52,075 sq mi land; pop. 2,522,819)

County	County seat or courthouse	1997 Pop.	1990 Pop.	Land area sq mi
Arkansas	DeWitt & Stuttgart	20,794	21,653	989
Ashley	Hamburg	24,421	24,319	921
Baxter	Mountain Home	36,578	31,186	554
Benton	Bentonville	130,006	97,499	843
Boone	Harrison	31,980	28,297	591
Bradley	Warren	11,558	11,793	651
Calhoun	Hampton	5,748	5,826	628
Carroll	Berryville & Eureka Springs	22,358	18,654	634
Chicot	Lake Village	15,121	15,713	644
Clark	Arkadelphia	22,119	21,437	866
Clay	Corning & Piggott	17,392	18,107	639
Cleburne	Heber Springs	22,454	19,411	553
Cleveland	Rison	8,322	7,781	598
Columbia	Magnolia	25,214	25,691	766
Conway	Morrilton	19,999	19,151	556
Craighead	Jonesboro & Lake City	76,932	68,956	711
Crawford	Van Buren	49,545	42,493	596
Crittenden	Marion	49,690	49,939	611
Cross	Wynne	19,484	19,225	616
Dallas	Fordyce	9,175	9,614	668
Desha	Arkansas City	15,256	16,798	765
Drew	Monticello	17,743	17,369	828
Faulkner	Conway	76,595	60,006	647
Franklin	Charleston & Ozark	16,470	14,897	610
Fulton	Salem	10,960	10,037	618
Garland	Hot Springs	83,201	73,397	678
Grant	Sheridan	15,688	13,948	632
Greene	Paragould	35,538	31,804	578
Hempstead	Hope	21,945	21,621	729
Hot Spring	Malvern	28,564	26,115	615
Howard	Nashville	13,867	13,569	588
Independence	Batesville	32,912	31,192	764
Izard	Melbourne	12,919	11,364	581
Jackson	Newport	17,751	18,944	634
Jefferson	Pine Bluff	82,259	85,487	885
Johnson	Clarksville	21,165	18,221	662
Lafayette	Lewisville	9,084	9,643	527
Lawrence	Walnut Ridge	17,458	17,455	587
Lee	Marianna	12,495	13,053	602
Lincoln	Star City	14,347	13,690	561
Little River	Ashdown	13,209	13,966	532
Logan	Booneville & Paris	21,245	20,557	710
Lonoke	Lonoke	49,270	39,268	766
Madison	Huntsville	13,132	11,618	837

County	County seat or courthouse	1997 Pop.	1990 Pop.	Land area sq mi
Marion	Yellville	14,419	12,001	598
Miller	Texarkana	39,708	38,467	624
Mississippi	Blytheville & Osceola	50,506	57,525	898
Monroe	Clarendon	10,359	11,333	607
Montgomery	Mount Ida	8,500	7,841	781
Nevada	Prescott	10,034	10,101	620
Newton	Jasper	8,110	7,666	823
Ouachita	Camden	28,120	30,574	733
Perry	Perryville	9,458	7,969	551
Phillips	Helena	27,632	28,830	693
Pike	Murfreesboro	10,490	10,086	603
Poinsett	Harrisburg	24,602	24,664	758
Polk	Mena	19,646	17,347	860
Pope	Russellville	51,219	45,883	812
Prairie	Des Arc & De Valls Bluff	9,285	9,518	646
Pulaski	Little Rock	350,426	349,569	771
Randolph	Pocahontas	17,702	16,558	652
Saint Francis	Forrest City	28,385	28,497	634
Saline	Benton	75,903	64,183	725
Scott	Waldron	10,850	10,205	894
Searcy	Marshall	7,785	7,841	667
Sebastian	Fort Smith & Greenwood	105,968	99,590	536
Sevier	De Queen	14,799	13,637	564
Sharp	Ash Flat	16,647	14,109	604
Stone	Mountain View	10,939	9,775	607
Union	El Dorado	45,488	46,719	1,039
Van Buren	Clinton	15,544	14,008	712
Washington	Fayetteville	136,974	113,409	950
White	Searcy	63,312	54,676	1,034
Woodruff	Augusta	8,957	9,520	587
Yell	Danville & Dardanelle	19,089	17,759	928

California

(58 counties, 155,973 sq mi land; pop. 32,268,301)

County	County seat or courthouse	1997 Pop.	1990 Pop.	Land area sq mi
Alameda	Oakland	1,371,067	1,304,346	738
Alpine	Markleeville	1,205	1,113	739
Amador	Jackson	34,506	30,039	593
Butte	Oroville	194,160	182,120	1,640
Calaveras	San Andreas	39,880	31,998	1,020
Colusa	Colusa	18,783	16,275	1,151
Contra Costa	Martinez	899,258	803,732	720
Del Norte	Crescent City	28,285	23,460	1,008
El Dorado	Placerville	155,617	125,995	1,712
Fresno	Fresno	754,396	667,490	5,963
Glenn	Willows	26,363	24,798	1,315
Humboldt	Eureka	123,389	119,118	3,573
Imperial	El Centro	143,706	109,303	4,175
Inyo	Independence	18,300	18,281	10,192
Kern	Bakersfield	628,605	544,981	8,142
Kings	Hanford	115,489	101,469	1,390
Lake	Lakeport	55,325	50,631	1,259
Lassen	Susanville	33,934	27,598	4,558
Los Angeles	Los Angeles	9,145,219	8,863,052	4,060
Madera	Madera	114,307	88,090	2,138
Marin	San Rafael	235,692	230,096	520
Mariposa	Mariposa	15,752	14,302	1,451
Mendocino	Ukiah	84,281	80,345	3,509
Merced	Merced	196,123	178,403	1,929
Modoc	Alturas	10,133	9,678	3,944
Mono	Bridgeport	10,535	9,956	3,045
Monterey	Salinas	361,907	355,660	3,322
Napa	Napa	119,269	110,765	754
Nevada	Nevada City	90,584	78,510	958
Orange	Santa Ana	2,674,091	2,410,668	790
Placer	Auburn	221,476	172,796	1,404
Plumas	Quincy	20,922	19,739	2,554
Riverside	Riverside	1,447,791	1,170,413	7,208
Sacramento	Sacramento	1,125,976	1,041,219	966
San Benito	Hollister	47,546	36,697	1,389
San Bernardino	San Bernardino	1,615,817	1,418,380	20,062
San Diego	San Diego	2,722,650	2,498,016	4,205
San Francisco	San Francisco	732,307	723,959	47
San Joaquin	Stockton	542,504	480,628	1,399
San Luis Obispo	San Luis Obispo	233,291	217,162	3,305
San Mateo	Redwood City	694,006	649,623	449
Santa Barbara	Santa Barbara	390,199	369,608	2,739
Santa Clara	San Jose	1,609,037	1,497,577	1,291
Santa Cruz	Santa Cruz	240,488	229,734	446
Shasta	Redding	163,178	147,036	3,786
Sierra	Downieville	3,437	3,318	953
Siskiyou	Yreka	44,260	43,531	6,287
Solano	Fairfield	371,020	339,471	828
Sonoma	Santa Rosa	428,609	388,222	1,576
Stanislaus	Modesto	421,818	370,522	1,495
Sutter	Yuba City	77,754	64,415	603
Tehama	Red Bluff	53,988	49,625	2,951
Trinity	Weaverville	13,197	13,063	3,179
Tulare	Visalia	353,175	311,921	4,824
Tuolumne	Sonora	53,368	48,456	2,236
Ventura	Ventura	725,968	669,016	1,846
Yolo	Woodland	152,797	141,210	1,012
Yuba	Marysville	61,561	58,228	631

Colorado

(63 counties, 103,729 sq mi land; pop. 3,892,644)

County	County seat or courthouse	1997 Pop.	1990 Pop.	Land area sq mi
Adams	Brighton	316,066	265,038	1,192
Alamosa	Alamosa	14,374	13,617	723
Arapahoe	Littleton	463,201	391,511	803
Archuleta	Pagosa Springs	8,515	5,345	1,349
Baca	Springfield	4,398	4,556	2,556
Bent	Las Animas	5,480	5,048	1,514
Boulder	Boulder	261,617	225,339	743
Chaffee	Salida	15,022	12,684	1,014
Cheyenne	Cheyenne Wells	2,277	2,397	1,782
Clear Creek	Georgetown	8,917	7,619	396
Conejos	Conejos	7,826	7,453	1,287
Costilla	San Luis	3,643	3,190	1,227
Crowley	Ordway	4,265	3,946	789
Custer	Westcliffe	3,292	1,926	739
Delta	Delta	25,820	20,980	1,142
Denver	Denver	498,985	467,610	153
Dolores	Dove Creek	1,706	1,504	1,067
Douglas	Castle Rock	126,248	60,391	840
Eagle	Eagle	31,950	21,928	1,688
Elbert	Kiowa	17,527	9,646	1,851
El Paso	Colorado Springs	480,041	397,014	2,127
Fremont	Canon City	42,956	32,273	1,533
Garfield	Glenwood Springs	37,627	29,974	2,948
Gilpin	Central City	3,967	3,070	150
Grand	Hot Sulphur Springs	9,843	7,966	1,850
Gunnison	Gunnison	12,198	10,273	3,239
Hinsdale	Lake City	698	467	1,118
Huerfano	Walsenburg	6,722	6,009	1,591
Jackson	Walden	1,533	1,605	1,613
Jefferson	Golden	496,656	438,430	772
Kiowa	Eads	1,666	1,688	1,771
Kit Carson	Burlington	7,174	7,140	2,161
Lake	Leadville	6,323	6,007	377
La Plata	Durango	40,145	32,284	1,692
Larimer	Fort Collins	226,021	186,136	2,601
Las Animas	Trinidad	14,488	13,765	4,773
Lincoln	Hugo	5,611	4,529	2,586
Logan	Sterling	18,102	17,567	1,839
Mesa	Grand Junction	110,681	93,145	3,328
Mineral	Creede	678	558	876
Moffat	Craig	12,291	11,357	4,743
Montezuma	Cortez	22,269	18,672	2,037
Montrose	Montrose	30,278	24,423	2,241
Morgan	Fort Morgan	25,149	21,939	1,286
Otero	La Junta	20,858	20,185	1,263
Ouray	Ouray	3,200	2,295	542
Park	Fairplay	12,730	7,174	2,201
Phillips	Holyoke	4,332	4,189	688
Pitkin	Aspen	13,577	12,661	970
Prowers	Lamar	13,652	13,347	1,641
Pueblo	Pueblo	132,901	123,051	2,389
Rio Blanco	Meeker	6,287	6,051	3,221
Rio Grande	Del Norte	11,403	10,770	913
Routt	Steamboat Springs	17,230	14,088	2,362
Saguache	Saguache	5,906	4,619	3,169
San Juan	Silverton	557	745	388
San Miguel	Telluride	5,322	3,653	1,287
Sedgwick	Julesburg	2,604	2,690	548
Summit	Breckenridge	18,468	12,881	608
Teller	Cripple Creek	19,790	12,468	557
Washington	Akron	4,627	4,812	2,521
Weld	Greeley	155,582	131,821	3,993
Yuma	Wray	9,372	8,954	2,366

Connecticut

(8 counties, 4,845 sq mi land; pop. 3,269,858)

County	County seat or courthouse	1997 Pop.	1990 Pop.	Land area sq mi
Fairfield	Bridgeport	833,315	827,645	626
Hartford	Hartford	825,141	851,783	736
Litchfield	Litchfield	181,082	174,092	920
Middlesex	Middletown	149,010	143,196	369
New Haven	New Haven	792,200	804,219	606
New London	Norwich	252,958	254,957	666
Tolland	Rockville	131,023	128,699	410
Windham	Putnam	105,129	102,525	513

Delaware

(3 counties, 1,955 sq mi land; pop. 731,581)

County	County seat or courthouse	1997 Pop.	1990 Pop.	Land area sq mi
Kent	Dover	122,709	110,993	591
New Castle	Wilmington	474,838	441,946	426
Sussex	Georgetown	134,034	113,229	938

District of Columbia

(61 sq mi land; pop. 528,964)

Florida

(67 counties, 53,937 sq mi land; pop. 14,653,945)

County	County seat or courthouse	1997 Pop.	1990 Pop.	Land area sq mi
Alachua	Gainesville	198,326	181,596	874
Baker	Macclenny	20,761	18,486	585
Bay	Panama City	146,223	126,994	764
Bradford	Starke	24,646	22,515	293
Brevard	Titusville	460,977	398,978	1,019
Broward	Fort Lauderdale	1,470,758	1,255,531	1,209
Calhoun	Blountstown	12,337	11,011	567
Charlotte	Punta Gorda	133,681	110,975	694
Citrus	Inverness	112,454	93,513	584
Clay	Green Cove Springs	135,179	105,986	601
Collier	Naples	195,731	152,099	2,026
Columbia	Lake City	52,856	42,613	797
De Soto	Arcadia	26,259	23,865	637
Dixie	Cross City	12,563	10,585	704
Duval	Jacksonville	732,622	672,971	774
Escambia	Pensacola	282,604	262,798	664
Flagler	Bunnell	46,128	28,701	485
Franklin	Apalachicola	10,133	8,967	534
Gadsden	Quincy	45,441	41,116	516
Gilchrist	Trenton	13,367	9,667	349
Glades	Moore Haven	9,698	7,591	774
Gulf	Port Saint Joe	13,926	11,504	565
Hamilton	Jasper	12,521	10,930	515
Hardee	Wauchula	22,113	19,499	637
Hendry	La Belle	31,634	25,773	1,153
Hernando	Brooksville	125,537	101,115	478
Highlands	Sebring	76,854	68,432	1,029
Hillsborough	Tampa	909,444	834,054	1,051
Holmes	Bonifay	18,382	15,778	483
Indian River	Vero Beach	99,215	90,208	503
Jackson	Marianna	45,706	41,375	916
Jefferson	Monticello	13,232	11,296	598
Lafayette	Mayo	6,289	5,578	543
Lake	Tavares	196,214	152,104	953
Lee	Fort Myers	387,091	335,113	804
Leon	Tallahassee	215,170	192,493	667
Levy	Bronson	32,254	25,912	1,118
Liberty	Bristol	6,703	5,569	836
Madison	Madison	17,558	16,569	692
Manatee	Bradenton	237,139	211,707	741
Marion	Ocala	237,308	194,835	1,579
Martin	Stuart	116,087	100,900	556
Miami-Dade	Miami	2,044,600	1,937,194	1,945
Monroe	Key West	81,919	78,024	997
Nassau	Fernandina Beach	54,096	43,941	652
Okaloosa	Crestview	167,580	143,777	936
Okeechobee	Okeechobee	33,102	29,627	774
Orange	Orlando	783,974	677,491	908
Osceola	Kissimmee	142,128	107,728	1,322
Palm Beach	West Palm Beach	1,018,524	863,503	1,974
Pasco	New Port Richey	320,253	281,131	745
Pinellas	Clearwater	871,766	851,659	280
Polk	Bartow	448,646	405,382	1,875
Putnam	Palatka	70,430	65,070	722
Saint Johns	Saint Augustine	112,707	83,829	609
Saint Lucie	Fort Pierce	179,559	150,171	573
Santa Rosa	Milton	114,481	81,608	1,016
Sarasota	Sarasota	301,644	277,776	572
Seminole	Sanford	344,729	287,521	308
Sumter	Bushnell	39,428	31,577	546
Suwannee	Live Oak	33,077	26,780	688
Taylor	Perry	18,718	17,111	1,042
Union	Lake Butler	12,359	10,252	240
Volusia	De Land	419,797	370,737	1,106
Wakulla	Crawfordville	19,172	14,202	607
Walton	De Funiak Springs	37,914	27,759	1,058
Washington	Chipley	20,221	16,919	580

Georgia

(159 counties, 57,919 sq mi land; pop. 7,486,242)

County	County seat or courthouse	1997 Pop.	1990 Pop.	Land area sq mi
Appling	Baxley	16,393	15,744	509
Atkinson	Pearson	7,082	6,213	338
Bacon	Alma	10,345	9,566	285
Baker	Newton	3,733	3,615	343
Baldwin	Milledgeville	41,939	39,530	259
Banks	Homer	12,432	10,308	234
Barrow	Winder	38,966	29,721	162
Bartow	Cartersville	69,181	55,915	460
Ben Hill	Fitzgerald	17,338	16,245	252
Berrien	Nashville	15,968	14,153	453
Bibb	Macon	155,975	150,137	250
Bleckley	Cochran	11,147	10,430	217
Brantley	Nahunta	13,380	11,077	444
Brooks	Quitman	16,668	15,398	494
Bryan	Pembroke	23,093	15,438	442
Bulloch	Statesboro	49,865	43,125	683
Burke	Waynesboro	22,725	20,579	831
Butts	Jackson	17,205	15,326	187
Calhoun	Morgan	5,071	5,013	280
Camden	Woodbine	45,153	30,167	630
Candler	Metter	8,909	7,744	247
Carroll	Carrollton	81,402	71,422	499
Catoosa	Ringgold	49,567	42,464	162
Charlton	Folkston	9,272	8,496	781
Chatham	Savannah	225,934	216,774	440
Chattahoochee	Cusseta	16,320	16,934	249
Chattooga	Summerville	22,922	22,242	314
Cherokee	Canton	126,838	90,204	424
Clarke	Athens	91,042	87,594	121
Clay	Fort Gaines	3,461	3,364	195
Clayton	Jonesboro	204,197	181,436	143
Clinch	Homerville	6,641	6,160	809
Cobb	Marietta	551,059	447,745	340
Coffee	Douglas	33,904	29,592	599
Colquitt	Moultrie	39,616	36,645	552
Columbia	Appling	88,812	66,031	290
Cook	Adel	14,627	13,456	229
Coweta	Newnan	80,658	53,853	443
Crawford	Knoxville	11,044	8,991	325
Crisp	Cordele	20,662	20,011	274
Dade	Trenton	14,664	13,147	174
Dawson	Dawsonville	13,875	9,429	211
Decatur	Bainbridge	26,614	25,517	597
De Kalb	Decatur	587,730	546,171	268
Dodge	Eastman	18,196	17,607	501
Dooly	Vienna	10,413	9,901	393
Dougherty	Albany	95,800	96,321	330
Douglas	Douglasville	86,653	71,120	199
Early	Blakely	12,152	11,854	511
Echols	Statenville	2,422	2,334	404
Effingham	Springfield	35,063	25,687	480
Elbert	Elberton	19,134	18,949	369
Emanuel	Swainsboro	21,008	20,546	686
Evans	Claxton	9,746	8,724	185
Fannin	Blue Ridge	18,090	15,992	386
Fayette	Fayetteville	85,047	62,415	197
Floyd	Rome	84,640	81,251	513
Forsyth	Cumming	75,749	44,083	226
Franklin	Carnesville	18,513	16,650	263
Fulton	Atlanta	722,540	648,779	529
Gilmer	Ellijay	17,891	13,368	427
Glascock	Gibson	2,490	2,357	144
Glynn	Brunswick	66,650	62,496	422
Gordon	Calhoun	40,290	35,067	355
Grady	Cairo	21,510	20,279	458
Greene	Greensboro	13,401	11,793	388
Gwinnett	Lawrenceville	500,816	352,910	433
Habersham	Clarkesville	31,197	27,622	278
Hall	Gainesville	116,047	95,434	394
Hancock	Sparta	8,990	8,908	473
Haralson	Buchanan	24,154	21,966	282
Harris	Hamilton	22,227	17,788	464
Hart	Hartwell	21,482	19,712	232
Heard	Franklin	9,969	8,628	296
Henry	McDonough	98,103	58,741	323
Houston	Perry	103,543	89,208	377
Irwin	Ocilla	8,968	8,649	357
Jackson	Jefferson	36,477	30,005	342
Jasper	Monticello	9,873	8,453	371
Jeff Davis	Hazlehurst	12,616	12,032	333
Jefferson	Louisville	17,845	17,408	528
Jenkins	Millen	8,413	8,247	350
Johnson	Wrightsville	8,343	8,329	304
Jones	Gray	22,634	20,739	394
Lamar	Barnesville	14,671	13,038	185
Lanier	Lakeland	6,818	5,531	187
Laurens	Dublin	43,502	39,988	813
Lee	Leesburg	21,874	16,250	356
Liberty	Hinesville	60,017	52,745	519
Lincoln	Lincolnton	8,095	7,442	211
Long	Ludowici	8,343	6,202	401
Lowndes	Valdosta	83,980	75,981	504
Lumpkin	Dahlonega	18,121	14,573	285
McDuffie	Thomson	21,588	20,119	260
McIntosh	Darien	9,935	8,634	434
Macon	Oglethorpe	13,253	13,114	403
Madison	Danielsville	24,416	21,050	284
Marion	Buena Vista	6,528	5,590	367
Meriwether	Greenville	22,908	22,411	503
Miller	Colquitt	6,280	6,280	283
Mitchell	Camilla	21,082	20,275	512
Monroe	Forsyth	19,269	17,113	396
Montgomery	Mount Vernon	7,747	7,379	245
Morgan	Madison	14,561	12,883	350
Murray	Chatsworth	31,944	26,147	344
Muscogee	Columbus	182,769	179,280	216
Newton	Covington	55,148	41,808	276
Oconee	Watkinsville	23,065	17,618	186
Oglethorpe	Lexington	11,243	9,763	441
Paulding	Dallas	68,962	41,611	314
Peach	Fort Valley	24,053	21,189	151

County	County seat or courthouse	1997 Pop.	1990 Pop.	Land area sq mi
Pickens	Jasper	18,574	14,432	232
Pierce	Blackshear	15,483	13,328	343
Pike	Zebulon	12,374	10,224	218
Polk	Cedartown	35,811	33,815	311
Pulaski	Hawkinsville	8,337	8,108	247
Putnam	Eatonton	16,861	14,137	345
Quitman	Georgetown	2,444	2,210	152
Rabun	Clayton	13,246	11,648	371
Randolph	Cuthbert	7,898	8,023	429
Richmond	Augusta	193,098	189,719	324
Rockdale	Conyers	67,050	54,091	131
Schley	Ellaville	3,835	3,590	168
Screven	Sylvania	14,402	13,842	649
Seminole	Donalsonville	9,824	9,010	238
Spalding	Griffin	56,972	54,457	198
Stephens	Toccoa	25,239	23,436	179
Stewart	Lumpkin	5,421	5,654	459
Sumter	Americus	31,685	30,232	485
Talbot	Talbotton	6,895	6,524	393
Taliaferro	Crawfordville	1,857	1,915	195
Tattnall	Reidsville	19,056	17,722	484
Taylor	Butler	8,215	7,642	378
Telfair	MacRae	11,465	11,000	441
Terrell	Dawson	11,097	10,653	336
Thomas	Thomasville	42,560	38,943	548
Tift	Tifton	36,892	34,998	265
Toombs	Lyons	25,614	24,072	367
Towns	Hiawassee	8,167	6,754	167
Treutlen	Soperton	5,959	5,994	201
Troup	La Grange	58,547	55,532	414
Turner	Ashburn	9,150	8,703	286
Twiggs	Jeffersonville	9,872	9,806	360
Union	Blairsville	15,675	11,993	323
Upson	Thomaston	27,231	26,300	326
Walker	La Fayette	61,848	58,340	446
Walton	Monroe	51,539	38,586	329
Ware	Waycross	35,817	35,471	903
Warren	Warrenton	6,038	6,078	286
Washington	Sandersville	19,999	19,112	681
Wayne	Jesup	25,068	22,356	645
Webster	Preston	2,255	2,263	210
Wheeler	Alamo	4,954	4,903	298
White	Cleveland	16,828	13,006	242
Whitfield	Dalton	81,317	72,462	290
Wilcox	Abbeville	7,308	7,008	380
Wilkes	Washington	10,549	10,597	471
Wilkinson	Irwinton	10,859	10,228	447
Worth	Sylvester	22,361	19,744	570

Hawaii

(5 counties, 6,423 sq mi land; pop. 1,186,602)

County	County seat or courthouse	1997 Pop.	1990 Pop.	Land area sq mi
Hawaii	Hilo	141,458	120,317	4,028
Honolulu	Honolulu	869,857	836,231	600
Kalawao[1]		81	130	13
Kauai	Lihue	56,423	51,177	623
Maui	Wailuku	118,783	100,374	1,159

(1) Administered by state government.

Idaho

(44 counties, 82,751 sq mi land; pop. 1,210,232)

County	County seat or courthouse	1997 Pop.	1990 Pop.	Land area sq mi
Ada	Boise	267,168	205,775	1,055
Adams	Council	3,859	3,254	1,365
Bannock	Pocatello	73,850	66,026	1,113
Bear Lake	Paris	6,577	6,084	971
Benewah	Saint Maries	8,967	7,937	776
Bingham	Blackfoot	41,621	37,583	2,095
Blaine	Hailey	17,213	13,552	2,645
Boise	Idaho City	5,026	3,509	1,903
Bonner	Sandpoint	34,771	26,622	1,738
Bonneville	Idaho Falls	80,294	72,207	1,869
Boundary	Bonners Ferry	9,882	8,332	1,269
Butte	Arco	3,141	2,918	2,233
Camas	Fairfield	843	727	1,075
Canyon	Caldwell	116,675	90,076	590
Caribou	Soda Springs	7,380	6,963	1,766
Cassia	Burley	21,441	19,532	2,567
Clark	Dubois	837	762	1,765
Clearwater	Orofino	9,455	8,505	2,462
Custer	Challis	4,242	4,133	4,926
Elmore	Mountain Home	24,880	21,205	3,078
Franklin	Preston	10,816	9,232	666
Fremont	Saint Anthony	11,818	10,937	1,867
Gem	Emmett	14,454	11,844	563
Gooding	Gooding	13,566	11,633	731
Idaho	Grangeville	15,082	13,768	8,485
Jefferson	Rigby	18,942	16,543	1,095
Jerome	Jerome	17,665	15,138	600
Kootenai	Coeur d'Alene	98,767	69,795	1,245
Latah	Moscow	32,532	30,617	1,077
Lemhi	Salmon	8,081	6,899	4,564
Lewis	Nez Perce	4,067	3,516	479
Lincoln	Shoshone	3,806	3,308	1,206
Madison	Rexberg	23,508	23,674	472
Minidoka	Rupert	20,655	19,361	760
Nez Perce	Lewiston	36,819	33,754	849
Oneida	Malad City	4,012	3,492	1,200
Owyhee	Murphy	10,227	8,392	7,678
Payette	Payette	20,220	16,434	408
Power	American Falls	8,294	7,086	1,406
Shoshone	Wallace	13,982	13,931	2,634
Teton	Driggs	5,310	3,439	450
Twin Falls	Twin Falls	61,298	53,580	1,925
Valley	Cascade	8,099	6,109	3,678
Washington	Weiser	10,090	8,550	1,456

Illinois

(102 counties, 55,593 sq mi land; pop. 11,895,849)

County	County seat or courthouse	1997 Pop.	1990 Pop.	Land area sq mi
Adams	Quincy	67,851	66,090	857
Alexander	Cairo	10,029	10,626	236
Bond	Greenville	17,070	14,991	380
Boone	Belvidere	37,922	30,806	281
Brown	Mount Sterling	6,345	5,836	306
Bureau	Princeton	35,606	35,688	869
Calhoun	Hardin	4,960	5,322	254
Carroll	Mount Carroll	16,941	16,805	444
Cass	Virginia	13,223	13,437	376
Champaign	Urbana	168,473	173,025	997
Christian	Taylorville	34,608	34,418	709
Clark	Marshall	17,572	15,921	502
Clay	Louisville	14,450	14,460	469
Clinton	Carlyle	35,367	33,944	474
Coles	Charleston	51,312	51,644	508
Cook	Chicago	5,076,786	5,105,044	946
Crawford	Robinson	21,070	19,464	444
Cumberland	Toledo	11,172	10,670	346
De Kalb	Sycamore	83,602	77,932	634
De Witt	Clinton	16,781	16,516	398
Douglas	Tuscola	19,782	19,464	417
Du Page	Wheaton	870,378	781,689	334
Edgar	Paris	19,905	19,595	624
Edwards	Albion	7,028	7,440	222
Effingham	Effingham	33,280	31,704	479
Fayette	Vandalia	21,604	20,893	717
Ford	Paxton	14,049	14,275	486
Franklin	Benton	40,679	40,319	412
Fulton	Lewiston	38,405	38,080	866
Gallatin	Shawneetown	6,671	6,909	324
Greene	Carrollton	15,639	15,317	543
Grundy	Morris	36,253	32,337	420
Hamilton	McLeansboro	8,621	8,499	435
Hancock	Carthage	21,146	21,373	795
Hardin	Elizabethtown	4,964	5,189	178
Henderson	Oquawka	8,637	8,096	379
Henry	Cambridge	51,453	51,159	823
Iroquois	Watseka	31,400	30,787	1,117
Jackson	Murphysboro	60,698	61,067	588
Jasper	Newton	10,559	10,609	494
Jefferson	Mount Vernon	38,966	37,020	571
Jersey	Jerseyville	21,248	20,539	369
Jo Daviess	Galena	21,678	21,821	601
Johnson	Vienna	13,074	11,347	346
Kane	Geneva	380,801	317,471	521
Kankakee	Kankakee	101,984	96,255	678
Kendall	Yorkville	49,856	39,413	321
Knox	Galesburg	55,559	56,393	716
Lake	Waukegan	594,799	516,418	448
La Salle	Ottawa	109,543	106,913	1,135
Lawrence	Lawrenceville	15,622	15,972	372
Lee	Dixon	35,777	34,392	725
Livingston	Pontiac	40,316	39,301	1,044
Logan	Lincoln	31,317	30,798	618
McDonough	Macomb	34,086	35,244	589
McHenry	Woodstock	236,952	183,241	604
McLean	Bloomington	140,797	129,180	1,184
Macon	Decatur	114,265	117,206	581
Macoupin	Carlinville	49,214	47,679	864
Madison	Edwardsville	258,641	249,238	725
Marion	Salem	42,035	41,561	572
Marshall	Lacon	12,858	12,846	386
Mason	Havana	16,885	16,269	539
Massac	Metropolis	15,420	14,752	239
Menard	Petersburg	12,345	11,164	314
Mercer	Aledo	17,544	17,290	561
Monroe	Waterloo	25,931	22,422	388
Montgomery	Hillsboro	30,992	30,728	704
Morgan	Jacksonville	36,056	36,397	569
Moultrie	Sullivan	14,433	13,930	336
Ogle	Oregon	50,199	45,957	759
Peoria	Peoria	182,657	182,827	620
Perry	Pinckneyville	21,368	21,412	441
Piatt	Monticello	16,498	15,548	440
Pike	Pittsfield	17,287	17,577	830

County	County seat or courthouse	1997 Pop.	1990 Pop.	Land area sq mi
Pope	Golconda	4,681	4,373	371
Pulaski	Mound City	7,209	7,523	201
Putnam	Hennepin	5,854	5,730	160
Randolph	Chester	34,082	34,583	578
Richland	Olney	16,843	16,545	360
Rock Island	Rock Island	148,277	148,723	427
Saint Clair	Belleville	263,866	262,852	664
Saline	Harrisburg	26,359	26,551	383
Sangamon	Springfield	191,597	178,386	868
Schuyler	Rushville	7,625	7,498	437
Scott	Winchester	5,591	5,644	251
Shelby	Shelbyville	22,593	22,261	759
Stark	Toulon	6,344	6,534	288
Stephenson	Freeport	49,354	48,052	564
Tazewell	Pekin	128,521	123,692	649
Union	Jonesboro	18,037	17,619	416
Vermilion	Danville	85,097	88,257	899
Wabash	Mount Carmel	12,731	13,111	224
Warren	Monmouth	18,777	19,181	543
Washington	Nashville	15,325	14,965	563
Wayne	Fairfield	17,011	17,241	714
White	Carmi	15,647	16,522	495
Whiteside	Morrison	68,073	60,186	685
Will	Joliet	444,469	357,313	837
Williamson	Marion	61,163	57,733	424
Winnebago	Rockford	266,653	252,913	514
Woodford	Eureka	34,776	32,653	528

Indiana

(92 counties, 35,870 sq mi land; pop. 5,864,108)

County	County seat or courthouse	1997 Pop.	1990 Pop.	Land area sq mi
Adams	Decatur	32,837	31,095	339
Allen	Fort Wayne	312,091	300,836	657
Bartholomew	Columbus	68,734	63,657	407
Benton	Fowler	9,557	9,441	406
Blackford	Hartford City	14,020	14,067	165
Boone	Lebanon	42,985	38,147	423
Brown	Nashville	15,591	14,080	312
Carroll	Delphi	19,989	18,809	372
Cass	Logansport	38,573	38,413	413
Clark	Jeffersonville	93,212	87,774	375
Clay	Brazil	26,531	24,705	358
Clinton	Frankfort	33,232	30,974	405
Crawford	English	10,499	9,914	306
Daviess	Washington	28,851	27,533	431
Dearborn	Lawrenceburg	46,576	38,835	305
Decatur	Greensburg	25,362	23,645	373
De Kalb	Auburn	38,722	35,324	363
Delaware	Muncie	117,625	119,659	393
Dubois	Jasper	39,139	36,616	430
Elkhart	Goshen	170,725	156,198	464
Fayette	Connersville	26,133	26,015	215
Floyd	New Albany	71,465	64,404	148
Fountain	Covington	18,235	17,808	396
Franklin	Brookville	21,582	19,580	386
Fulton	Rochester	20,351	18,840	369
Gibson	Princeton	31,948	31,913	489
Grant	Marion	72,818	74,169	414
Greene	Bloomfield	33,074	30,410	542
Hamilton	Noblesville	154,785	108,936	398
Hancock	Greenfield	53,071	45,527	306
Harrison	Corydon	33,999	29,890	485
Hendricks	Danville	92,291	75,717	408
Henry	New Castle	48,867	48,139	393
Howard	Kokomo	83,586	80,827	293
Huntington	Huntington	37,144	35,427	383
Jackson	Brownstown	40,884	37,730	509
Jasper	Rensselaer	28,697	24,960	560
Jay	Portland	21,692	21,512	384
Jefferson	Madison	31,292	29,797	361
Jennings	Vernon	27,217	23,661	377
Johnson	Franklin	106,888	88,109	320
Knox	Vincennes	39,686	39,884	516
Kosciusko	Warsaw	70,363	65,294	538
Lagrange	Lagrange	32,719	29,477	380
Lake	Crown Point	479,339	475,594	497
La Porte	La Porte	109,080	107,066	598
Lawrence	Bedford	45,539	42,836	449
Madison	Anderson	131,840	130,669	452
Marion	Indianapolis	813,670	797,159	396
Marshall	Plymouth	45,337	42,182	444
Martin	Shoals	10,510	10,369	336
Miami	Peru	33,199	36,897	376
Monroe	Bloomington	116,653	108,978	394
Montgomery	Crawfordsville	36,285	34,436	505
Morgan	Martinsville	64,787	55,920	407
Newton	Kentland	14,683	13,551	402
Noble	Albion	41,918	37,877	411
Ohio	Rising Sun	5,458	5,315	87
Orange	Paoli	19,378	18,409	400
Owen	Spencer	20,257	17,281	385
Parke	Rockville	16,446	15,410	445
Perry	Cannelton	19,306	19,107	381
Pike	Petersburg	12,758	12,509	336
Porter	Valparaiso	144,084	128,932	418
Posey	Mount Vernon	26,640	25,968	409
Pulaski	Winamac	13,212	12,643	434
Putnam	Greencastle	33,706	30,315	480
Randolph	Winchester	27,480	27,148	453
Ripley	Versailles	27,177	24,616	446
Rush	Rushville	18,236	18,129	408
Saint Joseph	South Bend	258,056	247,052	457
Scott	Scottsburg	22,818	20,991	190
Shelby	Shelbyville	43,151	40,307	413
Spencer	Rockport	20,690	19,490	399
Starke	Knox	23,759	22,747	309
Steuben	Angola	31,102	27,446	309
Sullivan	Sullivan	20,280	18,993	447
Switzerland	Vevay	8,636	7,738	221
Tippecanoe	Lafayette	138,307	130,598	500
Tipton	Tipton	16,395	16,119	260
Union	Liberty	7,272	6,976	162
Vanderburgh	Evansville	166,837	165,058	235
Vermillion	Newport	16,997	16,773	257
Vigo	Terre Haute	104,940	106,107	403
Wabash	Wabash	34,525	35,069	413
Warren	Williamsport	8,170	8,176	365
Warrick	Boonville	50,831	44,920	384
Washington	Salem	27,143	23,717	515
Wayne	Richmond	71,800	71,951	404
Wells	Bluffton	26,773	25,948	370
White	Monticello	25,041	23,265	505
Whitley	Columbia City	29,969	27,651	336

Iowa

(99 counties, 55,875 sq mi land; pop. 2,852,423)

County	County seat or courthouse	1997 Pop.	1990 Pop.	Land area sq mi
Adair	Greenfield	8,232	8,409	569
Adams	Corning	4,420	4,866	424
Allamakee	Waukon	13,991	13,855	640
Appanoose	Centerville	13,511	13,743	496
Audubon	Audubon	6,814	7,334	443
Benton	Vinton	25,019	22,429	717
Black Hawk	Waterloo	121,502	123,798	567
Boone	Boone	26,158	25,186	572
Bremer	Waverly	23,304	22,813	438
Buchanan	Independence	21,139	20,844	571
Buena Vista	Storm Lake	19,565	19,965	575
Butler	Allison	15,695	15,731	580
Calhoun	Rockwell City	11,426	11,508	570
Carroll	Carroll	21,703	21,423	569
Cass	Atlantic	14,743	15,128	564
Cedar	Tipton	17,969	17,444	580
Cerro Gordo	Mason City	46,371	46,733	568
Cherokee	Cherokee	13,418	14,098	577
Chickasaw	New Hampton	13,435	13,295	505
Clarke	Osceola	8,237	8,287	431
Clay	Spencer	17,600	17,585	569
Clayton	Elkader	18,791	19,054	779
Clinton	Clinton	50,224	51,040	695
Crawford	Denison	16,389	16,775	714
Dallas	Adel	35,765	29,755	587
Davis	Bloomfield	8,414	8,312	503
Decatur	Leon	8,190	8,338	532
Delaware	Manchester	18,449	18,035	578
Des Moines	Burlington	42,123	42,614	416
Dickinson	Spirit Lake	15,985	14,909	381
Dubuque	Dubuque	88,084	86,403	608
Emmet	Estherville	10,931	11,569	396
Fayette	West Union	21,995	21,843	731
Floyd	Charles City	16,472	17,058	501
Franklin	Hampton	10,874	11,364	583
Fremont	Sidney	7,840	8,226	511
Greene	Jefferson	10,043	10,045	568
Grundy	Grundy Center	12,280	12,029	503
Guthrie	Guthrie Center	11,432	10,935	591
Hamilton	Webster City	16,058	16,071	577
Hancock	Garner	12,038	12,638	571
Hardin	Eldora	18,512	19,094	569
Harrison	Logan	15,346	14,730	697
Henry	Mount Pleasant	19,948	19,226	435
Howard	Cresco	9,710	9,809	473
Humboldt	Dakota City	10,398	10,756	434
Ida	Ida Grove	7,935	8,365	432
Iowa	Marengo	15,468	14,630	587
Jackson	Maquoketa	20,097	19,950	636
Jasper	Newton	35,700	34,795	730
Jefferson	Fairfield	17,020	16,310	435
Johnson	Iowa City	102,318	96,119	615
Jones	Anamosa	20,281	19,444	575
Keokuk	Sigourney	11,495	11,624	579
Kossuth	Algona	17,908	18,591	973
Lee	Fort Madison & Keokuk	38,654	38,687	517
Linn	Cedar Rapids	181,704	168,767	718
Louisa	Wapello	11,934	11,592	402
Lucas	Chariton	9,067	9,070	431

County	County seat or courthouse	1997 Pop.	1990 Pop.	Land area sq mi
Lyon	Rock Rapids	11,960	11,952	588
Madison	Winterset	13,733	12,483	561
Mahaska	Oskaloosa	21,822	21,532	571
Marion	Knoxville	31,260	30,001	554
Marshall	Marshalltown	38,789	38,276	572
Mills	Glenwood	14,387	13,202	437
Mitchell	Osage	11,063	10,928	469
Monona	Onawa	9,998	10,034	693
Monroe	Albia	8,045	8,114	433
Montgomery	Red Oak	11,907	12,076	424
Muscatine	Muscatine	41,212	39,907	439
O'Brien	Primghar	14,920	15,444	573
Osceola	Sibley	6,999	7,267	399
Page	Clarinda	17,130	16,870	535
Palo Alto	Emmetsburg	10,074	10,669	564
Plymouth	Le Mars	24,649	23,388	864
Pocahontas	Pocahontas	8,835	9,525	578
Polk	Des Moines	354,232	327,140	570
Pottawattamie	Council Bluffs	85,405	82,628	954
Poweshiek	Montezuma	18,999	19,033	585
Ringgold	Mount Ayr	5,337	5,420	538
Sac	Sac City	11,890	12,324	576
Scott	Davenport	157,433	150,973	458
Shelby	Harlan	13,118	13,230	591
Sioux	Orange City	31,090	29,903	768
Story	Nevada	74,582	74,252	573
Tama	Toledo	17,636	17,419	721
Taylor	Bedford	7,146	7,114	534
Union	Creston	12,461	12,750	424
Van Buren	Keosauqua	7,825	7,676	485
Wapello	Ottumwa	35,358	35,696	432
Warren	Indianola	39,720	36,033	572
Washington	Washington	20,855	19,612	569
Wayne	Corydon	6,824	7,067	526
Webster	Fort Dodge	38,616	40,342	715
Winnebago	Forest City	12,060	12,122	401
Winneshiek	Decorah	20,895	20,847	690
Woodbury	Sioux City	102,092	98,276	873
Worth	Northwood	7,764	7,991	400
Wright	Clarion	14,178	14,269	581

Kansas

(105 counties, 81,823 sq mi land; pop. 2,594,840)

County	County seat or courthouse	1997 Pop.	1990 Pop.	Land area sq mi
Allen	Iola	14,442	14,638	503
Anderson	Garnett	8,021	7,803	583
Atchison	Atchison	16,319	16,932	432
Barber	Medicine Lodge	5,412	5,874	1,134
Barton	Great Bend	27,936	29,382	894
Bourbon	Fort Scott	15,227	14,966	637
Brown	Hiawatha	11,037	11,128	571
Butler	El Dorado	60,235	50,580	1,428
Chase	Cottonwood Falls	2,893	3,021	776
Chautauqua	Sedan	4,399	4,407	642
Cherokee	Columbus	22,547	21,374	587
Cheyenne	Saint Francis	3,208	3,243	1,020
Clark	Ashland	2,444	2,418	975
Clay	Clay Center	9,226	9,158	644
Cloud	Concordia	10,190	11,023	716
Coffey	Burlington	8,741	8,404	630
Comanche	Coldwater	2,021	2,313	788
Cowley	Winfield	36,716	36,915	1,126
Crawford	Girard	35,986	35,582	593
Decatur	Oberlin	3,527	4,021	894
Dickinson	Abilene	19,705	18,958	848
Doniphan	Troy	7,664	8,134	392
Douglas	Lawrence	91,093	81,798	457
Edwards	Kinsley	3,426	3,787	622
Elk	Howard	3,360	3,327	648
Ellis	Hays	26,342	26,004	900
Ellsworth	Ellsworth	6,284	6,586	716
Finney	Garden City	35,909	33,070	1,300
Ford	Dodge City	29,254	27,463	1,099
Franklin	Ottawa	23,790	21,994	574
Geary	Junction City	25,321	30,453	384
Gove	Gove	3,085	3,231	1,072
Graham	Hill City	3,248	3,543	898
Grant	Ulysses	7,896	7,159	575
Gray	Cimarron	5,493	5,396	869
Greeley	Tribune	1,728	1,774	778
Greenwood	Eureka	8,043	7,847	1,140
Hamilton	Syracuse	2,284	2,388	997
Harper	Anthony	6,497	7,124	802
Harvey	Newton	31,594	31,028	539
Haskell	Sublette	4,008	3,886	577
Hodgeman	Jetmore	2,229	2,177	860
Jackson	Holton	12,036	11,525	657
Jefferson	Oskaloosa	17,930	15,905	536
Jewell	Mankato	3,966	4,251	909
Johnson	Olathe	417,336	355,021	477
Kearny	Lakin	4,199	4,027	870
Kingman	Kingman	8,512	8,292	864
Kiowa	Greensburg	3,440	3,660	722
Labette	Oswego	22,852	23,693	649
Lane	Dighton	2,186	2,375	717
Leavenworth	Leavenworth	70,176	64,371	463
Lincoln	Lincoln	3,344	3,653	719
Linn	Mound City	9,064	8,254	599
Logan	Oakley	3,045	3,081	1,073
Lyon	Emporia	34,085	34,732	851
McPherson	McPherson	27,596	27,268	900
Marion	Marion	12,914	12,888	943
Marshall	Marysville	11,146	11,705	903
Meade	Meade	4,396	4,247	979
Miami	Paola	26,190	23,466	577
Mitchell	Beloit	7,002	7,203	700
Montgomery	Independence	37,144	38,816	645
Morris	Council Grove	6,197	6,198	697
Morton	Elkhart	3,374	3,480	730
Nemaha	Seneca	10,254	10,446	719
Neosho	Erie	16,951	17,035	572
Ness	Ness City	3,638	4,033	1,075
Norton	Norton	5,815	5,947	878
Osage	Lyndon	17,082	15,248	704
Osborne	Osborne	4,508	4,867	893
Ottawa	Minneapolis	5,825	5,634	721
Pawnee	Larned	7,240	7,555	754
Phillips	Phillipsburg	6,062	6,590	886
Pottawatomie	Westmoreland	18,206	16,128	844
Pratt	Pratt	9,705	9,702	735
Rawlins	Atwood	3,211	3,404	1,070
Reno	Hutchinson	62,920	62,389	1,255
Republic	Belleville	6,140	6,482	717
Rice	Lyons	9,991	10,610	727
Riley	Manhattan	63,186	67,139	610
Rooks	Stockton	5,724	6,039	888
Rush	LaCrosse	3,430	3,842	718
Russell	Russell	7,630	7,835	885
Saline	Salina	51,620	49,301	720
Scott	Scott City	4,991	5,289	718
Sedgwick	Wichita	438,679	403,662	1,000
Seward	Liberal	20,154	18,743	640
Shawnee	Topeka	164,932	160,976	550
Sheridan	Hoxie	2,747	3,043	896
Sherman	Goodland	6,600	6,926	1,056
Smith	Smith Center	4,659	5,078	896
Stafford	Saint John	5,101	5,365	792
Stanton	Johnson	2,330	2,333	680
Stevens	Hugoton	5,405	5,048	728
Sumner	Wellington	26,983	25,841	1,182
Thomas	Colby	8,183	8,258	1,075
Trego	WaKeeney	3,331	3,694	888
Wabaunsee	Alma	6,704	6,603	798
Wallace	Sharon Springs	1,800	1,821	914
Washington	Washington	6,598	7,073	899
Wichita	Leoti	2,703	2,758	719
Wilson	Fredonia	10,292	10,289	574
Woodson	Yates Center	3,973	4,116	501
Wyandotte	Kansas City	152,627	162,026	151

Kentucky

(120 counties, 39,732 sq mi land; pop. 3,908,124)

County	County seat or courthouse	1997 Pop.	1990 Pop.	Land area sq mi
Adair	Columbia	16,494	15,360	407
Allen	Scottsville	16,233	14,628	346
Anderson	Lawrenceburg	18,032	14,571	203
Ballard	Wickliffe	8,346	7,902	251
Barren	Glasgow	36,770	34,001	491
Bath	Owingsville	10,355	9,692	279
Bell	Pineville	29,784	31,506	361
Boone	Burlington	76,173	57,589	246
Bourbon	Paris	19,349	19,236	291
Boyd	Catlettsburg	49,865	51,150	160
Boyle	Danville	27,069	25,641	182
Bracken	Brooksville	8,291	7,766	203
Breathitt	Jackson	15,642	15,703	495
Breckinridge	Hardinsburg	17,299	16,312	572
Bullitt	Shepherdsville	58,005	47,567	299
Butler	Morgantown	11,757	11,245	428
Caldwell	Princeton	13,341	13,232	347
Calloway	Murray	33,072	30,735	386
Campbell	Newport	87,422	83,866	152
Carlisle	Bardwell	5,381	5,238	193
Carroll	Carrollton	9,585	9,292	130
Carter	Grayson	26,591	24,340	411
Casey	Liberty	14,531	14,211	446
Christian	Hopkinsville	73,229	68,941	721
Clark	Winchester	31,679	29,496	254
Clay	Manchester	22,544	21,746	471
Clinton	Albany	9,311	9,135	198
Crittenden	Marion	9,480	9,196	362
Cumberland	Burkesville	6,876	6,784	306
Daviess	Owensboro	91,011	87,189	462
Edmonson	Brownsville	11,135	10,357	303
Elliott	Sandy Hook	6,540	6,455	234
Estill	Irvine	15,487	14,614	254
Fayette	Lexington	239,874	225,366	285
Fleming	Flemingsburg	13,200	12,292	351
Floyd	Prestonsburg	43,343	43,586	394

County	County seat or courthouse	1997 Pop.	1990 Pop.	Land area sq mi
Franklin	Frankfort	46,226	44,143	211
Fulton	Hickman	7,630	8,271	209
Gallatin	Warsaw	6,771	5,393	99
Garrard	Lancaster	13,670	11,579	231
Grant	Williamstown	19,828	15,737	260
Graves	Mayfield	35,592	33,550	556
Grayson	Leitchfield	23,279	21,050	504
Green	Greensburg	10,570	10,371	289
Greenup	Greenup	37,125	36,742	346
Hancock	Hawesville	8,846	7,864	189
Hardin	Elizabethtown	90,001	89,240	628
Harlan	Harlan	35,362	36,574	467
Harrison	Cynthiana	17,352	16,248	310
Hart	Munfordville	16,555	14,890	416
Henderson	Henderson	44,621	43,044	440
Henry	New Castle	14,711	12,823	289
Hickman	Clinton	5,173	5,566	245
Hopkins	Madisonville	46,283	46,126	551
Jackson	McKee	12,829	11,955	346
Jefferson	Louisville	670,622	665,123	385
Jessamine	Nicholasville	36,038	30,508	173
Johnson	Paintsville	24,091	23,248	262
Kenton	Covington	146,224	142,031	163
Knott	Hindman	18,019	17,906	352
Knox	Barbourville	31,477	29,676	388
Larue	Hodgenville	12,888	11,679	263
Laurel	London	50,068	43,438	436
Lawrence	Louisa	15,434	13,998	419
Lee	Beattyville	7,972	7,422	210
Leslie	Hyden	13,538	13,642	404
Letcher	Whitesburg	26,623	27,000	339
Lewis	Vanceburg	13,568	13,029	485
Lincoln	Stanford	22,047	20,045	337
Livingston	Smithland	9,330	9,062	316
Logan	Russellville	26,163	24,416	556
Lyon	Eddyville	8,012	6,624	216
McCracken	Paducah	64,736	62,879	251
McCreary	Whitley City	16,557	15,603	428
McLean	Calhoun	9,701	9,628	254
Madison	Richmond	65,343	57,508	441
Magoffin	Salyersville	13,828	13,077	310
Marion	Lebanon	16,979	16,499	347
Marshall	Benton	29,832	27,205	305
Martin	Inez	12,231	12,526	231
Mason	Maysville	16,903	16,666	241
Meade	Brandenburg	28,140	24,170	309
Menifee	Frenchburg	5,620	5,092	204
Mercer	Harrodsburg	20,447	19,148	251
Metcalfe	Edmonton	9,470	8,963	291
Monroe	Tompkinsville	11,223	11,401	331
Montgomery	Mount Sterling	20,778	19,561	199
Morgan	West Liberty	13,480	11,648	381
Muhlenberg	Greenville	31,957	31,318	475
Nelson	Bardstown	35,152	29,710	423
Nicholas	Carlisle	7,036	6,725	197
Ohio	Hartford	21,957	21,105	594
Oldham	La Grange	43,248	33,263	189
Owen	Owenton	10,087	9,035	352
Owsley	Booneville	5,381	5,036	198
Pendleton	Falmouth	13,859	12,036	280
Perry	Hazard	31,110	30,283	342
Pike	Pikeville	72,561	72,584	788
Powell	Stanton	12,614	11,686	180
Pulaski	Somerset	55,616	49,489	662
Robertson	Mount Olivet	2,173	2,124	100
Rockcastle	Mount Vernon	15,744	14,803	318
Rowan	Morehead	22,021	20,353	281
Russell	Jamestown	16,318	14,716	254
Scott	Georgetown	29,446	23,867	285
Shelby	Shelbyville	28,836	24,824	384
Simpson	Franklin	16,175	15,145	236
Spencer	Taylorsville	9,157	6,801	186
Taylor	Campbellsville	22,912	21,146	270
Todd	Elkton	11,198	10,940	376
Trigg	Cadiz	12,072	10,361	443
Trimble	Bedford	7,294	6,090	149
Union	Morganfield	16,537	16,557	345
Warren	Bowling Green	86,525	77,720	545
Washington	Springfield	10,758	10,441	301
Wayne	Monticello	18,697	17,468	459
Webster	Dixon	13,529	13,955	335
Whitley	Williamsburg	35,583	33,326	440
Wolfe	Campton	7,325	6,503	223
Woodford	Versailles	22,344	19,955	191

Louisiana

(64 parishes, 43,566 sq mi land; pop. 4,351,769)

Parish	Parish seat or courthouse	1997 Pop.	1990 Pop.	Land area sq mi
Acadia	Crowley	57,691	55,882	655
Allen	Oberlin	23,908	21,226	765
Ascension	Donaldsonville	69,978	58,214	292
Assumption	Napoleonville	22,863	22,753	339
Avoyelles	Marksville	40,791	39,159	833
Beauregard	De Ridder	31,799	30,083	1,160
Bienville	Arcadia	15,827	16,201	811
Bossier	Benton	92,750	86,088	839
Caddo	Shreveport	243,391	248,253	882
Calcasieu	Lake Charles	178,874	168,134	1,071
Caldwell	Columbia	10,351	9,806	530
Cameron	Cameron	9,012	9,260	1,313
Catahoula	Harrisonburg	11,063	11,065	704
Claiborne	Homer	16,888	17,405	755
Concordia	Vidalia	20,741	20,828	696
De Soto	Mansfield	25,091	25,699	877
East Baton Rouge	Baton Rouge	394,249	380,105	456
East Carroll	Lake Providence	8,991	9,709	422
East Feliciana	Clinton	20,825	19,211	453
Evangeline	Ville Platte	34,108	33,274	664
Franklin	Winnsboro	22,068	22,387	623
Grant	Colfax	18,625	17,526	645
Iberia	New Iberia	72,092	68,297	575
Iberville	Plaquemine	31,129	31,049	619
Jackson	Jonesboro	15,550	15,924	570
Jefferson	Gretna	451,240	448,306	306
Jefferson Davis	Jennings	31,675	30,722	652
Lafayette	Lafayette	184,102	164,762	270
Lafourche	Thibodaux	88,037	85,860	1,085
La Salle	Jena	13,751	13,662	624
Lincoln	Ruston	41,952	41,745	471
Livingston	Livingston	85,470	70,523	648
Madison	Tallulah	12,987	12,463	624
Morehouse	Bastrop	31,734	31,938	794
Natchitoches	Natchitoches	37,285	37,199	1,256
Orleans	New Orleans	469,089	496,938	181
Ouachita	Monroe	147,055	142,191	611
Plaquemines	Pointe a la Hache	25,856	25,575	845
Pointe Coupee	New Roads	23,636	22,540	557
Rapides	Alexandria	126,491	131,556	1,323
Red River	Coushatta	9,696	9,518	389
Richland	Rayville	20,861	20,629	559
Sabine	Many	23,762	22,646	865
Saint Bernard	Chalmette	66,267	66,631	465
Saint Charles	Hahnville	47,704	42,437	284
Saint Helena	Greensburg	9,782	9,874	408
Saint James	Convent	20,991	20,879	246
Saint John the Baptist	Edgard	42,021	39,996	219
Saint Landry	Opelousas	83,465	80,312	929
Saint Martin	Saint Martinville	46,769	44,097	740
Saint Mary	Franklin	56,950	58,086	613
Saint Tammany	Covington	184,590	144,500	854
Tangipahoa	Amite	95,254	85,709	790
Tensas	Saint Joseph	6,747	7,103	603
Terrebonne	Houma	103,190	96,982	1,255
Union	Farmerville	21,788	20,796	878
Vermilion	Abbeville	51,693	50,055	1,174
Vernon	Leesville	51,832	61,961	1,329
Washington	Franklinton	43,087	43,185	670
Webster	Minden	42,597	41,989	596
West Baton Rouge	Port Allen	20,468	19,419	191
West Carroll	Oak Grove	12,196	12,093	359
West Feliciana	Saint Francisville	13,275	12,915	406
Winn	Winnfield	17,769	16,496	951

Maine

(16 counties, 30,865 sq mi land; pop. 1,242,051)

County	County seat or courthouse	1997 Pop.	1990 Pop.	Land area sq mi
Androscoggin	Auburn	101,045	105,259	470
Aroostook	Houlton	77,094	86,936	6,672
Cumberland	Portland	251,438	243,135	836
Franklin	Farmington	29,015	29,008	1,698
Hancock	Ellsworth	49,638	46,948	1,589
Kennebec	Augusta	115,885	115,904	868
Knox	Rockland	37,543	36,310	366
Lincoln	Wiscasset	31,601	30,357	456
Oxford	South Paris	53,776	52,602	2,078
Penobscot	Bangor	143,300	146,601	3,396
Piscataquis	Dover-Foxcroft	18,315	18,653	3,967
Sagadahoc	Bath	35,663	33,535	254
Somerset	Skowhegan	52,220	49,767	3,927
Waldo	Belfast	36,020	33,018	730
Washington	Machias	35,986	35,308	2,569
York	Alfred	173,512	164,587	991

Maryland

(23 counties, 1 ind. city, 9,775 sq mi land; pop. 5,094,289)

County	County seat or courthouse	1997 Pop.	1990 Pop.	Land area sq mi
Allegany	Cumberland	72,289	74,946	425
Anne Arundel	Annapolis	470,028	427,239	416
Baltimore	Towson	720,662	692,134	599
Calvert	Prince Frederick	69,413	51,372	215
Caroline	Denton	29,527	27,035	320
Carroll	Westminster	146,936	123,372	449

County	County seat or courthouse	1997 Pop.	1990 Pop.	Land area sq mi
Cecil	Elkton	80,768	71,347	348
Charles	La Plata	115,075	101,154	461
Dorchester	Cambridge	29,893	30,236	558
Frederick	Frederick	183,215	150,208	663
Garrett	Oakland	29,511	28,138	648
Harford	Bel Air	212,560	182,132	440
Howard	Ellicott City	228,797	187,328	252
Kent	Chestertown	19,067	17,842	279
Montgomery	Rockville	826,766	762,207	495
Prince George's	Upper Marlboro	770,633	723,373	486
Queen Anne's	Centreville	39,093	33,953	372
Saint Mary's	Leonardtown	85,684	75,974	361
Somerset	Princess Anne	24,474	23,440	327
Talbot	Easton	33,054	30,549	269
Washington	Hagerstown	128,155	121,393	458
Wicomico	Salisbury	79,318	74,339	377
Worcester	Snow Hill	42,115	35,028	473
Independent City				
Baltimore		657,256	736,014	81

Massachusetts

(14 counties, 7,838 sq mi land; pop. 6,117,520)

County	County seat or courthouse	1997 Pop.	1990 Pop.	Land area sq mi
Barnstable	Barnstable	205,128	186,605	396
Berkshire	Pittsfield	134,244	139,352	931
Bristol	Taunton	515,501	506,325	556
Dukes	Edgartown	13,578	11,639	104
Essex	Salem	691,400	670,080	498
Franklin	Greenfield	71,341	70,092	702
Hampden	Springfield	440,974	456,310	619
Hampshire	Northampton	150,136	146,568	529
Middlesex	East Cambridge	1,417,868	1,398,468	824
Nantucket	Nantucket	7,508	6,012	48
Norfolk	Dedham	639,243	616,087	400
Plymouth	Plymouth	462,159	435,276	661
Suffolk	Boston	642,900	663,906	59
Worcester	Worcester	725,540	709,705	1,513

Michigan

(83 counties, 56,809 sq mi land; pop. 9,773,892)

County	County seat or courthouse	1997 Pop.	1990 Pop.	Land area sq mi
Alcona	Harrisville	10,980	10,145	675
Alger	Munising	9,958	8,972	918
Allegan	Allegan	100,585	90,509	828
Alpena	Alpena	30,638	30,605	574
Antrim	Bellaire	20,975	18,185	477
Arenac	Standish	16,411	14,906	367
Baraga	L'Anse	8,448	7,954	904
Barry	Hastings	53,533	50,057	556
Bay	Bay City	110,423	111,723	444
Benzie	Beulah	14,290	12,200	321
Berrien	Saint Joseph	160,713	161,378	571
Branch	Coldwater	43,628	41,502	507
Calhoun	Marshall	141,821	135,982	709
Cass	Cassopolis	49,967	49,477	492
Charlevoix	Charlevoix	23,630	21,468	417
Cheboygan	Cheboygan	23,535	21,398	716
Chippewa	Sault Sainte Marie	37,900	34,604	1,561
Clare	Harrison	29,011	24,952	567
Clinton	Saint Johns	63,087	57,893	572
Crawford	Grayling	13,880	12,260	558
Delta	Escanaba	38,801	37,780	1,170
Dickinson	Iron Mountain	27,062	26,831	766
Eaton	Charlotte	100,173	92,879	577
Emmet	Petoskey	28,339	25,040	468
Genesee	Flint	435,393	430,459	640
Gladwin	Gladwin	24,879	21,896	507
Gogebic	Bessemer	17,439	18,052	1,102
Grand Traverse	Traverse City	73,161	64,273	465
Gratiot	Ithaca	40,024	38,982	570
Hillsdale	Hillsdale	46,240	43,431	599
Houghton	Houghton	35,810	35,446	1,012
Huron	Bad Axe	35,270	34,951	837
Ingham	Mason	284,089	281,912	559
Ionia	Ionia	61,112	57,024	573
Iosco	Tawas City	25,129	30,209	549
Iron	Crystal Falls	13,067	13,175	1,167
Isabella	Mount Pleasant	57,623	54,624	574
Jackson	Jackson	155,346	149,756	707
Kalamazoo	Kalamazoo	229,192	223,411	562
Kalkaska	Kalkaska	15,451	13,497	561
Kent	Grand Rapids	539,425	500,631	856
Keweenaw	Eagle River	2,078	1,701	541
Lake	Baldwin	10,153	8,583	568
Lapeer	Lapeer	86,893	74,768	654
Leelanau	Leland	18,755	16,527	349
Lenawee	Adrian	97,998	91,476	751
Livingston	Howell	141,914	115,645	568
Luce	Newberry	6,584	5,763	903
Mackinac	Saint Ignace	11,113	10,674	1,022
Macomb	Mount Clemens	783,451	717,400	480
Manistee	Manistee	23,179	21,265	544
Marquette	Marquette	61,792	70,887	1,821
Mason	Ludington	27,854	25,537	495
Mecosta	Big Rapids	39,178	37,308	556
Menominee	Menominee	24,443	24,920	1,044
Midland	Midland	81,248	75,651	521
Missaukee	Lake City	13,682	12,147	567
Monroe	Monroe	142,301	133,600	551
Montcalm	Stanton	59,647	53,059	708
Montmorency	Atlanta	9,980	8,936	548
Muskegon	Muskegon	165,882	158,983	509
Newaygo	White Cloud	45,059	38,206	842
Oakland	Pontiac	1,166,512	1,083,592	873
Oceana	Hart	24,599	22,455	541
Ogemaw	West Branch	20,955	18,681	564
Ontonagon	Ontonagon	8,117	8,854	1,312
Osceola	Reed City	22,028	20,146	566
Oscoda	Mio	8,844	7,842	565
Otsego	Gaylord	21,800	17,957	515
Ottawa	Grand Haven	220,403	187,768	566
Presque Isle	Rogers City	14,392	13,743	660
Roscommon	Roscommon	23,174	19,776	521
Saginaw	Saginaw	211,278	211,946	809
Saint Clair	Port Huron	157,704	145,607	725
Saint Joseph	Centreville	61,234	58,913	504
Sanilac	Sandusky	42,736	39,928	964
Schoolcraft	Manistique	8,748	8,302	1,178
Shiawassee	Corunna	72,236	69,770	539
Tuscola	Caro	58,087	55,498	813
Van Buren	Paw Paw	75,686	70,060	611
Washtenaw	Ann Arbor	299,503	282,937	710
Wayne	Detroit	2,127,087	2,111,687	614
Wexford	Cadillac	29,147	26,360	566

Minnesota

(87 counties, 79,617 sq mi land; pop. 4,685,549)

County	County seat or courthouse	1997 Pop.	1990 Pop.	Land area sq mi
Aitkin	Aitkin	13,868	12,425	1,819
Anoka	Anoka	286,673	243,641	424
Becker	Detroit Lakes	29,240	27,881	1,311
Beltrami	Bemidji	38,709	34,384	2,505
Benton	Foley	33,671	30,185	408
Big Stone	Ortonville	5,689	6,285	497
Blue Earth	Mankato	54,037	54,044	752
Brown	New Ulm	27,222	26,984	611
Carlton	Carlton	30,689	29,259	860
Carver	Chaska	63,198	47,915	357
Cass	Walker	25,746	21,791	2,018
Chippewa	Montevideo	13,019	13,228	583
Chisago	Center City	39,439	30,521	418
Clay	Moorhead	51,816	50,422	1,045
Clearwater	Bagley	8,201	8,309	995
Cook	Grand Marais	4,740	3,868	1,451
Cottonwood	Windom	12,257	12,694	640
Crow Wing	Brainerd	51,105	44,249	997
Dakota	Hastings	334,585	275,189	570
Dodge	Mantorville	17,002	15,731	440
Douglas	Alexandria	30,727	28,674	634
Faribault	Blue Earth	16,432	16,937	714
Fillmore	Preston	20,689	20,777	861
Freeborn	Albert Lea	31,562	33,060	708
Goodhue	Red Wing	42,706	40,690	759
Grant	Elbow Lake	6,141	6,246	547
Hennepin	Minneapolis	1,053,178	1,032,431	557
Houston	Caledonia	19,228	18,497	558
Hubbard	Park Rapids	16,758	14,939	923
Isanti	Cambridge	29,557	25,921	439
Itasca	Grand Rapids	43,555	40,863	2,665
Jackson	Jackson	11,700	11,677	702
Kanabec	Mora	14,042	12,802	525
Kandiyohi	Willmar	41,090	38,761	796
Kittson	Hallock	5,358	5,767	1,097
Koochiching	International Falls	15,682	16,299	3,102
Lac qui Parle	Madison	8,101	8,924	765
Lake	Two Harbors	10,716	10,415	2,099
Lake of the Woods	Baudette	4,539	4,076	1,297
Le Sueur	Le Center	24,885	23,239	449
Lincoln	Ivanhoe	6,552	6,890	537
Lyon	Marshall	24,518	24,789	714
McLeod	Glencoe	33,688	32,030	492
Mahnomen	Mahnomen	5,089	5,044	556
Marshall	Warren	10,525	10,993	1,772
Martin	Fairmont	22,243	22,914	709
Meeker	Litchfield	21,522	20,846	609
Mille Lacs	Milaca	20,670	18,670	575
Morrison	Little Falls	30,501	29,604	1,125
Mower	Austin	37,132	37,385	712
Murray	Slayton	9,527	9,660	705
Nicollet	Saint Peter	30,035	28,076	452
Nobles	Worthington	19,730	20,098	716
Norman	Ada	7,717	7,975	876
Olmsted	Rochester	114,619	106,470	653
Otter Tail	Fergus Falls	54,222	50,714	1,980
Pennington	Thief River Falls	13,547	13,306	617

County	County seat or courthouse	1997 Pop.	1990 Pop.	Land area sq mi
Pine	Pine City	23,574	21,264	1,411
Pipestone	Pipestone	10,083	10,491	466
Polk	Crookston	32,091	32,589	1,971
Pope	Glenwood	10,902	10,745	670
Ramsey	Saint Paul	484,354	485,783	156
Red Lake	Red Lake Falls	4,344	4,525	432
Redwood	Redwood Falls	16,656	17,254	880
Renville	Olivia	17,066	17,673	983
Rice	Faribault	53,590	49,183	498
Rock	Luverne	9,889	9,806	483
Roseau	Roseau	16,302	15,026	1,663
Saint Louis	Duluth	194,989	198,213	6,226
Scott	Shakopee	76,078	57,846	357
Sherburne	Elk River	57,867	41,945	437
Sibley	Gaylord	14,575	14,366	589
Stearns	Saint Cloud	127,540	119,324	1,345
Steele	Owatonna	31,531	30,729	430
Stevens	Morris	10,138	10,634	562
Swift	Benson	10,826	10,724	744
Todd	Long Prairie	23,967	23,363	942
Traverse	Wheaton	4,279	4,463	574
Wabasha	Wabasha	20,748	19,744	525
Wadena	Wadena	12,955	13,154	536
Waseca	Waseca	18,168	18,079	423
Washington	Stillwater	191,548	145,858	392
Watonwan	Saint James	11,742	11,682	435
Wilkin	Breckenridge	7,367	7,516	752
Winona	Winona	48,262	47,828	626
Wright	Buffalo	83,156	68,710	661
Yellow Medicine	Granite Falls	11,573	11,684	758

Mississippi

(82 counties, 46,914 sq mi land; pop. 2,730,501)

County	County seat or courthouse	1997 Pop.	1990 Pop.	Land area sq mi
Adams	Natchez	34,530	35,356	460
Alcorn	Corinth	32,740	31,722	400
Amite	Liberty	13,695	13,328	730
Attala	Kosciusko	18,392	18,481	735
Benton	Ashland	7,972	8,046	407
Bolivar	Cleveland & Rosedale	40,563	41,875	876
Calhoun	Pittsboro	15,038	14,908	587
Carroll	Carrollton & Vaiden	10,077	9,237	628
Chickasaw	Houston & Okolona	18,274	18,085	502
Choctaw	Ackerman	9,311	9,071	419
Claiborne	Port Gibson	11,731	11,370	487
Clarke	Quitman	17,998	17,313	691
Clay	West Point	21,571	21,120	409
Coahoma	Clarksdale	31,334	31,665	554
Copiah	Hazlehurst	28,896	27,592	777
Covington	Collins	17,507	16,527	414
De Soto	Hernando	92,019	67,910	478
Forrest	Hattiesburg	73,759	68,314	467
Franklin	Meadville	8,259	8,377	565
George	Lucedale	18,906	16,673	478
Greene	Leakesville	11,848	10,220	713
Grenada	Grenada	22,472	21,555	422
Hancock	Bay Saint Louis	39,261	31,760	477
Harrison	Gulfport	175,611	165,365	581
Hinds	Jackson & Raymond	247,492	254,441	869
Holmes	Lexington	21,424	21,604	756
Humphreys	Belzoni	11,308	12,134	418
Issaquena	Mayersville	1,637	1,909	413
Itawamba	Fulton	21,051	20,017	532
Jackson	Pascagoula	128,551	115,243	727
Jasper	Bay Springs & Paulding	17,615	17,114	676
Jefferson	Fayette	8,482	8,653	519
Jefferson Davis	Prentiss	13,965	14,051	408
Jones	Ellisville & Laurel	63,419	62,031	694
Kemper	De Kalb	10,419	10,356	766
Lafayette	Oxford	34,388	31,826	631
Lamar	Purvis	35,825	30,424	497
Lauderdale	Meridian	76,733	75,555	704
Lawrence	Monticello	12,946	12,458	431
Leake	Carthage	19,392	18,436	583
Lee	Tupelo	73,943	65,579	450
Leflore	Greenwood	37,179	37,341	592
Lincoln	Brookhaven	31,703	30,278	586
Lowndes	Columbus	61,202	59,308	502
Madison	Canton	70,888	53,794	719
Marion	Columbia	26,426	25,544	542
Marshall	Holly Springs	32,402	30,361	706
Monroe	Aberdeen	38,142	36,582	764
Montgomery	Winona	12,389	12,387	407
Neshoba	Philadelphia	27,138	24,800	570
Newton	Decatur	21,379	20,291	578
Noxubee	Macon	12,369	12,604	695
Oktibbeha	Starkville	39,172	38,375	458
Panola	Batesville & Sardis	32,852	29,996	684
Pearl River	Poplarville	45,592	38,714	812
Perry	New Augusta	11,790	10,865	647
Pike	Magnolia	37,992	36,882	409
Pontotoc	Pontotoc	24,754	22,237	497
Prentiss	Booneville	24,206	23,278	415
Quitman	Marks	9,824	10,490	405
Rankin	Brandon	107,003	87,161	775
Scott	Forest	25,121	24,137	609
Sharkey	Rolling Fork	6,615	7,066	428
Simpson	Mendenhall	25,206	23,953	589
Smith	Raleigh	15,140	14,798	636
Stone	Wiggins	12,875	10,750	445
Sunflower	Indianola	34,913	35,129	694
Tallahatchie	Charleston & Sumner	15,065	15,210	644
Tate	Senatobia	23,570	21,432	405
Tippah	Ripley	20,899	19,523	458
Tishomingo	Iuka	18,563	17,683	424
Tunica	Tunica	8,092	8,164	455
Union	New Albany	23,618	22,085	416
Walthall	Tylertown	14,332	14,352	404
Warren	Vicksburg	49,218	47,880	587
Washington	Greenville	65,812	67,935	724
Wayne	Waynesboro	20,112	19,517	810
Webster	Walthall	10,412	10,222	423
Wilkinson	Woodville	9,196	9,678	677
Winston	Louisville	19,267	19,433	607
Yalobusha	Coffeeville & Water Valley	12,329	12,033	467
Yazoo	Yazoo City	25,390	25,506	920

Missouri

(114 cos., 1 ind. city, 68,898 sq mi land; pop. 5,402,058)

County	County seat or courthouse	1997 Pop.	1990 Pop.	Land area sq mi
Adair	Kirksville	24,299	24,577	568
Andrew	Savannah	15,325	14,632	435
Atchison	Rockport	7,137	7,457	545
Audrain	Mexico	23,568	23,599	693
Barry	Cassville	32,686	27,547	779
Barton	Lamar	11,949	11,312	594
Bates	Butler	15,849	15,025	849
Benton	Warsaw	16,529	13,859	706
Bollinger	Marble Hill	11,512	10,619	621
Boone	Columbia	128,309	112,379	685
Buchanan	Saint Joseph	81,786	83,083	410
Butler	Poplar Buff	40,408	38,765	698
Caldwell	Kingston	8,691	8,380	429
Callaway	Fulton	36,932	32,809	839
Camden	Camdenton	33,250	27,495	655
Cape Girardeau	Jackson	66,010	61,633	579
Carroll	Carrollton	10,182	10,748	695
Carter	Van Buren	6,345	5,515	508
Cass	Harrisonville	77,896	63,808	699
Cedar	Stockton	13,029	12,093	476
Chariton	Keytesville	8,794	9,202	756
Christian	Ozark	46,960	32,644	563
Clark	Kahoka	7,504	7,547	507
Clay	Liberty	174,035	153,411	397
Clinton	Plattsburg	18,620	16,595	419
Cole	Jefferson City	68,814	63,579	392
Cooper	Boonville	16,094	14,835	565
Crawford	Steelville	22,011	19,173	743
Dade	Greenfield	7,944	7,449	490
Dallas	Buffalo	15,137	12,646	542
Daviess	Gallatin	7,789	7,865	567
De Kalb	Maysville	11,097	9,967	424
Dent	Salem	14,079	13,702	754
Douglas	Ava	12,299	11,876	815
Dunklin	Kennett	32,806	33,112	546
Franklin	Union	90,997	80,603	922
Gasconade	Hermann	14,763	14,006	520
Gentry	Albany	6,856	6,854	492
Greene	Springfield	225,577	207,949	675
Grundy	Trenton	10,243	10,536	436
Harrison	Bethany	8,395	8,469	725
Henry	Clinton	21,066	20,044	703
Hickory	Hermitage	8,636	7,335	399
Holt	Oregon	5,629	6,034	462
Howard	Fayette	9,773	9,631	466
Howell	West Plains	35,566	31,447	928
Iron	Ironton	11,017	10,726	551
Jackson	Kansas City	647,973	633,234	605
Jasper	Carthage	98,812	90,465	640
Jefferson	Hillsboro	193,210	171,380	657
Johnson	Warrensburg	47,356	42,514	831
Knox	Edina	4,368	4,482	506
Laclede	Lebanon	30,414	27,158	766
Lafayette	Lexington	32,524	31,107	629
Lawrence	Mount Vernon	32,850	30,236	613
Lewis	Monticello	10,159	10,233	505
Lincoln	Troy	35,181	28,892	631
Linn	Linneus	13,966	13,885	620
Livingston	Chillicothe	14,352	14,592	535
McDonald	Pineville	19,738	16,938	540
Macon	Macon	15,272	15,345	804
Madison	Fredericktown	11,581	11,127	497
Maries	Vienna	8,331	7,976	528
Marion	Palmyra	27,823	27,682	438
Mercer	Princeton	3,996	3,723	455

County	County seat or courthouse	1997 Pop.	1990 Pop.	Land area sq mi
Miller	Tuscumbia	22,592	20,700	592
Mississippi	Charleston	13,489	14,442	413
Moniteau	California	13,201	12,298	417
Monroe	Paris	9,029	9,104	646
Montgomery	Montgomery City	11,846	11,355	539
Morgan	Versailles	18,077	15,574	598
New Madrid	New Madrid	20,524	20,928	678
Newton	Neosho	48,315	44,445	627
Nodaway	Maryville	20,911	21,709	877
Oregon	Alton	9,957	9,470	792
Osage	Linn	12,529	12,018	606
Ozark	Gainesville	9,613	8,598	747
Pemiscot	Caruthersville	21,520	21,921	493
Perry	Perryville	17,478	16,648	475
Pettis	Sedalia	36,788	35,437	685
Phelps	Rolla	38,464	35,248	673
Pike	Bowling Green	16,141	15,969	673
Platte	Platte City	68,680	57,867	420
Polk	Bolivar	25,454	21,826	637
Pulaski	Waynesville	38,176	41,307	547
Putnam	Unionville	4,940	5,079	518
Ralls	New London	8,832	8,476	471
Randolph	Huntsville	23,888	24,370	482
Ray	Richmond	23,216	21,968	570
Reynolds	Centerville	6,702	6,661	811
Ripley	Doniphan	13,890	12,303	630
Saint Charles	Saint Charles	264,275	212,751	561
Saint Clair	Osceola	9,083	8,457	677
Sainte Genevieve	Sainte Genevieve	17,214	16,037	502
Saint Francois	Farmington	54,598	48,904	450
Saint Louis	Clayton	1,003,595	993,508	508
Saline	Marshall	22,890	23,523	756
Schuyler	Lancaster	4,374	4,236	308
Scotland	Memphis	4,829	4,822	439
Scott	Benton	40,312	39,376	421
Shannon	Eminence	8,157	7,613	1,004
Shelby	Shelbyville	6,818	6,942	501
Stoddard	Bloomfield	29,567	28,895	827
Stone	Galena	26,486	19,078	463
Sullivan	Milan	6,658	6,326	651
Taney	Forsyth	33,962	25,561	632
Texas	Houston	22,442	21,476	1,179
Vernon	Nevada	19,163	19,041	834
Warren	Warrenton	23,626	19,534	432
Washington	Potosi	22,686	20,380	760
Wayne	Greenville	12,859	11,543	761
Webster	Marshfield	28,443	23,753	593
Worth	Grant City	2,333	2,440	267
Wright	Hartville	19,468	16,758	682
Independent City				
Saint Louis		341,869	396,685	62

Montana

(56 counties, 145,556 sq mi land; pop. 878,810)

County	County seat or courthouse	1997 Pop.	1990 Pop.	Land area sq mi
Beaverhead	Dillon	9,012	8,424	5,543
Big Horn	Hardin	12,617	11,337	4,995
Blaine	Chinook	7,081	6,728	4,226
Broadwater	Townsend	4,083	3,318	1,192
Carbon	Red Lodge	9,425	8,080	2,048
Carter	Ekalaka	1,503	1,503	3,340
Cascade	Great Falls	79,134	77,691	2,698
Chouteau	Fort Benton	5,236	5,452	3,973
Custer	Miles City	12,115	11,697	3,783
Daniels	Scobey	2,057	2,266	1,426
Dawson	Glendive	9,048	9,505	2,373
Deer Lodge	Anaconda	9,995	10,356	737
Fallon	Baker	3,035	3,103	1,620
Fergus	Lewistown	12,498	12,083	4,339
Flathead	Kalispell	71,707	59,218	5,099
Gallatin	Bozeman	61,111	50,463	2,507
Garfield	Jordan	1,444	1,589	4,668
Glacier	Cut Bank	12,687	12,121	2,995
Golden Valley	Ryegete	1,051	912	1,175
Granite	Philipsburg	2,632	2,548	1,728
Hill	Havre	17,538	17,654	2,896
Jefferson	Boulder	9,878	7,939	1,657
Judith Basin	Stanford	2,316	2,282	1,870
Lake	Polson	25,341	21,041	1,494
Lewis & Clark	Helena	53,251	47,495	3,461
Liberty	Chester	2,391	2,295	1,430
Lincoln	Libby	18,772	17,481	3,613
McCone	Circle	2,035	2,276	2,643
Madison	Virginia City	6,899	5,989	3,587
Meagher	White Sulphur Springs	1,805	1,819	2,392
Mineral	Superior	3,725	3,315	1,220
Missoula	Missoula	88,818	78,687	2,598
Musselshell	Roundup	4,605	4,106	1,867
Park	Livingston	15,910	14,484	2,656
Petroleum	Winnett	518	519	1,654
Phillips	Malta	4,904	5,163	5,140
Pondera	Conrad	6,431	6,433	1,625
Powder River	Broadus	1,909	2,090	3,297
Powell	Deer Lodge	7,072	6,620	2,326
Prairie	Terry	1,335	1,383	1,737
Ravalli	Hamilton	34,554	25,010	2,394
Richland	Sidney	10,191	10,716	2,084
Roosevelt	Wolf Point	11,121	10,999	2,356
Rosebud	Forsyth	10,209	10,505	5,012
Sanders	Thompson Falls	10,253	8,669	2,762
Sheridan	Plentywood	4,341	4,732	1,677
Silver Bow	Butte	34,441	33,941	718
Stillwater	Columbus	7,835	6,536	1,795
Sweet Grass	Big Timber	3,400	3,154	1,855
Teton	Choteau	6,340	6,271	2,273
Toole	Shelby	4,818	5,046	1,911
Treasure	Hysham	839	874	979
Valley	Glasgow	8,295	8,239	4,921
Wheatland	Harlowton	2,333	2,246	1,423
Wibaux	Wibaux	1,106	1,191	889
Yellowstone	Billings	125,771	113,419	2,635
Yellowstone National Park[1]	NA	39	52	245

NA=Not applicable. (1) The area of Yellowstone National Park in Montana is not included in any county.

Nebraska

(93 counties, 76,878 sq mi land; pop. 1,656,870)

County	County seat or courthouse	1997 Pop.	1990 Pop.	Land area sq mi
Adams	Hastings	29,745	29,625	563
Antelope	Neligh	7,362	7,965	857
Arthur	Arthur	428	462	715
Banner	Harrisburg	866	852	746
Blaine	Brewster	638	675	711
Boone	Albion	6,379	6,667	687
Box Butte	Alliance	12,920	13,130	1,075
Boyd	Butte	2,636	2,835	540
Brown	Ainsworth	3,610	3,657	1,221
Buffalo	Kearney	40,200	37,447	968
Burt	Tekamah	7,888	7,868	493
Butler	David City	8,589	8,601	584
Cass	Plattsmouth	24,002	21,318	559
Cedar	Hartington	9,818	10,131	740
Chase	Imperial	4,247	4,381	895
Cherry	Valentine	6,405	6,307	5,961
Cheyenne	Sidney	9,544	9,494	1,196
Clay	Clay Center	7,153	7,123	573
Colfax	Schuyler	10,546	9,139	413
Cuming	West Point	9,973	10,117	572
Custer	Broken Bow	12,086	12,270	2,576
Dakota	Dakota City	18,731	16,742	264
Dawes	Chadron	9,038	9,021	1,396
Dawson	Lexington	23,134	19,940	1,013
Deuel	Chappell	2,025	2,237	440
Dixon	Ponca	6,417	6,143	476
Dodge	Fremont	35,125	34,500	535
Douglas	Omaha	441,006	416,444	331
Dundy	Benkelman	2,312	2,582	920
Fillmore	Geneva	6,891	7,103	577
Franklin	Franklin	3,820	3,938	576
Frontier	Stockville	3,180	3,101	975
Furnas	Beaver City	5,425	5,553	718
Gage	Beatrice	22,877	22,794	855
Garden	Oshkosh	2,224	2,460	1,705
Garfield	Burwell	2,080	2,141	570
Gosper	Elwood	2,288	1,928	458
Grant	Hyannis	735	769	776
Greeley	Greeley	2,936	3,006	570
Hall	Grand Island	51,675	48,925	546
Hamilton	Aurora	9,427	8,862	544
Harlan	Alma	3,773	3,810	553
Hayes	Hayes Center	1,085	1,222	713
Hitchcock	Trenton	3,417	3,750	710
Holt	O'Neill	12,215	12,599	2,413
Hooker	Mullen	717	793	721
Howard	Saint Paul	6,484	6,057	570
Jefferson	Fairbury	8,393	8,759	573
Johnson	Tecumseh	4,573	4,673	376
Kearney	Minden	6,679	6,629	516
Keith	Ogallala	8,622	8,584	1,061
Keya Paha	Springview	980	1,029	773
Kimball	Kimball	4,030	4,108	952
Knox	Center	9,375	9,564	1,108
Lancaster	Lincoln	233,319	213,641	839
Lincoln	North Platte	33,521	32,508	2,564
Logan	Stapleton	900	878	571
Loup	Taylor	676	683	570
McPherson	Tryon	556	546	859
Madison	Madison	34,860	32,655	573
Merrick	Central City	8,178	8,049	485
Morrill	Bridgeport	5,423	5,423	1,424
Nance	Fullerton	4,227	4,275	441
Nemaha	Auburn	7,816	7,980	409
Nuckolls	Nelson	5,366	5,786	575
Otoe	Nebraska City	14,582	14,252	616
Pawnee	Pawnee City	3,172	3,317	432

County	County seat or courthouse	1997 Pop.	1990 Pop.	Land area sq mi
Perkins	Grant	3,288	3,367	883
Phelps	Holdrege	9,911	9,715	540
Pierce	Pierce	7,910	7,827	574
Platte	Columbus	30,512	29,820	678
Polk	Osceola	5,628	5,668	439
Red Willow	McCook	11,386	11,705	717
Richardson	Falls City	9,557	9,937	554
Rock	Bassett	1,735	2,019	1,009
Saline	Wilber	13,026	12,715	575
Sarpy	Papillion	118,571	102,583	241
Saunders	Wahoo	19,152	18,285	754
Scotts Bluff	Gering	36,281	36,025	739
Seward	Seward	16,282	15,450	575
Sheridan	Rushville	6,620	6,750	2,441
Sherman	Loup City	3,580	3,718	566
Sioux	Harrison	1,513	1,549	2,067
Stanton	Stanton	6,199	6,244	430
Thayer	Hebron	6,273	6,635	575
Thomas	Thedford	799	851	713
Thurston	Pender	7,192	6,936	394
Valley	Ord	4,778	5,169	568
Washington	Blair	18,470	16,607	391
Wayne	Wayne	9,302	9,364	444
Webster	Red Cloud	4,026	4,279	575
Wheeler	Bartlett	952	948	575
York	York	14,607	14,428	576

Nevada

(16 counties, 1 ind. city, 109,806 sq mi land; pop. 1,676,809)

County	County seat or courthouse	1997 Pop.	1990 Pop.	Land area sq mi
Churchill	Fallon	22,752	17,938	4,929
Clark	Las Vegas	1,106,047	741,368	7,911
Douglas	Minden	36,096	27,637	710
Elko	Elko	45,400	33,463	17,182
Esmeralda	Goldfield	1,165	1,344	3,589
Eureka	Eureka	1,858	1,547	4,176
Humboldt	Winnemucca	17,473	12,844	9,648
Lander	Battle Mountain	7,113	6,266	5,494
Lincoln	Pioche	4,435	3,775	10,635
Lyon	Yerington	28,819	20,001	1,994
Mineral	Hawthorne	5,727	6,475	3,757
Nye	Tonopah	27,168	17,781	18,147
Pershing	Lovelock	5,381	4,336	6,009
Storey	Virginia City	2,999	2,526	264
Washoe	Reno	305,792	254,667	6,343
White Pine	Ely	10,216	9,264	8,877
Independent City				
Carson City		48,368	40,443	144

New Hampshire

(10 counties, 8,969 sq mi land; pop. 1,172,709)

County	County seat or courthouse	1997 Pop.	1990 Pop.	Land area sq mi
Belknap	Laconia	52,166	49,216	401
Carroll	Ossipee	38,890	35,410	934
Cheshire	Keene	71,538	70,121	708
Coos	Lancaster	33,198	34,828	1,801
Grafton	Woodsville	78,135	74,929	1,714
Hillsborough	Nashua	357,840	335,838	877
Merrimack	Concord	125,949	120,240	935
Rockingham	Exeter	267,105	245,845	695
Strafford	Dover	108,098	104,233	369
Sullivan	Newport	39,790	38,592	537

New Jersey

(21 counties, 7,419 sq mi land; pop. 8,052,849)

County	County seat or courthouse	1997 Pop.	1990 Pop.	Land area sq mi
Atlantic	Mays Landing	236,569	224,327	561
Bergen	Hackensack	851,344	825,380	234
Burlington	Mount Holly	417,930	395,066	805
Camden	Camden	504,591	502,824	222
Cape May	Cape May Courthouse	98,125	95,089	255
Cumberland	Bridgeton	140,907	138,053	489
Essex	Newark	750,842	777,964	126
Gloucester	Woodbury	246,070	230,082	325
Hudson	Jersey City	551,451	553,099	47
Hunterdon	Flemington	120,578	107,802	430
Mercer	Trenton	329,786	325,824	226
Middlesex	New Brunswick	708,118	671,811	311
Monmouth	Freehold	596,250	553,093	472
Morris	Morristown	454,154	421,361	469
Ocean	Toms River	480,721	433,203	636
Passaic	Paterson	484,049	470,864	185
Salem	Salem	66,040	65,294	338
Somerset	Somerville	276,826	240,245	305
Sussex	Newton	142,057	130,943	521
Union	Elizabeth	498,148	493,819	103
Warren	Belvidere	98,293	91,607	358

New Mexico

(33 counties, 121,364 sq mi land; pop. 1,729,751)

County	County seat or courthouse	1997 Pop.	1990 Pop.	Land area sq mi
Bernalillo	Albuquerque	526,088	480,577	1,166
Catron	Reserve	2,795	2,563	6,928
Chaves	Roswell	63,001	57,849	6,071
Cibola	Grants	25,928	23,794	4,540
Colfax	Raton	13,718	12,925	3,757
Curry	Clovis	46,737	42,207	1,406
DeBaca	Fort Sumner	2,311	2,252	2,325
Dona Ana	Las Cruces	168,470	135,510	3,807
Eddy	Carlsbad	53,256	48,605	4,182
Grant	Silver City	31,350	27,676	3,966
Guadalupe	Santa Rosa	4,079	4,156	3,031
Harding	Mosquero	899	987	2,126
Hidalgo	Lordsburg	6,354	5,958	3,446
Lea	Lovington	56,387	55,765	4,393
Lincoln	Carrizozo	16,000	12,219	4,831
Los Alamos	Los Alamos	18,275	18,115	109
Luna	Deming	23,922	18,110	2,965
McKinley	Gallup	67,644	60,686	5,449
Mora	Mora	4,778	4,264	1,931
Otero	Alamogordo	55,759	51,928	6,627
Quay	Tucumcari	10,107	10,823	2,875
Rio Arriba	Tierra Amarilla	37,780	34,365	5,858
Roosevelt	Portales	18,525	16,702	2,449
Sandoval	Bernalillo	85,823	63,319	3,710
San Juan	Aztec	103,520	91,605	5,514
San Miguel	Las Vegas	28,925	25,743	4,717
Santa Fe	Santa Fe	121,791	98,928	1,909
Sierra	Truth or Consequences	10,989	9,912	4,181
Socorro	Socorro	16,250	14,764	6,647
Taos	Taos	26,556	23,118	2,203
Torrance	Estancia	14,697	10,285	3,345
Union	Clayton	4,111	4,124	3,830
Valencia	Los Lunas	62,926	45,235	1,068

New York

(62 counties, 47,224 sq mi land; pop. 18,137,226)

County	County seat or courthouse	1997 Pop.	1990 Pop.	Land area sq mi
Albany	Albany	294,312	292,793	524
Allegany	Belmont	51,633	50,470	1,030
Bronx[1]	Bronx	1,187,984	1,203,789	42
Broome	Binghamton	198,734	212,160	707
Cattaraugus	Little Valley	85,247	84,234	1,310
Cayuga	Auburn	82,314	82,313	693
Chautauqua	Mayville	140,015	141,895	1,062
Chemung	Elmira	93,088	95,195	408
Chenango	Norwich	52,358	51,768	894
Clinton	Plattsburgh	80,659	85,969	1,039
Columbia	Hudson	64,082	62,982	636
Cortland	Cortland	48,844	48,963	500
Delaware	Delhi	46,555	47,225	1,446
Dutchess	Poughkeepsie	264,687	259,462	802
Erie	Buffalo	944,472	968,584	1,045
Essex	Elizabethtown	38,368	37,152	1,797
Franklin	Malone	48,929	46,540	1,632
Fulton	Johnstown	53,287	54,191	496
Genesee	Batavia	61,808	60,060	494
Greene	Catskill	47,853	44,739	648
Hamilton	Lake Pleasant	5,213	5,279	1,721
Herkimer	Herkimer	65,691	65,809	1,412
Jefferson	Watertown	113,131	110,943	1,272
Kings[1]	Brooklyn	2,240,384	2,300,664	71
Lewis	Lowville	28,199	26,796	1,276
Livingston	Geneseo	66,491	62,372	632
Madison	Wampsville	71,652	69,166	656
Monroe	Rochester	717,780	713,968	659
Montgomery	Fonda	51,453	51,981	405
Nassau	Mineola	1,303,686	1,287,444	287
New York[1]	New York	1,536,220	1,487,536	28
Niagara	Lockport	220,249	220,756	523
Oneida	Utica	233,187	250,836	1,213
Onondaga	Syracuse	461,490	468,973	780
Ontario	Canandaigua	99,976	95,101	644
Orange	Goshen	327,160	307,647	816
Orleans	Albion	44,734	41,846	391
Oswego	Oswego	125,315	121,785	953
Otsego	Cooperstown	61,480	60,517	1,003
Putnam	Carmel	92,382	83,941	232
Queens[1]	Jamaica	1,975,676	1,951,598	109
Rensselaer	Troy	154,364	154,429	654
Richmond[1]	Saint George	402,372	378,977	59
Rockland	New City	279,860	265,475	174
Saint Lawrence	Canton	114,180	111,974	2,686
Saratoga	Ballston Spa	196,584	181,276	812
Schenectady	Schenectady	147,224	149,285	206
Schoharie	Schoharie	32,483	31,859	622
Schuyler	Watkins Glen	19,162	18,662	329
Seneca	Ovid & Waterloo	32,819	33,683	325
Steuben	Bath	99,057	99,088	1,393

County	County seat or courthouse	1997 Pop.	1990 Pop.	Land area sq mi
Suffolk	Riverhead	1,362,616	1,321,768	911
Sullivan	Monticello	70,355	69,277	970
Tioga	Owego	52,964	52,337	519
Tompkins	Ithaca	96,646	94,097	476
Ulster	Kingston	166,933	165,304	1,127
Warren	Lake George	61,893	59,209	870
Washington	Hudson Falls	60,689	59,330	836
Wayne	Lyons	95,293	89,123	604
Westchester	White Plains	896,221	874,866	433
Wyoming	Warsaw	44,596	42,507	593
Yates	Penn Yan	24,137	22,810	338

(1) New York City consists of 5 counties: Bronx, Kings (Brooklyn), New York (Manhattan), Queens, and Richmond (Staten Island).

North Carolina

(100 counties, 48,718 sq mi land; pop. 7,425,183)

County	County seat or courthouse	1997 Pop.	1990 Pop.	Land area sq mi
Alamance	Graham	117,919	108,213	431
Alexander	Taylorsville	30,660	27,544	260
Alleghany	Sparta	9,756	9,590	235
Anson	Wadesboro	24,330	23,474	532
Ashe	Jefferson	23,954	22,209	426
Avery	Newland	15,654	14,867	247
Beaufort	Washington	44,224	42,283	828
Bertie	Windsor	20,443	20,388	699
Bladen	Elizabethtown	30,604	28,663	875
Brunswick	Bolivia	65,938	50,985	855
Buncombe	Asheville	192,784	174,819	656
Burke	Morganton	81,718	75,740	507
Cabarrus	Concord	116,001	98,935	364
Caldwell	Lenoir	75,619	70,709	472
Camden	Camden	6,681	5,904	241
Carteret	Beaufort	59,725	52,553	531
Caswell	Yanceyville	21,689	20,693	426
Catawba	Newton	130,371	118,412	400
Chatham	Pittsboro	44,860	38,759	683
Cherokee	Murphy	22,282	20,170	455
Chowan	Edenton	14,163	13,506	173
Clay	Hayesville	8,292	7,155	215
Cleveland	Shelby	91,921	84,713	464
Columbus	Whiteville	52,485	49,587	937
Craven	New Bern	87,367	81,613	696
Cumberland	Fayetteville	284,047	274,713	653
Currituck	Currituck	17,119	13,736	262
Dare	Manteo	27,875	22,746	382
Davidson	Lexington	139,159	126,677	552
Davie	Mocksville	31,198	27,859	265
Duplin	Kenansville	43,161	39,995	818
Durham	Durham	199,653	181,855	291
Edgecombe	Tarboro	55,598	56,692	505
Forsyth	Winston-Salem	285,807	265,878	410
Franklin	Louisburg	43,542	36,414	492
Gaston	Gastonia	183,368	175,093	357
Gates	Gatesville	10,005	9,305	341
Graham	Robbinsville	7,657	7,196	292
Granville	Oxford	42,141	38,341	531
Greene	Snow Hill	18,026	15,384	265
Guilford	Greensboro	381,916	347,420	650
Halifax	Halifax	56,708	55,516	725
Harnett	Lillington	80,620	67,833	595
Haywood	Waynesville	51,136	46,942	554
Henderson	Hendersonville	79,343	69,285	374
Hertford	Winton	22,382	22,523	354
Hoke	Raeford	29,393	22,856	391
Hyde	Swan Quarter	5,385	5,411	613
Iredell	Statesville	108,882	92,935	574
Jackson	Sylva	29,629	26,846	491
Johnston	Smithfield	101,908	81,306	792
Jones	Trenton	8,977	9,414	473
Lee	Sanford	48,439	41,370	257
Lenoir	Kinston	59,631	57,274	400
Lincoln	Lincolnton	57,209	50,319	299
McDowell	Marion	39,063	35,681	442
Macon	Franklin	27,610	23,499	517
Madison	Marshall	18,500	16,953	449
Martin	Williamston	26,324	25,078	463
Mecklenburg	Charlotte	613,310	511,481	527
Mitchell	Bakersville	14,820	14,433	222
Montgomery	Troy	24,282	23,352	491
Moore	Carthage	70,174	59,000	699
Nash	Nashville	89,973	76,677	540
New Hanover	Wilmington	147,642	120,284	199
Northampton	Jackson	21,227	20,798	536
Onslow	Jacksonville	143,013	149,838	767
Orange	Hillsborough	108,503	93,851	400
Pamlico	Bayboro	12,169	11,368	337
Pasquotank	Elizabeth City	34,224	31,298	227
Pender	Burgaw	38,019	28,855	871
Perquimans	Hertford	11,137	10,447	247
Person	Roxboro	33,242	30,180	392
Pitt	Greenville	121,057	108,480	652
Polk	Columbus	16,525	14,416	238
Randolph	Asheboro	119,534	106,546	788
Richmond	Rockingham	46,137	44,518	474
Robeson	Lumberton	114,257	105,170	949
Rockingham	Wentworth	90,083	86,064	567
Rowan	Salisbury	123,527	110,605	511
Rutherford	Rutherfordton	60,132	56,919	564
Sampson	Clinton	51,793	47,297	946
Scotland	Laurinburg	35,629	33,763	319
Stanly	Albemarle	55,579	51,765	395
Stokes	Danbury	42,705	37,223	452
Surry	Dobson	66,497	61,704	537
Swain	Bryson City	12,189	11,268	528
Transylvania	Brevard	27,880	25,520	378
Tyrrell	Columbia	3,763	3,856	390
Union	Monroe	106,326	84,210	637
Vance	Henderson	41,585	38,892	254
Wake	Raleigh	551,588	426,300	834
Warren	Warrenton	18,191	17,265	429
Washington	Plymouth	13,739	13,997	348
Watauga	Boone	40,727	36,952	313
Wayne	Goldsboro	111,981	104,666	553
Wilkes	Wilkesboro	62,454	59,393	757
Wilson	Wilson	67,782	66,061	371
Yadkin	Yadkinville	34,541	30,488	336
Yancey	Burnsville	16,396	15,419	312

North Dakota

(53 counties, 68,994 sq mi land; pop. 640,883)

County	County seat or courthouse	1997 Pop.	1990 Pop.	Land area sq mi
Adams	Hettinger	2,748	3,174	988
Barnes	Valley City	12,066	12,545	1,492
Benson	Minnewaukan	6,795	7,198	1,389
Billings	Medora	1,109	1,108	1,152
Bottineau	Bottineau	7,483	8,011	1,669
Bowman	Bowman	3,290	3,596	1,162
Burke	Bowbells	2,332	3,002	1,104
Burleigh	Bismarck	66,647	60,131	1,633
Cass	Fargo	114,580	102,874	1,766
Cavalier	Langdon	5,145	6,064	1,489
Dickey	Ellendale	5,636	6,107	1,131
Divide	Crosby	2,416	2,899	1,259
Dunn	Manning	3,641	4,005	2,010
Eddy	New Rockford	2,867	2,951	632
Emmons	Linton	4,372	4,830	1,510
Foster	Carrington	3,772	3,983	635
Golden Valley	Beach	1,901	2,108	1,002
Grand Forks	Grand Forks	69,609	70,683	1,438
Grant	Carson	3,043	3,549	1,660
Griggs	Cooperstown	2,834	3,303	709
Hettinger	Mott	2,966	3,445	1,132
Kidder	Steele	2,929	3,332	1,352
La Moure	La Moure	4,907	5,383	1,147
Logan	Napoleon	2,417	2,847	993
McHenry	Towner	6,168	6,528	1,874
McIntosh	Ashley	3,569	4,021	975
McKenzie	Watford City	5,771	6,383	2,742
McLean	Washburn	9,753	10,457	2,110
Mercer	Stanton	9,440	9,808	1,045
Morton	Mandan	24,397	23,700	1,926
Mountrail	Stanley	6,650	7,021	1,824
Nelson	Lakota	3,811	4,410	982
Oliver	Center	2,217	2,381	724
Pembina	Cavalier	8,617	9,238	1,119
Pierce	Rugby	4,567	5,052	1,018
Ramsey	Devils Lake	12,376	12,681	1,186
Ransom	Lisbon	5,826	5,921	863
Renville	Mohall	2,852	3,160	875
Richland	Wahpeton	18,222	18,148	1,437
Rolette	Rolla	14,130	12,772	903
Sargent	Forman	4,430	4,549	859
Sheridan	McClusky	1,784	2,148	972
Sioux	Fort Yates	4,088	3,761	1,094
Slope	Amidon	846	907	1,218
Stark	Dickinson	22,697	22,832	1,338
Steele	Finley	2,252	2,420	712
Stutsman	Jamestown	21,117	22,241	2,222
Towner	Cando	3,077	3,627	1,025
Traill	Hillsboro	8,630	8,752	862
Walsh	Grafton	13,671	13,840	1,282
Ward	Minot	58,747	57,921	2,013
Wells	Fessenden	5,261	5,864	1,271
Williams	Williston	20,412	21,129	2,071

Ohio

(88 counties, 40,953 sq mi land; pop. 11,186,331)

County	County seat or courthouse	1997 Pop.	1990 Pop.	Land area sq mi
Adams	West Union	28,480	25,371	584
Allen	Lima	107,979	109,755	405
Ashland	Ashland	52,010	47,507	424
Ashtabula	Jefferson	103,140	99,821	703
Athens	Athens	61,276	59,549	507
Auglaize	Wapakoneta	46,965	44,585	401

County	County seat or courthouse	1997 Pop.	1990 Pop.	Land area sq mi
Belmont	Saint Clairsville	69,595	71,074	537
Brown	Georgetown	40,243	34,966	492
Butler	Hamilton	326,749	291,479	467
Carroll	Carrollton	28,925	26,521	395
Champaign	Urbana	38,221	36,019	429
Clark	Springfield	146,185	147,548	400
Clermont	Batavia	173,163	150,167	452
Clinton	Wilmington	39,318	35,417	411
Columbiana	Lisbon	111,644	108,276	533
Coshocton	Coshocton	36,156	35,427	564
Crawford	Bucyrus	47,089	47,870	402
Cuyahoga	Cleveland	1,386,803	1,412,140	458
Darke	Greenville	54,318	53,619	600
Defiance	Defiance	39,932	39,350	411
Delaware	Delaware	87,396	66,929	443
Erie	Sandusky	78,745	76,779	255
Fairfield	Lancaster	121,457	103,472	506
Fayette	Washington Courthouse	28,599	27,466	407
Franklin	Columbus	1,017,274	961,437	540
Fulton	Wauseon	41,324	38,498	407
Gallia	Gallipolis	33,085	30,954	469
Geauga	Chardon	87,913	81,129	404
Greene	Xenia	139,704	136,731	415
Guernsey	Cambridge	40,782	39,024	522
Hamilton	Cincinnati	851,599	866,228	407
Hancock	Findlay	68,813	65,536	531
Hardin	Kenton	31,724	31,111	470
Harrison	Cadiz	16,159	16,085	404
Henry	Napoleon	29,893	29,108	417
Highland	Hillsboro	39,814	35,728	553
Hocking	Logan	28,755	25,533	423
Holmes	Millersburg	37,373	32,849	423
Huron	Norwalk	60,035	56,240	493
Jackson	Jackson	32,404	30,230	420
Jefferson	Steubenville	76,014	80,298	410
Knox	Mount Vernon	52,498	47,473	527
Lake	Painesville	223,715	215,499	228
Lawrence	Ironton	64,485	61,834	455
Licking	Newark	139,411	128,300	687
Logan	Bellefontaine	45,937	42,310	459
Lorain	Elyria	282,465	271,126	493
Lucas	Toledo	451,325	462,361	340
Madison	London	41,486	37,068	465
Mahoning	Youngstown	257,489	264,806	415
Marion	Marion	65,115	64,274	404
Medina	Medina	141,961	122,354	422
Meigs	Pomeroy	23,994	22,987	430
Mercer	Celina	40,984	39,443	463
Miami	Troy	97,742	93,182	407
Monroe	Woodsfield	15,331	15,497	456
Montgomery	Dayton	561,303	573,809	462
Morgan	McConnelsville	14,615	14,194	418
Morrow	Mount Gilead	31,080	27,749	406
Muskingum	Zanesville	84,539	82,068	665
Noble	Caldwell	12,304	11,336	399
Ottawa	Port Clinton	40,651	40,029	255
Paulding	Paulding	20,157	20,488	416
Perry	New Lexington	34,144	31,557	410
Pickaway	Circleville	53,218	48,244	502
Pike	Waverly	27,565	24,249	442
Portage	Ravenna	150,792	142,585	492
Preble	Eaton	42,862	40,113	425
Putnam	Ottawa	35,080	33,819	484
Richland	Mansfield	127,762	126,137	497
Ross	Chillicothe	75,195	69,330	689
Sandusky	Fremont	62,296	61,963	409
Scioto	Portsmouth	80,756	80,327	612
Seneca	Tiffin	60,025	59,733	551
Shelby	Sidney	47,415	44,915	409
Stark	Canton	373,719	367,585	576
Summit	Akron	531,650	514,990	413
Trumbull	Warren	226,082	227,813	616
Tuscarawas	New Philadelphia	88,209	84,090	568
Union	Marysville	38,634	31,969	437
Van Wert	Van Wert	30,278	30,464	410
Vinton	McArthur	12,034	11,098	414
Warren	Lebanon	140,080	113,927	400
Washington	Marietta	63,612	62,254	635
Wayne	Wooster	109,548	101,461	555
Williams	Bryan	37,870	36,956	422
Wood	Bowling Green	119,156	113,269	617
Wyandot	Upper Sandusky	22,709	22,254	406

Oklahoma

(77 counties, 68,679 sq mi land; pop. 3,317,091)

County	County seat or courthouse	1997 Pop.	1990 Pop.	Land area sq mi
Adair	Stillwell	20,112	18,421	576
Alfalfa	Cherokee	6,056	6,416	867
Atoka	Atoka	13,335	12,778	978
Beaver	Beaver	5,981	6,023	1,815
Beckham	Sayre	18,555	18,812	902
Blaine	Watonga	10,590	11,470	929
Bryan	Durant	34,183	32,089	909
Caddo	Anadarko	30,931	29,550	1,278
Canadian	El Reno	84,670	74,409	900
Carter	Ardmore	44,120	42,919	824
Cherokee	Tahlequah	38,295	34,049	751
Choctaw	Hugo	15,256	15,302	774
Cimarron	Boise City	3,082	3,301	1,835
Cleveland	Norman	197,164	174,253	536
Coal	Coalgate	6,058	5,780	518
Comanche	Lawton	113,957	111,486	1,069
Cotton	Walters	6,691	6,651	637
Craig	Vinita	14,442	14,104	761
Creek	Sapulpa	66,129	60,915	956
Custer	Arapaho	25,788	26,897	987
Delaware	Jay	33,879	28,070	741
Dewey	Taloga	5,038	5,551	1,000
Ellis	Arnett	4,223	4,497	1,229
Garfield	Enid	56,699	56,735	1,059
Garvin	Pauls Valley	27,016	26,605	809
Grady	Chickasha	45,403	41,747	1,101
Grant	Medford	5,399	5,689	1,001
Greer	Mangum	6,377	6,559	639
Harmon	Hollis	3,473	3,793	538
Harper	Buffalo	3,620	4,063	1,039
Haskell	Stigler	11,388	10,940	577
Hughes	Holdenville	13,101	13,014	807
Jackson	Altus	28,712	28,764	803
Jefferson	Waurika	6,669	7,010	759
Johnston	Tishomingo	10,270	10,032	645
Kay	Newkirk	46,837	48,056	919
Kingfisher	Kingfisher	13,480	13,212	903
Kiowa	Hobart	10,827	11,347	1,015
Latimer	Wilburton	10,285	10,333	722
Le Flore	Poteau	46,486	43,270	1,586
Lincoln	Chandler	31,083	29,216	959
Logan	Guthrie	30,607	29,011	745
Love	Marietta	8,596	7,788	515
McClain	Purcell	25,816	22,795	570
McCurtain	Idabel	34,435	33,433	1,852
McIntosh	Eufaula	18,798	16,779	620
Major	Fairview	7,772	8,055	957
Marshall	Madill	12,045	10,829	371
Mayes	Pryor	37,074	33,366	656
Murray	Sulphur	12,367	12,042	418
Muskogee	Muskogee	69,375	68,078	814
Noble	Perry	11,246	11,045	732
Nowata	Nowata	9,902	9,992	565
Okfuskee	Okemah	11,269	11,551	625
Oklahoma	Oklahoma City	630,388	599,611	709
Okmulgee	Okmulgee	38,193	36,490	697
Osage	Pawhuska	42,514	41,645	2,251
Ottawa	Miami	30,581	30,561	471
Pawnee	Pawnee	16,207	15,575	570
Payne	Stillwater	64,272	61,507	686
Pittsburg	McAlester	43,196	40,950	1,306
Pontotoc	Ada	34,809	34,119	720
Pottawatomie	Shawnee	61,859	58,760	788
Pushmataha	Antlers	11,506	10,997	1,397
Roger Mills	Cheyenne	3,602	4,147	1,142
Rogers	Claremore	65,654	55,170	675
Seminole	Wewoka	25,018	25,412	633
Sequoyah	Sallisaw	36,882	33,828	674
Stephens	Duncan	43,605	42,299	877
Texas	Guymon	18,081	16,419	2,037
Tillman	Frederick	9,656	10,384	872
Tulsa	Tulsa	535,896	503,341	570
Wagoner	Wagoner	54,203	47,883	563
Washington	Bartlesville	47,406	48,066	417
Washita	Cordell	11,686	11,441	1,004
Woods	Alva	8,251	9,103	1,287
Woodward	Woodward	18,664	18,976	1,242

Oregon

(36 counties, 96,002 sq mi land; pop. 3,243,487)

County	County seat or courthouse	1997 Pop.	1990 Pop.	Land area sq mi
Baker	Baker City	16,418	15,317	3,068
Benton	Corvallis	76,544	70,811	677
Clackamas	Oregon City	331,106	278,850	1,868
Clatsop	Astoria	35,546	33,301	827
Columbia	Saint Helens	43,751	37,557	657
Coos	Coquille	62,531	60,273	1,601
Crook	Prineville	16,958	14,111	2,980
Curry	Gold Beach	21,283	19,327	1,627
Deschutes	Bend	101,367	74,976	3,018
Douglas	Roseburg	101,818	94,649	5,037
Gilliam	Condon	1,955	1,717	1,204
Grant	Canyon City	8,002	7,853	4,529
Harney	Burns	7,033	7,060	10,135
Hood River	Hood River	19,618	16,903	522
Jackson	Medford	170,960	146,387	2,785
Jefferson	Madras	16,587	13,676	1,781
Josephine	Grants Pass	73,459	62,649	1,640

County	County seat or courthouse	1997 Pop.	1990 Pop.	Land area sq mi
Klamath	Klamath Falls	63,009	57,702	5,945
Lake	Lakeview	7,327	7,186	8,136
Lane	Eugene	311,356	282,912	4,554
Lincoln	Newport	45,587	38,889	980
Linn	Albany	103,440	91,227	2,291
Malheur	Vale	28,504	26,038	9,888
Marion	Salem	265,123	228,483	1,185
Morrow	Heppner	9,631	7,625	2,033
Multnomah	Portland	624,619	583,887	435
Polk	Dallas	60,130	49,541	741
Sherman	Moro	1,801	1,918	823
Tillamook	Tillamook	24,384	21,570	1,102
Umatilla	Pendleton	64,754	59,249	3,215
Union	La Grande	25,071	23,598	2,037
Wallowa	Enterprise	7,413	6,911	3,145
Wasco	The Dalles	23,252	21,683	2,381
Washington	Hillsboro	391,335	311,554	724
Wheeler	Fossil	1,603	1,396	1,715
Yamhill	McMinnville	80,212	65,551	716

Pennsylvania

(67 counties, 44,820 sq mi land; pop. 12,019,661)

County	County seat or courthouse	1997 Pop.	1990 Pop.	Land area sq mi
Adams	Gettysburg	85,754	78,274	520
Allegheny	Pittsburgh	1,280,624	1,336,449	730
Armstrong	Kittanning	73,572	73,478	654
Beaver	Beaver	185,682	186,093	435
Bedford	Bedford	49,253	47,919	1,015
Berks	Reading	354,057	336,523	859
Blair	Hollidaysburg	130,923	130,542	526
Bradford	Towanda	62,292	60,967	1,151
Bucks	Doylestown	582,633	541,174	608
Butler	Butler	169,197	152,013	789
Cambria	Ebensburg	157,419	163,062	688
Cameron	Emporium	5,719	5,913	397
Carbon	Jim Thorpe	58,844	56,846	383
Centre	Bellefonte	132,993	124,812	1,108
Chester	West Chester	416,541	376,396	756
Clarion	Clarion	41,820	41,699	603
Clearfield	Clearfield	80,656	78,097	1,147
Clinton	Lock Haven	36,885	37,182	891
Columbia	Bloomsburg	64,230	63,202	486
Crawford	Meadville	89,322	86,170	1,013
Cumberland	Carlisle	207,852	195,257	550
Dauphin	Harrisburg	245,793	237,813	525
Delaware	Media	543,010	547,651	184
Elk	Ridgway	34,911	34,878	829
Erie	Erie	279,401	275,572	802
Fayette	Uniontown	145,036	145,351	790
Forest	Tionesta	4,910	4,802	428
Franklin	Chambersburg	127,373	121,082	772
Fulton	McConnellsburg	14,457	13,837	438
Greene	Waynesburg	42,210	39,550	576
Huntingdon	Huntingdon	45,172	44,164	875
Indiana	Indiana	89,182	89,994	830
Jefferson	Brookville	46,567	46,083	656
Juniata	Mifflintown	21,898	20,625	392
Lackawanna	Scranton	210,464	219,097	459
Lancaster	Lancaster	454,063	422,822	949
Lawrence	New Castle	95,442	96,246	361
Lebanon	Lebanon	117,216	113,744	362
Lehigh	Allentown	297,703	291,130	347
Luzerne	Wilkes-Barre	317,560	328,149	891
Lycoming	Williamsport	118,405	118,710	1,235
McKean	Smethport	46,806	47,131	982
Mercer	Mercer	122,045	121,003	672
Mifflin	Lewistown	47,176	46,197	411
Monroe	Stroudsburg	122,531	95,709	607
Montgomery	Norristown	712,466	678,193	483
Montour	Danville	17,971	17,735	131
Northampton	Easton	257,289	247,105	374
Northumberland	Sunbury	95,100	96,771	460
Perry	New Bloomfield	44,164	41,172	554
Philadelphia	Philadelphia	1,451,372	1,585,577	135
Pike	Milford	39,108	27,966	547
Potter	Coudersport	17,160	16,717	1,081
Schuylkill	Pottsville	151,256	152,585	779
Snyder	Middleburg	38,279	36,680	331
Somerset	Somerset	80,255	78,218	1,075
Sullivan	Laporte	6,103	6,104	450
Susquehanna	Montrose	42,085	40,380	823
Tioga	Wellsboro	41,613	41,126	1,134
Union	Lewisburg	41,774	36,176	317
Venango	Franklin	58,067	59,381	675
Warren	Warren	44,228	45,049	884
Washington	Washington	205,807	204,584	857
Wayne	Honesdale	45,387	39,944	729
Westmoreland	Greensburg	374,673	370,321	1,023
Wyoming	Tunkhannock	29,387	28,076	397
York	York	370,518	339,574	905

Rhode Island

(5 counties, 1,045 sq mi land; pop. 987,429)

County	County seat or courthouse	1997 Pop.	1990 Pop.	Land area sq mi
Bristol	Bristol	48,970	48,859	25
Kent	East Greenwich	161,742	161,135	170
Newport	Newport	82,598	87,194	104
Providence	Providence	574,429	596,270	413
Washington	West Kingston	119,690	110,006	333

South Carolina

(46 counties, 30,111 sq mi land; pop. 3,760,181)

County	County seat or courthouse	1997 Pop.	1990 Pop.	Land area sq mi
Abbeville	Abbeville	24,409	23,862	508
Aiken	Aiken	133,980	120,991	1,073
Allendale	Allendale	11,570	11,722	408
Anderson	Anderson	158,251	145,177	718
Bamberg	Bamberg	16,614	16,902	393
Barnwell	Barnwell	21,830	20,293	549
Beaufort	Beaufort	106,582	86,425	587
Berkeley	Moncks Corner	134,311	128,776	1,100
Calhoun	Saint Matthews	13,769	12,753	380
Charleston	Charleston	284,815	295,041	917
Cherokee	Gaffney	48,357	44,506	393
Chester	Chester	33,713	32,170	581
Chesterfield	Chesterfield	40,039	38,575	799
Clarendon	Manning	30,683	28,450	607
Colleton	Walterboro	37,019	34,377	1,057
Darlington	Darlington	65,784	61,851	562
Dillon	Dillon	29,693	29,114	405
Dorchester	Saint George	90,730	83,060	575
Edgefield	Edgefield	19,750	18,360	502
Fairfield	Winnsboro	22,371	22,295	687
Florence	Florence	124,379	114,344	799
Georgetown	Georgetown	52,336	46,302	815
Greenville	Greenville	348,523	320,167	792
Greenwood	Greenwood	63,324	59,567	456
Hampton	Hampton	19,045	18,191	560
Horry	Conway	169,178	144,053	1,134
Jasper	Ridgeland	16,953	15,487	654
Kershaw	Camden	47,746	43,599	726
Lancaster	Lancaster	57,889	54,516	549
Laurens	Laurens	61,908	58,092	713
Lee	Bishopville	20,186	18,437	410
Lexington	Lexington	200,371	167,611	701
McCormick	McCormick	9,525	8,868	360
Marion	Marion	34,892	33,899	489
Marlboro	Bennettsville	29,550	29,716	480
Newberry	Newberry	34,243	33,172	631
Oconee	Walhalla	63,461	57,494	625
Orangeburg	Orangeburg	87,477	84,803	1,106
Pickens	Pickens	104,618	93,896	497
Richland	Columbia	303,577	286,321	757
Saluda	Saluda	16,795	16,357	451
Spartanburg	Spartanburg	244,980	226,793	811
Sumter	Sumter	106,589	101,276	666
Union	Union	30,558	30,337	514
Williamsburg	Kingstree	37,306	36,815	934
York	York	150,502	131,497	683

South Dakota

(66 counties, 75,896 sq mi land; pop. 737,973)

County	County seat or courthouse	1997 Pop.	1990 Pop.	Land area sq mi
Aurora	Plankinton	3,018	3,135	708
Beadle	Huron	17,976	18,253	1,259
Bennett	Martin	3,289	3,206	1,185
Bon Homme	Tyndall	7,677	7,089	563
Brookings	Brookings	26,186	25,207	795
Brown	Aberdeen	35,701	35,580	1,713
Brule	Chamberlain	5,545	5,485	819
Buffalo	Gannvalley	1,770	1,759	471
Butte	Belle Fourche	8,926	7,914	2,249
Campbell	Mound City	1,975	1,965	736
Charles Mix	Lake Andes	9,493	9,131	1,098
Clark	Clark	4,370	4,403	958
Clay	Vermillion	15,370	13,186	412
Codington	Watertown	25,452	22,698	688
Corson	McIntosh	4,275	4,195	2,473
Custer	Custer	6,966	6,179	1,558
Davison	Mitchell	18,807	17,503	436
Day	Webster	6,421	6,978	1,029
Deuel	Clear Lake	4,553	4,522	624
Dewey	Timber Lake	5,668	5,523	2,303
Douglas	Armour	3,573	3,746	434
Edmunds	Ipswich	4,248	4,356	1,146
Fall River	Hot Springs	7,123	7,353	1,740
Faulk	Faulkton	2,532	2,744	1,000
Grant	Milbank	8,048	8,372	683
Gregory	Burke	5,036	5,359	1,016
Haakon	Philip	2,469	2,624	1,813
Hamlin	Hayti	5,307	4,974	511

County	County seat or courthouse	1997 Pop.	1990 Pop.	Land area sq mi
Hand	Miller	4,191	4,272	1,437
Hanson	Alexandria	2,899	2,994	435
Harding	Buffalo	1,497	1,669	2,671
Hughes	Pierre	15,404	14,817	741
Hutchinson	Olivet	8,102	8,262	813
Hyde	Highmore	1,648	1,696	861
Jackson	Kadoka	2,926	2,811	1,869
Jerauld	Wessington Springs	2,278	2,425	530
Jones	Murdo	1,284	1,324	971
Kingsbury	De Smet	5,830	5,925	838
Lake	Madison	10,647	10,550	563
Lawrence	Deadwood	22,131	20,655	800
Lincoln	Canton	20,152	15,427	578
Lyman	Kennebec	3,926	3,638	1,640
McCook	Salem	5,686	5,688	575
McPherson	Leola	2,782	3,228	1,137
Marshall	Britton	4,625	4,844	839
Meade	Sturgis	21,999	21,878	3,471
Mellette	White River	1,983	2,137	1,307
Miner	Howard	2,926	3,272	570
Minnehaha	Sioux Falls	140,518	123,809	809
Moody	Flandreau	6,538	6,507	520
Pennington	Rapid City	87,190	81,343	2,776
Perkins	Bison	3,542	3,932	2,872
Potter	Gettysburg	2,925	3,190	867
Roberts	Sisseton	9,973	9,914	1,101
Sanborn	Woonsocket	2,760	2,833	569
Shannon	(Attached to Fall River)	12,010	9,902	2,094
Spink	Redfield	7,700	7,981	1,504
Stanley	Fort Pierre	2,923	2,453	1,443
Sully	Onida	1,539	1,589	1,007
Todd	(Attached to Tripp)	9,296	8,352	1,388
Tripp	Winner	6,883	6,924	1,614
Turner	Parker	8,633	8,576	617
Union	Elk Point	11,959	10,189	460
Walworth	Selby	5,620	6,087	708
Yankton	Yankton	21,013	19,252	522
Ziebach	Dupree	2,261	2,220	1,963

Tennessee

(95 counties, 41,219 sq mi land; pop. 5,368,198)

County	County seat or courthouse	1997 Pop.	1990 Pop.	Land area sq mi
Anderson	Clinton	71,429	68,250	338
Bedford	Shelbyville	34,162	30,411	474
Benton	Camden	16,311	14,524	395
Bledsoe	Pikeville	10,599	9,669	406
Blount	Maryville	100,377	85,969	559
Bradley	Cleveland	80,250	73,712	329
Campbell	Jacksboro	37,859	35,079	480
Cannon	Woodbury	12,039	10,467	266
Carroll	Huntingdon	28,904	27,514	599
Carter	Elizabethton	53,082	51,505	341
Cheatham	Ashland City	34,405	27,140	303
Chester	Henderson	14,524	12,819	289
Claiborne	Tazewell	28,999	26,137	434
Clay	Celina	7,331	7,238	236
Cocke	Newport	31,597	29,141	434
Coffee	Manchester	45,520	40,339	429
Crockett	Alamo	13,798	13,378	265
Cumberland	Crossville	43,120	34,736	682
Davidson	Nashville	533,689	510,786	502
Decatur	Decaturville	10,766	10,472	334
De Kalb	Smithville	15,801	14,360	305
Dickson	Charlotte	41,024	35,061	490
Dyer	Dyersburg	36,451	34,854	511
Fayette	Somerville	29,526	25,559	705
Fentress	Jamestown	15,903	14,669	499
Franklin	Winchester	37,146	34,725	553
Gibson	Trenton	48,108	46,315	603
Giles	Pulaski	28,478	25,741	611
Grainger	Rutledge	19,462	17,095	280
Greene	Greeneville	59,446	55,853	622
Grundy	Altamont	13,975	13,362	361
Hamblen	Morristown	53,737	50,480	161
Hamilton	Chattanooga	294,676	285,536	543
Hancock	Sneedville	6,805	6,739	222
Hardeman	Bolivar	24,155	23,377	668
Hardin	Savannah	24,746	22,633	578
Hawkins	Rogersville	48,777	44,565	487
Haywood	Brownsville	19,798	19,437	533
Henderson	Lexington	23,998	21,844	520
Henry	Paris	29,702	27,888	562
Hickman	Centerville	19,906	16,754	613
Houston	Erin	7,801	7,018	200
Humphreys	Waverly	16,797	15,813	532
Jackson	Gainesboro	9,553	9,297	309
Jefferson	Dandridge	42,054	33,016	274
Johnson	Mountain City	16,556	13,766	299
Knox	Knoxville	365,626	335,749	509
Lake	Tiptonville	8,190	7,129	163
Lauderdale	Ripley	24,161	23,491	471
Lawrence	Lawrenceburg	39,114	35,303	617
Lewis	Hohenwald	10,741	9,247	282
Lincoln	Fayetteville	29,203	28,157	570
Loudon	Loudon	38,234	31,255	229
McMinn	Athens	45,890	42,383	430
McNairy	Selmer	23,678	22,422	560
Macon	Lafayette	17,779	15,906	307
Madison	Jackson	84,795	77,982	557
Marion	Jasper	26,733	24,860	500
Marshall	Lewisburg	25,658	21,539	375
Maury	Columbia	68,099	54,812	613
Meigs	Decatur	9,697	8,033	195
Monroe	Madisonville	33,934	30,541	635
Montgomery	Clarksville	124,252	100,498	539
Moore	Lynchburg	5,227	4,721	129
Morgan	Wartburg	18,494	17,300	522
Obion	Union City	32,118	31,717	545
Overton	Livingston	19,136	17,636	433
Perry	Linden	7,487	6,612	415
Pickett	Byrdstown	4,605	4,548	163
Polk	Benton	14,703	13,643	435
Putnam	Cookeville	58,264	51,373	401
Rhea	Dayton	27,588	24,344	316
Roane	Kingston	49,909	47,227	361
Robertson	Springfield	51,482	41,492	477
Rutherford	Murfreesboro	159,543	118,570	619
Scott	Huntsville	19,788	18,358	532
Sequatchie	Dunlap	10,102	8,863	266
Sevier	Sevierville	62,602	51,043	592
Shelby	Memphis	865,970	826,330	755
Smith	Carthage	16,079	14,143	314
Stewart	Dover	11,257	9,479	458
Sullivan	Blountville	150,684	143,596	413
Sumner	Gallatin	121,836	103,281	529
Tipton	Covington	45,981	37,568	459
Trousdale	Hartsville	6,805	5,920	114
Unicoi	Erwin	17,259	16,549	186
Union	Maynardville	15,913	13,694	224
Van Buren	Spencer	4,994	4,846	274
Warren	McMinnville	35,779	32,992	433
Washington	Jonesboro	101,558	92,315	326
Wayne	Waynesboro	16,553	13,935	734
Weakley	Dresden	32,844	31,972	580
White	Sparta	22,167	20,090	377
Williamson	Franklin	111,373	81,021	583
Wilson	Lebanon	81,172	67,675	571

Texas

(254 counties, 261,914 sq mi land; pop. 19,439,337)

County	County seat or courthouse	1997 Pop.	1990 Pop.	Land area sq mi
Anderson	Palestine	52,540	48,024	1,071
Andrews	Andrews	14,072	14,338	1,501
Angelina	Lufkin	76,799	69,884	802
Aransas	Rockport	22,579	17,892	252
Archer	Archer City	8,276	7,973	910
Armstrong	Claude	2,172	2,021	914
Atascosa	Jourdanton	35,268	30,533	1,232
Austin	Bellville	22,903	19,832	653
Bailey	Muleshoe	6,831	7,064	827
Bandera	Bandera	15,005	10,562	792
Bastrop	Bastrop	49,031	38,263	889
Baylor	Seymour	4,165	4,385	871
Bee	Beeville	28,054	25,135	880
Bell	Belton	222,302	191,073	1,059
Bexar	San Antonio	1,332,547	1,185,394	1,247
Blanco	Johnson City	8,213	5,972	711
Borden	Gail	748	799	899
Bosque	Meridian	16,674	15,125	989
Bowie	Boston	83,672	81,665	888
Brazoria	Angleton	225,406	191,707	1,387
Brazos	Bryan	133,008	121,862	586
Brewster	Alpine	9,039	8,653	6,193
Briscoe	Silverton	1,982	1,971	900
Brooks	Falfurrias	8,458	8,204	943
Brown	Brownwood	36,903	34,371	944
Burleson	Caldwell	15,368	13,625	666
Burnet	Burnet	30,755	22,677	995
Caldwell	Lockhart	31,625	26,392	546
Calhoun	Port Lavaca	20,806	19,053	512
Callahan	Baird	12,816	11,859	899
Cameron	Brownsville	320,801	260,120	906
Camp	Pittsburg	10,978	9,904	198
Carson	Panhandle	6,698	6,576	923
Cass	Linden	30,518	29,982	938
Castro	Dimmitt	8,307	9,070	898
Chambers	Anahuac	23,545	20,088	599
Cherokee	Rusk	42,778	41,049	1,052
Childress	Childress	7,630	5,953	710
Clay	Henrietta	10,407	10,024	1,098
Cochran	Morton	3,978	4,377	775
Coke	Robert Lee	3,426	3,424	899
Coleman	Coleman	9,590	9,710	1,273
Collin	McKinney	401,352	264,036	848
Collingsworth	Wellington	3,330	3,573	919
Colorado	Columbus	18,880	18,383	963
Comal	New Braunfels	70,682	51,832	562
Comanche	Comanche	13,595	13,381	938
Concho	Paint Rock	3,104	3,044	992

County	County seat or courthouse	1997 Pop.	1990 Pop.	Land area sq mi
Cooke	Gainesville	32,989	30,777	874
Coryell	Gatesville	77,438	64,226	1,052
Cottle	Paducah	1,957	2,247	901
Crane	Crane	4,557	4,652	786
Crockett	Ozona	4,518	4,078	2,808
Crosby	Crosbyton	7,375	7,304	900
Culberson	Van Horn	3,136	3,407	3,813
Dallam	Dalhart	6,361	5,461	1,505
Dallas	Dallas	2,023,140	1,852,810	880
Dawson	Lamesa	14,793	14,349	902
Deaf Smith	Hereford	19,448	19,153	1,497
Delta	Cooper	4,941	4,857	277
Denton	Denton	365,058	273,525	889
DeWitt	Cuero	19,674	18,840	909
Dickens	Dickens	2,254	2,571	904
Dimmit	Carrizo Springs	10,486	10,433	1,331
Donley	Clarendon	3,810	3,696	930
Duval	San Diego	13,607	12,918	1,793
Eastland	Eastland	17,857	18,488	926
Ector	Odessa	124,727	118,934	901
Edwards	Rocksprings	3,738	2,266	2,120
Ellis	Waxahachie	100,627	85,167	940
El Paso	El Paso	701,576	591,610	1,013
Erath	Stephenville	31,275	27,991	1,086
Falls	Marlin	17,747	17,712	769
Fannin	Bonham	27,655	24,804	892
Fayette	La Grange	21,101	20,095	950
Fisher	Roby	4,352	4,842	901
Floyd	Floydada	8,213	8,497	992
Foard	Crowell	1,726	1,794	707
Fort Bend	Richmond	321,149	225,421	875
Franklin	Mount Vernon	9,589	7,802	286
Freestone	Fairfield	17,540	15,818	885
Frio	Pearsall	15,875	13,472	1,133
Gaines	Seminole	14,985	14,123	1,502
Galveston	Galveston	242,979	217,396	399
Garza	Post	4,632	5,143	896
Gillespie	Fredericksburg	19,909	17,204	1,061
Glasscock	Garden City	1,454	1,447	901
Goliad	Goliad	6,776	5,980	854
Gonzales	Gonzales	17,569	17,205	1,068
Gray	Pampa	23,719	23,967	928
Grayson	Sherman	101,541	95,019	934
Gregg	Longview	113,147	104,948	274
Grimes	Anderson	22,846	18,828	794
Guadalupe	Seguin	77,963	64,873	711
Hale	Plainview	36,603	34,671	1,005
Hall	Memphis	3,705	3,905	903
Hamilton	Hamilton	7,608	7,733	836
Hansford	Spearman	5,396	5,848	920
Hardeman	Quanah	4,701	5,283	695
Hardin	Kountze	48,403	41,320	894
Harris	Houston	3,158,095	2,818,101	1,729
Harrison	Marshall	59,687	57,483	899
Hartley	Channing	5,121	3,634	1,462
Haskell	Haskell	6,107	6,820	903
Hays	San Marcos	86,284	65,614	678
Hemphill	Canadian	3,618	3,720	910
Henderson	Athens	67,347	58,543	874
Hidalgo	Edinburg	510,922	383,545	1,569
Hill	Hillsboro	30,033	27,146	962
Hockley	Levelland	23,933	24,199	908
Hood	Granbury	36,205	28,981	422
Hopkins	Sulphur Springs	30,535	28,833	785
Houston	Crockett	21,884	21,375	1,231
Howard	Big Spring	32,562	32,343	903
Hudspeth	Sierra Blanca	3,328	2,915	4,571
Hunt	Greenville	69,309	64,343	841
Hutchinson	Stinnett	23,973	25,689	887
Irion	Mertzon	1,696	1,629	1,052
Jack	Jacksboro	7,314	6,981	917
Jackson	Edna	13,656	13,039	830
Jasper	Jasper	33,203	31,102	938
Jeff Davis	Fort Davis	2,234	1,946	2,265
Jefferson	Beaumont	241,940	239,389	904
Jim Hogg	Hebbronville	4,925	5,109	1,136
Jim Wells	Alice	39,842	37,679	865
Johnson	Cleburne	114,052	97,165	729
Jones	Anson	18,803	16,490	931
Karnes	Karnes City	12,501	12,455	750
Kaufman	Kaufman	63,857	52,220	786
Kendall	Boerne	20,394	14,589	663
Kenedy	Sarita	427	460	1,457
Kent	Jayton	863	1,010	902
Kerr	Kerrville	42,623	36,304	1,106
Kimble	Junction	4,199	4,122	1,251
King	Guthrie	348	354	912
Kinney	Brackettville	3,481	3,119	1,364
Kleberg	Kingsville	30,216	30,274	871
Knox	Benjamin	4,309	4,837	854
Lamar	Paris	45,772	43,949	917
Lamb	Littlefield	14,849	15,072	1,016
Lampasas	Lampasas	17,491	13,521	712
La Salle	Cotulla	5,935	5,254	1,489
Lavaca	Hallettsville	18,676	18,690	970
Lee	Giddings	14,792	12,854	629
Leon	Centerville	14,450	12,665	1,072
Liberty	Liberty	63,948	52,726	1,160
Limestone	Groesbeck	21,059	20,946	909
Lipscomb	Lipscomb	3,027	3,143	932
Live Oak	George West	10,157	9,556	1,036
Llano	Llano	13,104	11,631	935
Loving	Mentone	106	107	673
Lubbock	Lubbock	230,672	222,636	900
Lynn	Tahoka	6,591	6,758	892
McCulloch	Brady	8,778	8,778	1,069
McLennan	Waco	202,983	189,123	1,042
McMullen	Tilden	783	817	1,113
Madison	Madisonville	11,932	10,931	470
Marion	Jefferson	10,672	9,984	381
Martin	Stanton	5,078	4,956	915
Mason	Mason	3,650	3,423	932
Matagorda	Bay City	37,910	36,928	1,115
Maverick	Eagle Pass	47,877	36,378	1,280
Medina	Hondo	36,827	27,312	1,328
Menard	Menard	2,333	2,252	902
Midland	Midland	118,662	106,611	900
Milam	Cameron	24,266	22,946	1,017
Mills	Goldthwaite	4,771	4,531	748
Mitchell	Colorado City	8,768	8,016	910
Montague	Montague	18,290	17,274	931
Montgomery	Conroe	258,127	182,201	1,044
Moore	Dumas	19,510	17,865	900
Morris	Daingerfield	13,302	13,200	255
Motley	Matador	1,280	1,532	989
Nacogdoches	Nacogdoches	56,716	54,753	947
Navarro	Corsicana	41,366	39,926	1,071
Newton	Newton	14,418	13,569	933
Nolan	Sweetwater	16,486	16,594	912
Nueces	Corpus Christi	317,474	291,145	836
Ochiltree	Perryton	8,902	9,128	918
Oldham	Vega	2,219	2,278	1,501
Orange	Orange	84,648	80,509	356
Palo Pinto	Palo Pinto	25,494	25,055	953
Panola	Carthage	23,005	22,035	801
Parker	Weatherford	78,811	64,785	904
Parmer	Farwell	10,475	9,863	882
Pecos	Fort Stockton	16,196	14,675	4,764
Polk	Livingston	47,452	30,687	1,057
Potter	Amarillo	109,243	97,841	909
Presidio	Marfa	8,577	6,637	3,856
Rains	Emory	8,213	6,715	232
Randall	Canyon	98,922	89,673	915
Reagan	Big Lake	4,228	4,514	1,175
Real	Leakey	2,686	2,412	700
Red River	Clarksville	13,794	14,317	1,050
Reeves	Pecos	14,856	15,852	2,636
Refugio	Refugio	7,882	7,976	770
Roberts	Miami	988	1,025	924
Robertson	Franklin	15,534	15,511	855
Rockwall	Rockwall	35,923	25,604	129
Runnels	Ballinger	11,457	11,294	1,055
Rusk	Henderson	45,636	43,735	924
Sabine	Hemphill	10,565	9,586	490
San Augustine	San Augustine	8,184	7,999	528
San Jacinto	Coldspring	20,860	16,372	571
San Patricio	Sinton	69,626	58,749	692
San Saba	San Saba	6,424	5,401	1,135
Schleicher	Eldorado	3,047	2,990	1,311
Scurry	Snyder	18,185	18,634	903
Shackelford	Albany	3,335	3,316	914
Shelby	Center	22,652	22,034	794
Sherman	Stratford	2,905	2,858	923
Smith	Tyler	166,723	151,309	929
Somervell	Glen Rose	6,235	5,360	187
Starr	Rio Grande City	55,560	40,518	1,223
Stephens	Breckenridge	9,902	9,010	895
Sterling	Sterling City	1,385	1,438	923
Stonewall	Aspermont	1,807	2,013	919
Sutton	Sonora	4,437	4,135	1,454
Swisher	Tulia	8,347	8,133	901
Tarrant	Fort Worth	1,327,332	1,170,103	864
Taylor	Abilene	121,456	119,655	916
Terrell	Sanderson	1,189		2,358
Terry	Brownfield	13,003	13,218	890
Throckmorton	Throckmorton	1,704	1,880	912
Titus	Mount Pleasant	25,245	24,009	411
Tom Green	San Angelo	102,648	98,458	1,522
Travis	Austin	693,606	576,407	989
Trinity	Groveton	12,410	11,445	693
Tyler	Woodville	20,107	16,646	923
Upshur	Gilmer	35,416	31,370	588
Upton	Rankin	3,815	4,447	1,242
Uvalde	Uvalde	25,619	23,340	1,557
Val Verde	Del Rio	43,115	38,721	3,171
Van Zandt	Canton	42,998	37,944	849
Victoria	Victoria	82,024	74,361	883
Walker	Huntsville	54,528	50,917	788
Waller	Hempstead	26,792	23,389	514
Ward	Monahans	11,891	13,115	836
Washington	Brenham	29,033	26,154	609
Webb	Laredo	183,219	133,239	3,357
Wharton	Wharton	40,146	39,955	1,090
Wheeler	Wheeler	5,309	5,879	914

County	County seat or courthouse	1997 Pop.	1990 Pop.	Land area sq mi
Wichita	Wichita Falls	128,827	122,378	628
Wilbarger	Vernon	14,138	15,121	971
Willacy	Raymondville	19,662	17,705	597
Williamson	Georgetown	210,477	139,551	1,124
Wilson	Floresville	30,194	22,650	807
Winkler	Kermit	8,037	8,626	841
Wise	Decatur	42,387	34,679	905
Wood	Quitman	34,170	29,380	650
Yoakum	Plains	8,169	8,786	800
Young	Graham	17,575	18,126	922
Zapata	Zapata	11,266	9,279	997
Zavala	Crystal City	11,955	12,162	1,299

Utah

(29 counties, 82,168 sq mi land; pop. 2,059,148)

County	County seat or courthouse	1997 Pop.	1990 Pop.	Land area sq mi
Beaver	Beaver	5,861	4,765	2,590
Box Elder	Brigham City	41,102	36,485	5,724
Cache	Logan	84,818	70,183	1,165
Carbon	Price	20,932	20,228	1,479
Daggett	Manila	754	690	698
Davis	Farmington	226,062	187,941	305
Duchesne	Duchesne	14,442	12,645	3,238
Emery	Castle Dale	10,875	10,332	4,452
Garfield	Panguitch	4,205	3,980	5,175
Grand	Moab	8,118	6,620	3,682
Iron	Parowan	27,747	20,789	3,299
Juab	Nephi	7,248	5,817	3,392
Kane	Kanab	5,828	5,169	3,992
Millard	Fillmore	12,320	11,333	6,590
Morgan	Morgan	6,905	5,528	609
Piute	Junction	1,391	1,277	758
Rich	Randolph	1,816	1,725	1,029
Salt Lake	Salt Lake City	839,896	725,956	737
San Juan	Monticello	13,688	12,621	7,821
Sanpete	Manti	20,893	16,259	1,588
Sevier	Richfield	18,064	15,431	1,910
Summit	Coalville	25,752	15,518	1,871
Tooele	Tooele	31,410	26,601	6,946
Uintah	Vernal	25,513	22,211	4,477
Utah	Provo	328,142	263,590	1,998
Wasatch	Heber City	12,788	10,089	1,181
Washington	Saint George	78,614	48,560	2,427
Wayne	Loa	2,368	2,177	2,461
Weber	Ogden	181,596	158,330	576

Vermont

(14 counties, 9,249 sq mi land; pop. 588,978)

County	County seat or courthouse	1997 Pop.	1990 Pop.	Land area sq mi
Addison	Middlebury	34,958	32,953	770
Bennington	Bennington	35,955	35,845	676
Caledonia	Saint Johnsbury	28,692	27,846	651
Chittenden	Burlington	141,387	131,761	539
Essex	Guildhall	6,549	6,405	665
Franklin	Saint Albans	43,505	39,980	637
Grand Isle	North Hero	6,196	5,318	83
Lamoille	Hyde Park	21,442	19,735	461
Orange	Chelsea	27,798	26,149	689
Orleans	Newport	25,316	24,053	697
Rutland	Rutland	62,709	62,142	932
Washington	Montpelier	56,478	54,928	690
Windham	Newfane	42,843	41,588	789
Windsor	Woodstock	55,150	54,055	971

Virginia

(95 counties, 40 ind. cities, 39,598 sq mi land; pop. 6,733,996)

County	County seat or courthouse	1997 Pop.	1990 Pop.	Land area sq mi
Accomack	Accomac	32,096	31,703	455
Albemarle	Charlottesville	77,518	68,172	723
Alleghany	Covington	12,310	12,969	446
Amelia	Amelia Courthouse	10,264	8,787	357
Amherst	Amherst	29,965	28,578	475
Appomattox	Appomattox	12,943	12,298	334
Arlington	Arlington	172,580	170,897	26
Augusta	Staunton	61,814	54,677	972
Bath	Warm Springs	4,923	4,799	532
Bedford	Bedford	55,661	45,552	755
Bland	Bland	6,860	6,514	359
Botetourt	Fincastle	28,264	24,992	543
Brunswick	Lawrenceville	16,816	15,987	566
Buchanan	Grundy	29,361	31,333	504
Buckingham	Buckingham	14,572	12,873	581
Campbell	Rustburg	50,176	47,572	505
Caroline	Bowling Green	21,722	19,217	533
Carroll	Hillsville	27,976	26,565	477
Charles City	Charles City	6,969	6,282	183
Charlotte	Charlotte Courthouse	12,171	11,688	475
Chesterfield	Chesterfield	242,987	209,564	426
Clarke	Berryville	12,910	12,101	177
Craig	New Castle	4,887	4,372	330
Culpeper	Culpeper	32,581	27,791	381
Cumberland	Cumberland	7,823	7,825	299
Dickenson	Clintwood	17,195	17,620	333
Dinwiddie	Dinwiddie	24,333	22,319	504
Essex	Tappahannock	9,225	8,689	258
Fairfax	Fairfax	914,259	818,358	396
Fauquier	Warrenton	53,167	48,860	650
Floyd	Floyd	13,059	11,965	382
Fluvanna	Palmyra	17,768	12,429	287
Franklin	Rocky Mount	44,360	39,549	692
Frederick	Winchester	54,693	45,723	415
Giles	Pearisburg	16,172	16,366	358
Gloucester	Gloucester	34,456	30,131	217
Goochland	Goochland	17,597	14,163	285
Grayson	Independence	16,163	16,278	443
Greene	Stanardsville	13,427	10,297	157
Greensville	Emporia	11,433	8,630	296
Halifax	Halifax	37,097	36,030	820
Hanover	Hanover	78,939	63,306	473
Henrico	Henrico	243,841	217,849	238
Henry	Martinsville	56,001	56,942	382
Highland	Monterey	2,525	2,635	416
Isle of Wight	Isle of Wight	28,551	25,053	316
James City	Williamsburg	42,862	34,970	143
King and Queen	King and Queen Courthouse	6,536	6,289	316
King George	King George	16,942	13,527	180
King William	King William	12,471	10,913	275
Lancaster	Lancaster	11,285	10,896	133
Lee	Jonesville	24,053	24,496	437
Loudoun	Leesburg	133,493	86,129	520
Louisa	Louisa	23,840	20,325	498
Lunenburg	Lunenburg	12,182	11,419	432
Madison	Madison	12,498	11,949	322
Mathews	Mathews	9,112	8,348	86
Mecklenburg	Boydton	30,939	29,241	624
Middlesex	Saluda	9,554	8,653	130
Montgomery	Christiansburg	76,022	73,913	388
Nelson	Lovingston	13,756	12,778	472
New Kent	New Kent	12,261	10,445	210
Northampton	Eastville	12,790	13,061	207
Northumberland	Heathsville	11,431	10,524	192
Nottoway	Nottoway	15,021	14,993	315
Orange	Orange	24,965	21,421	342
Page	Luray	22,854	21,690	311
Patrick	Stuart	18,161	17,473	483
Pittsylvania	Chatham	57,588	55,672	971
Powhatan	Powhatan	21,215	15,328	261
Prince Edward	Farmville	18,884	17,320	353
Prince George	Prince George	29,741	27,394	266
Prince William	Manassas	254,464	215,677	338
Pulaski	Pulaski	34,389	34,496	321
Rappahannock	Washington	7,051	6,622	267
Richmond	Warsaw	8,575	7,273	192
Roanoke	Salem	81,320	79,294	251
Rockbridge	Lexington	19,413	18,350	600
Rockingham	Harrisonburg	63,763	57,482	851
Russell	Lebanon	29,016	28,667	475
Scott	Gate City	22,688	23,204	537
Shenandoah	Woodstock	34,280	31,636	512
Smyth	Marion	32,909	32,370	452
Southampton	Courtland	17,678	17,550	600
Spotsylvania	Spotsylvania	81,052	57,403	401
Stafford	Stafford	87,857	61,236	270
Surry	Surry	6,432	6,145	279
Sussex	Sussex	10,084	10,248	491
Tazewell	Tazewell	46,866	45,960	520
Warren	Front Royal	30,008	26,142	214
Washington	Abingdon	48,802	45,887	564
Westmoreland	Montross	16,297	15,480	229
Wise	Wise	39,288	39,573	403
Wythe	Wytheville	26,302	25,471	463
York	Yorktown	57,118	42,434	106
Independent Cities				
Alexandria		116,405	111,182	15
Bedford		6,296	6,177	7
Bristol		17,297	18,426	12
Buena Vista		6,136	6,406	7
Charlottesville		37,904	40,475	10
Chesapeake		195,616	151,982	341
Clifton Forge		4,403	4,679	3
Colonial Heights		16,680	16,064	8
Covington		6,954	7,198	4
Danville		51,014	53,056	43
Emporia		5,519	5,479	7
Fairfax		20,365	19,894	6
Falls Church		9,879	9,522	2
Franklin		8,806	7,864	8
Fredericksburg		21,088	19,027	11
Galax		6,886	6,699	8
Hampton		138,555	133,811	52
Harrisonburg		33,513	30,707	18
Hopewell		22,168	23,101	10
Lexington		7,195	6,959	3
Lynchburg		65,328	66,049	49

County	County seat or courthouse	1997 Pop.	1990 Pop.	Land area sq mi
Independent Cities				
Manassas		34,296	27,957	10
Manassas Park		8,469	6,734	2
Martinsville		15,793	16,162	11
Newport News		175,839	171,439	68
Norfolk		229,386	261,250	54
Norton		4,240	4,247	7
Petersburg		34,138	37,027	23
Poquoson		11,450	11,005	16
Portsmouth		99,503	103,910	33
Radford		15,320	15,940	10
Richmond		192,395	202,798	60
Roanoke		94,153	96,509	43
Salem		24,797	23,797	15
Staunton		23,327	24,461	20
Suffolk		61,033	52,143	400
Virginia Beach		432,545	393,089	248
Waynesboro		18,554	18,549	14
Williamsburg		11,800	11,409	9
Winchester		22,433	21,947	9

Washington

(39 counties, 66,581 sq mi land; pop. 5,610,362)

County	County seat or courthouse	1997 Pop.	1990 Pop.	Land area sq mi
Adams	Ritzville	15,541	13,603	1,925
Asotin	Asotin	21,171	17,605	636
Benton	Prosser	135,772	112,560	1,703
Chelan	Wenatchee	59,717	52,250	2,922
Clallam	Port Angeles	63,857	56,210	1,745
Clark	Vancouver	316,526	238,053	628
Columbia	Dayton	4,277	4,024	869
Cowlitz	Kelso	90,834	82,119	1,139
Douglas	Waterville	33,484	26,205	1,821
Ferry	Republic	7,256	6,295	2,204
Franklin	Pasco	47,027	37,473	1,242
Garfield	Pomeroy	2,279	2,248	711
Grant	Ephrata	69,719	54,798	2,676
Grays Harbor	Montesano	67,945	64,175	1,917
Island	Coupeville	70,664	60,195	209
Jefferson	Port Townsend	25,945	20,406	1,809
King	Seattle	1,632,852	1,507,305	2,126
Kitsap	Port Orchard	234,608	189,731	396
Kittitas	Ellensburg	31,383	26,725	2,297
Klickitat	Goldendale	19,069	16,616	1,873
Lewis	Chehalis	67,585	59,358	2,408
Lincoln	Davenport	9,802	8,864	2,311
Mason	Shelton	49,477	38,341	961
Okanogan	Okanogan	38,652	33,350	5,268
Pacific	South Bend	21,116	18,882	975
Pend Oreille	Newport	11,271	8,915	1,401
Pierce	Tacoma	664,776	586,203	1,676
San Juan	Friday Harbor	12,261	10,035	175
Skagit	Mount Vernon	97,705	79,545	1,735
Skamania	Stevenson	9,642	8,289	1,657
Snohomish	Everett	564,610	465,628	2,090
Spokane	Spokane	404,650	361,333	1,764
Stevens	Colville	39,243	30,948	2,478
Thurston	Olympia	200,362	161,238	727
Wahkiakum	Cathlamet	3,895	3,327	264
Walla Walla	Walla Walla	53,501	48,439	1,271
Whatcom	Bellingham	154,249	127,780	2,120
Whitman	Colfax	39,321	38,775	2,159
Yakima	Yakima	218,318	188,823	4,296

West Virginia

(55 counties, 24,087 sq mi land; pop. 1,815,787)

County	County seat or courthouse	1997 Pop.	1990 Pop.	Land area sq mi
Barbour	Philippi	16,207	15,699	341
Berkeley	Martinsburg	69,072	59,253	321
Boone	Madison	26,422	25,870	503
Braxton	Sutton	13,299	12,998	514
Brooke	Wellsburg	26,238	26,992	89
Cabell	Huntington	95,061	96,827	282
Calhoun	Grantsville	7,906	7,885	281
Clay	Clay	10,513	9,983	342
Doddridge	West Union	7,384	6,994	321
Fayette	Fayetteville	48,426	47,952	664
Gilmer	Glenville	7,179	7,669	340
Grant	Petersburg	11,087	10,428	477
Greenbrier	Lewisburg	35,502	34,693	1,021
Hampshire	Romney	18,896	16,498	642
Hancock	New Cumberland	34,473	35,233	83
Hardy	Moorefield	11,801	10,977	583
Harrison	Clarksburg	70,736	69,371	416
Jackson	Ripley	27,554	25,938	466
Jefferson	Charles Town	40,077	35,926	210
Kanawha	Charleston	203,646	207,619	903
Lewis	Weston	17,546	17,223	389
Lincoln	Hamlin	22,220	21,382	438
Logan	Logan	41,293	43,032	454
McDowell	Welch	30,613	35,233	535
Marion	Fairmont	56,876	57,249	310
Marshall	Moundsville	35,700	37,356	307
Mason	Point Pleasant	25,971	25,178	432
Mercer	Princeton	64,316	64,980	421
Mineral	Keyser	26,833	26,697	328
Mingo	Williamson	32,562	33,739	423
Monongalia	Morgantown	77,484	75,509	361
Monroe	Union	13,157	12,406	473
Morgan	Berkeley Springs	13,477	12,128	229
Nicholas	Summersville	27,580	26,775	649
Ohio	Wheeling	48,858	50,871	106
Pendleton	Franklin	8,003	8,054	698
Pleasants	St. Marys	7,487	7,546	131
Pocahontas	Marlinton	9,039	9,008	940
Preston	Kingwood	29,757	29,037	648
Putnam	Winfield	50,204	42,835	346
Raleigh	Beckley	78,995	76,819	607
Randolph	Elkins	28,779	27,803	1,040
Ritchie	Harrisville	10,264	10,233	454
Roane	Spencer	15,313	15,120	484
Summers	Hinton	13,775	14,204	361
Taylor	Grafton	15,345	15,144	173
Tucker	Parsons	7,714	7,728	419
Tyler	Middlebourne	10,063	9,796	258
Upshur	Buckhannon	23,823	22,867	355
Wayne	Wayne	42,077	41,636	506
Webster	Webster Springs	10,337	10,729	556
Wetzel	New Martinsville	18,506	19,258	359
Wirt	Elizabeth	5,664	5,192	233
Wood	Parkersburg	87,029	86,915	367
Wyoming	Pineville	27,648	28,990	501

Wisconsin

(72 counties, 54,314 sq mi land; pop. 5,169,677)

County	County seat or courthouse	1997 Pop.	1990 Pop.	Land area sq mi
Adams	Friendship	18,158	15,682	648
Ashland	Ashland	16,486	16,307	1,044
Barron	Barron	43,674	40,750	863
Bayfield	Washburn	15,228	14,008	1,476
Brown	Green Bay	214,244	194,594	529
Buffalo	Alma	14,187	13,584	685
Burnett	Siren	14,531	13,084	822
Calumet	Chilton	38,045	34,291	320
Chippewa	Chippewa Falls	54,249	52,360	1,011
Clark	Neillsville	32,995	31,647	1,216
Columbia	Portage	50,362	45,088	774
Crawford	Prairie du Chien	16,549	15,940	573
Dane	Madison	397,511	367,085	1,202
Dodge	Juneau	82,422	76,559	882
Door	Sturgeon Bay	26,897	25,690	483
Douglas	Superior	43,195	41,758	1,309
Dunn	Menomonie	38,755	35,909	852
Eau Claire	Eau Claire	89,237	85,183	638
Florence	Florence	5,219	4,590	488
Fond du Lac	Fond du Lac	94,329	90,083	723
Forest	Crandon	9,581	8,776	1,014
Grant	Lancaster	49,493	49,266	1,148
Green	Monroe	33,155	30,339	584
Green Lake	Green Lake	19,452	18,651	354
Iowa	Dodgeville	22,168	20,150	763
Iron	Hurley	6,479	6,153	757
Jackson	Black River Falls	17,617	16,588	987
Jefferson	Jefferson	73,375	67,783	557
Juneau	Mauston	23,991	21,650	768
Kenosha	Kenosha	142,872	128,181	273
Kewaunee	Kewaunee	19,678	18,878	343
La Crosse	La Crosse	102,279	97,904	453
Lafayette	Darlington	16,374	16,074	634
Langlade	Antigo	20,563	19,505	873
Lincoln	Merrill	29,633	26,993	883
Manitowoc	Manitowoc	82,221	80,421	592
Marathon	Wausau	122,450	115,400	1,545
Marinette	Marinette	43,017	40,548	1,402
Marquette	Montello	14,805	12,321	456
Menominee	Keshena	4,774	3,890	358
Milwaukee	Milwaukee	908,940	959,275	242
Monroe	Sparta	39,355	36,633	901
Oconto	Oconto	33,384	30,226	998
Oneida	Rhinelander	35,697	31,679	1,125
Outagamie	Appleton	154,175	140,510	640
Ozaukee	Port Washington	80,737	72,831	232
Pepin	Durand	7,191	7,107	232
Pierce	Ellsworth	35,194	32,765	577
Polk	Balsam Lake	38,276	34,773	917
Portage	Stevens Point	64,748	61,405	806
Price	Phillips	15,721	15,600	1,253
Racine	Racine	185,393	175,034	333
Richland	Richland Center	17,920	17,521	586
Rock	Janesville	150,332	139,510	721
Rusk	Ladysmith	15,313	15,079	913
Saint Croix	Hudson	57,310	50,251	722
Sauk	Baraboo	52,987	46,975	838
Sawyer	Hayward	15,984	14,181	1,257
Shawano	Shawano	38,495	37,157	893
Sheboygan	Sheboygan	109,896	103,877	514
Taylor	Medford	19,268	18,901	975

County	County seat or courthouse	1997 Pop.	1990 Pop.	Land area sq mi
Trempealeau	Whitehall	26,354	25,263	734
Vernon	Viroqua	27,178	25,617	795
Vilas	Eagle River	21,117	17,707	873
Walworth	Elkhorn	84,404	75,000	555
Washburn	Shell Lake	15,295	13,772	810
Washington	West Bend	112,694	95,328	431
Waukesha	Waukesha	348,808	304,715	556
Waupaca	Waupaca	50,041	46,104	751
Waushara	Wautoma	21,507	19,385	626
Winnebago	Oshkosh	149,934	140,320	439
Wood	Wisconsin Rapids	75,779	73,605	793

Wyoming

(23 counties, 97,105 sq mi land; pop. 479,743)

County	County seat or courthouse	1997 Pop.	1990 Pop.	Land area sq mi
Albany	Laramie	29,709	30,797	4,274
Big Horn	Basin	11,031	10,525	3,137
Campbell	Gillette	32,087	29,370	4,797
Carbon	Rawlins	15,845	16,659	7,897
Converse	Douglas	12,295	11,128	4,255
Crook	Sundance	5,794	5,294	2,859
Fremont	Lander	35,888	33,662	9,183
Goshen	Torrington	12,837	12,373	2,226
Hot Springs	Thermopolis	4,681	4,809	2,004
Johnson	Buffalo	6,786	6,145	4,166
Laramie	Cheyenne	78,473	73,142	2,686
Lincoln	Kemmerer	13,871	12,625	4,069
Natrona	Casper	63,638	61,226	5,340
Niobrara	Lusk	2,618	2,499	2,626
Park	Cody	25,671	23,178	6,943
Platte	Wheatland	8,540	8,145	2,085
Sheridan	Sheridan	25,199	23,562	2,523
Sublette	Pinedale	5,696	4,843	4,882
Sweetwater	Green River	39,738	38,823	10,426
Teton	Jackson	13,924	11,173	4,008
Unita	Evanston	20,287	18,705	2,082
Washakie	Worland	8,630	8,388	2,240
Weston	Newcastle	6,505	6,518	2,398

Population of Outlying Areas

Source: Bureau of the Census, U.S. Dept. of Commerce; World Almanac research

Population estimates for July 1, 1996, are given for Puerto Rican municipios; all other population counts and all land area figures are from the U.S. census conducted on Apr. 1, 1990. Because only selected areas are shown, the population and land area figures may not equal the total reported. ZIP codes with an asterisk (*) are general delivery ZIP codes. Consult the local postmaster for more specific delivery information. Wake Atoll, Johnston Atoll, and Midway Atoll receive mail through APO and FPO addresses. U.S. outlying areas that are not listed in this table may not receive U.S. mail delivery.

Commonwealth of Puerto Rico

ZIP code	Municipio	1996 Pop.	Land area sq mi
00601	Adjuntas	19,592	67
00602	Aguada	37,651	31
*00605	Aguadilla	65,207	37
00703	Aguas Buenas	30,062	31
00705	Aibonito	27,863	31
00610	Añasco	27,007	39
*00613	Arecibo	100,755	126
00714	Arroyo	19,549	15
00617	Barceloneta	26,480	23
00794	Barranquitas	28,702	34
*00958	Bayamón	231,845	44
00623	Cabo Rojo	47,365	70
*00726	Caguas	140,114	59
00627	Camuy	32,438	46
00729	Canóvanas	50,666	33
*00984	Carolina	188,427	45
*00963	Cataño	32,391	5
*00737	Cayey	50,728	52
00735	Ceiba	17,715	29
00638	Ciales	19,447	67
00739	Cidra	49,326	36
00769	Coamo	35,673	78
00782	Comerío	20,914	28
00783	Corozal	36,304	43
00775	Culebra	1,632	12
00646	Dorado	32,166	23
00738	Fajardo	38,383	30
00650	Florida	8,434	10
00653	Guánica	21,596	37
*00785	Guayama	41,994	65
00656	Guayanilla	27,316	42
*00970	Guaynabo	104,927	27
00778	Gurabo	32,003	28
00659	Hatillo	40,149	42
00660	Hormigüeros	16,121	11
*00791	Humacao	57,643	45
00662	Isabela	41,156	55
00664	Jayuya	16,791	45
00795	Juana Díaz	49,693	60
00777	Juncos	41,424	27
00667	Lajas	26,704	60
00669	Lares	32,282	62
00670	Las Marías	9,923	46
00771	Las Piedras	30,111	34
00772	Loíza	27,904	19
00773	Luquillo	18,407	26
00674	Manatí	38,781	45
00606	Maricao	5,979	37
00707	Maunabo	13,503	21
*00681	Mayagüez	100,937	78
00676	Moca	37,154	50
00687	Morovis	33,388	39
00718	Naguabo	24,517	52
00719	Naranjito	29,016	27
00720	Orocovis	24,075	64
00723	Patillas	21,259	47
00624	Peñuelas	26,595	45
*00732	Ponce	189,988	116
00678	Quebradillas	26,008	23
00677	Rincón	13,589	14
00745	Río Grande	48,997	61
00637	Sabana Grande	23,244	36
00751	Salinas	29,962	69
00683	San Germán	36,925	55
*00902	San Juan	433,705	48
00754	San Lorenzo	36,435	53
00685	San Sebastián	42,573	70
00757	Santa Isabel	19,546	34
*00954	Toa Alta	58,240	27
*00950	Toa Baja	92,702	23
*00976	Trujillo Alto	74,644	21
00641	Utuado	35,212	114
00692	Vega Alta	35,828	28
*00694	Vega Baja	61,401	46
00765	Vieques	9,503	51
00766	Villalba	22,695	36
00767	Yabucoa	40,602	55
00698	Yauco	42,879	68
Total		**3,782,862**	**3,427**

Commonwealth of the Northern Mariana Islands

ZIP code	Municipality	1990 Pop.	Land area sq mi
96950	Northern Islands	36	60
96951	Rota	2,295	33
96950	Saipan	38,896	47
96952	Tinian	2,118	39
Total		**43,345**	**179**

Other U.S. External Territories

American Samoa

ZIP code	Location	1990 Pop.	Land area sq mi
96799	American Samoa	46,773	77

Guam

ZIP code	Location	1990 Pop.	Land area sq mi
*96913	Agaña	1,139	1
96919	Agaña Hts.	3,646	1
96928	Agat	4,960	10
96922	Asan	2,070	6
*96913	Barrigada	8,846	9
96924	Chalan-Pago-Ordot	4,451	6
96912	Dededo	31,728	30
96917	Inarajan	2,469	19
96923	Mangilao	10,483	10
96916	Merizo	1,742	6
96927	Mongmong-Toto-Maite	5,845	2
96925	Piti	1,827	7
96915	Santa Rita	11,857	17
96926	Sinajana	2,658	1
96930	Talofofo	2,310	17
*96913	Tamuning	16,673	6
96918	Umatac	897	6
96929	Yigo	14,213	35
96914	Yona	5,338	20
Total		**133,152**	**210**

Virgin Islands

ZIP code	Location	1990 Pop.	Land area sq mi
00820	Saint Croix	50,139	83
*00820	Christiansted	2,555	
*00841	Frederiksted	1,064	
*00830	Saint John	3,504	20
*00801	Saint Thomas	48,166	31
00801	Charlotte Amalie	12,331	
Total		**101,809**	**134**

CITIES OF THE U.S.

Sources: Bureau of the Census: population, with rank in parentheses, estimated as of July 1996, and population growth. Bureau of Labor Statistics: employment (1997). Bureau of Economic Analysis: per capita personal income (1996).

Included here are the 100 most populous cities, based on July 1996 Census Bureau estimates (inc.=incorporated; est.=established). Most data are for the city proper. Some statistics, where noted, apply to the whole MSA (Metropolitan Statistical Area).
Note: Websites are as of Aug. 1998 and subject to change. Official sites are listed first, where available.

Akron, Ohio

Population: 216,882 (74); **Pop. density:** 3,487 per sq. mi; **Pop. growth (1990-96):** –2.8%. **Area:** 62.2 sq. mi. **Employment:** 106,582 employed, 6.2% unemployed. **Per capita income (MSA):** $24,371; % increase, 1990-96: 32.7.

History: settled 1825; inc. as city 1865; located on Ohio-Erie Canal and is a port of entry; since 1870, rubber capital of U.S.

Transportation: 1 airport; major trucking industry; Conrail; metro transit system. **Communications:** 7 radio stations. **Medical facilities:** 4 hosp.; specialized children's treatment center. **Educational facilities:** 4 univ. and colleges; 68 pub. schools. **Further information:** Akron Regional Development Board, Cascade Plaza, Akron, OH 44308.

Websites: http://www.ci.akron.oh.us
http://www.ardb.org

Albuquerque, New Mexico

Population: 419,681 (37); **Pop. density:** 3,175 per sq. mi; **Pop. growth (1990-96):** 9.0%. **Area:** 132.2 sq. mi. **Employment:** 228,743 employed, 4.1% unemployed. **Per capita income (MSA):** $22,353; % increase, 1990-96: 33.9.

History: founded 1706 by the Spanish; inc. 1890.

Transportation: 1 intl. airport; 1 railroad; 1 bus line. **Communications:** 8 TV, 38 radio stations. **Medical facilities:** 6 major hosp. **Educational facilities:** 1 univ., 13 colleges. **Further information:** Convention & Visitors Bureau, PO Box 26866, Albuquerque, NM 87125-6866.

Websites: http://www.abqcvb.org
http://www.cabq.org

Anaheim, California

Population: 288,945 (57); **Pop. density:** 6,522 per sq. mi; **Pop. growth (1990-96):** 8.5%. **Area:** 44.3 sq. mi. **Employment:** 146,527 employed, 3.8% unemployed. **Per capita income (MSA):** $28,936; % increase, 1990-96: 13.5.

History: founded 1857; inc. 1870; now known as home of Disneyland and the Mighty Ducks of Anaheim.

Transportation: access to 3 municipal airports; 4 railroads; Greyhound buses (MSA). **Communications:** 12 TV, 4 radio stations (MSA). **Medical facilities:** 5 hosp.; 4 medical centers (MSA). **Educational facilities:** 13 univ. and colleges; 47 elem., 10 junior high, 11 high schools (MSA). **Further information:** Chamber of Commerce, 100 South Anaheim Blvd., Ste. 300, Anaheim, CA 92805.

Website: http://www.anaheim.net

Anchorage, Alaska

Population: 250,505 (66); **Pop. density:** 148 per sq. mi; **Pop. growth (1990-96):** 10.7%. **Area:** 1,697.6 sq. mi. **Employment:** 130,381 employed, 5.8% unemployed. **Per capita income (MSA):** $28,908; % increase, 1990-96: 17.7.

History: founded 1914 as a construction camp for railroad; HQ of Alaska Defense Command, WWII; severely damaged in earthquake 1964, but now rebuilt and currently population center of Alaska.

Transportation: 1 intl. airport; 1 railroad; transit system. **Communications:** 9 TV, 22 radio stations. **Medical facilities:** 4 hosp. **Educational facilities:** 5 univ., 3 colleges. **Further information:** Chamber of Commerce, 441 W. 5th Ave., Ste. 300, Anchorage, AK 99501-2309.

Websites: http://www.ci.anchorage.ak.us
http://www.anchoragechamber.org

Arlington, Texas

Population: 294,816 (56); **Pop. density:** 3,170 per sq. mi; **Pop. growth (1990-96):** 12.6%. **Area:** 93 sq. mi. **Employment:** 173,409 employed, 3.2% unemployed. **Per capita income (MSA):** $23,690; % increase, 1990-96: 25.2.

History: settled in 1840s between Dallas and Ft. Worth; inc. 1884.

Transportation: Dallas/Ft. Worth airport is 20 min. away; 11 railway lines; intercity transport system in planning stage. **Communications:** 11 TV, 44 radio stations. **Medical facilities:** 2 hosp. **Educational facilities:** 1 univ., 1 junior college; 54 pub. schools. **Further information:** The Arlington Chamber, 316 W. Main St., Arlington, TX 76010.

Websites: http://www.ci.arlington.tx.us
http://www.chamber.arlingtontx.com

Atlanta, Georgia

Population: 401,907 (38); **Pop. density:** 3,049 per sq. mi; **Pop. growth (1990-96):** 2.0%. **Area:** 131.8 sq. mi. **Employment:** 205,062 employed, 6.2% unemployed. **Per capita income (MSA):** $27,241; % increase, 1990-96: 30.9.

History: founded as "Terminus" 1837; renamed Atlanta 1845; inc. 1847; played major role in Civil War; became permanent state capital 1877; birthplace of civil rights movement; host to 1996 Centennial Olympic Games.

Transportation: 1 intl. airport; 3 railroad lines; MARTA bus and rapid rail service. **Communications:** 11 TV, 49 radio stations; 26 cable TV cos. **Medical facilities:** 61 hosp.; VA hosp.; U.S. Centers for Disease Control and Prevention; American Cancer Society. **Educational facilities:** 40+ colleges, univ., seminaries, junior colleges. **Further information:** Metro Atlanta Chamber of Commerce, 235 Intl. Blvd. NW, Atlanta, GA 30303.

Websites: http://www.atlanta.org
http://www.metroatlantachamber.com

Aurora, Colorado

Population: 252,341 (65); **Pop. density:** 1,904 per sq. mi; **Pop. growth (1990-96):** 13.6%. **Area:** 132.5 sq. mi. **Employment:** 149,208 employed, 2.6% unemployed. **Per capita income (MSA):** $29,234; % increase, 1990-96: 34.8.

History: located 5 mi east of Denver; early growth stimulated by presence of military bases; fast-growing trade center.

Transportation: adjacent to new Denver Intl. Airport; 1 airport; 4 railroads; bus system. **Communications:** 1 TV station. **Medical facilities:** 2 private hosp.; 1 pub. hosp. **Educational facilities:** 1 univ., 1 community college, 2 technical colleges. **Further information:** Aurora Planning Dept., 1470 S. Havana St., Rm. 608, Aurora, CO 80012.

Websites: http://www.ci.aurora.co.us
http://www.mktplace.net/aurora/chamber

Austin, Texas

Population: 541,278 (22); **Pop. density:** 2,485 per sq. mi; **Pop. growth (1990-96):** 14.7%. **Area:** 217.8 sq. mi. **Employment:** 343,885 employed, 3.4% unemployed. **Per capita income (MSA):** $23,669; % increase, 1990-96: 34.6.

History: first permanent settlement 1835; capital of Rep. of Texas 1838; named after Stephen Austin; inc. 1840.

Transportation: 1 intl. airport; 4 railroads. **Communications:** 7 TV, 20 radio stations. **Medical facilities:** 11 hosp. **Educational facilities:** 8 univ. and colleges. **Further information:** Chamber of Commerce, PO Box 1967, Austin, TX 78767.

Websites: http://www.ci.austin.tx.us
http://www.austin-chamber.org

Bakersfield, California

Population: 205,508 (77); **Pop. density:** 2,239 per sq. mi; **Pop. growth (1990-96):** 16.6%. **Area:** 91.8 sq. mi. **Employment:** 90,079 employed, 8.9% unemployed. **Per capita income (MSA):** $17,810; % increase, 1990-96: 11.1.

History: named after Col. Thomas Baker, an early settler; inc. 1898.

Transportation: 1 airport; 3 railroads; Amtrak; Greyhound buses; local bus system. **Communications:** 5 TV, 34 radio stations. **Medical facilities:** 6 major hosp.; 9 convalescent, 1 psychiatric, 3 physical rehab., 5 urgent care facilities; 3 clinics. **Educational facilities:** 1 univ., 1 community college, 9 vocational schools, 1 adult school, 1 college of law. **Further information:** Greater Bakersfield Chamber of Commerce, 1033 Truxtun Ave., PO Box 1947, Bakersfield, CA 93303.

Website: http://www.bakersfield.org/chamber

Baltimore, Maryland

Population: 675,401 (15); **Pop. density:** 8,359 per sq. mi; **Pop. growth (1990-96):** –8.2%. **Area:** 80.8 sq. mi. **Employment:** 288,017 employed, 9.3% unemployed. **Per capita income (MSA):** $26,731; % increase, 1990-96: 24.0.

History: founded by Maryland legislature 1729; inc. 1797; bombing of Ft. McHenry (1814) inspired Francis Scott Key to

write "Star-Spangled Banner"; birthplace of America's railroads 1828; rebuilt after fire 1904; site of National Aquarium 1981.
Transportation: 1 major airport; 3 railroads; bus system; subway system; light rail system; Inner Harbor water taxi system; 2 underwater tunnels. **Communications:** 5 TV, 33 radio stations. **Medical facilities:** 29 hosp.; 2 major medical centers. **Educational facilities:** over 30 univ. and colleges; 183 pub. schools. **Further information:** Greater Baltimore Committee, 111 S. Calvert St., Ste. 1700, Baltimore, MD 21202-6180.
Websites: http://www.ci.baltimore.md.us
http://www.gbc.org

Baton Rouge, Louisiana

Population: 215,882 (75); **Pop. density:** 2,921 per sq. mi; **Pop. growth (1990-96):** –1.7%. **Area:** 73.9 sq. mi. **Employment:** 109,451 employed, 5.8% unemployed. **Per capita income (MSA):** $21,910; % increase, 1990-96: 32.2.
History: claimed by Spain at time of Louisiana Purchase 1803; est. independence by rebellion 1810; inc. as town 1817; became state capital 1849; Union-held most of Civil War.
Transportation: 1 airport, 5 airlines; 1 bus line; 3 railroad trunk lines. **Communications:** 5 TV, 19 radio stations. **Medical facilities:** 5 hosp. **Educational facilities:** 2 univ.; 92 pub., 39 private schools. **Further information:** Chamber of Commerce, PO Box 3217, Baton Rouge, LA 70821.
Websites: http://www.intersurf.com/~aevinc/aev2gbr.htm
http://www.brchamber.org

Birmingham, Alabama

Population: 258,543 (63); **Pop. density:** 1,741 per sq. mi; **Pop. growth (1990-96):** –2.6%. **Area:** 148.5 sq. mi. **Employment:** 125,805 employed, 5.3% unemployed. **Per capita income (MSA):** $24,227; % increase, 1990-96: 33.8.
History: settled as a result of discovery of elements needed for steel production; inc. 1871; named after Great Britain's steel-making center.
Transportation: 1 airport; 4 major rail freight lines, Amtrak; 1 bus line; 75 truck line terminals; 5 air cargo cos.; 7 barge lines; 4 interstate highways. **Communications:** 7 TV, 30 radio stations; 1 educational TV, 1 educational radio station. **Medical facilities:** Univ. of Alabama at Birmingham Medical Center; VA hosp. with organ transplant program; 15 other hosp. **Educational facilities:** 1 univ., 2 colleges, 2 junior colleges. **Further information:** Chamber of Commerce, 2027 First Ave. N, Birmingham, AL 35202.
Websites: http://www.birmingham.org/thechamber
http://www2.bham.net/bhamcity.html

Boston, Massachusetts

Population: 558,394 (20); **Pop. density:** 11,537 per sq. mi; **Pop. growth (1990-96):** –2.8%. **Area:** 48.4 sq. mi. **Employment:** 285,485 employed, 4.2% unemployed. **Per capita income (MSA):** $30,366; % increase, 1990-96: 28.9.
History: settled 1630 by John Winthrop; capital of Mass. Bay Colony; figured strongly in Am. Revolution, earning distinction as the "Cradle of Liberty"; inc. 1822.
Transportation: 1 major airport; 2 railroads; city rail and subway system; 3 underwater tunnels; port. **Communications:** 9 TV, 21 radio stations. **Medical facilities:** 13 hosp.; 8 major medical research centers. **Educational facilities:** 30 univ. and colleges. **Further information:** Greater Boston Chamber of Commerce, 1 Beacon St., 4th fl., Boston, MA 02108-3114.
Websites: http://www.bostonusa.com
http://www.gbcc.org

Buffalo, New York

Population: 310,548 (54); **Pop. density:** 7,649 per sq. mi; **Pop. growth (1990-96):** –5.4%. **Area:** 40.6 sq. mi. **Employment:** 132,660 employed, 8.5% unemployed. **Per capita income (MSA):** $23,588; % increase, 1990-96: 27.0.
History: founded 1790 by the Dutch; raided twice by British, War of 1812; served as western terminus for Erie Canal, became a center for trade and manufacturing; inc. 1832; last stop on the Underground Railroad; key point for Canada-U.S. political, trade, and social relations.
Transportation: 1 intl. airport; 4 major railroads; metro rail system; water service to Great Lakes-St. Lawrence Seaway system and Atlantic seaboard. **Communications:** 8 TV, 18 radio stations. **Medical facilities:** 14 hosp., 37 research centers. **Educational facilities:** 12 colleges and univ.; 111 pub. and private schools. **Further information:** Buffalo Niagara Partnership, 300 Main Place Tower, Buffalo, NY 14202-3797.
Websites: http://www.ci.buffalo.ny.us
http://www.gbpartnership.org

Charlotte, North Carolina

Population: 441,297 (32); **Pop. density:** 2,532 per sq. mi; **Pop. growth (1990-96):** 5.2%. **Area:** 174.3 sq. mi. **Employment:** 262,788 employed, 2.9% unemployed. **Per capita income (MSA):** $25,446; % increase, 1990-96: 33.1.
History: settled by Scotch-Irish immigrants 1740s; inc. 1768 and named after Queen Charlotte, George III's wife; scene of first major U.S. gold discovery 1799.
Transportation: 1 airport; 2 major railway lines; 2 bus lines; 238 trucking firms. **Communications:** 7 TV, 26 radio stations. **Medical facilities:** 12 hosp., 1 medical center. **Educational facilities:** 3 univ., 5 colleges. **Further information:** Chamber of Commerce, PO Box 32785, Charlotte, NC 28232.
Websites: http://www.charlottechamber.org
http://www.charweb.org

Chesapeake, Virginia

Population: 192,342 (87); **Pop. density:** 565 per sq. mi; **Pop. growth (1990-96):** 26.6%. **Area:** 340.7 sq. mi. **Employment:** 95,706 employed, 4.0% unemployed. **Per capita income (MSA):** $21,311; % increase, 1990-96: 23.9.
History: Battle of Great Bridge fought here 1775; inc. as a city 1963.
Transportation: Amtrak; bus service; deepwater ports. **Communications:** 13 TV, 6 city-access TV, 27 radio stations. **Medical facilities:** 1 hosp. **Educational facilities:** 1 college; 41 pub. schools. **Further information:** Chesapeake Chamber of Commerce, 400 Volvo Pky., Chesapeake, VA 23327.
Website: http://www.chesapeake.va.us

Chicago, Illinois

Population: 2,721,547 (3); **Pop. density:** 11,979 per sq. mi; **Pop. growth (1990-96):** –2.2%. **Area:** 227.2 sq. mi. **Employment:** 1,215,134 employed, 6.0% unemployed. **Per capita income (MSA):** $29,940; % increase, 1990-96: 32.4.
History: site acquired from Indians 1795; significant white settlement began with opening of Erie Canal 1825; chartered as city 1837; boomed with arrival of railroads from east and canal to Mississippi R.; about one-third of city destroyed by fire 1871; major grain & livestock market.
Transportation: 3 airports; major railroad system, trucking industry. **Communications:** 9 TV, 31 radio stations. **Medical facilities:** over 123 hosp. **Educational facilities:** 95 insts. of higher learning. **Further information:** Chicagoland Chamber of Commerce, 1 IBM Plaza, Ste. 2800, Chicago, IL 60611.
Websites: http://www.ci.chi.il.us
http://www.chicagolandchamber.org

Cincinnati, Ohio

Population: 345,818 (49); **Pop. density:** 4,480 per sq. mi; **Pop. growth (1990-96):** -5.0%. **Area:** 77.2 sq. mi. **Employment:** 167,254 employed, 5.1% unemployed. **Per capita income (MSA):** $25,359; % increase, 1990-96: 29.2.
History: founded 1788 and named after the Society of Cincinnati, an organization of Revolutionary War officers; chartered as village 1802; inc. as city 1819.
Transportation: 1 intl. airport; 3 railroads; 1 bus system. **Communications:** 9 TV, 27 radio stations. **Medical facilities:** 32 hosp.; Children's Hosp. Medical Center; VA hosp. **Educational facilities:** 4 univ.; 11 colleges, 8 technical & 2-year colleges. **Further information:** Chamber of Commerce, 300 Carew Tower, 441 Vine St., Cincinnati, OH 45202.
Websites: http://www.gccc.com
http://www.cincinnatigov.com

Cleveland, Ohio

Population: 498,246 (25); **Pop. density:** 6,471 per sq. mi; **Pop. growth (1990-96):** –1.5%. **Area:** 77 sq. mi. **Employment:** 188,696 employed, 9.2% unemployed. **Per capita income (MSA):** $26,529; % increase, 1990-96: 27.8.
History: surveyed in 1796; given recognition as village 1815, inc. as city 1836; annexed Ohio City 1854.
Transportation: 1 intl. airport; rail service; major port; rapid transit system. **Communications:** 9 TV, 21 radio stations. **Medical facilities:** 14 hosp. **Educational facilities:** 8 univ. and colleges; 127 pub. schools. **Further information:** Greater Cleveland Growth Assn., 200 Tower City Center, 50 Pub. Square, Cleveland, OH 44113-2291.
Websites: http://www.cleveland.oh.us
http://www.clevelandgrowth.com

Colorado Springs, Colorado

Population: 345,127 (50); **Pop. density:** 1,884 per sq. mi; **Pop. growth (1990-96):** 23.1%. **Area:** 183.2 sq. mi. **Employment:** 175,268 employed, 3.7% unemployed. **Per capita income (MSA):** $22,320; % increase, 1990-96: 30.9.

History: city founded in 1871 at the foot of Pike's Peak; inc. 1872.

Transportation: 1 municipal airport; 2 railroads; bus line. **Communications:** 9 TV, 28 radio stations. **Medical facilities:** 7 hosp. **Educational facilities:** 11 univ., 12 colleges. **Further information:** Chamber of Commerce, PO Box B, Colorado Springs, CO 80901.

Websites: http://www.coloradosprings-travel.com/ cscvb
http://www.cscc.org

Columbus, Georgia

Population: 182,828 (99); **Pop. density:** 846 per sq. mi; **Pop. growth (1990-96):** 2.3%. **Area:** 216.1 sq. mi. **Employment:** 78,993 employed, 5.2% unemployed. **Per capita income (MSA):** $19,890; % increase, 1990-96: 34.0.

History: settled, inc. 1828; port city on Chattahoochee R.

Transportation: 1 major airport; Metra bus system; bus line; 2 railroads. **Communications:** 5 TV, 13 radio stations. **Medical facilities:** 5 hosp. **Educational facilities:** 4 colleges; 50 pub. schools; 1 technical, 13 private schools. **Further information:** Chamber of Commerce, PO Box 1200, Columbus, GA 31902.

Website: http://www.columbusga.com

Columbus, Ohio

Population: 657,053 (16); **Pop. density:** 3,442 per sq. mi; **Pop. growth (1990-96):** 3.8%. **Area:** 190.9 sq. mi. **Employment:** 369,904 employed, 3.1% unemployed. **Per capita income (MSA):** $24,863; % increase, 1990-96: 31.6.

History: first settlement 1797; laid out as new capital 1812 with current name; became city 1834.

Transportation: 6 airports; 3 railroads; 4 intercity bus lines. **Communications:** 8 TV, 25 radio stations. **Medical facilities:** 18 hosp. **Educational facilities:** 11 univ. and colleges; 8 technical/2-year schools. **Further information:** Chamber of Commerce, 37 N. High St., Columbus, OH 43215.

Website: http://www.columbus.org

Corpus Christi, Texas

Population: 280,260 (59); **Pop. density:** 2,076 per sq. mi; **Pop. growth (1990-96):** 8.9%. **Area:** 135 sq. mi. **Employment:** 122,931 employed, 7.7% unemployed. **Per capita income (MSA):** $19,034; % increase, 1990-96: 27.7.

History: settled 1839 and inc. 1852.

Transportation: 1 intl. airport; 2 bus lines, metro bus system; 3 freight railroads. **Communications:** 6 TV, 17 radio stations. **Medical facilities:** 14 hosp. including a children's center. **Educational facilities:** 1 univ., 1 college. **Further information:** Greater Corpus Christi Business Alliance, PO Box 640, Corpus Christi, TX 78403.

Website: http://www.cctexas.org

Dallas, Texas

Population: 1,053,292 (9); **Pop. density:** 3,076 per sq. mi; **Pop. growth (1990-96):** 4.5%. **Area:** 342.4 sq. mi. **Employment:** 617,054 employed, 4.9% unemployed. **Per capita income (MSA):** $28,513; % increase, 1990-96: 32.2.

History: first settled 1841; platted 1846; inc. 1871; developed as the financial and commercial center of Southwest; headquarters for oil companies; major center for distribution and high-tech manufacturing.

Transportation: 1 intl. airport, 1 regional airport; Amtrak; transit system. **Communications:** 10 TV, 26 radio stations. **Medical facilities:** 15 general hosp.; major medical center. **Educational facilities:** 11 univ. and colleges, 3 community college campuses. **Further information:** Greater Dallas Chamber, Resource Center, 1201 Elm, Ste. 2000, Dallas, TX 75270.

Websites: http://www.dallaschamber.org
http://www.ci.dallas.tx.us

Denver, Colorado

Population: 497,840 (26); **Pop. density:** 3,248 per sq. mi; **Pop. growth (1990-96):** 6.5%. **Area:** 153.3 sq. mi. **Employment:** 268,102 employed, 3.8% unemployed. **Per capita income (MSA):** $29,234; % increase, 1990-96: 34.8.

History: settled 1858 by gold prospectors and miners; inc. 1861; became territorial capital 1867; growth spurred by gold and silver boom; financial, industrial, cultural center of Rocky Mt. region.

Transportation: 1 intl. airport, 3 corporate reliever airports; 5 rail freight lines, Amtrak; 1 bus line. **Communications:** 14 TV, 29 radio stations. **Medical facilities:** 20 hosp. **Educational facilities:** 15 four-yr. colleges and univ.; 8 two-yr. and community colleges. **Further information:** Denver Metro Chamber of Commerce, 1445 Market St., Denver, CO 80202-1729.

Website: http://www.den-chamber.org

Des Moines, Iowa

Population: 193,422 (85); **Pop. density:** 2,569 per sq. mi; **Pop. growth (1990-96):** 0.1%. **Area:** 75.3 sq. mi. **Employment:** 115,974 employed, 3.4% unemployed. **Per capita income (MSA):** $26,557; % increase, 1990-96: 31.8.

History: Fort Des Moines built 1843; settled and inc. 1851; chartered as city 1857.

Transportation: 1 intl. airport; 4 bus lines; 4 railroads; metro bus system. **Communications:** 5 TV, 17 radio stations. **Medical facilities:** 8 hosp. **Educational facilities:** 2 univ., 5 colleges. **Further information:** Greater Des Moines Chamber of Commerce Federation, 601 Locust St., Ste. 100, Des Moines, IA 50309.

Websites: http://www.dmchamber.com
http://www.ci.des-moines.ia.us

Detroit, Michigan

Population: 1,000,272 (10); **Pop. density:** 7,212 per sq. mi; **Pop. growth (1990-96):** –2.7%. **Area:** 138.7 sq. mi. **Employment:** 362,939 employed, 7.9% unemployed. **Per capita income (MSA):** $27,250; % increase, 1990-96: 29.4.

History: founded by French 1701; controlled by British 1760; acquired by U.S. 1796; destroyed by fire 1805; inc. as city 1824; capital of state 1837-47; auto manufacturing began 1899.

Transportation: 1 intl. airport; 10 railroads; major intl. port; pub. transit system. **Communications:** 9 TV, 37 radio stations. **Medical facilities:** 28 hosp.; major medical center. **Educational facilities:** 18 univ. and colleges. **Further information:** Detroit Regional Chamber, One Hoodward Ave., PO Box 33840, Detroit, MI 48232-0840.

Websites: http://www.detroitchamber.com
http://detroit.freenet.org

El Paso, Texas

Population: 599,865 (17); **Pop. density:** 2,444 per sq. mi; **Pop. growth (1990-96):** 16.4%. **Area:** 245.4 sq. mi. **Employment:** 233,028 employed, 10.7% unemployed. **Per capita income (MSA):** $14,480; % increase, 1990-96: 22.1.

History: first settled 1827; inc. 1873; arrival of railroad 1881 boosted city's population and industries.

Transportation: 1 intl. airport; 3 rail providers; 2 interstate highways; 4 intl. ports of entry. **Communications:** 12 TV, 20 radio stations. **Medical facilities:** 6 hosp.; 3 rehabilitation, 11 specialty centers. **Educational facilities:** 1 univ., 3 colleges (1 grad. only). **Further information:** Greater El Paso Chamber of Commerce, 10 Civic Center Plaza, El Paso, TX 79901.

Website: http://www.elpaso.org

Fort Wayne, Indiana

Population: 184,783 (96); **Pop. density:** 2,947 per sq. mi; **Pop. growth (1990-96):** –3.7%. **Area:** 62.7 sq. mi. **Employment:** 95,304 employed, 3.6% unemployed. **Per capita income (MSA):** $24,281; % increase, 1990-96: 31.9.

History: French fort 1680; U.S. fort 1794; settled by 1832; inc. 1840 prior to Wabash-Erie canal completion 1843.

Transportation: 2 airports; 3 railroads; 6 bus lines. **Communications:** 5 TV, 13 radio stations. **Medical facilities:** 3 regional hosp.; VA hosp. **Educational facilities:** 5 univ., 4 colleges, 2 bus. schools; 80 pub. schools. **Further information:** Chamber of Commerce, 826 Ewing Street, Fort Wayne, IN 46802-2182.

Websites: http://www.ft-wayne.in.us
http://www.fwchamber.org

Fort Worth, Texas

Population: 479,716 (28); **Pop. density:** 1,707 per sq. mi; **Pop. growth (1990-96):** 7.2%. **Area:** 281.1 sq. mi. **Employment:** 245,273 employed, 4.8% unemployed. **Per capita income (MSA):** $23,690; % increase, 1990-96: 25.2.

History: est. as military post 1849; inc. 1873; oil discovered 1917.

Transportation: 1 intl. airport; 9 major railroads, Amtrak; local bus service; 2 transcontinental, 2 intrastate bus lines. **Communications:** 14 TV, 11 local radio stations. **Medical facilities:** 25 hosp.; 1 children's hosp.; 4 government hosp. **Educational facilities:** 8 univ. and colleges. **Further information:** Chamber of Commerce, 777 Taylor St. #900, Fort Worth, TX 76102.

Website: http://www.fortworth.acn.net

Fremont, California

Population: 187,800 (94); **Pop. density:** 2,439 per sq. mi; **Pop. growth (1990-96):** 8.3%. **Area:** 77 sq. mi. **Employment:** 101,769 employed, 3.0% unemployed. **Per capita income (MSA):** $29,842; % increase, 1990-96: 25.5.

History: area first settled by Spanish 1769; inc. 1956 with consolidation of 5 communities.

Transportation: intracity bus line; Bay Area Rapid Transit System (southern terminal). **Communications:** 1 radio station. **Medical facilities:** 2 hosp. **Educational facilities:** 1 junior college; 43 pub. schools. **Further information:** Chamber of Commerce, 39488 Stevenson Place #100, Fremont, CA 94539.

Website: http://www.fremontbusiness.com

Fresno, California

Population: 396,011 (39); **Pop. density:** 3,996 per sq. mi; **Pop. growth (1990-96):** 11.9%. **Area:** 99.1 sq. mi. **Employment:** 169,365 employed, 11.9% unemployed. **Per capita income (MSA):** $18,727; % increase, 1990-96: 14.5.

History: founded 1872; inc. as city 1885.

Transportation: municipal airport; Amtrak; 1 bus line; intracity bus system. **Communications:** 13 TV, 23 radio stations. **Medical facilities:** 17 general hosp. **Educational facilities:** 9 colleges; 102 pub. schools. **Further information:** Chamber of Commerce, 2331 Fresno St., Fresno, CA 93721.

Websites: http://fresno-online.com/cvb
http://www.fresnochamber.com

Garland, Texas

Population: 190,055 (92); **Pop. density:** 3,317 per sq. mi; **Pop. growth (1990-96):** 5.2%. **Area:** 57.3 sq. mi. **Employment:** 116,872 employed, 3.2% unemployed. **Per capita income (MSA):** $28,513; % increase, 1990-96: 32.2.

History: settled 1850s; inc. 1891.

Transportation: 30 min. from Dallas/Ft. Worth Intl. Airport; 2 railroads. **Communications:** 14 local TV (Dallas/Ft. Worth), 25+ radio stations. **Medical facilities:** 2 hosp.; 329 beds. **Educational facilities:** 1 univ., 2 community colleges; 59 pub. schools. **Further information:** Chamber of Commerce, 914 S. Garland Ave., Garland, TX 75040.

Websites: http://www.ci.garland.tx.us
http://www.garlandtx.com

Glendale, Arizona

Population: 182,219 (100); **Pop. density:** 1,455 per sq. mi; **Pop. growth (1990-96):** 23.2%. **Area:** 56.5 sq. mi. **Employment:** 97,247 employed, 3.0% unemployed. **Per capita income (MSA):** $23,377; % increase, 1990-96: 27.7.

History: est. 1892; inc. 1910.

Transportation: 1 local airport, 30 min. from Phoenix Sky Harbor Intl. Airport. **Communications:** 12 TV stations, 40 radio stations. **Medical facilities:** 3 hosp. **Educational facilities:** 12 institutes of higher education, 9 pub. school districts. **Further information:** Chamber of Commerce, PO Box 249, 7105 N. 59th Ave., Glendale, AZ 85311.

Glendale, California

Population: 184,321 (97); **Pop. density:** 6,043 per sq. mi; **Pop. growth (1990-96):** 2.4%. **Area:** 30.5 sq. mi. **Employment:** 86,809 employed, 6.4% unemployed. **Per capita income (MSA):** $24,945; % increase, 1990-96: 15.7.

History: Became a town in 1887; inc. 1906.

Transportation: near Los Angeles Intl. airport; commuter trains, Amtrak; bus system. **Communications:** 21 TV, 70 radio stations. **Medical facilities:** 3 hosp; other facilities. **Educational facilities:** 1 community college; 27 pub. schools. **Further information:** City of Glendale Public Information Officer, 613 E. Broadway, Glendale, CA 91206.

Website: http://www.ci.glendale.ca.usa

Grand Rapids, Michigan

Population: 188,242 (93); **Pop. density:** 4,249 per sq. mi; **Pop. growth (1990-96):** –0.5%. **Area:** 44.3 sq. mi. **Employment:** 106,130 employed, 4.5% unemployed. **Per capita income (MSA):** $24,139; % increase, 1990-96: 35.2.

History: originally site of Ottawa Indian village; trading post 1826; became lumbering center and incorporated city 1850.

Transportation: 1 intl. airport; 3 rail carriers; Amtrak, 5 bus lines; transit bus system. **Communications:** 7 TV, 34 radio stations. **Medical facilities:** 9 hosp. **Educational facilities:** 15 colleges; 19 pub. schools, 9 charter schools. **Further information:** Chamber of Commerce, 111 Pearl St., NW, Grand Rapids, MI 49503.

Websites: http://www.grcvb.org
http://grand-rapids.mi.us

Greensboro, North Carolina

Population: 195,426 (83); **Pop. density:** 2,449 per sq. mi; **Pop. growth (1990-96):** 6.3%. **Area:** 79.8 sq. mi. **Employment:** 112,085 employed, 3.1% unemployed. **Per capita income (MSA):** $24,597; % increase, 1990-96: 29.6.

History: settled 1749; site of Revolutionary War conflict 1781 between Nathanael Greene and Cornwallis; inc. 1807.

Transportation: 1 regional airport; 2 railroads; Trailways/Greyhound bus service. **Communications:** all cable TV stations; 11 radio stations. **Medical facilities:** 4 hosp. **Educational facilities:** 2 univ., 3 colleges; 94 pub. schools. **Further information:** Chamber of Commerce, PO Box 3246, Greensboro, NC 27402.

Websites: http://www.ci.greensboro.nc.us
http://www.greensboro.org

Hialeah, Florida

Population: 204,684 (78); **Pop. density:** 9,304 per sq. mi; **Pop. growth (1990-96):** 8.9%. **Area:** 22 sq. mi. **Employment:** 96,247 employed, 7.4% unemployed. **Per capita income (MSA):** $22,370; % increase, 1990-96: 24.8.

History: founded 1917, inc. 1925; industrial and residential city NW of Miami; Hialeah Park Horse Racing Track.

Transportation: 5 mi from Miami Intl. Airport; access to Port of Miami; Amtrak; 2 rail freight lines; Metrorail, Metrobus systems. **Communications:** 5 TV, 7 radio stations. **Medical facilities:** 4 hosp. (30 more in the area). **Educational facilities:** 8 univ. and colleges. **Further information:** Hialeah-Dade Development, Inc., 501 Palm Ave., Hialeah, FL 33010.

Honolulu, Hawai'i

Population: 423,475 (35); **Pop. density:** 5,114 per sq. mi; **Pop. growth (1990-96):** 12.3%. **Area:** 82.8 sq. mi. **Employment (MSA):** 403,419 employed, 5.3% unemployed. **Per capita income (MSA):** $27,040; % increase, 1990-96: 18.9.

History: harbor entered by Europeans 1778; declared capital of kingdom by King Kamehameha III 1850; Pearl Harbor naval base attacked by Japanese Dec. 7, 1941.

Transportation: 1 major airport; large, active port for passengers and cargo. **Communications:** 10 TV, 30 radio stations. **Medical facilities:** 13 major medical centers. **Educational facilities:** 4 univ., 5 colleges; 246 pub. schools, 98 private schools. **Further information:** Hawaii Visitors and Convention Bureau, 2270 Kalakaua Avenue, Honolulu, HI 96815.

Websites: http://www.co.honolulu.hi.us
http://www.gohawaii.com

Houston, Texas

Population: 1,744,058 (4); **Pop. density:** 3,230 per sq. mi; **Pop. growth (1990-96):** 6.5%. **Area:** 539.9 sq. mi. **Employment:** 930,594 employed, 6.2% unemployed. **Per capita income (MSA):** $27,195; % increase, 1990-96: 30.3.

History: founded 1836; inc. 1837; capital of Repub. of Texas 1837-39; developed rapidly after construction of channel to Gulf of Mexico 1914; world center of oil and natural gas technology.

Transportation: 3 commercial airports; 2 mainline railroads; major bus transit system; major intl. port. **Communications:** 15 TV, 54 radio stations. **Medical facilities:** 62 hosp.; major medical center. **Educational facilities:** 24 univ. and colleges. **Further information:** Greater Houston Partnership, 1200 Smith St., Houston, TX 77002-4309.

Websites: http://www.houston.org
http://www.ci.houston.tx.us

Huntington Beach, California

Population: 190,751 (90); **Pop. density:** 7,225 per sq. **Pop. growth (1990-96):** 5.1%. **Area:** 26.4 sq. mi. **Employment:** 111,918 employed, 2.5% unemployed. **Per capita income (MSA):** $28,936; % increase, 1990-96: 13.5.

History: settled in early 1880s; inc. 1909; oil discovered 1920, led to city's development.

Transportation: 1 railroad; 2 bus lines. **Communications:** 2 TV stations. **Medical facilities:** 2 hosp. **Educational facilities:** 1 community college; 34 pub. schools. **Further information:** Chamber of Commerce, Seacliff Office Park, 2100 Main St., #200, Huntington Beach, CA 92648.

Websites: http://www.thebeach.com/cities/hb
http://www.hbchamber.org

Indianapolis, Indiana

Population: 746,737 (12); **Pop. density:** 2,065 per sq. mi; **Pop. growth (1990-96):** 2.1%. **Area:** 361.7 sq. mi. **Employment:** 405,194 employed, 3.2% unemployed. **Per capita income (MSA):** $25,898; % increase, 1990-96: 31.6.

History: settled 1820; became capital 1825.

Transportation: 1 intl. airport; 5 railroads; 3 interstate bus lines. **Communications:** 10 TV, 27 radio stations. **Medical facilities:** 17 hosp.; 1 major medical and research center. **Educational facilities:** 8 univ. and colleges; major pub. library system. **Further information:** Chamber of Commerce, 320 N. Meridian St., Indianapolis, IN 46204.

Websites: http://www.ci.indianapolis.in.us;
http://www.indychamber.com

Jackson, Mississippi

Population: 192,923 (86); **Pop. density:** 1,770 per sq. mi; **Pop. growth (1990-96):** –4.5%. **Area:** 109 sq. mi. **Employment:** 96,207 employed, 4.4% unemployed. **Per capita income (MSA):** $21,592; % increase, 1990-96: 29.1.

History: originally known as Le Fleur's Bluff; selected as capital 1822 and named for Andrew Jackson; inc. 1823; scene of secession convention 1861; captured by Sherman 1863.

Transportation: 9 airlines; 1 bus line; 2 railroads; 5 freight carriers. **Communications:** 5 TV, 20 radio stations. **Medical facilities:** 9 hosp. incl. a VA facility. **Educational facilities:** 2 univ., 4 colleges; 1 pub. school district. **Further information:** Metro Jackson Chamber of Commerce, PO Box 22548, Jackson, MS 39225-2548.

Website: http://www.metrojackson.com

Jacksonville, Florida

Population: 679,792 (14); **Pop. density:** 896 per sq. mi; **Pop. growth (1990-96):** 7.0%. **Area:** 758.7 sq. mi. **Employment:** 366,576 employed, 3.7% unemployed. **Per capita income (MSA):** $23,679; % increase, 1990-96: 28.6.

History: settled 1816 as Cowford; renamed after Andrew Jackson 1822; inc. 1832; rechartered 1851; scene of conflicts in Seminole and Civil wars.

Transportation: 1 intl. airport; 3 railroads; 2 interstate bus lines. **Communications:** 6 TV, 34 radio stations. **Medical facilities:** 11 hosp. **Educational facilities:** 3 univ., 4 colleges. **Further information:** Chamber of Commerce, 3 Independent Drive, Jacksonville, FL 32202-5092.

Websites: http://www.jacksonvillechamber.org
http://www.ci.jax.fl.us

Jersey City, New Jersey

Population: 229,039 (72); **Pop. density:** 15,372 per sq. mi; **Pop. growth (1990-96):** 0.2%. **Area:** 14.9 sq. mi. **Employment:** 102,419 employed, 9.7% unemployed. **Per capita income (MSA):** $24,456; % increase, 1990-96: 23.5.

History: site bought from Indians 1630; chartered as town by British 1668; scene of Revolutionary War conflict 1779; chartered under present name 1838; important station on Underground Railroad.

Transportation: bus and subway system. **Communications:** see New York, NY. **Medical facilities:** 4 hosp. **Educational facilities:** 3 colleges. **Further information:** Hudson County Chamber of Commerce, 574 Summit Ave., Ste. 404, Jersey City, NJ 07306.

Website: http://www.jerseycitynet.com

Kansas City, Missouri

Population: 441,259 (33); **Pop. density:** 1,417 per sq. mi; **Pop. growth (1990-96):** 1.5%. **Area:** 311.5 sq. mi. **Employment:** 247,784 employed, 4.6% unemployed. **Per capita income (MSA):** $25,949; % increase, 1990-96: 32.4.

History: settled by 1838 at confluence of the Missouri and Kansas rivers; inc. 1851.

Transportation: 1 intl. airport; a major rail center; 191 trunk lines; several barge cos. **Communications:** 7 TV, 29 radio stations. **Medical facilities:** 14 hosp.; VA facility. **Educational facilities:** 9 univ. and colleges. **Further information:** Greater Kansas City Chamber of Commerce, 911 Main St., Ste. 2600, Kansas City, MO 64105.

Websites: http://www.kansascity.com
http://www.kcchamber.com
http://www.kcmo.org

Las Vegas, Nevada

Population: 376,906 (41); **Pop. density:** 4,525 per sq. mi; **Pop. growth (1990-96):** 46.0%. **Area:** 83.3 sq. mi. **Employment:** 201,073 employed, 4.0% unemployed. **Per capita income (MSA):** $24,706; % increase, 1990-96: 29.9.

History: occupied by Mormons 1855-57; bought by railroad 1903; city of Las Vegas inc. 1911; gambling legalized 1931.

Transportation: 1 intl. airport; 2 railroads; bus system. **Communications:** 7 TV, 28 radio stations. **Medical facilities:** 12 hosp. **Educational facilities:** 1 univ., 5 colleges; 205 pub. schools in area. **Further information:** Chamber of Commerce, 3720 Howard Hughes Parkway, Las Vegas, NV 89109.

Website: http://www.lvchamber.com

Lexington, Kentucky

Population: 239,942 (68); **Pop. density:** 843 per sq. mi; **Pop. growth (1990-96):** 6.5%. **Area:** 284.5 sq. mi. **Employment:** 136,684 employed, 2.5% unemployed. **Per capita income (MSA):** $23,929; % increase, 1990-96: 31.7.

History: site was founded and named 1775 by hunters who heard of the Revolutionary War battle at Lexington, Mass.; settled 1779; chartered 1782; inc. as a city 1832.

Transportation: 11 comm. airlines; 2 railroads; city buses. **Communications:** 5 TV, 16 radio stations. **Medical facilities:** 5 general, 5 specialized hosp. **Educational facilities:** 2 univ., 4 colleges. **Further information:** Greater Lexington Chamber of Commerce, 330 E. Main St., Lexington, KY 40507.

Website: http://www.lexchamber.com

Lincoln, Nebraska

Population: 209,192 (76); **Pop. density:** 3,305 per sq. mi; **Pop. growth (1990-96):** 9.0%. **Area:** 63.3 sq. mi. **Employment:** 124,598 employed, 2.3% unemployed. **Per capita income (MSA):** $23,591; % increase, 1990-96: 33.5.

History: originally called Lancaster; chosen state capital 1867, renamed after Abraham Lincoln; inc. 1869.

Transportation: 1 airport; Greyhound; Amtrak, 2 railroads. **Communications:** 2 TV, 13 radio stations. **Medical facilities:** 5 hosp. including VA, rehabilitation facilities. **Educational facilities:** 3 univ., 3 voc.-tech./business colleges; 48 pub., 15 private schools. **Further information:** Chamber of Commerce, PO Box 83006, Lincoln, NE 68501.

Websites: http://www.lincoln.org
http://www.lcoc.com

Long Beach, California

Population: 421,904 (36); **Pop. density:** 8,438 per sq. mi; **Pop. growth (1990-96):** –1.7%. **Area:** 50 sq. mi. **Employment:** 196,433 employed, 6.4% unemployed. **Per capita income (MSA):** $24,945; % increase, 1990-96: 15.7.

History: settled as early as 1784 by Spanish; by 1884 present site developed on harbor; inc. 1888; oil discovered 1921.

Transportation: 1 airport; 3 railroads; major intl. port; 4 bus co. with 40 bus lines, light rail service. **Communications:** 1 radio station, 1 CATV franchise. **Medical facilities:** 10 hosp. **Educational facilities:** 1 univ., 1 community college (2 campuses); 85 pub. schools in district. **Further information:** Long Beach City Hall, 333 W. Ocean Blvd., Long Beach, CA 90802

Websites: http://www.ci.long-beach.ca.us
http://www.lbchamber.com

Los Angeles, California

Population: 3,553,638 (2); **Pop. density:** 7,572 per sq. mi; **Pop. growth (1990-96):** –2.0%. **Area:** 469.3 sq. mi. **Employment:** 1,664,682 employed, 7.8% unemployed. **Per capita income (MSA):** $24,945 % increase, 1990-96: 15.7.

History: founded by Spanish 1781; captured by U.S. 1846; inc. 1850; Hollywood a district of L.A.

Transportation: 1 intl. airport; 3 railroads; major freeway system; intracity transit system. **Communications:** 21 TV, 70 radio stations. **Medical facilities:** 822 hosp. and clinics in metropolitan area. **Educational facilities:** 192 univ. and colleges (incl. junior, community, and other); 1,678 pub. schools; 1,470 private schools. **Further information:** Chamber of Commerce, 350 S. Bixel St., PO Box 3696, Los Angeles, CA 90051-1696.

Websites: http://www.ci.la.ca.us
http://www.lachamber.com

Louisville, Kentucky

Population: 260,689 (61); **Pop. density:** 4,198 per sq. mi; **Pop. growth (1990-96):** –3.3%. **Area:** 62.1 sq. mi. **Employment:** 125,534 employed, 4.9% unemployed. **Per capita income (MSA):** $24,764; % increase, 1990-96: 32.7.

History: settled 1778; named for Louis XVI of France; inc. 1828; base for Union forces in Civil War.

Transportation: 1 municipal airport, 1 private-craft airport; 1 terminal, 4 trunk-line railroads; metro bus line, Greyhound station; 5 barge lines. **Communications:** 5 TV, 21 radio stations, 2 educational. **Medical facilities:** 23 hosp. **Educational facilities:** 10 univ. and colleges, 9 business colleges and technical schools. **Further information:** Greater Louisville, Inc. Metro Chamber of Commerce, 600 W. Main St., Louisville, KY 40202.

Website: http://www.greaterlouisville.com

Lubbock, Texas

Population: 193,565 (84); **Pop. density:** 1,859 per sq. mi; **Pop. growth (1990-96):** 4.0%. **Area:** 104.1 sq. mi. **Employment:** 99,294 employed, 4.0% unemployed. **Per capita income (MSA):** $21,065; % increase, 1990-96: 30.8.

History: settled 1879; laid out 1891; inc. 1909 through merger of two towns.

Transportation: 1 intl. airport; 2 railroads, bus line. **Communications:** 5 TV, 18 radio statons. **Medical facilities:** 7 hosp. **Educational facilities:** 3 univ., 1 junior college; 51 pub. schools. **Further information:** Chamber of Commerce, PO Box 561, Lubbock, TX 79408.

Websites: http://www.ci.lubbock.tx.us
http://www.lubbock.org

Madison, Wisconsin

Population: 197,630 (81); **Pop. density:** 3,419 per sq. mi; **Pop. growth (1990-96):** 3.6%. **Area:** 57.8 sq. mi. **Employment:** 126,929 employed, 1.9% unemployed. **Per capita income (MSA):** $28,087; % increase, 1990-96: 37.3.

History: first white settlement 1832; selected as site for state capital, named after James Madison, 1836; chartered 1856.

Transportation: 1 airport, 7 airlines; 1 intracity, 3 intercity bus systems; 3 freight rail lines. **Communications:** 5 TV, 24 radio stations, 3 cable providers. **Medical facilities:** 6 hosp., 92 clinics. **Educational facilities:** 7 colleges and univ., including main branch of Univ. of Wisconsin; 45 pub. schools. **Further information:** Greater Madison Chamber of Commerce, PO Box 71, Madison, WI 53701-0071.

Websites: http://www.ci.madison.wi.us
http://www.greatermadisonchamber.com

Memphis, Tennessee

Population: 596,725 (18); **Pop. density:** 2,118 per sq. mi; **Pop. growth (1990-96):** –3.5%. **Area:** 281.8 sq. mi. **Employment:** 288,958 employed, 5.7% unemployed. **Per capita income (MSA):** $24,945; % increase, 1990-96: 36.6.

History: French, Spanish, and U.S. forts by 1797; settled by 1819; inc. as town 1826, as city 1840; surrendered charter to state 1879 after yellow fever epidemics; rechartered as city 1893.

Transportation: 1 intl. airport; 5 railroads; bus system. **Communications:** 6 TV, 42 radio stations. **Medical facilities:** 21 hosp. **Educational facilities:** 14 univ. and colleges; 205 pub., 76 private schools. **Further information:** Memphis Area Chamber of Commerce, 22 N. Front St., Ste. 200, PO Box 224, Memphis, TN 38101-0224.

Websites: http://www.memphis.acn.net
http://www.ci.memphis.tn.us
http://www.memphischamber.com

Mesa, Arizona

Population: 344,764 (51); **Pop. density:** 3,175 per sq. mi; **Pop. growth (1990-96):** 19.2%. **Area:** 108.6 sq. mi. **Employment:** 179,052 employed, 2.5% unemployed. **Per capita income (MSA):** $23,377; % increase, 1990-96: 27.7.

History: founded by Mormons 1878; inc. 1883; 13 mi. from Phoenix; population boomed fivefold 1960-80.

Transportation: near Sky Harbor Intl. Airport in Phoenix; 2 railroads; bus line. **Medical facilities:** 4 major hosp. **Educational facilities:** 1 univ., 3 colleges; 70 pub. schools. **Further information:** Convention and Visitor's Bureau, 120 N. Center, Mesa, AZ 85201.

Websites: http://www.ci.mesa.az.us
http://www.arizonaguide.com\mesa

Miami, Florida

Population: 365,127 (44); **Pop. density:** 10,256 per sq. mi; **Pop. growth (1990-96):** 1.8%. **Area:** 35.6 sq. mi. **Employment:** 162,394 employed, 10.3% unemployed. **Per capita income (MSA):** $22,370; % increase, 1990-96: 24.8.

History: site of fort 1836; settlement began 1870; inc. 1896, modern city developed into resort and recreation center; land speculation in 1920s added to city's growth, as did Cuban, Central and South American, and Haitian immigration since 1960.

Transportation: 1 intl. airport; seaport; Amtrak, transit rail system; 2 bus lines; 65 truck lines. **Communications:** 9 commercial, 2 educational TV stations; 41 radio stations. **Medical facilities:** 36 hosp.; VA hosp. **Educational facilities:** 6 univ. and colleges. **Further information:** Miami-Dade Dept. of Planning, Development, and Regulation, Research Div., 111 NW 1st St., Ste. 1220, Miami, FL 33128.

Websites: http://ci.miami.fl.us
http://www.greatermiami.com
http://www.metro-dade.com

Milwaukee, Wisconsin

Population: 590,503 (19); **Pop. density:** 6,145 per sq. mi; **Pop. growth (1990-96):** –6.0%. **Area:** 96.1 sq. mi. **Employment:** 279,353 employed, 5.6% unemployed. **Per capita income (MSA):** $27,202; % increase, 1990-96: 33.6.

History: Indian trading post by 1674; settlement began 1835; inc. as city 1848; famous beer industry.

Transportation: 1 intl. airport; 3 railroads; major port; 4 bus lines. **Communications:** 12 TV, 37 radio stations. **Medical facilities:** 9 hosp.; major medical center. **Educational facilities:** 10 univ. and colleges. **Further information:** Metropolitan Milwaukee Association of Commerce, 756 N. Milwaukee Street, Milwaukee, WI 53202.

Websites: http://www.ci.mil.wi.us
http://www.milwaukee.org

Minneapolis, Minnesota

Population: 358,785 (46); **Pop. density:** 6,535 per sq. mi; **Pop. growth (1990-96):** –2.6%. **Area:** 54.9 sq. mi. **Employment:** 200,282 employed, 3.2% unemployed. **Per capita income (MSA):** $29,299; % increase, 1990-96: 32.2.

History: site visited by Hennepin 1680; included in area of military reservations 1819; inc. 1867.

Transportation: 1 intl. airport; 5 railroads. **Communications:** 7 TV, 30 radio stations. **Medical facilities:** 7 hosp., incl. leading heart hosp. at Univ. of Minnesota. **Educational facilities:** 10 univ. and colleges; 82 pub., 35 private schools. **Further information:** City of Minneapolis Office of Pub. Affairs, 323M City Hall, 350 S. 5th St., Minneapolis, MN 55415.

Website: http://www.ci.minneapolis.mn.us

Mobile, Alabama

Population: 202,581 (79); **Pop. density:** 1,717 per sq. mi; **Pop. growth (1990-96):** 3.2%. **Area:** 118 sq. mi. **Employment:** 100,338 employed, 5.7% unemployed. **Per capita income (MSA):** $19,508; % increase, 1990-96: 34.3.

History: settled by French 1711; occupied by U.S. 1813; inc. as town 1814, as city 1819; only seaport of Alabama.

Transportation: 4 rail freight lines, Amtrak; 3 airlines; 65 truck lines; leading river system. **Communications:** 7 TV, 21 radio stations. **Medical facilities:** 9 hosp. **Educational facilities:** 3 univ., 3 colleges. **Further information:** Chamber of Commerce, PO Box 2187, Mobile, AL 36652.

Websites: http://www.ci.mobile.al.us
http://www.mobcham.org

Montgomery, Alabama

Population: 196,363 (82); **Pop. density:** 1,455 per sq. mi; **Pop. growth (1990-96):** 3.2%. **Area:** 135 sq. mi. **Employment:** 97,197 employed, 4.5% unemployed. **Per capita income (MSA):** $21,973; % increase, 1990-96: 30.1.

History: inc. as town 1819, as city 1837; became state capital 1846; first capital of Confederacy 1861.

Transportation: 4 airlines; 2 railroads; 2 bus lines; Alabama R. navigable to Gulf of Mexico. **Communications:** 5 TV, 2 CATV, 15 radio stations. **Medical facilities:** 4 major hosp.; VA and 32 clinics. **Educational facilities:** 5 univ.; 49 pub., 28 private schools. **Further information:** Montgomery Area Chamber of Commerce, PO Box 79, Montgomery, AL 36101.

Website: http://www.montgomery.al.us

Nashville, Tennessee

Population: 511,263 (24); **Pop. density:** 1,080 per sq. mi; **Pop. growth (1990-96):** 4.7%. **Area:** 473.3 sq. mi. **Employment:** 290,487 employed, 3.4% unemployed. **Per capita income (MSA):** $26,262; % increase, 1990-96: 39.4.

History: settled 1779; first chartered 1806; became permanent state capital 1843; home of Grand Ole Opry.

Transportation: 1 airport; 1 railroad; bus line; transit system of buses and trolleys. **Communications:** 11 TV, 34 radio stations. **Medical facilities:** 14 hosp.; VA and speech-hearing center. **Educational facilities:** 16 universities and colleges. **Further information:** Chamber of Commerce, 161 4th Ave., Nashville, TN 37219.

Website: http://www.nashvillechamber.com

Newark, New Jersey

Population: 268,510 (60); **Pop. density:** 11,282 per sq. mi; **Pop. growth (1990-96):** –2.4%. **Area:** 23.8 sq. mi. **Employment:** 101,402 employed, 11.0% unemployed. **Per capita income (MSA):** $33,952; % increase, 1990-96: 28.6.

History: settled by Puritans 1666; used as supply base by Washington 1776; inc. as town 1833, as city 1836.

Transportation: 1 intl. airport; 2 railroads; bus system; 2 subways. **Communications:** 3 TV, 5 radio stations within city limits. **Medical facilities:** 6 hosp. **Educational facilities:** 5 univ. and colleges; 71 pub. schools. **Further information:** Regional Business Partnership, 1 Newark Center, 22d fl., Newark, NJ 07102-5265.

Websites: http://www.ci.newark.nj.us
http://www.rbp.org

New Orleans, Louisiana

Population: 476,625 (29); **Pop. density:** 2,639 per sq. mi; **Pop. growth (1990-96):** –4.1%. **Area:** 180.6 sq. mi. **Employment:** 190,878 employed, 6.6% unemployed. **Per capita income (MSA):** $22,179; % increase, 1990-96: 30.1.

History: founded by French 1718; became major seaport on Mississippi R.; acquired by U.S. as part of La. Purchase 1803; inc. as city 1805; Battle of New Orleans was last battle of War of 1812.

Transportation: 2 airports; major railroad center; major intl. port. **Communications:** 7 TV, 18 radio stations. **Medical facilities:** numerous hosp.; major research center. **Educational facilities:** 13 univ. and colleges. **Further information:** New Orleans Metropolitan Convention & Visitors Bureau, Inc., 1520 Sugar Bowl Dr., New Orleans, LA 70112.

Website: http://www.neworleanscvb.com

New York, New York

Population: 7,380,906 (1); **Pop. density:** 23,894 per sq. mi; **Pop. growth (1990-96):** 0.8%. **Area:** 308.9 sq. mi. **Employment:** 3,056,225 employed, 9.4% unemployed. **Per capita income (MSA):** $33,177; % increase, 1990-96: 29.8.

History: trading post established by Henry Hudson 1609; British took control from Dutch 1664 and named New York; briefly U.S. capital; Washington inaugurated as president 1789; under new charter, 1898, city expanded to include 5 boroughs: The Bronx, Brooklyn, Queens, and Staten Island, as well as Manhattan.

Transportation: 3 intl. airports serve area; 2 rail terminals; major subway network; ferry system; 4 underwater tunnels. **Communications:** 13 TV, 117 radio stations. **Medical facilities:** 81 hosp.; 5 academic medical centers. **Educational facilities:** 92 univ. and colleges; 1,100 pub. schools. **Further information:** Convention and Visitors Bureau, 810 Seventh Ave., New York, NY 10019.

Websites: http://www.ci.nyc.ny.us
http://www.nycvisit.com

Norfolk, Virginia

Population: 233,430 (70); **Pop. density:** 4,339 per sq. mi; **Pop. growth (1990-96):** –10.6%. **Area:** 53.8 sq. mi. **Employment:** 80,612 employed, 6.8% unemployed. **Per capita income (MSA):** $21,311; % increase, 1990-96: 23.9.

History: founded 1682; burned by patriots to prevent capture by British during Revolutionary War; rebuilt and inc. as town 1805, as city 1845; site of world's largest naval base.

Transportation: 1 intl. airport; 2 railroads; Amtrak; bus system. **Communications:** 13 TV, 6 city-access TV, 27 radio stations. **Medical facilities:** 6 hosp. **Educational facilities:** 2 univ., 1 college, 1 medical school; 58 pub. schools. **Further information:** Norfolk Convention and Visitors Bureau, 232 E. Main St., Norfolk, VA 23510.

Website: http://www.norfolk.va.us

Oakland, California

Population: 367,230 (43); **Pop. density:** 6,546 per sq. mi; **Pop. growth (1990-96):** –1.3%. **Area:** 56.1 sq. mi. **Employment:** 171,784 employed, 6.9% unemployed. **Per capita income (MSA):** $29,842; % increase, 1990-96: 25.5.

History: area settled by Spanish 1820; inc. as city under present name 1854.

Transportation: 1 intl. airport; western terminus for 3 railroads; underground, 75-mi underwater subway. **Communications:** 1 TV, 3 radio stations in city. **Medical facilities:** 10 hosp. in MSA. **Educational facilities:** 8 East Bay colleges and univ.; 94 pub. schools. **Further information:** Oakland Metropolitan Chamber of Commerce, 475 14th St., Oakland, CA 94612-1903.

Websites: http://oakweb.ci.oakland.ca.us
http://www.oaklandchamber.com

Oklahoma City, Oklahoma

Population: 469,852 (30); **Pop. density:** 773 per sq. mi; **Pop. growth (1990-96):** 5.7%. **Area.** 608.2 sq. mi. **Employment:** 234,366 employed, 3.6% unemployed. **Per capita income (MSA):** $21,148; % increase, 1990-96: 25.2.

History: settled during land rush in Midwest 1889; inc. 1890; became capital 1910; oil discovered 1928.

Transportation: 1 intl. airport; 3 railroads; pub. transit system; 5 major bus lines. **Communications:** 8 TV, 24 radio stations. **Medical facilities:** 20 hosp. **Educational facilities:** 17 univ. and colleges; 83 pub., 37 private schools. **Further information:** Chamber of Commerce, Economic Development Division, 123 Park Ave., Oklahoma City, OK 73102.

Websites: http://www.okcchamber.com
http://www.okccvb.org
http://www.ocbn.org

Omaha, Nebraska

Population: 364,253 (45); **Pop. density:** 3,621 per sq. mi; **Pop. growth (1990-96):** 6.2%. **Area:** 100.6 sq. mi. **Employment:** 195,797 employed, 3.1% unemployed. **Per capita income (MSA):** $25,291; % increase, 1990-96: 35.0.

History: founded 1854; inc. 1857; large food-processing, telecommunications, information-processing center; home of more than 20 insurance companies.

Transportation: 11 major airlines; 4 major railroads; intercity bus line. **Communications:** 8 TV, 22 radio stations. **Medical facilities:** 16 hosp.; institute for cancer research. **Educational facilities:** 5 univ., 4 colleges; 243 pub., 78 private schools. **Further information:** Greater Omaha Chamber of Commerce, 1301 Harney St., Omaha, NE 68102.

Websites: http://www.ci.omaha.ne.us
http://www.accessomaha.com

Philadelphia, Pennsylvania

Population: 1,478,002 (5); **Pop. density:** 10,940 per sq. mi; **Pop. growth (1990-96):** –6.8%. **Area:** 135.1 sq. mi. **Employment:** 607,602 employed, 6.8% unemployed. **Per capita income (MSA):** $28,447; % increase, 1990-96: 28.5.

History: first settled by Swedes 1638; Swedes surrendered to Dutch 1654; settled by English and Scottish Quakers 1678; named Philadelphia 1682; chartered 1701; Continental Congresses convened 1774, 1775; Declaration of Independence signed here 1776; national capital 1790-1800; state capital 1683-1799.

Transportation: 1 major airport; 3 railroads; major freshwater port; subway, el, rail commuter, bus, and streetcar system. **Communications:** 11 TV, 44 radio stations. **Medical facilities:** 47 hosp. **Educational facilities:** 25 degree-granting institutions; 10 community college campuses. **Further information:** Office of City Representative and City Commerce Director, 1600 Arch St., 13th fl., Philadelphia, PA 19103.

Websites: http://www.phila.gov
http://www.gpcc.com

Phoenix, Arizona

Population: 1,159,014 (7); **Pop. density:** 2,471 per sq. mi; **Pop. growth (1990-96):** 17.7%. **Area:** 469 sq. mi. **Employment:** 635,387 employed, 3.3% unemployed. **Per capita income (MSA):** $23,377; % increase, 1990-96: 27.7.

History: settled 1870; inc. as city 1881; became territorial capital 1889.

Transportation: 1 intl. airport; 5 railroads; transcontinental bus line; pub. transit system. **Communications:** 13 TV, 45 radio stations. **Medical facilities:** 20 hosp., 1 medical research center. **Educational facilities:** 88 institutions of higher learning; 186 pub. schools. **Further information:** Chamber of Commerce, 201 N. Central Ave., 27th fl., Phoenix, AZ 85073.

Websites: http://www.ci.phoenix.az.us
http://www.phoenixchamber.com

Pittsburgh, Pennsylvania

Population: 350,363 (48); **Pop. density:** 6,301 per sq. mi; **Pop. growth (1990-96):** –5.3%. **Area:** 55.6 sq. mi. **Employment:** 155,013 employed, 5.1% unemployed. **Per capita income (MSA):** $25,359; % increase, 1990-96: 30.6.

History: settled around Ft. Pitt 1758; inc. as city 1816; has one of the largest inland ports; by Civil War, already a center for iron production.

Transportation: 1 intl. airport; 20 railroads; 2 bus lines; trolley/subway system. **Communications:** 6 TV, 26 radio stations. **Medical facilities:** 35 hosp.; VA installation. **Educational facilities:** 3 univ., 6 colleges; 86 pub. schools. **Further information:** Greater Pittsburgh Convention & Visitors Bureau, 4 Gateway Ctr., Pittsburgh, PA 15222.

Websites: http://www.pittsburgh.net
http://www.pittsburgh-cvb.org

Plano, TX

Population: 192,280 (88); **Pop. density:** 2,595 per sq. mi; **Pop. growth (1990-96):** 50.4%. **Area:** 74.1 sq. mi. **Employment:** 111,801 employed, 2.1% unemployed. **Per capita income (MSA):** $28,513; % increase, 1990-96: 32.2.

History: settled 1846; inc. as city 1873.

Transportation: 1 bus line. **Communications:** 2 TV, 2 radio stations. **Medical facilities:** 5 hosp. **Educational facilities:** 2 institutes of higher learning, 51 pub. schools. **Further information:** Plano Chamber of Commerce, PO Drawer 940287, Plano, TX 75094.

Website: http://www.cin-co.com

Portland, Oregon

Population: 480,824 (27); **Pop. density:** 3,856 per sq. mi; **Pop. growth (1990-96):** 3.7%. **Area:** 124.7 sq. mi. **Employment:** 261,172 employed, 5.2% unemployed. **Per capita income (MSA):** $26,228; % increase, 1990-96: 33.8.

History: settled by pioneers 1845; developed as trading center, aided by California Gold Rush 1849; city chartered 1851.

Transportation: 1 intl. airport; 2 major rail freight lines, Amtrak; 2 intercity bus lines; 27-mi. frontage freshwater port; mass transit bus and rail system. **Communications:** 7 TV, 37 radio stations. **Medical facilities:** 16 hosp.; VA hosp. **Educational facilities:** 26 univ. and colleges, 1 community college. **Further information:** Portland Metropolitan Chamber of Commerce, 221 N.W. 2d Ave., Portland, OR 9720.

Website: http://www.pdxchamber.org

Raleigh, North Carolina

Population: 243,835 (67); **Pop. density:** 2,768 per sq. mi; **Pop. growth (1990-96):** 15.0%. **Area:** 88.1 sq. mi. **Employment:** 157,630 employed, 2.0% unemployed. **Per capita income (MSA):** $26,255; % increase, 1990-96: 24.3.

History: named after Sir Walter Raleigh; site chosen for capital 1788; laid out 1792; inc. 1795; occupied by Gen. Sherman 1865.

Transportation: 1 intl. airport, 11 airlines, 5 commuter airlines; 3 railroads; 2 bus lines. **Communications:** 8 TV, 30 radio stations. **Medical facilities:** 6 hosp. **Educational facilities:** 6 univ. and colleges; 1 community college; 107 pub. schools (county). **Further information:** Chamber of Commerce, 800 S. Salisbury St., PO Box 2978, Raleigh, NC 27602.

Websites: http://www.raleigh.acn.net
http://www.raleighchamber.org

Richmond, Virginia

Population: 198,267 (80); **Pop. density:** 3,299 per sq. mi; **Pop. growth (1990-96):** –2.2%. **Area:** 60.1 sq. mi. **Employment:** 93,493 employed, 4.8% unemployed. **Per capita income (MSA):** $26,974; % increase, 1990-96: 24.2.

History: first settled 1607; became capital of Commonwealth of Virginia, 1779; attacked by British under Benedict Arnold 1781; inc. as city 1782; capital of Confederate States of America, 1861-65.

Transportation: 1 intl. airport; 4 railroads; 3 intracity bus lines; deepwater terminal accessible to oceangoing ships. **Communications:** 6 TV, 26 radio stations. **Medical facilities:** Medical Coll. of Virginia renowned for heart and kidney transplants; 19 other hosp. incl. VA facility. **Educational facilities:** 9 univ. and colleges; 173 pub., 45 private schools. **Further information:** Chamber of Commerce, PO Box 12280, Richmond, VA 23241-2280.

Websites: http://www.ci.richmond.va.us
http://www.grcc.com

Riverside, California

Population: 255,069 (64); **Pop. density:** 3,283 per sq. mi; **Pop. growth (1990-96):** 12.6%. **Area:** 77.7 sq. mi. **Employment:** 126,127 employed, 7.5% unemployed. **Per capita income (MSA):** $19,090; % increase, 1990-96: 8.6.

History: founded 1870; inc. 1886; known for its citrus industry; home of the parent navel orange.

Transportation: municipal airport, intl. airport nearby; rail freight lines, commuter line; trolley/bus system. **Communications:** 15 TV, 47 radio stations. **Medical facilities:** 4 hosp.; many clinics. **Educational facilities:** 3 univ., 1 community college. **Further information:** Chamber of Commerce, 3985 University Ave., Riverside, CA 92501.

Websites: http://www.ci.riverside.ca.us
http://www.riverside-chamber.com

Rochester, New York

Population: 221,594 (73); **Pop. density:** 6,190 per sq. mi; **Pop. growth (1990-96):** –3.8%. **Area:** 35.8 sq. mi. **Employment:** 106,839 employed, 6.5% unemployed. **Per capita income (MSA):** $25,543; % increase, 1990-96: 22.6.

History: first permanent settlement 1812; inc. as village 1817, as city 1834; developed as Erie Canal town.

Transportation: 1 intl. airport; Amtrak; 3 bus lines; intracity transit service; Port of Rochester. **Communications:** 6 TV, 18 radio stations. **Medical facilities:** 8 general hosp. **Educational facilities:** 10 colleges, 3 community colleges. **Further information:** Greater Rochester Metro Chamber of Commerce, 55 St. Paul St., Rochester, NY 14604-1391.

Websites: http://www.rochester.lib.ny.us/cityhall
http://www.rnychamber.com

Sacramento, California

Population: 376,243 (42); **Pop. density:** 3,907 per sq. mi; **Pop. growth (1990-96):** 1.9%. **Area:** 96.3 sq. mi. **Employment:** 175,228 employed, 6.7% unemployed. **Per capita income (MSA):** $24,444; % increase, 1990-96: 21.9.

History: settled 1839; important trading center during California Gold Rush 1840s; became state capital 1854.

Transportation: international, executive, and cargo airports; 2 mainline transcontinental rail carriers; bus and light rail system; Port of Sacramento. **Communications:** 7 TV, 25 radio stations; 3 cable TV cos. **Medical facilities:** 8 hosp. **Educational facilities:** 2 univ., 4 community colleges. **Further information:** Metro Chamber of Commerce, 917 7th St., Sacramento, CA 95814.

Websites: http://www.ci.sacramento.ca.us
http://www.metrochamber.org

St. Louis, Missouri

Population: 351,565 (47); **Pop. density:** 5,680 per sq. mi; **Pop. growth (1990-96):** –11.4%. **Area:** 61.9 sq. mi. **Employment:** 154,073 employed, 7.2% unemployed. **Per capita income (MSA):** $26,337; % increase, 1990-96: 28.6.

History: founded 1764 as a fur trading post by French; acquired by U.S. 1803; chartered as city 1822; lies on Mississippi R., near confluence with Missouri R.

Transportation: 1 intl. airport; major rail center, 17 trunk-line railroads; major inland port; 14 bus lines; 14 barge lines. **Communications:** 7 TV, 35 radio stations. **Medical facilities:** 65 hosp. **Educational facilities:** 6 univ., 25 colleges and seminaries. **Further information:** St. Louis Community Development Agency, 1015 Locust St., Ste. 1200, St. Louis, MO 63101.

Websites: http://www.st-louis.mo.us
http://stlouis.missouri.org

St. Paul, Minnesota

Population: 259,606 (62); **Pop. density:** 4,917 per sq. mi; **Pop. growth (1990-96):** –4.6%. **Area:** 52.8 sq. mi. **Employment:** 135,975 employed, 3.3% unemployed. **Per capita income (MSA):** $29,299; % increase, 1990-96: 32.3.

History: founded in early 1840s as "Pig's Eye Landing"; became capital of the Minnesota territory 1849 and chartered as St. Paul 1854.

Transportation: 1 intl., 1 business airport; 6 major rail lines; 3 interstate bus lines; pub. transit system. **Communications:** 6 TV, 35 radio stations. **Medical facilities:** 6 hosp. **Educational facilities:** 3 univ., 4 colleges; 1 technical, 3 first professional colleges. **Further information:** St. Paul Area Chamber of Commerce, 332 Minnesota St., Ste. N-205, St. Paul, MN 55101.

Website: http://www.ci.stpaul.mn.us

St. Petersburg, Florida

Population: 235,988 (69); **Pop. density:** 3,986 per sq. mi; **Pop. growth (1990-96):** –1.8%. **Area:** 59.2 sq. mi. **Employment:** 124,759 employed, 4.0% unemployed. **Per capita income (MSA):** $23,984; % increase, 1990-96: 30.7.

History: founded 1888; inc. 1892.

Transportation: 2 airports (1 intl.); Amtrak bus connection; county-wide public bus system; 1 cruise port. **Communications:** 12 TV, 22 radio stations. **Medical facilities:** 4 major hosp.; VA hosp. **Educational facilities:** 1 univ., 1 college, 1 law school, 1 junior college; 119 pub. schools. **Further information:** St. Petersburg Area Chamber of Commerce, PO Box 1371, St. Petersburg, FL 33731.

Website: http://www.stpete.com

San Antonio, Texas

Population: 1,067,816 (8); **Pop. density:** 3,207 per sq. mi; **Pop. growth (1990-96):** 11.3%. **Area:** 333 sq. mi. **Employment:** 491,745 employed, 4.6% unemployed. **Per capita income (MSA):** $21,237; % increase, 1990-96: 33.4.

History: first Spanish garrison 1718; Battle at the Alamo fought here 1836; city subsequently captured by Texans; inc. 1837.

Transportation: 1 intl. airport; 4 railroads; 3 bus lines; pub. transit system. **Communications:** 9 TV, 34 radio stations. **Medical facilities:** 36 hosp.; major medical center. **Educational facilities:** 18 univ. and colleges; 16 pub. school districts. **Further information:** Chamber of Commerce, 602 E. Commerce, PO Box 1628, San Antonio, TX 78296.

Websites: http://www.tristero.com/usa/tx/
http://www.ci.sat.tx.us
http://www.sachamber.org

San Bernardino, California

Population: 183,474 (98); **Pop. density:** 3,330 per sq. mi; **Pop. growth (1990-96):** 7.9%. **Area:** 55.1 sq. mi. **Employment:** 69,307 employed, 9.1% unemployed. **Per capita income (MSA):** $19,090; % increase, 1990-96: 8.6.

History: Spanish missionaries arrived here 1810; Mormons est. first permanent settlement 1851; inc. 1854.

Transportation: 1 intl. airport; Amtrak; rail transit system; bus systems. **Communications:** 5 TV, 22 radio stations. **Medical facilities:** 4 hosp. **Educational facilities:** 1 univ., 1 community college; 59 pub. schools. **Further information:** San Bernardino Area Chamber of Commerce, 546 W. 6th St., PO Box 658, San Bernardino, CA 92402.

Website: http://www.ci.san-bernardino.ca.us

San Diego, California

Population: 1,171,121 (6); **Pop. density:** 3,615 per sq. mi; **Pop. growth (1990-96):** 5.4%. **Area:** 324 sq. mi. **Employment:** 562,377 employed, 4.3% unemployed. **Per capita income (MSA):** $24,282; % increase, 1990-96: 19.8.

History: claimed by the Spanish 1542; first mission est. 1769; scene of conflict during Mexican-American War 1846; inc. 1850.

Transportation: 1 major airport; 1 railroad; major freeway system; bus system; trolley system. **Communications:** 8 TV, 22 radio stations, 6 cable providers. **Medical facilities:** 28 hosp. **Educational facilities:** 5 univ., 7 colleges. **Further information:** Greater San Diego Chamber of Commerce, 402 W. Broadway, Ste. 1000, San Diego, CA 92101-3585.

Websites: http://www.sannet.gov
http://www.sdchamber.org

San Francisco, California

Population: 735,315 (13); **Pop. density:** 15,746 per sq. mi; **Pop. growth (1990-96):** 1.6%. **Area:** 46.7 sq. mi. **Employment:** 396,100 employed, 4.0% unemployed. **Per capita income (MSA):** $39,746; % increase, 1990-96: 28.4.

History: nearby Farallon Islands sighted by Spanish 1542; city settled by 1776; claimed by U.S. 1846; became a major city during California Gold Rush 1849; inc. as city 1850; earthquake devastated city 1906.

Transportation: 1 major airport; intracity railway system; 2 railway transit systems; bus and railroad service; ferry system; 1 underwater tunnel. **Communications:** 10 TV; 15 radio stations. **Medical facilities:** 16 medical centers. **Educational facilities:** 16 univ. and colleges. **Further information:** Convention & Visitors Bureau, 201 3d St., Ste. 900, San Francisco, CA 94103.

Websites: http://www.ci.sf.ca.us
http://www.sfchamber.com

San Jose, California

Population: 838,744 (11); **Pop. density:** 4,896 per sq. mi; **Pop. growth (1990-96):** 7.2%. **Area:** 171.3 sq. mi. **Employment:** 459,994 employed, 3.6% unemployed. **Per capita income (MSA):** $35,395; % increase, 1990-96: 37.9.

History: founded by the Spanish 1777 between San Francisco and Monterey; state cap. 1849-51; inc. 1850.

Transportation: 1 intl. airport; 2 railroads; bus system. **Communications:** 4 TV, 14 radio stations. **Medical facilities:** 6 hosp. **Educational facilities:** 3 univ. and colleges. **Further information:** Chamber of Commerce, 310 S. First St., San Jose, CA 95113.

Websites: http://www.ipac.net/csj
http://www.sjchamber.com

Santa Ana, California

Population: 302,419 (55); **Pop. density:** 11,159 per sq. mi; **Pop. growth (1990-96):** 2.9%. **Area:** 27.1 sq. mi. **Employment:** 145,354 employed, 5.9% unemployed. **Per capita income (MSA):** $28,936; % increase, 1990-96: 13.5.

History: founded 1869; inc. as city 1886.

Transportation: 1 airport; 5 major freeways including main Los Angeles-San Diego artery; Amtrak. **Communications:** 14 TV, 28 radio stations. **Medical facilities:** 4 hosp. **Educational facilities:** 1 community college. **Further information:** Santa Ana Chamber of Commerce, PO Box 205, Santa Ana, CA 92702.

Website: http://www.santaanacc.com

Seattle, Washington

Population: 524,704 (23); **Pop. density:** 6,254 per sq. mi; **Pop. growth (1990-96):** 1.6%. **Area:** 83.9 sq. mi. **Employment:** 336,561 employed, 3.9% unemployed. **Per capita income (MSA):** $31,372; % increase, 1990-96: 33.6.

History: settled 1851; inc. 1869; suffered severe fire 1889; played prominent role during Alaska Gold Rush 1897; growth followed opening of Panama Canal 1914; center of aircraft industry WWII.

Transportation: 1 intl. airport; 2 railroads; ferries serve Puget Sound, Alaska, Canada. **Communications:** 7 TV, 39 radio stations. **Medical facilities:** 40 hosp. **Educational facilities:** 7 univ., 6 colleges, 11 community colleges. **Further information:** Greater Seattle Chamber of Commerce, 1301 5th Ave., Ste. 2400, Seattle, WA 98101-2603.

Websites: http://www.ci.seattle.wa.us
http://www.seattlechamber.com

Shreveport, Louisiana

Population: 191,558 (89); **Pop. density:** 1,943 per sq. mi; **Pop. growth (1990-96):** –3.5%. **Area:** 98.6 sq. mi. **Employment:** 89,646 employed, 7.1% unemployed. **Per capita income (MSA):** $20,756; % increase, 1990-96: 33.7.

History: founded 1833 near site of a 160-mi logjam cleared by Capt. Henry Shreve; inc. 1839; oil discovered 1906.

Transportation: 2 airports; 1 bus line. **Communications:** 6 TV, 16 radio stations. **Medical facilities:** 16 hosp. **Educational facilities:** 4 univ., 1 college. **Further information:** Chamber of Commerce, PO Box 20074, Shreveport, LA 71120.
Website: http://www.shreveportchamber.org

Spokane, Washington

Population: 186,562 (95); **Pop. density:** 3,337 per sq. mi; **Pop. growth (1990-96):** 5.3%. **Area:** 55.9 sq. mi. **Employment:** 94,366 employed, 5.2% unemployed. **Per capita income (MSA):** $21,555; % increase, 1990-96: 29.4.
History: settled 1872; inc. as village of Spokane Falls 1881, destroyed in fire 1889; reinc. as city of Spokane 1891.
Transportation: 1 intl. airport; 2 railroads; bus system. **Communications:** 5 TV, 25 radio stations. **Medical facilities:** 6 major hosp. **Educational facilities:** 9 univ. and colleges; 14 pub. school districts, 16 high schools. **Further information:** Chamber of Commerce, 801 W. Riverside Ave., PO Box 2147, Spokane, WA 99210.
Website: http://www.spokane.net

Stockton, California

Population: 232,660 (71); **Pop. density:** 4,423 per sq. mi; **Pop. growth (1990-96):** 10.3%. **Area:** 52.6 sq. mi. **Employment:** 89,054 employed, 12.5% unemployed. **Per capita income (MSA):** $19,531; % increase, 1990-96: 17.5.
History: site purchased 1842; settled 1847; inc. 1850; chief distributing point for agric. products of San Joaquin Valley.
Transportation: 1 airport; deepwater inland seaport; 4 railroads; 2 bus lines, county bus system. **Communications:** 5 TV stations. **Medical facilities:** 4 hosp.; regional burn, cancer, heart centers. **Educational facilities:** 6 univ. and colleges; 58 pub. schools. **Further information:** Chamber of Commerce, 445 W. Weber Ave., Ste. 220, Stockton, CA 95203.
Websites: http://www.ci.stockton.ca.us
http://www.stocktonchamber.org

Tampa, Florida

Population: 285,206 (58); **Pop. density:** 2,624 per sq. mi; **Pop. growth (1990-96):** 1.9%. **Area:** 108.7 sq. mi. **Employment:** 155,899 employed, 4.2% unemployed. **Per capita income (MSA):** $23,984; % increase, 1990-96: 30.7.
History: U.S. army fort on site 1824; inc. 1855; Ybor City National Historical Landmark district.
Transportation: 1 intl. airport; Port of Tampa; CSX rail, bus system. **Communications:** 12 TV, 30 radio stations. **Medical facilities:** 17 hosp. **Educational facilities:** 3 univ. and colleges; 183 pub. schools. **Further information:** Chamber of Commerce, 401 E. Jackson St., PO Box 420, Tampa, FL 33601-0420.
Website: http://www.tampachamber.com

Toledo, Ohio

Population: 317,606 (53); **Pop. density:** 3,941 per sq. mi; **Pop. growth (1990-96):** –4.6%. **Area:** 80.6 sq. mi. **Employment:** 149,620 employed, 6.1% unemployed. **Per capita income (MSA):** $23,955; % increase, 1990-96: 31.2.
History: site of Ft. Industry 1794; Battles of Ft. Meigs and Ft. Timbers 1812; figured in "Toledo War" 1835-36 between Ohio and Michigan over borders; inc. 1837.
Transportation: 5 major airlines; 5 railroads; 81 motor freight lines; 4 interstate bus lines. **Communications:** 7 TV, 19 radio stations. **Medical facilities:** 7 major hosp. complexes. **Educational facilities:** 7 univ. and colleges. **Further information:** Toledo Area Chamber of Commerce, 300 Madison Ave., Ste. 200, Toledo, OH 43604.
Website: http://www.toledochamber.com

Tucson, Arizona

Population: 449,002 (31); **Pop. density:** 2,873 per sq. mi; **Pop. growth (1990-96):** 9.1%. **Area:** 156.3 sq. mi. **Employment:** 214,057 employed, 3.7% unemployed. **Per capita income (MSA):** $20,535; % increase, 1990-96: 30.6.
History: settled 1775 by Spanish as a presidio; acquired by U.S. in Gadsden Purchase 1853; inc. 1877.
Transportation: 1 intl. airport; 2 railroads; bus system. **Communications:** 9 TV, 27 radio stations. **Medical facilities:** 14 hosp. **Educational facilities:** 3 univ., 1 college; 165 pub. schools. **Further information:** Chamber of Commerce, PO Box 991, Tucson, AZ 85702.
Websites: http://www.ci.tucson.az.us
http://www.tucsonchamber.org

Tulsa, Oklahoma

Population: 378,491 (40); **Pop. density:** 2,063 per sq. mi; **Pop. growth (1990-96):** 3.0%. **Area:** 183.5 sq. mi. **Employment:** 204,043 employed, 3.6% unemployed. **Per capita income (MSA):** $23,141; % increase, 1990-96: 26.4.
History: settled in 1830s by Creek Indians; modern town founded 1882 and inc. 1898; oil discovered early 20th century.
Transportation: 1 intl. airport; 5 rail lines; 5 bus lines; transit bus system. **Communications:** 43 TV, 26 radio stations. **Medical facilities:** 10 hosp. **Educational facilities:** 8 univ. and colleges; 83 pub., 39 private schools. **Further information:** Metropolitan Tulsa Chamber of Commerce, 616 S. Boston Ave., Ste. 100, Tulsa, OK 74119-1298.
Website: http://www.tulsachamber.com

Virginia Beach, Virginia

Population: 430,385 (34); **Pop. density:** 1,733 per sq. mi; **Pop. growth (1990-96):** 9.5%. **Area:** 248.3 sq. mi. **Employment:** 199,779 employed, 4.0% unemployed. **Per capita income (MSA):** $21,311; % increase, 1990-96: 23.9.
History: area founded by Capt. John Smith 1607; formed by merger with Princess Anne Co. 1963.
Transportation: 1 airport; 2 railroads; 2 bus lines; pub. transit system. **Communications:** 6 TV, 41 radio stations. **Medical facilities:** 2 hosp. **Educational facilities:** 1 univ., 2 colleges; 83 pub. schools. **Further information:** Virginia Beach Dept. of Economic Development, One Columbus Center, Ste. 300, Virginia Beach, VA 23462.
Website: http://www.virginia-beach.va.us

Washington, District of Columbia

Population: 543,213 (21); **Pop. density:** 8,847 per sq. mi; **Pop. growth (1990-96):** –10.5%. **Area:** 61.4 sq. mi. **Employment:** 236,620 employed, 7.9% unemployed. **Per capita income (MSA):** $32,376; % increase, 1990-96: 24.7.
History: U.S. capital; site at Potomac R. chosen by George Washington 1790 on land ceded from VA and MD (portion S of Potomac returned to VA 1846); Congress first met 1800; inc. 1802; sacked by British, War of 1812.
Transportation: 3 intl. airports in area; Amtrak, 6 other passenger & cargo rail lines; Metrobus/Metrorail transit system; bus line. **Communications:** 5 TV, 61 radio stations. **Medical facilities:** 16 hosp. **Educational facilities:** 10 univ. and colleges. **Further information:** DC Chamber of Commerce, 1301 Pennsylvania Ave. NW, Ste. 309, Washington, DC 20004.
Websites: http://www.ci. washington.dc.us
http://www.dcchamber.org

Wichita, Kansas

Population: 320,395 (52); **Pop. density:** 2,784 per sq. mi; **Pop. growth (1990-96):** 5.4%. **Area:** 115.1 sq. mi. **Employment:** 166,642 employed, 3.7% unemployed. **Per capita income (MSA):** $23,753; % increase, 1990-96: 25.0.
History: founded 1864; inc. 1871.
Transportation: 2 airports; 3 major rail freight lines; 2 bus lines. **Communications:** 5 TV, 26 radio stations. **Medical facilities:** 7 hosp., 2 psychiatric rehab. centers. **Educational facilities:** 3 univ., 1 medical school; 96 pub. schools. **Further information:** Chamber of Commerce, 350 W. Douglas Ave., Wichita, KS 67202.
Websites: http://www.ci.wichita.ks.us
http://www.wacc.org

Yonkers, New York

Population: 190,316 (91); **Pop. density:** 10,515 per sq. mi; **Pop. growth (1990-96):** 1.2%. **Area:** 18.1 sq. mi. **Employment:** 86,203 employed, 5.1% unemployed. **Per capita income (MSA):** $33,177; % increase, 1990-96: 29.8.
History: founded 1641 by the Dutch; inc. as town 1855; chartered as city 1872; directly north of NYC.
Transportation: intracity bus system; rail service. **Communications:** see New York, NY. **Medical facilities:** 3 hosp. **Educational facilities:** 1 college; 32 pub. schools. **Further information:** Chamber of Commerce, 20 S. Broadway, 12th fl., Yonkers, NY 10701.
Websites: http://www.ci.yonkers.ny.us
http://www.yonkerschamber.com

WORLD EXPLORATION AND GEOGRAPHY

Early Explorers of the Western Hemisphere

Reviewed by Susan Skomal, PhD, editor, *Anthropology Newsletter*, American Anthropological Assn., and Paul B. Frederic, PhD, prof. of geography, Univ. of Maine at Farmington.

The first people to discover the New World, or western hemisphere, are believed to have traveled across a "land bridge" from Siberia to Alaska, an isthmus since broken by the Bering Strait. From Alaska, these early Native Americans could then have spread through North, Central, and South America. This theory is supported by archaeological and genetic evidence; a theory that the first Americans came by sea, landing in S. America, is no longer seriously considered by archaeologists, partly because of a lack of evidence of such early habitation in Polynesia.

In 1997, archaeologists confirmed evidence of human habitation in the Americas at least 12,500 years ago at a site in Chile known as Monte Verde. This site predates a previously discovered site in Clovis, NM, by over 1,000 years. The findings raise questions concerning the migratory path of these peoples, since a glacier covered most of N. America for a period between 20,000 years ago and some time after 13,000 years ago. The migration may have taken place in an ice-free corridor or along the west coast, perhaps in vessels along the water. An alternative possibility is that people had spread to S. America before the coming of the ice.

At first, these early Americans were hunters, using flint weapons and tools. In Mexico, about 7000-6000 BC, they founded farming cultures and developed crops, such as corn and squash. Eventually they created complex civilizations—the Olmec, Toltec, Aztec, Maya, and, in S. America, the Inca. Carbon-14 tests show that humans lived about 8000 BC near what are now Front Royal, VA; Kanawha, WV; and Dutchess Quarry, NY. The Hopewell Culture, based on farming, flourished about 1000 BC; remains of it are seen today in large mounds in Ohio and other states.

Norsemen (Norwegian Vikings sailing out of Iceland and Greenland), led by Leif Ericson, are credited by most scholars with having been the first Europeans to reach America, with at least 5 voyages occurring about AD 1000 to areas they called Helluland, Markland, and Vinland—possibly what are known today as Labrador, Nova Scotia or Newfoundland, and New England. L'Anse aux Meadows, on the northern tip of Newfoundland, is the only documented settlement.

Sustained contact between the hemispheres began with the first voyage of Christopher Columbus (born Cristoforo Colombo, c 1451, in or near Genoa, Italy). Columbus made trips to the New World while sailing for the Spanish.

His earliest voyage began when he left Palos, Spain, Aug. 3, 1492, with 88 (est.) men and landed at San Salvador (Watling Islands, Bahamas) on Oct. 12, 1492. His fleet consisted of 3 vessels—the *Niña, Pinta,* and *Santa María*. Stops were also made on Cuba and Hispaniola. A 2d expedition left Cadiz, Spain, Sept. 25, 1493, with 17 ships and 1,500 men, and reached the Lesser Antilles Nov. 3.

His 3d voyage brought him from Sanlucar, Spain (May 30, 1498, with 6 ships), to the north coast of S. America. A few years later a 4th voyage reached the mainland of Central America, after leaving Cadiz, Spain, May 9, 1502. Columbus died in 1506 convinced he had reached Asia by sailing west from Europe.

In N. America, John and Sebastian Cabot, Italian explorers sailing for the English, reached Newfoundland and possibly Nova Scotia in 1497. John's 2d voyage (1498), seeking a new trade route to Asia, resulted in the loss of his entire fleet.

During this period exploration in the western hemisphere was dominated by Spain and Portugal. In 1497 and 1499 Amerigo Vespucci (whom the Americas are named for), an Italian explorer sailing for the Spanish, passed along the N and E coasts of S America. He was the first to argue that the newly discovered lands were a continent other than Asia. The basic geography of the hemisphere became well understood by the early 1800s, as explorers from many countries helped fill in the map.

Year	Explorer	Nationality (employer, if different)	Area reached or explored
c1000	Leif Ericson	Norse	Newfoundland
1492-1502	Christopher Columbus	Italian (Spanish)	West Indies, S. and C. America
1497	John and Sebastian Cabot	Italian (English)	Atlantic Canada
1497-99	Amerigo Vespucci	Italian (Spanish)	E and N Coast of S. America
1499	Alonso de Ojeda	Spanish	N South American coast, Venezuela
1500, Feb.	Vicente Yañez Pinzon	Spanish	S. American coast, Amazon R.
1500, Apr.	Pedro Alvarez Cabral	Portuguese	Brazil
1500-02	Gaspar Corte-Real	Portuguese	Labrador
1501	Rodrigo de Bastidas	Spanish	Central America
1513	Vasco Nunez de Balboa	Spanish	Panama, Pacific Ocean
1513	Juan Ponce de Leon	Spanish	Florida, Yucatán Peninsula
1515	Juan de Solis	Spanish	Río de la Plata
1519	Alonso de Pineda	Spanish	Mouth of Mississippi R.
1519	Hernando Cortes	Spanish	Mexico
1519-20	Ferdinand Magellan	Portuguese (Spanish)	Straits of Magellan, Tierra del Fuego
1524	Giovanni da Verrazano	Italian (French)	Atlantic coast, inc. New York harbor
1528	Cabeza de Vaca	Spanish	Texas coast and interior
1532	Francisco Pizarro	Spanish	Peru
1534	Jacques Cartier	French	Canada, Gulf of St. Lawrence
1536	Pedro de Mendoza	Spanish	Buenos Aires
1539	Francisco de Ulloa	Spanish	California coast
1539-41	Hernando de Soto	Spanish	Mississippi R., near Memphis
1539	Marcos de Niza	Italian (Spanish)	SW United States
1540	Francisco de Coronado	Spanish	SW United States
1540	Hernando Alarcon	Spanish	Colorado R.
1540	Garcia de L. Cardenas	Spanish	Colorado, Grand Canyon
1541	Francisco de Orellana	Spanish	Amazon R.
1542	Juan Rodriguez Cabrillo	Portuguese (Spanish)	W Mexico, San Diego harbor
1565	Pedro Menéndez de Aviles	Spanish	St. Augustine, FL
1576	Sir Martin Frobisher	English	Frobisher's Bay, Canada
1577-80	Sir Francis Drake	English	California coast
1582	Antonio de Espejo	Spanish	Southwest U.S. (New Mexico)
1584	Amadas & Barlow (for Raleigh)	English	Virginia
1585-87	Sir Walter Raleigh's men	English	Roanoke Isl., NC
1595	Sir Walter Raleigh	English	Orinoco R.
1603-09	Samuel de Champlain	French	Canadian interior, Lake Champlain
1607	Capt. John Smith	English	Atlantic coast
1609-10	Henry Hudson	English (Dutch)	Hudson R., Hudson Bay
1634	Jean Nicolet	French	Lake Michigan, Wisconsin
1673	Jacques Marquette, Louis Jolliet	French	Mississippi R., S to Arkansas
1682	Robert Cavelier, sieur de La Salle	French	Mississippi R., S to Gulf of Mexico
1727-29	Vitus Bering	Danish (Russian)	Bering Strait and Alaska
1789	Sir Alexander Mackenzie	Canadian	NW Canada
1804-06	Meriwether Lewis and William Clark	American	Missouri R., Rocky Mts., Columbia R.

Arctic Exploration

Early Explorers

1587 — John Davis (Eng.). Davis Strait to Sanderson's Hope, 72°12′ N.

1596 — Willem Barents and Jacob van Heemskerck (Holland). Discovered Bear Isl., touched NW tip of Spitsbergen, 79°49′ N, rounded Novaya Zemlya, wintered at Ice Haven.

1607 — Henry Hudson (Eng.). North along Greenland's E coast to Cape Hold-with-Hope, 73°30′, then N of Spitsbergen to 80°23′. Returning he explored Hudson's Touches (Jan Mayen).

1616 — William Baffin and Robert Bylot (Eng.). Baffin Bay to Smith Sound.

1728 — Vitus Bering (Russ.). Proved Asia and America are separated, by sailing through strait that now bears his name.

1733-40 — Great Northern Expedition (Russ.). Surveyed Siberian Arctic coast.

1741 — Vitus Bering (Russ.). Sighted Alaska, named Mount St. Elias. His lieutenant, Chirikof, explored coast.

1771 — Samuel Hearne (Hudson's Bay Co.). Overland from Prince of Wales Fort (Churchill) on Hudson Bay to mouth of Coppermine R.

1778 — James Cook (Brit.). Through Bering Strait to Icy Cape, AK, and North Cape, Siberia.

1789 — Alexander Mackenzie (North West Co., Brit.). Montreal to mouth of Mackenzie River.

1806 — William Scoresby (Brit.). N of Spitsbergen to 81°30′.

1820-23 — Ferdinand von Wrangel (Russ.). Surveyed Siberian Arctic coast. His exploration joined James Cook's at North Cape, confirming separation of the continents.

1878-79 — (Nils) Adolf Erik Nordenskjöld (Swed.). The first to navigate the Northeast Passage—an ocean route connecting Europe's North Sea, along the Arctic coast of Asia and through the Bering Sea, to the Pacific Ocean.

1881 — The U.S. steamer *Jeannette*, led by Lt. Cmdr. George W. DeLong, was trapped in ice and crushed, June 1881. DeLong and 11 others died; 12 survived.

1888 — Fridtjof Nansen (Nor.) crossed Greenland's icecap.

1893-96 — Nansen in *Fram* drifted from New Siberian Isls. to Spitsbergen; tried polar dash in 1895, reached Franz Josef Land, 86°14′ N.

1897 — Salomon A. Andrée (Switz.) and 2 others started in balloon from Spitsbergen, July 11, to drift across pole to U.S., and disappeared. More than 33 yrs. later, Aug. 6, 1930, their frozen bodies were found on White Isl., 82°57′ N, 29°52′ E.

1903-6 — Roald Amundsen (Nor.) first sailed the Northwest Passage—an ocean route linking the Atlantic Ocean to the Pacific via Canada's marine waterways.

North Pole Exploration

Robert E. Peary explored Greenland's coast, 1891-92; tried for North Pole, 1893. In 1900 he reached N limit of Greenland and 83°50′ N; in 1902 he reached 84°06′ N; in 1906 he went from Ellesmere Isl. to 87°06′ N. He sailed in the *Roosevelt,* July 1908, to winter off Cape Sheridan, Grant Land. The dash for the North Pole began Mar. 1 from Cape Columbia, Ellesmere Isl. Peary reportedly reached the pole, 90° N, Apr. 6, 1909; however, subsequent research suggests that he may have miscalculated and fallen short of his goal by c. 30-60 mi. Peary had several supporting groups carrying supplies until the last group turned back at 87°47′ N. Peary, Matthew Henson, and 4 Eskimos proceeded with dog teams and sleds. They were said to have crossed the pole several times, then built an igloo there and remained 36 hours. Started south, Apr. 7 at 4 PM, for Cape Columbia.

1914 — Donald MacMillan (U.S.). Northwest, 200 mi, from Axel Heiberg Isl. to seek Peary's Crocker Land.

1915-17 — Vihjalmur Stefansson (Can.). Discovered Borden, Brock, Meighen, and Lougheed Isls.

1918-20 — Amundsen sailed the Northeast Passage.

1925 — Amundsen and Lincoln Ellsworth (U.S.) reached 87°44′ N in attempt to fly to North Pole from Spitsbergen.

1926 — Richard E. Byrd and Floyd Bennett (U.S.) reputedly flew over North Pole, May 9. (Claim to have reached the Pole is in dispute, however.)

1926 — Amundsen, Ellsworth, and Umberto Nobile (It.) flew from Spitsbergen over North Pole May 12, to Teller, AK, in dirigible *Norge.*

1928 — Nobile crossed North Pole in airship, May 24; crashed, May 25. Amundsen died attempting a rescue.

North Pole Exploration Records

On Aug. 3, 1958, the *Nautilus,* under Comdr. William R. Anderson, became the first ship to cross the North Pole beneath the Arctic ice.

In Aug. 1960, the nuclear-powered U.S. submarine *Seadragon* (Comdr. George P. Steele 2d) made the first E-W underwater transit through the Northwest Passage. Traveling submerged for the most part, it took 6 days to make the 850-mi trek from Baffin Bay to the Beaufort Sea.

On Aug. 16, 1977, the Soviet nuclear icebreaker *Arktika* reached the North Pole, becoming the first surface ship to break through the Arctic ice pack.

On Apr. 30, 1978, Naomi Uemura (Jap.) became the first person to reach the North Pole alone, traveling by dog sled in a 54-day, 600-mi trek over the frozen Arctic.

In Apr. 1982, Sir Ranulph Fiennes and Charles Burton, Brit. explorers, reached the North Pole and became the first to circle the earth from pole to pole. They had reached the South Pole 16 months earlier. The 52,000-mi trek took 3 years, involved 23 people, and cost an estimated $18 mil.

On May 2, 1986, 6 Amer. and Can. explorers reached the North Pole assisted only by dogs. They became the first to reach the pole without aerial logistics support since Robert E. Peary planted a flag there in 1909. The explorers, Amer. Will Steger, Paul Schurke, Anne Bancroft, and Geoff Carroll, and Can. Brent Boddy and Richard Weber, completed the 500-mi journey in 56 days.

On June 15, 1995, Weber and Russ. Mikhail Malakhov became the first pair to make it to the pole and back without any mechanical assistance. The 940-mi trip, made entirely on skis, took 121 days.

Antarctic Exploration

Antarctica has been approached since 1773-75, when Capt. James Cook (Brit.) reached 71° 10′ S. Many sea and landmarks bear names of early explorers. Fabian von Bellingshausen (Russ.) discovered Peter I and Alexander I Isls., 1819-21. Nathaniel Palmer (U.S.) traveled throughout Palmer Peninsula, 60° W, 1820, without realizing that this was a continent. Capt. John Davis (U.S.) made the first known landing on the continent on Feb. 7, 1821. Later, in 1823, James Weddell (Brit.) found Weddell Sea, 74° 15′ S, the southernmost point that had been reached.

First to announce existence of the continent of Antarctica was Charles Wilkes (U.S.), who followed the coast for 1,500 mi, 1840. Adelie Coast, 140° E, was found by Dumont d'Urville (Fr.), 1840. Ross Ice Shelf was found by James Clark Ross (Brit.), 1841-42.

1895 — Leonard Kristensen (Nor.) landed a party on the coast of Victoria Land. They were the first ashore on the main continental mass. C. E. Borchgrevink, a member of that party, returned in 1899 with a Brit. expedition, first to winter on Antarctica.

1902-4 — Robert F. Scott (Brit.) explored Edward VII Peninsula. He reached 82° 17′ S, 146° 33′ E from McMurdo Sound.

1908-9 — Ernest Shackleton (Brit.) introduced the use of Manchurian ponies in Antarctic sledging. He reached 88° 23′ S, discovering a route on to the plateau by way of the Beardmore Glacier and pioneering the way to the pole.

1911 — Roald Amundsen (Nor.) with 4 men and dog teams reached the South Pole, Dec. 14.

1912 — Scott reached the pole from Ross Isl., Jan. 18, with 4 companions. None of Scott's party survived. Their bodies and expedition notes were found, Nov. 12.

1928 — First person to use an airplane over Antarctica was Sir George Hubert Wilkins (Austral.).

1929 — Richard E. Byrd (U.S.) established Little America on Bay of Whales. On 1,600-mi airplane flight begun Nov. 28, he crossed South Pole, Nov. 29, with 3 others.

1934-35 — Byrd led 2d expedition to Little America, explored 450,000 sq mi, wintered alone at weather station, 80°08′ S.

1934-37 — John Rymill led British Graham Land expedition; discovered Palmer Penin. is part of mainland.

1935 — Lincoln Ellsworth (U.S.) flew S along E Coast of Palmer Penin., then crossed continent to Little America, making 4 landings on unprepared terrain in bad weather.

1939-41 — U.S. Antarctic Service Expedition built West Base on Ross Ice Shelf under Paul Siple, and East Base on Palmer Peninsula under Richard Black. U.S. Navy plane flights discovered about 150,000 sq mi of new land.

1940 — Byrd charted most of coast between Ross Sea and Palmer Penin.

1946-47 — U.S. Navy undertook Operation Highjump, commanded by Byrd, included 13 ships and 4,000 men. Airplanes photomapped coastline and penetrated beyond pole.

1946-48 — Ronne Antarctic Research Expedition Comdr., Finn Ronne, USNR, determined the Antarctic to be only one continent with no strait between Weddell Sea and Ross Sea; explored 250,000 sq mi of land by flights to 79° S. Mrs. Ronne and Mrs. H. Darlington were the first women to winter on Antarctica.

1955-57 — U.S. Navy's Operation Deep Freeze led by Adm. Byrd. Supporting U.S. scientific efforts for the International Geophysical Year (IGY), the operation was commanded by Rear Adm. George Dufek. It established 5 coastal stations fronting the Indian, Pacific, and Atlantic oceans and also 3 interior stations; explored more than 1,000,000 sq mi in Wilkes Land.

1957-58 — During the IGY, July 1957 through Dec. 1958, scientists from 12 countries conducted Antarctic research at a network of some 60 stations on Antarctica.

Dr. Vivian E. Fuchs led a 12-person Trans-Antarctic Expedition on the first land crossing of Antarctica. Starting from the Weddell Sea, they reached Scott Station, Mar. 2, 1958, after traveling 2,158 mi in 98 days.

1958 — A group of 5 U.S. scientists led by Edward C. Thiel, seismologist, moving by tractor from Ellsworth Station on Weddell Sea, identified a huge mountain range, 5,000 ft above the ice sheet and 9,000 ft above sea level. The range, originally seen by a Navy plane, was named the Dufek Massif, for Rear Adm. George Dufek.

1959 — Argentina, Australia, Belgium, Chile, France, Japan, New Zealand, Norway, South Africa, U.S.S.R., U.K, and U.S. signed a treaty suspending territorial claims for 30 yrs. and reserving the continent, S of 60° S, for research.

1961-62 — Scientists discovered the Bentley Trench, running from Ross Ice Shelf into Marie Byrd Land, near the end of the Ellsworth Mts., toward the Weddell Sea.

1962 — First nuclear power plant began operation at McMurdo Sound.

1963 — On Feb. 22, a U.S. plane made the longest nonstop flight ever in the South Pole area, covering 3,600 mi in 10 hr. The flight was from McMurdo Station S past the pole to Shackleton Mts., SE to the "Area of Inaccessibility," and back to McMurdo Station.

1964 — A Brit. survey team was landed by helicopter on Cook Island, the first recorded visit since 1775.

1964 — New Zealanders mapped the mountain area from Cape Adare W some 400 mi to Pennell Glacier.

1985 — Igor A. Zotikov, a Russian researcher, discovered sediments in the Ross Ice Shelf that seem to support the continental drift theory. Research by the Ocean Drilling Project off the Queen Maud Land coast indicated that the ice sheets of E Antarctica are 37 million yrs. old.

1989 — Victoria Murden and Shirley Metz became both the first women and the first Americans to reach the South Pole overland when they arrived with 9 others on Jan. 17, 1989. The 51-day trek on skis covered 740 mi.

1991 — 24 nations approved a protocol to the 1959 Antarctica Treaty, Oct. 4. New conservation provisions, including banning oil and other mineral exploration for 50 yrs.

1995 — On Dec. 22, a Norwegian, Borge Ousland, reached the South Pole in the fastest time on skis: 44 days.

1996-97 — Ousland became 1st person to traverse Antarctica alone; reached South Pole Dec. 19, 1996; traveled 1,675 mi in 64 days, ending Jan. 18, 1997.

Volcanoes

Sources: *Volcanoes of the World, 2d edition*, 1994, Geoscience Press; Global Volcanism Network, Smithsonian Institution

Roughly 540 volcanoes are known to have erupted during historical times. Nearly 75% of these historically active volcanoes lie along the so-called Ring of Fire, running along the W coast of the Americas from the southern tip of Chile to Alaska, down the E coast of Asia from Kamchatka to Indonesia, and continuing from New Guinea to New Zealand. The Ring of Fire marks the boundary between the mobile tectonic plates underlying the Pacific Ocean and those of the surrounding continents. Other active regions occur along rift zones, where plates pull apart, as in Iceland, or where molten material moves up from the mantle over local "hot spots," as in Hawaii. The vast majority of the earth's volcanism occurs at submarine rift zones. For more information on volcanoes visit the Smithsonian Institution's Global Volcanism Network Web site at http://www.nmnh.si.edu/gvp

Notable Volcanic Eruptions

Approximately 7,000 years ago, Mazama, a 9,900-ft volcano in southern Oregon, erupted violently, ejecting large amounts of ash and pumice and voluminous pyroclastic flows. The ash spread over the entire northwestern U.S. and as far away as Saskatchewan, Can. During the eruption, the top of the mountain collapsed, leaving a caldera 6 mi across and about a half mile deep, which filled with rainwater to form what is now called Crater Lake.

In AD 79, Vesuvio, or Vesuvius, a 4,190-ft volcano overlooking Naples Bay, became active after several centuries of apparent quiescence. On Aug. 24 of that year, a heated mud and ash flow swept down the mountain, engulfing the cities of Pompeii, Herculaneum, and Stabiae with debris more than 60 ft deep. About 10% of the population of the 3 towns were killed.

In 1883, an eruption similar to the Mazama eruption occurred on the island of Krakatau. At least 2,000 people died in pyroclastic flows on Aug. 26. The next day, the 2,640-ft peak of the volcano collapsed to 1,000 ft below sea level, sinking most of the island and killing over 3,000 people. A tsunami (tidal wave) generated by the collapse then killed more than 31,000 people in nearby Java and Sumatra and eventually reached England. Ash from the eruption colored sunsets around the world for 2 years. A similar, even more powerful eruption had taken place 68 years earlier at Mt. Tambora on the Indonesian island of Sumbawa.

Date	Volcano	Estimated Deaths	Date	Volcano	Estimated Deaths
Aug. 24, AD 79	Mt. Vesuvius, Italy	16,000	May 8, 1902	Mt. Pelée, Martinique	28,000
1586	Kelut, Java, Indon.	10,000	Jan. 30, 1911	Mt. Taal, Phil.	1,400
Dec. 15, 1631	Mt. Vesuvius, Italy	4,000	May 19, 1919	Mt. Kelud, Java, Indon.	5,000
Aug. 12, 1772	Mt. Papandayan, Java, Indon.	3,000	Jan. 17-21, 1951	Mt. Lamington, New Guinea	3,000
June 8, 1783	Laki, Iceland	9,350	May 18, 1980	Mt. St. Helens, U.S.	57
May 21, 1792	Mt. Unzen, Japan	14,500	Mar. 28, 1982	El Chichon, Mex.	1,880
Apr. 10-12, 1815	Mt. Tambora, Sumbawa, Indon.	92,000[1]	Nov. 13, 1985	Nevado del Ruiz, Colombia	23,000
Aug. 26-28, 1883	Krakatau, Indon.	36,000	Aug. 21, 1986	Lake Nyos, Cameroon	1,700
Apr. 24, 1902	Santa María, Guatemala	1,000[2]	June 15, 1991	Mt. Pinatubo, Luzon, Phil.	800

(1) Of these, 10,000 were directly related to the eruption; an additional 82,000 were the result of starvation and disease brought on by the event. (2) An additional 3,000 deaths due to a malaria outbreak are sometimes attributed to the eruption.

Notable Active Volcanoes

Active volcanoes display a wide range of activity. In this table, years are given for last display of eruptive activity, as of June 1998; list does not include submarine volcanoes. An eruption may involve explosive ejection of new or old fragmental material, escape of liquid lava, or both. Volcanoes are listed by height, which does not reflect eruptive magnitude.

Name (latest eruption)	Location	Height (ft)
Africa		
Mt. Cameroon (1982)	Cameroon	13,435
Nyiragongo (1994)	Congo	11,400
Nyamuragira (1994)	Congo	10,028
Ol Doinyo Lengai (1996)	Tanzania	9,469
Fogo (1995)	Cape Verde Isls.	9,281
Karthala (1991)	Comoros	8,000
Piton de la Fournaise (1998)	Réunion Isl., Indian Ocean	5,981
Lake Nyos (1986)	Cameroon	3,011
Erta-Ale (1998)	Ethiopia	1,650
Antarctica		
Erebus (1998)	Ross Isl.	12,450
Deception Island (1970)	S. Shetland Isl.	1,890
Asia-Oceania		
Kliuchevskoi (1990)	Kamchatka, Russia	15,863
Kerinci (1970)	Sumatra, Indon.	12,467
Fuji (1708)	Honshu, Japan	12,388
Tolbachik (1876)	Kamchatka, Russia	12,080
Semeru (1998)	Java, Indon.	12,060
Slamet (1989)	Java, Indon.	11,247
Raung (1997)	Java, Indon.	10,932
Shiveluch (1993)	Kamchatka, Russia	10,771
On-take (1980)	Honshu, Japan	10,049
Mayon (1993)	Luzon, Phil.	9,991
Merapi (1997)	Java, Indon.	9,550
Bezymianny (1998)	Kamchatka, Russia	9,455
Ruapehu (1996)	New Zealand	9,175
Peuet Sague (1979)	Sumatra, Indon.	9,120
Heard (1993)	Indian Ocean	9,006
Baitoushan (1702)	China/Korea	9,003
Asama (1990)	Honshu, Japan	8,300
Niigata Yake-yama (1989)	Honshu, Japan	8,111
Canlaon (1997)	Negros Isls., Phil.	8,070
Alaid (1996)	Kuril Isl., Russia	7,674
Ulawun (1993)	Papua New Guinea	7,532
Ngauruhoe (1977)	New Zealand	7,515
Chokai (1974)	Honshu, Japan	7,300
Galunggung (1984)	Java, Indon.	7,113
Azuma (1977)	Honshu, Japan	6,700
Bagana (1998)	Papua New Guinea	6,558
ySangeang Api (1988)	Lesser Sunda Isl., Indon.	6,351
Nasu (1963)	Honshu, Japan	6,210
Tiatia (1981)	Kuril Isl., Russia	6,013
Soputan (1996)	Sulawesi, Indon.	5,994
Bandai (1888)	Honshu, Japan	5,968
Manam (1998)	Papua New Guinea	5,928
Kuju (1996)	Kyushu, Japan	5,866
Karangetang-Api Siau (1995)	Sangihe, Indon.	5,853
Kelud (1990)	Java, Indon.	5,679
Adatara (1996)	Honshu, Japan	5,636
Gamalama (1993)	Halmahera, Indon.	5,627
Kirishima (1992)	Kyushu, Japan	5,577
Gamkonora (1987)	Halmahera, Indon.	5,364
Pinatubo (1995)	Luzon, Phil.	5,249
Aso (1995)	Kyushu, Japan	5,223
Lokon-Empung (1992)	Sulawesi, Indon.	5,187
Bulusan (1995)	Luzon, Phil.	5,115
Sarychev Peak (1989)	Kuril Isl., Russia	4,960
Karkar (1979)	Papua New Guinea	4,920
Akan (1997)	Hokkaido, Japan	4,917
Akademia (1996)	Kamchatka, Russia	4,875
Karymsky (1998)	Kamchatka, Russia	4,875
Lopevi (1996)	Vanuatu	4,755
Akita-Yake-yama (1998)	Japan	4,482
Unzen (1996)	Kyushu, Japan	4,462
Ambrym (1998)	Vanuatu	4,376
Langila (1998)	Papua New Guinea	4,363
Awu (1992)	Sangihe Isl., Indon.	4,350
Sakura-jima (1998)	Kyushu, Japan	3,665
Komaga-take (1996)	Hokkaido, Japan	3,740
Dukono (1998)	Halmahera, Indonesia	3,566
Krakatau (1995)	Indonesia	2,667
Suwanose-jima (1998)	Kyushu, Japan	2,621
Gaua (1982)	Vanuatu	2,614
Oshima (1990)	Izu Isls., Japan	2,487
Usu (1982)	Hokkaido, Japan	2,398
Rabaul (1998)	Papua New Guinea	2,257
Pagan (1993)	N. Mariana Isl.	1,870
Yasur (1998)	Tanna Island, Vanuatu	1,184
White Island (1998)	Bay of Plenty, New Zealand	1,053
Taal (1977)	Luzon, Phil.	984
McDonald Island (1997)	Indian Ocn., Australia	610
Central America—Caribbean		
Acatenango (1972)	Guatemala	12,992
Tacana (1986)	Guatemala	12,400
Santa María (1998)	Guatemala	12,375
Fuego (1987)	Guatemala	12,346
Irazú (1965)	Costa Rica	11,260
Turrialba (1866)	Costa Rica	10,958
Póas (1994)	Costa Rica	8,884
Pacaya (1998)	Guatemala	8,373
San Miguel (1986)	El Salvador	6,994
Rincón de la Vieja (1998)	Costa Rica	6,286
San Cristobal (1997)	Nicaragua	5,725
Arenal (1998)	Costa Rica	5,436
Concepción (1986)	Nicaragua	5,282
Soufrière Guadeloupe (1977)	Guadeloupe	4,813
Pelee (1932)	Martinique	4,583
Momotombo (1905)	Nicaragua	4,127
Soufriere St. Vincent (1979)	St. Vincent	3,865
Soufriere Hills (1998)	Montserrat	3,001
Masaya (1996)	Nicaragua	2,083
South America		
Llullaillaco (1877)	Chile	22,057
Guallatiri (1960)	Chile	19,918
Cotopaxi (1940)	Ecuador	19,347
El Misti (1870?)	Peru	19,101
Tupungatito (1986)	Chile	18,504
Láscar (1995)	Chile	18,346
Ruiz (1991)	Colombia	17,457
Sangay (1998)	Ecuador	17,021
Irruputuncu (1995)	Chile	16,939
Guagua Pichincha (1993)	Ecuador	15,696
Purace (1977)	Colombia	15,601
Galeras (1993)	Colombia	14,029
Llaima (1995)	Chile	10,253
Villarrica (1998)	Chile	9,340
Cerro Hudson (1991)	Chile	8,580
Fernandina (1995)	Galapagos Isls., Ecuador	4,905
Mid-Pacific		
Mauna Loa (1984)	Hawaii, HI	13,680
Kilauea (1998)	Hawaii, HI	4,009
Mid-Atlantic Ridge		
Jan Mayen (1985)	N. Atlantic Ocn., Norway	7,470
Grímsvötn (1996)	Iceland	5,659
Hekla (1991)	Iceland	4,892
Krafla (1984)	Iceland	2,145
Europe		
Etna (1998)	Italy	10,990
Vesuvius (1944)	Italy	4,203
Stromboli (1998)	Italy	3,038
Santorini (1950)	Greece	1,850
North America		
Pico de Orizaba (1687)	Mexico	18,555
Popocatépetl (1998)	Mexico	17,802
Rainier (1894?)	Washington	14,410
Wrangell (1907?)	Alaska	14,163
Shasta (1786)	California	14,162
Colima (1994)	Mexico	12,361
Redoubt (1990)	Alaska	10,197
Iliamna (1953)	Alaska	10,016
Shishaldin (1995)	Aleutian Isl., AK	9,373
Pavlof (1997)	Alaska	8,264
St. Helens (1991)	Washington	8,363
Veniaminof (1995)	Alaska	8,225
El Chichon (1982)	Mexico	7,300
Novarupta (Katmai) (1912)	Alaska	6,715
Makushin (1987)	Aleutian Isl., AK	6,680
Great Sitkin (1974)	Aleutian Isl., AK	5,710
Cleveland (1994)	Aleutian Isl., AK	5,675
Gareloi (1989)	Aleutian Isl., AK	5,161
Atka (1996)	Aleutian Isl., AK	5,029
Korovin (1998)	Aleutian Isl., AK	4,852
Akutan (1992)	Aleutian Isl., AK	4,275
Kiska (1990)	Aleutian Isl., AK	4,275
Augustine (1986)	Alaska	3,999
Okmok (1997)	Aleutian Isl., AK	3,520
Seguam (1993)	Aleutian Isl., AK	3,458

Mountains

Height of Mount Everest

Mt. Everest was considered 29,002 ft when Edmund Hillary and Tenzing Norgay scaled it in 1953. This triangulation figure had been accepted since 1850. In 1954 the Surveyor General of the Republic of India set the height at 29,028 ft, plus or minus 10 ft because of snow; this figure is used below. The National Geographic Society accepts it, but many mountaineering groups still use 29,002 ft.

In 1987, new calculations based on satellite measurements suggested that the Himalayan peak K-2 rose 29,064 ft above sea level and that Mt. Everest is 800 ft higher. The National Geographic Society kept to the figure of 29,028 ft.

United States, Canada, Mexico

Name	Place	Height (ft)
McKinley	AK	20,320
Logan	Yukon	19,850
Pico de Orizaba	Mexico	18,555
St. Elias	AK-Yukon	18,008
Popocatépetl	Mexico	17,930
Foraker	AK	17,400
Iztaccihuatl	Mexico	17,343
Lucania	Yukon	17,147
King	Yukon	16,971
Steele	Yukon	16,644
Bona	AK	16,550
Blackburn	AK	16,390
Kennedy	AK	16,286
Sanford	AK	16,237
Vancouver	AK-Yukon	15,979
South Buttress	AK	15,885
Wood	Yukon	15,885
Churchill	AK	15,638
Fairweather	AK-BC	15,300
Zinantecatl (Toluca)	Mexico	15,016
Hubbard	AK-Yukon	15,015
Bear	AK	14,831
Walsh	Yukon	14,780
East Buttress	AK	14,730
Matlalcueyetl	Mexico	14,636
Hunter	AK	14,573
Alverstone	AK-Yukon	14,565
Browne Tower	AK	14,530
Whitney	CA	14,494
Elbert	CO	14,433
Massive	CO	14,421
Harvard	CO	14,420
Rainier	WA	14,410
University Peak	AK	14,410
Williamson	CA	14,375
La Plata Peak	CO	14,361
Blanca Peak	CO	14,345
Uncompahgre Peak	CO	14,309
Crestone Peak	CO	14,294
Lincoln	CO	14,286
Grays Peak	CO	14,270
Antero	CO	14,269
Torreys Peak	CO	14,267
Castle Peak	CO	14,265
Quandary Peak	CO	14,265
Evans	CO	14,264
Longs Peak	CO	14,255
McArthur	Yukon	14,253
Wilson	CO	14,246
White Mt. Peak	CA	14,246
North Palisade	CA	14,242
Cameron	CO	14,238
Shavano	CO	14,229
Belford	CO	14,197
Princeton	CO	14,197
Crestone Needle	CO	14,197
Yale	CO	14,196
Bross	CO	14,172
Kit Carson	CO	14,165
Wrangell	AK	14,163
Shasta	CA	14,162
El Diente Peak	CO	14,159
Point Success	WA	14,158
Maroon Peak	CO	14,156
Tabeguache	CO	14,155
Oxford	CO	14,153
Sill	CA	14,153
Sneffels	CO	14,150
Democrat	CO	14,148
Capitol Peak	CO	14,130
Liberty Cap	WA	14,112
Pikes Peak	CO	14,110
Snowmass	CO	14,092
Russell	CA	14,088
Eolus	CO	14,083
Windom	CO	14,082
Columbia	CO	14,073
Augusta	AK	14,070

South America

Peak, country	Height (ft)
Aconcagua, Argentina	22,834
Ojos del Salado, Arg.-Chile	22,572
Bonete, Argentina	22,546
Tupungato, Argentina-Chile	22,310
Pissis, Argentina	22,241
Mercedario, Argentina	22,211
Huascaran, Peru	22,205
Llullaillaco, Argentina-Chile	22,057
El Libertador, Argentina	22,047
Cachi, Argentina	22,047
Incahuasi, Argentina-Chile	21,720
Yerupaja, Peru	21,709
Galan, Argentina	21,654
El Muerto, Argentina-Chile	21,457
Sajama, Bolivia	21,391
Nacimiento, Argentina	21,302
Illimani, Bolivia	21,201
Coropuna, Peru	21,083
Laudo, Argentina	20,997
Ancohuma, Bolivia	20,958
Ausangate, Peru	20,945
Toro, Argentina-Chile	20,932
Illampu, Bolivia	20,873
Tres Cruces, Argentina-Chile	20,853
Huandoy, Peru	20,852
Parinacota, Bolivia-Chile	20,768
Tortolas, Argentina-Chile	20,745
Ampato, Peru	20,702
El Condor, Argentina	20,669
Salcantay, Peru	20,574
Chimborazo, Ecuador	20,561
Huancarhuas, Peru	20,531
Famatina, Argentina	20,505
Pumasillo, Peru	20,492
Solo, Argentina	20,492
Polleras, Argentina	20,456
Pular, Chile	20,423
Chani, Argentina	20,341
Aucanquilcha, Chile	20,295
Juncal, Argentina-Chile	20,276
Negro, Argentina	20,184
Quela, Argentina	20,128
Condoriri, Bolivia	20,095
Palermo, Argentina	20,079
Solimana, Peru	20,068
San Juan, Argentina-Chile	20,049
Sierra Nevada, Arg.-Chile	20,023
Antofalla, Argentina	20,013
Marmolejo, Argentina-Chile	20,013
Chachani, Peru	19,931

The highest point in the West Indies is in the Dominican Republic, Pico Duarte (10,417 ft).

Africa

Peak, country/island	Height (ft)
Kilimanjaro, Tanzania	19,340
Kenya, Kenya	17,058
Margherita Pk., Uganda-Congo	16,763
Ras Dashan, Ethiopia	15,158
Meru, Tanzania	14,979
Karisimbi, Congo-Rwanda	14,787
Elgon, Kenya-Uganda	14,178
Batu, Ethiopia	14,131
Guna, Ethiopia	13,881
Gughe, Ethiopia	13,780
Toubkal, Morocco	13,661
Cameroon, Cameroon	13,435

Australia, New Zealand, SE Asian Islands

Peak, country/island	Height (ft)
Jaya, New Guinea	16,500
Trikora, New Guinea	15,585
Mandala, New Guinea	15,420
Wilhelm, New Guinea	14,793
Kinabalu, Malaysia	13,455
Kerinci, Sumatra, Indon.	12,467
Cook, New Zealand	12,349
Teide, Canary Isls.	12,198
Semeru, Java, Indon.	12,060
Kosciusko, Australia	7,310

Europe

Alps

Peak, country	Height (ft)
Mont Blanc, Fr.-It.	15,771
Monte Rosa (highest peak of group), Switz.	15,203
Dom, Switz.	14,911
Liskamm, It., Switz.	14,852
Weisshorn, Switz.	14,780
Taschhorn, Switz.	14,733
Matterhorn, It., Switz.	14,690
Dent Blanche, Switz.	14,293
Nadelhorn, Switz.	14,196
Grand Combin, Switz.	14,154
Lenzpitze, Switz.	14,088
Finsteraarhorn, Switz.	14,022
Castor, Switz.	13,865
Zinalrothorn, Switz.	13,849
Hohberghom, Switz.	13,842
Alphubel, Switz.	13,799
Rimpfischhom, Switz.	13,776
Aletschorn, Switz.	13,763
Strahlhorn, Switz.	13,747
Dent D'Herens, Switz.	13,686
Breithorn, It., Switz.	13,665
Bishorn, Switz.	13,645
Jungfrau, Switz.	13,642
Ecrins, Fr.	13,461
Monch, Switz.	13,448
Pollux, Switz.	13,422
Schreckhorn, Switz.	13,379
Ober Gabelhorn, Switz.	13,330
Gran Paradiso, It.	13,323
Bernina, It., Switz.	13,284
Fiescherhorn, Switz.	13,283
Grunhorn, Switz.	13,266
Lauteraarhorn, Switz.	13,261
Durrenhorn, Switz.	13,238
Allalinhorn, Switz.	13,213
Weissmies, Switz.	13,199
Lagginhorn, Switz.	13,156
Zupo, Switz.	13,120
Fletschhorn, Switz.	13,110
Adlerhorn, Switz.	13,081
Gletscherhorn, Switz.	13,068
Schalihorn, Switz.	13,040
Scerscen, Switz.	13,028
Eiger, Switz.	13,025
Jagerhorn, Switz.	13,024
Rottalhorn, Switz.	13,022

Pyrenees

Peak, country	Height (ft)
Aneto, Sp.	11,168
Posets, Sp.	11,073
Perdido, Sp.	11,007
Vignemale, Fr.-Sp.	10,820
Long, Sp.	10,479
Estats, Sp.	10,304
Montcalm, Sp.	10,105

Caucasus (Europe-Asia)

Peak, country	Height (ft)
Elbrus, Russia	18,841
Shkhara, Georgia	17,064
Dykh Tau, Russia	17,054
Kashtan Tau, Russia	16,877
Janqi, Georgia	16,565
Kazbek, Georgia	16,558

Asia (Mainland)

Peak	Place	Height (ft)
Everest	Nepal-Tibet	29,028
K2 (Godwin Austen)	Kashmir	28,250
Kanchenjunga	India-Nepal	28,208
Lhotse I (Everest)	Nepal-Tibet	27,923
Makalu I	Nepal-Tibet	27,824
Lhotse II (Everest)	Nepal-Tibet	27,560
Dhaulagiri	Nepal	26,810
Manaslu I	Nepal	26,760
Cho Oyu	Nepal-Tibet	26,750
Nanga Parbat	Kashmir	26,660
Annapurna I	Nepal	26,504
Gasherbrum	Kashmir	26,470
Broad	Kashmir	26,400
Gosainthan	Tibet	26,287
Annapurna II	Nepal	26,041
Gyachung Kang	Nepal-Tibet	25,910
Disteghil Sar	Kashmir	25,868
Himalchuli	Nepal	25,801
Nuptse (Everest)	Nepal-Tibet	25,726
Masherbrum	Kashmir	25,660
Nanda Devi	India	25,645
Rakaposhi	Kashmir	25,550
Kamet	India-Tibet	25,447
Namcha Barwa	Tibet	25,445
Gurla Mandhata	Tibet	25,355
Ulugh Muz Tagh	Xinjiang-Tibet	25,340
Kungur	Xinjiang	25,325
Tirich Mir	Pakistan	25,230
Makalu II	Nepal-Tibet	25,120
Minya Konka	China	24,900
Kula Gangri	Bhutan-Tibet	24,784
Changtzu (Everest)	Nepal-Tibet	24,780
Muz Tagh Ata	Xinjiang	24,757
Skyang Kangri	Kashmir	24,750
Communism Peak	Tajikistan	24,590
Jongsang Peak	India-Nepal	24,472
Jengish Chokusu	Xinjiang-Kyrgyzstan	24,406
Sia Kangri	Kashmir	24,350
Haramosh Peak	Pakistan	24,270
Istoro Nal	Pakistan	24,240
Tent Peak	India-Nepal	24,165
Chomo Lhari	Bhutan-Tibet	24,040
Chamlang	Nepal	24,012
Kabru	India-Nepal	24,002
Alung Gangri	Tibet	24,000
Baltoro Kangri	Kashmir	23,990
Mussu Shan	Xinjiang	23,890
Mana	India	23,860
Baruntse	Nepal	23,688
Nepal Peak	India-Nepal	23,500
Amne Machin	China	23,490
Gauri Sankar	Nepal-Tibet	23,440
Badrinath	India	23,420
Nunkun	Kashmir	23,410
Lenin Peak	Tajikistan	23,405
Pyramid	India-Nepal	23,400
Api	Nepal	23,399
Pauhunri	India-Tibet	23,385
Trisul	India	23,360
Kangto	India-Tibet	23,260
Nyenchhe Thanglha	Tibet	23,255
Trisuli	India	23,210
Pumori	Nepal-Tibet	23,190
Dunagiri	India	23,184
Lombo Kangra	Tibet	23,165
Saipal	Nepal	23,100
Macha Pucchare	Nepal	22,958
Numbar	Nepal	22,817
Kanjiroba	Nepal	22,580
Ama Dablam	Nepal	22,350
Cho Polu	Nepal	22,093
Lingtren	Nepal-Tibet	21,972
Khumbutse	Nepal-Tibet	21,785
Hlako Gangri	Tibet	21,266
Mt. Grosvenor	China	21,190
Thagchhab Gangri	Tibet	20,970
Damavand	Iran	18,606
Ararat	Turkey	16,804

Antarctica

Peak	Height (ft)
Vinson Massif	16,864
Tyree	16,290
Shinn	15,750
Gardner	15,375
Epperly	15,100
Kirkpatrick	14,855
Elizabeth	14,698
Markham	14,290
Bell	14,117
Mackellar	14,098
Anderson	13,957
Bentley	13,934
Kaplan	13,878
Andrew Jackson	13,750
Sidley	13,720
Ostenso	13,710
Minto	13,668
Miller	13,650
Long Gables	13,620
Dickerson	13,517
Giovinetto	13,412
Wade	13,400
Fisher	13,386
Fridtjof Nansen	13,350
Wexler	13,202
Lister	13,200
Shear	13,100
Odishaw	13,008
Donaldson	12,894
Ray	12,808
Sellery	12,779
Waterman	12,730
Anne	12,703
Press	12,566
Falla	12,549
Rucker	12,520
Goldthwait	12,510
Morris	12,500
Erebus	12,450
Campbell	12,434
Don Pedro Christophersen	12,355
Lysaght	12,326
Huggins	12,247
Sabine	12,200
Astor	12,175
Mohl	12,172
Frankes	12,064
Jones	12,040
Gjelsvik	12,008
Coman	12,000

Some Notable U.S. Mountains

Name	Place	Height (ft)
Gannett Peak	WY	13,804
Grand Teton	WY	13,766
Kings	UT	13,528
Cloud	WY	13,175
Wheeler	NM	13,161
Boundary	NV	13,140
Granite	MT	12,799
Borah	ID	12,662
Humphreys	AZ	12,633
Adams	WA	12,277
San Gorgonio	CA	11,502
Hood	OR	11,239
Lassen	CA	10,457
Granite	CA	10,321
Guadalupe	TX	8,749
Olympus	WA	7,965
Harney	SD	7,242
Mitchell	NC	6,684
Clingmans Dome	NC-TN	6,643
Washington	NH	6,288
Rogers	VA	5,729
Marcy	NY	5,344
Katahdin	ME	5,268
Spruce Knob	WV	4,862
Mansfield	VT	4,393
Black Mountain	KY	4,145

Important Islands and Their Areas

Reviewed by Laurel Duda, Marine Biological Laboratory/Woods Hole Oceanographic Inst. Library.

Figure in parentheses shows rank among the world's 10 largest individual islands. Because some islands have not been surveyed accurately, some areas shown are estimates. Figures are for total areas in square miles. Some "islands" listed are island groups. Only the largest islands in a group are listed individually. Only islands 10 sq. miles or larger are listed.

Antarctica

Adelaide	1,400
Alexander	16,700
Berkner	18,500
Roosevelt	2,900

Arctic Ocean

Akimiski, Northwest Territories	1,159
Amund Ringnes, NWT	2,029
Axel Heiberg, NWT	16,671
Baffin, NWT **(5)**	195,928
Banks, NWT	27,038
Bathurst, NWT	6,194
Bolshevik, Russia	4,368
Bolshoy Lyakhovsky, Russia	1,776
Borden, NWT	1,079
Bylot, NWT	4,273
Coats, NWT	2,123
Cornwallis, NWT	2,701
Devon, NWT	21,331
Disko, Greenland	3,312
Ellef Ringnes, NWT	4,361
Ellesmere, NWT **(10)**	75,767
Faddayevskiy, Russia	1,930
Franz Josef Land, Russia	8,000
Iturup (Etorofu), Russia	2,596
King William, NWT	5,062
Komsomolets, Russia	3,477
Kotelnyy, Russia	4,504
Mackenzie King, NWT	1,949
Mansel, NWT	1,228
Melville, NWT	16,274
Milne Land, Greenland	1,400
New Siberian Islands, Russia	14,500
Novaya Zemlya, Russia (2 isls.)	31,730
Oktyabrskoy, Russia	5,471
Prince Charles, NWT	3,676
Prince of Wales, NWT	12,872
Prince Patrick, NWT	6,119
Somerset, NWT	9,570
Southampton, NWT	15,913
Stefansson, NWT	1,723
Svalbard (tot. group)	23,957
Nordaustlandet	5,410
Spitsbergen	15,060
Traill, Greenland	1,300
Victoria, NWT **(9)**	83,897
Wrangel, Russia	2,800

Atlantic Ocean

Anticosti, Canada	3,068
Ascension, UK	34
Azores, Portugal (tot. group)	868
Faial	67
San Miguel	291
Bermuda Islands, UK	20
Bioko Isl., Equatorial Guinea	785
Block Islands, RI, US	21
Canary Islands, Spain (tot. group)	2,807
Fuerteventura	688
Gran Canaria	592
Tenerife	795
Cape Breton, Canada	3,981
Cape Verde Islands	1,557
Caviana, Para, Brazil	1,918
Channel Islands, UK (tot. group)	75
Guernsey	24
Jersey	45
Faroe Islands, Denmark	540
Falkland Islands, UK (tot. group)	4,700
East Falkland	2,550
West Falkland	1,750
Great Britain, UK **(8)**	84,200
Greenland, Denmark **(1)**	840,000
Gurupa, Para, Brazil	1,878
Hebrides, Scotland	2,744
Iceland	39,699
Ireland (tot. group)	32,589
Irish Republic	27,137
Northern Ireland	5,452
Isle of Man, UK	227
Isle of Wight, England	147
Long Island, NY, US	1,320
Madeira Islands, Portugal	306
Marajo, Brazil	15,444
Martha's Vineyard, MA, US	89
Mount Desert, ME, US	104
Nantucket, MA, US	45
Newfoundland, Canada	42,031
Orkney Islands, Scotland	390
Prince Edward, Canada	2,185
St. Helena, UK	47
Shetland Islands, Scotland	587
Skye, Scotland	670
South Georgia, UK	1,450
Tierra del Fuego, Chile, Arg.	18,800
Tristan da Cunha, UK	40

Baltic Sea

Aland Islands, Finland	590
Bornholm, Denmark	227
Gotland, Sweden	1,159

Caribbean Sea

Antigua	108
Aruba, Netherlands	75
Bahama Isls., Bahama (tot. group)	5,382
Andros, Bahamas	2,300
Barbados	166
Cuba	42,804
Isle of Youth	926
Cayman Islands	100
Curacao, Netherlands	171
Dominica	290
Guadeloupe, France	687
Hispaniola, Haiti and Dominican Rep.	29,389
Jamaica	4,244
Martinique, France	436
Puerto Rico, US	3,339
Tobago	116
Trinidad	1,864
Virgin Islands, UK	59
Virgin Islands, US	134

East Indies

Bali, Indonesia	2,171
Bangka, Indonesia	4,375
Borneo, Indonesia-Malaysia-Brunei **(3)**	280,100
Bougainville, Papua New Guinea	3,880
Buru, Indonesia	3,670
Celebes, Indonesia	69,000
Flores, Indonesia	5,500
Halmahera, Indonesia	6,865
Java (Jawa), Indonesia	48,900
Madura, Indonesia	2,113
Moluccas, Indonesia	32,307
New Britain, Papua New Guinea	14,093
New Guinea, Indon.-PNG **(2)**	306,000
New Ireland, PNG	3,707
Seram, Indonesia	6,621
Sumba, Indonesia	4,306
Sumbawa, Indonesia	5,965
Sumatra, Indonesia **(6)**	165,000
Timor, Indonesia	13,094
Yos Sudarsa, Indonesia	4,500

Indian Ocean

Andaman Isls., India	2,500
Kerguelen	2,247
Madagascar **(4)**	226,658
Mauritius	720
Pemba, Tanzania	380
Reunion, France	970
Seychelles	176
Sri Lanka	25,332
Zanzibar, Tanzania	640

Mediterranean Sea

Balearic Isls., Spain	1,927
Corfu, Greece	229
Corsica, France	3,369
Crete, Greece	3,189
Cyprus	3,572
Elba, Italy	86
Euboea, Greece	1,411
Malta	95
Rhodes, Greece	540
Sardinia, Italy	9,301
Sicily, Italy	9,926

Pacific Ocean

Admiralty, AK, US	1,709
Aleutian Isls., AK, US (tot. group)	6,912
Adak	275
Amchitka	116
Attu	350
Kanaga	142
Kiska	106
Tanaga	195
Umnak	686
Unalaska	1,051
Unimak	1,571
Baranof, AK, US	1,636
Chichagof, AK, US	2,062
Chiloe, Chile	3,241
Christmas, Kiribati	94
Diomede, Big, Russia	11
Easter Isl., Chile	69
Fiji (tot. group)	7,056
Vanua Levu	2,242
Viti Levu	4,109
Galapagos Isls., Ecuador	3,043
Graham Isl., British Columbia	2,456
Guadalcanal, Solomon Isls.	2,180
Guam, US	210
Hainan, China	13,000
Hawaiian Isls., HI, US (tot. group)	6,428
Hawaii	4,028
Oahu	600
Hong Kong, China	31
Hoste, Chile	1,590
Japan (tot. group)	145,850
Hokkaido	30,144
Honshu **(7)**	87,805
Kyushu	14,114
Okinawa	459
Shikoku	7,049
Kangaroo, South Australia	1,680
Kodiak, AK, US	3,485
Kupreanof, AK, US	1,084
Marquesas Isls., France	492
Marshall Isls.	70
Melville, Northern Territory, Australia	2,240
Micronesia	271
New Caledonia, France	6,530
New Zealand (tot. group)	104,454
Chatham Isls.	372
North	44,204
South	58,384
Stewart	674
North Mariana Isls., US	179
Nunivak, AK, US	1,600
Palau	188
Philippines (tot. group)	115,860
Leyte	2,787
Luzon	40,680
Mindanao	36,775
Mindoro	3,690
Negros	4,907
Palawan	4,554
Panay	4,446
Samar	5,050
Prince of Wales, AK, US	2,770
Revillagigedo, AK, US	1,134
Riesco, Chile	1,973
St. Lawrence, AK, US	1,780
Sakhalin, Russia	29,500
Samoa Isls. (tot. group)	1,177
American Samoa, US	77
Tutuila, US	55
Savail, Samoa	659
Upolu, Samoa	432
Santa Catalina, CA, US	75
Santa Ines, Chile	1,407
Tahiti, France	402
Taiwan, China (tot. group)	13,969
Jinmen Dao (Quemoy)	56
Tasmania, Australia	26,178
Tonga Isls.	290
Vancouver Isl., Brit. Columbia, Canada	12,079
Vanuatu	4,707
Wellington, Chile	2,549

Persian Gulf

Bahrain	217

Areas and Average Depths of Oceans, Seas, and Gulfs

Geographers and mapmakers recognize 4 major bodies of water: the Pacific, the Atlantic, the Indian, and the Arctic oceans. The Atlantic and Pacific oceans are considered divided at the equator into the N and S Atlantic and the N and S Pacific. The Arctic Ocean is the name for waters N of the continental landmasses in the region of the Arctic Circle.

	Area (sq mi)	Avg. depth (ft)
Pacific Ocean	64,186,300	12,925
Atlantic Ocean	33,420,000	11,730
Indian Ocean	28,350,500	12,598
Arctic Ocean	5,105,700	3,407
South China Sea	1,148,500	4,802
Caribbean Sea	971,400	8,448
Mediterranean Sea	969,100	4,926
Bering Sea	873,000	4,893
Gulf of Mexico	582,100	5,297
Sea of Okhotsk	537,500	3,192
Sea of Japan	391,100	5,468
Hudson Bay	281,900	305
East China Sea	256,600	620
Andaman Sea	218,100	3,667
Black Sea	196,100	3,906
Red Sea	174,900	1,764
North Sea	164,900	308
Baltic Sea	147,500	180
Yellow Sea	113,500	121
Persian Gulf	88,800	328
Gulf of California	59,100	2,375

Principal Ocean Depths

Source: National Imagery and Mapping Agency, U.S. Dept. of Defense

Name of area	Location (lat.)	Location (long.)	Depth (meters)	Depth (fathoms)	Depth (ft)
Pacific Ocean					
Mariana Trench	11°22′ N	142°36′ E	10,924	5,973	35,840
Tonga Trench	23°16′ S	174°44′ W	10,800	5,906	35,433
Philippine Trench	10°38′ N	126°36′ E	10,057	5,499	32,995
Kermadec Trench	31°53′ S	177°21′ W	10,047	5,494	32,963
Bonin Trench	24°30′ N	143°24′ E	9,994	5,464	32,788
Kuril Trench	44°15′ N	150°34′ E	9,750	5,331	31,988
Izu Trench	31°05′ N	142°10′ E	9,695	5,301	31,808
New Britain Trench	06°19′ S	153°45′ E	8,940	4,888	29,331
Yap Trench	08°33′ N	138°02′ E	8,527	4,663	27,976
Japan Trench	36°08′ N	142°43′ E	8,412	4,600	27,599
Peru-Chile Trench	23°18′ S	71°14′ W	8,064	4,409	26,457
Palau Trench	07°52′ N	134°56′ E	8,054	4,404	26,424
Aleutian Trench	50°51′ N	177°11′ E	7,679	4,199	25,194
New Hebrides Trench	20°36′ S	168°37′ E	7,570	4,139	24,836
North Ryukyu Trench	24°00′ N	126°48′ E	7,181	3,927	23,560
Mid. America Trench	14°02′ N	93°39′ W	6,662	3,643	21,857
Atlantic Ocean					
Puerto Rico Trench	19°55′ N	65°27′ W	8,605	4,705	28,232
S Sandwich Trench	55°42′ S	25°56′ E	8,325	4,552	27,313
Romanche Gap	0°13′ S	18°26′ W	7,728	4,226	25,354
Cayman Trench	19°12′ N	80°00′ W	7,535	4,120	24,721
Brazil Basin	09°10′ S	23°02′ W	6,119	3,346	20,076
Indian Ocean					
Java Trench	10°19′ S	109°58′ E	7,125	3,896	23,376
Ob' Trench	09°45′ S	67°18′ E	6,874	3,759	22,553
Diamantina Trench	35°50′ S	105°14′ E	6,602	3,610	21,660
Vema Trench	09°08′ S	67°15′ E	6,402	3,501	21,004
Agulhas Basin	45°20′ S	26°50′ E	6,195	3,387	20,325
Arctic Ocean					
Eurasia Basin	82°23′ N	19°31′ E	5,450	2,980	17,881
Mediterranean Sea					
Ionian Basin	36°32′ N	21°06′ E	5,150	2,816	16,896

Note: Greater depths have been reported in some areas but are not officially confirmed by research vessels.

Latitude, Longitude, and Altitude of World Cities

Source: National Imagery Mapping Agency, U.S. Dept. of Defense

City	Lat. °	Lat. ′	Long. °	Long. ′	Alt. (ft)
Athens, Greece	37	59 N	23	44 E	300
Bangkok, Thailand	13	45 N	100	31 E	0
Beijing, China	39	56 N	116	24 E	600
Berlin, Germany	52	31 N	13	25 E	110
Bogotá, Colombia	04	36 N	74	05 W	8,660
Bombay (Mumbai), India	18	58 N	72	50 E	27
Buenos Aires, Argentina	34	36 S	58	28 W	0
Cairo, Egypt	30	03 N	31	15 E	381
Jakarta, Indonesia	06	10 S	106	48 E	26
Jerusalem, Israel	31	46 N	35	14 E	2,500
Johannesburg, So. Afr.	26	12 S	28	05 E	5,740
Kathmandu, Nepal	27	43 N	85	19 E	4,500
Kiev, Ukraine	50	26 N	30	31 E	587
London, UK (Greenwich)	51	30 N	00	00	245
Manila, Philippines	14	35 N	120	00 E	0
Mecca, Saudi Arabia	21	27 N	39	49 E	6,562
Mexico City, Mexico	19	24 N	99	09 W	7,347
Moscow, Russia	55	45 N	37	35 E	394
New Delhi, India	28	36 N	77	12 E	770
Panama City, Panama	08	58 N	79	32 W	0
Paris, France	48	52 N	02	20 E	300
Quito, Ecuador	00	13 S	78	30 W	9,222
Rio de Janeiro, Brazil	22	43 S	43	13 W	30
Rome, Italy	41	53 N	12	30 E	95
Santiago, Chile	33	27 S	70	40 W	4,921
Seoul, South Korea	37	34 N	127	00 E	34
Sydney, Australia	33	53 S	151	12 E	25
Tehran, Iran	35	40 N	51	26 E	3,937
Tokyo, Japan	35	42 N	139	46 E	30
Tripoli, Libya	32	54 N	13	11 E	0
Warsaw, Poland	52	15 N	21	00 E	360
Wellington, New Zealand	41	18 S	174	47 E	0

Latitude, Longitude, and Altitude of U.S. and Canadian Cities

Source: U.S. geographic positions, U.S. altitudes provided by Geological Survey, U.S. Dept. of the Interior. Canadian geographic positions and altitudes provided by the Canada Flight Supplement, Natural Resources Canada.

City	Lat. N °	′	″	Long. W °	′	″	Elev. (ft)
Abilene, TX	32	26	55	99	43	58	1,718
Akron, OH	41	4	53	81	31	9	1,050
Albany, NY	42	39	9	73	45	24	20
Albuquerque, NM	35	5	4	106	39	2	4,955
Alert, N.W.T.	82	31	04	62	16	50	100
Allentown, PA	40	36	30	75	29	26	350
Amarillo, TX	35	13	19	101	49	51	3,685
Anchorage, AK	61	13	5	149	54	1	101
Ann Arbor, MI	42	16	15	83	43	35	880
Asheville, NC	35	36	3	82	33	15	2,134
Ashland, KY	38	28	42	82	38	17	558
Atlanta, GA	33	44	56	84	23	17	1,050
Atlantic City, NJ	39	21	51	74	25	24	8
Augusta, GA	33	28	15	81	58	30	414
Augusta, ME	44	18	38	69	46	48	45
Austin, TX	30	16	1	97	44	34	501
Bakersfield, CA	35	22	24	119	1	4	408
Baltimore, MD	39	17	25	76	36	45	100
Bangor, ME	44	48	4	68	46	42	158
Baton Rouge, LA	30	27	2	91	9	16	53
Battle Creek, MI	42	19	16	85	10	47	820
Bay City, MI	43	35	40	83	53	20	595
Beaumont, TX	30	5	9	94	6	6	20
Belleville, Ont.	44	11	32	77	18	34	320
Bellingham, WA	48	45	35	122	29	13	100
Berkeley, CA	37	52	18	122	16	18	150
Billings, MT	45	47	0	108	30	0	3,124
Biloxi, MS	30	23	45	88	53	7	25
Binghamton, NY	42	5	55	75	55	6	865
Birmingham, AL	33	31	14	86	48	9	600
Bismarck, ND	46	48	30	100	47	0	1,700
Bloomington, IL	40	29	3	88	59	37	829
Boise, ID	43	36	49	116	12	9	2,730
Boston, MA	42	21	30	71	3	37	20
Bowling Green, KY	36	59	25	86	26	37	510
Brandon, Man.	49	54	35	99	57	03	1,343
Brantford, Ont.	43	07	53	80	20	33	815
Brattleboro, VT	42	51	3	72	33	30	240
Bridgeport, CT	41	10	1	73	12	19	10
Brockton, MA	42	5	0	71	1	8	112
Buffalo, NY	42	53	11	78	52	43	585
Burlington, Ont.	43	26	33	79	51	03	640
Burlington, VT	44	28	33	73	12	45	113
Butte, MT	46	0	14	112	32	2	5,549
Calgary, Alta.	51	06	50	114	01	13	3,557
Cambridge, MA	42	22	30	71	6	22	30
Canton, OH	40	47	56	81	22	43	1,100
Carson City, NV	39	9	50	119	45	59	4,730
Cedar Rapids, IA	42	0	30	91	38	38	730
Central Islip, NY	40	47	26	73	12	8	88
Champaign, IL	40	6	59	88	14	36	740
Charleston, SC	32	46	35	79	55	52	118
Charleston, WV	38	20	59	81	37	58	606
Charlotte, NC	35	13	37	80	50	36	850
Charlottetown, P.E.I.	46	17	24	63	07	16	160
Chattanooga, TN	35	2	44	85	18	35	685
Cheyenne, WY	41	8	24	104	49	11	6,067
Chicago, IL	41	51	0	87	39	0	596
Churchill, Man.	58	44	14	94	03	26	94
Cincinnati, OH	39	9	43	84	27	25	683
Cleveland, OH	41	29	58	81	41	44	690
Colorado Springs, CO	38	50	2	104	49	15	6,008
Columbia, MO	38	57	6	92	20	2	758
Columbia, SC	34	0	2	81	2	6	314
Columbus, GA	32	27	39	84	59	16	300
Columbus, OH	39	57	40	82	59	56	800
Concord, NH	43	12	29	71	32	17	288
Corpus Christi, TX	27	48	1	97	23	46	35
Dallas, TX	32	47	0	96	48	0	463
Dawson, Yukon	64	02	35	139	07	40	1,214
Dayton, OH	39	45	32	84	11	30	750
Daytona Beach, FL	29	12	38	81	1	23	10
Decatur, IL	39	50	25	88	57	17	670
Denver, CO	39	44	21	104	59	3	5,260
Des Moines, IA	41	36	2	93	36	32	803
Detroit, MI	42	19	53	83	2	45	585
Dodge City, KS	37	45	10	100	1	0	2,550
Dubuque, IA	42	30	2	90	39	52	620
Duluth, MN	46	47	0	92	6	23	610
Durham, NC	35	59	38	78	53	56	394
Eau Claire, WI	44	48	41	91	29	54	850
Edmonton, Alta.	53	34	21	113	31	14	2,200
Elizabeth, NJ	40	39	50	74	12	40	38
El Paso, TX	31	45	31	106	29	11	3,695
Enid, OK	36	23	44	97	52	41	1,246
Erie, PA	42	7	45	80	5	7	650
Eugene, OR	44	3	8	123	5	8	419
Eureka, CA	40	48	8	124	9	45	44
Evansville, IN	37	58	29	87	33	21	388
Fairbanks, AK	64	50	16	147	42	59	440
Fall River, MA	41	42	5	71	9	20	200
Fargo, ND	46	52	38	96	47	22	900
Flagstaff, AZ	35	11	53	111	39	2	6,900
Flint, MI	43	0	45	83	41	15	750
Ft. Smith, AR	35	23	9	94	23	54	446
Ft. Wayne, IN	41	7	50	85	7	44	781
Ft. Worth, TX	32	43	31	97	19	14	670
Fredericton, N.B.	45	52	10	66	31	54	67
Fresno, CA	36	44	52	119	46	17	296
Gadsden, AL	34	0	51	86	0	24	554
Gainesville, FL	29	39	5	82	19	30	183
Gallup, NM	35	31	41	108	44	31	6,508
Galveston, TX	29	18	4	94	47	51	10
Gary, IN	41	35	36	87	20	47	600
Grand Junction, CO	39	3	50	108	33	0	4,597
Grand Rapids, MI.	42	57	48	85	40	5	610
Great Falls, MT	47	30	1	111	18	0	3,334
Green Bay, WI	44	31	9	88	1	11	594
Greensboro, NC	36	4	21	79	47	32	770
Greenville, SC	34	51	9	82	23	39	966
Guelph, Ont.	43	33	0	80	16	0	1,100
Gulfport, MS	30	22	2	89	5	34	25
Halifax, N.S.	44	52	51	63	30	31	477
Hamilton, OH	39	23	58	84	33	41	600
Hamilton, Ont.	43	10	19	79	55	53	780
Harrisburg, PA	40	16	25	76	53	5	320
Hartford, CT	41	45	49	72	41	8	40
Helena, MT	46	35	34	112	2	7	4,090
Hilo, HI	19	43	47	155	5	24	38
Honolulu, HI	21	18	25	157	51	30	18
Houston, TX	29	45	47	95	21	47	40
Huntsville, AL	34	43	49	86	35	10	641
Indianapolis, IN	39	46	6	86	9	29	717
Iowa City, IA	41	39	40	91	31	48	685
Jackson, MI	42	14	45	84	24	5	940
Jackson, MS	32	17	55	90	11	5	294
Jacksonville, FL	30	19	55	81	39	21	12
Jersey City, NJ	40	43	41	74	4	41	83
Johnstown, PA	40	16	42	76	19	0	521
Joplin, MO	37	5	3	94	30	47	990
Juneau, AK	58	18	7	134	25	11	50
Kalamazoo, MI	42	17	30	85	35	14	755
Kansas City, KS	39	6	51	94	37	38	750
Kansas City, MO	39	5	59	94	34	42	740
Kenosha, WI	42	35	5	87	49	16	610
Key West, FL	24	33	19	81	46	58	8
Kingston, Ont.	44	13	31	76	35	49	305
Kitchener, Ont.	43	27	32	80	23	04	1,040
Knoxville, TN	35	57	38	83	55	15	889
Lafayette, IN	40	25	0	86	52	31	567
Lancaster, PA	40	2	16	76	18	21	368
Lansing, MI	42	43	57	84	33	20	830
Laredo, TX	27	30	22	99	30	26	414
Las Vegas, NV	36	10	30	115	8	11	2,000
Lawrence, MA	42	42	25	71	9	49	50
Lethbridge, Alta.	49	37	49	112	47	59	3,047
Lexington, KY	37	59	19	84	28	40	955
Lihue, HI	21	58	52	159	22	16	206
Lima, OH	40	44	33	84	6	19	875

City	Lat. N °	′	″	Long. W °	′	″	Elev. (ft)
Lincoln, NE	40	48	0	96	40	0	1,150
Little Rock, AR	34	44	47	92	17	22	350
London, Ont.	42	57	31	81	13	33	875
Los Angeles, CA	34	3	8	118	14	34	330
Louisville, KY	38	15	15	85	45	34	462
Lowell, MA	42	38	0	71	19	0	102
Lubbock, TX	33	34	40	101	51	17	3,195
Macon, GA	32	50	26	83	37	57	400
Madison, WI	43	4	23	89	24	4	863
Manchester, NH	42	59	44	71	27	19	175
Marshall, TX	32	32	41	94	22	2	410
Medicine Hat, Alta.	50	01	08	110	43	15	2,352
Memphis, TN	35	8	58	90	2	56	254
Meriden, CT	41	32	17	72	48	27	190
Miami, FL	25	46	26	80	11	38	11
Milwaukee, WI	43	2	20	87	54	23	634
Minneapolis, MN	44	58	48	93	15	49	815
Minot, ND	48	13	57	101	17	45	1,555
Mobile, AL	30	41	39	88	2	35	16
Moncton, N.B.	46	06	44	64	40	57	232
Montgomery, AL	32	22	0	86	18	0	250
Montpelier, VT	44	15	36	72	34	33	525
Montréal, Que.	45	41	06	73	55	52	221
Moose Jaw, Sask.	50	19	48	105	33	29	1,892
Muncie, IN	40	11	36	85	23	11	952
Nashville, TN	36	9	57	86	47	4	440
Natchez, MS	31	33	37	91	24	11	230
Newark, NJ	40	44	8	74	10	22	95
New Britain, CT	41	39	40	72	46	48	200
New Haven, CT	41	18	29	72	55	43	40
New Orleans, LA	29	57	16	90	4	30	11
New York, NY	40	42	51	74	0	23	55
Niagara Falls, Ont.	43	07	0	79	04	0	589
Nome, AK	64	30	4	165	24	23	25
Norfolk, VA	36	50	48	76	17	8	10
North Bay, Ont.	46	26	0	79	28	0	1,200
Oakland, CA	37	48	16	122	16	11	42
Ogden, UT	41	13	23	111	58	23	4,299
Oklahoma City, OK	35	28	3	97	30	58	1,195
Omaha, NE	41	15	31	95	56	15	1,040
Orlando, FL	28	32	17	81	22	46	106
Ottawa, Ont.	45	19	09	76	01	20	382
Paducah, KY	37	5	0	88	36	0	345
Pasadena, CA	34	8	52	118	8	37	865
Paterson, NJ	40	55	0	74	10	20	70
Pensacola, FL	30	25	16	87	13	1	32
Peoria, IL	40	41	37	89	35	20	470
Peterborough, Ont.	44	13	48	78	21	48	628
Philadelphia, PA	39	57	8	75	9	51	40
Phoenix, AZ	33	26	54	112	4	24	1,090
Pierre, SD	44	22	6	100	21	2	1,484
Pittsburgh, PA	40	26	26	79	59	46	770
Pittsfield, MA	42	27	0	73	14	45	1,039
Pocatello, ID	42	52	17	112	26	41	4,464
Pt. Arthur, TX	29	53	55	93	55	43	10
Portland, ME	43	39	41	70	15	21	25
Portland, OR	45	31	25	122	40	30	50
Portsmouth, NH	43	4	18	70	45	47	21
Portsmouth, VA	36	50	7	76	17	55	10
Prince Rupert, B.C.	54	17	10	130	26	41	116
Providence, RI	41	49	26	71	24	48	80
Provo, UT	40	14	2	111	39	28	4,549
Pueblo, CO	38	15	16	104	36	31	4,662
Québec City, Que.	46	47	36	71	23	29	244
Racine, WI	42	43	34	87	46	58	630
Raleigh, NC	35	46	19	78	38	20	350
Rapid City, SD	44	4	50	103	13	50	3,247
Reading, PA	40	20	8	75	55	38	266
Regina, Sask.	50	25	55	104	39	57	1,894
Reno, NV	39	31	47	119	48	46	4,498
Richmond, VA	37	33	13	77	27	38	190
Roanoke, VA	37	16	15	79	56	30	940
Rochester, MN	44	1	18	92	28	11	990
Rochester, NY	43	9	17	77	36	57	515
Rockford, IL	42	16	16	89	5	38	715
Sacramento, CA	38	34	54	121	29	36	20
Saginaw, MI	43	25	10	83	57	3	595
St. Catharines, Ont.	43	11	30	79	10	18	321
St. Cloud, MN	45	33	39	94	9	44	1,040
St. John, N.B.	45	18	58	65	53	25	357
St. John's, Nfld.	47	37	07	52	45	07	461

City	Lat. N °	′	″	Long. W °	′	″	Elev. (ft)
St. Joseph, MO	39	46	7	94	50	47	850
St. Louis, MO	38	37	38	90	11	52	455
St. Paul, MN	44	56	40	93	5	35	780
St. Petersburg, FL	27	46	14	82	40	46	44
Salem, OR	44	56	35	123	2	2	154
Salina, KS	38	50	25	97	36	40	1,225
Salt Lake City, UT	40	45	39	111	53	25	4,266
San Antonio, TX	29	25	26	98	29	36	650
San Bernardino, CA	34	6	30	117	17	20	1,200
San Diego, CA	32	42	55	117	9	23	40
San Francisco, CA	37	46	30	122	25	6	63
San Jose, CA	37	20	22	121	53	38	87
San Juan, P.R.	18	28	6	66	6	22	8
Santa Barbara, CA	34	25	15	119	41	50	50
Santa Cruz, CA	36	58	27	122	1	47	20
Santa Fe, NM	35	41	13	105	56	14	6,989
Sarasota, FL	27	20	10	82	31	51	27
Saskatoon, Sask.	52	10	15	106	41	59	1,653
Sault Ste. Marie, Ont.	46	29	06	84	30	34	630
Savannah, GA	32	5	0	81	6	0	42
Schenectady, NY	42	48	51	73	56	24	245
Seattle, WA	47	36	23	122	19	51	350
Sheboygan, WI	43	45	3	87	42	52	630
Sherbrooke, Que.	45	26	17	71	41	26	792
Sheridan, WY	44	47	50	106	57	20	3,742
Shreveport, LA	32	31	30	93	45	0	209
Sioux City, IA	42	30	0	96	24	0	1,117
Sioux Falls, SD	43	33	0	96	42	0	1,442
South Bend, IN	41	41	0	86	15	0	725
Spartanburg, SC	34	56	58	81	55	56	816
Spokane, WA	47	39	32	117	25	30	2,000
Springfield, IL	39	48	6	89	38	37	610
Springfield, MA	42	6	5	72	35	25	70
Springfield, MO	37	12	55	93	17	53	1,300
Springfield, OH	39	55	27	83	48	32	1,000
Stamford, CT	41	3	12	73	32	21	35
Steubenville, OH	40	22	11	80	38	3	1,060
Stockton, CA	37	57	28	121	17	23	15
Sudbury, Ont.	46	37	30	80	47	56	1,140
Superior, WI	46	43	15	92	6	14	642
Sydney, N.S.	46	09	41	60	02	52	203
Syracuse, NY	43	2	53	76	8	52	400
Tacoma, WA	47	15	11	122	26	35	380
Tallahassee, FL	30	26	17	84	16	51	188
Tampa, FL	27	56	50	82	27	31	48
Terre Haute, IN	39	28	0	87	24	50	501
Texarkana, TX	33	25	30	94	2	51	324
Thunder Bay, Ont.	48	22	19	89	19	26	653
Timmins, Ont	48	34	11	81	22	36	967
Toledo, OH	41	39	50	83	33	19	615
Topeka, KS	39	2	54	95	40	40	1,000
Toronto, Ont.	43	37	39	79	23	46	251
Trenton, NJ	40	13	1	74	44	36	54
Trois-Rivières, Que.	46	21	10	72	40	46	198
Troy, NY	42	43	42	73	41	32	35
Tucson, AZ	32	13	18	110	55	33	2,390
Tulsa, OK	36	9	14	95	59	33	804
Urbana, IL	40	6	38	88	12	26	725
Utica, NY	43	6	3	75	13	59	415
Vancouver, B.C.	49	11	42	123	10	55	14
Victoria, B.C.	48	38	49	123	25	33	63
Waco, TX	31	32	57	97	8	47	405
Walla Walla, WA	46	3	53	118	20	31	1,000
Washington, DC	38	53	42	77	2	12	25
Waterloo, IA	42	29	34	92	20	34	850
West Palm Beach, FL	26	42	54	80	3	13	21
Wheeling, WV	40	3	50	80	43	16	672
Whitehorse, Yukon	60	42	36	135	04	06	2,305
White Plains, NY	41	2	2	73	45	48	220
Wichita, KS	37	41	32	97	20	14	1,305
Wilkes-Barre, PA	41	14	45	75	52	54	550
Wilmington, DE	39	44	45	75	32	49	100
Wilmington, NC	34	13	32	77	56	42	50
Windsor, Ont.	42	16	29	82	57	30	622
Winnipeg, Man.	49	54	39	97	14	36	783
Winston-Salem, NC	36	5	59	80	14	40	912
Worcester, MA	42	15	45	71	48	10	480
Yakima, WA	46	36	8	120	30	17	1,066
Yellowknife, N.W.T.	62	27	46	114	26	25	675
Youngstown, OH	41	5	59	80	38	59	861
Yuma, AZ	32	43	31	114	37	25	160
Zanesville, OH	39	56	25	82	0	48	710

Principal World Rivers

Reviewed by Laurel Duda, Marine Biological Laboratory, Woods Hole Oceanogr. Inst. Library. For N American rivers, see separate table.

Africa

River	Outflow	Length (mi)
Chari	Lake Chad	500
Congo	Atlantic Ocean	2,900
Gambia	Atlantic Ocean	700
Kasai	Congo River	1,000
Limpopo	Indian Ocean	1,100
Lualaba	Congo River	1,100
Niger	Gulf of Guinea	2,590
Nile	Mediterranean	4,160
Okavango	Okavango Delta	1,000
Orange	Atlantic Ocean	1,300
Senegal	Atlantic Ocean	1,020
Ubangi	Congo River	660
Zambezi	Indian Ocean	1,700

Asia

River	Outflow	Length (mi)
Amu Darya	Aral Sea	1,550
Amur	Tatar Strait	1,780
Angara	Yenisey River	1,151
Brahmaputra	Bay of Bengal	1,800
Chang	East China Sea	3,964
Euphrates	Shatt al-Arab	1,700
Ganges	Bay of Bengal	1,560
Godavari	Bay of Bengal	900
Hsi (see Xi)		
Huang	Yellow Sea	3,395
Indus	Arabian Sea	1,800
Irrawaddy	Andaman Sea	1,337
Jordan	Dead Sea	200
Kolyma	Arctic Ocean	1,323
Krishna	Bay of Bengal	800
Kura	Caspian Sea	848
Lena	Laptev Sea	2,734
Mekong	South China Sea	2,700
Narbada (see Narmada)		
Narmada	Arabian Sea	800
Ob	Gulf of Ob	2,268
Ob-Irtysh	Gulf of Ob	3,362
Salween	Gulf of Martaban	1,500
Songhua	Amur River	1,150
Sungari	Amur River	1,197
Sutlej	Indus River	900
Syr	Aral Sea	1,370
Tarim	Lop Nor Basin	1,261
Tigris	Shatt al-Arab	1,180
Xi	South China Sea	1,200
Yamuna	Ganges River	855
Yangtze (see Chang)		
Yellow (see Huang)		
Yenisey	Kara Sea	2,543

Australia

River	Outflow	Length (mi)
Murray-Darling	Indian Ocean	2,310
Murrumbidgee	Murray River	981

Europe

River	Outflow	Length (mi)
Bug, Northern	Wisla	481
Bug, Southern	Dnieper River	532
Danube	Black Sea	1,776
Don	Sea of Azov	1,224
Dori	Sea of Azov	1,224
Dnieper	Black Sea	1,420
Dniester	Black Sea	877
Drava	Danube River	447
Dvina, North	White Sea	824
Dvina, West	Gulf of Riga	634
Ebro	Mediterranean	565
Elbe	North Sea	724
Garonne	Bay of Biscay	357
Kama	Volga River	1,122
Loire	Bay of Biscay	634
Mame	Seine River	326
Meuse	North Sea	580
Oder	Baltic Sea	567
Oka	Volga River	932
Pechora	Barents Sea	1,124
Po	Adriatic Sea	405
Rhine	North Sea	820
Rhone	Gulf of Lions	505
Seine	English Channel	496
Shannon	Atlantic Ocean	230
Tagus	Atlantic Ocean	626
Thames	North Sea	210
Tiber	Tyrrhenian Sea	252
Tisza	Danube River	600
Ural	Caspian Sea	1,575
Volga	Caspian Sea	2,290
Weser	North Sea	454
Wisla	Gulf of Gdansk	675

South America

River	Outflow	Length (mi)
Amazon	Atlantic Ocean	4,000
Araguaia	Tocantins River	1,100
Iça (see Putumayo)		
Iguaça	Parana River	808
Japura	Amazon River	1,750
Madeira	Amazon River	2,013
Magdalena	Caribbean Sea	956
Negro	Amazon River	1,400
Orinoco	Atlantic Ocean	1,600
Paraguay	Parana River	1,584
Parana	Rio de la Plata	2,485
Pilcomayo	Paraguay River	1,000
Purus	Amazon River	2,100
Putumayo	Amazon River	1,000
Rio de la Plata	Atlantic Ocean	150
Rio Roosevelt	Aripuana	400
Sao Francisco	Atlantic Ocean	1,988
Tocantins	Para River	1,677
Ucayali	Marañón River	910
Uruguay	Rio de la Plata	1,000
Xingu	Amazon River	1,300

Major Rivers in North America

Reviewed by Laurel Duda, Marine Biological Laboratory, Woods Hole Oceanographic Inst. Library

River	Source or upper limit of length	Outflow	Length (mi)
Alabama	Gilmer County, GA	Mobile River	729
Albany	Lake St. Joseph, Ontario	James Bay	610
Allegheny	Potter County, PA	Ohio River	325
Altamaha-Ocrnulgee	Junction of Yellow and South Rivers, Newton County, GA	Atlantic Ocean	392
Apalachicola-Chattahoochee	Towns County, GA	Gulf of Mexico	524
Arkansas	Lake County, CO	Mississippi River	1,459
Assiniboine	Eastern Saskatchewan	Red River	450
Attawapiskat	Attawapiskat, Ontario	James Bay	465
Back (NWT)	Contwoyto Lake	Chantrey Inlet, Arctic Ocean	605
Big Black (MS)	Webster County, MS	Mississippi River	330
Brazos	Junction of Salt and Double Mountain Forks, Stonewall County, TX	Gulf of Mexico	950
Canadian	Las Animas County, CO	Arkansas River	906
Cedar (IA)	Dodge County, MN	Iowa River	329
Cheyenne	Junction of Antelope Creek and Dry Fork, Converse County, WY	Missouri River	290
Churchill, Man.	Methy Lake, Saskatchewan	Hudson Bay	1,000
Cimarron	Colfax County, NM	Arkansas River	600
Colorado (AZ)	Rocky Mountain Natl. Park, CO (90 mi in Mexico)	Gulf of California	1,450
Colorado (TX)	West Texas	Matagorda Bay	862
Columbia	Columbia Lake, British Columbia	Pacific Ocean, bet. OR and WA	1,243
Columbia, Upper	Columbia Lake, British Columbia	To mouth of Snake River	890
Connecticut	Third Connecticut Lake, NH	Long Island Sound, CT	407
Coppermine (NWT)	Lac de Gras	Coronation Gulf, Arctic Ocean	525
Cumberland	Letcher County, KY	Ohio River	720
Delaware	Schoharie County, NY	Liston Point, Delaware Bay	390
Fraser	Near Mount Robson (on Continental Divide)	Strait of Georgia	850
Gila	Catron County, NM	Colorado River	649
Green (UT-WY)	Junction of Wells and Trail Creeks, Sublette County, WY	Colorado River	730
Hamilton (Lab.)	Lake Ashuanipi	Atlantic Ocean	532
Hudson	Henderson Lake, Essex County, NY	Upper NY Bay	306
Illinois	St. Joseph County, IN	Mississippi River	420
James (ND-SD)	Wells County, ND	Missouri River	710
James (VA)	Junction of Jackson and Cowpasture Rivers, Botetourt County, VA	Hampton Roads	340
Kanawha-New	Junction of North and South Forks of New River, NC	Ohio River	352
Kentucky	Junction of North and Middle Forks, Lee County, KY	Ohio River	259
Klamath	Lake Ewauna, Klamath Falls, OR	Pacific Ocean	250
Kootenay	Kootenay Lake, British Columbia	Columbia River	485
Koyukuk	Endicott Mountains, AK	Yukon River	470

River	Source or upper limit of length	Outflow	Length (mi)
Kuskokwim	Alaska Range	Kuskokwim Bay	724
Liard	Southern Yukon, AK	Mackenzie River	693
Little Missouri	Crook County, WY	Missouri River	560
Mackenzie	Great Slave Lake, N.W.T.	Arctic Ocean	1,060
Milk	Junction of North and South Forks, Alberta	Missouri River	625
Minnesota	Big Stone Lake, MN	Mississippi River	332
Mississippi	Lake Itasca, MN	Gulf of Mexico	2,340
Mississippi-Missouri-Red Rock	Source of Red Rock, Beaverhead Co., MT	Gulf of Mexico	3,710
Missouri	Junction of Jefferson, Madison, and Gallatin Rivers, Madison County, MT	Mississippi River	2,315
Missouri-Red Rock	Source of Red Rock, Beaverhead Co., MT	Mississippi River	2,540
Mobile-Alabama-Coosa	Gilmer County, GA	Mobile Bay	774
Nelson (Man.)	Lake Winnipeg	Hudson Bay	410
Neosho	Morris County, KS	Arkansas River, OK	460
Niobrara	Niobrara County, WY	Missouri River, NE	431
North Canadian	Union County, NM	Canadian River, OK	800
North Platte	Junction of Grizzly and Little Grizzly Creeks, Jackson County, CO	Platte River, NE	618
Ohio	Junction of Allegheny and Monongahela Rivers, Pittsburgh, PA	Mississippi River	981
Ohio-Allegheny	Potter County, PA	Mississippi River	1,310
Osage	East-central Kansas	Missouri River	500
Ottawa	Lake Capimitchigama	St. Lawrence River	790
Ouachita	Polk County, AR	Black River	605
Peace	Stikine Mountains, B.C.	Slave River	1,210
Pearl	Neshoba County, MS	Gulf of Mexico	411
Pecos	Mora County, NM	Rio Grande	926
Pee Dee-Yadkin	Watauga County, NC	Winyah Bay	435
Pend Orelle-Clark Fork	Near Butte, MT	Columbia River	531
Platte	Junction of North and South Platte Rivers, NE	Missouri River	310
Porcupine	Ogilvie Mountains, AK	Yukon River, AK	569
Potomac	Garrett County, MD	Chesapeake Bay	383
Powder	Junction of South and Middle Forks, WY	Yellowstone River	375
Red (OK-TX-LA)	Curry County, NM	Mississippi River	1,290
Red River of the North	Junction of Otter Tail and Bois de Sioux Rivers, Wilkin County, MN	Lake Winnipeg	545
Republican	Junction of North Fork and Arikaree River, NE	Kansas River	445
Rio Grande	San Juan County, CO	Gulf of Mexico	1,900
Roanoke	Junction of N and S Forks, Montgomery Co., VA	Albemarle Sound	380
Rock (IL-WI)	Dodge County, WI	Mississippi River	300
Sabine	Junction of S and Caddo Forks, Hunt County, TX	Sabine Lake	380
Sacramento	Siskiyou County, CA	Suisun Bay	377
St. Francis	Iron County, MO	Mississippi River	425
St. John	Northwestern Maine	Bay of Fundy	418
St. Lawrence	Lake Ontario	Gulf of St. Lawrence, Atlantic Ocean	800
Saguenay	Lake St. John, Quebec	St. Lawrence River	434
Salmon (ID)	Custer County, ID	Snake River	420
San Joaquin	Junction of S and Middle Forks, Madera Co., CA	Suisun Bay	350
San Juan	Silver Lake, Archuleta County, CO	Colorado River	360
Santee-Wateree-Catawba	McDowell County, NC	Atlantic Ocean	538
Saskatchewan, North	Rocky Mountains	Saskatchewan R.	800
Saskatchewan, South	Rocky Mountains	Saskatchewan R.	865
Savannah	Junction of Seneca and Tugaloo Rivers, Anderson County, SC	Atlantic Ocean, GA-SC	314
Savern (Ont.)	Sandy Lake	Hudson Bay	610
Smokey Hill	Cheyenne County, CO	Kansas River, KS	540
Snake	Teton County, WY	Columbia River, WA	1,038
South Platte	Junction of S and Middle Forks, Park County, CO	Platte River	424
Susitna	Alaska Range	Cook Inlet	313
Susquehanna	Huyden Creek, Otsego County, NY	Chesapeake Bay	447
Tallahatchie	Tippah County, MS	Yazoo River	301
Tanana	Wrangell Mountains, AK	Yukon River	659
Tennessee	Junction of French Broad and Holston Rivers	Ohio River	652
Tennessee-French Broad	Courthouse Creek, Transylvania County, NC	Ohio River	886
Tombigbee	Prentiss County, MS	Mobile River	525
Trinity	North of Dallas, TX	Galveston Bay	360
Wabash	Darke County, OH	Ohio River	512
Washita	Hemphill County, TX	Red River, OK	500
White (AR-MO)	Madison County, AR	Mississippi River	722
Willamette	Douglas County, OR	Columbia River	309
Wind-Bighorn	Junction of Wind and Little Wind Rivers, Fremont Co., WY (Source of Wind R. is Togwotee Pass, Teton Co., WY)	Yellowstone River	338
Wisconsin	Lac Vieux Desert, Vilas County, WI	Mississippi River	430
Yellowstone	Park County, WY	Missouri River	682
Yukon	McNeil R., Yukon Territory	Bering Sea	1,979

Highest and Lowest Continental Altitudes

Source: National Geographic Society

Continent	Highest point	Elev. (ft)	Lowest point	ft below sea level
Asia	Mount Everest, Nepal-Tibet	29,028	Dead Sea, Israel-Jordan	1,312
South America	Mount Aconcagua, Argentina	22,834	Valdes Peninsula, Argentina	131
North America	Mount McKinley, AK	20,320	Death Valley, California	282
Africa	Kilimanjaro, Tanzania	19,340	Lake Assal, Djibouti	512
Europe	Mount Elbrus, Russia	18,510	Caspian Sea, Russia, Azerbaijan	92
Antarctica	Vinson Massif	16,864	Bentley Subglacial Trench	8,327[1]
Australia	Mount Kosciusko, New South Wales	7,310	Lake Eyre, South Australia	52

(1) Estimated level of the continental floor. Lower points that have yet to be discovered may exist further beneath the ice.

Major Natural Lakes of the World

Source: Geological Survey, U.S. Dept. of the Interior

A lake is generally defined as a body of water surrounded by land. By this definition some bodies of water that are called seas, such as the Caspian Sea and the Aral Sea, are really lakes. In the following table, the word *lake* is omitted when it is part of the name.

Name	Continent	Area (sq mi)	Length (mi)	Maximum depth (ft)	Elevation (ft)
Caspian Sea	Asia-Europe	143,244	760	3,363	–92
Superior	North America	31,700	350	1,330	600
Victoria	Africa	26,828	250	270	3,720
Aral Sea	Asia	24,904[1]	280	220	174
Huron	North America	23,000	206	750	579
Michigan	North America	22,300	307	923	579
Tanganyika	Africa	12,700	420	4,823	2,534
Baykal	Asia	12,162	395	5,315	1,493
Great Bear	North America	12,096	192	1,463	512
Nyasa (Malawi)	Africa	11,150	360	2,280	1,550
Great Slave	North America	11,031	298	2,015	513
Erie	North America	9,910	241	210	570
Winnipeg	North America	9,417	266	60	713
Ontario	North America	7,340	193	802	245
Balkhash	Asia	7,115	376	85	1,115
Ladoga	Europe	6,835	124	738	13
Chad	Africa	6,300	175	24	787
Maracaibo	South America	5,217	133	115	sea level
Onega	Europe	3,710	145	328	108
Eyre	Australia	3,600[2]	90	4	–52
Volta	Africa	3,276	250	....	....
Titicaca	South America	3,200	122	922	12,500
Nicaragua	Central America	3,100	102	230	102
Athabasca	North America	3,064	208	407	700
Reindeer	North America	2,568	143	720	1,106
Turkana (Rudolf)	Africa	2,473	154	240	1,230
Issyk Kul	Asia	2,355	115	2,303	5,279
Torrens	Australia	2,230	130	....	92
Vanern	Europe	2,156	91	328	144
Nettilling	North America	2,140	67	....	95
Winnipegosis	North America	2,075	141	38	830
Albert	Africa	2,075	100	168	2,030
Kariba	Africa	2,050	175	390	1,590
Nipigon	North America	1,872	72	540	1,050
Gairdner	Australia	1,840	90	....	112
Urmia	Asia	1,815	90	49	4,180
Manitoba	North America	1,799	140	12	813

(1) Probably less because of the diversion of feeder rivers. (2) Approximate figure, subject to great seasonal variation.

The Great Lakes

Source: National Ocean Service, U.S. Dept. of Commerce

The Great Lakes form the world's largest body of fresh water, and with their connecting waterways are the largest inland water transportation unit. Draining the great North Central basin of the U.S., they enable shipping to reach the Atlantic via their outlet, the St. Lawrence R., and to reach the Gulf of Mexico via the Illinois Waterway, from Lake Michigan to the Mississippi R. A 3d outlet connects with the Hudson R. and then the Atlantic via the New York State Barge Canal System. Traffic on the Illinois Waterway and the N.Y. State Barge Canal System is limited to recreational boating and small shipping vessels.

Only one of the lakes, Lake Michigan, is wholly in the U.S.; the others are shared with Canada. Ships move from the shores of Lake Superior to Whitefish Bay at the E end of the lake, then through the Soo (Sault Ste. Marie) locks, through the St. Mary's R. and into Lake Huron. To reach Gary and the Port of Indiana and South Chicago, IL, ships move W from Lake Huron to Lake Michigan through the Straits of Mackinac. Lake Superior is 601 ft above low water datum at Rimouski, Quebec, on the International Great Lakes Datum (1985). From Duluth, MN, to the E end of Lake Ontario is 1,156 mi.

	Superior	Michigan	Huron	Erie	Ontario
Length in mi	350	307	206	241	193
Breadth in mi	160	118	183	57	53
Deepest soundings in ft	1,333	923	750	210	802
Volume of water in cu mi	2,935	1,180	850	116	393
Area (sq mi) water surface—U.S.	20,600	22,300	9,100	4,980	3,460
Canada	11,100	.....	13,900	4,930	3,880
Area (sq mi) entire drainage basin—U.S.	16,900	45,600	16,200	18,000	15,200
Canada	32,400	.....	35,500	4,720	12,100
Total area (sq mi) U.S. and Canada	**81,000**	**67,900**	**74,700**	**32,630**	**34,850**
Low water datum above mean water level at Rimouski, Quebec, avg. level in ft (1985)	601.10	577.50	577.50	569.20	243.30
Latitude, N	46° 25′	41° 37′	43° 00′	41° 23′	43° 11′
	49° 00′	46° 06′	46° 17′	42° 52′	44° 15′
Longitude, W.	84° 22′	84° 45′	79° 43′	78° 51′	76° 03′
	92° 06′	88° 02′	84° 45′	83° 29′	79° 53′
National boundary line in mi	282.8	None	260.8	251.5	174.6
United States shoreline (mainland only) mi	863	1,400	580	431	300

Famous Waterfalls

Source: National Geographic Society

The earth has thousands of waterfalls, some of considerable magnitude. Their importance is determined not only by height but by volume of flow, steadiness of flow, crest width, whether the water drops sheerly or over a sloping surface, and whether it descends in one leap or a succession of leaps. A series of low falls flowing over a considerable distance is known as a cascade.

Estimated mean annual flow, in cubic feet per second, of major waterfalls are as follows: Niagara, 212,200; Paulo Afonso, 100,000; Urubupunga, 97,000; Iguazu, 61,000; Patos-Maribondo, 53,000; Victoria, 35,400; and Kaieteur, 23,400.

Elevation = total drop in feet in one or more leaps. #=falls of more than one leap; *= falls that diminish greatly seasonally; **= falls that reduce to a trickle or are dry for part of each year. If river names not shown, they are same as the falls. R. = river; L. = lake; (C) = cascade type.

Africa

Name and location	Elevation (ft)
Angola	
Ruacana, Cuene R.	406
Ethiopia	
Fincha	508
Lesotho	
Maletsunyane*	630
Zimbabwe-Zambia	
Victoria, Zambezi R.*	343
South Africa	
Augrabies, Orange R.*	480
Tugela#	2,014
Tanzania-Zambia	
Kalambo*	726

Asia

Name and location	Elevation (ft)
India	
Cauvery*	330
Jog (Gersoppa), Sharavathi R.*	830
Japan	
Kegon, Daiya R.*	330

Australia

Name and location	Elevation (ft)
Australia	
New South Wales	
Wentworth	614
Wollomombi	1,100
Queensland	
Tully	885
Wallaman, Stony Cr.#	1,137
New Zealand	
Helena	890
Sutherland, Arthur R.#	1,904

Europe

Name and location	Elevation (ft)
Austria	
Gastein#	492
Krimml#	1,312
France	
Gavarnie*	1,385
Great Britain	
Scotland	
Glomach	370
Wales	
Rhaiadr	240
Italy	
Frua, Toce R. (C)	470
Norway	
Mardalsfossen (Northern)	1,535
Mardalsfossen (Southern)#	2,149
Skjeggedal, Nybuai R.#**	1,378
Skykje**	984
Vetti, Morka-Koldedola R.	900
Sweden	
Handol#	427
Switzerland	
Giessbach (C)	984
Reichenbach#	656
Simmen#	459
Staubbach	984
Trummelbach#	1,312

North America

Name and location	Elevation (ft)
Canada	
Alberta	
Panther, Nigel Cr.	600
British Columbia	
Della#	1,443
Takakkaw, Daly Glacier#	1,200
Quebec	
Montmorency	274
Canada—United States	
Niagara: American	182
Horseshoe	173
United States	
California	
Feather, Fall R. *	640
Yosemite National Park	
Bridalveil*	620
Illilouette*	370
Nevada, Merced R.*	594
Ribbon**	1,612
Silver Strand, Meadow Br.**	1,170
Vernal, Merced R. *	317
Yosemite#**	2,425
Colorado	
Seven, South Cheyenne Cr.#	300
Hawaii	
Akaka, Kolekole Str.	442
Idaho	
Shoshone, Snake R.**	212
Kentucky	
Cumberland	68
Maryland	
Great, Potomac R. (C) *	71
Minnesota	
Minnehaha**	53
New Jersey	
Passaic	70
New York	
Taughannock*	215
Oregon	
Multnomah#	620
Tennessee	
Fall Creek	256
Washington	
Mt. Rainier Natl. Park	
Sluiskin, Paradise R.	300
Snoqualmie**	268
Wisconsin	
Big Manitou, Black R. (C)*	165
Wyoming	
Yellowstone Natl. Pk. Tower	132
Yellowstone (upper)*	109
Yellowstone (lower)*	308
Mexico	
El Salto	218

South America

Name and location	Elevation (ft)
Argentina-Brazil	
Iguazu	230
Brazil	
Glass	1,325
Patos-Maribondo, Grande R.	115
Paulo Afonso, Sao Francisco R.	275
Urubupunga, Parana R.	39
Colombia	
Catarata de Candelas, Cusiana R.	984
Tequendama, Bogota R.*	427
Ecuador	
Agoyan, Pastaza R.*	200
Guyana	
Kaieteur, Potaro R.	741
Great, Kamarang R.	1,600
Marina, Ipobe R.#	500
Venezuela	
Angel#*	3,212
Cuquenan	2,000

Notable Deserts of the World

Arabian (Eastern), 70,000 sq mi in Egypt between the Nile R and Red Sea, extending southward into Sudan

Atacama, 600-mi-long area rich in nitrate and copper deposits in N Chile

Chihuahuan, 140,000 sq mi in TX, NM, AZ, and Mexico

Dasht-e Kauir, approx. 300 mi long by approx. 100 mi wide in N central Iran

Dasht-e Lut, 20,000 sq mi in E Iran

Death Valley, 3,300 sq mi in CA and NV

Gibson, 120,000 sq mi in the interior of W Australia

Gobi, 500,000 sq mi in Mongolia and China

Great Sandy, 150,000 sq mi in W Australia

Great Victoria, 150,000 sq mi in SW Australia

Kalahari, 225,000 sq mi in S Africa

Kara Kum, 120,000 sq mi in Turkmenistan

Kyzyl Kum, 100,000 sq mi in Kazakhstan and Uzbekistan

Libyan, 450,000 sq mi in the Sahara, extending from Libya through SW Egypt into Sudan

Mojave, 15,000 sq mi in southern CA

Namib, long narrow area (varies from 30-100 mi wide) extending 800 mi along SW coast of Africa

Nubian, 100,000 sq mi in the Sahara in NE Sudan

Patagonia, 300,000 sq mi in S Argentina

Painted Desert, section of high plateau in northern AZ extending 150 mi

Rub al-Khali (Empty Quarter), 250,000 sq mi in the S Arabian Peninsula

Sahara, 3,500,000 sq mi in N Africa, extending westward to the Atlantic. Largest desert in the world

Sonoran, 70,000 sq mi in southwestern AZ and southeastern CA extending into NW Mexico

Syrian, 100,000-sq-mi arid wasteland extending over much of N Saudi Arabia, E Jordan, S Syria, and W Iraq

Taklimakan, 140,000 sq mi in Xinjiang Prov., China

Thar (Great Indian), 100,000-sq-mi arid area extending 400 mi along India-Pakistan border

PRESIDENTIAL ELECTIONS

Popular and Electoral Vote, 1992 and 1996

Source: Voter News Service; Federal Election Commission; totals are official.

	1996						1992					
	Electoral Vote			Democrat	Republican	Reform	Electoral Vote			Democrat	Republican	Independent
State	Clinton	Dole	Perot	Clinton	Dole	Perot	Clinton	Bush	Perot	Clinton	Bush	Perot
AL	0	9	0	662,165	769,044	92,149	0	9	0	690,080	804,283	183,109
AK	0	3	0	662,165	769,044	92,149	0	3	0	78,294	102,000	73,481
AZ	8	0	0	653,288	622,073	112,072	0	8	0	543,050	572,086	353,741
AR	6	0	0	475,171	325,416	69,884	6	0	0	505,823	337,324	99,132
CA	54	0	0	5,119,835	3,828,380	697,847	54	0	0	5,121,325	3,630,574	2,296,006
CO	0	8	0	671,152	691,848	99,629	8	0	0	629,681	562,850	366,010
CT	8	0	0	735,740	483,109	139,523	8	0	0	682,318	578,313	348,771
DE	3	0	0	140,355	99,062	28,719	3	0	0	126,054	102,313	59,213
DC	3	0	0	158,220	17,339	3,611	3	0	0	192,619	20,698	9,681
FL	25	0	0	2,545,968	2,243,324	483,776	0	25	0	2,071,651	2,171,781	1,052,481
GA	0	13	0	1,053,849	1,080,843	146,337	13	0	0	1,008,966	995,252	309,657
HI	4	0	0	205,012	113,943	27,358	4	0	0	179,310	136,822	53,003
ID	0	4	0	165,443	256,595	62,518	0	4	0	137,013	202,645	130,395
IL	22	0	0	2,341,744	1,587,021	346,408	22	0	0	2,453,350	1,734,096	840,515
IN	0	12	0	887,424	1,006,693	224,299	0	12	0	848,420	989,375	455,934
IA	7	0	0	620,258	492,644	105,159	7	0	0	586,353	504,891	253,468
KS	0	6	0	387,659	583,245	92,639	0	6	0	390,434	449,951	312,358
KY	8	0	0	636,614	623,283	120,396	8	0	0	665,104	617,178	203,944
LA	9	0	0	927,837	712,586	123,293	9	0	0	815,971	733,386	211,478
ME	4	0	0	312,788	186,378	85,970	4	0	0	263,420	206,504	206,820
MD	10	0	0	966,207	681,530	115,812	10	0	0	988,571	707,094	281,414
MA	12	0	0	1,571,509	718,058	227,206	12	0	0	1,318,639	805,039	630,731
MI	18	0	0	1,989,653	1,481,212	336,670	18	0	0	1,871,182	1,554,940	824,813
MN	10	0	0	1,120,438	766,476	257,704	10	0	0	1,020,997	747,841	562,506
MS	0	7	0	394,022	439,838	52,222	0	7	0	400,258	487,793	85,626
MO	11	0	0	1,025,935	890,016	217,188	11	0	0	1,053,873	811,159	518,741
MT	0	3	0	167,922	179,652	55,229	3	0	0	154,507	144,207	107,225
NE	0	5	0	236,761	363,467	71,278	0	5	0	216,864	343,678	174,104
NV	4	0	0	203,974	199,244	43,986	4	0	0	189,148	175,828	132,580
NH	4	0	0	246,166	196,486	48,387	4	0	0	209,040	202,484	121,337
NJ	15	0	0	1,652,361	1,103,099	262,134	15	0	0	1,436,206	1,356,865	521,829
NM	5	0	0	273,495	232,751	32,257	5	0	0	261,617	212,824	91,895
NY	33	0	0	3,756,177	1,933,492	503,458	33	0	0	3,444,450	2,346,649	1,090,721
NC	0	14	0	1,107,849	1,225,938	168,059	0	14	0	1,114,042	1,134,661	357,864
ND	0	3	0	106,905	125,050	32,515	0	3	0	99,168	136,244	71,084
OH	21	0	0	2,148,222	1,859,883	483,207	21	0	0	1,984,942	1,894,310	1,036,426
OK	0	8	0	488,105	582,315	130,788	0	8	0	473,066	592,929	319,878
OR	7	0	0	649,641	538,152	121,221	7	0	0	621,314	475,757	354,091
PA	23	0	0	2,215,819	1,801,169	430,984	23	0	0	2,239,164	1,791,841	902,667
RI	4	0	0	233,050	104,683	43,723	4	0	0	213,299	131,601	105,045
SC	0	8	0	506,283	573,458	64,386	0	8	0	479,514	577,507	138,872
SD	0	3	0	139,333	150,543	31,250	0	3	0	124,888	136,718	73,295
TN	11	0	0	909,146	863,530	105,918	11	0	0	933,521	841,300	199,968
TX	0	32	0	2,459,683	2,736,167	378,537	0	32	0	2,281,815	2,496,071	1,354,781
UT	0	5	0	221,633	361,911	66,461	0	5	0	183,429	322,632	203,400
VT	3	0	0	137,894	80,352	31,024	3	0	0	133,590	88,122	65,985
VA	0	13	0	1,091,060	1,138,350	159,861	0	13	0	1,038,650	1,150,517	348,639
WA	11	0	0	1,123,323	840,712	201,003	11	0	0	993,037	731,234	541,780
WV	5	0	0	327,812	233,946	71,639	5	0	0	331,001	241,974	108,829
WI	11	0	0	1,071,971	845,029	227,339	11	0	0	1,041,066	930,855	544,479
WY	0	3	0	77,934	105,388	25,928	0	3	0	68,160	79,347	51,263
Total	**379**	**159**	**0**	**47,401,185**	**39,197,469**	**8,085,294**	**370**	**168**	**0**	**44,908,254**	**39,102,343**	**19,741,065**

PRESIDENTIAL ELECTION RETURNS BY COUNTIES

All 1996 results are official. Results for New England states are for selected cities or towns because county results are not available. Totals are always statewide. D-Democrat; R-Republican; RF-Reform; I-Independent. (In 1996, Ross Perot was listed on the ballot in some states as "Independent.")

Source: Voter News Service; Federal Election Commission; Alaska Division of Elections

Alabama

County	1996 Clinton (D)	1996 Dole (R)	1996 Perot (RF)	1992 Clinton (D)	1992 Bush (R)	1992 Perot (I)
Autauga . .	5,015	9,509	813	4,819	8,715	1,916
Baldwin . .	12,776	29,487	4,520	12,195	26,270	7,656
Barbour . .	4,787	3,627	515	4,836	4,475	1,020
Bibb	2,775	3,037	455	2,900	3,124	686
Blount . . .	5,061	9,056	985	5,433	8,882	1,949
Bullock . .	3,078	1,154	111	3,259	1,253	266
Butler . . .	3,828	3,352	538	4,021	3,494	867
Calhoun .	15,725	18,088	2,613	16,453	20,623	4,717
Chambers	5,515	4,707	812	5,938	5,682	1,427
Cherokee	4,399	3,048	899	4,222	2,745	846
Chilton . .	5,354	7,910	929	4,946	8,126	1,363
Choctaw .	4,074	2,623	413	3,941	3,069	489
Clarke . . .	4,831	4,785	478	5,023	5,495	872
Clay	2,306	2,694	538	2,073	2,859	652
Cleburne .	1,737	2,063	385	2,144	2,425	630
Coffee . . .	5,168	7,805	1,042	5,776	7,591	2,021
Colbert . .	10,226	8,305	1,696	12,206	8,073	2,098
Conecuh .	2,903	2,093	445	3,155	2,463	552
Coosa . . .	2,121	1,721	262	2,330	1,973	476
Covington	4,543	6,035	1,098	5,004	6,840	1,880
Crenshaw	2,172	1,939	317	2,404	2,339	485
Cullman . .	9,544	14,308	2,440	10,451	14,411	4,113
Dale	4,732	8,288	1,216	5,098	8,123	2,423
Dallas . . .	10,507	6,612	477	11,053	7,394	1,110
DeKalb . .	6,544	9,823	1,609	8,245	10,519	2,741
Elmore . .	6,530	12,937	1,368	6,223	11,356	2,765
Escambia .	4,651	5,214	867	4,809	5,955	1,616
Etowah . .	17,976	16,835	2,529	20,558	17,467	4,277
Fayette . .	3,381	3,191	590	3,830	3,604	1,012
Franklin . .	5,028	4,449	966	5,953	4,794	1,075
Geneva . .	3,174	4,725	857	3,622	4,843	1,323
Greene . .	3,526	796	55	3,865	805	194
Hale	3,372	1,893	190	3,481	2,001	486
Henry . . .	3,019	3,082	515	2,804	2,970	667
Houston . .	8,791	17,476	1,653	8,857	17,360	3,492
Jackson .	8,204	5,650	1,573	10,628	5,711	2,462
Jefferson .	120,208	130,980	7,997	125,889	149,832	22,191
Lamar . . .	2,843	2,955	597	2,849	3,262	763
Lauderdale	13,619	14,058	2,574	15,936	13,728	4,009
Lawrence	5,254	3,893	964	6,364	3,576	1,624
Lee	12,919	17,985	1,949	13,770	16,885	4,572
Limestone	8,045	10,862	1,659	8,087	9,862	3,584
Lowndes .	3,970	1,369	72	3,500	1,328	284
Macon . . .	7,018	987	150	7,253	1,134	283
Madison . .	42,259	50,390	7,437	38,974	51,444	16,989
Marengo .	4,899	4,013	337	5,632	4,470	919
Marion . . .	5,049	4,742	979	6,167	5,692	1,389
Marshall . .	8,722	12,323	2,150	10,421	12,249	3,795
Mobile . . .	54,749	66,775	7,555	54,962	72,935	15,105
Monroe . .	3,815	4,382	486	3,872	4,919	759
Montgomery	38,382	37,784	2,036	37,342	40,742	7,647
Morgan . .	14,616	21,765	3,348	15,091	21,073	7,683
Perry . . .	4,053	1,703	119	3,712	1,829	213
Pickens . .	4,018	3,322	403	3,783	3,634	690
Pike	4,514	5,281	503	4,688	5,423	1,024
Randolph .	3,023	3,304	603	3,318	3,813	919
Russell . .	7,834	5,025	792	8,647	5,587	1,360
St. Clair . .	6,187	12,762	1,417	6,517	12,447	2,614
Shelby . .	11,280	37,090	2,035	10,317	32,736	5,022
Sumter . .	4,706	1,561	172	4,810	1,807	388
Talladega .	10,385	10,931	1,335	10,695	12,661	2,629
Tallapoosa	6,071	7,627	1,038	5,703	8,140	1,562
Tuscaloosa	23,067	27,939	3,048	23,495	27,454	7,011
Walker . .	12,929	9,837	2,012	14,831	11,301	3,344
Washington	3,935	2,900	819	4,046	3,270	829
Wilcox . . .	3,303	1,454	71	3,439	1,671	174
Winston . .	3,120	4,728	723	3,415	5,550	1,110
Totals . . .	**662,165**	**769,044**	**92,149**	**690,080**	**804,283**	**183,109**

Alabama Vote Since 1948

1948, Thurmond, States' Rights, 171,443; Dewey, Rep., 40,930; Wallace, Prog., 1,522; Watson, Proh., 1,085.

1952, Eisenhower, Rep., 149,231; Stevenson, Dem., 275,075; Hamblen, Proh., 1,814.

1956, Stevenson, Dem., 290,844; Eisenhower, Rep., 195,694; Independent electors, 20,323.

1960, Kennedy, Dem., 324,050; Nixon, Rep., 237,981; Faubus, States' Rights, 4,367; Decker, Proh., 2,106; King, Afro-Americans, 1,485; scattering, 236.

1964, Dem. (electors unpledged), 209,848; Goldwater, Rep., 479,085; scattering, 105.

1968, Nixon, Rep., 146,923; Humphrey, Dem., 196,579; Wallace, 3d Party, 691,425; Munn, Proh., 4,022.

1972, Nixon, Rep., 728,701; McGovern, Dem., 219,108 plus 37,815 Natl. Demo. Party of Alabama; Schmitz, Conservative, 11,918; Munn., Proh., 8,551.

1976, Carter, Dem., 659,170; Ford, Rep., 504,070; Maddox, Amer. Ind., 9,198; Bubar, Proh., 6,669; Hall, Com., 1,954; MacBride, Libertarian, 1,481.

1980, Reagan, Rep., 654,192; Carter, Dem., 636,730; Anderson, Independent, 16,481; Rarick, Amer. Ind., 15,010; Clark, Libertarian, 13,318; Bubar, Statesman, 1,743; Hall, Com., 1,629; DeBerry, Soc. Workers, 1,303; McReynolds, Socialist, 1,006; Commoner, Citizens, 517.

1984, Reagan, Rep., 872,849; Mondale, Dem., 551,899; Bergland, Libertarian, 9,504.

1988, Bush, Rep., 815,576; Dukakis, Dem., 549,506; Paul, Lib., 8,460; Fulani, Ind., 3,311.

1992, Bush, Rep., 804,283; Clinton, Dem., 690,080; Perot, Ind., 183,109; Marrou, Libertarian, 5,737; Fulani, New Alliance, 2,161.

1996, Dole, Rep., 769,044; Clinton, Dem., 662,165; Perot, Ind. (Ref.), 92,149; Browne, Libertarian, 5,290; Phillips, Ind., 2,365; Hagelin, Natural Law, 1,697; Harris, Ind., 516.

Alaska

Election District[1]	1996 Clinton (D)	1996 Dole (R)	1996 Perot (RF)	1992 Clinton (D)	1992 Bush (R)	1992 Perot (I)
No. 1 . . .	1,480	4,209	696	2,055	2,495	2,120
No. 2 . . .	2,563	3,247	912	2,565	2,916	2,137
No. 3 . . .	3,724	2,671	654	4,064	2,447	1,424
No. 4 . . .	3,037	3,336	694	2,688	2,894	1,561
No. 5 . . .	2,148	2,564	826	2,095	1,844	1,684
No. 6 . . .	1,576	2,707	557	1,546	2,345	1,748
No. 7 . . .	2,177	3,517	907	2,088	2,173	2,244
No. 8 . . .	1,643	3,624	826	1,509	2,499	2,325
No. 9 . . .	1,334	3,459	727	1,540	2,349	2,368
No. 10. . . .	2,203	4,184	642	1,947	3,548	1,899
No. 11. . . .	1,946	3,073	603	2,009	2,730	2,081
No. 12. . . .	1,825	3,568	543	1,831	2,999	2,039
No. 13. . . .	2,780	3,270	608	3,001	2,963	1,907
No. 14. . . .	1,471	3,005	458	1,423	3,013	1,599
No. 15. . . .	2,178	1,974	552	2,389	1,842	1,591
No. 16. . . .	1,629	1,328	414	1,814	1,375	1,320
No. 17. . . .	1,868	3,284	633	1,749	2,623	1,958
No. 18. . . .	2,708	4,245	694	2,483	3,629	2,134
No. 19. . . .	2,014	3,159	636	1,931	2,539	1,840
No. 20. . . .	2,144	3,025	545	2,383	2,914	1,823
No. 21. . . .	2,228	2,553	557	2,386	2,437	1,693
No. 22. . . .	2,511	3,887	624	2,253	3,164	1,713
No. 23. . . .	1,071	2,127	388	1,139	2,127	1,217
No. 24. . . .	1,914	3,653	548	1,876	3,441	1,930
No. 25. . . .	1,629	4,099	691	1,513	3,197	2,122
No. 26. . . .	1,519	3,913	883	1,439	2,675	2,419
No. 27. . . .	1,887	4,384	1,122	1,625	2,757	2,401
No. 28. . . .	1,645	4,202	1,333	1,522	2,459	2,825
No. 29. . . .	3,023	3,012	658	3,216	2,205	2,026
No. 30. . . .	1,794	2,785	601	1,860	2,434	1,912
No. 31. . . .	1,903	2,721	684	1,969	2,223	1,992
No. 32. . . .	1,275	2,736	675	1,150	2,339	1,724
No. 33. . . .	1,852	4,089	759	1,712	3,100	2,278
No. 34. . . .	1,388	3,677	734	1,455	3,408	2,201
No. 35. . . .	1,447	3,016	875	1,572	2,525	2,139
No. 36. . . .	2,321	1,992	453	1,748	2,081	1,322
No. 37. . . .	2,134	1,835	456	1,822	1,689	925
No. 38. . . .	2,436	1,716	393	1,897	2,011	850
No. 39. . . .	2,692	1,618	404	1,797	1,777	860
No. 40. . . .	1,260	1,280	368	1,211	1,786	1,122
Totals. . . .	**80,377**	**122,744**	**26,333**	**78,294**	**102,000**	**73,481**

(1) 1992 and 1996 results are not comparable because of a 1994 reapportionment of districts.

Alaska Vote Since 1960

1960, Kennedy, Dem., 29,809; Nixon, Rep., 30,953.

1964, Johnson, Dem., 44,329; Goldwater, Rep., 22,930.

1968, Nixon, Rep., 37,600; Humphrey, Dem., 35,411; Wallace, 3d Party, 10,024.

1972, Nixon, Rep., 55,349; McGovern, Dem., 32,967; Schmitz, Amer., 6,903.

1976, Carter, Dem., 44,058; Ford, Rep., 71,555; MacBride, Libertarian, 6,785.

1980, Reagan, Rep., 86,112; Carter, Dem., 41,842; Clark, Libertarian, 18,479; Anderson, Ind., 11,155; write-in, 857.

1984, Reagan, Rep., 138,377; Mondale, Dem., 62,007; Bergland, Libertarian, 6,378.

1988, Bush, Rep., 119,251; Dukakis, Dem., 72,584; Paul, Lib., 5,484; Fulani, New Alliance, 1,024.

1992, Bush, Rep., 102,000; Clinton, Dem., 78,294; Perot, Ind., 73,481; Gritz, Populist/America First, 1,379; Marrou, Libertarian, 1,378.

1996, Dole, Rep., 122,746; Clinton, Dem., 80,380; Perot, Ref., 26,333; Nader, Green, 7,597; Browne, Libertarian, 2,276; Phillips, Taxpayers, 925; Hagelin, Natural Law, 729.

Arizona

	1996			1992		
	Clinton	Dole	Perot	Clinton	Bush	Perot
County	(D)	(R)	(RF)	(D)	(R)	(I)
Apache . . .	12,394	4,761	1,296	11,218	4,588	1,979
Cochise . . .	13,782	14,365	3,346	12,701	12,202	7,857
Coconino . .	20,475	13,638	3,666	18,888	13,769	9,363
Gila	8,577	6,407	2,211	7,571	5,781	4,694
Graham . . .	3,938	4,222	1,034	3,391	4,169	1,860
Greenlee . .	1,755	1,159	426	1,695	1,451	794
La Paz . . .	1,964	1,902	597	1,808	1,599	1,488
Maricopa . .	363,991	386,015	58,479	285,457	360,049	221,475
Mohave . . .	16,629	17,997	6,369	13,255	13,684	12,706
Navajo . . .	12,912	9,262	2,461	10,882	7,994	4,787
Pima	137,983	104,121	18,809	128,569	97,036	53,925
Pinal	19,579	13,034	3,972	15,468	11,669	9,231
Santa Cruz	5,241	2,256	600	3,512	3,024	1,447
Yavapai . . .	21,801	29,921	6,649	18,268	23,419	16,409
Yuma	12,267	13,013	2,157	10,367	11,652	5,726
Totals	**653,288**	**622,073**	**112,072**	**543,050**	**572,086**	**353,741**

Arizona Vote Since 1948

1948, Truman, Dem., 95,251; Dewey, Rep., 77,597; Wallace, Prog., 3,310; Watson, Proh., 786; Teichert, Soc. Labor, 121.

1952, Eisenhower, Rep., 152,042; Stevenson, Dem., 108,528.

1956, Eisenhower, Rep., 176,990; Stevenson, Dem., 112,880; Andrews, Ind. 303.

1960, Kennedy, Dem., 176,781; Nixon, Rep., 221,241; Hass, Soc. Labor, 469.

1964, Johnson, Dem., 237,753; Goldwater, Rep., 242,535; Hass, Soc. Labor, 482.

1968, Nixon, Rep., 266,721; Humphrey, Dem., 170,514; Wallace, 3d Party, 46,573; McCarthy, New Party, 2,751; Halstead, Soc. Workers, 85; Cleaver, Peace and Freedom, 217; Blomen, Soc. Labor, 75.

1972, Nixon, Rep., 402,812; McGovern, Dem., 198,540; Schmitz, Amer., 21,208; Soc. Workers, 30,945. Because of ballot peculiarities in 3 counties (particularly Pima), thousands of voters cast ballots for the Soc. Workers Party *and* one of the major candidates. Court ordered both votes counted as official.

1976, Carter, Dem., 295,602; Ford, Rep., 418,642; McCarthy, Ind., 19,229; MacBride, Libertarian, 7,647; Camejo, Soc. Workers, 928; Anderson, Amer., 564; Maddox, Amer. Ind., 85.

1980, Reagan, Rep., 529,688; Carter, Dem., 246,843; Anderson, Ind., 76,952; Clark, Libertarian, 18,784; De Berry, Soc. Workers, 1,100; Commoner, Citizens, 551; Hall, Com., 25; Griswold, Workers World, 2.

1984, Reagan, Rep., 681,416; Mondale, Dem., 333,854; Bergland, Libertarian, 10,585.

1988, Bush, Rep., 702,541; Dukakis, Dem., 454,029; Paul, Lib., 13,351; Fulani, New Alliance, 1,662.

1992, Bush, Rep., 572,086; Clinton, Dem., 543,050; Perot, Ind., 353,741; Gritz, Populist/America First, 8,141; Marrou, Libertarian, 6,759; Hagelin, Natural Law, 2,267.

1996, Clinton, Dem., 653,288; Dole, Rep., 622,073; Perot, Ref., 112,072; Browne, Libertarian, 14,358.

Arkansas

	1996			1992		
	Clinton	Dole	Perot	Clinton	Bush	Perot
County	(D)	(R)	(RF)	(D)	(R)	(I)
Arkansas .	4,220	1,910	463	4,709	2,594	639
Ashley . . .	5,011	2,428	704	5,876	2,686	931
Baxter . . .	6,703	6,877	1,572	6,991	5,640	2,938
Benton. . .	17,205	23,748	4,147	15,774	21,126	6,128
Boone . . .	5,745	6,093	1,132	6,128	6,094	2,079
Bradley . .	2,566	1,146	221	2,954	1,482	391
Calhoun . .	1,306	727	237	1,389	1,047	257
Carroll . . .	3,689	3,957	986	3,769	3,535	1,500
Chicot . . .	3,090	1,056	233	3,504	1,242	347
Clark	5,281	2,112	567	5,767	2,403	714
Clay	3,848	1,512	464	4,848	1,647	568
Cleburne .	4,475	3,807	1,021	5,090	3,580	1,263
Cleveland .	1,741	990	268	1,893	1,127	337
Columbia .	4,730	3,376	678	4,747	3,702	1,090
Conway . .	4,055	2,307	746	4,898	2,719	803
Craighead.	13,284	9,210	1,778	13,931	9,104	2,274
Crawford .	6,749	7,182	1,683	6,656	6,882	2,442
Crittenden	8,415	4,673	554	9,683	5,910	848
Cross. . . .	3,631	2,000	466	4,058	2,303	602
Dallas . . .	2,118	1,041	236	2,107	1,458	345
Desha . . .	3,230	978	247	3,815	1,279	392
Drew	3,570	1,657	395	3,748	1,938	596
Faulkner. .	12,032	10,178	1,528	13,000	9,491	2,437
Franklin . .	3,269	2,246	626	3,217	2,495	987
Fulton . . .	2,361	1,351	455	2,827	1,258	631
Garland . .	19,211	13,662	2,769	18,811	12,886	3,475
Grant. . . .	2,948	1,925	557	3,190	2,272	702
Greene . .	6,622	3,757	1,014	7,541	3,510	1,213
Hempstead	4,983	2,021	501	5,476	2,387	1,022
Hot Spring	6,002	2,864	1,123	6,308	3,036	1,209
Howard . .	2,741	1,478	369	2,764	1,728	466
Independence	6,240	4,021	1,126	7,083	4,232	1,444
Izard	2,818	1,678	541	3,419	1,532	606
Jackson . .	4,304	1,525	611	4,944	1,864	673
Jefferson .	19,701	6,330	1,284	21,819	7,525	2,067
Johnson. .	3,585	2,367	757	3,951	2,563	1,013
Lafayette .	2,466	971	374	2,273	1,188	504
Lawrence .	3,652	1,823	609	4,146	2,124	636
Lee	3,267	1,013	257	3,436	1,293	308
Lincoln. . .	2,517	907	221	2,805	1,142	390
Little River	3,183	1,409	480	3,327	1,483	890
Logan . . .	3,832	2,966	1,048	3,995	3,408	1,220
Lonoke . .	8,049	6,414	1,369	7,963	6,253	1,554
Madison. .	2,504	2,303	461	2,415	2,238	598
Marion . . .	2,735	2,312	764	2,757	2,023	1,327
Miller. . . .	6,469	4,874	1,043	7,050	5,273	2,249
Mississippi	8,301	3,919	1,016	10,046	4,697	981
Monroe . .	2,247	973	202	2,578	1,324	355
Montgomery	1,830	1,137	427	1,904	1,205	576
Nevada . .	2,279	976	345	2,242	1,217	455
Newton . .	1,631	1,927	498	1,765	1,730	608
Ouachita .	6,635	3,136	733	7,411	3,711	1,238
Perry	1,873	1,143	395	1,906	1,162	412
Phillips. . .	5,715	2,205	461	6,456	2,695	634
Pike.	2,362	1,401	441	2,168	1,577	472
Poinsett . .	4,686	2,034	647	5,341	2,425	761
Polk.	2,824	2,852	876	3,162	2,757	1,225
Pope	8,433	8,243	1,891	7,704	8,056	1,989
Prairie . . .	2,211	1,025	305	2,366	1,154	434
Pulaski. . .	75,084	44,780	6,014	79,482	47,789	8,751
Randolph .	3,213	1,789	561	3,921	1,766	578
St. Francis	5,562	2,523	506	6,548	3,289	766
Saline . . .	14,027	11,695	2,612	12,671	10,105	2,751
Scott	2,259	1,426	513	2,228	1,695	610
Searcy. . .	1,669	1,786	381	1,679	1,772	503
Sebastian.	15,514	16,482	2,899	16,570	16,817	6,023
Sevier . . .	2,553	1,379	446	2,558	1,592	643
Sharp . . .	3,573	2,635	687	3,761	2,486	921
Stone. . . .	2,227	1,526	579	2,622	1,672	697
Union. . . .	8,373	6,053	1,073	8,786	7,305	1,919
Van Buren	3,521	2,345	830	3,819	2,612	888
Washington	20,419	19,476	3,133	22,029	20,292	5,304
White. . . .	10,204	8,659	1,828	10,494	8,538	2,366
Woodruff .	2,044	598	186	2,589	676	227
Yell	3,749	2,111	714	4,165	2,506	940
Totals . . .	**475,171**	**325,416**	**69,884**	**505,823**	**337,324**	**99,132**

Arkansas Vote Since 1948

1948, Truman, Dem., 149,659; Dewey, Rep., 50,959; Thurmond, States' Rights, 40,068; Thomas, Soc., 1,037; Wallace, Prog., 751; Watson, Proh., 1.

1952, Eisenhower, Rep., 177,155; Stevenson, Dem., 226,300; Hamblen, Proh., 886; MacArthur, Christian Nationalist, 458; Hass, Soc. Labor, 1.

1956, Stevenson, Dem., 213,277; Eisenhower, Rep., 186,287; Andrews, Ind., 7,008.

1960, Kennedy, Dem., 215,049; Nixon, Rep., 184,508; Natl. States' Rights, 28,952.

1964, Johnson, Dem., 314,197; Goldwater, Rep., 243,264; Kasper, Natl. States' Rights, 2,965.

1968, Nixon, Rep., 189,062; Humphrey, Dem., 184,901; Wallace, 3d Party, 235,627.

1972, Nixon, Rep., 445,751; McGovern, Dem., 198,899; Schmitz, Amer., 3,016.

1976, Carter, Dem., 498,604; Ford, Rep., 267,903; McCarthy, Ind., 639; Anderson, Amer., 389.

1980, Reagan, Rep., 403,164; Carter, Dem., 398,041; Anderson, Ind., 22,468; Clark, Libertarian, 8,970; Commoner, Citizens, 2,345; Bubar, Statesman, 1,350; Hall, Com., 1,244.

1984, Reagan, Rep., 534,774; Mondale, Dem., 338,646; Bergland, Libertarian, 2,220.

1988, Bush, Rep., 466,578; Dukakis, Dem., 349,237; Duke, Chr. Pop., 5,146; Paul, Lib., 3,297.

1992, Clinton, Dem., 505,823; Bush, Rep., 337,324; Perot, Ind., 99,132; Phillips, U.S. Taxpayers, 1,437; Marrou, Libertarian, 1,261; Fulani, New Alliance, 1,022.

1996, Clinton, Dem., 475,171; Dole, Rep., 325,416; Perot, Ref., 69,884; Nader, Ind., 3,649; Browne, Ind., 3,076; Phillips, Ind., 2,065; Forbes, Ind., 932; Collins, Ind., 823; Masters, Ind., 749; Hagelin, Ind., 729; Moorehead, Ind., 747; Hollis, Ind., 538; Dodge, Ind., 483.

California

	1996			1992		
	Clinton	Dole	Perot	Clinton	Bush	Perot
County	(D)	(R)	(RF)	(D)	(R)	(I)
Alameda . .	303,903	106,581	24,270	334,224	109,292	81,643
Alpine	258	264	63	215	222	186

County	1996 Clinton (D)	1996 Dole (R)	1996 Perot (RF)	1992 Clinton (D)	1992 Bush (R)	1992 Perot (I)
Amador . . .	5,868	6,870	1,267	5,286	5,477	4,553
Butte	30,651	38,961	6,393	32,489	31,608	20,231
Calaveras. .	6,646	8,279	1,612	5,989	6,006	4,848
Colusa. . . .	2,054	3,047	404	1,798	2,589	1,206
Contra Costa	196,512	123,954	20,416	194,960	112,965	72,518
Del Norte . .	3,652	3,670	1,225	3,639	3,083	2,575
El Dorado. .	22,957	32,759	5,077	21,012	25,906	17,503
Fresno. . . .	94,448	98,813	10,962	92,418	89,137	36,299
Glenn	2,841	5,041	788	2,666	3,812	2,278
Humboldt . .	24,628	19,803	5,811	28,854	18,299	12,340
Imperial . . .	14,591	9,705	1,778	11,109	9,759	4,247
Inyo.	2,601	3,924	811	2,695	3,689	1,999
Kern	62,658	92,151	13,452	60,510	80,762	36,891
Kings.	11,254	12,368	1,745	9,982	10,673	4,899
Lake	10,432	7,458	2,539	10,548	6,678	5,797
Lassen. . . .	3,318	5,194	1,080	3,388	3,836	3,004
Los Angeles.	1,430,629	746,544	157,752	1,446,529	799,607	488,624
Madera . . .	11,254	16,510	2,192	10,863	13,066	6,156
Marin.	67,406	32,714	6,559	76,158	30,479	22,986
Mariposa . .	2,920	3,976	729	3,023	2,982	2,211
Mendocino .	14,952	9,765	3,685	18,344	7,958	9,753
Merced . . .	21,786	20,847	3,427	20,133	17,981	10,914
Modoc	1,368	2,285	528	1,489	1,803	1,269
Mono.	1,580	1,882	447	1,489	1,570	1,248
Monterey . .	57,700	39,794	7,240	54,861	36,461	24,472
Napa.	24,588	17,439	4,254	24,215	15,662	13,150
Nevada . . .	15,369	21,784	3,330	15,433	17,343	11,072
Orange . . .	327,485	446,717	66,195	306,930	426,613	232,394
Placer	34,981	49,808	6,542	30,783	38,298	21,741
Plumas . . .	3,540	4,905	919	3,742	3,599	2,551
Riverside . .	168,579	178,611	35,481	166,241	159,457	102,233
Sacramento	203,019	166,049	23,856	197,540	160,366	91,412
San Benito .	7,030	5,384	1,044	5,354	4,112	3,182
San Bernardino	183,372	180,135	39,330	183,634	176,563	109,183
San Diego .	389,964	402,876	63,037	367,397	352,125	259,249
San Francisco .	209,777	45,479	9,659	233,263	57,352	29,018
San Joaquin	67,253	65,131	9,692	63,655	58,355	31,205
San Luis Obispo . . .	40,395	46,733	8,204	40,136	36,384	27,314
San Mateo .	152,304	73,508	15,047	149,232	75,080	50,465
Santa Barbara. . .	70,650	63,915	9,457	69,215	57,375	35,105
Santa Clara	297,639	168,291	34,908	296,265	170,870	128,895
Santa Cruz.	58,250	27,766	6,555	66,183	24,916	21,615
Shasta. . . .	20,848	34,736	5,875	21,605	28,190	17,990
Sierra	573	877	170	653	691	519
Siskiyou. . .	7,022	8,653	1,879	8,254	6,660	5,567
Solano. . . .	64,644	40,742	8,682	64,320	38,883	27,851
Sonoma. . .	100,738	53,555	13,862	104,334	47,619	43,859
Stanislaus .	53,738	52,403	8,360	52,415	47,275	27,651
Sutter	8,504	14,264	1,533	7,883	12,956	4,881
Tehama . . .	7,290	10,292	2,325	7,508	7,419	5,884
Trinity	2,203	2,530	856	1,967	1,886	2,092
Tulare	32,669	46,272	5,106	31,188	40,482	16,430
Tuolumne. .	8,950	10,386	1,925	9,216	8,525	6,294
Ventura . . .	110,772	109,202	23,054	99,011	94,911	71,844
Yolo	33,033	18,807	3,150	33,297	17,574	11,073
Yuba	5,789	7,971	1,308	5,785	7,333	3,637
Totals	**5,119,835**	**3,828,380**	**697,847**	**5,121,325**	**3,630,574**	**2,296,006**

California Vote Since 1948

1948, Truman, Dem., 1,913,134; Dewey, Rep., 1,895,269; Wallace, Prog., 190,381; Watson, Proh., 16,926; Thomas, Soc., 3,459; Thurmond, States' Rights, 1,228; Teichert, Soc. Labor, 195; Dobbs, Soc. Workers, 133.

1952, Eisenhower, Rep., 2,897,310; Stevenson, Dem., 2,197,548; Hallinan, Prog., 24,106; Hamblen, Proh., 15,653; MacArthur, (Tenny Ticket), 3,326; (Kellems Ticket) 178; Hass, Soc. Labor, 273; Hoopes, Soc., 206; scattered, 3,249.

1956, Eisenhower, Rep., 3,027,668; Stevenson, Dem., 2,420,136; Holtwick, Proh., 11,119; Andrews, Constitution, 6,087; Hass, Soc. Labor, 300; Hoopes, Soc., 123; Dobbs, Soc. Workers, 96; Smith, Christian Natl., 8.

1960, Kennedy, Dem., 3,224,099; Nixon, Rep., 3,259,722; Decker, Proh., 21,706; Hass, Soc. Labor, 1,051.

1964, Johnson, Dem., 4,171,877; Goldwater, Rep., 2,879,108; Hass, Soc. Labor, 489; DeBerry, Soc. Workers, 378; Munn, Proh., 305; Hensley, Universal, 19.

1968, Nixon, Rep., 3,467,664; Humphrey, Dem., 3,244,318; Wallace, 3d Party, 487,270; Peace and Freedom, 27,707; McCarthy, Alternative, 20,721; Gregory, write-in, 3,230; Mitchell, Com., 260; Munn, Proh., 59; Blomen, Soc. Labor, 341; Soeters, Defense, 17.

1972, Nixon, Rep., 4,602,096; McGovern, Dem., 3,475,847; Schmitz, Amer., 232,554; Spock, Peace and Freedom, 55,167; Hall, Com., 373; Hospers, Libertarian, 980; Munn, Proh., 53; Fisher, Soc. Labor, 197; Jenness, Soc. Workers, 574; Green, Universal, 21.

1976, Carter, Dem., 3,742,284; Ford, Rep., 3,882,244; MacBride, Libertarian, 56,388; Maddox, Amer. Ind., 51,098; Wright, People's, 41,731; Camejo, Soc. Workers, 17,259; Hall, Com., 12,766; write-in, McCarthy, 58,412; other write-in, 4,935.

1980, Reagan, Rep. 4,524,858; Carter, Dem., 3,083,661; Anderson, Ind., 739,833; Clark, Libertarian, 148,434; Commoner, Ind., 61,063; Smith, Peace and Freedom, 18,116; Rarick, Amer. Ind., 9,856.

1984, Reagan, Rep. 5,305,410; Mondale, Dem., 3,815,947; Bergland, Libertarian, 48,400.

1988, Bush, Rep., 5,054,917; Dukakis, Dem., 4,702,233; Paul, Lib., 70,105; Fulani, Ind., 31,181.

1992, Clinton, Dem., 5,121,325; Bush, Rep., 3,630,575; Perot, Ind., 2,296,006; Marrou, Libertarian, 48,139; Daniels, Ind., 18,597; Phillips, U.S. Taxpayers, 12,711.

1996, Clinton, Dem., 5,119,835; Dole, Rep., 3,828,380; Perot, Ref., 697,847; Nader, Green, 237,016; Browne, Libertarian, 73,600; Feinland, Peace & Freedom, 25,332; Phillips, Amer. Ind., 21,202; Hagelin, Natural Law, 15,403.

Colorado

County	1996 Clinton (D)	1996 Dole (R)	1996 Perot (RF)	1992 Clinton (D)	1992 Bush (R)	1992 Perot (I)
Adams. . . .	48,314	36,666	7,206	45,357	30,856	26,379
Alamosa. . .	2,330	2,038	437	1,928	1,572	1,089
Arapahoe . .	68,306	82,778	8,476	66,607	72,221	44,363
Archuleta . .	997	1,963	360	819	1,242	741
Baca	659	1,321	203	726	1,240	647
Bent	1,046	917	209	985	759	506
Boulder . . .	63,316	41,922	6,840	64,567	33,553	27,762
Chaffee . . .	2,768	3,052	538	2,284	2,419	1,549
Cheyenne. .	328	739	91	301	615	292
Clear Creek	1,863	1,746	365	1,744	1,356	1,308
Conejos . . .	1,726	1,149	245	1,705	1,160	578
Costilla . . .	1,168	333	112	1,180	366	199
Crowley . . .	559	680	114	570	602	276
Custer	412	920	164	343	651	368
Delta	3,584	6,047	1,060	3,424	4,359	2,627
Denver. . . .	120,312	58,529	8,777	121,961	55,418	37,298
Dolores . . .	276	417	95	242	315	285
Douglas . . .	16,232	32,120	2,662	9,991	18,592	11,329
Eagle.	5,094	4,637	1,193	3,870	3,100	3,821
Elbert	1,894	4,125	507	1,237	2,205	1,567
El Paso . . .	55,822	102,403	11,175	45,827	86,044	34,346
Fremont. . .	5,344	7,437	1,438	5,356	5,961	3,709
Garfield . . .	5,722	6,281	1,562	5,082	4,404	4,408
Gilpin.	799	682	184	726	462	545
Grand	2,012	2,264	473	1,678	1,763	1,454
Gunnison . .	2,812	2,230	570	2,389	1,662	1,671
Hinsdale. . .	185	289	56	151	188	136
Huerfano . .	1,483	996	210	1,224	685	385
Jackson . . .	222	486	107	216	422	326
Jefferson . .	89,494	101,517	12,967	80,834	82,705	58,404
Kiowa	246	549	74	290	472	267
Kit Carson .	1,073	2,068	235	925	1,801	919
Lake	1,338	728	274	1,426	605	863
La Plata . . .	6,509	8,057	1,403	5,913	5,522	4,083
Larimer . . .	40,965	45,935	6,823	38,232	35,995	24,879
Las Animas.	3,611	1,905	427	3,847	1,739	953
Lincoln. . . .	729	1,272	164	640	1,079	581
Logan	2,765	4,032	609	2,718	3,420	2,184
Mesa.	17,114	24,761	3,707	15,162	18,169	10,474
Mineral . . .	192	179	69	171	159	117
Moffat	1,635	2,466	649	1,386	1,809	1,875
Montezuma .	2,578	4,175	827	2,270	3,124	2,205
Montrose . .	4,019	6,730	1,187	3,713	4,847	3,093
Morgan . . .	3,347	4,557	687	2,985	3,724	2,175
Otero.	3,386	3,356	581	3,485	3,120	1,590
Ouray	569	984	167	461	653	466
Park	1,844	2,661	534	1,307	1,530	1,396
Philips	706	1,284	156	692	1,075	525
Pitkin.	3,949	1,969	535	3,820	1,686	1,907
Prowers. . .	1,745	2,504	342	1,770	2,371	1,184
Pueblo. . . .	28,791	17,402	3,374	30,261	16,120	9,841
Rio Blanco .	731	1,697	243	778	1,231	794
Rio Grande.	1,720	2,129	379	1,541	1,927	1,043
Routt.	3,660	3,019	859	3,188	2,358	2,564
Saguache. .	969	712	160	1,011	675	471
San Juan . .	133	153	50	147	118	183
San Miguel.	1,535	773	231	1,380	628	634
Sedgwick . .	519	715	101	397	447	295
Summit . . .	3,970	3,261	823	3,344	2,256	2,715
Teller.	2,312	4,458	707	1,873	3,050	1,927
Washington	649	1,566	190	660	1,266	671
Weld	21,325	26,518	4,347	19,295	20,958	13,571
Yuma.	1,439	2,589	319	1,269	2,019	1,197
Totals	**671,152**	**691,848**	**99,629**	**629,681**	**562,850**	**366,010**

Colorado Vote Since 1948

1948, Truman, Dem., 267,288; Dewey, Rep., 239,714; Wallace, Prog., 6,115; Thomas, Soc., 1,678; Dobbs, Soc. Workers, 228; Teichert, Soc. Labor, 214.

1952, Eisenhower, Rep., 379,782; Stevenson, Dem., 245,504; MacArthur, Constitution, 2,181; Hallinan, Prog., 1,919; Hoopes, Soc., 365; Hass, Soc. Labor, 352.

1956, Eisenhower, Rep., 394,479; Stevenson, Dem., 263,997; Hass, Soc. Lab., 3,308; Andrews, Ind., 759; Hoopes, Soc., 531.

1960, Kennedy, Dem., 330,629; Nixon, Rep., 402,242; Hass, Soc. Labor, 2,803; Dobbs, Soc. Workers, 572.
1964, Johnson, Dem., 476,024; Goldwater, Rep., 296,767; Hass, Soc. Labor, 302; DeBerry, Soc. Workers, 2,537; Munn, Proh., 1,356.
1968, Nixon, Rep., 409,345; Humphrey, Dem., 335,174; Wallace, 3d Party, 60,813; Blomen, Soc. Labor, 3,016; Gregory, New-party, 1,393; Munn, Proh., 275; Halstead, Soc. Workers, 235.
1972, Nixon, Rep., 597,189; McGovern, Dem., 329,980; Fisher, Soc. Labor, 4,361; Hospers, Libertarian, 1,111; Hall, Com., 432; Jenness, Soc. Workers, 555; Munn, Proh., 467; Schmitz, Amer., 17,269; Spock, Peoples, 2,403.
1976, Carter, Dem., 460,353; Ford, Rep., 584,367; McCarthy, Ind., 26,107; MacBride, Libertarian, 5,330; Bubar, Proh., 2,882.
1980, Reagan, Rep., 652,264; Carter, Dem., 367,973; Anderson, Ind., 130,633; Clark, Libertarian, 25,744; Commoner, Citizens, 5,614; Bubar, Statesman, 1,180; Pulley, Socialist, 520; Hall, Com., 487.
1984, Reagan, Rep., 821,817; Mondale, Dem., 454,975; Bergland, Libertarian, 11,257.
1988, Bush, Rep., 728,177; Dukakis, Dem., 621,453; Paul, Lib., 15,482; Dodge, Proh., 4,604.
1992, Clinton, Dem., 629,681; Bush, Rep., 562,850; Perot, Ind., 366,010; Marrou, Libertarian, 8,669; Fulani, New Alliance, 1,608.
1996, Dole, Rep., 691,848; Clinton, Dem., 671,152; Perot, Ref., 99,629; Nader, Green, 25,070; Browne, Libertarian, 12,392; Collins, Ind., 2,809; Phillips, Amer. Constitution, 2,813; Hagelin, Natural Law, 2,547; Hollis, Soc., 669; Moorehead, Workers World, 599; Templin, Amer., 557; Dodge, Proh., 375; Harris, Soc. Workers, 244.

Connecticut

City	1996 Clinton (D)	1996 Dole (R)	1996 Perot (RF)	1992 Clinton (D)	1992 Bush (R)	1992 Perot (I)
Bridgeport	22,883	6,785	2,367	22,321	13,149	6,263
Bristol . . .	13,616	6,560	3,049	11,872	8,407	7,890
Danbury . .	12,102	7,965	2,158	9,909	10,310	5,517
Fairfield . .	12,639	12,314	2,092	12,099	13,968	5,941
Greenwich	11,622	14,308	1,437	11,893	15,885	4,584
Hartford . .	22,929	3,082	1,010	26,971	6,180	3,390
New Britain	14,322	4,911	1,717	14,159	7,040	4,983
New Haven	26,161	4,822	1,555	29,774	8,931	4,130
Norwalk . .	17,354	10,800	2,237	16,488	14,743	6,046
Stamford .	25,005	14,696	2,595	23,185	19,809	6,763
Waterbury	18,901	12,075	3,169	16,366	16,155	9,188
West Hartford	19,037	10,781	1,890	19,623	12,266	5,017
Other	519,169	374,010	114,247	467,658	431,470	279,059
Totals . . .	**735,740**	**483,109**	**139,523**	**682,318**	**578,313**	**348,771**

Connecticut Vote Since 1948

1948, Truman, Dem., 423,297; Dewey, Rep., 437,754; Wallace, Prog., 13,713; Thomas, Soc., 6,964; Teichert, Soc. Labor, 1,184; Dobbs, Soc. Workers, 606.
1952, Eisenhower, Rep., 611,012; Stevenson, Dem., 481,649; Hoopes, Soc., 2,244; Hallinan, Peoples, 1,466; Hass, Soc. Labor, 535; write-in, 5.
1956, Eisenhower, Rep., 711,837; Stevenson, Dem., 405,079; scattered, 205.
1960, Kennedy, Dem., 657,055; Nixon, Rep., 565,813.
1964, Johnson, Dem., 826,269; Goldwater, Rep., 390,996; scattered, 1,313.
1968, Nixon, Rep., 556,721; Humphrey, Dem., 621,561; Wallace, 3d Party, 76,650; scattered, 1,300.
1972, Nixon, Rep., 810,763; McGovern, Dem., 555,498; Schmitz, Amer., 17,239; scattered, 777.
1976, Carter, Dem., 647,895; Ford, Rep., 719,261; Maddox, George Wallace Party, 7,101; LaRouche, U.S. Labor, 1,789.
1980, Reagan, Rep., 677,210; Carter, Dem., 541,732; Anderson, Ind., 171,807; Clark, Libertarian, 8,570; Commoner, Citizens, 6,130; scattered, 836.
1984, Reagan, Rep., 890,877; Mondale, Dem., 569,597.
1988, Bush, Rep., 750,241; Dukakis, Dem., 676,584; Paul, Lib., 14,071; Fulani, New Alliance, 2,491.
1992, Clinton, Dem., 682,318; Bush, Rep., 578,313; Perot, Ind., 348,771; Marrou, Libertarian, 5,391; Fulani, New Alliance, 1,363.
1996, Clinton, Dem., 735,740; Dole, Rep., 483,109; Perot, Ref., 139,523; Nader, Green, 24,321; Browne, Libertarian, 5,788; Phillips, Concerned Citizens, 2,425; Hagelin, Natural Law, 1,703.

Delaware

County	1996 Clinton (D)	1996 Dole (R)	1996 Perot (RF)	1992 Clinton (D)	1992 Bush (R)	1992 Perot (I)
Kent	18,327	15,932	4,705	15,364	15,562	8,916
New Castle .	98,837	60,943	17,748	91,516	66,311	37,581
Sussex. . . .	23,191	22,187	6,266	19,174	20,440	12,716
Totals	**140,355**	**99,062**	**28,719**	**126,054**	**102,313**	**59,213**

Delaware Vote Since 1948

1948, Truman, Dem., 67,813; Dewey, Rep., 69,688; Wallace, Prog., 1,050; Watson, Proh., 343; Thomas, Soc., 250; Teichert, Soc. Labor, 29.
1952, Eisenhower, Rep., 90,059; Stevenson, Dem., 83,315; Hass, Soc. Labor, 242; Hamblen, Proh., 234; Hallinan, Prog., 155; Hoopes, Soc., 20.
1956, Eisenhower, Rep., 98,057; Stevenson, Dem., 79,421; Oltwick, Proh., 400; Hass, Soc. Labor, 110.
1960, Kennedy, Dem., 99,590; Nixon, Rep., 96,373; Faubus, States' Rights, 354; Decker, Proh., 284; Hass, Soc. Labor, 82.
1964, Johnson, Dem., 122,704; Goldwater, Rep., 78,078; Hass, Soc. Labor, 113; Munn, Proh., 425.
1968, Nixon, Rep., 96,714; Humphrey, Dem., 89,194; Wallace, 3d Party, 28,459.
1972, Nixon, Rep., 140,357; McGovern, Dem., 92,283; Schmitz, Amer., 2,638; Munn, Proh., 238.
1976, Carter, Dem., 122,596; Ford, Rep., 109,831; McCarthy, non-partisan, 2,437; Anderson, Amer., 645; LaRouche, U.S. Labor, 136; Bubar, Proh., 103; Levin, Soc. Labor, 86.
1980, Reagan, Rep., 111,252; Carter, Dem., 105,754; Anderson, Ind., 16,288; Clark, Libertarian, 1,974; Greaves, Amer., 400.
1984, Reagan, Rep., 152,190; Mondale, Dem., 101,656; Bergland, Libertarian, 268.
1988, Bush, Rep., 139,639; Dukakis, Dem., 108,647; Paul, Lib., 1,162; Fulani, New Alliance, 443.
1992, Clinton, Dem., 126,054; Bush, Rep., 102,313; Perot, Ind., 59,213; Fulani, New Alliance, 1,105.
1996, Clinton, Dem., 140,355; Dole, Rep., 99,062; Perot, Ind. (Ref.), 28,719; Browne, Libertarian, 2,052; Phillips, Taxpayers, 348; Hagelin, Natural Law, 274.

District of Columbia

	1996 Clinton (D)	1996 Dole (R)	1996 Perot (RF)	1992 Clinton (D)	1992 Bush (R)	1992 Perot (I)
Totals	**158,220**	**17,339**	**3,611**	**192,619**	**20,698**	**9,681**

District of Columbia Vote Since 1964

1964, Johnson, Dem., 169,796; Goldwater, Rep., 28,801.
1968, Nixon, Rep., 31,012; Humphrey, Dem., 139, 566.
1972, Nixon, Rep., 35,226; McGovern, Dem., 127,627; Reed, Soc. Workers, 316; Hall, Com., 252.
1976, Carter, Dem., 137,818; Ford, Rep., 27,873; Camejo, Soc. Workers, 545; MacBride, Libertarian, 274; Hall, Com., 219; LaRouche, U.S. Labor, 157.
1980, Reagan, Rep., 23,313; Carter, Dem., 130,231; Anderson, Ind., 16,131; Commoner, Citizens, 1,826; Clark, Libertarian, 1,104; Hall, Com., 369; DeBerry, Soc. Workers, 173; Griswold, Workers World, 52; write-ins, 690.
1984, Mondale, Dem., 180,408; Reagan, Rep., 29,009; Bergland, Libertarian, 279.
1988, Bush, Rep., 27,590; Dukakis, Dem., 159,407; Fulani, New Alliance, 2,901; Paul, Lib., 554.
1992, Clinton, Dem., 192,619; Bush, Rep., 20,698; Perot, Ind., 9,681; Fulani, New Alliance, 1,459; Daniels, Ind., 1,186.
1996, Clinton, Dem., 158,220; Dole, Rep., 17,339; Perot, Ref., 3,611; Nader, Green, 4,780; Browne, Libertarian, 588; Hagelin, Natural Law, 283; Harris, Soc. Workers, 257.

Florida

County	1996 Clinton (D)	1996 Dole (R)	1996 Perot (RF)	1992 Clinton (D)	1992 Bush (R)	1992 Perot (I)
Alachua . .	40,144	25,303	8,072	37,876	22,806	15,293
Baker . . .	2,273	3,684	667	1,974	3,417	1,315
Bay	17,020	28,290	5,922	12,830	22,820	9,702
Bradford . .	3,356	4,038	819	3,040	3,671	1,572
Brevard . .	80,416	87,980	25,249	61,070	84,545	49,491
Broward . .	320,736	142,834	38,964	276,309	164,782	90,923
Calhoun . .	1,794	1,717	630	1,665	1,721	1,176
Charlotte .	27,121	27,836	7,783	22,904	24,302	14,711
Citrus . . .	22,042	20,114	7,244	15,935	16,402	12,310
Clay	13,246	30,332	3,281	10,597	26,313	8,414
Collier . . .	23,182	42,590	6,320	18,794	38,447	14,514
Columbia .	6,691	7,588	1,970	5,526	6,489	2,906
Dade[1] . . .	317,378	209,634	24,722	254,444	235,149	53,957
De Soto . .	3,219	3,272	965	2,646	3,070	1,687
Dixie	1,731	1,398	652	1,855	1,401	1,094
Duval. . . .	112,258	126,857	13,844	92,010	123,480	33,335
Escambia .	37,768	60,839	8,587	32,018	52,775	19,868
Flagler . . .	9,583	8,232	2,185	6,692	6,241	3,387
Franklin . .	2,095	1,563	878	1,534	1,660	1,143
Gadsden .	9,405	3,813	938	8,478	3,975	1,871
Gilchrist . .	1,985	1,939	841	1,511	1,395	1,090
Glades. . .	1,530	1,361	521	1,305	1,185	878
Gulf.	2,480	2,424	1,054	1,938	2,650	1,245

County	1996 Clinton (D)	1996 Dole (R)	1996 Perot (RF)	1992 Clinton (D)	1992 Bush (R)	1992 Perot (I)
Hamilton. .	1,734	1,518	406	1,622	1,402	695
Hardee. . .	2,417	2,926	851	2,017	2,898	1,498
Hendry. . .	3,882	3,855	1,135	2,690	3,279	2,032
Hernando .	28,520	22,039	7,272	19,171	17,896	11,845
Highlands .	14,244	15,608	3,739	11,234	14,497	6,592
Hillsborough	144,223	136,621	25,154	115,261	130,611	63,037
Holmes . .	2,310	3,248	1,208	1,877	3,196	1,426
Indian River	16,373	22,709	4,635	12,359	19,137	12,375
Jackson . .	6,665	7,187	1,602	5,481	6,720	2,447
Jefferson .	2,543	1,851	393	2,270	1,506	894
Lafayette .	829	1,166	316	866	1,037	612
Lake	29,750	35,089	8,813	23,199	30,818	15,606
Lee	65,692	80,882	18,389	53,656	73,423	38,446
Leon	50,058	33,914	6,672	47,770	31,964	17,207
Levy	4,938	4,299	1,774	4,330	3,796	2,784
Liberty . . .	868	913	376	820	1,126	617
Madison . .	2,791	2,195	578	2,644	2,006	1,174
Manatee. .	41,835	44,059	10,360	33,826	42,708	23,282
Marion . . .	37,033	41,397	11,340	30,823	35,438	20,524
Martin . . .	20,851	28,516	5,005	14,778	24,768	13,433
Monroe . .	15,219	12,021	4,817	10,435	9,891	8,306
Nassau . .	7,276	12,134	1,657	5,497	9,364	3,251
Okaloosa .	16,434	40,631	5,432	12,003	32,755	16,649
Okeechobee	4,824	3,415	1,666	3,418	3,298	2,645
Orange . .	105,513	106,026	18,191	82,656	108,738	44,827
Osceola . .	21,870	18,335	6,091	15,009	19,139	11,021
Palm Beach	230,621	133,762	30,739	187,840	140,317	76,223
Pasco . . .	66,472	48,346	18,011	53,125	47,721	34,650
Pinellas . .	184,728	152,125	36,990	160,217	158,733	101,150
Polk.	66,735	67,943	14,991	51,442	65,952	28,198
Putnam . .	12,008	9,781	3,272	10,707	8,909	5,975
St. Johns .	16,713	27,311	4,205	12,284	20,173	7,397
St. Lucie. .	36,168	28,892	8,482	23,873	24,397	19,813
Santa Rosa	10,923	26,244	4,957	6,526	17,229	8,735
Sarasota .	63,648	69,198	14,939	54,536	66,831	34,281
Seminole .	45,051	59,778	9,357	35,649	57,085	24,477
Sumter. . .	7,014	5,960	2,375	5,027	4,366	2,901
Suwannee	4,479	5,742	1,874	3,985	4,571	2,790
Taylor . . .	3,583	3,188	1,140	2,568	2,693	1,929
Union. . . .	1,388	1,636	425	1,247	1,543	770
Volusia. . .	78,905	63,067	17,319	65,213	59,155	30,813
Wakulla . .	3,054	2,931	1,091	2,319	2,586	1,790
Walton . . .	5,341	7,706	2,342	3,886	5,719	3,886
Washington	2,992	3,522	1,287	2,544	3,694	1,596
Totals . . .	**2,545,968**	**2,243,324**	**483,776**	**2,071,651**	**2,171,781**	**1,052,481**

(1) In 1997, Dade County changed its name to Miami-Dade County.

Florida Vote Since 1948

1948, Truman, Dem., 281,988; Dewey, Rep., 194,280; Thurmond, States' Rights, 89,755; Wallace, Prog., 11,620.

1952, Eisenhower, Rep., 544,036; Stevenson, Dem., 444,950; scattered, 351.

1956, Eisenhower, Rep., 643,849; Stevenson, Dem., 480,371.

1960, Kennedy, Dem., 748,700; Nixon, Rep., 795,476.

1964, Johnson, Dem., 948,540; Goldwater, Rep., 905,941.

1968, Nixon, Rep., 886,804; Humphrey, Dem., 676,794; Wallace, 3d Party, 624,207.

1972, Nixon, Rep., 1,857,759; McGovern, Dem., 718,117; scattered, 7,407.

1976, Carter, Dem., 1,636,000; Ford, Rep., 1,469,531; McCarthy, Ind., 23,643; Anderson, Amer., 21,325.

1980, Reagan, Rep., 2,046,951; Carter, Dem., 1,419,475; Anderson, Ind., 189,692; Clark, Libertarian, 30,524; write-ins, 285.

1984, Reagan, Rep., 2,728,775; Mondale, Dem., 1,448,344.

1988, Bush, Rep., 2,616,597; Dukakis, Dem., 1,655,851; Paul, Lib., 19,796, Fulani, New Alliance, 6,655.

1992, Bush, Rep., 2,171,781; Clinton, Dem., 2,071,651; Perot, Ind., 1,052,481; Marrou, Libertarian, 15,068.

1996, Clinton, Dem., 2,545,968; Dole, Rep., 2,243,324; Perot, Ref., 483,776; Browne, Libertarian, 23,312.

Georgia

County	1996 Clinton (D)	1996 Dole (R)	1996 Perot (RF)	1992 Clinton (D)	1992 Bush (R)	1992 Perot (I)
Appling . .	2,070	2,572	446	2,455	2,514	1,047
Atkinson. .	823	784	215	1,056	779	342
Bacon . . .	1,360	1,580	402	1,423	1,301	604
Baker. . . .	955	408	105	864	391	210
Baldwin . .	5,740	4,570	849	5,813	4,262	1,679
Banks . . .	1,536	1,925	595	1,530	1,551	583
Barrow. . .	3,928	5,342	942	3,991	4,328	1,633
Bartow. . .	6,853	9,250	1,770	6,675	7,742	2,500
Ben Hill . .	2,198	1,516	358	2,348	1,476	619
Berrien. . .	2,066	1,950	525	2,103	1,637	796
Bibb	26,727	20,778	2,268	28,070	19,847	6,021
Bleckley . .	1,365	1,632	300	1,710	1,570	662
Brantley . .	1,494	1,738	386	1,883	1,541	840
Brooks . . .	1,977	1,738	314	1,895	1,779	630
Bryan. . . .	2,152	3,577	513	2,031	2,789	1,095
Bulloch. . .	5,396	6,646	939	4,903	5,690	2,020
Burke. . . .	3,915	2,590	389	3,647	2,390	807
Butts	2,271	2,027	416	2,448	1,768	619
Calhoun . .	1,217	541	106	1,301	464	248
Camden. .	3,644	4,222	572	2,952	3,517	1,077
Candler . .	1,097	1,131	264	1,192	1,014	541
Carroll . . .	8,438	11,157	2,002	8,404	10,750	3,358
Catoosa . .	5,185	8,237	1,257	4,817	7,599	2,290
Charlton. .	1,368	1,374	280	1,127	1,333	427
Chatham .	35,781	31,987	3,028	31,533	31,925	8,269
Chattahoo- chee. . . .	565	398	115	604	413	177
Chattooga	3,003	2,513	796	2,976	2,439	965
Cherokee .	10,802	24,527	2,872	8,113	16,054	4,950
Clarke . . .	15,206	10,504	1,201	15,403	10,459	2,987
Clay	787	293	62	778	264	155
Clayton . .	30,687	20,625	3,494	25,890	23,965	7,942
Clinch . . .	973	789	182	759	790	286
Cobb. . . .	73,750	114,188	10,438	63,960	103,734	28,747
Coffee . . .	3,407	3,934	711	3,275	3,778	1,256
Colquitt . .	4,135	4,847	977	3,891	4,680	1,682
Columbia .	8,601	21,291	1,709	7,115	16,657	4,379
Cook. . . .	1,780	1,354	267	1,731	1,318	537
Coweta . .	7,794	13,058	1,949	7,093	9,814	3,587
Crawford .	1,534	1,290	270	1,648	974	549
Crisp	2,504	2,321	445	2,610	2,253	823
Dade. . . .	1,737	2,295	618	1,782	2,191	823
Dawson . .	1,434	2,343	473	1,399	1,696	790
Decatur . .	3,245	3,035	497	3,198	3,142	1,068
DeKalb . .	137,903	60,255	6,742	124,559	70,282	19,741
Dodge . . .	2,696	2,478	587	3,002	2,287	978
Dooly. . . .	1,951	990	207	1,993	1,034	350
Dougherty	15,600	11,144	1,072	15,236	12,455	3,178
Douglas . .	9,631	14,495	2,109	8,869	13,349	4,362
Early	1,648	1,374	246	1,970	1,457	652
Echols . . .	308	335	97	312	361	238
Effingham.	3,031	5,022	769	2,690	3,814	1,443
Elbert . . .	2,900	2,393	552	3,025	2,372	757
Emanuel .	2,947	2,451	450	2,951	2,662	755
Evans . . .	1,117	1,206	204	1,230	1,244	480
Fannin . . .	2,741	3,373	782	2,902	3,255	1,028
Fayette . .	9,875	21,005	2,016	8,430	17,576	5,598
Floyd. . . .	10,464	12,426	2,345	11,614	12,378	3,779
Forsyth . .	5,957	15,013	1,889	4,936	8,652	3,453
Franklin . .	2,338	2,364	665	2,505	2,391	1,014
Fulton . . .	143,306	89,809	7,720	147,459	85,451	23,578
Gilmer . . .	2,464	3,121	725	2,311	2,661	879
Glascock .	348	532	128	316	516	180
Glynn . . .	8,058	12,305	1,137	8,581	11,242	3,053
Gordon . .	4,239	5,232	1,284	4,103	5,265	1,818
Grady . . .	2,862	2,674	633	2,520	2,370	1,126
Greene . .	2,115	1,702	173	2,259	1,307	483
Gwinnett .	53,819	96,610	10,236	44,253	81,822	23,926
Habersham	3,170	4,730	1,149	3,098	4,569	1,444
Hall.	10,362	19,280	2,321	11,214	16,108	5,043
Hancock. .	2,135	438	71	2,461	506	189
Haralson .	2,850	3,260	808	3,281	3,142	1,167
Harris . . .	2,779	3,829	489	2,679	3,316	954
Hart.	3,486	2,884	767	3,614	2,607	1,376
Heard . . .	1,248	1,170	406	1,456	1,190	617
Henry . . .	9,498	16,968	2,320	7,817	12,634	3,769
Houston . .	12,760	17,050	2,730	12,270	14,119	6,263
Irwin	1,225	1,085	224	1,366	973	465
Jackson . .	3,746	4,782	899	3,792	3,976	1,381
Jasper . . .	1,553	1,423	243	1,485	1,153	373
Jeff Davis .	1,576	1,796	428	2,031	1,947	958
Jefferson .	3,404	2,077	298	3,220	2,077	685
Jenkins . .	1,336	955	166	1,401	929	394
Johnson. .	1,194	815	242	1,473	1,314	502
Jones . . .	3,195	3,272	497	3,338	2,770	1,159
Lamar . . .	2,125	1,988	409	2,065	1,707	600
Lanier . . .	818	519	160	811	600	298
Laurens . .	5,792	6,118	818	6,184	6,146	1,602
Lee	2,005	3,983	506	1,811	3,061	1,024
Liberty . . .	4,462	3,042	580	3,853	2,832	1,176
Lincoln. . .	1,334	1,391	208	1,327	1,149	479
Long	936	791	236	874	719	355
Lowndes .	9,470	10,578	1,518	9,019	10,276	2,864
Lumpkin. .	1,949	2,576	588	2,010	1,972	1,035
McDuffie .	2,725	3,254	395	2,640	2,955	860
McIntosh .	1,927	1,219	293	1,925	1,027	550
Macon . . .	2,618	1,006	159	2,491	944	363
Madison. .	2,571	3,992	868	2,393	3,351	1,129
Marion . . .	977	678	159	1,145	711	198
Meriwether	3,492	2,259	480	4,002	2,364	942
Miller. . . .	909	847	235	934	826	455
Mitchell . .	3,165	2,033	372	3,052	1,917	818
Monroe . .	2,768	3,054	488	2,774	2,423	949
Montgomery	1,233	1,163	284	1,185	1,009	416
Morgan . .	2,111	2,118	364	2,057	1,797	596
Murray. . .	2,861	3,289	938	2,764	3,256	1,186
Muscogee	24,867	19,360	1,891	25,476	21,386	4,327
Newton . .	6,759	7,274	1,258	5,811	5,804	1,998
Oconee . .	2,992	5,116	615	2,745	4,125	1,182
Oglethorpe	1,570	1,826	369	1,491	1,590	620
Paulding. .	5,699	10,152	1,603	5,212	7,180	2,654
Peach . . .	3,582	2,676	471	3,677	2,327	947
Pickens . .	2,693	3,041	783	2,359	2,332	1,037
Pierce . . .	1,420	2,319	333	1,852	1,899	708
Pike.	1,474	2,054	357	1,651	1,822	623

County	1996 Clinton (D)	1996 Dole (R)	1996 Perot (RF)	1992 Clinton (D)	1992 Bush (R)	1992 Perot (I)
Polk.	4,298	4,130	1,076	4,872	4,158	1,598
Pulaski. . .	1,554	1,196	268	1,756	1,075	614
Putnam . .	2,340	2,306	474	2,149	1,756	775
Quitman . .	514	224	59	523	284	113
Rabun . . .	1,943	2,213	585	1,878	1,902	825
Randolph .	1,438	816	126	1,756	887	315
Richmond.	30,738	23,670	2,310	28,910	24,227	6,290
Rockdale .	7,656	13,006	1,750	7,003	11,945	3,664
Schley . . .	576	470	123	601	511	180
Screven . .	2,087	1,862	263	1,940	1,705	709
Seminole .	1,265	1,003	250	1,193	850	468
Spalding. .	6,017	7,376	1,059	6,392	7,262	2,044
Stephens .	3,072	3,890	979	2,976	4,047	1,448
Stewart . .	1,537	525	152	1,540	1,186	175
Sumter. . .	4,239	3,358	451	4,489	3,616	1,046
Talbot . . .	1,579	652	111	1,768	671	238
Taliaferro .	615	235	36	755	269	80
Tattnall. . .	2,369	2,518	541	2,360	2,566	996
Taylor . . .	1,450	1,002	195	1,508	1,078	281
Telfair . . .	1,856	1,143	322	2,238	1,324	613
Terrell . . .	1,509	1,111	129	1,942	1,143	384
Thomas . .	5,183	5,649	667	4,841	5,500	1,591
Tift	4,198	5,613	728	3,930	4,485	1,139
Toombs . .	2,763	3,646	602	2,648	3,609	1,210
Towns . . .	1,664	2,030	459	1,487	1,674	537
Treutlen . .	912	723	122	1,116	898	318
Troup. . . .	5,940	8,716	1,090	6,412	8,118	2,488
Turner . . .	1,272	924	246	1,669	936	370
Twiggs. . .	1,927	958	210	2,097	853	432
Union. . . .	2,175	2,685	622	2,304	2,533	804
Upson . . .	3,491	3,783	731	3,740	4,053	1,186
Walker. . .	6,743	8,817	1,969	6,217	8,489	2,748
Walton . . .	5,618	7,934	1,323	4,821	5,619	1,923
Ware	4,171	4,746	636	4,573	4,573	1,263
Warren. . .	1,230	735	83	1,239	751	180
Washington	4,057	2,348	488	3,508	2,384	820
Wayne . . .	2,734	3,709	665	3,052	3,381	1,107
Webster . .	529	235	59	600	208	103
Wheeler . .	751	460	141	880	601	214
White. . . .	1,864	2,959	556	1,756	2,477	981
Whitfield . .	7,720	12,368	1,637	7,335	12,003	2,866
Wilcox . . .	1,067	882	171	1,365	916	433
Wilkes . . .	1,971	1,417	184	1,955	1,535	464
Wilkinson .	2,278	1,332	287	2,286	1,232	520
Worth . . .	2,300	2,752	521	2,578	2,344	905
Totals . . .	**1,053,849**	**1,080,843**	**146,337**	**1,008,966**	**995,252**	**309,657**

Georgia Vote Since 1948

1948, Truman, Dem., 254,646; Dewey, Rep., 76,691; Thurmond, States' Rights, 85,055; Wallace, Prog., 1,636; Watson, Proh., 732.

1952, Eisenhower, Rep., 198,979; Stevenson, Dem., 456,823; Liberty Party, 1.

1956, Stevenson, Dem., 444,388; Eisenhower, Rep., 222,778; Andrews, Ind., write-in, 1,754.

1960, Kennedy, Dem., 458,638; Nixon, Rep., 274,472; write-in, 239.

1964, Johnson, Dem., 522,557; Goldwater, Rep., 616,600.

1968, Nixon, Rep., 380,111; Humphrey, Dem., 334,440; Wallace, 3d Party, 535,550; write-in, 162.

1972, Nixon, Rep., 881,496; McGovern, Dem., 289,529; scattered, 2,935; Schmitz, Amer., 812.

1976, Carter, Dem., 979,409; Ford, Rep., 483,743; write-in, 4,306.

1980, Reagan, Rep., 654,168; Carter, Dem., 890,955; Anderson, Ind., 36,055; Clark, Libertarian, 15,627.

1984, Reagan, Rep., 1,068,722; Mondale, Dem., 706,628.

1988, Bush, Rep., 1,081,331; Dukakis, Dem., 714,792; Paul, Lib., 8,435; Fulani, New Alliance, 5,099.

1992, Clinton, Dem., 1,008,966; Bush, Rep., 995,252; Perot, Ind., 309,657; Marrou, Libertarian, 7,110.

1996, Dole, Rep., 1,080,843; Clinton, Dem., 1,053,849; Perot, Ref., 146,337; Browne, Libertarian, 17,870.

Hawaii

County	1996 Clinton (D)	1996 Dole (R)	1996 Perot (RF)	1992 Clinton (D)	1992 Bush (R)	1992 Perot (I)
Hawaii. . . .	27,262	13,516	5,137	25,725	15,460	8,889
Honolulu . .	143,793	85,779	17,389	123,908	103,937	35,728
Kauai	13,357	5,325	1,568	10,715	6,274	1,756
Maui	20,600	9,323	3,264	18,962	11,151	6,630
Totals. . . .	**205,012**	**113,943**	**27,358**	**179,310**	**136,822**	**53,003**

Hawaii Vote Since 1960

1960, Kennedy, Dem., 92,410; Nixon, Rep., 92,295.

1964, Johnson, Dem., 163,249; Goldwater, Rep., 44,022.

1968, Nixon, Rep., 91,425; Humphrey, Dem., 141,324; Wallace, 3d Party, 3,469.

1972, Nixon, Rep., 168,865; McGovern, Dem., 101,409.

1976, Carter, Dem., 147,375; Ford, Rep., 140,003; MacBride, Libertarian, 3,923.

1980, Reagan, Rep., 130,112; Carter, Dem., 135,879; Anderson, Ind., 32,021; Clark, Libertarian, 3,269; Commoner, Citizens, 1,548; Hall, Com., 458.

1984, Reagan, Rep., 184,934; Mondale, Dem., 147,098; Bergland, Libertarian, 2,167.

1988, Bush, Rep., 158,625; Dukakis, Dem., 192,364; Paul, Lib., 1,999; Fulani, New Alliance, 1,003.

1992, Clinton, Dem., 179,310; Bush, Rep., 136,822; Perot, Ind., 53,003; Gritz, Populist/America First, 1,452; Marrou, Libertarian, 1,119.

1996, Clinton, Dem., 205,012; Dole, Rep., 113,943; Perot, Ref., 27,358; Nader, Green, 10,386; Browne, Libertarian, 2,493; Hagelin, Natural Law, 570; Phillips, Taxpayers, 358.

Idaho

County	1996 Clinton (D)	1996 Dole (R)	1996 Perot (RF)	1992 Clinton (D)	1992 Bush (R)	1992 Perot (I)
Ada.	43,040	61,811	11,171	31,941	49,000	28,192
Adams . . .	537	1,053	311	457	754	695
Bannock. . .	12,806	14,058	4,158	11,091	12,016	8,116
Bear Lake .	805	1,583	396	562	1,419	684
Benewah . .	1,488	1,667	701	1,270	1,223	1,165
Bingham . .	4,304	8,391	2,021	3,565	7,333	4,144
Blaine	3,840	3,003	1,193	2,865	2,243	2,831
Boise	879	1,576	440	623	912	754
Bonner. . . .	5,294	6,207	2,669	4,995	3,937	4,645
Bonneville .	9,013	19,977	3,921	7,014	16,557	10,241
Boundary . .	1,194	1,937	626	1,095	1,479	1,136
Butte	507	741	233	433	602	392
Camas . . .	156	283	95	134	202	145
Canyon . . .	11,800	23,988	3,956	9,095	19,220	8,974
Caribou . . .	841	1,740	501	562	1,350	1,088
Cassia. . . .	1,596	4,663	976	1,351	4,052	1,785
Clark	117	266	45	95	195	119
Clearwater .	1,507	1,658	650	1,433	1,152	1,098
Custer	635	1,249	400	564	829	729
Elmore. . . .	2,324	3,668	845	1,858	3,087	1,867
Franklin . . .	807	2,435	589	524	2,115	890
Fremont . .	1,114	3,042	630	903	2,333	1,349
Gem	1,968	3,362	833	1,609	2,455	1,555
Gooding. . .	1,503	2,637	980	1,530	2,178	1,591
Idaho.	1,979	3,871	1,083	1,974	2,709	1,900
Jefferson . .	1,427	4,925	994	978	3,471	2,164
Jerome . . .	1,679	3,358	1,014	1,739	2,972	1,768
Kootenai . .	13,627	18,740	6,083	11,553	13,065	11,261
Latah.	7,741	6,311	1,828	7,233	5,353	3,602
Lemhi	1,015	2,334	461	996	1,540	1,175
Lewis	674	861	316	674	593	491
Lincoln . . .	478	734	319	514	656	441
Madison . .	1,216	5,706	744	741	4,591	1,920
Minidoka . .	1,977	4,008	977	1,815	3,304	1,875
Nez Perce .	7,491	6,675	2,385	7,069	5,431	4,363
Oneida . . .	429	993	285	351	713	590
Owyhee . . .	895	2,033	354	686	1,469	862
Payette . . .	2,119	3,901	906	1,656	2,895	2,055
Power	1,070	1,501	344	837	1,352	697
Shoshone. .	2,981	1,588	1,283	3,182	1,441	1,878
Teton	866	1,251	326	472	762	608
Twin Falls. .	6,826	12,393	3,383	6,593	10,335	6,043
Valley	1,564	2,089	568	1,259	1,548	1,313
Washington	1,314	2,318	525	1,122	1,802	1,204
Totals	**165,443**	**256,595**	**62,518**	**137,013**	**202,645**	**130,395**

Idaho Vote Since 1948

1948, Truman, Dem., 107,370; Dewey, Rep., 101,514; Wallace, Prog., 4,972; Watson, Proh., 628; Thomas, Soc., 332.

1952, Eisenhower, Rep., 180,707; Stevenson, Dem., 95,081; Hallinan, Prog., 443; write-in, 23.

1956, Eisenhower, Rep., 166,979; Stevenson, Dem., 105,868; Andrews, Ind., 126; write-in, 16.

1960, Kennedy, Dem., 138,853; Nixon, Rep., 161,597.

1964, Johnson, Dem., 148,920; Goldwater, Rep., 143,557.

1968, Nixon, Rep., 165,369; Humphrey, Dem., 89,273; Wallace, 3d Party, 36,541.

1972, Nixon, Rep., 199,384; McGovern, Dem., 80,826; Schmitz, Amer., 28,869; Spock, Peoples, 903.

1976, Carter, Dem., 126,549; Ford, Rep., 204,151; Maddox, Amer., 5,935; MacBride, Libertarian, 3,558; LaRouche, U.S. Labor, 739.

1980, Reagan, Rep., 290,699; Carter, Dem., 110,192; Anderson, Ind., 27,058; Clark, Libertarian, 8,425; Rarick, Amer., 1,057.

1984, Reagan, Rep., 297,523; Mondale, Dem., 108,510; Bergland, Libertarian, 2,823.

1988, Bush, Rep., 253,881; Dukakis, Dem., 147,272; Paul, Lib., 5,313; Fulani, Ind., 2,502.

1992, Clinton, Dem., 137,013; Bush, Rep., 202,645; Perot, Ind., 130,395; Gritz, Populist/America First, 10,281; Marrou, Libertarian, 1,167.

1996, Dole, Rep., 256,595; Clinton, Dem., 165,443; Perot, Ref., 62,518; Browne, Libertarian, 3,325; Phillips, Taxpayers, 2,230; Hagelin, Natural Law, 1,600.

Illinois

		1996			1992	
County	Clinton (D)	Dole (R)	Perot (RF)	Clinton (D)	Bush (R)	Perot (I)
Adams . . .	11,336	13,836	3,069	11,748	13,529	6,157
Alexander.	2,753	1,212	321	2,566	1,301	474
Bond	3,213	3,018	685	3,428	2,715	1,373
Boone . . .	5,345	6,181	1,377	5,114	5,589	2,880
Brown . . .	997	1,053	237	1,146	1,029	504
Bureau. . .	7,651	6,528	1,798	7,551	6,836	3,465
Calhoun . .	1,676	941	363	1,519	745	532
Carroll . . .	2,926	3,029	792	2,854	3,297	1,502
Cass	2,834	2,214	589	3,200	2,162	1,072
Champaign	32,454	28,232	4,806	35,003	27,096	13,571
Christian. .	7,431	5,563	1,727	9,042	5,087	3,401
Clark	2,995	3,409	781	3,338	3,175	1,450
Clay.	2,750	2,703	719	2,962	2,471	1,193
Clinton . . .	6,104	6,065	1,580	6,686	5,771	3,315
Coles. . . .	8,950	8,038	2,137	9,402	8,098	4,707
Cook	1,153,289	461,557	96,633	1,249,533	605,300	281,999
Crawford .	3,627	3,965	1,057	3,964	3,606	2,062
Cumberland	1,776	2,002	657	2,111	1,860	1,209
DeKalb. . .	12,715	12,380	3,009	13,744	12,655	7,680
DeWitt . . .	2,878	2,978	694	3,009	3,164	1,543
Douglas . .	2,955	3,272	740	3,341	3,309	1,600
DuPage . .	129,709	164,630	27,419	114,564	178,271	76,839
Edgar. . . .	3,552	3,746	935	4,014	3,790	1,930
Edwards. .	1,089	1,613	384	1,299	1,601	634
Effingham.	4,825	7,696	1,555	5,221	6,329	3,354
Fayette. . .	3,887	3,881	964	4,833	3,508	1,730
Ford	2,065	3,077	590	2,175	3,046	1,222
Franklin . .	9,814	5,354	2,096	12,744	5,504	3,180
Fulton . . .	8,857	5,155	1,610	9,725	5,062	2,874
Gallatin . .	2,113	856	527	2,371	990	568
Greene. . .	2,734	2,245	903	3,164	2,391	1,461
Grundy. . .	6,759	6,177	1,860	6,122	6,346	3,724
Hamilton. .	2,242	1,677	560	2,582	1,521	862
Hancock. .	4,001	3,961	1,148	4,213	3,714	2,091
Hardin . . .	1,323	790	485	1,665	985	515
Henderson	1,953	1,233	408	2,013	1,310	715
Henry. . . .	11,201	8,393	2,194	11,077	8,989	4,231
Iroquois . .	4,559	6,564	1,522	4,440	6,948	3,073
Jackson . .	12,214	7,422	2,082	13,373	6,899	3,995
Jasper . . .	2,038	2,234	641	2,284	1,996	1,160
Jefferson .	7,263	5,937	1,647	8,665	5,497	3,403
Jersey . . .	4,275	3,211	1,186	4,749	2,933	2,363
Jo Daviess	4,171	3,915	1,131	4,044	4,249	2,102
Johnson . .	2,009	2,241	640	2,299	2,124	944
Kane	47,902	54,375	11,270	44,568	55,684	27,179
Kankakee.	16,820	14,595	3,574	17,229	15,411	7,264
Kendall. . .	6,499	8,958	2,055	5,423	8,521	4,394
Knox	12,487	7,822	2,096	12,524	8,331	4,357
Lake	93,315	93,149	16,640	81,693	99,000	42,384
LaSalle. . .	21,643	15,299	5,259	23,276	16,078	10,434
Lawrence .	2,871	2,568	916	3,270	2,681	1,498
Lee	5,895	6,677	1,520	5,530	6,652	3,191
Livingston.	5,641	7,653	1,409	6,007	8,004	3,029
Logan . . .	4,618	6,518	1,141	5,169	6,567	2,420
McDonough	5,632	5,049	1,217	5,814	5,297	2,770
McHenry .	31,240	41,136	10,082	24,783	41,356	21,817
McLean . .	22,708	26,428	3,816	23,090	25,726	10,282
Macon . . .	24,256	18,161	4,540	27,449	18,684	9,236
Macoupin .	11,107	7,235	2,532	12,050	6,518	5,018
Madison. .	53,568	35,758	10,121	58,484	32,167	23,110
Marion . . .	7,792	5,999	1,825	9,669	5,764	3,407
Marshall . .	2,640	2,453	586	2,819	2,491	1,169
Mason . . .	3,385	2,430	600	3,969	2,473	1,245
Massac . .	2,841	2,507	675	3,347	2,754	892
Menard . .	2,204	3,106	534	2,264	2,834	1,179
Mercer. . .	4,278	2,688	889	3,990	2,983	1,535
Monroe . .	4,798	5,350	1,276	4,894	4,807	2,813
Montgomery	6,338	4,770	1,436	7,424	4,407	2,956
Morgan . .	6,150	6,352	1,633	6,351	6,566	3,317
Moultrie . .	2,629	2,199	596	3,056	2,065	1,322
Ogle	6,765	9,558	1,876	6,512	9,008	4,455
Peoria . . .	37,383	30,990	5,220	38,099	30,718	12,195
Perry	5,347	3,237	1,262	6,009	3,105	1,955
Piatt.	3,274	3,265	818	3,520	3,076	1,822
Pike.	3,604	3,225	1,039	4,016	3,342	1,643
Pope	915	850	277	1,063	951	391
Pulaski. . .	1,524	1,036	235	1,987	1,169	379
Putnam . .	1,425	987	322	1,574	969	752
Randolph .	7,419	5,422	1,698	8,529	4,899	3,092
Richland. .	2,679	3,137	927	3,286	3,053	1,689
Rock Island	34,822	20,626	5,135	37,412	23,212	10,416
St. Clair . .	53,405	33,066	7,027	57,625	31,951	17,592
Saline . . .	6,156	6,193	1,752	7,258	3,667	2,302
Sangamon	38,902	42,174	6,446	40,052	39,641	16,861
Schuyler. .	1,636	1,597	483	1,650	1,512	815
Scott	1,012	1,112	396	1,057	1,132	588
Shelby . . .	4,249	4,215	1,262	5,101	3,631	2,401
Stark	1,262	1,278	312	1,336	1,384	625
Stephenson	7,145	8,871	1,940	7,899	9,005	4,677
Tazewell. .	24,139	24,395	4,814	26,428	23,469	9,927
Union. . . .	4,252	3,147	832	4,681	3,003	1,373
Vermilion .	15,525	12,015	3,577	18,383	11,703	8,162
Wabash . .	2,177	2,381	683	2,436	2,485	1,302
Warren. . .	3,500	2,974	742	3,661	3,325	1,436
Washington	2,744	3,339	790	2,986	3,003	1,542
Wayne . . .	3,054	4,029	999	3,332	3,809	1,702
White. . . .	3,553	2,878	888	4,308	3,057	1,428
Whiteside .	11,913	8,859	2,436	12,329	10,146	4,589
Will	69,354	62,506	15,485	59,633	58,337	32,788
Williamson	12,510	9,734	2,877	14,361	9,462	4,779
Winnebago	46,264	44,479	8,192	48,298	42,221	21,227
Woodford .	5,270	8,527	1,170	5,490	8,032	2,733
Totals . . .	**2,341,744**	**1,587,021**	**346,408**	**2,453,350**	**1,734,096**	**840,515**

Illinois Vote Since 1948

1948, Truman, Dem., 1,994,715; Dewey, Rep., 1,961,103; Watson, Proh., 11,959; Thomas, Soc., 11,522; Teichert, Soc. Labor, 3,118.

1952, Eisenhower, Rep., 2,457,327; Stevenson, Dem., 2,013,920; Hass, Soc. Labor, 9,363; write-in, 448.

1956, Eisenhower, Rep., 2,623,327; Stevenson, Dem., 1,775,682; Hass, Soc. Labor, 8,342; write-in, 56.

1960, Kennedy, Dem., 2,377,846; Nixon, Rep., 2,368,988; Hass, Soc. Labor, 10,560; write-in, 15.

1964, Johnson, Dem., 2,796,833; Goldwater, Rep., 1,905,946; write-in, 62.

1968, Nixon, Rep., 2,174,774; Humphrey, Dem., 2,039,814; Wallace, 3d Party, 390,958; Blomen, Soc. Labor, 13,878; write-in, 325.

1972, Nixon, Rep. 2,788,179; McGovern, Dem., 1,913,472; Fisher, Soc. Labor, 12,344; Schmitz, Amer., 2,471; Hall, Com., 4,541; others, 2,229.

1976, Carter, Dem., 2,271,295; Ford, Rep., 2,364,269; McCarthy, Ind., 55,939; Hall, Com., 9,250; MacBride, Libertarian, 8,057; Camejo, Soc. Workers, 3,615; Levin, Soc. Labor, 2,422; LaRouche, U.S. Labor, 2,018; write-in, 1,968.

1980, Reagan, Rep., 2,358,049; Carter, Dem., 1,981,413; Anderson, Ind., 346,754; Clark, Libertarian, 38,939; Commoner, Citizens, 10,692; Hall, Com., 9,711; Griswold, Workers World, 2,257; DeBerry, Soc. Workers, 1,302; write-ins, 604.

1984, Reagan, Rep., 2,707,103; Mondale, Dem., 2,086,499; Bergland, Libertarian, 10,086.

1988, Bush, Rep., 2,310,939; Dukakis, Dem., 2,215,940; Paul, Lib., 14,944; Fulani, Solid., 10,276.

1992, Clinton, Dem., 2,453,350; Bush, Rep., 1,734,096; Perot, Ind., 840,515; Marrou, Libertarian, 9,218; Fulani, New Alliance, 5,267; Gritz, Populist/America First, 3,577; Hagelin, Natural Law, 2,751; Warren, Soc. Workers, 1,361.

1996, Clinton, Dem., 2,341,744; Dole, Rep., 1,587,021; Perot, Ref., 346,408; Browne, Libertarian, 22,548; Phillips, Taxpayers, 7,606; Hagelin, Natural Law, 4,606.

Indiana

		1996			1992	
County	Clinton (D)	Dole (R)	Perot (RF)	Clinton (D)	Bush (R)	Perot (I)
Adams. . . .	4,247	6,960	1,346	3,708	6,078	2,865
Allen	41,450	59,255	8,808	39,629	55,003	25,809
Bartholomew.	9,301	13,188	2,815	8,284	13,146	5,882
Benton. . . .	1,311	1,947	609	1,221	2,030	1,056
Blackford . .	2,335	2,070	681	2,088	2,347	1,319
Boone	4,625	11,338	1,498	3,982	9,485	3,826
Brown	2,413	2,988	802	2,029	2,633	1,635
Carroll	2,747	4,062	1,171	2,561	3,800	2,173
Cass	5,419	8,020	2,029	4,757	7,421	3,944
Clark	17,799	14,396	3,578	17,460	13,333	5,653
Clay	3,605	4,858	1,406	3,306	4,696	2,134
Clinton. . . .	3,949	6,156	1,355	3,490	6,141	2,535
Crawford . .	2,324	1,759	700	2,260	1,903	819
Daviess . . .	3,230	5,531	994	3,201	5,591	1,695
Dearborn . .	6,269	8,318	1,731	5,116	6,974	3,384
Decatur . . .	3,190	4,782	1,389	2,774	5,195	2,299
Dekalb. . . .	4,840	6,851	1,534	4,652	6,682	3,554
Delaware . .	20,385	18,126	6,042	19,556	20,473	10,453
Dubois. . . .	6,499	6,840	1,777	5,878	6,785	3,195
Elkhart. . . .	16,598	28,770	5,133	14,660	27,920	9,450
Fayette . . .	3,822	4,091	1,137	3,969	4,376	2,299
Floyd.	13,814	12,473	2,609	13,166	11,932	4,421
Fountain. . .	2,327	3,984	1,033	2,829	3,391	2,162
Franklin . . .	2,808	4,167	943	2,456	3,831	1,858
Fulton	2,956	3,934	1,143	2,552	3,982	1,963
Gibson. . . .	6,488	5,392	1,585	6,909	5,172	2,680
Grant.	9,818	13,443	3,008	9,211	13,806	5,597
Greene . . .	5,277	5,746	1,690	5,431	5,410	2,610
Hamilton . .	14,153	42,792	4,234	10,215	34,622	10,365
Hancock. . .	6,123	12,907	2,258	4,752	11,072	4,752
Harrison. . .	5,900	6,073	1,839	5,768	5,403	2,469
Hendricks. .	9,392	22,293	3,405	7,071	18,373	7,519
Henry	7,667	8,537	2,381	6,794	8,720	4,416
Howard . . .	11,999	16,771	4,172	10,288	15,306	8,575

County	1996 Clinton (D)	Dole (R)	Perot (RF)	1992 Clinton (D)	Bush (R)	Perot (I)
Huntington	4,287	8,275	1,400	3,855	9,093	2,967
Jackson	5,150	5,883	1,590	5,663	7,246	3,148
Jasper	3,554	5,173	1,271	3,033	4,809	2,019
Jay	3,356	3,584	1,022	3,208	3,609	1,994
Jefferson	5,441	4,827	1,438	5,510	4,937	2,565
Jennings	4,223	4,461	1,629	3,471	4,392	2,370
Johnson	11,278	23,733	3,975	8,712	20,353	8,246
Knox	7,003	6,395	2,022	6,718	6,683	3,719
Kosciusko	6,166	15,084	2,531	5,307	14,179	5,115
LaGrange	2,704	4,033	949	2,093	3,584	1,736
Lake	100,198	47,873	15,051	102,778	53,867	28,635
LaPorte	19,879	14,106	5,133	17,717	14,962	9,641
Lawrence	5,703	8,107	2,063	5,557	7,712	3,452
Madison	23,772	23,151	6,447	22,276	23,479	13,100
Marion	124,448	133,329	21,358	122,234	141,369	57,878
Marshall	5,486	8,158	1,698	4,912	8,048	3,522
Martin	1,848	2,281	485	2,018	2,523	883
Miami	4,260	6,719	1,657	3,967	6,416	3,428
Monroe	18,531	16,744	3,179	19,712	16,661	6,943
Montgomery	3,825	7,705	1,766	3,371	7,602	3,511
Morgan	5,812	12,872	2,755	4,690	10,939	5,375
Newton	1,897	2,075	801	1,757	2,295	1,274
Noble	5,101	6,782	1,521	4,411	5,883	3,328
Ohio	1,083	1,098	281	970	1,009	527
Orange	3,016	3,355	938	2,948	3,738	1,296
Owen	2,244	3,056	874	2,207	2,753	1,563
Parke	2,453	3,151	981	2,429	2,953	1,696
Perry	4,427	2,554	913	4,829	2,973	1,560
Pike	2,730	2,174	884	2,960	2,156	1,238
Porter	24,044	22,931	7,169	21,022	22,644	13,096
Posey	4,965	4,638	1,304	4,632	4,435	2,357
Pulaski	2,010	2,693	634	1,950	2,712	1,214
Putnam	3,962	5,958	1,619	3,487	5,341	3,174
Randolph	4,087	4,708	1,557	3,870	4,937	2,939
Ripley	4,097	5,303	1,216	3,480	5,033	2,406
Rush	2,578	3,827	973	2,168	3,873	1,948
St. Joseph	45,704	38,281	8,379	46,203	38,934	18,828
Scott	3,798	2,620	760	4,085	2,649	1,092
Shelby	5,374	7,778	1,874	4,560	8,075	3,521
Spencer	4,058	3,770	739	4,301	3,789	1,464
Starke	3,854	3,108	1,096	3,695	3,100	1,885
Steuben	4,124	5,513	1,390	3,630	4,868	2,896
Sullivan	4,076	3,207	1,178	4,211	3,052	1,857
Switzerland	1,496	1,266	403	1,535	1,211	636
Tippecanoe	17,232	22,556	5,394	17,343	23,050	9,684
Tipton	2,478	3,980	861	2,125	3,906	1,816
Union	1,019	1,334	364	898	1,394	664
Vanderburgh	30,934	28,509	6,132	33,799	30,271	12,513
Vermillion	3,251	2,334	1,029	3,652	2,360	1,794
Vigo	17,974	15,751	4,508	18,050	15,834	8,141
Wabash	4,577	6,990	1,294	4,518	7,062	3,424
Warren	1,394	1,678	560	1,367	1,601	1,020
Warrick	9,285	9,221	2,471	8,612	8,087	3,862
Washington	3,819	4,066	1,264	4,092	4,043	1,846
Wayne	10,905	12,188	2,525	9,960	12,221	5,095
Wells	3,752	6,322	1,157	3,282	5,799	2,890
White	3,396	4,642	1,610	2,988	4,622	2,582
Whitley	4,176	5,965	1,392	3,569	5,217	3,195
Totals	**887,424**	**1,006,693**	**224,299**	**848,420**	**989,375**	**455,934**

Indiana Vote Since 1948

1948, Truman, Dem., 807,833; Dewey, Rep., 821,079; Watson, Proh., 14,711; Wallace, Prog., 9,649; Thomas, Soc., 2,179; Teichert, Soc. Labor, 763.

1952, Eisenhower, Rep., 1,136,259; Stevenson, Dem., 801,530; Hamblen, Proh., 15,335; Hallinan, Prog., 1,222; Hass, Soc. Labor, 979.

1956, Eisenhower, Rep., 1,182,811; Stevenson, Dem., 783,908; Holtwick, Proh., 6,554; Hass, Soc. Labor, 1,334.

1960, Kennedy, Dem., 952,358; Nixon, Rep., 1,175,120; Decker, Proh., 6,746; Hass, Soc. Labor, 1,136.

1964, Johnson, Dem., 1,170,848; Goldwater, Rep., 911,118; Munn, Proh., 8,266; Hass, Soc. Labor, 1,374.

1968, Nixon, Rep., 1,067,885; Humphrey, Dem., 806,659; Wallace, 3d Party, 243,108; Munn, Proh., 4,616; Halstead, Soc. Workers, 1,293; Gregory, write-in, 36.

1972, Nixon, Rep., 1,405,154; McGovern, Dem., 708,568; Reed, Soc. Workers, 5,575; Fisher, Soc. Labor, 1,688; Spock, Peace and Freedom, 4,544.

1976, Carter, Dem., 1,014,714; Ford, Rep., 1,185,958; Anderson, Amer., 14,048; Camejo, Soc. Workers, 5,695; LaRouche, U.S. Labor, 1,947.

1980, Reagan, Rep., 1,255,656; Carter, Dem., 844,197; Anderson, Ind., 111,639; Clark, Libertarian, 19,627; Commoner, Citizens, 4,852; Greaves, Amer., 4,750; Hall, Com., 702; DeBerry, Soc., 610.

1984, Reagan, Rep., 1,377,230; Mondale, Dem., 841,481; Bergland, Libertarian, 6,741.

1988, Bush, Rep., 1,297,763; Dukakis, Dem., 860,643; Fulani, New Alliance, 10,215.

1992, Bush, Rep., 989,375; Clinton, Dem., 848,420; Perot, Ind., 455,934; Marrou, Libertarian, 7,936; Fulani, New Alliance, 2,583.

1996, Dole, Rep., 1,006,693; Clinton, Dem., 887,424; Perot, Ref., 224,299; Browne, Libertarian, 15,632.

Iowa

County	1996 Clinton (D)	Dole (R)	Perot (RF)	1992 Clinton (D)	Bush (R)	Perot (I)
Adair	1,802	1,655	458	1,655	1,713	814
Adams	1,070	920	320	1,034	863	679
Allamakee	2,551	2,457	680	2,362	2,627	1,543
Appanoose	2,747	2,233	554	2,810	2,346	1,161
Audubon	1,827	1,314	314	1,589	1,373	887
Benton	5,546	3,835	846	4,467	3,469	2,454
Black Hawk	29,651	19,322	3,623	29,584	21,398	10,182
Boone	6,446	4,293	987	5,913	4,148	2,070
Bremer	5,023	4,213	862	4,774	4,482	2,338
Buchanan	4,997	3,043	836	4,166	3,313	2,126
Buena Vista	3,420	3,636	831	3,374	3,863	1,955
Butler	3,061	3,036	489	2,548	3,209	1,333
Calhoun	2,193	2,077	462	2,140	2,169	946
Carroll	4,333	3,392	998	3,800	3,439	2,192
Cass	2,616	3,384	809	2,231	3,176	1,608
Cedar	3,856	2,966	756	3,296	2,965	1,945
Cerro Gordo	11,943	7,427	1,689	11,415	8,250	4,498
Cherokee	2,853	2,629	834	2,590	2,768	1,503
Chickasaw	3,355	2,191	759	2,913	2,129	1,566
Clarke	2,053	1,401	440	1,921	1,417	899
Clay	3,659	3,129	802	3,346	3,011	1,964
Clayton	4,284	2,944	912	3,742	3,044	2,309
Clinton	11,481	7,624	2,300	11,683	8,746	4,414
Crawford	3,140	2,686	847	3,004	2,693	1,905
Dallas	8,017	6,647	1,198	6,554	5,587	2,665
Davis	1,894	1,445	382	1,962	1,344	718
Decatur	1,846	1,287	452	1,866	1,316	786
Delaware	3,704	3,065	679	3,093	3,195	2,144
Des Moines	10,761	5,778	1,792	11,309	6,378	3,386
Dickinson	3,562	3,129	901	3,106	3,196	1,974
Dubuque	20,839	13,391	3,304	20,539	14,007	8,208
Emmet	2,270	1,641	470	2,239	1,749	1,010
Fayette	4,832	3,848	890	4,412	3,879	2,493
Floyd	3,769	2,379	689	3,688	2,404	1,611
Franklin	2,232	2,054	417	2,049	2,137	1,045
Fremont	1,481	1,576	480	1,422	1,459	1,003
Greene	2,519	1,861	396	2,422	1,952	956
Grundy	2,322	2,928	401	1,895	3,160	1,069
Guthrie	2,552	2,034	515	2,234	1,962	1,216
Hamilton	3,455	3,109	661	3,262	3,031	1,348
Hancock	2,399	2,353	529	2,175	2,428	1,170
Hardin	4,053	3,505	713	3,792	3,590	1,547
Harrison	2,576	3,070	820	2,349	2,763	1,691
Henry	3,798	3,478	914	3,544	3,435	1,522
Howard	2,303	1,528	555	2,099	1,516	1,193
Humboldt	2,080	2,236	590	1,765	2,299	1,093
Ida	1,589	1,684	436	1,449	1,714	1,061
Iowa	3,354	3,042	575	2,560	2,656	1,709
Jackson	4,609	2,827	936	4,421	2,673	2,096
Jasper	8,776	6,414	1,263	8,120	6,866	2,972
Jefferson	2,597	2,541	571	2,562	2,541	1,241
Johnson	27,888	13,402	2,313	28,656	14,041	8,625
Jones	4,668	3,083	765	3,508	3,071	2,306
Keokuk	2,545	2,080	432	2,329	1,981	1,238
Kossuth	4,031	3,477	932	3,660	3,464	1,906
Lee	8,831	4,932	1,734	9,366	4,777	2,920
Linn	45,497	30,958	5,607	38,567	30,215	19,643
Louisa	2,081	1,565	590	2,091	1,691	1,044
Lucas	2,168	1,586	433	2,072	1,734	848
Lyon	1,489	3,396	422	1,331	3,272	1,068
Madison	3,070	2,550	654	2,525	2,421	1,168
Mahaska	3,737	4,473	656	3,714	4,953	1,508
Marion	5,978	6,100	871	5,531	6,062	1,896
Marshall	8,669	7,017	1,455	8,303	6,784	3,100
Mills	2,068	2,958	683	1,798	2,699	1,638
Mitchell	2,596	1,877	563	2,177	1,933	1,199
Monona	1,952	1,674	580	1,939	1,660	1,231
Monroe	1,884	1,272	329	1,829	1,323	612
Montgomery	1,912	2,583	663	1,599	2,404	1,341
Muscatine	7,674	5,858	1,705	7,089	6,087	3,583
O'Brien	2,236	3,877	578	2,122	3,869	1,557
Osceola	1,010	1,736	274	990	1,756	813
Page	2,220	4,032	753	1,951	3,670	1,669
Palo Alto	2,371	1,817	477	2,374	1,789	1,186
Plymouth	3,745	5,117	997	3,171	5,196	2,039
Pocahontas	1,981	1,707	478	1,919	1,743	942
Polk	83,877	60,884	9,516	78,585	63,708	24,155
Pottawattamie	3,276	15,648	3,534	13,228	15,671	8,035
Poweshiek	4,183	3,221	681	4,056	3,245	1,680
Ringgold	1,439	967	310	1,341	967	551
Sac	2,170	2,209	579	1,896	2,138	1,157
Scott	32,694	26,751	4,991	33,765	28,844	11,423
Shelby	2,176	3,056	652	2,094	2,809	1,614
Sioux	2,392	10,864	718	2,226	10,637	1,771
Story	17,234	12,468	2,091	17,118	12,702	6,275
Tama	3,994	2,986	713	3,573	2,948	1,748
Taylor	1,458	1,419	379	1,430	1,200	910
Union	2,787	2,156	660	2,565	2,224	1,280
Van Buren	1,536	1,460	347	1,464	1,418	811
Wapello	8,437	4,828	1,376	8,670	4,852	2,513

County	1996 Clinton (D)	1996 Dole (R)	1996 Perot (RF)	1992 Clinton (D)	1992 Bush (R)	1992 Perot (I)
Warren. . . .	9,120	6,905	1,267	8,612	7,242	3,217
Washington .	3,828	3,600	636	3,384	3,576	1,994
Wayne. . . .	1,650	1,295	310	1,632	1,299	642
Webster . . .	8,380	6,275	1,580	8,562	6,992	3,272
Winnebago .	2,679	2,211	590	2,322	2,407	1,329
Winneshiek .	4,122	3,532	973	3,791	3,331	2,416
Woodbury. .	17,224	16,368	3,436	17,398	18,148	7,182
Worth	2,293	1,284	403	2,009	1,382	1,044
Wright	2,912	2,473	536	2,776	2,708	1,151
Totals	**620,258**	**492,644**	**105,159**	**586,353**	**504,891**	**253,468**

Iowa Vote Since 1948

1948, Truman, Dem., 522,380; Dewey, Rep., 494,018; Wallace, Prog., 12,125; Teichert, Soc. Labor, 4,274; Watson, Proh., 3,382; Thomas, Soc., 1,829; Dobbs, Soc. Workers, 26.

1952, Eisenhower, Rep., 808,906; Stevenson, Dem., 451,513; Hallinan, Prog., 5,085; Hamblen, Proh., 2,882; Hoopes, Soc., 219; Hass, Soc. Labor, 139; scattering, 29.

1956, Eisenhower, Rep., 729,187; Stevenson, Dem., 501,858; Andrews (A.C.P. of Iowa), 3,202; Hoopes, Soc., 192; Hass, Soc. Labor, 125.

1960, Kennedy, Dem., 550,565; Nixon, Rep., 722,381; Hass, Soc. Labor, 230; write-in, 634.

1964, Johnson, Dem., 733,030; Goldwater, Rep., 449,148; Hass, Soc. Labor, 182; DeBerry, Soc. Workers, 159; Munn, Proh., 1,902.

1968, Nixon, Rep., 619,106; Humphrey, Dem., 476,699; Wallace, 3d Party, 66,422; Munn, Proh., 362; Halstead, Soc. Workers, 3,377; Cleaver, Peace and Freedom, 1,332; Blomen, Soc. Labor, 241.

1972, Nixon, Rep., 706,207; McGovern, Dem., 496,206; Schmitz, Amer., 22,056; Jenness, Soc. Workers, 488; Fisher, Soc. Labor, 195; Hall, Com., 272; Green, Universal, 199; scattered, 321.

1976, Carter, Dem., 619,931; Ford, Rep., 632,863; McCarthy, Ind., 20,051; Anderson, Amer., 3,040; MacBride, Libertarian, 1,452.

1980, Reagan, Rep., 676,026; Carter, Dem., 508,672; Anderson, Ind., 115,633; Clark, Libertarian, 13,123; Commoner, Citizens, 2,273; McReynolds, Socialist, 534; Hall, Com., 298; DeBerry, Soc. Workers, 244; Greaves, Amer., 189; Bubar, Statesman, 150; scattering, 519.

1984, Reagan, Rep., 703,088; Mondale, Dem., 605,620; Bergland, Libertarian, 1,844.

1988, Bush, Rep., 545,355; Dukakis, Dem., 670,557; LaRouche, Ind., 3,526; Paul, Lib., 2,494.

1992, Clinton, Dem., 586,353; Bush, Rep., 504,891; Perot, Ind., 253,468; Hagelin, Natural Law, 3,079; Gritz, Populist/America First, 1,177; Marrou, Libertarian, 1,076.

1996, Clinton, Dem., 620,258; Dole, Rep., 492,644; Perot, Ref., 105,159; Nader, Green, 6,550; Hagelin, Natural Law, 3,349; Browne, Libertarian, 2,315; Phillips, Taxpayers, 2,229; Harris, Soc. Workers, 331.

Kansas

County	1996 Clinton (D)	1996 Dole (R)	1996 Perot (RF)	1992 Clinton (D)	1992 Bush (R)	1992 Perot (I)
Allen	2,299	2,797	793	2,312	2,351	1,746
Anderson . .	1,367	1,636	449	1,178	1,218	1,282
Atchison. . .	2,926	2,828	727	2,959	2,521	2,020
Barber	730	1,696	279	759	1,225	893
Barton	3,121	7,855	1,004	3,846	5,113	4,574
Bourbon . . .	2,491	3,318	760	2,509	2,876	1,763
Brown	1,529	2,688	497	1,476	2,203	1,603
Butler.	7,294	13,979	2,274	7,029	9,166	7,355
Chase	496	778	259	470	610	600
Chautauqua	568	1,142	222	598	853	607
Cherokee . .	3,771	4,138	1,072	4,083	3,589	2,067
Cheyenne .	422	1,211	174	407	863	477
Clark	334	855	109	293	676	341
Clay	963	2,793	389	947	2,198	1,434
Cloud.	1,615	2,743	609	1,720	2,131	1,578
Coffey	1,118	2,369	572	1,021	1,824	1,443
Comanche .	298	691	133	325	636	324
Cowley. . . .	5,588	7,872	1,904	5,405	5,422	4,911
Crawford . .	7,504	6,447	1,785	7,366	5,468	3,706
Decatur . . .	417	1,255	156	576	940	565
Dickinson . .	2,423	5,174	888	2,518	3,851	2,833
Doniphan . .	1,050	1,962	0	1,177	1,579	1,200
Douglas . . .	18,116	16,116	2,630	19,439	12,949	9,630
Edwards . .	539	1,088	180	567	769	584
Elk	488	933	206	485	748	503
Ellis.	4,142	6,809	894	4,544	3,985	3,887
Ellsworth . .	899	2,078	245	1,010	1,197	1,020
Finney	2,420	6,188	805	2,612	5,278	3,011
Ford	2,628	5,681	914	2,635	4,342	3,341
Franklin . . .	3,552	5,007	1,184	2,968	3,699	3,184
Geary	2,444	3,686	618	2,559	2,928	2,057
Gove	351	1,123	141	379	792	532
Graham . . .	432	1,031	152	554	752	603
Grant	633	1,772	250	619	1,561	835
Gray	404	1,457	164	443	1,039	686
Greeley . . .	161	567	47	191	504	175
Greenwood.	1,108	1,932	552	1,262	1,411	1,167
Hamilton . .	342	811	84	386	716	271
Harper . . .	836	1,941	355	845	1,371	1,151
Harvey. . . .	4,918	8,382	1,023	5,047	6,259	3,653
Haskell . . .	304	1,143	96	336	1,023	462
Hodgeman .	251	808	99	258	625	343
Jackson . . .	1,983	2,682	735	1,639	1,970	1,927
Jefferson . .	2,757	3,781	1,030	2,538	2,569	2,642
Jewell	417	1,374	188	546	1,050	698
Johnson. . .	68,129	110,368	10,425	59,573	85,418	49,136
Kearny . . .	335	1,041	106	384	943	376
Kingman . .	1,006	2,659	409	1,100	1,680	1,370
Kiowa	331	1,264	170	355	1,057	475
Labette . . .	3,931	4,283	1,091	4,196	3,368	2,577
Lane	271	865	86	265	674	356
Leavenworth .	9,098	10,778	2,419	8,077	7,738	7,306
Lincoln . . .	528	1,372	212	612	893	657
Linn.	1,590	2,077	535	1,353	1,413	1,358
Logan	296	1,155	112	355	905	446
Lyon	4,884	6,612	1,584	4,811	5,090	4,717
McPherson .	3,536	8,142	1,115	3,645	5,745	3,561
Marion	1,673	4,173	492	1,627	3,142	1,557
Marshall. . .	1,932	2,811	713	2,022	2,030	1,786
Meade . . .	426	1,443	173	430	1,135	592
Miami	4,237	5,256	1,339	3,835	3,528	3,701
Mitchell . . .	833	2,435	246	938	1,601	1,098
Montgomery.	5,269	7,428	1,528	5,453	6,848	3,570
Morris	965	1,553	451	957	1,071	1,071
Morton . . .	376	1,073	124	398	915	350
Nemaha. . .	1,648	3,014	676	1,580	2,220	1,804
Neosho . . .	2,527	3,409	907	2,799	2,926	2,136
Ness	428	1,336	186	565	967	678
Norton . . .	640	1,814	265	779	1,469	815
Osage	2,502	3,487	1,101	2,297	2,561	2,532
Osborne . .	608	1,582	191	779	1,003	819
Ottawa . . .	752	1,846	261	764	1,284	762
Pawnee . . .	932	1,927	275	1,118	1,357	1,097
Phillips . . .	758	2,005	242	843	1,579	955
Pottawatomie.	1,997	4,504	1,035	2,099	3,106	2,759
Pratt	1,367	2,591	408	1,466	1,779	1,528
Rawlins . . .	335	1,393	146	393	1,023	517
Reno	9,108	14,275	2,661	9,257	11,377	7,636
Republic . .	688	2,283	268	939	1,767	1,084
Rice	1,434	2,842	482	1,555	2,158	1,543
Riley	6,746	11,113	1,478	7,933	8,394	5,387
Rooks	650	1,864	251	771	1,249	1,063
Rush	547	1,239	185	689	756	665
Russell . . .	705	3,347	164	1,178	1,434	1,395
Saline	7,728	12,475	2,192	7,890	8,565	7,108
Scott	458	1,750	160	480	1,426	621
Sedgwick . .	59,643	93,397	11,875	62,670	75,577	47,238
Seward . . .	1,309	3,812	396	1,488	3,477	1,818
Shawnee . .	32,803	34,845	7,304	31,972	29,344	20,653
Sheridan . .	264	1,053	95	347	739	546
Sherman . .	736	2,110	220	810	1,630	828
Smith	638	1,628	213	789	1,236	816
Stafford . . .	651	1,604	276	777	1,064	910
Stanton . . .	189	628	60	224	556	214
Stevens . . .	405	1,548	213	390	1,408	674
Sumner . . .	3,638	5,952	1,260	3,564	4,087	3,887
Thomas . . .	866	2,725	295	932	1,849	1,129
Trego	548	1,205	209	608	727	574
Wabaunsee	966	1,884	479	851	1,254	1,258
Wallace . . .	160	738	65	164	679	219
Washington	804	2,397	326	893	1,740	1,054
Wichita . . .	239	796	80	241	681	303
Wilson	1,297	2,458	562	1,331	1,925	1,365
Woodson . .	598	953	269	590	662	604
Wyandotte .	31,252	14,011	3,931	34,397	12,872	13,620
Totals	**387,659**	**583,245**	**92,639**	**390,434**	**449,951**	**312,358**

Kansas Vote Since 1948

1948, Truman, Dem., 351,902; Dewey, Rep., 423,039; Watson, Proh., 6,468; Wallace, Prog., 4,603; Thomas, Soc., 2,807.

1952, Eisenhower, Rep., 616,302; Stevenson, Dem., 273,296; Hamblen, Proh., 6,038; Hoopes, Soc., 530.

1956, Eisenhower, Rep., 566,878; Stevenson, Dem., 296,317; Holtwick, Proh., 3,048.

1960, Kennedy, Dem., 363,213; Nixon, Rep., 561,474; Decker, Proh., 4,138.

1964, Johnson, Dem., 464,028; Goldwater, Rep., 386,579; Munn, Proh., 5,393; Hass, Soc. Labor, 1,901.

1968, Nixon, Rep., 478,674; Humphrey, Dem., 302,996; Wallace, 3d Party, 88,921; Munn, Proh., 2,192.

1972, Nixon, Rep., 619,812; McGovern, Dem., 270,287; Schmitz, Conservative, 21,808; Munn, Proh., 4,188.
1976, Carter, Dem., 430,421; Ford, Rep., 502,752; McCarthy, Ind., 13,185; Anderson, Amer., 4,724; MacBride, Libertarian, 3,242; Maddox, Conservative, 2,118; Bubar, Proh., 1,403.
1980, Reagan, Rep., 566,812; Carter, Dem., 326,150; Anderson, Ind., 68,231; Clark, Libertarian, 14,470; Shelton, Amer., 1,555; Hall, Com., 967; Bubar, Statesman, 821; Rarick, Conservative, 789.
1984, Reagan, Rep., 674,646; Mondale, Dem., 332,471; Bergland, Libertarian, 3,585.
1988, Bush, Rep., 554,049; Dukakis, Dem., 422,636; Paul, Ind., 12,553; Fulani, Ind., 3,806.
1992, Clinton, Dem., 390,434; Bush, Rep., 449,951; Perot, Ind., 312,358; Marrou, Libertarian, 4,314.
1996, Dole, Rep., 583,245; Clinton, Dem., 387,659; Perot, Ref., 92,639; Browne, Libertarian, 4,557; Phillips, Ind., 3,519; Hagelin, Ind., 1,655.

Kentucky

	1996			1992		
County	Clinton (D)	Dole (R)	Perot (RF)	Clinton (D)	Bush (R)	Perot (I)
Adair	1,821	3,876	790	2,044	3,740	617
Allen	1,781	3,032	393	2,040	2,747	606
Anderson	2,898	2,972	751	2,491	2,731	1,219
Ballard	2,255	1,064	411	2,268	1,108	500
Barren	5,044	5,700	1,065	5,688	5,467	1,778
Bath	1,886	1,229	428	2,229	1,259	694
Bell	5,058	3,917	940	5,745	4,501	1,193
Boone	8,379	15,085	1,900	6,514	12,306	4,676
Bourbon	3,030	2,592	603	2,895	2,707	1,290
Boyd	9,668	7,054	2,070	10,496	7,387	3,195
Boyle	3,877	4,157	709	3,894	4,019	1,335
Bracken	1,055	1,371	271	1,259	1,162	500
Breathitt	3,106	1,058	397	3,496	1,303	515
Breckinridge	2,956	3,151	670	3,113	2,941	945
Bullitt	7,651	8,697	1,973	7,830	7,745	3,333
Butler	1,260	2,531	348	1,468	2,729	596
Caldwell	2,434	2,067	637	3,000	1,966	670
Calloway	5,281	4,989	1,223	6,181	4,654	1,853
Campbell	11,957	16,640	2,312	10,673	16,382	5,659
Carlisle	1,355	816	245	1,383	844	309
Carroll	1,689	1,170	351	2,119	1,046	566
Carter	3,728	3,240	781	4,224	3,305	989
Casey	1,106	3,187	525	1,409	3,317	542
Christian	6,843	8,285	1,064	6,709	7,737	1,789
Clark	4,987	4,739	1,095	4,892	4,625	1,955
Clay	2,135	3,716	478	2,012	4,747	648
Clinton	1,072	2,521	350	1,241	2,830	348
Crittenden	1,480	1,509	400	1,740	1,576	495
Cumberland	753	1,654	227	917	1,866	268
Daviess	15,366	15,844	3,344	16,592	14,936	5,112
Edmonson	1,595	2,619	298	1,653	2,486	438
Elliott	1,298	421	284	1,796	444	273
Estill	1,724	2,220	479	1,837	2,453	736
Fayette	43,632	42,930	5,345	38,306	41,908	14,215
Fleming	1,913	2,313	522	2,257	2,045	815
Floyd	9,655	3,139	1,518	13,351	3,540	1,723
Franklin	11,251	7,132	1,873	9,896	7,591	3,340
Fulton	1,614	863	223	1,813	1,073	306
Gallatin	1,189	838	299	1,171	699	445
Garrard	1,486	2,540	337	1,730	2,359	697
Grant	2,541	2,697	661	2,097	2,128	1,149
Graves	6,991	5,130	1,596	8,001	5,311	1,943
Grayson	2,716	4,249	677	2,909	4,533	993
Green	1,285	2,763	475	1,760	2,709	500
Greenup	6,883	5,370	1,627	7,214	4,975	2,188
Hancock	1,547	1,356	418	1,714	1,261	551
Hardin	11,031	12,642	2,815	9,417	12,299	4,026
Harlan	5,874	3,337	884	6,796	3,970	1,391
Harrison	2,934	2,433	801	2,795	2,148	1,225
Hart	2,527	2,701	501	2,852	2,401	579
Henderson	8,051	5,092	1,556	8,270	5,125	2,678
Henry	2,324	2,110	564	2,838	1,640	720
Hickman	1,220	695	247	1,296	861	294
Hopkins	7,239	6,363	1,512	8,881	6,032	2,565
Jackson	960	3,045	299	776	3,398	341
Jefferson	144,207	114,860	19,413	152,728	116,566	39,822
Jessamine	4,428	6,686	1,040	3,764	6,474	2,059
Johnson	3,348	3,262	1,010	3,669	3,614	1,118
Kenton	19,407	28,579	3,680	16,344	27,261	9,336
Knott	4,842	1,201	517	5,500	1,243	560
Knox	3,736	4,502	811	3,787	5,011	972
Larue	2,040	2,140	469	2,190	2,154	582
Laurel	4,306	9,454	1,211	4,560	8,583	1,859
Lawrence	2,195	1,812	481	2,400	2,084	557
Lee	1,023	1,302	181	1,170	1,617	356
Leslie	1,466	2,296	304	1,591	2,879	450
Letcher	4,160	2,222	782	5,817	3,011	1,206
Lewis	1,415	2,365	561	1,713	2,493	673
Lincoln	2,550	3,006	526	2,532	2,624	762
Livingston	2,228	1,258	449	2,386	1,339	578
Logan	4,181	3,888	704	4,064	3,710	1,043
Lyon	1,641	999	284	1,583	820	293
McCracken	12,670	10,221	2,268	13,341	10,657	3,077
McCreary	1,710	2,527	488	1,934	3,588	624
McLean	1,834	1,368	385	2,223	1,355	529
Madison	8,142	9,212	1,613	8,005	8,719	3,038
Magoffin	2,249	1,434	337	3,261	1,992	440
Marion	2,922	2,013	757	3,403	2,091	805
Marshall	6,054	4,579	1,391	6,576	4,368	1,773
Martin	1,807	1,612	401	1,715	1,961	393
Mason	2,444	2,588	484	2,657	2,432	916
Meade	3,653	2,855	912	3,387	2,641	1,298
Menifee	979	608	179	1,311	557	254
Mercer	3,179	3,264	738	3,010	3,211	1,298
Metcalfe	1,349	1,651	355	1,703	1,683	409
Monroe	1,114	3,300	415	1,515	3,776	480
Montgomery	3,372	2,681	705	3,686	2,590	1,308
Morgan	1,843	1,439	380	2,655	1,239	498
Muhlenberg	6,564	3,569	1,218	7,901	3,551	1,624
Nelson	5,392	4,645	1,067	5,437	4,495	1,638
Nicholas	1,092	950	265	1,341	894	513
Ohio	3,487	3,475	1,076	4,022	3,385	1,423
Oldham	6,202	10,477	1,521	5,457	8,263	2,855
Owen	1,603	1,709	454	1,830	1,108	613
Owsley	647	920	153	678	1,437	209
Pendleton	1,926	2,177	462	1,740	1,810	1,086
Perry	6,015	3,382	894	6,619	4,128	1,308
Pike	14,126	7,160	2,148	17,358	8,212	2,444
Powell	2,156	1,526	523	2,323	1,809	874
Pulaski	5,340	11,945	1,420	5,465	11,423	2,449
Robertson	360	368	117	439	329	170
Rockcastle	1,160	3,106	338	1,144	3,287	446
Rowan	3,215	2,309	724	3,558	2,469	1,212
Russell	1,582	4,017	837	1,950	4,641	673
Scott	4,258	4,349	977	3,639	3,810	1,800
Shelby	4,629	5,307	780	4,398	4,550	1,451
Simpson	2,749	2,186	401	2,834	2,280	708
Spencer	1,404	1,614	341	1,383	1,305	466
Taylor	2,897	4,573	829	3,518	4,319	1,044
Todd	1,744	1,912	424	1,858	1,691	612
Trigg	2,087	1,975	394	2,438	1,820	573
Trimble	1,245	999	308	1,413	789	413
Union	2,913	1,554	598	3,325	1,605	794
Warren	11,642	15,784	1,835	11,529	14,748	3,533
Washington	1,639	2,116	383	2,008	2,098	542
Wayne	2,422	3,122	481	2,516	3,412	560
Webster	2,852	1,568	660	3,380	1,408	854
Whitley	4,174	5,402	1,027	4,600	5,998	1,533
Wolfe	1,297	772	202	1,674	697	297
Woodford	3,910	4,270	746	3,161	3,992	1,535
Totals	**636,614**	**623,283**	**120,396**	**665,104**	**617,178**	**203,944**

Kentucky Vote Since 1948

1948, Truman, Dem., 466,756; Dewey, Rep., 341,210; Thurmond, States' Rights, 10,411; Wallace, Prog., 1,567; Thomas, Soc., 1,284; Watson, Proh., 1,245; Teichert, Soc. Labor, 185.
1952, Eisenhower, Rep., 495,029; Stevenson, Dem., 495,729; Hamblen, Proh., 1,161; Hass, Soc. Labor, 893; Hallinan, Proh., 336.
1956, Eisenhower, Rep., 572,192; Stevenson, Dem., 476,453; Byrd, States' Rights, 2,657; Holtwick, Proh., 2,145; Hass, Soc. Labor, 358.
1960, Kennedy, Dem., 521,855; Nixon, Rep., 602,607.
1964, Johnson, Dem., 669,659; Goldwater, Rep., 372,977; Kasper, Natl. States Rights, 3,469.
1968, Nixon, Rep., 462,411; Humphrey, Dem., 397,547; Wallace, 3d Party, 193,098; Halstead, Soc. Workers, 2,843.
1972, Nixon, Rep., 676,446; McGovern, Dem., 371,159; Schmitz, Amer., 17,627; Jenness, Soc. Workers, 685; Hall, Com., 464; Spock, Peoples, 1,118.
1976, Carter, Dem., 615,717; Ford, Rep., 531,852; Anderson, Amer., 8,308; McCarthy, Ind., 6,837; Maddox, Amer. Ind., 2,328; MacBride, Libertarian, 814.
1980, Reagan, Rep., 635,274; Carter, Dem., 616,417; Anderson, Ind., 31,127; Clark, Libertarian, 5,531; McCormack, Respect For Life, 4,233; Commoner, Citizens, 1,304; Pulley, Socialist, 393; Hall, Com., 348.
1984, Reagan, Rep., 815,345; Mondale, Dem., 536,756.
1988, Bush, Rep., 734,281; Dukakis, Dem., 580,368; Duke, Pop., 4,494; Paul, Lib., 2,118.
1992, Clinton, Dem., 665,104; Bush, Rep., 617,178; Perot, Ind., 203,944; Marrou, Libertarian, 4,513.
1996, Clinton, Dem., 636,614; Dole, Rep., 623,283; Perot, Ref., 120,396; Browne, Libertarian, 4,009; Phillips, Taxpayers, 2,204; Hagelin, Natural Law, 1,493.

Louisiana

Parish	Clinton (D)	1996 Dole (R)	Perot (RF)	Clinton (D)	1992 Bush (R)	Perot (I)
Acadia	12,300	9,246	2,234	12,276	9,017	3,145
Allen	4,930	2,589	1,187	5,626	3,069	1,245
Ascension	15,263	10,885	3,027	13,036	10,275	4,295
Assumption	6,416	2,698	904	5,639	2,928	1,358
Avoyelles	9,689	4,433	1,937	8,696	4,851	2,139
Beauregard	4,925	5,526	1,834	5,037	5,119	2,103
Bienville	4,335	2,402	457	3,899	2,412	832
Bossier	15,504	16,852	2,660	11,313	15,628	4,863
Caddo	55,543	38,445	4,821	47,733	42,665	11,830
Calcasieu	38,238	26,494	8,281	33,570	24,847	10,980
Caldwell	2,117	1,842	514	2,061	1,752	653
Cameron	2,103	1,365	594	1,985	1,329	995
Catahoula	2,692	1,770	615	2,570	1,976	773
Claiborne	3,609	2,500	530	3,263	2,599	926
Concordia	4,565	3,134	855	4,283	3,223	1,317
DeSoto	6,221	3,526	646	5,671	3,643	1,358
E. Baton Rouge	83,493	77,811	7,990	68,622	81,072	16,102
East Carroll	2,149	1,008	186	1,835	1,142	283
East Feliciana	4,714	2,949	660	4,093	2,813	932
Evangeline	7,847	5,278	1,447	8,564	5,147	2,124
Franklin	4,076	3,961	814	4,127	3,889	1,311
Grant	2,980	3,117	1,055	3,122	3,214	1,174
Iberia	15,087	12,014	2,448	13,040	11,905	4,337
Iberville	9,553	4,031	1,076	8,218	5,211	1,543
Jackson	3,368	3,030	571	3,370	3,072	882
Jefferson	80,407	92,820	9,667	64,302	100,493	21,278
Jefferson Davis	6,897	4,311	1,543	7,022	4,513	2,221
Lafayette	32,504	36,419	4,631	28,583	32,406	9,124
Lafourche	18,810	12,105	2,984	16,182	12,744	5,077
LaSalle	2,543	2,925	947	2,389	3,068	993
Lincoln	7,903	6,973	761	7,205	7,220	1,751
Livingston	13,276	16,159	4,150	11,499	14,808	4,971
Madison	3,085	1,591	315	2,773	1,702	469
Morehouse	6,160	5,193	963	6,013	5,364	1,727
Natchitoches	8,296	5,471	1,053	6,974	5,694	1,606
Orleans	144,720	39,576	3,805	133,261	52,019	10,889
Ouachita	24,525	28,559	3,586	20,835	27,600	6,612
Plaquemines	5,348	4,493	856	4,467	5,018	1,729
Pointe Coupee	6,835	3,545	845	6,512	3,563	1,157
Rapides	23,004	21,548	4,670	20,873	22,783	6,599
Red River	2,641	1,344	268	2,360	1,649	566
Richland	4,143	3,765	645	3,706	3,808	1,054
Sabine	4,263	3,543	1,043	4,173	3,586	1,219
St. Bernard	14,312	13,549	2,664	12,305	16,131	4,308
St. Charles	10,612	9,316	1,307	8,810	9,158	2,593
St. Helena	3,692	1,455	417	3,416	1,515	589
St. James	7,247	2,832	608	6,609	3,339	993
St. John the Baptist	9,937	6,025	966	8,977	6,730	1,922
St. Landry	20,636	12,273	2,311	20,383	11,882	4,266
St. Martin	12,492	6,296	1,607	11,252	5,909	2,573
St. Mary	12,402	8,018	1,850	10,648	8,792	3,257
St. Tammany	24,281	44,761	4,741	19,735	37,839	9,005
Tangipahoa	18,617	15,517	3,144	15,194	14,128	4,612
Tensas	1,882	1,000	176	1,666	1,153	353
Terrebonne	18,550	13,944	3,359	13,325	14,662	5,505
Union	4,260	4,418	696	4,005	4,434	1,209
Vermilion	12,609	7,653	1,954	12,324	7,062	3,127
Vernon	6,195	5,449	2,068	6,005	5,912	2,313
Washington	9,603	6,642	1,643	9,095	7,227	2,303
Webster	9,688	6,153	1,324	8,380	6,640	2,629
W. Baton Rouge	5,697	3,254	799	5,131	3,522	1,249
West Carroll	1,853	2,366	461	2,068	2,082	771
W. Feliciana	2,416	1,616	388	2,328	1,501	516
Winn	3,779	2,803	735	3,537	2,932	843
Totals	**927,837**	**712,586**	**123,293**	**815,971**	**733,386**	**211,478**

Louisiana Vote Since 1948

1948, Thurmond, States' Rights, 204,290; Truman, Dem., 136,344; Dewey, Rep., 72,657; Wallace, Prog., 3,035.

1952, Eisenhower, Rep., 306,925; Stevenson, Dem., 345,027.

1956, Eisenhower, Rep., 329,047; Stevenson, Dem., 243,977; Andrews, States' Rights, 44,520.

1960, Kennedy, Dem., 407,339; Nixon, Rep., 230,890; States' Rights (unpledged), 169,572.

1964, Johnson, Dem., 387,068; Goldwater, Rep., 509,225.

1968, Nixon, Rep., 257,535; Humphrey, Dem., 309,615; Wallace, 3d Party, 530,300.

1972, Nixon, Rep., 686,852; McGovern, Dem., 298,142; Schmitz, Amer., 52,099; Jenness, Soc. Workers, 14,398.

1976, Carter, Dem., 661,365; Ford, Rep., 587,446; Maddox, Amer., 10,058; Hall, Com., 7,417; McCarthy, Ind., 6,588; MacBride, Libertarian, 3,325.

1980, Reagan, Rep., 792,853; Carter, Dem., 708,453; Anderson, Ind., 26,345; Rarick, Amer. Ind., 10,333; Clark, Libertarian, 8,240; Commoner, Citizens, 1,584; DeBerry, Soc. Work., 783.

1984, Reagan, Rep., 1,037,299; Mondale, Dem., 651,586; Bergland, Libertarian, 1,876.

1988, Bush, Rep., 883,702; Dukakis, Dem., 717,460; Duke, Pop., 18,612; Paul, Lib., 4,115.

1992, Clinton, Dem., 815,971; Bush, Rep., 733,386; Perot, Ind., 211,478; Gritz, Populist/America First, 18,545; Marrou, Libertarian, 3,155; Daniels, Ind., 1,663; Phillips, U.S. Taxpayers, 1,552; Fulani, New Alliance, 1,434; LaRouche, Ind., 1,136.

1996, Clinton, Dem., 927,837; Dole, Rep., 712,586; Perot, Ref., 123,293; Browne, Libertarian, 7,499; Nader, Liberty, Ecology, Community, 4,719; Phillips, Taxpayers, 3,366; Hagelin, Natural Law, 2,981; Moorehead, Workers World, 1,678.

Maine

City	Clinton (D)	1996 Dole (R)	Perot (RF)	Clinton (D)	1992 Bush (R)	Perot (I)
Auburn	5,750	3,060	1,484	5,025	3,653	3,964
Augusta	5,307	2,353	1,100	4,657	3,003	3,002
Bangor	7,609	4,476	1,399	6,826	5,185	4,689
Biddeford	5,653	1,768	1,019	4,945	2,533	2,717
Brunswick	5,258	2,850	841	4,686	3,058	2,282
Gorham	2,990	2,269	710	2,516	2,422	2,015
Lewiston	10,275	3,182	2,113	9,265	4,372	6,180
Orono	2,748	1,106	369	2,813	1,336	1,502
Portland	19,755	7,178	2,255	19,510	8,660	6,910
Presque Isle	2,015	1,491	594	1,750	1,709	1,318
Saco	4,506	2,140	834	4,000	2,769	2,303
Sanford	4,368	2,239	1,524	3,854	3,030	3,215
Scarborough	3,906	3,214	805	2,941	3,235	2,033
S. Portland	6,777	3,241	906	5,933	3,999	2,734
Waterville	4,219	1,478	750	3,868	1,832	2,257
Westbrook	4,373	2,186	864	3,665	2,904	2,512
Windham	3,251	2,396	898	2,444	2,603	2,250
York	2,970	2,525	649	2,445	2,740	1,648
Other	211,058	137,226	66,856	172,277	147,461	153,289
Totals	**312,788**	**186,378**	**85,970**	**263,420**	**206,504**	**206,820**

Maine Vote Since 1948

1948, Truman, Dem., 111,916; Dewey, Rep., 150,234; Wallace, Prog., 1,884; Thomas, Soc., 547; Teichert, Soc. Labor, 206.

1952, Eisenhower, Rep., 232,353; Stevenson, Dem., 118,806; Hallinan, Prog., 332; Hass, Soc. Labor, 156; Hoopes, Soc., 138; scattered, 1.

1956, Eisenhower, Rep., 249,238; Stevenson, Dem., 102,468.

1960, Kennedy, Dem., 181,159; Nixon, Rep., 240,608.

1964, Johnson, Dem., 262,264; Goldwater, Rep., 118,701.

1968, Nixon, Rep., 169,254; Humphrey, Dem., 217,312; Wallace, 3d Party, 6,370.

1972, Nixon, Rep., 256,458; McGovern, Dem., 160,584; scattered, 229.

1976, Carter, Dem., 232,279; Ford, Rep., 236,320; McCarthy, Ind., 10,874; Bubar, Proh., 3,495.

1980, Reagan, Rep., 238,522; Carter, Dem., 220,974; Anderson, Ind., 53,327; Clark, Libertarian, 5,119; Commoner, Citizens, 4,394; Hall, Com., 591; write-ins, 84.

1984, Reagan, Rep., 336,500; Mondale, Dem., 214,515.

1988, Bush, Rep., 307,131; Dukakis, Dem., 243,569; Paul, Lib., 2,700; Fulani, New Alliance, 1,405.

1992, Clinton, Dem., 263,420; Perot, Ind., 206,820; Bush, Rep., 206,504; Marrou, Libertarian, 1,681.

1996, Clinton, Dem., 312,788; Dole, Rep., 186,378; Perot, Ref., 85,970; Nader, Green, 15,279; Browne, Libertarian, 2,996; Phillips, Taxpayers, 1,517; Hagelin, Natural Law, 825.

Maryland

County	Clinton (D)	1996 Dole (R)	Perot (RF)	Clinton (D)	1992 Bush (R)	Perot (I)
Allegany	11,025	12,136	2,652	11,501	13,862	5,081
Anne Arundel	72,147	83,574	14,287	68,629	81,467	35,191
Baltimore	132,599	114,449	20,393	143,498	126,728	51,757
Calvert	10,008	11,509	1,932	8,619	10,026	4,499
Caroline	3,251	3,874	947	2,822	3,856	1,729
Carroll	17,122	30,316	4,873	15,447	28,405	10,965
Cecil	10,144	10,885	3,124	10,232	10,784	6,115
Charles	15,890	17,432	2,333	14,498	17,293	6,501
Dorchester	4,613	4,337	1,008	3,933	4,934	2,010
Frederick	25,081	34,494	4,989	21,848	31,290	11,373
Garrett	3,121	5,400	1,200	2,856	5,714	1,987
Harford	29,779	39,686	7,939	27,164	36,350	17,002
Howard	47,569	40,849	6,011	44,763	38,594	16,182
Kent	3,207	3,055	676	3,093	3,094	1,411
Montgomery	198,807	117,730	14,450	199,757	119,705	41,971
Prince George's	176,612	52,697	9,153	168,691	62,955	23,355
Queen Anne's	5,054	7,147	1,312	4,668	6,829	2,958
St. Mary's	9,988	11,835	1,827	8,931	11,485	4,550
Somerset	3,557	2,919	613	3,210	3,450	1,230

County	1996 Clinton (D)	1996 Dole (R)	1996 Perot (RF)	1992 Clinton (D)	1992 Bush (R)	1992 Perot (I)
Talbot	4,821	6,997	914	4,642	6,774	2,233
Washington	16,481	21,434	3,934	16,495	21,977	7,537
Wicomico	12,303	12,687	2,160	11,481	13,560	5,140
Worcester	7,587	7,621	1,612	6,040	7,237	3,256
City						
Baltimore	145,441	28,467	7,473	185,753	40,725	17,381
Totals	**966,207**	**681,530**	**115,812**	**988,571**	**707,094**	**281,414**

Maryland Vote Since 1948

1948, Truman, Dem., 286,521; Dewey, Rep., 294,814; Wallace, Prog., 9,983; Thomas, Soc., 2,941; Thurmond, States' Rights, 2,476; Wright, write-in, 2,294.

1952, Eisenhower, Rep., 499,424; Stevenson, Dem., 395,337; Hallinan, Prog., 7,313.

1956, Eisenhower, Rep., 559,738; Stevenson, Dem., 372,613.

1960, Kennedy, Dem., 565,800; Nixon, Rep., 489,538.

1964, Johnson, Dem., 730,912; Goldwater, Rep., 385,495; write-in, 50.

1968, Nixon, Rep., 517,995; Humphrey, Dem., 538,310; Wallace, 3d Party, 178,734.

1972, Nixon, Rep., 829,305; McGovern, Dem., 505,781; Schmitz, Amer., 18,726.

1976, Carter, Dem., 759,612; Ford, Rep., 672,661.

1980, Reagan, Rep., 680,606; Carter, Dem., 726,161; Anderson, Ind., 119,537; Clark, Libertarian, 14,192.

1984, Reagan, Rep., 879,918; Mondale, Dem., 787,935; Bergland, Libertarian, 5,721.

1988, Bush, Rep., 876,167; Dukakis, Dem., 826,304; Paul, Lib., 6,748; Fulani, New Alliance, 5,115.

1992, Clinton, Dem., 988,571; Bush, Rep., 707,094; Perot, Ind., 281,414; Marrou, Libertarian, 4,715; Fulani, New Alliance, 2,786.

1996, Clinton, Dem., 966,207; Dole, Rep., 681,530; Perot, Ref., 115,812; Browne, Libertarian, 8,765; Phillips, Taxpayers, 3,402; Hagelin, Natural Law, 2,517.

Massachusetts

City	1996 Clinton (D)	1996 Dole (R)	1996 Perot (RF)	1992 Clinton (D)	1992 Bush (R)	1992 Perot (I)
Boston	125,529	33,366	8,428	114,260	41,868	25,189
Brockton	16,361	6,972	2,738	13,209	8,863	7,579
Brookline	18,812	4,579	799	19,848	4,892	2,629
Cambridge	29,913	4,976	1,415	30,737	5,847	4,106
Chicopee	14,203	5,188	2,495	11,433	6,138	6,452
Fall River	22,796	4,287	2,612	18,652	5,456	6,922
Framingham	16,836	6,669	1,700	15,165	8,114	6,089
Lawrence	8,615	2,804	1,096	7,698	5,079	3,245
Lowell	16,912	5,896	2,911	14,492	8,467	8,893
Lynn	18,370	5,634	2,726	15,275	7,350	7,665
Medford	16,639	5,844	1,741	14,690	7,690	5,480
New Bedford	23,620	4,151	2,547	20,880	5,255	6,965
Newton	30,005	8,499	1,674	29,136	9,623	5,685
Quincy	23,182	9,824	3,066	18,891	12,306	9,068
Somerville	20,206	3,983	1,455	19,792	5,883	4,416
Springfield	31,266	9,110	3,407	27,302	12,200	10,361
Waltham	13,607	5,830	1,663	11,333	7,365	5,092
Weymouth	13,536	6,904	2,181	10,762	7,849	6,552
Worcester	35,607	12,879	3,925	32,326	17,228	10,488
Other	1,075,494	570,663	178,627	872,758	617,566	487,855
Totals	**1,571,509**	**718,058**	**227,206**	**1,318,639**	**805,039**	**630,731**

Massachusetts Vote Since 1948

1948, Truman, Dem., 1,151,788; Dewey, Rep., 909,370; Wallace, Prog., 38,157; Teichert, Soc. Labor, 5,535; Watson, Proh., 1,663.

1952, Eisenhower, Rep., 1,292,325; Stevenson, Dem., 1,083,525; Hallinan, Prog., 4,636; Hass, Soc. Labor, 1,957; Hamblen, Proh., 886; scattered, 69; blanks, 41,150.

1956, Eisenhower, Rep., 1,393,197; Stevenson, Dem., 948,190; Hass, Soc. Labor, 5,573; Holtwick, Proh., 1,205; others, 341.

1960, Kennedy, Dem., 1,487,174; Nixon, Rep., 976,750; Hass, Soc. Labor, 3,892; Decker, Proh., 1,633; others, 31; blank and void, 26,024.

1964, Johnson, Dem., 1,786,422; Goldwater, Rep., 549,727; Hass, Soc. Labor, 4,755; Munn, Proh., 3,735; scattered, 159; blank, 48,104.

1968, Nixon, Rep., 766,844; Humphrey, Dem., 1,469,218; Wallace, 3d Party, 87,088; Blomen, Soc. Labor, 6,180; Munn, Proh., 2,369; scattered, 53; blanks, 25,394.

1972, Nixon, Rep., 1,112,078; McGovern, Dem., 1,332,540; Jenness, Soc. Workers, 10,600; Fisher, Soc. Labor, 129; Schmitz, Amer., 2,877; Spock, Peoples, 101; Hall, Com., 46; Hospers, Libertarian, 43; scattered, 342.

1976, Carter, Dem., 1,429,475; Ford, Rep., 1,030,276; McCarthy, Ind., 65,637; Camejo, Soc. Workers, 8,138; Anderson, Amer., 7,555; La Rouche, U.S. Labor, 4,922; MacBride, Libertarian, 135.

1980, Reagan, Rep., 1,057,631; Carter, Dem., 1,053,802; Anderson, Ind., 382,539; Clark, Libertarian, 22,038; DeBerry, Soc. Workers, 3,735; Commoner, Citizens, 2,056; McReynolds, Soc., 62; Bubar, Statesman, 34; Griswold, Workers World, 19; scattered, 2,382.

1984, Reagan, Rep., 1,310,936; Mondale, Dem., 1,239,606.

1988, Bush, Rep., 1,194,635; Dukakis, Dem., 1,401,415; Paul, Lib., 24,251; Fulani, New Alliance, 9,561.

1992, Clinton, Dem., 1,318,639; Bush, Rep., 805,039; Perot, Ind., 630,731; Marrou, Libertarian, 9,021; Fulani, New Alliance, 3,172; Phillips, U.S. Taxpayers, 2,218; Hagelin, Natural Law, 1,812; LaRouche, Ind., 1,027.

1996, Clinton, Dem., 1,571,509; Dole, Rep., 718,058; Perot, Ref., 227,206; Browne, Libertarian, 20,424; Hagelin, Natural Law, 5,183; Moorehead, Workers World, 3,276.

Michigan

County	1996 Clinton (D)	1996 Dole (R)	1996 Perot (RF)	1992 Clinton (D)	1992 Bush (R)	1992 Perot (I)
Alcona	2,619	2,227	669	2,383	2,247	1,117
Alger	2,229	1,429	537	2,144	1,471	941
Allegan	14,361	20,859	3,269	12,823	19,077	8,742
Alpena	7,114	4,525	1,730	6,894	4,878	3,236
Antrim	4,226	4,630	1,129	3,431	3,984	2,528
Arenac	3,472	2,247	844	3,244	2,330	1,608
Baraga	1,601	1,209	460	1,695	1,160	754
Barry	9,467	11,139	2,282	8,652	9,489	6,303
Bay	27,835	16,038	5,410	26,492	16,383	11,258
Benzie	3,081	2,856	763	2,715	2,438	1,657
Berrien	24,614	28,254	5,958	25,840	29,252	14,056
Branch	6,567	6,321	1,779	5,850	5,976	4,683
Calhoun	26,287	20,953	4,765	25,542	19,791	13,058
Cass	8,207	7,373	2,241	8,047	7,391	4,756
Charlevoix	4,689	4,864	1,303	4,063	4,017	3,360
Cheboygan	5,018	4,244	1,462	4,459	3,864	2,495
Chippewa	6,532	5,137	1,453	5,434	5,462	2,706
Clare	6,311	3,742	1,531	5,346	3,916	2,812
Clinton	11,945	13,694	2,698	10,116	12,216	7,877
Crawford	2,666	2,157	840	2,252	2,193	1,442
Delta	8,561	5,925	1,543	8,387	6,027	3,485
Dickinson	5,614	4,408	1,478	5,689	4,273	3,022
Eaton	19,781	20,092	4,378	16,752	18,669	12,208
Emmet	4,892	6,002	1,512	4,245	5,312	3,576
Genesee	106,065	49,332	17,671	105,156	47,834	46,259
Gladwin	5,494	3,670	1,466	4,457	3,616	2,649
Gogebic	4,436	2,769	917	4,792	2,838	1,543
Grand Traverse	12,987	16,355	3,527	11,148	13,629	9,495
Gratiot	6,793	6,214	1,762	5,678	6,280	3,866
Hillsdale	5,955	7,947	2,262	5,244	7,579	4,968
Houghton	5,957	5,941	1,584	6,558	5,575	2,945
Huron	6,827	6,126	1,811	6,023	6,491	4,064
Ingham	63,584	43,096	8,640	61,596	43,926	27,683
Ionia	9,261	9,574	2,354	8,370	9,135	6,211
Iosco	6,240	4,410	1,710	5,369	4,912	3,131
Iron	3,232	2,014	755	3,648	1,971	1,344
Isabella	9,635	7,460	2,069	8,784	7,706	5,434
Jackson	24,633	24,987	5,968	23,686	25,424	15,194
Kalamazoo	45,644	40,703	5,867	43,568	38,035	21,666
Kalkaska	2,666	2,455	922	2,297	2,173	1,915
Kent	85,912	121,335	14,120	82,305	115,285	43,707
Keweenaw	572	491	169	582	378	212
Lake	2,606	1,213	552	2,351	1,194	981
Lapeer	14,308	13,369	4,793	11,982	12,326	10,541
Leelanau	4,019	5,155	924	3,445	3,993	2,685
Lenawee	16,924	14,168	4,167	15,399	14,297	9,517
Livingston	22,517	30,598	6,337	17,851	27,539	15,971
Luce	1,107	964	366	972	958	660
Mackinac	2,700	2,281	742	2,293	2,278	1,379
Macomb	151,430	120,616	29,859	130,732	147,795	67,954
Manistee	5,383	3,807	1,230	5,193	3,491	2,923
Marquette	15,168	8,805	2,492	16,038	9,665	5,768
Mason	5,597	5,066	1,525	4,829	5,102	3,096
Mecosta	6,370	5,289	1,373	6,097	6,047	3,612
Menominee	4,880	4,038	1,205	4,559	3,995	2,487
Midland	15,177	16,547	3,964	13,382	16,149	8,945
Missaukee	2,256	3,012	719	1,893	2,829	1,306
Monroe	26,072	19,678	6,315	24,957	20,250	13,551
Montcalm	10,053	8,679	2,530	8,730	8,420	5,504
Montmorency	2,120	1,760	682	1,903	1,794	1,077
Muskegon	35,328	21,873	5,794	32,515	23,769	15,268
Newaygo	7,614	7,868	2,047	6,455	7,333	4,056
Oakland	241,884	219,855	36,709	214,733	242,160	94,911
Oceana	4,419	3,947	1,286	3,846	3,944	2,713
Ogemaw	4,725	2,904	1,369	4,016	2,936	2,122
Ontonagon	2,080	1,523	604	2,451	1,463	805
Osceola	4,085	3,855	1,068	3,529	3,606	2,199
Oscoda	1,652	1,545	503	1,471	1,583	755
Otsego	3,351	3,638	1,280	3,129	3,393	2,635
Ottawa	27,024	61,436	6,275	22,180	56,862	16,855
Presque Isle	3,449	2,463	932	3,308	2,398	1,612
Roscommon	6,092	4,135	1,539	5,243	4,170	2,551
Saginaw	47,579	31,577	8,081	43,819	32,103	20,523
St. Clair	28,881	22,495	8,134	23,385	24,508	18,523
St. Joseph	8,529	9,764	2,319	7,817	9,836	6,209

County	1996 Clinton (D)	1996 Dole (R)	1996 Perot (RF)	1992 Clinton (D)	1992 Bush (R)	1992 Perot (I)
Sanilac. . . .	7,092	7,821	2,265	5,868	7,891	4,894
Schoolcraft .	2,187	1,200	460	2,139	1,253	721
Shiawassee .	14,662	11,714	3,703	12,629	10,930	8,632
Tuscola . . .	10,314	9,154	3,013	9,138	8,636	6,765
Van Buren .	13,355	11,347	2,946	12,466	10,357	7,255
Washtenaw.	73,106	40,097	8,020	73,325	41,386	21,889
Wayne. . . .	504,466	175,886	43,554	508,464	227,002	102,074
Wexford. . .	5,510	4,866	1,386	4,894	4,696	2,923
Totals	**1,989,653**	**1,481,212**	**336,670**	**1,871,182**	**1,554,940**	**824,813**

Michigan Vote Since 1948

1948, Truman, Dem., 1,003,448; Dewey, Rep., 1,038,595; Wallace, Prog., 46,515; Watson, Proh., 13,052; Thomas, Soc., 6,063; Teichert, Soc. Labor, 1,263; Dobbs, Soc. Workers, 672.

1952, Eisenhower, Rep., 1,551,529; Stevenson, Dem., 1,230,657; Hamblen, Proh., 10,331; Hallinan, Prog., 3,922; Hass, Soc. Labor, 1,495; Dobbs, Soc. Workers, 655; scattered, 3.

1956, Eisenhower, Rep., 1,713,647; Stevenson, Dem., 1,359,898; Holtwick, Proh., 6,923.

1960, Kennedy, Dem., 1,687,269; Nixon, Rep., 1,620,428; Dobbs, Soc. Workers, 4,347; Decker, Proh., 2,029; Daly, Tax Cut, 1,767; Hass, Soc. Labor, 1,718; Ind. Amer., 539.

1964, Johnson, Dem., 2,136,615; Goldwater, Rep., 1,060,152; DeBerry, Soc. Workers, 3,817; Hass, Soc. Labor, 1,704; Proh. (no candidate listed), 699; scattering, 145.

1968, Nixon, Rep., 1,370,665; Humphrey, Dem., 1,593,082; Wallace, 3d Party, 331,968; Halstead, Soc. Workers, 4,099; Blomen, Soc. Labor, 1,762; Cleaver, New Politics, 4,585; Munn, Proh., 60; scattering, 29.

1972, Nixon, Rep., 1,961,721; McGovern, Dem., 1,459,435; Schmitz, Amer., 63,321; Fisher, Soc. Labor, 2,437; Jenness, Soc. Workers, 1,603; Hall, Com., 1,210.

1976, Carter, Dem., 1,696,714; Ford, Rep., 1,893,742; McCarthy, Ind., 47,905; MacBride, Libertarian, 5,406; Wright, People's, 3,504; Camejo, Soc. Workers, 1,804; LaRouche, U.S. Labor, 1,366; Levin, Soc. Labor, 1,148; scattering, 2,160.

1980, Reagan, Rep., 1,915,225; Carter, Dem., 1,661,532; Anderson, Ind., 275,223; Clark, Libertarian, 41,597; Commoner, Citizens, 11,930; Hall, Com., 3,262; Griswold, Workers World, 30; Greaves, Amer., 21; Bubar, Statesman, 9.

1984, Reagan, Rep., 2,251,571; Mondale, Dem., 1,529,638; Bergland, Libertarian, 10,055.

1988, Bush, Rep., 1,965,486; Dukakis, Dem., 1,675,783; Paul, Lib., 18,336; Fulani, Ind., 2,513.

1992, Clinton, Dem., 1,871,182; Bush, Rep., 1,554,940; Perot, Ind., 824,813; Marrou, Libertarian, 10,175; Phillips, U.S. Taxpayers, 8,263; Hagelin, Natural Law, 2,954.

1996, Clinton, Dem., 1,989,653; Dole, Rep., 1,481,212; Perot, Ref., 336,670; Browne, Libertarian, 27,670; Hagelin, Natural Law, 4,254; Moorehead, Workers World, 3,153; White, Soc. Equality, 1,554.

Minnesota

County	1996 Clinton (D)	1996 Dole (R)	1996 Perot (RF)	1992 Clinton (D)	1992 Bush (R)	1992 Perot (I)
Aitkin	3,810	2,327	1,155	3,400	2,151	1,951
Anoka . . .	63,756	41,745	16,448	54,621	39,458	35,140
Becker . . .	5,911	5,461	1,813	4,958	5,430	3,238
Beltrami . .	8,006	5,806	1,635	7,210	5,204	3,473
Benton . . .	6,006	4,835	2,133	5,156	5,053	4,048
Big Stone .	1,619	990	368	1,610	1,052	740
Blue Earth.	12,420	9,082	3,324	11,531	8,813	7,299
Brown . . .	4,864	5,580	1,786	4,278	5,390	3,845
Carlton . . .	8,052	4,034	1,591	7,736	3,922	3,005
Carver . . .	11,554	12,380	3,781	8,349	10,201	7,942
Cass	5,437	4,791	1,620	4,901	4,276	2,939
Chippewa .	3,178	2,119	782	2,929	2,143	1,505
Chisago . .	8,611	5,984	2,812	7,077	4,813	5,098
Clay.	10,476	8,764	1,733	9,845	9,666	3,835
Clearwater	1,578	1,423	471	1,587	1,315	841
Cook	1,169	1,010	246	1,005	878	704
Cottonwood	2,737	2,633	741	2,382	2,481	1,749
Crow Wing	11,156	10,095	3,423	8,896	9,112	6,367
Dakota . . .	77,297	57,244	17,095	63,660	52,312	40,244
Dodge . . .	3,233	2,888	1,223	2,620	3,049	2,231
Douglas . .	6,450	6,747	2,093	5,252	6,356	4,138
Faribault. .	3,817	3,272	1,103	3,339	3,439	2,322
Fillmore . .	4,732	3,466	1,575	3,977	3,583	3,011
Freeborn. .	8,458	5,166	2,226	7,759	5,089	4,878
Goodhue .	9,931	7,293	2,806	7,916	7,321	5,790
Grant. . . .	1,806	1,284	434	1,561	1,201	885
Hennepin .	285,126	173,887	47,663	278,648	179,581	123,659
Houston . .	4,153	3,674	1,439	3,744	3,853	2,697
Hubbard . .	3,802	3,593	1,141	3,362	3,227	1,949
Isanti	6,041	4,450	2,242	5,386	3,988	3,898
Itasca. . . .	10,706	6,506	2,889	9,621	5,952	5,147
Jackson . .	2,727	2,153	908	2,481	1,824	1,918
Kanabec. .	2,927	1,924	996	2,532	1,876	1,836
Kandiyohi .	9,009	7,119	2,229	7,914	6,784	4,869
Kittson . . .	1,394	1,055	270	1,307	1,098	558
Koochiching	3,472	2,080	1,098	3,474	1,954	1,993
LacQuiParle	2,420	1,447	561	2,342	1,435	1,163
Lake	3,388	1,684	752	3,415	1,465	1,437
Lake of the Woods . .	888	814	287	794	762	629
Le Sueur .	5,457	3,902	1,699	4,662	3,858	3,363
Lincoln . . .	1,641	1,199	504	1,555	1,084	967
Lyon	5,062	4,932	1,351	4,481	4,591	3,180
McLeod . .	6,027	5,474	2,402	4,919	5,422	4,933
Mahnomen	1,026	877	270	1,035	854	483
Marshall . .	2,333	2,068	710	2,309	2,136	1,306
Martin . . .	4,718	4,303	1,405	4,019	4,438	3,089
Meeker. . .	4,531	3,428	1,571	3,861	3,497	3,120
Mille Lacs .	4,336	2,948	1,467	3,648	2,814	2,615
Morrison. .	5,728	5,054	2,310	5,588	5,038	3,710
Mower . . .	10,413	4,994	2,464	9,935	5,147	5,001
Murray . . .	2,173	1,907	753	1,993	1,609	1,588
Nicollet. . .	6,772	5,057	1,737	6,055	5,091	3,799
Nobles . . .	4,106	3,769	1,132	3,756	3,548	2,586
Norman . .	1,875	1,392	425	1,784	1,541	776
Olmsted . .	22,857	22,860	5,640	19,039	23,404	13,806
Otter Tail .	10,519	11,808	3,191	9,176	11,074	6,274
Pennington	2,814	2,129	910	2,578	2,155	1,598
Pine.	5,432	3,080	1,597	4,929	2,841	2,952
Pipestone .	1,999	2,096	599	1,773	1,953	1,429
Polk.	6,369	5,563	1,502	5,850	5,817	3,176
Pope	2,803	1,992	665	2,619	1,886	1,390
Ramsey . .	133,878	66,954	20,351	130,932	68,206	50,757
Red Lake .	1,053	695	334	1,020	691	472
Redwood .	2,997	3,700	1,053	2,740	3,408	2,710
Renville . .	3,956	2,887	1,311	3,414	2,852	2,598
Rice.	12,821	7,016	2,872	10,908	7,015	6,057
Rock	2,142	2,169	554	2,006	2,065	1,244
Roseau . .	2,759	2,988	1,081	2,346	2,785	2,099
St. Louis. .	60,736	25,553	11,308	61,813	24,579	21,714
Scott	14,657	12,734	4,886	11,225	10,936	9,881
Sherburne.	10,551	8,699	3,665	7,843	7,339	6,534
Sibley . . .	2,769	2,590	1,226	2,421	2,315	2,407
Stearns . .	24,238	21,474	8,150	21,451	22,502	14,834
Steele . . .	6,974	5,617	2,197	5,152	5,964	4,542
Stevens . .	2,741	2,141	467	2,466	2,229	1,086
Swift	3,054	1,541	690	2,980	1,603	1,359
Todd	4,520	4,078	1,958	4,059	3,990	2,976
Traverse. .	1,135	775	295	1,053	841	582
Wabasha .	4,523	3,452	1,474	3,736	3,397	3,012
Wadena . .	2,480	2,696	801	2,340	2,492	1,535
Waseca . .	3,819	3,171	1,385	3,146	3,118	2,621
Washington	45,119	31,219	10,106	35,820	26,568	22,585
Watonwan	2,534	1,997	711	2,100	1,871	1,574
Wilkin. . . .	1,319	1,508	358	1,122	1,626	748
Winona . .	10,272	7,955	2,907	9,707	8,585	5,993
Wright . . .	15,542	13,224	5,550	12,465	11,650	10,829
Yellow Medicine	2,741	2,006	818	2,593	1,909	1,645
Totals . . .	**1,120,438**	**766,476**	**257,704**	**1,020,997**	**747,841**	**562,506**

Minnesota Vote Since 1948

1948, Truman, Dem., 692,966; Dewey, Rep., 483,617; Wallace, Prog., 27,866; Thomas, Soc., 4,646; Teichert, Soc. Labor, 2,525; Dobbs, Soc. Workers, 606.

1952, Eisenhower, Rep., 763,211; Stevenson, Dem., 608,458; Hallinan, Prog., 2,666; Hass, Soc. Labor, 2,383; Hamblen, Proh., 2,147; Dobbs, Soc. Workers, 618.

1956, Eisenhower, Rep., 719,302; Stevenson, Dem., 617,525; Hass, Soc. Labor (Ind. Gov.), 2,080; Dobbs, Soc. Workers, 1,098.

1960, Kennedy, Dem., 779,933; Nixon, Rep., 757,915; Dobbs, Soc. Workers, 3,077; Industrial Gov., 962.

1964, Johnson, Dem., 991,117; Goldwater, Rep., 559,624; DeBerry, Soc. Workers, 1,177; Hass, Industrial Gov., 2,544.

1968, Nixon, Rep., 658,643; Humphrey, Dem., 857,738; Wallace, 3d Party, 68,931; scattered, 2,443; Halstead, Soc. Workers, 808; Blomen, Ind. Gov't., 285; Mitchell, Com., 415; Cleaver, Peace, 935; McCarthy, write-in, 585; scattered, 170.

1972, Nixon, Rep., 898,269; McGovern, Dem., 802,346; Schmitz, Amer., 31,407; Spock, Peoples, 2,805; Fisher, Soc. Labor, 4,261; Jenness, Soc. Workers, 940; Hall, Com., 662; scattered, 962.

1976, Carter, Dem., 1,070,440; Ford, Rep., 819,395; McCarthy, Ind., 35,490; Anderson, Amer., 13,592; Camejo, Soc. Workers, 4,149; MacBride, Libertarian, 3,529; Hall, Com., 1,092.

1980, Reagan, Rep., 873,268; Carter, Dem., 954,173; Anderson, Ind., 174,997; Clark, Libertarian, 31,593; Commoner, Citizens, 8,406; Hall, Com., 1,117; DeBerry, Soc. Workers, 711; Griswold, Workers World, 698; McReynolds, Soc., 536; write-ins, 281.

1984, Reagan, Rep., 1,032,603; Mondale, Dem., 1,036,364; Bergland, Libertarian, 2,996.

1988, Bush, Rep., 962,337; Dukakis, Dem., 1,109,471; McCarthy, Minn. Prog., 5,403; Paul, Lib., 5,109.
1992, Clinton, Dem., 1,020,997; Bush, Rep., 747,841; Perot, Ind., 562,506; Marrou, Libertarian, 3,373; Gritz, Populist/America First, 3,363; Hagelin, Natural Law, 1,406.
1996, Clinton, Dem., 1,120,438; Dole, Rep., 766,476; Perot, Ref., 257,704; Nader, Green, 24,908; Browne, Libertarian, 8,271; Peron, Grass Roots, 4,898; Phillips, Taxpayers, 3,416; Hagelin, Natural Law, 1,808; Birrenbach, Ind. Grass Roots, 787; Harris, Soc. Workers, 684; White, Soc. Equality, 347.

Mississippi

County	1996 Clinton (D)	1996 Dole (R)	1996 Perot (RF)	1992 Clinton (D)	1992 Bush (R)	1992 Perot (I)
Adams	8,218	5,378	779	8,255	5,831	1,753
Alcorn	4,964	4,960	929	6,373	6,249	1,349
Amite	2,824	2,521	351	2,608	2,561	498
Attala	3,092	3,130	383	3,015	3,520	529
Benton	1,944	993	209	2,402	1,253	293
Bolivar	8,670	4,027	320	8,801	4,752	593
Calhoun	2,178	2,470	351	2,462	3,191	607
Carroll	2,041	2,629	245	1,182	1,695	200
Chickasaw	2,971	2,535	401	3,220	3,150	629
Choctaw	1,247	1,715	247	1,435	2,026	298
Claiborne	3,739	784	103	3,302	935	161
Clarke	2,337	3,470	366	2,259	4,207	450
Clay	4,267	2,948	337	4,620	3,297	626
Coahoma	5,776	3,441	256	6,409	4,120	518
Copiah	4,415	4,138	375	4,397	4,600	409
Covington	2,628	3,219	417	2,775	3,525	654
DeSoto	10,282	18,135	2,399	8,833	16,104	2,569
Forrest	7,965	11,278	1,094	8,333	12,432	1,909
Franklin	1,381	1,586	329	1,587	1,942	393
George	1,888	3,311	710	2,650	4,141	1,335
Greene	1,347	1,947	322	1,664	2,406	559
Grenada	4,402	4,527	470	4,203	4,721	609
Hancock	4,303	5,820	1,143	4,651	6,422	2,302
Harrison	18,775	25,486	3,726	15,268	25,049	6,855
Hinds	45,410	35,653	2,929	43,434	45,031	5,341
Holmes	4,720	1,536	140	4,092	1,694	203
Humphreys	2,305	1,382	110	2,696	1,721	258
Issaquena	546	269	42	550	298	79
Itawamba	2,987	3,490	732	3,635	4,142	918
Jackson	13,598	24,918	2,947	13,017	25,321	6,484
Jasper	3,170	2,615	353	3,059	2,789	568
Jefferson	2,531	489	89	2,796	562	156
Jefferson Davis	2,663	1,890	264	2,991	2,228	382
Jones	7,360	13,020	1,362	8,035	13,824	2,523
Kemper	2,048	1,439	188	2,243	1,830	278
Lafayette	4,646	4,753	580	5,224	5,251	861
Lamar	3,169	8,609	925	3,208	8,259	1,543
Lauderdale	8,668	15,055	1,036	8,489	17,098	1,659
Lawrence	2,481	2,392	471	2,582	2,689	765
Leake	2,902	3,017	406	3,333	3,943	497
Lee	8,438	11,815	1,361	7,710	12,231	2,041
Leflore	6,853	4,456	240	6,374	5,298	611
Lincoln	4,294	5,960	778	4,744	7,040	1,281
Lowndes	6,220	9,169	750	6,552	10,509	1,716
Madison	9,354	14,467	759	9,386	12,810	1,478
Marion	4,334	5,023	585	4,654	5,776	1,162
Marshall	7,521	3,272	482	7,913	3,847	689
Monroe	5,184	5,206	889	4,933	5,994	1,255
Montgomery	1,970	1,943	197	2,076	2,324	370
Neshoba	2,646	4,545	560	3,090	6,135	794
Newton	2,163	4,223	464	2,146	5,128	494
Noxubee	2,801	1,287	119	3,188	1,623	203
Oktibbeha	5,923	6,142	395	5,726	6,381	984
Panola	5,408	3,701	513	6,066	4,644	729
Pearl River	4,892	8,212	1,190	4,683	7,726	2,352
Perry	1,413	2,178	450	1,490	2,538	462
Pike	6,302	5,403	683	6,279	6,005	1,380
Pontotoc	2,597	4,289	774	2,965	4,595	777
Prentiss	3,053	3,473	574	3,385	4,317	781
Quitman	2,186	1,121	126	2,422	1,451	210
Rankin	8,614	24,585	2,093	8,155	24,537	3,454
Scott	3,163	4,018	466	3,349	5,268	691
Sharkey	1,566	906	70	1,526	1,008	145
Simpson	2,851	4,455	525	3,213	5,358	726
Smith	1,858	3,371	522	1,968	4,106	680
Stone	1,551	2,288	417	1,447	2,295	447
Sunflower	4,960	2,926	290	5,050	3,726	600
Tallahatchie	2,990	1,676	251	2,902	2,213	380
Tate	3,195	3,694	406	3,519	4,196	634
Tippah	2,992	3,249	661	3,475	4,444	802
Tishomingo	2,709	2,766	609	3,910	3,393	751
Tunica	1,263	557	55	1,451	693	96
Union	3,316	4,375	788	3,714	5,173	816
Walthall	2,240	2,239	444	2,476	2,728	711
Warren	8,774	9,261	1,259	8,175	10,209	2,146
Washington	10,053	6,762	437	10,588	7,598	795
Wayne	2,652	3,219	595	3,064	3,874	824
Webster	1,379	2,254	255	1,746	2,791	444
Wilkinson	2,807	1,016	226	3,210	1,399	307
Winston	3,488	3,498	434	3,953	4,311	688
Yalobusha	2,437	1,711	332	2,617	2,179	438
Yazoo	4,754	4,152	362	4,880	5,113	669
Totals	**394,022**	**439,838**	**52,222**	**400,258**	**487,793**	**85,626**

Mississippi Vote Since 1948

1948, Thurmond, States' Rights, 167,538; Truman, Dem., 19,384; Dewey, Rep., 5,043; Wallace, Prog., 225.
1952, Eisenhower, Ind. vote pledged to Rep. candidate, 112,966; Stevenson, Dem., 172,566.
1956, Eisenhower, Rep., 56,372; Stevenson, Dem., 144,498; Black and Tan Grand Old Party, 4,313; total, 60,685; Byrd, Ind., 42,966.
1960, Kennedy, Dem., 108,362; Democratic unpledged electors, 116,248; Nixon, Rep., 73,561. Mississippi's victorious slate of 8 unpledged Democratic electors cast their votes for Sen. Harry F. Byrd (D, VA).
1964, Johnson, Dem., 52,618; Goldwater, Rep., 356,528.
1968, Nixon, Rep., 88,516; Humphrey, Dem., 150,644; Wallace, 3d Party, 415,349.
1972, Nixon, Rep., 505,125; McGovern, Dem., 126,782; Schmitz, Amer., 11,598; Jenness, Soc. Workers, 2,458.
1976, Carter, Dem., 381,309; Ford, Rep., 366,846; Anderson, Amer., 6,678; McCarthy, Ind., 4,074; Maddox, Ind., 4,049; Camejo, Soc. Workers, 2,805; MacBride, Libertarian, 2,609.
1980, Reagan, Rep., 441,089; Carter, Dem., 429,281; Anderson, Ind., 12,036; Clark, Libertarian, 5,465; Griswold, Workers World, 2,402; Pulley, Soc. Workers, 2,347.
1984, Reagan, Rep., 582,377; Mondale, Dem., 352,192; Bergland, Libertarian, 2,336.
1988, Bush, Rep., 557,890; Dukakis, Dem., 363,921; Duke, Ind., 4,232; Paul, Lib., 3,329.
1992, Bush, Rep., 487,793; Clinton, Dem., 400,258; Perot, Ind., 85,626; Fulani, New Alliance, 2,625; Marrou, Libertarian, 2,154; Phillips, U.S. Taxpayers, 1,652; Hagelin, Natural Law, 1,140.
1996, Dole, Rep., 439,838; Clinton, Dem., 394,022; Perot, Ind. (Ref.), 52,222; Browne, Libertarian, 2,809; Phillips, Taxpayers, 2,314; Hagelin, Natural Law, 1,447; Collins, Ind., 1,205.

Missouri

County	1996 Clinton (D)	1996 Dole (R)	1996 Perot (RF)	1992 Clinton (D)	1992 Bush (R)	1992 Perot (I)
Adair	4,441	4,656	1,170	4,232	4,141	2,224
Andrew	2,807	3,281	964	2,675	2,652	2,151
Atchison	1,266	1,327	367	1,208	1,140	840
Audrain	4,690	3,955	1,046	4,731	3,798	2,099
Barry	4,352	5,855	1,494	4,791	5,565	2,381
Barton	1,625	2,812	563	1,433	2,775	971
Bates	3,224	2,904	949	2,993	2,499	2,225
Benton	2,996	2,895	764	3,195	2,511	1,551
Bollinger	2,044	2,420	506	2,150	2,289	909
Boone	24,984	22,047	4,083	26,176	19,405	12,040
Buchanan	15,848	12,610	4,248	16,570	11,275	9,404
Butler	5,780	6,996	1,414	6,602	6,450	2,189
Caldwell	1,487	1,464	468	1,456	1,295	1,283
Callaway	5,880	5,567	1,530	5,799	4,880	3,266
Camden	5,566	7,190	1,809	5,140	5,554	3,891
Cape Girardeau	9,957	15,557	1,861	9,605	13,464	5,199
Carroll	2,080	1,839	580	2,100	1,774	1,495
Carter	1,172	1,180	301	1,169	1,101	405
Cass	11,743	13,495	3,474	10,246	10,349	9,216
Cedar	2,027	2,484	658	2,064	2,085	1,173
Chariton	2,072	1,508	423	2,141	1,378	1,067
Christian	6,627	9,477	2,301	6,242	7,422	3,422
Clark	1,749	1,081	458	1,815	1,039	725
Clay	32,603	28,935	7,048	30,565	23,798	20,951
Clinton	3,445	2,780	848	3,400	2,391	2,423
Cole	10,857	16,140	2,121	10,201	15,270	5,770
Cooper	2,753	2,900	891	2,709	2,867	1,735
Crawford	3,349	2,990	1,223	3,515	2,831	2,002
Dade	1,243	1,822	447	1,332	1,577	834
Dallas	2,277	2,554	787	2,533	2,116	1,392
Daviess	1,534	1,321	466	1,477	1,107	1,143
DeKalb	1,679	1,627	492	1,630	1,318	1,207
Dent	2,234	2,542	693	2,689	2,125	1,049
Douglas	1,744	2,601	775	2,126	2,569	1,081
Dunklin	5,428	3,766	934	6,277	4,024	1,166
Franklin	13,908	13,715	5,517	13,431	11,477	11,043
Gasconade	2,104	2,997	820	1,952	2,690	1,672
Gentry	1,493	1,361	416	1,519	1,272	921
Greene	39,300	48,193	8,569	41,137	46,457	17,770
Grundy	2,073	1,883	631	1,968	1,749	1,372
Harrison	1,628	1,737	484	1,590	1,563	1,059
Henry	4,579	3,260	1,231	4,232	2,681	2,807
Hickory	1,858	1,491	531	1,929	1,259	864
Holt	1,144	1,323	314	1,050	1,202	781
Howard	2,014	1,545	568	2,085	1,253	1,090
Howell	5,261	5,991	2,066	5,492	5,360	2,650

	1996			1992		
County	Clinton (D)	Dole (R)	Perot (RF)	Clinton (D)	Bush (R)	Perot (I)
Iron	2,221	1,328	568	2,507	1,276	841
Jackson	140,317	85,534	21,047	145,999	78,611	66,142
Jasper	11,462	18,361	3,545	11,727	17,592	6,440
Jefferson	32,073	23,877	8,893	32,569	20,637	20,057
Johnson	6,220	6,276	1,911	5,546	5,032	4,578
Knox	891	862	254	1,010	724	523
Laclede	4,047	5,887	1,459	4,179	5,176	2,852
Lafayette	6,118	5,489	1,516	5,213	4,651	3,561
Lawrence	4,465	6,099	1,613	4,666	5,608	2,570
Lewis	2,050	1,453	644	2,196	1,461	892
Lincoln	5,644	4,897	1,881	5,453	3,718	3,572
Linn	2,967	2,097	781	2,916	1,967	1,524
Livingston	2,913	2,384	777	2,505	2,370	1,976
McDonald	1,980	3,008	923	2,281	3,010	1,551
Macon	2,937	2,634	848	3,194	2,256	1,697
Madison	2,351	1,595	625	2,501	1,673	899
Maries	1,540	1,560	516	1,732	1,356	915
Marion	4,924	4,653	1,082	5,156	4,762	1,841
Mercer	700	660	208	843	626	378
Miller	3,110	4,387	1,185	2,905	4,175	2,391
Mississippi	3,235	1,595	380	3,226	1,675	776
Moniteau	2,129	2,603	693	2,018	2,566	1,499
Monroe	1,938	1,333	532	2,060	1,153	969
Montgomery	2,277	2,124	772	2,063	1,974	1,266
Morgan	3,006	3,059	1,006	2,906	2,819	2,028
New Madrid	4,451	2,417	663	4,883	2,431	962
Newton	5,840	10,067	1,995	5,987	8,804	3,567
Nodaway	3,966	3,362	1,043	3,723	3,147	2,484
Oregon	1,795	1,502	475	2,258	1,402	564
Osage	2,045	2,890	608	1,860	2,784	1,423
Ozark	1,445	1,882	595	1,581	1,772	906
Pemiscot	3,371	1,820	458	3,924	2,161	670
Perry	2,517	3,427	777	2,525	3,205	1,498
Pettis	6,057	7,336	1,716	5,314	6,823	4,278
Phelps	6,405	6,990	1,703	6,852	6,040	3,774
Pike	3,495	2,209	916	3,609	2,255	1,464
Platte	12,705	13,332	3,035	10,920	9,380	9,062
Polk	3,307	4,521	1,169	3,316	3,465	1,879
Pulaski	3,783	4,089	1,141	4,113	3,793	2,057
Putnam	857	1,091	276	838	1,143	522
Ralls	1,998	1,513	520	2,158	1,349	880
Randolph	4,502	3,274	1,130	4,951	3,025	2,212
Ray	4,714	2,884	1,113	4,457	2,563	2,567
Reynolds	1,631	903	386	2,014	776	532
Ripley	2,081	1,988	530	2,300	1,814	739
St. Charles	41,369	47,705	11,591	37,263	38,673	30,351
St. Clair	1,974	1,815	650	1,965	1,555	1,083
St. Francois	9,034	6,200	2,266	9,367	5,889	3,635
St. Louis	225,524	196,096	34,850	235,760	188,285	109,099
Ste. Genevieve	3,597	2,078	942	3,795	1,780	1,547
Saline	4,765	2,931	1,090	4,643	2,688	2,815
Schuyler	857	777	287	936	742	487
Scotland	990	773	326	1,070	798	617
Scott	7,011	6,641	1,483	7,452	6,265	2,763
Shannon	1,882	1,339	524	2,135	1,224	579
Shelby	1,410	1,213	413	1,435	1,169	786
Stoddard	4,883	5,020	1,185	5,720	4,608	1,977
Stone	3,497	5,223	1,353	3,256	4,035	1,884
Sullivan	1,402	1,275	340	1,510	1,326	596
Taney	4,623	6,844	1,580	4,682	6,081	2,395
Texas	3,897	4,065	1,335	4,597	3,470	1,900
Vernon	3,363	3,123	1,135	3,546	2,851	1,890
Warren	3,443	3,768	1,254	3,213	2,953	2,471
Washington	4,315	2,259	1,169	4,211	2,157	1,618
Wayne	2,754	2,172	674	3,073	2,101	837
Webster	3,855	4,958	1,214	4,149	4,361	2,108
Worth	572	540	150	599	483	328
Wright	2,280	3,754	890	2,814	3,427	1,425
City						
St. Louis	91,233	22,121	7,276	102,356	25,441	18,864
Totals	**1,025,935**	**890,016**	**217,188**	**1,053,873**	**811,159**	**518,741**

Missouri Vote Since 1948

1948, Truman, Dem., 917,315; Dewey, Rep., 655,039; Wallace, Prog., 3,998; Thomas, Soc., 2,222.

1952, Eisenhower, Rep., 959,429; Stevenson, Dem., 929,830; Hallinan, Prog., 987; Hamblen, Proh., 885; MacArthur, Christian Nationalist, 302; America First, 233; Hoopes, Soc., 227; Hass, Soc. Labor, 169.

1956, Stevenson, Dem., 918,273; Eisenhower, Rep., 914,299.

1960, Kennedy, Dem., 972,201; Nixon, Rep., 962,221.

1964, Johnson, Dem., 1,164,344; Goldwater, Rep., 653,535.

1968, Nixon, Rep., 811,932; Humphrey, Dem., 791,444; Wallace, 3d Party, 206,126.

1972, Nixon, Rep., 1,154,058; McGovern, Dem., 698,531.

1976, Carter, Dem., 999,163; Ford, Rep., 928,808; McCarthy, Ind., 24,329.

1980, Reagan, Rep., 1,074,181; Carter, Dem., 931,182; Anderson, Ind., 77,920; Clark, Libertarian, 14,422; DeBerry, Soc. Workers, 1,515; Commoner, Citizens, 573; write-ins, 31.

1984, Reagan, Rep., 1,274,188; Mondale, Dem., 848,583.

1988, Bush, Rep., 1,084,953; Dukakis, Dem., 1,001,619; Fulani, New Alliance, 6,656; Paul, write-in, 434.

1992, Clinton, Dem., 1,053,873; Bush, Rep., 811,159; Perot, Ind., 518,741; Marrou, Libertarian, 7,497.

1996, Clinton, Dem., 1,025,935; Dole, Rep., 890,016; Perot, Ref., 217,188; Phillips, Taxpayers, 11,521; Browne, Libertarian, 10,522; Hagelin, Natural Law, 2,287.

Montana

	1996			1992		
County	Clinton (D)	Dole (R)	Perot (RF)	Clinton (D)	Bush (R)	Perot (I)
Beaverhead	1,164	2,414	412	1,098	1,746	1,202
Big Horn	2,453	1,336	424	2,154	1,377	840
Blaine	1,316	1,127	435	1,355	971	699
Broadwater	603	1,029	318	491	830	505
Carbon	1,854	2,147	713	1,549	1,562	1,482
Carter	150	522	89	154	497	220
Cascade	15,707	14,291	4,749	14,719	12,494	9,151
Chouteau	1,039	1,660	434	959	1,380	870
Custer	2,115	2,467	695	1,968	2,105	1,505
Daniels	510	558	240	457	496	402
Dawson	1,903	1,890	842	1,785	1,679	1,370
Deer Lodge	3,331	883	772	3,174	832	1,207
Fallon	452	778	276	446	731	427
Fergus	1,866	3,671	605	1,615	2,736	1,934
Flathead	10,452	16,542	4,786	9,746	11,699	9,109
Gallatin	10,972	14,559	3,146	9,535	11,109	7,711
Garfield	107	562	69	125	403	281
Glacier	2,292	1,270	491	2,076	1,222	997
Golden Valley	128	284	73	142	192	157
Granite	429	733	228	358	556	386
Hill	3,517	2,601	950	3,618	2,408	2,017
Jefferson	1,775	2,248	729	1,415	1,541	1,172
Judith Basin	452	753	126	409	610	415
Lake	4,195	4,723	1,804	3,938	3,596	2,878
Lewis & Clark	11,535	11,665	3,140	11,117	9,351	5,560
Liberty	379	634	144	321	512	363
Lincoln	2,705	3,552	1,425	2,765	2,799	2,637
McCone	390	615	244	424	528	395
Madison	955	1,984	516	779	1,415	1,043
Meagher	281	505	142	260	422	310
Mineral	658	549	383	664	403	543
Missoula	21,874	16,034	5,586	20,347	12,898	9,735
Musselshell	652	1,121	291	648	876	691
Park	2,564	3,837	959	2,258	2,846	2,182
Petroleum	62	186	36	61	135	95
Phillips	705	1,392	401	634	1,026	949
Pondera	1,123	1,438	383	1,046	1,252	855
Powder River	236	663	137	258	547	340
Powell	952	1,274	531	989	1,058	872
Prairie	259	417	99	260	412	179
Ravalli	5,200	8,138	2,731	4,644	5,392	4,573
Richland	1,614	2,021	906	1,440	1,760	1,525
Roosevelt	2,118	1,209	645	1,827	1,212	1,089
Rosebud	1,681	1,413	547	1,669	1,130	1,099
Sanders	1,573	2,043	990	1,689	1,361	1,378
Sheridan	1,187	832	408	1,077	795	782
Silver Bow	11,199	3,909	2,447	9,960	3,491	4,570
Stillwater	1,282	1,871	618	1,178	1,390	1,056
Sweet Grass	469	1,109	186	395	880	507
Teton	1,188	1,701	416	1,043	1,364	969
Toole	874	1,203	386	854	943	903
Treasure	171	237	87	157	206	178
Valley	1,674	1,838	645	1,715	1,497	1,320
Wheatland	391	563	127	384	478	284
Wibaux	197	284	128	195	234	173
Yellowstone	22,992	26,367	6,139	20,163	22,822	13,133
Totals	**167,922**	**179,652**	**55,229**	**154,507**	**144,207**	**107,225**

Montana Vote Since 1948

1948, Truman, Dem., 119,071; Dewey, Rep., 96,770; Wallace, Prog., 7,313; Thomas, Soc., 695; Watson, Proh., 429.

1952, Eisenhower, Rep., 157,394; Stevenson, Dem., 106,213; Hallinan, Prog., 723; Hamblen, Proh., 548; Hoopes, Soc., 159.

1956, Eisenhower, Rep., 154,933; Stevenson, Dem., 116,238.

1960, Kennedy, Dem., 134,891; Nixon, Rep., 141,841; Decker, Proh., 456; Dobbs, Soc. Workers, 391.

1964, Johnson, Dem., 164,246; Goldwater, Rep., 113,032; Kasper, Natl. States' Rights, 519; Munn, Proh., 499; DeBerry, Soc. Workers, 332.

1968, Nixon, Rep., 138,835; Humphrey, Dem., 114,117; Wallace, 3d Party, 20,015; Halstead, Soc. Workers, 457; Munn, Proh., 510; Caton, New Reform, 470.

1972, Nixon, Rep., 183,976; McGovern, Dem., 120,197; Schmitz, Amer., 13,430.

1976, Carter, Dem., 149,259; Ford, Rep., 173,703; Anderson, Amer., 5,772.

1980, Reagan, Rep., 206,814; Carter, Dem., 118,032; Anderson, Ind., 29,281; Clark, Libertarian, 9,825.

1984, Reagan, Rep., 232,450; Mondale, Dem., 146,742; Bergland, Libertarian, 5,185.

1988, Bush, Rep., 190,412; Dukakis, Dem., 168,936; Paul, Lib., 5,047; Fulani, New Alliance, 1,279.

1992, Clinton, Dem., 154,507; Bush, Rep., 144,207; Perot, Ind., 107,225; Gritz, Populist/America First, 3,658.

1996, Dole, Rep., 179,652; Clinton, Dem., 167,922; Perot, Ref., 55,229; Browne, Libertarian, 2,526; Hagelin, Natural Law, 1,754.

Nebraska

County	Clinton (D) 1996	Dole (R) 1996	Perot (RF) 1996	Clinton (D) 1992	Bush (R) 1992	Perot (I) 1992
Adams	3,935	6,924	1,513	3,445	6,346	3,273
Antelope	884	2,005	457	650	1,979	1,134
Arthur	25	187	46	18	148	97
Banner	62	309	30	68	284	128
Blaine	53	284	39	64	256	130
Boone	806	1,695	424	604	1,588	956
Box Butte	1,782	2,458	695	1,935	2,198	1,508
Boyd	372	778	181	353	744	468
Brown	359	1,105	289	311	999	525
Buffalo	4,277	10,004	1,484	3,742	9,708	4,083
Burt	1,237	1,707	497	1,224	1,667	1,009
Butler	1,099	2,042	512	1,087	1,881	1,157
Cass	3,477	4,878	1,239	2,949	4,314	2,657
Cedar	1,218	2,171	739	1,007	1,981	1,507
Chase	365	1,277	197	398	1,000	674
Cherry	551	1,905	332	563	1,707	730
Cheyenne	1,059	2,571	287	967	2,197	1,061
Clay	880	1,982	425	802	1,818	952
Colfax	1,065	1,954	492	1,011	1,915	1,197
Cuming	1,033	2,520	503	835	2,711	1,192
Custer	1,293	3,453	615	1,126	3,180	1,492
Dakota	2,632	2,592	721	2,322	2,771	1,307
Dawes	1,108	1,991	442	987	1,961	1,103
Dawson	2,180	4,794	1,044	1,739	4,710	2,305
Deuel	245	629	111	232	558	327
Dixon	931	1,478	414	830	1,484	726
Dodge	5,181	7,484	1,894	4,665	7,269	4,432
Douglas	70,708	92,334	14,863	67,003	93,421	38,641
Dundy	224	752	112	244	664	332
Fillmore	1,058	1,696	321	988	1,495	993
Franklin	483	1,013	215	477	967	527
Frontier	310	901	169	302	785	479
Furnas	663	1,475	207	624	1,365	804
Gage	4,008	4,413	1,346	3,309	3,995	2,726
Garden	279	851	155	212	697	385
Garfield	249	625	111	221	595	270
Gosper	275	609	150	254	492	297
Grant	84	258	55	75	247	124
Greeley	472	642	155	435	587	395
Hall	6,708	10,183	2,403	5,519	9,264	5,822
Hamilton	1,172	2,623	457	992	2,379	1,213
Harlan	520	1,120	203	488	991	623
Hayes	87	439	39	85	362	207
Hitchcock	409	977	173	359	824	540
Holt	1,107	3,436	677	835	3,131	1,714
Hooker	115	308	83	70	283	102
Howard	853	1,294	417	778	1,138	940
Jefferson	1,520	1,979	495	1,506	1,783	1,177
Johnson	770	1,009	309	822	885	642
Kearney	782	1,953	296	644	1,751	844
Keith	830	2,504	460	731	2,019	1,130
Keya Paha	94	385	47	105	368	158
Kimball	527	1,011	212	408	931	440
Knox	1,266	2,123	531	968	2,112	1,166
Lancaster	43,339	44,812	8,595	41,207	41,400	21,783
Lincoln	5,165	7,482	2,043	5,142	7,025	3,384
Logan	79	294	72	80	271	98
Loup	74	229	28	58	233	96
McPherson	50	233	33	49	217	62
Madison	3,047	7,965	1,554	2,352	7,851	3,486
Merrick	997	2,084	449	864	1,854	1,072
Morrill	620	1,296	262	577	1,184	752
Nance	585	892	238	559	851	569
Nemaha	1,232	1,888	485	1,110	1,696	1,020
Nuckolls	757	1,383	306	834	1,277	825
Otoe	2,279	3,290	877	2,038	2,960	1,800
Pawnee	580	766	207	566	670	565
Perkins	352	1,018	163	300	842	522
Phelps	1,071	3,015	465	829	2,748	1,298
Pierce	697	1,923	446	611	1,853	1,084
Platte	3,010	7,948	1,353	2,409	7,712	3,656
Polk	750	1,504	268	661	1,435	812
Red Willow	1,365	3,112	499	1,164	2,488	1,660
Richardson	1,517	2,089	633	1,513	2,050	1,356
Rock	180	564	135	162	588	233
Saline	2,523	1,945	689	2,425	1,740	1,576
Sarpy	12,806	23,023	3,722	10,720	20,482	9,270
Saunders	2,777	4,514	1,223	2,509	4,037	2,567
Scotts Bluff	4,547	7,641	1,251	4,173	7,213	3,514
Seward	2,432	3,479	745	2,118	3,044	1,722
Sheridan	573	1,834	289	535	1,698	751
Sherman	567	822	266	568	736	582
Sioux	138	551	75	148	445	206
Stanton	577	1,457	386	496	1,274	786
Thayer	933	1,698	334	923	1,387	1,077
Thomas	64	303	62	69	283	115
Thurston	962	835	293	865	898	487
Valley	758	1,346	274	716	1,173	693
Washington	2,248	4,391	971	2,108	4,035	2,148
Wayne	1,048	2,150	440	921	2,122	1,047
Webster	621	1,094	236	624	972	657
Wheeler	106	241	69	88	246	127
York	1,653	4,266	559	1,385	3,783	1,825
Totals	**236,761**	**363,467**	**71,278**	**216,864**	**343,678**	**174,104**

Nebraska Vote Since 1948

1948, Truman, Dem., 224,165; Dewey, Rep., 264,774.

1952, Eisenhower, Rep., 421,603; Stevenson, Dem., 188,057.

1956, Eisenhower, Rep., 378,108; Stevenson, Dem., 199,029.

1960, Kennedy, Dem., 232,542; Nixon, Rep., 380,553.

1964, Johnson, Dem., 307,307; Goldwater, Rep., 276,847.

1968, Nixon, Rep., 321,163; Humphrey, Dem., 170,784; Wallace, 3d Party, 44,904.

1972, Nixon, Rep., 406,298; McGovern, Dem., 169,991; scattered, 817.

1976, Carter, Dem., 233,287; Ford, Rep., 359,219; McCarthy, Ind., 9,383; Maddox, Amer. Ind., 3,378; MacBride, Libertarian, 1,476.

1980, Reagan, Rep., 419,214; Carter, Dem., 166,424; Anderson, Ind., 44,854; Clark, Libertarian, 9,041.

1984, Reagan, Rep., 459,135; Mondale, Dem., 187,475; Bergland, Libertarian, 2,075.

1988, Bush, Rep., 397,956; Dukakis, Dem., 259,235; Paul, Lib., 2,534; Fulani, New Alliance, 1,740.

1992, Bush, Rep., 343,678; Clinton, Dem., 216,864; Perot, Ind., 174,104; Marrou, Libertarian, 1,340.

1996, Dole, Rep., 363,467; Clinton, Dem., 236,761; Perot, Ref., 71,278; Browne, Libertarian, 2,792; Phillips, Ind., 1,928; Hagelin, Natural Law, 1,189.

Nevada

County	Clinton (D) 1996	Dole (R) 1996	Perot (RF) 1996	Clinton (D) 1992	Bush (R) 1992	Perot (I) 1992
Churchill	2,282	4,369	821	1,770	3,789	1,964
Clark	127,963	103,431	23,177	124,586	97,403	75,364
Douglas	5,109	8,828	1,486	3,928	6,182	4,814
Elko	3,149	6,512	1,539	2,782	5,208	3,628
Esmeralda	140	277	91	118	221	220
Eureka	158	412	90	129	330	214
Humboldt	1,467	2,334	603	810	1,505	1,149
Lander	660	1,107	361	423	885	652
Lincoln	499	936	255	511	890	394
Lyon	3,419	4,753	1,104	2,777	3,509	2,716
Mineral	1,068	814	361	909	918	746
Nye	3,300	3,979	1,544	2,561	2,743	2,501
Pershing	565	743	203	467	643	429
Storey	614	705	244	488	458	550
Washoe	44,915	49,477	9,970	39,500	42,636	30,974
White Pine	1,397	1,399	546	1,354	1,206	1,070
City						
Carson City	7,269	9,168	1,591	6,035	7,302	5,195
Totals	**203,974**	**199,244**	**43,986**	**189,148**	**175,828**	**132,580**

Nevada Vote Since 1948

1948, Truman, Dem., 31,291; Dewey, Rep., 29,357; Wallace, Prog., 1,469.

1952, Eisenhower, Rep., 50,502; Stevenson, Dem., 31,688.

1956, Eisenhower, Rep., 56,049; Stevenson, Dem., 40,640.

1960, Kennedy, Dem., 54,880; Nixon, Rep., 52,387.

1964, Johnson, Dem., 79,339; Goldwater, Rep., 56,094.

1968, Nixon, Rep., 73,188; Humphrey, Dem., 60,598; Wallace, 3d Party, 20,432.

1972, Nixon, Rep., 115,750; McGovern, Dem., 66,016.

1976, Carter, Dem., 92,479; Ford, Rep., 101,273; MacBride, Libertarian, 1,519; Maddox, Amer. Ind., 1,497; scattered, 5,108.

1980, Reagan, Rep., 155,017; Carter, Dem., 66,666; Anderson, Ind., 17,651; Clark, Libertarian, 4,358.

1984, Reagan, Rep., 188,770; Mondale, Dem., 91,655; Bergland, Libertarian, 2,292.

1988, Bush, Rep., 206,040; Dukakis, Dem., 132,738; Paul, Lib., 3,520; Fulani, New Alliance, 835.

1992, Clinton, Dem., 189,148; Bush, Rep., 175,828; Perot, Ind., 132,580; Gritz, Populist/America First, 2,892; Marrou, Libertarian, 1,835.

1996, Clinton, Dem., 203,974; Dole, Rep., 199,244; Perot, Ref., 43,986; "None of These Candidates," 5,608; Nader, Green, 4,730; Browne, Libertarian, 4,460; Phillips, Ind. Amer., 1,732; Hagelin, Natural Law, 545.

New Hampshire

City	1996 Clinton (D)	1996 Dole (R)	1996 Perot (RF)	1992 Clinton (D)	1992 Bush (R)	1992 Perot (I)
Concord . . .	9,719	5,082	1,164	8,325	5,651	2,843
Derry	4,814	4,503	1,083	3,962	4,750	3,363
Dover	6,332	3,752	930	5,449	4,197	2,246
Hudson . . .	3,841	3,167	976	3,053	3,315	2,774
Keene	5,401	2,910	621	5,210	3,257	1,736
Laconia . . .	2,865	2,842	508	2,390	3,033	1,496
Londonderry	3,666	4,076	838	2,915	3,960	2,532
Manchester .	20,185	14,704	3,053	16,627	16,298	7,441
Merrimack . .	4,934	4,499	949	3,764	4,410	2,787
Nashua . . .	16,584	11,479	2,858	14,777	12,514	8,306
Portsmouth .	6,343	3,014	661	6,132	3,563	2,088
Rochester . .	5,489	3,650	1,108	4,588	4,272	2,541
Salem	5,164	4,257	1,241	4,184	4,864	3,382
Other	150,829	128,551	32,397	127,664	128,400	77,802
Totals	**246,166**	**196,486**	**48,387**	**209,040**	**202,484**	**121,337**

New Hampshire Vote Since 1948

1948, Truman, Dem., 107,995; Dewey, Rep., 121,299; Wallace, Prog., 1,970; Thomas, Soc., 86; Teichert, Soc. Labor, 83; Thurmond, States' Rights, 7.

1952, Eisenhower, Rep., 166,287; Stevenson, Dem., 106,663.

1956, Eisenhower, Rep., 176,519; Stevenson, Dem., 90,364; Andrews, Const., 111.

1960, Kennedy, Dem., 137,772; Nixon, Rep., 157,989.

1964, Johnson, Dem., 182,065; Goldwater, Rep., 104,029.

1968, Nixon, Rep., 154,903; Humphrey, Dem., 130,589; Wallace, 3d Party, 11,173; New Party, 421; Halstead, Soc. Workers, 104.

1972, Nixon, Rep., 213,724; McGovern, Dem., 116,435; Schmitz, Amer., 3,386; Jenness, Soc. Workers, 368; scattered, 142.

1976, Carter, Dem., 147,645; Ford, Rep., 185,935; McCarthy, Ind., 4,095; MacBride, Libertarian, 936; Reagan, write-in, 388; La Rouche, U.S. Labor, 186; Camejo, Soc. Workers, 161; Levin, Soc. Labor, 66; scattered, 215.

1980, Reagan, Rep., 221,705; Carter, Dem., 108,864; Anderson, Ind., 49,693; Clark, Libertarian, 2,067; Commoner, Citizens, 1,325; Hall, Com., 129; Griswold, Workers World, 76; DeBerry, Soc. Workers, 72; scattered, 68.

1984, Reagan, Rep., 267,051; Mondale, Dem., 120,377; Bergland, Libertarian, 735.

1988, Bush, Rep., 281,537; Dukakis, Dem., 163,696; Paul, Lib., 4,502; Fulani, New Alliance, 790.

1992, Clinton, Dem., 209,040; Bush, Rep., 202,484; Perot, Ind., 121,337; Marrou, Libertarian, 3,548.

1996, Clinton, Dem., 246,166; Dole, Rep., 196,486; Perot, Ref., 48,387; Browne, Libertarian, 4,214; Phillips, Taxpayers, 1,344.

New Jersey

County	1996 Clinton (D)	1996 Dole (R)	1996 Perot (RF)	1992 Clinton (D)	1992 Bush (R)	1992 Perot (I)
Atlantic . . .	44,434	29,538	8,261	39,633	34,279	15,890
Bergen . . .	191,085	141,164	25,512	171,104	178,223	52,082
Burlington .	85,086	57,337	18,407	72,845	63,709	35,322
Camden . .	114,962	52,791	17,433	104,915	67,205	37,144
Cape May .	19,849	19,357	4,978	17,324	21,502	9,798
Cumberland	25,444	14,744	5,348	22,220	19,253	9,901
Essex . . .	175,387	65,172	9,513	158,130	89,146	26,961
Gloucester	51,928	32,138	14,361	42,425	37,335	24,132
Hudson . .	116,121	38,288	8,965	99,799	66,505	14,569
Hunterdon	18,446	26,379	5,686	15,423	25,130	12,736
Mercer . . .	77,641	40,559	10,536	71,383	50,473	22,503
Middlesex .	145,201	82,433	24,643	128,824	108,701	45,055
Monmouth	120,414	99,975	22,754	101,750	117,715	45,445
Morris . . .	81,092	95,830	15,299	67,593	108,431	32,447
Ocean . . .	94,243	82,830	22,864	75,431	95,984	41,668
Passaic . .	85,879	53,584	10,944	70,030	71,147	21,494
Salem . . .	12,044	9,294	4,124	10,062	10,363	7,274
Somerset .	50,673	51,868	8,377	42,867	56,044	21,014
Sussex . . .	19,525	26,746	6,705	14,775	29,510	12,537
Union	108,102	65,912	12,432	96,671	87,742	23,991
Warren . . .	14,805	17,160	4,992	13,002	18,468	9,866
Totals . . .	**1,652,361**	**1,103,099**	**262,134**	**1,436,206**	**1,356,865**	**521,829**

New Jersey Vote Since 1948

1948, Truman, Dem., 895,455; Dewey, Rep., 981,124; Wallace, Prog., 42,683; Watson, Proh., 10,593; Thomas, Soc., 10,521; Dobbs, Soc. Workers, 5,825; Teichert, Soc. Labor, 3,354.

1952, Eisenhower, Rep., 1,373,613; Stevenson, Dem., 1,015,902; Hoopes, Soc., 8,593; Hass, Soc. Labor, 5,815; Hallinan, Prog., 5,589; Krajewski, Poor Man's, 4,203; Dobbs, Soc. Workers, 3,850; Hamblen, Proh., 989.

1956, Eisenhower, Rep., 1,606,942; Stevenson Dem., 850,337; Holtwick, Proh., 9,147; Hass, Soc. Labor, 6,736; Andrews, Cons., 5,317; Dobbs, Soc. Workers, 4,004; Krajewski, Amer. Third Party, 1,829.

1960, Kennedy, Dem., 1,385,415; Nixon, Rep., 1,363,324; Dobbs, Soc. Workers, 11,402; Lee, Cons., 8,708; Hass, Soc. Labor, 4,262.

1964, Johnson, Dem., 1,867,671; Goldwater, Rep., 963,843; DeBerry, Soc. Workers, 8,181; Hass, Soc. Labor, 7,075.

1968, Nixon, Rep., 1,325,467; Humphrey, Dem., 1,264,206; Wallace, 3d Party, 262,187; Halstead, Soc. Workers, 8,667; Gregory, Peace and Freedom, 8,084; Blomen, Soc. Labor, 6,784.

1972, Nixon, Rep., 1,845,502; McGovern, Dem., 1,102,211; Schmitz, Amer., 34,378; Spock, Peoples, 5,355; Fisher, Soc. Labor, 4,544; Jenness, Soc. Workers, 2,233; Mahalchik, Amer. First, 1,743; Hall, Com., 1,263.

1976, Carter, Dem., 1,444,653; Ford, Rep., 1,509,688; McCarthy, Ind., 32,717; MacBride, Libertarian, 9,449; Maddox, Amer., 7,716; Levin, Soc. Labor, 3,686; Hall, Com., 1,662; LaRouche, U.S. Labor, 1,650; Camejo, Soc. Workers, 1,184; Wright, People's, 1,044; Bubar, Proh., 554; Zeidler, Soc., 469.

1980, Reagan, Rep., 1,546,557; Carter, Dem., 1,147,364; Anderson, Ind., 234,632; Clark, Libertarian, 20,652; Commoner, Citizens, 8,203; McCormack, Right to Life, 3,927; Lynen, Middle Class, 3,694; Hall, Com., 2,555; Pulley, Soc. Workers, 2,198; McReynolds, Soc., 1,973; Gahres, Down With Lawyers, 1,718; Griswold, Workers World, 1,288; Wendelken, Ind., 923.

1984, Reagan, Rep., 1,933,630; Mondale, Dem., 1,261,323; Bergland, Libertarian, 6,416.

1988, Bush, Rep., 1,740,604; Dukakis, Dem., 1,317,541; Lewin, Peace and Freedom, 9,953; Paul, Lib., 8,421.

1992, Clinton, Dem., 1,436,206; Bush, Rep., 1,356,865; Perot, Ind., 521,829; Marrou, Libertarian, 6,822; Fulani, New Alliance, 3,513; Phillips, U.S. Taxpayers, 2,670; LaRouche, Ind., 2,095; Warren, Soc. Workers, 2,011; Daniels, Ind., 1,996; Gritz, Populist/America First, 1,867; Hagelin, Natural Law, 1,353.

1996, Clinton, Dem., 1,652,361; Dole, Rep., 1,103,099; Perot, Ref., 262,134; Nader, Green, 32,465; Browne, Libertarian, 14,763; Hagelin, Natural Law, 3,887; Phillips, Taxpayers, 3,440; Harris, Soc. Workers, 1,837; Moorehead, Workers World, 1,337; White, Soc. Equality, 537.

New Mexico

County	1996 Clinton (D)	1996 Dole (R)	1996 Perot (RF)	1992 Clinton (D)	1992 Bush (R)	1992 Perot (I)
Bernalillo . .	88,140	78,832	8,708	90,863	77,304	31,241
Catron	423	923	114	465	771	289
Chaves . . .	7,014	9,991	1,271	6,360	8,872	3,590
Cibola	4,030	2,245	488	3,334	2,051	847
Colfax	2,659	1,975	411	2,607	1,730	871
Curry	4,116	7,378	842	3,699	6,831	2,056
De Baca . . .	509	489	86	451	526	204
Dona Ana . .	22,766	17,541	2,269	19,894	16,308	7,682
Eddy	8,959	8,534	1,297	7,409	7,313	3,430
Grant	5,860	3,993	778	5,603	2,917	1,685
Guadalupe .	1,208	436	79	1,225	691	173
Harding . . .	264	321	28	268	312	98
Hidalgo . . .	943	789	209	995	871	442
Lea	5,393	7,661	1,465	5,047	7,921	3,233
Lincoln	2,209	3,396	666	1,730	2,669	1,431
Los Alamos .	3,983	4,999	560	3,897	4,320	2,339
Luna	3,001	2,616	598	2,637	2,166	1,445
McKinley . .	10,124	4,470	650	9,405	4,720	1,304
Mora	1,646	561	131	1,555	668	188
Otero	5,938	9,065	1,096	5,377	7,481	3,257
Quay	1,830	1,943	377	1,758	1,759	755
Rio Arriba . .	7,965	2,551	469	7,832	2,680	984
Roosevelt . .	2,097	3,245	467	2,172	3,215	1,085
Sandoval . .	13,081	11,015	1,482	10,951	8,491	3,954
San Juan . .	12,070	17,478	2,355	11,302	13,415	5,351
San Miguel .	6,995	1,938	405	6,186	2,183	965
Santa Fe . .	26,349	10,857	1,846	27,189	9,684	5,656
Sierra	2,154	2,140	431	1,771	1,562	1,055
Socorro . . .	3,374	2,315	455	2,908	2,186	918
Taos	6,635	2,126	545	7,051	2,260	1,300
Torrance . .	2,072	2,154	332	1,662	1,667	810
Union	519	995	125	519	975	355
Valencia . . .	9,169	7,779	1,222	7,495	6,305	2,902
Totals	**273,495**	**232,751**	**32,257**	**261,617**	**212,824**	**91,895**

New Mexico Vote Since 1948

1948, Truman, Dem., 105,464; Dewey, Rep., 80,303; Wallace, Prog., 1,037; Watson, Proh., 127; Thomas, Soc., 83; Teichert, Soc. Labor, 49.

1952, Eisenhower, Rep., 132,170; Stevenson, Dem., 105,661; Hamblen, Proh., 297; Hallinan, Ind. Prog., 225; MacArthur, Christian National, 220; Hass, Soc. Labor, 35.

1956, Eisenhower, Rep., 146,788; Stevenson, Dem., 106,098; Holtwick, Proh., 607; Andrews, Ind., 364; Hass, Soc. Labor, 69.

1960, Kennedy, Dem., 156,027; Nixon, Rep., 153,733; Decker, Proh., 777; Hass, Soc. Labor, 570.
1964, Johnson, Dem., 194,017; Goldwater, Rep., 131,838; Hass, Soc. Labor, 1,217; Munn, Proh., 543.
1968, Nixon, Rep., 169,692; Humphrey, Dem., 130,081; Wallace, 3d Party, 25,737; Chavez, 1,519; Halstead, Soc. Workers, 252.
1972, Nixon, Rep., 235,606; McGovern, Dem., 141,084; Schmitz, Amer., 8,767; Jenness, Soc. Workers, 474.
1976, Carter, Dem., 201,148; Ford, Rep., 211,419; Camejo, Soc. Workers, 2,462; MacBride, Libertarian, 1,110; Zeidler, Soc., 240; Bubar, Proh., 211.
1980, Reagan, Rep., 250,779; Carter, Dem., 167,826; Anderson, Ind., 29,459; Clark, Libertarian, 4,365; Commoner, Citizens, 2,202; Bubar, Statesman, 1,281; Pulley, Soc. Workers, 325.
1984, Reagan, Rep., 307,101; Mondale, Dem., 201,769; Bergland, Libertarian, 4,459.
1988, Bush, Rep., 270,341; Dukakis, Dem., 244,497; Paul, Lib., 3,268; Fulani, New Alliance, 2,237.
1992, Clinton, Dem., 261,617; Bush, Rep., 212,824; Perot, Ind., 91,895; Marrou, Libertarian, 1,615.
1996, Clinton, Dem., 273,495; Dole, Rep., 232,751; Perot, Ref., 32,257; Nader, Green, 13,218; Browne, Libertarian, 2,996; Phillips, Taxpayers, 713; Hagelin, Natural Law, 644.

New York

	1996			1992		
County	Clinton (D)	Dole (R)	Perot (RF)	Clinton (D)	Bush (R)	Perot (I)
Albany	85,993	39,785	11,957	80,641	49,452	24,064
Allegany	6,621	8,107	2,730	4,848	8,976	4,703
Bronx	248,276	30,435	7,186	225,038	63,310	15,115
Broome	44,407	31,327	9,114	43,444	34,653	21,280
Cattaraugus	13,029	12,971	5,151	10,150	13,944	10,662
Cayuga	15,879	11,093	4,420	13,088	12,065	10,279
Chautauqua	26,831	21,261	7,484	22,645	21,222	18,455
Chemung	16,977	14,287	3,967	15,099	16,088	7,493
Chenango	8,797	7,319	2,822	8,017	8,114	5,356
Clinton	15,386	9,759	3,488	12,881	13,455	5,389
Columbia	12,910	10,324	3,466	11,368	11,568	5,829
Cortland	9,130	7,606	2,398	7,815	7,782	5,098
Delaware	8,724	7,684	2,601	7,152	8,829	4,404
Dutchess	47,339	41,929	12,294	41,655	46,709	26,320
Erie	224,554	132,343	45,679	196,233	129,444	123,358
Essex	7,893	6,379	2,363	6,717	8,278	3,784
Franklin	8,494	5,072	2,499	7,654	6,635	3,857
Fulton	9,779	7,881	3,214	8,400	9,137	5,120
Genesee	10,074	10,821	2,996	8,071	11,663	6,192
Greene	8,251	8,712	2,790	6,924	9,390	4,689
Hamilton	1,228	1,841	492	963	2,038	793
Herkimer	11,910	10,085	4,235	10,880	12,052	6,866
Jefferson	16,783	12,362	4,561	13,380	14,227	9,461
Kings	432,232	81,406	15,031	411,183	133,344	33,014
Lewis	4,402	3,965	1,669	3,676	4,101	3,164
Livingston	10,868	10,981	2,889	8,648	12,122	5,775
Madison	11,832	11,324	3,379	10,099	11,293	7,391
Monroe	164,858	115,694	23,936	141,502	134,021	63,229
Montgomery	10,485	7,172	3,253	9,509	8,802	5,020
Nassau	303,587	196,820	36,122	282,593	246,881	77,097
New York	394,131	67,839	11,144	416,142	84,501	27,689
Niagara	44,203	31,438	12,564	35,649	30,401	30,126
Oneida	44,399	37,996	11,296	40,966	43,806	22,717
Onondaga	100,190	73,771	17,602	90,645	77,642	45,175
Ontario	19,156	17,237	4,391	16,064	18,995	9,571
Orange	54,995	45,956	11,778	45,946	53,493	22,499
Orleans	6,233	6,865	1,986	4,927	7,468	4,275
Oswego	20,440	17,159	7,499	16,990	18,530	14,853
Otsego	11,470	8,774	3,217	10,471	10,141	5,841
Putnam	16,173	17,452	4,032	14,048	18,934	8,011
Queens	372,925	107,650	22,288	349,520	157,561	46,014
Rensselaer	34,273	23,482	8,405	29,793	28,937	15,198
Richmond	64,684	52,207	8,968	56,901	70,707	19,678
Rockland	63,127	40,395	6,798	56,759	49,608	15,026
St. Lawrence	21,798	10,827	5,309	18,197	13,901	9,758
Saratoga	39,832	34,337	10,141	33,011	36,917	19,091
Schenectady	35,404	22,106	7,865	32,335	26,258	14,838
Schoharie	5,902	5,353	1,796	4,997	5,678	3,327
Schuyler	3,303	3,134	1,037	2,859	3,226	2,051
Seneca	6,825	5,004	1,889	5,810	5,432	3,660
Steuben	14,481	17,710	5,496	12,043	19,761	9,378
Suffolk	261,828	182,510	52,209	220,811	229,467	112,973
Sullivan	15,052	9,321	3,453	13,717	11,396	6,336
Tioga	8,769	9,416	2,721	7,791	9,287	5,867
Tompkins	20,772	11,532	2,623	23,197	11,520	6,704
Ulster	35,852	26,212	9,246	32,886	29,223	17,952
Warren	11,603	11,152	3,623	9,820	12,260	6,401
Washington	9,572	8,954	3,648	8,429	10,305	6,143
Wayne	15,145	15,837	4,619	11,866	18,019	9,188
Westchester	196,310	123,719	18,028	184,300	151,990	39,933
Wyoming	5,735	7,477	2,411	4,045	7,324	4,837
Yates	4,066	3,925	1,190	3,242	4,366	2,354
Totals	**3,756,177**	**1,933,492**	**503,458**	**3,444,450**	**2,346,649**	**1,090,721**

New York Vote Since 1948

1948, Truman, Dem., 2,557,642; Liberal, 222,562; total, 2,780,204; Dewey, Rep., 2,841,163; Wallace, Amer. Lab., 509,559; Thomas, Soc., 40,879; Teichert, Ind. Gov't., 2,729; Dobbs, Soc. Workers, 2,675.
1952, Eisenhower, Rep., 3,952,815; Stevenson, Dem., 2,687,890; Liberal, 416,711; total, 3,104,601; Hallinan, Amer. Lab., 64,211; Hoopes, Soc., 2,664; Dobbs, Soc. Workers, 2,212; Hass, Ind. Gov't., 1,560; scattering, 178; blank and void, 87,813.
1956, Eisenhower, Rep., 4,340,340; Stevenson, Dem., 2,458,212; Liberal, 292,557; total, 2,750,769; write-in votes for Andrews, 1,027; Werdel, 492; Hass, 150; Hoopes, 82; others, 476.
1960, Kennedy, Dem., 3,423,909; Liberal, 406,176; total, 3,830,085; Nixon, Rep., 3,446,419; Dobbs, Soc. Workers, 14,319; scattering, 256; blank and void, 88,896.
1964, Johnson, Dem., 4,913,156; Goldwater, Rep., 2,243,559; Hass, Soc. Labor, 6,085; DeBerry, Soc. Workers, 3,215; scattering, 188; blank and void, 151,383.
1968, Nixon, Rep., 3,007,932; Humphrey, Dem., 3,378,470; Wallace, 3d Party, 358,864; Blomen, Soc. Labor, 8,432; Halstead, Soc. Workers, 11,851; Gregory, Freedom and Peace, 24,517; blank, void, and scattering, 171,624.
1972, Nixon, Rep., 3,824,642; Cons., 368,136; McGovern, Dem., 2,767,956; Liberal, 183,128; Reed, Soc. Workers, 7,797; Fisher, Soc. Labor, 4,530; Hall, Com., 5,641; blank, void, or scattered, 161,641.
1976, Carter, Dem., 3,389,558; Ford, Rep., 3,100,791; MacBride, Libertarian, 12,197; Hall, Com., 10,270; Camejo, Soc. Workers, 6,996; LaRouche, U.S. Labor, 5,413; blank, void, or scattered, 143,037.
1980, Reagan, Rep., 2,893,831; Carter, Dem., 2,728,372; Anderson, Ind., 467,801; Clark, Libertarian, 52,648; McCormack, Right To Life, 24,159; Commoner, Citizens, 23,186; Hall, Com., 7,414; DeBerry, Soc. Workers, 2,068; Griswold, Workers World, 1,416; scattering, 1,064.
1984, Reagan, Rep., 3,664,763; Mondale, Dem., 3,119,609; Bergland, Libertarian, 11,949.
1988, Bush, Rep., 3,081,871; Dukakis, Dem., 3,347,882; Marra, Right to Life, 20,497; Fulani, New Alliance, 15,845.
1992, Clinton, Dem., 3,444,450; Bush, Rep., 2,346,649; Perot, Ind., 1,090,721; Warren, Soc. Workers, 15,472; Marrou, Libertarian, 13,451; Fulani, New Alliance, 11,318; Hagelin, Natural Law, 4,420.
1996, Clinton, Dem., 3,756,177; Dole, Rep., 1,933,492; Perot, Ind. (Ref.), 503,458; Nader, Green, 75,956; Phillips, Right to Life, 23,580; Browne, Libertarian, 12,220; Hagelin, Natural Law, 5,011; Harris, Soc. Workers, 2,762; Moorehead, Workers World, 3,473.

North Carolina

	1996			1992		
County	Clinton (D)	Dole (R)	Perot (RF)	Clinton (D)	Bush (R)	Perot (I)
Alamance	15,814	22,461	3,395	15,521	20,637	6,444
Alexander	3,955	6,748	1,004	4,849	6,764	2,002
Alleghany	1,801	1,936	458	2,271	1,853	600
Anson	4,890	2,193	512	5,269	2,334	921
Ashe	3,825	5,203	865	4,624	5,200	1,220
Avery	1,586	3,870	655	1,755	3,895	1,123
Beaufort	6,172	8,154	834	6,445	7,337	2,174
Bertie	4,202	1,745	316	4,382	1,756	600
Bladen	4,952	3,335	655	5,700	3,214	1,248
Brunswick	10,041	10,065	1,815	10,177	8,833	3,349
Buncombe	31,658	30,518	6,254	32,955	30,892	11,481
Burke	11,678	13,853	2,654	12,565	13,397	4,124
Cabarrus	14,447	23,035	3,626	13,513	21,281	6,251
Caldwell	8,050	12,653	2,099	9,033	12,543	3,965
Camden	1,186	1,074	293	1,153	1,039	479
Carteret	7,566	11,721	1,467	8,028	10,334	3,401
Caswell	4,312	3,310	510	4,725	2,793	827
Catawba	15,601	26,898	3,629	16,334	25,466	7,523
Chatham	9,353	7,731	1,113	9,520	6,568	2,425
Cherokee	3,129	3,883	785	3,686	4,021	1,040
Chowan	2,239	1,659	359	2,136	1,661	700
Clay	1,462	1,769	387	1,600	1,890	465
Cleveland	12,728	13,474	1,931	13,037	13,650	3,784
Columbus	9,019	6,017	1,170	11,469	5,462	1,963
Craven	10,317	13,264	1,528	9,998	11,575	3,679
Cumberland	32,739	29,804	3,776	30,291	27,139	6,792
Currituck	2,277	2,569	770	1,935	2,188	1,163
Dare	4,522	4,977	1,258	3,925	4,357	2,388
Davidson	13,593	24,797	3,698	16,462	24,869	8,324
Davie	3,525	8,141	915	3,675	6,796	1,903
Duplin	6,179	5,432	766	6,816	5,286	1,636
Durham	49,186	27,825	3,122	47,331	27,581	7,504
Edgecombe	10,568	6,010	660	11,174	6,275	2,175
Forsyth	46,543	59,160	5,747	49,006	52,787	14,262

County	Clinton (D)	1996 Dole (R)	Perot (RF)	Clinton (D)	1992 Bush (R)	Perot (I)
Franklin . . .	6,448	5,648	891	6,517	4,669	2,062
Gaston. . . .	19,458	33,149	3,921	19,121	34,714	7,490
Gates	2,155	1,072	307	2,206	1,158	466
Graham . . .	1,210	1,801	270	1,551	1,919	403
Granville. . .	6,747	5,498	432	6,178	4,538	1,321
Greene . . .	2,224	2,689	280	2,768	2,180	780
Guilford . . .	69,208	67,727	9,739	66,319	60,140	19,601
Halifax. . . .	9,551	5,700	816	9,960	5,769	2,047
Harnett. . . .	8,767	11,596	1,287	8,473	9,751	2,684
Haywood . .	9,350	7,995	2,594	10,385	7,292	3,303
Henderson .	10,626	19,182	2,679	10,747	17,010	5,260
Hertford . . .	4,856	1,823	356	4,609	2,208	846
Hoke	3,510	1,914	481	3,730	1,711	887
Hyde	1,109	782	143	1,206	740	340
Iredell	13,102	21,163	2,970	13,263	19,411	6,204
Jackson . . .	5,211	4,244	970	5,753	4,275	1,516
Johnston . .	11,175	18,704	2,163	11,284	15,418	4,939
Jones	1,829	1,682	197	1,962	1,438	444
Lee	6,290	7,321	980	5,852	6,658	2,125
Lenoir	8,635	9,433	822	8,793	8,932	2,107
Lincoln. . . .	7,721	11,439	1,619	8,150	11,018	3,142
McDowell . .	4,553	6,407	1,275	5,309	6,090	1,881
Macon	4,209	5,267	1,121	4,624	4,797	1,829
Madison . . .	3,333	3,110	538	3,980	3,121	857
Martin	4,500	3,590	445	4,069	2,958	981
Mecklenburg.	103,429	97,719	10,473	97,065	99,496	31,283
Mitchell . . .	1,496	3,874	549	1,727	4,405	877
Montgomery.	3,856	3,379	587	4,422	3,543	1,185
Moore	9,847	14,760	1,761	9,649	12,448	4,448
Nash	11,142	15,309	1,751	10,809	14,446	4,544
New Hanover	22,839	27,889	3,615	20,291	24,338	7,401
Northampton	5,207	1,881	402	5,195	1,845	916
Onslow . . .	8,685	13,396	1,857	8,045	11,842	4,387
Orange . . .	28,674	15,053	1,534	28,595	13,009	5,535
Pamlico . . .	2,204	2,270	297	2,229	1,929	809
Pasquotank .	4,233	2,999	565	4,709	3,419	1,434
Pender. . . .	5,409	5,538	945	5,825	4,857	1,725
Perquimans .	2,069	1,561	369	1,818	1,429	624
Person. . . .	4,540	4,883	591	4,323	4,460	1,431
Pitt	17,555	18,227	2,037	17,959	16,609	5,262
Polk.	2,704	3,516	493	2,939	3,448	1,134
Randolph . .	10,783	23,030	3,593	11,274	20,697	6,870
Richmond. .	7,564	3,973	1,230	9,163	4,356	2,015
Robeson . .	17,361	8,146	2,105	19,378	7,777	3,277
Rockingham.	12,096	14,255	2,528	13,880	12,678	4,671
Rowan. . . .	13,461	22,754	2,902	14,308	21,297	7,053
Rutherford .	7,162	9,792	1,585	7,855	9,748	2,695
Sampson . .	8,150	8,241	825	8,698	8,007	1,852
Scotland. . .	4,870	2,858	548	5,175	2,980	1,196
Stanly	7,131	11,446	1,690	7,735	11,030	2,855
Stokes. . . .	4,769	9,471	1,025	6,463	7,979	2,183
Surry	7,303	11,117	1,538	9,392	10,866	3,164
Swain	1,869	1,444	401	2,117	1,640	568
Transylvania	4,842	6,734	1,183	5,120	5,984	2,006
Tyrrell	908	488	112	928	553	189
Union.	11,525	18,802	2,477	10,789	16,542	4,601
Vance	6,385	4,651	575	6,598	4,747	1,444
Wake.	103,574	108,780	11,811	88,979	86,798	31,140
Warren. . . .	4,141	1,861	319	4,656	1,767	693
Washington .	2,790	1,562	171	2,902	1,780	563
Watauga . .	7,349	8,146	1,415	8,262	7,899	3,007
Wayne. . . .	11,580	16,588	1,178	10,307	14,397	2,798
Wilkes	6,793	12,395	1,967	7,991	12,547	3,307
Wilson	9,779	10,518	1,100	10,105	10,176	2,630
Yadkin	2,927	8,439	913	3,913	7,311	1,725
Yancey . . .	3,956	3,973	720	4,285	3,994	917
Totals	**1,107,849**	**1,225,938**	**168,059**	**1,114,042**	**1,134,661**	**357,864**

North Carolina Vote Since 1948

1948, Truman, Dem., 459,070; Dewey, Rep., 258,572; Thurmond, States' Rights, 69,652; Wallace, Prog., 3,915.

1952, Eisenhower, Rep., 558,107; Stevenson, Dem., 652,803.

1956, Eisenhower, Rep., 575,062; Stevenson, Dem., 590,530.

1960, Kennedy, Dem., 713,136; Nixon, Rep., 655,420.

1964, Johnson, Dem., 800,139; Goldwater, Rep., 624,844.

1968, Nixon, Rep., 627,192; Humphrey, Dem., 464,113; Wallace, 3d Party, 496,188.

1972, Nixon, Rep., 1,054,889; McGovern, Dem., 438,705; Schmitz, Amer., 25,018.

1976, Carter, Dem., 927,365; Ford, Rep., 741,960; Anderson, Amer., 5,607; MacBride, Libertarian, 2,219; LaRouche, U.S. Labor, 755.

1980, Reagan, Rep., 915,018; Carter, Dem., 875,635; Anderson, Ind., 52,800; Clark, Libertarian, 9,677; Commoner, Citizens, 2,287; DeBerry, Soc. Workers, 416.

1984, Reagan, Rep., 1,346,481; Mondale, Dem., 824,287; Bergland, Libertarian, 3,794.

1988, Bush, Rep., 1,237,258; Dukakis, Dem., 890,167; Fulani, New Alliance, 5,682; Paul, write-in, 1,263.

1992, Clinton, Dem., 1,114,042; Bush, Rep., 1,134,661; Perot, Ind., 357,864; Marrou, Libertarian, 5,171.

1996, Dole, Rep., 1,225,938; Clinton, Dem., 1,107,849; Perot, Ref., 168,059; Browne, Libertarian, 8,740; Hagelin, Natural Law, 2,771.

North Dakota

County	Clinton (D)	1996 Dole (R)	Perot (RF)	Clinton (D)	1992 Bush (R)	Perot (I)
Adams.	366	575	200	469	647	499
Barnes.	2,317	2,449	666	2,124	2,728	1,568
Benson	1,059	850	252	1,126	874	610
Billings.	116	281	107	123	279	270
Bottineau . . .	1,280	1,682	536	1,266	1,787	1,036
Bowman. . . .	489	710	261	506	712	678
Burke	416	483	176	458	551	506
Burleigh	10,679	15,464	3,535	8,940	16,484	6,780
Cass	21,693	24,238	4,116	18,077	25,312	9,513
Cavalier	941	1,188	326	866	1,527	723
Dickey	953	1,418	276	918	1,514	616
Divide	637	488	209	634	515	456
Dunn	587	830	304	667	784	637
Eddy	553	517	201	575	591	432
Emmons . . .	544	1,148	441	595	1,047	774
Foster	664	801	265	565	803	556
Golden Valley	235	520	163	255	503	352
Grand Forks	11,376	11,606	2,663	10,930	13,705	6,349
Grant.	300	760	295	415	900	629
Griggs	670	731	162	647	773	330
Hettinger . . .	418	765	238	465	854	500
Kidder	434	691	242	468	739	489
La Moure . . .	880	1,220	276	797	1,270	679
Logan	360	705	254	383	703	390
McHenry . . .	1,096	1,187	453	1,173	1,321	886
McIntosh . . .	470	1,005	295	450	1,134	454
McKenzie. . .	928	1,338	428	787	1,324	969
McLean	1,759	1,988	618	1,808	2,124	1,330
Mercer.	1,300	1,953	764	1,323	2,274	1,378
Morton.	3,745	4,699	1,566	3,594	5,042	2,787
Mountrail . . .	1,277	965	360	1,393	1,017	861
Nelson.	827	745	206	841	864	486
Oliver	333	499	183	306	503	407
Pembina . . .	1,191	1,678	400	1,186	1,917	991
Pierce	671	1,017	270	761	1,099	554
Ramsey	2,123	2,077	549	2,008	2,516	1,507
Ransom	1,199	920	303	1,166	1,102	625
Renville	562	576	210	580	655	429
Richland. . . .	2,890	3,345	782	2,688	3,873	1,698
Rolette.	2,299	823	448	2,002	895	660
Sargent	1,003	814	241	961	816	463
Sheridan . . .	252	566	121	276	589	304
Sioux.	393	207	82	463	264	244
Slope.	123	260	60	145	226	162
Stark	3,095	4,086	1,456	3,003	4,491	3,123
Steele	620	486	115	598	503	267
Stutsman . . .	3,589	3,784	1,141	3,313	4,039	2,580
Towner	649	542	187	748	600	402
Traill	1,822	1,820	380	1,638	2,019	875
Walsh	2,082	2,222	599	1,936	2,544	1,384
Ward	8,660	10,546	2,587	7,856	12,056	5,856
Wells.	962	1,192	373	888	1,171	850
Williams. . . .	3,018	3,590	1,174	3,008	3,664	3,180
Totals	**106,905**	**125,050**	**32,515**	**99,168**	**136,244**	**71,084**

North Dakota Vote Since 1948

1948, Truman, Dem., 95,812; Dewey, Rep., 115,139; Wallace, Prog., 8,391; Thomas, Soc., 1,000; Thurmond, States' Rights, 374.

1952, Eisenhower, Rep., 191,712; Stevenson, Dem., 76,694; MacArthur, Christian Nationalist, 1,075; Hallinan, Prog., 344; Hamblen, Proh., 302.

1956, Eisenhower, Rep., 156,766; Stevenson, Dem., 96,742; Andrews, Amer., 483.

1960, Kennedy, Dem., 123,963; Nixon, Rep., 154,310; Dobbs, Soc. Workers, 158.

1964, Johnson, Dem., 149,784; Goldwater, Rep., 108,207; DeBerry, Soc. Workers, 224; Munn, Proh., 174.

1968, Nixon, Rep., 138,669; Humphrey, Dem., 94,769; Wallace, 3d Party, 14,244; Halstead, Soc. Workers, 128; Munn, Prohibition, 38; Troxell, Ind., 34.

1972, Nixon, Rep., 174,109; McGovern, Dem., 100,384; Jenness, Soc. Workers, 288; Hall, Com., 87; Schmitz, Amer., 5,646.

1976, Carter, Dem., 136,078; Ford, Rep., 153,470; Anderson, Amer., 3,698; McCarthy, Ind., 2,952; Maddox, Amer. Ind., 269; MacBride, Libertarian, 256; scattering, 371.

1980, Reagan, Rep., 193,695; Carter, Dem., 79,189; Anderson, Ind., 23,640; Clark, Libertarian, 3,743; Commoner, Libertarian, 429; McLain, Natl. People's League, 296; Greaves, Amer., 235; Hall, Com., 93; DeBerry, Soc. Workers, 89; McReynolds, Soc., 82; Bubar, Statesman, 54.

1984, Reagan, Rep., 200,336; Mondale, Dem., 104,429; Bergland, Libertarian, 703.

1988, Bush, Rep., 166,559; Dukakis, Dem., 127,739; Paul, Lib., 1,315; LaRouche, Natl. Econ. Recovery, 905.

1992, Clinton, Dem., 99,168; Bush, Rep., 136,244; Perot, Ind., 71,084.

1996, Dole, Rep., 125,050; Clinton, Dem., 106,905; Perot, Ref., 32,515; Browne, Libertarian, 847; Phillips, Ind., 745; Hagelin, Natural Law, 349.

Ohio

		1996			1992	
County	Clinton (D)	Dole (R)	Perot (RF)	Clinton (D)	Bush (R)	Perot (I)
Adams	4,317	4,763	1,223	3,998	4,722	1,993
Allen	15,529	24,325	3,799	13,777	25,322	8,131
Ashland	6,573	10,402	2,630	5,985	9,864	4,950
Ashtabula	19,341	13,287	5,700	18,843	13,254	10,765
Athens	13,418	7,154	2,777	13,423	7,184	5,074
Auglaize	6,652	10,169	2,641	4,960	10,455	4,840
Belmont	17,705	8,213	4,452	18,527	8,614	6,142
Brown	6,318	6,970	1,941	5,540	5,912	3,676
Butler	43,690	67,023	10,540	39,682	63,375	27,527
Carroll	4,792	4,449	2,445	4,731	4,224	3,434
Champaign	5,990	6,568	2,219	5,201	7,004	3,992
Clark	27,890	22,297	7,083	26,692	24,011	12,571
Clermont	21,329	36,457	5,795	17,558	32,065	14,279
Clinton	5,303	7,504	1,588	4,638	7,290	3,402
Columbiana	20,716	15,386	7,127	19,765	15,016	12,611
Coshocton	6,005	6,018	2,183	6,212	5,705	4,081
Crawford	7,449	8,730	3,072	6,351	8,618	5,764
Cuyahoga	341,357	163,770	50,691	337,548	187,186	112,352
Darke	8,871	10,798	3,168	7,016	11,098	6,217
Defiance	6,343	7,469	1,929	5,735	7,195	4,187
Delaware	13,463	24,123	3,471	9,263	18,225	9,244
Erie	16,730	12,204	4,225	14,531	12,459	8,720
Fairfield	18,821	26,850	4,660	14,249	24,125	12,246
Fayette	3,665	4,831	1,047	2,976	4,916	2,162
Franklin	192,795	178,412	25,400	176,656	186,324	79,049
Fulton	6,662	8,703	2,412	5,576	8,358	4,798
Gallia	5,386	5,135	1,839	5,350	5,776	2,549
Geauga	14,143	19,662	4,848	11,466	18,200	10,577
Greene	25,082	30,677	5,246	20,139	27,651	11,459
Guernsey	6,731	5,970	2,251	6,428	5,749	4,103
Hamilton	160,458	186,493	21,335	148,409	192,447	60,145
Hancock	9,334	17,252	2,904	7,944	16,821	7,002
Hardin	4,930	5,506	1,365	4,364	5,851	2,867
Harrison	3,721	2,310	1,302	3,830	2,289	1,679
Henry	4,762	6,385	1,550	3,933	6,196	3,178
Highland	5,837	7,102	1,629	4,866	7,020	3,315
Hocking	4,646	4,017	1,564	3,935	3,761	2,831
Holmes	2,531	5,213	1,276	1,969	5,079	1,945
Huron	8,858	8,750	3,338	7,930	9,480	6,751
Jackson	5,538	4,922	1,529	5,016	5,422	2,389
Jefferson	19,402	10,212	4,748	20,978	10,764	6,910
Knox	7,562	10,159	2,138	7,259	9,044	5,282
Lake	43,186	40,974	12,507	37,682	40,766	26,878
Lawrence	11,595	8,832	3,232	12,325	10,044	4,536
Licking	22,624	28,276	6,516	18,898	26,918	13,806
Logan	6,397	8,325	2,264	4,889	9,364	4,472
Lorain	55,744	34,937	14,889	50,962	36,803	30,425
Lucas	104,911	58,120	17,282	99,989	63,297	38,108
Madison	5,072	6,871	1,386	3,998	6,865	3,170
Mahoning	72,716	31,397	13,213	64,731	31,191	29,417
Marion	10,482	11,112	2,897	9,444	11,675	6,471
Medina	23,727	26,120	8,700	18,995	24,090	17,290
Meigs	4,275	3,622	1,453	4,226	3,916	2,098
Mercer	6,300	8,832	2,361	4,883	8,683	4,913
Miami	15,540	19,509	4,599	12,547	19,741	10,544
Monroe	3,914	1,856	1,128	4,235	1,823	1,505
Montgomery	115,469	95,391	18,298	108,017	104,751	47,854
Morgan	2,385	2,566	922	2,402	2,719	1,551
Morrow	4,627	5,655	1,745	3,907	5,208	3,623
Muskingum	13,813	13,861	4,880	11,670	14,168	8,731
Noble	2,366	2,183	899	2,201	2,223	1,429
Ottawa	9,321	6,991	2,438	8,128	6,782	4,832
Paulding	3,449	3,760	1,292	3,293	3,652	2,510
Perry	5,819	4,606	1,854	4,972	4,712	3,810
Pickaway	7,042	8,666	1,702	5,765	8,690	4,319
Pike	5,542	3,759	1,402	5,057	4,094	2,192
Portage	29,441	18,939	9,178	26,325	18,447	17,065
Preble	6,611	8,139	2,235	5,557	8,023	4,460
Putnam	4,972	9,294	1,767	3,962	9,338	3,648
Richland	20,832	23,697	6,613	19,606	23,532	13,370
Ross	12,649	10,286	2,648	10,452	10,825	5,616
Sandusky	11,547	10,033	3,617	9,878	10,772	6,682
Scioto	15,041	11,679	4,418	14,715	11,931	6,860
Seneca	10,044	9,713	3,498	9,280	9,763	6,967
Shelby	6,729	8,773	2,686	5,262	8,854	5,835
Stark	73,437	60,212	23,004	70,064	61,863	42,413
Summit	112,050	73,555	27,723	107,881	77,530	55,151
Trumbull	55,604	24,811	13,563	54,591	25,831	26,791
Tuscarawas	15,244	13,388	5,682	14,787	13,179	8,785
Union	4,989	8,290	1,596	3,465	7,818	3,433
Van Wert	4,453	6,999	1,487	3,822	7,227	3,102
Vinton	2,350	1,673	728	2,308	1,975	1,050
Warren	17,089	33,210	4,689	13,542	27,998	11,115
Washington	10,945	11,965	2,832	10,380	12,204	5,415
Wayne	14,850	19,628	5,771	13,953	18,350	9,482
Williams	5,524	7,747	2,121	4,862	7,614	4,902
Wood	23,183	20,518	5,065	20,754	20,579	11,682
Wyandot	3,677	4,473	1,347	3,031	4,411	2,929
Totals	**2,148,222**	**1,859,883**	**483,207**	**1,984,942**	**1,894,310**	**1,036,426**

Ohio Vote Since 1948

1948, Truman, Dem., 1,452,791; Dewey, Rep., 1,445,684; Wallace, Prog., 37,596.

1952, Eisenhower, Rep., 2,100,391; Stevenson, Dem., 1,600,367.

1956, Eisenhower, Rep., 2,262,610; Stevenson, Dem., 1,439,655.

1960, Kennedy, Dem., 1,944,248; Nixon, Rep., 2,217,611.

1964, Johnson, Dem., 2,498,331; Goldwater, Rep., 1,470,865.

1968, Nixon, Rep., 1,791,014; Humphrey, Dem., 1,700,586; Wallace, 3d Party, 467,495; Gregory, 372; Munn, Proh., 19; Blomen, Soc. Labor, 120; Halstead, Soc. Workers, 69; Mitchell, Com., 23.

1972, Nixon, Rep., 2,441,827; McGovern, Dem., 1,558,889; Fisher, Soc. Labor, 7,107; Hall, Com., 6,437; Schmitz, Amer., 80,067; Wallace, Ind., 460.

1976, Carter, Dem., 2,011,621; Ford, Rep., 2,000,505; McCarthy, Ind., 58,258; Maddox, Amer. Ind., 15,529; MacBride, Libertarian, 8,961; Hall, Com., 7,817; Camejo, Soc. Workers, 4,717; LaRouche, U.S. Labor, 4,335; scattered, 130.

1980, Reagan, Rep., 2,206,545; Carter, Dem., 1,752,414; Anderson, Ind., 254,472; Clark, Libertarian, 49,033; Commoner, Citizens, 8,564; Hall, Com., 4,729; Congress, Ind., 4,029; Griswold, Workers World, 3,790; Bubar, Statesman, 27.

1984, Reagan, Rep., 2,678,559; Mondale, Dem., 1,825,440; Bergland, Libertarian, 5,886.

1988, Bush, Rep., 2,416,549; Dukakis, Dem., 1,939,629; Fulani, Ind., 12,017; Paul, Ind., 11,926.

1992, Clinton, Dem., 1,984,942; Bush, Rep., 1,894,310; Perot, Ind., 1,036,426; Marrou, Libertarian, 7,252; Fulani, New Alliance, 6,413; Gritz, Populist/America First, 4,699; Hagelin, Natural Law, 3,437; LaRouche, Ind., 2,446.

1996, Clinton, Dem., 2,148,222; Dole, Rep., 1,859,883; Perot, Ref., 483,207; Browne, Ind., 12,851; Moorehead, Ind., 10,813; Hagelin, Natural Law, 9,120; Phillips, Ind., 7,361.

Oklahoma

		1996			1992	
County	Clinton (D)	Dole (R)	Perot (RF)	Clinton (D)	Bush (R)	Perot (I)
Adair	2,792	2,956	751	2,645	2,994	914
Alfalfa	796	1,504	348	741	1,567	722
Atoka	2,281	1,542	532	2,336	1,561	1,255
Beaver	515	1,893	199	580	1,699	565
Beckham	2,797	2,912	817	2,947	2,913	1,929
Blaine	1,832	2,127	563	1,564	2,209	1,258
Bryan	5,962	3,943	1,396	6,259	3,452	3,713
Caddo	4,844	3,422	1,358	4,861	3,664	2,911
Canadian	8,977	18,139	3,297	7,215	16,756	8,985
Carter	6,979	6,769	1,997	7,171	5,947	5,188
Cherokee	6,817	5,046	1,777	6,794	4,977	3,297
Choctaw	3,198	1,580	589	3,413	1,641	1,298
Cimarron	361	986	102	395	965	254
Cleveland	26,038	36,457	6,785	24,404	35,561	20,352
Coal	1,205	734	323	1,448	714	618
Comanche	12,841	14,461	2,819	12,237	15,704	7,463
Cotton	1,258	1,042	381	1,314	910	853
Craig	2,649	2,058	758	2,780	2,106	1,316
Creek	9,674	9,861	2,837	9,118	10,055	5,984
Custer	4,027	4,723	1,101	3,540	5,362	2,741
Delaware	5,094	5,230	1,573	4,842	4,840	2,689
Dewey	816	1,179	292	845	1,244	684
Ellis	619	1,090	279	594	1,072	632
Garfield	7,504	11,712	2,523	6,720	13,095	5,559
Garvin	4,639	3,745	1,345	4,811	3,983	3,014
Grady	6,256	7,228	2,048	6,177	6,997	4,528
Grant	867	1,382	384	864	1,311	871
Greer	1,240	905	361	1,162	964	640
Harmon	729	448	143	783	496	326
Harper	511	1,036	219	486	1,038	501
Haskell	2,762	1,442	590	3,069	1,461	995
Hughes	2,748	1,510	730	2,850	1,522	1,158
Jackson	3,245	4,422	892	3,273	3,893	2,227
Jefferson	1,430	865	337	1,580	671	758
Johnston	1,998	1,229	532	2,096	1,191	1,040
Kay	6,882	9,741	2,785	6,643	9,115	6,984
Kingfisher	1,626	3,423	621	1,379	3,479	1,534

		1996			1992	
County	Clinton (D)	Dole (R)	Perot (RF)	Clinton (D)	Bush (R)	Perot (I)
Kiowa	1,973	1,638	510	2,143	1,635	1,114
Latimer . . .	2,222	1,189	578	2,606	1,212	1,049
Le Flore . . .	6,831	5,689	1,721	7,843	5,850	3,021
Lincoln. . . .	4,332	5,243	1,500	3,904	5,315	3,160
Logan	4,854	5,949	1,410	4,453	6,071	3,239
Love	1,675	1,224	385	1,708	922	1,033
McClain . . .	3,753	4,363	1,289	3,378	4,377	2,996
McCurtain. .	4,350	3,892	1,483	5,082	3,519	2,852
McIntosh . .	4,219	2,400	1,044	4,184	2,225	1,469
Major.	900	2,188	410	731	2,154	857
Marshall. . .	2,624	1,605	663	2,519	1,478	1,486
Mayes	6,377	5,268	1,617	6,432	5,445	3,235
Murray. . . .	2,620	1,712	723	2,594	1,536	1,447
Muskogee. .	12,963	8,974	3,163	13,619	8,782	5,454
Noble.	1,756	2,318	694	1,333	2,474	1,449
Nowata . . .	1,788	1,457	586	1,912	1,531	1,063
Okfuskee . .	2,074	1,380	536	2,141	1,580	889
Oklahoma. .	80,438	120,429	18,411	76,271	126,788	56,139
Okmulgee. .	7,555	4,246	1,487	7,767	4,586	3,013
Osage	7,342	5,827	1,938	6,894	5,891	4,477
Ottawa. . . .	5,844	4,127	1,496	6,304	4,141	2,721
Pawnee . . .	2,663	2,560	756	2,612	2,675	1,656
Payne	9,985	11,686	2,472	9,886	13,032	7,852
Pittsburg. . .	8,475	5,966	2,217	8,523	5,659	4,594
Pontotoc. . .	6,470	5,366	1,712	6,350	5,206	3,916
Pottawatomie.	9,141	9,802	2,724	8,616	10,350	6,520
Pushmataha	2,270	1,458	588	2,553	1,319	1,000
Roger Mills .	733	959	233	767	890	505
Rogers. . . .	9,544	12,883	3,022	8,257	12,455	7,101
Seminole . .	4,225	2,935	1,041	4,624	3,253	2,330
Sequoyah . .	5,665	4,733	1,673	6,092	4,925	2,486
Stephens . .	7,248	8,144	2,312	7,644	7,085	5,692
Texas	1,408	4,139	518	1,487	4,059	1,417
Tillman. . . .	1,827	1,346	471	1,749	1,377	1,039
Tulsa.	76,924	111,243	18,201	71,165	117,465	49,760
Wagoner . .	7,749	9,392	2,357	7,041	9,053	5,381
Washington .	6,732	11,605	2,255	6,593	11,342	5,664
Washita . . .	1,913	1,994	748	1,929	1,912	1,468
Woods	1,431	2,151	497	1,361	2,225	1,167
Woodward .	2,403	4,093	963	2,063	4,006	2,411
Totals	**488,105**	**582,315**	**130,788**	**473,066**	**592,929**	**319,878**

Oklahoma Vote Since 1948

1948, Truman, Dem., 452,782; Dewey, Rep., 268,817.
1952, Eisenhower, Rep., 518,045; Stevenson, Dem., 430,939.
1956, Eisenhower, Rep., 473,769; Stevenson, Dem., 385,581.
1960, Kennedy, Dem., 370,111; Nixon, Rep., 533,039.
1964, Johnson, Dem., 519,834; Goldwater, Rep., 412,665.
1968, Nixon, Rep., 449,697; Humphrey, Dem., 301,658; Wallace, 3d Party, 191,731.
1972, Nixon, Rep., 759,025; McGovern, Dem., 247,147; Schmitz, Amer., 23,728.
1976, Carter, Dem., 532,442; Ford, Rep., 545,708; McCarthy, Ind., 14,101.
1980, Reagan, Rep., 695,570; Carter, Dem., 402,026; Anderson, Ind., 38,284; Clark, Libertarian, 13,828.
1984, Reagan, Rep., 861,530; Mondale, Dem., 385,080; Bergland, Libertarian, 9,066.
1988, Bush, Rep., 678,367; Dukakis, Dem., 483,423; Paul, Lib., 6,261; Fulani, New Alliance, 2,985.
1992, Clinton, Dem., 473,066; Bush, Rep., 592,929; Perot, Ind., 319,878; Marrou, Libertarian, 4,486.
1996, Dole, Rep., 582,315; Clinton, Dem., 488,105; Perot, Ref., 130,788; Browne, Libertarian, 5,505.

Oregon

		1996			1992	
County	Clinton (D)	Dole (R)	Perot (RF)	Clinton (D)	Bush (R)	Perot (I)
Baker. . . .	2,547	3,975	900	2,395	2,862	2,191
Benton. . .	17,211	12,450	2,445	17,966	11,550	8,103
Clackamas	67,709	59,443	12,304	60,310	53,724	39,776
Clatsop . .	7,732	5,334	1,582	7,700	4,683	4,316
Columbia .	9,275	6,205	2,330	8,298	5,227	5,670
Coos	12,171	10,886	3,460	12,072	9,284	7,989
Crook . . .	2,607	3,250	948	2,508	2,703	2,024
Curry. . . .	4,202	4,790	1,560	3,841	3,809	3,310
Deschutes	17,151	21,135	5,306	15,693	15,655	12,293
Douglas . .	15,250	21,855	4,465	14,137	19,011	12,377
Gilliam . . .	485	398	143	374	377	283
Grant. . . .	1,180	2,110	432	1,135	1,496	1,302
Harney. . .	980	1,948	506	973	1,350	1,024
Hood River	3,654	2,794	721	3,106	2,453	2,235
Jackson . .	29,230	33,771	7,470	29,146	28,704	18,633
Jefferson .	2,555	2,634	813	2,161	1,962	1,741
Josephine.	11,113	16,048	3,546	11,007	13,003	8,426
Klamath . .	7,207	12,116	2,538	7,918	11,864	6,636
Lake	962	2,239	385	1,019	1,791	980
Lane	69,461	48,253	11,498	74,083	41,789	34,906
Lincoln. . . .	10,552	6,717	2,269	9,603	5,716	6,127
Linn.	17,041	18,331	4,773	15,399	16,461	13,256
Malheur . . .	2,827	6,045	844	2,539	5,374	2,654
Marion	48,637	46,415	8,802	41,137	42,145	26,156
Morrow . . .	1,426	1,381	455	1,174	1,187	1,089
Multnomah .	159,878	71,094	17,536	165,081	72,326	58,236
Polk.	10,942	11,478	2,093	9,551	10,082	5,818
Sherman . .	444	476	126	362	424	326
Tillamook . .	5,775	3,884	1,263	5,040	3,359	2,997
Umatilla . . .	8,774	9,703	2,500	6,787	7,095	5,581
Union.	4,379	5,414	1,241	3,990	4,223	3,305
Wallowa. . .	1,321	2,379	483	1,203	1,630	1,209
Wasco	4,967	3,662	1,004	4,663	3,242	3,008
Washington .	76,619	65,221	11,446	67,528	57,146	41,575
Wheeler . . .	299	418	121	267	357	227
Yamhill . . .	13,078	13,900	2,913	11,148	11,693	8,312
Totals	**649,641**	**538,152**	**121,221**	**621,314**	**475,757**	**354,091**

Oregon Vote Since 1948

1948, Truman, Dem., 243,147; Dewey, Rep., 260,904; Wallace, Prog., 14,978; Thomas, Soc., 5,051.
1952, Eisenhower, Rep., 420,815; Stevenson, Dem., 270,579; Hallinan, Ind., 3,665.
1956, Eisenhower, Rep., 406,393; Stevenson, Dem., 329,204.
1960, Kennedy, Dem., 367,402; Nixon, Rep., 408,060.
1964, Johnson, Dem., 501,017; Goldwater, Rep., 282,779; write-in, 2,509.
1968, Nixon, Rep., 408,433; Humphrey, Dem., 358,866; Wallace, 3d Party, 49,683; write-in, McCarthy, 1,496; N. Rockefeller, 69; others, 1,075.
1972, Nixon, Rep., 486,686; McGovern, Dem., 392,760; Schmitz, Amer., 46,211; write-in, 2,289.
1976, Carter, Dem., 490,407; Ford, Rep., 492,120; McCarthy, Ind., 40,207; write-in, 7,142.
1980, Reagan, Rep., 571,044; Carter, Dem., 456,890; Anderson, Ind., 112,389; Clark, Libertarian, 25,838; Commoner, Citizens, 13,642; scattered, 1,713.
1984, Reagan, Rep., 658,700; Mondale, Dem., 536,479.
1988, Bush, Rep., 560,126; Dukakis, Dem., 616,206; Paul, Lib., 14,811; Fulani, Ind., 6,487.
1992, Clinton, Dem., 621,314; Bush, Rep., 475,757; Perot, Ind., 354,091; Marrou, Libertarian, 4,277; Fulani, New Alliance, 3,030.
1996, Clinton, Dem., 649,641; Dole, Rep., 538,152; Perot, Ref., 121,221; Nader, Pacific, 49,415; Browne, Libertarian, 8,903; Phillips, Taxpayers, 3,379; Hagelin, Natural Law, 2,798; Hollis, Soc., 1,922.

Pennsylvania

		1996			1992	
County	Clinton (D)	Dole (R)	Perot (RF)	Clinton (D)	Bush (R)	Perot (I)
Adams. . . .	10,774	15,338	3,186	9,576	13,552	6,313
Allegheny . .	284,480	204,067	42,309	324,004	183,035	103,470
Armstrong .	11,130	11,052	3,452	12,995	9,122	6,166
Beaver. . . .	39,578	26,048	8,276	44,877	21,361	15,954
Bedford . . .	5,954	10,064	2,041	5,840	9,216	3,731
Berks.	49,887	56,289	13,788	46,031	52,939	31,663
Blair	15,036	21,282	4,014	14,857	21,447	8,284
Bradford. . .	7,736	10,393	2,712	6,903	10,221	5,452
Bucks	103,313	94,899	24,544	97,902	94,584	53,931
Butler	21,990	32,038	6,145	22,303	23,656	15,013
Cambria. . .	30,391	20,341	7,837	34,334	20,770	11,070
Cameron . .	822	1,113	283	824	1,173	676
Carbon . . .	9,457	7,193	2,992	9,072	7,243	5,222
Centre	21,145	20,935	4,173	21,177	20,478	9,356
Chester . . .	64,783	77,029	14,067	59,643	74,002	34,536
Clarion. . . .	5,954	6,916	2,064	5,584	6,477	3,619
Clearfield . .	11,991	12,987	3,758	12,247	11,553	6,989
Clinton. . . .	5,658	4,293	1,424	5,397	4,471	2,654
Columbia . .	8,379	8,234	3,654	8,261	9,742	5,683
Crawford . .	12,943	14,659	3,519	12,813	14,112	7,392
Cumberland.	28,749	43,943	5,669	26,635	43,447	14,344
Dauphin . . .	40,936	44,417	6,967	36,990	45,479	16,063
Delaware . .	115,946	92,628	21,883	111,210	108,587	43,728
Elk	5,749	4,889	2,293	5,016	4,908	3,885
Erie.	57,508	39,884	10,386	56,381	39,283	21,510
Fayette . . .	26,359	14,019	5,722	30,577	12,820	10,162
Forest	964	902	325	890	801	448
Franklin . . .	14,980	25,392	4,127	13,440	23,387	6,941
Fulton	1,620	2,665	554	1,588	2,558	869
Greene . . .	7,620	4,002	2,052	8,438	3,482	3,186
Huntingdon.	5,285	7,324	1,813	5,153	7,249	3,273
Indiana . . .	13,868	12,874	3,674	15,194	10,966	7,089
Jefferson . .	5,846	8,156	2,322	5,998	7,271	4,403
Juniata. . . .	2,896	4,128	911	2,601	3,980	1,819
Lackawanna	46,377	26,930	8,189	45,054	33,443	15,667
Lancaster. .	49,120	92,875	11,601	44,255	88,447	26,807
Lawrence . .	18,993	13,088	4,002	20,830	12,359	7,950
Lebanon. . .	14,187	21,885	4,235	12,350	21,512	9,005

County	1996 Clinton (D)	1996 Dole (R)	1996 Perot (RF)	1992 Clinton (D)	1992 Bush (R)	1992 Perot (I)
Lehigh	48,568	45,103	10,947	46,711	42,631	24,853
Luzerne . . .	60,174	43,577	12,424	56,623	49,285	21,007
Lycoming . .	13,516	21,535	3,855	13,315	20,536	9,170
McKean . . .	5,509	6,838	2,350	5,331	6,965	4,019
Mercer	23,003	17,213	5,108	23,264	16,081	10,277
Mifflin.	5,327	6,888	1,392	4,946	6,300	3,382
Monroe . . .	16,547	17,326	4,650	13,468	14,557	9,257
Montgomery	143,664	121,047	24,392	136,572	125,704	53,738
Montour . . .	2,183	2,785	784	2,150	3,096	1,373
Northampton	43,959	35,726	9,848	42,203	34,429	20,234
Northumberland.	13,418	13,551	5,173	12,814	15,057	7,782
Perry	4,611	8,156	1,609	4,086	7,871	3,334
Philadelphia .	412,988	85,345	29,329	434,904	133,328	65,455
Pike.	5,509	6,697	1,873	4,382	6,084	3,019
Potter	2,146	3,714	925	1,892	3,452	1,687
Schuylkill . .	24,860	22,920	8,471	23,679	25,780	13,398
Snyder. . . .	3,405	6,742	1,451	2,952	6,934	2,686
Somerset . .	12,719	14,735	3,968	12,493	13,858	6,333
Sullivan . . .	1,071	1,352	418	1,030	1,340	731
Susquehanna . . .	5,912	7,354	2,266	5,368	7,356	3,946
Tioga.	4,961	7,382	1,993	4,868	7,823	3,804
Union.	3,658	6,570	1,431	3,623	6,362	2,255
Venango . .	8,205	8,398	2,777	8,230	8,545	4,695
Warren. . . .	7,291	7,056	2,504	6,972	6,585	4,795
Washington .	40,952	27,777	8,661	46,143	21,977	16,083
Wayne	5,928	8,077	2,126	4,817	8,184	3,727
Westmoreland	63,686	62,058	16,230	69,817	47,315	37,036
Wyoming . .	4,049	4,888	1,414	3,158	5,143	2,525
York	49,596	65,188	11,652	46,113	60,130	27,743
Totals	**2,215,819**	**1,801,169**	**430,984**	**2,239,164**	**1,791,841**	**902,667**

Pennsylvania Vote Since 1948

1948, Truman, Dem., 1,752,426; Dewey, Rep., 1,902,197; Wallace, Prog., 55,161; Thomas, Soc., 11,325; Watson, Proh., 10,338; Dobbs, Militant Workers, 2,133; Teichert, Ind. Gov., 1,461.

1952, Eisenhower, Rep., 2,415,789; Stevenson, Dem., 2,146,269; Hamblen, Proh., 8,771; Hallinan, Prog., 4,200; Hoopes, Soc., 2,684; Dobbs, Militant Workers, 1,502; Hass, Ind. Gov., 1,347; scattered, 155.

1956, Eisenhower, Rep., 2,585,252; Stevenson, Dem., 1,981,769; Hass, Soc. Labor, 7,447; Dobbs, Militant Workers, 2,035.

1960, Kennedy, Dem., 2,556,282; Nixon, Rep., 2,439,956; Hass, Soc. Labor, 7,185; Dobbs, Soc. Workers, 2,678; scattering, 440.

1964, Johnson, Dem., 3,130,954; Goldwater, Rep., 1,673,657; DeBerry, Soc. Workers, 10,456; Hass, Soc. Labor, 5,092; scattering, 2,531.

1968, Nixon, Rep., 2,090,017; Humphrey, Dem., 2,259,405; Wallace, 3d Party, 378,582; Blomen, Soc. Labor, 4,977; Halstead, Soc. Workers, 4,862; Gregory, Peace and Freedom, 7,821; others, 2,264.

1972, Nixon, Rep., 2,714,521; McGovern, Dem., 1,796,951; Schmitz, Amer., 70,593; Jenness, Soc. Workers, 4,639; Hall, Com., 2,686; others, 2,715.

1976, Carter, Dem., 2,328,677; Ford, Rep., 2,205,604; McCarthy, Ind., 50,584; Maddox, Constitution, 25,344; Camejo, Soc. Workers, 3,009; LaRouche, U.S. Labor, 2,744; Hall, Com., 1,891; others, 2,934.

1980, Reagan, Rep., 2,261,872; Carter, Dem., 1,937,540; Anderson, Ind., 292,921; Clark, Libertarian, 33,263; DeBerry, Soc. Workers, 20,291; Commoner, Consumer, 10,430; Hall, Com., 5,184.

1984, Reagan, Rep., 2,584,323; Mondale, Dem., 2,228,131; Bergland, Libertarian, 6,982.

1988, Bush, Rep., 2,300,087; Dukakis, Dem., 2,194,944; McCarthy, Consumer, 19,158; Paul, Lib., 12,051.

1992, Clinton, Dem., 2,239,164; Bush, Rep., 1,791,841; Perot, Ind., 902,667; Marrou, Libertarian, 21,477; Fulani, New Alliance, 4,661.

1996, Clinton, Dem., 2,215,819; Dole, Rep., 1,801,169; Perot, Ref., 430,984; Browne, Libertarian, 28,000; Phillips, Constitutional, 19,552; Hagelin, Natural Law, 5,783.

Rhode Island

City	1996 Clinton (D)	1996 Dole (R)	1996 Perot (RF)	1992 Clinton (D)	1992 Bush (R)	1992 Perot (I)
Cranston . .	20,901	9,098	3,457	18,589	12,450	8,331
East Providence. . . .	12,846	4,199	1,971	11,701	5,843	4,661
Pawtucket .	14,719	3,877	2,508	14,177	6,322	6,244
Providence.	29,450	7,068	2,733	32,536	11,519	7,816
Warwick . .	23,152	10,414	4,541	20,504	13,348	10,526
Other	131,982	70,027	28,513	115,792	82,119	67,467
Totals. . . .	**233,050**	**104,683**	**43,723**	**213,299**	**131,601**	**105,045**

Rhode Island Vote Since 1948

1948, Truman, Dem., 188,736; Dewey, Rep., 135,787; Wallace, Prog., 2,619; Thomas, Soc., 429; Teichert, Soc. Labor, 131.

1952, Eisenhower, Rep., 210,935; Stevenson, Dem., 203,293; Hallinan, Prog., 187; Hass, Soc. Labor, 83.

1956, Eisenhower, Rep., 225,819; Stevenson, Dem., 161,790.

1960, Kennedy, Dem., 258,032; Nixon, Rep., 147,502.

1964, Johnson, Dem., 315,463; Goldwater, Rep., 74,615.

1968, Nixon, Rep., 122,359; Humphrey, Dem., 246,518; Wallace, 3d Party, 15,678; Halstead, Soc. Workers, 383.

1972, Nixon, Rep., 220,383; McGovern, Dem., 194,645; Jenness, Soc. Workers, 729.

1976, Carter, Dem., 227,636; Ford, Rep., 181,249; MacBride, Libertarian, 715; Camejo, Soc. Workers, 462; Hall, Com., 334; Levin, Soc. Labor, 188.

1980, Reagan, Rep., 154,793; Carter, Dem., 198,342; Anderson, Ind., 59,819; Clark, Libertarian, 2,458; Hall, Com., 218; McReynolds, Soc., 170; DeBerry, Soc. Workers, 90; Griswold, Workers World, 77.

1984, Reagan, Rep., 212,080; Mondale, Dem., 197,106; Bergland, Libertarian, 277.

1988, Bush, Rep., 177,761; Dukakis, Dem., 225,123; Paul, Lib., 825; Fulani, New Alliance, 280.

1992, Clinton, Dem., 213,299; Bush, Rep., 131,601; Perot, Ind., 105,045; Fulani, New Alliance, 1,878.

1996, Clinton, Dem., 233,050; Dole, Rep., 104,683; Perot, Ref., 43,723; Nader, Green, 6,040; Browne, Libertarian, 1,109; Phillips, Taxpayers, 1,021; Hagelin, Natural Law, 435; Moorehead, Workers World, 186.

South Carolina

County	1996 Clinton (D)	1996 Dole (R)	1996 Perot (RF)	1992 Clinton (D)	1992 Bush (R)	1992 Perot (I)
Abbeville . . .	3,493	3,054	537	3,968	3,317	1,036
Aiken.	14,314	26,539	1,984	14,802	25,731	6,056
Allendale . . .	2,222	941	87	2,159	1,049	212
Anderson . . .	17,460	24,137	3,896	16,072	24,793	6,966
Bamberg . . .	3,380	1,715	192	3,426	1,906	360
Barnwell. . . .	3,620	3,808	310	3,344	4,026	752
Beaufort. . . .	15,764	17,575	1,838	11,466	14,735	4,966
Berkeley. . . .	13,358	17,691	1,922	12,533	18,048	4,632
Calhoun	2,716	2,520	316	2,770	2,418	564
Charleston . .	43,571	48,675	3,514	40,095	47,403	10,354
Cherokee . . .	5,821	6,689	1,064	5,453	6,887	2,186
Chester	5,108	3,157	758	5,458	3,451	1,350
Chesterfield. .	5,734	4,028	768	5,691	4,183	1,315
Clarendon . .	5,930	3,841	395	6,033	4,147	744
Colleton	5,329	4,462	550	5,455	4,545	1,245
Darlington. . .	8,943	8,220	898	9,090	8,912	1,863
Dillon.	3,992	2,774	275	4,953	3,575	831
Dorchester . .	9,931	15,283	1,591	9,160	15,004	3,648
Edgefield . . .	3,576	3,640	244	3,433	3,339	596
Fairfield	4,719	2,414	284	4,867	2,518	652
Florence. . . .	15,804	18,490	1,563	15,569	19,802	3,499
Georgetown. .	8,298	7,023	950	7,494	6,870	1,840
Greenville. . .	41,605	71,210	6,761	34,651	65,066	13,699
Greenwood. .	8,193	8,865	985	7,621	9,079	2,101
Hampton . . .	4,828	2,111	344	4,332	2,402	564
Horry.	23,722	26,159	4,446	18,896	23,489	8,472
Jasper	4,053	2,024	348	3,453	1,725	549
Kershaw. . . .	6,764	8,513	996	6,585	8,499	2,150
Lancaster. . .	8,752	7,544	1,598	8,307	7,757	2,563
Laurens	7,055	8,057	1,341	6,638	8,347	2,157
Lee	3,588	1,973	320	4,454	2,730	611
Lexington . . .	18,907	39,658	3,703	18,312	41,759	8,652
McCormick . .	1,858	1,104	148	1,846	899	295
Marion	6,359	3,595	356	5,843	3,647	822
Marlboro . . .	5,348	2,148	494	5,111	2,526	895
Newberry . . .	4,804	5,670	682	4,896	5,980	1,393
Oconee	7,398	10,503	1,961	6,617	10,379	3,405
Orangeburg. .	18,610	10,494	1,112	18,440	11,328	2,383
Pickens	8,369	17,151	2,211	8,275	17,008	4,128
Richland. . . .	52,222	39,092	3,158	53,648	43,744	7,918
Saluda	2,486	2,825	371	2,393	2,968	833
Spartanburg. .	26,814	35,972	3,885	25,488	37,707	8,900
Sumter.	12,198	12,080	933	11,852	12,576	2,062
Union.	5,407	3,855	749	4,644	4,647	1,371
Williamsburg	6,987	3,957	375	8,077	5,289	864
York	16,873	22,222	3,173	15,844	21,297	6,418
Totals	**506,283**	**573,458**	**64,386**	**479,514**	**577,507**	**138,872**

South Carolina Vote Since 1948

1948, Thurmond, States' Rights, 102,607; Truman, Dem., 34,423; Dewey, Rep., 5,386; Wallace, Prog., 154; Thomas, Soc., 1.
1952, Eisenhower ran on two tickets. Under state law vote cast for two Eisenhower slates of electors could not be combined. Eisenhower, Ind., 158,289; Rep., 9,793; total, 168,082; Stevenson, Dem., 173,004; Hamblen, Proh., 1.
1956, Eisenhower, Rep., 75,700; Stevenson, Dem., 136,372; Byrd, Ind., 88,509; Andrews, Ind., 2.
1960, Kennedy, Dem., 198,129; Nixon, Rep., 188,558; write-in, 1.
1964, Johnson, Dem., 215,700; Goldwater, Rep., 309,048; write-ins: Nixon, 1, Wallace, 5; Powell, 1; Thurmond, 1.
1968, Nixon, Rep., 254,062; Humphrey, Dem., 197,486; Wallace, 3d Party, 215,430.
1972, Nixon, Rep., 477,044; McGovern, Dem., 184,559; United Citizens, 2,265; Schmitz, Amer., 10,075; write-in, 17.
1976, Carter, Dem., 450,807; Ford, Rep., 346,149; Anderson, Amer., 2,996; Maddox, Amer. Ind., 1,950; write-in, 681.
1980, Reagan, Rep., 439,277; Carter, Dem., 428,220; Anderson, Ind., 13,868; Clark, Libertarian, 4,807; Rarick, Amer. Ind., 2,086.
1984, Reagan, Rep., 615,539; Mondale, Dem., 344,459; Bergland, Libertarian, 4,359.
1988, Bush, Rep., 606,443; Dukakis, Dem., 370,554; Paul, Lib., 4,935; Fulani, United Citizens, 4,077.
1992, Clinton, Dem., 479,514; Bush, Rep., 577,507; Perot, Ind., 138,872; Marrou, Libertarian, 2,719; Phillips, U.S. Taxpayers, 2,680; Fulani, New Alliance, 1,235.
1996, Dole, Rep., 573,458; Clinton, Dem., 506,283; Perot, Ref./Patriot, 64,386; Browne, Libertarian, 4,271; Phillips, Taxpayers, 2,043; Hagelin, Natural Law, 1,248.

South Dakota

County	1996 Clinton (D)	1996 Dole (R)	1996 Perot (RF)	1992 Clinton (D)	1992 Bush (R)	1992 Perot (I)
Aurora	664	709	199	680	594	435
Beadle	3,984	3,670	842	3,925	3,363	1,819
Bennett	507	539	93	413	556	221
Bon Homme	1,569	1,428	391	1,294	1,212	836
Brookings	5,105	5,112	979	4,645	4,698	2,614
Brown	7,913	6,801	1,622	7,521	6,665	3,812
Brule	1,091	981	281	1,060	908	687
Buffalo	465	134	35	282	137	72
Butte	1,132	1,947	541	973	1,674	1,039
Campbell	202	623	140	222	574	252
Chas. Mix	1,913	1,711	390	1,639	1,570	886
Clark	956	998	272	799	803	761
Clay	2,980	2,008	505	2,826	1,869	1,303
Codington	4,722	4,995	1,239	3,701	3,943	3,262
Corson	539	533	216	444	483	321
Custer	1,122	1,740	418	1,078	1,422	845
Davison	3,364	3,371	737	3,285	3,111	1,706
Day	1,840	1,282	395	1,578	1,161	973
Deuel	1,090	955	275	880	778	761
Dewey	1,114	657	195	766	642	340
Douglas	524	1,210	161	481	1,175	403
Edmunds	973	1,055	263	894	944	415
Fall River	1,357	1,636	417	1,416	1,533	792
Faulk	493	726	165	488	658	281
Grant	1,805	1,782	471	1,484	1,595	1,018
Gregory	923	1,208	286	879	1,027	688
Haakon	284	887	110	209	860	245
Hamlin	1,101	1,352	285	826	1,133	774
Hand	803	1,187	250	785	1,130	624
Hanson	541	801	170	566	522	341
Harding	151	537	90	139	515	225
Hughes	2,788	4,469	531	2,578	4,325	1,160
Hutchinson	1,285	2,177	409	1,211	2,002	920
Hyde	309	493	95	301	440	211
Jackson/ Washabaugh	423	646	88	351	627	184
Jerauld	656	530	151	600	518	346
Jones	184	463	75	166	454	154
Kingsbury	1,357	1,297	320	1,267	1,113	744
Lake	2,526	1,966	593	2,388	1,890	1,299
Lawrence	3,568	4,430	1,308	3,157	3,770	2,673
Lincoln	3,643	4,201	682	2,943	3,365	1,593
Lyman	646	726	130	486	669	311
McCook	1,166	1,292	245	1,167	1,177	617
McPherson	463	1,080	182	478	945	322
Marshall	1,185	861	189	1,056	810	427
Meade	2,960	4,984	1,133	2,694	4,724	2,611
Mellette	302	417	67	277	417	140
Miner	739	571	170	698	543	332
Minnehaha	29,790	27,432	4,425	27,016	25,081	11,496
Moody	1,443	1,024	284	1,473	898	715
Pennington	12,784	19,293	3,149	11,106	18,052	8,358
Perkins	460	983	225	566	872	541
Potter	534	979	181	493	901	375
Roberts	2,186	1,646	474	1,716	1,437	954
Sanborn	647	630	151	632	595	376
Shannon	1,926	253	87	1,267	225	137
Spink	1,636	1,651	360	1,732	1,527	839
Stanley	454	795	121	427	719	240
Sully	321	592	106	273	565	167
Todd	1,380	482	108	915	456	246
Tripp	1,088	1,680	337	1,046	1,459	848
Turner	1,682	1,970	385	1,507	1,906	867
Union	2,378	2,234	555	2,210	1,784	1,085
Walworth	939	1,461	366	829	1,439	628
Yankton	3,775	3,885	1,073	3,404	3,430	2,511
Ziebach	483	375	62	280	328	117
Totals	**139,333**	**150,543**	**31,250**	**124,888**	**136,718**	**73,295**

South Dakota Vote Since 1948

1948, Truman, Dem., 117,653; Dewey, Rep., 129,651; Wallace, Prog., 2,801.
1952, Eisenhower, Rep., 203,857; Stevenson, Dem., 90,426.
1956, Eisenhower, Rep., 171,569; Stevenson, Dem., 122,288.
1960, Kennedy, Dem., 128,070; Nixon, Rep., 178,417.
1964, Johnson, Dem., 163,010; Goldwater, Rep., 130,108.
1968, Nixon, Rep., 149,841; Humphrey, Dem., 118,023; Wallace, 3d Party, 13,400.
1972, Nixon, Rep., 166,476; McGovern, Dem., 139,945; Jenness, Soc. Workers, 994.
1976, Carter, Dem., 147,068; Ford, Rep., 151,505; MacBride, Libertarian, 1,619; Hall, Com., 318; Camejo, Soc. Workers, 168.
1980, Reagan, Rep., 198,343; Carter, Dem., 103,855; Anderson, Ind., 21,431; Clark, Libertarian, 3,824; Pulley, Soc. Workers, 250.
1984, Reagan, Rep., 200,267; Mondale, Dem., 116,113.
1988, Bush, Rep., 165,415; Dukakis, Dem., 145,560; Paul, Lib., 1,060; Fulani, New Alliance, 730.
1992, Clinton, Dem., 124,888; Bush, Rep., 136,718; Perot, Ind., 73,295.
1996, Dole, Rep., 150,543; Clinton, Dem., 139,333; Perot, Ref., 31,250; Browne, Libertarian, 1,472; Phillips, Taxpayers, 912; Hagelin, Natural Law, 316.

Tennessee

County	1996 Clinton (D)	1996 Dole (R)	1996 Perot (RF)	1992 Clinton (D)	1992 Bush (R)	1992 Perot (I)
Anderson	13,457	11,943	1,817	13,482	11,838	3,149
Bedford	5,735	4,634	823	5,978	3,836	1,541
Benton	4,341	2,395	663	3,896	1,625	559
Bledsoe	1,621	1,626	251	1,884	1,776	352
Blount	14,687	19,310	2,556	14,655	18,415	4,468
Bradley	9,095	15,478	1,856	9,889	16,528	3,212
Campbell	6,122	4,393	785	6,756	4,897	1,240
Cannon	2,318	1,468	361	2,593	1,229	495
Carroll	4,912	4,206	697	5,741	4,842	1,139
Carter	6,218	10,540	1,383	6,502	10,712	1,898
Cheatham	4,883	4,283	705	4,817	3,496	1,433
Chester	1,922	2,746	203	2,317	2,834	439
Claiborne	3,861	4,023	727	4,509	4,065	860
Clay	1,559	1,108	316	1,922	1,072	223
Cocke	3,326	4,481	798	3,495	5,298	1,124
Coffee	7,951	7,038	1,205	8,534	6,047	2,420
Crockett	2,256	1,872	201	2,657	2,180	507
Cumberland	6,676	8,096	1,399	6,393	7,116	2,200
Davidson	110,805	78,453	9,018	106,355	76,567	20,184
Decatur	2,262	1,712	229	2,633	1,667	351
De Kalb	3,213	1,696	342	4,382	1,714	608
Dickson	7,458	5,283	996	7,863	4,450	1,730
Dyer	5,602	5,059	676	5,845	5,668	1,241
Fayette	4,655	4,406	416	4,211	3,713	657
Fentress	2,332	2,307	386	2,730	2,391	606
Franklin	6,929	5,296	1,057	7,773	4,507	1,837
Gibson	8,851	6,614	891	9,555	7,161	1,536
Giles	4,948	3,269	733	5,601	2,827	1,309
Grainger	2,162	2,875	382	2,242	2,772	513
Greene	6,885	9,779	1,604	7,857	9,912	2,930
Grundy	2,596	1,094	326	2,997	1,004	366
Hamblen	7,006	9,797	1,106	7,114	8,898	1,760
Hamilton	48,008	55,205	6,699	46,770	53,476	14,400
Hancock	760	1,259	116	1,000	1,274	151
Hardeman	4,859	2,961	346	4,832	3,122	594
Hardin	3,508	3,980	594	3,922	3,875	734
Hawkins	6,367	8,164	1,282	6,623	7,758	1,847
Haywood	3,565	2,293	154	3,511	2,518	331
Henderson	2,841	4,002	408	3,502	4,719	785
Henry	6,153	4,272	992	6,797	3,661	1,588
Hickman	3,917	2,002	460	4,093	1,820	795
Houston	1,868	742	182	2,012	648	280
Humphreys	3,675	1,892	423	3,875	1,641	609
Jackson	2,889	944	289	3,208	708	332
Jefferson	4,688	6,446	882	4,740	6,184	1,385
Johnson	1,698	3,137	489	1,781	3,170	574
Knox	61,158	70,761	6,402	59,702	66,607	15,669
Lake	1,273	589	110	1,449	680	151
Lauderdale	4,349	2,481	308	4,452	2,928	561
Lawrence	6,188	6,115	973	6,816	5,608	1,403

County	1996 Clinton (D)	1996 Dole (R)	1996 Perot (RF)	1992 Clinton (D)	1992 Bush (R)	1992 Perot (I)
Lewis. . . .	1,971	1,298	316	2,491	1,218	434
Lincoln. . .	4,361	4,551	761	5,063	3,814	1,371
Loudon . .	5,552	7,097	889	5,414	6,444	1,602
McMinn . .	5,987	7,655	1,033	6,682	7,453	1,812
McNairy . .	4,050	3,960	519	4,691	4,093	774
Macon . . .	2,240	2,481	421	2,961	2,299	443
Madison. .	13,577	14,908	968	13,629	14,869	2,634
Marion . . .	5,194	3,166	768	5,589	3,262	1,186
Marshall. .	4,447	2,781	603	4,491	2,516	1,050
Maury . . .	10,367	8,737	1,366	9,997	7,440	2,821
Meigs . . .	1,476	1,228	245	1,673	1,355	453
Monroe . .	4,872	5,257	713	5,384	6,025	936
Montgomery	16,498	15,133	1,781	14,507	13,011	3,753
Moore . . .	935	846	177	1,151	661	327
Morgan . .	2,767	2,070	446	3,190	2,306	658
Obion . . .	6,226	4,310	932	6,497	4,812	1,494
Overton . .	3,800	1,756	431	4,489	1,657	468
Perry	1,444	747	178	1,889	708	317
Pickett . . .	901	1,046	116	1,144	1,094	121
Polk.	2,450	1,910	377	2,583	1,584	419
Putnam . .	10,047	9,093	1,487	10,858	7,998	2,473
Rhea	3,969	4,476	694	4,289	4,860	1,163
Roane . . .	9,744	9,044	1,438	9,812	8,719	2,396
Robertson.	8,465	6,685	993	8,498	5,271	1,978
Rutherford	22,815	24,565	3,787	21,084	18,877	7,005
Scott	2,506	2,646	431	2,730	3,011	643
Sequatchie	1,598	1,391	288	1,754	1,381	405
Sevier . . .	7,136	11,847	1,650	6,719	11,714	2,760
Shelby . . .	179,663	136,315	8,307	191,322	153,310	20,223
Smith. . . .	3,812	1,857	346	5,061	1,482	486
Stewart . .	2,962	1,306	386	2,779	1,046	487
Sullivan . .	20,571	29,296	3,555	20,935	28,801	6,730
Sumner . .	19,205	20,863	2,783	19,387	17,401	5,177
Tipton . . .	6,596	7,585	799	5,652	6,757	1,279
Trousdale.	1,615	683	190	1,846	565	243
Unicoi . . .	2,131	3,122	447	2,375	3,344	709
Union. . . .	2,421	2,253	385	2,478	2,274	580
Van Buren	1,010	504	128	1,329	555	191
Warren. . .	6,389	4,226	917	7,189	3,704	1,415
Washington	13,259	18,960	2,237	13,071	18,206	4,002
Wayne . . .	1,574	2,715	323	1,868	2,955	424
Weakley. .	5,657	4,622	873	5,691	4,800	1,355
White. . . .	3,592	2,498	505	4,102	2,118	821
Williamson	15,231	27,699	2,071	13,053	22,015	5,026
Wilson . . .	13,655	13,817	1,841	13,861	12,061	3,848
Totals . . .	**909,146**	**863,530**	**105,918**	**933,521**	**841,300**	**199,968**

Tennessee Vote Since 1948

1948, Truman, Dem., 270,402; Dewey, Rep., 202,914; Thurmond, States' Rights, 73,815; Wallace, Prog., 1,864; Thomas, Soc., 1,288.

1952, Eisenhower, Rep., 446,147; Stevenson, Dem., 443,710; Hamblen, Proh., 1,432; Hallinan, Prog., 885; MacArthur, Christian Nationalist, 379.

1956, Eisenhower, Rep., 462,288; Stevenson, Dem., 456,507; Andrews, Ind., 19,820; Holtwick, Proh., 789.

1960, Kennedy, Dem., 481,453; Nixon, Rep., 556,577; Faubus, States' Rights, 11,304; Decker, Proh., 2,458.

1964, Johnson, Dem., 635,047; Goldwater, Rep., 508,965; write-in, 34.

1968, Nixon, Rep., 472,592; Humphrey, Dem., 351,233; Wallace, 3d Party, 424,792.

1972, Nixon, Rep., 813,147; McGovern, Dem., 357,293; Schmitz, Amer., 30,373; write-in, 369.

1976, Carter, Dem., 825,879; Ford, Rep., 633,969; Anderson, Amer., 5,769; McCarthy, Ind., 5,004; Maddox, Amer. Ind., 2,303; MacBride, Libertarian, 1,375; Hall, Com., 547; LaRouche, U.S. Labor, 512; Bubar, Proh., 442; Miller, Ind., 316; write-in, 230.

1980, Reagan, Rep., 787,761; Carter, Dem., 783,051; Anderson, Ind., 35,991; Clark, Libertarian, 7,116; Commoner, Citizens, 1,112; Bubar, Statesman, 521; McReynolds, Soc., 519; Hall, Com., 503; DeBerry, Soc. Workers, 490; Griswold, Workers World, 400; write-ins, 152.

1984, Reagan, Rep., 990,212; Mondale, Dem., 711,714; Bergland, Libertarian, 3,072.

1988, Bush, Rep., 947,233; Dukakis, Dem., 679,794; Paul, Ind., 2,041; Duke, Ind., 1,807.

1992, Clinton, Dem., 933,521; Bush, Rep., 841,300; Perot, Ind., 199,968; Marrou, Libertarian, 1,847.

1996, Clinton, Dem., 909,146; Dole, Rep., 863,530; Perot, Ind. (Ref.), 105,918; Nader, Ind., 6,427; Browne, Ind., 5,020; Phillips, Ind., 1,818; Collins, Ind., 688; Hagelin, Ind., 636; Michael, Ind., 408; Dodge, Ind., 324.

Texas

County	1996 Clinton (D)	1996 Dole (R)	1996 Perot (RF)	1992 Clinton (D)	1992 Bush (R)	1992 Perot (I)
Anderson . .	5,693	6,458	1,170	5,322	5,598	3,519
Andrews . .	1,181	2,360	431	1,081	2,266	875
Angelina . .	11,346	11,789	2,160	10,318	9,722	6,204
Aransas. . .	2,964	3,769	655	2,246	2,826	1,676
Archer	1,235	1,974	437	1,284	1,560	1,106
Armstrong .	272	582	75	278	561	187
Atascosa . .	4,259	4,102	813	3,766	3,806	2,035
Austin	2,719	4,669	577	2,278	4,015	1,585
Bailey	706	1,246	109	677	1,308	376
Bandera. . .	1,383	3,700	520	1,059	2,674	1,537
Bastrop . . .	6,773	6,323	1,342	6,252	4,980	3,240
Baylor	955	860	262	990	611	529
Bee.	4,561	3,611	539	4,083	3,633	1,367
Bell	22,638	30,348	3,666	18,684	24,936	11,026
Bexar	180,308	161,619	17,822	172,513	168,816	72,110
Blanco. . . .	1,028	1,919	330	891	1,370	830
Borden . . .	93	194	45	106	184	87
Bosque . . .	2,427	2,840	739	2,173	2,300	1,999
Bowie	13,657	12,750	2,760	11,825	11,776	6,659
Brazoria. . .	22,959	36,392	5,869	21,861	30,384	18,954
Brazos. . . .	13,968	22,082	2,215	14,819	23,943	10,372
Brewster . .	1,643	1,438	299	1,383	1,127	712
Briscoe . . .	408	416	65	430	360	164
Brooks. . . .	2,945	413	108	2,856	585	318
Brown	4,138	6,524	1,081	4,264	5,313	3,034
Burleson . .	2,419	2,174	347	2,511	2,013	1,179
Burnet	4,123	5,744	1,108	3,638	4,272	2,865
Caldwell. . .	3,961	3,239	545	3,794	2,749	1,776
Calhoun. . .	2,753	2,832	507	2,550	2,640	1,579
Callahan . .	1,666	2,480	534	1,694	2,134	1,452
Cameron . .	34,891	18,434	2,760	29,435	20,123	9,286
Camp	1,912	1,488	252	1,938	1,219	821
Carson . . .	742	1,742	227	825	1,647	578
Cass	5,691	4,066	1,038	5,476	3,999	2,168
Castro	1,107	1,231	144	1,113	1,307	485
Chambers .	2,876	4,101	818	2,832	3,398	2,122
Cherokee . .	5,185	6,483	971	5,003	5,847	3,273
Childress . .	719	1,072	165	881	1,033	421
Clay	1,690	1,997	465	1,919	1,586	1,397
Cochran. . .	541	667	127	454	750	255
Coke.	595	790	157	580	640	393
Coleman . .	1,488	1,793	349	1,579	1,462	1,095
Collin.	37,854	83,750	10,443	24,508	60,514	43,287
Collingsworth.	581	729	118	635	697	265
Colorado . .	2,795	3,381	574	2,442	3,286	1,421
Comal	7,132	16,763	1,903	6,312	12,651	5,841
Comanche .	2,138	2,123	511	2,296	1,666	1,281
Concho . . .	434	488	107	489	414	329
Cooke	3,782	7,320	1,150	3,105	5,299	4,658
Coryell. . . .	5,300	7,143	1,443	4,157	6,144	3,974
Cottle	404	331	77	542	245	235
Crane	616	984	201	514	918	412
Crockett. . .	684	714	147	653	623	368
Crosby . . .	1,122	968	189	1,010	1,006	313
Culberson .	804	329	99	424	251	171
Dallam. . . .	483	970	170	434	922	325
Dallas	255,766	260,058	36,759	231,412	256,007	170,571
Dawson . . .	1,612	2,319	232	1,639	2,691	518
Deaf Smith .	1,655	3,051	310	1,642	3,137	772
Delta	849	744	146	864	599	551
Denton . . .	36,138	65,313	9,294	27,891	48,492	39,653
DeWitt. . . .	2,074	3,577	483	2,127	3,238	1,346
Dickens . . .	509	421	117	536	373	250
Dimmit. . . .	2,242	604	128	3,172	844	361
Donley. . . .	495	988	97	578	893	260
Duval	3,958	543	136	4,006	698	326
Eastland . .	2,594	3,272	705	2,738	2,830	1,698
Ector.	12,017	17,746	2,511	11,130	18,161	6,668
Edwards . .	437	511	60	254	460	171
Ellis.	10,832	16,046	2,750	9,537	13,564	10,303
El Paso . . .	83,964	43,255	6,300	67,715	47,224	19,738
Erath.	3,664	4,750	1,134	3,531	3,835	3,046
Falls	3,256	2,260	479	2,761	1,826	1,185
Fannin. . . .	4,276	3,495	980	4,164	2,510	2,919
Fayette . . .	3,119	4,195	708	2,923	3,789	2,088
Fisher	1,142	537	170	1,242	539	442
Floyd.	986	1,530	126	947	1,676	385
Foard	355	166	52	435	207	152
Fort Bend. .	38,163	49,945	4,363	29,992	41,039	16,853
Franklin . . .	1,484	1,575	386	1,338	1,058	942
Freestone .	2,630	2,888	568	2,445	2,316	1,596
Frio.	2,593	1,225	253	2,377	1,275	654
Gaines. . . .	1,012	1,812	353	1,095	2,138	696
Galveston .	38,458	35,251	5,897	38,623	31,303	20,103
Garza	703	946	103	558	982	345
Gillespie . .	1,655	5,867	542	1,600	4,712	2,018
Glasscock .	70	382	30	100	379	93
Goliad	1,135	1,335	148	1,069	1,236	521
Gonzales . .	2,110	2,687	354	2,006	2,502	1,018
Gray	2,114	6,102	568	2,426	6,105	1,810
Grayson. . .	14,338	17,169	3,745	12,547	12,322	13,327
Gregg	13,659	21,611	2,079	12,797	20,542	8,437
Grimes . . .	2,584	2,564	538	2,594	2,402	1,213
Guadalupe .	8,079	14,254	1,811	6,567	10,818	5,618
Hale	3,204	5,905	605	2,761	6,098	1,357
Hall.	750	626	94	819	631	263
Hamilton . .	1,200	1,493	323	1,100	1,232	921
Hansford . .	343	1,493	105	345	1,660	398

County	1996 Clinton (D)	1996 Dole (R)	1996 Perot (RF)	1992 Clinton (D)	1992 Bush (R)	1992 Perot (I)
Hardeman	750	610	168	954	614	362
Hardin	7,179	8,529	2,112	6,753	5,885	4,129
Harris	386,726	421,462	42,364	360,171	406,778	172,922
Harrison	10,307	9,835	1,427	9,538	8,733	4,371
Hartley	463	1,242	101	406	1,081	308
Haskell	1,374	966	225	1,438	852	562
Hays	11,580	12,865	1,990	10,842	10,008	6,252
Hemphill	344	986	104	479	989	232
Henderson	10,085	10,345	2,274	9,105	8,368	6,746
Hidalgo	56,335	24,437	3,536	51,205	26,976	9,757
Hill	3,988	4,401	1,052	3,929	3,669	2,752
Hockley	2,170	4,230	519	2,301	4,261	1,291
Hood	5,459	7,575	1,445	4,359	5,313	4,457
Hopkins	4,522	4,341	1,034	4,085	3,398	3,147
Houston	3,383	3,443	585	3,250	3,067	1,690
Howard	3,732	5,007	1,037	3,735	5,129	1,984
Hudspeth	427	367	92	364	325	178
Hunt	8,801	10,746	2,225	7,452	9,739	7,387
Hutchinson	2,553	6,350	864	2,833	6,034	1,993
Irion	213	386	86	256	283	290
Jack	1,019	1,162	301	1,254	1,041	1,045
Jackson	1,785	2,533	309	1,722	2,451	976
Jasper	5,039	4,523	1,041	5,658	3,870	2,539
Jeff Davis	370	482	99	321	360	187
Jefferson	45,854	32,821	5,314	48,405	29,622	17,242
Jim Hogg	1,437	307	64	1,520	478	107
Jim Wells	7,116	2,989	430	7,812	3,311	1,413
Johnson	12,817	16,246	3,250	12,030	13,473	11,573
Jones	2,422	2,351	614	2,400	2,088	1,436
Karnes	2,154	1,869	291	1,897	1,990	802
Kaufman	7,383	8,697	1,831	6,498	6,578	5,913
Kendall	2,092	5,940	620	1,374	4,162	1,773
Kenedy	133	71	4	87	69	18
Kent	260	187	67	271	175	163
Kerr	4,192	11,173	1,236	3,707	8,787	3,790
Kimble	521	898	131	467	790	354
King	46	97	29	54	79	56
Kinney	503	650	97	598	634	299
Kleberg	5,136	3,391	431	5,109	3,897	1,470
Knox	785	599	149	854	521	438
Lamar	6,075	6,393	1,198	6,328	5,778	4,093
Lamb	1,683	2,593	283	1,737	2,998	709
Lampasas	1,819	3,008	509	1,508	2,233	1,432
LaSalle	1,522	570	85	1,522	586	211
Lavaca	2,575	3,697	551	2,700	3,362	1,696
Lee	2,008	2,354	421	1,847	2,108	1,088
Leon	2,217	2,839	499	2,042	2,212	1,251
Liberty	6,877	7,784	2,011	7,036	6,959	4,311
Limestone	3,236	2,691	693	3,188	2,358	1,505
Lipscomb	357	869	115	338	839	270
Live Oak	1,372	1,929	292	1,345	1,805	806
Llano	2,633	4,290	762	2,409	3,056	1,799
Loving	14	48	15	20	31	45
Lubbock	22,786	47,304	3,996	22,240	48,847	11,618
Lynn	903	1,151	136	902	1,233	291
McCulloch	1,231	1,465	296	1,393	1,108	986
McLennan	27,050	30,666	5,131	25,903	28,473	15,505
McMullen	117	274	35	78	274	89
Madison	1,470	1,576	293	1,553	1,544	778
Marion	2,028	1,260	353	2,156	1,245	882
Martin	643	973	140	641	986	356
Mason	618	949	151	570	776	364
Matagorda	5,374	5,876	1,190	4,759	5,328	3,045
Maverick	5,307	1,050	202	4,540	2,002	771
Medina	3,880	5,710	715	3,650	4,912	2,167
Menard	490	443	102	553	354	367
Midland	9,513	25,382	2,079	9,160	24,143	7,880
Milam	3,869	3,019	657	3,542	2,414	1,495
Mills	748	1,044	230	753	702	530
Mitchell	1,213	949	232	1,353	1,128	604
Montague	2,718	3,029	842	2,885	2,304	2,330
Montgomery	20,722	51,011	6,065	18,551	39,976	19,203
Moore	1,358	3,353	359	1,361	3,147	976
Morris	2,973	1,449	402	3,028	1,400	1,138
Motley	164	380	56	256	446	117
Nacogdoches	7,641	10,361	1,352	6,937	9,864	4,803
Navarro	6,078	5,236	1,140	6,006	4,897	3,800
Newton	2,554	1,409	474	3,249	1,212	1,032
Nolan	2,582	2,166	613	2,490	1,993	1,455
Nueces	50,009	37,470	5,103	46,317	36,781	17,374
Ochiltree	467	2,448	167	557	2,419	576
Oldham	213	583	77	225	583	177
Orange	13,741	12,560	2,836	15,305	9,793	7,321
Palo Pinto	3,938	3,666	1,011	3,392	2,852	3,010
Panola	4,168	4,008	777	3,950	3,473	1,906
Parker	9,447	14,580	2,703	7,934	10,321	9,148
Parmer	676	2,042	160	637	1,829	564
Pecos	1,816	1,730	369	1,778	1,836	895
Polk	6,360	6,473	1,347	5,942	5,390	2,884
Potter	9,273	14,995	1,799	9,527	13,510	4,655
Presidio	1,205	383	111	1,189	400	290
Rains	1,265	1,123	335	1,108	975	890
Randall	9,177	28,266	1,985	9,119	24,971	6,340
Reagan	407	645	101	337	651	259
Real	414	845	178	463	787	386
Red River	2,339	1,783	433	2,686	1,735	1,228
Reeves	2,279	1,007	245	2,569	1,244	734
Refugio	1,635	1,376	222	1,531	1,469	716
Roberts	122	421	40	126	391	99
Robertson	2,912	1,944	315	2,927	1,707	963
Rockwall	3,289	8,319	1,121	2,397	6,427	4,393
Runnels	1,417	1,941	396	1,401	1,653	1,279
Rusk	5,988	8,423	1,072	5,391	7,560	3,575
Sabine	1,913	1,660	334	2,288	1,490	894
San Augustine	1,924	1,296	324	1,737	1,243	667
San Jacinto	2,771	2,878	810	2,846	2,494	1,653
San Patricio	8,132	7,678	1,085	8,202	7,456	3,178
San Saba	726	991	194	716	723	660
Schleicher	505	587	111	420	452	355
Scurry	2,099	2,929	813	1,609	2,670	1,826
Shackelford	502	792	169	484	623	422
Shelby	3,720	3,482	815	3,986	3,217	1,487
Sherman	243	809	89	261	851	256
Smith	18,265	32,171	2,933	17,514	27,753	13,569
Somervell	993	1,099	273	782	872	903
Starr	6,312	756	157	7,668	1,209	345
Stephens	1,218	1,714	336	1,115	1,573	1,062
Sterling	186	394	86	127	322	182
Stonewall	487	323	105	561	242	322
Sutton	508	688	102	524	687	387
Swisher	1,224	1,159	195	1,413	989	541
Tarrant	170,431	208,312	28,715	156,230	183,387	129,998
Taylor	13,213	23,682	2,912	12,382	22,614	10,331
Terrell	278	185	47	325	176	128
Terry	1,272	2,013	269	1,461	2,309	619
Throckmorton	285	360	90	401	389	228
Titus	3,725	3,438	744	3,625	3,024	2,146
Tom Green	11,782	18,112	2,757	11,437	14,989	10,244
Travis	128,970	98,454	14,008	130,546	88,105	56,158
Trinity	2,774	2,058	460	2,784	1,988	1,133
Tyler	3,340	2,804	645	3,465	2,357	1,529
Upshur	5,032	5,174	1,086	4,776	4,511	2,896
Upton	424	685	88	489	908	313
Uvalde	3,397	3,494	403	3,482	3,635	1,387
Val Verde	5,623	4,357	548	4,748	4,102	2,093
Van Zandt	5,752	7,453	1,756	5,310	5,810	5,239
Victoria	8,238	14,457	1,197	7,604	13,086	5,136
Walker	6,088	7,177	1,186	5,619	6,662	3,619
Waller	4,535	3,559	499	4,270	3,065	1,692
Ward	1,644	1,620	446	1,695	1,769	948
Washington	3,460	6,319	601	3,283	5,817	1,738
Webb	18,997	4,712	936	14,509	7,789	2,517
Wharton	5,176	6,163	871	4,643	5,503	2,624
Wheeler	750	1,355	174	938	1,458	367
Wichita	15,775	20,495	3,371	17,021	17,956	11,478
Wilbarger	1,730	2,037	465	1,924	1,959	1,453
Willacy	3,789	1,332	241	3,359	1,490	652
Williamson	24,175	36,836	4,931	19,437	26,208	15,415
Wilson	3,713	4,530	760	3,711	3,766	2,105
Winkler	872	1,009	218	942	1,173	582
Wise	5,056	6,330	1,516	4,478	4,555	4,485
Wood	4,711	6,228	1,184	4,084	4,708	3,494
Yoakum	738	1,485	218	595	1,486	484
Young	2,394	3,647	639	2,464	2,894	2,302
Zapata	1,786	521	131	2,052	866	326
Zavala	2,629	463	91	3,058	571	237
Totals	**2,459,683**	**2,736,167**	**378,537**	**2,281,815**	**2,496,071**	**1,354,781**

Texas Vote Since 1948

1948, Truman, Dem., 750,700; Dewey, Rep., 282,240; Thurmond, States' Rights, 106,909; Wallace, Prog., 3,764; Watson, Proh., 2,758; Thomas, Soc., 874.

1952, Eisenhower, Rep., 1,102,878; Stevenson, Dem., 969,228; Hamblen, Proh., 1,983; MacArthur, Christian Nationalist, 833; MacArthur, Constitution, 730; Hallinan, Prog., 294.

1956, Eisenhower, Rep., 1,080,619; Stevenson, Dem., 859,958; Andrews, Ind., 14,591.

1960, Kennedy, Dem., 1,167,932; Nixon, Rep., 1,121,699; Sullivan, Constitution, 18,169; Decker, Proh., 3,870; write-in, 15.

1964, Johnson, Dem., 1,663,185; Goldwater, Rep., 958,566; Lightburn, Constitution, 5,060.

1968, Nixon, Rep., 1,227,844; Humphrey, Dem., 1,266,804; Wallace, 3d Party, 584,269; write-in, 489.

1972, Nixon, Rep., 2,298,896; McGovern, Dem., 1,154,289; Schmitz, Amer., 6,039; Jenness, Soc. Workers, 8,664; others, 3,393.

1976, Carter, Dem., 2,082,319; Ford, Rep., 1,953,300; McCarthy, Ind., 20,118; Anderson, Amer., 11,442; Camejo, Soc. Workers, 1,723; write-in, 2,982.

1980, Reagan, Rep., 2,510,705; Carter, Dem., 1,881,147; Anderson, Ind., 111,613; Clark, Libertarian, 37,643; write-in, 528.

1984, Reagan, Rep., 3,433,428; Mondale, Dem., 1,949,276.

1988, Bush, Rep., 3,036,829; Dukakis, Dem., 2,352,748; Paul, Lib., 30,355; Fulani, New Alliance, 7,208.

1992, Clinton, Dem., 2,281,815; Bush, Rep., 2,496,071; Perot, Ind., 1,354,781; Marrou, Libertarian, 19,699.

1996, Dole, Rep., 2,736,167; Clinton, Dem., 2,459,683; Perot, Ind. (Ref.), 378,537; Browne, Libertarian, 20,256; Phillips, Taxpayers, 7,472; Hagelin, Natural Law, 4,422.

Utah

County	1996 Clinton (D)	1996 Dole (R)	1996 Perot (RF)	1992 Clinton (D)	1992 Bush (R)	1992 Perot (I)
Beaver. . .	687	1,164	217	668	1,040	330
Box Elder.	3,170	8,373	1,578	2,186	7,712	4,507
Cache . . .	6,595	16,832	2,399	4,973	15,971	8,032
Carbon. . .	4,172	2,343	952	4,480	2,038	2,002
Daggett . .	131	237	55	122	172	117
Davis. . . .	19,301	42,768	7,495	14,924	39,087	24,105
Duchesne.	892	2,648	566	772	1,983	1,229
Emery . . .	1,371	2,033	663	1,349	1,643	1,138
Garfield . .	283	1,330	222	309	1,235	355
Grand . . .	1,199	1,384	432	1,160	1,100	991
Iron	1,887	6,550	716	1,537	5,616	1,693
Juab	928	1,290	353	823	1,237	616
Kane	304	1,682	290	295	1,241	534
Millard . . .	945	2,681	505	742	2,496	1,064
Morgan . .	859	1,659	337	520	1,339	851
Piute	176	475	59	169	429	146
Rich	179	523	88	154	525	187
Salt Lake .	117,951	127,951	27,620	100,082	117,247	91,968
San Juan .	1,675	2,139	271	1,639	2,004	576
Sanpete . .	1,568	3,631	801	1,302	2,995	1,742
Sevier . . .	1,327	4,031	670	1,039	3,160	1,671
Summit . .	4,177	3,867	971	3,013	3,133	3,060
Tooele . . .	3,992	3,881	1,244	3,270	3,676	3,011
Uintah . . .	1,714	4,743	899	1,374	3,505	2,250
Utah	18,291	69,653	8,106	14,090	61,398	24,558
Wasatch. .	1,374	2,222	558	1,042	1,822	1,234
Washington	4,816	17,637	2,069	3,364	11,310	4,623
Wayne . . .	265	741	121	236	706	251
Weber . . .	21,404	27,443	6,204	17,795	26,812	20,559
Totals . . .	**221,633**	**361,911**	**66,461**	**183,429**	**322,632**	**203,400**

Utah Vote Since 1948

1948, Truman, Dem., 149,151; Dewey, Rep., 124,402; Wallace, Prog., 2,679; Dobbs, Soc. Workers, 73.

1952, Eisenhower, Rep., 194,190; Stevenson, Dem., 135,364.

1956, Eisenhower, Rep., 215,631; Stevenson, Dem., 118,364.

1960, Kennedy, Dem., 169,248; Nixon, Rep., 205,361; Dobbs, Soc. Workers, 100.

1964, Johnson, Dem., 219,628; Goldwater, Rep., 181,785.

1968, Nixon, Rep., 238,728; Humphrey, Dem., 156,665; Wallace, 3d Party, 26,906; Halstead, Soc. Workers, 89; Peace and Freedom, 180.

1972, Nixon, Rep., 323,643; McGovern, Dem., 126,284; Schmitz, Amer., 28,549.

1976, Carter, Dem., 182,110; Ford, Rep., 337,908; Anderson, Amer., 13,304; McCarthy, Ind., 3,907; MacBride, Libertarian, 2,438; Maddox, Amer. Ind., 1,162; Camejo, Soc. Workers, 268; Hall, Com., 121.

1980, Reagan, Rep., 439,687; Carter, Dem., 124,266; Anderson, Ind., 30,284; Clark, Libertarian, 7,226; Commoner, Citizens, 1,009; Greaves, Amer., 965; Rarick, Amer. Ind., 522; Hall, Com., 139; DeBerry, Soc. Workers, 124.

1984, Reagan, Rep., 469,105; Mondale, Dem., 155,369; Bergland, Libertarian, 2,447.

1988, Bush, Rep., 428,442; Dukakis, Dem., 207,352; Paul, Lib., 7,473; Dennis, Amer., 2,158.

1992, Clinton, Dem., 183,429; Bush, Rep., 322,632; Perot, Ind., 203,400; Gritz, Populist/America First, 28,602; Marrou, Libertarian, 1,900; Hagelin, Natural Law, 1,319; LaRouche, Ind., 1,089.

1996, Dole, Rep., 361,911; Clinton, Dem., 221,633; Perot, Ref., 66,461; Nader, Green, 4,615; Browne, Libertarian, 4,129; Phillips, Taxpayers, 2,601; Templin, Ind. Amer., 1,290; Crane, Ind., 1,101; Hagelin, Natural Law, 1,085; Moorehead, Workers World, 298; Harris, Soc. Workers, 235; Dodge, Proh., 111.

Vermont

City	1996 Clinton (D)	1996 Dole (R)	1996 Perot (RF)	1992 Clinton (D)	1992 Bush (R)	1992 Perot (I)
Barre City. . .	1,890	1,107	376	1,807	1,508	1,035
Bennington. .	3,454	1,654	960	3,646	2,151	1,536
Brattleboro . .	3,016	1,195	395	3,519	1,447	847
Burlington. . .	11,600	3,762	1,309	12,508	4,462	3,241
Colchester . .	3,314	2,035	769	2,966	1,997	1,739
Essex	4,063	2,944	796	3,825	2,960	2,302
Hartford	2,106	1,290	400	2,034	1,564	793
Montpelier . .	2,458	1,118	269	2,490	1,407	657
Rutland City...	3,817	2,320	741	3,888	2,915	1,722
S. Burlington	3,929	2,274	548	3,730	2,131	1,359
Springfield . .	2,267	1,189	561	2,179	1,468	1,091
Other.	95,980	59,464	23,900	90,998	64,112	49,663
Totals	**137,894**	**80,352**	**31,024**	**133,590**	**88,122**	**65,985**

Vermont Vote Since 1948

1948, Truman, Dem., 45,557; Dewey, Rep., 75,926; Wallace, Prog., 1,279; Thomas, Soc., 585.

1952, Eisenhower, Rep., 109,717; Stevenson, Dem., 43,355; Hallinan, Prog., 282; Hoopes, Soc., 185.

1956, Eisenhower, Rep., 110,390; Stevenson, Dem., 42,549; scattered, 39.

1960, Kennedy, Dem., 69,186; Nixon, Rep., 98,131.

1964, Johnson, Dem., 107,674; Goldwater, Rep., 54,868.

1968, Nixon, Rep., 85,142; Humphrey, Dem., 70,255; Wallace, 3d Party, 5,104; Halstead, Soc. Workers, 295; Gregory, New Party, 579.

1972, Nixon, Rep., 117,149; McGovern, Dem., 68,174; Spock, Liberty Union, 1,010; Jenness, Soc. Workers, 296; scattered, 318.

1976, Carter, Dem., 77,798; Carter, Ind. Vermonter, 991; Ford, Rep., 100,387; McCarthy, Ind., 4,001; Camejo, Soc. Workers, 430; LaRouche, U.S. Labor, 196; scattered, 99.

1980, Reagan, Rep., 94,598; Carter, Dem., 81,891; Anderson, Ind., 31,760; Commoner, Citizens, 2,316; Clark, Libertarian, 1,900; McReynolds, Liberty Union, 136; Hall, Com., 118; DeBerry, Soc. Workers, 75; scattering, 413.

1984, Reagan, Rep., 135,865; Mondale, Dem., 95,730; Bergland, Libertarian, 1,002.

1988, Bush, Rep., 124,331; Dukakis, Dem., 115,775; Paul, Lib., 1,000; LaRouche, Ind., 275.

1992, Clinton, Dem., 133,590; Bush, Rep., 88,122; Perot, Ind., 65,985.

1996, Clinton, Dem., 137,894; Dole, Rep., 80,352; Perot, Ref., 31,024; Nader, Green, 5,585; Browne, Libertarian, 1,183; Hagelin, Natural Law, 498; Peron, Grass Roots, 480; Phillips, Taxpayers, 382; Hollis, Liberty Union, 292; Harris, Soc. Workers, 199.

Virginia

County	1996 Clinton (D)	1996 Dole (R)	1996 Perot (RF)	1992 Clinton (D)	1992 Bush (R)	1992 Perot (I)
Accomack. .	5,220	5,013	1,218	4,950	5,666	2,304
Albemarle. .	14,089	15,243	1,533	13,886	13,894	3,855
Alleghany . .	2,398	2,015	607	2,396	2,294	926
Amelia	1,625	2,119	323	1,534	2,062	574
Amherst . . .	4,864	5,094	835	4,101	5,482	1,268
Appomattox.	2,239	2,625	510	1,919	2,830	801
Arlington. . .	45,573	26,106	2,782	47,756	26,376	7,992
Augusta . . .	5,965	13,458	1,916	5,190	12,896	3,397
Bath	922	847	247	855	1,075	354
Bedford . . .	7,786	11,955	1,976	6,792	10,496	3,251
Bland.	939	1,167	385	1,001	1,368	408
Botetourt . .	4,576	6,404	1,138	4,349	5,904	1,819
Brunswick. .	3,442	2,059	340	3,687	2,480	479
Buchanan. .	6,551	2,785	858	7,405	3,297	815
Buckingham	2,374	1,974	392	2,193	2,368	459
Campbell . .	6,788	10,273	1,505	5,999	10,931	2,553
Caroline . . .	3,897	2,816	521	3,770	2,947	965
Carroll	3,611	5,088	1,158	3,790	5,664	1,388
Charles City	1,842	729	178	2,010	729	251
Charlotte . .	2,007	2,103	431	2,098	2,293	640
Chesterfield.	30,220	56,650	6,004	28,028	56,626	16,898
Clarke	1,906	2,201	379	1,811	1,994	802
Craig	895	979	262	965	1,008	304
Culpeper . .	3,907	5,688	787	3,444	5,226	1,640
Cumberland.	1,303	1,544	275	1,284	1,643	372
Dickenson .	3,913	2,229	660	4,839	2,574	660
Dinwiddie . .	3,871	3,503	666	3,624	3,648	1,198
Essex	1,668	1,627	188	1,583	1,897	382
Fairfax	170,150	176,033	16,134	160,186	170,488	53,012
Fauquier. . .	6,759	11,063	1,287	6,600	10,497	3,464
Floyd	1,909	2,374	545	2,026	2,575	672
Fluvanna . .	2,676	3,442	457	2,134	2,811	871
Franklin . . .	7,300	7,382	2,015	6,590	6,724	2,232
Frederick . .	5,976	10,608	1,599	4,942	9,425	2,981
Giles	3,196	2,566	841	3,346	3,023	1,142
Gloucester .	4,710	6,447	1,266	4,058	6,461	2,640
Goochland .	2,784	4,119	424	2,589	3,834	994
Grayson . . .	2,661	3,004	675	2,615	3,378	860
Greene. . . .	1,440	2,351	346	1,353	2,265	627
Greensville .	2,381	1,176	263	2,237	1,335	360
Halifax	5,599	6,490	876	4,752	5,199	1,140
Hanover . . .	9,880	22,086	2,447	8,021	20,336	5,674
Henrico	41,121	54,430	5,920	36,807	56,910	14,720
Henry.	9,061	9,110	2,370	9,296	9,005	3,212
Highland. . .	446	631	134	494	686	212
Isle of Wight.	4,952	5,416	893	4,380	5,370	1,536
James City .	7,247	10,120	1,116	6,536	8,781	2,675
King and Queen . . .	1,393	1,073	213	1,811	2,570	918
King George	1,875	2,597	341	1,363	1,206	323
King William	1,765	2,346	339	1,822	2,591	758
Lancaster . .	1,844	2,709	324	1,812	2,841	739
Lee	4,444	3,225	822	5,215	3,504	1,002
Loudoun. . .	19,942	25,715	3,082	14,462	19,290	7,391

County	1996 Clinton (D)	1996 Dole (R)	1996 Perot (RF)	1992 Clinton (D)	1992 Bush (R)	1992 Perot (I)
Louisa	3,761	3,768	693	3,399	3,461	1,381
Lunenburg	1,995	2,063	299	2,082	2,227	505
Madison	1,734	2,296	360	1,700	2,341	653
Mathews	1,602	2,206	403	1,402	2,179	884
Mecklenburg	4,408	4,933	789	4,273	5,401	1,128
Middlesex	1,704	2,141	350	1,597	2,224	768
Montgomery	10,867	10,517	2,594	10,658	10,606	3,449
Nelson	2,782	1,988	411	2,586	2,159	748
New Kent	1,859	2,852	520	1,738	2,708	1,017
Northampton	2,569	1,763	522	2,568	2,088	844
Northumberland	1,957	2,605	375	1,862	2,667	729
Nottoway	2,327	2,416	346	2,411	2,610	606
Orange	3,590	4,435	750	3,348	4,092	1,425
Page	2,868	3,876	640	3,010	4,203	1,163
Patrick	2,301	3,547	719	2,465	3,521	1,026
Pittsylvania	7,681	12,127	1,469	7,675	11,467	2,296
Powhatan	2,254	4,679	626	1,950	3,832	1,232
Prince Edward	2,678	2,530	403	2,775	2,858	635
Prince George	3,498	5,216	698	3,087	4,799	1,459
Prince William	33,462	39,292	4,881	26,486	35,432	13,190
Pulaski	5,333	5,387	1,399	5,633	6,148	2,066
Rappahannock	1,405	1,505	213	1,273	1,410	487
Richmond	1,101	1,424	201	1,034	1,609	366
Roanoke	15,387	20,700	2,934	14,704	20,667	5,477
Rockbridge	3,116	3,274	760	2,908	3,228	1,254
Rockingham	5,867	14,035	1,318	5,407	13,016	2,839
Russell	5,437	3,706	862	6,480	3,891	958
Scott	3,449	4,086	798	3,979	4,515	957
Shenandoah	4,224	7,440	1,353	3,956	7,746	2,063
Smyth	4,990	4,966	1,407	4,924	6,128	1,618
Southampton	3,454	2,275	564	3,199	2,844	754
Spotsylvania	10,342	13,786	1,860	8,133	11,829	3,918
Stafford	9,902	14,098	1,856	7,718	12,528	4,481
Surry	1,753	944	181	1,823	1,046	364
Sussex	2,089	1,378	256	2,193	1,527	446
Tazewell	7,500	6,131	1,554	8,586	6,375	1,872
Warren	3,814	4,657	904	3,554	4,319	1,650
Washington	6,939	9,098	1,654	7,269	9,150	2,288
Westmoreland	2,949	2,333	427	2,758	2,554	818
Wise	6,712	4,660	1,478	7,681	5,144	1,835
Wythe	3,275	4,274	955	3,616	5,121	1,557
York	7,731	11,396	1,469	6,218	10,197	3,426
Cities						
Alexandria	27,968	15,554	1,472	30,784	16,700	4,934
Bedford	1,065	990	212	963	1,091	313
Bristol	2,586	2,983	429	2,948	3,616	851
Buena Vista	1,090	713	216	1,023	849	291
Charlottesville	7,916	4,091	565	8,685	4,705	1,397
Chesapeake	28,713	29,251	4,456	23,495	28,909	9,237
Clifton Forge	974	486	147	958	632	251
Colonial Heights	1,782	4,632	518	1,721	5,298	1,312
Covington	1,394	763	255	1,442	995	402
Danville	8,168	9,254	762	8,134	9,584	1,679
Emporia	1,103	835	98	1,048	1,094	157
Fairfax	3,909	4,319	422	3,884	4,333	1,439
Falls Church	2,375	1,644	202	2,864	1,912	599
Franklin	1,962	1,200	201	1,696	1,347	272
Fredericksburg	3,215	2,579	300	3,266	2,819	738
Galax	1,033	910	221	957	1,087	276
Hampton	24,493	16,596	2,783	23,395	19,219	6,581
Harrisonburg	3,346	4,945	434	3,414	4,935	1,162
Hopewell	2,868	3,493	550	2,863	3,818	1,227
Lexington	1,059	850	112	1,128	894	228
Lynchburg	10,281	11,441	1,155	9,587	12,518	2,545
Manassas	4,378	5,799	670	3,647	5,453	1,971
Manassas Park	748	916	151	567	792	356
Martinsville	2,941	2,446	387	3,073	2,690	748
Newport News	27,678	23,072	3,090	25,743	26,779	8,217
Norfolk	37,655	18,693	3,435	37,602	22,362	8,732
Norton	802	416	138	871	472	182
Petersburg	8,105	2,261	423	8,671	3,125	834
Poquoson	1,409	3,422	400	1,086	3,354	960
Portsmouth	22,150	10,686	2,238	20,416	12,575	4,360
Radford	2,113	1,742	381	2,183	1,996	582
Richmond	42,273	20,993	2,762	47,642	24,341	6,992
Roanoke	17,282	12,283	2,169	17,724	13,443	3,753
Salem	4,282	4,936	796	4,028	5,143	1,430
S. Boston[1]	—	—	—	1,051	1,435	252
Staunton	3,162	4,526	605	2,851	4,989	1,146
Suffolk	10,827	8,572	1,266	9,196	8,697	2,150
Virginia Beach	52,142	63,741	9,328	44,294	68,936	24,087
Waynesboro	2,398	3,466	462	2,302	3,758	961
Williamsburg	1,820	1,560	162	1,856	1,349	445
Winchester	3,027	3,681	434	2,768	3,833	1,048
Totals	**1,091,060**	**1,138,350**	**159,861**	**1,038,650**	**1,150,517**	**348,639**

(1) South Boston merged with Halifax County in July 1996.

Virginia Vote Since 1948

1948, Truman, Dem., 200,786; Dewey, Rep., 172,070; Thurmond, States' Rights, 43,393; Wallace, Prog., 2,047; Thomas, Soc., 726; Teichert, Soc. Labor, 234.

1952, Eisenhower, Rep., 349,037; Stevenson, Dem., 268,677; Hass, Soc. Labor, 1,160; Hoopes, Soc. Dem., 504; Hallinan, Prog., 311.

1956, Eisenhower, Rep., 386,459; Stevenson, Dem., 267,760; Andrews, States' Rights, 42,964; Hoopes, Soc. Dem., 444; Hass, Soc. Labor, 351.

1960, Kennedy, Dem., 362,327; Nixon, Rep., 404,521; Coiner, Cons., 4,204; Hass, Soc. Labor, 397.

1964, Johnson, Dem., 558,038; Goldwater, Rep., 481,334; Hass, Soc. Labor, 2,895.

1968, Nixon, Rep., 590,319; Humphrey, Dem., 442,387; Wallace, 3d Party, *320,272; Blomen, Soc. Labor, 4,671; Munn, Proh., 601; Gregory, Peace and Freedom, 1,680.

*10,561 votes for Wallace were omitted in the count.

1972, Nixon, Rep., 988,493; McGovern, Dem., 438,887; Schmitz, Amer., 19,721; Fisher, Soc. Labor, 9,918.

1976, Carter, Dem., 813,896; Ford, Rep., 836,554; Camejo, Soc. Workers, 17,802; Anderson, Amer., 16,686; LaRouche, U.S. Labor, 7,508; MacBride, Libertarian, 4,648.

1980, Reagan, Rep., 989,609; Carter, Dem., 752,174; Anderson, Ind., 95,418; Commoner, Citizens, 14,024; Clark, Libertarian, 12,821; DeBerry, Soc. Workers, 1,986.

1984, Reagan, Rep., 1,337,078; Mondale, Dem., 796,250.

1988, Bush, Rep., 1,309,162; Dukakis, Dem., 859,799; Fulani, Ind., 14,312; Paul, Lib., 8,336.

1992, Clinton, Dem., 1,038,650; Bush, Rep., 1,150,517; Perot, Ind., 348,639; LaRouche, Ind., 11,937; Marrou, Libertarian, 5,730; Fulani, New Alliance, 3,192.

1996, Dole, Rep., 1,138,350; Clinton, Dem., 1,091,060; Perot, Ref., 159,861; Phillips, Taxpayers, 13,687; Browne, Libertarian, 9,174; Hagelin, Natural Law, 4,510.

Washington

County	1996 Clinton (D)	1996 Dole (R)	1996 Perot (RF)	1992 Clinton (D)	1992 Bush (R)	1992 Perot (I)
Adams	1,740	2,356	448	1,449	2,087	1,010
Asotin	3,349	2,860	936	3,239	2,425	1,849
Benton	20,783	26,664	5,311	16,459	22,883	12,878
Chelan	8,595	12,363	2,332	7,860	10,716	4,606
Clallam	12,585	12,432	3,187	10,820	9,765	7,775
Clark	52,254	46,794	9,663	42,648	36,906	26,163
Columbia	743	948	228	668	761	466
Cowlitz	18,054	11,221	3,441	15,052	10,000	9,246
Douglas	3,913	5,682	1,132	3,731	4,920	2,315
Ferry	1,197	1,091	408	963	773	762
Franklin	4,961	5,946	992	3,743	4,486	2,597
Garfield	497	623	117	473	620	222
Grant	8,065	10,895	2,496	7,278	9,503	4,898
Grays Harbor	14,082	7,635	3,757	12,599	6,904	7,460
Island	12,157	12,387	2,787	9,555	9,526	7,889
Jefferson	7,145	4,607	1,385	6,148	3,467	3,168
King	417,846	232,811	51,309	391,050	212,986	167,216
Kitsap	44,167	35,304	8,769	34,442	29,340	23,873
Kittitas	5,707	5,224	1,214	5,432	4,078	2,778
Klickitat	3,214	2,662	875	2,758	2,085	1,938
Lewis	10,331	13,238	3,373	7,810	12,316	6,684
Lincoln	1,806	2,587	518	1,653	2,152	1,098
Mason	10,088	7,149	2,816	8,076	5,776	5,577
Okanogan	4,810	5,890	1,797	5,015	4,265	3,541
Pacific	5,095	2,598	1,131	4,587	2,243	2,351
Pend Oreille	2,126	2,012	709	1,798	1,528	1,340
Pierce	120,893	89,295	22,051	102,243	77,410	59,523
San Juan	3,663	2,523	508	3,353	1,901	1,776
Skagit	18,295	16,397	4,818	15,936	13,388	10,973
Skamania	1,724	1,387	450	1,474	1,102	1,050
Snohomish	109,624	81,885	22,731	88,643	69,137	65,838
Spokane	71,727	66,628	16,532	69,526	59,984	38,251
Stevens	5,591	7,524	2,158	4,960	5,706	3,769
Thurston	45,522	29,835	7,622	38,293	25,643	19,551
Wahkiakum	924	619	215	696	488	584
Walla Walla	8,038	9,085	1,894	7,325	7,894	4,507
Whatcom	29,074	27,153	4,854	26,619	23,801	12,455
Whitman	7,262	6,734	1,315	7,637	6,428	3,220
Yakima	25,676	27,668	4,724	21,026	25,841	10,583
Totals	**1,123,323**	**840,712**	**201,003**	**993,037**	**731,234**	**541,780**

Washington Vote Since 1948

1948, Truman, Dem., 476,165; Dewey, Rep., 386,315; Wallace, Prog., 31,692; Watson, Proh., 6,117; Thomas, Soc., 3,534; Teichert, Soc. Labor, 1,133; Dobbs, Soc. Workers, 103.

1952, Eisenhower, Rep., 599,107; Stevenson, Dem., 492,845; MacArthur, Christian Nationalist, 7,290; Hallinan, Prog., 2,460; Hass, Soc. Labor, 633; Hoopes, Soc., 254; Dobbs, Soc. Workers, 119.

1956, Eisenhower, Rep., 620,430; Stevenson, Dem., 523,002; Hass, Soc. Labor, 7,457.

1960, Kennedy, Dem., 599,298; Nixon, Rep., 629,273; Hass, Soc. Labor, 10,895; Curtis, Constitution, 1,401; Dobbs, Soc. Workers, 705.

1964, Johnson, Dem., 779,699; Goldwater, Rep., 470,366; Hass, Soc. Labor, 7,772; DeBerry, Freedom Soc., 537.

1968, Nixon, Rep., 588,510; Humphrey, Dem., 616,037; Wallace, 3d Party, 96,990; Blomen, Soc. Labor, 488; Cleaver, Peace and Freedom, 1,609; Halstead, Soc. Workers, 270; Mitchell, Free Ballot, 377.

1972, Nixon, Rep., 837,135; McGovern, Dem., 568,334; Schmitz, Amer., 58,906; Spock, Ind., 2,644; Fisher, Soc. Labor, 1,102; Jenness, Soc. Workers, 623; Hall, Com., 566; Hospers, Libertarian, 1,537.

1976, Carter, Dem., 717,323; Ford, Rep., 777,732; McCarthy, Ind., 36,986; Maddox, Amer. Ind., 8,585; Anderson, Amer., 5,046; MacBride, Libertarian, 5,042; Wright, People's, 1,124; Camejo, Soc. Workers, 905; LaRouche, U.S. Labor, 903; Hall, Com., 817; Levin, Soc. Labor, 713; Zeidler, Soc., 358.

1980, Reagan, Rep., 865,244; Carter, Dem., 650,193; Anderson, Ind., 185,073; Clark, Libertarian, 29,213; Commoner, Citizens, 9,403; DeBerry, Soc. Workers, 1,137; McReynolds, Soc., 956; Hall, Com., 834; Griswold, Workers World, 341.

1984, Reagan, Rep., 1,051,670; Mondale, Dem., 798,352; Bergland, Libertarian, 8,844.

1988, Bush, Rep., 903,835; Dukakis, Dem., 933,516; Paul, Lib., 17,240; LaRouche, Ind., 4,412.

1992, Clinton, Dem., 993,037; Bush, Rep., 731,234; Perot, Ind., 541,780; Marrou, Libertarian, 7,533; Gritz, Populist/America First, 4,854; Hagelin, Natural Law, 2,456; Phillips, U.S. Taxpayers, 2,354; Fulani, New Alliance, 1,776; Daniels, Ind., 1,171.

1996, Clinton, Dem., 1,123,323; Dole, Rep., 840,712; Perot, Ref., 201,003; Nader, Ind., 60,322; Browne, Libertarian, 12,522; Hagelin, Natural Law, 6,076; Phillips, Taxpayers, 4,578; Collins, Ind., 2,374; Moorehead, Workers World, 2,189; Harris, Soc. Workers, 738.

West Virginia

County	1996 Clinton (D)	1996 Dole (R)	1996 Perot (RF)	1992 Clinton (D)	1992 Bush (R)	1992 Perot (I)
Barbour	3,076	2,155	784	3,467	2,322	1,153
Berkeley	8,321	9,859	2,291	7,159	9,134	3,645
Boone	6,048	1,917	927	6,576	2,021	1,037
Braxton	3,001	1,441	527	3,396	1,535	823
Brooke	5,338	2,741	1,375	5,693	2,582	2,103
Cabell	16,277	13,179	2,968	15,111	13,203	5,311
Calhoun	1,402	1,000	307	1,627	1,095	537
Clay	2,074	1,137	355	1,928	1,255	462
Doddridge	865	1,335	382	968	1,500	515
Fayette	9,471	3,669	1,552	9,574	3,991	2,002
Gilmer	1,390	933	316	1,576	1,085	484
Grant	1,206	2,599	481	1,011	2,762	519
Greenbrier	6,286	4,434	1,418	5,784	4,442	1,898
Hampshire	2,335	2,814	605	2,365	2,767	1,022
Hancock	7,521	4,268	2,158	7,830	3,897	3,267
Hardy	1,911	1,895	438	1,917	2,144	602
Harrison	14,746	8,857	3,135	15,480	9,687	5,131
Jackson	4,882	4,235	1,295	5,102	4,192	1,908
Jefferson	6,361	5,287	1,307	5,363	4,656	2,114
Kanawha	40,357	29,311	6,412	38,315	31,358	11,778
Lewis	2,868	2,285	974	2,931	2,413	1,197
Lincoln	4,994	2,530	696	4,502	2,637	787
Logan	10,840	2,627	1,532	11,095	3,336	1,835
McDowell	5,989	1,550	655	7,019	1,941	803
Marion	12,994	6,160	2,881	14,042	6,380	4,736
Marshall	7,045	4,460	2,202	7,298	4,463	3,402
Mason	5,284	3,581	1,533	5,331	3,808	2,045
Mercer	8,721	7,768	2,141	9,511	7,888	2,817
Mineral	3,487	4,380	1,170	3,992	4,837	1,884
Mingo	7,584	2,229	1,020	7,342	2,584	915
Monongalia	13,406	10,189	3,040	14,142	9,831	4,576
Monroe	2,382	2,131	559	2,418	2,311	685
Morgan	1,929	2,599	513	1,854	2,585	886
Nicholas	4,769	2,649	1,071	5,042	2,959	1,495
Ohio	8,781	7,267	2,065	9,522	7,421	3,632
Pendleton	1,591	1,431	276	1,626	1,589	362
Pleasants	1,478	1,265	416	1,387	1,248	731
Pocahontas	1,796	1,242	426	1,741	1,401	627
Preston	4,237	4,257	1,760	3,933	4,429	2,109
Putnam	8,029	8,803	1,901	6,817	7,653	2,910
Raleigh	12,547	8,628	2,355	13,171	8,700	3,247
Randolph	5,469	3,348	1,184	5,097	3,496	1,582
Ritchie	1,385	1,906	522	1,474	2,184	745
Roane	2,572	2,069	622	2,607	2,207	1,009
Summers	2,397	1,505	438	2,650	1,652	565
Taylor	2,692	1,977	844	2,843	2,022	1,242
Tucker	1,649	1,217	424	1,805	1,261	550
Tyler	1,459	734	563	1,587	1,593	1,013
Upshur	3,052	3,325	1,031	3,161	3,505	1,558
Wayne	8,300	5,492	1,633	8,392	5,729	2,199
Webster	2,292	654	369	2,320	811	436
Wetzel	3,209	2,037	1,004	3,753	2,271	1,550
Wirt	906	928	280	1,043	939	394
Wood	13,261	15,502	3,694	13,529	15,441	6,998
Wyoming	5,550	2,155	812	5,782	2,821	996
Totals	**327,812**	**233,946**	**71,639**	**331,001**	**241,974**	**108,829**

West Virginia Vote Since 1948

1948, Truman, Dem., 429,188; Dewey, Rep., 316,251; Wallace, Prog., 3,311.

1952, Eisenhower, Rep., 419,970; Stevenson, Dem., 453,578.

1956, Eisenhower, Rep., 449,297; Stevenson, Dem., 381,534.

1960, Kennedy, Dem., 441,786; Nixon, Rep., 395,995.

1964, Johnson, Dem., 538,087; Goldwater, Rep., 253,953.

1968, Nixon, Rep., 307,555; Humphrey, Dem., 374,091; Wallace, 3d Party, 72,560.

1972, Nixon, Rep., 484,964; McGovern, Dem., 277,435.

1976, Carter, Dem., 435,864; Ford, Rep., 314,726.

1980, Reagan, Rep., 334,206; Carter, Dem., 367,462; Anderson, Ind., 31,691; Clark, Libertarian, 4,356.

1984, Reagan, Rep., 405,483; Mondale, Dem., 328,125.

1988, Bush, Rep., 310,065; Dukakis, Dem., 341,016; Fulani, New Alliance, 2,230.

1992, Clinton, Dem., 331,001; Bush, Rep., 241,974; Perot, Ind., 108,829; Marrou, Libertarian, 1,873.

1996, Clinton, Dem., 327,812; Dole, Rep., 233,946; Perot, Ref., 71,639; Browne, Libertarian, 3,062.

Wisconsin

County	1996 Clinton (D)	1996 Dole (R)	1996 Perot (RF)	1992 Clinton (D)	1992 Bush (R)	1992 Perot (I)
Adams	4,119	2,450	1,122	3,539	2,465	2,003
Ashland	3,808	1,863	861	4,213	2,372	1,746
Barron	8,025	6,158	2,692	8,063	6,572	5,479
Bayfield	3,895	2,250	899	3,873	2,393	1,786
Brown	42,823	38,563	8,036	37,513	42,352	22,395
Buffalo	2,681	1,800	972	2,996	2,029	1,889
Burnet	3,625	2,452	962	3,172	2,340	1,855
Calumet	6,940	7,049	2,112	5,701	7,541	5,055
Chippewa	9,647	7,520	3,567	10,487	8,215	6,408
Clark	5,540	4,622	2,486	5,540	4,977	4,284
Columbia	10,336	8,377	2,377	9,348	9,099	5,439
Crawford	3,658	2,149	1,060	3,540	2,390	1,797
Dane	109,347	59,487	12,436	114,724	61,957	31,874
Dodge	12,625	12,890	3,322	11,438	14,971	9,136
Door	5,590	4,948	1,475	4,735	5,468	3,506
Douglas	10,976	5,167	2,001	12,319	5,679	4,150
Dunn	7,536	4,917	2,555	7,965	5,283	4,809
Eau Claire	20,298	13,900	5,160	21,221	15,915	9,783
Florence	869	927	316	978	942	719
Fond du Lac	15,542	16,488	4,204	13,757	19,785	10,660
Forest	2,092	1,166	678	1,904	1,393	1,062
Grant	9,203	7,021	2,648	8,914	7,678	6,405
Green	6,136	4,697	1,534	5,467	4,887	3,735
Green Lake	3,152	3,565	1,025	2,772	3,897	2,827
Iowa	4,690	2,866	1,071	4,467	3,288	2,341
Iron	1,725	1,260	469	1,762	1,273	835
Jackson	3,705	2,262	1,163	3,681	2,644	2,040
Jefferson	13,188	12,681	3,177	11,593	13,072	7,960
Juneau	4,331	3,226	1,393	4,177	4,051	2,670
Kenosha	27,964	18,296	6,507	27,341	19,854	14,232
Kewaunee	4,311	3,431	1,161	4,050	3,570	2,700
La Crosse	23,647	16,482	4,844	22,838	18,891	10,224
La Fayette	3,261	2,172	944	3,143	2,582	2,079
Langlade	4,074	3,206	1,249	3,630	3,890	2,444
Lincoln	6,166	4,076	1,800	5,297	4,321	3,605
Manitowoc	16,750	13,239	3,941	15,903	14,008	11,179
Marathon	24,012	19,874	6,749	21,482	20,948	14,600
Marinette	8,413	7,231	2,367	7,626	7,984	5,412
Marquette	2,859	2,208	915	2,533	2,322	1,818
Menominee	992	230	107	691	244	221
Milwaukee	216,620	119,407	26,027	235,521	151,314	76,039
Monroe	6,924	5,299	2,081	6,427	6,118	4,183
Oconto	6,723	5,389	1,655	5,898	5,720	4,405
Oneida	7,619	6,339	2,604	7,160	6,725	4,782
Outagamie	28,815	27,758	7,235	23,735	30,370	18,479
Ozaukee	13,269	22,078	2,774	11,879	22,805	8,002
Pepin	1,585	1,007	456	1,673	1,098	781
Pierce	7,970	4,599	2,074	7,824	4,844	4,492
Polk	8,334	5,387	2,369	7,746	5,446	4,753
Portage	15,901	9,631	3,410	15,553	10,914	7,083
Price	3,523	2,545	1,218	3,575	2,654	2,286
Racine	38,567	30,107	7,611	34,875	32,310	20,227
Richland	3,502	2,642	901	3,458	3,144	1,899
Rock	32,450	20,096	6,800	31,154	21,942	15,700
Rusk	2,941	2,219	1,331	3,376	2,430	2,085
St. Croix	11,384	8,253	3,180	10,281	8,114	7,125
Sauk	9,889	7,448	2,448	9,128	8,886	5,280

County	1996 Clinton (D)	1996 Dole (R)	1996 Perot (RF)	1992 Clinton (D)	1992 Bush (R)	1992 Perot (I)
Sawyer. . . .	2,773	2,603	962	2,796	2,658	1,861
Shawano . .	6,850	6,396	2,071	6,062	7,253	4,540
Sheboygan .	22,022	20,067	4,157	20,568	22,526	11,295
Taylor	3,253	3,108	1,457	3,305	3,415	2,590
Trempealeau	5,848	3,035	1,688	6,218	3,577	3,160
Vernon. . . .	5,572	3,796	1,523	5,673	4,072	2,890
Vilas	4,226	4,496	1,548	3,764	4,616	2,827
Walworth . .	13,283	15,099	3,729	11,825	15,727	9,029
Washburn. .	3,231	2,703	920	3,080	2,586	1,978
Washington .	17,154	25,829	4,786	13,339	22,739	13,045
Waukesha .	57,354	91,729	13,109	50,270	91,461	36,622
Waupaca . .	7,800	8,679	2,464	6,666	10,252	6,088
Waushara. .	3,824	3,573	1,264	3,402	4,045	2,829
Winnebago .	29,564	27,880	6,531	27,234	33,709	16,140
Wood.	14,650	12,666	4,599	13,208	13,843	8,822
Totals	**1,071,971**	**845,029**	**227,339**	**1,041,066**	**930,855**	**544,479**

Wisconsin Vote Since 1948

1948, Truman, Dem., 647,310; Dewey, Rep., 590,959; Wallace, Prog., 25,282; Thomas, Soc., 12,547; Teichert, Soc. Labor, 399; Dobbs, Soc. Workers, 303.

1952, Eisenhower, Rep., 979,744; Stevenson, Dem., 622,175; Hallinan, Ind., 2,174; Dobbs, Ind., 1,350; Hoopes, Ind., 1,157; Hass, Ind., 770.

1956, Eisenhower, Rep., 954,844; Stevenson, Dem., 586,768; Andrews, Ind., 6,918; Hoopes, Soc., 754; Hass, Soc. Labor, 710; Dobbs, Soc. Workers, 564.

1960, Kennedy, Dem., 830,805; Nixon, Rep., 895,175; Dobbs, Soc. Workers, 1,792; Hass, Soc. Labor, 1,310.

1964, Johnson, Dem., 1,050,424; Goldwater, Rep., 638,495; DeBerry, Soc. Workers, 1,692; Hass, Soc. Labor, 1,204.

1968, Nixon, Rep., 809,997; Humphrey, Dem., 748,804; Wallace, 3d Party, 127,835; Blomen, Soc. Labor, 1,338; Halstead, Soc. Workers, 1,222; scattered, 2,342.

1972 Nixon, Rep., 989,430; McGovern, Dem., 810,174; Schmitz, Amer., 47,525; Spock, Ind., 2,701; Fisher, Soc. Labor, 998; Hall, Com., 663; Reed, Ind., 506; scattered, 893.

1976, Carter, Dem., 1,040,232; Ford, Rep., 1,004,987; McCarthy, Ind., 34,943; Maddox, Amer. Ind., 8,552; Zeidler, Soc., 4,298; MacBride, Libertarian, 3,814; Camejo, Soc. Workers, 1,691; Wright, People's, 943; Hall, Com., 749; LaRouche, U.S. Lab., 738; Levin, Soc. Labor, 389; scattered, 2,839.

1980, Reagan, Rep., 1,088,845; Carter, Dem., 981,584; Anderson, Ind., 160,657; Clark, Libertarian, 29,135; Commoner, Citizens, 7,767; Rarick, Constitution, 1,519; McReynolds, Soc., 808; Hall, Com., 772; Griswold, Workers World, 414; DeBerry, Soc. Workers, 383; scattering, 1,337.

1984, Reagan, Rep., 1,198,584; Mondale, Dem., 995,740; Bergland, Libertarian, 4,883.

1988, Bush, Rep., 1,047,499; Dukakis, Dem., 1,126,794; Paul, Lib., 5,157; Duke, Pop., 3,056.

1992, Clinton, Dem., 1,041,066; Bush, Rep., 930,855; Perot, Ind., 544,479; Marrou, Libertarian, 2,877; Gritz, Populist/America First, 2,311; Daniels, Ind., 1,883; Phillips, U.S. Taxpayers, 1,772; Hagelin, Natural Law, 1,070.

1996, Clinton, Dem., 1,071,971; Dole, Rep., 845,029; Perot, Ref., 227,339; Nader, Green, 28,723; Phillips, Taxpayers, 8,811; Browne, Libertarian, 7,929; Hagelin, Natural Law, 1,379; Moorehead, Workers World, 1,333; Hollis, Soc., 848; Harris, Soc. Workers, 483.

Wyoming

County	1996 Clinton (D)	1996 Dole (R)	1996 Perot (RF)	1992 Clinton (D)	1992 Bush (R)	1992 Perot (I)
Albany	6,399	5,967	1,333	5,713	4,176	2,862
Big Horn. . .	1,438	2,821	545	1,216	2,216	1,236
Campbell . .	3,468	6,382	1,954	2,709	5,315	3,133
Carbon . . .	2,690	2,930	855	2,737	2,320	1,579
Converse . .	1,520	2,702	639	1,307	2,159	1,260
Crook	651	1,698	394	568	1,377	718
Fremont . . .	5,445	7,554	1,840	4,765	5,387	3,594
Goshen . . .	1,923	2,989	547	1,754	2,395	1,144
Hot Springs.	779	1,348	287	740	978	652
Johnson. . .	815	2,071	378	656	1,614	844
Laramie . . .	13,676	16,924	2,958	12,177	12,890	6,607
Lincoln. . . .	1,803	3,764	906	1,430	2,595	1,495
Natrona . . .	11,240	13,182	3,524	9,817	9,717	7,647
Niobrara. . .	325	757	209	298	635	355
Park	3,240	7,430	1,318	2,771	5,218	3,145
Platte.	1,631	2,155	579	1,398	1,668	956
Sheridan . .	4,594	5,892	1,414	4,139	4,303	3,035
Sublette . . .	677	1,829	401	536	1,168	828
Sweetwater.	7,088	5,591	2,792	6,417	4,476	3,879
Teton.	4,042	3,918	839	3,120	2,854	2,340
Uinta	2,414	3,471	1,242	2,047	2,701	2,041
Washakie. .	1,205	2,250	470	1,118	1,720	1,084
Weston . . .	871	1,763	504	727	1,465	829
Totals	**77,934**	**105,388**	**25,928**	**68,160**	**79,347**	**51,263**

Wyoming Vote Since 1948

1948, Truman, Dem., 52,354; Dewey, Rep., 47,947; Wallace, Prog., 931; Thomas, Soc., 137; Teichert, Soc. Labor, 56.

1952, Eisenhower, Rep., 81,047; Stevenson, Dem., 47,934; Hamblen, Proh., 194; Hoopes, Soc., 40; Haas, Soc. Labor, 36.

1956, Eisenhower, Rep., 74,573; Stevenson, Dem., 49,554.

1960, Kennedy, Dem., 63,331; Nixon, Rep., 77,451.

1964, Johnson, Dem., 80,718; Goldwater, Rep., 61,998.

1968, Nixon, Rep., 70,927; Humphrey, Dem., 45,173; Wallace, 3d Party, 11,105.

1972, Nixon, Rep., 100,464; McGovern, Dem., 44,358; Schmitz, Amer., 748.

1976, Carter, Dem., 62,239; Ford, Rep., 92,717; McCarthy, Ind., 624; Reagan, Ind., 307; Anderson, Amer., 290; MacBride, Libertarian, 89; Brown, Ind., 47; Maddox, Amer. Ind., 30.

1980, Reagan, Rep., 110,700; Carter, Dem., 49,427; Anderson, Ind., 12,072; Clark, Libertarian, 4,514.

1984, Reagan, Rep., 133,241; Mondale, Dem., 53,370; Bergland, Libertarian, 2,357.

1988, Bush, Rep., 106,867; Dukakis, Dem., 67,113; Paul, Lib., 2,026; Fulani, New Alliance, 545.

1992, Clinton, Dem., 68,160; Bush, Rep., 79,347; Perot, Ind., 51,263.

1996, Dole, Rep., 105,388; Clinton, Dem., 77,934; Perot, Ind. (Ref.), 25,928; Browne, Libertarian, 1,739; Hagelin, Natural Law, 582.

1996 Official Presidential General Election Results

Source: Voter News Service; *Congressional Quarterly*

Candidate (Party)	Popular Vote	Percent of Popular Vote
Bill Clinton (Democrat)	47,401,185	49.25
Bob Dole (Republican)	39,197,469	40.73
Ross Perot (Reform)	8,085,294	8.40
Ralph Nader (Green)	651,771	.68
Harry Browne (Libertarian)	485,120	.50
Howard Phillips (U.S. Taxpayers)	182,924	.19
John Hagelin (Natural Law)	112,978	.12
Monica Moorehead (Workers World)	29,082	.03
Marsha Feinland (Peace & Freedom)	25,332	.03
James Harris (Socialist Workers)	8,286	.01
Charles Collins (Independent)	7,899	.01
Dennis Peron (Grass Roots)	5,378	.01
Mary Cal Hollis (Socialist)	4,269	.00
Jerome White (Socialist Equality)	2,438	.00
Diane Beall Templin (American)	1,847	.00
Earl Dodge (Prohibition)	1,293	.00
A. Peter Crane (Independent)	1,101	.00
Ralph Forbes (Independent)	932	.00
John Birrenbach (Independent Grass Roots)	787	.00
Isabell Masters (Independent)	749	.00
Steve Michael (Independent)	408	.00
Write-in	24,475	.03
None of These Candidates (Nevada)	5,608	.01
Total	**96,236,625**	**100**

Note: Party designations may vary from one state to another.

Voter Turnout in Presidential Elections, 1932-96

Source: Federal Election Commission; Commission for Study of American Electorate; *Congressional Quarterly*

	Candidates	Voter Participation (% of voting-age population)		Candidates	Voter Participation (% of voting-age population)
1932	Roosevelt-Hoover	52.4	1968	Humphrey-Nixon	60.9
1936	Roosevelt-Landon	56.0	1972	McGovern-Nixon	55.2 (1)
1940	Roosevelt-Willkie	58.9	1976	Carter-Ford	53.5
1944	Roosevelt-Dewey	56.0	1980	Carter-Reagan	54.0
1948	Truman-Dewey	51.1	1984	Mondale-Reagan	53.1
1952	Stevenson-Eisenhower	61.6	1988	Dukakis-Bush	50.2
1956	Stevenson-Eisenhower	59.3	1992	Clinton-Bush-Perot	55.9
1960	Kennedy-Nixon	62.8	1996	Clinton-Dole-Perot	49.0
1964	Johnson-Goldwater	61.9			

(1) The sharp drop in 1972 follows the expansion of eligibility with the enfranchisement of 18- to 21-year-olds.

Electoral Votes for President

(based on 1990 Census)

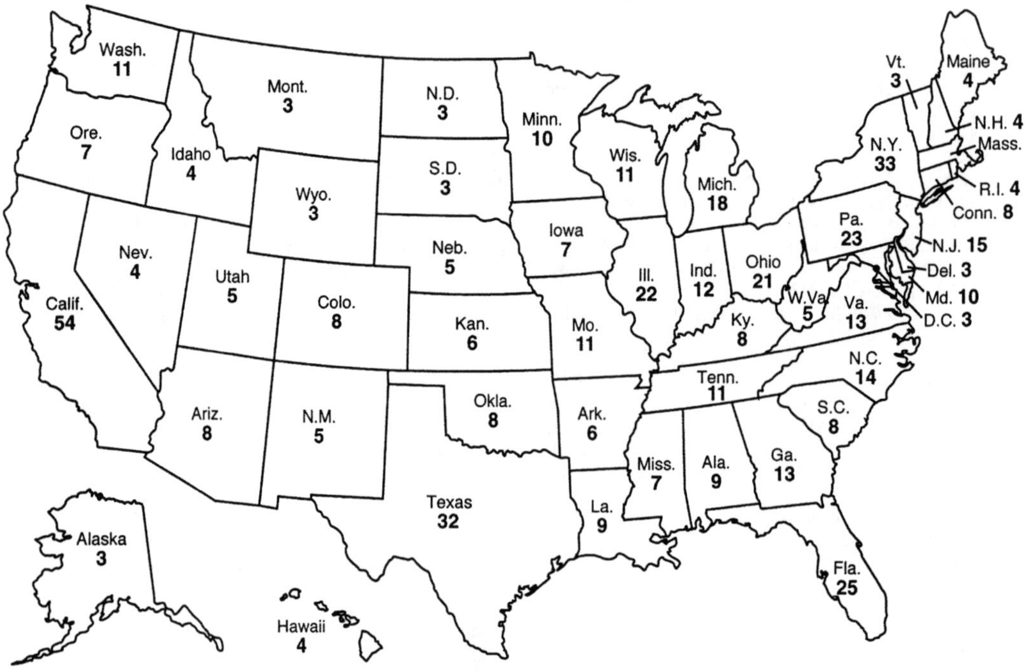

The Electoral College

The president and the vice president are the only elective federal officials not chosen by direct vote of the people. They are elected by the members of the Electoral College, an institution provided for in the U.S. Constitution.

On presidential election day, the first Tuesday after the first Monday in Nov. of every 4th year, each state chooses as many electors as it has senators and representatives in Congress. In 1964, for the first time, as provided by the 23d Amendment to the Constitution, the District of Columbia voted for 3 electors. Thus, with 100 senators and 435 representatives, there are 538 members of the Electoral College, with a majority of 270 electoral votes needed to elect the president and vice president.

Although political parties were not part of the original plan created by the Founding Fathers, today political parties customarily nominate their lists of electors at their respective state conventions. Some states print names of the candidates for president and vice president at the top of the Nov. ballot; others list only the electors' names. In either case, the electors of the party receiving the highest vote are elected.

The electors meet on the first Monday after the 2d Wednesday in Dec. in their respective state capitals or in some other place prescribed by state legislatures. By long-established custom, they vote for their party nominees, although this is not required by law.

The Constitution requires electors to cast a ballot for at least one person who is not an inhabitant of that elector's home state. This ensures that presidential and vice presidential candidates from the same party will not be from the same state. Also, an elector cannot be a member of Congress or hold federal office.

Certified and sealed lists of the votes of the electors in each state are sent to the president of the U.S. Senate, who then opens them in the presence of the members of the Senate and House of Representatives in a joint session held in early Jan., and the electoral votes of all the states are then officially counted. (The count was made on Jan. 9 in 1997.)

If no candidate for president has a majority, the House of Representatives chooses a president from the top 3 candidates, with all representatives from each state combining to cast one vote for that state. The House decided the outcome of the 1800 and 1824 presidential elections. If no candidate for vice president has a majority, the Senate chooses from the top 2, with the senators voting as individuals. The Senate chose the vice president following the 1836 election.

Under the electoral college system, a candidate who fails to be the top vote getter in the popular vote may still win a majority of electoral votes. This happened in the elections of 1876 and 1888.

In the 1996 election, Bill Clinton won 379 electoral votes, and Bob Dole won 159.

Third-Party and Independent Presidential Candidates

Although many "third party" candidates or independents have pursued the presidency, only 9 of these have polled more than a million votes. In most elections since 1860, fewer than one vote in 20 has been cast for a third-party candidate. In only 5 presidential elections since then have all non-major-party candidates combined polled more than 10% of the vote. The major vote getters in those elections were James B. Weaver (People's Party), 1892; former President Theodore Roosevelt (Progressive Party), 1912; Robert M. La Follette (Progressive Party), 1924; George C. Wallace (American Independent Party), 1968; and H. Ross Perot, as an independent in 1992.

Roosevelt outpolled the Republican candidate, William Howard Taft, in 1912, capturing 28% of the popular vote and 88 electoral votes. In 1948, Strom Thurmond was able to capture 39 electoral votes (from 5 Southern states); however, all third parties received only 5.75% of the popular vote in the election. Twenty years later, George Wallace's popularity in the same region allowed him to get 46 electoral votes and 13.5% of the popular vote. In 1992 Perot was able to capture 19% of the popular vote; however, he did not win a single state. In 1996, Perot (as the candidate of his newly formed Reform Party) won 8% of the vote; all third-party candidates combined won 10%.

Despite the difficulty in winning the presidency, independent and third-party candidates sometimes succeed in winning other offices and often bring the attention of all presidential candidates combined to particular issues.

Notable Third Party and Independent Campaigns by Year

Party	Presidential nominee	Year	Issues	Strength in . . .
Anti-Masonic	William Wirt	1832	Against secret societies and oaths	PA, VT
Liberty	James G. Birney	1844	Anti-slavery	North
Free Soil	Martin Van Buren	1848	Anti-slavery	NY, OH
American (Know-Nothing)	Millard Fillmore	1856	Anti-immigrant	Northeast, South
Greenback	Peter Cooper	1876	For "cheap money," labor rights	National
Greenback	James B. Weaver	1880	For "cheap money," labor rights	National
Prohibition	John P. St. John	1884	Anti-liquor	National
People's (Populists)	James B. Weaver	1892	For "cheap money," end of national banks	South, West
Socialist	Eugene V. Debs	1900-12; 1920	For public ownership	National
Progressive (Bull Moose)	Theodore Roosevelt	1912	Against high tariffs	Midwest, West
Progressive	Robert M. La Follette	1924	Farmer and labor rights	Midwest, West
Socialist	Norman Thomas	1928-48	Liberal reforms	National
Union	William Lemke	1936	Anti-New Deal	National
States' Rights (Dixiecrats)	Strom Thurmond	1948	For states' rights	South
Progressive	Henry A. Wallace	1948	Anti-cold war	NY, CA
American Independent	George C. Wallace	1968	For states' rights	South
American	John G. Schmitz	1972	For "law and order"	Far West, OH, LA
None (Independent)	John B. Anderson	1980	A 3d choice	National
None (Independent)	H. Ross Perot	1992	Federal budget deficit	National
Reform	H. Ross Perot	1996	Deficit; campaign finance	National

Major-Party Nominees for President and Vice President

Asterisk (*) denotes winning ticket

	Democratic		Republican	
Year	President	Vice President	President	Vice President
1856	James Buchanan*	John Breckinridge	John Frémont	William Dayton
1860	Stephen A. Douglas(1)	Herschel V. Johnson	Abraham Lincoln*	Hannibal Hamlin
1864	George McClellan	G.H. Pendleton	Abraham Lincoln*	Andrew Johnson
1868	Horatio Seymour	Francis Blair	Ulysses S. Grant*	Schuyler Colfax
1872	Horace Greeley	B. Gratz Brown	Ulysses S. Grant*	Henry Wilson
1876	Samuel J. Tilden	Thomas Hendricks	Rutherford B. Hayes*	William Wheeler
1880	Winfield Hancock	William English	James A. Garfield*	Chester A. Arthur
1884	Grover Cleveland*	Thomas Hendricks	James Blaine	John Logan
1888	Grover Cleveland	A.G. Thurman	Benjamin Harrison*	Levi Morton
1892	Grover Cleveland*	Adlai Stevenson	Benjamin Harrison	Whitelaw Reid
1896	William J. Bryan	Arthur Sewall	William McKinley*	Garret Hobart
1900	William J. Bryan	Adlai Stevenson	William McKinley*	Theodore Roosevelt
1904	Alton Parker	Henry Davis	Theodore Roosevelt*	Charles Fairbanks
1908	William J. Bryan	John Kern	William H. Taft*	James Sherman
1912	Woodrow Wilson*	Thomas Marshall	William H. Taft	James Sherman(2)
1916	Woodrow Wilson*	Thomas Marshall	Charles Hughes	Charles Fairbanks
1920	James M. Cox	Franklin D. Roosevelt	Warren G. Harding*	Calvin Coolidge
1924	John W. Davis	Charles W. Bryan	Calvin Coolidge*	Charles G. Dawes
1928	Alfred E. Smith	Joseph T. Robinson	Herbert Hoover*	Charles Curtis
1932	Franklin D. Roosevelt*	John N. Garner	Herbert Hoover	Charles Curtis
1936	Franklin D. Roosevelt*	John N. Garner	Alfred M. Landon	Frank Knox
1940	Franklin D. Roosevelt*	Henry A. Wallace	Wendell L. Willkie	Charles McNary
1944	Franklin D. Roosevelt*	Harry S. Truman	Thomas E. Dewey	John W. Bricker
1948	Harry S. Truman*	Alben W. Barkley	Thomas E. Dewey	Earl Warren
1952	Adlai E. Stevenson	John J. Sparkman	Dwight D. Eisenhower*	Richard M. Nixon
1956	Adlai E. Stevenson	Estes Kefauver	Dwight D. Eisenhower*	Richard M. Nixon
1960	John F. Kennedy*	Lyndon B. Johnson	Richard M. Nixon	Henry Cabot Lodge
1964	Lyndon B. Johnson*	Hubert H. Humphrey	Barry M. Goldwater	William E. Miller
1968	Hubert H. Humphrey	Edmund S. Muskie	Richard M. Nixon*	Spiro T. Agnew
1972	George S. McGovern	R. Sargent Shriver Jr.	Richard M. Nixon*	Spiro T. Agnew
1976	Jimmy Carter*	Walter F. Mondale	Gerald R. Ford	Bob Dole
1980	Jimmy Carter	Walter F. Mondale	Ronald Reagan*	George Bush
1984	Walter F. Mondale	Geraldine Ferraro	Ronald Reagan*	George Bush
1988	Michael S. Dukakis	Lloyd Bentsen	George Bush*	Dan Quayle
1992	Bill Clinton*	Al Gore	George Bush	Dan Quayle
1996	Bill Clinton*	Al Gore	Bob Dole	Jack Kemp

(1) Douglas and Johnson were nominated at the Baltimore convention. An earlier convention in Charleston, SC, failed to reach a consensus and resulted in a split in the party. The Southern faction of the Democrats nominated John Breckinridge for president and Joseph Lane for vice president. (2) Died Oct. 30; replaced on ballot by Nicholas Butler.

Popular and Electoral Vote for President

(D) Democrat; (DR) Democratic Republican; (F) Federalist; (LR) Liberal Republican; (NR) National Republican; (P) People's; (PR) Progressive; (R) Republican; (RF) Reform; (SR) States' Rights; (W) Whig; Asterisk (*)—See notes.

Year	President elected	Popular	Elec.	Major losing candidate(s)	Popular	Elec.
1789	George Washington (F)	Unknown	69	No opposition	—	—
1792	George Washington (F)	Unknown	132	No opposition	—	—
1796	John Adams (F)	Unknown	71	Thomas Jefferson (DR)	Unknown	68
1800*	Thomas Jefferson (DR)	Unknown	73	Aaron Burr (DR)	Unknown	73
1804	Thomas Jefferson (DR)	Unknown	162	Charles Pinckney (F)	Unknown	14
1808	James Madison (DR)	Unknown	122	Charles Pinckney (F)	Unknown	47
1812	James Madison (DR)	Unknown	128	DeWitt Clinton (F)	Unknown	89
1816	James Monroe (DR)	Unknown	183	Rufus King (F)	Unknown	34
1820	James Monroe (DR)	Unknown	231	John Quincy Adams (DR)	Unknown	1
1824*	John Quincy Adams (DR)	105,321	84	Andrew Jackson (DR)	155,872	99
				Henry Clay (DR)	46,587	37
				William H. Crawford (DR)	44,282	41
1828	Andrew Jackson (D)	647,231	178	John Quincy Adams (NR)	509,097	83
1832	Andrew Jackson (D)	687,502	219	Henry Clay (NR)	530,189	49
1836	Martin Van Buren (D)	762,678	170	William H. Harrison (W)	548,007	73
1840	William H. Harrison (W)	1,275,017	234	Martin Van Buren (D)	1,128,702	60
1844	James K. Polk (D)	1,337,243	170	Henry Clay (W)	1,299,068	105
1848	Zachary Taylor (W)	1,360,101	163	Lewis Cass (D)	1,220,544	127
				Martin Van Buren (Free Soil)	291,501	—
1852	Franklin Pierce (D)	1,601,474	254	Winfield Scott (W)	1,386,578	42
1856	James Buchanan (D)	1,927,995	174	John C. Fremont (R)	1,391,555	114
				Millard Fillmore (American)	873,053	8
1860	Abraham Lincoln (R)	1,866,352	180	Stephen A. Douglas (D)	1,375,157	12
				John C. Breckinridge (D)	845,763	72
				John Bell (Const. Union)	589,581	39
1864	Abraham Lincoln (R)	2,216,067	212	George McClellan (D)	1,808,725	21
1868	Ulysses S. Grant (R)	3,015,071	214	Horatio Seymour (D)	2,709,615	80
1872*	Ulysses S. Grant (R)	3,597,070	286	Horace Greeley (D-LR)*	2,834,079	—
1876*	Rutherford B. Hayes (R)	4,033,950	185	Samuel J. Tilden (D)	4,284,757	184
1880	James A. Garfield (R)	4,449,053	214	Winfield S. Hancock (D)	4,442,030	155
1884	Grover Cleveland (D)	4,911,017	219	James G. Blaine (R)	4,848,334	182
1888*	Benjamin Harrison (R)	5,444,337	233	Grover Cleveland (D)	5,540,050	168
1892	Grover Cleveland (D)	5,554,414	277	Benjamin Harrison (R)	5,190,802	145
				James Weaver (P)	1,027,329	22
1896	William McKinley (R)	7,035,638	271	William J. Bryan (D-P)	6,467,946	176
1900	William McKinley (R)	7,219,530	292	William J. Bryan (D)	6,358,071	155
1904	Theodore Roosevelt (R)	7,628,834	336	Alton B. Parker (D)	5,084,491	140
1908	William H. Taft (R)	7,679,006	321	William J. Bryan (D)	6,409,106	162
1912	Woodrow Wilson (D)	6,286,214	435	Theodore Roosevelt (PR)	4,216,020	88
				William H. Taft (R)	3,483,922	8
1916	Woodrow Wilson (D)	9,129,606	277	Charles E. Hughes (R)	8,538,221	254
1920	Warren G. Harding (R)	16,152,200	404	James M. Cox (D)	9,147,353	127
1924	Calvin Coolidge (R)	15,725,016	382	John W. Davis (D)	8,385,586	136
				Robert M. La Follette (PR)	4,822,856	13
1928	Herbert Hoover (R)	21,392,190	444	Alfred E. Smith (D)	15,016,443	87
1932	Franklin D. Roosevelt (D)	22,821,857	472	Herbert Hoover (R)	15,761,841	59
1936	Franklin D. Roosevelt (D)	27,751,597	523	Alfred Landon (R)	16,679,583	8
1940	Franklin D. Roosevelt (D)	27,243,466	449	Wendell Willkie (R)	22,304,755	82
1944	Franklin D. Roosevelt (D)	25,602,505	432	Thomas E. Dewey (R)	22,006,278	99
1948	Harry S. Truman (D)	24,105,812	303	Thomas E. Dewey (R)	21,970,065	189
				Strom Thurmond (SR)	1,169,021	39
				Henry A. Wallace (PR)	1,157,172	—
1952	Dwight D. Eisenhower (R)	33,936,252	442	Adlai E. Stevenson (D)	27,314,992	89
1956*	Dwight D. Eisenhower (R)	35,585,316	457	Adlai E. Stevenson (D)	26,031,322	73
1960*	John F. Kennedy (D)	34,227,096	303	Richard M. Nixon (R)	34,108,546	219
1964	Lyndon B. Johnson (D)	43,126,506	486	Barry M. Goldwater (R)	27,176,799	52
1968	Richard M. Nixon (R)	31,785,480	301	Hubert H. Humphrey (D)	31,275,166	191
				George C. Wallace (3d party)	9,906,473	46
1972*	Richard M. Nixon (R)	47,165,234	520	George S. McGovern (D)	29,170,774	17
1976*	Jimmy Carter (D)	40,828,929	297	Gerald R. Ford (R)	39,148,940	240
1980	Ronald Reagan (R)	43,899,248	489	Jimmy Carter (D)	35,481,435	49
				John B. Anderson (independent)	5,719,437	—
1984	Ronald Reagan (R)	54,281,858	525	Walter F. Mondale (D)	37,457,215	13
1988*	George Bush (R)	48,881,221	426	Michael S. Dukakis (D)	41,805,422	111
1992	Bill Clinton (D)	44,908,254	370	George Bush (R)	39,102,343	168
				H. Ross Perot (independent)	19,741,065	—
1996	Bill Clinton (D)	47,401,185	379	Bob Dole (R)	39,197,469	159
				H. Ross Perot (RF)	8,085,294	—

1800—Elected by House of Representatives because of tied electoral vote. **1824**—Elected by House of Representatives because no candidate had polled a majority. By 1824, the Democratic Republicans had become a loose coalition of competing political groups. By 1828, the supporters of Jackson were known as Democrats, and the John Q. Adams and Henry Clay supporters as National Republicans. **1872**—Greeley died Nov. 29, 1872. His electoral votes were split among 4 individuals. **1876**—FL, LA, OR, and SC election returns were disputed. Congress in joint session (Mar. 2, 1877) declared Hayes and Wheeler elected president and vice president. **1888**—Cleveland had more popular votes than Harrison, but since Harrison won 233 electoral votes as against 168 for Cleveland, Harrison won the presidency. **1956**—Democrats elected 74 electors, but one from Alabama refused to vote for Stevenson. **1960**—Sen. Harry F. Byrd (D, VA) received 15 electoral votes. **1972**—John Hospers of California received one vote from an elector of Virginia. **1976**—Ronald Reagan of CA received one vote from an elector of Washington. **1988**—Sen. Lloyd Bentsen (D, TX) received 1 vote from an elector of West Virginia.

Presidents of the U.S.

No.	Name	Politics	Born	in	Inaug.	at age	Died	at age
1.	George Washington	Fed.	1732, Feb. 22	VA	1789	57	1799, Dec. 14	67
2.	John Adams	Fed.	1735, Oct. 30	MA	1797	61	1826, July 4	90
3.	Thomas Jefferson	Dem.-Rep.	1743, Apr. 13	VA	1801	57	1826, July 4	83
4.	James Madison	Dem.-Rep.	1751, Mar. 16	VA	1809	57	1836, June 28	85
5.	James Monroe	Dem.-Rep.	1758, Apr. 28	VA	1817	58	1831, July 4	73
6.	John Quincy Adams	Dem.-Rep.	1767, July 11	MA	1825	57	1848, Feb. 23	80
7.	Andrew Jackson	Dem.	1767, Mar. 15	SC	1829	61	1845, June 8	78
8.	Martin Van Buren	Dem.	1782, Dec. 5	NY	1837	54	1862, July 24	79
9.	William Henry Harrison	Whig	1773, Feb. 9	VA	1841	68	1841, Apr. 4	68
10.	John Tyler	Whig	1790, Mar. 29	VA	1841	51	1862, Jan. 18	71
11.	James Knox Polk	Dem.	1795, Nov. 2	NC	1845	49	1849, June 15	53
12.	Zachary Taylor	Whig	1784, Nov. 24	VA	1849	64	1850, July 9	65
13.	Millard Fillmore	Whig	1800, Jan. 7	NY	1850	50	1874, Mar. 8	74
14.	Franklin Pierce	Dem.	1804, Nov. 23	NH	1853	48	1869, Oct. 8	64
15.	James Buchanan	Dem.	1791, Apr. 23	PA	1857	65	1868, June 1	77
16.	Abraham Lincoln	Rep.	1809, Feb. 12	KY	1861	52	1865, Apr. 15	56
17.	Andrew Johnson	(1)	1808, Dec. 29	NC	1865	56	1875, July 31	66
18.	Ulysses Simpson Grant	Rep.	1822, Apr. 27	OH	1869	46	1885, July 23	63
19.	Rutherford Birchard Hayes	Rep.	1822, Oct. 4	OH	1877	54	1893, Jan. 17	70
20.	James Abram Garfield	Rep.	1831, Nov. 19	OH	1881	49	1881, Sept. 19	49
21.	Chester Alan Arthur	Rep.	1830, Oct. 5	VT	1881	50	1886, Nov. 18	56
22.	Grover Cleveland	Dem.	1837, Mar. 18	NJ	1885	47	1908, June 24	71
23.	Benjamin Harrison	Rep.	1833, Aug. 20	OH	1889	55	1901, Mar. 13	67
24.	Grover Cleveland	Dem.	1837, Mar. 18	NJ	1893	55	1908, June 24	71
25.	William McKinley	Rep.	1843, Jan. 29	OH	1897	54	1901, Sept. 14	58
26.	Theodore Roosevelt	Rep.	1858, Oct. 27	NY	1901	42	1919, Jan. 6	60
27.	William Howard Taft	Rep.	1857, Sept. 15	OH	1909	51	1930, Mar. 8	72
28.	Woodrow Wilson	Dem.	1856, Dec. 28	VA	1913	56	1924, Feb. 3	67
29.	Warren Gamaliel Harding	Rep.	1865, Nov. 2	OH	1921	55	1923, Aug. 2	57
30.	Calvin Coolidge	Rep.	1872, July 4	VT	1923	51	1933, Jan. 5	60
31.	Herbert Clark Hoover	Rep.	1874, Aug. 10	IA	1929	54	1964, Oct. 20	90
32.	Franklin Delano Roosevelt	Dem.	1882, Jan. 30	NY	1933	51	1945, Apr. 12	63
33.	Harry S. Truman	Dem.	1884, May 8	MO	1945	60	1972, Dec. 26	88
34.	Dwight David Eisenhower	Rep.	1890, Oct. 14	TX	1953	62	1969, Mar. 28	78
35.	John Fitzgerald Kennedy	Dem.	1917, May 29	MA	1961	43	1963, Nov. 22	46
36.	Lyndon Baines Johnson	Dem.	1908, Aug. 27	TX	1963	55	1973, Jan. 22	64
37.	Richard Milhous Nixon (2)	Rep.	1913, Jan. 9	CA	1969	56	1994, Apr. 22	81
38.	Gerald Rudolph Ford	Rep.	1913, July 14	NE	1974	61		
39.	Jimmy Carter	Dem.	1924, Oct. 1	GA	1977	52		
40.	Ronald Reagan	Rep.	1911, Feb. 6	IL	1981	69		
41.	George Bush	Rep.	1924, June 12	MA	1989	64		
42.	Bill Clinton	Dem.	1946, Aug. 19	AR	1993	46		

(1) Andrew Johnson was a Democrat, nominated vice president by Republicans, and elected with Lincoln on National Union ticket.
(2) Resigned Aug. 9, 1974.

U.S. Presidents, Vice Presidents, Congresses

	President	Service		Vice President	Congress
1.	George Washington	Apr. 30, 1789—Mar. 3, 1797	1.	John Adams	1, 2, 3, 4
2.	John Adams	Mar. 4, 1797—Mar. 3, 1801	2.	Thomas Jefferson	5, 6
3.	Thomas Jefferson	Mar. 4, 1801—Mar. 3, 1805	3.	Aaron Burr	7, 8
	"	Mar. 4, 1805—Mar. 3, 1809	4.	George Clinton	9, 10
4.	James Madison	Mar. 4, 1809—Mar. 3, 1813		" (1)	11, 12
	"	Mar. 4, 1813—Mar. 3, 1817	5.	Elbridge Gerry(2)	13, 14
5.	James Monroe	Mar. 4, 1817—Mar. 3, 1825	6.	Daniel D. Tompkins	15, 16, 17, 18
6.	John Quincy Adams	Mar. 4, 1825—Mar. 3, 1829	7.	John C. Calhoun	19, 20
7.	Andrew Jackson	Mar. 4, 1829—Mar. 3, 1833		" (3)	21, 22
	"	Mar. 4, 1833—Mar. 3, 1837	8.	Martin Van Buren	23, 24
8.	Martin Van Buren	Mar. 4, 1837—Mar. 3, 1841	9.	Richard M. Johnson	25, 26
9.	William Henry Harrison(4)	Mar. 4, 1841—Apr. 4, 1841	10.	John Tyler	27
10.	John Tyler	Apr. 6, 1841—Mar. 3, 1845			27, 28
11.	James K. Polk	Mar. 4, 1845—Mar. 3, 1849	11.	George M. Dallas	29, 30
12.	Zachary Taylor(4)	Mar. 5, 1849—July 9, 1850	12.	Millard Fillmore	31
13.	Millard Fillmore	July 10, 1850—Mar. 3, 1853			31, 32
14.	Franklin Pierce	Mar. 4, 1853—Mar. 3, 1857	13.	William R. King(5)	33, 34
15.	James Buchanan	Mar. 4, 1857—Mar. 3, 1861	14.	John C. Breckinridge	35, 36
16.	Abraham Lincoln	Mar. 4, 1861—Mar. 3, 1865	15.	Hannibal Hamlin	37, 38
	" (4)	Mar. 4, 1865—Apr. 15, 1865	16.	Andrew Johnson	39
17.	Andrew Johnson	Apr. 15, 1865—Mar. 3, 1869			39, 40
18.	Ulysses S. Grant	Mar. 4, 1869—Mar. 3, 1873	17.	Schuyler Colfax	41, 42
	"	Mar. 4, 1873—Mar. 3, 1877	18.	Henry Wilson(6)	43, 44
19.	Rutherford B. Hayes	Mar. 4, 1877—Mar. 3, 1881	19.	William A. Wheeler	45, 46
20.	James A. Garfield(4)	Mar. 4, 1881—Sept. 19, 1881	20.	Chester A. Arthur	47
21.	Chester A. Arthur	Sept. 20, 1881—Mar. 3, 1885			47, 48
22.	Grover Cleveland(7)	Mar. 4, 1885—Mar. 3, 1889	21.	Thomas A. Hendricks(8)	49, 50
23.	Benjamin Harrison	Mar. 4, 1889—Mar. 3, 1893	22.	Levi P. Morton	51, 52
24.	Grover Cleveland(7)	Mar. 4, 1893—Mar. 3, 1897	23.	Adlai E. Stevenson	53, 54
25.	William McKinley	Mar. 4, 1897—Mar. 3, 1901	24.	Garret A. Hobart(9)	55, 56
	"(4)	Mar. 4, 1901—Sept. 14, 1901	25.	Theodore Roosevelt	57
26.	Theodore Roosevelt	Sept. 14, 1901—Mar. 3, 1905			57, 58
	"	Mar. 4, 1905—Mar. 3, 1909	26.	Charles W. Fairbanks	59, 60
27.	William H. Taft	Mar. 4, 1909—Mar. 3, 1913	27.	James S. Sherman(10)	61, 62
28.	Woodrow Wilson	Mar. 4, 1913—Mar. 3, 1921	28.	Thomas R. Marshall	63, 64, 65, 66

(continued)

U.S. Presidents, Vice Presidents, Congresses *(continued)*

	President	Service		Vice President	Congress
29.	Warren G. Harding(4)	Mar. 4, 1921—Aug. 2, 1923	29.	Calvin Coolidge	67
30.	Calvin Coolidge	Aug. 3, 1923—Mar. 3, 1925			68
	"	Mar. 4, 1925—Mar. 3, 1929	30.	Charles G. Dawes	69, 70
31.	Herbert C. Hoover	Mar. 4, 1929—Mar. 3, 1933	31.	Charles Curtis	71, 72
32.	Franklin D. Roosevelt(11)	Mar. 4, 1933—Jan. 20, 1941	32.	John N. Garner	73, 74, 75, 76
	"	Jan. 20, 1941—Jan. 20, 1945	33.	Henry A. Wallace	77, 78
	" (4)	Jan. 20, 1945—Apr. 12, 1945	34.	Harry S. Truman	79
33.	Harry S. Truman	Apr. 12, 1945—Jan. 20, 1949			79, 80
	"	Jan. 20, 1949—Jan. 20, 1953	35.	Alben W. Barkley	81, 82
34.	Dwight D. Eisenhower	Jan. 20, 1953—Jan. 20, 1961	36.	Richard M. Nixon	83, 84, 85, 86
35.	John F. Kennedy(4)	Jan. 20, 1961—Nov. 22, 1963	37.	Lyndon B. Johnson	87, 88
36.	Lyndon B. Johnson	Nov. 22, 1963—Jan. 20, 1965			88
	"	Jan. 20, 1965—Jan. 20, 1969	38.	Hubert H. Humphrey	89, 90
37.	Richard M. Nixon	Jan. 20, 1969—Jan. 20, 1973	39.	Spiro T. Agnew(12)	91, 92, 93
	" (13)	Jan. 20, 1973—Aug. 9, 1974	40.	Gerald R. Ford(14)	93
38.	Gerald R. Ford(15)	Aug. 9, 1974—Jan. 20, 1977	41.	Nelson A. Rockefeller(16)	93, 94
39.	Jimmy (James Earl) Carter	Jan. 20, 1977—Jan. 20, 1981	42.	Walter F. Mondale	95, 96
40.	Ronald Reagan	Jan. 20, 1981—Jan. 20, 1989	43.	George Bush	97, 98, 99, 100
41.	George Bush	Jan. 20, 1989—Jan. 20, 1993	44.	Dan Quayle	101, 102
42.	Bill Clinton	Jan. 20, 1993—	45.	Al Gore	103, 104, 105

(1) Died Apr. 20, 1812. (2) Died Nov. 23, 1814. (3) Resigned Dec. 28, 1832, to become U.S. senator. (4) Died in office. (5) Died Apr. 18, 1853. (6) Died Nov. 22, 1875. (7) Terms not consecutive. (8) Died Nov. 25, 1885. (9) Died Nov. 21, 1899. (10) Died Oct. 30, 1912. (11) First president to be inaugurated under 20th Amendment, Jan. 20, 1937. (12) Resigned Oct. 10, 1973. (13) Resigned Aug. 9, 1974. (14) First nonelected vice president, chosen under 25th Amendment procedure. (15) First president never elected president or vice president. (16) Second nonelected vice president, chosen under 25th Amendment.

Vice Presidents of the U.S.

The numerals given vice presidents do not coincide with those given presidents, because some presidents had none and some had more than one.

Name	Birthplace	Year	Home	Inaug.	Politics	Place of death	Year	Age
1. John Adams	Quincy, MA	1735	MA	1789	Fed.	Quincy, MA	1826	90
2. Thomas Jefferson	Shadwell, VA	1743	VA	1797	Dem.-Rep.	Monticello, VA	1826	83
3. Aaron Burr	Newark, NJ	1756	NY	1801	Dem.-Rep.	Staten Island, NY	1836	80
4. George Clinton	Ulster Co., NY	1739	NY	1805	Dem.-Rep.	Washington, DC	1812	73
5. Elbridge Gerry	Marblehead, MA	1744	MA	1813	Dem.-Rep.	Washington, DC	1814	70
6. Daniel D. Tompkins	Scarsdale, NY	1774	NY	1817	Dem.-Rep.	Staten Island, NY	1825	51
7. John C. Calhoun(1)	Abbeville, SC	1782	SC	1825	Dem.-Rep.	Washington, DC	1850	68
8. Martin Van Buren	Kinderhook, NY	1782	NY	1833	Dem.	Kinderhook, NY	1862	79
9. Richard M. Johnson(2)	Louisville, KY	1780	KY	1837	Dem.	Frankfort, KY	1850	70
10. John Tyler	Greenway, VA	1790	VA	1841	Whig	Richmond, VA	1862	71
11. George M. Dallas	Philadelphia, PA	1792	PA	1845	Dem.	Philadelphia, PA	1864	72
12. Millard Fillmore	Summerhill, NY	1800	NY	1849	Whig	Buffalo, NY	1874	74
13. William R. King	Sampson Co., NC	1786	AL	1853	Dem.	Dallas Co., AL	1853	67
14. John C. Breckinridge	Lexington, KY	1821	KY	1857	Dem.	Lexington, KY	1875	54
15. Hannibal Hamlin	Paris, ME	1809	ME	1861	Rep.	Bangor, ME	1891	81
16. Andrew Johnson	Raleigh, NC	1808	TN	1865	(3)	Carter Co., TN	1875	66
17. Schuyler Colfax	New York, NY	1823	IN	1869	Rep.	Mankato, MN	1885	62
18. Henry Wilson	Farmington, NH	1812	MA	1873	Rep.	Washington, DC	1875	63
19. William A. Wheeler	Malone, NY	1819	NY	1877	Rep.	Malone, NY	1887	68
20. Chester A. Arthur	Fairfield, VT	1830	NY	1881	Rep.	New York, NY	1886	57
21. Thomas A. Hendricks	Muskingum Co., OH	1819	IN	1885	Dem.	Indianapolis, IN	1885	66
22. Levi P. Morton	Shoreham, VT	1824	NY	1889	Rep.	Rhinebeck, NY	1920	96
23. Adlai E. Stevenson(4)	Christian Co., KY	1835	IL	1893	Dem.	Chicago, IL	1914	78
24. Garret A. Hobart	Long Branch, NJ	1844	NJ	1897	Rep.	Paterson, NJ	1899	55
25. Theodore Roosevelt	New York, NY	1858	NY	1901	Rep.	Oyster Bay, NY	1919	60
26. Charles W. Fairbanks	Unionville Centre, OH	1852	IN	1905	Rep.	Indianapolis, IN	1918	66
27. James S. Sherman	Utica, NY	1855	NY	1909	Rep.	Utica, NY	1912	57
28. Thomas R. Marshall	N. Manchester, IN	1854	IN	1913	Dem.	Washington, DC	1925	71
29. Calvin Coolidge	Plymouth, VT	1872	MA	1921	Rep.	Northampton, MA	1933	60
30. Charles G. Dawes	Marietta, OH	1865	IL	1925	Rep.	Evanston, IL	1951	85
31. Charles Curtis	Topeka, KS	1860	KS	1929	Rep.	Washington, DC	1936	76
32. John Nance Garner	Red River Co., TX	1868	TX	1933	Dem.	Uvalde, TX	1967	98
33. Henry Agard Wallace	Adair County, IA	1888	IA	1941	Dem.	Danbury, CT	1965	77
34. Harry S. Truman	Lamar, MO	1884	MO	1945	Dem.	Kansas City, MO	1972	88
35. Alben W. Barkley	Graves County, KY	1877	KY	1949	Dem.	Lexington, VA	1956	78
36. Richard M. Nixon	Yorba Linda, CA	1913	CA	1953	Rep.	New York, NY	1994	81
37. Lyndon B. Johnson	Johnson City, TX	1908	TX	1961	Dem.	San Antonio, TX	1973	64
38. Hubert H. Humphrey	Wallace, SD	1911	MN	1965	Dem.	Waverly, MN	1978	66
39. Spiro T. Agnew(5)	Baltimore, MD	1918	MD	1969	Rep.	Berlin, MD	1996	77
40. Gerald R. Ford(6)	Omaha, NE	1913	MI	1973	Rep.			
41. Nelson A. Rockefeller(7)	Bar Harbor, ME	1908	NY	1974	Rep.	New York, NY	1979	70
42. Walter F. Mondale	Ceylon, MN	1928	MN	1977	Dem.			
43. George Bush	Milton, MA	1924	TX	1981	Rep.			
44. Dan Quayle	Indianapolis, IN	1947	IN	1989	Rep.			
45. Al Gore	Washington, DC	1948	TN	1993	Dem.			

(1) John C. Calhoun resigned Dec. 28, 1832, having been elected to the Senate to fill a vacancy. (2) Richard M. Johnson was the only vice president to be chosen by the Senate because of a tied vote in the Electoral College. (3) Andrew Johnson was a Democrat, nominated vice president by Republicans, and elected with Lincoln on the National Union Ticket. (4) Adlai E. Stevenson, 23d vice president, was grandfather of Democratic candidate for president in 1952 and 1956. (5) Resigned Oct. 10, 1973. (6) First nonelected vice president, chosen under 25th Amendment procedure. (7) Second nonelected vice president, chosen under 25th Amendment procedure.

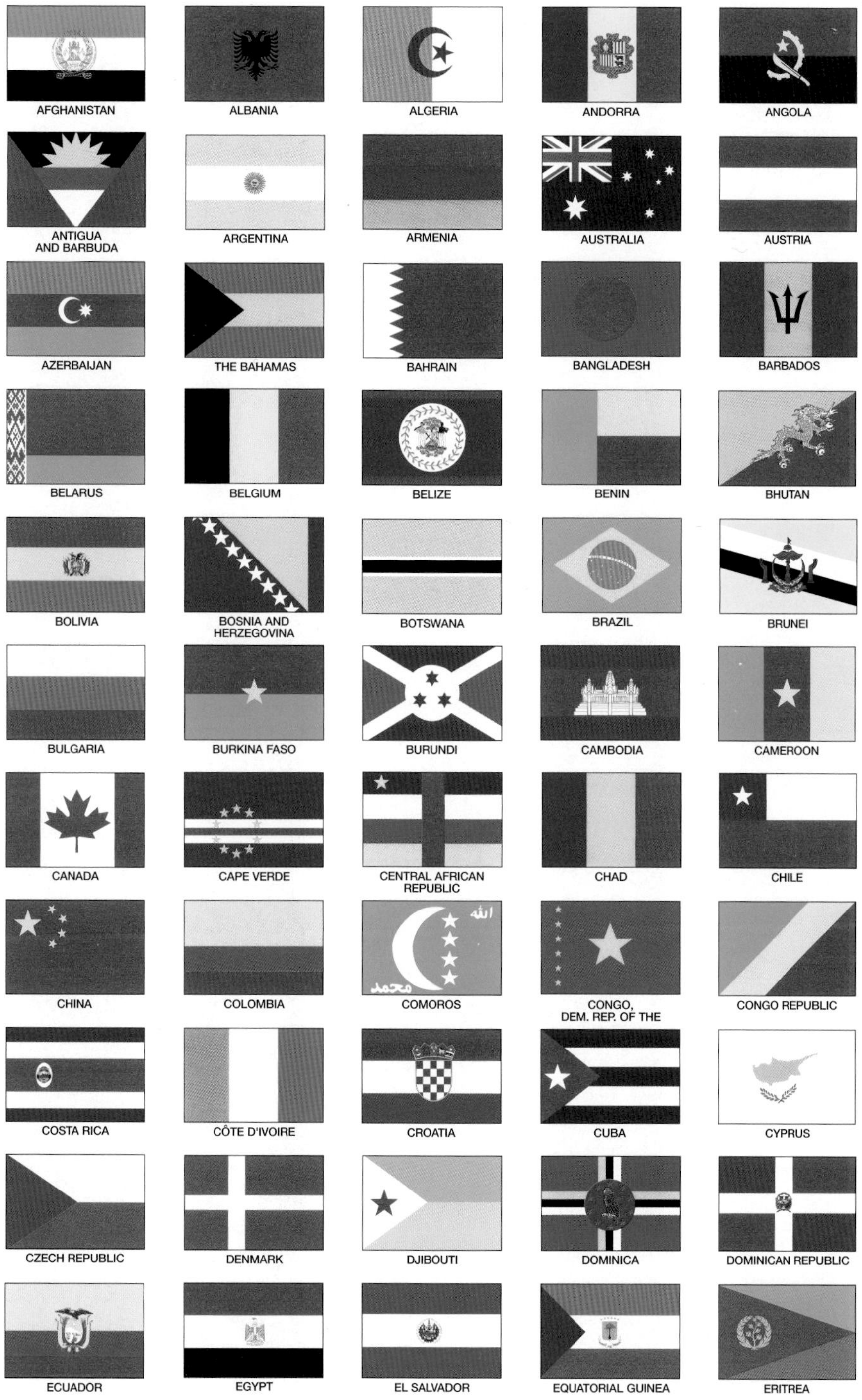
AFGHANISTAN
ALBANIA
ALGERIA
ANDORRA
ANGOLA
ANTIGUA AND BARBUDA
ARGENTINA
ARMENIA
AUSTRALIA
AUSTRIA
AZERBAIJAN
THE BAHAMAS
BAHRAIN
BANGLADESH
BARBADOS
BELARUS
BELGIUM
BELIZE
BENIN
BHUTAN
BOLIVIA
BOSNIA AND HERZEGOVINA
BOTSWANA
BRAZIL
BRUNEI
BULGARIA
BURKINA FASO
BURUNDI
CAMBODIA
CAMEROON
CANADA
CAPE VERDE
CENTRAL AFRICAN REPUBLIC
CHAD
CHILE
CHINA
COLOMBIA
COMOROS
CONGO, DEM. REP. OF THE
CONGO REPUBLIC
COSTA RICA
CÔTE D'IVOIRE
CROATIA
CUBA
CYPRUS
CZECH REPUBLIC
DENMARK
DJIBOUTI
DOMINICA
DOMINICAN REPUBLIC
ECUADOR
EGYPT
EL SALVADOR
EQUATORIAL GUINEA
ERITREA

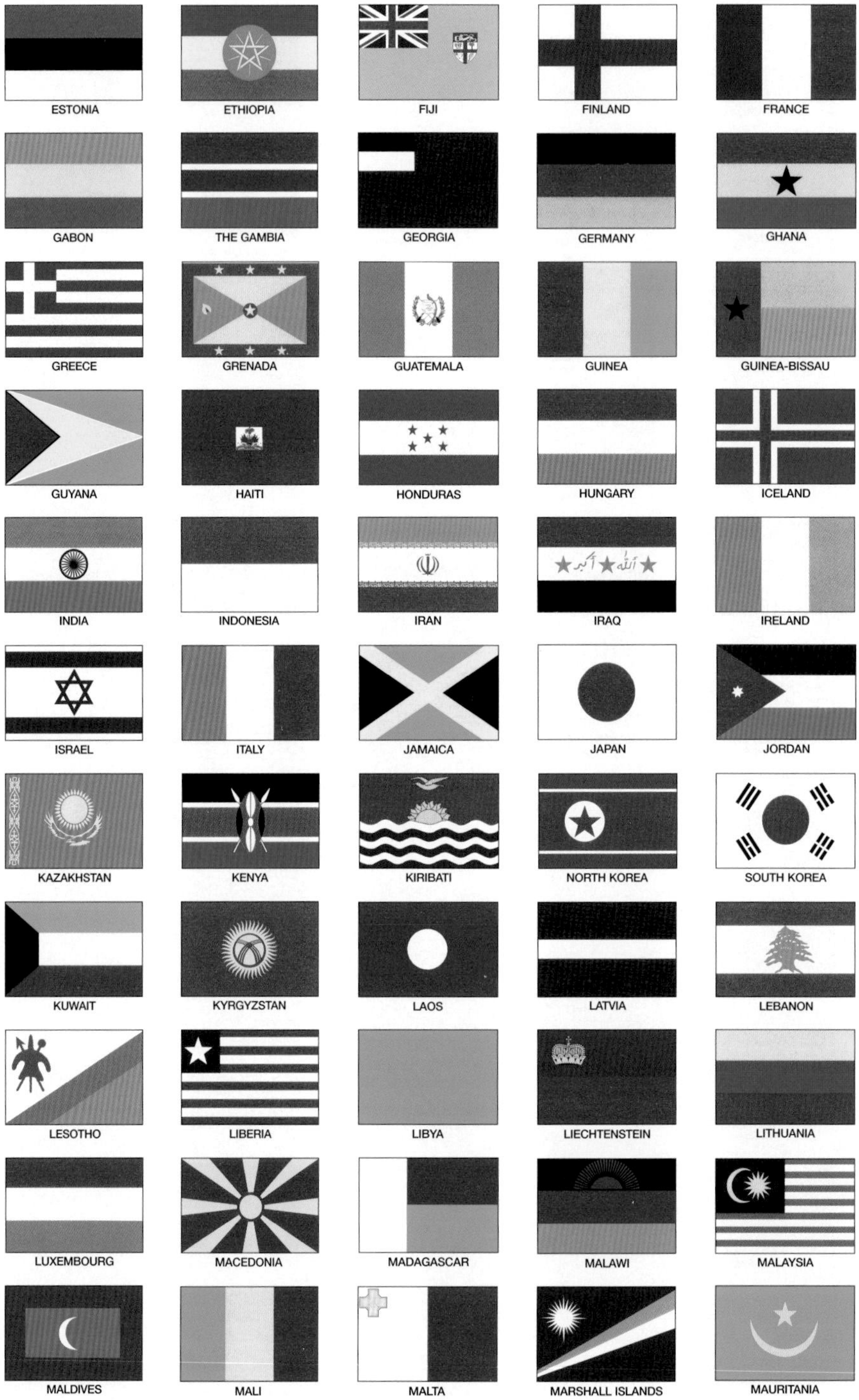
ESTONIA
ETHIOPIA
FIJI
FINLAND
FRANCE
GABON
THE GAMBIA
GEORGIA
GERMANY
GHANA
GREECE
GRENADA
GUATEMALA
GUINEA
GUINEA-BISSAU
GUYANA
HAITI
HONDURAS
HUNGARY
ICELAND
INDIA
INDONESIA
IRAN
IRAQ
IRELAND
ISRAEL
ITALY
JAMAICA
JAPAN
JORDAN
KAZAKHSTAN
KENYA
KIRIBATI
NORTH KOREA
SOUTH KOREA
KUWAIT
KYRGYZSTAN
LAOS
LATVIA
LEBANON
LESOTHO
LIBERIA
LIBYA
LIECHTENSTEIN
LITHUANIA
LUXEMBOURG
MACEDONIA
MADAGASCAR
MALAWI
MALAYSIA
MALDIVES
MALI
MALTA
MARSHALL ISLANDS
MAURITANIA

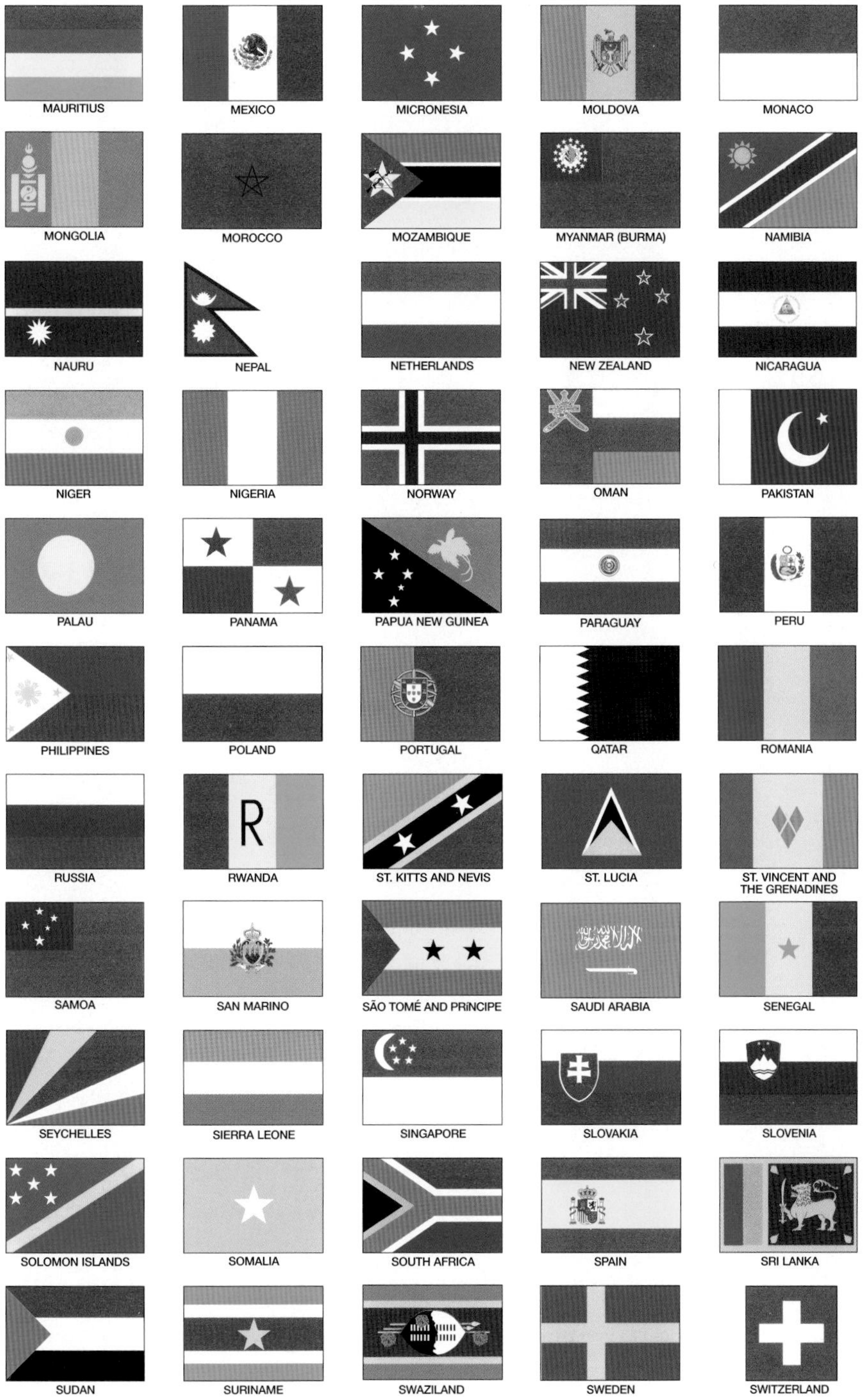
MAURITIUS
MEXICO
MICRONESIA
MOLDOVA
MONACO
MONGOLIA
MOROCCO
MOZAMBIQUE
MYANMAR (BURMA)
NAMIBIA
NAURU
NEPAL
NETHERLANDS
NEW ZEALAND
NICARAGUA
NIGER
NIGERIA
NORWAY
OMAN
PAKISTAN
PALAU
PANAMA
PAPUA NEW GUINEA
PARAGUAY
PERU
PHILIPPINES
POLAND
PORTUGAL
QATAR
ROMANIA
RUSSIA
R
RWANDA
ST. KITTS AND NEVIS
ST. LUCIA
ST. VINCENT AND THE GRENADINES
SAMOA
SAN MARINO
SÃO TOMÉ AND PRíNCIPE
SAUDI ARABIA
SENEGAL
SEYCHELLES
SIERRA LEONE
SINGAPORE
SLOVAKIA
SLOVENIA
SOLOMON ISLANDS
SOMALIA
SOUTH AFRICA
SPAIN
SRI LANKA
SUDAN
SURINAME
SWAZILAND
SWEDEN
SWITZERLAND

SYRIA

TAIWAN

TAJIKISTAN

TANZANIA

THAILAND

TOGO

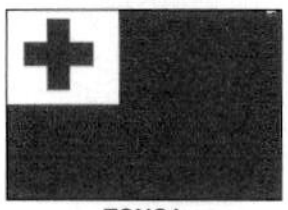
TONGA

TRINIDAD AND TOBAGO

TUNISIA

TURKEY

TURKMENISTAN

TUVALU

UGANDA

UKRAINE

UNITED ARAB EMIRATES

UNITED KINGDOM

UNITED STATES

URUGUAY

UZBEKISTAN

VANUATU

VATICAN CITY

VENEZUELA

VIETNAM

YEMEN

YUGOSLAVIA

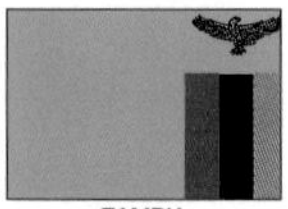
ZAMBIA

ZIMBABWE

INTERNATIONAL TIME ZONES

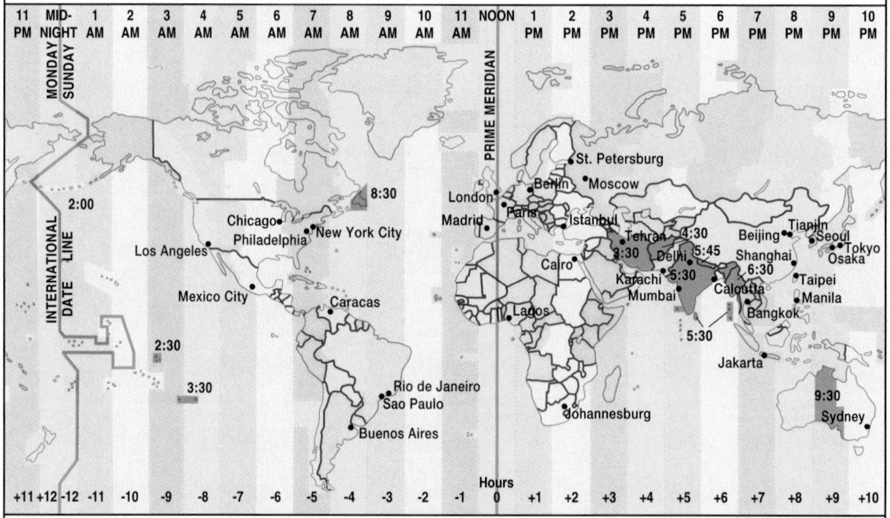

The world is divided into 24 time zones, each 15° longitude wide. The longitudinal meridian passing through Greenwich, England, is the starting point, and is called the *prime meridian.* The 12th zone is divided by the 180th meridian (International Date Line). When the line is crossed going west, the date is advanced one day; when crossed going east, the date becomes a day earlier.

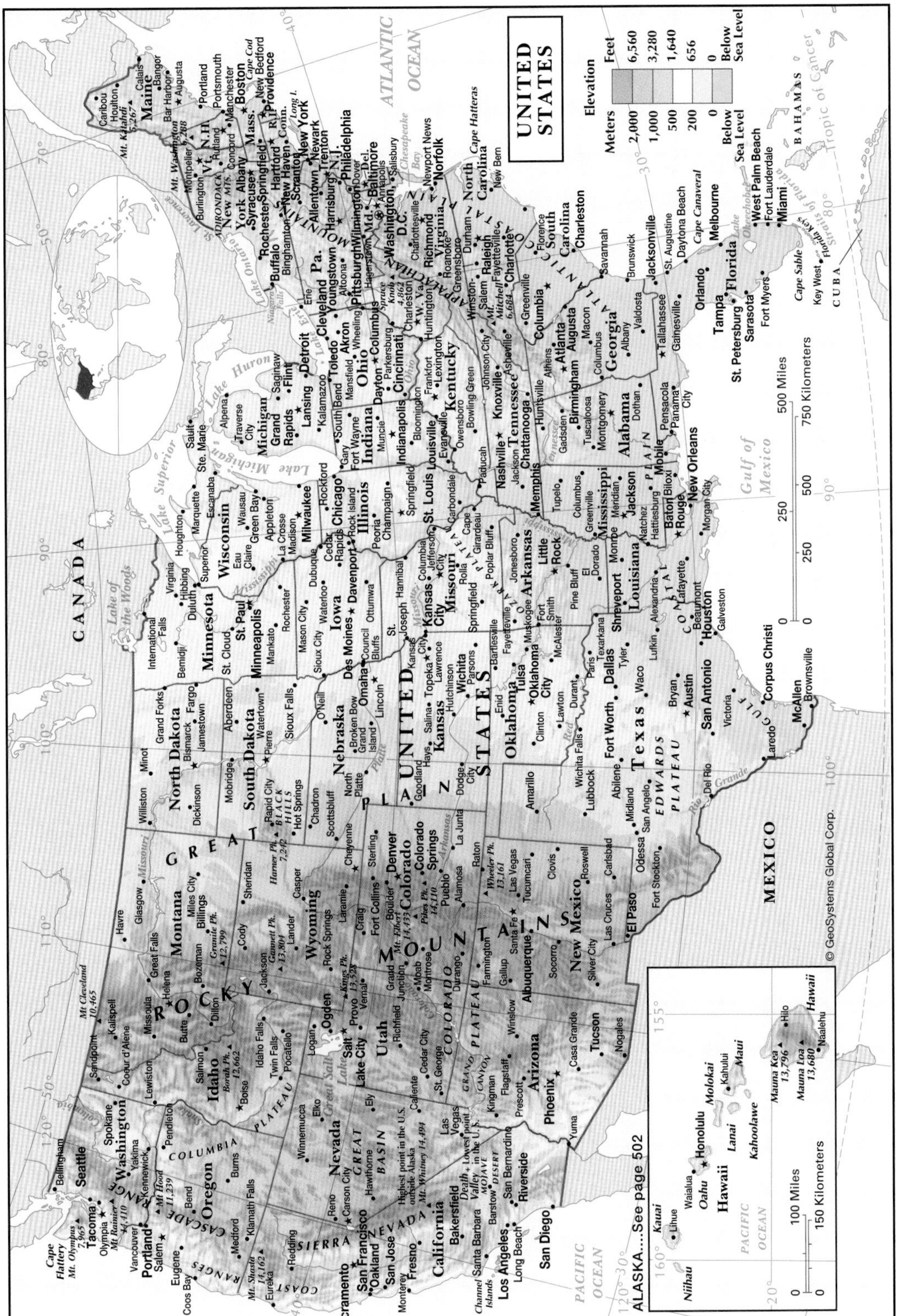

UNITED STATES
Elevation
Meters
Feet
2,000
6,560
1,000
3,280
500
1,640
200
656
0
0
Below Sea Level
Below Sea Level
CANADA
MEXICO
ATLANTIC OCEAN
PACIFIC OCEAN
Gulf of Mexico
GREAT PLAINS
ROCKY MOUNTAINS
APPALACHIAN MOUNTAINS
ATLANTIC COASTAL PLAIN
GULF COASTAL PLAIN
COLORADO PLATEAU
GREAT BASIN
COLUMBIA PLATEAU
CASCADE RANGE
SIERRA NEVADA
COAST RANGES
EDWARDS PLATEAU
OZARK PLATEAU
Washington
Oregon
California
Idaho
Nevada
Montana
Wyoming
Utah
Colorado
Arizona
New Mexico
North Dakota
South Dakota
Nebraska
Kansas
Oklahoma
Texas
Minnesota
Iowa
Missouri
Arkansas
Louisiana
Wisconsin
Illinois
Michigan
Indiana
Ohio
Kentucky
Tennessee
Mississippi
Alabama
Georgia
Florida
South Carolina
North Carolina
Virginia
W. Va.
Pa.
New York
Maine
Vt.
N.H.
Mass.
Conn.
R.I.
N.J.
Del.
Md.
D.C.
Hawaii
ALASKA....See page 502
0 250 500 Miles
0 250 500 750 Kilometers
0 100 Miles
0 150 Kilometers
© GeoSystems Global Corp.

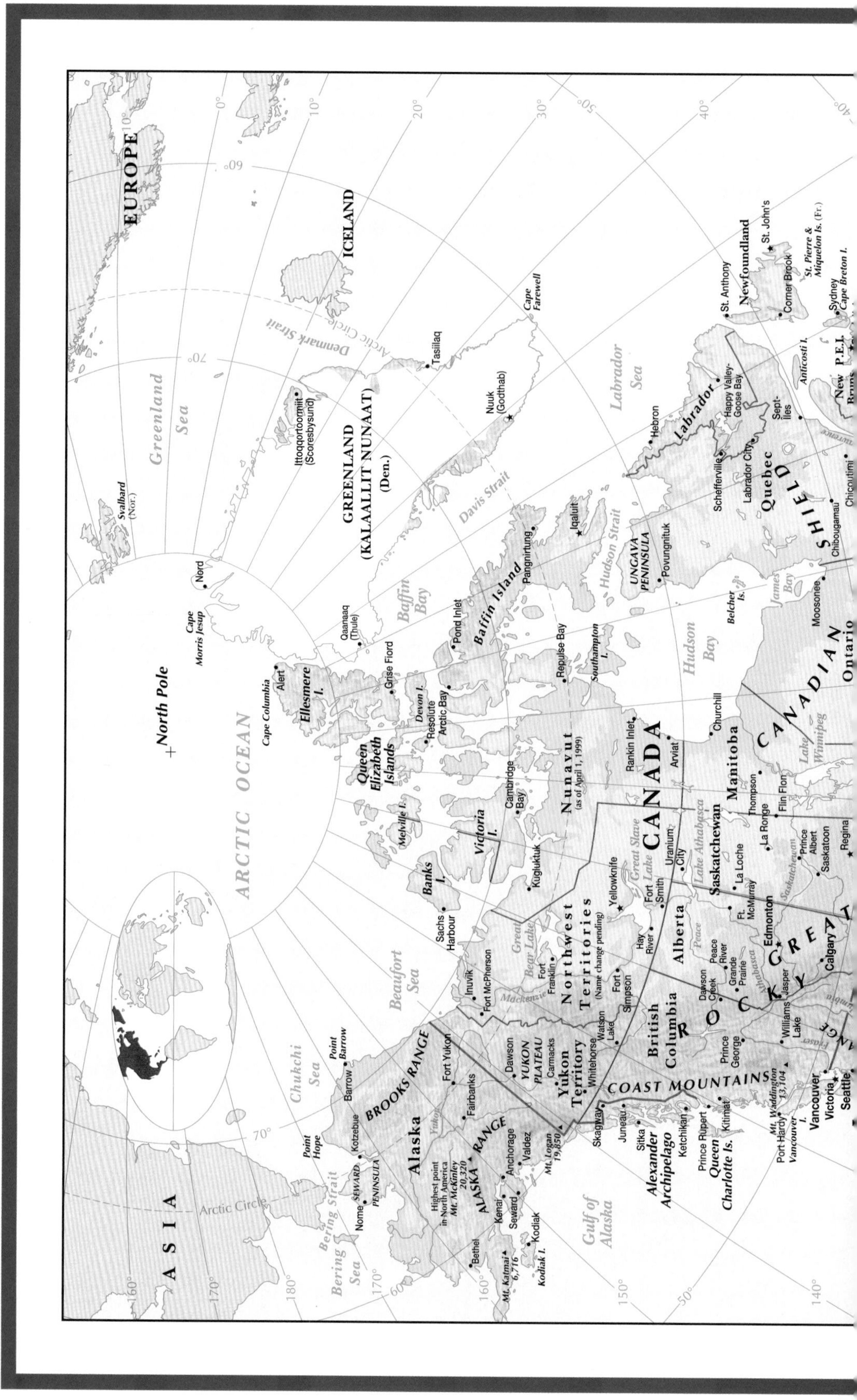
EUROPE
ICELAND
ASIA
ARCTIC OCEAN
North Pole
Greenland Sea
Svalbard (Nor.)
Denmark Strait
Arctic Circle
GREENLAND (KALAALLIT NUNAAT) (Den.)
Ittoqqortoormiit (Scoresbysund)
Tasiilaq
Cape Farewell
Nuuk (Godthab)
Nord
Cape Morris Jesup
Cape Columbia
Alert
Ellesmere I.
Qaanaaq (Thule)
Grise Fiord
Baffin Bay
Davis Strait
Labrador Sea
Devon I.
Resolute
Arctic Bay
Pond Inlet
Baffin Island
Pangnirtung
Iqaluit
Queen Elizabeth Islands
Melville I.
Banks I.
Victoria I.
Cambridge Bay
Kugluktuk
Sachs Harbour
Beaufort Sea
Chukchi Sea
Point Barrow
Barrow
Point Hope
Kotzebue
Bering Strait
Bering Sea
SEWARD PENINSULA
Nome
Bethel
BROOKS RANGE
Alaska
Fort Yukon
Fairbanks
ALASKA RANGE
Highest point in North America Mt. McKinley 20,320
Anchorage
Valdez
Kenai
Seward
Kodiak
Kodiak I.
Mt. Katmai 6,716
Mt. Logan 19,850
Gulf of Alaska
Inuvik
Fort McPherson
Dawson
YUKON PLATEAU
Carmacks
Yukon Territory
Whitehorse
Skagway
Juneau
Sitka
Alexander Archipelago
Ketchikan
Prince Rupert
Queen Charlotte Is.
Kitimat
Port Hardy
Vancouver I.
Mt. Waddington 13,104
COAST MOUNTAINS
Vancouver
Victoria
Seattle
Watson Lake
Fort Simpson
Fort Franklin
Great Bear Lake
Northwest Territories (Name change pending)
Yellowknife
Great Slave Lake
Hay River
Fort Smith
British Columbia
Prince George
Williams Lake
Dawson Creek
Peace River
Grande Prairie
Jasper
ROCKY
Alberta
Edmonton
Calgary
Ft. McMurray
La Loche
Uranium City
Lake Athabasca
Saskatchewan
La Ronge
Prince Albert
Saskatoon
Regina
CANADA
Nunavut (as of April 1, 1999)
Repulse Bay
Rankin Inlet
Arviat
Churchill
Southampton I.
Hudson Bay
Manitoba
Thompson
Flin Flon
Lake Winnipeg
CANADIAN
Ontario
Belcher Is.
James Bay
Moosonee
UNGAVA PENINSULA
Povungnituk
Hudson Strait
Hebron
Labrador
Schefferville
Labrador City
Happy Valley-Goose Bay
Quebec
SHIELD
Chibougamau
Chicoutimi
Sept-Iles
Anticosti I.
St. Anthony
Newfoundland
Corner Brook
St. John's
St. Pierre & Miquelon Is. (Fr.)
Sydney
Cape Breton I.
P.E.I.
New Bruns.

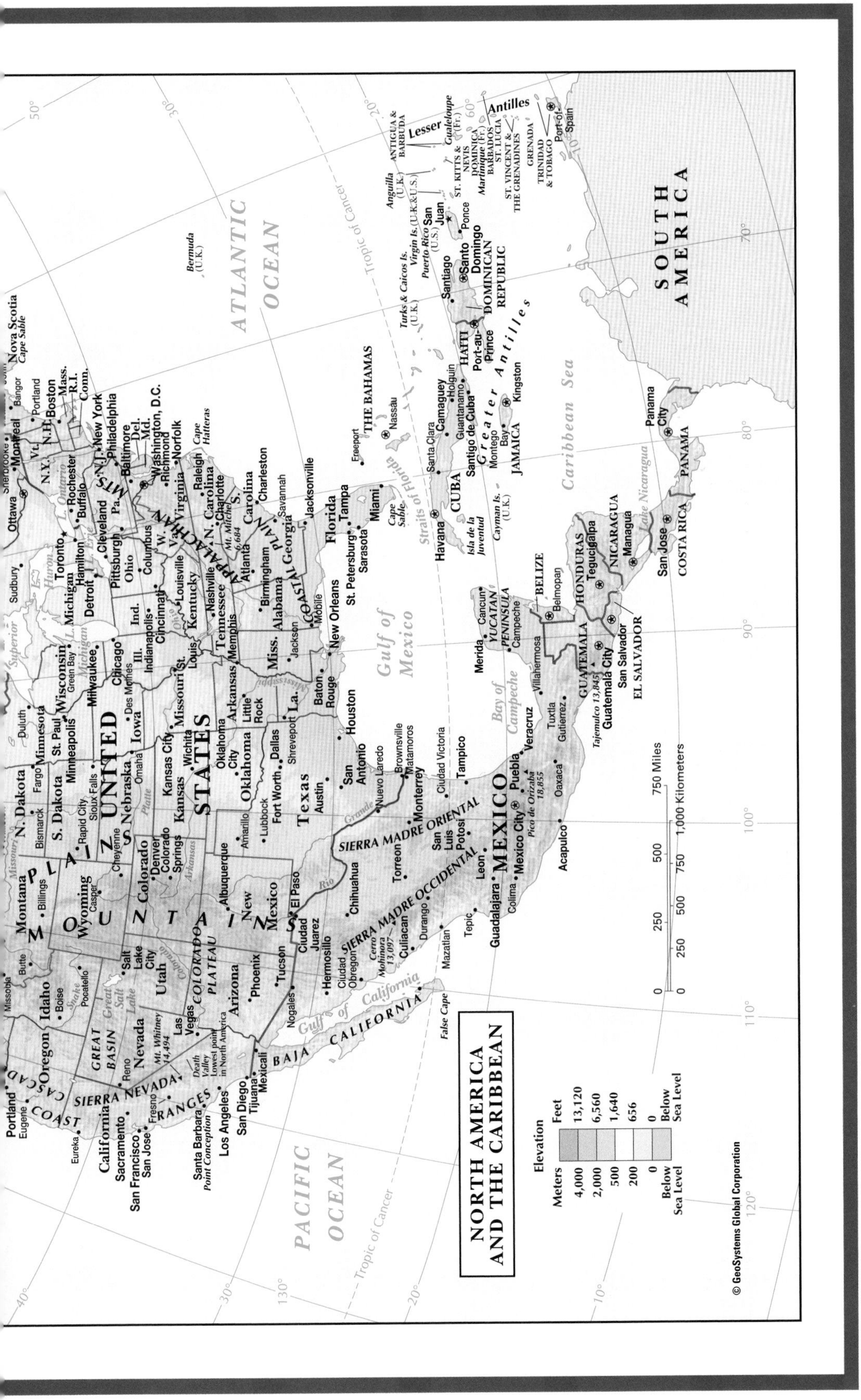

NORTH AMERICA
AND THE CARIBBEAN
Elevation
Meters
Feet
4,000
13,120
2,000
6,560
500
1,640
200
656
0
0
Below Sea Level
Below Sea Level
0
250
500
750 Miles
0
250
500
750
1,000 Kilometers
© GeoSystems Global Corporation
PACIFIC OCEAN
ATLANTIC OCEAN
Tropic of Cancer
UNITED STATES
MEXICO
CUBA
HAITI
DOMINICAN REPUBLIC
JAMAICA
THE BAHAMAS
BELIZE
GUATEMALA
HONDURAS
EL SALVADOR
NICARAGUA
COSTA RICA
PANAMA
SOUTH AMERICA
Gulf of Mexico
Caribbean Sea
Bay of Campeche
Gulf of California
Straits of Florida
Greater Antilles
Lesser Antilles
ROCKY MOUNTAINS
GREAT PLAINS
APPALACHIAN MTS.
COASTAL PLAIN
COAST RANGES
CASCADE
SIERRA NEVADA
GREAT BASIN
COLORADO PLATEAU
SIERRA MADRE ORIENTAL
SIERRA MADRE OCCIDENTAL
BAJA CALIFORNIA
YUCATAN PENINSULA
Bermuda (U.K.)
Turks & Caicos Is. (U.K.)
Cayman Is. (U.K.)
Puerto Rico (U.S.)
Virgin Is. (U.K.&U.S.)
Anguilla (U.K.)
ANTIGUA & BARBUDA
Guadeloupe (Fr.)
ST. KITTS & NEVIS
DOMINICA
Martinique (Fr.)
BARBADOS
ST. LUCIA
ST. VINCENT & THE GRENADINES
GRENADA
TRINIDAD & TOBAGO
Port-of-Spain
Isla de la Juventud
Mt. Whitney 14,494
Death Valley lowest point in North America
Mt. Mitchell 6,684
Pico de Orizaba 18,855
Tajemulco 13,845
Cerro Mohinora 13,097
Cape Hatteras
Cape Sable
False Cape
Point Conception
Havana
Nassau
Santo Domingo
Port-au-Prince
Kingston
Mexico City
Guatemala City
Tegucigalpa
Managua
San Jose
Panama City
San Salvador
Belmopan
Washington, D.C.
Ottawa

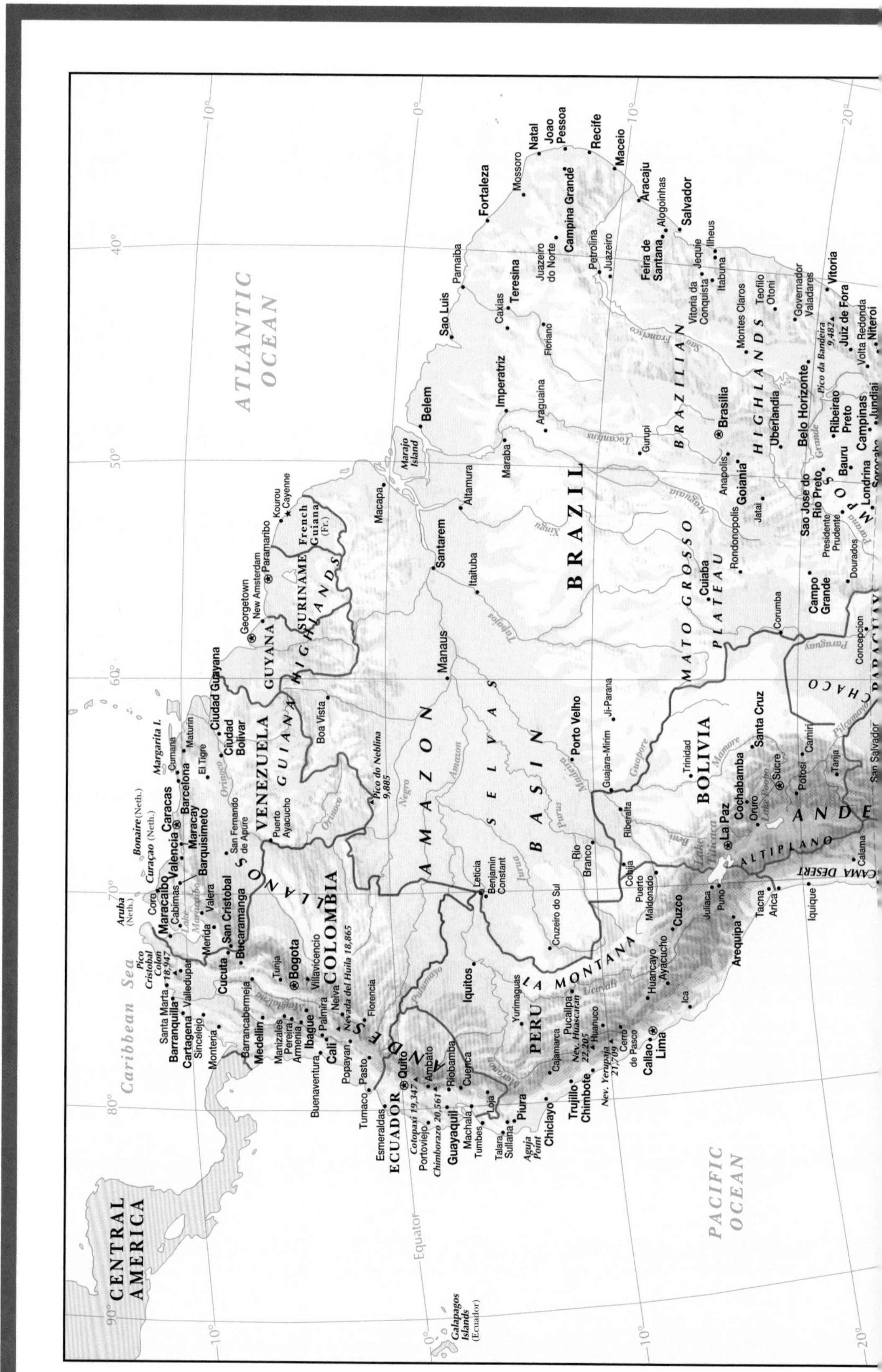

CENTRAL AMERICA
Caribbean Sea
ATLANTIC OCEAN
PACIFIC OCEAN
Equator
Galapagos Islands (Ecuador)
Aruba (Neth.)
Curaçao (Neth.)
Bonaire (Neth.)
Margarita I.
Pico Cristobal Colon 18,947
Santa Marta
Barranquilla
Cartagena
Sincelejo
Monteria
Valledupar
Maracaibo
Cabimas
Lake Maracaibo
Coro
Valencia
Caracas
Maracay
Barquisimeto
Barcelona
Cumana
Maturin
El Tigre
Ciudad Guayana
Ciudad Bolivar
San Fernando de Apure
Puerto Ayacucho
Merida
Valera
San Cristobal
Cucuta
Bucaramanga
Barrancabermeja
Medellin
Manizales
Pereira
Armenia
Ibague
Tunja
Bogota
Villavicencio
Neiva
Cali
Palmira
Buenaventura
Popayan
Pasto
Florencia
Nevada del Huila 18,865
Tumaco
Esmeraldas
VENEZUELA
COLOMBIA
LLANOS
GUYANA
Georgetown
New Amsterdam
SURINAME
Paramaribo
French Guiana (Fr.)
Kourou
Cayenne
GUIANA HIGHLANDS
Boa Vista
Pico do Neblina 9,885
Orinoco
Negro
Amazon
AMAZON BASIN
SELVAS
Macapa
Marajo Island
Belem
Santarem
Altamura
Itaituba
Manaus
Tapajos
Xingu
Tocantins
Araguaia
Madeira
Purus
Jurua
Guapore
Mamore
Beni
Porto Velho
Ji-Parana
Guajara-Mirim
Riberalta
Rio Branco
Cobija
Cruzeiro do Sul
Leticia
Benjamin Constant
Iquitos
Putumayo
Marañon
Ucayali
Yurimaguas
Pucallpa
Huanuco
Nev. Huascaran 22,205
Nev. Yerupaja 21,709
Cerro de Pasco
Huancayo
Ayacucho
Cuzco
Puerto Maldonado
Juliaca
Puno
Arequipa
Tacna
Arica
Iquique
Ica
Callao
Lima
Chimbote
Trujillo
Cajamarca
Chiclayo
Piura
Talara
Sullana
Tumbes
Aguja Point
PERU
LA MONTANA
ECUADOR
Quito
Cotopaxi 19,347
Ambato
Riobamba
Chimborazo 20,561
Portoviejo
Guayaquil
Machala
Cuenca
Loja
ANDES
BOLIVIA
Trinidad
La Paz
Lake Titicaca
Lake Poopo
Oruro
Cochabamba
Santa Cruz
Sucre
Potosi
Camiri
Tarija
San Salvador
Calama
ALTIPLANO
ATACAMA DESERT
CHACO
PARAGUAY
Paraguay
Pilcomayo
Concepcion
BRAZIL
MATO GROSSO PLATEAU
BRAZILIAN HIGHLANDS
Sao Francisco
Cuiaba
Rondonopolis
Corumba
Campo Grande
Dourados
Jatai
Goiania
Anapolis
Brasilia
Gurupi
Maraba
Araguaina
Imperatriz
Sao Luis
Parnaiba
Teresina
Caxias
Floriano
Fortaleza
Mossoro
Natal
Joao Pessoa
Campina Grande
Recife
Juazeiro do Norte
Petrolina
Juazeiro
Maceio
Aracaju
Alagoinhas
Salvador
Feira de Santana
Jequie
Ilheus
Itabuna
Vitoria da Conquista
Montes Claros
Teofilo Otoni
Governador Valadares
Vitoria
Uberlandia
Belo Horizonte
Pico da Bandeira 9,482
Juiz de Fora
Volta Redonda
Niteroi
Ribeirao Preto
Sao Jose do Rio Preto
Presidente Prudente
Bauru
Londrina
Campinas
Jundiai
Grande
Parana

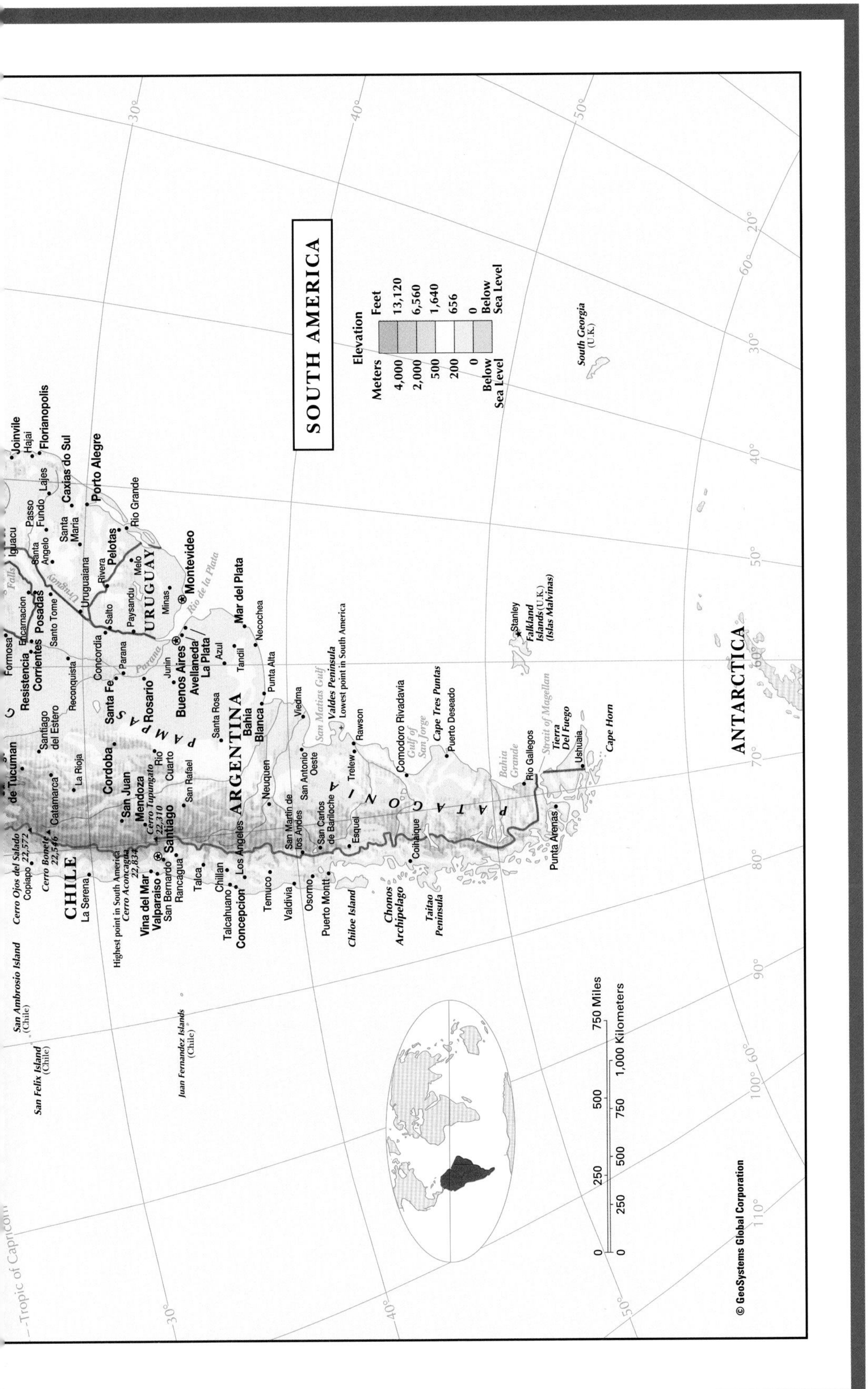

SOUTH AMERICA
Elevation
Meters
Feet
4,000
13,120
2,000
6,560
500
1,640
200
656
0
0
Below Sea Level
Below Sea Level
CHILE
ARGENTINA
URUGUAY
PAMPAS
PATAGONIA
ANTARCTICA
San Ambrosio Island (Chile)
San Felix Island (Chile)
Juan Fernandez Islands (Chile)
Cerro Ojos del Salado 22,572
Cerro Bonete 22,546
Highest point in South America Cerro Aconcagua 22,834
Cerro Tupungato 22,310
Copiapo
La Serena
Vina del Mar
Valparaiso
Santiago
San Bernardo
Rancagua
Talca
Chillan
Talcahuano
Concepcion
Los Angeles
Temuco
Valdivia
Osorno
Puerto Montt
Chiloe Island
Chonos Archipelago
Taitao Peninsula
Coihaique
Punta Arenas
de Tucuman
Catamarca
La Rioja
Santiago del Estero
Cordoba
San Juan
Mendoza
San Rafael
Rio Cuarto
Santa Fe
Rosario
Reconquista
Resistencia
Corrientes
Formosa
Encarnacion
Posadas
Santo Tome
Concordia
Parana
Salto
Paysandu
Uruguaiana
Rivera
Melo
Minas
Montevideo
Rio de la Plata
Buenos Aires
Avellaneda
La Plata
Junin
Azul
Tandil
Mar del Plata
Necochea
Punta Alta
Santa Rosa
Bahia Blanca
Neuquen
San Martin de los Andes
San Carlos de Bariloche
Esquel
San Antonio Oeste
Viedma
San Matias Gulf
Valdes Peninsula
Lowest point in South America
Trelew
Rawson
Comodoro Rivadavia
Gulf of San Jorge
Cape Tres Puntas
Puerto Deseado
Bahia Grande
Rio Gallegos
Strait of Magellan
Tierra Del Fuego
Ushuaia
Cape Horn
Stanley
Falkland Islands (U.K.) (Islas Malvinas)
South Georgia (U.K.)
Iguacu Falls
Santa Angelo
Passo Fundo
Santa Maria
Pelotas
Rio Grande
Porto Alegre
Caxias do Sul
Lajes
Florianopolis
Hajai
Joinvile
Uruguay
Parana
Tropic of Capricorn
750 Miles
1,000 Kilometers
© GeoSystems Global Corporation

EUROPE
Elevation
Meters
Feet
4,000
13,120
2,000
6,560
500
1,640
200
656
0
0
Below Sea Level
Below Sea Level
GREENLAND
(KALAALLIT NUNAAT)
(Denmark)
Arctic Circle
Isafjordhur
Keflavik
Reykjavik
ICELAND
Akureyri
Seydhisfjordhur
Norwegian Sea
Torshavn
Faroe Islands
(Den.)
Shetland Islands
(U.K.)
Orkney Islands
ATLANTIC OCEAN
North Sea
Hebrides
Thurso
Inverness
Scotland
Aberdeen
Dundee
Glasgow
Ayr
Edinburgh
Londonderry
Northern Ireland
Belfast
Galway
UNITED KINGDOM
Newcastle
IRELAND
Dublin
Limerick
Cork
Waterford
Liverpool
Leeds
Manchester
Kingston upon Hull
Sheffield
Birmingham
Coventry
Norwich
Wales
Swansea
Cardiff
Bristol
England
Thames
London
Plymouth
Land's End
Portsmouth
Dover
English Channel
Channel Is.
(U.K.)
Brest
Le Havre
Caen
Rouen
Paris
Seine
Rennes
Le Mans
Nantes
Loire
Orleans
Tours
Bay of Biscay
FRANCE
Limoges
Dijon
Bordeaux
Clermont-Ferrand
Lyon
Saint-Etienne
Grenoble
Garonne
Rhone
Toulouse
Montpellier
Marseille
Toulon
Nice
MONACO
Avignon
NETHERLANDS
Amsterdam
The Hague
Rotterdam
Antwerp
Brussels
Lille
BELGIUM
Liege
LUXEMBOURG
Luxembourg
Groningen
Bremen
Hamburg
Hannover
Bielefeld
Essen
Cologne
Bonn
GERMANY
Kassel
Wiesbaden
Frankfurt
Mannheim
Saarbrucken
Nancy
Strasbourg
Rhine
Stuttgart
Nurnberg
Augsburg
Munich
Basel
Zurich
Bern
SWITZERLAND
Geneva
Mt. Blanc
15,771
Matterhorn
14,690
ALPS
LIECHTENSTEIN
Milan
Verona
Torino
Genoa
Venice
Parma
Po
Bologna
Florence
Pisa
SAN MARINO
APENNINES
Ancona
Perugia
Tiber
Elba
Corsica
(Fr.)
Ajaccio
VATICAN CITY
Rome
ITALY
Naples
Vesuvius
4,202
Foggia
Salerno
Sassari
Sardinia
(It.)
Cagliari
Tyrrhenian Sea
Palermo
Messina
Etna
11,053
Sicily
(It.)
Catania
Reggio di Calabria
MALTA
Valletta
Mediterranean Sea
Adriatic Sea
A Coruna
Vigo
Gijon
Santander
Leon
Bilbao
Donostia–San Sebastian
Vitoria
Pamplona
Braga
Porto
Duero
Valladolid
Ebro
Pico de Aneto
11,168
PYRENEES
ANDORRA
Coimbra
IBERIAN
Salamanca
PORTUGAL
Lisbon
Setubal
Madrid
Zaragoza
Tagus
Badajoz
Toledo
SPAIN
Barcelona
Terragona
Castellon de la Plana
Valencia
PENINSULA
Majorca
Minorca
Palma de Mallorca
Balearic Is.
(Sp.)
Cape St. Vincent
Cordoba
Seville
Alicante
Murcia
Cadiz
Malaga
Granada
Almeria
Cartagena
Strait of Gibraltar
Gibraltar
(U.K.)
AFRICA
0
250
500 Miles
0
250
500
750 Kilometers
NORWAY
Bodo
Namsos
Trondheim
Molde
Alesund
Bergen
Haugesund
Stavanger
Oslo
Drammen
Skien
Kristiansand
Karlstad
Uppsa
Orebro
Stockh
Vanern
Vattern
Norrkoping
Linko
Jonkoping
Goteborg
Vaxjo
Halmstad
Helsingborg
Malmo
Alborg
Jutland
Arhus
Copenhagen
Esbjerg
Odense
DENMARK
Bornho
(Den.)
Kiel
Lubeck
Rostock
Szczecin
Elbe
Berlin
Magdeburg
Bydgos
Oder
Leipzig
Erfurt
Dresden
Chemnitz
Liberec
Prague
Plzen
CZECH. REP.
Regensburg
Brno
Linz
Danube
Salzburg
Innsbruck
Vienna
AUSTRIA
Graz
Klagenfurt
SLOVENIA
Udine
Trieste
Ljubljana
Zagreb
Rijeka
CROAT
DINARIC
Split
Dubrovn
Bari
Tara
40°
30°
20°
10°
0°
70°
60°
50°

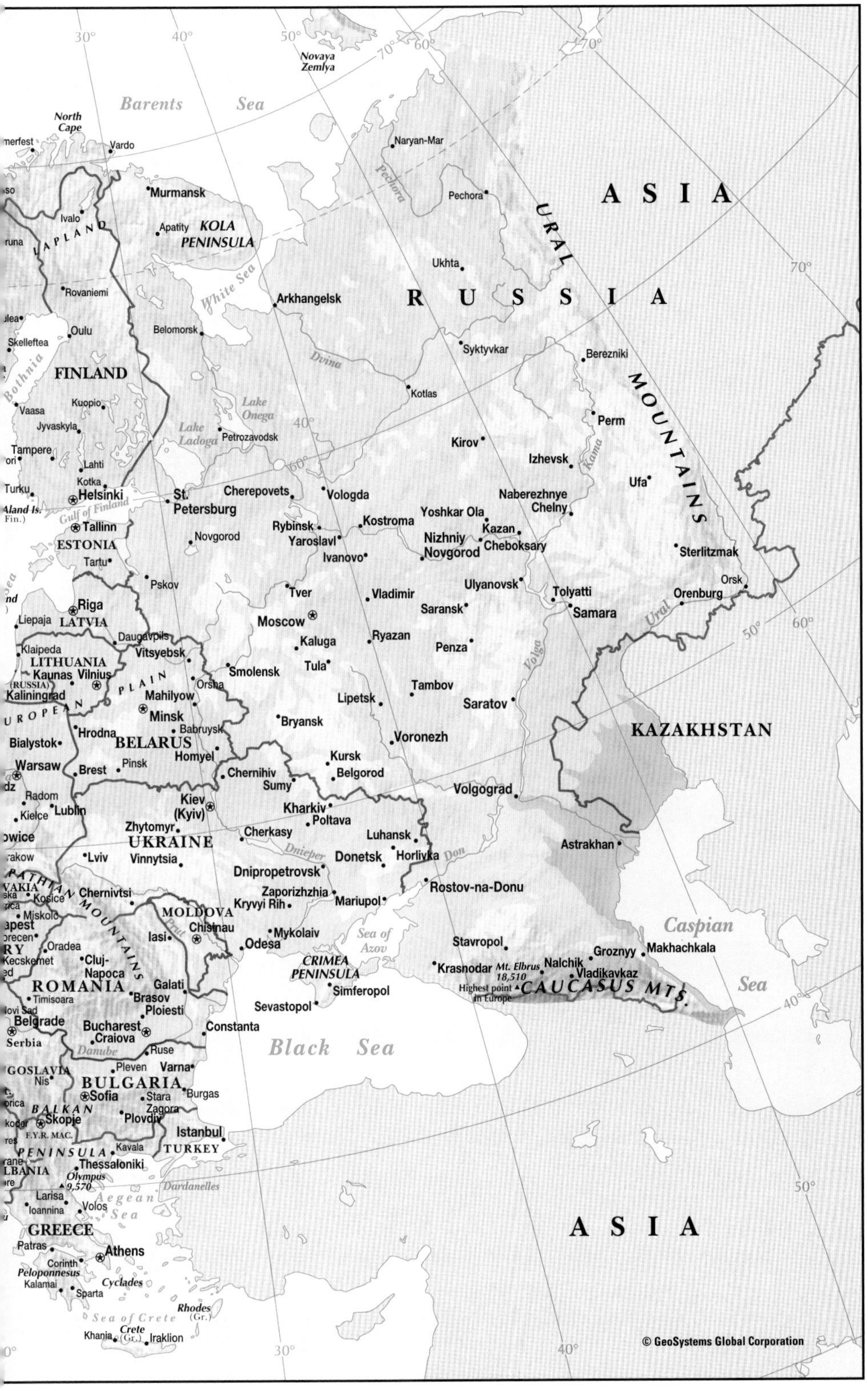
Novaya Zemlya
Barents Sea
North Cape
Vardo
Naryan-Mar
Pechora
Murmansk
Ivalo
LAPLAND
Apatity
KOLA PENINSULA
ASIA
URAL
Ukhta
Rovaniemi
White Sea
Arkhangelsk
RUSSIA
Oulu
Belomorsk
Skelleftea
Syktyvkar
Berezniki
Dvina
FINLAND
Kotlas
MOUNTAINS
Kuopio
Vaasa
Lake Onega
Perm
Jyvaskyla
Lake Ladoga
Petrozavodsk
Kirov
Kama
Tampere
Lahti
Izhevsk
Ufa
Kotka
Turku
Helsinki
St. Petersburg
Cherepovets
Vologda
Naberezhnye Chelny
Aland Is.
Gulf of Finland
Rybinsk
Kostroma
Yoshkar Ola
Tallinn
Novgorod
Yaroslavl
Kazan
ESTONIA
Nizhniy Novgorod
Cheboksary
Sterlitzmak
Tartu
Ivanovo
Pskov
Ulyanovsk
Orsk
Tver
Vladimir
Tolyatti
Orenburg
Riga
Samara
Ural
LATVIA
Moscow
Saransk
Liepaja
Daugavpils
Kaluga
Ryazan
Penza
Klaipeda
Vitsyebsk
LITHUANIA
Tula
Kaunas
Vilnius
Smolensk
(RUSSIA)
Kaliningrad
Orsha
Tambov
PLAIN
Mahilyow
Lipetsk
Saratov
Volga
Minsk
Bryansk
Babruysk
Hrodna
BELARUS
KAZAKHSTAN
Bialystok
Voronezh
Pinsk
Homyel
Kursk
Warsaw
Brest
Chernihiv
Belgorod
Sumy
Radom
Volgograd
Kiev (Kyiv)
Kharkiv
Kielce
Lublin
Poltava
Zhytomyr
Cherkasy
Luhansk
UKRAINE
Astrakhan
Lviv
Vinnytsia
Dnieper
Donetsk
Horlivka
Don
Dnipropetrovsk
Rostov-na-Donu
Kosice
Chernivtsi
Zaporizhzhia
Mariupol
Miskolc
MOLDOVA
Kryvyi Rih
Iasi
Chisinau
Mykolaiv
Sea of Azov
Caspian
Prut
Stavropol
Oradea
Odesa
Groznyy
Makhachkala
Cluj-Napoca
CRIMEA PENINSULA
Nalchik
Krasnodar
Mt. Elbrus 18,510
Highest point in Europe
Vladikavkaz
Galati
ROMANIA
Timisoara
Brasov
Simferopol
CAUCASUS MTS.
Sea
Ploiesti
Sevastopol
Belgrade
Bucharest
Constanta
Craiova
Serbia
Black Sea
Danube
Ruse
Pleven
Varna
Nis
BULGARIA
Sofia
Stara Zagora
Burgas
BALKAN
Skopje
Plovdiv
F.Y.R. MAC.
Istanbul
Kavala
TURKEY
PENINSULA
Thessaloniki
Olympus 9,570
Dardanelles
Aegean Sea
Larisa
Volos
Ioannina
ASIA
GREECE
Patras
Athens
Corinth
Peloponnesus
Cyclades
Kalamai
Sparta
Rhodes (Gr.)
Sea of Crete
Crete (Gr.)
Khania
Iraklion
30°
40°
50°
60°
70°
© GeoSystems Global Corporation

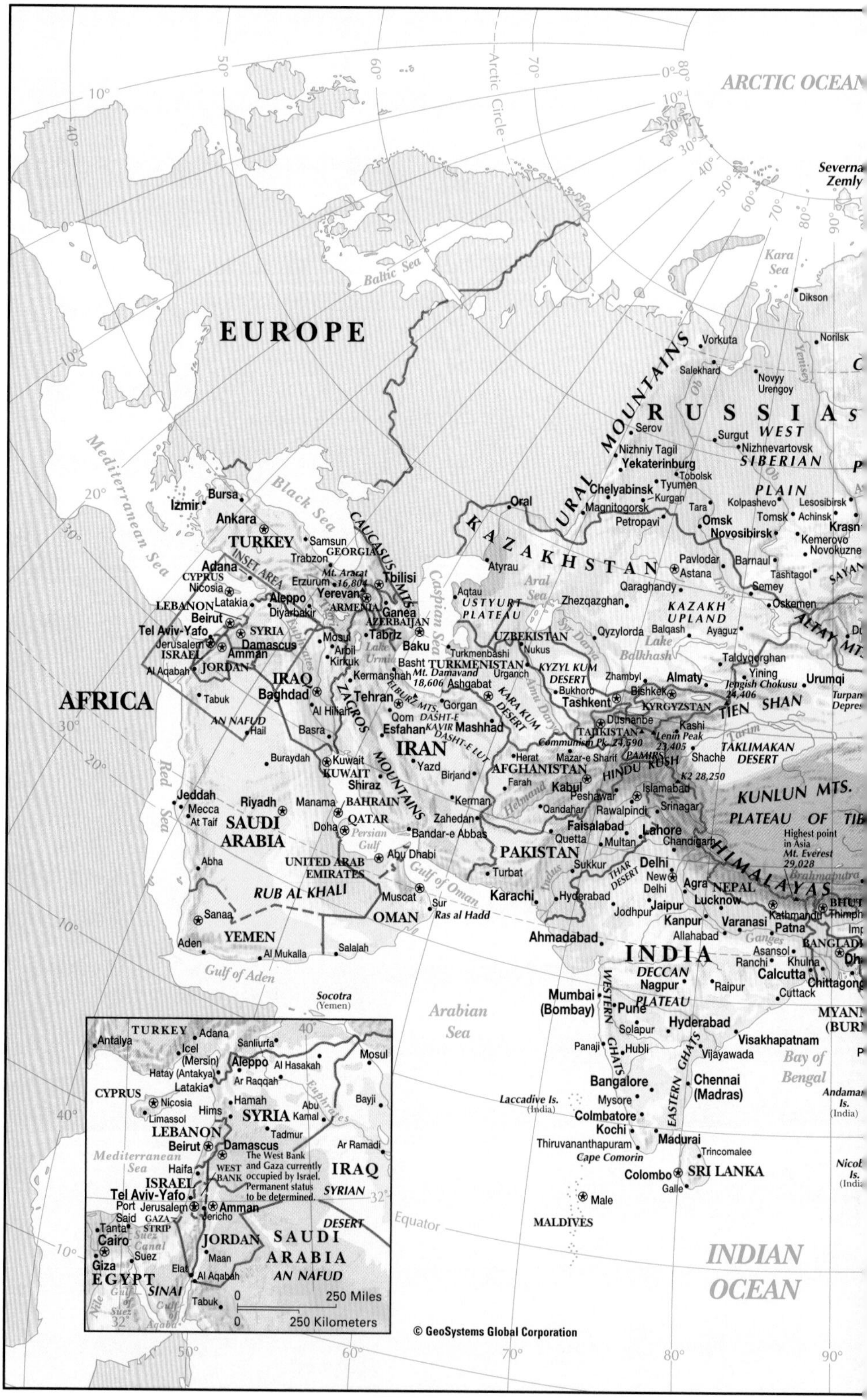
ARCTIC OCEAN
EUROPE
Baltic Sea
Black Sea
Mediterranean Sea
AFRICA
Red Sea
RUSSIA
WEST SIBERIAN PLAIN
URAL MOUNTAINS
KAZAKHSTAN
KAZAKH UPLAND
Kara Sea
Dikson
Norilsk
Vorkuta
Salekhard
Novyy Urengoy
Serov
Surgut
Nizhnevartovsk
Nizhniy Tagil
Yekaterinburg
Tobolsk
Tyumen
Chelyabinsk
Kurgan
Magnitogorsk
Tara
Kolpashevo
Lesosibirsk
Tomsk
Achinsk
Omsk
Novosibirsk
Kemerovo
Novokuzne
Petropavl
Oral
Pavlodar
Astana
Barnaul
Tashtagol
Semey
Oskemen
Qaraghandy
Zhezqazghan
Aral Sea
Atyrau
Aqtau
USTYURT PLATEAU
Caspian Sea
Qyzylorda
Balqash
Ayaguz
Lake Balkhash
Taldyqorghan
UZBEKISTAN
Nukus
Turkmenbashi
TURKMENISTAN
Urganch
KYZYL KUM DESERT
Bukhoro
Tashkent
KARA KUM DESERT
Amu Darya
Syr Darya
Zhambyl
Almaty
Bishkek
KYRGYZSTAN
Yining
Jengish Chokusu 24,406
Urumqi
TIEN SHAN
Dushanbe
TAJIKISTAN
Lenin Peak 23,405
Communism Pk. 24,590
PAMIRS
Kashi
Shache
TAKLIMAKAN DESERT
K2 28,250
KUNLUN MTS.
PLATEAU OF TIB
Highest point in Asia Mt. Everest 29,028
Herat
Mazar-e Sharif
AFGHANISTAN
HINDU KUSH
Farah
Kabul
Peshawar
Islamabad
Srinagar
Qandahar
Rawalpindi
Faisalabad
Lahore
Quetta
Multan
Chandigarh
HIMALAYAS
PAKISTAN
Sukkur
THAR DESERT
Delhi
New Delhi
Agra
NEPAL
Kathmandu
Thimphu
Turbat
Karachi
Hyderabad
Jaipur
Jodhpur
Lucknow
Kanpur
Varanasi
Patna
Allahabad
Ganges
Brahmaputra
Ahmadabad
INDIA
DECCAN PLATEAU
Nagpur
Raipur
Asansol
Ranchi
Khulna
Calcutta
Chittagong
Cuttack
Mumbai (Bombay)
Pune
Solapur
Hyderabad
Visakhapatnam
Vijayawada
Panaji
Hubli
WESTERN GHATS
EASTERN GHATS
Bangalore
Chennai (Madras)
Mysore
Coimbatore
Kochi
Madurai
Thiruvananthapuram
Cape Comorin
Trincomalee
Colombo
SRI LANKA
Galle
Male
MALDIVES
Laccadive Is. (India)
Arabian Sea
Bay of Bengal
INDIAN OCEAN
Andaman Is. (India)
Nicobar Is. (India)
Severnaya Zemlya
Izmir
Bursa
Ankara
TURKEY
Samsun
Trabzon
GEORGIA
CAUCASUS MTS.
Tbilisi
Adana
CYPRUS
Nicosia
INSET AREA
Erzurum
Mt. Ararat 16,804
Yerevan
ARMENIA
Ganca
AZERBAIJAN
LEBANON
Latakia
Aleppo
Diyarbakir
Beirut
SYRIA
Tel Aviv-Yafo
Damascus
Jerusalem
Amman
ISRAEL
JORDAN
Al Aqabah
Euphrates
Tigris
Mosul
Arbil
Kirkuk
Lake Urmia
Tabriz
Baku
Basht
IRAQ
Baghdad
Kermanshah
Mt. Damavand 18,606
Ashgabat
Tehran
ELBURZ MTS.
Gorgan
Qom
DASHT-E KAVIR
Mashhad
DASHT-E LUT
Al Hillah
ZAGROS MOUNTAINS
Esfahan
IRAN
Yazd
Birjand
Tabuk
AN NAFUD
Hail
Basra
Buraydah
Kuwait
KUWAIT
Shiraz
Kerman
Zahedan
Helmand
Jeddah
Mecca
At Taif
Riyadh
SAUDI ARABIA
Manama
BAHRAIN
QATAR
Doha
Persian Gulf
Bandar-e Abbas
Abu Dhabi
UNITED ARAB EMIRATES
Gulf of Oman
Abha
RUB AL KHALI
Muscat
Sur
Ras al Hadd
OMAN
Sanaa
YEMEN
Aden
Al Mukalla
Salalah
Gulf of Aden
Socotra (Yemen)
Arctic Circle
Equator
TURKEY
Antalya
Adana
Icel (Mersin)
Sanliurfa
Hatay (Antakya)
Aleppo
Al Hasakah
Mosul
Latakia
Ar Raqqah
CYPRUS
Nicosia
Hamah
Limassol
Hims
SYRIA
Abu Kamal
Bayji
LEBANON
Tadmur
Beirut
Damascus
Ar Ramadi
Mediterranean Sea
Haifa
WEST BANK
The West Bank and Gaza currently occupied by Israel. Permanent status to be determined.
IRAQ
ISRAEL
SYRIAN DESERT
Tel Aviv-Yafo
Port Said
Jerusalem
Amman
Jericho
GAZA STRIP
Tanta
Suez Canal
Cairo
JORDAN
SAUDI ARABIA
Suez
Maan
Giza
Elat
EGYPT
Al Aqabah
AN NAFUD
SINAI
Gulf of Suez
Gulf of Aqaba
Nile
Tabuk
0 250 Miles
0 250 Kilometers
© GeoSystems Global Corporation

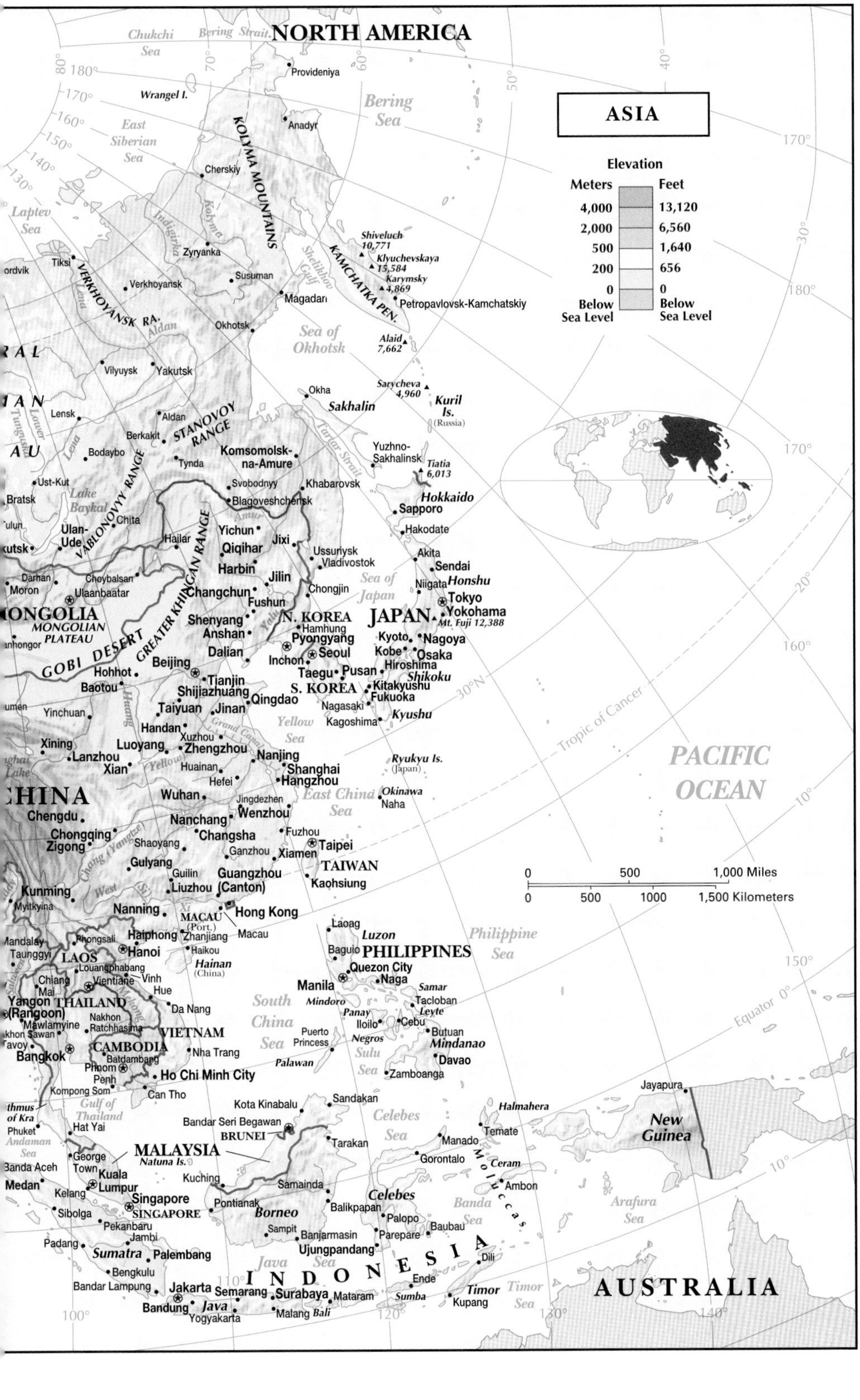

NORTH AMERICA
ASIA
Elevation
Meters
Feet
4,000
13,120
2,000
6,560
500
1,640
200
656
0
0
Below Sea Level
Below Sea Level
Chukchi Sea
Bering Strait
Provideniya
Wrangel I.
Bering Sea
Anadyr
East Siberian Sea
KOLYMA MOUNTAINS
Cherskiy
Laptev Sea
Kolyma
Indigirka
Zyryanka
Tiksi
VERKHOYANSK RA.
Lena
Verkhoyansk
Susuman
Magadan
Shelikhov Gulf
KAMCHATKA PEN.
Shiveluch 10,771
Klyuchevskaya 15,584
Karymsky 4,869
Petropavlovsk-Kamchatskiy
Okhotsk
Aldan
Sea of Okhotsk
Alaid 7,662
Vilyuysk
Yakutsk
Okha
Sarycheva 4,960
Sakhalin
Kuril Is.
(Russia)
Lensk
Aldan
Berkakit
STANOVOY RANGE
Tynda
Bodaybo
Komsomolsk-na-Amure
Tatar Strait
Yuzhno-Sakhalinsk
Tiatia 6,013
Ust-Kut
Svobodnyy
Khabarovsk
Bratsk
Lake Baykal
YABLONOVYY RANGE
Blagoveshchensk
Hokkaido
Sapporo
Chita
Ulan-Ude
Amur
Hakodate
Hailar
Yichun
Jixi
Qiqihar
Ussuriysk
Akita
Vladivostok
Sendai
Harbin
GREATER KHINGAN RANGE
Jilin
Darhan
Choybalsan
Moron
Ulaanbaatar
Chongjin
Sea of Japan
Niigata
Honshu
Changchun
Fushun
MONGOLIA
MONGOLIAN PLATEAU
N. KOREA
JAPAN
Tokyo
Yokohama
Mt. Fuji 12,388
Shenyang
Anshan
Hamhung
Pyongyang
GOBI DESERT
Dalian
Kyoto
Nagoya
Kobe
Osaka
Inchon
Seoul
Hiroshima
Hohhot
Beijing
Tianjin
Taegu
Pusan
Shikoku
Baotou
S. KOREA
Kitakyushu
Fukuoka
Shijiazhuang
Qingdao
Nagasaki
Yinchuan
Taiyuan
Jinan
Kyushu
Kagoshima
Yellow Sea
Handan
Grand Canal
Xuzhou
Xining
Luoyang
Zhengzhou
Nanjing
Lanzhou
Ryukyu Is.
(Japan)
Xian
Huainan
Shanghai
Hangzhou
Hefei
Tropic of Cancer
PACIFIC OCEAN
CHINA
Wuhan
Jingdezhen
East China Sea
Okinawa
Naha
Chengdu
Nanchang
Wenzhou
Chongqing
Changsha
Fuzhou
Zigong
Shaoyang
Taipei
Ganzhou
Xiamen
Gulyang
TAIWAN
Guilin
Guangzhou (Canton)
Kaohsiung
Kunming
Liuzhou
Myitkyina
Nanning
MACAU (Port.)
Hong Kong
Zhanjiang
Macau
Laoag
Luzon
Philippine Sea
Mandalay
Phongsali
Haiphong
Hanoi
Haikou
Baguio
PHILIPPINES
Taunggyi
LAOS
Hainan (China)
Louangphabang
Quezon City
Chiang Mai
Vientiane
Vinh
Manila
Naga
Hue
Samar
Yangon (Rangoon)
THAILAND
Mindoro
Tacloban
Da Nang
South China Sea
Leyte
Panay
Mawlamyine
Nakhon Ratchasima
Iloilo
Cebu
VIETNAM
Puerto Princesa
Negros
Butuan
Nakhon Sawan
Mindanao
Tavoy
CAMBODIA
Nha Trang
Bangkok
Batdambang
Sulu Sea
Davao
Phnom Penh
Palawan
Ho Chi Minh City
Zamboanga
Kompong Som
Can Tho
Sandakan
Jayapura
Kota Kinabalu
Halmahera
Gulf of Thailand
Celebes Sea
Isthmus of Kra
Bandar Seri Begawan
New Guinea
Phuket
Hat Yai
BRUNEI
Ternate
Andaman Sea
Tarakan
Manado
George Town
MALAYSIA
Natuna Is.
Gorontalo
Moluccas
Ceram
Banda Aceh
Kuala Lumpur
Kuching
Medan
Samainda
Ambon
Kelang
Singapore
Celebes
Pontianak
SINGAPORE
Balikpapan
Banda Sea
Arafura Sea
Sibolga
Borneo
Palopo
Pekanbaru
Sampit
Baubau
Jambi
Banjarmasin
Parepare
Padang
Sumatra
Palembang
Ujungpandang
INDONESIA
Dili
Java Sea
Bengkulu
Ende
Timor
Timor Sea
Bandar Lampung
Jakarta
Semarang
Surabaya
Mataram
Sumba
Kupang
AUSTRALIA
Bandung
Java
Malang
Bali
Yogyakarta
Equator 0°
0
500
1,000 Miles
0
500
1000
1,500 Kilometers

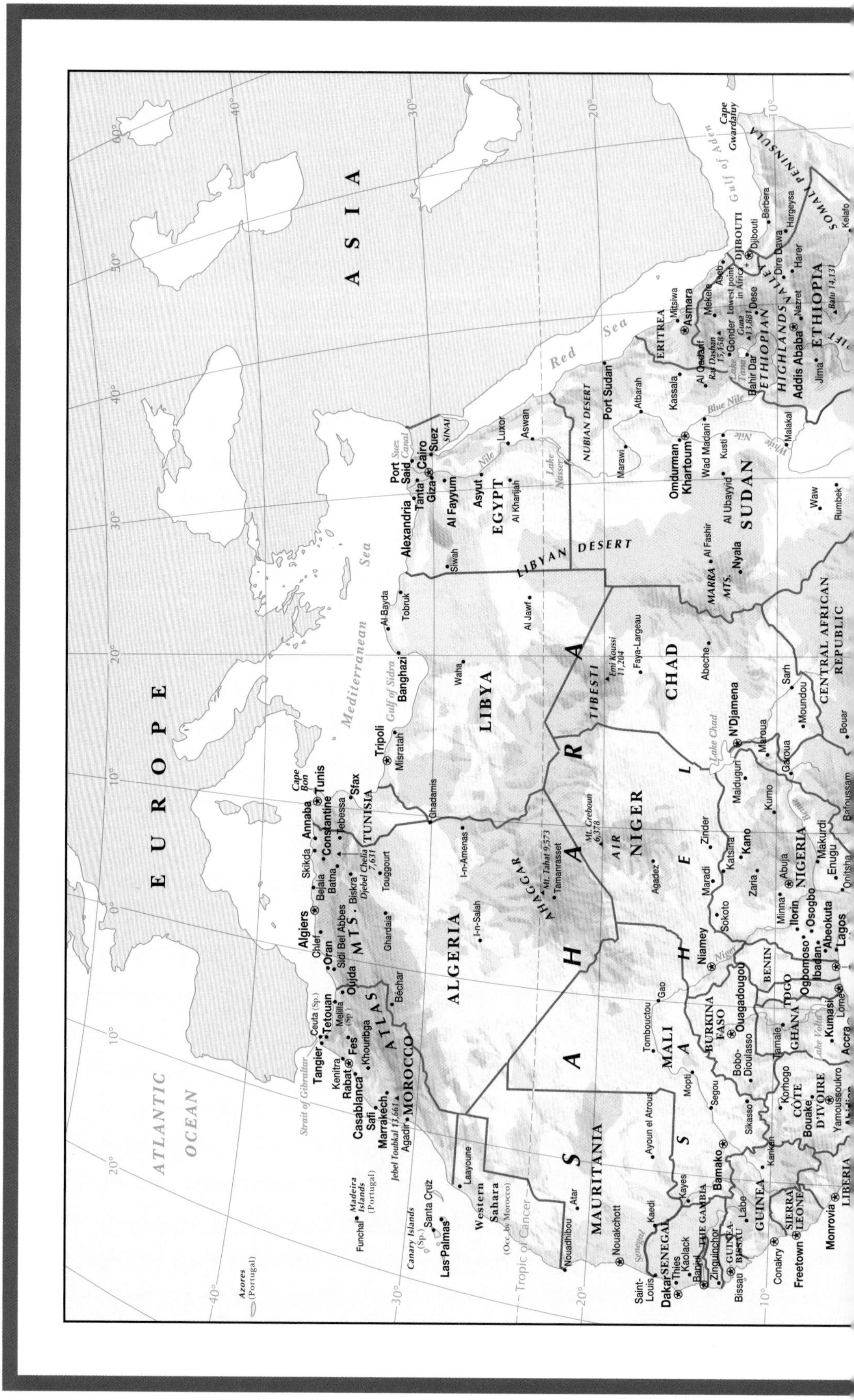
EUROPE
ASIA
ATLANTIC OCEAN
Mediterranean Sea
Red Sea
Gulf of Aden
Gulf of Sidra
Strait of Gibraltar
Tropic of Cancer
SAHARA
SAHEL
ATLAS MTS.
AHAGGAR
TIBESTI
AIR
LIBYAN DESERT
NUBIAN DESERT
MARRA MTS.
ETHIOPIAN HIGHLANDS
SOMALI PENINSULA
SINAI
Azores (Portugal)
Madeira Islands (Portugal)
Canary Islands (Sp.)
Cape Bon
Cape Gwardafuy
MOROCCO
ALGERIA
TUNISIA
LIBYA
EGYPT
SUDAN
CHAD
NIGER
MALI
MAURITANIA
Western Sahara (Occ. by Morocco)
SENEGAL
THE GAMBIA
GUINEA-BISSAU
GUINEA
SIERRA LEONE
LIBERIA
CÔTE D'IVOIRE
BURKINA FASO
GHANA
TOGO
BENIN
NIGERIA
CENTRAL AFRICAN REPUBLIC
ERITREA
DJIBOUTI
ETHIOPIA
Jebel Toubkal 13,661
Djebel Chelia 7,631
Mt. Tahat 9,573
Mt. Greboun 6,378
Emi Koussi 11,204
Ras Dashan 15,158
Guna 13,881
Batu 14,131
Lowest point in Africa
Nile
Blue Nile
White Nile
Niger
Benue
Senegal
Suez Canal
Lake Nasser
Lake Chad
Lake Tana
Lake Volta
Funchal
Santa Cruz
Las Palmas
Tangier
Ceuta (Sp.)
Tetouan
Melilla (Sp.)
Kenitra
Rabat
Fes
Khouribga
Casablanca
Safi
Marrakech
Agadir
Oujda
Oran
Sidi Bel Abbes
Chlef
Algiers
Bejaia
Skikda
Annaba
Constantine
Batna
Tebessa
Biskra
Touggourt
Ghardaia
Béchar
I-n-Salah
I-n-Amenas
Tamanrasset
Ghadamis
Tunis
Sfax
Tripoli
Misratah
Banghazi
Al-Bayda
Tobruk
Waha
Al Jawf
Siwah
Alexandria
Tanta
Port Said
Cairo
Giza
Suez
Al Fayyum
Asyut
Luxor
Aswan
Al Kharijah
Laayoune
Atar
Nouadhibou
Nouakchott
Kaedi
Saint-Louis
Dakar
Thies
Kaolack
Banjul
Ziguinchor
Bissau
Conakry
Freetown
Monrovia
Labe
Kankan
Kayes
Bamako
Segou
Sikasso
Mopti
Tombouctou
Gao
Ayoun el Atrous
Bobo-Dioulasso
Ouagadougou
Korhogo
Bouake
Yamoussoukro
Tamale
Kumasi
Accra
Lome
Niamey
Sokoto
Maradi
Agadez
Zinder
Katsina
Kano
Zaria
Maiduguri
Kumo
Minna
Abuja
Ilorin
Ogbomoso
Osogbo
Ibadan
Abeokuta
Lagos
Makurdi
Enugu
Onitsha
Bafoussam
Garoua
Maroua
N'Djamena
Moundou
Sarh
Bouar
Abeche
Faya-Largeau
Al Fashir
Nyala
Al Ubayyid
Kusti
Wad Madani
Omdurman
Khartoum
Marawi
Atbarah
Port Sudan
Kassala
Malakal
Waw
Rumbek
Al Qadarif
Gonder
Bahir Dar
Mekele
Mitsiwa
Asmara
Aseb
Djibouti
Dese
Addis Ababa
Nazret
Jima
Dire Dawa
Harer
Hargeysa
Berbera
Kelafo
60°
50°
40°
30°
20°
10°
0°

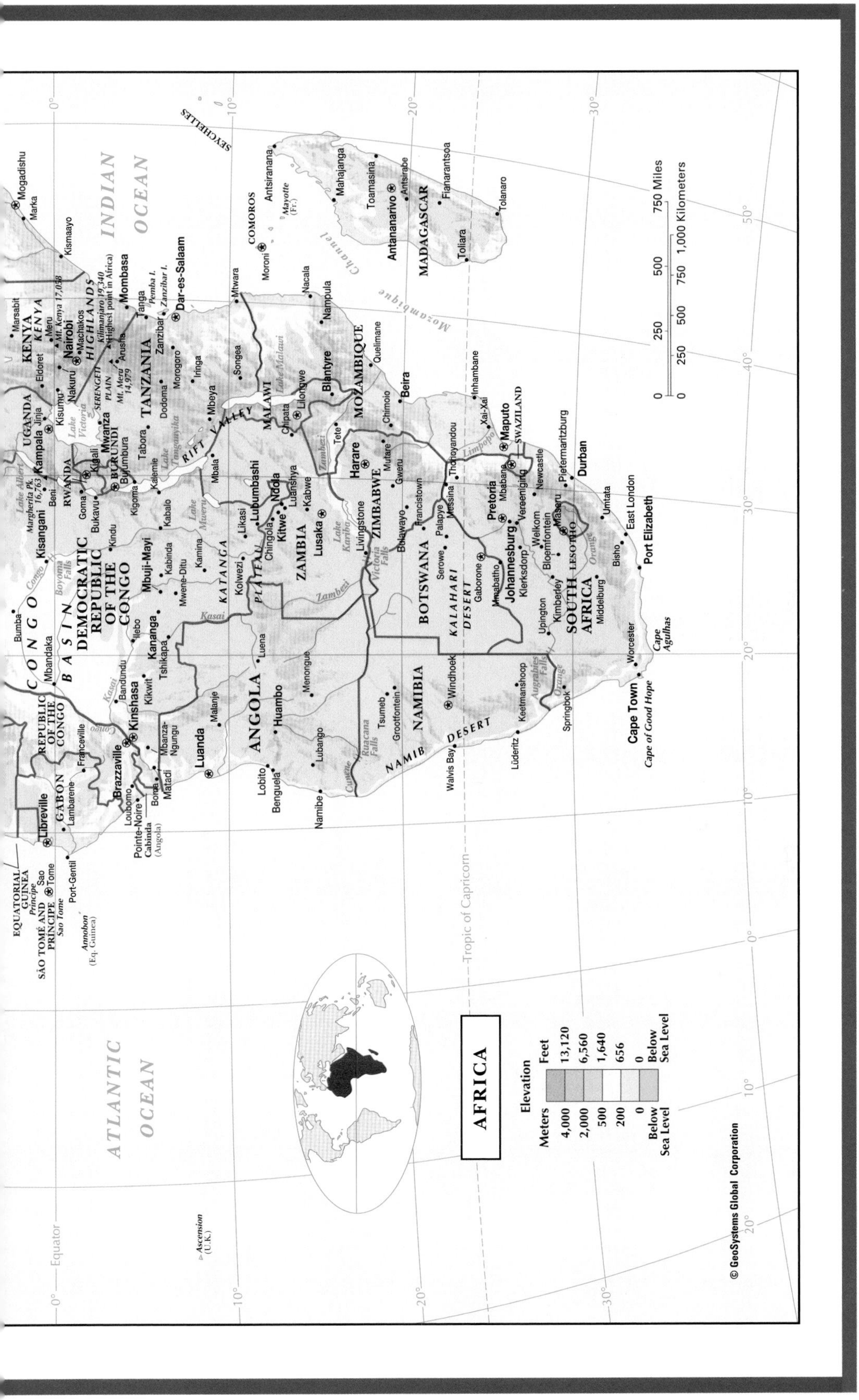

AFRICA
ATLANTIC OCEAN
INDIAN OCEAN
Equator
Tropic of Capricorn
Elevation
Meters
Feet
4,000
13,120
2,000
6,560
500
1,640
200
656
0
0
Below Sea Level
Below Sea Level
0 250 500 750 Miles
0 250 500 750 1,000 Kilometers
© GeoSystems Global Corporation
EQUATORIAL GUINEA
SÃO TOMÉ AND PRINCIPE
Principe
Sao Tome
Sao Tome
Annobon (Eq. Guinea)
Ascension (U.K.)
Port-Gentil
Libreville
GABON
Lambarene
REPUBLIC OF THE CONGO
Franceville
Brazzaville
Loubomo
Pointe-Noire
Cabinda (Angola)
Boma
Matadi
Kinshasa
Bandundu
Kikwit
Mbanza-Ngungu
Luanda
Malanje
ANGOLA
Huambo
Lobito
Benguela
Lubango
Namibe
Menongue
Luena
Tshikapa
Kananga
Ilebo
Mbandaka
Bumba
CONGO BASIN
DEMOCRATIC REPUBLIC OF THE CONGO
Kisangani
Boyoma Falls
Kindu
Mbuji-Mayi
Kabinda
Mwene-Ditu
Kamina
Kabalo
Kalemie
KATANGA PLATEAU
Kolwezi
Likasi
Lubumbashi
Chingola
Kitwe
Ndola
Luanshya
ZAMBIA
Lusaka
Kabwe
Livingstone
Victoria Falls
Lake Kariba
ZIMBABWE
Harare
Bulawayo
Gweru
Mutare
Francistown
BOTSWANA
KALAHARI DESERT
Gaborone
Serowe
Palapye
Mmabatho
NAMIBIA
Windhoek
Tsumeb
Grootfontein
Walvis Bay
NAMIB DESERT
Lüderitz
Keetmanshoop
Ruacana Falls
Augrabies Falls
Springbok
Upington
Kimberley
SOUTH AFRICA
Middelburg
Bloemfontein
Welkom
Klerksdorp
Johannesburg
Pretoria
Vereeniging
Messina
Thohoyandou
Maseru
LESOTHO
Bisho
East London
Port Elizabeth
Umtata
Durban
Pietermaritzburg
Newcastle
Mbabane
SWAZILAND
Maputo
Xai-Xai
Inhambane
Worcester
Cape Town
Cape of Good Hope
Cape Agulhas
MOZAMBIQUE
Beira
Chimoio
Tete
Quelimane
Nampula
Nacala
Blantyre
Lilongwe
Chipata
MALAWI
Lake Malawi
Mbeya
Mbala
RIFT VALLEY
Songea
Mtwara
Iringa
TANZANIA
Dodoma
Morogoro
Tabora
Kigoma
Lake Tanganyika
Lake Mweru
Mwanza
Lake Victoria
SERENGETI PLAIN
Mt. Meru 14,979
Arusha
Kilimanjaro 19,340 (highest point in Africa)
Tanga
Pemba I.
Zanzibar I.
Zanzibar
Dar-es-Salaam
Mombasa
BURUNDI
Bujumbura
RWANDA
Kigali
Goma
Bukavu
Beni
Margherita Pk. 16,763
Lake Albert
UGANDA
Kampala
Jinja
Kisumu
Nakuru
Eldoret
KENYA
KENYA HIGHLANDS
Nairobi
Machakos
Mt. Kenya 17,058
Meru
Marsabit
Kismaayo
Marka
Mogadishu
COMOROS
Moroni
Mayotte (Fr.)
Mozambique Channel
MADAGASCAR
Antsiranana
Mahajanga
Toamasina
Antananarivo
Antsirabe
Fianarantsoa
Toliara
Tolanaro
SEYCHELLES
Congo
Kasai
Zambezi
Limpopo
Orange
Cunene
0° 10° 20° 30° 40° 50°

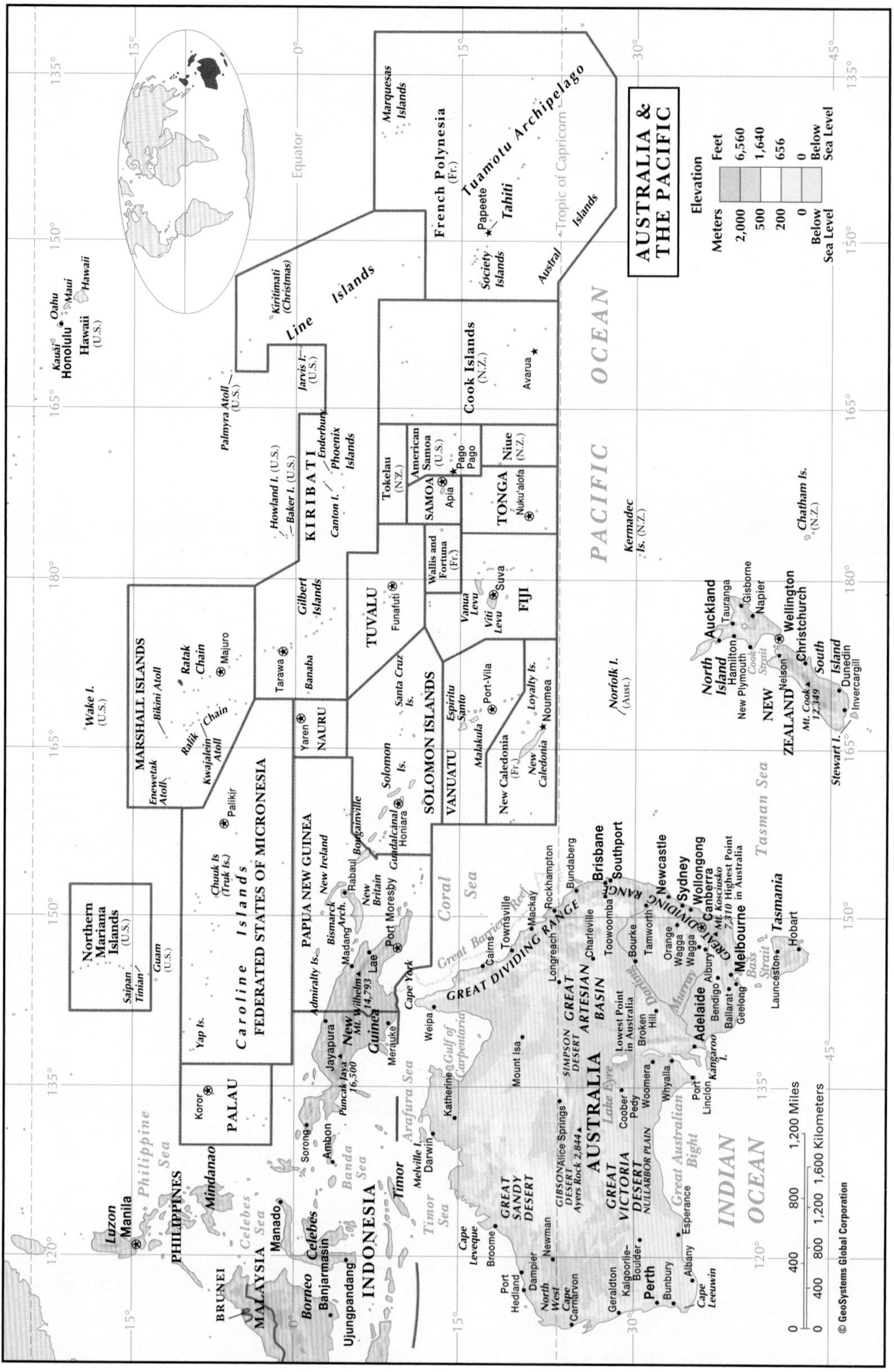
AUSTRALIA & THE PACIFIC
Elevation
Meters
Feet
2,000
6,560
500
1,640
200
656
0
0
Below Sea Level
Below Sea Level
0
400
800
1,200 Miles
0
400
800
1,200
1,600 Kilometers
© GeoSystems Global Corporation
PACIFIC
OCEAN
INDIAN
OCEAN
Equator
Tropic of Capricorn
AUSTRALIA
PAPUA NEW GUINEA
INDONESIA
PHILIPPINES
MALAYSIA
BRUNEI
PALAU
FEDERATED STATES OF MICRONESIA
MARSHALL ISLANDS
NAURU
KIRIBATI
TUVALU
SOLOMON ISLANDS
VANUATU
FIJI
TONGA
SAMOA
NEW ZEALAND
Northern Mariana Islands (U.S.)
Guam (U.S.)
Saipan
Tinian
Wake I. (U.S.)
Hawaii (U.S.)
Honolulu
Kauai
Oahu
Maui
Hawaii
Palmyra Atoll (U.S.)
Howland I. (U.S.)
Baker I. (U.S.)
Jarvis I. (U.S.)
Kiritimati (Christmas)
Line Islands
Phoenix Islands
Canton I.
Enderbury
Gilbert Islands
Tarawa
Banaba
Yaren
Funafuti
Tokelau (N.Z.)
American Samoa (U.S.)
Pago Pago
Apia
Wallis and Futuna (Fr.)
Niue (N.Z.)
Nuku'alofa
Suva
Vanua Levu
Viti Levu
Cook Islands (N.Z.)
Avarua
French Polynesia (Fr.)
Society Islands
Papeete
Tahiti
Tuamotu Archipelago
Marquesas Islands
Austral Islands
Kermadec Is. (N.Z.)
Chatham Is. (N.Z.)
Norfolk I. (Aust.)
New Caledonia (Fr.)
Noumea
Loyalty Is.
Port-Vila
Espiritu Santo
Malakula
Santa Cruz Is.
Solomon Is.
Guadalcanal
Honiara
Bougainville
Majuro
Ratak Chain
Ralik Chain
Bikini Atoll
Enewetak Atoll
Kwajalein Atoll
Palikir
Chuuk Is (Truk Is.)
Caroline Islands
Yap Is.
Koror
Philippine Sea
Luzon
Manila
Mindanao
Celebes Sea
Manado
Borneo
Celebes
Banjarmasin
Ujungpandang
Banda Sea
Ambon
Sorong
Timor
Timor Sea
Arafura Sea
Jayapura
Puncak Jaya 16,500
New Guinea
Mt. Wilhelm 14,793
Madang
Lae
Port Moresby
Admiralty Is.
Bismarck Arch.
New Ireland
New Britain
Rabaul
Merauke
Cape York
Weipa
Gulf of Carpentaria
Coral Sea
Great Barrier Reef
Cairns
Townsville
Mackay
Rockhampton
Bundaberg
Brisbane
Southport
Toowoomba
GREAT DIVIDING RANGE
Newcastle
Sydney
Wollongong
Canberra
Mt. Kosciusko 7,310 Highest Point in Australia
Melbourne
Geelong
Ballarat
Bendigo
Albury
Wagga Wagga
Orange
Tamworth
Bourke
Charleville
Longreach
GREAT ARTESIAN BASIN
SIMPSON DESERT
Lake Eyre
Lowest Point in Australia
Broken Hill
Darling
Murray
Adelaide
Kangaroo I.
Port Lincoln
Whyalla
Woomera
Coober Pedy
Alice Springs
Ayers Rock 2,844
Mount Isa
Katherine
Darwin
Melville I.
GIBSON DESERT
GREAT SANDY DESERT
GREAT VICTORIA DESERT
NULLARBOR PLAIN
Great Australian Bight
Cape Leveque
Broome
Port Hedland
Dampier
Newman
North West Cape
Carnarvon
Geraldton
Kalgoorlie-Boulder
Perth
Bunbury
Albany
Esperance
Cape Leeuwin
Bass Strait
Launceston
Hobart
Tasmania
Tasman Sea
North Island
Auckland
Tauranga
Hamilton
Gisborne
Napier
New Plymouth
Cook Strait
Wellington
Nelson
Christchurch
South Island
Mt. Cook 12,349
Dunedin
Invercargill
Stewart I.

UNITED STATES HISTORY

1492

Christopher Columbus and crew sighted land **Oct. 12** in the present-day Bahamas.

1497

John Cabot explored northeast coast to Delaware.

1513

Juan Ponce de León explored Florida coast.

1524

Giovanni da Verrazano led French expedition along coast from Carolina north to Nova Scotia; entered New York harbor.

1539

Hernando de Soto landed in Florida **May 28;** crossed Mississippi River, **1541.**

1540

Francisco Vásquez de Coronado explored Southwest north of Rio Grande. Hernando de Alarcón reached Colorado River; Don Garcia Lopez de Cardenas reached Grand Canyon. Others explored California coast.

1565

St. Augustine, FL, founded **Sept. 8** by Pedro Menéndez. Razed by Francis Drake **1586.**

1579

Francis Drake entered San Francisco Bay and claimed region for Britain.

1607

Capt. John Smith and 105 cavaliers in 3 ships landed on Virginia coast, started first permanent English settlement in New World at **Jamestown** in **May.**

1609

Henry Hudson, English explorer of Northwest Passage, employed by Dutch, sailed into New York harbor in **Sept.,** and up Hudson to Albany. **Samuel de Champlain** explored Lake Champlain, just to the north.

Spaniards settled **Santa Fe, NM.**

1619

House of Burgesses, first representative assembly in New World, elected **July 30** at Jamestown, VA.

First black laborers—indentured servants—in English N. American colonies, landed by Dutch at Jamestown in **Aug.** Chattel slavery legally recognized, **1650.**

1620

Plymouth Pilgrims, Puritan separatists, left Plymouth, England, **Sept. 16** on *Mayflower*. They reached Cape Cod **Nov. 19,** explored coast; 103 passengers landed **Dec. 26** at Plymouth. **Mayflower Compact** was agreement to form a government and abide by its laws. Half of colony died during harsh winter.

1624

Dutch colonies started in Albany and in New York area, where **New Netherland** was established in **May.**

1626

Peter Minuit bought Manhattan for Dutch from Man-a-hat-a Indians during summer for goods valued at $24; named island **New Amsterdam.**

1630

Settlement of **Boston** established by Massachusetts colonists led by John Winthrop.

1634

Maryland, founded as a Catholic colony, under a charter granted to Lord Baltimore. Religious toleration granted **1649.**

1636

Roger Williams founded Providence, RI, **June,** as a democratically ruled colony with separation of church and state. Charter granted, **1644.**

Harvard College founded **Oct. 28,** now oldest in U.S.; grammar school, compulsory education established at Boston.

1640

First book was printed in America, the so-called Bay Psalm Book.

1647

Liberal constitution drafted in Rhode Island.

1660

British Parliament passed First **Navigation Act Dec. 1,** regulating colonial commerce to suit English needs.

1664

British troops Sept. 8 seized New Netherland from Dutch. Charles II granted New Netherland and city of New Amsterdam to brother, Duke of York; both renamed **New York.** Dutch recaptured colony **1673,** but ceded it to Britain **Nov. 10, 1674.**

1673

Jacques **Marquette** and Louis **Jolliet** reached the upper **Mississippi** and traveled down it.

1676

Nathaniel Bacon led planters against autocratic British Gov. Sir William Berkeley, burned Jamestown, VA, **Sept. 19.** Rebellion collapsed when Bacon died; 23 followers executed.

Bloody **Indian war** in New England ended **Aug. 12.** King Philip, Wampanoag chief, and Narragansett Indians killed.

1682

Robert Cavelier, Sieur de La Salle, claimed lower Mississippi River country for France, called it Louisiana **Apr. 9.** Had French outposts built in Illinois and Texas, **1684.** Killed during mutiny **Mar. 19, 1687.**

William Penn arrived in **Pennsylvania.**

1683

William Penn signed treaty with Delaware Indians and made payment for Pennsylvania lands.

1692

Witchcraft delusion at Salem, MA; 20 alleged witches executed by special court.

1696

Capt. William Kidd settled in America, was hired by British to fight pirates and take booty, but himself became one. Arrested and sent to England; hanged **1701.**

1699

French settlements made in Mississippi, Louisiana.

1704

Indians attacked Deerfield, MA, **Feb. 28-29;** killed 40, carried off 100.

Boston News Letter, **first regular newspaper,** started by John Campbell, postmaster. (An earlier paper, *Publick Occurences*, was suppressed after one issue **1690.**)

1709

British-Colonial troops captured French fort, Port Royal, Nova Scotia, in **Queen Anne's War 1701-13.** France yielded Nova Scotia by treaty **1713.**

1712

Slaves revolted in New York **Apr. 6.** Six committed suicide; 21 were executed. Second rising, **1741;** 13 slaves hanged, 13 burned, 71 deported.

1716

First theater in colonies opened in Williamsburg, VA.

1726

Poor people **rioted** in Philadelphia.

Great Awakening religious revival began.

1732

Benjamin Franklin published the first *Poor Richard's Almanac;* published annually to **1757.**

Last of the 13 colonies, **Georgia,** chartered.

1735

Editor **John Peter Zenger acquitted** in New York of libeling British governor by criticizing his conduct in office.

1740-41

Capt. Vitus Bering reached Alaska.

1744

King George's War pitted British and colonials vs. French. Colonials captured Louisburg, Cape Breton Is., **June 17, 1745.** Returned to France **1748** by Treaty of Aix-la-Chapelle.

1752

Benjamin Franklin, flying kite in thunderstorm, proved lightning is electricity **June 15;** invented lightning rod.

1754

French and Indian War began when French occupied Ft. Duquesne (Pittsburgh). British moved Acadian French from Nova Scotia to Louisiana **Oct. 8, 1755.** British captured Québec **Sept. 18, 1759,** in battles in which French Gen. Joseph de Montcalm and British Gen. James Wolfe were killed. Peace pact signed **Feb. 10, 1763.** French lost Canada and Midwest.

1764

Sugar Act placed duties on lumber, foodstuffs, molasses, and rum in colonies, to pay French and Indian War debts.

1765

Stamp Act, enacted by Parliament **Mar. 22,** required revenue stamps to help fund royal troops. Nine colonies, at **Stamp Act Congress** in New York **Oct. 7-25,** adopted Declaration of Rights. Stamp Act **repealed Mar. 17, 1766.**

1767

Townshend Acts levied taxes on glass, painter's lead, paper, and tea. In **1770** all duties except those on tea were repealed.

1770

British troops fired **Mar. 5** into Boston mob, killed 5 including **Crispus Attucks,** a black man, reportedly leader of group; later called **Boston Massacre.**

1773

East India Co. tea ships turned back at Boston, New York, and Philadelphia in **May.** Cargo ship burned at Annapolis **Oct. 14;** cargo thrown overboard at **Boston Tea Party Dec. 16,** to protest the tea tax.

1774

"Intolerable Acts" of Parliament curtailed Massachusetts self-rule; barred use of Boston harbor till tea was paid for.

First Continental Congress held in Philadelphia **Sept. 5-Oct. 26;** called for civil disobedience against British.

Rhode Island abolished slavery.

1775

Patrick Henry addressed Virginia convention, **Mar. 23,** said "Give me liberty or give me death."

Paul Revere and William Dawes on night of **Apr. 18** rode to alert Patriots that British were on their way to Concord to destroy arms. At Lexington, MA, **Apr. 19,** Minutemen lost 8. On return from Concord, British took 273 casualties.

Col. Ethan Allen (joined by Col. Benedict Arnold) captured **Ft. Ticonderoga, NY, May 10;** also Crown Point. Colonials headed for **Bunker Hill,** fortified Breed's Hill, Charlestown, MA. Repulsed British under Gen. William Howe twice before retreating **June 17;** called Battle of Bunker Hill.

Continental Congress **June 15** named **George Washington** commander in chief.

1776

France and Spain each agreed **May 2** to provide arms.

In Continental Congress **June 7,** Richard Henry Lee (VA) moved "that these united colonies are and of right ought to be free and independent states." Resolution adopted July 2. **Declaration of Independence** approved **July 4.**

Col. William Moultrie's batteries at **Charleston, SC,** repulsed British sea attack **June 28.** Washington, with 10,000 men, lost **Battle of Long Island Aug. 27;** evacuated New York.

Nathan Hale executed as spy by British **Sept. 22.**

Brig. Gen. Arnold's **Lake Champlain** fleet was defeated at Valcour **Oct. 11,** but British returned to Canada. Howe failed to destroy Washington's army at **White Plains Oct. 28.** Hessians captured Ft. Washington, Manhattan, and 3,000 men **Nov. 16;** captured Ft. Lee, NJ, **Nov. 18.**

Washington, in Pennsylvania, recrossed **Delaware River Dec. 25-26,** defeated Hessians at Trenton, NJ, **Dec. 26.**

1777

Washington defeated Lord Cornwallis at **Princeton Jan. 3.** Continental Congress adopted Stars and Stripes.

Maj. Gen. John Burgoyne, force of 8,000 from Canada, captured **Ft. Ticonderoga July 6.** Americans beat back Burgoyne at Bemis Heights **Oct. 7,** cut off British escape route. Burgoyne surrendered 5,000 men at **Saratoga, NY, Oct. 17.**

Articles of Confederation adopted by Continental Congress **Nov. 15**; ratified **Mar. 1,** by last state, Maryland.

France recognized independence of 13 colonies **Dec. 17.**

1778

France signed treaty of aid with U.S. **Feb. 6.** Sent fleet; British evacuated Philadelphia in consequence **June 18.**

1779

John Paul Jones on the *Bonhomme Richard* defeated *Serapis* in British North Sea waters **Sept. 23.**

1780

Charleston, SC, fell to the British **May 12,** but a British force was defeated near **Kings Mountain, NC, Oct. 7** by militiamen.

Benedict Arnold found to be a traitor **Sept. 23.** Arnold escaped, made brigadier general in British army.

1781

Bank of North America incorporated **May 26.**

Cornwallis, sapped by Patriot victories, retired to **Yorktown, VA.** Adm. Francois Joseph de Grasse landed 3,000 French and stopped British fleet in Hampton Roads. Washington and Jean Baptiste de Rochambeau joined forces, arrived near Williamsburg **Sept. 26.** Siege of Cornwallis began **Oct. 6; Cornwallis surrendered Oct. 19.**

1782

New **British** cabinet agreed **in March** to **recognize U.S.** independence. Preliminary agreement signed in Paris **Nov. 30.**

1783

Massachusetts Supreme Court declared **slavery** illegal in that state.

Britain, U.S. signed Paris **peace treaty Sept. 3** recognizing American independence (Congress ratified it **Jan. 14, 1784).**

Washington ordered army disbanded Nov. 3, bade farewell to his officers at Fraunces Tavern, New York City, **Dec. 4.**

Noah Webster published *American Spelling Book.*

1784

Thomas Jefferson's proposal to **ban slavery** in new territory after 1802 was narrowly defeated **Mar. 1.**

First successful daily newspaper, ***Pennsylvania Packet & General Advertiser,*** published **Sept. 21.**

1786

Delegates from 5 states at **Annapolis, MD, Sept. 11-14** asked Congress to call convention in Philadelphia to write practical constitution for the 13 states.

1787

Shays's Rebellion of debt-ridden farmers in Massachusetts failed **Jan. 25.**

Northwest Ordinance adopted **July 13** by Continental Congress for Northwest Territory, N of Ohio River, W of New York; made rules for statehood. Guaranteed freedom of religion, support for schools, no slavery.

Constitutional convention opened at Philadelphia **May 25** with Washington presiding. Constitution accepted by delegates **Sept. 17;** ratification by 9th state, New Hampshire, **June 21, 1788,** meant adoption; declared in effect **Mar. 4, 1789.**

1789

George Washington chosen president by all electors voting (73 eligible, 69 voting, 4 absent); John Adams, vice president, got 34 votes. First Congress met at Federal Hall, New York City, **Mar. 4.** Washington inaugurated there **Apr. 30.** Supreme Court created by Federal Judiciary Act **Sept. 24.** Congress submitted Bill of Rights to states **Sept. 25.**

1790

Congress, **Mar. 1,** authorized decennial **U.S. census; Naturalization Act** (2-year residency) passed **Mar. 26.**

Congress met in Philadelphia, new temporary capital, **Dec. 6.**

1791

Bill of Rights went into effect **Dec. 15.**

1792

Coinage Act established **U.S. Mint** in Philadelphia **Apr. 2.**

Gen. **"Mad" Anthony Wayne** made commander in Ohio-Indiana area, trained "American Legion," established string of forts. Routed Indians at Fallen Timbers on Maumee River **Aug. 20, 1794,** checked British at Fort Miami, OH.

White House cornerstone laid **Oct. 13.**

1793

Eli Whitney invented **cotton gin,** reviving Southern slavery.

1794

Whiskey Rebellion, W Pennsylvania farmers protesting liquor tax of **1791,** was suppressed by federal militia **Sept. 1794.**

1795

U.S. bought peace from **Algerian pirates** by paying $1 mil ransom for 115 seamen **Sept. 5,** followed by annual tributes.

Gen. Wayne signed peace with Indians at Fort Greenville.

University of North Carolina became first operating state university.

1796

Washington's Farewell Address as president delivered **Sept. 19.** Gave strong warnings against permanent alliances with foreign powers, big public debt, large military establishment, and devices of "small, artful, enterprising minority."

1797

U.S. **frigate *United States*** launched at Philadelphia **July 10; *Constellation*** at Baltimore **Sept. 7; *Constitution*** (Old Ironsides) at Boston **Sept. 20.**

1798

Alien & Sedition Acts passed by Federalists **June-July;** intended to silence political opposition.

War with France threatened over French raids on U.S. shipping and rejection of U.S. diplomats. Navy (45 ships) and 365 privateers captured 84 French ships. *USS Constellation* took French warship *Insurgente* **1799.** Napoleon stopped French raids after becoming First Consul.

1800

Federal government moved to **Washington, DC.**

1801

John Marshall named Supreme Court chief justice, **Jan. 20.**

Tripoli declared war June 10 against U.S., which refused added tribute to commerce-raiding Arab corsairs. Land and naval campaigns forced Tripoli to negotiate **peace June 4, 1805.**

1803

Supreme Court, in **Marbury *v* Madison** case, for the first time overturned a U.S. law **Feb. 24.**

Napoleon sold all of **Louisiana,** stretching to Canadian border, to U.S., for $11,250,000 in bonds, plus $3,750,000 indemnities to American citizens with claims against France. U.S. took title **Dec. 20.** Purchase doubled U.S. area.

1804

Lewis and Clark expedition ordered by Pres. Thomas Jefferson to explore what is now northwest U.S. Started from St. Louis **May 14;** ended **Sept. 23, 1806.**

Vice Pres. **Aaron Burr shot Alexander Hamilton** in a duel **July 11** in Weehawken, NJ; Hamilton died the next day.

1807

Robert Fulton made first practical steamboat trip; left New York City **Aug. 17,** reached Albany, 150 mi, in 32 hr.

Embargo Act banned all trade with foreign countries, forbidding ships to set sail for foreign ports **Dec. 22.**

1808

Slave importation outlawed. Some 250,000 slaves were illegally imported **1808-60.**

1811

William Henry Harrison, governor of Indiana, defeated Indians under the Prophet, in battle of **Tippecanoe Nov. 7.**

Cumberland Road begun at Cumberland, MD; became important route to West.

1812

War of 1812 had 3 main causes: Britain seized U.S. ships trading with France; Britain seized 4,000 naturalized U.S. sailors by **1810;** Britain armed Indians who raided western border. U.S. stopped trade with Europe **1807** and **1809.** Trade with Britain only was stopped **1810.**

Unaware that Britain had raised the blockade against France 2 days before, **Congress declared war June 18.**

USS Essex captured *Alert* **Aug. 13;** *USS Constitution* destroyed *Guerriere* **Aug. 19;** *USS Wasp* took *Frolic* **Oct. 18;** *USS United States* defeated *Macedonian* off Azores **Oct. 25;** *Constitution* beat *Java* **Dec. 29.** British took Detroit **Aug. 16.**

1813

Oliver H. Perry defeated British fleet at Battle of Lake Erie, **Sept. 10.** U.S. won Battle of the Thames, Ontario, **Oct. 5,** but failed in Canadian invasion attempts. York (Toronto) and Buffalo were burned.

1814

British landed in Maryland in Aug., defeated U.S. force **Aug. 24, burned Capitol and White House.** Maryland militia stopped British advance **Sept. 12.** Bombardment of Ft. McHenry, Baltimore, for 25 hours, **Sept. 13-14,** by British fleet failed; Francis Scott Key wrote words to **"Star Spangled Banner."**

U.S. won naval Battle of **Lake Champlain Sept. 11.** Peace treaty signed at Ghent **Dec. 24.**

1815

Some 5,300 British, unaware of peace treaty, attacked U.S. entrenchments near **New Orleans, Jan. 8.** British had more than 2,000 casualties; Americans lost 71.

U.S. flotilla finally ended piracy by **Algiers, Tunis, Tripoli** by **Aug. 6.**

1816

Second **Bank of the U.S.** chartered.

1817

Rush-Bagot treaty signed **Apr. 28-29;** limited U.S., British armaments on the Great Lakes.

William Cullen Bryant's poem "Thanatopsis" published.

1819

Spain ceded **Florida** to U.S. **Feb. 22.**

American steamship *Savannah* made first part-steam-powered, part-sail-powered crossing of Atlantic, Savannah, GA, to Liverpool, England, 29 days.

1820

First organized **immigration of blacks to Africa** from U.S. began with 86 free blacks sailing **Feb.** to Sierra Leone.

Henry Clay's **Missouri Compromise** bill passed by Congress **Mar. 3.** Slavery was allowed in Missouri, but not elsewhere west of the Mississippi River north of 36° 30′ latitude (the southern line of Missouri). Repealed **1854.**

1821

Emma Willard founded Troy Female Seminary, first U.S. women's college.

1823

Monroe Doctrine, opposing European intervention in the Americas, enunciated by Pres. James Monroe **Dec. 2.**

1824

Pawtucket, RI, **weavers strike,** first such action by women.

1825

After a deadlocked election, John Quincy Adams was elected president by the U.S. House, **Feb. 9.**

Erie Canal opened; first boat left Buffalo **Oct. 26,** reached New York City **Nov. 4.** Canal cost $7 mil but opened Great Lakes area, made New York City chief Atlantic port.

John Stevens, of Hoboken, NJ, built and operated first experimental **steam locomotive** in U.S.

1826

Thomas Jefferson and John Adams both died **July 4.**

1828

South Carolina **Dec. 19** declared the right of state **nullification of federal laws,** opposing the "Tariff of Abominations."

Noah Webster published his *American Dictionary of the English Language.*

Baltimore & Ohio, 1st U.S. passenger railroad, was begun **July 4.**

1829

Andrew Jackson inaugurated as president, **Mar. 4.**

1830

Mormon church organized by Joseph Smith in Fayette, NY, **Apr. 6.**

1831

William Lloyd Garrison began abolitionist newspaper *The Liberator,* **Jan. 1.**

Nat Turner, black slave in Virginia, led local slave rebellion, starting **Aug. 21;** 57 whites killed. Troops called in, 100 slaves killed, Turner captured, tried, and hanged **Nov. 11.**

1832

Black Hawk War (IL-WI) **Apr.-Sept.** pushed Sauk and Fox Indians west across Mississippi.

South Carolina convention passed **Ordinance of Nullification Nov. 24** against permanent tariff, threatening to withdraw from Union. Congress **Feb. 1833** passed compromise tariff act, whereupon South Carolina repealed its act.

1833

Oberlin College became first in U.S. to adopt coeducation.

1835

Seminole Indians in Florida under Osceola began attacks **Nov. 1,** protesting forced removal. The unpopular 8-year war ended **Aug. 14, 1842;** Indians were sent to Oklahoma.

Texas proclaimed right to secede from Mexico; Sam Houston put in command of Texas army, **Nov. 2-4.**

Gold discovered on **Cherokee land** in Georgia. Indians forced to cede lands **Dec. 20** and to cross Mississippi.

Halley's Comet passed by the Earth.

1836

Texans besieged in Alamo in San Antonio by Mexicans under Santa Anna **Feb. 23-Mar. 6;** entire garrison killed. Texas independence declared, **Mar. 2.** At San Jacinto **Apr. 21,** Sam Houston and Texans defeated Mexicans.

Marcus Whitman, H. H. Spaulding, and wives reached Fort Walla Walla on Columbia River, OR. **First white women to cross plains.**

1838

Cherokee Indians made **"Trail of Tears,"** removed from Georgia to Oklahoma starting **Oct.**

1841

First emigrant **wagon train for California,** 47 persons, left Independence, MO, **May 1,** reached California **Nov. 4.**

Brook Farm commune set up by New England Transcendentalist intellectuals. Lasted to **1846.**

1842

Webster-Ashburton Treaty signed **Aug. 9,** fixing the U.S.-Canada border in Maine and Minnesota.

First use of **anesthetic** (sulfuric ether gas).

Settlement of Oregon began via **Oregon Trail.**

1843

More than 1,000 settlers left Independence, MO, for Oregon **May 22,** arrived **Oct.**

1844

First message over first **telegraph line** sent **May 24** by inventor Samuel F.B. Morse from Washington to Baltimore: "What hath God wrought!"

1845

Texas Congress **voted for annexation** by U.S. **July 4.** U.S. Congress admitted Texas to Union **Dec. 29.**

Edgar Allan Poe's poem "The Raven" published.

1846

Mexican War began after Pres. James K. Polk ordered Gen. Zachary Taylor to seize disputed Texan land settled by Mexicans. After border clash, U.S. declared war **May 13;** Mexico **May 23.**

Bear flag of Republic of California raised by American settlers at Sonoma **June 14.**

About 12,000 U.S. troops took Vera Cruz **Mar. 27, 1847,** and Mexico City **Sept. 14, 1847.** By **treaty,** signed **Feb. 2, 1848,** war was ended, and Mexico ceded claims to Texas, California, and other territory.

Treaty with Britain **June 15** set **boundary in Oregon** territory at 49th parallel (extension of existing line). Expansionists had used slogan "54° 40′ or fight."

Mormons, after violent clashes with settlers over polygamy, left Nauvoo, IL, for West under Brigham Young; settled **July 1847** at **Salt Lake City, UT.**

Elias Howe invented **sewing machine.**

1847

First **adhesive U.S. postage stamps** on sale **July 1;** Benjamin Franklin 5¢, Washington 10¢.

Ralph Waldo Emerson published first book of poems; **Henry Wadsworth Longfellow** published *Evangeline.*

1848

Gold discovered Jan. 24 in California; 80,000 prospectors emigrated in **1849.**

Lucretia Mott and Elizabeth Cady Stanton led **Seneca Falls, NY, Women's Rights Convention July 19-20.**

1850

Sen. Henry Clay's **Compromise of 1850** admitted California as 31st state **Sept. 9,** with slavery forbidden; made Utah and New Mexico territories; made Fugitive Slave Law more harsh; ended District of Columbia slave trade.

Nathaniel Hawthorne's *The Scarlet Letter* published.

1851

Herman Melville's *Moby-Dick* published.

1852

Uncle Tom's Cabin, by **Harriet Beecher Stowe,** published.

1853

Comm. Matthew C. Perry, U.S.N., received by Japan, **July 14; negotiated treaty to open Japan** to U.S. ships.

1854

Republican Party formed at Ripon, WI, **Feb. 28.** Opposed Kansas-Nebraska Act (became law **May 30**), which left issue of slavery to vote of settlers.

Henry David Thoreau published *Walden.*

Treaty ratified with Mexico **Apr. 25,** providing for purchase of a strip of land **(Gadsden Purchase).**

1855

Walt Whitman published *Leaves of Grass.*

First railroad train crossed Mississippi on the river's first bridge, Rock Island, IL, Davenport, IA, **Apr. 21.**

1856

Republican Party's first nominee for president, **John C. Fremont,** defeated. Abraham Lincoln made 50 speeches for him.

Lawrence, KS, sacked **May 21** by proslavery group; abolitionist **John Brown** led antislavery men against Missourians at **Osawatomie, KS, Aug. 30.**

1857

Dred Scott decision by Supreme Court **Mar. 6** held that slaves did not become free in a free state, Congress could not bar slavery from a territory, and blacks could not be citizens.

1858

First **Atlantic cable** was completed, by Cyrus W. Field **Aug. 5.**

Lincoln-Douglas debates in Illinois **Aug. 21-Oct. 15.**

1859

First commercially productive **oil well,** drilled near Titusville, PA, by Edwin L. Drake **Aug. 27.**

Abolitionist **John Brown,** with 21 men, seized U.S. Armory at **Harpers Ferry Oct. 16.** U.S. Marines captured raiders, killing several. Brown was hanged for treason **Dec. 2.**

1860

Approximately 20,000 **New England shoe workers** went on strike **Feb. 22** and won higher wages.

Abraham Lincoln, Republican, elected president **Nov. 6** in 4-way race.

First **Pony Express** between Sacramento, CA, and St. Joseph, MO, started **Apr. 3;** service ended **Oct. 24, 1861,** when first transcontinental telegraph line was completed.

1861

Seven southern states set up **Confederate States of America Feb. 8,** with Jefferson Davis as president, captured federal arsenals and forts. **Civil War** began as Confederates fired on **Ft. Sumter** in Charleston, SC, **Apr. 12,** capturing it **Apr. 14.**

Pres. **Lincoln called for 75,000 volunteers Apr. 15.** By **May,** 11 states had seceded. Lincoln blockaded Southern ports **Apr. 19,** cutting off vital exports, aid.

Confederates repelled Union forces at first **Battle of Bull Run July 21.**

First **transcontinental telegraph** was put in operation.

1862

Homestead Act approved **May 20;** it granted free family farms to settlers.

Land Grant Act approved **July 7,** providing for public land sale to benefit agricultural education; eventually led to establishment of state university systems.

Union forces were victorious in Western campaigns, took **New Orleans May 1.** Battles in East were inconclusive.

1863

Pres. Lincoln issued **Emancipation Proclamation Jan. 1,** freeing "all slaves in areas still in rebellion."

Entire **Mississippi River** was in Union hands by **July 4.** Union forces won a major victory at **Gettysburg, PA, July 1-3.** Lincoln read his **Gettysburg Address Nov. 19.**

In **draft riots** in New York City about 1,000 were killed or wounded; some blacks were hanged by mobs **July 13-16.**

1864

Gen. William Tecumseh **Sherman marched through Georgia,** taking Atlanta **Sept. 1,** Savannah **Dec. 22.**

Sand Creek massacre of Cheyenne and Arapaho Indians **Nov. 29.** Cavalry attacked Indians awaiting surrender terms.

1865

Gen. Robert E. Lee surrendered 27,800 Confederate troops to Gen. Ulysses S. Grant at Appomattox Court House, VA, **Apr. 9.** J. E. Johnston surrendered 31,200 to Sherman at Durham Station, NC, **Apr. 18.** Last rebel troops surrendered **May 26.**

Pres. Lincoln was shot Apr. 14 by John Wilkes Booth in Ford's Theater, Washington, DC; died the following morning. Vice Pres. **Andrew Johnson** was sworn in as president. Booth was hunted down; fatally wounded, perhaps by his own hand, **Apr. 26.** Four co-conspirators were hanged **July 7.**

13th Amendment, abolishing slavery, ratified **Dec. 6.**

1866

Ku Klux Klan formed secretly in South to terrorize blacks who voted. Disbanded **1869-71.** A 2d Klan organized **1915.**

Congress took control of Southern Reconstruction, backed freedmen's rights.

1867

Alaska sold to U.S. by Russia for $7.2 mil **Mar. 30** through efforts of Sec. of State William H. Seward.

Horatio Alger published first book, *Ragged Dick.*

The **Grange** was organized **Dec. 4,** to protect farmer interests.

1868

The World Almanac, a publication of the *New York World,* appeared for the first time.

Pres. **Johnson** tried to remove Edwin M. Stanton, secretary of war; was impeached by House **Feb. 24** for violation of Tenure of Office Act; acquitted by Senate **Mar.-May.**

1869

Financial **"Black Friday"** in New York **Sept. 24;** caused by attempt to "corner" gold.

Transcontinental railroad completed; golden spike driven at Promontory, UT, **May 10,** marking the junction of Central Pacific and Union Pacific.

Knights of Labor formed in Philadelphia. By **1886,** this labor union had 700,000 members nationally.

Woman suffrage law passed in Wyoming Territory **Dec. 10.**

1871

Great fire destroyed **Chicago Oct. 8-11.**

1872

Amnesty Act restored civil rights to citizens of the South **May 22** except for 500 Confederate leaders.

Congress founded first national park—**Yellowstone.**

1873

First U.S. **postal card** issued **May 1.**

Banks failed, panic began in **Sept.** Depression lasted 5 years.

"Boss" William Tweed of New York City convicted **Nov. 19** of stealing public funds. He died in jail in **1878.**

New York's Bellevue Hospital started **first nursing school.**

1875

Congress passed **Civil Rights Act Mar. 1,** giving equal rights to blacks in public accommodations and jury duty. Act invalidated in **1883** by Supreme Court.

First **Kentucky Derby** held **May 17.**

1876

Samuel J. Tilden, Democrat, received majority of popular votes for president over **Rutherford B. Hayes,** Republican, but 22 electoral votes were in dispute; issue left to Congress. Hayes given presidency in **Feb. 1877** after Republicans agreed to end Reconstruction of South.

Col. **George A. Custer** and 264 soldiers of the 7th Cavalry killed **June 25** in "last stand," Battle of the Little Big Horn, MT, in Sioux Indian War.

1877

Molly Maguires, Irish terrorist society in Scranton, PA, mining areas, was broken up by the hanging, **June 21,** of 11 leaders for murders of mine officials and police.

Pres. Rutherford B. Hayes sent troops in violent national **railroad strike.**

1878

First commercial **telephone** exchange opened, New Haven, CT, **Jan. 28.**

Thomas A. Edison founded **Edison Electric Light Co.** on **Oct. 15.**

1879

F. W. Woolworth opened his first five-and-ten store, in Utica, NY, **Feb. 22.**

Henry George published *Progress & Poverty,* advocating single tax on land.

1881

Pres. **James A. Garfield shot** in Washington, DC, **July 2;** died **Sept. 19.**

Booker T. Washington founded Tuskegee Institute for blacks.

Helen Hunt Jackson published *A Century of Dishonor,* about mistreatment of Indians.

1883

Pendleton Act passed **Jan. 16,** reformed civil service.

Brooklyn Bridge opened **May 24.**

1884

Mark Twain's masterpiece, *The Adventures of Huckleberry Finn,* appeared.

1886

Haymarket riot and bombing, **May 4,** followed bitter labor battles for 8-hour day in Chicago; 7 police and 4 workers died. Eight anarchists found guilty **Aug. 20,** 4 hanged **Nov. 11.**

Geronimo, Apache Indian, finally surrendered **Sept. 4.**

Statue of Liberty dedicated **Oct. 28.**

American Federation of Labor (AFL) formed **Dec. 8** by 25 craft unions.

1888

Great blizzard struck eastern U.S. **Mar. 11-14,** causing about 400 deaths.

1889

U.S. opened Oklahoma to white settlement **Apr. 22;** within 24 hours **claims for 2 mil acres** were staked by 50,000 settlers.

Johnstown, PA, flood May 31; 2,200 lives lost.

1890

Battle of **Wounded Knee, SD, Dec. 29,** the last major conflict between Indians and U.S. troops. About 200 Indian men, women, and children and 29 soldiers were killed.

Sherman Antitrust Act passed **July 2,** began federal effort to curb monopolies.

Jacob Riis published *How the Other Half Lives,* about city slums.

Poems of **Emily Dickinson** published posthumously.

1891

Forest Reserve Act Mar. 3 let president close public forest land to settlement for establishment of national parks.

1892

Ellis Island, in New York Bay, opened **Jan. 1** to receive immigrants.

Homestead, PA, strike at Carnegie steel mills; 7 guards and 11 strikers and spectators shot to death **July 6;** setback for unions.

1893

Financial panic began, led to 4-year depression.

1894

Thomas A. **Edison's kinetoscope** (motion pictures) (invented **1887**) given first public showing **Apr. 14.**

The **Pullman strike** began **May 11** at a railroad car plant in Chicago.

Jacob S. Coxey led army of unemployed from the Midwest, reaching Washington, DC, **Apr. 30.** Coxey arrested **May 1** for trespassing on Capitol grounds; his army disbanded.

1896

William Jennings Bryan delivered "Cross of Gold" speech **July 8;** won Democratic Party nomination.

Supreme Court, in **Plessy *v.* Ferguson,** approved racial segregation under the "separate but equal" doctrine.

1898

U.S. **battleship *Maine*** blown up **Feb. 15** at Havana; 260 killed.

U.S. blockaded Cuba Apr. 22 in aid of independence forces. U.S. declared war on Spain, **Apr. 24,** destroyed Spanish fleet in Philippines **May 1,** took Guam **June 20.**

Puerto Rico taken by U.S. **July 25-Aug. 12.** Spain agreed **Dec. 10** to cede Philippines, Puerto Rico, and Guam, and approved independence for Cuba.

Annexation of **Hawaii** signed by Pres. William McKinley, **July 7.**

1899

Filipino insurgents, unable to get recognition of independence from U.S., started guerrilla war **Feb. 4.** Their leader, Emilio Aguinaldo, captured **May 23, 1901.** Philippine Insurrection ended **1902.**

U.S. declared **Open Door Policy** to make China an open international market and to preserve its integrity as a nation.

John Dewey published *The School and Society,* advocating "progressive education."

1900

Carry Nation, Kansas antisaloon agitator, began raiding with hatchet.

U.S. helped suppress **"Boxers"** in Beijing.

International Ladies' Garment Workers Union was founded in New York City in **Nov.**

1901

Texas had first significant **oil strike, Jan. 10.**

Pres. **McKinley was shot Sept. 6** in Buffalo, NY, by an anarchist, Leon Czolgosz; died **Sept. 14.**

1903

Treaty between U.S. and Colombia to have U.S. dig **Panama Canal** signed **Jan. 22,** rejected by Colombia. Panama declared independence from Colombia with U.S. support **Nov. 3;** recognized by Pres. Theodore Roosevelt **Nov. 6.** U.S., Panama signed canal treaty **Nov. 18.**

Wisconsin set first **direct primary** voting system **May 23.**

First successful flight in heavier-than-air mechanically propelled airplane by **Orville Wright Dec. 17** near Kitty Hawk, NC, 120 ft in 12 secs. Fourth flight same day by **Wilbur Wright,** 852 ft in 59 secs. Improved plane patented, **1906.**

Great Train Robbery, pioneering film, produced.

1904

Ida Tarbell published muckraking *History of Standard Oil.*

1905

First **Rotary Club** founded in Chicago.

1906

San Francisco earthquake and fire **Apr. 18-19** left 503 dead, $350 mil damages.

Pure Food and Drug Act and Meat Inspection Act both passed **June 30.**

1907

Financial panic and depression started **Mar. 13.**

First round-world cruise of U.S. **"Great White Fleet";** 16 battleships, 12,000 men.

1908

Henry Ford introduced **Model T** car, priced at $850, **Oct. 1.**

1909

Adm. Robert E. Peary claimed to have reached **North Pole Apr. 6** on 6th attempt, accompanied by Matthew Henson, a black man, and 4 Eskimos; may have fallen short.

National Conference on the Negro convened **May 30,** leading to founding of National Association for the Advancement of Colored People.

1910

Boy Scouts of America founded **Feb. 8.**

1911

Supreme Court dissolved **Standard Oil Co. May 15.**

Building holding New York City's **Triangle Shirtwaist Co.** factory caught fire **Mar. 25;** 146 died.

First **transcontinental airplane flight** (with numerous stops) by C. P. Rodgers, New York to Pasadena, CA, **Sept. 17-Nov. 5;** time in air 82 hr, 4 min.

1912

American Girl Guides founded **Mar. 12;** name changed in **1913** to **Girl Scouts.**

U.S. sent Marines **Aug. 14** to **Nicaragua,** which was in default of loans to U.S. and Europe.

1913

NY Armory Show brought modern art to U.S. **Feb. 17.**

U.S. blockaded Mexico in support of revolutionaries.

Charles Beard published his *Economic Interpretation of the Constitution.*

Federal Reserve System was authorized **Dec. 23,** in a major reform of U.S. banking and finance.

1914

Ford Motor Co. raised basic wage rates from $2.40 for 9-hr day to $5 for 8-hr day **Jan. 5.**

When U.S. sailors were arrested at Tampico, Mexico, **Apr. 9,** Atlantic fleet was sent to **Veracruz,** occupied city.

Pres. Woodrow Wilson proclaimed **U.S. neutrality** in the European war **Aug. 4.**

Panama Canal was officially opened **Aug. 15.**

The **Clayton Antitrust Act** was passed **Oct. 15,** strengthening federal antimonopoly powers.

1915

First transcontinental **telephone call,** New York to San Francisco, completed **Jan. 25,** by Alexander Graham Bell and Thomas A. Watson.

British ship ***Lusitania*** sunk **May 7** by German submarine; 128 American passengers lost (Germany had warned passengers in advance). As a result of U.S. campaign, Germany issued apology and promise of payments **Oct. 5.** Pres. Wilson asked for a military fund increase **Dec. 7.**

U.S. troops landed in **Haiti July 28.** Haiti became a virtual U.S. protectorate under **Sept. 16** treaty.

1916

Gen. John J. **Pershing entered Mexico** to pursue Francisco (Pancho) Villa, who had raided U.S. border areas. Forces withdrawn **Feb. 5, 1917.**

Rural Credits Act passed **July 17,** followed by Warehouse Act **Aug. 11;** both provided financial aid to farmers.

Bomb exploded during **San Francisco** Preparedness Day parade **July 22,** killed 10. Thomas J. Mooney, labor organizer, and Warren K. Billings, shoe worker, were convicted **1917;** both later pardoned.

U.S. bought **Virgin Islands** from Denmark **Aug. 4.**

Jeannette Rankin (R, MT) elected as **first-ever female** member of U.S. **House.**

U.S. established military government in the **Dominican Republic Nov. 29.**

Trade and loans to **European allies** soared during the year.

Carl Sandburg published *Chicago Poems.*

1917

Germany, suffering from British blockade, declared almost unrestricted **submarine warfare Jan. 31.** U.S. cut diplomatic ties with Germany **Feb. 3,** and formally declared war **Apr. 6.**

Conscription law was passed **May 18.** First U.S. troops arrived in Europe **June 26.**

18th **(Prohibition)** Amendment to the Constitution was submitted to the states by Congress **Dec. 18.** On **Jan. 16, 1919,** the 36th state (Nevada) ratified it.

1918

Pres. Wilson set out his **14 Points** as basis for peace **Jan. 8.**

More than 1 mil **American troops** were in Europe by **July.** Allied counteroffensive launched at Château-Thierry **July 18.** War ended with signing of armistice **Nov. 11.**

Influenza epidemic killed an estimated 20 mil worldwide, 548,000 in U.S.

1919

First **transatlantic flight,** by U.S. Navy seaplane, left Rockaway, NY, **May 8,** stopped at Newfoundland, Azores, Lisbon **May 27.**

Boston police strike Sept. 9; National Guard breaks strike.

Sherwood Anderson published *Winesburg, Ohio.*

About 250 **alien radicals** were deported **Dec. 22.**

1920

In national **Red Scare,** some 2,700 Communists, anarchists, and other radicals were arrested **Jan.-May.**

Senate refused **Mar. 19** to ratify the **League of Nations Covenant.**

Radicals Nicola **Sacco** and Bartolomeo **Vanzetti** accused of killing 2 men in Massachusetts payroll holdup **Apr. 15.** Found guilty **1921.** A 6-year campaign for their release failed, and both were executed **Aug. 23, 1927.** Controversial verdict repudiated **1977,** by proclamation of Massachusetts Gov. Michael Dukakis.

First regular licensed **radio broadcasting** begun **Aug. 20.**

19th Amendment ratified **Aug. 18,** giving women right to vote.

League of Women Voters founded.

Wall St., New York City, **bomb** explosion killed 30, injured 100, did $2 mil damage **Sept. 16.**

Sinclair Lewis's *Main Street,* **F. Scott Fitzgerald's** *This Side of Paradise* published.

1921

Congress sharply curbed **immigration,** set national quota system **May 19.**

Joint congressional resolution declaring **peace with Germany, Austria,** and **Hungary** signed **July 2** by Pres. Warren G. Harding; treaties were signed in **Aug.**

Limitation of Armaments Conference met in Washington, DC, **Nov. 12-Feb. 6, 1922.** Major powers agreed to curtail naval construction, outlaw poison gas, restrict submarine attacks on merchant vessels, respect integrity of China.

Ku Klux Klan began revival with violence against Catholics in North, South, and Midwest.

1922

Violence during **coal-mine strike** at Herrin, IL, **June 22-23** cost 36 lives, including those of 21 nonunion miners.

Reader's Digest founded.

1923

First **sound-on-film motion picture,** *Phonofilm*, shown at Rivoli Theater, New York City, beginning in **April.**

1924

Law approved by Congress **June 15** making all **Indians citizens.**

Nellie Tayloe Ross elected governor of Wyoming **Nov. 9** as nation's first woman governor. **Miriam (Ma) Ferguson** elected governor of Texas **Nov. 9; installed Jan. 20, 1925.**

George Gershwin wrote *Rhapsody in Blue.*

1925

John T. Scopes found guilty of having taught **evolution** in Dayton, TN, high school, fined $100 and costs **July 24.**

1926

Dr. Robert H. Goddard demonstrated practicality of **rockets Mar. 16** at Auburn, MA, with first liquid-fuel rocket; rocket traveled 184 ft in 2.5 sec.

Congress established **Army Air Corps July 2.**

Air Commerce Act passed **Nov. 2,** providing federal aid for airlines and airports.

Ernest Hemingway's *The Sun Also Rises* published.

1927

About 1,000 **marines landed in China Mar. 5** to protect property in civil war.

Capt. **Charles A. Lindbergh** left Roosevelt Field, NY, **May 20** alone in plane *Spirit of St. Louis* on first New York-Paris nonstop flight. Reached Le Bourget airfield **May 21,** 3,610 mi in 33½ hours.

The Jazz Singer, with **Al Jolson,** demonstrated part-talking pictures in New York City **Oct. 6.**

Show Boat opened in New York **Dec. 27.**

O. E. Rolvaag published *Giants in the Earth.*

1928

Herbert Hoover elected president, defeating New York Gov. **Alfred E. Smith,** a Catholic.

Amelia Earhart became first woman to fly the Atlantic, **June 17.**

1929

"St. Valentine's Day massacre" in Chicago **Feb. 14;** gangsters killed 7 rivals.

Farm price stability aided by **Agricultural Marketing Act,** passed **June 15.**

Albert B. Fall, former secretary of the interior, was convicted of accepting bribe of $100,000 in the leasing of the **Elk Hills (Teapot Dome)** naval oil reserve; sentenced **Nov. 1** to a year in prison and fined $100,000.

Stock market crash Oct. 29 marked end of past prosperity as stock prices plummeted. Stock losses for 1929-31 estimated at $50 bil; worst American depression began.

Thomas Wolfe published *Look Homeward, Angel.* **William Faulkner** published *The Sound and the Fury.*

1930

London **Naval Reduction Treaty** signed by U.S., Britain, Italy, France, and Japan **Apr. 22;** in effect **Jan. 1, 1931;** expired **Dec. 31, 1936.**

Hawley-Smoot Tariff signed; rate hikes slash world trade.

1931

Empire State Building opened in New York City **May 1.**

Al Capone was convicted of tax evasion **Oct. 17.**

Pearl Buck published *The Good Earth.*

1932

Reconstruction Finance Corp. established **Jan. 22** to stimulate banking and business. Unemployment at 12 mil.

19-month-old **Charles Lindbergh Jr. was kidnapped Mar. 1;** found dead **May 12.** Bruno Hauptmann found guilty in trial **Jan.-Feb. 1935;** executed **Apr. 3, 1936.**

Bonus March on Washington, DC, launched **May 29** by World War I veterans demanding Congress pay their bonus in full.

Franklin D. Roosevelt elected president for the first time.

1933

Pres. Roosevelt named **Frances Perkins** U.S. secretary of labor; first woman in U.S. cabinet.

All **banks in the U.S. were ordered closed** by Pres. Roosevelt **Mar. 6.**

In a "100 days" special session, **Mar. 9-June 16,** Congress passed **New Deal** social and economic measures, including measures to regulate banks, distribute funds to the jobless, create jobs, raise agricultural prices, and set wage and production standards for industry.

Tennessee Valley Authority created by act of Congress, **May 18.**

Gold standard dropped by U.S.; announced by Pres. Roosevelt **Apr. 19,** ratified by Congress **June 5.**

Prohibition ended in the U.S. as 36th state ratified 21st Amendment **Dec. 5.**

U.S. foreswore armed intervention in **western hemisphere** nations **Dec. 26.**

1934

U.S. troops pulled out of **Haiti Aug. 6.**

1935

Works Progress Administration **(WPA)** instituted **May 6.** Rural Electrification Administration created **May 11.** National Industrial Recovery Act struck down by Supreme Court **May 27.**

Comedian **Will Rogers** and aviator **Wiley Post killed Aug. 15** in Alaska plane crash.

Social Security Act passed by Congress **Aug. 14.**

Huey Long, senator from Louisiana and national political leader, **assassinated Sept. 8.**

Porgy and Bess opened **Oct. 10** in New York.

Committee for Industrial Organization (CIO; later Congress of Industrial Organizations) formed to expand industrial unionism **Nov. 9.**

1936

Boulder Dam completed.

Margaret Mitchell published *Gone With the Wind.*

1937

Joe Louis knocked out James J. Braddock, became world heavyweight champ **June 22.**

Amelia Earhart, aviator, and copilot Fred Noonan lost **July 2** near Howland Island, in the Pacific.

Pres. Roosevelt asked for 6 additional Supreme Court justices; **"packing" plan** defeated.

Auto, steel labor unions won first big contracts.

1938

Naval Expansion Act passed **May 17.**

National minimum wage enacted **June 25.**

Orson Welles radio dramatization of **Martian invasion,** *War of the Worlds,* caused nationwide scare **Oct. 30.**

1939

Pres. Roosevelt asked for **defense budget hike Jan. 5, 12.**

New York World's Fair opened **Apr. 30,** closed **Oct. 31;** reopened **May 11, 1940,** and finally closed **Oct. 21.**

Albert Einstein alerted Pres. Roosevelt to **A-bomb** opportunity in **Aug. 2** letter.

U.S. declared its neutrality in European war **Sept. 5.**

Roosevelt proclaimed a limited **national emergency Sept. 8,** an unlimited emergency **May 27, 1941.** Both ended by Pres. Harry Truman **Apr. 28, 1952.**

John Steinbeck published *Grapes of Wrath.*

Gone With the Wind and *The Wizard of Oz* appeared on screen.

1940

U.S. okayed sale of **surplus war materiel** to Britain **June 3;** announced transfer of 50 overaged destroyers **Sept. 3.**

First **peacetime draft** approved **Sept. 14.**

Richard Wright published *Native Son.*

1941

Four Freedoms termed essential by Pres. Roosevelt in speech to Congress **Jan. 6:** freedom of speech and religion, freedom from want and fear.

Lend-Lease Act signed **Mar. 11** provided $7 bil in military credits for Britain. Lend-Lease for USSR approved in **Nov.**

U.S. occupied **Iceland July 7.**

The **Atlantic Charter,** 8-point declaration of principles, issued by Roosevelt and British Prime Min. Winston Churchill **Aug. 14.**

Japan attacked **Pearl Harbor,** Hawaii, 7:55 AM Hawaiian time, **Dec. 7;** 19 ships sunk or damaged, 2,300 dead. U.S. declared war on Japan **Dec. 8,** on Germany and Italy **Dec. 11.**

1942

Japanese troops took Bataan peninsula **Apr. 8,** Corregidor **May 6.**

Federal government forcibly moved 110,000 **Japanese-Americans** from West Coast to detention camps. Exclusion lasted 3 years.

Battle of **Midway June 4-7** was Japan's first major defeat.

Marines landed on **Guadalcanal Aug. 7;** last Japanese not expelled until **Feb. 9, 1943.**

U.S., Britain invaded North Africa **Nov. 8.**

First **nuclear chain reaction** (fission of uranium isotope U-235) produced at University of Chicago, under physicists Arthur Compton, Enrico Fermi, others **Dec. 2.**

1943

Oklahoma! opened **Mar. 31** on Broadway.

All war contractors barred from **racial discrimination, May 27.**

Pres. Roosevelt signed **June 10** pay-as-you-go income tax bill. Starting **July 1** wage and salary earners were subject to a **paycheck withholding** tax.

Race riot in Detroit June 21; 34 dead, 700 injured. Riot in Harlem section of New York City; 6 killed.

U.S., Britain invaded **Sicily July 9,** Italian **mainland Sept. 3.**

Marines advanced on **Gilbert Island in Nov.**

1944

U.S., Allied forces invaded Europe at **Normandy June 6** in greatest amphibious landing in history.

GI Bill of Rights signed **June 22,** providing veterans' benefits.

U.S. forces landed on **Leyte,** Philippines, **Oct. 20.**

1945

Yalta Conference met in the Crimea, USSR, **Feb. 4-11.** Roosevelt, Churchill, and Soviet leader Joseph Stalin agreed that their 3 countries, plus France, would occupy Germany and that the Soviet Union would enter war against Japan.

Marines landed on **Iwo Jima Feb. 19,** won control of Iwo Jima **Mar. 16** after heavy casualties. U.S. forces invaded **Okinawa Apr. 1,** captured Okinawa **June 21.**

Pres. Roosevelt, 63, died in Warm Springs, GA, **Apr. 12;** Vice Pres. **Harry S. Truman** became president.

Germany surrendered May 7; May 8 proclaimed V-E Day.

First **atomic bomb,** produced at Los Alamos, NM, exploded at Alamogordo, NM, **July 16.** Bomb dropped on **Hiroshima Aug. 6,** with about 75,000 people killed; bomb dropped on **Nagasaki Aug. 9,** killing about 40,000. Japan agreed to surrender, **Aug. 14;** formally surrendered **Sept. 2.**

At **Potsdam Conference, July 17-Aug. 2,** leaders of U.S., USSR, and Britain agreed on disarmament of Germany, occupation zones, war crimes trials.

U.S. forces entered **Korea** south of 38th parallel to displace Japanese **Sept. 8.**

Gen. Douglas MacArthur took over supervision of Japan **Sept. 9.**

1946

Strike by 400,000 **mine workers** began **Apr. 1;** other industries followed.

Philippines given independence by U.S. **July 4.**

1947

Pres. Truman asked Congress to aid Greece and Turkey to combat Communist terrorism **(Truman Doctrine), Mar. 12.** Approved **May 15.**

UN Security Council voted unanimously **Apr. 2** to place under **U.S. trusteeship** the Pacific islands formerly mandated to Japan.

Jackie Robinson joined the Brooklyn Dodgers **Apr. 11,** breaking the color barrier in major league baseball.

Taft-Hartley Labor Act curbing strikes was vetoed by Truman **June 20;** Congress overrode the veto.

Proposals known as the **Marshall Plan,** under which the U.S. would extend aid to European countries, were made by Sec. of State George C. Marshall **June 5.** Congress authorized some $12 bil in next 4 years.

1948

USSR halted all surface traffic into W. Berlin, **June 23;** in response, U.S. and British troops launched an airlift. Soviet blockade halted **May 12, 1949;** airlift ended **Sept. 30.**

Organization of American States founded **Apr. 30.**

Alger Hiss indicted **Dec. 15** for perjury, after denying he had passed secret documents to Whittaker Chambers for transmission to a Communist spy ring. Convicted **Jan. 21, 1950.**

Pres. Truman reelected Nov. 2, defeating Gov. Thomas E. Dewey in a historic upset.

Kinsey Report on sexuality in the human male published.

1949

U.S. troops withdrawn from **Korea June 29.**

NATO established **Aug. 24** by U.S., Canada, and 10 Western European nations, agreeing that an armed attack against one or more would be considered an attack against all.

Mrs. I. Toguri D'Aquino **(Tokyo Rose** of Japanese wartime broadcasts) was sentenced **Oct. 7** to 10 years in prison for treason. Paroled **1956,** pardoned **1977.**

Eleven leaders of **U.S. Communist Party** convicted **Oct. 14** of advocating violent overthrow of U.S. government; sentenced to prison. Supreme Court upheld convictions **1951.**

1950

Masked bandits robbed **Brink's, Inc.,** Boston express office, **Jan. 17** of $2.8 mil, of which $1.2 mil was in cash. Case solved **1956;** 8 sentenced to life.

Pres. Truman authorized production of **H-bomb Jan. 31.**

North Korea forces invaded **South Korea June 25.** UN asked for troops to restore peace.

Truman ordered Air Force and Navy to Korea **June 27.** Truman approved ground forces, air strikes against North Korea **June 30.**

U.S. sent 35 military advisers to **South Vietnam June 27,** and agreed to provide military and economic aid to anti-Communist government.

Army seized all railroads Aug. 27 on Truman's order to prevent a general strike; returned to owners in **1952.**

U.S. forces landed at Inchon Sept. 15; UN force took Pyongyang **Oct. 20,** reached China border **Nov. 20;** China sent troops across border **Nov. 26.**

Two members of **Puerto Rican nationalist** movement tried to kill Pres. Truman **Nov. 1.**

U.S. **Dec. 8** banned shipments to **Communist China** and to Asiatic ports trading with it.

1951

Sen. Estes Kefauver led Senate investigation into organized crime.

Julius Rosenberg, his wife, Ethel, and Morton Sobell found guilty **Mar. 29** of conspiracy to commit wartime espionage. Rosenbergs executed **June 19, 1953.** Sobell sentenced to 30 years; released **1969.**

Gen. Douglas MacArthur removed from Korea command **Apr. 11** by Pres. Truman, for having made unauthorized policy statements.

Korea cease-fire talks began in July; lasted 2 years. **Fighting ended July 27, 1953.**

Tariff concessions by the U.S. to the Soviet Union, Communist China, and all Communist-dominated lands were suspended **Aug. 1.**

The **U.S., Australia,** and **New Zealand** signed a mutual security pact **Sept. 1.**

Transcontinental television inaugurated **Sept. 4** with Pres. Truman's address at the Japanese Peace Treaty Conference in San Francisco.

Japanese peace treaty signed in San Francisco **Sept. 8** by U.S., Japan, and 47 other nations.

J. D. Salinger published *Catcher in the Rye.*

1952

U.S. **seizure of nation's steel mills** was ordered by Pres. Truman **Apr. 8** to avert a strike. Ruled illegal by Supreme Court **June 2.**

Peace contract between West Germany, U.S., Great Britain, and France was signed **May 26.**

The last racial and ethnic barriers to naturalization removed, **June 26-27,** with passage of **Immigration and Naturalization Act of 1952.**

First **hydrogen device** explosion **Nov. 1** at Eniwetok Atoll in Pacific.

1953

Pres. Dwight D. Eisenhower announced **May 8** that U.S. had given France $60 mil for **Indochina War.** More aid was announced in **Sept.**

Korean War armistice signed **July 27.**

1954

Nautilus, first atomic-powered submarine, was launched at Groton, CT, **Jan. 21.**

Five members of Congress were wounded in the House **Mar. 1** by 4 **Puerto Rican independence supporters** who fired at random from a spectators' gallery.

Sen. Joseph McCarthy (R, WI) led televised hearings **Apr. 22-June 17** into alleged Communist influence in the Army.

Racial segregation in public schools unanimously ruled unconstitutional by Supreme Court **May 17,** in *Brown* v. *Board of Education of Topeka.*

Southeast Asia Treaty Organization (**SEATO**) formed by defense pact signed in Manila **Sept. 8** by U.S., Britain, France, Australia, New Zealand, Philippines, Pakistan, and Thailand.

Condemnation of **Sen. McCarthy** voted by Senate, 67-22, **Dec. 2** for contempt of Senate subcommittee, abuse of its members, insults to Senate during Army investigation hearings.

1955

U.S. agreed **Feb. 12** to help train **South Vietnamese** army.

Supreme Court ordered **"all deliberate speed"** in integration of public schools **May 31.**

A **summit meeting** of leaders of U.S., Britain, France, and USSR took place **July 18-23** in Geneva, Switzerland.

Rosa Parks refused **Dec. 1** to give her seat to a white man on a **bus in Montgomery, AL.** Bus segregation ordinance declared unconstitutional by a federal court following boycott and NAACP protest.

America's 2 largest labor organizations merged **Dec. 5,** creating the AFL-CIO.

1956

Massive resistance to Supreme Court desegregation rulings was called for **Mar. 12** by 101 Southern congressmen.

Federal-Aid **Highway Act** signed **June 29,** inaugurating interstate highway system.

First transatlantic **telephone cable** activated **Sept. 25.**

1957

Congress approved first **civil rights bill** for blacks since Reconstruction **Apr. 29,** to protect voting rights.

National Guardsmen, called out by Arkansas Gov. Orval Faubus **Sept. 4,** barred 9 black students from entering all-white high school in **Little Rock.** Faubus complied **Sept. 21** with federal court order to remove Guardsmen, but the blacks were ordered to withdraw by local authorities. Pres. Eisenhower sent federal troops **Sept. 24** to enforce court order.

Jack Kerouac published *On the Road.*

1958

First U.S. **earth satellite** to go into orbit, **Explorer I,** launched by Army **Jan. 31** at Cape Canaveral, FL; discovered Van Allen radiation belt.

U.S. Marines sent to **Lebanon** to protect elected government from threatened overthrow **July-Oct.**

First domestic **jet airline** passenger service in U.S. opened by National Airlines **Dec. 10** between New York and Miami.

1959

Alaska admitted as 49th state **Jan. 3; Hawaii** admitted as 50th **Aug. 21.**

St. Lawrence Seaway opened **Apr. 25.**

Soviet **Premier Nikita Khrushchev** paid unprecedented visit to U.S. **Sept. 15-27,** made transcontinental tour.

1960

Sit-ins began **Feb. 1** when 4 black college students in Greensboro, NC, refused to move from a Woolworth lunch counter when denied service. By **Sept. 1961** more than 70,000 students, whites and blacks, had participated in sit-ins.

Congress approved a strong **voting rights act Apr. 21.**

A U.S. **U-2 reconnaissance plane** was shot down in the Soviet Union **May 1**; pilot Gary Powers captured. The incident led to cancellation of an imminent Paris summit conference.

Vice Pres. Richard Nixon and Sen. John F. Kennedy faced each other, **Sept. 26,** in the first in a series of televised **campaign debates. Kennedy defeated Nixon** to win the presidency, **Nov. 8.**

U.S. announced **Dec. 15** it backed rightist group in **Laos,** which took power the next day.

1961

U.S. severed diplomatic and consular relations with **Cuba Jan. 3,** after disputes over nationalizations of U.S. firms, U.S. military presence at Guantanamo base.

Invasion of Cuba's **"Bay of Pigs" Apr. 17** by Cuban exiles trained, armed, and directed by U.S., attempted to overthrow the regime of Premier Fidel Castro, unsuccessfully.

Peace Corps created by executive order, **Mar. 1.**

Commander Alan B. Shepard Jr. was rocketed from Cape Canaveral, FL, 116.5 mi above the earth in a Mercury capsule **May 5,** in first U.S.-crewed suborbital space flight.

"Freedom Rides" from Washington, DC, across deep South were launched **May 20** to **protest segregation** in interstate transportation.

1962

Lt. Col. John H. Glenn Jr. became first American in orbit **Feb. 20** when he circled the earth 3 times in the Mercury capsule ***Friendship 7.***

Pres. John F. Kennedy said **Feb. 14** U.S. military advisers in Vietnam would fire if fired upon.

Supreme Court **Mar. 26** backed **"one-man one-vote"** apportionment of seats in state legislatures.

James Meredith became first black student at University of Mississippi **Oct. 1** after 3,000 troops put down riots.

A Soviet **offensive missile buildup in Cuba** was revealed **Oct. 22** by Pres. Kennedy, who ordered a naval and air quarantine on shipment of offensive military equipment to the island. He and Soviet Premier Khrushchev agreed **Oct. 28** on a formula to end the crisis. Kennedy announced **Nov. 2** that Soviet missile bases in Cuba were being dismantled.

Rachel Carson's *Silent Spring* launched environmentalist movement.

1963

Supreme Court ruled **Mar. 18** that all **criminal defendants** must have counsel and that illegally acquired evidence was inadmissible in state as well as federal courts.

University of Alabama **desegregated** after Gov. **George Wallace** stepped aside when confronted by federally deployed National Guard troops, **June 11.**

Civil rights leader **Medgar Evers** assassinated **June 12.**

Supreme Court ruled, 8-1, **June 17** that laws requiring **recitation of the Lord's Prayer** or Bible verses in public schools were unconstitutional.

A limited **nuclear test-ban treaty** was agreed upon **July 25** by the U.S., the Soviet Union, and Britain.

March on Washington by 200,000 persons **Aug. 28** in support of **black demands** for equal rights. Highlight was "I have a dream" speech by **Dr. Martin Luther King Jr.**

Baptist church in Birmingham, AL, bombed **Sept. 15** in racial violence; 4 black girls killed.

South Vietnam Pres. **Ngo Dinh Diem assassinated Nov. 2;** U.S. had earlier withdrawn support.

Pres. Kennedy shot and fatally wounded Nov. 22 as he rode in a motorcade through downtown Dallas, TX. Vice Pres. **Lyndon B. Johnson sworn in** as president. **Lee Harvey Oswald arrested** and charged with the murder; he was shot and fatally wounded **Nov. 24.** Jack Ruby, a nightclub owner, was convicted of Oswald's murder; he died in **1967,** while awaiting retrial following reversal of his conviction.

Betty Friedan's *Feminine Mystique* ignited the women's movement.

1964

Panama suspended relations with U.S. **Jan. 9** after riots. U.S. offered **Dec. 18** to negotiate a new canal treaty.

Supreme Court ordered **Feb. 17** that **congressional districts** have equal populations.

U.S. reported **May 27** it was sending military planes to **Laos.**

Omnibus **civil rights bill** cleared by Congress **July 2,** signed same day by Pres. Johnson, banning discrimination in voting, jobs, public accommodations.

Three **civil rights workers** were reported missing in Mississippi **June 22;** found buried **Aug. 4.** Twenty-one white men were arrested. On **Oct. 20, 1967,** an all-white federal jury convicted 7 of conspiracy in the slayings.

Bill establishing **Medicare,** government health insurance program for persons over 65, signed **July 30.**

U.S. Congress **Aug. 7** passed **Tonkin Gulf Resolution,** authorizing presidential action in Vietnam, after N Vietnamese boats reportedly attacked 2 U.S. destroyers **Aug. 2.**

Congress approved **War on Poverty** bill **Aug. 11,** providing for a domestic Peace Corps (**VISTA**), a **Job Corps,** and antipoverty funding.

The **Warren Commission** released **Sept. 27** a report concluding that Lee Harvey Oswald was solely responsible for the Kennedy assassination.

Pres. Johnson was elected to a full term, **Nov. 3,** defeating Republican **Sen. Barry Goldwater** (AZ) in a landslide.

1965

Pres. Johnson in **Feb.** ordered continuous **bombing of North Vietnam** below 20th parallel.

Malcolm X assassinated **Feb. 21** at New York City rally.

Some 14,000 U.S. troops sent to **Dominican Republic** during civil war **Apr. 28.** All troops withdrawn by next year.

March from Selma to Montgomery, AL, **begun Mar. 21** by Rev. Martin Luther King Jr. to demand federal protection of **blacks' voting rights.** New **Voting Rights Act** signed **Aug. 6.**

Los Angeles riot by blacks living in **Watts** area resulted in 34 deaths and $200 mil in property damage **Aug. 11-16.**

National **immigration** quota system abolished **Oct. 3.**

Electric power failure blacked out most of northeastern U.S., parts of 2 Canadian provinces the night of **Nov. 9-10.**

U.S. forces in **S. Vietnam** reached 184,300 by year-end.

1966

U.S. forces began firing into **Cambodia May 1.**

Bombing of Hanoi area of N Vietnam by U.S. planes began **June 29.** By **Dec. 31,** 385,300 U.S. troops were stationed in S Vietnam, plus 60,000 offshore and 33,000 in Thailand.

Medicare began **July 1.**

Edward Brooke (R, MA) elected **Nov. 8** as first black U.S. senator in 85 years.

1967

Black U.S. Rep. **Adam Clayton Powell** (D, NY) was denied **Mar. 1** his seat because of charges he misused government funds. Reelected in **1968,** he was seated, but fined $25,000 and stripped of his seniority.

Pres. Johnson and Soviet Premier Aleksei Kosygin met **June 23 and 25** at **Glassboro State College** in NJ; agreed not to let any crisis push them into war.

The **25th Amendment,** providing for **presidential succession,** was ratified **Feb. 10.**

USS Liberty, an intelligence ship, was torpedoed by Israel in the Mediterranean, apparently by accident **June 8;** 34 killed.

Riots by blacks in **Newark, NJ, July 12-17** killed 26, injured 1,500; more than 1,000 arrested. In **Detroit, MI, July 23-30,** more than 40 died; 2,000 injured, 5,000 left homeless by rioting, looting, burning in city's black ghetto.

Thurgood Marshall was sworn in **Oct. 2** as first black U.S. Supreme Court Justice. **Carl B. Stokes** (D, Cleveland) and **Richard G. Hatcher** (D, Gary, IN) were elected first black mayors of major U.S. cities **Nov. 7.**

1968

USS Pueblo and 83-man crew seized in Sea of Japan **Jan. 23** by North Koreans; 82 men released **Dec. 22.**

"Tet offensive": Communist troops attacked Saigon, 30 province capitals **Jan. 30,** suffered heavy casualties.

Pres. Johnson **curbed bombing** of North Vietnam **Mar. 31.** Peace talks began in Paris **May 10.** All bombing of North halted **Oct. 31.**

Martin Luther King Jr., 39, assassinated Apr. 4 in Memphis, TN. **James Earl Ray,** an escaped convict, pleaded guilty to the slaying, was sentenced to 99 years.

Sen. Robert F. Kennedy (D, NY), 42, **shot June 5** in Hotel Ambassador, Los Angeles, after celebrating presidential primary victories. Died **June 6.** Sirhan Bishara Sirhan, convicted of murder, **1969;** death sentence commuted to life in prison, **1972.**

Vice Pres. **Hubert Humphrey nominated** for president by Democrats **at national convention in Chicago,** marked by clash between police and **antiwar protesters, Aug. 26-29.**

The Republican nominee, **Richard Nixon, won the presidency,** defeating Hubert Humphrey in a close race **Nov. 5.**

Rep. Shirley Chisholm (D, NY) became the first black woman elected to Congress.

1969

Expanded 4-party **Vietnam peace talks** began **Jan. 18.** U.S. force peaked at 543,400 in April. Withdrawal started **July 8.** Pres. Nixon set Vietnamization policy **Nov. 3.**

U.S. astronaut **Neil Armstrong,** commander of the Apollo 11 mission, became the first person to **set foot on the moon, July 20;** followed by astronaut **Edwin Aldrin;** astronaut **Michael Collins** remained aboard command module.

Woodstock music festival near Bethel, NY, drew 300,000-500,000 people, **Aug. 15-17.**

Anti-Vietnam War **demonstrations reached peak** in U.S.; some 250,000 marched in Washington, DC, **Nov. 15.**

Massacre of hundreds of civilians at **Mylai, South Vietnam,** in 1968 incident reported **Nov. 16.**

1970

United Mine Workers official **Joseph A. Yablonski,** his wife, and their daughter found shot to death **Jan. 5;** UMW chief W. A. (Tony) Boyle later convicted of the killing.

A federal jury **Feb. 18** found the **"Chicago 7"** antiwar activists innocent of conspiring to incite riots during the 1968 **Democratic National Convention.** However, 5 were convicted of crossing state lines with intent to incite riots.

Millions of Americans participated in antipollution demonstrations **Apr. 22** to mark the **first Earth Day.**

U.S. and South Vietnamese forces crossed **Cambodian** borders **Apr. 30** to get at enemy bases. Four students were killed **May 4** at **Kent State** University in Ohio by National Guardsmen during a protest against the war.

Two **women generals,** the first in U.S. history, were named by Pres. Nixon **May 15.**

A **postal reform** measure was signed **Aug. 12,** creating an independent U.S. Postal Service.

1971

Charles Manson and 3 of his cult followers were found guilty **Jan. 25** of first-degree murder in **1969** slaying of actress Sharon Tate and 6 others.

The 26th Amendment, lowering the **voting age to 18** in all elections, was ratified **June 20.**

A court-martial jury **Mar. 29** convicted **Lt. William L. Calley Jr.** of premeditated murder of 22 South Vietnamese at Mylai on **Mar. 16, 1968.** He was sentenced to life imprisonment **Mar. 31.** Sentence was reduced to 20 years **Aug. 20.**

Publication of classified **Pentagon papers** on U.S. involvement in Vietnam was begun **June 13** by the *New York Times.* In a 6-3 vote, U.S. Supreme Court **June 30** upheld the right of the *Times* and the *Washington Post* to publish the documents.

U.S. bombers struck massively in North Vietnam for 5 days starting **Dec. 26** in retaliation for alleged violations of agreements reached prior to the 1968 bombing halt.

1972

Pres. Nixon arrived in **Beijing Feb. 21** for an 8-day visit to China, which he called a "journey for peace."

By a vote of 84 to 8, the Senate, **Mar. 22,** approved banning **discrimination** on the basis of sex, and sent the measure to the states for ratification.

North Vietnamese forces launched the biggest attacks in 4 years across the demilitarized zone **Mar. 30.** The U.S. responded **Apr. 15** by resumption of bombing of Hanoi and Haiphong after a 4-year lull.

Pres. Nixon announced **May 8** the mining of **North Vietnam ports.** Last U.S. combat troops left **Aug. 11.**

Gov. George C. Wallace (AL), campaigning for the presidency at a Laurel, MD, shopping center **May 15, was shot** and seriously wounded. Arthur H. Bremer **convicted Aug. 4,** sentenced to 63 years for shooting Wallace and 3 bystanders.

In **first visit of a U.S. president to Moscow,** Pres. Nixon arrived **May 22** for a week of summit talks with Kremlin leaders that culminated in a landmark **strategic arms pact.**

Five men were arrested **June 17** for breaking into the offices of the Democratic National Committee in the **Watergate** office complex in Washington, DC.

Pres. **Nixon reelected Nov. 7** in a landslide, defeating Democratic Sen. George McGovern (SD).

The **Dow Jones** industrial average closed above 1,000 for the first time, **Nov. 14.**

Full-scale **bombing of North Vietnam** resumed after Paris peace negotiations reached an impasse **Dec. 18.**

1973

Five of 7 defendants in **Watergate** break-in trial pleaded guilty **Jan. 11 and 15;** the other 2 were convicted **Jan. 30.**

In ***Roe* v. *Wade,*** Supreme Court ruled, 7-2, **Jan. 22,** that states may not ban **abortions** during **first 3 months of pregnancy** and may regulate, but may not ban, abortions during 2d trimester.

Four-party **Vietnam peace pacts** were signed in Paris **Jan. 27,** and North Vietnam released some 590 U.S. prisoners by **Apr. 1.** Last U.S. troops left **Mar. 29.**

End of the military draft announced **Jan. 27.**

Top **Nixon aides** H. R. Haldeman, John D. Ehrlichman, and John Dean and Attorney Gen. Richard Kleindienst **resigned Apr. 30,** amid charges of White House efforts to obstruct justice in the Watergate case.

John Dean, former Nixon counsel, told Senate hearings **June 25** that Nixon, his staff and campaign aides, and the Justice Department had conspired to cover up Watergate facts.

The U.S. officially ceased bombing in **Cambodia** at midnight **Aug. 14** in accord with a June congressional action.

Vice Pres. Spiro T. Agnew Oct. 10 resigned and pleaded no contest to a charge of tax evasion on payments made to him by contractors when he was governor of Maryland. **Gerald R. Ford Oct. 12** became **first appointed vice president** under the 25th Amendment; sworn in **Dec. 6.**

A total ban on **oil exports** to the U.S. was imposed by Arab oil-producing nations **Oct. 19-21** after the outbreak of an Arab-Israeli war. The ban was lifted **Mar. 18, 1974.**

Attorney Gen. Elliot Richardson resigned, and his deputy William D. Ruckelshaus and **Watergate Special Prosecutor Archibald Cox** were **fired** by Pres. Nixon **Oct. 20,** when Cox threatened to secure a judicial ruling that Nixon was violating a court order to give tapes to Judge John Sirica. **Leon Jaworski** named **Nov. 1** by the Nixon administration to succeed Cox.

Congress overrode **Nov. 7** Pres. Nixon's veto of the **war powers** bill, which curbed president's power to commit armed forces to hostilities abroad without congressional approval.

1974

Impeachment hearings opened **May 9** against Pres. Nixon by the House Judiciary Committee.

John D. Ehrlichman and 3 **White House "plumbers"** found guilty **July 12** of conspiring to violate the civil rights of Pentagon Papers leaker Daniel Ellsberg's psychiatrist by breaking into his office.

U.S. Supreme Court ruled, 8-0, **July 24** that Nixon had to turn over **64 tapes** of White House conversations.

House Judiciary Committee, in televised hearings **July 24-30,** recommended 3 **articles of impeachment** against Pres. Nixon. The first, voted 27-11 **July 27,** charged conspiracy to obstruct justice in the Watergate cover-up. The 2d, voted 28-10 **July 29,** charged abuses of power. The 3d, voted 21-17 **July 30,** charged defiance of committee subpoenas. The House voted **Aug. 20,** 412-3, to accept the committee report, which included the impeachment articles.

Pres. Nixon announced his resignation, Aug. 8, and resigned Aug. 9; his support in Congress had begun to collapse **Aug. 5,** after release of tapes implicating him in Watergate cover-up. **Vice Pres. Gerald R. Ford was sworn in Aug. 9** as 38th U.S. president.

A **pardon** to ex-Pres. Nixon for any federal crimes he committed while president was issued by Pres. Ford **Sept. 8.**

1975

Found guilty of Watergate cover-up charges Jan. 1 were ex-Atty. Gen. John Mitchell, ex-presidential advisers H. R. Haldeman and John Ehrlichman.

U.S. launched **evacuation of American and some South Vietnamese from Saigon Apr. 29** as Communist forces completed takeover of South Vietnam; **South Vietnamese** government officially **surrendered Apr. 30.**

U.S. merchant ship ***Mayaguez*** and its crew of 39 were seized by Cambodian forces in Gulf of Siam **May 12.** In rescue operation, U.S. Marines attacked Tang Island, planes bombed air base; Cambodia surrendered ship and crew.

Congress voted $405 mil for **South Vietnam refugees May 16;** 140,000 were flown to the U.S.

Illegal CIA operations, including records on 300,000 persons and groups, and infiltration of agents into black, antiwar, and political movements, described by panel headed by Vice Pres. **Nelson Rockefeller June 10.**

Publishing heiress **Patricia (Patty) Hearst,** kidnapped **Feb. 5, 1974,** by "Symbionese Liberation Army" militants, was captured, in San Francisco **Sept. 18** with others. She was convicted **Mar. 20, 1976,** of bank robbery.

1976

U.S. celebrated **200th anniversary of independence July 4,** with festivals, parades, and New York City's Operation Sail, a gathering of tall ships from around the world.

"Legionnaire's disease" killed 29 persons who attended an American Legion convention **July 21-24** in Philadelphia.

Viking II set down on **Mars'** Utopia Plains **Sept. 3,** following the successful landing by *Viking I* **July 20.**

1977

Pres. Jimmy Carter **Jan. 21** pardoned most Vietnam War **draft evaders.**

Convicted murderer **Gary Gilmore executed** by a Utah firing squad **Jan. 17,** in the first exercise of capital punishment in the U.S. since **1967.**

Pres. Carter signed an act **Aug. 4** creating a new cabinet-level **Energy Department.**

1978

U.S. Senate voted **Apr. 18** to turn over **Panama Canal** to Panama Dec. 31, 1999; **Mar. 16** vote had given approval to a treaty guaranteeing the area's neutrality after the year 2000.

Californians, **June 6,** approved **Proposition 13,** a state constitutional amendment slashing property taxes.

U.S. Supreme Court, **June 28,** ruled against **racial quotas** in *Bakke* v. *University of California.*

1979

Partial meltdown released radioactive material **Mar. 28,** at nuclear reactor on **Three Mile Island** near Middletown, PA.

Federal government announced, **Nov. 1,** a $1.5 bil loan-guarantee plan to aid the ailing **Chrysler Corp.**

Some 90 people, including 63 Americans, **taken hostage, Nov. 4,** at **American embassy in Tehran,** Iran, by militant followers of Ayatollah Khomeini. He demanded return of former Shah Muhammad Reza Pahlavi, who was undergoing medical treatment in New York City.

1980

Pres. Carter announced, **Jan. 4, economic sanctions against the USSR,** in retaliation for Soviet invasion of Afghanistan. At Carter's request, **U.S. Olympic Committee** voted, **Apr. 12,** against U.S. participation in Moscow Summer Olympics.

Eight Americans killed and 5 wounded, **Apr. 24, in ill-fated** attempt to **rescue hostages** held by Iranian militants.

Mt. St. Helens, in Washington state, **erupted, May 18.** The blast, with others **May 25** and **June 12,** left 57 dead.

In a sweeping victory, **Nov. 4, Ronald Reagan** (R) was elected 40th president, defeating incumbent Pres. Carter. Republicans gained control of the Senate.

Former Beatle **John Lennon** was shot and killed, **Dec. 8,** in New York City.

1981

Minutes after **Reagan's inauguration Jan. 20,** the **52 Americans** held **hostage in Iran** for 444 days were freed.

Pres. Reagan was **shot and seriously wounded, Mar. 30,** in Washington, DC; also seriously wounded were a Secret Service agent, a policeman, and Press Sec. **James Brady. John W. Hinckley Jr.** arrested, found not guilty by reason of insanity in **1982,** and committed to mental institution.

World's first reusable spacecraft, the **space shuttle *Columbia,*** was sent into space, **Apr. 12.**

Congress, **July 29,** passed Pres. Reagan's **tax-cut legislation,** expected to save taxpayers $750 bil over 5 years.

Federal air traffic controllers, Aug. 3, began an illegal **nationwide strike.** Most defied a back-to-work order and were dismissed by Pres. Reagan **Aug. 5.**

In a 99-0 vote, the Senate confirmed, **Sept. 21,** appointment of **Sandra Day O'Connor** as an **associate justice of U.S. Supreme Court.** She was the first woman appointed to that body.

1982

The 13-year-old lawsuit against **AT&T** by the **Justice Dept.** was settled **Jan. 8.** AT&T agreed to give up the 22 Bell System companies and was allowed to expand business.

The Equal Rights Amendment was defeated after a 10-year struggle for ratification.

In Dec., **unemployment** hit 10.8%, highest since 1940.

A retired dentist, **Dr. Barney B. Clark,** 61, became first recipient of a **permanent artificial heart, Dec. 2.**

1983

On **Apr. 20, Pres. Reagan** signed a compromise bipartisan bill designed to save **Social Security** from bankruptcy.

Sally Ride became the first American **woman** to travel in **space, June 18,** when the **space shuttle *Challenger*** was launched from Cape Canaveral, FL.

On **Sept. 1, a South Korean passenger jet** infringing on Soviet air space was **shot down;** 269 people were killed.

On **Oct. 23,** 241 **U.S. Marines and sailors,** members of the multinational **peacekeeping force** in **Lebanon,** were killed when a TNT-laden suicide bomb blew up Marine headquarters at **Beirut** International Airport.

U.S. troops, with a small force from 6 **Caribbean** nations, invaded **Grenada Oct. 25.** After a few days, Grenadian militia and Cuban "construction workers" were overcome, U.S. citizens evacuated, and the **Marxist regime deposed.** Congress applied the War Powers Resolution, requiring U.S. troops to leave Grenada by **Dec. 24.**

1984

The space shuttle *Challenger* was launched on its 4th trip into space, **Feb. 3.** On **Feb. 7,** Navy Capt. Bruce McCandless, followed by Army Lt. Colonel Robert Stewart, **became first humans to fly free of a spacecraft.**

On **May 7,** American **Vietnam war** veterans reached an out-of-court **settlement with 7 chemical companies** in a class-action suit over the herbicide **Agent Orange.**

Former Vice Pres. **Walter Mondale** won the **Democratic presidential nomination, June 6; chose Rep. Geraldine Ferraro** (D, NY), as candidate for **vice president.**

Pres. **Ronald Reagan** was reelected **Nov. 6** in the greatest Republican **landslide** in history, carrying 49 states.

1985

"Live Aid," a rock concert broadcast around the world **July 13,** raised $70 mil for starving peoples of Africa.

On **June 14** a **TWA jet was seized** by terrorists after takeoff from Athens; 153 passengers and crew held hostage for 17 days; 1 U.S. serviceman killed.

On **Oct. 7, 4 Palestinian hijackers seized** Italian cruise ship, **Achille Lauro** at sea as it approached Port Said, Egypt. Over 400 passengers and crew were held hostage for 2 days; one American, Leon Klinghoffer, was killed.

1986

On **Jan. 20,** for the first time, the U.S. officially observed **Martin Luther King Jr. Day.**

Moments after liftoff, **Jan. 28,** the **space shuttle Challenger exploded, killing 6 astronauts and Christa McAuliffe,** a New Hampshire teacher, on board. Later investigations found NASA had taken inadequate safety precautions.

U.S. Congress, overriding Pres. Reagan's veto in **Sept.,** joined other nations in imposing **economic sanctions on South Africa,** pressuring the government to end apartheid.

U.S. Senate confirmed, **Sept. 17,** Pres. Reagan's nomination of **William Rehnquist** as chief justice and **Antonin Scalia** as associate justice of the Supreme Court.

Congress passed, in late **Sept.,** a major **tax reform law.**

In **congressional races, Nov. 4, Democrats** won a 55-45 Senate majority and enlarged their House majority.

Press reports in early **Nov.** broke first news of the **Iran-contra scandal,** involving secret U.S. sale of arms to Iran.

Ivan Boesky, accused of insider trading, agreed, **Nov. 14,** to plead guilty to an unspecified criminal count, pay a $100 mil fine, and return profits; he was barred for life from trading securities.

1987

Pres. Reagan produced the nation's first **trillion-dollar budget, Jan. 5.**

The stock market continued to rise, with the **Dow Jones closing** at 2002.25, **Jan. 8,** its **first finish above 2000.**

An **Iraqi warplane missile killed 37 sailors** on the frigate USS *Stark* in the Persian Gulf, **May 17.** Iraq called it an accident. The *Stark's* officers were found negligent.

Public hearings by Senate and House committees investigating the **Iran-contra affair** were held **May-Aug.** Lt. Col. **Oliver North** said he had believed all his activities were authorized by his superiors. Pres. Reagan, **Aug. 12,** denied knowing of the funds' diversion to the contras.

Wall Street crashed, Oct. 19, with the Dow Jones plummeting a record 508 points.

Pres. Reagan and Soviet leader **Mikhail Gorbachev, Dec. 8,** signed a **pact to dismantle** all 1,752 **U.S. and** 859 **Soviet missiles** with a 300- to 3,400-mi. range.

1988

Nearly **1.4 mil illegal aliens** met **May 4** deadline for applying for **amnesty** under a new federal policy.

A missile, fired from **U.S. Navy warship *Vincennes,*** in the Persian Gulf, mistakenly struck and **destroyed** a commercial **Iranian airliner, July 3,** killing all 290.

George Bush, vice president under Reagan, **elected** 41st U.S. **president, Nov. 8.** Bush decisively defeated the Democratic nominee, Gov. **Michael Dukakis** (MA).

Drexel Burnham Lambert agreed, **Dec. 21, to plead guilty to 6 violations of federal law,** including insider trading, stock manipulation, and falsified records, and **pay penalties of $650 mil,** the largest such settlement ever.

1989

One of the **largest oil spills in U.S. history** occurred after the ***Exxon Valdez*** struck Bligh Reef in Alaska's Prince William Sound, **Mar. 24.**

Former National Security Council staff member **Oliver North** was convicted, **May 4,** on charges related to the **Iran-contra** scandal. Conviction thrown out on appeal in **1991.**

A measure to **rescue the savings and loan industry** was signed into law, **Aug. 9,** by Pres. Bush.

Army Gen. Colin Powell was nominated **Aug. 10** by Pres. Bush, as **chairman of the Joint Chiefs of Staff;** he became the first black to hold the post.

Just before a World Series game, **Oct. 17,** an **earthquake struck the San Francisco Bay area,** causing 62 deaths.

L. Douglas Wilder (D) was elected governor of Virginia, the **first U.S. black governor** since Reconstruction.

U.S. troops invaded Panama, Dec. 20, overthrowing the government of **Manuel Noriega.** Noriega, wanted by U.S. authorities on drug charges, took refuge in the Vatican mission; he surrendered to the U.S. **Jan. 3, 1990.**

1990

Pres. Bush signed **Americans With Disabilities Act** on **July 26,** barring discrimination against handicapped.

Justice William Brennan announced, **July 20,** his resignation from the U.S. Supreme Court; in his place, Bush nominated **Judge David Souter,** who was confirmed **Sept. 27.**

Operation Desert Shield forces left for **Saudi Arabia, Aug. 7,** to defend that country following the **invasion** of its neighbor **Kuwait by Iraq,** Aug. 2.

Pres. Bush signed, **Nov. 5,** a bill to **reduce budget deficits** $500 bil over 5 years, by spending curbs and tax hikes.

1991

The **U.S. and its allies defeated Iraq** in the **Persian Gulf War** and liberated Kuwait, which Iraq had overrun in Aug. **1990.** On **Jan. 17,** the allies launched a devastating **attack on Iraq from the air.** In a **ground war** starting **Feb. 24,** which lasted just 100 hours, the U.S.-led attackers killed or captured many thousands of Iraqi soldiers and sent the rest into retreat before Pres. Bush ordered a cease-fire **Feb. 27.**

The **Dow Jones industrial average** finished above 3,000 for the first time, **Apr. 17.**

U.S. **House bank** ordered closed **Oct. 3** after revelations House members had written 8,331 bad checks.

The **Senate approved, Oct. 15, nomination of Clarence Thomas** to the Supreme Court, despite allegations of sexual harassment against him by **Anita Hill,** a former aide. He became the 2d African-American to serve on the Court, replacing retiring Justice **Thurgood Marshall,** the 1st black to do so.

Charles Keating convicted of securities fraud **Dec. 4.**

1992

Riots swept South-Central Los Angeles Apr. 29, after **jury acquitted 4 white policemen** on all but one count in the videotaped 1991 beating of black motorist **Rodney King.** The death toll in the L.A. violence was put at 52.

Bill Clinton (D) was **elected** 42d president, **Nov. 3,** defeating **Pres. George Bush** (R) and independent **Ross Perot.**

A UN-sanctioned military force, led by U.S. troops, arrived in **Somalia Dec. 9.**

1993

A bomb exploded in a parking garage beneath the **World Trade Center** in New York City, **Feb. 26,** killing 6 people.

Janet Reno became the first woman U.S. attorney general **Mar. 12.**

Four federal agents were killed, Feb. 28, during an unsuccessful raid on the **Branch Davidian compound near Waco, TX.** A 51-day siege of the compound by federal agents ended **Apr. 19,** when armored vehicles pumped tear gas into it; those inside responded with gunfire. The compound then **burned down,** leaving more than 70 cult members dead.

A federal jury, **Apr. 17, found 2 Los Angeles police officers guilty** and 2 not guilty of violating the civil rights of motorist **Rodney King** in 1991 beating incident.

"The Great Flood of 1993" inundated 8 mil acres in 9 Midwestern states in summer, leaving 50 dead.

Pres. Clinton, **July 19,** announced a "don't ask, don't tell, don't pursue" policy for **homosexuals** in the U.S. military.

Vincent Foster, deputy White House counsel, was found shot to death in a N Virginia park, an apparent suicide.

Judge Ruth Bader Ginsburg was sworn in, **Aug. 10,** as **107th justice of the U.S. Supreme Court,** replacing Associate Justice Byron White, who retired.

Pres. Clinton, **Aug. 10,** signed a compromise bill designed to **cut federal budget deficits** $496 bil over 5 years, through spending cuts and new taxes.

The **"Brady Bill,"** a major gun-control measure, was signed into law by Pres. Clinton **Nov. 30.**

1994

North American Free Trade Agreement took effect **Jan. 1.**

A predawn **earthquake struck the Los Angeles area, Jan. 17,** claiming 61 lives and causing heavy damage.

Attorney Gen. Janet Reno **Jan. 20** appointed Robert Fiske independent counsel to probe **Whitewater affair;** under a court ruling he was **replaced Aug. 5 by Kenneth Starr**. Congressional committees, **late July,** began Whitewater hearings.

Byron De La Beckwith convicted Feb. 5 of the 1963 murder of **civil rights leader Medgar Evers.**

Longtime CIA officer **Aldrich Ames** and his wife were **charged Feb. 21 with spying.** Under a plea bargain, he received life in prison, while she was sentenced to 63 months.

Eleven **Branch Davidian cult** members were acquitted **Feb. 26** of charges in the deaths of 4 federal agents in a 1993 shootout at the cult's compound near Waco, TX.

Four men were found guilty, **Mar. 4,** in the 1993 bombing of the **World Trade Center** in New York City.

A former Arkansas state employee, **Paula Jones, filed a suit, May 6,** that accused Pres. Clinton of sexual harassment while governor of Arkansas.

Major league **baseball players went on strike,** following **Aug. 11** games; strike ended **Apr. 25, 1995.**

Senate Majority Leader George Mitchell (D, ME), **Sept. 26,** dropped efforts to pass Clinton's **health-care reform** package.

Republicans won control of Congress in **Nov. 8** elections.

Pres. Clinton, **Dec. 8,** approved tariff-cutting provisions of the Uruguay Round of the General Agreement on Tariffs and Trade (GATT; renamed **World Trade Organization** [WTrO]).

1995

When the 104th Congress opened, **Jan. 4, Sen. Bob Dole** (R, KS) became **Senate majority leader** and **Rep. Newt Gingrich** (R, GA) was elected **House Speaker.** A bill to end Congress's exemption from federal labor laws, first in a series of measures in Republicans' **"Contract With America,"** cleared Congress **Jan. 17;** signed into law **Jan. 23.**

Clinton invoked emergency powers, **Jan. 31,** to extend a **$20 bil loan to help Mexico** avert financial collapse.

A bill making it more difficult for Congress to approve **"unfunded mandates"**—measures requiring but not funding actions by states—was signed by Pres. Clinton **Mar. 22.** A proposed constitutional **amendment mandating a balanced budget** passed the House **Jan. 26** but failed in the Senate **Mar. 2.** A proposed constitutional **amendment limiting terms** in Congress failed in the House, **Mar. 29.**

The **Dow Jones** industrial average passed 4,000 **Feb 23.**

The last UN peacekeeping troops withdrew from **Somalia Feb. 28-Mar. 3,** with the aid of U.S. Marines. In **Haiti,** peacekeeping responsibilities were transferred from U.S. to UN forces **Mar. 31,** with the U.S. providing 2,400 soldiers.

A truck **bomb** exploded outside **a federal office building in Oklahoma City Apr. 19, killing 168** people in all.

The U.S. space shuttle *Atlantis* made the first in a series of planned **dockings with** the Russian space station ***Mir,* June 29-July 4.**

A U.S. **F-16 fighter jet** piloted by Air Force Capt. **Scott O'Grady** was **shot down over Bosnia and Herzegovina June 2**; O'Grady was **rescued** by U.S. Marines 6 days later.

At least **800 people died** in the Midwest and Northeast from a **heat wave July 12-17.**

In his first veto, Clinton, June 7, struck down a bill cutting $16.4 bil from spending appropriated by Congress. On **July 27,** however, he signed a revised bill cutting $16.3 bil.

The U.S. announced on **July 11** that it was reestablishing **diplomatic relations with Vietnam.**

Shannon Faulkner was admitted to the all-male cadet corps of **The Citadel, Aug. 11,** but dropped out soon after.

Former football star **O. J. Simpson** was found **not guilty Oct. 3** of the June 1994 murders of his former wife, Nicole Brown Simpson, and her friend Ronald Goldman.

Hundreds of thousands of African-American men participated in **"Million Man March"** and rally in Washington, DC, **Oct. 16,** organized by Rev. Louis Farrakhan.

Billy Dale, discharged head of the White House travel office, was **acquitted of embezzlement Nov. 16.**

The federal **55-mile-per-hour speed limit** was **repealed** by a measure signed **Nov. 28.**

After talks outside Dayton, OH, **warring parties in Bosnia and Herzegovina reached agreement Nov. 21** to end their conflict; treaty was signed **Dec. 14,** after which first of some 20,000 **U.S. peacekeeping troops arrived in Bosnia.**

Five Americans were among 7 **killed, Nov. 13,** when **2 bombs exploded** at a military post **in Riyadh, Saudi Arabia.**

MILLENNIUM FACT BOX

Immigration to the United States

Source: U.S. Dept. of Commerce, Bureau of the Census; Immigration and Naturalization Service.

Immigration has been a major factor in the growth and development of the United States. The number of arrivals surged in the late 19th and early 20th century and has also risen sharply in recent years. Until 1890, most immigrants came from western or northern Europe, while from 1890 to 1910 the majority came from southern and eastern Europe. In recent decades, European immigration has been leveling off, while immigration from Asia and other parts of the world has soared.

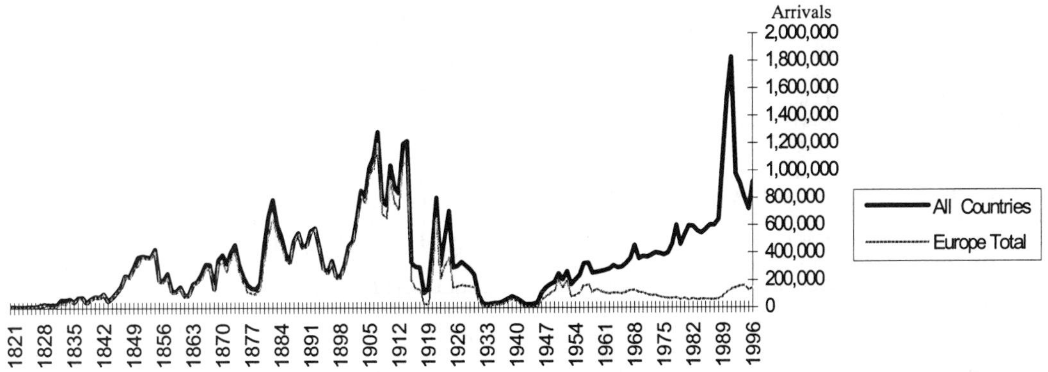

A budget impasse between Congress and Pres. Clinton led to a partial government shutdown, Nov. 14. Operations resumed Nov. 20 under continuing resolutions. On Dec. 6, Clinton vetoed a budget reconciliation bill including tax cuts and cuts in projected Medicare spending; the continuing resolution expired Dec. 16 and a longer shutdown began.

The **Dow Jones** industrial average, which passed 5,000 **Nov. 21,** closed **Dec. 29** at 5117.12, up 33.5% for the year.

1996

Long-sought records released by White House **Jan. 5** showed **Hillary Rodham Clinton** did 60 hours of work for an S&L linked to **Whitewater** scandal. Responding to a subpoena, she testified **Jan. 26** before a grand jury.

Senate, **Jan. 26,** approved, 87–4, the Second Strategic Arms Reduction Treaty, signed by Pres. Boris Yeltsin of Russia and Pres. Bush in **Jan. 1993.**

On **Feb. 24 Cuban jets shot down 2 unarmed planes** owned by a Cuban exile organization; all 4 persons on the planes were presumed killed. Pres. Clinton, **Mar. 12,** signed a bill strengthening U.S. economic embargo against Cuba.

John Salvi was found guilty, **Mar. 18,** in the **1994 murder** of receptionists **at 2 abortion clinics** in Brookline, MA.

Congress, in late **Mar.,** approved a **"line item veto"** bill allowing the president to veto parts of a spending bill while approving the rest. It was later struck down by the Supreme Court, **June 25, 1998.**

U.S. Commerce Sec. **Ron Brown** was killed **Apr. 3** in a plane crash in Croatia.

On **Apr. 3, Theodore Kaczynski** was arrested in Montana; later charged with being the notorious **Unabomber** who had killed 3 people in a series of bombings.

On **Apr. 10,** Pres. Clinton vetoed a bill that would have banned so-called **partial-birth abortions.**

An auction, **Apr. 23–26,** of items owned by former First Lady **Jacqueline Kennedy Onassis** brought in $34 mil.

James and Susan McDougal were convicted **May 28** of fraud and conspiracy. Arkansas Gov. **Jim Guy Tucker** was convicted of similar charges by the same jury.

The antitax **Freemen** surrendered to federal authorities **June 13** after an 81-day standoff at a ranch near Jordan, MT.

Republicans **June 12** chose Sen. **Trent Lott** (MS) as new majority leader to replace Sen. **Robert Dole,** who resigned, **June 11,** to focus on his presidential campaign.

The Republican majority and Democratic minority on the **Senate Whitewater Committee** issued separate final reports, **June 18,** based on their investigations.

A **bomb** exploded at a military complex near Dhahran, **Saudi Arabia, June 25,** killing 19 American servicemen.

TWA Flight 800, bound from New York to Paris, **crashed** into the Atlantic shortly after takeoff **July 17,** killing 230.

On **July 27 a bomb exploded** in an Atlanta park filled with people attending the **Olympics;** one person was directly killed.

The Senate, **July 30,** 78–21, and House, **July 31,** 328–101, approved a wide-ranging **welfare reform bill** which provided for welfare through block grants to states and ended federal guarantee of subsidies to poor people with children. Pres. Clinton signed it **Aug. 22,** though opposing some provisions.

Shannon Lucid, Sept. 26, completed a space voyage of 188 days, a record for women and for U.S. astronauts.

Dow Jones passed 6,000, **Oct. 14,** and closed **Dec. 31,** at 6448.27, a 26% advance for 1996.

Pres. Clinton reelected to 2d term, **Nov. 5,** carrying 31 states and District of Columbia.

A House subcommittee said, **Dec. 21,** that House Speaker **Newt Gingrich** had violated House ethics rules in use of tax-exempt funds to support a course he taught.

1997

Bombs were detonated at **2 abortion clinics** in Tulsa, OK, **Jan. 1,** in Atlanta on **Jan. 16,** and again at the first site in Tulsa on **Jan. 19.** Six people were injured.

Newt Gingrich (R, GA) was reelected Speaker of the U.S. House, **Jan. 7,** but received a reprimand from colleagues for alleged misuse of tax-exempt donations. Gingrich agreed to accept the reprimand and pay a $300,000 fine.

Pres. Bill Clinton awarded, **Jan 13,** the **Medal of Honor** to 7 black soldiers (6 of them deceased) for courage in action in Italy during World War II. This was the first time the medal was given to black World War II servicemen.

Madeleine Albright was sworn in as secretary of state **Jan. 23,** becoming the first woman to head the State Dept.

Ennis Cosby, 27, son of comedian **Bill Cosby,** was shot to death **Jan 16** in Los Angeles, as he changed a flat tire. Mikhail Markhasev was convicted of the murder, **July 7, 1998;** he was sentenced **Aug. 11,** to life without parole.

A civil jury, **Feb. 4,** found **O. J. Simpson** liable in the 1994 murders of his former wife, Nicole Brown Simpson, and her friend Ronald Goldman.

Harold Nicholson, a former CIA official, pleaded guilty, **Mar. 3,** to spying for Russia; he was sentenced to 23 years and 7 months in prison.

The full Senate, **Mar. 11,** voted, 99–0, to look into alleged improper fund-raising activities by the Democratic National Committee and the president and vice president.

The Liggett Group, Inc., the 5th-largest U.S. tobacco company, agreed, **Mar. 20,** to admit that smoking is addictive and causes health problems and that the industry had sought to sell its products to children as young as 14.

Thirty-nine members of the **Heaven's Gate religious cult** were found dead in a large house in Rancho Santa Fe, CA, **Mar. 26,** in an apparent mass suicide.

James McDougal, former partner with then-Gov. Bill Clinton in the Whitewater Development Corp., was sentenced **Apr. 14** to 3 years in prison for seeking to enrich himself with fraudulent loans. He died in prison, **Mar. 8, 1998.**

Attorney Gen. Janet Reno declined, **Apr. 14,** to appoint an independent counsel to investigate whether funds had been improperly raised for Pres. Clinton's 1996 reelection campaign.

The rising Red River, **Apr. 19,** drove residents of **Grand Forks,** ND, and East Grand Forks, MN, from their homes, many of which were destroyed.

Tiger Woods, a 21-year-old African-American golfer, won the Masters Tournament, **Apr. 13,** achieving many firsts in the process.

Actress **Ellen DeGeneres,** and her character in the TV sitcom *Ellen,* revealed their homosexuality in **Apr.**

White House and congressional negotiators reached an agreement, **May 2,** intended to result in a balanced federal budget by 2002.

FBI director Louis Freeh indicated, **May 4,** that "catastrophic mechanical failure" was the most likely cause of the crash of TWA Flight 800 in July 1996.

The Army's highest-ranking enlisted soldier, **Sgt. Maj. Gene McKinney,** was charged, **May 7,** with 18 offenses, including adultery, assault, obstruction of justice, and mistreatment of soldiers. He was convicted, **Mar. 13, 1998,** of only 1 count of obstruction of justice.

First Lt. Kelly Flinn, the Air Force's first woman B-52 bomber pilot, was discharged **May 29** after an investigation stemming from adultery charges against her.

Garry Kasparov, the world chess champion, was defeated by a computer, IBM's Deep Blue, in a 6-game match that concluded **May 11** in New York City.

Timothy McVeigh was convicted of conspiracy and murder, **June 2,** in 1995 bombing of federal office building in Oklahoma City that killed 168. Jurors, **June 13,** unanimously recommended death sentence.

Four major U.S. tobacco companies and several state attorneys general agreed, **June 20,** to a settlement that would cost the companies $368.5 bil, including $50 bil in punitive damages for concealing evidence of the dangers of smoking.

NASA's ***Pathfinder*** landed on Mars, **July 4.**

The Senate Governmental Affairs Committee began hearings, **July 8,** into potentially illegal fund-raising practices related to the 1994 and 1996 elections.

Fashion designer **Gianni Versace** was shot to death in Miami Beach, **July 15,** by serial murderer Andrew Phillip Cunanan, who later committed suicide.

On **July 16,** the **Dow Jones** passed 8,000 for the first time.

Autumn Jackson, 22, who claimed to be the out-of-wedlock daughter of comedian **Bill Cosby,** was convicted **July 25** of seeking to extort $40 mil from him.

The Teamsters Union, **Aug. 4-19,** carried out a strike against **United Parcel Service.**

Hundreds of thousands of Christian men from the **Promise Keepers** gathered on the Mall in Washington, DC, **Oct. 4,** to reaffirm faith in God and family values.

Scientists announced, **Oct. 7,** they had found, 25,000 light-years distant, one of the most massive stars known.

Major tobacco companies, **Oct. 10,** agreed to a settlement in the class-action suit brought against them by 60,000 present and former flight attendants.

On **Oct. 27,** the **Dow Jones** fell 554.26 points, the largest 1-day point decline yet. On **Oct. 28,** the Dow rebounded, surging 337.17 points, the largest-yet single-day point advance.

Pres. Jiang Zemin of China began a 9-day visit to the United States, **Oct. 26.**

The **Oct. 30** murder conviction of **Louise Woodward,** a British au pair, was overturned, **Nov. 10,** and her sentence, for involuntary manslaughter, was reduced to time served.

Islamic militants **Ramzi Ahmed Yousef** and **Eyad Ismoil Yousef** were convicted, **Nov. 12,** in the 1993 bombing of the World Trade Center in New York City.

On **Nov. 19, Bobbi McCaughey,** 29, in Des Moines, IA, delivered the first set of live septuplets (4 boys, 3 girls) to survive more than a month.

In a runoff election **Dec. 6,** Houston voters chose Lee Brown, a Democrat, as its first black mayor.

A preliminary injunction was filed against **Microsoft, Dec. 11,** ordering it to stop bundling its Windows 95 operating system with its Internet Explorer browser.

Terry Nichols was convicted **Dec. 23** on some charges related to the 1995 bombing of the Murrah Federal Building in Oklahoma City, which killed 168 people.

The **Dow Jones** industrial average closed **Dec. 31** at 7908.25, up by 1459.98 points for the year, a 22.6% advance.

The Mayflower Compact

The threat of James I to "harry them out of the land" sent a little band of religious dissenters from England to Holland in 1608. They were known as Separatists because they wished to cut all ties with the established church. In 1620, some of them, known now as the Pilgrims, joined with a larger group in England to set sail on the *Mayflower* for the New World. A joint stock company financed their venture.

In November, they sighted Cape Cod and decided to land an exploring party at Plymouth Harbor. A rebellious group picked up at Southampton and London troubled the Pilgrim leaders, however, and to control their actions 41 Pilgrims drew up the Mayflower Compact and signed it before going ashore. The voluntary agreement to govern themselves was America's first written constitution. It reads as follows:

In the name of God, Amen. We, whose names are underwritten, the Loyal Subjects of our dread Sovereign Lord, King *James,* by the Grace of God, of *Great Britain, France and Ireland,* King, *Defender of the Faith,* etc.

Having undertaken for the Glory of God, and Advancement of the Christian Faith, and the Honour of our King and Country, a voyage to plant the first colony in the northern Parts of Virginia; do by these Presents, solemnly and mutually in the Presence of God and one of another, covenant and combine ourselves together into a civil Body Politick, for our better Ordering and Preservation, and Furtherance of the Ends aforesaid; And by Virtue hereof to enact, constitute, and frame, such just and equal Laws, Ordinances, Acts, Constitutions and Offices, from time to time, as shall be thought most meet and convenient for the General good of the Colony; unto which we promise all due Submission and Obedience.

In Witness whereof we have hereunto subscribed our names at *Cape Cod* the eleventh of *November,* in the Reign of our Sovereign Lord, King *James* of *England, France* and *Ireland,* the eighteenth, and of *Scotland* the fifty-fourth. *Anno Domini, 1620.*

The Continental Congress: Meetings, Presidents

Meeting places	Dates of meetings	Congress presidents	Date elected
Philadelphia, PA	Sept. 5 to Oct. 26, 1774	Peyton Randolph, VA (1)	Sept. 5, 1774
"	"	Henry Middleton, SC	Oct. 22, 1774
Philadelphia, PA	May 10, 1775 to Dec. 12, 1776	Peyton Randolph, VA	May 10, 1775
"	"	John Hancock, MA	May 24, 1775
Baltimore, MD	Dec. 20, 1776 to Mar. 4, 1777	"	
Philadelphia, PA	Mar. 5 to Sept. 18, 1777	"	
Lancaster, PA	Sept. 27, 1777 (one day)	"	
York, PA	Sept. 30, 1777 to June 27, 1778	Henry Laurens, SC	Nov. 1, 1777(4)
Philadelphia, PA	July 2, 1778 to June 21, 1783	John Jay, NY	Dec. 10, 1778
"	"	Samuel Huntington, CT	Sept. 28, 1779
"	"	Thomas McKean, DE	July 10, 1781
"	"	John Hanson, MD (2)	Nov. 5, 1781
"	"	Elias Boudinot, NJ	Nov. 4, 1782
Princeton, NJ	June 30 to Nov. 4, 1783	Thomas Mifflin, PA	Nov. 3, 1783
Annapolis, MD	Nov. 26, 1783 to June 3, 1784	"	
Trenton, NJ	Nov. 1 to Dec. 24, 1784	Richard Henry Lee, VA	Nov. 30, 1784
New York City, NY	Jan. 11 to Nov. 4, 1785	"	
"	Nov. 7, 1785 to Nov. 3, 1786	John Hancock, MA (3)	Nov. 23, 1785
"	"	Nathaniel Gorham, MA	June 6, 1786
"	Nov. 6, 1786 to Oct. 30, 1787	Arthur St. Clair, PA	Feb. 2, 1787
"	Nov. 5, 1787 to Oct. 21, 1788	Cyrus Griffin, VA	Jan. 22, 1788
"	Nov. 3, 1788 to Mar. 2, 1789	"	

(1) Resigned Oct. 22, 1774. (2) Titled "President of the United States in Congress Assembled," John Hanson is considered by some the first U.S. president because he was the first to serve under the Articles of Confederation. He was, however, little more than presiding officer of the Congress, which retained full executive power. He could be considered the head of government, but not head of state. (3) Resigned May 29, 1786, without serving, because of illness. (4) Articles of Confederation agreed upon, Nov. 15, 1777; last ratification from Maryland, Mar. 1, 1781.

Patrick Henry's Speech to the Virginia Convention

The following is an excerpt from Patrick Henry's speech to the Virginia Convention on Mar. 23, 1775:

Gentlemen may cry, peace, peace—but there is no peace. The war is actually begun! The next gale that sweeps from the north will bring to our ears the clash of resounding arms! Our brethren are already in the field! Why stand we here idle? What is it that gentlemen wish? What would they have? Is life so dear, or peace so sweet, as to be purchased at the price of chains and slavery? Forbid it, Almighty God! I know not what course others may take; but as for me, give me liberty, or give me death!

How the Declaration of Independence Was Adopted

On June 7, 1776, Richard Henry Lee, who had issued the first call for a congress of the colonies, introduced in the Continental Congress at Philadelphia a resolution declaring "that these United Colonies are, and of right ought to be, free and independent states, that they are absolved from all allegiance to the British Crown, and that all political connection between them and the state of Great Britain is, and ought to be, totally dissolved."

The resolution, seconded by John Adams on behalf of the Massachusetts delegation, came up again on June 10 when a committee of 5, headed by Thomas Jefferson, was appointed to express the purpose of the resolution in a declaration of independence. The others on the committee were John Adams, Benjamin Franklin, Robert R. Livingston, and Roger Sherman.

Drafting the Declaration was assigned to Jefferson, who worked on a portable desk of his own construction in a room at Market and 7th Sts. The committee reported the result on June 28, 1776. The members of the Congress suggested a number of changes, which Jefferson called "deplorable." They didn't approve Jefferson's arraignment of the British people and King George III for encouraging and fostering the slave trade, which Jefferson called "an execrable commerce." They made 86 changes, eliminating 480 words and leaving 1,337. In the final form, capitalization was erratic. Jefferson had written that men were endowed with "inalienable" rights; in the final copy it came out as "unalienable" and has been thus ever since.

The Lee-Adams resolution of independence was adopted by 12 yeas on July 2—the actual date of the act of independence. The Declaration, which explains the act, was adopted July 4, in the evening.

After the Declaration was adopted, July 4, 1776, it was turned over to John Dunlap, printer, to be printed on broadsides. The original copy was lost and one of his broadsides was attached to a page in the journal of the Congress. It was read aloud July 8 in Philadelphia, PA, Easton, PA, and Trenton, NJ. On July 9 at 6 PM it was read by order of Gen. George Washington to the troops assembled on the Common in New York City (City Hall Park).

The Continental Congress of July 19, 1776, adopted the following resolution:

"Resolved, That the Declaration passed on the 4th, be fairly engrossed on parchment with the title and stile of 'The Unanimous Declaration of the thirteen United States of America' and that the same, when engrossed, be signed by every member of Congress."

Not all delegates who signed the engrossed Declaration were present on July 4. Robert Morris (PA), William Williams (CT), and Samuel Chase (MD) signed on Aug. 2; Oliver Wolcott (CT), George Wythe (VA), Richard Henry Lee (VA), and Elbridge Gerry (MA) signed in August and September; Matthew Thornton (NH) joined the Congress Nov. 4 and signed later. Thomas McKean (DE) rejoined Washington's army before signing and said later that he signed in 1781.

Charles Carroll of Carrollton was appointed a delegate by Maryland on July 4, 1776, presented his credentials July 18, and signed the engrossed Declaration on Aug. 2. Born Sept. 19, 1737, he was 95 years old and the last surviving signer when he died on Nov. 14, 1832.

Two Pennsylvania delegates who did not support the Declaration on July 4 were replaced.

The 4 New York delegates did not have authority from their state to vote on July 4. On July 9, the New York state convention authorized its delegates to approve the Declaration, and the Congress was so notified on July 15, 1776. The 4 signed the Declaration on Aug. 2.

The original engrossed Declaration is preserved in the National Archives Building in Washington.

Declaration of Independence

The Declaration of Independence was adopted by the Continental Congress in Philadelphia on July 4, 1776. John Hancock was president of the Congress, and Charles Thomson was secretary. A copy of the Declaration, engrossed on parchment, was signed by members of Congress on and after Aug. 2, 1776. On Jan. 18, 1777, Congress ordered that "an authenticated copy, with the names of the members of Congress subscribing the same, be sent to each of the United States, and that they be desired to have the same put upon record." Authenticated copies were printed in broadside form in Baltimore, where the Continental Congress was then in session. The following text is that of the original printed by John Dunlap at Philadelphia for the Continental Congress.

IN CONGRESS, July 4, 1776.

A DECLARATION

By the REPRESENTATIVES of the

UNITED STATES OF AMERICA,

In GENERAL CONGRESS assembled

When in the Course of human Events, it becomes necessary for one People to dissolve the Political Bands which have connected them with another, and to assume among the Powers of the Earth, the separate and equal Station to which the Laws of Nature and of Nature's God entitle them, a decent Respect to the Opinions of Mankind requires that they should declare the causes which impel them to the Separation.

We hold these Truths to be self-evident, that all Men are created equal, that they are endowed by their Creator with certain unalienable Rights, that among these are Life, Liberty, and the Pursuit of Happiness—That to secure these Rights, Governments are instituted among Men, deriving their just Powers from the Consent of the Governed, that whenever any Form of Government becomes destructive of these Ends, it is the Right of the People to alter or to abolish it, and to institute new Government, laying its Foundation on such Principles, and organizing its Powers in such Form, as to them shall seem most likely to effect their Safety and Happiness. Prudence, indeed, will dictate that Governments long established should not be changed for light and transient Causes; and accordingly all Experience hath shewn, that Mankind are more disposed to suffer, while Evils are sufferable, than to right themselves by abolishing the Forms to which they are accustomed. But when a long Train of Abuses and Usurpations, pursuing invariably the same Object, evinces a Design to reduce them under absolute Despotism, it is their Right, it is their Duty, to throw off such Government, and to provide new Guards for their future Security. Such has been the patient Sufferance of these Colonies; and such is now the Necessity which constrains them to alter their former Systems of Government. The History of the present King of Great-Britain is a History of repeated Injuries and Usurpations, all having in direct Object the Establishment of an absolute Tyranny over these States. To prove this, let Facts be submitted to a candid World.

He has refused his Assent to Laws, the most wholesome and necessary for the public Good.

He has forbidden his Governors to pass Laws of immediate and pressing Importance, unless suspended in their Operation till his Assent should be obtained; and when so suspended, he has utterly neglected to attend to them.

He has refused to pass other Laws for the Accommodation of large Districts of People, unless those People would relinquish the Right of Representation in the Legislature, a Right inestimable to them, and formidable to Tyrants only.

He has called together Legislative Bodies at Places unusual, uncomfortable, and distant from the Depository of their Public Records, for the sole Purpose of fatiguing them into Compliance with his Measures.

He has dissolved Representative Houses repeatedly, for opposing with manly Firmness his Invasions on the Rights of the People.

He has refused for a long Time, after such Dissolutions, to cause others to be elected; whereby the Legislative Powers, incapable of Annihilation, have returned to the People at large for their exercise; the State remaining in the mean time exposed to all the Dangers of Invasion from without, and Convulsions within.

He has endeavoured to prevent the Population of these States; for that Purpose obstructing the Laws for Naturalization of Foreigners; refusing to pass others to encourage their Migrations hither, and raising the Conditions of new Appropriations of Lands.

He has obstructed the Administration of Justice, by refusing his Assent to Laws for establishing Judiciary Powers.

He has made Judges dependent on his Will alone, for the Tenure of their Offices, and the Amount and payment of their Salaries.

He has erected a Multitude of new Offices, and sent hither Swarms of Officers to harrass our People, and eat out their Substance.

He has kept among us, in Times of Peace, Standing Armies, without the consent of our Legislatures.

He has affected to render the Military independent of, and superior to the Civil Power.

He has combined with others to subject us to a Jurisdiction foreign to our Constitution, and unacknowledged by our Laws; giving his Assent to their Acts of pretended Legislation:

For quartering large Bodies of Armed Troops among us:

For protecting them, by a mock Trial, from Punishment for any Murders which they should commit on the Inhabitants of these States:

For cutting off our Trade with all Parts of the World:

For imposing Taxes on us without our Consent:

For depriving us, in many Cases, of the Benefits of Trial by Jury:

For transporting us beyond Seas to be tried for pretended Offences:

For abolishing the free System of English Laws in a neighbouring Province, establishing therein an arbitrary Government, and enlarging its Boundaries, so as to render it at once an Example and fit Instrument for introducing the same absolute Rule into these Colonies:

For taking away our Charters, abolishing our most valuable Laws, and altering fundamentally the Forms of our Governments:

For suspending our own Legislatures, and declaring themselves invested with Power to legislate for us in all Cases whatsoever.

He has abdicated Government here, by declaring us out of his Protection and waging War against us.

He has plundered our Seas, ravaged our Coasts, burnt our towns, and destroyed the Lives of our People.

He is, at this Time, transporting large Armies of foreign Mercenaries to complete the works of Death, Desolation, and Tyranny, already begun with circumstances of Cruelty and Perfidy, scarcely paralleled in the most barbarous Ages, and totally unworthy the Head of a civilized Nation.

He has constrained our fellow Citizens taken Captive on the high Seas to bear Arms against their Country, to become the Executioners of their Friends and Brethren, or to fall themselves by their Hands.

He has excited domestic Insurrections amongst us, and has endeavoured to bring on the Inhabitants of our Frontiers, the merciless Indian Savages, whose known Rule of Warfare, is an undistinguished Destruction, of all Ages, Sexes and Conditions.

In every stage of these Oppressions we have Petitioned for Redress in the most humble Terms: Our repeated Petitions have been answered only by repeated Injury. A Prince, whose Character is thus marked by every act which may define a Tyrant, is unfit to be the Ruler of a free People.

Nor have we been wanting in Attentions to our British Brethren. We have warned them from Time to Time of Attempts by their Legislature to extend an unwarrantable Jurisdiction over us. We have reminded them of the Circumstances of our Emigration and Settlement here. We have appealed to their native Justice and Magnanimity, and we have conjured them by the Ties of our common Kindred to disavow these Usurpations, which, would inevitably interrupt our Connections and Correspondence. They too have been deaf to the Voice of Justice and of Consanguinity. We must, therefore, acquiesce in the Necessity, which denounces our Separation, and hold them, as we hold the rest of Mankind, Enemies in War, in Peace, Friends.

We, therefore, the Representatives of the UNITED STATES OF AMERICA, in General Congress, Assembled, appealing to the Supreme Judge of the World for the Rectitude of our Intentions, do, in the Name, and by Authority of the good People of these Colonies, solemnly Publish and Declare, That these United Colonies are, and of Right ought to be, Free and Independent States; that they are absolved from all Allegiance to the British Crown, and that all political Connection between them and the State of Great-Britain, is and ought to be totally dissolved; and that as Free and Independent States, they have full Power to levy War, conclude Peace, contract Alliances, establish Commerce, and to do all other Acts and Things which Independent States may of right do. And for the support of this declaration, with a firm Reliance on the Protection of Divine Providence, we mutually pledge to each other our lives, our Fortunes, and our sacred Honor.

JOHN HANCOCK, President

Attest.
CHARLES THOMSON, Secretary.

Signers of the Declaration of Independence

Delegate (state)	Occupation	Birthplace	Born	Died
Adams, John (MA)	Lawyer	Braintree (Quincy), MA	Oct. 30, 1735	July 4, 1826
Adams, Samuel (MA)	Political leader	Boston, MA	Sept. 27, 1722	Oct. 2, 1803
Bartlett, Josiah (NH)	Physician, judge	Amesbury, MA	Nov. 21, 1729	May 19, 1795
Braxton, Carter (VA)	Farmer	Newington Plantation, VA	Sept. 10, 1736	Oct. 10, 1797
Carroll, Chas. of Carrollton (MD)	Lawyer	Annapolis, MD	Sept. 19, 1737	Nov. 14, 1832
Chase, Samuel (MD)	Judge	Princess Anne, MD	Apr. 17, 1741	June 19, 1811
Clark, Abraham (NJ)	Surveyor	Roselle, NJ	Feb. 15, 1726	Sept. 15, 1794
Clymer, George (PA)	Merchant	Philadelphia, PA	Mar. 16, 1739	Jan. 23, 1813
Ellery, William (RI)	Lawyer	Newport, RI	Dec. 22, 1727	Feb. 15, 1820
Floyd, William (NY)	Soldier	Brookhaven, NY	Dec. 17, 1734	Aug. 4, 1821
Franklin, Benjamin (PA)	Printer, publisher	Boston, MA	Jan. 17, 1706	Apr. 17, 1790
Gerry, Elbridge (MA)	Merchant	Marblehead, MA	July 17, 1744	Nov. 23, 1814
Gwinnett, Button (GA)	Merchant	Down Hatherly, England	c. 1735	May 19, 1777
Hall, Lyman (GA)	Physician	Wallingford, CT	Apr. 12, 1724	Oct. 19, 1790
Hancock, John (MA)	Merchant	Braintree (Quincy), MA	Jan. 12, 1737	Oct. 8, 1793

Delegate (state)	Occupation	Birthplace	Born	Died
Harrison, Benjamin (VA)	Farmer	Berkeley, VA	Apr. 5, 1726	Apr. 24, 1791
Hart, John (NJ)	Farmer	Stonington, CT	c. 1711	May 11, 1779
Hewes, Joseph (NC)	Merchant	Princeton, NJ	Jan. 23, 1730	Nov. 10, 1779
Heyward, Thos. Jr. (SC)	Lawyer, farmer	St. Luke's Parish, SC	July 28, 1746	Mar. 6, 1809
Hooper, William (NC)	Lawyer	Boston, MA	June 28, 1742	Oct. 14, 1790
Hopkins, Stephen (RI)	Judge, educator	Providence, RI	Mar. 7, 1707	July 13, 1785
Hopkinson, Francis (NJ)	Judge, author	Philadelphia, PA	Sept. 21, 1737	May 9, 1791
Huntington, Samuel (CT)	Judge	Windham County, CT	July 3, 1731	Jan. 5, 1796
Jefferson, Thomas (VA)	Lawyer	Shadwell, VA	Apr. 13, 1743	July 4, 1826
Lee, Francis Lightfoot (VA)	Farmer	Westmoreland County, VA	Oct. 14, 1734	Jan. 11, 1797
Lee, Richard Henry (VA)	Farmer	Westmoreland County, VA	Jan. 20, 1732	June 19, 1794
Lewis, Francis (NY)	Merchant	Llandaff, Wales	Mar., 1713	Dec. 31, 1802
Livingston, Philip (NY)	Merchant	Albany, NY	Jan. 15, 1716	June 12, 1778
Lynch, Thomas Jr. (SC)	Farmer	Winyah, SC	Aug. 5, 1749	(at sea) 1779
McKean, Thomas (DE)	Lawyer	New London, PA	Mar. 19, 1734	June 24, 1817
Middleton, Arthur (SC)	Farmer	Charleston, SC	June 26, 1742	Jan. 1, 1787
Morris, Lewis (NY)	Farmer	Morrisania (Bronx County), NY.	Apr. 8, 1726	Jan. 22, 1798
Morris, Robert (PA)	Merchant	Liverpool, England	Jan. 20, 1734	May 9, 1806
Morton, John (PA)	Judge	Ridley, PA	1724	Apr., 1777
Nelson, Thos. Jr. (VA)	Farmer	Yorktown, VA	Dec. 26, 1738	Jan. 4, 1789
Paca, William (MD)	Judge	Abingdon, MD	Oct. 31, 1740	Oct. 23, 1799
Paine, Robert Treat (MA)	Judge	Boston, MA	Mar. 11, 1731	May 12, 1814
Penn, John (NC)	Lawyer	Near Port Royal, VA	May 17, 1741	Sept. 14, 1788
Read, George (DE)	Judge	Near North East, MD	Sept. 18, 1733	Sept. 21, 1798
Rodney, Caesar (DE)	Judge	Dover, DE	Oct. 7, 1728	June 29, 1784
Ross, George (PA)	Judge	New Castle, DE	May 10, 1730	July 14, 1779
Rush, Benjamin (PA)	Physician	Byberry, PA (Philadelphia)	Dec. 24, 1745	Apr. 19, 1813
Rutledge, Edward (SC)	Lawyer	Charleston, SC	Nov. 23, 1749	Jan. 23, 1800
Sherman, Roger (CT)	Lawyer	Newton, MA	Apr. 19, 1721	July 23, 1793
Smith, James (PA)	Lawyer	Dublin, Ireland	c. 1719	July 11, 1806
Stockton, Richard (NJ)	Lawyer	Near Princeton, NJ	Oct. 1, 1730	Feb. 28, 1781
Stone, Thomas (MD)	Lawyer	Charles County, MD	1743	Oct. 5, 1787
Taylor, George (PA)	Ironmaster	Ireland	1716	Feb. 23, 1781
Thornton, Matthew (NH)	Physician	Ireland	1714	June 24, 1803
Walton, George (GA)	Judge	Prince Edward County, VA	1741	Feb. 2, 1804
Whipple, William (NH)	Merchant, judge	Kittery, ME.	Jan. 14, 1730	Nov. 28, 1785
Williams, William (CT)	Merchant	Lebanon, CT	Apr. 23, 1731	Aug. 2, 1811
Wilson, James (PA)	Judge	Carskerdo, Scotland	Sept. 14, 1742	Aug. 28, 1798
Witherspoon, John (NJ)	Clergyman, educator	Gifford, Scotland	Feb. 5, 1723	Nov. 15, 1794
Wolcott, Oliver (CT)	Judge	Windsor, CT	Dec. 1, 1726	Dec. 1, 1797
Wythe, George (VA)	Lawyer	Elizabeth City Co. (Hampton), VA	1726	June 8, 1806

Origin of the Constitution

The War of Independence was conducted by delegates from the original 13 states, called the Congress of the United States of America and known as the Continental Congress. In 1777 the Congress submitted to the legislatures of the states the Articles of Confederation and Perpetual Union, which were ratified by New Hampshire, Massachusetts, Rhode Island, Connecticut, New York, New Jersey, Pennsylvania, Delaware, Virginia, North Carolina, South Carolina, and Georgia and finally, in 1781, by Maryland.

The first article read: "The stile of this confederacy shall be the United States of America." This did not signify a sovereign nation, because the states delegated only those powers they could not handle individually, such as to wage war, make treaties, and contract debts for general expenses (e.g. paying the army). Taxes for payment of such debts were levied by the individual states. The president signed himself "President of the United States in Congress assembled," but here the United States were considered in the plural, a cooperating group.

When the war was won, it became evident that a stronger federal union was needed. The Congress left the initiative to the legislatures. Virginia in Jan. 1786 appointed commissioners to meet with representatives of other states; delegates from Virginia, Delaware, New York, New Jersey, and Pennsylvania met at Annapolis. Alexander Hamilton prepared their call asking delegates from all states to meet in Philadelphia in May 1787 "to render the Constitution of the federal government adequate to the exigencies of the union." Congress endorsed the plan on Feb. 21, 1787. Delegates were appointed by all states except Rhode Island.

The convention met on May 14, 1787. George Washington was chosen president (presiding officer). The states certified 65 delegates, but 10 did not attend. The work was done by 55, not all of whom were present at all sessions. Of the 55 attending delegates, 16 failed to sign, and 39 actually signed Sept. 17, 1787, some with reservations. Some historians have said 74 delegates (9 more than the 65 actually certified) were named and 19 failed to attend. These 9 additional persons refused the appointment, were never delegates, and were never counted as absentees. Washington sent the Constitution to Congress, and that body, Sept. 28, 1787, ordered it sent to the legislatures, "in order to be submitted to a convention of delegates chosen in each state by the people thereof."

The Constitution was ratified by votes of state conventions as follows: Delaware, Dec. 7, 1787, unanimous; Pennsylvania, Dec. 12, 1787, 43 to 23; New Jersey, Dec. 18, 1787, unanimous; Georgia, Jan. 2, 1788, unanimous; Connecticut, Jan. 9, 1788, 128 to 40; Massachusetts, Feb. 6, 1788, 187 to 168; Maryland, Apr. 28, 1788, 63 to 11; South Carolina, May 23, 1788, 149 to 73; New Hampshire, June 21, 1788, 57 to 46; Virginia, June 25, 1788, 89 to 79; New York, July 26, 1788, 30 to 27. Nine states were needed to establish the operation of the Constitution "between the states so ratifying the same," and New Hampshire was the 9th state. The government did not declare the Constitution in effect until the first Wednesday in Mar. 1789, which was Mar. 4. After that, North Carolina ratified it on Nov. 21, 1789, 194 to 77; and Rhode Island, May 29, 1790, 34 to 32. Vermont in convention ratified it on Jan. 10, 1791, and by act of Congress approved on Feb. 18, 1791, was admitted into the Union as the 14th state, Mar. 4, 1791.

Constitution of the United States

The Original 7 Articles

The text of the Constitution (except for Amendment XXVII) is taken from the pocket-size edition of the Constitution published by the U.S. Government Printing Office under a U.S. House and Senate resolution to print the Constitution in its original form as amended through July 5, 1971. Text in **boldface** summarizes an article or amendment and was added by *The World Almanac*. Text in *italic* indicates that an item has been superseded or amended, or provides background information on amendments.

PREAMBLE

We, the People of the United States, in Order to form a more perfect Union, establish Justice, insure domestic Tranquility, provide for the common defence, promote the general Welfare, and secure the Blessings of Liberty to ourselves and our Posterity, do ordain and establish this Constitution for the United States of America.

ARTICLE I.

Section 1—Legislative powers; in whom vested:

All legislative Powers herein granted shall be vested in a Congress of the United States, which shall consist of a Senate and House of Representatives.

Section 2—House of Representatives, how and by whom chosen. Qualifications of a Representative. Representatives and direct taxes, how apportioned. Enumeration. Vacancies to be filled. Power of choosing officers, and of impeachment.

The House of Representatives shall be composed of Members chosen every second Year by the People of the several States, and the Electors in each State shall have the Qualifications requisite for Electors of the most numerous Branch of the State Legislature.

No person shall be a Representative who shall not have attained to the Age of twenty-five Years, and been seven Years a Citizen of the United States, and who shall not, when elected, be an Inhabitant of that State in which he shall be chosen.

(Representatives and direct taxes shall be apportioned among the several States which may be included within this Union, according to their respective Numbers, which shall be determined by adding to the whole Number of free Persons, including those bound to Service for a Term of Years, and excluding Indians not taxed, three-fifths of all other persons.) (The previous sentence was superseded by Amendment XIV, section 2.) The actual Enumeration shall be made within three Years after the first Meeting of the Congress of the United States, and within every subsequent Term of ten Years, in such Manner as they shall by Law direct. The Number of Representatives shall not exceed one for every thirty Thousand, but each State shall have at Least one Representative; and until such enumeration shall be made, the State of New Hampshire shall be entitled to chuse three, Massachusetts eight, Rhode-Island and Providence Plantations one, Connecticut five, New-York six, New Jersey four, Pennsylvania eight, Delaware one, Maryland six, Virginia ten, North Carolina five, South Carolina five, and Georgia three.

When vacancies happen in the Representation from any State, the Executive Authority thereof shall issue Writs of Election to fill such Vacancies.

The House of Representatives shall chuse their Speaker and other Officers; and shall have the sole Power of Impeachment.

Section 3—Senators, how and by whom chosen. How classified. Qualifications of a Senator. President of the Senate, his right to vote. President pro tem., and other officers of the Senate, how chosen. Power to try impeachments. When President is tried, Chief Justice to preside. Sentence.

The Senate of the United States shall be composed of two Senators from each State, *(chosen by the Legislature thereof) (the preceding five words were superseded by Amendment XVII, section 1)* for six Years; and each Senator shall have one Vote.

Immediately after they shall be assembled in Consequence of the first Election, they shall be divided as equally as may be into three Classes. The Seats of the Senators of the first Class shall be vacated at the Expiration of the second Year, of the second Class at the Expiration of the fourth Year, and of the third Class at the Expiration of the Sixth year, so that one-third may be chosen every second Year; *(and if Vacancies happen by Resignation, or otherwise, during the Recess of the Legislature of any State, the Executive thereof may make temporary Appointments until the next Meeting of the Legislature, which shall then fill such Vacancies.) (The words in parentheses were superseded by Amendment XVII, section 2.)*

No person shall be a Senator who shall not have attained to the Age of thirty Years, and been nine Years a Citizen of the United States, and who shall not, when elected, be an Inhabitant of that State for which he shall be chosen.

The Vice President of the United States shall be President of the Senate, but shall have no Vote, unless they be equally divided.

The Senate shall chuse their other Officers, and also a President pro tempore, in the absence of the Vice President, or when he shall exercise the Office of President of the United States.

The Senate shall have the sole Power to try all Impeachments. When sitting for that Purpose, they shall be on Oath or Affirmation. When the President of the United States is tried, the Chief Justice shall preside: And no Person shall be convicted without the Concurrence of two thirds of the Members present.

Judgment in Cases of Impeachment shall not extend further than to removal from Office, and disqualification to hold and enjoy any Office of honor, Trust or Profit under the United States: but the Party convicted shall nevertheless be liable and subject to Indictment, Trial, Judgment and Punishment, according to Law.

Section 4—Times, etc., of holding elections, how prescribed. One session each year.

The Times, Places and Manner of holding Elections for Senators and Representatives, shall be prescribed in each State by the Legislature thereof; but the Congress may at any time by Law make or alter such Regulations, except as to the Place of Chusing Senators.

The Congress shall assemble at least once in every Year, and such Meeting shall *(be on the first Monday in December,) (The words in parentheses were superseded by Amendment XX, section 2.)* unless they shall by Law appoint a different Day.

Section 5—Membership, quorum, adjournments, rules. Power to punish or expel. Journal. Time of adjournments, how limited, etc.

Each House shall be the Judge of the Elections, Returns and Qualifications of its own Members, and a Majority of each shall constitute a Quorum to do Business; but a smaller number may adjourn from day to day, and may be authorized to compel the Attendance of absent Members, in such manner, and under such Penalties as each House may provide.

Each House may determine the Rules of its Proceedings, punish its members for disorderly Behavior, and, with the Concurrence of two thirds, expel a Member.

Each House shall keep a Journal of its Proceedings, and from time to time publish the same, excepting such Parts as may in their Judgment require Secrecy; and the Yeas and Nays of the Members of either House on any question shall, at the Desire of one fifth of those Present, be entered on the Journal.

Neither House, during the Session of Congress, shall, without the Consent of the other, adjourn for more than three days, nor to any other Place than that in which the two Houses shall be sitting.

Section 6—Compensation, privileges, disqualifications in certain cases.

The Senators and Representatives shall receive a Compensation for their Services, to be ascertained by Law, and paid out of the Treasury of the United States. They shall in all Cases, except Treason, Felony and Breach of the Peace, be privileged from Arrest during their Attendance at the Session of their respective Houses, and in going to and returning from the same; and for any Speech or Debate in either House, they shall not be questioned in any other Place.

No Senator or Representative shall, during the Time for which he was elected, be appointed to any civil Office under the Authority of the United States, which shall have been created, or the Emoluments whereof shall have been encreased during such time; and no Person holding any Office under the United States, shall be a Member of either House during his Continuance in Office.

Section 7—House to originate all revenue bills. Veto. Bill may be passed by two-thirds of each House, notwithstanding, etc. Bill, not returned in ten days, to become a law. Provisions as to orders, concurrent resolutions, etc.

All bills for raising Revenue shall originate in the House of Representatives; but the Senate may propose or concur with Amendments as on other Bills.

Every Bill which shall have passed the House of Representatives and the Senate, shall, before it become a Law, be presented to the President of the United States; If he approve he shall sign it, but if not he shall return it, with his Objections to that House in which it shall have originated, who shall enter the Objections at large on their Journal, and proceed to reconsider it. If after such Reconsideration two thirds of that House shall agree to pass the Bill, it shall be sent, together with the Objections, to the other House, by which it shall likewise be reconsidered, and if approved by two thirds of that House, it shall become a Law. But in all such Cases the Votes of both Houses shall be determined by Yeas and Nays, and the Names of the Persons voting for and against the Bill shall be entered on the Journal of each House respectively. If any Bill shall not be returned by the President within ten Days (Sundays excepted) after it shall have been presented to him, the Same shall be a Law, in like Manner as if he had signed it, unless the Congress by their Adjournment prevent its Return, in which Case it shall not be a Law.

Every order, Resolution, or Vote to which the Concurrence of the Senate and House of Representatives may be necessary (except on a question of Adjournment) shall be presented to the President of the United States; and before the Same shall take Effect, shall be approved by him, or being disapproved by him, shall be repassed by two thirds of the Senate and House of Representatives, according to the Rules and Limitations prescribed in the Case of a Bill.

Section 8—Powers of Congress.

The Congress shall have Power To lay and collect Taxes, Duties, Imposts and Excises, to pay the Debts and provide for the common Defence and general Welfare of the United States; but all Duties, Imposts and Excises shall be uniform throughout the United States;

To borrow money on the credit of the United States;

To regulate Commerce with foreign Nations, and among the several States, and with the Indian Tribes;

To establish an uniform Rule of Naturalization, and uniform Laws on the subject of Bankruptcies throughout the United States;

To coin Money, regulate the Value thereof, and of foreign Coin, and fix the Standard of Weights and Measures;

To provide for the Punishment of counterfeiting the Securities and current Coin of the United States;

To establish Post Offices and post Roads;

To promote the Progress of Science and useful Arts, by securing for limited Times to Authors and Inventors the exclusive Right to their respective Writings and Discoveries;

To constitute Tribunals inferior to the supreme Court;

To define and punish Piracies and Felonies committed on the high Seas, and Offenses against the Law of Nations;

To declare War, grant Letters of Marque and Reprisal, and make Rules concerning Captures on Land and Water;

To raise and support Armies, but no Appropriation of Money to that Use shall be for a longer Term than two Years;

To provide and maintain a Navy;

To make Rules for the Government and Regulation of the land and naval Forces;

To provide for calling forth the Militia to execute the Laws of the Union, suppress Insurrections and repel Invasions;

To provide for organizing, arming, and disciplining the Militia, and for governing such Part of them as may be employed in the Service of the United States, reserving to the States respectively, the Appointment of the Officers, and the Authority of training the Militia according to the discipline prescribed by Congress;

To exercise exclusive Legislation in all Cases whatsoever, over such District (not exceeding ten Miles square) as may, by Cession of particular States, and the acceptance of Congress, become the Seat of the Government of the United States, and to exercise like Authority over all Places purchased by the Consent of the Legislature of the State in which the Same shall be, for the Erection of Forts, Magazines, Arsenals, dock-Yards, and other needful Buildings;—And

To make all Laws which shall be necessary and proper for carrying into Execution the foregoing Powers, and all other Powers vested by this Constitution in the Government of the United States, or in any Department or Officer thereof.

Section 9—Provision as to migration or importation of certain persons. Habeas corpus, bills of attainder, etc. Taxes, how apportioned. No export duty. No commercial preference. Money, how drawn from Treasury, etc. No titular nobility. Officers not to receive presents, etc.

The Migration or Importation of such Persons as any of the States now existing shall think proper to admit, shall not be prohibited by the Congress prior to the Year one thousand eight hundred and eight, but a tax or duty may be imposed on such Importation, not exceeding ten dollars for each Person.

The privilege of the Writ of Habeas Corpus shall not be suspended, unless when in Cases of Rebellion or Invasion the public Safety may require it.

No Bill of Attainder or ex post facto Law shall be passed.

No capitation, or other direct, Tax shall be laid, unless in Proportion to the Census or Enumeration herein before directed to be taken. *(Modified by Amendment XVI.)*

No Tax or Duty shall be laid on Articles exported from any State.

No Preference shall be given by any Regulation of Commerce or Revenue to the Ports of one State over those of another: nor shall Vessels bound to, or from, one State, be obliged to enter, clear, or pay Duties in another.

No Money shall be drawn from the Treasury, but in Consequence of Appropriations made by Law; and a regular Statement and Account of the Receipts and Expenditures of all public Money shall be published from time to time.

No Title of Nobility shall be granted by the United States: and no Person holding any Office of Profit or Trust under them, shall, without the Consent of the Congress, accept of any present, Emolument, Office, or Title, of any kind whatever, from any King, Prince, or foreign State.

Section 10—States prohibited from the exercise of certain powers.

No State shall enter into any Treaty, Alliance, or Confederation; grant Letters of Marque and Reprisal; coin Money; emit Bills of Credit; make any Thing but gold and silver Coin a Tender in Payment of Debts; pass any Bill of Attainder, ex post facto Law, or Law impairing the Obligation of Contracts, or grant any Title of Nobility.

No State shall, without the Consent of the Congress, lay any Imposts or Duties on Imports or Exports, except what may be absolutely necessary for executing its inspection Laws: and the net Produce of all Duties and Imposts, laid by any State on Imports or Exports, shall be for the Use of the Treasury of the United States; and all such Laws shall be subject to the Revision and Control of the Congress.

No State shall, without the Consent of Congress, lay any duty of Tonnage, keep Troops, or Ships of War in time of Peace, enter into any Agreement or Compact with another State, or with a foreign Power, or engage in War, unless actually invaded, or in such imminent Danger as will not admit of delay.

ARTICLE II.

Section 1—President: his term of office. Electors of President; number and how appointed. Electors to vote on same day. Qualification of President. On

whom his duties devolve in case of his removal, death, etc. President's compensation; oath of office.

The executive Power shall be vested in a President of the United States of America. He shall hold his Office during the Term of four Years, and, together with the Vice President, chosen for the same Term, be elected, as follows.

Each State shall appoint, in such Manner as the Legislature thereof may direct, a Number of Electors, equal to the whole Number of Senators and Representatives to which the State may be entitled in the Congress: but no Senator or Representative, or Person holding an Office of Trust or Profit under the United States, shall be appointed an Elector.

(The Electors shall meet in their respective States, and vote by Ballot for two persons, of whom one at least shall not be an Inhabitant of the same State with themselves. And they shall make a List of all the Persons voted for, and of the Number of Votes for each; which List they shall sign and certify, and transmit sealed to the Seat of the Government of the United States, directed to the President of the Senate. The President of the Senate shall, in the Presence of the Senate and House of Representatives, open all the Certificates, and the Votes shall then be counted. The Person having the greatest Number of Votes shall be the President, if such Number be a Majority of the whole Number of Electors appointed; and if there be more than one who have such Majority, and have an equal Number of Votes, then the House of Representatives shall immediately chuse by Ballot one of them for President; and if no Person have a Majority, then from the five highest on the List the said House shall in like Manner chuse the President. But in chusing the President, the Votes shall be taken by States, the Representation from each State having one Vote; a quorum for this Purpose shall consist of a Member or Members from two thirds of the States, and a Majority of all the States shall be necessary to a Choice. In every Case, after the Choice of the President, the Person having the greatest Number of Votes of the Electors shall be the Vice President. But if there should remain two or more who have equal Votes, the Senate shall chuse from them by Ballot the Vice-President.)

(This clause was superseded by Amendment XII.)

The Congress may determine the Time of chusing the Electors, and the Day on which they shall give their Votes; which Day shall be the same throughout the United States.

No person except a natural born Citizen, or a Citizen of the United States, at the time of the Adoption of this Constitution, shall be eligible to the Office of President; neither shall any Person be eligible to that Office who shall not have attained to the Age of thirty-five Years, and been fourteen Years a Resident within the United States.

(For qualification of the Vice President, see Amendment XII.)

In Case of the Removal of the President from Office, or of his Death, Resignation, or Inability to discharge the Powers and Duties of the said Office, the same shall devolve on the Vice President, and the Congress may by Law, provide for the Case of Removal, Death, Resignation or Inability, both of the President and Vice President, declaring what Officer shall then act as President, and such Officer shall act accordingly, until the Disability be removed, or a President shall be elected.

(This clause has been modified by Amendments XX and XXV.)

The President shall, at stated Times, receive for his Services, a Compensation, which shall neither be encreased nor diminished during the Period for which he shall have been elected, and he shall not receive within that Period any other Emolument from the United States, or any of them.

Before he enter on the Execution of his Office, he shall take the following Oath or Affirmation:–"I do solemnly swear (or affirm) that I will faithfully execute the Office of President of the United States, and will to the best of my Ability, preserve, protect and defend the Constitution of the United States."

Section 2—President to be Commander-in-Chief. He may require opinions of cabinet officers, etc., may pardon. Treaty-making power. Nomination of certain officers. When President may fill vacancies.

The President shall be Commander in Chief of the Army and Navy of the United States, and of the Militia of the several States, when called into the actual Service of the United States; he may require the Opinion in writing, of the principal Officer in each of the executive Departments, upon any subject relating to the Duties of their respective Offices, and he shall have Power to Grant Reprieves and Pardons for Offenses against the United States, except in Cases of Impeachment.

He shall have Power, by and with the Advice and Consent of the Senate, to make Treaties, provided two-thirds of the Senators present concur; and he shall nominate, and by and with the Advice and Consent of the Senate, shall appoint Ambassadors, other public Ministers and Consuls, Judges of the supreme Court, and all other Officers of the United States, whose Appointments are not herein otherwise provided for, and which shall be established by Law: but the Congress may by Law vest the Appointment of such inferior Officers, as they think proper, in the President alone, in the Courts of Law, or in the Heads of Departments.

The President shall have Power to fill up all Vacancies that may happen during the Recess of the Senate, by granting Commissions which shall expire at the End of their next Session.

Section 3—President shall communicate to Congress. He may convene and adjourn Congress, in case of disagreement, etc. Shall receive ambassadors, execute laws, and commission officers.

He shall from time to time give to the Congress Information of the State of the Union, and recommend to their Consideration such Measures as he shall judge necessary and expedient; he may, on extraordinary Occasions, convene both Houses, or either of them, and in Case of Disagreement between them, with Respect to the Time of Adjournment, he may adjourn them to such Time as he shall think proper; he shall receive Ambassadors and other public Ministers; he shall take Care that the Laws be faithfully executed, and shall Commission all the Officers of the United States.

Section 4—All civil offices forfeited for certain crimes.

The President, Vice President and all civil Officers of the United States, shall be removed from Office on Impeachment for, and Conviction of, Treason, Bribery, or other high Crimes and Misdemeanors.

ARTICLE III.

Section 1—Judicial powers, Tenure. Compensation.

The judicial Power of the United States, shall be vested in one supreme Court, and in such inferior Courts as the Congress may from time to time ordain and establish. The Judges, both of the supreme and inferior Courts, shall hold their Offices during good Behaviour, and shall, at stated Times, receive for their Services, a Compensation, which shall not be diminished during their Continuance in Office.

Section 2—Judicial power; to what cases it extends. Original jurisdiction of Supreme Court; appellate jurisdiction. Trial by jury, etc. Trial, where.

The judicial Power shall extend to all Cases, in Law and Equity, arising under this Constitution, the Laws of the United States, and Treaties made, or which shall be made, under their Authority;–to all Cases affecting Ambassadors, other public Ministers and Consuls;–to all Cases of admiralty and maritime Jurisdiction;–to Controversies to which the United States shall be a Party;–to Controversies between two or more States;–between a State and Citizens of another State;–between Citizens of different States;–between Citizens of the same State claiming Lands under Grants of different States, and between a State, or the Citizens thereof, and foreign States, Citizens or Subjects.

(This section is modified by Amendment XI.)

In all Cases affecting Ambassadors, other public Ministers and Consuls, and those in which a State shall be Party, the supreme Court shall have original Jurisdiction. In all the other Cases before mentioned, the supreme Court shall have appellate Jurisdiction, both as to Law and Fact, with such Exceptions, and under such Regulations as the Congress shall make.

The trial of all Crimes, except in Cases of Impeachment, shall be by Jury; and such Trial shall be held in the State where the said Crimes shall have been committed; but when not committed within any State, the Trial shall be at such Place or Places as the Congress may by Law have directed.

Section 3—Treason Defined, Proof of, Punishment of.

Treason against the United States, shall consist only in levying War against them, or in adhering to their Enemies, giving them Aid and Comfort. No Person shall be convicted of Treason unless on the Testimony of two Witnesses to the same overt Act, or on Confession in open Court.

The Congress shall have Power to declare the Punishment of Treason, but no Attainder of Treason shall work Corruption of Blood, or Forfeiture except during the Life of the Person attainted.

ARTICLE IV.

Section 1—Each State to give credit to the public acts, etc., of every other State.

Full Faith and Credit shall be given in each State to the public Acts, Records, and judicial Proceedings of every other State. And the Congress may by general Laws prescribe the Manner in which such Acts, Records and Proceedings shall be proved, and the Effect thereof.

Section 2—Privileges of citizens of each State. Fugitives from justice to be delivered up. Persons held to service having escaped, to be delivered up.

The Citizens of each State shall be entitled to all Privileges and Immunities of Citizens in the several States.

A Person charged in any State with Treason, Felony, or other Crime, who shall flee from Justice, and be found in another State, shall on demand of the executive Authority of the State from which he fled, be delivered up, to be removed to the State having Jurisdiction of the Crime.

(No Person held to Service or Labour in one State, under the Laws thereof, escaping into another, shall, in Consequence of any Law or Regulation therein, be discharged from such Service or Labour, but shall be delivered up on Claim of the Party to whom such Service or Labour may be due.) (This clause was superseded by Amendment XIII.)

Section 3—Admission of new States. Power of Congress over territory and other property.

New States may be admitted by the Congress into this Union; but no new State shall be formed or erected within the Jurisdiction of any other State; nor any State be formed by the Junction of two or more States, or parts of States, without the Consent of the Legislatures of the States concerned as well as of the Congress.

The Congress shall have Power to dispose of and make all needful Rules and Regulations respecting the Territory or other Property belonging to the United States; and nothing in this Constitution shall be so construed as to Prejudice any Claims of the United States, or of any particular State.

Section 4—Republican form of government guaranteed. Each state to be protected.

The United States shall guarantee to every State in this Union a Republican Form of Government, and shall protect each of them against Invasion; and on Application of the Legislature, or of the Executive (when the Legislature cannot be convened) against domestic Violence.

ARTICLE V.

Constitution: how amended; proviso.

The Congress, whenever two-thirds of both Houses shall deem it necessary, shall propose Amendments to this Constitution, or, on the Application of the Legislatures of two-thirds of the several States, shall call a Convention for proposing Amendments, which, in either Case, shall be valid to all Intents and Purposes, as part of this Constitution, when ratified by the Legislatures of three-fourths of the several States, or by Conventions in three-fourths thereof, as the one or the other Mode of Ratification may be proposed by the Congress: Provided that no Amendment which may be made prior to the Year One thousand eight hundred and eight shall in any Manner affect the first and fourth Clauses in the Ninth Section of the first Article; and that no State, without its Consent, shall be deprived of its equal Suffrage in the Senate.

ARTICLE VI.

Certain debts, etc., declared valid. Supremacy of Constitution, treaties, and laws of the United States. Oath to support Constitution, by whom taken. No religious test.

All Debts contracted and Engagements entered into, before the Adoption of this Constitution, shall be as valid against the United States under this Constitution, as under the Confederation.

This Constitution, and the Laws of the United States which shall be made in Pursuance thereof; and all Treaties made, or which shall be made, under the Authority of the United States, shall be the supreme Law of the Land; and the Judges in every State shall be bound thereby, any Thing in the Constitution or Laws of any State to the Contrary notwithstanding.

The Senators and Representatives before mentioned, and the Members of the several State Legislatures, and all executive and judicial Officers, both of the United States and of the several States, shall be bound by Oath or Affirmation, to support this Constitution; but no religious Test shall ever be required as a Qualification to any Office or public Trust under the United States.

ARTICLE VII.

What ratification shall establish Constitution.

The Ratification of the Conventions of nine States shall be sufficient for the Establishment of this Constitution between the States so ratifying the Same.

Done in Convention by the Unanimous Consent of the States present the Seventeenth Day of September in the Year of our Lord one thousand seven hundred and Eighty seven and of the Independence of the United States of America the Twelfth.

In Witness whereof We have hereunto subscribed our Names.

Go WASHINGTON, Presidt and deputy from Virginia
New Hampshire—John Langdon, Nicholas Gilman
Massachusetts—Nathaniel Gorham, Rufus King
Connecticut—Wm Saml Johnson, Roger Sherman
New York—Alexander Hamilton
New Jersey—Wil: Livingston, David Brearley, Wm Paterson, Jona: Dayton
Pennsylvania—B Franklin, Thomas Mifflin, Robt. Morris, Geo. Clymer, Thos. FitzSimons, Jared Ingersoll, James Wilson, Gouv Morris
Delaware—Geo: Read, Gunning Bedford jun, John Dickinson, Richard Bassett, Jaco: Broom
Maryland—James McHenry, Dan: of St Thos Jenifer, Danl Carrol
Virginia—John Blair, James Madison Jr.
North Carolina—Wm Blount, Richd. Dobbs Spaight, Hu Williamson
South Carolina—J. Rutledge, Charles Cotesworth Pinckney, Charles Pinckney, Pierce Butler
Georgia—William Few, Abr Baldwin
Attest: William Jackson, Secretary.

Ten Original Amendments: The Bill of Rights

In force Dec. 15, 1791

(The First Congress, at its first session in the City of New York, Sept. 25, 1789, submitted to the states 12 amendments to clarify certain individual and state rights not named in the Constitution. They are generally called the Bill of Rights.

(Influential in framing these amendments was the Declaration of Rights of Virginia, written by George Mason (1725-1792) in 1776. Mason, a Virginia delegate to the Constitutional Convention, did not sign the Constitution and opposed its ratification on the ground that it did not sufficiently oppose slavery or safeguard individual rights.

(In the preamble to the resolution offering the proposed amendments, Congress said: "The conventions of a number of the States having at the time of their adopting the Constitution, expressed a desire, in order to prevent misconstruction or abuse of its powers, that further declaratory and restrictive clauses should be added, and as extending the ground of public confidence in the government will best insure the beneficent ends of its institution, be it resolved," etc.

(Ten of these amendments, now commonly known as one to 10 inclusive, but originally 3 to 12 inclusive, were ratified by the states as follows: New Jersey, Nov. 20, 1789; Maryland, Dec. 19, 1789; North Carolina, Dec. 22, 1789; South Carolina, Jan. 19, 1790; New Hampshire, Jan. 25, 1790; Delaware, Jan. 28, 1790; New York, Feb. 27, 1790; Pennsylvania, Mar. 10, 1790; Rhode Island, June 7, 1790; Vermont, Nov. 3, 1791; Virginia, Dec. 15, 1791; Massachusetts, Mar. 2, 1939; Georgia, Mar. 18, 1939; Connecticut, Apr. 19, 1939. These original 10 ratified amendments follow as Amendments I to X inclusive.

(Of the two original proposed amendments that were not ratified promptly by the necessary number of states, the first related to apportionment of Representatives; the second, relating to compensation of members of Congress, was ratified in 1992 and became Amendment 27.)

AMENDMENT I.

Religious establishment prohibited. Freedom of speech, of press, right to assemble and to petition.

Congress shall make no law respecting an establishment of religion, or prohibiting the free exercise thereof; or abridging the freedom of speech, or of the press; or the right of the people peaceably to assemble, and to petition the Government for a redress of grievances.

AMENDMENT II.

Right to keep and bear arms.

A well regulated Militia, being necessary to the security of a free State, the right of the people to keep and bear Arms, shall not be infringed.

AMENDMENT III.

Conditions for quarters for soldiers.

No Soldier shall, in time of peace be quartered in any house, without the consent of the Owner, nor in time of war, but in a manner to be prescribed by law.

AMENDMENT IV.

Protection from unreasonable search and seizure.

The right of the people to be secure in their persons, houses, papers, and effects, against unreasonable searches and seizures, shall not be violated, and no Warrants shall issue, but upon probable cause, supported by Oath or affirmation, and particularly describing the place to be searched, and the persons or things to be seized.

AMENDMENT V.

Provisions concerning prosecution and due process of law. Double jeopardy restriction. Private property not to be taken without compensation.

No person shall be held to answer for a capital, or otherwise infamous crime, unless on a presentment or indictment of a Grand Jury, except in cases arising in the land or naval forces, or in the Militia, when in actual service in time of War or public danger; nor shall any person be subject for the same offence to be twice put in jeopardy of life or limb; nor shall be compelled in any criminal case to be a witness against himself, nor be deprived of life, liberty, or property, without due process of law; nor shall private property be taken for public use, without just compensation.

AMENDMENT VI.

Right to speedy trial, witnesses, etc.

In all criminal prosecutions, the accused shall enjoy the right to a speedy and public trial, by an impartial jury of the State and district wherein the crime shall have been committed, which district shall have been previously ascertained by law, and to be informed of the nature and cause of the accusation; to be confronted with the witnesses against him; to have compulsory process for obtaining witnesses in his favor, and to have the Assistance of Counsel for his defence.

AMENDMENT VII.

Right of trial by jury.

In suits at common law, where the value in controversy shall exceed twenty dollars, the right of trial by jury shall be preserved, and no fact tried by a jury, shall be otherwise reexamined in any Court of the United States, than according to the rules of the common law.

AMENDMENT VIII.

Excessive bail or fines; cruel and unusual punishment.

Excessive bail shall not be required, nor excessive fines imposed, nor cruel and unusual punishments inflicted.

AMENDMENT IX.

Rule of construction of Constitution.

The enumeration in the Constitution, of certain rights, shall not be construed to deny or disparage others retained by the people.

AMENDMENT X.

Rights of States under Constitution.

The powers not delegated to the United States by the Constitution, nor prohibited by it to the States, are reserved to the States respectively, or to the people.

Amendments Since the Bill of Rights

AMENDMENT XI.

Judicial powers construed.

The Judicial power of the United States shall not be construed to extend to any suit in law or equity, commenced or prosecuted against one of the United States by Citizens of another State, or by Citizens or Subjects of any Foreign State.

(This amendment was proposed to the Legislatures of the several States by the Third Congress on March. 4, 1794, and was declared to have been ratified in a message from the President to Congress, dated Jan. 8, 1798.

(It was on Jan. 5, 1798, that Secretary of State Pickering received from 12 of the States authenticated ratifications, and informed President John Adams of that fact.

(As a result of later research in the Department of State, it is now established that Amendment XI became part of the Constitution on Feb. 7, 1795, for on that date it had been ratified by 12 States as follows:

(1. New York, Mar. 27, 1794. 2. Rhode Island, Mar. 31, 1794. 3. Connecticut, May 8, 1794. 4. New Hampshire, June 16, 1794. 5. Massachusetts, June 26, 1794. 6. Vermont, between Oct. 9, 1794, and Nov. 9, 1794. 7. Virginia, Nov. 18,

1794. 8. Georgia, Nov. 29, 1794. 9. Kentucky, Dec. 7, 1794. 10. Maryland, Dec. 26, 1794. 11. Delaware, Jan. 23, 1795. 12. North Carolina, Feb. 7, 1795.

(On June 1, 1796, more than a year after Amendment XI had become a part of the Constitution—but before anyone was officially aware of this—Tennessee had been admitted as a State; but not until Oct. 16, 1797, was a certified copy of the resolution of Congress proposing the amendment sent to the Governor of Tennessee, John Sevier, by Secretary of State Pickering, whose office was then at Trenton, New Jersey, because of the epidemic of yellow fever at Philadelphia; it seems, however, that the Legislature of Tennessee took no action on Amendment XI, owing doubtless to the fact that public announcement of its adoption was made soon thereafter.

(Besides the necessary 12 States, one other, South Carolina, ratified Amendment XI, but this action was not taken until Dec. 4, 1797; the two remaining States, New Jersey and Pennsylvania, failed to ratify.)

AMENDMENT XII.

Manner of choosing President and Vice-President.

(Proposed by Congress Dec. 9, 1803; ratified June 15, 1804.)

The Electors shall meet in their respective states and vote by ballot for President and Vice-President, one of whom, at least, shall not be an inhabitant of the same state with themselves; they shall name in their ballots the person voted for as President, and in distinct ballots the person voted for as Vice-President, and they shall make distinct lists of all persons voted for as President, and of all persons voted for as Vice-President, and of the number of votes for each, which lists they shall sign and certify, and transmit sealed to the seat of the government of the United States, directed to the President of the Senate;–The President of the Senate shall, in presence of the Senate and House of Representatives, open all the certificates and the votes shall then be counted;—The person having the greatest number of votes for President, shall be the President, if such number be a majority of the whole number of Electors appointed; and if no person have such majority, then from the persons having the highest numbers not exceeding three on the list of those voted for as President, the House of Representatives shall choose immediately, by ballot, the President. But in choosing the President, the votes shall be taken by states, the representation from each state having one vote; a quorum for this purpose shall consist of a member or members from two-thirds of the states, and a majority of all the states shall be necessary to a choice. *(And if the House of Representatives shall not choose a President whenever the right of choice shall devolve upon them, before the fourth day of March next following, then the Vice-President shall act as President, as in the case of the death or other constitutional disability of the President.) (The words in parentheses were superseded by Amendment XX, section 3.)* The person having the greatest number of votes as Vice-President, shall be the Vice-President, if such number be a majority of the whole number of Electors appointed, and if no person have a majority, then from the two highest numbers on the list, the Senate shall choose the Vice-President; a quorum for the purpose shall consist of two-thirds of the whole number of Senators, and a majority of the whole number shall be necessary to a choice. But no person constitutionally ineligible to the office of President shall be eligible to that of Vice-President of the United States.

THE RECONSTRUCTION AMENDMENTS

(Amendments XIII, XIV, and XV are commonly known as the Reconstruction Amendments, inasmuch as they followed the Civil War, and were drafted by Republicans who were bent on imposing their own policy of reconstruction on the South. Post-bellum legislatures there—Mississippi, South Carolina, Georgia, for example—had set up laws which, it was charged, were contrived to perpetuate Negro slavery under other names.)

AMENDMENT XIII.

Slavery abolished.

(Proposed by Congress Jan. 31, 1865; ratified Dec. 6, 1865. The amendment, when first proposed by a resolution in Congress, was passed by the Senate, 38 to 6, on Apr. 8, 1864, but was defeated in the House, 95 to 66 on June 15, 1864. On reconsideration by the House, on Jan. 31, 1865, the resolution passed, 119 to 56. It was approved by President Lincoln on Feb. 1, 1865, although the Supreme Court had decided in 1798 that the President has nothing to do with the proposing of amendments to the Constitution, or their adoption.)

1. Neither slavery nor involuntary servitude, except as a punishment for crime whereof the party shall have been duly convicted, shall exist within the United States, or any place subject to their jurisdiction.

2. Congress shall have power to enforce this article by appropriate legislation.

AMENDMENT XIV.

Citizenship rights not to be abridged.

(The following amendment was proposed to the Legislatures of the several states by the 39th Congress, June 13, 1866, ratified July 9, 1868, and declared to have been ratified in a proclamation by the Secretary of State, July 28, 1868.

(The 14th amendment was adopted only by virtue of ratification subsequent to earlier rejections. Newly constituted legislatures in both North Carolina and South Carolina (respectively July 4 and 9, 1868), ratified the proposed amendment, although earlier legislatures had rejected the proposal. The Secretary of State issued a proclamation, which, though doubtful as to the effect of attempted withdrawals by Ohio and New Jersey, entertained no doubt as to the validity of the ratification by North and South Carolina. The following day (July 21, 1868), Congress passed a resolution which declared the 14th Amendment to be a part of the Constitution and directed the Secretary of State so to promulgate it. The Secretary waited, however, until the newly constituted Legislature of Georgia had ratified the amendment, subsequent to an earlier rejection, before the promulgation of the ratification of the new amendment.)

1. All persons born or naturalized in the United States, and subject to the jurisdiction thereof, are citizens of the United States and of the State wherein they reside. No State shall make or enforce any law which shall abridge the privileges or immunities of citizens of the United States; nor shall any State deprive any person of life, liberty, or property, without due process of law; nor deny to any person within its jurisdiction the equal protection of the laws.

2. Representatives shall be apportioned among the several States according to their respective numbers, counting the whole number of persons in each State, excluding Indians not taxed. But when the right to vote at any election for the choice of electors for President and Vice-President of the United States, Representatives in Congress, the Executive and Judicial officers of a State, or the members of the Legislature thereof, is denied to any of the male inhabitants of such State, being twenty-one years of age, and citizens of the United States, or in any way abridged, except for participation in rebellion, or other crime, the basis of representation therein shall be reduced in the proportion which the number of such male citizens shall bear to the whole number of male citizens twenty-one years of age in such State.

3. No person shall be a Senator or Representative in Congress, or elector of President and Vice-President, or hold any office, civil or military, under the United States, or under any State, who, having previously taken an oath, as a member of Congress, or as an officer of the United States, or as a member of any State legislature, or as an executive or judicial officer of any State, to support the Constitution of the United States, shall have engaged in insurrection or rebellion against the same, or given aid or comfort to the enemies thereof. But Congress may by a vote of two-thirds of each House, remove such disability.

4. The validity of the public debt of the United States, authorized by law, including debts incurred for payment of pensions and bounties for services in suppressing insurrection or rebellion, shall not be questioned. But neither the United States nor any State shall assume or pay any debt or obligation incurred in aid of insurrection or rebellion against the United

States, or any claim for the loss or emancipation of any slave; but all such debts, obligations and claims shall be held illegal and void.

The Congress shall have power to enforce, by appropriate legislation, the provisions of this article.

AMENDMENT XV.

Race no bar to voting rights.

(The following amendment was proposed to the legislatures of the several States by the 40th Congress, Feb. 26, 1869, and ratified Feb. 8, 1870.)

1. The right of citizens of the United States to vote shall not be denied or abridged by the United States or by any State on account of race, color, or previous condition of servitude–

2. The Congress shall have power to enforce this article by appropriate legislation.

AMENDMENT XVI.

Income taxes authorized.

(Proposed by Congress July 12, 1909; ratified Feb. 3, 1913.)

The Congress shall have power to lay and collect taxes on incomes, from whatever source derived, without apportionment among the several States, and without regard to any census or enumeration.

AMENDMENT XVII.

United States Senators to be elected by direct popular vote.

(Proposed by Congress May 13, 1912; ratified Apr. 8, 1913.)

The Senate of the United States shall be composed of two Senators from each State, elected by the people thereof, for six years; and each Senator shall have one vote. The electors in each State shall have the qualifications requisite for electors of the most numerous branch of the State legislatures.

When vacancies happen in the representation of any State in the Senate, the executive authority of such State shall issue writs of election to fill such vacancies: *Provided,* That the legislature of any State may empower the executive thereof to make temporary appointments until the people fill the vacancies by election as the legislature may direct.

This amendment shall not be so construed as to affect the election or term of any Senator chosen before it becomes valid as part of the Constitution.

AMENDMENT XVIII.

Liquor prohibition amendment.

(Proposed by Congress Dec. 18, 1917; ratified Jan. 16, 1919. Repealed by Amendment XXI, effective Dec. 5, 1933.)

1. After one year from the ratification of this article the manufacture, sale, or transportation of intoxicating liquors within, the importation thereof into, or the exportation thereof from the United States and all territory subject to the jurisdiction thereof for beverage purposes is hereby prohibited.

2. The Congress and the several States shall have concurrent power to enforce this article by appropriate legislation.

3. This article shall be inoperative unless it shall have been ratified as an amendment to the Constitution by the legislatures of the several States as provided in the Constitution, within seven years from the date of the submission hereof to the States by the Congress.

(The total vote in the Senates of the various States was 1,310 for, 237 against—84.6% dry. In the lower houses of the States the vote was 3,782 for, 1,035 against—78.5% dry.

(The amendment ultimately was adopted by all the States except Connecticut and Rhode Island.)

AMENDMENT XIX.

Giving nationwide suffrage to women.

(Proposed by Congress June 4, 1919; ratified Aug. 18, 1920.)

The right of citizens of the United States to vote shall not be denied or abridged by the United States or by any State on account of sex.

Congress shall have power to enforce this Article by appropriate legislation.

AMENDMENT XX.

Terms of President and Vice President to begin on Jan. 20; those of Senators, Representatives, Jan. 3.

(Proposed by Congress Mar. 2, 1932; ratified Jan. 23, 1933.)

1. The terms of the President and Vice President shall end at noon on the 20th day of January, and the terms of Senators and Representatives at noon on the 3d day of January, of the years in which such terms would have ended if this article had not been ratified; and the terms of their successors shall then begin.

2. The Congress shall assemble at least once in every year, and such meeting shall begin at noon on the 3d day of January, unless they shall by law appoint a different day.

3. If, at the time fixed for the beginning of the term of the President, the President elect shall have died, the Vice President elect shall become President. If a President shall not have been chosen before the time fixed for the beginning of his term, or if the President elect shall have failed to qualify, then the Vice President elect shall act as President until a President shall have qualified; and the Congress may by law provide for the case wherein neither a President elect nor a Vice President elect shall have qualified, declaring who shall then act as President, or the manner in which one who is to act shall be selected, and such person shall act accordingly until a President or Vice President shall have qualified.

4. The Congress may by law provide for the case of the death of any of the persons from whom the House of Representatives may choose a President whenever the right of choice shall have devolved upon them, and for the case of the death of any of the persons from whom the Senate may choose a Vice President whenever the right of choice shall have devolved upon them.

5. Sections 1 and 2 shall take effect on the 15th day of October following the ratification of this article (Oct. 1933).

6. This article shall be inoperative unless it shall have been ratified as an amendment to the Constitution by the legislatures of three-fourths of the several States within seven years from the date of its submission.

AMENDMENT XXI.

Repeal of Amendment XVIII.

(Proposed by Congress Feb. 20, 1933; ratified Dec. 5, 1933.)

1. The eighteenth article of amendment to the Constitution of the United States is hereby repealed.

2. The transportation or importation into any State, Territory, or possession of the United States for delivery or use therein of intoxicating liquors, in violation of the laws thereof, is hereby prohibited.

3. This article shall be inoperative unless it shall have been ratified as an amendment to the Constitution by conventions in the several States, as provided in the Constitution, within seven years from the date of the submission hereof to the States by the Congress.

AMENDMENT XXII.

Limiting Presidential terms of office.

(Proposed by Congress Mar. 24, 1947; ratified Feb. 27, 1951.)

1. No person shall be elected to the office of the President more than twice, and no person who has held the office of President, or acted as President, for more than two years of a term to which some other person was elected President shall be elected to the office of the President more than once. But this Article shall not apply to any person holding the office of

President when this Article was proposed by the Congress, and shall not prevent any person who may be holding the office of President, or acting as President, during the term within which this Article becomes operative from holding the office of President or acting as President during the remainder of such term.

2. This article shall be inoperative unless it shall have been ratified as an amendment to the Constitution by the legislatures of three-fourths of the several States within seven years from the date of its submission to the States by the Congress.

AMENDMENT XXIII.

Presidential vote for District of Columbia.

(Proposed by Congress June 16, 1960; ratified Mar. 29, 1961.)

1. The District constituting the seat of Government of the United States shall appoint in such manner as the Congress may direct:

A number of electors of President and Vice President equal to the whole number of Senators and Representatives in Congress to which the District would be entitled if it were a State, but in no event more than the least populous State; they shall be in addition to those appointed by the States, but they shall be considered, for the purposes of the election of President and Vice President, to be electors appointed by a State; and they shall meet in the District and perform such duties as provided by the twelfth article of amendment.

2. The Congress shall have power to enforce this article by appropriate legislation.

AMENDMENT XXIV.

Barring poll tax in federal elections.

(Proposed by Congress Aug. 27, 1962; ratified Jan. 23, 1964.)

1. The right of citizens of the United States to vote in any primary or other election for President or Vice President, for electors for President or Vice President, or for Senator or Representative in Congress, shall not be denied or abridged by the United States or any State by reason of failure to pay any poll tax or other tax.

2. The Congress shall have power to enforce this article by appropriate legislation.

AMENDMENT XXV.

Presidential disability and succession.

(Proposed by Congress July 6, 1965; ratified Feb. 10, 1967.)

1. In case of the removal of the President from office or of his death or resignation, the Vice President shall become President.

2. Whenever there is a vacancy in the office of the Vice President, the President shall nominate a Vice President who shall take office upon confirmation by a majority vote of both houses of Congress.

3. Whenever the President transmits to the President pro tempore of the Senate and the Speaker of the House of Representatives his written declaration that he is unable to discharge the powers and duties of his office, and until he transmits to them a written declaration to the contrary, such powers and duties shall be discharged by the Vice President as Acting President.

4. Whenever the Vice President and a majority of either the principal officers of the executive departments or of such other body as Congress may by law provide, transmit to the President pro tempore of the Senate and the Speaker of the House of Representatives their written declaration that the President is unable to discharge the powers and duties of his office, the Vice President shall immediately assume the powers and duties of the office as Acting President.

Thereafter, when the President transmits to the President pro tempore of the Senate and the Speaker of the House of Representatives his written declaration that no inability exists, he shall resume the powers and duties of his office unless the Vice President and a majority of either the principal officers of the executive department or of such other body as Congress may by law provide, transmit within four days to the President pro tempore of the Senate and the Speaker of the House of Representatives their written declaration that the President is unable to discharge the powers and duties of his office. Thereupon Congress shall decide the issue, assembling within forty-eight hours for that purpose if not in session. If the Congress, within twenty-one days after receipt of the latter written declaration, or, if Congress is not in session, within twenty-one days after Congress is required to assemble, determines by two-thirds vote of both Houses that the President is unable to discharge the powers and duties of his office, the Vice President shall continue to discharge the same as Acting President; otherwise, the President shall resume the powers and duties of his office.

AMENDMENT XXVI.

Lowering voting age to 18 years.

(Proposed by Congress Mar. 23, 1971; ratified July 1, 1971.)

1. The right of citizens of the United States, who are eighteen years of age or older, to vote shall not be denied or abridged by the United States or by any State on account of age.

2. The Congress shall have the power to enforce this article by appropriate legislation.

AMENDMENT XXVII.

Congressional pay.

(Proposed by Congress Sept. 25, 1789; ratified May 7, 1992.)

No law, varying the compensation for the services of the Senators and Representatives, shall take effect, until an election of Representatives shall have intervened.

How a Bill Becomes a Law

1. A senator or representative introduces a bill by sending it to the clerk of the House or the Senate, who assigns it a number and title. This procedure is termed the first reading. The clerk then refers the bill to the appropriate Senate or House committee.
2. If the committee opposes the bill, it will table, or kill, it. Otherwise, the committee holds hearings to listen to opinions and facts offered by members and other interested people. The committee then debates the bill and possibly offers amendments. A vote is taken, and if favorable, the bill is sent back to the clerk of the House or Senate.
3. The clerk reads the bill to the house—the second reading. Members may then debate the bill and suggest amendments.
4. After debate and possibly amendment, the bill is given a third reading, simply of the title, and put to a voice or roll-call vote.
5. If passed, the bill goes to the other house, where it may be defeated or passed, with or without amendments. If defeated, the bill dies. If passed with amendments, a conference committee made up of members of both houses works out the differences and arrives at a compromise.
6. After passage of the final version by both houses, the bill is sent to the president. If the president signs it, the bill becomes a law. The president may, however, veto the bill by refusing to sign it and sending it back to the house where it originated, with reasons for the veto.
7. The president's objections are then read and debated, and a roll-call vote is taken. If the bill receives less than a two-thirds majority, it is defeated. If it receives at least two-thirds, it is sent to the other house. If that house also passes it by at least a two-thirds majority, the veto is overridden, and the bill becomes a law.
8. If the president neither signs nor vetoes the bill within 10 days—not including Sundays—it automatically becomes a law even without the president's signature. However, if Congress has adjourned within those 10 days, the bill is automatically killed; this indirect rejection is termed a pocket veto.

Note: Under "line-item veto" legislation effective Jan. 1, 1997, the president was authorized, under certain circumstances, to veto a bill in part, but the legislation was found unconstitutional by the Supreme Court, June 25, 1998.

Confederate States and Secession

The American Civil War (1861-65) grew out of sectional disputes over the continued existence of slavery in the South and the contention of Southern legislators that the states retained many rights, including the right to secede.

The war was not fought by state against state but by one federal regime against another, the Confederate government in Richmond assuming control over the economic, political, and military life of the South, under protest from Georgia and South Carolina.

South Carolina voted an ordinance of secession from the Union, repealing its 1788 ratification of the U.S. Constitution on Dec. 20, 1860, to take effect on Dec. 24. Other states seceded in 1861. Their votes in conventions were: Mississippi, Jan. 9, 84-15; Florida, Jan. 10, 62-7; Alabama, Jan. 11, 61-39; Georgia, Jan. 19, 208-89; Louisiana, Jan. 26, 113-17; Texas, Feb. 1, 166-7, ratified by popular vote on Feb. 23 (for 34,794, against 11,325); Virginia, Apr. 17, 88-55, ratified by popular vote on May 23 (for 128,884; against 32,134); Arkansas, May 6, 69-1; Tennessee, May 7, ratified by popular vote on June 8 (for 104,019, against 47,238); North Carolina, May 21.

Missouri Unionists stopped secession in conventions Feb. 28 and Mar. 9. The legislature condemned secession Mar. 7. Under the protection of Confederate troops, secessionist members of the legislature adopted a resolution of secession at Neosho, Oct. 31. The Confederate Congress seated the secessionists' representatives.

Kentucky did not secede, and its government remained Unionist. In a part of the state occupied by Confederate troops, Kentuckians approved secession, and the Confederate Congress admitted their representatives.

The Maryland legislature voted against secession Apr. 27, 53-13. Delaware did not secede. Western Virginia held conventions at Wheeling, named a pro-Union governor on June 11, 1861, and was admitted to the Union as West Virginia on June 20, 1863. Its constitution provided for gradual abolition of slavery.

Confederate Government

Forty-two delegates from South Carolina, Georgia, Alabama, Mississippi, Louisiana, and Florida met in convention at Montgomery, AL, on Feb. 4, 1861. They adopted a provisional constitution of the Confederate States of America and elected Jefferson Davis (MS) as provisional president and Alexander H. Stephens (GA) as provisional vice president.

A permanent constitution was adopted Mar. 11. It abolished the African slave trade, but it did not bar interstate commerce in slaves. On July 20 the Congress moved to Richmond, VA. Davis was elected president in October and was inaugurated on Feb. 22, 1862.

The Congress adopted a flag, consisting of a red field with a white stripe, and a blue jack with a circle of white stars. Later the more popular flag was the red field with blue diagonal crossbars that held 13 white stars, for the 11 states in the Confederacy plus Kentucky and Missouri.

Lincoln's Address at Gettysburg, 1863

Fourscore and seven years ago our fathers brought forth on this continent a new nation, conceived in liberty and dedicated to the proposition that all men are created equal.

Now we are engaged in a great civil war, testing whether that nation or any nation so conceived and so dedicated can long endure. We are met on a great battle field of that war. We have come to dedicate a portion of that field, as a final resting-place for those who here gave their lives that that nation might live. It is altogether fitting and proper that we should do this.

But, in a larger sense, we can not dedicate—we can not consecrate—we can not hallow—this ground. The brave men, living and dead, who struggled here, have consecrated it, far above our poor power to add or detract. The world will little note, nor long remember, what we say here, but it can never forget what they did here. It is for us the living, rather, to be dedicated here to the unfinished work which they who fought here have thus far so nobly advanced. It is rather for us to be here dedicated to the great task remaining before us—that from these honored dead we take increased devotion to that cause for which they gave the last full measure of devotion—that we here highly resolve that these dead shall not have died in vain—that this nation, under God, shall have a new birth of freedom—and that government of the people, by the people, for the people, shall not perish from the earth.

Selected Landmark Decisions of the U.S. Supreme Court

1803: Marbury v. Madison. The Court ruled that Congress exceeded its power in the Judiciary Act of 1789; the Court thus established its power to review acts of Congress and declare invalid those it found in conflict with the Constitution.

1819: McCulloch v. Maryland. The Court ruled that Congress had the authority to charter a national bank, under the Constitution's granting of the power to enact all laws "necessary and proper" to responsibilities of government.

1819: Trustees of Dartmouth College v. Woodward. The Court ruled that a state could not arbitrarily alter the terms of a college's contract. (In later years the Court used a similar principle to limit the states' ability to interfere with business contracts.)

1857: Dred Scott v. Sanford. The Court declared unconstitutional the already-repealed Missouri Compromise of 1820 because it deprived a person of his or her property—a slave—without due process of law. The Court also ruled that slaves were not citizens of any state nor of the U.S. (The latter part of the decision was overturned by ratification of the 14th Amendment in 1868.)

1896: Plessy v. Ferguson. The Court ruled that a state law requiring federal railroad trains to provide separate but equal facilities for black and white passengers neither infringed upon federal authority to regulate interstate commerce nor violated the 13th and 14th Amendments. (The "separate but equal" doctrine remained effective until the 1954 **Brown v. Board of Education** decision.)

1904: Northern Securities Co. v. U.S. The Court ruled that a holding company formed solely to eliminate competition between two railroad lines was a combination in restraint of trade, violating the federal antitrust act.

1908: Muller v. Oregon. The Court upheld a state law limiting the working hours of women. (Instead of presenting legal arguments, Louis D. Brandeis, counsel for the state, brought forth evidence from social workers, physicians, and factory inspectors that the number of hours women worked affected their health and morals.)

1911: Standard Oil Co. of New Jersey et al. v. U.S. The Court ruled that the Standard Oil Trust must be dissolved because of its unreasonable restraint of trade.

1919: Schenck v. U.S. The Court sustained the Espionage Act of 1917, maintaining that freedom of speech and press could be constrained if "the words used . . . create a clear and present danger. . ."

1925: Gitlow v. New York. The Court ruled that the First Amendment prohibition against government abridgment of the freedom of speech applied to the states as well as to the federal government. The decision was the first of a number of rulings holding that the 14th Amendment extended the guarantees of the Bill of Rights to state action.

1935: Schechter Poultry Corp. v. U.S. The Court ruled that Congress exceeded its authority to delegate legislative powers and to regulate interstate commerce when it enacted the National Industrial Recovery Act, which afforded the U.S. president too much discretionary power.

1951: Dennis et al. v. U.S. The Court upheld convictions under the Smith Act of 1940 for invoking Communist theory that advocated the forcible overthrow of the government. (In the **1957 Yates v. U.S.** decision, the Court moderated this ruling by allowing such advocacy in the abstract, if not connected to action to achieve the goal.)

1954: Brown v. Board of Education of Topeka. The Court ruled that separate public schools for black and white students were inherently unequal, so that state-sanctioned segregation in public schools violated the equal protection guarantee of the 14th Amendment. And in **Bolling v. Sharpe** the Court ruled that the congressionally mandated segregated public school system in the District of Columbia violated the 5th Amendment's due process guarantee of personal liberty. (The Brown ruling also led to abolition of state-sponsored segregation in other public facilities.)

1957: Roth v. U.S., Alberts v. California. The Court ruled obscene material was not protected by First Amendment guarantees of freedom of speech and press, defining obscene as "utterly without redeeming social value" and appealing to "prurient interests" in the view of the average person. This definition was modified in later decisions, and the "average person" standard was replaced by the "local community" standard in **Miller v. California (1973).**

1961: Mapp v. Ohio. The Court ruled that evidence obtained in violation of the 4th Amendment guarantee against unreasonable search and seizure must be excluded from use at state as well as federal trials.

1962: Engel v. Vitale. The Court ruled that public school officials could not require pupils to recite a state-composed prayer, even if the prayer was nondenominational and voluntary, because this would be an unconstitutional attempt to establish religion.

1962: Baker v. Carr. The Court held that the constitutional challenges to the unequal distribution of voters among legislative districts could be resolved by federal courts, rejecting its own **1946** precedent.

1963: Gideon v. Wainwright. The Court ruled that the state as well as federal defendants who are charged with serious crimes must have access to an attorney, at state expense if necessary.

1964: New York Times Co. v. Sullivan. The Court ruled that the First Amendment guarantee of freedom of the press protected the press from libel suits for defamatory reports on public officials unless it was proved that the reports were made from malice, i.e., "with knowledge that [the defamatory statement] was false or with reckless disregard of whether it was false or not."

1965: Griswold v. Conn. The Court ruled that a state unconstitutionally interfered with personal privacy in the marriage relationship when it prohibited anyone, including married couples, from using contraceptives.

1966: Miranda v. Arizona. The Court ruled that, under the guarantee of due process, suspects in custody, before being questioned, must be informed that they have the right to remain silent, that anything they say may be used against them, and that they have the right to counsel.

1973: Roe v. Wade, Doe v. Bolton. The Court ruled that the fetus was not a "person" with constitutional rights and that a right to privacy inherent in the 14th Amendment's due process guarantee of personal liberty protected a woman's decision to have an abortion. During the first trimester of pregnancy, the Court maintained, the decision should be left entirely to a woman and her physician. Some regulation of abortion procedures was allowed in the 2d trimester, and some restriction of abortion in the 3d.

1974: U.S. v. Nixon. The Court ruled that neither the separation of powers nor the need to preserve the confidentiality of presidential communications could alone justify an absolute executive privilege of immunity from judicial demands for evidence to be used in a criminal trial.

1976: Gregg v. Georgia, Profitt v. Fla., Jurek v. Texas. The Court held that death, as a punishment for persons convicted of first degree murder, was not in and of itself cruel and unusual punishment in violation of the 8th Amendment. But the Court ruled that the sentencing judge and jury must consider the individual character of the offender and the circumstances of the particular crime.

1978: Regents of Univ. of Calif. v. Bakke. The Court ruled that a special admissions program for a state medical school, under which a set number of places were reserved for minorities, violated the 1964 Civil Rights Act, which forbids excluding anyone, because of race, from a federally funded program. However, the Court ruled that race could be considered as one of a complex of factors.

1986: Bowers v. Hardwick. The Court refused to extend any constitutional right of privacy to homosexual activity, upholding a Georgia law that in effect made such activity a crime. (Although the Georgia law specifically prohibited sodomy, whether heterosexual or homosexual, enforcement had been confined to homosexual sodomy.) In **Romer v. Evans (1996),** however, the Court struck down a Colorado constitutional provision that barred legislation protecting homosexuals from discrimination.

1990: Cruzan v. Missouri. The Court ruled that a person had the right to refuse life-sustaining medical treatment. However, the Court also ruled that, before treatment could be withheld from a comatose patient, a state could require "clear and convincing evidence" that the patient would not have wanted to live. And in 2 **1997** rulings, **Washington v. Glucksberg** and **Vacco v. Quill,** the Court ruled that states could ban doctor-assisted suicide.

1995: Adarand Constructors v. Peña. The Court held that federal programs that classify people by race, unless "narrowly tailored" to accomplish a "compelling governmental interest," may deny individuals the right to equal protection. Such federal programs, the Court maintained, must adhere to the same strict standards required of state-run affirmative action programs.

1995: U.S. Term Limits Inc. v. Thorton. The Court ruled that neither states nor Congress could limit terms of members of Congress, since the Constitution reserves to the people the right to choose federal lawmakers.

1997: Clinton v. Jones. Rejecting an appeal by Pres. Clinton in a sexual harassment suit, the Court ruled that a sitting president did not have temporary immunity from a lawsuit for actions outside the realm of official duties.

1997: City of Boerne v. Flores. The Court overturned a 1993 law that banned enforcement of laws that "substantially burden" religious practice unless there is a "compelling need" to do so. The Court held that the act was an unwarranted intrusion by Congress on states' prerogatives and an infringement of the judiciary's role.

1997: Reno v. ACLU. Citing the right to free expression, the Court overturned a provision making it a crime to display or distribute "indecent" or "patently offensive" material on the Internet. In **1998**, however, the Court ruled in **NEA v. Finley** that "general standards of decency" may be used as a criterion in federal arts funding.

1998: Clinton v. City of New York. The Court struck down the Line-Item Veto Act (1996), holding that it unconstitutionally gave the president "the unilateral power to change the text of duly enacted statutes."

1998: Faragher v. City of Boca Raton, Burlington Industries, Inc. v. Ellerth. The Court issued new guidelines for workplace sexual harassment suits, holding employers responsible for misconduct by supervisory employees. And in **Oncale v. Sundowner Offshore Services,** the Court ruled that the law against sexual harassment applies regardless of whether harasser and victim are the same sex.

Presidential Oath of Office

The Constitution (Article II) directs that the president shall take the following oath or affirmation: "I do solemnly swear (affirm) that I will faithfully execute the office of President of the United States, and will, to the best of my ability, preserve, protect, and defend the Constitution of the United States." (Custom decrees the use of the words "So help me God" at the end of the oath when taken by the president-elect, his or her left hand on the Bible for the duration of the oath, with his or her right hand slightly raised.)

Law on Succession to the Presidency

If by reason of death, resignation, removal from office, inability, or failure to qualify there is neither a president nor vice president to discharge the powers and duties of the office of president, then the speaker of the House of Representatives shall upon his resignation as speaker and as representative, act as president. The same rule shall apply in the case of the death, resignation, removal from office, or inability of an individual acting as president.

If at the time when a speaker is to begin the discharge of the powers and duties of the office of president there is no speaker, or the speaker fails to qualify as acting president, then the president pro tempore of the Senate, upon his resignation as president pro tempore and as senator, shall act as president.

An individual acting as president shall continue to act until the expiration of the then current presidential term, except that (1) if his discharge of the powers and duties of the office is founded in whole or in part in the failure of both the president-elect and the vice president-elect to qualify, then he shall act only until a president or vice president qualifies, and (2) if his discharge of the powers and duties of the office is founded in whole or in part on the inability of the president or vice president, then he shall act only until the removal of the disability of one of such individuals.

If, by reason of death, resignation, removal from office, or failure to qualify, there is no president pro tempore to act as president, then the officer of the United States who is highest on the following list, and who is not under any disability to discharge the powers and duties of president shall act as president; the secretaries of state, treasury, defense, attorney general; secretaries of interior, agriculture, commerce, labor, health and human services, housing and urban development, transportation, energy, education, veterans affairs.

(Legislation approved July 18, 1947; amended Sept. 9, 1965, Oct. 15, 1966, Aug. 4, 1977, and Sept. 27, 1979. See also Constitutional Amendment XXV.)

Origin of the United States National Motto

In God We Trust, designated as the U.S. National Motto by Congress in 1956, originated during the Civil War as an inscription for U. S. coins, although it was used by Francis Scott Key in a slightly different form when he wrote "The Star-Spangled Banner" in 1814. On Nov. 13, 1861, when Union morale had been shaken by battlefield defeats, the Rev. M. R. Watkinson, of Ridleyville, PA, wrote to Secy. of the Treasury Salmon P. Chase. "From my heart I have felt our national shame in disowning God as not the least of our present national disasters," the minister wrote, suggesting "recognition of the Almighty God in some form on our coins." Secy. Chase ordered designs prepared with the inscription *In God We Trust* and backed coinage legislation that authorized use of this slogan. It first appeared on some U.S. coins in 1864, disappeared and reappeared on various coins until 1955, when Congress ordered it placed on all paper money and all coins.

The Great Seal of the U.S.

On July 4, 1776, the Continental Congress appointed a committee consisting of Benjamin Franklin, John Adams, and Thomas Jefferson "to bring in a device for a seal of the United States of America." The designs submitted by this and a subsequent committee were considered unacceptable. After many delays, a third committee, appointed early in 1782, presented a design prepared by William Barton. Charles Thomson, the secretary of Congress, suggested certain changes, and Congress finally approved the design on June 20, 1782. The obverse side of the seal shows an American bald eagle. In its mouth is a ribbon bearing the motto *e pluribus unum* (one out of many). In the eagle's talons are the arrows of war and an olive branch of peace. The reverse side shows an unfinished pyramid with an eye (the eye of Providence) above it.

The American's Creed

William Tyler Page, Clerk of the U.S. House of Representatives, wrote "The American's Creed" in 1917. It was accepted by the House on behalf of the American people on April 3, 1918.

"I believe in the United States of America as a government of the people, by the people, for the people; whose just powers are derived from the consent of the governed; a democracy in a republic; a sovereign Nation of many sovereign States; a perfect union, one and inseparable; established upon those principles of freedom, equality, justice, and humanity for which American patriots sacrificed their lives and fortunes.

"I therefore believe it is my duty to my country to love it, to support its Constitution, to obey its laws, to respect its flag, and to defend it against all enemies."

The Flag of the U.S.—The Stars and Stripes

The 50-star flag of the United States was raised for the first time officially at 12:01 AM on July 4, 1960, at Fort McHenry National Monument in Baltimore, MD. The 50th star had been added for Hawaii; a year earlier the 49th, for Alaska. Before that, no star had been added since 1912, when New Mexico and Arizona were admitted to the Union.

The true history of the Stars and Stripes has become so cluttered by myth and tradition that the facts are difficult, and in some cases impossible, to establish. For example, it is not certain who designed the Stars and Stripes, who made the first such flag, or even whether it ever flew in any sea fight or land battle of the American Revolution.

All agree, however, that the Stars and Stripes originated as the result of a resolution offered by the Marine Committee of the Second Continental Congress at Philadelphia and adopted on June 14, 1777. It read:

Resolved: that the flag of the United States be thirteen stripes, alternate red and white; that the union be thirteen stars, white in a blue field, representing a new constellation.

Congress gave no hint as to the designer of the flag, no instructions as to the arrangement of the stars, and no information on its appropriate uses. Historians have been unable to find the original flag law.

The resolution establishing the flag was not even published until Sept. 2, 1777. Despite repeated requests, Washington did not get the flags until 1783, after the American Revolution was over. And there is no certainty that they were the Stars and Stripes.

Early Flags

Many historians consider the first flag of the U.S. to have been the Grand Union (sometimes called Great Union) flag, although the Continental Congress never officially adopted it. This flag was a modification of the British Meteor flag, which had the red cross of St. George and the white cross of St. Andrew combined in the blue canton. For the Grand Union flag, 6 horizontal stripes were imposed on the red field, dividing it into 13 alternating red and white stripes. On Jan. 1, 1776, when the Continental Army came into formal existence, this flag was unfurled on Prospect Hill, Somerville, MA. Washington wrote that "we hoisted the Union Flag in compliment to the United Colonies."

One of several flags about which controversy has raged for years is at Easton, PA. Containing the devices of the national flag in reversed order, this flag has been in the public library at Easton for more than 150 years. Some contend that this flag was actually the first Stars and Stripes, first displayed on July 8, 1776. This flag has 13 red and white stripes in the canton, 13 white stars centered in a blue field.

A flag was hastily improvised from garments by the defenders of Fort Schuyler at Rome, NY, Aug. 3-22, 1777. Historians believe it was the Grand Union Flag.

The Sons of Liberty had a flag of 9 red and white stripes, to signify 9 colonies, when they met in New York in 1765 to oppose the Stamp Tax. By 1775, the flag had grown to 13 red and white stripes, with a rattlesnake on it.

At Concord, Apr. 19, 1775, the minutemen from Bedford, MA, are said to have carried a flag having a silver arm with sword on a red field. At Cambridge, MA, the Sons of Liberty used a plain red flag with a green pine tree on it.

In June 1775, Washington went from Philadelphia to Boston to take command of the army, escorted to New York by the Philadelphia Light Horse Troop. It carried a yellow flag that had an elaborate coat of arms—the shield charged with 13 knots, the motto "For These We Strive"—and a canton of 13 blue and silver stripes.

In Feb. 1776, Col. Christopher Gadsden, a member of the Continental Congress, gave the South Carolina Provincial Congress a flag "such as is to be used by the commander-in-chief of the American Navy." It had a yellow field, with a rattlesnake about to strike and the words "Don't Tread on Me."

At the Battle of Bennington, Aug. 16, 1777, patriots used a flag of 7 white and 6 red stripes with a blue canton extending down 9 stripes and showing an arch of 11 white stars over the figure 76 and a star in each of the upper corners. The stars are 7-pointed. This flag is preserved in the Historical Museum at Bennington, VT.

At the Battle of Cowpens, Jan. 17, 1781, the 3d Maryland Regiment is said to have carried a flag of 13 red and white stripes, with a blue canton containing 12 stars in a circle around one star.

Who Designed the Flag? No one knows for certain. Francis Hopkinson, designer of a naval flag, declared he also had designed the flag and in 1781 asked Congress to reimburse him for his services. Congress did not do so. Dumas Malone of Columbia University wrote: "This talented man . . . designed the American flag."

Who Called the Flag "Old Glory"? The flag is said to have been named Old Glory by William Driver, a sea captain of Salem, MA. One legend has it that when he raised the flag on his brig, the *Charles Doggett*, in 1824, he said: "I name thee Old Glory." But his daughter, who presented the flag to the Smithsonian Institution, said he named it at his 21st birthday celebration on Mar. 17, 1824, when his mother presented the homemade flag to him.

The Betsy Ross Legend. The widely publicized legend that Mrs. Betsy Ross made the first Stars and Stripes in June 1776, at the request of a committee composed of George Washington, Robert Morris, and George Ross, an uncle, was first made public in 1870, by a grandson of Mrs. Ross. Historians have been unable to find a historical record of such a meeting or committee.

Adding New Stars

The flag of 1777 was used until 1795. Then, on the admission of Vermont and Kentucky to the Union, Congress passed and Pres. Washington signed an act that after May 1, 1795, the flag should have 15 stripes, alternating red and white, and 15 white stars on a blue field.

When new states were admitted, it became evident that the flag would become burdened with stripes. Congress thereupon ordered that after July 4, 1818, the flag should have 13 stripes, symbolizing the 13 original states; that the union have 20 stars, and that whenever a new state was admitted a new star should be added on the July 4 following admission. No law designates the permanent arrangement of the stars. However, since 1912, when a new state has been admitted, the new design has been announced by executive order. No star is specifically identified with any state.

Code of Etiquette for Display and Use of the U.S. Flag

Reviewed by National Flag Foundation

Although the Stars and Stripes originated in 1777, it was not until 146 years later that there was a serious attempt to establish a uniform code of etiquette for the U.S. flag. On Feb. 15, 1923, the War Department issued a circular on the rules of flag usage. These rules were adopted almost in their entirety June 14, 1923, by a conference of 68 patriotic organizations in Washington, D.C. Finally, on June 22, 1942, a joint resolution of Congress, amended by Public Law 94-344, July 7, 1976, codified "existing rules and customs pertaining to the display and use of the flag . . ."

When to Display the Flag—The flag should be displayed on all days, especially on legal holidays and other special occasions, on official buildings when in use, in or near polling places on election days, and in or near schools when in session. Citizens may fly the flag at any time. It is customary to display it only from sunrise to sunset on buildings and on stationary flagstaffs in the open. It may be displayed at night, however, on special occasions, preferably lighted. The flag now flies over the White House both day and night. It flies over the Senate wing of the Capitol when the Senate is in session and over the House wing when that body is in session. It flies day and night over the east and west fronts of the Capitol, without floodlights at night but receiving illumination from the Capitol Dome. It flies 24 hours a day at several other places, including the Fort McHenry National Monument in Baltimore, where it inspired Francis Scott Key to write "The Star Spangled Banner." The flag also flies 24 hours a day, properly illuminated, at U.S. Customs ports of entry.

Flying the Flag at Half-Staff—Flying the flag at half-staff, that is, halfway up the staff, is a signal of mourning. The flag should be hoisted to the top of the staff for an instant before being lowered to half-staff. It should be hoisted to the peak again before being lowered for the day or night.

As provided by presidential proclamation, the flag should fly at half-staff for 30 days from the day of death of a president or former president; for 10 days from the day of death of a vice president, chief justice or retired chief justice of the U.S., or speaker of the House of Representatives; from day of death until burial of an associate justice of the Supreme Court, cabinet member, former vice president, Senate president pro tempore, or majority or minority Senate or House leader; for a U.S. senator, representative, territorial delegate, or the resident commissioner of Puerto Rico, on day of death and the following day within the metropolitan area of the District of Columbia and from day of death until burial within the decedent's state, congressional district, territory or commonwealth; and for the death of the governor of a state, territory, or possession of the U.S., from day of death until burial.

On Memorial Day, the flag should fly at half-staff until noon and then be raised to the peak. The flag should also fly at half-staff on Korean War Veterans Armistice Day (July 27), National Pearl Harbor Remembrance Day (Dec. 7), and Peace Officers Memorial Day (May 15).

How to Fly the Flag—The flag should be hoisted briskly and lowered ceremoniously and should never be allowed to touch the ground or the floor. When the flag is hung over a sidewalk from a rope extending from a building to a pole, the union should be away from the building. When the flag is hung over the center of a street the union should be to the north in an east-west street and to the east in a north-south street. No other flag may be flown above or, if on the same level, to the right of the U.S. flag, except that at the United Nations Headquarters the UN flag may be placed above flags of all member nations and other national flags may be flown with equal prominence or honor with the flag of the U.S. At services by Navy chaplains at sea, the church pennant may be flown above the flag.

When 2 flags are placed against a wall with crossed staffs, the U.S. flag should be at right—its own right, and its staff should be in front of the staff of the other flag; when a number of flags are grouped and displayed from staffs, it should be at the center and highest point of the group.

Church and Platform Use—In an auditorium, the flag may be displayed flat, above and behind the speaker. When displayed from a staff in a church or in a public auditorium, the flag should hold the position of superior prominence, in advance of the audience, and in the position of honor at the speaker's right as she or he faces the audience. Any other flag so displayed should be placed on the left of the speaker or to the right of the audience.

When the flag is displayed horizontally or vertically against a wall, the stars should be uppermost and at the observer's left.

When used to cover a casket, the flag should be placed so that the union is at the head and over the left shoulder. It should not be lowered into the grave nor touch the ground.

How to Dispose of Worn Flags—When the flag is in such condition that it is no longer a fitting emblem for display, it should be destroyed in a dignified way, preferably by burning.

When to Salute the Flag—All persons present should face the flag, stand at attention, and salute on the following occasions: (1) when the flag is passing in a parade or in a review, (2) during the ceremony of hoisting or lowering, (3) when the national anthem is played, and (4) during the Pledge of Allegiance. Those present in uniform should render the military salute. Those not in uniform should place the right hand over the heart. A man wearing a hat should remove it with his right hand and hold it to his left shoulder during the salute.

Prohibited Uses of the Flag—The flag should not be dipped to any person or thing. (An exception—customarily, ships salute by dipping their colors.) It should never be displayed with the union down save as a distress signal. It should never be carried flat or horizontally, but always aloft and free.

It should not be displayed on a float, an automobile, or a boat except from a staff. It should never be used as a covering for a ceiling, nor have placed on it any word, design, or drawing. It should never be used as a receptacle for carrying anything. It should not be used to cover a statue or a monument.

The flag should never be used for advertising purposes, nor be embroidered on such articles as cushions or handkerchiefs, printed or otherwise impressed on boxes or anything that is designed for temporary use and discard; or used as a costume or athletic uniform. Advertising signs should not be fastened to its staff or halyard.

The flag should never be used as drapery of any sort, never festooned, drawn back, nor up, in folds, but always allowed to fall free. Bunting of blue, white, and red, always arranged with the blue above and the white in the middle, should be used for covering a speaker's desk, draping the front of a platform, and for decoration in general.

An act of Congress approved on Feb. 8, 1917, provided certain penalties for the desecration, mutilation, or improper use of the flag within the District of Columbia. A 1968 federal law provided penalties of as much as a year's imprisonment or a $1,000 fine or both for publicly burning or otherwise desecrating any U.S. flag. In addition, many states have laws against flag desecration. In 1989, the Supreme Court ruled that no laws could prohibit political protesters from burning the flag. The decision had the effect of declaring unconstitutional the flag desecration laws of 48 states, as well as a similar federal statute, in cases of peaceful political expression.

The Supreme Court, in June 1990, declared that a new federal law making it a crime to burn or deface the American flag violated the free-speech guarantee of the First Amendment. The 5-4 decision led to renewed calls in Congress for a constitutional amendment to make it possible to prosecute flag burners.

Pledge of Allegiance to the Flag

I pledge allegiance to the flag of the United States of America and to the republic for which it stands, one nation under God, indivisible, with liberty and justice for all.

This, the current official version of the Pledge of Allegiance, has developed from the original pledge, which was first published in the Sept. 8, 1892, issue of *Youth's Companion*, a weekly magazine then published in Boston. The original pledge contained the phrase "my flag," which was changed more than 30 years later to "flag of the United States of America." A 1954 act of Congress added the words "under God."

The authorship of the pledge had been in dispute for many years. The *Youth's Companion* stated in 1917 that the original draft was written by James B. Upham, an executive of the magazine who died in 1910. A leaflet circulated by the magazine later named Upham as the originator of the draft "afterwards condensed and perfected by him and his associates of the Companion force."

Francis Bellamy, a former member of *Youth's Companion* editorial staff, publicly claimed authorship of the pledge in 1923. In 1939, the United States Flag Association, acting on the advice of a committee named to study the controversy, upheld the claim of Bellamy, who had died 8 years earlier. In 1957 the Library of Congress issued a report attributing the authorship to Bellamy.

The History of the National Anthem

"The Star-Spangled Banner" was ordered played by the military and naval services by Pres. Woodrow Wilson in 1916. It was designated the national anthem by Act of Congress, Mar. 3, 1931. The words were written by Francis Scott Key, of Georgetown, MD, during the bombardment of Fort McHenry, Baltimore, Sept. 13-14, 1814. Key was a lawyer, a graduate of St. John's College, Annapolis, and a volunteer in a light artillery company. When a friend, Dr. Beanes, a Maryland physician, was taken aboard Admiral Cockburn's British squadron for interfering with ground troops, Key and J. S. Skinner, carrying a note from Pres. Madison, went to the fleet under a flag of truce on a cartel ship to ask Beanes's release. Cockburn consented, but as the fleet was about to sail up the Patapsco to bombard Fort McHenry, he detained them, first on HMS *Surprise* and then on a supply ship.

Key witnessed the bombardment from his own vessel. It began at 7 AM, Sept. 13, 1814, and lasted, with intermissions, for 25 hr. The British fired more than 1,500 shells, each weighing as much as 220 lb. They were unable to approach closely because the U.S. had sunk 22 vessels. Only 4 Americans were killed and 24 wounded. A British bomb-ship was disabled.

During the event, Key wrote a stanza on the back of an envelope. Next day at Indian Queen Inn, Baltimore, he wrote out the poem and gave it to his brother-in-law, Judge J. H. Nicholson. Nicholson suggested use of the tune, "Anacreon in Heaven" (attributed to a British composer named John Stafford Smith), and had the poem printed on broadsides, of which 2 survive. On Sept. 20 it appeared in the *Baltimore American*. Later Key made 3 copies; one is in the Library of Congress, and one in the Pennsylvania Historical Society. The copy Key wrote on Sept. 14 remained in the Nicholson family for 93 years. In 1907 it was sold to Henry Walters of Baltimore. In 1934 it was bought at auction by the Walters Art Gallery, Baltimore, for $26,400. In 1953 it was sold to the Maryland Historical Society for the same price.

The flag that Key saw during the bombardment is preserved in the Smithsonian Institution, Washington, DC. It is 30 by 42 ft and has 15 alternating red and white stripes and 15 stars, for the original 13 states plus Kentucky and Vermont. It was made by Mary Young Pickersgill. The Baltimore Flag House, a museum, occupies her premises, which were restored in 1953.

The Star-Spangled Banner

I

Oh, say can you see by the dawn's early light
What so proudly we hailed at the twilight's last gleaming?
Whose broad stripes and bright stars thru the perilous fight,
O'er the ramparts we watched were so gallantly streaming?
And the rocket's red glare, the bombs bursting in air,
Gave proof through the night that our flag was still there.
Oh, say does that star-spangled banner yet wave
O'er the land of the free and the home of the brave?

II

On the shore, dimly seen through the mists of the deep,
Where the foe's haughty host in dread silence reposes,
What is that which the breeze, o'er the towering steep,
As it fitfully blows, half conceals, half discloses?
Now it catches the gleam of the morning's first beam,
In full glory reflected now shines in the stream:
'Tis the star-spangled banner! Oh long may it wave
O'er the land of the free and the home of the brave!

III

And where is that band who so vauntingly swore
That the havoc of war and the battle's confusion,
A home and a country should leave us no more!
Their blood has washed out their foul footsteps' pollution.
No refuge could save the hireling and slave
From the terror of flight, or the gloom of the grave:
And the star-spangled banner in triumph doth wave
O'er the land of the free and the home of the brave!

IV

Oh! thus be it ever, when freemen shall stand
Between their loved home and the war's desolation!
Blest with victory and peace, may the heav'n rescued land
Praise the Power that hath made and preserved us a nation.
Then conquer we must, when our cause it is just,
And this be our motto: "In God is our trust."
And the star-spangled banner in triumph shall wave
O'er the land of the free and the home of the brave!

America
(My Country 'Tis of Thee)

First sung in public on July 4, 1831, at a service in the Park Street Church, Boston, the words were written by Rev. Samuel Francis Smith, a Baptist clergyman, who set them to a melody he found in a German songbook, unaware that it was the tune for the British anthem, "God Save the King/Queen."

My country, 'tis of thee,
Sweet land of liberty, Of thee I sing.
Land where my fathers died!
Land of the Pilgrims' pride!
From ev'ry mountainside,
Let freedom ring!

My native country, thee,
Land of the noble free,
Thy name I love.
I love thy rocks and rills,
Thy woods and templed hills;
My heart with rapture thrills
Like that above.

Let music swell the breeze,
And ring from all the trees
Sweet freedom's song.
Let mortal tongues awake;
Let all that breathe partake;
Let rocks their silence break,
The sound prolong.

Our fathers' God, to Thee,
Author of liberty,
To Thee we sing.
Long may our land be bright
With freedom's holy light;
Protect us by Thy might,
Great God, our King!

America, the Beautiful

Words composed by Katharine Lee Bates, a Massachusetts educator and author, in 1893, inspired by the view she experienced atop Pikes Peak. The final form was established in 1911, and it is set to the music of Samuel A. Ward's "Materna."

O beautiful for spacious skies,
For amber waves of grain,
For purple mountain majesties
Above the fruited plain.
America! America!
God shed His grace on thee,
And crown thy good with brotherhood
From sea to shining sea.

O beautiful for pilgrim feet
Whose stern impassion'd stress
A thorough-fare for freedom beat
Across the wilderness.
America! America!
God mend thine ev'ry flaw,
Confirm thy soul in self control,
Thy liberty in law.

O beautiful for heroes prov'd
In liberating strife,
Who more than self their country lov'd
And mercy more than life.
America! America!
May God thy gold refine
Till all success be nobleness,
And ev'ry gain divine.

O beautiful for patriot dream
That sees beyond the years,
Thine alabaster cities gleam,
Undimmed by human tears.
America! America!
God shed His grace on thee,
And crown thy good with brotherhood
From sea to shining sea.

The Liberty Bell: Its History and Significance

The Liberty Bell, in Independence National Historical Park, Philadelphia, is an object of great reverence to Americans because of its association with the historic events of the American Revolution.

The original Province bell was ordered by Assembly Speaker and Chairman of the State House Superintendents Isaac Norris and was ordered from Thomas Lester, Whitechapel Foundry, London. It reached Philadelphia at the end of August 1752. It bore an inscription from Leviticus 25:10: "PROCLAIM LIBERTY THROUGHOUT ALL THE LAND UNTO ALL THE INHABITANTS THEREOF."

The bell was cracked by a stroke of its clapper in Sept. 1752 while it hung on a truss in the State House yard for testing. Pass & Stow, Philadelphia founders, recast the bell, adding 1½ ounces of copper to a pound of the original "Whitechapel" metal to reduce its high tone and brittleness. It was found that the bell contained too much copper, injuring its tone, so Pass & Stow recast it again, this time successfully.

In June 1753 the bell was hung in the old wooden steeple of the State House. In use while the Continental Congress was in session in the State House, it rang out in defiance of British tax and trade restrictions, and it proclaimed the Boston Tea Party and the first public reading of the Declaration of Independence.

On Sept. 18, 1777, when the British Army was about to occupy Philadelphia, the bell was moved in a baggage train of the American Army to Allentown, PA, where it was hidden in the Zion Reformed Church until June 27, 1778. It was moved back to Philadelphia after the British left.

In July 1781 the wooden steeple became insecure and had to be taken down. The bell was lowered into the brick section of the tower, where it remained until 1828. Between 1828 and 1844 the old State House bell continued to ring during special occasions. It rang for the last time on Feb. 23, 1846. In 1852 it was placed on exhibition in the Declaration Chamber of Independence Hall.

In 1876, when many thousands of Americans visited Philadelphia for the Centennial Exposition, the bell was placed in its old wooden support in the tower hallway. In 1877 it was hung from the ceiling of the tower by a chain of 13 links. It was returned again to the Declaration Chamber and in 1896 taken back to the tower hall, where it occupied a glass case. In 1915 the case was removed so that the public might touch it. On Jan. 1, 1976, just after midnight to mark the opening of the Bicentennial Year, the bell was moved to a new glass and steel pavilion behind Independence Hall for easier viewing.

The measurements of the bell are: circumference around the lip, 12 ft ½ in; circumference around the crown, 6 ft 11¼ in; lip to the crown, 3 ft; height over the crown, 2 ft 3 in; thickness at lip, 3 in; thickness at crown, 1¼ in; weight, 2,080 lb; length of clapper, 3 ft 2 in.

The specific source of the crack in the bell is unknown.

Statue of Liberty National Monument

Since 1886, the Statue of Liberty Enlightening the World has stood as a symbol of freedom in New York harbor. It also commemorates French-American friendship, for it was given by the people of France and designed by French sculptor Frederic Auguste Bartholdi (1834-1904).

Edouard de Laboulaye, French historian, suggested the French present a monument to the U.S., the latter to provide pedestal and site. Bartholdi visualized a colossal statue at the entrance of New York harbor, welcoming the peoples of the world with the torch of liberty.

On Washington's Birthday, Feb. 22, 1877, Congress approved the use of a site on Bedloe's Island suggested by Bartholdi. This island of 12 acres had been owned in the 17th century by a Walloon named Isaac Bedloe. It was called Bedloe's until Aug. 3, 1956, when Pres. Eisenhower approved a resolution of Congress changing the name to Liberty Island.

The statue was finished on May 21, 1884, and formally presented to the U.S. minister to France, Levi Parsons Morton, July 4, 1884, by Ferdinand de Lesseps, head of the Franco-American Union, promoter of the Panama Canal, and builder of the Suez Canal.

On Aug. 5, 1884, the Americans laid the cornerstone for the pedestal. This was to be built on the foundations of Fort Wood, which had been erected by the government in 1811. The American committee had raised $125,000, but this was found to be inadequate. Joseph Pulitzer, owner of the *New York World,* appealed on Mar. 16, 1885, for general donations. By Aug. 11, 1885, he had raised $100,000.

The statue arrived dismantled, in 214 packing cases, from Rouen, France, in June 1885. The last rivet of the statue was driven on Oct. 28, 1886, when Pres. Grover Cleveland dedicated the monument.

The statue weighs 450,000 lb, or 225 tons. The copper sheeting weighs 200,000 lb. There are 167 steps from the land level to the top of the pedestal, 168 steps inside the statue to the head, and 54 rungs on the ladder leading to the arm that holds the torch.

A $2.5 million building housing the American Museum of Immigration was opened by Pres. Richard Nixon on Sept. 26, 1972, at the base of the statue. It houses a permanent exhibition of photos, posters, and artifacts tracing the history of American immigration. The Statue of Liberty National Monument is administered by the National Park Service.

Two years of restoration work was completed before the statue's centennial celebration on July 4, 1986. Among other repairs, the multimillion dollar project included replacing the 1,600 wrought iron bands that hold the statue's copper skin to its frame, replacing its torch, and installing an elevator.

A 4-day extravaganza of concerts, tall ships, ethnic festivals, and fireworks, July 3-6, 1986, celebrated the 100th anniversary. The festivities included Chief Justice Warren E. Burger's swearing-in of 5,000 new citizens on Ellis Island, while 20,000 others across the country were simultaneously sworn in through a satellite telecast.

The ceremonies were followed by others on Oct. 28, 1986, to mark the statue's exact 100th birthday.

Dimensions of the Statue	**Ft.**	**In.**
Height from base to torch (45.3 meters)	151	1
Foundation of pedestal to torch (91.5 meters)	305	1
Heel to top of head	111	1
Length of hand	16	5
Index finger	8	0
Size of finger nail	13x10 in.	
Head from chin to cranium	17	3
Head thickness from ear to ear	10	0
Length of nose	4	6
Right arm, length	42	0
Right arm, greatest thickness	12	0
Thickness of waist	35	0
Width of mouth	3	0
Tablet, length	23	7
Tablet, width	13	7
Tablet, thickness	2	0

Emma Lazarus's Famous Poem

A sonnet by Emma Lazarus is graven on a tablet within the pedestal on which the Statue of Liberty stands.

The New Colossus

Not like the brazen giant of Greek fame,
With conquering limbs astride from land to land;
Here at our sea-washed, sunset gates shall stand
A mighty woman with a torch, whose flame
Is the imprisoned lightning, and her name
Mother of Exiles. From her beacon-hand
Glows world-wide welcome; her mild eyes command
The air-bridged harbor that twin cities frame.
"Keep ancient lands, your storied pomp!" cries she
With silent lips. "Give me your tired, your poor,
Your huddled masses yearning to breathe free,
The wretched refuse of your teeming shore.
Send these, the homeless, tempest-tost to me,
I lift my lamp beside the golden door!"

Ellis Island

Ellis Island was the gateway to America for more than 12 million immigrants between 1892 and 1924. In the late 18th century, Samuel Ellis, a New York City merchant, purchased the island and gave it his name. From Ellis, it passed to New York State, and the U.S. government bought it in 1808. On Jan. 1, 1892 the government opened the first federal immigration center in the U.S. on the island. The 27½-acre site eventually supported more than 35 buildings, including the Main Building with its Great Hall, in which as many as 5,000 people a day were processed.

Closed as an immigration station in 1954, Ellis Island was proclaimed part of the Statue of Liberty National Monument in 1965 by Pres. Lyndon B. Johnson. After a 6-year $170 million restoration project funded by The Ellis Island Fdn. Inc., Ellis Island was reopened as a museum in 1990. Artifacts, historic photographs and documents, oral histories, and ethnic music depicting 400 years of American immigration are housed in the museum. The museum also includes The American Immigrant Wall of Honor (http://www.wallofhonor.com), inscribed with nearly 600,000 names. In May 1998, the Supreme Court ruled that nearly 90% of the island (the 24.2 acres which are landfill) lies in New Jersey, while the original 3.3 acres are in New York.

BIOGRAPHIES OF U.S. PRESIDENTS

George Washington (1789-97)

George Washington, first president, Federalist, was born on Feb. 22, 1732, in Wakefield on Pope's Creek, Westmoreland Co., VA, the son of Augustine and Mary Ball Washington. He spent his early childhood on a farm near Fredericksburg. His father died when George was 11. He studied mathematics and surveying, and when he was 16, he went to live with his elder half brother, Lawrence, who built and named Mount Vernon. George surveyed the lands of Thomas Fairfax in the Shenandoah Valley, keeping a diary. He accompanied Lawrence to Barbados, West Indies, where he contracted smallpox and was deeply scarred. Lawrence died in 1752, and George inherited his property. He valued land, and when he died, he owned 70,000 acres in Virginia and 40,000 acres in what is now West Virginia.

Washington's military service began in 1753, when Lt. Gov. Robert Dinwiddie of Virginia sent him on missions deep into Ohio country. He clashed with the French and had to surrender Fort Necessity on July 3, 1754. He was an aide to the British general Edward Braddock and was at his side when the army was ambushed and defeated (July 9, 1755) on a march to Fort Duquesne. He helped take Fort Duquesne from the French in 1758.

After Washington's marriage to Martha Dandridge Custis, a widow, in 1759, he managed his family estate at Mount Vernon. Although not at first for independence, he opposed the repressive measures of the British crown and took charge of the Virginia troops before war broke out. He was made commander of the newly created Continental Army by the Continental Congress on June 15, 1775.

The American victory was due largely to Washington's leadership. He was resourceful, a stern disciplinarian, and the one strong, dependable force for unity. Washington favored a federal government. He became chairman of the Constitutional Convention of 1787 and helped get the Constitution ratified. Unanimously elected president by the Electoral College, he was inaugurated Apr. 30, 1789, on the balcony of New York's Federal Hall.

He was reelected in 1792. Washington made an effort to avoid partisan politics as president.

Refusing to consider a 3d term, he retired to Mount Vernon in March 1797. He suffered acute laryngitis after a ride in snow and rain around his estate, was bled profusely, and died Dec. 14, 1799.

John Adams (1797-1801)

John Adams, 2d president, Federalist, was born on Oct. 30, 1735, in Braintree (now Quincy), MA, the son of John and Susanna Boylston Adams. He was a great-grandson of Henry Adams, who came from England in 1636. He graduated from Harvard in 1755 and then taught school and studied law. He married Abigail Smith in 1764. In 1765 he argued against taxation without representation before the royal governor. In 1770 he successfully defended in court the British soldiers who fired on civilians in the Boston Massacre. He was a delegate to the Continental Congress and a signer of the Declaration of Independence. In 1778, Congress sent Adams and John Jay to join Benjamin Franklin as diplomatic representatives in Europe. Because he ran second to Washington in Electoral College balloting in February 1789, Adams became the nation's first vice president; he was reelected in 1792.

In 1796 Adams was chosen president by the electors. His administration was marked by rivalry with Alexander Hamilton and a crisis in U.S.-French relations. He was extraordinarily unpopular for securing passage of the Alien and Sedition Acts in 1798. His foreign policy contributed significantly to the election of Thomas Jefferson in 1800.

Adams lived for a quarter century after he left office, during which time he wrote extensively. He died July 4, 1826, on the same day as Thomas Jefferson (the 50th anniversary of the Declaration of Independence).

Thomas Jefferson (1801-9)

Thomas Jefferson, 3d president, Democratic-Republican, was born on Apr. 13, 1743, in Shadwell in Goochland (now Albemarle) Co., VA, the son of Peter and Jane Randolph Jefferson. Peter died when Thomas was 14, leaving him 2,750 acres and his slaves. Jefferson attended (1760-62) the College of William and Mary, read Greek and Latin classics, and played the violin. In 1769 he was elected to the Virginia House of Burgesses. In 1770 he began building his home, Monticello, and in 1772 he married Martha Wayles Skelton, a wealthy widow. Jefferson helped establish the Virginia Committee of Correspondence. As a member of the Second Continental Congress he drafted the Declaration of Independence in late June 1776. He also was a member of the Virginia House of Delegates (1776-79) and was first elected governor of Virginia in 1779, succeeding Patrick Henry. He was reelected governor in 1780 but resigned in June 1781 after British troops invaded Virginia. During his term he wrote the statute on religious freedom. After his wife's death in 1782, Jefferson again became a delegate to the Congress, and in 1784 he drafted the report that was the basis for the Ordinances of 1784, 1785, and 1787. He was minister to France from 1785 to 1789, when George Washington appointed him secretary of state.

Jefferson's strong faith in the consent of the governed conflicted with the emphasis on executive control, favored by Alexander Hamilton, secretary of the Treasury, and Jefferson resigned on Dec. 31, 1793. In the 1796 election Jefferson was the Democratic-Republican candidate for president; John Adams won the election, and Jefferson became vice president. In 1800, Jefferson and Aaron Burr received equal Electoral College votes. The House of Representatives elected Jefferson president. Major events of his first term were the Louisiana Purchase (1803) and the Lewis and Clark Expedition. An important development during his second term was passage of the Embargo Act, barring U.S. ships from setting sail to foreign ports. Jefferson established the University of Virginia and designed its buildings. He died July 4, 1826, on the same day as John Adams (the 50th anniversary of the Declaration of Independence).

James Madison (1809-17)

James Madison, 4th president, Democratic-Republican, was born on Mar. 16, 1751, in Port Conway, King George Co., VA, the son of James and Eleanor Rose Conway Madison. Madison graduated from Princeton in 1771. He served in the Virginia Constitutional Convention (1776), and, in 1780, became a delegate to the Second Continental Congress. He was chief recorder at the Constitutional Convention in 1787 and supported ratification in the *Federalist Papers*, written with Alexander Hamilton and John Jay. In 1789, Madison was elected to the House of Representatives, where he helped frame the Bill of Rights and fought against passage of the Alien and Sedition Acts. In the 1790s, he helped found the Democratic-Republican Party, which ultimately became the Democratic Party. He became Jefferson's secretary of state in 1801.

Madison was elected president in 1808. His first term was marked by tensions with Great Britain, and his conduct of foreign policy was criticized by the Federalists and by his own party. Nevertheless, he was reelected in 1812, the year war was declared on Great Britain. The war that many considered a second American revolution ended with a treaty that settled none of the issues. Madison's most important action after the war was demilitarizing the U.S.-Canadian border.

In 1817, Madison retired to his estate, Montpelier, where he served as an elder statesman, "the last of the fathers." He edited his famous papers on the Constitutional Convention and helped found the University of Virginia, of which he became rector in 1826. He died June 28, 1836.

James Monroe (1817-25)

James Monroe, 5th president, Democratic-Republican, was born on Apr. 28, 1758, in Westmoreland Co., VA, the son of Spence and Eliza Jones Monroe. He entered the College of William and Mary in 1774 but left to serve in the 3d Virginia Regiment during the American Revolution. After the war, he studied law with Thomas Jefferson. In 1782 he was elected to the Virginia House of Delegates, and he served (1783-86) as a delegate to the Confederation Congress. He opposed ratification of the Constitution because it lacked a bill of rights. Monroe was elected to the U.S. Senate in 1790. In 1794 President George Washington appointed Monroe minister to France. He served twice as governor of Virginia (1799-1802, 1811). President Jefferson also sent him to France as minister (1803), and from 1803 to 1807 he served as minister to Great Britain.

In 1816 Monroe was elected president; he was reelected in 1820 with all but one Electoral College vote. His administration became known as the Era of Good Feeling. He obtained Florida from Spain, settled boundary disputes with Britain over Canada, and eliminated border forts. He supported the antislavery position that led to the Missouri Compromise. His most significant contribution was the Monroe Doctrine, which opposed European intervention in the Western Hemisphere and became a cornerstone of U.S. foreign policy.

Although Monroe retired to Oak Hill, VA, financial problems forced him to sell his property and move to New York City. He died there on July 4, 1831.

John Quincy Adams (1825-29)

John Quincy Adams, 6th president, independent Federalist, later Democratic-Republican, was born on July 11, 1767, in Braintree (now Quincy), MA, the son of John and Abigail Adams. His father was the 2d president. He studied abroad and at Harvard University from which he graduated in 1787. In 1803, he was elected to the U.S. Senate. President Monroe chose him as his secretary of state in 1817. In this capacity he negotiated the cession of the Floridas from Spain, supported exclusion of slavery in the Missouri Compromise, and helped formulate the Monroe Doctrine.

In 1824 Adams was elected president by the House of Representatives after he failed to win an Electoral College majority. His expansion of executive powers was strongly opposed, and in the 1828 election he lost to Andrew Jackson. In 1831 he entered the House of Representatives and served 17 years with distinction. He opposed slavery, the annexation of Texas, and the Mexican War. He helped establish the Smithsonian Institution. He suffered a stroke in the House and died in the Speaker's Room on Feb. 23, 1848.

Andrew Jackson (1829-37)

Andrew Jackson, 7th president, Democratic-Republican, later a Democrat, was born on Mar. 15, 1767, in the Waxhaw district, on the border of North Carolina and South Carolina, the son of Andrew and Elizabeth Hutchinson Jackson. At the age of 13, he joined the militia to fight in the American Revolution and was captured. Orphaned at the age of 14, Jackson was brought up by a well-to-do uncle. By age 20, he was practicing law, and he later served as prosecuting attorney in Nashville, TN. In 1796 he helped draft the constitution of Tennessee, and for a year he occupied its one seat in the House of Representatives. The next year he served in the U.S. Senate.

In the War of 1812, Jackson crushed (1814) the Creek Indians at Horseshoe Bend, AL, and, with an army consisting chiefly of backwoodsmen, defeated (1815) General Edward Pakenham's British troops at the Battle of New Orleans. In 1818 he briefly invaded Spanish Florida to quell Seminoles and outlaws who harassed frontier settlements. In 1824 he ran for president against John Quincy Adams. Although he won the most popular and electoral votes, he did not have a majority. The House of Representatives decided the election and chose Adams. In the 1828 election, however, Jackson defeated Adams, carrying the West and the South.

As president, Jackson introduced what became known as the spoils system—rewarding party members with government posts. Perhaps his most controversial act, however, was depositing federal funds in so-called pet banks, those directed by Democratic bankers, rather than in the Bank of the United States. "Let the people rule" was his slogan. In 1832, Jackson killed the congressional caucus for nominating presidential candidates and substituted the national convention. When South Carolina refused to collect imports under his protective tariff, he ordered army and naval forces to Charleston. After leaving office in 1837, he retired to the Hermitage, outside Nashville, where he died on June 8, 1845.

Martin Van Buren (1837-41)

Martin Van Buren, 8th president, Democrat, was born on Dec. 5, 1782, in Kinderhook, NY, the son of Abraham and Maria Hoes Van Buren. After attending local schools, he studied law and became a lawyer at the age of 20. A consummate politician, Van Buren began his career in the New York state senate and then served as state attorney general from 1816 to 1819. He was elected to the U.S. Senate in 1821. He helped swing eastern support to Andrew Jackson in the 1828 election and then served as Jackson's secretary of state from 1829 to 1831. In 1832 he was elected vice president. Known as the Little Magician, Van Buren was extremely influential in Jackson's administration. In the election of 1836 he defeated William Henry Harrison for president and took office as the financial panic of 1837 initiated a nationwide depression. Although he instituted the independent treasury system, his refusal to spend land revenues led to his defeat by William Henry Harrison in the election of 1840. In 1844 he lost the Democratic nomination to James Knox Polk. In 1848 he again ran for president on the Free Soil ticket but lost. He died in Kinderhook on July 24, 1862.

William Henry Harrison (1841)

William Henry Harrison, 9th president, Whig, who served only 31 days, was born on Feb. 9, 1773, in Berkeley, Charles City Co., VA, the son of Benjamin Harrison, a signer of the Declaration of Independence, and of Elizabeth Bassett Harrison. He attended Hampden-Sydney College. Harrison served as secretary of the Northwest Territory in 1798 and was its delegate to the House of Representatives in 1799. He was the first governor of the Indiana Territory and served as superintendent of Indian affairs. With 900 men he put down a Shawnee uprising at Tippecanoe, IN, on Nov. 7, 1811. A generation later, in 1840, he waged a rousing presidential campaign, using the slogan "Tippecanoe and Tyler too." The Tyler of the slogan was his running mate, John Tyler. Although born to one of the wealthiest, most prestigious, and most influential families in Virginia, Harrison was elected president with a "log cabin and hard cider" slogan. He caught pneumonia during the inauguration and died Apr. 4, 1841.

John Tyler (1841-45)

John Tyler, 10th president, independent Whig, was born on Mar. 29, 1790, in Greenway, Charles City Co., VA, the son of John and Mary Armistead Tyler. His father was governor of Virginia (1808-11). Tyler graduated from the College of William and Mary in 1807 and in 1811 was elected to the Virginia legislature. In 1816 he was chosen for the U.S. House of Representatives. He served in the Virginia legislature again from 1823 to 1825, when he was elected governor of Virginia. After a stint in the U.S. Senate (1827-36), he was elected vice president (1840). When William Henry Harrison died only a month after taking office, Tyler succeeded him. Because he was the first person to occupy the presidency without having been elected to that office, he was referred to as "His Accidency." Tyler gained passage of the Preemption Act of 1841, which gave squatters on government land the right to buy 160 acres at the minimum auction price. His last act as president was to sign the resolution annexing Texas. Tyler accepted renomination in 1844 from some Democrats but withdrew in favor of the official party candidate, James K. Polk. He died in Richmond, VA, on Jan. 18, 1862.

James Knox Polk (1845-49)

James Knox Polk, 11th president, Democrat, was born on Nov. 2, 1795, in Mecklenburg Co., NC, the son of Samuel and Jane Knox Polk. He graduated from the University of North Carolina in 1818 and served in the Tennessee state legislature from 1823 to 1825. He served in the U.S. House of Representatives from 1825 to 1839, the last 4 years as Speaker. He was governor of Tennessee from 1839 to 1841. In 1844, after the Democratic National Convention became deadlocked, it nominated Polk, who thus became the nation's first "dark horse" candidate for president. He was nominated primarily because he was known to favor annexation of Texas. As president, Polk reestablished the independent treasury system originated by Van Buren. He was so intent on acquiring California from Mexico that he sent troops under Zachary Taylor to the Mexican border and, when Mexicans attacked, declared that a state of war existed. The Mexican War ended with the annexation of California and much of the Southwest as part of America's "manifest destiny." Polk compromised on the Oregon boundary ("54-40 or fight!") by accepting the 49th parallel and yielding Vancouver Island to the British. A few weeks after leaving office, Polk died in Nashville, TN, on June 15, 1849.

Zachary Taylor (1849-50)

Zachary Taylor, 12th president, Whig, who served only 16 months, was born on Nov. 24, 1784, in Orange Co., VA, the son of Richard and Sarah Strother Taylor. He grew up on his father's plantation near Louisville, KY, where he was educated by private tutors. In 1808 Taylor joined the regular army and was commissioned first lieutenant. He fought in the War of 1812, the Black Hawk War (1832), and the second Seminole War (beginning in 1837). He was called "Old Rough and Ready." In 1846 President Polk sent him with an army to the Rio Grande. When the Mexicans attacked him, Polk declared war. Outnumbered 4-1, Taylor defeated (1847) Santa Anna at Buena Vista. A national hero, he received the Whig nomination in 1848 and was elected president, even though he had never bothered to vote. He resumed the spoils system and, though a slaveholder, worked to admit California as a free state. He fell ill and died in office on July 9, 1850.

Millard Fillmore (1850-53)

Millard Fillmore, 13th president, Whig, was born on Jan. 7, 1800, in Cayuga Co., NY, the son of Nathaniel and Phoebe Millard Fillmore. Although he had little schooling, he became a law clerk at the age of 22 and a year later was admitted to the bar. He was elected to the New York state assembly in 1828 and served until 1831. From 1833 until 1835 and again from 1837 to 1843, he represented his district in the U.S. House of Representatives. He opposed the entrance of Texas as a slave territory and voted for a protective tariff. In 1844 he was defeated for governor of New York. In 1848 he was elected vice president, and he succeeded as president after Taylor's death. Fillmore favored the Compromise of 1850 and signed the Fugitive Slave Law. His policies pleased neither expansionists nor slaveholders, and he was not renominated in 1852. In 1856 he was nominated by the American (Know-Nothing) Party, but despite the support of the Whigs, he was defeated by James Buchanan. He died in Buffalo, NY, on Mar. 8, 1874.

Franklin Pierce (1853-57)

Franklin Pierce, 14th president, Democrat, was born on Nov. 23, 1804, in Hillsboro, NH, the son of Benjamin Pierce, an American Revolutionary War general and governor of New Hampshire, and Anna Kendrick. He graduated from Bowdoin College in 1824 and was admitted to the bar in 1827. He was elected to the New Hampshire state legislature in 1829 and was chosen Speaker in 1831. He went to the U.S. House of Representatives in 1833 and was elected a U.S. senator in 1837. He enlisted in the Mexican War and became brigadier general under Gen. Winfield Scott. In 1852 Pierce was nominated as the Democratic presidential candidate on the 49th ballot. He decisively defeated Gen. Scott, his Whig opponent, in the election. Although against slavery, Pierce was influenced by pro-slavery Southerners. He supported the controversial Kansas-Nebraska Act, which left the question of slavery in the new territories of Kansas and Nebraska to popular vote. Pierce signed a reciprocity treaty with Canada and approved the Gadsden Purchase, a border area on a proposed railroad route, from Mexico. Denied renomination by the Democrats, he spent most of his remaining years in Concord, NH, where he died on Oct. 8, 1869.

James Buchanan (1857-61)

James Buchanan, 15th president, Federalist, later Democrat, was born on Apr. 23, 1791, near Mercersburg, PA, the son of James and Elizabeth Speer Buchanan. He graduated from Dickinson College in 1809 and was admitted to the bar in 1812. He fought in the War of 1812 as a volunteer. He was twice elected to the Pennsylvania general assembly, and in 1821 he entered the U.S. House of Representatives. After briefly serving (1832-33) as minister to Russia, he was elected U.S. senator from Pennsylvania. As Polk's secretary of state (1845-49), he ended the Oregon dispute with Britain and supported the Mexican War and annexation of Texas. As minister to Great Britain, he signed the Ostend Manifesto (1854), declaring a U.S. right to take Cuba by force should efforts to purchase it fail. Nominated by Democrats, Buchanan was elected president in 1856. On slavery he favored popular sovereignty and choice by state constitutions but did not consistently uphold this position. He denied the right of states to secede but opposed coercion and attempted to keep peace by not provoking secessionists. Buchanan left office having failed to deal decisively with the situation. He died at Wheatland, his estate, near Lancaster, PA, on June 1, 1868.

Abraham Lincoln (1861-65)

Abraham Lincoln, 16th president, Republican, was born on Feb. 12, 1809, in a log cabin on a farm then in Hardin Co., KY, now in Larue, the son of Thomas and Nancy Hanks Lincoln. The Lincolns moved to Spencer Co., IN, near Gentryville, when Abe was 7. After Abe's mother died, his father married (1819) Mrs. Sarah Bush Johnston. In 1830 the family moved to Macon Co., IL.

Defeated in 1832 in a race for the state legislature, Lincoln was elected on the Whig ticket 2 years later and served in the lower house from 1834 to 1842. In 1837 Lincoln was admitted to the bar and became partner in a Springfield, IL, law office. He soon won recognition as an effective and resourceful attorney. In 1846, he was elected to the House of Representatives, where he attracted attention during a single term for his opposition to the Mexican War and his position on slavery. In 1856 he campaigned for the newly founded Republican Party, and in 1858 he became its senatorial candidate against Stephen A. Douglas. Although he lost the election, Lincoln gained national recognition from his debates with Douglas.

In 1860, Lincoln was nominated for president by the Republican Party on a platform of restricting slavery. He ran against Douglas, a northern Democrat; John C. Breckinridge, a Southern proslavery Democrat; and John Bell, of the Constitutional Union Party. As a result of Lincoln's winning the election, South Carolina seceded from the Union on Dec. 20, 1860, followed in 1861 by 10 other Southern states.

The Civil War erupted when Fort Sumter, which Lincoln decided to resupply, was attacked by Confederate forces on Apr. 12, 1861. Lincoln called successfully for recruits from the North. On Sept. 22, 1862, 5 days after the Battle of Antietam, Lincoln announced that slaves in territory then in rebellion would be free Jan. 1, 1863, the date of the Emancipation Proclamation. His speeches, including his Gettysburg and Inaugural addresses, are remembered for their eloquence.

Lincoln was reelected, in 1864, over Gen. George B. McClellan, Democrat. Lee surrendered on Apr. 9, 1865. On Apr. 14, Lincoln was shot by actor John Wilkes Booth in Ford's Theater, in Washington, DC. He died the next day.

Andrew Johnson (1865-69)

Andrew Johnson, 17th president, Democrat, was born on Dec. 29, 1808, in Raleigh, NC, the son of Jacob and Mary McDonough Johnson. He was apprenticed to a tailor as a youth, but ran away after two years and eventually settled in Greeneville, TN. He became popular with the townspeople and in 1829 was elected councilman and later mayor. In 1835 he was sent to the state general assembly. In 1843 he was elected to the U.S. House of Representatives, where he served for 10 years. Johnson was governor of Tennessee from 1853 to 1857, when he was elected to the U.S. Senate. He supported John C. Breckinridge against Lincoln in the 1860 election. Although Johnson had held slaves, he opposed secession and tried to prevent Tennessee from seceding. In Mar. 1862, Lincoln appointed him military governor of occupied Tennessee.

In 1864, in order to balance Lincoln's ticket with a Southern Democrat, the Republicans nominated Johnson for vice president. He was elected vice president with Lincoln and then succeeded to the presidency upon Lincoln's death. Soon afterward, in a controversy with Congress over the president's power over the South, he proclaimed an amnesty to all Confederates, except certain leaders, if they would ratify the 13th Amendment abolishing slavery. States doing so added anti-

Negro provisions that enraged Congress, which restored military control over the South. When Johnson removed Edwin M. Stanton, secretary of war, without notifying the Senate, the House, in Feb. 1868, impeached him. Ostensibly charging him with thereby having violated the Tenure of Office Act, the House was actually responding to his opposition to harsh congressional Reconstruction, expressed in repeated vetoes. He was tried by the Senate, and in May, in two separate votes on different counts, was acquitted, both times by only one vote. Johnson was denied renomination but remained politically active. He was re-elected to the Senate in 1874. Johnson died July 31, 1875, at Carter Station, TN.

Ulysses Simpson Grant (1869-77)

Ulysses S. Grant, 18th president, Republican, was born on Apr. 27, 1822, in Point Pleasant, OH, the son of Jesse R. and Hannah Simpson Grant. The next year the family moved to Georgetown, OH. Grant was named Hiram Ulysses, but on entering West Point in 1839, his name was put down as Ulysses Simpson, and he adopted it. He graduated in 1843. During the Mexican War, Grant served under both Gen. Zachary Taylor and Gen. Winfield Scott. In 1854, he resigned his commission because of loneliness and drinking problems, and in the following years he engaged in generally unsuccessful farming and business ventures. With the start of the Civil War, he was named colonel and then brigadier general of the Illinois Volunteers. He took Forts Henry and Donelson and fought at Shiloh. His brilliant campaign against Vicksburg and his victory at Chattanooga made him so prominent that Lincoln placed him in command of all Union armies. Grant accepted Lee's surrender at Appomattox Court House on Apr. 9, 1865. President Johnson appointed Grant secretary of war when he suspended Stanton, but Grant was not confirmed. He was nominated for president by the Republicans in 1868 and elected over Horatio Seymour, Democrat. The 15th Amendment, amnesty bill, and the peaceful settlement of disputes with Great Britain were events of his administration. The Liberal Republicans and Democrats opposed him with Horace Greeley in the 1872 election, but Grant was reelected. His second administration was marked by many scandals, including widespread corruption in the Treasury Department and the Indian Service. An attempt by the Stalwarts (Old Guard Republicans) to nominate him in 1880 failed. In 1884 the collapse of Grant & Ward, an investment firm in which he was a partner, left him penniless. He wrote his personal memoirs while ill with cancer and completed them shortly before his death at Mt. McGregor, NY, on July 23, 1885.

Rutherford Birchard Hayes (1877-81)

Rutherford B. Hayes, 19th president, Republican, was born on Oct. 4, 1822, in Delaware, OH, the son of Rutherford and Sophia Birchard Hayes. He was reared by his uncle, Sardis Birchard. Hayes graduated from Kenyon College in 1842 and from Harvard Law School in 1845. He practiced law in Lower Sandusky (now Fremont), OH, and was city solicitor of Cincinnati from 1858 to 1861. During the Civil War, he was major of the 23d Ohio Volunteers. He was wounded several times, and by the end of the war he had risen to the rank of brevet major general. While serving (1865-67) in the U.S. House of Representatives, Hayes supported Reconstruction and Johnson's impeachment. He was twice elected governor of Ohio (1867, 1869). After losing a race for the U.S. House in 1872, he was reelected governor of Ohio in 1875. In 1876 he was nominated for president and believed he had lost the election to Samuel J. Tilden, Democrat. But a few Southern states submitted 2 sets of electoral votes, and the result was in dispute. An electoral commission, appointed by Congress and consisting of 8 Republicans and 7 Democrats, awarded all disputed votes to Hayes, allowing him to become president by one electoral vote. Hayes, keeping a promise to southerners, withdrew troops from areas still occupied in the South, ending the era of Reconstruction. He proposed civil service reforms, alienating those favoring the spoils system, and advocated repeal of the Tenure of Office Act restricting presidential power to dismiss officials. He supported sound money and specie payments. Hayes died in Fremont, OH, on Jan. 17, 1893.

James Abram Garfield (1881)

James A. Garfield, 20th president, Republican, was born on Nov. 19, 1831, in Orange, Cuyahoga Co., OH, the son of Abram and Eliza Ballou Garfield. His father died in 1833, and he was reared in poverty by his mother. He worked as a canal bargeman, a farmer, and a carpenter and managed to secure a college education. He taught at Hiram College and later became principal. In 1859 he was elected to the Ohio legislature. Antislavery and antisecession, he volunteered for military service in the Civil War, becoming colonel of the 42d Ohio Infantry and brigadier in 1862. He fought at Shiloh, was chief of staff for Gen. William Starke Rosecrans, and was made major general for gallantry at Chickamauga. He entered Congress as a radical Republican in 1863, calling for execution or exile of Confederate leaders, but he moderated his views after the Civil War. On the electoral commission in 1877 he voted for Hayes against Tilden on strict party lines. He was a senator-elect in 1880 when he became the Republican nominee for president. He was chosen as a compromise over Gen. Grant, James G. Blaine, and John Sherman, and won election despite some bitterness among Grant's supporters. On July 2, 1881, Garfield was shot and seriously wounded by a mentally disturbed office-seeker, Charles J. Guiteau, while entering a railroad station in Washington, DC. He died on Sept. 19, 1881, in Elberon, NJ.

Chester Alan Arthur (1881-85)

Chester A. Arthur, 21st president, Republican, was born on Oct. 5, 1829, in Fairfield, VT, the son of William and Malvina Stone Arthur. He graduated from Union College in 1848, taught school in Vermont, then studied law and opened a practice in New York City. In 1853 he argued in a fugitive slave case that slaves transported through New York state were thereby freed. In 1871, he was appointed to the lucrative post of collector of the Port of New York. President Hayes, an opponent of the spoils system, forced Arthur to resign in 1878. This made the New York machine strong enemies of Hayes. Arthur and the Stalwarts (Old Guard Republicans) tried to nominate Grant for a 3d term in 1880. When Garfield was nominated, Arthur was nominated for vice president in the interests of harmony. Upon Garfield's assassination, Arthur became president. Despite his past connections, he signed civil service reform legislation. Arthur tried to dissuade Congress from enacting the high protective tariff of 1883. He was defeated for renomination in 1884 by James G. Blaine. He died in New York City on Nov. 18, 1886.

Grover Cleveland (1885-89; 1893-97)

(According to a ruling of the State Dept., Grover Cleveland should be counted as both the 22d and the 24th president, because his 2 terms were not consecutive.)

Grover Cleveland, Democrat, was born Stephen Grover Cleveland on Mar. 18, 1837, in Caldwell, NJ, the son of Richard F. and Ann Neal Cleveland. When he was a small boy, his family moved to New York. Prevented by his father's death from attending college, he studied by himself and was admitted to the bar in Buffalo, NY, in 1859. In succession he became assistant district attorney (1863), sheriff (1871), mayor (1881), and governor of New York (1882). He was an independent, honest administrator who hated corruption. He was nominated for president over Tammany Hall opposition in 1884 and defeated Republican James G. Blaine. As president, he enlarged the civil service and vetoed many pension raids on the Treasury. In the 1888 election he was defeated by Benjamin Harrison, although his popular vote was larger. Reelected over Harrison in 1892, he faced a money crisis brought about by a lowered gold reserve, circulation of paper, and exorbitant silver purchases under the Sherman Silver Purchase Act. He obtained a repeal of the Sherman Act, but was unable to secure effective tariff reform. A severe economic depression and labor troubles racked his administration, but he refused to interfere in business matters and rejected Jacob Coxey's demand for unemployment relief. In 1894, he broke the Pullman strike. In 1896, the Democrats repudiated his administration and chose silverite William Jennings Bryan as their candidate. Cleveland died in Princeton, NJ, on June 24, 1908.

Benjamin Harrison (1889-93)

Benjamin Harrison, 23d president, Republican, was born on Aug. 20, 1833, in North Bend, OH, the son of John Scott and Elizabeth Irwin Harrison. His great-grandfather, Benjamin Harrison, was a signer of the Declaration of Independence; his grandfather, William Henry Harrison, was 9th president; his father was a member of Congress. He attended school on his father's farm and graduated from Miami University in Oxford, OH, in 1852. He was admitted to the bar in 1854 and practiced in Indianapolis. During the Civil War, he rose to the rank of brevet brigadier general and fought at Kennesaw Mountain, at Peachtree Creek, at Nashville, and in the Atlanta campaign. He lost the 1876 gubernatorial election in Indiana but succeeded in becoming a U.S. senator in 1881. In 1888 he defeated Cleveland for president despite receiving fewer popular votes. As president, he expanded the pension list and signed the McKinley high tariff bill, the Sherman Antitrust Act, and the Sherman Silver Purchase Act. During his administration, 6 states were admitted to the Union. He was defeated for reelection in 1892. He died in Indianapolis on Mar. 13, 1901.

William McKinley (1897-1901)

William McKinley, 25th president, Republican, was born on Jan. 29, 1843, in Niles, OH, the son of William and Nancy Allison McKinley. McKinley briefly attended Allegheny College. When the Civil War broke out in 1861, he enlisted and served for the duration. He rose to captain and in 1865 was made brevet major. After studying law in Albany, NY, he opened (1867) a law office in Canton, OH. He served twice in the U.S. House of Representatives (1877-83; 1885-91) and led the fight there for the McKinley Tariff, which was passed in 1890. However, he was not reelected to the House as a result. He served two terms (1892-96) as governor of Ohio. In 1896 he was elected president as a proponent of a protective tariff and sound money (gold standard), over William Jennings Bryan, the Democrat and a proponent of free silver. McKinley was reluctant to intervene in Cuba, but the loss of the battleship *Maine* at Havana crystallized opinion. He demanded Spain's withdrawal from Cuba; Spain made some concessions, but Congress announced a state of war as of Apr. 21, 1898. He was reelected in the 1900 campaign, defeating Bryan's anti-imperialist arguments with the promise of a "full dinner pail." McKinley was respected for his conciliatory nature and for his conservative stance on business issues. On Sept. 6, 1901, while welcoming citizens at the Pan-American Exposition, in Buffalo, NY, he was shot by Leon Czolgosz, an anarchist. He died Sept. 14.

Theodore Roosevelt (1901-9)

Theodore Roosevelt, 26th president, Republican, was born on Oct. 27, 1858, in New York City, the son of Theodore and Martha Bulloch Roosevelt. He was a 5th cousin of Franklin D. Roosevelt and an uncle of Eleanor Roosevelt. Roosevelt graduated from Harvard University in 1880. He attended Columbia Law School briefly but abandoned the study of law to enter politics. He was elected to the New York state assembly in 1881 and served until 1884. He spent the next 2 years ranching and hunting in the Dakota Territory. Back in politics in 1886, he ran unsuccessfully for mayor of New York City. He was Civil Service commissioner in Washington, DC, from 1889 to 1895. From 1895 to 1897, he served as New York City's police commissioner. He was assistant secretary of the navy under McKinley. The Spanish-American War made Roosevelt a nationally known figure. He organized the 1st U.S. Volunteer Cavalry (Rough Riders) and, as lieutenant colonel, led the charge up Kettle Hill in San Juan. Elected New York governor in 1898, he fought the spoils system and achieved taxation of corporation franchises.

Nominated for vice president in 1900, he became the nation's youngest president when McKinley was assassinated. He was reelected in 1904. As president he fought corruption of politics by big business, dissolved the Northern Securities Co. and others for violating antitrust laws, intervened in the 1902 coal strike on behalf of the public, obtained the Elkins Law (1903) forbidding rebates to favored corporations, and helped pass the Hepburn Railway Rate Act of 1906 (extending Jurisdiction of the Interstate Commerce Commission). He helped obtain passage of the Pure Food and Drug Act (1906), and employers' liability laws. Roosevelt vigorously organized conservation efforts. He mediated (1905) the peace between Japan and Russia, for which he won the Nobel Peace Prize. He abetted the 1903 revolution in Panama that led to U.S. acquisition of territory for the Panama Canal.

In 1908 Roosevelt obtained the nomination of William H. Taft, who was elected. Feeling that Taft had abandoned his policies, Roosevelt unsuccessfully sought the nomination in 1912. He bolted the party and ran on the Progressive "Bull Moose" ticket against Taft and Woodrow Wilson, splitting the Republicans and ensuring Wilson's election. He was shot during the campaign but recovered. In 1916, after unsuccessfully seeking the presidential nomination for himself, Roosevelt supported the Republican candidate, Charles E. Hughes. A strong friend of Britain, he fought for American intervention in World War I. He wrote some 40 books on many topics; his book *The Winning of the West* is perhaps best known. He died Jan. 6, 1919, at Sagamore Hill, Oyster Bay, NY.

William Howard Taft (1909-13)

William Howard Taft, 27th president, Republican, and 10th chief justice of the U.S., was born on Sept. 15, 1857, in Cincinnati, OH, the son of Alphonso and Louisa Maria Torrey Taft. His father was secretary of war and attorney general in Grant's cabinet and minister to Austria and Russia under Arthur. Taft graduated from Yale in 1878 and from Cincinnati Law School in 1880. After working as a law reporter for Cincinnati newspapers, he served as assistant prosecuting attorney (1881-82), assistant county solicitor (1885), judge, superior court (1887), U.S. solicitor-general (1890), and federal circuit judge (1892). In 1900 he became head of the U.S. Philippines Commission and was the first civil governor of the Philippines (1901-4). In 1904 he served as secretary of war, and in 1906 he was sent to Cuba to help avert a threatened revolution. He was groomed for the presidency by Theodore Roosevelt and elected over William Jennings Bryan in 1908. Taft vigorously continued Roosevelt's trust-busting, instituted the Department of Labor, and drafted the amendments calling for direct election of senators and the income tax. His tariff and conservation policies angered progressives. Although renominated in 1912, he was opposed by Roosevelt, who ran on the Progressive Party ticket; the result was Democrat Woodrow Wilson's election. Taft, with some reservations, supported the League of Nations. After leaving office, he was professor of constitutional law at Yale (1913-21) and chief justice of the U.S. (1921-30). Taft was the only person in U.S. history to have been both president and chief justice. Illness forced him to resign from the Court in Feb. 1930, and he died in Washington, DC, on Mar. 8, 1930.

Woodrow Wilson (1913-21)

Thomas Woodrow Wilson, 28th president, Democrat, was born on Dec. 28, 1856, in Staunton, VA, the son of Joseph Ruggles and Janet (Jessie) Woodrow Wilson. He grew up in Georgia and South Carolina. He attended Davidson College in North Carolina before graduating from Princeton University in 1879. He studied law at the University of Virginia and then studied political science at Johns Hopkins University, where he received his PhD in 1886. He taught at Bryn Mawr (1885-88) and then at Wesleyan (1888-90) before joining the faculty at Princeton. He was president of Princeton from 1902 until 1910, when he was elected governor of New Jersey. In 1912 he was nominated for president with the aid of William Jennings Bryan, who sought to block James "Champ" Clark and Tammany Hall. Wilson won the election because the Republican vote for Taft was split by the Progressives.

As president, Wilson protected American interests in revolutionary Mexico and fought for American rights on the high seas. He oversaw the creation of the Federal Reserve system, cut the tariff, and developed a reputation as a reformer. His sharp warnings to Germany led to the resignation of his secretary of state, Bryan, a pacifist. In 1916 he was reelected by a slim margin with the slogan, "He kept us out of war," although his attempts to mediate in the war failed. After several American ships had been sunk by the Germans, he secured a declaration of war against Germany on Apr. 6, 1917.

Wilson outlined his peace program on Jan. 8, 1918, in the Fourteen Points, a state paper that had worldwide influence. He enunciated a doctrine of self-determination for the settlement of territorial disputes. The Germans accepted his terms and an armistice on Nov. 11, 1918.

Wilson went to Paris to help negotiate the peace treaty, the crux of which he considered the League of Nations. The Senate demanded reservations that would not make the U.S. subordinate to the votes of other nations in case of war. Wilson refused to consider any reservations and toured the country to get support. He suffered a stroke in Oct. 1919. An invalid for months, he clung to his executive powers while his wife and doctors effectively functioned as president.

Wilson was awarded the 1919 Nobel Peace Prize, but the treaty embodying the League of Nations was ultimately rejected by the Senate in 1920. He left the White House in Mar. 1921. He died in Washington, DC, on Feb. 3, 1924.

Warren Gamaliel Harding (1921-23)

Warren Gamaliel Harding, 29th president, Republican, was born on Nov. 2, 1865, near Corsica (now Blooming Grove), OH, the son of George Tyron and Phoebe Elizabeth Dickerson Harding. He attended Ohio Central College, studied law, and became editor and publisher of a county newspaper. He entered the political arena as state senator (1901-4) and then served as lieutenant governor (1904-6). In 1910 he ran unsuccessfully for governor of Ohio; then in 1914 he was elected to the U.S. Senate. In the Senate he voted for antistrike legislation, woman suffrage, and the Volstead Prohibition Enforcement Act over President Wilson's veto. He opposed the League of Nations. In 1920 he was nominated for president and defeated James M. Cox in the election. The Republicans capitalized on war weariness and fear that Wilson's League of Nations would curtail U.S. sovereignty. Harding stressed a return to "normalcy" and worked for tariff revision and the repeal of excess profits law and high income taxes. His secretary of interior, Albert B. Fall, became involved in the Teapot Dome scandal. As rumors began to circulate about the corruption in his administration, Harding became ill while returning from a trip to Alaska, and he died in San Francisco on Aug. 2, 1923.

Calvin Coolidge (1923-29)

John Calvin Coolidge, 30th president, Republican, was born on July 4, 1872, in Plymouth, VT, the son of John Calvin and Victoria J. Moor Coolidge. Coolidge graduated from Amherst College in 1895. He entered Republican state politics and served as mayor of Northampton, MA, as state senator, as lieutenant governor, and, in 1919, as governor. In Sept. 1919, Coolidge attained national prominence by calling out the state guard in the Boston police strike. He declared: "There is no right to strike against the public safety by anybody, anywhere, anytime." This brought his name before the Republican convention of 1920, where he was nominated for vice president. He succeeded to the presidency on Harding's death. As president, he opposed the League of Nations and the soldiers' bonus bill, which was passed over his veto. In 1924 he was elected by a huge majority. He substantially reduced the national debt. He twice vetoed the McNary-Haugen farm bill, which would have provided relief to financially hard-pressed farmers. With Republicans eager to renominate him, Coolidge simply announced, Aug. 2, 1927: "I do not choose to run for president in 1928." He died in Northampton, MA, on Jan. 5, 1933.

Herbert Clark Hoover (1929-33)

Herbert Hoover, 31st president, Republican, was born on Aug. 10, 1874, in West Branch, IA, the son of Jesse Clark and Hulda Randall Minthorn Hoover. Hoover grew up in Indian Territory (now Oklahoma) and Oregon and graduated from Stanford University with a degree in engineering in 1895. He worked briefly with the U.S. Geological Survey and then managed mines in Australia, Asia, Europe, and Africa. While chief engineer of imperial mines in China, he directed food relief for victims of the Boxer Rebellion. He gained a reputation not only as an engineer but as a humanitarian as he directed the American Relief Committee, London (1914-15) and the U.S. Commission for Relief in Belgium (1915-19). He was U.S. Food Administrator (1917-19), American Relief Administrator (1918-23), and in charge of Russian Relief (1918-23). He served as secretary of commerce under both Harding and Coolidge. Some historians believe that he was the most effective secretary of commerce ever to hold that office.

In 1928 Hoover was elected president over Alfred E. Smith. In 1929 the stock market crashed, and the economy collapsed. During the depression, Hoover inaugurated some government assistance programs, but he was opposed to administration of aid through a federal bureaucracy. As the effects of the depression continued, he was defeated in the 1932 election by Franklin D. Roosevelt. President Truman named him coordinator of the European Food Program (1946) and chairman of the Commission on Organization of the Executive Branch (1947-49; 1953-55). Hoover died in New York City on Oct. 20, 1964.

Franklin Delano Roosevelt (1933-45)

Franklin D. Roosevelt, 32d president, Democrat, was born on Jan. 30, 1882, near Hyde Park, NY, the son of James and Sara Delano Roosevelt. He graduated from Harvard University in 1904. He attended Columbia University Law School without taking a degree and was admitted to the New York state bar in 1907. His political career began when he was elected to the New York state senate in 1910. In 1913 President Wilson appointed him assistant secretary of the navy, a post he held during World War I.

In 1920 Roosevelt ran for vice president with James Cox and was defeated. From 1921 to 1928 he worked in his New York law office and was also vice president of Fidelity & Deposit Co. of Maryland. In Aug. 1921, he was stricken with poliomyelitis, which left his legs paralyzed. As a result of therapy he was able to stand, or walk a few steps, with the aid of leg braces.

Roosevelt served 2 terms as governor of New York (1929-33). In 1932, W. G. McAdoo, pledged to John N. Garner, threw his votes to Roosevelt, who was nominated for president. The depression and the promise to repeal Prohibition ensured his election. He asked for emergency powers, proclaimed the New Deal, and put into effect a vast number of administrative changes. Foremost was the use of public funds for relief and public works, resulting in deficit financing. He greatly expanded the federal government's regulation of business and by an excess profits tax and progressive income taxes produced a redistribution of earnings on an unprecedented scale. The Wagner Act gave labor many advantages in organizing and collective bargaining. He promoted legislation establishing the Social Security system. He was the last president inaugurated on Mar. 4 (1933) and the first inaugurated on Jan. 20 (1937).

Roosevelt was the first president to use radio for "fireside chats." When the Supreme Court nullified some New Deal laws, he sought power to "pack" the court with additional justices, but Congress refused to give him the authority. He was the first president to break the "no 3d term" tradition (1940) and was elected to a 4th term in 1944, despite failing health. Roosevelt was openly hostile to fascist governments before World War II and launched a lend-lease program on behalf of the Allies. With British Prime Min. Winston Churchill he wrote a declaration of principles to be followed after Nazi defeat (the Atlantic Charter of Aug. 14, 1941) and urged the Four Freedoms (freedom of speech, of worship, from want, from fear) Jan. 6, 1941. When Japan attacked Pearl Harbor on Dec. 7, 1941, the U.S. entered the war. Roosevelt conferred with allied heads of state at Casablanca (Jan. 1943), Quebec (Aug. 1943), Tehran (Nov.-Dec. 1943), Cairo (Nov. and Dec. 1943), and Yalta (Feb. 1945). He did not, however, see the end of the war. He died of a cerebral hemorrhage in Warm Springs, GA, on Apr. 12, 1945.

Harry S. Truman (1945-53)

Harry S. Truman, 33d president, Democrat, was born on May 8, 1884, in Lamar, MO, the son of John Anderson and Martha Ellen Young Truman. A family disagreement on whether his middle name should be Shippe or Solomon, after names of 2 grandfathers, resulted in his using only the middle initial S. After graduating from high school in Independence, MO, he worked (1901) for the *Kansas City Star,* as a railroad timekeeper, and as a clerk in Kansas City banks until about 1905. He ran his family's farm from 1906 to 1917. He served in France during World War I. After the war he opened a haberdashery shop, was a judge on the Jackson Co. Court (1922-24), and attended Kansas City School of Law (1923-25).

Truman was elected to the U.S. Senate in 1934 and reelected in 1940. In 1944, with Roosevelt's backing, he was nominated for vice president and elected. On Roosevelt's death in 1945, Truman became president. In 1948, in a famous upset victory, he defeated Republican Thomas E. Dewey to win election to a new term.

Truman authorized the first uses of the atomic bomb (Hiroshima and Nagasaki, Aug. 6 and 9, 1945), bringing World War II to a rapid end. He was responsible for what came to be called the Truman Doctrine (to aid nations such as Greece and Turkey, threatened by Communist takeover), and his strong commitment to NATO and to the Marshall Plan helped bring them about. In 1948-49, he broke a Soviet blockade of West Berlin with a massive airlift. When Communist North Korea invaded South Korea (June 1950), he won UN approval for a "police action" and sent in forces under Gen. Douglas MacArthur. When MacArthur opposed his policy of limited objectives, Truman removed him.

Truman was responsible for a higher minimum-wage, increased Social Security, and aid-for-housing laws. He died in Kansas City, MO, on Dec. 26, 1972.

Dwight David Eisenhower (1953-61)

Dwight D. Eisenhower, 34th president, Republican, was born on Oct. 14, 1890, in Denison, TX, the son of David Jacob and Ida Elizabeth Stover Eisenhower. He grew up on a small farm in Abilene, KS, and graduated from West Point in 1915. He was on the staff of Gen. Douglas MacArthur in the Philippines from 1935 to 1939. In 1942, he was made commander of Allied forces landing in North Africa; the next year he was made full general. He became supreme Allied commander in Europe that same year and as such led the Normandy invasion (June 6, 1944). He was given the rank of general of the army on Dec. 20, 1944, which was made permanent in 1946. On May 7, 1945, Eisenhower received the surrender of Germany at Rheims. He returned to the U.S. to serve as chief of staff (1945-48). His war memoir, *Crusade in Europe* (1948), was a best-seller. In 1948 he became president of Columbia University; in 1950 he became Commander of NATO forces.

Eisenhower resigned from the army and was nominated for president by the Republicans in 1952. He defeated Adlai E. Stevenson in the 1952 election and again in 1956. Eisenhower called himself a moderate, favored the "free market system" vs. government price and wage controls, kept government out of labor disputes, reorganized the defense establishment, and promoted missile programs. He continued foreign aid, sped the end of the Korean War, endorsed Taiwan and SE Asia defense treaties, backed the UN in condemning the Anglo-French raid on Egypt, and advocated the "open skies" policy of mutual inspection with the USSR. He sent U.S. troops into Little Rock, AR, in Sept. 1957, during the segregation crisis.

Eisenhower died on Mar. 28, 1969, in Washington, DC.

John Fitzgerald Kennedy (1961-63)

John F. Kennedy, 35th president, Democrat, was born on May 29, 1917, in Brookline, MA, the son of Joseph P. and Rose Fitzgerald Kennedy. He graduated from Harvard University in 1940. While serving in the navy (1941-45), he commanded a PT boat in the Solomons and won the Navy and Marine Corps Medal. In 1956, while recovering from spinal surgery, he wrote *Profiles in Courage,* which won a Pulitzer Prize in 1957. He served in the House of Representatives from 1947 to 1953 and was elected to the Senate in 1952 and again in 1958. In 1960, Kennedy won the Democratic nomination for president and narrowly defeated Republican Vice Pres. Richard M. Nixon Kennedy was the youngest president ever elected and the first Roman Catholic.

In Apr. 1961, the new Kennedy administration suffered a severe setback when an invasion force of anti-Castro Cubans, trained and directed by the U.S. Central Intelligence Agency, failed to establish a beachhead at the Bay of Pigs in Cuba. By the same token, one of Kennedy's most important acts as president was his successful demand on Oct. 22, 1962, that the Soviet Union dismantle its missile bases in Cuba. Kennedy also defied Soviet attempts to force the Allies out of Berlin. He started the Peace Corps, and he backed civil rights and expanded medical care for the aged. Space exploration was greatly developed during his administration.

On Nov. 22, 1963, Kennedy was assassinated while riding in a motorcade in Dallas, TX.

Lyndon Baines Johnson (1963-69)

Lyndon B. Johnson, 36th president, Democrat, was born on Aug. 27, 1908, near Stonewall, TX, the son of Sam Ealy and Rebekah Baines Johnson. He graduated from Southwest Texas State Teachers College in 1930 and attended Georgetown University Law School. He taught public speaking in Houston (1930-31) and then served as secretary to Rep. R. M. Kleberg (1931-35). In 1937 Johnson won an election to fill the vacancy caused by the death of a U.S. representative and in 1938 was elected to the full term, after which he returned for 4 terms. During 1941 and 1942 he also served in the Navy in the Pacific, earning a Silver Star for bravery. He was elected U.S. senator in 1948 and reelected in 1954. He became Democratic leader of the Senate in 1953. Johnson had strong support for the Democratic presidential nomination at the 1960 convention, where the nominee, John F. Kennedy, asked him to run for vice president. His campaigning helped overcome religious bias against Kennedy in the South.

Johnson became president when Kennedy was assassinated. He was elected to a full term in 1964. Johnson's domestic program was of considerable importance. He won passage of major civil rights, anti-poverty, aid to education, and health-care (Medicare, Medicaid) legislation—the "Great Society" program. However, his escalation of the war in Vietnam came to overshadow the achievements of his administration. In the face of increasing division in the nation and in his own party over his handling of the war, Johnson declined to seek another term.

Johnson died on Jan. 22, 1973, in San Antonio, TX.

Richard Milhous Nixon (1969-74)

Richard M. Nixon, 37th president, Republican, was born on Jan. 9, 1913, in Yorba Linda, CA, the son of Francis Anthony and Hannah Milhous Nixon. He graduated from Whittier College in 1934 and from Duke University Law School in 1937. After practicing law in Whittier and serving briefly in the Office of Price Administration in 1942, he entered the navy and served in the South Pacific. Nixon was elected to the House of Representatives in 1946 and 1948. He achieved prominence as the House Un-American Activities Committee member who forced the showdown leading to the Alger Hiss perjury conviction. In 1950 he was elected to the Senate.

Nixon was elected vice president in the Eisenhower landslides of 1952 and 1956. He won the Republican nomination for president in 1960 but was narrowly defeated by John F. Kennedy. He ran unsuccessfully for governor of California in 1962. In 1968 he again won the GOP presidential nomination, then defeated Hubert Humphrey for the presidency.

Nixon appointed 4 Supreme Court justices, including the chief justice, moving the court to the right, and as a "new federalist" sought to shift responsibility to state and local governments. He dramatically altered relations with China, which he visited in 1972—the first president to do so. With foreign affairs adviser Henry Kissinger he pursued détente with the Soviet Union. He began a gradual withdrawal from Vietnam, but U.S. troops remained there through his first term. He ordered an incursion into Cambodia (1970) and the bombing of Hanoi and mining of Haiphong Harbor (1972). Reelected by a large majority in Nov. 1972, he secured a Vietnam cease-fire.

Nixon's 2d term was cut short by scandal, after disclosures relating to a June 1972 burglary of Democratic Party headquarters in the Watergate office complex. After it emerged that most of Nixon's office conversations and calls had been taped, the courts and Congress sought the tapes for criminal proceedings against former White House aides and for a House inquiry into possible impeachment. Nixon claimed executive privilege to keep the tapes secret, but the Supreme Court ruled against him. In late July the House Judiciary Committee recommended adoption of 3 impeachment articles charging him with obstruction of justice, abuse of power, and contempt of Congress. On Aug. 5, he released transcripts of conversations that linked him to cover-up activities. He resigned on Aug. 9, becoming the first president ever to do so. In later years, Nixon emerged as an elder statesman.

Nixon died Apr. 22, 1994, in New York City.

Gerald Rudolph Ford (1974-77)

Gerald R. Ford, 38th president, Republican, was born on July 14, 1913, in Omaha, NE, the son of Leslie and Dorothy Gardner King, and was named Leslie Jr. When he was 2, his parents were divorced, and his mother moved with the boy to Grand Rapids, MI. There she met and married Gerald R. Ford, who formally adopted him and gave him his own name. Ford graduated from the University of Michigan in 1935 and from Yale Law School in 1941. He began practicing law in Grand Rapids, but in 1942 joined the navy and served in the Pacific, leaving the service in 1946 as a lieutenant commander. He entered the House of Representatives in 1949 and spent 25 years in the House, 8 of them as Republican leader.

On Oct. 12, 1973, after Vice President Spiro T. Agnew resigned, Ford was nominated by President Nixon to replace him. It was the first use of the procedures set out in the 25th Amendment. When Nixon resigned, Aug. 9, 1974, Ford became president; he was the only president who was never elected either to the presidency or to the vice presidency. On Sept. 8, in a controversial move, he pardoned Nixon for any federal crimes he might have committed as president. Ford vetoed 48 bills in his first 21 months in office, mostly in the interest of fighting high inflation; he was less successful in curbing high unemployment. In foreign policy, Ford continued to pursue détente. He was narrowly defeated in the 1976 election by Democrat Jimmy Carter.

Jimmy (James Earl) Carter (1977-81)

Jimmy (James Earl) Carter, 39th president, Democrat, was the first president from the Deep South since before the Civil War. He was born on Oct. 1, 1924, in Plains, GA, the son of James and Lillian Gordy Carter.

Carter graduated from the U.S. Naval Academy in 1946 and in 1952 entered the navy's nuclear submarine program as an aide to Capt. (later Adm.) Hyman Rickover. He studied nuclear physics at Union College. Carter's father died in 1953, and he left the navy to take over the family businesses. He served in the Georgia state senate (1963-67) and as governor of Georgia (1971-75). In 1976, Carter won the Democratic nomination and defeated President Gerald R. Ford.

On his first full day in office, Carter pardoned all Vietnam draft evaders. He played a major role in the peace negotiations between Israel and Egypt. However, Carter was widely criticized for the poor state of the economy and was viewed by many as weak in his handling of foreign policy. In Nov. 1979, Iranian student militants attacked the U.S. embassy in Tehran and held members of the embassy staff hostage. Efforts to obtain release of the hostages were a major preoccupation during the rest of his term. He reacted to the Soviet invasion of Afghanistan by imposing a grain embargo and boycotting the Moscow Olympic Games.

Carter was defeated by Ronald Reagan in the 1980 election. Carter administration efforts finally resulted in the release of the hostages on Inauguration Day, 1981, just after Reagan officially became president. After leaving office, Carter was hailed for his humanitarian efforts and took a prominent role in mediating international disputes.

Ronald Wilson Reagan (1981-89)

Ronald Wilson Reagan, 40th president, Republican, was born on Feb. 6, 1911, in Tampico, IL, the son of John Edward and Nellie Wilson Reagan. Reagan graduated from Eureka College in 1932, after which he worked as a sports announcer in Des Moines, IA. He began a successful career as an actor in 1937, starring in numerous movies, and later in television, until the 1960s. He served as president of the Screen Actors Guild from 1947 to 1952 and in 1959-60. Reagan was elected governor of California in 1966 and reelected in 1970.

In 1980, Reagan gained the Republican presidential nomination and won a landslide victory over Jimmy Carter. He was easily reelected in 1984. Reagan successfully forged a bipartisan coalition in Congress, which led to enactment of his program of large-scale tax cuts, cutbacks in many government programs, and a major defense buildup. He signed a Social Security reform bill designed to provide for the long-term solvency of the system. In 1986, he signed into law a major tax-reform bill. He was shot and wounded in an assassination attempt in 1981.

In 1982, the U.S. joined France and Italy in maintaining a peacekeeping force in Beirut, Lebanon, and the next year Reagan sent a task force to invade the island of Grenada after 2 Marxist coups there. Reagan's opposition to international terrorism led to the U.S. bombing of Libyan military installations in 1986. He strongly supported El Salvador, the Nicaraguan contras, and other anti-communist governments and forces throughout the world. He also held 4 summit meetings with Soviet leader Mikhail Gorbachev. At the 1987 meeting in Washington, DC, a historic treaty eliminating short- and medium-range missiles from Europe was signed.

Reagan faced a crisis in 1986-87, when it was revealed that the U.S. had sold weapons to Iran in exchange for release of U.S. hostages being held in Lebanon and that subsequently some of the money was diverted to the Nicaraguan contras (Congress had barred aid to the contras). The scandal led to the resignation of leading White House aides. As Reagan left office in Jan. 1989, the nation was experiencing its 6th consecutive year of economic prosperity. Reagan, however, was unable to control the high budget deficits that plagued him throughout his administration.

In 1994, in a letter to the American people, Reagan revealed that he was suffering from Alzheimer's disease.

George Herbert Walker Bush (1989-93)

George Herbert Walker Bush, 41st president, Republican, was born on June 12, 1924, in Milton, MA, the son of Prescott and Dorothy Walker Bush. He served as a U.S. Navy pilot in World War II. After graduating from Yale University in 1948, he settled in Texas, where, in 1953, he helped found an oil company. After losing a bid for a U.S. Senate seat in Texas in 1964, he was elected to the House of Representatives in 1966 and 1968. He lost a 2d U.S. Senate race in 1970. Subsequently he served as U.S. ambassador to the United Nations (1971-73), headed the U.S. Liaison Office in Beijing (1974-75), and was director of central intelligence (1976-77).

Following an unsuccessful bid for the 1980 Republican presidential nomination, Bush was chosen by Ronald Reagan as his vice presidential running mate. He served as U.S. vice president from 1981 to 1989.

In 1988, Bush gained the Republican presidential nomination and defeated Democrat Michael Dukakis in the November elections. Bush took office faced with the ongoing U.S. budget and trade deficits as well as the rescue of insolvent U.S. savings and loan institutions. He faced a severe budget deficit annually, struggled with military cutbacks in light of reduced cold war tensions, and vetoed abortion-rights legislation. In 1990 he agreed to a budget deficit-reduction plan that included tax hikes.

Bush supported Soviet reforms and Eastern Europe democratization. He was criticized by some for keeping U.S. policy tied closely to Mikhail Gorbachev as the Soviet leader lost power and for underreaction to China's violent repression of pro-democracy demonstrators in 1989. In Dec. 1989, Bush sent troops to Panama; they overthrew the government and captured strongman Gen. Manuel Noriega.

Bush reacted to Iraq's Aug. 1990 invasion of Kuwait by sending U.S. forces to the Persian Gulf area and assembling a UN-backed coalition, including NATO and Arab League members. After a month-long air war, in Feb. 1991, Allied forces retook Kuwait in a 4-day ground assault. The quick victory, with light casualties, gave Bush one of the highest presidential approval ratings in history. His popularity plummeted by the end of 1991, however, as the economy struggled through a prolonged recession. He was defeated by his Democratic opponent, Bill Clinton, in the 1992 election.

Bill (William Jefferson) Clinton (1993-)

Bill Clinton, 42d president, Democrat, was born on Aug. 19, 1946, in Hope, AR, son of William Blythe and Virginia Cassidy Blythe, and was named William Jefferson Blythe IV. Blythe died in an automobile accident before his son was born. His widow married Roger Clinton, and at the age of 16, William Jefferson Blythe IV changed his name to Bill Clinton. Clinton graduated from Georgetown University in 1968, attended Oxford University as a Rhodes scholar, and earned a degree from Yale Law School in 1973.

Clinton worked on George McGovern's 1972 presidential campaign. He taught at the University of Arkansas from 1973 to 1976, when he was elected state attorney general. In 1978, he was elected governor, becoming the nation's youngest. Defeated for reelection in 1980, he was returned to office in 1982, 1984, 1986, and 1990. He married Hillary Rodham in 1975.

Despite attacks on his character, Clinton won most of the 1992 presidential primaries, moving his party toward the center as he tried to broaden his appeal; as the party's presidential nominee he defeated Pres. George Bush in November. In 1993, Clinton won passage of a measure to reduce the federal budget deficit and won congressional approval of the North American Free Trade Agreement. His plan for major health-care reform legislation died in Congress.

After 1994 midterm elections, Clinton faced Republican majorities in both houses of Congress. He followed a centrist course at home, sent troops to Bosnia to help implement a peace settlement, and cultivated relations with Russia and China.

Despite alleged improprieties in his involvement in an Arkansas real estate venture (Whitewater) and in other matters, Clinton easily won reelection in 1996. In 1997 he reached agreement with Congress on legislation to balance the federal budget by 2002. A strong economy helped him retain popularity through summer 1998 despite controversy over alleged sexual impropriety.

On Aug. 20, 1998, Clinton responded to bombings of U.S. embassies in Kenya and Tanzania by authorizing the launching of cruise missiles against targets in Sudan and Afghanistan allegedly linked to terrorism.

On Aug. 17, 1998, in videotaped testimony before a grand jury convened by independent counsel Kenneth Starr and in a speech to the nation, Clinton admitted having had an improper relationship with a White House intern, Monica Lewinsky, despite earlier denials. On Sept. 9, Starr presented a report to Congress asserting possible grounds for impeachment—including perjury and obstruction of justice—in the Lewinsky matter.

Wives and Children of the Presidents

Name (Born–died; married)	State	Sons/ daughters
Martha Dandridge Custis Washington (1731-1802; 1759)	VA	None
Abigail Smith Adams (1744-1818; 1764)	MA	3/2
Martha Wayles Skelton Jefferson (1748-82; 1772)	VA	1/5
Dorothea "Dolley" Payne Todd Madison (1768-1849; 1794)	NC	None
Elizabeth Kortright Monroe (1768-1830; 1786)	NY	. . ./2 (A)
Louisa Catherine Johnson Adams (1775-1852; 1797)	MD(B)	3/1
Rachel Donelson Robards Jackson (1767-1828; 1791)	VA	None
Hannah Hoes Van Buren (1783-1819; 1807)	NY	4/. . .
Anna Tuthill Symmes Harrison (1775-1864; 1795)	NJ	6/4
Letitia Christian Tyler (1790-1842; 1813)	VA	3/4 (A)
Julia Gardiner Tyler (1820-89; 1844)	NY	5/2
Sarah Childress Polk (1803-91; 1824)	TN	None
Margaret Mackall Smith Taylor (1788-1852; 1810)	MD	1/5
Abigail Powers Fillmore (1798-1853; 1826)	NY	1/1
Caroline Carmichael McIntosh Fillmore (1813-81; 1858)	NJ	None
Jane Means Appleton Pierce (1806-63; 1834)	NH	3/. . .
Mary Todd Lincoln (1818-82; 1842)	KY	4/. . .
Eliza McCardle Johnson (1810-76; 1827)	TN	3/2
Julia Boggs Dent Grant (1826-1902; 1848)	MO	3/1
Lucy Ware Webb Hayes (1831-89; 1852)	OH	7/1
Lucretia Rudolph Garfield (1832-1918; 1858)	OH	4/1
Ellen Lewis Herndon Arthur (1837-80; 1859)	VA	2/1
Frances Folsom Cleveland (1864-1947; 1886)	NY	2/3
Caroline Lavinia Scott Harrison (1832-92; 1853)	OH	1/1
Mary Scott Lord Dimmick Harrison (1858-1948; 1896)	PA	. . ./1
Ida Saxton McKinley (1847-1907; 1871)	OH	. . ./2
Alice Hathaway Lee Roosevelt (1861-84; 1880)	MA	. . ./1
Edith Kermit Carow Roosevelt (1861-1948; 1886)	CT	4/1
Helen Herron Taft (1861-1943; 1886)	OH	2/1
Ellen Louise Axson Wilson (1860-1914; 1885)	GA	. . ./3
Edith Bolling Galt Wilson (1872-1961; 1915)	VA	None
Florence Kling De Wolfe Harding (1860-1924; 1891)	OH	None
Grace Anna Goodhue Coolidge (1879-1957; 1905)	VT	2/. . .
Lou Henry Hoover (1875-1944; 1899)	IA	2/. . .
Anna Eleanor Roosevelt Roosevelt (1884-1962; 1905)	NY	4/1 (A)
Elizabeth Virginia "Bess" Wallace Truman (1885-1982; 1919)	MO	. . ./1
Mamie Geneva Doud Eisenhower (1896-1979; 1916)	IA	1/. . . (A)
Jacqueline Lee Bouvier Kennedy (1929-94; 1953)	NY	1/1 (A)
Claudia "Lady Bird" Alta Taylor Johnson (1912; 1934)	TX	. . ./2
Thelma Catherine Patricia Ryan Nixon (1912-1993; 1940)	NV	. . ./2
Elizabeth Bloomer Warren Ford (1918; 1948)	IL	3/1
Rosalynn Smith Carter (1927; 1946)	GA	3/1
Anne Frances "Nancy" Robbins Davis Reagan (1921; 1952)	NY	1/1 (C)
Barbara Pierce Bush (1925; 1945)	NY	4/2
Hillary Rodham Clinton (1947; 1975)	IL	. . ./1

James Buchanan, 15th president, was unmarried. (A) plus one infant, deceased. (B) Born in London, father a MD citizen. (C) Pres. Reagan married and divorced Jane Wyman; they had a daughter who died in infancy, and a son and daughter who both lived past infancy.

First Lady Hillary Rodham Clinton

Hillary Rodham Clinton was born in Chicago, Oct. 26, 1947, to Hugh and Dorothy Rodham. She graduated from Wellesley College and Yale Law School. She married Bill Clinton in 1975, and a daughter, Chelsea, was born in 1980. From 1977 to 1992, she was a partner in the Rose Law Firm in Little Rock, AR. In this capacity she did some work for an S&L linked to the Whitewater scandal. In 1988 and 1991, she was voted one of the "100 Most Influential Lawyers in America" by the *National Law Journal.*

In 1993-94, as first lady, she played a leading role in an unsuccessful effort to reform the U.S. health-care system. In 1995 her book *It Takes a Village*, about the needs of children, was published; her recording of the text won a Grammy in 1997. She was a critic of investigations by independent counsel Kenneth Starr aimed at the president and others, and she expressed loyalty to her husband after he admitted an improper extramarital relationship in Aug. 1998.

Burial Places of the Presidents

President	Burial Place
Washington	Mt. Vernon, VA
J. Adams	Quincy, MA
Jefferson	Charlottesville, VA
Madison	Montpelier Station, VA
Monroe	Richmond, VA
J. Q. Adams	Quincy, MA
Jackson	Nashville, TN
Van Buren	Kinderhook, NY
W. H. Harrison	North Bend, OH
Tyler	Richmond, VA
Polk	Nashville, TN
Taylor	Louisville, KY
Fillmore	Buffalo, NY
Pierce	Concord, NH
Buchanan	Lancaster, PA
Lincoln	Springfield, IL
A. Johnson	Greeneville, TN
Grant	New York, NY
Hayes	Fremont, OH
Garfield	Cleveland, OH
Arthur	Albany, NY
Cleveland	Princeton, NJ
B. Harrison	Indianapolis, IN
McKinley	Canton, OH
T. Roosevelt	Oyster Bay, NY
Taft	Arlington Natl. Cem.
Wilson	Wash. Natl. Cathedral
Harding	Marion, OH
Coolidge	Plymouth, VT
Hoover	West Branch, IA
F. Roosevelt	Hyde Park, NY
Truman	Independence, MO
Eisenhower	Abilene, KS
Kennedy	Arlington Natl. Cem.
L. B. Johnson	Johnson City, TX
Nixon	Yorba Linda, CA

Presidential Libraries

The libraries listed below, except for that of Richard Nixon (which is a private institution), are coordinated by the National Archives and Records Administration (NARA) in Washington, DC. Further information is available at the NARA Web site (http://www.nara.gov/nara/president/overview.html). NARA also has custody of the Nixon presidential historical materials. Materials for presidents prior to Herbert Hoover are held by private institutions.

Herbert Hoover Library
211 Parkside Dr., PO Box 488
West Branch, IA 52358-0488
PHONE: 319-643-5301
FAX: 319-643-5825
E-MAIL:library@hoover.nara.gov

Franklin D. Roosevelt Library
511 Albany Post Rd.
Hyde Park, NY 12538-1999
PHONE: 914-229-8114
FAX: 914-229-0872
E-MAIL: library@roosevelt.nara.gov

Harry S. Truman Library
500 West U.S. Hwy. 24
Independence, MO 64050-1798
PHONE: 816-833-1400
FAX: 816-833-4368
E-MAIL: library@truman.nara.gov

Dwight D. Eisenhower Library
200 S.E. 4th St.
Abilene, KS 67410-2900
PHONE: 785-263-4751
FAX: 785-263-4218
E-MAIL: library@eisenhower.nara.gov

John Fitzgerald Kennedy Library
Columbia Pt.
Boston, MA 02125-3398
PHONE: 617-929-4500
FAX: 617-929-4538
E-MAIL: library@kennedy.nara.gov

Lyndon Baines Johnson Library
2313 Red River St.
Austin, TX 78705-5702
PHONE: 512-916-5137
FAX: 512-478-9104
E-MAIL: library@johnson.nara.gov

Richard Nixon Library & Birthplace
18001 Yorba Linda Blvd.
Yorba Linda, CA 92886-3949
PHONE: 714-993-3393
FAX: 714-528-0544
WEB SITE: http://www.nixonfoundation.org
E-MAIL:stedman@chapman.edu

Gerald R. Ford Library
1000 Beal Ave.
Ann Arbor, MI 48109-2114
PHONE: 734-741-2218
FAX: 734-741-2341
E-MAIL: library@fordlib.nara.gov

Jimmy Carter Library
441 Freedom Pkwy.
Atlanta, GA 30307-1406
PHONE: 404-331-3942
FAX: 404-730-2215
E-MAIL: library@carter.nara.gov

Ronald Reagan Library
40 Presidential Dr.
Simi Valley, CA 93065-0666
PHONE: 805-522-8444
FAX: 805-522-9621
E-MAIL: library@reagan.nara.gov

George Bush Library
1000 George Bush Dr., West
College Station, TX 77482-0410
PHONE: 409-260-9552
FAX: 409-260-9557
E-MAIL: library@bush.nara.gov

Impeachment in U.S. History

The U.S. Constitution provides for impeachment and, upon conviction, removal from office of federal officials on grounds of "Treason, Bribery, or other high Crimes and Misdemeanors" (Article II, Sect. 4). Impeachment involves the bringing of charges by the House of Representatives, followed by a Senate trial; a two-thirds vote is needed for conviction and removal from office, which does not preclude criminal indictment and trial (Article I, Sect. 2, Para. 5; Sect. 3, Para. 6-7).

In July 1974, 3 articles of impeachment against Pres. Richard M. Nixon, for obstruction of justice, abuse of power, and contempt of Congress, were voted by the House Judiciary Committee. However, with congressional support collapsing, Nixon resigned Aug. 9, before the full House could vote on impeaching him. One prior president—Andrew Johnson—was impeached but not convicted. A list of impeached federal officials follows:

Name	Position Held	Senate Trial Began	Action Taken	Date
William Blount	Senator, TN	Dec. 17, 1798	Charges dismissed	Jan. 14, 1799
John Pickering	District Court Judge, NH	Mar. 3, 1803	Removed from office	Mar. 12, 1804
Samuel Chase	Supreme Court Assoc. Justice	Nov. 30, 1804	Acquitted	Mar. 1, 1805
James H. Peck	District Court Judge, MO	Apr. 26, 1830	Acquitted	Jan. 31, 1831
West H. Humphreys	District Court Judge, TN	May 7, 1862	Removed from office	June 26, 1862
Andrew Johnson	President	Feb. 25, 1868	Acquitted	May 26, 1868
William W. Belknap	Secretary of War	Mar. 3, 1876	Acquitted	Aug. 1, 1876
Charles Swayne	District Court Judge, FL	Dec. 14, 1904	Acquitted	Feb. 27, 1905
Robert W. Archbald	Commerce Court, Assoc. Judge	July 13, 1912	Removed from office	Jan. 13, 1913
George W. English	District Court Judge, IL	Nov. 4, 1926*	Charges dismissed	Nov. 4, 1926
Harold Louderback	District Court Judge, CA	May 15, 1933	Acquitted	May 24, 1933
Halsted L. Ritter	District Court Judge, FL	Apr. 6, 1936	Removed from office	Apr. 17, 1936
Harry E. Claiborne	District Court Judge, NV	Oct. 7, 1986	Removed from office	Oct. 9, 1986
Alcee L. Hastings	District Court Judge, FL	Oct. 18, 1989	Removed from office	Oct. 20, 1989
Walter L. Nixon	District Court Judge, MS	Nov. 1, 1989	Removed from office	Nov. 3, 1989

*Date of resignation, after which the impeachment charges were dismissed.

UNITED STATES FACTS

Superlative U.S. Statistics[1]

Source: U.S. Geological Survey, Dept. of the Interior; U.S. Bureau of the Census, Dept. of Commerce; World Almanac research

Area for 50 states and Washington, DC	Total Land, 3,536,278 sq mi; Water, 251,041 sq mi	3,787,319 sq mi
Largest state	Alaska	656,424 sq mi
Smallest state	Rhode Island	1,545 sq mi
Largest county (excluding Alaska)	San Bernardino County, CA	20,106 sq mi
Smallest county	Kalawao, HI	52 sq mi
Largest incorporated city	Sitka, AK	2,881 sq mi
Northernmost city	Barrow, AK	71°17′ N
Northernmost point	Point Barrow, AK	71°23′ N
Southernmost city	Hilo, HI	19°44′ N
Southernmost settlement	Naalehu, HI	19°03′ N
Southernmost point	Ka Lae (South Cape), Island of Hawaii	18°55′ N(155°41′ W)
Easternmost city	Eastport, ME	66°59′ 05″ W
Easternmost settlement[2]	Amchitka Isl., AK	179°15′ E
Easternmost point[2]	Pochnoi Point, on Semisopochnoi Isl., AK	179°46′ E
Westernmost city	Atka, AK	174°12′ W
Westernmost settlement	Adak Station, AK	176°39′ W
Westernmost point	Amatignak Isl., AK	179°06′ W
Highest settlement	Climax, CO	11,360 ft
Lowest settlement	Calipatria, CA	–184 ft
Highest point on Atlantic coast	Cadillac Mountain, Mount Desert Isl., ME	1,530 ft
Oldest national park	Yellowstone National Park (1872), WY, MT, ID	2,219,791 acres
Largest national park	Wrangell-St. Elias, AK	8,323,618 acres
Highest waterfall	Yosemite Falls—Total in 3 sections	2,425 ft
	Upper Yosemite Fall	1,430 ft
	Cascades in middle section	675 ft
	Lower Yosemite Fall	320 ft
Longest river system	Mississippi-Missouri-Red Rock	3,710 mi
Highest mountain	Mount McKinley, AK	20,320 ft
Lowest point	Death Valley, CA	–282 ft
Deepest lake	Crater Lake, OR	1,932 ft
Rainiest spot	Mount Waialeale, HI	Annual avg rainfall 460 in
Largest gorge	Grand Canyon, Colorado River, AZ	277 mi long, 600 ft to 18 mi wide, 1 mi deep
Deepest gorge	Hells Canyon, Snake River, OR-ID	7,900 ft
Strongest surface wind	Mount Washington, NH, recorded 1934	231 mph
Largest dam	New Cornelia Tailings, Ten Mile Wash, AZ[3]	274,026,000 cu yds material used
Tallest building	Sears Tower, Chicago, IL	1,450 ft
Largest building	Boeing 747 Manufacturing Plant, Everett, WA	205,600,000 cu ft; covers 47 acres
Tallest structure	TV tower, Blanchard, ND	2,063 ft
Longest bridge span	Verrazano-Narrows, NY	4,260 ft
Highest bridge	Royal Gorge, CO	1,053 ft above water
Deepest well	Gas well, Washita County, OK	31,441 ft

The 48 Contiguous States

Area for 48 states and Washington, DC	Total Land, 2,959,481 sq mi; Water, 160,483 sq mi	3,119,963 sq mi[4]
Largest state	Texas	268,601 sq mi
Northernmost city	Bellingham, WA	48°46′ N
Northernmost settlement	Angle Inlet, MN	49°21′ N
Northernmost point	Northwest Angle, MN	49°23′ N
Southernmost city	Key West, FL	24°33′ N
Southernmost mainland city	Florida City, FL	25°27′ N
Southernmost point	Key West, FL	24°33′ N
Easternmost settlement	Lubec, ME	66°58′49″ W
Easternmost point	West Quoddy Head, ME	66°57′ W
Westernmost town	La Push, WA	124°38′ W
Westernmost point	Cape Alava, WA	124°44′ W
Highest mountain	Mount Whitney, CA	14,494 ft

(1) All areas are total area, including water, unless otherwise noted. (2) Alaska's Aleutian Islands extend into the eastern hemisphere and thus technically contain the easternmost point and settlement in the U.S. (3) The New Cornelia Tailings Dam is a privately owned industrial dam composed of tailings, remnants of a mining process. (4) Does not add, because of rounding.

Geodetic Datum of North America

In July 1986, the National Oceanic and Atmospheric Administration's National Geodetic Survey (NGS), in cooperation with Canada and Mexico, completed readjustment and redefinition of the system of latitudes and longitudes. The resulting North American Datum of 1983 (NAD 83) replaces the North American Datum of 1927, as well as local reference systems for Hawaii and for Puerto Rico and the Virgin Islands. The change was prompted by Hawaii's increased need for accurate coordinate information. To facilitate use of satellite surveying and navigation systems, such as the Global Positioning System (GPS), the new datum was redefined using the Geodetic Reference System 1980 as the reference ellipsoid because this model more closely approximates the true size and shape of the earth. In addition, the origin of the coordinate system is referenced to the mass center of the earth to coincide with the orbital orientation of the GPS satellites. Positional changes resulting from the datum redefinition can reach 330 ft in the continental U.S., Canada, and Mexico. Changes that exceed 660 ft can be expected in Alaska, Puerto Rico, and the Virgin Islands. Hawaii's coordinates changed about 1,300 ft.

Additional Statistical Information About the U.S.

The annual *Statistical Abstract of the United States,* published by U.S. Dept. of Commerce, contains additional social, political, and economic data about the U.S. For information on this and other printed publications, write to: Superintendent of Documents, Government Printing Office, PO Box 371954, Pittsburgh, PA 15250-7954, or call (202) 512-1800. For information on electronic products, write to: U.S. Dept. of Commerce, Bureau of the Census, PO Box 277943, Atlanta, GA 30384-7943, or call (301) 457-4100. Parts of *The Statistical Abstract* can be viewed on the Internet. See Internet Directory to Selected Sites in the Internet and Computers chapter.

Highest and Lowest Altitudes in U.S. States and Territories

Source: U.S. Geological Survey, Dept. of the Interior

(Minus sign means below sea level.)

State/Terr.	Highest Point Name	County	Elev. (ft)	Lowest Point Name	County	Elev. (ft)
Alabama	Cheaha Mountain	Cleburne	2,405	Gulf of Mexico		Sea level
Alaska	Mount McKinley	Denali	20,320	Pacific Ocean		Sea level
Arizona	Humphreys Peak	Coconino	12,633	Colorado R	Yuma	70
Arkansas	Magazine Mountain	Logan	2,753	Ouachita R	Ashley-Union	55
California	Mount Whitney	Inyo-Tulare	14,494	Death Valley	Inyo	–282
Colorado	Mount Elbert	Lake	14,433	Arkansas R	Prowers	3,350
Connecticut	Mount Frissell	Litchfield	2,380	Long Island Sound		Sea level
Delaware	On Ebright Road	New Castle	448	Atlantic Ocean		Sea level
Dist. of Columbia	Tenleytown	N W part	410	Potomac R		1
Florida	Sec. 30, T6N, R20W[1]	Walton	345	Atlantic Ocean		Sea level
Georgia	Brasstown Bald	Towns-Union	4,784	Atlantic Ocean		Sea level
Guam	Mount Lamlam	Agat District	1,332	Pacific Ocean		Sea level
Hawaii	Mauna Kea	Hawaii	13,796	Pacific Ocean		Sea level
Idaho	Borah Peak	Custer	12,662	Snake R	Nez Perce	710
Illinois	Charles Mound	Jo Daviess	1,235	Mississippi R	Alexander	279
Indiana	Franklin Township	Wayne	1,257	Ohio R	Posey	320
Iowa	Sec. 29, T100N, R41W[1]	Osceola	1,670	Mississippi R	Lee	480
Kansas	Mount Sunflower	Wallace	4,039	Verdigris R	Montgomery	679
Kentucky	Black Mountain	Harlan	4,139	Mississippi R	Fulton	257
Louisiana	Driskill Mountain	Bienville	535	New Orleans	Orleans	–8
Maine	Mount Katahdin	Piscataquis	5,267	Atlantic Ocean		Sea level
Maryland	Backbone Mountain	Garrett	3,360	Atlantic Ocean		Sea level
Massachusetts	Mount Greylock	Berkshire	3,487	Atlantic Ocean		Sea level
Michigan	Mount Arvon	Baraga	1,979	Lake Erie	Monroe	571
Minnesota	Eagle Mountain	Cook	2,301	Lake Superior		600
Mississippi	Woodall Mountain	Tishomingo	806	Gulf of Mexico		Sea level
Missouri	Taum Sauk Mt.	Iron	1,772	St. Francis R	Dunklin	230
Montana	Granite Peak	Park	12,799	Kootenai R	Lincoln	1,800
Nebraska	Johnson Township	Kimball	5,424	Missouri R	Richardson	840
Nevada	Boundary Peak	Esmeralda	13,140	Colorado R	Clark	479
New Hampshire	Mt. Washington	Coos	6,288	Atlantic Ocean		Sea level
New Jersey	High Point	Sussex	1,803	Atlantic Ocean		Sea level
New Mexico	Wheeler Peak	Taos	13,161	Red Bluff Res.	Eddy	2,842
New York	Mount Marcy	Essex	5,344	Atlantic Ocean		Sea level
North Carolina	Mount Mitchell	Yancey	6,684	Atlantic Ocean		Sea level
North Dakota	White Butte	Slope	3,506	Red R	Pembina	750
Ohio	Campbell Hill	Logan	1,549	Ohio R	Hamilton	455
Oklahoma	Black Mesa	Cimarron	4,973	Little R	McCurtain	289
Oregon	Mount Hood	Clackamas-Hood R.	11,239	Pacific Ocean		Sea level
Pennsylvania	Mt. Davis	Somerset	3,213	Delaware R	Delaware	Sea level
Puerto Rico	Cerro de Punta	Ponce District	4,390	Atlantic Ocean		Sea level
Rhode Island	Jerimoth Hill	Providence	812	Atlantic Ocean		Sea level
Samoa	Lata Mountain	Tau Island	3,160	Pacific Ocean		Sea level
South Carolina	Sassafras Mountain	Pickens	3,560	Atlantic Ocean		Sea level
South Dakota	Harney Peak	Pennington	7,242	Big Stone Lake	Roberts	966
Tennessee	Clingmans Dome	Sevier	6,643	Mississippi R	Shelby	178
Texas	Guadalupe Peak	Culberson	8,749	Gulf of Mexico		Sea level
Utah	Kings Peak	Duchesne	13,528	Beaverdam Wash	Washington	2,000
Vermont	Mount Mansfield	Lamoille	4,393	Lake Champlain		95
Virginia	Mount Rogers	Grayson-Smyth	5,729	Atlantic Ocean		Sea level
Virgin Islands	Crown Mountain	St. Thomas Island	1,556	Atlantic Ocean		Sea level
Washington	Mount Rainier West	Pierce	14,410	Pacific Ocean		Sea level
West Virginia	Spruce Knob	Pendleton	4,861	Potomac R	Jefferson	240
Wisconsin	Timms Hill	Price	1,951	Lake Michigan		579
Wyoming	Gannett Peak	Fremont	13,804	Belle Fourche R.	Crook	3,099

(1) Sec.=section; T=township; R=range; N=north; W=west.

U.S. Coastline by States

Source: National Oceanic and Atmospheric Administration, U.S. Dept. of Commerce

(in statute miles)

State	Coastline[1]	Shoreline[2]
Atlantic coast	**2,069**	**28,673**
Connecticut	0	618
Delaware	28	381
Florida	580	3,331
Georgia	100	2,344
Maine	228	3,478
Maryland	31	3,190
Massachusetts	192	1,519
New Hampshire	13	131
New Jersey	130	1,792
New York	127	1,850
North Carolina	301	3,375
Pennsylvania	0	89
Rhode Island	40	384
South Carolina	187	2,876
Virginia	112	3,315
Gulf coast	**1,631**	**17,141**
Alabama	53	607
Florida	770	5,095
Louisiana	397	7,721
Mississippi	44	359
Texas	367	3,359
Pacific coast	**7,623**	**40,298**
Alaska	5,580	31,383
California	840	3,427
Hawaii	750	1,052
Oregon	296	1,410
Washington	157	3,026
Arctic coast, Alaska	**1,060**	**2,521**
United States	**12,383**	**88,633**

(1) Figures are lengths of general outline of seacoast. Measurements were made with a unit measure of 30 minutes of latitude on charts as near the scale of 1:1,200,000 as possible. Coastline of sounds and bays is included to a point where they narrow to width of unit measure, and includes the distance across at such point. (2) Figures obtained in 1939-40 with a recording instrument on the largest-scale charts and maps then available. Shoreline of outer coast, offshore islands, sounds, bays, rivers, and creeks is included to the head of tidewater or to a point where tidal waters narrow to a width of 100 ft.

States: Settled, Capitals, Entry Into Union, Area, Rank

The 13 colonies that seceded from Great Britain and fought the War of Independence (American Revolution) became the 13 original states. They were (in the order in which they ratified the Constitution): Delaware, Pennsylvania, New Jersey, Georgia, Connecticut, Massachusetts, Maryland, South Carolina, New Hampshire, Virginia, New York, North Carolina, and Rhode Island.

State	Settled[1]	Capital	Entered Union Date	Entered Union Order	Extent in miles Long (approx.)	Extent in miles Wide (mean)	Area in sq. mi Land	Area in sq. mi Inland Water	Area in sq. mi Total	Rank in area[2]
AL	1702	Montgomery	Dec. 14, 1819	22	330	190	50,750	1,486	52,237	30
AK	1784	Juneau	Jan. 3, 1959	49	1,480[3]	810[3]	570,374	44,856	615,230	1
AZ	1776	Phoenix	Feb. 14, 1912	48	400	310	113,642	364	114,006	6
AR	1686	Little Rock	June 15, 1836	25	260	240	52,075	1,107	53,182	28
CA	1769	Sacramento	Sept. 9, 1850	31	770	250	155,973	2,895	158,869	3
CO	1858	Denver	Aug. 1, 1876	38	380	280	103,729	371	104,100	8
CT	1634	Hartford	Jan. 9, 1788	5	110	70	4,845	698	5,544	48
DE	1638	Dover	Dec. 7, 1787	1	100	30	1,955	442	2,396	49
DC	NA	Washington	NA	NA	...	...	61	7	68	51
FL	1565	Tallahassee	Mar. 3, 1845	27	500	160	53,937	5,991	59,928	23
GA	1733	Atlanta	Jan. 2, 1788	4	300	230	57,919	1,058	58,977	24
HI	1820	Honolulu	Aug. 21, 1959	50	...	...	6,423	36	6,459	47
ID	1842	Boise	July 3, 1890	43	570	300	82,751	823	83,574	14
IL	1720	Springfield	Dec. 3, 1818	21	390	210	55,593	2,325	57,918	25
IN	1733	Indianapolis	Dec. 11, 1816	19	270	140	35,870	550	36,420	38
IA	1788	Des Moines	Dec. 28, 1846	29	310	200	55,875	401	56,276	26
KS	1727	Topeka	Jan. 29, 1861	34	400	210	81,823	459	82,282	15
KY	1774	Frankfort	June 1, 1792	15	380	140	39,732	679	40,411	37
LA	1699	Baton Rouge	Apr. 30, 1812	18	380	130	43,566	6,085	49,651	31
ME	1624	Augusta	Mar. 15, 1820	23	320	190	30,865	2,876	33,741	39
MD	1634	Annapolis	Apr. 28, 1788	7	250	90	9,775	2,522	12,297	42
MA	1620	Boston	Feb. 6, 1788	6	190	50	7,838	1,403	9,241	45
MI	1668	Lansing	Jan. 26, 1837	26	490	240	56,809	39,895	96,705	11
MN	1805	St. Paul	May 11, 1858	32	400	250	79,617	7,326	86,943	12
MS	1699	Jackson	Dec. 10, 1817	20	340	170	46,914	1,372	48,286	32
MO	1735	Jefferson City	Aug. 10, 1821	24	300	240	68,898	811	69,709	21
MT	1809	Helena	Nov. 8, 1889	41	630	280	145,556	1,490	147,046	4
NE	1823	Lincoln	Mar. 1, 1867	37	430	210	76,878	481	77,358	16
NV	1849	Carson City	Oct. 31, 1864	36	490	320	109,806	761	110,567	7
NH	1623	Concord	June 21, 1788	9	190	70	8,969	314	9,283	44
NJ	1660	Trenton	Dec. 18, 1787	3	150	70	7,419	796	8,215	46
NM	1610	Santa Fe	Jan. 6, 1912	47	370	343	121,364	234	121,598	5
NY	1614	Albany	July 26, 1788	11	330	283	47,224	6,766	53,989	27
NC	1660	Raleigh	Nov. 21, 1789	12	500	150	48,718	3,954	52,672	29
ND	1812	Bismarck	Nov. 2, 1889	39	340	211	68,994	1,710	70,704	18
OH	1788	Columbus	M a	17	220	220	40,953	3,875	44,828	34
OK	1889	Oklahoma City	Nov. 16, 1907	46	400	220	68,679	1,224	69,903	20
OR	1811	Salem	Feb. 14, 1859	33	360	261	96,002	1,129	97,132	10
PA	1682	Harrisburg	Dec. 12, 1787	2	283	160	44,820	1,239	46,058	33
RI	1636	Providence	May 29, 1790	13	40	30	1,045	186	1,231	50
SC	1670	Columbia	May 23, 1788	8	260	200	30,111	1,078	31,189	40
SD	1859	Pierre	Nov. 2, 1889	40	380	210	75,896	1,225	77,121	17
TN	1769	Nashville	June 1, 1796	16	440	120	41,219	926	42,146	36
TX	1682	Austin	Dec. 29, 1845	28	790	660	261,914	5,363	267,277	2
UT	1847	Salt Lake City	Jan. 4, 1896	45	350	270	82,168	2,736	84,904	13
VT	1724	Montpelier	Mar. 4, 1791	14	160	80	9,249	366	9,615	43
VA	1607	Richmond	June 25, 1788	10	430	200	39,598	2,729	42,326	35
WA	1811	Olympia	Nov. 11, 1889	42	360	240	66,581	4,055	70,637	19
WV	1727	Charleston	June 20, 1863	35	240	130	24,087	145	24,231	41
WI	1766	Madison	May 29, 1848	30	310	260	54,314	11,186	65,499	22
WY	1834	Cheyenne	July 10, 1890	44	360	280	97,105	714	97,818	9

Note: Land and water areas may not add to totals because of rounding. NA=Not applicable. (1) First permanent European settlement. (2) Rank is based on total area, including inland and coastal waters. (3) Aleutian Islands and Alexander Archipelago are not considered in these measurements.

The Continental Divide of the U.S.

The Continental Divide of the U.S., also known as the Great Divide, is located at the watershed created by the mountain ranges, or tablelands, of the Rocky Mountains. This watershed separates the waters that drain easterly into the Atlantic Ocean and its marginal seas, such as the Gulf of Mexico, from those that drain westerly into the Pacific Ocean. The majority of easterly flowing water drains into the Gulf of Mexico before reaching the Atlantic Ocean. The majority of westerly flowing water, before reaching the Pacific Ocean, either drains through the Columbia R. or through the Colorado R., which flows into the Gulf of California before reaching the Pacific Ocean.

The location and route of the Continental Divide across the U.S. can briefly be described as follows:

Beginning at point of crossing the U.S.-Mexican boundary, near long. 108°45′ W, the Divide, in a northerly direction, crosses New Mexico along the western edge of the Rio Grande drainage basin, entering Colorado near long. 106°41′ W.

From there by a very irregular route north across Colorado along the W summits of the Rio Grande and of the Arkansas, the South Platte, and the North Platte river basins, and across Rocky Mountain National Park, entering Wyoming near long. 106°52′ W.

From there in a northwesterly direction, forming the W rims of the North Platte, the Big Horn, and the Yellowstone river basins, crossing the SW portion of Yellowstone National Park.

From there in a westerly and then a northerly direction forming the common boundary of Idaho and Montana, to a point on said boundary near long. 114°00′ W.

From there northeasterly and northwesterly through Montana and the Glacier National Park, entering Canada near long. 114°04′ W.

Chronological List of Territories, With State Admissions to Union

Source: National Archives and Records Service

Name of territory	Date of Organic Act creating territory	Organic Act effective	Admission as state	Yrs. terr.
Northwest Territory[1]	July 13, 1787	No fixed date	Mar. 1, 1803[2]	16
Territory southwest of River Ohio	May 26, 1790	No fixed date	June 1, 1796[3]	6
Mississippi	Apr. 7, 1798	When president acted	Dec. 10, 1817	19
Indiana	May 7, 1800	July 4, 1800	Dec. 11, 1816	16
Orleans	Mar. 26, 1804	Oct. 1, 1804	Apr. 30, 1812[4]	7
Michigan	Jan. 11, 1805	June 30, 1805	Jan. 26, 1837	31
Louisiana-Missouri[5]	Mar. 3, 1805	July 4, 1805	Aug. 10, 1821	16
Illinois	Feb. 3, 1809	Mar. 1, 1809	Dec. 3, 1818	9
Alabama	Mar. 3, 1817	When MS became a state	Dec. 14, 1819	2
Arkansas	Mar. 2, 1819	July 4, 1819	June 15, 1836	17
Florida	Mar. 30, 1822	No fixed date	Mar. 3, 1845	23
Wisconsin	Apr. 20, 1836	July 3, 1836	May 29, 1848	12
Iowa	June 12, 1838	July 3, 1838	Dec. 28, 1846	8
Oregon	Aug. 14, 1848	Date of act	Feb. 14, 1859	10
Minnesota	Mar. 3, 1849	Date of act	May 11, 1858	9
New Mexico	Sept. 9, 1850	On president's proclamation	Jan. 6, 1912	61
Utah	Sept. 9, 1850	Date of act	Jan. 4, 1896	46
Washington	Mar. 2, 1853	Date of act	Nov. 11, 1889	36
Nebraska	May 30, 1854	Date of act	Mar. 1, 1867	12
Kansas	May 30, 1854	Date of act	Jan. 29, 1861	6
Colorado	Feb. 28, 1861	Date of act	Aug. 1, 1876	15
Nevada	Mar. 2, 1861	Date of act	Oct. 31, 1864	3
Dakota	Mar. 2, 1861	Date of act	Nov. 2, 1889	28
Arizona	Feb. 24, 1863	Date of act	Feb. 14, 1912	49
Idaho	Mar. 3, 1863	Date of act	July 3, 1890	27
Montana	May 26, 1864	Date of act	Nov. 8, 1889	25
Wyoming	July 25, 1868	When officers were qualified	July 10, 1890	22
Alaska[6]	May 17, 1884	No fixed date	Jan. 3, 1959	75
Oklahoma	May 2, 1890	Date of act	Nov. 16, 1907	17
Hawaii	Apr. 30, 1900	June 14, 1900	Aug. 21, 1959	59

(1) Included what is now Ohio, Indiana, Illinois, Michigan, Wisconsin, eastern Minnesota. (2) Whole territory admitted as the state of Ohio. (3) Admitted as the state of Tennessee. (4) Admitted as the state of Louisiana. (5) The organic act for Missouri Territory of June 4, 1812, became effective Dec. 7, 1812. (6) Although the May 17, 1884, act actually constituted Alaska as a district, it was often referred to as a territory, and unofficially administered as such. The Territory of Alaska was legally and formally organized by an act of Aug. 24, 1912.

Geographic Centers, U.S. and Each State

Source: U.S. Geological Survey, Dept. of the Interior

There is no generally accepted definition of geographic center and no uniform method for determining it. Following the U.S. Geological Survey, the geographic center of an area is defined here as the center of gravity of the surface, or that point on which the surface would balance if it were a plane of uniform thickness. All locations in the following list are approximate.

No marked or monumented point has been established by any government agency as the geographic center of the 50 states, the conterminous U.S. (48 states), or the North American continent. However, a group of citizens erected a monument in Lebanon, KS, marking it as geographic center of the conterminous U.S., and a cairn in Rugby, ND, designates that location as the center of the North American continent.

United States, including Alaska and Hawaii—W of Castle Rock, Butte County, South Dakota; lat. 44°58′N, long. 103°46′W
Conterminous U.S. (48 states)—Near Lebanon, Smith Co., Kansas, lat. 39°50′N, long. 98°35′W
North American continent—6 mi W of Balta, Pierce County, North Dakota; lat. 48°10′N, long. 100°10′W

State—county, locality of center

Alabama—Chilton, 12 mi SW of Clanton
Alaska—lat. 63°50′N, long. 152°W; approx. 60 mi NW of Mt. McKinley
Arizona—Yavapai, 55 mi E-SE of Prescott
Arkansas—Pulaski, 12 mi NW of Little Rock
California—Madera, 38 mi E of Madera
Colorado—Park, 30 mi NW of Pikes Peak
Connecticut—Hartford, at East Berlin
Delaware—Kent, 11 mi S of Dover
District of Columbia—Near 4th and L Sts. NW
Florida—Hernando, 12 mi N-NW of Brooksville
Georgia—Twiggs, 18 mi SE of Macon
Hawaii—Hawaii, lat. 20°15′N, long. 156°20′W, off Maui Isl.
Idaho—Custer, SW of Challis
Illinois—Logan, 28 mi NE of Springfield
Indiana—Boone, 14 mi N-NW of Indianapolis
Iowa—Story, 5 mi NE of Ames
Kansas—Barton, 15 mi NE of Great Bend
Kentucky—Marion, 3 mi N-NW of Lebanon
Louisiana—Avoyelles, 3 mi SE of Marksville
Maine—Piscataquis, 18 mi N of Dover
Maryland—Prince George's, 4.5 mi NW of Davidsonville
Massachusetts—Worcester, N part of city
Michigan—Wexford, 5 mi N-NW of Cadillac
Minnesota—Crow Wing, 10 mi SW of Brainerd
Mississippi—Leake, 9 mi W-NW of Carthage
Missouri—Miller, 20 mi SW of Jefferson City
Montana—Fergus, 11 mi W of Lewistown
Nebraska—Custer, 10 mi NW of Broken Bow
Nevada—Lander, 26 mi SE of Austin
New Hampshire—Belknap, 3 mi E of Ashland
New Jersey—Mercer, 5 mi SE of Trenton
New Mexico—Torrance, 12 mi S-SW of Willard
New York—Madison, 12 mi S of Oneida and 26 mi SW of Utica
North Carolina—Chatham, 10 mi NW of Sanford
North Dakota—Sheridan, 5 mi SW of McClusky
Ohio—Delaware, 25 mi N-NE of Columbus
Oklahoma—Oklahoma, 8 mi N of Oklahoma City
Oregon—Crook, 25 mi S-SE of Prineville
Pennsylvania—Centre, 2.5 mi SW of Bellefonte
Rhode Island—Kent, 1 mi S-SW of Crompton
South Carolina—Richland, 13 mi SE of Columbia
South Dakota—Hughes, 8 mi NE of Pierre
Tennessee—Rutherford, 5 mi NE of Murfreesboro
Texas—McCulloch, 15 mi NE of Brady
Utah—Sanpete, 3 mi N of Manti
Vermont—Washington, 3 mi E of Roxbury
Virginia—Buckingham, 5 mi SW of Buckingham
Washington—Chelan, 10 mi W-SW of Wenatchee
West Virginia—Braxton, 4 mi E of Sutton
Wisconsin—Wood, 9 mi SE of Marshfield
Wyoming—Fremont, 58 mi E-NE of Lander

International Boundary Lines of the U.S.

The length of the N boundary of the conterminous U.S.—the U.S.-Canadian border, excluding Alaska—is 3,987 mi according to the U.S. Geological Survey, Dept. of the Interior. The length of the Alaskan-Canadian border is 1,538 mi. The length of the U.S.-Mexican border, from the Gulf of Mexico to the Pacific Ocean, is approximately 1,933 mi (1963 boundary agreement).

Origins of the Names of U.S. States

Source: State officials, Smithsonian Institution, and Topographic Division, U.S. Geological Survey, Dept. of the Interior

Alabama—Indian for tribal town, later a tribe (Alabamas or Alibamons) of the Creek confederacy.

Alaska—Russian version of Aleutian (Eskimo) word, *alakshak*, for "peninsula," "great lands," or "land that is not an island."

Arizona—Spanish version of Pima Indian word for "little spring place," or Aztec *arizuma*, meaning "silver-bearing."

Arkansas—Algonquin name for the Quapaw Indians, meaning "south wind."

California—Bestowed by the Spanish conquistadors (possibly by Cortez). It was the name of an imaginary island, an earthly paradise, in *Las Serges de Esplandian*, a Spanish romance written by Montalvo in 1510. *Baja California* (Lower California, in Mexico) was first visited by Spanish in 1533. The present U.S. state was called *Alta* (Upper) *California*.

Colorado—From Spanish for "red," first applied to Colorado River.

Connecticut—From Mohican and other Algonquin words meaning "long river place."

Delaware—Named for Lord De La Warr, early governor of Virginia; first applied to river, then to Indian tribe (Lenni-Lenape), and the state.

District of Columbia—For Christopher Columbus, 1791.

Florida—Named by Ponce de Leon *Pascua Florida*, "Flowery Easter," on Easter Sunday, 1513.

Georgia—For King George II of England, by James Oglethorpe, colonial administrator, 1732.

Hawaii—Possibly derived from native word for homeland, *Hawaiki* or *Owhyhee*.

Idaho—Said to be a coined name with an invented meaning: "gem of the mountains"; originally suggested for the Pikes Peak mining territory (Colorado), then applied to the new mining territory of the Pacific Northwest. Another theory suggests *Idaho* may be a Kiowa Apache term for the Comanche.

Illinois—French for *Illini* or "land of *Illini*," Algonquin word meaning "men" or "warriors."

Indiana—Means "land of the Indians."

Iowa— Indian word variously translated as "here I rest" or "beautiful land." Named for the Iowa R., which was named for the Iowa Indians.

Kansas—Sioux word for "south wind people."

Kentucky—Indian word that is variously translated as "dark and bloody ground," "meadowland," and "land of tomorrow."

Louisiana—Part of territory called Louisiana by Sieur de La Salle for French King Louis XIV.

Maine—From Maine, ancient French province. Also: descriptive, referring to the mainland as distinct from the many coastal islands.

Maryland—For Queen Henrietta Maria, wife of Charles I of England.

Massachusetts—From Indian tribe named after "large hill place" identified by Capt. John Smith as being near Milton, MA.

Michigan—From Chippewa words, *mici gama*, meaning "great water," after the lake of the same name.

Minnesota—From Dakota Sioux word meaning "cloudy water" or "sky-tinted water" of the Minnesota River.

Mississippi—Probably Chippewa; *mici zibi*, "great river" or "gathering-in of all the waters." Also: Algonquin word, *messipi*.

Missouri—An Algonquin Indian term meaning "river of the big canoes."

Montana—Latin or Spanish for "mountainous."

Nebraska—From Omaha or Otos Indian word meaning "broad water" or "flat river," describing the Platte River.

Nevada—Spanish, meaning "snow-clad."

New Hampshire—Named, 1629, by Capt. John Mason of Plymouth Council for his home county in England.

New Jersey—The Duke of York, 1664, gave a patent to John Berkeley and Sir George Carteret to be called Nova Caesaria, or New Jersey, after England's Isle of Jersey.

New Mexico—Spaniards in Mexico applied term to land north and west of Rio Grande in the 16th century.

New York—For Duke of York and Albany, who received patent to New Netherland from his brother Charles II and sent an expedition to capture it, 1664.

North Carolina—In 1619 Charles I gave a large patent to Sir Robert Heath to be called Province of Carolana, from *Carolus*, Latin name for Charles. A new patent was granted by Charles II to Earl of Clarendon and others. Divided into North and South Carolina, 1710.

North Dakota—*Dakota* is Sioux for "friend" or "ally."

Ohio—Iroquois word for "fine or good river."

Oklahoma—Choctaw word meaning "red man," proposed by Rev. Allen Wright, Choctaw-speaking Indian.

Oregon—Origin unknown. One theory holds that the name may have been derived from that of the Wisconsin River, shown on a 1715 French map as "Ouaricon-sint."

Pennsylvania—William Penn, the Quaker who was made full proprietor of this area by King Charles II in 1681, suggested "Sylvania," or "woodland," for his tract. The king's government owed Penn's father, Admiral William Penn, £16,000, and the land was granted as partial settlement. Charles II added the "Penn" to Sylvania, against the desires of the modest proprietor, in honor of the admiral.

Puerto Rico—Spanish for "rich port."

Rhode Island—Exact origin is unknown. One theory notes that Giovanni de Verrazano recorded an island about the size of Rhodes in the Mediterranean in 1524, but others believe the state was named *Roode Eylandt* by Adriaen Block, Dutch explorer, because of its red clay.

South Carolina—See North Carolina.

South Dakota—See North Dakota.

Tennessee—*Tanasi* was the name of Cherokee villages on the Little Tennessee River. From 1784 to 1788 this was the State of Franklin, or Frankland.

Texas—Variant of word used by Caddo and other Indians meaning "friends" or "allies," and applied to them by the Spanish in eastern Texas. Also written *Texias*, *Tejas*, *Teysas*.

Utah—From a Navajo word meaning "upper," or "higher up," as applied to a Shoshone tribe called Ute. Spanish form is *Yutta*. The English is *Uta* or *Utah*. Proposed name *Deseret*, "land of honeybees," from Book of Mormon, was rejected by Congress.

Vermont—From French words *vert* (green) and *mont* (mountain). The Green Mountains were said to have been named by Samuel de Champlain. When the state was formed, 1777, Dr. Thomas Young suggested combining *vert* and *mont* into Vermont.

Virginia—Named by Sir Walter Raleigh, who fitted out the expedition of 1584, in honor of Queen Elizabeth, the Virgin Queen of England.

Washington—Named after George Washington. When the bill creating the Territory of Columbia was introduced in the 32d Congress, the name was changed to Washington because of the existence of the District of Columbia.

West Virginia—So named when western counties of Virginia refused to secede from the U.S. in 1863.

Wisconsin—An Indian name, spelled *Ouisconsin* and *Mesconsing* by early chroniclers. Believed to mean "grassy place" in Chippewa. Congress made it *Wisconsin*.

Wyoming—From the Algonquin words for "large prairie place," "at the big plains," or "on the great plain."

Territorial Sea of the U.S.

According to a Dec. 27, 1988, proclamation by Pres. Ronald Reagan: "The territorial sea of the United States henceforth extends to 12 nautical miles from the baselines of the United States determined in accordance with international law. In accordance with international law, as reflected in the applicable provisions of the 1982 United Nations Convention on the Law of the Sea, within the territorial sea of the United States, the ships of all countries enjoy the right of innocent passage and the ships and aircraft of all countries enjoy the right of transit passage through international straits."

Accession of Territory by the U.S.

Source: U.S. Dept. of the Interior; Bureau of the Census, U.S. Dept. of Commerce

	Acquisition date	Land area (sq mi)[1]
Total U.S.[2]	**NA**	**3,540,305**
50 states and Washington, DC.	NA	3,536,278
Territory in 1790[3]	NA	895,415
Louisiana Purchase[4]	1803	909,380
Purchase of Florida	1819	58,666

	Acquisition date	Land area (sq mi)[1]
Texas	1845	388,687
Oregon Territory	1846	286,541
Mexican Cession	1848	529,189
Gadsden Purchase	1853	29,670
Alaska	1867	570,374
Hawaii	1898	6,423

	Acquisition date	Land area (sq mi)[1]
Other areas:		
Puerto Rico[5]	1899	3,427
Guam[6]	1899	210
American Samoa[7]	1900	77
U.S. Virgin Islands	1917	134
N Mariana Islands	1986	179
All other[8]	NA	15

NA=not applicable. (1) Area figures from the Bureau of the Census, Apr. 1, 1990. As a result of independent rounding, the sum of these figures does not equal the total. (2) Includes outlying areas. (3) Includes that part of a drainage basin of Red River of the North, S of 49th parallel, sometimes considered part of Louisiana Purchase. (4) Also acquired areas W of the Mississippi River amounting to 22,834 sq mi, but relinquished to Spain 97,150 sq mi, or a net loss of 15,650 sq mi. (5) Ceded by Spain in 1898, ratified in 1899, and became the Commonwealth of Puerto Rico by Act of Congress on July 25, 1952. (6) Acquired 1898; ratified 1899. (7) Acquired 1899; ratified 1900. (8) Consisting of the following islands, with gross areas as indicated in sq mi: Midway (2), Wake (3), Palmyra (2), Navassa (3), Baker, Howland, and Jarvis (combined area, 3), Johnston Atoll (combined area, less than 1), and Kingman Reef (less than 0.5).

Federally Owned Land, by State, 1996

Source: Bureau of Land Management, U.S. Dept. of the Interior; as of Sept. 30, 1996

State	Federal acreage[1]	Total acreage of state[2]	Percentage of federally owned acreage[1]
AL	1,080,003.8	32,678,400	3.305
AK	171,787,844.1	365,481,600	47.003
AZ	31,336,525.9	72,688,000	43.111
AR	2,739,612.8	33,599,360	8.154
CA	44,757,446.9	100,206,720	44.665
CO	24,129,261.8	66,485,760	36.292
CT	6,909.8	3,135,360	0.220
DE	1,916.0	1,265,920	0.151
DC	9,153.6	39,040	23.447
FL	2,644,547.2	34,721,280	7.617
GA	1,459,961.4	37,295,360	3.915
HI	350,221.2	4,105,600	8.530
ID	32,991,883.8	52,933,120	62.328
IL	404,911.8	35,795,200	1.131
IN	394,186.1	23,158,400	1.702
IA	29,604.0	35,860,480	0.083
KS	349,708.0	52,510,720	0.666
KY	1,082,523.7	25,512,320	4.243
LA	744,782.4	28,867,840	2.580
ME	193,279.4	19,847,680	0.974
MD	157,271.6	6,319,360	2.489
MA	52,108.6	5,034,880	1.035
MI	3,979,625.4	36,492,160	10.905
MN	4,068,850.2	51,205,760	7.946
MS	1,276,341.8	30,222,720	4.223
MO	1,658,253.1	44,248,320	3.748

State	Federal acreage[1]	Total acreage of state[2]	Percentage of federally owned acreage[1]
MT	25,485,339.5	93,271,040	27.324
NE	514,978.6	49,031,680	1.050
NV	56,081,559.1	70,264,320	79.815
NH	734,448.1	5,768,960	12.731
NJ	101,564.1	4,813,440	2.110
NM	26,216,537.1	77,766,400	33.712
NY	196,618.5	30,680,960	0.641
NC	2,028,449.8	31,402,880	6.459
ND	1,412,803.4	44,452,480	3.178
OH	279,601.5	26,222,080	1.066
OK	677,614.5	44,087,680	1.537
OR	31,809,283.0	61,598,720	51.640
PA	622,551.0	28,804,480	2.161
RI	3,100.1	677,120	0.458
SC	934,567.5	19,374,080	4.824
SD	2,577,446.3	48,881,920	5.273
TN	1,576,100.7	26,727,680	5.897
TX	2,007,830.8	168,217,600	1.194
UT	33,898,255.1	52,696,960	64.327
VT	376,551.1	5,936,640	6.343
VA	2,279,369.0	25,496,320	8.940
WA	11,938,958.4	42,693,760	27.964
WV	1,077,285.4	15,410,560	6.991
WI	1,733,205.5	35,011,200	4.950
WY	30,878,165.7	62,343,040	49.530
Total	**563,128,918.2**	**2,271,343,360**	**24.793**

Note: Totals do not include inland water. (1) Excludes trust properties. (2) Bureau of the Census, U.S. Dept. of Commerce figures.

Special Recreation Areas Administered by the U.S. Forest Service, 1996

Source: U.S. Forest Service, Dept. of Agriculture

Area name	Location	Estab.	Acres
Admiralty Island	AK	1980	978,881
Allegheny	PA	1984	23,063
Arapaho	CO	1978	30,690
Beech Creek	OK	1988	7,500
Cascade Head	OR	1974	6,630
Columbia River Gorge	OR-WA	1986	63,150
Coosa Bald	GA	1991	7,100
Ed Jenkins	GA	1991	23,166
Flaming Gorge	WY-UT	1968	189,825
Grand Island	MI	1990	12,961
Hells Canyon	ID-OR	1975	536,648
Indian Nations	OK	1988	40,051
Jemez	NM	1993	57,000
Misty Fiords	AK	1980	2,293,428
Mono Basin	CA	1984	115,600
Mount Baker	WA	1984	8,473

Area name	Location	Estab.	Acres
Mount Pleasant	VA	1994	7,580
Mount Rogers	VA	1966	114,520
Mount St. Helens	WA	1989	112,593
Newberry	OR	1990	54,822
North Cascades	WA	1984	87,600
Oregon Dunes	OR	1972	27,212
Pine Ridge	NE	1986	6,600
Rattlesnake	MT	1980	59,119
Sawtooth	ID	1972	729,322
Smith River	CA	1990	305,169
Spring Mt.	NV	1993	312,683
Spruce Knob-Seneca Rocks	WV	1965	57,237
Whiskeytown-Shasta-Trinity	CA	1965	176,367
White Rocks	VT	1984	36,400
Winding Stair Mt.	OK	1988	25,890

National Parks, Other Areas Administered by National Park Service

Dates that the sites were authorized for initial protection by Congress or by presidential proclamation are given in parentheses. If different, the date the area was given its current designation, or was transferred to the National Park Service, follows. Gross area in acres, as of Dec. 31, 1997, follows date(s). More than 83 mil acres of federal land are now administered by the National Park Service.

National Parks

Acadia, ME (1916/1929) 47,678. Includes Mount Desert Isl., half of Isle au Haut, Schoodic Peninsula on mainland. Highest elevation on Eastern seaboard.

American Samoa, AS (1988) 9,000. Features a paleotropical rain forest and a coral reef. No federal facilities.

Arches, UT (1929/1971) 73,379. Contains giant red sandstone arches and other products of erosion.

Badlands, SD (1929/1978) 242,756. Prairie with bison, bighorn, and antelope. Contains animal fossils from 26 to 37 mil years ago.

Big Bend, TX (1935) 801,163. Rio Grande, Chisos Mts.

Biscayne, FL (1968/1980) 172,924. Aquatic park encompassing chain of islands south of Miami.

Bryce Canyon, UT (1923/1928) 35,835. Spectacularly colorful and unusual display of erosion effects.

Canyonlands, UT (1964) 337,570. At junction of Colorado and Green rivers; extensive evidence of prehistoric Indians.

Capitol Reef, UT (1937/1971) 241,904. A 70-mi uplift of sandstone cliffs dissected by high-walled gorges.

Carlsbad Caverns, NM (1923/1930) 46,766. Largest known caverns; not yet fully explored.

Channel Islands, CA (1938/1980) 256,334. Sea lion breeding place, nesting sea birds, unique plants.

Crater Lake, OR (1902) 183,224. Extraordinary blue lake in the crater of Mt. Mazama, a volcano that erupted about 7,700 years ago; deepest U.S. lake.

Death Valley, CA-NV (1933/1994) 3,367,628. Large desert area. Includes the lowest point in the Western Hemisphere; also includes Scottys Castle.

Denali, AK (1917/1980) 4,741,800. Name changed from Mt. McKinley NP. Contains highest mountain in U.S.; wildlife.

Dry Tortugas, FL (1935/1992) 64,700. Formerly Ft. Jefferson National Monument.

Everglades, FL (1934) 1,508,490. Largest remaining subtropical wilderness in continental U.S.

Gates of the Arctic, AK (1978/1984) 7,523,898. Vast wilderness in north central region. Limited federal facilities.

Glacier, MT (1910) 1,013,572. Superb Rocky Mt. scenery, numerous glaciers and glacial lakes. Part of Waterton-Glacier Intl. Peace Park established by U.S. and Canada in 1932.

Glacier Bay, AK (1925/1986) 3,225,484. Great tidewater glaciers that move down mountainsides and break up into the sea; much wildlife.

Grand Canyon, AZ (1893/1919) 1,217,403. Most spectacular part of Colorado River's greatest canyon.

Grand Teton, WY (1929) 310,027. Most impressive part of the Teton Mts., winter feeding ground of largest American elk herd.

Great Basin, NV (1922/1986) 77,180. Includes Wheeler Pk., Lexington Arch, and Lehman Caves.

Great Smoky Mountains, NC-TN (1926/1934) 521,621. Largest Eastern mountain range, magnificent forests.

Guadalupe Mountains, TX (1966) 86,416. Extensive Permian limestone fossil reef; tremendous earth fault.

Haleakala, HI (1916/1960) 28,091. Dormant volcano on Maui with large colorful craters.

Hawaii Volcanoes, HI (1916/1961) 209,695. Contains Kilauea and Mauna Loa, active volcanoes.

Hot Springs, AR (1832/1921) 5,549. Bathhouses are furnished with thermal waters from the park's 47 hot springs; these waters are used for bathing and drinking.

Isle Royale, MI (1931) 571,790. Largest island in Lake Superior, noted for its wilderness area and wildlife.

Joshua Tree, CA (1936/1994) 792,750. Desert region includes Joshua trees and other plant and animal life.

Katmai, AK (1918/1980) 3,674,541. "Valley of Ten Thousand Smokes," scene of 1912 volcanic eruption.

Kenai Fjords, AK (1978/1980) 652,048. Abundant marine mammals, birdlife; the Harding Icefield, one of the 4 major icecaps in U.S.

Kings Canyon, CA (1890/1940) 461,901. Mountain wilderness, dominated by Kings River Canyons and High Sierra; contains giant sequoias.

Kobuk Valley, AK (1978/1980) 1,750,737. Contains geological and recreational sites. Limited federal facilities.

Lake Clark, AK (1978/1980) 2,619,859. Across Cook Inlet from Anchorage. A scenic wilderness rich in fish and wildlife. Limited federal facilities.

Lassen Volcanic, CA (1907/1916) 106,372. Contains Lassen Peak, recently active volcano, and other volcanic phenomena.

Mammoth Cave, KY (1926/1941) 52,830. 144 mi of surveyed underground passages, beautiful natural formations, river 300 ft below surface.

Mesa Verde, CO (1906) 52,122. Most notable and best preserved prehistoric cliff dwellings in the U.S.

Mount Rainier, WA (1899) 235,613. Greatest single-peak glacial system in the U.S.

North Cascades, WA (1968) 504,781. Spectacular mountainous region with many glaciers, lakes.

Olympic, WA (1909/1938) 922,651. Mountain wilderness containing finest remnant of Pacific Northwest rain forest, active glaciers, Pacific shoreline, rare elk.

Petrified Forest, AZ (1906/1962) 93,533. Extensive petrified wood and Indian artifacts. Contains part of Painted Desert.

Redwood, CA (1968) 110,232. 40 mi of Pacific coastline, groves of ancient redwoods and world's tallest trees.

Rocky Mountain, CO (1915) 265,727. On the Continental Divide; includes peaks over 14,000 ft.

Saguaro, AZ (1933/1994) 91,444. Part of the Sonoran Desert; includes the giant saguaro cacti, unique to the region.

Sequoia, CA (1890) 402,482. Groves of giant sequoias, highest mountain in conterminous U.S.—Mt. Whitney (14,494 ft). World's largest tree.

Shenandoah, VA (1926) 197,506. Portion of the Blue Ridge Mts.; overlooks Shenandoah Valley; Skyline Drive.

Theodore Roosevelt, ND (1947/1978) 70,447. Contains part of T.R.'s ranch and scenic badlands.

Virgin Islands, VI (1956) 14,689. Authorized to cover 75% of St. John Isl. and Hassel Isl.; lush growth, lovely beaches, Carib Indian petroglyphs, evidence of colonial Danes.

Voyageurs, MN (1971) 218,200. Abundant lakes, forests, wildlife, canoeing, boating.

Wind Cave, SD (1903) 28,295. Limestone caverns in Black Hills. Extensive wildlife includes a herd of bison.

Wrangell-St. Elias, AK (1978/1980) 8,323,618. Largest area in park system, most peaks over 16,000 ft, abundant wildlife; day's drive east of Anchorage. Limited federal facilities.

Yellowstone, ID-MT-WY (1872) 2,219,791. World's first national park. World's greatest geyser area has about 10,000 geysers and hot springs; spectacular falls and impressive canyons of the Yellowstone River; grizzly bear, moose, and bison.

Yosemite, CA (1890) 761,236. Yosemite Valley, the nation's highest waterfall, grove of sequoias, and mountains.

Zion, UT (1909/1919) 146,598. Unusual shapes and landscapes have resulted from erosion and faulting; evidence of past volcanic activity; Zion Canyon, with sheer walls ranging up to 2,640 ft, is readily accessible.

National Historical Parks

Appomattox Court House, VA (1930/1954) 1,775. Where Lee surrendered to Grant.

Boston, MA (1974) 41. Includes Faneuil Hall, Old North Church, Bunker Hill, Paul Revere House.

Cane River Creole (and heritage area), LA (1994) 207. Preserves the Creole culture as it developed along the Cane R.

Chaco Culture, NM (1907/1980) 33,974. Ruins of pueblos built by prehistoric Indians.

Chesapeake and Ohio Canal, MD-DC-WV (1938/1971) 19,439. 184-mi historic canal; DC to Cumberland, MD.

Colonial, VA (1930/1936) 9,349. Includes most of Jamestown Isl., site of first successful English colony; Yorktown, site of Cornwallis's surrender to George Washington; and the Colonial Parkway.

Cumberland Gap, KY-TN-VA (1940) 20,454. Mountain pass of the Wilderness Road, which carried the first great migration of pioneers into America's interior.

Dayton Aviation Heritage, OH (1992) 86. Commemorates the area's aviation heritage.

George Rogers Clark, Vincennes, IN (1966) 26. Commemorates American defeat of British in West during Revolution.

Harpers Ferry, MD-VA-WV (1944/1963) 2,287. At the confluence of the Shenandoah and Potomac rivers, the site of John Brown's 1859 raid on the Army arsenal.

Hopewell Culture, OH (1923/1992) 1,245. Formerly Mound City Group National Monument.

Independence, PA (1948) 45. Contains several properties in Philadelphia associated with the American Revolution and the founding of the U.S. Includes Independence Hall.

Jean Laffite (and preserve), LA (1907/1978) 20,020. Includes Chalmette, site of 1815 Battle of New Orleans; French Quarter.

Kalaupapa, HI (1980) 10,779. Molokai's former leper colony site and other historic areas.

Kaloko-Honokohau, HI (1978) 1,161. Preserves the native culture of Hawaii. No federal facilities.

Keweenaw, MI (1992) 1,870. Site of first significant copper mine in U.S. Federal facilities are under development.

Klondike Gold Rush, AK-WA (1976) 13,191. Alaskan Trails in 1898 Gold Rush. Museum in Seattle.

Lowell, MA (1978) 139. Textile mills, canal, 19th-cent. structures; park shows planned city of Industrial Revolution.

Lyndon B. Johnson, TX (1969/1980) 1,570. President's birthplace, boyhood home, ranch.

Marsh-Billings, VT (1992) 643. Boyhood home of pioneer conservationist George Perkins Marsh. No federal facilities.

Minute Man, MA (1959) 967. Where the colonial Minute Men battled the British, Apr. 19, 1775. Also contains Nathaniel Hawthorne's home.

Morristown, NJ (1933) 1,684. Sites of important military encampments during the American Revolution; Washington's headquarters, 1777, 1779-80.

Natchez, MS (1988) 108. Mansions, townhouses, and villas related to history of Natchez.

New Bedford Whaling, MA (1996) 20. Preserves structures and relics associated with the city's 19th-century whaling industry.

New Orleans Jazz, LA (1994) Acreage undetermined. Preserves, educates, and interprets jazz as it has evolved in New Orleans.

Nez Perce, ID (1965) 2,123. Illustrates the history and culture of the Nez Perce Indian country (38 separate sites).

Pecos, NM (1965/1990) 6,671. Ruins of ancient Pueblo of Pecos, archaeological sites, and 2 associated Spanish colonial missions from the 17th and 18th centuries.

Pu'uhonua o Honaunau, HI (1955/1978) 182. Until 1819, a sanctuary for Hawaiians vanquished in battle and for those guilty of crimes or breaking taboos.

Salt River Bay (and ecological preserve), St. Croix, VI (1992) 945. The only site known where, 500 years ago, members of a Columbus party landed on what is now territory of the U.S.

San Antonio Missions, TX (1978) 819. Four of finest Spanish missions in U.S., 18th-cent. irrigation system.

San Francisco Maritime, CA (1988) 31. Artifacts, photographs, and historic vessels related to the development of the Pacific Coast.

San Juan Island, WA (1966) 1,752. Commemorates peaceful relations between the U.S., Canada, and Great Britain since the 1872 boundary disputes.

Saratoga, NY (1938) 3,394. Scene of a major 1777 battle that became a turning point in the American Revolution.

Sitka, AK (1910/1972) 107. Scene of last major resistance of the Tlingit Indians to the Russians, 1804.

Tumacacori, AZ (1908/1990) 47. Historic Spanish Catholic mission building stands near the site first visited by Jesuit Father Kino in 1691.

Valley Forge, PA (1976) 3,466. Continental Army campsite in 1777-78 winter.

War in the Pacific, GU (1978) 1,960. Seven distinct units illustrating the Pacific theater of WWII. Limited federal facilities.

Women's Rights, NY (1980) 7. Seneca Falls site where Lucretia Mott, Elizabeth Cady Stanton began rights movement in 1848.

National Battlefields

Antietam, MD (1890/1978) 3,256. Battle here ended first Confederate invasion of North, Sept. 17, 1862.

Big Hole, MT (1910/1963) 656. Site of major battle with Nez Perce Indians.

Cowpens, SC (1929/1972) 842. American Revolution battlefield.

Fort Donelson, TN-KY (1928/1985) 552. Site of first major Union victory.

Fort Necessity, PA (1931/1961) 903. Site of first battle of French and Indian War.

Monocacy, MD (1934/1976) 1,647. Civil War battle in defense of Washington, DC, fought here, July 9, 1864.

Moores Creek, NC (1926/1980) 88. 1776 battle between Patriots and Loyalists commemorated here.

Petersburg, VA (1926/1962) 2,659. Scene of 10-month Union campaigns, 1864-65.

Stones River, TN (1927/1960) 711. Scene of battle that began federal offensive to trisect the Confederacy.

Tupelo, MS (1929/1961) 1. Site of crucial battle over Sherman's supply line, 1865.

Wilson's Creek, MO (1960/1970) 1,750. Scene of Civil War battle for control of Missouri.

National Battlefield Parks

Kennesaw Mountain, GA (1917/1935) 2,884. Site of two major battles of Atlanta campaign in Civil War.

Manassas, VA (1940) 5,072. Scene of two battles in Civil War, 1861 and 1862.

Richmond, VA (1936) 1,058. Site of battles defending Confederate capital.

National Battlefield Site

Brices Cross Roads, MS (1929) 1. Civil War battlefield.

National Military Parks

Chickamauga and Chattanooga, GA-TN (1890) 8,119. Site of major Confederate victory, 1863.

Fredericksburg and Spotsylvania County, VA (1927/1933) 7,927. Sites of several major Civil War battles and campaigns.

Gettysburg, PA (1895/1933) 5,912. Site of decisive Confederate defeat in North and of Gettysburg Address.

Guilford Courthouse, NC (1917/1933) 220. American Revolution battle site.

Horseshoe Bend, AL (1956) 2,040. On Tallapoosa River, where Gen. Andrew Jackson's forces broke the power of the Upper Creek Indian Confederacy.

Kings Mountain, SC (1931/1933) 3,945. Site of American Revolution battle.

Pea Ridge, AR (1956) 4,300. Scene of Civil War battle.

Shiloh, TN (1894/1933) 3,973. Major Civil War battlesite; includes some well-preserved Indian burial mounds.

Vicksburg, MS (1899/1933) 1,736. Union victory gave North control of the Mississippi and split the Confederate forces.

National Memorials

Arkansas Post, AR (1960) 389. First permanent French settlement in the lower Mississippi River valley.

Arlington House, the Robert E. Lee Memorial, VA (1925/1972) 28. Lee's home overlooking the Potomac.

Chamizal, El Paso, TX (1966/1974) 55. Commemorates 1963 settlement of 99-year border dispute with Mexico.

Coronado, AZ (1941/1952) 4,750. Commemorates first European exploration of the Southwest.

DeSoto, FL (1948) 27. Commemorates 16th-cent. Spanish explorations.

Federal Hall, NY (1939/1955) 0.45. First seat of U.S. government under the Constitution.

Fort Caroline, FL (1950) 138. On St. Johns River, overlooks site of a French Huguenot colony.

Fort Clatsop, OR (1958) 125. Lewis and Clark encampment, 1805-6.

Franklin Delano Roosevelt, DC (1982) 7.5. Statues of Pres. Roosevelt and Eleanor Roosevelt, as well as waterfalls and gardens. Dedicated May 2, 1997.

General Grant, NY (1958) 0.76. Tomb of Grant and wife.

Hamilton Grange, NY (1962) 0.11. Home of Alexander Hamilton.

Jefferson National Expansion Memorial, St. Louis, MO (1935) 91. Commemorates westward expansion.

Johnstown Flood, PA (1964) 164. Commemorates tragic flood of 1889.

Korean War Veterans, DC (1986) 2. Dedicated in 1995; honors those who served in the Korean War.

Lincoln Boyhood, IN (1962) 200. Lincoln grew up here.

Lincoln Memorial, DC (1911/1933) 107. Marble statue of the 16th U.S. president.

Lyndon B. Johnson Grove on the Potomac, DC (1973) 17. Overlooks the Potomac R.; vista of the Capital.

Mount Rushmore, SD (1925) 1,278. World-famous sculpture of 4 presidents.

Oklahoma City National Memorial, OK (1997) 6. Commemorates site of April 19, 1995, bombing which killed 168.

Perry's Victory and International Peace Memorial, Put-in-Bay, OH (1936/1972) 25. The world's most massive Doric column, constructed 1912-15, promotes pursuit of international peace through arbitration and disarmament.

Roger Williams, Providence, RI (1965) 5. Memorial to founder of Rhode Island.

Thaddeus Kosciuszko, PA (1972) 0.02. Memorial to Polish hero of American Revolution.

Theodore Roosevelt Island, DC (1932/1933) 89. Statue of Roosevelt in wooded island sanctuary.

Thomas Jefferson Memorial, DC (1934) 18. Statue of Jefferson in an inscribed circular, colonnaded structure.

USS *Arizona*, HI (1980). 11. Memorializes American losses at Pearl Harbor.

Vietnam Veterans, DC (1980) 2. Black granite wall inscribed with names of those missing or killed in action in the Vietnam War.

Washington Monument, DC (1848/1933) 106. Obelisk honoring the first U.S. president.

Wright Brothers, NC (1927/1953) 428. Site of first powered flight.

National Historic Sites

Abraham Lincoln Birthplace, Hodgenville, KY (1916/1959) 117. Early 17th-cent. cabin.

Adams, Quincy, MA (1946/1952) 14. Home of Pres. John Adams, John Quincy Adams, and celebrated descendants.

Allegheny Portage Railroad, PA (1964) 1,249. Linked the Pennsylvania Canal system and the West.

Andersonville, Andersonville, GA (1970) 495. Noted Civil War prisoner-of-war camp.

Andrew Johnson, Greeneville, TN (1935/1963) 17. Two homes and the tailor shop of the 17th U.S. president.

Bent's Old Fort, CO (1960) 800. Reconstruction of S Plains outpost.

Boston African American, MA (1980) Acreage undetermined. Pre-Civil War black history structures.

Brown v. Board of Education, KS (1992) 2. Commemorates the landmark 1954 U.S. Supreme Court decision.

Carl Sandburg Home, Flat Rock, NC (1968) 264. Poet's home.

Charles Pinckney, SC (1988) 28. Statesman's farm.

Christiansted, St. Croix, VI (1952/1961) 27. Commemorates Danish colony.

Clara Barton, MD (1974) 9. Home of founder of American Red Cross.

Edgar Allan Poe, PA (1978/1980) 0.52. Writer's home.

Edison, West Orange, NJ (1955/1962) 21. Inventor's home and laboratory.

Eisenhower, Gettysburg, PA (1967) 690. Home of 34th president.

Eleanor Roosevelt, Hyde Park, NY (1977) 181. The former first lady's personal retreat.

Eugene O'Neill, Danville, CA (1976) 13. Playwright's home.

Ford's Theatre, DC (1866/1970) 0.29. Includes theater, now restored, where Lincoln was assassinated, house where he died, and Lincoln Museum.

Fort Bowie, AZ (1964) 1,000. Focal point of operations against Geronimo and the Apaches.

Fort Davis, TX (1961) 460. Key frontier outpost in West Texas.

Fort Laramie, WY (1938/1960) 833. Military post on Oregon Trail.

Fort Larned, KS (1964/1966) 718. Military post on Santa Fe Trail.

Fort Point, San Francisco, CA (1970) 29. West Coast fortification.

Fort Raleigh, NC (1941) 513. First attempted English settlement in North America.

Fort Scott, KS (1965/1978) 17. Commemorates U.S. frontier of 1840s and '50s.

Fort Smith, AR-OK (1961) 75. Active post during 1817-90.

Fort Union Trading Post, MT-ND (1966) 444. Principal fur-trading post on upper Missouri, 1829-67.

Fort Vancouver, WA (1948/1961) 209. Headquarters for Hudson's Bay Company in 1825. Early political seat.

Frederick Douglass, DC (1962/1988) 9. Home of famous black abolitionist, writer, and orator.

Frederick Law Olmsted, MA (1979) 2. Home of famous city planner.

Friendship Hill, PA (1978) 675. Home of Albert Gallatin, Jefferson's and Madison's secretary of treasury.

Golden Spike, UT (1957) 2,735. Commemorates completion of first transcontinental railroad in 1869.

Grant-Kohrs Ranch, MT (1972) 1,498. Ranch house and part of 19th-cent. ranch.

Hampton, MD (1948) 62. 18th-cent. Georgian mansion.

Harry S. Truman, MO (1983) 7. Home of Pres. Truman after 1919.

Herbert Hoover, West Branch, IA (1965) 187. Birthplace and boyhood home of 31st president.

Home of Franklin D. Roosevelt, Hyde Park, NY (1944) 290. FDR's birthplace, home, and "summer White House."

Hopewell Furnace, PA (1938/1985) 848. 19th-cent. iron-making village.

Hubbell Trading Post, AZ (1965) 160. Still active today.

James A. Garfield, Mentor, OH (1980) 8. Home of 20th president.

Jimmy Carter, GA (1987) 71. Birthplace and home of 39th president.

John Fitzgerald Kennedy, Brookline, MA (1967) 0.09. Birthplace and childhood home of 35th president.

John Muir, Martinez, CA (1964) 345. Home of early conservationist and writer.

Knife River Indian Villages, ND (1974) 1,758. Remnants of villages last occupied by Hidatsa and Mandan Indians.

Lincoln Home, Springfield, IL (1971) 12. Lincoln's residence at the time he was elected 16th president, 1860.

Longfellow, Cambridge, MA (1972) 2. Longfellow's home, 1837-82, and Washington's headquarters during Boston siege, 1775-76.

Maggie L. Walker, VA (1978) 1. Richmond home of black leader and bank president, daughter of an ex-slave.

Manzanar, Lone Pine, CA (1992) 814. Commemorates Manzanar War Relocation Ctr., a Japanese-American internment camp during WWII. No federal facilities.

Martin Luther King Jr., Atlanta, GA (1980) 37. Birthplace, grave, and church of the civil rights leader. Limited federal facilities.

Martin Van Buren, NY (1974) 40. Lindenwald, home of 8th president, near Kinderhook.

Mary McLeod Bethune Council House, DC (1982/1991) 0.07. Commemorates Bethune's leadership in the black women's movement.

Nicodemus, KS (1996) 161. Only remaining western town established by African-Americans during Reconstruction.

Ninety Six, SC (1976) 989. Colonial trading village.

Palo Alto Battlefield, TX (1978) 3,357. Scene of first battle of the Mexican War.

Pennsylvania Avenue, DC (1965) Acreage undetermined. Also includes area adjacent to the road between Capitol and White House, encompassing Ford's Theatre and a number of other federal structures.

Puukohola Heiau, HI (1972) 86. Ruins of temple built by King Kamehameha.

Sagamore Hill, Oyster Bay, NY (1962) 83. Home of Pres. Theodore Roosevelt from 1885 until his death in 1919.

Saint-Gaudens, Cornish, NH (1964) 148. Home, studio, and gardens of American sculptor Augustus Saint-Gaudens.

Saint Paul's Church, NY, NY (1943) 6. Site associated with John Peter Zenger's "freedom of press" trial.

Salem Maritime, MA (1938) 9. Only port never seized from the patriots by the British. Major fishing and whaling port.

San Juan, PR (1949) 75. 16th-cent. Span. fortifications.

Saugus Iron Works, MA (1974) 9. Reconstructed 17th-cent. colonial ironworks.

Springfield Armory, MA (1974) 55. Small-arms manufacturing center for nearly 200 years.

Steamtown, PA (1986) 62. Railyard, roadhouse, repair shops of former Delaware, Lackawanna, & Western Railroad.

Theodore Roosevelt Birthplace, New York, NY (1962) 0.11. Reconstructed brownstone.

Theodore Roosevelt Inaugural, Buffalo, NY (1966) 1. Wilcox House where he took oath of office, 1901.

Thomas Stone, MD (1978) 328. Home of signer of Declaration of Independence, built in 1771.

Tuskegee Institute, AL (1974) 58. College founded by Booker T. Washington in 1881 for blacks.

Ulysses S. Grant, St. Louis Co., MO (1989) 10. Home of Grant during pre-Civil War years.

Vanderbilt Mansion, Hyde Park, NY (1940) 212. Mansion of 19th-cent. financier.

Washita Battlefield, OK (1996) 315. Scene of Nov. 27, 1868, battle between Plains tribes and the U.S. army.

Weir Farm, Wilton, CT (1990) 61. Home and studio of American impressionist painter J. Alden Weir.

Whitman Mission, WA (1936/1963) 98. Site where Dr. and Mrs. Marcus Whitman ministered to the Indians until slain by them in 1847.

William Howard Taft, Cincinnati, OH (1969) 3. Birthplace and early home of the 27th president.

National Monuments

Name	State	Year[1]	Acreage
Agate Fossil Beds	NE	1965	3,055
Alibates Flint Quarries	TX	1965	1,371
Aniakchak[2]	AK	1978	137,176
Aztec Ruins	NM	1923	320
Bandelier	NM	1916	32,737
Black Canyon of the Gunnison	CO	1933	20,766
Booker T. Washington	VA	1956	224
Buck Island Reef	VI	1961	880
Cabrillo	CA	1913	137
Canyon de Chelly	AZ	1931	83,840
Cape Krusenstern[3]	AK	1978	650,000
Capulin Volcano	NM	1916	793
Casa Grande Ruins	AZ	1889	473
Castillo de San Marcos	FL	1924	21
Castle Clinton	NY	1946	1
Cedar Breaks	UT	1933	6,155
Chiricahua	AZ	1924	11,985
Colorado	CO	1911	20,454
Congaree Swamp	SC	1976	22,200
Craters of the Moon	ID	1924	53,440
Devils Postpile	CA	1911	798
Devils Tower	WY	1906	1,347
Dinosaur	CO-UT	1915	210,844
Effigy Mounds	IA	1949	1,481
El Malpais	NM	1987	114,277
El Morro	NM	1906	1,279
Florissant Fossil Beds	CO	1969	5,998
Fort Frederica	GA	1936	241
Fort Matanzas	FL	1924	228
Fort McHenry National Monument and Historic Shrine	MD	1925	43
Fort Pulaski	GA	1924	5,623
Fort Stanwix	NY	1935	16
Fort Sumter	SC	1948	195
Fort Union	NM	1954	721
Fossil Butte	WY	1972	8,198
George Washington Birthplace	VA	1930	550
George Washington Carver	MO	1943	210
Gila Cliff Dwellings	NM	1907	533
Grand Portage	MN	1951	710
Great Sand Dunes	CO	1932	38,662
Hagerman Fossil Beds[3]	ID	1988	4,346
Hohokam Pima[4]	AZ	1972	1,690
Homestead Natl. Monument of America	NE	1936	195
Hovenweep	CO-UT	1923	785
Jewel Cave	SD	1908	1,274
John Day Fossil Beds	OR	1974	14,057
Lava Beds	CA	1925	46,560
Little Big Horn Battlefield	MT	1879	765
Montezuma Castle	AZ	1906	858

Name	State	Year[1]	Acreage
Muir Woods	CA	1908	554
Natural Bridges	UT	1908	7,636
Navajo	AZ	1909	360
Ocmulgee	GA	1934	702
Oregon Caves	OR	1909	488
Organ Pipe Cactus	AZ	1937	330,689
Petroglyph	NM	1990	7,240
Pinnacles	CA	1908	16,265
Pipe Spring	AZ	1923	40
Pipestone	MN	1937	282
Poverty Point[2]	LA	1988	911
Rainbow Bridge[3]	UT	1910	160
Russell Cave	AL	1961	310
Salinas Pueblo Missions	NM	1909	1,071
Scotts Bluff	NE	1919	3,003
Statue of Liberty	NJ-NY	1924	58
Sunset Crater Volcano	AZ	1930	3,040
Timpanogos Cave	UT	1922	250
Tonto	AZ	1907	1,120
Tuzigoot	AZ	1939	801
Walnut Canyon	AZ	1915	3,579
White Sands	NM	1933	143,733
Wupatki	AZ	1924	35,422
Yucca House[4]	CO	1919	34

National Preserves

Aniakchak	AK	1978	465,603
Bering Land Bridge[3]	AK	1978	2,698,000
Big Cypress	FL	1974	720,533
Big Thicket	TX	1974	97,191
Denali	AK	1917	1,334,200
Gates of the Arctic	AK	1978	948,629
Glacier Bay	AK	1925	58,406
Katmai	AK	1918	418,699
Lake Clark	AK	1978	1,410,642
Little River Canyon[2]	AL	1992	13,633
Mojave	CA	1994	1,586,947
Noatak[3]	AK	1978	6,587,167
Tallgrass Prairie	KS	1996	10,894
Timucuan Ecological & Historic Preserve[3]	FL	1988	46,000
Wrangell-St. Elias	AK	1978	4,852,773
Yukon-Charley Rivers[3]	AK	1978	2,526,509

National Seashores

Assateague Island	MD-VA	1965	39,723
Canaveral	FL	1975	57,662
Cape Cod	MA	1961	44,294
Cape Hatteras	NC	1937	30,319
Cape Lookout	NC	1966	28,243
Cumberland Island	GA	1972	36,416
Fire Island	NY	1964	19,579
Gulf Islands	FL-MS	1971	137,961
Padre Island	TX	1962	130,434
Point Reyes	CA	1962	71,057

National Parkways

Blue Ridge	NC-VA	1933	88,432
George Washington Memorial	VA-MD-DC	1930	7,248
John D. Rockefeller Jr. Mem.	WY	1972	23,777
Natchez Trace	MS-AL-TN	1938	51,752

National Lakeshores

Apostle Islands	WI	1970	69,372
Indiana Dunes	IN	1966	15,135
Pictured Rocks	MI	1966	73,236
Sleeping Bear Dunes	MI	1970	71,193

National Reserves

Name	State	Year[1]	Acreage
City of Rocks[3]	ID	1988	14,407
Ebey's Landing[3]	WA	1978	19,000

National Rivers

Big South Fork Natl. R and Recreation Area	KY-TN	1976	125,000
Buffalo	AR	1972	94,308
Mississippi Natl. R and Recreation Area	MN	1988	53,775
New River Gorge	WV	1978	70,912
Niobrara	NE-SD	1991	NA
Ozark	MO	1964	80,790

National Wild and Scenic Rivers

Alagnak	AK	1980	30,800
Bluestone[2]	WV	1978	4,310
Delaware	NY-NJ-PA	1978	1,973
Great Egg Harbor	NJ	1992	NA
Missouri	NE-SD	1991	NA
Obed	TN	1976	5,157
Rio Grande[2]	TX	1978	9,600
Saint Croix	MN-WI	1968	67,458
Upper Delaware	NY-PA	1978	75,000

National Recreation Areas

Amistad	TX	1965	58,500
Bighorn Canyon	MT-WY	1966	120,296
Boston Harbor Islands	MA	1996	1,482
Chattahoochee R.	GA	1978	9,247
Chickasaw	OK	1902	9,889
Curecanti	CO	1965	41,972
Cuyahoga Valley	OH	1974	32,522
Delaware Water Gap	NJ-PA	1965	67,210
Gateway	NJ-NY	1972	26,601
Gauley R.[3]	WV	1988	11,344
Glen Canyon	AZ-UT	1958	1,236,880
Golden Gate	CA	1972	74,460
Lake Chelan	WA	1968	62,040
Lake Mead	AZ-NV	1936	1,495,666
Lake Meredith	TX	1965	44,978
Lake Roosevelt[5]	WA	1946	100,390
Ross Lake	WA	1968	117,575
Santa Monica Mts.[3]	CA	1978	151,144
Whiskeytown	CA	1965	42,503

National Scenic Trails

Appalachian	ME to GA	1968	213,705
Natchez Trace	MS-TN	1983	10,995
Potomac Heritage	MD-DC-VA-PA	1983	NA

Parks (no other classification)

Catoctin Mountain	MD	1954	5,770
Constitution Gardens	DC	1974	52
Fort Washington	MD	1930	341
Greenbelt	MD	1950	1,176
National Capital	DC	1933	6,544
National Mall	DC	1933	146
Piscataway	MD	1961	4,441
Prince William Forest	VA	1948	18,572
Rock Creek	DC	1890	1,754
White House	DC	1933	18
Wolf Trap Farm Park for the Performing Arts	VA	1966	130

International Historic Site

Saint Croix Island[3]	ME	1949	45

NA=Not available. (1) Year first designated. (2) No federal facilities. (3) Limited federal facilities. (4) Not open to the public. (5) Formerly Coulee Dam National Recreation Area.

20 Most-Visited Sites in the National Park System, 1997

Source: National Park Service, Dept. of the Interior

Attendance at all areas administered by the National Park Service in 1997 totaled 275,236,335 recreation visits.

Site (location)	Recreation visits
Blue Ridge Parkway (NC, VA)	18,373,279
Golden Gate National Recreation Area (CA)	13,803,382
Great Smoky Mountains National Park (TN, NC)	9,965,075
Lake Mead National Recreation Area (AZ, NV)	8,528,420
Gateway National Recreation Area (NY, NJ)	6,807,945
Natchez Trace National Parkway (MS, AL, TN)	5,992,978
George Washington Memorial National Parkway (VA, MD, DC)	5,844,294
Grand Canyon National Park (AZ)	4,791,668
Delaware Water Gap National Recreation Area (PA, NJ)	4,752,100
Statue of Liberty National Monument (NY, NJ)	4,738,388
Gulf Islands National Seashore (FL, MS)	4,697,014
Cape Cod National Seashore (MA)	4,608,454
Castle Clinton National Monument (NY)	4,109,013
Olympic National Park (WA)	3,846,709
Yosemite National Park (CA)	3,669,970
San Francisco Maritime National Historical Park (CA)	3,530,687
Cuyahoga Valley National Recreation Area (OH)	3,527,837
Jefferson National Expansion Memorial (MO)	3,420,076
Colonial National Historical Park (VA)	3,218,180
Independence National Historical Park (PA)	3,155,195

Federal Indian Reservations and Trust Lands[1]

Source: Tiller Research, Inc., Albuquerque, NM

State	No. of reser.	Tribally owned acreage[2]	Individually owned acreage[2]	No. of persons[2]	Major tribes and/or nations
Alabama	1	230	0	16,506	Poarch Creek
Alaska	1[4]	86,773	1,265,432	85,698	Aleut, Eskimo, Athabascan,[5] Haida, Tlingit, Tsimpshian
Arizona	23	19,775,959	311,579	203,527	Navajo, Apache, Papago, Hopi, Yavapai, Pima
California	96	520,049	66,769	242,164	Hoopa, Paiute, Yurok, Karok, Cherokee
Colorado	2	764,120	2,805	27,776	Ute
Connecticut	1	1,638	0	6,654	Mashantucket Pequot
Florida	4	153,874	0	36,335	Seminole, Miccosukee, Cherokee
Idaho	4	609,622	327,301	13,780	Shoshone, Bannock, Nez Perce
Iowa	1	3,550	0	7,349	Sac and Fox
Kansas	4	7,219	23,763	21,965	Potawatomi, Kickapoo, Iowa
Louisiana	3	415	0	18,541	Chitimacha, Coushatta, Tunica-Biloxi
Maine	3	191,511	0	5,998	Passamaquoddy, Penobscot, Maliseet
Massachusetts	1	157	0	12,241	Wampanoag
Michigan	8	14,411	9,276	55,638	Chippewa, Potawatomi, Ottawa, Cherokee
Minnesota	14	779,138	50,338	49,909	Chippewa, Sioux
Mississippi	1	20,486	0	8,525	Choctaw
Montana	7	2,663,385	2,911,450	47,679	Blackfoot, Crow, Sioux, Assiniboine, Cheyenne
Nebraska	3	23,792	43,208	12,410	Omaha, Winnebago, Santee Sioux
Nevada	19	1,147,088	78,529	19,637	Paiute, Shoshone, Washoe
New Mexico	25	7,252,326	630,293	134,355	Apache, Navajo, Pueblo
New York	8	118,199	0	62,651	Seneca, Mohawk, Onondaga, Oneida
North Carolina	1	56,509	0	80,155	Cherokee, Lumbee
North Dakota	3	214,006	627,289	25,917	Sioux, Chippewa, Mandan, Arikara, Hidatsa
Oklahoma	36[6]	96,839	1,000,165	252,420	Cherokee, Creek, Choctaw, Chickasaw, Osage, Cheyenne, Arapahoe, Kiowa, Comanche
Oregon	7	660,367	135,053	38,496	Warm Springs, Wasco, Paiute, Umatilla, Siletz
Rhode Island	1	1,800	0	4,071	Narragansett
South Carolina	1	639	0	8,246	Catawba
South Dakota	9	2,399,531	2,121,188	50,575	Sioux
Texas	3	4,726	0	65,877	Alabama-Coushatta, Tiwa, Kickapoo
Utah	4	2,286,448	32,838	24,283	Ute, Goshute, Southern Paiute, Navajo
Washington	27	2,250,731	467,785	81,483	Yakama, Lummi, Quinault
Wisconsin	11	338,097	80,345	39,387	Chippewa, Oneida, Winnebago
Wyoming	1	1,958,095	101,537	9,479	Shoshone, Arapahoe

(1) In Oct. 1993, the Bureau of Indian Affairs of the U.S. Dept. of the Interior published in the *Federal Register* (vol. 58, no. 202, pp. 54364-69) a comprehensive listing of 552 "Indian Entities Recognized and Eligible to Receive Services From the United States Bureau of Indian Affairs" (328 in the conterminous 48 states, 224 in Alaska). The term *Indian entities* includes Indian tribes, bands, villages, groups, and pueblos; also included are Eskimo and Aleut villages and tribes. All such entities have a government-to-government relationship with the U.S. Some reservation boundaries transcend state boundaries (e.g., Navajo, which is in Arizona, New Mexico, and Utah). For the purpose of "Number of Reservations," such reservations are counted in the state where their population is predominant and/or tribal headquarters are located. (2) Information provided by the Bureau of Indian Affairs; data current as of 1990. Acreages refer only to lands that are either owned by the tribes and individual members or are held in trust by the U.S. government. Many of these parcels are located off reservations. Not all lands within reservation boundaries are necessarily trust lands. Many are privately owned by tribes, tribal members, or non-Indians; others are the property of various governmental agencies. (3) Total Native American (Indian, Eskimo, or Aleut) population in each state with reservation/trust lands, including those persons living outside the Bureau of Indian Affairs service area. Populations as of 1990. (4) The only federally recognized reservation in Alaska is the Annette Island Reserve. In all other cases, the U.S. government's relationship to Native Americans in Alaska is set out by the Alaska Native Claims Settlement Act of 1971. The act provided for the establishment of regional and village corporations to conduct business for profit and nonprofit purposes; these corporations are also landowners. There are 12 regional corporations, each with organized village corporations, plus one regional corporation for Alaska Natives outside the state. (5) Aleuts and Eskimos are racially and linguistically related. Athabascans are related to the Navajo and Apache Indians. (6) There are 36 tribal entities in Oklahoma, each of which owns land in the state. Because of the way in which the state was formed out of the Oklahoma and Indian territories, the reservation status of land in the state is frequently disputed in both civil and criminal proceedings.

Largest American Indian Tribes

Source: Bureau of the Census, U.S. Dept. of Commerce, as of 1990 census

Tribe	Number	Percent	Tribe	Number	Percent
All American Indians	**1,937,391**	**100.0**	Chickasaw	21,522	1.1
Cherokee	369,035	19.0	Tohono O'Odham	16,876	0.9
Navajo	225,298	11.6	Potawatomi	16,719	0.9
Sioux	107,321 [1]	5.5	Seminole	15,564	0.8
Chippewa	105,988	5.5	Pima	15,074	0.8
Choctaw	86,231	4.5	Tlingit	14,417	0.7
Pueblo	55,330	2.9	Alaskan Athabaskans	14,198	0.7
Apache	53,330	2.8	Cheyenne	11,809	0.6
Iroquois[2]	52,557	2.7	Comanche	11,437	0.6
Lumbee	50,888	2.6	Paiute	11,369	0.6
Creek	45,872	2.4	Osage	10,430	0.5
Blackfoot	37,992	2.0	Puget Sound Salish	10,384	0.5
Canadian and Latin American	27,179	1.4	Yaqui	9,838	0.5

(1) Any entry from NC with the spelling "Siouan" in the 1990 census was miscoded to count as Sioux. (2) Reporting and/or processing problems in the 1990 census have affected accuracy of the data for this tribe.

WORLD HISTORY

Prehistory: Our Ancestors Emerge

Revised by Susan Skomal, Ph.D., Editor, Anthropology Newsletter, *American Anthropological Association*

Homo sapiens. The precise origins of *Homo sapiens,* the species to which all humans belong, are subject to broad speculation based on a small, but increasing, number of fossils, on genetic and anatomical studies, and on interpretation of the geological record. Most scientists at least agree that humans evolved from apelike primate ancestors in a process that began millions of years ago.

Current theories trace the first hominid (humanlike primate) to Africa, where at least 2 lines of hominids appeared 5 to 7 million years before the present (BP). In one line was *Australopithecus*, a social animal that lived from perhaps 5 million to 3 million years BP, then apparently died out. In the other, human line was *Homo habilis*, a large-brained specimen that walked upright and had a dextrous hand. *Homo habilis* appeared some 2.5 million years BP, lived in semipermanent camps, had a food-gathering economy, and probably produced stone tools.

Homo erectus, the nearest ancestor to humans, appeared in Africa perhaps 2 million years BP and began spreading into Asia and Europe soon after. It had a fairly large brain and a skeletal structure similar to that of modern humans. *Homo erectus* hunted, learned to control fire, and may have had some primitive language skills. Brain development to *Homo sapiens,* then to the subspecies *Homo sapiens sapiens,* occurred between 500,000 and 50,000 years BP in Africa. All modern humans are members of the subspecies *Homo sapiens sapiens.*

Humans have roamed widely over the globe throughout their development. There is increasing evidence that migration from Asia to Australia via the Timor Straits took place as early as 100,000 BP. Evidence of hominids in Siberia dates as early as 300,000 BP. First confirmed evidence for the crossing from Asia to the Americas, by land bridge, dates to the end of the last Ice Age, at 12,500 BP.

Earliest cultures. A variety of cultural modes—in toolmaking, diet, shelter, and possibly social arrangements and spiritual expression—arose as humans adapted to different geographic and climatic zones and the database of knowledge grew. Sites from all over the world show seasonal migration patterns and efficient exploitation of a wide range of plant and animal foods.

Archaeologists recognize 5 basic toolmaking traditions as arising and often coexisting from more than 2.5 million years ago to the near past: (1) the *chopper tradition*—also known as the Oldowan—found in Africa, producing crude chopping tools and simple flake tools; (2) the *biface* or handaxe tradition, found in Africa, W and S Europe, and S Asia, producing pointed hand axes chipped on both faces for cutting; (3) the *flake tradition*, found in Africa and Europe, producing small cutting and flaking tools; (4) the *blade tradition*, a more efficient technology characteristic of the Upper Paleolithic, found across Eurasia to Siberia and N Africa, producing many usable blades from a single stone; and (5) the *microlith tradition*, found throughout the inhabited world, producing specialized small tools for use as projectile points, in carving softer materials, and in making more complex tools.

Sketchy evidence remains for the stages in increasing control over the environment. Fire was used for heating and cooking by 465,000 BP in W France. Fire-hardened wooden spears, weighted and set with small stone blades, were fashioned by big-game hunters 400,000 years ago in Germany. Scraping tools found at certain sites (200,000-30,000 BP in Europe, N Africa, the Middle East, and Cen. Asia) suggest the treatment of skins for clothing. By the time Australia was settled, human ancestors had learned to navigate in boats over open water. The earliest bone tools found to date were developed 80,000 years ago in the Congo basin by fishermen, who created sophisticated fishing tackle to catch giant catfish.

Early human ancestors included artists and musicians. About 60,000 years ago the earliest immigrants to Australia carved and painted abstract designs on rocks. Painting and decoration flourished, along with stone and ivory sculpture, from 30,000 BP in Europe; more than 200 caves, mainly in S France and N Spain, show remarkable examples of naturalistic wall painting. Other examples have been found in Africa. Proto-religious rites are suggested by these works, and by evidence of ritual burial. A variety of musical instruments, including bone flutes with precisely bored holes, have been found in Paleolithic (early Stone Age) sites going back as far as 40,000-80,000 years BP.

Neolithic advances. Some time after 10,000 BC, among widely separated communities, a series of dramatic technological and social changes occurred, marking the Neolithic, or New Stone, Age. As the world climate became drier and warmer, humans learned to cultivate plants. This in turn encouraged growth of permanent settlements. Animals were domesticated. Manufacture of pottery and cloth began. These techniques permitted a dramatic increase in world population and social complexity, and accelerated humankind's ability to manipulate the environment.

Sites in N, Cen., and S America, SE Europe, and the Middle East show roughly contemporaneous (10,000-8000 BC) evidence of one or more Neolithic traits. Dates near 6000-3000 BC have been given for E and S Asian, W European, and sub-Saharan African Neolithic remains. The variety of crops—field grains, rice, maize, and roots—and varying mix of other characteristics suggest that this adaptation occurred independently in all these regions.

History Begins: 4000-1000 BC

Near Eastern cradle. If history began with writing, the first chapter opened in Mesopotamia, the Tigris-Euphrates river valley. The Sumerians used clay tablets with pictographs to keep records after 4000 BC. A **cuneiform** (wedge-shaped) script evolved by 3000 BC as a full syllabic alphabet. Neighboring peoples adapted the script to their own language.

Sumerian life centered, from 4000 BC, on large cities (Eridu, Ur, Uruk, Nippur, Kish, and Lagash) organized around temples and priestly bureaucracies, with surrounding plains watered by vast irrigation works and worked with traction plows. Sailboats, wheeled vehicles, potter's wheels, and kilns were used. Copper was smelted and tempered from c 4000 BC; bronze was produced not long after. Ores, as well as precious stones and metals, were obtained through long-distance ship and caravan trade. Iron was used from c 2000 BC. Improved ironworking, developed partly by the Hittites, became widespread by 1200 BC.

Sumerian political primacy passed among cities and their kingly dynasties. Semitic-speaking peoples, with cultures derived from the Sumerian, founded a succession of dynasties that ruled in Mesopotamia and neighboring areas for most of 1,800 years; among them were the **Akkadians** (first under Sargon I, c 2350 BC), the Amorites (whose laws, codified by **Hammurabi,** c 1792-1750 BC, have biblical parallels), and the Assyrians, with interludes of rule by the Hittites, Kassites, and Mitanni.

Mesopotamian learning, maintained by scribes and preserved in vast libraries, was practically oriented. Advances in mathematics related to construction, commerce, and administration. Lists of astronomical phenomena, plants, animals, and stones were kept; medical texts listed ailments and herbal cures. The Sumerians worshiped anthropomorphic gods representing natural forces, such as Anu, god of heaven, and Enlil (Ea), god of water. Sacrifices were made at **ziggurats**—huge stepped temples.

Paleontology: The History of Life

All dates are approximate, and are subject to change based on new fossil finds or new dating techniques, but the sequence of events is generally accepted. Dates are in years before the present.

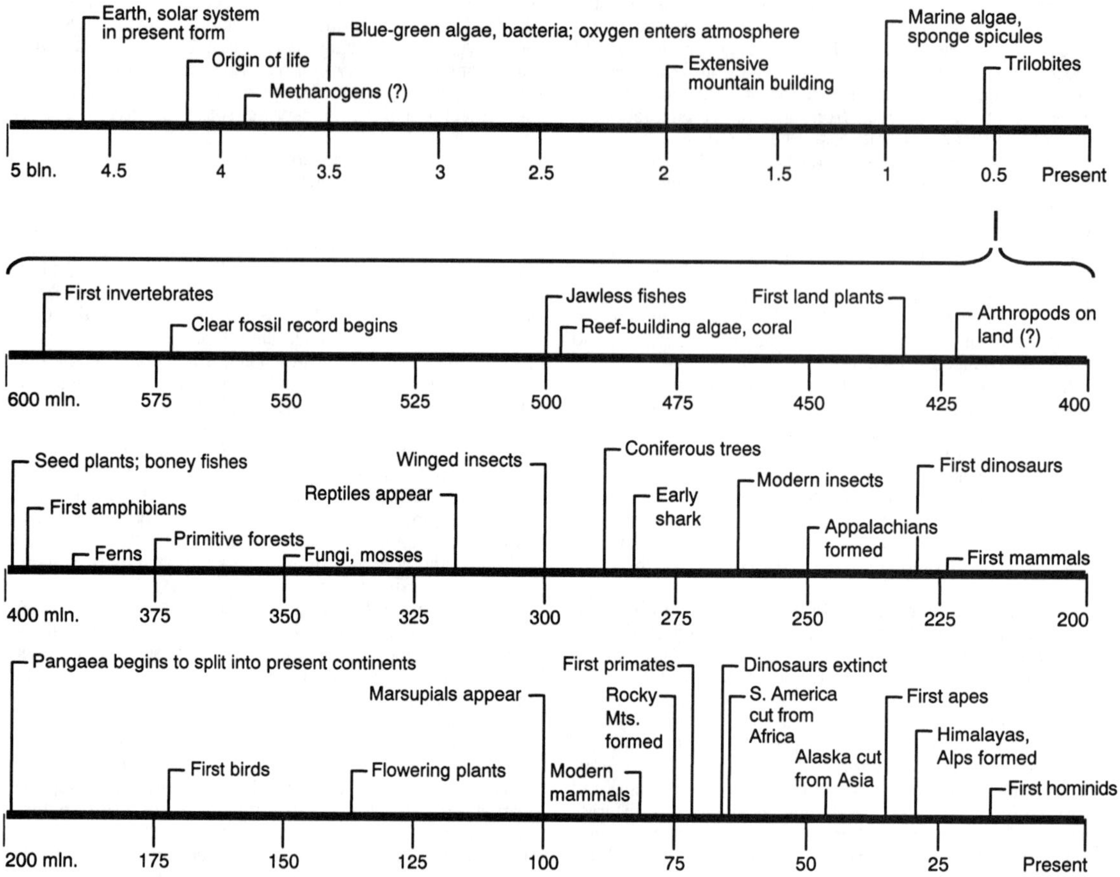

The Syria-Palestine area, site of some of the earliest urban remains (Jericho, 7000 BC), and of the recently uncovered **Ebla** civilization (fl 2500 BC), experienced Egyptian cultural and political influence along with Mesopotamian. The **Phoenician** coast was an active commercial center. A phonetic alphabet was invented here before 1600 BC. It became the ancestor of many other alphabets.

Egypt. Agricultural villages along the Nile were united by 3300 BC into 2 kingdoms, Upper and Lower Egypt, which were unified (c 3100 BC) under the pharaoh Menes. A bureaucracy supervised construction of canals and monuments (**pyramids** starting 2700 BC). Control over Nubia to the S was asserted from 2600 BC. Brilliant Old Kingdom Period achievements in architecture, sculpture, and painting, which reached their height during the 3d and 4th Dynasties, set the standards for subsequent Egyptian civilization. **Hieroglyphic writing** appeared by 3200 BC, recording a sophisticated literature that included religious writings, philosophies, history, and science. An ordered hierarchy of gods, including totemistic animal elements, was served by a powerful priesthood in Memphis. The pharaoh was identified with the falcon god Horus. Other trends included belief in an afterlife and short-lived quasi-monotheistic reforms introduced by the pharaoh **Akhenaton** (c 1379-1362 BC).

After a period of dominance by Semitic Hyksos from Asia (c 1700-1550 BC), the New Kingdom established an empire in Syria. Egypt became increasingly embroiled in Asiatic wars and diplomacy. Conquered by Persia in 525 BC, it eventually faded away as an independent culture.

India. An urban civilization with a so-far-undeciphered writing system stretched across the Indus Valley and along the Arabian Sea c 3000-1500 BC. Major sites are Harappa and **Mohenjo-Daro** in Pakistan, well-planned geometric cities with underground sewers and vast granaries. The entire region may have been ruled as a single state. Bronze was used, and arts and crafts were well developed. Religious life apparently took the form of fertility cults. Indus civilization was probably in decline when it was destroyed by **Aryan invaders** from the NW, speaking an Indo-European language from which most languages of Pakistan, N India, and Bangladesh descend. Led by a warrior aristocracy whose legendary deeds are in the **Rig Veda**, the Aryans spread E and S, bringing their sky gods, priestly (Brahman) ritual, and the beginnings of the caste system; local customs and beliefs were assimilated by the conquerors.

Europe. On Crete, the Bronze Age **Minoan civilization** emerged c 2500 BC. A prosperous economy and richly decorative art was supported by seaborne commerce. Mycenae and other cities in mainland Greece and Asia Minor (e.g., **Troy**) preserved elements of the culture until c 1200 BC. Cretan Linear A script (c 2000-1700 BC) remains undeciphered; Linear B script (c 1300-1200 BC) records an early Greek dialect. Unclear is the possible connection between Mycenaean monumental stonework and the megalithic monuments of W Europe, Iberia, and Malta (c 4000-1500 BC).

Major Gods & Goddesses of the Classical World

Greek	Roman	Relations	Sphere or Position
Aphrodite	Venus	Daughter of Zeus & Dione	Love
Apollo	——	Son of Zeus & Leto	Healing, poetry, light
Ares	Mars	Son of Zeus & Hera	War
Artemis	Diana	Daughter of Zeus & Leto	Hunting, chastity
Athena	Minerva	Daughter of Zeus & Metis	Wisdom, crafts, war
Cronus	Saturn	Father of Zeus	Titans' ruler
Demeter	Ceres	Sister of Zeus	Agriculture, fertility
Dionysus	Bacchus	Son of Zeus & Semele	Wine, fertility, ecstasy
Eros	Cupid	Son of Ares & Aphrodite	Love
Hades	Pluto	Brother of Zeus	The underworld, death
Hephaestus	Vulcan	Son of Zeus & Hera	Fire
Hera	Juno	Wife & sister of Zeus	Earth
Hermes	Mercury	Son of Zeus & Maia	Travel, commerce, gods' messenger
Hestia	Vesta	Sister of Zeus	The hearth
Pan	——	Son of Hermes & a wood nymph	Forests, flocks, shepherds
Persephone	Proserpina	Daughter of Zeus & Demeter	Grain
Poseidon	Neptune	Brother of Zeus	The sea
Rhea	Ops	Mother of Zeus	The earth
Uranus	Uranus	Father of Titans (elder gods)	The heavens
Zeus	Jupiter	Son of Cronus & Rhea	Ruler of the gods

China. Proto-Chinese neolithic cultures had long covered N and SE China when the first large political state was organized in the N by the **Shang dynasty** (c 1523 BC). Shang kings called themselves Sons of Heaven, and they presided over a cult of human and animal sacrifice to ancestors and nature gods. The Chou dynasty, starting c 1027 BC, expanded the area of the Son of Heaven's dominion, but feudal states exercised most temporal power. A writing system with 2,000 characters was already in use under the Shang, with **pictographs** later supplemented by phonetic characters. Many of its principles and symbols, despite changes in spoken Chinese, were preserved in later writing systems. Technical advances allowed urban specialists to create fine ceramic and jade products, and bronze casting after 1500 BC was the most advanced in the world. Bronze artifacts have recently been discovered in N Thailand dating from 3600 BC, hundreds of years before similar Middle Eastern finds.

Americas. Olmecs settled (1500 BC) on the Gulf coast of Mexico and soon developed the first civilization in the western hemisphere. Temple cities and huge stone sculpture date from 1200 BC. A rudimentary calendar and writing system existed. Olmec religion, centering on a jaguar god, and Olmec art forms influenced all later Meso-American cultures.

Classical Era of Old World Civilizations: 1000 BC-400 BC

Greece. After a period of decline during the Dorian Greek invasions (1200-1000 BC), Greece and the Aegean area developed a unique civilization. Drawing upon Mycenaean traditions, Mesopotamian learning (weights and measures, lunisolar calendar, astronomy, musical scales), the Phoenician alphabet (modified for Greek), and Egyptian art, the revived **Greek city-states** saw a rich elaboration of intellectual life. Homer's epics, the *Iliad* and the *Odyssey,* were probably composed around the 8th cent. BC. Long-range commerce was aided by metal coinage (introduced by the Lydians in Asia Minor before 700 BC); colonies were founded around the Mediterranean (Cumae in Italy in 760 BC; Massalia in France c 600 BC) and Black Sea shores.

Philosophy, starting with Ionian speculation on the nature of matter (Thales, c 634-546 BC), continued by other "Pre-Socratics" (e.g., Heraclitus, c 535-415 BC; Parmenides, born c 515 BC), reached a high point in Athens in the rationalist idealism of **Plato** (c 428-347 BC), a disciple of **Socrates** (c 469-399 BC; executed for alleged impiety), and in **Aristotle** (384-322 BC), a pioneer in many fields, from natural sciences to logic, ethics, and metaphysics. The **arts** were highly valued. Architecture culminated in the **Parthenon** (438 BC) by Phidias (fl 490-430 BC). Poetry (Sappho, c 610-580 BC; Pindar, c 518-438 BC) and **drama** (Aeschylus, 525-456 BC; Sophocles, c 496-406 BC; Euripides, c 484-406 BC) thrived. Male beauty and strength, a chief artistic theme, were enhanced at the gymnasium and celebrated at the national games at Olympia. Ruled by local tyrants or **oligarchies**, the Greeks were not politically united, but managed to resist inclusion in the Persian Empire—Persian king Darius was defeated at Marathon (490 BC), his son Xerxes at Salamis (480 BC), and the Persian army at Plataea (479 BC). Local warfare was common; the **Peloponnesian Wars** (431-404 BC) ended in Sparta's victory over Athens. Greek political power waned, but Greek cultural forms spread throughout the ancient world.

Hebrews. Nomadic Hebrew tribes entered Canaan before 1200 BC, settling among other Semitic peoples speaking the same language. They brought from the desert a **monotheistic** faith said to have been revealed to Abraham in Canaan c 1800 BC and Moses at Mt. Sinai c 1250 BC, after the Hebrews' escape from bondage in Egypt. David (r 1000-961 BC) and Solomon (r 961-922 BC) united them in a kingdom that briefly dominated the area. **Phoenicians** to the N founded Mediterranean colonies (Carthage, c 814 BC) and sailed into the Atlantic.

A temple in Jerusalem became the national religious center, with sacrifices performed by a hereditary priesthood. Polytheistic influences, especially of the fertility cult of Baal, were opposed by **prophets** (Elijah, Amos, Isaiah).

Divided into **two kingdoms** after Solomon, the Hebrews were unable to resist the revived Assyrian empire, which conquered Israel, the N kingdom, in 722 BC. Judah, the S kingdom, was conquered in 586 BC by the Babylonians under Nebuchadnezzar II. With the fixing of most of the biblical canon by the mid-4th cent. BC and the emergence of rabbis, Judaism successfully survived the loss of Hebrew autonomy. A Jewish kingdom was revived under the Hasmoneans (168-42 BC).

China. During the **Eastern Chou** dynasty (770-256 BC), Chinese culture spread E to the sea and S to the Yangtze R. Large feudal states on the periphery of the empire contended for preeminence, but continued to recognize the Son of Heaven (king), who retained a purely ritual role enriched with courtly music and dance. In the Age of Warring States (403-221 BC), when the first sections of the **Great Wall** were built, the Ch'in state in the W gained supremacy and finally united all of China.

Iron tools entered China c 500 BC, and casting techniques were advanced, aiding agriculture. Peasants owned their land and owed civil and military service to nobles. China's cities grew in number and size, although barter remained the chief trade medium.

Intellectual ferment among noble scribes and officials produced the Classical Age of Chinese literature and philosophy. **Confucius** (551-479 BC) urged a restoration of a supposedly harmonious social order of the past through proper conduct in accordance with one's station and through filial and ceremonial piety. The *Analects* attributed to him are revered throughout E Asia. **Mencius** (d 289 BC) added the view that the Mandate of Heaven can be removed from an unjust dynasty. The Legalists sought to curb the supposed natural wickedness of people through new institutions and harsh laws; they aided the Ch'in rise to power. The Naturalists emphasized the balance of opposites—yin, yang—in the world. **Taoists** sought mystical knowledge through meditation and disengagement.

India. The political and cultural center of India shifted from the Indus to the Ganges River Valley. Buddhism, Jainism, and mystical revisions of orthodox Vedism all developed c 500-300 BC. The *Upanishads,* last part of the *Veda*, urged escape from the physical world. Vedism remained the preserve of the Brahman caste. In contrast, **Buddhism**, founded by Siddarta Gautama (c 563-c 483 BC)—Buddha ("Enlightened One")—appealed to merchants in the urban centers and took hold at first (and most lastingly) on the geographic fringes of Indian civilization. The classic Indian epics were composed in this era: the **Ramayana** perhaps c 300 BC, the **Mahabharata** over a period starting 400 BC.

N India was divided into a large number of monarchies and aristocratic republics, probably derived from tribal groupings, when the Magadha kingdom was formed in Bihar c 542 BC. It soon became the dominant power. The **Maurya dynasty**, founded by Chandragupta c 321 BC, expanded the kingdom, uniting most of N India in a centralized bureaucratic empire. The third Mauryan king, **Asoka** (reigned c 274-236 BC), conquered most of the subcontinent. He converted to Buddhism and inscribed its tenets on pillars throughout India. He downplayed the caste system and tried to end expensive sacrificial rites.

Before its final decline in India, Buddhism developed into a popular worship of heavenly Bodhisattvas ("enlightened beings"); and produced a refined architecture (the Great Stupa [shrine] at Sanchi, AD 100) and sculpture (Gandhara reliefs, AD 1-400).

Persia. Aryan peoples (Persians, Medes) dominated the area of present Iran by the beginning of the 1st millennium BC. The prophet **Zoroaster** (born c 628 BC) introduced a dualistic religion in which the forces of good (Ahura Mazda, "Lord of Wisdom") and evil (Ahriam) battle for dominance; individuals are judged by their actions and earn damnation or salvation. Zoroaster's hymns (*Gathas*) are included in the *Avesta*, the Zoroastrian scriptures. A version of this faith became the established religion of the Persian Empire and probably influenced later monotheistic religions.

Africa. Nubia, periodically occupied by Egypt since about 2600 BC, ruled Egypt c 750-661 BC and survived as an independent Egyptianized kingdom (**Kush;** capital Meroe) for 1,000 years. The Iron Age Nok culture flourished c 500 BC- AD 200 on the Benue Plateau of **Nigeria**.

Americas. The Chavin culture controlled N Peru from 900 BC to 200 BC. Its ceremonial centers, featuring the jaguar god, survived long after. Chavin architecture, ceramics, and textiles influenced other Peruvian cultures. **Mayan civilization** began to develop in Central America as early as 1500 BC.

Great Empires Unite the Civilized World: 400 BC-AD 400

Persia and Alexander the Great. Cyrus, ruler of a small kingdom in Persia from 559 BC, united the Persians and Medes within 10 years and conquered Asia Minor and Babylonia in another 10. His son Cambyses, followed by **Darius** (r 522-486 BC), added vast lands to the E and N as far as the Indus Valley and Central Asia, as well as Egypt and Thrace. The whole empire was ruled by an international bureaucracy and army, with Persians holding the chief positions. The resources and styles of all the subject civilizations were exploited to create a rich syncretic art.

The kingdom of Macedon, which under Philip II dominated the Greek world and Egypt, was passed on to his son **Alexander** in 336 BC. Within 13 years, Alexander had conquered all the Persian dominions. Imbued by his tutor Aristotle with Greek ideals, Alexander encouraged Greek colonization, and Greek-style cities were founded. After his death in 323 BC, wars of succession divided the empire into 3 parts—**Macedon,** Egypt (ruled by the **Ptolemies**), and the **Seleucid** Empire.

In the ensuing 300 years (the **Hellenistic Era**), a cosmopolitan Greek-oriented culture permeated the ancient world from W Europe to the borders of India, absorbing native elites everywhere.

Hellenistic philosophy stressed the private individual's search for happiness. The Cynics followed Diogenes (c 372-287 BC), who stressed self-sufficiency and restriction of desires and expressed contempt for luxury and social convention. Zeno (c 335-c 263 BC) and the **Stoics** exalted reason, identified it with virtue, and counseled an ascetic disregard for misfortune. The **Epicureans** tried to build lives of moderate pleasure without political or emotional involvement. Hellenistic arts imitated life realistically, especially in sculpture and literature (comedies of Menander, 342-292 BC).

The sciences thrived, especially at Alexandria, where the Ptolemies financed a great library and museum. Fields of study included mathematics (**Euclid's** geometry, c 300 BC); astronomy (heliocentric theory of Aristarchus, 310-230 BC; Julian calendar, 45 BC; Ptolemy's *Almagest*, c AD 150); geography (world map of Eratosthenes, 276-194 BC); hydraulics (**Archimedes,** 287-212 BC); medicine (Galen, AD 130-200); and chemistry. Inventors refined uses for siphons, valves, gears, springs, screws, levers, cams, and pulleys.

A restored Persian empire under the **Parthians** (N Iranian tribesmen) controlled the eastern Hellenistic world from 250 BC to AD 229. The Parthians and the succeeding Sassanian dynasty (c AD 224- 651) fought with Rome periodically. The **Sassanians** revived Zoroastrianism as a state religion and patronized a nationalistic artistic and scholarly renaissance.

Rome. The city of Rome was founded, according to legend, by Romulus in 753 BC. Through military expansion and colonization, and by granting citizenship to conquered tribes, the city annexed all of Italy S of the Po in the 100-year period before 268 BC. The Latin and other Italic tribes were annexed first, followed by the **Etruscans** (founders of a great civilization, N of Rome) and the Greek colonies in the S. With a large standing army and reserve forces of several hundred thousand, Rome was able to defeat **Carthage** in the 3 **Punic Wars** (264-241, 218-201, 149-146 BC), despite the invasion of Italy (218 BC) by **Hannibal,** thus gaining Sicily and territory in Spain and N Africa.

New provinces were added in the E, as Rome exploited local disputes to conquer Greece and Asia Minor in the 2d cent. BC, and Egypt in the 1st (after the defeat and suicide of **Antony and Cleopatra**, 30 BC). All the Mediterranean civilized world up to the disputed Parthian border was now Roman and remained so for 500 years. Less civilized regions were added to the Empire: Gaul (conquered by **Julius Caesar**, 58-51 BC), Britain (AD 43), and Dacia NE of the Danube (AD 107).

The original aristocratic republican government, with democratic features added in the 5th and 4th cent. BC, deteriorated under the pressures of empire and class conflict (**Gracchus** brothers, social reformers, murdered in 133 BC and 121 BC; slave revolts in 135 BC and 73 BC). After a series of civil wars (Marius vs. Sulla 88-82 BC, Caesar vs. **Pompey** 49-45 BC, triumvirate vs. Caesar's assassins 44-43 BC, Antony vs. Octavian 32-30 BC), the empire came under the rule of a deified monarch (first emperor, **Augustus**, 27 BC- AD 14). Provincials (nearly all granted citizenship by Caracalla, AD 212) came to dominate the army and civil service. Traditional Roman law, systematized and interpreted by independent jurists, and local self-rule in provincial cities were supplanted by a vast tax-collecting bureaucracy in the 3d and 4th cent. The legal rights of women, children, and slaves were strengthened.

The Seven Wonders of the Ancient World

These ancient works of art and architecture were considered awe-inspiring in splendor and/or size by the Greek and Roman world of the Alexandrian epoch. Later classical writers disagreed as to which works made up the list of Wonders, but the following were usually included:

The Pyramids of Egypt: The only surviving ancient Wonder, these monumental structures of masonry, located at Giza on the W bank of the Nile R above Cairo, were built from c 2700 to 2500 BC as royal tombs. Three—Khufu (Cheops), Khafra (Chephren), and Menkaura (Mycerimus)—were often grouped as the first Wonder of the World. The largest, the Great Pyramid of Khufu, is a solid mass of limestone blocks covering 13 acres. It is estimated to contain 2.3 million blocks of stone, the stones themselves averaging 2½ tons and some weighing 30 tons. Its construction reputedly took 100,000 laborers 20 years.

The Hanging Gardens of Babylon: These gardens were laid out on a brick terrace about 400 ft square and 75 ft above the ground. To irrigate the trees, shrubs, and flowers, screws were turned to lift water from the Euphrates R. The gardens were probably built by King Nebuchadnezzar II about 600 BC. The Walls of Babylon, long, thick, and made of colorfully glazed brick, were considered by some among the Seven Wonders.

The Statue of Zeus (Jupiter) at Olympia: This statue of the king of the gods showed him seated on a throne. His flesh was made of ivory, his robe and ornaments of gold. Reputedly 40 ft high, the statue was made by Phidias and was placed in the great temple of Zeus in the sacred grove of Olympia about 457 BC.

The Colossus of Rhodes: A bronze statue of the sun god Helios, the Colossus was worked on for 12 years in the third cent. BC by the sculptor Chares. It was probably 120 ft high. A symbol of the city of Rhodes at its height, the statue stood on a promontory overlooking the harbor.

The Temple of Artemis (Diana) at Ephesus: This largest and most complex temple of ancient times was built about 550 BC and was made of marble except for its tile-covered wooden roof. It was begun in honor of a non-Hellenic goddess who later became identified with the Greek goddess of the same name. Ephesus was one of the greatest of the Ionian cities.

The Mausoleum at Halicarnassus: The source of our word *mausoleum*, this marble tomb was built in what is now SE Turkey by Artemisia for her husband Mausolus, king of Caria in Asia Minor, who died in 353 BC. About 135 ft high, the tomb was adorned with the works of 4 sculptors.

The Pharos (Lighthouse) of Alexandria: This structure was designed about 270 BC, during the reign of Ptolemy II, by the Greek architect Sostratos. Estimates of its height range from 200 to 600 ft.

Roman innovations in **civil engineering** included water mills, windmills, and rotary mills and use of cement that hardened under water. Monumental architecture (baths, theaters, temples) relied on the arch and the dome. The network of roads (some still standing) stretched 53,000 mi, passing through mountain tunnels as long as 3.5 mi. Aqueducts brought water to cities; underground sewers removed waste.

Roman art and literature were to a large extent derivative of Greek models. Innovations were made in sculpture (naturalistic busts, equestrian statues), decorative wall painting (as at Pompeii), satire (Juvenal, AD 60-127), history (Tacitus, AD 56-120), prose romance (Petronius, d AD 66). Gladiatorial contests dominated public amusements, which were supported by the state.

India. The **Gupta** monarchs reunited N India c AD 320. Their peaceful and prosperous reign saw a revival of Hindu religious thought and Brahman power. The old Vedic traditions were combined with devotion to many indigenous deities (who were seen as manifestations of Vedic gods). **Caste lines** were reinforced, and Buddhism gradually disappeared. The art (often erotic), architecture, and literature of the period, patronized by the Gupta court, are considered among India's finest achievements (Kalidasa, poet and dramatist, fl. c AD 400). Mathematical innovations included use of the zero and decimal numbers. Invasions by White Huns from the NW destroyed the empire c 550. Rich cultures also developed in S India in this era. Emotional Tamil religious poetry aided the Hindu revival. The Pallava kingdom controlled much of S India c 350-880 and helped spread Indian civilization to SE Asia.

China. The Ch'in ruler Shih Huang Ti (r 221-210 BC), known as the First Emperor, centralized political authority in China, standardized the written language, laws, weights, measures, and coinage, and conducted a census, but tried to destroy most philosophical texts. The **Han dynasty** (202 BC-AD 220) instituted the Mandarin bureaucracy, which lasted for 2,000 years. Local officials were selected by examination in the Confucian classics and trained at the imperial university and at provincial schools. The invention of **paper** facilitated this bureaucratic system. Agriculture was promoted, but the peasants bore most of the tax burden. Irrigation was improved, water clocks and sundials were used, astronomy and mathematics thrived, and landscape painting was perfected.

With the expansion S and W (to nearly the present borders of today's China), trade was opened with India, SE Asia, and the Middle East, over sea and caravan routes. Indian missionaries brought Mahayana Buddhism to China by the 1st cent. AD and spawned a variety of sects. Taoism was revived and merged with popular superstitions. Taoist and Buddhist monasteries and convents multiplied in the turbulent centuries after the collapse of the Han dynasty.

Monotheism Spreads: AD 1-750

Roman Empire. Polytheism was practiced in the Roman Empire, and religions indigenous to particular Middle Eastern nations became international. Roman citizens worshiped **Isis** of Egypt, **Mithras** of Persia, **Demeter** of Greece, and the great mother **Cybele** of Phrygia. Their cults centered on mysteries (secret ceremonies) and the promise of an afterlife, symbolized by the death and rebirth of the god. The Jews the empire preserved their monotheistic religion—Judaism, the world's oldest (c 1300 BC) continuous religion. Its teachings are contained in the Bible (the Old Testament). First-cent. Judaism embraced several sects, including the **Sadducees**, mostly drawn from the Temple priesthood, who were culturally Hellenized; the **Pharisees**, who upheld the full range of traditional customs and practices as of equal weight to literal scriptural law and elaborated synagogue worship; and the **Essenes**, an ascetic, millennarian sect. Messianic fervor led to repeated, unsuccessful rebellions against Rome (66-70, 135). As a result, the Temple in Jerusalem was destroyed and the population decimated; this event marked the beginning of the Diaspora (living in exile). To preserve the faith, a program of codification of law was begun at the academy of Yavneh. The work continued for some 500 years in Palestine and in Babylonia, ending in the final redaction (c 600) of the **Talmud**, a huge collection of legal and moral debates, rulings, liturgy, biblical exegesis, and legendary materials.

Christianity, which emerged as a distinct sect by the 2d half of the 1st cent., is based on the teachings of **Jesus**, whom believers considered the Savior (Messiah or Christ) and son of God. Missionary activities of the Apostles and such early leaders as **Paul of Tarsus** spread the faith. Intermittent persecution, as in Rome under Nero in AD 64, on grounds of suspected disloyalty, failed to disrupt the Christian communities. Each congregation, generally urban and of plebeian character, was tightly organized under a leader (bishop), elders (presbyters or priests), and assistants (deacons). The four **Gospels** (accounts of the life and teachings of Jesus) and the Acts of the Apostles were written down in the late 1st and early 2d cent. and circulated along with letters of Paul and other Christian leaders. An authoritative canon of these writings was not fixed until the 4th cent.

A school for priests was established at Alexandria in the 2d cent. Its teachers (**Origen** c 182-251) helped define doctrine and promote the faith in Greek-style philosophical works. Neoplatonism was given Christian coloration in the writings of Church Fathers such as **Augustine** (354-430). Christian hermits began to associate in monasteries, first in Egypt (St. Pachomius c 290-345), then in other eastern lands, then in the W (**St. Benedict's rule**, 529). Devotion to saints, especially Mary, mother of Jesus, spread. Under **Constantine** (r 306-37), Christianity became in effect the established religion of the Empire. Pagan temples were expropriated, state funds were used to build churches and support the hierarchy, and laws were adjusted in accordance with Christian ideas. Pagan worship was banned by the end of the 4th cent., and severe restrictions were placed on Judaism.

The newly established church was rocked by doctrinal disputes, often exacerbated by regional rivalries. Chief heresies (as defined by church councils, backed by imperial authority) were **Arianism**, which denied the divinity of Jesus; the **Monophysite** position denying the human nature of Christ; **Donatism**, which regarded as invalid any sacraments administered by sinful clergy; and **Pelagianism,** which denied the necessity of unmerited divine aid (grace) for salvation.

Islam. The earliest Arab civilization emerged by the end of the 2d millennium BC in the watered highlands of Yemen. Seaborne and caravan trade in frankincense and myrrh connected the area with the Nile and Fertile Crescent. The Minaean, Sabean (Sheba), and Himyarite states successively held sway. By Muhammad's time (7th cent. AD), the region was a province of Sassanian Persia. In the N, the Nabataean kingdom at Petra and the kingdom of Palmyra were Aramaicized, Romanized, and finally absorbed, as neighboring Judea had been, into the Roman Empire. Nomads shared the central region with a few trading towns and oases. Wars between tribes and raids on communities were common and were celebrated in a poetic tradition that by the 6th cent. helped establish a classic literary Arabic.

About 610, **Muhammad**, a 40-year-old Arab of Mecca, emerged as a prophet to his people. He proclaimed a revelation from the one true God, calling on contemporaries to abandon idolatry and restore the faith of Abraham. He introduced his religion as "Islam," meaning "submission" to the one God, Allah, as a continuation of the biblical faith of Abraham, Moses, and Jesus, all respected as prophets in this system. His teachings, recorded in the **Koran** (al-Qur'an in Arabic), in many ways were inclusive of Abrahamic monotheistic ideas known to the Jews and Christians in Arabia. A key aspect of the Abrahamic connection was insistence on justice in society, which led to severe opposition among the aristocrats in Mecca. As conditions worsened for Muhammad and his followers, he decided in 622 to make a ***hijra*** (emigration) to Medina, 200 mi. to the N. This event marks the beginning of the Muslim lunar calendar. Hostilities between Mecca and Medina increased, and in 629 Muhammad conquered Mecca. By his death in 632, nearly all the Arabian peninsula accepted his political and religious leadership.

After his death the majority of Muslims recognized the leadership of the **caliph** ("successor") Abu Bakr (632-34), followed by Umar (634-44), Uthman (644-56), and Ali (656-60). A minority, the **Shiites**, insisted instead on the leadership of Ali, Muhammad's cousin and son-in-law. By 644, **Muslim rule** over Arabia was confirmed. Muslim armies had threatened the Byzantine and Persian empires, which were weakened by wars and disaffection among subject peoples (including Coptic and Syriac Christians opposed to the Byzantine Orthodox establishment). Syria, Palestine, Egypt, Iraq, and Persia fell to Muslim armies. The new administration assimilated existing systems in the region; hence the conquered peoples participated in running of the empire. The Koran recognized the Peoples of the Book, i.e., Christians, Jews, and Zoroastrians, as tolerated monotheists, and Muslim policy was relatively tolerant to minorities living as "protected" peoples. An expanded tax system, based on conquests of the Persian and Byzantine empires, provided revenue to organize campaigns against neighboring non-Muslim regions.

Disputes over succession, and pious opposition to injustices in society, led to a number of oppositional movements, which also led to the factionalization of Muslim community. The **Shiites** supported leadership candidates descended from Muhammad, believing them to be carriers of some kind of divine authority. The **Kharijites** supported an egalitarian system derived from the Koran, opposing and even engaging in battle against those who did not agree with them.

Under the **Umayyads** (661-750) and **Abbasids** (750-1256), territorial expansion led Muslim armies across N Africa and into Spain (711). Muslim armies in the W were stopped at Tours (France) in 732 by the Frankish ruler **Charles Martel**. Asia Minor, the Indus Valley, and Transoxiana were conquered in the E. The conversion of conquered peoples to Islam was gradual. In many places the official Arabic language supplanted the local tongues. But in the eastern regions the Arab rulers and their armies adopted Persian cultures and language as part of their Muslim identity.

New Peoples Enter World History: 400-900

Barbarian invasions. Germanic tribes infiltrated S and E from their Baltic homeland during the 1st millennium BC, reaching S Germany by 100 BC and the Black Sea by AD 214. Organized into large federated tribes under elected kings, most resisted Roman domination and raided the empire in time of civil war (Goths took Dacia in 214, raided Thrace in 251-69). Germanic troops and commanders dominated the Roman armies by the end of the 4th cent. **Huns**, invaders from Asia, entered Europe in 372, driving more Germans into the W empire. Emperor Valens allowed Visigoths to cross the Danube in 376. Huns under Attila (d 453) raided Gaul, Italy, and the Balkans. The W empire, weakened by overtaxation and social stagnation, was overrun in the 5th cent. Gaul was effectively lost in 406-7, Spain in 409, Britain in 410, Africa in 429-39. Rome was sacked in 410 by Visigoths under Alaric and in 455 by Vandals. The last western emperor, Romulus Augustulus, was deposed in 476 by the Germanic chief Odovacar.

Celts. Celtic cultures, which in pre-Roman times covered most of W Europe, were confined almost entirely to the British Isles after the Germanic invasions. **St. Patrick** completed (c 457-92) the conversion of Ireland. A strong monastic tradition took hold. Irish monastic missionaries in Scotland, England, and the continent (Columba c 521-97; Columban c 543-615) helped restore Christianity after the Germanic invasions. Monasteries became centers of classic and Christian learning and presided over the recording of a Christianized Celtic mythology, elaborated by secular writers and bards. An intricate decorative art style developed, especially in book illumination (Lindisfarne Gospels, c 700; Book of Kells, 8th cent.).

Successor states. The Visigothic kingdom in Spain (from 419) and much of France (to 507) saw continuation of Roman administration, language, and law (Breviary of Alaric, 506) until its destruction by the Muslims (711). The Vandal kingdom in Africa (from 429) was conquered by the Byzantines in 533. Italy was ruled successively by an Ostrogothic kingdom under Byzantine suzerainty (489-554), direct Byzantine government, and German Lombards (568-774). The Lombards divided the peninsula with the Byzantines and papacy under the dynamic reformer **Pope Gregory the Great** (590-604) and successors.

King Clovis (r 481-511) united the Franks on both sides of the Rhine and, after his conversion to Christianity, defeated the Arian heretics, Burgundians (after 500), and Visigoths (507) with the support of native clergy and the papacy. Under the **Merovingian** kings, a feudal system emerged: Power was fragmented among hierarchies of military landowners. Social stratification, which in late Roman times had acquired legal, hereditary sanction, was reinforced. The Carolingians (747-987) expanded the kingdom and restored central power. **Charlemagne** (r 768-814) conquered nearly all the Germanic lands, including Lombard Italy, and was crowned Emperor by Pope Leo III in Rome in 800. A centuries-long decline in commerce and arts was reversed under Charlemagne's patronage. He welcomed Jews to his kingdom, which became a center of Jewish learning (Rashi, 1040-1105). He sponsored the Carolingian Renaissance of learning under the Anglo-Latin scholar Alcuin (c 732-804), who reformed church liturgy.

Byzantine Empire. Under **Diocletian** (r 284-305) the empire had been divided into 2 parts to facilitate administration and defense. **Constantine** founded (330) **Constantinople** (at old Byzantium) as a fully Christian city. Commerce and taxation financed a sumptuous, orientalized court, a class of hereditary bureaucratic families, and magnificent urban construction (Hagia Sophia, 532-37). The city's fortifications and naval innovations repelled assaults by Goths, Huns, Slavs, Bulgars, Avars, Arabs, and Scandinavians. Greek replaced Latin as the official language by c 700. Byzantine art, a solemn, sacral, and stylized variation of late classical styles (mosaics at the Church of San Vitale, Ravenna, Italy 526-48), was a starting point for medieval art in E and W Europe.

Justinian (r 527-65) reconquered parts of Spain, N Africa, and Italy, codified Roman law (Codex Justinianus [529] was medieval Europe's chief legal text), closed the Platonic Academy at Athens, and ordered all pagans to convert. Lombards in Italy and Arabs in Africa retook most of his conquests. The Isaurian dynasty from Anatolia (from 717) and the Macedonian dynasty (867-1054) restored military and commercial power. The Iconoclast controversy (726-843) over the permissibility of images helped alienate the Eastern Church from the papacy.

Abbasid Empire. Baghdad (est. 762), became seat of the **Abbasid dynasty** (est 750), while Ummayads continued to rule in Spain. A brilliant cosmopolitan civilization emerged, inaugurating a Muslim-Arab golden age. Arabic was the lingua franca of the empire; intellectual sources from Persian, Sanskrit, Greek, and Syriac were rendered into Arabic. Christians and Jews equally participated in this translation movement, which also involved interaction between Jewish legal thought and Islamic law, as much as between Christian theology and Muslim scholasticism. Persian-style court life, with art and music, flourished at the court of **Harun al-Rashid** (786-809), celebrated in the masterpiece known to English readers as *The Arabian Nights*. The sciences, medicine, and mathematics were pursued at Baghdad, Cordova, and Cairo (es.t 969). The culmination of this intellectual synthesis in Islamic civilization came with the scientific and philosophical works of **Avicenna** (Ibn Sina, 980-1037), **Averroes** (Ibn Rushd, 1126-98), and **Maimonides** (1135-1204), a Jew who wrote in Arabic. This intellectual tradition was translated into Latin and opened a new period in Christian thought.

The decentralization of the Abbasid empire, from 874, led to establishment of various Muslim dynasties under different ethnic groups. Persians, Berbers, and Turks ruled different regions, retaining connection with the Abbasid caliph at the religious level. The Abbasid period also saw various religious movements against the orthodox position held by governing authorities. This situation in religion led to establishment of different legal, theological and mystical schools of thought. The most influential mass movement was **Sufism**, which aimed at the reaching out of the average individual in quest of a spiritual path. Al-Ghazali (1058-1111) is credited with reconciling personal Sufism with orthodox Sunni tradition.

Africa. Immigrants from Saba in S Arabia helped set up the **Axum** kingdom in Ethiopia in the 1st cent. (their language, Ge'ez, is preserved by the Ethiopian Church). In the 3d cent., when the kingdom became Christianized, it defeated Kushite Meroe and expanded its influence into Yemen. Axum was the center of a vast ivory trade and controlled the Red Sea coast until c 1100. Arab conquest in Egypt cut Axum's political and economic ties with Byzantium.

The Iron Age entered W Africa by the end of the 1st millennium BC. **Ghana**, the first known sub-Saharan state, ruled in the upper Senegal-Niger region c 400-1240, controlling the trade of gold from mines in the S to trans-Sahara caravan routes to the N. The **Bantu** peoples, probably of W African origin, began to spread E and S perhaps 2,000 years ago, displacing the Pygmies and Bushmen of central and S Africa during a 1,500-year period.

Japan. The advanced Neolithic Yayoi period, when irrigation, rice farming, and iron and bronze casting techniques were introduced from China or Korea, persisted to c AD 400. The myriad Japanese states were then united by the **Yamato** clan, under an emperor who acted as chief priest of the animistic Shinto cult. Japanese political and military intervention by the 6th cent. in Korea, then under strong Chinese influence, quickened a Chinese cultural invasion of Japan, bringing Buddhism, the Chinese language (which long remained a literary and governmental medium), Chinese ideographs, and Buddhist styles in painting, sculpture, literature, and architecture (7th cent., Horyu-ji temple at Nara). The Taika Reforms (646) tried unsuccessfully to centralize Japan according to Chinese bureaucratic and Buddhist philosophical values. A nativist reaction against the Buddhist **Nara period** (710-94) ushered in the **Heian period** (794-1185) centered at the new capital, Kyoto. Japanese elegance and simplicity modified Chinese styles in architecture, scroll painting, and literature; the writing system was also simplified. The courtly novel *Tale of Genji* (1010-20) testifies to the enhanced role of women.

Southeast Asia. The historic peoples of SE Asia began arriving some 2,500 years ago from China and Tibet, displacing scattered aborigines. Their agriculture relied on rice and yams. Indian cultural influences were strongest; literacy and Hindu and Buddhist ideas followed the S India-China trade route. From the S tip of Indochina, the kingdom of **Funan** (1st-7th cent.) traded as far W as Persia. It was absorbed by Chenla, itself conquered by the **Khmer Empire** (600-1300). The Khmers, under Hindu god-kings (Suryavarman II, 1113-c 1150), built the monumental Angkor Wat temple center for the royal phallic cult. The **Nam-Viet** kingdom in Annam, dominated by China and Chinese culture for 1,000 years, emerged in the 10th cent., growing at the expense of the Khmers, who also lost ground in the NW to the new, highly organized **Thai** kingdom. On Sumatra, the **Srivijaya** Empire controlled vital sea lanes (7th to 10th cent.). A Buddhist dynasty, the Sailendras, ruled central **Java** (8th-9th cent.), building at Borobudur one of the largest stupas in the world.

China. The Sui dynasty (581-618) ushered in a period of commercial, artistic, and scientific achievement in China, continuing under the **Tang** dynasty (618-906). Inventions like the magnetic compass, gunpowder, the abacus, and printing were introduced or perfected. Medical innovations included cataract surgery. The state, from its cosmopolitan capital, Chang-an, supervised foreign trade, which exchanged Chinese silks, porcelains, and art for spices, ivory, etc., over Central Asian caravan routes and sea routes reaching Africa. A golden age of poetry bequeathed valuable works to later generations (Tu Fu, 712-70; Li Po, 701-62). Landscape painting flourished. Commercial and industrial expansion continued under the **Northern Sung** dynasty (960-1126), facilitated by paper money and credit notes. But commerce never achieved respectability; government monopolies expropriated successful merchants. The population, long stable at 50 million, doubled in 200 years with the introduction of early-ripening rice and the double harvest. In art, native Chinese styles were revived.

Americas. From 300 to 600 a Native American empire stretched from the Valley of Mexico to Guatemala, centering on the huge city **Teotihuacán** (founded 100 BC). To the S, in Guatemala, a high **Mayan** civilization developed (150-900) around hundreds of rural ceremonial centers. The Mayans improved on Olmec writing and the calendar and pursued astronomy and mathematics (using the idea of zero). In South America, a widespread pre-Inca culture grew from **Tiahuanacu,** Bolivia, near Lake Titicaca (Gateway of the Sun, c 700).

Christian Europe Regroups and Expands: 900-1300

Scandinavians. Pagan Danish and Norse (Viking) adventurers, traders, and pirates raided the coasts of the British Isles (Dublin, est. c 831), France, and even the Mediterranean for over 200 years beginning in the late 8th cent. Inland settlement in the W was limited to Great Britain (King Canute, 994-1035) and Normandy, settled (911) under Rollo, as a fief of France. Vikings also reached Iceland (874), Greenland (c 986), and North America (**Leif Eriksson,** c 1000). Norse traders

(**Varangians**) developed Russian river commerce from the 8th to the 11th cent. and helped set up a state at Kiev in the late 9th cent. Conversion to Christianity occurred in 10th cent., reaching Sweden 100 years later. In the 11th cent. Norman bands conquered S Italy and Sicily, and Duke **William of Normandy** conquered (1066) England, bringing feudalism and the French language, essential elements in later English civilization.

Central and East Europe. Slavs began to expand from about AD 150 in all directions in Europe, and by the 7th cent. they reached as far S as the Adriatic and Aegean seas. In the Balkan Peninsula they dislocated Romanized local populations or assimilated newcomers (Bulgarians, a Turkic people). The first Slavic states were Moravia (628) in Central Europe and the Bulgarian state (680) in the Balkans. Missions of St. Methodius and Cyril (whose Greek-based cyrillic alphabet is still used by some S and E Slavs) converted (863) Moravia.

The Eastern Slavs, part-civilized under the overlordship of the Turkish-Jewish **Khazar** trading empire (7th-10th cent.), gravitated toward Constantinople by the 9th cent. The **Kievan state** adopted (989) Eastern Christianity under Prince Vladimir. King Boleslav I (992-1025) began **Poland's** long history of eastern conquest. The Magyars (**Hungarians**), in present-day Hungary since 896, accepted (1001) Latin Christianity.

Germany. The German kingdom that emerged after the breakup of Charlemagne's W Empire remained a confederation of largely autonomous states. Otto I, a Saxon who was king from 936, established the **Holy Roman Empire**—a union of Germany and N Italy—in alliance with Pope John XII, who crowned (962) him emperor; he defeated (955) the Magyars. Imperial power was greatest under the **Hohenstaufens** (1138-1254), despite the growing opposition of the papacy, which ruled central Italy, and the Lombard League cities. Frederick II (1194-1250) improved administration and patronized the arts; after his death, German influence was removed from Italy.

Christian Spain. From its N mountain redoubts, Christian rule slowly migrated S through the 11th cent., when Muslim unity collapsed. After the capture (1085) of **Toledo**, the kingdoms of Portugal, Castile, and Aragon undertook repeated crusades of reconquest, finally completed in 1492. Elements of Islamic civilization persisted in recaptured areas, influencing all Western Europe.

Crusades. Pope Urban II called (1095) for a crusade to restore Asia Minor to Byzantium and to regain the Holy Land from the Turks. Some 10 crusades (to 1291) succeeded only in founding 4 temporary Frankish states in the Levant. The 4th crusade sacked (1204) Constantinople. In Rhineland (1096), England (1290), and France (1306), Jews were massacred or expelled, and wars were launched against Christian heretics (**Albigensian** crusade in France, 1229). Trade in eastern luxuries expanded, led by the Venetian naval empire.

Economy. The agricultural base of European life benefited from improvements in **plow design** (c 1000) and by draining of lowlands and clearing of forests, leading to a rural population increase. Towns grew in N Italy, Flanders, and N Germany (Hanseatic League). Improvements in **loom design** permitted factory textile production. **Guilds** dominated urban trades from the 12th cent. Banking (centered in Italy, 12th-15th cent.) facilitated long-distance trade.

The Church. The split between the Eastern and Western churches was formalized in 1054. Western and Central Europe was divided into 500 bishoprics under one united hierarchy, but conflicts between secular and church authorities were frequent (German **Investiture Controversy**, 1075-1122). Clerical power was first strengthened through the international monastic reform begun at Cluny in 910. Popular religious enthusiasm often expressed itself in heretical movements (Waldensians from 1173), but was channelled by the **Dominican** (1215) and **Franciscan** (1223) friars into the religious mainstream.

Arts. Romanesque architecture (11th-12th cent.) expanded on late Roman models, using the rounded arch and massed stone to support enlarged basilicas. Painting and sculpture followed Byzantine models. The literature of **chivalry** was exemplified by the epic (*Chanson de Roland*, c 1100) and by courtly love poems of the troubadours of Provence and minnesingers of Germany. **Gothic** architecture emerged in France (choir of St. Denis, c 1040) and spread as French cultural influence predominated in Europe. Rib vaulting and pointed arches were used to combine soaring heights with delicacy, and they freed walls for display of stained glass. Exteriors were covered with painted relief sculpture and embellished with elaborate architectural detail.

Learning. Law, medicine, and philosophy were advanced at independent **universities** (Bologna, late 11th cent.), originally corporations of students and masters. Twelfth-cent. translations of Greek classics, especially Aristotle, encouraged an analytic approach. Scholastic philosophy, from Anselm (1033-1109) to **Aquinas** (1225-74), attempted to understand revelation through reason.

Apogee of Central Asian Power; Islam Grows: 1250-1500

Turks. Turkic peoples, of Central Asian ancestry, were a military threat to the Byzantine and Persian Empires from the 6th cent. After several waves of invasions, during which most of the Turks adopted Islam, the **Seljuk Turks** took (1055) Baghdad. They ruled Persia, Iraq and, after 1071, Asia Minor, where massive numbers of Turks settled. The empire was divided in the 12th cent. into smaller states ruled by Seljuks, Kurds (**Saladin,** c 1137-93), and Mamluks (a military caste of former Turk, Kurd, and Circassian slaves), which governed Egypt and the Middle East until the Ottoman era (c 1290-1922).

Osman I (r c 1290-1326) and succeeding sultans united Anatolian Turkish warriors in a militaristic state that waged holy war against Byzantium and Balkan Christians. Most of the Balkans had been subdued, and Anatolia united, when Constantinople fell (1453). By the mid-16th cent., Hungary, the Middle East, and N Africa had been conquered. The Turkish advance was stopped at Vienna (1529) and at the naval battle of Lepanto (1571) by Spain, Venice, and the papacy.

The Ottoman state was governed in accordance with orthodox Muslim law. Greek, Armenian, and Jewish communities were segregated and were ruled by religious leaders responsible for taxation; they dominated trade. State offices and most army ranks were filled by slaves through a system of child conscription among Christians.

India. Mahmud of Ghazni (971-1030) led repeated Turkish raids into N India. Turkish power was consolidated in 1206 with the start of the **Sultanate at Delhi**. Centralization of state power under the early Delhi sultans went far beyond traditional Indian practice. Muslim rule of most of the subcontinent lasted until the British conquest some 600 years later.

Mongols. Genghis Khan (c 1167-1227) first united the feuding Mongol tribes, and built their armies into an effective offensive force around a core of highly mobile cavalry. He and his immediate successors created the largest land empire in history; by 1279 it stretched from the E coast of Asia to the Danube, from the Siberian steppes to the Arabian Sea. East-West trade and contacts were facilitated (Marco Polo, c 1254-1324). The W Mongols were Islamized by 1295; successor states soon lost their Mongol character by assimilation. They were briefly reunited under the Turk Tamerlane (1336-1405).

Kublai Khan ruled China from his new capital Beijing (est c 1264). Naval campaigns against Japan (1274, 1281) and Java (1293) were defeated, the latter by the Hindu-Buddhist maritime kingdom of Majapahit. The **Yuan** dynasty used

Mongols and other foreigners (including Europeans) in official posts and tolerated the return of Nestorian Christianity (suppressed 841-45) and the spread of Islam in the S and W. A native reaction expelled the Mongols in 1367-68.

Russia. The Kievan state in Russia, weakened by the decline of Byzantium and the rise of the Catholic Polish-Lithuanian state, was overrun (1238-40) by the Mongols. Only the northern trading republic of Novgorod remained independent. The grand dukes of Moscow emerged as leaders of a coalition of princes that eventually (by 1481) defeated the Mongols. After the fall of Constantinople in 1453, the **Tsars** (Caesars) at Moscow (from Ivan III, r 1462-1505) set up an independent Russian Orthodox Church. Commerce failed to revive. The isolated Russian state remained agrarian, with the peasant class falling into serfdom.

Persia. A revival of Persian literature, making use of the Arab alphabet and literary forms, began in the 10th cent. (epic of Firdausi, 935-1020). An art revival, influenced by Chinese styles introduced after the Mongols came to power in Iran, began in the 13th cent. Persian cultural and political forms, and often the Persian language, were used for centuries by Turkish and Mongol elites from the Balkans to India. Persian mystics from Rumi (1207-73) to Jami (1414-92) promoted **Sufism** in their poetry.

Africa. Two militant Islamic Berber dynasties emerged from the Sahara to carve out empires from the Sahel to central Spain—the **Almoravids** (c 1050-1140) and the fanatical **Almohads** (c 1125-1269). The Ghanaian empire was replaced in the upper Niger by Mali (c 1230-1340), whose Muslim rulers imported Egyptians to help make **Timbuktu** a center of commerce (in gold, leather, and slaves) and learning. The Songhay empire (to 1590) replaced Mali. To the S, forest kingdoms produced refined artworks (Ife terra cotta, **Benin** bronzes). Other Muslim states in Nigeria (Hausas) and Chad originated in the 11th cent. and continued in some form until the 19th-cent. European conquest. Less-developed Bantu kingdoms existed across central Africa.

Some 40 Muslim Arab-Persian trading colonies and city-states were established all along the E African coast from the 10th cent. (Kilwa, Mogadishu). The interchange with Bantu peoples produced the **Swahili** language and culture. Gold, palm oil, and slaves were brought from the interior, stimulating the growth of the Monamatapa kingdom of the Zambezi (15th cent.). The Christian Ethiopian empire (from 13th cent.) continued the traditions of Axum.

Southeast Asia. Islam was introduced into Malaya and the Indonesian islands by Arab, Persian, and Indian traders. Coastal Muslim cities and states (starting before 1300) soon dominated the interior. Chief among these was the **Malacca** state (c 1400-1511), on the Malay peninsula.

Arts and Statecraft Thrive in Europe: 1350-1600

Italian Renaissance and Humanism. Distinctive Italian achievements in the arts in the late Middle Ages (**Dante,** 1265-1321; Giotto, 1276-1337) led to the vigorous new styles of the Renaissance (14th-16th cent.). Patronized by the rulers of the quarreling petty states of Italy (**Medicis** in Florence and the papacy, c 1400-1737), the plastic arts perfected realistic techniques, including **perspective** (Masaccio, 1401-28, **Leonardo,** 1452-1519). Classical motifs were used in architecture, and increased talent and expense were put into secular buildings. The Florentine dialect was refined as a national literary language (**Petrarch,** 1304-74). Greek refugees from the E strengthened the respect of humanist scholars for the classic sources. Soon an international movement aided by the spread of **printing** (Gutenberg, c 1400-68), **humanism** was optimistic about the power of human reason (Erasmus of Rotterdam, 1466-1536, **More's** *Utopia*, 1516) and valued individual effort in the arts and in politics (**Machiavelli,** 1469-1527).

France. The French monarchy, strengthened in its repeated struggles with powerful nobles (Burgundy, Flanders, Aquitaine) by alliances with the growing commercial towns, consolidated bureaucratic control under Philip IV (r 1285-1314) and extended French influence into Germany and Italy (popes at Avignon, France, 1309-1417). The **Hundred Years War** (1337-1453) ended English dynastic claims in France (battles of Crécy, 1346, and Poitiers, 1356; Joan of Arc executed, 1431). A French Renaissance, dating from royal invasions (1494, 1499) of Italy, was encouraged at the court of Francis I (r 1515-47), who centralized taxation and law. French vernacular literature consciously asserted its independence (La Pléiade, 1549).

England. The evolution of England's unique political institutions began with the **Magna Carta** (1215), by which King John guaranteed the privileges of nobles and church against the monarchy and assured jury trial. After the **Wars of the Roses** (1455-85), the **Tudor dynasty** reasserted royal prerogatives (Henry VIII, r 1509-47), but the trend toward independent departments and ministerial government also continued. English trade (wool exports from c 1340) was protected by the nation's growing maritime power (**Spanish Armada** destroyed, 1588).

English replaced French and Latin in the late 14th cent. in law and literature (**Chaucer,** c 1340-1400) and English translation of the Bible began (Wycliffe, 1380s). **Elizabeth I** (r 1558-1603) presided over a confident flowering of poetry (Spenser, 1552-99), drama (**Shakespeare**, 1564-1616), and music.

German Empire. From among a welter of minor feudal states, church lands, and independent cities, the **Habsburgs** assembled a far-flung territorial domain, based in Austria from 1276. The family held the title Holy Roman Emperor from 1438 to the Empire's dissolution in 1806, but failed to centralize its domains, leaving Germany disunited for centuries. Resistance to Turkish expansion brought Hungary under Austrian control from the 16th cent. The Netherlands, Luxembourg, and Burgundy were added in 1477, curbing French expansion.

The Flemish painting tradition of naturalism, technical proficiency, and bourgeois subject matter began in the 15th cent. (**Jan Van Eyck,** c 1390-1441), the earliest northern manifestation of the Renaissance. Albrecht **Dürer** (1471-1528) typified the merging of late Gothic and Italian trends in 16th-cent. German art. Imposing civic architecture flourished in the prosperous commercial cities.

Spain. Despite the unification of Castile and Aragon in 1479, the 2 countries retained separate governments, and the nobility, especially in Aragon and Catalonia, retained many privileges. Spanish lands in Italy (Naples, Sicily) and the Netherlands entangled the country in European wars through the mid-17th cent., while explorers, traders, and conquerors built up a Spanish empire in the Americas and the Philippines. From the late 15th cent., a **golden age** of literature and art produced works of social satire (plays of Lope de Vega, 1562-1635; **Cervantes,** 1547-1616), as well as spiritual intensity (**El Greco,** 1541-1614; **Velazquez,** 1599-1660).

Black Death. The bubonic plague reached Europe from the E in 1348, killing as much as half the population by 1350. Labor scarcity forced a rise in wages and brought greater freedom to the peasantry, making possible **peasant uprisings** (Jacquerie in France, 1358; Wat Tyler's rebellion in England, 1381). In the *ciompi* revolt (1378), Florentine wage earners demanded a say in economic and political power.

Explorations. Organized European maritime exploration began, seeking to evade the Venice-Ottoman monopoly of E trade and to promote Christianity. Beginning in 1418, expeditions from Portugal explored the W coast of Africa, until Vasco da Gama rounded the Cape of Good Hope in 1497 and reached India. A Portuguese trading empire was consolidated by the seizure of Goa (1510) and Malacca (1551). Japan was reached in 1542. The voyages of Christopher **Columbus** (1492-1504) uncovered a world new to Europeans, which Spain hastened to subdue. Navigation schools in Spain and Portugal, the development of large sailing ships (carracks), and the invention (c 1475) of the rifle aided European penetration.

Mughals and Safavids. E of the Ottoman Empire, 2 Muslim dynasties ruled unchallenged in the 16th and 17th cent. The Mughal dynasty of India, founded by Persianized Turkish invaders from the NW under Babur, dates from their 1526 conquest of the Delhi Sultanate. The dynasty ruled most of India for more than 200 years, surviving nominally until 1857. **Akbar** (r 1556-1605) consolidated administration at his glorious court, where the Urdu language (Persian-influenced Hindi) developed. Trade relations with Europe increased. Under Shah Jahan (1629-58), a secularized art fusing Hindu and Muslim element flourished in miniature painting and in architecture (**Taj Mahal**). **Sikhism** (founded c 1519) combined elements of both faiths. Suppression of Hindus and Shi'ite Muslims in S India in the late 17th cent. weakened the empire.

Fanatical devotion to the Shi'ite sect characterized the Safavids (1502-1736) of Persia and led to hostilities with the Sunni Ottomans for more than a century. The prosperity and the strength of the empire are evidenced by the mosques at its capital city, **Isfahan**. The Safavids enhanced Iranian national consciousness.

China. The **Ming** emperors (1368-1644), the last native dynasty in China, wielded unprecedented personal power, while the Confucian bureaucracy began to suffer from inertia. European trade (Portuguese monopoly through **Macao** from 1557) was strictly controlled. Jesuit scholars and scientists (Matteo Ricci, 1552-1610) introduced some Western science; their writings familiarized the West with China. Chinese technological inventiveness declined from this era, but the arts thrived, especially painting and ceramics.

Japan. After the decline of the first hereditary shogunate (chief generalship) at **Kamakura** (1185-1333), fragmentation of power accelerated, as did the consequent social mobility. Under Kamakura and the Ashikaga shogunate (1338-1573), the daimyos (lords) and samurai (warriors) grew more powerful and promoted a martial ideology. Japanese pirates and traders plied the China coast. Popular Buddhist movements included the nationalist Nichiren sect (from c 1250) and **Zen** (brought from China, 1191), which stressed meditation and a disciplined esthetic (tea ceremony, gardening, martial arts, No drama).

Reformed Europe Expands Overseas: 1500-1700

Reformation begun. Theological debate and protests against real and perceived clerical corruption existed in the medieval Christian world, expressed by such dissenters as John **Wycliffe** (c 1320-84) and his followers, the Lollards, in England, and **Huss** (burned as a heretic, 1415) in Bohemia.

Martin **Luther** (1483-1546) preached that faith alone leads to salvation, without the mediation of clergy or good works. He attacked the authority of the pope, rejected priestly celibacy, and recommended individual study of the Bible (which he translated c 1525). His 95 Theses (1517) led to his excommunication (1521). John **Calvin** (1509-64) said that God's elect were predestined for salvation and that good conduct and success were signs of election. Calvin in Geneva and John Knox (1505-72) in Scotland established theocratic states.

Henry VIII asserted English national authority and secular power by breaking away (1534) from the Catholic Church. Monastic property was confiscated, and some Protestant doctrines given official sanction.

Religious wars. A century and a half of religious wars began with a S German peasant uprising (1524), repressed with Luther's support. Radical sects—democratic, pacifist, millennarian—arose (Anabaptists ruled Münster in 1534-35) and were suppressed violently. Civil war in France from 1562 between **Huguenots** (Protestant nobles and merchants) and Catholics ended with the 1598 **Edict of Nantes,** tolerating Protestants (revoked 1685). Habsburg attempts to restore Catholicism in Germany were resisted in 25 years of fighting; the 1555 Peace of Augsburg guarantee of religious independence to local princes and cities was confirmed only after the **Thirty Years War** (1618-48), when much of Germany was devastated by local and foreign armies (Sweden, France).

A Catholic Reformation, or **Counter Reformation**, met the Protestant challenge, clearly defining an official theology at the Council of Trent (1545-63). The **Jesuit** order (Society of Jesus), founded in 1534 by Ignatius Loyola (1491-1556), helped reconvert large areas of Poland, Hungary, and S Germany and sent missionaries to the New World, India, and China, while the Inquisition helped suppress heresy in Catholic countries. A revival of piety appeared in the devotional literature (Teresa of Avila, 1515-82) and grandiose Baroque art (Bernini, 1598-1680) of Roman Catholic countries.

Scientific Revolution. The late nominalist thinkers (Ockham, c 1300-49) of Paris and Oxford challenged Aristotelian orthodoxy, allowing for a freer scientific approach. At the same time, metaphysical values, such as the Neoplatonic faith in an orderly, mathematical cosmos, still motivated and directed inquiry. Nicolaus **Copernicus** (1473-1543) promoted the heliocentric theory, which was confirmed when Johannes Kepler (1571-1630) discovered the mathematical laws describing the orbits of the planets. The traditional Christian-Aristotelian belief that heavens and earth were fundamentally different collapsed when **Galileo** (1564-1642) discovered moving sunspots, irregular moon topography, and moons around Jupiter. He and Sir Isaac **Newton** (1642-1727) developed a mechanics that unified cosmic and earthly phenomena. Newton and Gottfried von Leibniz (1646-1716) invented calculus, and René Descartes (1596-1650) invented analytic geometry.

An explosion of **observational science** included the discovery of blood circulation (Harvey, 1578-1657) and microscopic life (Leeuwenhoek, 1632-1723) and advances in anatomy (Vesalius, 1514-64, dissected corpses) and chemistry (Boyle, 1627-91). Scientific research institutes were founded: Florence (1657), London (**Royal Society**, 1660), Paris (1666). Inventions proliferated (Savery's steam engine, 1696).

Arts. Mannerist trends of the High Renaissance (**Michelangelo**, 1475-1564) exploited virtuosity, grace, novelty, and exotic subjects and poses. The notion of artistic genius was promoted, in contrast to the anonymous medieval artisan. Private connoisseurs entered the art market. These trends were elaborated in the 17th cent. **Baroque** era on a grander scale. Dynamic movement in painting and sculpture was emphasized by sharp lighting effects, use of rich materials (colored marble, gilt), and realistic details. Curved facades, broken lines, rich, deep-cut detail, and ceiling decoration characterized Baroque architecture, especially in Germany. Monarchs, princes, and prelates, usually Catholic, used Baroque art to enhance and embellish their authority, as in royal portraits (Velazquez, 1599-1660; Van Dyck, 1599-1641).

National styles emerged. In France, a taste for rectilinear order and serenity (Poussin, 1594-1665), linked to the new rational philosophy, was expressed in classical forms. The influence of **classical values** in French literature (tragedies of **Racine**, 1639-99) gave rise to the "battle of the Ancients and Moderns." New forms included the essay (**Montaigne**, 1533-92) and novel (*Princesse de Cleves*, La Fayette, 1678).

Dutch painting of the 17th cent. was unique in its wide social distribution. The Flemish tradition of undemonstrative realism reached its peak in **Rembrandt** (1606-69) and Jan Vermeer (1632-75).

Economy. European economic expansion was stimulated by the new trade with the East, by New World gold and silver, and by a doubling of population (50 million in 1450, 100 million in 1600). New business and financial techniques were developed and refined, such as joint-stock companies, insurance, and letters of credit and exchange. The Bank of Amsterdam (1609) and the Bank of England (1694) broke the old monopoly of private banking families. The rise of a business mentality was typified by the spread of clock towers in cities in the 14th cent. By the mid-15th cent., portable clocks were available; the first watch was invented in 1502.

By 1650, most governments had adopted the **mercantile system**, in which they sought to amass metallic wealth by protecting their merchants' foreign and colonial trade monopolies. The rise in prices and the new coin-based economy undermined the craft guild and feudal manorial systems. Expanding industries (clothweaving, mining) benefited from technical advances. Coal replaced disappearing wood as the chief fuel; it was used to fuel new 16th-cent. blast furnaces making cast iron.

New World. The **Aztecs** united much of the Meso-American culture area in a militarist empire by 1519, from their capital, Tenochtitlán (pop. 300,000), which was the center of a cult requiring ritual human sacrifice. Most of the civilized areas of South America were ruled by the centralized Inca Empire (1476-1534), stretching 2,000 mi from Ecuador to NW Argentina. Lavish and sophisticated traditions in pottery, weaving, sculpture, and architecture were maintained in both regions.

These empires, beset by revolts, fell in 2 short campaigns to gold-seeking Spanish forces based in the Antilles and Panama. Hernan **Cortes** took Mexico (1519-21); Francisco **Pizarro,** Peru (1532-35). From these centers, land and sea expeditions claimed most of North and South America for Spain. The Indian high cultures did not survive the impact of Christian missionaries and the new upper class of whites and mestizos. In turn, New World silver and such Indian products as potatoes, tobacco, corn, peanuts, chocolate, and rubber exercised a major economic influence on Europe. Although the Spanish administration intermittently concerned itself with the welfare of Indians, the population remained impoverished at most levels. European diseases reduced the native population.

Brazil, which the Portuguese reached in 1500 and settled after 1530, and the Caribbean colonies of several European nations developed a plantation economy where sugarcane, tobacco, cotton, coffee, rice, indigo, and lumber were grown by slaves. From the early 16th to late 19th cent., c 10 million Africans were transported to **slavery** in the New World.

Netherlands. The urban, Calvinist N provinces of the Netherlands rebelled (1568) against Habsburg Spain and founded an oligarchic mercantile republic. Their strategic control of the Baltic grain market enabled them to exploit Mediterranean food shortages. Religious refugees—French and Belgian Protestants, Iberian Jews—added to the cosmopolitan commercial talent pool. After Spain absorbed Portugal in 1580, the Dutch seized Portuguese possessions and created a vast, though short-lived commercial empire in Brazil, the Antilles, Africa, India, Ceylon, Malacca, Indonesia, and Taiwan and challenged or supplanted Portuguese traders in China and Japan. Revolution in 1640 restored Portuguese independence.

England. Anglicanism became firmly established under **Elizabeth I** after a brief Catholic interlude under "Bloody Mary" (1553-58). But religious and political conflicts led to a rebellion (1642) by Parliament. Roundheads (Puritans) defeated Cavaliers (Royalists); Charles I was beheaded (1649). The new Commonwealth was ruled as a military dictatorship by Oliver **Cromwell,** who also brutally crushed (1649-51) an Irish rebellion. Conflicts within the Puritan camp (democratic Levelers defeated, 1649) aided the Stuart restoration (1660), but Parliament was strengthened and the peaceful **"Glorious Revolution"** (1688) advanced political and religious liberties (writings of **Locke,** 1632-1704). British privateers (Drake, 1540-96) challenged Spanish control of the New World and penetrated Asian trade routes (Madras taken, 1639). North American colonies (Jamestown, 1607; Plymouth, 1620) provided an outlet for religious dissenters from Europe.

France. Emerging from the religious civil wars in 1628, France regained military and commercial great power status (under the ministries of **Richelieu**, Mazarin, and Colbert). Under **Louis XIV** (reigned 1643-1715), royal absolutism triumphed over nobles and local *parlements* (defeat of Fronde, 1648-53). Permanent colonies were founded in Canada (1608), the Caribbean (1626), and India (1674).

Sweden. Sweden seceded from the Scandinavian Union in 1523. The thinly populated agrarian state (with copper, iron, and timber exports) was united by the Vasa kings, whose conquests by the mid-17th cent. made Sweden the dominant Baltic power. The empire collapsed in the Great Northern War (1700-21).

Poland. After the union with Lithuania in 1447, Poland ruled vast territories from the Baltic to the Black Sea, resisting German and Turkish incursions. Catholic nobles failed to gain the loyalty of their Orthodox Christian subjects in the E; commerce and trades were practiced by German and Jewish immigrants. The bloody 1648-49 Cossack uprising began the kingdom's dismemberment.

China. A new dynasty, the **Manchus,** invaded from the NE, seized power in 1644, and expanded Chinese control to its greatest extent in Central and SE Asia. Trade and diplomatic contact with Europe grew, carefully controlled by China. New crops (sweet potato, maize, peanut) allowed an economic and population growth (pop. 300 million, in 1800). Traditional arts and literature were pursued with increased sophistication (*Dream of the Red Chamber*, novel, mid-18th cent.).

Japan. Tokugawa Ieyasu, shogun from 1603, finally unified and pacified feudal Japan. Hereditary daimyos and samurai monopolized government office and the professions. An urban merchant class grew, literacy spread, and a cultural renaissance occurred (**haiku,** a verse innovation of the poet Basho, 1644-94). Fear of European domination led to persecution of Christian converts from 1597 and to stringent isolation from outside contact from 1640.

Philosophy, Industry, and Revolution: 1700-1800

Science and Reason. Greater faith in human reason and empirical observation as a source of truth and a means to improve the physical and social environment, espoused since the Renaissance (Francis Bacon, 1561-1626), was bolstered by scientific discoveries in spite of theological opposition (Galileo's forced retraction, 1633). René **Descartes** (1596-1650) used a rationalistic approach modeled on geometry to discover "self-evident" truths as a foundation of knowledge. Sir Isaac **Newton** emphasized induction from experimental observation. Baruch de **Spinoza** (1632-77), who called for political and intellectual freedom, developed a systematic rationalistic philosophy in his classic work *Ethics*.

French philosophers assumed leadership of the **Enlightenment** in the 18th cent. Montesquieu (1689-1755) used British history to support his notions of limited government. **Voltaire**'s (1694-1778) diaries and novels of exotic travel illustrated the intellectual trends toward secular ethics and relativism. Jean-Jacques **Rousseau's** (1712-1778) radical concepts of the **social contract** and of the inherent goodness of the common man gave impetus to antimonarchical republicanism. The *Encyclopedia* (1751-72, edited by Diderot and d'Alembert), designed as a monument to reason, was largely devoted to practical technology.

In England, ideals of political and religious liberty were connected with empiricist philosophy and science in the followers of Locke. But British empiricism, especially as developed by the skeptical David **Hume** (1711-76), radically reduced the role of reason in philosophy, as did the evolutionary approach to law and politics of Edmund Burke (1729-97) and the utilitarian ethics of Jeremy Bentham (1748-1832). Adam Smith (1723-90) and other **physiocrats** called for a rationalization of economic activity by removing artificial barriers to a supposedly natural free exchange of goods.

German writers participated in the new philosophical trends popularized by Christian von Wolff (1679-1754). Immanuel **Kant's** (1724-1804) transcendental idealism, unifying an empirical epistemology with a priori moral and logical concepts, directed German thought away from skepticism. Italian contributions included work on electricity by (Galvani, 1737-98;

Volta, 1745-1827), the pioneer historiography of Vico (1668-1744), and writings on penal reform (Beccaria, 1738-94). Benjamin Franklin (1706-90) was celebrated in Europe for his varied achievements.

The growth of the **press** (*Spectator*, 1711-12) and the wide distribution of realistic but sentimental **novels** attested to the increase of a large bourgeois public.

Arts. Rococo art, characterized by extravagant decorative effects, asymmetries copied from organic models, and artificial pastoral subjects, was favored by the continental aristocracy for most of the cent. (Watteau, 1684-1721) and had musical analogies in the ornamentalized polyphony of late Baroque. The **Neoclassical** art after 1750, associated with the new scientific archaeology, was more streamlined and was infused with the supposed moral and geometric rectitude of the Roman Republic (David, 1748-1825). In England, **town planning** on a grand scale began.

Industrial Revolution in England. Agricultural improvements, such as the sowing drill (1701) and livestock breeding, were implemented on the large fields provided by enclosure of common lands by private owners. Profits from agriculture and from colonial and foreign trade (1800 volume, £54 million) were channeled through hundreds of banks and the **Stock Exchange** (est 1773) into new industrial processes.

The Newcomen steam pump (1712) aided coal mining. Coal fueled the new efficient steam engines patented by James Watt in 1769, and coke-smelting produced cheap, sturdy iron for machinery by the 1730s. The **flying shuttle** (1733) and **spinning jenny** (c 1764) were used in the large new cotton textile factories, where women and children were much of the work force. Goods were transported cheaply over **canals** (2,000 mi; built 1760-1800).

American Revolution. The British colonies in North America attracted a mass immigration of religious dissenters and poor people throughout the 17th and 18th cent., coming from the British Isles, Germany, the Netherlands, and other countries. The population reached 3 million non-natives by the 1770s. The small native population was greatly reduced by European diseases and by wars with and between the various colonies. British attempts to control colonial trade and to tax the colonists to pay for the costs of colonial administration and defense clashed with traditions of local self-government and eventually provoked the colonies to rebellion.

Central and East Europe. The monarchs of the three states that dominated E Europe—Austria, Prussia, and Russia—accepted the advice and legitimation of philosophes in creating more modern, centralized institutions in their kingdoms, enlarged by the division (1772-95) of Poland.

Under **Frederick II** (r 1740-86) Prussia, with its efficient modern army, doubled in size. State monopolies and tariff protection fostered industry, and some legal reforms were introduced. Austria's heterogeneous realms were unified under **Maria Theresa** (r 1740-80) and **Joseph II** (r 1780-90). Reforms in education, law, and religion were enacted, and the Austrian serfs were freed (1781). With its defeat in the Seven Years' War in 1763, Austria failed to regain Silesia, which had been seized by Prussia, but it was compensated by expansion to the E and S (Hungary, Slavonia, 1699; Galicia, 1772).

Russia, whose borders continued to expand in all directions, adopted some Western bureaucratic and economic policies under **Peter I** (r 1682-1725) and **Catherine II** (r 1762-96). Trade and cultural contacts with the West multiplied from the new Baltic Sea capital, **St. Petersburg** (est 1703).

French Revolution. The growing French middle class lacked political power and resented aristocratic tax privileges, especially in light of the successful American Revolution. Peasants lacked adequate land and were burdened with feudal obligations to nobles. War with Britain led to the loss of French Canada and drained the treasury, finally forcing the king to call the **Estates-General** in 1789 (first time since 1614), in an atmosphere of food riots (poor crop in 1788).

Aristocratic resistance to absolutism was soon overshadowed by the reformist Third Estate (middle class), which proclaimed itself the **National Constituent Assembly** June 17 and took the "Tennis Court oath" on June 20 to secure a constitution. The storming of the **Bastille** on July 14 by Parisian artisans was followed by looting and seizure of aristocratic property throughout France. Assembly reforms included abolition of class and regional privileges, a Declaration of Rights, suffrage by taxpayers (75% of males), and the **Civil Constitution of the Clergy** providing for election and loyalty oaths for priests. A republic was declared Sept. 22, 1792, in spite of royalist pressure from Austria and Prussia, which had declared war in April (joined by Britain the next year). Louis XVI was beheaded Jan. 21, 1793, Queen Marie Antoinette was beheaded Oct. 16, 1793.

Royalist uprisings in La Vendée and military reverses led to a **reign of terror** in which tens of thousands of opponents of the Revolution and criminals were executed. Radical reforms in the **Convention** period (Sept. 1793-Oct. 1795) included the abolition of colonial slavery, economic measures to aid the poor, support of public education, and a short-lived de-Christianization.

Division among radicals (execution of Hebert, Danton, and Robespierre, 1794) aided the ascendance of a moderate **Directory**, which consolidated military victories. **Napoleon Bonaparte** (1769-1821), a popular young general, exploited political divisions and participated in a coup Nov. 9, 1799, making himself first consul (dictator).

India. Sikh and Hindu rebels (Rajputs, Marathas) and Afghans destroyed the power of the Mughals during the 18th cent. After France's defeat (1763) in the Seven Years' War, Britain was the primary European trade power in India. Its control of inland **Bengal and Bihar** was recognized (1765) by the Mughal shah, who granted the **British East India Co.** (under Clive, 1725-74) the right to collect land revenue there. Despite objections from Parliament (1784 India Act), the company's involvement in local wars and politics led to repeated acquisitions of new territory. The company exported Indian textiles, sugar, and indigo.

Change Gathers Steam: 1800-40

French ideals and empire spread. Inspired by the ideals of the French Revolution, and supported by the expanding French armies, new republican regimes arose near France: the **Batavian** Republic in the Netherlands (1795-1806), the **Helvetic** Republic in Switzerland (1798-1803), the **Cisalpine** Republic in N Italy (1797-1805), the **Ligurian** Republic in Genoa (1797-1805), and the **Parthenopean** Republic in S Italy (1799). A Roman Republic existed briefly in 1798 after Pope Pius VI was arrested by French troops. In Italy and Germany, new nationalist sentiments were stimulated both in imitation of and in reaction to developments in France (anti-French and anti-Jacobin peasant uprisings in Italy, 1796-99).

From 1804, when Napoleon declared himself emperor, to 1812, a succession of military victories (Austerlitz, 1805; Jena, 1806) extended his control over most of Europe, through puppet states (**Confederation of the Rhine** united W German states for the first time and **Grand Duchy of Warsaw** revived Polish national hopes), expansion of the empire, and alliances.

Among the lasting reforms initiated under Napoleon's absolutist reign were: establishment of the Bank of France, centralization of tax collection, codification of law along Roman models (Code Napoléon), and reform and extension of secondary and university education. In an 1801 concordat, the papacy recognized the effective autonomy of the French Catholic Church. Some 400,000 French soldiers were killed in the Napoleonic Wars, along with 600,000 foreign troops.

Last gasp of old regime. France's coastal blockade of Europe (**Continental System**) failed to neutralize Britain. The disastrous 1812 invasion of Russia exposed Napoleon's overextension. After Napoleon's 1814 exile at Elba, his armies were defeated (1815) at **Waterloo**, by British and Prussian troops.

At the **Congress of Vienna**, the monarchs and princes of Europe redrew their boundaries, to the advantage of Prussia (in Saxony and the Ruhr), Austria (in Illyria and Venetia), and Russia (in Poland and Finland). British conquest of Dutch and

French colonies (S Africa, Ceylon, Mauritius) was recognized, and France, under the restored Bourbons, retained its expanded 1792 borders. The settlement brought 50 years of international peace to Europe.

But the Congress was unable to check the advance of liberal ideals and of nationalism among the smaller European nations. The 1825 **Decembrist uprising** by liberal officers in Russia was easily suppressed. But an independence movement in **Greece**, stirred by commercial prosperity and a cultural revival, succeeded in expelling Ottoman rule by 1831, with the aid of Britain, France, and Russia.

A constitutional monarchy was secured in France by the **1830 Revolution**; Louis Philippe became king. The revolutionary contagion spread to **Belgium**, which gained its independence (1830) from the Dutch monarchy, to **Poland**, whose rebellion was defeated (1830-31) by Russia, and to Germany.

Romanticism. A new style in intellectual and artistic life began to replace Neoclassicism and Rococo after the mid-18th cent. By the early 19th cent., this style, Romanticism, had prevailed in the European world.

Rousseau had begun the reaction against rationalism; in education (*Émile*, 1762) he stressed subjective spontaneity over regularized instruction. German writers (Lessing, 1729-81; Herder, 1744-1803) favorably compared the German folk song to classical forms and began a cult of Shakespeare, whose passion and "natural" wisdom was a model for the romantic *Sturm und Drang* (Storm and Stress) movement. **Goethe's** *Sorrows of Young Werther* (1774) set the model for the tragic, passionate genius.

A new interest in **Gothic architecture** in England after 1760 (Walpole, 1717-97) spread through Europe, associated with an aesthetic Christian and mystic revival (**Blake,** 1757-1827). Celtic, Norse, and German mythology and folk tales were revived or imitated (Macpherson's Ossian translation, 1762; Grimm's Fairy Tales, 1812-22). The medieval revival (Scott's *Ivanhoe*, 1819) led to a new interest in history, stressing national differences and organic growth (**Carlyle,** 1795-1881; Michelet, 1798-1874), corresponding to theories of natural evolution (Lamarck's *Philosophie Zoologique*, 1809; Lyell's *Geology*, 1830-33). A reaction against classicism characterized the English **romantic poets** (beginning with **Wordsworth,** 1770-1850). Revolution and war fed an emphasis on freedom and conflict, expressed by both poets (**Byron**, 1788-1824; **Hugo**, 1802-85) and philosophers (**Hegel**, 1770-1831).

Wild gardens replaced the formal French variety, and painters favored rural, stormy, and mountainous landscapes (**Turner**, 1775-1851; **Constable**, 1776-1837). Clothing became freer, with wigs, hoops, and ruffles discarded. Originality and genius were expected in the life as well as the work of inspired artists (Murger's *Scenes from Bohemian Life*, 1847-49). Exotic locales and themes (as in Gothic horror stories) were used in art and literature (Delacroix, 1798-1863; **Poe**, 1809-49).

Music exhibited the new dramatic style and a breakdown of classical forms (**Beethoven,** 1770-1827). The use of folk melodies and modes aided the growth of distinct national traditions (Glinka in Russia, 1804-57).

Latin America. Francois **Toussaint L'Ouverture** led a successful slave revolt in Haiti, which subsequently became the first Latin American state to achieve independence (1804). The mainland Spanish colonies won their independence (1810-24), under such leaders as Simon **Bolivar** (1783-1830). Brazil became an independent empire (1822) under the Portuguese prince regent. A new class of military officers divided power with large landholders and the church.

United States. Heavy immigration and exploitation of ample natural resources fueled rapid economic growth. The spread of the franchise, public education, and antislavery sentiment were signs of a widespread democratic ethic.

China. Failure to keep pace with Western arms technology exposed China to greater European influence and hampered efforts to bar imports of opium, which had damaged Chinese society and drained wealth overseas. In the **Opium War** (1839-42), Britain forced China to expand trade opportunities and to cede Hong Kong.

Triumph of Progress: 1840-80

Idea of Progress. As a result of the cumulative scientific, economic, and political changes of the preceding eras, the idea took hold among literate people in the West that continuing growth and improvement was the usual state of human and natural life.

Darwin's statement of the **theory of evolution** and survival of the fittest (*Origin of Species*, 1859), defended by intellectuals and scientists against theological objections, was taken as confirmation that progress was the natural direction of life. The controversy helped define popular ideas of the dedicated scientist and ever-expanding human knowledge of and control over the world (Foucault's demonstration of earth's rotation, 1851; **Pasteur's** germ theory, 1861).

Liberals following Ricardo (1772-1823) in their faith that unrestrained competition would bring continuous economic expansion sought to adjust political life to the new social realities and believed that unregulated competition of ideas would yield truth (**Mill,** 1806-73). In England, successive reform bills (1832, 1867, 1884) gave representation to the new industrial towns and extended the franchise to the middle and lower classes and to Catholics, Dissenters, and Jews. On both sides of the Atlantic, reformists tried to improve conditions for the mentally ill (**Dix,** 1802-87), women (Anthony, 1820-1906), and prisoners. Slavery was barred in the British Empire (1833); the U.S. (1865); and Brazil (1888).

Socialist theories based on ideas of human perfectibility or progress were widely disseminated. Utopian socialists such as Saint-Simon (1760-1825) envisaged an orderly, just society directed by a technocratic elite. A model factory town, New Lanark, Scotland, was set up by utopian Robert Owen (1771-1858), and communal experiments were tried in the U.S. (Brook Farm, Mass., 1841-47). Bakunin's (1814-76) anarchism represented the opposite utopian extreme of total freedom. Karl **Marx** (1818-83) posited the inevitable triumph of socialism in industrial countries through a dialectical process of class conflict.

Spread of industry. The technical processes and managerial innovations of the English industrial revolution spread to Europe (especially Germany) and the U.S., causing an explosion of industrial production, demand for raw materials, and competition for markets. Inventors, both trained and self-educated, provided the means for larger-scale production (Bessemer steel, 1856; sewing machine, 1846). Many inventions were shown at the 1851 London Great Exhibition at the **Crystal Palace,** the theme of which was universal prosperity.

Local specialization and long-distance trade were aided by a revolution in transportation and communication. Railroads were first introduced in the 1820s in England and the U.S. More than 150,000 mi of track had been laid worldwide by 1880, with another 100,000 mi laid in the next decade. Steamships were improved (*Savannah* crossed Atlantic, 1819). The **telegraph**, perfected by 1844 (Morse), connected the Old and New Worlds by cable in 1866 and quickened the pace of international commerce and politics. The first commercial **telephone** exchange went into operation in the U.S. in 1878.

The new class of industrial workers, uprooted from their rural homes, lacked job security and suffered from dangerous overcrowded conditions at work and at home. Many responded by organizing **trade unions** (legalized in England, 1824; France, 1884). The U.S. Knights of Labor had 700,000 members by 1886. The First International (1864-76) tried to unite workers internationally around a Marxist program. The quasi-Socialist Paris Commune uprising (1871) was violently suppressed. Factory Acts to reduce child labor and regulate conditions were passed (1833-50 in England). Social security measures were introduced by the Bismarck regime (1883-89) in Germany.

Revolutions of 1848. Among the causes of the continent-wide revolutions were an international collapse of credit and resulting unemployment, bad harvests in 1845-47, and a cholera epidemic. The new urban proletariat and expanding bourgeoisie demanded a greater political role. Republics were proclaimed in France, Rome, and Venice. Nationalist feelings reached fever pitch in the Habsburg empire, as Hungary declared independence under Kossuth, as a Slav Congress demanded equality, and as Piedmont tried to drive Austria from Lombardy. A national liberal assembly at Frankfurt called for German unification.

But riots fueled bourgeois fears of socialism (**Marx and Engels**, *Communist Manifesto*, 1848), and peasants remained conservative. The old establishment—the Papacy, the Habsburgs with the help of the Czarist Russian army —was able to rout the revolutionaries by 1849. The French Republic succumbed to a renewed monarchy by 1852 (Emperor Napoleon III).

Great nations unified. Using the "blood and iron" tactics of Bismarck from 1862, Prussia controlled N Germany by 1867 (war with Denmark, 1864; Austria, 1866). After defeating France in 1870 (annexation of Alsace-Lorraine), it won the allegiance of S German states. A new **German Empire** was proclaimed (1871). **Italy**, inspired by Giuseppe Mazzini (1805-72) and Giuseppe Garibaldi (1807-82), was unified by the reformed Piedmont kingdom through uprisings, plebiscites, and war.

The **U.S.**, its area expanded after the 1846-48 Mexican War, defeated (1861-65) a secession attempt by slave states. The Canadian provinces were united in an autonomous **Dominion of Canada** (1867). Control in **India** was removed from the East India Co. and centralized under British administration after the 1857-58 Sepoy rebellion, laying the groundwork for the modern Indian State. Queen Victoria was named Empress of India (1876).

Europe dominates Asia. The Ottoman Empire began to collapse in the face of Balkan nationalisms and European imperial incursions in N Africa (**Suez Canal**, 1869). The Turks had lost control of most of both regions by 1882. Russia completed its expansion S by 1884 (despite the temporary setback of the **Crimean War** with Turkey, Britain, and France, 1853-56), taking Turkestan, all the Caucasus, and Chinese areas in the E and sponsoring Balkan Slavs against the Turks. A succession of reformist and reactionary regimes presided over a slow modernization (serfs freed, 1861). Persian independence suffered as Russia and British India competed for influence.

China was forced to sign a series of unequal treaties with European powers and Japan. Overpopulation and an inefficient dynasty brought misery and caused rebellions (Taiping, Muslims) leaving tens of millions dead. **Japan** was forced by the U.S. (Commodore Perry's visits, 1853-54) and Europe to end its isolation. The Meiji restoration (1868) gave power to a Westernizing oligarchy. Intensified empire-building gave Burma to Britain (1824-85) and Indochina to France (1862-95). Christian missionary activity followed imperial and trade expansion in Asia.

Respectability. The fine arts were expected to reflect and encourage the good morals and manners among the Victorians. Prudery, exaggerated delicacy, and familial piety were heralded by **Bowdler's** expurgated edition (1818) of Shakespeare. Government-supported mass education inculcated a work ethic as a means to escape poverty (**Horatio Alger,** 1832-99).

The official **Beaux Arts** school in Paris set an international style of imposing public buildings (Paris Opera, 1861-74; Vienna Opera, 1861-69) and uplifting statues (Bartholdi's Statue of Liberty, 1884). Realist painting, influenced by photography (Daguerre, 1837), appealed to a new mass audience with social or historical narrative (Wilkie, 1785-1841; Poynter, 1836-1919) or with serious religious, moral, or social messages (pre-Raphaelites, Millet's *Angelus*, 1858) often drawn from ordinary life. The **Impressionists** (Monet, 1840-1926; Pissarro, 1830-1903; Renoir, 1841-1919) rejected the formalism, sentimentality, and precise techniques of academic art in favor of a spontaneous, undetailed rendering of the world through careful representation of the effect of natural light on objects.

Realistic **novelists** presented the full panorama of social classes and personalities, but retained sentimentality and moral judgment (**Dickens,** 1812-70; **Eliot,** 1819-80; **Tolstoy,** 1828-1910; **Balzac,** 1799-1850).

Veneer of Stability: 1880-1900

Imperialism triumphant. The vast **African** interior, visited by European explorers (Barth, 1821-65; Livingstone, 1813-73), was conquered by the European powers in rapid, competitive thrusts from their coastal bases after 1880, mostly for domestic political and international strategic reasons. W African Muslim kingdoms (Fulani), Arab slave traders (Zanzibar), and Bantu military confederations (Zulu) were alike subdued. Only Christian Ethiopia (defeat of Italy, 1896) and Liberia resisted successfully. France (W Africa) and Britain ("Cape to Cairo," **Boer War,** 1899-1902) were the major beneficiaries. The ideology of "the white man's burden" (Kipling, *Barrack Room Ballads*, 1892) or of a "civilizing mission" (France) justified the conquests.

W European foreign capital investment soared to nearly $40 billion by 1914, but most was in E Europe (France, Germany), the Americas (Britain), and the Europeans' colonies. The foundation of the modern interdependent world economy was laid, with cartels dominating raw material trade.

An industrious world. Industrial and technological proficiency characterized the 2 new great powers—Germany and the **U.S.** Coal and iron deposits enabled Germany to reach 2d or 3d place status in iron, steel, and shipbuilding by the 1900s. German electrical and chemical industries were world leaders. The U.S. post-Civil War boom (interrupted by "panics"—1884, 1893, 1896) was shaped by massive immigration from S and E Europe from 1880, government subsidy of railroads, and huge private monopolies (Standard Oil, 1870; U.S. Steel, 1901). The **Spanish-American War**, 1898 (Philippine Insurrection, 1899-1902), and the **Open Door policy** in China (1899) made the U.S. a world power.

England led in **urbanization** (72% by 1890), with **London** the world capital of finance, insurance, and shipping. Sewer systems (Paris, 1850s), electric subways (London, 1890), parks, and bargain department stores helped improve living standards for most of the urban population of the industrial world.

Westernization of Asia. Asian reaction to European economic, military, and religious incursions took the form of imitation of Western techniques and adoption of Western ideas of progress and freedom. The Chinese "self-strengthening" movement of the 1860s and 1870s included rail, port, and arsenal improvements and metal and textile mills. Reformers such as **K'ang Yu-wei** (1858-1927) won liberalizing reforms in 1898, right after the European and Japanese "scramble for concessions."

A universal education system in Japan and importation of foreign industrial, scientific, and military experts aided Japan's unprecedented rapid modernization after 1868, under the authoritarian Meiji regime. Japan's victory in the **Sino-Japanese War** (1894-95) put Formosa and Korea in its power.

In India, the British alliance with the remaining princely states masked reform sentiment among the Westernized urban elite; higher education had been conducted largely in English for 50 years. The **Indian National Congress**, founded in 1885, demanded a larger government role for Indians.

***Fin-de-siècle* sophistication. Naturalist** writers pushed realism to its extreme limits, adopting a quasi-scientific attitude and writing about formerly taboo subjects such as sex, crime, extreme poverty, and corruption (Flaubert, 1821-80; Zola, 1840-1902; Hardy, 1840-1928). Unseen or repressed psychological motivations were explored in the clinical and theoretical works of Sigmund **Freud** (1856-1939) and in fiction (**Dostoyevsky,** 1821-81; James, 1843-1916; Schnitzler, 1862-1931; others).

A contempt for bourgeois life or a desire to shock a complacent audience was shared by the French **symbolist** poets (Verlaine, 1844-96; Rimbaud, 1854-91), by neopagan English writers (Swinburne, 1837-1909), by continental dramatists (**Ibsen,** 1828-1906), and by satirists (Wilde, 1854-1900). Friedrich **Nietzsche** (1844-1900) was influential in his elitism and pessimism.

Postimpressionist art neglected long-cherished conventions of representation (Cézanne, 1839-1906) and showed a willingness to learn from primitive and non-European art (Gauguin, 1848-1903; Japanese prints).

Racism. Gobineau (1816-82) gave a pseudobiological foundation to modern racist theories, which spread in the latter 19th cent., along with **Social Darwinism**, the belief that societies are and should be organized as a struggle for survival of the fittest. The medieval period was interpreted as an era of natural Germanic rule (Chamberlain, 1855-1927), and notions of superiority were associated with German national aspirations (Treitschke, 1834-96). **Anti-Semitism**, with a new racist rationale, became a significant political force in Germany (Anti-Semitic Petition, 1880), Austria (Lueger, 1844-1910), and France (Dreyfus case, 1894-1906).

Last Respite: 1900-9

Alliances. While the peace of Europe (and its dependencies) continued to hold (1907 **Hague Conference** extended the rules of war and international arbitration procedures), imperial rivalries, protectionist trade practices (in Germany and France), and the escalating arms race (British *Dreadnought* battleship launched; Germany widens Kiel canal, 1906) exacerbated minor disputes (German-French Moroccan "crises," 1905, 1911).

Security was sought through alliances: **Triple Alliance** (Germany, Austria-Hungary, Italy; renewed in 1902 and 1907); Anglo-Japanese Alliance (1902), Franco-Russian Alliance (1899), **Entente Cordiale** (Britain, France, 1904), Anglo-Russian Treaty (1907), German-Ottoman friendship.

Ottomans decline. The inefficient, corrupt Ottoman government was unable to resist further loss of territory. Nearly all European lands were lost in 1912 to Serbia, Greece, Montenegro, and Bulgaria. Italy took Libya and the Dodecanese islands the same year, and Britain took Kuwait (1899) and the Sinai (1906). The **Young Turk** revolution in 1908 forced the sultan to restore a constitution, and it introduced some social reform, industrialization, and secularization.

British Empire. British trade and cultural influence remained dominant in the empire, but constitutional reforms presaged its eventual dissolution: The colonies of **Australia** were united in 1901 under a self-governing commonwealth. **New Zealand** acquired dominion status in 1907. The old Boer republics joined Cape Colony and Natal in the self-governing **Union of South Africa** in 1910.

The 1909 Indian Councils Act enhanced the role of elected province legislatures in **India**. The Muslim League (founded 1906) sought separate communal representation.

East Asia. Japan exploited its growing industrial power to expand its empire. Victory in the 1904-5 war against Russia (naval battle of Tsushima, 1905) assured Japan's domination of **Korea** (annexed 1910) and Manchuria (Port Arthur taken, 1905).

In China, central authority began to crumble (empress died, 1908). Reforms (Confucian exam system ended 1905, modernization of the army, building of railroads) were inadequate, and secret societies of reformers and nationalists, inspired by the Westernized **Sun Yat-sen** (1866-1925) fomented periodic uprisings in the S.

Siam, whose independence had been guaranteed by Britain and France in 1896, was split into spheres of influence by those countries in 1907.

Russia. The population of the Russian Empire approached 150 million in 1900. Reforms in education, in law, and in local institutions (*zemstvos*) and an industrial boom starting in the 1880s (oil, railroads) created the beginnings of a modern state, despite the autocratic tsarist regime. Liberals (1903 Union of Liberation), Socialists (Social Democrats founded 1898, Bolsheviks split off 1903), and populists (Social Revolutionaries founded 1901) were periodically repressed, and national minorities were persecuted (anti-Jewish pogroms, 1903, 1905-6).

An industrial crisis after 1900 and harvest failures aggravated poverty among urban workers, and the 1904-5 defeat by Japan (which checked Russia's Asian expansion) sparked **the Revolution of 1905-6.** A **Duma** (parliament) was created, and an agricultural reform (under Stolypin, prime minister 1906-11) created a large class of landowning peasants (kulaks).

The world shrinks. Developments in transportation and communication and mass population movements helped create an awareness of an interdependent world. Early **automobiles** (Daimler, Benz, 1885) were experimental or were designed as luxuries. Assembly-line mass production (Ford Motor Co., 1903) made the invention practicable, and by 1910 nearly 500,000 motor vehicles were registered in the U.S. alone. **Heavier-than-air flights** began in 1903 in the U.S. (Wright brothers), preceded by glider, balloon, and model plane advances in several countries. Trade was advanced by improvements in **ship design** (gyrocompass, 1910), speed (*Lusitania* crossed Atlantic in 5 days, 1907), and reach (Panama Canal begun, 1904).

The first transatlantic **radio** telegraphic transmission occurred in 1901, 6 years after Marconi discovered radio. Radio transmission of human speech had been made in 1900. Telegraphic transmission of photos was achieved in 1904, lending immediacy to news reports. **Phonographs**, popularized by Caruso's recordings (starting 1902), made for quick international spread of musical styles (ragtime). **Motion pictures**, perfected in the 1890s (Dickson, Lumière brothers), became a popular and artistic medium after 1900; newsreels appeared in 1909.

Emigration from crowded European centers soared in the decade: 9 million migrated to the U.S., and millions more went to Siberia, Canada, Argentina, Australia, South Africa, and Algeria. Some 70 million Europeans emigrated in the cent. before 1914. Several million Chinese, Indians, and Japanese migrated to SE Asia, where their urban skills often enabled them to take a predominant economic role.

Social reform. The social and economic problems of the poor were kept in the public eye by realist fiction writers (Dreiser's *Sister Carrie*, 1900; Gorky's *Lower Depths*, 1902; Sinclair's *The Jungle*, 1906), journalists (U.S. **muckrakers**—Steffens, Tarbell), and artists (Ashcan school). Frequent labor strikes and occasional assassinations by anarchists or radicals (Empress Elizabeth of Austria, 1898; King Umberto I of Italy, 1900; U.S. Pres. McKinley, 1901; Russian Interior Minister Plehve, 1904; Portugal's King Carlos, 1908) added to social tension and fear of revolution.

But democratic reformism prevailed. In Germany, Bernstein's (1850-1932) **revisionist Marxism**, downgrading revolution, was accepted by the powerful Social Democrats and trade unions. The British Fabian Society (the Webbs, Shaw) and the Labour Party (founded 1906) worked for reforms such as Social Security and union rights (1906), while woman suffragists grew more militant. U.S. **progressives** fought big business (Pure Food and Drug Act, 1906). In France, the 10-hour work day (1904) and separation of church and state (1905) were reform victories, as was universal suffrage in Austria (1907).

Arts. An unprecedented period of experimentation, centered in France, produced several new **painting** styles: Fauvism exploited bold color areas (Matisse, *Woman With Hat*, 1905); expressionism reflected powerful inner emotions (the Brücke group, 1905); cubism combined several views of an object on one flat surface (Picasso's *Demoiselles*, 1906-7); futurism tried to depict speed and motion (Italian Futurist Manifesto, 1910). **Architects** explored new uses of steel structures, with facades either neoclassical (Adler and Sullivan in U.S.); curvilinear Art Nouveau (Gaudi's Casa Mila, 1905-10); or functionally streamlined (Wright's Robie House, 1909).

Music and dance shared the experimental spirit. Ruth St. Denis (1877-1968) and Isadora Duncan (1878-1927) pioneered modern dance, while Sergei Diaghilev in Paris revitalized classic ballet from 1909. Composers explored atonal music (Debussy, 1862-1918) and dissonance (Schoenberg, 1874-1951) or revolutionized classical forms (Stravinsky, 1882-1971), often showing jazz or folk music influences.

The Seven Natural Wonders of the Modern World

This list names features of significance noted by world travelers during recent centuries.

Mt. Everest: The highest peak in the world, Mt. Everest is in S central Asia, in the Himalaya range, on the frontier of Nepal and Tibet. Controversy surrounds its actual elevation. A 1954 Indian government survey placed it at 29,028 ft above sea level; however, more recent surveys cast some doubt on this figure. The summit was first scaled in 1953.

Victoria Falls: This 400-ft waterfall is on the Zambezi R in S central Africa on the border between Zimbabwe and Zambia. The river here is about 1 mi wide. A railroad bridge, completed in 1905, spans the gorge below the falls.

The Grand Canyon: This exceptionally deep (more than 1 mi) and extremely beautiful steep-walled chasm in NW Arizona is about 217 mi long and up to 18 mi wide. Excavated by the Colorado R, it is of relatively recent origin; apparently, erosion began a little more than a million years ago. The canyon contains towering buttes, mesas, and valleys within its main gorge.

The Great Barrier Reef: This chain of coral reefs is in the Coral Sea, off the E coast of Queensland, Australia. It is the largest known deposit of coral and extends in a NW direction more than 1200 mi. The reef serves as a barrier to disturbances in the Coral Sea, thus affording a sheltered passage for ships.

The Northern Lights: Also known as aurora borealis, the Northern Lights consists of rapidly shifting patches and dancing columns of light of various hues. The aurora assumes an endless variety of forms, including the arch, the band, filaments and streamers at right angles to the arch or band, the corona, clouds, the glow, and curtains, fans, flames, or streamers of various shapes.

Paricutin: This volcano is one of the world's youngest. It was discovered in 1943 west of Mexico City.

The Harbor at Rio de Janeiro, Brazil (as seen from the sea): One of the world's most beautiful natural harbors, the harbor at Rio is surrounded by low mountain ranges whose spurs extend almost to the waterside, and thus divide the city.

War and Revolution: 1910-19

War threatens. Germany under Wilhelm II sought a political and imperial role consonant with its industrial strength, challenging Britain's world supremacy and threatening France, which was still resenting the loss (1871) of Alsace-Lorraine. Austria wanted to curb an expanded Serbia (after 1912) and the threat it posed to its own Slav lands. Russia feared Austrian and German political and economic aims in the Balkans and Turkey. An accelerated arms race resulted: The German standing army rose to more than 2 million men by 1914. Russia and France had more than a million each, and Austria and the British Empire nearly a million each. Dozens of enormous battleships were built by the powers after 1906.

The **assassination of Austrian Archduke Franz Ferdinand** by a Serbian, June 28, 1914, was the pretext for war. The system of alliances made the conflict Europe-wide; Germany's invasion of Belgium to outflank France forced Britain to enter the war. Patriotic fervor was nearly unanimous among all classes in most countries.

World War I. German forces were stopped in France in one month. The rival armies dug **trench networks.** Artillery and improved machine guns prevented either side from any lasting advance despite repeated assaults (600,000 dead at **Verdun,** Feb.-July 1916). Poison gas, used by Germany in 1915, proved ineffective. The entrance of more than 1 million U.S. troops tipped the balance after mid-1917, forcing Germany to sue for peace the next year. The formal armistice was signed at 5 AM, Nov. 11, 1918.

In the E, the Russian armies were thrown back (battle of **Tannenberg,** Aug. 20, 1914), and the war grew unpopular in Russia. An allied attempt to relieve Russia through Turkey failed (**Gallipoli,** 1915). The **Russian Revolution** (1917) abolished the monarchy. The new Bolshevik regime signed the capitulatory Brest-Litovsk peace in March 1918. Italy entered the war on the allied side in May 1915 but was pushed back by Oct. 1917. A renewed offensive with Allied aid in Oct.-Nov. 1918 forced Austria to surrender.

The British Navy successfully blockaded Germany, which responded with submarine U-boat attacks; **unrestricted submarine warfare** against neutrals after Jan. 1917 helped bring the U.S. into the war. Other battlefields included Palestine and Mesopotamia, both of which Britain wrested from the Turks in 1917, and the African and Pacific colonies of Germany, most of which fell to Britain, France, Australia, Japan, and South Africa.

From 1916, the civilian populations and economies of both sides were mobilized to an unprecedented degree. Hardships intensified among fighting nations in 1917 (French mutiny crushed in May). More than 10 million soldiers died in the war.

Settlement. At the **Paris Peace Conference** (Jan.-June 1919), concluded by the **Treaty of Versailles,** and in subsequent negotiations and local wars (Russian-Polish War, 1920), the map of Europe was redrawn with a nod to U.S. Pres. Wilson's principle of self-determination. Austria and Hungary were separated, and much of their land was given to Yugoslavia (formerly Serbia), Romania, Italy, and the newly independent Poland and Czechoslovakia. Germany lost territory in the W, N, and E, while Finland and the Baltic states were detached from Russia. Turkey lost nearly all its Arab lands to British-sponsored Arab states or to direct French and British rule. Belgium's sovereignty was recognized.

A huge **reparations** burden and partial demilitarization were imposed on Germany. Pres. Wilson obtained approval for a League of Nations, but the U.S. Senate refused to allow the U.S. to join.

Russian revolution. Military defeats and high casualties caused a contagious lack of confidence in Tsar Nicholas, who was forced to abdicate Mar. 1917. A liberal provisional government failed to end the war, and massive desertions, riots, and fighting between factions followed. A moderate socialist government under Aleksandr Kerensky was overthrown (Nov. 1917) in a violent coup by the **Bolsheviks** in Petrograd under **Lenin,** who later disbanded the elected Constituent Assembly.

The Bolsheviks brutally suppressed all opposition and ended the war with Germany in Mar. 1918. **Civil war** broke out in the summer between the Red Army, including the Bolsheviks and their supporters, and monarchists, anarchists, nationalities (Ukrainians, Georgians, Poles), and others. Small U.S., British, French, and Japanese units also opposed the Bolsheviks (1918-19; Japan in Vladivostok to 1922). The civil war, anarchy, and pogroms devastated the country until the 1920 Red Army victory. The wartime total monopoly of political, economic, and police power by the Communist Party leadership was retained.

Other European revolutions. An unpopular monarchy in **Portugal** was overthrown in 1910. The new republic took severe anticlerical measures in 1911.

After a century of Home Rule agitation, during which **Ireland** was devastated by famine (1 million dead, 1846-47) and emigration, republican militants staged an unsuccessful uprising in Dublin during Easter 1916. The execution of the leaders and mass arrests by the British won popular support for the rebels. The Irish Free State, comprising all but the 6 N counties, achieved dominion status in 1922.

In the aftermath of the world war, radical revolutions were attempted in Germany (**Spartacist** uprising, Jan. 1919), **Hungary** (Kun regime, 1919), and elsewhere. All were suppressed or failed for lack of support.

Chinese revolution. The Manchu Dynasty was overthrown and a republic proclaimed in Oct. 1911. First Pres. Sun Yat-sen resigned in favor of strongman Yuan Shih-k'ai. Sun organized the parliamentarian **Kuomintang** party.

Students launched protests on May 4, 1919, against League of Nations concessions in China to Japan. Nationalist, liberal, and socialist ideas and political groups spread. The **Communist Party** was founded in 1921. A Communist regime took power in Mongolia with Soviet support in 1921.

India restive. Indian objections to British rule erupted in nationalist riots as well as in the nonviolent tactics of Mahatma **Gandhi** (1869-1948). Nearly 400 unarmed demonstrators were shot at **Amritsar** in Apr. 1919. Britain approved limited self-rule that year.

Mexican revolution. Under the long Diaz dictatorship (1877-1911) the economy advanced, but Indian and mestizo lands were confiscated, and concessions to foreigners (mostly U.S.) damaged the middle class. A **revolution in 1910** led to civil wars and U.S. intervention (1914, 1916-17). Land reform and a more democratic constitution (1917) were achieved.

The Aftermath of War: 1920-29

U.S. Easy credit, technological ingenuity, and war-related industrial decline in Europe caused a long economic boom, in which ownership of the new products—**autos, phones, radios**—became democratized. Prosperity, an increase in women workers, woman suffrage (1920), and drastic change in fashion (flappers, mannish bob for women, clean-shaven men) created a wide perception of social change, despite prohibition of alcoholic beverages (1919-33). Union membership and strikes increased. Fear of radicals led to Palmer raids (1919-20) and the Sacco/Vanzetti case (1921-27).

Europe sorts itself out. Germany's liberal **Weimar constitution** (1919) could not guarantee a stable government in the face of rightist violence (Rathenau assassinated, 1922) and Communist refusal to cooperate with Socialists. Reparations and Allied occupation of the Rhineland caused staggering inflation that destroyed middle-class savings, but economic expansion resumed after mid-decade, aided by U.S. loans. A sophisticated, **innovative culture** developed in architecture and design (Bauhaus, 1919-28), film (Lang, *M*, 1931), painting (Grosz), music (Weill, *Threepenny Opera*, 1928), theater (Brecht, *A Man's a Man*, 1926), criticism (Benjamin), philosophy (Jung), and fashion. This culture was considered decadent and socially disruptive by rightists.

England elected its first Labour governments (Jan. 1924, June 1929). A 10-day general strike in support of coal miners failed in May 1926. In **Italy**, strikes, political chaos, and violence by small Fascist bands culminated in the Oct. 1922 Fascist March on Rome, which established Mussolini's dictatorship. Strikes were outlawed (1926), and Italian influence was pressed in the Balkans (Albania a protectorate, 1926). A conservative dictatorship was also established in **Portugal** in a 1926 military coup.

Czechoslovakia, the only stable democracy to emerge from the war in Central or East Europe, faced opposition from Germans (in the Sudetenland), Ruthenians, and some Slovaks. As the industrial heartland of the old Habsburg empire, it remained fairly prosperous. With French backing, it formed the Little Entente with Yugoslavia (1920) and **Romania** (1921) to block Austrian or Hungarian irredentism. Hungary remained dominated by the landholding classes and expansionist feeling. Croats and Slovenes in **Yugoslavia** demanded a federal state until King Alexander I proclaimed (1929) a royal dictatorship. Poland faced nationality problems as well (Germans, Ukrainians, Jews); Pilsudski ruled as dictator from 1926. The Baltic states were threatened by traditionally dominant ethnic Germans and by Soviet-supported Communists.

An economic collapse and famine in **Russia** (1921-22) claimed 5 million lives. The New Economic Policy (1921) allowed landownership by peasants and some private commerce and industry. Stalin was absolute ruler within 4 years of Lenin's death (1924). He inaugurated a brutal collectivization program (1929-32) and used foreign Communist parties for Soviet state advantage.

Internationalism. Revulsion against World War I led to pacifist agitation, to the Kellogg-Briand Pact renouncing aggressive war (1928), and to **naval disarmament** pacts (Washington, 1922; London, 1930). But the League of Nations was able to arbitrate only minor disputes (Greece-Bulgaria, 1925).

Middle East. Mustafa Kemal (**Ataturk**) led **Turkish** nationalists in resisting Italian, French, and Greek military advances (1919-23). The sultanate was abolished (1922), and elaborate reforms were passed, including secularization of law and adoption of the Latin alphabet. Ethnic conflict led to persecution of **Armenians** (more than 1 million dead in 1915, 1 million expelled), Greeks (forced Greek-Turk population exchange, 1923), and Kurds (1925 uprising).

With evacuation of the Turks from **Arab** lands, the puritanical Wahabi dynasty of E Arabia conquered (1919-25) what is now Saudi Arabia. British, French, and Arab dynastic and nationalist maneuvering resulted in the creation of 2 more Arab monarchies in 1921—Iraq and Transjordan (both under British control)—and 2 French mandates—Syria and Lebanon. Jewish immigration into British-mandated **Palestine**, inspired by the Zionist movement, was resisted by Arabs, at times violently (1921, 1929 massacres).

Reza Khan ruled **Persia** after his 1921 coup (shah from 1925), centralized control, and created the trappings of a modern secular state.

China. The Kuomintang under **Chiang Kai-shek** (1887-1975) subdued the warlords by 1928. The Communists were brutally suppressed after their alliance with the Kuomintang was broken in 1927. Relative peace thereafter allowed for industrial and financial improvements, with some Russian, British, and U.S. cooperation.

Arts. Nearly all bounds of subject matter, style, and attitude were broken in the arts of the period. **Abstract** art first took inspiration from natural forms or narrative themes (Kandinsky from 1911) and then worked free of any representational aims (Malevich's suprematism, 1915-19; Mondrian's geometric style from 1917). The **Dada** movement (from 1916) mocked artistic pretension with absurd collages and constructions (Arp, Tzara, from 1916). Paradox, illusion, and psychological taboos were exploited by **surrealists** by the latter 1920s (Dali, Magritte). Architectural schools celebrated industrial values, whether vigorous abstract constructivism (Tatlin, *Monument to 3rd International*, 1919) or the machined, streamlined **Bauhaus** style, which was extended to many design fields (Helvetica typeface).

Prose writers explored revolutionary narrative modes related to dreams (Kafka's *Trial*, 1925), internal monologue (Joyce's **Ulysses**, 1922), and word play (Stein's *Making of Americans*, 1925). Poets and novelists wrote of modern alienation (Eliot's ***Waste Land***, 1922) and aimlessness (Lost Generation).

Sciences. Scientific specialization prevailed by the 20th cent. Advances in knowledge and technological aptitude increased with the geometric rise in the number of practitioners. Physicists challenged common-sense views of causality, observation, and a mechanistic universe, putting science further beyond popular grasp (**Einstein's** general theory of relativity, 1915; Bohr's quantum mechanics, 1913; Heisenberg's uncertainty principle, 1927).

Rise of Totalitarians: 1930-39

Depression. A worldwide financial panic and economic depression began with the Oct. 1929 U.S. stock market crash and the May 1931 failure of the Austrian Credit-Anstalt. A credit crunch caused international bankruptcies and **unemployment**: 12 million jobless by 1932 in the U.S., 5.6 million in Germany, 2.7 million in England. Governments responded with

tariff restrictions (Smoot-Hawley Act, 1930; Ottawa Imperial Conference, 1932), which dried up world trade. Government public works programs were vitiated by deflationary budget balancing.

Germany. Years of agitation by violent extremists were brought to a head by the Depression. Nazi leader Adolf **Hitler** was named chancellor in Jan. 1933 and given dictatorial power by the Reichstag in March. Opposition parties were disbanded, strikes banned, and all aspects of economic, cultural, and religious life were brought under central government and Nazi party control and manipulated by sophisticated propaganda. Severe persecution of Jews began (**Nuremberg Laws,** Sept. 1935). Many Jews, political opponents, and others were sent to concentration camps (Dachau, 1933), where thousands died or were killed. Public works, renewed conscription (1935), arms production, and a 4-year plan (1936) all but ended unemployment.

Hitler's expansionism started with reincorporation of the Saar (1935), occupation of the **Rhineland** (Mar. 1936), and annexation of Austria (Mar. 1938). At **Munich** (Sept. 1938) an indecisive Britain and France sanctioned German dismemberment of Czechoslovakia.

Russia. Urbanization and education advanced. Rapid industrialization was achieved through successive **5-year-plans** starting in 1928, using severe labor discipline and mass forced labor. Industry was financed by a decline in living standards and exploitation of agriculture, which was almost totally collectivized by the early 1930s (*kolkhoz*, collective farm; *sovkhoz*, state farm, often in newly worked lands). Successive **purges** increased the role of professionals and management at the expense of workers. Millions perished in a series of manufactured disasters: extermination (1929-34) of kulaks (peasant landowners), severe famine (1932-33), party purges and show trials (Great Purge, 1936-38), suppression of nationalities, and poor conditions in labor camps.

Spain. An industrial revolution during World War I created an urban proletariat, which was attracted to socialism and anarchism; Catalan nationalists challenged central authority. The 5 years after King Alfonso left Spain in Apr. 1931 were dominated by tension between intermittent leftist and anticlerical governments and clericals, monarchists, and other rightists. Anarchist and Communist rebellions were crushed, but a July 1936 extreme right rebellion led by Gen. Francisco **Franco** and aided by Nazi Germany and Fascist Italy succeeded, after a 3-year **civil war** (more than 1 million dead in battles and atrocities). The war polarized international public opinion.

Italy. Despite propaganda for the ideal of the Corporate State, few domestic reforms were attempted. An entente with Hungary and Austria (Mar. 1934), a pact with Germany and Japan (Nov. 1937), and intervention by 50,000-75,000 troops in Spain (1936-39) sealed Italy's identification with the fascist bloc (anti-Semitic laws after Mar. 1938). Ethiopia was conquered (1935-36), and Albania annexed (Jan. 1939) in conscious imitation of ancient Rome.

East Europe. Repressive regimes fought for power against an active opposition (liberals, socialists, Communists, peasants, Nazis). Minority groups and Jews were restricted within national boundaries that did not coincide with ethnic population patterns. In the destruction of **Czechoslovakia**, Hungary occupied S Slovakia (Nov. 1938) and Ruthenia (Mar. 1939), and a pro-Nazi regime took power in the rest of Slovakia. Other boundary disputes (e.g., Poland-Lithuania, Yugoslavia-Bulgaria, Romania-Hungary) doomed attempts to build joint fronts against Germany or Russia. Economic depression was severe.

East Asia. After a period of liberalism in **Japan**, nativist militarists dominated the government with peasant support. Manchuria was seized (Sept. 1931-Feb. 1932), and a puppet state was set up (Manchukuo). Adjacent Jehol (Inner Mongolia) was occupied in 1933. China proper was invaded in July 1937; large areas were conquered by Oct. 1938. Hundreds of thousands of rapes, murders, and other atrocities were attributed to the Japanese.

In **China** Communist forces left Kuomintang-besieged strongholds in the S in a Long March (1934-35) to the N. The Kuomintang-Communist civil war was suspended in Jan. 1937 in the face of threatening Japan.

The democracies. The Roosevelt Administration, in office Mar. 1933, embarked on an extensive program of **New Deal** social reform and economic stimulation, including protection for labor unions (heavy industries organized), Social Security, public works, wage-and-hour laws, and assistance to farmers. Isolationist sentiment (1937 Neutrality Act) prevented U.S. intervention in Europe, but military expenditures were increased in 1939.

French political instability and polarization prevented resolution of economic and international security questions. The **Popular Front** government under Leon Blum (June 1936-Apr. 1938) passed social reforms (40-hour week) and raised arms spending. National coalition governments, which ruled Britain from Aug. 1931, brought some economic recovery but failed to define a consistent international policy until Chamberlain's government (from May 1937), which practiced deliberate **appeasement** of Germany and Italy.

India. Twenty years of agitation for autonomy and then for independence (Gandhi's **salt march**, 1930) achieved some constitutional reform (extended provincial powers, 1935) despite Muslim-Hindu strife. Social issues assumed prominence with peasant uprisings (1921), strikes (1928), Gandhi's efforts for untouchables (1932 "fast unto death"), and social and agrarian reform by the provinces after 1937.

Arts. The streamlined, geometric design motifs of Art Deco (from 1925) prevailed through the 1930s. **Abstract art** flourished (Moore sculptures from 1931) alongside a new **realism** related to social and political concerns (Socialist Realism, the official Soviet style from 1934; Mexican muralist Rivera, 1886-1957; and Orozco, 1883-1949), which were also expressed in fiction and poetry (Steinbeck's *Grapes of Wrath*, 1939; Sandburg's *The People, Yes*, 1936). Modern architecture (International Style, 1932) was unchallenged in its use of artificial materials (concrete, glass), lack of decoration, and monumentality (Rockefeller Center, 1929-40). U.S.-made films captured a worldwide audience with their larger-than-life fantasies (*Gone With the Wind*, *The Wizard of Oz,* both 1939).

War, Hot and Cold: 1940-49

War in Europe. The Nazi-Soviet nonaggression pact (Aug. 1939) freed Germany to attack Poland (Sept.). Britain and France, which had guaranteed Polish independence, declared war on Germany. Russia seized E Poland (Sept.), attacked Finland (Nov.), and took the Baltic states (July 1940). Mobile German forces staged *blitzkrieg* attacks during Apr.-June 1940, conquering neutral Denmark, Norway, and the Low Countries and defeating France; 350,000 British and French troops were evacuated at **Dunkirk** (May). The **Battle of Britain** (June-Dec. 1940) denied Germany air superiority. German-Italian campaigns won the Balkans by Apr. 1941. Three million Axis troops **invaded Russia** in June 1941, marching through Ukraine to the Caucasus, and through White Russia and the Baltic republics to Moscow and Leningrad.

Russian winter counterthrusts (1941-42 and 1942-43) stopped the German advance (**Stalingrad,** Sept. 1942-Feb. 1943). With British and U.S. Lend-Lease aid and sustaining great casualties, the Russians drove the Axis from all E Europe and the Balkans in the next 2 years. Invasions of N Africa (Nov. 1942), Italy (Sept. 1943), and **Normandy** (launched on D-Day, June 6, 1944) brought U.S., British, Free French, and allied troops to Germany by spring 1945. Germany surrendered May 7, 1945.

War in Asia-Pacific. Japan occupied Indochina in Sept. 1940, dominated Thailand in Dec. 1941, and attacked Hawaii (**Pearl Harbor**), the Philippines, Hong Kong, Malaya on Dec. 7, 1941 (precipitating U.S. entrance into the war). Indonesia was attacked in Jan. 1942, and Burma was conquered in Mar. 1942. The Battle of **Midway** (June 1942) turned back the Japanese advance. "Island-hopping" battles (**Guadalcanal,** Aug. 1942-Jan. 1943; **Leyte Gulf,** Oct. 1944; **Iwo Jima,** Feb.-Mar. 1945; **Okinawa,** Apr. 1945) and massive bombing raids on Japan from June 1944 wore out Japanese defenses. U.S. atom bombs, dropped Aug. 6 and 9 on **Hiroshima** and Nagasaki, forced Japan to agree, on Aug. 14, to surrender; formal surrender was on Sept. 2, 1945.

Atrocities. The war brought 20th-cent. cruelty to its peak. The Nazi regime systematically killed an estimated 5-6 million Jews, including some 3 million who died in death camps (e.g., **Auschwitz**). Gypsies, political opponents, sick and retarded people, and others deemed undesirable were also murdered by the Nazis, as were vast numbers of Slavs, especially leaders.

Civilian deaths. German bombs killed 70,000 British civilians. More than 100,000 Chinese civilians were killed by Japanese forces in the capture and occupation of Nanking. Severe retaliation by the Soviet army, E European partisans, Free French, and others took a heavy toll. U.S. and British bombing of Germany killed hundreds of thousands, as did U.S. bombing of Japan (80,000-200,000 at Hiroshima alone). Some 45 million people lost their lives in the war.

Settlement. The **United Nations** charter was signed in San Francisco on June 26, 1945, by 50 nations. The International Tribunal at **Nuremberg** convicted 22 German leaders for war crimes in Sept. 1946; 23 Japanese leaders were convicted in Nov. 1948. Postwar border changes included large gains in territory for the USSR, losses for Germany, a shift to the W in Polish borders, and minor losses for Italy. Communist regimes, supported by Soviet troops, took power in most of E Europe, including Soviet-occupied Germany (GDR proclaimed Oct. 1949). Japan lost all overseas lands.

Recovery. Basic political and social changes were imposed on Japan and W Germany by the western allies (Japan constitution adopted, Nov. 1946; W German basic law, May 1949). U.S. **Marshall Plan** aid ($12 billion, 1947-51) spurred W European economic recovery after a period of severe inflation and strikes in Europe and the U.S. The British Labour Party introduced a national health service and nationalized basic industries in 1946.

Cold War. Western fears of further Soviet advances (Cominform formed in Oct. 1947; Czechoslovakia coup, Feb. 1948; Berlin blockade, Apr. 1948-Sept. 1949) led to the formation of **NATO.** Civil War in Greece and Soviet pressure on Turkey led to U.S. aid under the **Truman Doctrine** (Mar. 1947). Other anti-Communist security pacts were the Organization of American States (Apr. 1948) and the SE Asia Treaty Organization (Sept. 1954). A new wave of **Soviet purges** and repression intensified in the last years of Stalin's rule, extending to E Europe (Slansky trial in Czechoslovakia, 1951). Only Yugoslavia resisted Soviet control (expelled by Cominform, June 1948; U.S. aid, June 1949).

China, Korea. Communist forces emerged from World War II strengthened by the Soviet takeover of industrial Manchuria. In 4 years of fighting, the Kuomintang was driven from the mainland; the People's Republic was proclaimed Oct. 1, 1949. Korea was divided by USSR and U.S. occupation forces. Separate republics were proclaimed in the 2 zones in Aug.-Sept. 1948.

India. India and Pakistan became independent dominions on Aug. 15, 1947. Millions of Hindu and Muslim refugees were created by the partition; riots (1946-47) took hundreds of thousands of lives; Mahatma **Gandhi** was assassinated in Jan. 1948. Burma became completely independent in Jan. 1948; Ceylon took dominion status in Feb.

Middle East. The UN approved partition of Palestine into Jewish and Arab states. **Israel** was proclaimed a state, May 14, 1948. Arabs rejected partition, but failed to defeat Israel in war (May 1948-July 1949). Immigration from Europe and the Middle East swelled Israel's Jewish population. British and French forces left Lebanon and Syria in 1946. Transjordan occupied most of Arab Palestine.

Southeast Asia. Communists and others fought against restoration of French rule in Indochina from 1946; a non-Communist government was recognized by France in Mar. 1949, but fighting continued. Both Indonesia and the Philippines became independent; the former in 1949 after 4 years of war with Netherlands, the latter in 1946. Philippine economic and military ties with the U.S. remained strong; a Communist-led peasant rising was checked in 1948.

Arts. New York became the center of the world art market; **abstract expressionism** was the chief mode (Pollock from 1943, de Kooning from 1947). Literature and philosophy explored **existentialism** (Camus's *Stranger*, 1942; Sartre's *Being and Nothingness*, 1943). Non-Western attempts to revive or create regional styles (Senghor's Négritude, Mishima's novels) only confirmed the emergence of a universal culture. Radio and phonograph records spread American popular music (swing, bebop) around the world.

The American Decade: 1950-59

Polite decolonization. The peaceful decline of European political and military power in Asia and Africa accelerated in the 1950s. Nearly all of **N Africa** was freed by 1956, but France fought a bitter war to retain Algeria, with its large European minority, until 1962. **Ghana**, independent in 1957, led a parade of new black African nations (more than 2 dozen by 1962), which altered the political character of the UN. Ethnic disputes often exploded in the new nations after decolonization (UN troops in Cyprus, 1964; **Nigerian civil war**, 1967-70). Leaders of the new states, mostly sharing socialist ideologies, tried to create an Afro-Asian bloc (Bandung Conference, 1955), but Western economic influence and U.S. political ties remained strong (Baghdad Pact, 1955).

Trade. World trade volume soared, in an atmosphere of monetary stability assured by international accords (**Bretton Woods,** 1944). In Europe, economic integration advanced (**European Economic Community,** 1957; European Free Trade Association, 1960). Comecon (1949) coordinated the economies of Soviet-bloc countries.

U.S. Economic growth produced an abundance of consumer goods (9.3 million motor vehicles sold, 1955). Suburban housing tracts changed life patterns for middle and working classes (Levittown, 1946-51). Pres. Dwight **Eisenhower's** landslide election victories (1952, 1956) reflected consensus politics. Senate condemnation of Senator Joseph **McCarthy** (Dec. 1954) curbed the political abuse of anti-Communism. A system of alliances and military bases bolstered U.S. influence on all continents. Trade and payments surpluses were balanced by overseas investments and foreign aid ($50 billion, 1950-59).

USSR. In the "thaw" after Stalin's death in 1953, relations with the West improved (evacuation of Vienna, Geneva summit conference, both 1955). Repression of scientific and cultural life eased, and many prisoners were freed or rehabilitated culminating in **de-Stalinization** (1956). **Nikita Khrushchev's** leadership aimed at consumer sector growth, but farm production lagged, despite the virgin lands program (from 1954). Soviet crushing of the 1956 Hungarian revolution, the 1960 U-2 spy plane episode, and other incidents renewed East-West tension and domestic curbs.

East Europe. Resentment of Russian domination and Stalinist repression combined with nationalist, economic, and religious factors to produce periodic violence. E Berlin workers rioted (1953), Polish workers rioted in Poznan (June 1956), and a broad-based **revolution** broke out **in Hungary** (Oct. 1956). All were suppressed by Soviet force or threats (at least 7,000 dead in Hungary). But Poland was allowed to restore private ownership of farms, and a degree of personal and economic freedom returned to Hungary. Yugoslavia experimented with worker self-management and a market economy.

Korea. The 1945 division of Korea along the 38th parallel left industry in the N, which was organized into a militant regime and armed by the USSR. The S was politically disunited. More than 60,000 N Korean troops invaded the S on June 25, 1950. The U.S., backed by the UN Security Council, sent troops. UN troops reached the Chinese border in Nov. Some 200,000 Chinese troops crossed the Yalu R. and drove back UN forces. By spring 1951 battle lines had become stabilized near the original 38th parallel border, but heavy fighting continued. Finally, an armistice was signed on July 27, 1953. U.S. troops remained in the S, and U.S. economic and military aid continued. The war stimulated rapid economic recovery in Japan.

China. Starting in 1952, industry, agriculture, and social institutions were forcibly collectivized. In a massive purge, as many as several million people were executed as Kuomintang supporters or as class and political enemies. The **Great Leap Forward** (1958-60) unsuccessfully tried to force the pace of development by substituting labor for investment.

Indochina. Ho Chi Minh's forces, aided by the USSR and the new Chinese Communist government, fought French and pro-French Vietnamese forces to a standstill and captured the strategic **Dienbienphu** camp in May 1954. The Geneva Agreements divided Vietnam in half pending elections (never held) and recognized Laos and Cambodia as independent. The U.S. aided the anti-Communist Republic of Vietnam in the S.

Middle East. Arab revolutions placed leftist, militantly nationalist regimes in power in Egypt (1952) and Iraq (1958). But Arab unity attempts failed (United Arab Republic joined Egypt, Syria, Yemen, 1958-61). Arab refusal to recognize Israel (Arab League economic blockade began Sept. 1951) led to a permanent state of war, with repeated incidents (Gaza, 1955). Israel occupied Sinai, and Britain and France took (Oct. 1956) the Suez Canal, but were replaced by the UN Emergency Force. The Mossadegh government in Iran nationalized (May 1951) the British-owned oil industry May, but was overthrown (Aug. 1953) in a U.S.-aided coup.

Latin America. Argentinian dictator Juan **Perón,** in office 1946, enforced land reform, some nationalization, welfare state measures, and curbs on the Roman Catholic Church, and crushed opposition. A Sept. 1955 coup deposed Perón. The 1952 revolution in Bolivia brought land reform, nationalization of tin mines, and improvement in the status of Indians, who nevertheless remained poor. The Batista regime in Cuba was overthrown (Jan. 1959) by Fidel **Castro,** who imposed a Communist dictatorship, aligned Cuba with the USSR, but improved education and health care. A U.S.-backed anti-Castro invasion (**Bay of Pigs**, Apr. 1961) was crushed. Self-government advanced in the British Caribbean.

Technology. Large outlays on research and development in the U.S. and the USSR focused on military applications (H-bomb in U.S., 1952; USSR, 1953; Britain, 1957; intercontinental missiles, late 1950s). Soviet launching of the **Sputnik** satellite (Oct. 4, 1957) spurred increases in U.S. science education funds (National Defense Education Act).

Literature and film. Alienation from social and literary conventions reached an extreme in the theater of the absurd (Beckett's *Waiting for Godot,* 1952), the "new novel" (Robbe-Grillet's *Voyeur,* 1955), and avant-garde film (Antonioni's *L'Avventura,* 1960). U.S. beatniks (Kerouac's *On the Road,* 1957) and others rejected the supposed conformism of Americans (Riesman's *The Lonely Crowd,* 1950).

Rising Expectations: 1960-69

Economic boom. The longest sustained economic boom on record spanned almost the entire decade in the capitalist world; the closely watched GNP figure doubled (1960-70) in the U.S., fueled by Vietnam War–related budget deficits. The **General Agreement on Tariffs and Trade** (1967) stimulated W European prosperity, which spread to peripheral areas (Spain, Italy, E Germany). Japan became a top economic power. Foreign investment aided the industrialization of Brazil. There were limited Soviet economic reform attempts.

Reform and radicalization. Pres. John F. **Kennedy**, inaugurated 1961, emphasized youthful idealism and vigor; his assassination Nov. 22, 1963, was a national trauma. A series of political and social reform movements took root in the U.S., later spreading to other countries. Blacks demonstrated nonviolently and with partial success against segregation and poverty (1963 March on Washington; 1964 **Civil Rights Act**), but some urban ghettos erupted in extensive riots (Watts, 1965; Detroit, 1967; Martin Luther King assassination, Apr. 4, 1968). New concern for the poor (Harrington's *Other America*, 1963) helped lead to Pres. Lyndon Johnson's **"Great Society"** programs (Medicare, Water Quality Act, Higher Education Act, all 1965). Concern with the **environment** surged (Carson's *Silent Spring*, 1962). **Feminism** revived as a cultural and political movement (Friedan's *Feminine Mystique*, 1963; National Organization for Women founded 1966), and a movement for homosexual rights emerged (Stonewall riot in NYC, 1969). Pope John XXIII called the **Second Vatican Council** (1962-65), which liberalized Roman Catholic liturgy and some other aspects of Catholicism.

Opposition to U.S. involvement in Vietnam, especially among university students (**Moratorium** protest, Nov. 1969), turned violent (Weatherman Chicago riots, Oct. 1969). **New Left** and Marxist theories became popular, and membership in radical groups (Students for a Democratic Society, Black Panthers) increased. Maoist groups, especially in Europe, called for total transformation of society. In France, students sparked a nationwide strike affecting 10 million workers in May-June 1968, but an electoral reaction barred revolutionary change.

Arts and styles. The boundary between fine and popular arts was blurred to some extent by Pop Art (Warhol) and rock musicals (*Hair*, 1968). Informality and exaggeration prevailed in fashion (beards, miniskirts). A nonpolitical "counterculture" developed, rejecting traditional bourgeois life goals and personal habits, and use of marijuana and hallucinogens spread (**Woodstock** festival, Aug. 1969). Indian influence was felt in religion (Ram Dass) and fashion, and The **Beatles,** who brought unprecedented sophistication to rock music, became for many a symbol of the decade.

Science. Achievements in space (**humans on the moon,** July 1969) and electronics (lasers, integrated circuits) encouraged a faith in scientific solutions to problems in agriculture ("green revolution"), medicine (heart transplants, 1967), and other areas. Harmful technology, it was believed, could be controlled (1963 nuclear weapon test ban treaty, 1968 nonproliferation treaty).

China. Mao's revolutionary militancy caused disputes with the USSR under "revisionist" Khrushchev, starting in 1960. The 2 powers exchanged fire in 1969 border disputes. China used force to capture (1962) areas disputed with India. The **"Great Proletarian Cultural Revolution"** tried to impose a utopian egalitarian program in China and spread revolution abroad; political struggle, often violent, convulsed China in 1965-68.

Indochina. Communist-led guerrillas aided by N Vietnam fought from 1960 against the S Vietnam government of Ngo Dinh Diem (killed 1963). The U.S. military role increased after the 1964 **Tonkin Gulf** incident. U.S. forces peaked at 543,400 in Apr. 1969. Massive numbers of N Vietnamese troops also fought. Laotian and Cambodian neutrality were threatened by Communist insurgencies, with N Vietnamese aid, and U.S. intrigues.

Third World. A bloc of authoritarian leftist regimes among the newly independent nations emerged in political opposition to the U.S.-led Western alliance and came to dominate the conference of nonaligned nations (Belgrade, 1961; Cairo, 1964; Lusaka, 1970). Soviet political ties and military bases were established in Cuba, Egypt, Algeria, Guinea, and other countries whose leaders were regarded as revolutionary heroes by opposition groups in pro-Western or colonial countries. Some leaders were ousted in coups by pro-Western groups—Zaire's Patrice Lumumba (killed 1961), Ghana's Kwame Nkrumah (exiled 1966), and Indonesia's Sukarno (effectively ousted in 1965 after a Communist coup failed).

MILLENNIUM FACT BOX

Some Famous Dates of the Second Millennium

Below are a few dates marking key events in the history of the world since AD 1000.

1066 William, Duke of Normandy, conquered England.
1095 Pope Urban II called for the First Crusade.
1211 Genghis Khan invaded China, as he built the largest empire in history.
1215 England's King John accepted the Magna Carta, limiting royal power.
1325 The Aztecs founded their capital city of Tenochtitlan.
1348 The Black Death (bubonic plague) reached Europe from the East.
1453 Constantinople fell to the Ottoman Turks.
1455 Johann Gutenberg printed 200 Bibles, launching a technological revolution.
1492 Christopher Columbus reached the New World.
1517 Martin Luther made public his Ninety-five Theses, starting the Protestant Reformation.
1769 James Watt patented the steam engine, initiating the Industrial Revolution.
1776 The American colonies declared independence.
1789 The French Revolution was inaugurated with the storming of the Bastille.
1796 Edward Jenner discovered a vaccine for smallpox, laying foundation for modern immunology.
1815 Napoleon was defeated at Waterloo.
1821 Simon Bolivar freed Venezuela from Spanish rule, in a campaign that led to widespread independence in South America.
1868 Japan opened its trade to the West after Commodore Matthew Perry arrived with gunships in Tokyo Bay.
1869 The Suez Canal opened.
1914 The assassination of Austrian Archduke Franz Ferdinand precipitated World War I.
1917 The Bolsheviks took power in Russia in a violent coup.
1933 Adolf Hitler assumed power in Germany.
1945 The U.S. dropped atom bombs on Hiroshima and Nagasaki, precipitating the surrender of Japan and end of World War II.
1949 The People's Republic of China was established, after the defeat of Nationalist forces.
1969 Neil Armstrong became the first human to walk on the Moon.
1989 The Berlin Wall was opened, heralding the end of the Cold War and the coming collapse of the Soviet Union.

Middle East. Arab-Israeli tension erupted into a brief war June 1967. Israel emerged from the war as a major regional power. Military shipments before and after the war brought much of the Arab world into the Soviet political sphere. Most Arab states broke U.S. diplomatic ties, while Communist countries cut their ties to Israel. Intra-Arab disputes continued: Egypt and Saudi Arabia supported rival factions in a bloody Yemen civil war 1962-70; Lebanese troops fought Palestinian commandos 1969.

East Europe. To stop the large-scale exodus of citizens, E German authorities built (Aug. 1961) a **fortified wall across Berlin.** Soviet sway in the Balkans was weakened by Albania's support of China (USSR broke ties in Dec. 1961) and Romania's assertion (1964) of industrial and foreign policy autonomy. Liberalization (spring 1968) in Czechoslovakia was crushed with massive force by troops of 5 Warsaw Pact countries. W German treaties (1970) with the USSR and Poland facilitated the transfer of German technology and confirmed postwar boundaries.

Disillusionment: 1970-79

U.S.: Caution and neoconservatism. A relatively sluggish economy, energy and resource shortages (natural gas crunch, 1975; gasoline shortage, 1979), and environmental problems contributed to a **"limits of growth"** philosophy. Suspicion of science and technology killed or delayed major projects (supersonic transport dropped, 1971; Seabrook nuclear power plant protests, 1977-78) and was fed by the Three Mile Island nuclear reactor accident (Mar. 1979).

There were signs of growing mistrust of big government and weakened support for government reform plans. School busing and racial quotas were opposed (Bakke decision, June 1978); the proposed Equal Rights Amendment for women languished; civil rights for homosexuals were opposed (Dade County referendum, June 1977).

Completion of Communist forces' takeover of **South Vietnam** (evacuation of U.S. civilians, Apr. 1975), revelations of Central Intelligence Agency misdeeds (Rockefeller Commission report, June 1975), and **Watergate** scandals (Nixon resigned in Aug. 1974) reduced faith in U.S. moral and material capacity to influence world affairs. Revelations of Soviet crimes (Solzhenitsyn's *Gulag Archipelago,* 1974) and Soviet intervention in Africa helped foster a revival of anti-Communist sentiment.

Economy sluggish. The 1960s boom faltered in the 1970s; a severe recession in the U.S. and Europe (1974-75) followed a huge oil price hike (Dec. 1973). Monetary instability (U.S. cut ties to gold in Aug. 1971), the decline of the dollar, and protectionist moves by industrial countries (1977-78) threatened trade. Business investment and spending for research declined. Severe inflation plagued many countries (25% in Britain, 1975; 18% in U.S., 1979).

China picks up pieces. After the 1976 deaths of Mao Zedong and Zhou Enlai, struggle for the leadership succession was won by pragmatists. A nationwide purge of orthodox Maoists was carried out, and the **Gang of Four,** led by Mao's widow, Chiang Ching, arrested. The new leaders freed more than 100,000 political prisoners and reduced public adulation of Mao. Political and trade ties were expanded with Japan, Europe, and the U.S. in the late 1970s, as relations worsened with the USSR, Cuba, and Vietnam (4-week invasion by China, 1979). Ideological guidelines in industry, science, education, and the armed forces, which the ruling faction said had caused chaos and decline, were reversed (bonuses to workers, Dec. 1977; exams for college entrance, Oct. 1977). Severe restrictions on cultural expression were eased.

Europe. European unity moves (EEC-EFTA trade accord, 1972) faltered as economic problems appeared (Britain floated pound, 1972; France floated franc, 1974). Germany and Switzerland curbed guest workers from southern Europe. Greece and Turkey quarreled over Cyprus and Aegean oil rights.

All non-Communist Europe was under democratic rule after free elections were held (June 1976) in **Spain** 7 months after the death of Franco. The conservative, colonialist regime in **Portugal** was overthrown in Apr. 1974. In **Greece** the 7-year-old military dictatorship yielded power in 1974. Northern Europe, though ruled mostly by Socialists (**Swedish** Socialists unseated in 1976 after 44 years in power), turned more conservative. The **British** Labour government imposed (1975) wage curbs and suspended nationalization schemes. Terrorism in **Germany** (1972 Munich Olympics killings) led to laws curbing some civil liberties. **French** "new philosophers" rejected leftist ideologies, and the shaky Socialist-Communist coalition lost a 1978 election bid.

Religion and politics. The improvement in **Muslim** countries' political fortunes by the 1950s (with the exception of Central Asia under Soviet and Chinese rule) and the growth of Arab oil wealth were followed by a resurgence of traditional religious fervor. Libyan dictator Muammar al-Qaddafi mixed Islamic laws with socialism and called for Muslim return to

Spain and Sicily. The illegal Muslim Brotherhood in **Egypt** was accused of violence, while extreme groups bombed (1977) theaters to protest secular values.

In **Turkey**, the National Salvation Party was the first Islamic group to share (1974) power since secularization in the 1920s. In **Iran, Ayatollah Ruhollah Khomeini,** led a revolution that deposed the secular shah (Jan. 1979) and created an Islamic republic there. Religiously motivated Muslims took part in an insurrection in Saudi Arabia that briefly seized (1979) the Grand Mosque in Mecca. Muslim puritan opposition to **Pakistan** Pres. Zulfikar Ali-Bhutto helped lead to his overthrow in July 1977. Muslim solidarity, however, could not prevent Pakistan's eastern province (**Bangladesh**) from declaring (Dec. 1971) independence after a bloody civil war.

Muslim and Hindu resentment of coerced sterilization in **India** helped defeat the Gandhi government, which was replaced (Mar. 1977) by a coalition including religious Hindu parties. Muslims in the S **Philippines**, aided by Libya, rebelled against central rule from 1973.

Evangelical Protestant groups grew in numbers and prosperity in the U.S. A revival of interest in Orthodox Christianity occurred among **Russian** intellectuals (Solzhenitsyn). The secularist **Israeli** Labor party, after decades of rule, was ousted in 1977 by conservatives led by Menachem Begin; religious militants founded settlements on the disputed West Bank, part of biblically promised Israel. U.S. Reform Judaism revived many previously discarded traditional practices.

The Buddhist Soka Gakkai movement launched (1964) the Komeito party in **Japan,** which became a major opposition party in 1972 and 1976 elections.

Old-fashioned religious wars raged intermittently in **Northern Ireland** (Catholic vs. Protestant, 1969-) and **Lebanon** (Christian vs. Muslim, 1975-), while religious militancy complicated the Israel-Arab dispute (1973 Israel-Arab war). Despite a 1979 **peace treaty between Egypt and Israel,** increased militancy on the West Bank impeded further progress.

Latin America. Repressive conservative regimes strengthened their hold on most of the continent, with a violent coup against the elected (Sept. 1973) Allende government in **Chile**, a 1976 military coup in **Argentina**, and coups against reformist regimes in **Bolivia** (1971, 1979) and **Peru** (1976). In Central America increasing liberal and leftist militancy led to the ouster (1979) of the Somoza regime of **Nicaragua** and to civil conflict in **El Salvador**.

Indochina. Communist victories in Vietnam, Cambodia, and Laos by May 1975 led to new turmoil. The **Pol Pot regime** ordered millions of city-dwellers to resettle in rural areas, in a program of forced labor, combined with terrorism, that cost more than 1 million lives (1975-79) and caused hundreds of thousands of ethnic Chinese and others to flee Vietnam ("boat people," 1979). The Vietnamese invasion of Cambodia swelled the refugee population and contributed to widespread starvation in that devastated country.

Russian expansion. Soviet influence, checked in some countries (troops ousted by Egypt, 1972), was projected farther afield, often with the use of Cuban troops (Angola, 1975-89; Ethiopia, 1977-88) and aided by a growing navy, a merchant fleet, and international banking ability. **Détente** with the West—1972 Berlin pact, 1972 strategic arms pact (**SALT**)—gave way to a more antagonistic relationship in the late 1970s, exacerbated by the Soviet invasion (1979) of **Afghanistan.**

Africa. The last remaining European colonies were granted independence (**Spanish Sahara**, 1976; **Djibouti,** 1977) and, after 10 years of civil war and many negotiation sessions, a black government took over (1979) in Zimbabwe (Rhodesia); white domination remained in **South Africa**. Great power involvement in local wars (Russia in **Angola, Ethiopia**; France in **Chad, Zaire, Mauritania**) and the use of tens of thousands of Cuban troops were denounced by some African leaders. Ethnic or tribal clashes made Africa a locus of sustained warfare during the late 1970s.

Arts. Traditional modes of painting, architecture, and music, pursued in relative obscurity for much of the 20th cent., received increased popular and critical attention in the 1970s. The pictorial emphasis in neorealist and photorealist painting, the return of many architects to detail, decoration, and natural materials, and the concern with ordered structure in musical composition were, ironically, novel experiences for artistic consumers after the exhaustion of experimental possibilities. These more conservative styles, however, coexisted with modernist works in an atmosphere of increased variety and tolerance.

Revitalization of Capitalism, Demand for Democracy: 1980-89

USSR, Eastern Europe. A troublesome 1980-85 for the USSR was followed by 5 years of astonishing change: the surrender of the Communist monopoly, remaking of the Soviet state, and the beginning of the disintegration of the Soviet empire. After the deaths of Leonid **Brezhnev** (1982) and 2 successors (Andropov in 1984 and Chernenko in 1985), the harsh treatment of dissent and restriction of emigration, and the Soviet invasion (Dec. 1979) of Afghanistan, Gen. Sec. Mikhail **Gorbachev** (in office 1985-1991) promoted *glasnost* and *perestroika*—economic, political, and social reform. Supported by the Communist Party (July 1988), he signed (Dec. 1987) the INF disarmament treaty, and he pledged (1988) to cut the military budget. Military withdrawal from Afghanistan was completed in Feb. 1989, democratization was not hindered in Poland and Hungary, and the Soviet people chose (Mar. 1989) part of the new Congress from competing candidates. By decade's end the **Cold War** appeared to be fading away, with much of the credit given to Gorbachev.

In **Poland, Solidarity**, the labor union founded (1980) by Lech **Walesa**, was outlawed in 1982 and then legalized in 1988, after years of unrest. Poland's first free election since the Communist takeover brought Solidarity victory (June 1989); Tadeusz Mazowiecki, a Walesa adviser, became (Aug. 1989) prime minister in a government with the Communists. In the fall of 1989 the failure of Marxist economies in **Hungary, East Germany, Czechoslovakia, Bulgaria,** and **Romania** brought the collapse of the Communist monopoly and a demand for democracy. In a historic step, the **Berlin Wall** was opened in Nov. 1989.

U.S. "The Reagan Years" (1981-88) brought the **longest economic boom** yet in U.S. history via budget and tax cuts, deregulation, "junk bond" financing, leveraged buyouts, and mergers and takeovers. However, there was a stock market crash (Oct. 1987), and federal budget deficits and the trade deficit increased. Foreign policy showed a **strong anti-Communist stance**, via increased defense spending, aid to anti-Communists in Central America, invasion of Cuba-threatened Grenada, and championing of the MX missile system and "Star Wars" missile defense program. Four Reagan-Gorbachev summits (1985-88) climaxed in the INF treaty (1987), as the Cold War began to wind down. The Iran-contra affair (North's TV testimony, July 1987) was a major political scandal. Homelessness and drug abuse (especially "crack" cocaine) were growing social problems. In 1988, Vice Pres. George Bush was elected to succeed Ronald Reagan as president.

Middle East. The Middle East remained militarily unstable, with sharp divisions along economic, political, racial, and religious lines. In **Iran**, the Islamic revolution of 1979 created a strong anti-U.S. stance (hostage crisis, Nov. 1979-Jan. 1981). In Sept. 1980, **Iraq** repudiated its border agreement with Iran and began major hostilities that led to an 8-year war in which millions were killed.

Libya's support for international terrorism induced the U.S. to close (May 1981) its diplomatic mission there and embargo (Mar. 1982) Libyan oil. The U.S. accused Libyan leader Muammar al-Qaddafi of aiding (Dec. 1985) terrorists in Rome and of Vienna airport attacks, and retaliated by bombing Libya (Apr. 1986).

Israel affirmed (July 1980) all Jerusalem as its capital, destroyed (1981) an Iraqi atomic reactor, and invaded (1982) Lebanon, forcing the PLO to agree to withdraw. A **Palestinian uprising**, including women and children hurling rocks and bottles at troops, began (Dec. 1987) in Israeli-occupied Gaza and spread to the West Bank; troops responded with force, killing 300 by the end of 1988, with 6,000 more in detention camps.

Israeli withdrawal from **Lebanon** began in Feb. 1985 and ended in June 1985, as Lebanon continued torn by military and political conflict. Artillery duels (Mar.-Apr. 1989) between Christian East Beirut and Muslim West Beirut left 200 dead and 700 wounded. At decade's end, violence still dominated.

Latin America. In **Nicaragua**, the leftist Sandinista National Liberation Front, in power after the 1979 civil war, faced problems as a result of Nicaragua's military aid to leftist guerrillas in El Salvador and U.S. backing of antigovernment contras. The U.S. CIA admitted (1984) having directed the mining of Nicaraguan ports, and the U.S. sent humanitarian (1985) and military (1986) aid. Profits from secret arms sales to Iran were found (1987) diverted to contras. Cease-fire talks between the Sandinista government and contras came in 1988, and elections were held in Feb. 1990.

In **El Salvador**, a military coup (Oct. 1979) failed to halt extreme right-wing violence and left-wing terrorism. Archbishop Oscar Romero was assassinated in Mar. 1980; from Jan. to June some 4,000 civilians reportedly were killed in the civil unrest. In 1984, newly elected Pres. José Napoleon Duarte worked to stem human rights abuses, but violence continued.

In **Chile**, Gen. Augusto Pinochet yielded the presidency after a democratic election (Dec. 1989), but remained as head of the army. He had ruled the country since 1973, imposing harsh measures against leftists and dissidents; at the same time he introduced economic programs that restored prosperity to Chile.

Africa. 1980-85 marked a rapid decline in the economies of virtually all African countries, a result of accelerating desertification, the world economic recession, heavy indebtedness to overseas creditors, rapid population growth, and political instability. Some 60 million Africans faced prolonged hunger in 1981; much of Africa had one of the worst droughts ever in 1983, and by year's end **150 million faced near-famine.** "Live Aid," a marathon rock concert, was presented in July 1985, and the U.S. and Western nations sent aid in Sept. 1985. Economic hardship fueled political unrest and coups. Wars in Ethiopia and Sudan and military strife in several other nations continued. AIDS took a heavy toll.

South Africa. Antiapartheid sentiment gathered force; demonstrations and violent police response grew. South African white voters approved (Nov. 1983) the first constitution to give Coloureds and Asians a voice, while still excluding blacks (70% of the population). The U.S. imposed economic sanctions in Aug. 1985, and 11 Western nations followed in September. P. W. **Botha**, 1980s president, was succeeded by F. W. **de Klerk**, in Sept. 1989, who promised "evolutionary" change via negotiation with the black population.

China. During the 1980s the Communist government and paramount leader **Deng Xiaoping** pursued **far-reaching changes**, expanding commercial and technical ties to the industrialized world and increasing the role of market forces in stimulating urban development. Apr. 1989 brought new demands for democratization: student demonstrators camped out in Tiananmen Sq., Beijing, in a massive peaceful protest. Some 100,000 students and workers marched, and at least 20 other cities saw protests. In response, martial law was imposed; army troops crushed the demonstration in and around Tiananmen Square on June 3-4, with death toll estimates at 500-7,000, as many as 10,000 injured, up to 10,000 dissidents arrested, 31 people tried and executed. The conciliatory Communist Party chief was ousted; the Politburo adopted (July) reforms against official corruption.

Japan. Japan's relations with other nations, especially the U.S., were dominated by **trade imbalances favoring Japan.** In 1985 the U.S. trade deficit with Japan was $49.7 billion, one-third of the total U.S. trade deficit. After Japan was found (Apr. 1986) to sell semiconductors and computer memory chips below cost, the U.S. was assured a "fair share" of the market, but charged (Mar. 1987) Japan with failing to live up to the agreement.

European Community. With the addition of Greece, Portugal, and Spain, the EC became a **common market of more than 300 million people**, the West's largest trading entity. Margaret **Thatcher** became the first British prime minister in the 20th century to win a 3d consecutive term (1987). France elected (1981) its first socialist president, François **Mitterrand**, who was reelected in 1988. Italy elected (1983) its first socialist premier, Bettino **Craxi.**

International terrorism. With the 1979 overthrow of the shah of Iran, terrorism became a prominent political tactic. It increased through the 1980s, but with fewer high-profile attacks after 1985. In 1979-81, Iranian militants held 52 Americans hostage in Iran for 444 days; in 1983 a TNT-laden suicide terrorist blew up U.S. Marine headquarters in Beirut, killing 241 Americans, and a truck bomb blew up a French paratroop barracks, killing 58. The *Achille Lauro* cruise ship was hijacked in 1986, and an American passenger killed; the U.S. subsequently intercepted the Egyptian plane flying the terrorists to safety. Incidents rose to 700 in 1985, and to 1,000 in 1988. **Assassinated leaders** included Egypt's Pres. Anwar al-**Sadat** (1981), India's Prime Min. Indira **Gandhi** (1984), and Lebanese Premier Rashid **Karami** (1987).

Post-Cold-War World: 1990-97

Soviet Empire breakup. The world community witnessed the extraordinary spectacle of a superpower's disintegration when the **Soviet Union** broke apart into 15 independent states. The 1980s had already seen internal reforms and a decline of Communist power both within the Soviet Union and in Eastern Europe. The Soviet breakup began in earnest with the declarations of independence adopted by the Baltic republics of **Lithuania, Latvia,** and **Estonia** during an abortive coup against reformist leader Mikhail **Gorbachev** (Aug. 1991). The other republics soon took the same step. In Dec. 1991, **Russia, Ukraine,** and **Belarus** declared the Soviet Union dead; Gorbachev resigned, and the Soviet Parliament went out of existence. Most of the former republics formed a loose confederation called the **Commonwealth of Independent States.** The Warsaw Pact and the Council for Mutual Economic Assistance (Comecon) were disbanded. **Russia** remained the predominant country after the breakup, but its people soon suffered severe economic hardship as the nation, under Pres. Boris **Yeltsin,** moved to revamp the economy and to adopt a free market system. In Oct. 1993, **anti-Yeltsin forces** occupied the Parliament building and were ousted by the army; about 140 people died in the fighting.

The Muslim republic of **Chechnya** declared independence from the rest of Russia, but this was met with an invasion by Russian troops (Dec. 1994). Vicious fighting continued for almost 21 months. A cease-fire finally took hold (1996), and after the Russian withdrawal, Chechnya held elections, making a former guerrilla leader president (1997).

Europe. Yugoslavia also broke apart, and hostilities ensued among the republics along ethnic and religious lines. **Croatia, Slovenia,** and **Macedonia** declared independence (1991), followed by **Bosnia-Herzegovina** (1992). **Serbia** and **Montenegro** remained as the republic of Yugoslavia. Bitter fighting went on for 5 years, especially in Bosnia, in which the civilian population was targeted. Serbia and the Bosnian Serbs were accused of engaging in "ethnic cleansing" of the

Muslim population. The UN and NATO intervened in an attempt at pacification. A peace plan (Dayton accord), brokered by the United States, was signed by **Bosnia, Serbia**, and **Croatia** (Dec. 1995), with NATO troops responsible for policing its implementation. Czechoslovakia also broke apart, but peacefully (Jan. 1, 1993), becoming the **Czech Republic** and **Slovakia**.

The two **Germanys** were reunited after 45 years (Oct. 1990). The union was greeted with jubilation, but stresses became apparent when free market principles were applied to the aging East German industries, resulting in many plant closings and rising unemployment. In **Poland**, Lech **Walesa** was elected president (Dec. 1991) but was unsuccessful in seeking a 2d term, being defeated (Nov. 1995) by a former Communist, Aleksandr Kwasniewski.

NATO approved the Partnership for Peace Program (Jan. 1994) coordinating the defense of **Eastern** and **Central European** countries; Russia joined that program later that year. NATO signed a pact with **Russia** (1997) providing for NATO expansion into the former Soviet-bloc countries; a similar treaty was set up with **Ukraine**. NATO later approved the entry of the **Czech Republic, Hungary**, and **Poland** by 1999. Efforts toward European unity continued a shaky progress with adoption of a single market (Jan. 1993) and conversion of the European Community to the **European Union** as the Maastricht Treaty took effect (Nov. 1993).

An intraparty revolt forced Margaret **Thatcher** out as prime minister of **Great Britain**, to be succeeded by John Major (Nov. 1990); 7 years later, Major suffered an overwhelming defeat at the hands of the new Labour Party leader, Tony Blair (May 1997). The divorce of Prince Charles and Princess Diana, followed by the death of Diana in a car accident (Aug. 1997), made headlines around the world. A priority of the Labour government was an aggressive pursuit of **peace** in **Northern Ireland**. Peace talks that included participation of Sinn Fein, political arm of the IRA, were begun under the chairmanship of former U.S. Sen. George Mitchell. (Agreement was later reached on a peace plan, which was approved in an all-Ireland vote May 1998.) In **Scotland** voters overwhelmingly approved the establishment of a regional legislature (1997), and in **Wales** voters narrowly approved the establishment of a local assembly (1997). In a historic innovation, the Church of England ordained 32 women as priests (Mar. 1994).

Middle East. Another war in the Persian Gulf began when **Iraq's Saddam Hussein** ordered his troops to invade **Kuwait** (Aug. 1990). The UN approved military action against Iraq (Nov. 1990), and U.S. Pres. George **Bush** put together an international military force. U.S. and allied planes bombed Iraq (Jan. 1991) and launched a land attack, quickly crushing the invasion (Feb. 1991). In the course of the conflict, Iraq fired Scud missiles into **Israel**. Iraq formally accepted a cease-fire (Apr. 1991). U.S. troops withdrew, but "no-fly" zones were set up over northern Iraq to protect the Kurds and over southern Iraq to protect Shiite Muslims. The UN imposed sanctions on Iraq for failure to abide by the cease-fire; tensions continued between the Iraqi regime and UN arms inspectors charged with finding and destroying weapons of mass destruction.

Last Western hostages were freed in **Lebanon**, June 1992. After months of negotiations, **Israel** and the **Palestine Liberation Organization** signed a peace accord (Sept. 1993) providing for Palestinian self-government in the West Bank and the Gaza Strip. Prime Minister Yitzhak **Rabin** and Foreign Minister Shimon Peres of Israel and Yasir **Arafat** of the PLO received the Nobel Peace Prize for their efforts (1994). Six Arab nations relaxed their boycott against Israel (1994), and Israel and **Jordan** signed a peace treaty (Oct. 1994). Rabin was assassinated (Nov. 1995) by an Israeli student opposed to the peace settlement with the PLO. After new elections (May 1996), Benjamin Netanyahu became prime minister of Israel and adopted a harder line on implementation of the peace accord. Arafat was elected to the presidency of the Palestinian Authority (Jan. 1996). Israel agreed to return control of Hebron to the Palestinian Authority (Jan. 1997), but demanded that the PLO take stronger action against terrorism.

Asia. Hong Kong was returned to **China** (July 1997) after being a British colony for 156 years. China, which emerged in the decade as a major developing economic power, had agreed to follow a policy of "one country, two systems" in Hong Kong. **Jiang Zemin**, general secretary of the Chinese Communist Party, assumed the additional post of president of China (Mar. 1993) and was the apparent key leader after the influence of paramount leader **Deng Xiaoping** ended with his death (Feb. 1997). China released from prison—and exiled—some well-known dissidents but continued to be criticized for detention of others and other alleged human rights abuses, including persecutions of Christians and forced abortions.

After years of economic prosperity, **Thailand, Indonesia**, and **South Korea** in 1997 began to suffer severe economic reverses that were to have a worldwide ripple effect. Each of the countries was the recipient of billion-dollar IMF bailout packages. In **South Korea**, former dissident Kim Dae Jung was elected president (Dec. 1997). Two previous presidents, Roh Tae Woo and Chun Doo Hwan, were both convicted of crimes committed while in office but were given amnesty by the new president.

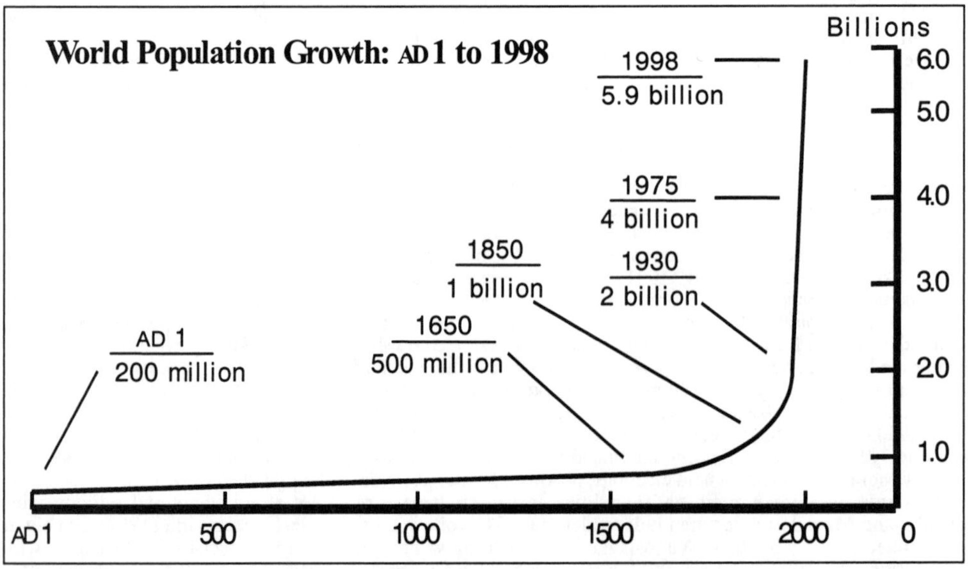

Japan was the victim of urban terrorism when members of a religious cult, Aum Shinrikyo, released the nerve gas sarin on 5 Tokyo subway cars, killing 12 people and injuring more than 5,500 (Mar. 1995). Arrests of cult members and their leader followed. Tamil rebels continued their armed conflict in **Sri Lanka**, and in **Afghanistan** warring Islamic factions fought for control of the country, with the Taliban, an extreme fundamentalist group, gaining control of Kabul (Sept. 1996) and, eventually, most of the rest of the country.

In **North Korea**, longtime dictator **Kim Il Sung** died (July 1994), to be succeeded by his son. In the same year the country signed an agreement with the United States setting a timetable for North Korea to eliminate its nuclear program. The country also suffered a severe drought, and many were estimated to have died of starvation. (Uneasy relations between **India** and **Pakistan** reached a new level when both nations conducted nuclear tests, May 1998.)

Africa. South Africa was transformed as the white-dominated government abandoned apartheid and the country made the transition to a nonracial democratic government. Pres. F. W. **de Klerk** released Nelson **Mandela** from prison (Feb. 1990), after he had been held by the government for 27 years, and lifted the ban on the African National Congress. The white government repealed its apartheid laws (1990, 1991). Mandela was elected president (Apr. 1994), and a new constitution became law (Dec. 1996).

The decades-long rule of Mobutu Sese Seko in **Zaire** came to an end (May 1997) at the hands of rebel forces led by Laurent Kabila; an ailing Mobutu fled the country and soon after died. Kabila changed the country name back to **Democratic Republic of the Congo**; economic and political conditions remained unstable. After the presidents of **Burundi** and **Rwanda** were killed in an airplane crash (Apr. 1994), violence erupted in Rwanda between Hutu and Tutsi factions; tens of thousands of people were slain. The conflict spread to refugee camps in neighboring Zaire and Burundi. Factional fighting also erupted in **Somalia** after Pres. Muhammad Siad Barre was ousted (Jan. 1991). The UN sent a U.S.-led peacekeeping force, but it was unsuccessful in restoring order. Some soldiers of the peacekeeping force were killed, including 23 Pakistanis (June 1993) and 18 U.S. Rangers (Oct. 1993). The UN ended its mission (Mar. 1995) with no durable formal government in place. **Liberia** endured similar factional fighting that lasted almost 5 years and claimed 150,000 lives. A cease-fire was finally concluded (Aug. 1995), and one of the faction leaders, Charles Taylor, was elected president (July 1997). The World Health Organization reported (1995) that Africa accounted for 70% of AIDS cases worldwide.

A 16-year civil war came to an end in **Angola** (May 1991) when the government signed a peace accord with the rebel UNITA faction. The country remained unstable, however, even after the inauguration of a national unity government (Apr. 1997). **Namibia** officially became an independent country in Mar. 1990. Claimed by South Africa since 1919 and placed under UN authority in 1971, it had long been a focus of colonial rivalries. In **Algeria,** the army cancelled a 2d round of parliamentary elections (Jan. 1992) after the Islamic party won a first round. Islamic fundamentalists then began a terrorist campaign that, along with killings by pro-government squads, eventually claimed thousands of lives.

North America. The **North American Free Trade Agreement** (NAFTA), liberalizing trade between the United States, Canada, and Mexico, went into effect Jan. 1, 1994. In **Canada**, the Progressive Conservative Party suffered a crushing defeat in general elections (Oct. 1993), and liberal Jean Chrétien became prime minister.

In the **United States**, in the 1992 presidential election, Democrat Bill **Clinton** defeated Pres. Bush, but in 1994 congressional elections Republicans gained control of both houses of Congress for the first time in 40 years. Congress passed a welfare reform act under which federal protection for welfare recipients was ended and funds were turned over to the states to implement their own programs. Clinton reached agreement with Congress on measures to eliminate the federal deficit. With the U.S. economy strong, Clinton easily won reelection in 1996, defeating Republican Bob Dole, but the new administration was plagued by continuing scandals, probed by special prosecutors.

The U.S. Army and Navy were torn by sexual scandals involving abuse of women personnel. The **CIA** suffered embarrassment with the discovery of espionage by agents (Aldrich Ames, Harold Nicholson).

In **Mexico,** Ernesto Zedillo of the ruling PRI party was elected president (July 1994) after the party's first candidate was assassinated. The country soon faced a crisis affecting the value of the peso, but was able to recover after receiving a bailout package from the United States. A peasant revolt spearheaded by the **Zapatista National Liberation Army** erupted in the state of Chiapas (Jan. 1994). The initial outbreak was suppressed, but the movement remained in existence.

Central America. In **Haiti**, Jean-Bertrand Aristide, a Catholic priest and politician, was elected president (Dec. 1990) but was ousted in a military coup after 9 months in office. The UN approved a U.S.-led invasion of Haiti to restore the elected leader; shortly before the troops arrived, a delegation headed by former U.S. president Jimmy Carter arranged (Sept. 1994) for the military junta to step aside for Aristide. In **Nicaragua**, Violetta Chamarro defeated Daniel Ortega in the presidential election (Feb. 1990), thus ousting the Sandanistas. In **Panama**, U.S. troops invaded and overthrew the government of Manuel Noriega (Dec. 1989), who was wanted on drug charges; Noriega was captured Jan. 1990. In **El Salvador** (1991) and **Guatemala** (1996) the governments signed agreements with rebel factions to end long-running civil conflicts.

South America. Alberto Fujimori was elected president of **Peru** in June 1990 and despite his suppression of the constitution (1992) was reelected in 1995. Peru succeeded in capturing (Sept. 1992) the leader of the Shining Path guerrilla movement, Abimael Guzmán Reynoso, and sentenced him to life imprisonment. Leftist guerrillas took hostages at an ambassador's residence in Lima (Dec. 1996); one hostage was killed during a government assault rescuing the rest (Apr. 1997). In **Ecuador**, the Congress took the unusual step of ousting a president, Abdalá Bucaran (nicknamed El Loco), for "mental incapacity" (Feb. 1997). The UN Conference on Environment and Development, or the **Earth Summit**, was held (June 1992) in **Rio de Janeiro, Brazil**. Delegates from 178 nations convened to pursue means of economic development that would protect the Earth's nonrenewable resources and to aid **Third World** nations in this endeavor.

Crime and terrorism. A court in Rostov-on-Don, **Russia**, convicted and sentenced to death (Oct. 1992) Andrei Chikatilo, a 56-year-old former schoolteacher reputed to be the worst serial killer in modern times. He was estimated to have killed at least 52 young women and children.

Terrorism, often linked to Mideastern sources and with the U.S. as object, continued. A terrorist bomb exploded in a garage beneath New York City's World Trade Center, killing 6 people (Feb. 1993). Bombings of a U.S. military training center (Nov. 1995) and a barracks holding U.S. airmen (June 1996), both in **Saudi Arabia,** killed 7 and 19, respectively. In an act not associated with Mideastern terrorists, the Alfred P. Murrah Federal Building in Oklahoma City, OK, was destroyed by a bomb that killed 168 people (Apr. 1995). A 27-year-old U.S. army veteran was convicted and sentenced to death for this crime (1997).

Science. The **Hubble Space Telescope** was launched in Apr. 1990, but flaws were discovered in its mirrors and solar panels. After repairs by space-walking astronauts (Dec. 1993), an extraordinary amount of information about the solar system and beyond became available to scientists. The U.S. space shuttle ***Atlantis*** docked with the orbiting Russian space station ***Mir*** (June 1995) for the first time, in the first of several joint missions in a spirit of post-Cold-War cooperation.

Scottish scientist Ian Wilmot announced (Feb. 1997) the **cloning** of a sheep, nicknamed Dolly—the first mammal successfully cloned from a cell from an adult animal.

HISTORICAL FIGURES

Ancient Greeks and Latins

Greeks

Aeschines, orator, 389-314BC.
Aeschylus, dramatist, 525-456BC.
Aesop, fableist, c620-c560BC.
Alcibiades, politician, 450-404BC.
Anacreon, poet, c582-c485BC.
Anaxagoras, philosopher, c500-428BC.
Anaximander, philosopher, 611-546BC.
Anaximenes, philosopher, c570-500BC.
Antiphon, speechwriter, c480-411BC.
Apollonius, mathematician, c265-170BC.
Archimedes, math. 287-212BC.
Aristophanes, dramatist, c448-380BC.
Aristotle, philosopher, 384-322BC.
Athenaeus, scholar, fl. c200.
Callicrates, architect, fl. 5th cent.BC.
Callimachus, poet, c305-240BC.
Cratinus, comic dramatist, 520-421BC.
Democritus, philosopher, c460-370BC.
Demosthenes, orator, 384-322BC.
Diodorus, historian, fl. 20BC.
Diogenes, philosopher, 372-c287BC.
Dionysius, historian, d. c7BC.
Empedocles, philosopher, c490-430BC.
Epicharmus, dramatist, c530-440BC.
Epictetus, philosopher, c55-c135.
Epicurus, philosopher, 341-270BC.
Eratosthenes, scientist, 276-194BC.
Euclid, mathematician, fl. c300BC.
Euripides, dramatist, c484-406BC.
Galen, physician, 130-200.
Heraclitus, philosopher, c540-c475BC.
Herodotus, historian, c484-420BC.
Hesiod, poet, 8th cent. BC.
Hippocrates, physician, c460-377BC.
Homer, poet, fl. c700BC(?).
Isocrates, orator, 436-338BC.
Menander, dramatist, 342-292BC.
Parmenides, philosopher, b c515BC.
Pericles, statesman, c495-429BC.
Phidias, sculptor, c500-435BC.
Pindar, poet, c518-c438BC.
Plato, philosopher, c428-347BC.
Plutarch, biographer, c46-120.
Polybius, historian, c200-c118BC.
Praxiteles, sculptor, 400-330BC.
Pythagoras, phil., math., c580-c500BC.
Sappho, poet, c610-c580BC.
Simonides, poet, 556-c468BC.
Socrates, philosopher, 469-399BC.
Solon, statesman, 640-560BC.
Sophocles, dramatist, c496-406BC.
Strabo, geographer, c63BC-AD24.
Thales, philosopher, c634-546BC.
Themistocles, politician, c524-c460BC.
Theocritus, poet, c310-250BC.
Theophrastus, phil., c372-c287BC.
Thucydides, historian, fl. 5th cent.BC.
Timon, philosopher, c320-c230BC.
Xenophon, historian, c434-c355BC.
Zeno, philosopher, c495-c430BC.

Latins

Ammianus, historian, c330-395.
Apuleius, satirist, c124-c170.
Boethius, scholar, c480-524.
Caesar, Julius, leader, 100-44BC.
Catilina, politician, c108-62BC.
Cato (Elder), statesman, 234-149BC.
Catullus, poet, c84-54BC.
Cicero, orator, 106-43BC.
Claudian, poet, c370-c404.
Ennius, poet, 239-170BC.
Gellius, author, c130-c165.
Horace, poet, 65-8BC.
Juvenal, satirist, 60-127.
Livy, historian, 59BC-AD17.
Lucan, poet, 39-65.
Lucilius, poet, c180-c102BC.
Lucretius, poet, c99-c55BC.
Martial, epigrammatist, c38-c103.
Nepos, historian, c100-c25BC.
Ovid, poet, 43BC-AD17.
Persius, satirist, 34-62.
Plautus, dramatist, c254-c184BC.
Pliny the Elder, scholar, 23-79.
Pliny the Younger, author, 62-113.
Quintilian, rhetorician, c35-c97.
Sallust, historian, 86-34BC.
Seneca, philosopher, 4BC-AD65.
Silius, poet, c25-101.
Statius, poet, c45-c96.
Suetonius, biographer, c69-c122.
Tacitus, historian, 56-120.
Terence, dramatist, 185-c159BC.
Tibullus, poet, c55-c19BC.
Virgil, poet, 70-19BC.
Vitruvius, architect, fl. 1st cent.BC.

Rulers of England and Great Britain

England

Name		Began	Died	Age	Rgd
	Saxons and Danes				
Egbert	King of Wessex, won allegiance of all English	**829**	**839**	—	10
Ethelwulf	Son, King of Wessex, Sussex, Kent, Essex	**839**	**858**	—	19
Ethelbald	Son of Ethelwulf, displaced father in Wessex	**858**	**860**	—	2
Ethelbert	2d son of Ethelwulf, united Kent and Wessex	**860**	**866**	—	6
Ethelred I	3d son, King of Wessex, fought Danes	**866**	**871**	—	5
Alfred	The Great, 4th son, defeated Danes, fortified London	**871**	**899**	52	28
Edward	The Elder, Alfred's son, united English, claimed Scotland	**899**	**924**	55	25
Athelstan	The Glorious, Edward's son, King of Mercia, Wessex	**924**	**940**	45	16
Edmund	3d son of Edward, King of Wessex, Mercia	**940**	**946**	25	6
Edred	4th son of Edward	**946**	**955**	32	9
Edwy	The Fair, eldest son of Edmund, King of Wessex	**955**	**959**	18	3
Edgar	The Peaceful, 2d son of Edmund, ruled all English	**959**	**975**	32	17
Edward	The Martyr, eldest son of Edgar, murdered by stepmother	**975**	**978**	17	4
Ethelred II	The Unready, 2d son of Edgar, married Emma of Normandy	**978**	**1016**	48	37
Edmund II	Ironside, son of Ethelred II, King of London	**1016**	**1016**	27	0
Canute	The Dane, gave Wessex to Edmund, married Emma	**1016**	**1035**	40	19
Harold I	Harefoot, natural son of Canute	**1035**	**1040**	—	5
Hardecanute	Son of Canute by Emma, Danish King	**1040**	**1042**	24	2
Edward	The Confessor, son of Ethelred II (canonized 1161)	**1042**	**1066**	62	24
Harold II	Edward's brother-in-law, last Saxon King	**1066**	**1066**	44	0
	House of Normandy				
William I	The Conqueror, defeated Harold at Hastings	**1066**	**1087**	60	21
William II	Rufus, 3d son of William I, killed by arrow	**1087**	**1100**	43	13
Henry I	Beauclerc, youngest son of William I	**1100**	**1135**	67	35
	House of Blois				
Stephen	Son of Adela, daughter of William I, and Count of Blois	**1135**	**1154**	50	19
	House of Plantagenet				
Henry II	Son of Geoffrey Plantagenet (Angevin) by Matilda, daughter of Henry I	**1154**	**1189**	56	35
Richard I	Coeur de Lion, son of Henry II, crusader	**1189**	**1199**	42	10
John	Lackland, son of Henry II, signed Magna Carta, 1215	**1199**	**1216**	50	17
Henry III	Son of John, acceded at 9, under regency until 1227	**1216**	**1272**	65	56
Edward I	Longshanks, son of Henry III	**1272**	**1307**	68	35
Edward II	Son of Edward I, deposed by Parliament, 1327	**1307**	**1327**	43	20
Edward III	Of Windsor, son of Edward II	**1327**	**1377**	65	50
Richard II	Grandson of Edward III, minor until 1389, deposed 1399	**1377**	**1400**	33	22
	House of Lancaster				
Henry IV	Son of John of Gaunt, Duke of Lancaster, son of Edward III	**1399**	**1413**	47	13
Henry V	Son of Henry IV, victor of Agincourt	**1413**	**1422**	34	9
Henry VI	Son of Henry V, deposed 1461, died in Tower	**1422**	**1471**	49	39

Name		Began	Died	Age	Rgd
	House of York				
Edward IV	Great-great-grandson of Edward III, son of Duke of York	**1461**	**1483**	40	22
Edward V	Son of Edward IV, murdered in Tower of London	**1483**	**1483**	13	0
Richard III	Crookback, brother of Edward IV, fell at Bosworth Field	**1483**	**1485**	32	2
	House of Tudor				
Henry VII	Son of Edmund Tudor, Earl of Richmond, whose father had married the widow of Henry V; descended from Edward III through his mother, Margaret Beaufort via John of Gaunt. By marriage with daughter of Edward IV he united Lancaster and York	**1485**	**1509**	53	24
Henry VIII	Son of Henry VII, by Elizabeth, daughter of Edward IV	**1509**	**1547**	56	38
Edward VI	Son of Henry VIII, by Jane Seymour, his 3d queen. Ruled under regents. Was forced to name Lady Jane Grey his successor. Council of State proclaimed her queen July 10, 1553. Mary Tudor won Council, was proclaimed queen July 19, 1553. Mary had Lady Jane Grey beheaded for treason, Feb., 1554	**1547**	**1553**	16	6
Mary I	Daughter of Henry VIII, by Catherine of Aragon	**1553**	**1558**	43	5
Elizabeth I	Daughter of Henry VIII, by Anne Boleyn	**1558**	**1603**	69	44

Great Britain

Name		Began	Died	Age	Rgd
	House of Stuart				
James I	James VI of Scotland, son of Mary, Queen of Scots. *First to call himself King of Great Britain. This became official with the Act of Union, 1707*	**1603**	**1625**	59	22
Charles I	Only surviving son of James I; beheaded Jan. 30, 1649	**1625**	**1649**	48	24
	Commonwealth, 1649-1660				
	Council of State, 1649; Protectorate, 1653				
The Cromwells	Oliver Cromwell, Lord Protector	**1653**	**1658**	59	—
	Richard Cromwell, son, Lord Protector, resigned May 25, 1659	**1658**	**1712**	86	—
	House of Stuart (Restored)				
Charles II	Eldest son of Charles I, died without issue	**1660**	**1685**	55	25
James II	2d son of Charles I. Deposed 1688. Interregnum Dec. 11, 1688, to Feb. 13, 1689	**1685**	**1701**	68	3
William III	Son of William, Prince of Orange, by Mary, daughter of Charles I	**1689**	**1702**	51	13
and Mary II	Eldest daughter of James II and wife of William III		**1694**	33	6
Anne	2d daughter of James II	**1702**	**1714**	49	12
	House of Hanover				
George I	Son of Elector of Hanover, by Sophia, granddaughter of James I	**1714**	**1727**	67	13
George II	Only son of George I, married Caroline of Brandenburg	**1727**	**1760**	77	33
George III	Grandson of George II, married Charlotte of Mecklenburg	**1760**	**1820**	81	59
George IV	Eldest son of George III, Prince Regent, from Feb. 1811	**1820**	**1830**	67	10
William IV	3d son of George III, married Adelaide of Saxe-Meiningen	**1830**	**1837**	71	7
Victoria	Daughter of Edward, 4th son of George III; married (1840) Prince Albert of Saxe-Coburg and Gotha, who became Prince Consort	**1837**	**1901**	81	63
	House of Saxe-Coburg and Gotha				
Edward VII	Eldest son of Victoria, married Alexandra, Princess of Denmark	**1901**	**1910**	68	9
	House of Windsor				
	Name Adopted July 17, 1917				
George V	2d son of Edward VII, married Princess Mary of Teck	**1910**	**1936**	70	25
Edward VIII	Eldest son of George V; acceded Jan. 20, 1936, abdicated Dec. 11	**1936**	**1972**	77	1
George VI	2d son of George V; married Lady Elizabeth Bowes-Lyon	**1936**	**1952**	56	15
Elizabeth II	Elder daughter of George VI, acceded Feb. 6, 1952	**1952**	**—**	—	—

Rulers of Scotland

Kenneth I MacAlpin was the first Scot to rule both Scots and Picts, AD 846.

Duncan I was the first general ruler, 1034. Macbeth seized the kingdom 1040, was slain by Duncan's son, Malcolm III MacDuncan (Canmore), 1057.

Malcolm married Margaret, Saxon princess who had fled from the Normans. Queen Margaret introduced English language and English monastic customs. She was canonized, 1250. Her son Edgar, 1097, moved the court to Edinburgh. His brothers Alexander I and David I succeeded. Malcolm IV, the Maiden, 1153, grandson of David I, was followed by his brother, William the Lion, 1165, whose son was Alexander II, 1214. The latter's son, Alexander III, 1249, defeated the Norse and regained the Hebrides. When he died, 1286, his granddaughter, Margaret, child of Eric of Norway and grandniece of Edward I of England, known as the Maid of Norway, was chosen ruler, but died 1290, aged 8.

John Baliol, 1292-1296. (Interregnum, 10 years.)

Robert Bruce (The Bruce), 1306-1329, victor at Bannockburn, 1314.

David II, only son of Robert Bruce, ruled 1329-1371.

Robert II, 1371-1390, grandson of Robert Bruce, son of Walter, the Steward of Scotland, was called The Steward, first of the so-called Stuart line.

Robert III, son of Robert II, 1390-1406.

James I, son of Robert III, 1406-1437.

James II, son of James I, 1437-1460.

James III, eldest son of James II, 1460-1488.

James IV, eldest son of James III, 1488-1513.

James V, eldest son of James IV, 1513-1542.

Mary, daughter of James V, born 1542, became queen when one week old; was crowned 1543. Married, 1558, Francis, son of Henry II of France, who became king 1559, died 1560. Mary ruled Scots 1561 until abdication, 1567. She also married Henry Stewart, Lord Darnley (1565), and James, Earl of Bothwell (1567). Imprisoned by Elizabeth I, Mary was beheaded 1587.

James VI, 1566-1625, son of Mary and Lord Darnley, became King of England on death of Elizabeth in 1603. Although the thrones were thus united, the legislative union of Scotland and England was not effected until the Act of Union, May 1, 1707.

Prime Ministers of Great Britain

Designations in parentheses describe each government;
W=Whig; T=Tory; Cl=Coalition; P=Peelite; L=Liberal; C=Conservative; La=Labour.

Sir Robert Walpole (W)	1721-1742
Earl of Wilmington (W)	1742-1743
Henry Pelham (W)	1743-1754
Duke of Newcastle (W)	1754-1756
Duke of Devonshire (W)	1756-1757
Duke of Newcastle (W)	1757-1762
Earl of Bute (T)	1762-1763
George Grenville (W)	1763-1765
Marquess of Rockingham (W)	1765-1766
William Pitt the Elder (Earl of Chatham) (W)	1766-1768
Duke of Grafton (W)	1768-1770
Frederick North (Lord North) (T)	1770-1782
Marquess of Rockingham (W)	1782
Earl of Shelburne (W)	1782-1783
Duke of Portland (Cl)	1783
William Pitt the Younger (T).	1783-1801
Henry Addington (T)	1801-1804
William Pitt the Younger (T).	1804-1806
William Wyndham Grenville, Baron Grenville (W)	1806-1807
Duke of Portland (T)	1807-1809
Spencer Perceval (T)	1809-1812
Earl of Liverpool (T)	1812-1827
George Canning (T)	1827
Viscount Goderich (T)	1827-1828
Duke of Wellington (T)	1828-1830
Earl Grey (W)	1830-1834
Viscount Melbourne (W)	1834
Sir Robert Peel (T)	1834-1835
Viscount Melbourne (W)	1835-1841
Sir Robert Peel (T)	1841-1846
Lord (later Earl) John Russell (W)	1846-1852
Earl of Derby (T)	1852
Earl of Aberdeen (P)	1852-1855
Viscount Palmerston (Li)	1855-1858
Earl of Derby (C)	1858-1859
Viscount Palmerston (Li)	1859-1865
Earl Russell (Li)	1865-1866
Earl of Derby (C)	1866-1868
Benjamin Disraeli (C)	1868
William E. Gladstone (Li)	1868-1874
Benjamin Disraeli (C)	1874-1880
William E. Gladstone (Li)	1880-1885
Marquess of Salisbury (C)	1885-1886
William E. Gladstone (Li)	1886
Marquess of Salisbury (C)	1886-1892
William E. Gladstone (Li)	1892-1894
Earl of Rosebery (Li)	1894-1895
Marquess of Salisbury (C)	1895-1902
Arthur J. Balfour (C)	1902-1905
Sir Henry Campbell-Bannerman (Li)	1905-1908
Herbert H. Asquith (Li)	1908-1915
Herbert H. Asquith (Cl)	1915-1916
David Lloyd George (Cl)	1916-1922
Andrew Bonar Law (C)	1922-1923
Stanley Baldwin (C)	1923-1924
James Ramsay MacDonald (La)	1924
Stanley Baldwin (C)	1924-1929
James Ramsay MacDonald (La)	1929-1931
James Ramsay MacDonald (Cl)	1931-1935
Stanley Baldwin (Cl)	1935-1937
Neville Chamberlain (Cl)	1937-1940
Winston Churchill (Cl)	1940-1945
Winston Churchill (C)	1945
Clement Attlee (La)	1945-1951
Sir Winston Churchill (C)	1951-1955
Sir Anthony Eden (C)	1955-1957
Harold Macmillan (C)	1957-1963
Sir Alec Douglas-Home (C)	1963-1964
Harold Wilson (La)	1964-1970
Edward Heath (C)	1970-1974
Harold Wilson (La)	1974-1976
James Callaghan (La)	1976-1979
Margaret Thatcher (C)	1979-1990
John Major (C)	1990-1997
Tony Blair (La)	1997-

Historical Periods of Japan

Yamato	c. 300-592	Conquest of Yamato plain c. AD 300.
Asuka	592-710	Accession of Empress Suiko, 592.
Nara	710-794	Completion of Heijo (Nara), 710; the capital moves to Nagaoka, 784.
Heian	794-1185	Completion of Heian (Kyoto), 794.
Fujiwara	858-1160	Fujiwara-no-Yoshifusa becomes regent, 858.
Taira	1160-1185	Taira-no-Kiyomori assumes control, 1160; Minamoto-no-Yoritomo victor over Taira, 1185.
Kamakura	1192-1333	Yoritomo becomes shogun, 1192.
Namboku	1334-1392	Restoration of Emperor Godaigo, 1334; Southern Court established by Godaigo at Yoshino, 1336.
Ashikaga	1338-1573	Ashikaga Takauji becomes shogun, 1338.
Muromachi	1392-1573	Unification of Southern and Northern Courts, 1392.
Sengoku	1467-1600	Beginning of the Onin war, 1467.
Momoyama	1573-1603	Oda Nobunaga enters Kyoto, 1568; Nobunaga deposes last Ashikaga shogun, 1573; Tokugawa Ieyasu victor at Sekigahara, 1600.
Edo	1603-1867	Ieyasu becomes shogun, 1603.
Meiji	1868-1912	Enthronement of Emperor Mutsuhito (Meiji), 1867; Meiji Restoration and Charter Oath, 1868.
Taisho	1912-1926	Accession of Emperor Yoshihito, 1912.
Showa	1926-1989	Accession of Emperor Hirohito, 1926.
Heisei	1989-	Accession of Emperor Akihito, 1989.

Rulers of France: Kings, Queens, Presidents

Caesar to Charlemagne

Julius Caesar subdued the Gauls, native tribes of Gaul (France), 58 to 51 BC. The Romans ruled 500 years. The Franks, a Teutonic tribe, reached the Somme from the East c. AD 250. By the 5th century the Merovingian Franks ousted the Romans. In 451, with the help of Visigoths, Burgundians and others, they defeated Attila and the Huns at Chalons-sur-Marne.

Childeric I became leader of the Merovingians 458. His son Clovis I (Chlodwig, Ludwig, Louis), crowned 481, founded the dynasty. After defeating the Alemanni (Germans) 496, he was baptized a Christian and made Paris his capital. His line ruled until Childeric III was deposed, 751.

The West Merovingians were called Neustrians, the eastern Austrasians. Pepin of Herstal (687-714), major domus, or head of the palace, of Austrasia, took over Neustria as dux (leader) of the Franks. Pepin's son, Charles, called Martel (the Hammer), defeated the Saracens at Tours-Poitiers, 732; was succeeded by his son, Pepin the Short, 741, who deposed Childeric III and ruled as king until 768.

His son, Charlemagne, or Charles the Great (742-814), became king of the Franks, 768, with his brother Carloman, who died 771. Charlemagne ruled France, Germany, parts of Italy, Spain, and Austria, and enforced Christianity. Crowned Emperor of the Romans by Pope Leo III in St. Peter's, Rome, Dec. 25, 800. Succeeded by son, Louis I the Pious, 814. At death, 840, Louis left empire to sons, Lothair (Roman emperor); Pepin I (king of Aquitaine); Louis II (of Germany); Charles the Bald (France). They quarreled and, by the peace of Verdun, 843, divided the empire.

Date in bold is year of accession.

The Carolingians

843 Charles I (the Bald); Roman Emperor, 875
877 Louis II (the Stammerer), son
879 Louis III (died 882) and Carloman, brothers
885 Charles II (the Fat); Roman Emperor, 881
888 Eudes (Odo), elected by nobles
898 Charles III (the Simple), son of Louis II, defeated by
922 Robert, brother of Eudes, killed in war
923 Rudolph (Raoul), Duke of Burgundy
936 Louis IV, son of Charles III
954 Lothair, son, aged 13, defeated by Capet
986 Louis V (the Sluggard), left no heirs

The Capets

987 Hugh Capet, son of Hugh the Great
996 Robert II (the Wise), his son
1031 Henry I, his son
1060 Philip I (the Fair), son
1108 Louis VI (the Fat), son
1137 Louis VII (the Younger), son
1180 Philip II (Augustus), son, crowned at Reims
1223 Louis VIII (the Lion), son
1226 Louis IX, son, crusader; Louis IX (1214-1270) reigned 44 years, arbitrated disputes with English King Henry III; led crusades, 1248 (captured in Egypt 1250) and 1270, when he died of plague in Tunis. Canonized 1297 as St. Louis.
1270 Philip III (the Hardy), son
1285 Philip IV (the Fair), son, king at 17
1314 Louis X (the Headstrong), son. His posthumous son, John I, lived only 7 days
1316 Philip V (the Tall), brother of Louis X
1322 Charles IV (the Fair), brother of Louis X

House of Valois

1328 Philip VI (of Valois), grandson of Philip III
1350 John II (the Good), his son, retired to England
1364 Charles V (the Wise), son
1380 Charles VI (the Beloved), son
1422 Charles VII (the Victorious), son. In 1429 Joan of Arc (Jeanne d'Arc) promised Charles to oust the English, who occupied northern France. Joan won at Orleans and Patay and had Charles crowned at Reims, July 17, 1429. Joan was captured May 24, 1430, and executed May 30, 1431, at Rouen for heresy. Charles ordered her rehabilitation, effected 1455.
1461 Louis XI (the Cruel), son, civil reformer
1483 Charles VIII (the Affable), son
1498 Louis XII, great-grandson of Charles V
1515 Francis I, of Angouleme, nephew, son-in-law. Francis I (1494-1547) reigned 32 years, fought 4 big wars, was patron of the arts, aided Cellini, del Sarto, Leonardo da Vinci, Rabelais, embellished Fontainebleau.
1547 Henry II, son, killed at a joust in a tournament. He was the husband of Catherine de Medicis (1519-1589) and the lover of Diane de Poitiers (1499-1566). Catherine was born in Florence, daughter of Lorenzo de Medici. By her marriage to Henry II she became the mother of Francis II, Charles IX, Henry III and Queen Margaret (Reine Margot), wife of Henry IV. She persuaded Charles IX to order the massacre of Huguenots on the Feast of St. Bartholomew, Aug. 24, 1572, the day her daughter was married to Henry of Navarre.
1559 Francis II, son. In 1548, Mary, Queen of Scots since infancy, was betrothed when 6 to Francis, aged 4. They were married 1558. Francis died 1560, aged 16; Mary ruled Scotland, abdicated 1567.
1560 Charles IX, brother
1574 Henry III, brother, assassinated

House of Bourbon

1589 Henry IV, of Navarre, assassinated. Henry IV made enemies when he gave tolerance to Protestants by Edict of Nantes, 1598. He was grandson of Queen Margaret of Navarre, literary patron. He married Margaret of Valois, daughter of Henry II and Catherine de Medicis; was divorced; in 1600 married Marie de Medicis, who became Regent of France, 1610-1617, for her son, Louis XIII, but was exiled by Richelieu, 1631.
1610 Louis XIII (the Just), son. Louis XIII (1601-1643) married Anne of Austria. His ministers were Cardinals Richelieu and Mazarin.
1643 Louis XIV (The Grand Monarch), son. Louis XIV was king 72 years. He exhausted a prosperous country in wars for thrones and territory. By revoking the Edict of Nantes (1685) he caused the emigration of the Huguenots. He said: "I am the state."
1715 Louis XV, great-grandson. Louis XV married a Polish princess; lost Canada to the English. His favorites, Mme. Pompadour and Mme. Du Barry, influenced policies. Noted for saying "After me, the deluge."
1774 Louis XVI, grandson; married Marie Antoinette, daughter of Empress Maria Therese of Austria. King and queen beheaded by Revolution, 1793. Their son, called Louis XVII, died in prison, never ruled.

First Republic

1792 National Convention of the French Revolution
1795 Directory, under Barras and others
1799 Consulate, Napoleon Bonaparte, first consul. Elected consul for life, 1802.

First Empire

1804 Napoleon I (Napoleon Bonaparte), emperor. Josephine (de Beauharnais), empress, 1804-1809; Marie Louise, empress, 1810-1814. Her son, Francois (1811-1832), titular King of Rome, later Duke de Reichstadt and "Napoleon II," never ruled. Napoleon abdicated 1814, died 1821.

Bourbons Restored

1814 Louis XVIII, king; brother of Louis XVI
1824 Charles X, brother; reactionary; deposed by the July Revolution, 1830

House of Orleans

1830 Louis-Philippe, the "citizen king"

Second Republic

1848 Louis Napoleon Bonaparte, president, nephew of Napoleon I.

Second Empire

1852 Napoleon III (Louis Napoleon Bonaparte), emperor; Eugenie (de Montijo), empress. Lost Franco-Prussian war, deposed 1870. Son, Prince Imperial (1856-1879), died in Zulu War. Eugenie died 1920.

Third Republic—Presidents

1871 Thiers, Louis Adolphe (1797-1877)
1873 MacMahon, Marshal Patrice M. de (1808-1893)
1879 Grevy, Paul J. (1807-1891)
1887 Sadi-Carnot, M. (1837-1894), assassinated
1894 Casimir-Perier, Jean P. P. (1847-1907)
1895 Faure, François Felix (1841-1899)
1899 Loubet, Emile (1838-1929)
1906 Fallieres, C. Armand (1841-1931)
1913 Poincare, Raymond (1860-1934)
1920 Deschanel, Paul (1856-1922)
1920 Millerand, Alexandre (1859-1943)
1924 Doumergue, Gaston (1863-1937)
1931 Doumer, Paul (1857-1932), assassinated
1932 Lebrun, Albert (1871-1950), resigned 1940
1940 Vichy govt. under German armistice: Henri Philippe Petain (1856-1951), Chief of State, 1940-1944. Provisional govt. after liberation: Charles de Gaulle (1890-1970), Oct. 1944-Jan. 21, 1946; Felix Gouin (1884-1977), Jan. 23, 1946; Georges Bidault (1899-1983), June 24, 1946.

Fourth Republic—Presidents

1947 Auriol, Vincent (1884-1966)
1954 Coty, Rene (1882-1962)

Fifth Republic—Presidents

1959 De Gaulle, Charles Andre J. M. (1890-1970)
1969 Pompidou, Georges (1911-1974)
1974 Giscard d'Estaing, Valery (1926-)
1981 Mitterrand, François (1916-1996)
1995 Chirac, Jacques (1932-)

Rulers of Middle Europe; Rise and Fall of Dynasties; Rulers of Germany

Carolingian Dynasty

Charles the Great, or Charlemagne, ruled France, Italy, and Middle Europe; established Ostmark (later Austria); crowned Roman emperor by pope in Rome, AD 800; died 814.

Louis I (Ludwig) the Pious, son; crowned by Charlemagne 814; died 840.

Louis II, the German, son; succeeded to East Francia (Germany) 843-876.

Charles the Fat, son; inherited East Francia and West Francia (France) 876, reunited empire, crowned emperor by pope 881, deposed 887.

Arnulf, nephew, 887-899. Partition of empire.

Louis the Child, 899-911, last direct descendant of Charlemagne.

Conrad I, duke of Franconia, first elected German king, 911-918, founded House of Franconia.

Saxon Dynasty; First Reich

Henry I, the Fowler, duke of Saxony, 919-936.

Otto I, the Great, 936-973, son; crowned Holy Roman Emperor by pope, 962.

Otto II, 973-983, son; failed to oust Greeks and Arabs from Sicily.

Otto III, 983-1002, son; crowned emperor at 16.

Henry II, the Saint, duke of Bavaria, 1002-1024, great-grandson of Otto the Great.

House of Franconia

Conrad II, 1024-1039, elected king of Germany.

Henry III, the Black, 1039-1056, son; deposed 3 popes; annexed Burgundy.

Henry IV, 1056-1106, son; regency by his mother, Agnes of Poitou. Banned by Pope Gregory VII, he did penance at Canossa.

Henry V, 1106-1125, son; last of Salic House.

Lothair, duke of Saxony, 1125-1137. Crowned emperor in Rome, 1134.

House of Hohenstaufen

Conrad III, duke of Swabia, 1138-1152. In 2d Crusade.

Frederick I, Barbarossa, 1152-1190; Conrad's nephew.

Henry VI, 1190-1196, took lower Italy from Normans. Son became king of Sicily.

Philip of Swabia, 1197-1208, brother.

Otto IV, of House of Welf, 1198-1215; deposed.

Frederick II, 1215-1250, son of Henry VI; king of Sicily; crowned king of Jerusalem in 5th Crusade.

Conrad IV, 1250-1254, son; lost lower Italy to Charles of Anjou.

Conradin, 1252-1268, son, king of Jerusalem and Sicily, beheaded. Last Hohenstaufen.

Interregnum, 1254-1273, Rise of the Electors.

Transition

Rudolph I of Hapsburg, 1273-1291, defeated King Ottocar II of Bohemia. Bequeathed duchy of Austria to eldest son, Albert.

Adolph of Nassau, 1292-1298, killed in war with Albert of Austria.

Albert I, king of Germany, 1298-1308, son of Rudolph.

Henry VII, of Luxemburg, 1308-1313, crowned emperor in Rome. Seized Bohemia, 1310.

Louis IV of Bavaria (Wittelsbach), 1314-1347. Also elected was Frederick of Austria, 1314-1330 (Hapsburg). Abolition of papal sanction for election of Holy Roman Emperor.

Charles IV, of Luxemburg, 1347-1378, grandson of Henry VII, German emperor and king of Bohemia, Lombardy, Burgundy; took Mark of Brandenburg.

Wenceslaus, 1378-1400, deposed.

Rupert, Duke of Palatine, 1400-1410.

Sigismund, 1411-1437.

Hungary

Stephen I, house of Arpad, 997-1038. Crowned king 1000; converted Magyars; canonized 1083. After several centuries of feuds Charles Robert of Anjou became Charles I, 1308-1342.

Louis I, the Great, son, 1342-1382; joint ruler of Poland with Casimir III, 1370. Defeated Turks.

Mary, daughter, 1382-1395, ruled with husband. Sigismund of Luxemburg, 1387-1437, also king of Bohemia. As bro. of Wenceslaus he succeeded Rupert as Holy Roman Emperor, 1410.

Albert, 1438-1439, son-in-law of Sigismund; also Roman emperor as Albert II *(see under Hapsburg)*.

Ulaszlo I of Poland, 1440-1444.

Ladislaus V, posthumous son of Albert II, 1444-1457. John Hunyadi (Hunyadi Janos), governor (1446-1452), fought Turks, Czechs; died 1456.

Matthias I (Corvinus), son of Hunyadi, 1458-1490. Shared rule of Bohemia, captured Vienna, 1485, annexed Austria, Styria, Carinthia.

Ulaszlo II (king of Bohemia), 1490-1516.

Louis II, son, aged 10, 1516-1526. Wars with Suleiman, Turk. In 1527 Hungary split between Ferdinand I, Archduke of Austria, bro.-in-law of Louis II, and John Zapolya of Transylvania. After Turkish invasion, 1547, Hungary split between Ferdinand, Prince John Sigismund (Transylvania), and the Turks.

House of Hapsburg

Albert V of Austria, Hapsburg, crowned king of Hungary, Jan. 1438, Roman emperor, March 1438, as Albert II; died 1439.

Frederick III, cousin, 1440-1493. Fought Turks.

Maximilian I, son, 1493-1519. Assumed title of Holy Roman Emperor (German), 1493.

Charles V, grandson, 1519-1556. King of Spain with mother co-regent; crowned Roman emperor at Aix, 1520. Confronted Luther at Worms; attempted church reform and religious conciliation; abdicated 1556.

Ferdinand I, king of Bohemia, 1526, of Hungary, 1527; disputed. German king, 1531. Crowned Roman emperor on abdication of brother Charles V, 1556.

Maximilian II, son, 1564-1576.

Rudolph II, son, 1576-1612.

Matthias, brother, 1612-1619, king of Bohemia and Hungary.

Ferdinand II of Styria, king of Bohemia, 1617, of Hungary, 1618, Roman emperor, 1619. Bohemian Protestants deposed him, elected Frederick V of Palatine, starting Thirty Years War.

Ferdinand III, son, king of Hungary, 1625, Bohemia, 1627, Roman emperor, 1637. Peace of Westphalia, 1648, ended war. Leopold I, 1658-1705; Joseph I, 1705-1711; Charles VI, 1711-1740.

Maria Theresa, daughter, 1740-1780, Archduchess of Austria, queen of Hungary; ousted pretender, Charles VII, crowned 1742; in 1745 obtained election of her husband Francis I as Roman emperor and co-regent (d. 1765). Fought Seven Years' War with Frederick II of Prussia. Mother of Marie Antoinette.

Joseph II, son, 1765-1790, Roman emperor, reformer; powers restricted by Empress Maria Theresa until her death, 1780. First partition of Poland. Leopold II, 1790-1792.

Francis II, son, 1792-1835. Fought Napoleon. Proclaimed first hereditary emperor of Austria, 1804. Forced to abdicate as Roman emperor, 1806; last use of title. Ferdinand I, son, 1835-1848, abdicated during revolution.

Austro-Hungarian Monarchy

Francis Joseph I, nephew, 1848-1916, emperor of Austria, king of Hungary. Dual monarchy of Austria-Hungary formed, 1867. After assassination of heir, Archduke Francis Ferdinand, June 28, 1914, Austrian diplomacy precipitated World War I.

Charles I, grand-nephew, 1916-1918, last emperor of Austria and king of Hungary. Abdicated Nov. 11-13, 1918, died 1922.

Rulers of Prussia

Nucleus of Prussia was the Mark of Brandenburg. First margrave Albert the Bear (Albrecht), 1134-1170. First Hohenzollern margrave was Frederick, burgrave of Nuremberg, 1417-1440.

Frederick William, 1640-1688, the Great Elector. Son, Frederick III, 1688-1713, crowned King Frederick of Prussia, 1701.

Frederick William I, son, 1713-1740.

Frederick II, the Great, son, 1740-1786, annexed Silesia, part of Austria.

Frederick William II, nephew, 1786-1797.

Frederick William III, son, 1797-1840. Napoleonic wars.

Frederick William IV, son, 1840-1861. Uprising of 1848 and first parliament and constitution.

Second and Third Reich

William I, 1861-1888, brother. Annexation of Schleswig and Hanover; Franco-Prussian war, 1870-1871, proclamation of German Reich, Jan. 18, 1871, at Versailles; William, German emperor (Deutscher Kaiser), Bismarck, chancellor.

Frederick III, son, 1888.

William II, son, 1888-1918. Led Germany in World War I, abdicated as German emperor and king of Prussia, Nov. 9, 1918. Died in exile in Netherlands, June 4, 1941. Minor rulers of Bavaria, Saxony, Wurttemberg also abdicated.

Germany proclaimed republic at Weimar, July 1, 1919. Presidents included: Frederick Ebert, 1919-1925; Paul von Hindenburg-Beneckendorff, 1925, reelected 1932, d. Aug. 2, 1934. Adolf Hitler, chancellor, chosen successor as Leader-Chancellor (Fuehrer-Reichskanzler) of Third Reich. Annexed Austria, Mar. 1938. Precipitated World War II, 1939-1945. Suicide Apr. 30, 1945.

Germany After 1945

Following World War II, Germany was split between democratic West and Soviet-dominated East. West German chancellors: Konrad Adenauer, 1949-1963; Ludwig Erhard, 1963-1966; Kurt Georg Kiesinger, 1966-1969; Willy Brandt, 1969-1974; Helmut Schmidt, 1974-1982; Helmut Kohl, 1982-1990. East German Communist party leaders: Walter Ulbricht, 1946-1971; Erich Honecker, 1971-1989; Egon Krenz, 1989-1990.

Germany reunited Oct. 3, 1990. Post-reunification chancellors: Helmut Kohl, 1990-1998; Gerhard Schröder, 1998- .

Rulers of Poland

House of Piasts

Miesko I, 962?-992; Poland Christianized 966. Expansion under 3 Boleslavs: I, 992-1025, son, crowned king 1024; II, 1058-1079, great-grandson, exiled after killing bishop Stanislav who became chief patron saint of Poland; III, 1106-1138, nephew, divided Poland among 4 sons, eldest suzerain.

1138-1306, feudal division. 1226 founding in Prussia of military order Teutonic Knights. 1226 invasion by Tartars/Mongols.

Vladislav I, 1306-1333, reunited most Polish territories, crowned king 1320. Casimir III the Great, 1333-1370, son, developed economic, cultural life, foreign policy.

House of Anjou

Louis I, 1370-1382, nephew/was also Louis I of Hungary.

Jadwiga, 1384-1399, daughter, married 1386 Jagiello, Grand Duke of Lithuania.

House of Jagiellonians

Vladislav II, 1386-1434, Christianized Lithuania, founded personal union between Poland & Lithuania. Defeated 1410 Teutonic Knights at Grunwald.

Vladislav III, 1434-1444, son, simultaneously king of Hungary. Fought Turks, killed 1444 in battle of Varna.

Casimir IV, 1446-1492, brother, competed with Hapsburgs, put son Vladislav on throne of Bohemia, later also of Hungary (Ulaszlo II).

Sigismund I, 1506-1548, son, patronized science and arts, his and son's reign "Golden Age."

Sigismund II, 1548-1572, son, established 1569 real union of Poland and Lithuania (lasted until 1795).

Elective Kings

Polish nobles in 1572 proclaimed Poland a republic headed by king to be elected by whole nobility.

Stephen Batory, 1576-1586, duke of Transylvania, married Ann, sister of Sigismund II August. Fought Russians.

Sigismund III Vasa, 1587-1632, nephew of Sigismund II. 1592-1598 also king of Sweden. His generals fought Russians, Turks.

Vladislav II Vasa, 1632-1648, son. Fought Russians.

John II Casimir Vasa, 1648-1668, brother. Fought Cossacks, Swedes, Russians, Turks, Tatars (the "Deluge"). Abdicated 1668.

John III Sobieski, 1674-1696. Won Vienna from besieging Turks, 1683.

Stanislav II, 1764-1795, last king. Encouraged reforms; 1791 1st modern Constitution in Europe. 1772, 1793, 1795 Poland partitioned among Russia, Prussia, Austria. Unsuccessful insurrection against foreign invasion 1794 under Kosciuszko, American-Polish general.

1795-1918: Poland Under Foreign Rule

1807-1815 Grand Duchy of Warsaw created by Napoleon I, Frederick August of Saxony grand duke.

1815 Congress of Vienna proclaimed part of Poland "Kingdom" in personal union with Russia.

Polish uprisings: 1830 against Russia; 1846, 1848 against Austria; 1863 against Russia—all repressed.

1918-1939: Second Republic

1918-1922 Head of State Jozef Pilsudski. Presidents: Gabriel Narutowicz 1922, assassinated; Stanislav Wojciechowski 1922-1926, had to abdicate after Pilsudski's coup d'état; Ignacy Moscicki, 1926-1939, ruled (with Pilsudski until his death, 1935) as virtual dictator.

1939-1945: Poland Under Foreign Occupation

Nazi aggression Sept. 1939. Polish government-in-exile, first in France, then in England. Vladislav Raczkiewicz president; Gen. Vladislav Sikorski, then Stanislav Mikolajczyk, prime ministers. Soviet-sponsored Polish Committee of National Liberation proclaimed at Lublin July 1944, transformed into government Jan. 1, 1945.

Poland After 1945

In the late 1940s, Poland came increasingly under Soviet control. Communist party ruled in Poland until Aug. 1989, when democratic Solidarity party gained control of government. Solidarity leader Lech Walesa was elected president, Nov. 1990; succeeded by former Communist Aleksander Kwasniewski, Nov. 1995.

Rulers of Denmark, Sweden, Norway

Denmark

Earliest rulers invaded Britain; King Canute, who ruled in London 1016-1035, was most famous. The Valdemars furnished kings until the 15th century. In 1282 the Danes won the first national assembly, Danehof, from King Erik V.

Most redoubtable medieval character was Margaret, daughter of Valdemar IV, born 1353, married at 10 to King Haakon VI of Norway. In 1376 she had her first infant son Olaf made king of Denmark. After his death, 1387, she was regent of Denmark and Norway. In 1388 Sweden accepted her as sovereign. In 1389 she made her grand-nephew, Duke Erik of Pomerania, titular king of Denmark, Sweden, and Norway, with herself as regent. In 1397 she effected the Union of Kalmar of the three kingdoms and had Erik VII crowned. In 1439 the three kingdoms deposed him and elected, 1440, Christopher of Bavaria king (Christopher III). On his death, 1448, the union broke up.

Succeeding rulers were unable to enforce their claims as rulers of Sweden until 1520, when Christian II conquered Sweden. He was thrown out 1522, and in 1523 Gustavus Vasa united Sweden. Denmark continued to dominate Norway until the Napoleonic wars, when Frederick VI, 1808-1839, joined the Napoleonic cause after Britain had destroyed the Danish fleet, 1807. In 1814 he was forced to cede Norway to Sweden and Helgoland to Britain, receiving Lauenburg. Successors Christian VIII, 1839; Frederick VII, 1848; Christian IX, 1863; Frederick VIII, 1906; Christian X, 1912; Frederick IX, 1947; Margrethe II, 1972.

Sweden

Early kings ruled at Uppsala, but did not dominate the country. Sverker, c1130-c1156, united the Swedes and Goths. In 1435 Sweden obtained the Riksdag, or parliament. After the Union of Kalmar, 1397, the Danes either ruled or harried the country until Christian II of Denmark conquered it anew, 1520. This led to a rising under Gustavus Vasa, who ruled Sweden 1523-1560, and established an independent kingdom. Charles IX, 1599-1611, crowned 1604, conquered Moscow. Gustavus II Adolphus, 1611-1632, was called the Lion of the North. Later rulers: Christina, 1632; Charles X Gustavus, 1654; Charles XI, 1660; Charles XII (invader of Russia and Poland, defeated at Poltava, June 28, 1709), 1697; Ulrika Eleanora, sister, elected queen 1718; Frederick I (of Hesse), her husband, 1720; Adolphus Frederick, 1751; Gustavus III, 1771; Gustavus IV Adolphus, 1792; Charles XIII, 1809. (Union with Norway began 1814.) Charles XIV John, 1818 (he was Jean Bernadotte, Napoleon's Prince of Ponte Corvo, elected 1810 to succeed Charles XIII); he founded the present dynasty: Oscar I, 1844; Charles XV, 1859; Oscar II, 1872; Gustavus V, 1907; Gustav VI Adolf, 1950; Carl XVI Gustaf, 1973.

Norway

Overcoming many rivals, Harald Haarfager, 872-930, conquered Norway, Orkneys, and Shetlands; Olaf I, great-grandson, 995-1000, brought Christianity into Norway, Iceland, and Greenland. In 1035 Magnus the Good also became king of Denmark. Haakon V, 1299-1319, had married his daughter to Erik of Sweden. Their son, Magnus, became ruler of Norway and Sweden at 6. His son, Haakon VI, married Margaret of Denmark; their son Olaf IV became king of Norway and Denmark, followed by Margaret's regency and the Union of Kalmar, 1397.

In 1450 Norway became subservient to Denmark. Christian IV, 1588-1648, founded Christiania, now Oslo. After Napoleonic wars, when Denmark ceded Norway to Sweden, a strong nationalist movement forced recognition of Norway as an independent kingdom united with Sweden under the Swedish kings, 1814-1905. In 1905 the union was dissolved and Prince Charles of Denmark became Haakon VII. He died Sept. 21, 1957; succeeded by son, Olav V. Olav V died Jan. 17, 1991; succeeded by son, Harald V.

Rulers of the Netherlands and Belgium

The Netherlands (Holland)

William Frederick, Prince of Orange, led a revolt against French rule, 1813; crowned king, 1815. Belgium seceded Oct. 4, 1830, after a revolt. The secession was ratified by the two kingdoms by treaty, Apr. 19, 1839.

Succession: William II, son, 1840; William III, son, 1849; Wilhelmina, daughter of William III and his 2d wife Princess Emma of Waldeck, 1890; Wilhelmina abdicated, Sept. 4, 1948, in favor of daughter, Juliana. Juliana abdicated, Apr. 30, 1980, in favor of daughter, Beatrix.

Belgium

A national congress elected Prince Leopold of Saxe-Coburg as king; he took the throne July 21, 1831, as Leopold I. Succession: Leopold II, son, 1865; Albert I, nephew of Leopold II, 1909; Leopold III, son of Albert, 1934; Prince Charles, Regent 1944; Leopold returned 1950, yielded powers to son Baudouin, Prince Royal, Aug. 6, 1950, abdicated July 16, 1951. Baudouin I took throne July 17, 1951, died July 31, 1993; succeeded by brother, Albert II.

Roman Rulers

Listed up to the end of the Empire in the West. Rulers in the East sat in Constantinople and, briefly, in Nicaea, until the capture of Constantinople by the Turks in 1453, when Byzantium was succeeded by the Ottoman Empire.

BC

The Kingdom

753 Romulus (Quirinus)
716 Numa Pompilius
673 Tullus Hostilius
640 Ancus Marcius
616 L. Tarquinius Priscus
578 Servius Tullius
534 L. Tarquinius Superbus

The Republic

509 Consulate established
509 Quaestorship instituted
498 Dictatorship introduced
494 Plebeian Tribunate created
494 Plebeian Aedileship created
444 Consular Tribunate organized
435 Censorship instituted
366 Praetorship established
366 Curule Aedileship created
362 Military Tribunate elected
326 Proconsulate introduced
311 Naval Duumvirate elected
217 Dictatorship of Fabius Maximus
133 Tribunate of Tiberius Gracchus
123 Tribunate of Gaius Gracchus
82 Dictatorship of Sulla
60 First Triumvirate formed (Caesar, Pompeius, Crassus)
46 Dictatorship of Caesar
43 Second Triumvirate formed (Octavianus, Antonius, Lepidus)

The Empire

27 Augustus (Gaius Julius Caesar Octavianus)

AD

14 Tiberius I
37 Gaius Caesar (Caligula)
41 Claudius I
54 Nero
68 Galba
69 Galba; Otho, Vitellius
69 Vespasianus
79 Titus
81 Domitianus
96 Nerva
98 Trajanus
117 Hadrianus
138 Antoninus Pius
161 Marcus Aurelius and Lucius Verus
169 Marcus Aurelius (alone)
180 Commodus
193 Pertinax; Julianus I
193 Septimius Severus
211 Caracalla and Geta
212 Caracalla (alone)
217 Macrinus
218 Elagabalus (Heliogabalus)
222 Alexander Severus
235 Maximinus I (the Thracian)
238 Gordianus I and Gordianus II; Pupienus and Balbinus
238 Gordianus III
244 Philippus (the Arabian)
249 Decius
251 Gallus and Volusianus
253 Aemilianus
253 Valerianus and Gallienus
258 Gallienus (alone)
268 Claudius Gothicus
270 Quintillus
270 Aurelianus
275 Tacitus
276 Florianus
276 Probus
282 Carus
283 Carinus and Numerianus
284 Diocletianus
286 Diocletianus and Maximianus
305 Galerius and Constantius I
306 Galerius, Maximinus II, Severus I
307 Galerius, Maximinus II, Constantinus I, Licinius, Maxentius
311 Maximinus II, Constantinus I, Licinius, Maxentius
314 Maximinus II, Constantinus I, Licinius
314 Constantinus I and Licinius
324 Constantinus I (the Great)
337 Constantinus II, Constans I, Constantius II
340 Constantius II and Constans I
350 Constantius II
361 Julianus II (the Apostate)
363 Jovianus

West (Rome) and East (Constantinople)

364 Valentinianus I (West) and Valens (East)
367 Valentinianus I with Gratianus (West) and Valens (East)
375 Gratianus with Valentinianus II (West) and Valens (East)
378 Gratianus with Valentinianus II (West), Theodosius I (East)
383 Valentinianus II (West) and Theodosius I (East)
394 Theodosius I (the Great)
395 Honorius (West) and Arcadius (East)
408 Honorius (West) and Theodosius II (East)
423 Valentinianus III (West) and Theodosius II (East)
450 Valentinianus III (West) and Marcianus (East)
455 Maximus (West), Avitus (West); Marcianus (East)
456 Avitus (West), Marcianus (East)
457 Majorianus (West), Leo I (East)
461 Severus II (West), Leo I (East)
467 Anthemius (West), Leo I (East)
472 Olybrius (West), Leo I (East)
473 Glycerius (West), Leo I (East)
474 Julius Nepos (West), Leo II (East)
475 Romulus Augustulus (West) and Zeno (East)
476 End of Empire in West; Odovacar, King, drops title of Emperor; murdered by King Theodoric of Ostrogoths, 493

MILLENNIUM FACT BOX

The 10 Most Influential People of the Second Millennium

By Arthur M. Schlesinger Jr.

Arthur M. Schlesinger Jr., the Pulitzer Prize-winning historian and writer, is the Albert Schweitzer Professor in the Humanities at the City University of New York. He served as special assistant to the president in the Kennedy administration.

As we anticipate the advent of the third millennium, *The World Almanac* asked Professor Schlesinger whom he considered to be the 10 most influential people of the second millennium. Here are the names he listed, in order of importance.

	Name	Born	Died
1.	William Shakespeare	1564	1616
2.	Isaac Newton	1642	1727
3.	Charles Darwin	1809	1882
4.	Nicolaus Copernicus	1473	1543
5.	Galileo Galilei	1564	1642
6.	Albert Einstein	1879	1955
7.	Christopher Columbus	1451	1506
8.	Abraham Lincoln	1809	1865
9.	Johann Gutenberg	c. 1397	1468
10.	William Harvey	1578	1657

Rulers of Modern Italy

After the fall of Napoleon in 1814, the Congress of Vienna, 1815, restored Italy as a political patchwork, comprising the Kingdom of Naples and Sicily, the Papal States, and smaller units. Piedmont and Genoa were awarded to Sardinia, ruled by King Victor Emmanuel I of Savoy.

United Italy emerged under the leadership of Camillo, Count di Cavour (1810-1861), Sardinian prime minister. Agitation was led by Giuseppe Mazzini (1805-1872) and Giuseppe Garibaldi (1807-1882), soldier; Victor Emmanuel I abdicated 1821. After a brief regency for a brother, Charles Albert was king 1831-1849, abdicating when defeated by the Austrians at Novara. Succeeded by Victor Emmanuel II, 1849-1861.

In 1859 France forced Austria to cede Lombardy to Sardinia, which gave rights to Savoy and Nice to France. In 1860 Garibaldi led 1,000 volunteers in a spectacular campaign, took Sicily and expelled the King of Naples. In 1860 the House of Savoy annexed Tuscany, Parma, Modena, Romagna, the Two Sicilys, the Marches, and Umbria. Victor Emmanuel assumed the title of King of Italy at Turin Mar. 17, 1861. In 1866 he allied with Prussia in the Austro-Prussian War, with Prussia's victory received Venetia. On Sept. 20, 1870, his troops under Gen. Raffaele entered Rome and took over the Papal States, ending the temporal power of the Roman Catholic Church.

Succession: Umberto I, 1878, assassinated 1900; Victor Emmanuel III, 1900, abdicated 1946, died 1947; Humbert II, 1946, ruled a month. In 1921 Benito Mussolini (1883-1945) formed the Fascist party; he became prime minister Oct. 31, 1922. He entered World War II as an ally of Hitler. He was deposed July 25, 1943.

At a plebiscite June 2, 1946, Italy voted for a republic; Premier Alcide de Gasperi became chief of state June 13, 1946. On June 28, 1946, the Constituent Assembly elected Enrico de Nicola, Liberal, provisional president. Successive presidents: Luigi Einaudi, elected May 11, 1948; Giovanni Gronchi, Apr. 29, 1955; Antonio Segni, May 6, 1962; Giuseppe Saragat, Dec. 28, 1964; Giovanni Leone, Dec. 29, 1971; Alessandro Pertini, July 9, 1978; Francesco Cossiga, July 9, 1985; Oscar Luigi Scalfaro, May 28, 1992.

Rulers of Spain

From 8th to 11th centuries Spain was dominated by the Moors (Arabs and Berbers). The Christian reconquest established small kingdoms (Asturias, Aragon, Castile, Catalonia, Leon, Navarre, and Valencia). In 1474 Isabella, b. 1451, became Queen of Castile & Leon. Her husband, Ferdinand, b. 1452, inherited Aragon 1479, with Catalonia, Valencia, and the Balearic Islands, became Ferdinand V of Castile. By Isabella's request Pope Sixtus IV established the Inquisition, 1478. Last Moorish kingdom, Granada, fell 1492. Columbus opened New World of colonies, 1492. Isabella died 1504, succeeded by her daughter, Juana "the Mad," but Ferdinand ruled until his death 1516.

Charles I, b. 1500, son of Juana, grandson of Ferdinand and Isabella, and of Maximilian I of Hapsburg; succeeded later as Holy Roman Emperor, Charles V, 1520; abdicated 1556. Philip II, son, 1556-1598, inherited only Spanish throne; conquered Portugal, fought Turks, sent Armada vs. England. Married to Mary I of England, 1554-1558. Succession: Philip III, 1598-1621; Philip IV, 1621-1665; Charles II, 1665-1700, left Spain to Philip of Anjou, grandson of Louis XIV, who as Philip V, 1700-1746, founded Bourbon dynasty; Ferdinand VI, 1746-1759; Charles III, 1759-1788; Charles IV, 1788-1808, abdicated.

Napoleon now dominated politics and made his brother Joseph King of Spain 1808, but the Spanish ousted him in 1813. Ferdinand VII, 1808, 1814-1833, lost American colonies; succeeded by daughter Isabella II, aged 3, with wife Maria Christina of Naples regent until 1843. Isabella deposed by revolution 1868. Elected king by the Cortes, Amadeo of Savoy, 1870; abdicated 1873. First republic, 1873-74. Alphonso XII, son of Isabella, 1875-85. His posthumous son was Alphonso XIII, with his mother, Queen Maria Christina regent; Spanish-American war, Spain lost Cuba, gave up Puerto Rico, Philippines, Sulu Is., Marianas. Alphonso took throne 1902, aged 16, married British Princess Victoria Eugenia of Battenberg. Dictatorship of Primo de Rivera, 1923-30, precipitated revolution of 1931. Alphonso agreed to leave without formal abdication. Monarchy abolished; the second republic established, with socialist backing. Niceto Alcala Zamora was president until 1936, when Manuel Azaña was chosen.

In July 1936, the army in Morocco revolted against the government and General Francisco Franco led the troops into Spain. The revolution succeeded by Feb. 1939, when Azaña resigned. Franco became chief of state.

Alphonso XIII died in Rome Feb. 28, 1941, aged 54. His property and citizenship had been restored.

A law restoring the monarchy was approved in a 1947 referendum. Prince Juan Carlos, b. 1938, grandson of Alphonso XIII, was designated by Franco and the Cortes (Parliament) in 1969 as future king and chief of state. Franco died Nov. 20, 1975; Juan Carlos proclaimed king, Nov. 22.

Leaders in the South American Wars of Liberation

Here are some of the heroes in the early 19th century struggles of South American nations for independence:

Francisco Antonio Gabriel Miranda (1750-1816), Venezuelan. Served with the French in the American Revolution, commanded parts of French Revolutionary armies in the Netherlands. In 1806 attempted to start a revolt in Venezuela and failed. In 1810 became dictator until Britain and U.S. withdrew support. Overthrown, died 1816 in a Spanish prison.

Jose Francisco de San Martin (1778-1850), born in Argentina. Served in Spanish campaigns in Europe and Africa, 1789-1811. Joined Argentina's independence movement, 1812; invaded Chile, 1817; with Gen. Bernardo O'Higgins (1778-1842) defeated the Spaniards at Chacabuco, 1817. O'Higgins was named Liberator, became first director of Chile, 1817-23. In 1821 San Martin occupied Lima and Callao, Peru, and became protector of Peru.

Simon Bolivar (1783-1830), greatest leader of South American liberation from Spain, born to an aristocratic family in Venezuela. First served under Miranda, 1812; captured Caracas, named Liberator, 1813. Forced out by civil strife, led campaign that captured Bogota, 1814. In 1817 was again in control of Venezuela, named dictator. Organized Nueva Granada with help of Gen. Francisco de Paula Santander (1792-1840). By joining Nueva Granada, Venezuela, and the area that is now Panama and Ecuador, the republic of Colombia was formed, with Bolivar president. After numerous setbacks he decisively defeated the Spaniards, June 24, 1821. In May 1822, Gen. Antonio Jose de Sucre (1795-1830), Bolivar's lieutenant, took Quito. Bolivar conferred with San Martin, who resigned as protector of Peru and withdrew from politics. With a new army of Colombians and Peruvians Bolivar defeated the Spaniards in 1824 and cleared Peru. De Sucre organized Charcas (Upper Peru) as Republica Bolivar (now Bolivia), acted as president in place of Bolivar, who wrote its constitution. De Sucre defeated the Spanish faction of Peru at Ayacucho, Dec. 19, 1824. Continued civil strife led to breakup of the Colombian federation. Santander turned against Bolivar, but was defeated and banished. In 1828 Bolivar gave up the presidency he had held precariously for 14 years. He became ill from tuberculosis and died Dec. 17, 1830.

Rulers of Russia; Leaders of the USSR and Russian Federation

First ruler to consolidate Slavic tribes was Rurik, leader of the Russians who established himself at Novgorod, AD 862. He and his immediate successors had Scandinavian affiliations. They moved to Kiev after 972 and ruled as Dukes of Kiev. In 988 Vladimir was converted and adopted the Byzantine Greek Orthodox service, later modified by Slav influences. Important as organizer and lawgiver was Yaroslav, 1019-1054, whose daughters married kings of Norway, Hungary, and France. His grandson, Vladimir II (Monomakh), 1113-1125, was progenitor of several rulers, but in 1169 Andrew Bogolubski overthrew Kiev and began the line known as Grand Dukes of Vladimir.

Of the Grand Dukes of Vladimir, Alexander Nevsky, 1246-1263, had a son, Daniel, first to be called Duke of Muscovy (Moscow), who ruled 1294-1303. His successors became Grand Dukes of Muscovy. After Dmitri III Donskoi defeated the Tatars in 1380, they also became Grand Dukes of all Russia. Independence of the Tatars and considerable territorial expansion were achieved under Ivan III, 1462-1505.

Tsars of Muscovy—Ivan III was referred to in church ritual as Tsar. He married Sofia, niece of the last Byzantine emperor. His successor, Basil III, died in 1533 when Basil's son Ivan was only 3. He became Ivan IV, "the Terrible"; crowned 1547 as Tsar of all the Russias, ruled until 1584. Under the weak rule of his son, Feodor I, 1584-1598, Boris Godunov had control. The dynasty died, and after years of tribal strife and intervention by Polish and Swedish armies, the Russians united under 17-year-old Michael Romanov, distantly related to the first wife of Ivan IV. He ruled 1613-1645 and established the Romanov line. Fourth ruler after Michael was Peter I.

Tsars, or Emperors, of Russia (Romanovs)—Peter I, 1682-1725, known as Peter the Great, took title of Emperor in 1721. His successors and dates of accession were: Catherine, his widow, 1725; Peter II, his grandson, 1727; Anne, Duchess of Courland, 1730, daughter of Peter the Great's brother, Tsar Ivan V; Ivan VI, 1740, great-grandson of Ivan V, child, kept in prison and murdered 1764; Elizabeth, daughter of Peter I, 1741; Peter III, grandson of Peter I, 1761, deposed 1762 for his consort, Catherine II, former princess of Anhalt Zerbst (Germany) who is known as Catherine the Great; Paul I, her son, 1796, killed 1801; Alexander I, son of Paul, 1801, defeated Napoleon; Nicholas I, his brother, 1825; Alexander II, son of Nicholas, 1855, assassinated 1881 by terrorists; Alexander III, son, 1881. Nicholas II, son, 1894-1917, last Tsar of Russia, was forced to abdicate by the Revolution that followed losses to Germany in WWI. The Tsar, the Empress, the Tsarevich (Crown Prince), and the Tsar's 4 daughters were murdered by the Bolsheviks in Yekaterinburg, July 16, 1918.

Provisional Government—Prince Georgi Lvov and Alexander Kerensky, premiers, 1917.

Union of Soviet Socialist Republics

Bolshevik Revolution, Nov. 7, 1917, displaced Kerensky; council of People's Commissars formed, Lenin (Vladimir Ilyich Ulyanov), premier. Lenin died Jan. 21, 1924. Aleksei Rykov (executed 1938) and V. M. Molotov held the office, but actual ruler was Joseph Stalin (Joseph Vissarionovich Djugashvili), general secretary of the Central Committee of the Communist Party. Stalin became president of the Council of Ministers (premier) May 7, 1941, died Mar. 5, 1953. Succeeded by Georgi M. Malenkov, as head of the Council and premier, and Nikita S. Khrushchev, first secretary of the Central Committee. Malenkov resigned Feb. 8, 1955, became deputy premier, was dropped July 3, 1957. Marshal Nikolai A. Bulganin became premier Feb. 8, 1955; was demoted and Khrushchev became premier Mar. 27, 1958.

Khrushchev was ousted Oct. 14-15, 1964, replaced by Leonid I. Brezhnev as first secretary of the party and by Aleksei N. Kosygin as premier. On June 16, 1977, Brezhnev also took office as president. He died Nov. 10, 1982; 2 days later the Central Committee elected former KGB head Yuri V. Andropov president. Andropov died Feb. 9, 1984; on Feb. 13, Konstantin U. Chernenko chosen by Central Committee as its general secretary. Chernenko died Mar. 10, 1985; on Mar. 11, he was succeeded as general secretary by Mikhail Gorbachev, who replaced Andrei Gromyko as president on Oct. 1, 1988. Gorbachev resigned Dec. 25, 1991, and the Soviet Union officially disbanded the next day. A loose Commonwealth of Independent States, made up of most of the 15 former Soviet constituent republics, was created.

Post-Soviet Russia

After adopting a degree of sovereignty, the Russian Republic had held elections in June 1991. Boris Yeltsin was sworn in, July 10, 1991, as Russia's first elected president. After the Dec. 1991 dissolution of the Soviet Union, Yeltsin remained as president of Russia (officially Russian Federation).

Governments of China

(Until 221 BC and frequently thereafter, China was not a unified state. Where dynastic dates overlap, the rulers or events referred to appeared in different areas of China.)

Hsia	c1994 BC	-	c1523 BC
Shang	c1523	-	c1028
Western Chou	c1027	-	770
Eastern Chou	770	-	256
Warring States	403	-	222
Ch'in (first unified empire)	221	-	206
Han	202 BC	-	AD 220
Western Han (expanded Chinese state beyond the Yellow and Yangtze River valleys)	202 BC	-	AD 9
Hsin (Wang Mang, usurper)	AD 9	-	AD 23
Eastern Han (expanded Chinese state into Indochina and Turkestan)	25	-	220
Three Kingdoms (Wei, Shu, Wu)	220	-	265
Chin (western)	265	-	317
(eastern)	317	-	420
Northern Dynasties (followed several short-lived governments by Turks, Mongols, etc.)	386	-	581
Southern Dynasties (capital: Nanjing)	420	-	589
Sui (reunified China)	581	-	618
Tang (a golden age of Chinese culture; capital: Xian)	618	-	906
Five Dynasties (Yellow River basin)	902	-	960
Ten Kingdoms (southern China)	907	-	979
Liao (Khitan Mongols; capital at site of Beijing)	947	-	1125
Sung	960	-	1279
Northern Sung (reunified central and southern China)	960	-	1126
Western Hsai (non-Chinese rulers in northwest)	990	-	1227
Chin (Tatars; drove Sung out of central China)	1115	-	1234
Yuan (Mongols; Kublai Khan est. capital at site of Beijing, c. 1264)	1271	-	1368
Ming (China reunified under Chinese rule; capital: Nanjing, then Beijing in 1420)	1368	-	1644
Ch'ing (Manchus, descendents of Tatars)	1644	-	1911
Republic (disunity; provincial rulers, warlords)	1912	-	1949
People's Republic of China	1949	-	—

Leaders of China Since 1949

Mao Zedong	Chairman, Central People's Administrative Council, Communist Party (CPC), 1949-1976
Zhou Enlai	Premier, foreign minister, 1949-1976
Deng Xiaoping	Vice Premier, 1952-1966, 1973-1976, 1977-1980; "paramount leader," 1978-1997
Liu Shaoqi	President, 1959-1969
Hua Guofeng	Premier, 1976-1980; CPC Chairman, 1976-1981
Zhao Ziyang	Premier, 1980-1988; CPC General Secretary, 1987-1989
Hu Yaobang	CPC Chairman, 1981-1982; CPC General Secretary 1982-1987
Li Xiannian	President, 1983-1988
Yang Shangkun	President, 1988-1993
Li Peng	Premier, 1988-
Jiang Zemin	CPC General Secretary, 1989- ; President, 1993-

SCIENCE AND TECHNOLOGY

Inventions

Inventions	Date	Inventor	Nationality
Adding machine	1642	Pascal	French
Adding machine	1885	Burroughs	U.S.
Aerosol spray	1926	Rotheim	Norwegian
Airbag	1974	General Motors	U.S.
Air brake	1868	Westinghouse	U.S.
Air conditioning	1902	Carrier	U.S.
Air pump	1654	Guericke	German
Airplane, automatic pilot	1912	Sperry	U.S.
Airplane, experimental	1896	Langley	U.S.
Airplane, hydro	1911	Curtiss	U.S.
Airplane jet engine	1939	Ohain	German
Airplane with motor	1903	Wright Bros.	U.S.
Airship	1852	Giffard	French
Airship, rigid dirigible	1900	Zeppelin	German
Arc welder	1919	Thomson	U.S.
Aspartame	1965	Schlatter	U.S.
Autogyro	1920	de la Cierva	Spanish
Automobile, differential gear	1885	Benz	German
Automobile, electric	1892	Morrison	U.S.
Automobile, exp'mtl	1864	Marcus	Austrian
Automobile, gasoline	1889	Daimler	German
Automobile, gasoline	1892	Duryea	U.S.
Automobile magneto	1897	Bosch	German
Automobile muffler	1904	Pope	U.S.
Automobile self-starter	1911	Kettering	U.S.
Babbitt metal	1839	Babbitt	U.S.
Bakelite	1907	Baekeland	Belgium, U.S.
Balloon	1783	Montgolfier	French
Barometer	1643	Torricelli	Italian
Bicycle, modern	1885	Starley	English
Bifocal lens	1780	Franklin	U.S.
Block signals, railway	1867	Hall	U.S.
Bomb, depth	1916	Tait	U.S.
Bottle machine	1895	Owens	U.S.
Braille printing	1829	Braille	French
Bubble gum	1928	Diemer	U.S.
Burner, gas	1855	Bunsen	German
Calculating machine	1833	Babbage	English
Calculator, electronic pocket	1972	Merryman, Van Tassel	U.S.
Camera, Kodak	1888	Eastman, Walker	U.S
Camera, Polaroid Land	1948	Land	U.S.
Car coupler	1873	Janney	U.S.
Carburetor, gasoline	1893	Maybach	German
Card time recorder	1894	Cooper	U.S.
Carding machine	1797	Whittemore	U.S.
Carpet sweeper	1876	Bissell	U.S.
Cash register	1879	Ritty	U.S.
Cassette, audio	1963	Philips Co.	Dutch
Cassette, videotape	1969	Sony	Japanese
Cathode-ray tube	1897	Braun	German
CAT, or CT, scan	1973	Hounsfield	English
Cellophane	1908	Brandenberger	Swiss
Celluloid	1870	Hyatt	U.S.
Cement, Portland	1824	Aspdin	English
Chronometer	1761	Harrison	English
Circuit breaker	1925	Hilliard	U.S.
Circuit, integrated	1959	Kilby, Noyce, Texas Instr.	U.S.
Clock, pendulum	1657	Huygens	Dutch
Coaxial cable system	1929	Affel, Espensched	U.S.
Coke oven	1893	Hoffman	Austrian
Compressed air rock drill	1871	Ingersoll	U.S.
Comptometer	1887	Felt	U.S.
Computer, automatic sequence	1944	Aiken, et al.	U.S.
Computer, electronic	1942	Atanasoff, Berry	U.S.
Computer, laptop	1987	Sinclair	English
Computer, mini	1960	Digital Corp	U.S.
Condenser microphone (telephone)	1916	Wente	U.S.
Contact lens, corneal	1948	Tuohy	U.S.
Contraceptive, oral	1954	Pincus, Rock	U.S.
Corn, hybrid	1917	Jones	U.S.
Correction fluid	1951	Nesmith	U.S.
Cotton gin	1793	Whitney	U.S.
Cream separator	1878	DeLaval	Swedish
Cultivator, disc	1878	Mallon	U.S.
Cystoscope	1878	Nitze	German
Diesel engine	1895	Diesel	German
Disc, compact	1972	RCA	U.S.
Disc player, compact	1979	Sony, Philips Co.	Japan., Dutch
Disk, floppy	1970	IBM	U.S.
Disk, video	1972	Philips Co.	Dutch
Dynamite	1866	Nobel	Swedish
Dynamo, continuous current	1871	Gramme	Belgian
Dynamo, hydrogen cooled	1915	Schuler	U.S.
Electric battery	1800	Volta	Italian
Electric fan	1882	Wheeler	U.S.
Electrocardiograph	1903	Einthoven	Dutch
Electroencephalograph	1929	Berger	German
Electromagnet	1824	Sturgeon	English
Electron spectrometer	1944	Deutsch, Elliott, Evans	U.S.
Electron tube multigrid	1913	Langmuir	U.S.
Electroplating	1805	Brugnatelli	Italian
Electrostatic generator	1929	Van de Graaff	U.S.
Elevator brake	1852	Otis	U.S.
Elevator, push button	1922	Larson	U.S.
Engine, automatic transmission	1910	Fottinger	German
Engine, coal-gas 4-cycle	1876	Otto	German
Engine, compression ignition	1883	Daimler	German
Engine, electric ignition	1883	Benz	German
Engine, gas, compound	1926	Eickemeyer	U.S.
Engine, gasoline	1872	Brayton, Geo.	U.S.
Engine, gasoline	1889	Daimler	German
Engine, jet	1930	Whittle	English
Engine, steam, piston	1705	Newcomen	English
Engine, steam, piston	1769	Watt	Scottish
Engraving, half-tone	1852	Talbot	U.S.
Fiberglass	1938	Owens-Corning	U.S.
Fiber optics	1955	Kapany	English
Filament, tungsten	1913	Coolidge	U.S.
Flanged rail	1831	Stevens	U.S.
Flatiron, electric	1882	Seely	U.S.
Food, frozen	1924	Birdseye	U.S.
Freon	1930	Midgley, et al.	U.S.
Furnace (for steel)	1858	Siemens	German
Galvanometer	1820	Sweigger	German
Gas discharge tube	1922	Hull	U.S.
Gas lighting	1792	Murdoch	Scottish
Gas mantle	1885	Welsbach	Austrian
Gasoline (lead ethyl)	1922	Midgley	U.S.
Gasoline, cracked	1913	Burton	U.S.
Gasoline, high octane	1930	Ipatieff	Russian
Geiger counter	1913	Geiger	German
Glass, laminated safety	1909	Benedictus	French
Glider	1853	Cayley	English
Gun, breechloader	1811	Thornton	U.S.
Gun, Browning	1897	Browning	U.S.
Gun, magazine	1875	Hotchkiss	U.S.
Gun, silencer	1908	Maxim, H.P.	U.S.
Guncotton	1847	Schoenbein	German
Gyrocompass	1911	Sperry	U.S.
Gyroscope	1852	Foucault	French
Harvester-thresher	1818	Lane	U.S.
Heart, artificial	1982	Jarvik	U.S.
Helicopter	1939	Sikorsky	U.S.
Hydrometer	1768	Baume	French
Iron lung	1928	Drinker, Slaw	U.S.
Kaleidoscope	1817	Brewster	Scottish
Kinetoscope	1889	Edison	U.S.
Lacquer, nitrocellulose	1921	Flaherty	U.S.
Lamp, arc	1847	Staite	English
Lamp, fluorescent	1938	General Electric, Westinghouse	U.S.
Lamp, incandescent	1879	Edison	U.S.
Lamp, incand., frosted	1924	Pipkin	U.S.
Lamp, incand., gas	1913	Langmuir	U.S.
Lamp, klieg	1911	Kliegl, A. & J.	U.S.
Lamp, mercury vapor	1912	Hewitt	U.S.
Lamp, miner's safety	1816	Davy	English
Lamp, neon	1909	Claude	French
Lathe, turret	1845	Fitch	U.S.
Launderette	1934	Cantrell	U.S.
Lens, achromatic	1758	Dollond	English
Lens, fused bifocal	1908	Borsch	U.S.
Leyden jar (condenser)	1745	von Kleist	German
Lightning rod	1752	Franklin	U.S.
Linoleum	1860	Walton	English
Linotype	1884	Mergenthaler	U.S.
Lock, cylinder	1851	Yale	U.S.
Locomotive, electric	1851	Vail	U.S.
Locomotive, exp'mtl	1802	Trevithick	English
Locomotive, exp'mtl	1812	Fenton, et al.	English
Locomotive, exp'mtl	1813	Hedley	English
Locomotive, exp'mtl	1814	Stephenson	English
Locomotive, practical	1829	Stephenson	English
Locomotive, 1st U.S.	1830	Cooper, P.	U.S.
Loom, power	1785	Cartwright	English
Loudspeaker, dynamic	1924	Rice, Kellogg	U.S.
Machine gun	1862	Gatling	U.S.
Machine gun, improved	1872	Hotchkiss	U.S.
Machine gun (Maxim)	1883	Maxim, H.S.	U.S., Eng.
Magnet, electro	1828	Henry	U.S.
Mantle, gas	1885	Welsbach	Austrian
Mason jar	1858	Mason, J.	U.S.
Match, friction	1827	Walker, J.	English
Mercerized textiles	1843	Mercer, J.	English
Meter, induction	1888	Shallenberg	U.S.
Metronome	1816	Malezel	German
Microcomputer	1973	Truong, et al.	French
Micrometer	1636	Gascoigne	English
Microphone	1877	Berliner	U.S.
Microprocessor	1971	Intel Corp.	U.S.
Microscope, compound	1590	Janssen	Dutch
Microscope, electronic	1931	Knoll, Ruska	German
Microscope, field ion	1951	Mueller	German
Microwave oven	1947	Spencer	U.S.
Monitor, warship	1861	Ericsson	U.S.

(continued)

Inventions *(continued)*

Inventions	Date	Inventor	Nationality
Monotype	1887	Lanston	U.S.
Motor, AC	1892	Tesla	U.S.
Motor, DC	1837	Davenport	U.S.
Motor, induction	1887	Tesla	U.S.
Motorcycle	1885	Daimler	German
Movie machine	1894	Jenkins	U.S.
Movie, panoramic	1952	Waller	U.S.
Movie, talking	1927	Warner Bros.	U.S.
Mower, lawn	1831	Budding, Ferrabee	English
Mowing machine	1822	Bailey	U.S.
Neoprene	1930	Carothers	U.S.
Nylon	1937	Du Pont lab	U.S.
Nylon synthetic	1930	Carothers	U.S.
Oil cracking furnace	1891	Gavrilov	Russian
Oil filled power cable	1921	Emanueli	Italian
Oleomargarine	1869	Mege-Mouries	French
Ophthalmoscope	1851	Helmholtz	German
Pacemaker	1952	Zoll	U.S.
Paper	105	Ts'ai	Chinese
Paper machine	1809	Dickinson	U.S.
Parachute	1785	Blanchard	French
Pen, ballpoint	1888	Loud	U.S.
Pen, fountain	1884	Waterman	U.S.
Pen, steel	1780	Harrison	English
Pendulum	1583	Galileo	Italian
Percussion cap	1807	Forsythe	Scottish
Phonograph	1877	Edison	U.S.
Photo, color	1892	Ives	U.S.
Photo film, celluloid	1893	Reichenbach	U.S.
Photo film, transparent	1884	Eastman, Goodwin	U.S.
Photoelectric cell	1895	Elster	German
Photocopier	1938	Carlson	U.S.
Photographic paper	1835	Talbot	English
Photography	1816	Niepce	French
Photography	1835	Talbot	English
Photography	1835	Daguerre	French
Photophone	1880	Bell	U.S.-Scot.
Phototelegraphy	1925	Bell Labs	U.S.
Piano	1709	Cristofori	Italian
Piano, player	1863	Fourneaux	French
Pin, safety	1849	Hunt	U.S.
Pistol (revolver)	1836	Colt	U.S.
Plow, cast iron	1785	Ransome	English
Plow, disc	1896	Hardy	U.S.
Pneumatic hammer	1890	King	U.S.
Post-it note	1974	Fry	U.S.
Powder, smokeless	1884	Vieille	French
Printing press, rotary	1845	Hoe	U.S.
Printing press, web	1865	Bullock	U.S.
Propeller, screw	1804	Stevens	U.S.
Propeller, screw	1837	Ericsson	Swedish
Pulsars	1967	Bell	English
Punch card accounting	1889	Hollerith	U.S.
Quasars	1963	Schmidt	U.S.
Radar	1940	Watson-Watt	Scottish
Radio, magnetic detector	1902	Marconi	Italian
Radio, signals	1895	Marconi	Italian
Radio amplifier	1906	De Forest	U.S.
Radio beacon	1928	Donovan	U.S.
Radio crystal oscillator	1918	Nicolson	U.S.
Radio receiver, cascade tuning	1913	Alexanderson	U.S.
Radio receiver, heterodyne	1913	Fessenden	U.S.
Radio transmitter triode modulation	1914	Alexanderson	U.S.
Radio tube diode	1905	Fleming	English
Radio tube oscillator	1915	De Forest	U.S.
Radio tube triode	1906	De Forest	U.S.
Radio FM, 2-path	1933	Armstrong	U.S.
Rayon (acetate)	1895	Cross	English
Rayon (cuprammonium)	1890	Despeissis	French
Rayon (nitrocellulose)	1884	Chardonnet	French
Razor, electric	1917	Schick	U.S.
Razor, safety	1895	Gillette	U.S.
Reaper	1834	McCormick	U.S.
Record, cylinder	1887	Bell, Tainter	U.S.
Record, disc	1887	Berliner	U.S.
Record, long playing	1947	Goldmark	U.S.
Record, wax cylinder	1888	Edison	U.S.
Refrigerator car	1868	David	U.S.
Resin, synthetic	1931	Hill	English
Richter scale	1935	Richter	U.S.
Rifle, repeating	1860	Spencer	U.S.
Rocket engine	1926	Goddard	U.S.
Rubber, vulcanized	1839	Goodyear	U.S.
Saccharin	1879	Remsen, Fahlberg	U.S.
Saw, band	1808	Newberry	English
Saw, circular	1777	Miller	English
Scotch tape	1930	Drew	U.S.
Seat belt	1959	Volvo	Swedish
Sewing machine	1846	Howe	U.S.
Shoe-lasting machine	1883	Matzeliger	U.S.
Shoe-sewing machine	1860	McKay	U.S.
Shrapnel shell	1784	Shrapnel	English
Shuttle, flying	1733	Kay	English
Sleeping-car	1865	Pullman	U.S.
Slide rule	1620	Oughtred	English
Soap, hardwater	1928	Bertsch	German
Spectroscope	1859	Kirchoff, Bunsen	German
Spectroscope (mass)	1918	Dempster	U.S.
Spinning jenny	c.1764	Hargreaves	English
Spinning mule	1779	Crompton	English
Steamboat, exp'mtl	1778	Jouffroy	French
Steamboat, exp'mtl	1785	Fitch	U.S.
Steamboat, exp'mtl	1787	Rumsey	U.S.
Steamboat, exp'mtl	1788	Miller	Scottish
Steamboat, exp'mtl	1803	Fulton	U.S.
Steamboat, exp'mtl	1804	Stevens	U.S.
Steamboat, practical	1802	Symington	Scottish
Steamboat, practical	1807	Fulton	U.S.
Steam car	1770	Cugnot	French
Steam turbine	1884	Parsons	English
Steel (converter)	1856	Bessemer	English
Steel alloy	1891	Harvey	U.S.
Steel alloy, high-speed	1901	Taylor, White	U.S.
Steel, electric	1900	Heroult	French
Steel, manganese	1884	Hadfield	English
Steel, stainless	1916	Brearley	English
Stereoscope	1838	Wheatstone	English
Stethoscope	1819	Laennec	French
Stethoscope, binaural	1840	Cammann	U.S.
Stock ticker	1870	Edison	U.S.
Storage battery, rechargeable	1859	Plante	French
Stove, electric	1896	Hadaway	U.S.
Submarine	1891	Holland	U.S.
Submarine, even keel	1894	Lake	U.S.
Submarine, torpedo	1776	Bushnell	U.S.
Superconductivity	1957	Bardeen, Cooper, Schreiffer	U.S.
Synthesizer	1964	Moog	U.S.
Tank, military	1914	Swinton	English
Tape recorder, magnetic	1899	Poulsen	Danish
Teflon	1938	Du Pont	U.S.
Telegraph, magnetic	1837	Morse	U.S.
Telegraph, quadruplex	1864	Edison	U.S.
Telegraph, railroad	1887	Woods	U.S.
Telegraph, wireless high frequency	1895	Marconi	Italian
Telephone	1876	Bell	U.S.-Scot.
Telephone, automatic	1891	Strowger	U.S.
Telephone, cellular	1947	Bell Labs	U.S.
Telephone, radio	1900	Poulsen, Fessenden	Danish
Telephone, radio	1906	De Forest	U.S.
Telephone, radio, l. d.	1915	AT&T	U.S.
Telephone, recording	1898	Poulsen	Danish
Telephone, wireless	1899	Collins	U.S.
Telephone amplifier	1912	De Forest	U.S.
Telescope	1608	Lippershey	Neth.
Telescope	1609	Galileo	Italian
Telescope, astronomical	1611	Kepler	German
Teletype	1928	Morkrum, Kleinschmidt	U.S.
Television, color	1928	Baird	Scottish
Television, electronic	1927	Farnsworth	U.S.
Television, iconoscope	1923	Zworykin	U.S.
Television, mech. scanner	1923	Baird	Scottish
Thermometer	1593	Galileo	Italian
Thermometer	1730	Reaumur	French
Thermometer, mercury	1714	Fahrenheit	German
Time, self-regulator	1918	Bryce	U.S.
Time recorder	1890	Bundy	U.S.
Tire, double-tube	1845	Thomson	Scottish
Tire, pneumatic	1888	Dunlop	Scottish
Toaster, automatic	1918	Strite	U.S.
Toilet, flush	1589	Harington	English
Tool, pneumatic	1865	Law	English
Torpedo, marine	1804	Fulton	U.S.
Tractor, crawler	1904	Holt	U.S.
Transformer, AC	1885	Stanley	U.S.
Transistor	1947	Shockley, Brattain, Bardeen	U.S.
Trolley car, electric	1884-87	Van DePoele, Sprague	U.S.
Tungsten, ductile	1912	Coolidge	U.S.
Tupperware	1945	Tupper	U.S.
Turbine, gas	1849	Bourdin	French
Turbine, hydraulic	1849	Francis	U.S.
Turbine, steam	1884	Parsons	English
Type, movable	1447	Gutenberg	German
Typewriter	1867	Sholes, Soule, Glidden	U.S.
Vacuum cleaner, electric	1907	Spangler	U.S.
Vacuum evaporating pan	1846	Rillieux	U.S.
Velcro	1948	de Mestral	Swiss
Video game ("Pong")	1972	Buschnel	U.S.
Video home system (VHS)	1975	Matsushita, JVC	Japan.
Washer, electric	1901	Fisher	U.S.
Welding, atomic hydrogen	1924	Langmuir, Palmer	U.S.
Welding, electric	1877	Thomson	U.S.
Windshield wiper	1903	Anderson	U.S.
Wind tunnel	1912	Eiffel	French
Wire, barbed	1874	Glidden	U.S.
Wire, barbed	1875	Haish	U.S.
Wrench, double-acting	1913	Owen	U.S.
X-ray tube	1913	Coolidge	U.S.
Zeppelin	1900	Zeppelin	German

MILLENNIUM FACT BOX

The Telephone

When Alexander Graham Bell received the patent for the telephone on Mar. 7, 1876, and then made the first telephone call 3 days later to his assistant Thomas Watson ("Mr. Watson, come here—I want you"), he could not have envisioned the incredible changes his invention would undergo. The following is a chronological list of some telephone milestones:

- 1st telephone call, Alexander Graham Bell, 1876
- Bell Telephone Company founded, 1877
- 1st commercial switchboard, New Haven, CT, 1878
- 1st long-distance call, between New York and Boston, 1884
- Public, coin-operated telephone patented, 1889
- 1st automatic telephone exchange, 1891
- 1st long-distance call between New York and Chicago, 1892
- 1st transcontinental call, between New York and San Francisco, 1915
- 1st pagers used, by Detroit Police Dept., 1921
- Rotary-dial telephone patented, 1923
- 1st transatlantic call, between New York and Britain, 1923
- 2-way video telephone demonstrated, 1930
- Cellular telephone originated, Bell Laboratories, 1947
- 1st transcontinental direct-dial service, 1951
- 1st transatlantic telephone cable, 1956
- AT&T offers Touch-Tone telephones, 1963
- 100,000,000th telephone installed in the U.S., 1967
- 1st 911 emergency system, in Haleyville, AL, 1968
- 1st commercial Picturephone service, Pittsburgh, 1970
- Cellular telephone 1st demonstrated, 1977
- 1st cellular telephone service, in Chicago, 1983
- Breakup of AT&T, 1984

Discoveries and Innovations: Chemistry, Physics, Biology, Medicine

	Date	Discoverer	Nationality
Acetylene gas	1862	Berthelot	French
ACTH	1927	Evans, Long	U.S.
Adrenalin	1901	Takamine	Japanese
Aluminum, electrolytic process	1886	Hall	U.S.
Aluminum, isolated	1825	Oersted	Danish
Anesthesia, ether	1842	Long	U.S.
Anesthesia, local	1885	Koller	Austrian
Anesthesia, spinal	1898	Bier	German
Aniline dye	1856	Perkin	English
Anti-rabies	1885	Pasteur	French
Antiseptic surgery	1867	Lister	English
Antitoxin, diphtheria	1891	Von Behring	German
Argyrol	1897	Bayer	German
Arsphenamine	1910	Ehrlich	German
Aspirin	1853	Gerhardt	French
Atabrine	1932	Mietzsch, et al.	German
Atomic numbers	1913	Moseley	English
Atomic theory	1803	Dalton	English
Atomic time clock	1948	Lyons	U.S.
Atomic time clock, cesium beam	1948	Essen	English
Atom-smashing theory	1919	Rutherford	English
Bacitracin	1943	Johnson, Meleneyl.	U.S.
Bacteria, description	1676	Leeuwenhoek	Dutch
Barbital	1903	Fischer	German
Bleaching powder	1798	Tennant	English
Blood, circulation	1628	Harvey	English
Blood plasma storage (blood banks)	1940	Drew	U.S.
Bordeaux mixture	1885	Millardet	French
Bromine from the sea	1826	Balard	French
Calcium carbide	1888	Wilson	U.S.
Calculus	1670	Newton	English
Camphor synthetic	1896	Haller	French
Canning (food)	1804	Appert	French
Carbomycin	1952	Tanner	U.S.
Carbon oxides	1925	Fisher	German
Chemotherapy	1909	Ehrlich	German
Chloamphenicol	1947	Burkholder	U.S.
Chlorine	1774	Scheele	Swedish
Chloroform	1831	Guthrie, S.	U.S.
Chlortetracycline	1948	Duggen	U.S.
Classification of plants and animals	1735	Linnaeus	Swedish
Cloning, mammal	1996	Wilmut, et al.	Scottish
Cocaine	1860	Niermann	German
Combustion explained	1777	Lavoisier	French
Conditioned reflex	1914	Pavlov	Russian
Cortisone	1936	Kendall	U.S.
Cortisone, synthesis	1946	Sarett	U.S.
Cosmic rays	1910	Gockel	Swiss
Cyanamide	1905	Frank, Caro	German
Cyclotron	1930	Lawrence	U.S.
DDT (not applied as insecticide until 1939)	1874	Zeidler	German
Deuterium	1932	Urey, Brickwedde, Murphy	U.S.
DNA (structure)	1951	Crick Watson Wilkins	English U.S. English
Electric resistance, law of	1827	Ohm	German
Electric waves	1888	Hertz	German
Electrolysis	1852	Faraday	English
Electromagnetism	1819	Oersted	Danish
Electron	1897	Thomson, J.	English
Electron diffraction	1936	Thomson, G. Davisson	English U.S.
Electroshock treatment	1938	Cerletti, Bini	Italian
Erythromycin	1952	McGuire	U.S.
Evolution, natural selection	1858	Darwin	English
Falling bodies, law of	1590	Galileo	Italian
Gases, law of combining volumes	1808	Gay-Lussac	French
Geometry, analytic	1619	Descartes	French
Gold, cyanide process for extraction	1887	MacArthur, Forest	British
Gravitation, law	1687	Newton	English
Holograph	1948	Gabor	British
Human heart transplant	1967	Barnard	S. African
Human immunodeficiency virus identified	1984	Mortagnier Gallo	French U.S.
Indigo, synthesis of	1880	Baeyer	German
Induction, electric	1830	Henry	U.S.
Insulin	1922	Banting, Best, Macleod	Canadian, Scottish
Intelligence testing	1905	Binet, Simon	French
In vitro fertilization	1978	Steptoe, Edwards	English
Isoniazid	1952	Hoffmann-LaRoche Domagk	U.S. German
Isotopes, theory	1912	Soddy	English
Laser (light amplification by stimulated emission of radiation)	1957	Gould	U.S.
Light, velocity	1675	Roemer	Danish
Light, wave theory	1690	Huygens	Dutch
Lithography	1796	Senefelder	Bohemian
Lobotomy	1935	Egas Moniz	Portuguese
Logarithms	1614	Napier	Scottish
LSD-25	1943	Hoffman	Swiss
Mendelian laws	1866	Mendel	Austrian
Mercator projection (map)	1568	Mercator (Kremer)	Flemish
Methanol	1661	Boyle	Irish
Milk condensation	1853	Borden	U.S.
Molecular hypothesis	1811	Avogadro	Italian
Motion, laws of	1687	Newton	English
Neomycin	1949	Waksman, Lechevalier	U.S.
Neutron	1932	Chadwick	English
Nitric acid	1648	Glauber	German
Nitric oxide	1772	Priestley	English
Nitroglycerin	1846	Sobrero	Italian
Oil cracking process	1891	Dewar	U.S.
Oxygen	1774	Priestley	English
Oxytetracycline	1950	Finlay, et al.	U.S.
Ozone	1840	Schonbein	German
Paper, sulfite process	1867	Tilghman	U.S.
Paper, wood pulp, sulfate process	1884	Dahl	German
Penicillin	1928	Fleming	Scottish
practical use	1941	Florey, Chain	English
Periodic law and table of elements	1869	Mendeleyev	Russian
Physostigmine synthesis	1935	Julian	U.S.
Planetary motion, laws	1609	Kepler	German
Plutonium fission	1940	Kennedy, Wahl, Seaborg, Segre	U.S.
Polymyxin	1947	Ainsworth	English
Positron	1932	Anderson	U.S.
Proton	1919	Rutherford	N. Zealand
Psychoanalysis	1900	Freud	Austrian
Quantum theory	1900	Planck	German
Quasars	1963	Matthews, Sandage	U.S.
Quinine synthetic	1946	Woodward, Doering	U.S.
Radioactivity	1896	Becquerel	French
Radiocarbon dating	1947	Libby	U.S.

(continued)

Discoveries and Innovations *(continued)*

	Date	Discoverer	Nationality
Radium	1898	Curie, Pierre	French
		Curie, Marie	Pol.-Fr.
Relativity theory	1905	Einstein	German
Reserpine	1949	Jal Vaikl	Indian
Schick test	1913	Schick	U.S.
Silicon	1823	Berzelius	Swedish
Smallpox eradication	1979	World Health Org.	UN
Streptomycin	1944	Waksman, et al	U.S.
Sulfanilamide	1935	Bovet, Trefouel	French
Sulfanilamide theory	1908	Gelmo	German
Sulfapyridine	1938	Ewins, Phelps	English
Sulfathiazole	1939	Fosbinder, Walter	U.S.
Sulfuric acid	1831	Phillips	English
Sulfuric acid, lead	1746	Roebuck	English
Syphilis test	1906	Wassermann	German
Thiacetazone	1950	Belmisch, Mietzsch, Domagk	German
Tuberculin	1890	Koch	German
Uranium fission theory	1939	Hahn, Meitner, Strassmann	German
		Bohr	Danish
		Fermi	Italian
		Einstein, Pegram, Wheeler	U.S.
Uranium fission, atomic reactor	1942	Fermi, Szilard	U.S.
Vaccine, measles	1963	Enders	U.S.
Vaccine, meningitis (first conjugate)	1987	Gordon, et al., Connaught Lab.	U.S.
Vaccine, polio	1954	Salk	U.S.
Vaccine, polio, oral	1960	Sabin	U.S.
Vaccine, rabies	1885	Pasteur	French
Vaccine, smallpox	1796	Jenner	English
Vaccine, typhus	1909	Nicolle	French
Vaccine, varicella	1974	Takahashi	Japanese
Van Allen belts, radiation	1958	Van Allen	U.S.
Vitamin A	1913	McCollum, Davis	U.S.
Vitamin B	1916	McCollum	U.S.
Vitamin C	1928	Szent-Gyorgyi, King	U.S.
Vitamin D	1922	McCollum	U.S.
Vitamin K	1935	Dam, Doisy	U.S.
Xerography	1938	Carlson	U.S.
X ray	1895	Roentgen	German

Top 20 Corporations Receiving U.S. Patents in 1997

Source: *Technology Assessment and Forecast Report,* U.S. Patent and Trademark Office, U.S. Department of Commerce

Rank	Company	Number of patents
1.	International Business Machines Corp.	1,724
2.	Canon K. K.	1,381
3.	NEC Corp.	1,095
4.	Motorola, Inc.	1,058
5.	Fujitsu, Ltd.	903
5.	Hitachi, Ltd.	903
7.	Mitsubishi Denki K. K.	892
8.	Toshiba Corp.	862
9.	Sony Corp.	859
10.	Eastman Kodak Company	795
11.	Lucent Technologies Inc.	768
12.	Matsushita Electric Industrial Co., Ltd.	746
13.	General Electric Company	664
14.	Texas Instruments, Inc.	607
15.	Xerox Corp.	606
16.	Samsung Electronics Co., Ltd.	582
17.	Minnesota Mining & Manufacturing Co.	548
18.	Hewlett-Packard Company	530
19.	Nikon Corp.	479
20.	U.S. Philips Corp.	473

Breaking the Sound Barrier; Speed of Sound

The prefix **Mach** is used to describe supersonic speed. It was named for Ernst Mach (1838-1916), a Czech-born Austrian physicist, who contributed to the study of sound. When a plane moves at the speed of sound, it is Mach 1. When the plane is moving at twice the speed of sound, it is Mach 2. When it is moving below the speed of sound, the speed can be designated accordingly—for example, Mach 0.90. Mach is defined as "the ratio of the velocity of a rocket or a jet to the velocity of sound in the medium being considered."

When a plane passes the sound barrier—flying faster than sound travels—listeners in the area hear thunderclaps, but the pilot of the plane does not hear them.

Sound is produced by vibrations of an object and is transmitted by alternate increase and decrease in pressures that radiate outward through a material media of molecules—somewhat like waves spreading out on a pond after a rock has been tossed into it.

The **frequency of sound** is determined by the number of times the vibrating waves undulate per second and is measured in cycles per second. The slower the cycle of waves, the lower the frequency. As frequencies increase, the sound is higher in pitch.

Sound is audible to human beings only if the frequency falls within a certain range. The human ear is usually not sensitive to frequencies of fewer than 20 vibrations per second or greater than about 20,000 vibrations per second—although this range varies among individuals. Any sound at a pitch higher than the human ear can hear is termed ultrasonic.

Intensity, or loudness, is the strength of the pressure of these radiating waves and is measured in decibels. The human ear responds to intensity in a range from zero to 120 decibels. Any sound with a pressure of more than 120 decibels is painful to the human ear.

The **speed of sound** is generally defined as 1,088 feet per second at sea level at 32°F. It varies in other temperatures and in different media. Sound travels faster in water than in air, and even faster in iron and steel. It takes 5 seconds to travel a mile in air, and 1 second to move a mile under water, and sound travels through iron in 1/3 second. It travels through ice-cold vapor at approximately 4,708 feet per second; ice-cold water, 4,938; granite, 12,960; hardwood, 12,620; brick, 11,960; glass, 16,410 to 19,690; silver, 8,658; gold, 5,717.

Light; Colors of the Spectrum

Light, a form of electromagnetic radiation similar to radiant heat, radio waves, and X rays, is emitted from a source in straight lines and spreads out over a larger and larger area as it travels; the light per unit area diminishes as the square of the distance.

The English mathematician and physicist Sir Isaac Newton (1642-1727) described light as an **emission of particles**; the Dutch astronomer, mathematician, and physicist Christiaan Huygens (1629-95) developed the theory that light travels by a **wave motion.** It is now believed that these 2 theories are essentially complementary, and the development of quantum theory has led to results where light acts like a series of particles in some experiments and like a wave in others.

The **speed of light** was first measured in a laboratory experiment by the French physicist Armand Hippolyte Louis Fizeau (1819-96). Today the speed of light is known very precisely as 299,792.458 km per sec (or 186,282.396 mi per sec) in a vacuum. The velocity of light in air varies slightly with color, averaging about 3% less than in a vacuum; the speed in water is about 25% less, and in glass, 33% less.

Color sensations are produced through the excitation of the retina of the eye by light vibrating at different frequencies. The different colors of the spectrum may be produced by viewing a light beam that is refracted by passage through a prism, which breaks the light into its wavelengths.

Customarily, the **primary colors** of the spectrum are taken to be the 6 monochromatic colors that occupy relatively large areas of the spectrum: red, orange, yellow, green, blue, and violet. However, Newton named a 7th color, indigo, situated between blue and violet on the spectrum. Aubert estimated (1865) the solar spectrum to contain approximately 1,000 distinguishable hues; of the hues, according to Rood (1881), 2 million tints and shades can be distinguished. Luckiesh stated (1915) that 55 distinctly different hues have been seen in a single spectrum.

Many physicists recognize only 3 primary colors: red, yellow, and blue (Mayer, 1775); red, green, and violet (Thomas Young, 1801); or red, green, and blue (Clerk Maxwell, 1860).

The color sensation of **black** is due to complete lack of stimulation of the retina, that of **white** to complete stimulation. The **infrared and ultraviolet rays**, below the red (long) end of the spectrum and above the violet (short) end respectively, are invisible to the naked eye. Heat is the principal effect of the infrared rays, and chemical action that of the ultraviolet rays.

Weight or Mass of Water

	Weight, at 20°C	
1	cubic inch	0.0360 pound
12	cubic inches	0.433 pound
1	cubic foot	62.4 pounds
1	cubic foot	7.48052 U.S. gal
1.8	cubic feet	112.0 pounds
35.96	cubic feet	2240.0 pounds
1	U.S. gallon	8.33 pounds
13.45	U.S. gallons	112.0 pounds
269.0	U.S. gallons	2240.0 pounds
	Mass, at 4°C (Maximum Density)	
1	cubic centimeter	1 gram
1	liter	1 kilogram
1	cubic meter	1 metric ton

Density of Gases and Vapors

at 0°C and 760 mmHg; kilograms per cubic meter

Gas	Mass	Gas	Mass	Gas	Mass
Acetylene	1.171	Ethylene	1.260	Methyl fluoride	1.545
Air	1.293	Fluorine	1.696	Mono methylamine	1.38
Ammonia	0.759	Helium	0.178	Neon	0.900
Argon	1.784	Hydrogen	0.090	Nitric oxide	1.341
Arsine	3.48	Hydrogen bromide	3.50	Nitrogen	1.250
Butane-iso	2.60	Hydrogen chloride	1.639	Nitrosyl chloride	2.99
Butane-n	2.519	Hydrogen iodide	5.724	Nitrous oxide	1.997
Carbon dioxide	1.977	Hydrogen selenide	3.66	Oxygen	1.429
Carbon monoxide	1.250	Hydrogen sulfide	1.539	Phosphine	1.48
Carbon oxysulfide	2.72	Krypton	3.745	Propane	2.020
Chlorine	3.214	Methane	0.717	Silicon tetrafluoride	4.67
Chlorine monoxide	3.89	Methyl chloride	2.25	Sulfur dioxide	2.927
Ethane	1.356	Methyl ether	2.091	Xenon	5.897

Chemical Elements, Atomic Weights, Discoverers

Source: Glenn T. Seaborg, Ph.D., Lawrence Berkeley National Laboratory, Berkeley, CA

Atomic weights, based on the exact number 12 as the assigned atomic mass of the principal isotope of carbon, carbon 12, are provided through the courtesy of the International Union of Pure and Applied Chemistry (IUPAC) and Butterworth Scientific Publications. For the radioactive elements, with the exception of uranium and thorium, the mass number of either the isotope of longest half-life (*) or the better known isotope (**) is given.

Chemical element	Symbol	Atomic number	Atomic weight	Year discov.	Discoverer
Actinium	Ac	89	227.03	1899	Debierne
Aluminum	Al	13	26.9815	1825	Oersted
Americium	Am	95	243*	1944	Seaborg, et al.
Antimony	Sb	51	121.75	1450	Valentine
Argon	Ar	18	39.948	1894	Rayleigh, Ramsay
Arsenic	As	33	74.9216	13th c.	Albertus Magnus
Astatine	At	85	210*	1940	Corson, et al.
Barium	Ba	56	137.33	1808	Davy
Berkelium	Bk	97	249**	1949	Thompson, Ghiorso, Seaborg
Beryllium	Be	4	9.0122	1798	Vauquelin
Bismuth	Bi	83	208.980	15th c.	Valentine
Bohrium	Bh	107	264*	1981	Münzenberg, et al.
Boron	B	5	10.811[a]	1808	Gay-Lussac, Thenard
Bromine	Br	35	79.904[b]	1826	Balard
Cadmium	Cd	48	112.41	1817	Stromeyer
Calcium	Ca	20	40.08	1808	Davy
Californium	Cf	98	251*	1950	Thompson, et al.
Carbon	C	6	12.01115[a]	BC	unknown
Cerium	Ce	58	140.12	1803	Klaproth
Cesium	Cs	55	132.905	1860	Bunsen, Kirchhoff
Chlorine	Cl	17	35.453[b]	1774	Scheele
Chromium	Cr	24	51.996[b]	1797	Vauquelin
Cobalt	Co	27	58.9332	1735	Brandt
Copper	Cu	29	63.546[b]	BC	unknown
Curium	Cm	96	247*	1944	Seaborg, James, Ghiorso
Dysprosium	Dy	66	162.50*	1886	Boisbaudran
Einsteinium	Es	99	254**	1952	Ghiorso, et al.
Erbium	Er	68	167.26	1843	Mosander
Europium	Eu	63	151.96	1901	Demarcay
Fermium	Fm	100	257*	1953	Ghiorso, et al.
Fluorine	F	9	18.9984	1771	Scheele
Francium	Fr	87	223*	1939	Perey
Gadolinium	Gd	64	157.25	1886	Marignac
Gallium	Ga	31	69.72	1875	Boisbaudran
Germanium	Ge	32	72.59	1886	Winkler
Gold	Au	79	196.967	BC	unknown

(continued)

Chemical element	Symbol	Atomic number	Atomic weight	Year discov.	Discoverer
Hafnium	Hf	72	178.49	1923	Coster, Hevesy
Hahnium[1]	Ha	105	262*	1970	Ghiorso, et al.
Hassium	Hs	108	269*	1984	Münzenberg, et al.
Helium	He	2	4.0026	1868	Janssen, Lockyer
Holmium	Ho	67	164.930	1878	Soret, Delafontaine
Hydrogen	H	1	1.00797[a]	1766	Cavendish
Indium	In	49	114.82	1863	Reich, Richter
Iodine	I	53	126.9044	1811	Courtois
Iridium	Ir	77	192.22	1804	Tennant
Iron	Fe	26	55.847[b]	BC	unknown
Krypton	Kr	36	83.80	1898	Ramsay, Travers
Lanthanum	La	57	138.91	1839	Mosander
Lawrencium	Lr	103	262*	1961	Ghiorso, T. Sikkeland, A.E. Larsh, and R.M. Latimer
Lead	Pb	82	207.19	BC	unknown
Lithium	Li	3	6.939	1817	Arfvedson
Lutetium	Lu	71	174.97	1907	Welsbach, Urbain
Magnesium	Mg	12	24.312	1829	Bussy
Manganese	Mn	25	54.9380	1774	Gahn
Meitnerium	Mt	109	268*	1982	Münzenberg, et al.
Mendelevium	Md	101	258*	1955	Ghiorso, et al.
Mercury	Hg	80	200.59	BC	unknown
Molybdenum	Mo	42	95.94	1782	Hjelm
Neodymium	Nd	60	144.24	1885	Welsbach
Neon	Ne	10	20.183	1898	Ramsay, Travers
Neptunium	Np	93	237.05*	1940	McMillan, Abelson
Nickel	Ni	28	58.70	1751	Cronstedt
Niobium[2]	Nb	41	92.906	1801	Hatchett
Nitrogen	N	7	14.0067	1772	Rutherford
Nobelium	No	102	259*	1958	Ghiorso, et al.
Osmium	Os	76	190.2	1804	Tennant
Oxygen	O	8	15.9994a	1774	Priestley, Scheele
Palladium	Pd	46	106.4	1803	Wollaston
Phosphorus	P	15	30.9738	1669	Brand
Platinum	Pt	78	195.09	1735	Ulloa
Plutonium	Pu	94	242**	1940	Seaborg, et al.
Polonium	Po	84	210**	1898	P. and M. Curie
Potassium	K	19	39.102	1807	Davy
Praseodymium	Pr	59	140.907	1885	Welsbach
Promethium	Pm	61	147**	1945	Glendenin, Marinsky, Coryell
Protactinium	Pa	91	231.04*	1917	Hahn, Meitner
Radium	Ra	88	226.03*	1898	P. and M. Curie, Bemont
Radon	Rn	86	222*	1900	Dorn
Rhenium	Re	75	186.21	1925	Noddack, Tacke, Berg
Rhodium	Rh	45	102.905	1803	Wollaston
Rubidium	Rb	37	85.47	1861	Bunsen, Kirchhoff
Ruthenium	Ru	44	101.07	1845	Klaus
Rutherfordium	Rf	104	261*	1969	Ghiorso, et al.
Samarium	Sm	62	150.35	1879	Boisbaudran
Scandium	Sc	21	44.956	1879	Nilson
Seaborgium	Sg	106	266*	1974	Ghiorso, et al.
Selenium	Se	34	78.96	1817	Berzelius
Silicon	Si	14	28.086a	1823	Berzelius
Silver	Ag	47	107.868b	BC	unknown
Sodium	Na	11	22.9898	1807	Davy
Strontium	Sr	38	87.62	1790	Crawford
Sulfur	S	16	32.064a	BC	unknown
Tantalum	Ta	73	180.948	1802	Ekeberg
Technetium	Tc	43	99**	1937	Perrier, Segre
Tellurium	Te	52	127.60	1782	Von Reichenstein
Terbium	Tb	65	158.9324	1843	Mosander
Thallium	Tl	81	204.37	1861	Crookes
Thorium	Th	90	232.038	1828	Berzelius
Thulium	Tm	69	168.934	1879	Cleve
Tin	Sn	50	118.69	BC	unknown
Titanium	Ti	22	47.90	1791	Gregor
Tungsten (Wolfram)	W	74	183.85	1783	d'Elhujar
Uranium	U	92	238.03	1789	Klaproth
Vanadium	V	23	50.942	1830	Sefstrom
Xenon	Xe	54	131.30	1898	Ramsay, Travers
Ytterbium	Yb	70	173.04	1878	Marignac
Yttrium	Y	39	88.905	1794	Gadolin
Zinc	Zn	30	65.37	BC	unknown
Zirconium	Zr	40	91.22	1789	Klaproth

Note: 109 elements are listed here. In addition, elements 110-112 were discovered recently at the Gesellschaft für Schwerionenforschung (GSI) at Darmstadt, Germany, by a team led by Dr. Sigurd Hofmann; these elements have not yet been named. Elements 110 and 111, discovered in 1994, have atomic weights 273 and 272, respectively; element 112, discovered in 1996, has atomic weight 277. (1) The name Dubnium (Db) has been approved by IUPAC, but the name Hahnium is commonly used. (2) Formerly Columbium. (a) Atomic weights so designated are known to be variable because of natural variations in isotopic composition. The observed ranges are: hydrogen±0.0001; boron±0.003; carbon±0.005; oxygen±0.0001; silicon±0.001; sulfur±0.003. (b) Atomic weights so designated are believed to have the following experimental uncertainties: chlorine±0.001; chromium±0.001; iron±0.003; copper±0.001; bromine±0.001; silver±0.001.

Periodic Table of the Elements

Source: © 1996 Lawrence Berkeley National Laboratory

Parentheses indicate undiscovered elements.

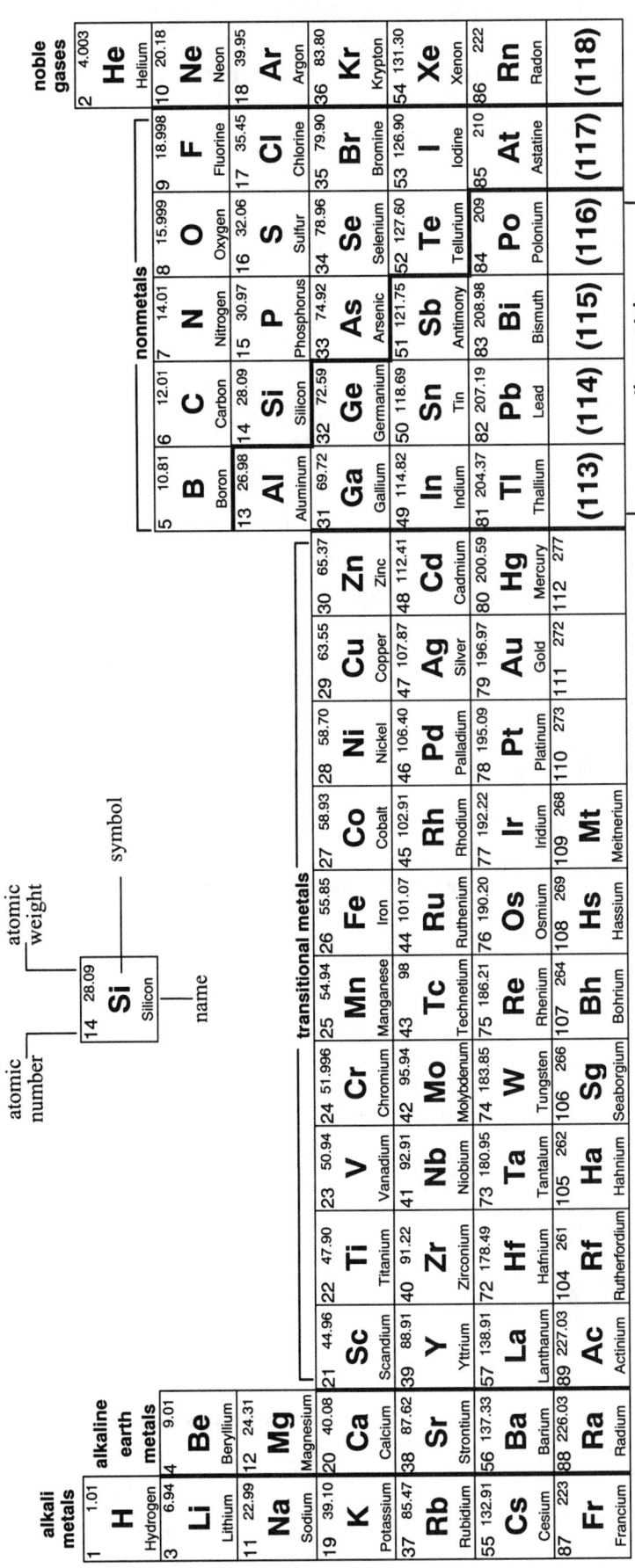

atomic number — 14 | atomic weight — 28.09 | symbol — Si | name — Silicon

Groups: alkali metals; alkaline earth metals; transitional metals; nonmetals; other metals; noble gases

1 1.01 H Hydrogen																	2 4.003 He Helium
3 6.94 Li Lithium	4 9.01 Be Beryllium											5 10.81 B Boron	6 12.01 C Carbon	7 14.01 N Nitrogen	8 15.999 O Oxygen	9 18.998 F Fluorine	10 20.18 Ne Neon
11 22.99 Na Sodium	12 24.31 Mg Magnesium											13 26.98 Al Aluminum	14 28.09 Si Silicon	15 30.97 P Phosphorus	16 32.06 S Sulfur	17 35.45 Cl Chlorine	18 39.95 Ar Argon
19 39.10 K Potassium	20 40.08 Ca Calcium	21 44.96 Sc Scandium	22 47.90 Ti Titanium	23 50.94 V Vanadium	24 51.996 Cr Chromium	25 54.94 Mn Manganese	26 55.85 Fe Iron	27 58.93 Co Cobalt	28 58.70 Ni Nickel	29 63.55 Cu Copper	30 65.37 Zn Zinc	31 69.72 Ga Gallium	32 72.59 Ge Germanium	33 74.92 As Arsenic	34 78.96 Se Selenium	35 79.90 Br Bromine	36 83.80 Kr Krypton
37 85.47 Rb Rubidium	38 87.62 Sr Strontium	39 88.91 Y Yttrium	40 91.22 Zr Zirconium	41 92.91 Nb Niobium	42 95.94 Mo Molybdenum	43 98 Tc Technetium	44 101.07 Ru Ruthenium	45 102.91 Rh Rhodium	46 106.40 Pd Palladium	47 107.87 Ag Silver	48 112.41 Cd Cadmium	49 114.82 In Indium	50 118.69 Sn Tin	51 121.75 Sb Antimony	52 127.60 Te Tellurium	53 126.90 I Iodine	54 131.30 Xe Xenon
55 132.91 Cs Cesium	56 137.33 Ba Barium	57 138.91 La Lanthanum	72 178.49 Hf Hafnium	73 180.95 Ta Tantalum	74 183.85 W Tungsten	75 186.21 Re Rhenium	76 190.20 Os Osmium	77 192.22 Ir Iridium	78 195.09 Pt Platinum	79 196.97 Au Gold	80 200.59 Hg Mercury	81 204.37 Tl Thallium	82 207.19 Pb Lead	83 208.98 Bi Bismuth	84 209 Po Polonium	85 210 At Astatine	86 222 Rn Radon
87 223 Fr Francium	88 226.03 Ra Radium	89 227.03 Ac Actinium	104 261 Rf Rutherfordium	105 262 Ha Hahnium	106 266 Sg Seaborgium	107 264 Bh Bohrium	108 269 Hs Hassium	109 268 Mt Meitnerium	110 273	111 272	112 277	(113)	(114)	(115)	(116)	(117)	(118)

Lanthanide series	58 140.12 Ce Cerium	59 140.91 Pr Praseodymium	60 144.24 Nd Neodymium	61 145 Pm Promethium	62 150.35 Sm Samarium	63 151.96 Eu Europium	64 157.25 Gd Gadolinium	65 158.93 Tb Terbium	66 162.50 Dy Dysprosium	67 164.93 Ho Holmium	68 167.26 Er Erbium	69 168.93 Tm Thulium	70 173.04 Yb Ytterbium	71 174.97 Lu Lutetium
Actinide series	90 232.04 Th Thorium	91 231.04 Pa Protactinium	92 238.03 U Uranium	93 237.05 Np Neptunium	94 244 Pu Plutonium	95 243 Am Americium	96 247 Cm Curium	97 247 Bk Berkelium	98 251 Cf Californium	99 252 Es Einsteinium	100 257 Fm Fermium	101 258 Md Mendelevium	102 259 No Nobelium	103 262 Lr Lawrencium

WEIGHTS AND MEASURES

Source: National Institute of Standards and Technology, U.S. Dept. of Commerce

The International System of Units (SI)

Two systems of weights and measures coexist in the U.S. today: the U.S. Customary System and the International System of Units (SI, after the initials of Système International). SI, commonly identified with the metric system, is actually a more complete, coherent version of it. Throughout U.S. history, the Customary System (inherited from, but now different from, the British Imperial System) has been generally used; federal and state legislation has given it, through implication, standing as the primary weights and measures system. The metric system, however, is the only system that Congress has ever specifically sanctioned. An 1866 law reads:

> It shall be lawful throughout the United States of America to employ the weights and measures of the metric system; and no contract or dealing, or pleading in any court, shall be deemed invalid or liable to objection because the weights or measures expressed or referred to therein are weights or measures of the metric system.

Since that time, use of the metric system in the U.S. has slowly and steadily increased, particularly in the scientific community, in the pharmaceutical industry, and in the manufacturing sector—the last motivated by the practice in international commerce, in which the metric system is now predominantly used.

On Feb. 10, 1964, the National Bureau of Standards (now known as the National Institute of Standards and Technology) issued the following statement:

> Henceforth it shall be the policy of the National Bureau of Standards to use the units of the International System (SI), as adopted by the 11th General Conference on Weights and Measures (October 1960), except when the use of these units would obviously impair communication or reduce the usefulness of a report.

On Dec. 23, 1975, Pres. Gerald R. Ford signed the Metric Conversion Act of 1975. It defines the metric system as being the International System of Units as interpreted in the U.S. by the secretary of commerce. The Trade Act of 1988 and other legislation declare the metric system the preferred system of weights and measures for U.S. trade and commerce, call for the federal government to adopt metric specifications, and mandate the Commerce Dept. to oversee the program. However, the metric system has still not become the system of choice for most Americans' daily use.

The following 7 units serve as the base units for the International System: **length**—meter; **mass**—kilogram; **time**—second; **electric current**—ampere; **thermodynamic temperature**—kelvin; **amount of substance**—mole; and **luminous intensity**—candela.

Prefixes

The following prefixes, in combination with the basic unit names, provide the multiples and submultiples in the International System. For example, the unit name *meter*, with the prefix *kilo* added, produces *kilometer*, meaning "1,000 meters."

Prefix	Symbol	Multiples	Equivalent
yotta	Y	10^{24}	septillionfold
zetta	Z	10^{21}	sextillionfold
exa	E	10^{18}	quintillionfold
peta	P	10^{15}	quadrillionfold
tera	T	10^{12}	trillionfold
giga	G	10^{9}	billionfold
mega	M	10^{6}	millionfold
kilo	k	10^{3}	thousandfold
hecto	h	10^{2}	hundredfold
deka	da	10	tenfold

Prefix	Symbol	Submultiples	Equivalent
deci	d	10^{-1}	tenth part
centi	c	10^{-2}	hundredth part
milli	m	10^{-3}	thousandth part
micro	µ	10^{-6}	millionth part
nano	n	10^{-9}	billionth part
pico	p	10^{-12}	trillionth part
femto	f	10^{-15}	quadrillionth part
atto	a	10^{-18}	quintillionth part
zepto	z	10^{-21}	sextillionth part
yocto	y	10^{-24}	septillionth part

Tables of Metric Weights and Measures

(**Note:** The SI generally uses the term *mass* instead of *weight*. Mass is a measure of an object's inertial property, or the amount of matter it contains. Weight is a measure of the force exerted on an object by gravity or the force needed to support it. Also, the SI does not make a distinction between "dry volume" and "liquid volume.")

Length

10 millimeters (mm)	= 1 centimeter (cm)
10 centimeters	= 1 decimeter (dm) = 100 millimeters
10 decimeters	= 1 meter (m) = 1,000 millimeters
10 meters	= 1 dekameter (dam)
10 dekameters	= 1 hectometer (hm) = 100 meters
10 hectometers	= 1 kilometer (km) = 1,000 meters

Area

100 square millimeters (mm^2)	= 1 square centimeter (cm^2)
10,000 square centimeters	= 1 square meter (m^2) = 1,000,000 square millimeters
100 square meters	= 1 are (a)
100 ares	= 1 hectare (ha) = 10,000 square meters
100 hectares	= 1 square kilometer (km^2) = 1,000,000 square meters

Volume

10 milliliters (mL)	= 1 centiliter (cL)
10 centiliters	= 1 deciliter (dL) = 100 milliliters
10 deciliters	= 1 liter (L) = 1,000 milliliters
10 liters	= 1 dekaliter (daL)
10 dekaliters	= 1 hectoliter (hL) = 100 liters
10 hectoliters	= 1 kiloliter (kL) = 1,000 liters

Volume (Cubic Measure)

1,000 cubic millimeters (mm^3)	= 1 cubic centimeter (cm^3)
1,000 cubic centimeters	= 1 cubic decimeter (dm^3) = 1,000,000 cubic millimeters
1,000 cubic decimeters	= 1 cubic meter (m^3) = 1 stere = 1,000,000 cubic centimeters = 1,000,000,000 cubic millimeters

Weight (Mass)

10 milligrams (mg)	= 1 centigram (cg)
10 centigrams	= 1 decigram (dg) = 100 milligrams
10 decigrams	= 1 gram (g) = 1,000 milligrams
10 grams	= 1 dekagram (dag)
10 dekagrams	= 1 hectogram (hg) = 100 grams
10 hectograms	= 1 kilogram (kg) = 1,000 grams
1,000 kilograms	= 1 metric ton (t)

Table of U.S. Customary Weights and Measures

Length

12 inches (in)	= 1 foot (ft)
3 feet	= 1 yard (yd)
5 ½ yards	= 1 rod (rd), pole, or perch (16 ½ feet)
40 rods	= 1 furlong (fur)=220 yards= 660 feet
8 furlongs	= 1 statute mile (mi) = 1,760 yards = 5,280 feet
3 miles	= 1 league = 5,280 yards = 15,840 feet
6076.11549 feet	= 1 international nautical mile

Volume (Liquid Measure)

When necessary to distinguish the liquid pint or quart from the dry pint or quart, the word *liquid* or the abbreviation *liq* is used in combination with the name or abbreviation of the liquid unit.

4 gills (gi)	= 1 pint (pt) = 28.875 cubic inches
2 pints	= 1 quart (qt) = 57.75 cubic inches
4 quarts	= 1 gallon (gal) = 231 cubic inches = 8 pints = 32 gills

Volume (Dry Measure)

When necessary to distinguish the dry pint or quart from the liquid pint or quart, the word *dry* is used in combination with the name or abbreviation of the dry unit.

2 pints (pt)	= 1 quart (qt) = 67.2006 cubic inches
8 quarts	= 1 peck (pk) = 537.605 cubic inches = 16 pints
4 pecks	= 1 bushel (bu) = 2,150.42 cubic inches = 32 quarts

Area

Squares and cubes of units are sometimes abbreviated by using superscripts. For example, ft^2 means square foot, and ft^3 means cubic foot.

144 square inches	= 1 square foot (ft^2)
9 square feet	= 1 square yard (yd^2) = 1,296 square inches
30 ¼ square yards	= 1 square rod (rd^2) = 272 ¼ square feet
160 square rods	= 1 acre = 4,840 square yards = 43,560 square feet
640 acres	= 1 square mile (mi^2)
1 mile square	= 1 section (of land)
6 miles square	= 1 township = 36 sections = 36 square miles

Cubic Measure

1 cubic foot (ft^3)	= 1,728 cubic inches (in^3)
27 cubic feet	= 1 cubic yard (yd^3)

Gunter's, or Surveyor's, Chain Measure

7.92 inches (in)	= 1 link
100 links	= 1 chain (ch) = 4 rods = 66 feet
80 chains	= 1 statute mile (mi) = 320 rods = 5,280 feet

Avoirdupois Weight

When necessary to distinguish the avoirdupois ounce or pound from the troy ounce or pound, the word *avoirdupois* or the abbreviation *avdp* is used in combination with the name or abbreviation of the avoirdupois unit. The *grain* is the same in avoirdupois and troy weight.

27 11/32 grains	= 1 dram (dr)
16 drams	= 1 ounce (oz) = 437 ½ grains
16 ounces	= 1 pound (lb) = 256 drams = 7,000 grains
100 pounds	= 1 hundredweight (cwt)*
20 hundredweights	= 1 ton = 2,000 pounds*

In *gross* or *long* measure, the following values are recognized.

112 pounds	= 1 gross or long hundredweight*
20 gross or long hundredweights	= 1 gross or long ton = 2,240 pounds*

*When the terms *hundredweight* and *ton* are used unmodified, they are commonly understood to mean the 100-pound hundredweight and the 2,000-pound ton, respectively; these units may be designated *net* or *short* when necessary to distinguish them from the corresponding units in gross or long measure.

Troy Weight

24 grains	= 1 pennyweight (dwt)
20 pennyweights	= 1 ounce troy (oz t) = 480 grains
12 ounces troy	= 1 pound troy (lb t) = 240 pennyweights = 5,760 grains

Tables of Equivalents

In this table it is necessary to distinguish between the *international* and the *survey* foot. The international foot, defined in 1959 as exactly equal to 0.3048 meter, is shorter than the old survey foot by exactly 2 parts in one million. The survey foot is still used in data expressed in feet in geodetic surveys within the U.S. In this table the survey foot is italicized.

When the name of a unit is enclosed in brackets, e.g., [1 hand], either (1) the unit is not in general current use in the U.S. or (2) the unit is believed to be based on custom and usage rather than on formal definition.

Equivalents involving decimals are, in most instances, rounded to the 3d decimal place; exact equivalents are so designated.

Lengths

1 angstrom (Å)	= 0.1 nanometer (exactly)
	= 0.000 1 micrometer (exactly)
	= 0.000 000 1 millimeter (exactly)
	= 0.000 000 004 inch
1 cable's length	= 120 fathoms (exactly)
	= 720 *feet* (exactly)
	= 219 meters
1 centimeter (cm)	= 0.3937 inch
1 chain (ch) (Gunter's or surveyor's)	= 66 *feet* (exactly)
	= 20.1168 meters
1 chain (engineer's)	= 100 feet
	= 30.48 meters (exactly)
1 decimeter (dm)	= 3.937 inches
1 degree (geographical)	= 364,566.929 feet
	= 69.047 miles (avg.)
	= 111.123 kilometers (avg.)
-of latitude	= 68.708 miles at equator
	= 69.403 miles at poles
-of longitude	= 69.171 miles at equator
1 dekameter (dam)	= 32.808 feet
1 fathom	= 6 *feet* (exactly)
	= 1.8288 meters
1 foot (ft)	= 0.3048 meters (exactly)
1 furlong (fur)	= 10 chains (surveyors) (exactly)
	= 660 *feet* (exactly)
	= 1/8 statute mile (exactly)
	= 201.168 meters
[1 hand] (height measure for horses from ground to top of shoulders)	= 4 inches
1 inch (in)	= 2.54 centimeters (exactly)
1 kilometer (km)	= 0.621371 mile
	= 3,280.8 feet
1 league (land)	= 3 statute miles (exactly)
	= 4.828 kilometers
1 link (Gunter's or surveyor's)	= 7.92 inches (exactly)
	= 0.201 meter
1 link (engineer's)	= 1 foot
	= 0.305 meter
1 meter (m)	= 39.37 inches
	= 1.09361 yards
1 micrometer (μm) [the Greek letter mu]	= 0.001 millimeter (exactly)
	= 0.00003937 inch
1 mil	= 0.001 inch (exactly)
	= 0.0254 millimeter (exactly)
1 mile (mi) (statute or land)	= 5,280 *feet* (exactly)
	= 1.609344 kilometers (exactly)
1 international nautical mile (nmi)	= 1.852 kilometers (exactly)
	= 1.150779 statute miles
	= 6,076.11549 feet
1 millimeter (mm)	= 0.03937 inch
1 nanometer (nm)	= 0.001 micrometer (exactly)
	= 0.00000003937 inch
1 pica (typography)	= 12 points
1 point (typography)	= 0.013 837 inch (exactly)
	= 0.351 millimeter
1 rod (rd), pole, or perch	= 16½ *feet* (exactly)
	= 5.029 meters
1 yard (yd)	= 0.9144 meter (exactly)

Areas or Surfaces

1 acre	= 43,560 square *feet* (exactly)
	= 4,840 square yards
	= 0.405 hectare
1 are (a)	= 119.599 square yards
	= 0.025 acre

(continued)

1 bolt (cloth measure):
  length = 100 yards (on modern looms)
  width = 45 or 60 inches
1 hectare (ha) = 2.471 acres
[1 square (building)] = 100 square feet
1 square centimeter (cm^2) = 0.155 square inch
1 square decimeter (dm^2) = 15.500 square inches
1 square foot (ft^2) = 929.030 square centimeters
1 square inch (in^2) = 6.4516 square centimeters (exactly)
1 square kilometer (km^2) = 247.104 acres
  = 0.386102 square mile
1 square meter (m^2) = 1.196 square yards
  = 10.764 square feet
1 square mile (mi^2) = 258.999 hectares
1 square millimeter (mm^2) = 0.002 square inch
1 square rod (rd^2), sq. pole, or sq. perch = 25.293 square meters
1 square yard (yd^2) = 0.836127 square meter

Capacities or Volumes

1 barrel (bbl), liquid = 31 to 42 gallons*

*There are a variety of "barrels" established by law or usage. For example: federal taxes on fermented liquors are based on a barrel of 31 gallons; many state laws fix the "barrel for liquids" as 31½ gallons; one state fixes a 36-gallon barrel for cistern measurement; federal law recognizes a 40-gallon barrel for "proof spirits"; by custom, 42 gallons constitute a barrel of crude oil or petroleum products for statistical purposes, and this equivalent is recognized "for liquids" by 4 states.

1 barrel (bbl), standard for fruits, vegetables, and other dry commodities except dry cranberries = 7,056 cubic inches
  = 105 dry quarts
  = 3.281 bushels, struck measure
1 barrel (bbl), standard, cranberry = 5,826 cubic inches
  = 86 45/64 dry quarts
  = 2.709 bushels, struck measure
1 board foot (lumber measure) = a foot-square board 1 inch thick
1 bushel (bu) (U.S.) (struck measure) = 2,150.42 cubic inches (exactly)
  = 35.239 liters
[1 bushel, heaped (U.S.)] = 2,747.715 cubic inches
  = 1.278 bushels, struck measure*

*Frequently recognized as 1¼ bushels, struck measure.

[1 bushel (bu) (British Imperial) (struck measure)] = 1.032 U.S. bushels, struck measure
  = 2,219.36 cubic inches
1 cord (cd) firewood = 128 cubic feet (exactly)
1 cubic centimeter (cm^3) = 0.061 cubic inch
1 cubic decimeter (dm^3) = 61.024 cubic inches
1 cubic inch (in^3) = 0.554 fluid ounce
  = 4.433 fluid drams
  = 16.387 cubic centimeters
1 cubic foot (ft^3) = 7.481 gallons
  = 28.317 cubic decimeters
1 cubic meter (m^3) = 1.308 cubic yards
1 cubic yard (yd^3) = 0.765 cubic meter
1 cup, measuring = 8 fluid ounces (exactly)
  = ½ liquid pint (exactly)
[1 drachm, fluid (fl dr) (British)] = 0.961 U.S. fluid dram
  = 0.217 cubic inch
  = 3.552 milliliters
1 dekaliter (daL) = 2.642 gallons
  = 1.135 pecks
1 gallon (gal) (U.S.) = 231 cubic inches (exactly)
  = 3.785 liters
  = 0.833 British gallon
  = 128 U.S. fluid ounces (exactly)
[1 gallon (gal) British Imperial] = 277.42 cubic inches
  = 1.201 U.S. gallons
  = 4.546 liters
  = 160 British fluid ounces (exactly)
1 gill (gi) = 7.219 cubic inches
  = 4 fluid ounces (exactly)
  = 0.118 liter
1 hectoliter (hL) = 26.418 gallons
  = 2.838 bushels
1 liter (L) (1 cubic decimeter exactly) = 1.057 liquid quarts
  = 0.908 dry quart
  = 61.024 cubic inches
1 milliliter (mL) (1 cu cm exactly) = 0.271 fluid dram
  = 16.231 minims
  = 0.061 cubic inch
1 ounce, liquid (U.S.) = 1.805 cubic inches
  = 29.574 milliliters
  = 1.041 British fluid ounces
[1 ounce, fluid (fl oz) (British)] = 0.961 U.S. fluid ounce
  = 1.734 cubic inches
  = 28.412 milliliters
1 peck (pk) = 8.810 liters
1 pint (pt), dry = 33.600 cubic inches
  = 0.551 liter
1 pint (pt), liquid = 28.875 cubic inches (exactly)
  = 0.473 liter
1 quart (qt), dry (U.S.) = 67.201 cubic inches
  = 1.101 liters
  = 0.969 British quart
1 quart (qt), liquid (U.S.) = 57.75 cubic in (exactly)
  = 0.946 liter
  = 0.833 British quart
[1 quart (qt) (British)] = 69.354 cubic inches
  = 1.032 U.S. dry quarts
  = 1.201 U.S. liquid quarts
1 tablespoon = 3 teaspoons* (exactly)
  = 4 fluid drams
  = ½ fluid ounce (exactly)
1 teaspoon = 1/3 tablespoon* (exactly)
  = 1 1/3 fluid drams*

*The equivalent "1 teaspoon=1 1/3 fluid drams" has been found to correspond more closely with the actual capacities of teaspoons in use than the equivalent "1 teaspoon=1 fluid dram" which is given by many dictionaries.

Weights or Masses

1 assay ton** (AT) = 29.167 grams

**Used in assaying. The assay ton bears the same relation to the milligram that a ton of 2,000 pounds avoirdupois bears to the ounce troy; hence, the weight in milligrams of precious metal obtained from one assay ton of ore gives directly the number of troy ounces to the net ton.

1 bale (cotton measure) = 500 pounds in U.S.
  = 750 pounds in Egypt
1 carat (c) = 200 milligrams (exactly)
  = 3.086 grains
1 dram avoirdupois (dr avdp) = 27 11/32 (=27.344) grains
  = 1.772 grams
1 gamma (γ) = 1 microgram (exactly), see below
1 grain = 64.7989 milligrams
1 gram = 15.432 grains
  = 0.035 ounce, avoirdupois
1 hundredweight, gross or long*** (gross cwt) = 112 pounds (exactly)
  = 50.802 kilograms
1 hundredweight, net or short (cwt or net cwt) = 100 pounds (exactly)
  = 45.359 kilograms
1 kilogram (kg) = 2.20462 pounds
1 microgram (μg [the Greek letter mu in combination with the letter g]) = 0.000001 gram (exactly)
1 milligram (mg) = 0.015 grain
1 ounce, avoirdupois (oz avdp) = 437.5 grains (exactly)
  = 0.911 troy ounce
  = 28.3495 grams
1 ounce, troy (oz t) = 480 grains (exactly)
  = 1.097 avoirdupois ounces
  = 31.103 grams
1 pennyweight (dwt) = 1.555 grams
1 pound, avoirdupois (lb avdp) = 7,000 grains (exactly)
  = 1.215 troy pounds
  = 453.59237 grams (exactly)
1 pound, troy (lb t) = 5,760 grains (exactly)
  = 0.823 pound, avoirdupois
  = 373.242 grams
1 ton, gross or long*** (gross ton) = 2,240 pounds (exactly)
  = 1.12 net tons (exactly)
  = 1.016 metric tons

***The gross or long ton and hundredweight are used commercially in the U.S. to only a limited extent, usually in restricted industrial fields. These units are the same as the British ton and hundredweight.

1 ton, metric (t) = 2,204.623 pounds
  = 0.984 gross ton
  = 1.102 net tons
1 ton, net or short (sh ton) = 2,000 pounds (exactly)
  = 0.893 gross ton
  = 0.907 metric ton

Tables of Interrelation of Units of Measurement

Units of length and area of the international and survey measures are included in the following tables. Units unique to the survey measure are *italicized*. See Tables of Equivalents, 1st paragraph.

1 international foot = 0.999 998 survey foot (exactly)
1 survey foot = 1200/3937 meter (exactly)
1 international foot = 12 × 0.0254 meter (exactly)

Boldface type indicates exact values.

Units of Length

Units	Inches	*Links*	Feet	Yards	*Rods*	*Chains*	Miles	Cm	Meters
1 inch=	1	0.126 263	0.083 333	0.027 778	0.005 051	0.001 263	0.000 016	**2.54**	**0.025 4**
1 *link*=	**7.92**	1	**0.66**	**0.22**	**0.04**	0.01	0.000 125	20.117	0.201 168
1 foot=	**12**	1.515 152	1	0.333 333	0.060 606	0.015 152	0.000 189	**30.48**	**0.304 8**
1 yard=	**36**	4.545 45	**3**	1	0.181 818	0.045 455	0.000 568	**91.44**	**0.914 4**
1 *rod*=	**198**	**25**	**16.5**	**5.5**	1	**0.25**	**0.003 125**	502.92	5.029 2
1 *chain*=	**792**	**100**	**66**	**22**	**4**	1	**0.012 5**	2011.68	20.116 8
1 mile=	**63 360**	**8000**	**5280**	**1760**	**320**	**80**	1	**160 934.4**	**1609.344**
1 cm=	0.3937	0.049 710	0.032 808	0.010 936	0.001 988	0.000 497	0.000 006	1	**0.01**
1 meter=	39.37	4.970 960	3.280 840	1.093 613	0.198 838	0.049 710	0.000 621	**100**	1

Units of Area

Units	Sq. inches	*Sq. links*	Sq. feet	Sq. yards	*Sq. rods*	*Sq. chains*
1 sq. inch=	1	0.015 942 3	0.006 944	0.000 771 605	0.000 025 5	0.000 001 594
1 sq. *link*=	62.726 4	1	**0.435 6**	**0.0484**	**0.0016**	0.000 1
1 sq. foot=	**144**	2.295 684	1	0.111 111 1	0.003 673 09	0.000 229 568
1 sq. yard=	**1296**	20.661 16	**9**	1	0.033 057 85	0.002 066 12
1 sq. *rod*=	**39 204**	**625**	**272.25**	**30.25**	1	0.062 5
1 sq. *chain*=	**627 264**	**10 000**	**4356**	**484**	**16**	1
1 *acre*=	**6 272 640**	**100 000**	**43 560**	**4840**	**160**	**10**
1 sq. mile=	**4 014 489 600**	**64 000 000**	**27 878 400**	**3 097 600**	**102 400**	**6400**
1 sq. cm=	0.155 000 3	0.002 471 05	0.001 076	0.000 119 599	0.000 003 954	0.000 000 247
1 sq. meter=	1550.003	24.710 44	10.763 91	1.195 990	0.039 536 70	0.002 471 044
1 *hectare*=	15 500 031	247 104	107 639.1	11 959.90	395.367 0	**24.710 44**

Units	*Acres*	Sq. miles	Sq. cm	Sq. meters	*Hectares*
1 sq. inch=	0.000 000 159 423	0.000 000 000 249 10	**6.451 6**	**0.000 645 16**	0.000 000 065
1 sq. *link*=	**0.000 01**	**0.000 000 015 625**	404.685 642 24	0.040 468 56	0.000 004 047
1 sq. foot=	0.000 022 956 84	0.000 000 035 870 06	929.034 1	0.092 903 41	0.000 009 290
1 sq. yard=	0.000 206 611 6	0.000 000 322 830 6	**8361.273 6**	0.836 127 36	0.000 083 613
1 sq. *rod*=	**0.006 25**	**0.000 009 765 625**	252 929.5	25.292 95	0.002 529 295
1 sq. *chain*=	**0.1**	**0.000 156 25**	4 046 873	404.687 3	0.040 468 73
1 *acre*=	1	**0.001 562 5**	40 468 730	4046.873	0.404 687 3
1 sq. mile=	**640**	1	25 899 881 103	2 589 988.11	258.998 811 034
1 sq. cm=	0.000 000 024 711	0.000 000 000 038 610	1	**0.000 1**	**0.000 000 01**
1 sq. meter=	0.000 247 104 4	0.000 000 386 102 2	**10 000**	1	**0.0001**
1 *hectare*=	2.471 044	0.003 861 006	**100 000 000**	**10 000**	1

Units of Weight or Mass Not Greater Than Pounds and Kilograms

Units	Grains	Pennyweights	Avdp drams	Avdp ounces
1 grain=	1	0.041 666 67	0.036 571 43	0.002 285 71
1 pennyweight=	**24**	1	0.877 714 3	0.054 857 14
1 dram avdp=	**27.343 75**	1.139 323	1	**0.062 5**
1 ounce avdp=	**437.5**	18.229 17	**16**	1
1 ounce troy=	**480**	**20**	17.554 29	1.097 143
1 pound troy=	**5760**	**240**	210.651 4	13.165 71
1 pound avdp=	**7000**	291.666 7	**256**	**16**
1 milligram=	0.015 432	0.000 643 015	0.000 564 383	0.000 035 274
1 gram=	15.432 36	0.643 014 9	0.564 383 4	0.035 273 96
1 kilogram=	15 432.36	643.014 9	564.383 4	35.273 96

Units	Troy ounces	Troy pounds	Avdp pounds	Milligrams	Grams	Kilograms
1 grain=	0.002 083 33	0.000 173 611	0.000 142 857	**64.798 91**	**0.064 798 91**	0.000 064 799
1 pennywt.=	**0.05**	0.004 166 667	0.003 428 571	**1555.173 84**	**1.555 173 84**	0.001 555 174
1 dram avdp=	0.056 966 15	0.004 747 179	0.003 906 25	1771.845 195	1.771 845 195	0.001 771 845
1 oz avdp=	0.911 458 3	0.075 954 86	0.062 5	**28 349.523 125**	**28.349 523 125**	0.028 349 52
1 oz troy=	1	0.083 333 333	0.068 571 43	**31 103.476 8**	**31.103 476 8**	0.031 103 48
1 lb troy=	**12**	1	0.822 857 1	**373 241.721 6**	**373.241 721 6**	0.373 241 722
1 lb avdp=	14.583 33	1.215 278	1	**453 592.37**	**453.592 37**	**0.453 592 37**
1 milligram=	0.000 032 151	0.000 002 679	0.000 002 205	1	**0.001**	**0.000 001**
1 gram=	0.032 150 75	0.002 679 229	0.002 204 623	**1000**	1	**0.001**
1 kilogram=	32.150 75	2.679 229	2.204 623	**1 000 000**	**1000**	1

Units of Weight or Mass Not Less Than Avoirdupois Ounces

Units	Avdp oz	Avdp lb	Short cwt	Short tons	Long tons	Kilograms	Metric tons
1 oz avdp=	1	**0.0625**	**0.000 625**	**0.000 031 25**	0.000 027 902	0.028 349 523	0.000 028 350
1 lb avdp=	**16**	1	**0.01**	**0.000 5**	0.000 446 429	**0.453 592 37**	0.000 453 592
1 sh cwt=	**1600**	**100**	1	**0.05**	0.044 642 86	**45.359 237**	**0.045 359 237**
1 sh ton=	**32 000**	**2000**	**20**	1	0.892 857 1	**907.184 74**	**0.907 184 74**
1 long ton=	**35 840**	**2240**	**22.4**	**1.12**	1	**1 016.046 908 8**	1.016 046 909
1 kg=	35.273 96	2.204 623	0.022 046 23	0.001 102 311	0.000 984 207	1	**0.001**
1 metric ton=	35 273.96	2204.623	22.046 23	1.102 311	0.984 206 5	**1000**	1

Units of Volume

Units	Cubic inches	Cubic feet	Cubic yards	Cubic cm	Cubic dm	Cubic meters
1 cubic inch=	1	0.000 578 704	0.000 021 433	**16.387 064**	0.016 387	0.000 016 387
1 cubic foot=	**1728**	1	0.037 037 04	**28 316.846 592**	28.316 847	0.028 316 847
1 cubic yard=	**46 656**	**27**	1	**764 554.857 984**	764.554 858	0.764 554 858
1 cubic cm=	0.061 023 74	0.000 035 315	0.000 001 308	1	**0.001**	**0.000 001**
1 cubic dm=	61.023 74	0.035 314 67	0.001 307 951	**1000**	1	**0.001**
1 cubic meter=	61 023.74	35.314 67	1.307 951	**1 000 000**	**1000**	1

Units of Capacity (Liquid Measure)

Units	Minims	Fluid drams	Fluid ounces	Gills	Liquid pint
1 minim=	1	0.016 666 7	0.002 083 33	0.000 520 833	0.000 130 208
1 fluid dram=	**60**	1	**0.125**	**0.031 25**	**0.007 812 5**
1 fluid ounce=	**480**	**8**	1	**0.25**	**0.062 5**
1 gill=	**1920**	**32**	**4**	1	**0.25**
1 liquid pint=	**7680**	**128**	**16**	**4**	1
1 liquid quart=	**15 360**	**256**	**32**	**8**	**2**
1 gallon=	**61 440**	**1024**	**128**	**32**	**8**
1 cubic inch=	265.974	4.432 900	0.554 112 6	0.138 528 1	0.034 632 03
1 cubic foot=	459 603.1	7660.052	957.506 5	239.376 6	59.844 16
1 liter=	16 230.73	270.512 18	33.814 02	8.453 506	2.113 376

Units	Liquid quarts	Gallons	Cubic inches	Cubic feet	Liters
1 minim=	0.000 065 104 17	0.000 016 276 04	0.003 759 766	0.000 002 175 790	0.000 061 611 52
1 flu. dram=	**0.003 906 25**	**0.000 976 562 5**	0.225 585 9	0.000 130 547 4	0.003 696 691
1 fluid oz=	**0.031 25**	**0.007 812 5**	**1.804 687 5**	0.001 044 379	0.029 573 53
1 gill=	**0.125**	**0.031 25**	**7.218 75**	0.004 177 517	0.118 294 118
1 liquid pt=	**0.5**	**0.125**	**28.875**	0.016 710 07	0.473 176 473
1 liquid qt=	1	**0.25**	**57.75**	0.033 420 14	0.946 352 946
1 gallon=	**4**	1	**231**	0.133 680 6	3.785 411 784
1 cubic inch=	0.017 316 02	0.004 329 004	1	0.000 578 703 7	0.016 387 064
1 cubic foot=	29.922 08	7.480 519	**1728**	1	**28.316 846 592**
1 liter=	1.056 688	0.264 172 05	61.023 74	0.035 314 67	1

Units of Capacity (Dry Measure)

Units	Dry pints	Dry quarts	Pecks	Bushels	Cubic in.	Liters
1 dry pint=	1	0.5	**0.062 5**	**0.015 625**	**33.600 312 5**	0.550 610 47
1 dry quart=	**2**	1	**0.125**	**0.031 25**	**67.200 625**	1.101 220 9
1 peck=	**16**	**8**	1	**0.25**	**537.605**	8.809 767 5
1 bushel=	**64**	**32**	**4**	1	**2150.42**	35.239 07
1 cubic inch=	0.029 761 6	0.014 880 8	0.001 860 10	0.000 465 025	1	0.016 387 06
1 liter=	1.816 166	0.908 083	0.113 510 37	0.028 377 59	61.023 74	1

Miscellaneous Measures

Caliber—the diameter of a gun bore. In the U.S., caliber is traditionally expressed in hundredths of inches, e.g., .22 or .30. In Britain, caliber is often expressed in thousandths of inches, e.g., .270 or .465. Now it is commonly expressed in millimeters, e.g., the 5.56 mm M16 rifle. Heavier weapons' caliber has long been expressed in millimeters, e.g., the 81 mm mortar, the 105 mm howitzer (light), the 155 mm howitzer (medium or heavy).

Naval guns' caliber refers to the barrel length as a multiple of the bore diameter. A 5-inch, 50-caliber naval gun has a 5-inch bore and a barrel length of 250 inches.

Karat or carat—a measure of fineness for gold equal to 1/24 part of pure gold in an alloy. Thus 24-karat gold is pure; 18-karat gold is 1/4 alloy. (A *carat* is also a unit of weight for precious stones, equal to 200 milligrams.)

Decibel (dB)—a measure of the relative loudness or intensity of sound. A 20-decibel sound is 10 times louder than a 10-decibel sound; 30 decibels is 100 times louder; 40 decibels is 1,000 times louder, etc. One decibel is the smallest difference between sounds detectable by the human ear. A 120-decibel sound is painful.

10 decibels	–	a light whisper
20	–	quiet conversation
30	–	normal conversation
40	–	light traffic
50	–	typewriter, loud conversation
60	–	noisy office
70	–	normal traffic, quiet train
80	–	rock music, subway
90	–	heavy traffic, thunder
100	–	jet plane at takeoff

Em—a printer's measure designating the square width of any given type size. Thus, an em of 10-point type is 10 points. An en is half an em.

Gauge—a measure of shotgun bore diameter. Gauge numbers originally referred to the number of lead balls just fitting the gun barrel diameter required to make a pound. Thus, a 16-gauge shotgun's bore was smaller than a 12-gauge shotgun's. Today, an international agreement assigns millimeter measures to each gauge, e.g.:

Gauge	Bore diameter (in mm)
6	23.34
10	19.67
12	18.52
14	17.60
16	16.81
20	15.90

Horsepower—the power needed to lift 550 pounds 1 foot in 1 second or to lift 33,000 pounds 1 foot in 1 minute. Equivalent to 746 watts or 2,546.0756 Btu/h.

Knot—a measure of the speed of ships. A knot equals 1 nautical mile per hour.

Quire—25 sheets of paper

Ream—500 sheets of paper

Electrical Units

The **watt** is the unit of power (electrical, mechanical, thermal, etc.). Electrical power is given by the product of the voltage and the current.

Energy is sold by the **joule,** but in common practice the billing of electrical energy is expressed in terms of the **kilowatt-hour,** which is 3,600,000 joules or 3.6 megajoules.

The **horsepower** is a nonmetric unit sometimes used in mechanics. It is equal to 746 watts.

The **ohm** is the unit of electrical resistance and represents the physical property of a conductor that offers a resistance to the flow of electricity, permitting just 1 ampere to flow at 1 volt of pressure.

Ancient Measures

Biblical

Cubit	=	21.8 inches
Omer	=	0.45 peck
	=	3.964 liters
Ephah	=	10 omers
Shekel	=	0.497 ounce
	=	14.1 grams

Greek

Cubit	=	18.3 inches
Stadion	=	607.2 or 622 feet
Obolos	=	715.38 milligrams
Drachma	=	4.2923 grams
Mina	=	0.9463 pound
Talent	=	60 mina

Roman

Cubit	= 17.5 inches
Stadium	= 202 yards
As, libra, pondus	= 325.971 grams
	= 0.71864 pound

Spirits Measures

Pony	= 0.5 jigger	Quart	= 32 shots	For champagne only:	
Shot	= 0.666 jigger		= 1.25 fifths		
	= 1.0 ounce	Magnum	= 2 quarts	Rehoboam	= 3 magnums
Jigger	= 1.5 shots		= 2.49797 bottles (wine)	Methuselah	= 4 magnums
Pint	= 16 shots			Salmanazar	= 6 magnums
	= 0.625 fifth	For champagne and brandy only:		Balthazar	= 8 magnums
Fifth	= 25.6 shots			Nebuchadnezzar	= 10 magnums
	= 1.6 pints	Jeroboam	= 6.4 pints		
	= 0.8 quart		= 1.6 magnum	Wine bottle (standard)	= 0.800633 quart
	= 0.75706 liter		= 0.8 gallon		= 0.7576778 liter

Temperature Conversion Table

The numbers in **boldface type** refer to the temperatures either in degrees Celsius or Fahrenheit that are to be converted. If converting from degrees Fahrenheit to Celsius, refer to the column on the left; if converting from degrees Celsius to Fahrenheit, consult the column on the right.

For temperatures not shown. To convert Fahrenheit to Celsius by formula, subtract 32 degrees and divide by 1.8; to convert Celsius to Fahrenheit, multiply by 1.8 and add 32 degrees.

Note: Although the term *centigrade* is still frequently used, the International Committee on Weights and Measures and the National Institute of Standards and Technology have recommended since 1948 that this scale be called Celsius.

Celsius		Fahrenheit	Celsius		Fahrenheit	Celsius		Fahrenheit
–273.2	**–459.7**	......	–17.8	**0**	32	35.0	**95**	203
–184	**–300**	......	–12.2	**10**	50	36.7	**98**	208.4
–169	**–273**	– 459.4	– 6.67	**20**	68	37.8	**100**	212
–157	**–250**	– 418	– 1.11	**30**	86	43	**110**	230
–129	**–200**	– 328	4.44	**40**	104	49	**120**	248
–101	**–150**	– 238	10.0	**50**	122	54	**130**	266
– 73.3	**–100**	– 148	15.6	**60**	140	60	**140**	284
– 45.6	**– 50**	– 58	21.1	**70**	158	66	**150**	302
– 40.0	**– 40**	– 40	23.9	**75**	167	93	**200**	392
– 34.4	**– 30**	– 22	26.7	**80**	176	121	**250**	482
– 28.9	**– 20**	– 4	29.4	**85**	185	149	**300**	572
– 23.3	**– 10**	14	32.2	**90**	194			

Boiling and Freezing Points

Water boils at 212°F at sea level. For every 550 feet above sea level, boiling point of water is lower by about 1°F. Methyl alcohol boils at 148°F. Average human oral temperature, 98.6°F. Water freezes at 32°F.

Compound Interest

Compounded Annually

Principal	Period	4%	5%	6%	7%	8%	9%	10%	12%	14%	16%
$100	1 day	0.011	0.014	0.016	0.019	0.022	0.025	0.027	0.033	0.038	0.044
	1 week	0.077	0.096	0.115	0.134	0.153	0.173	0.192	0.230	0.268	0.307
	6 mos.	2.00	2.50	3.00	3.50	4.00	4.50	5.00	6.00	7.00	8.00
	1 year	4.00	5.00	6.00	7.00	8.00	9.00	10.00	12.00	14.00	16.00
	2 years	8.16	10.25	12.36	14.49	16.64	18.81	21.00	25.44	29.96	34.56
	3 years	12.49	15.76	19.10	22.50	25.97	29.50	33.10	40.49	48.15	56.09
	4 years	16.99	21.55	26.25	31.08	36.05	41.16	46.41	57.35	68.90	81.06
	5 years	21.67	27.63	33.82	40.26	46.93	53.86	61.05	76.23	92.54	110.03
	6 years	26.53	34.01	41.85	50.07	58.69	67.71	77.16	97.38	119.50	143.64
	7 years	31.59	40.71	50.36	60.58	71.38	82.80	94.87	121.07	150.23	182.62
	8 years	36.86	47.75	59.38	71.82	85.09	99.26	114.36	147.60	185.26	227.84
	9 years	42.33	55.13	68.95	83.85	99.90	117.19	135.79	177.31	225.19	280.30
	10 years	48.02	62.89	79.08	96.72	115.89	136.74	159.37	210.58	270.72	341.14
	12 years	60.10	79.59	101.22	125.22	151.82	181.27	213.84	289.60	381.79	493.60
	15 years	80.09	107.89	139.66	175.90	217.22	264.25	317.72	447.36	613.79	826.55
	20 years	119.11	165.33	220.71	286.97	366.10	460.44	572.75	864.63	1,274.35	1,846.08

Common Fractions Reduced to Decimals

8ths	16ths	32ds	64ths	
			1	= 0.015625
		1	2	= 0.03125
			3	= 0.046875
	1	2	4	= 0.0625
			5	= 0.078125
		3	6	= 0.09375
			7	= 0.109375
1	2	4	8	= 0.125
			9	= 0.140625
		5	10	= 0.15625
			11	= 0.171875
	3	6	12	= 0.1875
			13	= 0.203125
		7	14	= 0.21875
			15	= 0.234375
2	4	8	16	= 0.25
			17	= 0.265625
		9	18	= 0.28125
			19	= 0.296875
	5	10	20	= 0.3125
			21	= 0.328125
		11	22	= 0.34375

8ths	16ths	32ds	64ths	
			23	= 0.359375
3	6	12	24	= 0.375
			25	= 0.390625
		13	26	= 0.40625
			27	= 0.421875
	7	14	28	= 0.4375
			29	= 0.453125
		15	30	= 0.46875
			31	= 0.484375
4	8	16	32	= 0.5
			33	= 0.515625
		17	34	= 0.53125
			35	= 0.546875
		18	36	= 0.5625
			37	= 0.578125
		19	38	= 0.59375
			39	= 0.609375
5	10	20	40	= 0.625
			41	= 0.640625
		21	42	= 0.65625
			43	= 0.671875

8ths	16ths	32ds	64ths	
	11	22	44	= 0.6875
			45	= 0.703125
		23	46	= 0.71875
			47	= 0.734375
6	12	24	48	= 0.75
			49	= 0.765625
		25	50	= 0.78125
			51	= 0.796875
	13	26	52	= 0.8125
			53	= 0.828125
		27	54	= 0.84375
			55	= 0.859375
7	14	28	56	= 0.875
			57	= 0.890625
		29	58	= 0.90625
			59	= 0.921875
	15	30	60	= 0.9375
			61	= 0.953125
		31	62	= 0.96875
			63	= 0.984375
8	16	32	64	= 1.0

Measures of Force and Pressure

Dyne = force necessary to accelerate a 1-gram mass 1 centimeter per second squared = 0.000072 poundal

Poundal = force necessary to accelerate a 1-pound mass 1 foot per second squared = 13,825.5 dynes = 0.138255 newtons

Newton = force needed to accelerate a 1-kilogram mass 1 meter per second squared

Pascal (pressure) = 1 newton per square meter = 0.020885 pound per square foot

Atmosphere (air pressure at sea level) = 2,116.102 pounds per square foot = 14.6952 pounds per square inch = 1.0332 kilograms per square centimeter = 101,323 newtons per square meter

Mathematical Formulas

Note: The value of π (the Greek letter pi) is approximately 3.14159265 (equal to the ratio of the circumference of a circle to the diameter), typically rounded further to 3.1416 or 3.14.

To find the CIRCUMFERENCE of a:

Circle — Multiply the diameter by π.

To find the AREA of a:

Circle — Multiply the square of the radius (equal to ½ the diameter) by π.

Rectangle — Multiply the length of the base by the height.

Sphere (surface) — Multiply the square of the radius by π and multiply by 4.

Square — Square the length of one side.

Trapezoid — Add the two parallel sides, multiply by the height, and divide by 2.

Triangle — Multiply the base by the height, divide by 2.

To find the VOLUME of a:

Cone — Multiply the square of the radius of the base by π, multiply by the height, and divide by 3.

Cube — Cube the length of one edge.

Cylinder— Multiply the square of the radius of the base by π and multiply by the height.

Pyramid — Multiply the area of the base by the height and divide by 3.

Rectangular Prism — Multiply the length by the width by the height.

Sphere —Multiply the cube of the radius by π, multiply by 4, and divide by 3.

Playing Cards and Dice Chances

5-Card Poker Hands

Hand	Number possible	Odds against
Royal flush	4	649,739 to 1
Other straight flush	36	72,192 to 1
Four of a kind	624	4,164 to 1
Full house	3,744	693 to 1
Flush	5,108	508 to 1
Straight	10,200	254 to 1
Three of a kind	54,912	46 to 1
Two pairs	123,552	20 to 1
One pair	1,098,240	4 to 3 (1.37 to 1)
Nothing	1,302,540	1 to 1
Total	**2,598,960**	

Note: Although there are only 13 4-of-a-kind combinations, the above numbers take into account the total possibilities when a fifth card is figured in to make a five-card hand.

Dice

(probabilities of consecutive winning plays)

No. consecutive wins	By 7,11, or point	No. consecutive wins	By 7, 11, or point
1	244 in 495	6	1 in 70
2	6 in 25	7	1 in 141
3	3 in 25	8	1 in 287
4	1 in 17	9	1 in 582
5	1 in 34		

Dice

(probabilities on 2 dice)

Total	Odds against (single toss)	Total	Odds against (single toss)
2	35 to 1	8	31 to 5
3	17 to 1	9	8 to 1
4	11 to 1	10	11 to 1
5	8 to 1	11	17 to 1
6	31 to 5	12	35 to 1
7	5 to 1		

Pinochle Auction

(odds against finding in "widow" of 3 cards)

Open places	Odds	Open places	Odds
1	5 to 1 against	4	1½ to 1 for
2	2 to 1 against	5	2 to 1 for
3	Even	6	3 to 1 for

Bridge

The odds—against suit distribution in a hand of 4-4-3-2 are about 4 to 1, against 5-4-2-2 about 8 to 1, against 6-4-2-1 about 20 to 1, against 7-4-1-1 about 254 to 1, against 8-4-1-0 about 2,211 to 1, and against 13-0-0-0 about 158,753,389,899 to 1.

Large Numbers

U.S.	Number of zeros	British[1], French, German
million	6	million
billion	9	milliard
trillion	12	billion
quadrillion	15	1,000 billion
quintillion	18	trillion
sextillion	21	1,000 trillion
septillion	24	quadrillion
octillion	27	1,000 quadrillion
nonillion	30	quintillion
decillion	33	1,000 quintillion
undecillion	36	sextillion
duodecillion	39	1,000 sextillion
tredecillion	42	septillion
quattuordecillion	45	1,000 septillion
quindecillion	48	octillion
sexdecillion	51	1,000 octillion
septendecillion	54	nonillion
octodecillion	57	1,000 nonillion
novemdecillion	60	decillion
vigintillion	63	1,000 decillion
googol	100	googol
centillion	303	—
—	600	centillion
googolplex	googol	googolplex

(1) In recent years, it has become more common in Britain to use American terminology for large numbers.

Roman Numerals

I — 1	VI — 6	XI — 11	L — 50	CD — 400	$\overline{X}$ — 10,000
II — 2	VII — 7	XIX — 19	LX — 60	D — 500	$\overline{L}$ — 50,000
III — 3	VIII — 8	XX — 20	XC — 90	CM — 900	$\overline{C}$ — 100,000
IV — 4	IX — 9	XXX— 30	C — 100	M — 1,000	$\overline{D}$ — 500,000
V — 5	X — 10	XL — 40	CC — 200	$\overline{V}$ — 5,000	$\overline{M}$ — 1,000,000

THE INTERNET AND COMPUTERS

What Is the Internet?

The **Internet** is a vast computer network of computer networks. In 1994, 3 million people (most of them in the United States) made use of it. In 1998, 100 million people around the world were using the Internet, and it is estimated that by 2005, some 1 billion people may be connected.

Some other facts about the Internet and computing:

- Recent research estimates that there are now 320 million pages on the Web.
- UUNET, a large Internet backbone, estimates that traffic on the Internet doubles every 100 days.
- By December 1996, about 627,000 Internet domain names had been registered. By October 1998, 2.3 million had been registered.
- Radio existed 38 years before 50 million people tuned in. It took television 13 years to reach 50 million viewers. After the introduction of the first personal computer kit, it took 16 years before 50 million people were using one. But within only 4 years of the Internet's being opened to the general public, 50 million people were connected.
- Today, a strand of optical fiber as thin as a human hair can transmit the equivalent of 90,000 volumes of an encyclopedia in a single second.

(You can find information such as this, and more, in *The Emerging Digital Economy,* a study released by the U.S. Department of Commerce in May 1998. The entire text is available at `http://www.ecommerce.gov`)

The Internet is not owned or funded by any one institution, organization, or government. It does not have a CEO and is not a commercial service. The Internet is, however, directed by the Internet Society (ISOC), composed of volunteers. The ISOC appoints a subcouncil, the Internet Architecture Board (IAB), which works out issues of standards, network resources, network addresses, and so on. Another volunteer group, the Internet Engineering Task Force (IETF), handles day-to-day issues of Internet operation.

Practically speaking, the Internet is composed of people, hardware, and software. With the proper equipment on both ends, you can sit at your computer and communicate with someone anyplace in the world. You can also use the Internet to access vast amounts of information, including text, graphics, sound, and video. From your computer you can send e-mail, "chat" with others on another continent, do your banking, purchase stocks, buy books, flowers, cars, and so on, work with others on an electronic whiteboard, and, with the appropriate equipment, video-conference.

How Did It Originate?

The Internet grew out of a series of developments in the academic, governmental, and information technology communities. Listed below are some of the major milestones:

- In 1969, ARPAnet, an experimental 4-computer network, was established by the Advanced Research Projects Agency (ARPA) of the U.S. Department of Defense so that research scientists could communicate.
- By 1971, ARPAnet linked almost 2 dozen sites, including MIT and Harvard. By 1974, there were over 200 sites.
- During the 1980s, more and more computers using different operating systems were connected. In 1983, the military portion of ARPAnet was moved onto the MILnet, and ARPAnet was officially disbanded in 1990.
- In the late 1980s, the National Science Foundation's NSFnet began its own network and allowed everyone to access it. It was, however, primarily the domain of "techies," computer-science graduates, and university professors.
- In 1991, Al Gore, then a U.S. senator, proposed widening the NSFnet to include more schools and colleges. Resulting legislation expanded NSFnet, renamed it NREN (National Research and Educational Network), and allowed businesses to purchase part of the network for commercial uses. The mass commercialization of today's Internet is a result of this legislation.
- In 1992, the World Wide Web system and software were released, in 1993, the National Center for Supercomputing Applications released versions of Mosaic (the first graphical Web browser) for Microsoft Windows, for Unix systems running the X Window System, and for the Apple Macintosh.
- In 1994, Netscape Communications released the Netscape Navigator browser, and in 1995, Microsoft released Internet Explorer. By mid-1997, these browsers were in head-to-head competition for a place on each Internet user's computer.
- In 1998, the U.S. Department of Justice and the attorneys general from several states filed suit against Microsoft, claiming that the inclusion of Internet Explorer in Windows 98 was in violation of antitrust guidelines.

How Can You Get There?

First, you need the equipment. Basic Internet access is possible with any computer that has a **modem** connected to a phone line. However, to take advantage of the World Wide Web, you need a PC that has an 80486 or higher CPU and the following:

- At least 8 megabytes of RAM
- A 250-megabyte hard drive
- A 14.4-kbps modem (28.8 or faster is better)

Modem speed is critical to your Internet travels. The higher the modem's baud rate, the faster Web pages appear on your computer screen. For example, a 3.5-minute video clip will download in 46 minutes if you are using a 28.8-kbps modem. (Obviously, then, you would not want to attempt this using a 14.4-kbps modem.) With a 128-kbps ISDN line, the same video clip will download in 10 minutes, and with a 10-mbps cable modem, it will take only 8 seconds.

The proposed 1999 U.S. federal budget calls for investing $110 million in the Next Generation Internet Initiative, intended to create a research network 100 to 1,000 times faster than today's Internet. Its primary focus will be to support new applications such as telemedicine and distance learning.

An **Internet service provider** is a company that provides access to the Internet; some also provide content and e-mail. The best-known ISPs are the commercial online services such as America Online, CompuServe, Prodigy, and MSN (The Microsoft Network), but many national companies (such as MCI and AT&T) and local and regional companies also provide Internet access. ISPs generally charge a monthly subscription rate. Some may charge additionally for longer connect time included in the monthly rate, but many commonly charge a set monthly fee for unlimited access, including e-mail and access to a news server.

Internet Resources

What you can do on the Internet depends on which resource you access.

E-mail. Electronic mail is probably the most popular and widely used resource on the Internet. To use it you must accurately input the recipient's address. An e-mail address consists of a **username,** a **service,** and a **domain.** For example, in `Walmanac@aol.com` (The World Almanac's e-mail address), `Walmanac` is the username, `aol` the service (in this case, America Online), and `com` the domain (in this case, a commercial organization). Domains are identified in the Domain Name System.

The registration of domain names has been the ultimate responsibility of the federal government and has been administered by Network Solutions Inc., under contract. In June 1998, the Clinton Administration proposed the establishment of a new nonprofit corporation to oversee the Domain Name System in place of the government, with administration of the registration process to be opened up to other companies. The new nonprofit corporation was expected to be set up in late 1998.

In mid-1998 registration of domain names cost $70 for 2 years, and $35 per year thereafter and could be initiated online through `http://rs.internic.net`

Here are the most familiar top-level domains as of mid-1998 (subject to future change and additions):

Domain	What It Is
.com	generally a commercial organization, business, or company
.edu	a 4-year higher-educational institution
.gov	a nonmilitary government entity
.int	an international organization
.mil	a military organization
.net	suggested for a network administration
.org	suggested for a nonprofit organization

Outside the U.S., the final part of a domain name represents the name of the country where the site is located—for example, `jp` for Japan, `uk` for United Kingdom, and `ru` for Russia.

FAQs. Frequently Asked Questions documents contain the answers to common Internet questions. Reading some of these documents should help Internet newcomers.

FTP. File Transfer Protocol is a method of transferring files on the Internet and a type of Internet site. Using FTP, you log on to a remote site (usually a server), view the available files, and copy them to your computer. The address for an FTP site begins with `ftp.`

Newsgroups. Newsgroups, a classic institution of the Internet, are found on the part of the Internet called Usenet. In a newsgroup, messages concerning a particular topic are posted in a public forum. You can simply read the postings, or you can post something yourself.

The World Wide Web. The Web may be the most complete realization of the Internet to date. It was developed in the early 1990s at the European Center for Nuclear Research as an environment in which scientists in Geneva, Switzerland, could share information. It has evolved into a medium that consists of text, graphics, audio, animation, and video. The address of a **website** usually begins with `http://www.` The World Wide Web is a graphical environment that can be navigated through **hyperlinks**. From one site you click on hyperlinks to go to any number of related sites.

How the World Wide Web Works

The Internet involves 3 fundamental elements: server, client, and network. A **server** is a computer program that makes data available to other programs on the same or other computers—it "serves" them. A **client** is a computer that requests data from a server. A **network** is an interconnected system in which multiple computers can communicate. The communication may be via copper wire, coaxial cable, fiber-optic cable, satellite transmission, etc. The software by which you access Internet resources is the **browser**. When you go to a site on the World Wide Web, you access the site's files.

Here are the steps in opening and accessing a file:

- In the browser, specify the address, or **URL,** of the website.
- The browser sends your request to the Internet service provider's server.
- That server sends the request to the server at the specified URL.
- The file is sent to the Internet service provider's server, which sends the file back to the browser, which displays the file.

How the Internet Is Being Used

Using credit cards, 10 million people in the United States and Canada had bought something over the Internet by the end of 1997, more than doubling the number of people who shopped the Internet 6 months earlier. But not only can you make purchases over the Internet, you can also receive the goods. Software programs, newspapers, and music CDs all are available over the Internet.

The number of Americans accessing the Internet to read news is growing rapidly. In 1996, only 6 percent went online for news; in 1998, that number increased to 20 percent. Nearly 90 percent of Web users access the Internet for news and information, which is available from around the world and is usually free. More than 2,700 newspapers have online businesses, and all but 3 of the top 50 U.S. magazines had a Web presence by January 1998. In addition, more than 800 U.S. television stations have websites.

According to a survey by the Travel Industry Assocation of America that was released in late 1997, 13.8 million Americans planned trips using the Internet, and 6.3 million used the Internet to make reservations for airline tickets, hotel rooms, rental cars, cruises, and so on. The largest online travel business is the sale of airline tickets, and for good reason. If you purchase your ticket through a travel agent, it costs the airline $8. If you buy it over the Internet, it costs the airline $1.

Online banking, though still in its infancy, is a growing segment of the Internet. Banks that offer online banking allow customers to check their balances, transfer funds, and pay bills while seated at their home computer. Again, for good reason. An online transaction costs the bank about a penny; a face-to-face interaction with a bank's teller costs the bank about a dollar. By the year 2000, 16 million households are expected to be banking online.

Safety and Security on the Internet

The responsibility for safety and security on the Internet rests with those who use it. Common sense dictates some basic rules of conduct:

- If you encounter an area that you find offensive—for example, a newsgroup or a chat room—remove that area from your list of places to visit.
- If you feel someone is being threatening or dangerous, inform your Internet service provider, which can issue a warning or can even withdraw entirely the person's online privileges.
- Be conscious of your privacy needs, as you would in any other situation where you interact with strangers. Children, especially, should not give out their phone number, address, or other personal information.
- Be extremely careful about giving out credit card numbers. They will not be 100% secure.
- The two major browsers, Netscape Navigator and Internet Explorer, both contain features that let you filter the content that can be viewed on your computer.

Netparents.org is an association devoted to providing information about such resources. Check out its website at `http://www.netparents.org`

Searching the Internet

A **search engine** is a special website you can use to locate information based on specific keywords. Many of the newer search engines actively search the Web, checking that existing URLs in their giant databases still work and adding information about new sites. The programs that do this are called **Web crawlers,** spiders, or bots (short for robots). Some search engines store only the title and URL of sites; others index every word of a site's content.

Of the 25 most-visited websites, 9 are search engines. Some of the most popular are described below.

AltaVista, sponsored by Digital Equipment Corp., has a growing index of more than 125 million unique Web pages. You can use AltaVista to search in English, Chinese, Japanese, Korean, Russian, French, German, and Italian. An instant translation service translates words, phrases, and entire websites into a variety of languages. Find AltaVista at `http://www.altavista.digital.com`

Excite lets you search more than 50 million Web pages, 140,000 website listings, and thousands of Usenet postings. You can search either by keyword or by concept. Excite gets about 16 million visitors each month. Find Excite at `http://www.excite.com`

HotBot features a menu-driven search engine. You can search Usenet, the Yellow Pages, the White Pages, e-mail addresses, domain names, stocks, classifieds, and so on. You can access HotBot at `http://www.hotbot.com`

InfoSeek is a full-text search system that you can search by phrase or keyword. You can use InfoSeek to find e-mail addresses, street maps, and investing opportunities as well as to track UPS packages. Enter a word or a question, or choose from a category to search. Access InfoSeek at `http://www2.infoseek.com`

Lycos is a search service and more. Use it to find personal home pages, to locate the best websites in a particular country, and to track UPS packages. Find Lycos at `http://www.lycos.com`

WebCrawler is also much more than a search service. In addition to searching the Web, you can find people, get your horoscope, search Yellow Pages, get stock quotes, and more. Access WebCrawler at `http://webcrawler.com`

Yahoo is perhaps the best known and most often used of all the search services, with about 32 million visitors each month. In addition to the standard search options, you can now get free e-mail through Yahoo, get stock quotes, the weather, and sports scores, and peruse the classifieds and personals. Find Yahoo at `http://www.yahoo.com`

Although these sites originally functioned strictly as search sites, and searching is still one of their major features, all of them now include numerous other features, such as free e-mail, chat, news services, stock updates, weather reports, real estate listings, yellow pages, people finders, movie listings, message boards, shopping, and even the tools to create and post your own Web page. These sites are now referred to as Web supersites, megasites, or portals. In addition, other sites are getting on the portal bandwagon. Two of the most popular are Netscape's Netcenter at `http://home.netscape.com` and Microsoft's Internet Start at `http://www.start.com`

Internet Lingo

The following abbreviations are sometimes used in Internet documents and in e-mail.

BTW By the way
F2F Face to face; a personal meeting
FCOL For crying out loud
FWIW For what it's worth
FYI For your information
GOK God only knows
HHOK Ha, ha—only kidding
HHOS Ha, ha—only serious
IMHO In my humble opinion
IMO In my opinion
LOL Laughing out loud
OTOH On the other hand
ROFL or **ROTFL** Rolling on the floor laughing
TAFN That's all for now

Emoticons, or **smileys**, are a series of typed characters that, when turned sideways, resemble a face and express an emotion. Here are some smileys that are often encountered on the Internet.

:-)	Smile	**:-***	Kiss	**:-b...**	Drooling
;-)	Wink	:-(	Unhappy	**=:o**	Argh!
:-D	Laugh	**:-o**	Shouting	**{*}**	A hug and a kiss

Internet Directory to Selected Sites

The e-mail and site addresses listed are but a small sampling of what is available on the Internet. For some other websites, see the Where to Get Help directory in the Health chapter, the Business Directory in the Consumer Information chapter, the website listings in the Travel and Tourism chapter, the Directory of Sports Organizations, and chapters on Associations and Societies, U.S. Cities, U.S. States, and Nations of the World. Sites or products are not endorsed by *The World Almanac.*

When you enter an address, you must type it exactly as written, including capital and lowercase letters, any nonalphanumeric characters, and spaces. You may be unable to connect to a site for the following reasons: (1) You have mistyped the address; (2) the site is busy; (3) as often happens, the site has moved or no longer exists.

Online Service Providers

America Online
`http://www.aol.com`
CompuServe
`http://www.compuserve.com`
The Microsoft Network
`http://home.microsoft.com`
Prodigy
`http://www.prodigy.com`
Internet Service Providers
`http://thelist.internet.com`

Security Information

The National Fraud Information Center
`http://www.fraud.org`
The Secure Electronic Transaction Standard (general information about electronic commerce)
`http://www.visa.com/cgi-bin/vee/nt/ecomm/main.html?2+0`

Directory Services

(Online directories that contain names, addresses, phone numbers, and e-mail addresses)

Bigfoot (e-mail addresses and white page listings)
`http://www.bigfoot.com`
Four11, the Internet White Pages
`http://www.four11.com`
InfoSpace, the Ultimate Directory
`http://www.infospace.com`
People Search
`http://www.yahoo.com/search/people`
Switchboard, the People and Business Directory
`http://www.switchboard.com`
WhoWhere?
`http://www.whowhere.com`

Bookstores

Amazon.com Inc.
`http://www.amazon.com`
Barnes and Noble
`http://www.barnesandnoble.com`
Books.Com
`http://www.books.com/scripts/news.exe`
Borders.Com
`http://www.borders.com`
The Complete Guide to Online Bookstores
`http://www.bookarea.com`

U.S. Government

To send e-mail to the president, the vice president, or the first lady, use the following addresses:

`president@whitehouse.gov`
`vice.president@whitehouse.gov`
`first.lady@whitehouse.gov`

To take a virtual tour of the White House, connect to:

`http://www.whitehouse.gov`

The White House FAQ is at the following address:

`http://www.whitehouse.gov/WH/html/faq.html`

You can access the text of the U.S. Constitution online at:

`http://www.house.gov/Constitution/Constitution.html`

For a complete list of links to all U.S. government servers and an e-mail address for each one, go to:

`http://www.sbaonline.sba.gov/world/federal-servers.html`

U.S. House of Representatives
`http://www.house.gov`
U.S. Senate
`http://www.senate.gov`

U.S. Supreme Court
http://supct.law.cornell.edu/supct
Department of Agriculture
http://www.usda.gov
Department of Commerce
http://www.doc.gov
Department of Defense
http://www.defenselink.mil
Department of Education
http://www.ed.gov
Department of Energy
http://apollo.osti.gov
Department of Health and Human Services
http://www.os.dhhs.gov
Department of Housing and Urban Development
http://www.hud.gov
Department of the Interior
http://www.doi.gov
Department of Justice
http://www.usdoj.gov
Department of Labor
http://www.dol.gov
Department of State
http://www.state.gov
Department of Transportation
http://www.dot.gov
Department of the Treasury
http://www.ustreas.gov
Department of Veterans Affairs
http://www.va.gov
Census Bureau
http://www.census.gov
Central Intelligence Agency
http://www.odci.gov/cia/index.html
Environmental Protection Agency
http://www.epa.gov
Federal Bureau of Investigation
http://www.fbi.gov
Federal Emergency Management Agency
http://www.fema.gov
Federal Trade Commisssion
http://www.ftc.gov
Library of Congress
http://www.loc.gov
NASA
http://www.nasa.gov
National Institutes of Health
http://www.nih.gov
Postal Service
http://www.usps.gov
Social Security Administration
http://www.ssa.gov
THOMAS: Legislative Information
http://thomas.loc.gov

Economic Data

Bureau of Economic Analysis
http://www.bea.doc.gov
Bureau of Labor Statistics
http://www.bls.gov
Economics Statistics Briefing Room
http://www.whitehouse.gov/fsbr/prices.html
Economy at a Glance
http://stats.bls.gov/eag.table.html
Government Information Sharing Project
http://govinfo.kerr.orst.edu
Office of Management and Budget
http://www.access.gpo.gov/omb/omb003.html
Statistical Abstract of the United States (a sampling of selective data)
http://www.census.gov:80/stat_abstract
STAT-USA/Internet (a subscription-based govt. service)
http://www.stat-usa.gov/stat-usa.html

Personal Finance

Internal Revenue Service
http://www.irs.gov
Wall Street Journal
http://www.wsj.com
American Stock Exchange
http://www.amex.com
NASDAQ
http://www.nasdaq.com
New York Stock Exchange
http://www.nyse.com
Automobile Buying/Leasing Calculator
http://www.financenter.com/autos.htm
Debt Calculator
http://www.uclending.com/debt_calculators.asp
Electric Bill Calculator
http://www.ue.com/meter/calculate.html
Insurance Calculator
http://www.financenter.com/insure.htm
Investment Calculator
http://www.financenter.com/invest.htm
Mortgage Calculator
http://www.weichert.com/mortgage
Retirement Calculator
http://www.worldi.com/calcltee.htm
Wealth Calculator
http://www.interest.com/hugh/calc/wealth.cgi

Weather

National Weather Service Home Page
http://www.nws.noaa.gov
National Weather Service Office of Meteorology
http://www.nws.noaa.gov/om/omhome
National Center for Environmental Prediction
http://www.ncep.noaa.gov
National Drought Mitigation Center
http://enso.unl.edu/ndmc
Office of Hydrology (flooding)
http://www.nws.noaa.gov/oh
Storm Prediction Center
http://www.nssl.noaa.gov/~spc
Tropical Prediction Center
http://www.nhc.noaa.gov
Ultraviolet (UV) Index Forecast
http://nic.fb4.noaa.gov/products/stratosphere/uv_index
Weather Calculator
http://nwselp.epcc.edu/elp/wxcalc.html

What's New Sites

Nerd World: What's New
http://www.nerdworld.com/whatsnew.html
Net-happenings
http://scout.cs.wisc.edu/scout/net-hap
Netscape's What's New
http://home.netscape.com/netcenter/new.html
The Scout Report (new sites of interest to researchers and educators)
http://wwwscout.cs.wisc.edu/scout/report
Starting Point New Sites
http://www.stpt.com/general/newsite.html
What's New (a search engine that provides access to new sites submitted over the previous 6 weeks)
http://www.whatsnu.com
What's New Too!
http://newtoo.manifest.com
Yahoo! What's New (listing of every new site each day; sometimes thousands)
http://www.yahoo.com/new

Chat Sites

Excite
http://www.excite.com/communities
The Globe
http://www.theglobe.com
IVILLAGE: The Women's Network
http://www.ivillage.com
Lycos
http://chat.lycos.com

Star Media (in Spanish and Portuguese)
http://www.starmedia.com
Yahoo
http://www.yahoo.com

Sites for Kids

Goosebumps
http://place.scholastic.com/goosebumps/index.htm
The John Newbery Medal
http://www.ala.org/alsc/newbery.html
Judy Blume's Home Base
http://www.judyblume.com/home.html
Little League Baseball
http://www.littleleague.org
Major League Baseball
http://www.majorleaguebaseball.com
National Basketball Association
http://www.nba.com
National Football League
http://www.nfl.com
National Hockey League
http://www.nhl.com
Major League Soccer
http://www.mlsnet.com
Rock and Roll Hall of Fame and Museum
http://www.rockhall.com
Seussville
http://www.randomhouse.com/seussville
Special Olympics
http://www.specialolympics.org
SuperSite for Kids
http://www.bonus.com
Weekly Reader
http://www.weeklyreader.com
White House for Kids
http://www.whitehouse.gov/WH/kids/html/home.html
Yahooligans (guide to homework help sites)
http://www.yahooligans.com

Resources for Families

Family.Com
http://family.disney.com
Family Internet
http://www.familyinternet.com
Kidshop Online
http://www.kidshoponline.com
KidSource Online
http://www.kidsource.com
ParenthoodWeb
http://www.parenthoodweb.com
Parent Soup
http://www.parentsoup.com
ParentsPlace.com
http://parentsplace.com
ParentTime
http://parenttime.com
Screen It!
http://www.screenit.com

Reference

BookWire—The First Place to Look for Book Information
http://www.bookwire.com
CIA Publications and Handbooks
http://odci.gov/cia/publications/pubs.html
Internet Search Tools, The Library of Congress
http://lcweb.loc.gov/global/search.html
Libweb—Library Servers via WWW
http://sunsite.berkeley.edu/Libweb
Liszt, the Mailing List Directory
http://www.liszt.com
Miriam-Webster Online
http://www.m-w.com/mw
On-line Dictionaries, A Web of
http://www.facstaff.bucknell.edu/rbeard/diction.html

Percent of U.S. Households With Online Service, by Selected Characteristics, 1997

Source: National Telecommunications and Information Administration, U.S. Dept. of Commerce

	U.S.	Rural	Urban	Central city
Race				
White, not Hispanic	21.2	15.6	23.5	23.3
Black, not Hispanic	7.7	5.5	7.9	5.8
Other not Hispanic	25.2	16.1	26.4	23.5
Hispanic	8.7	7.3	8.9	7.0
Age of householder				
Under 25 years	17.1	12.1	18.0	19.2
25-34 years	22.0	15.7	23.6	22.6
35-44 years	24.7	21.0	25.9	20.9
45-54 years	25.8	21.6	27.3	22.2
55+ years	8.8	6.7	9.5	7.8
Educational attainment				
Elementary	1.8	1.2	2.1	2.2
Some high school	3.1	2.5	3.4	2.5
High school diploma or GED	9.6	9.2	9.8	7.9
Some college	21.9	20.5	22.3	19.7
Bachelor's degree or more	38.4	35.6	39.0	36.1
Region				
Northeast	18.4	19.7	18.0	12.6
Midwest	17.3	13.9	18.6	16.7
South	17.4	12.7	19.4	17.0
West	22.4	17.8	23.1	21.7

Percent of U.S. Households With a Computer, by Selected Characteristics, 1994, 1997

Source: National Telecommunications and Information Administration, U.S. Dept. of Commerce

	1994	1997	'94-'97 change
Race			
White, not Hispanic	27.1	40.8	13.7
Black, not Hispanic	10.3	19.3	9.0
Other not Hispanic	32.6	47.0	14.4
Hispanic	12.3	19.4	7.1
Age of householder			
Under 25 years	18.1	28.0	9.9
25-34 years	25.1	40.0	14.9
35-44 years	34.1	49.0	14.9
45-54 years	33.6	48.0	14.4
55+ years	12.7	21.0	8.3
Educational attainment			
Elementary	2.6	6.8	4.2
Some high school	6.0	10.9	4.9
High school diploma or GED	14.8	25.7	10.9
Some college	28.9	43.4	14.5
Bachelor's degree or more	48.4	63.2	14.8
Annual income			
Under $5,000	8.4	16.5	8.1
$5,000-$9,999	6.1	9.9	3.8
$10,000-$14,999	8.2	12.9	4.7
$15,000-$19,999	11.7	17.4	5.7
$20,000-$24,999	15.2	23.0	7.8
$25,000-$34,999	19.8	31.7	11.9
$35,000-$49,999	33.0	45.6	12.6
$50,000-$74,999	46.0	60.6	14.6
$75,000+	60.9	75.9	15.0
Region			
Northeast	22.9	35.2	12.3
Midwest	24.1	36.5	12.4
South	20.9	33.4	12.5
West	30.6	43.4	12.8
Household type			
Married couple with children under 18	46.0	57.2	11.2
Male householder with children under 18	25.8	30.5	4.7
Female householder with children under 18	19.3	25.0	5.7
Family households without children	26.6	36.4	9.8
Nonfamily households	15.0	23.5	8.5

Percent of All U.S. Households With Selected Facilities, 1994, 1997

Source: National Telecommunications and Information Administration, U.S. Dept. of Commerce

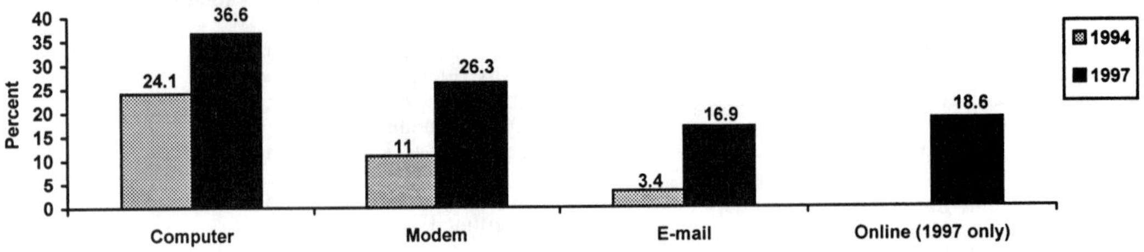

Top-Selling Software, 1998

Source: PC Data, Reston, VA

(based on average U.S. sales, Jan.-June 1998)

CD-ROM, All Categories

1. TurboTax, Intuit
2. TurboTax Deluxe, Intuit
3. Microsoft Windows 98 Upgrade, Microsoft
4. Taxcut, Block Financial
5. Deer Hunter, GT Interactive
6. Starcraft, Cendant Software
7. VirusScan 3, Network Associates
8. TurboTax Multi State, Intuit
9. Microsoft Windows 95 Upgrade, Microsoft
10. Quicken Deluxe, Intuit

Windows 95 Software

1. TurboTax, Intuit
2. TurboTax Deluxe, Intuit
3. Microsoft Windows 98 Upgrade, Microsoft
4. TurboTax Multi State, Intuit
5. Taxcut, Block Financial
6. Deer Hunter, GT Interactive
7. Microsoft Windows 95 Upgrade, Microsoft
8. Starcraft, Cendant Software
9. VirusScan 3, Network Associates
10. Quicken Deluxe, Intuit

PC Games (Windows/Win95/MS-DOS)

1. Deer Hunter, GT Interactive
2. Starcraft, Cendant Software
3. Myst, Brøderbund
4. Titanic: Adventure out of Time, Cyberflix
5. Microsoft Flight Simulator, Microsoft
6. Riven: The Sequel to Myst, Brøderbund
7. Quake II, Activision
8. Cabela's Big Game Hunter, Head Games Publishing
9. Wild Turkey Hunt, GT Interactive
10. Microsoft Age Of Empires, Microsoft

Games (Macintosh)

1. 7th Guest, Virgin
2. Myst, Brøderbund
3. Myth: The Fallen Lords, Bungie
4. Diablo, Cendant Software
5. Civilization 2, GT Interactive
6. Play to Win Casino, GT Interactive
7. Monopoly Game, Hasbro Interactive
8. Mac Pack Blitz, Aztech New Media
9. Mac Cubed, Aztech New Media
10. Quake, GT Interactive

Reference Software

1. Encyclopaedia Britannica 98, Brøderbund
2. Microsoft Encarta Encyclopedia, Microsoft
3. Collier's Encyclopedia '98, Cendant Software
4. Microsoft Encarta Encyclopedia Deluxe, Microsoft
5. Microsoft Encarta Reference Suite, Microsoft

Home Education (Windows/Win95/MS-DOS)

1. Math Blaster Ages 6-9, Cendant Software
2. Fisher Price Ready For School Toddler, Cendant Software
3. Math Blaster Ages 9-12, Cendant Software
4. Sesame Street Toddler Deluxe, Learning Company
5. Jumpstart Kindergarten II, Cendant Software
6. Clue Finders 3rd Grade Adventures, Learning Company
7. Reader Rabbit 1st Grade, Learning Company
8. Sesame Street Elmo's Preschool, Learning Company
9. Jumpstart First Grade, Cendant Software
10. Jumpstart Preschool, Cendant Software

Home Education (Macintosh)

1. Mavis Beacon Teaches Typing 5, Learning Company
2. Winnie The Pooh Animated Storybook, Disney
3. Guitar Method, Emedia
4. ClarisWorks For Kids, Apple Computer
5. Microsoft Magic School Bus: Body, Microsoft
6. A.D.A.M. Inside Story, Learning Company
7. Lion King Activity Center, Disney
8. Guitar Method 2, Emedia
9. Pocahontas Animated Storybook, Disney
10. Kid Pix, Brøderbund

Personal Productivity (Windows/Win95/MS-DOS)

1. TurboTax, Intuit
2. TurboTax Deluxe, Intuit
3. TurboTax Multi State, Intuit
4. Taxcut, Block Financial
5. Quicken Deluxe, Intuit
6. Print Shop Premier, Brøderbund
7. Taxcut Deluxe, Block Financial
8. Printmaster Gold Deluxe, Learning Company
9. Quicken, Intuit
10. Taxcut – Multi-State, Block Financial

Personal Productivity (Macintosh)

1. MacInTax, Intuit
2. MacInTax Deluxe, Intuit
3. Quicken Deluxe, Intuit
4. MacInTax Multistate, Intuit
5. Quicken, Intuit

Business Software (Windows/Win95/NT)

1. Microsoft Windows 98 Upgrade, Microsoft
2. Microsoft Windows 95 Upgrade, Microsoft
3. VirusScan 3, Network Associates
4. Norton Antivirus 4, Symantec
5. Norton Utilities 3.0, Symantec

Business Software (Macintosh)

1. Norton Utilities, Symantec
2. Mac Os 8.1, Apple Computer
3. Adobe Photoshop 5.0 Upgrade, Adobe
4. Microsoft Office 98 Upgrade, Microsoft
5. Norton Utilities Upgrade, Symantec

The Year 2000 Problem (Y2K), or The Millennium Bug

When computer systems were originally created, programmers decided to save memory in their coding by representing the year with only the last 2 digits. Because of this lack of foresight, many computers will be unable to interpret dates past the year 1999. For example, the year 2000, shown as "00," will be read as 1900. This is what technical people call the year 2000 problem, or Y2K for short. Many governments and corporations will be affected, and if needed corrections are not done in time, the general public could suffer in many ways, from inaccessible bank accounts to flight delays to delays in receiving Social Security checks. Home computers could be affected depending on the model or software used. Programmers are hard at work fixing the problem, and for some larger companies that means millions of lines of coding need to be reviewed. In mid-1998, Wall Street firms ran a test by setting the clocks on their computers ahead to Dec. 30, 1999, and making mock trades through Jan. 4, 2000; they did not encounter any major problems.

The Office of Management and Budget estimates the cost to correct federal computers will be $4.7 billion. The total cost for fixing it everywhere could reach $600 billion worldwide according to some estimates, and it is possible that half of all companies that need to make adjustments will not be ready in time.

Glossary of Computer and Internet Terms

application A program designed to assist in the performance of a specific task, such as word processing, accounting, or inventory management.

artificial intelligence (AI) The branch of computer science concerned with enabling computers to simulate such aspects of human intelligence as speech recognition, deduction, inference, creative response, and the ability to learn from experience.

ASCII Pronounced "askee." An acronym for American Standard Code for Information Interchange, a coding scheme using 7 or 8 bits that assigns numeric values to up to 256 characters, including letters, numerals, punctuation marks, control characters, and other symbols.

authenticode Security feature of Internet Explorer that allows vendors to attach digital certificates to their products to assure end users that the code is from the original developer and has not been altered. *See* **digital certificate**.

backup (noun); back up (verb) As a noun, a duplicate copy of a program, a disk, or data. As a verb, to make a duplicate copy of a program, a disk, or data.

bandwidth Data transfer capacity of a digital communications system.

baud rate Speed at which a modem can transmit data.

BBS An abbreviation for bulletin board system, a computer system equipped with one or more modems or other means of network access that serves as an information and message-passing center for remote users.

bit Short for binary digit; the smallest unit of information handled by a computer. One bit expresses a 1 or a 0 in a binary numeral, or a true or a false logical condition, and is represented physically by an element such as a high or low voltage at one point in a circuit or a small spot on a disk magnetized one way or the other.

boot The process of starting or resetting a computer.

browser *See* **Web browser.**

bug An error in coding or logic that causes a program to malfunction or to produce incorrect results. Also, a recurring physical problem that prevents a system or set of components from working together properly.

bulletin board system *See* **BBS.**

byte Short for binary term. A unit of data, today almost always consisting of 8 bits. A byte can represent a single character, such as a letter, a digit, or a punctuation mark.

CD-ROM Acronym for compact disc read-only memory, a form of storage characterized by high capacity (roughly 650 megabytes) and the use of laser optics rather than magnetic means for reading data.

central processing unit (CPU) The computational and control unit of a computer; the device that interprets and executes instructions.

Certificate Authority An issuer of digital certificates, the cyberspace equivalent of ID cards.

chat Real-time conversation via computer. Also, an Internet utility program that supports chat.

chip *See* **integrated circuit.**

client On a local area network, a computer that accesses shared network resources provided by another computer (called a server). *See also* **server.**

computer Any machine that does three things: accepts structured input, processes it according to prescribed rules, and produces the results as output.

CPU *See* **central processing unit.**

cracker A person who overcomes the security measures of a computer system and gains unauthorized access. *See also* **hacker.**

crash The failure of either a program or a disk drive. A program crash results in the loss of all unsaved data and can leave the operating system unstable enough to require restarting the computer.

cursor A special on-screen indicator, such as a blinking underline or rectangle, that marks the place of which keystrokes will appear when typed.

cyberspace The universe of environments, such as the Internet, in which persons interact by means of connected computers.

cyberspeak Terminology and language (often jargon, slang, and acronyms) relating to the Internet—computer-connected—environment, that is, cyberspace. Most words prefixed by *cyber-* have the same meaning as their "real-world" counterparts, but specifically indicate their use in the online culture of the Internet and the World Wide Web. Examples: cybercafé, cybercash, cybercrop.

database A file composed of records, each of which contains fields, together with a set of operations for searching, sorting, recombining, and other functions.

data compression A means of reducing the space or bandwidth needed to store or transmit a block of data.

debug To detect, locate, and correct logical or syntactical errors in a program or malfunctions in hardware.

desktop publishing The use of a computer and specialized software to combine text and graphics to create a document that can be printed on either a laser printer or a typesetting machine.

dial-up access Connection to a data communications network through the public switched telecommunication network.

dictation software Computer programs that can recognize spoken words as input. Used as alternatives to keyboard input.

Digerati Cyberspace populace that can be roughly compared to *literati.* Digerati are renowned as or claiming to be knowledgeable about topics and issues related to the digital revolution; more specifically, they are "in the know" about the Internet and online activities.

digital certificate 1. An assurance that software downloaded from the Internet comes from a reputable source. 2. A user identity card or "driver's license" for cyberspace. Issued by a certificate authority.

directory service A service on a network that returns mail addresses of other users or enables a user to locate hosts and services.

disk A round, flat piece of flexible plastic (floppy disk) or inflexible metal (hard disk) coated with a magnetic material that can be electrically influenced to hold information recorded in digital (binary) format.

disk drive An electromechanical device that reads from and writes to disks.

disk operating system Abbreviated DOS. A generic term describing any operating system that is loaded from disk devices when the system is started or rebooted.

distance learning Broadly, any educational or learning process or system in which the teacher/instructor is separated geographically or in time from his or her students; or in which students are separated from other students or educational resources.

DOS *See* **disk operating system.**

download In communications, to transfer a copy of a file from a remote computer to the requesting computer by means of a modem or network. *See also* **upload.**

dynamic HTML A technology designed to add richness, interactivity, and graphical interest to Web pages by providing those pages with the ability to change and update themselves in response to user actions, without the need for repeated downloads from a server.

encryption The process of encoding data to prevent unauthorized access, especially during transmission. The U.S. National Bureau of Standards created a complex encryption standard, DES (Data Encryption Standard), that provides almost unlimited ways to encrypt documents.

FAQ An abbreviation for Frequently Asked Questions, a document listing common questions and answers on a particular subject. FAQs are often posted on Internet newsgroups where new participants ask the same questions that regular readers have answered many times.

field A location in a record in which a particular type of data is stored.
file A complete, named collection of information, such as a program, a set of data used by a program, or a user-created document.
firewall A security system intended to protect an organization's network against external threats, such as hackers, from another network. *See also* **proxy server.**
flame An abusive or personally insulting e-mail message or newsgroup posting.
format In general, the structure or appearance of a unit of data. As a verb, to change the appearance of selected text or the contents of a selected cell in a spreadsheet.
forum A medium provided by an online service or BBS for users to carry on written discussions of a topic by posting messages and replying to them.
FTP An abbreviation for File Transfer Protocol, the protocol used for copying files to and from remote computer systems on a network using TCP/IP such as the Internet.
gigabyte Abbreviated GB; 1024 megabytes. *See* **megabyte.**
graphical user interface Abbreviated GUI (pronounced "gooey"). A type of environment that represents programs, files, and options by means of icons, menus, and dialog boxes on the screen. The user can select and activate these options by pointing and clicking with a mouse or, often, with the keyboard. *See also* **icon.**
hacker A computerphile—a person who is engrossed in computer technology and programming or who likes to examine the code of operating systems and other programs to see how they work. Also, a person who uses computer expertise for illicit ends, such as for gaining access to computer systems without permission and tampering with programs and data. *See also* **cracker.**
hard copy Printed output on paper, film, or other permanent medium.
hit Retrieval of a document, such as a home page, from a website.
home page A document intended to serve as a starting point in a hypertext system, especially the World Wide Web. Also, an entry page for a set of Web pages and other files in a website.
host The main computer in a system of computers or terminals connected by communications links.
HTML An abbreviation for HyperText Markup Language, the markup language used for documents on the World Wide Web.
HTTP An abbreviation for HyperText Transfer Protocol, the client/server protocol used to access information on the Web.
hyperlink A connection between an element in a hypertext document, such as a word, phrase, symbol, or image, and a different element in the document, another hypertext document, a file, or a script. The user activates the link by clicking on the linked element, which is usually highlighted in some way.
hypermedia The integration of any combination of text, graphics, sound, and video into a primarily associative system of information storage and retrieval in which users jump from subject to related subject.
hypertext Text linked together in a complex, nonsequential web of associations in which the user can browse through related topics.
icon A small image displayed on the screen to represent an object that can be manipulated by the user.
import To bring information from one system or program into another.
integrated circuit Also called a chip. A device consisting of a number of connected circuit elements, such as transistors and resistors, fabricated on a single chip of silicon crystal or other semiconductor material.
interactive Characterized by conversational exchange of input and output, as when a user enters a question or command the system immediately responds.
Internet The worldwide collection of networks and gateways that use the TCP/IP suite of protocols to communicate with each other. At the heart of the Internet is a backbone of high-speed data communication lines between major nodes or host computers, consisting of thousands of commercial, government, educational, and other computer systems, that route data and messages.
intranet A TCP/IP network designed for information processing within a company or organization. It usually employs Web pages for information dissemination and Internet applications, such as Web browsers.
IP address Short for Internet Protocol address, a 32-bit (4-byte) binary number that uniquely identifies a host (computer) connected to the Internet to other Internet hosts, for the purposes of communication through the transfer of packets.
Java A programming language, developed by Sun Microsystems, Inc., that can be run on any platform.
kilobyte Abbreviated K, KB, or Kbyte; 1,024 bytes.
LAN Rhymes with "can." Acronym for local area network, a group of computers and other devices dispersed over a limited area and connected by a communications link that enables any device to interact with any other on the network.
laptop A small, portable computer that runs on either batteries or AC power, designed for use during travel. Laptops have flat screens and small keyboards. Some weigh as little as 5 pounds.
legacy system A computer, software program, network, or other computer equipment that remains in use after a business or organization installs new systems.
link *See* **hyperlink.**
logon The process of identifying oneself to a computer after connecting to it over a communications line. Also called *login.*
lurk To receive and read articles or messages in a newsgroup or other online conference without contributing anything to the ongoing conversation.
mailing list A list of names and e-mail addresses that are grouped under a single name. When a user places the name of the mailing list in a mail client's To: field, the client automatically sends the same message to the machine where the mailing list resides, and that machine sends the message to all the addresses on the list.
mainframe computer A high-level computer designed for the most intensive computational tasks.
megabyte Abbreviated MB. Usually 1,048,576 bytes (2^{20}); sometimes interpreted as 1 million bytes.
memory Circuitry that allows information to be stored and retrieved. In common usage it refers to the fast semiconductor storage (RAM) directly connected to the processor. *See also* **RAM**.
menu A list of options from which a program user can make a selection in order to perform a desired action, such as choosing a command or applying a format.
microcomputer A computer built around a single-chip microprocessor.
microprocessor A central processing unit (CPU) on a single chip. *See also* **integrated circuit.**
minicomputer A mid-level computer built to perform complex computations while dealing efficiently with a high level of input and output from users connected via terminals.
modem A communications device that enables a computer to transmit information over a standard telephone line.
monitor The device on which images generated by the computer's video adapter are displayed.
motherboard The main circuit board containing the primary components of a computer system.
mouse A common pointing device. It has a flat-bottomed casing designed to be gripped by one hand.
multitasking A mode of operation offered by an operating system in which a computer works on more than one task at a time.
Net Short for Internet.
netiquette Short for network etiquette.
netizen A person who participates in online communication through the Internet and other networks, especially conference and chat services.
network A group of computers and associated devices that are connected by communications facilities.
newbie An inexperienced user on the Internet.

newsgroup A forum on the Internet for threaded discussions on a specified range of subjects. A newsgroup consists of articles and follow-up posts. *See* **post, thread.**
online Activated and ready for operating; capable of communicating with or being controlled by a computer.
operating system The software that controls the allocation and usage of hardware resources such as memory, CPU time, disk space, and peripheral devices.
optical scanner An input device that uses light-sensing equipment to scan paper or another medium, translating the pattern of light and dark or color into a digital signal that can be manipulated by either optical character recognition software or graphics software.
packet A unit of information transmitted as a whole from one device to another on a network.
password A unique string of characters that a user types in as an identification code.
PC Abbreviation for personal computer, a microcomputer that conforms to the standard developed by IBM for personal computers, which uses an Intel microprocessor (or one that is compatible).
peripheral A device, such as a disk drive, printer, modem, or joystick, that is connected to a computer and is controlled by the computer's microprocessor.
ping packet An "are you there" message sent from one node to the IP address of a network computer to determine whether that node is able to send and receive transmissions.
pixel Short for picture element; also called *pel*. One spot in a rectilinear grid of thousands of such spots that are individually "painted" to form an image produced on the screen by a computer or on paper by a printer.
post To submit an article in a newsgroup or other online conference. *See* **thread**.
program A sequence of instructions that can be executed by a computer.
protocol A set of rules or standards designed to enable computers to communicate with one another and to exchange information with as little error as possible.
proxy server A firewall component that manages Internet traffic to and from a local area network and can provide other features, such as document caching and access control.
push In networks and the Internet, to send data or a program from a server to a client at the instigation of the server.
RAM Pronounced "ram." An acronym for random access memory. Semiconductor-based memory that can be read and written by the CPU or other hardware devices.
routing table In data communications, a table of information that provides network hardware (bridges and routers) with the directions needed to forward packets of data to locations on other networks.
search engine On the Internet, a program that searches for keywords in files and documents.
server On a local area network (LAN), a computer running administrative software that controls access to the network and its resources, such as printers and disk drives. On the Internet or other network, a computer or program that responds to commands from a client. *See* **client, LAN.**
sleep mode A power management mode that shuts down all unnecessary computer operations to save energy; also known as suspend mode.
snail mail A phrase popular on the Internet for referring to mail services provided by the United States Postal Service and similar agencies in other countries.
software Computer programs; instructions that make hardware work.
spam An unsolicited e-mail message sent to many recipients at one time, or a news article posted simultaneously to many newsgroups. Electronic junk mail.
spreadsheet program An application commonly used for budgets, forecasting, and other finance-related tasks that organizes data values using cells, where the relationships between cells are defined by formulas.
supercomputer A large, extremely fast, and expensive computer used for complex or sophisticated calculations.
system administrator The person responsible for administering use of a multiuser computer system, communications system, or both.
TCP/IP An abbreviation for Transmission Control Protocol/Internet Protocol, a protocol developed by the Department of Defense for communications between computers. It has become the de facto standard for data transmission over networks, including the Internet.
technophobe A person who is afraid of or dislikes technological advances, especially computers.
telecommute To work in one location (often, at home) and communicate with a main office at a different location through a personal computer.
teleconferencing The use of audio, video, or computer equipment linked through a communications system to enable geographically separated individuals to participate in a meeting or discussion.
teleworker A businessperson who substitutes information technologies for work-related travel. Teleworkers include home-based and small business workers who use computer and communications technologies to interact with customers and/or colleagues.
thread In electronic mail and Internet newsgroups, a series of messages and replies related to a specific topic.
ubiquitous computing A computing environment so pervasive in daily life that it is invisible to the user. Household appliances such as VCRs and microwave ovens are contemporary low-level examples of ubiquitous computing, which is considered the third stage in the evolution of computing technology, after the mainframe and the personal computer.
upload In communications, the process of transferring a copy of a file from a local computer to a remote computer by means of a modem or network.
URL An abbreviation for Uniform Resource Locator, an address for a resource on the Internet.
Usenet A worldwide network of Unix systems that has a decentralized administration and is used as a bulletin board system by special-interest discussion groups.
user interface The portion of a program with which a user interacts.
user-friendly Easy to learn and easy to use.
virus An intrusive program that infects computer files by inserting in those files copies of itself.
Web *See* **World Wide Web.**
Web browser A client application that enables a user to view HTML documents, follow the hyperlinks among them, transfer files, and execute some programs.
webcasting Popular term for broadcasting information via the World Wide Web, using push and pull technologies to move selected information from a server to a client.
webmaster The person or persons responsible for creating and maintaining a site on the World Wide Web.
website A group of related HTML documents and associated files, scripts, and databases that is served up by an HTTP server on the World Wide Web.
wide area network (WAN) A communications network that connects geographically separated areas.
window In applications and graphical interfaces, a portion of the screen that can contain its own document or message.
word processor A program for manipulating text-based documents; the electronic equivalent of paper, pen, typewriter, eraser, and, most likely, dictionary and thesaurus.
workstation A combination of input, output, and computing hardware used for work by an individual.
World Wide Web (WWW) The total set of interlinked hypertext documents residing on Web, or HTTP, servers all around the world.
WYSIWYG Pronounced "wizzywig." An acronym for "What you see is what you get." A display method that shows documents and graphics characters on the screen as they will appear when printed.
Zip drive A disk drive developed by Iomega that uses 3.5-inch removable disks (Zip disks) capable of storing 100 megabytes of data apiece. *See also* **disk drive.**

BUILDINGS, BRIDGES, TUNNELS, AND DAMS

Notable Tall Buildings in North American Cities

Source: Council on Tall Buildings and Urban Habitat; World Almanac research

Lists include some structures that do not have stories and are not technically considered "buildings." Height is generally measured from sidewalk to roof, including penthouse and tower if enclosed as integral part of structure; stories generally counted from street level. Asterisk (*) denotes building still under construction. Year in parentheses is date of completion.

Atlanta, GA

Building	Ht. (ft.)	Stories
NationsBank Plaza (1992)	1,023	55
Sun Trust Bank Tower (1992)	880	63
One Peachtree Center (1992)	867	60
One Atlantic Center (1988)	820	50
Georgia-Pacific Corporation (1982)	754	52
191 Peachtree (1992)	740	50
Peachtree Plaza Hotel (1975)	723	70
Promenade Two (1989)	691	40
Bell South Telephone (1980)	677	47
GLG Grand (1993)	609	53
Concourse Tower #5 (1988)	570	32
First National Bank (1967)	562	44
State of Georgia Tower (1968)	556	44
Marriott Marquis (1985)	554	52
Concourse Tower #6 (1991)	553	32
Equitable Bldg. (1969)	453	34
101 Marietta Tower (1975)	446	36
Ravinia #3 (1991)	444	34
National Bank of Georgia (1961)	439	32
AT&T Long Line Bldg. (1975)	433	NA
Bell South Enterprises (1990)	428	28
Atlanta Plaza I (1986)	425	32
Park Place, 2660 Peachtree (1986)	420	40
Club Towers Apts. (1989)	410	38
One Park Tower (1961)	409	32
Peachtree Summit Number 1 (1976)	406	31
North Avenue Tower (1979)	403	26
Tower Place (1975)	401	29

Baltimore, MD

Building	Ht. (ft.)	Stories
U.S. Fidelity & Guaranty Co. (1973)	529	40
Maryland National Bank (1929)	509	34
William Donald Schaefer Tower	493	29
Commerce Place	454	30
World Trade Center Bldg. (1977)	405	32

Boston, MA

Building	Ht. (ft.)	Stories
John Hancock Tower (1976)	788	60
Prudential Center (1964)	750	52
Federal Reserve Bldg. (1977)	604	32
Boston Company County Bldg.(1970)	601	41
One International Place	600	46
One Financial Center	598	47
First National Bank of Boston	591	37
Exchange Place, 53 State Street	554	40
John Hancock Bldg	528	36
One Post Office Square	525	40
Shawmut Bank Bldg.	520	38
Sixty State Bldg.	509	38
Employers' Commercial Union Company	507	40
New England Merchant Bank Bldg.	500	40
U.S. Custom House, State Street	496	32
John Hancock Bldg. (1973)	495	26
State Street Bank Bldg.	477	34
100 Summer Street	450	33
Two International Place	433	33
McCormack Bldg.	401	22
Keystone Custodian Funds Bldg. (1971)	400	32
Harbor Towers (2 bldgs.) (1972) 85 E. India	400	40
65 E. India	396	40

Calgary, Alberta

Building	Ht. (ft.)	Stories
Petro-Canada I (1984)	689	52
Bankers Hall (1989)	645	50
Calgary Tower (1988)	626	–
Canterra Tower (1988)	580	46
First Canadian Place (1982)	530	41
Calgary Eatons Centre	530	40
Norcen Tower (1976)	508	33
Western Canadian Place (1983)	507	41
Scotia Centre (1975)	504	38
Nova Bldg., 801 7th Ave. SW	500	37
Petro-Canada Centre, E. Tower (1984)	469	33
Two Bow Valley Square (1974)	468	39
Toronto Dominion Square- North (1976)	463	34
Canada Trust Tower (1991)	462	40
Shell Tower (1977)	460	34
Petro-Canada II (1983)	455	32
Toronto Dominion Square- South (1976)	449	33
Esso Plaza (twin towers)	435	34
Three Bow Valley Square (1979)	432	35
Fifth & Fifth Bldg. (1980)	410	34
Sovereign Life Bldg.	410	33
Pan Canadian Bldg.	410	28
Norcen Tower	408	33
Alberta Stock Exchange Bldg.	407	33

Charlotte, NC

Building	Ht. (ft.)	Stories
NationsBank Corporate Center (1992)	871	60
One First Union Center (1988)	587	42
North Carolina NationsBank Plaza (1974)	503	40
Interstate Tower (1990)	459	32
IJL Financial Center (1998)	450	30
Jefferson First Union Tower (1971)	433	32
Wachovia Center (1974)	420	32

Chicago, IL

Building	Ht. (ft.)	Stories
Sears Tower (1974)	1,450	110
Amoco Bldg. (1973)	1,136	80
John Hancock Center (1969)	1,127	100
AT&T Corporate Center (1989)	1,007	60
Two Prudential Plaza (1990)	978	64
311 South Wacker Drive (1990)	959	65
900 North Michigan Ave. (1989)	871	66
Water Tower Place (1976)	859	74
One First National Plaza (1969)	850	60
Three First National Plaza (1981)	753	57
Chicago Title and Trust (1992)	742	51
Olympia Centre (1981)	725	63
One IBM Plaza (1973)	695	52
181 West Madison Street (1990)	680	50
77 West Wacker Drive (1992)	668	50
One Magnificent Mile (1983)	660	58
Civic Center (1965)	648	31
Lake Point Tower (1968)	645	70
1000 Lake Shore Plaza (1964)	640	55
Leo Burnett Bldg. (1989)	635	46
NBC Chicago Cityfront Center (1989)	627	34
Chicago Place (1990)	605	43
Prudential Plaza Bldg. (1955)	601	41
Heller International Tower (1992)	600	45
Marina City Twin Towers (1962)	588	61
Mid-Continental Plaza (1972)	582	50
North Pier Apartments (1990)	581	61
55 East Monroe Street	580	50
Madison Plaza (1983)	580	41
One Park Place (1984)	576	38
Stone Container Bldg. (1984)	575	40
190 South LaSalle Street (1986)	573	42
Onterie Center (1985)	570	58
Palmolive Bldg. (1929)	565	37
Newberry Plaza (1972)	560	56
Huron Plaza Apartments (1983)	560	54
C. N. A. Towers (1972)	560	40
Morton International Bldg. (1990)	560	36
Harbor Point (1975)	558	59
Pittsfield Bldg. (1927)	557	38
Chicago Temple (1923)	556	21
Kemper Bldg. (1929)	555	45
Civic Opera Bldg. (1929)	554	45
75 East Wacker Drive (1928)	554	42
Boulevard Towers South (1985)	553	44
30 North LaSalle Street (1975)	553	43
Xerox Center (1979)	550	45
Two First National Bank (1972)	550	40
Brunswick Bldg. (1965)	550	38
Kluczynski Bldg. (1971)	547	42
One South Wacker Dr. (1983)	540	40
LaSalle Natl. Bank (1934)	535	44
Frontier Towers (1973)	533	55
10 & 30 South Wacker Drive (1988)	525	38
River Plaza (1978)	524	56
Chicago Board of Trade Bldg. (1930)	524	45
Parkshore Tower (1991)	523	61
Pure Oil Bldg. (1978)	523	40
35 East Wacker Drive (1926)	523	40
United Insurance Company (1978)	522	41
111 East Chestnut Street (1972)	520	57
175 North Harbor Drive (1991)	520	55

Building	Ht. (ft.)	Stories
Northwestern Atrium Center (1987)	516	40
One Financial Place (1984)	515	40
Hotel Inter-Continental Chicago (1929)	513	42
Quaker Tower (1987)	510	35
200 South Wacker Drive (1981)	505	38
Carbide & Carbon Bldg. (1929)	503	37
LaSalle-Wacker (1934)	491	41
American National. Bank (1929)	479	40
Park Tower (1974)	476	54
Bankers Bldg. (1927)	476	41
American Furniture Mart (1926)	476	24
Continental Companies	475	45
310 Center (1924)	475	37
333 West Wacker Drive (1983)	475	36
Sheraton Hotel (1961)	474	42
666 North Lake Shore Drive (1923)	474	30
City Place (1990)	470	40
Harris Bank III (1976)	470	35
919 North Michigan Ave. (1929)	468	37
188 Randolph Tower	465	45
Tribune Tower (1925)	462	36
Chicago Marriott Hotel (1981)	460	45
Olympic Towers (1984)	460	45
Equitable Life Bldg. (1964)	457	35
Roanoke Bldg.	452	37
Gateway Center III (1972)	450	35

Cincinnati, OH

Building	Ht. (ft.)	Stories
Carew Tower (1930)	574	49
First National Bank Center	545	28
Central Trust Tower (1913)	495	34
312 Walnut Street (1990)	468	36
Fifth Third Center (1970)	460	31
Atrium Two (1984)	428	30
DuBois Tower	423	32
Chemed Center (1990)	410	32

Cleveland, OH

Building	Ht. (ft.)	Stories
Society Tower (1991)	950	57
Terminal Tower (1930)	708	52
BP America (1986)	658	45
Standard Oil Co. of Ohio	630	45
Erieview Plaza Tower (1964)	529	40
*Federal Courthouse (2000)	460	25
One Cleveland Center (1983)	450	31
Bank One Center (1991)	446	28
A. J. Celebreeze Federal Bldg. (1968)	440	32
Justice Center (1976)	420	26
*Federal Bldg..	419	32
National City Center (1980)	410	35

Columbus, OH

Building	Ht. (ft.)	Stories
James Rhodes State Office Tower (1973)	592	41
LeVeque Tower	555	47
Ohio Bureau of Worker's Compensation & Ind. Comm. (1990)	530	33
Huntington Center	512	37
Verne-Riffe State Office Tower	503	33
Nationwide Plaza	485	40
Franklin County Courthouse	464	27
One Riverside Plaza	456	31
Borden Bldg. (1974)	438	34
Three Nationwide Plaza (1989)	408	27

Dallas, TX

Building	Ht. (ft.)	Stories
NationsBank Plaza (1985)	921	72
Renaissance Tower (1975)	886	56
Bank One Center (1987)	787	60
Texas Commerce Tower (1987)	738	55
Fountain Place (1986)	721	60
First Interstate Bank (1986)	716	62
L T V Center (1985)	686	54
Trammell Crow Center (1987)	686	49
First City Center (1982)	655	50
Thanksgiving Tower (1982)	645	50
Arco Tower (1983)	629	49
First National Bank (1964)	625	52
Elm Place (1965)	625	50
Republic Bank Tower (1964)	598	50
Republic Bank Tower 2 (1980)	598	50
Lincoln Plaza (1984)	579	45
One Lincoln Plaza	574	45
Harwood @Bryan Corp. Center (1982)	562	36
Cityplace Center (1989)	560	42
Southland Life Insurance Bldg. (1958)	550	41
Maxus Energy Tower (1980)	550	34
2001 Bryan Street Tower (1972)	512	40
Olympia & York Tower (1982)	483	36
San Jacinto Tower (1982)	456	33
Republic Bank Bldg. (1954)	452	36
M-Bank Bldg. (1943)	452	31
Stouffer Hotel	451	29
One Dallas Centre (1979)	448	30
One Main Place (1968)	445	34
1600 Pacific Bldg. (1964)	434	32
L T V Tower (1964)	434	32
Mobil Bldg. (1921)	430	31
Mercantile National Bank (1937)	430	31
Magnolia Bldg. (1923)	430	27
Fidelity Union Tower (1959)	400	33

Dayton, OH

Building	Ht. (ft.)	Stories
Kettering Tower (1970)	405	30
Winters Bank Bldg. (1970)	404	30

Denver, CO

Building	Ht. (ft.)	Stories
Republic Plaza (1984)	714	56
City Center 4 (1982)	709	54
One Norwest Center (1983)	698	52
Anaconda Bldg. (1978)	580	40
1999 Broadway (1985)	544	43
MCI Tower (1982)	527	42
Brooks Tower (1965)	504	42
Amoco Bldg.(1980)	450	36
17th Street Plaza (1982)	438	32
First of Denver (1974)	431	32
One Denver Place (1983)	428	34
One Tabor Center (1984)	408	30
Manville Plaza (1989)	404	29

Detroit, MI

Building	Ht. (ft.)	Stories
Renaissance Center Complex (1977)	739	73
One Detroit Center (1990)	620	43
City National Bank Bldg. (1928)	562	47
Penobscot Bldg. (1928)	557	46
Renaissance Center II-V(4 bldgs.) (1976)	534	40
Guardian (1928)	485	40
Book Tower (1925)	472	35
Madden Bldg. (1988)	470	26
Prudential 3000 Town Center	448	32
Cadillac Tower (1928)	437	40
David Stott (1930)	436	38
Consolidated Gas Co.	430	32
ANR Bldg. (1962) 1 Woodward	430	30
Isher (1928)	420	28
Town Center (1975)	405	32

Edmonton, Alberta

Building	Ht. (ft.)	Stories
Manulife Place (1983)	479	36
AGT Tower (1971)	441	33
Canada Trust Tower (1982)	440	31
Commerce Place (1990)	409	30
Toronto Dominion Bank Tower (1976)	400	30

Fort Worth, TX

Building	Ht. (ft.)	Stories
City Center Tower II (1984)	546	38
Burnett Plaza (1983)	538	40
Continental Plaza (1982)	520	40
Texas Commerce Tower(1982)	475	33
Bank One Tower (1975)	457	35
Fort Worth National Bank	454	37
Texas Bldg. (1955)	420	30

Hartford, CT

Building	Ht. (ft.)	Stories
City Place (1983)	535	38
Travelers Ins. Co. Bldg. (1919)	527	34
Goodwin Square (1990)	522	30
Hartford Plaza (1967)	420	22

Honolulu, HI

Building	Ht. (ft.)	Stories
First Hawaiian Bank (1995)	430	27
Waterfront Towers (1990)	400	46
Nauru Tower (1991)	400	45
Imperial Plaza (1992)	400	40

Houston, TX

Building	Ht. (ft.)	Stories
Texas Commerce Tower (1982)	1,000	75
First Interstate Plaza (1983)	972	71
Transco Tower (1983)	901	64

(continued)

Houston, TX *(continued)*

Building	Ht. (ft.)	Stories
NationsBank Center (1984)	780	56
Heritage Plaza, (1987)	762	53
1100 Louisiana Bldg. (1980)	748	55
InterFirst Plaza (1980)	744	55
Houston Industries Plaza	741	53
1600 Smith Street (1984)	732	55
Gulf Tower (1982)	725	52
One Shell Plaza (1971) (not incl. 285-ft. TV tower)	714	50
Enron Bldg. (1983)	692	50
Four Allen Center (1984)	691	50
Three Allen Center (1980)	686	50
One Houston Center (1978)	682	46
First City Tower (1981)	663	49
First City, Tex. Financial Center (1984)	662	47
Brookhollow Central Two	656	15
1100 Milam Bldg. (1974)	651	47
San Felipe Plaza (1984)	625	45
Exxon Bldg. (1964)	606	44
The America Tower (1983)	590	42
Two Houston Center (1974)	581	40
Marathon Oil Tower (1983)	562	41
1200 Milam Bldg.	558	NA
United Bank Plaza (1984)	550	45
1415 Louisiana Tower (1983)	550	44
Dresser Tower (1974)	550	40
MW Kellogg Tower (1973)	550	40
Pennzoil Place (1976) (2 bldgs.)	522	36
Two Allen Center (1978)	521	36
Entex Bldg. (1971)	518	35
1201 Louisiana (1971)	518	35
The Huntington (1982)	503	34
Tenneco Bldg. (1963)	500	32
Conoco Bldg. (1973)	465	32
One Allen Center (1973)	452	34

Indianapolis, IN

Building	Ht. (ft.)	Stories
Bank One Center (1989)	700	51
AUL Tower (1981)	533	38
Market Tower (1988)	515	32
National Bank Tower (1971)	504	37
Riley Towers (1963) (2 bldgs.)	427	30
300 North Meridian Bldg. (1988)	408	28

Jacksonville, FL

Building	Ht. (ft.)	Stories
Barnett Center (1990)	617	42
Independent Life and Accident Insur. (1974)	535	37
Southern Bell (1983)	447	32
Gulf Life Tower (1967)	433	27

Kansas City, MO

Building	Ht. (ft.)	Stories
One Kansas City Place (1988)	626	42
AT&T Town Pavilion (1986)	590	38
Hyatt Regency (1980)	504	40
Kansas City Power and Light Bldg.(1931)	476	33
City Hall (1936)	443	29
Fidelity Bank and Trust Bldg. (1931)	426	35
1201 Walnut (1991)	425	30
Federal Office Bldg.(1946)	417	36
Commerce Tower (1963)	407	31
City Center Square (1977)	402	30

Las Vegas, NV

Building	Ht. (ft.)	Stories
Stratosphere Tower (1996)	1,049	114
New York-New York Hotel & Casino (1997)	525	48

Little Rock, AR

Building	Ht. (ft.)	Stories
TCBY Towers (1986)	546	40
First National Bank (1975)	454	33

Los Angeles, CA

Building	Ht. (ft.)	Stories
First Interstate World Center (1989)	1,018	75
First Interstate Tower (1974)	858	62
Two California Plaza (1992)	750	52
Gas Company Tower (1991)	749	50
333 South Hope Bldg. (1975)	743	55
Wells Fargo Tower (1983)	740	54
777 Tower	725	52
Sanwa Bank Plaza (1990)	717	53
Atlantic Richfield Tower	699	52
Bank of America Tower	699	52
444 South Flower Street	625	48
Crocker Citizens Tower (1969)	620	42
Jay Square	597	48
One California Plaza	578	42
Theme Towers (1974) (2 bldgs.)	576	43
Century Plaza Towers (2 bldgs.)	571	44
IBM Tower	560	45
Citicorp Plaza	534	42
1999 Ave. of the Stars (1989)	533	39
Manulife Tower (1990)	517	37
Union Bank Plaza (1966)	512	41
MCA-Getty	506	36
WTC Bldg.	496	36
Fox Plaza	492	34
ARCO Center	462	32
Equitable Life (1969)	454	34
City Hall (1927)	454	29
Occidental Life (1965)	452	32
Mutual Benefit Life Bldg. (1970)	435	31
Warner Center Plaza III	415	25
Broadway Plaza (1973)	414	32

Louisville, KY

Building	Ht. (ft.)	Stories
Providian Center (1992)	549	35
First National Bank	512	40
National City Tower (1972)	495	40
Citizens Fidelity Bank (1972)	420	30
Humana Bldg.(1985)	417	30

Mexico City, Mexico

Building	Ht. (ft.)	Stories
Petrolaos Mexicanos (1984)	702	52
Latin American Tower (1956)	668	55
Hotel de Mexico (1972)	573	48
Nonoalco Tlateloco Tower (1962)	417	25

Miami, FL

Building	Ht. (ft.)	Stories
Southeast Financial Center (1983)	738	55
International Place (1987)	562	35
Metro-Dade Administration Bldg.	510	30
Florida National Tower (1986)	484	35
One Biscayne Corporation	456	40
Barnett Tower (1986)	450	33
Courthouse Center (1986)	405	30

Milwaukee, WI

Building	Ht. (ft.)	Stories
First Wisconsin Bank (1973)	625	42
Faison Bldg., 100 East (1989)	549	37
Milwaukee Center (1987)	426	29
411 Bldg., 411 East Wisconsin (1983)	408	30

Minneapolis, MN

Building	Ht. (ft.)	Stories
IDS Center (1972)	775	57
Norwest (1988)	774	57
First Bank Place (1992)	774	53
Multifoods Tower (1983)	608	51
Piper Jaffray Tower (1984)	627	42
Dain Bosworth Plaza	539	40
Pillsbury Bldg.(1981)	529	40
150 South Fifth	498	36
Metropolitan Center (1987)	496	31
Plaza VII, 45 South 7th (1987)	468	36
Foshay Tower (1929) (not incl. 160-ft. antenna tower)	447	32
Hennepin County Convention Center (1974)	403	24

Montreal, Quebec

Building	Ht. (ft.)	Stories
1100 Rue de la Gauchetiere	669	45
1250 Boulevard Rene Levesque	640	45
Place Ville Marie (1962)	630	47
Place Victoria (1964)	624	47
Royal Bank Bldg. (1961)	612	54
Canadian Imperial Bank of Commerce (1962)	590	45
Place Desjardins (1976) (3 bldgs.)		
La Tour du Sud	498	40
La Tour du L'Est	428	32
La Tour du Nord	355	27
Le Chateau Champlain (1967)	480	38
Les Cooperants (1987)	479	34
CIL House (1962)	450	33
Holiday Inn Hotel (1977)	450	38
Place Montreal Trust (1988)	449	32
Le Port Royal (1964)	425	33
Le Cartier Apts. (1964)	425	32
Tour Terminal (1966)	400	30

Nashville, TN

Building	Ht. (ft.)	Stories
South Central Bell Bldg.	617	33
Third National Financial Center	490	30
National Life and Accident Insur. Co.	452	31
Landmark Center	409	30
Nashville City Center (1987)	402	27

Newark, NJ

Building	Ht. (ft.)	Stories
Natl. Newark & Essex Bank	465	36
Raymond-Commerce Bldg.	448	36
Park Plaza Bldg.	400	26

New Orleans, LA

Building	Ht. (ft.)	Stories
One Shell Square (1972)	697	51
Place St. Charles (1985)	645	53
Plaza Tower (1970)	531	45
Energy Centre (1984)	530	39
LL&E Tower (1987)	481	36
Sheraton Hotel (1985)	478	47
Marriott Hotel (1974)	450	42
Texaco Bldg. (1983)	442	33
Canal Place One (1979)	439	32
Bank of New Orleans (1970)	438	31
International Trade Mart (1967)	407	33

New York, NY

Building	Ht. (ft.)	Stories
One World Trade Center (1972)	1,368	110
Two World Trade Center (1973)	1,362	110
Empire State Bldg. (1931)	1,250	102
(incl. 164-ft. TV tower)	1,414	–
Chrysler Bldg. (1930)	1,046	77
American International Bldg.(1932)	950	66
40 Wall Street (1930)	927	70
Citicorp Center (1977)	915	59
G.E. Bldg. (1933)	850	70
Cityspire (1989)	814	72
One Chase Manhattan Plaza (1961)	813	60
Met Life (1963)	808	59
Woolworth Bldg. (1913)	792	57
One Worldwide Plaza (1989)	778	47
Carnegie Hall Tower (1991)	757	60
Equitable Tower (1985)	752	51
One Penn Plaza (1972)	750	57
1251 Ave. of Americas (1972)	750	54
J. P. Morgan Headquarters (1989)	745	50
One Liberty Plaza (1973)	743	54
20 Exchange Place (Citibank) (1931)	741	55
World Financial Center (1984)	739	53
One Astor Plaza (1972)	730	54
Metropolitan Life Insurance Tower (1909)	720	52
Metropolitan Tower (1985)	716	68
Union Carbide Bldg. (1960)	707	52
General Motors Bldg. (1968)	705	50
500 5th Ave. (1930)	700	60
Nine West 57th Street (1974)	689	50
Marine Midland Bldg. (1966)	688	52
55 Water Street (1972)	687	53
Chemical Bank World Headquarters (1963)	685	50
Ulris Bldg. (1972)	685	50
Four Seasons Hotel (1993)	682	52
Chanin Bldg.(1929)	680	55
Trump International Hotel and Tower (1970)	679	52
Lincoln (1939)	673	53
Citicorp (Queens) (1990)	673	50
McGraw Hill (1972)	670	51
Trump Tower (1982)	664	58
599 Lexington Ave. (1988)	653	47
Museum Tower Apts. (1985)	650	58
712 5th Ave. (1990)	650	56
550 Madison Ave. (1983)	648	37
American Brands Bldg. (1967)	647	47
AT&T Headquarters (1932)	647	27
Irving Trust (1931)	645	50
World Financial Center Tower B (1986)	645	50
RCA Bldg. (1931)	642	51
345 Park Ave. (1968)	634	44
One New York Plaza (1969)	630	50
Grace Plaza (1972)	630	50
Home Insurance Co. Bldg. (1966)	630	45
New York Telephone.(1975)	630	40
Central Park Place (1988)	628	56
One Dag Hammarskjold Plaza (1972)	628	50
888 7th Ave. (1971)	628	45
Burlington House (1969)	625	50
Waldorf-Astoria (1931)	623	47
Olympic Tower (1976)	620	51
10 East 40th Street (1929)	620	48
101 Park Ave. (1982)	618	46
General Electric Bldg. (1930)	616	50
750 7th Ave.	615	35
New York Life (1928)	615	33
Righhga Royal Hotel	610	54
17 State Street	610	41
Penney Bldg. (1964)	609	46
IBM Headquarters (1983)	603	43
780 3d Ave.	600	50
Jacob K. Javits Federal Bldg. (1960)	593	45
Celanese Bldg. (1973)	592	45
U.S. Court House (1976)	590	37
Kalikow Hotel	588	58
Millennium Hilton Hotel	587	58
Time & Life Bldg. (1959)	587	48
Federal Office Bldg. (1968)	587	41
Millennium Broadway(1995)	580	46
Stevens Tower	580	42
1185 Avenue of the Americas (1971)	580	42
Cooper Bregstein Bldg. (1969)	580	38
Municipal Bldg. (1914)	580	34
520 Madison Ave. (1983)	577	42
One Madison Square Plaza (1973)	576	42
Park Ave. Plaza (1981)	575	44
World Financial Center Tower A (1986)	575	42
One Financial Square (1987)	575	37
Marriott Marquis Hotel (1985)	574	50
Westvaco Bldg. (1967)	574	42
Socony Mobil Bldg. (1956)	572	42
780 3d Ave. (1983)	570	49
Sperry Rand Bldg. (1963)	570	43
600 3d Ave. (1971)	570	42
One Bankers Trust Plaza (1974)	565	40
New York General (1928)	565	35
Hemsley Palace Hotel (1980)	563	51
30 Broad Street (1932)	562	48
Park Ave. Tower (1986)	561	36
Sherry-Netherland Bldg. (1927)	560	40
Continental Can Company (1962)	557	41
Three Park Ave. (1975)	556	42
Continental Corp	555	41
Sperry & Hutchinson (1964)	555	41
Galleria (1975), 117 East 57th Street	552	57
Interchem Bldg.	552	45
919 3d Ave.	550	47
NYNEX (1979)	550	45
Burroughs Bldg. (1963)	550	44
151 East 44th Street	550	44

Oklahoma City, OK

Building	Ht. (ft.)	Stories
Liberty Tower (1971)	500	36
First National Bank (1974)	493	33
City National Bank Tower (1985)	440	32
First Oklahoma Tower (1982)	434	31

Omaha, NE

Building	Ht. (ft.)	Stories
Woodmen Tower (1970)	440	30
Enron Bldg. (1960)	400	18

Orlando, FL

Building	Ht. (ft.)	Stories
Sun Bank Center Tower (1988)	441	35
Orange County Courthouse (1997)	416	24
Barnett Bank Center (1988)	404	28

Philadelphia, PA

Building	Ht. (ft.)	Stories
One Liberty Place (1987)	945	61
Two Liberty Place (1990)	848	58
Mellon Bank Center (1990)	792	54
Bell Atlantic Tower (1991)	739	53
Blue Cross Tower (1990)	700	50
Commerce Sq., #1 (1990)	572	40
Commerce Sq., #2 (1992)	572	40
City Hall Tower (1901), (incl. 37-ft. statue of William Penn)	548	7
1818 Market St. (1974)	500	40
Phila. Saving Fund Society (1932)	492	39
Fidelity Mutual Life Bldg. (1971)	492	38
Meridan Bank (1972)	492	38
Provident Mutual Life (1983)	491	40
PSFS Bldg. (1932)	491	36
Central Penn Natl. Bank (1970)	490	36
5 Penncenter (1970)	488	36
Industrial Valley Bank Bldg. (1969)	482	32
Philadelphia National Bank (1930)	475	25
Two Mellon Plaza (1930)	450	30
Centre Square (2 towers) (1973)	490/416	38/32

(continued)

Philadelphia, PA *(continued)*

Building	Ht. (ft.)	Stories
Two Logan Square (1987)	435	34
2000 Market Street (1973)	435	29
Two Girard Plaza (1930)	412	30
Fidelity Bank (1927)	405	30
Two Girard Plaza	404	30
Lewis Tower (1929)	400	33
One Logan Square (1982)	400	32

Phoenix, AZ

Building	Ht. (ft.)	Stories
Valley Bank Center (1972)	483	40
Arizona Bank Downtown (1976)	407	31

Pittsburgh, PA

Building	Ht. (ft.)	Stories
USX Tower (1970)	841	64
One Mellon Bank Center (1983)	725	54
One PPG Place	635	40
Fifth Avenue Place (1987)	616	31
One Oxford Centre	615	45
Gulf Bldg.	582	38
University of Pittsburgh (1936)	535	42
Mellon Bank Bldg. (1951)	520	41
One Oliver Plaza (1968)	511	40
Grant (1928)	485	40
Koppers (1929)	475	34
Two PNC Plaza	445	34
Equibank Bldg. (1975)	442	34
CNG Tower (1987)	430	32
Pittsburgh National Bldg. (1972)	428	30
One PNC Plaza	424	30
Alcoa Bldg. (1953)	410	30

Portland, OR

Building	Ht. (ft.)	Stories
Wells Fargo Tower	546	40
First National Bank of Oregon (1973)	536	40
Koin Tower Plaza	509	35

Richmond, VA

Building	Ht. (ft.)	Stories
James Monroe Bldg.	450	29
City Hall (incl. penthouse)	425	17
Crestar Bank HQ. Bldg.	400	24

St. Louis, MO

Building	Ht. (ft.)	Stories
Gateway Arch (1965)	630	–
Metropolitan Square Tower (1988)	593	42
One Bell Center (1984)	588	44
Mercantile Trust Bldg. (1975)	485	35
Boatmen's Plaza (1982)	420	30
Laclede Gas. Bldg. (1969)	400	34

St. Paul, MN

Building	Ht. (ft.)	Stories
Minnesota World Trade Center	471	36
Galtier Plaza's Jackson Tower	440	46
First Natl. Bank Bldg.	417	32

San Antonio, TX

Building	Ht. (ft.)	Stories
Tower of the Americas (1968)	622	–
Marriott Rivercenter (1988)	546	38
Weston Centre (1988)	444	32
Tower Life (1929)	404	30

San Diego, CA

Building	Ht. (ft.)	Stories
One American Plaza (1991)	500	34
Symphony Tower (1989)	499	34
Hyatt Regency San Diego (1992)	495	39
Emerald-Shapery Center (1991)	450	30
One Harbor Drive (1992)	424	41

San Francisco, CA

Building	Ht. (ft.)	Stories
Transamerica Pyramid (1972)	853	48
Bank of America (1969)	779	52
345 California Bldg.	615	48
101 California Street (1986)	600	48
California Center (1983)	600	47
Pacific Gas and Electric Bldg. (1970)	598	35
Embarcadero Center, No. 4 (1982)	570	45
Security Pacific Bank (1970)	569	45
One Market Plaza, Spear Street (1976)	565	43
Southern Pacific (1975)	564	43
Wells Fargo Bldg. (1966)	561	43
Standard Oil Bldg. (1948)	551	37
One Sansome-Citicorp	550	39
Shaklee Bldg. (1981)	537	38
Crocker Plaza (1967)	532	38

Building	Ht. (ft.)	Stories
AETNA Bldg. (1969)	529	38
525 Market Street (1973)	529	38
First and Market Bldg.	529	38
Metropolitan Life Bldg. (1973)	524	38
Crocker National Bank	500	38
333 Bush Street	495	40
Hilton Hotel (1971)	493	46
Pacific Gas & Electric (1970)	492	34
Union Bank Bldg. (1972)	490	37
Pacific Insurance Co. Bldg. (1972)	476	34
Bechtel Bldg. (1977)	475	33
333 Market Bldg. (1979)	474	33
Hartford Insurance (1965)	446	33
Mutual Benefit Life (1969)	438	32
Russ Bldg. (1928)	435	31
Telephone Bldg. (1925)	435	26
Pacific Gateway (1983)	416	30
Levi Strauss Bldg. (1974)	412	31
Embarcadero Center Complex III (1976)	412	31
101 Montgomery Street	405	28

Seattle, WA

Building	Ht. (ft.)	Stories
Columbia Seafirst Center (1985)	943	76
Two Union Square (1989)	740	56
Washington Mutual Tower (1988)	735	55
AT&T Gateway Tower (1989)	722	62
Key Tower	722	62
Seattle First National Bank (1969)	609	50
Space Needle (1962)	605	–
Pacific First Center (1989)	580	44
First Interstate Center (1983)	574	48
Rainier National Bank (1976)	569	51
Bank of California (1974)	543	43
Seafirst 5th Ave. Plaza (1981)	543	42
L. C. Smith Tower (1925)	520	42
Security Pacific Bank Tower (1977)	514	42
Henry M. Jackson Federal Bldg. (1974)	514	34
Federal Office Bldg. (1973)	499	38
520 Pike Tower (1984)	498	29
Key Tower (1986)	493	40
Federal Office Bldg.	487	37
1600 Bell Plaza	480	33
US West Communications	466	33
One Union Square (1981)	456	38
1111 3d Ave. Bldg. (1980)	454	38
Westin Bldg. (1981)	409	34

Tampa, FL

Building	Ht. (ft.)	Stories
100 N. Tampa (1992)	579	42
Barnett Plaza (1986)	577	42
One Tampa Center (1981)	537	39
SunTrust Financial Centre (1992)	525	36
First Financial Tower (1973)	458	36
NationsBank Plaza (1988)	454	33

Toledo, OH

Building	Ht. (ft.)	Stories
One SeaGate (1962)	404	30
Owens Illinois Headquarters Bldg. (1982)	404	30
Owens-Corning Fiberglas Tower (1970)	400	30

Toronto, Ontario

Building	Ht. (ft.)	Stories
CN Tower (1975) (world's tallest self-supporting structure)	1,821	–
First Canadian Place (1975)	952	72
Scotia Plaza (1989)	902	68
Canada Trust Tower (1990)	863	51
Commerce Court West (1973)	784	57
Toronto-Dominion Bank Tower (1967)	731	56
Bay-Wellington Tower (1990)	705	47
Royal Trust Tower (1969)	609	46
Royal Bank Plaza(1976)	567	41
Manu-Life Centre (1975)	525	51
Eaton Centre (1990)	494	34
AETNA Life Bldg. (1986)	489	36
Workers' Compensation Bldg. (1995)	487	33
Two Bloor Street West (1974)	480	34
Old Bank Of Commerce (1930)	477	34
Exchange Tower (1981)	475	36
Cadillac/Fairview Tower (1982)	466	36
Continental Bank (1980)	465	35
Commerce Court North- C.I.B.C. (1930)	464	34
Cadillac-Fairview Tower (1982)	460	36
Palace Place (1992)	455	46
Palace Pier (1978)	453	46
Richmond Adelaide Centre (1980)	450	35

Building	Ht. (ft.)	Stories
Sheraton Centre (1972)	443	43
Hudson's Bay Centre (1974)	442	35
Two Bloor Street East (1974)	442	34
Royal York Hotel (1929)	439	26
Harbour Castle Hotel	438	38
Ernst & Young Tower (TD Centre) (1990)	438	31
Four Seasons Sheraton Hotel (1972)	428	43
Leaside Towers (2 bldgs.) (1970)	423	44
Commercial Union Tower (TD Centre) (1974)	420	32
Metro Hall (1991)	420	27
Commercial Union Tower (1974)	419	32
Hotel Plaza II	415	41
Leaside Towers (1970)	410	43
Young-Eglinton Centre—Triathlon Tower	408	30
Harbour Square Apts.	403	34

Tulsa, OK

Building	Ht. (ft.)	Stories
Bank of Oklahoma Tower	667	52
Cityplex Towers	640	60
First National Tower	516	41
Mid-Continent Tower	513	36
Fourth National Bank of Tulsa	412	21
National Bank of Tulsa	400	24

Vancouver, British Columbia

Building	Ht. (ft.)	Stories
Harbour Centre (1976)	479	28
Royal Bank Tower (1973)	468	37
Granville Square	466	28
Vancouver Center (1977)	462	36
Scotiabank Tower	451	36
Bentall IV (1981)	450	35
Park Place (1984)	450	35
Toronto Dominion Bank	440	30
Harbour Centre (1977)	426	21
200 Granville Square	403	30
Bentall III (1974)	400	31

Winnipeg, Manitoba

Building	Ht. (ft.)	Stories
Trizec (1980)	494	32
Richardson Bldg. (1969)	439	34
Toronto Dominion Centre (1989)	413	33

Winston-Salem, NC

Building	Ht. (ft.)	Stories
Wachovia Bldg. (1995)	460	28
Wachovia Bldg. (1965)	410	27

Some Other Notable Tall Buildings in North American Cities

Building	City	Ht. (ft.)	Stories
Skylon	Niagara Falls, Ont.	774	–
Principal Fin'l. Group Bldg.	Des Moines, IA	630	44
Office Tower, S. Mall (1973)	Albany, NY	589	44
Vehicle Assembly Bldg	Cape Canaveral, FL.	552	40
Marine Midland Ctr. (1970)	Buffalo, NY	529	40
State Capitol (1932)	Baton Rouge, LA	460	34
Southtrust Tower (1986)	Birmingham, AL	454	34
Xerox Tower (1967)	Rochester, NY	443	30
One Summit Square	Fort Wayne, IN.	442	26
State Capitol	Lincoln, NE	432	40
BB & T/2 Hanover Sq. (1991)	Raleigh, NC	431	29
100 N. Main Bldg.	Memphis, TN	430	37
Taj Mahal	Atlantic City, NJ.	429	51
Industrial Trust Bldg. (1927)	Providence, RI	428	26
First Natl. Bank	Mobile, AL	420	33
L.D.S. Church Office Bldg.	Salt Lake City, UT	420	30
Century Twenty One	Hamilton, Ont.	418	43
Complex G (1972)	Quebec City, Que.	415	33
Lexington Financial Ctr.	Lexington, KY	410	30
Ordway Bldg.(1985)	Oakland, CA	404	28
Wells Fargo Center	Sacramento, CA	402	30
United American Bank	Knoxville, TN	400	30

Notable International Buildings

Source: Council on Tall Buildings and Urban Habitat, Lehigh Univ.; World Almanac research

List includes some structures that do not have stories and are not technically considered buildings.

Building (yr. completed or to be completed)	Ht. (ft.)	Stories
Oriental Pearl Television Tower (1995), Shanghai, China	1,535	–
Petronas Tower I (1997), Kuala Lumpur, Malaysia.	1,483	88
Petronas Tower II (1997), Kuala Lumpur, Malaysia.	1,483	88
Jin Mao Bldg. (1998), Shanghai, China*	1,379	88
Plaza Rakyat (1998), Kuala Lumpur, Malaysia*	1,254	77
Central Plaza (1992), Hong Kong, China	1,227	78
Bank of China Tower (1989), Hong Kong, China.	1,209	70
T & C Tower (1997), Kaoshiung, Taiwan	1,140	85
Shun Hing Square (1996), Shenzen, China	1,066	81
Sky Central Plaza (1997), Guangzhou, China	1,056	80
Chicago Beach Tower Hotel (1998), Dubai, UAE*	1,053	60
Baiyoke Tower II (1997), Bangkok, Thailand	1,050	90
BDNI Ctr.-TowerA (1999), Jakarta, Indonesia*	1,040	62
Eiffel Tower (1889), Paris, France	984	–
Ryugyong Hotel (1995), Pyongyang, N. Korea	984	105
Landmark Tower (1993), Yokohama, Japan.	971	70
Jubilee St./Queen's Rd. Central (1998), Hong Kong, China*	958	69
Overseas Union Bank Centre(1986), Singapore	919	66
United Overseas Bank Plaza (1992), Singapore	919	66
Republic Plaza (1995), Singapore	919	66
Commerzbank Tower (1997), Frankfurt, Germany	850	60
Messeturm. Bldg. (1990), Frankfurt, Germany	843	63
Gate Tower (1996), Osaka, Japan	833	56
World Trade Center (1995), Osaka, Japan.	827	55
BNI City Tower (1995), Jakarta, Indonesia.	820	46
Korea Life Ins. Co. (1985), Seoul, S. Korea	817	60
Kompleks Tun Abdul Razak Bldg. (1985), Penang, Malaysia	804	65
Shin Kong Life Tower (1993), Taipei, Taiwan.	801	51
Malayan Bank(1988), Kuala Lumpur, Malaysia	799	50
Metropolitan Gov't. Bldg. (1991), Tokyo, Japan	797	48
Rialto Tower (1985), Melbourne, Australia	794	56
BDNI Ctr.-Tower B (1999), Jakarta, Indonesia*	788	45
JR Central Towers (1999), Nagoya, Japan*	787	53
Graha Kuningan (1998), Jakarta, Indonesia*	784	52
Moscow State Univ. (1953), Moscow, Russia.	784	26
Empire Tower (1994), Kuala Lumpur, Malaysia	781	62
One Canada Square, London	774	50
Singapore Treasury Bldg. (1986), Singapore	771	52
Opera City Tower (1997), Tokyo, Japan	768	54
Shinjuku Park Tower (1994), Tokyo, Japan	764	52
Palace of Culture & Science (1955), Warsaw, Poland	758	42
MLC Centre (1978), Sydney, Australia	748	65

* still under construction.

Notable Bridges in America

Source: Federal Highway Administration, Bridge Division, U.S. Dept. of Transportation; World Almanac research

Asterisk (*) designates railroad bridge. Double asterisk (**) designates bridge under construction. Span of a bridge is the distance between its supports.

Suspension

Year	Bridge	Location	Main span (ft.)
1964	Verrazano-Narrows	New York, NY.	4,260
1937	Golden Gate	San Fran. Bay, CA	4,200
1957	Mackinac Straits	Sts. of Mackinac, MI	3,800
1931	Geo. Washington.	Hudson R., NY–NJ	3,500
1950	Tacoma Narrows	Tacoma, WA.	2,800
1936	San. Fran.-Oakland Bay[1]	San Fran. Bay, CA	2,310
1939	Bronx-Whitestone	East R., NY	2,300
1970	Pierre Laporte	Quebec, Canada.	2,190
1960	Seaway Skyway	Ogdensburg, NY.	2,150
1968	Del. Memorial	Wilmington, DE.	2,150
1957	Walt Whitman	Philadelphia, PA	2,000
1929	Ambassador.	Detroit, MI–Can.	1,850
1917	Quebec	Quebec, Canada	1,800
1961	Throgs Neck	Long Is. Sound, NY.	1,800
1926	Benjamin Franklin.	Philadelphia, PA	1,750
1924	Bear Mt.	Hudson R., NY.	1,632
1903	Williamsburg	East R., NY	1,600
1952	Wm. Preston La. Mem.[2]	Sandy Point, MD	1,600
1952	Chesapeake Bay	Sandy Point, MD	1,600
1969	Newport.	Narragansett Bay, RI	1,600
1883	Brooklyn	East R., NY	1,595
1939	Lion's Gate	Burrard Inlet, BC	1,550
1930	Mid-Hudson	Poughkeepsie, NY.	1,500

(continued)

Suspension (*continued*)

Year	Bridge	Location	Main span (ft.)
1963	Vincent Thomas	L. A. Harbor, CA	1,500
1909	Manhattan	East R., NY	1,470
1955	MacDonald Bridge	Halifax, Nova Scotia	1,447
1970	A. Murray Mackay	Halifax, Nova Scotia	1,400
1936	Triborough	East R., NY	1,380
1931	St. Johns	Portland, OR	1,207
1929	Mount Hope	RI	1,200
1960	Ogdensburg	St. Lawrence R., NY	1,150
1965	Bidwell Bar Bridge	Oroville, CA	1,108
1964	Middle Fork Feather	CA	1,105
1939	Deer Isle	ME	1,080
1931	Simon Kenton Memorial	Ohio R., Maysville, KY	1,060
1936	Ile d'Orleans	St. Lawrence R., Quebec	1,059
1867	John A. Roebling	Ohio R., KY	1,057
1971	Dent	Clearwater Co., ID	1,050
1900	Miampimi	Mexico	1,030
1849	Wheeling	Ohio R., WV	1,010

Cantilever

Year	Bridge	Location	Main span (ft.)
1917	Québec Bridge	St. Lawrence R., Quebec	1,800
1988	Greater New Orleans Bridge	Mississippi R., New Orleans, LA	1,575
1995	Gramercy Bridge	Mississippi R., Gramercy, LA	1,460
1936	Transbay	San Fran. Bay, CA	1,400
1968	Baton Rouge Bridge	Mississippi R., Baton Rouge, LA	1,235
1955	Tappan Zee	Hudson R., NY	1,212
1930	Lewis and Clark	Longview, WA–OR	1,200
1976	Patapsco River	Baltimore, MD	1,200
1909	Queensboro	East R., NY	1,182
1927	Carquinez Strait	CA	1,100
1958	Parallel Span	CA	1,100
1930	Jacques Cartier	Montreal, Quebec	1,097
1968	Isaiah D. Hart	Jacksonville, FL	1,088
1956	Richmond[3]	San Fran. Bay, CA	1,070
1929	Grace Memorial	Charleston, SC	1,050
1980	Newburgh-Beacon	Hudson R., NY	1,000
1949	Martin Luther King	St. Louis, MO	963
1975	Caruthersville	Mississippi R., MO–TN	920
1969	Silver Memorial	Pt. Pleasant, WV–OH	900
1977	Saint Marys	Saint Marys, WV–OH	900
1981	Ravenswood	WV	900
1987	Carl Perkins	Ohio R., KY	900
1988	Mississippi R.	Natchez, MS	875
1938	Blue Water	Pt. Huron, MI	871
1972	Mississippi R.	Vicksburg, MS	870
1972	N. Fork American R.	Auburn, CA	862
1940	*Baton Rouge	Mississippi R., LA	848
1899	*Cornwall	St. Lawrence R.	843
1940	Rte. 82	Mississippi R., AR	840
1961	Mississippi R.	Greenville, MS	840
1961	Rte. 49	Mississippi R., AR	840
1963	Brent Spence	KY–OH	830
1940	Mississippi R.	Vicksburg, MS	825
1963	Mississippi R.	Donaldsonville, LA	825
1929	Clark Memorial	Ohio R., KY	820
1961	Campbellton-Cross Pt.	New Brunswick, Can.	815
1932	Washington Mem.	Seattle, WA	800
1935	Rip Van Winkle	Catskill, NY	800
1938	Cairo	Ohio R., IL–KY	800
1936	McCullough	Coos Bay, OR	793
1892	Memphis	Mississippi R., TN	790
1935	Huey P. Long[4]	New Orleans, LA	790
1949	Rte. 55	Mississippi R, AR–TN	790
1910	*P&LE RR Bridge	Ohio R., PA	750
1932	Bi-State Vietnam Gold Star	Henderson, KY	720
1904	*Norfolk Southern RR	Ohio R., OH	700
1943	*Pit River	Redding, CA	620
1941	Columbia R.	Kettle Falls, WA	600
1954	Columbia R.	Umatilla, OR	600
1954	Columbia R.	The Dalles, OR	576
1968	W. 17th St.	Huntington, WV	562

Simple Truss

Year	Bridge	Location	Main span (ft.)
1976	Chester	Chester, WV	745
1929	Irvin S. Cobb	Ohio R.,IL–KY	716
1922	*Tanana R.	Nenana, AK	700
1967	I-77, Ohio R.	Williamstown, WV	650
1917	MacArthur[4]	St. Louis, IL–MO	647
1992	St. Charles	Missouri R, MO	625
1933	Atchafalaya	Morgan City, LA	608
1924	*Castleton	Hudson R., NY	598
1937	Delaware R.	Easton, PA	550
1930	Swindell Bridge	Pittsburgh, PA	545
1952	Allegheny R. Tpk.	Pittsburgh, PA	534
1930	*Martinez	Martinez, CA	528

Year	Bridge	Location	Main span (ft.)
1951	Rankin	Pittsburgh, PA	525
1914	Old Brownsville	Brownsville, PA	520
1906	Donora-Webster	Donora-Webster, PA	515
1909	Hulton	Pittsburgh, PA	505
1967	Tanana R.	AK	500

Steel Truss

Year	Bridge	Location	Main span (ft.)
1988	Glade Creek	Raleigh Co., WV	784
1973	Atchafalaya R.	Krotz Springs, LA	780
1972	Piscataqua R.	NH–ME	756
1972	Atchafalaya R.	Simmesport, LA	720
1957	SR-3, Rappahannock R.	Middlesex Co., VA	648
1978	Atchafalaya R.	Morgan City, LA	607
1959	Summit	Summit, DE	600
1969	Reedy Point	Delaware City, DE	600
1938	US-22	Delaware R., NJ	540
1955	Interstate (I-5)	Columbia R., OR–WA	531
1910	McKinley, St. Louis[4]	Mississippi R., MO	517
1972	Mississippi R.	Muscatine, IA	512
1896	Newport	Ohio R., KY	511
1989	US 190, Atchafalaya R.	Krotz Springs, LA	506
1931	Lucy Jefferson Lewis	Cumberland R., KY	500
1958	Lake Oahe	Gettysburg, SD	500
1958	Lake Oahe	Mobridge, SD	500
1970	Lake Koocanusa	Lincoln Co., MT	500

Continuous Truss

Year	Bridge	Location	Main span (ft.)
1966	Columbia R. (Astoria)	OR–WA	1,232
1977	Francis Scott Key	Baltimore, MD	1,200
1981	Ravenswood/Ohio R.	Ravenswood, WV	902
1995	**Central	Ohio R., KY–OH	850
1943	Dubuque	Mississippi R., IA	845
1966	Charles Braga	Fall River, MA	840
1956	Earl C. Clements[5]	Ohio R., IL–KY	825
1929	U.S. 31	Ohio R., IN–KY	820
1953	John E. Mathews	Jacksonville, FL	810
1950	Maurice J. Tobin	Boston, MA	801
1940	Gov. Nice Memorial	Potomac River, MD	800
1957	Kingston-Rhinecliff	Hudson R., NY	800
1992	Mark Clark Expwy. I-526	Cooper R., Charleston,SC	800
1986	Rochester-Monaca	Rochester-Monaca,PA	780
1940	U.S. 231	Ohio R., IN	750
1974	Carroll L. Cropper	Ohio R., IN–KY	750
1981	Sewickley	Sewickley, PA	750
1984	13th St. Bridge, Ohio R.	Ashland, KY	740
1959	Monaca-E. Rochester	Monaca-E. Rochester, PA	730
1976	Betsy Ross	Philadelphia, PA	729
1929	U.S. 421	Ohio R., IN–KY	727
1967	Matthew E. Welsh[6]	Mauckport, IN	725
1962	U.S. 41	Ohio R., IN–KY	720
1994	6th St.	Huntington, WV	720
1970	Vanport	Vanport, PA	715
1962	Champlain	Montreal, Que.	707
1962	John F. Kennedy[7]	Ohio R., IN–KY	701
1973	Girard Point	Philadelphia, PA	700
1954	PA Tpk., Delaware R.	Philadelphia, PA	682
1938	Port Arthur-Orange	TX	680
1949	George Platt	Philadelphia, PA	680
1926	Cape Girardeau	Mississippi R., MO	677
1929	*Cincinnati	Ohio R., OH	675
1946	Chester	Mississippi R, IL	670
1970	Gulfgate	Port Arthur, TX	664
1994	Williamstown-Marietta	Williamstown, WV	650
1955	Jefferson City	Missouri R., MO	640
1930	Quincy	Mississippi R., IL	628
1959	US 181, over harbor	Corpus Christi, TX	620
1961	Shippingport	Shippingport, PA	620
1935	Bourne-Sagamore	Cape Cod Canal, MA	616
1965	Clarion R. (I-80)	Clarion, PA	612
1975	Donora-Monessen	Donora-Monessen, PA	608
1957	Blatnik	Duluth, MN	600
1965	Rio Grande Gorge	Taos, NM	600
1991	Hoffstadt Creek	Mt. St. Helens, WA	600
1991	Jefferson City	Missouri R., MO	596
1962	W. Branch Feather R.	Oroville, CA	576
1967	Glenwood	Pittsburgh, PA	567
1936	Mark Twain Mem.	Hannibal, MO	562
1957	Mackinac	Mackinac Straits, MI	560
1932	Pulaski Skyway	Passaic R.-Hackensack R., NJ	550
1966	Emlenton	Emlenton, PA	540
1973	Gold Star Memorial	New London, CT	540
1936	Homestead High Level	Pittsburgh, PA	534
1959	Martinez	Benicia-Martinez, CA	528
1960	Brownsville High Level	Brownsville, PA	518
1971	Grandad	Elk River, ID	504
1945	Mansfield-Dravosburg	Pittsburgh, PA	500

Continuous Box and Plate Girder

Year	Bridge	Location	Main span (ft.)
1967	San Mateo-Hayward #2	San Fran. Bay, CA . . .	750
1976	Intracoastal Canal	Forked Is., LA	750
1977	Intracoastal Canal	Gibbstown, LA	750
1982	Houston Ship Chan . . .	Houston, TX	750
1969	San Diego-Coronado[8] . .	San Diego Bay, CA . . .	660
1987	Umatilla, Columbia R. .	OR–WA	660
1994	Acosta	Jacksonville, FL	630
1981	Douglas	Juneau, AK	620
1976	Wax L. Outlet	Calumet, LA	618
1963	Poplar St.	St. Louis, MO	600
1981	Glenn Jackson (I-205) .	Columbia R., OR–WA .	600
1976	Stanislaus River	Sonora, CA.	580
1982	Illinois R..	Pekin, IL.	550
1982	I-440.	Arkansas R., AR.	540
1980	US-64, Tennessee R. .	Savannah, TN.	525
1965	McDonald-Cartier	Ottawa, Ont.	520
1988	Mon City	Monongahela, PA	520
1984	Columbia R.	Richland, WA	450
1986	Veterans	Pittsburgh, PA.	440
1987	SR 76, Cumberland R..	Dover, TN.	440
1987	SR 20, Tennessee R.. .	Perryville, TN	440
1970	Willamette R., I-205 . . .	West Linn, OR	430
1974	I-430.	Arkansas R., AR.	430
1965	I-24, Tennessee R. . . .	Marion Co., TN	420
1974	Dunbar-S. Charleston .	S. Charleston, WV. . . .	420
1975	36th St..	Charleston, WV.	420
1978	Snake R..	Clarkston, WA.	420
1984	FAU 3456, TN R..	Chattanooga, TN.	420

Continuous Plate

Year	Bridge	Location	Main span (ft.)
1973	Ship Channel (I-610) . .	Houston, TX	630
1971	W. Atchafalaya	Henderson, LA	573
1992	State Route 76	Paris, TN	525
1981	Illinois 23	Illinois R., IL	510
1968	Trinity R..	Dallas, TX	480
1978	San Joaquin R.	Antioch, CA	460
1977	Thomas Johnson Mem.	Solomons, MD	451
1967	Mississippi R.	La Crosse, WI.	450
1975	I-129.	Missouri R., IA–NE . . .	450
1979	Lewis	St. Louis, MO	450
1992	Cuba Landing Bridge . .	Tennessee R., TN. . . .	450
1966	I-480.	Missouri R., IA–NE . . .	425
1972	Whiskey Bay Pilot	Ramah, LA.	425
1972	I-80	Missouri R., IA–NE . . .	425
1972	I-635, Kansas City	Missouri R., KS–MO . .	425
1983	US-36.	Missouri R., KS–MO. .	425
1987	I-435.	Missouri R., KS–MO. .	425
1978	I-24	Cumberland R., KY . . .	420
1993	Bob Michael Bridge . . .	Peoria, IL	360

Cable-Stayed

Year	Bridge	Location	Main span (ft.)
1986	Annacis (Alex Fraser) .	Vancouver, BC	1,526
1993	Quetzalapa Bridge . . .	Quetzalapa, Mexico . .	1,391
1988	Dames Point	Jacksonville, FL	1,300
1995	Houston Ship Channel.	Baytown,TX.	1,250
1983	Hale Boggs Memorial. .	Luling, LA.	1,222
1987	Sunshine Skyway	Tampa Bay, FL.	1,200
1988	Tampico/Panuco R. . .	Mexico	1,181
1988	ALRT Fraser River Bridge	Vancouver, BC	1,115
1990	Talmadge Mem.	Savannah, GA	1,100
1993	Mezcala	Mex. City/Acapulco. Hwy..	1,024
1978	Pasco-Kennewick	Columbia R., WA	981
1984	Coatzacoalcos R.	Mexico	919
1985	E. Huntington	E. Huntington, WV. . . .	900
1987	Bayview Bridge	Quincy, IL.	900
1970	Burton Bridge	New Brunswick, Canada	850
1990	Weirton-Steubenville . .	WV–OH	820
1969	Papineau-Leblanc . . .	Montreal, Que.	790
1991	Cochrane	Mobile, AL	780
1994	Clark Bridge	Alton, IL	756
1995	Chesapeake & Delaware Canal Bridge	Dover-Wilmington, DE	750
1966	Longs Creek.	New Brunswick, Canada	713
1967	Hawkshaw.	New Brunswick, Canada	713
1993	Quetzalapa Bridge . . .	Quetzalapa, Mexico . .	699
1993	Burlington Bridge.	Burlington, IA	660
1991	Neches R..	Port Arthur-Orange,TX	640
1989	James River Bridge. . .	Richmond, VA.	630

I-Beam Girder

Year	Bridge	Location	Main span (ft.)
1980	Interstate 20	Shreveport, LA	438
1988	Route 18.	Weston's Mill Pond, NJ	276

Steel Arch

Year	Bridge	Location	Main span (ft.)
1977	New River Gorge	Fayetteville, WV.	1,700
1931	Bayonne (Kill Van Kull) .	Bayonne, NJ	1,652
1973	Fremont.	Portland, OR	1,255
1964	Port Mann	Vancouver, BC.	1,200
1967	Trois-Rivieres.	St. Lawrence R., Que.	1,100
1967	Lavioleete	Three Rivers, Canada	1,100
1992	Roosevelt Lake	Roosevelt Lake, AZ . . .	1,080
1959	Glen Canyon	Page., AZ	1,028
1962	Lewiston-Queenston. . .	Niagara R., Ont..	1,000
1976	Perrine	Twin Falls, ID.	993
1941	Rainbow Bridge	Niagara Falls, NY.	984
1917	*Hell Gate	East R., N.Y.	977
1977	Moundsville	Ohio R., WV	912
1992	I-255, Miss. R.	St. Louis, MO.	909
1972	I-40, Miss. R.[9].	AR– TN.	900
1936	Henry Hudson	Harlem R., NY	840
1967	Lincoln Trail Bridge. . . .	Ohio R., IN–KY	825
1978	I-57, Miss. R.	Cairo , IL.	821
1961	I-64, Ohio R.	IN	800
1980	I-65, Mobile R.	Mobile, AL	800
1930	West End.	Pittsburgh, PA	780
1978	I-470 Bridge, Ohio R. . .	Wheeling, WV	780
1996	Navajo Bridge	Glen Canyon, AZ	726

Concrete Arch

Year	Bridge	Location	Main span (ft.)
1993	Natchez Trace Pkwy. . .	Franklin, TN.	582
1993	Lake Street Bridge	St. Paul, MN	556
1971	Selah Creek (twin)	Selah, WA.	549
1968	Cowlitz R.	Mossyrock, WA	520
1931	Westinghouse	Pittsburgh, PA	460
1923	Cappelen.	Minneapolis, MN	435
1930	Jack's Run.	Pittsburgh, PA	400

Segmental Concrete

Year	Bridge	Location	Main span (ft.)
1997	Confederation Bridge . .	Prince Edward Isl., NB	820
1982	Jesse H, Jones Memorial	Houston, TX	750
1978	Shubenacadie River . . .	S. Maitland, Nova Scotia	790
1992	Narragansett Bay Crossing	Jamestown, RI.	674
1986	WB I-82 (Columbia R.) .	Umatilla, OR	660
1976	Stanislaus River	Parrets Ferry. CA	640
1992	Jamestown-Verranzzano	Jamestown, RI	636
1981	Gastineau Channel Br. .	Juneau, AK	620
1991	Veterans Memorial Centennial Bridge.	Coeur d'Alene, ID.	520
1974	Pine Valley Creek.	Pine Valley, CA	450
1988	Zilwaukee Bridge (twin) .	Zilwaukee, MI	392
1985	Red River Bridge	Boyce, LA	370

Twin Concrete Trestle[10]

Year	Bridge	Location	Total length
1979	I-55/I-10.	Manchac, LA..	181,157
1969	L. Pontchartrain Cswy. .	Mandeville, LA.	126,720
1972	Atchafalaya Flwy.	Baton Rouge, LA	93,984
1963	L. Pontchartrain	Slidell, LA	28,547
1983	Interstate 310.	Kenner, LA	25,925

Concrete Slab Dam[10]

Year	Bridge	Location	Total length
1927	Conowingo Dam.	MD	4,611
1952	SR-4, Roanoke R.	Mecklenburg Co., VA .	2,785
1936	Hoover Dam.	Lake Mead, NV	1,324

Drawbridges

Vertical Lift

Year	Bridge	Location	Main span (ft.)
1959	*Arthur Kill.	NY–NJ	558
1965	Pennsylvania Railroad .	Kirkwood-Mt. Pleasant, DE	548
1935	*Cape Cod Canal.	Cape Cod, MA.	544
1961	*Delair.	Delaware R., NJ.	542
1931	Burlington-Bristol	Delaware R., NJ–PA. .	540
1937	Marine Parkway	Jamaica Bay, NY	540
1908	*Willamette R.	Portland, OR	521
1968	Second Narrows.	Vancouver, B.C..	493
1912	*A-S-B Fratt.	Kansas City, MO	428
1945	*Harry S Truman	Kansas City, MO	427
1955	Roosevelt Island.	East R., NY	418
1980	US-17, James R.	Isle of Wight, Co., VA .	415
1932	*M-K-T R.R..	Missouri R., MO	414
1969	Cape Fear Mem.	Wilmington, NC	408
1930	Aerial.	Duluth, MN	386
1962	Burlington	Ontario, Can.	370
1922	*Cincinnati.	Ohio R., OH.	365
1941	Main Street	Jacksonville, FL	365

(continued)

Vertical Lift (continued)

Year	Bridge	Location	Main span (ft.)
1967	SR-156, James R.	Prince George Co., VA	364
1950	Red R.	Moncla, LA	360
1957	Industrial Canal	New Orleans, LA	360
1936	Tribo	Harlem R., NY	344
1961	Corpus Christi Harbor[4]	Corpus Christi, TX	344
1939	U.S. 1&9, Passaic R.	Newark, NJ	333
1930	*Martinez	Martinez, CA	328
1960	St. Andrews Bay	Panama City, FL	327
1929	*Penn-Lehigh	Newark Bay, PA	322
1987	Industrial Canal	New Orleans, LA	320
1920	*Chattanooga	Tennessee R., TN	310

Bascule

Year	Bridge	Location	Main span (ft.)
1940	Lorain	Black R., OH	333
1917	SR-8, Tennessee R.	Chattanooga, TN	306
1956	Duwamish R.	Seattle, WA	300
1955	Chehalis R.	Aberdeen, WA	288
1968	Elizabeth R.	Chesapeake, VA	280
1913	Broadway	Portland, OR	278
1954	Fuller Warren	Jacksonville, FL	267

Swing Bridges

Year	Bridge	Location	Main span (ft.)
1927	Fort Madison[4]	Mississippi R., IA	545
1991	SW. Spokane St.	Seattle, WA	480
1930	Rigolets Pass	New Orleans, LA	400
1950	Douglass Memorial	Washington, DC	386
1945	Lord Delaware	Mattaponi R., VA	252

Swing Span

Year	Bridge	Location	Main span (ft.)
1952	US-17	York R., VA	500
1897	*Duluth	St. Louis Bay, MN	486
1899	*C.M.&N.R.R.	Chicago, IL	474
1913	Rt. 82, Conn-R.	E. Haddam, CT	465
1914	*Coos Bay	OR	458

Floating Pontoon

Year	Bridge	Location	Floating length
1963	Evergreen Pt.	Seattle, WA	7,578
1961	Hood Canal	Pt. Gamble, WA	6,521
1993	Lacey V. Murrow[11]	Seattle, WA	6,620
1989	Third Lake Washington	Seattle, WA	5,811

(1) Swing span bridge with 2 spans of 2,310 ft. each. (2) A second bridge in parallel was completed in 1973. (3) The Richmond Bridge has twin spans 1,070 ft. each. (4) Railroad and vehicular bridge. (5) Two spans each 825 ft. (6) Two spans each 707 ft. (7) Two spans each 700 ft. (8) Two spans each 660 ft. (9) Two spans each 900 ft. (10) Length listed is total length of bridge. (11) Replaces the original Lacey V. Murrow bridge, which opened in 1940 and sank in 1990.

Oldest U.S. Bridges in Continuous Use

Built in 1697, the stone-arch Frankford Ave. Bridge crosses Pennypack Creek in Philadelphia, PA. A 3-span bridge with a total length of 75 ft., it was constructed as part of the King's Road, which eventually connected Philadelphia to New York.

The oldest covered bridge, completed in 1827, is the double-span, 278-ft. Haverhill Bath Bridge, which spans the Ammonoosuc River, between the towns of Bath and Haverhill, NH.

Some Notable International Bridges

Span of bridge is the distance between its supports. Asterisk (*) designates under construction as of Sept. 1998.

Suspension

Year	Bridge	Location	Main span (ft.)
1998	Akashi Kaikyo	Japan	6,570
1998	Storebælt (East Bridge)	Denmark	5,328
1981	Humber	England	4,626
1999*	Jiangyin Yangtze	China	4,544
1997	Tsing Ma[1]	China	4,518
1997	Hoga Kusten	Sweden	3,970
1988	Minami Bisan-Seto	Japan	3,609
1988	Bosphorus II	Turkey	3,576
1973	Bosphorus I	Turkey	3,524
1999*	Kurushima III	Japan	3,379
1999*	Kurushima II	Japan	3,346
1966	Tagus River[2]	Portugal	3,323
1964	Forth Road	Scotland	3,300
1988	Kita Bisan-Seto	Japan	3,248
1966	Severn	England	3,241
1988	Shimotsui Strait	Japan	3,084

Cantilever

Year	Bridge	Location	Main span (ft.)
1890	Forth[3] (rail)	Scotland	1,710
1974	Nanko	Japan	1,673

Steel Arch

Year	Bridge	Location	Main span (ft.)
1932	Sydney Harbour	Australia	1,650
1967	Zdakov	Czech Republic	1,244
1962	Thatcher	Panama Canal Zone	1,128
1961	Runcorn-Widnes	England	1,082
1935	Birchenough	Zimbabwe	1,080

Concrete Arch

Year	Bridge	Location	Main span (ft.)
1980	Krk I	Croatia.	1,280
1964	Gladesville	Australia	1,000
1964	Amizade	Brazil	951
1963	Arrabida	Portugal	886
1943	Sando	Sweden	866

Steel Plate and Box Girder

Year	Bridge	Location	Main span (ft.)
1974	President Costa e Silva	Brazil	984
1956	Sava I	Yugoslavia	856
1966	Zoobrüke	Germany	850

Cable-Stayed

Year	Bridge	Location	Main span (ft.)
1999*	Tatara	Japan	2,920
1995	Pont de Normandie	France	2,808
1996	Quingzhou Minjang	China	1,985
1993	Yangpu	China	1,975
1997	Xupu	China	1,936
1998*	Meiko Chuo	Japan	1,936
1991	Skarnsundet	Norway	1,739
1995	Tsurumi Tsubasa	Japan	1,673
2000*	Oresund	Denmark/Sweden	1,614
1991	Ikuchi	Japan	1,608
1994	Higashi Kobe	Japan	1,591
1997	Ting Kau	China	1,558

(1) Double-decked road and rail bridge. (2) Railroad and highway bridge. (3) Two spans of 1,710 ft. each.

Underwater Vehicular Tunnels in North America

(more than 5,000 ft. in length; year in parentheses is year of completion)

Name	Location	Waterway	Feet
Brooklyn-Battery (1950) (twin)	New York, NY	East River	9,117
Holland Tunnel (1927) (twin)	New York, NY	Hudson River	8,557
Ted Williams Tunnel (1995)	Boston, MA	Boston Harbor	8,448
Lincoln Tunnel (1937, 1945, 1957) (3 tubes)	New York, NY	Hudson River	8,216
Thimble Shoal Channel (1964)	Northampton Co., VA	Chesapeake Bay	8,187
Chesapeake Channel (1964)	Northampton Co., VA	Chesapeake Bay	7,941
Fort McHenry Tunnel (1985) (twin)	Baltimore, MD	Baltimore Harbor	7,920
Hampton Roads (1957) (twin)	Hampton, VA	Hampton Roads	7,479
Baltimore Harbor Tunnel (1957) (twin)	Baltimore, MD	Patapsco River	7,392
Queens Midtown (1940) (twin)	New York, NY	East River	6,414
Sumner Tunnel (1934)	Boston, MA	Boston Harbor	5,653
Louis-Hippolyte Lafontaine Tunnel	Montreal, Que.	St. Lawrence R.	5,280
Detroit-Windsor (1930)	Detroit, MI	Detroit River	5,160
Callahan Tunnel (1961)	Boston, MA	Boston Harbor	5,070

Land Vehicular Tunnels in the U.S.

(more than 3,000 ft. in length)

Name	Location	Feet
E. Johnson Memorial	I-70, CO	8,959
Eisenhower Memorial	I-70, CO	8,941
Allegheny (twin)	PA Turnpike	6,072
Liberty Tubes	Pittsburgh, PA	5,920
Zion Natl. Park	Rte. 9, UT	5,766
East River Mt. (twin)	VA–WV	5,412
Tuscarora (twin)	PA Turnpike	5,400
Tetsuo Harano (twin)	H-3, HI	5,165
Kittatinny (twin)	PA Turnpike	4,660
Cumberland Gap (twin)	KY–TN	4,600
Blue Mountain (twin)	PA Turnpike	4,435
Lehigh (twin)	PA Turnpike	4,379
Wawona	Yosemite Natl. Park, CA.	4,233
Big Walker Mt.	Bland Co., VA	4,229
Squirrel Hill	Pittsburgh, PA	4,225
Hanging Lake (twin)	Glenwood Canyon, CO.	4,000
Caldecott (3 tubes)	Oakland, CA	3,616
Fort Pitt (twin)	Pittsburgh, PA	3,560
Dingess Tunnel	Mingo Co., WV	3,400
Mall Tunnel	Dist. of Columbia	3,400
Cody No. 1	U.S. 14, 16, 20, WY	3,202

World's Longest Railway Tunnels

Source: Railway Directory & Year Book.

Tunnel	Date	Miles	Operating railway	Country
Seikan	1985	33.50	Japanese Railway	Japan
English Channel Tunnel	1994	31.04	Eurotunnel	United Kingdom-France
Dai-shimizu	1979	14.00	Japanese Railway	Japan
Simplon No. 1 and 2	1906, 1922	12.00	Swiss Fed. & Italian St.	Switzerland-Italy
Kanmon	1975	12.00	Japanese Railway	Japan
Apennine	1934	11.00	Italian State	Italy
Rokko	1972	10.00	Japanese Railway	Japan
Mt. MacDonald	1989	9.10	Canadian Pacific	Canada
Gotthard	1882	9.00	Swiss Federal	Switzerland
Lotschberg	1913	9.00	Bern-Lotschberg-Simplon	Switzerland
Hokuriku	1962	9.00	Japanese Railway	Japan
Mont Cenis (Frejus)	1871	8.00	Italian State	France-Italy
Shin-Shimizu	1961	8.00	Japanese Railway	Japan
Aki	1975	8.00	Japanese Railway	Japan
Cascade	1929	8.00	Burlington Northern	United States
Flathead	1970	8.00	Burlington Northern	United States

World's Largest-Capacity Hydro Plants

Source: U.S. Committee on Large Dams of the Intl. Commission on Large Dams, 1998

Rank order	Name	Country	Rated capacity now (MW)	Rated capacity planned (MW)
1.	Turukhansk (Lower Tungu-ska)*	Russia	—	20,000
2.	Three Gorges Dam*	China	—	18,200
3.	Itaipu	Brazil/Paraguay	7,400	13,320
4.	Grand Coulee	U.S.	6,495	10,830
5.	Guri (Raúl Leoni)	Venezuela	10,300	10,300
6.	Tucuruí	Brazil	2,640	7,260
7.	Sayano-Shushensk*	Russia	—	6,400
8.	Corpus Posadas	Argentina/Paraguay	4,700	6,000
8.	Krasnoyarsk	Russia	6,000	6,000
10.	La Grande 2	Canada	5,328	5,328
11.	Churchill Falls	Canada	5,225	5,225
12.	Xingo	Brazil	3,012	5,020
13.	Tarbela	Pakistan	1,750	4,678
14.	Bratsk	Russia	4,500	4,500
14.	Ust-Ilim	Russia	3,675	4,500
16.	Cabora Bassa	Mozambique	2,425	4,150
17.	Boguchany*	Russia	—	4,000
18.	Rogun*	Tajikistan	3,600	3,600
18.	Oak Creek	U.S.	3,600	3,600
20.	Paulo Afonso I	Brazil	1,524	3,409
21.	Pati*	Argentina	—	3,300
22.	Ilha Solteira	Brazil	3,200	3,200
23.	Chapetón*	Argentina	—	3,000
24.	Gezhouba	China	2,715	2,715

*Planned or under construction.

Major Dams of the World

Source: U.S. Committee on Large Dams of the Intl. Commission on Large Dams, 1998

World's Highest Dams

Rank order	Name	Country	Height above lowest formation (m)
1.	Rogun*	Tajikistan	335
2.	Nurek	Tajikistan	300
3.	Grand Dixence	Switzerland	285
4.	Inguri	Georgia	272
5.	Vajont	Italy	262
6.	Manuel M. Torres	Mexico	261
7.	Tehri*	India	261
8.	Alvaro Obregon	Mexico	260
9.	Mauvoisin	Switzerland	250
10.	Alberto Lleraso*	Colombia	243
11.	Mica	Canada	243
12.	Sayano-Shushensk	Russia	242
13.	Ertan*	China	240
14.	La Esmeralda	Colombia	237
15.	Kishau*	India	236
16.	El Cajón	Honduras	234
17.	Chirkei	Russia	233
18.	Oroville	U.S.	230
19.	Bhakra	India	226
20.	Hoover	U.S.	221

* Under construction.

World's Largest-Volume Embankment Dams

Rank order	Name	Country	Volume cubic meters × 1000
1.	Tarbela	Pakistan	148,500
2.	Fort Peck	U.S.	96,050
3.	Tucurui	Brazil	85,200
4.	Ataturk*	Turkey	85,000
5.	Yacireta*	Argentina	81,000
6.	Rogun*	Tajikistan	75,500
7.	Oahe	U.S.	70,339
8.	Guri	Venezuela	70,000
9.	Parambikulam	India	69,165
10.	High Island West	China	67,000
11.	Gardiner	Canada	65,000
12.	Afsluitdijk	Netherlands	63,400
13.	Mangla	Pakistan	63,379
14.	Oroville	U.S.	59,635
15.	San Luis	U.S.	59,559
16.	Nurek	Tajikistan	58,000
17.	Tanda	Pakistan	57,250
18.	Garrison	U.S.	50,843
19.	Cochiti	U.S.	50,228
20.	Oosterschelde	Netherlands	50,000

*Under construction.

World's Largest-Capacity Reservoirs

Source: U.S. Committee on Large Dams of the Intl. Commission on Large Dams, Oct. 1998

Rank order	Name	Country	Capacity cubic meters × 100,000
1.	Owen Falls	Uganda	204,800
2.	Kariba	Zimbabwe/Zambia	180,600
3.	Bratsk	Russia	169,000
4.	High Aswan	Egypt	162,000
5.	Akosombo	Ghana	147,960
6.	Daniel Johnson	Canada	141,851
7.	Xinfeng	China	138,960
8.	Guri	Venezuela	135,000
9.	W A C Bennett	Canada	74,300
10.	Krasnoyarsk	Russia	73,300
11.	Zeya	Russia	68,400
12.	La Grande 2	Canada	61,715
13.	La Grande 3	Canada	60,020
14.	Ust-Ilim	Russia	59,300
15.	Boguchany*	Russia	58,200
16.	Kuibyshev	Russia	58,000
17.	Serra de Mesa	Brazil	54,400
18.	Caniapiscau Barrage KA 3	Canada	53,790
19.	Cahora Bassa	Mozambique	52,000
20.	Bukhtarma	Kazakhstan	49,800

*Under construction.

Major U.S. Dams and Reservoirs

Source: Committee on Register of Dams, Corps of Engineers, U.S. Army, Oct. 1998

Highest U.S. Dams

Rank Order	Dam name	River	State	Type	Height Feet	Height Meters	Year completed
1.	Oroville	Feather	California	E	754	230	1968
2.	Hoover	Colorado	Nevada	A	725	221	1936
3.	Dworshak	N. Fork Clearwater	Idaho	G	718	219	1973
4.	Glen Canyon	Colorado	Arizona	A	708	216	1966
5.	New Bullards Bar	North Yuba	California	A	636	194	1970
6.	New Melones	Stanislaus	California	R	626	191	1979
7.	Swift	Lewis	Washington	E	610	186	1958
8.	Mossyrock	Cowlitz	Washington	A	607	185	1968
9.	Shasta	Sacramento	California	G	600	183	1945
10.	Don Pedro	Tuolumne	California	E	567	173	1971

E= Embankment, Earthfill; R= Embankment, Rockfill; G= Gravity; A= Arch.

Largest U.S. Embankment Dams

Rank Order	Dam name	River	State	Type	Volume Cubic yards × 1000	Volume Cubic meters × 1000	Year completed
1.	Fort Peck	Missouri	Montana	E	125,624	96,050	1937
2.	Oahe	Missouri	South Dakota	E	91,996	70,339	1958
3.	Oroville	Feather	California	E	77,997	59,635	1968
4.	San Luis	San Luis Creek	California	E	77,897	59,559	1967
5.	Garrison	Missouri	North Dakota	E	66,498	50,843	1953
6.	Cochiti	Rio Grande	New Mexico	E	65,693	50,228	1975
7.	Fort Randall	Missouri	South Dakota	E	49,962	38,200	1952
8.	Castaic	Castaic Creek	California	E	43,998	33,640	1973
9.	Ludington P/S	Lake Michigan	Michigan	E	37,699	28,824	1973
10.	Kingsley	N. Platte	Nebraska	E	31,999	24,466	1941

E= Embankment, Earthfill.

Largest U.S. Reservoirs

Rank Order	Dam name, location	Reservoir name	Location	Reservoir capacity Acre-Feet	Reservoir capacity Cubic meters × 1000	Year completed
1.	Hoover, NV	Lake Mead	AZ/NV	28,253,000	34,850,000	1936
2.	Glen Canyon, AZ	Lake Powell	AZ/UT	26,997,000	33,300,000	1966
3.	Garrison, ND	Lake Sakakawea	ND	22,635,000	27,920,000	1953
4.	Oahe, SD	Lake Oahe	ND/SD	22,238,000	27,430,000	1958
5.	Fort Peck, MT	Fort Peck Lake	MT	17,933,000	22,120,000	1937
6.	Grand Coulee, WA	F. D. Roosevelt Lake	WA	9,558,000	11,790,000	1942
7.	Libby, MT	Lake Koocanusa	MT/B.C.	5,813,000	7,170,000	1973
8.	Fort Randall, SD	Lake Francis Case	SD	4,621,000	5,700,000	1952
9.	Shasta, CA	Lake Shasta	CA	4,548,000	5,610,000	1945
10.	Toledo Bend, LA	Toledo Bend Lake	LA/TX	4,475,000	5,520,000	1968

1 acre-foot = 1 acre of water, 1 foot deep

STATES AND OTHER AREAS OF THE U.S.

Sources: Population: Commerce Dept., Bureau of the Census (July 1997 est., including armed forces stationed in the state). Area: Bureau of the Census, Geography Division; forested land: Agriculture Dept., Forest Service. Lumber production: Bureau of the Census, Industry Division; mineral production: Dept. of Interior, Office of Mineral Information; commercial fishing: Commerce Dept., Natl. Marine Fisheries Service; value of construction: McGraw-Hill Information Systems Co., F.W. Dodge Division. Personal per capita income: Commerce Dept., Bureau of Economic Analysis; sales tax: CCH Inc.; unemployment: Labor Dept., Bureau of Labor Statistics. Tourism: Tourism Industries/ITA, Tourism Works for America Report. Lottery figures (not all states have a lottery): *La Fleur's Lottery World.* Finance: Federal Deposit Insurance Corp. Federal employees: Labor Dept., Office of Personnel Management. Energy: Energy Dept., Energy Information Administration. Other information from sources in individual states.

Note: Categories under racial/ethnic or employment distrib. do not necessarily converge or add to 100%. Nonfuel mineral values for some states exclude small amounts to avoid disclosing proprietary data. Famous Persons lists may include some nonnatives associated with the state as well as persons born there. Website addresses listed may not be official state sites; all are subject to change.

Alabama

Heart of Dixie, Camellia State

People. Population (1997): 4,319,154; rank: 23; **net change** (1990-97): 2.3%. **Pop. density** (1990): 79.6 per sq mi. **Racial/ethnic distrib.** (1990): 73.6% white; 25.3% black; 0.6% Hispanic.

Geography. Total area: 52,237 sq mi; rank: 30. **Land area:** 50,750 sq mi; rank: 28. **Acres forested:** 21,974,000. **Location:** East South Central state extending N-S from Tenn. to the Gulf of Mexico; E of the Mississippi River. **Climate:** long, hot summers; mild winters; generally abundant rainfall. **Topography:** coastal plains, including Prairie Black Belt, give way to hills, broken terrain; highest elevation, 2,407 ft. **Capital:** Montgomery.

Economy. Chief industries: pulp & paper, chemicals, electronics, apparel, textiles, primary metals, lumber and wood products, food processing, fabricated metals, automotive tires, oil and gas exploration. **Chief manuf. goods:** electronics, cast iron & plastic pipe, fabricated steel products, ships, paper products, chemicals, steel, mobile homes, fabrics, poultry processing, soft drinks, furniture, tires. **Chief crops**: cotton, greenhouse & nursery, peanuts, sweet potatoes, potatoes and other vegetables. **Livestock** (Jan. 1998): 1.5 mil cattle/calves; 7,000 sheep/lambs; (Dec. 1997) 190,000 hogs/pigs; (Dec. 1997) 16.1 mil chickens (excl. broilers); (Dec. 1996) 873.3 mil broilers. **Timber/lumber** (1997): pine, hardwoods; 2.5 bil bd. ft. **Nonfuel minerals** (est. 1997): $805 mil; mostly portland cement, crushed stone, lime, sand & gravel, masonry cement. **Commercial fishing** (1997): $38.3 mil. **Chief port:** Mobile. **Value of construction** (1997): $4.8 bil. **Gross state product** (1996): $99.2 bil. **Employment distrib.** (May 1998): 23.1% trade; 23.3% serv; 20.0% mfg.; 18.3% govt. **Per cap. pers. income** (1997): $20,842. **Sales tax** (1998): 4%. **Unemployment** (1997): 5.1%. **Tourism expends.** (1996): $4.4 bil.

Finance. FDIC-insured commercial banks (1997): 175. **Deposits:** $72.7 bil. **FDIC-insured savings institutions** (1997): 12. **Assets:** $2.0 bil.

Federal govt. Fed. civ. employees (Mar. 1997): 37,790. **Avg. salary:** $43,359. **Notable fed. facilities:** George C. Marshall NASA Space Center; Gunter Annex & Maxwell AFB; Ft. Rucker; Ft. McClellan; Natl. Fertilizer Develop. Center; Navy Station & U.S. Corps of Engineers; Redstone Arsenal.

Energy. Electricity production (1997, kWh, by source): Coal: 71.6 bil; Petroleum: 119 mil; Gas: 885 mil; Hydroelectric: 11.5 bil; Nuclear: 29.6 bil.

State data. Motto: We dare defend our rights. **Flower:** Camellia. **Bird:** Yellowhammer. **Tree:** Southern pine. **Song:** Alabama. **Entered union** Dec. 14, 1819; rank, 22d. **State fair:** Regional and county fairs held in Sept. and Oct.; no state fair.

History. Alabama was inhabited by the Creek, Cherokee, Chickasaw, Alabama, and Choctaw peoples when the Europeans arrived. The first Europeans were Spanish explorers in the early 1500s. The French made the first permanent settlement on Mobile Bay, 1702. France later gave up the entire region to England under the Treaty of Paris, 1763. Spanish forces took control of the Mobile Bay area, 1780, and it remained Spanish until U.S. troops seized the area, 1813. Most of present-day Alabama was held by the Creeks until Gen. Andrew Jackson broke their power, 1814, and they were removed to Oklahoma Territory. The state seceded, 1861, and the Confederate states were organized Feb. 4, at Montgomery, the first capital; it was readmitted, 1868.

Tourist attractions. First White House of the Confederacy, Civil Rights Memorial, Alabama Shakespeare Festival, all Montgomery; Ivy Green, Helen Keller's birthplace, Tuscumbia; Civil Rights Museum, statue of Vulcan, Birmingham; Carver Museum, Tuskegee; W. C. Handy Home & Museum, Florence; Alabama Space and Rocket Center, Huntsville; Moundville State Monument, Moundville; Pike Pioneer Museum, Troy; USS *Alabama* Memorial Park, Mobile; Russell Cave Natl. Monument, near Bridgeport: a detailed record of occupancy by humans from about 10,000 BC to AD 1650.

Famous Alabamians. Hank Aaron, Tallulah Bankhead, Hugo L. Black, Paul "Bear" Bryant, George Washington Carver, Nat King Cole, William C. Handy, Bo Jackson, Helen Keller, Coretta Scott King, Harper Lee, Joe Louis, Willie Mays, John Hunt Morgan, Jesse Owens, George Wallace, Booker T. Washington, Hank Williams.

Tourist information. Bureau of Tourism and Travel, 401 Adams Avenue, Suite 126, Montgomery, AL 36104. **Toll-free travel information.** 1-800-ALABAMA out of state.

Website. http://alaweb.asc.edu

Tourism website. http://www.touralabama.org

Alaska

The Last Frontier (unofficial)

People. Population (1997): 609,311; rank: 48; **net change** (1990-97): 10.8%. **Pop. density** (1990): 1.0 per sq mi. **Racial/ethnic distrib.** (1990): 75.5% white; 4.1% black; 15.6% Amer. Indian, Eskimo or Aleut; 3.6% Asian or Pacific Is.; 3.2% Hispanic.

Geography. Total area: 615,230 sq mi; rank: 1. **Land area:** 570,374 sq mi; rank: 1. **Acres forested:** 129,131,000. **Location:** NW corner of North America, bordered on E by Canada. **Climate:** SE, SW, and central regions, moist and mild; far north extremely dry. Extended summer days, winter nights, throughout. **Topography:** includes Pacific and Arctic mountain systems, central plateau, and Arctic slope. Mt. McKinley, 20,320 ft, is the highest point in North America. **Capital:** Juneau.

Economy. Chief industries: petroleum, tourism, fishing, mining, forestry, transportation, aerospace. **Chief manuf. goods:** fish products, lumber & pulp, furs. **Agriculture: Chief crops:** greenhouse products, barley, oats, hay, potatoes, lettuce, aquaculture. **Livestock** (Jan. 1998): 12,500 cattle/calves; 1,400 sheep/lambs; (Dec. 1997) 2,000 hogs/pigs. **Timber/lumber:** spruce, yellow cedar, hemlock. **Nonfuel minerals** (est. 1997): $827 mil; mostly zinc, lead, gold, sand & gravel, silver. **Commercial fishing** (1997): $1.1 bil. **Chief ports:** Anchorage, Dutch Harbor, Kodiak, Seward, Skagway, Juneau, Sitka, Valdez, Wrangell. **Internat. airports at:** Anchorage, Fairbanks, Juneau. **Value of construction** (1997): $1.0 bil. **Gross state product** (1996): $24.2 bil. **Employment distrib.** (May 1998): 26.8% govt.; 24.7% serv.; 20.9% trade; 5.1% mfg. **Per cap. pers. income** (1997): $25,305. **Sales tax**: none. **Unemployment** (1997): 7.9%. **Tourism expends.** (1996): $1.4 bil.

Finance. FDIC-insured commercial banks (1997): 6. **Deposits:** $3.5 bil. **FDIC-insured savings institutions** (1997): 2. **Assets:** $252 mil.

Federal govt. Fed. civ. employees (Mar. 1997): 11,643. **Avg. salary:** $42,530.

Energy. Electricity production (1997, kWh, by source): Coal: 237 mil; Petroleum: 741 mil; Gas: 3.0 bil; Hydroelectric: 1.1 bil.

State data. Motto: North to the future. **Flower:** Forget-Me-Not. **Bird:** Willow ptarmigan. **Tree:** Sitka spruce. **Song:** Alaska's Flag. **Entered union** Jan. 3, 1959; rank, 49th. **State fair** at Palmer; late Aug.-early Sept.

History. Early inhabitants were the Tlingit-Haida people and tribes of the Athabascan family. The Aleut and Inuit (Eskimo), who arrived about 4,000 years ago from Siberia, lived in the coastal areas. Vitus Bering, a Danish explorer working for Russia, was the first European to land in Alaska, 1741. The first permanent Russian settlement was established on Kodiak Island, 1784. In 1799, the Russian-American Co. controlled the region, and the first chief manager, Aleksandr Baranov, set up headquarters at Archangel, near present-day Sitka. Sec. of State William H. Seward bought Alaska from Russia for $7.2 mil in 1867, a bargain some called "Seward's Folly." In 1896, gold was discovered in the Klondike region, and the famed gold rush began. Alaska became a territory in 1912.

Tourist attractions. Inside Passage; Portage Glacier; Mendenhall Glacier; Ketchikan Totems; Glacier Bay Natl. Park and Preserve; Denali Natl. Park, one of N. America's great wildlife sanctuaries, surrounding Mt. McKinley, N. America's highest peak; Mt. Roberts Tramway, Juneau; Pribilof Islands fur seal rookeries; restored St. Michael's Russian Orthodox Cathedral, Sitka; Katmai Natl. Park & Preserve.

Famous Alaskans. Tom Bodett, Susan Butcher, Ernest Gruening, Gov. Tony Knowles, Sydney Laurence, Libby Riddles, Jefferson "Soapy" Smith.

Tourist information. Alaska Division of Tourism, PO Box 110801, Juneau, AK 99811-0801; 1-907-465-2010.

Website. http://www.state.ak.us

Tourism website. http://www.commerce.state.ak.us/tourism

Arizona

Grand Canyon State

People. Population (1997): 4,554,966; rank: 21; **net change** (1990-97): 24.3%. **Pop. density** (1990): 32.3 per sq mi. **Racial/ethnic distrib.** (1990): 80.8% white; 3.0% black; 5.6% American Indian; 18.8% Hispanic.

Geography. Total area: 114,006 sq mi; rank: 6. **Land area:** 113,642 sq mi; rank: 6. **Acres forested:** 19,596,000. **Location:** in the southwestern U.S. **Climate:** clear and dry in the southern regions and northern plateau; high central areas have heavy winter snows. **Topography:** Colorado plateau in the N, containing the Grand Canyon; Mexican Highlands running diagonally NW to SE; Sonoran Desert in the SW. **Capital:** Phoenix.

Economy. Chief industries: manufacturing, construction, tourism, mining, agriculture. **Chief manuf. goods:** electronics, printing & publishing, foods, prim. & fabric. metals, aircraft and missiles, apparel. **Chief crops:** cotton, lettuce, cauliflower, broccoli, sorghum, barley, corn, wheat, citrus fruits. **Livestock** (Jan. 1998): 800,000 cattle/calves; 120,000 sheep/lambs; (Dec. 1997) 145,000 hogs/pigs. **Timber/lumber** (1997): pine, fir, spruce; 115 mil bd. ft. **Nonfuel minerals** (est. 1997): $3.52 bil; mostly copper, sand & gravel, cement, molybdenum, lime. **Internat. airports at:** Phoenix, Tucson, Yuma. **Value of construction** (1997): $10.0 bil. **Gross state product** (1996): $111.5 bil. **Employment distrib.** (May 1998): 30.6% services; 24.3% trade; 16.2% govt.; 10.4% mfg. **Per cap. pers. income** (1997): $22,364. **Sales tax** (1998): 5%. **Unemployment** (1997): 4.6%. **Tourism expends.** (1996): $8.4 bil. **Lottery** (1997): total sales: $249.8 mil; net income: $78.3 mil.

Finance. FDIC-insured commercial banks (1997): 41. **Deposits**: $22.8 bil. **FDIC-insured savings institutions** (1997): 2. **Assets:** $600 mil.

Federal govt. Fed. civ. employees (Mar. 1997): 27,251. **Avg. salary:** $38,943. **Notable fed. facilities:** Luke, Davis-Monthan AF bases; Ft. Huachuca Army Base; Yuma Proving Grounds.

Energy. Electricity production (1997, kWh, by source): Coal: 34.2 bil; Petroleum: 61 mil; Gas: 2.1 bil; Hydroelectric: 12.4 bil; Nuclear: 29.3 bil.

State data. Motto: Ditat Deus (God enriches). **Flower:** Blossom of the Saguaro cactus. **Bird:** Cactus wren. **Tree:** Paloverde. **Song:** Arizona. **Entered union** Feb. 14, 1912; rank, 48th. **State fair** at Phoenix; late Oct.-early Nov.

History. Anasazi, Mogollon, and Hohokam civilizations inhabited the area c 300 BC-AD 1300, later Pueblo peoples; Navajo and Apache came c 15th cent. Marcos de Niza, a Franciscan, and Estevanico, a former black slave, explored, 1539; Spanish explorer Francisco Vásquez de Coronado visited, 1540. Eusebio Francisco Kino, a Jesuit missionary, taught Indians 1692-1711, and left missions. Tubac, a Spanish fort, became the first European settlement, 1752. Spain ceded Arizona to Mexico, 1821. The U.S. took over, 1848, after the Mexican War. The area below the Gila River was obtained from Mexico in the Gadsden Purchase, 1853. Arizona became a territory, 1863. Apache wars ended with Geronimo's surrender, 1886.

Tourist attractions. The Grand Canyon of the Colorado; Painted Desert; Petrified Forest Natl. Park; Canyon de Chelly; Meteor Crater; London Bridge, Lake Havasu City; Biosphere 2, Oracle; Navajo Natl. Monument; Sedona.

Famous Arizonans. Bruce Babbitt, Cochise, Geronimo, Barry Goldwater, Zane Grey, Carl Hayden, George W. P. Hunt, Helen Jacobs, Percival Lowell, William H. Pickering, John J. Rhodes, Morris Udall, Stewart Udall, Frank Lloyd Wright.

Tourist information. Arizona Office of Tourism, Ste. 4015, 2702 N. 3rd St., Phoenix, AZ 85004.

Website. http://www.state.az.us

Tourism website. http://www.arizonaguide.com

Arkansas

The Natural State, The Razorback State

People. Population (1997): 2,522,819; rank: 33; **net change** (1990-97): 7.3%. **Pop. density** (1990): 45.1 per sq mi. **Racial/ethnic distrib.** (1990): 82.7% white; 15.9% black; 0.8% Hispanic.

Geography. Total area: 53,182 sq mi; rank: 28. **Land area:** 52,075 sq mi; rank: 27. **Acres forested:** 17,864,000. **Location:** in the west south-central U.S. **Climate:** long, hot summers, mild winters; generally abundant rainfall. **Topography:** eastern delta and prairie, southern lowland forests, and the northwestern highlands, which include the Ozark Plateaus. **Capital:** Little Rock.

Economy. Chief industries: manufacturing, agriculture, tourism, forestry. **Chief manuf. goods:** food products, chemicals, lumber, paper, plastics, electric motors, furniture, auto components, airplane parts, apparel, machinery, steel. **Chief crops:** rice, soybeans, cotton, tomatoes, grapes, apples, commercial vegetables, peaches, wheat. **Livestock** (Jan. 1998): 1.8 mil cattle/calves; (Dec. 1997) 850,000 hogs/pigs; (Dec. 1997) 23.1 mil chickens (excl. broilers); (Dec. 1996) 1.2 bil broilers. **Timber/lumber** (1997): oak, hickory, gum, cypress, pine; 2.4 bil bd. ft. **Nonfuel minerals** (est. 1997): $535 mil; mostly bromine, crushed stone, portland cement, sand & gravel. **Chief ports:** Little Rock, Pine Bluff, Osceola, Helena, Fort Smith, Van Buren, Camden, Dardanelle, North Little Rock, West Memphis, Crossett, McGehee, Morrilton. **Value of construction** (1997): $3.0 bil. **Gross state product** (1996): $56.4 bil. **Employment distrib.** (May 1998): 22.7% mfg.; 22.8% trade; 23.4% serv.; 16.4% govt. **Per cap. pers. income** (1997): $19,585. **Sales tax** (1998): 4.63%. **Unemployment** (1997): 5.3%. **Tourism expends.** (1996): $3.3 bil.

Finance. FDIC-insured commercial banks (1997): 226. **Deposits:** $24.7 bil. **FDIC-insured savings institutions** (1997): 14. **Assets:** $3.5 bil.

Federal govt. Fed. civ. employees (Mar. 1997): 11,049. **Avg. salary:** $37,519. **Notable fed. facilities:** Nat'l. Center for Toxicological Research, Jefferson; Pine Bluff Arsenal, Little Rock AFB.

Energy. Electricity production (1997, kWh, by source): Coal: 22.8 bil; Petroleum: 67 mil; Gas: 2.2 bil; Hydroelectric: 3.5 bil; Nuclear: 14.2 bil.

State data. Motto: Regnat Populus (The people rule). **Flower:** Apple blossom. **Bird:** Mockingbird. **Tree:** Pine. **Song:** Arkansas. **Entered union** June 15, 1836; rank, 25th. **State fair** at Little Rock; late Sept.-early Oct.

History. Quapaw, Caddo, Osage, Cherokee, and Choctaw peoples lived in the area at the time of European contact. The first European explorers were de Soto, 1541; Marquette and Jolliet, 1673; and La Salle, 1682. The first settlement was by the French under Henri de Tony, 1686, at Arkansas Post. In 1762, the area was ceded by France to Spain, then given back again, 1800, and was part of the Louisiana Purchase, 1803. It was made a territory, 1819. Arkansas seceded in 1861, only after the Civil War began; more than 10,000 Arkansans fought on the Union side.

Tourist attractions. Hot Springs Natl. Park (water ranging from 95°F-147°F); Eureka Springs; Ozark Folk Center, Blanchard Caverns, both near Mountain View; Crater of Diamonds (only U.S. diamond mine) near Murfreesboro; Toltec Mounds Archeological State Park, Little Rock; Buffalo Natl. River; Mid-America Museum, Hot Springs; Pea Ridge National Military Park, Pead Ridge; Tanyard Springs, Morrilton; Wiederkehr Wine Village, Wiederkehr Village.

Famous Arkansans. Daisy Bates, Dee Brown, Paul "Bear" Bryant, Glen Campbell, Johnny Cash, Hattie Caraway, Bill Clinton, "Dizzy" Dean, Orval Faubus, James W. Fulbright, John H. Johnson, John Grisham, Douglas MacArthur, John L. McClellan, James S. McDonnel, Scottie Pipen, Dick Powell, Winthrop Rockefeller, Mary Steenburgen, Edward Durell Stone, Archibald Yell.

Tourist Information. Arkansas Dept. of Parks & Tourism, One Capitol Mall, Little Rock, AR 72201

Toll-free travel information. 1-800-NATURAL.

Website. http://www.state.ar.us

Tourism website. http://www.arkansas.com

California

Golden State

People. Population (1997): 32,268,301; rank: 1; **net change** (1990-97): 8.3%. **Pop. density** (1990): 190.8 per sq mi. **Racial/ethnic distrib.** (1990): 69.0% white; 7.4% black; 9.6% Asian; 25.8% Hispanic.

Geography. Total area: 158,869 sq mi; rank: 3. **Land area:** 155,973 sq mi; rank: 3. **Acres forested:** 37,263,000. **Location:** on western coast of the U.S. **Climate:** moderate temperatures and rainfall along the coast; extremes in the interior. **Topography:** long mountainous coastline; central valley; Sierra Nevada on the east; desert basins of the southern interior; rugged mountains of the north. **Capital:** Sacramento.

Economy. Chief industries: agriculture, tourism, apparel, electronics, telecommunications, entertainment. **Chief manuf. goods:** electronic and electrical equip., computers, industrial machinery, transportation equip. and instruments, food. **Chief farm products**: milk and cream, grapes, cotton, flowers, oranges, rice, nursery products, hay, tomatoes, lettuce, strawberries, almonds, asparagus. **Livestock** (Jan. 1998): 4.6 mil cattle/calves; 870,000 sheep/lambs; (Dec. 1997) 190,000 hogs/pigs; (Dec. 1997) 30.5 mil chickens (excl. broilers); (Dec. 1996) 234.2 mil broilers. **Timber/lumber** (1997): fir, pine, redwood, oak; 3.5 bil bd. ft. **Nonfuel minerals** (est. 1997): $2.81 bil; mostly portland cement, sand & gravel, boron, crushed stone, gold. **Commercial fishing** (1997): $178.3 mil. **Chief ports:** Long Beach, Los Angeles, San Diego, Oakland, San Francisco, Sacramento, Stockton. **Internat. airports at:** Fresno, Los Angeles, Sacramento, San Francisco, San Jose, San Diego. **Value of construction** (1997): $36.7 bil. **Gross state product** (1996): $962.7 bil. **Employment distrib.** (May 1998): 31.1% serv.; 23.1% trade; 14.4% mfg.; 16.1% govt. **Per cap. pers. income** (1997): $26,570. **Sales tax** (1998): 6%. **Unemployment** (1997): 6.3%. **Tourism expends.** (1996): $62.6 bil. **Lottery** (1997): total sales: $2.06 bil; net income: $727.6 mil.

Finance. FDIC-insured commercial banks (1997): 336. **Deposits**: $361.4 bil. **FDIC-insured savings institutions** (1997): 58. **Assets:** $273.6 bil.

Federal govt. Fed. civ. employees (Mar. 1997): 161,971. **Avg. salary: $43,485. Notable fed. facilities:** Vandenberg, Beale, Travis, McClellan AF bases; San Francisco Mint.

Energy. Electricity production (1997, kWh, by source): Petroleum: 142 mil; Gas: 36.3 bil; Hydroelectric: 39.8 bil; Nuclear: 30.5 bil.

State data. Motto: Eureka (I have found it). **Flower:** Golden poppy. **Bird:** California valley quail. **Tree:** California redwood. **Song:** I Love You, California. **Entered union** Sept. 9, 1850; rank, 31st. **State fair** at Sacramento; late Aug.-early Sept.

History. Early inhabitants included more than 100 different Native American tribes with multiple dialects. The first European explorers were Cabrillo, 1542, and Drake, 1579. The first settlement was the Spanish Alto California mission at San Diego, 1769, first in a string founded by Franciscan Father Junípero Serra. U.S. traders and settlers arrived in the 19th cent. and staged the Bear Flag revolt, 1846, in protest against Mexican rule; later that year U.S. forces occupied California. At the end of the Mexican War, Mexico ceded the territory to the U.S., 1848; that same year gold was discovered, and the famed gold rush began.

Tourist attractions. The *Queen Mary*, Long Beach; Palomar Mountain; Disneyland, Anaheim; Getty Center, Los Angeles; Tournament of Roses and Rose Bowl, Pasadena; Universal Studios, Hollywood; Long Beach Aquarium of the Pacific; Golden State Museum, Sacramento; San Diego Zoo; Yosemite Valley; Lassen and Sequoia-Kings Canyon natl. parks; Lake Tahoe; Mojave and Colorado deserts; San Francisco Bay; Napa Valley; Monterey Peninsula; oldest living things on earth believed to be a stand of Bristlecone pines in the Inyo National Forest, est. 4,700 years old; world's tallest tree, 365-ft "National Geographic Society" coast redwood, in Humboldt Redwoods State Park.

Famous Californians. Edmund G. (Pat) Brown, Jerry Brown, Luther Burbank, Ted Danson, Leonardo DiCaprio, John C. Fremont, Tom Hanks, Helen Hunt, Bret Harte, William Randolph Hearst, Jack Kemp, Jack London, Mark McGuire, Aimee Semple McPherson, John Muir, Richard M. Nixon, George S. Patton Jr., Sally K. Ride, William Saroyan, Father Junípero Serra, Leland Stanford, John Steinbeck, Shirley Temple, Earl Warren.

California Division of Tourism. P.O. Box 1499, Sacramento, CA 95812-1499.

Toll-free travel information. 1-800-862-2543.

Website. http://www.ca.gov/s

Tourism website. http://gocalif.ca.gov

Colorado

Centennial State

People. Population (1997): 3,892,644; rank: 25; **net change** (1990-97): 18.2%. **Pop. density** (1990): 31.8 per sq mi. **Racial/ethnic distrib.** (1990): 88.2% white; 4.0% black; 12.9% Hispanic.

Geography. Total area: 104,100 sq mi; rank: 8. **Land area:** 103,729 sq mi; rank: 8. **Acres forested:** 21,338,000. **Location:** in W central U.S. **Climate:** low relative humidity, abundant sunshine, wide daily, seasonal temp. ranges; alpine conditions in the high mountains. **Topography:** eastern dry high plains; hilly to mountainous central plateau; western Rocky Mountains of high ranges, with broad valleys, deep, narrow canyons. **Capital:** Denver.

Economy. Chief industries: manufacturing, construction, government, tourism, agriculture, aerospace, electronics equipment. **Chief manuf. goods:** computer equip. & instruments, foods, machinery, aerospace products. **Chief crops:** corn, wheat, hay, sugar beets, barley, potatoes, apples, peaches, pears, dry edible beans, sorghum, onions, oats, sunflowers, vegetables. **Livestock** (Jan. 1998): 3.1 mil cattle/calves; 575,000 sheep/lambs; (Dec. 1997) 790,000 hogs/pigs; (Dec. 1997) 4.6 mil chickens (excl. broilers). **Timber/lumber** (1997): oak, ponderosa pine, Douglas fir; 114 mil bd. ft. **Nonfuel minerals** (est. 1997): $521 mil; mostly sand & gravel, portland cement, molybdenum, crushed stone, gold. **Internat. airport at:** Denver. **Value of construction** (1997): $9.2 bil. **Gross state product** (1996): $116.2 bil. **Employment distrib.** (May 1998): 30.3% serv.; 24.4% trade; 15.7% govt.; 10.2% mfg. **Per cap. pers. income** (1997): $27,051. **Sales tax** (1998): 3%. **Unemployment** (1997): 3.3%. **Tourism expends.** (1996): $8.3 bil. **Lottery** (1997): total sales: $360.9 mil; net income: $94.6 mil.

Finance. FDIC-insured commercial banks (1997): 216. **Deposits:** $29.3 bil. **FDIC-insured savings institutions** (1997): 12. **Assets:** $2.5 bil.

Federal govt. Fed. civ. employees (Mar. 1997): 34,349. **Avg. salary:** $44,156. **Notable fed. facilities:** U.S. Air Force Academy; U.S. Mint; Ft. Carson; Natl. Renewable Energy Labs; U.S. Rail Transportation Test Center; N. American Aerospace Defense Command; Consolidated Space Operations Ctr.; Denver Federal Center; Natl. Center for Atmospheric Research; Natl. Instit. for Standards in Technology; Natl. Oceanic and Atmospheric Administration.

Energy. Electricity production (1997, kWh, by source): Coal: 32.0 bil; Petroleum: 15 mil; Gas: 424 mil; Hydroelectric: 1.9 bil.

State data. Motto: Nil Sine Numine (Nothing Without Providence). **Flower:** Rocky Mountain columbine. **Bird:** Lark bunting. **Tree:** Colorado blue spruce. **Song:** Where the Columbines Grow. **Entered union** Aug. 1, 1876; rank 38th. **State fair** at Pueblo; mid-Aug. - early Sept.

History. Early civilization centered around the Mesa Verde c 2,000 years ago, later, Ute, Pueblo, Cheyenne, and Arapaho peoples lived in the area. The region was claimed by Spain, but passed to France. The U.S. acquired eastern Colorado in the Louisiana Purchase, 1803. Lt. Zebulon M. Pike explored the area, 1806, discovering the peak that bears his name. After the Mexican War, 1846-48, U.S. immigrants settled in the east, former Mexicans in the south. Gold was discovered in 1858, causing a population boom. Displaced Native Americans protested, resulting in the so-called Sand Creek Massacre, 1864, where more than 200 Cheyenne and Arapaho were killed. All Native Americans were later removed to Oklahoma Territory.

Tourist attractions. Rocky Mountain Natl. Park; Aspen Ski Resort; Garden of the Gods, Colorado Springs; Great Sand Dunes, Dinosaur, Black Canyon of the Gunnison, and Colorado natl. monuments; Pikes Peak and Mt. Evans highways; Mesa Verde Natl. Park (ancient Anasazi Indian cliff dwellings); Grand Mesa Natl. Forest; mining towns of Central City, Silverton, Cripple Creek; Burlington's Old Town; Bent's Fort, outside La Junta; Georgetown Loop Historic Mining Railroad Park, Cumbres & Toltec Scenic Railroad; limited stakes gaming in Central City, Blackhawk, Cripple Creek, Ignacio, and Towaoe.

Famous Coloradans. Tim Allen, Frederick Bonfils, Henry Brown, Molly Brown, William N. Byers, M. Scott Carpenter, Jack Dempsey, Mamie Eisenhower, Douglas Fairbanks, Barney Ford, Scott Hamilton, Chief Ourey, "Baby Doe" Tabor, Lowell Thomas, Byron R. White, Paul Whiteman.

State Chamber of Commerce. 1776 Lincoln, Ste. 1200, Denver, CO 80203. Phone:: 303-831-7411

Tourist information. Colorado Travel and Tourism Authority, P. O. Box 3524, Englewood, CO 80155.

Toll-free travel information. 1-800-COLORADO.

Website. http://www.state.co.us

Tourism website. http://www.colorado.com

Connecticut

Constitution State, Nutmeg State

People. Population (1997): 3,269,858; rank: 28; **net change** (1990-97): -0.5%. **Pop. density** (1990): 678.4 per sq mi. **Racial/ethnic distrib.** (1990): 87.0% white; 8.3% black; 6.5% Hispanic.

Geography. Total area: 5,544 sq mi; rank: 48. **Land area:** 4,845 sq mi; rank: 48. **Acres forested:** 1,819,000. **Location:** New England state in NE corner of the U.S. **Climate:** moderate; winters avg. slightly below freezing; warm, humid summers. **Topography:** western upland, the Berkshires, in the NW, highest elevations; narrow central lowland N-S; hilly eastern upland drained by rivers. **Capital:** Hartford.

Economy. Chief industries: manufacturing, retail trade, government, services, finances, insurance, real estate. **Chief manuf. goods:** aircraft engines and parts, submarines, helicopters, machinery and computer equipment, electronics and electrical equipment, medical instruments, pharmaceuticals. **Chief crops:** nursery stock, Christmas trees, mushrooms, vegetables, sweet corn, tobacco, apples. **Livestock** (Jan. 1998): 68,000 cattle/calves; 7,000 sheep/lambs; (Dec. 1997) 3,000 hogs/pigs; (Dec. 1997) 4.3 mil chickens (excl. broilers). **Timber/lumber** (1997): oak, birch, beech, maple; 48 mil bd. ft. **Nonfuel minerals** (est. 1997): $65 mil; mostly crushed stone, sand & gravel, dimension stone, clays, gemstones. **Commercial fishing** (1997): $49.5 mil. **Chief ports:** New Haven, Bridgeport, New London. **Internat. airport at:** Windsor Locks. **Value of construction** (1997): $3.8 bil. **Gross state product** (1996): $124.0 bil. **Employment distrib.** (May 1998): 31.0% serv.; 21.9% trade; 16.9% mfg.; 13.7% govt. **Per cap. pers. income** (1997): $36,263. **Sales tax** (1998): 6%. **Unemployment** (1997): 5.1%. **Tourism expends.** (1996): $4.3 bil. **Lottery** (1997): total sales: $769.8 mil; net income: $253.5 mil.

Finance. FDIC-insured commercial banks (1997): 26. **Deposits:** $4.0 bil. **FDIC-insured savings institutions** (1997): 52. **Assets**: $38.8 bil.

Federal govt. Fed. civ. employees (Mar. 1997): 7,903. **Avg. salary:** $44,311. **Notable fed. facilities:** U.S. Coast Guard Academy; U.S. Navy Submarine Base.

Energy. Electricity production (1997, kWh, by source): Coal: 2.6 bil; Petroleum: 8.4 bil; Gas: 1.5 bil; Hydroelectric: 367 mil; Nuclear: –125 mil.

State data. Motto: Qui Transtulit Sustinet (He who transplanted still sustains). **Flower:** Mountain laurel. **Bird:** American robin. **Tree:** White oak. **Song:** Yankee Doodle. **Fifth** of the 13 original states to ratify the Constitution, Jan. 9, 1788. **State Fair:** largest fair at Durham, late Sept.; no state fair.

History. At the time of European contact, inhabitants of the area were Algonquian peoples, including the Mohegan and Pequot. Dutch explorer Adriaen Block was the first European visitor, 1614. By 1634, settlers from Plymouth Bay had started colonies along the Connecticut River; in 1637 they defeated the Pequots. The Colony of Connecticut was chartered by England, 1662, adding New Haven, 1665. In the American Revolution, Connecticut Patriots fought in most major campaigns, while Connecticut privateers captured British merchant ships.

Tourist attractions. Mark Twain House, Hartford; Yale University's Art Gallery, Peabody Museum, both in New Haven; Mystic Seaport; Mystic Marine Life Aquarium; P. T. Barnum Museum, Bridgeport; Gillette Castle, Hadlyme; U.S.S. *Nautilus* Memorial, Groton (1st nuclear-powered submarine); Mashantucket Pequot Museum & Research Center, Foxwoods Resort & Casino, both; Ledyard, Mohegan Sun, Uncasville; Lake Compounce, Bristol.

Famous "Nutmeggers." Ethan Allen, Phineas T. Barnum, Samuel Colt, Jonathan Edwards, Nathan Hale, Katharine Hepburn, Isaac Hull, Robert Mitchum, J. Pierpont Morgan, Israel Putnam, Wallace Stevens, Harriet Beecher Stowe, Mark Twain, Noah Webster, Eli Whitney.

Tourist information. Dept. of Economic and Community Development, 505 Hudson St., Hartford, CT 06106.

Toll-free travel information. 1-800-CTBOUND

Website. http://www.state.ct.us

Tourism website. http://www.state.ct.us/tourism

Delaware

First State, Diamond State

People. Population (1997): 731,581; rank: 46; **net change** (1990-97): 9.8%. **Pop. density** (1990): 340.8 per sq mi. **Racial/ethnic distrib.** (1990): 80.3% white; 16.9% black; 2.4% Hispanic.

Geography. Total area: 2,396 sq mi; rank: 49. **Land area:** 1,955 sq mi; rank: 49. **Acres forested:** 398,000. **Location:** occupies the Delmarva Peninsula on the Atlantic coastal plain. **Climate:** moderate. **Topography:** Piedmont plateau to the N, sloping to a near sea-level plain. **Capital:** Dover.

Economy. Chief industries: chemicals, agriculture, finance, poultry, shellfish, tourism, auto assembly, food processing, transportation equipment. **Chief manuf. goods:** nylon, apparel, luggage, foods, autos, processed meats and vegetables, railroad & aircraft equipment. **Chief crops:** soybeans, potatoes, corn, mushrooms, lima beans, green peas, barley, cucumbers, wheat, corn, grain sorghum, greenhouse & nursery. **Livestock** (Jan. 1998): 29,000 cattle/calves; (Dec. 1997) 18,000 hogs/pigs; (Dec. 1997) 425,000 chickens (excl. broilers); (Dec. 1996) 257.6 mil broilers. **Timber/lumber** (1997): hardwoods and softwoods (except for southern yellow pine); 15 mil bd. ft. **Nonfuel minerals** (est. 1997): $6.5 mil; mostly magnesium compounds, sand & gravel, gemstones. **Commercial fishing** (1997): $5.3 mil. **Chief ports:** Wilmington. **Internat. airport at:** Philadelphia/Wilmington. **Value of construction** (1997): $935 mil. **Gross state product** (1996): $28.3 bil. **Employment distrib.** (May 1998): 28.0% serv; 21.8% trade; 14.8% mfg.; 13.7 % govt. **Per cap. pers. income** (1997): $29,022. **Sales tax:** none. **Unemployment** (1997): 4.0%. **Tourism expends.** (1996): $1.0 bil. **Lottery** (1997): total sales: $359.2 mil; net income: $127.8 mil.

Finance. FDIC-insured commercial banks (1997): 34. **Deposits:** $50.8 bil. **FDIC-insured savings institutions** (1997): 6. **Assets:** $3.5 bil.

Federal govt. Fed. civ. employees (Mar. 1997): 2,667. **Avg. salary:** $40,159. **Notable fed. facilities:** Dover Air Force Base, Federal Wildlife Refuge, Bombay Hook.

Energy. Electricity production (1997, kWh, by source): Coal: 3.9 bil; Petroleum: 833 mil; Gas: 1.8 bil.

State data. Motto: Liberty and independence. **Flower:** Peach blossom. **Bird:** Blue hen chicken. **Tree:** American holly. **Song:** Our Delaware. **First** of original 13 states to ratify the Constitution, Dec. 7, 1787. **State fair** at Harrington; end of July.

History. The Lenni Lenape (Delaware) people lived in the region at the time of European contact. Henry Hudson located the Delaware R., 1609, and in 1610, English explorer Samuel Argall entered Delaware Bay, naming the area after Virginia's governor, Lord De La Warr. The Dutch first settled near present Lewes, 1631, but the colony was destroyed by Indians. Swedes settled at Fort Christina (now Wilmington), 1638. Dutch settled anew, 1651, near New Castle and seized the Swedish settlement, 1655, only to lose all Delaware and New Netherland to the British, 1664. After 1682, Delaware became part of Pennsylvania, and in 1704 it was granted its own assembly. In 1776, it adopted a constitution as the state of Delaware. Although it remained in the Union during the Civil War, Delaware retained slavery until abolished by the 13th Amendment in 1865.

Tourist attractions. Ft. Christina Monument, site of founding of New Sweden, Holy Trinity (Old Swedes) Church, erected 1698, the oldest Protestant church in the U.S. still in use, Wilmington; Hagley Museum, Winterthur Museum and Gardens, both near Wilmington; historic district, New Castle; John Dickinson "Penman of the Revolution" home, Dover; Rehoboth Beach, "nation's summer capital," Rehoboth; Dover Downs Intl. Speedway.

Famous Delawareans. Thomas F. Bayard, Henry Seidel Canby, E. I. du Pont, John P. Marquand, Howard Pyle, Caesar Rodney.

Chamber of Commerce. 1200 N. Orange St., Ste. 200, Wilmington, DE 19899-0671.

Toll-free travel information. 1-800-441-8846.

Website. http://www.state.de.us

Tourism website. http://www.state.de.us/tourism/intro.htm

Florida

Sunshine State

People. Population (1997): 14,653,945; rank: 4; **net change** (1990-97): 13.3%. **Pop. density** (1990): 239.6 per sq mi. **Racial/ethnic distrib.** (1990): 83.1% white; 13.6% black; 12.2% Hispanic.

Geography. Total area: 59,928 sq mi; rank: 23. **Land area:** 53,937 sq mi; rank: 26. **Acres forested:** 16,549,000. **Location:** peninsula jutting southward 500 mi between the Atlantic and the Gulf of Mexico. **Climate:** subtropical N of Bradenton-Lake Okeechobee-Vero Beach line; tropical S of line. **Topography:** land is flat or rolling; highest point is 345 ft in the NW. **Capital:** Tallahassee.

Economy. Chief industries: tourism, agriculture, manufacturing, construction, services, international trade. **Chief manuf. goods:** electric & electronic equipment, transportation equipment, food, printing & publishing, chemicals, instruments, industrial machinery. **Chief crops:** citrus fruits, vegetables, melons, greenhouse and nursery products, potatoes, sugarcane, strawberries. **Livestock** (Jan. 1998): 1.9 mil cattle/calves; (Dec. 1997) 60,000 hogs/pigs; (Dec. 1997) 13.0 mil chickens (excl. broilers); (Dec. 1996) 131.4 mil broilers. **Timber/lumber** (1997): pine, cypress, cedar; 807 mil bd. ft. **Nonfuel minerals** (est. 1997): $1.74 bil; mostly phosphate rock, crushed stone, portland cement, sand & gravel, titanium. **Commercial fishing** (1997): $209.2 mil. **Chief ports:** Pensacola, Tampa, Manatee, Miami, Port Everglades, Jacksonville, St. Petersburg, Canaveral. **Internat. airports at:** Ft. Lauderdale/Hollywood, Daytona Beach, Ft. Myers, Key West, Jacksonville, Miami, Orlando, St. Petersburg/Clearwater, Panama City, Tampa, Sarasota/Bradenton, West Palm Beach. **Value of construction** (1997): $25.2 bil. **Gross state product** (1996): $360.5 bil. **Employment distrib.** (May 1998): 36.0% services, 25.4% trade, 14.4% govt., 7.4% mfg. **Per cap. pers. income** (1997): $25,255. **Sales tax** (1998): 6%. **Unemployment** (1997): 4.8% **Tourism expends.** (1996): $48.1 bil. **Lottery** (1997): total sales: $2.07 bil; net income: $817.5 mil.

Finance. FDIC-insured commercial banks (1997): 266. **Deposits:** $92.1 bil. **FDIC-insured savings institutions** (1997): 47. **Assets:** $18.3 bil.

Federal govt. Fed. civ. employees (Mar. 1997): 61,772. **Avg. salary:** $42,047. **Notable fed. facilities:** John F. Kennedy Space Center, NASA-Kennedy Space Center's Spaceport USA; Eglin Air Force Base; Pensacola Naval Training Center; MacDill Air Force Base, Tampa.

Energy. Electricity production (1997, kWh, by source): Coal: 66.0 bil; Petroleum: 25.7 bil; Gas: 33.0 bil; Hydroelectric: 241 mil; Nuclear: 23.0 bil.

State data. Motto: In God we trust. **Flower:** Orange blossom. **Bird:** Mockingbird. **Tree:** Sabal palmetto palm. **Song:** Old Folks at Home. **Entered union** Mar. 3, 1845; rank, 27th. **State fair** at Tampa; early Feb.

History. The original inhabitants of Florida included the Timucua, Apalachee, and Calusa peoples. Later the Seminole migrated from Georgia to Florida, becoming dominant there in the early 18th cent. The first European to see Florida was Ponce de León, 1513. France established a colony, Fort Caroline, on the St. John River, 1564. Spain settled St. Augustine, 1565, and Spanish troops massacred most of the French. Britain's Sir Francis Drake burned St. Augustine, 1586. In 1763, Spain ceded Florida to Great Britain, which held the area briefly, 1763-83, before returning it to Spain. After Andrew Jackson led a U.S. invasion, 1818, Spain ceded Florida to the U.S., 1819. The Seminole War, 1835-42, resulted in removal of most Native Americans to Oklahoma Territory. Florida seceded from the Union, 1861, and was readmitted in 1868.

Tourist attractions. Miami Beach; St. Augustine, oldest permanent European settlement in U.S.; Castillo de San Marcos, St. Augustine; Walt Disney World's Magic Kingdom, EPCOT Center, and Disney-MGM Studios, Animal Kingdom all near Orlando; Sea World, Universal Studios, near Orlando; Spaceport USA, Kennedy Space Center; Everglades Natl. Park; Ringling Museum of Art, Ringling Museum of the Circus, both in Sarasota; Cypress Gardens, Winter Haven; Busch Gardens, Tampa; U.S. Astronaut Hall of Fame, Mariana Caverns; Church St. Station, Orlando; Silver Springs, Ocala.

Famous Floridians. Marjory Stoneman Douglas, Henry M. Flagler, James Weldon Johnson, MacKinlay Kantor, Chief Osceola, Claude Pepper, Henry B. Plant, A. Philip Randolph, Marjorie Kinnan Rawlings, Joseph W. Stilwell, Charles P. Summerall.

Tourist information. Visit Florida, P.O. Box 1100, Tallahassee, FL 32302-1100, 1-850-488-5607.

Toll free number. 1-888-735-2872 (1-888-7FLA-USA)

Website. http://www.state.fl.us

Tourism website. http://www.flausa.com

Georgia

Empire State of the South, Peach State

People. Population (1997): 7,486,242; rank: 10; **net change** (1990-97): 15.6%. **Pop. density** (1990): 111.9 per sq mi. **Racial/ethnic distrib.** (1990): 71.0% white; 27.0% black; 1.7% Hispanic.

Geography. Total area: 58,977 sq mi; rank: 24. **Land area:** 57,919 sq mi; rank: 21. **Acres forested:** 24,137,000. **Location:** South Atlantic state. **Climate:** maritime tropical air masses dominate in summer; polar air masses in winter; E central area drier. **Topography:** most southerly of the Blue Ridge Mts. cover NE and N central; central Piedmont extends to the fall line of rivers; coastal plain levels to the coast flatlands. **Capital:** Atlanta.

Economy. Chief industries: services, manufacturing, retail trade. **Chief manuf. goods:** textiles, apparel, food, and kindred products, pulp & paper products. **Chief crops:** peanuts, cotton, corn, tobacco, hay, soybeans. **Livestock** (Jan. 1998): 1.5 mil cattle/calves; (Dec. 1997) 720,000 hogs/pigs; (Dec. 1997) 29.9 mil chickens (excl. broilers); (Dec. 1996) 1.2 bil broilers. **Timber/lumber** (1997): pine, hardwood; 3.2 bil bd. ft. **Nonfuel minerals** (est. 1997): $1.77 bil; mostly clays (kaolin), crushed stone, portland cement, clays (fuller's earth), sand & gravel. **Commercial fishing** (1997): $27.4 mil. **Chief ports:** Savannah, Brunswick. **Internat. airports at:** Atlanta. **Value of construction** (1997): $13.6 bil. **Gross state product** (1996): $216.0 bil. **Employment distrib.** (May 1998): 26.4% serv.; 25.3% retail trade; 15.9% mfg.; 15.8% govt. **Per cap. pers. income** (1997): $24,061. **Sales tax** (1998): 4%. **Unemployment**

(1997): 4.5%. **Tourism expends.** (1996): $12.1 bil. **Lottery** (1997): total sales: $1.65 bil; net income: $568.2 mil.

Finance. FDIC-insured commercial banks (1997): 353. **Deposits:** $46.9 bil. **FDIC-insured savings institutions** (1997): 31. **Assets:** $5.8 bil.

Federal govt. Fed. civ. employees (Mar. 1997): 63,355. **Avg. salary:** $40,562. **Notable fed. facilities:** Dobbins AFB; Fts. Benning, Gordon, Fort Gillen; Fort Stewart; King's Bay Naval Base; Moody Air Force Base; Navy Supply Corps School; McPherson; Fed. Law Enforcement Training Ctr., Glynco, Warner Robins AFB; Centers for Disease Control.

Energy. Electricity production (1997, kWh, by source): Coal: 66.2 bil; Petroleum: 201 mil; Gas: 568 mil; Hydroelectric: 4.4 bil; Nuclear: 30.4 bil.

State data. Motto: Wisdom, justice and moderation. **Flower:** Cherokee rose. **Bird:** Brown thrasher. **Tree:** Live oak. **Song:** Georgia On My Mind. **Fourth** of the 13 original states to ratify the Constitution, Jan. 2, 1788. **State fair** at Perry, 5th Friday after Labor Day.

History. Creek and Cherokee peoples were early inhabitants of the region. The earliest known European settlement was the Spanish mission of Santa Catalina, 1566, on Saint Catherines Island. Gen. James Oglethorpe established a colony at Savannah, 1733, for the poor and religiously persecuted. Oglethorpe defeated a Spanish army from Florida at Bloody Marsh, 1742. In the American Revolution, Georgians seized the Savannah armory, 1775, and sent the munitions to the Continental Army. They fought seesaw campaigns with Cornwallis's British troops, twice liberating Augusta and forcing final evacuation by the British from Savannah, 1782. The Cherokee were removed to Oklahoma Territory, 1832-38, and thousands died on the long march, known as the Trail of Tears. Georgia seceded from the Union, 1861, and was invaded by Union forces, 1864, under Gen. William T. Sherman, who took Atlanta, Sept. 2, and proceeded on his famous "march to the sea," ending in Dec., in Savannah. Georgia was readmitted, 1870.

Tourist attractions. State Capitol, Stone Mt. Park, Six Flags Over Georgia, Kennesaw Mt. Natl. Battlefield Park, Martin Luther King Jr. Natl. Historic Site, Underground Atlanta, Jimmy Carter Library & Museum, all Atlanta; Chickamauga and Chattanooga Natl. Military Park, near Dalton; Chattahoochee Natl. Forest; alpine village of Helen; Dahlonega, site of America's first gold rush; Brasstown Bald Mt.; Lake Lanier; Franklin D. Roosevelt's Little White House, Warm Springs; Callaway Gardens, Pine Mt.; Andersonville Natl. Historic Site; Okefenokee Swamp, near Waycross; Jekyll Island; St. Simons Island; Cumberland Island Natl. Seashore; historic riverfront district, Savannah.

Famous Georgians. Griffin Bell, James Bowie, James Brown, Erskine Caldwell, Jimmy Carter, Ray Charles, Lucius D. Clay, Ty Cobb, James Dickey, John C. Fremont, Newt Gingrich, Joel Chandler Harris, "Doc" Holiday, Martin Luther King Jr., Gladys Knight, Sidney Lanier, Little Richard, Juliette Gordon Low, Margaret Mitchell, Flannery O'Connor, Otis Redding, Jackie Robinson, Clarence Thomas, Alice Walker, Joseph Wheeler, Joanne Woodward, Andrew Young.

Chamber of Commerce. 235 International Blvd., Atlanta, GA 30303; (404) 880-9000.

Toll-free travel information. 1-800-VISITGA.

Website. http://www.state.ga.us

Tourism website. http://www.georgia.org

Hawai'i

Aloha State

People. Population (1997): 1,186,602; rank: 41; **net change** (1990-97): 7.1%. **Pop. density** (1990): 172.5 per sq mi. **Racial/ethnic distrib.** (1990): 33.4% white; 2.5% black; 61.8% Asian or Pacific Is.; 7.3% Hispanic.

Geography. Total area: 6,459 sq mi; rank: 47. **Land area:** 6,423 sq mi; rank: 47. **Acres forested:** 1,748,000. **Location:** Hawaiian Islands lie in the North Pacific, 2,397 mi SW from San Francisco. **Climate:** subtropical, with wide variations in rainfall; Waialeale, on Kaua'i, wettest spot in U.S. (annual rainfall 460 in.) **Topography:** islands are tops of a chain of submerged volcanic mountains; active volcanoes: Mauna Loa, Kilauea. **Capital:** Honolulu.

Economy. Chief industries: tourism, defense, sugar, pineapples. **Chief manuf. goods:** processed sugar, canned pineapple, clothing, foods, printing & publishing. **Chief crops:** sugar, pineapples, macadamia nuts, fruits, coffee, vegetables, floriculture. **Livestock** (Jan. 1998): 164,000 cattle/calves; (Dec. 1997) 27,000 hogs/pigs; (Dec. 1997) 863,000 chickens (excl. broilers); (Dec. 1996) 950,000 broilers. **Nonfuel minerals** (est. 1997): $100 mil; mostly crushed stone, portland cement, masonry cement, gemstones. **Commercial fishing** (1997): $68.7 mil. **Chief ports:** Honolulu, Nawiliwili, Barbers Point, Kahului, Hilo. **Internat. airport at:** Honolulu. **Value of construction** (1997): $1.7 bil. **Gross state product** (1996): $36.3 bil. **Employment distrib.** (May 1998): 32.1% serv.; 25.1% trade; 21.2% govt.; 3.1% mfg. **Per cap. pers. income** (1997): $26,034. **Sales tax** (1998): 4%. **Unemployment** (1997): 6.4%. **Tourism expenditures** (1996): $14.0 bil.

Finance. FDIC-insured commercial banks (1997): 14. **Deposits:** $15.7 bil. **FDIC-insured savings institutions** (1997): 4. **Assets:** $8.0 bil.

Federal govt. Fed. civ. employees (Mar. 1997): 20,221. **Avg. salary:** $39,984. **Notable fed. facilities:** Pearl Harbor Naval Shipyard; Hickam AFB; Schofield Barracks; Ft. Shafter; Marine Corps Base-Kaneohe Bay; Barbers Point NAS; Wheeler AFB; Prince Kuhio Federal Building.

Energy. Electricity production (1997, kWh, by source): Petroleum: 6.2 bil; Hydroelectric: 19 mil.

State data. Motto: The life of the land is perpetuated in righteousness. **Flower:** Yellow hibiscus. **Bird:** Hawaiian goose. **Tree:** Kukui (Candlenut). **Song:** Hawai'i Pono'i. **Entered union** Aug. 21, 1959; rank, 50th. **State fair:** at O'ahu, late June.

History. Polynesians from islands 2,000 mi to the south settled the Hawaiian Islands, probably between AD 300 and AD 600. The first European visitor was British captain James Cook, 1778. Between 1790 and 1810, the islands were united politically under the leadership of a native king, Kamehameha I, whose five successors—all bearing the name Kamehameha—ruled the kingdom from his death, 1819, until the end of the dynasty, 1872. Missionaries arrived, 1820, bringing Western culture. King Kamehameha III and his chiefs created the first constitution and a legislature that set up a public school system. Sugar production began, 1835, and it became the dominant industry. In 1893, Queen Liliuokalani was deposed, and a republic was instituted, 1894, headed by Sanford B. Dole. Annexation by the U.S. came in 1898. The Japanese attack on Pearl Harbor, Dec. 7, 1941, brought the U.S. into World War II.

Tourist attractions. Hawaii Volcanoes, Haleakala natl. parks; Natl. Memorial Cemetery of the Pacific, Waikiki Beach, Diamond Head, Honolulu; U.S.S. *Arizona* Memorial, Pearl Harbor; Hanauma Bay; Polynesian Cultural Center, Laie; Nu'uanu Pali; Waimea Canyon; Wailoa and Wailuku River state parks.

Famous Islanders. Bernice Pauahi Bishop, Tia Carrera, Father Damien de Veuster, Don Ho, Duke Kahanamoku, King Kamehameha, Brook Mahealani Lee, Daniel K. Inouye, Jason Scott Lee, Queen Liliuokalani, Bette Midler, Ellison Onizuka.

Chamber of Commerce of Hawaii. 1132 Bishop St., Suite 200, Honolulu, HI 96813; phone: (808) 545-4300.

Toll free travel information. 1-800-464-2924.

Website. http://www.hawaii.gov

Tourism website. http://www.gohawaii.com

Idaho

Gem State

People. Population (1997): 1,210,232; rank: 40; **net change** (1990-97): 20.2%. **Pop. density** (1990): 12.2 per sq mi. **Racial/ethnic distrib.** (1990): 94.4% white; 0.3% black; 5.3% Hispanic.

Geography. Total area: 83,574 sq mi; rank: 14. **Land area:** 82,751 sq mi; rank: 11. **Acres forested:** 21,621,000. **Location:** northwestern Mountain state bordering on British Columbia. **Climate:** tempered by Pacific westerly winds; drier, colder, continental climate in SE; altitude an important factor. **Topography:** Snake R. plains in the S; central region of mountains, canyons, gorges (Hells Canyon, 7,900 ft, deepest in N. America); subalpine northern region. **Capital:** Boise.

Economy. Chief industries: manufacturing, agriculture, tourism, lumber, mining, electronics. **Chief manuf. goods:** electronic components, computer equipment, processed foods, lumber and wood products, chemical products, primary metals, fabricated metal products, machinery. **Chief crops:** potatoes, peas, dry beans, sugar beets, alfalfa seed, lentils, wheat, hops, barley, plums and prunes, mint, onions, corn, cherries, apples, hay. **Livestock** (Jan. 1998): 1.8 mil cattle/calves; 285,000 sheep/lambs; (Dec. 1997) 38,000 hogs/pigs; (Dec. 1997) 1.2 mil chickens (excl. broilers). **Timber/lumber** (1997): yellow, white pine; Douglas fir; white spruce; 2.1 bil bd. ft. **Nonfuel minerals** (est. 1997): $442 mil; mostly phosphate rock, gold, sand & gravel, molybdenum, silver. **Chief port:** Lewiston. **Value of construction** (1997) $1.8 bil. **Gross state product** (1996): $27.9 bil. **Employment distrib.** (May 1998): 25.4% trade; 23.5% serv., 19.6% govt.; 14.8% mfg. **Per cap. pers. income** (1997): $20,478. **Sales tax** (1998): 5%. **Unemployment** (1997): 5.3%. **Tourism expenditures** (1996): $1.9 bil. **Lottery** (1997): total sales: $87.0 mil; net income: $18.4 mil.

Finance. FDIC-insured commercial banks (1997): 16. **Deposits:** $1.2 bil. **FDIC-insured savings institutions** (1997): 4. **Assets:** $675 mil.

Federal govt. Fed. civ. employees (Mar. 1997): 7,421. **Avg. salary:** $40,580. **Notable fed. facilities:** Idaho Natl. Engineering Lab; Mt. Home Air Force Base.

Energy. Electricity production (1997, kWh, by source): Hydroelectric: 13.5 bil.

State data. Motto: Esto Perpetua (It is perpetual). **Flower:** Syringa. **Bird:** Mountain bluebird. **Tree:** White pine. **Song:** Here We Have Idaho. **Entered union** July 3, 1890; rank, 43d. **State fair** at Boise, late Aug.; at Blackfoot, early Sept.

History. Early inhabitants were Shoshone, Northern Paiute, Bannock, and Nez Percé peoples. White exploration of the region began with Lewis and Clark, 1805-6. Next came fur traders, setting up posts, 1809-34, and missionaries, 1830s-50s. Mormons made their first permanent settlement at Franklin, 1860. Idaho's gold rush began the same year and brought thousands of permanent settlers. Most remarkable of the Indian wars was the 1,700-mi trek, 1877, of Chief Joseph and the Nez Percé, pursued by U.S. troops through 3 states and caught just short of the Canadian border. The Idaho territory was organized, 1863. Idaho adopted a progressive constitution and became a state, 1890.

Tourist attractions. Hells Canyon, deepest gorge in N. America; World Center for Birds of Prey; Craters of the Moon; Sun Valley, in Sawtooth Mts.; Crystal Falls Cave; Shoshone Falls; Lava Hot Springs; Lake Pend Oreille; Lake Coeur d'Alene; Sawtooth Natl. Recreation Area; River of No Return Wilderness Area; Redfish Lake.

Famous Idahoans. William E. Borah, Frank Church, Fred T. Dubois, Ezra Pound, Chief Joseph, Sacagawea.

Tourist information. Department of Commerce, 700 W. State St., Boise, ID 83720.

Toll-free travel information. 1-800-VISIT-ID.

Website. http://www.state.id.us

Tourism website. http://www.visitid.org

Illinois

Prairie State

People. Population (1997): 11,895,849; rank: 6; **net change** (1990-97): 4.1%. **Pop. density** (1990): 205.6 per sq mi. **Racial/ethnic distrib.** (1990): 78.3% white; 14.8% black; 7.9% Hispanic.

Geography. Total area: 57,918 sq mi; rank: 25. **Land area:** 55,593 sq mi; rank: 24. **Acres forested:** 4,266,000. **Location:** East North Central state; western, southern, and eastern boundaries formed by Mississippi, Ohio, and Wabash rivers, respectively. **Climate:** temperate; typically cold, snowy winters, hot summers. **Topography:** prairie and fertile plains throughout; open hills in the southern region. **Capital:** Springfield.

Economy. Chief industries: services, manufacturing, travel, wholesale and retail trade, finance, insurance, real estate, construction, health care, agriculture. **Chief manuf. goods:** machinery, electric and electronic equipment, prim. & fabric. metals, chemical products, printing & publishing, food and kindred products. **Chief crops:** corn, soybeans, wheat, sorghum, hay. **Livestock** (Jan. 1998): 1.7 mil cattle/calves; 79,000 sheep/lambs; (Dec. 1997) 4.8 mil hogs/pigs; (Dec. 1997) 3.8 mil chickens (excl. broilers). **Timber/lumber** (1997): oak, hickory, maple, cottonwood; 93 mil bd. ft. **Nonfuel minerals** (est. 1997): $880 mil; mostly crushed stone, portland cement, sand & gravel, lime. **Commercial fishing** (1997): $241,000. **Chief ports:** Chicago. **Internat. airport at:** Chicago. **Value of construction** (1997): $12.5 bil. **Gross state product** (1996): $370.8 bil. **Employment distrib.** (May 1998): 29.5% serv.; 22.9% trade; 16.7% mfg.; 13.7% govt. **Per cap. pers. income** (1997): $28,202. **Sales tax** (1998): 6.25%. **Unemployment** (1997): 4.7%. **Tourism expends.** (1996): $18.4 bil. **Lottery** (1997): total sales: $1.57 bil; net income: $587.2 mil.

Finance. FDIC-insured commercial banks (1997): 784. **Deposits:** $194.8 bil. **FDIC-insured savings institutions** (1997): 129. **Assets:** $45.1 bil.

Federal govt. Fed. civ. employees (Mar. 1997): 44,568. **Avg. salary:** $44,846. **Notable fed. facilities:** Fermi Natl. Accelerator Lab; Argonne Natl. Lab; Rock Island Arsenal; Great Lakes, Naval Training Station, Scott AFB.

Energy. Electricity production (1997, kWh, by source): Coal: 76.1 bil; Petroleum: 495 mil; Gas: 3.4 bil; Hydroelectric: 17 mil; Nuclear: 51.1 bil.

State data. Motto: State sovereignty—national union. **Flower:** Native violet. **Bird:** Cardinal. **Tree:** White oak. **Song:** Illinois. **Entered union** Dec. 3, 1818; rank, 21st. **State fair** at Springfield, mid-Aug.; DuQuoin, late Aug.

History. Seminomadic Algonquian peoples, including the Peoria, Illinois, Kaskaskia, and Tamaroa, lived in the region at the time of European contact. Fur traders were the first Europeans in Illinois, followed shortly by Jolliet and Marquette, 1673, and La Salle, 1680, who built a fort near present-day Peoria. The first settlements were French, at Cahokia, near present-day St. Louis, 1699, and Kaskaskia, 1703. France ceded the area to Britain, 1763, and in 1778, American Gen. George Rogers Clark took Kaskaskia from the British without a shot. Defeat of Native American tribes in Black Hawk War, 1832, and growth of railroads brought change to the area. In 1787, it became part of the Northwest Territory. Post-Civil War Illinois became a center for the labor movement as bitter strikes, such as the Haymarket Square riot, occurred in 1885-86.

Tourist attractions: Chicago museums and parks; Lincoln shrines at Springfield, New Salem, Sangamon County; Cahokia Mounds, Collinsville; Starved Rock State Park; Crab Orchard Wildlife Refuge; Mormon settlement at Nauvoo; Fts. Kaskaskia, Chartres, Massac (parks); Shawnee Natl. Forest, Southern Illinois; Illinois State Museum, Springfield; Dickson Mounds Museum, between Havana and Lewistown.

Famous Illinoisans. Jane Addams, Saul Bellow, Jack Benny, Ray Bradbury, Gwendolyn Brooks, William Jennings Bryan, St. Frances Xavier Cabrini, Hillary Rodham Clinton, Clarence Darrow, John Deere, Stephen A. Douglas, James T. Farrell, George W. Ferris, Marshall Field, Betty Friedan, Benny Goodman, Ulysses S. Grant, Ernest Hemingway, Wild Bill Hickok, Henry J. Hyde, Abraham Lincoln, Vachel Lindsay, Edgar Lee Masters, Oscar Mayer, Cyrus McCormick, Ronald Reagan, Carl Sandburg, Adlai Stevenson, Frank Lloyd Wright, Philip Wrigley.

Tourist information. Illinois Dept. of Commerce and Community Affairs, 620 E. Adams St., Springfield, IL 62701.

Toll-free travel information: 1-800-2-CONNECT.

Website. http://www.state.il.us

Tourism website. http://www.enjoyillinois.com

Indiana

Hoosier State

People. Population (1997): 5,864,108; rank: 14; **net change** (1990-97): 5.8%. **Pop. density** (1990): 154.6 per sq mi. **Racial/ethnic distrib.** (1990): 90.6% white; 7.8% black; 1.8% Hispanic.

Geography. Total area: 36,420 sq mi; rank: 38. **Land area:** 35,870 sq mi; rank: 38. **Acres forested:** 4,439,000. **Location:** East North Central state; Lake Michigan on N border. **Climate:** 4 distinct seasons with a temperate climate. **Topography:** hilly southern region; fertile rolling plains of central region; flat, heavily glaciated north; dunes along Lake Michigan shore. **Capital:** Indianapolis.

Economy: Chief industries: manufacturing, services, agriculture, government, wholesale and retail trade, transportation and public utilities. **Chief manuf. goods:** primary metals, transportation equipment, motor vehicles & equip., industrial machinery & equipment, electronic & electric equipment. **Chief crops:** corn, soybeans, wheat, nursery and greenhouse products, vegetables, popcorn, fruit, hay, tobacco, mint. **Livestock** (Jan. 1998): 1.1 mil cattle/calves; 55,000 sheep/lambs; (Dec. 1997) 3.8 mil hogs/pigs; (Dec. 1997) 27.2 mil chickens (excl. broilers). **Timber/lumber** (1997): oak, tulip, beech, sycamore; 370 mil bd. ft. **Nonfuel minerals** (est. 1997): $669 mil; mostly crushed stone, portland cement, sand & gravel, lime, masonry cement. **Commercial fishing** (1997): $327,000 **Chief ports:** Burns Harbor, Portage; Southwind Maritime, Mt. Vernon; Clark Maritime, Jeffersonville. **Internat. airports at:** Indianapolis, Ft. Wayne. **Value of construction** (1997): $9.2 bil. **Gross state product** (1996): $155.8 bil. **Employment distrib.** (May 1998): 23.6% trade; 23.5% mfg.; 24.2% serv; 13.7% govt. **Per cap. pers. income** (1997): $23,604. **Sales tax** (1998): 5%. **Unemployment** (1997): 3.5%. **Tourism expends.** (1996): $5.2 bil. **Lottery** (1997): total sales: $578.9 mil; net income: $176.3 mil.

Finance. FDIC-insured commercial banks (1997): 185. **Deposits:** $50.9 bil. **FDIC-insured savings institutions** (1997): 71. **Assets:** $15.1 bil.

Federal govt. Fed. civ. employees (Mar. 1997): 19,031. **Avg. salary:** $40,718. **Notable fed. facilities:** Naval Air Warfare Center; Ft. Benjamin Harrison; Del. Grissom AFB; Naval Surface Warfare Center.

Energy. Electricity production (1997, kWh, by source): Coal: 108.9 bil; Petroleum: 607 mil; Gas: 386 mil; Hydroelectric: 562 mil.

State data. Motto: Crossroads of America. **Flower:** Peony. **Bird:** Cardinal. **Tree:** Tulip poplar. **Song:** On the Banks of the Wabash, Far Away. **Entered union** Dec. 11, 1816; rank, 19th. **State fair** at Indianapolis; mid-Aug.

History. When the Europeans arrived, Miami, Potawatomi, Kickapoo, Piankashaw, Wea, and Shawnee peoples inhabited the area. A French trading post was built, 1731-32, at Vincennes. La Salle visited the present South Bend area, 1679 and 1681. The first French fort was built near present-day Lafayette, 1717. France ceded the area to Britain, 1763. During the American Revolution, American Gen. George Rogers Clark captured Vincennes, 1778, and defeated British forces, 1779. At war's end, Britain ceded the area to the U.S. Miami Indians defeated U.S. troops twice, 1790, but were beaten, 1794, at Fallen Timbers by Gen. Anthony Wayne. At Tippecanoe, 1811, Gen. William H. Harrison defeated Tecumseh's Indian confederation. The Delaware, Potawatomi, and Miami were moved farther west, 1820-1850.

Tourist attractions. Lincoln Log Cabin Historic Site, near Charleston; George Rogers Clark Park, Vincennes; Wyandotte Cave; Tippecanoe Battlefield Memorial Park; Benjamin Harrison home; Indianapolis 500 raceway and museum, all Indianapolis; Indiana Dunes, near Chesterton; National College Football Hall of Fame, South Bend; Hoosier Nat'l. Forest, south-central Indiana.

Famous "Hoosiers." Larry Bird, Ambrose Burnside, Hoagy Carmichael, Jim Davis, James Dean, Eugene V. Debs, Theodore Dreiser, Paul Dresser, Gil Hodges, David Letterman, Jane Pauley, Cole Porter, Dan Quayle, Gene Stratton Porter, Ernie Pyle, James Whitcomb Riley, Oscar Robertson, Red Skelton, Booth Tarkington, Kurt Vonnegut, Lew Wallace, Wendell L. Willkie, Wilbur Wright.

Chamber of Commerce. One North Capital, Suite 200, Indianapolis, IN 46204.

Toll-free travel information. 1-800-289-6646.

Website. http://www.ai.org

Tourism website. http://www.state.in.us/tourism

Iowa

Hawkeye State

People. Population (1997): 2,852,423; rank: 30; **net change** (1990-97): 2.7%. **Pop. density** (1990): 49.7 per sq mi. **Racial/ethnic distrib.** (1990): 96.6% white; 1.7% black; 1.2% Hispanic.

Geography. Total area: 56,276 sq mi; rank: 26. **Land area:** 55,875 sq mi; rank: 23. **Acres forested:** 2,050,000. **Location:** West North Central state bordered by Mississippi R. on the E and Missouri R. on the W. **Climate:** humid, continental. **Topography:** Watershed from NW to SE; soil especially rich and land level in the N central counties. **Capital:** Des Moines.

Economy. Chief industries: agriculture, communications, construction, finance, insurance, trade, services, manufacturing. **Chief manuf. goods:** processed food products, tires, farm machinery, electronic products, appliances, household furniture, chemicals, fertilizers, auto accessories. **Chief crops:** silage and grain corn, soybeans, oats, hay. **Livestock** (Jan. 1998): 3.8 mil cattle/calves; 235,000 sheep/lambs; (Dec. 1997) 14.0 hogs/pigs; (Dec. 1997) 25.7 mil chickens (excl. broilers); (Dec. 1996) 17.2 mil broilers. **Timber/lumber** (1997): red cedar; 77 mil bd. ft. **Nonfuel minerals** (est. 1997): $493 mil; mostly crushed stone, portland cement, sand & gravel, gypsum, lime. **Internat. airport at:** Des Moines. **Value of construction** (1997): $3.2 bil. **Gross state product** (1996): $76.3 bil. **Employment distrib.** (May 1998): 26.2% serv.; 24.3% trade; 18.0% mfg.; 16.5% govt. **Per cap. pers. income** (1997): $23,102. **Sales tax** (1998): 5%. **Unemployment** (1997): 3.3%. **Tourism expends.** (1996): $3.6 bil. **Lottery** (1997): total sales: $173.7 mil; net income: $43.4 mil.

Finance. FDIC-insured commercial banks (1997): 453. **Deposits:** $36.0 bil. **FDIC-insured savings institutions** (1997): 26. **Assets:** $4.9 bil.

Federal govt. Fed. civ. employees (Mar. 1997): 6,981. **Avg. salary:** $39,512.

Energy. Electricity production (1997, kWh, by source): Coal: 28.7 bil; Petroleum: 82 mil; Gas: 277 mil; Hydroelectric: 795 mil; Nuclear: 4.1 bil.

State data. Motto: Our liberties we prize, and our rights we will maintain. **Flower:** Wild rose. **Bird:** Eastern goldfinch. **Tree:** Oak. **Rock:** Geode. **Entered union** Dec. 28, 1846; rank, 29th. **State fair** at Des Moines; mid-Aug.

History. Early inhabitants were Mound Builders who dwelt on Iowa's fertile plains. Later, Woodland tribes including the Iowa and Yankton Sioux lived in the area. The first Europeans, Marquette and Jolliet, gave France its claim to the area, 1673. In 1762, France ceded the region to Spain, but Napoleon took it back, 1800. It became part of the U.S. through the Louisiana Purchase, 1803. Native American Sauk and Fox tribes moved into the area from states farther east but relinquished their land in defeat, after the 1832 uprising led by the Sauk chieftain Black Hawk. By mid-19th cent. they were forced to move on to Kansas. Iowa became a territory in 1838, and entered as a free state, 1846, strongly supporting the Union.

Tourist attractions. Herbert Hoover birthplace and library, West Branch; Effigy Mounds Natl. Monument, prehistoric Indian burial site, Marquette; Amana Colonies; Grant Wood's paintings and memorabilia, Davenport Municipal Art Gallery; Living History Farms, Des Moines; Adventureland, Altoona; Boone & Scenic Valley Railroad, Boone; Greyhound Parks, in Dubuque and Council Bluffs; Prairie Meadows horse racing, Altoona; riverboat cruises and casino gambling, Mississippi and Missouri Rivers; Iowa Great Lakes, Okoboji.

Famous Iowans. Tom Arnold, Johnny Carson, Marquis Childs, Buffalo Bill Cody, Mamie Dowd Eisenhower, George Gallup, Susan Glaspell, James Norman Hall, Harry Hansen, Herbert Hoover, Ann Landers, Glenn Miller, Lillian Russell, Billy Sunday, James A. Van Allen, Carl Van Vechten, Henry Wallace, John Wayne, Meredith Willson, Grant Wood.

Tourist information. Division of Tourism, Iowa Dept. of Economic Development, 200 E. Grand Ave., Des Moines, IA 50309.

Toll-free travel information. 1-800-345-IOWA.

Website. http://www.state.ia.us

Tourism website. http://www.state.ia.us/tourism/index.html

Kansas

Sunflower State

People. Population (1997): 2,594,840; rank: 32; **net change** (1990-97): 4.7%. **Pop. density** (1990): 30.3 per sq mi. **Racial/ethnic distrib.** (1990): 90.1% white; 5.8% black; 3.8% Hispanic.

Geography. Total area: 82,282 sq mi; rank: 15. **Land area:** 81,823 sq mi; rank: 13. **Acres forested:** 1,359,000. **Location:** West North Central state, with Missouri R. on E. **Climate:** temperate but continental, with great extremes between summer and winter. **Topography:** hilly Osage Plains in the E; central region level prairie and hills; high plains in the W. **Capital:** Topeka.

Economy. Chief industries: manufacturing, finance, insurance, real estate, services. **Chief manuf. goods:** transportation equipment, machinery & computer equipment, food and kindred products, printing & publishing. **Chief crops:** wheat, sorghum, corn, hay, soybeans, sunflowers. **Livestock** (Jan. 1998): 6.6 mil cattle/calves; 120,000 sheep/lambs; (Dec. 1997) 1.4 mil hogs/pigs; (Dec. 1997) 1.9 mil chickens (excl. broilers). **Timber/lumber:** (1997) oak, walnut; 10 mil bd. ft. **Nonfuel minerals** (est. 1997): $547 mil; mostly portland cement, salt, crushed stone, helium, sand & gravel. **Chief ports:** Kansas City. **Internat. airports at:** Wichita. **Value of construction** (1997): $3.8 bil. **Gross state product** (1996): $68.0 bil. **Employment distrib.** (May 1998): 25.2% serv.; 24.4% trade; 18.5% govt.; 16.2% mfg. **Per cap. pers. income** (1997): $24,379. **Sales tax** (1998): 4.9%. **Unemployment** (1997): 3.8%. **Tourism expends.** (1996): $3.1 bil. **Lottery** (1997): total sales: $185.4 mil; net income: $56.8 mil.

Finance. FDIC-insured commercial banks (1997): 403. **Deposits**: $26.7 bil. **FDIC-insured savings institutions** (1997): 19. **Assets** : $8.3 bil.

Federal govt. Fed. civ. employees (Mar. 1997): 14,986. **Avg. salary:** $39,936. **Notable fed. facilities:** Fts. Riley, Leavenworth; Leavenworth Federal Penitentiary; Colmery-O'Neal Veterans Hospital.

Energy. Electricity production (1997, kWh, by source): Coal: 27.2 bil; Petroleum: 110 mil; Gas: 2.1 bil; Nuclear: 8.4 bil.

State data. Motto: Ad Astra per Aspera (To the stars through difficulties). **Flower:** Native sunflower. **Bird:** Western meadowlark. **Tree:** Cottonwood. **Song:** Home on the Range. **Entered union** Jan. 29, 1861; rank, 34th. **State fair** at Hutchinson; begins Friday after Labor Day.

History. When Coronado first explored the area, Wichita, Pawnee, Kansa, and Osage peoples lived there. These Native Americans—hunters who also farmed—were joined on the Plains by the nomadic Cheyenne, Arapaho, Comanche, and Kiowa about 1800. French explorers established trading between 1682 and 1739, and the U.S. took over most of the area in the Louisiana Purchase, 1803. After 1830, thousands of eastern Native Americans were removed to Kansas. Kansas became a territory, 1854. Violent incidents between pro- and antislavery settlers caused the territory to be known as "Bleeding Kansas." It eventually entered the Union as a free state, 1861. Railroad construction after the war made Abilene and Dodge City terminals of large cattle drives from Texas.

Tourist attractions. Eisenhower Center, Abilene; Agricultural Hall of Fame and Natl. Center, Bonner Springs; Dodge City-Boot Hill & Frontier Town; Old Cowtown Museum, Wichita; Ft. Scott and Ft. Larned, restored 1800s cavalry forts; Kansas Cosmosphere and Space Center, Hutchinson; Woodlands Racetrack, Kansas City; U.S. Cavalry Museum, Ft. Riley; NCAA Visitors Center, Shawnee; Heartland Park Raceway, Topeka.

Famous Kansans. Ed Asner, Roscoe "Fatty" Arbuckle, Thomas Hart Benton, John Brown, George Washington Carver, Wilt Chamberlain, Walter P. Chrysler, Glen Cunningham, John Stuart Curry, Robert Dole, Amelia Earhart, Wyatt Earp, Dwight D. Eisenhower, Ron Evans, Wild Bill Hickok, Cyrus Holliday, Dennis Hopper, William Inge, Walter Johnson, Nancy Landon Kassebaum, Buster Keaton, Emmett Kelly, Alf Landon, Edgar Lee Masters, Hattie McDaniel, Oscar Micheaux, Carrie Nation, Georgia Neese-Gray, Charlie Parker, Gordon Parks, Jim Ryun, Barry Sanders, Vivian Vance, William Allen White, Jess Willard.

Tourist information. Kansas Dept. of Commerce & Housing, Travel and Tourism Div., 700 SW Harrison, Suite 1300, Topeka, KS 66601; 1-913-296-2009.

Toll-free travel information. 1-800-2KANSAS.

Website. http://www.ink.org

Tourism website. http://kansascommerce.com

Kentucky

Bluegrass State

People. Population (1997): 3,908,124; rank: 24; **net change** (1990-97): 6.0%. **Pop. density** (1990): 92.8 per sq mi. **Racial/ethnic distrib.** (1990): 92.0% white; 7.1% black; 0.6% Hispanic.

Geography. Total area: 40,411 sq mi; rank: 37. **Land area:** 39,732 sq mi; rank: 36. **Acres forested:** 12,714,000. **Location:** East South Central state, bordered on N by Illinois, Indiana, Ohio; on E by West Virginia and Virginia; on S by Tennessee; on W by Missouri. **Climate:** moderate, with plentiful rainfall. **Topography:** mountainous in E; rounded hills of the Knobs in the N; Bluegrass, heart of state; wooded rocky hillsides of the Pennyroyal; Western Coal Field; the fertile Purchase in the SW. **Capital:** Frankfort.

Economy. Chief industries: manufacturing, services, finance, insurance and real estate, retail trade, public utilities. **Chief manuf. goods:** transportation & industrial machinery, apparel, printing & publishing, food products, electric & electronic equipment. **Chief crops:** tobacco, corn, soybeans. **Livestock** (Jan. 1998): 2.4 mil cattle/calves; 17,000 sheep/lambs; (Dec. 1997) 590,000 hogs/pigs; (Dec. 1997) 4.6 mil chickens (excl. broilers); (Dec. 1996) 77.0 mil broilers. **Timber/lumber** (1997): hardwoods, pines; 723 mil bd. ft. **Nonfuel minerals** (est. 1997): $476 mil; mostly crushed stone, lime, portland cement, sand & gravel, clays. **Chief ports:** Paducah, Louisville, Covington, Owensboro, Ashland, Henderson County, Lyon County, Hickman-Fulton County. **Internat. airports at:** Covington and Louisville. **Value of construction** (1997): $4.8 bil. **Gross state product** (1996): $95.4 bil. **Employment distrib.** (May 1998): 25.2% serv.; 24% trade; 18.1% mfg.; 16.6% govt. **Per cap. pers. income** (1997): $20,657. **Sales tax** (1998): 6%. **Unemployment** (1997): 5.4%. **Tourism expends.** (1996): $4.4 bil. **Lottery** (1997): total sales: $569.1 mil; net income: $153.7 mil.

Finance. FDIC-insured commercial banks (1997): 271. **Deposits:** $38.2 bil. **FDIC-insured savings institutions** (1997): 42. **Assets:** $6.8 bil.

Federal govt. Fed. civ. employees (Mar. 1997): 21,350. **Avg. salary:** $35,722. **Notable fed. facilities:** U.S. Gold Bullion Depository, Fort Knox; Federal Correctional Institution, Lexington.

Energy. Electricity production (1997, kWh, by source): Coal: 87.9 bil; Petroleum: 126 mil; Gas: 177 mil; Hydroelectric: 3.4 bil.

State data. Motto: United we stand, divided we fall. **Flower:** Goldenrod. **Bird:** Cardinal. **Tree:** Tulip Poplar. **Song:** My Old Kentucky Home. **Entered union** June 1, 1792; rank, 15th. **State fair** at Louisville, late Aug.

History. The area was predominantly hunting grounds for Shawnee, Wyandot, Delaware, and Cherokee peoples. Explored by Americans Thomas Walker and Christopher Gist, 1750-51, Kentucky was the first area west of the Alleghenies settled by American pioneers. The first permanent settlement was Harrodsburg, 1744. Daniel Boone blazed the Wilderness Trail through the Cumberland Gap and founded Ft. Boonesborough, 1775. Conflicts with Native Americans, spurred by the British, were unceasing until, during the American Revolution, Gen. George Rogers Clark captured British forts in Indiana and Illinois, 1778. In 1792, Virginia dropped its claims to the region, and it became the 15th state. Although officially a Union state, Kentuckians had divided loyalties during the Civil War and were forced to choose sides; its slaves were freed only after the adoption of the 13th Amendment to the U.S. Constitution, 1865.

Tourist attractions. Kentucky Derby; Louisville; Land Between the Lakes Natl. Recreation Area, Kentucky Lake and Lake Barkley; Mammoth Cave Natl. Park; Echo River, 360 ft below ground; Lake Cumberland; Lincoln's birthplace, Hodgenville; My Old Kentucky Home State Park, Bardstown; Cumberland Gap Natl. Historical Park, Middlesboro; Kentucky Horse Park, Lexington; Shaker Village, Pleasant Hill.

Famous Kentuckians. Muhammad Ali, John James Audubon, Alben W. Barkley, Daniel Boone, Louis D. Brandeis, John C. Breckinridge, Kit Carson, Albert B. "Happy" Chandler, Henry Clay, Jefferson Davis, D. W. Griffith, "Casey" Jones, Abraham Lincoln, Mary Todd Lincoln, Thomas Hunt Morgan, Carrie Nation, Col. Harland Sanders, Diane Sawyer, Jesse Stuart, Adlai Stevenson, Zachary Taylor, Robert Penn Warren, Whitney Young Jr.

Tourist Information. Kentucky Dept. of Travel, 500 Mero St., #2200, Frankfort, KY 40601.

Toll-free travel information. 1-800-225-TRIP.

Website. http://www.state.ky.us

Tourism website. http://www.kentuckytourism.com

Louisiana

Pelican State

People. Population (1997): 4,351,769; rank: 22; **net change** (1990-97): 3.1%. **Pop. density** (1990): 96.9 per sq mi. **Racial/ethnic distrib.** (1990): 67.3% white; 30.8% black; 2.2% Hispanic.

Geography. Total area: 49,651 sq mi; rank: 31. **Land area:** 43,566 sq mi; rank: 33. **Acres forested:** 13,864,000. **Location:** West South Central state on the Gulf Coast. **Climate:** subtropical, affected by continental weather patterns. **Topography:** lowlands of marshes and Mississippi R. flood plain; Red R. Valley lowlands; upland hills in the Florida Parishes; average elevation, 100 ft. **Capital:** Baton Rouge.

Economy. Chief industries: wholesale and retail trade, tourism, manufacturing, construction, transportation, communication, public utilities, finance, insurance, real estate, mining. **Chief manuf. goods:** chemical products, foods, transportation equipment, electronic equipment, petroleum products, lumber, wood, and paper. **Chief crops:** soybeans, sugarcane, rice, corn, cotton, sweet potatoes, pecans, sorghum, aquaculture. **Livestock** (Jan. 1998): 1.0 mil cattle/calves; 13,500 sheep/lambs; (Dec. 1997) 32,000 hogs/pigs; (Dec. 1997) 2.5 mil chickens (excl. broilers). **Timber/lumber** (1997): pines, hardwoods, oak; 1.3 bil bd. ft. **Nonfuel minerals** (est. 1997): $379 mil; mostly salt, sulfur, sand & gravel, crushed stone. **Commercial fishing** (1997): $318.8 mil. **Chief ports:** New Orleans, Baton Rouge, Lake Charles, Port of S. Louisiana (La Place), Shreveport, Plaquemine, St. Bernard, Alexandria. **Internat. airports at:** New Orleans, Alexandria. **Value of construction** (1997): $4.7 bil. **Gross state product** (1996): $121.1 bil. **Employment distrib.** (May 1998): 27.2% serv.; 23.2% trade; 19.5% govt.; 10.1% mfg. **Per cap. pers. income** (1997): $20,680. **Sales tax** (1998): 4%. **Unemployment** (1997): 6.1%. **Tourism expends.** (1996): $7.0 bil. **Lottery** (1997): total sales: $280.7 mil; net income: $101.6 mil.

Finance. FDIC-insured commercial banks (1997): 158. **Deposits**: $37.6 bil. **FDIC-insured savings institutions** (1997): 34. **Assets:** $4.1 bil.

Federal govt. Fed. civ. employees (Mar. 1997): 20,277. **Avg. salary:** $39,153. **Notable federal facilities:** Strategic Petroleum Reserve, Michoud Assembly Plant, Southeast U.S. Agricultural Research Ctr., U.S. Army Corps of Engineers, all New Orleans; Ft. Polk military bases, Barksdale; U.S. Public Service Hospital, Carville; Naval Air Station, Chalmette; V.A. Hospital, Pineville.

Energy. Electricity production (1997, kWh, by source): Coal: 21.0 bil; Petroleum: 646 mil; Gas: 26.0 bil; Nuclear: 13.5 bil.

State data. Motto: Union, justice, and confidence. **Flower:** Magnolia. **Bird:** Eastern brown pelican. **Tree:** Cypress. **Song:** Give Me Louisiana. **Entered union** Apr. 30, 1812; rank, 18th. **State fair** at Shreveport; Oct.

History. Caddo, Tunica, Choctaw, Chitimacha, and Chawash peoples lived in the region at the time of European contact. Europeans Cabeza de Vaca and Panfilo de Narvaez first visited, 1530. The region was claimed for France by La Salle, 1682. The first permanent settlement was by the French at Biloxi, now in Mississippi, 1699. France ceded the region to Spain, 1762, took it back, 1800, and sold it to the U.S., 1803, in the Louisiana Purchase. During the American Revolution, Spanish Louisiana aided the Americans. Admitted as a state in 1812, Louisiana was the scene of the Battle of New Orleans, 1815.

Louisiana Creoles are descendants of early French and/or Spanish settlers. About 4,000 Acadians, French settlers in Nova Scotia, Canada, were forcibly transported by the British to Louisiana in 1755 (an event commemorated in Longfellow's "Evangeline") and settled near Bayou Teche; their descendants became known as Cajuns. Another group, the Islenos, were descendants of Canary Islanders brought to Louisiana by a Spanish governor in 1770. Traces of Spanish and French survive in local dialects.

Tourist attractions. Mardi Gras, French Quarter, Superdome, Dixieland jazz, Aquarium of the Americas, Audubon Zoo & Gardens, all New Orleans; Battle of New Orleans site; Longfellow-Evangeline Memorial Park, St. Martinville; Kent House Museum, Alexandria; Hodges Gardens, Natchitoches, USS Kidd Memorial, Baton Rouge.

Famous Louisianans. Louis Armstrong, Pierre Beauregard, Judah P. Benjamin, Braxton Bragg, Kate Chopin, Lillian Hellman, Grace King, Huey Long, Winton Marsalis, Leonidas K. Polk, Anne Rice, Henry Miller Shreve, Edward D. White Jr.

Tourist information. Louisiana Office of Tourism, PO Box 94291, Baton Rouge, LA 70804-9291.

Toll-free travel information. 1-800-677-4082.

Website. http://www.state.la.us

Tourism website. http://www.louisianatravel.com

Maine

Pine Tree State

People. Population (1997): 1,242,051; rank: 39; **net change** (1990-97): 1.2%. **Pop. density** (1990): 39.8 per sq mi. **Racial/ethnic distrib.** (1990): 98.4% white; 0.4% black; 0.6% Hispanic.

Geography. Total area: 33,741 sq mi; rank: 39. **Land area:** 30,865 sq mi; rank: 39. **Acres forested:** 17,533,000. **Location:** New England state at northeastern tip of U.S. **Climate:** Southern interior and coastal, influenced by air masses from the S and W; northern clime harsher, avg. over 100 in. snow in winter. **Topography:** Appalachian Mts. extend through state; western borders have rugged terrain; long sand beaches on southern coast; northern coast mainly rocky promontories, peninsulas, fjords. **Capital:** Augusta.

Economy. Chief industries: manufacturing, agriculture, fishing, services, trade, government, finance, insurance, real estate, construction. **Chief manuf. goods:** paper & wood products, transportation equipment. **Chief crops:** potatoes, aquaculture products. **Livestock** (Jan. 1998): 107,000 cattle/calves; 11,000 sheep/lambs; (Dec. 1997) 6,000 hogs/pigs; (Dec. 1997) 6.9 mil chickens (excl. broilers). **Timber/lumber** (1997): pine, spruce, fir; 1.1 bil bd. ft. **Nonfuel minerals** (est. 1997): $88.2 mil; mostly sand & gravel, portland cement, crushed stone, peat, masonry cement. **Commercial fishing** (1997): $223.2 mil. **Chief ports:** Searsport, Portland, Eastport. **Internat. airports at:** Portland, Bangor. **Value of construction** (1997): $1.1 bil. **Gross state product** (1996): $28.9 bil. **Employment distrib.** (May 1998): 29.1% serv.; 25.1% trade; 16.3% govt.; 15.5% mfg. **Per cap. pers. income (1997)**: $22,078. **Sales tax** (1998): 6%. **Unemployment** (1997): 5.4%. **Tourism expends.** (1996): $1.9 bil. **Lottery** (1997): total sales: $146.3 mil; net income: $41.8 mil.

Finance. FDIC-insured commercial banks (1997): 17. **Deposits**: $3.7 bil. **FDIC-insured savings institutions** (1997): 28. **Assets**: $9.1 bil.

Federal govt. Fed. civ. employees (Mar. 1997): 7,827. **Avg. salary:** $40,079. **Notable fed. facilities:** Kittery Naval Shipyard; Brunswick Naval Air Station.

Energy. Electricity production (1997, kWh, by source): Petroleum: 1.4 bil; Hydroelectric: 1.8 bil.

State data. Motto: Dirigo (I direct). **Flower:** White pine cone and tassel. **Bird:** Chickadee. **Tree:** Eastern white pine. **Song:** State of Maine Song. **Entered union** Mar. 15, 1820; rank, 23d. **State fair:** at Bangor, late July; at Skowhegon, mid-Aug.

History. When the Europeans arrived, Maine was inhabited by Algonquian peoples including the Abnaki, Penobscot, and Passamaquoddy. Maine's rocky coast was believed to have been explored by the Cabots, 1498-99. French settlers arrived, 1604, at the St. Croix River, English, c 1607, on the Kennebec; both settlements failed. Maine was made part of Massachusetts, 1691. In the American Revolution, a Maine regiment fought at Bunker Hill. A British fleet destroyed Falmouth (now Portland), 1775, but the British ship *Margaretta* was captured near Machiasport. In 1820, Maine broke off and became a separate state.

Tourist attractions. Acadia Natl. Park, Bar Harbor, on Mt. Desert Island; Old Orchard Beach; Portland's Old Port; Kennebunkport; Common Ground Country Fair; Portland Headlight; Baxter State Pk.; Freeport/L. L. Bean.

Famous "Down Easters." James G. Blaine, Cyrus H. K. Curtis, Hannibal Hamlin, Sarah Jewett, Stephen King, Henry Wadsworth Longfellow, Sir Hiram and Hudson Maxim, Edna St. Vincent Millay, George Mitchell, Edmund Muskie, Edwin Arlington Robinson, Kate Douglas Wiggin, Ben Ames Williams.

Chamber of Commerce and Industry. Maine Chamber & Business Alliance, 7 Community Dr., Augusta, ME 04330.

Toll-free travel information. 1-888-624-6345 (from within the United States and Canada).

Website. http://www.state.me.us

Tourism website. http://www.visitmaine.com

Maryland

Old Line State, Free State

People. Population (1997): 5,094,289; rank: 19; **net change** (1990-97): 6.6%. **Pop. density** (1990): 489.2 per sq mi. **Racial/ethnic distrib.** (1990): 71.0% white; 24.9% black; 2.9% Asian; 2.6% Hispanic.

Geography. Total area: 12,297 sq mi; rank: 42. **Land area:** 9,775 sq mi; rank: 42. **Acres forested:** 2,700,000. **Location:** South Atlantic state stretching from the Ocean to the Allegheny Mts. **Climate:** continental in the west; humid subtropical in the east. **Topography:** Eastern Shore of coastal plain and Maryland Main of coastal plain, piedmont plateau, and the Blue Ridge, separated by the Chesapeake Bay. **Capital:** Annapolis.

Economy. Chief industries: manufacturing, biotechnology and information technology, services, tourism. **Chief manuf. goods:** electric and electronic equipment; food and kindred products, chemicals and allied products, printed materials. **Chief crops:** greenhouse and nursery products, soybeans, corn. **Livestock** (Jan. 1998): 265,000 cattle/calves; 33,000 sheep/lambs; (Dec. 1997) 73,000 hogs/pigs; (Dec. 1997) 4.1 mil chickens (excl. broilers); (Dec. 1996) 294.8 mil broilers. **Timber/lumber:** (1997) hardwoods; 250 mil bd. ft. **Nonfuel minerals** (est. 1997): $401 mil; mostly crushed stone, portland cement, sand & gravel, masonry cement, dimension stone. **Commercial fishing** (1997): $64.3 mil. **Chief port:** Baltimore. **Internat. airport at:** Baltimore-Washington Intl. **Value of construction** (1997): $5.9 bil. **Gross state product** (1996): $143.2 bil. **Employment distrib.** (May 1998): 33.6% serv.; 23.7% trade; 18.5% govt.; 7.7% mfg. **Per cap. pers. income** (1997): $28,969. **Sales tax** (1998): 5%. **Unemployment** (1997): 5.1%. **Tourism expends.** (1996): $6.4 bil. **Lottery** (1997): total sales: $1.04 bil; net income: $393.4 mil.

Finance. FDIC-insured commercial banks (1997): 83. **Deposits:** $26.9 bil. **FDIC-insured savings institutions** (1997): 65. **Assets:** $8.3 bil.

Federal govt. Fed. civ. employees (Mar. 1997): 99,407. **Avg. salary:** $50,757. **Notable fed. facilities:** U.S. Naval Academy; Natl. Agriculture Research Center; Ft. George G. Meade, Aberdeen Proving Ground; Goddard Space Flight Center; Natl. Institutes of Health; Natl. Institute of Standards & Technology; Food & Drug Administration; Bureau of the Census.

Energy. Electricity production (1997, kWh, by source): Coal: 27.4 bil; Petroleum: 1.5 bil; Gas: 879 mil; Hydroelectric: 1.6 bil; Nuclear: 13.2 bil.

State data. Motto: Fatti Maschii, Parole Femine (Manly deeds, womanly words). **Flower:** Black-eyed Susan. **Bird:** Baltimore oriole. **Tree:** White oak. **Song:** Maryland, My Maryland. **Seventh** of the original 13 states to ratify Constitution, Apr. 28, 1788. **State fair** at Timonium; late Aug.-early Sept.

History. Europeans encountered Algonquian-speaking Nanticoke and Piscataway and Iroquois-speaking Susquehannock when they first visited the area. Italian explorer Verrazano visited the Chesapeake region in the early 16th cent. English Capt. John Smith explored and mapped the area, 1608. William Claiborne set up a trading post on Kent Island in Chesapeake Bay, 1631. King Charles I granted land to Cecilius Calvert, Lord Baltimore, 1632; Calvert's brother Leonard, with about 200 settlers, founded St. Marys, 1634. The bravery of Maryland troops in the American Revolution, as at the Battle of Long Island, won the state its nickname "The Old Line State." In the War of 1812, when a British fleet tried to take Ft. McHenry, Marylander Francis Scott Key wrote "The Star Spangled Banner," 1814. Although a slaveholding state, Maryland remained with the Union during the Civil War and was the site of the battle of Antietam, 1862, which halted Gen. Robert E. Lee's march north.

Tourist attractions. The Preakness at Pimlico track, Baltimore; The Maryland Million at Laurel Race Course; Ocean City; restored Ft. McHenry, near which Francis Scott Key wrote "The Star-Spangled Banner"; Edgar Allan Poe house, Ravens Football at Memorial Stadium, Camden Yards, Natl. Aquarium, Harborplace, all Baltimore; Antietam Battlefield, near Hagerstown; South Mountain Battlefield; U.S. Naval Academy, Annapolis; Maryland State House, Annapolis, 1772, the oldest still in legislative use in the U.S.

Famous Marylanders. John Astin, Benjamin Banneker, Tom Clancy, Jonathan Demme, Francis Scott Key, H. L. Mencken, Charles Willson Peale, William Pinkney, Edgar Allan Poe, Babe Ruth, Upton Sinclair, Roger B. Taney, John Waters.

Maryland Dept. of Business & Economic Development. 217 E. Redwood St., Baltimore, MD 21202; (410) 767-6870.

Toll-free travel information. 1-800-543-1036.

Website. http://www.state.md.us

Tourism website. http//www.mdisfun.org

Massachusetts

Bay State, Old Colony

People. Population (1997): 6,117,520; rank: 13; **net change** (1990-97): 1.7%. **Pop. density** (1990): 767.6 per sq mi. **Racial/ethnic distrib.** (1990): 89.8% white; 5.0% black; 2.4% Asian; 4.8% Hispanic.

Geography. Total area: 9,241 sq mi; rank: 45. **Land area:** 7,838 sq mi; rank: 45. **Acres forested:** 3,203,000. **Location:** New England state along Atlantic seaboard. **Climate:** temperate, with colder and drier clime in western region. **Topography:** jagged indented coast from Rhode Island around Cape Cod; flat land yields to stony upland pastures near central region and gentle hilly country in west; except in west, land is rocky, sandy, and not fertile. **Capital:** Boston.

Economy. Chief industries: services, trade, manufacturing. **Chief manuf. goods:** electric and electronic equipment, instruments, industrial machinery and equipment, printing and publishing, fabricated metal products. **Chief crops:** cranberries, greenhouse, nursery, vegetables. **Livestock** (Jan. 1998): 60,000 cattle/calves; 11,000 sheep/lambs; (Dec. 1997) 15,500 hogs/pigs; (Dec. 1997) 704,000 chickens (excl. broilers). **Timber/lumber** white pine, oak, other hard woods. **Nonfuel minerals** (est. 1997): $213 mil; mostly crushed stone, sand & gravel, dimension stone, lime, clays. **Commercial fishing** (1997): $214.7 mil. **Chief ports:** Boston, Fall River, New Bedford, Salem, Gloucester, Plymouth. **Internat. airport at:** Boston. **Value of construction** (1997): $10.3 bil. **Gross state product** (1996): $208.6 bil. **Employment distrib.** (May 1998): 35.8% serv.; 22.8% trade; 14.1% mfg.; 12.8% govt. **Per cap. pers. income** (1997): $31,524. **Sales tax** (1998): 5%. **Unemployment** (1997): 4.0%. **Tourism expends.** (1996): $10.2 bil. **Lottery** (1997): total sales: $3.2 bil; net income: $720 mil.

Finance. FDIC-insured commercial banks (1997): 46. **Deposits:** $84.2 bil. **FDIC-insured savings institutions** (1997): 200. **Assets:** $56.6 bil.

Federal govt. Fed. civ. employees (Mar. 1997): 26,424. **Avg. salary:** $44,421. **Notable fed. facilities:** Thomas P. O'Neill Jr. Federal Bldg., J.W. McCormack Bldg., John Fitzgerald Kennedy Federal Bldg., Q.M. Laboratory, Natick.

Energy. Electricity production (1997, kWh, by source): Coal: 12.5 bil; Petroleum: 11.6 bil; Gas: 5.2 bil; Hydroelectric: 300 mil; Nuclear: 4.3 bil.

State data. Motto: Ense Petit Placidam Sub Libertate Quietem (By the sword we seek peace, but peace only under liberty). **Flower:** Mayflower. **Bird:** Chickadee. **Tree:** American elm. **Song:** All Hail to Massachusetts. **Sixth** of the original 13 states to ratify Constitution, Feb. 6, 1788. **State Fair** at Topsfield, early Oct.

History. Early inhabitants were the Algonquian Nauset, Wampanoag, Massachuset, Pennacook, Nipmuc, and Pocumtuc peoples. Pilgrims settled in Plymouth, 1620, giving thanks for their survival with the first Thanksgiving Day, 1621. About 20,000 new settlers arrived, 1630-40. Native American relations with the colonists deteriorated leading to King Philip's War, 1675-76, which the colonists won, ending Native American resistance. Demonstrations against British restrictions set off the Boston Massacre, 1770, and the Boston Tea Party, 1773. The first bloodshed of American Revolution was at Lexington, 1775.

Tourist attractions. Provincetown artists' colony; Cape Cod; Plymouth Rock, Plymouth Plantation, Mayflower II, all Plymouth; Freedom Trail, Museum of Fine Arts, Children's Museum, Museum of Science, New England Aquarium, JFK Library, Boston Ballet, Boston Pops, Boston Symphony Orchestra, all Boston; Tanglewood, Jacob's Pillow Dance Festival, Hancock Shaker Village Berkshire Railway Museum, all in the Berkshires; Salem; Old Sturbridge Village; Deerfield Historic District; Walden Pond; Naismith Memorial Basketball Hall of Fame, Springfield.

Famous "Bay Staters." John Adams, John Quincy Adams, Samuel Adams, Louisa May Alcott, Horatio Alger, Susan B. Anthony, Crispus Attucks, Clara Barton, Alexander Graham Bell, Stephen Breyer, George Bush, John Cheever, E. E. Cummings, Emily Dickinson, Charles Eliot, Ralph Waldo Emerson, William Lloyd Garrison, Edward Everett Hale, John Hancock, Nathaniel Hawthorne, Oliver Wendell Holmes, Winslow Homer, Elias Howe, John F. Kennedy, James Russell Lowell, Cotton Mather, Samuel F. B. Morse, Edgar Allan Poe, Paul Revere, Dr. Seuss, Henry David Thoreau, James McNeil Whistler, John Greenleaf Whittier.

Tourist information. Massachusetts Office of Travel & Tourism, 100 Cambridge St., 13th Floor, Boston, MA 02202.

Toll-free travel information. 1-800-227-6277.

Website. http://www.state.ma.us

Tourism website. http://www.mass-vacation.com

Michigan

Great Lakes State, Wolverine State

People. Population (1997): 9,773,892; rank: 8; **net change** (1990-97): 5.1%. **Pop. density** (1990): 163.6 per sq mi. **Racial/ethnic distrib.** (1990): 83.4% white; 13.9% black; 2.2% Hispanic.

Geography. Total area: 96,705 sq mi; rank: 11. **Land area:** 56,809 sq mi; rank: 22. **Acres forested:** 18,253,000. **Location:** East North Central state bordering on 4 of the 5 Great Lakes, divided into an Upper and Lower Peninsula by the Straits of Mackinac, which link lakes Michigan and Huron. **Climate:** well-defined seasons tempered by the Great Lakes. **Topography:** low rolling hills give way to northern tableland of hilly belts in Lower Peninsula; Upper Peninsula is level in the east, with swampy areas; western region is higher and more rugged. **Capital:** Lansing.

Economy. Chief industries: manufacturing, services, tourism, agriculture, forestry/lumber. **Chief manuf. goods:** automobiles, transportation equipment, machinery, fabricated metals, food products, plastics, office furniture. **Chief crops:** corn, wheat, soybeans, dry beans, hay, potatoes, sweet corn, apples, cherries, sugar beets, blueberries, cucumbers, Niagra grapes. **Livestock** (Jan. 1998): 1.1 mil cattle/calves; 90,000 sheep/lambs; (Dec. 1997) 1.0 mil hogs/pigs; (Dec. 1997) 6.2 mil chickens (excl. broilers); (Dec. 1996) 550,000 broilers. **Timber/lumber** (1997): maple, oak, aspen; 673 mil bd. ft. **Nonfuel minerals** (est. 1997): $1.56 bil; mostly portland cement, iron ore, sand & gravel, magnesium compounds, crushed stone. **Commercial fishing** (1997): $9.6 mil. **Chief ports:** Detroit, Saginaw River, Escanaba, Muskegon, Sault Ste. Marie, Port Huron, Marine City. **Internat. airports at:** Detroit, Grand Rapids, Flint, Kalamazoo, Lansing, Saginaw. **Value of construction** (1997): $10.7 bil. **Gross state product** (1996): $263.3 bil. **Employment distrib.** (May 1998): 27.7% serv.; 21.6% mfg.; 23.5% trade; 14.4% govt. **Per cap. pers. income** (1997): $25,560. **Sales tax** (1998): 6%. **Unemployment** (1997): 4.2%. **Tourism expends.** (1996): $9.6 bil. **Lottery** (1997): total sales: $1.6 bil; net income: $595.1 mil.

Finance. FDIC-insured commercial banks (1997): 163. **Deposits:** $85.3 bil. **FDIC-insured savings institutions** (1997): 23. **Assets:** $26.0 bil.

Federal govt. Fed. civ. employees (Mar. 1997): 22,044. **Avg. salary:** $44,538. **Notable fed. facilities:** Isle Royal, Sleeping Bear Dunes national parks.

Energy. Electricity production (1997, kWh, by source): Coal: 65.5 bil; Petroleum: 602 mil; Gas: 838 mil; Hydroelectric: 658 mil; Nuclear: 21.9 bil.

State data. Motto: Si Quaeris Peninsulam Amoenam, Circumspice (If you seek a pleasant peninsula, look about you). **Flower:** Apple blossom. **Bird:** Robin. **Tree:** White pine. **Song:** Michigan, My Michigan. **Entered union** Jan. 26, 1837; rank, 26th. **State fair** at Detroit, late Aug.–early Sept.; Upper Peninsula (Escanaba), mid-Aug.

History. Early inhabitants were the Ojibwa, Ottawa, Miami, Potawatomi, and Huron. French fur traders and missionaries visited the region, 1616, set up a mission at Sault Ste. Marie, 1641, and a settlement there, 1668. French settlements were taken over, 1763, by the British, who crushed a Native American uprising led by Ottawa chieftain Pontiac that same year. Treaty of Paris ceded territory to U.S., 1783, but British remained until 1796. The British seized Ft. Mackinac and Detroit, 1812. After Oliver H. Perry's Lake Erie victory and William H. Harrison's victory near the Thames River, 1813, the British retreated to Canada. The opening of the Erie Canal, 1825, and new land laws and Native American cessions led the way for a flood of settlers.

Tourist attractions. Henry Ford Museum, Greenfield Village, both in Dearborn; Michigan Space Center, Jackson; Tahquamenon *(Hiawatha)* Falls; DeZwaan windmill and Tulip Festival, Holland; "Soo Locks," St. Mary's Falls Ship Canal, Sault Ste. Marie, Kalamazoo Aviation History Museum; Mackinac Island; Kellogg's Cereal City USA, Battle Creek; Museum of African-American History, Motown Historical Museum, both Detroit.

Michigan's Famous People. Ralph Bunche, Paul de Kruif, Thomas A. Edison, Edna Ferber, Gerald R. Ford, Henry Ford, Aretha Franklin, Edgar Guest, Lee Iacocca, Robert Ingersoll, Magic Johnson, Will Kellogg, Ring Lardner, Elmore Leonard, Charles Lindbergh, Joe Louis, Madonna, Jack Paar, Pontiac, Diana Ross, Tom Selleck, John Smoltz, Lily Tomlin, Stewart Edward White, Malcolm X.

State Chamber of Commerce. 600 S. Walnut, Lansing, MI 48933. Phone: 517-371-2100

Toll-free travel information. 1-888-784-7328.

Website. http://www.migov.state.mi.us

Tourism website. http://www.michigan.org

Minnesota

North Star State, Gopher State

People. Population (1997): 4,685,549; rank: 20; **net change** (1990-97): 7.1%. **Pop. density** (1990): 55.0 per sq mi. **Racial/ethnic distrib.** (1990): 94.4% white; 2.2% black; 1.8% Asian; 1.2% Hispanic.

Geography. Total area: 86,943 sq mi; rank: 12. **Land area:** 79,617 sq mi; rank: 14. **Acres forested:** 16,718,000. **Location:** West North Central state bounded on the E by Wisconsin and Lake Superior, on the N by Canada, on the W by the Dakotas, and on the S by Iowa. **Climate:** northern part of state lies in the moist Great Lakes storm belt; the western border lies at the edge of the semi-arid Great Plains. **Topography:** central hill and lake region covering approx. half the state; to the NE, rocky ridges and deep lakes; to the NW, flat plain; to the S, rolling plains and deep river valleys. **Capital:** St. Paul.

Economy. Chief industries: agribusiness, forest products, mining, manufacturing, tourism. **Chief manuf. goods:** food, chemical and paper products, industrial machinery, electric and electronic equipment, computers, printing & publishing, scientific and medical instruments, fabricated metal products, forest products. **Chief crops:** corn, soybeans, wheat, sugar beets, hay, barley, potatoes, sunflowers. **Livestock** (Jan. 1998): 2.6 mil cattle/calves; 170,000 sheep/lambs; (Dec. 1997) 5.4 mil hogs/pigs; (Dec. 1997) 147 mil chickens (excl. broilers); (Dec. 1996) 47.5 mil broilers. **Timber/lumber** (1997): needle-leaves and hardwoods; 337 mil bd. ft. **Nonfuel minerals** (est. 1997): $1.60 bil; mostly iron ore, sand & gravel, crushed stone, dimension stone. **Commercial fishing** (1997): $236,000. **Chief ports:** Duluth, St. Paul, Minneapolis. **Internat. airport at:** Minneapolis-St. Paul. **Value of construction** (1997): $6.2 bil. **Gross state product** (1996): $141.6 bil. **Employment distrib.** (May 1998): 28.5% serv.; 23.9% trade; 17.4% mfg.; 15.0% govt. **Per cap. pers. income** (1997): $26,797. **Sales tax** (1998): 6.5%. **Unemployment** (1997): 3.3%. **Tourism expends.** (1996): $5.8 bil. **Lottery** (1997): total sales: $368.5 mil; net income: $88.6 mil.

Finance. FDIC-insured commercial banks (1997): 520. **Deposits**: $97.9 bil. **FDIC-insured savings institutions** (1997): 23. **Assets**: $2.6 bil.

Federal govt. Fed. civ. employees (Mar. 1997): 13,188. **Avg. salary:** $43,280.

Energy. Electricity production (1997, kWh, by source): Coal: 27.1 bil; Petroleum: 764 mil; Gas: 512 mil; Hydroelectric: 697 mil; Nuclear: 10.8 bil.

State data. Motto: L'Etoile du Nord (The star of the north). **Flower:** Pink and white lady's-slipper. **Bird:** Common loon. **Tree:** Red pine. **Song:** Hail! Minnesota. **Entered union** May 11, 1858; rank, 32d. **State fair** at St. Paul/Minneapolis; late Aug.-early Sept.

History. Dakota Sioux were early inhabitants of the area, and in the 16th cent., the Ojibwa began moving in from the east. French fur traders Médard Chouart and Pierre Esprit Radisson entered the region in the mid-17th cent. In 1679, French explorer Daniel Greysolon, sieur Duluth, claimed the entire region in the name of France. Britain took the area east of the Mississippi, 1763. The U.S. took over that portion after the American Revolution and in 1803, gained the western area in the Louisiana Purchase. The U.S. built Ft. St. Anthony (now Ft. Snelling), 1819, and in 1837, bought Native American lands, spurring an influx of settlers from the east. In 1849, the Territory of Minnesota was created. Sioux Indians staged a bloody uprising, the Battle of Woods Lake, 1862, and were driven from the state.

Tourist attractions. Minneapolis Institute of Arts, Walker Art Center, Minneapolis Sculpture Garden, Minnehaha Falls (inspiration for Longfellow's *Hiawatha),* Guthrie Theater, Minneapolis; Ordway Theater, St. Paul; Voyageurs Natl. Park; Mayo Clinic, Rochester; St. Paul Winter Carnival; North Shore (of Lake Superior).

Famous Minnesotans. Warren Burger, William O. Douglas, Bob Dylan, F. Scott Fitzgerald, Judy Garland, Cass Gilbert, Hubert Humphrey, Garrison Keillor, Sister Elizabeth Kenny, Sinclair Lewis, Paul Manship, Roger Maris, E. G. Marshall, William and Charles Mayo, Eugene McCarthy, Walter F. Mondale, Charles Schulz, Harold Stassen, Thorstein Veblen.

Chamber of Commerce. 30 East 7th St., Suite 1700, St. Paul, MN 55101-4901.

Toll-free travel information. 1-800-657-3700.

Website. http://www.state.mn.us

Tourism website. http://www.dted.state.mn.us/explore/explore.html

Mississippi

Magnolia State

People. Population (1997): 2,730,501; rank: 31; **net change** (1990-97): 6.0%. **Pop. density** (1990): 54.9 per sq mi. **Racial/ethnic distrib.** (1990): 63.5% white; 35.6% black; 0.6% Hispanic.

Geography. Total area: 48,286 sq mi; rank: 32. **Land area:** 46,914 sq mi; rank: 31. **Acres forested:** 17,000,000. **Location:** East South Central state bordered on the W by the Mississippi R. and on the S by the Gulf of Mexico. **Climate:** semi-tropical, with abundant rainfall, long growing season, and extreme temperatures unusual. **Topography:** low, fertile delta between the Yazoo and Mississippi rivers; loess bluffs stretching around delta border; sandy gulf coastal terraces followed by piney woods and prairie; rugged, high sandy hills in extreme NE followed by Black Prairie Belt, Pontotoc Ridge, and flatwoods into the north central highlands. **Capital:** Jackson.

Economy. Chief industries: warehousing & distribution, services, manufacturing, government, wholesale and retail trade. **Chief manuf. goods:** chemicals & plastics, food & kindred products, furniture, lumber & wood products, electrical machinery, transportation equipment. **Chief crops:** cotton, rice, soybeans. **Livestock** (Jan. 1998): 1.3 mil cattle/calves; (Dec. 1997) 240,000 hogs/pigs; (Dec. 1997) 11.1 mil chickens (excl. broilers); (Dec. 1996) 676.0 mil broilers. **Timber/lumber** (1997): pine, oak, hardwoods; 2.8 bil bd. ft. **Nonfuel minerals** (est. 1997): $137 mil; mostly sand & gravel, portland cement, clays, crushed stone. **Commercial fishing** (1997): $42 mil. **Chief ports:** Pascagoula, Vicksburg, Gulfport, Natchez, Greenville. **Value of construction** (1997): $2.6 bil. **Gross state product** (1996): $56.4 bil. **Employment distrib.** (May 1998): 23.6% serv.; 21.6% mfg.; 21.3% trade; 19.8% govt. **Per cap. pers. income** (1997): $18,272. **Sales tax** (1998): 7%. **Unemployment** (1997): 5.7%. **Tourism expends.** (1996): $3.5 bil.

Finance. FDIC-insured commercial banks (1997): 107. **Deposits:** $27.8 bil. **FDIC-insured savings institutions** (1997): 13. **Assets:** $1.4 bil.

Federal govt. Fed. civ. employees (Mar. 1997): 17,160. **Avg. salary:** $39,495. **Notable fed. facilities:** Columbus, Keesler AF bases; Meridian Naval Air Station, John C. Stennis Space Center; U.S. Army Corps of Engineers Waterway Experiment Station.

Energy. Electricity production (1997, kWh, by source): Coal: 12.5 bil; Petroleum: 2.6 bil; Gas: 5.3 bil; Nuclear: 10.8 bil.

State data. Motto: Virtute et Armis (By valor and arms). **Flower:** Magnolia. **Bird:** Mockingbird. **Tree:** Magnolia. **Song:** Go, Mississippi! **Entered union** Dec. 10, 1817; rank, 20th. **State fair** at Jackson; early Oct.

History. Early inhabitants of the region were Choctaw, Chickasaw, and Natchez peoples. Hernando de Soto explored the area, 1540, and sighted the Mississippi River, 1541. Robert La Salle traced the river from Illinois to its mouth and claimed the entire valley for France, 1682. The first settlement was the French Ft. Maurepas, near Ocean Springs, 1699. The area was ceded to Britain, 1763; American settlers followed. During the American Revolution, Spain seized part of the area, remaining even after the U.S. acquired title at the end of the conflict; Spain finally moved out, 1798. The Territory of Mississippi was formed, 1798. Mississippi seceded, 1861. Union forces captured Corinth and Vicksburg and destroyed Jackson and much of Meridian. Mississippi was readmitted to the Union in 1870.

Tourist attractions. Vicksburg Natl. Military Park and Cemetery, other Civil War sites; Hattiesburg; Natchez Trace; Indian mounds; Antebellum homes; pilgrimages in Natchez and some 25 other cities; Smith Robertson Museum, Mynelle Gardens, both Jackson; Mardi Gras and Shrimp Festival, both in Biloxi; Gulf Islands Natl. Seashore; Casinos on the Mississippi River; the Mississippi Coast.

Famous Mississippians. Dana Andrews, Margaret Walker Alexander, Jimmy Buffett, Hodding Carter III, Bo Diddley, William Faulkner, Brett Favre, Shelby Foote, Morgan Freeman, John Grisham, Fannie Lou Hamer, Jim Henson, Robert Johnson, James Earl Jones, B. B. King, L. Q. C. Lamar, Trent Lott, Gerald McRaney, Willie Morris, Walter Payton, Elvis Presley, Leontyne Price, Charley Pride, LeAnn Rimes, Muddy Waters, Eudora Welty, Tennessee Williams, Oprah Winfrey, Johnny Winter, Richard Wright, Tammy Wynette.

Tourist Information. Dept. of Economic & Community Development. PO Box 849, Jackson, MS 39205-0849.

Toll-free travel information. 1-800-WARMEST.

Website. http://www.state.ms.us

Tourism website. http://www.decd.state.ms.us/tourism.htm

Missouri

Show Me State

People. Population (1997): 5,402,058; rank: 16; **net change** (1990-97): 5.6%. **Pop. density** (1990): 74.3 per sq mi. **Racial/ethnic distrib.** (1990): 87.7% white; 10.7% black; 1.2% Hispanic.

Geography. Total area: 69,709 sq mi; rank: 21. **Land area:** 68,898 sq mi; rank: 18. **Acres forested:** 14,007,000. **Location:** West North Central state near the geographic center of the conterminous U.S.; bordered on the E by the Mississippi R., on the NW by the Missouri R. **Climate:** continental, susceptible to cold Canadian air, moist, warm gulf air, and drier SW air. **Topography:** rolling hills, open, fertile plains, and well-watered prairie N of the Missouri R.; south of the river land is rough and hilly with deep, narrow valleys; alluvial plain in the SE; low elevation in the west. **Capital:** Jefferson City.

Economy. Chief industries: agriculture, manufacturing, aerospace, tourism. **Chief manuf. goods:** transportation equipment, food and related products, electrical and electronic equipment, chemicals. **Chief crops:** soybeans, corn, wheat, hay. **Livestock** (Jan. 1998): 4.3 mil cattle/calves; 65,000 sheep/lambs; (Dec. 1997) 3.5 mil hogs/pigs; (Dec. 1997) 9.4 mil chickens (excl. broilers); (Dec. 1996) 246.3 mil broilers. **Timber/lumber** (1997): oak, hickory; 583 mil bd. ft. **Nonfuel minerals** (est. 1997): $1.32 bil; mostly crushed stone, lead, portland cement, lime, zinc. **Chief ports:** St.

Louis, Kansas City. **Internat. airports at:** St. Louis, Kansas City. **Value of construction** (1997): $5.9 bil. **Gross state product** (1996): $145.1 bil. **Employment distrib.** (May 1998): 28% services; 23.7% trade; 15.8% mfg.; 15.7% govt. **Per cap. pers. income** (1997): $24,001. **Sales tax** (1998): 4.23%. **Unemployment** (1997): 4.2%. **Tourism expends.** (1996): $7.9 bil. **Lottery** (1997): total sales: $439.6 mil; net income: $132.7 mil.

Finance. FDIC-insured commercial banks (1997): 404. **Deposits**: $53.5 bil. **FDIC-insured savings institutions** (1997): 45. **Assets**: $6.9 bil.

Federal govt. Fed. civ. employees (Mar. 1997): 34,997. **Avg. salary:** $39,880. **Notable fed. facilities:** Federal Reserve banks; Ft. Leonard Wood; Jefferson Barracks; Whiteman AFB.

Energy. Electricity production (1997 kWh, by source): Coal: 59.9 bil; Petroleum: 125 mil; Gas: 570 mil; Hydroelectric: 1.5 bil; Nuclear: 9.0 bil.

State data. Motto: Salus Populi Suprema Lex Esto (The welfare of the people shall be the supreme law). **Flower:** Hawthorn. **Bird:** Bluebird. **Tree:** Dogwood. **Song:** Missouri Waltz. **Entered union** Aug. 10, 1821; rank, 24th. **State fair** at Sedalia; 3d week in Aug.

History. Early inhabitants of the region were Algonquian Sauk, Fox, and Illinois and Siouan Osage, Missouri, Iowa, and Kansa peoples. Hernando de Soto visited 1541. French hunters and lead miners made the first settlement c 1735, at Ste. Genevieve. The territory was ceded to Spain by the French, 1763, then returned to France, 1800. The U.S. acquired Missouri as part of the Louisiana Purchase, 1803. The influx of white settlers drove Native American tribes to the Kansas and Oklahoma territories; most were gone by 1836. The fur trade and the Santa Fe Trail provided prosperity; St. Louis became the gateway for pioneers heading West. Missouri entered the Union as a slave state, 1821. Though it remained with the Union, pro- and anti-slavery forces battled there during the Civil War.

Tourist attractions. Silver Dollar City, Branson; Mark Twain Area, Hannibal; Pony Express Museum, St. Joseph; Harry S. Truman Library, Independence; Gateway Arch, St. Louis; Worlds of Fun, Kansas City; Lake of the Ozarks; Churchill Mem., Fulton; State Capitol, Jefferson City.

Famous Missourians. Maya Angelou, Robert Altman, Burt Bacharach, Josephine Baker, Scot Bakula, Thomas Hart Benton, Tom Berenger, Chuck Berry, George Caleb Bingham, Daniel Boone, Omar Bradley, Kate Capshaw, Dale Carnegie, George Washington Carver, Bob Costas, Walter Cronkite, Walt Disney, T. S. Eliot, Richard Gephardt, John Goodman, Betty Grable, Edwin Hubble, Jesse James, Marianne Moore, Reinhold Niebuhr, J. C. Penney, John J. Pershing, Brad Pitt, Joseph Pulitzer, Ginger Rogers, Bess Truman, Harry S. Truman, Kathleen Turner, Tina Turner, Mark Twain, Dick Van Dyke, Tennessee Williams, Lanford Wilson, Shelley Winters, Jane Wyman.

Chamber of Commerce. 428 E. Capitol, Jefferson City, MO 65101.

Toll-free travel information. 1-888-925-3875, ext. 124.

Website. http://www.ecodev.state.mo.us

Tourism website. http://www.missouritourism.org

Montana

Treasure State

People. Population (1997): 878,810; rank: 44; **net change** (1990-97): 10.0%. **Pop. density** (1990): 5.5 per sq mi. **Racial/ethnic distrib.** (1990): 92.7% white; 0.3% black; 6.0% Amer. Indian; 1.5% Hispanic.

Geography. Total area: 147,046 sq mi; rank: 4. **Land area:** 145,556 sq mi; rank: 4. **Acres forested:** 22,512,000. **Location:** Mountain state bounded on the E by the Dakotas, on the S by Wyoming, on the SSW by Idaho, and on the N by Canada. **Climate:** colder, continental climate with low humidity. **Topography:** Rocky Mts. in western third of the state; eastern two-thirds gently rolling northern Great Plains. **Capital:** Helena.

Economy. Chief industries: agriculture, timber, mining, tourism, oil and gas. **Chief manuf. goods:** food products, wood & paper products, primary metals, printing & publishing, petroleum and coal products. **Chief crops:** wheat, barley, sugar beets, hay, oats. **Livestock** (Jan. 1998): 2.6 mil cattle/calves; 410,000 sheep/lambs; (Dec. 1997) 175,000 hogs/pigs; (Dec. 1997) 390,000 chickens (excl. broilers). **Timber/lumber** (1997): Douglas fir, pines, larch; 1.4 bil bd. ft. **Nonfuel minerals** (est. 1997): $498 mil; mostly copper, gold, portland cement, palladium metal, molybdenum. **Internat. airports at:** Great Falls, Billings, Kalispell, Missoula. **Value of construction** (1997): $827 mil. **Gross state product** (1996): $18.5 bil. **Employment distrib.** (May 1998): 28.8% serv.; 26.7% trade; 21.2% govt.; 6.7% mfg. **Per cap. pers. income** (1997): $20,046. **Sales tax**: none. **Unemployment** (1997): 5.4%. **Tourism expends.** (1996): $1.7 bil. **Lottery** (1997): total sales: $28.2 mil; net income: $6.6 mil.

Finance. FDIC-insured commercial banks (1997): 96. **Deposits**: $7.5 bil. **FDIC-insured savings institutions** (1997): 9. **Assets**: $2.0 bil.

Federal govt. Fed. civ. employees (Mar. 1997): 7,869. **Avg. salary:** $39,562. **Notable fed. facilities:** Malmstrom AFB; Ft. Peck, Hungry Horse, Libby, Yellowtail dams; numerous missile silos.

Energy. Electricity production (1997, kWh, by source): Coal: 14.4 bil; Petroleum: 17 mil; Gas: 32 mil; Hydroelectric: 13.3 bil.

State data. Motto: Oro y Plata (Gold and silver). **Flower:** Bitterroot. **Bird:** Western meadowlark. **Tree:** Ponderosa pine. **Song:** Montana. **Entered union** Nov. 8, 1889; rank, 41st. **State fair** at Great Falls; late July-early Aug.

History. Cheyenne, Blackfoot, Crow, Assiniboin, Salish (Flatheads), Kootenai, and Kalispel peoples were early inhabitants of the area. French explorers visited the region, 1742. The U.S. acquired the area partly through the Louisiana Purchase, 1803, partly through explorations of Lewis and Clark, 1805-6. Fur traders and missionaries established posts early 19th cent. Gold was discovered, 1863, and the Montana territory was established, 1864. Indian uprisings reached their peak with the Battle of Little Bighorn, 1876. Chief Joseph and the Nez Percé tribe surrendered here, 1877, after long trek across the state. Mining activity and the coming of the Northern Pacific Railway, 1883, brought population growth. Copper wealth from the Butte pits resulted in the turn of the century "War of Copper Kings" as factions fought for control of "the richest hill on earth."

Tourist attractions. Glacier Natl. Park; Yellowstone Natl. Park; Museum of the Rockies, Bozeman; Museum of the Plains Indian, Blackfeet Reservation, near Browning; Little Bighorn Battlefield Natl. Monument and Custer Natl. Cemetery; Flathead Lake; Helena; Lewis and Clark Caverns State Park, near Whitehall; Lewis and Clark Interpretive Center, Great Falls.

Famous Montanans. Gary Cooper, Marcus Daly, Chet Huntley, Will James, Myrna Loy, Mike Mansfield, Brent Musburger, Jeannette Rankin, Charles M. Russell, Lester Thurow.

Chamber of Commerce. 2030 11th Ave., PO Box 1730, Helena, MT 59624.

Toll-free travel information. 1-800-VISITMT.

Website. http://www.mt.gov

Tourism website. http://travel.mt.gov

Nebraska

Cornhusker State

People. Population (1997): 1,656,870; rank: 38; **net change** (1990-97): 5.0%. **Pop. density** (1990): 20.5 per sq mi. **Racial/ethnic distrib.** (1990): 93.8% white; 3.6% black; 2.3% Hispanic.

Geography. Total area: 77,358 sq mi; rank: 16. **Land area:** 76,878 sq mi; rank: 15. **Acres forested:** 722,000. **Location:** West North Central state with the Missouri R. for a NE and E border. **Climate:** continental semi-arid. **Topography:** till plains of the central lowland in the eastern third rising to the Great Plains and hill country of the north central and NW. **Capital:** Lincoln.

Economy. Chief industries: agriculture, manufacturing. **Chief manuf. goods:** processed foods, industrial machinery, printed materials, electric and electronic equipment, primary and fabricated metal products, transportation equipment. **Chief crops:** corn, sorghum, soybeans, hay, wheat, dry beans, oats, potatoes, sugar beets. **Livestock** (Jan. 1998): 6.7 mil cattle/calves; 100,000 sheep/lambs; (Dec. 1997) 3.6 mil hogs/pigs; (Dec. 1997) 12.1 mil chickens (excl. broilers);

(Dec. 1996) 2.3 mil broilers. **Timber/lumber** (1997): oak, hickory, and elm; 25 mil bd. ft. **Nonfuel minerals** (est. 1997): $161 mil; mostly portland cement, sand & gravel, crushed stone, masonry cement, clays. **Chief ports:** Omaha, Sioux City, Brownville, Blair, Plattsmouth, Nebraska City. **Value of construction** (1997): $2.0 bil. **Gross state product** (1996): $47.2 bil. **Employment distrib.** (May 1998): 27% serv.; 24.4% trade; 17.3% govt.; 13.7% mfg. **Per cap. pers. income** (1997): $23,803. **Sales tax** (1998): 4.5%. **Unemployment** (1997): 2.6%. **Tourism expends.** (1996): $2.3 bil. **Lottery** (1997): total sales: $76.6 mil; net income: $20.6 mil.

Finance. FDIC-insured commercial banks (1997): 326. **Deposits**: $21.6 bil. **FDIC-insured savings institutions** (1997): 13. **Assets**: $9.2 bil.

Federal govt. Fed. civ. employees (Mar. 1997): 7,994. **Avg. salary:** $39,952. **Notable fed. facilities:** Offutt AFB.

Energy. Electricity production (1997, kWh, by source): Coal: 17.2 bil; Petroleum: 31 mil; Gas: 206 mil; Hydroelectric: 1.7 mil; Nuclear: 9.3 bil.

State data. Motto: Equality before the law. **Flower:** Goldenrod. **Bird:** Western meadowlark. **Tree:** Cottonwood. **Song:** Beautiful Nebraska. **Entered union** Mar. 1, 1867; rank, 37th. **State fair** at Lincoln; Aug.- Sept.

History. When the Europeans first arrived, Pawnee, Ponca, Omaha, and Oto peoples lived in the region. Spanish and French explorers and fur traders visited the area prior to its acquisition in the Louisiana Purchase, 1803. Lewis and Clark passed through, 1804-6. The first permanent settlement was Bellevue, near Omaha, 1823. The region was gradually settled, despite the 1834 Indian Intercourse Act, which declared Nebraska Indian country and excluded white settlement. Conflicts with settlers eventually forced Native Americans to move to reservations. Many Civil War veterans settled under free land terms of the 1862 Homestead Act; as agriculture grew, struggles followed between homesteaders and ranchers.

Tourist attractions. State Museum (Elephant Hall), State Capitol, both Lincoln; Stuhr Museum of the Prairie Pioneer, Grand Island; Museum of the Fur Trade, Chadron; Henry Doorly Zoo, Joslyn Art Museum, both Omaha; Ashfall Fossil Beds, Strategic Air Command Museum, Ashland; Boys Town, west of Omaha; Arbor Lodge State Park, Nebraska City; Buffalo Bill Ranch State Hist. Park, North Platte; Pioneer Village, Minden; Oregon Trail landmarks; Scotts Bluff Natl. Monument; Chimney Rock Historic Site; Ft. Robinson; Hastings Museum, Hastings.

Famous Nebraskans. Fred Astaire, Marlon Brando, Charles W. Bryan, William Jennings Bryan, Warren Buffett, Johnny Carson, Willa Cather, Dick Cavett, William F. "Buffalo Bill" Cody, Loren Eiseley, Rev. Edward J. Flanagan, Henry Fonda, Gerald R. Ford, Bob Gibson, Rollin Kirby, Harold Lloyd, Malcolm X, J. Sterling Morton, John Neihardt, Nick Nolte, George Norris, John J. Pershing, Roscoe Pound, Chief Red Cloud, Mari Sandoz, Robert Taylor, Daryl F. Zannuck.

Chamber of Commerce and Industry. 1320 Lincoln Mall, Ste. 201, Lincoln, NE 68508; 402-474-4422

Toll-free travel information. 1-800-228-4307.

Website. http://www.state.ne.us

Tourism website. http://www.visitnebraska.org

Nevada

Sagebrush State, Battle Born State, Silver State

People. Population (1997): 1,676,809; rank: 37; **net change** (1990-97): 39.5%. **Pop. density** (1990): 10.9 per sq mi. **Racial/ethnic distrib.** (1990): 84.3% white; 6.6% black; 3.2% Asian; 10.4% Hispanic.

Geography. Total area: 110,567 sq mi; rank: 7. **Land area:** 109,806 sq mi; rank: 7. **Acres forested:** 8,938,000. **Location:** Mountain state bordered on N by Oregon and Idaho, on E by Utah and Arizona, on SE by Arizona, and on SW and W by California. **Climate:** semi-arid and arid. **Topography:** rugged N-S mountain ranges; highest elevation, Boundary Peak, 13,140 ft; southern area is within the Mojave Desert; lowest elevation, Colorado River at southern tip of state, 479 ft. **Capital:** Carson City.

Economy. Chief industries: gaming, tourism, mining, manufacturing, government, retailing, warehousing, trucking. **Chief manuf. goods:** food products, plastics, chemicals, aerospace products, lawn and garden irrigation equipment, seismic and machinery-monitoring devices. **Chief crops:** hay, alfalfa seed, potatoes, onions, garlic, barley, wheat. **Livestock** (Jan. 1998): 510,000 cattle/calves; 80,000 sheep/lambs; (Dec. 1997) 8,000 hogs/pigs. **Timber/lumber:** piñon, juniper, other pines. **Nonfuel minerals** (est. 1997): $3.03 bil; mostly gold, copper, silver, sand & gravel, diatomite. **Internat. airports at:** Las Vegas, Reno. **Value of construction** (1997): $6.7 bil. **Gross state product** (1996): $53.7 bil. **Employment distrib.** (May 1998): 42.6% serv.; 20.2% trade; 11.9% govt.; 4.6% mfg. **Per cap. pers. income** (1997): $26,791. **Sales tax** (1998): 6.5%. **Unemployment** (1997): 4.1%. **Tourism expends.** (1996): $17.6 bil.

Finance. FDIC-insured commercial banks (1997): 25. **Deposits**: $8.1 bil.

Federal govt. Fed. civ. employees (Mar. 1997): 7,141. **Avg. salary:** $43,066. **Notable fed. facilities:** Nevada Test Site; Hawthorne Army Ammunition Plant, Nellis Air Force Base and Gunnery Range; Fallon Naval Air Station; Palomino Valley Wild Horse and Burro Placement Center.

Energy. Electricity production (1997, kWh, by source): Coal: 15.3 bil; Petroleum: 31 mil; Gas: 5.0 bil; Hydroelectric: 2.6 bil.

State data. Motto: All for our country. **Flower:** Sagebrush. **Bird:** Mountain bluebird. **Trees:** Single-leaf piñon and bristlecone pine. **Song:** Home Means Nevada. **Entered union** Oct. 31, 1864; rank, 36th. **State fair** at Reno; late Aug.

History. Shoshone, Paiute, Bannock, and Washoe peoples lived in the area at the time of European contact. Nevada was first explored by Spaniards, 1776. Hudson's Bay Co. trappers explored the north and central region, 1825; trader Jedediah Smith crossed the state, 1826-27. The area was acquired by the U.S., 1848, at the end of the Mexican War. The first settlement, Mormon Station, now Genoa, was established, 1849. Discovery of the Comstock Lode, rich in gold and silver, 1859, spurred a population boom. In the early 20th cent., Nevada adopted progressive measures such as the initiative, referendum, recall, and woman suffrage.

Tourist attractions. Legalized gambling at: Lake Tahoe, Reno, Las Vegas, Laughlin, Elko County, and elsewhere. Hoover Dam; Lake Mead; Great Basin Natl. Park; Valley of Fire State Park; Virginia City; Red Rock Canyon Natl. Conservation Area; Liberace Museum, the Las Vegas Strip, Guinness World of Records Museum, Lost City Museum, Overton, Lamoille Canyon, Pyramid Lake, all Las Vegas. Skiing near Lake Tahoe.

Famous Nevadans. Walter Van Tilburg Clark, George Ferris, Sarah Winnemucca Hopkins, Paul Laxalt, Dat So La Lee, John William Mackay, Anne Martin, Pat McCarran, Key Pittman, William Morris Stewart.

Tourist information. Commission on Tourism, 5151 S. Carson St., Carson City, NV 89701.

Toll-free travel information. 1-800-638-2328.

Website. http://www.state.nv.us

Tourism website. http://www.travelnevada.com

New Hampshire

Granite State

People. Population (1997): 1,172,709; rank: 42; **net change** (1990-97): 5.7%. **Pop. density** (1990): 123.7 per sq mi. **Racial/ethnic distrib.** (1990): 98.0% white; 0.6% black; 1.0% Hispanic.

Geography. Total area: 9,283 sq mi; rank: 44. **Land area:** 8,969 sq mi; rank: 44. **Acres forested:** 4,981,000. **Location:** New England state bounded on S by Massachusetts, on W by Vermont, on N and NW by Canada, on E by Maine and the Atlantic Ocean. **Climate:** highly varied, due to its nearness to high mountains and ocean. **Topography:** low, rolling coast followed by countless hills and mountains rising out of a central plateau. **Capital:** Concord.

Economy. Chief industries: tourism, manufacturing, agriculture, trade, mining. **Chief manuf. goods:** machinery, electrical and electronic products, plastics, fabricated metal products. **Chief crops:** dairy products, nursery & greenhouse products, hay, vegetables, fruit, maple syrup & sugar products. **Livestock** (Jan. 1998): 37,000 cattle/calves; 7,000 sheep/lambs; (Dec. 1997) 2,500 hogs/pigs; (Dec. 1997) 218,000 chickens (excl. broilers). **Timber/lumber** (1997): white pine, hemlock, oak, birch; 294 mil bd. ft. **Nonfuel minerals** (est. 1997): $60.2 mil; mostly sand & gravel, crushed and dimension stone, gemstones. **Commercial fishing** (1997): $12.6 mil. **Chief ports:** Portsmouth, Hampton, Rye. **Value of construction** (1997): $1.3 bil. **Gross state product** (1996): $34.1 bil. **Employment distrib.** (May 1998): 26.1% trade; 28.9% serv.; 18.8% mfg.; 13.8% govt. **Per cap. pers. income** (1997): $28,047. **Sales**

tax: none. **Unemployment** (1997): 3.1%. **Tourism expends.** (1996): $1.8 bil. **Lottery** (1997): total sales: $176.8 mil; net income: $54.2 mil.

Finance. FDIC-insured commercial banks (1997): 21. **Deposits:** $8.5 bil. **FDIC-insured savings institutions** (1997): 21. **Assets**: $9.9 bil.

Federal govt. Fed. civ. employees (Mar. 1997): 3,338. **Avg. salary:** $47,655.

Energy. Electricity production (1997, kWh, by source): Coal: 4.1 bil; Petroleum: 1.0 bil; Gas: 35 mil; Hydroelectric: 1.2 bil; Nuclear: 8.0 bil.

State data. Motto: Live free or die. **Flower:** Purple lilac. **Bird:** Purple finch. **Tree:** White birch. **Song:** Old New Hampshire. **Ninth** of the original 13 states to ratify the Constitution, June 21, 1788. **State Fair:** Many agricultural fairs statewide, July through Sept.; no State fair

History. Algonquian-speaking peoples, including the Pennacook, lived in the region when the Europeans arrived. The first explorers to visit the area were England's Martin Pring, 1603, and France's Champlain, 1605. The first settlement was Odiorne's Point (now port of Rye), 1623. Native American conflicts were ended, 1759, by Robert Rogers' Rangers. Before the American Revolution, New Hampshire residents seized a British fort at Portsmouth, 1774, and drove the royal governor out, 1775. New Hampshire became the first colony to adopt its own constitution, 1776. Three regiments served in the Continental Army, and scores of privateers raided British shipping.

Tourist attractions. Mt. Washington, highest peak in Northeast; Lake Winnipesaukee; White Mt. National Forest; Crawford, Franconia—famous for the Old Man of the Mountain, described by Hawthorne as the Great Stone Face, Pinkham notches, all White Mt. region; the Flume, a spectacular gorge; the aerial tramway, Cannon Mt.; Strawbery Banke, Portsmouth; Shaker Village, Canterbury; Saint-Gaudens, natl. historic site, Cornish; Mt. Monadnock.

Famous New Hampshirites. Salmon P. Chase, Ralph Adams Cram, Mary Baker Eddy, Daniel Chester French, Robert Frost, Horace Greeley, Sarah Buell Hale, Franklin Pierce, Augustus Saint-Gaudens, David H. Souter, Daniel Webster.

Tourist information. Division of Travel & Tourism Development, PO Box 1856, Concord, NH 03302-1856.

Toll-free travel information. 1-800-386-4664.

Website. http://www.state.nh.us

Tourism website. http://www.visitnh.gov

New Jersey

Garden State

People. Population (1997): 8,052,849; rank: 9; **net change** (1990-97): 3.9%. **Pop. density** (1990): 1,042.0 per sq mi. **Racial/ethnic distrib.** (1990): 79.3% white; 13.4% black; 3.5% Asian; 9.6% Hispanic.

Geography. Total area: 8,215 sq mi; rank: 46. **Land area:** 7,419 sq mi; rank: 46. **Acres forested:** 2,007,000. **Location:** Middle Atlantic state bounded on N and E by New York and Atlantic Ocean, on S and W by Delaware and Pennsylvania. **Climate:** moderate, with marked difference bet. NW and SE extremities. **Topography:** Appalachian Valley in the NW also has highest elevation, High Pt., 1,801 ft; Appalachian Highlands, flat-topped NE-SW mountain ranges; Piedmont Plateau, low plains broken by high ridges (Palisades) rising 400-500 ft; Coastal Plain, covering three-fifths of state in SE, rises from sea level to gentle slopes. **Capital:** Trenton.

Economy. Chief industries: pharmaceuticals/drugs, telecommunications, biotechnology, printing & publishing. **Chief manuf. goods:** chemicals, electronic equipment, food. **Chief crops:** nursery/greenhouse, tomatoes, blueberries, peaches, peppers, cranberries, soybeans. **Livestock** (Jan. 1998): 67,000 cattle/calves; 17,000 sheep/lambs; (Dec. 1997) 16,000 hogs/pigs; (Dec. 1997) 2.1 mil chickens (excl. broilers). **Timber/lumber:** (1997) pine, cedar, mixed hardwoods; 8 mil bd. ft. **Nonfuel minerals** (est. 1997): $296 mil; mostly crushed stone, sand & gravel, greensand marl, peat. **Commercial fishing** (1997): $98 mil. **Chief ports:** Newark, Elizabeth, Hoboken, Camden. **Internat. airport at:** Newark. **Value of construction** (1997): $8.3 bil. **Gross state product** (1996): $276.4 bil. **Employment distrib.** (May 1998): 31.9% serv.; 23.5% trade; 14.9% govt.; 12.7% mfg. **Per cap. pers. income** (1997): $32,654. **Sales tax** (1998): 6%. **Unemployment** (1997): 5.1%. **Tourism expends.** (1996): $13.2 bil. **Lottery** (1997): total sales: $1.56 bil; net income: $647.6 mil.

Finance. FDIC-insured commercial banks (1997): 71. **Deposits**: $62.4 bil. **FDIC-insured savings institutions** (1997): 87. **Assets**: $46.3 bil.

Federal govt. Fed. civ. employees (Mar. 1997): 30,939. **Avg. salary:** $46,692. **Notable fed. facilities:** McGuire AFB; Fort Dix; Fort Monmouth; Picatinny Arsenal; Lakehurst Naval Air Engineering Center.

Energy. Electricity production (1997, kWh, by source): Coal: 6.8 bil; Petroleum: 384 mil; Gas: 2.8 bil; Hydroelectric: –130 mil; Nuclear: 13.9 bil.

State data. Motto: Liberty and prosperity. **Flower:** Purple violet. **Bird:** Eastern goldfinch. **Tree:** Red oak. **Third** of the original 13 states to ratify the Constitution, Dec. 18, 1787. **State fair** at Cherry Hill; late July-early Aug.

History. The Lenni Lenape (Delaware) peoples lived in the region and had mostly peaceful relations with European colonists, who arrived after the explorers Verrazano, 1524, and Hudson, 1609. The first permanent European settlement was Dutch, at Bergen (now Jersey City), 1660. When the British took New Netherland, 1664, the area between the Delaware and Hudson Rivers was given to Lord John Berkeley and Sir George Carteret. During the American Revolution, New Jersey was the scene of nearly 100 battles, large and small, including Trenton, 1776; Princeton, 1777; Monmouth, 1778.

Tourist attractions. 127 mi of beaches; Miss America Pageant, Atlantic City; Grover Cleveland birthplace, Caldwell; Cape May Historic District; Edison Natl. Historic Site, W. Orange; Six Flags Great Adventure, Jackson; Liberty State Park, Jersey City; Meadowlands Sports Complex, E. Rutherford; Pine Barrens wilderness area; Princeton University; numerous Revolutionary War historical sites; State Aquarium, Camden.

Famous New Jerseyans. Count Basie, Judy Blume, Bill Bradley, Jon Bon Jovi, Aaron Burr, Grover Cleveland, James Fenimore Cooper, Stephen Crane, Thomas Edison, Albert Einstein, Allen Ginsberg, Alexander Hamilton, Whitney Houston, Buster Keaton, Joyce Kilmer, George McClellan, Thomas Paine, Dorothy Parker, Molly Pitcher, Paul Robeson, Philip Roth, Wally Schirra, H. Norman Schwarzkopf, Frank Sinatra, Bruce Springsteen, Martha Stewart, Meryl Streep, Walt Whitman, William Carlos Williams, Woodrow Wilson.

Chamber of Commerce. 50 W. State St., Trenton, NJ 08608.

Toll-free travel information. 1-800-JERSEY7.

Website. http://www.state.nj.us

Tourism website. http://www.state.nj.us/travel

New Mexico

Land of Enchantment

People. Population (1997): 1,729,751; rank: 36; **net change** (1990-97): 14.2%. **Pop. density** (1990): 12.5 per sq mi. **Racial/ethnic distrib.** (1990): 75.6% white; 2.0% black; 8.9% Amer. Indian; 38.2% Hispanic.

Geography. Total area: 121,598 sq mi; rank: 5. **Land area:** 121,364 sq mi rank: 5. **Acres forested:** 15,296,000. **Location:** southwestern state bounded by Colorado on the N, Oklahoma, Texas, and Mexico on the E and S, and Arizona on the W. **Climate:** dry, with temperatures rising or falling 5° F with every 1,000 ft elevation. **Topography:** eastern third, Great Plains; central third, Rocky Mts. (85% of the state is over 4,000-ft elevation); western third, high plateau. **Capital:** Santa Fe.

Economy. Chief industries: government, services, trade. **Chief manuf. goods:** foods, machinery, apparel, lumber, printing, transportation equipment, electronics, semiconductors. **Chief crops:** hay, onions, chiles, greenhouse nursery, pecans, cotton. **Livestock** (Jan. 1998): 1.4 mil cattle/calves; 240,000 sheep/lambs; (Dec. 1997) 5,000 hogs/pigs; (Dec. 1997) 1.4 mil chickens (excl. broilers). **Timber/lumber** (1997): ponderosa pine, Douglas fir; 119 mil bd. ft. **Nonfuel minerals** (est. 1997): $994 mil; mostly copper, potash, sand & gravel, portland cement, perlite. **Internat. airports at:** Albuquerque. **Value of construction** (1997): $1.9 bil. **Gross state product** (1996): $42.7 bil. **Employment distrib.** (May 1998): 27.8% serv.; 24.8% govt. 23.9% trade; 6.3% mfg. **Per cap. pers. income** (1997): $19,587. **Sales tax** (1998): 5%. **Unemployment** (1997): 6.2%. **Tourism expends.** (1996): $3.3 bil. **Lottery** (1997): total sales: $82.1 mil; net income: $20.3 mil.

Finance. FDIC-insured commercial banks (1997): 58. **Deposits**: $9.0 bil. **FDIC-insured savings institutions** (1997): 10. **Assets**: $1.8 bil.

Federal govt. Fed. civ. employees (Mar. 1997): 21,867. **Avg. salary:** $40,424. **Notable fed. facilities:** Kirtland, Cannon, Holloman AF bases; Los Alamos Scientific Laboratory; White Sands Missile Range; Natl. Solar Observatory; Natl. Radio Astronomy Observatory, Sandia National Laboratories.

Energy. Electricity production (1997, kWh, by source): Coal: 27.1 bil; Petroleum: 21 mil; Gas: 3.2 bil; Hydroelectric: 259 mil.

State data. Motto: Crescit Eundo (It grows as it goes). **Flower:** Yucca. **Bird:** Roadrunner. **Tree:** Piñon. **Song:** O, Fair New Mexico; Asi Es Nuevo Mexico. **Entered union** Jan. 6, 1912; rank, 47th. **State fair** at Albuquerque; mid-Sept.

History. Early inhabitants were peoples of the Mogollon and Anasazi civilizations, followed by the Pueblo peoples, Anasazi descendants. The nomadic Navajo and Apache tribes arrived c 15th cent. Franciscan Marcos de Niza and a former black slave, Estevanico, explored the area, 1539, seeking gold. First settlements were at San Juan Pueblo, 1598, and Santa Fe, 1610. Settlers alternately traded and fought with the Apache, Comanche, and Navajo. Trade on the Santa Fe Trail to Missouri started, 1821. The Mexican War was declared in May 1846; Gen. Stephen Kearny took Santa Fe without firing a shot, Aug. 18, 1846, declaring New Mexico part of the U.S. All Hispanic New Mexicans and Pueblo became U.S. citizens by terms of the 1848 treaty ending the war, but Congress denied the area statehood and created the territory of New Mexico, 1850. Pancho Villa raided Columbus, 1916, and U.S. troops were sent to the area. The world's first atomic bomb was exploded near Alamogordo, south of Santa Fe, 1945.

Tourist attractions. Carlsbad Caverns Natl. Park, with the largest natural underground chamber in the world; Santa Fe, oldest capital in U.S.; White Sands Natl. Monument, the largest gypsum deposit in the world; Chaco Culture National Historical Park; Acoma Pueblo, the "sky city," built atop a 357-ft mesa; Taos; Taos Art Colony; Taos Ski Valley; Ute Lake State Park; Shiprock.

Famous New Mexicans. Ben Abruzzo, Maxie Anderson, Billy (the Kid) Bonney, Kit Carson, Bob Foster, Peter Hurd, Archbishop Jean Baptiste Lamy, Nancy Lopez, Bill Mauldin, Georgia O'Keeffe, Kim Stanley, Al Unser, Bobby Unser, Lew Wallace.

Tourist information. New Mexico Dept. of Tourism, PO Box 20002, Santa Fe, NM 87503.

Toll-free travel information. 1-800-545-2040, ext. 751

Website. http://www.state.nm.us

Tourism website. http://www.newmexico.org

New York

Empire State

People. Population (1997): 18,137,226; rank: 3; **net change** (1990-97): 0.8%. **Pop. density** (1990): 381.0 per sq mi. **Racial/ethnic distrib.** (1990): 74.4% white; 15.9% black; 3.9% Asian; 12.3% Hispanic.

Geography. Total area: 53,989 sq mi; rank: 27. **Land area:** 47,224 sq mi; rank: 30. **Acres forested:** 18,713,000. **Location:** Middle Atlantic state, bordered by the New England states, Atlantic Ocean, New Jersey and Pennsylvania, Lakes Ontario and Erie, and Canada. **Climate:** variable; the SE region moderated by the ocean. **Topography:** highest and most rugged mountains in the NE Adirondack upland; St. Lawrence-Champlain lowlands extend from Lake Ontario NE along the Canadian border; Hudson-Mohawk lowland follows the flows of the rivers N and W, 10-30 mi wide; Atlantic coastal plain in the SE; Appalachian Highlands, covering half the state westward from the Hudson Valley, include the Catskill Mts., Finger Lakes; plateau of Erie-Ontario lowlands. **Capital:** Albany.

Economy. Chief industries: manufacturing, finance, communications, tourism, transportation, services. **Principal manufactured goods:** books & periodicals, clothing & apparel, pharmaceuticals, machinery, instruments, toys & sporting goods, electronic equipment, automotive & aircraft components. **Chief crops:** apples, grapes, strawberries, cherries, pears, onions, potatoes, cabbage, sweet corn, green beans, cauliflower, field corn, hay, wheat, oats, dry beans. **Products:** milk, cheese, maple syrup, wine. **Livestock** (Jan. 1998): 1.5 mil cattle/calves; 65,000 sheep/lambs; (Dec. 1997) 67,000 hogs/pigs; (Dec. 1997) 4.5 mil chickens (excl. broilers); (Dec. 1996) 1.5 mil broilers. **Timber/lumber** (1997): birch, sugar and red maple, basswood, hemlock, pine, oak, ash; 565 mil bd. ft. **Nonfuel minerals** (est. 1997): $904 mil; mostly crushed stone, portland cement, salt, sand & gravel, zinc. **Commercial fishing** (1997): $96.8 mil. **Chief ports:** New York, Buffalo, Albany. **Internat. airports at:** New York, Buffalo, Syracuse, Massena, Ogdensburg, Watertown, Niagara Falls, Newburgh. **Value of construction** (1997): $15.8 bil. **Gross state product** (1996): $613.3 bil. **Employment distrib.** (May 1998): 34.1% serv.; 20.4% trade; 16.9% govt.; 11.3% mfg. **Per cap. pers. income** (1997): $30,752. **Sales tax** (1998): 4%. **Unemployment** (1997): 6.4%. **Tourism expends.** (1996): $31.3 bil. **Lottery** (1997): total sales: $4.0 bil; net income: $1.5 bil.

Finance. FDIC-insured commercial banks (1997): 153. **Deposits:** $630.7 bil. **FDIC-insured savings institutions** (1997): 97. **Assets:** $115.1 bil.

Federal govt. Fed. civ. employees (Mar. 1997): 59,557. **Avg. salary:** $42,827. **Notable fed. facilities:** West Point Military Academy; Merchant Marine Academy; Ft. Drum; Rome Labs.; Watervliet Arsenal.

Energy. Electricity production (1997, kWh, by source): Coal: 21.8 bil; Petroleum: 8.1 bil; Gas: 20.7 bil; Hydroelectric: 27.9 bil; Nuclear: 29.6 bil.

State data. Motto: Excelsior (Ever upward). **Flower:** Rose. **Bird:** Bluebird. **Tree:** Sugar maple. **Song:** I Love New York. **Eleventh** of the original 13 states to ratify the Constitution, July 26, 1788. **State fair** at Syracuse; late Aug.-early Sept.

History. Algonquians including the Mahican, Wappinger, and Lenni Lenape inhabited the region, as did the Iroquoian Mohawk, Oneida, Onondaga, Cayuga, and Seneca tribes, who established the League of the Five Nations. In 1609, Henry Hudson visited the river named for him, and Champlain explored the lake named for him. The first permanent settlement was Dutch, near present-day Albany, 1624. New Amsterdam was settled, 1626, at the S tip of Manhattan Island. A British fleet seized New Netherland, 1664. Ninety-two of the 300 or more engagements of the American Revolution were fought in New York, including the Battle of Bemis Heights-Saratoga, 1777, a turning point of the war. Completion of Erie Canal, 1825, established the state as a gateway to the West. The first woman's rights convention was held in Seneca Falls, 1848.

Tourist attractions. New York City; Adirondack and Catskill Mts.; Finger Lakes; Great Lakes; Thousand Islands; Niagara Falls; Saratoga Springs; Philipsburg Manor, Sunnyside (Washington Irving's home), the Dutch Church of Sleepy Hollow, all in Tarrytown area; Corning Glass Center and Steuben factory, Corning; Fenimore House, Natl. Baseball Hall of Fame and Museum, both in Cooperstown; Ft. Ticonderoga overlooking Lakes George and Champlain; Empire State Plaza, Albany; Lake Placid; Franklin D. Roosevelt Natl. Historic Site, including the Roosevelt Library, Hyde Park; Long Island beaches; Theodore Roosevelt estate, Sagamore Hill, Oyster Bay; Turning Stone Casino.

Famous New Yorkers. Woody Allen, Susan B. Anthony, James Baldwin, Lucille Ball, Benjamin Cardozo, De Witt Clinton, Peter Cooper, Aaron Copland, George Eastman, Millard Fillmore, Lou Gehrig, George and Ira Gershwin, Ruth Bader Ginsberg, Rudolph Giuliani, Julia Ward Howe, Charles Evans Hughes, Washington Irving, Henry and William James, John Jay, Edward Koch, Fiorello La Guardia, Herman Melville, J. Pierpont Morgan Jr., Joyce Carol Oates, Eugene O'Neill, Colin Powell, Nancy Reagan, John D. Rockefeller, Nelson Rockefeller, Eleanor Roosevelt, Franklin D. Roosevelt, Theodore Roosevelt, J. D. Salinger, Jerry Seinfeld, Paul Simon, Alfred E. Smith, Elizabeth Cady Stanton, Donald Trump, William (Boss) Tweed, Martin Van Buren, Gore Vidal, Edith Wharton, Walt Whitman.

Tourist information. Empire State Development, Travel Information Center, 1 Commerce Plaza, Albany, NY 12245.

Toll-free travel information. 1-800-CALLNYS from U.S. states and territories and Canada; 1-518-474-4116 from other areas.

Website. http://www.empire.state.ny.us

Tourism website. http://www.iloveny.state.ny.us

North Carolina

Tar Heel State, Old North State

People. Population (1997): 7,425,183; rank: 11; **net change** (1990-97): 12.0%. **Pop. density** (1990): 136.1 per sq mi. **Racial/ethnic distrib.** (1990): 75.6% white; 22.0% black; 1.2% Amer. Indian; 1.2% Hispanic.

Geography. Total area: 52,672 sq mi; rank: 29. **Land area:** 48,718 sq mi; rank: 29. **Acres forested:** 19,278,000. **Location:** South Atlantic state bounded by Virginia, South Carolina, Georgia, Tennessee, and the Atlantic Ocean. **Climate:** sub-tropical in SE, medium-continental in mountain region; tempered by the Gulf Stream and the mountains in W. **Topography:** coastal plain and tidewater, two-fifths of state, extending to the fall line of the rivers; piedmont plateau, another two-fifths, of gentle to rugged hills; southern Appalachian Mts. contains the Blue Ridge and Great Smoky Mts. **Capital:** Raleigh.

Economy. Chief industries: manufacturing, agriculture, tourism. **Chief manuf. goods:** food products, textiles, industrial machinery and equipment, electrical and electronic equipment, furniture, tobacco products, apparel. **Chief crops:** tobacco, cotton, soybeans, corn, food grains, wheat, peanuts, sweet potatoes. **Livestock** (Jan. 1998): 1.1 mil cattle/calves; 11,000 sheep/lambs; (Dec. 1997) 9.7 mil hogs/pigs; (Dec. 1997) 17.2 mil chickens (excl. broilers); (Dec. 1996) 681.1 mil broilers. **Timber/lumber** (1997): yellow pine, oak, hickory, poplar, maple; 2.4 bil bd. ft. **Nonfuel minerals** (est. 1997): $758 mil; mostly crushed stone, phosphate rock, sand & gravel, clays. **Commercial fishing** (1997): $101.7 mil. **Internat. airports at:** Charlotte/Douglas, Raleigh/Durham. **Chief ports:** Morehead City, Wilmington. **Value of construction** (1997): $14.0 bil. **Gross state product** (1996): $204.2 bil. **Employment distrib.** (May 1998): 24.5% serv.; 22.2% mfg.; 22.6% trade; 15.9% govt. **Per cap. pers. income** (1997): $23,345. **Sales tax** (1998): 4%. **Unemployment** (1997): 3.6%. **Tourism expends.** (1996): $10.2 bil.

Finance. FDIC-insured commercial banks (1997): 60. **Deposits**: $270.9 bil. **FDIC-insured savings institutions** (1997): 59. **Assets:** $8.0 bil.

Federal govt. Fed. civ. employees (Mar. 1997): 31,028. **Avg. salary:** $38,466. **Notable fed. facilities:** Ft. Bragg; Camp LeJeune Marine Base; U.S. EPA Research and Development Labs, Cherry Point Marine Corps Air Station; Natl. Humanities Center; Natl. Inst. of Environmental Health Science; Natl. Center for Health Statistics Lab, Research Triangle Park.

Energy. Electricity production (1997, kWh, by source): Coal: 70.2 bil; Petroleum: 212 mil; Gas: 377 mil; Hydroelectric: 4.1 bil; Nuclear: 32.5 bil.

State data. Motto: Esse Quam Videri (To be rather than to seem). **Flower:** Dogwood. **Bird:** Cardinal. **Tree:** Pine. **Song:** The Old North State. **Twelfth** of the original 13 states to ratify the Constitution, Nov. 21, 1789. **State fair** at Raleigh; mid-Oct.

History. Algonquian, Siouan, and Iroquoian peoples lived in the region at the time of European contact. The first English colony in America was the first of 2 established by Sir Walter Raleigh on Roanoke Island, 1585 and 1587. The first group returned to England; the second, the "Lost Colony," disappeared without a trace. Permanent settlers came from Virginia, c 1660. Roused by British repression, the colonists drove out the royal governor, 1775. The province's congress was the first to vote for independence; ten regiments were furnished to the Continental Army. Cornwallis's forces were defeated at Kings Mountain, 1780, and forced out after Guilford Courthouse, 1781. The state seceded in 1861, and provided more troops to the Confederacy than any other state; readmitted in 1868.

Tourist attractions. Cape Hatteras and Cape Lookout natl. seashores; Great Smoky Mts.; Guilford Courthouse and Moore's Creek parks; 66 American Revolution battle sites; Bennett Place, near Durham, where Gen. Joseph Johnston surrendered the last Confederate army to Gen. William Sherman; Ft. Raleigh, Roanoke Island, where Virginia Dare, first child of English parents in the New World, was born Aug. 18, 1587; Wright Brothers Natl. Memorial, Kitty Hawk; Battleship *North Carolina*, Wilmington; NC Zoo, Asheboro; NC Symphony, NC Museum, Raleigh; Carl Sandburg Home, Hendersonville, Biltmore House & Gardens, Asheville.

Famous North Carolinians. David Brinkley, Shirley Caesar, John Coltrane, Elizabeth Dole, Ava Gardner, Richard J. Gatling, Billy Graham, Andy Griffith, O. Henry, Andrew Jackson, Andrew Johnson, Michael Jordan, Wm. Rufus King, Charles Kuralt, Dolley Madison, Theolonius Monk, Edward R. Murrow, Arnold Palmer, Richard Petty, James K. Polk, Carl Sandburg, Enos Slaughter, Dean Smith, James Taylor, Thomas Wolfe, Orville and Wilbur Wright.

Tourist information. North Carolina Division of Tourism, Film & Sports Development, 301 N. Wilmington St., Raleigh, NC 27601.

Toll-free travel information. 1-800-VISITNC.

Website. http://www.state.nc.us

Tourism website. http://www.visitnc.com

North Dakota

Peace Garden State

People. Population (1997): 640,883; rank: 47; **net change** (1990-97): 0.3%. **Pop. density** (1990): 9.3 per sq mi. **Racial/ethnic distrib.** (1990): 94.6% white; 0.6% black; 4.1% Amer. Indian; 0.7% Hispanic.

Geography. Total area: 70,704 sq mi; rank: 18. **Land area:** 68,994 sq mi; rank: 17. **Acres forested:** 462,000. **Location:** West North Central state, situated exactly in the middle of North America, bounded on the N by Canada, on the E by Minnesota, on the S by South Dakota, on the W by Montana. **Climate:** continental, with a wide range of temperature and moderate rainfall. **Topography:** Central Lowland in the E comprises the flat Red River Valley and the Rolling Drift Prairie; Missouri Plateau of the Great Plains on the W. **Capital:** Bismarck.

Economy. Chief industries: agriculture, mining, tourism, manufacturing, telecommunications, energy, food processing. **Chief manuf. goods:** farm equipment, processed foods, fabricated metal, high-tech. electronics. **Chief crops:** spring wheat, durum, barley, flaxseed, oats, potatoes, dry edible beans, honey, soybeans, sugar beets, sunflowers, hay. **Livestock** (Jan. 1998): 1.8 mil cattle/calves; 110,000 sheep/lambs; (Dec. 1997) 165,000 hogs/pigs; (Dec. 1997) 310,000 chickens (excl. broilers). **Timber/lumber:** (1997) oak, ash, cottonwood, aspen; 1 mil bd. ft. **Nonfuel minerals** (est. 1997): $31.6 mil; mostly sand & gravel, lime, clays, gemstones. **Internat. airports at:** Fargo, Grand Forks, Bismarck, Minot, Pembina, Dunseith. **Value of construction** (1997): $788 mil. **Gross state product** (1996): $15.7 bil. **Employment distrib.** (May 1998): 28.1% serv.; 25.4% trade; 22.2% govt.; 7.6% mfg. **Per cap. pers. income** (1997): $20,271. **Sales tax** (1998): 5%. **Unemployment** (1997): 2.5%. **Tourism expends.** (1996): $1.1 bil.

Finance. FDIC-insured commercial banks (1997): 117. **Deposits:** $7.6 bil. **FDIC-insured savings institutions** (1997): 2. **Assets:** $658 mil.

Federal govt. Fed. civ. employees (Mar. 1997): 4,935. **Avg. salary:** $37,702. **Notable fed. facilities:** Strategic Air Command Base; Northern Prairie Wildlife Research Center; Garrison Dam; Theodore Roosevelt Natl. Park; Grand Forks Energy Research Center; Ft. Union Natl. Historic Site.

Energy. Electricity production (1997, kWh, by source): Coal: 26.3 bil; Petroleum: 86 mil; Hydroelectric: 3.3 bil.

State data. Motto: Liberty and union, now and forever, one and inseparable. **Flower:** Wild prairie rose. **Bird:** Western meadowlark. **Tree:** American elm. **Song:** North Dakota Hymn. **Entered union** Nov. 2, 1889; rank, 39th. **State fair** at Minot; July.

History. At the time of European contact, the Ojibwa, Yanktonai and Teton Sioux, Mandan, Arikara, and Hidatsa peoples lived in the region. Pierre de Varennes was the first French fur trader in the area, 1738, followed later by the English. The U.S. acquired half the territory in the Louisiana Purchase, 1803. Lewis and Clark built Ft. Mandan, near present-day Stanton, 1804-5, and wintered there. In 1818, American ownership of the other half was confirmed by agreement with Britain. The first permanent settlement was at Pembina, 1812. Missouri River steamboats reached the area, 1832, the first railroad, 1873, bringing many homesteaders. The "bonanza farm" craze of the 1870s-80s attracted many settlers. The state was first to hold a national Presidential primary, 1912.

Tourist attractions. North Dakota Heritage Center, Bismarck; Bonanzaville, Fargo; Ft. Union Trading Post Natl. Historic Site; Lake Sakakawea; Intl. Peace Garden; Theodore Roosevelt Natl. Park, including Elkhorn Ranch, Badlands; Ft. Abraham Lincoln State Park and Museum, near Mandan; Dakota Dinosaur Museum, Dickinson; Knife River Indian Villages-National Historic Site.

Famous North Dakotans. Maxwell Anderson, Angie Dickinson, John Bernard Flannagan, Phil Jackson, Louis L'Amour, Peggy Lee, Eric Sevareid, Vilhjalmur Stefansson, Lawrence Welk.

Greater North Dakota Association (Chamber of Commerce). PO Box 2639, 2000 Schafer St., Bismarck, ND 58501.

Toll-free travel information. 1-800-HELLO-ND

Website. http://www.state.nd.us

Tourism website. http//www.glness.com/tourism

Ohio

Buckeye State

People. Population (1997): 11,186,331; rank: 7; **net change** (1990-97): 3.1%. **Pop. density** (1990): 264.9 per sq mi. **Racial/ethnic distrib.** (1990): 87.8% white; 10.6% black; 1.3% Hispanic.

Geography. Total area: 44,828 sq mi; rank: 34. **Land area:** 40,953 sq mi; rank: 35. **Acres forested:** 7,863,000. **Location:** East North Central state bounded on the N by Michigan and Lake Erie; on the E and S by Pennsylvania, West Virginia, and Kentucky; on the W by Indiana. **Climate:** temperate but variable; weather subject to much precipitation. **Topography:** generally rolling plain; Allegheny plateau in E; Lake Erie plains extend southward; central plains in the W. **Capital:** Columbus.

Economy. Chief industries: manufacturing, trade, services. **Chief manuf. goods:** transportation equipment, machinery, primary and fabricated metal products. **Chief crops:** corn, hay, winter wheat, oats, soybeans. **Livestock** (Jan. 1998): 1.4 mil cattle/calves; 117,000 sheep/lambs; (Dec. 1997) 1.6 hogs/pigs; (Dec. 1997) 33.1 mil chickens (excl. broilers); (Dec. 1996) 48.6 mil broilers. **Timber/lumber** (1997): oak, ash, maple, walnut, beech; 401 mil bd. ft. **Nonfuel minerals** (est. 1997): $984 mil; mostly crushed stone, sand & gravel, salt, lime, portland cement. **Commercial fishing** (1997): $2.2 mil. **Chief ports:** Toledo, Conneaut, Cleveland, Ashtabula. **Internat. airports at:** Cleveland, Cincinnati, Columbus, Dayton. **Value of construction** (1997): $14.7 bil. **Gross state product** (1996): $304.4 bil. **Employment distrib.** (May 1998): 27.7% serv.; 24.2% trade; 20% mfg.; 14% govt. **Per cap. pers. income** (1997): $24,661. **Sales tax** (1998): 5%. **Unemployment** (1997): 4.6%. **Tourism expends.** (1996): $11.1 bil. **Lottery** (1997): total sales: $2.3 bil; net income: $752 mil.

Finance. FDIC-insured commercial banks (1997): 235. **Deposits:** $154.4 bil. **FDIC-insured savings institutions** (1997): 150. **Assets:** $59.4 bil.

Federal govt. Fed. civ. employees (Mar. 1997): 45,409. **Avg. salary:** $44,790. **Notable fed. facilities:** Wright Patterson AFB; Defense Construction Supply Center; Lewis Research Ctr.; Portsmouth Gaseous Diffusion Plant.

Energy. Electricity production (1997, kWh, by source): Coal: 124.9 bil; Petroleum: 273 mil; Gas: 228 mil; Hydroelectric: 507 mil; Nuclear: 15.3 mil.

State data. Motto: With God, all things are possible. **Flower:** Scarlet carnation. **Bird:** Cardinal. **Tree:** Buckeye. **Song:** Beautiful Ohio. **Entered union** Mar. 1, 1803; rank, 17th. **State fair** at Columbus; Aug.

History. Wyandot, Delaware, Miami, and Shawnee peoples sparsely occupied the area when the first Europeans arrived. La Salle visited the region, 1669, and France claimed the area, 1682. Around 1730, traders from Pennsylvania and Virginia entered the area; the French and their Native American allies sought to drive them out. France ceded its claim, 1763, to Britain. During the American Revolution, George Rogers Clark seized British posts and held the region, until Britain gave up its claim, 1883, in the Treaty of Paris. The region became U.S. territory after the American Revolution. First organized settlement was at Marietta, 1788. Indian warfare ended with Anthony Wayne's victory at Fallen Timbers, 1794. In the War of 1812, Oliver Hazard Perry's victory on Lake Erie and William Henry Harrison's invasion of Canada, 1813, ended British incursions.

Tourist attractions. Mound City Group Natl. Monuments, a group of 24 prehistoric Indian burial mounds; Neil Armstrong Air and Space Museum, Wapakoneta; Air Force Museum, Dayton; Pro Football Hall of Fame, Canton; King's Island amusement park, Mason; Lake Erie Islands, Cedar Point amusement park, both Sandusky; birthplaces, homes of, and memorials to U.S. Pres.s W. H. Harrison, Grant, Garfield, Hayes, McKinley, Harding, Taft, Benjamin Harrison; Amish Region, Tuscarawas/Holmes counties; German Village, Columbus; Sea World, Aurora; Jack Nicklaus Sports Center, Mason; Bob Evans Farm, Rio Grande; Rock and Roll Hall of Fame and Museum, Cleveland.

Famous Ohioans. Sherwood Anderson, Neil Armstrong, George Bellows, Ambrose Bierce, Erma Bombeck, Hart Crane, George Coster, Clarence Darrow, Paul Laurence Dunbar, Thomas Edison, Clark Gable, John Glenn, Bob Hope, William Dean Howells, Toni Morrison, Jack Nicklaus, Jesse Owens, Pontiac, Eddie Rickenbacker, John D. Rockefeller Sr. and Jr., Roy Rogers, Pete Rose, Arthur Schlesinger Jr., Gen. William Sherman, Steven Spielberg, Gloria Steinem, Harriet Beecher Stowe, Charles Taft, Robert A. Taft, William H. Taft, Tecumseh, James Thurber, Orville and Wilbur Wright.

Chamber of Commerce. PO Box 15159. 230 E. Town St., Columbus, OH 43215-0159.

Toll-free travel information. 1-800-BUCKEYE.

Website. http://www.state.oh.us

Tourism website. http://www.ohiotourism.com

Oklahoma

Sooner State

People. Population (1997): 3,317,091; rank: 27; **net change** (1990-97): 5.5%. **Pop. density** (1990): 45.8 per sq mi. **Racial/ethnic distrib.** (1990): 82.1% white; 7.4% black; 8.0% Amer. Indian; 2.7% Hispanic.

Geography. Total area: 69,903 sq mi; rank: 20. **Land area:** 68,679 sq mi; rank: 19. **Acres forested:** 7,539,000. **Location:** West South Central state bounded on the N by Colorado and Kansas; on the E by Missouri and Arkansas; on the S and W by Texas and New Mexico. **Climate:** temperate; southern humid belt merging with colder northern continental; humid eastern and dry western zones. **Topography:** high plains predominate in the W, hills and small mountains in the E; the east central region is dominated by the Arkansas R. Basin, and the Red R. Plains, in the S. **Capital:** Oklahoma City.

Economy. Chief industries: manufacturing, mineral and energy exploration and production, agriculture, services. **Chief manuf. goods:** nonelectrical machinery, transportation equipment, food products, fabricated metal products. **Chief crops:** wheat, cotton, hay, peanuts, grain sorghum, soybeans, corn, pecans. **Livestock** (Jan. 1998): 5.5 mil cattle/calves; 70,000 sheep/lambs; (Dec. 1997) 1.6 hogs/pigs; (Dec. 1997) 4.8 mil chickens (excl. broilers); (Dec. 1996) 204.0 mil broilers. **Timber/lumber:** pine, oak, hickory. **Nonfuel minerals** (est. 1997): $411 mil; mostly crushed stone, portland cement, sand & gravel, iodine. **Chief ports:** Catoosa, Muskogee. **Internat. airports at:** Oklahoma City, Tulsa. **Value of construction** (1997): $3.1 bil. **Gross state product** (1996): $72.8 bil. **Employment distrib.** (May 1998): 27.6% serv.; 23% trade; 19.8% govt.; 13% mfg. **Per cap. pers. income** (1997): $20,556. **Sales tax** (1998): 4.5%. **Unemployment** (1997): 4.1%. **Tourism expends.** (1996): $3.3 bil.

Finance. FDIC-insured commercial banks (1997): 320. **Deposits:** $28.0 bil. **FDIC-insured savings institutions** (1997): 12. **Assets:** $6.4 bil.

Federal govt. Fed. civ. employees (Mar. 1997): 31,272. **Avg. salary:** $39,311. **Notable fed. facilities:** Federal Aviation Agency and Tinker AFB, Oklahoma City; Ft. Sill, Lawton; Altus AFB; Vance AFB.

Energy. Electricity production (1997, kWh, by source): Coal: 33.0 bil; Petroleum: 13 mil; Gas: 12.5 bil; Hydroelectric: 2.8 bil.

State data. Motto: Labor Omnia Vincit (Labor conquers all things). **Flower:** Mistletoe. **Bird:** Scissor-tailed flycatcher. **Tree:** Redbud. **Song:** Oklahoma! **Entered union** Nov. 16, 1907; rank, 46th. **State fair** at Oklahoma City; last 2 full weeks of Sept.

History. The region was sparsely inhabited by Native American tribes when Coronado, the first European, arrived in 1541; in the 16th and 17th cent., French traders visited. Part of the Louisiana Purchase, 1803, Oklahoma was established as Indian Territory (but not given territorial government). It became home to the "Five Civilized Tribes"—Cherokee, Choctaw, Chickasaw, Creek, and Seminole—after the forced removal of Indians from the eastern U.S., 1828-46. The land was also used by Comanche, Osage, and other Plains Indians. As white settlers pressed west, land was opened for homesteading by runs and lottery, the first run on Apr. 22, 1889. The most famous run was to the Cherokee Outlet, 1893.

Tourist attractions. Cherokee Heritage Center, Tahlequah; White Water Bay and Frontier City theme pks., both Oklahoma City; Will Rogers Memorial, Claremore; Natl. Cowboy Hall of Fame and Remington Park Race Track, both Oklahoma City; Ft. Gibson Stockade, near Muskogee; Ouachita Natl. Forest; Tulsa's art deco district; Wichita Mts. Wildlife Refuge, Lawton; Woolaroc Museum & Wildlife Preserve, Bartlesville; Sequoyah's Home Site, near Sallisaw; Philbrook Museum of Art and Gilcrease Museum, both Tulsa.

Famous Oklahomans. Troy Aikman, Carl Albert, Gene Autry, Johnny Bench, Garth Brooks, William "Hopalong Cassidy" Boyd, Lon Chaney, Walter Cronkite, L. Gordon Cooper, Jerome "Dizzy" Dean, Ralph Ellison, John Hope Franklin, James Garner, Geronimo, Woody Guthrie, Paul Harvey, Ron Howard, Gen. Patrick J. Hurley, Jeane Kirkpatrick, Louis L'Amour, Shannon Lucid, Mickey Mantle, Reba McEntire, Wiley Post, Tony Randall, Oral Roberts, Will Rogers, Maria Tallchief, Jim Thorpe.

Chamber of Commerce. Chamber of Commerce, 330 NE 10th, Oklahoma City, OK 73104.

Tourism Dept. PO Box 60789, Oklahoma City, OK 73146-0789.

Toll-free travel information. 1-800-652-6552.

Website. http://www.state.ok.us

Tourism website. http://www.otrd.state.ok.us

Oregon

Beaver State

People. Population (1997): 3,243,487; rank: 29; **net change** (1990-97): 14.1%. **Pop. density** (1990): 29.6 per sq mi. **Racial/ethnic distrib.** (1990): 92.8% white; 1.6% black; 4.0% Hispanic.

Geography. Total area: 97,132 sq mi; rank: 10. **Land area:** 96,002 sq mi; rank: 10. **Acres forested:** 27,997,000. **Location:** Pacific state, bounded on N by Washington; on E by Idaho; on S by Nevada and California; on W by the Pacific. **Climate:** coastal mild and humid climate; continental dryness and extreme temperatures in the interior. **Topography:** Coast Range of rugged mountains; fertile Willamette R. Valley to E and S; Cascade Mt. Range of volcanic peaks E of the valley; plateau E of Cascades, remaining two-thirds of state. **Capital:** Salem.

Economy. Chief industries: manufacturing, services, trade, finance, insurance, real estate, government, construction. **Chief manuf. goods:** electronics & semiconductors, lumber & wood products metals, transportation equipment, processed food, paper. **Chief crops:** greenhouse, hay, wheat, grass seed, potatoes, onions, Christmas trees, pears, mint. **Livestock** (Jan. 1998): 1.4 mil cattle/calves; 265,000 sheep/lambs; (Dec. 1997) 35,000 hogs/pigs; (Dec. 1997) 3.6 mil chickens (excl. broilers); (Dec. 1996) 21.3 mil broilers. **Timber/lumber** (1997): Douglas fir, hemlock, ponderosa pine; 5.9 bil bd. ft. **Nonfuel minerals** (est. 1997): $272 mil; mostly sand & gravel, crushed stone, portland cement, diatomite, lime. **Commercial fishing** (1997): $80.4 mil. **Chief ports:** Portland, Astoria, Coos Bay. **Internat. airports at:** Portland, Klamath Falls. **Value of construction** (1997): $6.0 bil. **Gross state product** (1996): $87.0 bil. **Employment distrib.** (May 1998): 26.5% serv.; 24.8% trade; 16.5% govt.; 15.8% mfg. **Per cap. pers. income** (1997): $24,393. **Sales tax:** none. **Unemployment** (1997): 5.8%. **Tourism expends.** (1996): $4.9 bil. **Lottery** (1997): total sales: $688.8 mil; net income: $301.2 mil.

Finance. FDIC-insured commercial banks (1997): 41. **Deposits:** $4.7 bil. **FDIC-insured savings institutions** (1997): 7. **Assets:** $14.8 bil.

Federal govt. Fed. civ. employees (Mar. 1997): 17,966. **Avg. salary:** $41,756. **Notable fed. facilities:** Bonneville Power Administration.

Energy. Electricity production (1997, kWh, by source): Coal: 1.5 bil; Petroleum: 11 mil; Gas: 1.3 bil; Hydroelectric: 46.3 bil.

State data. Motto: She flies with her own wings. **Flower:** Oregon grape. **Bird:** Western meadowlark. **Tree:** Douglas fir. **Song:** Oregon, My Oregon. **Entered union** Feb. 14, 1859; rank, 33d. **State fair** at Salem; 12 days ending with Labor Day.

History. More than 100 Native American tribes inhabited the area at the time of European contact, including the Chinook, Yakima, Cayuse, Modoc, and Nez Percé. Capt. Robert Gray sighted and sailed into the Columbia River, 1792; Lewis and Clark, traveling overland, wintered at its mouth, 1805-6; John Jacob Astor established a trading post in the Columbia River region, 1811. Settlers arrived in the Willamette Valley, 1834. In 1843, the first large wave of settlers arrived via the Oregon Trail. Early in the 20th cent., the "Oregon System"—political reforms that included the initiative, referendum, recall, direct primary, and woman suffrage—was adopted.

Tourist attractions. John Day Fossil Beds Natl. Monument; Columbia River Gorge; Timberline Lodge, Mt. Hood Natl. Forest; Crater Lake Natl. Park; Oregon Dunes Natl. Recreation Area; Ft. Clatsop Natl. Memorial; Oregon Caves Natl. Monument; Oregon Museum of Science and Industry, Portland; Shakespearean Festival, Ashland; High Desert Museum, Bend; Multnomah Falls; Diamond Lake.

Famous Oregonians. Ernest Bloch, Raymond Carver, Ernest Haycox, Chief Joseph, Phil Knight, Edwin Markham, Tom McCall, Dr. John McLoughlin, Joaquin Miller, Bob Packwood, Linus Pauling, John Reed, Alberto Salazar, Mary Decker Slaney, William Simon U'Ren.

Tourist information. Economic Development Department, 775 Summer St. NE, Salem, OR 97310.

Toll-free travel information. 1-800-547-7842.

Website. http://www.state.or.us

Tourism website. http://www.traveloregon.com

Pennsylvania

Keystone State

People. Population (1997): 12,019,661; rank: 5; **net change** (1990-97): 1.2%. **Pop. density** (1990): 265.1 per sq mi. **Racial/ethnic distrib.** (1990): 88.5% white; 9.2% black; 2.0% Hispanic.

Geography. Total area: 46,058 sq mi; rank: 33. **Land area:** 44,820 sq mi; rank: 32. **Acres forested:** 16,969,000. **Location:** Middle Atlantic state, bordered on the E by the Delaware R.; on the S by the Mason-Dixon Line; on the W by West Virginia and Ohio; on the N/NE by Lake Erie and New York. **Climate:** continental with wide fluctuations in seasonal temperatures. **Topography:** Allegheny Mts. run SW to NE, with Piedmont and Coast Plain in the SE triangle; Allegheny Front a diagonal spine across the state's center; N and W rugged plateau falls to Lake Erie Lowland. **Capital:** Harrisburg.

Economy. Chief industries: agribusiness, advanced manufacturing, health care, travel & tourism, depository institutions, biotechnology, printing & publishing, research & consulting, trucking & warehousing, transportation by air, engineering & management, legal services. **Chief manuf. goods:** fabricated metal products; industrial machinery & equipment, transportation equipment, rubber & plastics, electronic equipment, chemicals & pharmaceuticals, lumber & wood products, stone, clay, & glass products. **Chief crops:** corn, hay, mushrooms, apples, potatoes, winter wheat, oats, vegetables, tobacco, grapes, peaches. **Livestock** (Jan. 1998): 1.8 mil cattle/calves; 94,000 sheep/lambs; (Dec. 1997) 1.0 mil hogs/pigs; (Dec. 1997) 27.0 mil chickens (excl. broilers); (Dec. 1996) 128.2 mil broilers. **Timber/lumber** (1997): pine, oak, maple; 1.1 bil bd. ft. **Nonfuel minerals** (est. 1997): $1.24 bil; mostly crushed stone, portland cement, lime, sand & gravel, masonry cement. **Commercial fishing** (1997): $11,000. **Chief ports:** Philadelphia, Pittsburgh, Erie. **Internat. airports at:** Allentown, Erie, Harrisburg, Philadelphia, Pittsburgh, Wilkes-Barre/Scranton. **Value of construction** (1997): $10.1 bil. **Gross state product** (1996): $328.5 bil. **Employment distrib.** (May 1998): 31.8% serv.; 22.5% trade; 17.2% mfg.; 13.1% govt. **Per cap. pers. income** (1997): $26,058. **Sales tax** (1998): 6%. **Unemployment** (1997): 5.2%. **Tourism expends.** (1996): $13.1 bil. **Lottery** (1997): total sales: $1.71 bil; net income: $701.6 mil.

Finance. FDIC-insured commercial banks (1997): 212. **Deposits:** $194.9 bil. **FDIC-insured savings institutions** (1997): 117. **Assets:** $52.3 bil.

Federal govt. Fed. civ. employees (Mar. 1997): 64,954. **Avg. salary:** $39,768. **Notable fed. facilities:** Carlisle Barracks; Army War College; Naval Inventory Control Point, Phila. and Mechanicsbrg; Defense Personnel Supply Center, Phila.; Defense Distribution Center, New Cumberland; Tobyhanna Army Depot; Letterkenny Army Depot; NAS Willow Grove; 911th Air Wing, Pittsburgh; Naval Surface Warfare Center, Phila.; Charles E. Kelly Support Facility.

Energy. Electricity production (1997, kWh, by source): Coal: 105.4 bil; Petroleum: 2.3 bil; Gas: 611 mil; Hydroelectric: 1.1 bil; Nuclear: 67.7 bil.

State data. Motto: Virtue, liberty and independence. **Flower:** Mountain laurel. **Bird:** Ruffed grouse. **Tree:** Hemlock. **Second** of the original 13 states to ratify the Constitution, Dec. 12, 1787. **State fair** at Harrisburg; 2d week in Jan. at State Farm Show Building.

History. At the time of European contact, Lenni Lenape (Delaware), Shawnee and Iroquoian Susquehannocks, Erie, and Seneca occupied the region. Swedish explorers established the first permanent settlement, 1643, on Tinicum Island. In 1655, the Dutch seized the settlement but lost it to the British, 1664. The region was given by Charles II to William Penn, 1681. Philadelphia ("brotherly love") was the capital of the colonies during most of the American Revolution, and of the U.S., 1790-1800. Philadelphia was taken by the British, 1777; Washington's troops encamped at Valley Forge in the bitter winter of 1777-78. The Declaration of Independence, 1776, and the Constitution, 1787, were signed in Philadelphia. The Civil War battle of Gettysburg, July 1-3, 1863, marked a turning point, favoring Union forces.

Tourist attractions. Independence Natl. Historic Park, Franklin Institute Science Museum, Philadelphia Museum of Art, all in Philadelphia; Valley Forge Natl. Historic Park; Gettysburg Natl. Military Park; Pennsylvania Dutch Country; Hershey; Duquesne Incline, Carnegie Institute, Heinz Hall, all in Pittsburgh; Pocono Mts.; Pennsylvania's Grand Canyon, Tioga County; Allegheny Natl. Forest; Laurel Highlands; Presque Isle State Park; Fallingwater, Ligonier; Johnstown; SteamTown U.S.A., Scranton; State Flagship Niagara, Erie; Oil Heritage Region, Northwest PA.

Famous Pennsylvanians. Marian Anderson, Maxwell Anderson, James Buchanan, Andrew Carnegie, Rachel Carson, Thomas Eakins, Stephen Foster, Benjamin Franklin, Robert Fulton, Martha Graham, Milton Hershey, Gene Kelly, Grace Kelly (Princess Grace of Monaco), George C. Marshall, John J. McCloy, Margaret Mead, Andrew W. Mellon, Robert E. Peary, John O'Hara, Mary Roberts Rinehart, Betsy Ross, Will Smith, Jimmy Stewart, Jim Thorpe, John Updike, Benjamin West.

Chamber of Business and Industry. 417 Walnut St., Harrisburg, PA 17120; 717-255-3252.

Toll-free travel information. 1-800-VISITPA.

Website. http://www.state.pa.us

Tourism website. http://www.state.pa.us/visit

Rhode Island

Little Rhody, Ocean State

People. Population (1997): 987,429; rank: 43; **net change** (1990-97): -1.6%. **Pop. density** (1990): 960.3 per sq mi. **Racial/ethnic distrib.** (1990): 91.4% white; 3.9% black; 4.6% Hispanic.

Geography. Total area: 1,231 sq mi; rank: 50. **Land area:** 1,045 sq mi; rank: 50. **Acres forested:** 401,000. **Location:** New England state. **Climate:** invigorating and changeable. **Topography:** eastern lowlands of Narragansett Basin; western uplands of flat and rolling hills. **Capital:** Providence.

Economy. Chief industries: services, manufacturing. **Chief manuf. goods:** costume jewelry, toys, machinery, textiles, electronics. **Chief crops:** nursery products, turf & vegetable production. **Livestock** (Jan. 1998): 6,500 cattle/calves; (Dec. 1997) 2,600 hogs/pigs; (Dec. 1997) 90,000 chickens (excl. broilers). **Timber/lumber:** (1997) oak; 11 mil bd. ft. **Nonfuel minerals** (est. 1997): $22.6 mil; mostly sand & gravel, crushed stone, gemstones. **Commercial fishing** (1997): $74.8 mil. **Chief ports:** Providence, Quonset Point, Newport. **Value of construction** (1997): $773 mil. **Gross state product** (1996): $25.6 bil. **Employment distrib.** (May 1998): 33.4% services; 21.7% trade; 17.3% mfg.; 14.5% govt. **Per cap. pers. income** (1997): $25,760. **Sales tax** (1998): 7%. **Unemployment** (1997): 5.3%. **Tourism expends.** (1996): $922 mil. **Lottery** (1997): total sales: $548.7 mil; net income: $100 mil.

Finance. FDIC-insured commercial banks (1997): 9. **Deposits:** $54.8 bil. **FDIC-insured savings institutions** (1997): 6. **Assets:** $1.6 bil.

Federal govt. Fed. civ. employees (Mar. 1997): 6,076. **Avg. salary:** $45,971. **Notable fed. facilities:** Naval War College; Naval Underwater Warfare Center; Natl. Marine Fisheries Laboratory; EPA Environmental Research Laboratory.

Energy. Electricity production (1997, kWh, by source): Petroleum: 17 mil; Gas: 3.5 bil.

State data. Motto: Hope. **Flower:** Violet. **Bird:** Rhode Island red. **Tree:** Red maple. **Song:** Rhode Island. **Thirteenth** of original 13 states to ratify the Constitution, May 29, 1790. **State fair** at Richmond; mid-Aug.

History. When the Europeans arrived Narragansett, Niantic, Nipmuc, and Wampanoag peoples lived in the region. Verrazano visited the area, 1524. The first permanent settlement was founded at Providence, 1636, by Roger Williams, who was exiled from the Massachusetts Bay Colony; Anne Hutchinson, also exiled, settled Portsmouth, 1638. Quaker and Jewish immigrants seeking freedom of worship began arriving, 1650s-60s. The colonists broke the power of the Narragansett in the Great Swamp Fight, 1675, the decisive battle in King Philip's War. British trade restrictions angered colonists, and they burned the British customs vessel *Gaspee*, 1772. The colony became the first to formally renounce all allegiance to King George III, May 4, 1776. Initially opposed to joining the Union, Rhode Island was the last of the 13 colonies to ratify the Constitution, 1790.

Tourist attractions. Newport mansions; yachting races including Newport to Bermuda; Block Island; Touro Synagogue, oldest in U.S., Newport; first Baptist Church in America, Providence; Slater Mill Historic Site, Pawtucket; Gilbert Stuart birthplace, Saunderstown.

Famous Rhode Islanders. Ambrose Burnside, George M. Cohan, Nelson Eddy, Jabez Gorham, Nathanael Greene, Christopher and Oliver La Farge, Matthew C. and Oliver Hazard Perry, Gilbert Stuart.

Tourist Information. Rhode Island Economic Development Corporation, One W. Exchange St., Providence, RI 02903.

Toll-free travel information. 1-800-556-2484.

Website. http://www.state.ri.us

Tourism website. http://visitrhodeisland.com

South Carolina

Palmetto State

People. Population (1997): 3,760,181; rank: 26; **net change** (1990-97): 7.9%. **Pop. density** (1990): 115.8 per sq mi. **Racial/ethnic distrib.** (1990): 69.0% white; 29.8% black; 0.9% Hispanic.

Geography. Total area: 31,189 sq mi; rank: 40. **Land area:** 30,111 sq mi; rank: 40. **Acres forested:** 12,257,000. **Location:** South Atlantic state, bordered by North Carolina on the N; Georgia on the SW and W; the Atlantic Ocean on the E, SE, and S. **Climate:** humid subtropical. **Topography:** Blue Ridge province in NW has highest peaks; piedmont lies between the mountains and the fall line; coastal plain covers two-thirds of the state. **Capital:** Columbia.

Economy. Chief industries: tourism, agriculture, manufacturing. **Chief manuf. goods:** textiles, chemicals and allied products, machinery and fabricated metal products, apparel and related products. **Chief crops:** tobacco, cotton, soybeans, corn, wheat, peaches, tomatoes. **Livestock** (Jan. 1998): 510,000 cattle/calves; (Dec. 1997) 290,000 hogs/pigs; (Dec. 1997) 5.7 mil chickens (excl. broilers); (Dec. 1996) 177.5 mil broilers. **Timber/lumber** (1997): pine, oak; 1.5 bil bd. ft. **Nonfuel minerals** (est. 1997): $507 mil; mostly portland cement, crushed stone, gold, sand & gravel, masonry cement. **Commercial fishing** (1997): $31.5 mil. **Chief ports:** Charleston, Georgetown, Beaufort/ Port Royal. **Internat. airport at:** Charleston. **Value of construction** (1997): $6.0 bil. **Gross state product** (1996): $89.5 bil. **Employment distrib.** (May 1998): 24.5% trade; 23.3% serv.; 20.4% mfg.; 17% govt. **Per cap. pers. income** (1997): $20,755. **Sales tax** (1998): 5%. **Unemployment** (1997): 4.5%. **Tourism expends.** (1996): $6.2 bil.

Finance. FDIC-insured commercial banks (1997): 80. **Deposits:** $14.5 bil. **FDIC-insured savings institutions** (1997): 32. **Assets:** $8.0 bil.

Federal govt. Fed. civ. employees (Mar. 1997): 16,377. **Avg. salary:** $38,601. **Notable fed. facilities:** Polaris Submarine Base; Barnwell Nuclear Power Plant; Ft. Jackson; Parris Island; Savannah River Plant.

Energy. Electricity production (1997, kWh, by source): Coal: 31.0 bil.; Petroleum: 188 mil; Gas: 181 mil; Hydroelectric: 2.0 bil; Nuclear: 44.9 bil.

State data. Motto: Dum Spiro Spero (While I breathe, I hope). **Flower:** Yellow jessamine. **Bird:** Carolina wren. **Tree:** Palmetto. **Song:** Carolina. **Eighth** of the original 13 states to ratify the Constitution, May 23, 1788. **State fair** at Columbia; mid-Oct.

History. At the time of European settlement, Cherokee, Catawba, and Muskogean peoples lived in the area. The first English colonists settled near the Ashley River, 1670, and moved to the site of Charleston, 1680. The colonists seized the government, 1775, and the royal governor fled. The British took Charleston, 1780, but were defeated at Kings Mountain that same year, and at Cowpens and Eutaw Springs, 1781. In the 1830s, South Carolinians, angered by federal protective tariffs, adopted the Nullification

Doctrine, holding that a state can void an act of Congress. The state was the first to secede from the Union, 1861, and Confederate troops fired on and forced the surrender of U.S. troops at Ft. Sumter, in Charleston Harbor, launching the Civil War. South Carolina was readmitted,1868.

Tourist attractions. Historic Charleston; Ft. Sumter Natl. Monument, in Charleston Harbor; Charleston Museum, est. 1773, oldest museum in U.S.; Middleton Place, Magnolia Plantation, Cypress Gardens, Drayton Hall, all near Charleston; other gardens at Brookgreen, Edisto, Glencairn; Myrtle Beach; Hilton Head Island; Revolutionary War battle sites; Andrew Jackson State Park & Museum; South Carolina State Museum, Columbia; Riverbanks Zoo, Columbia.

Famous South Carolinians. Charles Bolden, James F. Byrnes, John C. Calhoun, DuBose Heyward, Ernest F. Hollings, Andrew Jackson, Jesse Jackson, James Longstreet, Francis Marion, Ronald McNair, Charles Pinckney, John Rutledge, Thomas Sumter, Strom Thurmond, John B. Watson.

Tourist information. S. Carolina Dept. of Parks, Recreation, & Tourism; 803-734-0122.

Toll-free travel information. 1-800-346-3634.

Website. http://www.state.sc.us

Tourism website. http://www.sccsi.com/sc

South Dakota

Coyote State, Mount Rushmore State

People. Population (1997): 737,973; rank: 45; **net change** (1990-97): 6.0%. **Pop. density** (1990): 9.2 per sq mi. **Racial/ethnic distrib.** (1990): 91.6% white; 0.5% black; 7.3% Amer. Indian; 0.8% Hispanic.

Geography. Total area: 77,121 sq mi; rank: 17. **Land area:** 75,896 sq mi; rank: 16. **Acres forested:** 1,690,000. **Location:** West North Central state bounded on the N by North Dakota; on the E by Minnesota and Iowa; on the S by Nebraska; on the W by Wyoming and Montana. **Climate:** characterized by extremes of temperature, persistent winds, low precipitation and humidity. **Topography:** Prairie Plains in the E; rolling hills of the Great Plains in the W; the Black Hills, rising 3,500 ft, in the SW corner. **Capital:** Pierre.

Economy. Chief industries: agriculture, services, manufacturing. **Chief manuf. goods:** food and kindred products, machinery, electric and electronic equipment. **Chief crops:** corn, soybeans, oats, wheat, sunflowers, sorghum. **Livestock** (Jan. 1998): 3.6 mil cattle/calves; 400,000 sheep/lambs; (Dec. 1997) 1.3 hogs/pigs; (Dec. 1997) 2.6 mil chickens (excl. broilers). **Timber/lumber** ponderosa pine. **Nonfuel minerals** (est. 1997): $340 mil; mostly gold, portland cement, sand & gravel, lime. **Value of construction** (1997): $742 mil. **Gross state product** (1996): $20.3 bil. **Employment distrib.** (May 1998): 26.5% serv.; 24.8% trade; 19.6% govt.; 13.6% mfg. **Per cap. pers. income** (1997): $21,447. **Sales tax** (1998): 4%. **Unemployment** (1997): 3.1%. **Tourism expends.** (1996) $1.0 bil. **Lottery** (1997): total sales: $533.2 mil; net income: $95.9 mil.

Finance. FDIC-insured commercial banks (1997): 106. **Deposits:** $11.8 bil. **FDIC-insured savings institutions** (1997): 5. **Assets:** $886 mil.

Federal govt. Fed. civ. employees (Mar. 1997): 6,723. **Avg. salary:** $36,899. **Notable fed. facilities:** Ellsworth AFB, Corp of Engineers, Nat'l Park Service.

Energy. Electricity production (1997, kWh, by source): Coal: 3.3 bil; Petroleum: 7 mil; Gas: 117 mil; Hydroelectric: 9.0 bil.

State data. Motto: Under God, the people rule. **Flower:** Pasqueflower. **Bird:** Chinese ring-necked pheasant. **Tree:** Black Hills spruce. **Song:** Hail, South Dakota. **Entered union** Nov. 2, 1889; rank, 40th. **State fair** at Huron; late Aug.-early Sept.

History. At the time of first European contact, Mandan, Hidatsa, Arikara and Sioux lived in the area. The French Verendrye brothers explored the region, 1742-43. The U.S. acquired the area, 1803, in the Louisiana Purchase. Lewis and Clark passed through the area, 1804-6. In 1817 a trading post was opened at Fort Pierre, which later became the site of the first European settlement in South Dakota. Gold was discovered, 1874, in the Black Hills on the great Sioux reservation; the "Great Dakota Boom" began in 1879. Conflicts with Native Americans led to the Great Sioux Agreement, 1889, which established reservations and opened up more land for white settlement. The massacre of Native American families at Wounded Knee, 1890, ended Sioux resistance.

Tourist attractions. Black Hills; Mt. Rushmore; Needles Highway; Harney Peak, tallest E. of Rockies; Deadwood, 1876 Gold Rush town; Custer State Park; Jewel Cave Natl. Monument; Badlands Natl. Park "moonscape"; "Great Lakes of S. Dakota"; Ft. Sisseton; Great Plains Zoo & Museum, Sioux Falls; Corn Palace, Mitchell; Wind Cave Natl. Park; Crazy Horse Memorial, mountain carving in progress.

Famous South Dakotans. Sparky Anderson, Tom Brokaw, Crazy Horse, Thomas Daschle, Myron Floren, Mary Hart, Cheryl Ladd, Dr. Ernest O. Lawrence, George McGovern, Billy Mills, Allen Neuharth, Pat O'Brien, Sitting Bull.

Tourist information. Department of Tourism, Capitol Lake Plaza, 711 E. Wells Ave., c/o 500 E. Capitol Ave., Pierre, SD 57501-5070.

Toll-free travel information. 1-800-SDAKOTA.

Website. http://www.state.sd.us

Tourism website. http://www.state.sd.us/tourism

Tennessee

Volunteer State

People. Population (1997): 5,368,198; rank: 17; **net change** (1990-97): 10.1%. **Pop. density** (1990): 118.3 per sq mi. **Racial/ethnic distrib.** (1990): 83.0% white; 16.0% black; 0.7% Hispanic.

Geography. Total area: 42,146 sq mi; rank: 36. **Land area:** 41,219 sq mi; rank: 34. **Acres forested:** 13,612,000. **Location:** East South Central state bounded on the N by Kentucky and Virginia; on the E by North Carolina; on the S by Georgia, Alabama, and Mississippi; on the W by Arkansas and Missouri. **Climate:** humid continental to the N; humid subtropical to the S. **Topography:** rugged country in the E; the Great Smoky Mts. of the Unakas; low ridges of the Appalachian Valley; the flat Cumberland Plateau; slightly rolling terrain and knobs of the Interior Low Plateau, the largest region; Eastern Gulf Coastal Plain to the W, laced with streams; Mississippi Alluvial Plain, a narrow strip of swamp and flood plain in the extreme W. **Capital:** Nashville.

Economy. Chief industries: manufacturing, trade, services, tourism, finance, insurance, real estate. **Chief manuf. goods:** chemicals, food, transportation equipment, industrial machinery & equipment, fabricated metal products, rubber/plastic products, paper & allied products, printing & publishing. **Chief crops:** tobacco, cotton, lint, soybeans, grain, corn. **Livestock** (Jan. 1998): 2.3 mil cattle/calves; 11,000 sheep/lambs; (Dec. 1997) 340,000 hogs/pigs; (Dec. 1997) 2.0 mil chickens (excl. broilers); (Dec. 1996) 134.0 mil broilers. **Timber/lumber** (1997): red oak, white oak, yellow poplar, hickory; 943 mil bd. ft. **Nonfuel minerals** (est. 1997): $786 mil; mostly crushed stone, zinc, portland cement, sand & gravel, clays. **Chief ports:** Memphis, Nashville, Chattanooga, Knoxville. **Internat. airports at:** Memphis, Nashville. **Value of construction** (1997): $8.2 bil. **Gross state product** (1996): $140.8 bil. **Employment distrib.** (May 1998): 26.7% serv.; 23.7% trade; 19.6% mfg.; 14.7% govt. **Per cap. pers. income** (1997): $23,018. **Sales tax** (1998): 6%. **Unemployment** (1997): 5.4%. **Tourism expends.** (1996): $8.4 bil.

Finance. FDIC-insured commercial banks (1997): 232. **Deposit:** $56.3 bil. **FDIC-insured savings institutions** (1997): 24. **Assets:** $4.3 bil.

Federal govt. Fed. civ. employees (Mar. 1997): 34,241. **Avg. salary:** $42,084. **Notable fed. facilities:** Tennessee Valley Authority; Oak Ridge Nat'l. Laboratories; Arnold Engineering Development Center; Ft. Campbell Army Base; Millington Naval Station.

Energy. Electricity production (1997, kWh, by source): Coal: 58.9 bil; Petroleum: 193 mil; Gas: 152 mil; Hydroelectric: 9.4 bil; Nuclear: 24.6 bil.

State data. Motto: Agriculture and commerce. **Flower:** Iris. **Bird:** Mockingbird. **Tree:** Tulip poplar. **Song:** The Tennessee Waltz. **Entered union** June 1, 1796; rank, 16th. **State fair** at Nashville; mid-Sept.

History. When the first European explorers arrived, Creek and Yuchi peoples lived in the area; the Cherokee moved into the region in the early 18th cent. Spanish explorers first visited the area, 1541. English traders crossed the Great Smokies from the east while France's Marquette and Jolliet sailed down the Mississippi on the west, 1673. The first permanent settlement was by Virginians on the Watauga River, 1769. During the American Revolution, the colonists helped win the Battle of Kings Mountain (NC), 1780, and joined other eastern campaigns. The state seceded from the Union, 1861, and saw many Civil War engagements, but 30,000 soldiers fought for the Union. Tennessee was re-admitted in 1866, the only former Confederate state not to have a postwar military government.

Tourist attractions. Reelfoot Lake; Lookout Mountain, Chattanooga; Fall Creek Falls; Great Smoky Mountains Natl. Park; Lost Sea, Sweetwater; Cherokee Natl. Forest; Cumberland Gap Natl. Park; Andrew Jackson's home, the Hermitage, near Nashville; homes of Pres.s Polk and Andrew Johnson; American Museum of Science and Energy, Oak Ridge; Parthenon, Grand Old Opry, Opryland USA, all Nashville; Dollywood theme park, Pigeon Forge; Tennessee Aquarium, Chattanooga; Graceland, home of Elvis Presley, Memphis; Alex Haley Home and Museum, Henning; Casey Jones Home and Museum, Jackson.

Famous Tennesseans. Roy Acuff, Davy Crockett, David Farragut, Ernie Ford, Aretha Franklin, Morgan Freeman, Al Gore Jr., Alex Haley, William C. Handy, Sam Houston, Cordell Hull, Andrew Jackson, Andrew Johnson, Casey Jones, Estes Kefauver, Grace Moore, Dolly Parton, Minnie Pearl, James Polk, Elvis Presley, Dinah Shore, Bessie Smith, Alvin York.

Tourist information. Dept. of Tourist Development, 5th Floor, Rachel Jackson Bldg., 320 6th Ave. N., Nashville, TN 37202.

Toll-free travel information. 1-800-TENN200.

Website. http://www.state.tn.us

Tourism website. http://www.state.tn.us/tourdev

Texas

Lone Star State

People. Population (1997): 19,439,337; rank: 2; **net change** (1990-97): 14.4%. **Pop. density** (1990): 64.9 per sq mi. **Racial/ethnic distrib.** (1990): 75.2% white; 11.9% black; 25.5% Hispanic.

Geography. Total area: 267,277 sq mi; rank: 2. **Land area:** 261,914 sq mi; rank: 2. **Acres forested:** 19,193,000. **Location:** Southwestern state, bounded on the SE by the Gulf of Mexico; on the SW by Mexico, separated by the Rio Grande; surrounding states are Louisiana, Arkansas, Oklahoma, New Mexico. **Climate:** extremely varied; driest region is the Trans-Pecos; wettest is the NE. **Topography:** Gulf Coast Plain in the S and SE; North Central Plains slope upward with some hills; the Great Plains extend over the Panhandle, are broken by low mountains; the Trans-Pecos is the southern extension of the Rockies. **Capital:** Austin.

Economy. Chief industries: manufacturing, trade, oil and gas extraction, services. **Chief manuf. goods:** industrial machinery and equipment, foods, electrical and electronic products, chemicals and allied products, apparel. **Chief crops:** cotton, grains (wheat), sorghum grain, vegetables, citrus and other fruits, greenhouse/nursery, pecans, peanuts. **Chief farm products:** milk, eggs **Livestock** (Jan. 1998): 14.3 mil cattle/calves; 1.5 mil sheep/lambs; (Dec. 1997) 560,000 hogs/pigs; (Dec. 1997) 22.7 mil chickens (excl. broilers); (Dec. 1996) 419.2 mil broilers. **Timber/lumber** (1997): pine, cypress; 1.6 bil bd. ft. **Nonfuel minerals** (est. 1997): $1.70 bil; mostly portland cement, crushed stone, sand & gravel, magnesium metal, salt. **Commercial fishing** (1997): $203.1 mil. **Chief ports:** Houston, Galveston, Brownsville, Beaumont, Port Arthur, Corpus Christi. **Major Internat. airports at:** Houston, Dallas/Ft. Worth, San Antonio. **Value of construction** (1997): $27.2 bil. **Gross state product** (1996): $551.8 bil. **Employment distrib.** (May 1998): 28.2% serv.; 23.6% trade; 17% govt.; 12.4% mfg. **Per cap. pers. income** (1997): $23,656. **Sales tax** (1998): 6.25%. **Unemployment** (1997): 5.4%. **Tourism expends.** (1996): $27.6 bil. **Lottery** (1997): total sales: $3.75 bil; net income: $1.2 bil.

Finance. FDIC-insured commercial banks (1997): 839. **Deposits:** $191.8 bil. **FDIC-insured savings institutions** (1997): 48. **Assets:** $48.2 bil.

Federal govt. Fed. civ. employees (Mar. 1997): 111,498. **Avg. salary:** $39,994. **Notable fed. facilities:** Fort Hood, Kelly AFB, and Ft. Sam Houston.

Energy. Electricity production (1997, kWh, by source): Coal: 135.7 bil; Petroleum: 188 mil; Gas: 102.2 bil; Hydroelectric: 1.8 bil; Nuclear: 37.4 bil.

State data. Motto: Friendship. **Flower:** Bluebonnet. **Bird:** Mockingbird. **Tree:** Pecan. **Song:** Texas, Our Texas. **Entered union** Dec. 29, 1845; rank, 28th. **State fair** at Dallas; mid-Oct.

History. At the time of European contact, Native American tribes in the region were numerous and diverse in culture. Coahuiltecan, Karankawa, Caddo, Jumano, and Tonkawa peoples lived in the area, and during the 19th cent., the Apache, Comanche, Cherokee, and Wichita arrived. Spanish explorer Pineda sailed along the Texas coast, 1519; Cabeza de Vaca and Coronado visited the interior, 1541. Spaniards made the first settlement at Ysleta, near El Paso, 1682. Americans moved into the land early in the 19th cent. Mexico, of which Texas was a part, won independence from Spain, 1821; Santa Anna became dictator in 1835; Texans rebelled. Santa Anna wiped out defenders of the Alamo, 1836; Sam Houston's Texans defeated Santa Anna at San Jacinto, and independence was proclaimed that same year. The Republic of Texas, with Sam Houston as its first president, functioned as a nation until 1845, when it was admitted to the Union.

Tourist attractions. Padre Island Natl. Seashore; Big Bend, Guadalupe Mts. natl. parks; The Alamo; Ft. Davis; Six Flags Amusement Park; Sea World and Fiesta Texas, both in San Antonio; San Antonio Missions Natl. Park; Cowgirl Hall of Fame, Fort Worth; Lyndon B. Johnson Natl. Park, marking his birthplace, boyhood home, and ranch, near Johnson City; Lyndon B. Johnson Library and Museum, Austin; Texas State Aquarium, Corpus Christi; Kimball Art Museum, Fort Worth; George Bush Library, College Station.

Famous Texans. Stephen F. Austin, Lloyd Bentsen, James Bowie, Carol Burnett, George Bush, J. Frank Dobie, Dwight D. Eisenhower, Farrah Fawcett, Sam Houston, Howard Hughes, Lyndon B. Johnson, Tommy Lee Jones, Janis Joplin, Mary Martin, Chester Nimitz, Sandra Day O'Connor, H. Ross Perot, Katharine Ann Porter, Dan Rather, Sam Rayburn, Ann Richards, Sissy Spacek, Kenneth Starr, George Strait.

Chamber of Commerce. 900 Congress, Suite 501, Austin, TX 78701.

Toll-free travel information. 1-800-8888TEX.

Website. http://www.state.tx.us

Tourism website. http://www.traveltex.com

Utah

Beehive State

People. Population (1997): 2,059,148; rank: 34; **net change** (1990-97): 19.5%. **Pop. density** (1990): 21.0 per sq mi. **Racial/ethnic distrib.** (1990): 93.8% white; 0.7% black; 4.9% Hispanic.

Geography. Total area: 84,904 sq mi; rank: 13. **Land area:** 82,168 sq mi; rank: 12. **Acres forested:** 16,234,000. **Location:** Middle Rocky Mountain state; its southeastern corner touches Colorado, New Mexico, and Arizona, and is the only spot in the U.S. where 4 states join. **Climate:** arid; ranging from warm desert in SW to alpine in NE. **Topography:** high Colorado plateau is cut by brilliantly colored canyons of the SE; broad, flat, desert-like Great Basin of the W; the Great Salt Lake and Bonneville Salt Flats to the NW; Middle Rockies in the NE run E-W; valleys and plateaus of the Wasatch Front. **Capital:** Salt Lake City.

Economy. Chief industries: services, trade, manufacturing, government, transportation, utilities. **Chief manuf. goods:** medical instruments, electronic components, food products, fabricated metals, transportation equipment, steel and copper. **Chief crops:** hay, corn, wheat, barley, apples, potatoes, cherries, onions, peaches, pears. **Livestock** (Jan. 1998): 870,000 cattle/calves; 350,000 sheep/lambs; (Dec. 1997) 295,000 hogs/pigs; (Dec. 1997) 1.9 mil chickens (excl. broilers). **Timber/lumber:** (1997) aspen, spruce, pine; 27 mil bd. ft. **Nonfuel minerals** (est. 1997): $1.76 bil; mostly copper, gold, molybdenum, magnesium metal, sand & gravel. **Internat. airports at:** Salt Lake City. **Value of construction** (1997): $5.3 bil. **Gross state product** (1996): $50.4 bil. **Employment distrib.** (May 1998): 27.2% serv.; 23.8% trade; 13.2% mfg.; 17.4% govt. **Per cap. pers. income** (1997): $20,432. **Sales tax** (1998): 4.75%. **Unemployment** (1997): 3.1%. **Tourism expends.** (1996): $3.6 bil.

Finance. FDIC-insured commercial banks (1997): 49. **Deposits:** $20.2 bil. **FDIC-insured savings institutions** (1997): 2. **Assets:** $1.3 bil.

Federal govt. Fed. civ. employees (Mar. 1997): 23,705. **Avg. salary:** $37,793. **Notable fed. facilities:** Hill AFB; Tooele Army Depot; IRS Western Service Center.

Energy. Electricity production (1997, kWh, by source): Coal: 32.1 bil; Petroleum: 29 mil; Gas: 297 mil; Hydroelectric: 1.3 bil.

State data. Motto: Industry. **Flower:** Sego lily. **Bird:** Seagull. **Tree:** Blue spruce. **Song:** Utah, We Love Thee. **Entered union** Jan. 4, 1896; rank, 45th. **State fair** at Salt Lake City; Sept.

History. Ute, Gosiute, Southern Paiute, and Navajo peoples lived in the region at the time of European contact. Spanish Franciscans visited the area, 1776; American fur traders followed. Permanent settlement began with the arrival of the Mormons, 1847; they made the arid land bloom and created a prosperous economy. The State of Deseret was organized in 1849, and asked admission to the Union. In 1850, Congress established the region as the territory of Utah, and Brigham Young was appointed governor. The Union and Pacific Railroads met near Promontory, May 10, 1869, creating the first transcontinental railroad. Statehood was not achieved until 1896, after a long period of controversy over the Mormon Church's doctrine of polygamy, which it discontinued in 1890.

Tourist attractions. Temple Square, Mormon Church headquarters, Salt Lake City; Great Salt Lake; Natural Zion, Canyonlands, Bryce Canyon, Arches, and Capitol Reef natl. parks; Dinosaur, Rainbow Bridge, Timpanogos Cave, and Natural Bridges natl. monuments; Lake Powell; Flaming Gorge Natl. Recreation Area.

Famous Utahans. Maude Adams, Ezra Taft Benson, John Moses Browning, Mariner Eccles, Philo Farnsworth, James Fletcher, David M. Kennedy, J. Willard Marriott, Merlin Olsen, Osmond family, Ivy Baker Priest, George Romney, Brigham Young, Loretta Young.

Tourist information. Utah Travel Council, Council Hall, Salt Lake City, UT 84114; 801-538-1030.

Toll-free travel information. 1-800-200-1160

Website. http://www.state.ut.us

Tourism website. http://www.utah.com

Vermont

Green Mountain State

People. Population (1997): 588,978; rank: 49; **net change** (1990-97): 4.7%. **Pop. density** (1990): 60.8 per sq mi. **Racial/ethnic distrib.** (1990): 98.6% white; 0.3% black; 0.6% Asian; 0.7% Hispanic.

Geography. Total area: 9,615 sq mi; rank: 43. **Land area:** 9,249 sq mi; rank: 43. **Acres forested:** 4,538,000. **Location:** northern New England state. **Climate:** temperate, with considerable temperature extremes; heavy snowfall in mountains. **Topography:** Green Mts. N-S backbone 20-36 mi wide; avg. altitude 1,000 ft. **Capital:** Montpelier.

Economy. Chief industries: manufacturing, tourism, agriculture, trade, finance, insurance, real estate, government. **Chief manuf. goods:** machine tools, furniture, scales, books, computer components, speciality foods. **Chief crops:** dairy products, apples, maple syrup, greenhouse/nursery, vegetables and small fruits. **Livestock** (Jan. 1998): 305,000 cattle/calves; 14,000 sheep/lambs; (Dec. 1997) 2,200 hogs/pigs; (Dec. 1997) 185,000 chickens (excl. broilers). **Timber/lumber** (1997): pine, spruce, fir, hemlock; 277 mil bd. ft. **Nonfuel minerals** (est. 1997): $68.2 mil; mostly dimension stone, crushed stone, sand & gravel, talc & pyrophyllite, gemstones. **Internat. airport at:** Burlington. **Value of construction** (1997): $622 mil. **Gross state product** (1996): $14.6 bil. **Employment distrib.** (May 1998): 30.4% serv.; 23.2% trade; 15.9% govt.; 17% mfg. **Per cap. pers. income** (1997): $23,401. **Sales tax** (1998): 5%. **Unemployment** (1997): 4.0%. **Tourism expends.** (1996): $1.3 bil. **Lottery** (1997): total sales: $77.3 mil; net income: $23.7 mil.

Finance. FDIC-insured commercial banks (1997): 21. **Deposits:** $5.9 bil. **FDIC-insured savings institutions** (1997): 5. **Assets:** $870 mil.

Federal govt. Fed. civ. employees (Mar. 1997): 2,693. **Avg. salary:** $39,748.

Energy. Electricity production (1997, kWh, by source): Petroleum: 10 mil; Hydroelectric: 896 mil; Nuclear: 4.3 bil.

State data. Motto: Freedom and unity. **Flower:** Red clover. **Bird:** Hermit thrush. **Tree:** Sugar maple. **Song:** Hail, Vermont. **Entered union** Mar. 4, 1791; rank, 14th. **State fair** at Rutland; early Sept.

History. Before the arrival of the Europeans, Abnaki and Mahican peoples lived in the region. Champlain explored the lake that bears his name, 1609. The first American settlement was Ft. Dummer, 1724, near Brattleboro. During the American Revolution, Ethan Allen and the Green Mountain Boys captured Ft. Ticonderoga (NY), 1775; John Stark defeated part of Burgoyne's forces near Bennington, 1777. In the War of 1812, Thomas MacDonough defeated a British fleet on Lake Champlain off Plattsburgh (NY), 1814.

Tourist attractions. Shelburne Museum; Rock of Ages Quarry, Graniteville; Vermont Marble Exhibit, Proctor; Bennington Battle Monument; Pres. Calvin Coolidge homestead, Plymouth; Maple Grove Maple Museum, St. Johnsbury; Ben & Jerry's Factory, Waterbury.

Famous Vermonters. Ethan Allen, Chester A. Arthur, Calvin Coolidge, George Dewey, John Dewey, Stephen A. Douglas, Dorothy Canfield Fisher, James Fisk.

Chamber of Commerce. PO Box 37, Montpelier, VT 05601.

Tourist information. Vermont Dept. of Tourism and Marketing, 6 Baldwin St., Drawer 33, Montpelier, VT 05633-1301.

Toll-free travel information. 1-800-VERMONT

Website. http://www.state.vt.us

Tourism website. http://www.travel-vermont.com

Virginia

Old Dominion

People. Population (1997): 6,733,996; rank: 12; **net change** (1990-97): 8.8%. **Pop. density** (1990): 156.3 per sq mi. **Racial/ethnic distrib.** (1990): 77.4% white; 18.8% black; 2.6% Asian; 2.6% Hispanic.

Geography. Total area: 42,326 sq mi; rank: 35. **Land area:** 39,598 sq mi; rank: 37. **Acres forested:** 15,858,000. **Location:** South Atlantic state bounded by the Atlantic Ocean on the E and surrounded by North Carolina, Tennessee, Kentucky, West Virginia, and Maryland. **Climate:** mild and equable. **Topography:** mountain and valley region in the W, including the Blue Ridge Mts.; rolling piedmont plateau; tidewater, or coastal plain, including the eastern shore. **Capital:** Richmond.

Economy. Chief industries: services, trade, government, manufacturing, tourism, agriculture. **Chief manuf. goods:** food processing, transportation equipment, printing, textiles, electronic & electrical equipment, industrial machinery & equipment, lumber & wood products, chemicals, rubber & plastics, furniture. **Chief crops:** tobacco, grain corn, soybeans, winter wheat, peanuts, lint & seed cotton. **Livestock** (Jan. 1998): 1.8 mil cattle/calves; 81,000 sheep/lambs; (Dec. 1997) 420,000 hogs/pigs; (Dec. 1997) 4.7 mil chickens (excl. broilers); (Dec. 1996) 259.1 mil broilers. **Timber/lumber** (1997): pine and hardwoods; 1.3 bil bd. ft. **Nonfuel minerals** (est. 1997): $600 mil; mostly crushed stone, sand & gravel, portland cement, lime, kyanite. **Commercial fishing** (1997): $105 mil. **Chief ports:** Hampton Roads, Richmond, Alexandria. **Internat. airports at:** Norfolk, Dulles, Richmond, Newport News. **Value of construction** (1997): $10.1 bil. **Gross state product** (1996): $197.8 bil. **Employment distrib.** (May 1998): 30.9% serv.; 22.2% trade; 18% govt.; 12.2% mfg. **Per cap. pers. income** (1997): $26,438. **Sales tax** (1998): 3.5%. **Unemployment** (1997): 4.0%. **Tourism expends.** (1996): $11.0 bil. **Lottery** (1997): total sales: $920.8 mil; net income: $342.5 mil.

Finance. FDIC-insured commercial banks (1997): 151. **Deposits:** $55.9 bil. **FDIC-insured savings institutions** (1997): 28. **Assets:** $15.9 bil.

Federal govt. Fed. civ. employees (Mar. 1997): 120,876. **Avg. salary:** $48,650. **Notable fed. facilities:** Pentagon; Norfolk Naval Station, Norfolk Naval Air Station; Naval Shipyard; Marine Corps Base; Langley AFB; NASA at Langley.

Energy. Electricity production (1997, kWh, by source): Coal: 29.7 bil; Petroleum: 858 mil; Gas: 1.3 bil; Hydroelectric: 76 mil; Nuclear: 27.1 bil.

State data. Motto: Sic Semper Tyrannis (Thus always to tyrants). **Flower:** Dogwood. **Bird:** Cardinal. **Tree:** Dogwood. **Song Emeritus:** Carry Me Back to Old Virginia. **Tenth** of the original 13 states to ratify the Constitution, June 25, 1788. **State fair** at Richmond; late Sept.-early Oct.

History. Living in the area at the time of European contact were the Cherokee and Susquehanna and the Algonquians of the Powhatan Confederacy. English settlers founded Jamestown, 1607. Virginians took over much of the government from royal governor Dunmore, 1775, forcing him to flee. Virginians under George Rogers Clark freed the Ohio-Indiana-Illinois area of British forces. Benedict Arnold burned Richmond and Petersburg for the British, 1781. That same year, Britain's Cornwallis was trapped at Yorktown and surrendered, ending the American Revolution. Virginia seceded from the Union, 1861, and Richmond became the capital of the Confederacy. Hampton Roads, off the Virginia coast, was the site of the famous naval battle of the USS *Monitor* and CSS *Virginia* (Merrimac), 1862. Virginia was readmitted, 1870.

Tourist attractions. Colonial Williamsburg; Busch Gardens, Williamsburg; Wolf Trap Farm, near Falls Church; Arlington Natl. Cemetery; Mt. Vernon, home of George Washington; Jamestown Festival Park; Yorktown; Jefferson's Monticello, Charlottesville; Robert E. Lee's birthplace, Stratford Hall, and grave, Lexington; Appomattox; Shenandoah Natl. Park; Blue Ridge Parkway; Virginia Beach; Paramount's King's Dominion, near Richmond.

Famous Virginians. Richard E. Byrd, James B. Cabell, Henry Clay, Jerry Falwell, William Henry Harrison, Patrick Henry, Thomas Jefferson, Joseph E. Johnston, Robert E. Lee, Meriwether Lewis and William Clark, James Madison, John Marshall, George Mason, James Monroe, Pocahontas, Edgar Allan Poe, John Randolph, Walter Reed, John Smith, William Styron, Zachary Taylor, John Tyler, Maggie Walker, Booker T. Washington, George Washington, Woodrow Wilson.

Chamber of Commerce. 9 South Fifth St., Richmond, VA 23219.

Toll-free travel information. 1-800-VISITVA.

Website. http://www.state.va.us

Tourism website. http://www.virginia.org

Washington

Evergreen State

People. Population (1997): 5,610,362; rank: 15; **net change** (1990-97): 15.3%. **Pop. density** (1990): 73.1 per sq mi. **Racial/ethnic distrib.** (1990): 88.5% white; 3.1% black; 4.3% Asian; 4.4% Hispanic.

Geography. Total area: 70,637 sq mi; rank: 19. **Land area:** 66,581 sq mi; rank: 20. **Acres forested:** 20,483,000. **Location:** Pacific state bordered by Canada on the N; Idaho on the E; Oregon on the S; and the Pacific Ocean on the W. **Climate:** mild, dominated by the Pacific Ocean and protected by the Cascades. **Topography:** Olympic Mts. on NW peninsula; open land along coast to Columbia R.; flat terrain of Puget Sound Lowland; Cascade Mts. region's high peaks to the E; Columbia Basin in central portion; highlands to the NE; mountains to the SE. **Capital:** Olympia.

Economy. Chief industries: advanced technology, aerospace, biotechnology, intl. trade, forestry, tourism, recycling, agriculture & food processing. **Chief manuf. goods:** computer software, aircraft, pulp & paper, lumber and plywood, aluminum, processed fruits and vegetables, machinery, electronics. **Chief crops:** apples, potatoes, hay, farm forest products. **Livestock** (Jan. 1998): 1.2 mil cattle/calves; 62,000 sheep/lambs; (Dec. 1997) 39,000 hogs/pigs; (Dec. 1997) 7.0 mil chickens (excl. broilers); (Dec. 1996) 40.0 mil broilers. **Timber/lumber** (1997): Douglas fir, hemlock, cedar, pine; 4.3 bil bd. ft. **Nonfuel minerals** (est. 1997): $522 mil; mostly sand & gravel, magnesium metal, crushed stone, portland cement, gold. **Commercial fishing** (1997): $139.6 mil. **Chief ports:** Seattle, Tacoma, Vancouver, Kelso-Longview. **Internat. airports at:** Seattle/Tacoma, Spokane, Boeing Field. **Value of construction** (1997): $8.5 bil. **Gross state product** (1996): $159.6 bil. **Employment distrib.** (May 1998): 27.4% serv.; 24.2% trade; 17.7% govt.; 14.6% mfg. **Per cap. pers. income** (1997): $26,718. **Sales tax** (1998): 6.5%. **Unemployment** (1997): 4.8%. **Tourism expends.** (1996): $7.5 bil. **Lottery** (1997): total sales: $408.2 mil; net income: $94.6.

Finance. FDIC-insured commercial banks (1997): 80. **Deposits:** $9.9 bil. **FDIC-insured savings institutions** (1997): 20. **Assets:** $42.6 bil.

Federal govt. Fed. civ. employees (Mar. 1997): 43,935. **Avg. salary:** $42,838. **Notable fed. facilities:** Bonneville Power Admin.; Ft. Lewis; McChord AFB; Hanford Nuclear Reservation; Bremerton Naval Shipyards.

Energy. Electricity production (1997, kWh, by source): Coal: 7.0 bil; Petroleum: 16 mil; Gas: 229 mil; Hydroelectric: 103.7 bil; Nuclear: 6.2 bil.

State data. Motto: Alki (By and by). **Flower:** Western rhododendron. **Bird:** Willow goldfinch. **Tree:** Western hemlock. **Song:** Washington, My Home. **Entered union** Nov. 11, 1889; rank, 42d. **State fairs:** 5 area fairs, in Aug. and Sept.; no state fair.

History. At the time of European contact, many Native American tribes lived in the area, including the Nez Percé, Spokan, Yakima, Cayuse, Okanogan, Walla Walla, and Colville peoples, who lived in the interior region, and the Nooksak, Chinook, Nisqually, Clallam, Makah, Quinault, and Puyallup peoples, who inhabited the coastal area. Spain's Bruno Hezeta sailed the coast, 1775. In 1792, British naval officer George Vancouver mapped Puget Sound area, and that same year, American Capt. Robert Gray sailed up the Columbia River. Canadian fur traders set up Spokane House, 1810. Americans under John Jacob Astor established a post at Ft. Okanogan, 1811, and missionary Marcus Whitman settled near Walla Walla, 1836. Final agreement on the border of Washington and Canada was made with Britain, 1846, and Washington became part of the Oregon Territory, 1848. Gold was discovered, 1855.

Tourist attractions. Seattle Waterfront, Seattle Center and Space Needle, Museum of Flight, all Seattle; Mt. Rainier, Olympic, and North Cascades natl. parks; Mt. St. Helens; Puget Sound; San Juan Islands; Grand Coulee Dam; Columbia R. Gorge Natl. Scenic Area; Spokane's Riverfront Park.

Famous Washingtonians. Bing Crosby, William O. Douglas, Bill Gates, Henry M. Jackson, Gary Larson, Mary McCarthy, Robert Motherwell, Edward R. Murrow, Theodore Roethke, Marcus Whitman, Minoru Yamasaki.

Tourist information. WA State Tourism Division, PO Box 42500, Olympia, WA 98504-2500.

Toll-free travel information. 1-800-544-1800. ext. 101

Website. http://www.wa.gov/wahome.html

Tourism website. http://www.tourism.wa.gov

West Virginia

Mountain State

People. Population (1997): 1,815,787; rank: 35; **net change** (1990-97): 1.2%. **Pop. density** (1990): 74.5 per sq mi. **Racial/ethnic distrib.** (1990): 96.2% white; 3.1% black; 0.5% Hispanic.

Geography. Total area: 24,231 sq mi; rank: 41. **Land area:** 24,087 sq mi; rank: 41. **Acres forested:** 12,128,000. **Location:** South Atlantic state bounded on the N by Ohio, Pennsylvania, Maryland; on the S and W by Virginia, Kentucky, Ohio; on the E by Maryland and Virginia. **Climate:** humid continental climate except for marine modification in the lower panhandle. **Topography:** ranging from hilly to mountainous; Allegheny Plateau in the W, covers two-thirds of the state; mountains here are the highest in the state, over 4,000 ft. **Capital:** Charleston.

Economy. Chief industries: manufacturing, services, mining, tourism. **Chief manuf. goods:** machinery, plastic & hardwood prods., fabricated metals, chemicals, aluminum, automotive parts, steel. **Chief crops:** apples, peaches, hay, tobacco, corn, wheat, oats. **Chief farm products:** dairy products, eggs. **Livestock** (Jan. 1998): 420,000 cattle/calves; 40,000 sheep/lambs; (Dec. 1997) 14,000 hogs/pigs; (Dec. 1997) 1.8 mil chickens (excl. broilers); (Dec. 1996) 89.7 mil broilers. **Timber/lumber** (1997): oak, yellow poplar, hickory, walnut, cherry; 701 mil bd. ft. **Nonfuel minerals** (est. 1997): $190 mil; mostly crushed stone, portland cement, sand & gravel, lime, salt. **Chief port:** Huntington. **Value of construction** (1997): $1.2 bil. **Gross state product** (1996): $37.2 bil. **Employment distrib.** (May 1998): 28.1% serv.; 22.5% trade; 20.8% govt.; 11.5% mfg. **Per cap. pers. income** (1997): $18,957. **Sales tax** (1998): 6%. **Unemployment** (1997): 6.9%. **Tourism expends.** (1996): $1.6 bil. **Lottery** (1997): total sales: $245.1 mil; net income: $72.8 mil.

Finance. FDIC-insured commercial banks (1997): 100. **Deposits:** $17.5 bil. **FDIC-insured savings institutions** (1997): 8. **Assets:** $1.1 bil.

Federal govt. Fed. civ. employees (Mar. 1997): 11,112. **Avg. salary:** $40,066. **Notable fed. facilities:** National Radio Astronomy Observatory; Bureau of Public Debt Bldg.; Harpers Ferry Natl. Park; Correctional Institution for Women; FBI Identification Center.

Energy. Electricity production (1997, kWh, by source): Coal: 87.7 bil; Petroleum: 171 mil; Gas: 21 mil; Hydroelectric: 377 mil.

State data. Motto: Montani Semper Liberi (Mountaineers are always free). **Flower:** Big rhododendron. **Bird:** Cardinal. **Tree:** Sugar maple. **Songs:** The West Virginia Hills; This Is My West Virginia; West Virginia, My Home, Sweet Home. **Entered union** June 20, 1863; rank, 35th. **State fair** at Lewisburg (Fairlea); late Aug.

History. Sparsely inhabited at the time of European contact, the area was primarily Native American hunting grounds. British explorers Thomas Batts and Robert Fallam reached the New River, 1671. Early American explorers included George Washington, 1753, and Daniel Boone. In the fall of 1774, frontiersmen defeated an allied Indian uprising at Point Pleasant. The area was part of Virginia and often objected to rule by the eastern part of the state. When Virginia seceded in 1861, the Wheeling Convention repudiated the act and created a new state, Kanawha, later renamed West Virginia. It was admitted to the Union 1863.

Tourist attractions. Harpers Ferry Natl. Historic Park; Science and Cultural Center, Charleston; White Sulphur (in Greenbrier) and Berkeley Springs mineral water spas; New River Gorge, Fayetteville; Winter Place, Exhibition Coal Mine, both Beckley; Monongahela Natl. Forest; Fenton Glass, Williamstown; Viking Glass, New Martinsville; Blenko Glass, Milton; Sternwheel Regatta, Charleston; Mountain State Forest Festival; Snowshoe Ski Resort, Slaty Fork; Canaan State Park, Davis; Mountain State Arts & Crafts Fair, Ripley; Ogle Bay, Wheeling; White water rafting, several locations.

Famous West Virginians. Newton D. Baker, Pearl Buck, John W. Davis, Thomas "Stonewall" Jackson, Don Knotts, Dwight Whitney Morrow, Michael Owens, Walter Reuther, Cyrus Vance, Charles "Chuck" Yeager.

Tourist information. Dept. of Commerce, West Virginia Division of Tourism, State Capitol, Charleston WV 25305.

Toll-free travel information. 1-800-CALLWVA.

Website. http://www.state.wv.us

Tourism website. http://wvweb.com/www/travel_recreation

Wisconsin

Badger State

People. Population (1997): 5,169,677; rank: 18; **net change** (1990-97): 5.7%. **Pop. density** (1990): 90.1 per sq mi. **Racial/ethnic distrib.** (1990): 92.2% white; 5.0% black; 1.9% Hispanic.

Geography. Total area: 65,499 sq mi; rank: 22. **Land area:** 54,314 sq mi; rank: 25. **Acres forested:** 15,513,000. **Location:** East North Central state, bounded on the N by Lake Superior and Upper Michigan; on the E by Lake Michigan; on the S by Illinois; on the W by the St. Croix and Mississippi rivers. **Climate:** long, cold winters and short, warm summers tempered by the Great Lakes. **Topography:** narrow Lake Superior Lowland plain met by Northern Highland, which slopes gently to the sandy crescent Central Plain; Western Upland in the SW; 3 broad parallel limestone ridges running N-S are separated by wide and shallow lowlands in the SE. **Capital:** Madison.

Economy. Chief industries: services, manufacturing, trade, government, agriculture, tourism. **Chief manuf. goods:** food products, motor vehicles & equip., paper products, medical instruments and supplies, printing, plastics. **Chief crops:** corn, hay, soybeans, potatoes, cranberries, sweet corn, peas, oats, snap beans. **Chief products:** milk, butter, cheese, canned and frozen vegetables. **Livestock** (Jan. 1998): 3.6 mil cattle/calves; 70,000 sheep/lambs; (Dec. 1997) 730,000 hogs/pigs; (Dec. 1997) 5.0 mil chickens (excl. broilers); (Dec. 1996) 32.4 mil broilers. **Timber/lumber** (1997): maple, birch, oak, evergreens; 659 mil bd. ft. **Nonfuel minerals** (est. 1997): $389 mil; mostly crushed stone, sand & gravel, copper, lime. **Commercial fishing** (1997): $4.1 mil. **Chief ports:** Superior, Ashland, Milwaukee, Green Bay, Kewaunee, Pt. Washington, Manitowoc, Sheboygan, Marinette, Kenosha. **Internat. airports at:** Milwaukee. **Value of construction** (1997): $6.1 bil. **Gross state product** (1996): $139.2 bil. **Employment distrib.** (May 1998): 25.9% serv.; 22.9% mfg.; 22.7% trade; 14.5% govt. **Per cap. pers. income** (1997): $24,475. **Sales tax** (1998): 5%. **Unemployment** (1997): 3.7%. **Tourism expends.** (1996): $5.4 bil. **Lottery** (1997): total sales: $431.1 mil; net income: $137.7 mil.

Finance. FDIC-insured commercial banks (1997): 361. **Deposits:** $55.4 bil. **FDIC-insured savings institutions** (1997): 46. **Assets:** $21.8 bil.

Federal govt. Fed. civ. employees (Mar. 1997): 11,522. **Avg. salary:** $39,432. **Notable fed. facilities:** Ft. McCoy.

Energy. Electricity production (1997, kWh, by source): Coal: 40.8 bil; Petroleum: 170 mil; Gas: 1.1 bil; Hydroelectric: 2.2 bil; Nuclear: 3.9 bil.

State data. Motto: Forward. **Flower:** Wood violet. **Bird:** Robin. **Tree:** Sugar maple. **Song:** On, Wisconsin! **Entered union** May 29, 1848; rank, 30th. **State fair** at State Fair Park, West Allis; July-Aug.

History. At the time of European contact, Ojibwa, Menominee, Winnebago, Kickapoo, Sauk, Fox, and Potawatomi peoples inhabited the region. Jean Nicolet was the first European to see the Wisconsin area, arriving in Green Bay, 1634; French missionaries and fur traders followed. The British took over, 1763. The U.S. won the land after the American Revolution, but the British were not ousted until after the War of 1812. Lead miners came next, then farmers. In 1816, the U.S. government built a fort at Prairie du Chien on Wisconsin's border with Iowa. Native Americans in the area rebelled against the seizure of their tribal lands in the Black Hawk War of 1832, but treaties from 1829 to 1848, transferred all land titles in Wisconsin to the U.S. government. Railroads were started in 1851, serving growing wheat harvests and iron mines. Some 96,000 soldiers served the Union cause during the Civil War.

Tourist attractions. Old Wade House and Carriage Museum, Greenbush; Villa Louis, Prairie du Chien; Circus World Museum, Baraboo; Wisconsin Dells; Old World Wisconsin, Eagle; Door County peninsula; Chequamegon and Nicolet national forests; Lake Winnebago; House on the Rock, Dodgeville; Monona Terrace, Madison.

Famous Wisconsinites. Carrie Chapman Catt, Edna Ferber, King Camp Gillette, Harry Houdini, Robert La Follette, Alfred Lunt, Pat O'Brien, Georgia O'Keeffe, William H. Rehnquist, John Ringling, Donald K. "Deke" Slayton, Spencer Tracy, Thorstein Veblen, Orson Welles, Laura Ingalls Wilder, Thornton Wilder, Frank Lloyd Wright.

Tourist information. Wisconsin Dept. of Tourism, 201 W. Washington Ave., PO Box 7976, Madison, WI 53707-7976.

Toll-free travel information. 1-800-432-8747.

Website. http://www.state.wi.us

Tourism website. http://tourism.state.wi.us

Wyoming

Equality State, Cowboy State

People. Population (1997): 479,743; rank: 50; **net change** (1990-97): 5.8%. **Pop. density** (1990): 4.7 per sq mi. **Racial/ethnic distrib.** (1990): 94.2% white; 0.8% black; 2.1% Amer. Indian; 5.7% Hispanic.

Geography. Total area: 97,818 sq mi; rank: 9. **Land area:** 97,105 sq mi; rank: 9. **Acres forested:** 9,966,000. **Location:** Mountain state lying in the high western plateaus of the Great Plains. **Climate:** semi-desert conditions throughout; true desert in the Big Horn and Great Divide basins. **Topography:** the eastern Great Plains rise to the foothills of the Rocky Mts.; the Continental Divide crosses the state from the NW to the SE. **Capital:** Cheyenne.

Economy. Chief industries: mineral extraction, oil, natural gas, tourism and recreation, agriculture. **Chief manuf. goods:** refined petroleum, wood, stone, clay products, foods, electronic devices, sporting apparel, and aircraft. **Chief crops:** wheat, beans, barley, oats, sugar beets, hay. **Livestock** (Jan. 1998): 1.5 mil cattle/calves; 680,000 sheep/lambs; (Dec. 1997) 95,000 hogs/pigs; (Dec. 1997) 17,000 chickens (excl. broilers). **Timber/lumber** (1997): ponderosa & lodgepole pine, Douglas fir, Engelmann spruce; 226 mil bd. ft. **Nonfuel minerals** (est. 1997): $996 mil; mostly soda ash, clays, helium, portland cement, crushed stone. **Internat. airport at:** Casper. **Value of construction** (1997): $655 mil. **Gross state product** (1996): $16.8 bil. **Employment distrib.** (May 1998): 25.6% govt.; 23.2% trade; 22% serv.; 4.9% mfg. **Per cap. pers. income** (1997): $22,648. **Sales tax** (1998): 4%. **Unemployment** (1997): 5.1%. **Tourism expends.** (1996): $1.5 bil.

Finance. FDIC-insured commercial banks (1997): 52. **Deposits:** $7.2 bil. **FDIC-insured savings institutions** (1997): 4. **Assets:** $358 mil.

Federal govt. Fed. civ. employees (Mar. 1997): 4,420. **Avg. salary:** $38,686. **Notable fed. facilities:** Warren AFB.

Energy. Electricity production (1997, kWh, by source): Coal: 39.3 bil; Petroleum: 59 mil; Gas: 10 mil; Hydroelectric: 1.4 bil.

State data. Motto: Equal Rights. **Flower:** Indian Paintbrush. **Bird:** Western Meadowlark. **Tree:** Plains Cottonwood. **Song:** Wyoming. **Entered union** July 10, 1890; rank, 44th. **State fair** at Douglas; late Aug.

History. Shoshone, Crow, Cheyenne, Oglala Sioux, and Arapaho peoples lived in the area at the time of European contact. France's François and Louis La Verendrye were the first Europeans to see the region, 1743. John Colter, an American, was first to traverse Yellowstone area, 1807-8. Trappers and fur traders followed in the 1820s. Forts Laramie and Bridger became important stops on the pioneer trails to the West Coast. Population grew after the Union Pacific crossed the state, 1868. Women won the vote, for the first time in the U.S., from the Territorial Legislature, 1869. Disputes between large land owners and small ranchers culminated in the Johnson County Cattle War, 1892; federal troops were called in to restore order.

Tourist attractions. Yellowstone Natl. Park, the first U.S. national park, est. 1872; Grand Teton Natl. Park; Natl. Elk Refuge; Devils Tower Natl. Monument; Fort Laramie Natl. Historic Site and nearby pioneer trail ruts; Buffalo Bill Historical Center, Cody; Cheyenne Frontier Days, Cheyenne.

Famous Wyomingites. James Bridger, William F. "Buffalo Bill" Cody, Esther Hobart Morris, Nellie Tayloe Ross.

Tourist information. Division of Tourism & State Marketing, I-25 at College Dr., Cheyenne, WY 82002.

Toll-free travel information. 1-800-CALLWYO.

Website. http://www.state.wy.us

Tourism website. http://commerce.state.wy.us/tourismindex.htm

District of Columbia

People. Population (1997): 528,964; **net change** (1990-97): -12.8%. **Pop. density** (1990): 9,882.8 per sq mi.

Geography. Total area: 68 sq mi; rank: 51. **Land area:** 61 sq mi; rank: 51. **Location:** at the confluence of the Potomac and Anacostia rivers, flanked by Maryland on the N, E, and SE and by Virginia on the SW. **Climate:** hot humid summers, mild winters. **Topography:** low hills rise toward the N away from the Potomac R. and slope to the S; highest elevation, 410 ft, lowest Potomac R., 1 ft.

Economy. Chief industries: government, service, tourism. **Value of construction** (1997): $673 mil. **Gross state product** (1996): $51.2 bil. **Employment distrib.** (May 1998): 43.6% serv.; 37.5% govt.; 7.9% trade; 2.1% mfg. **Per cap. pers. income** (1997): $35,852. **Sales tax** (1998): 5.75%. **Unemployment** (1997): 7.9%. **Tourism expenditures** (1996): $5.1 bil. **Lottery** (1997) total sales: $202.9 mil; net income: $69.3 mil.

Finance. FDIC-insured commercial banks & trust companies (1997): 6. **Deposits:** $864 mil. **FDIC-insured savings institutions** (1997): 1. **Assets:** $270 mil.

Federal govt. No. of federal employees (Mar. 1997): 144,679. **Avg. salary:** $56,726.

Energy. Electricity production (1997, kWh, by source): Petroleum: 71 mil.

District data. Motto: Justitia omnibus (Justice for all). **Flower:** American beauty rose. **Tree:** Scarlet oak. **Bird:** Wood thrush.

History. The District of Columbia, coextensive with the city of Washington, is the seat of the U.S. federal government. It lies on the west central edge of Maryland on the Potomac River, opposite Virginia. Its area was originally 100 sq mi taken from the sovereignty of Maryland and Virginia. Virginia's portion south of the Potomac was given back to that state in 1846.

The 23d Amendment (1961) granted residents the right to vote for president and vice president for the first time since 1800 and gave them 3 members in the Electoral College. The first such votes were cast in Nov. 1964.

Congress, which has legislative authority over the District under the Constitution, established in 1874 a government of 3 commissioners appointed by the president. The Reorganization Plan of 1967 substituted a single appointive commissioner (also called mayor), assistant, and 9-member City Council. Funds were still appropriated by Congress; residents had no vote in local government, except to elect school board members. In Sept. 1970, Congress approved legislation giving the District one delegate to the House of Representatives, who can vote in committee but not on the floor. The first delegate was elected 1971.

In May 1974 voters approved a congressionally drafted charter giving them the right to elect their own mayor and a 13-member city council; the first took office Jan. 2, 1975. The district won the right to levy taxes; Congress retained power to veto council actions and approve the city budget.

Proposals for a "federal town" for the deliberations of the Continental Congress were made in 1783, 4 years before the adoption of the Constitution. Rivalry between Northern and Southern delegates over the site appeared in the First Congress, 1789. John Adams, presiding officer of the Senate, cast the deciding vote of that body for Germantown, PA. In 1790 Congress compromised by making Philadelphia the temporary capital for 10 years. The Virginia members of the House wanted a permanent capital on the eastern bank of the Potomac, while the Southerners opposed having the nation assume the war debts of the 13 original states as provided under the Assumption Bill, fathered by Alexander Hamilton. Hamilton and Jefferson arranged a compromise: the Virginia men voted for the Assumption Bill, and the Northerners conceded the capital to the Potomac. Pres. Washington chose the site in Oct. 1790 and persuaded landowners to sell their holdings to the government. The capital was named Washington.

Washington appointed Pierre Charles L'Enfant, a Frenchman, to plan the capital on an area not more than 10 mi square. The L'Enfant plan, for streets 100 to 110 ft. wide and one avenue 400 ft. wide and a mile long, seemed grandiose and foolhardy, but Washington endorsed it. When L'Enfant ordered a wealthy landowner to remove his new manor house because it obstructed a vista, and demolished it when the owner refused, Washington stepped in and dismissed the architect. Andrew Ellicott, who was working on surveying the area, finished the official map and design of the city. Ellicott was assisted by Benjamin Banneker, a distinguished black architect and astronomer.

On Sept. 18, 1793, Pres. Washington laid the cornerstone of the north wing of the Capitol. On June 3, 1800, Pres. John Adams moved to Washington, and on June 10, Philadelphia ceased to be the temporary capital. The City of Washington was incorporated in 1802; the District of Columbia was created as a municipal corporation in 1874, embracing Washington, Georgetown, and Washington County.

Tourist attractions: *See* Washington, DC, Capital of the U.S., which follows Outlying U.S. Areas.

Tourist information. Washington, DC Convention and Visitors Association, 1212 New York Ave. NW, #600, Washington, DC 20005; phone: 202-789-7000.

Website. http://dcpages.ari.net

Tourism website. http://www.washington.org

OUTLYING U.S. AREAS

American Samoa

People. Population (1997 est.): 61,819. **Population growth rate** (1997 est.): 3.72%. **Major ethnic group:** Samoan (Polynesian), Caucasian, Tongan. **Languages:** Samoan, English.

Land area: 77 sq. mi. **Total area:** 90 sq mi. **Capital:** Pago Pago, Island of Tutuila. **Motto:** Samoa Muamua le Atua (In Samoa, God Is First). **Song:** Amerika Samoa. **Flower:** Paogo (Ula-fala). **Plant:** Ava.

Public education. Student-teacher ratio (1995): 20.0.

Boasting spectacular scenery and delightful South Seas climate, American Samoa is the most southerly of all lands under U.S. sovereignty. It is an unincorporated territory consisting of 7 small islands of the Samoan group: **Tutuila, Aunu'u, Manu'a Group (Ta'u, Olosega, Ofu), Rose,** and **Swains Island.** The islands are 2,300 mi SW of Honolulu.

Economy. Chief industries: tuna processing, trade, services, tourism. **Chief crops:** vegetables, nuts, melons and other fruits. **Livestock** (1990): 179 cattle; 7,580 hogs/pigs; 27,401 chickens.

Finance. FDIC-insured commercial banks (1997): 1. **Deposits:** $44 mil.

A tripartite agreement between Great Britain, Germany, and the U.S. in 1899 gave the U.S. sovereignty over the eastern islands of the Samoan group; these islands became American Samoa. Local chiefs ceded Tutuila and Aunu'u to the U.S. in 1900, and the Manu'a group and Rose in 1904; Swains Island was annexed in 1925. Samoa (Western), comprising the larger islands of the Samoan group, was a New Zealand mandate and UN Trusteeship until it became independent Jan. 1, 1962 (now called Samoa).

Tutuila and Aunu'u have an area of 53 sq mi. Ta'u has an area of 17 sq mi, and the islets of Ofu and Olosega, 5 sq mi with a population of a few thousand. Swains Island has nearly 2 sq mi and a population of about 100.

About 70% of the land is bush and mountains. Chief exports are fish products. Taro, breadfruit, yams, coconuts, pineapples, oranges, and bananas are also produced.

From 1900 to 1951, American Samoa was under the jurisdiction of the U.S. Navy. Since 1951, it has been under the Interior Dept. On Jan. 3, 1978, the first popularly elected Samoan governor and lieutenant governor were inaugurated. Previously, the governor was appointed by the Secretary of the Interior. American Samoa has a bicameral legislature and elects a delegate to the House of Representatives, with no vote except in committees.

The American Samoans are of Polynesian origin. They are nationals of the U.S.; approximately 20,000 live in Hawaii, 65,000 in California and Washington.

Website. http://www.samoanet.com

Guam

Where America's Day Begins

People. Population (1997 est.): 160,595. **Population growth rate** (1997): 2.5%. **Pop. density** (1990): 631.6 per sq mi. **Major ethnic groups** Chamorro, Filipino, Caucasian, Chinese, Japanese, Korean. (Native Guamanians, ethnically Chamorros, are basically of Indonesian stock, with a mixture of Spanish and Filipino; in addition to the official language, they speak the native Chamorro). **Languages:** English, Chamorro, Japanese. **Migration** (1990): About 52% of population were born elsewhere; of these, 48% in Asia, 40% in U.S.

Geography. Total area: 217 sq mi. **Land area:** 210 sq. mi. **Location:** largest and southernmost of the Mariana Islands in the West Pacific, 3,700 mi W of Hawaii. **Climate:** tropical, with temperatures from 70° to 90° F; avg. annual rainfall, about 70 in. **Topography:** coralline limestone plateau in the N; southern chain of low volcanic mountains sloping gently to the W, more steeply to coastal cliffs on the E; general elevation, 500 ft; highest point, Mt. Lamlam, 1,334 ft. **Capital:** Hagatna.

Economy. Chief industries: tourism, U.S. military, construction, banking, printing & publishing. **Chief manuf. goods:** textiles, foods. **Chief crops:** cabbages, eggplants, cucumber, long beans, tomatoes, bananas, coconuts, watermelon, yams, cantaloupe, papayas, maize, sweet potatoes. **Livestock** (1992): 388 cattle; 2,038 hogs/pigs; 12,206 chickens. **Chief port:** Apra Harbor. **Internat. airport at:** Hagatna. **Value of construction** (1994): $614.3 mil. **Employment distrib.** (1994): 64.9% govt.; 20.2% trade; 19.5% serv. **Per capita income** (1992): $10,834. **Unemployment** (1994): 6.7%. **Tourism expends.** (1995): $4.9 bil.

Finance. FDIC-insured commercial banks (1997): 2. **Deposits:** $734 mil. **FDIC-insured savings institutions** (1997): 2. **Assets:** $276 mil.

Federal govt. Federal employees (1990): 7,200. **Notable fed. facilities:** Anderson AFB; naval, air, and port bases.

Public education. Student-teacher ratio (1995): 18.3.

Misc. data. Flower: Puti Tai Nobio (Bougainvillea). **Bird:** Toto (Fruit dove). **Tree:** Ifit (Intsiabijuga). **Song:** Stand Ye Guamanians.

History. Guam was probably settled by voyagers from the Indonesian-Philippine archipelago by 3d cent. BC. Pottery, rice cultivation, and megalithic technology show strong East Asian cultural influence. Centralized, village clan-based communities engaged in agriculture and offshore fishing. The estimated population by the early 16th cent. was 50,000-75,000. Magellan arrived in the Marianas Mar. 6, 1521. They were colonized in 1668 by Spanish missionaries, who named them the Mariana Islands in honor of Maria Anna, queen of Spain. When Spain ceded Guam to the U.S., it sold the other Marianas to Germany. Japan obtained a League of Nations mandate over the German islands in 1919; in Dec. 1941 it seized Guam, which was retaken by the U.S. in July-August 1944.

Guam is a self-governing organized unincorporated U.S. territory. The Organic Act of 1950 provided for a governor, elected to a 4-year term, and a 21-member unicameral legislature, elected biennially by the residents, who are American citizens. In 1970, the first governor was elected. In 1972, a U.S. law gave Guam one delegate to the U.S. House of Representatives who has a voice but no vote, except in committees.

Guam's quest to change its status to a U.S. Commonwealth began in the late 1970s. The Guam Commission on Self-Determination, created in 1984, developed a draft Commonwealth Act. In 1993, legislation proposing a change of status was submitted to the U.S. Congress. In 1994, the U.S. Congress passed legislation transferring 3,200 acres of land on Guam from federal to local control.

Tourist attractions. Tropical climate, oceanic marine environment; annual mid-Aug. Merizo Water Festival; Tarzan Falls; beaches; water sports; duty-free port shopping.

Website. http://www.gov.gu

Tourism website. http://www.chamarro.com

Commonwealth of the Northern Mariana Islands

People. Population (1997 est.): 53,552. **Major ethnic Groups:** Chamorro, Carolinians and other Micronesians, Caucasian, Japanese, Chinese, Korean. **Languages:** English, Chamorro, Carolinian.

Total area: 189 sq. mi. **Land area:** 179 sq. mi. Located in the perpetually warm climes between Guam and the Tropic of Cancer, the 14 islands of the Northern Marianas form a 300-mil-long archipelago. The indigenous population in 1990 was concentrated on the 3 largest of the 6 inhabited islands: **Saipan,** the seat of government and commerce (38,896), **Rota** (2,295), and **Tinian** (2,118).

Economy. Chief industries: trade, services, and tourism. **Chief manuf. goods:** apparel, stone, clay and glass products. **Chief crops:** melons, vegetables, horticulture, fruits and nuts. **Livestock** (1990) 4,513 cattle; 1,260 hogs/pigs; 9,580. **Employment distrib.** (1992): 53% trade; 33% serv.; 8% const.; 6% manuf.

Education. Pupil-teacher ratio (1995): 20.9.

The people of the Northern Marianas are predominantly of Chamorro cultural extraction, although Carolinians and immigrants from other areas of E. Asia and Micronesia have also settled in the islands. English is among the several languages commonly spoken. Pursuant to the Covenant of 1976, which established the Northern Marianas as a commonwealth in political union with the U.S., most of the indigenous population and many domiciliaries of these islands achieved U.S. citizenship on Nov. 3, 1986, when the U.S. terminated its administration of the UN trusteeship as it affected the Northern Marianas. From July 18, 1947, the U.S. had administered the Northern Marianas under a trusteeship agreement with the UN Security Council.

The Northern Mariana Islands has been self-governing since 1978, when a constitution drafted and adopted by the people became effective and a popularly elected bicameral legislature (2-year term), with offices of governor (4-year term) and lieut. governor, was inaugurated.

Commonwealth of Puerto Rico

(Estado Libre Asociado de Puerto Rico)

People. Population (1997 est): 3,828,506 (about 2.7 mil more Puerto Ricans reside in the mainland U.S.). **net change** (1990-96): 7.4% **Pop. density** (1990): 1,035 per sq mi. **Urban** (1990): 66.8%. **Ethnic distribution** (1990): 99.9% Hispanic. **Languages:** Spanish and English are joint official languages.

Geography. Total area: 3,508 sq. mi. **Land area:** 3,339 sq mi. **Location:** island lying between the Atlantic to the N and the Caribbean to the S; it is easternmost of the West Indies group called the Greater Antilles, of which Cuba, Hispaniola, and Jamaica are the larger islands. **Climate:** mild, with a mean temperature of 77° F. **Topography:** mountainous throughout three-fourths of its rectangular area, surrounded by a broken coastal plain; highest peak, Cerro de Punto, 4,390 ft. **Capital:** San Juan.

Economy. Chief industries: manufacturing, service. **Chief manuf. goods:** pharmaceuticals, apparel, electronics & other electric equipment, industrial machinery. **Gross domestic product:** (1995) $28.4 bil. **Chief crops:** coffee, plantains, pineapples, tomatoes, sugarcane, bananas, mangos, ornamental plants. **Livestock** (1996): 370,655 cattle; 182,247 hogs; 12.6 mil poultry. **Nonfuel minerals** (1996): $31.1 mil, mostly portland cement, crushed stone. **Commercial fishing** (1996): $15.7 mil. **Chief ports/river shipping:** San Juan, Ponce, Mayagüez. **Major airports at:** San Juan, Ponce, Mayagüez, Aguadilla. **Value of construction** (1996): $4.1 bil. **Employment distrib.** (1996): 32.6% public admin.; 23.1% serv.; 19.9% trade; 16.3% mfg. **Per capita income** (1996): $7,882. **Unemployment** (1997): 13.5%. **Tourism expends.** (1995): $1.9 mil.

Finance. FDIC-insured commercial banks (1997): 13. **Deposits:** $21.6 bil. **FDIC-insured savings institutions** (1997): 1. **Assets:** $30 mil.

Federal govt. Fed. civ. employees (1997): 13,874. **Notable fed. facilities:** U.S. Naval Station at Roosevelt Roads; P.R. National Guard Training Area at Camp

Santiago, and at Ft. Allen, Juana Diaz; Sabana SECA Communications Center (U.S. Navy); U.S. Army Station at Ft. Buchanan.

Energy. Electricity production (1996): 15.9 bil kWh.

Public education. Student-teacher ratio (1995): 16.0. **Min. teachers' salary** (1997): $1,500 monthly.

Misc. data. Motto: Joannes Est Nomen Eius (John is his name). **Flower:** Maga. **Bird:** Reinita. **Tree:** Ceiba. **National anthem:** La Borinqueña.

History. Puerto Rico (or Borinquen, after the original Arawak Indian name, Boriquen) was visited by Columbus on his second voyage, Nov. 19, 1493. In 1508, the Spanish arrived.

Sugarcane was introduced, 1515, and slaves were imported 3 years later. Gold mining petered out, 1570. Spaniards fought off a series of British and Dutch attacks; slavery was abolished, 1873. Under the treaty of Paris, Puerto Rico was ceded to the U.S. after the Spanish-American War, 1898. In 1952 the people voted in favor of Commonwealth status.

The Commonwealth of Puerto Rico is a self-governing part of the U.S. with a primarily Hispanic culture. The island's citizens have virtually the same control over their internal affairs as do the 50 states of the U.S. However, they do not vote in national general elections, only in national primaries.

Puerto Rico is represented in the U.S. House of Representatives by a delegate who has a voice but no vote, except in committees.

No federal income tax is collected from residents on income earned from local sources in Puerto Rico. Nevertheless, as part of the U.S. legal system, Puerto Rico is subject to the provisions of the U.S. Constitution; most federal laws apply as they do in the 50 states.

Puerto Rico's famous "Operation Bootstrap," begun in the late 1940s, succeeded in changing the island from "The Poorhouse of the Caribbean" to an area with the highest per capita income in Latin America. This program encouraged manufacturing and development of the tourist trade by selective tax exemption, low-interest loans, and other incentives. Despite the marked success of Puerto Rico's development efforts over an extended period of time, per capita income in Puerto Rico is low in comparison to that of the U.S.

Tourist attractions. Ponce Museum of Art; Forts El Morro and San Cristobal; Old Walled City of San Juan; Arecibo Observatory; Cordillera Central and state parks; El Yunque Rain Forest; San Juan Cathedral; Porta Coeli Chapel and Museum of Religious Art, Interamerican Univ., San Germán; Condado Convention Center; Casa Blanca, Ponce de León family home, Puerto Rican Family Museum of 16th and 17th centuries, and Fine Arts Center all in San Juan.

Cultural facilities and events. Festival Casals classical music concerts, mid-June; Puerto Rico Symphony Orchestra at Music Conservatory; Botanical Garden and Museum of Anthropology, Art, and History at the University of Puerto Rico; Institute of Puerto Rican Culture, at the Dominican Convent; and many popular festivals.

Famous Puerto Ricans. Julia de Burgos, Marta Casals Istomin, Pablo Casals, José Celso Barbosa, Orlando Cepeda, Roberto Clemente, José de Diego, José Feliciano, Doña Felisa Rincón de Gautier, Luis A. Ferré, José Ferrer, Commodore Diégo E. Hernández, Miguel Hernández Agosto, Rafael Hernández (El Jibarito), Rafael Hernández Colón, Raúl Juliá, René Marqués, Concha Meléndez, Rita Moreno, Luis Muñoz Marín, Luis Palés Matos, Adm. Horacio Rivero.

Chamber of Commerce. 100 Tetuán, PO Box S-3789, San Juan, PR 00902.

Website. http://fortaleza.govpr.org

Tourism website. http://www.discoverpuertorico.com

Virgin Islands

St. John, St. Croix, St. Thomas

People. Population (1997 est.): 97,240. **Population growth rate** (1994 est.): –0.52%. **Major ethnic groups:** West Indian, French, Hispanic. **Languages:** English (official), Spanish, Creole.

Geography. Total area: 171 sq mi. **Land area:** 134 sq mi. **Location:** 3 larger and 50 smaller islands and cays in the S and W of the V.I. group (British V.I. colony to the N and E), which is situated 70 mi E of Puerto Rico, located W of the Anegada Passage, a major channel connecting the Atlantic Ocean and the Caribbean Sea. **Climate:** subtropical; the sun tempered by gentle trade winds; humidity is low; average temperature, 78° F. **Topography:** St. Thomas is mainly a ridge of hills running E and W, and has little tillable land; St. Croix rises abruptly in the N but slopes to the S to flatlands and lagoons; St. John has steep, lofty hills and valleys with little level tillable land. **Capital:** Charlotte Amalie, St. Thomas.

Economy. Chief industries: tourism, rum, alumina, petroleum refining, watches, textiles, electronics, printing & publishing. **Chief manuf. goods:** rum, textiles, pharmaceuticals, perfumes, stone, glass & clay products. **Chief crops:** vegetables, horticulture, fruits and nuts. **Livestock** (1992): 7,132 cattle; 1,311 hogs/pigs; 9,087 chickens. **Minerals:** sand, gravel. **Chief ports:** Cruz Bay, St. John; Frederiksted and Christiansted, St. Croix; Charlotte Amalie, St. Thomas. **Internat. airports on:** St. Thomas, St. Croix. **Value of construction** (1992): $168.9 mil. **Employment distrib.** (1992): 50% trade; 43% serv. **Per capita income** (1989): $11,052. **Unemployment** (1992): 2.8%. **Tourism expends.** (1995): $792 mil.

Finance. FDIC-insured savings institutions (1997): 2. **Deposits:** $72 mil. **FDIC-insured savings institutions** (1997): 1. **Assets:** 54 mil.

Energy. Electricity production (1992): 565 mil kWh.

Public education. Student-teacher ratio (1995): 14.0.

Misc. data. Flower: Yellow elder or yellow trumpet, local designation Ginger Thomas. **Bird:** Yellow breast. **Song:** Virgin Islands March.

History. The islands were visited by Columbus in 1493. Spanish forces, 1555, defeated the Caribes and claimed the territory; by 1596 the native population was annihilated. First permanent settlement in the U.S. territory, 1672, by the Danes; U.S. purchased the islands, 1917, for defense purposes.

The Virgin Islands has a republican form of government, headed by a governor and lieut. governor elected, since 1970, by popular vote for 4-year terms. There is a 15-member unicameral legislature, elected by popular vote for a 2-year term. Residents of the V.I. have been U.S. citizens since 1927. Since 1973 they have elected a delegate to the U.S. House of Representatives, who has a voice but no vote, except in committees.

Tourist attractions. Magens Bay, St. Thomas; duty-free shopping; Virgin Islands Natl. Park, beaches, Indian relics, and evidence of colonial Danes.

Tourist information. Dept. of Economic Development & Agriculture: St. Thomas, PO Box 6400, St. Thomas, VI 00801; St. Croix, PO Box 4535, Christiansted, St. Croix 00820.

Website. http://www.usvi.net

Other Islands

Navassa lies between Jamaica and Haiti, 100 mi south of Guantanamo Bay, Cuba, in the Caribbean; it covers about 3 sq mi, is reserved by the U.S. for a lighthouse, and is uninhabited. It is administered by the U.S. Coast Guard.

Wake Atoll, and its neighboring atolls, **Wilkes** and **Peale,** lie in the Pacific Ocean on the direct route from Hawaii to Hong Kong, about 2,300 mi W of Honolulu and 1,290 mi E of Guam. The group is 4.5 mi long, 1.5 mi wide, and totals less than 3 sq mi. in land area. The U.S. flag was hoisted over Wake Atoll, July 4, 1898; formal possession taken Jan. 17, 1899. Wake was administered by the U.S. Air Force, 1972-94. The population consists of about 200 persons.

Midway Atoll, acquired in 1867, consist of 2 atolls, **Sand** and **Eastern,** in N Pacific 1,150 mi. NW of Honolulu, with an area of about 2 sq mi, administered by the U.S. Navy. There is no indigenous population; total pop. is about 450. **Johnston Atoll,** 717 mi WSW of Honolulu, area 1 sq mi, is operated by the Defense Nuclear Agency, and the Fish and Wildlife Service, U.S. Dept. of the Interior; its population is about 1,200. **Kingman Reef,** 920 mi S of Hawaii, is under Navy control. **Howland, Jarvis,** and **Baker Islands,** 1,400-1,650 mi SW of Honolulu, uninhabited since World War II, are under the Interior Dept. **Palmyra** is an atoll about 1,000 mi S of Hawaii, 2 sq mi. Privately owned, it is under the Interior Dept.

Washington, DC, Capital of the U.S.

Most attractions are free. All times are subject to change. For more details call the Washington, DC, Convention and Visitors Association at 202-789-7000, or check out the website at: http://www.washington.org

Bureau of Engraving and Printing

The **Bureau of Engraving and Printing** of the U.S. Treasury Dept. is the headquarters for the making of U.S. paper money. Free 35-minute self-guided tours (tickets required) Mon.-Fri., 9 AM-2 PM year-round; extended hours, June-Aug., 5 PM-6:40 PM. Closed federal holidays. 14th and C Sts. SW. Phone: 202-874-3019.

Capitol

The **United States Capitol** was originally designed by Dr. William Thornton, an amateur architect, who submitted a plan in 1793 that won him $500 and a city lot.

The south, or House, wing was completed in 1807 under the direction of Benjamin H. Latrobe.

The present Senate and House wings and the iron dome were designed and constructed by Thomas U. Walter, 4th architect of the Capitol, between 1851 and 1863.

The present cast iron dome at its greatest exterior measures 135 ft 5 in., and it is topped by the bronze Statue of Freedom that stands 19½ ft and weighs 14,985 lb. On its base are the words *E Pluribus Unum* (Out of Many, One).

The Capitol is open from 9 AM to 8 PM, March-Aug., and 9 AM to 4:30 PM, Sept.-Feb., daily. It is closed Jan. 1, Thanksgiving Day, and Dec. 25. Tours through the Capitol, including the House and Senate galleries, are conducted Mon.-Sat.

To observe debate in the House or Senate while Congress is in session, individuals living in the U.S. may obtain tickets to the visitor's galleries from their U.S. representative or senator. Visitors from other countries may obtain passes at the Capitol. Between Constitution & Independence Ave., at Pennsylvania Ave. Phone: 202-225-6827.

Federal Bureau of Investigation

The **Federal Bureau of Investigation** offers guided one-hour tours of its headquarters, beginning with a videotape presentation. Visitors learn about the history of the FBI and see such things as the weapons confiscated from famous gangsters, photos of the most-wanted fugitives, the DNA laboratory, goods forfeited and seized in narcotics operations, and a sharpshooting demonstration.

Tours are conducted Mon.-Fri., 8:45 AM-4:15 PM, except Jan. 1, Dec. 25, and other federal holidays. Tickets may be obtained at the FBI on day of tour or through a U.S. representative or senator. J. Edgar Hoover Bldg., Pennsylvania Ave., between 9th and 10th Sts. NW. Phone: 202-324-3447.

Folger Shakespeare Library

The **Folger Shakespeare Library,** on Capitol Hill, is a research institution holding rare books and manuscripts of the Renaissance period and the largest collection of Shakespearean materials in the world, including 79 copies of the First Folio. The library's museum and performing arts programs are presented in the Elizabethan Theatre, which resembles an innyard theater of Shakespeare's day.

Exhibit may be visited Mon.-Sat., 10 AM-4 PM., 201 E. Capitol St., SE , Phone: 202-544-7077.

Holocaust Memorial Museum

The **U.S. Holocaust Memorial Museum** opened on Apr. 21, 1993. The museum documents, through permanent and temporary displays, interactive videos, and special lectures, the events of the Holocaust beginning in 1933 and continuing World War II. The permanent exhibition is not recommended for children under the age of 11.

The museum is open daily, 10 AM-5:30 PM, except Yom Kippur and Dec. 25, and extended hours (8 AM-10 PM) Apr. 3-Sept. 2. A limited number of free tickets are available on day of visit; advance tickets may be ordered for a small fee. 100 Raoul Wallenberg Pl. SW. Phone: 202-488-0400.

Jefferson Memorial

Dedicated in 1943, the **Thomas Jefferson Memorial** stands on the south shore of the Tidal Basin in West Potomac Park. It is a circular stone structure, with Vermont marble on the exterior and Georgia white marble inside, and combines architectural elements of the dome of the Pantheon in Rome and the rotunda designed by Jefferson for the University of Virginia.

The memorial, on the south edge of the Tidal Basin, is open daily, 8 AM-midnight. An elevator and curb ramps for the handicapped are in service. Phone: 202-426-6841.

John F. Kennedy Center

The **John F. Kennedy Center for the Performing Arts,** designated by Congress as the National Cultural Center and the official memorial in Washington, DC, to Pres. John F. Kennedy, opened Sept. 8, 1971. Designed by Edward Durell Stone, the center includes an opera house, a concert hall, several theaters, 2 restaurants, and a library.

Free tours are available daily, 10 AM-1 PM. 2700 F St. NW. Phone: 202-416-8340, or 1-800-444-1324.

Korean War Veterans Memorial

Dedicated on July 27, 1995, the **Korean War Veterans Memorial** honors all Americans who served in the Korean War. Situated at the west end of the Mall, across the reflecting pool from the Vietnam Memorial, the triangular-shaped stone and steel memorial features a multiservice formation of 19 troops clad in ponchos with the wind at their back, ready for combat. A granite wall, with images of the men and women who served, juts into a pool of water, the Pool of Remembrance, and is inscribed with the words *Freedom Is Not Free.*

The $18 mil memorial, which was funded by private donations, is open 8 AM-midnight. Independence Ave. at Lincoln Memorial. Phone: 202-619-7222.

Library of Congress

Established by and for Congress in 1800, the **Library of Congress** has extended its services over the years to other government agencies and other libraries, to scholars, and to the general public, and it now serves as the national library. It contains more than 80 million items in 470 languages.

The library's exhibit halls are open to the public Mon.-Fri., 8:30 AM-9:30 PM; Sat., 8:30 AM-6 PM. The library is closed Jan. 1 and Dec. 25. 101 Independence Ave., SE. Phone: 202-707-8000.

Lincoln Memorial

Designed by Henry Bacon, the **Lincoln Memorial** in West Potomac Park, on the axis of the Capitol and the Washington Monument, consists of a large marble hall enclosing a heroic statue of Abraham Lincoln in meditation sitting on a large armchair. The memorial was dedicated on May 30, 1922. The statue was designed by Daniel Chester French and sculpted by French and the Piccirilli brothers. Murals and ornamentation on the bronze ceiling beams are by Jules Guerin. The text of the Gettysburg Address is in the south chamber; that of Lincoln's Second Inaugural speech is in the north chamber. Each is engraved on a stone tablet.

The memorial is open 24 hr daily. An elevator for the handicapped is in service. W. Potomac Park at 23rd St. NW. Phone: 202-619-7222.

National Archives and Records

Original copies of the Declaration of Independence, the Constitution, and the Bill of Rights are on permanent display in the **National Archives** Exhibition Hall. The National Archives also holds other valuable U.S. government records and historic maps, photographs, and manuscripts.

Central Research and Microfilm Research Rooms are also available to the public for genealogical research.

The Exhibition Hall is open daily, 10 AM-5:30 PM; closed Dec. 25. 7th & Pennsylvania Ave. NW. Phone: 202-501-5000.)

National Gallery of Art

The **National Gallery of Art**, situated on the north side of the Mall facing Constitution Avenue, was established by Congress, Mar. 24, 1937, and opened Mar. 17, 1941. The original West building was designed by John Russell Pope. The East building, opened in 1978, was designed by I. M. Pei. The National Gallery is separate from, but maintains a relationship with, the Smithsonian Institution.

Open daily, 10 AM-5 PM; Sunday, 11 AM-6 PM. Closed Jan. 1 and Dec. 25. 4th & Constitution Ave NW. Phone: 202-737-4215.

Franklin Delano Roosevelt Memorial

Opened May 2, 1997, by Pres. Bill Clinton, the **FDR Memorial** features 9 bronze sculptural ensembles depicting FDR, Eleanor Roosevelt (the first First Lady to be honored in a national memorial), and events from the Great Depression and World War II. This 7.5-acre memorial is located near the Tidal Basin in a park-like setting and includes waterfalls, quiet pools, and reddish Dakota granite upon which some of Pres. Roosevelt's well-known words are carved. The monument is wheelchair accessible.

Grounds, staffed daily, 8 AM-midnight, except Dec. 25. 1850 W. Basin Dr. SW. Phone: (202) 619-7222.

Smithsonian Institution

The **Smithsonian Institution,** established in 1846, is the world's largest museum complex and consists of 14 museums and the National Zoo. It holds some 100 mil. artifacts and specimens in its trust. Nine museums are on the National Mall between the Washington Monument and the Capitol; 5 other museums and the zoo are elsewhere in Washington (the Cooper-Hewitt Museum and the National Museum of the American Indian, also administered by the Smithsonian, are in New York City). The **Smithsonian Information Center,** is located in "the Castle" on the Mall. Also on the Mall are the **National Museum of American History,** the **National Museum of Natural History,** the **National Air and Space Museum,** the **Hirshhorn Museum and Sculpture Garden,** the **Arthur M. Sackler Gallery,** the **National Museum of African Art,** the **Freer Gallery of Art,** and the **Arts and Industries Building.** Near the Sackler Gallery is the **Enid A. Haupt Garden.** Located nearby are the **National Postal Museum,** the **National Museum of American Art,** the **National Portrait Gallery,** and the **Renwick Gallery.** Farther away, at 1901 Fort Place SE, is the **Anacostia Museum.**

Most museums are open daily, except Dec. 25, 10 AM-5:30 PM. Phone: 202-357-2700.

Vietnam Veterans Memorial

Originally dedicated on Nov. 13, 1982, the **Vietnam Veterans Memorial** is a recognition of the men and women who served in the armed forces in the Vietnam War. On a V-shaped black-granite wall, designed by Maya Ying Lin, are inscribed the names of the more than 58,000 Americans who lost their lives or remain missing.

Since 1982, 2 additions have been made to the Memorial. The 1st, dedicated on Nov. 11, 1984, is the Frederick Hart sculpture *Three Servicemen*. On Nov. 11, 1993, the Vietnam Women's Memorial was dedicated, honoring the more than 11,500 women who served in Vietnam. The bronze sculpture, portraying 3 women helping a wounded male soldier, was designed by Glenna Goodacre.

The memorial is open 24 hr daily. Constitution Ave. & Bacon Dr. NW. Phone: 202-634-1568.

Washington Monument

The **Washington Monument,** dedicated in 1885, is a tapering shaft, or obelisk, of white marble, 555 ft, 5 1/8 inches in height and 55 ft, 1½ in. square at base. Eight small windows, 2 on each side, are located at the 500-ft level, where points of interest are indicated.

Open daily (except Dec. 25), 9 AM-4:30 PM; 8 AM-midnight, Apr.-Labor Day. Free timed passes are available; passes are available in advance for a small fee. 15th & Constitution Ave. NW. Phone: 202-426-6841.

White House

The **White House,** the President's residence, stands on 18 acres on the south side of Pennsylvania Ave., between the Treasury and the old Executive Office Building. The walls are of sandstone, quarried at Aquia Creek, VA. The exterior walls were painted, causing the building to be termed the "White House." On Aug. 24, 1814, during Madison's administration, the house was burned by the British. James Hoban rebuilt it by Oct. 1817.

The White House is normally open for free self-guided tours Tues.-Sat., 10 AM-noon (passes, necessary mid-March-mid-Sept., are available at White House Visitor's Center, 8 AM-noon, located at 1450 Pennsylvania Ave., NW). Only the public rooms on the ground floor and state floor may be visited. Free reserved tickets for guided congressional tours can be obtained 8 to 10 weeks in advance from your local U.S. representative or senator. 1600 Pennsylvania Ave. Phone: 202-456-7041.

Attractions Near Washington, DC

Arlington National Cemetery

Arlington National Cemetery, on the former Custis estate in Arlington, VA, is the site of the **Tomb of the Unknowns** and is the final resting place of Pres. John Fitzgerald Kennedy, who was buried there on Nov. 25, 1963. His wife, Jacqueline Bouvier Kennedy Onassis, was buried at the same site on May 23, 1994. An eternal flame burns over the grave site. In an adjacent area is the grave of Pres. Kennedy's brother Sen. Robert F. Kennedy (NY), interred on June 8, 1968. Many other famous Americans are also buried at Arlington, as well as more than 200,000 American soldiers from every major war.

North of the National Cemetery, approximately 350 yd, stands the **U.S. Marine Corps War Memorial**, also known as Iwo Jima. The memorial is a bronze statue of the raising of the U.S. flag on Mt. Suribachi, Feb. 23, 1945, during World War II, executed by Felix de Weldon from the photograph by Joe Rosenthal.

On the southern side of the Memorial Bridge, near the cemetery entrance, a memorial honoring the women in the military was dedicated, Oct. 18, 1997. The **Women in Military Service for America Memorial** is a half-circle granite monument, 30 ft. high and 226 ft. in diameter, with the Great Seal of the United States in the center.

Open daily, 8 AM-5 PM (8 AM-7 PM., Apr.-Sept.), Arlington, VA. Phone: 703-697-4967.

Mount Vernon

Mount Vernon, George Washington's estate, is on the south bank of the Potomac R., 16 mi below Washington, DC, in northern Virginia. The present house is an enlargement of one apparently built on the site by Augustine Washington, who lived there 1735-38. His son Lawrence came there in 1743, and renamed the plantation Mount Vernon in honor of Admiral Vernon, under whom he had served in the West Indies. Lawrence Washington died in 1752 and was succeeded as proprietor by his half-brother, George Washington. The estate has been restored to its 18th-century appearance and includes many original furnishings. Washington and his wife, Martha, are buried on the grounds.

Open 365 days, 8 AM-5 PM, Apr.-Aug., 9 AM-5 PM, Sept., Oct., Mar.; 9 AM-4 PM, Nov.-Feb. Phone: 703-780-2000, or 1-800-429-1520. Admission: adults $8, seniors (62+) $7.50, children (6-11) $4, age 5 and under free.

The Pentagon

The **Pentagon,** headquarters of the Department of Defense, is one of the world's largest office buildings. Situated in Arlington, VA, it houses more than 23,000 employees in offices that occupy 3,707,745 sq ft.

Free tours (about every 2 hrs) are available Mon.-Fri. (excluding federal holidays), starting at 9 AM; last tour begins at 3:20 PM. Arlington, VA (I-395 South to Boundary Channel Drive exit). Phone: 703-695-1776.

AWARDS — MEDALS — PRIZES

The Alfred B. Nobel Prize Winners

Alfred B. Nobel (1833-96), inventor of dynamite, bequeathed $9 mil, the interest to be distributed yearly to those judged to have had most benefited humankind in physics, chemistry, medicine-physiology, literature, and promotion of peace. These prizes were first awarded in 1901. The first Nobel Memorial Prize in Economic Science was awarded in 1969, funded by the central bank of Sweden. If the year is omitted, no award was given. For 1998 winners, see separate section, The 1998 Nobel Prizes. In 1998, each prize was worth more than $1 mil.

Physics

- 1997 Steven Chu, William D. Phillips, both U.S.; Claude Cohen-Tannoudji, Fr.
- 1996 David M. Lee, Douglas D. Osheroff, Robert C. Richardson, all U.S.
- 1995 Martin Perl, Frederick Reines, both U.S.
- 1994 Bertram N. Brockhouse, Can.; Clifford G. Shull, U.S.
- 1993 Joseph H. Taylor, Russell A. Hulse, both U.S.
- 1992 Georges Charpak, Pol.-Fr.
- 1991 Pierre-Giles de Gennes, Fr.
- 1990 Richard E. Taylor, Can.; Jerome I. Friedman, Henry W. Kendall, both U.S.
- 1989 Norman F. Ramsey, U.S.; Hans G. Dehmelt, Ger.-U.S.; Wolfgang Paul, Ger.
- 1988 Leon M. Lederman, Melvin Schwartz, Jack Steinberger, all U.S.
- 1987 K. Alex Müller, Swiss; J. Georg Bednorz, Ger.
- 1986 Ernest Ruska, Ger.; Gerd Binnig, Ger.; Heinrich Rohrer, Swiss
- 1985 Klaus von Klitzing, Ger.
- 1984 Carlo Rubbia, It.; Simon van der Meer, Dutch
- 1983 Subrahmanyan Chandrasekhar, William A. Fowler, both U.S.
- 1982 Kenneth G. Wilson, U.S.
- 1981 Nicolaas Bloembergen, Arthur Schaalow, both U.S.; Kai M. Siegbahn, Swed.
- 1980 James W. Cronin, Val L. Fitch, both U.S.
- 1979 Steven Weinberg, Sheldon L. Glashow, both U.S.; Abdus Salam, Pakistani
- 1978 Pyotr Kapitsa, USSR; Arno Penzias, Robert Wilson, both U.S.
- 1977 John H. Van Vleck, Philip W. Anderson, both U.S.; Nevill F. Mott, Br.
- 1976 Burton Richter, Samuel C.C. Ting, both U.S.
- 1975 James Rainwater, U.S.; Ben Mottelson, U.S.-Dan.; Aage Bohr, Dan.
- 1974 Martin Ryle, Antony Hewish, both Br.
- 1973 Ivar Giaever, U.S.; Leo Esaki, Jpn.; Brian D. Josephson, Br.
- 1972 John Bardeen, Leon N. Cooper, John R. Schrieffer, all U.S.
- 1971 Dennis Gabor, Br.
- 1970 Louis Neel, Fr.; Hannes Alfven, Swed.
- 1969 Murray Gell-Mann, U.S.
- 1968 Luis W. Alvarez, U.S.
- 1967 Hans A. Bethe, U.S.
- 1966 Alfred Kastler, Fr.
- 1965 Richard P. Feynman, Julian S. Schwinger, both U.S.; Shinichiro Tomonaga, Jpn.
- 1964 Nikolai G. Basov, Aleksander M. Prochorov, both USSR; Charles H. Townes, U.S.
- 1963 Maria Goeppert-Mayer, Eugene P. Wigner, both U.S.; J. Hans D. Jensen, Ger.
- 1962 Lev. D. Landau, USSR
- 1961 Robert Hofstadter, U.S.; Rudolf L. Mossbauer, Ger.
- 1960 Donald A. Glaser, U.S.
- 1959 Owen Chamberlain, Emilio G. Segre, both U.S.
- 1958 Pavel Cherenkov, Ilya Frank, Igor Y. Tamm, all USSR
- 1957 Tsung-dao Lee, Chen Ning Yang, both U.S.
- 1956 John Bardeen, Walter H. Brattain, William Shockley, all U.S.
- 1955 Polykarp Kusch, Willis E. Lamb, both U.S.
- 1954 Max Born, Br.; Walter Bothe, Ger.
- 1953 Frits Zernike, Dutch
- 1952 Felix Bloch, Edward M. Purcell, both U.S.
- 1951 Sir John D. Cockroft, Br.; Ernest T. S. Walton, Ir.
- 1950 Cecil F. Powell, Br.
- 1949 Hideki Yukawa, Jpn.
- 1948 Patrick M. S. Blackett, Br.
- 1947 Sir Edward V. Appleton, Br.
- 1946 Percy W. Bridgman, U.S.
- 1945 Wolfgang Pauli, U.S.
- 1944 Isidor Isaac Rabi, U.S.
- 1943 Otto Stern, U.S.
- 1939 Ernest O. Lawrence, U.S.
- 1938 Enrico Fermi, It.-U.S.
- 1937 Clinton J. Davisson, U.S.; Sir George P. Thomson, Br.
- 1936 Carl D. Anderson, U.S.;Victor F. Hess, Aus.
- 1935 Sir James Chadwick, Br.
- 1933 Paul A. M. Dirac, Br.; Erwin Schrodinger, Austria
- 1932 Werner Heisenberg, Ger.
- 1930 Sir Chandrasekhara V. Raman, Indian
- 1929 Prince Louis-Victor de Broglie, Fr.
- 1928 Owen W. Richardson, Br.
- 1927 Arthur H. Compton, U.S.; Charles T. R. Wilson, Br.
- 1926 Jean B. Perrin, Fr.
- 1925 James Franck, Gustav Hertz, both Ger.
- 1924 Karl M. G. Siegbahn, Swed.
- 1923 Robert A. Millikan, U.S.
- 1922 Niels Bohr, Dan.
- 1921 Albert Einstein, Ger.-U.S.
- 1920 Charles E. Guillaume, Fr.
- 1919 Johannes Stark, Ger.
- 1918 Max K. E. L. Planck, Ger.
- 1917 Charles G. Barkla, Br.
- 1915 Sir William H. Bragg, Sir William L. Bragg, both Br.
- 1914 Max von Laue, Ger.
- 1913 Heike Kamerlingh-Onnes, Dutch
- 1912 Nils G. Dalen, Swed.
- 1911 Wilhelm Wien, Ger.
- 1910 Johannes D. van der Waals, Dutch
- 1909 Carl F. Braun, Ger.; Guglielmo Marconi, It.
- 1908 Gabriel Lippmann, Fr.
- 1907 Albert A. Michelson, U.S.
- 1906 Sir Joseph J. Thomson, Br.
- 1905 Philipp E. A. von Lenard, Ger.
- 1904 John W. Strutt, Lord Rayleigh, Br.
- 1903 Antoine Henri Becquerel, Pierre Curie, both Fr.; Marie Curie, Pol.-Fr.
- 1902 Hendrik A. Lorentz, Pieter Zeeman, both Dutch
- 1901 Wilhelm C. Roentgen, Ger.

Chemistry

- 1997 Paul D. Boyer, U.S., & John E. Walker, Br.; Jens C. Skou, Dan.
- 1996 Harold W. Kroto, Br.; Robert F. Curl Jr., Richard E. Smalley, both U.S.
- 1995 Paul Crutzen, Dutch; Mario Molina, Mex.-U.S.; Sherwood Rowland, U.S.
- 1994 George A. Olah, U.S.
- 1993 Kary B. Mullis, U.S.; Michael Smith, Br.-Can.
- 1992 Rudolph A. Marcus, Can.-U.S.
- 1991 Richard R. Ernst, Swiss
- 1990 Elias James Corey, U.S.
- 1989 Thomas R. Cech, Sidney Altman, both U.S.
- 1988 Johann Deisenhofer, Robert Huber, Hartmut Michel, all Ger.
- 1987 Donald J. Cram, Charles J. Pedersen, both U.S.; Jean-Marie Lehn, Fr.
- 1986 Dudley Herschbach, Yuan T. Lee, both U.S.; John C. Polanyi, Can.
- 1985 Herbert A. Hauptman, Jerome Karle, both U.S.
- 1984 Bruce Merrifield, U.S.
- 1983 Henry Taube, Can.
- 1982 Aaron Klug, S. Afr.
- 1981 Kenichi Fukui, Jpn.; Roald Hoffmann, U.S.
- 1980 Paul Berg, Walter Gilbert, both U.S.; Frederick Sanger, Br.
- 1979 Herbert C. Brown, U.S.; George Wittig, Ger.
- 1978 Peter Mitchell, Br.
- 1977 Ilya Prigogine, Belg.
- 1976 William N. Lipscomb, U.S.
- 1975 John Cornforth, Austral.-Br.; Vladimir Prelog, Yugo.-Swiss
- 1974 Paul J. Flory, U.S.
- 1973 Ernst Otto Fischer, Ger.; Geoffrey Wilkinson, Br.
- 1972 Christian B. Anfinsen, Stanford Moore, William H. Stein, all U.S.
- 1971 Gerhard Herzberg, Canadian
- 1970 Luis F. Leloir, Arg.
- 1969 Derek H. R. Barton, Br.; Odd Hassel, Nor.
- 1968 Lars Onsager, U.S.
- 1967 Manfred Eigen, Ger.; Ronald G. W. Norrish, George Porter, both Br.
- 1966 Robert S. Mulliken, U.S.
- 1965 Robert B. Woodward, U.S.
- 1964 Dorothy C. Hodgkin, Br.
- 1963 Giulio Natta, It.; Karl Ziegler, Ger.
- 1962 John C. Kendrew, Max F. Perutz, both Br.
- 1961 Melvin Calvin, U.S.
- 1960 Willard F. Libby, U.S.
- 1959 Jaroslav Heyrovsky, Czech.
- 1958 Frederick Sanger, Br.
- 1957 Sir Alexander R. Todd, Br.
- 1956 Sir Cyril N. Hinshelwood, Br.; Nikolai N. Semenov, USSR
- 1955 Vincent du Vigneaud, U.S.
- 1954 Linus C. Pauling, U.S.
- 1953 Hermann Staudinger, Ger.
- 1952 Archer J. P. Martin, Richard L. M. Synge, both Br.
- 1951 Edwin M. McMillan, Glenn T. Seaborg, both U.S.
- 1950 Kurt Alder, Otto P. H. Diels, both Ger.
- 1949 William F. Giauque, U.S.
- 1948 Arne W. K. Tiselius, Swed.
- 1947 Sir Robert Robinson, Br.
- 1946 James B. Sumner, John H. Northrop, Wendell M. Stanley, all U.S.
- 1945 Artturi I. Virtanen, Fin.
- 1944 Otto Hahn, Ger.
- 1943 Georg de Hevesy, Hung.
- 1939 Adolf F. J. Butenandt, Ger.; Leopold Ruzicka, Swiss
- 1938 Richard Kuhn, Ger.
- 1937 Walter N. Haworth, Br.; Paul Karrer, Swiss
- 1936 Peter J. W. Debye, Dutch
- 1935 Frederic & Irene Joliot-Curie, both Fr.
- 1934 Harold C. Urey, U.S.
- 1932 Irving Langmuir, U.S.
- 1931 Friedrich Bergius, Karl Bosch, both Ger.
- 1930 Hans Fischer, Ger.
- 1929 Sir Arthur Harden, Br.; Hans von Euler-Chelpin, Swed.
- 1928 Adolf O. R. Windaus, Ger.
- 1927 Heinrich O. Wieland, Ger.
- 1926 Theodor Svedberg, Swed.
- 1925 Richard A. Zsigmondy, Ger.
- 1923 Fritz Pregl, Austrian
- 1922 Francis W. Aston, Br.
- 1921 Frederick Soddy, Br.
- 1920 Walther H. Nernst, Ger.

1918 Fritz Haber, Ger.
1915 Richard M. Willstatter, Ger.
1914 Theodore W. Richards, U.S.
1913 Alfred Werner, Swiss
1912 Victor Grignard, Paul Sabatier, both Fr.
1911 Marie Curie, Pol.-Fr.
1910 Otto Wallach, Ger.
1909 Wilhelm Ostwald, Ger.
1908 Ernest Rutherford, Br.
1907 Eduard Buchner, Ger.
1906 Henri Moissan, Fr.
1905 Adolf von Baeyer, Ger.
1904 Sir William Ramsay, Br.
1903 Svante A. Arrhenius, Swed.
1902 Emil Fischer, Ger.
1901 Jacobus H. van't Hoff, Dutch

Physiology or Medicine

1997 Stanley B. Prusiner, U.S.
1996 Peter C. Doherty, Austral.; Rolf M. Zinkernagel, Swiss
1995 Edward B. Lewis, Eric F. Wieschaus, both U.S.; Christiane Nuesslein-Volhard, Ger.
1994 Alfred G. Gilman, Martin Rodbell, both U.S.
1993 Phillip A. Sharp, U.S.; Richard J. Roberts, Br.
1992 Edmond H. Fisher, Edwin G. Krebs, both U.S.
1991 Edwin Neher, Bert Sakmann, both Ger.
1990 Joseph E. Murray, E. Donnall Thomas, both U.S.
1989 J. Michael Bishop, Harold E. Varmus, both U.S.
1988 Gertrude B. Elion, George H. Hitchings, both U.S; Sir James Black, Br.
1987 Susumu Tonegawa, Jpn.
1986 Rita Levi-Montalcini, It.-U.S., Stanley Cohen, U.S.
1985 Michael S. Brown, Joseph L. Goldstein, both U.S.
1984 Cesar Milstein, Br.-Arg.; Georges J. F. Koehler, Ger.; Niels K. Jerne, Br.-Dan.
1983 Barbara McClintock, U.S.
1982 Sune Bergstrom, Bengt Samuelsson, both Swed.; John R. Vane, Br.
1981 Roger W. Sperry, David H. Hubel, Tosten N. Wiesel, all U.S.
1980 Baruj Benacerraf, George Snell, both U.S.; Jean Dausset, Fr.
1979 Allan M. Cormack, U.S.; Godfrey N. Hounsfield, Br.
1978 Daniel Nathans, Hamilton O. Smith, both U.S.; Werner Arber, Swiss
1977 Rosalyn S. Yalow, Roger C.L. Guillemin, Andrew V. Schally, all U.S.
1976 Baruch S. Blumberg, Daniel Carleton Gajdusek, both U.S.
1975 David Baltimore, Howard Temin, both U.S.; Renato Dulbecco, It.-U.S.
1974 Albert Claude, Lux.-U.S.; George Emil Palade, Rom.-U.S.; Christian Rene de Duve, Belg.
1973 Karl von Frisch, Ger.; Konrad Lorenz, Ger.-Aus.; Nikolaas Tinbergen, Br.
1972 Gerald M. Edelman, U.S.; Rodney R. Porter, Br.
1971 Earl W. Sutherland Jr., U.S.
1970 Julius Axelrod, U.S.; Sir Bernard Katz, Br.; Ulf von Euler, Swed.
1969 Max Delbrück, Alfred D. Hershey, Salvador Luria, all U.S.
1968 Robert W. Holley, H. Gobind Khorana, Marshall W. Nirenberg, all U.S.
1967 Ragnar Granit, Swed.; Haldan Keffer Hartline, George Wald, both U.S.
1966 Charles B. Huggins, Francis Peyton Rous, both U.S.
1965 François Jacob, Andre Lwoff, Jacques Monod, all Fr.
1964 Konrad E. Bloch, U.S.; Feodor Lynen, Ger.
1963 Sir John C. Eccles, Austral.; Alan L. Hodgkin, Andrew F. Huxley, both Br.
1962 Francis H. C. Crick, Maurice H. F. Wilkins, both Br.; James D. Watson, U.S.
1961 Georg von Bekesy, U.S.
1960 Sir F. MacFarlane Burnet, Austral.; Peter B. Medawar, Br.
1959 Arthur Kornberg, Severo Ochoa, both U.S.
1958 George W. Beadle, Edward L. Tatum, Joshua Lederberg, all U.S.
1957 Daniel Bovet, It.
1956 Andre F. Cournand, Dickinson W. Richards Jr., both U.S.; Werner Forssmann, Ger.
1955 Alex H. T. Theorell, Swed.
1954 John F. Enders, Frederick C. Robbins, Thomas H. Weller, all U.S.
1953 Hans A. Krebs, Br.; Fritz A. Lipmann, U.S.
1952 Selman A. Waksman, U.S.
1951 Max Theiler, U.S.
1950 Philip S. Hench, Edward C. Kendall, both U.S.; Tadeus Reichstein, Swiss
1949 Walter R. Hess, Swiss; Antonio Moniz, Port.
1948 Paul H. Müller, Swiss
1947 Carl F. Cori, Gerty T. Cori, both U.S.; Bernardo A. Houssay, Arg.
1946 Hermann J. Muller, U.S.
1945 Ernst B. Chain, Sir Alexander Fleming, Sir Howard W. Florey, all Br.
1944 Joseph Erlanger, Herbert S. Gasser, both U.S.
1943 Henrik C. P. Dam, Dan.; Edward A. Doisy, U.S.
1939 Gerhard Domagk, Ger.
1938 Corneille J. F. Heymans, Belg.
1937 Albert Szent-Gyorgyi, Hung.-U.S.
1936 Sir Henry H. Dale, Br.; Otto Loewi, U.S.
1935 Hans Spemann, Ger.
1934 George R. Minot, William P. Murphy, G. H. Whipple, all U.S.
1933 Thomas H. Morgan, U.S.
1932 Edgar D. Adrian, Sir Charles S. Sherrington, both Br.
1931 Otto H. Warburg, Ger.
1930 Karl Landsteiner, U.S.
1929 Christiaan Eijkman, Dutch; Sir Frederick G. Hopkins, Br.
1928 Charles J. H. Nicolle, Fr.
1927 Julius Wagner-Jauregg, Austrian
1926 Johannes A. G. Fibiger, Dan.
1924 Willem Einthoven, Dutch
1923 Frederick G. Banting, Can.; John J. R. Macleod, Scot.
1922 Archibald V. Hill, Br.; Otto F. Meyerhof, Ger.
1920 Schack A. S. Krogh, Dan.
1919 Jules Bordet, Belg.
1914 Robert Barany, Aus.
1913 Charles R. Richet, Fr.
1912 Alexis Carrel, Fr.
1911 Allvar Gullstrand, Swed.
1910 Albrecht Kossel, Ger.
1909 Emil T. Kocher, Swiss
1908 Paul Ehrlich, Ger.; Elie Metchnikoff, Fr.
1907 Charles L. A. Laveran, Fr.
1906 Camillo Golgi, It.; Santiago Ramon y Cajal, Span.
1905 Robert Koch, Ger.
1904 Ivan P. Pavlov, Russ.
1903 Niels R. Finsen, Dan.
1902 Sir Ronald Ross, Br.
1901 Emil A. von Behring, Ger.

Literature

1997 Dario Fo, It.
1996 Wislawa Szymborska, Pol.
1995 Seamus Heaney, Ir.
1994 Kenzaburo Oe, Jpn.
1993 Toni Morrison, U.S.
1992 Derek Walcott, W. Ind.
1991 Nadine Gordimer, S. Afr.
1990 Octavio Paz, Mex.
1989 Camilo José Cela, Span.
1988 Naguib Mahfouz, Egy.
1987 Joseph Brodsky, USSR-U.S.
1986 Wole Soyinka, Nig.
1985 Claude Simon, Fr.
1984 Jaroslav Siefert, Czech.
1983 William Golding, Br.
1982 Gabriel Garcia Marquez, Colombian-Mex.
1981 Elias Canetti, Bulg.-Br.
1980 Czeslaw Milosz, Pol.-U.S.
1979 Odysseus Elytis, Gk.
1978 Isaac Bashevis Singer, U.S.
1977 Vicente Aleixandre, Span.
1976 Saul Bellow, U.S.
1975 Eugenio Montale, It.
1974 Eyvind Johnson, Harry Edmund Martinson, both Swed.
1973 Patrick White, Austral.
1972 Heinrich Böll, Ger.
1971 Pablo Neruda, Chil.
1970 Aleksandr I. Solzhenitsyn, USSR
1969 Samuel Beckett, Ir.
1968 Yasunari Kawabata, Jpn.
1967 Miguel Angel Asturias, Guat.
1966 Samuel Joseph Agnon, Isr.; Nelly Sachs, Swed.
1965 Mikhail Sholokhov, USSR
1964 Jean Paul Sartre, Fr. (declined)
1963 Giorgos Seferis, Gk.
1962 John Steinbeck, U.S.
1961 Ivo Andric, Yugo.
1960 Saint-John Perse, Fr.
1959 Salvatore Quasimodo, It.
1958 Boris L. Pasternak, USSR (declined)
1957 Albert Camus, Fr.
1956 Juan Ramon Jimenez, Span.
1955 Halldor K. Laxness, Ice.
1954 Ernest Hemingway, U.S.
1953 Sir Winston Churchill, Br.
1952 Francois Mauriac, Fr.
1951 Par F. Lagerkvist, Swed.
1950 Bertrand Russell, Br.
1949 William Faulkner, U.S.
1948 T.S. Eliot, Br.
1947 Andre Gide, Fr.
1946 Hermann Hesse, Ger.-Swiss
1945 Gabriela Mistral, Chil.
1944 Johannes V. Jensen, Dan.
1939 Frans E. Sillanpaa, Fin.
1938 Pearl S. Buck, U.S.
1937 Roger Martin du Gard, Fr.
1936 Eugene O'Neill, U.S.
1934 Luigi Pirandello, It.
1933 Ivan A. Bunin, USSR
1932 John Galsworthy, Br.
1931 Erik A. Karlfeldt, Swed.
1930 Sinclair Lewis, U.S.
1929 Thomas Mann, Ger.
1928 Sigrid Undset, Nor.
1927 Henri Bergson, Fr.
1926 Grazia Deledda, It.
1925 George Bernard Shaw, Ir.-Br.
1924 Wladyslaw S. Reymont, Pol.
1923 William Butler Yeats, Ir.
1922 Jacinto Benavente, Span.
1921 Anatole France, Fr.
1920 Knut Hamsun, Nor.
1919 Carl F. G. Spitteler, Swiss
1917 Karl A. Gjellerup, Henrik Pontoppidan, both Dan.
1916 Verner von Heidenstam, Swed.
1915 Romain Rolland, Fr.
1913 Rabindranath Tagore, Ind.
1912 Gerhart Hauptmann, Ger.
1911 Maurice Maeterlinck, Belg.
1910 Paul J. L. Heyse, Ger.
1909 Selma Lagerlof, Swed.
1908 Rudolf C. Eucken, Ger.
1907 Rudyard Kipling, Br.
1906 Giosue Carducci, It.
1905 Henryk Sienkiewicz, Pol.
1904 Frederic Mistral, Fr.; Jose Echegaray, Span.
1903 Bjornsterne Bjornson, Nor.
1902 Theodor Mommsen, Ger.
1901 Rene F. A. Sully Prudhomme, Fr.

Peace

1997 Jody Williams, U.S.; International Campaign to Ban Landmines
1996 Bishop Carlos Ximenes Belo, José Ramos-Horta, both Timorese
1995 Joseph Rotblat, Pol.-Br.; Pugwash Conference
1994 Yasir Arafat, Pal.; Shimon Peres, Yitzhak Rabin, both Isr.
1993 Frederik W. de Klerk, Nelson Mandela, both S. Afr.
1992 Rigoberta Menchú, Guat.
1991 Aung San Suu Kyi, Myanmarese
1990 Mikhail S. Gorbachev, USSR
1989 Dalai Lama, Tibet
1988 UN Peacekeeping Forces
1987 Oscar Arias Sanchez, Costa Rican
1986 Elie Wiesel, Rom.-U.S.
1985 Intl. Physicians for the Prevention of Nuclear War, U.S.
1984 Bishop Desmond Tutu, S. Afr.
1983 Lech Walesa, Pol.
1982 Alva Myrdal, Swed.; Alfonso Garcia Robles, Mex.
1981 Office of UN High Com. for Refugees
1980 Adolfo Perez Esquivel, Arg.
1979 Mother Teresa of Calcutta, Alb.-Ind.
1978 Anwar Sadat, Egy.; Menachem Begin, Isr.
1977 Amnesty International
1976 Mairead Corrigan, Betty Williams, both N. Ir.
1975 Andrei Sakharov, USSR
1974 Eisaku Sato, Jpn.; Sean MacBride, Ir.
1973 Henry Kissinger, U.S.; Le Duc Tho, N. Viet. (Tho declined)
1971 Willy Brandt, Ger.
1970 Norman E. Borlaug, U.S.
1969 Intl. Labor Organization
1968 Rene Cassin, Fr.
1965 UN Children's Fund (UNICEF)
1964 Martin Luther King Jr., U.S.
1963 International Red Cross, League of Red Cross Societies
1962 Linus C. Pauling, U.S.
1961 Dag Hammarskjold, Swed.
1960 Albert J. Luthuli, S. Afr.
1959 Philip J. Noel-Baker, Br.
1958 Georges Pire, Belg.
1957 Lester B. Pearson, Can.
1954 Office of UN High Com. for Refugees
1953 George C. Marshall, U.S.
1952 Albert Schweitzer, Fr.
1951 Leon Jouhaux, Fr.
1950 Ralph J. Bunche, U.S.
1949 Lord John Boyd Orr of Brechin Mearns, Br.
1947 Friends Service Council, Br.; Amer. Friends Service Committee, U.S.
1946 Emily G. Balch, John R. Mott, both U.S.
1945 Cordell Hull, U.S.
1944 International Red Cross
1938 Nansen International Office for Refugees
1937 Viscount Cecil of Chelwood, Br.
1936 Carlos de Saavedra Lamas, Arg.
1935 Carl von Ossietzky, Ger.
1934 Arthur Henderson, Br.
1933 Sir Norman Angell, Br.
1931 Jane Addams, Nicholas Murray Butler, both U.S.
1930 Nathan Soderblom, Swed.
1929 Frank B. Kellogg, U.S.
1927 Ferdinand E. Buisson, Fr.; Ludwig Quidde, Ger.
1926 Aristide Briand, Fr.; Gustav Stresemann, Ger.
1925 Sir J. Austen Chamberlain, Br.; Charles G. Dawes, U.S.
1922 Fridtjof Nansen, Nor.
1921 Karl H. Branting, Swed.; Christian L. Lange, Nor.
1920 Leon V.A. Bourgeois, Fr.
1919 Woodrow Wilson, U.S.
1917 International Red Cross
1913 Henri La Fontaine, Belg.
1912 Elihu Root, U.S.
1911 Tobias M.C. Asser, Dutch; Alfred H. Fried, Austrian
1910 Permanent Intl. Peace Bureau
1909 Auguste M. F. Beernaert, Belg.; Paul H. B. B. d'Estournelles de Constant, Fr.
1908 Klas P. Arnoldson, Swed.; Fredrik Bajer, Dan.
1907 Ernesto T. Moneta, It.; Louis Renault, Fr.
1906 Theodore Roosevelt, U.S.
1905 Baroness Bertha von Suttner, Austrian
1904 Institute of International Law
1903 Sir William R. Cremer, Br.
1902 Elie Ducommun, Charles A. Gobat, both Swiss
1901 Jean H. Dunant, Swiss; Frederic Passy, Fr.

Nobel Memorial Prize in Economic Science

1997 Robert C. Merton, U.S.; Myron S. Scholes, Can.-U.S.
1996 James A. Mirrlees, Br.; William Vickrey, Can.-U.S.
1995 Robert E. Lucas Jr., U.S.
1994 John C. Harsanyi, John F. Nash, both U.S.; Reinhard Selten, Ger.
1993 Robert W. Fogel, Douglass C. North, both U.S.
1992 Gary S. Becker, U.S.
1991 Ronald H. Coase, Br.-U.S.
1990 Harry M. Markowitz, William F. Sharpe, Merton H. Miller, all U.S.
1989 Trygve Haavelmo, Nor.
1988 Maurice Allais, Fr.
1987 Robert M. Solow, U.S.
1986 James M. Buchanan, U.S.
1985 Franco Modigliani, It.-U.S.
1984 Richard Stone, Br.
1983 Gerard Debreu, Fr.-U.S.
1982 George J. Stigler, U.S.
1981 James Tobin, U.S.
1980 Lawrence R. Klein, U.S.
1979 Theodore W. Schultz, U.S.; Sir Arthur Lewis, Br.
1978 Herbert A. Simon, U.S.
1977 Bertil Ohlin, Swed.; James E. Meade, Br.
1976 Milton Friedman, U.S.
1975 Tjalling Koopmans, Dutch-U.S.; Leonid Kantorovich, USSR
1974 Gunnar Myrdal, Swed.; Friedrich A. von Hayek, Austrian
1973 Wassily Leontief, U.S.
1972 Kenneth J. Arrow, U.S.; John R. Hicks, Br.
1971 Simon Kuznets, U.S.
1970 Paul A. Samuelson, U.S.
1969 Ragnar Frisch, Nor.; Jan Tinbergen, Dutch

Pulitzer Prizes in Journalism, Letters, and Music

The Pulitzer Prizes were endowed by Joseph Pulitzer (1847-1911), publisher of the *New York World*, in a bequest to Columbia Univ. and have been awarded annually, in years shown, for work the year before. Prizes are now $5,000 in each category, except Meritorious Public Service, for which a medal is given. If a year is omitted, no award was given that year.

Journalism

Meritorious Public Service

1918—New York Times. Also special award to Minna Lewinson and Henry Beetle Hough
1919—Milwaukee Journal
1921—Boston Post
1922—New York World
1923—Memphis (TN) Commercial Appeal
1924—New York World
1926—Enquirer-Sun, Columbus, GA
1927—Canton (OH) Daily News
1928—Indianapolis (IN) Times
1929—New York Evening World
1931—Atlanta (GA) Constitution
1932—Indianapolis (IN) News
1933—New York World-Telegram
1934—Medford (OR) Mail-Tribune
1935—Sacramento (CA) Bee
1936—Cedar Rapids (IA) Gazette
1937—St.Louis Post-Dispatch
1938—Bismarck (ND) Tribune
1939—Miami (FL) Daily News
1940—Waterbury (CT) Republican and American
1941—St.Louis Post-Dispatch
1942—Los Angeles Times
1943—Omaha World Herald
1944—New York Times
1945—Detroit Free Press
1946—Scranton (PA) Times.
1947—Baltimore Sun
1948—St. Louis Post-Dispatch
1949—Nebraska State Journal
1950—Chicago Daily News; St. Louis Post-Dispatch
1951—Miami (FL) Herald and Brooklyn Eagle
1952—St. Louis Post-Dispatch
1953—Whiteville (NC) News Reporter; Tabor City (NC) Tribune
1954—Newsday (Long Island, NY)
1955—Columbus (GA) Ledger and Sunday Ledger-Enquirer
1956—Watsonville (CA) Register-Pajaronian
1957—Chicago Daily News
1958—Arkansas Gazette, Little Rock
1959—Utica (NY) Observer-Dispatch and Utica Daily Press
1960—Los Angeles Times
1961—Amarillo (TX) Globe-Times
1962—Panama City (FL) News-Herald
1963—Chicago Daily News
1964—St.Petersburg (FL) Times
1965—Hutchinson (KS) News
1966—Boston Globe
1967—Louisville (KY) Courier-Journal; Milwaukee Journal
1968—Riverside (CA) Press-Enterprise
1969—Los Angeles Times
1970—Newsday (Long Island, NY)
1971—Winston Salem (NC) Journal & Sentinel
1972—New York Times
1973—Washington Post
1974—Newsday (Long Island, NY)
1975—Boston Globe
1976—Anchorage (AK) Daily News
1977—Lufkin (TX) News
1978—Philadelphia Inquirer

1979—Point Reyes (CA) Light
1980—Gannett News Service
1981—Charlotte (NC) Observer
1982—Detroit News
1983—Jackson (MS) Clarion-Ledger
1984—Los Angeles Times
1985—Ft. Worth (TX) Star-Telegram
1986—Denver Post
1987—Pittsburgh Press
1988—Charlotte (NC) Observer
1989—Anchorage (AK) Daily News
1990—Philadelphia Inquirer, Gilbert M. Gaul; Washington (NC) Daily News
1991—Des Moines Register, Jane Schorer
1992—Sacramento (CA) Bee, Tom Knudson
1993—Miami (FL) Herald
1994—Akron (OH) Beacon Journal
1995—Virgin Islands Daily News, St. Thomas
1996—News & Observer, Raleigh (NC)
1997— New Orleans Times-Picayune
1998—Grand Forks (ND) Herald

Reporting

This category originally embraced all fields. Later, separate categories were made for national and international reporting.

1917—Herbert Bayard Swope, New York World
1918—Harold A. Littledale, New York Evening Post
1920—John J. Leary Jr., New York World
1921—Louis Seibold, New York World
1922—Kirke L. Simpson, Associated Press (AP)
1923—Alva Johnston, New York Times
1924—Magner White, San Diego Sun
1925—James W. Mulroy, Alvin H. Goldstein, Chicago Daily News
1926—William Burke Miller, Louisville (KY) Courier-Journal
1927—John T. Rogers, St. Louis Post-Dispatch
1929—Paul Y. Anderson, St. Louis Post-Dispatch
1930—Russell D. Owens, New York Times. Also $500 to W.O. Dapping, Auburn (NY) Citizen
1931—A.B. MacDonald, Kansas City Star
1932—W.C. Richards, D.D. Martin, J.S. Pooler, F.D. Webb, J.N.W. Sloan, Detroit Free Press
1933—Francis A. Jamieson, AP
1934—Royce Brier, San Francisco Chronicle
1935—William H. Taylor, New York Herald Tribune
1936—Lauren D. Lyman, New York Times
1937—John J. O'Neill, NY Herald Tribune; William L. Laurence, NY Times; Howard W. Blakeslee, AP; Gobind Behari Lal, Universal Service; and David Dietz, Scripps-Howard Newspapers
1938—Raymond Sprigle, Pittsburgh Post-Gazette
1939—Thomas L. Stokes, Scripps-Howard Newspaper Alliance
1940—S. Burton Heath, New York World-Telegram
1941—Westbrook Pegler, New York World-Telegram
1942—Stanton Delaplane, San Francisco Chronicle
1943—George Weller, Chicago Daily News
1944—Paul Schoenstein, New York Journal-American
1945—Jack S. McDowell, San Francisco Call-Bulletin
1946—William L. Laurence, New York Times
1947—Frederick Woltman, New York World-Telegram
1948—George E. Goodwin, Atlanta Journal
1949—Malcolm Johnson, New York Sun
1950—Meyer Berger, New York Times
1951—Edward S. Montgomery, San Francisco Examiner
1952—George de Carvalho, San Francisco Chronicle

(1) General or Spot; (2) Special or Investigative

1953—(1) Providence (RI) Journal and Evening Bulletin; (2) Edward J. Mowery, New York World-Telegram & Sun
1954—(1) Vicksburg (MS) Sunday Post-Herald; (2) Alvin Scott McCoy, Kansas City Star
1955—(1) Mrs. Caro Brown, Alice (TX) Daily Echo; (2) Roland K. Towery, Cuero (TX) Record
1956—(1) Lee Hills, Detroit Free Press; (2) Arthur Daley, New York Times
1957—(1) Salt Lake Tribune; (2) Wallace Turner and William Lambert, Portland Oregonian
1958—(1) Fargo, (ND) Forum; (2) George Beveridge, Washington (DC) Evening Star
1959—(1) Mary Lou Werner, Washington (DC) Evening Star; (2) John Harold Brislin, Scranton (PA) Tribune, and The Scrantonian
1960—(1) Jack Nelson, Atlanta Constitution; (2) Miriam Ottenberg, Washington (DC) Evening Star
1961—(1) Sanche de Gramont, New York Herald Tribune; (2) Edgar May, Buffalo (NY) Evening News
1962—(1) Robert D. Mullins, Deseret News, Salt Lake City; (2) George Bliss, Chicago Tribune
1963—(1) Sylvan Fox, William Longgood, Anthony Shannon, New York World-Telegram & Sun; (2) Oscar Griffin Jr., Pecos (TX) Independent and Enterprise
1964—(1) Norman C. Miller, Wall Street Journal; (2) James V. Magee, Albert V. Gaudiosi, Frederick A. Meyer, Philadelphia Bulletin
1965—(1) Melvin H. Ruder, Hungry Horse News, Columbia Falls, MT; (2) Gene Goltz, Houston Post
1966—(1) Los Angeles Times staff; (2) John A. Frasca, Tampa (FL) Tribune
1967—(1) Robert V. Cox, Chambersburg (PA) Public Opinion; (2) Gene Miller, Miami (FL) Herald
1968—(1) Detroit Free Press staff; (2) J. Anthony Lukas, New York Times
1969—(1) John Fetterman, Louisville Courier-Journal and Times; (2) Albert L. Delugach, St. Louis Globe Democrat, and Denny Walsh, Life
1970—(1) Thomas Fitzpatrick, Chicago Sun-Times; (2) Harold Eugene Martin, Montgomery Advertiser & Alabama Journal
1971—(1) Akron (OH) Beacon Journal staff; (2) William Hugh Jones, Chicago Tribune
1972—(1) Richard Cooper, John Machacek, Rochester (NY) Times-Union; (2) Timothy Leland, Gerard M. O'Neill, Stephen A. Kurkjian, Anne De Santis, Boston Globe
1973—(1) Chicago Tribune; (2) Sun Newspapers of Omaha
1974—(1) Hugh F. Hough, Arthur M. Petacque, Chicago Sun-Times; (2) William Sherman, New York Daily News
1975—(1) Xenia (OH) Daily Gazette; (2) Indianapolis Star
1976—(1) Gene Miller, Miami (FL) Herald; (2) Chicago Tribune
1977—(1) Margo Huston, Milwaukee Journal; (2) Acel Moore, Wendell Rawls Jr., Philadelphia Inquirer
1978—(1) Richard Whitt, Louisville (KY) Courier-Journal; (2) Anthony R. Dolan, Stamford (CT) Advocate
1979—(1) San Diego (CA) Evening Tribune; (2) Gilbert M. Gaul, Elliot G. Jaspin, Pottsville (PA) Republican
1980—(1) Philadelphia Inquirer; (2) Stephen A. Kurkjian, Alexander B. Hawes Jr., Nils Bruzelius, Joan Vennochi, Robert M. Porterfield, Boston Globe
1981—(1) Longview (WA) Daily News staff; (2) Clark Hallas, Robert B. Lowe, Arizona Daily Star
1982—(1) Kansas City Star, Kansas City Times; (2) Paul Henderson, Seattle Times
1983—(1) Fort Wayne (IN) News-Sentinel; (2) Loretta Tofani, Washington Post
1984—(1) New York Newsday; (2) Boston Globe
1985—(1) Thomas Turcol, Virginian-Pilot and Ledger-Star, Norfolk, VA; (2) William K. Marimow, Philadelphia Inquirer; Lucy Morgan, Jack Reed, St. Petersburg (FL) Times
1986—(1) Edna Buchanan, Miami (FL) Herald; (2) Jeffrey A. Marx, Michael M. York, Lexington (KY) Herald-Leader
1987—(1) Akron (OH) Beacon Journal; (2) Daniel R. Biddle, H.G. Bissinger, Fredric N. Tulsky, Philadelphia Inquirer; John Woestendiek, Philadelphia Inquirer
1988—(1) Alabama Journal; Lawrence (MA) Eagle-Tribune; (2) Walt Bogdanich, Wall Street Journal
1989—(1) Louisville (KY) Courier-Journal; (2) Bill Dedman, Atlanta Journal and Constitution
1990—(1) San Jose (CA) Mercury News; (2) Lon Kilzer, Chris Ison, Minneapolis-St. Paul Star Tribune
1991—(1) Miami (FL) Herald; (2) Joseph T. Hallinan, Susan M. Headden, Indianapolis Star
1992—(1) New York Newsday; (2) Lorraine Adams, Dan Malone, Dallas Morning News
1993—(1) Los Angeles Times; Jeff Brazil, Steve Berry, Orlando (FL) Sentinel
1994—(1) New York Times staff; (2) Providence (RI) Journal-Bulletin staff
1995—(1) Los Angeles Times staff; (2) Brian Donovan, Stephanie Saul, New York Newsday
1996—(1) New York Times, Robert D. McFadden; (2) Orange County (CA) Register staff
1997—(1) Long Island (NY) Newsday, staff; (2) Eric Nalder, Deborah Nelson, Alex Tizon, Seattle Times
1998—(1) Los Angeles Times staff; (2) Gary Cohn, Will Englund, Baltimore Sun

Criticism (1) or Commentary (2)

1970—(1) Ada Louise Huxtable, New York Times; (2) Marquis W. Childs, St. Louis Post-Dispatch
1971—(1) Harold C. Schonberg, New York Times; (2) William A. Caldwell, The Record, Hackensack, NJ
1972—(1) Frank Peters Jr., St. Louis Post-Dispatch; (2) Mike Royko, Chicago Daily News
1973—(1) Ronald Powers, Chicago Sun-Times; (2) David S. Broder, Washington Post
1974—(1) Emily Genauer, New York Newsday; (2) Edwin A. Roberts Jr., National Observer
1975—(1) Roger Ebert, Chicago Sun Times; (2) Mary McGrory, Washington Star
1976—(1) Alan M. Kriegsman, Washington Post; (2) Walter W. (Red) Smith, New York Times
1977—(1)William McPherson, Washington Post; (2) George F. Will, Washington Post Writers Group
1978—(1) Walter Kerr, New York Times; (2) William Safire, New York Times
1979—(1) Paul Gapp, Chicago Tribune; (2) Russell Baker, New York Times

(continued)

1980—(1) William A. Henry III, Boston Globe; (2) Ellen Goodman, Boston Globe
1981—(1) Jonathan Yardley, Washington Star; (2) Dave Anderson, New York Times
1982—(1) Martin Bernheimer, Los Angeles Times; (2) Art Buchwald, Los Angeles Times Syndicate
1983—(1) Manuela Hoelterhoff, Wall Street Journal; (2) Claude Sitton, Raleigh (NC) News & Observer
1984—(1) Paul Goldberger, New York Times; (2) Vermont Royster, Wall Street Journal
1985—(1) Howard Rosenberg, Los Angeles Times; (2) Murray Kempton, New York Newsday
1986—(1) Donal J. Henahan, New York Times; (2) Jimmy Breslin, New York Daily News
1987—(1) Richard Eder, Los Angeles Times; (2) Charles Krauthammer, Washington Post
1988—(1) Tom Shales, Washington Post; (2) Dave Barry, Miami (FL) Herald
1989—(1) Michael Skube, Raleigh, NC, News and Observer; (2) Clarence Page, Chicago Tribune
1990—(1) Allan Temko, San Francisco Chronicle; (2) Jim Murray, Los Angeles Times
1991—(1) David Shaw, Los Angeles Times; (2) Jim Hoagland, Washington Post
1992—(1) No award; (2) Anna Quindlen, New York Times
1993—(1) Michael Dirda, Washington Post; (2) Liz Balmaseda, Miami (FL) Herald
1994—(1) Lloyd Schwartz, Boston Phoenix; (2) William Raspberry, Washington Post
1995—(1) Margo Jefferson, New York Times; (2) Jim Dwyer, New York Newsday
1996—(1) Robert Campbell, Boston Globe; (2) E.R. Shipp, New York Daily News
1997—(1) Tim Page, Washington Post; (2) Eileen McNamara, Boston Globe
1998—(1) Michiko Kakutani, New York Times; (2) Mike McAlary, New York Daily News

National Reporting

1942—Louis Stark, New York Times
1944—Dewey L. Fleming, Baltimore Sun
1945—James B. Reston, New York Times
1946—Edward A. Harris, St. Louis Post-Dispatch
1947—Edward T. Folliard, Washington Post
1948—Bert Andrews, New York Herald Tribune; Nat S. Finney, Minneapolis Tribune
1949—Charles P. Trussell, New York Times
1950—Edwin O. Guthman, Seattle Times
1952—Anthony Leviero, New York Times
1953—Don Whitehead, AP
1954—Richard Wilson, Des Moines Register
1955—Anthony Lewis, Washington Daily News
1956—Charles L. Bartlett, Chattanooga (TN) Times
1957—James Reston, New York Times
1958—Relman Morin, AP; Clark Mollenhoff, Des Moines Register & Tribune
1959—Howard Van Smith, Miami (FL) News
1960—Vance Trimble, Scripps-Howard, Washington, DC
1961—Edward R. Cony, Wall Street Journal
1962—Nathan G. Caldwell, Gene S. Graham, Nashville Tennessean
1963—Anthony Lewis, New York Times
1964—Merriman Smith, UPI
1965—Louis M. Kohlmeier, Wall Street Journal
1966—Haynes Johnson, Washington (DC) Evening Star
1967—Monroe Karmin, Stanley Penn, Wall Street Journal
1968—Howard James, Christian Science Monitor; Nathan K. Kotz, Des Moines Register
1969—Robert Cahn, Christian Science Monitor
1970—William J. Eaton, Chicago Daily News
1971—Lucinda Franks, Thomas Powers, UPI
1972—Jack Anderson, United Feature Syndicate
1973—Robert Boyd, Clark Hoyt, Knight Newspapers
1974—James R. Polk, Washington (DC) Star-News; Jack White, Providence (RI) Journal-Bulletin
1975—Donald L. Barlett, James B. Steele, Philadelphia Inquirer
1976—James Risser, Des Moines Register
1977—Walter Mears, AP
1978—Gaylord D. Shaw, Los Angeles Times
1979—James Risser, Des Moines Register
1980—Charles Stafford, Bette Swenson Orsini, St. Petersburg (FL) Times
1981—John M. Crewdson, New York Times
1982—Rick Atkinson, Kansas City Times
1983—Boston Globe
1984—John Noble Wilford, New York Times
1985—Thomas J. Knudson, Des Moines Register
1986—Craig Flournoy, George Rodrigue, Dallas Morning News; Arthur Howe, Philadelphia Inquirer
1987—Miami (FL) Herald; New York Times
1988—Tim Weiner, Philadelphia Inquirer
1989—Donald L. Barlett, James B. Steele, Philadelphia Inquirer
1990—Ross Anderson, Bill Dietrich, Mary Ann Gwinn, Eric Nalder, Seattle Times
1991—Marjie Lundstrom, Rochelle Sharpe, Gannett News Service
1992—Jeff Taylor, Mike McGraw, Kansas City Star
1993—David Maraniss, Washington Post
1994—Eileen Welsome, Albuquerque Tribune
1995—Tony Horwitz, Wall Street Journal
1996—Alix M. Freedman, Wall Street Journal
1997—Wall Street Journal staff
1998—Russell Carollo, Jeff Nesmith, Dayton (OH) Daily News

International Reporting

1942—Laurence Edmund Allen, AP
1943—Ira Wolfert, North American Newspaper Alliance
1944—Daniel DeLuce, AP
1945—Mark S. Watson, Baltimore Sun
1946—Homer W. Bigart, New York Herald Tribune
1947—Eddy Gilmore, AP
1948—Paul W. Ward, Baltimore Sun
1949—Price Day, Baltimore Sun
1950—Edmund Stevens, Christian Science Monitor
1951—Keyes Beech, Fred Sparks, Chicago Daily News; Homer Bigart, Marguerite Higgins, New York Herald Tribune; Relman Morin, Don Whitehead, AP
1952—John M. Hightower, AP
1953—Austin C. Wehrwein, Milwaukee Journal
1954—Jim G. Lucas, Scripps-Howard Newspapers
1955—Harrison Salisbury, New York Times
1956—William Randolph Hearst Jr., Frank Conniff, Hearst Newspapers; Kingsbury Smith, INS
1957—Russell Jones, UPI
1958—New York Times
1959—Joseph Martin, Philip Santora, New York Daily News
1960—A.M. Rosenthal, New York Times
1961—Lynn Heinzerling, AP
1962—Walter Lippmann, New York Herald Tribune Syndicate
1963—Hal Hendrix, Miami (FL) News
1964—Malcolm W. Browne, AP; David Halberstam, New York Times
1965—J.A. Livingston, Philadelphia Bulletin
1966—Peter Arnett, AP
1967—R. John Hughes, Christian Science Monitor
1968—Alfred Friendly, Washington Post
1969—William Tuohy, Los Angeles Times
1970—Seymour M. Hersh, Dispatch News Service
1971—Jimmie Lee Hoagland, Washington Post
1972—Peter R. Kann, Wall Street Journal
1973—Max Frankel, New York Times
1974—Hedrick Smith, New York Times
1975—William Mullen and Ovie Carter, Chicago Tribune
1976—Sydney H. Schanberg, New York Times
1978—Henry Kamm, New York Times
1979—Richard Ben Cramer, Philadelphia Inquirer
1980—Joel Brinkley, Jay Mather, Louisville (KY) Courier-Journal
1981—Shirley Christian, Miami (FL) Herald
1982—John Darnton, New York Times
1983—Thomas L. Friedman, New York Times; Loren Jenkins, Washington Post
1984—Karen Elliot House, Wall Street Journal
1985—Josh Friedman, Dennis Bell, Ozler Muhammad, New York Newsday
1986—Lewis M. Simons, Pete Carey, Katherine Ellison, San Jose (CA) Mercury News
1987—Michael Parks, Los Angeles Times
1988—Thomas L. Friedman, New York Times
1989—Glenn Frankel, Wash. Post; Bill Keller, NY Times
1990—Nicholas D. Kirstof, Sheryl WuDunn, NY Times
1991—Caryle Murphy, Washington Post; Serge Schmemann, New York Times
1992—Patrick J. Sloyan, New York Newsday
1993—John F. Burns, NY Times; Roy Gutman, NY Newsday
1994—Dallas Morning News team
1995—Mark Fritz, AP
1996—David Rohde, Christian Science Monitor
1997—John F. Burns, New York Times
1998—New York Times staff

Washington or Foreign Correspondence

Category was merged with others in 1948.

1929—Paul Scott Mowrer, Chicago Daily News
1930—Leland Stowe, New York Herald Tribune
1931—H.R. Knickerbocker, Philadelphia Public Ledger and New York Evening Post
1932—Walter Duranty, New York Times; Charles G. Ross, St. Louis Post-Dispatch
1933—Edgar Ansel Mowrer, Chicago Daily News
1934—Frederick T. Birchall, New York Times
1935—Arthur Krock, New York Times
1936—Wilfred C. Barber, Chicago Tribune
1937—Anne O'Hare McCormick, New York Times
1938—Arthur Krock, New York Times
1939—Louis P. Lochner, AP
1940—Otto D. Tolischus, New York Times

1941—Bronze plaque to commemorate work of American correspondents on war fronts
1942—Carlos P. Romulo, Philippines Herald
1943—Hanson W. Baldwin, New York Times
1944—Ernest Taylor Pyle, Scripps-Howard Newspaper Alliance
1945—Harold V. (Hal) Boyle, AP
1946—Arnaldo Cortesi, New York Times
1947—Brooks Atkinson, New York Times

Editorial Writing

1917—New York Tribune
1918—Louisville (KY) Courier-Journal
1920—Harvey E. Newbranch, Omaha Evening World-Herald
1922—Frank M. O'Brien, New York Herald
1923—William Allen White, Emporia (KS) Gazette
1924—Frank Buxton, Boston Herald, Special Prize; Frank I. Cobb, New York World
1925—Robert Lathan, Charleston (SC) News and Courier
1926—Edward M. Kingsbury, New York Times
1927—F. Lauriston Bullard, Boston Herald
1928—Grover C. Hall, Montgomery (AL) Advertiser
1929—Louis Isaac Jaffe, Norfolk Virginian-Pilot
1931—Chas. Ryckman, Fremont (NE) Tribune
1933—Kansas City Star
1934—E. P. Chase, Atlantic (IA) News Telegraph
1936—Felix Morley, Washington Post; George B. Parker, Scripps-Howard Newspapers
1937—John W. Owens, Baltimore Sun
1938—W.W. Waymack, Des Moines Register & Tribune
1939—Ronald G. Callvert, Portland Oregonian
1940—Bart Howard, St. Louis Post-Dispatch
1941—Reuben Maury, New York Daily News
1942—Geoffrey Parsons, New York Herald Tribune
1943—Forrest W. Seymour, Des Moines Register & Tribune
1944—Henry J. Haskell, Kansas City Star
1945—George W. Potter, Providence (RI) Journal-Bulletin
1946—Hodding Carter, Greenville (MS) Delta Democrat-Times
1947—William H. Grimes, Wall Street Journal
1948—Virginius Dabney, Richmond (VA) Times-Dispatch
1949—John H. Crider, Boston Herald; Herbert Elliston, Washington Post
1950—Carl M. Saunders, Jackson (MI) Citizen-Patriot
1951—William H. Fitzpatrick, New Orleans States
1952—Louis LaCoss, St. Louis Globe Democrat
1953—Vermont C. Royster, Wall Street Journal
1954—Don Murray, Boston Herald
1955—Royce Howes, Detroit Free Press
1956—Lauren K. Soth, Des Moines Register & Tribune
1957—Buford Boone, Tuscaloosa (AL) News
1958—Harry S. Ashmore, Arkansas Gazette
1959—Ralph McGill, Atlanta Constitution
1960—Lenoir Chambers, Norfolk Virginian-Pilot
1961—William J. Dorvillier, San Juan (Puerto Rico) Star
1962—Thomas M. Storke, Santa Barbara (CA) News-Press
1963—Ira B. Harkey Jr., Pascagoula (MS) Chronicle
1964—Hazel Brannon Smith, Lexington (MS) Advertiser
1965—John R. Harrison, Gainesville (FL) Sun
1966—Robert Lasch, St. Louis Post-Dispatch
1967—Eugene C. Patterson, Atlanta Constitution
1968—John S. Knight, Knight Newspapers
1969—Paul Greenberg, Pine Bluff (AR) Commercial
1970—Philip L. Geyelin, Washington Post
1971—Horance G. Davis Jr., Gainesville (FL) Sun
1972—John Strohmeyer, Bethlehem (PA) Globe-Times
1973—Roger B. Linscott, Berkshire Eagle, Pittsfield, MA
1974—F. Gilman Spencer, Trenton (NJ) Trentonian
1975—John D. Maurice, Charleston (WV) Daily Mail
1976—Philip Kerby, Los Angeles Times
1977—Warren L. Lerude, Foster Church, Norman F. Cardoza, Reno Evening Gazette and Nevada State Journal
1978—Meg Greenfield, Washington Post
1979—Edwin M. Yoder, Washington Star
1980—Robert L. Bartley, Wall Street Journal
1982—Jack Rosenthal, New York Times
1983—Editorial board, Miami Herald
1984—Albert Scardino, Georgia Gazette
1985—Richard Aregood, Philadelphia Daily News
1986—Jack Fuller, Chicago Tribune
1987—Jonathan Freedman, Tribune (San Diego)
1988—Jane Healy, Orlando (FL) Sentinel
1989—Lois Wille, Chicago Tribune
1990—Thomas J. Hylton, Pottstown (PA) Mercury
1991—Ron Casey, Harold Jackson, Joey Kennedy, Birmingham (AL) News
1992—Maria Henson, Lexington (KY) Herald-Leader
1994—R. Bruce Dold, Chicago Tribune
1995—Jeffrey Good, St. Petersburg (FL) Times
1996—Robert B. Semple Jr., New York Times
1997—Michael Gartner, Ames (IA) Daily Tribune
1998—Bernard L. Stein, Riverdale (NY) Press

Editorial Cartooning

1922—Rollin Kirby, New York World
1924—Jay N. Darling, Des Moines Register
1925—Rollin Kirby, New York World
1926—D. R. Fitzpatrick, St. Louis Post-Dispatch
1927—Nelson Harding, Brooklyn Eagle
1928—Nelson Harding, Brooklyn Eagle
1929—Rollin Kirby, New York World
1930—Charles Macauley, Brooklyn Eagle
1931—Edmund Duffy, Baltimore Sun
1932—John T. McCutcheon, Chicago Tribune
1933—H. M. Talburt, Washington Daily News
1934—Edmund Duffy, Baltimore Sun
1935—Ross A. Lewis, Milwaukee Journal
1937—C. D. Batchelor, New York Daily News
1938—Vaughn Shoemaker, Chicago Daily News
1939—Charles G. Werner, Daily Oklahoman
1940—Edmund Duffy, Baltimore Sun
1941—Jacob Burck, Chicago Times
1942—Herbert L. Block, Newspaper Enterprise Assn.
1943—Jay N. Darling, Des Moines Register
1944—Clifford K. Berryman, Washington Star
1945—Bill Mauldin, United Feature Syndicate
1946—Bruce Alexander Russell, Los Angeles Times
1947—Vaughn Shoemaker, Chicago Daily News
1948—Reuben L. (Rube) Goldberg, New York Sun
1949—Lute Pease, Newark (NJ) Evening News
1950—James T. Berryman, Washington Star
1951—Reginald W. Manning, Arizona Republic
1952—Fred L. Packer, New York Mirror
1953—Edward D. Kuekes, Cleveland Plain Dealer
1954—Herbert L. Block, Washington Post & Times-Herald
1955—Daniel R. Fitzpatrick, St. Louis Post-Dispatch
1956—Robert York, Louisville (KY) Times
1957—Tom Little, Nashville Tennessean
1958—Bruce M. Shanks, Buffalo Evening News
1959—Bill Mauldin, St. Louis Post-Dispatch
1961—Carey Orr, Chicago Tribune
1962—Edmund S. Valtman, Hartford Times
1963—Frank Miller, Des Moines Register
1964—Paul Conrad, Denver Post
1966—Don Wright, Miami (FL) News
1967—Patrick B. Oliphant, Denver Post
1968—Eugene Gray Payne, Charlotte (NC) Observer
1969—John Fischetti, Chicago Daily News
1970—Thomas F. Darcy, New York Newsday
1971—Paul Conrad, Los Angeles Times
1972—Jeffrey K. MacNelly, Richmond News-Leader
1974—Paul Szep, Boston Globe
1975—Garry Trudeau, Universal Press Syndicate
1976—Tony Auth, Philadelphia Inquirer
1977—Paul Szep, Boston Globe
1978—Jeffrey K. MacNelly, Richmond News Leader
1979—Herbert L. Block, Washington Post
1980—Don Wright, Miami (FL) News
1981—Mike Peters, Dayton (OH) Daily News
1982—Ben Sargent, Austin American-Statesman
1983—Richard Locher, Chicago Tribune
1984—Paul Conrad, Los Angeles Times
1985—Jeffrey K. MacNelly, Chicago Tribune
1986—Jules Feiffer, Village Voice (NY)
1987—Berke Breathed, Washington Post
1988—Doug Marlette, Atlanta Constitution, Charlotte (NC) Observer
1989—Jack Higgins, Chicago Sun-Times
1990—Tom Toles, Buffalo News
1991—Jim Borgman, Cincinnati Enquirer
1992—Signe Wilkinson, Philadelphia Daily News
1993—Stephen R. Benson, Arizona Republic
1994—Michael P. Ramirez, Commercial Appeal, Memphis, TN
1995—Mike Luckovich, Atlanta Constitution
1996—Jim Morin, Miami (FL) Herald
1997—Walt Handelsman, New Orleans Times-Picayune
1998—Stephen P. Breen, Asbury Park Press, Neptune, NJ

Spot News Photography

1942—Milton Brooks, Detroit News
1943—Frank Noel, AP
1944—Frank Filan, AP; Earl L. Bunker, Omaha World-Herald
1945—Joe Rosenthal, AP
1947—Arnold Hardy, amateur, Atlanta, GA
1948—Frank Cushing, Boston Traveler
1949—Nathaniel Fein, New York Herald Tribune
1950—Bill Crouch, Oakland (CA) Tribune
1951—Max Desfor, AP
1952—John Robinson, Don Ultang, Des Moines Register & Tribune
1953—William M. Gallagher, Flint (MI) Journal
1954—Mrs. Walter M. Schau, amateur
1955—John L. Gaunt Jr., Los Angeles Times
1956—New York Daily News
1957—Harry A. Trask, Boston Traveler
1958—William C. Beall, Washington Daily News
1959—William Seaman, Minneapolis Star

(continued)

1960—Andrew Lopez, UPI
1961—Yasushi Nagao, Mainichi Newspapers, Tokyo
1962—Paul Vathis, AP
1963—Hector Rondon, La Republica, Caracas, Venezuela
1964—Robert H. Jackson, Dallas Times-Herald
1965—Horst Faas, AP
1966—Kyoichi Sawada, UPI
1967—Jack R. Thornell, AP
1968—Rocco Morabito, Jacksonville (FL) Journal
1969—Edward Adams, AP
1970—Steve Starr, AP
1971—John Paul Filo, Valley Daily News & Daily Dispatch of Tarentum & New Kensington, PA
1972—Horst Faas, Michel Laurent, AP
1973—Huynh Cong Ut, AP
1974—Anthony K. Roberts, AP
1975—Gerald H. Gay, Seattle Times
1976—Stanley Forman, Boston Herald American
1977—Neal Ulevich, AP; Stanley Forman, Boston Herald American
1978—John H. Blair, UPI
1979—Thomas J. Kelly III, Pottstown (PA) Mercury
1980—UPI
1981—Larry C. Price, Ft. Worth (TX) Star-Telegram
1982—Ron Edmonds, AP
1983—Bill Foley, AP
1984—Stan Grossfeld, Boston Globe
1985—The Register, Santa Ana, CA
1986—Carol Guzy, Michel duCille, Miami (FL) Herald
1987—Kim Komenich, San Francisco Examiner
1988—Scott Shaw, Odessa (TX) American
1989—Ron Olshwanger, St. Louis Post-Dispatch
1990—Oakland (CA) Tribune photo staff
1991—Greg Marinovich, AP
1992—Associated Press staff
1993—Ken Geiger, William Snyder, Dallas Morning News
1994—Paul Watson, Toronto Star
1995—Carol Guzy, Washington Post
1996—Charles Porter IV, AP
1997—Annie Wells, Santa Rosa (CA) Press Democrat
1998—Martha Rial, Pittsburgh Post-Gazette

Feature Photography

1968—Toshio Sakai, UPI
1969—Moneta Sleet Jr., Ebony
1970—Dallas Kinney, Palm Beach (FL) Post
1971—Jack Dykinga, Chicago Sun-Times
1972—Dave Kennerly, UPI
1973—Brian Lanker, Topeka (KS) Capitol-Journal
1974—Slava Veder, AP
1975—Matthew Lewis, Washington Post
1976—Louisville (KY) Courier-Journal and Louisville Times
1977—Robin Hood, Chattanooga (TN) News-Free Press
1978—J. Ross Baughman, AP
1979—Staff photographers, Boston Herald American
1980—Erwin H. Hagler, Dallas Times-Herald
1981—Taro M. Yamasaki, Detroit Free Press
1982—John H. White, Chicago Sun-Times
1983—James B. Dickman, Dallas Times-Herald
1984—Anthony Suad, Denver Post
1985—Stan Grossfeld, Boston Globe; Larry C. Price, Phila. Inquirer
1986—Tom Gralish, Philadelphia Inquirer
1987—David Peterson, Des Moines Register
1988—Michel duCille, Miami (FL) Herald
1989—Manny Crisostomo, Detroit Free Press
1990—David C. Turnley, Detroit Free Press
1991—William Snyder, Dallas Morning News
1992—John Kaplan, Block Newspapers (Toledo, OH)
1993—AP staff
1994—Kevin Carter, New York Times
1995—AP staff
1996—Stephanie Welsh, Newhouse News Service
1997—Alexander Zemlianichenko, AP
1998—Clarence Williams, Los Angeles Times

Special Citation

1930—William O. Dapping, Auburn (NY) Citizen
1938—Edmonton (Alberta) Journal, bronze plaque
1941—New York Times
1944—Byron Price and Mrs. William Allen White
1945—American Press cartographers, for war maps
1947—(Pulitzer centennial year) Columbia Univ. and the Graduate School of Journalism; St. Louis Post-Dispatch
1948—Dr. Frank Diehl Fackenthal
1951—C(yrus) L. Sulzberger, New York Times
1952—Max Kase, New York Journal-American; Kansas City Star
1953—New York Times, Lester Markel
1958—Walter Lippmann, New York Herald Tribune
1964—Gannett Newspapers, "The Road to Integration"
1976—Prof. John Hohenberg, Admin. of Pulitzer Prizes
1978—Richard Lee Strout, Christian Science Monitor and New Republic
1987—Joseph Pulitzer Jr.
1996—Herb Caen, San Francisco Chronicle

Feature Writing

1979—Jon D. Franklin, Baltimore Evening Sun
1980—Madeleine Blais, Miami (FL) Herald Tropic Magazine;
1981—Teresa Carpenter, Village Voice, New York City
1982—Saul Pett, AP
1984—Peter M. Rinearson, Seattle Times
1985—Alice Steinbach, Baltimore Sun
1986—John Camp, St. Paul Pioneer Press & Dispatch
1987—Steve Twomey, Philadephia Inquirer
1988—Jacqui Banaszynski, St. Paul Pioneer Press Dispatch
1989—David Zucchino, Philadephia Inquirer
1990—Dave Curtin, Colorado Springs Gazette Telegraph
1991—Sheryl James, St. Petersburg (FL) Times
1992—Howell Raines, New York Times
1993—George Lardner Jr., Washington Post
1994—Isabel Wilkerson, New York Times
1995—Ron Suskind, Wall Street Journal
1996—Rick Bragg, New York Times
1997—Lisa Pollak, Baltimore Sun
1998—Thomas French, St. Petersburg (FL)Times

Explanatory Reporting

1985—Jon Franklin, Baltimore Evening Sun
1986—New York Times staff
1987—Jeff Lyon, Peter Gorner, Chicago Tribune
1988—Daniel Hertzberg, James B. Stewart, Wall Street Journal
1989—David Hanners, William Snyder, Karen Blessen, Dallas Morning News
1990—David A. Vise, Steve Coll, Washington Post
1991—Susan C. Faludi, Wall Street Journal
1992—Robert S. Capers, Eric Lipton, Hartford (CT) Courant
1993—Mike Toner, Atlanta Journal-Constitution
1994—Ronald Kotulak, Chicago Tribune
1995—Leon Dash, Lucian Perkins, Washington Post
1996—Laurie Garrett, New York Newsday
1997—Michael Vitez, Ron Cortes, April Saul, Philadelphia Inquirer
1998—Paul Salopek, Chicago Tribune

Specialized Reporting (1985-90)

1985—Randall Savage, Jackie Crosby, Macon (GA) Tel. & News
1986—Andrew Schneider & Mary Pat Flaherty, Pittsburgh Press
1987—Alex S. Jones, New York Times
1988—Dean Baquet, William Gaines, Ann Marie Lipinski, Chicago Tribune
1989—Edward Humes, Orange County (CA) Register
1990—Tamar Stieber, Albuquerque Journal

Beat Reporting

1991—Natalie Angier, New York Times
1992—Deborah Blum, Sacramento (CA) Bee
1993—Paul Ingrassia, Joseph B. White, Wall Street Journal
1994—Eric Freedman, Jim Mitzelfeld, Detroit News
1995—David Shribman, Boston Globe
1996—Bob Keeler, New York Newsday
1997—Byron Acohido, Seattle Times
1998—Linda Greenhouse, New York Times

Letters

Fiction

1918—Ernest Poole, *His Family*
1919—Booth Tarkington, *The Magnificent Ambersons*
1921—Edith Wharton, *The Age of Innocence*
1922—Booth Tarkington, *Alice Adams*
1923—Willa Cather, *One of Ours*
1924—Margaret Wilson, *The Able McLaughlins*
1925—Edna Ferber, *So Big*
1926—Sinclair Lewis, *Arrowsmith* (refused prize)
1927—Louis Bromfield, *Early Autumn*
1928—Thornton Wilder, *Bridge of San Luis Rey*
1929—Julia M. Peterkin, *Scarlet Sister Mary*
1930—Oliver LaFarge, *Laughing Boy*
1931—Margaret Ayer Barnes, *Years of Grace*
1932—Pearl S. Buck, *The Good Earth*
1933—T. S. Stribling, *The Store*
1934—Caroline Miller, *Lamb in His Bosom*
1935—Josephine W. Johnson, *Now in November*
1936—Harold L. Davis, *Honey in the Horn*
1937—Margaret Mitchell, *Gone With the Wind*
1938—John P. Marquand, *The Late George Apley*
1939—Marjorie Kinnan Rawlings, *The Yearling*
1940—John Steinbeck, *The Grapes of Wrath*
1942—Ellen Glasgow, *In This Our Life*
1943—Upton Sinclair, *Dragon's Teeth*
1944—Martin Flavin, *Journey in the Dark*
1945—John Hersey, *A Bell for Adano*
1947—Robert Penn Warren, *All the King's Men*
1948—James A. Michener, *Tales of the South Pacific*
1949—James Gould Cozzens, *Guard of Honor*
1950—A. B. Guthrie Jr., *The Way West*
1951—Conrad Richter, *The Town*

1952—Herman Wouk, *The Caine Mutiny*
1953—Ernest Hemingway, *The Old Man and the* Sea
1955—William Faulkner, *A Fable*
1956—MacKinlay Kantor, *Andersonville*
1958—James Agee, *A Death in the Family*
1959—Robert Lewis Taylor, *The Travels of Jaimie McPheeters*
1960—Allen Drury, *Advise and Consent*
1961—Harper Lee, *To Kill a Mockingbird*
1962—Edwin O'Connor, *The Edge of Sadness*
1963—William Faulkner, *The Reivers*
1965—Shirley Ann Grau, *The Keepers of the House*
1966—Katherine Anne Porter, *Collected Stories*
1967—Bernard Malamud, *The Fixer*
1968—William Styron, *The Confessions of Nat Turner*
1969—N. Scott Momaday, *House Made of Dawn*
1970—Jean Stafford, *Collected Stories*
1972—Wallace Stegner, *Angle of Repose*
1973—Eudora Welty, *The Optimist's Daughter*
1975—Michael Shaara, *The Killer Angels*
1976—Saul Bellow, *Humboldt's Gift*
1978—James Alan McPherson, *Elbow Room*
1979—John Cheever, *The Stories of John Cheever*
1980—Norman Mailer, *The Executioner's Song*
1981—John Kennedy Toole, *A Confederacy of Dunces*
1982—John Updike, *Rabbit Is Rich*
1983—Alice Walker, *The Color Purple*
1984—William Kennedy, *Ironweed*
1985—Alison Lurie, *Foreign Affairs*
1986—Larry McMurtry, *Lonesome Dove*
1987—Peter Taylor, *A Summons to Memphis*
1988—Toni Morrison, *Beloved*
1989—Anne Tyler, *Breathing Lessons*
1990—Oscar Hijuelos, *The Mambo Kings Play Songs of Love*
1991—John Updike, *Rabbit at Rest*
1992—Jane Smiley, *A Thousand Acres*
1993—Robert Olen Butler, *A Good Scent From a Strange Mountain*
1994—E. Annie Proulx, *The Shipping News*
1995—Carol Shields, *The Stone Diaries*
1996—Richard Ford, *Independence Day*
1997—Steven Millhauser, *Martin Dressler: The Tale of an American Dreamer*
1998—Philip Roth, *American Pastoral*

Drama

1918—Jesse Lynch Williams, *Why Marry?*
1920—Eugene O'Neill, *Beyond the Horizon*
1921—Zona Gale, *Miss Lulu Bett*
1922—Eugene O'Neill, *Anna Christie*
1923—Owen Davis, *Icebound*
1924—Hatcher Hughes, *Hell-Bent for Heaven*
1925—Sidney Howard, *They Knew What They Wanted*
1926—George Kelly, *Craig's Wife*
1927—Paul Green, *In Abraham's Bosom*
1928—Eugene O'Neill, *Strange Interlude*
1929—Elmer Rice, *Street Scene*
1930—Marc Connelly, *The Green Pastures*
1931—Susan Glaspell, *Alison's House*
1932—George S. Kaufman, Morrie Ryskind, and Ira Gershwin, *Of Thee I Sing*
1933—Maxwell Anderson, *Both Your Houses*
1934—Sidney Kingsley, *Men in White*
1935—Zoe Akins, *The Old Maid*
1936—Robert E. Sherwood, *Idiot's Delight*
1937—George S. Kaufman and Moss Hart, *You Can't Take It With You*
1938—Thornton Wilder, *Our Town*
1939—Robert E. Sherwood, *Abe Lincoln in Illinois*
1940—William Saroyan, *The Time of Your Life*
1941—Robert E. Sherwood, *There Shall Be No Night*
1943—Thornton Wilder, *The Skin of Our Teeth*
1945—Mary Chase, *Harvey*
1946—Russel Crouse and Howard Lindsay, *State of the Union*
1948—Tennessee Williams, *A Streetcar Named Desire*
1949—Arthur Miller, *Death of a Salesman*
1950—Richard Rodgers, Oscar Hammerstein 2d and Joshua Logan, *South Pacific*
1952—Joseph Kramm, *The Shrike*
1953—William Inge, *Picnic*
1954—John Patrick, *Teahouse of the August Moon*
1955—Tennessee Williams, *Cat on a Hot Tin Roof*
1956—Frances Goodrich and Albert Hackett, *The Diary of Anne Frank*
1957—Eugene O'Neill, *Long Day's Journey Into Night*
1958—Ketti Frings, *Look Homeward, Angel*
1959—Archibald MacLeish, *J. B.*
1960—George Abbott, Jerome Weidman, Sheldon Harnick, and Jerry Bock, *Fiorello!*
1961—Tad Mosel, *All the Way Home*
1962—Frank Loesser and Abe Burrows, *How to Succeed in Business Without Really Trying*
1965—Frank D. Gilroy, *The Subject Was Roses*
1967—Edward Albee, *A Delicate Balance*
1969—Howard Sackler, *The Great White Hope*
1970—Charles Gordone, *No Place to Be Somebody*
1971—Paul Zindel, *The Effect of Gamma Rays on Man-in-the-Moon Marigolds*
1973—Jason Miller, *That Championship Season*
1975—Edward Albee, *Seascape*
1976—Michael Bennett, James Kirkwood, Nicholas Dante, Marvin Hamlisch, and Edward Kleban, *A Chorus Line*
1977—Michael Cristofer, *The Shadow Box*
1978—Donald L. Coburn, *The Gin Game*
1979—Sam Shepard, *Buried Child*
1980—Lanford Wilson, *Talley's Folly*
1981—Beth Henley, *Crimes of the Heart*
1982—Charles Fuller, *A Soldier's Play*
1983—Marsha Norman, *'night, Mother*
1984—David Mamet, *Glengarry Glen Ross*
1985—Stephen Sondheim and James Lapine, *Sunday in the Park With George*
1987—August Wilson, *Fences*
1988—Alfred Uhry, *Driving Miss Daisy*
1989—Wendy Wasserstein, *The Heidi Chronicles*
1990—August Wilson, *The Piano Lesson*
1991—Neil Simon, *Lost in Yonkers*
1992—Robert Schenkkan, *The Kentucky Cycle*
1993—Tony Kushner, *Angels in America: Millennium Approaches*
1994—Edward Albee, *Three Tall Women*
1995—Horton Foote, *The Young Man From Atlanta*
1996—Jonathan Larson, *Rent*
1998—Paula Vogel, *How I Learned to Drive*

History (U.S.)

1917—J. J. Jusserand, *With Americans of Past and Present Days*
1918—James Ford Rhodes, *History of the Civil War*
1920—Justin H. Smith, *The War With Mexico*
1921—William Sowden Sims, *The Victory at Sea*
1922—James Truslow Adams, *The Founding of New England*
1923—Charles Warren, *The Supreme Court in United States History*
1924—Charles Howard McIlwain, *The American Revolution: A Constitutional Interpretation*
1925—Frederick L. Paxton, *A History of the American Frontier*
1926—Edward Channing, *A History of the U.S.*
1927—Samuel Flagg Bemis, *Pinckney's Treaty*
1928—V. L Parrington, *Main Currents in American Thought*
1929—Fred A. Shannon, *The Organization and Administration of the Union Army, 1861-65*
1930—Claude H. Van Tyne, *The War of Independence*
1931—Bernadotte E. Schmitt, *The Coming of the War, 1914*
1932—Gen. John J. Pershing, *My Experiences in the World War*
1933—Frederick J. Turner, *The Significance of Sections in American History*
1934—Herbert Agar, *The People's Choice*
1935—Charles McLean Andrews, *The Colonial Period of American History*
1936—Andrew C. McLaughlin, *The Constitutional History of the United States*
1937—Van Wyck Brooks, *The Flowering of New England*
1938—Paul Herman Buck, *The Road to Reunion, 1865-1900*
1939—Frank Luther Mott, *A History of American Magazines*
1940—Carl Sandburg, *Abraham Lincoln: The War Years*
1941—Marcus Lee Hansen, *The Atlantic Migration, 1607-1860*
1942—Margaret Leech, *Reveille in Washington*
1943—Esther Forbes, *Paul Revere and the World He Lived In*
1944—Merle Curti, *The Growth of American Thought*
1945—Stephen Bonsal, *Unfinished Business*
1946—Arthur M. Schlesinger Jr., *The Age of Jackson*
1947—James Phinney Baxter 3d, *Scientists Against Time*
1948—Bernard De Voto, *Across the Wide Missouri*
1949—Roy F. Nichols, *The Disruption of American Democracy*
1950—O. W. Larkin, *Art and Life in America*
1951—R. Carlyle Buley, *The Old Northwest: Pioneer Period 1815-1840*
1952—Oscar Handlin, *The Uprooted*
1953—George Dangerfield, *The Era of Good Feelings*
1954—Bruce Catton, *A Stillness at Appomattox*
1955—Paul Horgan, *Great River: The Rio Grande in North American History*
1956—Richard Hofstadter, *The Age of Reform*
1957—George F. Kennan, *Russia Leaves the War*
1958—Bray Hammond, *Banks and Politics in America—From the Revolution to the Civil War*
1959—Leonard D. White and Jean Schneider, *The Republican Era; 1869-1901*
1960—Margaret Leech, *In the Days of McKinley*
1961—Herbert Feis, *Between War and Peace: The Potsdam Conference*
1962—Lawrence H. Gibson, *The Triumphant Empire: Thunderclouds Gather in the West*
1963—Constance McLaughlin Green, *Washington: Village and Capital, 1800-1878*
1964—Sumner Chilton Powell, *Puritan Village: The Formation of a New England Town*
1965—Irwin Unger, *The Greenback Era*

1966—Perry Miller, *Life of the Mind in America*
1967—William H. Goetzmann, *Exploration and Empire: The Explorer and Scientist in the Winning of the American West*
1968—Bernard Bailyn, *The Ideological Origins of the American Revolution*
1969—Leonard W. Levy, *Origin of the Fifth Amendment*
1970—Dean Acheson, *Present at the Creation: My Years in the State Department*
1971—James McGregor Burns, *Roosevelt: The Soldier of Freedom*
1972—Carl N. Degler, *Neither Black nor White*
1973—Michael Kammen, *People of Paradox: An Inquiry Concerning the Origins of American Civilization*
1974—Daniel J. Boorstin, *The Americans: The Democratic Experience*
1975—Dumas Malone, *Jefferson and His Time*
1976—Paul Horgan, *Lamy of Santa Fe*
1977—David M. Potter, *The Impending Crisis*
1978—Alfred D. Chandler Jr., *The Visible Hand: The Managerial Revolution in American Business*
1979—Don E. Fehrenbacher, *The Dred Scott Case: Its Significance in American Law and Politics*
1980—Leon F. Litwack, *Been in the Storm So Long*
1981—Lawrence A. Cremin, *American Education: The National Experience, 1783-1876*
1982—C. Vann Woodward, ed., *Mary Chesnut's Civil War*
1983—Rhys L. Issac, *The Transformation of Virginia, 1740-1790*
1985—Thomas K. McCraw, *Prophets of Regulation*
1986—Walter A. McDougall, *The Heavens and the Earth*
1987—Bernard Bailyn, *Voyagers to the West*
1988—Robert V. Bruce, *The Launching of Modern American Science, 1846-1876*
1989—Taylor Branch, *Parting the Waters: America in the King Years, 1954-63*; and James M. McPherson, *Battle Cry of Freedom: The Civil War Era*
1990—Stanley Karnow, *In Our Image: America's Empire in the Philippines*
1991—Laurel Thatcher Ulrich, *A Midwife's Tale: The Life of Martha Ballard,* based on her diary, 1785-1812
1992—Mark E. Neely Jr., *The Fate of Liberty: Abraham Lincoln and Civil Liberties*
1993—Gordon S. Wood, *The Radicalism of the American Revolution*
1995—Doris Kearns Goodwin, *No Ordinary Time: Franklin and Eleanor Roosevelt: The Home Front in World War II*
1996—Alan Taylor, *William Cooper's Town: Power and Persuasion on the Frontier of the Early American Republic*
1997—Jack N. Rakove, *Original Meanings: Politics and Ideas in the Making of the Constitution*
1998—Edward J. Larson, *Summer for the Gods: The Scopes Trial and America's Continuing Debate Over Science and Religion*

Biography or Autobiography

1917—Laura E. Richards and Maude Howe Elliott, assisted by Florence Howe Hall, *Julia Ward Howe*
1918—William Cabell Bruce, *Benjamin Franklin, Self-Revealed*
1919—Henry Adams, *The Education of Henry Adams*
1920—Albert J. Beveridge, *The Life of John Marshall*
1921—Edward Bok, *The Americanization of Edward Bok*
1922—Hamlin Garland, *A Daughter of the Middle Border*
1923—Burton J. Hendrick, *The Life and Letters of Walter H. Page*
1924—Michael Pupin, *From Immigrant to Inventor*
1925—M. A. DeWolfe Howe, *Barrett Wendell and His Letters*
1926—Harvey Cushing, *Life of Sir William Osler*
1927—Emory Holloway, *Whitman: An Interpretation in Narrative*
1928—Charles Edward Russell, *The American Orchestra and Theodore Thomas*
1929—Burton J. Hendrick, *The Training of an American: The Earlier Life and Letters of Walter H. Page*
1930—Marquis James, *The Raven* (Sam Houston)
1931—Henry James, *Charles W. Eliot*
1932—Henry F. Pringle, *Theodore Roosevelt*
1933—Allan Nevins, *Grover Cleveland*
1934—Tyler Dennett, *John Hay*
1935—Douglas Southall Freeman, *R. E. Lee*
1936—Ralph Barton Perry, *The Thought and Character of William James*
1937—Allan Nevins, *Hamilton Fish: The Inner History of the Grant Administration*
1938—Divided between Odell Shepard, *Pedlar's Progress* (Bronson Alcott) and Marquis James, *Andrew Jackson*
1939—Carl Van Doren, *Benjamin Franklin*
1940—Ray Stannard Baker, *Woodrow Wilson, Life and Letters*
1941—Ola Elizabeth Winslow, *Jonathan Edwards*
1942—Forrest Wilson, Crusader in Crinoline (Harriet Beecher Stowe)
1943—Samuel Eliot Morison, *Admiral of the Ocean Sea* (Christopher Columbus)
1944—Carleton Mabee, *The American Leonardo: The Life of Samuel F. B. Morse*
1945—Russell Blaine Nye, *George Bancroft: Brahmin Rebel.*
1946—Linny Marsh Wolfe, *Son of the Wilderness* (John Muir)
1947—William Allen White, *Autobiography of William Allen White*
1948—Margaret Clapp, *Forgotten First Citizen: John Bigelow*
1949—Robert E. Sherwood, *Roosevelt and Hopkins*
1950—Samuel Flag Bemis, *John Quincy Adams and the Foundations of American Foreign Policy*
1951—Margaret Louise Coit, *John C. Calhoun: American Portrait*
1952—Merlo J. Pusey, *Charles Evans Hughes*
1953—David J. Mays, *Edmund Pendleton, 1721-1803*
1954—Charles A. Lindbergh, *The Spirit of St. Louis*
1955—William S. White, *The Taft Story*
1956—Talbot F. Hamlin, *Benjamin Henry Latrobe*
1957—John F. Kennedy, *Profiles in Courage*
1958—Douglas Southall Freeman (Vols. I-VI) and John Alexander Carroll and Mary Wells Ashworth (Vol. VII), *George Washington*
1959—Arthur Walworth, *Woodrow Wilson: American Prophet*
1960—Samuel Eliot Morison, *John Paul Jones*
1961—David Donald, *Charles Sumner and the Coming of the Civil War*
1963—Leon Edel, *Henry James: Vols. 2-3*
1964—Walter Jackson Bate, *John Keats*
1965—Ernest Samuels, *Henry Adams*
1966—Arthur M. Schlesinger Jr., *A Thousand Days*
1967—Justin Kaplan, *Mr. Clemens and Mark Twain*
1968—George F. Kennan, *Memoirs (1925-1950)*
1969—B. L. Reid, *The Man From New York: John Quinn and His Friends*
1970—T. Harry Williams, *Huey Long*
1971—Lawrence Thompson, *Robert Frost: The Years of Triumph, 1915-1938*
1972—Joseph P. Lash, *Eleanor and Franklin*
1973—W. A. Swanberg, *Luce and His Empire*
1974—Louis Sheaffer, *O'Neill, Son and Artist*
1975—Robert A. Caro, *The Power Broker: Robert Moses and the Fall of New York*
1976—R.W.B. Lewis, *Edith Wharton: A Biography*
1977—John E. Mack, *A Prince of Our Disorder: The Life of T. E. Lawrence*
1978—Walter Jackson Bate, *Samuel Johnson*
1979—Leonard Baker, *Days of Sorrow and Pain: Leo Baeck and the Berlin Jews*
1980—Edmund Morris, *The Rise of Theodore Roosevelt*
1981—Robert K. Massie, *Peter the Great: His Life and World*
1982—William S. McFeely, *Grant: A Biography*
1983—Russell Baker, *Growing Up*
1984—Louis R. Harlan, *Booker T. Washington*
1985—Kenneth Silverman, *The Life and Times of Cotton Mather*
1986—Elizabeth Frank, *Louise Bogan: A Portrait*
1987—David J. Garrow, *Bearing the Cross: Martin Luther King Jr. and the Southern Christian Leadership Conference*
1988—David Herbert Donald, *Look Homeward: A Life of Thomas Wolfe*
1989—Richard Ellmann, *Oscar Wilde*
1990—Sebastian de Grazia, *Machiavelli in Hell*
1991—Steven Naifeh and Gregory White Smith, *Jackson Pollock: An American Saga*
1992—Lewis B. Puller Jr., *Fortunate Son: The Healing of a Vietnam Vet*
1993—David McCullough, *Truman*
1994—David Levering Lewis, *W.E.B. DuBois: Biography of a Race, 1868-1919*
1995—Joan D. Hedrick, *Harriet Beecher Stowe: A Life*
1996—Jack Miles, *God: A Biography*
1997—Frank McCourt, *Angela's Ashes: A Memoir*
1998—Katharine Graham, *Personal History*

American Poetry

Before 1922, awards were funded by the Poetry Society: **1918**—*Love Songs*, by Sara Teasdale; **1919**—*Old Road to Paradise*, by Margaret Widdemer; *Corn Huskers*, by Carl Sandburg.
1922—Edwin Arlington Robinson, *Collected Poems*
1923—Edna St. Vincent Millay, *The Ballad of the Harp-Weaver; A Few Figs From Thistles; other works*
1924—Robert Frost, *New Hampshire: A Poem With Notes and Grace Notes*
1925—Edwin Arlington Robinson, *The Man Who Died Twice*
1926—Amy Lowell, *What's O'Clock*
1927—Leonora Speyer, *Fiddler's Farewell*
1928—Edwin Arlington Robinson, *Tristram*
1929—Stephen Vincent Benet, *John Brown's Body*
1930—Conrad Aiken, *Selected Poems*
1931—Robert Frost, *Collected Poems*
1932—George Dillon, *The Flowering Stone*
1933—Archibald MacLeish, *Conquistador*
1934—Robert Hillyer, *Collected Verse*
1935—Audrey Wurdemann, *Bright Ambush*
1936—Robert P. Tristram Coffin, *Strange Holiness*
1937—Robert Frost, *A Further Range*
1938—Marya Zaturenska, *Cold Morning Sky*
1939—John Gould Fletcher, *Selected Poems*
1940—Mark Van Doren, *Collected Poems*
1941—Leonard Bacon, *Sunderland Capture*
1942—William Rose Benet, *The Dust Which Is God*
1943—Robert Frost, *A Witness Tree*
1944—Stephen Vincent Benet, *Western Star*

1945—Karl Shapiro, *V-Letter and Other Poems*
1947—Robert Lowell, *Lord Weary's Castle*
1948—W. H. Auden, *The Age of Anxiety*
1949—Peter Viereck, *Terror and Decorum*
1950—Gwendolyn Brooks, *Annie Allen*
1951—Carl Sandburg, *Complete Poems*
1952—Marianne Moore, *Collected Poems*
1953—Archibald MacLeish, *Collected Poems*
1954—Theodore Roethke, *The Waking*
1955—Wallace Stevens, *Collected Poems*
1956—Elizabeth Bishop, *Poems, North and South*
1957—Richard Wilbur, *Things of This World*
1958—Robert Penn Warren, *Promises: Poems 1954-1956*
1959—Stanley Kunitz, *Selected Poems 1928-1958*
1960—W. D. Snodgrass, *Heart's Needle*
1961—Phyllis McGinley, *Times Three: Selected Verse From Three Decades*
1962—Alan Dugan, *Poems*
1963—William Carlos Williams, *Pictures From Breughel*
1964—Louis Simpson, *At the End of the Open Road*
1965—John Berryman, *77 Dream Songs*
1966—Richard Eberhart, *Selected Poems*
1967—Anne Sexton, *Live or Die*
1968—Anthony Hecht, *The Hard Hours*
1969—George Oppen, *Of Being Numerous*
1970—Richard Howard, *Untitled Subjects*
1971—William S. Merwin, *The Carrier of Ladders*
1972—James Wright, *Collected Poems*
1973—Maxine Winokur Kumin, *Up Country*
1974—Robert Lowell, *The Dolphin*
1975—Gary Snyder, *Turtle Island*
1976—John Ashbery, *Self-Portrait in a Convex Mirror*
1977—James Merrill, *Divine Comedies*
1978—Howard Nemerov, *Collected Poems*
1979—Robert Penn Warren, *Now and Then: Poems 1976-1978*
1980—Donald Justice, *Selected Poems*
1981—James Schuyler, *The Morning of the Poem*
1982—Sylvia Plath, *The Collected Poems*
1983—Galway Kinnell, *Selected Poems*
1984—Mary Oliver, *American Primitive*
1985—Carolyn Kizer, *Yin*
1986—Henry Taylor, *The Flying Change*
1987—Rita Dove, *Thomas and Beulah*
1988—William Meredith, *Partial Accounts: New and Selected Poems*
1989—Richard Wilbur, *New and Collected Poems*
1990—Charles Simic, *The World Doesn't End*
1991—Mona Van Duyn, *Near Changes*
1992—James Tate, *Selected Poems*
1993—Louise Glück, *The Wild Iris*
1994—Yusef Komunyakaa, *Neon Vernacular*
1995—Philip Levine, *The Simple Truth*
1996—Jorie Graham, *The Dream of the Unified Field*
1997—Lisel Mueller, *Alive Together: New and Selected Poems*
1998—Charles Wright, *Black Zodiac*

General Nonfiction

1962—Theodore H. White, *The Making of the President 1960*
1963—Barbara W. Tuchman, *The Guns of August*
1964—Richard Hofstadter, *Anti-Intellectualism in American Life*
1965—Howard Mumford Jones, *O Strange New World*
1966—Edwin Way Teale, *Wandering Through Winter*
1967—David Brion Davis, *The Problem of Slavery in Western Culture*
1968—Will and Ariel Durant, *Rousseau and Revolution*
1969—Norman Mailer, *The Armies of the Night*; Rene Jules Dubos, *So Human an Animal: How We Are Shaped by Surroundings and Events*
1970—Eric H. Erikson, *Gandhi's Truth*
1971—John Toland, *The Rising Sun*
1972—Barbara W. Tuchman, *Stilwell and the American Experience in China, 1911-1945*
1973—Frances FitzGerald, *Fire in the Lake: The Vietnamese and the Americans in Vietnam*; Robert Coles, *Children of Crisis,* Volumes II & III
1974—Ernest Becker, *The Denial of Death*
1975—Annie Dillard, *Pilgrim at Tinker Creek*
1976—Robert N. Butler, *Why Survive? Being Old in America*
1977—William W. Warner, *Beautiful Swimmers*
1978—Carl Sagan, *The Dragons of Eden*
1979—Edward O. Wilson, *On Human Nature*
1980—Douglas R. Hofstadter, *Gödel, Escher, Bach: An Eternal Golden Braid*
1981—Carl E. Schorske, *Fin-de-Siecle Vienna: Politics and Culture*
1982—Tracy Kidder, *The Soul of a New Machine*
1983—Susan Sheehan, *Is There No Place on Earth for Me?*
1984—Paul Starr, *Social Transformation of American Medicine*
1985—Studs Terkel, *The Good War*
1986—Joseph Lelyveld, *Move Your Shadow*; J. Anthony Lukas, *Common Ground*
1987—David K. Shipler, *Arab and Jew*
1988—Richard Rhodes, *The Making of the Atomic Bomb*
1989—Neil Sheehan, *A Bright Shining Lie: John Paul Vann and America in Vietnam*
1990—Dale Maharidge and Michael Williamson, *And Their Children After Them*
1991—Bert Holldobler and Edward O. Wilson, *The Ants*
1992—Daniel Yergin, *The Prize: The Epic Quest for Oil*
1993—Garry Wills, *Lincoln at Gettysburg*
1994—David Remnick, *Lenin's Tomb: The Last Days of the Soviet Empire*
1995—Jonathan Weiner, *The Beak of the Finch: A Story of Evolution in Our Time*
1996—Tina Rosenberg, *The Haunted Land: Facing Europe's Ghosts After Communism*
1997—Richard Kluger, *Ashes to Ashes: America's Hundred-Year Cigarette War, the Public Health, and the Unabashed Triumph of Philip Morris*
1998—Jared Diamond, *Guns, Germs, and Steel: The Fates of Human Societies*

Special Citations

1944—Richard Rodgers and Oscar Hammerstein II, for *Oklahoma!*
1957—Kenneth Roberts, for his historical novels
1960—*The Armada*, by Garrett Mattingly
1961—*American Heritage Picture History of the Civil War*
1973—*George Washington, Vols. I-IV*, by James Thomas Flexner
1977—Alex Haley, for *Roots*
1978—E.B. White
1984—Theodore Seuss Geisel (Dr. Seuss)
1992—Art Spiegleman, for *Maus*

Music

1943—William Schuman, *Secular Cantata No. 2, A Free Song*
1944—Howard Hanson, *Symphony No. 4, Op. 34*
1945—Aaron Copland, *Appalachian Spring*
1946—Leo Sowerby, *The Canticle of the Sun*
1947—Charles E. Ives, *Symphony No. 3*
1948—Walter Piston, *Symphony No. 3*
1949—Virgil Thomson, *Louisiana Story*
1950—Gian-Carlo Menotti, *The Consul*
1951—Douglas Moore, *Giants in the Earth*
1952—Gail Kubik, *Symphony Concertante*
1954—Quincy Porter, *Concerto for Two Pianos and Orchestra*
1955—Gian-Carlo Menotti, *The Saint of Bleecker Street*
1956—Ernest Toch, *Symphony No. 3*
1957—Norman Dello Joio, *Meditations on Ecclesiastes*
1958—Samuel Barber, *Vanessa*
1959—John La Montaine, *Concerto for Piano and Orchestra*
1960—Elliott Carter, *Second String Quartet*
1961—Walter Piston, *Symphony No. 7*
1962—Robert Ward, *The Crucible*
1963—Samuel Barber, *Piano Concerto No. 1*
1966—Leslie Bassett, *Variations for Orchestra*
1967—Leon Kirchner, *Quartet No. 3*
1968—George Crumb, *Echoes of Time and The River*
1969—Karel Husa, *String Quartet No. 3*
1970—Charles W. Wuorinen, *Time's Encomium*
1971—Mario Davidovsky, *Synchronisms No. 6*
1972—Jacob Druckman, *Windows*
1973—Elliott Carter, *String Quartet No. 3*
1974—Donald Martino, *Notturno*
1975—Dominick Argento, *From the Diary of Virginia Woolf*
1976—Ned Rorem, *Air Music*
1977—Richard Wernick, *Visions of Terror and Wonder*
1978—Michael Colgrass, *Deja Vu for Percussion and Orchestra*
1979—Joseph Schwantner, *Aftertones of Infinity*
1980—David Del Tredici, *In Memory of a Summer Day*
1982—Roger Sessions, *Concerto for Orchestra*
1983—Ellen T. Zwilich, *Three Movements for Orchestra*
1984—Bernard Rands, *Canti del Sole*
1985—Stephen Albert, *Symphony, RiverRun*
1986—George Perle, *Wind Quintet IV*
1987—John Harbison, *The Flight Into Egypt*
1988—William Bolcom, *12 New Etudes for Piano*
1989—Roger Reynolds, *Whispers Out of Time*
1990—Mel Powell, *Duplicates: A Concerto for Two Pianos and Orchestra*
1991—Shulamit Ran, *Symphony*
1992—Wayne Peterson, *The Face of the Night, The Heart of the Dark*
1993—Christopher Rouse, *Trombone Concerto*
1994—Gunther Schuller, *Of Reminiscences and Reflections*
1995—Morton Gould, *Stringmusic*
1996—George Walker, *Lilacs*
1997—Wynton Marsalis, *Blood on the Fields*
1998—Aaron Jay Kernis, *String Quartet No. 2*

Special Citation

1974—Roger Sessions
1976—Scott Joplin
1982—Milton Babbitt
1985—William Schuman
1998—George Gershwin

Miscellaneous Book Awards

Year in parentheses is year awarded

Academy of American Poets Awards (1997). Lenore Marshall Prize, $10,000: Robert Pinsky; Raiziss/de Palchi Translation Award (book prize) $5,000: Michael Palma, *The Man I Pretend to Be: The Colloquies and Selected Poems of Guido Gozzano.* (1998) Tanning Prize, $100,000: A.R. Ammons; James Laughlin Award, $5,000: Sandra Alocosser, *Except by Nature*; Walt Whitman Award, $5,000: Jan Heller Levi, *Once I Gazed at You in Wonder;* Landon Translation Award, $1,000: Louis Simpson, *Modern Poets of France: A Bilingual Anthology*; Academy Fellowship, $20,000 stipend: Charles Simic

American Academy of Arts and Letters (1998). Gold Medal for Drama: Horton Foote; Award of Merit for Poetry, $5,000: Thom Gunn. Academy Awards in Literature ($7,500 each): fiction: Albert Guerard, Bradford Morrow; translation: Edward Snow; poetry: Edward Hirsch, Mary Ruefle, Gjertrud Schnackenberg; nonfiction: Annie Dillard, Robert D. Richardson Jr. Rosenthal Foundation Award in Literature, $5,000: Joseph Skibell, *A Blessing On the Moon;* Sue Kaufman Prize for First Fiction, $2,500: Charles Frazier, *Cold Mountain;* Harold D. Vursell Memorial Award, $5,000: Howard Bahr, *The Black Flower*, Morton Dauwen Zabel Award, $5,000: Yusef Komunyakaa; Witter Bynner Poetry Prize, $2,500: Elizabeth Spires; E. M. Forster Award, $15,000: Kate Atkinson; Addison Metcalf Award in Literature: Rick Moody, *The Ice Storm* and *Purple America*; Mildred and Harold Strauss Livings in Literature, $50,000 stipend for a 5-year period: Marilynne Robinson and W.D. Wetherell

Booker Prize (1997). British award for fiction, $35,000: Arundhati Roy, *The God of Small Things*

Christopher Awards (1998), by The Christophers, for expression of highest values of human spirit, bronze medallion each: Robert Ellsberg, *All Saints: Daily Reflections on Saints, Prophets, and Witnesses for Our Time*; Joseph Cardinal Bernardin, *The Gift of Peace: Personal Reflections*; Kathryn Spink, *Mother Teresa: A Complete Authorized Biography*, David L. Parker with Lee Engfer and Robert Conrow, *Stolen Dreams: Portraits of Working Children;* Mitch Albom, *Tuesdays With Morrie: An Old Man, a Young Man, and Life's Greatest Lesson*

Golden Kite Awards (1998), by Society of Children's Book Writers and Illustrators. Fiction: Donna Jo Napoli, *Stones In Water;* nonfiction: Arlene Schulman, *Carmine's Story: A Book About a Boy Living With AIDS;* picture-illustration: Robert Sabuda, *The Paper Dragon*; picture book text: Marguerite W. Davol, *The Paper Dragon*

Hugo Awards (1998), by the World Science Fiction Convention: Novel: *Forever Peace,* Joe Haldeman; novella: *...Where Angels Fear to Tread,* Allen Steele; novelette: *We Will Drink a Fish Together,* Bill Johnson; short story: *The 43 Antarean Dynasties,* Mike Resnick.

Coretta Scott King Award (1998), by the American Library Assn. for African American authors and illustrators of outstanding books for children and young adults: Author: Sharon M. Draper, *Forged by Fire;* Illustrator: Javaka Steptoe, *In Daddy's Arms I Am Tall.*

Lincoln Prize (1998), by Lincoln and Soldiers Institute at Gettysburg College, for lifetime contribution to Civil War studies, $30,000 and a bronze bust of Lincoln: James M. McPherson, *For Cause and Comrades: Why Men Fought in the Civil War.*

National Book Awards (1997), by National Book Foundation, $10,000 each. Fiction: Charles Frazier, *Cold Mountain;* nonfiction: Joseph Ellis, *American Sphinx: The Character of Thomas Jefferson*; poetry: William Meredith, *Effort at Speech: New and Selected Poems*; young people's literature: Han Nolan, *Dancing on the Edge*; Medal for Distinguished Contribution to American Letters: Studs Terkel

National Book Critics Circle Awards (1998). Fiction: Penelope Fitzgerald, *The Blue Flower;* nonfiction: Anne Fadiman, *The Spirit Catches You and You Fall Down;* criticism: Mario Vargas Llosa, *Making Waves;* biography: James Tobin, *Ernie Pyle's War: America's Eyewitness to World War II;* poetry: Charles Wright, *Black Zodiac;* Nona Balakian Citation for Excellence in Reviewing: Thomas Mallon; Ivan Sandrof Award, Contribution to American Arts & Letters: Leslie Fiedler

PEN/Faulkner Award (1998) for fiction, $15,000: Rafi Zabor, *The Bear Comes Home*

Edgar Allan Poe Awards (1998), by the Mystery Writers of America: Grand Master award: Barbara Mertz (aka Elizabeth Peters & Barbara Michaels); best novel: *Cimarron Rose*, James Lee Burke; best short story: "Keller on the Spot," Lawrence Block

Newbery Medal Books

The Newbery Medal is awarded annually by the Association for Library Service to Children, a division of the American Library Association, to the author of the most distinguished contribution to American literature for children.

Year Given	Book, Author
1922	*The Story of Mankind,* Hendrik Willem van Loon
1923	*The Voyages of Dr. Dolittle,* Hugh Lofting
1924	*The Dark Frigate,* Charles Boardman Hawes
1925	*Tales From Silver Lands,* Charles Joseph Finger
1926	*Shen of the Sea,* Arthur Bowie Chrisman
1927	*Smoky, the Cowhorse,* Will James
1928	*Gay-Neck,* Dhan Gopal Mukerji
1929	*The Trumpeter of Krakow,* Eric P. Kelly
1930	*Hitty, Her First Hundred Years,* Rachel Field
1931	*The Cat Who Went to Heaven,* Elizabeth Coatsworth
1932	*Waterless Mountain,* Laura Adams Armer
1933	*Young Fu of the Upper Yangtze,* Elizabeth Foreman Lewis
1934	*Invincible Louisa,* Cornelia Lynde Meigs
1935	*Dobry,* Monica Shannon
1936	*Caddie Woodlawn,* Carol Ryrie Brink
1937	*Roller Skates,* Ruth Sawyer
1938	*The White Stag,* Kate Seredy
1939	*Thimble Summer,* Elizabeth Enright
1940	*Daniel Boone,* James Daugherty
1941	*Call It Courage,* Armstrong Sperry
1942	*The Matchlock Gun,* Walter D. Edmonds
1943	*Adam of the Road,* Elizabeth Janet Gray
1944	*Johnny Tremain,* Esther Forbes
1945	*Rabbit Hill,* Robert Lawson
1946	*Strawberry Girl,* Lois Lenski
1947	*Miss Hickory,* Carolyn S. Bailey
1948	*Twenty-One Balloons,* William Pène Du Bois
1949	*King of the Wind,* Marguerite Henry
1950	*The Door in the Wall,* Marguerite de Angeli
1951	*Amos Fortune, Free Man,* Elizabeth Yates
1952	*Ginger Pye,* Eleanor Estes
1953	*Secret of the Andes,* Ann Nolan Clark
1954	*. . . And Now Miguel,* Joseph Krumgold
1955	*The Wheel on the School,* Meindert DeJong
1956	*Carry On, Mr. Bowditch,* Jean Lee Latham
1957	*Miracles on Maple Hill,* Virginia Sorensen
1958	*Rifles for Watie,* Harold Keith
1959	*The Witch of Blackbird Pond,* Elizabeth George Speare
1960	*Onion John,* Joseph Krumgold
1961	*Island of the Blue Dolphins,* Scott O'Dell
1962	*The Bronze Bow,* Elizabeth George Speare
1963	*A Wrinkle in Time,* Madeleine L'Engle
1964	*It's Like This, Cat,* Emily Cheney Neville
1965	*Shadow of a Bull,* Maja Wojciechowska
1966	*I, Juan de Pareja,* Elizabeth Borton de Trevino
1967	*Up a Road Slowly,* Irene Hunt
1968	*From the Mixed-Up Files of Mrs. Basil E. Frankweiler,* E. L. Konigsburg
1969	*The High King,* Lloyd Alexander
1970	*Sounder,* William H. Armstrong
1971	*The Summer of the Swans,* Betsy Byars
1972	*Mrs. Frisby and the Rats of NIMH,* Robert C. O'Brien
1973	*Julie of the Wolves,* Jean George
1974	*The Slave Dancer,* Paula Fox
1975	*M. C. Higgins the Great,* Virginia Hamilton
1976	*Grey King,* Susan Cooper
1977	*Roll of Thunder, Hear My Cry,* Mildred D. Taylor
1978	*Bridge to Terabithia,* Katherine Paterson
1979	*The Westing Game,* Ellen Raskin
1980	*A Gathering of Days,* Joan Blos
1981	*Jacob Have I Loved,* Katherine Paterson
1982	*A Visit to William Blake's Inn: Poems for Innocent and Experienced Travelers,* Nancy Willard
1983	*Dicey's Song,* Cynthia Voigt
1984	*Dear Mr. Henshaw,* Beverly Cleary
1985	*The Hero and the Crown,* Robin McKinley
1986	*Sarah, Plain and Tall,* Patricia MacLachlan
1987	*The Whipping Boy,* Sid Fleischman
1988	*Lincoln: A Photobiography,* Russell Freedman

Year Given	Book, Author
1989	*Joyful Noise: Poems for Two Voices,* Paul Fleischman
1990	*Number the Stars,* Lois Lowry
1991	*Maniac Magee,* Jerry Spinelli
1992	*Shiloh,* Phyllis Reynolds Naylor
1993	*Missing May,* Cynthia Rylant
1994	*The Giver,* Lois Lowry
1995	*Walk Two Moons,* Sharon Creech
1996	*The Midwife's Apprentice,* Karen Cushman
1997	*The View From Saturday,* E. L. Konigsburg
1998	*Out of the Dust,* Karen Hesse

Caldecott Medal Books

The Caldecott Medal is awarded annually by the Association for Library Service to Children, a division of the American Library Association, to the illustrator of the most distinguished American picture book for children.

Year Given	Book, Illustrator
1938	*Animals of the Bible,* Dorothy P. Lathrop
1939	*Mei Li,* Thomas Handforth
1940	*Abraham Lincoln,* Ingri & Edgar Parin d'Aulaire
1941	*They Were Strong and Good,* Robert Lawson
1942	*Make Way for Ducklings,* Robert McCloskey
1943	*The Little House,* Virginia Lee Burton
1944	*Many Moons,* Louis Slobodkin
1945	*Prayer for a Child,* Elizabeth Orton Jones
1946	*The Rooster Crows,* Maude & Miska Petersham
1947	*The Little Island,* Leonard Weisgard
1948	*White Snow, Bright Snow,* Roger Duvoisin
1949	*The Big Snow,* Berta & Elmer Hader
1950	*Song of the Swallows,* Leo Politi
1951	*The Egg Tree,* Karherine Milhous
1952	*Finders Keepers,* Nicolas, pseud. (Nicholas Mordvinoff)
1953	*The Biggest Bear,* Lynd Ward
1954	*Madeline's Rescue,* Ludwig Bemelmans
1955	*Cinderella, or the Little Glass Slipper,* Marcia Brown
1956	*Frog Went A-Courtin',* Feodor Rojankovsky
1957	*A Tree Is Nice,* Marc Simont
1958	*Time of Wonder,* Robert McCloskey
1959	*Chanticleer and the Fox,* Barbara Cooney
1960	*Nine Days to Christmas,* Marie Hall Ets
1961	*Baboushka and the Three Kings,* Nicolas Sidjakov
1962	*Once a Mouse,* Marcia Brown
1963	*The Snowy Day,* Ezra Jack Keats
1964	*Where the Wild Things Are,* Maurice Sendak
1965	*May I Bring a Friend?,* Beni Montressor
1966	*Always Room for One More,* Nonny Hogrogian
1967	*Sam, Bang, and Moonshine,* Evaline Ness
1968	*Drummer Hoff,* Ed Emberley
1969	*The Fool of the World and the Flying Ship,* Uri Shulevitz
1970	*Sylvester and the Magic Pebble,* William Steig
1971	A Story A Story, Gail E. Haley
1972	*One Fine Day,* Nonny Hogrogian
1973	*The Funny Little Woman,* Blair Lent
1974	*Duffy and the Devil,* Margot Zemach
1975	*Arrow to the Sun,* Gerald McDermott
1976	*Why Mosquitoes Buzz in People's Ears,* Leo & Diane Dillon
1977	*Ashanti to Zulu: African Traditions,* Leo & Diane Dillon
1978	*Noah's Ark,* Peter Spier
1979	*The Girl Who Loved Wild Horses,* Paul Goble
1980	*Ox-Cart Man,* Barbara Cooney
1981	*Fables,* Arnold Lobel
1982	*Jumanji,* Chris Van Allsburg
1983	*Shadow,* Marcia Brown
1984	*The Glorious Flight: Across the Channel with Louis Bleriot,* Alice and Martin Provensen
1985	*Saint George and the Dragon,* Trina Schart Hyman
1986	*The Polar Express,* Chris Van Allsburg
1987	*Hey, Al,* Richard Egielski
1988	*Owl Moon,* John Schoenherr
1989	*Song and Dance Man,* Stephen Grammell
1990	*Lon Po Po: A Red-Riding Hood Story From China,* Ed Young
1991	*Black and White,* David Macaulay
1992	*Tuesday,* David Wiesner
1993	*Mirette on the High Wire,* Emily Arnold McCully
1994	*Grandfather's Journey,* Allen Say
1995	*Smoky Night,* David Diaz
1996	*Officer Buckle and Gloria,* Peggy Rathmann
1997	*Golem,* David Wisniewski
1998	*Rapunzel,* Paul O. Zelinsky

Journalism

Year in parentheses is year awarded

National Journalism Awards (1998), by Scripps Howard Foundation, $2,500 each. Editorial writing: Daniel P. Henninger, *Wall Street Journal*; human interest writing: John Balzar, *LA Times*; environmental reporting (over 100,000 circ.): *Sacramento (CA) Bee*; environmental reporting (under 100,000 circ.): *Cape Cod Times*, Hyannis MA; public service reporting (over 100,000 circ.): Asbury Park Press, Neptune, NJ; public service reporting (under 100,000 circ.): *Pensacola (FL) News Journal*; commentary: Donald Kaul, *Des Moines Register*; photojournalism: Martha Rial, *Pittsburgh Post-Gazette*; college cartoonist: Brian Fairrington, Arizona State Univ. Distinguished service to literacy: (dual) *Knoxville News-Sentinel* and Betty J. Frey, Tucson Adult Literacy Volunteers Inc.; service to First Amendment: (dual) Jeff Montgomery, *News Journal*, Dover, DE, and *Palm Beach Post*; excellence in electronic media: WABC-TV, NY; WANE-TV, Fort Wayne, IN; Westwood One-Mutual/NBC, Arlington, VA; Alabama Public Radio, Tuscaloosa, AL

National Magazine Awards (1998), by American Society of Magazine Editors and Columbia Univ. Graduate School of Journalism. Gen. excel., circ. over 1 mil: *Rolling Stone*; 400,000-
1 mil: *Outside*; 100,000-400,000: *Preservation*; under 100,000: *DoubleTake*. Single topic issue: *The Sciences;* spec. interests: *Entertainment Weekly*; feature writing: *Harper's Mag.*; fiction: *The New Yorker;* design: *Entertainment Weekly;* photography: *W;* reporting: *Rolling Stone;* personal service: *Men's Journal;* public interest: *The Atlantic Monthly;* essays & criticism: *The New Yorker;* gen. excel., new media: *The Sporting News Online*

Overseas Press Club Awards (1998), for journalism abroad. Hal Boyle Award (newspaper or wire service reporting): Mark Bowden, *Philadelphia Inquirer*, "Blackhawk Down"; Bob Considine Award (newspaper or wire-service interpretation): *NY Times*, Howard W. French, James C. McKinley Jr., "Reports From Africa"; Robert Capa Gold Medal (photographic reporting requiring exceptional courage and enterprise) and Olivier Rebbot Award (photography in mags. and books): Horst Faas, Tim Page, *Requiem: By the Photographers Who Died in Vietnam and Indochina*; John Faber Award (photography in newspapers and wire services): John Moore, *AP*, "Zaire Refugees." Lowell Thomas Award (radio news or interpretation): Jennifer Glasse, Hank Weinbloom, *ABC News Radio*, "Perspective: Zaire"; David Kaplan Award (TV spot news reporting): Ron Allen, David Doss, Babak Behnam, *NBC Nightly News*, "Zaire Becomes the Congo"; Edward R. Murrow Award (TV interpretation or documentary): Fergal Keane, Mike Robinson, Michael Sullivan, David Fanning, *Frontline/WGBH Boston and BBC Panorama*, "Valentina's Nightmare"; Ed Cunningham Memorial Award (mag. reporting): Steven Strasser, Dorinda Elliott, Melinda Liu, and the *Newsweek* team, "Hong Kong's Handover to China"; Thomas Nast Award (cartooning): Robert L. Ariail, *The State,* Columbia, SC. Morton Frank Award (business reporting): *Business Week* Asia Team, "Asia in Crisis"; Malcolm Forbes Award (business reporting in newspapers or wire service): Wall Street Journal team, "The Asia Shock: The Economic Crisis That's Jolting the World"; Carl Spielvogel Award (business reporting in broadcast media): Julie McCarthy, Michael Sullivan, Loren Jenkins, *National Public Radio*, "Asian Economic Crisis." Cornelius Ryan Award (nonfiction book): Patrick Smith, *Japan: A Reinterpretation;* Madeline Dane Ross Award (foreign reporting concerned with human condition): (shared) Vanora Bennett, *LA Times,* "Victims of the Revolution: The Oppressed and Neglected of Post-Communist Russia," and Carol J. Williams, *LA Times*, "Life on the Edge: Russia's Far-flung Regions Struggle With Reforms"; Eric and Amy Burger Award (reporting on human rights): (shared) Brian Ross, Rhonda Schwartz, David Rummel, Phyllis McGrady, *ABC News*, "Blood Money," and Peter Van Sant, Randall Joyce, Nick Turner, Tomas Vavrusa, with Gordana Igric, *CBS News—Public Eye*, "In Plain Sight"; Whitman Bassow Award (reporting on internat. environmental issues): Gary Cohn, Will Englund, Perry Thorsvik, *Baltimore Sun*, "The Shipbreakers: Scrapping Ships, Sacrificing Men"; Robert Spiers Benjamin Award (reporting on Latin America): Mary Beth Sheridan, *LA Times*, "Mexico: Beyond the Myth"

George Foster Peabody Awards (1998), by the Univ. of Georgia. *State Farm: Good Neighbor or Bad Faith?*, KGO Radio, San Francisco; *Flood of the Century*, KFGO, Fargo, ND; *Will the Circle Be Unbroken?*, Southern Regional Council, Atlanta; *Dietrich Bonhoeffer: The Cost of Freedom*, Focus on the Family, Colorado Springs, CO; *Jazz From Lincoln Center*, Murray Street Enterprise, NY, for National Public Radio; *Military Medicine*, WRAL-TV, Raleigh, NC; *The Trial of Pol Pot*, ABC

News/Nightline; *Richard Rodriguez, Essays on American Life*, The NewsHour with Jim Lehrer; *The Castro*, KQED-TV, San Francisco; *Liberty! The American Revolution*, KTCA Twin Cities Public Television, St. Paul, MN, in assoc. with Middlemarch Films; *Hello Mr. President*, Barraclough Carey Productions for Channel 4, London, and The History Channel, NY; *A Healthy Baby Girl*, P.O.V./The American Documentary, a co-presentation with the Independent Television Service; *Look for Me Here: 299 Days in the Life of Nora Lenihan*, New England Cable News, Newton, MA; *In the Land of the Deaf*, Les Films d'Ici, La Sept-Cinema, Centre European Cinematographique RhoneAlpes, on Bravo/The Independent Film Channel; *Blue Note: A History of Modern Jazz*, Euroarts Entertainment, OHG & SDR artz, in assoc. with Bravo and Denmark Radio; *Divided Highways: The Interstates and the Transformation of American Life*, Florentine Films/Hott Productions and WETA-TV, Washington, DC; *The American Experience: The Presidents Series*, WGBH-TV, Boston; *The American Experience: Troublesome Creek—A Midwestern*, WGBH-TV, Boston; *The Nazis: A Warning From History*, BBC, London; *Body Doubles: The Twin Experience*, HBO and Carlton Television, in assoc. with Canadian Broadcasting Corp.; *City Arts*, Thirteen/WNET, NY; *Ellen—The Puppy Episode*, ABC, The Black/Marlens Company, in assoc. with Touchstone Television; *Homicide: Life on the Street*, NBC, Fatima Productions, NY; *Nothing Sacred*, ABC, Sarabande Productions, in assoc. with 20th Century Fox; *Mobil Masterpiece Theatre: The Tenant of Wildfell Hall*, WGBH-TV, Boston, BBC, London; *Don King: Only in America*, HBO Pictures and the Thomas Carter Company; *George Wallace*, TNT, a Mark Carliner Production; *The Eddie Files*, FASE Productions, LA, for PBS; *Wishbone*, Big Feats! Entertainment, a unit of Lyrick Studios, for PBS; *Nickelodeon: The Big Help*, Nickelodeon, NY; *CBS News: Sunday Morning*, CBS, NY; *CBS News: 60 Minutes*, CBS, NY. Carol Marin and Ted Turner each received a personal Peabody Award

George Polk Awards (1998), by Long Island Univ., for excellence in journalism. Career award: *Pittsburgh Courier*; foreign reporting: Laurie Garrett, *NY Newsday*; network TV reporting: Brian Ross and Rhonda Schwartz, *Prime Time Live*; military affairs reporting: *Dayton Daily News*; medical reporting: *Wall Street Journal*; business reporting: Kurt Eichenwald and Martin Gottlieb, *NY Times*; national reporting: Keith Bradsher, *NY Times;* local reporting: *Pensacola (FL) News Journal*; environmental reporting: Will Englund, Gary Cohn, Perry Thorsvik, *Baltimore Sun*; book award: *Requiem*, Horst Faas and Tim Page, editors, Random House; sports reporting: *Kansas City Star*; internat. reporting: Michael Dobbs, *Washington Post*; mag. reporting: Adam Gopnik, *The New Yorker*

Reuben Award, by National Cartoonists Society. Best cartoonist of 1998: Scott Adams

The Spingarn Medal

The Spingarn Medal has been awarded annually since 1915 (except in 1938) by the National Assoc. for the Advancement of Colored People for the highest achievement by a black American in the previous year.

1915	Ernest E. Just
1916	Charles Young
1917	Harry T. Burleigh
1918	William S. Braithwaite
1919	Archibald H. Grimké
1920	W. E. B. Du Bois
1921	Charles S. Gilpin
1922	Mary B. Talbert
1923	George W.Carver
1924	Roland Hayes
1925	James W. Johnson
1926	Carter G. Woodson
1927	Anthony Overton
1928	Charles W. Chesnutt
1929	Mordecai W. Johnson
1930	Henry A. Hunt
1931	Richard B. Harrison
1932	Robert R. Moton
1933	Max Yergan
1934	William T. B. Williams
1935	Mary McLeod Bethune
1936	John Hope
1937	Walter White
1939	Marian Anderson
1940	Louis T. Wright
1941	Richard Wright
1942	A. Philip Randolph
1943	William H. Hastie
1944	Charles Drew
1945	Paul Robeson
1946	Thurgood Marshall
1947	Dr. Percy L. Julian
1948	Channing H. Tobias
1949	Ralph J. Bunche
1950	Charles H. Houston
1951	Mabel K. Staupers
1952	Harry T. Moore
1953	Paul R. Williams
1954	Theodore K. Lawless
1955	Carl Murphy
1956	Jack R. Robinson
1957	Martin Luther King Jr.
1958	Daisy Bates and the Little Rock Nine
1959	Edward Kennedy (Duke) Ellington
1960	Langston Hughes
1961	Kenneth B. Clark
1962	Robert C. Weaver
1963	Medgar W. Evers
1964	Roy Wilkins
1965	Leontyne Price
1966	John H. Johnson
1967	Edward W. Brooke
1968	Sammy Davis Jr.
1969	Clarence M. Mitchell Jr.
1970	Jacob Lawrence
1971	Leon H. Sullivan
1972	Gordon Parks
1973	Wilson C. Riles
1974	Damon Keith
1975	Henry (Hank) Aaron
1976	Alvin Ailey
1977	Alex Haley
1978	Andrew Young
1979	Rosa L. Parks
1980	Dr. Rayford W. Logan
1981	Coleman Young
1982	Dr. Benjamin E. Mays
1983	Lena Horne
1984	Thomas Bradley
1985	Bill Cosby
1986	Dr. Benjamin L. Hooks
1987	Percy E. Sutton
1988	Frederick D. Patterson
1989	Jesse Jackson
1990	L. Douglas Wilder
1991	Gen. Colin L. Powell
1992	Barbara Jordan
1993	Dorothy I. Height
1994	Maya Angelou
1995	John Hope Franklin
1996	A. Leon Higginbotham
1997	Carl T. Rowan
1998	Myrlie Evers-Williams

Miscellaneous Awards

Year in parentheses is year awarded

American Academy of Arts and Letters (1998). Gold Medal for Graphic Art: Frank Stella*;* Award for Distinguished Service to the Arts: Agnus Gund; Arnold W. Brunner Memorial Prize in Architecture: Alvaro Siza; Academy Awards, $7,500 each, in Architecture: Laurie Olin; in Art: James O. Clark, David Deutsch, Charles LeDray, Ken Price, Terry Winters; in Music: Cindy Cox, Daniel S. Godfrey, Ingram D. Marshall, Jorge Martin. Jimmy Ernst Award in Art: Herman Rose; Walter Hinrichsen Award in Music: Albert Glinsky; Wladimir and Rhoda Lakond Award in Music: Wendell Logan; Willard L. Metcalf Award in Art: Nari Ward; Rosenthal Award in Art, $5,000: Sam Reveles. Richard Rodgers Development Awards for the Musical Theater: Erik Haagensen and Paul Schwartz, *Summer*, Alison Hubbard, Allan Knee, and Kim Oler, *Little Women*

National Medal of Humanities (formerly Charles Frankel Prizes), by National Endowment for the Humanities, for those who have increased public awareness of the humanities, $5,000 each (1997): Nina M. Archabal, David A. Berry, Richard J. Franke, William Friday, Don Henley, Maxine Hong Kingston, Luis Leal, Martin E. Marty, Paul Mellon, Studs Terkel

Intel Science Talent Search (formerly given by Westinghouse) (1998). 1st place, $40,000 schol.: Christopher Mihelich, Carmel, IN; 2d place, $30,000 schol.: Ravi Shah, Tempe, AZ; 3d place, $20,000 schol.: Parker Conrad, New York, NY

National Inventor of the Year Awards (1998), by Intellectual Property Owners: Antonette C. Allen; Christopher P. Alvares; Brenda S. Critz, Patricia D. Murphy; Sheri J. Olson, Denise (Schelter) Thurber; Bin Zeng, Oncormed, Inc.

John F. Kennedy Center for the Performing Arts Awards (1998): Bill Cosby, John Kander and Fred Ebb, Willie Nelson, André Previn, Shirley Temple (Black)

1998 Library of the Year Award, by Gale Research, Inc., and Library Journal: Medina County District Library, OH

National Medal of the Arts (1997) by White House: Edward Albee, Sarah Caldwell, Harry Callahan, Zelda Fichlander, Eduardo "Lalo" Guerrero, Lionel Hampton, Bella Lewitzky, Vera List, Robert Redford, Maurice Sendak, Stephen J. Sondheim, Boys Choir of Harlem

National Medals of Freedom (1998), by White House: Louise Bourgeois, Betty Carter, Agnes Gund, Daniel Urban Kiley, Angela Lansbury, James Levine, Tito Puente, Jason Robards, Edward Villella, Doc Watson, The MacDowell Colony

Pritzker Architecture Prize (1998) by the Hyatt Foundation, $100,000: Renzo Piano

1998 Teacher of the Year, by Council of Chief State School Officers and Scholastic Inc.: Philip Bigler, Fairfax County, VA

Templeton Prize for Progress in Religion (1998) by Templeton Foundation, about $1.2 million: Sir Sigmund Sternberg

Miss America Winners, 1921-1999

1921	Margaret Gorman, Washington, DC
1922-23	Mary Campbell, Columbus, Ohio
1924	Ruth Malcolmson, Philadelphia, Pennsylvania
1925	Fay Lamphier, Oakland, California
1926	Norma Smallwood, Tulsa, Oklahoma
1927	Lois Delander, Joliet, Illinois
1933	Marion Bergeron, West Haven, Connecticut
1935	Henrietta Leaver, Pittsburgh, Pennsylvania
1936	Rose Coyle, Philadelphia, Pennsylvania
1937	Bette Cooper, Bertrand Island, New Jersey
1938	Marilyn Meseke, Marion, Ohio
1939	Patricia Donnelly, Detroit, Michigan
1940	Frances Marie Burke, Philadelphia, Pennsylvania
1941	Rosemary LaPlanche, Los Angeles, California
1942	Jo-Caroll Dennison, Tyler, Texas
1943	Jean Bartel, Los Angeles, California

1944 Venus Ramey, Washington, D.C.
1945 Bess Myerson, New York City, New York
1946 Marilyn Buferd, Los Angeles, California
1947 Barbara Walker, Memphis, Tennessee
1948 BeBe Shopp, Hopkins, Minnesota
1949 Jacque Mercer, Litchfield, Arizona
1951 Yolande Betbeze, Mobile, Alabama
1952 Coleen Kay Hutchins, Salt Lake City, Utah
1953 Neva Jane Langley, Macon, Georgia
1954 Evelyn Margaret Ay, Ephrata, Pennsylvania
1955 Lee Meriwether, San Francisco, California
1956 Sharon Ritchie, Denver, Colorado
1957 Marian McKnight, Manning, South Carolina
1958 Marilyn Van Derbur, Denver, Colorado
1959 Mary Ann Mobley, Brandon, Mississippi
1960 Lynda Lee Mead, Natchez, Mississippi
1961 Nancy Fleming, Montague, Michigan
1962 Maria Fletcher, Asheville, North Carolina
1963 Jacquelyn Mayer, Sandusky, Ohio
1964 Donna Axum, El Dorado, Arkansas
1965 Vonda Kay Van Dyke, Phoenix, Arizona
1966 Deborah Irene Bryant, Overland Park, Kansas
1967 Jane Anne Jayroe, Laverne, Oklahoma
1968 Debra Dene Barnes, Moran, Kansas
1969 Judith Anne Ford, Belvidere, Illinois
1970 Pamela Anne Eldred, Birmingham, Michigan
1971 Phyllis Ann George, Denton, Texas
1972 Laurie Lea Schaefer, Columbus, Ohio
1973 Terry Anne Meeuwsen, DePere, Wisconsin
1974 Rebecca Ann King, Denver, Colorado
1975 Shirley Cothran, Fort Worth, Texas
1976 Tawney Elaine Godin, Yonkers, New York
1977 Dorothy Kathleen Benham, Edina, Minnesota
1978 Susan Perkins, Columbus, Ohio
1979 Kylene Barker, Galax, Virginia
1980 Cheryl Prewitt, Ackerman, Mississippi
1981 Susan Powell, Elk City, Oklahoma
1982 Elizabeth Ward, Russellville, Arkansas
1983 Debra Maffett, Anaheim, California
1984 Vanessa Williams*, Milwood, New York
Suzette Charles, Mays Landing, New Jersey
1985 Sharlene Wells, Salt Lake City, Utah
1986 Susan Akin, Meridian, Mississippi
1987 Kellye Cash, Memphis, Tennessee
1988 Kaye Lani Rae Rafko, Monroe, Michigan
1989 Gretchen Carlson, Anoka, Minnesota
1990 Debbye Turner, Columbia, Missouri
1991 Marjorie Vincent, Oak Park, Illinois
1992 Carolyn Suzanne Sapp, Honolulu, Hawaii
1993 Leanza Cornett, Jacksonville, Florida
1994 Kimberly Aiken, Columbia, South Carolina
1995 Heather Whitestone, Birmingham, Alabama
1996 Shawntel Smith, Muldrow, Oklahoma
1997 Tara Dawn Holland, Overland Park, Kansas
1998 Kate Shindle, Evanston, Illinois
1999 Nicole Johnson, Roanoke, Virginia

* Resigned July 23, 1984.

Entertainment Awards

1997-98 Emmy Awards

Prime-Time Emmy Awards

Drama series: *The Practice*, ABC
Comedy series: *Frasier*, NBC
Miniseries: *From the Earth to the Moon*, HBO
Variety, music or comedy series: *Late Show With David Letterman*, CBS
Variety, music or comedy special: *The 1997 Tony Awards*, CBS
Made-for-television movie: *Don King: Only in America*, HBO
Lead actor, drama series: Andre Braugher, *Homicide*, NBC
Lead actress, drama series: Christine Lahti, *Chicago Hope*, CBS
Lead actor, comedy series: Kelsey Grammer, *Frasier*, NBC
Lead actress, comedy series: Helen Hunt, *Mad About You*, NBC
Lead actor, miniseries/special: Gary Sinise, *George Wallace*, TNT
Lead actress, miniseries/special: Ellen Barkin, *Before Women Had Wings*, ABC
Supporting actor, drama series: Gordon Clapp, *N.Y.P.D. Blue*, ABC
Supporting actress, drama series: Camryn Manheim, *The Practice*, ABC
Supporting actor, comedy series: David Hyde Pierce, *Frasier*, NBC
Supporting actress, comedy series: Lisa Kudrow, *Friends*, NBC
Supporting actor, miniseries/special: George C. Scott, *12 Angry Men*, Showtime
Supporting actress, miniseries/special: Mare Winningham, *George Wallace*, TNT
Individual performance, variety/music program: Billy Crystal, *The 70th Annual Academy Awards*, ABC

Daytime Emmy Awards

Drama series: *All My Children*, ABC
Actress: Cynthia Watros, *Guiding Light*, CBS
Actor: Eric Braeden, *The Young and the Restless*, CBS
Supporting actress: Julia Barr, *All My Children*, ABC
Supporting actor: Steve Burton, *General Hospital*, ABC
Younger actress: Sarah Brown, *General Hospital*, ABC
Younger actor: Jonathan Jackson, *General Hospital*, ABC
Directing team: *The Young and the Restless*, CBS
Writing team: *All My Children*, ABC
Game/audience participation show: *Jeopardy!*, SYN
Game show host: Pat Sajak
Preschool children's series: *Sesame Street*, PBS
Children's special: *In His Father's Shoes*, SHO
Animated children's program: *Arthur*, PBS
Performer in a children's series: Bill Nye, *Disney Presents: Bill Nye the Science Guy*, SYN
Talk show: *The Rosie O'Donnell Show*, SYN
Talk show host: (tie) Rosie O'Donnell and Oprah Winfrey

Tony (Antoinette Perry) Awards (for Broadway Theater)

Tony Awards Given in 1998

Play: *Art*, by Yasmina Reza
Musical: *The Lion King*
Book of a musical: *Ragtime*, by Terrence McNally
Actor, play: Anthony LaPaglia, *A View From the Bridge*
Actress, play: Marie Mullen, *The Beauty Queen of Leenane*
Actor, musical: Alan Cumming, *Cabaret*
Actress, musical: Natasha Richardson, *Cabaret*
Musical score: *Ragtime*, Stephen Flaherty and Lynn Ahrens
Director, play: Garry Hynes, *The Beauty Queen of Leenane*
Director, musical: Julie Taymor, *The Lion King*
Play revival: *A View From the Bridge*
Musical revival: *Cabaret*
Featured actor, play: Tom Murphy, *The Beauty Queen of Leenane*
Featured actress, play: Anna Manahan, *The Beauty Queen of Leenane*
Featured actor, musical: Ron Rifkin, *Cabaret*
Featured actress, musical: Audra McDonald, *Ragtime*
Choreography: Garth Fagan, *The Lion King*
Costume design: Julie Taymor, *The Lion King*
Scenic design: Richard Hudson, *The Lion King*
Lighting design: Donald Holder, *The Lion King*
Orchestration: William David Brohn, *Ragtime*

Tony Awards, 1948-1998

Year	Play	Musical
1948	Mister Roberts	No Award
1949	Death of a Salesman	Kiss Me Kate
1950	The Cocktail Party	South Pacific
1951	The Rose Tatoo	Guys and Dolls
1952	The Fourposter	The King and I
1953	The Crucible	Wonderful Town
1954	The Teahouse of the August Moon	Kismet
1955	The Desperate Hours	The Pajama Game
1956	The Diary of Anne Frank	Damn Yankees
1957	Long Day's Journey Into Night	My Fair Lady
1958	Sunrise at Campobello	The Music Man
1959	J.B.	Redhead
1960	The Miracle Worker	(tie) Fiorello!, The Sound of Music
1961	Becket	Bye, Bye Birdie
1962	A Man for All Seasons	How to Succeed in Business Without Really Trying
1963	Who's Afraid of Virginia Woolf?	A Funny Thing Happened on the Way to the Forum
1964	Luther	Hello, Dolly!
1965	The Subject Was Roses	Fiddler on the Roof
1966	Marat/Sade	Man of La Mancha
1967	The Homecoming	Cabaret
1968	Rosencrantz and Guildenstern Are Dead	Hallelujah, Baby!
1969	The Great White Hope	1776
1970	Borstal Boy	Applause
1971	Sleuth	Company
1972	Sticks and Bones	Two Gentleman of Verona
1973	That Championship Season	A Little Night Music
1974	The River Niger	Raisin

Year	Play	Musical
1975	Equus	The Wiz
1976	Travesties	A Chorus Line
1977	The Shadow Box	Annie
1978	Da	Ain't Misbehavin'
1979	The Elephant Man	Sweeney Todd
1980	Children of a Lesser God	Evita
1981	Amadeus	42nd Street
1982	The Life and Adventures of Nicholas Nickelby	Nine
1983	Torch Song Trilogy	Cats
1985	Biloxi Blues	Big River
1986	I'm Not Rappaport	The Mystery of Edwin Drood
1987	Fences	Les Miserables
1988	M. Butterfly	Phantom of the Opera
1989	The Heidi Chronicles	Jerome Robbins' Broadway
1990	The Grapes of Wrath	City of Angels
1991	Lost in Yonkers	The Will Rogers Follies
1992	Dancing at Lughnasa	Crazy for You
1993	Angels in America: Millennium Approaches	Kiss of the Spider Woman
1994	Angels in America: Perestroika	Passion
1995	Love! Valour! Compassion!	Sunset Boulevard
1996	Master Class	Rent
1997	The Last Night of Ballyhoo	Titanic
1998	Art	The Lion King

1998 Golden Globe Awards

(Awarded for work in 1997)

Film

Drama: *Titanic*
Musical/comedy: *As Good As It Gets*
Actress, drama: Judi Dench, *Mrs. Brown*
Actor, drama: Peter Fonda, *Ulee's Gold*
Actress, musical/comedy: Helen Hunt, *As Good As It Gets*
Actor, musical/comedy: Jack Nicholson, *As Good As It Gets*
Supp. actress, drama: Kim Basinger, *L.A. Confidential*
Supp. actor, drama: Burt Reynolds, *Boogie Nights*
Director: James Cameron, *Titanic*
Screenplay: Matt Damon and Ben Affleck, *Good Will Hunting*
Foreign-language film: *My Life in Pink* (Belgium)
Original score: James Horner, *Titanic*
Original song: "My Heart Will Go On," *Titanic*
Cecil B. De Mille award for lifetime achievement: Shirley MacLaine

Television

Series, drama: *The X-Files*, Fox
Actress, drama: Christine Lahti, *Chicago Hope*
Actor, drama: Anthony Edwards, *ER*
Series, musical/comedy: *Ally McBeal*, Fox
Actress, musical/comedy: Calista Flockhart, *Ally McBeal*
Actor, musical/comedy: Michael J. Fox, *Spin City*
Miniseries, movie made for TV: *George Wallace*, TNT
Actress, miniseries, movie made for TV: Alfre Woodard, *Miss Evers' Boys*
Actor, miniseries, movie made for TV: Ving Rhames, *Don King: Only in America*
Supporting actress, miniseries, movie made for TV: Angelina Jolie, *George Wallace*
Supporting actor, miniseries, movie made for TV: George C. Scott, *12 Angry Men*

Academy Awards (Oscars) for 1927-1997

1927-28

Picture: *Wings*
Actor: Emil Jannings, *The Way of All Flesh*
Actress: Janet Gaynor, *Seventh Heaven*
Director: Frank Borzage, *Seventh Heaven;* Lewis Milestone, *Two Arabian Knights*

1928-29

Picture: *Broadway Melody*
Actor: Warner Baxter, *In Old Arizona*
Actress: Mary Pickford, *Coquette*
Director: Frank Lloyd, *The Divine Lady*

1929-30

Picture: *All Quiet on the Western Front*
Actor: George Arliss, *Disraeli*
Actress: Norma Shearer, *The Divorcee*
Director: Lewis Milestone, *All Quiet on the Western Front*

1930-31

Picture: *Cimarron*
Actor: Lionel Barrymore, *Free Soul*
Actress: Marie Dressler, *Min and Bill*
Director: Norman Taurog, *Skippy*

1931-32

Picture: *Grand Hotel*
Actor: Fredric March, *Dr. Jekyll and Mr. Hyde;* Wallace Beery, *The Champ* (tie)
Actress: Helen Hayes, *The Sin of Madelon Claudet*
Director: Frank Borzage, *Bad Girl*
Special: Walt Disney, *Mickey Mouse*

1932-33

Picture: *Cavalcade*
Actor: Charles Laughton, *The Private Life of Henry VIII*
Actress: Katharine Hepburn, *Morning Glory*
Director: Frank Lloyd, *Cavalcade*

1934

Picture: *It Happened One Night*
Actor: Clark Gable, *It Happened One Night*
Actress: Claudette Colbert, *It Happened One Night*
Director: Frank Capra, *It Happened One Night*

1935

Picture: *Mutiny on the Bounty*
Actor: Victor McLaglen, *The Informer*
Actress: Bette Davis, *Dangerous*
Director: John Ford, *The Informer*

1936

Picture: *The Great Ziegfeld*
Actor: Paul Muni, *Story of Louis Pasteur*
Actress: Luise Rainer, *The Great Ziegfeld*
Sup. Actor: Walter Brennan, *Come and Get It*
Sup. Actress: Gale Sondergaard, *Anthony Adverse*
Director: Frank Capra, *Mr. Deeds Goes to Town*

1937

Picture: *Life of Emile Zola*
Actor: Spencer Tracy, *Captains Courageous*
Actress: Luise Rainer, *The Good Earth*
Sup. Actor: Joseph Schildkraut, *Life of Emile Zola*
Sup. Actress: Alice Brady, *In Old Chicago*
Director: Leo McCarey, *The Awful Truth*

1938

Picture: *You Can't Take It With You*
Actor: Spencer Tracy, *Boys Town*
Actress: Bette Davis, *Jezebel*
Sup. Actor: Walter Brennan, *Kentucky*
Sup. Actress: Fay Bainter, *Jezebel*
Director: Frank Capra, *You Can't Take It With You*

1939

Picture: *Gone With the Wind*
Actor: Robert Donat, *Goodbye, Mr. Chips*
Actress: Vivien Leigh, *Gone With the Wind*
Sup. Actor: Thomas Mitchell, *Stage Coach*
Sup. Actress: Hattie McDaniel, *Gone With the Wind*
Director: Victor Fleming, *Gone With the Wind*

1940

Picture: *Rebecca*
Actor: James Stewart, *The Philadelphia Story*
Actress: Ginger Rogers, *Kitty Foyle*
Sup. Actor: Walter Brennan, *The Westerner*
Sup. Actress: Jane Darwell, *The Grapes of Wrath*
Director: John Ford, *The Grapes of Wrath*

1941

Picture: *How Green Was My Valley*
Actor: Gary Cooper, *Sergeant York*
Actress: Joan Fontaine, *Suspicion*
Sup. Actor: Donald Crisp, *How Green Was My Valley*
Sup. Actress: Mary Astor, *The Great Lie*
Director: John Ford, *How Green Was My Valley*

1942

Picture: *Mrs. Miniver*
Actor: James Cagney, *Yankee Doodle Dandy*
Actress: Greer Garson, *Mrs. Miniver*
Sup. Actor: Van Heflin, *Johnny Eager*
Sup. Actress: Teresa Wright, *Mrs. Miniver*
Director: William Wyler, *Mrs. Miniver*

1943

Picture: *Casablanca*
Actor: Paul Lukas, *Watch on the Rhine*
Actress: Jennifer Jones, *The Song of Bernadette*
Sup. Actor: Charles Coburn, *The More the Merrier*
Sup. Actress: Katina Paxinou, *For Whom the Bell Tolls*
Director: Michael Curtiz, *Casablanca*

1944

Picture: *Going My Way*
Actor: Bing Crosby, *Going My Way*
Actress: Ingrid Bergman, *Gaslight*
Sup. Actor: Barry Fitzgerald, *Going My Way*
Sup. Actress: Ethel Barrymore, *None But the Lonely Heart*
Director: Leo McCarey, *Going My Way*

1945

Picture: *The Lost Weekend*
Actor: Ray Milland, *The Lost Weekend*
Actress: Joan Crawford, *Mildred Pierce*
Sup. Actor: James Dunn, *A Tree Grows in Brooklyn*
Sup. Actress: Anne Revere, *National Velvet*
Director: Billy Wilder, *The Lost Weekend*

1946

Picture: *The Best Years of Our Lives*
Actor: Fredric March, *The Best Years of Our Lives*
Actress: Olivia de Havilland, *To Each His Own*
Sup. Actor: Harold Russell, *The Best Years of Our Lives*
Sup. Actress: Anne Baxter, *The Razor's Edge*
Director: William Wyler, *The Best Years of Our Lives*

1947

Picture: *Gentleman's Agreement*
Actor: Ronald Colman, *A Double Life*
Actress: Loretta Young, *The Farmer's Daughter*
Sup. Actor: Edmund Gwenn, *Miracle on 34th Street*
Sup. Actress: Celeste Holm, *Gentleman's Agreement*
Director: Elia Kazan, *Gentleman's Agreement*

1948

Picture: *Hamlet*

Actor: Laurence Olivier, *Hamlet*
Actress: Jane Wyman, *Johnny Belinda*
Sup. Actor: Walter Huston, *Treasure of Sierra Madre*
Sup. Actress: Claire Trevor, *Key Largo*
Director: John Huston, *Treasure of Sierra Madre*

1949
Picture: *All the King's Men*
Actor: Broderick Crawford, *All the King's Men*
Actress: Olivia de Havilland, *The Heiress*
Sup. Actor: Dean Jagger, *Twelve O'Clock High*
Sup. Actress: Mercedes McCambridge, *All the King's Men*
Director: Joseph L. Mankiewicz, *Letter to Three Wives*

1950
Picture: *All About Eve*
Actor: Jose Ferrer, *Cyrano de Bergerac*
Actress: Judy Holliday, *Born Yesterday*
Sup. Actor: George Sanders, *All About Eve*
Sup. Actress: Josephine Hull, *Harvey*
Director: Joseph L. Mankiewicz, *All About Eve*

1951
Picture: *An American in Paris*
Actor: Humphrey Bogart, *The African Queen*
Actress: Vivien Leigh, *A Streetcar Named Desire*
Sup. Actor: Karl Malden, *A Streetcar Named Desire*
Sup. Actress: Kim Hunter, *A Streetcar Named Desire*
Director: George Stevens, *A Place in the Sun*

1952
Picture: *The Greatest Show on Earth*
Actor: Gary Cooper, *High Noon*
Actress: Shirley Booth, *Come Back, Little Sheba*
Sup. Actor: Anthony Quinn, *Viva Zapata!*
Sup. Actress: Gloria Grahame, *The Bad and the Beautiful*
Director: John Ford, *The Quiet Man*

1953
Picture: *From Here to Eternity*
Actor: William Holden, *Stalag 17*
Actress: Audrey Hepburn, *Roman Holiday*
Sup. Actor: Frank Sinatra, *From Here to Eternity*
Sup. Actress: Donna Reed, *From Here to Eternity*
Director: Fred Zinnemann, *From Here to Eternity*

1954
Picture: *On the Waterfront*
Actor: Marlon Brando, *On the Waterfront*
Actress: Grace Kelly, *The Country Girl*
Sup. Actor: Edmond O'Brien, *The Barefoot Contessa*
Sup. Actress: Eva Marie Saint, *On the Waterfront*
Director: Elia Kazan, *On the Waterfront*

1955
Picture: *Marty*
Actor: Ernest Borgnine, *Marty*
Actress: Anna Magnani, *The Rose Tattoo*
Sup. Actor: Jack Lemmon, *Mister Roberts*
Sup. Actress: Jo Van Fleet, *East of Eden*
Director: Delbert Mann, *Marty*

1956
Picture: *Around the World in 80 Days*
Actor: Yul Brynner, *The King and I*
Actress: Ingrid Bergman, *Anastasia*
Sup. Actor: Anthony Quinn, *Lust for Life*
Sup. Actress: Dorothy Malone, *Written on the Wind*
Director: George Stevens, *Giant*

1957
Picture: *The Bridge on the River Kwai*
Actor: Alec Guinness, *The Bridge on the River Kwai*
Actress: Joanne Woodward, *The Three Faces of Eve*
Sup. Actor: Red Buttons, *Sayonara*
Sup. Actress: Miyoshi Umeki, *Sayonara*
Director: David Lean, *The Bridge on the River Kwai*

1958
Picture: *Gigi*
Actor: David Niven, *Separate Tables*
Actress: Susan Hayward, *I Want to Live*
Sup. Actor: Burl Ives, *The Big Country*
Sup. Actress: Wendy Hiller, *Separate Tables*
Director: Vincente Minnelli, *Gigi*

1959
Picture: *Ben-Hur*
Actor: Charlton Heston, *Ben-Hur*
Actress: Simone Signoret, *Room at the Top*
Sup. Actor: Hugh Griffith, *Ben-Hur*
Sup. Actress: Shelley Winters, *Diary of Anne Frank*
Director: William Wyler, *Ben-Hur*

1960
Picture: *The Apartment*
Actor: Burt Lancaster, *Elmer Gantry*
Actress: Elizabeth Taylor, *Butterfield 8*
Sup. Actor: Peter Ustinov, *Spartacus*
Sup. Actress: Shirley Jones, *Elmer Gantry*
Director: Billy Wilder, *The Apartment*

1961
Picture: *West Side Story*
Actor: Maximilian Schell, *Judgment at Nuremberg*
Actress: Sophia Loren, *Two Women*
Sup. Actor: George Chakiris, *West Side Story*
Sup. Actress: Rita Moreno, *West Side Story*
Director: Jerome Robbins, Robert Wise, *West Side Story*

1962
Picture: *Lawrence of Arabia*
Actor: Gregory Peck, *To Kill a Mockingbird*
Actress: Anne Bancroft, *The Miracle Worker*
Sup. Actor: Ed Begley, *Sweet Bird of Youth*
Sup. Actress: Patty Duke, *The Miracle Worker*
Director: David Lean, *Lawrence of Arabia*

1963
Picture: *Tom Jones*
Actor: Sidney Poitier, *Lilies of the Field*
Actress: Patricia Neal, *Hud*
Sup. Actor: Melvyn Douglas, *Hud*
Sup. Actress: Margaret Rutherford, *The V.I.P.s*
Director: Tony Richardson, *Tom Jones*

1964
Picture: *My Fair Lady*
Actor: Rex Harrison, *My Fair Lady*
Actress: Julie Andrews, *Mary Poppins*
Sup. Actor: Peter Ustinov, *Topkapi*
Sup. Actress: Lila Kedrova, *Zorba the Greek*
Director: George Cukor, *My Fair Lady*

1965
Picture: *The Sound of Music*
Actor: Lee Marvin, *Cat Ballou*
Actress: Julie Christie, *Darling*
Sup. Actor: Martin Balsam, *A Thousand Clowns*
Sup. Actress: Shelley Winters, *A Patch of Blue*
Director: Robert Wise, *The Sound of Music*

1966
Picture: *A Man for All Seasons*
Actor: Paul Scofield, *A Man for All Seasons*
Actress: Elizabeth Taylor, *Who's Afraid of Virginia Woolf?*
Sup. Actor: Walter Matthau, *The Fortune Cookie*
Sup. Actress: Sandy Dennis, *Who's Afraid of Virginia Woolf?*
Director: Fred Zinnemann, *A Man for All Seasons*

1967
Picture: *In the Heat of the Night*
Actor: Rod Steiger, *In the Heat of the Night*
Actress: Katharine Hepburn, *Guess Who's Coming to Dinner*
Sup. Actor: George Kennedy, *Cool Hand Luke*
Sup. Actress: Estelle Parsons, *Bonnie and Clyde*
Director: Mike Nichols, *The Graduate*

1968
Picture: *Oliver!*
Actor: Cliff Robertson, *Charly*
Actress: Katharine Hepburn, *The Lion in Winter*; Barbra Streisand, *Funny Girl* (tie)
Sup. Actor: Jack Albertson, *The Subject Was Roses*
Sup. Actress: Ruth Gordon, *Rosemary's Baby*
Director: Sir Carol Reed, *Oliver!*

1969
Picture: *Midnight Cowboy*
Actor: John Wayne, *True Grit*
Actress: Maggie Smith, *The Prime of Miss Jean Brodie*
Sup. Actor: Gig Young, *They Shoot Horses, Don't They?*
Sup. Actress: Goldie Hawn, *Cactus Flower*
Director: John Schlesinger, *Midnight Cowboy*

1970
Picture: *Patton*
Actor: George C. Scott, *Patton* (refused)
Actress: Glenda Jackson, *Women in Love*
Sup. Actor: John Mills, *Ryan's Daughter*
Sup. Actress: Helen Hayes, *Airport*
Director: Franklin Schaffner, *Patton*

1971
Picture: *The French Connection*
Actor: Gene Hackman, *The French Connection*
Actress: Jane Fonda, *Klute*
Sup. Actor: Ben Johnson, *The Last Picture Show*
Sup. Actress: Cloris Leachman, *The Last Picture Show*
Director: William Friedkin, *The French Connection*

1972
Picture: *The Godfather*
Actor: Marlon Brando, *The Godfather* (refused)
Actress: Liza Minnelli, *Cabaret*
Sup. Actor: Joel Grey, *Cabaret*
Sup. Actress: Eileen Heckart, *Butterflies Are Free*
Director: Bob Fosse, *Cabaret*

1973
Picture: *The Sting*
Actor: Jack Lemmon, *Save the Tiger*
Actress: Glenda Jackson, *A Touch of Class*
Sup. Actor: John Houseman, *The Paper Chase*
Sup. Actress: Tatum O'Neal, *Paper Moon*
Director: George Roy Hill, *The Sting*

1974
Picture: *The Godfather, Part II*
Actor: Art Carney, *Harry and Tonto*
Actress: Ellen Burstyn, *Alice Doesn't Live Here Anymore*
Sup. Actor: Robert DeNiro, *The Godfather, Part II*
Sup. Actress: Ingrid Bergman, *Murder on the Orient Express*
Director: Francis Ford Coppola, *The Godfather, Part II*

1975
Picture: *One Flew Over the Cuckoo's Nest*
Actor: Jack Nicholson, *One Flew Over the Cuckoo's Nest*
Actress: Louise Fletcher, *One Flew Over the Cuckoo's Nest*
Sup. Actor: George Burns, *The Sunshine Boys*
Sup. Actress: Lee Grant, *Shampoo*
Director: Milos Forman, *One Flew Over the Cuckoo's Nest*

1976
Picture: *Rocky*
Actor: Peter Finch, *Network*
Actress: Faye Dunaway, *Network*
Sup. Actor: Jason Robards, *All the President's Men*

(continued)

Sup. Actress: Beatrice Straight, *Network*
Director: John G. Avildsen, *Rocky*

1977

Picture: *Annie Hall*
Actor: Richard Dreyfuss, *The Goodbye Girl*
Actress: Diane Keaton, *Annie Hall*
Sup. Actor: Jason Robards, *Julia*
Sup. Actress: Vanessa Redgrave, *Julia*
Director: Woody Allen, *Annie Hall*

1978

Picture: *The Deer Hunter*
Actor: Jon Voight, *Coming Home*
Actress: Jane Fonda, *Coming Home*
Sup. Actor: Christopher Walken, *The Deer Hunter*
Sup. Actress: Maggie Smith, *California Suite*
Director: Michael Cimino, *The Deer Hunter*

1979

Picture: *Kramer vs. Kramer*
Actor: Dustin Hoffman, *Kramer vs. Kramer*
Actress: Sally Field, *Norma Rae*
Sup. Actor: Melvyn Douglas, *Being There*
Sup. Actress: Meryl Streep, *Kramer vs. Kramer*
Director: Robert Benton, *Kramer vs. Kramer*

1980

Picture: *Ordinary People*
Actor: Robert DeNiro, *Raging Bull*
Actress: Sissy Spacek, *Coal Miner's Daughter*
Sup. Actor: Timothy Hutton, *Ordinary People*
Sup. Actress: Mary Steenburgen, *Melvin & Howard*
Director: Robert Redford, *Ordinary People*

1981

Picture: *Chariots of Fire*
Actor: Henry Fonda, *On Golden Pond*
Actress: Katharine Hepburn, *On Golden Pond*
Sup. Actor: John Gielgud, *Arthur*
Sup. Actress: Maureen Stapleton, *Reds*
Director: Warren Beatty, *Reds*

1982

Picture: *Gandhi*
Actor: Ben Kingsley, *Gandhi*
Actress: Meryl Streep, *Sophie's Choice*
Sup. Actor: Louis Gossett Jr., *An Officer and a Gentleman*
Sup. Actress: Jessica Lange, *Tootsie*
Director: Richard Attenborough, *Gandhi*

1983

Picture: *Terms of Endearment*
Actor: Robert Duvall, *Tender Mercies*
Actress: Shirley MacLaine, *Terms of Endearment*
Sup. Actor: Jack Nicholson, *Terms of Endearment*
Sup. Actress: Linda Hunt, *The Year of Living Dangerously*
Director: James L. Brooks, *Terms of Endearment*

1984

Picture: *Amadeus*
Actor: F. Murray Abraham, *Amadeus*
Actress: Sally Field, *Places in the Heart*
Sup. Actor: Haing S. Ngor, *The Killing Fields*
Sup. Actress: Peggy Ashcroft, *A Passage to India*
Director: Milos Forman, *Amadeus*

1985

Picture: *Out of Africa*
Actor: William Hurt, *Kiss of the Spider Woman*
Actress: Geraldine Page, *The Trip to Bountiful*
Sup. Actor: Don Ameche, *Cocoon*
Sup. Actress: Anjelica Huston, *Prizzi's Honor*
Director: Sydney Pollack, *Out of Africa*

1986

Picture: *Platoon*
Actor: Paul Newman, *The Color of Money*
Actress: Marlee Matlin, *Children of a Lesser God*
Sup. Actor: Michael Caine, *Hannah and Her Sisters*
Sup. Actress: Dianne Wiest, *Hannah and Her Sisters*
Director: Oliver Stone, *Platoon*

1987

Picture: *The Last Emperor*
Actor: Michael Douglas, *Wall Street*
Actress: Cher, *Moonstruck*
Sup. Actor: Sean Connery, *The Untouchables*
Sup. Actress: Olympia Dukakis, *Moonstruck*
Director: Bernardo Bertolucci, *The Last Emperor*

1988

Picture: *Rain Man*
Actor: Dustin Hoffman, *Rain Man*
Actress: Jodie Foster, *The Accused*
Sup. Actor: Kevin Kline, *A Fish Called Wanda*
Sup. Actress: Geena Davis, *The Accidental Tourist*
Director: Barry Levinson, *Rain Man*

1989

Picture: *Driving Miss Daisy*
Actor: Daniel Day-Lewis, *My Left Foot*
Actress: Jessica Tandy, *Driving Miss Daisy*
Sup. Actor: Denzel Washington, *Glory*
Sup. Actress: Brenda Fricker, *My Left Foot*
Director: Oliver Stone, *Born on the Fourth of July*

1990

Picture: *Dances With Wolves*
Actor: Jeremy Irons, *Reversal of Fortune*
Actress: Kathy Bates, *Misery*
Sup. Actor: Joe Pesci, *Goodfellas*
Sup. Actress: Whoopi Goldberg, *Ghost*
Director: Kevin Costner, *Dances With Wolves*

1991

Picture: *The Silence of the Lambs*
Actor: Anthony Hopkins, *The Silence of the Lambs*
Actress: Jodie Foster, *The Silence of the Lambs*
Sup. Actor: Jack Palance, *City Slickers*
Sup. Actress: Mercedes Ruehl, *The Fisher King*
Director: Jonathan Demme, *The Silence of the Lambs*

1992

Picture: *Unforgiven*
Actor: Al Pacino, *Scent of a Woman*
Actress: Emma Thompson, *Howards End*
Sup. Actor: Gene Hackman, *Unforgiven*
Sup. Actress: Marisa Tomei, *My Cousin Vinny*
Director: Clint Eastwood, *Unforgiven*

1993

Picture: *Schindler's List*
Actor: Tom Hanks, *Philadelphia*
Actress: Holly Hunter, *The Piano*
Sup. Actor: Tommy Lee Jones, *The Fugitive*
Sup. Actress: Anna Paquin, *The Piano*
Director: Steven Spielberg, *Schindler's List*

1994

Picture: *Forrest Gump*
Actor: Tom Hanks, *Forrest Gump*
Actress: Jessica Lange, *Blue Sky*
Sup. Actor: Martin Landau, *Ed Wood*
Sup. Actress: Dianne Wiest, *Bullets Over Broadway*
Director: Robert Zemeckis, *Forrest Gump*

1995

Picture: *Braveheart*
Actor: Nicolas Cage, *Leaving Las Vegas*
Actress: Susan Sarandon, *Dead Man Walking*
Sup. Actor: Kevin Spacey, *The Usual Suspects*
Sup. Actress: Mira Sorvino, *Mighty Aphrodite*
Director: Mel Gibson, *Braveheart*

1996

Picture: *The English Patient*
Actor: Geoffrey Rush, *Shine*
Actress: Frances McDormand, *Fargo*
Sup. Actor: Cuba Gooding Jr., *Jerry Maguire*
Sup. Actress: Juliette Binoche, *The English Patient*
Director: Anthony Minghella, *The English Patient*

1997

Picture: *Titanic*
Actor: Jack Nicholson, *As Good As It Gets*
Actress: Helen Hunt, *As Good As It Gets*
Sup. Actor: Robin Williams, *Good Will Hunting*
Sup. Actress: Kim Basinger, *L.A. Confidential*
Director: James Cameron, *Titanic*
Foreign Film: *Character*, Netherlands
Original Screenplay: Matt Damon and Ben Affleck, *Good Will Hunting*
Adapted Screenplay: Brian Helgeland and Curtis Hanson, *L.A. Confidential*
Cinematography: Russell Carpenter, *Titanic*
Art Direction: Peter Lamont (art direction) and Michael Ford (set direction), *Titanic*
Film Editing: Conrad Buff, James Cameron, Richard A. Harris, *Titanic*
Original Song: "My Heart Will Go On," *Titanic*, James Horner and Will Jennings
Original musical or comedy score: Anne Dudley, *The Full Monty*
Original dramatic score: James Horner, *Titanic*
Costume: Deborah L. Scott, *Titantic*
Makeup: Rick Baker, David LeRoy Anderson, *Men in Black*
Sound: Gary Rydstrom, Tom Johnson, Gary Summers, Mark Ulano, *Titantic*
Documentary Feature: *The Long Way Home*
Documentary Short Subject: *A Story of Healing*
Short Film, Live: Chris Donahue, Chris Tashima, *Visas and Virtue*
Short Film, Animated: Jan Pinkava, *Geri's Game*
Visual Effects: Robert Legato, Mark Lasoff, Thomas L. Fisher, Michael Kanfer, *Titanic*
Sound Effects Editing: Tom Bellfort, Christopher Boyes, *Titanic*
Scientific and Technical Oscar: Gunnar P. Michelson
Honorary Award: Stanley Donen, choreographer/director
Gordon E. Sawyer Award: Don Iwerks

Other Film Awards

Year in parentheses is year awarded

Cannes Film Festival Awards (1998). Palme d'Or: *Eternity and a Day,* Theo Angelopoulos (Gk.); Grand Prix: *Life Is Beautiful,* Roberto Benigni (It.); best actress: (shared), Elodie Bouchez and Natacha Regier (both Fr.), *The Dream Life of Angels*; best actor: Peter Mullan (Br.), *My Name Is Joe*; best director: John Boorman (Br.), *The General*; best screenplay: Hal Hartley (U.S.), *Henry Fool.* Special Jury Prize: (shared) *The Class Trip*, Claude Miller (Fr.), and *Celebration*, Thomas Vinterber (Dan.). Golden Camera (best first-time director): Marc Levin (U.S.), *Slam*; best artistic contribution: *Velvet Goldmine*, Todd Haynes (U.S.)

Directors Guild of America Awards (1998). Feature film: James Cameron, *Titanic*; documentary: Michael Uys & Lexy

Lovell, *Riding the Rails*; 1998 D.W. Griffith Award (career achievement in motion picture directing): Francis Ford Coppola

Sundance Film Festival Awards (1998). Grand Jury Prize: (drama) *Slam*, Mark Levin; (docu.) *The Farm*, Jonathan Stack and Liz Garbus, and *Frat House*, Todd Phillips and Andrew Gurland (split). Directing Award: (drama) *π (Pi)*, Darren Aronofsky; (docu.) *Moment of Impact*, Julia Loktev. Audience Award: (drama) *Smoke Signals*, Chris Eyre; (docu.) *Out of the Past*, Jeff Dupre. Filmmakers Trophy: (drama) *Smoke and Signals*; (docu.) *Divine Trash*, Steve Yeager. Screenwriting Award: *High Art*, Lisa Cholodenko; Freedom of Expression Award: *The Decline of Western Civilization, Part III*, Penelope Spheeris. Latin Amer. Cinema Award: *Who the Hell Is Juliette?*, Carlos Marcovich. Short Filmmaking Award: *Snake Feed*, Debra Granik. Special Jury Prize for acting: Andrea Hart, *Miss Monday*.

Grammy Awards

Source: National Academy of Recording Arts & Sciences

Selected Grammy Awards for 1997

Single record: "Sunny Came Home," Shawn Colvin
Album: *Time Out of Mind*, Bob Dylan
Song: "Sunny Came Home," Shawn Colvin, John Leventhal
New artist: Paula Cole
Female pop vocalist: Sarah McLachlan, "Building a Mystery"
Male pop vocalist: Elton John, "Candle in the Wind 1997"
Pop album: *Hourglass*, James Taylor
Group or duo pop perf. with vocal: Jamiroquai, "Virtual Insanity"
Traditional pop album: *Tony Bennett on Holiday*, Tony Bennett
Rock vocalist, female: Fiona Apple, "Criminal"
Rock vocalist, male: Bob Dylan, "Cold Irons Bound"
Rock, duo or group: The Wallflowers, "One Headlight"
Rock song: "One Headlight," Jakob Dylan
Rock album: *Blue Moon Swamp*, John Fogerty
R & B vocalist, female: Erykah Badu, "On and On"
R & B vocalist, male: R. Kelly, "I Believe I Can Fly"
R & B, duo or group: Blackstreet, "No Diggity"
R & B song: "I Believe I Can Fly," R. Kelly
R & B album: *Baduizm*, Erykah Badu
Rap solo: "Men in Black," Will Smith
Rap, duo or group: Puff Daddy and Faith Evans featuring 112, "I'll Be Missing You"
Rap album: *No Way Out*, Puff Daddy and the Family
Jazz vocalist: Dee Dee Bridgewater, "Dear Ella"
Contemporary jazz performance: *Into the Sun*, Randy Brecker
Contemporary blues album: *Señor Blues*, Taj Mahal
Traditional blues album: *Don't Look Back*, John Lee Hooker
Country vocalist, female: Trisha Yearwood, "How Do I Live"
Country vocalist, male: Vince Gill, "Pretty Little Adriana"
Country, duo or group: Alison Krauss and Union Station, "Looking in the Eyes of Love"
Country song: "Butterfly Kisses," Bob Carlisle, Jeff Carson, and the Raybon Brothers
Country album: *Unchained*, Johnny Cash
Contemporary folk album: *Time Out of Mind*, Bob Dylan
Traditional folk album: *L'Amour ou la Folie*, Beausoleil
Reggae album: *Fallen Is Babylon*, Ziggy Marley and the Melody Makers
Non-musical album: *Charles Kuralt's Spring*, Charles Kuralt
Producer, non-classical, Babyface; classical, Steven Epstein
Opera album: *Wagner: Die Meistersinger von Nurnberg*, Chicago Symphony Orchestra and Chorus, Sir Georg Solti, conductor
Classical vocalist: Cecilia Bartoli, *An Italian Songbook*
Classical album: *Premieres: Cello Concertos*, Phil. Orch.

Grammy Awards for 1958-96

Single Record	Year	Album
Domenico Modugno, "Nel Blu Dipinto Di Blu (Volare)"	**1958**	Henry Mancini, *The Music From Peter Gunn*
Bobby Darin, "Mack the Knife"	**1959**	Frank Sinatra, *Come Dance With Me*
Percy Faith, "Theme From a Summer Place"	**1960**	Bob Newhart, *Button Down Mind*
Henry Mancini, "Moon River"	**1961**	Judy Garland, *Judy at Carnegie Hall*
Tony Bennett, "I Left My Heart in San Francisco"	**1962**	Vaughn Meader, *The First Family*
Henry Mancini, "The Days of Wine and Roses"	**1963**	Barbra Streisand, *The Barbra Streisand Album*
Stan Getz, Astrud Gilberto, "The Girl From Ipanema"	**1964**	Stan Getz, Astrud Gilberto, *Getz/Gilberto*
Herb Alpert, "A Taste of Honey"	**1965**	Frank Sinatra, *September of My Years*
Frank Sinatra, "Strangers in the Night"	**1966**	Frank Sinatra, *A Man and His Music*
5th Dimension, "Up, Up and Away"	**1967**	The Beatles, *Sgt. Pepper's Lonely Hearts Club Band*
Simon & Garfunkel, "Mrs. Robinson"	**1968**	Glen Campbell, *By the Time I Get to Phoenix*
5th Dimension, "Aquarius/Let the Sunshine In"	**1969**	Blood Sweat and Tears, *Blood, Sweat and Tears*
Simon & Garfunkel, "Bridge Over Troubled Water"	**1970**	Simon & Garfunkel, *Bridge Over Troubled Water*
Carole King, "It's Too Late"	**1971**	Carole King, *Tapestry*
Roberta Flack, "The First Time Ever I Saw Your Face"	**1972**	George Harrison and friends, *The Concert for Bangla Desh*
Roberta Flack, "Killing Me Softly With His Song"	**1973**	Stevie Wonder, *Innervisions*
Olivia Newton-John, "I Honestly Love You"	**1974**	Stevie Wonder, *Fulfillingness' First Finale*
Captain & Tennille, "Love Will Keep Us Together"	**1975**	Paul Simon, *Still Crazy After All These Years*
George Benson, "This Masquerade"	**1976**	Stevie Wonder, *Songs in the Key of Life*
Eagles, "Hotel California"	**1977**	Fleetwood Mac, *Rumours*
Billy Joel, "Just the Way You Are"	**1978**	Bee Gees, *Saturday Night Fever*
The Doobie Brothers, "What a Fool Believes"	**1979**	Billy Joel, *52nd Street*
Christopher Cross, "Sailing"	**1980**	Christopher Cross, *Christopher Cross*
Kim Carnes, "Bette Davis Eyes"	**1981**	John Lennon, Yoko Ono, *Double Fantasy*
Toto, "Rosanna"	**1982**	Toto, *Toto IV*
Michael Jackson, "Beat It"	**1983**	Michael Jackson, *Thriller*
Tina Turner, "What's Love Got to Do With It"	**1984**	Lionel Richie, *Can't Slow Down*
USA for Africa, "We Are the World"	**1985**	Phil Collins, *No Jacket Required*
Steve Winwood, "Higher Love"	**1986**	Paul Simon, *Graceland*
Paul Simon, "Graceland"	**1987**	U2, *The Joshua Tree*
Bobby McFerrin, "Don't Worry, Be Happy"	**1988**	George Michael, *Faith*
Bette Midler, "Wind Beneath My Wings"	**1989**	Bonnie Raitt, *Nick of Time*
Phil Collins, "Another Day in Paradise"	**1990**	Quincy Jones, *Back on the Block*
Natalie Cole, with Nat "King" Cole, "Unforgettable"	**1991**	Natalie Cole, with Nat "King" Cole, *Unforgettable*
Eric Clapton, "Tears in Heaven"	**1992**	Eric Clapton, *Unplugged*
Whitney Houston, "I Will Always Love You"	**1993**	Whitney Houston, *The Bodyguard*
Sheryl Crow, "All I Wanna Do"	**1994**	Tony Bennett, *MTV Unplugged*
Seal, "Kiss From a Rose"	**1995**	Alanis Morissette, *Jagged Little Pill*
Eric Clapton, "Change the World"	**1996**	Celine Dion, *Falling Into You*

1998 MTV Music Video Awards

Video of the Year: Madonna, "Ray of Light"
Best Male Video: Will Smith, "Just the Two of Us"
Best Female Video: Madonna, "Ray of Light"
Best Group Video: Backstreet Boys, "Everybody (Backstreet's Back)"
Best Rap Video: Will Smith, "Gettin' Jiggy Wit It"
Best Dance Video: Prodigy, "Smack My Bitch Up"
Best Rock Video: Aerosmith, "Pink"
Best Alternative Music Video: Green Day, "Time of Your Life (Good Riddance)"
Best New Artist: Natalie Imbruglia, "Torn"
Breakthrough Video: Prodigy, "Smack My Bitch Up"
Best R&B Video: Wyclef Jean featuring Refugee Allstars, "Gone 'Til November"
Best Video From a Film: Aerosmith, "I Don't Want to Miss a Thing," from *Armageddon*
Best Direction: Madonna, "Ray of Light" (Jonas Akerlund, director)
Best Choreography: Madonna, "Ray of Light"
Best Special Effects: Madonna, "Frozen"
Best Art Direction: Bjork, "Bachelorette"
Best Editing: Madonna, "Ray of Light"
Best Cinematography: Fiona Apple, "Criminal"
Viewers' Choice: Puff Daddy & The Family, "It's All About the Benjamins (Rock Remix)"

RELIGIOUS INFORMATION

Membership of Religious Groups in the U.S.

Source: *1998 Yearbook of American & Canadian Churches,* © National Council of the Churches of Christ in the USA; World Almanac research

These membership figures generally are based on reports made by officials of each group, and not on any religious census. Figures from other sources may vary. Many groups keep careful records; others only estimate. Not all groups report annually. Christian church membership figures reported in this table are inclusive and refer to *all* "members," not simply full communicants or confirmed members. Definitions of "member," however, vary from one denomination to another. Only data reported within the past 10 years are included.

The number of houses of worship appears in parentheses. * Indicates that the group declines to make the figure public. Groups reporting fewer than 5,000 members are not included; where membership numbers are not available, only those groups with 50 or more houses of worship are listed.

Religious Group	Members
Adventist churches:	
Advent Christian Ch. (318)	26,522
Ch. of God Gen. Conf. (Oregon, IL; Morrow, GA) (89)	5,096
Seventh-day Adventists (4,363)	809,159
American Rescue Workers (15)	**10,000**
Apostolic Christian Church of America (91)	**12,200**
Bahá'í Faith (7,200)	**133,000**[1]
Baptist churches:	
American Baptist Assn. (1,705)	300,000
American Baptist Chs. in the U.S.A. (5,807)	1,503,267
Baptist Bible Fellowship Intl. (3,600)	1,500,000
Baptist General Conference (875)	136,120
Baptist Missionary Assn. of America (1,349)	232,069
Conservative Baptist Assn. of America (1,084)	200,000
Free Will Baptists, Natl. Assn. of (2,491)	210,305
General Assn. of General Baptists (830)	67,881
General Assn. of Regular Baptist Chs. (1,440)	115,950
Natl. Baptist Convention, U.S.A., Inc. (33,000)	8,200,000
Natl. Missionary Baptist Convention of America	2,500,000
North American Baptist Conference (263)	43,928
Progressive National Baptist Convention (2,000)	2,500,000
Separate Baptists in Christ (100)	8,000
Southern Baptist Convention (40,565)	15,691,964
Brethren in Christ (199)	**18,424**
Brethren (German Baptists):	
Brethren Ch. (Ashland, OH) (119)	13,746
Church of the Brethren (1,106)	141,811
Grace Brethren Chs., Fellowship of (270)	34,500
Old German Baptist Brethren (57)	5,623
Buddhist Churches of America (62)	**780,000**[1]
Christian Brethren (Plymouth Brethren) (1,150)	**100,000**
Christian Church (Disciples of Christ) (3,840)	**910,297**
Christian Ch. of N.A., Gen. Council (350)	**31,558**
Christian Congregation, Inc. (1,437)	**114,685**
Christian and Missionary Alliance (1,850)	**311,612**
Christian Union, Churches of Christ in (240)	**10,400**
Church of Christ Scientist (2,200)	*
Church of the United Brethren in Christ (234)	**24,137**
Churches of Christ (14,000)	**2,250,000**
Churches of God:	
Chs. of God, General Conference (350)	31,558
Ch. of God (Anderson, IN) (2,327)	229,240
Ch. of God (Seventh Day), Denver, CO (170)	6,500
Ch. of God by Faith (145)	8,235
Ch. of God, Mountain Assembly (118)	6,140
Church of the Nazarene (5,135)	**608,008**
Community Churches, Intl. Council of (517)	**250,000**
Congregational Christian Chs., Nat'l Assoc. of (429)	**68,865**
Conservative Congregational Christian Conference (219)	**38,788**
Eastern Orthodox churches:	
American Carpatho-Russian Orthodox Greek Catholic Ch. (78)	12,541
Antiochian Orthodox Christian Diocese of North America (16)	50,000
Apostolic Catholic Assyrian Ch. of the East, N.A. Diocese (22)	120,000
Armenian Apostolic Ch. (28)	180,000
Diocese of America, Armenian Church (72)	414,000
Coptic Orthodox Ch. (85)	180,000
Greek Orthodox Archdiocese of North and South America (532)	1,950,000
Orthodox Ch. in America (600)	2,000,000
Romanian Orthodox Episcopate of America (37)	65,000
Russian Orthodox Ch. in U.S.A, Patriarchal Parishes (38)	9,780
Russian Orthodox Church Outside of Russia (153)	*
Syrian Orthodox Ch. of Antioch (17)	32,500
Episcopal Church (7,415)	**2,536,550**
Evangelical Church (134)	**12,352**
Evangelical Congregational Church (148)	**23,091**
Evangelical Covenant Church of America (615)	**93,136**
Evangelical Free Church of America (1,224)	**242,619**
Friends:	
Evangelical Friends Intl.-North American Region (92)	8,666
Friends General Conference (600)	33,000
Friends United Meeting (580)	43,800
Religious Society of Friends (Conservative) (1,200)	104,000
Full Gospel Fellowship of Churches and Ministers Intl. (650)	**195,000**
General Church of the New Jerusalem (34)	**8,568**
Grace Gospel Fellowship (128)	**60,000**
Hindu	**1,285,000**[1]
Independent Fundamental Churches of America (670)	**69,857**
Islam	**3,332,000**[1]
Jehovah's Witnesses (10,671)	**975,829**
Jewish organizations:	
Union of American Hebrew Congregations (Reform) (880)	1,500,000[1]
Union of Orthodox Jewish Congregations of America (800)	500,000[1]
United Synagogues of Conservative Judaism, The (760)	1,500,000[1]
Latter-day Saints:	
Ch. of Jesus Christ of Latter-day Saints (Mormon) (11,000)	4,800,000
Reorganized Ch. of Jesus Christ of Latter-day Saints (1,160)	177,779
Liberal Catholic Ch.—Province of the U.S.A. (16)	**6,500**
Lutheran churches:	
Apostolic Lutheran Ch. of America (60)	7,700
Ch. of the Lutheran Brethren of America (117)	13,442
Ch. of the Lutheran Confession (72)	8,958
Evangelical Lutheran Ch. in America (10,936)	5,180,910
Evangelical Lutheran Synod (135)	22,046
Free Lutheran Congregations, Assn. of (230)	30,769
Latvian Evangelical Lutheran Church in America (57)	12,097
Lutheran Ch.—Missouri Synod (6,154)	2,594,555
Lutheran Chs., American Assn. of (90)	19,629
Wisconsin Evangelical Lutheran Synod (1,252)	412,478
Mennonite churches:	
Beachy Amish Mennonite Chs. (138)	8,399
Church of God in Christ (Mennonite) (97)	11,286
Hutterian Brethren (398)	41,600
Mennonite Brethren Chs., Gen. Conf. (368)	82,130
Mennonite Church (1,004)	90,959
Mennonite Ch., General Conference of (265)	35,353
Old Order Amish Ch. (898)	80,820
Methodist churches:	
African Methodist Episcopal Ch. (8,000)	3,500,000
African Methodist Episcopal Zion Ch. (3,098)	1,252,369
Christian Methodist Episcopal Ch. (2,340)	718,922
Evangelical Methodist Ch. (132)	8,500
Free Methodist Ch. of North America (1,050)	74,855
Primitive Methodist Ch. in the U.S.A. (75)	7,200
Southern Methodist Ch. (125)	7,885
United Methodist Ch. (36,361)	8,495,378
The Wesleyan Church (1,580)	118,021
Metropolitan Community Churches, Universal Fellowship of (285)	**46,000**
Missionary Church (325)	**31,548**
Moravian churches:	
Moravian Ch. in America, Northern Prov. (94)	27,318
Moravian Ch. in America, Southern Prov. (56)	21,513
Natl. Organization of the New Apostolic Ch. of North America (554)	**41,863**
Pentecostal churches:	
Apostolic Faith Mission Ch. of God (26)	11,350
Apostolic Overcoming Holy Church of God (146)	12,871
Assemblies of God (11,884)	2,467,588
Bible Church of Christ (6)	6,850
Bible Fellowship Church (58)	7,132

Religious Group	Members
Church of God (Cleveland, TN) (6,060)	753,230
Church of God in Christ (15,300)	5,499,875
Church of God of Prophecy (1,910)	69,974
Elim Fellowship (170)	21,038
Intl. Ch. of the Foursquare Gospel (1,773)	229,643
Intl. Pentecostal Church of Christ (73)	5,411
Intl. Pentecostal Holiness Church (1,658)	164,132
Open Bible Standard Chs. (359)	45,988
Pentecostal Assemblies of the World (1,760)	1,000,000
Pentecostal Church of God (1,230)	111,900
Pentecostal Free Will Baptist Ch. (157)	16,000
United Pentecostal Ch. Intl. (3,600)	700,000
Polish National Catholic Church (143)	**50,000**
Presbyterian churches:	
Associate Reformed Presbyterian Ch. (General Synod) (215)	39,840
Cumberland Presbyterian Ch. (774)	88,066
Cumberland Presbyterian Ch. in America (152)	15,142
Evangelical Presbyterian Ch. (183)	57,502
Korean Presbyterian Church in America (203)	26,988
Orthodox Presbyterian Ch. (192)	21,820
Presbyterian Ch. in America (1,299)	267,764
Presbyterian Ch. (U.S.A.) (11,328)	3,637,375
Reformed Presbyterian Ch. of N. America (70)	5,657
Reformed churches:	
Christian Reformed Ch. in N. America (737)	201,795
Hungarian Reformed Ch. in America (27)	9,780
Protestant Reformed Churches in America (27)	6,391
Reformed Ch. in America (909)	304,113
United Church of Christ (6,110)	1,452,565
Reformed Episcopal Church (102)	**6,084**
Roman Catholic Church (22,728)	**61,207,914**
Salvation Army (1,264)	**453,150**
Unitarian Universalist Assn. of N. A. (40)	**215,000**

(1) Estimate; figures from other sources may vary.

Headquarters of Selected Religious Groups in the U.S.

Source: *1998 Yearbook of American & Canadian Churches*, © National Council of the Churches of Christ in the USA; World Almanac research

Year organized in parentheses

African Methodist Episcopal Church, (1787), 1134 11th St. NW, Washington, DC 20001; Senior Bishop, Bishop John H. Adams

African Methodist Episcopal Zion Church (1796), PO Box 32843, Charlotte, NC 28232; Pres., Marshall A. Strickland I

American Baptist Churches in the U.S.A. (1907), PO Box 851, Valley Forge, PA 19482; http://www.abc-usa.org; Pres., James B. Johnson

American Rescue Workers (1890), 643 Elmira St., Williamsport, PA 17701; http://www.arwus.com; Commander-in-Chief & Pres., Gen. Claude S. Astin Jr., Rev.

Antiochian Orthodox Christian Archdiocese of North America (1895), 358 Mountain Rd., Englewood, NJ 07631; http://www.archdiocese@antiochian.org; Primate, Metropolitan Philip Saliba

Armenian Apostolic Church of America (1887), **Eastern Prelacy**: 138 E. 39th St., New York, NY 10016; http://www.armprelacy.org; Prelate, Archbishop Mesrob Ashjian; **Western Prelacy**: 4401 Russel Ave., Los Angeles, CA 90027; Prelate, Very Rev. Moushegh Maedizossian

Assemblies of God (1914), 1445 Boonville Ave., Springfield, MO 65802; http://www.agifellowship.org; Gen. Supt., Thomas E. Trask

Bahá'í Faith, National Spiritual Assembly of the Bahá'í's of the U.S., 536 Sheridan Rd., Wilmette, IL 60091; http://www.us.bahai.org; Secy. Gen., Dr. Robert Henderson

Baptist Bible Fellowship Intl. (1950), Baptist Bible Fellowship Missions Bldg., 720 E. Kearney St., Springfield, MO 65803; Pres., Sam Davison

Baptist Convention, Progressive (1961), 601 50th St., NE, Washington, DC 20019; http://www.pribc.org; Pres., Dr. Bennett W. Smith Sr.

Baptist Convention, Southern (1845), 901 Commerce St., Ste. 750, Nashville, TN 37203; http://www.sbcnet.org; Pres., Tom Eliff

Baptist Convention, U.S.A., National 1700 Baptist World Center Dr., Nashville, TN 37207; Pres., Dr. Henry J. Lyons

Baptist Convention of America, Inc., National (1880), 777 S. R. L. Thornton Freeway, Ste. 205, Dallas, TX 75203; http://www.greatertempleofgod.com; Pres., Dr. E. Edward Jones

Baptist Convention of America, Natl. Missionary (1988), 1404 E. Firestone, Los Angeles, CA 90001; Pres., Dr. W. T. Snead Sr.

Baptist General Conference (1852), 2002 S. Arlington Heights Rd., Arlington Heights, IL 60005; http://www.ngc.bethel.edu; Pres., Dr. Robert S. Ricker

Brethren in Christ Church (1778), PO Box 290, Grantham, PA 17027; Moderator, Rev. Harvey R. Sider

Buddhist Churches of America (1899), 1710 Octavia St., San Francisco, CA 94109; Presiding Bishop, Hakubun Watanabe

Christian Church (Disciples of Christ) (1809), 130 E. Washington St., PO Box 1986, Indianapolis, IN 46206; http://www.disciples.org; Gen. Minister and Pres., Richard L. Hamm

Christian Churches and Churches of Christ, 4210 Bridgetown Rd., Box 11326, Cincinnati, OH 45211; http://www.nacc-online.org

Christian Congregation, Inc., The (1887), 804 W. Hemlock St., LaFollette, TN 37766; Gen. Supt., Rev. Ora W. Eads, D.D.

Christian Methodist Episcopal Church (1870), 4466 Elvis Presley Blvd., Memphis, TN 38116; Executive Secretary, Dr. W. Clyde Williams

Christian and Missionary Alliance (1897), PO Box 35000, Colorado Springs, CO 80935; http://www.cmalliance.org; Pres., Rev. Peter Nanfelt, D.D.

Christian Reformed Church in North America (1857), 2850 Kalamazoo Ave. SE, Grand Rapids, MI 49560; http://www.crcna.org; Gen. Secy., Dr. David H. Engelhard

Church of the Brethren (1708), 1451 Dundee Ave., Elgin, IL 60120; Moderator, David M. Wine

Church of Christ (1830), PO Box 472, Independence, MO 64051; Council of Apostles Sec., Apostle Smith N. Brickhouse

Church of God (Anderson, IN) (1881), Box 2420, Anderson, IN 46018; http://www.chog.org; Gen. Secy., Edward L. Foggs

Church of God (Cleveland, TN) (1886), PO Box 2430, Cleveland, TN 37320; Gen. Overseer, Paul L. Walker

Church of God in Christ (1907), Mason Temple, 939 Mason St., Memphis, TN 38126; Presiding Bishop, Bishop Chandler D. Owens

Church of Jesus Christ (Bickertonites) (1862), 6th & Lincoln Sts., Monongahela, PA 15063; Pres., Dominic Thomas

Church of Jesus Christ of Latter-day Saints (Mormon), The (1830), 50 E. North Temple St., Salt Lake City, UT 84150; http://www.lds.org; Pres., Gordon B. Hinckley

Church of the Nazarene (1907), 6401 The Paseo, Kansas City, MO 64131; Gen. Secy., Jack Stone

Community Churches, Internat. Council of (1950), 21116 Washington Pkwy., Frankfort, IL 60423; Pres., J. Ronald Miller

Conservative Judaism, United Synagogues of, 155 5th Ave., New York, NY 10010; http://www.uscj.org; Pres., Rabbi Jerome Epstein

Coptic Orthodox Church, 427 West Side Ave., Jersey City, NJ 07304

Cumberland Presbyterian Church (1810), 1978 Union Ave., Memphis, TN 38104; webmaster@cumberland.org; Moderator, Elder Lewis Wynn

Episcopal Church (1789), 815 Second Ave., New York, NY 10017; http://www.ecysa.angelican.org; Presiding Bishop, Most Rev. Frank Tracy Griswold III

Evangelical Free Church of America (1884), 901 E. 78th St., Minneapolis, MN 55420; Pres., Rev. William Hamel

Evangelical Lutheran Church in America (1987), 8765 W. Higgins Rd., Chicago, IL 60631; http://www.elca.org; Bishop, Rev. Dr. H. George Anderson

Fellowship of Grace Brethren Churches (1882), PO Box 386, Winona Lake, IN 46590; http://www.grace-brethren.org; Moderator, Don Rough

First Church of Christ, Scientist, The (1879), 175 Huntington Ave., Boston, MA 02115; http://www.tfccs.com; Pres., Thomas J. Black

Free Methodist Church of North America (1860), World Ministries Center, 770 N. High School Rd., Indianapolis, IN 46214

Friends General Conference (1900), 1216 Arch St. 2B, Philadelphia, PA 19107; Gen. Secy., Bruce Birchard

Greek Orthodox Archdiocese of America (1922), 8-10 E. 79th St., New York, NY 10021; http://www.goarch.org; Primate of Greek Orthodox Church in America, Archbishop Spyridon

Hebrew Congregations, Union of American (Reform), 633 3rd Ave., New York, NY 10017; http://www.uahc.org; Pres., Rabbi Eric H. Yoffie

International Church of the Foursquare Gospel (1927), 1910 W. Sunset Blvd., Ste. 200, PO Box 26902, Los Angeles, CA 90026; http://www.foursquare.org; Pres., Dr. John R. Holland

Islamic Associations in the U.S. and Canada, Federation of, 25351 Five Mile Rd., Redford Township, MI 48239; Secy., Nihad Hamed

Jehovah's Witnesses, 25 Columbia Heights, Brooklyn, NY 11201; Pres., Milton G. Henschel

Lutheran Church—Missouri Synod (1847), 1333 S. Kirkwood Rd., St. Louis, MO 63122; Pres., Dr. A. L. Barry

Mennonite Brethren Churches, General Conference of(1860), 4812 E. Butler Ave., Fresno CA 93727; Moderator, Ed Boschman

Mennonite Church (1893), 421 S. Second St., Ste. 600, Elkhart, IN 46516; http://www.mennonites.org; Moderator, Dwight McFadden, Jr.

Mennonite Church, The General Conference (1860), 722 Main, P.O. Box 347, Newton, KS 67114; www2.southwind.net/~gcmc; Moderator, Darrell Fast

Moravian Church in America (1735), **Northern Prov.:** 1021 Center St., PO Box 1245, Bethlehem, PA 18016; http://www.moravian.org; Pres., Rev. Dr. Gordon L. Sommers; **Southern Prov.:** 459 S. Church St., Winston-Salem, NC 27101; Pres., Rev. Dr. Robert E. Sawyer; **Alaska Prov.**: PO Box 545, Bethel, AK 99559; Pres., Rev. Frank Chingliak

Orthodox Church in America (1794), PO Box 675, Syosset, NY 11791; http://www.oca.org; Primate, Most Blessed Theodosius

Orthodox Jewish Congregations in America, Union of 333 7th Ave., New York, NY 10001; http://www.ou.org; Pres., Mandell I. Ganchrow, M.D.

Pentecostal Assemblies of the World, 3939 Meadows Dr., Indianapolis, IN 46205; Presiding Bishop, Paul A. Bowers

Presbyterian Church in America (1973), 1852 Century Pl., Atlanta, GA 30345; http://www.pcanet.org; Moderator, Hon. Samuel J. Duncan

Presbyterian Church (USA), (1983), 100 Witherspoon St., Louisville, KY 40202; http://www.pcusa.org; Moderator, Patricia G. Brown

Reformed Church in America (1628), 475 Riverside Dr., New York, NY 10115; http://www.rca.org; Pres., Charles Van Engen

Reorganized Church of Jesus Christ of Latter-day Saints (1830), PO Box 1059, Independence, MO 64051; Pres. W. Grant McMurray

Roman Catholic Church (1634), National Conference of Catholic Bishops, 3211 Fourth St., Washington, DC 20017; Pres., Most Rev. Anthony M. Pilla

Romanian Orthodox Episcopate of America (1929), PO Box 309, Grass Lake, MI 49240; http://www.roea.org; Ruling Bishop, His Grace Bishop Nathaniel Popp

Salvation Army (1865), 615 Slaters Lane, Alexandria, VA 22313; National Comdr., Commissioner Robert A. Watson

Seventh-Day Adventist Ch. (1863), 12501 Old Columbia Pike, Silver Spring, MD 20904; Pres., Robert S. Folkenberg

Southern Baptist convention (1845), 901 Commerce St., Suite 750, Nashville, TN 37203; http://www.sbcnet.org; Pres., Tom Eliff

Swedenborgian Church (1792), 48 Sargent St., Newton, MA 02158; http://www.swedenborg.org; Pres., Rev. Edwin G. Capon

Unitarian Universalist Association of North America (1793), 25 Beacon St., Boston, MA 02108; http://www.uua.org; Pres., John Buehrens

United Church of Christ (1957), 700 Prospect Ave., Cleveland, OH 44115; http://www.apk.net/ucc; Pres., Rev. Paul H. Sherry

United Methodist Church (1968), PO Box 320, Nashville, TN 37202; Pres. Council of Bishops, Bishop George W. Bashore

United Pentecostal Church Intl. (1925), 8855 Dunn Rd., Hazelwood, MO 63042; http://www.upcimain@aol.com; Gen. Superintendent, The Rev. Nathaniel A. Urshan

Volunteers of America (1896), 110 S. Union St., Alexandria, VA 22314; Chairperson, Jean Galloway

Wesleyan Church (1968), PO Box 50434, Indianapolis, IN 46250; http://www.wesleyan.org; Gen. Supts., Dr. Earle L. Wilson, Dr. Lee M. Haines, Dr. Thomas E. Armiger

Membership of Religious Groups in Canada

Source: *1998 Yearbook of American and Canadian Churches*; World Almanac research

Figures are generally based on reports of all-inclusive number of "members" by officials of each group. Some groups keep careful records; others only estimate. Not all groups report annually. The number of houses of worship appears in parentheses. * Indicates the group declines to make membership figures public. Groups reporting fewer than 5,000 members are not included. Where membership numbers are not available, only groups with 50 or more houses of worship are listed.

Religious Group	Members
Anglican Church of Canada (1,740)	780,897
Antiochian Orthodox Christian Archdiocese of North America (215)	350,000
Apostolic Church of Pentecost of Canada Inc. (160)	13,500
Armenian Holy Apostolic Church (Canadian Diocese) (10)	75,000
Associated Gospel Churches (126)	9,284
Bahá'í Faith[1] (1,480)	28,500
Baptist Conference, North American (122)	17,613
Baptist Convention of Ontario and Quebec (388)	57,428
Baptist Ministries, Canadian (1,133)	129,055
Baptist Union of Western Canada (161)	20,006
Christian and Missionary Alliance in Canada (376)	87,197
Christian Brethren (also known as Plymouth Brethren) (600)	*
Christian Reformed Church in North America (244)	79,235
Church of God (Cleveland, TN) (115)	8,908
Church of Jesus Christ of Latter-day Saints in Canada (391)	130,000
Church of the Nazarene Canada (182)	11,931
Churches of Christ in Canada (145)	6,950
Estonian Evangelical Lutheran Church (12)	6,159
Evangelical Baptist Churches in Canada, Fellowship of (506)	*
Evangelical Free Church of Canada (133)	22,528
Evangelical Lutheran Church in Canada (650)	198,751
Evangelical Mennonite Conference of Canada (53)	6,508
Evangelical Missionary Church of Canada (145)	12,217
Free Methodist Church in Canada (129)	5,360
Greek Orthodox Diocese of Toronto (Canada) (76)	350,000
Hindu[1]	90,000
Islam[1]	120,000
Jehovah's Witnesses (1,366)	112,960
Jewish congregations[1] (250+)	250,000
Lutheran Church–Canada (329)	79,844
Mennonite Brethren Churches, Canadian Conference of (207)	30,281
Mennonite Church (Canada) (117)	8,172
Mennonites in Canada, Conference of (223)	35,995
Old Order Amish Church (930)	*
Orthodox Church in America (Canada Section) (606)	1,000,000
Pentecostal Assemblies of Canada (1,100)	218,782
Pentecostal Assemblies of Newfoundland (157)	30,992
Presbyterian Church in Canada (1,010)	211,075
Reformed Church in Canada (41)	6,490
Reformed Churches, Canadian and American (46)	14,583
Reorganized Church of Jesus Christ of Latter-day Saints (75)	11,264
Roman Catholic Church in Canada (5,706)	12,498,605
Salvation Army in Canada (370)	95,763
Seventh-Day Adventist Church in Canada (335)	46,113
Southern Baptists, Canadian Convention of (128)	7,957
United Baptist Convention of the Atlantic Provinces (554)	61,220
United Church of Canada (3,872)	1,835,215
United Pentecostal Church in Canada (196)	*

(1) Estimates; figures from other sources may vary.

Headquarters of Selected Religious Groups in Canada

Source: *1998 Yearbook of American & Canadian Churches,* © National Council of the Churches of Christ in the USA; World Almanac research

(Year organized in parentheses)

Anglican Church of Canada (1700), Church House, 600 Jarvis St., Toronto, ON M4Y 2J6; Primate, Most Rev. Michael G. Peers

Bahá'í National Centre of Canada, 7200 Leslie St., Thornhill, ON L3T 6L8; Gen'l.-Secy., Reginald Newkirk

Baptist Ministries, Can., 7185 Millcreek Dr., Mississauga, ON L5N 5R4; http://www.cbmin.org; Pres., Dr. Carmine Moir

Christian and Missionary Alliance in Canada (1887), 300 Steeles Ave. E., Thornhill, ON L3T 1A7; http://www.cmacan.org; Pres., Dr. Arnold Cook

Church of Jesus Christ of Latter-day Saints (Mormon), The (1830), 50 E. North Temple St., Salt Lake City, UT 84150

Church of the Nazarene (1902), 20 Regan Rd. Unit 9, Brampton, ON L7A 1C3; http://web.1-888.com.nazarene/national; Natl. Dir., Dr. William E. Stewart

Evangelical Baptist Churches in Canada, Fellowship of (1953), 679 Southgate Dr., Guelph, ON N1G 4S2; Pres., Rev. Terry D. Cuthbert

Evang. Lutheran Church in Canada (1985), 1512 St. James St., Winnipeg, MB R3H OL2; Bishop, Rev. Telmor G. Sartison

Evang. Missionary Church in Canada (1993), #550 1212 31st Ave. NE, Calgary, AB T2E 7S8; Pres., Rev. David Crouse

Greek Orthodox Metropolis of Toronto, 86 Overlea Blvd., Toronto, ON M4H 1C6; http://www.gocanada.org; His Eminence Metropolitan Archbishop Sotirios

Jehovah's Witnesses (1879), Canadian office: Box 4100, Halton Hills, ON L7G 4Y4; Pres., Milton Henschel

Jewish Congress, Canadian (1919), 1590 Ave. Docteur Penfield, Montreal, Que. H3G 1C5; http://www.cjc.ca; Nat. Exec. Dir., Jack Silverstone (Nonrel. umbrella org. of Jewish groups)

Lutheran Church—Canada (1959), 3074 Portage Ave., Winnipeg, MB R3K OY2; Pres., Ralph Mayan

Mennonite Church (1898), 421 S. Second St., Ste. 600, Elkhart, IN 46516; Mod., Dwight Mcfadden Jr.

Muslim Communities in Canada, Council of, 1250 Ramsey View Ct., Ste. 504, Sudbury, ON P3E 2E7; Dir., Mir Iqbal Ali

North American Shi'a Muslim Communities Organization (NASIMCO), Super Center Postal Outlet, Box 76559, Markham, ON L3R ON5; Pres., Ahmad Bhalloo

Pentecostal Assemblies of Canada (1919), 6745 Century Ave., Mississauga, ON L5N 6P7; http://www.paoc.org; Gen. Supt., Rev. William D. Morrow

Presbyterian Church (1925), 50 Wynford Dr., North York, ON M3C 1J7; http://www.presbycan.ca; Mod., William Klempa

Roman Catholic Church, Canadian Conference of Catholic Bishops, 90 Parent Ave., Ottawa, ON K1N 7B1; Pres., Most Rev. Francis J. Spence

Salvation Army (1865), 2 Overlea Blvd., Toronto, ON M4H 1P4; http://www.sallynet.org; Territorial Cmdr., Commissioner Donald O. Kerr

Seventh-Day Adventist Church, 1148 King St., E. Oshawa, ON L1H 1H8; Pres., Orville Parchment

Ukranian Orthodox Church (1918), Consistory, Office of the, 9 St. John's Ave., Winnipeg, MB R2W 1G8; http://home.istar.ca/-visnyk; Primate, Most Rev. Metropolitan Wasyly Fedzk

United Brethren Church (1767) 302 Lake St., Huntington, IN 46750; Pres., Rev. Brian Magnus

United Church of Canada (1925), The United Church House, 3250 Bloor St. W., Etobicoke, ON M8X 2Y4; http://www.uccan.org; Mod., William F. Phipps

Wesleyan Church (1889), The Wesleyan Church Intl. Center, PO Box 50434, Indianapolis, IN 46250; Dist. Supt., Rev. Donald E. Hodgins

Adherents of All Religions by Six Continental Areas, Mid-1997

Source: *1998 Encyclopædia Britannica Book of the Year*

	Africa	Asia	Europe	Latin America	Northern America	Oceania	World
Atheists	423,000	117,789,000	24,038,000	2,612,000	1,385,000	368,000	146,615,000
Baha'is	2,263,000	3,606,000	104,000	880,000	740,000	73,000	7,666,000
Buddhists	136,000	348,559,000	1,478,000	645,000	2,132,000	191,000	353,141,000
Chinese folk religionists	28,000	362,013,000	216,000	184,000	832,000	61,000	363,334,000
Christians	350,892,000	289,784,000	552,183,000	455,882,000	257,129,000	24,117,000	1,929,987,000
Roman Catholics	117,990,000	111,215,000	286,902,000	442,657,000	73,880,000	7,710,000	1,040,354,000
Protestants	87,190,000	44,654,000	85,924,000	41,829,000	95,063,000	6,253,000	360,913,000
Orthodox	32,880,000	15,403,000	166,908,000	620,000	6,698,000	695,000	223,204,000
Anglicans	20,551,000	641,000	24,338,000	874,000	3,145,000	5,236,000	54,785,000
Other Christians	68,357,000	125,213,000	5,645,000	40,231,000	47,585,000	826,000	287,857,000
Confucianists	0	6,078,000	10,000	0	0	24,000	6,112,000
Ethnic religionists	90,365,000	138,469,000	1,220,000	1,060,000	331,000	249,000	231,694,000
Hindus	2,378,000	740,633,000	1,520,000	776,000	1,129,000	361,000	746,797,000
Jains	65,000	3,946,000	0	0	5,000	0	4,016,000
Jews	290,000	4,497,000	2,932,000	1,173,000	5,904,000	94,000	14,890,000
Mandeans	0	40,000	0	0	0	0	40,000
Muslims	306,606,000	803,605,000	31,347,000	1,632,000	4,066,000	238,000	1,147,494,000
New-Religionists	27,000	97,263,000	122,000	611,000	649,000	27,000	98,699,000
Nonreligious	4,798,000	597,804,000	113,165,000	15,144,000	26,127,000	3,242,000	760,280,000
Shintoists	0	2,611,000	0	7,000	54,000	0	2,672,000
Sikhs	52,000	21,464,000	497,000	0	491,000	14,000	22,518,000
Spiritists	3,000	2,000	78,000	11,229,000	148,000	7,000	11,467,000
Zoroastrians	1,000	268,000	0	0	3,000	0	272,000
Other religionists	67,000	23,000	259,000	94,000	593,000	9,000	1,045,000
Non-Christians	407,502,000	3,248,670,000	176,986,000	36,047,000	44,589,000	4,958,000	3,918,752,000
Total Population	**758,394,000**	**3,538,454,000**	**729,169,000**	**491,929,000**	**301,718,000**	**29,075,000**	**5,848,739,000**

Adherents. As defined and enumerated in *World Christian Encyclopedia* (1982), projected to mid-1997, adjusted for recent data.

Continents. These follow current UN demographic practice, which divides the world into the 6 major areas shown above and 21 regions. "Asia" now includes the former USSR Central Asian republics. "Europe" extends eastward to Vladivostok, the Sea of Japan, and the Bering Strait.

Christians. Followers of Jesus Christ affiliated with churches (church members, including children: 1,782,809,000) plus persons professing in censuses or polls though not so affiliated.

Other Christians. Catholics (non-Roman), marginal Protestants, crypto-Christians, and adherents of African, Asian, black, and Latin-American indigenous churches.

Atheists. Persons professing atheism, skepticism, disbelief, or irreligion, including antireligious (opposed to all religion).

Buddhists. 56% Mahayana, 38% Theravada (Hinayana), 6% Tantrayana (Lamaism).

Chinese folk religionists. Followers of traditional Chinese religion (local deities, ancestor veneration, Confucian ethics, Taoism, universism, divination, some Buddhist elements).

Confucians. Non-Chinese followers of Confucius and Confucianism, mostly Koreans in Korea.

Hindus. 70% Vaishnavites, 25% Shaivites, 2% neo-Hindus and reform Hindus.

Jews. Adherents of Judaism.

Muslims. 83% Sunni Muslims, 16% Shia Muslims (Shi'ites), 1% other schools.

New-Religionists. Followers of Asian 20th-cent. New Religions, New Religious movements, radical new crisis religions, and non-Christian syncretistic mass religions, all founded since 1800 and most since 1945.

Nonreligious. Persons professing no religion, nonbelievers, agnostics, freethinkers, dereligionized secularists indifferent to all religion.

Other religionists. Including 70 minor world religions and a large number of spiritist religions, New Age religions, quasi-religions, pseudo religions, parareligions, religious or mystic systems, and religious and semireligious brotherhoods of numerous varieties.

Total Population. UN medium variant figures for mid-1997, as given in *World Population Prospects*: *The 1996 Revision* (1997).

Episcopal Church Liturgical Colors and Calendar

Source: Church Publishing Incorporated, New York

The liturgical colors in the Episcopal Church are as follows: **White**—from Christmas Day through the First Sunday after Epiphany; Maundy Thursday (as an alternative to crimson at the Eucharist); from the Vigil of Easter to the Day of Pentecost (Whitsunday); Trinity Sunday; Feasts of the Lord (except Holy Cross Day); the Confession of St. Peter; the Conversion of St. Paul; St. Joseph; St. Mary Magdalene; St. Mary the Virgin; St. Michael and All Angels; All Saints' Day; St. John the Evangelist; memorials of other saints who were not martyred; Independence Day and Thanksgiving Day; weddings and funerals. **Red**—the Day of Pentecost; Holy Cross Day; feasts of apostles and evangelists (except those listed above); feasts and memorials of martyrs (including Holy Innocents' Day). **Violet**—Advent and Lent. **Crimson** (dark red)—Holy Week. **Green**—the seasons after Epiphany and after Pentecost. **Black**—optional alternative for funerals. Alternative colors used in some churches: **Blue**—Advent; **Lenten White**—Ash Wednesday to Palm Sunday.

In the Episcopal Church the days of fasting are Ash Wednesday and Good Friday. Other days of special devotion (penitence) are the 40 days of Lent and all Fridays of the year, except those in Christmas and Easter seasons and any Feasts of the Lord that occur on a Friday or during Lent. Ember Days (optional) are days of prayer for the church's ministry. They fall on the Wednesday, Friday, and Saturday after the first Sunday in Lent, the Day of Pentecost, Holy Cross Day, and the Third Sunday of Advent. Rogation Days (also optional), the 3 days before Ascension Day, are days of prayer for God's blessing on the crops, on commerce and industry, and for conservation of the earth's resources.

Days, etc.	1998	1999	2000	2001	2002
Golden Number	4	5	6	7	8
Sunday Letter	D	C	B & A	G	F
Sundays after Epiphany	7	6	9	8	5
Ash Wednesday	Feb. 25	Feb. 17	Mar. 8	Feb. 28	Feb. 13
First Sunday in Lent	Mar. 1	Feb. 21	Mar. 12	Mar. 4	Feb. 17
Passion/Palm Sunday	Apr. 5	Mar. 28	Apr. 16	Apr. 8	Mar. 24
Good Friday	Apr. 10	Apr. 2	Apr. 21	Apr. 13	Mar. 29
Easter Day	Apr. 12	Apr. 4	Apr. 23	Apr. 15	Mar. 31
Ascension Day	May 21	May 13	June 1	May 24	May 9
The Day of Pentecost	May 31	May 23	June 11	June 3	May 19
Trinity Sunday	June 7	May 30	June 18	June 10	May 26
Numbered Proper of 2 Pentecost	#6	#5	#7	#6	#4
First Sunday of Advent	Nov. 29	Nov. 28	Dec. 3	Dec. 2	Dec. 1

Greek Orthodox Movable Ecclesiastical Dates, 1998-2002

This 5-year chart has the dates of feast days and fasting days, which are determined annually on the basis of the date of Holy Pascha (Easter). This ecclesiastical cycle begins with the first day of the Triodion and ends with the Sunday of All Saints, a total of 18 weeks.

	1998	1999	2000	2001	2002
Triodion begins	Feb. 8	Jan. 31	Feb. 20	Feb. 4	Feb. 24
Sat. of Souls	Feb. 21	Feb. 13	Mar. 4	Feb. 17	Mar. 9
Meat Fare	Feb. 22	Feb. 14	Mar. 5	Feb. 18	Mar. 10
2d Sat. of Souls	Feb. 28	Feb. 20	Mar 11	Feb. 24	Mar. 16
Lent Begins	Mar. 2	Feb. 22	Mar. 13	Feb. 26	Mar. 18
St. Theodore—3d Sat. of Souls	Mar. 7	Feb. 27	Mar. 18	Mar. 3	Mar. 23
Sunday of Orthodoxy	Mar. 8	Feb. 28	Mar. 19	Mar. 4	Mar. 24
Sat. of Lazarus	Apr. 11	Apr. 3	Apr. 22	Apr. 7	Apr. 27
Palm Sunday	Apr. 12	Apr. 4	Apr. 23	Apr. 8	Apr. 28
Holy (Good) Friday	Apr. 17	Apr. 9	Apr. 28	Apr. 13	May 3
Western Easter	Apr. 12	Apr. 4	Apr. 23	Apr. 15	Mar. 31
Orthodox Easter	Apr. 19	Apr. 11	Apr. 30	Apr. 15	May 5
Ascension	May 28	May 20		May 24	June 13
Sat. of Souls	June 6	May 29	June 17	June 2	June 22
Pentecost	June 7	May 30	June 18	June 3	June 23
All Saints	June 14	June 6	June 25	June 10	June 30

Important Islamic Dates, 1997-2002 (1418-22)

Source: Imad-ad-Dean, Inc., Bethesda, MD 20814

The Islamic calendar is a strict lunar calendar reckoned from the year of the Hijra (Muhammad's flight from Mecca to Medina). Each year consists of 12 lunar months of 29 or 30 days beginning and ending with each new moon's visible crescent. Common years have 354 days; leap years have 355 days. Some Muslim countries employ a conventionalized calendar with the leap day added to the last month, Dhûl Hijah, but for religious purposes the leap date is taken into account by tracking each new moon sighting. The dates given below are based on the convention that the first new moon must be seen before the following dawn on the East Coast of the Americas. Actual (local) Western Hemisphere sightings may occur a day later, but never a day earlier, than these dates reflect.

	1997-98 (1418)	1998-99 (1419)	1999-2000 (1420)	2000-01 (1421)	2001-02 (1422)
New Year's Day (Muharram 1)	May 8, 1997	Apr. 27, 1998	Apr. 17,1999	Apr. 6, 2000	Mar. 26, 2001
Ashura (Muharram 10)	May 17, 1997	May 6, 1998	Apr. 26, 1999	Apr. 15, 2000	Apr. 4, 2001
Mawlid (Rabi'l 12)	July 17, 1997	July 6, 1998	June 26, 1999	June 14, 2000	June 4, 2001
Ramadan 1	Dec. 31, 1997	Dec. 20, 1998	Dec. 9, 1999	Nov. 27, 2000	Nov. 16, 2001
Id al-Fitr (Shawwal)	Jan. 29, 1998	Jan. 19, 1999	Jan. 8, 2000	Dec. 27, 2000	Dec. 16, 2001
Id al-Adha (Dhûl-Hijjah 10)	Apr. 7, 1998	Mar. 28, 1999	Mar. 16, 2000	Mar. 5, 2001	Feb. 22, 2002

Jewish Holy Days, Festivals, and Fasts, 1998-2002

	1998 (5758-59)		1999 (5759-60)		2000 (5760-61)		2001 (5761-62)		2002 (5762-63)	
Tu B'Shvat	Feb. 11	Wed.	Feb. 1	Mon.	Jan. 22	Sat.	Feb. 8	Thu.	Jan. 28	Mon.
Ta'anis Esther (Fast of Esther)	Mar. 11	Wed.	Mar. 1	Mon.	Mar. 20	Mon.	Mar. 8	Thu.	Feb. 25	Mon.
Purim	Mar. 12	Thu.	Mar. 2	Tue.	Mar. 21	Tue.	Mar. 9	Fri.	Feb. 26	Tue.
Pesach (Passover)	Apr. 11 Apr. 18	Sat. Sat.	Apr. 1 Apr. 8	Thu. Thu.	Apr. 20 Apr. 27	Thu. Thu.	Apr. 8 Apr. 15	Sun. Sun.	Mar. 28 Apr. 4	Thu. Sat.
Lag B'Omer	May 14	Thu.	May 4	Tue.	May 23	Tue.	May 11	Fri.	Apr. 30	Tue.
Shavuot (Pentecost)	May 31 June 1	Sun. Mon.	May 21 May 22	Fri. Sat.	June 9 June 10	Fri. Sat.	May 28 May 29	Mon. Tue.	May 17 May 18	Fri. Sat.
Fast of the 17th Day of Tammuz	July 12	Sun.*	July 1	Thu.	July 20	Thu.	July 8	Sun.	June 27	Thu.
Fast of the 9th Day of Av	Aug. 2	Sun.*	July 22	Thu.	Aug. 10	Thu.	July 29	Sun.	July 18	Thu.
Rosh Hashanah (Jewish New Year)	Sept. 21 Sept. 22	Mon. Tue.	Sept. 11 Sept. 12	Sat. Sun.	Sept. 30 Oct. 1	Sat. Sun.	Sept. 18 Sept. 19	Tue. Wed.	Sept. 7 Sept. 8	Sat. Sun.
Fast of Gedalya	Sept. 23	Wed.	Sept. 13	Mon.	Oct. 2	Mon.	Sept. 20	Thu.	Sept. 9	Mon.
Yom Kippur (Day of Atonement)	Sept. 30	Wed.	Sept. 20	Mon.	Oct. 9	Mon.	Sept. 27	Thu.	Sept. 16	Mon.
Sukkot	Oct. 5 Oct. 11	Mon. Sun.	Sept. 25 Oct. 1	Sat. Fri.	Oct. 14 Oct. 20	Sat. Fri.	Oct. 2 Oct. 8	Tue. Mon.	Sept. 21 Sept. 27	Sat. Fri.
Shmini Atzeret	Oct. 12 Oct. 13	Mon. Tue.	Oct. 2 Oct. 3	Sat. Sun.	Oct. 21 Oct. 22	Sat. Sun.	Oct. 9 Oct. 10	Tue. Wed.	Sept. 28 Sept. 29	Sat. Sun.
Hanukkah	Dec. 14 Dec. 21	Mon. Mon.	Dec. 4 Dec. 11	Sat. Sat.	Dec. 22 Dec. 29	Fri. Fri.	Dec. 10 Dec. 17	Mon. Mon.	Nov. 30 Dec. 7	Sat. Sat.
Fast of the 10th of Tevet	Dec. 29	Tue.	Dec. 19	Sun.	Jan. 5, 2001	Fri.	Dec. 25	Tue.	Jan. 15, 2003	Sun.

The months of the Jewish year are: 1) Tishri; 2) Cheshvan (also Marcheshvan); 3) Kislev; 4) Tevet (also Tebeth); 5) Shebat (also Shebhat); 6) Adar; 6a) Adar Sheni (II) added in leap years; 7) Nisan; 8) Iyar; 9) Sivan; 10) Tammuz; 11) Av (also Abh); 12) Elul. All Jewish holy days, etc., begin at sunset on the previous day. *Date changed to avoid Sabbath.

Ash Wednesday and Easter Sunday (Western churches), 1901-2100

Year	Ash Wed.	Easter Sunday	Year	Ash Wed.	Easter Sunday	Year	Ash Wed.	Easter Sunday	Year	Ash Wed.	Easter Sunday
1901	Feb. 20	Apr. 7	1951	Feb. 7	Mar. 25	2001	Feb. 28	Apr. 15	2051	Feb. 15	Apr. 2
1902	Feb. 12	Mar. 30	1952	Feb. 27	Apr. 13	2002	Feb. 13	Mar. 31	2052	Mar. 6	Apr. 21
1903	Feb. 25	Apr. 12	1953	Feb. 18	Apr. 5	2003	Mar. 5	Apr. 20	2053	Feb. 19	Apr. 6
1904	Feb. 17	Apr. 3	1954	Mar. 3	Apr. 18	2004	Feb. 25	Apr. 11	2054	Feb. 11	Mar. 29
1905	Mar. 8	Apr. 23	1955	Feb. 23	Apr. 10	2005	Feb. 9	Mar. 27	2055	Mar. 3	Apr. 18
1906	Feb. 28	Apr. 15	1956	Feb. 15	Apr. 1	2006	Mar. 1	Apr. 16	2056	Feb. 16	Apr. 2
1907	Feb. 13	Mar. 31	1957	Mar. 6	Apr. 21	2007	Feb. 21	Apr. 8	2057	Mar. 7	Apr. 22
1908	Mar. 4	Apr. 19	1958	Feb. 19	Apr. 6	2008	Feb. 6	Mar. 23	2058	Feb. 27	Apr. 14
1909	Feb. 24	Apr. 11	1959	Feb. 11	Mar. 29	2009	Feb. 25	Apr. 12	2059	Feb. 12	Mar. 30
1910	Feb. 9	Mar. 27	1960	Mar. 2	Apr. 17	2010	Feb. 17	Apr. 4	2060	Mar. 3	Apr. 18
1911	Mar. 1	Apr. 16	1961	Feb. 15	Apr. 2	2011	Mar. 9	Apr. 24	2061	Feb. 23	Apr. 10
1912	Feb. 21	Apr. 7	1962	Mar. 7	Apr. 22	2012	Feb. 22	Apr. 8	2062	Feb. 8	Mar. 26
1913	Feb. 5	Mar. 23	1963	Feb. 27	Apr. 14	2013	Feb. 13	Mar. 31	2063	Feb. 28	Apr. 15
1914	Feb. 25	Apr. 12	1964	Feb. 12	Mar. 29	2014	Mar. 5	Apr. 20	2064	Feb. 20	Apr. 6
1915	Feb. 17	Apr. 4	1965	Mar. 3	Apr. 18	2015	Feb. 18	Apr. 5	2065	Feb. 11	Mar. 29
1916	Mar. 8	Apr. 23	1966	Feb. 23	Apr. 10	2016	Feb. 10	Mar. 27	2066	Feb. 24	Apr. 11
1917	Feb. 21	Apr. 8	1967	Feb. 8	Mar. 26	2017	Mar. 1	Apr. 16	2067	Feb. 16	Apr. 3
1918	Feb. 13	Mar. 31	1968	Feb. 28	Apr. 14	2018	Feb. 14	Apr. 1	2068	Mar. 7	Apr. 22
1919	Mar. 5	Apr. 20	1969	Feb. 19	Apr. 6	2019	Mar. 6	Apr. 21	2069	Feb. 27	Apr. 14
1920	Feb. 18	Apr. 4	1970	Feb. 11	Mar. 29	2020	Feb. 26	Apr. 12	2070	Feb. 12	Mar. 30
1921	Feb. 9	Mar. 27	1971	Feb. 24	Apr. 11	2021	Feb. 17	Apr. 4	2071	Mar. 4	Apr. 19
1922	Mar. 1	Apr. 16	1972	Feb. 16	Apr. 2	2022	Mar. 2	Apr. 17	2072	Feb. 24	Apr. 10
1923	Feb. 14	Apr. 1	1973	Mar. 7	Apr. 22	2023	Feb. 22	Apr. 9	2073	Feb. 8	Mar. 26
1924	Mar. 5	Apr. 20	1974	Feb. 27	Apr. 14	2024	Feb. 14	Mar. 31	2074	Feb. 28	Apr. 15
1925	Feb. 25	Apr. 12	1975	Feb. 12	Mar. 30	2025	Mar. 5	Apr. 20	2075	Feb. 20	Apr. 7
1926	Feb. 17	Apr. 4	1976	Mar. 3	Apr. 18	2026	Feb. 18	Apr. 5	2076	Mar. 4	Apr. 19
1927	Mar. 2	Apr. 17	1977	Feb. 23	Apr. 10	2027	Feb. 10	Mar. 28	2077	Feb. 24	Apr. 11
1928	Feb. 22	Apr. 8	1978	Feb. 8	Mar. 26	2028	Mar. 1	Apr. 16	2078	Feb. 16	Apr. 3
1929	Feb. 13	Mar. 31	1979	Feb. 28	Apr. 15	2029	Feb. 14	Apr. 1	2079	Mar. 8	Apr. 23
1930	Mar. 5	Apr. 20	1980	Feb. 20	Apr. 6	2030	Mar. 6	Apr. 21	2080	Feb. 21	Apr. 7
1931	Feb. 18	Apr. 5	1981	Mar. 4	Apr. 19	2031	Feb. 26	Apr. 13	2081	Feb. 12	Mar. 30
1932	Feb. 10	Mar. 27	1982	Feb. 24	Apr. 11	2032	Feb. 11	Mar. 28	2082	Mar. 4	Apr. 19
1933	Mar. 1	Apr. 16	1983	Feb. 16	Apr. 3	2033	Mar. 2	Apr. 17	2083	Feb. 17	Apr. 4
1934	Feb. 14	Apr. 1	1984	Mar. 7	Apr. 22	2034	Feb. 22	Apr. 9	2084	Feb. 9	Mar. 26
1935	Mar. 6	Apr. 21	1985	Feb. 20	Apr. 7	2035	Feb. 7	Mar. 25	2085	Feb. 28	Apr. 15
1936	Feb. 26	Apr. 12	1986	Feb. 12	Mar. 30	2036	Feb. 27	Apr. 13	2086	Feb. 13	Mar. 31
1937	Feb. 10	Mar. 28	1987	Mar. 4	Apr. 19	2037	Feb. 18	Apr. 5	2087	Mar. 5	Apr. 20
1938	Mar. 2	Apr. 17	1988	Feb. 17	Apr. 3	2038	Mar. 10	Apr. 25	2088	Feb. 25	Apr. 11
1939	Feb. 22	Apr. 9	1989	Feb. 8	Mar. 26	2039	Feb. 23	Apr. 10	2089	Feb. 16	Apr. 3
1940	Feb. 7	Mar. 24	1990	Feb. 28	Apr. 15	2040	Feb. 15	Apr. 1	2090	Mar. 1	Apr. 16
1941	Feb. 26	Apr. 13	1991	Feb. 13	Mar. 31	2041	Mar. 6	Apr. 21	2091	Feb. 21	Apr. 8
1942	Feb. 18	Apr. 5	1992	Mar. 4	Apr. 19	2042	Feb. 19	Apr. 6	2092	Feb. 13	Mar. 30
1943	Mar. 10	Apr. 25	1993	Feb. 24	Apr. 11	2043	Feb. 11	Mar. 29	2093	Feb. 25	Apr. 12
1944	Feb. 23	Apr. 9	1994	Feb. 16	Apr. 3	2044	Mar. 2	Apr. 17	2094	Feb. 17	Apr. 4
1945	Feb. 14	Apr. 1	1995	Mar. 1	Apr. 16	2045	Feb. 22	Apr. 9	2095	Mar. 9	Apr. 24
1946	Mar. 6	Apr. 21	1996	Feb. 21	Apr. 7	2046	Feb. 7	Mar. 25	2096	Feb. 29	Apr. 15
1947	Feb. 19	Apr. 6	1997	Feb. 12	Mar. 30	2047	Feb. 27	Apr. 14	2097	Feb. 13	Mar. 31
1948	Feb. 11	Mar. 28	1998	Feb. 25	Apr. 12	2048	Feb. 19	Apr. 5	2098	Mar. 5	Apr. 20
1949	Mar. 2	Apr. 17	1999	Feb. 17	Apr. 4	2049	Mar. 3	Apr. 18	2099	Feb. 25	Apr. 12
1950	Feb. 22	Apr. 9	2000	Mar. 8	Apr. 23	2050	Feb. 23	Apr. 10	2100	Feb. 10	Mar. 28

The Ten Commandments

According to Judeo-Christian tradition, as related in the Bible, the Ten Commandments were revealed by God to Moses and form the basic moral component of God's covenant with Israel. The Ten Commandments appear in 2 places in the Old Testament—Exodus 20:1-17 and Deuteronomy 5:6-21; the phrasing is similar but not identical.

Following is abridged text of the Ten Commandments in Exodus 20:1-17:

I. I am the Lord your God, who brought you out of the land of Egypt, out of the house of bondage. You shall have no other gods before me.
II. You shall not make for yourself a graven image. You shall not bow down to them or serve them.
III. You shall not take the name of the Lord your God in vain.
IV. Remember the sabbath day, to keep it holy.
V. Honor your father and your mother.
VI. You shall not kill.
VII. You shall not commit adultery.
VIII. You shall not steal.
IX. You shall not bear false witness against your neighbor.
X. You shall not covet.

Most Protestant, Anglican, and Orthodox Christians follow Jewish tradition, which considers the introduction ("I am the Lord...") the first commandment and makes the prohibition against idolatry the second. Roman Catholic and Lutheran traditions follow a division used by St. Augustine, which combines I and II and splits the last commandment into 2 that separately prohibit coveting of a neighbor's wife and a neighbor's goods. This arrangement alters the numbering of the other commandments by one.

Books of the Bible

Old Testament—Standard Protestant List

Genesis	II Chronicles	Daniel
Exodus	Ezra	Hosea
Leviticus	Nehemiah	Joel
Numbers	Esther	Amos
Deuteronomy	Job	Obadiah
Joshua	Psalms	Jonah
Judges	Proverbs	Micah
Ruth	Ecclesiastes	Nahum
I Samuel	Song of Solomon	Habakkuk
II Samuel	Isaiah	Zephaniah
I Kings	Jeremiah	Haggai
II Kings	Lamentations	Zechariah
I Chronicles	Ezekiel	Malachi

New Testament List

Matthew	Ephesians	Hebrews
Mark	Phillippians	James
Luke	Colossians	I Peter
John	I Thessalonians	II Peter
Acts	II Thessalonians	I John
Romans	I Timothy	II John
I Corinthians	II Timothy	III John
II Corinthians	Titus	Jude
Galatians	Philemon	Revelation

The standard Protestant Old Testament consists of the same 39 books as in the Bible of Judaism, but the latter is organized differently. The Old Testament used by Roman Catholics has 7 additional "deuterocanonical" books, plus some additional parts of books. The 7 are: **Tobit, Judith, Wisdom, Sirach (Ecclesiasticus), Baruch, I Maccabees,** and **II Maccabees**. Both Catholic and Protestant versions of the New Testament have 27 books, with the same names.

Roman Catholic Hierarchy

Source: U.S. Catholic Conference; as of mid-1998

Supreme Pontiff

At the head of the Roman Catholic Church is the supreme pontiff, Pope John Paul II, Karol Wojtyla, born at Wadowice (Kraków), Poland, May 18, 1920; ordained priest Nov. 1, 1946; appointed bishop July 4, 1958; promoted to archbishop of Kraków Jan. 13, 1964; proclaimed cardinal June 26, 1967; elected pope as successor of Pope John Paul I Oct. 16, 1978; installed as pope Oct. 22, 1978.

College of Cardinals

Members of the Sacred College of Cardinals are chosen by the pope to be his chief assistants and advisers in the administration of the church. Among their duties is the election of the pope when the Holy See becomes vacant.

In its present form, the College of Cardinals dates from the 12th century. The first cardinals, from about the 6th century, were deacons and priests of the leading churches of Rome and were bishops of neighboring dioceses. The title of cardinal was limited to members of the college in 1567. The number of cardinals was set at 70 in 1586 by Pope Sixtus V. From 1959 Pope John XXIII began to increase the number; however, the number of cardinals eligible to participate in papal elections was limited to 120. There were lay cardinals until 1918, when the Code of Canon Law specified that all cardinals must be priests. Pope John XXIII in 1962 established that all cardinals must be bishops. The first age limits were set in 1971 by Pope Paul VI, who decreed that at age 80 cardinals must retire from curial departments and offices and from participation in papal elections.

North American Cardinals

Name	Office	Born	Named Cardinal
Aloysius M. Ambrozic	Archbishop of Toronto	1930	1998
Luis Apone Martinez	Archbishop of San Juan	1922	1973
William W. Baum	Major Penitentiary of Apostolic Penitentiary, the Vatican	1926	1976
Anthony J. Bevilacqua	Archbishop of Philadelphia	1923	1991
G. Emmett Carter[1]	Archbishop emeritus of Toronto	1912	1979
Ernesto Corripio Ahumada	Archbishop emeritus of Mexico	1919	1979
Edouard Gagnon	Pres. of Pontifical Commission of Intl. Eucharistic Congresses	1918	1985
Francis E. George	Archbishop of Chicago	1937	1998
James A. Hickey	Archbishop of Washington, DC	1920	1988
William Henry Keeler	Archbishop of Baltimore	1931	1994
Bernard F. Law	Archbishop of Boston	1931	1985
Roger Mahony	Archbishop of Los Angeles	1936	1991
Adam Joseph Maida	Archbishop of Detroit	1930	1994
John J. O'Connor	Archbishop of New York	1920	1985
Norberto Rivera Carrera	Archbishop of Mexico City	1942	1998
Juan Sandoval Iniquez	Archbishop of Guadalajara	1933	1994
James F. Stafford	President of the Pontifical Council for the Laity	1932	1998
Adolfo Antonio Suarez Rivera	Archbishop of Monterrey	1927	1994
Edmund C. Szoka	Pres. of Prefecture of Economic Affairs of Holy See, the Vatican	1927	1988
Jean-Claude Turcotte	Archbishop of Montreal	1936	1994
Louis-Albert Vachon[1]	Archbishop emeritus of Quebec	1912	1985

(1) Ineligible to take part in papal elections.

Chronological List of Popes

Source: Annuario Pontificio. Table lists year of accession of each pope.

The Roman Catholic Church named the Apostle Peter as founder of the church in Rome and the first pope. He arrived there c 42, was martyred there c 67, and was ultimately canonized as a saint.

The pope's temporal title is: Sovereign of the State of Vatican City. **The pope's spiritual titles are:** Bishop of Rome, Vicar of Jesus Christ, Successor of St. Peter, Prince of the Apostles, Supreme Pontiff of the Universal Church, Patriarch of the West, Primate of Italy, Archbishop and Metropolitan of the Roman Province.

The names of antipopes are in *italics.* Antipopes were illegitimate claimants of or pretenders to the papal throne.

Year	Pope
	St. Peter
67	St. Linus
76	St. Anacletus or Cletus
88	St. Clement I
97	St. Evaristus
105	St. Alexander I
115	St. Sixtus I
125	St. Telesphorus
136	St. Hyginus
140	St. Pius I
155	St. Anicetus
166	St. Soter
175	St. Eleutherius
189	St. Victor I
199	St. Zephyrinus
217	St. Callistus I
217	*St. Hippolytus*
222	St. Urban I
230	St. Pontian
235	St. Anterus
236	St. Fabian
251	St. Cornelius
251	*Novatian*
253	St. Lucius I
254	St. Stephen I
257	St. Sixtus II
259	St. Dionysius
269	St. Felix I
275	St. Eutychian
283	St. Caius
296	St. Marcellinus
308	St. Marcellus I
309	St. Eusebius
311	St. Melchiades
314	St. Sylvester I
336	St. Marcus
337	St. Julius I
352	Liberius
355	*Felix II*
366	St. Damasus I
366	*Ursinus*
384	St. Siricius
399	St. Anastasius I
401	St. Innocent I
417	St. Zosimus
418	St. Boniface I
418	*Eulalius*
422	St. Celestine I
432	St. Sixtus III
440	St. Leo I
461	St. Hilary
468	St. Simplicius
483	St. Felix III (II)
492	St. Gelasius I
496	Anastasius II
498	St. Symmachus
498	*Lawrence (501-505)*
514	St. Hormisdas
523	St. John I, Martyr
526	St. Felix IV (III)
530	Boniface II
530	*Dioscorus*
533	John II
535	St. Agapitus I
536	St. Silverius, Martyr
537	Vigilius
556	Pelagius I
561	John III
575	Benedict I
579	Pelagius II
590	St. Gregory I
604	Sabinian
607	Boniface III
608	St. Boniface IV
615	St. Deusdedit or Adeodatus
619	Boniface V
625	Honorius I
640	Severinus
640	John IV
642	Theodore I
649	St. Martin I, Martyr
654	St. Eugene I
657	St. Vitalian
672	Adeodatus II
676	Donus
678	St. Agatho
682	St. Leo II
684	St. Benedict II
685	John V
686	Conon
687	*Theodore*
687	*Paschal*
687	St. Sergius I
701	John VI
705	John VII
708	Sisinnius
708	Constantine
715	St. Gregory II
731	St. Gregory III
741	St. Zachary
752	Stephen II (III)
757	St. Paul I
767	*Constantine*
768	*Philip*
768	Stephen III (IV)
772	Adrian I
795	St. Leo III
816	Stephen IV (V)
817	St. Paschal I
824	Eugene II
827	Valentine
827	Gregory IV
844	*John*
844	Sergius II
847	St. Leo IV
855	Benedict III
855	*Anastasius*
858	St. Nicholas I
867	Adrian II
872	John VIII
882	Marinus I
884	St. Adrian III
885	Stephen V (VI)
891	Formosus
896	Boniface VI
896	Stephen VI (VII)
897	Romanus
897	Theodore II
898	John IX
900	Benedict IV
903	Leo V
903	*Christopher*
904	Sergius III
911	Anastasius III
913	Landus
914	John X
928	Leo VI
928	Stephen VII (VIII)
931	John XI
936	Leo VII
939	Stephen VIII (IX)
942	Marinus II
946	Agapitus II
955	John XII
963	Leo VIII
964	Benedict V
965	John XIII
973	Benedict VI
974	*Boniface VII*
974	Benedict VII
983	John XIV
985	John XV
996	Gregory V
997	*John XVI*
999	Sylvester II
1003	John XVII
1004	John XVIII
1009	Sergius IV
1012	Benedict VIII
1012	*Gregory*
1024	John XIX
1032	Benedict IX
1045	Sylvester III
1045	Benedict IX
1045	Gregory VI
1046	Clement II
1047	Benedict IX
1048	Damasus II
1049	St. Leo IX
1055	Victor II
1057	Stephen IX (X)
1058	*Benedict X*
1059	Nicholas II
1061	Alexander II
1061	*Honorius II*
1073	St. Gregory VII
1080	*Clement III*
1086	Bl. Victor III
1088	Bl. Urban II
1099	Paschal II
1100	*Theodoric*
1102	*Albert*
1105	*Sylvester IV*
1118	Gelasius II
1118	*Gregory VIII*
1119	Callistus II
1124	Honorius II
1124	*Celestine II*
1130	Innocent II
1130	*Anacletus II*
1138	*Victor IV*
1143	Celestine II
1144	Lucius II
1145	Bl. Eugene III
1153	Anastasius IV
1154	Adrian IV
1159	Alexander III
1159	*Victor IV*
1164	*Paschal III*
1168	*Callistus III*
1179	*Innocent III*
1181	Lucius III
1185	Urban III
1187	Clement III
1187	Gregory VIII
1191	Celestine III
1198	Innocent III
1216	Honorius III
1227	Gregory IX
1241	Celestine IV
1243	Innocent IV
1254	Alexander IV
1261	Urban IV
1265	Clement IV
1271	Bl. Gregory X
1276	Bl. Innocent V
1276	Adrian V
1276	John XXI
1277	Nicholas III
1281	Martin IV
1285	Honorius IV
1288	Nicholas IV
1294	St. Celestine V
1294	Boniface VIII
1303	Bl. Benedict XI
1305	Clement V
1316	John XXII
1328	*Nicholas V*
1334	Benedict XII
1342	Clement VI
1352	Innocent VI
1362	Bl. Urban V
1370	Gregory XI
1378	Urban VI
1378	*Clement VII*
1389	Boniface IX
1394	*Benedict XIII*
1404	Innocent VII
1406	Gregory XII
1409	*Alexander V*
1410	*John XXII*
1417	Martin V
1431	Eugene IV
1439	*Felix V*
1447	Nicholas V
1455	Callistus III
1458	Pius II
1464	Paul II
1471	Sixtus IV
1484	Innocent VIII
1492	Alexander VI
1503	Pius III
1503	Julius II
1513	Leo X
1522	Adrian VI
1523	Clement VII
1534	Paul III
1550	Julius III
1555	Marcellus II
1555	Paul IV
1559	Pius IV
1566	St. Pius V
1572	Gregory XIII
1585	Sixtus V
1590	Urban VII
1590	Gregory XIV
1591	Innocent IX
1592	Clement VIII
1605	Leo XI
1605	Paul V
1621	Gregory XV
1623	Urban VIII
1644	Innocent X
1655	Alexander VII
1667	Clement IX
1670	Clement X
1676	Bl. Innocent XI
1689	Alexander VIII
1691	Innocent XII
1700	Clement XI
1721	Innocent XIII
1724	Benedict XIII
1730	Clement XII
1740	Benedict XIV
1758	Clement XIII
1769	Clement XIV
1775	Pius VI
1800	Pius VII
1823	Leo XII
1829	Pius VIII
1831	Gregory XVI
1846	Pius IX
1878	Leo XIII
1903	St. Pius X
1914	Benedict XV
1922	Pius XI
1939	Pius XII
1958	John XXIII
1963	Paul VI
1978	John Paul I
1978	John Paul II

Major Christian Denominations:

Italics indicate some features that tend to

Denomination	Origins	Organization	Authority	Special rites
Baptists	In radical Reformation, objections to infant baptism, demands for church and state separation; John Smyth, English Separatist, in 1609; Roger Williams, 1638, Providence, RI.	Congregational; each local church is autonomous.	Scripture; some Baptists, particularly in the South, interpret the Bible literally.	*Baptism, usually early teen years and after, by total immersion;* Lord's Supper.
Church of Christ (Disciples)	Among evangelical Presbyterians in KY (1804) and PA (1809), in distress over Protestant factionalism and decline of fervor; organized in 1832.	Congregational.	*"Where the Scriptures speak, we speak; where the Scriptures are silent, we are silent."*	Adult baptism; Lord's Supper (weekly).
Episcopalians	Henry VIII separated English Catholic Church from Rome, 1534, for political reasons; Protestant Episcopal Church in U.S. founded in 1789.	*Diocesan bishops, in apostolic succession, are elected by parish representatives; the national Church is headed by General Convention and Presiding Bishop; part of the Anglican Communion.*	Scripture as interpreted by tradition, especially *39 Articles* (1563); not dogmatic; tri-annual convention of bishops, priests, and laypeople.	Infant baptism, Eucharist, and other sacraments; sacrament taken to be symbolic, but as having real spiritual effect.
Jehovah's Witnesses	Founded in 1870 in PA by Charles Taze Russell; incorporated as Watch Tower Bible and Tract Society of PA, 1884; name Jehovah's Witnesses adopted in 1931.	A governing body located in NY coordinates worldwide activities; each congregation cared for by a body of elders; each Witness considered a minister.	The Bible.	Baptism by immersion; annual Lord's Meal ceremony.
Latter-day Saints (Mormons)	In a vision of the Father and the Son reported by Joseph Smith (1820s) in NY. Smith also reported receiving new scripture on golden tablets: The Book of Mormon.	Theocratic; 1st Presidency (church president, 2 counselors), 12 Apostles preside over international church. Local congregations headed by lay priesthood leaders.	Revelation to living prophet (church president). The Bible, Book of Mormon, and other revelations to Smith and his successors.	Baptism, at age 8; laying on of hands (which confers the gift of the Holy Ghost); Lord's Supper; temple rites: baptism for the dead, marriage for eternity, others.
Lutherans	Begun by Martin Luther in Wittenberg, Germany in 1517; objection to Catholic doctrine of salvation and sale of indulgences; break complete, 1519.	Varies from congregational to episcopal; in U.S., a combination of regional synods and congregational polities is most common.	Scripture alone. The Book of Concord (1580), which includes the three Ecumenical Creeds, is subscribed to as a correct exposition of Scripture.	Infant baptism; Lord's Supper; Christ's true body and blood present "in, with, and under the bread and wine."
Methodists	Rev. John Wesley began movement in 1738, within Church of England; first U.S. denomination, Baltimore (1784).	Conference and superintendent system*; in United Methodist Church, general superintendents are bishops—not a priestly order, only an office—who are elected for life.*	Scripture as interpreted by tradition, reason, and experience.	Baptism of infants or adults; Lord's Supper commanded; other rites include marriage, ordination, solemnization of personal commitments.
Orthodox	Developed in original Christian proselytizing; broke with Rome in 1054, after centuries of doctrinal disputes and diverging traditions	Synods of bishops in autonomous, usually national, churches elect a patriarch, archbishop, or metropolitan; these men, as a group, are the heads of the church.	Scripture, tradition, and the first 7 church councils up to Nicaea II in 787; bishops in council have authority in doctrine and policy.	Seven sacraments: infant baptism and anointing, Eucharist, ordination, penance, and marriage.
Pentecostal	In Topeka, KS (1901) and Los Angeles (1906), in reaction to perceived loss of evangelical fervor among Methodists and others.	Originally a movement, not a formal organization, Pentecostalism now has a variety of organized forms and continues also as a movement.	Scripture; individual charismatic leaders, the teachings of the Holy Spirit.	*Spirit baptism, especially as shown in "speaking in tongues"; healing and sometimes exorcism;* adult baptism; Lord's Supper.
Presbyterians	In 16th-cent. Calvinist Reformation; differed with Lutherans over sacraments, church government; John Knox founded Scotch Presbyterian church about 1560.	*Highly structured representational system of ministers and laypersons (presbyters) in local, regional, and national bodies (synods).*	Scripture.	Infant baptism; Lord's Supper; bread and wine symbolize Christ's spiritual presence.
Roman Catholics	Traditionally, founded by Jesus who named St. Peter the 1st vicar; developed in early Christian proselytizing, especially after the conversion of imperial Rome in the 4th cent.	Hierarchy with supreme power vested in pope elected by cardinals; councils of bishops advise on matters of doctrine and policy.	*The pope, when speaking for the whole church in matters of faith and morals; and tradition (which is partly recorded in Scripture and expressed in church councils).*	Mass; 7 sacraments: baptism, reconciliation, Eucharist, confirmation, marriage, ordination, and anointing of the sick (unction).
United Church of Christ	*By ecumenical union, in 1957, of Congregationalists and Evangelical & Reformed, representing both Calvinist* and *Lutheran traditions.*	Congregational; a General Synod, representative of all congregations, sets general policy.	Scripture.	Infant baptism; Lord's Supper.

How Do They Differ?

distinguish a denomination sharply from others.

Practice	Ethics	Doctrine	Other	Denomination
Worship style varies from staid to evangelistic; extensive missionary activity.	Usually opposed to alcohol and tobacco; some tendency toward a perfectionist ethical standard.	*No creed; true church is of believers only, who are all equal.*	Believing no authority can stand between the believer and God, the Baptists are strong supporters of church and state separation.	**Baptists**
Tries to avoid any rite not considered part of the 1st-century church; some congregations may reject instrumental music.	Some tendency toward perfectionism; increasing interest in social action programs.	Simple New Testament faith; avoids any elaboration not firmly based on Scripture.	Highly tolerant in doctrinal and religious matters; strongly supportive of scholarly education.	**Church of Christ (Disciples)**
Formal, based on *Book of Common Prayer,* updated 1979; services range from austerely simple to highly liturgical.	Tolerant, sometimes permissive; some social action programs.	Scripture; the "historic creeds," which include the Apostles, Nicene, and Athanasian, and the *Book of Common Prayer*; ranges from Anglo-Catholic to low church, with Calvinist influences.	Strongly ecumenical, holding talks with many branches of Christendom.	**Episcopalians**
Meetings are held in Kingdom Halls and members' homes for study and worship; extensive door-to-door visitations.	High moral code; stress on marital fidelity and family values; avoidance of tobacco and blood transfusions.	*God, by his first creation, Christ, will soon destroy all wickedness; 144,000 faithful ones will rule in heaven with Christ over others on a paradise earth.*	Total allegiance proclaimed only to God's kingdom or heavenly government by Christ; politically neutral; main periodical, *The Watchtower* is printed in 115 languages.	**Jehovah's Witnesses**
Simple service with prayers, hymns, sermon; private temple ceremonies may be more elaborate.	Temperance; strict moral code; tithing; a strong work ethic with communal self-reliance; strong missionary activity; strong family emphasis.	Jesus Christ is the Son of God, the Eternal Father. Jesus' atonement saves all humans; those who are obedient to God's laws may become joint-heirs with Christ in God's kingdom.	Mormons believe theirs is the true church of Jesus Christ, restored by God through Joseph Smith. Official name: The Church of Jesus Christ of Latter-day Saints.	**Latter-day Saints (Mormons)**
Relatively simple, formal liturgy with emphasis on the sermon.	Generally conservative in personal and social ethics; doctrine of "2 kingdoms" (worldly and holy) supports conservatism in secular affairs.	Salvation by grace alone through faith; Lutheranism has made major contributions to Protestant theology.	Though still somewhat divided along ethnic lines (German, Swedish, etc.), main divisions are between fundamentalists and liberals.	**Lutherans**
Worship style varies widely by denomination, local church, geography.	Originally pietist and perfectionist; always strong social activist elements.	No distinctive theological development; 25 Articles abridged from Church of England's 39, not binding.	In 1968, The United Methodist Church was formed by the union of The Methodist Church and The Evangelical United Brethren Church.	**Methodists**
Elaborate liturgy, usually in the vernacular, though extremely traditional; the liturgy is the essence of Orthodoxy; veneration of icons.	Tolerant; little stress on social action; divorce, remarriage permitted in some cases; bishops are celibate; priests need not be.	Emphasis on Christ's resurrection, rather than crucifixion; the Holy Spirit proceeds from God the Father only.	Orthodox Church in America originally under Patriarch of Moscow, was granted autonomy in 1970; Greek Orthodox do not recognize this autonomy.	**Orthodox**
Loosely structured service with rousing hymns and sermons, culminating in spirit baptism.	Usually, emphasis on perfectionism with varying degrees of tolerance.	Simple traditional beliefs, usually Protestant, with emphasis on the immediate presence of God in the Holy Spirit.	Once confined to lower-class "holy rollers," Pentecostalism now appears in mainline churches and has established middle-class congregations.	**Pentecostal**
A simple, sober service in which the sermon is central.	Traditionally, a tendency toward strictness with firm church- and self-discipline; otherwise tolerant.	Emphasizes the sovereignty and justice of God; no longer dogmatic.	Although traces of belief in predestination (that God has foreordained salvation for the"elect") remain, this idea is no longer a central element in Presbyterianism.	**Presbyterians**
Relatively elaborate ritual centered on the Mass; also rosary recitation, novenas, etc.	Traditionally strict, but increasingly tolerant in practice; divorce and remarriage not accepted, but annulments sometimes granted; celibate clergy, except in Eastern rite.	Highly elaborated; salvation by merit gained through grace; dogmatic; special veneration of Mary, the mother of Jesus	Relatively rapid change followed Vatican Council II; Mass now in vernacular; more stress on social action, tolerance, ecumenism.	**Roman Catholics**
Usually simple services with emphasis on the sermon.	Tolerant; some social action emphasis.	Standard Protestant; *Statement of Faith* (1959) is not binding.	The 2 main churches in the 1957 union represented earlier unions with small groups of almost every Protestant denomination.	**United Church of Christ**

Major Non-Christian World Religions

Source: Reviewed by Anthony Padovano, PhD, STD, prof. of literature & relig. studies, Ramapo College, NJ, adj. prof. of theol., Fordham U., NYC; and (Islam) by Abdulaziz Sachedina, PhD, prof. of Islamic studies, Univ. of Virginia

Buddhism

Founded: About 525 BC, reportedly near Benares, India.
Founder: Gautama Siddhartha (c 563-483 BC), the Buddha, who achieved enlightenment through intense meditation.
Sacred Texts: The *Tripitaka*, a collection of the Buddha's teachings, rules of monastic life, and philosophical commentaries on the teachings; also a vast body of Buddhist teachings and commentaries, many of which are called *sutras.*
Organization: The basic institution is the *sangha*, or monastic order, through which the traditions are passed to from generation to generation. Monastic life tends to be democratic and anti-authoritarian. Large lay organizations have developed in some sects.
Practice: Varies widely according to the sect, and ranges from austere meditation to magical chanting and elaborate temple rites. Many practices, such as exorcism of devils, reflect pre-Buddhist beliefs.
Divisions: A variety of sects grouped into 3 primary branches: Theravada (sole survivor of the ancient Hinayana schools), which emphasizes the importance of pure thought and deed; Mahayana (includes Zen and Soka-gakkai), which ranges from philosophical schools to belief in the saving grace of higher beings or ritual practices and to practical meditative disciplines; and Tantrism, a combination of belief in ritual magic and sophisticated philosophy.
Location: Throughout Asia, from Sri Lanka to Japan. Zen and Soka-gakkai have several thousand adherents in the U.S.
Beliefs: Life is misery and decay, and there is no ultimate reality in it or behind it. The cycle of endless birth and rebirth continues because of desire and attachment to the unreal "self." Right meditation and deeds will end the cycle and achieve Nirvana, the Void, nothingness.

Hinduism

Founded: About 500 BC by Aryan invaders of India where their Vedic religion intermixed with the practices and beliefs of the natives.
Sacred texts: The *Veda,* including the *Upanishads,* a collection of rituals and mythological and philosophical commentaries; a vast number of epic stories about gods, heroes, and saints, including the *Bhagavadgita,* a part of the *Mahabharata,* and the *Ramayana;* and a great variety of other literature.
Organization: None, strictly speaking. Generally, rituals should be performed or assisted by Brahmins, the priestly caste, but in practice, simpler rituals can be performed by anyone. Brahmins are the final judges of ritual purity, the vital element in Hindu life. Temples and religious organizations are usually presided over by Brahmins.
Practice: A variety of private rituals, primarily passage rites (e.g., initiation, marriage, death, etc.) and daily devotions, and a similar variety of public rites in temples. Of the public rites, the *puja,* a ceremonial dinner for a god, is the most common.
Divisions: There is no concept of orthodoxy in Hinduism, which presents a variety of sects, most of them devoted to the worship of one of the many gods. The 3 major living traditions are those devoted to the gods Vishnu and Shiva and to the goddess Shakti; each is divided into further subsects. Numerous folk beliefs and practices, often in amalgamation with the above groups, exist side by side with sophisticated philosophical schools and exotic cults.
Location: Mainly India, Nepal, Malaysia, Guyana, Suriname, and Sri Lanka.
Beliefs: There is only one divine principle; the many gods are only aspects of that unity. Life in all its forms is an aspect of the divine, but it appears as a separation from the divine, a meaningless cycle of birth and rebirth (*samsara*) determined by the purity or impurity of past deeds (*karma*). To improve one's *karma* or escape *samsara* by pure acts, thought, and/or devotion is the aim of every Hindu.

Islam

Founded: About AD 622 in Mecca, Arabian Peninsula.
Founder: Muhammad (c 570-632), the Prophet.
Sacred texts: The *Koran* (al-Qur'an), the Word of God; *Sunna*, collections of *adth*, describing what Muhammad said or did.
Organization: Since the founder was both a prophet and a statesman, Muslim leadership has combined the civil and moral function of a state. Within the larger community, there are cultural and national groups, held together by a common religious law, the *Shari'a*, enforced uniformly in matters of religion only. In social transactions the community has often departed from traditional formulations. Although Islam is basically egalitarian and suspicious of authoritarianism, Muslim culture tends to be dominated by the conservative spirit of its religious establishment, the *ulema.*
Practice: Besides the general moral guidance that determines everyday life, there are "Five Pillars of Islam": profession of faith (oneness of God and prophethood of Muhammad); prayer 5 times a day; alms *(zakat)* from one's savings and estate; dawn-to-dusk fasting in the month of Ramadan; and once in a lifetime, pilgrimage to Mecca, if possible.
Divisions: There are 2 major groups: the majority known as Sunni and the minority Shiites. Shiites believe in Twelve Imams (perfect teachers) after the Prophet, of whom the last Imam has lived an invisible existence since 874, continuing to guide his community. Sunni Muslims believe in God's overpowering will over their affairs and tend to be predestinarian; Shiites believe in free will and give a substantial role to human reason in daily life. Sufism (mystical dimension of Islam) is prevalent among both Sunni and Shiites. Sufis emphasize personal relation to God and obedience informed by love of God.
Location: W Africa to Philippines, across band including E Africa, Central Asia and W China, India, Malaysia, Indonesia. Islam has several million adherents in North America.
Beliefs: Strictly monotheistic. God is creator of the universe, omnipotent, omniscient, just, forgiving, and merciful. The human is God's highest creation, but weak and egocentric, prone to forget the goal of life, constantly tempted by the Satan, an evil being. God revealed the Koran to Muhammad to guide humanity to truth and justice. Those who repent and sincerely "submit" (literal meaning of "islam") to God attain salvation. The forgiven enter the Paradise, and the wicked burn in Hell.

Judaism

Founded: About 1300 BC.
Founder: Abraham is regarded as the founding patriarch, but the Torah of Moses is the basic source of the teachings.
Sacred Texts: The 5 books of Moses constitute the written Torah. Special sanctity is also assigned other writings of the Hebrew Bible—the teachings of oral Torah are recorded in the Talmud, in the Midrash, and in various commentaries.
Organization: Originally theocratic, Judaism has evolved a congregational polity. The basic institution is the local synagogue, operated by the congregation and led by a rabbi of their choice. Chief rabbis in France and Great Britain have authority only over those who accept it; in Israel, the 2 chief rabbis have civil authority in family law.
Practice: Among traditional practicioners, almost all areas of life are governed by strict religious discipline. Sabbath and holidays are marked by special observances, and attendance at public worship is considered especially important then. Chief annual observances are Passover, celebrating liberation of the Israelites from Egypt and marked by the Seder meal in homes, and the 10 days from Rosh Hashana (New Year) to Yom Kippur (Day of Atonement), a period of fasting and penitence.
Divisions: Judaism is an unbroken spectrum from ultraconservative to ultraliberal, largely reflecting different points of view regarding the binding character of the prohibitions and duties—particularly the dietary and Sabbath observations—traditionally prescribed for the daily life of the Jew.
Location: Almost worldwide, with concentrations in Israel and the U.S.
Beliefs: Strictly monotheistic. God is the creator and absolute ruler of the universe. Men and women are free to choose to rebel against God's rule. God established a particular relationship with the Hebrew people: by obeying a divine law God gave them, they would be a special witness to God's mercy and justice. Judaism stresses ethical behavior (and, among the traditional, careful ritual obedience) as true worship of God.

LANGUAGE

New Words in English

The following words and definitions were provided by Merriam-Webster Inc., publishers of *Merriam-Webster's Collegiate Dictionary, Tenth Edition.* The words or meanings are among those that the Merriam-Webster editors decided had achieved enough currency in English to be entered in the 1998 copyright revision of the dictionary.

aerobicize: to engage in aerobics

audiobook: a recording of a reading of a book or magazine designed chiefly for the use of the blind

bioregion: a region whose limits are naturally defined by topographic and biological features (as mountains and ecosystems)

bottom-feeder: (1) a fish that feeds at the bottom; (2) one that is of the lowest status or rank; (3) an opportunist who seeks quick profit, usually at the expense of others or from their misfortune

buffalo wing: a deep-fried chicken wing coated with a spicy sauce and usually served with a blue cheese dressing

challenged: having a disability or deficiency

charter school: a tax-supported school established by a charter between a granting body (as a school board) and an outside group (as of teachers and parents) which operates the school without most local and state regulations so as to achieve set goals

chat room: an on-line interactive discussion group on the Internet

comfort food: food prepared in a traditional style having a usually nostalgic or sentimental appeal

domestic partner: (1) a company especially in a developing country that joins in a commercial venture with an international company; (2) either one of an unmarried heterosexual or homosexual cohabiting couple, especially when considered as to eligibility for spousal benefits

ecoterrorism: (1) sabotage intended to hinder activities that are considered damaging to the environment (2); political terrorism intended to damage an enemy's natural environment

edge city: a suburb that has developed its own political, economic, and commercial base independent of the central city

family leave: a usually unpaid leave of absence for an employee to attend to family concerns (as care of an infant or a serious illness)

feng shui; a Chinese practice in which a structure or site is chosen and configured so as to harmonize with the spiritual forces that inhabit it; also: auspicious orientation, placement, or arrangement as determined by feng shui

frisée, ***also*** **frisé:** curly chicory leaves used in a salad

hantavirus; any of a group of closely related RNA-containing arboviruses causing some forms of hemorrhagic fever and pneumonia

homeschooler: (1) one who teaches his or her children at home; (2) a child who is homeschooled

mad cow disease: a fatal disease of cattle affecting the nervous system, resembling or identical with scrapie of sheep and goats, and probably caused by a prion transmitted by infected tissue in food—also called *bovine spongiform encephalopathy*

medigap: supplemental health insurance that covers costs (as of medical care or a hospital stay) not covered by medicare

mesclun: a salad consisting of a mixture of young tender greens (as lettuces, arugula, and chicory)

plyometrics: exercise involving repeated rapid stretching and contracting of muscles (as of jumping and rebounding) to increase muscle power

ramen: quick-cooking noodles usually served in a broth with bits of meat and vegetables

trash talk: disparaging, taunting, or boastful comments esp. between opponents trying to intimidate each other

Eponyms

(words named for people)

Bloody Mary—a vodka and tomato juice drink; after the nickname of Mary I, Queen of England (1553-58), notorious for persecution of Protestants

bloomers—full, loose trousers that are gathered at the knee; after Amelia Bloomer, an American social reformer who advocated (1851) such clothing

bobbies—in Great Britain, police officers; after Sir Robert Peel, the statesman who organized the London police force, 1850

bowdlerize—to delete written matter considered indelicate; after Thomas Bowdler, English editor of an expurgated Shakespeare (1825)

boycott—to avoid trade or dealings with, as a protest; after Charles C. Boycott, an English land agent in County Mayo, Ireland, ostracized in 1880 for refusing to reduce rents

Braille—a system of writing for the blind; after Louis Braille, the French teacher of the blind who invented it (1853)

Casanova—a man who is a promiscuous and unscrupulous lover; after Giovanni Giacomo Casanova (1725-98), an Italian adventurer

chauvinist—excessively patriotic; after Nicolas Chauvin, a character in a 19th-cent. play who is devoted to Napoleon

derby—a stiff felt hat with a dome-shaped crown and rather narrow rolled brim; after Edward Stanley, 12th earl of Derby, who in 1780 founded the Derby horse race, to which these hats are worn

diesel—a type of internal combustion engine or a vehicle driven by it; after Rudolf Diesel (1858-1913), who built the first successful diesel engine

gerrymander—to draw an election district in such a way as to favor a political party; after Elbridge Gerry, who created (1812) just such an election district (shaped like a salamander) during his governorship of Massachusetts

guillotine—a machine for beheading; after Joseph Guillotin, a French physician who proposed its use in 1789 as more humane than hanging

leotard—a close-fitting garment for the torso, worn by dancers, acrobats, and the like; after Julius Leotard, a 19th-century French aerial gymnast

sandwich—2 or more slices of bread with a filling in between; after John Montagu, 4th earl of Sandwich (1718-92), who supposedly ate food in this form so that he would not have to leave the gaming table

silhouette—an outline image; from Étienne de Silhouette (1709-67), a close-fisted French finance minister

National Spelling Bee

The Scripps Howard National Spelling Bee, conducted by Scripps Howard Newspapers and other leading newspapers since 1939, was instituted by the Louisville (KY) *Courier-Journal* in 1925. Children under 16 years old and not beyond 8th grade are eligible to compete for cash prizes at the finals, held annually in Washington, DC. The 1998 winners were: 1st prize, Jody-Anne Maxwell, Kingston, Jamaica; 2d prize, Prem Murthy Trivedi, Morganville, NJ (2d year in a row); 3d prize, Hirsh Sandesara, Glenview, IL

Here are the last words given, and spelled correctly, in each of the years 1979-98 at the national spelling bee.

1979 — maculature	1984 — luge	1989 — spoliator	1994 — antediluvian
1980 — elucubrate	1985 — milieu	1990 — fibranne	1995 — xanthosis
1981 — sarcophagus	1986 — odontalgia	1991 — antipyretic	1996 — vivisepulture
1982 — psoriasis	1987 — staphylococci	1992 — lyceum	1997 — euonym
1983 — purim	1988 — elegiacal	1993 — kamikaze	1998 — chiaroscurist

Foreign Words and Phrases

(L=Latin; F=French; Y=Yiddish; G=Greek; I=Italian; S=Spanish)

ad hoc (L; ad HOK): for the end or purpose at hand
ad infinitum (L; ad in-fi-NITE-um): without end; forever
ad nauseam (L; ad NAWZ-ee-um): to a sickening degree
apropos (F; ap-ruh-POH): relevant
bête noire (F; BET NWAHR): a thing or person viewed with particular dislike or fear
bon appétit (F; BOH nap-uh-teet): have a good meal!
bona fide (L; BOH nuh-feyed): genuine; in good faith
carte blanche (F; kahrt BLANNSH): full discretionary power
cause célèbre (F; kawz suh-LEB-ruh): a notorious incident
c'est la vie (F; se lah VEE): that's life
chutzpah (Y; KHOOT-spuh): nerve bordering on arrogance
coup de grâce (F; kooh duh GRAHS): the final blow
coup d'état (F; kooh day TAH): overthrow of an existing government by a small group
crème de la crème (F; KREM duh luh KREM): the best of the best
cum laude/magna cum laude/summa cum laude (L; KUHM loud-ay; MAGN-ya ...; SOO-ma ...): with praise or honor/with great praise or honor/with the highest praise or honor
de facto (L; di FAK-toh): in fact, though not by right
déjà vu (F; DAY-zhah VOOH): the sensation that something happening has happened before
de jure (L; dee JOOR-ee, day YOOR-ay): in accordance with right or law; officially
de rigueur (F; duh ree-GUR): necessary according to convention or etiquette
détente (F; day-TAHNT): an easing of strained relations
éminence grise (F; ay-meh-NAHNN-suh GREEZ): one who wields power behind the scenes
enfant terrible (F; ahnn-FAHNN te-REE-bluh): one whose unconventional behavior causes embarrassment
en masse (F; ahn MAHS): in a large body
ergo (L; ER-goh): therefore
esprit de corps (F; es-PREE duh KAWR): group spirit; feeling of camaraderie
ex post facto (L; eks pohst FAK-toh): retroactive(ly)
fait accompli (F; fayt uh-kom-PLEE): an accomplished fact
faux pas (F; fowe PAH): a social blunder
hoi polloi (G; hoy puh-LOY): the masses
in loco parentis (L; in LOH-koh puh-REN-tis): in place of a parent
in memoriam (L; in muh-MAWR-ee-uhm): in memory of
in situ (L; in SEYE-tyooh): in the original place or position
in toto (L; in TOH-toh): totally
je ne sais quoi (F; zhuh nuh say KWAH): I don't know what; the little something that eludes description
joie de vivre (F; zhwah duh VEEV-ruh): zest for life
mea culpa (L; MAY-uh CUL-puh): through my fault
modus operandi (L; MOH-duhs op-uh-RAN-dee): method of operation
noblesse oblige (F; noh-BLES uh-BLEEZH): the obligation of nobility to help the less fortunate
non compos mentis (L; non KOM-puhs MEN-tis): not of sound mind
nouveau riche (F; nooh-voh REESH): a person newly rich; perhaps one who spends money conspicuously
persona non grata (L; per-SOH-nah non GRAH-tah): unwelcome person
postmortem (L; pohst-MORE-tuhm): after death; autopsy; analysis after an event
prima donna (I; pree-muh DAH-nuh): a principal female opera singer; temperamental person
pro tempore (L; proh TEM-puh-ree): for the time being
que sera sera (S; keh sair-ah sair-AH): what will be will be
quid pro quo (L; kwid proh KWOH): something given or received for something else
raison d'être (F; RAY-zohnn DET-ruh): reason for being
savoir faire (F; sav-wahr-FAIR): dexterity in social affairs
schlemiel (Y; shleh-MEEL): an unlucky, bungling person
semper fidelis (L; SEM-puhr fee-DAY-lis): always faithful
status quo (L; STAY-tus QWOH): existing order of things
terra firma (L; TER-uh FUR-muh): solid ground
tour de force (F; TOOR duh FAWRS): feat accomplished through great skill
verbatim (L; ver-BAY-tuhm): word for word
vis-à-vis (F; vee-ZUH-VEE): compared with; with regard to; with respect to

Some Common Abbreviations and Acronyms

Acronyms are pronounceable words formed from first letters (or syllables) of other words. Some abbreviations below (e.g., AIDS, NATO) are thus acronyms. Some acronyms are words coined as abbreviations and written in lower case (e.g., *radar*, *yuppie);* these are among abbreviations that may be more familiar than the terms they stand for. Acronyms do not have periods; usage for other abbreviations varies, but periods have become less common. Capitalization usage may vary from what is shown here. Italicized words preceding parenthetical definitions below are Latin unless otherwise noted. *See also* other chapters, including Internet and Computers; Weights and Measures.

AA=Alcoholics Anonymous
AAA=American Automobile Association
AARP=American Association of Retired Persons
ABA=American Bar Association
AC=alternating current
AD=*anno Domini* (in the year of the Lord)
AFL-CIO=American Federation of Labor and Congress of Industrial Organizations
AIDS=acquired immune deficiency syndrome
AM=*ante meridiem* (before noon)
AMA=American Medical Association
anon=anonymous
APO=army post office
ASAP=as soon as possible
ASCAP=American Society of Composers, Authors, and Publishers
ASPCA=American Society for Prevention of Cruelty to Animals
ATM=automated teller machine
Ave.=Avenue
AWOL=absent without leave
BA=Bachelor of Arts
bbl=barrel(s)
BC=before Christ
BCE=before Common Era
bpd=barrels per day
BS=Bachelor of Science
Btu=British thermal unit(s)
bu=bushel(s)
C= Celsius, centigrade
c=*circa* (about), copyright
Capt.=Captain
CE=Common Era
CEO=chief executive officer
CFO=chief financial officer
CIA=Central Intelligence Agency
cm=centimeter(s)
COD=cash (or collect) on delivery
Col.=Colonel
COLA=cost of living allowance
CPA=certified public accountant
Cpl.=Corporal
CPR=cardiopulmonary resuscitation
DA=district attorney
DAR=Daughters of the American Revolution
DC=direct current
DD=Doctor of Divinity
DDS=Doctor of Dental Science (or Surgery)
DNA=deoxyribonucleic acid
DNR=do not resuscitate
DOA=dead on arrival
DWI=driving while intoxicated
ed.=edited, edition, editor
e.g.=*exempli gratia* (for example)
EKG=electrocardiogram
EPA=Environmental Protection Agency

ESP=extrasensory perception
et al.=*et alii* (and others)
etc.=*et cetera* (and so forth)
EU=European Union
F=Fahrenheit
FBI=Federal Bureau of Investigation
FICA=Federal Insurance Contributions Act (Social Security)
FOB=free on board
ft=foot, feet
FY=fiscal year
FYI=for your information
gal=gallon(s)
GB=gigabyte(s)
GDP=gross domestic product
Gen.=General
GIGO=garbage in, garbage out
GNP=gross national product
GOP=Grand Old Party (Republican Party)
Hon.=the Honorable
HOV=high-occupancy vehicle
hr=hour(s)
ht=height
HVAC=heating, ventilating, and air-conditioning
i.e.=*id est* (that is)
IMF=International Monetary Fund
in.=inch(es)
IQ=intelligence quotient
IRA=individual retirement account, Irish Republican Army
IRS=Internal Revenue Service
ISBN=International Standard Book Number
JD=*Juris Doctor* (doctor of laws)
JP=Justice of the Peace
K=Kelvin
k=karat
KB=kilobyte(s)
kg=kilogram(s)
km=kilometer(s)
kw=kilowatt(s)
kwh=kilowatt-hour(s)
l=liter(s)
lb=*libra* (pound or pounds)
Lieut. or Lt.=Lieutenant
LLB=*Legum Baccalaureus* (bachelor of laws)
m=meter(s)
MA=Master of Arts
Maj.=Major
MB=megabyte(s)
MD=*Medicinae Doctor* (doctor of medicine)
MFN=most favored nation
mi=mile(s)
MIA=missing in action
min=minute(s)
ml=milliliter(s)
mm=millimeter(s)
mph=miles per hour
MS=Master of Science
MSG=monosodium glutamate
Msgr.=Monsignor
MVP=most valuable player
NAACP=National Association for the Advancement of Colored People
NASA=National Aeronautics and Space Administration
NAFTA=North American Free Trade Agreement
NATO=North Atlantic Treaty Organization
NB=*nota bene* (note carefully)
NCAA=National Collegiate Athletic Association
no=*numero* (number)
NOW=National Organization for Women
op=*opus* (work)
OPEC=Organization of Petroleum Exporting Countries
oz=ounce(s)
p, pp=page(s)
PAC=political action committee
PC=personal computer
PhD=*Philosophiae Doctor* (doctor of philosophy)
PIN=Personal Identification Number
PM=*post meridiem* (afternoon)
PO=post office
POW=prisoner of war
PS=*post scriptum* (postscript)
pt=part(s), pint(s), point(s)
Pvt.=Private
qt=quart(s)
q.v.=*quod vide* (which see)
radar=radio detecting and ranging
REM=rapid eye movement
Rev.=Reverend
RFD=rural free delivery
RIP=*requiescat in pace* (May he/she rest in peace)
RN=registered nurse
RNA=ribonucleic acid
ROTC=Reserve Officers' Training Corps
rpm=revolutions per minute
RR=railroad
RSVP=*répondez s'il vous plaît* (Fr.) (Please reply)
SASE=self-addressed stamped envelope
sec=second(s)
Sgt.=Sergeant
SIDS=sudden infant death syndrome
S.J.=Society of Jesus (Jesuits)
SRO=standing room only
St.=Saint, Street
TGIF=Thank God it's Friday
UFO=unidentified flying object
UHF=ultrahigh frequency
UNESCO=United Nations Educational, Social, and Cultural Organization
UNICEF=United Nations (International) Children's (Emergency) Fund
UPC=Universal Product Code
USS=United States ship
v (or vs)=*versus* (against)
VCR=videocassette recorder
VHF=very high frequency
VISTA=Volunteers in Service to America
W=watt(s)
Wasp=white Anglo-Saxon Protestant
WHO=World Health Organization
yd=yard(s)
yuppie=young urban professional
ZIP=zone improvement plan (U.S. Postal Service)

Names of the Days

ENGLISH	RUSSIAN	HEBREW	FRENCH	ITALIAN	SPANISH	GERMAN	JAPANESE
Sunday	Voskresenje	Yom rishon	Dimanche	Domenica	Domingo	Sonntag	Nichiyo\bi
Monday	Ponedeljnic	Yom sheni	Lundi	Lunedì	Lunes	Montag	Getsuyo\bi
Tuesday	Vtornik	Yom shlishi	Mardi	Martedì	Martes	Dienstag	Kayo\bi
Wednesday	Sreda	Yom ravii	Mercredi	Mercoledì	Miércoles	Mittwoch	Suiyo\bi
Thursday	Chetverg	Yom hamishi	Jeudi	Giovedì	Jueves	Donnerstag	Mokuyo\bi
Friday	Pjatnitsa	Yom shishi	Vendredi	Venerdì	Viernes	Freitag	Kin-yo\bi
Saturday	Subbota	Shabbat	Samedi	Sabato	Sábado	Samstag	Doyo\bi

Names for Animal Young

The young of many animals have come to be called by special names. Many of these are listed below.

bunny: rabbit
calf: cattle, elephant, antelope, rhino, hippo, whale, others
cheeper: grouse, partridge, quail
chick, chicken: fowl
cockerel: rooster
codling, sprag: codfish
colt: horse (male)
cub: lion, bear, shark, fox, others
cygnet: swan
duckling: duck
eaglet: eagle
elver: eel
eyas: hawk, others
fawn: deer
filly: horse (female)
fingerling: fish generally
flapper: wild fowl
fledgling: birds generally
foal: horse, zebra, others
fry: fish generally
gosling: goose
heifer: cow
joey: kangaroo, others
kid: goat
kit: fox, beaver, rabbit, cat
kitten, kitty, catling: cats, other small mammals
lamb, lambkin, cosset, hog: sheep
leveret: hare
nestling: birds generally
owlet: owl
parr, smolt, grilse: salmon
piglet, shoat, farrow, suckling: pig
polliwog, tadpole: frog
poult: turkey
pullet: hen
pup: dog, seal, sea lion, fox
puss, pussy: cat
spike, blinker, tinker: mackerel
squab: pigeon
squeaker: pigeon, others
whelp: dog, tiger, beasts of prey
yearling: cattle, sheep, horse, others

MILLENNIUM FACT BOX

Top 10 First Names of Americans by Decade of Birth

Source: Dr. Cleveland Kent Evans, Bellevue University, Bellevue, NE

Dr. Evans, a noted onomastician, or expert in name forms and origins, prepared these lists with data from his own research, as well as data supplied to him by the Social Security Administration.

Boys:	1900-1909	John, William, James, George, Joseph, Charles, Robert, Frank, Walter, Edward
	1910-1919	John, William, James, Robert, Joseph, Charles, George, Edward, Frank, Thomas
	1920-1929	John, Robert, James, William, Charles, George, Joseph, Richard, Thomas, Donald
	1930-1939	Robert, James, John, William, Richard, Charles, Donald, George, Thomas, David
	1940-1949	James, Robert, John, William, Richard, David, Charles, Thomas, Michael, Ronald
	1950-1959	Michael, Robert, James, John, David, William, Richard, Thomas, Mark, Steven
	1960-1969	Michael, David, John, James, Robert, William, Mark, Richard, Thomas, Jeffrey
	1970-1979	Michael, Christopher, David, Jason, James, John, Robert, Brian, Matthew, William
	1980-1989	Michael, Christopher, Matthew, David, Joshua, Daniel, James, Jason, Robert, Andrew
	1990-1997	Michael, Christopher, Matthew, Joshua, Nicholas, Tyler, Brandon, Zachary, Jacob, Andrew
Girls:	1900-1909	Mary, Helen, Margaret, Anna, Ruth, Elizabeth, Dorothy, Marie, Mildred, Florence
	1910-1919	Mary, Helen, Dorothy, Margaret, Ruth, Anna, Mildred, Elizabeth, Frances, Marie
	1920-1929	Mary, Dorothy, Helen, Betty, Margaret, Ruth, Virginia, Doris, Mildred, Elizabeth
	1930-1939	Mary, Barbara, Betty, Patricia, Shirley, Dorothy, Maria, Joan, Margaret, Helen
	1940-1949	Mary, Barbara, Patricia, Linda, Carol, Maria, Sandra, Nancy, Susan, Betty
	1950-1959	Deborah, Mary, Linda, Susan, Patricia, Maria, Barbara, Karen, Nancy, Donna
	1960-1969	Lisa, Maria, Mary, Susan, Karen, Kimberly, Deborah, Patricia, Michelle, Linda
	1970-1979	Jennifer, Amy, Michelle, Melissa, Angela, Lisa, Heather, Kimberly, Jessica, Maria
	1980-1989	Jessica, Jennifer, Amanda, Ashley, Sarah, Nicole, Stephanie, Melissa, Brittany, Elizabeth
	1990-1997	Ashley, Sarah, Jessica, Kaitlyn, Brittany, Emily, Megan, Samantha, Brianna, Kayla

Origins of Popular American Given Names

Source: Dr. Cleveland Kent Evans, Bellevue University, Bellevue, NE

Boys

Andrew: Gr. *andreios*, "man, manly"
Austin: Eng. form of Lat. *Augustinus*, "magnificent"
Brandon: Eng. place name, "gorse-covered hill"
Brian: Irish, perhaps Celtic *Brigonos*, "high, noble"
Charles: Ger. *ceorl*, "free man"
Christopher: Gr. *Khristophoros*, "bearing Christ [in one's heart]"
Daniel: Heb. "God is my judge"
David: Heb. *Dodavehu*, perhaps "darling"
Donald: Scots Gaelic *Domhnall*, "world rule"
Edward: Old Eng. *Eadweard*, "wealth-guard"
Frank: Ger. "Frenchman"
George: Gr. *georgos*, "soil tiller, farmer"
Jacob: Heb. *Yaakov,* "God protects" or "supplanter"
James: Late Lat. *Iacomus*, form of Jacob
Jason: Gr. *Iason*, "healer"
Jeffrey: Norman Fr. , from Ger. *Gaufrid*, "land-peace," or *Gisfrid*, "pledge-peace"
John: Heb. *Yohanan*, "God is gracious"
Joseph: Heb. *Yosef*, "[God] shall add"
Joshua: Heb. *Yoshua*, "God saves"
Mark: Lat. *Marcus*, perhaps "of Mars, the war god"
Matthew: Heb. *Mattathia*, "gift of God"
Michael: Heb. "Who could ever be like God?"
Nicholas: Gr. *Nikolaos*, "victory-people"
Richard: Ger. "power-hardy"
Robert: Ger. *Hrodberht*, "fame-bright"
Ronald: Scots form of Old Norse *Rögnvaldr*, "advice-ruler"
Steven: Gr. *stephanos*, "crown, garland"
Thomas: Aramaic "twin"
Tyler: Old Eng. *tigeler*, "tile layer"
Walter: Ger. *Waldheri*, "rule-army"
William: Ger. *Wilhelm*, "will-helmut"
Zachary: Eng. form of Heb. *Zechariah*, "God has remembered"

Girls

Amanda: 17th-cent. invention from Lat., "lovable"
Amy: Old Fr. *Amee*, "beloved"
Angela: Gr. *angelos*, "messenger [of God]"
Anna: Lat. and Gr. form of Hannah
Ashley: Eng. place name, "ash grove"
Barbara: Gr. *barbarus*, "foreign"
Betty: 18th-cent. pet form of Elizabeth
Brianna: modern fem. form of Brian
Brittany: place name, Fr. province settled by Britons
Caitlin: Irish form of Katherine, from *Aikaterine*, Egyptian name later modified to resemble Gr. *katharos*, "pure"
Carol: form of Charles
Deborah: Heb. "bee"
Donna: Ital. "lady"
Doris: Gr. "woman of the Dorian tribe," name of a sea nymph
Dorothy: Gr. *Dorothea*, "gift of God"
Elizabeth: Heb. *Elisheba*, perhaps "God is my oath" or "God is good fortune"
Emily: Roman *Aemilia*, possibly from Lat. *aemulus*, "rival"
Florence: Lat. *florens*, "flourishing"
Frances: fem. form of Francis, "a Frenchman"
Haley: Eng. place name, "hay clearing"
Hannah: Heb. "He has favored me"
Heather: Middle Eng. *hathir*, "heather"
Helen: Gr. *Helene,* possibly "sunbeam"
Jennifer: Cornish form of Welsh *Gwenhwyfar*, "fair-smooth"
Jessica: Shakespearean invention, probably fem. form of Jesse, Heb. "God exists"
Joan: Middle Eng. fem. form of John
Kaitlyn: modern American spelling of Caitlin
Karen: Danish form of Katherine [see Caitlin]
Kayla: modern invention; or Yiddish form of Kelila, Heb. "crown of laurel"
Kimberly: Eng. place name, "Cyneburgh's clearing"
Linda: Sp. "pretty" or Ger. "tender"
Lisa: pet form of Elizabeth
Madison: Middle Eng. surname, "son of Madeline or Maud"
Margaret: Gr. *margaron*, "pearl"
Maria: Lat. form of Mary
Marie: Fr. form of Mary
Mary: Eng. form of Heb. *Maryam*, perhaps "seeress" or "wished-for child"
Megan: Welsh form of Margaret
Melissa: Gr. "bee"
Michelle: Fr. fem. form of Michael
Mildred: Old Eng. *Mildthryth*, "mild-strength"
Nancy: medieval Eng. pet form of Agnes, Gr. *hagnos*, "holy"; later also used as pet form for Ann
Nicole: Fr. fem. form of Nicholas
Patricia: Lat. *Patricius*, "belonging to the noble class"
Ruth: Heb., perhaps "companion"
Samantha: colonial American invention, probably combining Sam from Samuel [Heb. "name of God"] with -antha from Gr. *anthos,* "flower"
Sandra: short form of Alessandra, Ital. fem. of Alexander, Gr. "defend-man"
Sarah: Heb., "princess"
Shirley: Eng. place name, "bright clearing" or "shire meadow"
Stephanie: Fr. fem. form of Steven
Susan: Eng. form of Heb. *Shoshana*, "lily"
Taylor: Anglo-Norman *taillour*, "tailor"
Virginia: Lat., "virgin-like"

Pen Names

Shalom Aleichem (Solomon J. Rabinowitz)
Woody Allen (Allen Stewart Konigsberg)
Currer, Ellis, and Acton Bell (Charlotte, Emily, and Anne Brontë)
John le Carré (David John Moore Cornwell)
Lewis Carroll (Charles Lutwidge Dodgson)
Colette (Sidonie Gabrielle Colette)
Isak Dinesen (Karen Blixen)
Elia (Charles Lamb)
George Eliot (Mary Ann or Marian Evans)
Maksim Gorky (Aleksey Maksimovich Peshkov)
O. Henry (William Sydney Porter)
James Herriot (James Alfred Wight)
P. D. James (Phyllis Dorothy James White)
[John] Ross Macdonald (Kenneth Millar)
André Maurois (Émile Herzog)
Molière (Jean Baptiste Poquelin)
Frank O'Connor (Michael Donovan)
George Orwell (Eric Arthur Blair)
Ellery Queen (Frederic Dannay and Manfred B. Lee)
Mary Renault (Mary Challans)
Françoise Sagan (Françoise Quoirez)
Saki (Hector Hugh Munro)
George Sand (Amandine Lucie Aurore Dupin)
Dr. Seuss (Theodor Seuss Geisel)
Stendhal (Marie Henri Beyle)
Mark Twain (Samuel Clemens)
Voltaire (François Marie Arouet)
Tom Wolfe (Thomas Kennerly Jr.)

Forms of Address

Addressee	Address	Salutation
Government		
President of the U.S.	The President, The White House, Washington, DC 20500; also, The President and Mrs. ____ or The President and Mr. ____	Dear Sir or Madam; Mr. President or Madam President; Dear Mr. President or Dear Madam President
U.S. Vice President	The Vice President, The White House, Washington, DC 20500; also, The Vice President and Mrs. ____ or The Vice President and Mr. ____	Dear Sir or Madam; Mr. Vice President or Madam Vice President; Dear Mr. Vice President or Dear Madam Vice President
Chief Justice	The Hon. *Firstname Surname*, Chief Justice of the U.S., The Supreme Court, Washington, DC 20543	Dear Sir or Madam; Dear Mr. or Madam Chief Justice
Associate Justice	The Hon. Justice *Firstname Surname,* The Supreme Court, Washington, DC 20543	Dear Sir or Madam; Dear Justice *Surname*
Judge	The Hon. *Firstname Surname*, Associate Judge, U.S. District Court	Dear Judge *Surname*
Attorney General	The Hon. *Firstname Surname,* Attorney General, Dept. of Justice, Constitution Ave. & 10th St. NW, Washington, DC 20530	Dear Sir or Madam; Dear Mr. or Ms. Attorney General
Cabinet Officer	The Hon. *Firstname Surname*, Secretary of ____	Dear Mr. or Madam Secretary; or Dear Mr. or Ms. *Surname*
Senator	The Hon. or Sen. *Firstname Surname*, U.S. Senate, Washington, DC 20510	Dear Mr. or Madam Senator, or Dear Mr. or Ms. *Surname*
Representative	The Hon. or Rep. *Firstname Surname*, House of Representatives, Washington, DC 20515	Dear Mr. or Madam *Surname*
Speaker of the House	The Hon. Speaker of the House of Representatives, House of Representatives, Washington, DC 20515	Dear Mr. or Madam Speaker
Ambassador, U.S.	The Hon. *Firstname Surname*, American Ambassador[1]	Sir or Madam; Dear Mr. or Madam Ambassador
Ambassador, Foreign	His or Her Excellency[2] *Firstname Surname*, Ambassador of ______	Excellency;[2] Dear Mr. or Madam Ambassador
Governor	The Hon. *Firstname Surname*, Governor of *State*; or in some states, His or Her Excellency, the Governor of *State*	Sir or Madam; Dear Governor *Surname*
Mayor	The Hon. *Firstname Surname*, Mayor of *City*	Sir or Madam; Dear Mayor *Surname*
Military Personnel		
All Titles	Full or abbreviated rank + full name + comma + abbreviation for branch of service. *Example*: Adm. John Smith, USN	Dear *Rank Surname*
Religious		
Clergy, Protestant	The Reverend *Firstname Surname*[3]	Dear Ms. or Mr. *Surname*
Pope	His Holiness Pope *Name* or His Holiness the Pope	Your Holiness or Most Holy Father
Priest	The Reverend *Firstname Surname* or The Reverend Father *Surname*	Reverend Father, Dear Father *Surname*, or Dear Father
Rabbi	Rabbi *Firstname Surname*	Dear Rabbi *Surname*
Royalty and Nobility		
King/Queen	His or Her Majesty, King or Queen of *Country*	Sir or Madam, or May it please Your Majesty

(1) If in Canada or Latin America, The Ambassador of the United States of America. (2) An American ambassador is not properly addressed as His or Her Excellency. (3) A member of the Protestant clergy who has a doctorate may be so addressed; for example, The Reverend Firstname Surname, DD, and Dear Dr. Surname.

Commonly Misspelled English Words

accidentally
accommodate
acknowledgment
acquainted
all right
already
amateur
appearance
appropriate
bureau
business
character
commitment
committee
conscientious
conscious
convenience
deceive
defendant
describe
description
desirable
despair
desperate
eliminate
embarrass
environment
existence
fascinating
February
finally
fluorine
foreign
forty
government
grammar
harass
humorous
hurrying
incidentally
independent
indispensable
inoculate
irresistible
judgment
laboratory
license
lightning
liquefy
maintenance
marriage
millennium
miniature
misspelled
mysterious
necessary
noticeable
occasionally
occurrence
opportunity
optimistic
parallel
performance
permanent
perseverance
privilege
receive
receipt
rhythm
ridiculous
separate
seize
similar
sincerely
supersede
transferred
weird
Wednesday

Commonly Confused English Words

adverse: unfavorable
averse: opposed

affect: to influence
effect: to bring about

allusion: an indirect reference
illusion: an unreal impression

appraise: to set a value on
apprise: to inform

capital: the seat of government
capitol: building where a legislature meets

complement: to make complete; something that completes
compliment: to praise; praise

denote: to mean
connote: to suggest beyond the explicit meaning

discreet: prudent
discrete: separate, distinct

disinterested: impartial
uninterested: without interest

elicit: to draw or bring out
illicit: illegal

emigrate: to leave for another place of residence
immigrate: to come to another place of residence

grisly: inspiring horror or great fear
grizzly: sprinkled or streaked with gray

historic: important in history
historical: relating to history

imminent: ready to take place
eminent: standing out

imply: to suggest but not explicitly; to entail
infer: to assume or understand information not relayed explicitly

include: used when the items following are part of a whole
comprise: used when the items following are all of a whole

incredible: unbelievable
incredulous: skeptical

ingenious: clever
ingenuous: innocent

oral: spoken, as opposed to written
verbal: relating to language

prostrate: stretched out face down
prostate: relating to prostate gland

The Principal Languages of the World

Source: Prof. Sidney Culbert, 351525, University of Washington, Seattle, WA 98195; data as of mid-1998

Languages Spoken by the Most People

	Speakers (millions) Native[1]	Speakers (millions) Total
Mandarin	874	1,052
Hindi	366	487
Spanish	358	417
English	341	508
Bengali	207	211
Arabic	206	246
Portuguese	176	191
Russian	167	277
Japanese	125	126
German	100	128
French	77	128
Malay-Indonesian	60	177

(1) A native speaker is one for whom the language is his or her first language.

Languages Spoken by at Least 1 Million People

Total number of speakers (native plus nonnative) of languages spoken by at least 1 million speakers. A native speaker is one for whom the language is his or her first language. Locations in parentheses are principal areas where the language is spoken.

Note: Languages are distinguished here according to consistent criteria commonly accepted by linguists and may sometimes be more narrowly defined than others may suppose. For example, Neapolitan, Piedmontese, Sardinian, Sicilian, and Venetian, all spoken in Italy, are here regarded as distinct languages, so their speakers are not counted as Italian speakers. In some cases nonlinguistic criteria supervene, as in the case of Arabic here, where speakers of many variants are, according to custom, included under one broad term, "Arabic."

Achinese (N Sumatra, Indonesia)	3
Afghan (see Pashtu)	
Afrikaans (S. Africa)	10
Akan (or Twi-Fanti) (Ghana)	8
Albanian (Albania; Kosovo, Yugoslavia)	5
Amharic (Ethiopia)	21
Arabic (see also above)	246
Armenian (Armenia)	6
Assamese[1] (India; Bangladesh)	10
Aymara (Bolivia; Peru)	2
Azeri (Azerbaijan)	15
Balinese (Bali, Indonesia)	3
Baluchi (Baluchistan, in SW Pakistan and SE Iran)	5
Bashkir (Bashkortostan, Russia)	1
Batak Toba (Indonesia)	4
Baule (Côte d'Ivoire)	2
Beja (Spoken Arabic dialect group)	5
Bemba (Zambia)	2
Bengali[1] (see also above)	211
Berber[2]	3
Beti (Cameroon; Gabon; Eq. Guinea)	2
Bhili (India)	6
Bikol (SE Luzon, Philippines)	4
Brahui (Pakistan)	2
Bugis (Indonesia; Malaysia)	4
Bulgarian (Bulgaria)	9
Burmese (Myanmar)	32
Buyi (S Guizhou, S China)	2
Byelorussian (Belarus)	10
Cantonese (China)	71
Catalan (NE Spain; Balearic Is.; S France; Andorra)	10
Cebuano (Bohol Sea, Philippines)	13
Chagga (Kilimanjaro area, Tanzania)	1
Chiga (Uganda)	1
Chinese[3]	
Chuvash (Chuvash, Russia)	2
Czech (Czech Republic)	12
Danish (Denmark)	5
Dimli (E Cent. Turkey)	1
Dogri (Jammu-Kashmir, CE India)	1
Dong (S Cent. China)	2
Dutch-Flemish (Netherlands; Belgium; NE France)	21
Dyerma (SW Niger)	2
Edo (Bendel, S Nigeria)	1
Efik (incl. Ibibio) (SE Nigeria)	6
English (see also above)	508
Esperanto	2
Estonian (Estonia)	1
Ewe (SE Ghana; S Togo)	3
Fang-Bulu (dialects of Beti, q. v.)	
Farsi (see Persian)	
Finnish (Finland; Sweden)	6
Fon (S Cent. Benin; S Togo)	1
French (see also above)	128
Fula (or Peulh) (Cameroon; Nigeria)	13
Fulakunda (Senegal; Gambia; Guinea-Bissau)	2
Futa Jalon (Guinea; Sierra Leone)	3
Galician (Galicia, NW Spain)	4
Galla (see Oromo)	
Ganda (or Luganda) (S Uganda)	4
Georgian (Georgia)	4
German (see also above)	128
Gilaki (Gilan, NW Iran)	2
Gogo (Riff Valley, Tanzania)	1
Gondi (Cent. India)	2
Greek (Greece)	12
Guarani (Paraguay)	5
Gujarati[1] (W Cent. India; S Pakistan)	44
Gusii (Kisii District, Nyanza, Kenya)	2
Gypsy (see Romany)	
Hadiyya (Arusi, Ethiopia)	1
Haitian-Creole French	8
Hakka (or Kejia) (SE China)	33
Hausa (N Nigeria; Niger; Cameroon)	39
Haya (Kagera, NW Tanzania)	1
Hebrew (Israel)	5
Hindi[1,4] (see also above)	487
Hmong (S China; SE Asia)	6
Ho (Bihar and Orissa States, India)	1
Hungarian (or Magyar) (Hungary)	14
Iban (Indonesia; Malaysia)	1
Ibibio (see Efik)	
Igbo (or Ibo) (lower Niger, Nigeria)	18
Ijaw (Niger River delta, Nigeria)	2
Ilocano (NW Luzon, Philippines)	7
Indonesian (see Malay-Indonesian)	
Italian (Italy)	62
Japanese (see also above)	126
Javanese (Java, Indonesia)	64
Kabyle (W Kabylia, N Algeria)	3
Kamba (E Kenya)	3
Kannada (S India)	44
Kanuri (Nigeria; Niger; Chad; Cameroon)	4
Karen (see Sgaw)	
Karo-Dairi (N Sumatra, Indonesia)	1
Kashmiri[1] (N India; NE Pakistan)	4
Kazak (Kazakhstan)	8
Khalka (see Mongolian)	
Khmer (Cambodia; Vietnam; Thai.)	8
Khmer, Northern (Thailand)	1
Kikuyu (or Gekoyo) (WC Kenya)	5
Kituba (Bas-Congo, Bandundu, Congo)	4
Kongo (W Congo[5]; S Congo Rep.; NW Angola)	3
Konkani (Maharashtra and SW India)	4
Korean (Korea; China; Japan)	78
Kurdish (Iran; Iraq; Turkey)	11
Kurukh (or Oraon) (Cent. and E India)	2
Kyrgyz (Kyrgyzstan)	3
Lampung (Sumatra, Indonesia)	2
Lao[6] (Laos)	4
Latvian (Latvia)	2
Lingala (incl. Bangala) (Congo[5])	7
Lithuanian (Lithuania)	3
Luba-Lulua (or Chiluba) (Congo[5])	7
Luba-Shaba (Shaba, Congo[5])	1
Luhya (W Kenya)	2
Luo (Kenya; Nyanza, Tanzania)	4
Luri (SW Iran; Iraq)	4
Lwena (E Angola; W Zambia)	1
Macedonian (Macedonia)	2
Madurese (Madura, Indonesia)	10
Magindanaon (S Philippines)	1
Makassar (S Sulawesi, Indonesia)	2
Makua (S Tanzania; N Mozambique)	4
Malagasy (Madagascar)	10
Malay-Indonesian (see also above)	177
Malay, Pattani (SE Thailand)	1
Malayalam[1] (Kerala, S India)	35
Malinke-Bambara-Dyula (W Africa)	9

Mandarin (China; Taiwan; see also above)	1,052
Marathi[1] (Maharashtra, India)	71
Mazandarani (N Iran)	3
Mbundu (Luanda, Bengladesh)	3
Meithei (NE India; Bangladesh)	1
Mende (Sierra Leone)	2
Meru (Eastern Province, Cent. Tanzania)	2
Mien (China; Viet.; Laos; Thailand)	1
Min (SE China; Taiwan; Malaysia)	50
Minangkabau (W Sumatra, Indon.)	6
Moldavian (incl. with Romanian)	
Mongolian (Mongolia; NE China)	6
Moré (Cent. Burkina Faso)	5
Nepali (Nepal; NE India; Bhutan)	16
Ngulu (Mozambique; Malawi)	3
Nkole (Western Prov., Uganda)	2
Norwegian (Norway)	5
Nung (NE of Hanoi, Vietnam; China)	1
Nupe (Kwara, Niger States, Nigeria)	1
Nyamwezi-Sukuma (NW Tanzania)	6
Nyanja (Malawi; Zambia; Zimbabwe)	10
Oriya[1] (Cent. and E India)	31
Oromo (W Ethiopia; N Kenya)	10
Pampangan (NW of Manila, Philip.)	2
Panay-Hiligaynon (Philippines)	7
Pangasinan (Lingayen G., Philip.)	2
Pashtu (Pakistan; Afghanistan; Iran)	19
Pedi (see Sotho, Northern)	
Persian (Iran; Afghanistan)	36
Polish (Poland)	44
Portuguese (see also above)	191
Provençal (S France)	3
Punjabi[1] (Punjab, Pakistan; India)	94
Pushto (see Pashtu)	
Quechua A (Peru; Boliv.; Ecuad.; Arg.)	8
Rejang (SW Sumatra, Indonesia)	1
Riff (N Morocco; Algerian coast)	1
Romanian (Romania; Moldova)	26
Romany[7]	2
Ruanda (Rwanda; Uganda; Congo[5])	5
Rundi (Burundi)	6
Russian (see also above)	277
Samar-Leyte (Cent. E Philippines)	3
Sango (Cent. African Republic)	4
Santali (E India; Nepal)	5
Sasak (Lombok, Alas Strait, Indon.)	2
Serbo-Croatian (Croatia; Serbia; other former Yugoslav republics and autonomous regions)	21
Sgaw (SW Myanmar)	2
Shan (E Myanmar)	3
Shilha (W Algeria; S Morocco)	2
Shona (Zimbabwe)	7
Sidamo (Sidamo, S Ethiopia)	2
Sindhi[1] (SE Pakistan; W India)	19
Sinhalese (Sri Lanka)	13
Slovak (Slovakia)	6
Slovene (Slovenia)	2
Soga (Busoga, Uganda)	1
Somali (Som.; Eth.; Ken.; Djibouti)	5
Songye (Kasai Or., NW Shaba, Congo[5])	2
Soninke (Mali; countries to W S E)	1
Sotho, Northern (So. Africa)	3
Sotho, Southern (So. Afr.; Lesotho)	4
Spanish (see also above)	417
Sundanese (Sunda Strait, Indonesia)	26
Swahili (Kenya; Tanzania; Congo[5]; Uganda)	49
Swati (Swaziland; South Africa)	2
Swedish (Sweden; Finland)	9
Sylhetti (Bangladesh)	5
Tagalog (Philippines)	57
Tajiki (Tajikistan; Uzbek.; Kyrgyz.)	5
Tamazight (N Morocco; W Algeria)	3
Tamil[1] (Tamil Nadu, India; Sri Lanka)	74
Tartar (Tartarstan, Russia)	8
Tausug (Philippines; Malaysia)	1
Telugu[1] (Andhra Pradesh, SE India)	75
Temne (central Sierra Leone)	2
Thai[6] (Thailand)	52
Tho (N Vietnam; S China)	2
Thonga (Mozambique; So. Africa)	3
Tibetan (SW China; N India; Nepal)	5
Tigrinya (S Eritrea; Tigre, Ethiopia)	4
Tiv (SE Nigeria; Cameroon)	2
Tong (see Dong)	
Tonga (SW Zambia; NW Zimbabwe)	2
Tswana (Botswana; South Africa)	4
Tulu (S India)	2
Tumbuka (N Malawi; NE Zambia)	2
Turkish (Turkey)	61
Turkmen (Turkmenistan; Afghanistan)	4
Twi-Fante (see Akan)	
Uighur (Xinjiang, NW China)	8
Ukrainian (Ukraine; Russia; Poland)	47
Urdu[1,4] (Pakistan; India)	104
Uzbek (Uzbekistan)	18
Vietnamese (Vietnam)	68
Wolaytta (SE Ethiopia)	2
Wolof (Senegal)	7
Wu (Shanghai region, China)	70
Xhosa (SW Cape Prov., South Africa)	8
Yao (see Mien)	
Yao (Malawi; Tanzania; Mozamb.)	1
Yi (S and SW China)	7
Yiddish[8]	4
Yoruba (SW Nigeria; Zou, Benin)	22
Zande (NE Congo[5]; SW Sudan)	1
Zhuang (S China)	10
Zulu (N. Natal, South Africa; Lesotho)	9

(1) One of the 15 languages under the constitution of India. (2) See Kabyle, Kabyle, Tamazight, Shilha, Riff. (3) See Mandarin, Cantonese, Wu, Min, and Hakka. The "common speech" (Putonghua) or the "national language" (Guoyu) is a standardized form of Mandarin as spoken in the area of Beijing. (4) Hindi and Urdu are essentially the same language, Hindustani. As the official language of Pakistan, it is written in a modified Arabic script and called Urdu. As the official language of India, it is written in the Devanagari script and called Hindi. (5) Congo refers to the Democratic Republic of the Congo (formerly Zaire), as distinct from the smaller Congo Republic. (6) The distinction between some Thai dialects and Lao are political rather than linguistic. (7) Mainly in Cent., E, and SE Europe and Turkey; some in the U.S. (8) Yiddish is usually considered a variant of German, but it has its own standard grammar and dictionaries, has a highly developed literature, and is written in Hebrew characters.

American Manual Alphabet

In the American Manual Alphabet, each letter of the alphabet is represented by a position of the fingers. This system was originally developed in France by Abbe Charles Michel De I'Epee in the late 1700s. It was brought to the U.S. by Laurent Clerce (1785-1869), a Frenchman who taught deaf or hearing-impaired people.

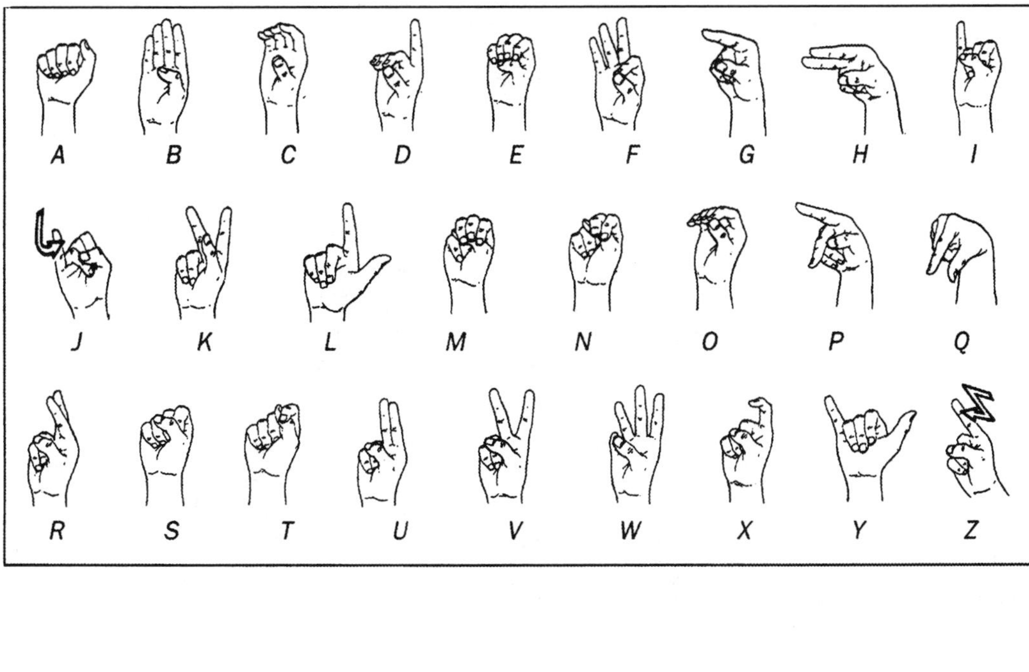

TRADE AND TRANSPORTATION

U.S. Trade With Selected Countries and Major Areas, 1997

Source: Office of Trade and Econ. Analysis, U.S. Dept. of Commerce

(in millions of dollars; trade bal. ranked by size of deficit)

Country/Area	U.S. trade balance with	Rank	Exports to	Rank	Imports from	Rank
Japan	$-56,114.8	1	$65,548.5	3	$121,663.2	2
China	-49,695.3	2	12,862.3	14	62,557.6	4
Germany	-18,663.2	3	24,458.3	6	43,121.5	5
Canada	-16,434.2	4	151,766.7	1	168,200.9	1
Mexico	-14,549.1	5	71,388.4	2	85,937.5	3
Taiwan	-12,262.8	6	20,365.7	7	32,628.5	7
Italy	-10,412.8	7	8,994.7	17	19,407.5	11
Malaysia	-7,246.7	8	10,780.0	16	18,026.7	12
Venezuela	-6,875.6	9	6,601.6	22	13,477.2	13
Nigeria	-5,536.4	10	813.1	58	6,349.4	26
Thailand	-5,252.1	11	7,349.4	21	12,601.5	14
France	-4,671.5	12	15,964.9	10	20,636.4	9
Indonesia	-4,666.1	13	4,522.3	28	9,188.4	19
Sweden	-3,984.8	14	3,314.1	35	7,298.9	24
India	-3,714.8	15	3,607.6	32	7,322.4	23
Philippines	-3,027.6	16	7,417.3	20	10,445.0	15
Angola	-2,498.6	17	280.6	82	2,779.1	34
Singapore	-2,378.4	18	17,696.2	9	20,074.6	10
Gabon	-2,117.7	19	84.5	114	2,202.3	43
Norway	-2,030.7	20	1,721.3	46	3,752.0	33
Algeria	-1,747.9	21	691.6	61	2,439.5	36
Sri Lanka	-1,465.3	22	154.7	96	1,620.0	51
Bangladesh	-1,420.4	23	259.0	84	1,679.4	50
Israel	-1,331.0	24	5,994.9	23	7,326.0	22
Ireland	-1,224.4	25	4,642.2	27	5,866.6	27
North America	-30,983.2	NA	223,155.2	NA	254,138.4	NA
Organization for Economic Cooperation & Development (OECD) in Europe	-17,624.7	NA	154,548.7	NA	172,173.4	NA
Western Europe	-17,572.9	NA	155,383.9	NA	172,956.8	NA
European Union (EU)	-16,754.5	NA	140,773.4	NA	157,527.8	NA
European Free Trade Association	-2,284.6	NA	10,219.9	NA	12,504.4	NA
Eastern Europe	-594.3	NA	7,888.6	NA	8,482.9	NA
Former Soviet Republics	-159.4	NA	5,190.8	NA	5,350.1	NA
Pacific Rim Countries	-121,627.4	NA	193,740.4	NA	315,367.7	NA
Assn. of Southeast Asian Nations (ASEAN)	-22,448.7	NA	47,943.2	NA	70,391.9	NA
Asia—Newly Industrialized Countries (NICS)	-7,938.9	NA	78,225.1	NA	86,164.0	NA
Asia—South	-6,888.0	NA	5,299.6	NA	12,187.5	NA
Asia—Near East	524.6	NA	20,927.1	NA	20,402.5	NA
Latin American Free Trade Association (LAFTA)	-8,103.2	NA	114,515.7	NA	122,618.9	NA
Twenty Latin American Republics	-7,975.1	NA	127,947.1	NA	135,922.2	NA
Central American Common Market	-958.4	NA	7,462.7	NA	8,421.2	NA
South/Central America	9,324.2	NA	63,021.1	NA	53,696.9	NA
North Atlantic Treaty Organization (NATO) Allies	-27,697.8	NA	286,209.4	NA	313,907.2	NA
Organization of Petroleum Exporting Countries (OPEC)	-18,499.8	NA	25,525.6	NA	44,025.3	NA
Unidentified	340.9	NA	340.9	NA	(-)	NA
Total	**$-181,488.2**	**NA**	**$689,182.4**	**NA**	**$870,670.7**	**NA**

NA – Not applicable. **Note:** Details may not equal totals because of rounding.

Definitions of areas as used in the above table:

North America—Canada, Mexico.

OECD—Austria, Belgium, Denmark, Finland, France, Germany, Greece, Iceland, Ireland, Italy, Liechtenstein, Luxembourg, Monaco, Netherlands, Norway, Portugal, San Marino, Spain, Svalbard/Jan Mayen Island, Sweden, Switzerland, Turkey, United Kingdom.

Western Europe—Andorra, Austria, Belgium, Bosnia and Herzegovina, Croatia, Cyprus, Denmark, Faroe Islands, Finland, France, Germany, Gibraltar, Greece, Iceland, Ireland, Italy, Liechtenstein, Luxembourg, Macedonia, Malta and Gozo, Monaco, Netherlands, Norway, Portugal, San Marino, Slovenia, Spain, Svalbard/Jan Mayen Island, Sweden, Switzerland, Turkey, United Kingdom, Vatican City, Yugoslavia.

European Union—Belgium, Denmark, France, Germany, Greece, Ireland, Italy, Luxembourg, Netherlands, Portugal, Spain, United Kingdom.

European Free Trade Association —Austria, Finland, Iceland, Liechtenstein, Norway, Sweden, Switzerland.

Eastern Europe—Albania, Armenia, Azerbaijan, Belarus, Bulgaria, Czech Republic, Estonia, Georgia, Hungary, Kazakhstan, Kyrgyzstan, Latvia, Lithuania, Moldova, Poland, Romania, Russia, Slovakia, Tajikistan, Turkmenistan, Ukraine, Uzbekistan.

Former Soviet Republics—Armenia, Azerbaijan, Belarus, Estonia, Georgia, Kazakhstan, Kyrgyzstan, Latvia, Lithuania, Moldova, Russia, Tajikistan, Turkmenistan, Ukraine, Uzbekistan.

Pacific Rim Countries/Territories—Australia, Brunei, China, Hong Kong (now part of China), Indonesia, Japan, South Korea, Macao, Malaysia, New Zealand, Papua New Guinea, Philippines, Singapore, Taiwan.

ASEAN—Brunei, Indonesia, Malaysia, Philippines, Singapore, Thailand.

Asia—Newly Industrialized Countries (NICS)—Hong Kong (now part of China), Korea, Singapore, Taiwan.

Asia—South—Afghanistan, Bangladesh, India, Nepal, Pakistan, Sri Lanka.

Asia—Near East—Bahrain, Iran, Iraq, Israel, Jordan, Kuwait, Lebanon, Oman, Qatar, Saudi Arabia, Syria, United Arab Emirates, Yemen.

LAFTA—Argentina, Bolivia, Brazil, Chile, Colombia, Ecuador, Mexico, Paraguay, Peru, Uruguay, Venezuela.

Twenty Latin American Republics—Argentina, Bolivia, Brazil, Chile, Colombia, Costa Rica, Cuba, Dominican Republic, Ecuador, El Salvador, Guatemala, Haiti, Honduras, Mexico, Nicaragua, Panama, Paraguay, Peru, Uruguay, Venezuela.

Central American Common Market—Costa Rica, El Salvador, Guatemala, Honduras, Nicaragua.

South/Central America—Anguilla, Antigua and Barbuda, Argentina, Aruba, Bahamas, Barbados, Belize, Bermuda, Bolivia, Brazil, British Virgin Islands, Cayman Islands, Chile, Colombia, Costa Rica, Cuba, Dominica, Dominican Republic, Ecuador, El Salvador, Falkland Islands, French Guiana, Grenada, Guadeloupe, Guatemala, Guyana, Haiti, Honduras, Jamaica, Martinique, Montserrat, Netherland Antilles, Nicaragua, Panama, Paraguay, Peru, St. Kitts and Nevis, St. Lucia, St. Vincent and the Grenadines, Suriname, Trinidad and Tobago, Turks and Caicos Islands, Uruguay, Venezuela.

NATO Allies—Belgium, Canada, Denmark, France, Germany, Greece, Iceland, Ireland, Italy, Liechtenstein, Luxembourg, Monaco, Netherlands, Norway, Portugal, San Marino, Spain, Svalbard/Jan Mayan Island, Sweden, Switzerland, Turkey, United Kingdom.

OPEC—Algeria, Gabon, Indonesia, Iran, Iraq, Kuwait, Libya, Nigeria, Qatar, Saudi Arabia, United Arab Emirates, Venezuela.

U.S. Exports and Imports by Principal Commodity Groupings, 1997

Source: Office of Trade and Economic Analysis, U.S. Dept. of Commerce

(millions of dollars)

Item	Exports	Imports
Total	**$689,182**	**$870,671**
Agricultural commodities	**55,639**	**35,164**
Animal feeds	4,621	648
Cereal flour	1,241	1,328
Coffee	7	3,575
Corn	5,426	103
Cotton, raw and linters	2,716	20
Hides and skins	1,503	130
Meat and preparations	6,885	2,656
Oils/fats, vegetable	1,398	1,381
Rice	933	217
Soybeans	7,479	86
Sugar	3	956
Tobacco, unmanufactured	1,548	1,129
Vegetables and fruit	7,472	7,752
Wheat	4,196	359
Manufactured goods	**550,629**	**728,928**
ADP equipment; office machinery	43,698	74,993
Airplanes	25,552	4,557
Airplane parts	13,266	4,917
Aluminum	3,768	5,558
Artwork/antiques	1,120	3,587
Basketware, etc.	2,494	3,364
Chemicals - cosmetics	4,873	2,677
Chemicals - dyeing	3,294	2,485
Chemicals - fertilizers	3,123	1,374
Chemicals - inorganic	5,264	5,132
Chemicals - medicinal	8,087	8,748
Chemicals - organic	16,408	16,874
Chemicals - plastics	17,274	8,237
Chemicals - other[1]	11,160	4,821
Clothing	8,396	48,408
Copper	1,441	3,254
Electrical machinery	65,816	80,370
Footwear	800	14,026
Furniture and bedding	3,942	11,144
Gem diamonds	108	7,595
General industrial machinery	30,603	26,321
Glass	2,125	1,750
Glassware	813	1,553
Gold, nonmonetary	5,673	3,035
Iron and steel mill products	5,637	11,285
Jewelry	729	4,588
Lighting, plumbing	$1,535	$2,944
Metal manufactures	10,309	12,242
Metalworking machinery	5,702	7,325
Nickel	347	1,144
Optical goods	1,697	2,493
Paper and paperboard	10,283	11,697
Photographic equipment	3,865	5,759
Plastic articles	5,092	6,676
Platinum	437	1,973
Pottery	101	1,683
Power generating machinery	27,221	24,601
Printed materials	4,605	2,871
Records/magnetic media	6,815	4,137
Rubber articles[1]	1,256	1,553
Rubber tires and tubes	2,394	3,417
Scientific instruments	24,039	13,969
Ships, boats	1,366	875
Silver and bullion	641	472
Spacecraft	994	239
Specialized industrial machinery	29,162	21,182
Televisions, VCRs, etc.	24,093	36,771
Textile yarn, fabric	8,975	11,951
Toys/games/sporting goods	3,827	17,374
Travel goods	330	3,841
Vehicles	55,669	112,926
Watches/clocks/parts	310	2,838
Wood manufactures	1,958	4,668
Mineral fuels	**12,682**	**78,277**
Coal	3,586	655
Crude oil	1,040	54,226
Liquefied propane/butane	298	1,158
Mineral fuels, other	3,355	1,864
Natural gas	275	5,477
Petroleum preparations	3,899	13,904
Selected commodities:		
Alcoholic bev., distilled	385	2,188
Cigarettes	4,417	75
Cork, wood, lumber	5,146	8,179
Crude fertilizers	1,621	1,334
Fish and preparations	2,624	7,687
Metal ores; scrap	4,662	4,156
Pulp and waste paper	3,868	2,639

Note: Not all products are listed in each commodity group. (1) Those not specified elsewhere.

MILLENNIUM FACT BOX

Trends in U.S. Foreign Trade Since 1790[1]

Source: Office of Trade and Economic Analysis, U.S. Dept. of Commerce

In 1790, U.S. exports and imports combined came to $43 million and there was a $3 million trade deficit. By 1997, U.S. exports and imports combined amounted to more than $1.5 trillion, and the trade deficit, which had generally been climbing in recent years (after a century of trade surpluses), reached more than $181 billion.

(in millions of dollars)

Year	Exports	Imports	Trade Balance
1790	$20	$23	$–3
1795	48	70	–22
1800	71	91	–20
1805	96	121	–25
1810	67	85	–19
1815	53	113	–60
1820	70	74	–5
1825	91	90	1
1830	72	63	9
1835	115	137	–22
1840	124	98	25
1845	106	113	–7
1850	144	174	–29
1855	219	258	–39
1860	334	354	–20
1865	166	239	–73
1870	393	436	–43
1875	513	533	–20
1880	836	668	168
1885	742	578	165
1890	858	789	69
1895	808	732	76
1900	$1,394	$850	$545
1905	1,519	1,118	401
1910	1,745	1,557	188
1915	2,769	1,674	1,094
1920	8,228	5,278	2,950
1925	4,910	4,227	683
1930	3,843	3,061	782
1935	2,283	2,047	235
1940	4,021	2,625	1,396
1945	9,806	4,159	5,646
1950	9,997	8,954	1,043
1955	14,298	11,566	2,732
1960	19,659	15,073	4,586
1965	26,742	21,520	5,222
1970	42,681	40,356	2,325
1975	107,652	98,503	9,149
1980	220,626	244,871	–24,245
1985	213,133	345,276	–132,143
1990	394,030	495,042	–101,012
1995	584,742	743,445	–158,703
1996	625,075	795,289	–170,214
1997	689,182	870,671	–181,489

(1) Because of rounding, not all totals add.

The North American Free Trade Agreement (NAFTA)

NAFTA, a comprehensive plan for free trade between the U.S., Canada, and Mexico, took effect on Jan. 1, 1994. Major provisions are as follows:

Agriculture—Tariffs on all farm products are to be eliminated over 15 years. Domestic price-support systems may continue provided they do not distort trade.

Automobiles—After 8 years, at least 62.5% of an automobile's value must have been produced in North America for it to qualify for duty-free status. Tariffs are to be phased out over 10 years.

Banking—U.S. and Canadian banks may acquire Mexican commercial banks accounting for as much as 8% of the industry's capital. All limits on ownership end in 2004.

Disputes—Special judges have jurisdiction to resolve disagreements within strict timetables.

Energy—Mexico continues to bar foreign ownership of its oil fields but, starting in 2004, U.S. and Canadian companies can bid on contracts offered by Mexican oil and electricity monopolies.

Environment—The agreement cannot be used to overrule national and state environmental, health, or safety laws.

Immigration—All 3 countries must ease restrictions on the movement of business executives and professionals.

Jobs—Barriers designed to limit Mexican migration to the U.S. remain in force.

Patent and copyright protection—Mexico strengthened its laws providing protection to intellectual property.

Tariffs—Tariffs on 10,000 customs goods are to be eliminated over 15 years. One-half of U.S. exports to Mexico are to be considered duty-free within 5 years.

Textiles—A "rule of origin" provision requires most garments to be made from yarn and fabric produced in North America. Most tariffs are being phased out over 5 years.

Trucking—Trucks are to have free access on crossborder routes and throughout the 3 countries by 1999.

U.S. Trade With Canada and Mexico, 1992-97

Source: Office of Trade and Economic Analysis, U.S. Dept. of Commerce

(millions of dollars)

MEXICO

Year	Exports	Imports	Trade Balance[1]
1992	$40,592	$35,211	$5,381
1993	41,581	39,917	1,664
1994[2]	50,844	49,494	1,350
1995	46,292	61,685	–15,393
1996	56,792	74,297	–17,506
1997	71,388	85,938	–14,549

CANADA

Year	Exports	Imports	Trade Balance[1]
1992	$90,594	$98,630	$–8,0361
1993	100,444	111,216	–10,772
1994[2]	114,439	128,406	–13,968
1995	127,226	145,349	–18,123
1996	134,210	155,893	–21,682
1997	151,767	168,201	–16,434

(1) Totals may not add due to rounding. (2) NAFTA provisions began to take effect Jan. 1, 1994.

50 Busiest U.S. Ports, 1996

Source: Corps of Engineers, Dept. of the Army, U.S. Dept. of Defense

(ports ranked by tonnage handled; all figures in tons)

Rank	Port	Total	Domestic	Foreign	Imports	Exports
1.	South Louisiana, LA, Port of	189,814,564	106,045,081	83,769,483	25,172,134	106,045,081
2.	Houston, TX	148,182,876	61,124,588	87,058,288	58,041,465	61,124,588
3.	New York, NY and NJ	131,601,244	75,115,630	56,485,614	48,472,360	75,115,630
4.	New Orleans, LA	83,726,470	36,813,969	46,912,501	20,840,444	36,813,969
5.	Baton Rouge, LA	81,009,253	45,222,690	35,788,563	24,803,274	45,222,690
6.	Corpus Christi, TX	80,460,088	23,841,943	56,618,145	49,158,007	23,841,943
7.	Valdez, AK	77,116,459	74,962,144	2,154,315	28,006	74,962,144
8.	Plaguemines, LA, Port of	66,910,237	46,221,107	20,689,130	6,394,967	46,221,107
9.	Long Beach, CA	58,395,243	22,367,442	36,027,801	17,586,084	22,367,442
10.	Texas City, TX	56,393,758	21,062,739	35,331,019	32,895,245	21,062,739
11.	Pittsburgh, PA	50,874,367	50,874,367	0	0	50,874,367
12.	Mobile, AL	50,863,944	25,368,474	25,495,470	13,133,946	25,368,474
13.	Tampa, FL	49,292,651	32,455,085	16,837,566	5,603,848	32,455,085
14.	Norfolk Harbor, VA	49,260,972	10,373,161	38,887,811	5,831,442	10,373,161
15.	Lake Charles, LA	49,096,325	19,745,486	29,350,839	24,779,328	19,745,486
16.	Los Angeles, CA	45,689,232	17,930,742	27,758,490	14,303,313	17,930,742
17.	Baltimore, MD	43,552,356	13,995,253	29,557,103	14,297,979	13,995,253
18.	Philadelphia, PA	41,882,200	13,015,275	28,866,925	28,221,332	13,015,275
19.	Duluth-Superior, MN & WI	41,398,293	30,247,130	11,151,163	1,087,294	30,247,130
20.	Port Arthur, TX	37,157,786	6,499,492	30,658,294	26,945,691	6,499,492
21.	Beaumont, TX	35,705,109	16,885,875	18,819,234	15,806,368	16,885,875
22.	St. Louis, MO & IL	30,161,905	30,161,905	0	0	30,161,905
23.	Portland, OR	29,733,913	13,185,558	16,548,355	3,058,501	13,185,558
24.	Pasquagoula, MS	29,342,671	9,049,918	20,292,753	17,450,158	9,049,918
25.	Chicago, IL	27,886,169	23,520,362	4,365,807	3,540,314	23,520,362
26.	Huntington, WV	27,478,215	27,478,215	0	0	27,478,215
27.	Paulsboro, NJ	25,038,524	10,122,925	14,915,599	14,610,448	10,122,925
28.	Newport News, VA	24,787,261	6,149,406	18,637,855	1,904,438	6,149,406
29.	Freeport, TX	24,570,954	5,372,850	19,198,104	17,474,251	5,372,850
30.	Seattle, WA	23,546,789	6,529,777	17,017,012	6,876,446	6,529,777
31.	Richmond, CA	21,802,748	16,435,324	5,367,424	3,344,985	16,435,324
32.	Tacoma, WA	21,490,783	7,254,817	14,235,966	4,087,540	7,254,817
33.	Boston, MA	20,103,978	9,414,556	10,689,422	10,035,099	9,414,556
34.	Port Everglades, FL	18,896,571	11,353,779	7,542,792	5,884,738	11,353,779
35.	Detroit, MI	18,603,745	12,310,105	6,293,640	5,646,698	12,310,105
36.	Savannah, GA	17,598,389	3,201,301	14,397,088	7,296,269	3,201,301
37.	Memphis, TN	17,299,836	17,299,836	0	0	17,299,836
38.	Indiana Harbor, IN	16,892,858	16,085,713	807,145	645,409	16,085,713
39.	Jacksonville, FL	16,736,773	9,264,866	7,471,907	5,970,161	9,264,866
40.	Cleveland, OH	16,720,837	12,743,288	3,977,549	3,367,610	12,743,288
41.	Lorain, OH	15,997,949	15,856,002	121,947	121,947	15,856,002
42.	Portland, ME	15,242,802	1,873,565	13,369,237	13,289,315	1,873,565
43.	San Juan, PR	15,112,223	10,324,064	4,788,159	3,991,274	10,324,064
44.	Anacortes, WA	13,843,669	11,829,632	2,014,037	547,053	11,829,632
45.	Toledo, OH	13,031,631	7,037,464	5,994,167	1,459,893	7,037,464
46.	Cincinnati, OH	12,803,247	12,803,247	0	0	12,803,247
47.	Marcus Hook, PA	12,365,946	7,200,109	5,165,837	5,125,343	7,200,109
48.	Honolulu, HI	12,010,003	10,350,170	1,659,833	1,470,971	10,350,170
49.	Galveston, TX	11,640,754	3,980,977	7,659,777	2,726,346	3,980,977
50.	Oakland, CA	11,229,862	2,580,330	8,649,532	2,948,029	2,580,330

Major Merchant Fleets of the World

Source: Maritime Administration, U.S. Dept of Commerce

Fleets of oceangoing steam and motor ships totaling 1,000 gross tons or more as of April 1998. Excludes ships operating exclusively on the Great Lakes and inland waterways and special types such as channel ships, icebreakers, cable ships, and merchant ships owned by any military force. Gross tonnage is a volume measurement; each cargo gross ton represents 100 cubic ft of enclosed space. Deadweight (Dwt) tonnage is carrying capacity of a ship in long tons (2,240 lb). Only some major types of vessels are shown separately. Tonnage figures may not add, because of rounding.

(tonnage in thousands)

	ALL VESSELS[1]			TYPE OF VESSEL: Tanker			Dry Bulk			Containership		
	No. of ships	Gross tons	Dwt tons	No. of ships	Gross tons	Dwt tons	No. of ships	Gross tons	Dwt tons	No. of ships	Gross tons	Dwt tons
All countries	28,073	483,757	748,601	6,917	178,202	311,057	5,821	160,304	281,010	2,238	50,431	57,237
United States	473	12,295	16,774	158	5,383	9,556	14	321	538	84	2,872	2,829
Privately owned	281	9,567	13,211	130	4,892	8,670	14	321	538	80	2,801	2,759
Government owned	192	2,728	3,563	28	491	886	—	—	—	4	71	70
Algeria	73	891	1,082	24	494	495	9	172	289	—	—	—
Antigua & Barbuda	386	2,105	2,723	10	27	39	10	180	296	81	903	1,149
Bahamas	990	24,854	38,917	239	12,184	22,346	153	4,746	8,281	45	950	942
Belize	321	1,407	2,137	40	354	672	19	179	266	5	32	32
Bermuda	93	4,727	7,679	32	2,657	4,631	20	1,771	2,249	17	589	549
Brazil	179	4,218	6,993	81	2,002	3,391	46	1,706	3,007	11	193	237
Bulgaria	100	1,075	1,552	12	168	282	34	532	834	5	58	67
Cambodia	94	373	534	1	1	3	10	133	206	1	2	3
China	1,503	14,707	22,402	258	2,063	3,329	328	6,390	10,762	99	1,393	1,709
Cyprus	1,461	23,340	36,858	171	4,111	7,240	514	11,881	20,509	114	2,097	2,465
Denmark (DIS)[2]	316	5,086	7,079	67	1,533	2,667	13	522	965	64	2,446	2,772
Egypt (UAR)	111	1,195	1,901	16	210	366	22	618	1057	—	—	—
Finland	91	1,193	1,105	16	344	570	6	80	121	—	—	—
Germany	472	6,753	8,364	19	185	282	—	—	—	253	5,553	7,036
Greece	769	24,096	43,185	263	12,619	24,042	330	9,417	16,805	40	1,030	1,107
Honduras	252	611	941	33	118	218	12	86	144	4	5	7
Hong Kong	186	5,965	10,029	6	175	324	106	4,343	8,055	41	888	1,008
India	291	6,399	10,704	94	2,895	5,011	131	2,958	4,957	6	84	111
Indonesia	499	2,265	3,508	136	830	1,333	23	343	549	7	68	90
Iran	122	3,297	5,828	27	1,764	3,430	47	1,024	1,704	3	10	12
Isle of Man	147	4,584	7,712	66	2,911	5,330	23	830	1,529	21	393	467
Italy	341	5,012	7,026	190	2,132	3,357	29	1,300	2,430	14	378	395
Japan	818	14,319	20,821	372	7,232	10,722	176	4,344	7,993	33	936	931
Korea (North)	100	566	774	4	5	9	9	105	174	—	—	—
Korea (South)	489	6,544	9,813	130	576	976	117	3,469	6,312	59	1,354	1,593
Liberia	1,609	59,070	96,068	667	31,791	55,929	480	17,754	31,505	158	3,813	4,420
Malaysia	386	4,688	6,859	118	1,986	2,760	54	1,327	2,323	43	599	720
Malta	1,279	22,996	38,281	329	9,643	17,660	372	8,747	15,016	43	700	783
Marshall Islands	124	6,140	10,527	38	3,406	6,432	42	1,597	2,886	22	995	1,066
Netherlands	489	4,001	4,718	67	613	966	8	177	289	40	1,177	1,223
Norway	126	1,940	3,070	42	1,635	2,869	7	19	21	—	—	—
Norway (NIS)[3]	662	19,944	31,261	295	11,572	20,741	109	4,064	7,225	5	67	89
Panama	4,406	91,927	140,565	963	26,160	45,304	1,293	39,787	69,776	436	10,838	12,004
Philippines	565	7,988	12,529	79	195	300	216	5,803	10,026	12	194	246
Poland	79	1,471	2,332	4	16	22	62	1,341	2,222	—	—	—
Portugal	105	805	1,276	30	466	759	9	130	243	3	15	19
Romania	209	2,084	3,127	9	243	421	38	834	1,358	2	16	16
Russia	1,513	7,177	8,957	274	1,635	2,428	117	1,366	2,017	25	278	308
Saint Vincent	808	7,868	12,102	107	1,339	2,402	142	3,180	5,516	24	129	150
Singapore	861	18,589	29,177	376	8,805	15,416	122	4,142	7,639	158	3,002	3,514
Spain	116	917	1,420	36	577	1,012	9	38	65	16	82	124
Sweden	177	2,165	1,850	63	523	864	8	29	41	—	—	—
Syria	129	385	551	—	—	—	2	13	20	—	—	—
Taiwan	197	5,709	8,791	17	904	1,554	53	2,372	4,408	85	2,290	2,617
Thailand	317	1,933	3,132	111	427	781	41	533	890	9	90	123
Turkey	542	5,923	9,812	81	615	1,057	177	4,121	7,148	8	65	91
Ukraine	293	1,707	1,853	24	71	97	11	241	393	4	51	48
United Kingdom	144	2,552	2,519	65	912	1,264	5	55	88	22	872	931
Vanuatu	81	1,244	1,530	10	115	162	27	603	1,007	—	—	—
Vietnam	126	470	726	12	33	57	9	92	149	—	—	—

(1) Includes combination passenger and cargo ships and other type of vessels not listed separately. (2) Danish international ship registry. (3) Norwegian international ship registry.

World Trade Organization (WTO)

Following World War II, the major economic powers of the world negotiated a set of rules for reducing and limiting trade barriers and for settling trade disputes. These rules were called the General Agreement on Tariffs and Trade (GATT). Headquarters to oversee the administration of the GATT were established in Geneva, Switzerland. Periodically, rounds of multilateral trade negotiations under the GATT were carried out. The 8th round, begun in 1986 in Punta del Este, Uruguay, and dubbed the Uruguay Round, concluded on Dec. 15, 1993, when 117 countries completed a new trade-liberalization agreement. The name for the GATT was changed to the World Trade Organization (WTO), which officially came into being Jan. 1, 1995.

New Passenger Cars Imported Into the U.S., by Country of Origin,[1] 1968-97

Source: Bureau of the Census, Foreign Trade Division

	Japan	Germany[2]	Italy	United Kingdom	Sweden	France	South Korea	Mexico	Canada	Total[3]
1968	169,849	707,972	33,843	96,787	52,515	39,551	NA	NA	500,881	1,620,452
1969	260,005	642,157	41,569	104,050	41,008	24,457	NA	NA	691,146	1,846,717
1970	381,338	674,945	42,523	76,257	57,844	37,114	NA	NA	692,783	2,013,420
1971	703,672	770,807	51,469	106,710	61,925	23,316	NA	0	802,281	2,587,484
1972	697,788	676,967	64,614	72,038	64,541	14,713	NA	9	842,300	2,485,901
1973	624,805	677,465	56,102	64,140	58,626	8,219	NA	4,469	871,557	2,437,345
1974	791,791	619,757	107,071	72,512	60,817	21,331	NA	3,914	817,559	2,572,557
1975	695,573	370,012	102,344	67,106	51,993	15,647	NA	0	733,766	2,074,653
1976	1,128,936	349,804	82,500	77,190	37,466	21,916	NA	0	825,590	2,536,749
1977	1,341,530	423,492	55,437	56,889	39,370	19,215	NA	NA	849,814	2,790,144
1978	1,563,047	416,231	69,689	54,478	56,140	28,502	NA	6	833,061	3,024,982
1979	1,617,328	495,565	72,456	46,911	65,907	27,887	NA	4	677,008	3,005,523
1980	1,991,502	338,711	46,899	32,517	61,496	47,386	NA	1	594,770	3,116,448
1981	1,911,525	234,052	21,635	12,728	68,042	42,477	NA	1	563,943	2,856,286
1982	1,801,185	259,385	9,402	13,023	89,231	50,032	NA	27	702,495	2,926,407
1983	1,871,192	239,807	5,442	17,261	114,726	40,823	NA	2	835,665	3,133,836
1984	1,948,714	335,032	8,582	19,833	114,854	37,788	NA	NA	1,073,425	3,559,427
1985	2,527,467	473,110	8,689	24,474	142,640	42,882	NA	13,647	1,144,805	4,397,679
1986	2,618,711	451,699	11,829	27,506	148,700	10,869	169,309	41,983	1,162,226	4,691,297
1987	2,417,509	377,542	8,648	50,059	138,565	26,707	399,856	126,266	926,927	4,589,010
1988	2,123,051	264,249	6,053	31,636	108,006	15,990	455,741	148,065	1,191,357	4,450,213
1989	2,051,525	216,881	9,319	29,378	101,571	4,885	270,609	133,049	1,151,122	4,042,728
1990	1,867,794	245,286	11,045	27,271	93,084	1,976	201,475	215,986	1,220,221	3,944,602
1991	1,762,347	171,097	2,886	14,862	62,905	1,727	186,740	249,498	1,109,248	3,612,665
1992	1,598,919	205,248	1,791	10,997	76,832	65	130,110	266,111	1,119,223	3,447,200
1993	1,501,953	180,383	1,178	20,029	58,742	23	122,943	299,634	1,371,856	3,604,361
1994	1,488,159	178,774	1,010	28,217	63,867	58	213,962	360,367	1,525,746	3,909,079
1995	1,114,360	204,932	1,031	42,450	82,593	14	131,718	462,800	1,552,691	3,624,428
1996	1,012,785	234,381	1,125	43,890	86,593	5	140,572	550,620	1,589,980	3,698,604
1997	1,387,419	300,013	1,530	43,325	79,725	18	222,539	543,494	1,727,542	4,372,227

(1) Excludes passenger cars assembled in U.S. foreign trade zones. (2) Figures prior to 1991 are for West Germany. (3) Includes countries not shown separately.

Passenger Car Production, U.S. Plants[1]

Source: American Automobile Manufacturers Assn.

	1996	1997
Chrysler Corp.		
Neon	100,358	80,617
Breeze	85,347	74,483
Prowler	0	463
Total Plymouth	**185,705**	**155,563**
Cirrus	37,870	38,057
Neon	12,992	6,039
Concorde	1,209	0
Total Chrysler-Plymouth	**237,776**	**199,659**
Neon	133,906	124,831
Stratus	109,550	114,437
Intrepid	35,291	0
Viper	1,669	1,790
Total Dodge	**280,416**	**241,058**
Total Chrysler Corp.	**518,192**	**440,717**
Ford Motor Co.		
Contour	154,962	186,329
Thunderbird	77,094	47,073
Taurus	436,786	371,861
Escort	236,718	238,981
Mustang	130,488	119,196
Total Ford	**1,036,048**	**913,440**
Cougar	34,495	24,019
Mystique	52,624	43,501
Sable	119,727	123,873
Lincoln Town Car	94,695	94,594
Mark	15,415	17,467
Continental	34,925	34,421
Tracer	37,890	38,473
Total Lincoln-Mercury	**389,711**	**376,348**
Total Ford Motor Co.	**1,425,769**	**1,289,788**
General Motors Corp.		
Caprice	66,263	0
Corvette	12,282	24,673
Beretta-Corsica	109,656	0
Cavalier	272,403	331,925
Geo Prizm	65,557	60,873
Malibu	11,550	233,349
Total Chevrolet	**537,711**	**650,820**
Grand Prix	108,939	163,911
Grand Am	244,066	237,531
Bonneville H	82,820	75,842
Sunfire	106,019	123,222
Total Pontiac	**641,844**	**600,506**
DeVille (K)	95,464	115,263
Fleetwood	9,411	0
Eldorado	20,113	21,783
Seville	37,261	32,866
Total Cadillac	**162,249**	**169,912**
Aurora	28,967	27,812
Delta 88	59,762	75,087
Oldsmobile 98	8,520	16
Achieva	40,187	58,116
Cutlass	2,935	40,171
Cutlass Supreme	87,475	21,737
Ciera	72,186	34
Intrigue	0	54,113
Total Oldsmobile	**300,032**	**277,086**
LeSabre	146,761	150,276
Roadmaster	14,007	0
Park Avenue	48,671	72,329
Riviera	21,593	13,604
Century	59,893	0
Skylark	51,613	51,446
Total Buick	**342,538**	**287,655**
Saturn	313,937	271,612
Toyota Cavalier	11,701	12,033
Total General Motors Corp.	**2,210,012**	**2,269,624**
Diamond Star		
Mitsubishi Eclipse	65,049	67,622
Mitsubishi Galant	57,013	42,820
Dodge Avenger	33,638	29,330
Chrysler Sebring	26,727	34,447
Eagle Talon	10,534	10,456
Total Mitsubishi Motor	**192,961**	**184,675**
BMW		
3 Series	9,666	0
Z3 Roadster	40,880	58,293
Total BMW	**50,546**	**58,293**
Honda		
Accord	424,462	415,588
Civic/Acura EL	186,838	201,439
Acura CL	23,048	31,241
Total Honda	**634,348**	**648,268**
Auto Alliance		
Probe	33,716	9,286
Mazda MX-6/626	95,726	90,830
Total Auto Alliance	**129,442**	**100,116**
Nissan		
Altima	141,714	163,934
Sentra	105,612	87,764
200 SX	30,543	27,812
Total Nissan	**277,869**	**279,510**
Subaru Legacy	**98,747**	**102,180**
Toyota		
Avalon	78,759	79,722
Corolla	158,974	149,147
Camry	307,618	325,241
Total Toyota	**545,351**	**554,110**
TOTAL Passenger Cars	**6,083,227**	**5,927,281**

(1) Not all models are listed.

Cars Registered in the U.S., 1900-96[1]

Source: American Automobile Manufacturers Assn.

(includes automobiles for public and private use)

Year	Cars Registered	Year	Cars Registered	Year	Cars Registered
1900	8,000	1945	25,796,985	1985	131,664,029
1905	77,400	1950	40,339,077	1990	143,549,627
1910	458,377	1955	52,144,739	1991	142,955,623
1915	2,332,426	1960	61,671,390	1992	144,213,429
1920	8,131,522	1965	75,257,588	1993	146,314,296
1925	17,481,001	1970	89,243,557	1994	133,929,662
1930	23,034,753	1975	106,705,934	1995	136,066,045
1935	22,567,827	1980	121,600,843	1996	129,728,341
1940	27,465,826				

1) There were no publicly owned vehicles before 1925; statistics also exclude military vehicles for all years. Alaska and Hawaii data included since 1960.

Domestic and Imported Retail Car Sales in the U.S., 1980-97

Source: American Automobile Manufacturers Assn.

Calendar year	Domestic	IMPORTS From Japan	From Germany	From other countries	Total imports	Total U.S. sales	Import % Total	Japan	U.S.-sponsored imports
1980	6,581,307	1,905,968	305,219	186,700	2,397,887	8,979,194	26.7	21.2	223,310
1981	6,208,760	1,858,896	282,881	185,502	2,327,279	8,536,039	27.3	21.8	174,665
1982	5,758,586	1,801,969	247,080	174,508	2,223,557	7,982,143	27.9	22.6	139,767
1983	6,795,295	1,915,621	279,748	191,403	2,386,772	9,182,067	26.0	20.9	136,798
1984	7,951,523	1,906,206	344,416	188,220	2,438,842	10,390,365	23.5	18.3	116,965
1985	8,204,542	2,217,837	423,983	195,925	2,837,745	11,042,287	25.7	20.1	206,252
1986	8,214,897	2,382,614	443,721	418,286	3,244,621	11,459,518	28.3	20.8	314,358
1987	7,080,858	2,190,405	347,881	657,465	3,195,751	10,276,609	31.1	21.3	348,154
1988	7,526,038	2,022,602	280,099	700,991	3,003,692	10,529,730	28.5	19.2	393,412
1989	7,072,902	1,897,143	248,561	553,660	2,699,364	9,772,266	27.6	19.4	340,425
1990	6,896,888	1,719,384	265,116	418,823	2,403,323	9,300,211	25.8	18.5	296,778
1991	6,136,757	1,500,309	192,776	344,814	2,037,899	8,174,656	24.9	18.4	280,673
1992	6,276,557	1,451,766	200,851	283,938	1,936,555	8,213,112	23.6	17.7	228,927
1993	6,741,667	1,328,445	186,177	261,570	1,776,192	8,517,859	20.9	15.6	185,284
1994	7,255,303	1,239,450	192,241	303,489	1,735,214	8,990,517	19.3	13.8	95,399
1995	7,128,712	981,462	207,555	317,269	1,506,257	8,634,964	17.4	11.4	99,657
1996	7,253,582	726,940	237,984	308,247	1,273,171	8,526,753	14.9	8.5	72,166
1997	6,916,769	726,104	297,028	332,173	1,355,305	8,272,074	16.4	8.8	87,107

Sport Utility Vehicle Sales in the U.S., 1988-97

Source: American Automobile Manufacturers Assn.

In 1988, 960,852 sport utility vehicles (SUVs) were sold in the United States, accounting for 6.3% of all sales of light vehicles (SUVs, minivans, vans, pickup trucks, and trucks under 14,000 lbs.). By 1997, sales of SUVs in the U.S. increased to 2,435,301, accounting for 16.1% of total light vehicle sales.

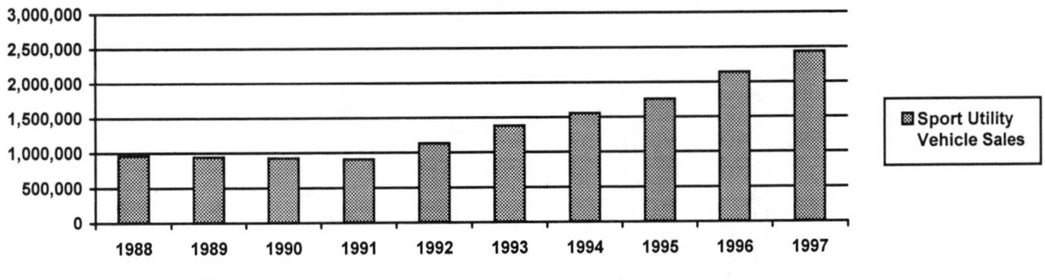

U.S. Car Sales by Type of Buyer, 1960-97

Source: American Automobile Manufacturers Assn.

Year	SALES IN THOUSANDS Consumer	Business	Government	Total[1]	% OF TOTAL SALES Consumer	Business
1997	3,880	4,233	131	8,245	47.1	51.3
1996	4,065	4,328	134	8,527	47.4	50.7
1995	4,313	4,211	162	8,686	49.7	48.5
1994	4,612	4,255	124	8,991	51.3	47.3
1993	4,669	3,941	108	8,718	53.6	45.2
1992	4,558	3,683	113	8,354	54.6	44.1
1991	4,538	3,752	97	8,387	54.1	44.8
1990	5,768	3,567	149	9,484	60.8	37.6
1989	6,375	3,402	136	9,913	64.3	34.3
1988	6,802	3,699	138	10,639	63.9	34.8
1987	6,748	3,395	135	10,278	65.7	33.0
1986	7,658	3,666	127	11,450	66.9	32.0
1985	7,083	3,822	134	11,039	64.2	34.6
1980	6,062	2,791	126	8,979	67.5	31.1
1975	5,907	2,508	123	8,538	69.2	29.4
1970	6,252	2,056	94	8,403	74.4	24.5
1965	7,106	2,149	89	9,344	76.0	23.0
1960	4,950	1,616	66	6,632	74.6	24.4

(1) Totals may not add, because of independent rounding.

U.S. Car Sales by Vehicle Size and Type, 1983, 1993, and 1997

Source: American Automobile Manufacturers Assn.

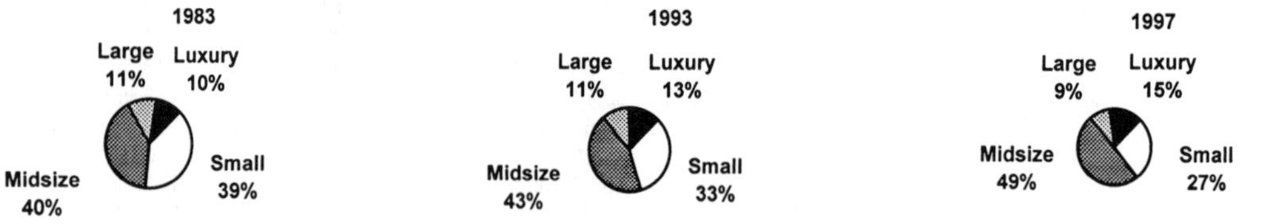

Top-Selling Passenger Cars in the U.S. by Calendar Year, 1993-97 (Domestic and Import)

Source: American Automobile Manufacturers Assn.

1997

Rank	Car	Sales
1.	Toyota Camry	397,156
2.	Honda Accord	384,609
3.	Ford Taurus	357,162
4.	Honda Civic	315,546
5.	Chevrolet Cavalier	302,161
6.	Ford Escort	283,898
7.	Saturn	250,810
8.	Chevrolet Lumina	228,451
9.	Toyota Corolla	218,461
10.	Pontiac Grand Am	204,078
11.	Chevrolet Malibu	164,654
12.	Ford Contour	151,060
13.	Buick LeSabre	150,744
14.	Nissan Altima	144,483
15.	Pontiac Grand Prix	142,018
16.	Nissan Maxima	123,215
17.	Nissan Sentra	122,468
18.	Dodge Neon	121,854
19.	Dodge Intrepid	118,537
20.	Ford Mustang	116,610

1996

Rank	Car	Sales
1.	Ford Taurus	401,049
2.	Honda Accord	382,298
3.	Toyota Camry	359,433
4.	Honda Civic	286,350
5.	Ford Escort	284,644
6.	Saturn	278,574
7.	Chevrolet Cavalier	277,222
8.	Chevrolet Lumina	237,973
9.	Pontiac Grand Am	222,477
10.	Toyota Corolla	209,048
11.	Ford Contour	174,187
12.	Chevrolet Corsica/Beretta	149,117
13.	Nissan Altima	147,910
14.	Dodge Intrepid	145,402
15.	Dodge Neon	139,831
16.	Buick LeSabre	131,316
17.	Nissan Sentra	129,596
18.	Nissan Maxima	128,395
19.	Ford Mustang	122,674
20.	Mercury Sable	114,164

1995

Rank	Car	Sales
1.	Ford Taurus	366,266
2.	Honda Accord	341,384
3.	Toyota Camry	328,595
4.	Honda Civic	289,435
5.	Saturn	285,674
6.	Ford Escort	285,570
7.	Dodge/Plymouth Neon	240,189
8.	Pontiac Grand Am	234,226
9.	Chevrolet Lumina	214,595
10.	Toyota Corolla	213,636

1994

Rank	Car	Sales
1.	Ford Taurus	397,031
2.	Honda Accord	367,615
3.	Ford Escort	336,967
4.	Toyota Camry	321,979
5.	Saturn	286,003
6.	Honda Civic	267,023
7.	Pontiac Grand Am	262,310
8.	Chevrolet Corsica/Beretta	222,129
9.	Toyota Corolla	210,926
10.	Chevrolet Cavalier	187,263

1993

Rank	Car	Sales
1.	Ford Taurus	360,448
2.	Honda Accord	330,030
3.	Toyota Camry	299,737
4.	Chevrolet Cavalier	273,617
5.	Ford Escort	269,034
6.	Honda Civic	255,579
7.	Saturn	229,356
8.	Chevrolet Lumina	219,683
9.	Ford Tempo	217,644
10.	Pontiac Grand Am	214,761

World Motor Vehicle Production, 1950-97

Source: American Automobile Manufacturers Assn.

(in thousands)

Year	United States	Canada	Europe	Japan	Other	World total	U.S. % of world total
1997	12,119	2,571	17,773	10,975	10,024	53,463	22.7
1996	11,799	2,397	17,550	10,346	9,241	51,332	23.0
1995	11,985	2,408	17,045	10,196	8,349	49,983	24.0
1994	12,263	2,321	16,195	10,554	8,167	49,500	24.8
1993	10,898	2,246	15,208	11,228	7,205	46,785	23.3
1992	9,729	1,961	17,628	12,499	6,269	48,088	20.2
1991	8,811	1,888	17,804	13,245	5,180	46,928	18.8
1990	9,783	1,928	18,866	13,487	4,496	48,554	20.1
1985	11,653	1,933	16,113	12,271	2,939	44,909	25.9
1980	8,010	1,324	15,496	11,043	2,692	38,565	20.8
1970	8,284	1,160	13,049	5,289	1,637	29,419	28.2
1960	7,905	398	6,837	482	866	16,488	47.9
1950	8,006	388	1,991	32	160	10,577	75.7

Note: As far as can be determined, production refers to vehicles locally manufactured.

Motor Vehicle Production by Selected Countries, 1997

Source: American Automobile Manufacturers Assn.

Country	Passenger cars	Commercial vehicles	Total
Argentina	366,466	79,579	446,045
Australia	320,000	29,000	349,000
Austria	97,774	10,215	107,989
Belgium	355,779	73,902	429,681
Brazil	1,679,644	387,808	2,067,452
Canada	1,373,561	1,197,561	2,571,122
China	481,611	1,096,287	1,577,898
Czech Republic	321,498	47,200	368,698
France	2,258,782	322,360	2,581,142
Germany	4,678,022	344,906	5,022,928
India	409,896	336,255	746,151
Italy	1,562,865	253,645	1,816,510
Japan	8,491,440	2,483,647	10,975,087
Korea, South	2,308,476	509,799	2,818,275
Malaysia	280,000	0	280,000
Mexico	854,809	503,304	1,358,113
Netherlands	197,225	20,428	217,653
Poland	294,767	27,050	321,817
Portugal	186,010	81,153	267,163
Romania	107,711	20,530	128,241
Russia	981,887	191,890	1,173,777
Spain	2,342,248	219,829	2,562,077
Sweden	375,705	104,034	479,739
Taiwan	268,060	113,043	381,103
Turkey	242,780	101,572	344,352
Ukraine	1,085	1,401	2,486
United Kingdom	1,698,015	237,703	1,935,718
United States	5,927,281	6,191,888	12,119,169
Yugoslavia, Fed. Rep.	11,124	2,379	13,503
Total	**38,474,521**	**14,988,368**	**53,462,889**

Licensed Drivers, by Age

Source: Federal Highway Administration, U.S. Dept. of Transportation

Age	1995 Male	1995 Female	1995 Total	1996 Male	1996 Female	1996 Total	1986 Total	Percent change total drivers 1986-96
under 16	30,833	27,827	58,660	15,343	13,651	28,994	96,000[1]	-69.80[1]
16	811,717	751,854	1,563,571	800,288	750,087	1,550,375	1,739,000	-10.85
17	1,169,351	1,081,243	2,250,594	1,198,089	1,114,889	2,312,978	2,397,000	-3.55
18	1,341,761	1,221,265	2,563,026	1,342,413	1,211,750	2,554,163	2,714,000	-5.89
19	1,407,905	1,280,369	2,688,274	1,454,111	1,333,378	2,787,489	2,975,000	-6.30
(19 and under)	4,761,567	4,362,558	9,124,125	4,810,244	4,423,755	9,234,000	2,921,000	-6.92
20	1,501,614	1,378,437	2,880,051	1,497,405	1,386,884	2,884,289	3,128,000	-7.82
21	1,510,552	1,402,840	2,913,392	1,502,939	1,413,063	2,916,002	3,392,000	-14.03
22	1,549,402	1,453,907	3,003,309	1,558,185	1,463,833	3,022,019	3,662,000	-17.48
23	1,645,621	1,555,962	3,201,583	1,604,854	1,513,211	3,118,065	3,836,000	-18.69
24	1,809,413	1,717,698	3,527,110	1,702,213	1,616,730	3,318,942	3,907,000	-15.05
(20-24)	8,016,601	7,508,844	15,525,445	7,865,595	7,393,721	15,259,317	17,925,000	-14.87
25-29	9,234,547	8,822,290	18,056,837	9,356,328	8,945,634	18,301,962	20,514,000	-10.78
30-34	10,255,668	10,028,055	20,283,723	10,120,589	9,870,916	19,991,504	19,599,000	2.00
35-39	10,381,712	10,277,348	20,659,060	10,520,825	10,438,935	20,959,760	17,777,000	17.90
40-44	9,512,860	9,465,126	18,977,987	9,775,750	9,751,892	19,527,642	14,095,000	38.54
45-49	8,469,713	8,401,960	16,871,673	8,754,215	8,710,255	17,464,470	11,167,000	56,39
50-54	6,493,069	6,397,959	12,891,029	6,839,745	6,763,244	13,602,989	9,872,000	37.79
55-59	5,167,725	5,057,785	10,225,511	5,341,398	5,258,010	10,599,409	9,766,000	8.54
60-64	4,530,005	4,428,256	8,958,261	4,565,061	4,485,658	9,050,719	9,276,000	-2.43
65-69	4,248,092	4,234,797	8,482,889	4,234,471	4,230,660	8,465,131	7,790,000	8.67
70-74	3,582,678	3,702,020	7,284,698	3,604,445	3,749,142	7,353,587	11,785,000	44.95
75-79	2,465,550	2,577,527	5,043,077	2,562,955	2,716,477	5,279,432	NA	NA
80-84	1,358,182	1,439,180	2,797,361	1,400,321	1,515,635	2,915,955	NA	NA
85 and over	736,399	710,409	1,446,808	766,714	766,750	1,533,464	NA	NA
TOTAL	**89,214,367**	**87,414,115**	**176,628,482**	**90,518,656**	**89,020,684**	**179,539,340**	**159,486,000**	**12.57**

(1) Comparisons between "licensed" drivers under age 16 in 1986 and in 1996 are not entirely valid because of a change in definition in 1990, which interpreted "licensed" drivers more strictly than before. NA = not available.

Highway Speed Limits, by State

Source: National Motorists Association

Under the National Highway System Designation Act, signed Nov. 28, 1995, by Pres. Bill Clinton, states were allowed to set their own highway speed limits, as of Dec. 8, 1995. Under federal legislation enacted in 1974 during the energy crisis, states had been, in effect, restricted to a National Maximum Speed Limit (NMSL) of 55 miles per hour (raised in 1987 to 65 mph on rural interstates). New maximum speed limits by state are given in the table below; all speeds are given in miles per hour. Most data current as of Sept. 1, 1998. For more information visit the National Motorists Association's website at http://www.motorists.org

State	Cars Interstate	Cars Other Primary	Trucks Interstate	Trucks Other Primary
AL	70	65	70	65
AK	65	55	65	55
AZ	75	55	75	55
AR	70	55	65	55
CA	70	65	55	55
CO	75	65	75	65
CT	65	65	65	65
DE	65	50	65	50
FL	70	65	70	65
GA	70	65	70	65
HI	55	55	55	55
ID	75	65	65	65
IL	65	65	55	65
IN	65	55	60	55
IA	65	65	65	65
KS	70	65	70	65
KY	65	55	65	55
LA	70	65	70	65
ME	65	55	65	55
MA	65	55	65	55
MA	65	65	65	65
MI	70	70	55	55
MN	70	65	70	65
MS	70	70	70	70
MO	70	70	70	70
MT	*/65	*/55	65[1]	60[1]/55
NE	75	65	75	65
NV	75	70	75	70
NH	65	55	65	55
NJ	65	65	65	65
NM	75	65	75	65
NY	65	55	65[2]	55
NC	70	55	70	55
ND	70	65/55	70	65/55
OH	65	65	55	55
OK	75	70	75	70
OR	65	55	55	55
PA	65	55	65	55
RI	65	55	65	55
SC	65	55	65	55
SD	75	65	65	55
TN	65	65	65	65
TX	70/65	70/65	60/55	60/55
UT	75	65	75	65
VT	65	50	65	50
VA	65	55	65	55
WA	70	55	60	55
WV	70	55	70	55
WI	65	65	65	65
WY	75	65	75	65

(1) 55 mph for triple-trailer trucks. (2) 55 mph for double-trailer trucks on the Thruway.

Note: Where two speeds are given, the first is for daytime and the second for nighttime. "Daytime" means from one-half hour before sunrise to one-half hour after sunset; "nighttime" means at any other hour.

* Denotes that drivers are required to restrict themselves to "reasonable and prudent" speeds, i.e., they must operate on a public street or highway in a careful and prudent manner, and at a rate of speed no greater than is reasonable and proper under the conditions existing at the point of operation, taking into account the amount and character of traffic, condition of brakes, weight of vehicle, grade and width of highway, condition of surface, and freedom of obstruction to view ahead, and they must not drive so as to unduly or unreasonably endanger the life, limb, property, or other rights of a person entitled to the use of the street or highway.

The Most Popular Colors, by Type of Vehicle, 1997 Model Year

Source: American Automobile Manufacturers Assn.

Luxury cars		Full size/ intermediate cars		Compact/sports cars		Light trucks and vans	
Color	**%**	**Color**	**%**	**Color**	**%**	**Color**	**%**
Light brown	19.8	Med./dark Green	17.5	Med./dark Green	20.3	White	23.2
Med./dark Green	13.0	White	17.0	White	13.9	Med./dark Green	18.5
White Metallic	12.6	Light Brown	14.4	Black	12.9	Black	11.2
Black	11.0	Black	8.0	Light Brown	12.8	Bright Red	7.6
White	10.1	Medium Red	7.4	Bright Red	9.1	Medium Red	7.5
Silver	6.7	Medium Grey	6.6	Medium Red	7.5	Light Brown	6.1
Light Green	5.7	Dark Red	5.2	Silver	5.7	Dark Red	5.2
Medium Red	5.2	Silver	4.8	Med./dark Blue	5.4	Silver	3.7
Dark Red	4.6	Bright Red	4.0	Purple	3.4	Med./dark Blue	2.9
Dark Blue	4.0	Medium Blue	3.9	Bright Blue	2.7	Teal/Aqua	2.6
Other	7.3	Other	11.2	Other	6.3	Other	11.8

Selected Motor Vehicle Statistics

Source: Federal Highway Administration; U.S. Dept. of Transportation; Insurance Institute for Highway Safety; 1996 figures where not otherwise specified.

State	Driver's age (Jan 1, 1997) Regular[1]	Driver's age (Jan 1, 1997) Learner's Permit	State gas tax cents/ gal. (July 1 1998)	Safety belt use law[8]	Lic. drivers per 1,000 resident pop.	Regist. motor vehicles per 1,000 pop.	Licensed drivers per motor vehicle	Gals. of fuel used per vehicle	Miles per gal.	Annual miles driven per vehicle	Vehicle miles per licensed driver
Alabama	16	15	18	S	734	778	0.94	880	17.58	15,475	16,389
Alaska	16	14	8	S	725	875	0.83	633	12.25	7,749	9,355
Arizona	16	15y, 7m	18	S	616	674	0.91	869	16.26	14,123	15,445
Arkansas	16	14	18.6	S	698	651	1.07	1,115	15.29	17,045	15,888
California	17	15	18	P	635	791	0.80	612	18.02	11,027	13,731
Colorado	16	15y, 3m	22	S	721	898	0.80	598	17.59	10,527	13,110
Connecticut	16y,6m[2]	16	33	P	716	797	0.90	576	18.71	10,785	12,004
Delaware	15y, 10 m[3]	16y, 10m[3]	23	S	730	818	0.89	687	18.81	12,927	14,484
Dist. of Col.	16	16	20	P	614	437	1.40	767	18.22	13,967	9,945
Florida	18	15	13	S	792	756	1.05	698	17.11	11,939	11,404
Georgia	18	15	7.5	P	675	854	0.79	858	16.53	14,187	17,947
Hawaii	15	15	16	P	620	664	0.93	526	19.41	10,217	10,948
Idaho	15	15	25	S	689	892	0.77	715	17.09	12,214	15,812
Illinois	17	15	19	S	642	744	0.86	654	16.76	10,971	12,712
Indiana	18	15	15	P	634	893	0.71	736	17.26	12,697	17,877
Iowa	17[4]	14[4]	20	P	686	1,006	0.68	661	14.17	9,368	13,745
Kansas	16	14	18	S	695	820	0.85	765	16.08	12,296	14,507
Kentucky	16y, 6 m	16	16.4	S	661	694	0.95	881	17.93	15,796	16,593
Louisiana	17	15	20	P	603	763	0.79	784	14.65	11,481	14,517
Maine	16	15	19	S	703	771	0.91	788	16.97	13,372	14,672
Maryland	17y, 7m[3]	15y, 9m[3]	23.5	P	666	717	0.93	693	18.34	12,708	13,675
Massachusetts	18	16	21	S	715	772	0.93	598	17.76	10,624	11,471
Michigan	17	14y, 9m	19	S	700	835	0.84	667	16.88	11,262	13,431
Minnesota	17[4,5]	15[4]	20	S	608	829	0.73	711	16.19	11,517	15,711
Mississippi	16	15	18.4	S	626	803	0.78	830	16.87	14,008	17,976
Missouri	16	15y, 6m	17	S	700	812	0.86	835	16.83	14,059	16,313
Montana	15	14y, 6m	27	S	652	1,107	0.59	629	15.42	9,707	16,464
Nebraska	17[4]	15[4]	24.6	S	702	895	0.78	762	14.42	10,982	14,000
Nevada	16	15y, 6m	24.75	S	697	683	1.02	920	14.04	12,922	12,677
New Hampshire	18	16	19.5	No	787	957	0.82	574	17.22	9,879	12,002
New Jersey	17	16	10.5	S	687	729	0.94	718	14.90	10,707	11,362
New Mexico	15	15	18.875	P	688	901	0.76	739	18.84	13,926	18,240
New York	18[6]	16[7]	22.65	P	577	585	0.99	599	18.63	11,155	11,317
North Carolina	16y, 6m	15	21.6	P	708	786	0.90	772	17.75	13,706	15,217
North Dakota	16	14	20	S	698	1,055	0.66	704	14.11	9,927	15,006
Ohio	17[4]	15y, 6m[4]	22	S	703	874	0.80	618	17.09	10,551	13,128
Oklahoma	16	15y, 6m	17	P	726	934	0.78	756	16.92	12,794	16,457
Oregon	16	15	24	P	816	890	0.92	645	16.48	10,634	11,605
Pennsylvania	18[6]	16	25.9	S	682	717	0.95	685	16.32	11,186	11,756
Rhode Island	17[4]	16[4]	29	S	676	703	0.96	605	16.92	10,231	10,644
South Carolina	16y, 3m	15	16	S	696	754	0.92	871	16.35	14,247	15,442
South Dakota	14	14	21	S	708	1,025	0.69	728	14.30	10,408	15,074
Tennessee	16	15	20	S	715	908	0.79	712	16.99	12,097	15,355
Texas	16	15	20	P	657	705	0.93	855	16.08	13,746	14,750
Utah	16	16	24.5	S	659	722	0.91	783	17.27	13,521	14,811
Vermont	16	15	20	S	797	855	0.93	796	15.93	12,674	13,601
Virginia	16	15	17.5	S	703	835	0.84	727	17.59	12,787	15,196
Washington	16	15	23	S	706	832	0.85	661	16.24	10,733	12,641
West Virginia	16	15	25.35	S	698	770	0.91	681	18.48	12,581	13,883
Wisconsin	16	15y, 6m	23.8	S	722	770	0.94	735	18.07	13,290	14,175
Wyoming	16	15	14	S	713	1,168	0.61	981	13.35	13,095	21,452
Average					**677**	**778**	**0.87**	**711**	**16.92**	**12,028**	**13,825**

Note: Many states are moving toward graduated licensing systems that phase in full driving privileges. During the learner's phase, driving generally is not permitted unless there is an adult supervisor. In an intermediate phase, young licensees not yet having unrestricted licenses may be allowed to drive unsupervised under certain conditions but not others. (1) Unrestricted operation of private passenger car. (2) Applicant may get an unrestricted license at age 16, 4 mo., upon completion of an approved driver education course. (3) Effective 7/1/99. (4) Effective 1/1/99. (5) Sixteen-year-olds with provisional licenses have no restrictions on when or where they can drive but are subject to sanctions that do not apply to regular license holders. (6) Applicant may get an unrestricted license at age 17 upon completion of an approved driver education course. (7) Driving in New York City is prohibited; driving in Nassau and Suffolk Counties is limited. (8) As of Sept. 1, 1998. P = officer may stop vehicle for a violation (primary); S = an officer may issue seat belt citation only when vehicle is stopped for another moving violation (secondary).

Road Mileage Between Selected U.S. Cities

	Atlanta	Boston	Chicago	Cincinnati	Cleveland	Dallas	Denver	Des Moines	Detroit	Houston
Atlanta, Ga.	...	1,037	674	440	672	795	1,398	870	699	789
Boston, Mass.	1,037	...	963	840	628	1,748	1,949	1,280	695	1,804
Chicago, Ill.	674	963	...	287	335	917	996	327	266	1,067
Cincinnati, Oh.	440	840	287	...	244	920	1,164	571	259	1,029
Cleveland, Oh.	672	628	335	244	...	1,159	1,321	652	170	1,273
Dallas Tex.	795	1,748	917	920	1,159	...	781	684	1,143	243
Denver, Col.	1,398	1,949	996	1,164	1,321	781	...	669	1,253	1,019
Detroit, Mich.	699	695	266	259	170	1,143	1,253	584	...	1,265
Houston, Tex.	789	1,804	1,067	1,029	1,273	243	1,019	905	1,265	...
Indianapolis, Ind.	493	906	181	106	294	865	1,058	465	278	987
Kansas City, Mo.	798	1,391	499	591	779	489	600	195	743	710
Los Angeles, Cal.	2,182	2,979	2,054	2,179	2,367	1,387	1,059	1,727	2,311	1,538
Memphis, Tenn.	371	1,296	530	468	712	452	1,040	599	713	561
Milwaukee, Wis.	761	1,050	87	374	422	991	1,029	361	353	1,142
Minneapolis, Minn.	1,068	1,368	405	692	740	936	841	252	671	1,157
New Orleans, La.	479	1,507	912	786	1,030	496	1,273	978	1,045	356
New York, N.Y.	841	206	802	647	473	1,552	1,771	1,119	637	1,608
Omaha, Neb.	986	1,412	459	693	784	644	537	132	716	865
Philadelphia, Pa.	741	296	738	567	413	1,452	1,691	1,051	573	1,508
Pittsburgh, Pa.	687	561	452	287	129	1,204	1,411	763	287	1,313
Portland Ore.	2,601	3,046	2,083	2,333	2,418	2,009	1,238	1,786	2,349	2,205
St. Louis, Mo.	541	1,141	289	340	529	630	857	333	513	779
San Francisco	2,496	3,095	2,142	2,362	2,467	1,753	1,235	1,815	2,399	1,912
Seattle, Wash.	2,618	2,976	2,013	2,300	2,348	2,078	1,307	1,749	2,279	2,274
Tulsa, Okla.	772	1,537	683	736	925	257	681	443	909	478
Washington, DC	608	429	671	481	346	1,319	1,616	984	506	1,375

	Indianapolis	Kansas City	Los Angeles	Louisville	Memphis	Milwaukee	Minneapolis	New Orleans	New York	Omaha
Atlanta, Ga.	493	798	2,182	382	371	761	1,068	479	841	986
Boston, Mass.	906	1,391	2,979	941	1,296	1,050	1,368	1,507	206	1,412
Chicago, Ill.	181	499	2,054	292	530	87	405	912	802	459
Cincinnati, Oh.	106	591	2,179	101	468	374	692	786	647	693
Cleveland Oh.	294	779	2,367	345	712	422	740	1,030	473	784
Dallas, Tex.	865	489	1,387	819	452	991	936	496	1,552	644
Denver, Col.	1,058	600	1,059	1,120	1,040	1,029	841	1,273	1,771	537
Detroit, Mich.	278	743	2,311	360	713	353	671	1,045	637	716
Houston, Tex.	987	710	1,538	928	561	1,142	1,157	356	1,608	865
Indianapolis, Ind.	...	485	2,073	111	435	268	586	796	713	587
Kansas City, Mo.	485	...	1,589	520	451	537	447	806	1,198	201
Los Angeles, Cal.	2,073	1,589	...	2,108	1,817	2,087	1,889	1,883	2,786	1,595
Memphis, Tenn.	435	451	1,817	367	...	612	826	390	1,100	652
Milwaukee, Wis.	268	537	2,087	379	612	...	332	994	889	493
Minneapolis, Minn.	586	447	1,889	697	826	332	...	1,214	1,207	357
New Orleans, La.	796	806	1,883	685	390	994	1,214	...	1,311	1,007
New York, N.Y.	713	1,198	2,786	748	1,100	889	1,207	1,311	...	1,251
Omaha, Neb.	587	201	1,595	687	652	493	357	1,007	1,251	...
Philadelphia, Pa.	633	1,118	2,706	668	1,000	825	1,143	1,211	100	1,183
Pittsburgh, Pa.	353	838	2,426	388	752	539	857	1,070	368	895
Portland, Ore.	2,272	1,809	959	2,320	2,259	2,010	1,678	2,505	2,885	1,654
St. Louis, Mo.	235	257	1,845	263	285	363	552	673	948	449
San Francisco	2,293	1,835	379	2,349	2,125	2,175	1,940	2,249	2,934	1,683
Seattle, Wash.	2,194	1,839	1,131	2,305	2,290	1,940	1,608	2,574	2,815	1,638
Tulsa, Okla.	631	248	1,452	659	401	757	695	647	1,344	387
Washington, DC	558	1,043	2,631	582	867	758	1,076	1,078	233	1,116

	Philadelphia	Pittsburgh	Portland	St. Louis	Salt Lake City	San Francisco	Seattle	Toledo	Tulsa	Wash., DC
Atlanta, Ga.	741	687	2,601	541	1,878	2,496	2,618	640	772	608
Boston, Mass.	296	561	3,046	1,141	2,343	3,095	2,976	739	1,537	429
Chicago, Ill.	738	452	2,083	289	1,390	2,142	2,013	232	683	671
Cincinnati, Oh.	567	287	2,333	340	1,610	2,362	2,300	200	736	481
Cleveland Oh.	413	129	2,418	529	1,715	2,467	2,348	111	925	346
Dallas, Tex.	1,452	1,204	2,009	630	1,242	1,753	2,078	1,084	257	1,319
Denver, Col.	1,691	1,411	1,238	857	504	1,235	1,307	1,218	681	1,616
Detroit, Mich.	576	287	2,349	513	1,647	2,399	2,279	59	909	506
Houston, Tex.	1,508	1,313	2,205	779	1,438	1,912	2,274	1,206	478	1,375
Indianapolis, Ind.	633	353	2,272	235	1,504	2,293	2,194	219	631	558
Kansas City, Mo.	1,118	838	1,809	257	1,086	1,835	1,839	687	248	1,043
Los Angeles, Cal.	2,706	2,426	959	1,845	715	379	1,131	2,276	1,452	2,631
Memphis, Tenn.	1,000	752	2,259	285	1,535	2,125	2,290	654	401	867
Milwaukee, Wis.	825	539	2,010	363	1,423	2,175	1,940	319	757	758
Minneapolis, Minn.	1,143	857	1,678	552	1,186	1,940	1,608	637	695	1,076
New Orleans, La.	1,211	1,070	2,505	673	1,738	2,249	2,574	986	647	1,078
New York, N.Y.	100	368	2,885	948	2,182	2,934	2,815	578	1,344	233
Omaha, Neb.	1,183	895	1,654	449	931	1,683	1,638	681	387	1,116
Philadelphia, Pa.	...	288	2,821	868	2,114	2,866	2,751	514	1,264	133
Pittsburgh, Pa.	288	...	2,535	588	1,826	2,578	2,465	228	984	221
Portland, Ore.	2,821	2,535	...	2,060	767	636	172	2,315	1,913	2,754
St. Louis, Mo.	868	588	2,060	...	1,337	2,089	2,081	454	396	793
San Francisco	2,866	2,578	636	2,089	752	...	808	2,364	1,760	2,799
Seattle, Wash.	2,751	2,465	172	2,081	836	808	...	2,245	1,982	2,684
Tulsa, Okla.	1,264	984	1,913	396	1,172	1,760	1,982	850	...	1,189
Washington, DC	133	221	2,754	793	2,047	2,799	2,684	447	1,189	...

Air Distances Between Selected World Cities in Statute Miles

Point-to-point measurements are usually from City Hall.

	Bangkok	Beijing	Berlin	Cairo	Cape Town	Caracas	Chicago	Hong Kong	Hono-lulu	Lima
Bangkok	...	2,046	5,352	4,523	6,300	10,555	8,570	1,077	6,609	12,244
Beijing	2,046	...	4,584	4,698	8,044	8,950	6,604	1,217	5,077	10,349
Berlin	5,352	4,584	...	1,797	5,961	5,238	4,414	5,443	7,320	6,896
Cairo	4,523	4,698	1,797	...	4,480	6,342	6,141	5,066	8,848	7,726
Cape Town	6,300	8,044	5,961	4,480	...	6,366	8,491	7,376	11,535	6,072
Caracas	10,555	8,950	5,238	6,342	6,366	...	2,495	10,165	6,021	1,707
Chicago	8,570	6,604	4,414	6,141	8,491	2,495	...	7,797	4,256	3,775
Hong Kong	1,077	1,217	5,443	5,066	7,376	10,165	7,797	...	5,556	11,418
Honolulu	6,609	5,077	7,320	8,848	11,535	6,021	4,256	5,556	...	5,947
London	5,944	5,074	583	2,185	5,989	4,655	3,958	5,990	7,240	6,316
Los Angeles	7,637	6,250	5,782	7,520	9,969	3,632	1,745	7,240	2,557	4,171
Madrid	6,337	5,745	1,165	2,087	5,308	4,346	4,189	6,558	7,872	5,907
Melbourne	4,568	5,643	9,918	8,675	6,425	9,717	9,673	4,595	5,505	8,059
Mexico City	9,793	7,753	6,056	7,700	8,519	2,234	1,690	8,788	3,789	2,639
Montreal	8,338	6,519	3,740	5,427	7,922	2,438	745	7,736	4,918	3,970
Moscow	4,389	3,607	1,006	1,803	6,279	6,177	4,987	4,437	7,047	7,862
New York	8,669	6,844	3,979	5,619	7,803	2,120	714	8,060	4,969	3,639
Paris	5,877	5,120	548	1,998	5,786	4,732	4,143	5,990	7,449	6,370
Rio de Janeiro	9,994	10,768	6,209	6,143	3,781	2,804	5,282	11,009	8,288	2,342
Rome	5,494	5,063	737	1,326	5,231	5,195	4,824	5,774	8,040	6,750
San Francisco	7,931	5,918	5,672	7,466	10,248	3,902	1,859	6,905	2,398	4,518
Singapore	883	2,771	6,164	5,137	6,008	11,402	9,372	1,605	6,726	11,689
Stockholm	5,089	4,133	528	2,096	6,423	5,471	4,331	5,063	6,875	7,166
Tokyo	2,865	1,307	5,557	5,958	9,154	8,808	6,314	1,791	3,859	9,631
Warsaw	5,033	4,325	322	1,619	5,935	5,559	4,679	5,147	7,366	7,215
Washington, DC	8,807	6,942	4,181	5,822	7,895	2,047	596	8,155	4,838	3,509

	London	Los An-geles	Madrid	Mel-bourne	Mexico City	Mon-treal	Moscow	New Delhi	New York	Paris
Bangkok	5,944	7,637	6,337	4,568	9,793	8,338	4,389	1,813	8,669	5,877
Beijing	5,074	6,250	5,745	5,643	7,753	6,519	3,607	2,353	6,844	5,120
Berlin	583	5,782	1,165	9,918	6,056	3,740	1,006	3,598	3,979	548
Cairo	2,185	7,520	2,087	8,675	7,700	5,427	1,803	2,758	5,619	1,998
Cape Town	5,989	9,969	5,308	6,425	8,519	7,922	6,279	5,769	7,803	5,786
Caracas	4,655	3,632	4,346	9,717	2,234	2,438	6,177	8,833	2,120	4,732
Chicago	3,958	1,745	4,189	9,673	1,690	745	4,987	7,486	714	4,143
Hong Kong	5,990	7,240	6,558	4,595	8,788	7,736	4,437	2,339	8,060	5,990
Honolulu	7,240	2,557	7,872	5,505	3,789	4,918	7,047	7,412	4,969	7,449
London	...	5,439	785	10,500	5,558	3,254	1,564	4,181	3,469	214
Los Angeles	5,439	...	5,848	7,931	1,542	2,427	6,068	7,011	2,451	5,601
Madrid	785	5,848	...	10,758	5,643	3,448	2,147	4,530	3,593	655
Melbourne	10,500	7,931	10,758	...	8,426	10,395	8,950	6,329	10,359	10,430
Mexico City	5,558	1,542	5,643	8,426	...	2,317	6,676	9,120	2,090	5,725
Montreal	3,254	2,427	3,448	10,395	2,317	...	4,401	7,012	331	3,432
Moscow	1,564	6,068	2,147	8,950	6,676	4,401	...	2,698	4,683	1,554
New York	3,469	2,451	3,593	10,359	2,090	331	4,683	7,318	...	3,636
Paris	214	5,601	655	10,430	5,725	3,432	1,554	4,102	3,636	...
Rio de Janeiro	5,750	6,330	5,045	8,226	4,764	5,078	7,170	8,753	4,801	5,684
Rome	895	6,326	851	9,929	6,377	4,104	1,483	3,684	4,293	690
San Francisco	5,367	347	5,803	7,856	1,887	2,543	5,885	7,691	2,572	5,577
Singapore	6,747	8,767	7,080	3,759	10,327	9,203	5,228	2,571	9,534	6,673
Stockholm	942	5,454	1,653	9,630	6,012	3,714	716	3,414	3,986	1,003
Tokyo	5,959	5,470	6,706	5,062	7,035	6,471	4,660	3,638	6,757	6,053
Warsaw	905	5,922	1,427	9,598	6,337	4,022	721	3,277	4,270	852
Washington, DC	3,674	2,300	3,792	10,180	1,885	489	4,876	7,500	205	3,840

	Rio de Janeiro	Rome	San Fran-cisco	Singa-pore	Stock-holm	Tehran	Tokyo	Vienna	Warsaw	Wash., DC
Bangkok	9,994	5,494	7,931	883	5,089	3,391	2,865	5,252	5,033	8,807
Beijing	10,768	5,063	5,918	2,771	4,133	3,490	1,307	4,648	4,325	6,942
Berlin	6,209	737	5,672	6,164	528	2,185	5,557	326	322	4,181
Cairo	6,143	1,326	7,466	5,137	2,096	1,234	5,958	1,481	1,619	5,822
Cape Town	3,781	5,231	10,248	6,008	6,423	5,241	9,154	5,656	5,935	7,895
Caracas	2,804	5,195	3,902	11,402	5,471	7,320	8,808	5,372	5,559	2,047
Chicago	5,282	4,824	1,859	9,372	4,331	6,502	6,314	4,698	4,679	596
Hong Kong	11,009	5,774	6,905	1,605	5,063	3,843	1,791	5,431	5,147	8,155
Honolulu	8,288	8,040	2,398	6,726	6,875	8,070	3,859	7,632	7,366	4,838
London	5,750	895	5,367	6,747	942	2,743	5,959	771	905	3,674
Los Angeles	6,330	6,326	347	8,767	5,454	7,682	5,470	6,108	5,922	2,300
Madrid	5,045	851	5,803	7,080	1,653	2,978	6,706	1,128	1,427	3,792
Melbourne	8,226	9,929	7,856	3,759	9,630	7,826	5,062	9,790	9,598	10,180
Mexico City	4,764	6,377	1,887	10,327	6,012	8,184	7,035	6,320	6,337	1,885
Montreal	5,078	4,104	2,543	9,203	3,714	5,880	6,471	4,009	4,022	489
Moscow	7,170	1,483	5,885	5,228	716	1,532	4,660	1,043	721	4,876
New York	4,801	4,293	2,572	9,534	3,986	6,141	6,757	4,234	4,270	205
Paris	5,684	690	5,577	6,673	1,003	2,625	6,053	645	852	3,840
Rio de Janeiro	...	5,707	6,613	9,785	6,683	7,374	11,532	6,127	6,455	4,779
Rome	5,707	...	6,259	6,229	1,245	2,127	6,142	477	820	4,497
San Francisco	6,613	6,259	...	8,448	5,399	7,362	5,150	5,994	5,854	2,441
Singapore	9,785	6,229	8,448	...	5,936	4,103	3,300	6,035	5,843	9,662
Stockholm	6,683	1,245	5,399	5,936	...	2,173	5,053	780	494	4,183
Tokyo	11,532	6,142	5,150	3,300	5,053	4,775	...	5,689	5,347	6,791
Warsaw	6,455	820	5,854	5,843	494	1,879	5,689	347	...	4,472
Washington, DC	4,779	4,497	2,441	9,662	4,183	6,341	6,791	4,438	4,472	...

TRAVEL AND TOURISM

World Tourism Receipts, 1988-97

Source: World Tourism Organization

(in billions)

Global spending on travel and tourism has more than doubled over the decade as the standard of living for most people in the world has risen and more countries have become accessible to tourists.

1988	$204.7	1990	$269.2	1992	$315.5	1994	$353.5	1996	$438.8
1989	221.0	1991	277.6	1993	322.3	1995	403.6	1997	447.7

World's Top 10 Tourist Destinations, 1997

(number of arrivals in millions; excluding same-day visitors)

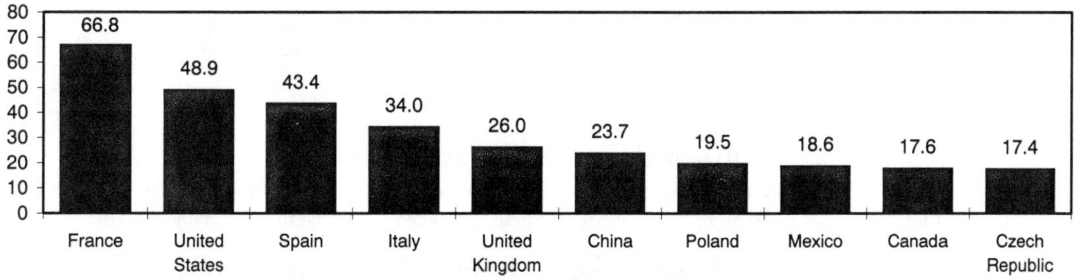

International Travel to the U.S., 1986-97

Source: Dept. of Commerce, Tourism Industries, International Trade Adm.

(Visitors each year, in millions; 1997 total is estimated)

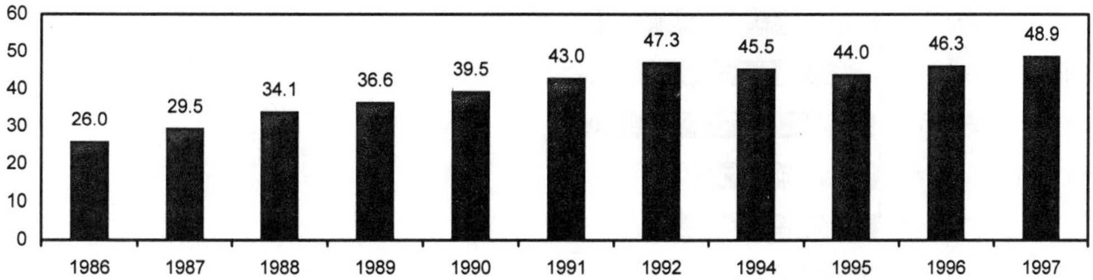

International Visitors to the U.S., 1996[1]

Source: Tourism Industries, International Trade Administration, Dept. of Commerce

Country of origin	Visitors (thousands)	Expenditures (millions)[2]	Expenditures per visitor
Canada	15,301	$6,763.0	$442
Mexico	8,530	3,001.0	352
Japan	5,047	13,163.0	2,608
United Kingdom	3,105	7,306.0	2,353
Germany	1,973	4,573.0	2,318
France	990	2,255.0	2,278
Brazil	891	NA	—
South Korea	796	NA	—
Italy	552	$1,440.0	$2,609
Australia	461	1,819.0	3,946
All countries	**46,324**	**69,908.0**[3]	**1,509**

(1) Excludes cruise travel. (2) Excludes international passenger fare payments. (3) Does not include international traveler spending on U.S. carriers for transactions made outside the U.S. NA=not available.

Traveler Spending in the U.S., 1987-96

Source: Tourism Industries, International Trade Administration, Dept. of Commerce

(in billions)

	Domestic Travelers	International Travelers
1987	$235	$31
1988	258	38
1989	273	47
1990	291	58
1991	$296	$64
1992	308	71
1993	322	75
1994	$339	$78
1995	360	80
1996	383	90[1]

(1) Includes international traveler spending on U.S. carriers for transactions made outside the U.S.

U.S. Pleasure Travel Overview

Source: TIA Research Dept., *Tourism Works for America Report* by Travel Industry Assn. of America

Pleasure travel by U.S. residents in 1996 amounted to 807.8 mil person-trips, about the same as in 1995 (809.5 mil person-trips), and accounted for 70% of all U.S. resident travel. Pleasure travel volume has grown 40% since 1986 (576.1 mil person-trips). About 50% of pleasure travelers in 1996 visited friends and relatives as their primary purpose; some 36% traveled for general entertainment purposes, and about 13% mainly for outdoor recreation purposes Overwhelmingly, pleasure travelers went by auto—car/truck/RV or rental car (83%). About 43% of pleasure travelers stayed overnight in a hotel or motel, for an average stay of 3.3 nights per trip. About 39% stayed with friends or relatives, for an average of 4.2 nights per trip.

U.S. Resident Pleasure Travel Volume, 1986-97

(in millions of person-trips of 100 mi or more, one-way)

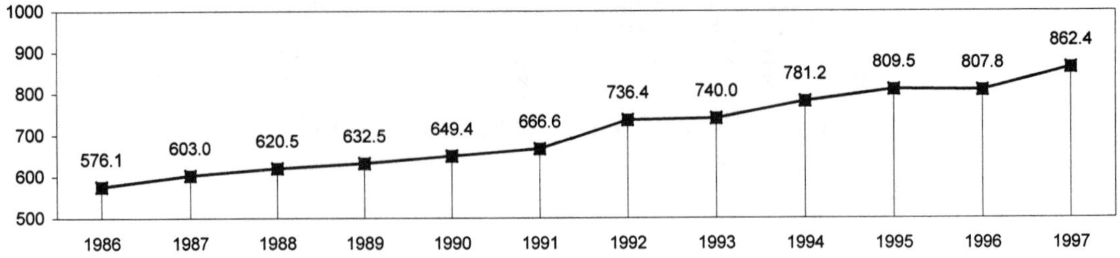

Activities of U.S. Resident Travelers, 1997

Source: TIA TravelScope® Cooperative Travel Survey, *Tourism Works for America Report* by Travel Industry Assn. of America

(In % of total person-trips 50 mi or more, one-way. Some respondents reported more than one activity.)

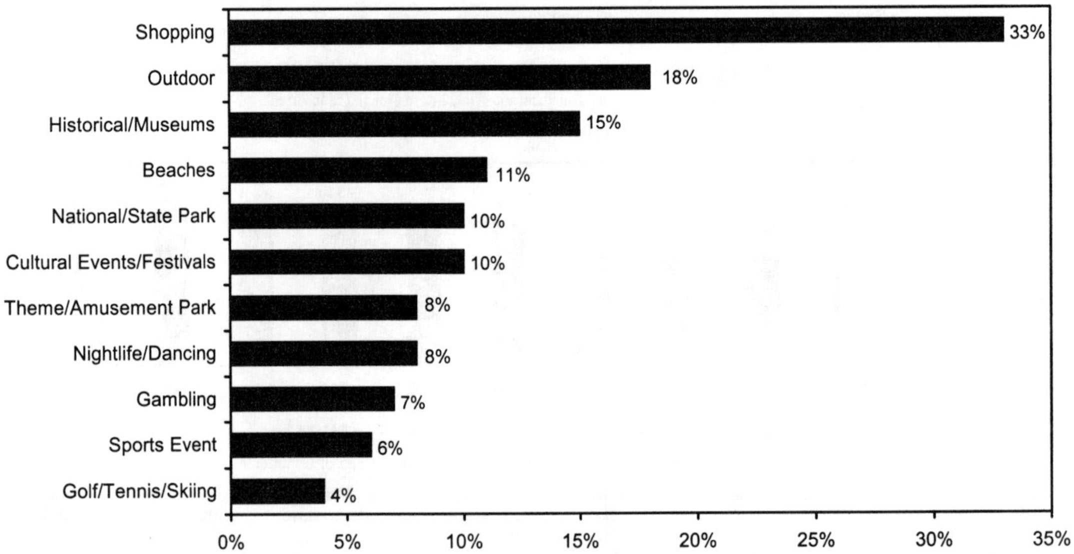

Top U.S. States by Total Traveler Spending, 1996

Source: *Tourism Works for America Report*, by Travel Industry Assn. of America; includes spending (in mil) in states by domestic and intl. travelers

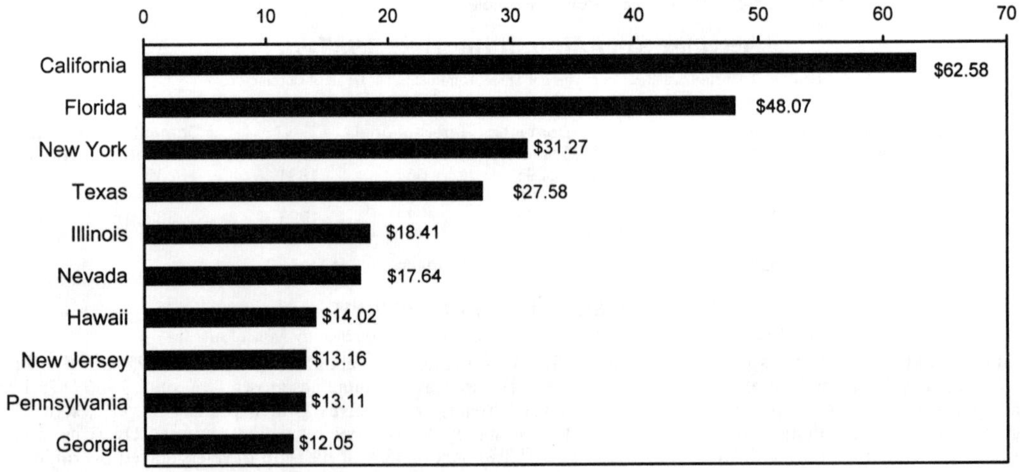

Travel Websites

The following websites are representative of the travel and tourism industry. Inclusion here does not represent endorsement by *The World Almanac.* Websites listed under "Maps" enable the user to plot a route to a destination.

AIRLINES

American Airlines
http://www.americanair.com

America West Airlines
http://www.americawest.com

Continental Airlines
http://www.flycontinental.com

Delta Air Lines
http://www.delta-air.com

Northwest Airlines
http://www.nwa.com

Southwest Airlines
http://www.iflyswa.com

Trans World Airlines
http://www.twa.com

United Airlines
http://www.ual.com

USAirways
http://www.usair.com

HOTELS/RESORTS

Best Western Int'l.
http://www.bestwestern.com/bwi.html

Choice Hotels Int'l., Clarion Hotels & Resorts, Comfort Inns, Econo Lodges, Quality Inns, Rodeway Inns, Sleep Inns
http://www.hotelchoice.com

Days Inn of America
http://www.daysinn.com

Doubletree Hotels
http://www.doubletreehotels.com

Embassy Suites
http://www.embassy-suites.com

Four Seasons Hotels
http://www.fshr.com

Hilton Hotels
http://www.hilton.com

Holiday Inn Worldwide
http://www.holiday-inn.com

Hyatt Hotels and Resorts
http://www.hyatt.com

Inter-Continental Hotels
http://www.travelweb.com/thisco/intercon/common/intercon.html

Loews Hotels
http://www.loewshotels.com

Marriott Int'l.
http://www.marriott.com

Radisson Hotels Int'l.
http://www.radisson.com

Sheraton Hotels & Resorts
http://www.sheraton.com

Westin Hotels & Resorts
http://www.westin.com

Wyndham Hotels & Resorts
http://www.wyndham.com

MAPS

http://www.freetrip.com
http://www.mapquest.com
http://www.mapsonus.com

CRUISE LINES

Carnival Cruise Lines
http://www.carnival.com

Celebrity Cruises
http://www.celebrity-cruises.com

Costa Cruise Lines
http://www.costacruises.com

Cunard Line
http://www.cunardline.com

Holland America Line
http://www.hollandamerica.com

Norwegian Cruise Line
http://www.ncl.inter.net

Princess Cruises
http://www.princesscruises.com

Renaissance Cruises
http://www.renaissancecruises.com

Royal Caribbean Intl.
http://www.royalcaribbean.comv

Windjammer Barefoot Cruises
http://www.windjammer.com

TRAINS

Amtrak
http://www.amtrak.com

BC Rail (Canada)
http://www.bcrail.com

Britrail Travel Int'l.
http://www.britrail.co.uk

Rail Europe
http://www.raileurope.com

CAR RENTALS

Alamo Rent A Car
http://www.goalamo.com

Avis Rent-A-Car
http://www.avis.com

Budget Rent A Car
http://www.budgetrentacar.com

Dollar Rent A Car
http://www.dollarcar.com

Enterprise Rent-A-Car
http://www.erac.com

Hertz
http://www.hertz.com

National Car Rental
http://www.nationalcar.com

Rent-A-Wreck
http://www.rent-a-wreck.com/raw

Thrifty Rent-A-Car
http://www.thrifty.com

BUSES

Gray Line Worldwide
http://www.grayline.com

Greyhound Lines
http://www.greyhound.com

Peter Pan Bus Lines
http://www.peterpan-bus.com

Customs Exemptions for Travelers

Source: U.S. Dept. of the Treasury, U.S. Customs Service

U.S. residents returning after a stay abroad of at least 48 hours are usually granted customs exemptions of $400 each (this and all exemptions figured according to fair retail value). The duty-free articles must accompany the traveler at the time of return, be for personal or household use, have been acquired as an incident of the trip, and be properly declared to Customs. No more than 1 liter of alcoholic beverages or more than 100 cigars and 200 cigarettes (1 carton) may be included in the $400 exemption. The exemption for alcoholic beverages holds only if the returning resident is at least 21 years old at the time of arrival. Cuban cigars may be included only if purchased in Cuba.

If a U.S. resident arrives directly or indirectly from a U.S. island possession—American Samoa, Guam, or U.S. Virgin Islands—a customs exemption of $1,200 is allowed. Up to 1,000 cigarettes may be included, but only 200 of them may have been purchased elsewhere. If a U.S. resident returns from any one of the following places, the exemption is $600: Antigua and Barbuda, Aruba, Bahamas, Barbados, Belize, British Virgin Islands, Costa Rica, Dominica, Dominican Republic, El Salvador, Grenada, Guatemala, Guyana, Haiti, Honduras, Jamaica, Montserrat, Netherlands Antilles, Nicaragua, Panama, St. Kitts and Nevis, St. Lucia, St. Vincent and the Grenadines, Trinidad and Tobago.

The $400, $600, or $1,200 exemption may be granted only if the exemption has not been used in whole or part within the preceding 30-day period and only if the stay abroad was for at least 48 hours. The 48-hr absence requirement does not apply to travelers returning from Mexico or U.S. Virgin Islands. Travelers who cannot claim the $400, $600, or $1,200 exemption because of the 30-day or 48-hr provisions may bring in free of duty and tax articles acquired abroad for personal or household use up to a value of $25.

There are also allowances for goods when shipped. Goods shipped for personal use may be imported free of duty and tax if the total value is no more than $200. This exemption does not apply to perfume containing alcohol if it is valued at more than $5 retail, to alcoholic beverages, or to cigars and cigarettes. The $200 mail exemption does not apply to merchandise subject to absolute or tariff-rate quotas unless the item is for personal use. Tailor-made suits ordered from Hong Kong, however, are subject to quota/visa requirements even if imported for personal use.

Bona fide gifts of not more than $100 in value, when shipped, can be received in the U.S. free of duty and tax, provided that the same person does not receive more than $100 in gift shipments in one day. The limit is increased to $200 for bona fide gift items shipped from U.S. Virgin Islands, American Samoa, or Guam. (Shipping of alcoholic beverages, including wine and beer, by mail is prohibited by U.S. postal laws.) These gifts are not declared by the traveler upon return to the U.S.

The U.S. Customs Service booklet *Know Before You Go* answers frequently asked customs questions and is available free by writing U.S. Customs Services, KBYG, PO Box 7407, Washington, DC 20044. Online information can be obtained at the U.S. Customs website—http://www.custom.ustreas.gov

Passports, Health Regulations, and Travel Warnings for Foreign Travel

Source: Bureau of Consular Affairs, U.S. Dept. of State

Passports are issued by the U.S. Department of State to citizens and nationals of the U.S. for the purpose of documenting them for foreign travel and identifying them as U.S. citizens. For U.S. citizens traveling on business or as tourists, especially in Europe, a U.S. passport is often sufficient to gain admission for a limited stay. For many countries, however, a **visa** must also be obtained before entering. It is the responsibility of the traveler to check in advance and obtain any visas where required, from the appropriate embassy or nearest consulate of each country.

Each country has its own specific guidelines concerning length and purpose of visit, etc. Some may require visitors to display proof that they (1) have sufficient funds to stay for the intended time period and (2) have onward/return tickets.

Some countries, including **Canada, Mexico,** and some **Caribbean** islands, do not require a passport or a visa for limited stays. Such countries do require proof of U.S. citizenship, and may have other requirements that must be met. For further information, check with the embassy or nearest consulate of the country you plan to visit.

How to Obtain a Passport

Those who have never been issued a passport in their own name must apply in person before (1) a passport agent; (2) a clerk of any federal court or state court of record or a clerk or judge of a probate court accepting applications; (3) a postal clerk at a post office that is authorized to accept passport applications; or (4) a U.S. diplomatic or consular officer abroad.

A DSP-11 is the correct form to use for those who must apply in person. All persons are required to obtain individual passports in their own name. However, a parent or legal guardian must execute the application for children under 13.

Persons who possess their most recent passport issued within the last 12 years and after their 18th birthday, may be eligible to apply for a new passport by mail. The form DSP-82, *Application for Passport by Mail,* must be filled out and mailed to the address shown on the form, together with the previous passport, 2 recent identical photographs (see below), and a fee of $55. The DSP-82 may not be used if the most recent passport has been altered or mutilated.

Proof of citizenship—A full validity passport previously issued to the applicant or one in which he or she was included will be accepted as proof of U.S. citizenship. If the applicant has no prior passport and was born in the U.S., a certified copy of the birth certificate generally must be presented. It must generally show the given name and surname, the date and place of birth, and that the birth record was filed shortly after birth. A delayed birth certificate (filed more than 1 year after date of birth) is acceptable if it shows that acceptable secondary evidence was used for creating this record.

If a birth certificate is not obtainable, a notice from a state registrar must be submitted stating that no birth record exists. It must be accompanied by the best obtainable secondary evidence, such as a baptismal certificate or hospital birth record.

A naturalized citizen with no previous passport must present a Certificate of Naturalization. A person born abroad claiming U.S. citizenship through either a native-born or a naturalized citizen parent must normally submit a Certificate of Citizenship issued by the Immigration and Naturalization Service or a Consular Report of Birth or Certification of Birth Abroad issued by the Dept. of State. If such a document has not been obtained, evidence of citizenship of the parent(s) through whom citizenship is claimed and evidence that would establish the parent/child relationship must be submitted. Additionally, if citizenship is derived through birth to citizen parent(s), the applicant must submit parents' marriage certificate plus an affidavit from parent(s) showing periods and places of residence or presence in the U.S. and abroad, and specifying periods spent abroad in the employment of the U.S. government, including the armed forces, or with certain international organizations. If citizenship is derived through naturalization of parents, evidence of admission to the U.S. for permanent residence also is required.

It is important to apply for a passport as far in advance as possible. Passport offices are busiest between March and September. It can take several weeks to receive a passport.

Photographs—Passport applicants must submit 2 identical photographs that are recent (normally not more than 6 months old) and that are a good likeness of and satisfactorily identify the applicant. Photographs should be 2 × 2 in. in size. The image size, from bottom of chin to top of head (including hair), should not be less than 1 inch or more than 1-3/8 in. Photographs should be portrait-type prints. They must be clear, front view, full face, with a plain white or off-white background. Photos that depict the applicant as relaxed and smiling are encouraged.

Identity—Applicants must establish their identity to the satisfaction of the authorities. Generally acceptable documents of identity include a previous U.S. passport, a Certificate of Naturalization, a Certificate of Citizenship, a valid driver's license, or a government identification card. Applicants may not use a Social Security card, learner's or temporary driver's license, credit card, or expired ID card. Extremely old documents cannot be used by themselves.

Applicants unable to establish identity must present some documentation in their own name and be accompanied by a person who has known them at least 2 years and is a U.S. citizen or legal U.S. permanent resident alien. That person must sign an affidavit before the individual who executes the application, and must establish his or her own identity.

Fees—For persons under 16 years of age, the basic passport fee is $40. These passports are valid for 5 years from the date of issue. The basic fee is $60 for passports issued to persons 16 and older. These passports are valid for 10 years from date of issuance. To receive a passport within 10 days or less, a $35 expedite fee is required. An additional fee of $10 is charged for the execution of the application. There is no execution fee when using DSP-82, *Application for Passport by Mail.* Applicants eligible to use this form pay only a $55 passport fee.

Passport loss—The loss or theft of a valid passport should be reported immediately in writing to Passport Services, 1111 19th St., NW, Dept. of State, Washington, DC 20524-1705, telephone: (202) 647-0518, or to the nearest passport agency or nearest U.S. embassy or consulate when abroad.

Health Regulations

Under the regulations adopted by the World Health Organization, a country may require International Certificates of Vaccination against yellow fever. A cholera immunization may be required for travelers from infected areas. Check with health care providers or your records to see that other immunizations (e.g., for tetanus and polio) are up-to-date.

Prophylactic medication for malaria and certain other preventive measures are advisable for travel to some countries. No immunizations are needed to return to the U.S. An increasing number of countries have established regulations regarding AIDS testing, particularly for longtime visitors. Detailed information is included in *Health Information for International Travel,* available from the U.S. Government Printing Office, Washington, DC 20402, for $14. Information may also be obtained from your local health department or physician, or by calling the Centers for Disease Control and Prevention at (404) 332-4559.

General information—The booklets *Passports—Applying for the Easy Way* and *Foreign Entry Requirements* are available for 50¢ each from the Consumer Information Center, Pueblo, CO 81009. For online information, go to the Consular Affairs website—http://www.custom.ustreas.gov

Travel Warnings

Travel Warnings are issued when the State Dept. decides, based on relevant information, to recommend that Americans avoid travel to a certain country; these are subject to change. As of Oct. 1, 1998, travel warnings were in effect for the following countries: Afghanistan, Albania, Algeria, Angola, Bosnia and Herzegovina, Burundi, Cambodia, Central African Republic, Colombia, Congo, Congo Republic, Eritrea, Guinea-Bissau, Iran, Iraq, Lebanon, Lesotho, Liberia, Libya, Nigeria, Pakistan, Rwanda, Sierra Leone, Somalia, Sudan, Tajikistan, and Yugoslavia.

HEALTH

Basic First Aid

Knowing what to do for an injured victim until a doctor or other trained person gets to the accident scene can save a life, especially in cases of stoppage of breathing, severe bleeding, and shock.

People with special medical problems, such as diabetes, cardiovascular disease, epilepsy, or allergy, are urged to wear some sort of emblem identifying the problem, as a safeguard against receiving medication that might be harmful or even fatal. Emblems may be obtained from Medic Alert Foundation, 2323 Colorado Ave., Turlock, CA 95382; 800-344-3226.

It is important to get medical assistance as soon as possible.

Animal bite — Wash wound with soap under running water and apply antibiotic ointment and dressing. When possible, the animal should be caught alive for rabies testing.

Asphyxiation — Start rescue breathing immediately after getting patient to fresh air.

Bleeding — Elevate the wound above the heart if possible. Press hard on wound with sterile compress until bleeding stops. Send for doctor if bleeding is severe.

Burn — If mild, with skin unbroken and no blisters, put into ice water until pain subsides. Apply a dry dressing if necessary. If severe, send for doctor. Apply sterile compresses and keep patient comfortably warm until doctor's arrival. Do not try to clean burn or break blisters.

Chemical in eye — With patient lying down, pour cupfuls of water immediately into corner of eye, letting it run to other side to remove chemicals thoroughly. Cover with sterile compress. Get medical attention immediately.

Choking — See **Abdominal Thrust**.

Convulsions — Place person on back on bed or rug. Loosen clothing. Turn head to side. Do not place a blunt object between the patient's teeth. If convulsions do not stop, get medical attention immediately.

Cut (minor) — Apply mild antiseptic and sterile compress after washing with soap under warm running water.

Fainting — If victim feels faint, lower head to knees. Lay patient down on back with head turned to side if he or she becomes unconscious. Elevate the legs 8 to 10 inches. Loosen clothing and open windows. Keep patient lying quietly for at least 15 minutes after he or she regains consciousness. Call doctor if faint lasts for more than a few minutes.

Foreign body in eye — Touch object with moistened corner of handkerchief if it can be seen. If it cannot be seen or does not come out after a few attempts, take patient to doctor. Do not rub the eye.

Frostbite— Handle frostbitten area gently. Do not rub. Soak affected area in water no warmer than 105°F. Do not allow frostbitten area to touch the container. Soak until frostbitten part looks red and feels warm. Loosely bandage. If fingers or toes are frostbitten, put gauze between them.

Heat Stroke and Heat Exhaustion — Remove the patient from the heat. Loosen any tight clothing and apply cool, wet cloths to the skin. Give the victim cool water, to drink slowly. Call an ambulance if the victim refuses water, vomits, or experiences changes in consciousness.

Hypothermia — Move victim to a warm place. Remove wet clothing and dry victim, if necessary. Warm patient gradually by wrapping the person in warm blankets or clothing. Apply heat pads or other heat sources if available, but not directly to the body. Give the victim warm liquids. Call an ambulance if breathing is slowed or stopped or if the pulse is slow or irregular.

Loss of Limb — If a limb is severed, it is important to properly protect the limb so that it can possibly be reattached. After the patient is cared for, the limb should be wrapped in a sterile gauze or clean material and placed in a clean plastic bag, garbage can, or other suitable container. Pack ice around the limb on the OUTSIDE of the bag to keep the limb cold. Call ahead to the hospital to alert staff there of the situation.

Poisoning — Call doctor. Use antidote listed on label if container is found. Call local Poison Control Center if possible. Do not give the victim any food or drink or induce vomiting, unless specified on the label or by a medical professional.

Shock (injury-related) — Keep the victim lying down; if uncertain as to his or her injuries, keep the patient flat on the back. Maintain normal body temperature; if the weather is cold or damp, place blankets or extra clothing over and under the victim; if weather is hot, provide shade.

Snakebite —Wash the injury. Keep the area still and at a lower level than the heart. Keep the victim quiet. Use a snakebite kit if available.

Sprains and fractures — Apply ice to reduce swelling and pain. Do not try to straighten or move broken limbs. Apply a splint to immobilize the injured area if the victim must be transported.

Sting from insect — If possible, remove stinger. Wash the area with soap and water; cover it to keep it clean. Apply a cold pack to reduce pain and swelling. Call physician immediately if body swells or patient collapses.

Unconsciousness — Send for doctor and place person on his or her back. Start rescue breathing if victim stops breathing. Never give food or liquids.

Abdominal Thrust (Heimlich Maneuver)

The American Red Cross and the American Heart Association both agree that the recommended first aid for choking victims is the abdominal thrust, also known as the Heimlich maneuver, after its creator, Dr. Henry Heimlich. Slaps on the back are no longer advised and may even prove detrimental to a choking victim.

- Get behind the victim and wrap your arms around him or her above the waist.
- Make a fist with one hand and place it, with the thumb knuckle pressing inward, just below the point of the "v" of the rib cage.
- Grasp the wrist with the other hand and give one or more upward thrusts or hugs.
- Start rescue breathing if breathing stops.

Rescue Breathing

Stressing that your breath can save a life, the American Red Cross gives the following directions for rescue breathing if the victim is not breathing:

- Determine consciousness by tapping the victim on the shoulder and asking loudly, "Are you okay?"
- Tilt the victim's head back so that the chin is pointing upward. Do not press on the soft tissue under the chin, as this might obstruct the airway. If you suspect that an accident victim might have neck or back injuries, open the airway by placing the tips of your index and middle fingers on the corners of the person's jaw to lift it forward without tilting the head.
- Place your cheek and ear close to the victim's mouth and nose. Look at the chest to see if it rises and falls. Listen and feel for air to be exhaled for about 5 seconds.
- If there is no breathing, pinch the victim's nostrils shut with the thumb and index finger of your hand that is pressing on the victim's forehead. Another way to prevent leakage of air when the lungs are inflated is to press your cheek against the victim's nose.
- Blow air into the mouth by taking a deep breath and then sealing your mouth tightly around the victim's mouth. Initially, give 2, quick (approx. 1.5 seconds each), full breaths without allowing the lungs to deflate completely between each breath.
- Watch the patient's chest to see if it rises.
- Stop when the chest is expanded. Raise your mouth; turn your head to the side and listen for exhalation.
- Watch the chest to see if it falls.
- Repeat the blowing cycle until the victim starts breathing.

Note: Infants (up to 1 year) and children (1 to 8 years) should be treated as described above, except for the following:

- Do not tilt the head as far back as an adult's head.
- Both the mouth and nose of an infant should be sealed by the mouth.
- Give breaths to a child once every 3 seconds.
- Blow into the infant's mouth and nose once every 3 seconds with less pressure and volume than for a child.

Nutritive Value of Food (Calories, Proteins, etc.)

Source: *Home and Garden Bulletin No. 72;* U.S. Dept. of Agriculture

Food	Measure	Grams	Food Energy (calories)	Protein (grams)	Fat (grams)	Saturated fats (grams)	Carbohydrate (grams)	Calcium (milligrams)	Iron (milligrams)	Sodium (milligrams)	Vitamin A (I.U.)	Ascorbic Acid (milligrams)
Dairy products												
Cheese, cheddar, cut pieces	1 oz.	28	115	7	9	6.0	T	204	0.2	176	300	0
Cheese, cottage, small curd	1 cup	210	215	26	9	6.0	6	126	0.3	850	340	T
Cheese, cream	1 oz.	28	100	2	10	6.2	1	23	0.3	84	400	0
Cheese, Swiss	1 oz.	28	95	7	7	4.5	1	219	0.2	388	230	0
Half-and-half	1 tbsp.	15	20	T	2	1.1	1	16	T	6	70	T
Cream, sour	1 tbsp.	12	25	T	3	1.6	1	14	T	6	90	T
Milk, whole	1 cup	244	150	8	8	5.1	11	291	0.1	120	310	2
Milk, nonfat (skim)	1 cup	245	85	8	T	0.3	12	302	0.1	126	500	2
Milkshake, chocolate	10 oz.	283	355	9	8	4.8	60	374	0.9	314	240	0
Ice cream, hardened	1 cup	133	270	5	14	8.9	32	176	0.1	116	540	1
Sherbet	1 cup	193	270	2	4	2.4	59	103	0.3	88	190	4
Yogurt, fruit-flavored	8 oz.	227	230	10	2	1.6	43	345	0.2	133	100	1
Eggs												
Fried in margarine	1	46	90	6	7	1.9	1	25	0.7	162	390	0
Hard-cooked	1	50	75	6	5	1.6	1	25	0.6	62	280	0
Scrambled (milk added) in margarine	1	61	100	7	7	2.2	1	44	0.7	171	420	T
Fats & oils												
Butter, salted	1 tbsp.	14	100	T	11	7.1	T	3	T	116	430	0
Margarine, salted	1 tbsp.	14	100	T	11	2.2	T	4	T	132	460	T
Olive oil	1 tbsp.	14	125	0	14	1.9	0	0	0	0	0	0
Salad dressing, blue cheese	1 tbsp.	15	75	1	8	1.5	1	12	T	164	30	T
Salad dressing, French, regular	1 tbsp.	16	85	T	9	1.4	1	2	T	188	T	T
Salad dressing, French, low calorie	1 tbsp.	16	25	T	2	0.2	2	6	T	306	T	T
Salad dressing, Italian	1 tbsp.	15	80	T	9	1.3	1	1	T	162	30	T
Mayonnaise	1 tbsp.	14	100	T	11	1.7	T	3	0.1	80	40	0
Fish, meat, poultry												
Clams, raw, meat only	3 oz.	85	65	11	1	0.3	2	59	2.6	102	90	9
Crabmeat, canned	1 cup	135	135	23	3	0.5	1	61	1.1	1,350	50	0
Fish sticks, frozen, reheated	1 fish stick	28	70	6	3	0.8	4	11	0.3	53	20	0
Salmon canned (pink), solids and liquid	3 oz.	85	120	17	5	0.9	0	167	0.7	443	60	0
Sardines, Atlantic, canned in oil, drained solids	3 oz.	85	175	20	9	2.1	0	371	2.6	425	190	0
Shrimp, French fried	3 oz.	85	200	16	10	2.5	11	61	2.0	384	90	0
Trout, broiled, with butter and lemon juice	3 oz.	85	175	21	9	4.1	T	26	1.0	122	230	1
Tuna, canned in oil	3 oz.	85	165	24	7	1.4	0	7	1.6	303	70	0
Bacon, broiled or fried crisp	3 slices	19	110	6	9	3.3	T	2	0.3	303	0	6
Ground beef, broiled, regular	3 oz.	85	245	20	18	6.9	0	9	2.1	70	T	0
Roast beef, relatively lean (lean only)	2.6 oz.	75	135	22	5	1.9	0	3	1.5	46	T	0
Beef steak, lean and fat	3 oz.	85	240	23	15	6.4	0	9	2.6	53	T	0
Beef & vegetable stew	1 cup	245	220	16	11	4.4	15	29	2.9	292	5,690	17
Lamb, chop, broiled loin, lean and fat	2.8 oz.	80	235	22	16	7.3	0	16	1.4	62	T	0
Liver, beef, fried	3 oz.	85	185	23	7	2.5	7	9	5.3	90	30,690	23
Ham, light cure, roasted, lean and fat	3 oz.	85	205	18	14	5.1	0	6	0.7	1,009	0	0
Pork, chop, broiled, lean and fat	3.1 oz.	87	275	24	19	7.0	0	3	0.7	61	10	T
Bologna	2 slices	57	180	7	16	6.1	2	7	0.9	581	0	12
Frankfurter, pork, cooked	1	45	145	5	13	4.8	1	5	0.5	504	0	12
Sausage, pork link, cooked	1 link	13	50	3	4	1.4	T	4	0.2	168	0	T
Veal, cutlet, braised or broiled	3 oz.	85	185	23	9	4.1	0	9	0.8	56	T	0
Chicken, drumstick, fried, bones removed	2.5 oz.	72	195	16	11	3.0	6	12	1.0	194	60	0
Chicken, roasted, half breast, without skin	3 oz.	86	140	27	3	0.9	0	13	0.9	64	20	0
Turkey, roasted, chopped light and dark meat	1 cup	140	240	41	7	2.3	0	35	2.5	98	0	0
Frankfurter, chicken, cooked	1	45	115	6	9	2.5	3	43	0.9	616	60	0
Fruits & fruit products												
Apple, raw, 2-3/4 in. diam.	1	138	80	T	T	0.1	21	10	0.2	T	70	8
Apple juice	1 cup	248	115	T	T	T	29	17	0.9	7	T	2
Apricots, raw	3	106	50	1	T	T	12	15	0.6	1	2,770	11
Banana, raw	1	114	105	1	1	0.2	27	7	0.4	1	90	10
Cherries, sweet, raw	10	68	50	1	1	0.1	11	10	0.3	T	150	5
Cranberry juice cocktail, sweetened	1 cup	253	145	T	T	T	38	8	0.4	10	10	108
Fruit cocktail, canned, in heavy syrup	1 cup	255	185	1	T	T	48	15	0.7	15	520	5
Grapefruit, raw, medium, white	1/2	120	40	1	T	T	10	14	0.1	T	10	41
Grapes, Thompson seedless	10	50	35	T	T	0.1	9	6	0.1	1	40	5
Lemonade, frozen, unsweetened	6 oz.	244	55	1	1	0.1	16	20	0.3	2	30	77
Cantaloupe, 5-in. diam.	1/2	267	95	2	1	0.1	22	29	0.6	24	8,610	113
Orange, 2-5/8 in. diam.	1	131	60	1	T	T	15	52	0.1	T	270	70
Orange juice, frozen, diluted	1 cup	249	110	2	T	T	27	22	0.2	2	190	97
Peach, raw, 2-1/2 in. diam.	1	87	35	1	T	T	10	4	0.1	T	470	6
Raisins, seedless	1 cup	145	435	5	1	0.2	115	71	3.0	17	10	5
Strawberries, whole	1 cup	149	45	1	1	T	10	21	0.6	1	40	84
Watermelon, 4 by 8 in. wedge	1 piece	482	155	3	2	0.3	35	39	0.8	10	1,760	46
Grain products												
Bagel, plain	1	68	200	7	2	0.3	38	29	1.8	245	0	0
Biscuit, 2 in. diam., from home recipe	1	28	100	2	5	1.2	13	47	0.7	195	10	T
Bread, pita, enriched, white, 6-1/2 in. diam	1 pita	60	165	6	1	0.1	12	15	0.7	124	0	0
Bread, white, enriched	1 slice	25	65	2	1	0.3	12	32	0.7	129	T	T
Bread, whole-wheat	1 slice	28	70	3	1	0.4	13	20	1.0	180	T	T
Oatmeal or rolled oats, without added salt	1 cup	234	145	6	2	0.4	25	19	1.6	2	40	0
Bran flakes (40% bran), added sugar, salt, iron, vitamins	1 oz.	28	90	4	1	0.1	22	14	8.1	264	1,250	0
Corn flakes, added sugar, salt, iron, vitamins	1 oz.	28	110	2	T	T	24	1	1.8	351	1,250	15
Rice, puffed, added iron, thiamine, niacin	1 oz.	28	110	2	T	T	25	4	1.8	340	1,250	15
Wheat, shredded, plain, 1 biscuit or 2/3 cup	1 oz.	28	100	3	1	0.1	23	11	1.2	3	0	0
Bulgur, uncooked	1 cup	170	600	19	3	1.2	129	49	9.5	7	0	0
Cake, angel food, 1/12 of cake	1	53	125	3	T	T	29	44	0.2	269	0	0
Cupcake, 2-1/2 in. diam., with chocolate icing	1	35	120	2	4	1.8	20	21	0.7	92	50	T

Food	Measure	Grams	Food Energy (calories)	Protein (grams)	Fat (grams)	Saturated fats (grams)	Carbohydrate (grams)	Calcium (miligrams)	Iron (miligrams)	Sodium (miligrams)	Vitamin A (I.U.)	Ascorbic Acid (miligrams)
Plain sheet cake with white, uncooked frosting, 1/9 of cake	1	121	445	4	14	4.6	77	61	1.2	275	240	T
Fruitcake, dark, 1/32 of loaf	1	43	165	2	7	1.5	25	41	1.2	67	50	16
Cake, pound, 1/17 of loaf	1	29	110	2	5	3.0	15	8	0.5	108	160	0
Cheesecake, 1/12 of 9-in. diam. cake	1	92	280	5	18	9.9	26	52	0.4	204	230	5
Brownies, with nuts, from commercial recipe.	1	25	100	1	4	1.6	16	13	0.6	59	70	T
Cookies, chocolate chip, from home recipe	4	40	185	2	11	3.9	26	13	1.0	82	20	0
Crackers, graham, 2-1/2 in. squares	2	14	60	1	1	0.4	11	6	0.4	86	0	0
Crackers, saltines	4	12	50	1	1	0.5	9	3	0.5	165	0	0
Danish pastry, round piece	1	57	220	4	12	3.6	26	60	1.1	218	60	T
Doughnut, cake type	1	50	210	3	12	2.8	24	22	1.0	192	20	T
Macaroni, firm stage (hot)	1 cup	130	190	7	1	0.1	39	14	2.1	1	0	0
Muffin, bran, commercial mix	1	45	140	3	4	1.3	24	27	1.7	385	100	0
Muffin, corn, from home recipe	1	45	145	3	5	1.5	21	66	0.9	169	80	T
Noodles, enriched, cooked	1 cup	160	200	7	2	0.5	37	16	2.6	3	110	0
Pie, apple, 1/6 of pie	1	158	405	3	18	4.6	60	13	1.6	476	50	2
Pie, cherry, 1/6 of pie	1	158	410	4	18	4.7	61	22	1.6	480	700	0
Pie, lemon meringue, 1/6 of pie	1	140	355	5	14	4.3	53	20	1.4	395	240	4
Pie, pecan, 1/6 of pie	1	138	575	7	32	4.7	71	65	4.6	305	220	0
Popcorn, air-popped, plain	1 cup	8	30	1	T	T	6	1	0.2	T	10	0
Pretzels, stick	10	3	10	T	T	T	2	1	0.1	48	0	0
Rolls, enriched, brown & serve	1	28	85	2	2	0.5	14	33	0.8	155	T	T
Rolls, frankfurter & hamburger	1	40	115	3	2	0.5	20	54	1.2	241	T	T
Tortillas, corn	1	30	65	2	1	0.1	13	42	0.6	1	80	0
Legumes, nuts, seeds												
Beans, Black	1 cup	171	225	15	1	0.1	41	47	2.9	1	T	0
Beans, Great Northern, cooked	1 cup	180	210	14	1	0.1	38	90	4.9	13	0	0
Peanuts, roasted in oil, salted	1 cup	145	840	39	71	9.9	27	125	2.8	626	0	0
Peanut butter	1 tbsp.	16	95	5	8	1.4	3	5	0.3	75	0	0
Refried beans, canned	1 cup	290	295	18	3	0.4	51	141	5.1	1,228	0	17
Tofu	1 piece	120	85	9	5	0.7	3	108	2.3	8	0	0
Sunflower seeds, hulled	1 oz.	28	160	6	14	1.5	5	33	1.9	1	10	T
Mixed foods												
Chop suey with beef and pork, home recipe	1 cup	250	300	26	17	4.3	13	60	4.8	1,053	600	33
Enchilada	1	230	235	20	16	7.7	24	97	3.3	1,332	2,720	T
Pizza, cheese, 1/8 of 15 in.-diam. pie	1	120	290	15	9	4.1	39	220	1.6	699	750	2
Spaghetti with meatballs & tomato sauce	1 cup	248	330	19	12	3.9	39	124	3.7	1,009	1,590	22
Sugars & sweets												
Candy, caramels	1 oz.	28	115	1	3	2.2	22	42	0.4	64	T	T
Candy, milk chocolate	1 oz.	28	145	2	9	5.4	16	50	0.4	23	30	T
Fudge, chocolate	1 oz.	28	115	1	3	2.1	21	22	0.3	54	T	T
Gelatin dessert, from prepared powder	1/2 cup	120	70	2	0	0.0	17	2	T	55	0	0
Candy, hard	1 oz.	28	110	0	0	0.0	28	T	0.1	7	0	0
Honey	1 tbsp.	21	65	T	0	0.0	17	1	0.1	1	0	T
Jams & Preserves	1 tbsp.	20	55	T	T	0.0	14	4	0.2	2	T	T
Popsicle, 3 fl. oz.	1	95	70	0	0	0.0	18	0	T	11	0	0
Sugar, white, granulated	1 tbsp.	12	45	0	0	0.0	12	T	T	T	0	0
Vegetables												
Asparagus, spears, cooked from raw	4 spears	60	15	2	T	T	3	14	0.4	2	500	16
Beans, green, from frozen, cuts	1 cup	135	35	2	T	T	8	61	1.1	18	710	11
Broccoli, cooked from raw	1 spear	180	50	5	1	0.1	10	82	2.1	20	2,540	113
Cabbage, raw, coarsely shredded or sliced	1 cup	70	15	1	T	T	4	33	0.4	13	90	33
Carrots, raw, 7-1/2 by 1-1/8 in.	1	72	30	1	T	T	7	19	0.4	25	20,250	7
Cauliflower, cooked, drained, from raw	1 cup	125	30	2	T	T	6	34	0.5	8	20	69
Celery, raw	1 stalk	40	5	T	T	T	1	14	0.2	35	50	3
Collards, cooked from raw	1 cup	190	25	2	T	0.1	5	148	0.8	36	4,220	19
Corn, sweet, yellow, cooked from raw	1 ear	77	85	3	1	0.2	19	2	0.5	13	170	5
Eggplant, cooked, steamed	1 cup	96	25	1	T	T	6	6	0.3	3	60	1
Lettuce, iceberg, chopped	1 cup	55	5	1	T	T	1	10	0.3	5	180	2
Lettuce, looseleaf (such as romaine)	1 cup	56	10	1	T	T	2	38	0.8	5	1,060	10
Mushrooms, raw	1 cup	70	20	1	T	T	3	4	0.9	3	0	2
Onions, raw, chopped	1 cup	160	55	2	T	0.1	12	40	0.6	3	0	13
Peas, green, frozen, cooked	1 cup	160	125	8	T	0.1	23	38	2.5	139	1,070	16
Potatoes, baked, peeled	1	156	145	3	T	T	34	8	0.5	8	0	20
Potatoes, frozen, French fried (oven-heated)	10	50	110	2	4	2.1	17	5	0.7	16	0	5
Potatoes, mashed, milk added	1 cup	210	160	4	1	0.7	37	55	0.6	636	40	14
Potato chips	10	20	105	1	7	1.8	10	5	0.2	94	0	8
Potato salad	1 cup	250	360	7	21	3.6	28	48	1.6	1,323	520	25
Spinach, drained, cooked from raw	1 cup	180	40	5	T	0.1	7	245	6.4	126	14,740	18
Sweet potatoes, baked in skin, peeled	1	114	115	2	T	T	28	32	0.5	11	24,880	28
Tomatoes, raw	1	123	25	1	T	T	5	9	0.6	10	1,390	22
Vegetable juice cocktail, canned	1 cup	242	45	2	T	T	11	27	1.0	883	2,830	67
Miscellaneous												
Beer, regular	12 fl. oz.	360	150	1	0	0.0	13	14	0.1	18	0	0
Gin, rum, vodka, whisky, 86 proof	1-1/2 fl. oz.	42	105	0	0	0.0	T	T	T	T	0	0
Wine, table, white	3-1/2 fl. oz.	102	80	T	0	0.0	3	9	0.3	5	(1)	0
Cola-type beverage	12 fl. oz.	369	160	0	0	0.0	41	11	0.2	18	0	0
Ginger ale	12 fl. oz	366	125	0	0	0.0	32	11	0.1	29	0	0
Coffee, brewed	6 fl. oz.	180	T	T	T	T	T	4	T	2	0	0
Tea, brewed	8 fl. oz.	240	T	T	T	T	T	0	T	1	0	0
Catsup	1 tbsp.	15	15	T	T	T	4	3	0.1	156	210	2
Mustard, prepared, yellow	1 tsp.	5	5	T	T	T	T	4	0.1	63	0	T
Olives, canned, green	4 medium	13	15	T	2	0.2	T	8	0.2	312	40	0
Pickles, dill, whole	1	65	5	T	T	T	1	17	0.7	928	70	4
Relish, finely chopped, sweet	1 tbsp.	15	20	T	T	T	5	3	0.1	107	20	1
Soup, tomato, prepared with milk	1 cup	248	160	6	6	2.9	22	159	1.8	932	850	68
Soup, chicken noodle, prepared with water	1 cup	241	75	4	2	0.7	9	17	0.8	1,106	710	T
Soup, green pea, prepared with water	1 cup	250	165	9	3	1.4	27	28	2.0	988	200	2
Soup, vegetarian, prepared with water	1 cup	241	70	2	2	0.3	12	22	1.1	822	3,010	1

T — Indicates trace (1) — Value not determined. **Note:** Values shown here for these foods may be from several different manufacturers and, therefore, may differ somewhat from the values provided by one source.

Food and Nutrition

The U.S. Dept. of Health and Human Services and the Dept. of Agriculture reissued guidelines in 1996 that offer dietary and exercise advice for children age 2 and over, as well as for adults. Recommended were: (1) no more than 30 percent of calories from fat, or about 65 grams of fat in a 2,000-calorie daily diet; with no more than 10 % of calories, or 20 grams of fat, from saturated fats; (2) maximum alcohol consumption of about 1 drink a day for women, 2 for men; (3) daily consumption of vegetables, 3-5 servings; fruits, 2-4; pastas, cereals, or breads, 6-11; milk, 2-3; meat, poultry, fish, beans, and eggs, 2-3. (For vegetables, 1 serving equals about 1 cup raw leafy greens or one-half cup other kinds; fruit, 1 medium apple, banana, or orange, or ¾ cup of fruit juice; grains, 1 slice of bread, ½ cup of pasta, or 1 oz. cereal; milk, 1 cup or 1.5 oz. of cheese; meat and poultry, 2-3 oz. cooked lean beef or chicken without skin; cooked dry beans, ½ cup.)

Protein

Proteins, composed of amino acids, are essential to good nutrition. They build, maintain, and repair the body. Best sources: eggs, milk, fish, meat, poultry, soybeans, nuts. High-quality proteins such as eggs, meat, or fish supply all 8 amino acids needed in the diet. Plant foods can be combined to meet protein needs as well: whole grain breads and cereals, rice, oats, soybeans, other beans, split peas, and nuts.

Fats

Fats provide energy by furnishing calories to the body, and they also carry vitamins A, D, E, and K. They are the most concentrated source of energy in the diet. Best sources of polyunsaturated and monounsaturated fats: margarine, vegetable/plant oils, nuts. Meats, cheeses, butter, cream, egg yolks, lard are concentrated sources of saturated fats.

Carbohydrates

Carbohydrates provide energy for body function and activity by supplying immediate calories. The carbohydrate group includes sugars, starches, fiber, and starchy vegetables. Best sources: grains, legumes, potatoes, vegetables, fruits.

Fiber

The portion of plant foods that our bodies cannot digest is known as fiber. There are 2 basic types: insoluble ("roughage") and soluble. Insoluble fibers help move food materials through the digestive tract; soluble fibers tend to slow them down. Both types absorb water, thus prevent and treat constipation by softening and increasing the bulk of the undigested food components passing through the digestive tract. Soluble fibers have also been reported to be helpful in reducing blood cholesterol levels. Best sources: beans, bran, fruits, whole grains, vegetables.

Water

Water dissolves and transports other nutrients throughout the body, aiding the processes of digestion, absorption, circulation, and excretion. It helps regulate body temperature.

Vitamins

Vitamin A—promotes good eyesight and helps keep the skin and mucous membranes resistant to infection. Best sources: liver, sweet potatoes, carrots, kale, cantaloupe, turnip greens, collard greens, broccoli, fortified milk.

Vitamin B_1 (thiamine)—prevents beriberi. Essential to carbohydrate metabolism and health of nervous system. Best sources: pork, enriched cereals, grains, soybeans, nuts.

Vitamin B_2 (riboflavin)—protects skin, mouth, eyes, eyelids, and mucous membranes. Essential to protein and energy metabolism. Best sources: milk, meat, poultry, cheese, broccoli, spinach.

Vitamin B_6 (pyridoxine)—important in the regulation of the central nervous system and in protein metabolism. Best sources: whole grains, meats, fish, poultry, nuts, brewers' yeast.

Vitamin B_{12} (cobalamin)—needed to form red blood cells. Best sources: meat, fish, poultry, eggs, dairy products.

Niacin—maintains health of skin, tongue, digestive system. Best sources: poultry, peanuts, fish, enriched flour and bread.

Folic acid (folacin)—required for normal blood cell formation, growth, and reproduction and for important chemical reactions in body cells. Best sources: yeast, orange juice, green leafy vegetables, wheat germ, asparagus, broccoli, nuts.

Other B vitamins—biotin, pantothenic acid.

Vitamin C (ascorbic acid)—maintains collagen, a protein necessary for the formation of skin, ligaments, and bones. It helps heal wounds and mend fractures and aids in resisting some types of viral and bacterial infections. Best sources: citrus fruits and juices, cantaloupe, broccoli, brussels sprouts, potatoes and sweet potatoes, tomatoes, cabbage.

Vitamin D—important for bone development. Best sources: sunlight, fortified milk and milk products, fish-liver oils, egg yolks.

Vitamin E (tocopherol)—helps protect red blood cells. Best sources: vegetable oils, wheat germ, whole grains, eggs, peanuts, margarine, green leafy vegetables.

Vitamin K—necessary for formation of prothrombin, which helps blood to clot. Also made by intestinal bacteria. Best dietary sources: green leafy vegetables, tomatoes.

Minerals

Calcium—works with phosphorus in building and maintaining bones and teeth. Best sources: milk and milk products, cheese, blackstrap molasses, some types of tofu.

Phosphorus—performs more functions than any other mineral, and plays a part in nearly every chemical reaction in the body. Best sources: cheese, milk, meats, poultry, fish, tofu.

Iron—Necessary for the formation of myoglobin, which is a reservoir of oxygen for muscle tissue, and hemoglobin, which transports oxygen in the blood. Best sources: lean meats, beans, green leafy vegetables, shellfish, enriched breads and cereals, whole grains.

Other minerals—chromium, cobalt, copper, fluorine, iodine, magnesium, manganese, molybdenum, potassium, selenium, sodium, sulfur, and zinc.

Understanding Food Label Claims

Source: Food Labeling Education Information Center, Beltville, Md.

The federal Nutrition Labeling and Education Act of 1990 provides that manufacturers can make certain claims on processed food labels only if they meet the definitions specified here:

Sugar

Sugar free: less than 0.5 g per serving

No added sugar; Without added sugar; No sugar added:

- No sugars added during processing or packing, including ingredients that contain sugars (for example, fruit juices, applesauce, or dried fruit).
- Processing does not increase the sugar content above the amount naturally present in the ingredients. (A functionally insignificant increase in sugars is acceptable from processes used for purposes other than increasing sugar content.)
- The food for which it substitutes normally contains added sugars.

Reduced sugar: at least 25% less sugar than reference food

Calories

Calorie free: fewer than 5 calories per serving

Low calorie: 40 calories or less per serving; if the serving is 30 g or less or 2 tablespoons or less, 40 calories or less per 50 g of food

Reduced or Fewer calories: at least 25% fewer calories than reference food

Fat

Fat free: less than 0.5 g of fat per serving

Saturated fat free: less than 0.5 g of saturated fat per serving, and the level of trans fatty acids does not exceed 1% of total fat

Low fat: 3 g or less per serving and, if the serving is 30 g or less or 2 tbs or less, per 50 g of the food

Low saturated fat: 1 g or less per serving and not more than 15% of calories from saturated fatty acids

Reduced or Less fat: at least 25% less per serving than reference food

Cholesterol

Cholesterol free: less than 2 mg of cholesterol and 2 g or less of saturated fat per serving

Low cholesterol: 20 mg or less and 2 g or less of saturated fat per serving and, if the serving is 30 g or less or 2 tbs or less, per 50 g of the food

Reduced or Less cholesterol: at least 25% less than reference food

Sodium

Sodium free: less than 5 mg per serving

Low sodium: 140 mg or less per serving and, if the serving is 30 g or less or 2 tbs or less, per 50 g of the food

Very low sodium: 35 mg or less per serving and, if the serving is 30 g or less or 2 tbs or less, per 50 g of the food

Reduced or Less sodium: at least 25% less per serving than reference food

Fiber

High fiber: 5 g or more per serving. (Also, must meet low-fat definition, or must state level of total fat.)

Good source of fiber: 2.5 g to 4.9 g per serving

More or Added fiber: at least 2.5 g more per serving than reference food

Dietary Requirements

In April 1998, the Institute of Medicine of the Food and Nutrition Board, National Academy of Sciences, released a report on Dietary Reference Intakes (DRIs), which updated and expanded dietary requirements previously set for thiamin, riboflavin, niacin, B_6, folate, B_{12}, pantothenic acid, biotin, and choline. A year earlier, the Institute updated the requirements for calcium, phosphorus, magnesium, vitamin D, and fluoride. All these new values are based on the latest knowledge relevant to optimizing health at all stages of life, not simply protecting against nutritional deficiencies. Reports on other nutrients are under development. In the meantime, the previously established Recommended Dietary Allowances (RDAs) for these nutrients apply.

The new DRIs include 4 categories for daily consumption: **RDA**—the intake that meets the nutrient requirements of almost all (97-98%) healthy individuals in a specified group; **Estimated Average Requirement (EAR)**—the intake that meets the estimated nutrient need of half the individuals in a specified group; **Adequate Intake (AI)**—the intake specified when sufficient broad scientific evidence is not available to calculate an EAR (for healthy breast-fed infants, the AI is the mean intake; the AI for other life stage groups is believed to cover their needs, but lack of data or uncertainty in the data prevent clear specification of this coverage); and **Tolerable Upper Intake Level (UL)**—the maximum intake that is unlikely to pose risks of adverse health effects in almost all healthy individuals in a specified group. RDAs and AIs may both be used as goals for individual intake. The UL is not recommended as a goal.

Recommended Levels for B Vitamins and Choline

Source: Food and Nutrition Board, National Academy of Sciences—Institute of Medicine, 1998

Group	Thiamin (mg/d)	Riboflavin (mg/d)	Niacin (mg/d)[1]	B_6 (mg/d)	Folate (μg/d)[2]	B_{12} (μg/d)	Pantothenic Acid (mg/d)	Biotin (μg/d)	Choline[3] (mg/d)
Infants									
0-5 mos	0.2*	0.3*	2*	0.1*	65*	0.4*	1.7*	5*	125*
6-11 mos	0.3*	0.4*	3*	0.3*	80*	0.5*	1.8*	6*	150*
Children									
1-3 yrs	0.5	0.5	6	0.5	150	0.9	2*	8*	200*
4-8 yrs	0.6	0.6	8	0.6	200	1.2	3*	12*	250*
Males									
9-13 yrs	0.9	0.9	12	1.0	300	1.8	4*	20*	375*
14-18 yrs	1.2	1.3	16	1.3	400	2.4	5*	25*	550*
19-30 yrs	1.2	1.3	16	1.3	400	2.4	5*	30*	550*
31-50 yrs	1.2	1.3	16	1.3	400	2.4	5*	30*	550*
51-70 yrs	1.2	1.3	16	1.7	400	2.4[4]	5*	30*	550*
over 70 yrs	1.2	1.3	16	1.7	400	2.4[4]	5*	30*	550*
Females									
9-13 yrs	0.9	0.9	12	1.0	300	1.8	4*	20*	375*
14-18 yrs	1.0	1.0	14	1.2	400[5]	2.4	5*	25*	400*
19-30 yrs	1.1	1.1	14	1.3	400[5]	2.4	5*	30*	425*
31-50 yrs	1.1	1.1	14	1.3	400[5]	2.4	5*	30*	425*
51-70 yrs	1.1	1.1	14	1.5	400[5]	2.4[4]	5*	30*	425*
over 70 yrs	1.1	1.1	14	1.5	400	2.4[4]	5*	30*	425*
Pregnant (all ages)	1.4	1.4	18	1.9	600[6]	2.6	6*	30*	450*
Lactating (all ages)	1.5	1.6	17	2.0	500	2.8	7*	35*	550*

mg/d=milligrams/day. μg/d=micrograms/day. **Note:** Adequate Intakes are followed by an asterisk. (1) As niacin equivalents. 1 mg of niacin = 60 mg of tryptophan. (2) As dietary folate equivalents (DFE). 1 DFE = 1 μg food folate = 0.6 μg of folic acid (from fortified food or supplement) consumed with food = 0.5 μg of synthetic (supplemental) folic acid taken on an empty stomach. (3) Although AIs have been set for choline, there is little evidence to assess whether a dietary supply of choline is needed at all stages of the life cycle, and it may be that the body can produce the required amount at some of these stages. (4) Since 10-30% of older people may malabsorb food-bound B_{12}, it is advisable for those over 50 yrs to meet this RDA mainly by taking foods fortified with B_{12} or a B_{12}-containing supplement. (5) In view of evidence linking folate intake with neural tube defects in the fetus, it is recommended that all women capable of becoming pregnant consume 400 μg of synthetic folic acid from fortified foods and/or supplements in addition to taking in food folate from a varied diet. (6) It is assumed that women will continue taking 400 μg of folic acid until their pregnancy is confirmed and they enter prenatal care, which ordinarily occurs after the critical time for formation of the neural tube.

Recommended Levels for Calcium, Phosphorus, Magnesium, Vitamin D, and Fluoride

Source: Food and Nutrition Board, National Academy of Sciences—Institute of Medicine, 1997

Group	Calcium AI[1]	Calcium UL[2]	Phosphorus EAR[1]	Phosphorus RDA[1]	Phosphorus AI[1]	Phosphorus UL[2]	Magnesium EAR[1] m	Magnesium EAR[1] f	Magnesium RDA[1] m	Magnesium RDA[1] f	Magnesium AI[1] m	Magnesium AI[1] f	Magnesium UL[1,3]	Vitamin D AI[4,5]	Vitamin D UL[4]	Fluoride AI[1] m	Fluoride AI[1] f	Fluoride UL[1]
Infants																		
0-6 mos	210	ND	—	—	100	ND	—	—	—	—	30	30	ND	5	25	0.01	0.01	0.7
6-12 mos	270	ND	—	—	275	ND	—	—	—	—	75	75	ND	5	25	0.50	0.50	0.9
Children																		
1-3 yrs	500	2.5	380	460	—	3.0	65	65	80	80	—	—	65	5	50	0.70	0.70	1.3
4-8 yrs	800	2.5	405	500	—	3.0	110	110	130	130	—	—	110	5	50	1.10	1.10	2.2
9-13 yrs	1,300	2.5	1,055	1,250	—	4.0	200	200	240	240	—	—	350	5	50	2.00	2.00	10.0
14-18 yrs	1,300	2.5	1,055	1,250	—	4.0	340	300	410	360	—	—	350	5	50	3.20	2.90	10.0
Adults																		
19-30 yrs	1,000	2.5	580	700	—	3.0	330	255	400	310	—	—	350	5	50	3.80	3.10	10.0
31-50 yrs	1,000	2.5	580	700	—	3.0	350	265	420	320	—	—	350	5	50	3.80	3.10	10.0
51-70 yrs	1,200	2.5	580	700	—	3.0	350	265	420	320	—	—	350	10	50	3.80	3.10	10.0
over 70 yrs	1,200	2.5	580	700	—	3.0	350	265	420	320	—	—	350	15	50	3.80	3.10	10.0
Pregnant																		
18 yrs or less	1,300	2.5	1,055	1,250	—	3.5	—	335	—	400	—	—	350	5	50	—	2.90	10.0
19-50 yrs	1,000	2.5	580	700	—	3.5	—	290	—	350	—	—	350	—	50	—	3.10	10.0
Lactating																		
18 yrs or less	1,300	2.5	1,055	1,250	—	4.0	—	300	—	360	—	—	350	5	50	—	2.90	10.0
19-50 yrs	1,000	2.5	580	700	—	4.0	—	255	—	310	—	—	350	—	50	—	3.10	10.0

m=male. f=female. ND=Not determinable, because of a lack of data on adverse effects in this age group and a concern over body's lack of ability to handle excess amounts. Source of intake in this case should be from food only. (1) mg/day. (2) g/day. (3) The UL for magnesium represents intake from a pharmacological agent only and does not include intake from food and water. (4) μg/day (microgram/day). (5) In the absence of adequate exposure to sunlight.

Recommended Dietary Allowances (RDAs)

Source: Food and Nutrition Board, National Academy of Sciences—Institute of Medicine, 1989

		Weight (lbs)	Protein (g)	Fat soluble vitamins: Vitamin A[1]	Fat soluble vitamins: Vitamin E[2]	Fat soluble vitamins: Vitamin K (μg)	Vitamin C[3] (mg)	Minerals: Iron (mg)	Minerals: Zinc (mg)	Minerals: Iodine (μg)	Minerals: Selenium (μg)
Infants	to 5 mos.	13	13	375	3	5	30	6	5	40	10
	to 1 yr.	20	14	375	4	10	35	10	5	50	15
Children	1-3	29	16	400	6	15	40	10	10	70	20
	4-6	44	24	500	7	20	45	10	10	90	20
	7-10	62	28	700	7	30	45	10	10	120	30
Males	11-14	99	45	1000	10	45	50	12	15	150	40
	15-18	145	59	1000	10	65	60	12	15	150	50
	19-24	160	58	1000	10	70	60	10	15	150	70
	25-50	174	63	1000	10	80	60	10	15	150	70
	51+	170	63	1000	10	80	60	10	15	150	70
Females	11-14	101	46	800	8	45	50	15	12	150	45
	15-18	120	44	800	8	55	60	15	12	150	50
	19-24	128	46	800	8	60	60	15	12	150	55
	25-50	138	50	800	8	65	60	15	12	150	55
	51+	143	50	800	8	65	60	10	12	150	55

g=grams. μg=micrograms. (1) Retinol equivalents. (2) Milligrams alpha-tocopherol equivalents. (3) Vitamin C is a water soluble vitamin.

Weight Guidelines for Adults

Source: *Clinical Guidelines on the Identification, Evaluation, and Treatment of Overweight and Obesity in Adults,* National Heart, Lung, and Blood Institute, National Institutes of Health, 1998

Guidelines on identification, evaluation, and treatment of overweight and obesity in adults were released in June 1998 by the National Heart, Lung, and Blood Institute (NHLBI), in cooperation with the National Institute of Diabetes and Digestive and Kidney Diseases. The guidelines, based on research into risk factors in heart disease, stroke, and other conditions, define degrees of overweight and obesity in terms of **body mass index (BMI)**, which is based on weight and height and is strongly correlated with total body fat content. A BMI of 25-29 is said to indicate **overweight**; a BMI of 30 or above is said to indicate **obesity**. Weight reduction is advised for persons with a BMI of 25 or higher, about 55% of the adult population. (Previous guidelines have been less stringent.) Factors such as large waist circumference, high blood pressure or cholesterol, and a family history of obesity-related disease may increase risk. The table below shows the BMI for certain heights and weights. For weight reduction tips, while they last, write NHLBI Information Center, PO Box 30105, Bethesda, MD 20824-0105. See also the NHLBI website: http://www.nhlbi.nih.gov/nhlbi/nhlbi.htm

Weight (lbs)

Height	Healthy						Overweight					Obese								
4'10"	91	96	100	105	110	115	119	124	129	134	138	143	148	153	158	162	167	172	177	181
4'11"	94	99	104	109	114	119	124	128	133	138	143	148	153	158	163	168	173	178	183	188
5'0"	97	102	107	112	118	123	128	133	138	143	148	153	158	163	168	174	179	184	189	194
5'1"	100	106	111	116	122	127	132	137	143	148	153	158	164	169	174	180	185	190	195	201
5'2"	104	109	115	120	126	131	136	142	147	153	158	164	169	175	180	186	191	196	202	207
5'3"	107	113	118	124	130	135	141	146	152	158	163	169	175	180	186	191	197	203	208	214
5'4"	110	116	122	128	134	140	145	151	157	163	169	174	180	186	192	197	204	209	215	221
5'5"	114	120	126	132	138	144	150	156	162	168	174	180	186	192	198	204	210	216	222	228
5'6"	118	124	130	136	142	148	155	161	167	173	179	186	192	198	204	210	216	223	229	235
5'7"	121	127	134	140	146	153	159	166	172	178	185	191	198	204	211	217	223	230	236	242
5'8"	125	131	138	144	151	158	164	171	177	184	190	197	203	210	216	223	230	236	243	249
5'9"	128	135	142	149	155	162	169	176	182	189	195	203	209	216	223	230	236	243	250	257
5'10"	132	139	146	153	160	167	174	181	188	195	202	209	216	222	229	236	243	250	257	264
5'11"	136	143	150	157	165	172	179	186	193	200	208	215	222	229	236	243	250	257	265	272
6'0"	140	147	154	162	169	177	184	191	199	206	213	221	228	235	242	250	258	265	272	279
6'1"	144	151	159	166	174	182	189	197	204	212	219	227	235	242	250	257	265	272	280	288
6'2"	148	155	163	171	179	186	194	202	210	218	225	233	241	249	256	264	272	280	287	295
6'3"	152	160	168	176	184	192	200	208	216	224	232	240	248	256	264	272	279	287	295	303
6'4"	156	164	172	180	189	197	205	213	221	230	238	246	254	263	271	279	287	295	304	312
BMI[1]	**19**	**20**	**21**	**22**	**23**	**24**	**25**	**26**	**27**	**28**	**29**	**30**	**31**	**32**	**33**	**34**	**35**	**36**	**37**	**38**

(1) The BMI numbers apply to both men and women. Some very muscular people may have a high BMI without health risks.

MILLENNIUM FACT BOX

Childhood Vaccinations

In the past century, scientists have been able to put a virtual end to some childhood diseases in much of the world by developing vaccines to prevent them. Listed below are a few major diseases and the results of vaccines for them.

Disease	Discoverer of vaccine	Year	Results of the vaccine
Diphtheria[1]	Gaston Ramon	1923	In 1921, there were about 200,000 cases of diphtheria in the U.S. Only 2 cases were reported in 1996.
Measles	John F. Enders	1963	In 1960, there were about 450,000 cases of measles reported in the U.S.; in 1996, only about 500 cases were reported.
Polio	Jonas E. Salk	1954	The greatest incidence of polio occurred from 1942 to 1952; there were nearly 60,000 cases in the U.S. in 1952. In 1996, only 5 cases were reported.
	Albert Sabin	1960	Sabin's oral vaccine is also used today.

(1) A vaccine developed by Emil von Behring in 1913 was not widely used; Ramon's vaccine was more effective.

U.S. Recommended Childhood Immunization Schedule

Source: Advisory Committee on Immunization Practices (ACIP), Amer. Acad. of Pediatrics, and Amer. Acad. of Family Physicians (AAFP), 1998

Vaccines are listed under the routinely recommended ages[1]. Bars indicate the range of recommended ages. Catch-up immunization should be done when feasible. Bars with dotted rules indicate vaccines to be given during the early adolescent years when necessary.

Age → / Vaccine ↓	Birth	1 mo	2 mos	4 mos	6 mos	12 mos	15 mos	18 mos	4-6 yrs	11-12 yrs	14-16 yrs
Hepatitis B[2,3]	Hep B-1										
		Hep B-2			Hep B-3					Hep B[3]	
Diphtheria, Tetanus, Pertussis (whooping cough)[4]			DTaP or DTP	DTaP or DTP	DTaP or DTP		DTaP or DTP[4]		DTaP or DTP	Td	
H. influenzae type b[5]			Hib	Hib	Hib	Hib					
Polio[6]			Polio[6]	Polio		Polio[6]			Polio		
Measles, Mumps, Rubella (German measles)[7]						MMR			MMR[7]	MMR[7]	
Varicella (chickenpox)[8]						Var				Var[8]	

1) This schedule indicates the recommended age for administration of childhood vaccines. Combination vaccines may be used whenever administration of all components of the vaccine is called for.

(2) **Infants born to mothers who do not have hepatitis B** should receive 2.5 μg (micrograms) of Merck vaccine (Recombivax HB) or 10 μg of Smithkline Beecham (SB) vaccine (Engerix-B). The 2d dose should be given at least 1 month after the 1st. The 3d dose should be given at least 2 months after the 2d, but not before 6 months of age.
Infants born to mothers who have hepatitis B should receive 0.5 mL (milliliters) of hepatitis B immune globulin (HBIG) within 12 hours of birth, and either 5 μg of Merck vaccine (Recombivax HB) or 10 μg of SB vaccine (Engerix-B). The 2d dose is recommended at 1-2 months of age, the 3d at 6 months.
Infants born to mothers whose hepatitis B status is unknown should receive either 5 μg of Merck vaccine (Recombivax HB) or 10 μg of SB vaccine (Engerix-B) within 12 hours of birth. The 2d dose is recommended at 1 month and the 3d at 6 months. Blood should be drawn at the time of delivery to determine if the mother has hepatitis B; if so, the infant should receive HBIG as soon as possible (no later than 1 week of age). The dosage and timing of later vaccine doses should be based upon the mother's hepatitis B-status.

(3) **Children and adolescents not vaccinated against hepatitis B** in infancy may begin the series at any time. Those who have not previously received 3 doses of hepatitis B vaccine should initiate or complete the series at the age of 11 or 12; unvaccinated older adolescents should be vaccinated whenever possible. The 2d dose should be given at least 1 month after the 1st, and the 3d at least 4 months after the 1st and at least 2 months after the 2d.

(4) **DTaP** (diphtheria and tetanus toxoids and acellular pertussis vaccine) is the preferred vaccine for all doses in this vaccination series, including completion of the series in children who have received 1 or more doses of whole-cell DTP vaccine. Whole-cell DTP is an acceptable alternative to DTaP. The 4th dose of the vaccine may be given as early as 12 months of age, provided 8 months have elapsed since the 3d dose. Td (tetanus and diphtheria toxoids) is recommended at 11-12 years of age if at least 5 years have elapsed since the last dose of DTP, DTaP, or DT. Boosters are recommended every 10 years.

(5) ***Haemophilus influenzae* type b** is a bacterium that can cause such serious infectious diseases as meningitis and pneumonia. Three *H. influenzae* type b (Hib) conjugate vaccines are licensed for infant use. If PRP-OMP (PedvaxHIB [Merck]) is administered at 2 and 4 months of age, a dose at 6 months is not required.

(6) Two **poliovirus vaccines** are currently licensed in the U.S.: inactivated poliovirus vaccine (IPV) and oral poliovirus vaccine (OPV). The following schedules are all acceptable; parents and physicians may choose among these options:
(a) 2 doses of IPV followed by 2 doses of OPV.
(b) 4 doses of IPV.
(c) 4 doses of OPV.
The ACIP recommends 2 doses of IPV at 2 and 4 months of age, followed by 2 doses of OPV at 12-18 months and 4-6 years. IPV is the only poliovirus vaccine recommended for people with impaired or weakened immune systems and their household contacts.

(7) The 2d dose of the **measles, mumps, rubella vaccine** (MMR) is recommended routinely at 4-6 years of age but may be administered at any time, provided that at least 1 month has elapsed since the 1st dose and both doses are administered beginning at or after 12 months of age. Those who have not previously received the 2d dose should complete the schedule by the age of 11 or 12.

(8) Children susceptible to **chickenpox** may receive Varicella vaccine (Var) any time after their 1st birthday, and those who lack a reliable history of chickenpox should be immunized at age 11 or 12. Susceptible children 13 years of age or older should receive 2 doses, at least 1 month apart.

Allergies and Asthma

Source: Asthma and Allergy Foundation of America, 1125 15th St., N.W., Suite 502, Washington, DC 20005; phone: (800) 7-ASTHMA

One out of every five Americans suffers from allergies. People with allergies have extra-sensitive immune systems that react to normally harmless substances. Allergens that sometimes produce this reaction include plant pollen, dust mites, or animal dander; plants such as poison ivy; certain drugs, such as penicillin; and certain foods such as eggs, milk, nuts, or seafood.

The tendency to develop a particular kind of allergy is inherited, and allergies usually begin to appear in childhood, but they can show up at any age. Common allergies for infants include food allergies and eczema (patches of dry skin). Older children and adults may often develop allergic rhinitis (hay fever), a reaction to an inhaled allergen; common symptoms include nasal congestion, runny nose, and sneezing.

It is best to avoid contact with the allergen, if feasible. In some cases, medications such as antihistamines are used to decrease the reaction, and there are treatments aimed at gradually desensitizing the patient. Other effective allergy treatments include decongestants, eye drops, and ointments.

Some people with allergies also have asthma, and allergens are a common asthma trigger. Asthma is a disease of chronic inflammation, affecting the passages that carry air into and out of the lungs. It is most often seen in children but can develop at any age.

People with asthma have inflamed, supersensitive airways that tighten and become filled with mucus during an asthma episode. Wheezing, difficulty in breathing, tightening of the chest, and coughing are common symptoms. Asthma can progress through stages to become life-threatening if not controlled. Emergency symptoms of asthma include a bluish cast to the face and lips, severe anxiety, increased pulse rate, and sweating.

Besides common allergens, tobacco smoke, cold air, and air pollutants can trigger an asthma attack, as can respiratory infections or physical exercise that taxes the breathing. Of course, an accurate diagnosis by a physician is important. Besides avoidance of triggers, treatment for asthma can include preventive medications and allergy immunotherapy, as well as bronchodilators and anti-inflammatory agents to better control the breathing.

Cancer Prevention

Source: American Cancer Society, 1599 Clifton Road NE, Atlanta, GA 30329-4251; phone: (800) 227-2345

PRIMARY PREVENTION: Modifiable determinants of cancer risk.

Smoking Lung cancer mortality rates are 23 times higher for current male smokers, and 13 times higher for current female smokers, than for those who have never smoked. Smoking accounts for about 29% of all cancer deaths and about 20% of all deaths in the U.S. Smoking is associated with cancer of the lungs, mouth, pharynx, larynx, esophagus, pancreas, uterine cervix, kidney, and bladder.

Nutrition and Diet Risk for colon, rectum, breast (among postmenopausal women), kidney, prostate, and endometrial cancers increases in obese people. A diet high in fat may be a factor in the development of certain cancers, particularly cancer of the breast, colon, and prostate. High-fiber foods may help reduce risk of colon cancer. Eating 5 or more servings of fruits and vegetables each day, and eating other foods from plant sources (especially grains and beans), may reduce risk for many cancers. Physical activity can help protect against some cancers.

Sunlight Many of the one million skin cancers that are expected to be diagnosed in 1998 could have been prevented by protection from the sun's rays. Epidemiological evidence shows that sun exposure is a major factor in the development of melanoma and that the incidence rates are increasing around the world.

Alcohol Heavy drinking, especially when accompanied by cigarette smoking or smokeless tobacco use, increases risk of cancers of the mouth, larynx, throat, esophagus, and liver. Studies have also noted an association between alcohol consumption and an increased risk of breast cancer.

Smokeless Tobacco Use of chewing tobacco or snuff increases risk of cancers of the mouth, larynx, throat, and esophagus. The excess risk of cancer of the cheek and gum may reach nearly 50-fold among long-term snuff users.

Estrogen Estrogen treatment to control menopausal symptoms can increase risk of endometrial cancer. However, including progesterone in estrogen replacement therapy helps to minimize this risk. Use of estrogen by menopausal women needs careful discussion by the woman and her physician, while research continues.

Radiation Excessive exposure to ionizing radiation can increase cancer risk. Medical and dental X rays are adjusted to deliver the lowest dose possible without sacrificing image quality. Excessive radon exposure in the home may increase lung cancer risk, especially in cigarette smokers. If levels are found to be too high, remedial actions should be taken.

Environmental Hazards Exposure to various chemicals (including benzene, asbestos, vinyl chloride, arsenic, and aflatoxin) increases risk of various cancers. Risk of lung cancer from asbestos is greatly increased when combined with smoking. Pesticides, low-frequency radiation, toxic wastes, and proximity to nuclear power plants have not been proven to cause cancer.

SECONDARY PREVENTION: Steps to diagnose a cancer or precursor as early as possible after it has developed.

CANCER-DETECTION GUIDELINES

A cancer-related checkup is recommended every 3 years for people aged 20-40 and every year for people 40 years of age and older. This exam should include health counseling and, depending on a person's age, might include examinations for cancers of the thyroid, oral cavity, skin, lymph nodes, testes, prostate, and ovaries, as well as for some nonmalignant diseases. Special tests for certain cancer sites are recommended as outlined below:

Breast Cancer
- Breast self-exam monthly, beginning at age 20.
- Breast clinical physical examination for women aged 20-39, every 3 years; 40 and over, every year.
- Mammography for women aged 40 and over, every year.

Cervical Cancer Annual Pap test and pelvic exam for women who are or have been sexually active or have reached age 18. After 3 or more consecutive satisfactory normal annual exams, the Pap test may be performed less frequently at the discretion of the physician.

Colorectal Cancer Beginning at age 50, both men and women should follow this testing schedule:
- Yearly fecal occult blood test, plus flexible sigmoidoscopy and digital rectal examination every 5 years, or
- Colonoscopy and digital rectal examination every 10 years, or
- Double-contrast barium enema and digital rectal examination every 5-10 years.

Endometrial Cancer Sampling of asymptomatic women at high risk of developing endometrial cancer should begin at menopause and may be indicated at various intervals thereafter, depending on the degree of risk and other factors determined by the physician. Factors that contribute to increased endometrial cancer risk include history of infertility, obesity, previous abnormal uterine bleeding, estrogen therapy opposed by progestin intake, diabetes, gall bladder disease, hypertension, and tamoxifen therapy.

Oral Cancer Regular checkups by dentists and primary care physicians will show any abnormalities.

Prostate Cancer Both Prostate-Specific Antigen (PSA) and Digital Rectal Examination (DRE) should be offered annually, beginning at age 50, to men who have at least a 10-year life expectancy, and should be offered to younger men who are at high risk. Information should be provided to patients regarding potential risks and benefits of intervention.
- Men who choose to undergo screening should begin at age 50. However, men in high-risk groups, such as those with a strong familial predisposition (e.g., 2 or more affected first-degree relatives) or African Americans may begin at a younger age (e.g., 45 years). More data on the precise age to start prostate cancer screening are needed for men at high risk.
- Screening for prostate cancer in men without any symptoms of prostate disease can help detect cancers at an earlier stage. Cancers found by screening care, on average, are smaller and have spread less than cancers discovered because of symptoms they cause.
- An abnormal PSA test result has been defined as a value of above 4.0 ng (nanogram)/ml. Conditions such as benign prostatic hyperplasia (noncancerous prostate enlargement) and prostatitis (inflammation of the prostate) can cause a borderline or high test result.
- The DRE of the prostate should be performed by health care workers skilled in recognizing subtle prostate abnormalities, including those of symmetry and consistency, as well as the more classic findings of marked induration or nodules. DRE is less effective in detecting prostate cancer than is PSA; therefore, the American Cancer Society guidelines recommend use of both tests.

Skin Cancer Skin exam for men and women over 20, every 3 years; for men and women over 40, every year.

Breast Cancer

Source: American Cancer Society, Inc., 1599 Clifton Road NE, Atlanta, GA 30329-4251; phone: (800) 227-2345

In 1998, in the United States, about 180,000 women and 1,600 men will be diagnosed with breast cancer; about 43,500 women and 400 men will die from it. Breast cancer is the second largest cause of cancer death for women in the U.S. (lung cancer ranks first), but mortality rates are declining, especially among younger women, probably because of earlier detection and improved treatment.

Breast cancer is often manifested first in an abnormality that appears on a mammogram. Physical signs and symptoms that show up later, and may be detectable by a woman or her physician, include a breast lump, thickening, swelling, distortion, or tenderness; skin irritation or dimpling; and nipple pain, scaliness, or retraction. Breast pain is more commonly associated with benign (noncancerous) conditions.

Studies show that early detection increases survival and treatment options. The American Cancer Society (ACS) recommends that women 40 and older should have an annual mammogram, have an annual clinical breast exam by a health care professional, and perform monthly breast self-examinations. The ACS recommends that women ages 20-39 should have a clinical breast exam every 3 years and should also perform monthly breast self-examinations. Although most breast lumps that are detected are noncancerous, any suspicious lump needs to be biopsied.

The risk for breast cancer increases as a woman ages. The risk is also higher for women with a personal or family history of the disease; early start of menstruation; late menopause; recent use of oral contraceptives or postmenopausal estrogens; no children or no live birth until a late age; and relatively high education and socioeconomic status. Other possible risk factors are pesticides and other chemicals, alcohol consumption, weight gain, and physical inactivity. Research is continuing into the genes BRCA1 and BRCA2, which have been found to predispose women who carry them to breast cancer.

Treatment for breast cancer may involve lumpectomy (local removal of a tumor) and removal of the lymph nodes under the arm, mastectomy (surgical removal of the breast) and removal of the lymph nodes under the arm, radiation therapy, chemotherapy, or hormone therapy. For early-stage breast cancer, long-term survival rates following lumpectomy plus radiation therapy are similar to survival rates after modified radical mastectomy.

Numerous drugs that may prevent breast cancer or improve its treatment are being studied. One is tamoxifen, a synthetic hormone that blocks the action of estrogen in the breast. Already used for treating breast cancer, it has been shown to reduce the likelihood of developing the disease in women who are considered high risk. Unfortunately, tamoxifen also has dangerous side effects, such as increased risk of uterine cancer and blood clots in the lungs. Research is also being done on another drug, Taxol, which is derived from the yew tree. Formerly used only for treating advanced breast cancer, it has now been proven to be effective for treating early as well as advanced breast cancer when given as part of chemotherapy after surgery. Another drug, Herceptin, which has been shown to delay the progression of breast cancer in women with advanced cases, was approved by the FDA in Sept. 1998.

Trends in Daily Use of Cigarettes, for U.S. 8th, 10th, and 12th Graders

Source: *Monitoring the Future,* Univ. of Michigan Inst. for Social Research and National Inst. on Drug Abuse

(percent who smoked daily in last 30 days)

	8th grade						10th grade						12th grade					
	1993	1994	1995	1996	1997	'96-'97 change	1993	1994	1995	1996	1997	'96-'97 change	1993	1994	1995	1996	1997	'96-'97 change
Total	**8.3**	**8.8**	**9.3**	**10.4**	**9.0**	**−1.4**	**14.2**	**14.6**	**16.3**	**18.3**	**18.0**	**−0.3**	**19.0**	**19.4**	**21.6**	**22.2**	**24.6**	**+2.4**
Sex																		
Male	8.8	9.5	9.2	10.5	9.0	−1.5	13.8	15.2	16.3	18.1	17.2	−0.9	19.4	20.4	21.7	22.2	24.8	+2.6
Female	7.8	8.0	9.2	10.1	8.7	−1.4	14.3	13.7	16.1	18.6	18.5	−0.1	18.2	18.1	20.8	21.8	23.6	+1.8
College plans																		
None or under 4 yrs.	21.5	22.6	22.5	26.0	25.4	−0.6	28.9	28.9	32.7	34.3	35.4	+1.1	27.8	29.8	33.7	33.2	35.6	+2.4
Complete 4 yrs.	6.4	6.8	7.5	8.0	6.9	−1.1	11.0	11.5	13.3	15.5	15.0	−0.5	15.9	15.7	17.4	18.9	20.6	+1.7
Region																		
Northeast	7.1	8.6	9.2	11.0	8.8	−2.2	16.3	14.1	15.8	18.8	18.0	−0.8	23.5	21.3	22.5	27.0	29.4	+2.4
North central	8.5	9.4	11.0	12.4	10.3	−2.1	15.1	16.9	17.6	20.6	19.5	−1.1	21.3	23.8	25.7	26.1	28.0	+1.9
South	9.3	9.4	9.4	10.4	9.5	−0.9	13.9	15.5	19.3	20.5	20.5	0	18.5	19.3	21.7	20.5	22.6	+2.1
West	7.4	7.4	7.0	7.5	6.8	−0.7	10.9	9.7	9.4	10.7	11.1	+0.4	13.0	12.4	14.5	13.8	17.5	+3.7
Race[1]																		
White	8.8	9.7	10.5	11.7	11.4	−0.3	15.3	16.5	17.6	20.0	21.4	+1.4	21.4	22.9	23.9	25.4	27.8	+2.4
Black	1.8	2.6	2.8	3.2	3.7	+0.5	3.1	3.8	4.7	5.1	5.6	+0.5	4.1	4.9	6.1	7.0	7.2	+0.2
Hispanic	7.2	9.0	9.2	8.0	8.1	+0.1	8.9	8.1	9.9	11.6	10.8	−0.8	11.8	10.6	11.6	12.9	14.0	+1.1

(1) For each racial group, data for the specified year and previous year have been combined to increase subgroup sample size and thus provide a more reliable estimate.

Some Benefits of Quitting Smoking

Source: American Cancer Society, phone: (800) 227-2345; U.S. Centers for Disease Control and Prevention

Within 20 Minutes
- Blood pressure drops to normal
- Pulse rate drops to normal
- Body temperature of hands and feet increases to normal

Within 8 Hours
- Carbon monoxide level in blood drops to normal
- Oxygen level in blood increases to normal

Within 24 Hours
- Chance of heart attack decreases

Within 48 Hours
- Nerve endings start regrowing
- Ability to smell and taste is enhanced

Within 2 Weeks to 3 Months
- Circulation improves
- Walking becomes easier
- Lung function increases up to 30%

Within 1 to 9 Months
- Coughing, sinus congestion, fatigue, and shortness of breath decrease
- Cilia regrow in lungs, increasing ability to handle mucus, clean the lungs, reduce infection
- Body's overall energy increases

Within 1 Year
- Excess risk of coronary heart disease is cut by half

Within 5 Years
- Lung cancer death rate for average former smoker (one pack a day) decreases by almost half
- Stroke risk is reduced to that of a nonsmoker 5-15 years after quitting
- Risk of cancer of the mouth, throat, and esophagus is half that of a smoker's

Within 10 Years
- Lung cancer death rate similar to that of nonsmokers
- Precancerous cells are replaced
- Risk of cancer of the mouth, throat, esophagus, bladder, kidney, and pancreas decreases

Within 15 Years
- Risk of coronary heart disease is that of a nonsmoker

Diabetes

Source: American Diabetes Association, 1660 Duke St., Alexandria, VA 22314; phone: (800) 342-2383

Diabetes is a chronic disease in which the body does not produce or properly use insulin, a hormone needed to convert sugar, starches, and other foods into energy necessary for daily life. Both genetics and environment appear to play roles in the onset of diabetes. This disease, which has no cure, is the 6th-leading cause of death by disease in the U.S. According to death certificate data, diabetes contributed to more than 187,000 deaths in 1995.

In 1997, the American Diabetes Association issued new guidelines for diagnosing diabetes. The recommendations include: lowering the acceptable level of blood sugar from 140 mg of glucose/deciliter of blood to 126 mg/deciliter, possibly identifying 2 million more people with the disease; testing all adults 45 years and older, and then every 3 years if normal; and testing at a younger age, or more frequently, in high-risk individuals. The American Diabetes Association believes that detection at an earlier stage will help prevent or delay complications of diabetes.

There are 2 major types of diabetes:

- **Type 1 (formerly known as insulin dependent)**—The body produces very little or no insulin; disease most often begins in childhood or early adulthood. People with type 1 diabetes must take daily insulin injections to stay alive.
- **Type 2 (formerly known as non-insulin dependent)**—The body does not produce enough or cannot properly use insulin. It is the most common form of the disease (90-95% of cases in people over age 20) and often begins later in life.

Warning Signs of Diabetes

Type 1 Diabetes (usually occurs suddenly):

- frequent urination
- unusual thirst
- extreme hunger
- unusual weight loss
- extreme fatigue
- irritability

Type 2 Diabetes (occurs less suddenly):

- any type 1 symptoms
- frequent infections
- blurred vision
- cuts/bruises slow to heal
- tingling/numbness in hands or feet
- recurring skin, gum, or bladder infections

Complications of Diabetes

More than one-third of all individuals with diabetes do not know that they have the disease until one of its life-threatening complications occurs. Potential complications include:

Blindness. Diabetes is the leading cause of blindness in people ages 20-74. Each year, from 12,000 to 24,000 people lose their sight because of diabetes.

Kidney disease. 10% to 21% of all people with diabetes develop kidney disease. In 1995, more than 27,900 people initiated treatment for end-stage renal disease (kidney failure) because of diabetes.

Amputations. Diabetes is the most frequent cause of nontraumatic lower limb amputations. The risk of a leg amputation is 15 to 40 times greater for a person with diabetes than for the average American. Each year, 56,000 people lose a foot or leg to complications brought on by diabetes.

Heart disease and stroke. People with diabetes are 2 to 4 times more likely to have heart disease (more than 77,000 deaths due to heart disease annually). And they are 2 to 4 times more likely to suffer a stroke.

Health-care and related costs for the treatment of the disease, added to the cost of lost productivity, total nearly $100 billion annually in the U.S.

Alzheimer's Disease

Source: Alzheimer's Association, 919 N Michigan Ave., Suite 1000, Chicago, IL 60611-1676; phone: (800) 272-3900

Alzheimer's disease is a progressive, degenerative disease of the brain in which brain cells die and are not replaced. It results in impaired memory, thinking, and behavior, and is the most common form of dementing illness. The debilitating nature of the disease renders patients susceptible to infections (such as pneumonia and urinary tract infections) as they become emaciated, incontinent, immobile, or enter a persistent vegetative state.

Alzheimer's disease afflicts an estimated 4 million Americans, striking equally among men and women of all races. Although most people diagnosed with Alzheimer's are older than age 60, the disease can occur in people in their 40s and 50s. Ten percent of those 65 years of age or older, and almost half of those over age 85, have the disease. It is estimated that the cost of diagnosis, treatment, and long-term care for patients with the disease amounts to $100 billion per year in the U.S.

The rate of the progression of Alzheimer's disease from the onset of symptoms until death ranges from 3 to 20 years; the average is 8 years. Eventually, patients become totally incapable of caring for themselves.

Diagnosis is complicated by the lack of a single, simple test to identify the disease. Through a series of diagnostic tests by a qualified physician, possible causes of symptoms, such as depression, drug interactions, nutrient imblances, or other forms of dementia, such as those associated with stroke, Huntington's disease, Parkinson's disease, Pick's disease, and infections (AIDS, meningitis, syphilis) are ruled out, yielding a diagnosis of Alzheimer's disease that is 80-90% accurate. A definitive diagnosis is possible only with a brain biopsy or an autopsy.

No treatment has proven successful in reversing the course of the disease, and providing care for patients with Alzheimer's disease is very physically and psychologically demanding. Nearly 70% of those afflicted with the disease live at home and are cared for by family and friends. In the last stages of the disease, it is often necessary for those afflicted to be cared for in a nursing home. Nearly half of all nursing home patients in the United States suffer from Alzheimer's disease.

People with Alzheimer's disease need a safe, stable environment and a regular daily schedule. Physical exercise and social activity are important, as is proper nutrition. A bracelet identifying the person's name and condition may be helpful in case the person wanders away.

The causes of the disease are unknown.

Warning Signs

- Recent memory loss that affects job performance
- Inability to learn new information
- Difficulty with everyday tasks such as cooking or dressing oneself
- Inability to remember simple words
- Use of inappropriate words when communicating
- Disorientation of time and place
- Poor or decreased judgment
- Problems with abstract thinking
- Misplacing objects in inappropriate places
- Rapid changes in mood or behavior
- Increased irritability, anxiety, depression, confusion, and restlessness
- Prolonged loss of initiative

Heart and Blood Vessel Disease

Source: American Heart Association, 7272 Greenville Ave., Dallas, TX 75231-4596; phone: (800) 242-8721

Warning Signs

Of Heart Attack

- Uncomfortable pressure, fullness, squeezing, or pain in the center of the chest lasting 2 minutes or longer
- Pain may radiate to the shoulder, arm, neck, or jaw
- Sweating may accompany pain or discomfort
- Nausea and vomiting may also occur
- Shortness of breath, dizziness, or fainting may accompany other signs

The American Heart Association advises immediate action at the onset of these symptoms. The association points out that more than half of heart attack victims die within 1 hour of the onset of symptoms and before they have reached the hospital.

Of Stroke

- Sudden temporary weakness or numbness of face or limbs on one side of the body
- Temporary loss of speech, or trouble speaking or understanding speech
- Temporary dim or lost vision, especially in one eye
- Unexplained dizziness, unsteadiness, or sudden falls

Some Major Risk Factors

Blood pressure—High blood pressure increases the risk of stroke, heart attack, kidney failure, and congestive heart failure.

Cholesterol—A blood cholesterol level over 240 mg/dl (milligrams of cholesterol per deciliter of blood) approximately doubles the risk of coronary heart disease; about 20% of the U.S. adult population (39.4 mil) have a cholesterol level over 240 mg/dl. Levels between 200 and 240 mg/dl are in a zone of moderate and increasing risk. An estimated 6.5 mil (10.8% of) youths age 4-19 have levels of 200 mg/dl or higher.

Cigarettes—Cigarette smokers have more than twice the risk of heart attack and 2-4 times the risk of sudden cardiac death as nonsmokers. Young smokers have a higher risk for early death from stroke.

Obesity—Using a body mass index (BMI) of 25-29 for overweight and 30 and higher for obesity, 104.4 mil Americans age 20 and over are overweight and 42.5 mil are obese.

Understanding Blood Pressure

High blood pressure, or hypertension, affects people of all races, sexes, ethnic origins, and ages. Various causes can trigger this often symptomless disease. Since hypertension can increase one's risk for stroke, heart attack, kidney failure, and congestive heart failure, it is recommended that individuals have a blood pressure reading at least once every 2 years (more often if advised by a physician).

A blood pressure reading is really two measurements in one, with one written over the other, such as 122/78. The **upper number (systolic pressure)** represents the amount of pressure in the blood vessels when the heart contracts (beats) and pushes blood through the circulatory system. The **lower number (diastolic pressure)** represents the pressure in the blood vessels between beats, when the heart is resting. According to National Institutes of Health guidelines, normal blood pressure is below 130/85 and "high normal" is between 130/85 and 139/89. High blood pressure is divided into 3 stages, based on severity:

- **Stage 1** high blood pressure is from 140/90 through 159/99
- **Stage 2** is from 160/100 through 179/109
- **Stage 3** is 180/110 or greater

The diagnosis of hypertension can be based on either the systolic or the diastolic reading.

High blood pressure usually cannot be cured, but it can be controlled in a variety of ways, including lifestyle modifications and medication. Treatment should always be at the direction and under the supervision of a physician.

Examples of Moderate[1] Amounts of Exercise

Source: *Physical Activity and Health: A Report of the Surgeon General*, U.S. Dept. of Health and Human Services, 1996

Activity	Duration[2] (min)	Activity	Duration[2] (min)
Washing and waxing a car	45-60	Raking leaves	30
Washing windows or floors	45-60	Walking 2 mi (15 min/mi)	30
Playing touch football	30-45	Swimming laps	20
Wheeling self in wheelchair	30-40	Basketball (playing a game)	15-20
Walking 1¾ mi (20 min/mi)	35	Bicycling 4 mi	15
Basketball (shooting baskets)	30	Jumping rope	15
Bicycling 5 mi	30	Running 1½ mi (10 min/mi)	15
Dancing fast (social)	30	Shoveling snow	15

Note: The activities are arranged from less vigorous, and using more time, to more vigorous, and using less time. (1) A "moderate" amount of physical activity uses about 150 calories (kcal), or 1,000 if done daily for a week. (2) Activities can be performed at various intensities; the suggested durations are based on the expected intensity of effort.

Finding Your Target Heart Rate

Source: Carole Casten, EdD, *Aerobics Today;* Peg Jordan, RN, Aerobics and Fitness Assoc. of America

The target heart rate is the heartbeat rate a person should have during aerobic exercise (such as running, fast walking, cycling, or cross-country skiing) to get the full benefit of the exercise for cardiovascular conditioning.

First, determine the intensity level at which one would like to exercise. A sedentary person may want to begin an exercise regimen at the 60% level and work up gradually to the 70% level. Athletes and highly fit individuals must work at the 85-95% level to receive benefits.

Second, calculate the target heart rate. One common way of doing this is by using the American College of Sports Medicine Method.

To obtain cardiovascular fitness benefits from aerobic exercise, it is recommended that an individual participate in an aerobic activity at least 3-5 times a week for 20-30 minutes per session, although cardiac patients and very sedentary individuals can obtain benefits with shorter periods (15-20 minutes). Generally, training changes occur in 4-6 weeks, but they can occur in as little as 2 weeks.

The American College of Sports Medicine Method

Using the American College of Sports Medicine Method to calculate one's target heart rate, an individual should subtract his or her age from 220, then multiply by the desired intensity level of the workout. Then divide the answer by 6 for a 10-second pulse count. (The 10-second pulse count is useful for checking whether the target heart rate is being achieved during the workout. One can easily check one's pulse—at the wrist or side of the neck—counting the number of beats in 10 seconds.)

For example, a 20-year-old wishing to exercise at 70% intensity would employ the following steps:

Maximum Heart Rate	220 − 20 = 200
Target Heart Rate	200 × .70 =140
10-second Pulse Count	140 ÷ 6 =23

To work at the desired level of intensity, this 20-year-old would strive for a target heart rate of 140 beats per minute, or a 10-second pulse count of 23.

Arthritis

Source: Arthritis Foundation, 1330 West Peachtree Street, Atlanta, GA 30309; phone: (800) 283-7800

The name *arthritis* refers to more than 100 different diseases that cause pain, stiffness, swelling, and restricted movement in joints and connective tissue. The condition is usually chronic. More than 40 million people in the U.S. have some form of arthritis—about 23 million are women and 285,000 are children. The cause for most types of arthritis is unknown; scientists are studying the roles played by genetics, lifestyle, and the environment.

Symptoms of arthritis may develop either slowly or suddenly. A visit to the doctor is indicated when pain, stiffness, or swelling in a joint or difficulty in moving a joint persists for more than two weeks. The doctor analyzes the patient's symptoms, to see if they are consistent with those of arthritis. The doctor examines joint movement, looks for any swelling, and checks for skin rashes. Finally, the doctor may test the blood, urine, or joint fluid, or take X rays of the joints.

Medications to treat arthritis include drugs that relieve pain and swelling, such as analgesics, anti-inflammatory drugs, or glucocorticoids; disease modifiers, which tend to slow the disease process; and sleep medications, which promote deeper sleep and help relax muscles. Most treatment programs call for exercise; use of heat or cold; and joint-protection techniques (such as avoiding excess stress on joints, using assistive devices, and controlling weight). In some cases, surgery can help when other treatments fail.

Of the three most prevalent forms of arthritis, osteoarthritis is the most common, affecting more than 20 million Americans; it usually occurs after age 45. In this type, which is also called degenerative arthritis, the cartilage and bones deteriorate, causing pain and stiffness as bones rub against each other. It usually occurs in the fingers, knees, feet, hips, and back.

Fibromyalgia, another common type of arthritis, affects more than 2 million Americans and affects more women than men. In this form, widespread pain and tenderness occur in muscles and their attachments to the bone. Common symptoms include fatigue, disturbed sleep, stiffness, and psychological distress.

Rheumatoid arthritis, which also affects more than 2 million people in the U.S., is one of the most serious and disabling forms of the disease. In this type, which is also more common in women, the joints become inflamed because of an abnormality in the body's immune system. The chronic inflammation may then damage the cartilage and bone. The areas of the body that can be affected are the hands, wrists, feet, knees, ankles, shoulders neck, jaw, and elbows.

Other forms of arthritis and related conditions include lupus, gout, ankylosing spondylitis, and scleroderma; also related are bursitis and tendinitis, which result from injuring or overusing a joint.

Alternative Medicine

Source: Office of Alternative Medicine, National Institutes of Health (NIH)

Alternative medicine comprises a wide variety of healing philosophies, approaches, and therapies. It includes treatments and health care practices not widely taught in medical schools, not generally used in hospitals, and not usually reimbursed by health insurance companies. The NIH cautions people not to seek alternative therapies without the consultation of a licensed health care provider.

Some alternative therapies are described as holistic—meaning that the practitioner considers the whole person, including physical, mental, emotional, and spiritual aspects. Some therapies are known as preventive, meaning that the practitioner stresses preventing health problems before they arise.

People may use an alternative therapy alone, along with other alternative therapies, or in combination with more standard therapies. Worldwide, only about 10-30% of health care is provided by conventional practitioners; the remaining 70-90% involves alternative practices. An estimated 1 in 3 Americans uses some form of alternative medicine.

An advisory panel to the Office of Alternative Medicine at the National Institutes of Health developed a classification of alternative health care practices. This list is broken down into 7 general fields of practice:

Alternative systems of medical practice range from self-care based on folk traditions to care given by practitioners according to established procedures. Included are such therapies as acupuncture, Ayurveda (India's traditional system of natural medicine), environmental medicine (treatment of certain illnesses believed to be caused by exposure to particular foods or chemicals), homeopathic medicine (use of remedies made from naturally occurring plant, animal, or mineral substances), Native American practices, naturopathic medicine (integration of traditional, natural therapeutics with modern scientific medicine), and traditional Oriental medicine.

Bioelectromagnetic applications explore how living things interact with electromagnetic fields. Such therapies include blue light treatment and artificial lighting, electroacupuncture, and electrostimulation.

Diet, nutrition, and lifestyle changes are intended to prevent illness, maintain good health, and reverse the effects of chronic disease. Examples include use of macrobiotics, nutritional supplements, and megavitamins.

Herbal medicine employs plants and plant products for pharmacological use. Some common plants used are echinacea, garlic, ginkgo biloba, ginseng, and St. John's wort.

Manual healing uses touch and manipulation with the hands therapeutically. Some types are acupressure, chiropractic medicine, massage therapy, osteopathy, and reflexology.

Mind/body control explores the mind's ability to affect the body. Therapies include counseling, hypnotherapy, meditation, relaxation techniques, support groups, and yoga.

Pharmacological and biological treatments involve drugs and vaccines that are not accepted by mainstream medicine. These include anti-oxidizing agents, metabolic therapy, and oxidizing agents.

Alternative Health Services in the U.S., 1996

Source: *Nutrition Business Journal;* American Osteopathic Assn; *Service Annual Survey: 1996,* U.S. Census Bureau, U.S. Dept. of Commerce

Health care practice	Licensed practitioners	Lay or other practitioners	Total revenues[1]
Acupuncture	8,000	7,000	$1,150
Chiropractic	55,000	NA	8,000
Homeopathy	1,000	2,000	240
Massage therapy	200,000	200,000	6,600
Naturopathy	1,500	1,000	200
Osteopathy	41,600[2]	0	$4,249
Traditional Oriental medicine	NA	9,000	990
Other[3]	NA	30,000	900
Total	**307,100**	**249,000**	**$22,329**

NA = Not available. (1) In millions of dollars. (2) Figure is for 1997. (3) Includes aromatherapy, Ayurveda, Bach flower remedies, biofeedback, colon therapy, crystal therapy, detox therapy, faith healing, fasting/juice therapy, guided imagery, herbal medicine, hydrotherapy, hypnotherapy, meditation/relaxation, and yoga, as well as mainstream practice providing alternative health services.

Top-Selling Medicinal Herbs in the U.S., 1995-97

Source: *Nutrition Business Journal*

Herb	Sales in 1995[1]	Sales in 1997[1]	% change 1995-97
Echinacea	$180	$310	72
Garlic[2]	150	200	33
Ginkgo biloba	160	240	50
Ginseng	210	270	29
St. John's wort	$10	$200	1,900
All other	1,800	2,430	35
Total	**$2,510**	**$3,650**	**45**

(1) In millions of dollars. (2) Does not include nonmedicinal use.

Where to Get Help

Source: Based on Health & Medical Year Book. Copyright © by Collier Newfield, Inc.; additional data, World Almanac research

Listed here are some of the major U.S. and Canadian organizations providing information about good health practices generally, or about specific conditions and how to deal with them. (Canadian sources are identified as such.) Where a toll-free number is not available, an address is given when possible.

Some entries conclude with an e-mail address for the organization and/or an address for its Internet site, where you can also obtain useful information. When inputting an e-mail or Internet address, be certain to type it exactly as it appears, including capital and lowercase letters, nonalphanumeric characters, and spaces (generally none). In addition to these selected sites, there is a vast array of medical information on the Internet; however, it is very important to be certain that the source of information is reliable and accurate. Always check with a physician before embarking on any new health-related venture.

General Sources

Centers for Disease Control and Prevention Voice Information System
888-232-3228
Recorded information about public health topics, such as AIDS and Lyme disease. Also, you can request to talk with a CDC expert or have information faxed to you.
Website: http://www.cdc.gov

National Health Information Center
800-336-4797; in Maryland, 301-565-4167
Phone numbers for more than 1,000 health-related organizations in the United States. Printed materials offered.
E-mail: nhicinfo@health.org

National Institutes of Health
Bethesda, MD 20892
301-496-4000
Free information, including the latest research findings, on many diseases.
Website: http://www.nih.gov

Tel-Med
Check the phone book for local listings or call Tel-Med at 909-825-6034.
Recorded information on over 600 health topics. Sponsored by local medical societies, health organizations, or hospitals.
E-mail: telmed@ix.netcom.com
Website: http://www.tel-med.com

Aging

National Association of Area Agencies on Aging's Eldercare Locator Line
800-677-1116
Information and assistance on a wide range of services and programs including adult day-care and respite services, consumer fraud, hospital and nursing home information, legal services, elder abuse/protective services, Medicaid/Medigap information, tax assistance, and transportation.

National Institute on Aging
800-222-2225
Information and publications about disabling conditions, support groups, and community resources.
E-mail: niainfo@access.digex.net
Website: http://www.nih.gov/nia

AIDS

AIDS Clinical Trials Information Service
800-874-2572
Information on federally and privately sponsored clinical trials for patients with AIDS or HIV.
E-mail: actis@actis.org
Website: http://www.actis.org

Canadian AIDS Society
800-499-1986, in Canada only
Written materials and referrals in the Toronto area.

Centers for Disease Control and Prevention National AIDS/HIV Hotline
800-342-AIDS 24 hours; in Spanish, 800-344-SIDA, M-F, 8 AM-2 AM
for the hearing impaired, 800-AIDS-TTY; M-F, 10 AM-10 PM
Information on the prevention and spread of AIDS, along with referrals.
Website: http://www.ashastd.org

HIV-AIDS Treatment Information Service
800-HIV-0440
Treatment information to people with AIDS, their families, and health care providers.

Alcoholism and Drug Abuse

Alcohol and Drug Helpline
800-821-4357, 24 hours
Referrals to local facilities

Alcoholics Anonymous
212-870-3400
Worldwide support groups for alcoholics. Check phone book for local chapters.
Website: http://www.alcoholics-anonymous.org

American Council on Alcoholism
800-527-5344
Treatment referrals and counseling for recovering alcoholics.
Website: http://www.aca-usa.org

National Clearinghouse for Alcohol and Drug Information
800-729-6686
Provides written materials on alcohol and drug-related subjects.
Website: http://www.health.org

National Council on Alcoholism and Drug Dependence Hopeline
800-622-2255
An answering machine for callers to request information.

National Health Lines
800-262-2463
Answers questions on substance abuse and provides referrals to treatment centers. Operates 24 hours.

Alzheimer's Disease

Alzheimer's Association
800-272-3900
Gives referrals to local chapters and support groups; offers information on publications available from the association.
E-mail: info@alz.org
Website: http://www.alz.org

Alzheimer's Society of Canada
20 Eglinton Ave., W., Suite 1200
Toronto, ON M4R 1K8
416-488-8772
Gives phone numbers for local support chapters. Publishes support materials.
E-mail: info@alzheimer.ca
Website: http://www.alzheimer.ca

Amyotrophic Lateral Sclerosis

ALS Association
800-782-4747; in the San Fernando Valley, 818-340-7500
Information about ALS (Lou Gehrig's Disease) and referrals to ALS specialists, local chapters and support groups.
Website: http://www.alsa.org

Arthritis

Arthritis Foundation
800-283-7800
Information, publications, and referrals to local groups.
Website: http://www.arthritis.org

Arthritis Society (Canada)
393 University Ave., Suite 1700
Toronto, ON M5G 1E6
416-979-7228; in Ontario only, 800-321-1433
Phone numbers for local chapters.
E-mail: info@arthritis.ca
Website: http://www.arthritis.ca

National Arthritis and Musculoskeletal and Skin Diseases Information Clearinghouse
301-495-4484
Subject searches and resource referrals.
Website: http://www.nih.gov/niams

Asthma and Allergies
See also *Lung Diseases*

Asthma and Allergy Foundation Information Clearinghouse
800-7-ASTHMA
Written information.

American Academy of Allergy, Asthma, and Immunology Referral Line
800-822-ASMA, 24 hours
Written materials on asthma and allergies.
Website: http://www.aaaai.org

Blindness and Eye Care

Canadian National Institute for the Blind
1929 Bayview Avenue
Toronto, ON M4G 3E8
416-486-2500 or contact your local chapter.
National office offers training and library with braille books and audiotapes. Local chapters provide core services: orientation in mobility, sight enhancement, counseling, referrals, career aid, technology services.
Website: http://www.cnib.ca

Foundation Fighting Blindness
800-683-5555; in Maryland, 410-785-1414; for the hearing impaired, 800-683-5551
Answers questions about retinal degenerative diseases; has written materials.
Website: http://www.blindness.org

Library of Congress National Service for the Blind and Physically Handicapped
800-424-9100; in Spanish, 800-345-8901; in Washington, DC, 202-707-5100
Information on libraries that offer talking books and books in braille.
Website: http://lcweb.loc.gov/nls/nls.html

National Association for Parents of the Visually Impaired
800-562-6265
Support and information for parents of individuals who are visually impaired.

Blood Disorders

Cooley's Anemia Foundation
800-522-7222
Information on patient care and support groups; makes referrals to local chapters.
E-mail: ncaf@aol.com
Website: http://www.thalassemia.org

Sickle Cell Disease Association of America
800-421-8453; in California, 310-216-6363
Genetic counseling and information packet.
E-mail: lascdaa@aol.com

Burns

Phoenix Society
800-888-2876
Counseling for burn survivors and information on self-help services for burn survivors and their families.
E-mail: info@burns-phoenix-society.org
Website: http://www.burns-phoenix-society.org

Cancer

American Cancer Society
800-ACS-2345
Publications and information about cancer and coping with cancer; makes referrals to local chapters for support services.
Website: http://www.cancer.org

Canadian Cancer Information Service
800-263-6750, in Canada only
Written materials, videos, support services, and referrals.

National Cancer Institute's Cancer Information Service
800-4-CANCER
Information about clinical trials, treatments, symptoms, prevention, referrals to support groups, and screening.
Website: http://wwwicic.nci.nih.gov

Y-Me Breast Cancer Support Program
800-221-2141, 24 hours; in Illinois, 312-986-8228
Information and literature on breast cancer, counseling, and referrals.
Website: http://www.y-me.org

Cerebral Palsy

Ontario Federation for Cerebral Palsy
1630 Lawrence Avenue West, Suite 104
Toronto, ON M6L 1C5
416-244-9686
Canada does not have a national cerebral palsy organization, but the provincial organizations offer information on housing, services, and coping with life, and each one will provide contact numbers for the others.
E-mail: ofcp@ofcp.on.ca
Website: http://www.ofcp.on.ca

United Cerebral Palsy Associations
800-USA-5UCP; in Washington, DC, 202-776-0406
Written materials.
Website: http://www.ucpa.org

Child Abuse
See *Domestic Violence*

Children

American Academy of Pediatrics
847-228-5005
Child-care publications and materials; referrals to pediatricians.
Website: http://www.aap.org

Childhelp's USA National Child Abuse Hotline
800-4-A-CHILD
Crisis intervention, professional counseling, referrals to local groups and to shelters for runaways, and literature. Operates 24 hours.

National Center for Missing and Exploited Children
800-843-5678; for the hearing impaired, 800-826-7653
Hotline for reporting missing children and sightings of missing children.

Chronic Fatigue Syndrome

CFIDS Association of America
800-442-3437
Literature and a list of support groups.
E-mail: info@cfids.org
Website: http://www.cfids.org

Crisis

National Runaway Switchboard
800-621-4000
Crisis intervention and referrals for runaways. Runaways can leave messages for parents, and vice versa. Operates 24 hours.

Cystic Fibrosis

Canadian Cystic Fibrosis Foundation
416-485-9149; in Canada only, 800-378-2233
Information and brochures; makes referrals to local chapters.
Website: http://www.ccff.ca/~cfwww/index.html

Cystic Fibrosis Foundation
800-FIGHT-CF
Answers questions and offers literature and referrals to local clinics.
Website: http://www.cff.org

Diabetes

American Diabetes Association
800-ADA-DISC; in Virginia and Washington, DC, 703-549-1500
Information about diabetes, nutrition, exercise, and treatment; offers referrals to diabetes specialists.
Website: http://www.diabetes.org

Canadian Diabetes Association
15 Toronto Street, Suite 800, Toronto, ON M5C 2E3
416-363-3373; in Ontario only, 800-361-1306
Information and publications.
Website: http://www.diabetes.ca

Juvenile Diabetes Foundation Hotline
800-223-1138 or 800-533-2873
Answers questions, provides literature (some in Spanish), and offers referrals to local chapters, physicians, and clinics.
Website: http://www.jdfcure.org

Digestive Diseases

Crohn's and Colitis Foundation of America
800-932-2423; in New York, 212-685-3440
Educational materials; offers referrals to local chapters, which can provide referrals to support groups and physicians.
Website: http://www.ccfa.org

Crohn's Colitis Foundation of Canada
21 St. Clair Avenue East, Suite 301, Toronto, ON M4T 1L9
416-920-5035; in Canada only, 800-387-1479
Will send educational materials on request.
Website: http://www.ccfc.ca

Domestic Violence

National Council on Child Abuse and Family Violence
800-222-2000;
in Washington, DC, 202-429-6695
A recording provides toll-free numbers to call for information or referrals.
E-mail: nccafv@aol.com

Down Syndrome

National Down Syndrome Congress
800-232-6372; in Georgia, 404-633-1555
Answers questions on all aspects of Down syndrome; referrals.
E-mail: ndsccenter@aol.com
Website: http://members.carol.net/ndsc

National Down Syndrome Society
800-221-4602; in New York City, 212-460-9330
Information; referrals to local programs for newborns.
Website: http://www.ndss.org

Drug Abuse
See *Alcoholism and Drug Abuse*

Dyslexia

International Dyslexia Association
800-ABCD-123; in Maryland, 410-296-0232
Information on testing, tutoring, and computers used to aid people with dyslexia and related disorders.
E-mail: info@interdys.org

Eating Disorders

National Association of Anorexia Nervosa and Associated Disorders
Box 7, Highland Park, IL 60035
847-831-3438
Written materials, referrals, and telephone counseling.
E-mail: anad20@aol.com
Website: http://members.aol.com/anad20/index.html

Endometriosis

Endometriosis Association
800-992-ENDO; in Canada, 800-426-2END
An answering machine for callers to request information.

Epilepsy

Epilepsy and Seizure Disorder Service at the Epilepsy Foundation of America
800-332-1000
Information and referrals to local chapters.
Website: http://www.efa.org

Food Safety and Nutrition

Meat and Poultry Hotline of the U.S. Department of Agriculture's Food, Safety, and Inspection Service
800-535-4555
Information on proper handling, preparation, storage, and cooking of meat, poultry, and eggs.

FDA Center for Food Safety and Applied Nutrition
800-FDA-4010; in Washington, DC, 202-205-4314
Information on how to buy and use seafood products and on their proper handling and storage. Callers may speak to food specialists, Mon. through Fri., 12 noon to 4 PM (EST).
Website: http://www.fda.gov

Headaches

National Headache Foundation
800-843-2256
Literature on headaches and treatment.
Website: http://www.headaches.org

Heart Disease and Stroke

American Heart Association
800-242-8721
Information, publications, and referrals to organizations.
Website: http://www.amhrt.org

National Institute of Neurological Disorders and Stroke
800-352-9424
Literature and information.
Website: http://www.ninds.nih.gov

National Stroke Association
800-787-6537
Information on support networks for stroke victims and their families; referrals to local support groups.
Website: http://www.stroke.org

Hospices

Children's Hospice International
800-242-4453; in Virginia, 703-684-0330
Information; referrals to children's hospices.
E-mail: chiorg@aol.com
Website: http://www.chionline.org

Hospice Education Institute Hospicelink
800-331-1620; in Connecticut, 860-767-1620
General information about hospice care and referrals to local programs.
E-mail: hospiceall@aol.com
Website: http://www.hospiceworld.org

Huntington's Disease

Huntington's Disease Society of America
800-345-4372; in New York, 212-242-1968
Information and referrals to physicians and support groups.
Website: http://hdsa.mgh.harvard.edu

Huntington Society of Canada
P.O. Box 1269,13 Water Street North, Cambridge, ON N1R 7G6
519-622-1002
Information, including telephone numbers of local services; publications and referrals.
E-mail: info@hsc-ca.org

Impotence

Impotence Information Center
800-843-4315
Information on the causes and treatment of impotence, incontinence, and prostate problems.

Impotence World Institute Hotline
800-669-1603
Written materials, physician referrals, and telephone numbers of local Impotents Anonymous chapters.

Kidney Diseases

Kidney Foundation of Canada
514-369-4806; in Canada only, 800-361-7494
Educational materials and general information.
Website: http://www.kidney.ca

National Kidney and Urologic Diseases Information Clearinghouse
3 Information Way
Bethesda, MD 20892-3580
301-654-4415
Information about kidney and urologic diseases and referrals to organizations.
Website: http://www.niddk.nih.gov

National Kidney Foundation
800-622-9010
Information and referrals.
Website: http://www.kidney.org

Lead Exposure

National Lead Information Center
800-LEAD-FYI
Recommendations (in English and Spanish) for reducing a child's exposure to lead. Referrals to state and local agencies.
Website: http://www.nsc.org/ehc/lead.htm

Liver Diseases

American Liver Foundation
800-223-0179; in New Jersey, 201-256-2550
Information on hepatitis, liver disease, and gallbladder disease.
Website: http://www.liverfoundation.org

Lung Diseases
See also *Asthma and Allergies*

American Lung Association
Check the phone book for local listings or call the national office at 800-LUNG-USA for automatic connection to the office nearest you. Answers questions about asthma and lung diseases; publications and referrals.
Website: http://www.lungusa.org

Lung Line Information Service at the National Jewish Medical and Research Center
800-222-LUNG; in Denver, 303-355-LUNG
Answers questions on asthma, emphysema, allergies, smoking, and other respiratory and immune system disorders.
Website: http://www.njc.org

Lupus

Lupus Foundation of America
800-558-0121; in Colorado, 303-670-9292
Sends information to those who leave name and address on answering machine.

Lyme Disease

Lyme Disease Foundation
800-886-LYME, 24 hours
Written information; doctor referrals.

Mental Health

National Clearinghouse on Family Support and Children's Mental Health
800-628-1696, 24 hours
Publications, computerized databank, and state-by-state resource file.

National Depressive and Manic Depressive Association
800-826-3632
Support for patients and families, provides publications, and makes referrals to affiliated organizations.
Website: http://www.ndmda.org

National Foundation for Depressive Illness
800-248-4344, 24 hours
Recorded message describing the symptoms of depression and offering an address for more information and physician referral.

National Institute of Mental Health
5600 Fisher's Lane, Room 7C02, MSC 8030, Bethesda, MD 20892-8030
301-443-4513
Information on a range of topics, from children's mental disorders to schizophrenia, depression, eating disorders, and others.
Website: http://www.nimh.nih.gov

National Mental Health Association
800-969-6642
Referrals to mental health groups.

Multiple Sclerosis

Multiple Sclerosis Society of Canada
800-268-7582, in Canada only
Counseling, literature, and referrals to local chapters.

National Multiple Sclerosis Society
800-344-4867
Information about local chapters.
Website: http://www.nmss.org

Muscular Dystrophy

Muscular Dystrophy Association
800-572-1717
Written materials on 40 neuromuscular diseases, including muscular dystrophy. Will give information over the phone about such matters as MDA clinics, support groups, summer camps, and wheelchair purchase assistance.
Website: http://www.mdausa.org

Nutrition
See *Food Safety and Nutrition*

Organ Donation

Living Bank
800-528-2971, 24 hours
A registry and referral service for people wanting to commit organs to transplantation or research.
Website: http://www.thelivingbank.org

Osteoporosis

National Osteoporosis Foundation
800-223-9994, in Washington, DC, 202-223-2226
Information packet available on request.
Website: http://www.nof.org

Pain

National Chronic Pain Outreach Association
540-997-5004
Information packet available on request.

Parkinson's Disease

National Parkinson Foundation
800-327-4545; in Florida, 800-433-7022; in Miami, 305-547-6666
Answers questions, makes physician referrals, and provides written information in English and Spanish.
E-mail: mailbox@npf.med.miami.edu
Website: http://www.parkinson.org

Parkinson Foundation of Canada
800-565-3000, in Canada only
Information; referrals to support groups.

Plastic Surgery

Plastic Surgery Information Service
800-635-0635
Referrals to board-certified plastic surgeons in the U.S. and Canada; general information.
Website: http://www.plasticsurgery.org

Polio

International Polio Network
4207 Lindell Blvd., #110
St. Louis, MO 63108
314-534-0475
Information on coping with the late effects of polio; referrals to other organizations.
E-mail: gini_intl@msn.com
Website: http://www.postpolio.org

Prostate Problems

Prostate Information Line
800-543-9632
Advice on treatment.

Rare Disorders

National Organization for Rare Disorders
800-999-6673
Information on diseases and networking programs; referrals to organizations for specific disorders.
Website: http://www.nord-rdb.com

Rehabilitation

National Rehabilitation Information Center
800-34-NARIC; in Maryland, 301-588-9284
Research referrals and information on rehabilitation issues.
Website: http://www.cais.net/naric

Scleroderma

United Scleroderma Foundation
800-722-4673
Referrals to local support groups and treatment centers, as well as information on scleroderma and related skin disorders.
E-mail: sclerofed@aol.com
Website: http://www.scleroderma.com

Sexually Transmitted Diseases
See also *AIDS*

National STD Hotline
800-227-8922
Information; confidential referrals.
Website: http://www.ashastd.org

Sjogren's Syndrome

Sjogren's Syndrome Foundation
800-4-SJOGREN; in New York, 516-933-6365
Provides an answering machine for callers to request treatment literature.

Skin Problems

National Psoriasis Foundation
800-723-9166
Information and referrals.
Website: http://www.psoriasis.org

Speech and Hearing

American Speech-Language-Hearing Association Helpline
800-638-8255 (also TTY); in Maryland, 301-897-8628
Materials on speech and language disorders and hearing impairment; referrals.
Website: http://www.asha.org

Canadian Hard of Hearing Association
2435 Holly Lane, Suite 205
Ottawa, ON K1V 7P2
613-526-1584; TTY 613-526-2692
Publications; answers general questions.
E-mail: chhanational@cyberuf.ca

Dial a Hearing Screening Test
800-222-EARS
Answers questions on hearing problems. Makes referrals to local telephone numbers for a two-minute hearing test. Also to ear, nose, and throat specialists and to organizations that can provide specialized ear and hearing aid information.
E-mail: dahst@aol.com

Hearing Aid Helpline
800-521-5247
Information and distributes a directory of hearing aid specialists certified by the International Hearing Society.
Website: http://www.hearingihs.org

National Center for Stuttering
800-221-2483; in New York, 212-532-1460
Information on stuttering in all age groups.
Website: http://www.stuttering.com

Stuttering Foundation of America
800-992-9392
Referrals to speech pathologists; resource lists, publications.
E-mail: stutterssa@aol.com

Spinal Injuries

National Spinal Cord Injury Association
800-962-9629; in Maryland, 301-588-6959
Peer counseling; referrals to local chapters and other organizations.
Website: http://www.spinalcord.org

National Spinal Cord Injury Hotline
800-526-3456
Written materials on spinal cord injuries; referrals to organizations and support groups.
Website: http://users.aol.com/scihotline

Stroke
See *Heart Disease and Stroke*

Sudden Infant Death Syndrome

American Sudden Infant Death Syndrome Institute
800-232-SIDS; in Georgia, 800-847-7437
Answers questions; literature; referrals to other organizations.
E-mail: prevent@sids.org
Website: http://www.sids.org

National SIDS Foundation
800-221-SIDS; in Maryland, 410-653-8226
Literature on medical information, referrals, and support groups.

Tourette Syndrome

Tourette Syndrome Association
800-237-0717; in New York, 718-224-2999
Printed information.
E-mail: tourette@ix.netcom.com

Urinary Incontinence

National Association for Continence
800-BLADDER
Information on bladder control, services available for incontinence, and assistive devices.
Website: http://www.nafc.org

Simon Foundation for Continence
800-23-SIMON
Support and literature on incontinence.

Women's Health

National Women's Health Network
514 10th Street NW, Suite 400
Washington, DC 20004
202-347-1140; 202-628-7814 (clearinghouse)
Information and referrals on more than 70 women's health concerns.

National Women's Health Resource Center
5255 Loughboro Road
Washington, DC 20016
202-537-4015
A national clearinghouse for women's health information.

POSTAL INFORMATION

(Based on information available Sept. 1998 from U.S. Postal Service, unless otherwise indicated)

U.S. Postal Service

The Postal Reorganization Act, creating a government-owned postal service under the executive branch and replacing the old Post Office Department, was signed into law by Pres. Richard Nixon Aug. 12, 1970. The service officially came into being on July 1, 1971.

The U.S. Postal Service is governed by an 11-person Board of Governors. Nine members are appointed to 9-year terms by the president with Senate approval. These 9, in turn, choose a postmaster general. The board and the postmaster general choose the 11th member, who serves as deputy postmaster general. An independent Postal Rate Commission of 5 members, appointed by the president, reviews and rules on proposed postal rate increases submitted by the Board of Governors.

As of Feb. 28, 1998, there were 38,019 post offices throughout the U.S., including both stations and branches.

U.S. Domestic Rates

Domestic rates apply to the U.S., to its territories and possessions, and to APOs and FPOs. On Jan. 10, 1999, many changes for domestic postal rates and fees will take effect.

First Class

First Class includes written matter such as letters, postal cards, and postcards (private mailing cards) plus all other matter wholly or partly in writing, whether sealed or unsealed, except book manuscripts, periodical articles and music, manuscript copy accompanying proofsheets or corrected proofsheets of the same, and the writing authorized by law on matter of other classes. Also included: matter sealed or closed against inspection, bills, and statements of accounts.

Mailing written letters and matter sealed against inspection will cost 33¢ as of Jan. 10, 1999 (32¢ before then), for first ounce or fraction, 22¢ (23¢ before then) for each additional ounce or fraction up to and including 13 oz (11 oz before Jan. 10, 1999). U.S. Postal Service cards and private postcards alike cost 20¢ single, 40¢ double. Presort and automation-compatible mail can qualify for lower rates if certain piece minimums, mailing permits, and other requirements are met.

Express Mail

Express Mail Service is available for any mailable article up to 70 lb, and guarantees delivery between major U.S. cities within a specified time frame or your money back. Articles received by the acceptance time authorized by the postmaster at a postal facility offering Express Mail are delivered by 3 PM the next day to some locations or by noon the next day to other destinations. Or, if you prefer, you can pick up the package yourself, as early as 10 AM the next business day. Second-day service is available to locations not on the Next Day Delivery Network. Rates include insurance, shipment receipt, and record of delivery at the destination post office.

The basic rate for Express Mail weighing up to 8 oz is $11.75 as of Jan. 10, 1999 ($10.75 before then). Consult postmaster for other Express Mail Services and rates. The Postal Service will refund, upon application to originating office, the postage for any Express Mail shipments not meeting the service standard, except for those delayed by strike or work stoppage, delay or cancellation of flights, or government action beyond the control of the Postal Service.

Periodicals

Periodicals include newspapers and magazines.

For the general public, the applicable Standard Mail or First-Class postage is paid for periodicals.

For publishers, rates vary according to (1) whether item is sent to same county, (2) percentage of reading and advertising matter, (3) weight, (4) distance, (5) level of presort, (6) automation compatibility.

Standard Mail (A)

Standard Mail (A) is limited to 16 ounces and bulk mailings (at least 200 pieces or 50 lbs.) of such items as solicitations, newsletters, and advertising materials.

For single-piece mailing of publications, small parcels, printed matter, booklets, and catalogs (service no longer available after Jan. 10, 1999), first ounce or fraction is 32¢; each additional ounce or fraction up to 11 oz is 23¢; the flat fee for pieces over 11 oz up to 13 oz is $2.90 and for pieces over 13 oz up to 16 oz is $2.95.

For mailing Standard Mail (A) in bulk (at least 200 pieces or 50 lb of such items as solicitations, newsletters, advertising materials, books, and cassettes, each item of which individually weighs less than 1 lb.), the minimum rate per piece, basic, non-letter, is $0.304 as of Jan. 10, 1999 ($0.306 before then), for pieces weighing 3.3087 oz or less; for pieces weighing more than 3.3087 oz, the rate is $0.164 as of Jan. 10, 1999 ($0.166 before then), per piece plus $0.677 per pound. Contact your post office for the discounts offered for presorted, letter-shaped, destination entry, and automation-compatible mail.

Separate rates are available for some nonprofit organizations provided with a permit. The permit requires a one-time imprint fee of $100 as of Jan. 10, 1999 ($85 before then) plus an annual (calendar year) fee of $100 ($85 before Jan. 10, 1999).

Parcel Post—Standard Mail (B)

Any matter that weighs 16 oz or more and is not included in First Class or Periodicals goes as Parcel Post, or Standard Mail (B). The post office determines Parcel Post charges according to the weight of the package in pounds and the zone distance it is being shipped. All fractions of a pound are counted as a full pound.

Forwarding Addresses

To obtain a forwarding address, the mailer must write on the envelope or cover the words "Address Correction Requested." The destination post office then will check for a forwarding address on file and provide it for 50¢ per manual correction, 20¢ per automated correction.

Priority Mail Flat Rate

The most expeditious handling and transportation available will be used for fast delivery by "Priority Mail." If the item fits into a special Postal Service flat-rate envelope, the rate is $3.20 as of Jan. 10, 1999 ($3.00 before then) regardless of weight.

Pickup service for Priority Mail is available for $8.25 as of Jan. 10, 1999 ($4.95 before then) per stop (not per package) by the Postal Service.

Priority Mail by Weight

Priority Mail may include packages up to 70 lb and not over 108 in. in length and girth combined, whether sealed or unsealed, including written and other First Class material. Fractions of a pound are rounded up to the next full pound.

	Up to 2 lb	3 lb	4 lb	5 lb
As of Jan. 10, 1999	$3.20	$4.30	$5.40	$6.50
Prior to Jan. 10, 1999	$3.00	$4.00	$5.00	$6.00

For parcels over 5 lb, rates by zone apply. The mileage between the specific geographic locations of 3-digit ZIP codes determines the zone number used. The mileage range by zone number is: Zone 1—up to 50 mi; 2—51 to 150 mi; 3—151 to 300 mi; 4—301 to 600 mi; 5—601 to 1,000 mi; 6—1,001 to 1,400 mi; 7—1,401 to 1,800 mi; 8—over 1,800 mi.

Parcels weighing less than 15 lb and measuring over 84 in. in length or girth, but not exceeding 108 in. in length and girth combined, cost the same as a 15-lb parcel mailed to the same zone.

Special Handling

Parcel Post parcels—and Standard Mail (A) before Jan. 10, 1999—can be given special, expedited handling upon payment of the following surcharge: up to 10 lb, $5.40; over 10 lb, $7.50. Such parcels must be marked for "Special Handling."

Bound Printed Matter Rates

(single-piece zone rate)
(effective Jan. 10, 1999)

Weight (lbs)	Local	Zones 1&2	3	4	5	6	7	8
1.5	$1.14	$1.54	$1.57	$1.63	$1.72	$1.81	$1.92	$2.02
2	1.16	1.57	1.61	1.69	1.81	1.93	2.08	2.21
2.5	1.18	1.60	1.66	1.76	1.90	2.06	2.24	2.40
3	1.20	1.63	1.70	1.82	1.99	2.18	2.40	2.60
3.5	1.22	1.66	1.74	1.88	2.08	2.30	2.56	2.79
4	1.24	1.70	1.79	1.94	2.18	2.42	2.72	2.98
4.5	1.26	1.73	1.83	2.01	2.27	2.55	2.88	3.17
5	1.28	1.76	1.88	2.07	2.36	2.67	3.05	3.37
6	1.31	1.82	1.96	2.20	2.54	2.92	3.37	3.75
7	1.35	1.89	2.05	2.32	2.73	3.16	3.69	4.14
8	1.39	1.95	2.14	2.45	2.91	3.41	4.01	4.52
9	1.43	2.02	2.22	2.57	3.10	3.65	4.33	4.91
10	1.47	2.08	2.31	2.70	3.28	3.90	4.65	5.29
11	1.51	2.14	2.40	2.83	3.46	4.15	4.97	5.68
12	1.55	2.21	2.48	2.95	3.65	4.39	5.29	6.06
13	1.59	2.27	2.57	3.08	3.83	4.64	5.61	6.45
14	1.63	2.34	2.66	3.20	4.02	4.88	5.93	6.83
15	1.67	2.40	2.75	3.33	4.20	5.13	6.26	7.22

(Includes both catalogs and similar bound printed matter.)

(Bound printed matter must weigh at least 1 lb and not more than 15 lb. Bound printed matter includes catalogs, directories, and books not eligible for special Parcel Post rates.)

Domestic Mail Special Services

Registry—Only matter prepaid with postage at First Class postage rates may be registered. Stamps or meter stamps must be attached. The face of the article must be at least 5″ long, 3½″ high. The mailer is required to declare the value of mail presented for registration.

Registered Mail

Declared Value	Fee as of Jan. 10, 1999 (1)	Fee prior to Jan. 10, 1999 (1)
$0.00	$6.00 (2)	$4.85 (2)
$0.01 to $100	6.20	4.95
$100.01 to $500	6.75	5.40
$500.01 to $1,000	7.30	5.85
$1,000.01 to $2,000	7.85	6.30
$2,000.01 to $3,000	8.40	6.75
$3,000.01 to $4,000	8.95	7.20
$4,000.01 to $5,000	9.50	7.65
$5,000.01 to $6,000	10.05	8.10
$6,000.01 to $7,000	10.60	8.55
$7,000.01 to $8,000	11.15	9.00
$8,000.01 to $9,000	11.70	9.45
$9,000.01 to $10,000	12.25	9.90

Consult postmaster for registry fees above $10,000.

(1) Fee for articles with declared value over $0.00 includes insurance; fee is in addition to postage. (2) Without insurance.

C.O.D.: Unregistered: Applicable to First Class, Priority Mail, Standard Mail, and Express Mail matter. Such mail must be sent as bona fide orders or be in conformity with agreements between senders and addressees. **Registered:** For details, consult postmaster.

Insurance: Applicable to Standard Mail matter. Matter for sale addressed to prospective purchasers who have not ordered it or authorized its sending cannot be insured.

Insured Mail Fees

Declared Value	Fee as of Jan. 10, 1999	Fee prior to Jan. 10, 1999
$0.01 to $50	$0.85	$0.75
$50.01 to $100	1.80	1.60
$100.01 to $200	2.75	2.50
$200.01 to $300	3.70	3.40
$300.01 to $400	4.65	4.30
$400.01 to $500	5.60	5.20
$500.01 to $600	6.55	6.10

Add $0.95 for each additional portion of $100 over $600 up to $5,000 in coverage. (Liability for insured mail is limited to $5,000.)

Certified mail: This service is available for any matter having no intrinsic value on which First Class or Priority Mail postage is paid. Receipt is furnished at time of mailing, and evidence of delivery is obtained. The basic fee is $1.40 as of Jan. 10, 1999 ($1.35 before then) in addition to postage. Return receipt and restricted delivery are available upon payment of additional fees. No indemnity.

Special Standard Mail

(limit 70 lb)

Applies only to: Books of at least 8 printed pages consisting wholly of reading matter or scholarly bibliography, or reading matter with incidental blank spaces for notations and containing no advertising matter other than incidental announcements of books; 16-mm or narrower-width films in final form and catalogs of such films of 24 pages or more (at least 22 of which are printed) except films and film catalogs sent to or from commercial theaters; printed music in bound or sheet form; printed objective test materials; sound recordings, playscripts, and manuscripts for books, periodicals, and music; printed educational reference charts; loose-leaf pages and binders consisting of medical information for distribution to doctors, hospitals, medical schools, and medical students; computer-readable media containing prerecorded information and guides for use with such media. Package must be marked "Special Standard Class Rate" and must state what it contains. The rates are: first pound or fraction, $1.13 as of Jan. 10, 1999 ($1.24 before then) [64¢ (70¢ before Jan. 10, 1999) if 500 pieces or more of special rate matter are presorted to 5-digit ZIP code, or 95¢ ($1.04 before Jan. 10, 1999) if 500 pieces or more are presorted to Bulk Mail Centers]; each additional pound or fraction through 7 lb, 45¢ (50¢ before Jan. 10, 1999); each additional pound, 28¢ (31¢ before Jan. 10, 1999).

Library Mail

(limit 70 lb)

Library Mail includes the following: books when loaned or exchanged between and sent to or from schools, colleges, public libraries, and certain nonprofit organizations; books, printed music, bound academic theses, periodicals, sound recordings, other library materials, museum materials (specimens, collections), scientific or mathematical kits, instruments or other devices; also catalogs, guides, or scripts for some of these materials. Also qualifying for library rate are books mailed from publishers or distributors to schools, libraries, colleges, or universities or to bookstores owned, operated, and controlled by schools, colleges, or universities. All such packages must be marked "Library Mail." The rate is: first pound, $1.13 as of Jan. 10, 1999 ($1.12 before then); each additional pound through 7 lb, 45¢ as of Jan. 10, 1999 (42¢ before then); each additional pound, 28¢ as of Jan. 10, 1999 (22¢ before then).

Parcel Post Rate Schedule

(Inter BMC/ASF ZIP codes only, machinable parcels, no discount, no surcharge)
(effective Jan. 10, 1999)

Weight up to but not exceeding—(pounds)	Zones 1 and 2	3	4	5	6	7	8
2	$3.15	$3.15	$3.15	$3.15	$3.15	$3.15	$3.15
3	3.59	3.90	4.25	4.25	4.25	4.25	4.25
4	3.73	4.16	4.91	5.35	5.35	5.35	5.35
5	3.86	4.39	5.33	6.45	6.45	6.45	6.45
6	3.99	4.62	5.71	7.10	7.40	7.60	8.15
7	4.11	4.82	6.07	7.72	8.35	8.75	9.85
8	4.24	5.01	6.38	8.26	9.30	9.90	11.55
9	4.33	5.19	6.71	8.76	10.25	11.05	13.25
10	4.45	5.36	6.99	9.23	10.92	12.20	14.95
11	4.54	5.53	7.27	9.66	11.47	13.30	16.10
12	4.64	5.68	7.53	10.06	11.97	14.30	17.35
13	4.73	5.81	7.77	10.44	12.44	15.17	18.65
14	4.82	5.97	8.01	10.80	12.89	15.74	19.90
15	4.90	6.10	8.24	11.13	13.31	16.28	21.15
16	4.98	6.23	8.45	11.45	13.70	16.77	21.85
17	5.07	6.34	8.66	11.74	14.08	17.25	22.49
18	5.14	6.46	8.85	12.02	14.42	17.69	23.10
19	5.23	6.58	9.04	12.29	14.76	18.12	23.67
20	5.29	6.68	9.20	12.54	15.07	18.52	24.21
21	5.36	6.80	9.37	12.79	15.38	18.90	24.72
22	5.43	6.89	9.54	13.02	15.66	19.26	25.21
23	5.50	7.01	9.71	13.23	15.93	19.60	25.67
24	5.55	7.10	9.85	13.45	16.19	19.94	26.12
25	5.62	7.19	10.01	13.64	16.44	20.24	26.54

Postal Union Mail Special Services

Registration: Available to practically all countries. Fee $4.85. The maximum indemnity payable—generally only in case of complete loss (of both contents and wrapper)—is $42.30. To Canada only, the fee is $4.95, providing indemnity for loss up to $100, $5.40 for loss up to $500, and $5.85 for loss up to $1,000.

Return receipt: Shows to whom and date delivered; $1.25 ($1.10 before Jan. 10, 1999).

Special delivery: As of June 8, 1997, this service was no longer available.

Marking: An article that is intended for special delivery service must have affixed to the cover near the name of the country of destination "EXPRES" (special delivery) label, obtainable at the post office, or the word "EXPRES" (special delivery) may be marked on the cover boldly in red letters.

Air mail: Available daily to practically all countries.

Prepayment of replies from other countries: A mailer who wishes to prepay a reply by letter from another country may do so by sending one or more international reply coupons, available at U.S. post offices. These should be accepted in any country in exchange for stamps to prepay an air mail letter of the first unit of weight to the U.S.

Insurance: Available to many countries for loss of or damage to items paid at parcel post rate. Consult postmaster for indemnity limits for individual countries.

Limit of indemnity Not over	Fees Canada[1]	All other countries[1]
$50	$0.75	$1.60
100	1.60	2.45
200	2.50	3.35
300	3.40	4.25
400	4.30	5.15
500	5.20	6.05
600	6.10	6.95
700		7.40
800		7.85
900		8.30
1,000		8.75
1,100		9.20
1,200		9.65

(1) Not all countries insure items up to the amounts listed in the table. Canada does not insure items for more than $600.

Restricted delivery: Available to many countries for registered mail; some limitations. Fee: $2.75.

Post Office-Authorized 2-Letter State Abbreviations

The abbreviations below are approved by the U.S. Postal Service for use in addresses for the 50 states, the District of Columbia, Puerto Rico, the U.S. Virgin Islands, American Samoa, Guam, and certain other areas in the Pacific.

Alabama	AL	Hawaii	HI	Missouri	MO	Pennsylvania	PA
Alaska	AK	Idaho	ID	Montana	MT	Puerto Rico	PR
American Samoa	AS	Illinois	IL	Nebraska	NE	Rhode Island	RI
Arizona	AZ	Indiana	IN	Nevada	NV	South Carolina	SC
Arkansas	AR	Iowa	IA	New Hampshire	NH	South Dakota	SD
California	CA	Kansas	KS	New Jersey	NJ	Tennessee	TN
Colorado	CO	Kentucky	KY	New Mexico	NM	Texas	TX
Connecticut	CT	Louisiana	LA	New York	NY	Utah	UT
Delaware	DE	Maine	ME	North Carolina	NC	Vermont	VT
Dist. of Col.	DC	Marshall Islands[1]	MH	North Dakota	ND	Virgin Islands	VI
Federated States of Micronesia[1]	FM	Maryland	MD	Northern Mariana Is.	MP	Virginia	VA
Florida	FL	Massachusetts	MA	Ohio	OH	Washington	WA
Georgia	GA	Michigan	MI	Oklahoma	OK	West Virginia	WV
Guam	GU	Minnesota	MN	Oregon	OR	Wisconsin	WI
		Mississippi	MS	Palau[1]	PW	Wyoming	WY

(1) Although an independent nation, this country is currently subject to domestic rates and fees.

Canadian Province and Territory Postal Abbreviations

Source: Canada Post

Alberta	AB	Newfoundland and Labrador	NF	Prince Edward Island	PE
British Columbia	BC	Northwest Territories	NT	Quebec	QC[1]
Manitoba	MB	Nova Scotia	NS	Saskatchewan	SK
New Brunswick	NB	Ontario	ON	Yukon Territory	YT

(1) PQ is also acceptable.

U.S. First Class Stamp Rates Since 1900

At the beginning of the 20th century the cost to send a letter that weighed 1 oz or less was 2 cents. The following table shows the changing rates for first class stamps and the date on which each new rate became effective.

Date	Cost	Date	Cost	Date	Cost	Date	Cost
Nov. 2, 1917	$0.03	Jan. 7, 1963	$0.05	Dec. 31, 1975	$0.13	Feb. 17, 1985	$0.22
July 1, 1919	0.02	Jan. 7, 1968	0.06	May 29, 1978	0.15	Apr. 3, 1988	0.25
July 6, 1932	0.03	May 16, 1971	0.08	Mar. 22, 1981	0.18	Feb. 3, 1991	0.29
Aug. 1, 1958	0.04	Mar. 2, 1974	0.10	Nov. 1, 1981	0.20	Jan. 1, 1995	0.32
						Jan. 10, 1999	0.33

International Air Mail Rates

Aerogrammes — 50¢ from U.S. to all countries.
Air mail postcards (single) — 50¢ to all countries except Canada (40¢ each) and Mexico (35¢ each).
International letters and letter packages: to Canada and Mexico (by air mail; there are no surface rates to these countries)—weight not over 0.5 oz, 46¢ to Canada, 40¢ to Mexico; not over 1.0 oz, 52¢ to Canada, 46¢ to Mexico; not over 2 oz, 72¢ to Canada, 86¢ to Mexico; not over 3 oz, 95¢ to Canada, $1.26 to Mexico.

Air Mail, Letter, and Letter Package Rates to Countries Other Than Canada and Mexico

(weight limit: 64 oz [4 lb])

Weight not over	Rate	Weight not over	Rate	Weight not over	Rate	Weight not over	Rate
0.5 oz	$0.60	12.5 oz	$10.20	24.5 oz	$19.80	41 oz	$29.40
1.0	1.00	13.0	10.60	25.0	20.20	42	29.80
1.5	1.40	13.5	11.00	25.5	20.60	43	30.20
2.0	1.80	14.0	11.40	26.0	21.00	44	30.60
2.5	2.20	14.5	11.80	26.5	21.40	45	31.00
3.0	2.60	15.0	12.20	27.0	21.80	46	31.40
3.5	3.00	15.5	12.60	27.5	22.20	47	31.80
4.0	3.40	16.0	13.00	28.0	22.60	48	32.20
4.5	3.80	16.5	13.40	28.5	23.00	49	32.60
5.0	4.20	17.0	13.80	29.0	23.40	50	33.00
5.5	4.60	17.5	14.20	29.5	23.80	51	33.40
6.0	5.00	18.0	14.60	30.0	24.20	52	33.80
6.5	5.40	18.5	15.00	30.5	24.60	53	34.20
7.0	5.80	19.0	15.40	31.0	25.00	54	34.60
7.5	6.20	19.5	15.80	31.5	25.40	55	35.00
8.0	6.60	20.0	16.20	32.0	25.80	56	35.40
8.5	7.00	20.5	16.60	33.0	26.20	57	35.80
9.0	7.40	21.0	17.00	34.0	26.60	58	36.20
9.5	7.80	21.5	17.40	35.0	27.00	59	36.60
10.0	8.20	22.0	17.80	36.0	27.40	60	37.00
10.5	8.60	22.5	18.20	37.0	27.80	61	37.40
11.0	9.00	23.0	18.60	38.0	28.20	62	37.80
11.5	9.40	23.5	19.00	39.0	28.60	63	38.20
12.0	9.80	24.0	19.40	40.0	29.00	64	38.60

Air Mail Parcel Post Rates

Weight	Canada	Mexico	Cost, depending on country's rate group A	B	C	D	E
First pound	$7.00[1]	$6.50[2]	$6.50	$8.25	$9.75	$11.20	$12.80
Each additional pound or fraction up to 5 lb	1.28	2.56	3.36	4.00	5.28	5.76	6.40
Each additional pound or fraction up to 10 lb	1.20	2.24	2.88	3.20	4.32	5.28	5.44
Each additional pound or fraction up to 20 lb	1.12	1.92	2.72	2.88	4.00	4.32	4.48
Each additional pound or fraction up to 30 lb	1.12	1.60	2.24	2.56	3.84	4.16	4.32
Each additional pound or fraction over 30 lb	1.12	1.60	1.92	2.24	3.68	4.00	4.16

(1) Fee up to 2 lbs. is $7.00. (2) Rate for each additional pound or fraction up to 3 lb is $3.20.

Country Rate Groups

(For further information, consult your local post office.)

Country or territory	Rate group	Maximum weight limit (lbs)
Afghanistan[1]	D	44
Albania	C	44
Algeria	D	66
Andorra	B	44
Angola	E	22
Anguilla	A	22
Antigua & Barbuda	A	22
Argentina	D	44
Armenia	E	44
Aruba	A	44
Ascension	no air service	44 (surface)
Australia	D	44
Austria	B	44
Azerbaijan	E	22
Azores	C	44
Bahamas	A	44
Bahrain	D	44
Bangladesh	E	22
Barbados	B	44
Belarus	E	44
Belgium	D	44
Belize	A	44
Benin	C	44
Bermuda	A	44
Bhutan	E	44
Bolivia	B	44
Bosnia and Herzegovina	C	33
Botswana	E	44
Brazil	E	44
British Virgin Islands	A	44
Brunei	D	44
Bulgaria	D	44
Burkina Faso	D	44
Burma	see Myanmar	
Burundi	E	44
Cambodia[2]	E	44 (air only)
Cameroon	D	44
Cape Verde	D	44
Cayman Islands	A	44
Central African Republic	E	44
Chad[3]	D	44 (air only)
Chile	D	44
China (People's Republic of)	D	44
Colombia	B	44
Comoros	E	44
Congo, Dem. Rep. of (Zaire)	E	44
Congo Republic	D	44
Corsica	E	44
Costa Rica	A	44
Côte d'Ivoire	D	44
Croatia	C	44
Cuba[2]	no parcel post	

Country or territory	Rate group	Maximum weight limit (lbs)
Cyprus	C	44
Czech Republic	C	33
Denmark	C	66
Djibouti	D	44
Dominica	A	44
Dominican Republic	A	44
East Timor	see Indonesia	
Ecuador	C	44
Egypt	D	44
El Salvador	B	44
Equatorial Guinea	D	44
Eritrea	D	44
Estonia	E	44
Ethiopia	D	44
Faroe Islands	C	66
Falkland Islands[2]	no air PP	44 (surface)
Fiji	B	44
Finland	D	44
France	E	44
French Guiana	C	44
French Polynesia	D	44
Gabon[3]	D	44
Gambia, The	B	22
Georgia, Republic of	E	22
Germany	B	44
Ghana	D	44
Gibraltar	C	44
Great Britain and Northern Ireland	C	66
Greece	C	44
Greenland	D	66
Grenada	A	44
Guadeloupe	A	44
Guatemala	A	44
Guinea	B	44
Guinea-Bissau	B	22
Guyana	B	44
Haiti	A	44
Honduras	B	44
Hong Kong	C	44
Hungary	C	44
Iceland	C	44
India	D	44
Indonesia[4]	E	44
Iran	D	44
Iraq[2]	D	44
Ireland	C	66
Israel[5]	C	44
Italy	C	44
Ivory Coast	see Côte d'Ivoire	
Jamaica	A	22
Japan	E	44
Jordan	C	44
Kazakhstan	E	44
Kenya	D	44
Kiribati	B	44
Korea, Democratic People's Rep. of (North)[2]	no parcel post	
Korea, Republic of (South)	C	44
Kuwait[3]	C	44 (air only)
Kyrgyzstan	E	22
Laos	E	44
Latvia	E	44
Lebanon[2,3]	C	22 (air only)
Lesotho	E	44
Liberia[3]	C	44
Libya[2]	D	44
Liechtenstein	B	66
Lithuania	E	44
Luxembourg	B	44
Macao	C	44
Macedonia	C	33
Madagascar	E	44
Madeira Islands	B	44
Malawi	D	44
Malaysia	D	22
Maldives	D	22
Mali	C	44
Malta	C	22
Martinique	A	44
Mauritania	D	44
Mauritius	E	22
Moldova	E	44
Monaco	E	44
Mongolia	no parcel post	
Montserrat	A	44
Morocco	C	44
Mozambique	E	44
Myanmar	D	22
Namibia	D	44
Nauru	C	44
Nepal	D	44 (surface) 11 (air)
Netherlands	C	44
Netherlands Antilles	A	44
New Caledonia	D	44
New Zealand	D	44
Nicaragua	B	44
Niger	D	44
Nigeria	C	44
Norway	D	44
Oman	D	44
Pakistan	D	44
Panama	A	44
Papua New Guinea[2]	D	44
Paraguay	D	44
Peru	B	44
Philippines	D	44
Pitcairn Island	B	22
Poland	B	33
Portugal	C	44
Qatar	C	44
Reunion	E	44
Romania	C	44
Russia	E	22
Rwanda[2]	D	44
Saint Helena	C	44
Saint Kitts & Nevis	A	44
Saint Lucia	A	44
Saint Pierre & Miquelon	A	44
Saint Vincent & the Grenadines	A	22
Samoa	B	44
San Marino	C	44
São Tomé & Príncipe	D	44
Saudi Arabia	D	44
Senegal	D	44
Seychelles	D	44
Sierre Leone	D	44
Singapore	D	44
Slovakia	C	33
Slovenia	C	33
Solomon Islands	C	44
Somalia[1]	D	44
South Africa	D	44
Spain	C	44
Sri Lanka	D	44
Sudan	D	44
Suriname	B	44
Swaziland	D	44
Sweden	D	44
Switzerland	B	66
Syria	C	44
Taiwan	C	44
Tajikistan	E	22
Tanzania	E	44
Thailand	D	44
Togo	D	44
Tonga	B	44
Trinidad & Tobago	B	22
Tristan da Cunha	E	22
Tunisia	C	44
Turkey	C	44
Turkmenistan	E	22
Turks and Caicos Islands	A	22
Tuvalu	B	44
Uganda	D	44
Ukraine	E	44
United Arab Emirates	D	44
United Kingdom	C	66
Uruguay	B	44
Uzbekistan	E	22
Vanuatu	B	44
Vatican City	C	44
Venezuela	B	44
Vietnam	E	44
Wallis & Futuna Islands	D	44
Yemen	E	44
Yugoslavia[2]	C	33
Zambia	E	44
Zimbabwe	E	44

(1) All mail service suspended. (2) Mail service restrictions apply. (3) Surface mail service suspended. (4) Includes East Timor. (5) West Bank and Gaza Strip are same rate group as Israel.

CONSUMER INFORMATION

Business Directory

Listed below are major U.S. corporations offering products and services to consumers. Listings generally include examples of products offered. When there is no hyphen or other punctuation at the end of a line in a website address, no spacing or punctuation should be added.

Company Name...Address...Telephone number...Website... Top executive...Business.

Abbott Laboratories...100 Abbott Park Rd., North Chicago, IL 60064...(708) 937-6100...Website: http:// www.abbott.com... Duane L. Burnham...health care prods. (Murine, Selsun Blue).

Aetna, Inc....151 Farmington Ave., Hartford, CT 06156...(203) 273-0123...Website: http://www.aetna.com...Ronald E. Compton...health insurance, financial services.

H. F. Ahmanson & Co....4900 Rivergrade Rd., Irwindale, CA 91706...(818) 814-7986...Charles Rinehart...1 of the largest thrift-holding cos. in U.S. (Home Savings of America).

Alberto Culver...2525 Armitage Ave., Melrose Park, IL 60160...(708) 450-3000...Website: http://www.alberto.com... Leonard H. Lavin...hair care (VO5), consumer prods. (Mrs. Dash, Sugar Twin), personal care prods. (St. Ives), Sally Beauty Supply stores.

Albertson's, Inc....250 Parkcenter Blvd., Boise, ID 83726...(208) 395-6200...Website: http:// www.albertsons.com...Gary Michael...supermarkets. (Co. announced 8/3/98 it would merge with American Stores Co., making Albertson's, Inc., the largest retail food and drug co. in the U.S.)

Allegheny Teledyne, Inc....1000 Six PPG Pl., Pittsburgh, PA 15222-5479...(412) 394-2800...Website: http://www.alleghenyteledyne.com...Richard P. Simmons...electronics, aerospace, industrial, consumer prods. (Water Pik); specialty metals.

AlliedSignal...Morristown, NJ 07960...(973) 455-2000...Website: http://www.alliedsignal.com...Lawrence A. Bossidy... aerospace, engineered materials, automotive prods.

Allstate Corp....Allstate Plaza, Northbrook, IL 60062...(847) 402-5000...Website: http://www.allstate.com...Jerry Choate... property/casualty, life insurance.

Aluminum Co. of America (Alcoa)...425 6th Ave., Pittsburgh, PA 15219...(412) 553-3042...Paul O'Neill...world's largest aluminum producer.

Amerada Hess Corp....1185 Ave. of the Americas, NY, NY 10036...(212) 997-8500...Website: http://www.hess.com...J. B. Hess...integrated petroleum co.

American Express Co....200 Vesey St., NY, NY 10285... (212) 640-2000...Website: http://www.americanexpress.com... Harvey Golub...travel, financial, and information services.

American Greetings Corp....1 American Rd., Cleveland, OH 44144...(216) 252-7300...Website: http://www.americangreetings.com...Morry Weiss...greeting cards, stationery, party goods, gift items.

American Home Prods. Corp....5 Giralda Farms, Madison, NJ 07940...(201) 660-5000...Website: http://www.ahp.com... John R. Stafford...prescription and over-the-counter drugs (Advil, Anacin, Dristan, Robitussin).

American Intl. Group...70 Pine St., NY, NY 10270...(212) 770-7000...Website: http://www.aig.com...Maurice R. Greenberg...insurance, financial services.

American Stores Co....709 E. South Temple, Salt Lake City, UT 84102...(801) 961-3000...Website: http://www.americanstores.com...Victor Lund...food markets (Lucky), dept. (Acme) & drug stores (American, Osco, Sav-On). (Co. announced 8/3/98 it would merge with Albertson's, Inc.)

Ameritech...30 S. Wacker Dr., Chicago, IL 60606...(312) 750-5000...Website: http://www.ameritech.com...Richard C. Notebaert...communications services.

Amoco Corp....200 E. Randolph Dr., Chicago, IL 60601... (312) 856-6111...Website: http://www.amoco.com...H. L. Fuller...integrated petroleum co.

AMP, Inc....Eisenhower Blvd., Harrisburg, PA 17105...(717) 564-0100...Website: http://www.amp.com...James E. Marley...designs, produces electronic connection devices.

AMR Corp....PO Box 619616, Dallas/Ft. Worth Airport, TX 75261...(817) 963-1234...Website: http://www.amrcorp.com... Donald J. Carty...air transportation (American Airlines, American Eagle).

Anheuser-Busch Cos., Inc....1 Busch Place, St. Louis, MO 63118...(314) 577-2000...Website: http://www.budweiser.com...August A. Busch 3d...world's largest brewer (Budweiser, Michelob, BudLight, Natural Light, Busch, O'Doul's), aluminum can manuf. and recycling, theme parks.

Apple Computer, Inc....1 Infinite Loop, Cupertino, CA 95014-2084...(408) 996-1010...Website: http://www.apple.com... Steve Jobs...manuf. personal computers, software, peripherals.

Aramark Corp....Aramark Tower, Philadelphia, PA 19107...(215) 238-3000...Joseph Neubauer...food, health, leisure services.

Archer Daniels Midland Co....4666 Faries Pkwy., Decatur, IL 62525...(217) 424-5200...Website: http://www.admworld.com...Dwayne O. Andreas...agricultural commodities and prods.

Armstrong World Industries, Inc....313 W. Liberty St., Lancaster, PA 17604...(717) 397-0611...Website: http://www.armstrong.com...George A. Lorch...interior furnishings, specialty prods.

Arvin Industries, Inc....1531 13th St., Columbus, IN 47201...(812) 379-3000...Website: http://www.arvin.com... Byron O. Pond...auto emission & ride control systems.

Ashland Inc....PO Box 391, Ashland, KY 41101...(606) 329-3333...Website: http://www.ashland.com...Paul W. Chellgren...petroleum producer and refiner (Valvoline), chemicals, road construction.

Atlantic Richfield Co....515 S. Flower St., Los Angeles, CA 90071-2256...(213) 486-3511...Website: http://www.arco.com...M. R. Bowlin...integrated oil and gas producer.

AT&T Corp....32 Ave. of the Americas, NY, NY 10013-2412... (212) 387-5400...Website: http://www.att.com...C. Michael Armstrong...communications, global information management. (Co. announced 6/24/98 it had agreed to acquire Tele-Communications, Inc. for approx. $69.9 bil.)

Avon Prods., Inc....9 W. 57th St., NY, NY 10019...(212) 546-6015...Website: http://www.avon.com...James E. Preston... cosmetics, fragrances, toiletries, fashion jewelry, gift items, casual apparel, lingerie.

BankAmerica Corp....NationsBank Corporate Center, Charlotte, NC 28255...(704) 386-5000...Website: http://www.bankamerica.com...http://www.NationsBank.com...Hugh McColl Jr...now the largest U.S. bank. (Co. completed merger 9/30/98 with NationsBank, under the name BankAmerica.)

Bausch & Lomb...1 Chase Square, Rochester, NY 14601... (716) 338-6000...Website: http://www.bausch.com...William H. Waltrip...vision & health-care prods., accessories.

Baxter International Inc....1 Baxter Pkwy., Deerfield, IL 60015...(847) 948-2000...Website: http://www.baxter.com... Vernon R. Loucks Jr...health care prods. & services.

Bear Stearns Cos. Inc....245 Park Ave., NY, NY 10167...(212) 272-2000...Website: http://www.bearstearns.com...Alan C. Greenberg...investment banking, securities trading, brokerage.

Becton, Dickinson & Co....1 Becton Dr., Franklin Lakes, NJ 07417...(201) 847-6800...Website: http://www.bd.com... C. Castellini...medical, laboratory, diagnostic prods.

Bell Atlantic Corp....1717 Arch St., Philadelphia, PA 19103... (215) 963-6000...Website: http://www.bell-atl.com...Raymond W. Smith...telephone service in mid-Atlantic region, worldwide wireless. (Co. announced 7/28/98 it had agreed to acquire GTE Corp. for $70.9 bil.)

BellSouth Corp....1155 Peachtree St. NE, Atlanta, GA 30309... (404) 249-2000...Website: http://www.bellsouth.com...John L. Clendenin...telephone service in southern U.S.

Best Buy Co., Inc....7075 Flying Cloud Dr., Eden Prairie, MN 55344...(612) 947-2000...Website: http://www.bestbuy.com... R. M. Schulze...retailer of software, appliances, electronics, cameras, home office equipment.

Bestfoods...International Plaza, Englewood Cliffs, NJ 07632...(201) 894-4000...Website: http://www.bestfoods.com...Charles R. Shoemate...food (Hellmann's, Best Foods mayonnaise, Skippy peanut butter, Knorr soups, Thomas' English muffins, Mueller pasta, Freihofer's, Boboli, Arnold breads, Mazola oils and margarine, Entenmann's cakes).

Bethlehem Steel Corp....1170 8th Ave., Bethlehem, PA 18016...(610) 694-2424...Website: http://www.bethsteel.com...Curtis H. Barnette...steel & steel prods.

Black & Decker Corp....701 E. Joppa Rd., Towson, MD 21204...(410) 716-3900...Website: http://www.blackanddecker.com...Nolan D. Archibald...manuf. power tools (DeWalt), household prods. (Kwikset, Price Pfister), small appliances (Black & Decker).

H & R Block, Inc....4410 Main St., Kansas City, MO 64111... (816) 753-6900...Website: http://www.hrblock.com...Henry Bloch...tax return preparation.

Boeing Co....7755 E. Marginal Way, Seattle, WA 98108... (206) 655-2121...Website: http://www.boeing.com...Philip M. Condit...aerospace, aircraft manuf., defense systems. (Co. acquired McDonnell Douglas Corp. 8/1/97.)

Boise Cascade Corp....1111 W. Jefferson St., Boise, ID 83728...(208) 384-6161...Website: http://www.bc.com... George J. Harad...timber; paper, wood prods.

Borden, Inc....180 E. Broad St., Columbus OH 43215-3707... (614) 225-4000...C. Robert Kidder...snacks (Wise, Cheez Doodles), adhesives (Elmer's, Krazy Glue), pasta (Prince, Creamette, Goodman's), pasta sauce (Aunt Millie's, Classico), Wyler's bouillon, Soup Starter; Corning Consumer Prods. (Corningware, Corelle, Pyrex, Revere).

Bristol-Myers Squibb Co....345 Park Ave., NY, NY 10022... (212) 546-4000...Website: http://www.bms.com...Charles A. Heimhold...toiletries (Ban antiperspirant), haircare (Clairol), drugs (Bufferin, Comtrex, Excedrin), infant formula (Enfamil).

Brown-Forman Corp....PO Box 1080, Louisville, KY 40201-1080...(502) 585-1100...Website: http://www.brown-forman.com...Owsley Brown 2d...distilled spirits (Jack Daniel's, Southern Comfort), wines (Bolla, Fetzer, Korbel), china and crystal (Dansk, Lenox), Gorham, Kirk Steiff silver prods., Hartmann luggage.

Brown Group, Inc....8300 Maryland Ave., St. Louis, MO 63166...(314) 854-4000...Website: http://www.browngroup.com...B. A. Bridgewater Jr...manuf. & retailer (Famous Footwear) of women's, men's, and children's shoes (Buster Brown, Naturalizer).

Brunswick Corp....1 N. Field Ct., Lake Forest, IL 60045-4811...(847) 735-4700...P. N. Larson...largest U.S. maker of leisure & recreation prods., marine, camping, fitness and fishing equip., bowling centers & equip.

Burlington Northern Santa Fe Inc....2650 Lou Menk Dr., Ft. Worth, TX 76131-2830...(817) 333-2000...Website: http://www.bnsf.com...Robert Krebs...one of the largest U.S. rail transportation cos.

Campbell Soup Co....Campbell Pl., Camden, NJ 08103... (609) 342-4800...Website: http://www.campbellsoups.com... David W. Johnson...soups, Franco-American spaghetti, V-8 vegetable juice, Godiva chocolates, Swanson frozen dinners, Prego spaghetti sauce, Pepperidge Farm.

Carter-Wallace, Inc....1345 Ave. of the Americas, NY, NY 10105...(212) 339-5000...H. H. Hoyt...personal care (Arrid, Rise, Pearl Drops, Nair, Trojan condoms).

Caterpillar Inc....100 N.E. Adams St., Peoria, IL 61629... (309) 675-1000...Website: http://www.cat.com...Donald Fites...world's largest producer of earth-moving equip.

Chase Manhattan Corp....270 Park Ave., NY, NY 10017... (212) 270-6000...Website: http://www.chase.com...Walter V. Shipley...largest bank-holding company in U.S.

Chevron Corp....475 Market St., San Francisco, CA 94105... (415) 894-7700...Website: http://www.chevron.com... Kenneth T. Derr...integrated oil co.

Chiquita Brands International, Inc....250 E. 5th St., Cincinnati, OH 45202...(513) 784-8000...Website: http://www.chiquita.com...Carl H. Lindner...bananas, fruits, vegetables.

Chrysler Corp....1000 Chrysler Dr., Auburn Hills, MI 48288... (248) 576-5741...Website: http://www.chryslercorp.com... Robert J. Eaton...cars, trucks, auto parts. (Co. announced 5/7/98 it had agreed to merge with Daimler-Benz of Germany to form Daimler Chrysler.)

Church & Dwight Co., Inc....469 N. Harrison St., Princeton, NJ 08543...(609) 683-5900...Website: http://www.armhammer.com...D. C. Minton...world's largest producer of sodium bicarbonate (Arm & Hammer), Brillo.

CIGNA Corp....1 Liberty Pl., Philadelphia, PA 19103... (215) 761-1000...Website: http://www.cigna.com...Wilson H. Taylor...insurance holding co.

Circuit City Stores, Inc....9950 Mayland Dr., Richmond, VA 23233-1464...(804) 527-4000...Website: http://www.circuitcity.com...Richard L. Sharp...retailer of electronic, audio/video equip., consumer appliances; new and used-car stores (CarMax).

Circus Circus Enterprises, Inc....2880 Las Vegas Blvd. S, Las Vegas, NV 89109...(702) 734-0410...Website: http://www.circuscircus.org...Michael Ensign...casino-resort operator (Excalibur, Luxor).

Citicorp...399 Park Ave., NY, NY 10043...(212) 559-1000... Website: http://www.citibank.com...J. S. Reed...one of the largest U.S. banking companies. (Co. announced 9/24/98 it would merge with Travelers Group as of 10/8/98, with the new name of Citigroup.)

Clorox Co....1221 Broadway, Oakland, CA 94612... (510) 271-7000...Website: http://www.clorox.com...G. Craig Sullivan...retail consumer prods. (Clorox, Formula 409, Pine-Sol, S.O.S., Soft Scrub cleansers; Kingsford charcoal briquets, Combat and Black Flag insecticides, Hidden Valley Ranch dressing, Brita water systems).

Coastal Corp....9 Greenway Plaza, Houston, TX 77046...(713) 877-1400...David A. Arledge...natural gas pipeline systems, oil refineries.

Coca-Cola Co....1 Coca-Cola Plaza, Atlanta, GA 30313... (404) 676-2121...Website: http://www.cocacola.com...M. Douglas Ivester...world's largest soft drink co. (Coca-Cola, Sprite, Nestea), world's largest dist. of juice prods. (Minute Maid, Five Alive, Hi-C, Fruitopia).

Colgate-Palmolive Co....300 Park Ave., NY, NY 10022... (212) 310-2000...Website: http://www.colgate.com...Reuben Mark...soap (Palmolive, Irish Spring), detergent (Fab, Ajax, Fresh Start), toothpaste (Colgate, Ultra Brite), Hill's pet food.

Columbia/HCA Healthcare Corp....1 Park Plaza, Nashville, TN 37203...(615) 344-9551...Website: http://www.columbia.net...T.F. Frist Jr...largest hospital mgmt. co. in the U.S.

Compaq Computer Corp....20555 SH 249, Houston, TX 77070...(281) 370-0670...Website: http://www.compaq.com...Benjamin M. Rosen...laptop and desktop computers. (Co. acquired Digital Equipment Corp. 6/98.)

CompUSA Inc....14951 N. Dallas Pkwy., Dallas, TX 75240... (972) 982-4000...Website: http://www.compusa.com... G. H. Bateman...largest U.S. superstore retailer of microcomputers and peripherals.

Computer Sciences Corp....2100 E. Grand Ave., El Segundo, CA 90245...(310) 615-0311...Website: http://www.csc.com...Van B. Honeycutt...technology services.

ConAgra...1 ConAgra Dr., Omaha, NE 68102...(402) 595-4000...Website: http://www.healthychoice.com...Philip B. Fletcher...2d largest U.S. food processor.

Continental Airlines, Inc....2929 Allen Pkwy., Houston, TX 77019...(713) 834-2950...Website: http://www.flycontinental.com...Gordon M. Bethune...air transportation.

Adolph Coors Co....Golden, CO 80401...(303) 279-6565... William K. Coors...brewer (Killian's, Zima).

Corning, Inc....1 Riverfront Plaza, Corning, NY 14831...(607) 974-9000...Website: http://www.corning.com...Roger G. Ackerman...specialty materials, optical fiber and cable.

Costco Cos., Inc....999 Lake Dr., Issaquah, WA 98027... (206) 313-8100...Website: http://www.pricecostco.com...James D. Sinegal...wholesale warehouses.

Crane Co....100 First Stamford Pl., Stamford, CT 06902... (203) 363-7300...Website: http://www.crane.com...R. S. Evans...manuf. fluid control devices, vending machines, fiberglass panels, aircraft brakes.

A. T. Cross Co....1 Albion Rd., Lincoln, RI 02865...(401) 333-1200...Website: http://www.cross.com...Bradford R. Boss...writing instruments.

Crown Cork & Seal Co....1 Crown Way, Philadelphia, PA 19154-4599...(215) 698-5100...Website: http://www.crowncork.com...William J. Avery...world's leading supplier of packaging prods.

CSX Corp....901 E. Cary St., Richmond, VA 23219... (804) 782-1400...Website: http://www.csx.com...John W. Snow...rail, ocean, barge freight transport.

CVS Corp....1 CVS Dr., Woonsocket, RI 02895...(401) 765-1500...Website: http://www.CVS.com...Stanley P. Goldstein...drugstore chain.

Dana Corp....4500 Dorr St., Toledo, OH 43615...(419) 535-4500...Website: http://www.dana.com...Southwood J. Morcott...truck and auto parts, supplies.

Dayton Hudson Corp....777 Nicollet Mall, Minneapolis, MN 55402...(612) 370-6948...Website: http:/www.dhc.com...Robert J. Ulrich...department, specialty stores (Marshall Fields, Target, Hudsons).

Deere & Co....John Deere Rd., Moline, IL 61265...(309) 765-8000...Website: http://www.deere.com...Hans W. Becherer... world's largest manuf. of farm equip.; industrial equip.; lawn and garden tractors.

Dell Computer Corp....1 Dell Way, Round Rock, TX 78682... (512) 338-4400...Website: http://www.dell.com...Michael S. Dell...laptop and desktop computers.

Delta Air Lines, Inc....Hartsfield Atlanta Intl. Airport, Atlanta, GA 30320...(404) 715-2600...Website: http://www.delta-air.com... Gerald Grinstein...air transportation.

Dial Corp....15501 N. Dial Blvd., Scottsdale, AZ 85260...(602) 754-3425...Website: http://www.dialcorp.com...Malcolm Jozoff... consumer prods. (Dial, Tone soap, Breck Shampoo, Armour Star meats, Renuzit air fresheners).

Diebold, Inc....PO Box 8230, Canton, OH 44711...(330) 490-4000...Website: http://www.diebold.com...Robert W. Mahoney... manuf. automatic teller machines, security systems and prods.

Dillard's...1600 Cantrell Rd., Little Rock, AR 72201...(501) 376-5200...Website: http://www.azstarnet.com/dillards...William Dillard...large dept. store chain.

Walt Disney Co....500 S. Buena Vista St., Burbank, CA 91521-7320...(818) 560-1000...Website: http://www.disney.com... Michael D. Eisner...motion pictures, television (ESPN, ABC, A&E, Lifetime), radio stations, theme parks (Walt Disney

World, Disneyland) and resorts, publishing, recordings, retailing (Disney Stores).

Dole Food Co., Inc....31365 Oak Crest Dr., Westlake Village, CA 91361...(818) 879-6600...Website: http://www.dole.com... David H. Murdock...food prods., fresh fruits and vegetables.

R. R. Donnelley & Sons Co....77 W. Wacker Dr., Chicago, IL 60601-8375...(312) 326-8000...Website: http://www.rrdonnelley.com...William L. Davis...world's largest commercial printer.

Dow Chemical Co....2030 Dow Center, Midland, MI 48674...(517) 636-1000...Website: http://www.dow.com... W. Stavropoulos...chemicals, plastics.

Dow Jones & Co., Inc....200 Liberty St., NY, NY 10281... (212) 416-2000...Website: http://www.dowjones.com...Peter R. Kann...financial news service, publishing (*Wall Street Journal, Barron's*, Ottaway Newspapers).

Dun & Bradstreet Corp....1 Diamond Hill Rd., Murray Hill, NJ 07974...(908) 665-5000...Website: http://www.dnb.com...Volney Taylor...business information, publishing (Moody's, "Yellow Pages" phone books).

E. I. du Pont de Nemours & Co....1007 Market St., Wilmington, DE 19898...(302) 774-1000...Website: http://www.dupont.com...J. Krol...largest U.S. chemical co.; petroleum, consumer prods.

Eastman Kodak Co....343 State St., Rochester, NY 14650...(716) 724-5492...Website: http://www.kodak.com... G. Fisher...world's largest producer of photographic prods.

Eaton Corp....1111 Superior Ave., Cleveland, OH 44114... (216) 523-5000...Website: http://www.eaton.com...Steven R. Hardis...manuf. of vehicle powertrain components, controls.

Emerson Electric Co....8000 W. Florissant Ave., St. Louis, MO 63136...(314) 553-2000...Website: http://www.emersonelectric.com...C. F. Knight...electrical, electronics prods. & systems.

Exxon Corp....5959 Las Colinas Blvd., Irving, TX 75039-2298...(972) 444-1000...Website: http://www.exxon.com... Lee R. Raymond...world's largest publicly owned integrated oil co.

Fabri-Centers of America, Inc....5555 Darrow Rd., Hudson, OH 44236...(330) 656-2600...Website: http://www.joann.com... Alan Rosskamm...specialty fabric stores (Jo-Ann Fabric and Crafts).

FDX Corp....Box 727, Memphis, TN 38194...(901) 369-3600...Website: http://www.fedex.com...F. W. Smith...express delivery service.

Fedders Corp....505 Martinsville Rd., Liberty Corner, NJ 07938...(908) 604-8686...Website: http://www.fedderslloyd.com...Salvatore Giordano Jr...manuf. of room air conditioners (Fedders, Airtemp), dehumidifiers.

Federal Home Loan Mortgage Corp. (Freddie Mac)...8200 Jones Branch Dr., McLean, VA 22102...(703) 903-2000...Website: http://www.freddiemac.com...Leland C. Brendsel...residential mortgage provider.

Federal National Mortgage Assn. (Fannie Mae)...3900 Wisconsin Ave. NW, Washington, DC 20016...(202) 752-7000...Website: http://www.fanniemae.com...James A. Johnson...largest U.S. provider of residential mortgage funds.

Federated Dept. Stores...7 W. 7th St., Cincinnati, OH 45202...(513) 579-7000...Website: http://www.federated-fds.com...James Zimmerman...Macy's, Bloomingdale's, Stern's dept. stores.

Fieldcrest Cannon, Inc....1 Lake Dr., Kannapolis, NC 28081...(704) 939-2000...James M. Fitzgibbons...household textile prods.

First Brands Corp....83 Wooster Hts. Rd., Danbury, CT 06813-1911...(203) 731-2300...Website: http://www.firstbrands.com...William V. Stephenson...consumer prods. (Glad plastic bags, Scoop-Away cat litter, STP auto prods.).

First Data Corp....401 Hackensack Ave., Hackensack, NJ 07601...(800) 735-3362...Website: http://www.firstdatacorp.com...Henry C. Duques...info. retrieval, data processing.

Fleetwood Enterprises, Inc....3125 Myers St., Riverside, CA 92503...(909) 351-3500...Website: http://www.fleetwood.com... Glenn F. Kummer...manufactured homes, recreational vehicles.

Fleming Cos. Inc....6301 Waterford Blvd., PO Box 26647, Oklahoma City, OK 73126...(405) 840-7200...Website: http://www.fleming.com...Robert E. Stauth...largest U.S. wholesale food distrib.

Fluor Corp....3333 Michelson Dr., Irvine, CA 92730... (714) 975-6961...Website: http://www.fluor.com...Philip J. Carroll...largest international engineering and construction co. in U.S.

Ford Motor Co....American Rd., Dearborn, MI 48121... (313) 845-8540...Website: http://www.ford.com...Alexander Trotman...motor vehicle sales (Ford, Lincoln-Mercury), rentals (Hertz).

Fortune Brands, Inc....1700 E. Putnam Ave., Old Greenwich, CT 06870...(203) 698-5000...Website: http://www.fortunebrands.com...Thomas C. Hays...whiskey (Jim Beam), hardware, office prods. (Swingline), golf and leisure prods. (Titleist, Cobra, Foot-Joy).

Fruit of the Loom, Inc....5000 Sears Tower, Chicago, IL 60606...(312) 876-1724...Website: http://www.fruit.com... William Farley...manuf. of underwear, activewear.

Gannett Co., Inc....1100 Wilson Blvd., Arlington, VA 22234... (703) 284-6000...Website: http://www.gannett.com...J. J. Curley...newspaper publishing (*USA Today*), network and cable TV.

The Gap, Inc....1 Harrison St., San Francisco, CA 94105... (415) 952-4400...Website: http://www.gap.com...Donald G. Fisher...casual and activewear retailer (Gap, Banana Republic, Old Navy).

General Dynamics...3190 Fairview Park Dr., Falls Church, VA 22042-4523...(703) 876-3000...Nicholas D. Chabraja... nuclear submarines (Trident, Seawolf), armored vehicles.

General Electric Co....3135 Easton Tpke., Fairfield, CT 06431...(203) 373-2211...Website: http://www.ge.com... John F. Welch...electrical, electronic equip., radio and television broadcasting (NBC), aircraft engines, power generation, appliances.

General Mills, Inc....PO Box 1113, Minneapolis, MN 55440... (612) 540-2444...Website: http://www.genmills.com...S. W. Sanger...foods (Total, Wheaties, Cheerios, Chex, Hamburger Helper, Betty Crocker, Bisquick).

General Motors...3044 W. Grand Blvd., Detroit, MI 48202-3091...(313) 556-5000...Website: http://www.gm.com...John F. Smith Jr...world's largest auto manuf. (Chevrolet, Pontiac, Cadillac, Buick).

Genuine Parts Co....2999 Circle 75 Pkwy., Atlanta, GA 30339...(404) 953-1700...Website: http://www.genpt.com... Larry L. Prince...distributes auto replacement parts (NAPA).

Georgia-Pacific Corp....133 Peachtree St. NE, Atlanta, GA 30303...(404) 521-5210...Website: http://www.gp.com... A. D. Correll...manuf. of paper and wood prods.

Gillette...Prudential Tower Bldg., Boston, MA 02199... (617) 463-3000...Website: http://www.gillette.com...Alfred Zeien...stationery prods. (PaperMate, Parker, Waterman pens), personal care prods. (Sensor, Atra razors, Right Guard, Soft and Dri), appliances (Braun), batteries (Duracell).

The Goodyear Tire & Rubber Co....1144 E. Market St., Akron, OH 44316...(330) 796-2121...Website: http://www.goodyear.com...Samir F. Gibara...world's largest rubber manuf.; tires and other auto prods.

W. R. Grace & Co....1 Town Center Rd., Boca Raton, FL 33486...(561) 362-2000...Albert J. Costello...chemicals, construction prods.

Great Atlantic & Pacific Tea Co. (A&P)...2 Paragon Dr., Montvale, NJ 07645...(201) 573-9700...Website: http://www.aptea.com...James Wood...supermarkets (A&P, Waldbaum's, Kohl's, Dominion).

GTE Corp....1 Stamford Forum, Stamford, CT 06904... (203) 965-2000...Website: http://www.gte.com...Charles R. Lee...large telecommunications co., cellular telephone provider. (Co. announced 7/28/98 it had agreed to be acquired by Bell Atlantic Corp. for $70.9 bil.)

Halliburton Co....500 N. Akard St., Dallas, TX 75201...(214) 978-2600...Website: http://www.halliburton.com...Richard Cheney...energy, engineering, and construction services.

Harley-Davidson, Inc....3700 W. Juneau Ave., Milwaukee, WI 53208...(414) 343-4680...Website: http://www.harley-davidson.com...Jeffrey Bleustein...manuf. of motorcycles, parts and accessories.

Harrah's Entertainment, Inc....1023 Cherry Rd., Memphis, TN 38117...(901) 762-8600...Website: http://www.harrahs.lv.com...Philip G. Satre...casino-hotels. (The co. announced 8/10/98 it had agreed to acquire Rio Hotel & Casino Inc., for $518 mil.)

Hartford Finl. Svces. Group, Inc....Hartford Plaza, Hartford, CT 06115...(860) 547-2403...Website: http://www.thehartford.com...Ramani Ayer...property/casualty, life insurance.

Hartmarx...101 N. Wacker Dr., Chicago, IL 60606...(312) 372-6300...Elbert O. Hand...apparel manuf. (Hart Schaffner & Marx, Hickey Freeman, Claiborne, Tommy Hilfiger, Pierre Cardin, Perry Ellis).

Hasbro, Inc....1027 Newport Ave., Pawtucket, RI 02862... (401) 431-8697...Website: http://www.hasbro.com...Alan G. Hassenfeld...toy and game manuf. (Milton Bradley, Playskool, G. I. Joe, Parker Bros., Tiger Electronics, Play-Doh).

H. J. Heinz Co....PO Box 57, Pittsburgh, PA 15230...(412) 456-6014...Website: http://www.heinz.com...William R. Johnson...foods (Star-Kist, Ore-Ida, 57 Varieties), pet food (Ken-L Ration, 9 Lives), Weight Watchers.

Hershey Foods Corp....100 Crystal A Dr., Hershey, PA 17033... (717) 534-6799...Website: http://www.hershey.com...Kenneth L. Wolfe...largest U.S. producer of chocolate and confectionery prods. (Reese's, Kit Kat, Mounds, Almond Joy, Cadbury, Jolly Rancher, Twizzler, Milk Duds, Good 'n' Plenty), pasta (San Giorgio, Ronzoni).

Hewlett-Packard Co....3000 Hanover St., Palo Alto, CA 94304...(650) 857-1501...Website: http://www.hp.com... Lewis E. Platt...manuf. computers, electronic prods. and systems.

Hillenbrand Industries, Inc....700 State Rte. 46, Batesville, IN 47006...(812) 934-7000...Website: http://www.hillenbrand.com...D. A. Hillenbrand...manuf. caskets, adjustable hospital beds, locks (Medeco).

Hilton Hotels Corp....9336 Civic Center Dr., Beverly Hills, CA 90210...(310) 278-4321...Website: http://www.hilton.com... Barron Hilton...hotels, casinos.

Home Depot, Inc....2455 Paces Ferry Rd. NW, Atlanta, GA 30339...(770) 433-8211...Website: http://www.homedepot.com...Bernard Marcus...retail building supply, home improvement warehouse stores.

Honeywell Inc....Honeywell Plaza, Minneapolis, MN 55408... (612) 951-1000...Website: http://www.honeywell.com... Michael R. Bonsignore...industrial and home control systems, aerospace guidance systems.

Hormel Foods Corp....1 Hormel Pl., Austin, MN 55912... (507) 437-5611...Website: http://www.hormel.com...Joel W. Johnson...meat processor, pork and beef prods. (SPAM, Dinty Moore, Little Sizzlers).

Houghton Mifflin Co....222 Berkeley St., Boston, MA 02116... (617) 351-5000...Website: http://www.hmco.com...Nader F. Darehshori...publisher of textbooks, reference, general interest books.

Huffy Corp....225 Byers Rd., Miamisburg, OH 45342... (937) 866-6251...Website: http://www.huffy.com...Don R. Graber...largest U.S. bicycle manuf., sports and hardware equip,

Humana, Inc....500 W. Main St., Louisville, KY 40201-1438... (502) 580-1000...Website: http://www.humana.com...David A. Jones...healthcare service provider, financial services.

IBP, Inc....IBP Ave., PO Box 515, Dakota City, NE 68731... (402) 494-2061...Website: http://www.ibpinc.com...Robert L. Peterson...world's largest processor of fresh beef and pork.

Ingersoll-Rand...Woodcliff Lake, NJ 07675...(201) 573-0123... Website: http://www.ingersoll-rand.com...J. E. Perella... industrial machinery.

Intel Corp....2200 Mission College Blvd., Santa Clara, CA 95052-8119...(408) 765-8080...Website: http://www.intc.com...A. S. Grove...manuf. integrated circuits (Pentium).

International Business Machines Corp. (IBM)...New Orchard Rd., Armonk, NY 10504...(914) 499-7777...Website: http://www.ibm.com...Louis V. Gerstner Jr....world's largest supplier of advanced information processing technology equip., services.

International Paper Co....2 Manhattanville Rd., Purchase, NY 10577...(914) 397-1500...Website: http://www.internationalpaper.com...John T. Dillon...world's largest paper/forest prods. co., chemicals, minerals.

Interstate Bakeries Corp....12 E. Armour Blvd., Kansas City, MO 64111...(816) 502-4000...Website: http://www.twinkies.com...Charles A. Sullivan...baked goods wholesaler, distributor (Wonder, Hostess, Dolly Madison, Beefsteak, Home Pride).

S.C. Johnson & Son, Inc....1515 Howe St., Racine, WI 53403...(414) 631-2000...Website: http://www.scjbrands.com...W.D. Perez...cleaning and other household prods. (Johnson's Wax, Windex, Pledge, Ziploc bags).

Johnson & Johnson...1 Johnson & Johnson Plaza, New Brunswick, NJ 08933...(732) 524-0400...Website: http://www.jnj.com...Ralph S. Larsen...surgical dressings (Band-Aid), pharmaceuticals (Tylenol), toiletries (Neutrogena).

Johnson Controls...5757 N. Green Bay Ave., Milwaukee, WI 53201...(414) 228-1200...Website: http://www.jci.com... James H. Keyes...fire protection services, auto seats and batteries.

Jostens Inc....5501 Norman Center Dr., Minneapolis, MN 55437...(612) 830-3300...Website: http://www.jostens.com... Robert P. Jensen...school rings, yearbooks, plaques.

Kellogg Co....1 Kellogg Sq., Battle Creek, MI 49016... (616) 961-2000...Website: http://www.kelloggs.com...Arnold G. Langbo...world's largest mfgr. of ready-to-eat cereals, other food prods. (Frosted Flakes, Rice Krispies, Froot Loops, Pop-Tarts, Nutri-Grain, Eggo).

Kimberly-Clark Corp....PO Box 619100, Dallas, TX 75261-9100...(972) 281-1200...Website: http://www.kimberly-clark.com...Wayne R. Sanders...personal care prods. (Kleenex, Scott, Cottonelle, Huggies, Viva, Kotex).

King World Productions, Inc....1700 Broadway, NY, NY 10019...(212) 315-4000...Website: http://www.kingworld.com...Roger King...distributor of TV programs (*Oprah Winfrey Show, Wheel of Fortune, Jeopardy!, Inside Edition*).

Kmart Corp....3100 W. Big Beaver Rd., Troy, MI 48084...(248) 643-1000...Website: http://www.kmart.com...Floyd Hall... discount stores, home improvement centers (Builders Square).

KnightRidder, Inc....1 Herald Plaza, Miami, FL 33101... (305) 376-3838...Website: http://www.kri.com...P. A. Ridder...newspaper publishing.

Kroger Co....1014 Vine St., Cincinnati, OH 45202...(513) 762-4000...Website: http://www.foodcoop.com/kroger...Joseph A. Pichler...2d largest U.S. grocery chain.

(Estee) Lauder Cos....767 5th Ave., NY, NY 10153... (212) 572-4200...Leonard A. Lauder...cosmetics (Clinique), fragrance prods. (Aramis, Aveda, Tommy Hilfiger).

La-Z-Boy Inc....1284 N. Telegraph Rd., Monroe, MI 48161...(313) 242-1444...Website: http://www.lazboy.com... Patrick H. Norton...reclining chairs, other furniture.

Leggett & Platt, Inc....No. 1 Leggett Rd., Carthage, MO 64836...(417) 358-8131...Website: http://www.leggett.com... Harry M. Cornell Jr...furniture and furniture components.

Lehman Bros. Holdings, Inc....3 World Financial Ctr., NY, NY 10285...(212) 526-7000...Website: http://www.lehman.com... Richard S. Fuld Jr...investment bank.

Levi Strauss Associates...1155 Battery St., San Francisco, CA 94111...(415) 544-6000...Website: http://www.levistrauss.com...Robert D. Haas...blue jeans, casual apparel.

Eli Lilly and Company...Lilly Corporate Center, Indianapolis, IN 46285...(317) 276-2000...Website: http://www.lilly.com... R. L. Tobias...pharmaceuticals (Axid, Ceclor, Prozac) and animal health prods.

The Limited, Inc....3 Limited Pkwy., Columbus, OH 43216... (614) 479-7000...Website: http://www.limited.com...Leslie H. Wexner...women's apparel stores (Lane Bryant, Lerner, Limited, Express, Structure, Victoria's Secret).

Litton Industries, Inc....21240 Burbank Blvd., Woodland Hills, CA 91367...(818) 598-5000...Website: http://www.littoncorp.com...John M. Leonis...advanced electronic systems, electronic and electrical prods., marine engineering, radar warning devices, warships.

Liz Claiborne, Inc....1441 Broadway, NY, NY 10018... (212) 354-4900...Website: http://www.lizclaiborne.com...P. Charron...apparel, accessories.

Lockheed Martin Corp....6801 Rockledge Dr., Bethesda, MD 20817...(301) 897-6000...Website: http://www.lmco.com... Vance Coffman...commercial and military aircraft, electronics, missiles.

Loews Corp....667 Madison Ave., NY, NY 10021...(212) 545-2000...Laurence A. Tisch...tobacco prods. (Kent, True, Newport), watches (Bulova), hotels, insurance (CNA Fin'l.), offshore drilling.

Longs Drug Stores, Inc....141 N. Civic Dr., Walnut Creek, CA 94596...(510) 937-1170...Website: http://www.long.com... R. M. Long...drug store chain.

Lowe's Cos., Inc....Box 1111, N. Wilkesboro, NC 28656... (336) 658-4000...Website: http://www.lowes.com...Robert L. Tillman...building materials and home improvement superstores.

Luby's Cafeterias, Inc....2211 NE Loop 410, San Antonio, TX 78265...(210) 654-9000...Website: http://www.lubys.com... Barry Parker...operates cafeterias in S and SW.

Lucent Technologies, Inc....600 Mountain Ave., Murray Hill, NJ 07974...(908) 582-8500...Website: http://www.lucent.com... Richard A. McGinn...leading developer, designer, and manuf. of telecommunications systems, software, and prods.

Manpower Inc....5301 N. Ironwood Rd., Milwaukee, WI 53201... (414) 961-1000...Website: http://www.manpower.com... Mitchell S. Fromstein...largest non-gov't. employment services co. in the world.

Marriott International, Inc....10400 Fernwood Rd., Bethesda, MD 20817...(301) 380-3000...Website: http://www.marriott.com...John Willard Marriott Jr...hotels, retirement communities, food service dist.

Masco Corp....21001 Van Born Rd., Taylor, MI 48180...(313) 274-7400...Website: http://www.masco.com...Richard A. Manoogian...manuf. kitchen, bathroom prods. (Delta, Peerless faucets; Fieldstone, Merillat cabinets).

Mattel, Inc....333 Continental Blvd., El Segundo, CA 90245...(310) 252-2000...Website: http://www.mattelmedia.com...Jill E. Barad...largest U.S. toymaker (Barbie, Fisher-Price, Hot Wheels, Matchbox, Polly Pocket). (Co. announced 6/98 it had agreed to acquire Pleasant Co., maker of the American Girls Collection, for $700 mil.)

May Department Stores Co....611 Olive St., St. Louis, MO 63101...(314) 342-6300...Website: http://www.maycompany.com...Jerome T. Loeb...department stores (Hecht's, Lord & Taylor, Filene's, Foley's).

Maytag Corp....Newton, IA 50208...(515) 792-8000...Website: http://www.maytagcorp.com...Leonard A. Hadley...major appliance mfgr. (Magic Chef, Admiral, Jenn-Air), Hoover vacuum cleaners, floor care systems.

McDonald's Corp....1 McDonald's Plaza, Oak Brook, IL 60521...(630) 623-7428...Website: http://www.mcdonalds.com...Jack Greenberg...fast-food restaurants.

McGraw-Hill Cos....1221 Ave. of the Americas, NY, NY 10020...(212) 512-2000...Website: http://www.mcgraw-hill.com...Joseph L. Dionne...book, textbooks, magazine publishing (*Business Week*), information and financial services (Standard and Poor's), TV stations.

MCI WorldCom, Inc....515 E. Amite St., Jackson, MS 39201-2702...(601) 360-8600...Website: http://www.mciworld.com...Bernard Ebbes...long-distance telephone service. (Co. formed 9/14/98 from merger of MCI and WorldCom.)

McKesson Corp....1 Post St., San Francisco, CA 94104...(415) 983-8300...http://www.mckesson.com...Alan Seelenfreund...largest distributor of drugs and toiletries in U.S.; bottled water.

Mead Corporation...Courthouse Plaza NE, Dayton, OH 45463...(937) 495-6323...Website: http://www.mead.com...Jerome F. Tatar...printing and writing paper, paperboard, packaging, shipping containers.

Medtronic, Inc....7000 Central Ave. NE, Minneapolis, MN 55432...(612) 514-4000...Website: http://www.medtronic.com...W. W. George...world's largest manuf. of implantable biomedical devices.

Merck & Co., Inc....PO Box 100, Whitehouse Station, NJ 08889-0100...(908) 423-1000...Raymond V. Gilmartin...pharmaceuticals (Pepcid, Zocor), animal health care prods.

Meredith Corp....1716 Locust St., Des Moines, IA 50336...(515) 284-3000...Website: http://www.meredith.com...William T. Kerr...magazine publishing (*Better Homes and Gardens, Ladies Home Journal*), book publishing, broadcasting.

Merrill Lynch & Co., Inc....World Financial Ctr., N. Tower, NY, NY 10281-1332...(212) 449-1000...Website: http://www.ml.com...David H. Komansky...securities broker, financial services.

Metropolitan Life Ins. Co....1 Madison Ave., NY, NY 10010-3603...(212) 578-2211...Website: http://www.metlife.com...Harry P. Kamen...insurance, financial services.

Microsoft Corp....1 Microsoft Way, Redmond, WA 98052-6399...(206) 882-8080...Website: http://www.microsoft.com...William H. Gates...largest independent software maker (Windows, Word, Excel).

Minnesota Mining & Manuf. Co....3M Center, St. Paul, MN 55144-1000...(612) 733-1110...Website: http://www.mmm.com...L. D. DeSimone...abrasives, adhesives, electrical, health care, cleaning (Scotch-Brite, O-Cel-O sponges), printing, consumer prods. (Scotch Tape, Post-It).

Mirage Resorts, Inc....3400 Las Vegas Blvd. S, Las Vegas, NV 89109...(702) 791-7111...Website: http://www.themirage.com...Stephen A. Wynn...hotel-casino operator (Mirage, Treasure Island, Golden Nugget).

Mobil Corp....3225 Gallows Rd., Fairfax, VA 22037...(703) 846-3000...Website: http://www.mobile.com...Lucio A. Noto...integrated international oil and petrochemical co.

Monsanto Company...800 N. Lindbergh Blvd., St. Louis, MO 63167...(314) 694-1000...Website: http://www.monsanto.com...Robert B. Shapiro...agricultural prods., pharmaceuticals, consumer prods. (Equal, NutraSweet).

J. P. Morgan & Co....60 Wall St., NY, NY 10260...(212) 483-2323...Website: http://www.jpmorgan.com...Douglas A. Warner...global financial firm.

Morgan Stanley Dean Witter & Co....1585 Broadway, NY, NY 10036...(212) 761-4000...Website: http://www.msdw.com...Phillip J. Purcell...diversified financial services, largest U.S. credit-card issuer.

Motorola, Inc....1303 E. Algonquin Rd., Schaumburg, IL 60196...(847) 576-5000...Website: http://www.mot.com...G. L. Tooker...electronic equipment and components.

National Semiconductor Corp....2900 Semiconductor Dr., Santa Clara, CA 95052-8090...(408) 721-5000...Website: http://www.national.com...B. Halla...manuf. of semiconductors, integrated circuits.

Navistar Intl. Corp....455 N. Cityfront Plaza Dr., Chicago, IL 60611...(312) 836-2000...Website: http://www.navistar.com...John R. Horne...manuf. heavy-duty trucks, parts, school buses.

New York Times Co....229 W. 43d St., NY, NY 10036...(212) 556-3660...Website: http://www.nytimes.com...A. O. Sulzberger Jr...newspapers (*Boston Globe*), radio and TV stations, magazines (*Golf Digest*).

Nike, Inc....1 Bowerman Dr., Beaverton, OR 97005...(503) 671-6453...Website: http://www.info.nike.com...Philip H. Knight...athletic and leisure footware, apparel.

Nordstrom, Inc....1501 5th Ave., Seattle, WA 98101...(206) 628-2111...Website: http://www.nordstrom-pta.com...John J. Whitacre...upscale dept. store chain.

Norfolk Southern Corp....3 Commercial Pl., Norfolk, VA 23510...(757) 629-2600...Website: http://www.nscorp.com...David R. Goode...operates railway, freight carrier.

Northrop Grumman Corp....1840 Century Park East, Los Angeles, CA 90067...(310) 553-6262...Website: http://www.northgrum.com...Kent Kresa...aircraft, electronics, data systems, missiles.

Northwest Airlines Corp....2700 Lone Oak Pkwy., Eagan, MN 55121...(612) 726-2111...Website: http://www.nwa.com...John H. Dasburg...air transportation.

Occidental Petroleum Corp....10889 Wilshire Blvd., Los Angeles, CA 90024...(310) 208-8800...Website: http://www.oxy.com...Ray R. Irani...oil, natural gas, chemicals, fertilizers.

Office Depot, Inc....2200 Old Germantown Rd., Delray Beach, FL 33445...(561) 278-4800...Website: http://www.officedepot.com...David I. Fuente...retail office supply stores. (Co. announced 5/18/98 it would acquire Viking Office Prods.)

Owens Corning...Fiberglass Towers, Toledo, OH 43659...(419) 248-8000...Website: http://www.owenscorning.com...Glen H. Hiner...world leader in advanced glass and composite materials.

Owens-Illinois...1 SeaGate, Toledo, OH 43666...(419) 247-5000...J. H. Lemieux...world's largest producer of glass bottles.

Pacific Gas & Electric Corp. (PG&E)...77 Beale St., San Francisco, CA 94106...(800) 367-7731...Website: http://www.pgecorp.com...Robert D. Glynn Jr...energy supplier.

PaineWebber Group, Inc....1285 Ave. of the Americas, NY, NY 10019-6028...Website: http://www.painewebber.com...Donald B. Marron...controls full-service securities firm.

J. C. Penney Co....6501 Legacy Dr., Plano, TX 75024...(214) 431-1000...Website: http://www.jcpenny.com...James E. Oesterreicher...dept. stores, catalog sales, drug stores (Eckerd, Fay's), insurance.

Pennzoil Co....1 Pennzoil Pl., Houston, TX 77252-8000...(713) 546-4000...Website: http://www.pennzoil.com...J. L. Pate...integrated oil and gas co., franchises Jiffy Lube service centers. (Co. announced 4/15/98 it would merge with Quaker State.)

PepsiCo, Inc....700 Anderson Hill Rd., Purchase, NY 10577...(914) 253-2000...Website: http://www.pepsico.com...Roger A. Enrico...soft drinks (Pepsi-Cola, Mountain Dew), snacks (Ruffles, Lay's, Fritos, Doritos, Rold Gold). (Co. announced 7/21/98 it had agreed to acquire Tropicana from Seagram Co. for $3.3 bil cash.)

Pfizer, Inc....235 E. 42d St., NY, NY 10017...(212) 573-2323...Website: http://www.pfizer.com...W. C. Steere Jr...pharmaceuticals (Viagra, Zithromax), hospital, agricultural, chemical prods., consumer prods. (Visine eye drops, Ben-Gay pain relief).

Pharmacia & Upjohn, Inc....700 Portage Rd., Kalamazoo, MI 49001...(616) 323-4000...Website: http://www.upjohn.com...Soren Gyll...pharmaceuticals (Motrin, Rogaine, Halcion, Xanax), chemicals, agricultural, health-care prods.

Philip Morris Cos. Inc....120 Park Ave., NY, NY 10017...(212) 880-5000...Geoffrey C. Bible...cigarettes (Marlboro, Merit, Virginia Slims), beer (Miller, Molson, Red Dog), Kraft Foods products (Jell-O, Maxwell House coffee, Kool-Aid, Oscar Mayer, Tang, Cheez Whiz and Velveeta cheese prods., Post cereals, Lender's Bagels, Tombstone Pizza, and Toblerone chocolate).

Phillips Petroleum Co....Bartlesville, OK 74004...(918) 661-6600...Website: http://www.phillips66.com...W. W. Allen...integrated oil and petrochemical co.

Pitney Bowes, Inc....Walter H. Wheeler Jr. Dr., Stamford, CT 06926...(203) 356-5000...Website: http://www.pitneybowes.com...Michael J. Critelli...world's largest mfgr. of postage meters, mailing equip.

Polaroid Corp....Technology Sq., Cambridge, MA 02139...(617) 386-2000...Website: http://www.polaroid.com...Gary T. DiCamillo...photographic equip. and supplies, optical goods.

PPG Industries, Inc....1 PPG Place, Pittsburgh, PA 15272...(412) 434-3131...Website: http://www.ppg.com...Raymond W. LeBoeuf...glass prods., fiberglass, chemicals; world's leading supplier of automobile/industrial coatings.

Premark Intl....1717 Deerfield Rd., Deerfield, IL 60015...(847) 405-6000...Website: http://www.premarkintl.com...Jim Ringler...food equip. (Hobart), home appliances and cookware (West Bend).

PRIMEDIA Inc....745 Fifth Avenue, New York, NY 10151... (212) 745-0100...Website: http://www.primediainc.com... William F. Reilly...consumer magazines (*New York, Seventeen, Modern Bride, American Baby, Soap Opera Digest*), professional magazines, classroom learning (*Weekly Reader,* Channel One), workplace learning, consumer and school/library reference (*The World Almanac, Funk & Wagnalls New Encyclopedia,* Facts on File News Services), business directories.

Procter & Gamble Co....1 Procter & Gamble Plaza, Cincinnati, OH 45202...(513) 983-1100...Website: http://www.pg.com... John Pepper...soaps and detergents (Ivory, Cheer, Tide, Mr. Clean, Comet, Spic and Span, Zest), toiletries (Crest, Scope, Prell, Head and Shoulders, Noxzema, Oil of Olay, Old Spice), pharmaceuticals (Pepto-Bismol); Pampers and Luvs disposable diapers, Cover Girl and Max Factor cosmetics, Folger's coffee, Hawaiian Punch, Charmin toilet tissues, Bounty towels, Vicks cough medicines, Crisco shortening, Tampax tampons, Pringles.

Prudential Ins. Co. of America...751 Broad St., Newark, NJ 07102-3777...(973) 802-6000...Website: http://www.prudential.com...Arthur F. Ryan...insurance, financial services.

Quaker Oats Co....PO Box 049001, Chicago, IL 60604... (312) 222-7818...Website: http://www.quakeroats.com... Robert S. Morrison...cereal (Life, Cap'n Crunch), foods (Aunt Jemima, Rice-A-Roni), beverages (Gatorade).

Quaker State Corp....255 E. John Carpenter Fwy., Irving, TX 75062...(972) 868-0438...Website: http://www.quakerstate.com...Herbert M. Baum...markets petroleum and car-care prods., quick-change oil centers. (Co. announced 4/15/98 it would merge with Pennzoil.)

Ralcorp Holdings, Inc....800 Market St., St. Louis, MO 63101...(314) 877-7000...Website: http://www.ralcorp.com... Joe R. Micheletto...private-label snack foods, baby food (Beech-Nut).

Ralston Purina Group...Checkerboard Sq., St. Louis, MO 63164...(314) 982-2161...Website: http://www.ralston.com... W. P. Stiritz...world's largest producer of dog and cat food (Purina), and dry-cell batteries (Eveready, Energizer).

Raytheon Co....141 Spring St., Lexington, MA 02173...(617) 862-6600...Website: http://www.raytheon.com...Dennis J. Picard...defense systems, electronics.

Reader's Digest Assn., Inc....Pleasantville, NY 10570...(914) 238-1000...Website: http://www.readersdigest.com...Thomas Ryder...magazines, books, music and video prods.

Reebok Intl., Ltd....100 Technology Ctr. Dr., Stoughton, MA 02072...(781) 401-5000...Website: http://www.reebok.com... P. Fireman...athletic and leisure footwear, apparel.

Revlon Consumer Prods. Corp....625 Madison Ave., NY, NY 10022...(212) 527-4000...Website: http://www.revlon.com... Jerry W. Levin...cosmetics, beauty aids, skin care.

Reynolds Metals Co....6601 W. Broad St., Richmond, VA 23230...(804) 281-2000...Website: http://www.rmc.com... Jeremiah J. Sheehan...aluminum prods.

Rite Aid Corp....30 Hunter Lane, Camp Hill, PA 17011-2404... (717) 761-2633...Website: http://www.RiteAid.com...Martin Grass...discount drug stores.

RJR Nabisco Holdings Corp....1301 Ave. of the Americas, NY, NY 10019...(212) 258-5600...Website: http://www.rjrnabisco.com...Steven F. Goldstone...cigarettes (Winston, Salem, Camel), largest U.S. mfgr. of cookies and crackers (Oreo, Chips Ahoy!, Newton, SnackWell's, Ritz, Premium, Triscuit); condiments (Grey Poupon, A-1); confections (Life Savers, Breath Savers, Bubble Yum, Carefree), Milk-Bone dog biscuits, Parkay margarine, Planters peanuts.

Rockwell Intl. Corp....600 Anton Blvd., Suite 700, Costa Mesa, CA 92628-5090...(714) 424-4200...Website: http://www.rockwell.com...Donald H. Davis...diversified high-technology co.

Rubbermaid Inc....1147 Akron Rd., Wooster, OH 44691...(330) 264-6464...Website: http://www.rubbermaid.com...Wolfgang R. Schmitt...rubber and plastic consumer prods. (Little Tykes).

Ryder System, Inc....3600 NW 82d Ave., Miami, FL 33166... (305) 593-3726...Website: http://www.ryder.inter.net/ryder...M. Anthony Burns...truck-leasing service.

Safeway Inc....5918 Stoneridge Mall Rd., Pleasanton, CA 94588-3229...(510) 467-3000...Website: http://www.safeway.com...Steven A. Burd...supermarkets.

Salomon Smith Barney Inc....7 World Trade Ctr., NY, NY 10048...(212) 783-7000...Website: http://www.smithbarney.com...Robert E. Denham...investment banking, securities and commodities trading.

Sara Lee Corp....3 First National Plaza, Chicago, IL 60602... (312) 726-2600...Website: http://www.saralee.com...John H. Bryan Jr...baked goods, fresh and processed meats (Ball Park, Jimmy Dean, Hillshire Farms, Kahn's), hosiery, intimate apparel and knitwear (Hanes, L'eggs, Playtex, Champion), Coach leather goods.

SBC Communications, Inc....175 E. Houston, San Antonio, TX 78205...(210) 821-4105...Website: http://www.sbc.com... Edward Whitacre Jr...telephone services (Southwestern Bell, Pacific Bell).

Schering-Plough Corp....1 Giralda Farms, Madison, NJ 07940... (201) 822-7000...Website: http://www.sch-plough.com...R.J. Kogan...pharmaceuticals (Claritin, Proventil), consumer prods. (Afrin, Coppertone), animal health prods.

Seagate Technology...920 Disc Dr., Scotts Valley, CA 95066...(408) 438-6550...Website: http://www.seagate.com...Alan F. Shugart...manuf. disk drives.

Sears, Roebuck and Co....3333 Beverly Rd., Hoffman Estates, IL 60179...(847) 286-2500...Website: http://www.sears.com... Arthur Martinez...department, specialty stores.

Service Merchandise Co., Inc....PO Box 24600, Nashville, TN 37202-4600...(615) 660-6000...Website: http://www. servicemerchandise.com...Raymond Zimmerman...largest catalog showroom retailer in U.S.

Shaw Industries, Inc....616 E. Walnut Ave., Dalton, GA 30720...(706) 278-3812...Website: http://www.shawinds.com... Robert E. Shaw...world's largest carpet mfgr. (Armstrong, Magee, Cabin Craft).

Sherwin-Williams Co....101 Prospect Ave. NW, Cleveland, OH 44115...(216) 566-2000...Website: http://www.sherwin.com...John G. Breen...largest North American paint and varnish producer (Dutch Boy, Pratt & Lambert, Minwax).

J. M. Smucker Co....Strawberry Lane, Orrville, OH 44667... (216) 682-3000...Website: http://www.smuckers.com...T. P. Smucker...preserves, jams, jellies (Dickinson's), toppings (Magic Shell), syrups, juices.

Sprint Corp....PO Box 11315, Kansas City, MO 64112...(913) 624-3000...Website: http://www.sprint.com...William T. Esrey...long-distance and local telecommunications.

Staples, Inc....1 Research Dr., Westborough, MA 01581... (508) 370-8500...Website: http://www.staples.com...Thomas Stemberg...office-supply superstores.

Starwood Hotels and Resorts Worldwide...777 Westchester Ave., White Plains, NY 10604...(914) 640-8100... Website: http://www.starwoodlodging.com...Richard D. Nanula ...casinos and hotels (Caesars, Sheraton, Westin), largest real estate investment trust in U.S.

State Farm Mutual Automobile Ins. Co....1 State Farm Plaza, Bloomington, IL 61701...(309) 766-2311...Website: http://www.statefarm.com...Edward B. Rust Jr...major insurance co.

Stone Container...150 N. Michigan Ave., Chicago, IL 60601... (312) 346-6600...Website: http://www.stonecontainer.com... R. W. Stone...industry leader for corrugated containers, paper bags and sacks.

Stride Rite Corp....191 Spring St., Lexington, MA 02173...(617) 824-6000...Website: http://www.striderite.com...Robert Siegel... adult's and children's footwear (Keds, Sperry Top-Sider).

Sun Company, Inc....1801 Market St., Philadelphia, PA 19103-1699...(215) 977-3000...R. H. Campbell...energy resources co., markets Sunoco gasoline.

Sun Microsystems, Inc....2550 Garcia Ave., Mountain View, CA 94043...(415) 960-1300...Website: http://www.sun.com...Scott G. McNealy...supplier of network-based distributed computer systems (Java programming language).

SUPERVALU Inc....PO Box 990, Minneapolis, MN 55440... (612) 828-4000...Website: http://www.supervalu.com...Michael W. Wright...food wholesaler, retailer.

Sysco Corp....1390 Enclave Pkwy, Houston, TX 77077-2099...(281) 584-1390...Website: http://www.sysco.com... John F. Baugh...largest U.S. food distributor.

Tandy Corp....100 Throckmorton St., Suite 1800, Fort Worth, TX 76102...(817) 390-3700...Website: http://www.tandy.com... J. V. Roach...consumer electronics retailer (Computer City, Radio Shack).

Tenneco, Inc....1275 King St., Greenwich, CT 06831...(203) 863-1000...Website: http://www.tenneco.com...Dana G. Mead...packaging materials, (Hefty, Baggies), automotive parts (Monroe, Walker).

Texaco Inc....2000 Westchester Ave., White Plains, NY 10650...(914) 253-4000...Website: http://www.texaco.com... Peter I. Bijur...integrated international oil co.

Texas Instruments Inc....13500 N. Central Expressway, Dallas, TX 75265...(214) 995-3773...Website: http://www.ti.com...T. J. Engibous...electronics.

Textron, Inc....40 Westminster St., Providence, RI 02903 ...(401) 421-2800...Website: http://www. textron.com...J. F. Hardymon...aerospace, industrial, automotive prods., financial services.

Times Mirror Publishing Co....Times Mirror Sq., Los Angeles, CA 90053...(213) 237-3700...Website: http://www.tm.com... R. F. Erburu...newspapers, magazines (*Field & Stream, Popular Science*), professional books (Matthew Bender).

Time Warner Inc....75 Rockefeller Plaza, NY, NY 10020...(212) 522-1212...Website: http://www.timewarner.com...Gerald M. Levin...magazine publishing (*Time, Sports Illustrated, Fortune, Money, People,* DC Comics), TV and CATV (WB Network, HBO, Cinemax, CNN, TBS, TNT), book publishing (Little, Brown; Warner Books), motion pictures (Warner Bros.), recordings, sports teams (Atlanta Braves, Atlanta Hawks), retailing (Warner Bros. stores).

The TJX Cos., Inc....770 Cochituate Rd., Framingham, MA 01701...(508) 390-1000...John Nelson...world's largest off-price apparel retailer (T.J. Maxx, Marshalls).

Tootsie Roll Industries, Inc....7401 S. Cicero Ave., Chicago, IL 60629...(773) 838-3400...M. J. Gordon...candy (Tootsie Roll, Mason Dots, Charms, Sugar Daddy, Charleston Chew, Junior Mints).

Toro Co....8111 Lyndale Ave. S, Bloomington, MN 55420...(612) 888-8801...Website: http://www.toro.com...Kendrick B. Melrose...lawn and turf maintenance (Lawn-Boy), snow removal equipment, lighting and irrigation systems.

Toys "R" Us...461 From Rd., Paramus, NJ 07652...(201) 262-7800...Website: http://www.toysrus.com...Michael Goldstein...world's largest children's specialty retailer (Toys "R" Us, Kids "R" Us).

Transamerica Corp....600 Montgomery St., San Francisco, CA 94111...(415) 983-4000...Website: http://www.transamerica.com...Frank C. Herringer...insurance, financial services.

Travelers Group Inc....388 Greenwich St., NY, NY 10013...(212) 816-8000...Website: http://www.travelers.com...Sanford I. Weill...insurance, financial services (Salomon Smith Barney, Primerica). (Co. announced 9/24/98 it would merge with Citicorp as of 10/8/98, under the new name Citigroup.)

Triarc Cos., Inc....280 Park Ave., NY, NY 10017....(212) 451-3000...Nelson Peltz...fast-food restaurants (Arby's), beverages (Royal Crown, Mystic, Nehi, Snapple, Stewart's).

Tribune Co....435 N. Michigan Ave., Chicago, IL 60611...(312) 222-9100...Website: http://www.tribune.com...J. W. Madigan...newspaper and book publishing, broadcasting, Chicago Cubs baseball team.

TRICON Global Restaurants, Inc....1441 Gardiner Lane, Louisville, KY 40213...(502) 456-8300...Website: http://www.triglobal.com...Andrall E. Pearson...fast food (Pizza Hut, KFC, Taco Bell).

Trinity Industries, Inc....2525 Stemmons Freeway, Dallas, TX 75207...(214) 631-4420...W. Ray Wallace...manufactures metal prods., rail and freight prods.

TRW Inc....1900 Richmond Rd., Cleveland, OH 44124...(216) 291-7000...Website: http://www.trw.com...J. T. Gorman...car and truck operations, electronics, space and defense systems.

Tyco Intl., Ltd....1 Tyco Pk., Exeter, NH 03833...(603) 778-9700...Website: http://www.tycoint.com...L. D. Kozlowski...fire protection systems, pipes, power cables, medical supplies, packaging.

Tyson Foods, Inc....2210 W. Oaklawn, Springdale, AR 72764...(501) 290-4000...Website: http://www.tyson.com...Leland Tollett...fresh and processed poultry and seafood prods. (Holly Farms, Weaver, Louis Kemp).

UAL Corp....1200 E. Algonquin Rd., Elk Grove Twp., IL 60007...(708) 952-4000...Website: http://www.ual.com...Gerald Greenwald...air transportation (United Airlines).

Union Carbide Corp....39 Old Ridgebury Rd., Danbury, CT 06817...(203) 794-6440...Website: http://www.unioncarbide.com...William H. Joyce...chemicals.

Union Pacific Corp....1717 Main St., Dallas, TX 75201...(214) 743-5600...Website: http://www.uprr.com...Richard Davidson...largest railroad, trucking co. in U.S.

Unisys Corp....PO Box 500, Blue Bell, PA 19424-0001...(215) 986-5777...Website: http://www.unisys.com...Lawrence A. Weinbach...designs, manuf. computer information systems and related prods..

United HealthCare Corp....9900 Bren Rd. East, Minnetonka, MN 55343...(612) 936-1300...Website: http://www.uhc.com...William W. McGuire...owns, manages health maintenance organizations.

United Parcel Service of America, Inc....55 Glenlake Pkwy. NE, Atlanta, GA 30328...(770) 828-6000...Website: http://www.ups.com...James P. Kelley...courier services, truck rentals.

United Technologies Corp....1 Financial Plaza, Hartford, CT 06101...(860) 728-7000...Website: http://www.utc.com...George David...aerospace, industrial prods. and services (Otis Elevator, Pratt & Whitney, Sikorsky Aircraft).

Unocal Corp....2141 Rosecrans Ave., Ste. 4000, El Segundo, CA 90245...(310) 726-7667...Website: http://www.unocal.com...Roger Beach...integrated oil co.

US Airways Group, Inc....2345 Crystal Dr., Arlington, VA 22202...(703) 872-5306...Website: http://www.usairways.com...Stephen M. Wolf...air transportation.

UST Inc....100 W. Putnam Ave., Greenwich, CT 06830...(203) 661-1100...Vincent A. Gierer Jr....smokeless tobacco (Copenhagen, Skoal), pipe tobacco, wine (Chateau St. Michelle, Conn Creek, Columbia Crest).

USX-Marathon Group...600 Grant St., Pittsburgh, PA 15230...(412) 433-1121...Website: http://www.marathon.com...Thomas J. Usher...integrated oil co.

Venator Group...233 Broadway, NY, NY 10279...(212) 553-2000...Website: http://www.venatorgroup.com...Roger Farah...shoes (Kinney), apparel (Northern group), athletic footwear (Foot Locker), athletic merchandise (Champs), San Francisco Music Box Company.

V.F. Corp....1047 N. Park Rd., Wyomissing, PA 19610...(610) 378-1151...Website: http://www.threads.vfc.com...L. R. Pugh...apparel (Lee, Wrangler jeans, Vanity Fair, Healthtex, Jantzen).

Viacom, Inc....1515 Broadway, NY, NY 10036...(212) 258-6000...Website: http://www.viacom.com...Sumner M. Redstone...TV broadcast stations and cable systems, channels (Showtime, MTV, VH-1, Nickelodeon); book publishing (Simon & Schuster, Macmillan); produces, distributes movies, TV shows (Paramount); video rental stores (Blockbuster), theme parks.

Walgreen Co....200 Wilmot Rd., Deerfield, IL 60015...(847) 940-2500...Website: http://www.walgreens.com...Charles R. Walgreen 3d...nation's largest drugstore chain.

Wal-Mart Stores, Inc....Box 116, Bentonville, AR 72716...(501) 273-4000...Website: http://www.wal-mart.com...S. Robson Walton...world's largest retailer; discount stores, wholesale clubs.

Warner-Lambert Co....201 Tabor Rd., Morris Plains, NJ 07950-2693...(201) 540-2000...Website: http://www.warner-lambert.com...M. R. Goodes...personal health care and consumer prods. (Benadryl, Listerine, Schick, Dentyne, Trident gum, Chiclets, Efferdent dental cleanser, Certs mints, Halls lozenges).

Washington Post Co....1150 15th St. NW, Washington, DC 20071...(202) 334-6000...D. E. Graham...newspapers, *Newsweek* magazine, TV and CATV stations, Stanley H. Kaplan Educational Centers.

Waste Management, Inc....3003 Butterfield Rd., Oak Brook, IL 60521...(630) 572-8800...Website: http://www.wastemanagement.com...Robert S. Miller...world's largest solid waste collection and disposal co.

Wells Fargo & Co....420 Montgomery St., San Francisco, CA 94163...(415) 396-3606...Website: http://www.wellsfargo.com...Paul Hazen...bank holding co.

Wendy's Intl., Inc....4288 W. Dublin-Granville Rd., Dublin, OH 43017...(614) 764-3100...Website: http://www.wendys.com...Gordon F. Teter...quick-service restaurants.

Westinghouse Electric Corp....11 Stanwix St., Pittsburgh, PA 15222...(412) 244-2000...Website: http://www.westinghouse.com...Michael H. Jordan...manuf. electrical, mechanical equip.; radio and television stations (CBS); power generation, energy services.

Weyerhaeuser Co....Tacoma, WA 98477...(253) 924-2345...Website: http://www.weyerhaeuser.com...George H. Weyerhaeuser...world's largest private owner of softwood timber, distrib. paper and wood prods.

Whirlpool Corp....Benton Harbor, MI 49022...(616) 923-5000...Website: http://www.whirlpool.com...David Whitwam...world's largest mfgr. of major home appliances (KitchenAid, Kenmore, Roper).

Whitman Corp....3501 Algonquin Rd., Rolling Meadows, IL 60008...(708) 818-5000...Website: http://www.whitmancorp.com...Bruce S. Chelberg...beverage bottler (Pepsi-Cola).

Winn-Dixie Stores, Inc....5050 Edgewood Ct., Jacksonville, FL 32205...(904) 783-5000...Website: http://www.winn-dixie.com...A. Dano Davis...supermarkets.

Winnebago Industries, Inc....PO Box 152, Forest City, IA 50436...(515) 582-3535...Website: http://www.winnebago.com...Bruce D. Hertzke...manuf. and financing of motor homes, recreation vehicles.

Wm. Wrigley Jr. Co....410 N. Michigan Ave., Chicago, IL 60611...(312) 644-2121...Website: http://www.wrigley.com...William Wrigley...world's largest mfgr. of chewing gum.

Xerox Corp....PO Box 1600, Stamford, CT 06904...(203) 968-3000...Website: http://www.xerox.com...Paul Allaire...copiers, printers, document publishing equip.

Who Owns What: Familiar Consumer Products

Listed below are consumer products and their parent companies. For company address see Business Directory.

A-1 steak sauce: RJR Nabisco
ABC broadcasting: Walt Disney
Admiral appliances: Maytag
Advil: American Home Products
Ajax cleanser: Colgate-Palmolive
Almond Joy candy bar: Hershey
Anacin: American Home Products
Arm & Hammer: Church & Dwight
Arnold breads: Bestfoods
Arrid antiperspirant: Carter-Wallace
Aunt Millie's pasta sauce: Borden
Baggies: Tenneco
Ban antiperspirant: Bristol-Myers Squibb
Banana Republic stores: The Gap
Barbie dolls: Mattel
Beech Aircraft: Raytheon
Beech-Nut baby food: Ralcorp
Ben-Gay: Pfizer
Betty Crocker prods.: General Mills
Black Flag insecticides: Clorox
Blockbuster video stores: Viacom
Bounce fabric softener: Procter & Gamble
Breck shampoo: Dial
Brillo soap pads: Church & Dwight
Brita water systems: Clorox
Bubble Yum gum: RJR Nabisco
Budweiser beer: Anheuser-Busch
Bufferin: Bristol-Myers Squibb
Bulova watches: Lowes
Business Week magazine: McGraw-Hill
Buster Brown shoes: Brown Group
BVD underwear: Fruit of the Loom
Cadbury: Hershey
Cap'n Crunch cereal: Quaker Oats
Carrier air conditioners: United Technologies
CBS broadcasting: Westinghouse
Certs mints: Warner-Lambert
Charmin toilet tissue: Procter & Gamble
Cheer detergent: Procter & Gamble
Cheerios cereal: General Mills
Cheez Whiz: Philip Morris
Cinemax: Time Warner
Clairol hair prods.: Bristol-Myers Squibb
Clorets breath mints: Warner-Lambert
CNN: Time Warner
Coach leather goods: Sara Lee
Combat insecticides: Clorox
Comet cleanser: Procter & Gamble
Coppertone sun care prods.: Schering-Plough
Crest toothpaste: Procter & Gamble
Crisco shortening: Procter & Gamble
Doritos chips: PepsiCo
Dristan: American Home Prods.
Duracell batteries: Gillette
Dutch Boy paints: Sherwin-Williams
Efferdent dental cleanser: Warner-Lambert
Elmer's glue: Borden
ESPN: Walt Disney
Eveready batteries: Ralston Purina
Excedrin: Bristol-Myers Squibb
Fab detergent: Colgate-Palmolive
Foamy shaving cream: Gillette
Folger's coffee: Procter & Gamble
Formula 409 spray cleaner: Clorox
Franco-American spaghetti: Campbell Soup
Frito-Lay snacks: PepsiCo
Fruitopia drinks: Coca-Cola
Gatorade: Quaker Oats
Glad plastic wrap: First Brands
Godiva chocolate: Campbell Soup
Halcion: Pharmacia & Upjohn
Hamburger Helper: General Mills
Handy Wipes: Colgate-Palmolive
Hanes hosiery: Sara Lee
Hawaiian Punch: Procter & Gamble
HBO: Time Warner
Head and Shoulders shampoo: Procter & Gamble
Healthtex: V.F. Corp.
Hellmann's mayonnaise: Bestfoods
Hi-C fruit drinks: Coca-Cola
Hidden Valley prods.: Clorox
Hillshire Farms meats: Sara Lee
Holly Farms: Tyson
Hostess cakes: Interstate Bakeries
Huggies diapers: Kimberly-Clark
Ivory soap: Procter & Gamble
Jack Daniel's Whiskey: Brown-Forman
Java programming language: Sun Microsystems
Jell-O: Philip Morris
Jenn-Air stoves: Maytag
Jif peanut butter: Procter & Gamble
Jim Beam bourbon: Fortune Brands
Keds footwear: Stride Rite
Ken-L-Ration pet foods: H. J. Heinz
Kent cigarettes: Loews
KFC restaurants: TRICON
Kinney shoe stores: Venator Group
KitchenAid appliances: Whirlpool
Kit Kat candy: Hershey's
Kleenex: Kimberly-Clark
Knorr soups: Bestfoods
Kool-Aid: Philip Morris
Krazy Glue: Borden
Kwikset doorknobs: Black & Decker
Ladies Home Journal magazine: Meredith
Lee jeans: V.F. Corp.
L'eggs hosiery: Sara Lee
Lender's bagels: Phillip Morris
Lenox china: Brown-Forman
Lerner stores: The Limited
Life Savers candy: RJR Nabisco
Listerine mouthwash: Warner-Lambert
Log Cabin syrup: Philip Morris
Lord & Taylor: May Dept. Stores
Marlboro cigarettes: Philip Morris
Maxwell House coffee: Philip Morris
Mazola oils and margarine: Bestfoods
Michelob beer: Anheuser-Busch
Miller beer: Philip Morris
Milton Bradley games: Hasbro
Minute Maid beverages: Coca-Cola
MTV: Viacom
Nature Valley granola bars: General Mills
NBC broadcasting: General Electric
Neutrogena soap: Johnson & Johnson
Newsweek magazine: Washington Post
9 Lives cat food: H.J. Heinz
North American Van Lines: Norfolk Southern
Oil of Olay: Procter & Gamble
Oreo cookies: RJR Nabisco
Oscar Mayer meats: Philip Morris
Pampers: Procter & Gamble
PaperMate pens: Gillette
People magazine: Time Warner
Pepperidge Farm prods.: Campbell Soup
Pepto-Bismol: Procter & Gamble
Pine-Sol cleaner: Clorox
Pizza Hut restaurants: TRICON
Planters nuts: RJR Nabisco
Playskool toys: Hasbro
Playtex apparel: Sara Lee
Post cereals: Philip Morris
Post-It stickers: Minn. Mining & Manuf.
Prego pasta sauce: Campbell Soup
Prell shampoo: Procter & Gamble
Prentice Hall publishing: Viacom
Prozac: Eli Lilly
Radio Shack retail outlets: Tandy
Reese's peanut butter cups: Hershey
Rice-A-Roni: Quaker Oats
Rice krispies: Kellogg
Right Guard deodorant: Gillette
Ritz crackers: RJR Nabisco
Robitussin: American Home Products
Rogaine hair growth aide: Pharmacia & Upjohn
Rolaids antacid: Warner-Lambert
Ronzoni pasta: Hershey
Ruffles chips: PepsiCo
San Francisco Music Box Co.: Venator Group
San Giorgio pasta: Hershey
Schick razors: Warner-Lambert
Scholl's foot prods.: Schering-Plough
Scope mouthwash: Procter & Gamble
Scotch tape: Minn. Mining & Manuf.
Seventeen magazine: PRIMEDIA
Simon & Schuster publishing: Viacom
Skippy peanut butter: Bestfoods
SnackWell's cookies: RJR Nabisco
Snapple beverages: Triarc
Southern Comfort liquor: Brown-Forman
SPAM meat: Hormel
Sports Illustrated magazine: Time Warner
Sprite soda: Coca-Cola
Star-Kist tuna: H.J. Heinz
Sugar Twin: Alberto Culver
Swanson frozen dinners: Campbell Soup
Taco Bell restaurants: TRICON
Tampax tampons: Procter & Gamble
Thomas' English muffins: Bestfoods
Tide detergent: Procter & Gamble
Titleist: Fortune Brands
Tombstone pizza: Philip Morris
Trident gum: Warner-Lambert
Trojan condoms: Carter-Wallace
Tylenol: Johnson & Johnson
Ultra Brite toothpaste: Colgate-Palmolive
USA Today newspaper: Gannett
V-8 vegetable juice: Campbell Soup
Vanity Fair apparel: V.F. Corp.
Velveeta cheese prods.: Philip Morris
Viagra: Pfizer
Vicks cough medicines: Procter & Gamble
Victoria's Secret stores: The Limited
Visine eye drops: Pfizer
Wall Street Journal: Dow Jones
Weight Watchers: H.J. Heinz
Wheaties cereal: General Mills
Windows software applications: Microsoft
Wise snacks: Borden
Wonder bread: Interstate Bakeries
Zest soap: Procter & Gamble
Ziploc storage bags: S.C. Johnson

At-Home Shopping—Consumer Tips and Rights

Source: Federal Trade Commission, Consumer Information Center; American Express

Tips

• Deal only with reliable firms. Check with your local consumer protection agency or the Better Business Bureau (BBB) nearest the business.

• Review the advertising offer carefully.

• Inquire about warranty, refund, and exchange policies.

• Never send cash. Pay by money order, check, charge, or credit card so that you have a record of your purchase.

• Keep the ad you responded to and a copy of the order form. If there is no order form, record the company's name, address, phone number, date, the item you purchased, amount paid, and the promised delivery date.

• Never give out your credit, debit, charge card, or bank account number unless you have checked out the company or have done business with it before.

Rights

Late deliveries. By federal law, a company must ship your order within 30 days, unless the advertisement promises a different shipping time. If the company cannot ship in time, it must give you an "Option Notice." You can either wait longer or cancel and get a prompt refund. If you cancel and your order was paid by charge or credit card, the seller has one billing cycle to tell the card issuer to credit your account.

The following are exceptions to this rule:

(1) If a company does not promise a shipping time and if you are applying for credit to pay for your purchase, the company has 50 days after receiving your order to ship.

(2) Other exceptions include spaced deliveries such as magazine subscriptions (except for 1st shipment), items that continue until you cancel (for example, book or record clubs), cash on delivery (COD) orders, services, and seeds or growing plants.

Unordered merchandise. If you are shipped a product that you did not order, it's yours. It is illegal for a company to pressure you to pay for it or to return it.

Damaged or spoiled items. If damage is obvious, and if you decide not to accept the package, write "REFUSED" on the wrapper and return it unopened to the seller. No new postage is needed, unless the package came by insured, registered, certified, or COD mail and you signed for it.

Disputes or billing errors. If there is a problem with your order—you were billed the wrong amount, you never got the product, the goods were damaged or merchandise or services were misrepresented—follow these steps:

(1) Write immediately to the company, explaining the problem and asking for a specific resolution. Be sure to include your name, address, and daytime phone number, your order or invoice number, a copy of the canceled check, and any other helpful information.

(2) If you charged your purchase to a charge or credit card account or if you arranged for the payment to be automatically withdrawn from a bank account, send a copy of your letter to the card issuer or bank.

You usually have 60 days to dispute charges.

Postal rules allow you to write a check payable to the sender, rather than to the delivery company, on COD orders. If, after examining the merchandise, you believe that there has been misrepresentation or fraud, you can then stop payment on the check and file a complaint with the U.S. Postal Inspector's Office.

On the Internet

Here are special tips for shopping on the Internet:

• Consider using a secured browser, which will encrypt or scramble purchase information that can be intercepted.

• If you do not have encryption software, consider shopping by mail, fax, or phone.

• If you are unfamiliar with a company, ask the company for a paper brochure or catalog in the mail.

• Be cautious about giving out personal information. It is rarely necessary to give your Social Security number. Never give out your Internet password.

• Print out a copy of your order and confirmation number for your records.

For further questions, contact: The Federal Trade Commission, Public Reference, Washington, DC 20580; 202-326-2222; or website at http://www.ftc.gov

Consumer Information Catalog

Source: Consumer Information Center, U.S. General Services Administration

The *Consumer Information Catalog* is a free listing of more than 200 federal consumer publications. The topics range from financial planning to planning a diet, from federal benefits to getting an education, from buying a computer to choosing a healthcare plan. Many of these booklets are available free.

The catalog is published quarterly by the Consumer Information Center (CIC) of the U.S. General Services Administration. For a free copy of the latest edition, send your name and address to Consumer Information Catalog, Pueblo, CO 81009, or phone 1-888-8PUEBLO. Educators, librarians, and members of nonprofit groups who can distribute 20 or more copies of the catalog on a quarterly basis should request an application to be placed on the bulk mailing list.

Publications listed in the *Consumer Information Catalog* are also available online, along with other consumer news, updates, and information, at the following website: http://www.pueblo.gsa.gov; Electronic BBS: 202-208-7679. For detailed instructions on connecting to CIC, send e-mail to catalog.pueblo@gsa.gov with the words "SEND INFO" in the message.

The Cost of Raising a Child

Source: Family Economics Research Group, U.S. Dept. of Agriculture

Estimated annual expenditures in 1997 dollars for a child born in 1997, by income group. Estimates are for the younger child in a 2-parent family with 2 children, for the overall U.S.

		Income group[1]		
Year	Age of child	Low	Middle	High
1997	under 1	$5,820	$8,060	$11,990
1998	1	6,110	8,460	12,590
1999	2	6,420	8,890	13,220
2000	3	6,850	9,570	14,160
2001	4	7,200	10,050	14,870
2002	5	7,560	10,550	15,610
2003	6	8,130	11,190	16,320
2004	7	8,540	11,750	17,140
2005	8	8,970	12,340	18,000
2006	9	$9,450	$12,910	$18,760
2007	10	9,920	13,550	19,690
2008	11	10,420	14,230	20,680
2009	12	12,360	16,250	23,220
2010	13	12,970	17,070	24,380
2011	14	13,620	17,920	25,600
2012	15	14,120	19,060	27,570
2013	16	14,820	20,020	28,940
2014	17	15,560	21,020	30,390
TOTAL		**$178,840**	**$242,890**	**$353,130**

(1) In 1997, low annual income is less than $35,500 (average in this range=$22,100); middle income is $35,500-$59,700 (average=$47,200); high income is $59,700 or more (average=$89,300). Projected annual inflation rate is 5%.

Interest Laws and Consumer Finance Loan Rates

Source: Revised by Christian T. Jones, Editor, *Consumer Finance Law Bulletin*, Evansville, IN

All states have laws regulating interest rates. These laws fix a legal or conventional rate, which applies when there is no contract for interest. They also fix a general maximum contract rate, but there are so many exceptions that the general contract maximum actually applies to few cases. Also, federal law has preempted state limits on first home mortgages, subject to each state's right to reinstate its own law, and has given depository institutions parity with other state lenders.

Legal rate of interest. The legal or conventional rate of interest applies to money obligations when no interest rate is contracted for, and also to judgments. The rate is usually somewhat below the general contract interest rate.

General maximum contract rates. General interest laws in most states set the maximum contract rate between 8% and 16% per year. Loans to corporations are frequently exempted or subject to a higher maximum. In recent years, it has also been common to provide special rates for home mortgage loans and variable usury rates that are indexed to market rates.

Specific enabling acts. In many states special statutes permit industrial loan companies, second mortgage lenders, and banks to charge 1.5% a month or more. Laws regulating revolving loans, charge accounts, and credit cards generally limit rates to 1.5%-2% per month, plus annual fees for credit cards. Rates for installment sales contracts in most states are somewhat higher. Credit unions generally charge 1%-1.5% a month. Pawnbrokers' rates vary widely. Savings and loan associations and loans insured by federal agencies are also specially regulated. A number of states allow regulated lenders and credit sellers to charge any rate agreed to with the customer for all credit or for credit over a certain amount.

Consumer finance loan statutes. Most consumer finance loan statutes are based on early models drafted by the Russell Sage Foundation (1916-42) to provide small loans to wage earners under license and other protective regulations. Since 1969, the model has frequently been the Uniform Consumer Credit Code, which applies to credit sales and loans for consumer purposes. In general, licensed lenders may charge 3% per month, with reduced rates for higher amounts. An add-on of 17% ($17 per $100) per year amounts to about 2.5% per month if paid in equal monthly installments (add-on rates are computed on the original principal, not taking into account reduced balances as payments are made). Discount rates are computed on the whole balance of the loan, including interest, to determine how much cash is paid out; thus, for a $1,000 loan at 10% interest the borrower would receive only $900.

In the table here, unless otherwise stated, monthly and annual rates are based on reducing principal balances, annual add-on rates are based on the original principal for the full term, and 2 or more rates apply to different portions of the balance or original principal.

Loan Regulations by State

(maximum monthly rates, unless otherwise indicated; as of Aug. 1998)

AL.........Yearly add-on: 15% to $750, 10% to $2,000 (min. 1.5% on unpaid balances). Higher rates to $749. Over $2,000, any agreed rate. Fee: 6% to $2,000; 5% for 2d mortgages.
AK.........3% to $850, 2% to $10,000. Over $10,000, any agreed rate.
AZ.........To $1,000: 3%. Over $1,000: 3% to $500, 2% to $10,000. Over $10,000, any agreed rate. Fee: 4% for 2d mortgages.
CA 2.5% to $225, 2% to $900, 1.5% to $1,650, 1% to $2,500 (1.6% min.). Over $2,500, any agreed rate. 5% fee (max. $50-$75) to $5,000.
CO.........36% per year to $630, 21% to $2,100, 15% to $25,000 (21% min.).
CT.........Annual add-on: 17% to $600, 11% to $5,000; 11% over $1,800 to $15,000 for certain secured loans. Any agreed rate for 2d mortgages; 8% fee.
DE.........Any agreed rate; 10% fee.
DC.........24% per year.
FL.........30% per year to $2,000, 24% to $3,000, 18% to $25,000; $10 fee.
GA.........10% per year discount to 18 months, add-on to 36½ months; 8% fee to $600, 4% on excess plus $2 per month. Over $3,000, any agreed rate.
HI.........3.5% to $100, 2.5% to $300; 2% on entire balance over $300 or discount rates.
ID.........Any agreed rate.
IL.........Any agreed rate. Fee: 3% for 2d mortgages.
IN.........36% per year to $930, 21% to $3,100, 15% to $25,000 (21% min.). Fee: 2% for 2d mortgages.
IA.........3% to $1,000, 2% to $2,800, 1.5% to $10,000; or equivalent flat rate. Over $10,000, 21% per year.
KS.........36% per year to $860, 21% to $2,860, 14.45% to $25,000 (18% min.). Fee: 2% (max. $100); 3% for 2d mortgages.
KY.........3% to $1,000, 2% to $3,000. Over $3,000, 2%.
LA.........36% per year to $1,400, 27% to $4,000, 24% to $7,000, 21% over $7,000, plus $25 fee. Higher rates to $500.
ME.........30% per year to $2,000, 24% to $4,000, 15% to $8,000; 18% on entire balance over $8,000 to $35,000.
MD.........2.75% to $1,000, 2% to $2,000. Over $2,000, 2%.
MA.........23% per year plus $20 annual fee to $6,000; any agreed rate over $6,000.
MI.........25% per year to $15,000; 25% for 2d mortgages, plus 5% fee.
MN.........33% per year to $750, 19% over $750 (21.75% min.) plus $25 fee to $4,230.
MS.........36% per year to $1,000, 33% to $1,800, 24% to $5,000, 14% over $5,000. Over $25,000, 18%; 2% fee (max. $50).
MO.........No limits, plus 5% fee (maximum $50 for non-real estate loans). Special rates to $500.
MT.........Any agreed rate.
NE.........24% per year to $1,000. 21% over $1,000, plus fee of 7% to $2,000 and 5% over $2,000 (max. $500). Any agreed rate for real estate loans of $7,500 or more or all loans over $25,000.
NV.........Any agreed rate.
NH.........2% to $600, 1.5% to $1,500; any agreed rate over $1,500 or for real estate mortgages.
NJ.........30% per year to $5,000 and for 2d mortgages.
NM.........Any agreed rate.
NY.........25% per year.
NC.........2.5% to $1,000, 1.5% to $7,500; 1.5% on entire amount to $10,000. 1.5% or variable plus 2% fee for 2d mortgages. Higher rates to $3,000.
ND.........2.5% to $250, 2% to $500, 1.75% to $750, 1.5% to $1,000; any agreed rate for amounts over $1,000 up to $35,000.
OH.........28% per year to $1,000, 22% to $5,000; 25% on entire amount over $5,000; plus fee.
OK.........30% per year to $1,120, 21% to $3,400, 15% to $45,000 (21% min.). Higher rates to $680.
OR.........Any agreed rate.
PA.........9.5% per year discount to 48 months, 6% for remaining time plus 2% fee (max. $100); or 2% on unpaid balances; 1.85% for 2d mortgages over $5,000, plus 2% fee.
PR.........21% per year to $2,000.
RI.........3% to $300, 2.5% for loans between $300 and $800; 2% for larger loans to $5,000. 1.75% over $5,000.
SC.........Any agreed and posted rate.
SD.........Any agreed rate.
TN.........Over $100, 24% per year or discount rates plus fees.
TX.........Annual add-on: 18% to $1,380, 8% to $11,5000 or formula rate (currently 18% per year on unpaid balances). Higher rates to $460.
UT.........Any agreed rate.
VT.........2% to $1,000, 1% to $3,000 (min. 1.5%); 1.5% for 2d mortgages.
VA.........3% to $2,500; any agreed rate to $6,000. Any agreed rate for 2d mortgages, plus 5% fee.
WA.........25% per year plus fees.
WV.........31% per year to $2,000, 27% per year to $10,000, 18% per year to $45,000; fees included in rates.
WI.........Any agreed rate.
WY.........36% per year to $1,000, 21% to $50,000. No limit over $50,000.

How to Check Your Credit File

Any individual can investigate the contents of his or her credit file by directly contacting one or more of the approximately 2,000 credit bureaus, or consumer credit clearinghouses, in the U.S. The nearest ones can be found by calling a local Better Business Bureau or by looking in the telephone Yellow Pages under "Credit Rating or Reporting Agencies."

Although the Fair Credit Reporting Act requires that a bureau give a person no more than an oral or written credit history review, many bureaus will go beyond the technical requirements of the law and furnish the same computer-generated compilation of facts that they give the banks, retailers, and other companies that subscribe to their service. An individual who has been denied credit on the basis of negative information from a credit bureau can obtain a review free of charge within 30 days of the denial.

After inspecting this record of past credit behavior, a consumer can question any item believed to be inaccurate, misleading, or vague. The credit bureau must then investigate and remove any item that cannot be substantiated.

When a bureau affirms, rather than removes, a questionable item, an individual can present a 100-word explanation that must be placed in his or her file. Whenever an adverse item is deleted from the file or an explanatory statement is added, a consumer may request that the credit bureau inform every credit grantor who received a report within the last 6 months.

Credit Card Rates

Source: Christian T. Jones, Editor, *Consumer Finance Law Bulletin*, Evansville, IN; as of Aug. 1, 1998

Nearly all states have special laws dealing with rates charged for credit cards issued by state banks and other financial institutions. Although some state laws apply only to banks, under federal parity law the same charges can be made by other financial institutions. A bank can charge the highest rates and charges allowed for revolving credit extended by any other creditor for similar types of credit in the state where the bank is located. These rates and charges may also be charged to residents of any other state. Maximum rates and fees are shown below; rates are yearly unless otherwise stated.

AL	No limit.
AK	17% plus fee.
AZ	No limit.
AR	5% over FRB discount rate (max. 17%).
CA	No limit.
CO	21%.
CT	No limit.
DC	24%.
DE	No limit.
FL	No limit.
GA	No limit.
HI	24%.
ID	No limit.
IL	No limit.
IN	36% to $930, 21% to $3,100, then 15%; or 21%.
IA	No limit.
KS	18% to $1,000 then 14.45%.
KY	21%; $20 annual fee.
LA	18%; 4% cash advance and $12 annual fee.
ME	No limit; plus annual fee.
MD	24%; 2% fee.
MA	18% or formula rate.
MI	No limit.
MN	18%; $50 annual fee.
MS	21%; or 18% plus $12 annual fee; no limit over $2,000.
MO	22% to $1,000, then 10%.
MT	No limit.
NE	No limit; plus fees.
NV	No limit.
NH	No limit.
NJ	30%; $15 annual fee or $50 over $5,000.
NM	No limit.
NY	25% plus annual fee.
NC	18%; $24 annual fee.
ND	No limit.
OH	25% plus fee.
OK	30% to $1,020, 21% to $3,400, then 15%; or 21%.
OR	No limit.
PA	Variable rate, plus fees.
PR	26% per year.
RI	No limit.
SC	No limit.
SD	No limit.
TN	24%.
TX	Set by rule (max. 22%, min. 14%).
UT	No limit.
VT	No limit.
VA	No limit.
WA	25% loan; no limit for purchases; fees.
WV	18%.
WI	No limit.
WY	36% to $1,000, then 21%; no limit over $50,000.

Telephone Area Codes

Source: Lockheed Martin IMS—NANPA

Sorted by number

Area Code	Location or Service
201	New Jersey
202	Dist. of Columbia
203	Connecticut
204	Manitoba
205	Alabama
206	Washington
207	Maine
208	Idaho
209	California
210	Texas
212	New York
213	California
214	Texas
215	Pennsylvania
216	Ohio
217	Illinois
218	Minnesota
219	Indiana
225	Louisiana
228	Mississippi
240	Maryland
242	Bahamas
246	Barbados
248	Michigan
250	British Columbia
252	North Carolina
253	Washington
254	Texas
255	Louisiana
256	Alabama
264	Anguilla
267	Pennsylvania
268	Antigua/Barbuda
281	Texas
284	British Virgin Is.
301	Maryland
302	Delaware
303	Colorado
304	West Virginia
305	Florida
306	Saskatchewan
307	Wyoming
308	Nebraska
309	Illinois
310	California
312	Illinois
313	Michigan
314	Missouri
315	New York
316	Kansas
317	Indiana
318	Louisiana
319	Iowa
320	Minnesota
323	California
330	Ohio
334	Alabama
336	North Carolina
340	US Virgin Islands
345	Cayman Islands
352	Florida
360	Washington
401	Rhode Island
402	Nebraska
403	Alberta
404	Georgia
405	Oklahoma
406	Montana
407	Florida
408	California
409	Texas
410	Maryland
412	Pennsylvania
413	Massachusetts
414	Wisconsin
415	California
416	Ontario
417	Missouri
418	Quebec
419	Ohio
423	Tennessee
424	California
425	Washington
435	Utah
440	Ohio
441	Bermuda
443	Maryland
450	Quebec
456	Inbound International
473	Grenada
484	Pennyslvania
500	Personal Comm. Svcs.
501	Arkansas
502	Kentucky
503	Oregon
504	Louisiana
505	New Mexico
506	New Brunswick
507	Minnesota
508	Massachusetts
509	Washington
510	California
512	Texas
513	Ohio
514	Quebec
515	Iowa
516	New York
517	Michigan
518	New York
519	Ontario
520	Arizona
530	California
540	Virginia
541	Oregon
559	California
561	Florida
562	California
570	Pennsylvania
573	Missouri
580	Oklahoma
600	Canada (Services)
601	Mississippi
602	Arizona
603	New Hampshire
604	British Columbia
605	South Dakota
606	Kentucky
607	New York
608	Wisconsin
609	New Jersey
610	Pennsylvania
612	Minnesota
613	Ontario
614	Ohio
615	Tennessee
616	Michigan
617	Massachusetts
618	Illinois
619	California
626	California
630	Illinois
649	Turks & Caicos Islands
650	California
651	Minnesota
660	Missouri
661	California
664	Montserrat
670	N. Mariana Isls.
671	Guam

(continued)

678 . . .	Georgia	758. . .	St. Lucia	815. . .	Illinois	904 . . .	Florida
700 . . .	Pay per call service	760. . .	California	816. . .	Missouri	905 . . .	Ontario
701 . . .	North Dakota	765. . .	Indiana	817. . .	Texas	906 . . .	Michigan
702 . . .	Nevada	767. . .	Dominica	818. . .	California	907 . . .	Alaska
703 . . .	Virginia	770. . .	Georgia	819. . .	Quebec	908 . . .	New Jersey
704 . . .	North Carolina	773. . .	Illinois	828. . .	North Carolina	909 . . .	California
705 . . .	Ontario	775. . .	Nevada	830. . .	Texas	910 . . .	North Carolina
706 . . .	Georgia	780. . .	Alberta	831. . .	California	912 . . .	Georgia
707 . . .	California	781. . .	Massachusetts	843. . .	South Carolina	913 . . .	Kansas
708 . . .	Illinois	784. . .	St. Vincent & Gren.	847. . .	Illinois	914 . . .	New York
709 . . .	Newfoundland	785. . .	Kansas	850. . .	Florida	915 . . .	Texas
710 . . .	U.S. Government	786. . .	Florida	860. . .	Connecticut	916 . . .	California
712 . . .	Iowa	787. . .	Puerto Rico	864. . .	South Carolina	917 . . .	New York
713 . . .	Texas	800. . .	Toll free service	867. . .	Yukon & NW Terr.	918 . . .	Oklahoma
714 . . .	California	801. . .	Utah	868. . .	Trinidad and Tobago	919 . . .	North Carolina
715 . . .	Wisconsin	802. . .	Vermont	869. . .	St. Kitts & Nevis	920 . . .	Wisconsin
716 . . .	New York	803. . .	South Carolina	870. . .	Arkansas	925 . . .	California
717 . . .	Pennsylvania	804. . .	Virginia	876. . .	Jamaica	931 . . .	Tennessee
718 . . .	New York	805. . .	California	877. . .	Toll free service	937 . . .	Ohio
719 . . .	Colorado	806. . .	Texas	880. . .	Paid service	940 . . .	Texas
720 . . .	Colorado	807. . .	Ontario	881. . .	Paid service	941 . . .	Florida
724 . . .	Pennsylvania	808. . .	Hawaii	882. . .	Paid service	949 . . .	California
727 . . .	Florida	809. . .	Caribbean Islands	888. . .	Toll free service	954 . . .	Florida
732 . . .	New Jersey	810. . .	Michigan	900. . .	Paid service	956 . . .	Texas
734 . . .	Michigan	812. . .	Indiana	901. . .	Tennessee	970 . . .	Colorado
740 . . .	Ohio	813. . .	Florida	902. . .	Nova Scotia	972 . . .	Texas
757 . . .	Virginia	814. . .	Pennsylvania	903. . .	Texas	973 . . .	New Jersey
						978 . . .	Massachusetts

Copyright Law of the United States

Source: Copyright Office, Library of Congress, Sept. 1998

Note: Legislation enacted in Oct. 1998 extends by 20 additional years the copyright protections described below; other legislation passed in Oct. limits liability for certain uses of copyrighted materials on the Internet when these are unwitting and not for financial gain.

What Copyright Is

Copyright is a form of protection provided by the laws of the U.S. (title 17, U.S. Code) to "original works of authorship," including literary, dramatic, musical, artistic, and certain other intellectual works. This protection is available to both published and unpublished works. Section 106 of the Copyright Act generally gives the owner of copyright the exclusive right to do and to authorize other parties to do the following:

Reproduce the copyrighted work in copies or phono records;

Prepare derivative works based upon the copyrighted work;

Distribute copies or phono records of the copyrighted work to the public by sale or other transfer of ownership, or by rental, lease, or lending;

Perform the copyrighted work publicly, in the case of literary, musical, dramatic, and choreographic works, pantomimes, and motion pictures and other audiovisual works; and

Display the copyrighted work publicly, in the case of literary, musical, dramatic, and choreographic works, pantomimes, and pictorial, graphic, or sculptural works, including individual images of a motion picture or other audiovisual work.

Perform the work publicly by means of a digital audio transmission, in the case of sound recordings.

It is illegal for anyone to violate any of the rights provided by the act to the owner of copyright. However, sections 107 through 120 of the Copyright Act establish limitations on these rights. In some cases, these limitations are specified exemptions from copyright liability; a major limitation is the doctrine of "fair use," which is given a statutory basis by section 107 of the act. In other instances, the limitation takes the form of a "compulsory license," under which certain limited uses of copyrighted works are permitted upon payment of specified royalties and compliance with statutory conditions.

Copyright protection subsists from the time the work is created in fixed form. The copyright in the work of authorship *immediately* becomes the property of the author who created it. Only the author or those deriving their rights from the author can rightfully claim copyright.

The employer and not the employee is considered the author of any "work made for hire," that is:

(1) a work prepared by an employee within the scope of his or her employment; or (2) a work specially ordered or commissioned for use as a contribution to a collective work, as a part of a motion picture or other audiovisual work, as a translation, as a supplementary work, as a compilation, as an instructional text, as a test, as answer material for a test, or as an atlas, if the parties expressly agree in a written instrument signed by them that the work shall be considered a work made for hire.

The authors of a joint work are co-owners of the copyright, unless there is an agreement to the contrary.

Copyright in each separate contribution to a periodical or other collective work is distinct from copyright in the collective work as a whole and vests initially with the author of the contribution.

Copyright protection is available for all unpublished works, regardless of the author's nationality or domicile.

Published works are eligible for copyright protection in the U.S. if any of the following conditions is met:

• On the date of first publication, one or more of the authors is a national or domiciliary of the U.S. or is a national, domiciliary, or sovereign authority of a foreign nation that is a party to a copyright treaty to which the U.S. is also a party, or is a stateless person; or

• The work is first published in the U.S. or in a foreign nation that, on the date of first publication, is a party to the Universal Copyright Convention; or the work comes within the scope of a Presidential proclamation; or

• The work is first published on or after Mar. 1, 1989, in a foreign nation that on the date of first publication, is a party to the Berne Convention; or, if the work is *not* first published in a country party to the Berne Convention, it is published (on or after Mar. 1, 1989) within 30 days of first publication in a country that is party to the Berne Convention; or the work, first published on or after Mar. 1, 1989, is a pictorial, graphic, or sculptural work that is incorporated in a permanent structure located in the U.S.; or if the work, first published on or after Mar. 1, 1989, is a published audiovisual work, all the authors are legal entities with headquarters in the U.S.

• The work is a foreign work that was in the public domain in the U.S. prior to 1996 and its copyright was restored under the Uruguay Round Agreements Act. Request Circular 38b for further information.

Which Works Are Protected

Copyright protects "original works of authorship" that are fixed in a tangible form of expression. The fixation need not be directly perceptible, as long as it may be communicated with the aid of a machine or device. Copyrightable works include the following categories:

(1) literary works; (2) musical works, including any accompanying words; (3) dramatic works, including any accompanying music; (4) pantomimes and choreographic works; (5) pictorial, graphic, and sculptural works; (6) motion pictures and other audiovisual works; (7) sound recordings; and (8) architectural works.

These categories should be viewed quite broadly: for example, computer programs and most "compilations" can be registered as "literary works"; maps and architectural plans are registrable as "pictorial, graphic, and sculptural works."

Which Works Are Not Protected

Several categories of material are generally not eligible for statutory copyright protection. These include among others:

• Works that have not been fixed in a tangible form of expression. For example: choreographic works that have not been notated or recorded, or improvisational speeches or performances that have not been written or recorded.

• Titles, names, short phrases, and slogans; familiar symbols or designs; mere variations of typographic ornamentation, lettering, or coloring; mere listings of ingredients or contents.

• Ideas, procedures, methods, systems, processes, concepts, principles, discoveries, or devices, as distinguished from a description, explanation, or illustration.

• Works consisting entirely of information that is common property and containing no original authorship. For example: standard calendars, height and weight charts, tape measures and rulers, and lists or tables taken from public documents.

Notice of Copyright

For works first published on or after Mar. 1, 1989, use of the copyright notice is optional, though highly recommended. Before Mar. 1, 1989, use of the notice was mandatory on all published works, and any work first published before that date *must* bear a notice or risk loss of copyright protection.

Use of the notice is recommended because it informs the public that the work is protected by copyright, identifies the copyright owner, and shows the year of first publication. Furthermore, in the event that a work is infringed, if the work carries a proper notice, the court will not allow a defendant to claim "innocent infringement"—that is, that he or she did not realize that the work is protected. (A successful innocent infringement claim may result in reduced damages.)

The use of the copyright notice is the responsibility of the copyright owner and does not require advance permission from, or registration with, the Copyright Office.

For visually perceptible copies, the notice consists of the following: © (the letter C in a circle), the word "Copyright," or "Copr.," and the year of first publication, and the name of the owner of copyright in the work. Example: © 1999 Judy Smith. The notice must be affixed in such manner and location as to give reasonable notice of the claim of copyright.

The notice of copyright prescribed for all published phono records of sound recordings consists of the following: ℗ (the letter P in a circle), the year of first publication of the sound recording, and the name of the owner of copyright in the sound recording. Example: ℗ 1999 XYZ Records, Inc. The notice on phono records may appear on the surface of the phono record or on the phono record label or container, provided the manner of placement and location give reasonable notice of the claim.

How Long Copyright Protection Endures

Works Originally Created on or after Jan. 1, 1978

A work that is created (fixed in tangible form for the first time) on or after Jan. 1, 1978, is automatically protected from the moment of its creation and is ordinarily given a term enduring for the author's life, plus an additional 50 years after the author's death. In the case of "a joint work prepared by 2 or more authors who did not work for hire," the term lasts for 50 years after the last surviving author's death. For works made for hire and for anonymous and pseudonymous works (unless the author's identity is revealed in Copyright Office records) the duration of copyright is 75 years from publication or 100 years from creation, whichever is shorter.

Works that were created but not published or registered for copyright before Jan. 1, 1978, have been automatically brought under the statute and are now given Federal copyright protection. The duration of copyright in these works will generally be computed in the same way as for works created on or after Jan. 1, 1978: the life-plus-50 or 75/100-year terms will apply to them as well. The law provides that in no case will the term of copyright for works in this category expire before Dec. 31, 2002, and for works published on or before Dec. 31, 2002, the term of copyright will not expire before Dec. 31, 2027.

Works Created and Published or Registered Before Jan. 1, 1978

Under the law in effect before 1978, copyright was secured either on the date a work was published or on the date of registration if the work was registered in unpublished form. In either case, the copyright endured for a first term of 28 years from the date it was secured. During the last (28th) year of the first term, the copyright was eligible for renewal. The current copyright law has extended the renewal term from 28 to 47 years for copyrights subsisting on Jan. 1, 1978, making these works eligible for a total term of protection of 75 years. In 1992 an amendment to the Copyright Law automatically extended the term of copyrights secured between Jan. 1, 1964, and Dec. 31, 1977, to a further term of 47 years and increased the filing fee from $12 to $20.

PL 102-307 makes renewal registration optional. An author need not file the renewal in order to extend the original 28-year copyright term to the full 75 years. It may be beneficial, however, to file a renewal registration during the 28th year of the original term. (For more information on copyright renewal, request Circular 15 from the Copyright Office.)

International Copyright Protection

There is no such thing as an "international copyright" that will in itself protect an author's writings throughout the world. Protection against unauthorized use in a particular country basically depends on the laws of that country. However, most countries do offer protection to foreign works under certain conditions which have been greatly simplified by international copyright treaties and conventions. There are 2 principal international copyright conventions, the Berne Union for the Protection of Literary and Artistic Property (Berne Convention) and the Universal Copyright Convention (UCC). The United States became a member of the Berne Convention on Mar. 1, 1989. It has been a member of the UCC since Sept. 16, 1955.

Generally, works of an author who is a national or domiciliary of a country subscribing to these treaties, or works first published in a member country, or works published in a Berne Union country within 30 days of first publication may claim protection. There are no formal requirements under the Berne Convention. Under the UCC, any formality in a national law may be satisfied by the use of a copyright notice in the form and position specified in the UCC. A UCC notice should consist of the symbol © accompanied by the year of first publication and the name of the copyright proprietor (example: © 1999 John Doe). This notice must be placed in such a manner and location as to give reasonable notice of the claim to copyright. Since the Berne Convention prohibits formal requirements that affect the "exercise and enjoyment" of the copyright, the U.S. changed its law on Mar. 1, 1989, to make the use of a copyright notice optional. However, U.S. law still provides certain advantages for use of a copyright notice; for example, its use can defeat a defense of "innocent infringement" brought by an alleged copyright violator.

Even if the work cannot be brought under an international convention, protection may be available in other countries by virtue of a bilateral agreement between the U.S. and other countries or under specific provision of a country's laws. (See Circular 38a, *International Copyright Relations of the United States*).

An author who wishes copyright protection in a particular country should first determine the extent of protection available to works of foreign authors there. If possible, this should be done before the work is published anywhere, because protection may depend on the facts existing at the time of first publication.

There are some countries that offer little or no copyright protection to any foreign works. For current information on the requirements and protection provided by specific countries, it is advisable to consult an expert familiar with foreign copyright laws.

Copyright Registration

Copyright registration is a legal formality intended to make a public record of the basic facts of a particular copyright. Except in specific situations, registration is not a condition for protection, but the copyright law provides several inducements or advantages to encourage copyright owners to register. Among these are the following:

• Registration establishes a public record of the copyright.

• Before an infringement suit may be filed in court, registration is necessary for works of U.S. origin and for foreign works not originating in a Berne Union country. (For more information on when a work is of U.S. origin, request Circular 93 from the Copyright Office.)

• If made before or within 5 years of publication, registration will establish prima facie evidence in court of the validity of the copyright and of the facts stated in the certificate.

• If registration is made within 3 months after publication of the work or prior to an infringement of the work, statutory damages and attorney's fees will be available to the copyright owner in court actions. Otherwise, only an award of actual damages and profits is available to the copyright owner.

Copyright registration allows the owner of the copyright to record the registration with the U.S. Customs Service for protection against the importation of infringing copies. For additional information, request Publication No. 563 from Commissioner of Customs, ATTN: IPR Branch, Rm 2104, U.S. Customs Service, 1301 Constitution Ave. NW, Washington, DC 20229.

Registration may be made at any time within the life of the copyright. When a work has been registered in unpublished form, making another registration when the work becomes published is unnecessary (although the copyright owner may register the published edition, if desired).

The process of registration is simple. Request an appropriate form from the Copyright Office and complete it. Returned it to the Copyright Office along with a $20 nonrefundable filing fee and the appropriate deposit(s) of the work for which registration is sought. In a common example—a published book—the deposit is 2 copies of the best edition of the book. The Copyright Office sends a certificate of registration when the paperwork is completed, a process that usually takes 12 to 16 weeks because of the large volume of registrations the Office must handle (over 500,000 annually).

Although a copyright registration is not required, the Copyright Act establishes a mandatory deposit requirement for works published in the U.S. In general, the owner of copyright or the owner of the exclusive right of publication in the work has a legal obligation to deposit in the Copyright Office, within 3 months of publication in the U.S., 2 copies (or, in the case of sound recordings, 2 phono records) for the use of the Library of Congress. Failure to deposit these copies can result in fines and other penalties but does not affect copyright protection. Certain categories of works are exempt entirely from the mandatory deposit requirements, and the obligation is reduced for certain other categories.

Information on registration and application forms may be obtained free of charge by writing the Copyright Office, Information Section, LM-401, Library of Congress, Washington, DC 20559. Registration application forms and circulars may be ordered on a 24-hr basis by calling (202) 707-9100. Request Circular 1 for additional general information on copyright, including a list of which application forms to use when registering specific types of works.

For more information on copyright laws, visit the Copyright Office website— http://www.loc.gov/copyright

Median Price of Existing Single-Family Homes

Source: National Association of REALTORS®

City[1]	1996	1997	First Quarter 1998
Akron, OH	$ 98,800	$ 105,900	$ 106,200
Albany, NY	106,900	105,300	105,400
Albuquerque, NM	122,300	126,700	126,200
Amarillo, TX	73,700	76,800	77,200
Anaheim/Santa Ana, CA[2]	213,400	229,800	243,200
Appleton/Oshkosh, WI	85,800	88,200	89,100
Atlanta, GA	100,700	108,400	110,800
Atlantic City, NJ	108,000	109,700	110,500
Aurora, IL	137,000	141,800	138,400
Austin, TX	108,100	NA	NA
Baltimore, MD	113,000	118,200	115,500
Baton Rouge, LA	87,800	92,300	97,100
Beaumont/Port Arthur, TX	68,100	69,000	73,200
Biloxi/Gulfport, MS	78,300	81,100	81,800
Birmingham, AL	114,100	118,900	121,300
Boise City, ID	101,200	102,500	105,800
Boston, MA	189,300	196,200	205,200
Bradenton, FL	95,100	94,900	100,200
Buffalo/Niagara Falls, NY	82,900	82,000	83,200
Canton, OH	89,300	94,300	87,500
Cedar Rapids, IA	91,200	94,800	95,600
Champaign, IL	79,800	84,500	90,600
Charleston, SC	94,900	103,600	113,400
Charleston, WV	90,400	87,800	90,000
Charlotte, NC	116,800	124,200	131,800
Chattanooga, TN	89,500	92,200	94,900
Chicago, IL	153,200	158,900	161,100
Cincinnati, OH/KY/IN	104,800	110,500	115,400
Cleveland, OH	111,900	116,800	117,000
Colorado Springs, CO	126,600	130,500	132,600
Columbia, SC	93,400	99,100	100,100
Columbus, OH	108,200	117,600	118,200
Corpus Christi, TX	79,600	81,800	83,100
Dallas, TX	103,500	112,000	116,400
Davenport, IA/IL	69,400	72,600	75,000
Dayton/Springfield, OH	95,100	96,700	96,800
Daytona Beach, FL	73,300	75,500	76,000
Denver, CO	133,400	140,600	147,000
Des Moines, IA	92,400	98,900	104,000
Detroit, MI	111,400	119,600	128,900
El Paso, TX	76,200	75,900	77,400
Eugene, OR	116,200	119,400	120,800
Fargo, ND/MN	83,200	86,000	89,400
Ft. Lauderdale, FL	112,300	123,700	122,000
Ft. Myers, FL	78,700	85,700	86,400
Ft. Wayne, IN	80,100	85,800	87,800
Ft. Worth/Arlington, TX	86,500	91,800	93,100
Gainesville, FL	93,600	99,600	97,700
Gary/Hammond, IN	95,000	97,300	101,000
Grand Rapids, MI	87,200	93,600	96,100
Green Bay, WI	96,100	100,900	103,700
Greensboro, NC	112,700	117,300	119,800
Greenville, NC	105,500	112,800	117,200
Hartford, CT	139,200	138,100	134,600
Honolulu, HI	335,000	307,000	288,500
Houston, TX	$ 84,700	$ 90,900	$ 92,000
Indianapolis, IN	98,000	103,700	107,000
Jacksonville, FL	88,400	86,400	89,600
Kalamazoo, MI	90,000	97,200	95,700
Kansas City, MO/KS	98,800	106,800	110,100
Knoxville, TN	98,700	99,900	102,800
Lake County, IL	144,700	153,500	157,800
Lansing, MI	84,700	89,600	95,500
Las Vegas, NV	118,500	123,200	125,500
Lexington/Fayette, KY	95,700	100,600	106,200
Lincoln, NE	87,200	92,800	95,800
Little Rock, AR	83,700	85,600	92,400
Los Angeles, CA[2]	172,900	176,500	176,500
Louisville, KY/IN	91,300	96,800	105,700
Madison, WI	122,200	126,800	128,600
Melbourne, FL	81,600	85,900	78,200
Memphis, TN/AR/MS	96,100	103,700	106,700
Miami, FL	113,200	117,700	117,800
Milwaukee, WI	119,400	125,300	132,200
Minneapolis, MN/WI	113,900	118,400	121,900
Mobile, AL	83,200	87,200	92,000
Montgomery, AL	90,100	94,100	98,600
Nashville, TN	112,700	115,200	117,600
New Haven, CT	133,300	134,100	130,300
New Orleans, LA	87,000	93,300	96,900
New York, NY	174,500	177,900	178,200
Norfolk/Virginia Bch, VA	110,200	NA	108,200
Ocala, FL	63,600	64,300	67,000
Oklahoma City, OK	74,600	77,000	81,200
Omaha, NE	88,300	93,600	102,100
Orlando, FL	92,400	94,500	99,300
Pensacola, FL	84,500	88,900	90,800
Peoria, IL	74,500	79,700	78,900
Philadelphia, PA/NJ	NA	NA	NA
Phoenix, AZ	105,300	113,700	117,300
Pittsburgh, PA	84,800	87,000	85,400
Portland, ME	91,000	94,500	94,600
Portland, OR	141,500	152,400	155,400
Providence, RI	118,100	119,600	119,500
Raleigh/Durham, NC	145,400	152,800	154,300
Reno, NV	140,000	143,400	144,900
Richland, WA	101,300	102,600	110,000
Richmond, VA	108,700	114,200	118,300
Riverside/San Bern.,CA[2]	115,200	114,300	118,400
Rochester, NY	86,200	86,800	84,900
Rockford, IL	88,700	88,800	89,000
Sacramento, CA[2]	115,300	116,100	116,900
Saginaw, MI	66,400	71,300	76,000
St. Louis, MO/IL	91,200	96,900	95,800
Salt Lake City, UT	122,700	128,600	132,600
San Antonio, TX	84,900	86,800	84,100
San Diego, CA[2]	174,500	185,200	192,300
San Francisco, CA[2]	266,700	292,600	292,600
Sarasota, FL	107,700	114,100	120,700
Seattle, WA	164,600	171,300	191,600

City[1]	1996	1997	First Quarter 1998	City[1]	1996	1997	First Quarter 1998
Shreveport, LA	$ 77,600	$ 78,200	$ 81,900	Topeka, KS	$ 73,900	$ 77,000	$ 78,400
Sioux Falls, SD	87,400	90,200	NA	Tenton, NJ	136,400	137,700	127,200
South Bend, IN	76,700	78,100	77,100	Tucson, AZ	105,500	106,800	108,800
Spokane, WA	101,200	102,700	96,300	Tulsa, OK	82,200	84,600	85,700
Springfield, IL	82,100	83,800	85,900	Washington, DC/MD/VA	160,700	166,300	163,000
Springfield, MA	106,000	106,500	114,700	Waterloo/Cedar Falls,IA	60,600	65,200	63,600
Springfield, MO	79,200	82,200	85,300	W. Palm Beach, FL	126,600	133,400	132,100
Syracuse, NY	79,100	79,000	78,700	Wichita, KS	80,700	83,200	83,700
Tacoma, WA	125,400	NA	138,000	Wilmington, DE/NJ/MD	NA	NA	NA
Tallahassee, FL	109,800	111,700	115,600	Worcester, MA	131,200	135,800	138,100
Tampa, FL	81,300	83,900	84,800	Youngstown, OH	69,700	73,900	75,800
Toledo, OH	84,200	87,300	89,600				

(1) All areas are metropolitan statistical areas (MSAs) as defined by the U.S. Office of Management and Budget. They include the named central city and surrounding areas. (2) Data provided by the California Association of REALTORS®. NA= not available.

Housing Affordability

Source: National Association of REALTORS®

Year	Median-priced existing home	Average mortgage rate[1]	Monthly principal and interest payment	Payment as percentage of median income	Year	Median-priced existing home	Average mortgage rate[1]	Monthly principal and interest payment	Payment as percentage of median income
1987	$85,600	9.28%	$565	21.9%	1993	$106,800	7.16%	$578	18.8%
1988	90,600	9.31	591	22.0	1994	109,900	7.47	613	19.0
1989	93,100	10.11	660	23.1	1995	113,100	7.85	654	19.3
1990	97,500	10.04	673	22.7	1996	118,200	7.71	675	19.2
1991	99,700	9.51	671	22.3	1997	124,100	7.68	706	19.3
1992	103,700	8.11	615	20.0	1998[2]	134,600	7.19	730	19.5

(1) The average mortgage rate is based on the effective rate on loans closed on existing homes monitored by the Federal Housing Finance Board. (2) Preliminary figures for June 1998.

Mortgage Loan Calculator

Source: Joyce E. Boulanger, Mortgage Access Corp.

To determine monthly payments, divide loan amount by 1,000 and then multiply the resulting figure by the appropriate factor from this table. To find the appropriate factor use the mortgage term in years and the interest rate percentage. More information on calculating mortgages can be found at http://www.weichert.com/mortgage

EXAMPLE: For a 30-year mortgage at 6.75%, the factor would be 6.49. If the mortgage amount is $220,000, divide by 1,000, which comes to 220. 220 x 6.49 (factor) = $1,427.80 monthly mortgage payment of principal and interest only (there will also be property taxes, home insurance, and other possible costs).

MORTGAGE TERM IN YEARS

INTEREST RATE	5	10	15	20	25	30	35	40
5.00	18.88	10.61	7.91	6.60	5.85	5.37	5.05	4.83
5.25	18.99	10.73	8.04	6.74	6.00	5.53	5.21	4.99
5.50	19.11	10.86	8.18	6.88	6.15	5.68	5.38	5.16
5.75	19.22	10.98	8.31	7.03	6.30	5.84	5.54	5.33
6.00	19.33	11.10	8.44	7.16	6.44	6.00	5.70	5.50
6.25	19.45	11.23	8.57	7.31	6.60	6.16	5.87	5.68
6.50	19.57	11.35	8.71	7.46	6.75	6.32	6.04	5.85
6.75	19.68	11.48	8.85	7.60	6.91	6.49	6.21	6.03
7.00	19.80	11.61	8.99	7.75	7.07	6.65	6.39	6.21
7.25	19.92	11.74	9.13	7.90	7.23	6.82	6.56	6.40
7.50	20.04	11.87	9.27	8.06	7.39	6.99	6.74	6.58
7.75	20.16	12.00	9.41	8.21	7.55	7.16	6.92	6.77
8.00	20.28	12.13	9.56	8.36	7.72	7.34	7.10	6.95
8.25	20.40	12.27	9.70	8.52	7.88	7.51	7.28	7.14
8.50	20.52	12.40	9.85	8.68	8.06	7.69	7.47	7.34
8.75	20.64	12.54	10.00	8.84	8.23	7.87	7.66	7.53
9.00	20.76	12.67	10.15	9.00	8.40	8.05	7.84	7.72
9.25	20.88	12.81	10.30	9.16	8.57	8.23	8.03	7.91
9.50	21.01	12.94	10.45	9.33	8.74	8.41	8.22	8.11
9.75	21.13	13.08	10.60	9.49	8.92	8.60	8.41	8.30
10.00	21.25	13.22	10.75	9.66	9.09	8.78	8.60	8.50
10.25	21.38	13.36	10.90	9.82	9.27	8.97	8.79	8.69
10.50	21.50	13.50	11.06	9.99	9.45	9.15	8.99	8.89
10.75	21.62	13.64	11.21	10.16	9.63	9.34	9.18	9.09
11.00	21.75	13.78	11.37	10.33	9.81	9.53	9.37	9.29
11.25	21.87	13.92	11.53	10.50	9.99	9.72	9.57	9.49
11.50	22.00	14.06	11.69	10.67	10.17	9.91	9.77	9.69
11.75	22.12	14.21	11.85	10.84	10.35	10.10	9.96	9.89
12.00	22.25	14.35	12.01	11.02	10.54	10.29	10.16	10.09
12.25	22.38	14.50	12.17	11.19	10.72	10.48	10.36	10.29
12.50	22.50	14.64	12.33	11.37	10.91	10.68	10.56	10.49
12.75	22.63	14.79	12.49	11.54	11.10	10.87	10.76	10.70
13.00	22.76	14.94	12.66	11.72	11.28	11.07	10.96	10.90
13.25	22.89	15.08	12.82	11.90	11.47	11.26	11.16	11.10
13.50	23.01	15.23	12.99	12.08	11.66	11.46	11.36	11.31
13.75	23.14	15.38	13.15	12.26	11.85	11.66	11.56	11.51
14.00	23.27	15.53	13.32	12.44	12.04	11.85	11.76	11.72

Leasing a Car

Source: Consumer Information Center, U.S. General Services Administration

Leasing a car instead of buying it has become an increasingly common option in recent years. In 1985, only 3.5% of all private vehicles were leased; by 1997, 29.3% were leased. Under the federal Consumer Leasing Act, consumers have a right to information about the costs and terms of a vehicle lease. The following information can help you compare lease offers and negotiate a lease that best fits your needs, budget, and driving patterns. (The information is mainly for a closed-end lease, the most common type.)

Here are some differences between buying and leasing:

Buying: You own the vehicle and get to keep it at the end of the financing term.

Leasing: You do not own the vehicle. You get to use it but must return it at the end of the lease unless you choose to buy it.

Buying: Up-front costs include the cash price or a down payment, taxes, registration and other fees, and various other charges.

Leasing: Up-front costs may include the first month's payment, a refundable security deposit, a capitalized cost reduction (like a down payment), taxes, registration and other fees, and other charges.

Buying: Monthly loan payments are usually higher than monthly lease payments because you are paying for the entire purchase price of the vehicle, plus interest and other finance charges, taxes, and fees.

Leasing: Monthly lease payments are usually lower because you pay only for depreciation during the lease term, plus rent charges (like interest), taxes, and various fees.

Buying: You are responsible for any pay-off amount if you end the loan early.

Leasing: You may have to pay substantial early termination charges if you end the lease early.

Buying: You may have to sell or trade the vehicle when you decide you want a different vehicle.

Leasing: You may return the vehicle at lease end, pay any end-of-lease costs, and "walk away."

Buying: You have the risk of the vehicle's market value when you trade or sell it.

Leasing: The lessor has the risk of the future market value of the vehicle.

Buying: You may drive as many miles as you want, but higher mileage will lower the vehicle's trade-in or resale value.

Leasing: You may have to pay extra for mileage above a certain limit—12,000-15,000 per year—if you return the vehicle. You can negotiate a higher mileage limit and pay a higher monthly payment.

Buying: There are no limits or charges for excessive wear to the vehicle, but excessive wear will lower the vehicle's trade-in or resale value.

Leasing: Most leases limit wear to the vehicle during the lease term; standards for excess wear, such as for body damage or worn tires, are in your lease agreement. You will likely have to pay extra charges for exceeding those limits if you return the vehicle.

Buying: At the end of the loan term (typically 4-6 years), you have no further loan payments.

Leasing: At the end of the lease (typically 2-4 years), you may have a new payment either to finance the purchase of the existing vehicle or to lease another vehicle.

During the lease, you will have to pay any additional taxes not included in the payment, such as sales, use, and personal property taxes; insurance premiums; ongoing maintenance costs and inspections; and any fees for late payment. At the end of the lease, if you don't buy the vehicle, you may have to pay a disposition fee and charges for excess miles and excess wear.

Among other things to consider when negotiating different lease offers and terms, consider the option to purchase either at lease end or earlier; also check whether your lease includes "gap" coverage, which protects you if the vehicle is stolen or totaled in an accident. Ask for alternatives to advertised specials and other lease offerings.

When you lease a vehicle, you have the right to take advantage of any warranties, recalls, or other services that apply to the vehicle.

For more information on leasing a car, contact your dealer, manufacturer, leasing company, or financial institution. For more information on consumer rights not covered in your lease agreement, contact your state's consumer protection agency or Attorney General's office.

How to Obtain Birth, Marriage, Death Records

The pamphlet *Where to Write for Vital Records: Births, Deaths, Marriages, and Divorces* (Stock # 017-022-01196-4) is available from the Superintendent of Documents, PO Box 371954, Pittsburgh, PA 15250-7954; advance payment of $2.25 is required. Orders can also be placed by calling (202) 512-1800 or via fax, (202) 512-2250, using a credit card.

Wedding Anniversaries

The traditional names for wedding anniversaries go back many years in social usage. As names like *wooden, crystal, silver*, and *golden* were applied to anniversary years, it was considered proper to present the married couple with gifts made of these products or of something related. Traditional products for gifts are listed here, with a few allowable revisions in parentheses, followed by common modern gifts in each category.

1st	PAPER, clocks	**9th**	POTTERY (CHINA), leather goods	**25th**	SILVER, sterling silver
2d	COTTON, china	**10th**	TIN, ALUMINUM, diamond	**30th**	PEARL, diamond
3d	LEATHER, crystal, glass	**11th**	STEEL, fashion jewelry	**35th**	CORAL (JADE), jade
4th	LINEN (SILK), appliances	**12th**	SILK, pearls, colored gems	**40th**	RUBY, ruby
5th	WOOD, silverware	**13th**	LACE, textiles, furs	**45th**	SAPPHIRE, sapphire
6th	IRON, wood objects	**14th**	IVORY, gold jewelry	**50th**	GOLD, gold
7th	WOOL (COPPER), desk sets	**15th**	CRYSTAL, watches	**55th**	EMERALD, emerald
8th	BRONZE, linens, lace	**20th**	CHINA, platinum	**60th**	DIAMOND, diamond

Birthstones

Source: Jewelry Industry Council

MONTH	Ancient	Modern	MONTH	Ancient	Modern
January	Garnet	Garnet	**July**	Onyx	Ruby
February	Amethyst	Amethyst	**August**	Carnelian	Sardonyx or Peridot
March	Jasper	Bloodstone or Aquamarine	**September**	Chrysolite	Sapphire
April	Sapphire	Diamond	**October**	Aquamarine	Opal or Tourmaline
May	Agate	Emerald	**November**	Topaz	Topaz
June	Emerald	Pearl, Moonstone, or Alexandrite	**December**	Ruby	Turquoise or Zircon

Marriage Laws*

Source: Gary N. Skoloff, Skoloff & Wolfe, Livingston, NJ; as of Aug. 1998

STATE	Age with parental consent		Age without consent		Physical exam & blood test for male and female		Waiting period	
	Male	Female	Male	Female	Max. period between exam and license	Scope of medical exam	Before license	After license issuance (expiration)
Alabama**	14a,t	14a,t	18	18	—	—	—	30 days
Alaska	16z	16z	18	18	—	—	3 days, w	—
Arizona	16z	16z	18	18	—	—	—	1 yr.
Arkansas	17c, z	16c, z	18	18	—	—	v	—
California	aa	aa	18	18	30 days, w, h	—	—	90 days
Colorado**[y]	16z	16z	18	18	—	—	—	30 days
Connecticut	16z	16z	18	18	—	bb	4 days, w	65 days
Delaware	18c	16c	18	18	—	—	24 hr, e	30 days
Florida	16a, c	16a, c	18	18	—	—	—	—
Georgia**	16j	16j	18	18	—	bb	3 days, g	30 days
Hawaii	15j	15j	18	18	—	—	—	—
Idaho**	16z	16z	18	18	—	s, zzz	—	—
Illinois	16pp	16pp	18	18	—	n	1 day	60 days
Indiana	17c	17c	18	18	—	rr	—	60 days
Iowa**	18j	18j	18	18	—	—	3 days	20 days
Kansas**[y]	14j	12j	18	18	—	—	3 days, w	—
Kentucky	18j	18j	18	18	—	—	—	—
Louisiana[xx]	18z	18z	18	18	10 days	—	—	—
Maine	16z	16z	18	18	—	—	3 days, v, w	90 days
Maryland	18c, f	18c, f	18	18	—	—	48 hr, w	6 mo
Massachusetts	14j	12j	18	18	3-60 days, u	—	3 days, v	—
Michigan	16	16	18	18	—	—	3 days, w	—
Minnesota	16j	16j	18	18	—	—	5 days, w	—
Mississippi	aa, j	aa, j	17	15	30 days	b	3 days, w	—
Missouri	15d	15d	18	18	—	—	—	—
Montana**[yy]	16j	16j	18	18	—	b	—	180 days
Nebraska[yy]	17	17	19	19	—	bb	—	1 yr
Nevada	16z	16z	18	18	—	—	—	1 yr
New Hampshire	18k	18k	18	18	—	—	3 days, v, w	90 days
New Jersey	16z, c	16z, c	18	18	—	—	72 hr, w	30 days
New Mexico	16d, c	16d, c	18	18	30 days	b	—	—
New York	16k	16k	18	18	—	nn	24 hr	60 days
North Carolina	16c	16c	18	18	—	—	—	—
North Dakota	16	16	18	18	—	—	—	60 days
Ohio	18, j	16c, z	18	18	—	—	5 days,w, r	60 days
Oklahoma**	16c, z	16c, z	18	18	30 days, w	b	ff	30 days
Oregon	17tt	17tt	18	18	—	—	3 days, w	—
Pennsylvania**	16d	16d	18	18	30 days	b	3 days, w	60 days
Rhode Island**	18d	16d	18	18	—	rrr	—	—
South Carolina**	16c	14c	18	18	—	—	1 day	—
South Dakota	16c	16c	18	18	—	—	—	20 days
Tennesee	16d	16d	18	18	—	—	3 days, cc, w	30 days
Texas**[y]	14j, k	14j, k	18	18	—	—	zzzz	30 days
Utah**	14a	14a	18x	18x	—	—	—	30 days
Vermont	16j	16j	18	18	30 days, w	b	1 day, w	—
Virginia	16a, c	16a, c	18	18	—	zz	—	60 days
Washington	17d	17d	18	18	—	bbb	3 days	60 days
West Virginia	18c	18c	18	18	—	b	3 days, w	—
Wisconsin	16	16	18	18	—	zzz	5 days, w	30 days
Wyoming	16d	16d	18	18	—	bb	—	—
Dist. of Columbia**	16a	16a	18	18	30 days	b	3 days, w	—
Puerto Rico	18c, d, z	16c, d, z	21	21c	—	b	—	—

*Most states have other laws as well as qualifications of the laws shown here and have proposed legislation pending. It would be advisable to consult a lawyer in conjunction with the use of this chart. **Indicates common-law marriage recognized. (a)Parental consent not required if minor was previously married. (aa)No age limits. (b)Venereal diseases. In WV and OK, Circuit Court judge may waive requirement. (bb)Venereal diseases and rubella (for female). (bbb)No exam required, but parties must file affidavit of non-affliction with contagious venereal disease. (c)Younger parties may obtain license in case of pregnancy or birth of child. (cc)Unless parties are over 18 yr of age. (d)Younger parties may obtain license in special circumstances. (e)Residents, before expiration of 24-hr waiting period; non-residents, before expiration of 96-hr waiting period. (f)If parties are at least 16 yr of age, proof of age and consent of parents in person are required. If a parent is ill, an affidavit by the incapacitated parent and a physician's affidavit required. (ff)If one or both parties are below the age for marriage without parental consent, 3-day waiting period. (g)Unless parties are 18 yr of age or more, or female is pregnant, or applicants are the parents of a living child born out of wedlock. (h)When unmarried man and unmarried woman, not minors, have been living together as man and wife, they may, without health certificate, be married upon issuance of appropriate authorization. (j)Parental consent and/or permission of judge required. (jj)Medical examination for syphilis (and for female, rubella), with required offer of HIV test. (k)Below age of consent parties need parental consent and permission of judge, no younger than 14 for males and 13 for females. (l)Medical examination not required but certificate evidencing HIV counseling required. (m)Mental incompetence, infectious tuberculosis, venereal diseases. (n)Venereal diseases; test for sickle cell anemia given at request of examining physician. (nn)Tests for sickle cell anemia may be required. (p)Rubella for female, except under limited circumstances. (pp)Judicial consent may be given when parents refuse to consent. (r)Applicants under age 18 must state that they have had marriage counseling. (rr)Any unsterilized female under 50 must submit with application for license a medical report stating whether she has immunological response to rubella, or a written record that the rubella vaccine was administered on or after her 1st birthday. Judge may by order dispense with these requirements. (rrr)Physical examination and blood test required; offer of HIV counseling required. (s)Rubella for female; there are certain exceptions, and district judge may waive medical examination on proof that emergency exists. (t)Other statutory requirements apply. (tt)If a party has no parent residing within state, and one party has residence within state for 6 mo, no permission required. (u)Doctor's certificate must be filed 30 days prior to notice of intention. (v)Parties must file notice of intention to marry with local clerk. (w)Waiting period may be avoided. (x)Authorizes counties to provide for premarital counseling as a requisite to issuance of license to persons under 19 and persons previously divorced. (xx) The "covenant marriage" bill, which went into effect Aug. 15, 1997, provides for an optional, voluntary form of marriage that is more difficult to dissolve. The covenant marriage requires pre-marriage counseling and limits grounds for divorce to such issues as spousal or child abuse, imprisonment, or adultery. (y)Marriages by proxy are valid. (yy) Proxy marriages are valid under certain conditions. (z)Younger parties may marry with parental consent and/or permission of judge. In CT, judicial approval. (zz)Required offer of HIV test, and/or must be provided with information on AIDS and tests available. (zzz)Applicants must receive information on AIDS and certify having read it. (zzzz)72-hr waiting period following issuance of license.

Divorce Laws

Source: Gary N. Skoloff, Skoloff & Wolfe, Livingston, NJ; as of Aug. 1998

Note: Almost all states also have other laws as well as qualifications of the laws shown here and have proposed divorce-reform laws pending. It would be advisable to consult a lawyer in conjunction with the use of this chart.

Some Grounds for Divorce[1]

	Residence	Adultery	Mental or physical cruelty	Desertion	Alcoholism	Impotency	Non-support	Insanity	Bigamy	Felony conviction or imprisonment	Drug addiction	Fraud, force, duress
AL	6 mo*	Yes	Yes	1 yr	Yes	Yes	2 yr	5 yr, A	A	2 yr*	Yes	A
AK	30 days*	Yes	Yes	1 yr	1 yr	Yes	No	18 mo	A	Yes	Yes	A
AZ	90 days	No	No	No	No	No	No	No	No	No	No	No
AR	60 days*	Yes	Yes	No	1 yr	Yes	Yes	3 yr	No	Yes	No	A
CA	6 mo*	No	No	No	No	A	No	Yes*	A	No	No	A
CO	90 days	No	No	No	No	A	No	No	A	No	No	A
CT	1 yr*	Yes	Yes	1 yr	Yes	No	Yes	5 yr	A	life*	No	Yes
DE	6 mo	Yes	Yes	Yes	Yes	A	No	Yes	Yes	Yes	Yes	A
FL	6 mo	No	No	No	No	No	No	3 yr	No	No	No	A
GA	6 mo	Yes	Yes	1 yr	Yes	Yes	No	2 yr	A	Yes*	Yes	Yes
HI	6 mo	No	No	No	No	No	No	No	A	No	No	A
ID	6 wk	Yes	Yes	Yes	Yes	A	Yes	3 yr	A	Yes	No	A
IL	90 days	Yes	Yes	1 yr	2 yr	Yes	No	No	Yes	Yes	2 yr	No
IN	6 mo*	No	No	No	No	Yes	No	2 yr	A	Yes	No	A
IA	1 yr*	No	No	No	No	A	No	A	A	No	No	No
KS	60 days	No	No	No	No	Yes	Yes	2 yr	A	No	No	A
KY	180 days	No	No	No	No	A	No	No	No	No	No	A
LA	6 mo*	Yes	No	No	No	No	No	No	A	Yes*	No	A
ME	6 mo*	Yes	Yes	3 yr	Yes	Yes	Yes	7 yr, A	A	No	Yes	No
MD	*	Yes	D	1 yr, D	No	No	No	3 yr	A	1 yr*	No	No
MA	1 yr*	Yes	Yes	1 yr	Yes	Yes	No†	A	A	5 yr*	Yes	No
MI	180 days*	No	No	No	No	No	No	No	No	No	No	A
MN	180 days	No	No	No	No	No	No	No	No	No	No	A
MS	6 mo	Yes	Yes	1 yr	Yes	Yes, A	No	3 yr, A	A	Yes	Yes	A
MO	90 days	No	No	No	No	No	No	No	A	No	No	A
MT	90 days	No	No	No	No	A	No	No	A	No	No	A
NE	1 yr*	No	No	No	No	A	No	A	A	No	No	A
NV	6 wk	No	No	No	No	No	No	2 yr	A	No	No	A
NH	1 yr*	Yes	Yes	2 yr	2 yr	Yes	2 yr	No	A	1 yr*	No	No
NJ	1 yr*	Yes	Yes	1 yr	1 yr	A	No	2 yr	A	18 mo	1 yr	A
NM	6 mo	Yes	Yes	Yes	No	No	No	No	No	No	No	No
NY	1 yr*	Yes, D	Yes	1 yr, D	No	No	D	A	A	3 yr, D	No	A
NC	6 mo	No, D	No, D	No, D	1 yr, D	A	No	3 yr	A	No	No, D	No
ND	6 mo	Yes	Yes	1 yr	No	A	1 yr	5 yr	A	Yes	No	A
OH	6 mo	Yes, D	Yes, D	1 yr, D	Yes, D	No	Yes, D	No	Yes, D	Yes, D	No	Yes, D
OK	6 mo	Yes	Yes	1 yr	Yes	Yes	Yes	5 yr	Yes	Yes	No	Yes
OR	6 mo*	No	No	No	No	No	No	No	No	No	Yes	A
PA	6 mo	Yes	Yes	1 yr	No	No	No	18 mo*	Yes	Yes	No	No
RI	1 yr	Yes	Yes	5 yr*	Yes	Yes	1 yr	No	No	Yes	Yes	No
SC	1 yr*	Yes	Yes	1 yr	Yes	No	No	No	A	No	Yes	No
SD	*	Yes, D	Yes, D	1 yr, D	1 yr, D	A	1 yr, D	5 yr, D	A	Yes, D	No	A
TN	6 mo*	Yes	Yes	1 yr	Yes	Yes	D	No	Yes	Yes	Yes	A
TX	6 mo*	Yes	Yes	1 yr	No	A	No	3 yr	No	1 yr	No	A
UT	3 mo*	Yes	Yes	1 yr	Yes	Yes	Yes	Yes*	A	Yes	No	No
VT	6 mo*	Yes	Yes	7 yr	No	No	Yes	5 yr, D	A	3 yr	No	A
VA	6 mo*	Yes	Yes, D	1 yr, D	No	A	D	A	A	1 yr	No	A
WA	bona fide resident	No	No	No	No	No	No	No	A*	No	No	A
WV	1 yr*	Yes	Yes	6 mo	Yes	A	No	3 yr	A	Yes	Yes	No
WI	6 mo	No	No	No	No	A	No	No	A	No	No	A
WY	2 mo*	No	No	No	No	No	No	2 yr	A	No	No	A
DC	6 mo	No	No	No	No	A	No	A	A	No	No	A
PR	1 yr	Yes	Yes	1 yr	Yes	Yes	No	Yes	A	Yes*	Yes	No

(1) Almost all states have "no-fault" divorce laws. Conduct that constitutes "no-fault" divorce may vary from state to state. (*) indicates qualification; check local statutes. (A) indicates grounds for annulment. (D) indicates grounds for divorce or legal separation.

SOCIAL SECURITY

Social Security Programs

Source: Social Security Administration; data as of Aug. 1998

Old-Age, Survivors, and Disability Insurance; Medicare; Supplemental Security Income

Social Security Benefits

Social Security benefits are based on a worker's primary insurance amount (PIA), which is related by law to the average indexed monthly earnings (AIME) on which Social Security contributions have been paid. The full PIA is payable to a retired worker who becomes entitled to benefits at age 65 and to an entitled disabled worker at any age. Spouses and children of retired or disabled workers and survivors of deceased workers receive set proportions of the PIA subject to a family maximum amount. The PIA is calculated by applying varying percentages to succeeding parts of the AIME. The formula is adjusted annually to reflect changes in average annual wages.

Automatic increases in Social Security benefits are initiated for Dec. of each year, assuming the Consumer Price Index (CPI) for the 3d calendar quarter of the year increased relative to the base quarter, which is either the 3d calendar quarter of the preceding year or the quarter in which an increase legislated by Congress became effective. The size of the benefit increase is determined by the actual percentage rise of the CPI between the quarters measured.

The average monthly benefit payable to all retired workers amounts to $780 in Dec. 1998. The average benefit for disabled workers in that month amounts to $733.

Minimum and maximum monthly retired-worker benefits payable to individuals who retired at age 65[1]

Year of attainment of age 65	Minimum benefit[2] Payable at retirement	Payable effective Dec. 1998	Maximum benefit[2] Payable at retirement Men	Women[3]	Payable effective Dec. 1998 Men	Women[3]
1970 . . .	$64.00	$300.10	$189.80	$196.40	$878.90	$922.00
1980 . . .	133.90	300.10	572.00	—	1,267.50	—
1990 . . .	(4)	(4)	975.00	—	1,247.50	—
1993 . . .	(4)	(4)	1,128.80	—	1,283.10	—
1994 . . .	(4)	(4)	1,147.50	—	1,271.30	—
1995 . . .	(4)	(4)	1,199.10	—	1,292.30	—
1996 . . .	(4)	(4)	1,248.90	—	1,312.00	—
1997 . . .	(4)	(4)	1,326.60	—	1,353.80	—
1998 . . .	(4)	(4)	1,342.80	—	—	—

(1) Assumes retirement at beginning of year. (2) The final benefit amount payable is rounded to next lower $1 (if not already a multiple of $1). (3) Benefits for women are the same as for men except where shown. (4) Minimum eliminated for workers who reach age 62 after 1981.

Amount of Work Required

To qualify for benefits, the worker generally must have worked a certain length of time in covered employment. Just how long depends on when the worker reaches age 62 or, if earlier, when he or she dies or becomes disabled.

A person is fully insured who has 1 quarter of coverage for every year after 1950 (or year age 21 is reached, if later) up to but not including the year the worker reaches 62, dies, or becomes disabled. In 1998, a person earns 1 quarter of coverage for each $700 of annual earnings in covered employment, up to 4 quarters per year.

The law permits special monthly payments under the Social Security program to certain very old persons who are not eligible for regular benefits since they had little or no opportunity to earn work credits during their working lifetime (so-called special age-72 beneficiaries).

To receive disability benefits, the worker, in addition to being fully insured, must generally have credit for 20 quarters of coverage out of the 40 calendar quarters before he or she became disabled. A disabled blind worker need meet only the fully insured requirement. Persons disabled before age 31 can qualify with a briefer period of coverage. Certain survivor benefits are payable if the deceased worker had 6 quarters of coverage in the 13 quarters preceding death.

Work credit for fully insured status for benefits

Born after 1929; die, become disabled, or reach age 62 in	Years needed	Born after 1929; die, become disabled, or reach age 62 in	Years needed
1983.	8	1987	9
1984.	8¼	1988	9¼
1985.	8½	1989	9½
1986.	8¾	1990	9¾
		1991 and after . .	10

Contribution and benefit base

Calendar year	OASDI[1]	HI[2]
1990.	$51,300	$51,300
1991.	53,400	125,000
1992.	55,500	130,200
1993.	57,600	135,000
1994.	60,600	no limit
1995.	61,200	no limit
1996.	62,700	no limit
1997.	65,400	no limit
1998.	68,400	no limit
1999.	72,600	no limit

(1) Old-Age, Survivors, and Disability Insurance. (2) Hospital Insurance.

Tax-rate schedule
(percentage of covered earnings)

Year	Total (for employees and employers, each)	OASDI	HI
1979-80.	6.13	5.08	1.05
1981	6.65	5.35	1.30
1982-83.	6.70	5.40	1.30
1984	7.00	5.70	1.30
1985	7.05	5.70	1.35
1986-87.	7.15	5.70	1.45
1988-89.	7.51	6.06	1.45
1990 and after	7.65	6.20	1.45
	For self-employed		
1979-80.	8.10	7.05	1.05
1981	9.30	8.00	1.30
1982-83.	9.35	8.05	1.30
1984	14.00	11.40	2.60
1985	14.10	11.40	2.70
1986-87.	14.30	11.40	2.90
1988-89.	15.02	12.12	2.90
1990 and after	15.30	12.40	2.90

What Aged Workers Receive

When a person has enough work in covered employment and reaches retirement age (currently age 65 for full benefit, age 62 for reduced benefit), he or she may retire and receive monthly old-age benefits. The age when unreduced benefits become payable will increase gradually from 65 to 67 over a 21-year period beginning with workers age 62 in the year 2000 (reduced benefits will still be available as early as age 62, but with a larger reduction at that age). If a person age 65-69 has earnings of over $14,500 in 1998, $1 in benefits will be withheld for every $3 above $13,500. For those under 65, the annual exempt amount is $9,120 in 1998, with $1 in benefits withheld for every $2 in earnings above the exempt amount. However, an eligible worker age 70 or over receives the full benefit regardless of earnings. The annual exempt amount has been raised automatically as the general earnings level rises. However, legislation enacted in 1996 provided for bigger increases in the annual exempt amount for persons aged 65-69, rising to $14,500 in 1998 and to $30,000 by 2002. After 2002, the annual exempt amount for those 65-69 will be raised automatically as general earnings levels rise.

For workers who reached age 65 between 1982 and 1989, Social Security benefits are raised by 3% for each year for which the worker between ages 65 and 70 (72 before 1984) failed to receive benefits, whether because of earnings from work or because the worker had not applied for benefits. The delayed retirement credit is 1% per year for workers who reached age 65 before 1982. The delayed retirement credit will gradually rise to 8% per year by 2008. The rate for workers who reached age 65 in 1996-97 is 5%. The rate for reaching age 65 in 1998-99 will be 5.5%.

Effective Dec. 1997, the special benefit for persons aged 72 or over who do not meet the regular coverage requirements became $203 a month. Like other monthly benefits, these payments are subject to cost-of-living increases. They are not made to persons on the public assistance or supplemental security income rolls.

Workers retiring before age 65 have their benefits permanently reduced by $5/9$ of 1% for each month they receive benefits before that age. Thus, workers entitled to benefits in the month they reach age 62 receive 80% of the PIA, while a worker retiring at age 65 receives a benefit equal to 100% of the PIA. The nearer to age 65 the worker is when he or she begins collecting a benefit, the larger the benefit will be.

Benefits for Worker's Spouse

The spouse of a worker who is getting Social Security retirement or disability payments may become entitled to an insurance benefit of one-half of the worker's PIA, when he or she reaches 65. Reduced spouse's benefits are available at age 62 ($^{25}/_{36}$ of 1% reduction for each month of entitlement before age 65). Benefits are also payable to the aged divorced spouse of an insured worker if he or she was married to the worker for at least 10 years.

Benefits for Children of Workers

If a retired or disabled worker has a child under age 18, the child will get a benefit equal to half of the worker's unreduced benefit. So will the worker's spouse, even if under age 62, if he or she is caring for an entitled child of the worker who is under 16 or became disabled before age 22. Total benefits paid on a worker's earnings record are subject to a maximum; if the total that would be paid to a family exceeds that maximum, the dependents' benefits are adjusted downward. (Total monthly benefits paid to the family of a worker who retired in Jan. 1997 at age 65 and always had the maximum earnings creditable under Social Security cannot exceed $2,349.90.)

When entitled children reach age 18, their benefits generally stop, but a child disabled before age 22 may get a benefit as long as the disability meets the definition in the law. Benefits will be paid until age 19 to a child attending elementary or secondary school full-time.

Benefits may also be paid to a grandchild or step-grandchild of a worker or of his or her spouse, in special circumstances.

OASDI	May 1998	May 1997	May 1996
Monthly beneficiaries, total (in thousands)[1]	**44,080**	**43,796**	**43,463**
Aged 65 and over, total	31,806	31,641	31,401
Retired workers	24,873	24,498	24,226
Survivors and dependents	6,933	7,143	7,174
Special age-72 beneficiaries	(2)	1	1
Under age 65, total	12,274	12,155	12,062
Retired workers	2,458	2,457	2,459
Disabled workers	4,458	4,407	4,273
Survivors and dependents	5,235	5,291	5,330
Total monthly benefits (in millions)	**$30,603**	**$29,542**	**$28,275**

(1) Totals may not add because of rounding. (2) Under 500.

What Disabled Workers Receive

A worker who becomes so disabled as to be unable to work may be eligible for a monthly disability benefit. Benefits continue until it is determined that the individual is no longer disabled. When a disabled-worker beneficiary reaches age 65, the disability benefit becomes a retired-worker benefit.

Benefits generally like those for dependents of retired-worker beneficiaries may be paid to dependents of disabled beneficiaries. However, the maximum family benefit in disability cases is generally lower than in retirement cases.

Survivor Benefits

If an insured worker should die, one or more types of benefits may be payable to survivors, again subject to a maximum family benefit as described above.

1. If claiming benefits at age 65, the surviving spouse will receive a benefit equal to 100% of the deceased worker's PIA. The surviving spouse may choose to get the benefit as early as age 60, but it is then reduced by $^{19}/_{40}$ of 1% for each month it is paid before age 65. However, for those whose spouses claimed their benefits before age 65, these are limited to the reduced amount the worker would be getting if alive, but not less than 82$^{1}/_{2}$% of the worker's PIA. Marriage after the worker's death ends the surviving spouse's benefit rights. However, if the widow(er) marries and the marriage is ended, he or she regains benefit rights. (A marriage after age 60, age 50 if disabled, is deemed not to have occurred for benefit purposes.) Survivor benefits may also be paid to a divorced spouse if the marriage lasted for at least 10 years.

Disabled widows and widowers may under certain circumstances qualify for benefits after attaining age 50 at the rate of 71.5% of the deceased worker's PIA. The widow or widower must have become totally disabled before or within 7 years after the spouse's death or the last month in which he or she received mother's or father's insurance benefits.

2. There is a benefit for each child until the child reaches age 18. The monthly benefit for each child of a deceased worker is three-quarters of the amount the worker would have received if he or she had lived and drawn full retirement benefits. A child with a disability that began before age 22 may also receive benefits. Also, a child may receive benefits until reaching age 19 if he or she is in full-time attendance at an elementary or secondary school.

3. There is a mother's or father's benefit for the widow(er) if children of the worker under age 16 are in his or her care. The benefit is 75% of the PIA, and it continues until the youngest child reaches age 16, at which time payments stop even if the child's benefit continues. However, if the widow(er) has a disabled child beneficiary age 16 or over in care, benefits may continue.

4. Dependent parents may be eligible for benefits if they have been receiving at least half their support from the worker before his or her death, have reached age 62, and (except in certain circumstances) have not remarried since the worker's death. Each parent gets 75% of the worker's PIA; if only one parent survives, the benefit is 82 $^{1}/_{2}$%.

5. A lump sum cash payment of $255 is made when there is a spouse who was living with the worker or a spouse or child who is eligible for immediate monthly survivor benefits.

Self-Employed Workers

A self-employed person who has net earnings of $400 or more in a year must report such earnings for Social Security tax and credit purposes. The person reports net returns from the business. Income from real estate, savings, dividends, loans, pensions, or insurance policies are not included unless it is part of the business.

A self-employed person receives 1 quarter of coverage for each $700 (for 1998), up to a maximum of 4 quarters.

The nonfarm self-employed have the option of reporting their earnings as $^{2}/_{3}$ of their gross income from self-employment, but not more than $1,600 a year and not less than their actual net earnings. This option can be used only if actual net earnings from self-employment income are less than $1,600, and may be used only 5 times. Also, the self-employed person must have actual net earnings of $400 or more in 2 of the 3 taxable years immediately preceding the year in which he or she uses the option.

When a person has both taxable wages and earnings from self-employment, wages are credited for Social Security purposes first; only as much self-employment income as brings total earnings up to the current taxable maximum becomes subject to the self-employment tax.

Farm Owners and Workers

Self-employed farmers whose gross annual earnings from farming are $2,400 or less may report $^{2}/_{3}$ of their gross earnings instead of net earnings for Social Security purposes. Farmers whose gross income is over $2,400 and whose net earnings are less than $1,600 can report $1,600. Cash or crop shares received from a tenant or share farmer count if the owner participated materially in production or management. The self-employed farmer pays contributions at the same rate as other self-employed persons.

Agricultural employees. A worker's earnings from farm work count toward benefits (1) if the employer pays the worker $150 or more in cash during the year; or (2) if the employer spends $2,500 or more in the year for agricultural labor. Under these rules a person gets credit for 1 calendar quarter for each $670 in cash pay in 1997 up to 4 quarters.

Foreign farm workers admitted to the U.S. on a temporary basis are not covered.

Household Workers

Anyone 18 or older employed as maid, cook, laundry worker, nurse, babysitter, chauffeur, gardener, or other worker in the house of another is covered by Social Security if paid $1,100 or more in cash in a calendar year by any one employer. Room and board do not count, but transportation costs count if paid in cash. The job need not be regular or full-time. The employee should get a Social Security card at the Social Security office and show it to the employer.

The employer deducts the amount of the employee's Social Security tax from the worker's pay, adds an identical amount as the employer's Social Security tax, and sends the total amount to the federal government.

Medicare Coverage

The Medicare health insurance program provides acute-care coverage for Social Security and Railroad Retirement beneficiaries age 65 and over, for persons entitled for 24 months to receive Social Security or Railroad Retirement disability benefits, and for certain persons with end-stage kidney disease.

The basic Medicare plan, available nationwide, is a fee-for-service arrangement, where the beneficiary may use any provider accepting Medicare; some services are not covered and there are some out-of-pocket costs.

Under "Medicare + Choice," persons eligible for Medicare, depending on where they live, may also have the option of getting services through a health maintenance organization (HMO) or other managed care plan. Any such plan must provide at least the same benefits, except for hospice services, and may provide added benefits—such as lower or no deductibles and coverage for some prescription drugs—but is usually subject to restrictions in choice of doctors, hospitals, and other providers. In some plans services by outside providers are still covered for an extra out-of-pocket cost. Also available as options in some areas are Medicare-approved private fee-for-service plans and Medicare medical savings accounts.

Hospital insurance (Part A). The basic hospital insurance program pays covered services for hospital and posthospital care as follows:

- All necessary inpatient hospital care for the first 60 days of each benefit period, except for a deductible ($764 in 1998). For days 61-90, Medicare pays for services over and above a coinsurance amount ($191 per day in 1998). After 90 days, the beneficiary has 60 reserve days for which Medicare helps pay. The coinsurance amount for reserve days was $382 in 1998.
- Up to 100 days' care in a skilled-nursing facility in each benefit period. Hospital insurance pays for all covered services for the first 20 days; for the 21-100th day, the beneficiary pays coinsurance ($95.50 a day in 1998).
- Visits by nurses or other health workers (not doctors) from a home health agency.
- Hospice care for terminally ill individuals.

Medical insurance (Part B). Aged persons can receive benefits under this supplementary program only if they sign up for them and agree to a monthly premium ($43.80 in 1998). The federal government pays the rest of the cost.

The medical insurance program usually pays 80% of the approved amount (after the first $100 in each calendar year) for the following services:

- Covered services received from a doctor in his or her office, in a hospital, in a skilled-nursing facility, at home, or in other locations.
- Medical and surgical services, including anesthesia.
- Diagnostic tests and procedures that are part of the patient's treatment.
- Radiology and pathology services by doctors while the individual is a hospital inpatient or outpatient.
- Other services such as X-rays, services of a doctor's office nurse, drugs and biologicals that cannot be self-administered, transfusions of blood and blood components, medical supplies, physical/occupational therapy and speech pathology services.
- Treatment of mental illness. Medicare payments are limited; services may be obtained from doctors, comprehensive outpatient rehabilitation facilities (CORFs), physician assistants, psychologists, and clinical social workers.

In addition to the above, certain other tests or preventive measures are now covered without an additional premium. These include mammograms, bone mass measurement, colorectal cancer screening, and flu shots.

Note: The services for nonhospital treatment of a mental illness are subject to a special payment rule. In effect, once the annual deductible is met, Medicare pays only 50% (not 80%) of approved charges. On assigned claims (those in which the service provider agrees to the fee set by Medicare), beneficiaries are responsible for the remaining 50%. For unassigned claims, beneficiaries may have to pay more.

Partial hospitalization services for treatment of mental illness are not subject to this special payment rule. Also, brief office visits for the sole purpose of monitoring or changing drug prescriptions used in the treatment of mental illness are not subject to this special payment rule.

To get medical insurance protection, persons approaching age 65 may enroll in the 7-month period that includes 3 months before the 65th birthday, the month of the birthday, and 3 months after the birthday, but if they wish coverage to begin in the month they reach age 65, they must enroll in the 3 months before their birthday. Persons not enrolling within their first enrollment period may enroll later, during the first 3 months of each year (coverage begins July 1), but their premium may be 10% higher for each 12-month period elapsed since they first could have enrolled.

The monthly premium is deducted from the cash benefit for persons receiving Social Security, Railroad Retirement, or Civil Service retirement benefits. Income from the medical premiums and the federal matching payments are put in a Supplementary Medical Insurance Trust Fund, from which benefits and administrative expenses are paid. *Further details are available* on the Internet at http://www.medicare.gov or by calling 1-800-638-6833.

Medicare card. Persons qualifying for hospital insurance under Social Security receive a health insurance card similar to cards now used by Blue Cross and other health insurers. The card indicates whether the individual has taken out medical insurance protection. It is to be shown to the hospital, skilled-nursing facility, home health agency, doctor, or whoever provides the covered services.

Payments are generally made only in the 50 states, Puerto Rico, Virgin Islands, Guam, and American Samoa.

Social Security Financing

Social Security is paid for by a tax on certain earnings (for 1998, on earnings up to $68,400) for Old Age, Survivors, and Disability Insurance and on all earnings (no upper limit) for Hospital Insurance with the Medicare Program; the taxable earnings base for OASDI has been adjusted annually to reflect increases in average wages. The employed worker and his or her employer share Social Security taxes equally.

Employers remit amounts withheld from employee wages for Social Security and income taxes to the Internal Revenue Service; employer Social Security taxes are also payable at the same time. (Self-employed workers pay Social Security taxes when filing their regular income tax forms.) The Social Security taxes (along with revenues arising from partial taxation of the Social Security benefits of certain high-income people) are transferred to the Social Security Trust Funds—the Federal Old-Age and Survivors Insurance (OASI) Trust Fund, the Federal Disability Insurance (DI) Trust Fund, and the Federal Hospital Insurance (HI) Trust Fund; they can be used only to pay benefits, the cost of rehabilitation services, and administrative expenses. Money not immediately needed for these purposes is by law invested in obligations of the federal government, which must pay interest on the money borrowed and must repay the principal when the obligations are redeemed or mature.

Supplemental Security Income

On Jan. 1, 1974, the Supplemental Security Income (SSI) program established by the 1972 Social Security Act amendments replaced the former federal grants to states for aid to the needy aged, blind, and disabled in the 50 states and the District of Columbia. The program provides both for federal payments, based on uniform national standards and eligibility requirements, and for state supplementary payments varying from state to state. The Social Security Administration administers the federal payments financed from general funds of the Treasury—and the state supplements as well, if the state elects to have its supplementary program federally administered. States may supplement the federal payment for all recipients and must supplement it for persons otherwise adversely affected by the transition from the former public assistance programs. In May 1998, the number of persons receiving federally administered payments was 6,551,526, and the payments totaled $2.55 billion.

The maximum monthly federal SSI payment for individuals with no other countable income, living in their own household, was $494 in 1998. For couples it was $741.

Obtaining Earnings and Benefits Statements

To obtain Personal Earnings and Benefit Estimates Statements (PEBES) from the Social Security Administration (SSA) through the mail, you may call 1-800-772-1213 and request a PEBES form. The SSA also provide PEBES information online via its Internet home page; you may request a PEBES form at the Internet web site. For more information on services and data available from the SSA, visit its website at http://www.ssa.gov

Examples of Monthly Benefits Available

Description of benefit or beneficiary	For low earnings ($12,552 in 1998)[1]	For avg. earnings ($27,894 in 1998)[2]	For max. earnings ($68,400 in 1998)
Primary insurance amount (worker retiring at 65)	$568.30	$938.00	$1,342.80
Maximum family benefit (worker retiring at 65)	852.60	1,709.30	2,349.80
Maximum family disability benefit (worker disabled at 55; in 1996)*	825.30	1,451.20	2,164.20
Disabled worker (worker disabled at 55):			
Worker alone	587.30	967.50	1,442.80
Worker, spouse, and 1 child	825.00	1,449.00	2,162.00
Retired worker claiming benefits at age 62:			
Worker alone[3]	470.00	774.00	1,109.00
Worker with spouse claiming benefits at—			
Age 65 or over	763.00	1,258.00	1,802.00
Age 62[3]	690.00	1,137.00	1,679.00
Widow or widower claiming benefits at—			
Age 65 or over[4]	568.00	938.00	1,342.00
Age 60 (spouse died at 65 without receiving reduced benefits)	406.00	670.00	960.00
Disabled widow or widower claiming benefits at age 50-59[5]	406.00	670.00	960.00
1 surviving child	426.00	703.00	1,007.00
Widow or widower age 65 or over and 1 child[6]	852.00	1,708.00	2,349.00
Widowed mother or father and 1 child[6]	852.00	1,406.00	2,014.00
Widowed mother or father and 2 children[6]	852.00	1,707.00	2,349.00

Effective Jan. 1997, for beneficiaries with first entitlement in 1977. *Assumes work beginning at age 22. (1) 45% of average. (2) Estimate. (3) Assumes maximum reduction. (4) A widow(er)'s benefit amount is limited to the amount the spouse would have been receiving if still living, but not less than 82.5% of the PIA. (5) Effective Jan. 1984, disabled widow(er)s claiming a benefit at ages 50-59 receive a benefit equal to 71.5% of the PIA. (6) Based on worker dying at age 65.

Social Security Trust Funds

Old-Age and Survivors Insurance Trust Fund, 1940-97

(in millions)

Fiscal year[1]	INCOME: Total	INCOME: Net contributions[2]	INCOME: Income from taxing benefits	INCOME: Payments from the Treasury fund[3]	INCOME: Net interest[4]	DISBURSEMENTS: Total	DISBURSEMENTS: Benefit payments[5]	DISBURSEMENTS: Administrative expenses	DISBURSEMENTS: Transfers to Railroad Retirement program	Interfund borrowing transfers[6]	Net increase in fund	Fund at end of period
1940	$592	$550	—	—	$42	$28	$16	$12	—	—	$564	$1,745
1950	2,367	2,106	—	$4	257	784	727	57	—	—	1,583	12,893
1960	10,360	9,843	—	—	517	11,073	10,270	202	$600	—	–713	20,829
1970	31,746	29,955	—	442	1,350	27,321	26,268	474	579	—	4,425	32,616
1980	100,051	97,608	—	557	1,886	103,228	100,626	1,160	1,442	—	–3,177	24,566
1990	278,607	261,506	$2,924	34	14,143	223,481	218,948	1,564	2,969	—	55,126	203,445
1995	326,067	289,529	5,114	7	31,417	294,456	288,607	1,797	4,052	—	31,611	447,946
1996	356,843	317,157	5,785	–124	34,026	305,311	299,968	1,788	3,554	—	51,533	499,479
1997	386,465	342,312	6,462	3	37,689	318,548	312,862	1,998	3,688	—	67,916	567,395

(1) Fiscal years 1977 and later consist of the 12 months ending on Sept. 30 of each year. Fiscal years prior to 1977 consisted of the 12 months ending on June 30 of each year. (2) Beginning in 1983, includes transfers from general fund of Treasury representing contributions that would have been paid on deemed wage credits for military service in 1957 and later, if such credits were considered covered wages. (3) Includes payments (a) in 1947-52 and in 1967 and later, for costs of noncontributory wage credits for military service performed before 1957; (b) in 1972-83, for costs of deemed wage credits for military service performed after 1956; and (c) in 1969 and later, for costs of benefits to certain uninsured persons who attained age 72 before 1968. (4) Net interest includes net profits or losses on marketable investments. Beginning in 1967, administrative expenses were charged currently to the trust fund on an estimated basis, with a final adjustment, including interest, made in the next fiscal year. The amounts of these interest adjustments are included in net interest. For years prior to 1967, the method of accounting for administrative expenses is described in the 1970 Annual Report. Beginning in Oct. 1973, the figures shown include relatively small amounts of gifts to the fund. During 1983-91, interest paid from the trust fund to the general fund on advance tax transfers is reflected. (5) Beginning in 1967, includes payments for vocational rehabilitation services furnished to disabled persons receiving benefits because of their disabilities. Beginning in 1983, amounts are reduced by amount of reimbursement for unnegotiated benefit checks. (6) Negative figures represent amounts repaid from the OASI Trust Fund to the DI and HI Trust Funds.

Disability Insurance Trust Fund, 1970-97

(in millions)

Fiscal year[1]	INCOME: Total	INCOME: Net contributions[2]	INCOME: Income from taxation of benefits	INCOME: Payments from the Treasury fund[3]	INCOME: Net interest[4]	DISBURSEMENTS: Total	DISBURSEMENTS: Benefit payments[5]	DISBURSEMENTS: Administrative expenses	DISBURSEMENTS: Transfers to Railroad Retirement program	Net increase in fund	Fund at end of period
1970	$4,380	$4,141	—	$16	$223	$2,954	$2,795	$149	$10	$1,426	$5,104
1980	17,376	16,805	—	118	453	15,320	14,998	334	–12	2,056	7,680
1990	28,215	27,291	$158	—	766	25,124	24,327	717	80	3,091	11,455
1995	70,209	67,987	335	—	1,888	41,374	40,234	1,072	68	28,835	35,206
1996	59,220	56,571	370	–203	2,482	44,343	43,266	1,074	2	14,877	50,083
1997	60,088	56,162	400	—	3,526	46,689	45,419	1,211	59	13,399	63,483

(1) Fiscal years 1977 and later consist of the 12 months ending Sept. 30 of each year. Fiscal years prior to 1977 consisted of the 12 months ending June 30 of each year. (2) Beginning in 1983, includes transfers from general fund of Treasury representing contributions that would have been paid on deemed wage credits for military service in 1957 and later, if such credits were considered to be covered wages. (3) Includes payments (a) for costs of noncontributory wage credits for military service performed before 1957; and (b) in 1972-83, for costs of deemed wage credits for military service performed after 1956. (4) Net interest includes net profits or losses on marketable investments. Administrative expenses are charged currently to the trust fund on an estimated basis, with a final adjustment, including interest, made in the following fiscal year. Figures shown include relatively small amounts of gifts to the fund. During the years 1983-91, interest paid from the trust fund to the general fund on advance tax transfers is reflected. (5) Includes payments for vocational rehabilitation services. Beginning in 1983, amounts are reduced by amount of reimbursement for unnegotiated benefit checks. NOTE: Totals may not add because of rounding.

Supplementary Medical Insurance Trust Fund, 1975-97

(in millions)

	INCOME				DISBURSEMENTS			
Fiscal year[1]	Premium from participants	Government contributions[2]	Interest and other income[3]	Total Income	Benefit payments	Administrative expenses	Total disbursements	Balance in fund at end of year[4]
1975	$1,887	$2,330	$105	$4,322	$3,765	$405	$4,170	$1,424
1980	2,928	6,932	415	10,275	10,144	593	10,737	4,532
1990	11,494[5]	33,210	1,434[5]	46,138[5]	41,498	1,524[5]	43,022[5]	14,527[5]
1995	19,244	36,988	1,937	58,169	63,491	1,722	65,213	13,874
1996	18,931	61,702	1,392	82,025	67,176	1,771	68,946	26,953
1997	19,141	59,471	2,193	80,806	71,133	1,420	72,553	35,206

(1) Fiscal year 1975 consists of the 12 months ending on June 30, 1975; fiscal years 1980 and later consist of the 12 months ending on September 30 of each year. (2) General fund matching payments, plus certain interest-adjustment items. (3) Other income includes recoveries of amounts reimbursed from the trust fund that are not obligations of the trust fund and other miscellaneous income. (4) The financial status of the program depends on both the assets and the liabilities of the program. (5) Includes the impact of the Medicare Catastrophic Coverage Act of 1988 (PL 100-360). NOTE: Totals do not necessarily equal the sums of rounded components.

Hospital Insurance Trust Fund, 1975-97

(in millions)

	INCOME								DISBURSEMENTS				
Fiscal year[1]	Payroll taxes	Income from taxation of benefits	Transfers from railroad retirement acct.	Reimbursement for uninsured persons	Premiums from voluntary enrollees	Pymts. for military wage credits	Interest on investments and other income[2]	Total income	Benefit pymts.[3]	Administrative expense[4]	Total disbursements	Net increase in fund	Fund at end of year
1975	$11,291	—	$132	$481	$6	$48	$609	$12,568	$10,353	$259	$10,612	$1,956	$9,870
1980	23,244	—	244	697	17	141	1,072	25,415	23,790	497	24,288	1,127	14,490
1990	70,655	—	367	413	113	107	7,908	79,563	65,912	774	66,687	12,876	95,631
1995	98,053	3,913	396	462	998	61	10,963	114,847	113,583	1,300	114,883	-36	129,520
1996	106,934	4,069	401	419	1,107	-2,293[5]	10,496	121,135	124,088	1,229	125,317	-4,182	125,338
1997	112,725	3,558	419	481	1,279	70	9,970	128,501	136,175	1,613	137,789	-9,287	125,338

(1) Fiscal year 1975 consists of the 12 months ending on June 30, 1975; fiscal years 1980 and later consist of the 12 months ending Sept. 30 of each year. (2) Other income includes recoveries of amounts reimbursed from the trust fund that are not obligations of the trust fund and a small amount of miscellaneous income, including amounts from the fraud and abuse control system. (3) Includes costs of Peer Review Organizations (beginning with the implementation of the Prospective Payment System on Oct. 1, 1983). (4) Includes costs of experiments and demonstration projects. Beginning in 1997, includes fraud and abuse control expenses, as provided for by PL 104-191. (5) Includes the lump-sum general revenue adjustment of $-2,366 mil, as provided for by PL 98-21. NOTE: Totals do not necessarily equal the sums of rounded components.

MILLENNIUM FACT BOX

Fewer and Fewer Workers Per Beneficiary

Source: Social Security Administration

In the first years of Social Security, there were a very large number of workers paying payroll taxes to support each person currently receiving benefits—in 1945, an estimated 42 workers per beneficiary. By 1955 there were only 8.6 workers per beneficiary; today there are 3.4. It is estimated that there will only be 2.0 workers per beneficiary by 2030. Given these estimates and current tax and benefit provisions, revenues taken in would fall short of fully covering benefits by around 2012. Trust fund reserves would make up the difference until around 2029, when current revenues would cover only about 75% of benefits.

The bars below show estimated covered workers and beneficiaries for selected years, with projections for the future based on mid-range assumptions. Years before 1958 include the Old Age and Survivors Insurance (OASI) program only; starting in 1958, disabled workers also received benefits and are included as well (OASDI).

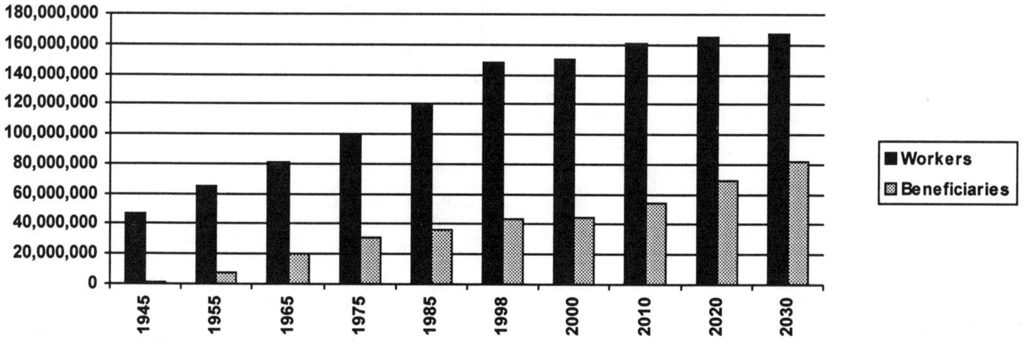

Note: Totals for beneficiaries exclude some uninsured persons, generally having fewer than 3 quarters of coverage, costs for whom are mostly reimbursed by the general fund of the Treasury.

NATIONS OF THE WORLD

Initials used include: AL (Arab League), CIS (Commonwealth of Independent States), EU (European Union), FAO (UN Food & Agriculture Org.), ILO (Intl. Labor Org.), IMF (Intl. Monetary Fund), IMO (Intl. Maritime Org.), NATO (North Atlantic Treaty Org.), OAS (Org. of American States), OAU (Org. of African Unity), OECD (Org. for Economic Cooperation and Development), OECS (Org. of Eastern Caribbean States), OSCE (Org. for Security and Cooperation in Europe), UN (United Nations), WHO (World Health Org.), WTrO (World Trade Org., formerly GATT). FY = fiscal year.

Sources: American Automobile Manufacturers Assn.; (U.S.) Census Bureau: Intl. Data Base; (U.S.) Central Intelligence Agency: *The World Factbook;* (U.S.) Dept. of Commerce; (U.S.) Dept. of Energy; Intl. Institute for Strategic Studies: *The Military Balance;* Intl. Monetary Fund; (U.S.) Dept. of State; UN Demographic Yearbook; UN Food and Agriculture Organization; UN Population Division: *World Urbanization Prospects;* UN Statistical Yearbook; World Tourism Organization; Encyclopaedia Britannica Book of the Year; The Europa World Year Book; The Statesman's Yearbook. Telephone data supplied by the Intl. Telecommunication Union, from the World Telecommunication Indicators database, copyright ITU.

Note: Because of rounding or incomplete enumeration, some percentages may not add to 100%. National population and health figures are mid-1998 estimates, unless otherwise noted. An * after city figures indicates 1995 urban agglomeration. Defense figures are for 1996 unless otherwise noted. Livestock figures are 1997. Gross domestic product estimates are based on purchasing power parity calculations, which involve use of intl. dollar price weights applied to quantities of goods and services produced. Tourism figures are 1997 and represent receipts from international tourism. Budget figures are for expenditures, unless otherwise noted. Motor vehicle statistics are for 1996; comm. (commercial) vehicles include trucks and buses. Per-person figures in communications data are post-1994. Literacy rates are 1995 est., unless otherwise noted. Literacy rates given generally measure the percent of population able to read and write on a lower elementary school level, not the (smaller) percent able to read instructions necessary for a job or license. Embassy addresses are Wash., DC, area code (202), unless otherwise noted.

See pages 497-512 for full-color maps and flags.

Afghanistan

Islamic State of Afghanistan

People: Population: 24,792,375. **Age distrib.** (%): <15: 42.9; 65+: 2.7. **Pop. density:** 98 per sq. mi. **Urban:** 20%. **Ethnic groups:** Pashtun 38%, Tajik 25%, Hazara 19%, Uzbek 6%. **Principal languages:** Pashtu 35%, Afghan (Dari) 50% (both official), Turkic (incl. Uzbek, Turkmen) 11%. **Chief religions:** Sunni Muslim 84%, Shi'a Muslim 15%.

Geography: Area: 251,825 sq. mi. **Location:** In SW Asia, NW of the Indian subcontinent. **Neighbors:** Pakistan on E, S; Iran on W; Turkmenistan, Tajikistan, Uzbekistan on N. The NE tip touches China. **Topography:** The country is landlocked and mountainous, much of it over 4,000 ft. above sea level. The Hindu Kush Mts. tower 16,000 ft. above Kabul and reach a height of 25,000 ft. to the E. Trade with Pakistan flows through the 35-mile-long Khyber Pass. The climate is dry, with extreme temperatures, and there are large desert regions, though mountain rivers produce intermittent fertile valleys. **Capital:** Kabul: 2,029,000*.

Government: Type: In transition. **Local divisions:** 32 provinces. **Defense:** 15.4% of GDP. **Active troop strength:** 429,000.

Economy: Industries: Textiles, soap, furniture, cement. **Chief crops:** Nuts, wheat, fruits. **Minerals:** Gas, oil, copper, coal, zinc, iron. **Other resources:** Wool, karakul pelts, mutton. **Arable land:** 12%. **Livestock** (1997): sheep: 14.30 mil; chickens: 7.20 mil; goats: 2.20 mil; cattle: 1.50 mil. **Electricity prod.** (1996): 540 mil kWh. **Labor force:** 67% agric.

Finance: Monetary unit: Afghani (Sept. 1998: 4,750.00 = $1 U.S.). **Gross domestic product** (1996 est.): $18.1 bil. **Per capita GDP:** $800. **Imports** (1996 est.): $150 mil; partners: Japan 14%, EU 11%. **Exports** (1996 est.): $80 mil; partners: EU 10%. **Tourism:** $1 mil.

Transport: Railroad: Length: 16 mi. **Motor vehicles in use:** 35,000 passenger cars, 32,000 comm. vehicles. **Civil aviation:** 177.9 mil passenger-mi; 33 airports.

Communications: Television sets: 10 per 1,000 pop. **Radios:** 73.7 per 1,000 pop. **Telephones:** 29,000 main lines. **Daily newspaper circ.:** 11 per 1,000 pop.

Health: Life expectancy at birth: 47.4 male; 46.3 female. **Births** (per 1,000 pop.): 42. **Deaths** (per 1,000 pop.): 17. **Natural increase:** 2.50%. **Hospital beds** (1993): 1 per 2,945 persons. **Physicians** (1993): 1 per 6,690 persons. **Infant mortality** (per 1,000 live births): 144.

Education: Compulsory: ages 7-13. **Literacy:** 31.5%.

Major International Organizations: UN (FAO, IBRD, ILO, IMF, WHO).

Embassy: 2341 Wyoming Ave. NW 20008; 234-3770.

Afghanistan, occupying a favored invasion route since antiquity, has been variously known as Ariana or Bactria (in ancient times) and Khorasan (in the Middle Ages). Foreign empires alternated rule with local emirs and kings until the 18th century, when a unified kingdom was established. In 1973, a military coup ushered in a republic.

Pro-Soviet leftists took power in a bloody 1978 coup and concluded an economic and military treaty with the USSR. In Dec. 1979 the USSR began a massive airlift into Kabul and backed a new coup, leading to installation of a more pro-Soviet leader. Soviet troops fanned out over Afghanistan and waged a protracted guerrilla war with Muslim rebels, in which some 15,000 Soviet troops reportedly died.

A UN-mediated agreement was signed Apr. 14, 1988, providing for withdrawal of Soviet troops, a neutral Afghan state, and repatriation of refugees. Afghan rebels rejected the pact, vowing to continue fighting while "Soviets and their puppets" remained in Afghanistan. The Soviets completed their troop withdrawal Feb. 15, 1989; fighting between Afghan rebels and government forces ensued.

Communist Pres. Najibullah resigned Apr. 16, 1992, as competing guerrilla forces advanced on Kabul. The rebels achieved power Apr. 28, ending 14 years of Soviet-backed regimes. More than 2 million Afghans had been killed and 6 million had left the country since 1979.

Following the rebel victory there were clashes between moderates and Islamic fundamentalist forces. Burhanuddin Rabbani, a guerrilla leader, became president June 28, 1992, but fierce fighting continued around Kabul and elsewhere. The Taliban, an insurgent Islamic fundamentalist faction, gained increasing control and in Sept. 1996 captured Kabul and set up a government. The Taliban executed former President Najibullah and empowered Islamic religious police to enforce codes of dress and behavior that were especially restrictive to women. Rabbani and other ousted leaders fled to the north.

Victories in the northern cities of Mazar-e Sharif, Aug. 8, 1998, and Taloqan, Aug. 11, gave the Taliban control over more than 90% of the country; the killing of several Iranian diplomats during the Mazar-e Sharif takeover heightened tensions with Iran. On Aug. 20, U.S. cruise missiles struck SE of Kabul, hitting facilities the U.S. alleged were terrorist training camps run by a wealthy Saudi businessman, Osama bin Laden.

Albania

Republic of Albania

People: Population: 3,330,754. **Age distrib.** (%): <15: 33.2; 65+: 5.9. **Pop. density:** 300 per sq. mi. **Urban:** 38%. **Ethnic groups:** Albanians (Gegs in N, Tosks in S) 95%, Greeks 3%. **Principal languages:** Albanian (official; Tosk is the official dialect), Greek. **Chief religions:** Muslim 70%, Albanian Orthodox 20%, Roman Catholic 10%.

Geography: Area: 11,100 sq. mi. **Location:** SE Europe, on SE coast of Adriatic Sea. **Neighbors:** Greece on S, Yugoslavia on N, Macedonia on E. **Topography:** Apart from a narrow coastal plain, Albania consists of hills and mountains covered with scrub forest, cut by small E-W rivers. **Capital:** Tiranë (1995 est.): 270,000.

Government: Type: Republic. **Head of state:** Pres. Rexhep Mejdani; in office: July 24, 1997. **Head of government:** Prem. Pandeli Majko; in office Oct. 2, 1998. **Local divisions:** 26 districts. **Defense:** 6.7% of GDP. **Active troop strength:** 54,000.

Economy: Industries: Cement, textiles, food processing. **Chief crops:** Corn, wheat, potatoes, tobacco, fruits. **Minerals:** Chromium, coal, oil, gas. **Crude oil reserves** (1997): 165 mil bbls. **Other resources:** Timber. **Arable land:** 21%. **Livestock** (1997): chickens: 4.30 mil; sheep: 2.50 mil; goats: 1.90 mil; cattle: 850,000; pigs: 100,000;. **Electricity prod.** (1996): 5.1 bil kWh. **Labor force:** 49.5% agric.

Finance: Monetary unit: Lek (Sept. 1998: 148.00 = $1 U.S.). **Gross domestic product** (1996 est.): $4.4 bil. **Per**

capita GDP: $1,290. **Imports** (1995): $680 mil; partners: Italy 38%, Greece 27%. **Exports** (1995): $205 mil; partners: Italy 52%, Greece 10%. **National budget** (1997): $996 mil. **International reserves less gold** (May 1998): $353.76 mil. **Gold:** 120,000 oz t. **Consumer prices** (change in 1997): 32.2%. **Tourism:** $10 mil.

Transport: Railroad: Length: 419.1 mi. **Chief ports:** Durres, Sarande Vlore. **Civil aviation:** 5.6 mil passenger-mi; 1 airport.

Communications: Television sets: 89 per 1,000 pop. **Radios:** 157 per 1,000 pop. **Telephones:** 63,850 main lines. **Daily newspaper circ.:** 54 per 1,000 pop.

Health: Life expectancy at birth: 65.6 male; 71.9 female. **Births** (per 1,000 pop.): 21. **Deaths** (per 1,000 pop): 7. **Natural increase:** 1.39%. **Hospital beds** (1994): 1 per 333 persons. **Physicians** (1994): 1 per 552 persons. **Infant mortality** (per 1,000 live births): 45.

Major International Organizations: UN (IBRD, ILO, IMF, IMO, WHO), OSCE.

Education: Free and compulsory: ages 6-14. **Literacy** (1993): 100%.

Embassy: 1511 K St. NW 20005; 223-4942.

Websites: http:/www.undp.tirana.al
http://www.tirana.al/minjash

Ancient Illyria was conquered by Romans, Slavs, and Turks (15th century); the latter Islamized the population. Independent Albania was proclaimed in 1912, republic was formed in 1920. King Zog I ruled 1925-39, until Italy invaded.

Communist partisans took over in 1944, allied Albania with USSR, then broke with USSR in 1960 over de-Stalinization. Strong political alliance with China followed, leading to several billion dollars in aid, which was curtailed after 1974. China cut off aid in 1978 when Albania attacked its policies after the death of Chinese ruler Mao Zedong. Large-scale purges of officials occurred during the 1970s.

Enver Hoxha, the nation's ruler for 4 decades, died Apr. 11, 1985. Eventually the new regime introduced some liberalization, including measures in 1990 providing for freedom to travel abroad. Efforts were begun to improve ties with the outside world. Mar. 1991 elections left the former Communists in power, but a general strike and urban opposition led to the formation of a coalition cabinet including non-Communists.

Albania's former Communists were routed in elections Mar. 1992, amid economic collapse and social unrest. Sali Berisha was elected as the first non-Communist president since World War II. Berisha's party claimed a landslide victory in disputed parliamentary elections, May 26 and June 2, 1996. Public protests over the collapse of fraudulent investment schemes in Jan. 1997 led to armed rebellion and anarchy. The UN Security Council, Mar. 28, authorized a 7,000-member force to restore order. Socialists and their allies won parliamentary elections, June 29 and July 6, and international peacekeepers completed their pullout by Aug. 11. Thousands of refugees from the civil war in Kosovo flooded into Albania in 1998.

Algeria

Democratic and Popular Republic of Algeria

People: Population: 30,480,793. **Age distrib.** (%): <15: 38.2; 65+: 3.8. **Pop. density:** 33 per sq. mi. **Urban:** 56%. **Ethnic groups:** Arab-Berber 99%. **Principal languages:** Arabic (official), French, Berber dialects. **Chief religion:** Sunni Muslim (state religion) 99%.

Geography: Area: 919,595 sq. mi. **Location:** In NW Africa, from Mediterranean Sea into Sahara Desert. **Neighbors:** Morocco on W; Mauritania, Mali, Niger on S; Libya, Tunisia on E. **Topography:** The Tell, located on the coast, comprises fertile plains 50-100 miles wide, with a moderate climate and adequate rain. Two major chains of the Atlas Mts., running roughly E-W and reaching 7,000 ft., enclose a dry plateau region. Below lies the Sahara, mostly desert with major mineral resources. **Capital:** Algiers (El Djazair): 3,705,000*.

Government: Type: Republic. **Head of state:** Pres. Liamine Zeroual; b July 3, 1941; in office: Jan. 31, 1994. **Head of government:** Prime Min. Ahmed Ouyahia; b July 2, 1952; in office: Dec. 31, 1995. **Local divisions:** 48 provinces. **Defense:** 4.0% of GDP. **Active troop strength:** 123,700.

Economy: Industries: Oil, natural gas, light industries, food processing. **Chief crops:** Grains, grapes, citrus, olives. **Minerals:** Iron, oil, gas, phosphates, zinc, lead. **Crude oil reserves** (1997): 9.2 bil bbls. **Arable land:** 3%. **Livestock** (1997): chickens: 132.00 mil; sheep: 16.75 mil; goats: 3.12 mil; cattle: 1.26 mil. **Fish catch** (1996): 99,678 metric tons. **Electricity prod.** (1996): 18.4 bil kWh. **Labor force:** 30% govt.; 27% ind., serv., commerce; 22% agric.

Finance: Monetary unit: Dinar (Sept. 1998: 58.47 = $1 U.S.). **Gross domestic product** (1996 est.): $115.9 bil. **Per capita GDP:** $4,000. **Imports** (1996 est.): $10.5 bil; partners: France 29%, Spain 11%. **Exports** (1996 est.): $11 bil; partners: Italy 19%, U.S. 15%. **National budget** (1995 est.): $17.9 bil. **International reserves less gold** (June 1998): $8.3 bil. **Gold:** 5.58 mil oz t. **Consumer prices** (change in 1996): 21.6%. **Tourism:** $20 mil.

Transport: Railroad: Length: 2,963.4 mi. **Motor vehicles in use:** 500,000 passenger cars, 420,000 comm. vehicles. **Civil aviation:** 1.78 bil passenger-mi; 28 airports. **Chief ports:** Algiers, Annaba, Oran.

Communications: Television sets: 71 per 1,000 pop. **Radios:** 122 per 1,000 pop. **Telephone:** 1,278,142 main lines. **Daily newspaper circ.:** 52 per 1,000 pop.

Health: Life expectancy at birth: 67.8 male; 70.1 female. **Births** (per 1,000 pop.): 28. **Deaths** (per 1,000 pop.): 6. **Natural increase:** 2.19%. **Hospital beds** (1994): 1 per 513 persons. **Physicians** (1994): 1 per 1,066 persons. **Infant mortality** (per 1,000 live births): 45.

Education: Compulsory: ages 6-15. **Literacy:** 62%.

Major International Organizations: UN (FAO, IBRD, ILO, IMF, IMO, WHO), AL, OAU, OPEC.

Embassy: 2118 Kalorama Rd. NW 20008; 265-2800.

Earliest known inhabitants were ancestors of Berbers, followed by Phoenicians, Romans, Vandals, and, finally, Arabs. Turkey ruled 1518 to 1830, when France took control.

Large-scale European immigration and French cultural inroads did not prevent an Arab nationalist movement from launching guerrilla war. Peace, and French withdrawal, was negotiated with French Pres. Charles de Gaulle. One million Europeans left. Independence came July 5, 1962. Ahmed Ben Bella was the victor of infighting and ruled until 1965, when an army coup installed Col. Houari Boumedienne as leader; Boumedienne led until his death from a blood disease, 1978.

In 1967, Algeria declared war on Israel, broke ties with U.S., and moved toward eventual military and political ties with the USSR. Some 500 died in riots protesting economic hardship in 1988. In 1989, voters approved a new constitution, which cleared the way for a multiparty system.

The government canceled the Jan. 1992 elections that Islamic fundamentalists were expected to win, and banned all nonreligious activities at Algeria's 10,000 mosques. Pres. Mohammed Boudiaf was assassinated June 29, 1992. There were repeated attacks on high-ranking officials, security forces, foreigners, and others by militant Muslim fundamentalists over the next 6 years; pro-government death squads also were active.

Liamine Zeroual won the presidential election of Nov. 16, 1995. A new constitution banning Islamic political parties and increasing the president's powers passed in a referendum on Nov. 28, 1996. Pro-government parties won the parliamentary election of June 6, 1997. The estimated death toll in the civil war was 70,000 by mid-1998. On Sept. 11, Zeroual called an early election for Feb. 1999, pledging not to run.

Andorra

Principality of Andorra

People: Population: 64,716. **Age distrib.** (%): <15: 14.4; 65+: 12.3. **Pop. density:** 358 per sq. mi. **Urban:** 95%. **Ethnic groups:** Spanish 61%, Andorran 30%, French 6%. **Principal languages:** Catalan (official), French, Castilian. **Chief religion:** Predominently Roman Catholic.

Geography: Area: 181 sq. mi. **Location:** SW Europe, in Pyrenees Mts. **Neighbors:** Spain on S, France on N. **Topography:** High mountains and narrow valleys cover the country. **Capital:** Andorra la Vella (1995 est.): 21,984.

Government: Type: Parliamentary co-principality. **Heads of state:** President of France & Bishop of Urgel (Spain), as co-princes. **Head of government:** Marc Forné Molné; in office: Dec. 21, 1994. **Local divisions:** 7 parishes. **Defense:** Responsibility of France and Spain.

Economy: Industries: Tourism, sheep, tobacco products. **Minerals:** Iron, lead. **Arable land:** 2%.

Finance: Monetary unit: French Franc (Sept. 1998: 5.81 = $1 U.S.). Spanish Peseta (Sept. 1998: 147.17 = $1 U.S.). **Gross domestic product** (1995 est.): $1.2 bil. **Per capita GDP:** $18,000. **Imports** (1995): $1 bil; partners: France, Spain. **Exports** (1995): $47 mil; partners: France 49%, Spain 47%. **National budget** (1993): $177 mil.

Transport: Motor vehicles in use: 35,358 passenger cars, 4,238 comm. vehicles.

Communications: Television sets: 315 per 1,000 pop. **Radios:** 156 per 1,000 pop. **Telephones:** 30,000 main lines. **Daily newspaper circ.:** 62 per 1,000 pop.

Health: Life expectancy at birth: 80.5 male; 86.5 female. **Births** (per 1,000 pop.): 10. **Deaths** (per 1,000 pop.): 5. **Natural increase:** 0.51%. **Hospital beds** (1993): 1 per 556 persons. **Physicians** (1994): 1 per 491 persons. **Infant mortality** (per 1,000 live births): 4.

Education: Free and compulsory: ages 6-16. **Literacy** (1997): 100%.

Major International Organizations: UN.
Embassy: 2 UN Plaza, 25th floor, New York, NY 10017; (212) 750-8064.
Website: http://www.andorra.ad/cniauk.html

Andorra was a co-principality, with joint sovereignty by France and the bishop of Urgel, from 1278 to 1993.

Tourism, especially skiing, is the economic mainstay. A free port, allowing for an active trading center, draws some 13 million tourists annually. Andorran voters chose to end a feudal system that had been in place for 715 years and adopt a parliamentary system of government Mar. 14, 1993.

Angola

Republic of Angola

People: Population: 10,864,512. **Age distrib.** (%): <15: 44.9; 65+: 2.7. **Pop. density:** 23 per sq. mi. **Urban:** 32%. **Ethnic groups:** Ovimbundu 37%, Kimbundu 25%, Bakongo 13%. **Principal languages:** Portuguese (official), various Bantu and other African languages. **Chief religions:** Indigenous beliefs 47%, Roman Catholic 38%, Protestant 15%.

Geography: Area: 481,351 sq. mi. **Location:** In SW Africa on Atlantic coast. **Neighbors:** Namibia on S, Zambia on E, Congo-Kinshasa (formerly Zaire) on N; Cabinda, an enclave separated from rest of country by short Atlantic coast of Congo-Kinshasa, borders Congo-Brazzaville. **Topography:** Most of Angola consists of a plateau elevated 3,000 to 5,000 feet above sea level, rising from a narrow coastal strip. There is also a temperate highland area in the west-central region, a desert in the S, and a tropical rain forest covering Cabinda. **Capital:** Luanda: 2,081,000*.

Government: Type: Republic. **Head of state:** Pres. José Eduardo dos Santos; b Aug. 28, 1942; in office: Sept. 20, 1979. **Head of government:** Prime Min. Fernando Franca van Dunem; in office: June 8, 1996. **Local divisions:** 18 provinces. **Defense:** 6.4% of GDP. **Active troop strength:** 97,000.

Economy: Industries: Food processing, textiles, mining, brewing, oil. **Chief crops:** Coffee, sugarcane, bananas. **Minerals:** Iron, diamonds (over 1 mil carats a year), gold, phosphates, oil. **Livestock** (1997): chickens: 6.55 mil; cattle: 3.56 mil; goats: 1.48 mil; pigs: 830,000; sheep: 250,000. **Crude oil reserves** (1997): 5.4 bil bbls. **Arable land:** 2%. **Fish catch** (1996): 72,841 metric tons. **Electricity prod.** (1996): 1.9 bil. kWh. **Labor force:** 85% agric., 15% industry.

Finance: Monetary unit: Readjusted Kwanza (Sept. 1998: 257,128.00 = $1 U.S.). **Gross domestic product** (1996 est.): $8.3 bil. **Per capita GDP:** $800. **Imports** (1995 est.): $1.7 bil; partners: Portugal 30%, U.S. 11%, France 10%. **Exports** (1996 est.): $4 bil; partners: U.S. 70%. **Tourism:** $9 mil. **National budget** (1992 est.): $2.5 bil.

Transport: Railroad: Length: 1,739 mi. **Motor vehicles in use:** 197,000 passenger cars, 26,000 comm. vehicles. **Civil aviation:** 546.5 mil passenger-mi; 17 airports. **Chief ports:** Cabinda, Lobito, Luanda.

Communications: Television sets: 48 per 1,000 pop. **Radios:** 39 per 1,000 pop. **Telephones:** 52,440 main lines. **Daily newspaper circ.:** 11 per 1,000 pop.

Health: Life expectancy at birth: 45.6 male; 50.2 female. **Births** (per 1,000 pop.): 44. **Deaths** (per 1,000 pop.): 17. **Natural increase:** 2.68%. **Infant mortality** (per 1,000 live births): 132.

Education: Free and compulsory: ages 7-15. **Literacy** (1992): 40%.

Major International Organizations: UN (FAO, IBRD, ILO, IMF, IMO, WHO, WTrO), OAU.

Embassy: 1050 Connecticut Avenue NW, Suite 760 20036; 785-1156.

Website: http://www.angola.org

From the early centuries AD to 1500, Bantu tribes penetrated most of the region. Portuguese came in 1583, allied with the Bakongo kingdom in the north, and developed the slave trade. Large-scale colonization did not begin until the 20th century, when 400,000 Portuguese immigrated.

A guerrilla war begun in 1961 lasted until 1975, when Portugal granted independence. Fighting then erupted between three rival rebel groups—the National Front, based in Zaire (now Congo), the Soviet-backed Popular Movement for the Liberation of Angola (MPLA), and the National Union for the Total Independence of Angola (UNITA), aided by the U.S. and South Africa. The civil war killed thousands of blacks, drove most whites to emigrate, and completed economic ruin. Cuban troops and Soviet aid helped the MPLA win control of most of the country by 1976, although fighting continued through the 1980s. A peace accord between the MPLA government and UNITA was signed May 1, 1991.

Elections were held in Sept. 1992, but fighting again broke out, as UNITA rejected the results. Large numbers of civilians died from war-related causes, especially starvation. UNITA signed a new peace treaty with the government, Nov. 20, 1994, but the rebels were slow to demobilize. The UN Security Council voted, Aug. 28, 1997, to impose sanctions on UNITA. In Aug. 1998, Angola sent thousands of troops into Congo-Kinshasa (formerly Zaire) to support Laurent Kabila's regime.

Antigua and Barbuda

People: Population: 64,006. **Age distrib.** (%): <15: 26.1; 65+: 5.6. **Pop. density:** 377 per sq. mi. **Urban:** 36%. **Ethnic groups:** Primarly black. **Principal language:** English (official). **Chief religion:** Predominantly Anglican.

Geography: Area: 170 sq. mi. **Location:** Eastern Caribbean. **Neighbors:** St. Kitts & Nevis to W, Guadeloupe (Fr.) to S. **Capital:** Saint John's (1991): 35,635.

Government: Type: Constitutional monarchy with British-style parliament. **Head of state:** Queen Elizabeth II; represented by Gov.-Gen. James Carlisle; b Aug. 5, 1937; in office: June 10, 1993. **Head of government:** Prime Min. Lester Bird; b Feb. 21, 1938; in office: Mar. 9, 1994. **Local divisions:** 6 parishes, 2 dependencies. **Defense:** 0.8% of GDP. **Active troop strength:** 200.

Economy: Industries: Tourism, manufacturing, construction. **Arable land:** 18%. **Electricity prod.** (1996): 95 mil kWh. **Labor force:** 82% commerce & serv.; 11% agric.; 7% ind.

Finance: Monetary unit: East Caribbean Dollar (Sept. 1998: 2.70 = $1 U.S.). **Gross domestic product** (1996 est.): $446 mil. **Per capita GDP:** $6,800. **Imports** (1996 est.): $350.8 mil; partners: U.S. 27%, U.K. 16%. **Exports** (1996 est.): $45 mil; partners: OECS 26%, Barbados 15%. **Tourism:** $260 mil. **National budget** (1995): $135.4 mil.

Transport: Railroad: Length: 47.8 mi. **Motor vehicles in use:** 13,250 passenger cars, 1,423 comm. vehicles. **Civil aviation:** 165.8 mil passenger-mi; 2 airports.

Communications: Television sets: 435 per 1,000 pop. **Radios:** 776 per 1,000 pop. **Telephone:** 28,000 main lines.

Health: Life expectancy at birth: 68.6 male; 73.7 female. **Births** (per 1,000 pop.): 17. **Deaths** (per 1,000 pop.): 6. **Natural increase:** 1.09%. **Hospital beds** (1992): 1 per 173 persons. **Physicians** (1992): 1 per 1,083 persons. **Infant mortality** (per 1,000 live births): 21.

Education: Compulsory: ages 5-16. **Literacy** (1992): 90%.

Major International Organizations: UN (FAO, IBRD, ILO, IMF, IMO, WHO, WTrO), Caricom, the Commonwealth, OAS, OECS.

Embassy: 3216 New Mexico Ave. NW 20016; 362-5211.

Website: http://www.antigua-barbuda.com

Columbus landed on Antigua in 1493. The British colonized it in 1632.

The British associated state of Antigua achieved independence as Antigua and Barbuda on Nov. 1, 1981. The government maintains close relations with the U.S., United Kingdom, and Venezuela. The country was hit hard by Hurricane Luis, Sept. 1995. About 3,000 refugees fleeing a volcanic eruption on Montserrat have settled in Antigua since 1995.

Argentina

Argentine Republic

People: Population: 36,265,463. **Age distrib.** (%): <15: 27.5; 65+: 10.2. **Pop. density:** 34 per sq. mi. **Urban:** 88%. **Ethnic groups:** White 85% (mostly Spanish, Italian); mestizo, Amerindian, other nonwhites 15%. **Principal languages:** Spanish (official), English, Italian. **Chief religion:** Nominally Roman Catholic 90%.

Geography: Area: 1,073,518 sq. mi., second largest country in South America. **Location:** Occupies most of S South America. **Neighbors:** Chile on W; Bolivia, Paraguay on N; Brazil, Uruguay on NE. **Topography:** Mountains in the W are: the Andean, Central, Misiones, and Southern. Aconcagua is the highest peak in the western hemisphere, alt. 22,834 ft. E of the Andes are heavily wooded plains, called the Gran Chaco in the N, and the fertile, treeless Pampas in the central region. Patagonia, in the S, is bleak and arid. Rio de la Plata, an estuary in the NE, 170 by 140 mi., is mostly fresh water, from 2,485-mi Parana and 1,000-mi Uruguay rivers. **Capital:** Buenos Aires (the Senate has approved moving the capital to the Patagonia Region). **Cities:** Buenos Aires 11,802,000; Cordoba 1,294,000; Rosario 1,155,000*.

Government: Type: Republic. **Head of state:** Pres. Carlos Saúl Menem; b July 2, 1930; in office: July 8, 1989. **Local divisions:** 23 provinces, 1 federal district. **Defense:** 1.5% of GDP. **Active troop strength:** 72,500.

Economy: Industries: Food processing, autos, chemicals, textiles, printing. **Chief crops:** Grains, corn, sugar beets, sorghum, soybeans. **Minerals:** Oil, lead, zinc, iron, copper, tin, uranium. **Crude oil reserves** (1997): 2.6 bil bbls. **Arable land:** 9%. **Livestock** (1997): chickens: 55.00 mil; cattle: 51.70 mil; sheep: 17.30 mil; goats: 3.37 mil; pigs: 3.20 mil. **Fish catch** (1996): 1.24 mil metric tons. **Electricity prod.** (1996): 64.7 bil kWh. **Labor force:** 57% services; 31% ind.; 12% agric.

Finance: Monetary unit: Peso (Sept. 1998: 1.00 = $1 U.S.). **Gross domestic product** (1996 est.): $296.9 bil. **Per capita GDP:** $8,600. **Imports** (1996): $23.7 bil; partners: Brazil 21%, U.S. 21%, Germany 6%, Italy 6%. **Exports** (1996): $23.8 bil; partners: Brazil; 26%, U.S. 9%. **Tourism:** $5.07 bil. **National budget** (1995 est.): $51.7 bil. **International reserves less gold** (June 1998): $27.77 bil. **Gold:** 361,000 oz t. **Consumer prices** (change in 1997): 0.5%.

Transport: Railroad: Length: 21,015 mi. **Motor vehicles in use:** 4.78 mil passenger cars, 1.29 mil comm. vehicles. **Civil aviation:** 8.30 bil passenger-mi; 39 airports. **Chief ports:** Buenos Aires, Bahia Blanca, La Plata.

Communications: Television sets: 347 per 1,000 pop. **Radios:** 614 per 1,000 pop. **Telephones:** 6,119,555 main lines. **Daily newspaper circ.:** 137 per 1,000 pop.

Health: Life expectancy at birth: 70.9 male; 78.3 female. **Births** (per 1,000 pop.): 20. **Deaths** (per 1,000 pop.): 8. **Natural increase:** 1.23%. **Hospital beds** (1992): 1 per 227 persons. **Physicians** (1992): 1 per 376 persons. **Infant mortality** (per 1,000 live births): 19.

Education: Free and compulsory: ages 6-14. **Literacy:** 96%.

Major International Organizations: UN (FAO, IBRD, ILO, IMF, IMO, WHO, WTrO), OAS.

Embassy: 1600 New Hampshire Ave. NW 20009; 939-6400.

Website: http://www.indec.mecon.ar/idefault.htm

Nomadic Indians roamed the Pampas when Spaniards arrived, 1515-16, led by Juan Diaz de Solis. Nearly all the Indians were killed by the late 19th century. The colonists won independence, 1816, and a long period of disorder ended in a strong centralized government.

Large-scale Italian, German, and Spanish immigration in the decades after 1880 spurred modernization. Social reforms were enacted in the 1920s, but military coups prevailed 1930-46, until the election of Gen. Juan Perón as president.

Perón, with his wife, Eva Duarte (d 1952), effected labor reforms, but also suppressed speech and press freedoms, closed religious schools, and ran the country into debt. A 1955 coup exiled Perón, who was followed by a series of military and civilian regimes. Perón returned to Argentina in 1973, and was once more elected president. He died 10 months later, succeeded by his wife Isabel, who had been elected vice president, and who became the first woman head of state in the western hemisphere.

A military junta ousted Mrs. Perón in 1976 amid charges of corruption. Under a continuing state of siege, the army battled guerrillas and leftists, killed 5,000 people, and jailed and tortured others. On Dec. 9, 1985, after a trial of 5 months and nearly 1,000 witnesses, 5 former junta members were found guilty of murder and human rights abuses.

Argentine troops seized control of the British-held Falkland Islands on Apr. 2, 1982. Both countries had claimed sovereignty over the islands, located 250 miles off the Argentine coast, since 1833. The British dispatched a task force and declared a total air and sea blockade around the Falklands. Fighting began May 1; several hundred lost their lives as the result of the destruction of a British destroyer and the sinking of an Argentine cruiser.

British troops landed on East Falkland Island May 21 and eventually surrounded Stanley, the capital city and Argentine stronghold. The Argentine troops surrendered, June 14; Argentine Pres. Leopoldo Galtieri resigned June 17.

Democratic rule returned to Argentina in 1983 as Raul Alfonsín's Radical Civic Union party gained an absolute majority in the presidential electoral college and Congress. By 1989 the nation was plagued by severe financial and political problems, as hyperinflation sparked looting and rioting in several cities. The government of Perónist Pres. Carlos Saúl Menem, installed 1989, introduced harsh economic measures designed to curtail inflation, control government spending, and restructure the foreign debt.

About 100 people were killed in the terrorist bombing of a Jewish cultural center in Buenos Aires, July 18, 1994. Following passage of a new constitution in Aug. 1994, Menem was reelected president on May 14, 1995.

Armenia

Republic of Armenia

People: Population: 3,421,775. **Age distrib.** (%): <15: 26.4; 65+: 8.4. **Pop. density:** 297 per sq. mi. **Urban:** 69%. **Ethnic groups:** Armenian 93%, Azeri 3%, Russian 2%, Kurd and others 2%. **Principal language:** Armenian (official). **Chief religion:** Armenian Orthodox 94%.

Geography: Area: 11,506 sq. mi. **Location:** SW Asia. **Neighbors:** Georgia on N, Azerbaijan on E, Iran on S, Turkey on W. **Topography:** Mountainous with many peaks above 10,000 ft. **Capital:** Yerevan: 1,278,000*.

Government: Type: Republic. **Head of state:** Pres. Robert Kocharian; b Aug. 31 1954; in office: Apr. 9, 1998. **Head of government:** Prime Min. Armen Darbinian; b 1965; in office: Apr. 10, 1998. **Local divisions:** 10 provinces, 1 capital. **Defense:** 6.2% of GDP. **Active troop strength:** 57,400.

Economy: Industries: Manufacturing, machinery, chemicals. **Chief crops:** Vegetables, grapes. **Minerals:** Copper, gold, zinc. **Arable land:** 17%. **Livestock** (1997): chickens: 2.70 mil; sheep: 400,000; cattle; 350,000. **Electricity prod.** (1996): 7.6 bil kWh.

Finance: Monetary unit: Dram (Aug. 1998: 503.00 = $1 U.S.). **Gross domestic product** (1996 est.): $9.7 bil. **Per capita GDP:** $2,800. **Imports** (1996): $830 mil. **Exports** (1996): $273 mil. **Tourism:** $12 mil. **International reserves less gold** (June 1998): $296.4 mil. **Consumer prices** (change in 1997): 13.9%.

Transport: Railroad: Length: 512.3 mi. **Civil aviation:** 463.6 mil passenger-mi; 1 airport.

Communications: Telephones: 579,500 main lines. **Daily newspaper circ.:** 23 per 1,000 pop.

Health: Life expectancy at birth: 62.5 male; 71.2 female. **Births** (per 1,000 pop.): 14. **Deaths** (per 1,000 pop.): 9. **Natural increase:** 0.47%. **Hospital beds** (1994): 1 per 125 persons. **Physicians** (1994): 1 per 288 persons. **Infant mortality** (per 1,000 live births): 41.

Education: Compulsory: ages 6-17. **Literacy** (1989): 99%.

Major International Organizations: UN (FAO, IBRD, ILO, IMF, WHO), CIS, OSCE.

Embassy: 2225 R St. NW 20008; 319-1976.

Ancient Armenia extended into parts of what are now Turkey and Iran. Present-day Armenia was set up as a Soviet republic Apr. 2, 1921. It joined Georgian and Azerbaijan SSRs Mar. 12, 1922, to form the Transcaucasian SFSR, which became part of the USSR Dec. 30, 1922. Armenia became a constituent republic of the USSR Dec. 5, 1936. An earthquake struck Armenia Dec. 7, 1988; approximately 55,000 were killed and several cities and towns were left in ruins.

Armenia declared independence Sept. 23, 1991, and became an independent state when the USSR disbanded Dec. 26, 1991. Fighting between mostly Christian Armenia and mostly Muslim Azerbaijan escalated in 1992 and continued through 1993. Each country claimed Nagorno-Karabakh, an enclave in Azerbaijan that has a majority population of ethnic Armenians. A temporary cease-fire was announced in May 1994, with Armenian forces in control of the enclave. Voters approved, July 5, 1995, a new constitution strengthening presidential powers. Pres. Levon Ter-Petrosian won reelection on Sept. 22, 1996, amid claims of fraud; he resigned Feb. 3, 1998, in a conflict over Nagorno-Karabakh. Robert Kocharian, a nationalist born in the disputed region, won the presidency on Mar. 30, 1998.

Australia

Commonwealth of Australia

People: Population: 18,613,087. **Age distrib.** (%): <15: 21.2; 65+: 12.4. **Pop. density:** 6 per sq. mi. **Urban:** 85%. **Ethnic groups:** Caucasian 95%, Asian 4%, aboriginal (including mixed) 1%. **Principal languages:** English (official), aboriginal languages. **Chief religions:** Anglican 26%, Roman Catholic 26%, other Christian 24%.

Geography: Area: 2,967,893 sq. mi. **Location:** SE of Asia, Indian O. is W and S, Pacific O. (Coral, Tasman seas) is E; they meet N of Australia in Timor and Arafura seas. Tasmania lies 150 mi. S of Victoria state, across Bass Strait. **Neighbors:** Nearest are Indonesia, Papua New Guinea on N; Solomons, Fiji, and New Zealand on E. **Topography:** An island continent. The Great Dividing Range along the E coast has Mt. Kosciusko, 7,310 ft. The W plateau rises to 2,000 ft., with arid areas in the Great Sandy and Great Victoria deserts. The NW part of Western Australia and Northern Terr. are arid and hot. The NE has heavy rainfall and Cape York Peninsula has jungles. **Capital:** Canberra. **Cities** (1995 est.): Sydney 3.8 mil; Melbourne 3.2 mil; Brisbane 1.5 mil; Perth 1.3 mil; Adelaide 1.1 mil.

Government: Type: Democratic, federal state system. **Head of state:** Queen Elizabeth II, represented by Gov.-Gen. Sir William Patrick Deane; b July 4, 1931; in office: Feb. 15, 1996. **Head of government:** Prime Min. John Howard; b July 26, 1939; in office: Mar. 8, 1996. **Local divisions:** 6 states, 2 territories. **Defense:** 2.2% of GDP. **Active troop strength:** 57,800.

Economy: Industries: Mining, steel, industrial & transportation equip., chemicals, food processing. **Chief crops:** Wheat (a leading export), barley, fruit, sugar. **Minerals:** Bauxite, coal, copper, iron, lead, tin, uranium, zinc. **Crude oil reserves** (1997): 1.8 bil bbls. **Other resources:** Wool (world's leading producer), beef. **Arable land:** 6%. **Livestock** (1997): sheep: 123.33 mil; chickens: 72.06 mil; cattle: 26.35 mil; pigs: 2.68 mil; goats: 200,000. **Fish catch** (1996): 191,533 metric tons. **Electricity prod.** (1996): 166.7 bil kWh. **Labor force:** 36% trade, manuf. & ind.; 34% finance & services; 6% agric.

Finance: Monetary unit: Dollar (Sept. 1998: 1.73 = $1 U.S.). **Gross domestic product** (1996 est.): $430.5 bil. **Per capita GDP:** $23,600. **Imports** (1996): $59.7 bil; partners: U.S. 22%, Japan 17%, UK 6%. **Exports** (1996): $59.5 bil; partners: Japan 24%, S. Korea 8%, New Zealand 7%. **Tourism:** $9.32 bil. **National budget** (FY 1995-96 est.): $95.15 bil. **International reserves less gold** (June 1998): $14.84 bil. **Gold:** 2.56 mil oz t. **Consumer prices** (change in 1997): 0.3%.

Transport: Railroad: Length: 23,947.6 mi. **Motor vehicles in use:** 8.7 mil passenger cars, 2.05 mil comm. vehicles. **Civil aviation:** 45.08 bil passenger-mi; 400 airports. **Chief ports:** Sydney, Melbourne, Brisbane, Adelaide, Fremantle, Geelong.

Communications: Television sets: 641 per 1,000 pop. **Radios:** 1,148 per 1,000 pop. **Telephones:** 9,500,000 main lines. **Daily newspaper circ.:** 258 per 1,000 pop.

Health: Life expectancy at birth: 77.0 male; 83.0 female. **Births** (per 1,000 pop.): 13. **Deaths** (per 1,000 pop.): 7. **Natural increase:** 0.66%. **Hospital beds** (1995): 1 per 226 persons. **Physicians** (1996): 1 per 400 persons. **Infant mortality** (per 1,000 live births): 5.

Education: Free and compulsory: ages 6-15. **Literacy** (1993): 100%.

Major International Organizations: UN and all of its specialized agencies, APEC, the Commonwealth, OECD.

Embassy: 1601 Massachusetts Ave. NW 20036; 797-3000.

Website: http://www.australia.com

Australia harbors many plant and animal species not found elsewhere, including kangaroos, koalas, platypuses, dingos (wild dogs), Tasmanian devils (raccoon-like marsupials), wombats (bear-like marsupials), and barking and frilled lizards.

Capt. James Cook explored the E coast in 1770, when the continent was inhabited by a variety of different tribes. The first settlers, beginning in 1788, were mostly convicts, soldiers, and government officials. By 1830, Britain had claimed the entire continent, and the immigration of free settlers began to accelerate. The Commonwealth was proclaimed Jan. 1, 1901. Northern Terr. was granted limited self-rule July 1, 1978.

State/Territory, Capital	Area (sq. mi.)	Population (1996 est.)
New South Wales, Sydney	309,500	6,190,000
Victoria, Melbourne	87,900	4,541,000
Queensland, Brisbane	666,990	3,355,000
Western Australia, Perth	975,100	1,763,000
South Australia, Adelaide	379,900	1,479,000
Tasmania, Hobart	26,200	473,000
Australian Capital Terr., Canberra	900	308,000
Northern Terr., Darwin	519,800	178,000

Racially discriminatory immigration policies were abandoned in 1973, after 3 million Europeans (half British) had entered since 1945. The 50,000 aborigines and 150,000 part-aborigines are mostly detribalized, but there are several preserves in the Northern Territory. They remain economically disadvantaged.

Australia's agricultural success makes the country among the top exporters of beef, lamb, wool, and wheat. Major mineral deposits have been developed, largely for export. Industrialization has been completed. The nation endured a deep recession 1990-93 but has rebounded strongly.

The Labor Party won a majority in Feb. 1983 general elections and was reelected in 1984, 1987, 1990, and 1993. After an election that focused mainly on economic issues, conservatives swept into power in elections Mar. 2, 1996. Constitutional convention delegates voted Feb. 13, 1998, to have a native Australian as head of state, subject to a referendum in 1999.

Prime Min. John Howard retained power, but with a reduced majority in parliamentary elections Oct. 3, 1998.

Australian External Territories

Norfolk Isl., area 13.3 sq. mi., pop. (1996 est.) 2,209, was taken over, 1914. The soil is very fertile, suitable for citrus, bananas, and coffee. Many of the inhabitants are descendants of the *Bounty* mutineers, moved to Norfolk 1856 from Pitcairn Isl. Australia offered the island limited home rule in 1978.

Coral Sea Isls. Territory, area 1 sq. mi., is administered from Norfolk Isl.

Territory of Ashmore and Cartier Isls., area 2 sq. mi., in the Indian O., came under Australian authority 1934 and are administered as part of Northern Territory. **Heard Isl. and McDonald Isls.,** area 159 sq. mi., are administered by the Dept. of Science.

Cocos (Keeling) Isls., 27 small coral islands in the Indian O. 1,750 mi. NW of Australia. Pop. (1996 est.) 609; area 5.5 sq. mi. The residents voted to become part of Australia, Apr. 1984.

Christmas Isl., area 52 sq. mi., pop. (1996 est.) 813; 230 mi. S of Java, was transferred by Britain in 1958. It has phosphate deposits.

Australian Antarctic Territory was claimed by Australia in 1933, including 2,362,000 sq. mi. of territory S of 60th parallel S Lat. and between 160th-45th meridians E Long. It does not include Adelie Coast.

Austria

Republic of Austria

People: Population: 8,133,611. **Age distrib.** (%): <15: 17; 65+: 15.5. **Pop. density:** 251 per sq. mi. **Urban:** 64%. **Ethnic groups:** German 99%, Croatian, Slovene. **Principal language:** German (official). **Chief religions:** Roman Catholic 85%, Protestant 6%.

Geography: Area: 32,374 sq. mi. **Location:** In S Central Europe. **Neighbors:** Switzerland, Liechtenstein on W; Germany, Czech Rep. on N; Slovakia, Hungary on E; Slovenia, Italy on S. **Topography:** Austria is primarily mountainous, with the Alps and foothills covering the western and southern provinces. The eastern provinces and Vienna are located in the Danube River Basin. **Capital:** Vienna: 2,060,000*.

Government: Type: Parliamentary democracy. **Head of state:** Pres. Thomas Klestil; b Nov. 4, 1932; in office: July 8, 1992. **Head of government:** Chancellor Viktor Klima; b June 4, 1947; in office: Jan. 28, 1997. **Local divisions:** 9 bundeslaender (states), each with a legislature. **Defense:** 0.9% of GDP. **Active troop strength:** 55,800.

Economy: Industries: Steel, machinery, autos, electrical equip., tourism, mining, paper, textiles, chemicals, food. **Chief crops:** Grains, fruits, potatoes, sugar beets. **Minerals:** Iron ore, oil, magnesite. **Crude oil reserves** (1997): 90 mil bbls. **Other resources:** Forests, hydropower. **Arable land:** 17%. **Livestock** (1997): chickens: 13.95 mil; pigs: 3.68 mil; cattle: 2.20 mil; sheep: 384,000. **Electricity prod.** (1996): 52.2 bil kWh. **Labor force:** 56% services; 35% ind. & crafts; 8% agric.

Finance: Monetary unit: Schilling (Sept. 1998: 12.18 = $1 U.S.). **Gross domestic product** (1996 est.): $157.6 bil. **Per capita GDP:** $19,700. **Imports** (1996 est.): $65.8 bil; partners: Germany 40%. **Exports** (1996 est.): $55.5 bil; partners: Germany 38%. **Tourism:** $12.39 bil. **National budget** (1997): $71 bil. **International reserves less gold** (June 1998): $19.82 bil. **Gold:** 7.77 mil oz t. **Consumer prices** (change in 1997): 1.3%.

Transport: Railroad: Length: 3,492.5 mi. **Motor vehicles in use:** 3.69 mil passenger cars, 787,324 comm. vehicles. **Civil aviation:** 5.46 bil passenger-mi; 6 airports. **Chief ports:** Linz, Vienna.

Communications: Television sets: 336 per 1,000 pop. **Radios:** 584 per 1,000 pop. **Telephones:** 3,778,993 main lines. **Daily newspaper circ.:** 465 per 1,000 pop.

Health: Life expectancy at birth: 74.1 male; 80.7 female. **Births** (per 1,000 pop.): 10. **Deaths** (per 1,000 pop.): 10. **Natural increase:** –0.02%. **Hospital beds** (1996): 1 per 117 persons. **Physicians** (1996): 1 per 289 persons. **Infant mortality** (per 1,000 live births): 5.

Education: Free and compulsory: ages 6-15. **Literacy** (1994): 100%.

Major International Organizations: UN and all of its specialized agencies, EU, OECD, OSCE.

Embassy: 3524 International Ct. NW 20008; 895-6700.

Website: http://www.austria.org

Rome conquered Austrian lands from Celtic tribes around 15 BC. In 788 the territory was incorporated into Charlemagne's empire. By 1300, the House of Hapsburg had gained control; they added vast territories in all parts of Europe to their realm in the next few hundred years.

Austrian dominance of Germany was undermined in the 18th century and ended by Prussia by 1866. But the Congress of Vienna, 1815, confirmed Austrian control of a large empire in southeast Europe consisting of Germans, Hungarians, Slavs,

Italians, and others. The dual Austro-Hungarian monarchy was established in 1867, giving autonomy to Hungary and almost 50 years of peace.

World War I, started after the June 28, 1914, assassination of Archduke Franz Ferdinand, the Hapsburg heir, by a Serbian nationalist, destroyed the empire. By 1918 Austria was reduced to a small republic, with the borders it has today.

Nazi Germany invaded Austria Mar. 13, 1938. The republic was reestablished in 1945, under Allied occupation. Full independence and neutrality were restored in 1955. Austria joined the European Union Jan. 1, 1995.

Azerbaijan

Azerbaijani Republic

People: Population: 7,855,576. **Age distrib.** (%): <15: 32.4; 65+: 6.4. **Pop. density:** 235 per sq. mi. **Urban:** 56%. **Ethnic groups:** Azeri 90%, Dagestani Peoples 3%, Russian 2.5%, Armenian 2%. **Principal languages:** Azeri (official) 89%, Russian 3%, Armenian 2%. **Chief religions:** Muslim 93%, Orthodox 5%.

Geography: Area: 33,436 sq. mi. **Location:** SW Asia. **Neighbors:** Russia, Georgia on N; Iran on S; Armenia on W; Caspian Sea on E. **Capital:** Baku: 1,848,000*.

Government: Type: Republic. **Head of state:** Pres. Haydar A. Aliyev; b May 10, 1923; in office: June 30, 1993. **Head of government:** Prime Min. Artur Rasizade; b Feb. 26, 1935; in office: Nov. 26, 1996. **Local division:** 59 rayons, 11 cities, 1 autonomous republic. **Defense:** 5.8% of GDP. **Active troop strength:** 70,700.

Economy: Industries: Oil refining, chemicals, textiles. **Chief crops:** Grain, rice, cotton, grapes. **Minerals:** Oil, gas, iron. **Crude oil reserves** (1997): 1.2 bil bbls. **Arable land:** 18%. **Livestock** (1997): chickens: 13.20 mil; sheep: 5.20 mil; cattle: 1.83 mil; buffalo: 303,000; goats: 275,000. **Electricity prod.** (1996): 16.0 bil kWh.

Finance: Monetary unit: Manat (Sept. 1998: 3,950.00 = $1 U.S.). **Gross domestic product** (1996 est.): $11.9 bil. **Per capita GDP:** $1,550. **Imports** (1996 est.): $900 mil. **Exports** (1996 est.): $700 mil. **Tourism:** $156 mil. **National budget** (1995 est.): $682 mil.

Transport: Railroad: Length: 1,319.6 mi. **Motor vehicles in use:** 289,000 passenger cars; 89,000 comm. vehicles. **Civil aviation:** 1.08 bil passenger-mi; 3 airports. **Chief port:** Baku.

Communications: Television sets: 212 per 1,000 pop. **Daily newspaper circ.:** 28 per 1,000 pop.

Health: Life expectancy at birth: 59.0 male; 67.8 female. **Births** (per 1,000 pop.): 22. **Deaths** (per 1,000 pop.): 9. **Natural increase:** 1.28%. **Hospital beds** (1994): 1 per 100 persons. **Physicians** (1994): 1 per 256 persons. **Infant mortality** (per 1,000 live births): 82.

Education: Compulsory: ages 6-17. **Literacy** (1995): 100%.

Major International Organizations: UN (FAO, IBRD, ILO, IMF, IMO, WHO), CIS, OSCE.

Embassy: 927 15th St. NW 20005; 842-0001.

Website: http://www.president.az/azerbaijan/azerbaijan.htm

Azerbaijan was the home of Scythian tribes and part of the Roman Empire. Overrun by Turks in the 11th century and conquered by Russia in 1806 and 1813, it joined the USSR Dec. 30, 1922, and became a constituent republic in 1936. Azerbaijan declared independence Aug. 30, 1991, and became an independent state when the Soviet Union disbanded Dec. 26, 1991.

Fighting between mostly Muslim Azerbaijan and mostly Christian Armenia escalated in 1992 and continued in 1993 and 1994. Each country claimed Nagorno-Karabakh, an enclave in Azerbaijan with a majority population of ethnic Armenians. A temporary cease-fire was announced in May 1994, with Armenian forces in control of the enclave.

A National Council ousted Communist Pres. Mutaibov and took power May 19, 1992. Abulfez Elchibey became the nation's first democratically elected president June 7, but was ousted from office by Surat Huseynov, commander of a private militia, June 30, 1993. Huseynov became prime minister, and Haydar Aliyev, a pro-Russian former Communist, became president. Huseynov fled the country after his supporters staged an unsuccessful coup attempt Oct. 1994. Voters approved a new constitution expanding presidential powers, Nov. 12, 1995. Pres. Aliyev was reelected Oct. 11, 1998, but international monitors called the election seriously flawed.

The Bahamas

The Commonwealth of The Bahamas

People: Population: 279,833. **Age distrib.** (%): <15: 27.9; 65+: 5.5. **Pop. density:** 52 per sq. mi. **Urban:** 87%. **Ethnic groups:** Black 85%, white (British, Canadian, U.S.) 15%. **Principal languages:** English (official), Creole. **Chief religions:** Baptist 32%, Anglican 20%, Roman Catholic 19%, other Christian 24%.

Geography: Area: 5,382 sq. mi. **Location:** In Atlantic O., E of Florida. **Neighbors:** Nearest are U.S. on W, Cuba on S. **Topography:** Nearly 700 islands (29 inhabited) and over 2,000 islets in the W Atlantic O. extend 760 mi. NW to SE. **Capital:** Nassau. **Cities** (1990 est.): Nassau 172,196; Grand Bahama 40,898.

Government: Type: Independent commonwealth. **Head of state:** Queen Elizabeth II, represented by Gov.-Gen. Orville A. Turnquest; b July 19, 1929; in office: Jan. 2, 1995. **Head of government:** Prime Min. Hubert Ingraham; b Aug. 4, 1947; in office: Aug. 21, 1992. **Local divisions:** 21 districts. **Defense:** 0.6% of GDP. **Active troop strength:** 900.

Economy: Industries: Tourism (more than 50% of GDP), rum, cement, banking, pharmaceuticals. **Chief crops:** Citrus, vegetables. **Minerals:** Salt, aragonite. **Other resources:** Lobsters. **Arable land:** 1%. **Livestock** (1997): chickens: 3.20 mil. **Electricity prod.** (1996): 1.0 bil kWh. **Labor force:** 40% tourism; 30% govt.; 10% serv.; 5% agric.

Finance: Monetary unit: Dollar (Sept. 1998: 1.00 = $1 U.S.). **Gross domestic product** (1995 est.): $4.8 bil. **Per capita GDP:** $18,700. **Imports** (1995): $1.17 bil; partners: U.S. 29%, Finland 10%, Iran 10%. **Exports** (1995): $267.5 mil; partners: U.S. 24%, Spain 14%, UK 7%, Norway 7%. **Tourism:** $1.57 bil. **National budget** (FY 1995-96 est.): $725 mil. **International reserves less gold** (June 1998): $330.0 mil. **Consumer prices** (change in 1997): 0.5%.

Transport: Motor vehicles in use: 69,000 passenger cars, 14,000 comm. vehicles. **Civil aviation:** 145.1 mil passenger-mi; 22 airports. **Chief ports:** Nassau, Freeport.

Communications: Television sets: 179 per 1,000 pop. **Radios:** 282 per 1,000 pop. **Telephones:** 89,463 main lines. **Daily newspaper circ.:** 126 per 1,000 pop.

Health: Life expectancy at birth: 70.7 male; 77.4 female. **Births** (per 1,000 pop.): 21. **Deaths** (per 1,000 pop.): 5. **Natural increase:** 1.56%. **Hospital beds** (1993): 1 per 249 persons. **Physicians** (1992): 1 per 709 persons. **Infant mortality** (per 1,000 live births): 19.

Education: Compulsory: ages 5-14. **Literacy** (1995): 98%.

Major International Organizations: UN (FAO, IBRD, ILO, IMF, IMO, WHO), Caricom, the Commonwealth, OAS.

Embassy: 2220 Massachusetts Ave. NW 20008; 319-2660.

Website: http://www.bahamas.net.bs/government

Christopher Columbus first set foot in the New World on San Salvador (Watling Isl.) in 1492, when Arawak Indians inhabited the islands. British settlement began in 1647; the islands became a British colony in 1783. Internal self-government was granted in 1964; full independence within the Commonwealth was attained July 10, 1973.

International banking and investment management have become major industries alongside tourism.

Bahrain

State of Bahrain

People: Population: 616,342. **Age distrib.** (%): <15: 30.7; 65+: 2.8. **Pop. density:** 2,300 per sq. mi. **Urban:** 91%. **Ethnic groups:** Bahraini 63%, Asian 13%, other Arab 10%, Iranian 8%. **Principal languages:** Arabic (official), English, Farsi, Urdu. **Chief religions:** Shi'a Muslim 75%, Sunni Muslim 25%.

Geography: Area: 268 sq. mi. **Location:** SW Asia, in Persian Gulf. **Neighbors:** Nearest are Saudi Arabia on W, Qatar on E. **Topography:** Bahrain Island, and several adjacent, smaller islands, are flat, hot, and humid, with little rain. **Capital:** Manama (1995 est.): 148,000.

Government: Type: Traditional monarchy. **Head of state:** Emir Isa bin Sulman al-Khalifa; b July 3, 1933; in office: Nov. 2, 1961. **Head of government:** Prime Min. Kahlifa bin Sulman al-Khalifa; b 1935; in office: Jan. 19, 1970. **Local divisions:** 12 municipalities. **Defense:** 5.5% of GDP. **Active troop strength:** 11,000.

Economy: Industries: Oil products, aluminum smelting. **Chief crops:** Fruits, vegetables. **Minerals:** Oil, gas. **Crude oil reserves** (1997): 210 mil bbls. **Arable land:** 1%. **Livestock** (1997): chickens: 700,000. **Electricity prod.** (1996): 4.7 bil kWh. **Labor force:** 85% ind. and commerce; 5% agric.; 5% services; 3% govt.

Finance: Monetary unit: Dinar (Sept. 1998: 0.38 = $1 U.S.). **Gross domestic product** (1995 est.): $7.3 bil. **Per capita GDP:** $12,000. **Imports** (1996 est.): $3.5 bil; partners: Saudi Arabia 40%, U.S. 13%. **Exports** (1996 est.): $4.2 bil; partners: India 22%, Japan 12%. **Tourism:** $260 mil. **National budget** (1995): $1.67 bil. **International reserves less gold** (June 1998): $1.19 bil. **Gold:** 150,000 oz t. **Consumer prices** (change in 1997): -0.2%.

Transport: Motor vehicles in use: 141,901 passenger cars, 30,243 comm. vehicles. **Civil aviation:** 1.71 bil passenger-mi; 1 airport. **Chief ports:** Manama, Sitrah.

Communications: Television sets: 442 per 1,000 pop. **Radios:** 555 per 1,000 pop. **Telephones:** 144,391 main lines. **Daily newspaper circ.:** 128 per 1,000 pop.

Health: Life expectancy at birth: 72.4 male; 77.6 female. **Births** (per 1,000 pop.): 22. **Deaths** (per 1,000 pop.): 3. **Natural increase:** 1.92%. **Hospital beds** (1993): 1 per 352 persons. **Physicians** (1993): 1 per 1,115 persons. **Infant mortality** (per 1,000 live births): 16.

Education: Free and compulsory: ages 6-17. **Literacy** (1995): 85%.

Major International Organizations: UN (FAO, IBRD, ILO, IMF, IMO, WHO, WTrO), AL.

Embassy: 3502 International Dr. NW 20008; 342-0741.

Website: http://www.uob.bh

Long ruled by the Khalifa family, Bahrain was a British protectorate from 1861 to Aug. 15, 1971, when it regained independence.

Pearls, shrimp, fruits, and vegetables were the mainstays of the economy until oil was discovered in 1932. By the 1970s, oil reserves were depleted; international banking thrived.

Bahrain took part in the 1973-74 Arab oil embargo against the U.S. and other nations. The government bought controlling interest in the oil industry in 1975. Shiite dissidents have clashed with the Sunni-led government since 1996.

Bangladesh

People's Republic of Bangladesh

People: Population: 127,567,002. **Age distrib.** (%): <15: 37.4; 65+: 3.2. **Pop. density:** 2,294 per sq. mi. **Urban:** 19%. **Ethnic groups:** Bengali 98%, Bihari, tribals. **Principal languages:** Bangla (official), English. **Chief religions:** Muslim 88%, Hindu 11%.

Geography: Area: 55,598 sq. mi. **Location:** In S Asia, on N bend of Bay of Bengal. **Neighbors:** India nearly surrounds country on W, N, E; Myanmar on SE. **Topography:** The country is mostly a low plain cut by the Ganges and Brahmaputra rivers and their delta. The land is alluvial and marshy along the coast, with hills only in the extreme SE and NE. A tropical monsoon climate prevails, among the rainiest in the world. **Capital:** Dhaka. **Cities:** Dhaka 8,545,000; Chittagong 2,477,000; Khulna 1,071,000*.

Government: Type: Parliamentary democracy. **Head of state:** Pres. Shahabuddin Ahmed; b 1930; in office: Oct. 9, 1996. **Head of government:** Prime Min. Hasina Wazed; b Sept. 27, 1947; in office: June 24, 1996. **Local divisions:** 6 divisions. **Defense:** 1.7% of GDP. **Active troop strength:** 117,500.

Economy: Industries: Food processing, jute, textiles, fertilizers, steel. **Chief crops:** Jute, rice, tea. **Minerals:** Natural gas. **Crude oil reserves** (1997): 5.4 mil bbls. **Arable land:** 73%. **Livestock** (1997): chickens: 152.88 mil; goats: 34.48 mil; cattle: 23.96 mil; sheep: 1.16 mil; buffalo: 854,000. **Fish catch** (1996): 874,347 metric tons. **Electricity prod.** (1996): 11.3 bil kWh. **Labor force:** 65% agric.; 21% services; 14% ind. & mining.

Finance: Monetary unit: Taka (Sept. 1998: 47.10 = $1 U.S.). **Gross domestic product** (1996 est.): $155.1 bil. **Per capita GDP:** $1,260. **Imports** (FY1995-96 est.): $6.8 bil; partners: India 21%, China 10%. **Exports** (FY1995-96 est.): $3.9 bil; partners: Western Europe 42%, U.S. 30%. **Tourism:** $42 mil. **National budget** (FY 1995-96 est.): $6 bil. **International reserves less gold** (June 1998): $1.72 bil. **Gold:** 105,000 oz t. **Consumer prices** (change in 1997): 5.7%.

Transport: Railroad: Length: 1,681 mi. **Motor vehicles in use:** 152,000 passenger cars, 73,000 comm. vehicles. **Civil aviation:** 1.86 bil passenger-mi; 8 airports. **Chief ports:** Chittagong, Dhaka, Chalna Port.

Communications: Television sets: 5 per 1,000 pop. **Radios:** 65 per 1,000 pop. **Telephones:** 316,081 main lines. **Daily newspaper circ.:** 0.4 per 1,000 pop.

Health: Life expectancy at birth: 56.7 male; 56.6 female. **Births** (per 1,000 pop.): 29. **Deaths** (per 1,000 pop.): 11. **Natural increase:** 1.83%. **Hospital beds** (1994): 1 per 3,312 persons. **Physicians** (1994): 1 per 4,759 persons. **Infant mortality** (per 1,000 live births): 98.

Education: Free and compulsory: ages 6-11. **Literacy:** 38%.

Major International Organizations: UN (FAO, IBRD, ILO, IMF, IMO, WHO, WTrO), the Commonwealth.

Embassy: 2201 Wisconsin Ave. NW 20007; 342-8372.

Website: http://www.undp.org:81/missions/bangladesh

Muslim invaders conquered the formerly Hindu area in the 12th century. British rule lasted from the 18th century to 1947, when East Bengal became part of Pakistan.

Charging West Pakistani domination, the Awami League, based in the East, won National Assembly control in 1971. Assembly sessions were postponed; riots broke out. Pakistani troops attacked Mar. 25; Bangladesh independence was proclaimed the next day. In the ensuing civil war, one million died and 10 million fled to India.

War between India and Pakistan broke out Dec. 3, 1971. Pakistan surrendered in the East on Dec. 16. Mujibur Rahman, known as Sheikh Mujib, became prime minister; he was killed in a coup Aug. 15, 1975. During the 1970s the country moved into the Indian and Soviet orbits in response to U.S. support of Pakistan, and much of the economy was nationalized.

On May 30, 1981, Pres. Ziaur Rahman was killed in an unsuccessful coup attempt by army rivals. Vice Pres. Abdus Sattar assumed the presidency but was ousted in a coup led by army chief of staff Gen. H. M. Ershad, Mar. 1982. Ershad declared Bangladesh an Islamic Republic in 1988; a parliamentary system of government was adopted in 1991.

Bangladesh is subject to devastating storms and floods that kill thousands. A cyclone struck Apr. 1991, killing over 131,000 people and causing $2.7 billion in damages. Chronic destitution in the densely crowded population has been worsened by the decline of jute as a world commodity.

Political turmoil led to the resignation, Mar. 30, 1996, of Prime Minister Khaleda Zia, the widow of Ziaur Rahman. Sheikh Mujib's daughter, Hasina Wazed (known as Sheikh Hasina), led the country after the June 12, 1996 election. Bangladesh and India signed a treaty, Dec. 12, resolving their long-standing dispute over the use of water from the Ganges River. A cyclone in May 1997 left an estimated 800,000 people homeless. Floods in July-Sept. 1998 inundated most of the country, killed over 1,400 people (many through disease), and stranded at least 30 million.

Barbados

People: Population: 259,025. **Age distrib.** (%): <15: 23.3; 65+: 10.1. **Pop. density:** 1,560 per sq. mi. **Urban:** 48%. **Ethnic groups:** Black 80%, white 4%, other 16%. **Principal language:** English (official). **Chief religions:** Protestant 67%, Roman Catholic 4%.

Geography: Area: 166 sq. mi. **Location:** In Atlantic O., farthest E of West Indies. **Neighbors:** Nearest are St. Lucia and St. Vincent & the Grenadines to the W. **Topography:** The island lies alone in the Atlantic almost completely surrounded by coral reefs. Highest point is Mt. Hillaby, 1,115 ft. **Capital:** Bridgetown (1990 met.): 97,516.

Government: Type: Parliamentary democracy. **Head of state:** Queen Elizabeth II, represented by Gov.-Gen. Sir Clifford Husbands; b Aug. 5, 1926; in office: June 1, 1996. **Head of government:** Prime Min. Owen Arthur; b Oct. 17, 1949; in office: Sept. 7, 1994. **Local divisions:** 11 parishes and Bridgetown. **Defense:** 0.7% of GDP. **Active troop strength:** 600.

Economy: Industries: Sugar, tourism. **Chief crops:** Sugar, vegetables, cotton. **Minerals:** Oil, gas. **Crude oil reserves** (1997): 3.0 mil bbls. **Other resources:** Fish. **Arable land:** 37%. **Livestock** (1997): chickens: 3.40 mil. **Electricity prod.** (1996): 600 mil kWh. **Labor force:** 41% serv. & govt.; 18% manuf. & constr.; 15% commerce; 6% agric.

Finance: Monetary unit: Dollar (Sept. 1998: 2.01 = $1 U.S.). **Gross domestic product** (1996 est.): $2.65 bil. **Per capita GDP:** $10,300. **Imports** (1995): $763 mil; partners: U.S. 36%, UK 11%, Trin. & Tob. 11%. **Exports** (1995): $235 mil; partners: U.S. 13%, UK 10%, Trin. & Tob. 9%. **Tourism:** $688 mil. **National budget** (FY 1995-96 est.): $710 mil. **International reserves less gold** (June 1998): $314.1 mil. **Consumer prices** (change in 1997): 7.7%.

Transport: Motor vehicles in use: 45,000 passenger cars; 3,500 comm. vehicles. **Civil aviation:** 204.9 mil passenger-mi; 1 airport. **Chief port:** Bridgetown.

Communications: Television sets: 287 per 1,000 pop. **Radios:** 1,134 per 1,000 pop. **Telephones:** 96,547 main lines. **Daily newspaper circ.:** 157 per 1,000 pop.

Health: Life expectancy at birth: 72.0 male; 77.6 female. **Births** (per 1,000 pop.): 15. **Deaths** (per 1,000 pop.): 8. **Natural increase:** 0.67%. **Hospital beds** (1992): 1 per 134 persons. **Physicians** (1992): 1 per 842 persons. **Infant mortality** (per 1,000 live births): 17.

Education: Compulsory: ages 5-16. **Literacy:** 97%.

Major International Organizations: UN (FAO, IBRD, ILO, IMF, IMO, WHO, WTrO), Caricom, the Commonwealth, OAS.

Embassy: 2144 Wyoming Ave. NW 20008; 939-9218.

Website: http://www.barbados.org

Barbados was probably named by Portuguese sailors in reference to bearded fig trees. An English ship visited in 1605, and British settlers arrived on the uninhabited island in 1627. Slaves worked the sugar plantations until slavery was abolished in 1834. Self-rule came gradually, with full independence proclaimed Nov. 30, 1966. British traditions have remained.

Belarus

Republic of Belarus

People: Population: 10,409,050. **Age distrib.** (%): <15: 20.0; 65+: 13.4. **Pop. density:** 130 per sq. mi. **Urban:** 72%. **Ethnic groups:** Byelorussian 78%, Russian 13%, Polish 4%. **Principal languages:** Byelorussian (official), Russian. **Chief religions:** Eastern Orthodox 80%, Roman Catholic, Muslim, other 20%.

Geography: Area: 80,154 sq. mi. **Location:** E Europe. **Neighbors:** Poland on W; Latvia, Lithuania on N; Russia on E; Ukraine on S. **Capital:** Minsk: 1,784,000*.

Government: Republic. **Head of state:** Pres. Aleksandr Lukashenko; b Aug. 30, 1954; in office: July 1994. **Head of government:** Prime Min. Sergei Ling; b May 7, 1937; in office, Nov. 18, 1996. **Local divisions:** 6 voblastsi and 1 municipality. **Defense:** 4.2% of GDP (1996). **Active troop strength:** 85,500.

Economy: Industries: Manufacturing, chemical fibers, textiles, agricultural & industrial machinery. **Chief crops:** Grain, vegetables, potatoes. **Crude oil reserves** (1997): 198 mil bbls. **Arable land:** 29%. **Livestock** (1997): chickens: 39.80; cattle: 4.85 mil; pigs: 3.72 mil; sheep: 155,300. **Electricity prod.** (1996): 21.0 bil kWh. **Labor force:** 45% services; 36% ind. & const.; 19% agric. & forestry.

Finance: Monetary unit: Ruble (Aug. 1998: 58,500.00 = $1 U.S.). **Gross domestic product** (1996 est.): $51.9 bil. **Per capita GDP:** $5,000. **Imports** (1996): $6.8 bil; partnersRussia 46%. **Exports** (1996): $5.2 bil; partners: Russia 47%. **Tourism:** $49 mil. **National budget** (1996 est.): $5.5 bil. **Consumer prices** (change in 1997): 63.9%.

Transport: Railroad: Length: 3,480 mi. **Motor vehicles in use:** 842,500 passenger cars, 10,000 comm. vehicles. **Civil aviation:** 265.3 mil passenger-mi; 1 airport. **Chief port:** Mazyr.

Communications: Television sets: 265 per 1,000 pop. **Radios:** 311 per 1,000 pop. **Telephones:** 2,127,972 main lines. **Daily newspaper circ.:** 187 per 1,000 pop.

Health: Life expectancy at birth: 62.3 male; 74.6 female. **Births** (per 1,000 pop.): 10. **Deaths** (per 1,000 pop.): 13. **Natural increase:** –0.38%. **Hospital beds** (1995): 1 per 81 persons. **Physicians** (1995): 1 per 224 persons. **Infant mortality** (per 1,000 live births): 14.

Education: Compulsory: ages 6-17. **Literacy** (1994) 98%.

Major International Organizations: UN (IBRD, ILO, IMF, WHO), CIS, OSCE.

Embassy: 1619 New Hampshire Ave. NW 20009; 986-1604.

The region was subject to Lithuanians and Poles in medieval times, and was a prize of war between Russia and Poland beginning in 1503. It became part of the USSR in 1922 although the western part of the region was controlled by Poland. Belarus was overrun by German armies in 1941; recovered by Soviet troops in 1944. Following World War II, Belarus increased in area through Soviet annexation of part of NE Poland. Belarus declared independence Aug. 25, 1991. It became an independent state when the Soviet Union disbanded Dec. 26, 1991.

A new constitution was adopted, Mar. 15, 1994, and a new president was chosen in elections concluding July 1. Russia and Belarus signed a pact Apr. 2, 1996, linking their political and economic systems. An authoritarian constitution enacted in Nov. gave Pres. Aleksandr Lukashenko vast new powers. Lukashenko's insistence on tightening ties with Russia resulted in the signing of new accords Apr. 2 and May 23, 1997.

Belgium

Kingdom of Belgium

People: Population: 10,174,922. **Age distrib.** (%): <15: 17.3; 65+: 16.8. **Pop. density:** 864 per sq. mi. **Urban:** 97%. **Ethnic groups:** Fleming 55%, Walloon 33%. **Principal languages:** Flemish (Dutch) 56%, French 32%, German 1% (all official). **Chief religions:** Roman Catholic 75%, Protestant and other 25%.

Geography: Area: 11,780 sq. mi. **Location:** In W Europe, on North Sea. **Neighbors:** France on W and S, Luxembourg on SE, Germany on E, Netherlands on N. **Topography:** Mostly flat, the country is trisected by the Scheldt and Meuse, major commercial rivers. The land becomes hilly and forested in the SE (Ardennes) region. **Capital:** Brussels. **Cities** (1995 met. est.): Antwerp 1,628,710; Ghent 1,349,382; Brussels 951,580.

Government: Type: Parliamentary democracy under a constitutional monarch. **Head of state:** King Albert II; b June 6, 1934; in office: Aug. 9, 1993. **Head of government:** Premier Jean-Luc Dehaene; b Aug. 7, 1940; in office: Mar. 7, 1992. **Local divisions:** 10 provinces and Brussels. **Defense:** 1.6% of GDP. **Active troop strength:** 46,300.

Economy: Industries: Metal products, glassware, autos, textiles, chemicals. **Chief crops:** Wheat, fruits, sugar beets, potatoes. **Minerals:** Coal, gas. **Arable land:** 24%. **Livestock** (1997): chickens: 43.00 mil; pigs: 7.05 mil; cattle: 3.28 mil; sheep: 121,000. **Fish catch** (1996): 30,823 metric tons. **Electricity prod.** (1996): 71.1 bil kWh. **Labor force:** 70% services; 27% industry; 3% agric.

Finance: Monetary unit: Franc (Sept. 1998: 35.74 = $1 U.S.). **Gross domestic product** (1996 est.): $204.8 bil. **Per capita GDP** $20,300. *Note:* Import/Export data include Luxembourg. **Imports** (1994): $140 bil; partners: EU 68%, U.S. 9%. **Exports** (1994): $108 bil; partners: EU 67%, U.S. 6%. **Tourism:** $5.99 bil. **National budget** (1994): $69.36 bil. **International reserves less gold** (June 1998): $19.74 bil. **Gold:** 7.62 mil oz t. **Consumer prices** (change in 1997): 1.6%.

Transport: Railroad: Length: 2,108.9 mi. **Motor vehicles in use:** 4.31 mil passenger cars, 530,627 comm. vehicles. **Civil aviation:** 5.60 bil passenger-mi; 2 airports. **Chief ports:** Antwerp, Zeebrugge, Ghent.

Communications: Television sets: 464 per 1,000 pop. **Radios:** 757 per 1,000 pop. **Telephones:** 4,725,496 main lines. **Daily newspaper circ.:** 304 per 1,000 pop.

Health: Life expectancy at birth: 74.1 male; 80.7 female. **Births** (per 1,000 pop.): 10. **Deaths** (per 1,000 pop.): 10. **Natural increase:** –0.02%. **Hospital beds** (1994): 1 per 131 persons. **Physicians** (1996): 1 per 264 persons. **Infant mortality** (per 1,000 live births): 6.

Education: Compulsory: ages 6-18. **Literacy** (1995): 99%.

Major International Organizations: UN and all of its specialized agencies, EU, NATO, OECD, OSCE.

Embassy: 3330 Garfield St. NW 20008; 333-6900.

Website: http://belgium.fgov.be

Belgium derives its name from the Belgae, the first recorded inhabitants, probably Celts. The land was conquered by Julius Caesar, and was ruled for 1800 years by conquerors, including Rome, the Franks, Burgundy, Spain, Austria, and France. After 1815, Belgium was made a part of the Netherlands, but it became an independent constitutional monarchy in 1830.

Belgian neutrality was violated by Germany in both world wars. King Leopold III surrendered to Germany, May 28, 1940. After the war, he was forced by political pressure to abdicate in favor of his son, King Baudouin. Baudouin was succeeded by his brother, Albert II, Aug. 9, 1993.

The Flemings of northern Belgium speak Dutch, while French is the language of the Walloons in the south. The language difference has been a perennial source of controversy and led to antagonism between the 2 groups. Parliament has passed measures aimed at transferring power from the central government to 3 regions—Wallonia, Flanders, and Brussels. Constitutional changes in 1993 made Belgium a federal state.

Belize

People: Population: 230,160. **Age distrib.** (%): <15: 42.2; 65+: 3.6. **Pop. density:** 26 per sq. mi. **Urban:** 46%. **Ethnic groups:** Mestizo 44%, Creole 30%, Maya 11%, Garifuna 7%. **Principal languages:** English (official), Spanish, Mayan, Garifuna (Carib). **Chief religions:** Roman Catholic 62%, Protestant 30%.

Geography: Area: 8,865 sq. mi. **Location:** Eastern coast of Central America. **Neighbors:** Mexico on N, Guatemala on W and S. **Capital:** Belmopan (1996 est.): 6,490.

Government: Type: Parliamentary democracy. **Head of state:** Queen Elizabeth II, represented by Gov.-Gen. Colville Young; b Nov. 20, 1932; in office: Nov. 17, 1993. **Head of government:** Prime Min. Manuel Esquivel; b May 2, 1940; in office: July 2, 1993. **Local divisions:** 6 districts. **Defense:** 2.5% of GDP. **Active troop strength:** 1,100.

Economy: Industries: Garments, food processing, tourism. **Chief crops:** Sugar (main export), citrus, bananas. **Arable land:** 2%. **Livestock** (1997): chickens: 1.30 mil. **Electricity prod.** (1996): 145 mil kWh.

Finance: Monetary unit: Dollar (Sept. 1998: 2.00 = $1 U.S.). **Gross domestic product** (1996 est.): $649 mil. **Per capita GDP:** $2,960. **Imports** (1996): $264 mil; partners: U.S. 53%. **Exports** (1996): $204 mil; partners: U.S. 38%. **Tourism:** $88 mil. **National budget** (FY1996-97): $180 mil. **International reserves less gold** (June 1998): $67.60 mil. **Consumer prices** (change in 1997): 1.0%.

Transport: Motor vehicles in use: 2,300 passenger cars, 3,100 comm. vehicles. **Chief ports:** Belize City, Big Creek. **Civil aviation:** 9 airports.

Communications: Television sets: 109 per 1,000 pop. **Radios:** 133 per 1,000 pop. **Telephones:** 29,600 main lines.

Health: Life expectancy at birth: 67.0 male; 71.0 female. **Births** (per 1,000 pop.): 31. **Deaths** (per 1,000 pop.): 6. **Natural increase:** 2.56%. **Hospital beds** (1993): 1 per 350 persons. **Physicians** (1995): 1 per 1,546 persons. **Infant mortality** (per 1,000 live births): 32.

Education: Compulsory: ages 5-14. **Literacy** (1993): 93%.
Major International Organizations: UN (FAO, IBRD, ILO, IMF, IMO, WHO, WTrO), Caricom, the Commonwealth, OAS.
Embassy: 2535 Massachusetts Ave. NW 20008; 332-9636.
Website: http://www.belize.gov.bz/bis.htm

Belize (formerly British Honduras) was Britain's last colony on the American mainland; independence was achieved Sept. 21, 1981. Relations with neighboring Guatemala, initially tense, have improved in recent years. Belize has become a center for drug trafficking between Colombia and the U.S.

Benin

Republic of Benin

People: Population: 6,100,799. **Age distrib.** (%): <15: 47.9; 65+: 2.3. **Pop. density:** 140 per sq. mi. **Urban:** 39%. **Ethnic groups:** African (Fon, Adja, Bariba, Yoruba) 99%. **Principal languages:** French (official), Fon, Yoruba. **Chief religions:** Indigenous beliefs 70%, Muslim 15%, Christian 15%.
Geography: Area: 43,483 sq. mi. **Location:** In W Africa on Gulf of Guinea. **Neighbors:** Togo on W; Burkina Faso, Niger on N; Nigeria on E. **Topography:** Most of Benin is flat and covered with dense vegetation. The coast is hot, humid, and rainy. **Capital:** Porto-Novo. **Cities** (1994 est.): Cotonou 750,000, Porto-Novo 200,000.
Government: Type: Republic. **Head of state:** Pres. Mathieu Kerekou; b Sept. 2, 1933; in office: Apr. 4, 1996. **Local divisions:** 12 departments. **Defense:** 1.4% of GDP. **Active troop strength:** 4,800.
Economy: Chief crops: Palm oil, cassava, peanuts, cotton, corn, rice. **Minerals:** Oil, limestone, marble. **Crude oil reserves** (1997): 6.2 mil bbls. **Arable land:** 13%. **Livestock** (1997): cattle: 1.40 mil; chickens: 27.00 mil; goats: 1.02 mil; pigs: 600,000; sheep: 605,000. **Fish catch** (1996): 42,000 metric tons. **Electricity prod.** (1996): 6 mil kWh. **Labor force:** 55% agric.; 29% transport, commerce, public services.
Finance: Monetary unit: CFA Franc (Sept. 1998: 580.94 = $1 U.S.). **Gross domestic product** (1996 est.): $8.2 bil. **Per capita GDP:** $1,440. **Imports** (1995): $380 mil; partners: France 27%, Thailand 9%. **Exports** (1995): $300 mil; partners: Brazil 18%, Portugal 14%. **Tourism:** $29 mil. **National budget** (1993 est.): $375 mil. **International reserves less gold** (Mar. 1998): $258.8 mil. **Consumer prices** (change in 1997): 3.5%.
Transport: Railroad: Length: 358.9 mi. **Motor vehicles in use:** 35,600 passenger cars, 19,300 comm. vehicles. **Civil aviation:** 139.6 mil passenger-mi; 1 airport. **Chief port:** Cotonou.
Communications: Television sets: 4 per 1,000 pop. **Radios:** 73 per 1,000 pop. **Telephones:** 32,679 main lines. **Daily newspaper circ.:** 2 per 1,000 pop.
Health: Life expectancy at birth: 51.6 male; 55.7 female. **Births** (per 1,000 pop.): 46. **Deaths** (per 1,000 pop.): 13. **Natural increase:** 3.31%. **Hospital beds** (1993): 1 per 4,182 persons. **Physicians** (1993): 1 per 14,216 persons. **Infant mortality** (per 1,000 live births): 100.
Education: Free and compulsory: ages 6-12. **Literacy:** 37%.
Major International Organizations: UN (FAO, IBRD, ILO, IMF, IMO, WHO, WTrO), OAU.
Embassy: 2737 Cathedral Ave. NW 20008; 232-6656.

The Kingdom of Abomey, rising to power in wars with neighboring kingdoms in the 17th century, came under French domination in the late 19th century and was incorporated into French West Africa by 1904.

Under the name Dahomey, the country gained independence Aug. 1, 1960; it became Benin in 1975. In the fifth coup since independence Col. Ahmed Kerekou took power in 1972; two years later he declared a socialist state with a "Marxist-Leninist" philosophy. In Dec. 1989, Kerekou announced Marxism-Leninism would no longer be the state ideology.

In Mar. 1991, Kerekou lost to Nicéphore Soglo in Benin's first free presidential election in 30 years. Kerekou defeated Soglo in Mar. 1996 to reclaim the presidency.

Bhutan

Kingdom of Bhutan

People: Population: 1,908,307. **Age distrib.** (%): <15: 40.1; 65+: 3.9. **Pop. density:** 105 per sq. mi. **Urban:** 6%. **Ethnic groups:** Bhote 50%, Nepalese 35%. **Principal languages:** Dzongkha (official), Tibetan, Nepalese dialects. **Chief religions:** Lamaistic Buddhist (state religion) 75%, Hindu 25%.
Geography: Area: 18,147 sq. mi. **Location:** S Asia, in eastern Himalayan Mts. **Neighbors:** India on W (Sikkim) and S, China on N. **Topography:** Bhutan is comprised of very high mountains in the N, fertile valleys in the center, and thick forests in the Duar Plain in the S. **Capital:** Thimphu (1993 est.): 30,300.
Government: Type: Monarchy. **Head of state:** King Jigme Singye Wangchuk; b Nov. 11, 1955; in office: July 21, 1972. **Local divisions:** 18 districts.
Economy: Industries: Cement, wood products. **Chief crops:** Rice, corn, citrus. **Other resources:** Timber, hydropower. **Livestock** (1997): cattle: 435,000; chickens: 310,000. **Arable land:** 2%. **Electricity prod.** (1996): 1.7 bil kWh. **Labor force:** 93% agric.; 5% services.
Finance: Monetary unit: Ngultrum (Sept. 1998: 42.52 = $1 U.S.; Indian Rupee also used). **Gross domestic product** (1995 est.): $1.3 bil. **Per capita GDP:** $730. **Tourism** (1994): 4.0 mil. **Imports** (FY 1994-95 est.): $113.6 mil; partners: India 77%. **Exports** (FY 1994-95 est.): $70.9 mil; partners: India 94%. **Tourism:** $6 mil. **National budget** (FY 1993-94): $150 mil. **International reserves less gold** (Jan. 1998): $190.94 mil. **Consumer prices** (change in 1997): 7.4%.
Transport: Civil aviation: 28.6 mil passenger-mi; 1 airport.
Communications: Radios: 27 per 1,000 pop. **Telephones:** 6,074 main lines.
Health: Life expectancy at birth: 52.8 male; 51.8 female. **Births** (per 1,000 pop.): 37. **Deaths** (per 1,000 pop.): 15. **Natural increase:** 2.27%. **Hospital beds** (1994): 1 per 825 persons. **Physicians** (1994): 1 per 8,000 persons. **Infant mortality** (per 1,000 live births): 112.
Education: Not compulsory. **Literacy:** 42%.
Major International Organizations: UN (FAO, IBRD, IMF, WHO).
Website: http://www.bhutan.org

The region came under Tibetan rule in the 16th century. British influence grew in the 19th century. A monarchy, set up in 1907, became a British protectorate by a 1910 treaty. The country became independent in 1949, with India guiding foreign relations and supplying aid. Most of the population engages in subsistence agriculture.

Bolivia

Republic of Bolivia

People: Population: 7,826,352. **Age distrib.** (%): <15: 39.4; 65+: 4.5. **Pop. density:** 18 per sq. mi. **Urban:** 61%. **Ethnic groups:** Quechua 30%, mestizo 25-30%, Aymara 25%, European 5-15%. **Principal languages:** Spanish, Quechua, Aymara (all official). **Chief religion:** Roman Catholic 95%.
Geography: Area: 424,162 sq. mi. **Location:** In W central South America, in the Andes Mts. (one of 2 landlocked countries in South America). **Neighbors:** Peru and Chile on W, Argentina and Paraguay on S, Brazil on E and N. **Topography:** The great central plateau, at an altitude of 12,000 ft., over 500 mi. long, lies between two great cordilleras having 3 of the highest peaks in South America. Lake Titicaca, on Peruvian border, is highest lake in world on which steamboats ply (12,506 ft.). The E central region has semitropical forests; the llanos, or Amazon-Chaco lowlands are in E. **Capitals:** La Paz (administrative), Sucre (judicial). **Cities:** La Paz 1,250,000; Santa Cruz 850,000*.
Government: Type: Republic. **Head of state:** Pres. Hugo Banzer Suárez; b May 10, 1926; in office: Aug. 6, 1997. **Local divisions:** 9 departments. **Defense:** 2.1% of GDP. **Active troop strength:** 33,500.
Economy: Industries: Mining, smelting, tobacco, handicrafts, clothing. **Chief crops:** Coffee, sugarcane, potatoes, cotton, corn, coca. **Minerals:** Antimony, tin, tungsten, silver, zinc, oil, gas, iron. **Crude oil reserves** (1997): 132 mil bbls. **Other resources:** Timber. **Arable land:** 2%. **Livestock** (1997): chickens: 65.00 mil; sheep: 8.23 mil; cattle: 6.24 mil; pigs: 2.57 mil; goats: 1.50 mil. **Electricity prod.** (1996): 3 bil kWh.
Finance: Monetary unit: Boliviano (Sept. 1998: 5.55 = $1 U.S.). **Gross domestic product** (1996 est.): $21.5 bil. **Per capita GDP:** $3,000. **Imports** (1995): $1.4 bil; partners: U.S. 18%. **Exports** (1995): $1.1 bil; partners: U.S. 26% Argentina 17%, UK 15%. **Tourism:** $180 mil. **National budget** (1995 est.): $3.75 bil. **International reserves less gold** (June 1998): $977.9 mil. **Gold:** 939,000 oz t. **Consumer prices** (change in 1997): 4.7%.
Transport: Railroad: Length: 2,292.1 mi. **Motor vehicles in use:** 199,309 passenger cars, 230,245 comm. vehicles. **Civil aviation:** 1.01 bil passenger-mi; 14 airports.
Communications: Television sets: 202 per 1,000 pop. **Radios:** 560 per 1,000 pop. **Telephones:** 327,570 main lines. **Daily newspaper circ.:** 69 per 1,000 pop.
Health: Life expectancy at birth: 58.0 male; 63.9 female. **Births** (per 1,000 pop.): 31. **Deaths** (per 1,000 pop.): 10. **Natural increase:** 2.15%. **Hospital beds** (1994): 1 per 1,005 persons. **Physicians** (1994): 1 per 3,663 persons. **Infant mortality** (per 1,000 live births): 64.

Education: Free and compulsory: ages 6-14. **Literacy:** 83%.
Major International Organizations: UN (FAO, IBRD, ILO, IMF, IMO, WHO, WTrO), OAS.
Embassy: 3014 Massachusetts Ave. NW 20008; 483-4410.
Website: http:/www.ine.gov.bo

The Incas conquered the region from earlier Indian inhabitants in the 13th century. Spanish rule began in the 1530s and lasted until Aug. 6, 1825. The country is named after Simon Bolivar, independence fighter.

In a series of wars, Bolivia lost its Pacific coast to Chile, the oil-bearing Chaco to Paraguay, and rubber-growing areas to Brazil, 1879-1935.

Economic unrest, especially among the militant mine workers, has contributed to continuing political instability. A reformist government under Victor Paz Estenssoro, 1951-64, nationalized tin mines and attempted to improve conditions for the Indian majority but was overthrown by a military junta. A long series of coups and countercoups continued until constitutional government was restored in 1982.

U.S. pressure on the government to reduce the country's output of coca, the raw material for cocaine, has led to clashes between police and coca growers and increased anti-U.S. feeling among Bolivians. Gen. Hugo Banzer Suárez, who ruled as a dictator, 1971-78, became president in Aug. 1997. More than 80 people were killed in earthquakes near Aiquile May 22, 1998.

Bosnia and Herzegovina

Republic of Bosnia and Herzegovina

People: Population: 3,365,727. **Age distrib.** (%): <15: 17.8; 65+: 11.7. **Pop. density:** 170 per sq. mi. **Urban:** 42%. **Ethnic groups:** Serb 40%, Muslim 38%, Croat 22%. **Principal language:** Serbo-Croatian (official) 99%. **Chief religions:** Muslim 40%, Orthodox 31%, Catholic 15%.
Geography: Area: 19,781 sq. mi. **Location:** On Balkan Peninsula in SE Europe. **Neighbors:** Yugoslavia on E and SE, Croatia on N and W. **Topography:** Hilly with some mountains. About 36% of the land is forested. **Capital:** Sarajevo (1993 est.): 300,000.
Government: Type: Republic. **Heads of state:** Collective Pres., Alija Izetbegovic (Muslim), b Aug. 8, 1925; Zivko Radisic (Serb); Ante Jelavic (Croat); elected: Sept. 12-13, 1998. **Local divisions:** Muslim-Croat Federation, divided into 10 cantons; Republika Srpska. **Defense**: 6.3% of GDP. **Active troop strength:** 92,000.
Economy: Industries: Steel, mining, textiles, timber. **Chief crops:** Corn, wheat, fruits, vegetables. **Minerals:** Bauxite, iron, coal. **Arable land:** 14%. **Livestock** (1997): chickens: 3.87 mil; sheep: 275,600; cattle: 260,000. **Electricity prod.** (1996): 2.3 bil kWh.
Finance: Monetary unit: Yugoslav New Dinar (Sept. 1998: 10.50 = $1 U.S.). **Gross domestic product** (1995 est.): $1.9 bil. **Per capita GDP:** $600. **Imports** (1996): $1.88 bil; partners: Croatia 32%. **Exports** (1996): $171 mil; partners: Croatia 34%, Italy 26%. **Tourism:** $15 mil.
Communications: Television sets: 94 per 1,000 pop. **Telephones:** 325,975 main lines. **Daily newspaper circ.:** 150 per 1,000 pop.
Transport: Railroad: Length: 344 mi. **Chief port:** Bosanski Brod. **Civil aviation:** 1 airport.
Health: Life expectancy at birth: 58.4 male; 68.0 female. **Births** (per 1,000 pop.): 9. **Deaths** (per 1,000 pop.): 12. **Natural increase:** –0.36%. **Physicians** (1996): 1 per 703 persons. **Infant mortality** (per 1,000 live births): 31.
Education: Free and compulsory: ages 7-15. **Literacy** (1991): 86%.
Major International Organizations: UN (FAO, IBRD, ILO, IMF, IMO, WHO), OSCE.
Embassy: 1707 L St. NW, Suite 760, 20036; 833-3612.
Website: http://www.bosnianembassy.org

Bosnia was ruled by Croatian kings c. AD 958, and by Hungary 1000-1200. It became organized c. 1200 and later took control of Herzegovina. The kingdom disintegrated from 1391, with the southern part becoming the independent duchy Herzegovina. It was conquered by Turks in 1463 and made a Turkish province. The area was placed under control of Austria-Hungary in 1878, and made part of the province of **Bosnia and Herzegovina,** which was formally annexed to Austria-Hungary 1908; Bosnia became a province of Yugoslavia in 1918. It was reunited with Herzegovina as a federated republic in the 1946 Yugoslavian constitution.

Bosnia and Herzegovina declared sovereignty Oct. 15, 1991. A referendum for independence was passed Feb. 29, 1992. Ethnic Serbs' opposition to the referendum spurred violent clashes and bombings. The U.S. and EU recognized the republic Apr. 7. Fierce three-way fighting continued between Bosnia's Serbs, Muslims, and Croats. Serb forces massacred thousands of Bosnian Muslims and engaged in "ethnic cleansing" (the expulsion of Muslims and other non-Serbs from areas under Bosnian Serb control). The capital, Sarajevo, was surrounded and besieged by Bosnian Serb forces. Muslims and Croats in Bosnia reached a cease fire Feb. 23, 1994, and signed an accord, Mar. 18, to create a Muslim-Croat confederation in Bosnia. However, by mid-1994, Bosnian Serbs controlled over 70% of the country.

As fighting continued in 1995, the balance of power began to shift toward the Muslim-Croat alliance. Massive NATO air strikes at Bosnian Serb targets beginning Aug. 30 triggered a new round of peace talks, and the siege of Sarajevo was lifted Sept. 15. The new talks produced an agreement in principle to create autonomous regions within Bosnia, with the Serb region (Republika Srpska) constituting 49% of the country. A Croat-Muslim offensive in Sept. recaptured significant territory, leaving the Bosnian Serbs in control of approximately that percentage.

A peace agreement initialed in Dayton, Ohio, Nov. 21, 1995, was signed in Paris, Dec. 14, by leaders of Bosnia, Croatia, and Serbia. Some 60,000 NATO troops (about 20,000 from the U.S.) moved in to police the accord. Meanwhile, a UN tribunal began bringing charges against suspected war criminals. Elections were held Sept. 14, 1996, for a 3-person collective presidency, for seats in a federal parliament, and for regional offices. In Dec. a revamped NATO "stabilization force" of some 30,000 members (more than 8,000 from the U.S.) received an 18-month mandate, which was later extended. A hardline Serb nationalist, Nikola Poplasen, was elected president of the Republika Srpska, Sept. 12-13, 1998, defeating the U.S.-backed Biljana Plavsic.

Botswana

Republic of Botswana

People: Population: 1,448,454. **Age distrib.** (%): <15: 42.3; 65+: 3.8. **Pop. density:** 6 per sq. mi. **Urban:** 63%. **Ethnic groups:** Batswana 95%, Kalanga, Basarwa, Kgalagadi. **Principal languages:** English (official), Setswana. **Chief religions:** Indigenous beliefs 50%, Christian 50%.
Geography: Area: 224,607 sq. mi. **Location:** In southern Africa. **Neighbors:** Namibia on N and W, South Africa on S, Zimbabwe on NE; Botswana claims border with Zambia on N. **Topography:** The Kalahari Desert, supporting nomadic Bushmen and wildlife, spreads over SW; there are swamplands and farming areas in N, and rolling plains in E where livestock are grazed. **Capital:** Gaborone (1995 est.): 182,000.
Government: Type: Parliamentary republic. **Head of state:** Pres. Festus Mogae; b Aug. 21, 1939; in office: Apr. 1, 1998. **Local divisions:** 10 districts, 4 town councils. **Defense:** 6.7% of GDP. **Active troop strength:** 7,500.
Economy: Industries: Livestock processing, mining, tourism. **Chief crops:** Maize, sorghum, millet, pulses, beans. **Minerals:** Copper, coal, nickel, diamonds salt, silver. **Arable land:** 1%. **Livestock** (1997): chickens: 1.40 mil; cattle: 2.30 mil; goats: 1.85 mil; sheep: 240,000. **Electricity prod.** (1996): 990 mil kWh. **Labor force:** 22% agric.; 19% manuf. & constr.; 16% serv.
Finance: Monetary unit: Pula (Sept. 1998: 4.67 = $1 U.S.). **Gross domestic product** (1996 est.): $4.6 bil. **Per capita GDP:** $3,100. **Imports** (1995 est.): $1.5 bil. **Exports** (1995 est.): $2.1 bil. **Tourism:** $181 mil. **National budget** (FY 1995-96): $1.9 bil. **International reserves less gold** (Mar. 1997): $5.37 bil. **Consumer prices** (change in 1997): 9.3%.
Transport: Railroad: Length: 603 mi. **Motor vehicles in use:** 80,000 passenger cars, 19,869 comm. vehicles. **Civil aviation:** 30.0 mil passenger-mi; 4 airports.
Communications: Television sets: 24 per 1,000 pop. **Radios:** 821 per 1,000 pop. **Telephones:** 72,189 main lines. **Daily newspaper circ.:** 29 per 1,000 pop.
Health: Life expectancy at birth: 39.5 male; 40.8 female. **Births** (1,000 pop.): 32. **Deaths** (per 1,000 pop.): 21. **Natural increase:** 1.11%. **Hospital beds** (1993): 1 per 434 persons. **Physicians** (1994): 1 per 4,395 persons. **Infant mortality** (per 1,000 live births): 59.
Education: Not compulsory. **Literacy:** 70%.
Major International Organizations: UN (FAO, IBRD, ILO, IMF, WHO, WTrO), the Commonwealth, OAU.
Embassy: 3400 International Dr. NW, Suite 7M, 20008; 244-4990.

First inhabited by bushmen, then Bantus, the region became the British protectorate of Bechuanaland in 1886, halting encroachment by Boers and Germans from the south and southwest. The country became fully independent Sept. 30, 1966, as Botswana. Cattle raising and mining (diamonds, copper, nickel) have contributed to economic growth; economy is closely tied to South Africa.

Brazil

Federative Republic of Brazil

People: Population: 169,806,557. **Age distrib.** (%): <15: 30.2; 65+: 5.1. **Pop. density:** 52 per sq. mi. **Urban:** 79%. **Ethnic groups:** White (incl. Portuguese, German, Italian, Spanish, Polish) 55%, mixed black and white 38%, black 6%. **Principal languages:** Portuguese (official), Spanish, English, French. **Chief religion:** Roman Catholic 70%.

Geography: Area: 3,286,470 sq. mi., largest country in South America. **Location:** Occupies E half of South America. **Neighbors:** French Guiana, Suriname, Guyana, Venezuela on N; Colombia, Peru, Bolivia, Paraguay, Argentina on W; Uruguay on S. **Topography:** Brazil's Atlantic coastline stretches 4,603 miles. In N is the heavily wooded Amazon basin covering half the country. Its network of rivers is navigable for 15,814 mi. The Amazon itself flows 2,093 miles in Brazil, all navigable. The NE region is semiarid scrubland, heavily settled and poor. The S central region, favored by climate and resources, has almost half of the population, produces 75% of farm goods and 80% of industrial output. The narrow coastal belt includes most of the major cities. Almost the entire country has a tropical or semitropical climate. **Capital:** Brasília. **Cities:** São Paulo 16,533,000; Rio de Janeiro 10,181,000; Belo Horizonte 3,775,000*.

Government: Type: Federal republic. **Head of state:** Pres. Fernando Henrique Cardoso; b June 18, 1931; in office: Jan. 1, 1995. **Local divisions:** 26 states, 1 federal district (Brasília). **Defense:** 2.1% of GDP. **Active troop strength:** 295,000.

Economy: Industries: Steel, autos, textiles, shoes, chemicals, machinery. **Chief crops:** Coffee (leading grower), soybeans, sugarcane, cocoa, rice, corn, citrus. **Minerals:** Iron (largest producer in the world), manganese, phosphates, uranium, gold, nickel, tin, bauxite, oil. **Crude oil reserves** (1997): 4.8 bil bbls. **Arable land:** 5%. **Livestock** (1997): chickens: 970.00 mil; cattle: 163.00 mil; pigs: 36.90 mil; sheep: 18.00 mil; goats: 10.50 mil; buffalo: 1.70 mil. **Fish catch** (1996): 798,719 metric tons. **Electricity prod.** (1996): 285.7 bil kWh. **Labor force:** 56% services; 25% agric.; 19% ind.

Finance: Monetary unit: Real (Sept. 1998: 1.18 = $1 U.S.). **Gross domestic product** (1996 est.): $1.022 tril. **Per capita GDP:** $6,300. **Imports** (1996): $53.3 bil; partners: EU 26%,. U.S. 24%. **Exports** (1995): $46.5 bil; partners: EU 28%, U.S. 17%. **Tourism:** $2.60 bil. **National budget** (1995): $90 bil. **International reserves less gold** (May 1998): $71.38 bil. **Gold:** 3.12 mil oz t. **Consumer prices** (change in 1997): 6.9%.

Transport: Railroad: Length: 18,578 mi. **Motor vehicles in use:** 12.8 mil passenger cars, 3.26 mil comm. vehicles. **Civil aviation:** 23.40 bil passenger-mi; 139 airports. **Chief ports:** Santos, Rio de Janeiro, Vitoria, Salvador, Rio Grande, Recife.

Communications: Television sets: 193 per 1,000 pop. **Radios:** 348 per 1,000 pop. **Telephones:** 15,105,886 main lines. **Daily newspaper circ.:** 47 per 1,000 pop.

Health: Life expectancy at birth: 59.4 male; 69.6 female. **Births** (per 1,000 pop.): 21. **Deaths** (per 1,000 pop.): 9. **Natural increase:** 1.24%. **Hospital beds** (1993): 1 per 298 persons. **Physicians** (1993): 1 per 681 persons. **Infant mortality** (per 1,000 live births): 37.

Education: Free and compulsory: ages 7-14. **Literacy:** 83%.

Major International Organizations: UN and most of its specialized agencies, OAS.

Embassy: 3006 Massachusetts Ave. NW 20008; 238-2700.

Website: http://www.ibge.gov.br

Pedro Alvares Cabral, a Portuguese navigator, is generally credited as the first European to reach Brazil, in 1500. The country was thinly settled by various Indian tribes. Only a few have survived to the present, mostly in the Amazon basin.

In the next centuries, Portuguese colonists gradually pushed inland, bringing along large numbers of African slaves. (Slavery was not abolished until 1888.)

The King of Portugal, fleeing before Napoleon's army, moved the seat of government to Brazil in 1808. Brazil thereupon became a kingdom under Dom Joao VI. After his return to Portugal, his son Pedro proclaimed the independence of Brazil, Sept. 7, 1822, and was crowned emperor. The second emperor, Dom Pedro II, was deposed in 1889, and a republic proclaimed, called the United States of Brazil. In 1967 the country was renamed the Federative Republic of Brazil.

A military junta took control in 1930; dictatorial power was assumed by Getulio Vargas, until finally forced out by the military in 1945. A democratic regime prevailed 1945-64, during which time the capital was moved from Rio de Janeiro to Brasília. In 1964, Pres. Joao Belchoir Marques Goulart instituted economic policies that aggravated Brazil's inflation; he was overthrown by an army revolt. The next 5 presidents were all military leaders. Censorship was imposed, and much of the opposition was suppressed amid charges of torture.

Since 1930, successive governments have pursued industrial and agricultural growth and interior area development. Exploiting vast natural resources and a huge labor force, Brazil became the leading industrial power of Latin America by the 1970s, while agricultural output soared. By the 1990s, Brazil had one of the world's largest economies; income was poorly distributed, however, and more than one out of four Brazilians continued to survive on less than $1 a day. Despite protective environmental legislation, development has destroyed much of the Amazon ecosystem. Brazil hosted delegates from 178 countries at the Earth Summit, June 3-14, 1992.

Democratic presidential elections were held in 1985 as the nation returned to civilian rule. Fernando Collor de Mello was elected president in Dec. 1989. In Sept. 1992, Collor was impeached for corruption. He resigned on Dec. 29 as his trial was beginning, and Itamar Franco, who had been acting president, was sworn in as president. In elections held on Oct. 3, 1994, Fernando Henrique Cardoso was elected president.

He won reelection Oct. 4, 1998, as Brazil faced a financial crisis.

Brunei

State of Brunei Darussalam

People: Population: 315,292. **Age distrib.** (%): <15: 33.0; 65+: 4.4. **Pop. density:** 142 per sq. mi. **Urban:** 70%. **Ethnic groups:** Malay 64%, Chinese 20%. **Principal languages:** Malay (official), English, Chinese. **Chief religions:** Muslim (official) 63%, Buddhist 14%, Christian 8%.

Geography: Area: 2,228 sq. mi. **Location:** In SE Asia, on the N coast of the island of Borneo; it is surrounded on its landward side by the Malaysian state of Sarawak. **Capital:** Bandar Seri Begawan (1994 met. est.): 187,000.

Government: Type: Independent sultanate. **Head of government:** Sultan Sir Muda Hassanal Bolkiah Mu'izzadin Waddaulah; b July 15, 1946; in office: Jan. 1, 1984. **Local divisions:** 4 districts. **Defense:** 6.5% of GDP. **Active troop strength:** 5,000.

Economy: Industries: Oil & gas (more than 40% of GDP. is derived from oil and gas exports). **Chief crops:** Rice, bananas, cassava. **Crude oil reserves** (1997): 1.35 bil bbls. **Arable land:** 1%. **Livestock** (1997): chickens: 3.00 mil. **Electricity prod.** (1996): 1.5 bil kWh.

Finance: Monetary unit: Dollar (Sept. 1998: 1.76 = $1 U.S.). **Gross domestic product** (1995 est.): $4.6 bil. **Per capita GDP:** $15,800. **Imports** (1995 est.): $2 bil; partners: Singapore 29%, UK 1990. **Exports** (1995 est.): $2.7 bil. partners: Japan 50%, UK 19%. **National budget** (1995 est.): $2.6 bil. **Tourism:** $39 mil.

Transport: Railroad: Length: 12 mi. **Motor vehicles in use:** 146,000 passenger cars, 17,780 comm. vehicles. **Civil aviation:** 1.68 bil passenger-mi; 1 airport.

Communications: Television sets: 308 per 1,000 pop. **Radios:** 417 per 1,000 pop. **Telephones:** 78,794 main lines. **Daily newspaper circ.:** 70 per 1,000 pop.

Health: Life expectancy at birth: 70.2 male; 73.3 female. **Births** (per 1,000 pop.): 25. **Deaths** (per 1,000 pop.): 5. **Natural increase:** 1.98%. **Hospital beds** (1993): 1 per 285 persons. **Physicians** (1993): 1 per 1,398 persons. **Infant mortality** (per 1,000 live births): 23.

Education: Free and compulsory: ages 5-17. **Literacy:** 88%.

Major International Organizations: UN and some of its specialized agencies, APEC, ASEAN, the Commonwealth.

Embassy: 2600 Virginia Ave. NW, suite 300, 20037; 342-0159.

Website: http://brunet.bn

The Sultanate of Brunei was a powerful state in the early 16th century, with authority over all of the island of Borneo as well as parts of the Sulu Islands and the Philippines. In 1888, a treaty placed the state under the protection of Great Britain.

Brunei became a fully sovereign and independent state on Jan. 1, 1984.

Bulgaria

Republic of Bulgaria

People: Population: 8,240,426. **Age distrib.** (%): <15: 16.5; 65+: 115.9. **Pop. density:** 192 per sq. mi. **Urban:** 69%. **Ethnic groups:** Bulgarian 85%, Turk 9%. **Principal languages:** Bulgarian (official), Turkish. **Chief religions:** Bulgarian Orthodox 85%, Muslim 13%.

Geography: Area: 42,822 sq. mi. **Location:** SE Europe, in E Balkan Peninsula on Black Sea. **Neighbors:** Romania on N; Yugoslavia, Macedonia on W; Greece, Turkey on S. **Topography:** The Stara Planina (Balkan) Mts. stretch E-W across the center of the country, with the Danubian plain on N, the

Rhodope Mts. on SW, and Thracian Plain on SE. **Capital:** Sofia. **Cities** (1996 est.): Plovdiv 344,326; Sofia 1,116,823.

Government: Type: Republic. **Head of state:** Pres. Petar Stoyanov; b May 25, 1952; in office: Jan. 19, 1997. **Head of government:** Prime Min. Ivan Kostov; b Dec. 23, 1949; in office: May 21, 1997. **Local divisions:** 9 provinces. **Defense:** 3.3% of GDP. **Active troop strength:** 103,500.

Economy: Industries: Chemicals, machinery, metals, textiles, food processing. **Chief crops:** Grain, fruit, oilseed, vegetables, tobacco. **Minerals:** Bauxite, copper, zinc, lead, coal. **Crude oil reserves** (1997): 15 mil bbls. **Arable land:** 37%. **Livestock** (1997): chickens: 15.13 mil; sheep: 3.02 mil; pigs: 1.50 mil; goats: 874,000; cattle: 582,000. **Fish catch** (1996): 12,723 metric tons. **Electricity prod.** (1996): 41.6 bil kWh. **Labor force:** 41% ind.; 18% agric.

Finance: Monetary unit: Lev (Sept. 1998: 1726.78 = $1 U.S.). **Gross domestic product** (1996 est.): $39.9 bil. **Per capita GDP:** $4,630. **Imports** (1996): $4.1 bil; partners: OECD 46%, CIS 41%. **Exports** (1996 est.): $4.2 bil; partners: OECD 50%, CIS 32.4%. **Tourism:** $391 mil. **National budget** (1996 est.): $4.1 bil. **International reserves less gold** (June 1998): $2.67 bil. **Gold:** 1.03 mil oz t.

Transport: Railroad: Length: 4,043 mi. **Motor vehicles in use:** 1.65 mil passenger cars, 264,196 comm. vehicles. **Civil aviation:** 1.12 bil passenger-mi; 3 airports. **Chief ports:** Burgas, Varna.

Communications: Television sets: 359 per 1,000 pop. **Telephones:** 2,647,459 main lines. **Daily newspaper circ.:** 141 per 1,000 pop.

Health: Life expectancy at birth: 68.4 male; 75.7 female. **Births** (per 1,000 pop.): 8. **Deaths** (per 1,000 pop.): 13. **Natural increase:** –0.52%. **Hospital beds** (1995): 1 per 94 persons. **Physicians** (1995): 1 per 288 persons. **Infant mortality** (per 1,000 live births): 13.

Education: Free and compulsory: ages 6-16. **Literacy** (1995): 98%.

Major International Organizations: UN (FAO, IBRD, ILO, IMF, IMO, WHO, WTrO), OSCE.

Embassy: 1621 22d St. NW 20008; 387-7969.

Bulgaria was settled by Slavs in the 6th century. Turkic Bulgars arrived in the 7th century, merged with the Slavs, became Christians by the 9th century, and set up powerful empires in the 10th and 12th centuries. The Ottomans prevailed in 1396 and remained for 500 years.

A revolt in 1876 led to an independent kingdom in 1908. Bulgaria expanded after the first Balkan War but lost its Aegean coastline in World War I, when it sided with Germany. Bulgaria joined the Axis in World War II but withdrew in 1944. Communists took power with Soviet aid; the monarchy was abolished Sept. 8, 1946.

On Nov. 10, 1989, Communist Party leader and head of state Todor Zhivkov, who had held power for 35 years, resigned. Zhivkov was imprisoned, Jan. 1990, and convicted, Sept. 1992, of corruption and abuse of power. In Jan. 1990, Parliament voted to revoke the constitutionally guaranteed dominant role of the Communist Party. A new constitution took effect July 13, 1991. An economic austerity program was launched in May 1996. Former Prime Min. Andrei Lukanov, a longtime Communist leader, was assassinated Oct. 2 in Sofia. Petar Stoyanov won a presidential runoff election Nov. 3. Bulgaria's deteriorating economy provoked nationwide strikes and demonstrations in Jan. 1997. The Union of Democratic Forces, an anti-Communist group, won parliamentary elections on Apr. 19, 1997.

Burkina Faso

People: Population: 11,266,393. **Age distrib.** (%): <15: 48.0; 65+ 3.0. **Pop. density:** 106 per sq. mi. **Urban:** 16%. **Ethnic groups:** Mossi, Gurunsi, Senufo, Lobi, Bobo, Mande, Fulani. **Principal languages:** French (official), Sudanic tribal languages. **Chief religions:** Muslim 50%, indigenous beliefs 40%, Christian (mostly Roman Catholic) 10%.

Geography: Area: 105,869 sq. mi. **Location:** In W Africa, S of the Sahara. **Neighbors:** Mali on NW; Niger on NE; Benin, Togo, Ghana, Côte d'Ivoire on S. **Topography:** Landlocked Burkina Faso is in the savanna region of W Africa. The N is arid, hot, and thinly populated. **Capital:** Ouagadougou 824,000*.

Government: Type: Republic. **Head of state:** Pres. Blaise Compaoré; b 1951; in office: Oct. 15, 1987. **Local divisions:** 30 provinces. **Defense:** 2.4% of GDP. **Active troop strength:** 5,800.

Economy: Industries: Agricultural processing, beverages, soap, textiles. **Chief crops:** Millet, sorghum, rice, peanuts, cotton. **Minerals:** Manganese, limestone, marble. **Arable land:** 13%. **Livestock** (1997): chickens: 20.52 mil; goats: 7.91 mil; sheep: 6.21 mil; cattle: 4.52 mil; pigs: 586,600. **Electricity prod.** (1996): 220 mil kWh. **Labor force:** 80% agric.; 15% ind.

Finance: Monetary unit: CFA Franc (Sept. 1998: 580.94 = $1 U.S.). **Gross domestic product** (1996 est.): $8 bil. **Per capita GDP:** $740. **Imports** (1995 est.): $500 mil; partners: France 25%, Côte d'Ivôire 18%. **Exports** (1995 est.): $298 mil; partners: Côte d' Ivôire 35%, France 21%. **Tourism:** $391 mil. **National budget** (1992): $548 mil. **International reserves less gold** (Mar. 1998): $343.9 mil. **Gold:** 11,000 oz t. **Consumer prices** (change in 1997): 2.3%.

Transport: Railroad: Length: 386.3 mi. **Motor vehicles in use:** 35,460 passenger cars, 19,473 comm. vehicles. **Civil aviation:** 160.3 mil passenger-mi; 2 airports.

Communications: Television sets: 4.4 per 1,000 pop. **Radios:** 48.3 per 1,000 pop. **Telephones:** 34,055 main lines.

Health: Life expectancy at birth: 45.4 male; 46.9 female. **Births** (per 1,000 pop.): 46. **Deaths** (per 1,000 pop.): 18. **Natural increase:** 2.86%. **Hospital beds** (1991): 1 per 1,837 persons. **Physicians** (1991): 1 per 27,158 persons. **Infant mortality** (per 1,000 live births): 109.

Education: Free and compulsory: ages 7-14. **Literacy:** 19%.

Major International Organizations: UN and many of its specialized agencies, OAU.

Embassy: 2340 Massachusetts Ave. NW 20008; 332-5577.

The Mossi tribe entered the area in the 11th to 13th centuries. Their kingdoms ruled until defeated by the Mali and Songhai empires.

French control came by 1896, but Upper Volta (renamed Burkina Faso on Aug. 4, 1984) was not established as a separate territory until 1947. Full independence came Aug. 5, 1960, and a pro-French government was elected. The military seized power in 1980. A 1987 coup established the current regime, which instituted a multiparty democracy in the early 1990s.

Several hundred thousand farm workers migrate each year to Côte d'Ivoire and Ghana. Burkina Faso is heavily dependent on foreign aid.

Burma

(See Myanmar)

Burundi

Republic of Burundi

People: Population: 5,537,387. **Age distrib.** (%): <15: 47.4; 65+: 3.0. **Pop. density:** 515 per sq. mi. **Urban:** 8%. **Ethnic groups:** Hutu (Bantu) 85%, Tutsi 14%, Twa (Pygmy) 1%. **Principal languages:** Kirundi, French (both official), Swahili. **Chief religions:** Roman Catholic 62%, indigenous beliefs 32%, Protestant 5%.

Geography: Area: 10,745 sq. mi. **Location:** In central Africa. **Neighbors:** Rwanda on N, Dem. Rep. of the Congo (formerly Zaire) on W, Tanzania on E and S. **Topography:** Much of the country is grassy highland, with mountains reaching 8,900 ft. The southernmost source of the White Nile is located in Burundi. Lake Tanganyika is the second deepest lake in the world. **Capital:** Bujumbura (1994 est.): 300,000.

Government: Type: In transition. **Head of state:** Pres. Pierre Buyoya; b 1949; in office: July 25, 1996. **Head of government:** Prime Min. Pascal Firmin Ndimira; in office: July 31, 1996. **Local divisions:** 15 provinces. **Defense:** 4.1% of GDP. **Active troop strength:** 18,500.

Economy: Industries: Light consumer goods, food processing. **Chief crops:** Coffee (80% of exports), cotton, tea. **Minerals:** Nickel, uranium. **Arable land:** 44%. **Livestock** (1997): chickens: 4.00 mil; goats: 910,000; cattle: 400,000; sheep: 330,000. **Electricity prod.** (1996): 122 mil kWh. **Labor force:** 93% agric.

Finance: Monetary unit: Franc (Sept. 1998: 446.77 = $1 U.S.). **Gross domestic product** (1995 est.): $4 bil. **Per capita GDP:** $600. **Imports** (1995 est.): $234 mil; partners: EU 47%. **Exports** (1995 est.): $117 mil; partners: EU 60%, U.S. 17%. **Tourism:** $1 mil. **National budget** (1995 est.): $258 mil. **International reserves less gold** (June 1998): $87.57 mil. **Gold:** 17,000 oz t. **Consumer prices** (change in 1997): 31.1%.

Transport: Motor vehicles in use: 8,200 passenger cars, 11,800 comm. vehicles. **Civil aviation:** 1.2 mil passenger-mi; 1 airport. **Chief port:** Bujumbura.

Communications: Television sets: 7 per 1,000 pop. **Radios:** 50 per 1,000 pop. **Telephones:** 15,181 main lines.

Health: Life expectancy at birth: 43.8 male; 47.4 female. **Births** (per 1,000 pop.): 42. **Deaths** (per 1,000 pop.): 17. **Natural increase:** 2.42%. **Infant mortality** (per 1,000 live births): 101.

Education: Free and compulsory: ages 7-13. **Literacy:** 35%.

Major International Organizations: UN (FAO, IBRD, ILO, IMF, WHO, WTrO), OAU.
Embassy: 2233 Wisconsin Ave. NW 20007; 342-2574.

The pygmy Twa were the first inhabitants, followed by Bantu Hutus, who were conquered in the 16th century by the Tutsi (Watusi), probably from Ethiopia. Under German control in 1899, the area fell to Belgium in 1916, which exercised successively a League of Nations mandate and UN trusteeship over Ruanda-Urundi (now the two countries of Rwanda and Burundi). Burundi became independent July 1, 1962.

An unsuccessful Hutu rebellion in 1972-73 left 10,000 Tutsi and 150,000 Hutu dead. Over 100,000 Hutu fled to Tanzania and Zaire (now Congo). In the 1980s, Burundi's Tutsi-dominated regime pledged itself to ethnic reconciliation and democratic reform. In the nation's first democratic presidential election, in June 1993, a Hutu, Melchior Ndadaye, was elected. He was killed in an attempted coup, Oct. 21, 1993. At least 150,000 Burundians died as a result of ethnic conflict during the next three years. Pres. Cyprien Ntaryamira, elected Jan. 1994, was killed with the president of Rwanda in a mysterious plane crash, Apr. 6. The incident sparked massive carnage in Rwanda; violence in Burundi, initially far more limited, intensified in 1995. Ethnic strife continued after a military coup, July 25, 1996.

Cambodia

Kingdom of Cambodia

People: Population: 11,339,562. **Age distrib.** (%): <15: 45.4; 65+: 3.0. **Pop. density:** 162 per sq. mi. **Urban:** 21%. **Ethnic groups:** Khmer 90%, Vietnamese 5%, Chinese 1%. **Principal languages:** Khmer (official), French. **Chief religion:** Theravada Buddhism 95%.

Geography: Area: 69,900 sq. mi. **Location:** SE Asia, on Indochina Peninsula. **Neighbors:** Thailand on W and N, Laos on NE, Vietnam on E. **Topography:** The central area, formed by the Mekong R. basin and Tonle Sap lake, is level. Hills and mountains are in SE, a long escarpment separates the country from Thailand on NW. 76% of the area is forested. **Capital:** Phnom Penh (1994 est.): 920,000.

Government: Type: Constitutional monarchy. **Head of state:** King Norodom Sihanouk; b Oct. 31, 1922; in office: Sept. 24, 1993. **Head of government:** Co-Prime Mins. Hun Sen; b Apr. 4, 1952; in office: Sept. 24, 1993; Ung Huot; in office: Aug. 6, 1997. **Local divisions:** 22 provinces and 1 municipality. **Defense:** 5.7% of GDP. **Active troop strength:** 87,700.

Economy: Industries: Rice milling, wood & wood products, fishing. **Chief crops:** Rice, corn, rubber. **Minerals:** Gemstones, phosphates, manganese. **Other resources:** Timber. **Arable land:** 13%. **Livestock** (1997): chickens: 11.41 mil; cattle: 2.90 mil; pigs: 2.15 mil; buffalo: 770,000. **Fish catch** (1996): 94,710 metric tons. **Electricity prod.** (1996): 195 mil kWh. **Labor force:** 80% agric.

Finance: Monetary unit: Riel (Sept. 1998: 4,015.00 = $1 U.S.). **Gross domestic product** (1996 est.): $7.7 bil. **Per capita GDP:** $710. **Imports** (1996 est.): $1.4 bil. **Exports** (1996 est.): $464 mil. **Tourism:** $145 mil. **National budget** (1995 est.): $496 mil. **International reserves less gold** (June 1998): $284.87 mil. **Consumer prices** (change in 1997): 3.2%.

Transport: Railroad: Length: 374.5 mi. **Motor vehicles in use:** 15,000 passenger cars, 15,000 comm. vehicles. **Civil aviation:** 8 airports. **Chief port:** Kompong Som (Sihanoukville).

Communications: Television sets: 8 per 1,000 pop. **Radios:** 124 per 1,000 pop. **Telephones:** 8,054 main lines.

Health: Life expectancy at birth: 46.6 male; 49.4 female. **Births** (per 1,000 pop.): 42. **Deaths** (per 1,000 pop.): 16. **Natural increase:** 2.51%. **Physicians** (1994): 1 per 7,900 persons. **Infant mortality** (per 1,000 live births): 107.

Education: Compulsory: ages 6-12. **Literacy** (1993): 65%.
Major International Organizations: UN (FAO, IBRD, ILO, IMF, IMO, WHO).
Embassy: 4500 16th St. NW 20011; 726-7742.
Website: http://www.cambodia.org

Early kingdoms dating from that of Funan in the 1st century AD culminated in the great Khmer empire that flourished from the 9th century to the 13th, encompassing present-day Thailand, Cambodia, Laos, and southern Vietnam. The peripheral areas were lost to invading Siamese and Vietnamese, and France established a protectorate in 1863. Independence came in 1953.

Prince Norodom Sihanouk, king 1941-1955 and head of state from 1960, tried to maintain neutrality. Relations with the U.S. were broken in 1965, after South Vietnam planes attacked Vietcong forces within Cambodia. Relations were restored in 1969, after Sihanouk charged Viet Communists with arming Cambodian insurgents.

In 1970, pro-U.S. Prem. Lon Nol seized power, demanding removal of 40,000 North Viet troops; the monarchy was abolished. Sihanouk formed a government-in-exile in Beijing, and open war began between the government and the Communist Khmer Rouge guerrillas. The U.S. provided heavy military and economic aid.

Khmer Rouge forces captured Phnom Penh Apr. 17, 1975. The new government evacuated all cities and towns, and shuffled the rural population, sending virtually the entire population to clear jungle, forest, and scrub. Over one million people were killed in executions and enforced hardships.

Severe border fighting broke out with Vietnam in 1978 and developed into a full-fledged Vietnamese invasion. Formation of a Vietnamese-backed government was announced, Jan. 8, 1979, one day after the Vietnamese capture of Phnom Penh. Thousands of refugees flowed into Thailand, and widespread starvation was reported.

On Jan. 10, 1983, Vietnam launched an offensive against rebel forces in the west. They overran a refugee camp, Jan. 31, driving 30,000 residents into Thailand. In March, Vietnam launched a major offensive against camps on the Cambodian-Thailand border, engaged Khmer Rouge guerrillas, and crossed the border, instigating clashes with Thai troops. Vietnam withdrew nearly all its troops by Sept. 1989.

Following UN-sponsored elections in Cambodia that ended May 28, 1993, the 2 leading parties agreed to share power in an interim government until a new constitution was adopted. On Sept. 21, a constitution reestablishing a monarchy was adopted by the National Assembly. It took effect Sept. 24, with Sihanouk as king. The Khmer Rouge, which had boycotted the elections, opposed the new government, and armed violence continued in the mid-1990s. Ieng Sary, a Khmer Rouge leader, broke with the guerrillas, formed a rival group, and announced his support for the monarchy in Aug. 1996, as Khmer Rouge strength rapidly diminished.

Co-Prime Min. Hun Sen staged a coup July 5, 1997, ousting his rival, Prince Norodom Ranariddh. Pol Pot, the Khmer Rouge leader who held power during the late 1970s, was denounced by his former comrades at a show trial, July 25, and sentenced to house arrest; he died Apr. 15, 1998. Hun Sen's party won parliamentary elections on July 26.

Cameroon

Republic of Cameroon

People: Population: 15,029,433. **Age distrib.** (%): <15: 45.9; 65+: 3.3. **Pop. density:** 82 per sq. mi. **Urban:** 46%. **Ethnic groups:** Cameroon Highlander 31%, Equatorial Bantu 19%, Kirdi 11%, Fulani 10%, NW Bantu 8%. **Principal languages:** English, French (both official), numerous African groups. **Chief religions:** Indigenous beliefs 51%, Christian 33%, Muslim 16%.

Geography: Area: 183,567 sq. mi. **Location:** Between W and central Africa. **Neighbors:** Nigeria on NW; Chad, Central African Republic on E; Congo, Gabon, Equatorial Guinea on S. **Topography:** A low coastal plain with rain forests is in S; plateaus in center lead to forested mountains in W, including Mt. Cameroon, 13,350 ft.; grasslands in N lead to marshes around Lake Chad. **Capital:** Yaoundé. **Cities:** Douala 1,320,000; Yaoundé 1,119,000*.

Government: Type: Republic. **Head of state:** Pres. Paul Biya; b Feb. 13, 1933; in office: Nov. 6, 1982. **Head of government:** Prime Min. Peter Mafani Musonge; b Dec. 3, 1942; in office: Sept. 19, 1996. **Local divisions:** 10 provinces. **Defense:** 2.4% of GDP. **Active troop strength:** 13,100.

Economy: Industries: Oil production and refining, food processing, light consumer goods. **Chief crops:** Cocoa, coffee, cotton. **Crude oil reserves** (1997): 400 mil bbls. **Minerals:** Oil, bauxite, iron. **Other resources:** Timber. **Arable land:** 13%. **Livestock** (1997): chickens: 20.00 mil; cattle: 4.90 mil; sheep: 3.80 mil; goats: 3.80 mil; pigs: 1.41 mil. **Fish catch** (1996): 83,984 metric tons. **Electricity prod.** (1996): 2.7 bil kWh. **Labor force:** 74% agric.; 11% ind. & transport.

Finance: Monetary unit: CFA Franc (Sept. 1998: 580.94 = $1 U.S.). **Gross domestic product** (1996 est.): $17.5 bil. **Per capita GDP:** $1,230. **Imports** (1995): $1.3 bil; partners: France 42%. **Exports** (1995): $1.9 bil; partners: EU about 50%. **Tourism:** $39 mil. **National budget** (FY 1996-97 est.): $2.23 bil. **International reserves less gold** (Mar. 1998): $1.47 mil. **Gold:** 30,000 oz t. **Consumer prices** (change in 1997): 4.4%.

Transport: Railroad: Length: 685.6 mi. **Motor vehicles in use:** 92,200 passenger cars, 60,800 comm. vehicles. **Civil aviation:** 403.0 mil passenger-mi; 5 airports. **Chief port:** Douala, Kribi.

Communications: Television sets: 72 per 1,000 pop. **Radios:** 325 per 1,000 pop. **Telephones:** 70,558 main lines.

Health: Life expectancy at birth: 49.9 male; 53.0 female. **Births** (per 1,000 pop.): 42. **Deaths** (per 1,000 pop.): 14. **Natural increase:** 2.81%. **Infant mortality** (per 1,000 live births): 77.

Education: Free and compulsory: ages 6-12. **Literacy:** 63%.

Major International Organizations: UN (FAO, IBRD, ILO, IMF, IMO, WHO, WTrO), the Commonwealth, OAU.

Embassy: 2349 Massachusetts Ave. NW 20008; 265-8790.

Website: http://www.camnet.cm

Portuguese sailors were the first Europeans to reach Cameroon, in the 15th century. The European and American slave trade was very active in the area. German control lasted from 1884 to 1916, when France and Britain divided the territory, later receiving League of Nations mandates and UN trusteeships. French Cameroon became independent Jan. 1, 1960; one part of British Cameroon joined Nigeria in 1961, the other part joined Cameroon. Stability has allowed for development of roads, railways, agriculture, and petroleum production.

Pres. Paul Biya retained his office in Oct. 1992 elections, but the results were widely disputed. A new constitution won legislative approval in Dec. 1995. Fraud charges accompanied legislative elections, May 17, 1997, which Biya's party won.

Canada

People: Population: 30,675,398. **Age distrib.** (%): <15: 19.8; 65+: 12.5. **Pop. density:** 8 per sq. mi. **Urban:** 77%. **Ethnic groups:** British Isles 40%, French 27%, other European 20%, indigenous Indian and Eskimo 1.5%, other (mostly Asian) 11.5%. **Principal languages:** English, French (both official). **Chief religions:** Roman Catholic 45%, United Church 12%, Anglican 8%.

Geography: Area: 3,849,674 sq. mi., the largest country in land size in the western hemisphere. **Topography:** Canada stretches 3,426 miles from east to west and extends southward from the North Pole to the U.S. border. Its seacoast includes 36,356 miles of mainland and 115,133 miles of islands, including the Arctic islands almost from Greenland to near the Alaskan border. **Climate:** While generally temperate, varies from freezing winter cold to blistering summer heat. **Capital:** Ottawa. **Cities** (met. 1996 cen.): Toronto 4.3 mil; Montreal 3.3 mil; Vancouver 1.8 mil; Ottawa-Hull 1.0 mil; Edmonton 862,600; Calgary 821,600; Quebec 671,900; Winnipeg 667,200.

Government: Type: Confederation with parliamentary democracy. **Head of state:** Queen Elizabeth II, represented by Gov.-Gen. Roméo A. LeBlanc; b Dec. 18, 1927; in office: Feb. 8, 1995. **Head of government:** Prime Min. Jean Chrétien; b Jan. 11, 1934; in office: Nov. 4, 1993. **Local divisions:** 10 provinces, 2 territories. **Defense:** 1.5% of GDP. **Active troop strength:** 70,500.

Economy: Industries: Mining, wood and food prods., transport equip., chemicals, oil, gas. **Minerals:** Nickel, zinc, copper, gold, lead, molybdenum, potash, silver. **Crude oil reserves** (1997): 4.9 bil barrels. **Arable land:** 5%. **Livestock** (1997): chickens: 139.00 mil; cattle: 13.34 mil; pigs: 12.11 mil; sheep: 628,300. **Fish catch** (1996): 900,806 metric tons. **Electricity prod.** (1996): 549.2 bil kWh. **Labor force:** 74% services, 15% manufacturing, 3% agric.

Finance: Monetary unit: Dollar (Sept. 1998: 1.53 = $1 U.S.). **Gross domestic product** (1996 est.): $721 bil. **Per capita GDP:** $25,000. **Imports** (1996 est.): $169.5 bil; partners: U.S. 67%. **Exports** (1996 est.): $195.4 bil; partners: U.S. 82%. **Tourism:** $8.93 bil. **National budget** (FY 1995-96 est.): $115.2 bil. **International reserves less gold** (June 1998): $19.83 bil. **Gold:** 3.09 mil oz t. **Consumer prices** (change in 1997): 1.6%.

Transport: Railroad: Length: 44,182 mi. **Motor vehicles in use:** 13.3 mil passenger cars, 3.52 mil comm. vehicles. **Civil aviation:** 34.79 bil passenger-mi: 269 airports. **Chief ports:** Halifax, Montreal, Quebec, Saint John, Toronto, Vancouver.

Communications: Television sets: 647 per 1,000 pop. **Radios:** 919 per 1,000 pop. **Telephones:** 18,050,804 main lines. **Daily newspaper circ.:** 215 per 1,000 pop.

Health: Life expectancy at birth: 75.9 male; 82.6 female. **Births** (per 1,000 pop.): 12. **Deaths** (per 1,000 pop.): 7. **Natural increase:** 0.49%. **Hospital beds** (1993): 1 per 177 persons. **Physicians** (1994): 1 per 534 persons. **Infant mortality** (per 1,000 live births): 6.

Education: Compulsory primary education. **Literacy** (1994): 97%.

Major International Organizations: UN and all of its specialized agencies, APEC, the Commonwealth, NATO, OAS, OECD, OSCE.

Embassy: 501 Pennsylvania Ave. NW 20001; 682-1740.

Websites: http://www.statcan.ca
http://canada.gc.ca/main_e.html

French explorer Jacques Cartier, who reached the Gulf of St. Lawrence in 1534, is generally regarded as Canada's founder. But English seaman John Cabot sighted Newfoundland in 1497, and Vikings are believed to have reached the Atlantic coast centuries before either explorer.

Canadian settlement was pioneered by the French who established Quebec City (1608) and Montreal (1642) and declared New France a colony in 1663.

Britain acquired Acadia (later Nova Scotia) in 1717 and, through military victory over French forces in Canada, captured Quebec (1759) and obtained control of the rest of New France in 1763. The French, through the Quebec Act of 1774, retained the rights to their own language, religion, and civil law. The British presence in Canada increased during the American Revolution when many colonials, proudly calling themselves United Empire Loyalists, moved north to Canada. Fur traders and explorers led Canadians westward across the continent. Sir Alexander Mackenzie reached the Pacific in 1793 and scrawled on a rock by the ocean, "from Canada by land."

In Upper and Lower Canada (later called Ontario and Quebec) and in the Maritimes, legislative assemblies appeared in the 18th century and reformers called for responsible government. But the War of 1812 intervened. The war, a conflict between Great Britain and the United States fought mainly in Upper Canada, ended in a stalemate in 1814.

In 1837 political agitation for more democratic government culminated in rebellions in Upper and Lower Canada. Britain sent Lord Durham to investigate; in a famous report (1839), he recommended union of the 2 parts into one colony called Canada. The union lasted until Confederation, July 1, 1867, when proclamation of the British North America (BNA) Act (now known as the Constitution Act, 1867) launched the Dominion of Canada, consisting of Ontario, Quebec, and the former colonies of Nova Scotia and New Brunswick.

Since 1840 the Canadian colonies had held the right to internal self-government. The BNA Act, which was the basis for the country's written constitution, established a federal system of government on the model of a British parliament and cabinet structure under the crown. Canada was proclaimed a self-governing Dominion within the British Empire in 1931. With the ratification of the Constitution Act, 1982, Canada severed its last formal legislative link with Britain by obtaining the right to amend its constitution.

The so-called Meech Lake Agreement was signed (subject to provincial ratification) June 3, 1987. The accord would have assured constitutional protection for Quebec's efforts to preserve its French language and culture. Critics charged it did not make any provision for other minority groups and it gave Quebec too much power, which might enable Quebec to override the nation's 1982 Charter of Rights and Freedoms (an integral part of the constitution). The accord died June 22, 1990.

Its failure sparked a separatist revival in Quebec, which culminated in Aug. 1992 in the Charlottetown agreement. This called for changes to the constitution, such as recognition of Quebec as a "distinct society" within the Canadian confederation. It was defeated in a national referendum Oct. 26, 1992.

In May 1992 voters in the Northwest Territories approved the creation of a self-governing homeland for the 17,500 Inuit living there. The area—to be known as Nunavut, "Our Land"—would cover an area of 136,493 sq. mi. and take effect by 1999.

Canada became the first nation to ratify the North American Free Trade Agreement between Canada, Mexico, and the U.S. June 23, 1993. It went into effect Jan. 1, 1994.

On Feb. 24, 1993, Brian Mulroney resigned as prime minister after more than 8 years in office; he was succeeded by Kim Campbell. In elections Oct. 25, 1993, the ruling Conservatives were defeated in a landslide that left them only 2 of the 295 seats in the House of Commons. Jean Chrétien became prime minister. In a Quebec referendum held Oct. 30, 1995, proponents of secession lost by a razor-thin margin. The elections of June 2, 1997, left the Liberals with a slim majority.

On Jan. 7, 1998, the government apologized to native peoples for 150 years of mistreatment and pledged to set up a "healing fund." Canada's highest court ruled, Aug. 20, that Quebec cannot secede unilaterally, even if a majority of the province approves.

Provinces/Territories	Area (sq. mi.)	Population (1996 cen.)
Alberta	255,287	2,696,826
British Columbia	365,948	3,724,500
Manitoba	250,947	1,113,898
New Brunswick	28,355	738,133
Newfoundland	156,649	551,792
Nova Scotia	21,425	909,282
Ontario	412,581	10,753,573
Prince Edward Island	2,185	134,557
Quebec	594,860	7,138,795
Saskatchewan	251,866	990,237
Northwest Territories	1,322,910	64,402
Yukon Territory	186,661	30,766

Prime Ministers of Canada

Canada is a constitutional monarchy with a parliamentary system of government. It is also a federal state. Canada's official head of state, Queen Elizabeth II, is represented by a resident Governor-General. However, in practice the nation is governed by the Prime Minister, leader of the party that commands the support of a majority of the House of Commons, dominant chamber of Canada's bicameral Parliament.

Name	Party	Term
Sir John A. MacDonald	Conservative	1867-1873
Alexander Mackenzie	Liberal	1873-1878
Sir John A. MacDonald	Conservative	1878-1891
Sir John J. C. Abbott	Conservative	1891-1892
Sir John S. D. Thompson	Conservative	1892-1894
Sir Mackenzie Bowell	Conservative	1894-1896
Sir Charles Tupper	Conservative	1896[1]
Sir Wilfrid Laurier	Liberal	1896-1911
Sir Robert Laird Borden	Cons./Union.[2]	1911-1920
Arthur Meighen	Unionist	1920-1921
W. L. Mackenzie King	Liberal	1921-1926
Arthur Meighen	Conservative	1926[3]
W. L. Mackenzie King	Liberal	1926-1930
Richard Bedford Bennett	Conservative	1930-1935
W. L. Mackenzie King	Liberal	1935-1948
Louis St. Laurent	Liberal	1948-1957
John G. Diefenbaker	Prog. Cons.	1957-1963
Lester Bowles Pearson	Liberal	1963-1968
Pierre Elliott Trudeau	Liberal	1968-1979
Joe Clark	Prog. Cons.	1979-1980
Pierre Elliott Trudeau	Liberal	1980-1984
John Napier Turner	Liberal	1984[4]
Brian Mulroney	Prog. Cons.	1984-1993
Kim Campbell	Prog. Cons.	1993[5]
Jean Chrétien	Liberal	1993-

(1) May-July. (2) Conservative 1911-1917, Unionist 1917-1920. (3) June-Sept. (4) June-Sept. (5) June-Oct.

Cape Verde

Republic of Cape Verde

People: Population: 399,857. **Age distrib.** (%): <15: 45.7; 65+: 6.1. **Pop. density:** 257 per sq. mi. **Urban:** 56%. **Ethnic groups:** Creole (mulatto) 71%, African 28%, **Principal languages:** Portuguese (official), Crioulo. **Chief religion:** Roman Catholic 96%.

Geography: Area: 1,556 sq. mi. **Location:** In Atlantic O., off W tip of Africa. **Neighbors:** Nearest are Mauritania, Senegal to E. **Topography:** Cape Verde Islands are 15 in number, volcanic in origin (active crater on Fogo). The landscape is eroded and stark, with vegetation mostly in interior valleys. **Capital:** Praia (1995 est.): 68,000.

Government: Type: Republic. **Head of state:** Pres. Antonio Mascarenhas Monteiro; b Feb. 16, 1944; in office: Mar. 22, 1991. **Head of government:** Prime Min. Carlos Veiga; b 1949; in office: Apr. 4, 1991. **Local divisions:** 16 districts. **Defense:** 1.7% of GDP. **Active troop strength:** 1,100.

Economy: Chief crops: Bananas, coffee, sweet potatoes, corn, beans. **Minerals:** Salt. **Other resources:** Fish. **Arable land:** 11%. **Livestock** (1997): chickens: 430,000; pigs: 470,000; goats: 110,000. **Electricity prod.** (1996): 40 mil kWh.

Finance: Monetary unit: Escudo (Sept. 1998: 99.69 = $1 U.S.). **Gross domestic product** (1995 est.): $472 mil. **Per capita GDP:** $1,000. **Imports** (1995 est.): $211.8 mil; partners: Portugal 45%. **Exports** (1995 est.): $10 mil; partners: Portugal 50%. **Tourism:** $10 mil. **National budget** (FY1996-97 est.): $276 mil.

Transport: Motor vehicles in use: 11,000 passenger cars, 7,000 comm. vehicles. **Civil aviation:** 116.4 mil passenger-mi; 9 airports. **Chief ports:** Mindelo, Praia.

Communications: Television sets: 2.6 per 1,000 pop. **Radios:** 146 per 1,000 pop. **Telephones:** 25,232 main lines.

Health: Life expectancy at birth: 67.2 male; 73.9 female. **Births** (per 1,000 pop.): 34. **Deaths** (per 1,000 pop.): 7. **Natural increase:** 2.74%. **Infant mortality** (per 1,000 live births): 48.

Education: Compulsory: ages 7-11. **Literacy:** 72%.

Major International Organizations: UN (FAO, IBRD, ILO, IMF, IMO, WHO), OAU.

Embassy: 3415 Massachusetts Ave. NW 20007; 965-6820.

The uninhabited Cape Verdes were discovered by the Portuguese in 1456 or 1460. The first Portuguese colonists landed in 1462; African slaves were brought soon after, and most Cape Verdeans descend from both groups. Cape Verde independence came July 5, 1975. Antonio Mascarenhas Monteiro won the nation's first free presidential election Feb. 17, 1991; he was reelected without opposition five years later.

Central African Republic

People: Population: 3,375,771. **Age distrib.** (%): <15: 43.9; 65+: 3.6. **Pop. density:** 14 per sq. mi. **Urban:** 40%. **Ethnic groups:** Baya 34%, Banda 27%, Mandjia 21%, Sara 10%. **Principal languages:** French (official), Sangho (national), Arabic, Hunsa, Swahili. **Chief religions:** Protestant 25%, Roman Catholic 25%, indigenous beliefs 24%, Muslim 15%.

Geography: Area: 240,533 sq. mi. **Location:** In central Africa. **Neighbors:** Chad on N, Cameroon on W, Congo-Brazzaville and Congo-Kinshasa (formerly Zaire) on S, Sudan on E. **Topography:** Mostly rolling plateau, average altitude 2,000 ft., with rivers draining S to the Congo and N to Lake Chad. Open, well-watered savanna covers most of the area, with an arid area in NE, and tropical rain forest in SW. **Capital:** Bangui (1995 est.): 553,000.

Government: Type: Republic. **Head of state:** Pres. Ange-Félix Patassé; b Jan. 25, 1937; in office: Oct. 22, 1993. **Head of government:** Prime Min. Michel Gbezera-Bria; b 1946; in office: Jan. 30, 1997. **Local divisions:** 14 prefectures, 2 economic prefectures, and 1 commune. **Defense:** 2.4% of GDP. **Active troop strength:** 2,700.

Economy: Industries: Textiles, breweries, sawmills, diamond mining. **Chief crops:** Cotton, coffee, corn, tobacco, yams. **Minerals:** Diamonds (chief export), uranium. **Other resources:** Timber. **Arable land:** 3%. **Livestock** (1997): chickens: 3.60 mil; cattle: 2.93 mil; goats: 2.21 mil; pigs: 596,000; sheep: 191,000. **Electricity prod.** (1996): 100 mil kWh. **Labor force:** 80% agric.

Finance: Monetary unit: CFA Franc (Sept. 1998: 580.94 = $1 U.S.). **Gross domestic product** (1995 est.): $2.5 bil. **Per capita GDP:** $800. **Imports** (1995 est.): $176 mil; partners: France 37%.; Japan 24. **Exports** (1995 est.): $181 mil; partners: Belg.-Lux. 40%, France 16%. **Tourism:** $5 mil. **National budget** (1994 est.): $1.9 bil. **International reserves less gold** (Mar. 1998): $170.57 mil. **Gold:** 11,000 oz t. **Consumer prices** change in 1997): 1.2%.

Transport: Motor vehicles in use: 11,000 passenger cars, 9,000 comm. vehicles. **Civil aviation:** 139.6 mil passenger-mi; 1 airport. **Chief port:** Bangui.

Communications: Television sets: 5 per 1,000 pop. **Radios:** 75 per 1,000 pop. **Telephones:** 9,704 main lines.

Health: Life expectancy at birth: 45.0 male; 48.7 female. **Births** (per 1,000 pop.): 39. **Deaths** (per 1,000 pop.): 17. **Natural increase:** 2.20%. **Hospital beds** (1991): 1 per 672 persons. **Physicians** (1992): 1 per 18,660 persons. **Infant mortality** (per 1,000 live births): 106.

Education: Compulsory: ages 6-14. **Literacy:** 60%.

Major International Organizations: UN (FAO, IBRD, ILO, IMF, WHO, WTrO), OAU.

Embassy: 1618 22d St. NW 20008; 483-7800.

Various Bantu tribes migrated through the region for centuries before French control was asserted in the late 19th century, when the region was named Ubangi-Shari. Complete independence was attained Aug. 13, 1960.

All political parties were dissolved in 1960, and the country became a center for Chinese political influence in Africa. Relations with China were severed after 1965. Pres. Jean-Bedel Bokassa, who seized power in a 1965 military coup, proclaimed himself constitutional emperor of the renamed Central African Empire Dec. 1976.

Bokassa's rule was characterized by ruthless and cruel authoritarianism and human rights violations. He was ousted in a bloodless coup aided by the French government, Sept. 20, 1979. In 1981, Gen. André Kolingba became head of state in another bloodless coup. Multiparty legislative and presidential elections were held in Oct. 1992 but were canceled by the government when Kolingba was losing. New elections were ultimately held in Aug. and Sept. 1993, leading to the installation of a civilian government. French troops intervened to suppress an army mutiny in May 1996. A month later, a 21-member government of national unity was formed. Another mutiny ended Jan. 25, 1997, after French intervention.

Chad

Republic of Chad

People: Population: 7,359,512. **Age distrib.** (%): <15: 44.2; 65+: 3.0. **Pop. density:** 15 per sq. mi. **Urban:** 23%. **Ethnic groups:** Sara 28%, Sudan & Arab 12%, many others. **Principal languages:** French, Arabic (both official), Sara, Sango, more than 100 other languages. **Chief religions:** Muslim 50%, Christian 25%, indigenous beliefs 25%.

Geography: Area: 495,752 sq. mi. **Location:** In central N Africa. **Neighbors:** Libya on N; Niger, Nigeria, Cameroon on W; Central African Republic on S; Sudan on E. **Topography:** Wooded savanna, steppe, and desert in the S; part of the Sahara in the N. Southern rivers flow N to Lake Chad, surrounded by marshland. **Capital:** N'Djamena 826,000*.

Government: Type: Republic. **Head of state:** Pres. Idriss Déby; in office: Dec. 4, 1990. **Head of government:** Prime Min. Nassour Guelengdoussia Ouaido; in office: May 17, 1997. **Local divisions:** 14 prefectures. **Defense:** 2.7% of GDP. **Active troop strength:** 25,400.

Economy: Industries Cotton textiles, meat packing, beer brewing, soap. **Chief crops:** Cotton, sorghum, millet. **Minerals:** Uranium. **Arable land:** 3%. **Livestock** (1997): chickens: 4.70 mil; cattle: 5.08 mil; goats: 3.80 mil; sheep: 2.59 mil. **Fish catch** (1996): 100,000 metric tons. **Electricity prod.** (1996): 90 mil kWh. **Labor force:** 85% agric.

Finance: Monetary unit: CFA Franc (Sept. 1998: 580.94 = $1 U.S.). **Gross domestic product** (1995 est.): $3.3 bil. **Per capita GDP:** $600. **Imports** (1995 est.): $225 mil; partners: France 34%, Cameroon 24%. **Exports** (1995): $226 mil; partners: Portugal 30%, Germany 18%. **Tourism:** $9 mil. **National budget** (1994 est.): $222 mil. **International reserves less gold** (Mar. 1998): $116.87 mil. **Gold:** 11,000 oz t. **Consumer prices** (change in 1997): 5.7%.

Transport: Motor vehicles in use: 9,630 passenger cars, 14,360 comm. vehicles. **Civil aviation:** 144.4 mil passenger-mi; 1 airport.

Communications: Television sets: 8 per 1,000 pop. **Radios:** 206 per 1,000 pop. **Telephones:** 6,004 main lines.

Health: Life expectancy at birth: 45.8 male; 50.7 female. **Births** (per 1,000 pop.): 43. **Deaths** (per 1,000 pop.): 17. **Natural increase:** 2.66%. **Hospital beds** (1993): 1 per 1,521 persons. **Physicians** (1993): 1 per 27,765 persons. **Infant mortality** (per 1,000 live births): 117.

Education: Compulsory: ages 6-14. **Literacy:** 48%.

Major International Organizations: UN (FAO, IBRD, ILO, IMF, WHO, WTrO), OAU.

Embassy: 2002 R St. NW 20009; 462-4009.

Chad was the site of paleolithic and neolithic cultures before the Sahara Desert formed. A succession of kingdoms and Arab slave traders dominated Chad until France took control around 1900. Independence came Aug. 11, 1960.

Northern Muslim rebels have fought animist and Christian southern government and French troops from 1966, despite numerous cease-fires and peace pacts.

Libyan troops entered the country at the request of a pro-Libyan Chad government, Dec. 1980. The troops were withdrawn from Chad in Nov. 1981. Rebel forces, led by Hissène Habré, captured the capital and forced Pres. Goukouni Oueddei to flee the country in June 1982.

In 1983, France sent some 3,000 troops to Chad to assist Pres. Habré in opposing Libyan-backed rebels. France and Libya agreed to a simultaneous withdrawal of troops from Chad in Sept. 1984, but Libyan forces remained in the north until Mar. 1987, when Chad forces drove them from their last major stronghold. In Dec. 1990, Habré was overthrown by a Libyan-supported insurgent group, the Patriotic Salvation Movement.

On Feb. 3, 1994, the World Court dismissed a long-standing territorial claim by Libya to the mineral-rich Aozou Strip, on the Libyan border. Libyan troops reportedly withdrew at the end of May. Following approval of a new constitution in March 1996, Chad's first multiparty presidential election was held in June and July. The U.S. Peace Corps withdrew from Chad in Apr. 1998 because of clashes between rebels and Chad government forces.

Chile

Republic of Chile

People: Population: 14,787,781. **Age distrib.** (%): <15: 28.3; 65+: 7.0. **Pop. density:** 51 per sq. mi. **Urban:** 84%. **Ethnic groups:** European and European-Indian 95%, Indian 3%. **Principal language:** Spanish (official). **Chief religions:** Roman Catholic 89%, Protestant 11%.

Geography: Area: 292,258 sq. mi. **Location:** Occupies western coast of S South America. **Neighbors:** Peru on N, Bolivia on NE, Argentina on E. **Topography:** Andes Mts. on E border incl. some of the world's highest peaks; on W is 2,650-mile Pacific coast. Width varies between 100 and 250 miles. In N is Atacama Desert, in center are agricultural regions, in S, forests and grazing lands. **Capital:** Santiago 4,891,000*.

Government: Type: Republic. **Head of state:** Pres. Eduardo Frei Ruiz-Tagle; b June 24, 1942; in office: Mar. 11, 1994. **Local divisions:** 13 regions. **Defense:** 3.5% of GDP. **Active troop strength:** 89,700.

Economy: Industries: Fish processing, wood products, iron, steel. **Chief crops:** Grain, grapes, fruits, beans, potatoes, sugar beets. **Minerals:** Copper (world's largest producer and exporter), molybdenum, nitrates, iron, gold. **Crude oil reserves** (1997): 150 mil bbls. **Other resources:** Timber. **Arable land:** 5%. **Livestock** (1997): chickens: 68.00 mil; cattle: 4.14 mil; sheep: 3.71 mil; pigs: 1.72 mil; goats: 738,200. **Fish catch** (1996): 6.69 mil metric tons. **Electricity prod.** (1996): 35.8 bil kWh. **Labor force:** 38% serv.; 34% ind. & commerce; 19% agric., forestry, fishing.

Finance: Monetary unit: Peso (Sept. 1998: 472.92 = $1 U.S.). **Gross domestic product** (1996 est.): $120.6 bil. **Per capita GDP:** $8,400. **Imports** (1996 est.): $16.5 bil; partners: U.S. 25%, EU 18%. **Exports** (1996 est.): $15.2 bil; partners: Asia 34%, EU 25%, U.S. 15%. **Tourism:** $1.08 bil. **National budget** (1996 est.): $17 bil. **International reserves less gold** (June 1998): $15.13 bil. **Gold:** 1.54 mil oz. t. **Consumer prices** (change in 1997): 6.1%.

Transport: Railroad: Length: 4,084 mi. **Motor vehicles in use:** 900,000 passenger cars, 475,000 comm. vehicles. **Civil aviation:** 4.21 bil passenger-mi; 23 airports. **Chief ports:** Valparaiso, Arica, Antofagasta.

Communications: Television sets: 280 per 1,000 pop. **Radios:** 305 per 1,000 pop. **Telephones:** 2,247,982 main lines. **Daily newspaper circ.:** 101 per 1,000 pop.

Health: Life expectancy at birth: 72.0 male; 78.5 female. **Births** (per 1,000 pop.): 18. **Deaths** (per 1,000 pop.): 6. **Natural increase:** 1.27%. **Hospital beds** (1994): 1 per 326 persons. **Physicians** (1994): 1 per 875 persons. **Infant mortality** (per 1,000 live births): 10.

Education: Free and compulsory, from age 6 or 7, for 8 years. **Literacy:** 95%.

Major International Organizations: UN and all of its specialized agencies, APEC, OAS.

Embassy: 1732 Massachusetts Ave. NW 20036; 785-1746.

Website: http://www.segegob.cl/seg-ingl/index2i.html

Northern Chile was under Inca rule before the Spanish conquest, 1536-40. The southern Araucanian Indians resisted until the late 19th century. Independence was gained 1810-18, under José de San Martin and Bernardo O'Higgins; the latter, as supreme director 1817-23, sought social and economic reforms until deposed. Chile defeated Peru and Bolivia in 1836-39 and 1879-84, gaining mineral-rich northern land.

In 1970, Salvador Allende Gossens, a Marxist, became president with a third of the national vote. His government improved conditions for the poor, but illegal and violent actions by extremist supporters of the government, the regime's failure to attain majority support, and poorly planned socialist economic programs led to political and financial chaos.

A military junta seized power Sept. 11, 1973, and said Allende had killed himself. The junta, headed by Gen. Augusto Pinochet Ugarte, named a mostly military cabinet and announced plans to "exterminate Marxism." Repression continued during the 1980s with little sign of any political liberalization.

In a plebiscite held Oct. 5, 1988, voters rejected the incumbent president, Pinochet. He agreed to presidential elections. In Dec. 1989 voters elected a civilian president, although Pinochet continued to head the army until Mar. 10, 1998. In Mar. 1994 a Chilean human rights group estimated that human rights violations had claimed more than 3,100 lives during Pinochet's rule. After a request by Spanish authorities, in a highly unusual move, Pinochet was arrested by British police in London Oct. 17, 1998, for questioning for "crimes of genocide and terrorism that include murder." Britain had 40 days to decide whether to extradite Pinochet to face charges in Spain.

Tierra del Fuego is the largest (18,800 sq. mi.) island in the archipelago of the same name at the southern tip of South America, an area of majestic mountains, tortuous channels, and high winds. It was visited 1520 by Magellan and named the Land of Fire because of its many Indian bonfires. Part of the island is in Chile, part in Argentina. Punta Arenas, on a mainland peninsula, is a center of sheep raising and the world's southernmost city (pop. about 70,000); Puerto Williams is the southernmost settlement.

China

People's Republic of China

(Statistical data on China do not include Hong Kong.)

People: Population: 1,236,914,658. **Age distrib.** (%): <15: 25.8; 65+: 6.6. **Pop. density:** 335 per sq. mi. **Urban:** 29%. **Ethnic groups:** Han Chinese 92%, Tibetan, Mongol, Korean, Manchu, others. **Principal languages:** Mandarin (official), Yue, Wu, Haka, Xiang, Gan, Minbei, Minnan. **Chief religions:** Officially atheist; Buddhism, Taoism; some Muslims, Christians.

Geography: Area: 3,696,100 sq. mi. **Location:** Occupies most of the habitable mainland of E Asia. **Neighbors:** Mongolia on N; Russia on NE and NW; Afghanistan, Pakistan, Tajikistan, Kazakhstan on W; India, Nepal, Bhutan, Myanmar, Laos, Vietnam on S; North Korea on NE. **Topography:** Two-thirds of the vast territory is mountainous or desert; only one-tenth is cultivated. Rolling topography rises to high elevations in the N in the Daxinganlingshanmai separating Manchuria and Mongolia; the Tien Shan in Xinjiang; the Himalayan and Kunlunshanmai in the SW and in Tibet. Length is 1,860 mi. from N to S, width E to W is more than 2,000 mi. The eastern half of China is one of the world's best-watered lands. Three great river systems, the Chang (Yangtze), Huang (Yellow), and Xi, provide water for vast farmlands. **Capital:** Beijing. **Cities:** Shanghai 13,584,000; Beijing 11,299,000; Tianjin 9,415,000; Shenyang 5,116,000; Guangzhou 4,492,000*.

Government: Type: Communist Party-led state. **Head of state:** Pres. Jiang Zemin; b Aug. 17, 1926; in office: Mar. 27, 1993. **Head of government:** Premier Zhu Rongji; b Oct. 1, 1928; in office: Mar. 17, 1998. **Local divisions:** 22 provinces (not including Taiwan), 5 autonomous regions, and 4 municipalities, plus (as of July 1, 1997) the special administrative region of Hong Kong. **Defense:** 5.7% of GDP. **Active troop strength:** 2.935 mil.

Economy: Industries: Iron and steel, textiles and apparel, machine building, armaments. **Chief crops:** Grain, rice, cotton, potatoes, tea. **Minerals:** Tungsten, antimony, coal, oil, mercury, iron, lead, manganese, molybdenum, tin. **Crude oil reserves** (1997): 24 bil bbls. **Other resources:** Hydropower silk. **Arable land:** 10%. **Livestock** (1997): chickens: 3.01 bil; cattle: 116.46 mil; pigs: 468.06 mil; goats: 170.99 mil; sheep: 132.69 mil; buffalo: 23.52 mil. **Fish catch** (1996): 14.22 mil metric tons. **Electricity prod.** (1996): 1.0 tril kWh. **Labor force:** 54% agric. & forestry; 26% ind. & commerce.

Finance: Monetary unit: Renminbi (Yuan) (Sept. 1998: 8.28 = $1 U.S.). **Gross domestic product** (1996 est.): $3.39 tril. **Per capita GDP:** $2,800. **Imports** (1995): $132.1 bil; partners: Japan 22%, U.S. 12%, Taiwan 11%. **Exports** (1996): $151.1 bil; partners: Hong Kong 24%, Japan 19%, U.S. 17%. **Tourism:** $12.07 bil. **National budget** (1994): $13.7 bil deficit. **International reserves less gold** (June 1998): $143.96 bil. **Gold:** 12.7 mil oz t. **Consumer prices** (change in 1997): 2.8%.

Transport: Railroad: Length: 45,319 mi. **Motor vehicles in use:** 4.7 mil passenger cars, 6.75 mil comm. vehicles. **Civil aviation:** 43.80 bil passenger-mi, 113 airports. **Chief ports:** Shanghai, Qinhuangdao, Dalian, Guangzhou (Canton).

Communications: Television sets: 189 per 1,000 pop. **Radios:** 177 per 1,000 pop. **Telephones:** 54,947,000 main lines. **Daily newspaper circ.:** 23 per 1,000 pop.

Health: Life expectancy at birth: 68.3 male; 71.1 female. **Births** (per 1,000 pop.): 16. **Deaths** (per 1,000 pop.): 7. **Natural increase:** 0.87%. **Hospital beds** (1995): 1 per 384 persons. **Physicians** (1995): 1 per 628 persons. **Infant mortality** (per 1,000 live births): 45.

Education: Compulsory 7-17. **Literacy** (1995): 82%.

Major International Organizations: UN (FAO, IBRD, ILO, IMF, IMO, WHO), APEC.

Embassy: 2300 Conn. Ave. NW 20008; 328-2500.

Website: http://www.china-embassy.org

Remains of various humanlike creatures who lived as early as several hundred thousand years ago have been found in many parts of China. Neolithic agricultural settlements dotted the Huang (Yellow) R. basin from about 5000 BC. Their language, religion, and art were the sources of later Chinese civilization.

Bronze metallurgy reached a peak and Chinese pictographic writing, similar to today's, was in use in the more developed culture of the Shang Dynasty (c. 1500 BC-c. 1000 BC), which ruled much of North China.

A succession of dynasties and interdynastic warring kingdoms ruled China for the next 3,000 years. They expanded Chinese political and cultural domination to the south and west, and developed a brilliant technologically and a culturally advanced society. Rule by foreigners (Mongols in the Yuan Dynasty, 1271-1368, and Manchus in the Ch'ing Dynasty, 1644-1911) did not alter the underlying culture.

A period of relative stagnation left China vulnerable to internal and external pressures in the 19th century. Rebellions left tens of millions dead, and Russia, Japan, Britain, and other powers exercised political and economic control in large parts of the country. China became a republic Jan. 1, 1912, following the Wuchang Uprising inspired by Dr. Sun Yat-sen, founder of the Kuomintang (Nationalist) party. By 1928, the Kuomintang, led by Chiang Kai-shek, succeeded in nominal reunification of China. About the same time, a bloody purge of Communists from the ranks of the Kuomintang fomented hostilities between the two groups that would continue for decades.

For a period of 50 years, 1894-1945, China was involved in conflicts with Japan. In 1895, China ceded Korea, Taiwan, and other areas. On Sept. 18, 1931, Japan seized the Northeastern Provinces (Manchuria) and set up a puppet state called Manchukuo. The border province of Jehol was cut off as a buffer state in 1933. Japan invaded China proper July 7, 1937. After its defeat in World War II, Japan gave up all seized land.

Following World War II, internal conflicts involving the Kuomintang, Communists, and other factions resumed. China came under domination of Communist armies, 1949-1950. The Kuomintang government moved to Taiwan, Dec. 8, 1949.

The Chinese People's Political Consultative Conference convened Sept. 21, 1949; The People's Republic of China was proclaimed in Beijing (Peking) Oct. 1, 1949, under Mao Zedong. China and the USSR signed a 30-year treaty of "friendship, alliance and mutual assistance," Feb. 15, 1950. The U.S. refused recognition of the new regime. On Nov. 26, 1950, the People's Republic sent armies into Korea against U.S. troops and forced a stalemate in the Korean War.

After an initial period of consolidation, 1949-52, industry, agriculture, and social and economic institutions were forcibly molded according to Maoist ideals. However, frequent drastic changes in policy and violent factionalism interfered with economic development. In 1957, Mao admitted an estimated 800,000 people had been executed 1949-54; opponents claimed much higher figures.

The Great Leap Forward, 1958-60, tried to force the pace of economic development through intensive labor on huge new rural communes, and through emphasis on ideological purity. The program caused resistance and was largely abandoned.

By the 1960s, relations with the USSR deteriorated, with disagreements on borders, ideology, and leadership of world Communism. The USSR canceled aid accords, and China, with Albania, launched anti-Soviet propaganda drives.

The Great Proletarian Cultural Revolution, 1965, was an attempt to oppose pragmatism and bureaucratic power and instruct a new generation in revolutionary principles. Massive purges took place. A program of forcibly relocating millions of urban teenagers into the countryside was launched. By 1968 the movement had run its course; many purged officials returned to office in subsequent years, and reforms that had placed ideology above expertise were gradually weakened.

On Oct. 25, 1971, the UN General Assembly ousted the Taiwan government from the UN and seated the People's Republic in its place. The U.S. had supported the mainland's admission but opposed Taiwan's expulsion.

U.S. Pres. Richard Nixon visited China Feb. 21-28, 1972, on invitation from Premier Zhou Enlai, ending years of antipathy between the 2 nations. China and the U.S. opened liaison offices in each other's capitals, May-June 1973. The U.S., Dec. 15, 1978, formally recognized the People's Republic of China as the sole legal government of China; diplomatic relations between the 2 nations were established, Jan. 1, 1979.

Mao died Sept. 9, 1976. By 1978, Vice Premier Deng Xiaoping had consolidated his power, succeeding Mao as "paramount leader" of China. The new ruling group modified Maoist policies in education, culture, and industry, and sought better ties with non-Communist countries. During this "reassessment" of Mao's policies his widow, Jiang Qing, and other "Gang of Four" leftists were convicted of "committing crimes during the 'Cultural Revolution,' " Jan. 25, 1981.

By the mid-1980s, China had enacted far-reaching economic reforms, deemphasizing centralized planning and incorporating market-oriented incentives. Some 100,000 students and workers staged a march in Beijing to demand political reforms, May 4, 1989. The demonstrations continued during a visit to Beijing by Soviet leader Mikhail Gorbachev May 15-18; it was the first Sino-Soviet summit since 1959. As the unrest spread, martial law was imposed, May 20. Troops entered Beijing, June 3-4, and crushed the pro-democracy protests, as tanks and armored personnel carriers rolled through Tiananmen Square. It is estimated that 5,000 died, 10,000 were injured, and hundreds of students and workers were arrested.

China had one of the world's fastest-growing economies in the 1990s. Although human rights violations have persisted, the U.S. has continued to renew China's most-favored-nation trading status. Deng died Feb. 19, 1997, leaving his chosen successor, Jiang Zemin, in firm control as president. Pres. Jiang paid a state visit to the U.S., Oct. 26-Nov. 3, and U.S. Pres. Clinton visited China, June 25-July 3, 1998. Floods in

July and Aug. killed at least 3,000 people, left millions homeless, and caused an estimated $20 billion in property damage.

By agreement with Great Britain, Hong Kong reverted to Chinese sovereignty on July 1, 1997. Portugal has agreed to return Macau to China in 1999. Although China and Taiwan remain diplomatic rivals, they tightened economic ties in the 1990s.

Manchuria. Home of the Manchus, rulers of China 1644-1911, Manchuria has accommodated millions of Chinese settlers in the 20th century. Under Japanese rule 1931-45, the area became industrialized. The region is divided into the 3 NE provinces of Heilongjiang, Jilin, and Liaoning.

Guangxi is in SE China, bounded on N by Guizhou and Hunan provinces, E and S by Guangdong, on SW by Vietnam, and on W by Yunnan. It produces rice in the river valleys and has valuable forest products.

Inner Mongolia was organized by the People's Republic in 1947. Its boundaries have undergone frequent changes, reaching its greatest extent in 1956 (and restored in 1979), with an area of 454,600 sq. mi., allegedly in order to dilute the minority Mongol population. Chinese settlers outnumber the Mongols more than 10 to 1. Pop. (1996 est.): 23.07 mil. Capital: Hohhot.

Xinjiang, in Central Asia, is 635,900 sq. mi., pop. (1996 est.): 16.89 mil (75% Uygurs, a Turkic Muslim group, with a heavy Chinese increase in recent years). Capital: Urumqi. It is China's richest region in strategic minerals.

Tibet, 471,700 sq. mi., is a thinly populated region of high plateaus and massive mountains, the Himalayas on the S, the Kunluns on the N. High passes connect with India and Nepal; roads lead into China proper. Capital: Lhasa. Average altitude is 15,000 ft. Jiachan, 15,870 ft., is believed to be the highest inhabited town on earth. Agriculture is primitive. Pop. (1996 est.): 2.44 mil (of whom about 500,000 are Chinese). Another 4 million Tibetans form the majority of the population of vast adjacent areas that have long been incorporated into China.

China ruled all of Tibet from the 18th century, but independence came in 1911. China reasserted control in 1951, and a Communist government was installed in 1953, revising the theocratic Lamaist Buddhist rule. Serfdom was abolished, but all land remained collectivized.

A Tibetan uprising within China in 1956 spread to Tibet in 1959. The rebellion was crushed with Chinese troops, and Buddhism was almost totally suppressed. The Dalai Lama and 100,000 Tibetans fled to India.

Hong Kong

Hong Kong (Xianggang), located at the mouth of the Zhu Jiang (Pearl R.) in SE China, 90 mi. S of Canton (Guangzhou), was a British dependency from 1842 until July 1, 1997, when it became a Special Administrative Region of China. Its nucleus is Hong Kong Isl., 31 sq. mi., occupied by the British in 1841 and formally ceded to them in 1842, on which is located the seat of government. Opposite is Kowloon Peninsula, 3 sq. mi., and Stonecutters Isl., added to the territory in 1860. An additional 355 sq. mi. known as the New Territories, a mainland area and islands, were leased from China, 1898, for 99 years. Total area 415 sq. mi.; pop. (1998 est.) 6.7 million, including fewer than 20,000 British.

Hong Kong is a major center for trade and banking. Per capita GDP, $26,500 (1996 est.), is among the highest in the world. Principal industries are textiles and apparel; also tourism ($9.24 bil expenditures in 1997), electronics, shipbuilding, iron and steel, fishing, cement, and small manufactures. Hong Kong's spinning mills are among the best in the world.

Hong Kong harbor was long an important British naval station and one of the world's great transshipment ports. The colony was often a place of refuge for exiles from mainland China. It was occupied by Japan during World War II.

From 1949 to 1962 Hong Kong absorbed more than a million refugees fleeing Communist China. Starting in the 1950s, cheap labor led to a boom in light manufacturing, while liberal tax policies attracted foreign investment; Hong Kong became one of the wealthiest, most productive areas in the Far East. Poor living and working conditions and low wages for many led to political unrest in the 1960s, but legislation and public works programs raised the standard of living by the 1970s.

With the end of the 99-year lease on the New Territories drawing near, Britain and China signed an agreement, Dec. 19, 1984, under which all of Hong Kong was to be returned to China in 1997; under this agreement Hong Kong was to be allowed to keep its capitalist system for 50 years. In Dec. 1996, an electoral college appointed by China chose a shipping magnate, Tung Chee-hwa, to be Hong Kong's chief executive when it reverted to Chinese control.

The July 1 transfer of government was marked by an elaborate ceremony. In the immediate wake of the changeover, Hong Kong retained its street names and its currency, the Hong Kong dollar (but without the queen's picture). Official languages remained Chinese (Cantonese dialect) and English. The Legislative Council was disbanded, and an appointed Provisional Legislature installed in its place. The new legislature imposed limits on opposition activities and sharply cut back the number of people eligible to vote in legislative elections; despite the restrictions, pro-democracy candidates did well in the balloting on May 24, 1998.

Colombia

Republic of Colombia

People: Population: 38,580,949. **Age distrib.** (%): <15: 33.2; 65+: 4.5. **Pop. density:** 88 per sq. mi. **Urban:** 73%. **Ethnic groups:** Mestizo 58%, white 20%, mulatto 14%, black 4%. **Principal language:** Spanish (official). **Chief religion:** Roman Catholic 95%.

Geography: Area: 440,762 sq. mi. **Location:** At the NW corner of South America. **Neighbors:** Panama on NW, Ecuador and Peru on S, Brazil and Venezuela on E. **Topography:** Three ranges of Andes Western, Central, and Eastern Cordilleras—run through the country from N to S. The eastern range consists mostly of high tablelands, densely populated. The Magdalena R. rises in the Andes, flows N to Caribbean, through a rich alluvial plain. Sparsely settled plains in E are drained by Orinoco and Amazon systems. **Capital:** Bogotá. (Full name: Santa Fe de Bogotá.) **Cities:** Bogotá 6,079,000; Medellin 3,291,000; Cali 1,870,000*.

Government: Type: Republic. **Head of state:** Pres. Andrés Pastrana Arango; b Aug. 17, 1954; in office: Aug. 7, 1998. **Local divisions:** 32 departments, capital district of Bogota. **Defense:** 2.6% of GDP. **Active troop strength:** 146,300.

Economy: Industries: Textiles, food processing, clothing, cement, chemicals. **Chief crops:** Coffee, rice, bananas, oilseeds, corn, cotton, sugar, tobacco, coca. **Minerals:** Oil, gas, emeralds, gold, copper, coal, iron, nickel. **Crude oil reserves** (1997): 2.8 bil bbls. **Other resources:** Forest products, cut flowers, hydropower. **Arable land:** 4%. **Livestock** (1997): chickens: 110.00; cattle: 26.35 mil; pigs: 2.48 mil; sheep: 2.42 mil; goats: 915,000. **Fish catch** (1996): 129,661 metric tons. **Electricity prod.** (1996): 53.7 bil kWh. **Labor force:** 46% services; 30% agric.; 24% ind.

Finance: Monetary unit: Peso (Sept. 1998: 1,540.00 = $1 U.S.). **Gross domestic product** (1996 est.): $201.4 bil. **Per capita GDP:** $5,400. **Imports** (1996 est.): $12.4 bil; partners: U.S. 36%, EC 18%. **Exports** (1996 est.): $10.3 bil; partners: U.S. 39%, EC 26%. **Tourism:** $955 mil. **National budget** (1997 est.): $30 bil. **International reserves less gold** (June 1998): $8.69 bil. **Gold:** 359,000 oz t. **Consumer prices** (change in 1997): 18.5%.

Transport: Railroad: Length: 2,102.7 mi. **Motor vehicles in use:** 1.15 mil passenger cars, 550,000 comm. vehicles. **Civil aviation:** 3.72 bil passenger-mi; 43 airports. **Chief ports:** Buenaventura, Barranquilla, Cartagena.

Communications: Television sets: 188 per 1,000 pop. **Radios:** 155 per 1,000 pop. **Telephones:** 4,645,453 main lines. **Daily newspaper circ.:** 55 per 1,000 pop.

Health: Life expectancy at birth: 66.2 male; 74.1 female. **Births** (per 1,000 pop.): 25. **Deaths** (per 1,000 pop.): 6. **Natural increase:** 1.92%. **Physicians** (1992): 1 per 1,078 persons. **Infant mortality** (per 1,000 live births): 25.

Education: Free and compulsory for 5 years between ages 6-12. **Literacy:** 91%.

Major International Organizations: UN (FAO, IBRD, ILO, IMF, IMO, WHO, WTrO), OAS.

Embassy: 2118 Leroy Pl. NW 20008; 387-8338.

Spain subdued the local Indian kingdoms (Funza, Tunja) by the 1530s and ruled Colombia and neighboring areas as New Granada for 300 years. Independence was won by 1819. Venezuela and Ecuador broke away in 1829-30, and Panama withdrew in 1903.

Colombia is plagued by rural and urban violence. "La Violencia" of 1948-58 claimed 200,000 lives; since 1987, according to human rights groups, political violence has resulted in more than 30,000 deaths. Attempts at land and social reform and progress in industrialization have not reduced massive social problems.

The government's increased activity against local drug traffickers sparked a series of retaliation killings. On Aug. 18, 1989, Luis Carlos Galán, the ruling party's presidential hopeful for the 1990 election, was assassinated. In 1990, 2 other presidential candidates were assassinated, as drug traffickers carried on a campaign of intimidation. Pablo Escobar, head of the Medellín drug cartel, escaped from prison in July 1992, allegedly with aid from military and prison officials. He was killed by government troops Dec. 1, 1993.

Charges that Ernesto Samper Pizano's 1994 campaign received money from the Cali drug cartel engulfed his administration in scandal, although the legislature voted, June 12, 1996, not to impeach him. Andrés Pastrana Arango, son of former Pres. Misael Pastrana Borrero (in office 1970-74), won a presidential runoff election, June 21, 1998.

Comoros

Federal Islamic Republic of the Comoros

People: Population: 545,528. **Age. distrib.** (%): <15: 42.6; 65+: 2.9. **Pop. density:** 759 per sq. mi. **Urban:** 31%. **Ethnic groups:** Antalote, Cafre, Makoa, Oimatsaha, Sakalava. **Principal languages:** Arabic, French, Comorian (all official). **Chief religions:** Sunni Muslim 86%, Roman Catholic 14%.

Geography: Area: 719 sq. mi. **Location:** 3 islands—Grande Comore (Njazidja), Anjouan (Nzwani), and Moheli (Mwali)—in the Mozambique Channel between NW Madagascar and SE Africa. **Neighbors:** Nearest are Mozambique on W, Madagascar on E. **Topography:** The islands are of volcanic origin, with an active volcano on Grande Comore. **Capital:** Moroni (1992 met. est.): 30,000.

Government: Type: In transition. **Head of state:** Pres. Mohamed Taki Abdul-Karim; in office: Mar. 1996. **Local divisions:** 3 main islands with 4 municipalities.

Economy: Industries: Perfume, textiles. **Chief crops:** Vanilla, copra, perfume essences, cloves. **Arable land:** 35%. **Livestock** (1997): chickens: 440,000; goats: 128,000. **Electricity prod.** (1996): 15 mil kWh. **Labor force:** 80% agric.

Finance: Monetary unit: Franc (Sept. 1998: 435.71 = $1 U.S.). **Gross domestic product** (1995 est.): $370 mil. **Per capita GDP:** $650. **Imports** (1993 est.): $40.9 mil; partners: France 60%. **Exports** (1995 est.): $11.2 mil; partners: France 54%, Germany 18%. **Tourism:** $20 mil. **National budget** (1992): $92 mil.

Transport: Civil aviation: 2.1 mil passenger-mi; 2 airports. **Chief ports:** Fomboni, Moroni, Mutsamudu.

Communications: Radios: 122 per 1,000 pop. **Telephones:** 4,980 main lines.

Health: Life expectancy at birth: 58.0 male; 62.8 female. **Births** (per 1,000 pop.): 41. **Deaths** (per 1,000 pop.): 10. **Natural increase:** 3.10%. **Infant mortality** (per 1,000 live births): 85.

Education: Compulsory: ages 7-16. **Literacy:** 57%.

Major International Organizations: UN (FAO, IBRD, ILO, IMF, WHO), AL, OAU.

Embassy: 336 E. 45th St., 2d Fl., New York, NY 10017; (212) 972-8010.

Website: http://www.ksu.edu/sasw/comoros/comoros.html

The islands were controlled by Muslim sultans until the French acquired them 1841-1909. They became a French overseas territory in 1947. A 1974 referendum favored independence, with only the Christian island of Mayotte preferring association with France. The French National Assembly decided to allow each of the islands to decide its own fate. The Comore Chamber of Deputies declared independence July 6, 1975, with Ahmed Abdallah as president. In a referendum in 1976, Mayotte voted to remain French.

A leftist regime that seized power from Abdallah in 1975 was deposed in a pro-French 1978 coup in which he regained the presidency. In Nov. 1989, Pres. Abdallah was assassinated; soon after, a multiparty system was instituted. A Sept. 1995 military coup, assisted by French mercenaries, ousted Pres. Said Mohamed Djohar. French troops invaded, Oct. 4, and forced coup leaders to surrender. Djohar returned from exile in Jan. 1996, and in Mar. a new presidential election was held. A hijacked Ethiopian Airlines Boeing 767 crashed offshore on Nov. 23, killing 123 of the 175 people on board. Seeking to resume ties with France, Anjouan seceded from the Comoros, Aug. 3, 1997. Comorian troops were unable to put down the rebellion, which was joined by Moheli.

Congo (*formerly* Zaire)

Democratic Republic of the Congo

(Congo, officially Democratic Republic of the Congo, is also known as Congo-Kinshasa. It should not be confused with Republic of the Congo, commonly called Congo Republic, and also known as Congo-Brazzaville.)

People: Population: 49,000,511. **Age distrib.** (%): <15: 48.2; 65+: 2.6. **Pop. density:** 54 per sq. mi. **Urban:** 29%. **Ethnic groups:** More than 200 tribes, mostly Bantu. **Principal languages:** French (official), more than 400 dialects. **Chief religions:** Roman Catholic 59%, Protestant 20%, Muslim 10%, Kimbanguist 10%.

Geography: Area: 905,563 sq. mi. **Location:** In central Africa. **Neighbors:** Congo-Brazzaville on W; Central African Republic, Sudan on N; Uganda, Rwanda, Burundi, Tanzania on E; Zambia, Angola on S. **Topography:** Congo includes the bulk of the Congo R. basin. The vast central region is a low-lying plateau covered by rain forest. Mountainous terraces in the W, savannas in the S and SE, grasslands toward the N, and the high Ruwenzori Mts. on the E surround the central region. A short strip of territory borders the Atlantic O. The Congo R. is 2,718 mi. long. **Capital:** Kinshasa. **Cities:** Kinshasa 4,241,000; Lubumbashi 810,000*.

Government: Type: Republic with strong presidential authority (in transition). **Head of state:** Pres. Laurent Kabila; b 1940; in office: May 29, 1997. **Local divisions:** 11 provinces. **Defense:** 2.8% of GDP. **Active troop strength:** 28,100.

Economy: Industries: Mining, consumer prods., food processing. **Chief crops:** Coffee, sugar, palm oil, rubber, tea. **Minerals:** Cobalt (65% of world reserves), copper, cadmium, oil, diamonds, gold, silver, tin, germanium, zinc, iron, manganese, uranium, radium. **Crude oil reserves** (1997): 187 mil bbls. **Other resources:** Forests. **Arable land:** 3%. **Livestock** (1997): chickens: 25.00 mil; goats: 4.09 mil; pigs: 1.18 mil; cattle: 1.10 mil; sheep: 1.02 mil. **Fish catch** (1996): 162,261 metric tons. **Electricity prod.** (1996): 6.4 bil kWh. **Labor force:** 65% agric.; 19% services; 16% industry.

Finance: Monetary unit: New Zaire (Sept. 1998: 118,750.00 = $1 U.S.). **Gross domestic product** (1995 est.): $16.5 bil. **Per capita GDP:** $400. **Imports** (1995 est.): $1.25 bil; partners: Belg.-Lux. 15%, U.S. 7%. **Exports** (1995 est.): $1.47 bil; partners: Belg.-Lux. 36%, U.S. 17%. **Tourism:** $2 mil. **National budget** (1996 est.): $479 mil. **International reserves less gold** (Dec. 1996): $82.5 mil **Consumer prices** (change in 1997): 176%.

Transport: Railroad: Length: 3,190.7 mi. **Motor vehicles in use:** 330,000 passenger cars, 200,000 comm. vehicles. **Civil aviation:** 173.2 mil passenger-mi; 22 airports. **Chief ports:** Matadi, Boma, Kinshasa.

Communications: Radios: 79.3 per 1,000 pop. **Telephones:** 36,000 main lines. **Daily newspaper circ.:** 3 per 1,000 pop.

Health: Life expectancy at birth: 47.3 male; 51.4 female. **Births** (per 1,000 pop.): 47. **Deaths** (per 1,000 pop.): 15. **Natural increase:** 3.16%. **Infant mortality** (per 1,000 live births): 102.

Education: Compulsory: ages 6-12. **Literacy** (1995): 77%.

Major International Organizations: UN and most of its specialized agencies, OAU.

Embassy: 1800 New Hampshire Ave. NW 20009; 234-7690.

The earliest inhabitants of Congo may have been the pygmies, followed by Bantus from the E and Nilotic tribes from the N. The large Bantu Bakongo kingdom ruled much of Congo and Angola when Portuguese explorers visited in the 15th century.

Leopold II, king of the Belgians, formed an international group to exploit the Congo region in 1876. In 1877 Henry M. Stanley explored the Congo, and in 1878 the king's group sent him back to organize the region and win over the native chiefs. The Conference of Berlin, 1884-85, organized the Congo Free State with Leopold as king and chief owner. Exploitation of native laborers on the rubber plantations caused international criticism and led to granting of a colonial charter, 1908; the colony became known as the Belgian Congo.

Belgian and Congolese leaders agreed Jan. 27, 1960, the Congo would become independent in June. In the first general elections, May 31, the National Congolese movement of Patrice Lumumba won 35 of 137 seats in the National Assembly. He was appointed premier June 21, and formed a coalition cabinet. The Republic of the Congo was proclaimed June 30.

Widespread violence caused Europeans and others to flee. The UN Security Council, Aug. 9, 1960, called on Belgium to withdraw its troops and sent a UN contingent. Pres. Joseph Kasavubu removed Lumumba as premier in Sept.; Lumumba was murdered in Feb. 1961.

The last UN troops left the Congo June 30, 1964, and Moise Tshombe became president.

On Sept. 7, 1964, leftist rebels set up a "People's Republic" in Stanleyville (now Kisangani). Tshombe hired foreign mercenaries and sought to rebuild the Congolese Army. In Nov. and Dec. 1964 rebels killed scores of white hostages and thousands of Congolese; Belgian paratroopers, dropped from U.S. transport planes, rescued hundreds. By July 1965 the rebels had lost their effectiveness.

In late 1965 Gen. Joseph D. Mobutu was named president. He later changed his name to Mobutu Sese Seko. The country became the Democratic Republic of the Congo (1966) and the Republic of Zaire (1971).

Economic decline and government corruption plagued Zaire in the 1980s and worsened in the 1990s. In 1990, Pres. Mobutu announced an end to a 20-year ban on multiparty politics. He sought to retain power despite mounting international pressure and internal opposition.

During 1994, Zaire was inundated with refugees from the massive ethnic bloodshed in Rwanda. Ethnic violence spread to E Zaire in 1996. In Oct. militant Hutus, who dominated in the refugee camps, fought against rebels (mostly Tutsis) in Zaire, precipitating intervention by government troops. As a result of the fighting, Rwandan refugees abandoned the camps; hundreds of thousands returned to Rwanda, while hundreds of thousands more were dispersed throughout E Zaire. The rebels, led by Gen. Laurent Kabila—a former Marxist and longtime opponent of Mobutu—gained momentum and began to move W across Zaire. As turmoil engulfed his nation, Mobutu stayed in W Europe for most of the last 4 months of 1996, receiving treatment for prostate cancer.

With Mobutu out of the country, the Zairean army put up little resistance; the rebels were aided by several of Mobutu's enemies, notably Rwanda and Uganda. Mobutu returned to Zaire in March 1997, but attempts to negotiate with Kabila were ineffectual. On May 17, Kabila's troops entered Kinshasa and Mobutu went into exile. The country again assumed the name Democratic Republic of the Congo. Mobutu died Sept. 7 in Rabat, Morocco.

Kabila, who ruled by decree, alienated UN officials, international aid donors, and former allies. Rebels assisted by Rwanda and Uganda threatened Kinshasa in Aug. 1998, but the revolt was put down with help from Angola, Namibia, and Zimbabwe.

Congo Republic

Republic of the Congo

(Congo Republic, officially Republic of the Congo, is also known as Congo-Brazzaville. It should not be confused with Democratic Republic of the Congo [formerly Zaire], now commonly called Congo, and also known as Congo-Kinshasa.)

People: Population: 2,658,123. **Age distrib.** (%): <15: 42.6; 65+: 3.4. **Pop. density:** 20 per sq. mi. **Urban:** 59%. **Ethnic groups:** Kongo 48%, Sangha 20%, Teke 17%, M'Bochi 12%. **Principal languages:** French (official); Lingala, Kikongo, other African languages. **Chief religions:** Christian 50%, indigenous beliefs 48%, Muslim 2%.

Geography: Area: 132,046 sq. mi. **Location:** In W central Africa. **Neighbors:** Gabon and Cameroon on W, Central African Republic on N, Congo-Kinshasa (formerly Zaire) on E, Angola on SW. **Topography:** Much of the Congo is covered by thick forests. A coastal plain leads to the fertile Niari Valley. The center is a plateau; the Congo R. basin consists of flood plains in the lower and savanna in the upper portion. **Capital:** Brazzaville: 1,004,000*.

Government: Type: Republic. **Head of state:** Pres. Denis Sassou-Nguesso; b 1943; in office: Oct. 25, 1997. **Local divisions:** 10 regions, 6 communes. **Defense:** 1.9% of GDP. **Active troop strength:** 10,000.

Economy: Industries: Oil, wood products, brewing. **Chief crops:** Cassava (90% of food output), rice, corn, sugar, cocoa, coffee. **Minerals:** Oil, potash, lead, copper, zinc. **Crude oil reserves** (1997): 1.5 bil bbls. **Livestock** (1997): chickens: 1.95 mil; goats: 286,000; sheep: 115,000. **Fish catch** (1996): 33,785 metric tons. **Electricity prod.** (1996): 438 mil kWh. **Labor force:** 59% agric.; 28% comm., ind., govt.

Finance: Monetary unit: CFA Franc (Sept. 1998: 580.94 = $1 U.S.). **Gross domestic product** (1995 est.): $4.9 bil. **Per capita GDP:** $1,960. **Imports** (1995): $600 mil; partners: France 32%. **Exports** (1995): $1 bil; partners: U.S. 23%, Italy 15%. **Tourism:** $3 mil. **National budget** (1997 est.): $970 mil. **International reserves less gold** (Mar. 1998): $59.94 mil.

Transport: Railroad: Length: 493.7 mi. **Motor vehicles in use:** 26,000 passenger cars, 21,100 comm. vehicles. **Civil aviation:** 10 airports. **Chief ports:** Pointe-Noire, Brazzaville.

Communications: Television sets: 17 per 1,000 pop. **Radios:** 312 per 1,000 pop. **Telephones:** 22,000 main lines.

Health: Life expectancy at birth: 45.3 male; 48.9 female. **Births** (per 1,000 pop.): 39. **Deaths** (per 1,000 pop.): 16. **Natural increase:** 2.21%. **Infant mortality** (per 1,000 live births): 103.

Education: Compulsory: ages 6-16. **Literacy:** 75%.

Major International Organizations: UN (FAO, IBRD, ILO, IMF, IMO, WHO), OAU.

Embassy: 4891 Colorado Ave. NW 20011; 726-5500.

Website: http://lcweb2.loc.gov/frd/cs/zrtoc.html

The Loango Kingdom flourished in the 15th century, as did the Anzico Kingdom of the Batekes; by the late 17th century they had become weakened. By 1885, France established control of the region, then called the Middle Congo. Republic of the Congo gained independence Aug. 15, 1960.

After a 1963 coup sparked by trade unions, the country adopted a Marxist-Leninist stance, with the USSR and China vying for influence. France remained a dominant trade partner and source of technical assistance, however, and French-owned private enterprise retained a major economic role. In 1970, the country was renamed People's Republic of the Congo.

In 1990, Marxism was renounced and opposition parties legalized. In 1991 the country's name was changed back to Republic of the Congo, and a new constitution was approved. A democratically elected government came into office in 1992; one of its key problems was a resurgence of ethnic and regional hostilities. Factional fighting broke out in Brazzaville, June 5, 1997, and intensified during the summer, devastating the capital and forcing international aid workers to flee. Pres. Pascal Lissouba fled the capital Oct. 14. The civil war ended Oct. 15, when rebel forces (aided by Angola) took the city, restoring former Marxist dictator Denis Sassou-Nguesso to power.

Costa Rica

Republic of Costa Rica

People: Population: 3,604,642. **Age distrib.** (%): <15: 33.6; 65+: 5.0. **Pop. density:** 183 per sq. mi. **Urban:** 50%. **Ethnic groups:** White and mestizo 96%. **Principal language:** Spanish (official). **Chief religion:** Roman Catholic 95%.

Geography: Area: 19,730 sq. mi. **Location:** In Central America. **Neighbors:** Nicaragua on N, Panama on S. **Topography:** Lowlands by the Caribbean are tropical. The interior plateau, with an altitude of about 4,000 ft., is temperate. **Capital:** San José: 920,000*.

Government: Type: Republic. **Head of state:** Pres. Miguel Angel Rodríguez Echeverría; b Jan. 9, 1940; in office: May 8, 1998. **Local divisions:** 7 provinces. **Defense:** 0.6% of GDP. **Active troop strength:** 7,000 paramilitary.

Economy: Industries: Food processing, textiles, construction materials, fertilizer, plastics. **Chief crops:** Coffee, bananas, sugar, rice, potatoes. **Minerals:** Gold, limestone. **Other resources:** Fish, forests. **Arable land:** 6%. **Livestock** (1997): chickens: 16.50 mil; cattle: 1.53 mil; pigs: 350,000. **Fish catch** (1996): 24,203 metric tons. **Electricity prod.** (1996): 4.8 bil kWh. **Labor force:** 54% serv. & govt.; 22% agric.

Finance: Monetary unit: Colon (Sept. 1998: 261.65 = $1 U.S.). **Gross domestic product** (1996 est.): $19 bil. **Per capita GDP:** $5,500. **Imports** (1996): $3.86 bil; partners: U.S. 44%. **Exports** (1996): $3.82 bil; partners: U.S. 50%. **Tourism:** $713 mil. **International reserves less gold** (June 1998): $1.17 bil. **Gold:** 2,000 oz t. **Consumer prices** (change in 1997): 13.2%.

Transport: Railroad: Length: 590.0 mi. **Motor vehicles in use:** 48,684 passenger cars, 70,308 comm. vehicles. **Civil aviation:** 1.22 bil passenger-mi; 14 airports. **Chief ports:** Limon, Puntarenas, Golfito.

Communications: Television sets: 102 per 1,000 pop. **Radios:** 224 per 1,000 pop. **Telephones:** 525,682 main lines. **Daily newspaper circ.:** 102 per 1,000 pop.

Health: Life expectancy at birth: 73.5 male; 78.5 female. **Births** (per 1,000 pop.): 23. **Deaths** (per 1,000 pop.): 4. **Natural increase:** 1.87%. **Hospital beds** (1996): 1 per 566 persons. **Physicians** (1996): 1 per 763 persons. **Infant mortality** (per 1,000 live births): 13.

Education: Free and compulsory: ages 6-15. **Literacy:** 95%.

Major International Organizations: UN (FAO, IBRD, ILO, IMF, IMO, WHO, WTrO), OAS.

Embassy: 2114 S St. NW 20008; 234-2945.

Guaymi Indians inhabited the area when Spaniards arrived, 1502. Independence came in 1821. Costa Rica seceded from the Central American Federation in 1838. Since the civil war of 1948-49, there has been little violent social conflict, and free political institutions have been preserved. During 1993 there was an unusual wave of kidnappings and hostage-taking, some of it related to the international cocaine trade.

Costa Rica, though still a largely agricultural country, has achieved a relatively high standard of living, and land ownership is widespread. Tourism is growing rapidly.

Côte d'Ivoire

Republic of Ivory Coast

People: Population: 15,446,231. **Age distrib.** (%): <15: 46.7; 65+: 2.2. **Pop. density:** 124 per sq. mi. **Urban:** 44%. **Ethnic groups:** Baoule 23%, Bete 18%, Senoufou 15%, Malinke 11%, Agni, foreign Africans. **Principal languages:** French (official), Dioula and other native dialects. **Chief religions:** Muslim 60%, indigenous beliefs 25%, Christian 12%.

Geography: Area: 124,502 sq. mi. **Location:** On S coast of W Africa. **Neighbors:** Liberia, Guinea on W; Mali, Burkina Faso on N; Ghana on E. **Topography:** Forests cover the W half of the country, and range from a coastal strip to halfway to the N on the E. A sparse inland plain leads to low mountains in NW. **Capital:** Yamoussoukro (official); Abidjan (de facto). **Cities:** Abidjan 2,793,000*.

Government: Type: Republic. **Head of state:** Henri Konan Bédié; b 1934; in office: Dec. 7, 1993. **Head of government:** Prime Min. Daniel Kablan Duncan; b June 30, 1943; in office: Dec. 15, 1993. **Local divisions:** 50 departments. **Defense:** 0.9% of GDP (1996). **Active troop strength:** 8,400.

Economy: Industries: Food processing, vehicles, textiles. **Chief crops:** Coffee, cocoa, rubber, palm kernels. **Minerals:** Oil, diamonds, manganese. **Crude oil reserves** (1997): 100 mil bbls. **Other resources:** Timber. **Arable land:** 8%. **Livestock** (1997): chickens: 31.06 mil; sheep: 1.35 mil; cattle: 1.31 mil; goats: 1.05 mil; pigs: 271,100. **Fish catch** (1996): 70,650 metric tons. **Electricity prod.** (1996): 1.9 bil kWh. **Labor force:** 51% agric.; 12% manuf. & mining.

Finance: Monetary unit: CFA Franc (Sept. 1998: 580.94 = $1 U.S.). **Gross domestic product** (1996 est.): $23.9 bil. **Per capita GDP:** $1,620. **Imports** (1995): $2.4 bil; partners: France 32%, Nigeria 20%. **Exports** (1995): $3.7 bil; partners: France 18%, Germany 11%. **Tourism:** $68 mil. **National budget** (1993): $3.4 bil. **International reserves less gold** (Mar. 1998): $811.3 mil. **Gold:** 45,000 oz t. **Consumer prices** (change in 1997): 5.6%.

Transport: Railroad: Length: 409.9 mi. **Motor vehicles in use:** 160,000 passenger cars, 95,000 comm. vehicles. **Civil aviation:** 190.5 mil passenger-mi; 5 airports. **Chief ports:** Abidjan, Dabou, San-Pédro.

Communications: Television sets: 57 per 1,000 pop. **Radios:** 112 per 1,000 pop. **Telephones:** 129,808 main lines.

Health: Life expectancy at birth: 44.7 male; 47.8 female. **Births** (per 1,000 pop.): 42. **Deaths** (per 1,000 pop.): 16. **Natural increase:** 2.60%. **Hospital beds** (1993): 1 per 1,698 persons. **Infant mortality** (per 1,000 live births): 96.

Education: Free and compulsory: ages 7-13. **Literacy:** 40%.

Major International Organizations: UN and all of its specialized agencies, OAU.

Embassy: 2424 Massachusetts Ave. NW 20008; 797-0300.

Website: http://lcweb2.loc.gov/frd/cs/citoc.html

A French protectorate from 1842, Côte d'Ivoire became independent in 1960. It is the most prosperous of all the tropical African nations, as a result of diversification of agriculture for export, close ties to France, and encouragement of foreign investment. About 20% of the population are workers from neighboring countries. Côte d'Ivoire officially changed its name from Ivory Coast in Oct. 1985.

Students and workers protested, Feb. 1990, demanding the ouster of longtime Pres. Félix Houphouët-Boigny and multiparty democracy. Côte d'Ivoire held its first multiparty presidential election Oct. 1990, and Houphouët-Boigny retained his office. He died Dec. 7, 1993. The National Assembly named a successor, Henri Konan Bédié, who was reelected Oct. 22, 1995.

Croatia

Republic of Croatia

People: Population: 4,671,584. **Age distrib.** (%): <15: 17.1; 65+: 14.7. **Pop. density:** 214 per sq. mi. **Urban:** 56%. **Ethnic groups:** Croat 78%, Serb 12%. **Principal language:** Serbo-Croatian (official) 96%. **Chief religions:** Catholic 77%, Orthodox 11%.

Geography: Area: 21,829 sq. mi. **Location:** SE Europe, on the Balkan Peninsula. **Neighbors:** Slovenia, Hungary on N; Bosnia and Herzegovina, Yugoslavia on E. **Topography:** Flat plains in NE; highlands, low mtns. along Adriatic coast. **Capital:** Zagreb: 981,000*.

Government: Type: Parliamentary democracy. **Head of state:** Pres. Franjo Tudjman; b May 14, 1922; in office: May 30, 1990. **Head of government:** Prime Min. Zlatko Matesa; b June 17, 1949; in office: Nov. 4, 1995. **Local divisions:** 21 counties. **Defense:** 6.8% of GDP. **Active troop strength:** 64,700.

Economy: Industries: Chemicals, plastics, machine tools, aluminum, steel, paper. **Chief crops:** Olives, wheat, corn, sugar beets, fruits. **Minerals:** Oil, bauxite, iron, coal. **Crude oil reserves** (1997): 55.1 mil bbls. **Arable land:** 21%. **Livestock** (1997): chickens: 9.98 mil; pigs: 1.18 mil; sheep: 452,130; cattle: 451,266. **Electricity prod.** (1996): 10.7 bil kWh.

Finance: Monetary unit: Kuna (Sept. 1998: 6.36 = $1 U.S.). **Gross domestic product** (1996 est.): $21.4 bil. **Per capita GDP:** $4,300. **Imports** (1995): $7.6 bil; partners: Germany 21%, Italy 19%. **Exports** (1995): $4.6 bil; partners: Germany 22%, Italy 21%, Slovenia 18%. **Tourism:** $2.17 bil. **National budget** (1994 est.): $3.72 bil. **International reserves less gold** (June 1998): $2.69 bil. **Consumer prices** (change in 1997): 4.1%.

Transport: Railroad: Length: 1,676.1 mi. **Motor vehicles in use:** 698,000 passenger cars, 54,000 comm. vehicles. **Civil aviation:** 301.5 mil passenger-mi; 4 airports. **Chief ports:** Rijeka, Split, Dubrovnik.

Communications: Television sets: 230 per 1,000 pop. **Radios:** 230 per 1,000 pop. **Telephones:** 1,389,026 main lines. **Daily newspaper circ.:** 575 per 1,000 pop.

Health: Life expectancy at birth: 70.4 male; 77.3 female. **Births** (per 1,000 pop.): 10. **Deaths** (per 1,000 pop.): 11. **Natural increase:** –0.07%. **Hospital beds** (1994): 1 per 169 persons. **Physicians** (1994): 1 per 524 persons. **Infant mortality** (per 1,000 live births): 8.

Education: Free and compulsory: ages 7-15. **Literacy** (1993): 97%.

Major International Organizations: UN (FAO, IBRD, ILO, IMF, IMO, WHO), OSCE.

Embassy: 2343 Massachusetts Ave. NW 20008; 588-5899.

From the 7th century the area was inhabited by Croats, a south Slavic people. It was formed into a kingdom under Tomislav in 924, and joined with Hungary in 1102. The Croats became westernized and separated from Slavs under Austro-Hungarian influence. The Croats retained autonomy under the Hungarian crown. Slavonia was taken by Turks in the 16th century; the northern part was restored by the Treaty of Karlowitz in 1699. Croatia helped Austria put down the Hungarian revolution 1848-49 and as a result was set up with Slavonia as the separate Austrian crownland of Croatia and Slavonia, which was reunited to Hungary as part of Ausgleich in 1867. It united with other Yugoslav areas to proclaim the Kingdom of Serbs, Croats, and Slovenes in 1918. At the reorganization of Yugoslavia in 1929, Croatia and Slavonia became Savska county, which in 1939 was united with Primorje county to form the county of Croatia. A nominally independent state between 1941 and 1945, it became a constituent republic in the 1946 constitution.

On June 25, 1991, Croatia declared independence from Yugoslavia. Fighting began between ethnic Serbs and Croats, with the former gaining control of about 30% of Croatian territory. A cease-fire was declared in Jan. 1992, but new hostilities broke out in 1993. A cease-fire with Serb rebels forming a self-declared republic of Krajina was agreed to Mar. 30, 1994. Croatian government troops recaptured most of the Serb-held territory Aug. 1995. Pres. Franjo Tudjman signed a peace accord with leaders of Bosnia and Serbia in Paris, Dec. 14. Tudjman won reelection June 15, 1997; international monitors called the vote "free but not fair." The last Serb-held enclave, E Slavonia, returned to Croatian control Jan. 15, 1998.

Cuba

Republic of Cuba

People: Population: 11,050,729. **Age distrib.** (%): <15: 22.0; 65+: 9.5. **Pop. density:** 258 per sq. mi. **Urban:** 76%. **Ethnic groups:** Mulatto 51%, white 37%, black 11%. **Principal language:** Spanish (official). **Chief religion:** Roman Catholic 85% prior to Castro.

Geography: Area: 42,803 sq. mi. **Location:** In the Caribbean, westernmost of West Indies. **Neighbors:** Bahamas and U.S. to N, Mexico to W, Jamaica to S, Haiti to E. **Topography:** The coastline is about 2,500 miles. The N coast is steep and rocky, the S coast low and marshy. Low hills and fertile valleys cover more than half the country. Sierra Maestra, in the E, is the highest of 3 mountain ranges. **Capital:** Havana 2,221,000*.

Government: Type: Communist state. **Head of state:** Pres. Fidel Castro Ruz; b Aug. 13, 1926; in office: Dec. 3, 1976 (formerly prime min. since Feb. 16, 1959). **Local divisions:** 14 provinces, 1 special municipality. **Defense:** 5.4% of GDP. **Active troop strength:** 100,000.

Economy: Industries: Oil, food and tobacco processing, sugar. **Chief crops:** Sugar, tobacco, rice, coffee, fruit. **Minerals:** Cobalt, nickel, iron, copper, manganese, salt. **Crude oil reserves** (1997): 255 mil bbls. **Other resources:** Timber. **Arable land:** 24%. **Livestock** (1997): chickens: 19.00 mil; cattle: 4.65 mil; pigs: 1.50 mil; sheep: 310,000. **Fish catch** (1996): 80,234 metric tons. **Electricity prod.** (1996): 10.6 bil kWh.

Finance: Monetary unit: Cuban Peso (Sept. 1998: 23.00 = $1 U.S.). **Gross domestic product** (1996 est.): $16.2 bil. **Per capita GDP:** $1,480. **Imports** (1996 est.): $3.5 bil; partners: Russia 14%, Spain 13%, Mexico 11%. **Exports** (1996 est.): $2.1 bil; partners: Canada 23%, Russia 21%. **Tourism:** $1.34 bil.

Transport: Railroad: Length: 3,033 mi. **Motor vehicles in use:** 16,500 passenger cars, 30,000 comm. vehicles. **Civil aviation:** 1.65 bil passenger-mi; 14 airports. **Chief ports:** Havana, Matanzas, Cienfuegos, Santiago de Cuba.

Communications: Television sets: 200 per 1,000 pop. **Radios:** 327 per 1,000 pop. **Telephones:** 356,158 main lines. **Daily newspaper circ.:** 122 per 1,000 pop.

Health: Life expectancy at birth: 73.3 male; 78.1 female. **Births** (per 1,000 pop.): 13. **Deaths** (per 1,000 pop.): 7. **Natural increase:** 0.58%. **Hospital beds** (1992): 1 per 134 persons. **Physicians:** 1 per 231 persons. **Infant mortality** (per 1,000 live births): 8.

Education: Free and compulsory: ages 6-11. **Literacy:** 96%.

Major International Organizations: UN (FAO, ILO, IMO, WHO, WTrO).

Website: http://www.cubanet.org

Some 50,000 Indians lived in Cuba when it was reached by Columbus in 1492. Its name derives from the Indian Cubanacan. Except for British occupation of Havana, 1762-63, Cuba remained Spanish until 1898. A slave-based sugar plantation economy developed from the 18th century, aided by early mechanization of milling. Sugar remains the chief product and chief export despite government attempts to diversify.

A ten-year uprising ended in 1878 with guarantees of rights by Spain, which Spain failed to carry out. A full-scale movement under Jose Marti began Feb. 24, 1895.

The U.S. declared war on Spain in Apr. 1898, after the sinking of the USS *Maine* in Havana harbor, and defeated it in the Spanish-American War. Spain gave up all claims to Cuba. U.S. troops withdrew in 1902, but under 1903 and 1934 agreements, the U.S. leases a site at Guantánamo Bay in the SE as a naval base. U.S. and other foreign investments acquired a dominant role in the economy. In 1952, former Pres. Fulgencio Batista seized control and established a dictatorship, which grew increasingly harsh and corrupt. Fidel Castro assembled a rebel band in 1956; guerrilla fighting intensified in 1958. Batista fled Jan. 1, 1959, and in the resulting political vacuum Castro took power, becoming premier Feb. 16.

The government began a program of sweeping economic and social changes, without restoring promised liberties. Opponents were imprisoned, and some were executed. Some 700,000 Cubans emigrated in the first years after the Castro takeover, mostly to the U.S.

Cattle and tobacco lands were nationalized, while a system of cooperatives was instituted. By 1960 all banks and industrial companies had been nationalized, including over $1 billion worth of U.S.-owned properties, mostly without compensation.

Poor sugar crops resulted in farm collectivization, tight labor controls, and rationing, despite continued aid from the USSR and other Communist nations. A U.S.-imposed export embargo in 1962 severely damaged the economy.

In 1961, some 1,400 Cubans, trained and backed by the U.S. Central Intelligence Agency, unsuccessfully tried to invade and overthrow the regime. In the fall of 1962, the U.S. learned the USSR had brought nuclear missiles to Cuba. After an Oct. 22 warning from Pres. John F. Kennedy, the missiles were removed.

In 1977, Cuba and the U.S. signed agreements to exchange diplomats, without restoring full ties, and to regulate offshore fishing. In 1978, and again in 1980, the U.S. agreed to accept political prisoners released by Cuba, some of whom were criminals and mental patients. A 1987 agreement provided for 20,000 Cubans to emigrate to the U.S. each year; Cuba agreed to take back some 2,500 jailed in the U.S. since 1980.

In 1975-78, Cuba sent troops to aid one faction in the Angola civil war; the last Cuban troops were withdrawn by May 1991. Cuba's involvement in Central America, Africa, and the Caribbean contributed to poor relations with the U.S.

Cuba's economy, dependent on aid from other Communist countries, was severely shaken by the collapse of the Communist bloc in the late 1980s. Stiffer trade sanctions enacted by the U.S. in 1992 made things worse. Antigovernment demonstrations in Aug. 1994 prompted Castro to loosen emigration restrictions. A new U.S.-Cuba accord in Sept. ended the exodus of "boat people" after more than 30,000 had left Cuba. In another policy shift, the U.S. announced May 2, 1995, it would admit 20,000 Cuban refugees held at the Guantánamo base but would send further boat people back to Cuba.

The U.S. imposed additional sanctions after Cuba, Feb. 24, 1996, shot down 2 aircraft operated by an anti-Castro exile group based in Miami. Cuba blamed exile groups for bombings at Havana tourist hotels, July-Sept. 1997. Pope John Paul II visited Cuba, Jan. 21-25, 1998, denouncing U.S. trade sanctions while at the same time pressing Castro to release political prisoners and allow full political and religious freedom.

Cyprus

Republic of Cyprus

(†Figures do not include Turkish-held area—Turkish Republic of Northern Cyprus)

People: Population: 748,982. **Age distrib.** (%): <15: 24.5; 65+: 10.4. **Pop. density:** 210 per sq. mi. **Urban:** 55%. **Ethnic groups:** Greek 78%, Turkish 18%. **Principal languages:** Greek, Turkish (both official), English. **Chief religions:** Greek Orthodox 78%, Muslim 18%.

Geography: Area: 3,571 sq. mi. **Location:** In eastern Mediterranean Sea, off Turkish coast. **Neighbors:** Nearest are Turkey on N, Syria and Lebanon on E. **Topography:** Two mountain ranges run E-W, separated by a wide, fertile plain. **Capital:** Nicosia (1994 est.): 186,400†.

Government: Type: Republic. **Head of state:** Pres. Glafcos Clerides; b Apr. 24, 1919; in office: Mar. 1, 1993. **Local divisions:** 6 districts. **Defense:** 5.2% of GDP. **Active troop strength†:** 10,000.

Economy: Industries: Food, beverages, textiles. **Chief crops:** Barley, grapes, vegetables, citrus, potatoes, olives. **Minerals:** Copper, pyrites, asbestos. **Arable land:** 12%. **Livestock** (1997): chickens: 3.45 mil; pigs: 379,100; sheep: 250,000; goats: 220,000. **Electricity prod.** (1996): 2.2 bil. kWh. **Labor force†:** 62% serv., 25% ind., 13% agric.

Finance: Monetary unit: Pound (Sept. 1998: 1.90 = $2.13 U.S.). **Gross domestic product†** (1996 est.): $8.8 bil. **Per capita GDP†:** $13,700. **Imports†** (1996): $4 bil; partners: U.S. 16%, UK 11%, Italy 9%. **Exports†** (1996): $1.4 bil; partners: Russia 17%, UK 11%, **Tourism:** $1.61 bil. **National budget†** (1996): $3.3 bil. **International reserves less gold** (May 1998): $1.32 bil. **Gold:** 462,000 oz t. **Consumer prices** (change in 1997): 3.6%.

Transport: Motor vehicles†: in use: 226,832 passenger cars, 106,844 comm. vehicles. **Civil aviation†:** 1.59 bil passenger-mi; 2 airports. **Chief ports:** Famagusta, Limassol.

Communications: Television sets†: 160 per 1000 pop. **Radios:** 287 per 1,000 pop. **Telephones†:** 1 per 2.1 persons. **Daily newspaper circ.†:** 135 per 1,000 pop.

Health: Life expectancy at birth: 74.6 male; 79.1 female. **Births** (per 1,000 pop.): 14. **Deaths** (per 1,000 pop.): 8. **Natural increase:** 0.64%. **Hospital** beds† (1993): 1 per 191 persons. **Physicians†** (1993): 1 per 433 persons. **Infant mortality** (per 1,000 live births): 8.

Education: Free and compulsory: ages 5½-15. **Literacy** (1994): 95%.

Major International Organizations: UN (FAO, IBRD, ILO, IMF, IMO, WHO, WTrO), the Commonwealth, OSCE.

Embassy: 2211 R St. NW 20008; 462-5772.

Agitation for enosis (union) with Greece increased after World War II, with the Turkish minority opposed, and broke into violence in 1955-56. In 1959, Britain, Greece, Turkey, and Cypriot leaders approved a plan for an independent republic, with constitutional guarantees for the Turkish minority and permanent division of offices on an ethnic basis. Greek and Turkish Communal Chambers dealt with religion, education, and other matters.

Archbishop Makarios III, formerly the leader of the enosis movement, was elected president, and full independence became final Aug. 16, 1960. Further communal strife led the United Nations to send a peacekeeping force in 1964; its mandate has been repeatedly renewed.

The Cypriot National Guard, led by officers from the army of Greece, seized the government July 15, 1974. On July 20, Turkey invaded the island; Greece mobilized its forces but did not intervene. A cease-fire was arranged but collapsed. By Aug. 16, Turkish forces had occupied the NE 40% of the island, despite the presence of UN peacekeeping forces.

Turkish Cypriots voted overwhelmingly, June 8, 1975, to form a separate Turkish Cypriot federated state. A president and assembly were elected in 1976. Some 200,000 Greeks have been expelled from the Turkish-controlled area, replaced by thousands of Turks, some from the mainland.

Turkish Republic of Northern Cyprus

A declaration of independence was announced by Turkish-Cypriot leader Rauf Denktash, Nov. 15, 1983. The state is not internationally recognized, although it does have trade relations with some countries. Area of TRNC: 1,295 sq mi.; pop. (1995 est.): 134,000, 99% Turkish; capital: Lefkosa (Nicosia).

Czech Republic

People: Population: 10,286,470. **Age distrib.** (%): <15: 17.2; 65+: 13.7. **Pop. density:** 339 per sq. mi. **Urban:** 66%. **Ethnic groups:** Czech 94%, Slovak 3%. **Principal languages:** Czech (official), Slovak. **Chief religions:** Atheist 40%, Roman Catholic 39%, Protestant 5%, Orthodox 3%.

Geography: Area: 30,387 sq. mi. **Location:** In E central Europe. **Neighbors:** Poland on N, Germany on N and W, Austria on S, Slovakia on E and SE. **Topography:** Bohemia, in W, is a plateau surrounded by mountains; Moravia is hilly. **Capital:** Prague. **Cities** (1996 est.): Prague 1,209,855; Brno 388,899; Ostrava 324,813.

Government: Type: Republic. **Head of state:** Vaclav Havel; b Oct. 5, 1936; in office: Feb. 15, 1993. **Head of government:** Prime Min. Milos Zeman; b Sept. 28, 1944; in office: Jul. 17, 1998. **Local divisions:** 8 regions. **Defense:** 2.4% of GDP. **Active troop strength:** 70,000.

Economy: Industries: Machinery, oil products, iron and steel, glass, motor vehicles. **Chief crops:** Wheat, sugar beets, potatoes, hops, fruit. **Minerals:** Coal, kaolin. **Arable land:** 41%. **Crude oil reserves** (1997): 6.0 mil bbls. **Livestock:** (1997): chickens: 26.49; pigs: 4.08 mil; cattle: 1.87 mil; sheep: 120,900. **Electricity prod.** (1996): 60.2 bil kWh. **Labor force:** 33% ind.; 9% constr.; 7% agric.

Finance: Monetary unit: Koruna (Sept. 1998: 30.98 = $1 U.S.). **Gross domestic product** (1996 est.): $114.3 bil. **Per capita GDP:** $11,100. **Imports** (1996 est.): $27.8 bil; partners: EU 56%, Slovakia 13%. **Exports** (1996 est.): $21.9 bil; partners: EU 55%, Slovakia 16%. **Tourism:** $3.70 bil. **National budget** (1996 est.): $18.4 bil. **International reserves less gold** (Apr. 1998): $11.09 bil. **Gold:** 1.28 mil oz t. **Consumer prices** (change in 1997): 8.4%.

Transport: Railroad: Length: 5,845.5 mi. **Motor vehicles in use:** 4.41 mil passenger cars, 514,589 comm. vehicles. **Civil aviation:** 1.47 bil passenger-mi; 2 airports. **Chief ports:** Decin, Prague, Usti nad Labem.

Communications: Television sets: 407 per 1,000 pop. **Telephones:** 2,817,215 main lines. **Daily newspaper circ.:** 219 per 1,000 pop.

Health: Life expectancy at birth: 70.8 male; 77.7 female. **Births** (per 1,000 pop.): 9. **Deaths** (per 1,000 pop.): 11. **Natural increase:** –0.20. **Hospital beds** (1995): 1 per 138 persons. **Physicians** (1995): 1 per 268 persons. **Infant mortality** (per 1,000 live births): 7.

Education: Compulsory: ages 6-14. **Literacy** (est.): 99%.

Major International Organizations: UN (FAO, IBRD, ILO, IMF, IMO, WHO, WTrO), OECD, OSCE.

Embassy: 3900 Spring of Freedom St. NW 20008; 274-9101.

Bohemia and Moravia were part of the Great Moravian Empire in the 9th century and later became part of the Holy Roman Empire. Under the kings of Bohemia, Prague in the 14th century was the cultural center of Central Europe. Bohemia and Hungary became part of Austria-Hungary.

In 1914-18 Thomas G. Masaryk and Eduard Benes formed a provisional government with the support of Slovak leaders including Milan Stefanik. They proclaimed the Republic of Czechoslovakia Oct. 28, 1918.

Czechoslovakia

By 1938 Nazi Germany had worked up disaffection among German-speaking citizens in Sudetenland and demanded its cession. British Prime Min. Neville Chamberlain, with the acquiescence of France, signed with Hitler at Munich, Sept. 30, 1938, an agreement to the cession, with a guarantee of peace by Hitler and Mussolini. Germany occupied Sudetenland Oct. 1-2.

Hitler on Mar. 15, 1939, dissolved Czechoslovakia, made protectorates of Bohemia and Moravia, and supported the autonomy of Slovakia, proclaimed independent Mar. 14, 1939.

Soviet troops with some Czechoslovak contingents entered eastern Czechoslovakia in 1944 and reached Prague in May 1945; Benes returned as president. In May 1946 elections, the Communist Party won 38% of the votes, and Benes accepted Klement Gottwald, a Communist, as prime minister.

In Feb. 1948, the Communists seized power in advance of scheduled elections. In May 1948 a new constitution was approved. Benes refused to sign it. On May 30 the voters were offered a one-slate ballot and the Communists won full control. Benes resigned June 7 and Gottwald became president. The country was renamed the Czechoslovak Socialist Republic. A harsh Stalinist period followed, with complete and violent suppression of all opposition.

In Jan. 1968 a liberalization movement spread explosively through Czechoslovakia. Antonin Novotny, long the Stalinist ruler of the nation, was deposed as party leader and succeeded by Alexander Dubcek, a Slovak, who supported democratic reforms. On Mar. 22 Novotny resigned as president and was succeeded by Gen. Ludvik Svoboda. On Apr. 6, Prem. Joseph Lenart resigned and was succeeded by Oldrich Cernik, a reformer.

In July 1968 the USSR and 4 Warsaw Pact nations demanded an end to liberalization. On Aug. 20, the Soviet, Polish, East German, Hungarian, and Bulgarian armies invaded Czechoslovakia. Despite demonstrations and riots by students and workers, press censorship was imposed, liberal leaders were ousted from office and promises of loyalty to Soviet policies were made by some old-line Communist Party leaders.

On Apr. 17, 1969, Dubcek resigned as leader of the Communist Party and was succeeded by Gustav Husak. In Jan. 1970, Cernik was ousted. Censorship was tightened, and the Communist Party expelled a third of its members. In 1973, amnesty was offered to some of the 40,000 who fled the country after the 1968 invasion, but repressive policies continued.

More than 700 leading Czechoslovak intellectuals and former party leaders signed a human rights manifesto in 1977, called Charter 77, prompting a renewed crackdown by the regime.

The police crushed the largest antigovernment protests since 1968, when tens of thousands of demonstrators took to the streets of Prague, Nov. 17, 1989. As protesters demanded free elections, the Communist Party leadership resigned Nov. 24; millions went on strike Nov. 27.

On Dec. 10, 1989, the first cabinet in 41 years without a Communist majority took power; Vaclav Havel, playwright and human rights campaigner, was chosen president, Dec. 29. In Mar. 1990 the country was officially renamed the Czech and Slovak Federal Republic. Havel failed to win reelection July 3, 1992; his bid was blocked by a Slovak-led coalition.

Slovakia declared sovereignty, July 17. Czech and Slovak leaders agreed, July 23, on a basic plan for a peaceful division of Czechoslovakia into 2 independent states.

Czech Republic

Czechoslovakia split into 2 separate states—the Czech Republic and Slovakia—on Jan. 1, 1993. Havel was elected president of the Czech Republic on Jan. 26. On July 8, 1997, NATO invited the Czech Republic to become a full member of the alliance within 2 years. Record floods in July caused more than $1.7 billion in damage.

Denmark

Kingdom of Denmark

People: Population: 5,333,617. **Age distrib.** (%): <15: 18.2; 65+: 14.9. **Pop. density:** 321 per sq. mi. **Urban:** 85%. **Ethnic groups:** Scandinavian, Eskimo, Faroese, German. **Principal languages:** Danish (official), Faroese. **Chief religion:** Evangelical Lutheran 91%.

Geography: Area: 16,639 sq. mi. **Location:** In N Europe, separating the North and Baltic seas. **Neighbors:** Germany on S, Norway on NW, Sweden on NE. **Topography:** Denmark consists of the Jutland Peninsula and about 500 islands, 100 inhabited. The land is flat or gently rolling and is almost all in productive use. **Capital:** Copenhagen: 1,326,000*.

Government: Type: Constitutional monarchy. **Head of state:** Queen Margrethe II; b Apr. 16, 1940; in office: Jan. 14, 1972. **Head of government:** Prime Min. Poul Nyrup Rasmussen; b June 15, 1943; in office: Jan. 25, 1993. **Local divisions:** 14 counties and 1 city (Copenhagen). **Defense:** 1.7% of GDP. **Active troop strength:** 32,900.

Economy: Industries: Food processing, machinery, textiles, furniture, electronics. **Chief crops:** Grains, potatoes, sugar beets. **Minerals:** Oil, gas, salt. **Crude oil reserves** (1997): 862 mil bbls. **Arable land:** 60%. **Livestock** (1997): chickens: 19.22 mil; cattle: 2.03 mil; pigs: 11.10 mil; sheep: 170,000. **Fish catch** (1996): 1.68 mil metric tons. **Electricity prod.** (1996): 50.6 bil kWh. **Labor force:** 70% serv. & govt.; 19% manuf. & mining; 6% constr.

Finance: Monetary unit: Krone (Sept. 1998: 6.59 = $1 U.S.). **Gross domestic product** (1996 est.): $118.2 bil. **Per capita GDP:** $22,700. **Imports** (1996 est.): $42.4 bil; partners: Germany 22%, Sweden 12%. **Exports** (1996 est.): $47.6 bil; partners: Germany 23%, Sweden 10%. **Tourism:** $3.16 bil. **National budget** (1996 est.): $66.4 bil. **International reserves less gold** (June 1998): $16.71 bil. **Gold:** 2.0 mil oz t. **Consumer prices** (change in 1997): 2.2%.

Transport: Railroad: Length: 1,768.6 mi. **Motor vehicles in use:** 1.74 mil passenger cars, 348,571 comm. vehicles. **Civil aviation:** 3.39 bil passenger-mi; 13 airports. **Chief ports:** Copenhagen, Alborg, Arhus, Odense.

Communications: Television sets: 516 per 1,000 pop. **Radios:** 988 per 1,000 pop. **Telephones:** 3,251,189 main lines. **Daily newspaper circ.:** 308 per 1,000 pop.

Health: Life expectancy at birth: 73.6 male; 79.1 female. **Births** (per 1,000 pop.): 12. **Deaths** (per 1,000 pop.): 11. **Natural increase:** 0.11%. **Hospital beds** (1994): 1 per 199 persons. **Physicians** (1994): 1 per 358 persons. **Infant mortality** (per 1,000 live births): 5.

Education: Compulsory: ages 7-16. **Literacy** (1997): 100%.

Major International Organizations: UN and all of its specialized agencies, EU, NATO, OECD, OSCE.

Embassy: 3200 Whitehaven St. NW 20008; 234-4300.

Website: http://www.denmark.org

The origin of Copenhagen dates back to ancient times, when the fishing and trading place named Havn (port) grew up on a cluster of islets, but Bishop Absalon (1128-1201) is regarded as the actual founder of the city.

Danes formed a large component of the Viking raiders in the early Middle Ages. The Danish kingdom was a major north European power until the 17th century, when it lost its land in southern Sweden. Norway was separated in 1815, and Schleswig-Holstein in 1864. Northern Schleswig was returned in 1920.

Voters ratified the Maastricht Treaty, the basic document of the European Union, in May 1993, after rejecting it in 1992.

The **Faroe Islands** in the North Atlantic, about 300 mi. NW of the Shetlands, and 850 mi. from Denmark proper, 18 inhabited, have an area of 540 sq. mi. and pop. (1997 est.) of 43,057. They are an administrative division of Denmark, self-governing in most matters. Torshavn is the capital.

Greenland (Kalaallit Nunaat)

Greenland, a huge island between the North Atlantic and the Polar Sea, is separated from the North American continent by Davis Strait and Baffin Bay. Its total area is 840,000 sq. mi., 84% of which is ice-capped. Most of the island is a lofty plateau 9,000 to 10,000 ft. in altitude. The average thickness of the cap is 1,000 ft. The population (1998 est.) is 59,309. Under the 1953 Danish constitution the colony became an integral part of the realm with representatives in the Folketing (Danish legislature). The Danish parliament, 1978, approved home rule for Greenland, effective May 1, 1979. With home rule, Greenlandic place names came into official use. The technically correct name for Greenland is now Kalaallit Nunaat; its capital is Nuuk, rather than Godthab. Fish is the principal export (115,940 metric tons in 1996).

Djibouti

Republic of Djibouti

People: Population: 440,727. **Age distrib.** (%): <15: 42.8; 65+: 2.6. **Pop. density:** 52 per sq. mi. **Urban:** 82%. **Ethnic groups:** Somali 60%, Afar 35%. **Principal languages:** French, Arabic (both official); Afar, Somali. **Chief religions:** Muslim 94%, Christian 6%.

Geography: Area: 8,494 sq. mi. **Location:** On E coast of Africa, separated from Arabian Peninsula by the strategically vital strait of Bab el-Mandeb. **Neighbors:** Ethiopia on W and SW, Eritrea on NW, Somalia on SE. **Topography:** The territory, divided into a low coastal plain, mountains behind, and an interior plateau, is arid, sandy, and desolate. The climate is generally hot and dry. **Capital:** Djibouti (1995): 383,000.

Government: Type: Republic. **Head of state:** Pres. Hassan Gouled Aptidon; b 1916; in office: June 24, 1977. **Head of government:** Prem. Barkat Gourad Hamadou; in office: Sept. 30, 1978. **Local divisions:** 5 districts. **Defense:** 5.2% of GDP. **Active troop strength:** 8,400.

Economy: Based on service activities. **Livestock** (1997): goats: 507,000; sheep: 470,000; cattle: 190,000. **Electricity prod.** (1996): 175 mil kWh.

Finance: Monetary unit: Franc (Sept. 1998: 177.72 = $1 U.S.). **Gross domestic product** (1995 est.): $500 mil. **Per capita GDP:** $1,200. **Imports** (1994 est.): $384 mil; partners: France 13%, Thailand 15%. **Exports** (1994 est.): $184 mil; partners: Somalia 48%, Yemen 42%. **Tourism:** $4 mil. **National budget** (1995 est.): $181 mil. **International reserves less gold** (Apr. 1998): $64.78 mil.

Transport: Railroad: Length: 60.2 mi. **Motor vehicles in use:** 13,000 passenger cars, 3,000 comm. vehicles. **Civil aviation:** 1 airport. **Chief port:** Djibouti.

Communications: Television sets: 43 per 1,000 pop. **Radios:** 80 per 1,000 pop. **Telephones:** 8,151 main lines.

Health: Life expectancy at birth: 49.1 male; 53.2 female. **Births** (per 1,000 pop.): 42. **Deaths** (per 1,000 pop.): 15. **Natural increase:** 2.71%. **Infant mortality** (per 1,000 live births): 102.

Education: Literacy (1995): 46%.

Major International Organizations: UN (FAO, IBRD, ILO, IMF, IMO, WHO, WTrO), AL, OAU.

Embassy: Suite 515, 1156 15th St. NW 20005; 331-0270.

Website: http://www.djibouti.org

France gained control of the territory in stages between 1862 and 1900. As French Somaliland it became an overseas territory of France in 1945; in 1967 it was renamed the French Territory of the Afars and the Issas.

Ethiopia and Somalia have renounced their claims to the area, but each has accused the other of trying to gain control. There were clashes between Afars (ethnically related to Ethiopians) and Issas (related to Somalis) in 1976. Immigrants from both countries continued to enter the country up to independence, which came June 27, 1977.

French aid is the mainstay of the economy, as well as assistance from Arab countries. A peace accord Dec. 1994 ended a 3-year-long uprising by Afar rebels.

Dominica

Commonwealth of Dominica

People: Population: 65,777. **Age distrib.:** (%): <15: 27.1; 65+: 9.5. **Pop. density:** 227 per sq. mi. **Urban:** 70%. **Ethnic groups:** Nearly all African, some Carib. **Principal languages:** English (official), French patois. **Chief religions:** Roman Catholic 77%, Protestant 15%.

Geography: Area: 290 sq. mi. **Location:** In Eastern Caribbean, most northerly Windward Isl. **Neighbors:** Guadeloupe to N, Martinique to S. **Topography:** Mountainous, a central ridge running from N to S, terminating in cliffs; volcanic in origin, with numerous thermal springs; rich deep topsoil on leeward side, red tropical clay on windward coast. **Capital:** Roseau (1991 est.): 15,900.

Government: Type: Parliamentary democracy. **Head of state:** Pres. Crispin Anselm Sorhaindo; b 1931; in office: Oct. 25, 1993. **Head of government:** Prime Min. Edison Chenfil James; b Oct. 18, 1943; in office: June 14, 1995. **Local divisions:** 10 parishes.

Economy: Industries: Soap, tourism. **Chief crops:** Bananas, citrus mangoes, coconuts. **Other resources:** Forests. **Arable land:** 9%. **Livestock** (1997): chickens: 190,000. **Electricity prod.** (1996): 40 mil kWh. **Labor force:** 40% agric.; 32% ind. & commerce; 28% services.

Finance: Monetary unit: East Caribbean Dollar (Sept. 1998: 2.70 = $1 U.S.). **Gross domestic product** (1996 est.): $208 mil. **Per capita GDP:** $2,500. **Imports** (1996): $122 mil; partners: U.S. 25%. **Exports** (1996): $40 mil; partners: UK 55%. **Tourism:** $37 mil. **National budget** (FY 1995-96 est.): $95.8 mil. **International reserves less gold** (Mar. 1998): $24.77 mil. **Consumer prices** (change in 1997): 2.4%.

Transport: Motor vehicles in use: 2,800 passenger cars, 2,900 comm. vehicles. **Civil aviation:** 2 airports. **Chief port:** Roseau.

Communications: Television sets: 70 per 1,000 pop. **Radios:** 875 per 1,000 pop. **Telephones:** 18,737 main lines.

Health: Life expectancy at birth: 74.9 male; 80.8 female. **Births** (per 1,000 pop.): 17. **Deaths** (per 1,000 pop.): 6. **Natural increase:** 1.11%. **Hospital beds** (1992): 1 per 298 persons. **Physicians** (1993): 1 per 2,952 persons. **Infant mortality** (per 1,000 live births): 9.

Education: Free and compulsory: ages 5-15. **Literacy** (1993): 90%.

Major International Organizations: UN (FAO, IBRD, ILO, IMF, IMO, WHO, WTrO), Caricom, the Commonwealth, OAS, OECS.

Embassy: 3216 New Mexico Ave. NW 20016; 364-6781

A British colony since 1805, Dominica was granted self-government in 1967. Independence was achieved Nov. 3, 1978.

Hurricane David struck, Aug. 30, 1979, devastating the island and destroying the banana plantations, Dominica's economic mainstay. Coups were attempted in 1980 and 1981.

Dominica participated in the 1983 U.S.-led invasion of Grenada.

Dominican Republic

People: Population: 7,998,766. **Age distrib.** (%): <15: 35.2; 65+: 4.4. **Pop. density:** 425 per sq. mi. **Urban:** 63%. **Ethnic groups:** Mixed 73%, white 16%, black 11%. **Principal language:** Spanish (official). **Chief religion:** Roman Catholic 95%.

Geography: Area: 18,815 sq. mi. **Location:** In West Indies, sharing isl. of Hispaniola with Haiti. **Neighbors:** Haiti on W, Puerto Rico (U.S.) to E. **Topography:** The Cordillera Central range crosses the center of the country, rising to over 10,000 ft., highest in the Caribbean. The Cibao Valley to the N is major agricultural area. **Capital:** Santo Domingo. **Cities:** Santo Domingo 3,166,000; Santiago de los Caballeros 1,289,000*.

Government: Type: Republic. **Head of state:** Pres. Leonel Fernández Reyna; b Dec. 26, 1953; in office: Aug. 16, 1996.

Local divisions: 29 provinces and national district. **Defense:** 1.1% of GDP. **Active troop strength:** 24,500.

Economy: Industries: Sugar refining, cement, tourism. **Chief crops:** Sugar, cocoa, coffee, cotton, rice. **Minerals:** Nickel, bauxite, gold, silver. **Arable land:** 23%. **Livestock** (1997): chickens: 42.95; cattle: 2.48 mil; pigs: 960,000; goats: 570,000; sheep: 135,000. **Electricity prod.** (1996): 6.7 bil kWh. **Labor force:** 50% agric.; 32% serv. & govt.; 18% ind.

Finance: Monetary unit: Peso (Sept. 1998: 15.40 = $1 U.S.). **Gross domestic product** (1996 est.): $29.8 bil. **Per capita GDP:** $3,670. **Imports** (1996 est.): $5.3 bil; partners: U.S. 44% EU 16%. **Exports** (1996 est.): $3.1 bil; partners: U.S. 45%, EU 34%. **Tourism:** $2.11 bil. **National budget** (1994 est.): $2.2 bil. **International reserves less gold** (May 1998): $294.9 mil. **Gold:** 18,000 oz t. **Consumer prices** (change in 1997): 8.3%.

Transport: Railroad: Length: 1,083 mi. **Motor vehicles in use:** 113,835 passenger cars, 92,198 comm. vehicles. **Civil aviation:** 8.6 mil passenger-mi; 7 airports. **Chief ports:** Santo Domingo, San Pedro de Macoris, Puerto Plata.

Communications: Television sets: 97 per 1,000 pop. **Radios:** 154 per 1,000 pop. **Telephones:** 665,013 main lines. **Daily newspaper circ.:** 35 per 1,000 pop.

Health: Life expectancy at birth: 67.5 male; 72.0 female. **Births** (per 1,000 pop.): 26. **Deaths** (per 1,000 pop.): 6. **Natural increase:** 2.07%. **Hospital beds** (1994): 1 per 858 persons. **Physicians** (1994): 1 per 1,052 persons. **Infant mortality** (per 1,000 live births): 44.

Education: Compulsory: ages 6-14. **Literacy** (1995): 82%.

Major International Organizations: UN (FAO, IBRD, ILO, IMF, IMO, WHO, WTrO), OAS.

Embassy: 1715 22d St. NW 20008; 332-6280.

Carib and Arawak Indians inhabited the island of Hispaniola when Columbus landed in 1492. The city of Santo Domingo, founded 1496, is the oldest settlement by Europeans in the hemisphere and has the supposed ashes of Columbus in an elaborate tomb in its ancient cathedral.

The western third of the island was ceded to France in 1697. Santo Domingo itself was ceded to France in 1795. Haitian leader Toussaint L'Ouverture seized it, 1801. Spain returned intermittently 1803-21, as several native republics came and went. Haiti ruled again, 1822-44, and Spanish occupation occurred 1861-63.

The country was occupied by U.S. Marines from 1916 to 1924, when a constitutionally elected government was installed.

In 1930, Gen. Rafael Leonidas Trujillo Molina was elected president. Trujillo ruled brutally until his assassination in 1961. Pres. Joaquín Balaguer, appointed by Trujillo in 1960, resigned under pressure in 1962.

Juan Bosch, elected president in the first free elections in 38 years, was overthrown in 1963. On Apr. 24, 1965, a revolt was launched by followers of Bosch and others, including a few Communists. Four days later U.S. Marines intervened against pro-Bosch forces. Token units were later sent by 5 South American countries as a peacekeeping force. A provisional government supervised a June 1966 election, in which Balaguer defeated Bosch. Balaguer remained in office for most of the next 28 years, but his May 1994 reelection was widely denounced as fraudulent. He cut short his term and on June 30, 1996, Leonel Fernández Reyna was elected.

Hurricane Georges struck Sept. 22, 1998, causing extensive property damage and claiming more than 200 lives.

Ecuador

Republic of Ecuador

People: Population: 12,336,572. **Age distrib.** (%): <15: 35.9; 65+: 4.4. **Pop. density:** 117 per sq. mi. **Urban:** 60%. **Ethnic groups:** Mestizo 55%, Amerindian 25%, Spanish 10%, black 10%. **Principal languages:** Spanish (official), Quechua, other Amerindian. **Chief religion:** Roman Catholic 95%.

Geography: Area: 105,037 sq. mi. **Location:** In NW South America, on Pacific coast, astride the Equator. **Neighbors:** Colombia on N, Peru on E and S. **Topography:** Two ranges of Andes run N and S, splitting the country into 3 zones: hot, humid lowlands on the coast; temperate highlands between the ranges; and rainy, tropical lowlands to the E. **Capital:** Quito. **Cities:** Guayaquil 1,831,000; Quito 1,298,000*.

Government: Type: Republic. **Head of state:** Pres. Jamil Mahuad Witt; b July 29, 1949; in office: Aug. 10, 1998. **Local divisions:** 21 provinces. **Defense:** 3.4% of GDP. **Active troop strength:** 57,100.

Economy: Industries: Oil, food processing, metalwork, textiles. **Chief crops:** Bananas, cocoa coffee, rice, sugar, potatoes. **Minerals:** Oil, gold. **Crude oil reserves** (1997): 2.1 bil bbls. **Other resources:** Forests (leading balsawood producer), seafood (world's 2d lgst. shrimp producer.). **Arable land:** 6%. **Livestock** (1997): chickens: 64.74 mil; cattle: 5.15 mil; pigs: 2.71 mil; sheep: 1.93 mil; goats: 307,000. **Fish catch** (1996): 684,806 metric tons. **Electricity prod.** (1996): 8.5 bil kWh. **Labor force:** 38% services/other activities; 29% agric.; 18% manuf.; 15% commerce.

Finance: Monetary unit: Sucre (Sept. 1998: 5,525.50 = $1 U.S.). **Gross domestic product** (1996 est.): $47 bil. **Per capita GDP:** $4,100. **Imports** (1995): $3.7 bil; partners: Latin America 35%, U.S. 32%. **Exports** (1996): $4.9 bil; partners: U.S. 39%, Latin America 25%. **Tourism:** $289 mil. **National budget** (1996 est.): $3.6 bil. **International reserves less gold** (June 1998): $1.83 bil. **Gold:** 414,000 oz t. **Consumer prices** (change in 1997): 30.6%.

Transport: Railroad: Length: 599.3 mi. **Motor vehicles in use:** 255,640 passenger cars, 424,120 comm. vehicles. **Civil aviation:** 1.03 bil passenger-mi; 14 airports. **Chief ports:** Guayaquil, Manta, Esmeraldas, Puerto Bolivar.

Communications: Television sets: 79 per 1,000 pop. **Radios:** 277 per 1,000 pop. **Telephones:** 857,000 main lines. **Daily newspaper circ.:** 72 per 1,000 pop.

Health: Life expectancy at birth: 69.2 male; 74.5 female. **Births** (per 1,000 pop.): 23. **Deaths** (per 1,000 pop.): 5. **Natural increase:** 1.80%. **Hospital beds** (1992): 1 per 623 persons. **Physicians** (1993): 1 per 904 persons. **Infant mortality** (per 1,000 live births): 32.

Education: Free and compulsory for 6 years between ages 6-14. **Literacy** (1995): 90%.

Major International Organizations: UN (FAO, IBRD, ILO, IMF, IMO, WHO, WTrO), OAS.

Embassy: 2535 15th St. NW 20009; 234-7200.

The region, which was the northern Inca empire, was conquered by Spain in 1533. Liberation forces defeated the Spanish May 24, 1822, near Quito. Ecuador became part of the Great Colombia Republic but seceded, May 13, 1830.

Since 1972, the economy has revolved around petroleum exports; oil revenues have declined since 1982, causing severe economic problems. Ecuador suspended interest payments for 1987 on its estimated $8.2 billion foreign debt following a Mar. 5-6 earthquake that left 20,000 homeless and destroyed a stretch of the country's main oil pipeline.

Ecuadoran Indians staged protests in the 1990s to demand greater rights. A border war with Peru flared from Jan. 26, 1995, until a truce took effect Mar. 1. Vice-Pres. Alberto Dahik resigned and fled Ecuador, Oct. 11, 1995, to avoid arrest on corruption charges. Elected president in a runoff, July 7, 1996, Abdalá Bucaram—a populist known as El Loco, or "The Crazy One"—imposed stiff price increases and other austerity measures. His rising unpopularity and erratic behavior led the National Congress, Feb. 6, 1997, to dismiss him for "mental incapacity." Bucaram went into exile, and Congress, on Feb. 11, confirmed its leader, Fabián Alarcón, as president for 18 months. Voters endorsed the actions in a referendum May 25. Jamil Mahuad Witt, mayor of Quito, won a presidential runoff election July 12, 1998. On Sept. 14 he imposed emergency measures to rescue Ecuador's ailing economy.

The **Galapagos Islands,** pop. (1996 est.) 14,000, about 600 mi. to the W, are the home of huge tortoises and other unusual animals.

Egypt

Arab Republic of Egypt

People: Population: 66,050,004. **Age distrib** (%) <15: 36.1; 65+: 3.7. **Pop. density:** 171 per sq. mi. **Urban:** 45%. **Ethnic groups:** Eastern Hamitic stock (Egyptian, Bedouin, Berber) 99%. **Principal languages:** Arabic (official), English, French. **Chief religions:** Muslim (mostly Sunni) 94%, Coptic Christian and other 6%.

Geography: Area: 385,229 sq. mi. **Location:** Northeast corner of Africa. **Neighbors:** Libya on W, Sudan on S, Israel and Gaza Strip on E. **Topography:** Almost entirely desolate and barren, with hills and mountains in E and along Nile. The Nile Valley, where most of the people live, stretches 550 miles. **Capital:** Cairo. **Cities:** Cairo 9,690,000; Alexandria 3,584,000; Shubra El-Khemia 1,204,000*.

Government: Type: Republic. **Head of state:** Pres. Hosni Mubarak; b May 4, 1928; in office: Oct. 14, 1981. **Head of government:** Prime Min. Kamal al-Ganzouri; b Jan. 12, 1933; in office: Jan. 4, 1996. **Local divisions:** 26 governorates. **Defense:** 4.5% of GDP. **Active troop strength:** 440,000.

Economy: Industries: Textiles, tourism, chemicals, oil, food processing, cement. **Chief crops:** Cotton, rice, beans, fruits, wheat, vegetables, corn. **Minerals:** Oil, gas, phosphates, gypsum, iron, manganese, limestone. **Crude oil reserves** (1997): 3.8 bil bbls. **Arable land:** 2%. **Livestock** (1997): chickens: 85.00 mil; sheep: 4.30 mil; goats: 3.20 mil; buffalo: 3.15 mil; cattle 3.00 mil. **Fish catch** (1996): 265,196 metric tons.

Electricity prod. (1996): 46 bil kWh. **Labor force:** 40% agric.; 38% serv. & gov't.

Finance: Monetary unit: Pound (Sept. 1998: 3.41 = $1 U.S.). **Gross domestic product** (1996 est.): $183.9 bil. **Per capita GDP:** $2,900. **Imports** (FY 1995-96 est.): $13.8 bil; partners: U.S. 19%, Germany 10%. **Exports** (FY 1995-96 est.): $4.6 bil; partners: Italy 19%, U.S. 11%. **Tourism:** $3.85 bil. **National budget** (FY 1995-96): $18.8 bil. **International reserves less gold** (May 1998): $18.47 bil. **Gold:** 2.43 mil oz t. **Consumer prices** (change in 1997): 4.6%.

Transport: Railroad: Length: 2,950.4 mi. **Motor vehicles in use:** 1.28 mil passenger cars, 423,300 comm. vehicles. **Civil aviation:** 5.43 bil passenger-mi; 11 airports. **Chief ports:** Alexandria, Port Said, Suez.

Communications: Television sets: 110 per 1,000 pop. **Radios:** 312 per 1,000 pop. **Telephones:** 3,024,947 main lines. **Daily newspaper circ.:** 43 per 1,000 pop.

Health: Life expectancy at birth: 60.1 male; 64.1 female. **Births** (per 1,000 pop.): 27. **Deaths** (per 1,000 pop.): 8. **Natural increase:** 1.89%. **Hospital beds** (1994): 1 per 515 persons. **Physicians** (1996): 1 per 472 persons. **Infant mortality** (per 1,000 live births): 69.

Education: Compulsory for 5 years between ages 6-13. **Literacy** (1995): 51%.

Major International Organizations: UN (FAO, IBRD, ILO, IMF, IMO, WHO, WTrO), AL, OAU.

Embassy: 3521 International Ct. NW 20008; 895-5400.

Website: http://www.idsc.gov.eg

Archaeological records of ancient Egyptian civilization date back to 4000 BC. A unified kingdom arose around 3200 BC and extended its way south into Nubia and as far north as Syria. A high culture of rulers and priests was built on an economic base of serfdom, fertile soil, and annual flooding of the Nile.

Imperial decline facilitated conquest by Asian invaders (Hyksos, Assyrians). The last native dynasty fell in 341 BC to the Persians, who were in turn replaced by Greeks (Alexander and the Ptolemies), Romans, Byzantines, and Arabs, who introduced Islam and the Arabic language. The ancient Egyptian language is preserved only in Coptic Christian liturgy.

Egypt was ruled as part of larger Islamic empires for several centuries. The Mamluks, a military caste of Caucasian origin, ruled Egypt from 1250 until defeat by the Ottoman Turks in 1517. Under Turkish sultans the khedive as hereditary viceroy had wide authority. Britain intervened in 1882 and took control of administration, though nominal allegiance to the Ottoman Empire continued until 1914.

The country was a British protectorate from 1914 to 1922. A 1936 treaty strengthened Egyptian autonomy, but Britain retained bases in Egypt and a condominium over the Sudan. Britain fought German and Italian armies from Egypt, 1940-42. In 1951 Egypt abrogated the 1936 treaty; the Sudan became independent in 1956.

The uprising of July 23, 1952 was led by the Society of Free Officers, who named Maj. Gen. Mohammed Naguib commander in chief and forced King Farouk to abdicate. When the republic was proclaimed June 18, 1953, Naguib became its first president and premier. Lt. Col. Gamal Abdel Nasser removed Naguib and became premier in 1954. In 1956, he was voted president. Nasser died in 1970 and was replaced by Vice Pres. Anwar Sadat.

The Aswan High Dam, completed 1971, provides irrigation for more than a million acres of land. Artesian wells, drilled in the Western Desert, reclaimed 43,000 acres, 1960-66.

When the state of Israel was proclaimed in 1948, Egypt joined other Arab nations invading Israel and was defeated.

After terrorist raids across its border, Israel invaded Egypt's Sinai Peninsula, Oct. 29, 1956. Egypt rejected a cease-fire demand by Britain and France; on Oct. 31 the 2 nations dropped bombs and on Nov. 5-6 landed forces. Egypt and Israel accepted a UN cease-fire; fighting ended Nov. 7.

A UN Emergency Force guarded the 117-mile-long border between Egypt and Israel until May 19, 1967, when it was withdrawn at Nasser's demand. Egyptian troops entered the Gaza Strip and the heights of Sharm el Sheikh and 3 days later closed the Strait of Tiran to all Israeli shipping. Full-scale war broke out June 5; before it ended under a UN cease-fire June 10, Israel had captured Gaza and the Sinai Peninsula, controlled the east bank of the Suez Canal, and reopened the gulf. After sporadic fighting, Israel and Egypt agreed, Aug. 7, 1970, to a new cease-fire.

In a surprise attack Oct. 6, 1973, Egyptian forces crossed the Suez Canal into the Sinai. (At the same time, Syrian forces attacked Israelis on the Golan Heights.) Egypt was supplied by a USSR military airlift; the U.S. responded with an airlift to Israel. Israel counterattacked, crossed the canal, surrounded Suez City. A UN cease-fire took effect Oct. 24.

Under an agreement signed Jan. 18, 1974, Israeli forces withdrew from the canal's W bank; limited numbers of Egyptian forces occupied a strip along the E bank. A second accord was signed in 1975, with Israel yielding Sinai oil fields. Pres. Sadat's surprise visit to Jerusalem, Nov. 1977, opened the prospect of peace with Israel. On Mar. 26, 1979, Egypt and Israel signed a formal peace treaty, ending 30 years of war, and establishing diplomatic relations. Israel returned control of the Sinai to Egypt in Apr. 1982.

Tension between Muslim fundamentalists and Christians in 1981 caused street riots and culminated in a nationwide security crackdown in Sept. Pres Sadat was assassinated on Oct. 6; he was succeeded by Hosni Mubarak.

Egypt was a political and military supporter of the Allied forces in their defeat of Iraq in the Persian Gulf War, 1991.

Egypt saw a rising tide of Islamic fundamentalist violence in the 1990s. Egyptian security forces conducted raids against Islamic militants, some of whom were executed for terrorism. Naguib Mahfouz, winner of the 1988 Nobel Prize for Literature, was stabbed by Islamic militants Oct. 14, 1994. Pres. Mubarak escaped assassination in Ethiopia, June 26, 1995; Egypt blamed Sudan for the attack. On Nov. 17, 1997, near Luxor, Muslim extremists killed 58 foreign tourists and 4 Egyptians.

The **Suez Canal,** 103 mi. long, links the Mediterranean and Red seas. It was built by a French corporation 1859-69, but Britain obtained controlling interest in 1875. The last British troops were removed June 13, 1956. On July 26, Egypt nationalized the canal.

El Salvador

Republic of El Salvador

People: Population: 5,752,067. **Age distrib.** (%): <15: 37.0; 65+: 5.2. **Pop. density:** 708 per sq. mi. **Urban:** 45%. **Ethnic groups:** Mestizo 94%, Amerindian 5%. **Principal language:** Spanish (official). **Chief religions:** Roman Catholic 75%, many Protestant groups.

Geography: Area: 8,124 sq. mi. **Location:** In Central America. **Neighbors:** Guatemala on W, Honduras on N. **Topography:** A hot Pacific coastal plain in the south rises to a cooler plateau and valley region, densely populated. The N is mountainous, including many volcanoes. **Capital:** San Salvador: 1,214,000*.

Government: Type: Republic. **Head of state:** Pres. Armando Calderón Sol; b June 24, 1948; in office: June 1, 1994. **Local divisions:** 14 departments. **Defense:** 1.5% of GDP. **Active troop strength:** 28,400.

Economy: Industries: Food and beverages, oil products, chemicals. **Chief crops:** Coffee, corn, sugar, rice. **Other resources:** Hydropower. **Arable land:** 27%. **Livestock** (1997): chickens: 5.05 mil; cattle: 1.18 mil; pigs: 316,400. **Electricity prod.** (1996): 3.6 bil kWh. **Labor force:** 40% agric.; 16% commerce; 15% manuf.; 13% govt.

Finance: Monetary unit: Colon (Sept. 1998: 8.76 = $1 U.S.). **Gross domestic product** (1996 est.): $12.2 bil. **Per capita GDP:** $2,080. **Imports** (1996): $3.2 bil; partners: U.S. 42%, Guatemala 11%. **Exports** (1996): $1.8 bil; partners: U.S. 23%, Guatemala 22%. **Tourism:** $67 mil. **National budget** (1997 est.): $1.82 bil. **International reserves less gold** (May 1998): $1.58 bil. **Gold:** 469,000 oz t. **Consumer prices** (change in 1997): 4.5%.

Transport: Railroad: Length: 349 mi. **Motor vehicles in use:** 35,300 passenger cars, 44,800 comm. vehicles. **Civil aviation:** 1.35 bil passenger-mi; 1 airport. **Chief ports:** La Union, Acajutla, La Libertad.

Communications: Television sets: 91 per 1,000 pop. **Radios:** 373 per 1,000 pop. **Telephones:** 325,259 main lines. **Daily newspaper circ.:** 53 per 1,000 pop.

Health: Life expectancy at birth: 66.3 male; 73.2 female. **Births** (per 1,000 pop.): 27. **Deaths** (per 1,000 pop.): 6. **Natural increase:** 2.04%. **Hospital beds** (1993): 1 per 588 persons. **Physicians** (1993): 1 per 1,219 persons. **Infant mortality** (per 1,000 live births): 29.

Education: Free and compulsory: ages 7-16. **Literacy** (1995): 71%.

Major International Organizations: UN (FAO, IBRD, ILO, IMF, IMO, WHO, WTrO), OAS.

Embassy: 2308 California St. NW 20008; 265-9671.

El Salvador became independent of Spain in 1821, and of the Central American Federation in 1839.

A fight with Honduras in 1969 over the presence of 300,000 Salvadoran workers left 2,000 dead.

A military coup overthrew the government of Pres. Carlos Humberto Romero in 1979, but the ruling military-civilian junta failed to quell a rebellion by leftist insurgents, armed by Cuba and Nicaragua. Extreme right-wing death squads organized to eliminate suspected leftists were blamed for thousands of deaths in the 1980s. The Reagan administration staunchly supported the government with military aid.

Voters turned out in large numbers in the May 1984 presidential election. Christian Democrat José Napoleon Duarte, a moderate, was victorious, with 54% of the vote.

The 12-year civil war ended Jan. 16, 1992, as the government and leftist rebels signed a formal peace treaty. The civil war had taken the lives of some 75,000 people. The treaty provided for military and political reforms.

Nine soldiers, including 3 officers, were indicted Jan. 1990 in the Nov. 1989 slaying of 6 Jesuit priests in San Salvador. Two of the officers received maximum 30-year jail sentences. They were released Mar. 20, 1993, when the National Assembly passed a sweeping amnesty.

Equatorial Guinea

Republic of Equatorial Guinea

People: Population: 454,001. **Age distrib.** (%): <15: 43.1; 65+: 3.8. **Pop. density:** 42 per sq. mi. **Urban:** 43%. **Ethnic groups:** Fang 83%, Bubi 10%. **Principal languages:** Spanish (official), Fang, Bubi. **Chief religion:** Predominantly Roman Catholic.

Geography: Area: 10,830 sq. mi. **Location:** Bioko Isl. off W Africa coast in Gulf of Guinea, and Rio Muni, mainland enclave. **Neighbors:** Gabon on S, Cameroon on E and N. **Topography:** Bioko Isl. consists of 2 volcanic mountains and a connecting valley. Rio Muni, with over 90% of the area, has a coastal plain and low hills beyond. **Capital:** Malabo (1991 est.): 58,000.

Government: Type: Republic. **Head of state:** Pres. Teodoro Obiang Nguema Mbasogo; b June 5, 1942; in office: Oct. 10, 1979. **Head of government:** Prime Min. Angel Serafin Seriche Dougan; in office: Mar. 29, 1996. **Local divisions:** 7 provinces. **Defense:** 1.0% of GDP. **Active troop strength:** 1,300.

Economy: Industries: Fishing, sawmilling. **Chief crops:** Cocoa, coffee, rice, bananas, yams. **Minerals:** Oil. **Other resources:** Timber. **Crude oil reserves** (1997): 12.0 mil bbls. **Arable land:** 5%. **Livestock** (1997): chickens: 250,000. **Electricity prod.** (1996): 19 mil kWh. **Labor force:** 66% agric.; 23% serv.; 11% ind.

Finance: Monetary unit: CFA Franc (Sept. 1998: 580.94 = $1 U.S.). **Gross domestic product** (1995 est.): $328 mil. **Per capita GDP:** $800. **Imports** (1995): $52.3 mil; partners: Spain 51%, Cameroon 21%, **Exports** (1995): $83.5 mil; partners: U.S. 34%, Japan 16%, Spain 15%. **Tourism:** $2 mil. **National budget** (1994): $34.1 mil.

Transport: Motor vehicles in use: 4,000 passenger cars, 3,600 comm. vehicles. **Civil aviation:** 4.6 mil passenger-mi; 1 airport. **Chief ports:** Malabo, Bata.

Communications: Television sets: 88 per 1,000 pop. **Radios:** 464 per 1,000 pop. **Telephones:** 3,668 main lines.

Health: Life expectancy at birth: 51.6 male; 56.3 female. **Births** (per 1,000 pop.): 39. **Deaths** (per 1,000 pop.): 13. **Natural increase:** 2.56%. **Infant mortality** (per 1,000 live births): 93.

Education: Free and compulsory: ages 6-11. **Literacy** (1995): 78%.

Major International Organizations: UN (FAO, IBRD, ILO, IMF, IMO, WHO), OAU.

Embassy: Suite 405, 1511 K St. NW 20005; 393-0525.

Fernando Po (now Bioko) Island was reached by Portugal in the late 15th century and ceded to Spain in 1778. Independence came Oct. 12, 1968. Riots occurred in 1969 over disputes between the island and the more backward Rio Muni province on the mainland. Masie Nguema Biyogo, a mainlander, became president for life in 1972.

Masie's reign was one of the most brutal in Africa, resulting in a bankrupted nation. Most of the nation's 7,000 Europeans emigrated. He was ousted in a military coup, Aug. 1979, and Teodoro Mbasogo, leader of the coup, became president. His regime eventually agreed to elections, held Nov. 21, 1993. These were nominally won by the ruling party, but boycotted by opposition parties that maintained the rules were rigged. A presidential election Feb. 25, 1996, was similarly flawed.

Eritrea

State of Eritrea

People: Population: 3,842,436. **Age distrib.** (%): <15: 42.8; 65+: 3.3. **Pop. density:** 82 per sq. mi. **Urban:** 17%. **Ethnic groups:** Tigrinya 50%, Tigre and Kunama 40%, Afar 4%. **Principal languages:** Tigrinya, Tigre. **Chief religions:** Approx. 50% each, Muslim and Christian.

Geography: Area: 46,842 sq. mi. **Location:** In E Africa, on SW coast of Red Sea. **Neighbors:** Ethiopia on S, Djibouti on SE, Sudan on W. **Topography:** Includes many islands of the Dahlak Archipelago, low coastal plains in S, mountain range with peaks to 9,000 ft. in N. **Capital:** Asmara (1995 est.): 431,000.

Government: Type: In transition. **Head of state:** Isaias Afwerki; b Feb. 2, 1946; in office: May 24, 1993. **Local divisions:** 6 administrative regions. **Defense:** 7.5% of GDP. **Active troop strength:** 55,000.

Economy: Industries: Food processing, textiles, fishing. **Chief crops:** Cotton, coffee, tobacco, lentils, sorghum. **Minerals:** Gold, potash, zinc, copper. **Arable land:** 12%. **Livestock** (1997): chickens: 4.30 mil; sheep: 1.53 mil; goats: 1.40 mil; cattle: 1.32 mil.

Finance: Monetary unit: Birr (Aug. 1998: 7.46 = $1 U.S.); the changeover to a new currency, the nakfa, began Nov. 1997. **Gross domestic product** (1995 est.): $2 bil. **Per capita GDP:** $570. **Imports** (1995 est.): $404 mil; partners: Saudi Arabia 30%, Italy 18%. **Exports** (1995 est.): $81 mil; partners: Ethiopia 63%. **National budget** (1995 est.): $397 mil. **Tourism:** $75 mil.

Transport: Railroad: Length: 190.6 mi. **Civil aviation:** 2 airports. **Chief ports:** Mitsiwa, Aseb.

Communications: Television sets: 6 per 1,000 pop. **Telephones:** 18,919 main lines .

Health: Life expectancy at birth: 53.2 male; 57.5 female. **Births** (per 1,000 pop.): 43. **Deaths** (per 1,000 pop.): 13. **Natural increase:** 3.00%. **Physicians** (1993): 1 per 36,000 persons. **Infant mortality** (per 1,000 live births): 79.

Education: Free and compulsory: ages 7-13. **Literacy** (1994): 20%.

Major International Organizations: UN (FAO, IBRD, ILO, IMF, IMO, WHO), OAU.

Embassy: 1708 New Hampshire Ave. NW 20009; 319-1991.

Website: http://www.NetAfrica.org/eritrea

Eritrea was part of the Ethiopian kingdom of Aksum. It was an Italian colony from 1890 to 1941, when it was captured by the British. Following a period of British and UN supervision, Eritrea was awarded to Ethiopia as part of a federation in 1952. Ethiopia annexed Eritrea as a province in 1962. This led to a 31-year struggle for independence, which ended when Eritrea formally declared itself an independent nation May 24, 1993. A border war with Ethiopia erupted in June 1998.

Estonia

Republic of Estonia

People: Population: 1,421,335. **Age distrib.** (%): <15: 18.8; 65+: 14.3. **Pop. density:** 81 per sq. mi. **Urban:** 73%. **Ethnic groups:** Estonian 64%, Russian 29%. **Principal languages:** Estonian (official), Latvian, Lithuanian, Russian. **Chief religion:** Evangelical Lutheran.

Geography: Area: 17,462 sq. mi. **Location:** E Europe, bordering the Baltic Sea and Gulf of Finland. **Neighbors:** Russia on E, Latvia on S. **Capital:** Tallinn (1996 est.): 427,500.

Government: Type: Republic. **Head of state:** Pres. Lennart Meri; b Mar. 29, 1929; in office: Oct. 5, 1992. **Head of government:** Prime Min. Mart Siimann; b 1946; in office: Feb. 27, 1997. **Local divisions:** 15 counties. **Defense:** 2.4% of GDP. **Active troop strength:** 3,500.

Economy: Industries: Shipbuilding, electric motors, cement. **Chief crops:** Potatoes, fruits, vegetables. **Minerals:** Shale oil, phosphorites. **Other resources:** Dairy prods., peat. **Arable land:** 27%. **Livestock** (1997): chickens: 2.86 mil; pigs: 315,200; cattle: 347,500. **Fish catch** (1996): 107,130 metric tons. **Electricity prod.** (1996): 8.6 bil kWh. **Labor force:** 42% ind. & constr., 20% agric. & forestry.

Finance: Monetary unit: Kroon (Sept. 1998: 13.99 = $1 U.S.). **Gross domestic product** (1996 est.): $8.1 bil. **Per capita GDP:** $5,560. **Imports** (1996): $3.1 bil; partners: Finland 29%, Russia 13%. **Exports** (1996): $2 bil; partners: Finland 18%, Russia 16%. **Tourism:** $475 mil. **National budget** (Jan.-Oct. 1995): $582 mil. **International reserves less gold** (June 1998): $815.79 mil. **Gold:** 8,000 oz. t. **Consumer prices** (change in 1997): 11.2%.

Transport: Railroad: Length: 632.2 mi. **Motor vehicles in use:** 338,000 passenger cars, 60,000 comm. vehicles. **Civil aviation:** 70.7 mil passenger-mi; 1 airport. **Chief port:** Tallinn.

Communications: Television sets: 411 per 1,000 pop. **Telephones:** 438,811 main lines. **Daily newspaper circ.:** 242 per 1,000 pop.

Health: Life expectancy at birth: 62.5 male; 74.8 female. **Births** (per 1,000 pop.): 9. **Deaths** (per 1,000 pop.): 14. **Natural increase:** –0.51%. **Hospital beds** (1994): 1 per 119 persons. **Physicians** (1994): 1 per 319 persons. **Infant mortality** (per 1,000 live births): 14.

Education: Compulsory: ages 7-16. **Literacy** (1994): 100%.

Major International Organizations: UN (FAO, IBRD, ILO, IMF, IMO, WHO), OSCE.

Embassy: 2131 Massachusetts Ave. NW 20008; 588-0101.

Website: http://www.ciesin.ee/undp/nhdr97/eng/index.html

Estonia was a province of imperial Russia before World War I, was independent between World Wars I and II. It was conquered by the USSR in 1940 and was incorporated as the Estonian SSR. Estonia declared itself an "occupied territory," and proclaimed itself a free nation Mar. 1990. During an abortive Soviet coup, Estonia declared immediate full independence, Aug. 20, 1991; the Soviet Union recognized its independence in Sept. 1991. The first free elections in over 50 years were held Sept. 20, 1992. The last occupying Russian troops were withdrawn by Aug. 31, 1994.

Ethiopia

Federal Democratic Republic of Ethiopia

People: Population: 58,390,351. **Age distrib.** (%): <15: 46.0; 65+: 2.8. **Pop. density:** 134 per sq. mi. **Urban:** 16%. **Ethnic groups:** Oromo 40%, Amhara and Tigrean 32%, Sidamo 9%. **Principal languages:** Amharic (official), Tigrinya, Orominga. **Chief religions:** Muslim 45-50%, Ethiopian Orthodox 35-40%, animist 12%.

Geography: Area: 435,184 sq. mi. **Location:** In East Africa. **Neighbors:** Sudan on W, Kenya on S, Somalia and Djibouti on E, Eritrea on N. **Topography:** A high central plateau, between 6,000 and 10,000 ft. high, rises to higher mountains near the Great Rift Valley, cutting in from the SW. The Blue Nile and other rivers cross the plateau, which descends to plains on both W and SE. **Capital:** Addis Ababa: 2,431,000*.

Government: Type: Federal republic. **Head of state:** Pres. Negasso Gidada; b Sept. 8, 1943; in office: Aug. 22, 1995. **Head of government:** Prime Min. Meles Zenawi; b May 8, 1955; in office: Aug. 23, 1995. **Local divisions:** 10 administrative regions. **Defense:** 2.0% of GDP. **Active troop strength:** 120,000.

Economy: Industries: Food processing, chemicals, textiles. **Chief crops:** Coffee (66% of export earnings), oilseeds, grains. **Minerals:** Platinum, gold, copper. **Arable land:** 12%. **Livestock** (1997): chickens: 55.00 mil; cattle: 29.90 mil; sheep: 21.85 mil; goats: 16.85 mil. **Electricity prod.** (1996): 1.3 bil kWh. **Labor force:** 89% agric.

Finance: Monetary unit: Birr (Sept. 1998: 6.99 = $1 U.S.). **Gross domestic product** (1995 est.): $24.8 bil. **Per capita GDP:** $430. **Imports** (1995 est.): $1.15 bil; partners: Saudi Arabia 13%, Italy 12%. **Exports** (1995 est.): $423 mil; partners: Germany 18%, Japan 13%. **Tourism:** $36 mil. **National budget** (FY 1996-97): $1.48 bil. **International reserves less gold** (June 1998): $439.4 mil. **Gold:** 2,000 oz t. **Consumer prices** (change in 1997): –3.7%.

Transport: Railroad: Length: 486 mi. **Motor vehicles in use:** 45,559 passenger cars, 20,462 comm. vehicles. **Civil aviation:** 1.17 bil passenger-mi; 31 airports.

Communications: Television sets: 4 per 1,000 pop. **Radios:** 153 per 1,000 pop. **Telephones:** 148,739 main lines.

Health: Life expectancy at birth: 39.8 male; 42.0 female. **Births** (per 1,000 pop.): 45. **Deaths** (per 1,000 pop.): 21. **Natural increase:** 2.34%. **Infant mortality** (per 1,000 live births): 126.

Education: Free and compulsory: ages 7-13. **Literacy** (1995): 36%.

Major International Organizations: UN (FAO, IBRD, ILO, IMF, IMO, WHO), OAU.

Embassy: 2134 Kalorama Rd. NW 20008; 234-2281.

Ethiopian culture was influenced by Egypt and Greece. The ancient monarchy was invaded by Italy in 1880 but maintained its independence until another Italian invasion in 1936. British forces freed the country in 1941.

The last emperor, Haile Selassie I, established a parliament and judiciary system in 1931 but barred all political parties.

A series of droughts in the 1970s killed hundreds of thousands. An army mutiny, strikes, and student demonstrations led to the dethronement of Selassie in 1974; he died Aug. 1975, while being held by the ruling junta. The junta pledged to form a one-party socialist state and instituted a successful land reform; opposition was violently suppressed. The influence of the Coptic Church, embraced in AD 330, was curbed, and the monarchy was abolished in 1975.

The regime, torn by bloody coups, faced uprisings by tribal and political groups in part aided by Sudan and Somalia. Ties with the U.S., once a major ally, deteriorated, while cooperation accords were signed with the USSR in 1977. In 1978, Soviet advisers and Cuban troops helped defeat Somalian forces. Ethiopia and Somalia signed a peace agreement in 1988.

A worldwide relief effort began in 1984, as an extended drought threatened the country with famine; up to a million people may have died as a result of starvation and disease.

The Ethiopian People's Revolutionary Democratic Front (EPRDF), an umbrella group of 6 rebel armies, launched a major push against government forces, Feb. 1991. In May, Pres. Mengistu Haile Mariam resigned and left the country. The EPRDF took over and set up a transitional government. Ethiopia's first multiparty general elections were held in 1995.

Eritrea, a province on the Red Sea, declared its independence May 24, 1993. Fighting along the border with Eritrea erupted in June 1998.

Fiji

Republic of Fiji

People: Population: 802,611. **Age distrib.** (%): <15: 34.1; 65+: 3.2. **Pop. density:** 114 per sq. mi. **Urban:** 41%. **Ethnic groups:** Fijian (Melanesian-Polynesian) 49%, Indian 46%. **Principal languages:** English (official), Fijian, Hindustani. **Chief religions:** Christian 52%, Hindu 38%, Muslim 8%.

Geography: Area: 7,054 sq. mi. **Location:** In western South Pacific O. **Neighbors:** Nearest are Vanuatu to W, Tonga to E. **Topography:** 322 islands (106 inhabited), many mountainous, with tropical forests and large fertile areas. Viti Levu, the largest island, has over half the total land area. **Capital:** Suva (1990 met.): 167,421.

Government: Type: Republic. **Head of state:** Pres. Ratu Sir Kamisese Mara; b May 13, 1920; in office: Jan. 18, 1994. **Head of government:** Prime Min. Sitiveni Rabuka; b Sept. 13, 1948; in office: June 2, 1992. **Local divisions:** 4 divisions comprising 14 provinces and 1 dependency. **Defense:** 2.6% of GDP. **Active troop strength:** 3,600.

Economy: Industries: Sugar refining, light industry, tourism. **Chief crops:** Sugarcane, cassava, coconuts. **Minerals:** Gold, copper. **Other resources:** Timber, fish. **Arable land:** 10%. **Livestock** (1997): chickens: 3.70 mil; cattle: 360,000; goats: 206,900; pigs: 125,000. **Electricity prod.** (1996): 545 mil kWh. **Labor force:** 67% subsistence agric.

Finance: Monetary unit: Dollar (Sept. 1998: 2.07 = $1.00 U.S.). **Gross domestic product** (1996 est.): $4.1 bil. **Per capita GDP:** $6,500. **Imports** (1995): $864 mil; partners: Australia 30%, N.Z. 17%, Japan 13%. **Exports** (1995): $607 mil; partners: EU 26%, Australia 15%. **Tourism:** $308 mil. **National budget** (1997 est.): $742.6 mil. **International reserves less gold** (May 1998): $359.62 mil. **Gold:** 1,000 oz t. **Consumer prices** (change in 1997): 3.4%.

Transport: Railroad: Length: 370.7 mi. **Motor vehicles in use:** 30,000 passenger cars, 29,000 comm. vehicles. **Civil aviation:** 755.8 mil passenger-mi; 13 airports. **Chief ports:** Suva, Lautoka.

Communications: Television sets: 89 per 1,000 pop. **Radios:** 561 per 1,000 pop. **Telephones:** 70,015 main lines. **Daily newspaper circ.:** 68 per 1,000 pop.

Health: Life expectancy at birth: 63.9 male; 68.8 female. **Births** (per 1,000 pop.): 23. **Deaths** (per 1,000 pop.): 6. **Natural increase:** 1.67%. **Hospital beds** (1993): 1 per 438 persons. **Physicians** (1994): 1 per 2,576 persons. **Infant mortality** (per 1,000 live births): 17.

Education: Free: ages 6-14. **Literacy** (1995): 92%.

Major International Organizations: UN (FAO, IBRD, ILO, IMF, IMO, WHO, WTrO), the Commonwealth.

Embassy: 2233 Wisconsin Ave. NW 20007; 337-8320.

A British colony since 1874, Fiji became an independent parliamentary democracy Oct. 10, 1970. Cultural differences between the Indian community (descendants of contract laborers brought to the islands in the 19th century) and indigenous Fijians have led to political polarization.

In 1987, a military coup ousted the government; order was restored May 21 under a compromise granting Lt. Col. Sitiveni Rabuka, the coup's leader, increased power. Rabuka staged a second coup Sept. 25 and declared Fiji a republic. Civilian government was restored in Dec. A new constitution favoring indigenous Fijians was issued July 25, 1990; amendments enacted in July 1997 made the constitution more equitable.

Finland

Republic of Finland

People: Population: 5,149,242. **Age distrib.** (%): <15: 18.6; 65+: 14.6. **Pop. density:** 40 per sq. mi. **Urban:** 64%. **Ethnic groups:** Finn 93%, Swede 6%. **Principal languages:** Finnish, Swedish (both official). **Chief religion:** Evangelical Lutheran 89%.

Geography: Area: 130,127 sq. mi. **Location:** In northern Europe. **Neighbors:** Norway on N, Sweden on W, Russia on E. **Topography:** South and central Finland are mostly flat areas with low hills and many lakes. The N has mountainous areas, 3,000-4,000 ft. **Capital:** Helsinki. **Cities** (1997 est.): Helsinki 532,053; Espoo 196,260; Tampere 186,026.

Government: Type: Constitutional republic. **Head of state:** Pres. Martti Ahtisaari; b June 23, 1937; in office: Mar. 1, 1994.

Head of government: Prime Min. Paavo Lipponen; b Apr. 23, 1941; in office: Apr. 13, 1995. **Local divisions:** 12 laanit (provinces). **Defense:** 2.0% of GDP. **Active troop strength:** 32,500.

Economy: Industries: Metal prods., shipbuilding, wood processing, chemicals, textiles. **Chief crops:** Grains, sugar beets, potatoes. **Minerals:** Copper, iron, silver, zinc. **Other resources:** Timber, dairy prods. **Arable land:** 8%. **Livestock** (1997): chickens: 5.23 mil; pigs: 1.39 mil; cattle: 1.15 mil; sheep: 110,800. **Fish catch** (1996): 177,984 metric tons. **Electricity prod.** (1996): 67.5 bil kWh. **Labor force:** 46% ind., commerce & finance; 30% public serv.; 9% agric.

Finance: Monetary unit: Markka (Sept. 1998: 5.27 = $1 U.S.). **Gross domestic product** (1996 est.): $97.1 bil. **Per capita GDP:** $19,000. **Imports** (1994): $23.2 bil; partners: Germany 15%. **Exports** (1994): $29.7 bil; partners: Germany 13%. **Tourism:** $1.63 bil. **National budget** (1995 est.): $35 bil. **International reserves less gold** (June 1998): $8.64 bil. **Gold:** 1.6 mil oz t. **Consumer prices** (change in 1997): 1.2%.

Transport: Railroad: Length: 3,660.8 mi. **Motor vehicles in use:** 1.94 mil passenger cars, 286,470 comm. vehicles. **Civil aviation:** 5.42 bil passenger-mi; 24 airports. **Chief ports:** Helsinki, Turku.

Communications: Television sets: 372 per 1,000 pop. **Radios:** 966 per 1,000 pop. **Telephone:** 2,813,000 main lines. **Daily newspaper circ.:** 464 per 1,000 pop.

Health: Life expectancy at birth: 73.6 male; 80.8 female. **Births** (per 1,000 pop.): 11. **Deaths** (per 1,000 pop.): 10. **Natural increase:** 0.16. **Hospital beds** (1994): 1 per 102 persons. **Physicians** (1995): 1 per 371 persons. **Infant mortality** (per 1,000 live births): 4.

Education: Free and compulsory: ages 7-16. **Literacy** (1997): 100%.

Major International Organizations: UN (FAO, IBRD, ILO, IMF, IMO, WHO, WTrO), EU, OECD, OSCE.

Embassy: 3301 Massachusetts Ave. NW 20008; 298-5800.

Website: http://www.finland.org

The early Finns probably migrated from the Ural area at about the beginning of the Christian era. Swedish settlers brought the country into Sweden, 1154 to 1809, when Finland became an autonomous grand duchy of the Russian Empire. Russian exactions created a strong national spirit; on Dec. 6, 1917, Finland declared its independence and in 1919 became a republic.

On Nov. 30, 1939, the Soviet Union invaded, and the Finns were forced to cede 16,173 sq. mi. of territory. After World War II, further cessions were exacted. In 1948, Finland signed a treaty of mutual assistance with the USSR; Finland and Russia nullified this treaty with a new pact in Jan. 1992.

Following approval by Finnish voters in an advisory referendum Oct. 16, 1994, Finland joined the European Union effective Jan. 1, 1995.

Aland or **Ahvenanmaa,** constituting an autonomous province, is a group of small islands, 590 sq. mi., in the Gulf of Bothnia, 25 mi. from Sweden, 15 mi. from Finland. Mariehamn is the principal port.

France

French Republic

People: Population: 58,804,944. **Age distrib.** (%): <15: 18.9; 65+: 15.8. **Pop. density:** 278 per sq. mi. **Urban:** 74%. **Ethnic groups:** Celtic and Latin; Teutonic, Slavic, North African, Indochinese, Basque minorities. **Principal language:** French (official). **Chief religion:** Roman Catholic 90%.

Geography: Area: 211,208 sq. mi. **Location:** In western Europe, between Atlantic O. and Mediterranean Sea. **Neighbors:** Spain on S; Italy, Switzerland, Germany on E; Luxembourg, Belgium on N. **Topography:** A wide plain covers more than half of the country, in N and W, drained to W by Seine, Loire, Garonne rivers. The Massif Central is a mountainous plateau in center. In E are Alps (Mt. Blanc is tallest in W Europe, 15,771 ft.), the lower Jura range, and the forested Vosges. The Rhone flows from Lake Geneva to Mediterranean. Pyrenees are in SW, on border with Spain. **Capital:** Paris. **Cities:** Paris 9,523,000; Lyon 1,319,000; Marseilles 1,234,000; Lille 976,000*.

Government: Type: Republic. **Head of state:** Pres. Jacques Chirac; b Nov. 29, 1932; in office: May 17, 1995. **Head of government:** Prime Min. Lionel Jospin; b July 12, 1937; in office: June 3, 1997. **Local divisions:** 22 administrative regions containing 96 departments. **Defense:** 3.1% of GDP. **Active troop strength:** 398,900.

Economy: Industries: Steel, chemicals, textiles, tourism, wine, perfume, aircraft, machinery, electronic equipment. **Chief crops:** Grains, sugar beets, winegrapes, fruits, vegetables. France is largest food producer, exporter, in W Europe. **Minerals:** Bauxite, iron, coal. **Crude oil reserves** (1997): 127 mil bbls. **Other resources:** Timber, dairy. **Arable land:** 33%. **Livestock** (1997): chickens: 231.00 mil; cattle: 20.56 mil; pigs: 15.35 mil; sheep: 10.13 mil; goats: 1.11 mil. **Fish catch** (1996): 542,187 metric tons. **Electricity prod.** (1996): 480.8 bil kWh. **Labor force:** 69% services; 26% ind.; 5% agric.

Finance: Monetary unit: Franc (Sept. 1998: 5.81 = $1 U.S.). **Gross domestic product** (1996 est.): $1.22 tril. **Per capita GDP:** $20,900. **Imports** (1996): $255.5 bil; partners: Germany 17%, Italy 10%, U.S. 8%. **Exports** (1996): $275 bil; partners: Germany 12%, Italy 9%, UK 9%. **Tourism:** $28.32 bil. **National budget** (1996 est.): $300.1 bil. **International reserves less gold** (Apr. 1998): $36.54 bil. **Gold:** 81.89 mil oz t. **Consumer prices** (change in 1997): 1.2%.

Transport: Railroad: Length: 19,847 mi. **Motor vehicles:** in use: 25.50 mil passenger cars, 5.26 mil comm. vehicles. **Civil aviation:** 48.36 bil passenger-mi; 61 airports. **Chief ports:** Marseille, Le Havre, Bordeaux, Rouen.

Communications: Television sets: 579 per 1,000 pop. **Radios:** 860 per 1,000 pop. **Telephones:** 32,900,000 main lines. **Daily newspaper circ.:** 235 per 1,000 pop.

Health: Life expectancy at birth: 74.6 male; 82.6 female. **Births** (per 1,000 pop.): 12. **Deaths** (per 1,000 pop.): 9. **Natural increase:** 0.26%. **Hospital beds** (1995): 1 per 86 persons. **Physicians** (1994): 1 per 361 persons. **Infant mortality** (per 1,000 live births): 6.

Education: Free and compulsory: ages 6-16. **Literacy** (1994): 99%.

Major International Organizations: UN and most of its specialized agencies, EU, NATO, OECD, OSCE.

Embassy: 4101 Reservoir Rd. NW 20007; 944-6000.

Website: http://www.france.org

Celtic Gaul was conquered by Julius Caesar 58-51 BC; Romans ruled for 500 years. Under Charlemagne, Frankish rule extended over much of Europe. After his death France emerged as one of the successor kingdoms.

The monarchy was overthrown by the French Revolution (1789-93) and succeeded by the First Republic; followed by the First Empire under Napoleon (1804-15), a monarchy (1814-48), the Second Republic (1848-52), the Second Empire (1852-70), the Third Republic (1871-1946), the Fourth Republic (1946-58), and the Fifth Republic (1958 to present).

France suffered severe losses in manpower and wealth in the World War I, when it was invaded by Germany. By the Treaty of Versailles, France exacted return of Alsace and Lorraine, provinces seized by Germany in 1871. Germany invaded France again in May 1940, and signed an armistice with a government based in Vichy. After France was liberated by the Allies Sept. 1944, Gen. Charles de Gaulle became head of the provisional government, serving until 1946.

De Gaulle again became premier in 1958, during a crisis over Algeria, and obtained voter approval for a new constitution, ushering in the Fifth Republic. He became president Jan. 1959. Using strong executive powers, he promoted French economic and technological advances in the context of the European Economic Community and guarded French foreign policy independence.

France had withdrawn from Indochina in 1954, and from Morocco and Tunisia in 1956. Most of its remaining African territories were freed 1958-62. In 1966, France withdrew all its troops from the integrated military command of NATO, though 60,000 remained stationed in Germany.

In May 1968 rebellious students in Paris and other centers rioted, battled police, and were joined by workers who launched nationwide strikes. The government awarded pay increases to the strikers May 26. De Gaulle resigned from office in Apr. 1969, after losing a nationwide referendum on constitutional reform. Georges Pompidou, who was elected to succeed him, continued De Gaulle's emphasis on French independence from the two superpowers. After Pompidou's death, in 1974, Valery Giscard d'Estaing was elected president; he continued the basically conservative policies of his predecessors.

On May 10, 1981, France elected François Mitterrand, a Socialist, president. Under Mitterrand the government nationalized 5 major industries and most private banks. After 1986, however, when rightists won a narrow victory in the National Assembly, Mitterrand chose conservative Jacques Chirac as premier. A 2-year period of "cohabitation" ensued, and France began to pursue a privatization program in which many state-owned companies were sold. After Mitterrand was elected to a 2d 7-year term in 1988, he appointed a Socialist as premier. The center-right won a large majority in 1993 legislative elections, ushering in another period of "cohabitation" with a conservative premier.

In 1993, France set tighter rules for entry into the country and made it easier for the government to expel foreigners. In 1994, France sent troops to Rwanda in an effort to help protect civilians there from ongoing massacres. The international terrorist known as Carlos the Jackal (Ilich Ramirez Sánchez) was arrested in Sudan in Aug. 1994 and extradited to France, where he had been sentenced in absentia to life imprisonment.

Former conservative Prime Min. Jacques Chirac won the presidency in a runoff May 7, 1995. A series of terrorist bombings and bombing attempts began in summer 1995; Islamic extremists, opposed to France's support of the Algerian government and its struggle with Islamic fundamentalists, were believed responsible. In Sept. 1995, France stirred widespread protests by resuming nuclear tests in the South Pacific, after a 3-year moratorium; the tests ended Jan. 1996.

Chirac cut government spending to help the French economy meet the budgetary goals set for the introduction of a common European currency. With unemployment at nearly 13%, legislative elections completed June 1, 1997, produced a decisive victory for the leftist parties. The result was a new period of "cohabitation," this time between a conservative president and a Socialist prime minister, Lionel Jospin.

The island of **Corsica,** in the Mediterranean W of Italy and N of Sardinia, is a territorial collectivity and region of France comprising 2 departments. It elects a total of 2 senators and 3 deputies to the French Parliament. Area: 3,369 sq. mi.; pop. (1996 est.): 258,000. The capital is Ajaccio, birthplace of Napoleon. Violence by Corsican separatist groups has hurt tourism, a leading industry on the island.

Overseas Departments

French Guiana is on the NE coast of South America with Suriname on the W and Brazil on the E and S. Its area is 33,399 sq. mi.; pop. (1998 est.): 162,547. Guiana sends one senator and 2 deputies to the French Parliament. Guiana is administered by a prefect and has a Council General of 16 elected members; capital is Cayenne.

The famous penal colony, Devil's Island, was phased out between 1938 and 1951. The European Space Agency maintains a satellite-launching center (established by France in 1964) in the city of Kourou.

Immense forests of rich timber cover 88% of the land. Fishing (especially shrimp), forestry, and gold mining are the most important industries.

Guadeloupe, in the West Indies' Leeward Islands, consists of 2 large islands, Basse-Terre and Grande-Terre, separated by the Salt River, plus Marie Galante and the Saintes group to the S and, to the N, Desirade, St. Barthelemy, and over half of St. Martin (the Netherlands' portion is called St. Maarten). A French possession since 1635, the department is represented in the French Parliament by 2 senators and 4 deputies; administration consists of a prefect (governor) and an elected general and regional councils.

Area of the islands is 687 sq. mi.; pop. (1998 est.) 416,439, mainly descendants of slaves; capital is Basse-Terre on Basse-Terre Island. The land is fertile; sugar, rum, and bananas are exported. Tourism is an important industry.

Martinique, the northernmost of the Windward Islands, in the West Indies, has been a possession since 1635, and a department since Mar. 1946. It is represented in the French Parliament by 2 senators and 4 deputies. The island was the birthplace of Napoleon's Empress Josephine.

It has an area of 436 sq. mi.; pop. (1998 est.) 407,284, mostly descendants of slaves. The capital is Fort-de-France (pop. 1991: 101,000). It is a popular tourist stop. The chief exports are rum, bananas, and petroleum products.

Réunion is a volcanic island in the Indian O. about 420 mi. E of Madagascar, and has belonged to France since 1665. Area, 970 sq. mi.; pop. (1998 est.) 705,053, 30% of French extraction. Capital: Saint-Denis. The chief export is sugar. It elects 5 deputies, 3 senators to the French Parliament.

Overseas Territorial Collectivities

Mayotte, claimed by Comoros and administered by France, voted in 1976 to become a territorial collectivity of France. An island NW of Madagascar, area is 144 sq. mi., pop. (1998 est.) 141,944. The capital is Mamoutzou.

St. Pierre and Miquelon, formerly an overseas territory (1816-1976) and department (1976-85), made the transition to territorial collectivity in 1985. It consists of 2 groups of rocky islands near the SW coast of Newfoundland, inhabited by fishermen. The exports are chiefly fish products. The St. Pierre group has an area of 10 sq. mi.; Miquelon, 83 sq. mi. Total pop. (1998 est.), 6,914. The capital is St. Pierre.

Both Mayotte and St. Pierre and Miquelon elect a deputy and a senator to the French Parliament.

Overseas Territories

Territory of **French Polynesia** comprises 130 islands widely scattered among 5 archipelagos in the South Pacific; administered by a Council of Ministers (headed by a president). Territorial Assembly and the Council have headquarters at Papeete, on Tahiti, one of the **Society Islands** (which include the **Windward** and **Leeward** islands). Two deputies and a senator are elected to the French Parliament.

Other groups are the **Marquesas Islands,** the **Tuamotu Archipelago,** including the **Gambier Islands,** and the **Austral Islands.**

Total area of the islands administered from Tahiti is 1,544 sq. mi.; pop. (1998 est.), 237,844, more than half on Tahiti. Tahiti is picturesque and mountainous with a productive coastline bearing coconuts, citrus, pineapples, and vanilla. Cultured pearls are also produced.

Tahiti was visited by Capt. James Cook in 1769 and by Capt. Bligh in the *Bounty*, 1788-89. Its beauty impressed Herman Melville, Paul Gauguin, and Charles Darwin. Tahitians angered by French nuclear testing rioted Sept. 1995.

Territory of the **French Southern and Antarctic Lands** comprises **Adelie Land,** on Antarctica, and 4 island groups in the Indian O. Adelie, reached 1840, has a research station, a coastline of 185 mi., and tapers 1,240 mi. inland to the South Pole. The U.S. does not recognize national claims in Antarctica. There are 2 huge glaciers, Ninnis, 22 mi. wide, 99 mi. long, and Mentz, 11 mi. wide, 140 mi. long. The Indian O. groups are:

Kerguelen Archipelago, visited 1772, consists of one large and 300 small islands. The chief is 87 mi. long, 74 mi. wide, and has Mt. Ross, 6,429 ft. tall. Principal research station is Port-aux-Français. Seals often weigh 2 tons; there are blue whales, coal, peat, semiprecious stones. **Crozet Archipelago,** reached 1772, covers 195 sq. mi. Eastern Island rises to 6,560 ft. **Saint Paul,** in southern Indian O., has warm springs with earth at places heating to 120° to 390° F. **Amsterdam** is nearby; both produce cod and rock lobster.

Territory of **New Caledonia** and Dependencies is a group of islands in the Pacific O. about 1,115 mi. E of Australia and approx. the same distance NW of New Zealand. Dependencies are the **Loyalty Islands, Isle of Pines, Belep Archipelago,** and **Huon Islands.**

The largest island, New Caledonia, is 6,530 sq. mi. Total area of the territory is 8,548 sq. mi.; population (1998 est.) 194,197. The group was acquired by France in 1853.

The territory is administered by a High Commissioner. There is a popularly elected Territorial Congress. Two deputies and a senator are elected to the French Parliament. Capital: Noumea.

Mining is the chief industry. New Caledonia is one of the world's largest nickel producers. Other minerals found are chrome, iron, cobalt, manganese, silver, gold, lead, and copper. Agricultural products include yams, sweet potatoes, potatoes, manioc (cassava), corn, and coconuts.

In 1987, New Caledonian voters chose by referendum to remain within the French Republic. There were clashes between French and Melanesians (Kanaks) in 1988. An agreement Apr. 21, 1998, between France and rival New Caledonian factions specified a 15- to 20-year period of "shared sovereignty." The French constitution was amended, July 6, to allow the territory a gradual increase in autonomy.

Territory of the **Wallis and Futuna Islands** comprises 2 island groups in the SW Pacific S of Tuvalu, N of Fiji, and W of Western Samoa; became an overseas territory July 29, 1961. The islands have a total area of 106 sq. mi. and population (1997 est.) of 14,974. **Alofi,** attached to Futuna, is uninhabited. Capital: Mata-Utu. Chief products are copra, yams, taro roots, bananas, and coconuts. A senator and a deputy are elected to the French Parliament.

Gabon

Gabonese Republic

People: Population: 1,207,844. **Age distrib.** (%): <15: 33.5; 65+: 5.5. **Pop. density:** 12 per sq. mi. **Urban:** 51%. **Ethnic groups:** Fang, Eshira, Bapounou, Bateke, other Bantu, other Africans, Europeans. **Principal languages:** French (official), Bantu dialects. **Chief religions:** Christian 80%, traditional 19%.

Geography: Area: 103,347 sq. mi. **Location:** On Atlantic coast of W central Africa. **Neighbors:** Equatorial Guinea and Cameroon on N, Congo on E and S. **Topography:** Heavily forested, the country consists of coastal lowlands; plateaus in N, E, and S; mountains in N, SE, and center. The Ogooue R. system covers most of Gabon. **Capital:** Libreville (1993): 362,386.

Government: Type: Republic. **Head of state:** Pres. Omar Bongo; b Dec. 30, 1935; in office: Dec. 2, 1967. **Head of government:** Prime Min. Paulin Obame-Nguema; b Dec. 28, 1934; in office: Nov. 2, 1994. **Local divisions:** 9 provinces. **Defense:** 2.0% of GDP. **Active troop strength:** 4,700.

Economy: Industries: Oil products, textiles, food and beverages. **Chief crops:** Cocoa, coffee, palm products. **Minerals:** Oil, manganese, uranium, iron, gold. **Crude oil reserves** (1997): 2.5 bil bbls. **Other resources:** Timber. **Arable land:**

1%. **Livestock** (1997): chickens: 2.70 mil; pigs: 208,000; sheep: 173,000. **Electricity prod.** (1996): 930 mil kWh. **Labor force:** 65% agric.; 30% ind. & commerce.

Finance: Monetary unit: CFA Franc (Sept. 1998: 580.94 = $1 U.S.). **Gross domestic product** (1996 est.): $6.3 bil. **Per capita GDP:** $5,400. **Imports** (1995): $700 mil; partners: France 39%. **Exports** (1995): $2.7 bil; partners: U.S. 59%. **Tourism:** $7 mil. **National budget** (1993 est.): $1.6 bil. **International reserves less gold** (Mar. 1998): $209.35 mil. **Gold:** 13,000 oz t. **Consumer prices** (change in 1997): 3.7%.

Transport: Railroad: Length: 403 mi. **Motor vehicles in use:** 23,800 passenger cars, 15,700 comm. vehicles. **Civil aviation:** 452.1 mil passenger-mi; 17 airports. **Chief ports:** Port-Gentil, Owendo, Libreville.

Communications: Television sets: 35 per 1,000 pop. **Radios:** 173 per 1,000 pop. **Telephones:** 35,000 main lines.

Health: Life expectancy at birth: 53.6 male; 59.6 female. **Births** (per 1,000 pop.): 28. **Deaths** (per 1,000 pop.): 13. **Natural increase:** 1.48%. **Infant mortality** (per 1,000 live births): 85.

Education: Compulsory: ages 6-16. **Literacy** (1995): 63%.

Major International Organizations: UN (FAO, IBRD, ILO, IMF, IMO, WHO, WTrO), OAU.

Embassy: Suite 200, 2034 20th St. NW 20009; 797-1000.

France established control over the region in the second half of the 19th century. Gabon became independent Aug. 17, 1960. A multiparty political system was introduced in 1990, and a new constitution was enacted Mar. 14, 1991. However, the reelection of longtime Pres. Omar Bongo, on Dec. 5, 1993, prompted rioting and charges of vote fraud. Under a revised constitution approved by referendum July 23, 1995, parliamentary elections were held in Dec. 1996.

Gabon is one of the most prosperous black African countries, thanks to abundant natural resources, foreign private investment, and government development programs.

The Gambia

Republic of The Gambia

People: Population: 1,291,858. **Age distrib.** (%): <15: 45.8; 65+: 2.7. **Pop. density:** 296 per sq. mi. **Urban:** 30%. **Ethnic groups:** Mandinka 42%, Fula 18%, Wolof 16%, other African. **Principal languages:** English (official), Mandinka, Wolof. **Chief religions:** Muslim 90%, Christian 9%.

Geography: Area: 4,363 sq. mi. **Location:** On Atlantic coast near W tip of Africa. **Neighbors:** Surrounded on 3 sides by Senegal. **Topography:** A narrow strip of land on each side of the lower Gambia R. **Capital:** Banjul (1993): 42,407.

Government: Type: Republic. **Head of state and government:** Yahya Jammeh; b May 25, 1965; in office: July 23, 1994. **Local divisions:** 6 divisions and Banjul. **Defense:** 3.9% of GDP. **Active troop strength:** 800.

Economy: Industries: Tourism, peanut processing. **Chief crops:** Peanuts (main export), rice. **Arable land:** 18%. **Livestock** (1997): chickens: 740,000; cattle: 346,300; goats: 250,200; sheep: 181,600. **Fish catch** (1996): 31,521 metric tons. **Electricity prod.** (1996): 70 mil kWh. **Labor force:** 75% agric.; 19% ind., comm., serv.

Finance: Monetary unit: Dalasi (Sept. 1998: 10.78 = $1.00 U.S.). **Gross domestic product** (1995 est.): $1.1 bil. **Per capita GDP:** $1,100. **Imports** (1995 est.): $201 mil; partners: China 25%. **Exports** (1995 est.): $127 mil; partners: Belg-Lux 50%. **Tourism:** $22 mil. **National budget** (FY 1996-97 est.): $98.2 mil. **International reserves less gold** (May 1998): $98.61 mil. **Consumer prices** (change in 1997): 2.8%.

Transport: Motor vehicles in use: 8,000 passenger cars, 1,000 comm. vehicles. **Civil aviation:** 31.1 mil passenger-mi; 1 airport. **Chief port:** Banjul.

Communications: Radios: 126 per 1,000 pop. **Telephones:** 21,319 main lines.

Health: Life expectancy at birth: 51.6 male; 56.3 female. **Births** (per 1,000 pop.): 43. **Deaths** (per 1,000 pop.): 13. **Natural increase:** 3.04%. **Infant mortality** (per 1,000 live births): 77.

Education: Free: ages 7-13. **Literacy** (1995): 39%.

Major International Organizations: UN (FAO, IBRD, ILO, IMF, IMO, WHO, WTrO), the Commonwealth, OAU.

Embassy: Suite 1000, 1155 15th St. NW 20005; 785-1399.

Website: http://www.Gambia.com

The tribes of Gambia were at one time associated with the West African empires of Ghana, Mali, and Songhay. The area became Britain's first African possession in 1588.

Independence came Feb. 18, 1965; republic status within the Commonwealth was achieved in 1970. The country suffered from severe famine in the 1970s. After a coup attempt in 1981, The Gambia formed the confederation of Senegambia with Senegal that lasted until 1989.

On July 23, 1994, after 24 years in power, Pres. Dawda K. Jawara was deposed in a bloodless coup by a military officer, Yahya Jammeh. Jammeh barred political activity, detained potential opponents, and governed by decree. A new constitution was approved by referendum, Aug. 8, 1996. On Sept. 27 Jammeh won the presidential election. Parliamentary balloting on Jan. 2, 1997, completed the nominal return to civilian rule, but Jammeh retained a firm grip on power.

Georgia

Republic of Georgia

People: Population: 5,108,527. **Age distrib.** (%): <15: 21.6; 65+: 12.1. **Pop. density:** 190 per sq. mi. **Urban:** 59%. **Ethnic groups:** Georgian 70%, Armenian 8%, Russian 6%. **Principal languages:** Georgian (official), Russian. **Chief religions:** Georgian Orthodox 65%, Muslim 11%, Russian Orthodox 10%.

Geography: Area: 26,911 sq. mi. **Location:** SW Asia, on E coast of Black Sea. **Neighbors:** Russia on N and NE, Turkey and Armenia on S, Azerbaijan on SE. **Topography:** Separated from Russia on NE by main range of the Caucasus Mts. **Capital:** Tbilisi (1994 est.): 1,342,000*.

Government: Type: Republic. **Head of state:** Pres. Eduard A. Shevardnadze; b Jan. 25, 1928; in office: Nov. 6, 1992. **Local divisions:** 9 districts and Tbilisi; 2 autonomous republics. **Defense:** 3.4% of GDP. **Active troop strength:** 10,000.

Economy: Industries: Manganese mining, steel, machinery. **Chief crops:** Citrus and other fruits, potatoes, corn, grapes, tea. **Minerals:** Manganese, iron, coal. **Crude oil reserves** (1997): 35.0 mil bbls. **Arable land:** 9%. **Livestock** (1997): chickens: 12.00 mil; cattle: 813,000; sheep: 580,000; pigs: 280,000. **Electricity prod.** (1996): 6.8 bil kWh. **Labor force:** 31% ind. & constr.; 25% agric. & forestry.

Finance: Monetary unit: Lavi (Aug. 1998: 1.33 = $1 U.S.). **Gross domestic product** (1996 est.): $7.1 bil. **Per capita GDP:** $1,350. **Imports** (1995): $647 mil; partners: Turkmenistan 71%, Turkey 13%. **Exports** (1995): $356 mil; partners: Russia 46%, Turkey 18%.

Transport: Railroad: Length: 975 mi. **Motor vehicles in use:** 442,000 passenger cars, 50,000 comm. vehicles. **Civil aviation:** 223.7 mil passenger-mi; 1 airport. **Chief ports:** Batumi, Sukhumi, Poti.

Communications: Television sets: 220 per 1,000 pop. **Telephones:** 567,400 main lines.

Health: Life expectancy at birth: 61.4 male; 68.4 female. **Births** (per 1,000 pop.): 12. **Deaths** (per 1,000 pop.): 14. **Natural increase:** –0.24%. **Hospital beds** (1993): 1 per 95 persons. **Physicians** (1993): 1 per 182 persons. **Infant mortality** (per 1,000 live births): 51.

Education: Compulsory: ages 6-14. **Literacy** (1995): 99%.

Major International Organizations: UN (FAO, IBRD, ILO, IMF, IMO, WHO), CIS, OSCE.

Embassy: Suite 424, 1511 K St. NW 20005; 393-5959.

Website: http://www.parliament.ge

The region, which contained the ancient kingdoms of Colchis and Iberia, was Christianized in the 4th century and conquered by Arabs in the 8th century. It expanded to include an area from the Black Sea to the Caspian and parts of Armenia and Persia before its disintegration under the impact of Mongol and Turkish invasions. Annexation by Russia in 1801 led to the Russian war with Persia, 1804-1813. Georgia entered the USSR in 1922 and became a constituent republic in 1936.

Georgia declared independence Apr. 9, 1991. It became an independent state when the Soviet Union disbanded Dec. 26, 1991. There was fighting during 1991 between rebel forces and loyalists of Pres. Zviad Gamsakhurdia, who fled the capital Jan. 6, 1992. The ruling Military Council picked former Soviet Foreign Minister Eduard A. Shevardnadze to chair a newly created State Council. An attempted coup by forces loyal to Gamsakhurdia was crushed June 24, 1992. Shevardnadze was later elected president. Gamsakhurdia died Jan. 1994, reportedly by suicide.

In Abkhazia, an autonomous republic within Georgia, ethnic Abkhazis, reportedly aided by Russia, launched a bloody military campaign and, by late 1993, had gained control of much of the region. A cease-fire providing for Russian peacekeepers was signed in Moscow May 14, 1994. Intermittent clashes continued into the late 1990s.

On Feb. 3, 1994, Georgia signed agreements with Russia for economic and military cooperation. On Mar. 1, Georgia's Supreme Council ratified membership by Georgia in the Commonwealth of Independent States.

Shevardnadze was wounded by a car bomb Aug. 29, 1995, while on his way to Parliament to sign a new constitution. He was reelected president Nov. 5. Shevardnadze escaped another assassination attempt, Feb. 9, 1998, when gunmen ambushed his motorcade.

Germany

Federal Republic of Germany

People: Population: 82,079,454. **Age distrib.** (%): <15: 15.6; 65+: 15.9. **Pop. density:** 596 per sq. mi. **Urban:** 87%. **Ethnic groups:** German 92%, Turkish 2%. **Principal language:** German (official). **Chief religions:** Protestant 38%, Roman Catholic 34%.

Geography: Area: 137,803 sq. mi. **Location:** In central Europe. **Neighbors:** Denmark on N; Netherlands, Belgium, Luxembourg, France on W; Switzerland, Austria on S; Czech Rep., Poland on E. **Topography:** Germany is flat in N, hilly in center and W, and mountainous in Bavaria in the S. Chief rivers are Elbe, Weser, Ems, Rhine, and Main, all flowing toward North Sea, and Danube, flowing toward Black Sea. **Capital:** Berlin. **Cities:** Essen 6,482,000; Frankfurt 3,605,000; Berlin 3,317,000; Düsseldorf 3,030,000; Cologne 2,984,000*.

Government: Type: Federal republic. **Head of state:** Pres. Roman Herzog; b Apr. 5, 1934; in office: July 1, 1994. **Head of government:** Chan. Gerhard Schröder; b Apr. 7, 1944; elected: Sept. 27, 1998. **Local divisions:** 16 laender (states) **Defense:** 1.7% of GDP. **Active troop strength:** 358,400.

Economy: Industries: Steel, ships, vehicles, machinery, electronics, coal, chemicals, iron, cement, food and beverages. **Chief crops:** Grains, potatoes, sugar beets. **Minerals:** Coal, potash, lignite, iron, uranium. **Crude oil reserves** (1997): 410 mil bbls. **Arable land:** 33%. **Livestock** (1997): chickens: 102.73 mil; pigs: 24.28 mil; cattle: 15.76 mil; sheep: 2.32 mil. **Fish catch** (1996): 236,573 metric tons. **Electricity prod.** (1996): 515.1 bil kWh. **Labor force:** 41% ind.; 3% agric., 56% services.

Finance: Monetary unit: Mark (Sept. 1998: 1.73 = $1 U.S.). **Gross domestic product** (1996 est.): $1.7 tril. **Per capita GDP:** $20,400. **Imports** (1996 est.): $430.7 bil; partners: EU 56. **Exports** (199 est.): $501.3 bil; partners: EU 58%. **Tourism:** $16.42 bil. **National budget** (1995): $832.1 bil. **International reserves less gold** (June 1998): $79.78 bil. **Gold:** 95.18 mil oz t. **Consumer prices** (change in 1997): 1.8%.

Transport: Railroad: Length: 54,994 mi. **Motor vehicles in use:** 41.05 mil passenger cars, 3.12 mil comm. vehicles. **Civil aviation:** 48.29 bil passenger-mi; 35 airports. **Chief ports:** Hamburg, Bremen, Bremerhaven, Lubeck, Rostock.

Communications: Television sets: 551 per 1,000 pop. **Radios:** 1,836 per 1,000 pop. **Telephones:** 44,100,000 main lines. **Daily newspaper circ.:** 375 per 1,000 pop.

Health: Life expectancy at birth: 73.8 male; 80.3 female. **Births** (per 1,000 pop.): 9. **Deaths** (per 1,000 pop.): 11. **Natural increase:** –0.19%. **Hospital beds** (1996): 1 per 130 persons. **Physicians** (1996): 1 per 293 persons. **Infant mortality** (per 1,000 live births): 5.

Education: Compulsory: ages 6-15. **Literacy** (1993): 100%.

Major International Organizations: UN and all of its specialized agencies, EU, NATO, OECD, OSCE.

Embassy: 4645 Reservoir Rd. NW 20007; 298-4000.

Website: http://www.undp.org/missions/germany

Germany is a central European nation originally composed of numerous states, with a common language and traditions, that were united in one country in 1871; Germany was split into 2 countries from the end of World War II until 1990, when it was reunified.

History and government. Germanic tribes were defeated by Julius Caesar, 55 and 53 BC, but Roman expansion N of the Rhine was stopped in AD 9. Charlemagne, ruler of the Franks, consolidated Saxon, Bavarian, Rhenish, Frankish, and other lands; after him the eastern part became the German Empire. The Thirty Years' War, 1618-1648, split Germany into small principalities and kingdoms. After Napoleon, Austria contended with Prussia for dominance, but lost the Seven Weeks' War to Prussia, 1866. Otto von Bismarck, Prussian chancellor, formed the North German Confederation, 1867.

In 1870 Bismarck maneuvered Napoleon III into declaring war. After the quick defeat of France, Bismarck formed the **German Empire** and on Jan. 18, 1871, in Versailles, proclaimed King Wilhelm I of Prussia German emperor (Deutscher kaiser).

The German Empire reached its peak before World War I in 1914, with 208,780 sq. mi., plus a colonial empire. After that war Germany ceded Alsace-Lorraine to France; West Prussia and Posen (Poznan) province to Poland; part of Schleswig to Denmark; lost all of its colonies and the ports of Memel and Danzig.

Republic of Germany, 1919-1933, adopted the Weimar constitution; met reparation payments and elected Friedrich Ebert and Gen. Paul von Hindenburg presidents.

Third Reich, 1933-1945, Adolf Hitler led the National Socialist German Workers' (Nazi) party after World War I. In 1923 he attempted to unseat the Bavarian government and was imprisoned. Pres. von Hindenburg named Hitler chancellor Jan. 30, 1933; on Aug. 3, 1934, the day after Hindenburg's death, the cabinet joined the offices of president and chancellor and made Hitler fuehrer (leader). Hitler abolished freedom of speech and assembly, and began a long series of persecutions climaxed by the murder of millions of Jews and others.

He repudiated the Versailles treaty and reparations agreements, remilitarized the Rhineland (1936), and annexed Austria (Anschluss, 1938). At Munich he made an agreement with Neville Chamberlain, British prime minister, which permitted Germany to annex part of Czechoslovakia. He signed a nonaggression treaty with the USSR, 1939 and declared war on Poland Sept. 1, 1939, precipitating World War II. With total defeat near, Hitler committed suicide in Berlin Apr. 1945. The victorious Allies voided all acts and annexations of Hitler's Reich.

Division of Germany. Germany was sectioned into 4 zones of occupation, administered by the Allied Powers (U.S., USSR, U.K., and France). The USSR took control of many E German states. The territory E of the so-called Oder-Neisse line was assigned to, and later annexed by, Poland. Northern East Prussia (now Kaliningrad) was annexed by the USSR. Administration of the remaining regions, in the W and S (which make up about two-thirds of present-day Germany), was split among the Western Allies.

There was also created the area of Greater Berlin, within but not part of the Soviet zone, administered by the 4 occupying powers under the Allied Command. In 1948 the USSR withdrew, established its single command in East Berlin, and cut off supplies. The Western Allies utilized a gigantic airlift to bring food to West Berlin, 1948-49.

In 1949, 2 separate German states were established; in May the zones administered by the Western Allies became West Germany, capital: Bonn; in Oct. the Soviet sector became East Germany, capital: East Berlin. West Berlin was considered an enclave of West Germany, although its status was disputed by the Soviet bloc.

East Germany. The German Democratic Republic (East Germany) was proclaimed in the Soviet sector of Berlin Oct. 7, 1949. It was proclaimed fully sovereign in 1954, but Soviet troops remained on grounds of security and the 4-power Potsdam agreement.

Coincident with the entrance of West Germany into the European defense community in 1952, the East German government decreed a prohibited zone 3 miles deep along its 600-mile border with West Germany and cut Berlin's telephone system in two. Berlin was further divided by erection of a fortified wall in 1961, after over 3 million East Germans had emigrated West; an exodus of refugees to the West continued, though on a smaller scale.

East Germany suffered severe economic problems at least until the mid-1960s. Then a "new economic system" was introduced, easing central planning controls and allowing factories to make profits provided they were reinvested in operations or redistributed to workers as bonuses. By the early 1970s, the economy was highly industrialized, and the nation was credited with the highest standard of living among Warsaw Pact countries. But growth slowed in the late 1970s, because of shortages of natural resources and labor, and a huge debt to lenders in the West. Comparison with the lifestyle in the West caused many young people to leave the country.

The government firmly resisted following the USSR's policy of *glasnost,* but by Oct. 1989, was faced with nationwide demonstrations demanding reform. Pres. Erich Honecker, in office since 1976, was forced to resign, Oct. 18. On Nov. 4, the border with Czechoslovakia was opened and permission granted for refugees to travel to the West. On Nov. 9, the East German government announced its decision to open the border with the West, signaling the end of the "Berlin Wall," which was the supreme emblem of the cold war. On Aug. 23, 1990, the East German parliament agreed to formal unification with West Germany; this occurred Oct. 3.

West Germany. The Federal Republic of Germany (West Germany) was proclaimed May 23, 1949, in Bonn, after a constitution had been drawn up by a consultative assembly formed by representatives of the 11 laender (states) in the French, British, and American zones. Later reorganized into 9 units, the laender numbered 10 with the addition of the Saar, 1957. Berlin also was granted land (state) status, but the 1945 occupation agreements placed restrictions on it.

The occupying powers, the U.S., Britain, and France, restored civil status, Sept. 21, 1949. The Western Allies ended the state of war with Germany in 1951 (the U.S. resumed diplomatic relations July 2), while the USSR did so in 1955. The powers lifted controls and the republic became fully independent May 5, 1955.

Dr. Konrad Adenauer, Christian Democrat, was made chancellor Sept. 15, 1949, reelected 1953, 1957, 1961. Willy Brandt, heading a coalition of Social Democrats and Free

Democrats, became chancellor Oct. 21, 1969. (He resigned May 1974 because of a spy scandal.)

In 1970 Brandt signed friendship treaties with the USSR and Poland. In 1971, the U.S., Britain, France, and the USSR signed an agreement on Western access to West Berlin. In 1972 East and West Germany signed their first formal treaty, implementing the agreement easing access to West Berlin. In 1973 a West Germany-Czechoslovakia pact normalized relations and nullified the 1938 "Munich Agreement."

West Germany experienced strong economic growth starting in the 1950s. The country led Europe in provisions for worker participation in the management of industry.

A NATO decision to deploy medium-range nuclear missiles in Western Europe sparked a demonstration by some 400,000 protesters in 1983. In 1989, Chancellor Helmut Kohl's call for early negotiations with the Soviets on reducing short-range missiles caused a rift with NATO allies.

In 1989, the changes in the East German government and opening of the Berlin Wall sparked talk of reunification of the 2 Germanys. In 1990, under Chancellor Kohl's leadership, West Germany moved rapidly to reunite with East Germany.

A New Era. As Communism was being rejected in East Germany, talks began concerning German reunification. At a meeting in Ottawa, Feb. 1990, the foreign ministers of the World War II "Big Four" Allied nations and of East Germany and West Germany reached agreement on a format for high-level talks on German reunification.

In May, NATO ministers adopted a package of proposals on reunification, including the inclusion of the united Germany as a full member of NATO and the barring of the new Germany from having its own nuclear, chemical, or biological weapons. In July, the USSR agreed to conditions that would allow Germany to become a member of NATO.

The 2 nations agreed to monetary unification under the West German mark beginning in July. The merger of the 2 Germanys took place Oct. 3, and the first all-German elections since 1932 were held Dec. 2. In 1991, Berlin again became the capital of Germany; the seat of government was scheduled to shift from Bonn to Berlin over the course of about 10 years.

In 1992, neo-Nazi groups intensified their campaign against refugees. Parliament approved constitutional changes to restrict foreigners' rights to seek asylum in Germany, May 1993.

Germany's highest court ruled, July 12, 1994, that German troops could participate in international military missions abroad, when approved by Parliament. Ceremonies were held marking the final withdrawal of Russian troops from Germany, Aug. 31, 1994. Ceremonies were held the following week marking the final withdrawal of American, British, and French troops from Berlin. General elections Oct. 16, 1994, left Chancellor Helmut Kohl's governing coalition with a slim parliamentary majority. Eastern Germany received more than $1 trillion in public and private funds from western Germany between 1990 and 1995. On Oct. 31, 1996, after more than 14 years in office, Kohl surpassed Adenauer as Germany's longest-serving chancellor in the 20th century. Unemployment hit a postwar high of 12.6% in Jan. 1998. The Kohl era ended with the defeat of the Christian Democrats in parliamentary elections Sept. 27; Gerhard Schröder, of the Social Democratic Party, became chancellor.

Helgoland, an island of 130 acres in the North Sea, was taken from Denmark by a British Naval Force in 1807 and later ceded to Germany to become part of Schleswig-Holstein province in return for rights in East Africa. The heavily fortified island was surrendered to UK, May 23, 1945, demilitarized in 1947, and returned to West Germany, Mar. 1, 1952. It is a free port.

Ghana

Republic of Ghana

People: Population: 18,497,206. **Age distrib.** (%): <15: 42.9; 65+: 3.1. **Pop. density:** 201 per sq. mi. **Urban:** 36%. **Ethnic groups:** Akan 44%, Moshi-Dagomba 16%, Ewe 13%, Ga 8%. **Principal languages:** English (official), Akan, Moshi-Dagomba, Ewe, Ga. **Chief religions:** Indigenous beliefs 38%, Muslim 30%, Christian 24%.

Geography: Area: 92,100 sq. mi. **Location:** On southern coast of W Africa. **Neighbors:** Côte d'Ivoire on W, Burkina Faso on N, Togo on E. **Topography:** Most of Ghana consists of low fertile plains and scrubland, cut by rivers and by the artificial Lake Volta. **Capital:** Accra: 1,673,000*.

Government: Type: Republic. **Head of state and government:** Pres. Jerry Rawlings; b June 22, 1947; in office: Dec. 31, 1981. **Local divisions:** 10 regions. **Defense:** 1.4% of GDP. **Active troop strength:** 7,000.

Economy: Industries: Aluminum, light manufacturing. **Chief crops:** Cocoa, coffee, rice, cassava, peanuts, corn. **Minerals:** Gold, manganese, industrial diamonds, bauxite. **Crude oil reserves** (1997): 16.5 mil bbls. **Other resources:** Timber, rubber. **Arable land:** 12%. **Livestock** (1997): chickens: 13.30 mil; goats: 2.20 mil; sheep: 2.10 mil; cattle: 1.15 mil; pigs: 395,000. **Fish catch** (1996): 476,623 metric tons. **Electricity prod.** (1996): 6.1 bil kWh. **Labor force:** 55% agric., fishing; 19% ind.; 15% sales, clerical.

Finance: Monetary unit: Cedi (Sept. 1998: 2,325.00 = $1 U.S.). **Gross domestic product** (1996 est.): $27 bil. **Per capita GDP:** $1,530. **Imports** (1995): $1.84 bil; partners: Germany 14%, UK 12%, U.S. 12%. **Exports** (1995 est.): $1.43 bil; partners: U.K. 16%, Italy 8%. **Tourism:** $256 mil. **National budget** (1993): $1.2 bil. **International reserves less gold** (Nov. 1997): $480.4 mil. **Gold:** 275,000 oz t. **Consumer prices** (change in 1997): 27.9%.

Transport: Railroad: Length: 591.8 mi. **Motor vehicles in use:** 90,000 passenger cars, 45,000 comm. vehicles. **Civil aviation:** 406.8 mil passenger-mi; 1 airport. **Chief ports:** Tema, Takoradi.

Communications: Television sets: 15.3 per 1,000 pop. **Radios:** 249 per 1,000 pop. **Telephones:** 77,886 main lines. **Daily newspaper circ.:** 64.4 per 1,000 pop.

Health: Life expectancy at birth: 54.8 male; 58.9 female. **Births** (per 1,000 pop.): 33. **Deaths** (per 1,000 pop.): 11. **Natural increase:** 2.22%. **Hospital beds** (1994): 1 per 638 persons. **Physicians** (1994): 1 per 22,970 persons. **Infant mortality** (per 1,000 live births): 78.

Education: Compulsory: ages 6-16. **Literacy** (1995): 64%.

Major International Organizations: UN and all of its specialized agencies, the Commonwealth, OAU.

Embassy: 3512 International Dr. NW 20008; 686-4520.

Named for an African empire along the Niger River, AD 400-1240, Ghana was ruled by Britain for 113 years as the Gold Coast. The UN in 1956 approved merger with the British Togoland trust territory. Independence came Mar. 6, 1957, and republic status within the Commonwealth in 1960.

Pres. Kwame Nkrumah built hospitals and schools, promoted development projects like the Volta R. hydroelectric and aluminum plants but ran the country into debt, jailed opponents, and was accused of corruption. A 1964 referendum gave Nkrumah dictatorial powers and set up a one-party socialist state. Nkrumah was overthrown in 1966 by a police-army coup, which expelled Chinese and East German teachers and technicians. Elections were held in 1969, but 4 further coups occurred in 1972, 1978, 1979, and 1981. The 1979 and 1981 coups, led by Flight Lieut. Jerry Rawlings, were followed by suspension of the constitution and banning of political parties. A new constitution, allowing multiparty politics, was approved in April 1992.

In Feb. 1993 more than 1,000 people were killed in ethnic clashes in northern Ghana. Rawlings won the presidential election of Dec. 7, 1996. Kofi Annan, a career UN diplomat from Ghana, became UN secretary general on Jan. 1, 1997. U.S. Pres. Clinton opened a 12-day African tour with a speech, Mar. 23, 1998, to an Accra audience estimated at over 500,000.

Greece

Hellenic Republic

People: Population: 10,662,138. **Age distrib.** (%): <15: 16.1; 65+: 16.5. **Pop. density:** 209 per sq. mi. **Urban:** 59%. **Ethnic groups:** Greek 98%. (**Note:** Greek govt. states there are no ethnic divisions in Greece.) **Principal languages:** Greek (official), English, French. **Chief religion:** Greek Orthodox 98% (official).

Geography: Area: 50,942 sq. mi. **Location:** Occupies southern end of Balkan Peninsula in SE Europe. **Neighbors:** Albania, Macedonia, Bulgaria on N; Turkey on E. **Topography:** About 3/4 of Greece is nonarable, with mountains in all areas. Pindus Mts. run through the country N to S. The heavily indented coastline is 9,385 mi. long. Of over 2,000 islands, only 169 are inhabited, among them Crete, Rhodes, Milos, Kerkira (Corfu), Chios, Lesbos, Samos, Euboea, Delos, Mykonos. **Capital:** Athens. **Cities:** Athens 3,093,000; Thessaloníki 987,000*.

Government: Type: Parliamentary republic. **Head of state:** Pres. Costis Stefanopoulos; b 1926; in office: Mar. 8, 1995. **Head of government:** Prime Min. Costas Simitis; b June 23, 1936; in office: Jan. 18, 1996. **Local divisions:** 13 regions comprising 51 prefectures. **Defense:** 4.8% of GDP. **Active troop strength:** 168,300.

Economy: Industries: Tourism, textiles, chemicals, metals, wine, food processing. **Chief crops:** Grains, corn, sugar beets, cotton, tobacco, olives, grapes, citrus and other fruits, tomatoes. **Minerals:** Bauxite, lignite, magnesite, marble, oil. **Crude oil reserves** (1997): 10 mil bbls. **Arable land:** 19%. **Livestock** (1997): chickens: 28.50; sheep: 9.24 mil; goats: 5.67 mil; pigs: 904,000; cattle: 541,700. **Fish catch** (1996): 162,123 metric tons. **Electricity prod.** (1996): 40.0 bil kWh. **Labor force:** 52% services; 25% ind.; 23% agric.

Finance: Monetary unit: Drachma (Sept. 1998: 297.32 = $1 U.S.). **Gross domestic product** (1996 est.): $106.9 bil. **Per capita GDP:** $10,000. **Imports** (1995): $20.3 bil; partners: Italy 18%, Germany 16%. **Exports** (1995): $5.9 bil; partners: Germany 22%, Italy 14%. **Tourism:** $3.80 bil. **National budget** (1996 est.): $45 bil. **International reserves less gold** (June 1998): $18.65 bil. **Gold:** 3.62 mil oz t. **Consumer prices** (change in 1997): 5.5%.

Transport: Railroad: Length: 1,536.4 mi. **Motor vehicles in use:** 2.34 mil passenger cars, 939,923 comm. vehicles. **Civil aviation:** 5.30 bil passenger-mi; 36 airports. **Chief ports:** Piraeus, Thessaloníki, Patrai.

Communications: Television sets: 442 per 1,000 pop. **Radios:** 402 per 1,000 pop. **Telephones:** 5,328,794 main lines. **Daily newspaper circ.:** 135 per 1,000 pop.

Health: Life expectancy at birth: 75.8 male; 81.0 female. **Births** (per 1,000 pop.): 10. **Deaths** (per 1,000 pop.): 9. **Natural increase:** 0.03. **Hospital beds** (1993): 1 per 199 persons. **Physicians** (1994): 1 per 258 persons. **Infant mortality** (per 1,000 live births): 7.

Education: Free and compulsory: ages 6-15. **Literacy** (1993): 95%.

Major International Organizations: UN (FAO, IBRD, ILO, IMF, IMO, WHO, WTrO), EU, NATO, OECD, OSCE.

Embassy: 2221 Massachusetts Ave. NW 20008; 939-5800.

Website: http://www.hiway.gr/gi

The achievements of ancient Greece in art, architecture, science, mathematics, philosophy, drama, literature, and democracy became legacies for succeeding ages. Greece reached the height of its glory and power, particularly in the Athenian city-state, in the 5th century BC. Greece fell under Roman rule in the 2d and 1st centuries BC. In the 4th century AD it became part of the Byzantine Empire and, after the fall of Constantinople to the Turks in 1453, part of the Ottoman Empire.

Greece won its war of independence from Turkey 1821-1829, and became a kingdom. A republic was established 1924; the monarchy was restored, 1935, and George II, King of the Hellenes, resumed the throne. In Oct. 1940, Greece rejected an ultimatum from Italy. Nazi support resulted in its defeat and occupation by Germans, Italians, and Bulgarians. By the end of 1944 the invaders withdrew. Communist resistance forces were defeated by Royalist and British troops. A plebiscite again restored the monarchy.

Communists waged guerrilla war 1947-49 against the government but were defeated with the aid of the U.S. A period of reconstruction and rapid development followed, mainly with conservative governments under Premier Constantine Karamanlis. The Center Union, led by George Papandreou, won elections in 1963 and 1964, but King Constantine, who acceded in 1964, forced Papandreou to resign. A period of political maneuvers ended in the military takeover of April 21, 1967, by Col. George Papadopoulos. King Constantine tried to reverse the consolidation of the harsh dictatorship Dec. 13, 1967, but failed and fled to Italy. Papadopoulos was ousted Nov. 25, 1973.

Greek army officers serving in the National Guard of Cyprus staged a coup on the island July 15, 1974. Turkey invaded Cyprus a week later, precipitating the collapse of the Greek junta, which was implicated in the Cyprus coup. Democratic government returned (and in 1975 the monarchy was abolished).

The 1981 electoral victory of the Panhellenic Socialist Movement (Pasok) of Andreas Papandreou brought about substantial changes in Greece's internal and external policies. A scandal centered on George Kostokas, a banker and publisher, led to the arrest or investigation of leading Socialists, implicated Papandreou, and contributed to the defeat of the Socialists at the polls in 1989. However, Papandreou, who was narrowly acquitted Jan. 1992 of corruption charges, led the Socialists to a comeback victory in general elections Oct. 10, 1993.

Tensions between Greece and the Former Yugoslav Republic of Macedonia eased when the 2 countries agreed to normalize relations Sept. 13, 1995. The ailing Papandreou was replaced as prime minister by Costas Simitis, Jan. 18, 1996. Simitis led the Socialists to victory in the election of Sept. 22. The International Olympic Committee, Sept. 5, 1997, chose Athens to host the Summer Games in 2004.

Grenada

People: Population: 96,217. **Age distrib.** (%): <15: 43.1; 65+: 4.6. **Pop. density:** 734 per sq. mi. **Urban:** 36%. **Ethnic groups:** Mostly black African. **Principal languages:** English (official), French patois. **Chief religions:** Roman Catholic 53%, Protestant 33%.

Geography: Area: 131 sq. mi. **Location:** In Caribbean, 90 mi. N of Venezuela. **Neighbors:** Venezuela, Trinidid & Tobago to S; St. Vincent & the Grenadines to N. **Topography:** Main island is mountainous; country includes Carriacou and Petit Martinique islands. **Capital:** Saint George's (1991): 4,439.

Government: Type: Parliamentary democracy. **Head of state:** Queen Elizabeth II, represented by Gov.-Gen. Daniel Williams; b Nov. 4, 1935; in office: Aug. 8, 1996. **Head of government:** Prime Min. Keith Mitchell; b Nov. 12, 1946; in office: June 22, 1995. **Local divisions:** 6 parishes, 1 dependency.

Economy: Industries: Tourism, textiles, food & beverages. **Chief crops:** Nutmeg, bananas, cocoa, mace. **Resources:** Timber. **Arable land:** 15%. **Livestock** (1997): chickens: 280,000. **Electricity prod.** (1996): 70 mil kWh. **Labor force:** 31% services; 24% agric.

Finance: Monetary unit: East Caribbean dollar (Sept. 1998: 2.70 = $1 U.S.). **Gross domestic product** (1996 est.): $300 mil. **Per capita GDP:** $3,160. **Imports** (1996 est.): $128 mil; partners: U.S. 31%, Caricom 24%, UK 14%. **Exports** (1996 est.): $24 mil; partners: Caricom 32%; UK 20%. **Tourism:** $61 mil. **National budget** (1996 est.): $126.7 mil. **International reserves less gold** (Mar. 1998): $41.04 mil. **Consumer prices** (change in 1997): 1.2%.

Transport: Civil aviation: 2 airports. **Chief ports:** Saint George's, Grenville.

Communications: Television sets: 154 per 1,000 pop. **Radios:** 460 per 1,000 pop. **Telephones:** 24,100 main lines.

Health: Life expectancy at birth: 68.8 male; 74.0 female. **Births** (per 1,000 pop.): 28. **Deaths** (per 1,000 pop.): 5. **Natural increase:** 2.28%. **Hospital beds** (1996): 1 per 223 persons. **Physicians** (1992): 1 per 2,045 persons. **Infant mortality** (per 1,000 live births): 11.

Education: Free and compulsory: ages 5-16. **Literacy** (1994): 85%.

Major International Organizations: UN (FAO, IBRD, ILO, IMF, WHO, WTrO), Caricom, the Commonwealth, OAS, OECS.

Embassy: 1701 New Hampshire Ave. NW 20009; 265-2561.

Website: http://www.grenada.org

Columbus sighted Grenada in 1498. First European settlers were French, 1650. The island was held alternately by France and England until final British occupation, 1784. Grenada became fully independent Feb. 7, 1974, during a general strike. It is the smallest independent nation in the western hemisphere.

On Oct. 14, 1983, a military coup ousted Prime Minister Maurice Bishop, who was put under house arrest, later freed by supporters, rearrested, and, finally, on Oct. 19, executed. U.S. forces, with a token force from 6 area nations, invaded Grenada, Oct. 25. Resistance from the Grenadian army and Cuban advisors was quickly overcome as most people welcomed the invading forces. U.S. troops left Grenada in June 1985. Cuban Pres. Castro received an enthusiastic greeting when visiting Grenada Aug. 2-3, 1998.

Guatemala

Republic of Guatemala

People: Population: 12,007,580. **Age distrib.** (%): <15: 42.9; 65+: 3.5. **Pop. density:** 286 per sq. mi. **Urban:** 39%. **Ethnic groups:** Mestizo 56%, Amerindian 44%. **Principal languages:** Spanish (official), Mayan languages. **Religion:** Mostly Roman Catholic, some Protestant, traditional Mayan.

Geography: Area: 42,042 sq. mi. **Location:** In Central America. **Neighbors:** Mexico on N and W, El Salvador on S, Honduras and Belize on E. **Topography:** The central highland and mountain areas are bordered by the narrow Pacific coast and the lowlands and fertile river valleys on the Caribbean. There are numerous volcanoes in S, more than half a dozen over 11,000 ft. **Capital:** Guatemala City: 2,205,000*.

Government: Type: Republic. **Head of state and government:** Pres. Alvaro Arzú Irigoyen; b Mar. 14, 1946; in office: Jan. 14, 1996. **Local divisions:** 22 departments. **Defense:** 1.4% of GDP. **Active troop strength:** 44,200.

Economy: Industries: Furniture, rubber, textiles. **Chief crops:** Coffee, sugar, bananas, corn, cardamom. **Minerals:** Oil, nickel. **Crude oil reserves** (1997): 200 mil bbls. **Other resources:** Rare woods, fish, chicle. **Arable land:** 12%. **Livestock** (1997): chickens: 23.00 mil; cattle: 1.77 mil; pigs: 801,500; sheep: 551,100; goats: 109,200. **Electricity prod.** (1996): 3.1 bil kWh. **Labor force:** 58% agric.; 14% serv.; 14% manuf.

Finance: Monetary unit: Quetzal (Sept. 1998: 6.52 = $1 U.S.). **Gross domestic product** (1996 est.): $39 bil. **Per capita GDP:** $3,460. **Imports** (1996): $3.11 bil; partners: U.S. 44%. **Exports** (1996): $1.8 bil; partners: U.S. 30%. **Tourism:** $325 mil. **National budget** (1996 est.): $1.88 bil. **International reserves less gold** (June 1998): $1.03 bil. **Gold:** 214,000 oz t. **Consumer prices** (change in 1997): 9.2%.

Transport: Railroad: Length: 549 mi. **Motor vehicles in use:** 102,000 passenger cars, 97,000 comm. vehicles. **Civil aviation:** 329.1 mil passenger-mi; 2 airports. **Chief ports:** Puerto Barrios, San Jose.

Communications: Television sets: 45 per 1,000 pop. **Radios:** 52 per 1,000 pop. **Telephones:** 342,046 main lines. **Daily newspaper circ.:** 29 per 1,000 pop.

Health: Life expectancy at birth: 63.4 male; 68.8 female. **Births** (per 1,000 pop.): 36. **Deaths** (per 1,000 pop.): 7. **Natural increase:** 2.91%. **Infant mortality** (per 1,000 live births): 48.

Education: Free and compulsory: ages 7-14. **Literacy:** (1995): 56%.

Major International Organizations: UN (FAO, IBRD, ILO, IMF, IMO, WHO, WTrO), OAS.

Embassy: 2220 R St. NW 20008; 745-4952.

The old Mayan Indian empire flourished in what is today Guatemala for over 1,000 years before the Spanish.

Guatemala was a Spanish colony 1524-1821; briefly a part of Mexico and then of the U.S. of Central America, the republic was established in 1839.

Since 1945 when a liberal government was elected to replace the long-term dictatorship of Jorge Ubico, the country has seen a variety of military and civilian governments and periods of civil war. Dissident army officers seized power Mar. 23, 1982, denouncing a presidential election as fraudulent and pledging to restore "authentic democracy" to the nation. Political violence caused large numbers of Guatemalans to seek refuge in Mexico. Another military coup occurred Oct. 8, 1983. The nation returned to civilian rule in 1986.

The crisis-ridden government of Pres. Jorge Serrano Elías was ousted by the military June 1, 1993. Ramiro de León Carpio was elected president by Congress June 6. A UN report in March 1995 blamed state authorities for a majority of human rights violations in Guatemala.

A conservative businessman, Alvaro Arzú Irigoyen, won the presidency, Jan. 7, 1996. On Sept. 19 the Guatemalan government and leftist rebels approved a peace accord; the final agreement was signed Dec. 29. During more than 35 years of armed conflict, over 100,000 people were killed, another 40,000 "disappeared" and are presumed dead, and a million more became refugees. Violent episodes in 1998 included the daylight ambush of a busload of U.S. college students, Jan. 16, resulting in the rape of five young women, and the murder of Bishop Juan José Girardi, a human rights activist, Apr. 26.

Guinea

Republic of Guinea

People: Population: 7,477,110. **Age distrib.** (%): <15: 43.9; 65+: 2.7. **Pop. density:** 79 per sq. mi. **Urban:** 30%. **Ethnic groups:** Peuhl 40%, Malinke 30%, Soussou 20%, smaller tribes 10%. **Principal languages:** French (official), tribal languages. **Chief religions:** Muslim 85%, Christian 8%.

Geography: Area: 94,927 sq. mi. **Location:** On Atlantic coast of W Africa. **Neighbors:** Guinea-Bissau, Senegal, Mali on N; Côte d'Ivoire on E; Liberia on S. **Topography:** A narrow coastal belt leads to the mountainous middle region, the source of the Gambia, Senegal, and Niger rivers. Upper Guinea, farther inland, is a cooler upland. The SE is forested. **Capital:** Conakry: 1,558,000*.

Government: Type: Republic. **Head of state and government:** Pres. Gen. Lansana Conté; b 1934; in office: Apr. 5, 1984. **Local divisions:** 33 prefectures and 1 national capital. **Defense:** 1.9% of GDP. **Active troop strength:** 9,700.

Economy: Industries: Mining, light manufacturing, agricultural processing. **Chief crops:** Bananas, pineapples, rice, palm kernels, coffee, cassava. **Minerals:** Bauxite, iron, diamonds, gold. **Arable land:** 2%. **Livestock** (1997): chickens: 7.40 mil; cattle: 2.30 mil; sheep: 625,000; goats: 770,000. **Fish catch** (1996): 64,580 metric tons. **Electricity prod.** (1996) 525 mil kWh. **Labor force:** 80% agric.; 11% ind. & commerce.

Finance: Monetary unit: Franc (Sept. 1998: 1,243.00 = $1 U.S.). **Gross domestic product** (1996 est.): $7.1 bil. **Per capita GDP:** $950. **Imports** (1995 est.): $775 mil; partners: France 20% Côted' Ivoire 16%. **Exports** (1995 est.): $725 mil; partners: Belg.-Lux. 27%, U.S. 15%. **Tourism:** $5 mil. **National budget** (1995 est.): $947 mil. **International reserves less gold** (Apr. 1998): $209.34 mil.

Transport: Railroad: Length: 411 mi. **Motor vehicles in use:** 13,700 passenger cars, 19,300 comm. vehicles. **Civil aviation:** 33.9 mil passenger-mi; 1 airport. **Chief port:** Conakry.

Communications: Television sets: 9.7 per 1,000 pop. **Radios:** 34.3 per 1,000 pop. **Telephones:** 16,206 main lines.

Health: Life expectancy at birth: 43.6 male; 48.5 female. **Births** (per 1,000 pop.): 41. **Deaths** (per 1,000 pop.): 18. **Natural increase:** 2.35%.

Education: Free and compulsory: ages 7-13. **Literacy:** (1995): 36%.

Major International Organizations: UN and most of its specialized agencies, OAU.

Embassy: 2112 Leroy Pl. NW 20008; 483-9420.

Part of the ancient West African empires, Guinea fell under French control 1849-98. Under Sékou Touré, it opted for full independence in 1958, and France withdrew all aid.

Touré turned to Communist nations for support and set up a militant one-party state. Thousands of opponents were jailed in the 1970s, in the aftermath of an unsuccessful Portuguese invasion. Many were tortured and killed.

The military took control in a bloodless coup after the March 1984 death of Touré. A new constitution was approved in 1991, but movement toward democracy was slow. When presidential elections were finally held, in Dec. 1993, the incumbent, Gen. Lansana Conté, was the official winner; outside monitors called the elections flawed. Parliamentary elections June 11, 1995, raised similar complaints. Conté suppressed an army mutiny in Conakry, Feb. 2-3, 1996.

Guinea-Bissau

Republic of Guinea-Bissau

People: Population: 1,206,311. **Age distrib.** (%): <15: 42.4; 65+: 2.8. **Pop. density:** 87 per sq. mi. **Urban:** 22%. **Ethnic groups:** Balanta 30%, Fula 20%, Manjaca 14%, Mandinga 13%. **Principal languages:** Portuguese (official), Criolo, tribal languages. **Chief religions:** Indigenous beliefs 65%, Muslim 30%, Christian 5%.

Geography: Area: 13,946 sq. mi. **Location:** On Atlantic coast of W Africa. **Neighbors:** Senegal on N, Guinea on E and S. **Topography:** A swampy coastal plain covers most of the country; to the east is a low savanna region. **Capital:** Bissau (1995 est.): 233,000.

Government: Type: Republic. **Head of state:** Pres. Joao Bernardo Vieira; b Apr. 27, 1939; in office: Nov. 14, 1980. **Head of government:** Prime Min. Carlos Correia; in office: June 6, 1997. **Local divisions:** 9 regions. **Defense:** 2.9% of GDP. **Active troop strength:** 7,300.

Economy: Chief crops: Peanuts, cashews, fruits, cotton, rice. **Minerals:** Bauxite, phosphates. **Arable land:** 11%. **Livestock** (1997): chickens: 850,000; cattle: 475,000; pigs: 310,000; goats: 270,000; sheep: 255,000. **Electricity prod.** (1996): 40 mil kWh. **Labor force:** 90% agric.

Finance: Monetary unit: CFA Franc (Sept. 1998: 580.94 = $1 U.S.). **Gross domestic product** (1996 est.): $1.1 bil. **Per capita GDP:** $950. **Imports** (1996): $63 mil; partners: Thailand 27%, Portugal 23%. **Exports** (1996): $25.8 mil; partners: Spain 35%. India 30%. **National budget** (1991 est.): $44.8 mil. **International reserves less gold** (Mar. 1997): $16.41 mil. **Consumer prices** (change in 1997): 49.1%.

Transport: Motor vehicles in use: 3,500 passenger cars, 2,500 comm. vehicles. **Civil aviation:** 6.2 mil passenger-mi; 2 airports. **Chief port:** Bissau.

Communications: Radios: 42 per 1,000 pop. **Telephones:** 7,926 main lines.

Health: Life expectancy at birth: 47.5 male; 50.9 female. **Births** (per 1,000 pop.): 39. **Deaths** (per 1,000 pop.): 15. **Natural increase:** 2.32%. **Hospital beds** (1993): 1 per 797 persons. **Infant mortality** (per 1,000 live births): 112.

Education: Compulsory: ages 7-13. **Literacy** (1995): 55%.

Major International Organizations: UN (FAO, IBRD, ILO, IMF, IMO, WHO, WTrO), OAU.

Embassy: 918 16th St. NW 20006; 872-4222.

Portuguese mariners explored the area in the mid-15th century; the slave trade flourished in the 17th and 18th centuries, and colonization began in the 19th.

Beginning in the 1960s, an independence movement waged a guerrilla war and formed a government in the interior that had international support. Independence came Sept. 10, 1974, after the Portuguese regime was overthrown.

The November 1980 coup gave Vieira absolute power. Vieira eventually initiated political liberalization; multiparty elections were held July 3, 1994. An army uprising June 7, 1998, triggered a civil war, with Senegal and Guinea aiding the Vieira regime; a cease-fire was declared July 26.

Guyana

Co-operative Republic of Guyana

People: Population: 707,954. **Age distrib.** (%): <15: 31.1; 65+: 4.6. **Pop. density:** 9 per sq. mi. **Urban:** 36%. **Ethnic groups:** East Indian 51%, black and mixed 43%, Amerindian 4%. **Principal languages:** English (official), Amerindian dialects. **Chief religions:** Christian 57%, Hindu 33%, Muslim 9%.

Geography: Area: 83,000 sq. mi. **Location:** On N coast of South America. **Neighbors:** Venezuela on W, Brazil on S, Suriname on E. **Topography:** Dense tropical forests cover much of the land, although a flat coastal area up to 40 mi. wide, where 90% of the population lives, provides rich alluvial soil for agriculture. A grassy savanna divides the 2 zones. **Capital:** Georgetown (1995 est.): 254,000.

Government: Type: Republic. **Head of state:** Pres. Janet Jagan; b Oct. 20, 1920; in office: Dec. 19, 1997. **Head of government:** Prime Min. Samuel Hinds; b Dec. 27, 1943; in office: Dec. 22, 1997. **Local divisions:** 10 regions. **Defense:** 1.0% of GDP. **Active troop strength:** 1,600.

Economy: Industries: Mining, textiles. **Chief crops:** Sugar, rice, coconuts, citrus, fruits. **Minerals:** Bauxite, gold, diamonds. **Other resources:** Timber, shrimp, dairy prods. **Arable land:** 2%. **Livestock** (1997): chickens: 11.50 mil; cattle: 250,000; sheep: 130,000. **Electricity prod.** (1996): 325 mil kWh. **Labor force:** 44.5% ind. & commerce; 34% agric.; 22% services.

Finance: Monetary unit: Dollar (Sept. 1998: 152.30 = $1 U.S.). **Gross domestic product** (1996 est.): $1.8 bil. **Per capita GDP:** $2,490. **Imports** (1996 est.): $589 mil; partners: U.S. 29%, Neitherlands 17%, Trin. & Tob. 17%. **Exports** (1996 est.): $565 mil; partners: Canada 33%, U.S. 24%. **Tourism:** $39 mil. **National budget** (1995 est): $303 mil. **International reserves less gold** (May 1998): $277.09 mil.

Transport: Railroad: Length: 116 mi. **Motor vehicles in use:** 24,000 passenger cars, 9,000 comm. vehicles. **Civil aviation:** 154.0 mil passenger-mi; 1 airport. **Chief port:** Georgetown.

Communications: Television sets: 197 per 1,000 pop. **Radios:** 454 per 1,000 pop. **Telephones:** 50,190 main lines. **Daily newspaper circ.:** 585 per 1,000 pop.

Health: Life expectancy at birth: 59.5 male; 65.3 female. **Births** (per 1,000 pop.): 18. **Deaths** (per 1,000 pop.): 9. **Natural increase:** 0.98%. **Physicians** (1993): 1 per 3,148 persons. **Infant mortality** (per 1,000 live births): 49.

Education: Free and compulsory: ages 6-14. **Literacy** (1995): 98%.

Major International Organizations: UN (FAO, IBRD, ILO, IMF, IMO, WHO, WTrO), Caricom the Commonwealth, OAS.

Embassy: 2490 Tracy Pl. NW 20008; 265-6900.

Guyana became a Dutch possession in the 17th century, but sovereignty passed to Britain in 1815. Indentured servants from India soon outnumbered African slaves. Ethnic tension has affected political life.

Guyana became independent May 26, 1966. A Venezuelan claim to the western half of Guyana was suspended in 1970 but renewed in 1982; an agreement was reached in 1989. The Suriname border is disputed. The government has nationalized most of the economy, which has remained severely depressed.

The Port Kaituma ambush of U.S. Rep. Leo J. Ryan and others investigating mistreatment of American followers of the Rev. Jim Jones's People's Temple cult triggered a mass suicide-execution of 911 cultists at Jonestown in the Guyana jungle, Nov. 18, 1978.

The People's National Congress, the party in power since Guyana became independent, was voted out of office with the election of Cheddi Jagan in Oct. 1992. When Pres. Jagan died Mar. 6, 1997, Prime Min. Samuel Hinds succeeded him; his widow, Janet Jagan, became prime min. Mar. 17. She won the presidency in a disputed election Dec. 15.

Haiti

Republic of Haiti

People: Population: 6,780,501. **Age distrib.** (%): <15: 42.6; 65+: 4.1. **Pop. density:** 633 per sq. mi. **Urban:** 32%. **Ethnic groups:** Black 95%. **Principal languages:** Haitian Creole, French (both official). **Chief religions:** Roman Catholic 80%, Protestant 16%; Voodoo widely practiced.

Geography: Area: 10,714 sq. mi. **Location:** In Caribbean, occupies western third of Isl. of Hispaniola. **Neighbors:** Dominican Republic on E, Cuba to W. **Topography:** About two-thirds of Haiti is mountainous. Much of the rest is semiarid. Coastal areas are warm and moist. **Capital:** Port-au-Prince: 1,461,000*.

Government: Type: Republic. **Head of state:** Pres. René Préval; b Jan. 17, 1943; in office Feb. 7, 1996. **Local divisions:** 9 departments. **Defense:** 3.5% of GDP. **Active security forces:** 3,000-4,000.

Economy: Industries: Sugar refining, textiles. **Chief crops:** Coffee, sugar, mangoes, corn, rice. **Minerals:** Bauxite. **Arable land:** 20%. **Livestock** (1997): chickens: 3.80 mil; goats: 1.44 mil; cattle: 1.27 mil; pigs: 600,000; sheep: 160,500. **Electricity prod.** (1996): 415 mil kWh. **Labor force:** 57% agric.

Finance: Monetary unit: Gourde (Sept. 1998: 16.46 = $1 U.S.). **Gross domestic product** (1996 est.): $6.8 bil. **Per capita GDP:** $1,000. **Imports** (1996): $666 mil; partners: U.S. 65%. **Exports** (1996): $123 mil; partners: U.S. 74%. **Tourism:** $80 mil. **National budget** (FY 1994-95): $250 mil. **International reserves less gold** (May 1998): $60.1 mil. **Gold:** 20,000 oz t. **Consumer prices** (change in 1997): 20.6%.

Transport: Railroad: Length: 24.8 mi. **Motor vehicles in use:** 32,000 passenger cars, 21,000 comm. vehicles. **Civil aviation:** 2 airports. **Chief ports:** Port-au-Prince, Cayes, Cap-Haitien.

Communications: Television sets: 3.9 per 1,000 pop. **Radios:** 41 per 1,000 pop. **Telephones:** 60,000 main lines. **Daily newspaper circ.:** 7 per 1,000 pop.

Health: Life expectancy at birth: 49.3 male; 53.6 female. **Births** (per 1,000 pop.): 33. **Deaths** (per 1,000 pop.): 14. **Natural increase:** 1.87%. **Hospital beds** (1994): 1 per 975 persons. **Physicians** (1994): 1 per 9,846 persons. **Infant mortality rate** (per 1,000 live births): 99.

Education: Compulsory: ages 6-12. **Literacy** (1995): 45%.

Major International Organizations: UN and most of its specialized agencies, OAS.

Embassy: 2311 Massachusetts Ave. NW 20008; 332-4090.

Website: http://www.haiti.org/embassy/

Haiti, visited by Columbus, 1492, and a French colony from 1697, attained its independence, 1804, following the rebellion led by former slave Toussaint L'Ouverture. Following a period of political violence, the U.S. occupied the country 1915-34.

Francois Duvalier was elected president in Sept. 1957; in 1964 he was named president for life. Upon his death in 1971, he was succeeded by his son, Jean Claude. Drought in 1975-77 brought famine, and Hurricane Allen in 1980 destroyed most of the rice, bean, and coffee crops. Following several weeks of unrest, President Jean Claude Duvalier fled Haiti aboard a U.S. Air Force jet Feb. 7, 1986, ending the 28-year dictatorship by the Duvalier family.

A military-civilian council headed by Gen. Henri Namphy assumed control. In 1987, voters approved a new constitution, but the Jan. 1988 elections were marred by violence and boycotted by the opposition. Gen. Namphy seized control, June 20, but was ousted by a military coup in Sept.

Father Jean-Bertrand Aristide was elected president Dec. 1990. In Sept. 1991, Aristide was arrested by the military and expelled from the country. Some 35,000 Haitian refugees were intercepted by the U.S. Coast Guard as they tried to enter the U.S., 1991-92. Most were returned to Haiti. There was a new upsurge of refugees starting in late 1993.

The UN imposed a worldwide oil, arms, and financial embargo on Haiti June 23, 1993. The embargo was suspended when the military agreed to Aristide's return to power on Oct. 30, but the military effectively blocked his return. After renewed sanctions, the UN Security Council authorized, July 31, 1994, an invasion of Haiti by a multinational force. With U.S. troops already en route, an invasion was averted, Sept. 18, by a new agreement for military leaders to step down and Aristide to resume office. As part of the agreement, thousands of U.S. troops began arriving in Haiti, Sept. 19. Aristide returned to Haiti and was restored in office Oct. 15. A UN peacekeeping force exercised responsibility in Haiti from Mar. 31, 1995 to Nov. 30, 1997.

Aristide transferred power to his elected successor, René Préval, on Feb. 7, 1996. Prime Min. Rosny Smarth announced his resignation June 9, 1997, and quit running the government Oct. 20, but Préval and parliament deadlocked on a successor. At least 140 people died and more than 160,000 became homeless when Hurricane Georges struck Haiti Sept. 22.

Honduras

Republic of Honduras

People: Population: 5,861,955. **Age distrib.** (%): <15: 41.8; 65+: 3.4. **Pop. density:** 135 per sq. mi. **Urban:** 44%. **Ethnic groups:** Mestizo 90%, Amerindian 7%. **Principal language:** Spanish (official). **Chief religion:** Roman Catholic 97%.

Geography: Area: 43,278 sq. mi. **Location:** In Central America. **Neighbors:** Guatemala on W, El Salvador and Nicaragua on S. **Topography:** The Caribbean coast is 500 mi. long. Pacific coast, on Gulf of Fonseca, is 40 mi. long. Honduras is mountainous, with wide fertile valleys and rich forests. **Capital:** Tegucigalpa: 995,000*.

Government: Type: Republic. **Head of State:** Pres. Carlos Flores Facusse; b Mar. 1, 1950; in office: Jan. 27, 1998. **Local divisions:** 18 departments. **Defense:** 1.3% of GDP. **Active troop strength:** 18,800.

Economy: Industries: Textiles, wood prods. **Chief crops:** Bananas, coffee, citrus. **Minerals:** Gold, silver, copper, lead, zinc, iron, antimony, coal. **Other resources:** Timber, fish. **Arable land:** 15%. **Livestock** (1997): chickens: 17.00 mil; cattle: 2.20 mil; pigs: 600,000. **Electricity prod.** (1996): 2.7 bil kWh. **Labor force:** 62% agric.; 20% services; 9% manuf.

Finance: Monetary unit: Lempira (Sept. 1998: 13.60 = $1 U.S.). **Gross domestic product** (1996 est.): $11.5 bil. **Per capita GDP:** $2,000. **Imports** (1996): $3.13 bil; partners: U.S. 50%. **Exports** (1996): $2.4 bil; partners: U.S. 65%. **Tourism:** $120 mil. **National budget** (1997 est.): $850 mil. **International reserves less gold** (June 1998): $730.79 mil. **Gold:** 21,000 oz t. **Consumer prices** (change in 1997): 20.2%.

Transport: Railroad: Length: 614 mi. **Motor vehicles in use:** 80,000 passenger cars, 105,000 comm. vehicles. **Civil aviation:** 189.5 mil passenger-mi; 8 airports. **Chief ports:** Puerto Cortes, La Ceiba.

Communications: Television sets: 29 per 1,000 pop. **Radios:** 337 per 1,000 pop. **Telephones:** 190,236 main lines. **Daily newspaper circ.:** 45 per 1,000 pop.

Health: Life expectancy at birth: 63.3 male; 66.8 female. **Births** (per 1,000 pop.): 32. **Deaths** (per 1,000 pop.): 7. **Natural increase:** 2.48%. **Hospital beds** (1994): 1 per 1,126 persons. **Infant mortality** (per 1,000 live births): 42.

Education: Free and compulsory: ages 7-13. **Literacy** (1995): 73%.

Major International Organizations: UN, (FAO, IBRD, ILO, IMF, IMO, WHO, WTrO), OAS.

Embassy: 3007 Tilden St. NW 20008; 966-7702.

Website: http://www.honduras.com

Mayan civilization flourished in Honduras in the 1st millennium AD. Columbus arrived in 1502. Honduras became independent after freeing itself from Spain, 1821, and from the Fed. of Central America, 1838.

Gen. Oswaldo Lopez Arellano, president for most of the period 1963-75 by virtue of one election and 2 coups, was ousted by the army in 1975 over charges of pervasive bribery by United Brands Co. of the U.S. An elected civilian government took power in 1982. Some 3,200 U.S. troops were sent to Honduras after the Honduran border was violated by Nicaraguan forces, Mar. 1988.

Honduras is one of the poorest countries in the western hemisphere.

Hungary

Republic of Hungary

People: Population: 10,208,127. **Age distrib.** (%): <15: 17.5; 65+: 14.4. **Pop. density:** 284 per sq. mi. **Urban:** 65%. **Ethnic groups:** Hungarian 90%, Gypsy 4%, German 3%. **Principal language:** Hungarian (Magyar; official). **Chief religions:** Roman Catholic 68%, Calvinist 20%, Lutheran 5%.

Geography: Area: 35,919 sq. mi. **Location:** In E central Europe. **Neighbors:** Slovakia, Ukraine on N; Austria on W; Slovenia, Yugoslavia, Croatia on S; Romania on E. **Topography:** The Danube R. forms the Slovak border in the NW, then swings S to bisect the country. The eastern half of Hungary is mainly a great fertile plain, the Alfold; the W and N are hilly. **Capital:** Budapest. **Cities** (1997 est.): Budapest 1,885,000; Debrecen 210,000; Miskolc 178,000.

Government: Type: Parliamentary democracy. **Head of state:** Pres. Arpad Goncz; b Feb. 10, 1922; in office: May 2, 1990. **Head of government:** Prime Min. Viktor Orbán; b May 31, 1963; in office: July 8, 1998. **Local divisions:** 19 counties, 1 capital. **Defense:** 1.7% of GDP. **Active troop strength:** 64,300.

Economy: Industries: Iron and steel, construction materials, processed foods, pharmaceuticals, vehicles. **Chief crops:** Wheat, corn, sunflowers, potatoes, sugar beets. **Minerals:** Bauxite, coal, gas. **Livestock** (1997): chickens: 27.83 mil; pigs: 5.29 mil; sheep: 872,000; cattle: 909,000. **Crude oil reserves** (1997): 128 mil bbls. **Arable land:** 51%. **Electricity prod.** (1996): 33.2 bil kWh. **Labor force:** 59% services; 35% ind.; 17% agric.

Finance: Monetary unit: Forint (Sept. 1998: 221.93 = $1 U.S.). **Gross domestic product** (1996 est.): $74.7 bil. **Per capita GDP:** $7,500. **Imports** (1996): $16.8 bil; partners: Germany 24%, Russia 15%, Austria 12%. **Exports** (1996): $14.2 bil; partners: Germany 29%, Austria 10%. **National budget** (1995): $11 bil. **Tourism:** $2.57 bil. **International reserves less gold** (Apr. 1998): $10.08 bil. **Gold:** 101,000 oz t. **Consumer prices** (change in 1997): 18.3%.

Transport: Railroad: Length: 8,190 mi. **Motor vehicles in use:** 2.28 mil passenger cars, 319,424 comm. vehicles. **Civil aviation:** 1.29 bil. passenger-mi; 1 airport.

Communications: Television sets: 444 per 1,000 pop. **Radios:** 590 per 1,000 pop. **Telephones:** 2,661,600 main lines. **Daily newspaper circ.:** 228 per 1,000 pop.

Health: Life expectancy at birth: 66.5 male; 75.4 female. **Births** (per 1,000 pop.): 11. **Deaths** (per 1,000 pop.): 13. **Natural increase:** –0.28%. **Hospital beds** (1995): 1 per 104 persons. **Physicians** (1995): 1 per 280 persons. **Infant mortality** (per 1,000 live births): 10.

Education: Compulsory: ages 6-16. **Literacy:** (1993): 99%.

Major International Organizations: UN (FAO, IBRD, ILO, IMF, IMO, WHO, WTrO), OECD, OSCE.

Embassy: 3910 Shoemaker St. NW 20008; 362-6730.

Website: http://www.hungaryemb.org

Earliest settlers, chiefly Slav and Germanic, were overrun by Magyars from the E. Stephen I (997-1038) was made king by Pope Sylvester II in AD 1000. The country suffered repeated Turkish invasions in the 15th-17th centuries. After the defeats of the Turks, 1686-1697, Austria dominated, but Hungary obtained concessions until it regained internal independence in 1867, with the emperor of Austria as king of Hungary in a dual monarchy with a single diplomatic service. Defeated with the Central Powers in 1918, Hungary lost Transylvania to Romania, Croatia and Bacska to Yugoslavia, Slovakia and Carpatho-Ruthenia to Czechoslovakia, all of which had large Hungarian minorities. A republic under Michael Karolyi and a bolshevist revolt under Bela Kun were followed by a vote for a monarchy in 1920 with Admiral Nicholas Horthy as regent.

Hungary joined Germany in World War II, and was allowed to annex most of its lost territories. Russian troops captured the country, 1944-1945. By terms of an armistice with the Allied powers Hungary agreed to give up territory acquired by the 1938 dismemberment of Czechoslovakia and to return to its borders of 1937.

A republic was declared Feb. 1, 1946; Zoltan Tildy was elected president. In 1947 the Communists forced Tildy out. Premier Imre Nagy, who had been in office since mid-1953, was ousted for his moderate policy of favoring agriculture and consumer production, April 18, 1955.

In 1956, popular demands to oust Erno Gero, Communist Party secretary, and for formation of a government by Nagy, resulted in the latter's appointment Oct. 23; demonstrations against Communist rule developed into open revolt. On Nov. 4 Soviet forces launched a massive attack against Budapest with 200,000 troops, 2,500 tanks and armored cars.

About 200,000 persons fled the country. Thousands were arrested and executed, including Nagy in June 1958. In spring 1963 the regime freed many captives from the 1956 revolt.

Hungarian troops participated in the 1968 Warsaw Pact invasion of Czechoslovakia. Major economic reforms were launched early in 1968, switching from a central planning system to one based on market forces and profit.

In 1989 Parliament passed legislation legalizing freedom of assembly and association as Hungary shifted away from communism. In Oct. the Communist Party was formally dissolved. The last Soviet troops left Hungary June 19, 1991. On July 8, 1997, NATO invited Hungary to become a full member of the alliance within 2 years.

Iceland

Republic of Iceland

People: Population: 271,033. **Age distrib.** (%): <15: 23.6; 65+: 11.7. **Pop. density:** 7 per sq. mi. **Urban:** 92%. **Ethnic groups:** Homogeneous descendants of Norwegians, Celts. **Principal language:** Icelandic (Islenska; official). **Chief religion:** Evangelical Lutheran 96%.

Geography: Area: 39,768 sq. mi. **Location:** Isl. at N end of Atlantic O. **Neighbors:** Nearest is Greenland (Den.), to W. **Topography:** Recent volcanic origin. Three-quarters of the surface is wasteland: glaciers, lakes, a lava desert. There are geysers and hot springs, and the climate is moderated by the Gulf Stream. **Capital:** Reykjavík (1996 est.): 105,487.

Government: Type: Constitutional republic. **Head of state:** Pres. Olafur Ragnar Grímsson; b May 14, 1943; in office: Aug. 1, 1996. **Head of government:** Prime Min. David Oddsson; Jan. 17, 1948; in office: Apr. 30, 1991. **Local divisions:** 165 municipalities, including 31 towns. **Defense:** Icelandic Defense Force provided by the U.S.

Economy: Industries: Fish products (64% of exports), aluminum. **Chief crops:** Potatoes, turnips. **Livestock** (1997): chickens: 190,000; sheep: 450,000. **Fish catch** (1996): 2.06 mil metric tons. **Electricity prod.** (1996): 5.5 bil kWh. **Labor force:** 60% commerce & services; 13% manuf.; 12% fish.

Finance: Monetary unit: Krona (Sept. 1998: 70.56 = $1 U.S.). **Gross domestic product** (1995 est.): $5 bil. **Per capita GDP:** $18,800. **Imports** (1995): $1.62 bil; partners: Germany 11%, Norway 10%, UK 10%. **Exports** (1995): $1.67 bil; partners: UK 19%, Germany 14%. **Tourism:** $156 mil. **National budget** (1994 est.): $2.1 bil. **International reserves less gold** (June 1998): $465.1 mil. **Gold:** 49,000 oz t. **Consumer prices** (change in 1997): 1.7%.

Transport: Motor vehicles in use: 124,909 passenger cars, 16,623 comm. vehicles. **Civil aviation:** 1.78 bil passenger-mi; 24 airports. **Chief port:** Reykjavík.

Communications: Television sets: 285 per 1,000 pop. **Radios:** 733 per 1,000 pop. **Telephones:** 155,400 main lines. **Daily newspaper circ.:** 515 per 1,000 pop.

Health: Life expectancy at birth: 76.8 male; 81.1 female. **Births** (per 1,000 pop.): 15. **Deaths** (per 1,000 pop.): 7. **Natural increase:** 0.81%. **Hospital beds** (1993): 1 per 95 persons. **Physicians** (1995): 1 per 335 persons. **Infant mortality** (per 1,000 live births): 5.

Education: Free and compulsory: ages 7-15. **Literacy** (1997): 100%.

Major International Organizations: UN (FAO, IBRD, ILO, IMF, IMO, WHO, WTrO), EFTA, NATO, OECD, OSCE.

Embassy: Suite 1200, 1156 15th St. NW 20005; 265-6653.

Website: http://www.iceland.org

Iceland was an independent republic from 930 to 1262, when it joined with Norway. Its language has maintained its purity for 1,000 years. Danish rule lasted from 1380-1918; the last ties with the Danish crown were severed in 1941. The Althing, or assembly, is the world's oldest surviving parliament.

India

Republic of India

People: Population: 984,003,683. **Age distrib.** (%): <15: 34.5; 65+: 4.6. **Pop. density:** 805 per sq. mi. **Urban:** 27%. **Ethnic groups:** Indo-Aryan 72%, Dravidian 25%. **Principal languages:** Hindi (official), English (associate official), 14 regional languages. **Chief religions:** Hindu 80%, Muslim 14%.

Geography: Area: 1,222,243 sq. mi. **Location:** Occupies most of the Indian subcontinent in S Asia. **Neighbors:** Pakistan on W; China, Nepal, Bhutan on N; Myanmar, Bangladesh on E. **Topography:** The Himalaya Mts., highest in world, stretch across India's northern borders. Below, the Ganges Plain is wide, fertile, and among the most densely populated regions of the world. The area below includes the Deccan Peninsula. Close to one quarter of the area is forested. The climate varies from tropical heat in S to near-Arctic cold in N. Rajasthan Desert is in NW; NE Assam Hills get 400 in. of rain a year. **Capital:** New Delhi. **Cities:** Mumbai (Bombay) 15,138,000; Calcutta 11,923,000; Delhi 9,948,000; Chennai (Madras) 6,002,000; Hyderabad 5,477,000; Bangalore 4,799,000*.

Government: Type: Federal republic. **Head of state:** Pres. Kocheril Raman Narayanan; b Oct. 17, 1920; in office: July 25, 1997. **Head of government:** Prime Min. Atal Bihari Vajpayee; b Dec. 25, 1924; in office Mar. 19, 1998. **Local divisions:** 25 states, 7 union territories. **Defense:** 2.8% of GDP. **Active troop strength:** 1.145 mil.

Economy: Industries: Textiles, steel, processed foods, cement, machinery, chemicals, mining, autos. **Chief crops:** Rice, grains, sugar, spices, tea, cashews, cotton, potatoes, jute, linseed. **Minerals:** Coal (4th largest reserves in the world), iron, manganese, mica, bauxite, titanium, chromite, diamonds, gas, oil. **Crude oil reserves** (1997): 4.3 bil bbls. **Other resources:** Timber. **Arable land:** 56%. **Livestock** (1997): chickens: 342.50; cattle: 209.08 mil; goats: 120.60 mil; buffalo: 92.19 mil; sheep: 56.47 mil; pigs: 15.42 mil. **Fish catch** (1996): 3.49 mil metric tons. **Electricity prod.** (1996): 404.5 bil kWh. **Labor force:** 65% agric.

Finance: Monetary unit: Rupee (Sept. 1998: 42.52 = $1 U.S.). **Gross domestic product** (1996 est.): $1.54 tril. **Per capita GDP:** $1,600. **Imports** (1995): $34.5 bil; partners: U.S. 11%, Germany 9%, Japan 7%. **Exports** (1995): $30.5 bil; partners: U.S. 17%, Japan 7%, UK 6%. **Tourism:** $3.15 bil. **National budget** (FY 1995-96): $52.3 bil. **International reserves less gold** (June 1998): $24.30 bil. **Gold:** 11.49 mil oz t. **Consumer prices** (change in 1997): 7.2%.

Transport: Railroad: Length: 38,788.9 mi. **Motor vehicles in use:** 4.25 mil passenger cars, 2.51 mil comm. vehicles. **Civil aviation:** 13.86 bil passenger-mi; 66 airports. **Chief ports:** Calcutta, Mumbai (Bombay), Chennai (Madras), Vishakhapatnam, Kandla.

Communications: Television sets: 21 per 1,000 pop. **Radios:** 117 per 1,000 pop. **Telephones:** 14,542,651 main lines. **Daily newspaper circ.:** 21 per 1,000 pop.

Health: Life expectancy at birth: 62.1 male; 63.7 female. **Births** (per 1,000 pop.): 26. **Deaths** (per 1,000 pop.): 9. **Natural increase:** 1.72%. **Hospital beds** (1992): 1 per 1,357 persons. **Physicians** (1992): 1 per 2,173 persons. **Infant mortality** (per 1,000 live births): 63.

Education: Theoretically compulsory in 23 states to age 14. **Literacy** (1995): 52%.

Major International Organizations: UN (FAO, IBRD, ILO, IMF, IMO, WHO, WTrO), the Commonwealth.

Embassy: 2107 Massachusetts Ave. NW 20008; 939-7000.

Website: http://www.nic.in/htm/ug.htm

India has one of the oldest civilizations in the world. Excavations trace the Indus Valley civilization back for at least 5,000 years. Paintings in the mountain caves of Ajanta, richly carved temples, the Taj Mahal in Agra, and the Kutab Minar in Delhi are among relics of the past.

Aryan tribes, speaking Sanskrit, invaded from the NW around 1500 BC, and merged with the earlier inhabitants to create classical Indian civilization.

Asoka ruled most of the Indian subcontinent in the 3d century BC, and established Buddhism. But Hinduism revived and eventually predominated. During the Gupta kingdom, 4th-6th century AD, science, literature, and the arts enjoyed a "golden age."

Arab invaders established a Muslim foothold in the W in the 8th century, and Turkish Muslims gained control of North India by 1200. The Mogul emperors ruled 1526-1857.

Vasco da Gama established Portuguese trading posts 1498-1503. The Dutch followed. The British East India Co. sent Capt. William Hawkins, 1609, to get concessions from the Mogul emperor for spices and textiles. Operating as the East India Co. the British gained control of most of India. The British parliament assumed political direction; under Lord Bentinck, 1828-35, rule by rajahs was curbed. After the Sepoy troops mutinied, 1857-58, the British supported the native rulers.

Nationalism grew rapidly after World War I. The Indian National Congress and the Muslim League demanded constitutional reform. A leader emerged in Mohandas K. Gandhi (called Mahatma, or Great Soul), born Oct. 2, 1869, assassinated Jan. 30, 1948. He advocated self-rule, nonviolence, and removal of the caste system of untouchability. In 1930 he launched a program of civil disobedience, including a boycott of British goods and rejection of taxes without representation.

In 1935 Britain gave India a constitution providing a bicameral federal congress. Muhammad Ali Jinnah, head of the Muslim League, sought creation of a Muslim nation, Pakistan.

The British government partitioned British India into the dominions of India and Pakistan. India became a member of the UN in 1945, a self-governing member of the Commonwealth in 1947, and a democratic republic, Jan. 26, 1950. More than 12 million Hindu and Muslim refugees crossed the India-Pakistan borders in a mass transferral of some of the 2 peoples during 1947; about 200,000 were killed in communal fighting.

After Pakistan troops began attacks on Bengali separatists in East Pakistan, Mar. 25, 1971, some 10 million refugees fled into India. India and Pakistan went to war Dec. 3, 1971, on both the East and West fronts. Pakistan troops in the east surrendered Dec. 16; Pakistan agreed to a cease-fire in the west Dec. 17.

Indira Gandhi, India's prime minister since Jan. 1966, invoked emergency powers in June 1975. Thousands of opponents were arrested and press censorship imposed. These and other actions, including enforcement of coercive birth control measures in some areas, were widely resented. Opposition parties, united in the Janata coalition, turned Gandhi's New Congress Party from power in federal and state parliamentary elections in 1977.

Gandhi became prime minister for the second time, Jan. 14, 1980. She was assassinated by 2 of her Sikh bodyguards Oct. 31, 1984, in response to the government suppression of a Sikh uprising in Punjab in June 1984, which included an assault on the Golden Temple at Amritsar, the holiest Sikh shrine. Widespread rioting followed the assassination. Thousands of Sikhs were killed and some 50,000 left homeless.

Rajiv, Indira Gandhi's son, replaced her as prime minister. He was swept from office in 1989 amid charges of incompetence and corruption, and assassinated May 21, 1991, while campaigning to recapture the prime ministership.

Sikhs ignited several violent clashes during the 1980s. The government's May 1987 decision to bring the state of Punjab under rule of the central government led to violence. Many died during a government siege of the Golden Temple, May 1988. Another trouble spot was Assam in NW India, where thousands were killed in ethnic violence in Feb. 1993; a renewed outburst in July 1994 led to more than 60 deaths.

Nationwide riots followed the destruction of a 16th-century mosque by Hindu militants in Dec. 1992. In the biggest wave of criminal violence in Indian history, a series of bombs jolted Bombay and Calcutta, Mar. 12-19, 1993, killing over 300.

Corruption scandals dominated Indian politics in the mid-1990s. After an inconclusive election, a Hindu nationalist party was unable to form a government, and a center-left coalition took office June 1, 1996. An aircraft collision in midair near New Delhi killed 349 passengers and crew on Nov. 12.

India's 1st lowest-caste pres., K. R. Narayanan, took office July 25, 1997. Mother Teresa of Calcutta, renowned for her work among the poor, died Sept. 5. Parliamentary elections in Feb. 1998 resulted in a Hindu nationalist victory, and Atal Bihari Vajpayee was sworn in as prime minister Mar. 19. India conducted a series of nuclear tests in mid-May, drawing worldwide condemnation and raising tensions with Pakistan. A cyclone June 9 left more than 1,000 people dead in Gujarat state.

Sikkim, bordered by Tibet, Bhutan, and Nepal, formerly British protected, became a protectorate of India in 1950. Area,

2,740 sq. mi; pop., 1994 est., 444,000; capital: Gangtok. In Sept. 1974, India's parliament voted to make Sikkim an associate Indian state, absorbing it into India.

Kashmir, a predominantly Muslim region in the NW, has been in dispute between India and Pakistan since 1947. A cease-fire was negotiated by the UN Jan. 1, 1949; it gave Pakistan control of one-third of the area, in the west and northwest, and India the remaining two-thirds, the Indian state of **Jammu and Kashmir**, which enjoys internal autonomy.

In the 1990s there were repeated clashes between Indian army troops and pro-independence demonstrators triggered by India's decision to impose central government rule; by 1996 the conflict had claimed at least 30,000 lives. The clashes strained relations between India and Pakistan, which India charged was aiding the Muslim separatists. In Sept. 1996, a pro-Indian-government party won a majority in assembly elections, the first held since separatist fighting began.

France, 1952-54, peacefully yielded to India its 5 colonies, former French India, comprising Pondicherry, Karikal, Mahe, Yanaon (which became **Pondicherry Union Territory**, area 190 sq. mi; pop., 1994 est., 894,000) and Chandernagor (which was incorporated into the state of **West Bengal**).

Indonesia

Republic of Indonesia

People: Population: 212,941,810. **Age distrib.** (%): <15: 30.8; 65+: 4.0. **Pop. density:** 287 per sq. mi. **Urban:** 36%. **Ethnic groups:** Javanese 45%, Sundanese 14%, Madurese 8%, Malay 8%. **Principal languages:** Bahasa Indonesian (official), English, Dutch, Javanese. **Chief religions:** Muslim 87%, Protestant 6%.

Geography: Area: 741,096 sq. mi. **Location:** Archipelago SE of Asian mainland along the Equator. **Neighbors:** Malaysia on N, Papua New Guinea on E. **Topography:** Indonesia comprises over 13,500 islands (6,000 inhabited), including Java (one of the most densely populated areas in the world with over 2,000 persons per sq. mi.), Sumatra, Kalimantan (most of Borneo), Sulawesi (Celebes), and West Irian (Irian Jaya, the W half of New Guinea). Also: Bangka, Billiton, Madura, Bali, Timor. The mountains and plateaus on the major islands have a cooler climate than the tropical lowlands. **Capital:** Jakarta. **Cities:** Jakarta 8,621,000; Bandung 2,896,000; Surabaya 2,253,000*.

Government: Type: Republic. **Head of state:** Pres. Bacharuddin Jusuf Habibie; b June 25, 1936; in office: May 21, 1998. **Local divisions:** 24 provinces, 2 special regions, 1 capital district. **Defense:** 2.1% of GDP. **Active troop strength:** 299,200.

Economy: Industries: Oil, gas, food processing, textiles, cement, mining. **Chief crops:** Rice, cocoa, peanuts. **Minerals:** Nickel, tin, oil, bauxite, copper, gas. **Crude oil reserves** (1997): 5.0 bil bbls. **Other resources:** Rubber, timber. **Arable land:** 10%. **Livestock** (1997): chickens: 1.20 bil; goats: 14.40 mil; cattle: 12.00 mil; pigs: 8.20 mil; sheep: 8.10 mil; buffalo: 3.14 mil. **Fish catch** (1996): 3.73 mil metric tons. **Electricity prod.** (1996): 66.8 bil kWh. **Labor force:** 55% agric.; 10% manuf.

Finance: Monetary unit: Rupiah (Sept. 1998: 10,750.00 = $1 U.S.). **Gross domestic product** (1996 est.): $779.7 bil. **Per capita GDP:** $3,770. **Imports** (1996): $42.9 bil; partners: Japan 23%, U.S. 12%, **Exports** (1996): $49.8 bil; partners: Japan 27%, U.S. 14%. **Tourism:** $6.59 bil. **National budget** (FY 1997-98 est.): $41.5 bil. **International reserves less gold** (June 1998): $17.95 bil. **Gold:** 3.10 mil oz t. **Consumer prices** (change in 1997): 11.6%.

Transport: Railroad: Length: 4,010.4 mi. **Motor vehicles in use:** 2.41 mil passenger cars, 2.03 mil comm. vehicles. **Civil aviation:** 15.58 bil passenger-mi; 81 airports. **Chief ports:** Jakarta, Surabaya, Palembang, Semarang, Ujungpandang.

Communications: Television sets: 145 per 1,000 pop. **Radios:** 132 per 1,000 pop. **Telephones:** 4,186,030 main lines. **Daily newspaper circ.:** 20 per 1,000 pop.

Health: Life expectancy at birth: 60.3 male; 64.8 female. **Births** (per 1,000 pop.): 23. **Deaths** (per 1,000 pop.): 8. **Natural increase:** 1.49%. **Hospital beds** (1994): 1 per 1,630 persons. **Physicians** (1994): 1 per 6,570 persons. **Infant mortality** (per 1,000 live births): 59.

Education: Compulsory: ages 7-16. **Literacy** (1995): 84%.

Major International Organizations: UN and all of its specialized agencies, APEC, ASEAN, OPEC.

Embassy: 2020 Massachusetts Ave. NW 20036; 775-5200.

Hindu and Buddhist civilization from India reached Indonesia nearly 2,000 years ago, taking root especially in Java. Islam spread along the maritime trade routes in the 15th century, and became predominant by the 16th century. The Dutch replaced the Portuguese as the area's most important European trade power in the 17th century, securing territorial control over Java by 1750. The outer islands were not finally subdued until the early 20th century, when the full area of present-day Indonesia was united under one rule for the first time.

Following Japanese occupation, 1942-45, nationalists led by Sukarno and Hatta declared independence. The Netherlands ceded sovereignty Dec. 27, 1949, after 4 years of fighting. A republic was declared, Aug. 17, 1950, with Sukarno as president. West Irian, on New Guinea, remained under Dutch control. After the Dutch in 1957 rejected proposals for new negotiations over West Irian, Indonesia stepped up the seizure of Dutch property. In 1963 the UN turned the area over to Indonesia, which promised a plebiscite. In 1969, voting by tribal chiefs favored staying with Indonesia, despite an uprising and widespread opposition.

Sukarno suspended Parliament in 1960, and was named president for life in 1963. He made close alliances with Communist governments. Russian-armed Indonesian troops staged raids in 1964 and 1965 into Malaysia, whose formation Sukarno had opposed. (In 1966 Indonesia and Malaysia signed an agreement ending hostility.)

In 1965 an attempted coup in which several military officers were murdered was successfully put down. The regime blamed the coup on the Communist Party, some of whose members were known to have been involved. In its wake more than 300,000 alleged Communists were killed in army-initiated massacres.

Gen. Suharto, head of the army, was named president in 1968. With military backing he developed a strong government party, restricted the opposition, and allied the country with the West; meanwhile, oil exports spurred economic growth. During Aug.-Nov. 1997, haze from forest fires in Indonesia blanketed large areas of SE Asia. A plane crash near Medan airport, Sept. 26, 1997, killed 234 persons.

Parliament reelected Suharto to a 7th consecutive 5-year term Mar. 10, 1998, as a severe economic downturn focused public anger on nepotism, cronyism, and corruption in the Suharto regime. Price increases in May sparked mass protests and then mob violence in Jakarta and other cities, claiming some 500 lives. Suharto resigned May 21 and was succeeded by his vice-president, Bacharuddin Jusuf Habibie.

In Dec. 1975, Indonesia invaded **East Timor** as Portuguese rule collapsed there. Indonesia annexed it in 1976, despite international condemnation. Timorese opposition to continued Indonesian rule has been ruthlessly suppressed.

Iran

Islamic Republic of Iran

People: Population: 68,959,931. **Age distrib.** (%): <15: 43.3; 65+: 4.1. **Pop. density:** 109 per sq. mi. **Urban:** 60%. **Ethnic groups:** Persian 51%, Azerbaijani 24%, Kurd 7%. **Principal languages:** Persian (Farsi; official), Turkic, Kurdish, Luri. **Chief religions:** Shi'a Muslim 89%, Sunni Muslim 10%.

Geography: Area: 632,457 sq. mi. **Location:** Between the Middle East and S Asia. **Neighbors:** Turkey, Iraq on W; Armenia, Azerbaijan, Turkmenistan on N; Afghanistan, Pakistan on E. **Topography:** Interior highlands and plains surrounded by high mountains, up to 18,000 ft. Large salt deserts cover much of area, but there are many oases and forest areas. Most of the population inhabits the N and NW. **Capital:** Tehran. **Cities:** Tehran 6,836,000; Mashhad 2,016,000; Esfahan 1,924,000*.

Government: Type: Islamic republic. **Religious head:** Ayatollah Sayyed Ali Khamenei; b 1940; in office: June 4, 1989. **Head of state:** Pres. Mohammad Khatami; b 1943; in office: Aug. 3, 1997. **Local divisions:** 26 provinces. **Defense:** 5.0% of GDP. **Active troop strength:** 513,000.

Economy: Industries: Oil, petrochemicals, cement, sugar refining, carpets. **Chief crops:** Grains, rice, fruits, nuts, sugar beets, cotton. **Minerals:** Chromium, coal, oil, gas. **Crude oil reserves** (1997): 93 bil bbls **Arable land:** 10%. **Livestock** (1997): chickens: 210.00 mil; sheep: 52.00 mil; goats: 26.00 mil; cattle: 8.60 mil; buffalo: 465,000. **Fish catch** (1996): 351,723 metric tons. **Electricity prod.** (1996): 79.5 bil kWh.

Finance: Monetary unit: Rial (Sept. 1998: 3,000 = $1 U.S.). **Gross domestic product** (1996 est.): $343.5 bil. **Per capita GDP:** $5,200. **Imports** (1996 est.): $13.3 bil; partners: Germany 19%, Italy 9%. **Exports** (1996 est.): $21.3 bil; partners: Japan 15%, U.S. 14%. **Tourism:** $248 mil. **National budget** (1990): $80 bil. **Consumer prices** (change in 1997): 17.2%.

Transport: Railroad: Length: 4,527 mi. **Motor vehicles in use:** 1.63 mil passenger cars, 609,000 comm. vehicles. **Civil**

aviation: 4.12 bil passenger-mi; 19 airports. **Chief port:** Bandar-e Abbas.

Communications: Television sets: 117 per 1,000 pop. **Radios:** 213 per 1,000 pop. **Telephones:** 5,824,968 main lines. **Daily newspaper circ.:** 20 per 1,000 pop.

Health: Life expectancy at birth: 66.8 male; 69.7 female. **Births** (per 1,000 pop.): 31. **Deaths** (per 1,000 pop.): 6. **Natural increase:** 2.52%. **Hospital beds** (1995): 1 per 650 persons. **Physicians** (1994): 1 per 1,600 persons. **Infant mortality** (per 1,000 live births): 49.

Education: Free and compulsory: ages 6-10. **Literacy** (1994): 72%.

Major International Organizations: UN (FAO, IBRD, ILO, IMF, IMO, WHO), OPEC.

Iran was once called Persia. The Iranians, who supplanted an earlier agricultural civilization, came from the E during the 2d millennium BC; they were an Indo-European group related to the Aryans of India.

In 549 BC Cyrus the Great united the Medes and Persians in the Persian Empire, conquered Babylonia in 538 BC, and restored Jerusalem to the Jews. Alexander the Great conquered Persia in 333 BC, but Persians regained their independence in the next century under the Parthians, themselves succeeded by Sassanian Persians in AD 226. Arabs brought Islam to Persia in the 7th century, replacing the indigenous Zoroastrian faith. After Persian political and cultural autonomy was reasserted in the 9th century, the arts and sciences flourished.

Turks and Mongols ruled Persia in turn from the 11th century to 1502, when a native dynasty reasserted full independence. The British and Russian empires vied for influence in the 19th century; Afghanistan was severed from Iran by Britain in 1857.

Reza Khan abdicated as shah, 1941, and was succeeded by his son, Mohammad Reza Pahlavi. He brought economic and social change to Iran, but political opposition was not tolerated.

Conservative Muslim protests led to 1978 violence. Martial law was declared in 12 cities Sept. 8. A military government was appointed Nov. 6 to deal with striking oil workers. The shah, who left Iran Jan. 16, 1979, appointed Prime Min. Shahpur Bakhtiar to head a regency council in his absence.

Exiled religious leader Ayatollah Ruhollah Khomeini named a provisional government council in preparation for his return to Tehran, Feb. 1. Clashes between Khomeini's supporters and government troops culminated in a rout of Iran's elite Imperial Guard Feb. 11, leading to the fall of Bakhtiar's government.

The Iranian revolution was marked by revolts among the ethnic minorities and by a continuing struggle between the clerical forces and westernized intellectuals and liberals. The Islamic Constitution established final authority to be vested in a Faghi, the Ayatollah Khomeini.

Iranian militants seized the U.S. embassy, Nov. 4, 1979, and took hostages including 62 Americans. Despite international condemnations and U.S. efforts, including an abortive Apr. 1980 rescue attempt, the crisis continued. The U.S. broke diplomatic relations with Iran, Apr. 7. The shah died in Egypt, July 27. The hostage drama ended Jan. 21, 1981, when an accord, involving the release of frozen Iranian assets, was reached.

A dispute over the Shatt al-Arab waterway that divides the two countries brought Iran and Iraq, Sept. 22, 1980, into open warfare. Iraqi planes attacked Iranian airfields including Tehran airport. Iranian planes bombed Iraqi bases. Iraqi troops occupied Iranian territory, including the port city of Khorramshahr in October. Iranian troops recaptured the city and drove Iraqi troops back across the border, May 1982. Iraq, and later Iran, attacked several oil tankers in the Persian Gulf during 1984.

In Nov. 1986 it became known that senior U.S. officials had secretly visited Iran and that the U.S. had provided arms in exchange for Iran's help in obtaining the release of U.S. hostages held by terrorists in Lebanon. The revelation sparked a major scandal in the Reagan administration.

A U.S. Navy warship shot down an Iranian commercial airliner, July 3, 1988, after mistaking it for an F-14 fighter jet; all 290 aboard the plane died. In Aug. 1988, Iran agreed to accept a UN resolution calling for a cease-fire with Iraq.

An earthquake struck northern Iran June 21, 1990, killing more than 45,000, injuring 100,000, and leaving 400,000 homeless. Some one million Kurdish refugees fled from Iraq to Iran following the Persian Gulf War. To curb Iran's alleged support for international terrorism, the U.S. in 1996 authorized sanctions on foreign companies that invest there.

Mohammad Khatami, a moderate Shiite Muslim cleric, was elected president on May 23, 1997, winning nearly 70% of the vote; his government was repeatedly challenged by religious conservatives. Tensions with the Taliban led Iran to mass 200,000 troops on the Afghan border in Sept. 1998.

Iraq

Republic of Iraq

People: Population: 21,722,287. **Age distrib.** (%): <15: 44.1; 65+: 3.2. **Pop. density:** 129 per sq. mi. **Urban:** 75%. **Ethnic groups:** Arab 75-80%, Kurd 15-20%, Turkoman. **Principal languages:** Arabic (official), Kurdish. **Chief religions:** Muslim 97% (Shi'a 60-65%, Sunni 32-37%).

Geography: Area: 167,975 sq. mi. **Location:** In the Middle East, occupying most of historic Mesopotamia. **Neighbors:** Jordan and Syria on W, Turkey on N, Iran on E, Kuwait and Saudi Arabia on S. **Topography:** Mostly an alluvial plain, including the Tigris and Euphrates rivers, descending from mountains in N to desert in SW. Persian Gulf region is marshland. **Capital:** Baghdad. **Cities:** Baghdad 4,336,000; Arbil 1,743,000; Mosul 879,000*.

Government: Type: Republic. **Head of state:** Pres. Saddam Hussein; b. Apr. 29, 1937; in office: July 16, 1979; also assumed post of prime minister, May 29, 1994. **Local divisions:** 18 governorates (3 in Kurdish Autonomous Region). **Defense:** 8.3% of GDP. **Active troop strength:** 382,500.

Economy: Industries: Textiles, chemicals, oil refining, cement. **Chief crops:** Grains, dates, cotton. **Minerals:** Oil, gas. **Crude oil reserves** (1997): 112.5 bil bbls. **Other resources:** Wool, hides. **Arable land:** 12%. **Livestock** (1997): chickens: 48.00 mil; sheep: 6.58 mil; cattle: 1.30 mil; goats: 1.47 mil. **Electricity prod.** (1996): 27.6 bil kWh.

Finance: Monetary unit: Dinar (Sept. 1998: 3.22 = $1 U.S.). **Gross domestic product** (1995 est.): $42 bil. **Per capita GDP:** $2,000. **Imports** (1996 est.): $1.9 bil; partners: Jordan 49%. **Exports** (1994 est.): $450 mil; partners: Jordan 98%. **Tourism:** $13 mil. **National budget** (1990): $35 bil.

Transport: Railroad: Length: 1,261.9 mi. **Motor vehicles in use:** 672,000 passenger cars, 368,000 comm. vehicles. **Civil aviation:** 12.4 mil passenger-mi. **Chief port:** Basra.

Communications: Television sets: 48 per 1,000 pop. **Radios:** 167 per 1,000 pop. **Telephones:** 675,000 main lines. **Daily newspaper circ.:** 27 per 1,000 pop.

Health: Life expectancy at birth: 65.5 male; 67.6 female. **Births** (per 1,000 pop.): 39. **Deaths** (per 1,000 pop.): 7. **Natural increase:** 3.20%. **Hospital beds** (1993): 1 per 704 persons. **Physicians** (1993): 1 per 2,181 persons. **Infant mortality** (per 1,000 live births): 62.

Education: Free and compulsory: ages 6-12. **Literacy** (1995): 58%.

Major International Organizations: UN (FAO, IBRD, ILO, IMF, IMO, WHO), AL, OPEC.

Website: http://www.undp.org/missions/iraq

The Tigris-Euphrates valley, formerly called Mesopotamia, was the site of one of the earliest civilizations in the world. The Sumerian city-states of 3,000 BC originated the culture later developed by the Semitic Akkadians, Babylonians, and Assyrians.

Mesopotamia ceased to be a separate entity after the Persian, Greek, and Arab conquests. The latter founded Baghdad, from where the caliph ruled a vast empire in the 8th and 9th centuries. Mongol and Turkish conquests led to a decline in population, economy, cultural life, and the irrigation system.

Britain secured a League of Nations mandate over Iraq after World War I. Independence under a king came in 1932. A leftist, pan-Arab revolution established a republic in 1958, which oriented foreign policy toward the USSR. Most industry has been nationalized, and large land holdings broken up.

A local faction of the international Baath Arab Socialist party has ruled by decree since 1968. The USSR and Iraq signed an aid pact in 1972, and arms were sent along with several thousand advisers. The 1978 execution of 21 Communists and a shift of trade to the West signalled a more neutral policy, straining relations with the USSR. In the 1973 Arab-Israeli war Iraq sent forces to aid Syria. Within a month of assuming power, Saddam Hussein instituted a bloody purge in the wake of a reported coup attempt against the new regime.

Years of battling with the Kurdish minority resulted in total defeat for the Kurds in 1975, when Iran withdrew support. The fighting led to Iraqi bombing of Kurdish villages in Iran, causing relations with Iran to deteriorate.

After skirmishing intermittently for 10 months over the sovereignty of the disputed Shatt al-Arab waterway that divides the two countries, Iraq and Iran entered into open warfare on Sept. 22, 1980. In the following days, there was heavy ground fighting around Abadan and the port of Khorramshahr, as Iraq launched an attack on Iran's oil-rich province of Khuzistan.

Israeli airplanes destroyed a nuclear reactor near Baghdad on June 7, 1981, claiming it could be used to produce nuclear weapons.

Iraq and Iran expanded their war to the Persian Gulf in Apr. 1984. There were several attacks on oil tankers. An Iraqi warplane launched a missile attack on the USS *Stark*, a U.S. Navy frigate on patrol in the Persian Gulf, May 17, 1987; 37 U.S.

sailors died. Iraq apologized for the attack, claiming it was inadvertent. The fierce war ended Aug. 1988, when Iraq accepted a UN resolution for a cease-fire.

Iraq attacked and overran Kuwait Aug. 2, 1990, sparking an international crisis. The UN, Aug. 6, imposed a ban on all trade with Iraq and called on member countries to protect the assets of the legitimate government of Kuwait. Iraq declared Kuwait its 19th province, Aug. 28.

A U.S.-led coalition launched air and missile attacks on Iraq, Jan. 16, 1991, after the expiration of a UN Security Council deadline for Iraq to withdraw from Kuwait. Iraq retaliated by firing scud missiles at Saudi Arabia and Israel. The coalition began a ground attack to retake Kuwait Feb. 23. Iraqi forces showed little resistance and were soundly defeated in 4 days. Some 175,000 Iraqis were taken prisoner, and casualties were estimated at over 85,000. As part of the cease-fire agreement, Iraq agreed to scrap all poison gas and germ weapons and allow UN observers to inspect the sites. UN trade sanctions would remain in effect until Iraq complied with all terms.

In the aftermath of the war, there were revolts against Pres. Saddam Hussein throughout Iraq. In Feb., Iraqi troops drove Kurdish insurgents and civilians to the Iran and Turkey borders, causing a refugee crisis. The U.S. and allies established havens inside Iraq for the Kurds. Iraqi cooperation with UN weapons inspection teams was intermittent.

The U.S. launched a missile attack aimed at Iraq's intelligence headquarters in Baghdad June 26, 1993. The U.S. justified the attack by citing evidence that Iraq had sponsored a plot to kill former Pres. George Bush during his visit to Kuwait in Apr. 1993. In Aug. 1995, two of Saddam Hussein's sons-in-law, who held high positions in the Iraqi military, defected to Jordan; both were killed after returning to Iraq in Feb. 1996. After fighting between two Kurdish factions (one allied with Iraq, the other with Iran) erupted in the protected zone of northern Iraq, the Baghdad government intervened in the conflict by sending troops into Arbil, Aug. 31, 1996. The U.S. retaliated with missile strikes against air defense sites in the south. On Dec. 9 the UN allowed Baghdad to begin selling limited amounts of oil for food and medicine. Saddam Hussein's son Odai was seriously wounded in an assassination attempt in Baghdad Dec. 12.

Iraqi resistance to unrestricted UN access to suspected weapons sites led to diplomatic crises in Nov. 1997 and Feb. 1998. Threatened with imminent air strikes by the U.S., Iraq on Feb. 22 embraced peace proposals brought to Baghdad by UN Secretary General Kofi Annan. Iraq balked again in Aug., as disputes over continued sanctions surfaced in the Security Council.

Ireland

People: Population: 3,619,480. **Age distrib.** (%): <15: 21.9; 65+: 11.3. **Pop. density:** 133 per sq. mi. **Urban:** 58%. **Ethnic groups:** Celtic, English minority. **Principal languages:** English predominates, Irish (Gaelic) spoken by minority (both official). **Chief religions:** Roman Catholic 93%, Anglican 3%.

Geography: Area: 27,135 sq. mi. **Location:** In the Atlantic O. just W of Great Britain. **Neighbors:** United Kingdom (Northern Ireland) on E. **Topography:** Ireland consists of a central plateau surrounded by isolated groups of hills and mountains. The coastline is heavily indented by the Atlantic O. **Capital:** Dublin. **Cities** (1996): Dublin 480,996; Cork 127,092.

Government: Type: Parliamentary republic. **Head of state:** Pres. Mary McAleese; b June 27, 1951; in office: Nov. 11, 1997. **Head of government:** Prime Min. Bertie Ahern; b Sept. 12, 1951; in office: June 26, 1997. **Local divisions:** 26 counties. **Defense:** 1.1% of GDP. **Active troop strength:** 12,700.

Economy: Industries: Food processing, textiles, chemicals, brewing, machinery, crystal. **Chief crops:** Potatoes, grains, sugar beets, turnips. **Minerals:** Zinc, lead, gas, oil. **Arable land:** 13%. **Livestock** (1997): chickens: 11.49 mil; cattle: 6.76 mil; sheep: 5.39 mil; pigs: 1.66 mil. **Fish catch** (1996): 332,878 metric tons. **Electricity prod.** (1996): 17.8 bil kWh. **Labor force:** 62% services; 26% manuf. & constr.; 11% agric. & fish.

Finance: Monetary unit: Pound (Sept. 1998: 1.45 = $1 U.S.). **Gross domestic product** (1996 est.): $59.9 bil. **Per capita GDP:** $16,800. **Imports** (1995): $32.7 bil; partners: UK 37%, U.S. 17%. **Exports** (1995): $43.3 bil; partners: UK 26%, Germany 14%. **Tourism:** $3.25 bil. **National budget** (1995): $23.6 bil. **International reserves less gold** (June 1998): $7.74 bil. **Gold:** 360,000 oz t. **Consumer prices** (change in 1997): 1.4%.

Transport: Railroad: Length: 1,207.2 mi. **Motor vehicles in use:** 1.06 mil passenger cars, 161,355 comm. vehicles. **Civil aviation:** 4.18 bil passenger-mi; 9 airports. **Chief ports:** Dublin, Cork.

Communications: Television sets: 279 per 1,000 pop. **Radios:** 597 per 1,000 pop. **Telephones:** 1,390,000 main lines. **Daily newspaper circ.:** 151 per 1,000 pop.

Health: Life expectancy at birth: 73.4 male; 79.1 female. **Births** (per 1,000 pop.): 13. **Deaths** (per 1,000 pop.): 9. **Natural increase:** 0.50%. **Hospital beds** (1994): 1 per 301 persons. **Infant mortality** (per 1,000 live births): 6.

Education: Compulsory: ages 6-15. **Literacy** (1993): 100%.

Major International Organizations: UN (FAO, IBRD, ILO, IMF, IMO, WHO, WTrO), EU, OECD, OSCE.

Embassy: 2234 Massachusetts Ave. NW 20008; 462-3939.

Website: http://www.cso.ie/index.html

Celtic tribes invaded the islands about the 4th century BC; their Gaelic culture and literature flourished and spread to Scotland and elsewhere in the 5th century AD, the same century in which St. Patrick converted the Irish to Christianity. Invasions by Norsemen began in the 8th century, ended with defeat of the Danes by the Irish King Brian Boru in 1014. English invasions started in the 12th century; for over 700 years the Anglo-Irish struggle continued with bitter rebellions and savage repressions.

The Easter Monday Rebellion in 1916 failed but was followed by guerrilla warfare and harsh reprisals by British troops called the "Black and Tans." The Dail Eireann, (Irish parliament), reaffirmed independence in Jan. 1919. The British offered dominion status to Ulster (6 counties) and southern Ireland (26 counties) Dec. 1921. The constitution of the Irish Free State, a British dominion, was adopted Dec. 11, 1922. Northern Ireland remained part of the United Kingdom.

A new constitution adopted by plebiscite came into operation Dec. 29, 1937. It declared the name of the state Eire in the Irish language (Ireland in the English) and declared it a sovereign democratic state.On Dec. 21, 1948, an Irish law declared the country a republic rather than a dominion and withdrew it from the Commonwealth. The British Parliament recognized both actions, 1949, but reasserted its claim to incorporate the 6 northeastern counties in the United Kingdom. This claim has not been recognized by Ireland *(see United Kingdom — Northern Ireland)*.

Irish governments have favored peaceful unification of all Ireland and have cooperated with Britain against terrorist groups. On Dec. 15, 1993, the Irish and British governments agreed on outlines of a peace plan to resolve the Northern Ireland issue. On Aug. 31, 1994, the Irish Republican Army announced a cease-fire; when peace talks lagged, however, the IRA returned to its terror campaign on Feb. 9, 1996. The IRA proclaimed a new cease-fire as of July 20, 1997, and peace talks resumed Sept. 15.

Ireland's first woman president, Mary Robinson, resigned Sept. 12 to become UN high commissioner for human rights. She was succeeded by Mary McAleese, a law professor from Northern Ireland and the first northerner to hold the office. After negotiators in Northern Ireland approved a peace settlement on Good Friday, April 10, 1998, voters in the Irish Republic endorsed the accord on May 22.

Israel

State of Israel

People: Population: 5,643,966. **Age distrib.** (%): <15: 28.2; 65+: 9.9. **Pop. density:** 704 per sq. mi. **Urban:** 91%. **Ethnic groups:** Jewish 82%, non-Jewish (mostly Arab) 18%. **Principal languages:** Hebrew (official), Arabic (used officially for Arab minority), English. **Chief religions:** Jewish 82%, Muslim (mostly Sunni) 14%.

Geography: Area: 8,019 sq. mi. **Location:** Middle East, on E end of Mediterranean Sea. **Neighbors:** Lebanon on N; Syria, West Bank, and Jordan on E; Gaza Strip and Egypt on W. **Topography:** The Mediterranean coastal plain is fertile and well-watered. In the center is the Judean Plateau. A triangular-shaped semi-desert region, the Negev, extends from south of Beersheba to an apex at the head of the Gulf of Aqaba. The E border drops sharply into the Jordan Rift Valley, including Lake Tiberias (Sea of Galilee) and the Dead Sea, which is 1,312 ft. below sea level, lowest point on the earth's surface. **Capital:** Jerusalem (most countries maintain their embassy in Tel Aviv). **Cities** (1997 est.): Jerusalem 591,400; Tel Aviv-Yafo 355,900; Haifa 255,300.

Government: Type: Republic. **Head of state:** Pres. Ezer Weizman; b June 15, 1924; in office: May 13, 1993. **Head of government:** Prime Min. Benjamin Netanyahu; b Oct. 21, 1949; in office: June 18, 1996. **Local divisions:** 6 districts. **Defense:** 12.1% of GDP. **Active troop strength:** 175,000.

Economy: Industries: Diamond cutting, textiles, electronics, food processing. **Chief crops:** Citrus, fruit, vegetables, cotton. **Minerals:** Copper, phosphates, bromide, potash, clay. **Crude oil reserves** (1997): 4.0 mil bbls. **Arable land:** 17%. **Livestock** (1997): chickens: 23.00 mil; cattle: 410,000; sheep: 340,000; pigs: 104,800. **Electricity prod.** (1996): 28.0 bil kWh. **Labor force:** 29% public services; 22% mfg.; 14% commerce.

Finance: Monetary unit: New Shekel (Sept. 1998: 3.85 = $1 U.S.). **Gross domestic prod.** (1996 est.): $85.7 bil. **Per capita GDP:** $16,400. **Imports** (1996): $28.3 bil; partners: U.S. 20%, Belgium 12%. **Exports** (1996): $20.3 bil; partners: U.S. 31%. **Tourism:** $2.80 bil. **National budget** (1996): $53 bil. **International reserves less gold** (June 1998): $21.32 bil. **Gold:** 9,000 oz t. **Consumer prices** (change in 1997): 9.0%.

Transport: Railroad: Length: 379 mi. **Motor vehicles in use:** 1.18 mil passenger cars, 289,094 comm. vehicles. **Civil aviation:** 7.32 bil passenger-mi; 7 airports. **Chief ports:** Haifa, Ashdod, Elat.

Communications: Television sets: 290 per 1,000 pop. **Radios:** 489 per 1,000 pop. **Telephones:** 2,539,117 main lines. **Daily newspaper circ.:** 271 per 1,000 pop.

Health: Life expectancy at birth: 76.5 male; 80.4 female. **Births** (per 1,000 pop.): 20. **Deaths** (per 1,000 pop.): 6. **Natural increase:** 1.38%. **Hospital beds** (1997): 1 per 165 persons. **Physicians** (1997): 1 per 206 persons. **Infant mortality** (per 1,000 live births): 8.

Education: Free and compulsory: ages 5-15. **Literacy** (1994): 95%.

Major International Organizations: UN (FAO, IBRD, ILO, IMF, IMO, WHO, WTrO).

Embassy: 3514 International Dr. NW 20008; 364-5500.

Websites: http://www.cbs.gov.il/engindex.htm
http://www.israel.org

Occupying the SW corner of the ancient Fertile Crescent, Israel contains some of the oldest known evidence of agriculture and of primitive town life. A more advanced civilization emerged in the 3d millennium BC. The Hebrews probably arrived early in the 2d millennium BC. Under King David and his successors (c.1000 BC-597 BC), Judaism was developed and secured. After conquest by Babylonians, Persians, and Greeks, an independent Jewish kingdom was revived, 168 BC, but Rome took effective control in the next century, suppressed Jewish revolts in AD 70 and AD 135, and renamed Judea Palestine, after the earlier coastal inhabitants, the Philistines.

Arab invaders conquered Palestine in 636. The Arabic language and Islam prevailed within a few centuries, but a Jewish minority remained. The land was ruled from the 11th century as a part of non-Arab empires by Seljuks, Mamluks, and Ottomans (with a crusader interval, 1098-1291).

After 4 centuries of Ottoman rule, during which the population declined to a low of 350,000 (1785), the land was taken in 1917 by Britain, which pledged in the Balfour Declaration to support a Jewish national homeland there. In 1920 a British Palestine Mandate was recognized; in 1922 the land east of the Jordan was detached.

Jewish immigration, begun in the late 19th century, swelled in the 1930s with refugees from the Nazis; heavy Arab immigration from Syria and Lebanon also occurred. Arab opposition to Jewish immigration turned violent in 1920, 1921, 1929, and 1936. The UN General Assembly voted in 1947 to partition Palestine into an Arab and a Jewish state. Britain withdrew in May 1948.

Israel was declared an independent state May 14, 1948; the Arabs rejected partition. Egypt, Jordan, Syria, Lebanon, Iraq, and Saudi Arabia invaded, but failed to destroy the Jewish state, which gained territory. Separate armistices with the Arab nations were signed in 1949; Jordan occupied the West Bank, Egypt occupied Gaza; neither granted Palestinian autonomy.

After persistent terrorist raids, Israel invaded Egypt's Sinai, Oct. 29, 1956, aided briefly by British and French forces. A UN cease-fire was arranged Nov. 6.

An uneasy truce between Israel and the Arab countries, supervised by a UN Emergency Force, prevailed until May 19, 1967, when the UN force withdrew at Egypt's demand. Egyptian forces reoccupied the Gaza Strip and closed the Gulf of Aqaba to Israeli shipping. In a 6-day war that started June 5, the Israelis took the Gaza Strip, occupied the Sinai Peninsula to the Suez Canal, and captured East Jerusalem, Syria's Golan Heights, and Jordan's West Bank. The fighting was halted June 10 by UN-arranged cease-fire agreements.

Egypt and Syria attacked Israel, Oct. 6, 1973 (Yom Kippur, most solemn day on the Jewish calendar). Israel counterattacked, driving the Syrians back, and crossed the Suez Canal. A cease-fire took effect Oct. 24; a UN peacekeeping force went to the area. Under a disengagement agreement signed Jan. 18, 1974, Israel withdrew from the canal's west bank.

Israeli forces raided Entebbe, Uganda, July 3, 1976, and rescued 103 hostages seized by Arab and German terrorists.

In 1977, the conservative opposition, led by Menachem Begin, was voted into office for the first time. Egypt's Pres. Anwar al-Sadat visited Jerusalem Nov. 1977, and on Mar. 26, 1979, Egypt and Israel signed a formal peace treaty, ending 30 years of war and establishing diplomatic relations. Israel returned the Sinai to Egypt in 1982.

Israel invaded S Lebanon, Mar. 1978, following a Lebanon-based terrorist attack in Israel. Israel withdrew in favor of a 6,000-man UN force, but continued to aid Lebanese Christian militiamen. Israel affirmed the whole of Jerusalem as its capital, July 1980, encompassing the annexed East Jerusalem.

On June 7, 1981, Israeli jets destroyed an Iraqi atomic reactor near Baghdad that, Israel claimed, would have enabled Iraq to manufacture nuclear weapons. Israeli forces invaded Lebanon, June 6, 1982, to destroy PLO strongholds there. After massive Israeli bombing of West Beirut, the PLO agreed to evacuate the city. Israeli troops entered West Beirut after newly elected Lebanese Pres. Bashir Gemayel was assassinated on Sept. 14. Israel drew widespread condemnation when Lebanese Christian forces, Sept. 16, entered two West Beirut refugee camps and slaughtered hundreds of Palestinian refugees.

In 1989, violence escalated over the Israeli military occupation of the West Bank and Gaza Strip. In a series of uprisings known as the intifada, Palestinian protesters defied Israeli troops, who forcibly retaliated. Israeli police and stone-throwing Palestinians clashed, Oct. 8, 1990, around the al-Aqsa mosque on the Temple Mount in Jerusalem; some 20 Palestinians died.

During the Persian Gulf War in early 1991, Iraq fired a series of scud missiles at Israel. The Labor Party of Yitzhak Rabin won a clear victory in elections held June 23, 1992.

Ongoing peace talks led to historic agreements between Israel and the PLO, Sept. 1993. The PLO recognized Israel's right to exist; Israel recognized the PLO as the Palestinians' representative; the two sides then signed, Sept. 13, an agreement for limited Palestinian self-rule and the West Bank and Gaza.

Israel and Jordan signed, July 25, 1994, in Washington, DC, a declaration ending their 46-year state of war. A formal peace treaty was signed Oct. 26.

Arab and Jewish extremists repeatedly challenged the peace process. A Jewish gunman opened fire on Arab worshippers at a mosque in Hebron, Feb. 25, 1994, killing at least 29 before he himself was killed. On Nov. 4, 1995, an Orthodox Jewish Israeli assassinated Rabin as he left a peace rally in Tel Aviv.

Support for Rabin's successor, Shimon Peres, was shaken by a series of suicide bombings and rocket attacks against Israel by Islamic militants. In Apr. 1996, Israel attacked suspected guerrilla bases in southern Lebanon. Emphasizing security issues, the candidate of the conservative Likud bloc, Benjamin Netanyahu, was elected prime minister on May 29.

On Sept. 24, 1996, Israel opened a tunnel entrance near a sacred Muslim site in Jerusalem, setting off several days of violence between Israeli soldiers and Palestinian demonstrators and police. Pres. Clinton hosted a summit meeting between Netanyahu and PLO leader Yasir Arafat soon after, on Oct. 1-2, and peace talks were resumed.

Two suicide bombings in a Jerusalem market July 30, 1997, left 15 people dead and more than 170 wounded. The parliament (Knesset) reelected Ezer Weizman as president Mar. 4, 1998, despite opposition from Netanyahu.

Under an interim accord brokered by Clinton and signed by Netanyahu and Arafat at the White House, Oct. 23, 1998, Israel yielded more West Bank territory to the Palestinians, in exchange for new security guarantees.

Gaza Strip

The Gaza Strip, also known as Gaza, extends NE from the Sinai Peninsula for 40 km (25 mi), with the Mediterranean Sea to the W and Israel to the E. The Palestinian Authority is responsible for civil government, but Israel retains control over security. Nearly all the inhabitants are Palestinian Arabs, more than 35% of whom live in refugee camps. Population (1998 est.): 1,054,173. Area: 140 sq. mi.

Israel captured Gaza from Egypt in the 1967 war. It remained under Israeli occupation until May 1994, when the Israel Defense Forces withdrew. Agreements between Israel and the PLO in 1993 and 1994 provided for interim self-rule in Gaza, pending the completion of final status negotiations.

West Bank

Located W of the Jordan R. and Dead Sea, the West Bank is bounded by Jordan on the E and by Israel on the N, W, and S. The Palestinian Authority administers several major cities, but Israel retains control over much land, including Jewish settlements. Population (1998 est.): 1,556,919. Area: 2,270 sq. mi.

Israel captured the West Bank from Jordan in the 1967 war. A 1974 Arab summit conference designated the PLO as sole representative of West Bank Arabs. In 1988 Jordan cut legal and administrative ties with the territory. Jericho was returned to Palestinian control in May 1994. An accord between Israel and the PLO expanding Palestinian self-rule in the West Bank was signed Sept. 28, 1995. Israel and the PLO agreed Jan. 15, 1997, on a partial Israeli pullout from Hebron.

Italy
Italian Republic

People: Population: 56,782,748. **Age distrib.** (%): <15: 14.4; 65+: 17.6. **Pop. density:** 488 per sq. mi. **Urban:** 67%. **Ethnic groups:** Italian, small minorities of German, French, Slovene, Albanian. **Principal languages:** Italian (official), German, French, Slovene. **Chief religion:** Roman Catholic 98%.

Geography: Area: 116,305 sq. mi. **Location:** In S Europe, jutting into Mediterranean Sea. **Neighbors:** France on W, Switzerland and Austria on N, Slovenia on E. **Topography:** Occupies a long boot-shaped peninsula, extending SE from the Alps into the Mediterranean, with the islands of Sicily and Sardinia offshore. The alluvial Po Valley drains most of N. The rest of the country is rugged and mountainous, except for intermittent coastal plains, like the Campania, S of Rome. Apennine Mts. run down through center of peninsula. **Capital:** Rome. **Cities:** Milan 4,251,000; Naples 3,012,000; Rome 2,688,000; Turin 1,294,000*.

Government: Type: Republic. **Head of state:** Pres. Oscar Luigi Scalfaro; b Sept. 9, 1918; in office: May 28, 1992. **Head of government:** Prime Min. Massimo D'Alema; b Apr. 20, 1949; in office: Oct. 21, 1998. **Local divisions:** 20 regions divided into 94 provinces. **Defense:** 2.2% of GDP. **Active troop strength:** 325,200.

Economy: Industries: Tourism, steel, machinery, autos, textiles, shoes, clothing, chemicals. **Chief crops:** Grapes, olives, fruits, vegetables, grain. **Minerals:** Mercury, potash, marble, sulphur. **Crude oil reserves** (1997): 729 mil bbls. **Arable land:** 31%. **Livestock** (1997): chickens: 138.00 mil; sheep: 10.92 mil; pigs: 8.09 mil; cattle: 7.24 mil; goats: 1.39 mil; buffalo: 150,000. **Fish catch** (1996): 358,736 metric tons. **Electricity prod.** (1996): 226.7 bil kWh. **Labor force:** 61% services; 32% ind.; 7% agric.

Finance: Monetary unit: Lira (Sept. 1998: 1,710.20 = $1 U.S.). **Gross domestic product** (1996 est.): $1.12 tril. **Per capita GDP:** $19,600. **Imports** (1996 est.): $205 bil; partners: EU 56%, U.S. 5%. **Exports** (1996 est.): $250.0 bil; partners: EU 53%, U.S. 8%. **Tourism:** $30.00 bil. **National budget** (1996 est.): $506 bil. **International reserves less gold** (June 1998): $46.66 bil. **Gold:** 66.67 mil oz t. **Consumer prices** (change in 1997): 2.0%.

Transport: Railroad: Length: 9,944 mi. **Motor vehicles:** in use: 30.60 mil passenger cars, 2.92 mil comm. vehicles. **Civil aviation:** 22.45 bil passenger-mi; 34 airports. **Chief ports:** Genoa, Venice, Trieste, Palermo, Naples, La Spezia.

Communications: Television sets: 436 per 1,000 pop. **Radios:** 790 per 1,000 pop. **Telephones: Daily newspaper circ.:** 126 per 1,000 pop.

Health: Life expectancy at birth: 75.3 male; 81.7 female. **Births** (per 1,000 pop.): 9. **Deaths** (per 1,000 pop.): 10. **Natural increase:** –0.11%. **Hospital beds** (1993): 1 per 147 persons. **Physicians** (1993): 1 per 193 persons. **Infant mortality** (per 1,000 live births): 6.

Education: Free and compulsory: ages 6-13. **Literacy** (1994): 97%.

Major International Organizations: UN and all of its specialized agencies, EU, NATO, OECD, OSCE.

Embassy: 1601 Fuller St. NW 20009; 328-5500.

Website: http://www.istat.it

Rome emerged as the major power in Italy after 500 BC, dominating the Etruscans to the N and Greeks to the S. Under the Empire, which lasted until the 5th century AD, Rome ruled most of Western Europe, the Balkans, the Middle East, and N Africa. In 1988, archaeologists unearthed evidence showing Rome as a dynamic society in the 6th and 7th centuries BC.

After the Germanic invasions, lasting several centuries, a high civilization arose in the city-states of the N, culminating in the Renaissance. But German, French, Spanish, and Austrian intervention prevented the unification of the country. In 1859 Lombardy came under the crown of King Victor Emmanuel II of Sardinia. By plebiscite in 1860, Parma, Modena, Romagna, and Tuscany joined, followed by Sicily and Naples, and by the Marches and Umbria. The first Italian Parliament declared Victor Emmanuel king of Italy Mar. 17, 1861. Mantua and Venetia were added in 1866 as an outcome of the Austro-Prussian war. The Papal States were taken by Italian troops Sept. 20, 1870, on the withdrawal of the French garrison. The states were annexed to the kingdom by plebiscite. Italy recognized Vatican City as independent Feb. 11, 1929.

Fascism appeared in Italy Mar. 23, 1919, led by Benito Mussolini, who took over the government at the invitation of the king Oct. 28, 1922. Mussolini acquired dictatorial powers. He made war on Ethiopia and proclaimed Victor Emmanuel III emperor, defied the sanctions of the League of Nations, sent troops to fight for Franco against the Republic of Spain, and joined Germany in World War II.

After Fascism was overthrown in 1943, Italy declared war on Germany and Japan and contributed to the Allied victory. It surrendered conquered lands and lost its colonies. Mussolini was killed by partisans Apr. 28, 1945. Victor Emmanuel III abdicated May 9, 1946; his son Humbert II was king until June 10, when Italy became a republic after a referendum, June 2-3.

Since World War II, Italy has enjoyed growth in industrial output and living standards, in part a result of membership in the European Community (now European Union). Political stability has not kept pace with economic prosperity, and organized crime and corruption have been persistent problems.

Christian Democratic leader and former Prime Min. Aldo Moro was abducted and murdered in 1978 by Red Brigade terrorists. The wave of left-wing political violence, including other kidnappings and assassinations, continued into the 1980s.

In the early 1990s, scandals implicated some of Italy's most prominent politicians. In Mar. 1994 voting, under reformed election rules, right-wing parties won a majority, dislodging Italy's long-powerful Christian Democratic Party. After a series of short-lived governments, a coalition of center-left parties won the election of Apr. 21, 1996. Italy led a 7,000-member international peacekeeping force in Albania, Apr.-Aug. 1997. Two earthquakes in central Italy Sept. 26 killed 11 people, left about 12,000 homeless, and damaged priceless frescoes in Assisi.

On Feb. 3, 1998, a low-flying U.S. military aircraft severed a gondola cable at a ski resort in N Italy, killing 20 people. Implementation of a deficit reduction plan enabled Italy to qualify in May to adopt the euro, a common European currency.

Sicily, 9,926 sq. mi., pop. (1994 est.) 5,025,000, is an island 180 by 120 mi., seat of a region that embraces the island of **Pantelleria,** 32 sq. mi., and the **Lipari** group, 44 sq. mi., including 2 active volcanoes: **Vulcano,** 1,637 ft., and **Stromboli,** 3,038 ft. From prehistoric times Sicily has been settled by various peoples; a Greek state had its capital at Syracuse. Rome took Sicily from Carthage 215 BC. **Mt. Etna,** an 11,053-ft. active volcano, is its tallest peak.

Sardinia, 9,301 sq. mi., pop. (1994 est.) 1,657,000, lies in the Mediterranean, 115 mi. W of Italy and 7½ mi. S of Corsica. It is 160 mi. long, 68 mi. wide, and mountainous, with mining of coal, zinc, lead, copper. In 1720 Sardinia was added to the possessions of the Dukes of Savoy in Piedmont and Savoy to form the Kingdom of Sardinia. Giuseppe Garibaldi is buried on the nearby isle of Caprera. **Elba,** 86 sq. mi., lies 6 mi. W of Tuscany. Napoleon I lived in exile on Elba 1814-1815.

Jamaica

People: Population: 2,634,678. **Age distrib.** (%): <15: 31.6; 65+: 6.8. **Pop. density:** 621 per sq. mi. **Urban:** 54%. **Ethnic groups:** African 76%, Afro-European 15%, white, Chinese. **Principal languages:** English (official), Jamaican Creole. **Chief religions:** Protestant 56%, Roman Catholic 5%, spiritual cults and other 39%.

Geography: Area: 4,243 sq. mi. **Location:** In West Indies. **Neighbors:** Nearest are Cuba to N, Haiti to E. **Topography:** Four-fifths of Jamaica is covered by mountains. **Capital:** Kingston (1991 met.): 103,771.

Government: Type: Parliamentary democracy. **Head of state:** Queen Elizabeth II, represented by Gov.-Gen. Sir Howard Cooke; b Nov. 13, 1915; in office: Aug. 1, 1991. **Head of government:** Prime Min. Percival J. Patterson; b Apr. 10, 1935; in office: Mar. 30, 1992. **Local divisions:** 14 parishes. **Defense:** 0.6% of GNP. **Active troop strength:** 3,300.

Economy: Industries: Bauxite mining, tourism. **Chief crops:** Sugar, coffee, bananas, potatoes, citrus. **Minerals:** Bauxite, limestone, gypsum. **Arable land:** 14%. **Livestock** (1997): chickens: 7.50 mil; cattle: 420,000; goats: 440,000; pigs: 180,000. **Fish catch** (1996): 12,843 metric tons. **Electricity prod.** (1996): 6.1 bil kWh. **Labor force:** 26% services; 19% agric.; 18% trade.

Finance: Monetary unit: Dollar (Sept. 1998: 35.80 = $1 U.S.). **Gross domestic product** (1996 est.): $8.4 bil. **Per capita GDP:** $3,260. **Imports** (1996 est.): $2.8 bil; partners: U.S. 54%. **Exports** (1996 est.): $1.4 bil; partners: U.S. 47%. **Tourism:** $1.20 bil. **National budget** (FY 1995-96 est.): $2 bil. **International reserves less gold** (Dec. 1997): $682.1 mil. **Consumer prices** (change in 1997): 9.7%.

Transport: Railroad: Length: 129 mi. **Motor vehicles in use:** 43,500 passenger cars, 15,400 comm. vehicles. **Civil aviation:** 1.31 bil passenger-mi; 4 airports. **Chief ports:** Kingston, Montego Bay.

Communications: Television sets: 306 per 1,000 pop. **Radios:** 739 per 1,000 pop. **Telephones:** 1 per 8.7 persons.

Health: Life expectancy at birth: 73.0 male; 77.8 female. **Births** (per 1,000 pop.): 21. **Deaths** (per 1,000 pop.): 5.

Natural increase: 1.55%. **Hospital beds** (1993): 1 per 492 persons. **Physicians** (1995): 1 per 6,043 persons. **Infant mortality** (per 1,000 live births): 14.

Education: Free and compulsory: ages 6-12. **Literacy** (1995): 85%.

Major International Organizations: UN (FAO, IBRD, ILO, IMF, IMO, WHO, WTrO), Caricom, the Commonwealth, OAS.

Embassy: 1520 New Hampshire Ave. NW 20036; 452-0660.

Website: http://www.jamaica.com

Jamaica was visited by Columbus, 1494, and ruled by Spain (under whom Arawak Indians died out) until seized by Britain, 1655. Jamaica won independence Aug. 6, 1962.

In 1974 Jamaica sought an increase in taxes paid by U.S. and Canadian bauxite mines. The socialist government acquired 50% ownership of the companies' Jamaican interests in 1976, and was reelected that year. Rudimentary welfare state measures were passed. Relations with the U.S. improved greatly in the 1980s following the election of Edward Seaga, which marked the beginning of a more conservative era.

Japan

People: Population: 125,931,533. **Age distrib.** (%): <15: 15.2; 65+: 16. **Pop. density:** 863 per sq. mi. **Urban:** 78%. **Ethnic groups:** Japanese 99.4%. **Principal language:** Japanese (official). **Chief religions:** Buddhism, Shintoism shared by 84%.

Geography: Area: 145,882 sq. mi. **Location:** Archipelago off E coast of Asia. **Neighbors:** Russia to N, South Korea to W. **Topography:** Japan consists of 4 main islands: Honshu ("mainland"), 87,805 sq. mi.; Hokkaido, 30,144 sq. mi.; Kyushu, 14,114 sq. mi.; and Shikoku, 7,049 sq. mi. The coast, deeply indented, measures 16,654 mi. The northern islands are a continuation of the Sakhalin Mts. The Kunlun range of China continues into southern islands, the ranges meeting in the Japanese Alps. In a vast transverse fissure crossing Honshu E-W rises a group of volcanoes, mostly extinct or inactive, including 12,388 ft. Mt. Fuji (Fujiyama) near Tokyo. **Capital:** Tokyo. **Cities:** Tokyo 26,959,000; Osaka 10,609,000; Nagoya 3,213,000; Sapporo 1,710,000; Kyoto 1,703,000*.

Government: Type: Parliamentary democracy. **Head of state:** Emp. Akihito; b Dec. 23, 1933; in office: Jan. 7, 1989. **Head of government:** Prime Min. Keizo Obuchi; b June 25, 1937; in office: July 30, 1998. **Local divisions:** 47 prefectures. **Defense:** 1.0% of GDP. **Active troop strength:** 235,500.

Economy: Industries: Electrical & electronic equip., vehicles, machinery, metallurgy, chemicals, fishing. **Chief crops:** Rice, potatoes, sugar beets, vegatables, fruits. **Crude oil reserves** (1997): 60 mil bbls. **Arable land:** 11%. **Livestock** (1997): chickens: 309.00 mil; pigs: 9.81 mil; cattle: 4.75 mil. **Fish catch** (1996): 5.96 mil metric tons. **Electricity prod.** (1996): 948.6 bil kWh. **Labor force:** 50% services & trade; 33% manuf., mining, & constr.; 7% agric. & fish.

Finance: Monetary unit: Yen (Sept. 1998: 135.78 = $1 U.S.). **Gross domestic product** (1996 est.): $2.85 tril. **Per capita GDP:** $22,700. **Imports** (1996 est.): $329 bil; partners: SE Asia 24%, U.S. 22%, China 12%. **Exports** (1996 est.): $385 bil; partners: SE Asia 37%, U.S. 27%. **Tourism:** $4.32 bil. **National budget** (FY1997-98 est.): $673 bil. **International reserves less gold** (May 1998): $205.83 bil. **Gold:** 24.23 mil oz t. **Consumer prices** (change in 1997): 1.7%.

Transport: Railroad: Length: 12,511 mi. **Motor vehicles in use:** 46.87 mil passenger cars, 21.93 mil comm. vehicles. **Civil aviation:** 88.07 bil passenger-mi; 73 airports. **Chief ports:** Tokyo, Kobe, Osaka, Nagoya, Chiba, Kawasaki, Hakodate.

Communications: Television sets: 619 per 1,000 pop. **Radios:** 799 per 1,000 pop. **Telephones:** 1 per 2.0 persons. **Daily newspaper circ.:** 578 per 1,000 pop.

Health: Life expectancy at birth: 76.9 male; 83.3 female. **Births** (per 1,000 pop.): 10. **Deaths** (per 1,000 pop.): 8. **Natural increase:** 0.23%. **Hospital beds** (1992): 1 per 74 persons. **Physicians** (1994): 1 per 546 persons. **Infant mortality** (per 1,000 live births): 4.

Education: Free and compulsory: ages 6-15. **Literacy** (1997): 100%.

Major International Organizations: UN and all its specialized agencies, APEC, OECD.

Embassy: 2520 Massachusetts Ave. NW 20008; 939-6700.

Website: http://www.japan.com

According to Japanese legend, the empire was founded by Emperor Jimmu, 660 BC, but earliest records of a unified Japan date from 1,000 years later. Chinese influence was strong in the formation of Japanese civilization. Buddhism was introduced before the 6th century AD.

A feudal system, with locally powerful noble families and their samurai warrior retainers, dominated from 1192. Central power was held by successive families of shoguns (military dictators), 1192-1867, until recovered by Emperor Meiji, 1868. The Portuguese and Dutch had minor trade with Japan in the 16th and 17th centuries; U.S. Commodore Matthew C. Perry opened it to U.S. trade in a treaty ratified 1854. Japan fought China, 1894-95, gaining Taiwan. After war with Russia, 1904-5, Russia ceded S half of Sakhalin and gave concessions in China. Japan annexed Korea 1910. In World War I Japan ousted Germany from Shandong in China, took over German Pacific islands. Japan took Manchuria 1931, started war with China 1932. Japan launched war against the U.S. by attack on Pearl Harbor Dec. 7, 1941. The U.S. dropped atomic bombs on Hiroshima, Aug. 6, and Nagasaki, Aug. 9, 1945. Japan surrendered Aug. 14, 1945. Japan apologized Aug. 15, 1995, for its acts of "colonial rule and aggression" during World War II.

In a new constitution adopted May 3, 1947, Japan renounced the right to wage war; the emperor gave up claims to divinity; the Diet became the sole law-making authority.

The U.S. and 48 other non-Communist nations signed a peace treaty and the U.S. a bilateral defense agreement with Japan, in San Francisco Sept. 8, 1951, restoring Japan's sovereignty as of April 28, 1952.

On June 26, 1968, the U.S. returned to Japanese control the Bonin Isls., Volcano Isls. (including Iwo Jima), and Marcus Isls. On May 15, 1972, Okinawa, the other Ryukyu Isls., and the Daito Isls. were returned by the U.S.; it was agreed the U.S. would continue to maintain military bases on Okinawa.

Industrialization was begun in the late 19th century. After World War II, Japan emerged as one of the most powerful economies in the world, and as a leader in technology.

The U.S. and EU member nations have criticized Japan for its restrictive policy on imports, which has given Japan a substantial trade surplus.

The Recruit scandal, the nation's worst political scandal since World War II, which involved illegal political donations and stock trading, led to the resignation of Premier Noboru Takeshita in May 1989. A series of scandals rocked Japan's financial sector in 1991.

Following new political scandals, the Liberal Democratic Party (LDP) was denied a majority in general elections July 18, 1993. The LDP had held power since it was founded in 1955. Morihiro Hosokawa was chosen prime minister Aug. 6; he initiated reforms but resigned Apr. 8, 1994, because of controversy over his financial connections. His replacement, Tsutomu Hata, resigned June 25, to be replaced by Japan's first Socialist premier since 1947-48, Tomiichi Murayama.

An earthquake in the Kobe area in Jan. 1995 claimed more than 5,000 lives, injured nearly 35,000, and caused over $90 billion in property damage. On Mar. 20, a nerve gas attack in the Tokyo subway (blamed on a religious cult) killed 12 and injured thousands. Public anger at the rape of a 12-year-old Okinawa schoolgirl by 3 U.S. servicemen, Sept. 4, led the U.S. to begin reducing its military presence there.

Murayama resigned as prime minister, Jan. 5, 1996, and was replaced by Ryutaro Hashimoto of the LDP. He signed a joint security declaration with U.S. Pres. Bill Clinton in Tokyo, Apr. 17, 1996. Nagano hosted the Winter Olympics, Feb. 7-22, 1998. With Japan mired in recession, the LDP suffered a sharp rebuke in elections for parliament's upper house, July 12. Hashimoto resigned, and on July 24 the LDP chose Keizo Obuchi to become Japan's 23d prime minister since World War II.

Jordan

Hashemite Kingdom of Jordan

People: Population: 4,434,978. **Age distrib.** (%): <15: 43.3; 65+: 2.9. **Pop. density:** 129 per sq. mi. **Urban:** 72%. **Ethnic groups:** Arab 98%. **Principal language:** Arabic (official). **Chief religions:** Sunni Muslim 92%, Christian 8%.

Geography: Area: 34,445 sq. mi. **Location:** In Middle East. **Neighbors:** Israel and West Bank on W, Saudi Arabia on S, Iraq on E, Syria on N. **Topography:** About 88% of Jordan is arid. Fertile areas are in W. Only port is on short Aqaba Gulf coast. Country shares Dead Sea (1,312 ft. below sea level) with Israel. **Capital:** Amman. **Cities:** Amman 483,000*.

Government: Type: Constitutional monarchy. **Head of state:** King Hussein I; b Nov. 14, 1935; in office: Aug. 11, 1952. **Head of government:** Prime Min. Fayed Tarawneh; b May 1, 1949; in office: Aug. 20, 1998. **Local divisions:** 12 governorates. **Defense:** 5.6% of GDP. **Active troop strength:** 98,700.

Economy: Industries: Oil refining, cement, light manufacturing. **Chief crops:** Grains, olives, fruits. **Minerals:** Phosphates, potash. **Arable land:** 4%. **Livestock** (1997): chickens: 78.00 mil; sheep: 2.10 mil; goats: 555,000. **Electricity prod.** (1996): 5.5 bil kWh. **Labor force:** 11% ind., commerce; 10% constr.; 9% transport, communications; 7% agric.; 52% other services.

Finance: Monetary unit: Dinar (Sept. 1998: 0.71 = $1 U.S.). **Gross domestic product** (1996 est.): $20.9 bil. **Per capita GDP:** $5,000. **Imports** (1996): $4.1 bil; partners: Iraq 12%, U.S. 10%. **Exports** (1996): $1.9 bil; partners: Saudi Arabia 13%, Iraq 9%. **Tourism:** $760 mil. **National budget** (1997 est.): $2.8 bil. **International reserves less gold** (June 1998): $2.12 bil. **Gold:** 821,000 oz t. **Consumer prices** (change in 1997): 3.0%.

Transport: Railroad: Length: 419.8 mi. **Motor vehicles in use:** 175,000 passenger cars, 90,000 comm. vehicles. **Civil aviation:** 2.95 bil passenger-mi; 2 airports. **Chief port:** Al Aqabah.

Communications: Television sets: 176 per 1,000 pop. **Radios:** 224 per 1,000 pop. **Telephones:** 1 per 14 persons. **Daily newspaper circ.:** 62 per 1,000 pop.

Health: Life expectancy at birth: 71.0 male; 74.8 female. **Births** (per 1,000 pop.): 35. **Deaths** (per 1,000 pop.): 4. **Natural increase:** 3.13%. **Hospital beds** (1995): 1 per 567 persons. **Physicians** (1995): 1 per 616 persons. **Infant mortality** (per 1,000 live births): 33.

Education: Free and compulsory: ages 6-16. **Literacy** (1995): 87%.

Major International Organizations: UN (FAO, IBRD, ILO, IMF, IMO, WHO), AL.

Embassy: 3504 International Dr. NW 20008; 966-2664.

Websites: http://www.iconnect.com/jordan
http://www.nic.gov.jo

From ancient times to 1922 the lands to the E of the Jordan River were culturally and politically united with the lands to the W. Arabs conquered the area in the 7th century; the Ottomans took control in the 16th. Britain's 1920 Palestine Mandate covered both sides of the Jordan. In 1921, Abdullah, son of the ruler of Hejaz in Arabia, was installed by Britain as emir of an autonomous Transjordan, covering two-thirds of Palestine. An independent kingdom was proclaimed, 1946.

During the 1948 Arab-Israeli war the West Bank and East Jerusalem were added to the kingdom, which changed its name to Jordan. All these territories were lost to Israel in the 1967 war, which swelled the number of Arab refugees on the East Bank.

Some 700,000 refugees entered Jordan following Iraq's invasion of Kuwait, Aug. 1990. Jordan was viewed as supporting Iraq during the 1990-1991 Persian Gulf crisis.

Jordan and Israel officially agreed, July 25, 1994, to end their state of war; a formal peace treaty was signed Oct. 26. In July 1998, King Hussein was diagnosed with lymphoma and began receiving chemotherapy treatments in the U.S.

Kazakhstan

Republic of Kazakhstan

People: Population: 16,846,808. **Age distrib.** (%): <15: 29.1; 65+: 7.0. **Pop. density:** 16 per sq. mi. **Urban:** 60%. **Ethnic groups:** Kazakh 46%, Russian 35%, Ukrainian 5% **Principal languages:** Kazakh, Russian (both official). **Chief religions:** Muslim 47%, Russian Orthodox 44%.

Geography: Area: 1,052,100 sq. mi. **Location:** In Central Asia. **Neighbors:** Russia on N; China on E; Kyrgyzstan, Uzbekistan, Turkmenistan on S; Caspian Sea on W. **Topography:** Extends from the lower reaches of Volga in Europe to the Altay Mts. on the Chinese border. **Capital:** Astana (1998 est.): 130,000.

Government: Type: Republic. **Head of state:** Pres. Nursultan A. Nazarbayev; b July 6, 1940; in office: Apr. 1990. **Head of government:** Prime Min. Nurlan Balgimbaev; b Nov. 20, 1947; in office: Oct. 10, 1997. **Local divisions:** 14 oblystar, 2 cities. **Defense:** 2.6% of GDP. **Active troop strength:** 40,000.

Economy: Industries: Oil, steel, mining, agricultural machinery. **Chief crops:** Grain, cotton. **Minerals:** Oil, gas, coal, iron, manganese, chrome ore, copper. **Crude oil reserves** (1997): 5.4 bil bbls. **Arable land:** 12%. **Livestock** (1997): chickens: 15.30 mil; sheep: 13.00 mil; cattle: 5.41 mil; pigs: 1.04 mil; goats: 742,000; buffalo: 100,000. **Electricity prod.** (1996): 57.6 bil kWh. **Labor force:** 27% industry; 23% agric., forestry.

Finance: Monetary unit: Tenge (Aug. 1998: 78.40 = $1 U.S.). **Gross domestic product** (1996 est.): $48.6 bil. **Per capita GDP:** $2,880. **Imports** (1996 est.): $6 bil; partners: Russia 65%. **Exports** (1996 est.): $5.7 bil; partners: Russia 64%. **International reserves less gold** (Mar. 1998): $1.41 bil. **Gold:** 1.81 mil oz t. **Consumer prices** (change in 1997): 17.4%.

Transport: Railroad: Length: 8,595.3 mi. **Motor vehicles:** 1.0 mil passenger cars, 515,000 comm. vehicles. **Civil aviation:** 825.9 mil passenger-mi; 20 airports. **Chief ports:** Aqtau, Atyrau.

Communications: Television: 275 per 1,000 pop. **Telephones:** 1 per 8.5 persons.

Health: Life expectancy at birth: 58.1 male; 69.3 female. **Birth rate** (per 1,000 pop.): 17. **Death rate** (per 1,000 pop.): 10. **Natural increase:** 0.71%. **Hospital beds** (1995): 1 per 86 persons. **Physicians** (1995): 1 per 267 persons. **Infant mortality** (per 1,000 live births): 58.

Education: Free and compulsory: ages 7-18. **Literacy** (1992): 98%.

Major International Organizations: UN (IBRD, ILO, IMF, IMO, WHO), CIS, OSCE.

Embassy: 3421 Massachusetts Ave. NW 20008; 333-4504.

Website: http://www.undp.org/missions/kazakhstan

The region came under the Mongols in the 13th century and gradually came under Russian rule, 1730-1853. It was admitted to the USSR as a constituent republic 1936. Kazakhstan declared independence Dec. 16, 1991. It became an independent state when the Soviet Union dissolved Dec. 26, 1991. The party chief, Nursultan Nazarbayev, was elected president unopposed. In legislative elections Mar. 7, 1994, criticized by international monitors, his party won a sweeping victory. Kazakhstan agreed, Feb. 14, to dismantle nuclear missiles and adhere to the 1968 Nuclear Nonproliferation Treaty; the U.S. pledged increased aid. A referendum Apr. 29, 1995, extended Nazarbayev's term to Dec. 2000; a new draft constitution was approved in a referendum Aug. 30. Private land ownership was legalized Dec. 26, 1995.

Astana (formerly Akmola) was dedicated as the nation's new capital on June 9, 1998.

Kenya

Republic of Kenya

People: Population: 28,337,071. **Age distrib.** (%): <15: 43.6; 65+: 2.7. **Pop. density:** 126 per sq. mi. **Urban:** 30%. **Ethnic groups:** Kikuyu 22%, Luhya 14%, Luo 13%, Kalenjin 12%, Kamba 11%, others including Asian, Arab, European. **Principal languages:** Swahili, English (both official), numerous indigenous languages. **Chief religions:** Protestant 38%, Roman Catholic 28%, indigenous beliefs 26%.

Geography: Area: 224,961 sq. mi. **Location:** E Africa, on coast of Indian O. **Neighbors:** Uganda on W, Tanzania on S, Somalia on E, Ethiopia on N, Sudan on NW. **Topography:** The northern three-fifths of Kenya is arid. To the S, a low coastal area and a plateau varying from 3,000 to 10,000 ft. The Great Rift Valley enters the country N-S, flanked by high mountains. **Capital:** Nairobi. **Cities** (1991 est.): Nairobi 2,000,000; Mombasa 600,000.

Government: Type: Republic. **Head of state:** Pres. Daniel arap Moi; b Sept. 2, 1924; in office: Aug. 22, 1978. **Local divisions:** Nairobi and 7 provinces. **Defense:** 2.2% of GDP. **Active troop strength:** 24,200.

Economy: Industries: Tourism, light industry, agricultural processing, oil refining. **Chief crops:** Coffee, corn, tea. **Minerals:** Gold, limestone, salt, rubies, fluorspar, garnets. **Other resources:** Hides, dairy products, cut flowers (world's 4th lgst. exporter). **Arable land:** 7%. **Livestock** (1997): chickens: 28.90 mil; cattle: 13.41 mil; goats: 7.60 mil; sheep: 5.80 mil; pigs: 180,000. **Fish catch** (1996): 178,354 metric tons. **Electricity prod.** (1996): 3.8 bil kWh. **Labor force:** 75-80% agric.

Finance: Monetary unit: Shilling (Sept. 1998: 59.63 = $1 U.S.). **Gross domestic product** (1996 est.): $39.2 bil. **Per capita GDP:** $1,400. **Imports** (1995 est.): $2.6 bil; partners: UK 21%, UAE 18%. **Exports** (1995 est.): $1.9 bil; partners: Uganda 23%, UK 20%, Tanzania 19%. **Tourism:** $400 mil. **National budget** (FY 1995-96): $2.7 bil. **International reserves less gold** (June 1998): $665.1 mil. **Gold:** 80,000 oz t. **Consumer prices** (change in 1997): 12.0%.

Transport: Railroad: Length: 1,646.9 mi. **Motor vehicles in use:** 271,000 passenger cars, 75,900 comm. vehicles. **Civil aviation:** 1.14 bil passenger-mi; 11 airports. **Chief port:** Mombasa.

Communications: Television sets: 18 per 1,000 pop. **Radios:** 103 per 1,000 pop. **Telephones:** 1 per 111 persons.

Health: Life expectancy at birth: 47.0 male; 48.1 female. **Births** (per 1,000 pop.): 32. **Deaths** (per 1,000 pop.): 14. **Natural increase:** 1.75%. **Hospital beds** (1994): 1 per 734 persons. **Physicians** (1994): 1 per 5,999 persons. **Infant mortality** (per 1,000 live births): 59.

Education: Free and compulsory: ages 6-14. **Literacy:** 78%.

Major International Organizations: UN and all of its specialized agencies, the Commonwealth, OAU.

Embassy: 2249 R St. NW 20008; 387-6101.

Website: http://www.embassyofkenya.com

Arab colonies exported spices and slaves from the Kenya coast as early as the 8th century. Britain obtained control in the 19th century. Kenya won independence Dec. 12, 1963, 4 years after the end of the violent Mau Mau uprising.

Kenya had steady growth in industry and agriculture under a modified private enterprise system, and enjoyed a relatively free political life. But stability was shaken in 1974-75, with opposition charges of corruption and oppression. Jomo Kenyatta, the country's leader since independence, died Aug. 22, 1978. He was succeeded by his vice president, Daniel arap Moi.

During the first half of the 1990s, Kenya suffered widespread unemployment and high inflation. Tribal clashes in the western provinces claimed thousands of lives and left tens of thousands homeless. Pres. Moi won a third term in Dec. 1992 elections, which were marred by violence and fraud. Clashes in the Mombasa region, Aug. 1997, left more than 40 people dead. Pres. Moi was reelected Dec. 29, in an election again plagued by irregularities.

A truck bomb explosion at the U.S. embassy in Nairobi, Aug. 7, 1998, killed more than 200 people and injured about 5,000. The U.S. blamed the attack on Islamic terrorists associated with a wealthy Saudi businessman, Osama bin Laden.

Kiribati

Republic of Kiribati

People: Population: 83,976. **Pop. density:** 268 per sq. mi. **Urban:** 36%. **Ethnic groups:** Micronesian. **Principal languages:** English (official), Gilbertese. **Chief religions:** Roman Catholic 53%, Protestant 41%.

Geography: Area: 313 sq. mi. **Location:** 33 Micronesian islands (the Gilbert, Line, and Phoenix groups) in the mid-Pacific scattered in a 2-mil sq. mi. chain around the point where the International Date Line formerly cut the Equator. In 1997 the Date Line was moved to follow Kiribati's E border. **Neighbors:** Nearest are Nauru to SW, Tuvalu and Tokelau Isls. to S. **Topography:** Except Banaba (Ocean) Isl., all are low-lying, with soil of coral sand and rock fragments, subject to erratic rainfall. **Capital:** Tarawa (1990): 25,000.

Government: Type: Republic. **Head of state and government:** Pres. Teburoro Tito; b 1953; in office: Oct. 1, 1994. **Local divisions:** 3 units, 6 districts.

Economy: Industries: Fishing, handicrafts. **Chief crops:** Copra, taro, breadfruit, sweet potatoes, vegetables. **Livestock** (1997): chickens: 300,000. **Electricity prod.** (1996): 7 mil kWh.

Finance: Monetary unit: Australian Dollar (Sept. 1998: 1.73 = $1 U.S.). **Gross domestic product** (1996 est.): $62 mil. **Per capita GDP:** $800. **Imports** (1995 est.): $38.6 mil; partners: Australia 40%. **Exports** (1995 est.): $6.3 mil; partners: Japan 33%. **Tourism:** $2 mil. **National budget** (1995 est.): $54.3 mil.

Transport: Chief port: Tarawa. **Civil aviation:** 6.9 mil passenger-mi., 17 airports.

Communications: Radios: 75 per 1,000 pop. **Telephones:** 1 per 39 persons.

Health: Life expectancy at birth: 60.8 male; 64.7 female. **Births** (per 1,000 pop.): 26. **Deaths** (per 1,000 pop.): 8. **Natural increase:** 1.88%. **Physicians** (1993): 1 per 7,687 persons. **Infant mortality** (per 1,000 live births): 50.

Education: Free and compulsory: ages 6-14. **Literacy** (1995): 90%.

Major International Organizations: IBRD, IMF, WHO, the Commonwealth.

A British protectorate since 1892, the Gilbert and Ellice Islands colony was completed with the inclusion of the Phoenix Islands, 1937. Self-rule was granted 1971; the Ellice Islands separated from the colony 1975 and became independent Tuvalu, 1978. Kiribati (pronounced *Kiribass)* independence was attained July 12, 1979. Under a treaty of friendship the U.S. relinquished its claims to several Line and Phoenix islands, including Christmas (Kiritimati), Canton, and Enderbury.

Tarawa Atoll was the scene of some of the bloodiest fighting in the Pacific during World War II.

Korea, North

Democratic People's Republic of Korea

People: Population: 21,234,387. **Age distrib.** (%): <15: 25.8; 65+: 6.0. **Pop. density:** 456 per sq. mi. **Urban:** 62%. **Ethnic group:** Korean. **Principal language:** Korean (official). **Chief religions:** Activities almost nonexistent; traditionally Buddhism, Confucianism, Chondogyo.

Geography: Area: 46,540 sq. mi. **Location:** In northern E Asia. **Neighbors:** China and Russia on N, South Korea on S. **Topography:** Mountains and hills cover nearly all the country, with narrow valleys and small plains in between. The N and the E coasts are the most rugged areas. **Capital:** Pyongyang (1987 est.): 2.4 mil.

Government: Type: Communist state. **Leader:** Kim Jong Il; b Feb. 16, 1948; officially assumed post Oct. 8, 1997. **Local divisions:** 9 provinces, 3 special cities. **Defense:** 27.2% of GDP. **Active troop strength:** 1.054 mil.

Economy: Industries: Textiles, chemicals, machinery, food processing. **Chief crops:** Corn, potatoes, soybeans, rice. **Minerals:** Coal, lead, tungsten, zinc, graphite, magnesite, iron, copper, gold, salt. **Arable land:** 14%. **Livestock** (1997): chickens: 14.00 mil; pigs: 3.10 mil; cattle: 1.15 mil; sheep: 355,000; goats: 265,000. **Fish catch** (1996): 1.73 mil metric tons. **Electricity prod.** (1996): 34.0 bil kWh. **Labor force:** 36% agric.

Finance: Monetary unit: Won (Sept. 1998: 2.20 = $1 U.S.). **Gross domestic product** (1996 est.): $20.9 bil. **Per capita GDP:** $900. **Imports** (1995 est.): $1.24 bil; partners: China 30%, Japan 16%. **Exports** (1995 est.): $805 mil; partners: Japan 31%, Austria 17%. **National budget** (1992 est.): $19.3 bil.

Transport: Railroad: Length: 5,302 mi. **Civil aviation:** 128.4 mil passenger-mi; 1 airport. **Chief ports:** Chongjin, Hamhung, Nampo.

Communications: Television sets: 85.1 per 1,000 pop. **Radios:** 200 per 1,000 pop. **Daily newspaper circ.:** 213 per 1,000 pop.

Health: Life expectancy at birth: 48.9 male; 53.9 female. **Births** (per 1,000 pop.): 15. **Deaths** (per 1,000 pop.): 16. **Natural increase:** –0.03%. **Infant mortality** (per 1,000 live births): 88.

Education: Free and compulsory: ages 6-17. **Literacy** (1992): 95%.

Major International Organizations: UN (FAO, IMO, WHO).

The Democratic People's Republic of Korea was founded May 1, 1948, in the zone occupied by Russian troops after World War II. Its armies tried to conquer the south, 1950. After 3 years of fighting, with Chinese and U.S. intervention, a cease-fire was proclaimed. For the next four decades, a hard-line Communist regime headed by Kim Il Sung kept tight control over the nation's political, economic, and cultural life. The nation used its abundant mineral and hydroelectric resources to develop its military strength and heavy industry..

In Mar. 1993, North Korea became the first nation to formally withdraw from the Nuclear Nonproliferation Treaty, the international pact designed to limit the spread of nuclear weapons. The nation suspended its withdrawal in June in reaction to threats of UN economic sanctions, but was widely believed to be developing nuclear weapons. The U.S. and North Korea reached an interim agreement, Aug. 13, 1994, intended to resolve the nuclear issue, and further negotiations followed.

Kim Il Sung died July 8, 1994. He was succeeded by his son, Kim Jong Il. North Korea suffered from defections by high officials, a deteriorating economy, and severe food shortages in the late 1990s.

Korea, South

Republic of Korea

People: Population: 46,416,796. **Age distrib.** (%): <15: 22.4; 65+: 6.4. **Pop. density:** 1,221 per sq. mi. **Urban:** 83%. **Ethnic group:** Korean. **Principal language:** Korean (official). **Chief religions:** Christianity 49%, Buddhism 47%.

Geography: Area: 38,023 sq. mi. **Location:** In northern E Asia. **Neighbors:** North Korea on N. **Topography:** The country is mountainous, with a rugged east coast. The western and southern coasts are deeply indented, with many islands and harbors. **Capital:** Seoul. **Cities:** Seoul 11,609,000; Pusan 4,038,000; Taegu 2,432,000*.

Government: Type: Republic, with power centralized in a strong executive. **Head of state:** Pres. Kim Dae Jung; b Dec. 3, 1925; in office: Dec. 18, 1997. **Head of government:** Prime Min. Kim Jong Pil; b 1926; in office: Aug. 17, 1998 (acting prime min. from Mar. 3). **Local divisions:** 9 provinces and 6 special cities. **Defense:** 3.3% of GDP. **Active troop strength:** 660,000.

Economy: Industries: Electronics, autos, chemicals, ships, textiles, clothing. **Chief crops:** Rice, barley, vegetables. **Minerals:** Tungsten, coal, graphite. **Arable land:** 19%. **Livestock** (1997): chickens: 88.25 mil; pigs: 7.10 mil; cattle: 3.40 mil; goats: 663,200. **Fish catch:** (1996): 2.41 mil metric tons. **Electricity prod.** (1996): 194.2 bil kWh. **Labor force:** 52% services & other; 27% manuf. & mining; 21% agric.

Finance: Monetary unit: Won (Sept. 1998: 1,331.25 = $1 U.S.). **Gross domestic product** (1996 est.): $647.2 bil. **Per capita GDP:** $14,200. **Imports** (1995): $150.2 bil; partners:

U.S. 22%, Japan 21%. **Exports** (1996): $130.9 bil; partners: U.S. 17%, Japan 12%. **Tourism** (1994): $3.8 bil. **National budget** (1995 est.): $67 bil. **International reserves less gold** (June 1998): $40.84 bil. **Gold:** 432,000 oz t. **Consumer prices** (change in 1997): 4.4%.

Transport: Railroad: Length: 1,925.7 mi. **Motor vehicles in use:** 6.89 mil passenger cars, 2.66 mil comm. vehicles. **Civil aviation:** 34.62 bil passenger-mi; 14 airports. **Chief ports:** Pusan, Inchon.

Communications: Television sets: 233 per 1,000 pop. **Radios:** 928 per 1,000 pop. **Daily newspaper circ.:** 405 per 1,000 pop.

Health: Life expectancy at birth: 70.4 male; 78.0 female. **Births** (per 1,000 pop.): 16. **Deaths** (per 1,000 pop.): 6. **Natural increase:** 1.04%. **Hospital beds** (1995): 1 per 229 persons. **Physicians** (1995): 1 per 784 persons. **Infant mortality** (per 1,000 live births): 8.

Education: Free and compulsory: ages 6-12. **Literacy** (1995): 98%.

Major International Organizations: UN (FAO, IBRD, ILO, IMF, IMO, WHO, WTrO), APEC, OECD.

Embassy: 2450 Massachusetts Ave. NW 20008; 939-5600.

Korea, once called the Hermit Kingdom, has a recorded history since the 1st century BC. It was united in a kingdom under the Silla Dynasty, AD 668. It was at times associated with the Chinese empire; the treaty that concluded the Sino-Japanese war of 1894-95 recognized Korea's complete independence. In 1910 Japan forcibly annexed Korea as Chosun.

At the Potsdam conference, July 1945, the 38th parallel was designated as the line dividing the Soviet and the American occupation. Russian troops entered Korea Aug. 10, 1945; U.S. troops entered Sept. 8, 1945. The Soviet military organized socialists and Communists and blocked efforts to let the Koreans unite their country.

The South Koreans formed the Republic of Korea in May 1948 with Seoul as the capital. Dr. Syngman Rhee was chosen president. A separate, Communist regime was formed in the N; its army attacked the S in June 1950, initiating the Korean War. UN troops, under U.S. command, supported the S in the war, which ended in an armistice (July 1953) leaving Korea divided by a "no-man's land" along the 38th parallel.

Rhee's authoritarian rule became increasingly unpopular, and a movement spearheaded by college students forced his resignation Apr. 26, 1960. In an army coup May 16, 1961, Gen. Park Chung Hee became chairman of a ruling junta. He was elected president, 1963; a 1972 referendum allowed him to be reelected for an unlimited series of 6-year terms. Park was assassinated by the chief of the Korean CIA, Oct. 26, 1979. In May 1980, Gen. Chun Doo Hwan, head of military intelligence, reinstated full martial law and ordered the brutal suppression of pro-democracy demonstrations in Kwangju.

In July 1972 South and North Korea agreed on a common goal of reunifying the 2 nations by peaceful means. But there was no sign of a thaw in relations between the two regimes until 1985, when they agreed to discuss economic issues.

On June 10, 1987, middle-class office workers, shopkeepers, and business executives joined students in antigovernment protests in Seoul calling for democratic reforms. Following weeks of rioting and violence, Chun, July 1, agreed to permit election of the next president by direct popular vote and other reforms. In Dec., Roh Tae Woo was elected president. In 1990, the nation's 3 largest political parties merged; some 100,000 students protested the merger as undemocratic.

Kim Young Sam took office in 1993 as the first civilian president since 1961. Convicted of mutiny, treason, and corruption, Chun was sentenced to death by a Seoul court, Aug. 26, 1996, for his role in the 1979 coup and 1980 Kwangju massacre; Roh received a 22-1/2 year prison sentence. On Dec. 16, Chun's term was reduced to life in prison, and Roh's to 17 years.

The collapse in Jan. 1997 of the Hanbo steel firm triggered a new round of corruption scandals. With currency and stock values plummeting, the nation averted default by agreeing, Dec. 4, on a $57 billion bailout from the IMF. Kim Dae Jung, a longtime dissident, won the presidential election Dec. 18. Chun and Roh were released and pardoned Dec. 22, 1997.

Kuwait

State of Kuwait

People: Population: 1,913,285. **Age distrib.** (%): <15: 32.3; 65+: 2.0. **Pop. density:** 278 per sq. mi. **Urban:** 97%. **Ethnic groups:** Kuwaiti 45%, other Arab 35%. **Principal language:** Arabic (official). **Chief religion:** Muslim 85%.

Geography: Area: 6,880 sq. mi. **Location:** In Middle East, at N end of Persian Gulf. **Neighbors:** Iraq on N, Saudi Arabia on S. **Topography:** The country is flat, very dry, and extremely hot. **Capital:** Kuwait City. **Cities** (1995 est.): Kuwait City 276,915; al-Jahra 228,457.

Government: Type: Constitutional monarchy. **Head of state:** Emir Sheikh Jabir al-Ahmad al-Jabir as-Sabah; b 1928; in office: Jan. 1, 1978. **Head of government:** Prime Min. Sheikh Saad Abdulla as-Salim as-Sabah; b 1930; in office: Feb. 8, 1978. **Local divisions:** 5 governorates. **Defense:** 12.9% of GDP. **Active troop strength:** 15,300.

Economy: Industries: Oil products. **Minerals:** Oil, gas. **Crude oil reserves** (1997): 94 bil bbls. **Livestock** (1997): chickens: 22.00 mil; sheep: 320,000. **Electricity prod.** (1996): 23 bil kWh. **Labor force:** 50% gov't. and social services; 25% industry and agric.

Finance: Monetary unit: Dinar (Sept. 1998: 0.31 = $1 U.S.). **Gross domestic product** (1996 est.): $32.5 bil. **Per capita GDP:** $16,700. **Imports** (1996 est.): $8.4 bil; partners: U.S. 24%, UK 14%. **Exports** (1996 est.): $13.6 bil; partners: Japan 23%, India 16%. **Tourism:** $140 mil. **National budget** (FY 1996-97 est.): $14 bil. **International reserves less gold** (June 1998): $4.01 bil. **Gold:** 2.54 mil oz t. **Consumer prices** (change in 1997): 3.2%.

Transport: Motor vehicles in use: 538,000 passenger cars, 155,000 comm. vehicles. **Civil aviation:** 3.77 bil passenger-mi; 1 airport. **Chief port:** Mina al-Ahmadi.

Communications: Television sets: 456 per 1,000 pop. **Radios:** 592 per 1,000 pop. **Telephones:** 1 per 4.4 persons. **Daily newspaper circ.:** 397 per 1,000 pop.

Health: Life expectancy at birth: 74.8 male; 78.9 female. **Births** (per 1,000 pop.): 21. **Deaths** (per 1,000 pop.): 2. **Natural increase:** 1.87%. **Hospital beds** (1995): 1 per 357 persons. **Physicians** (1995): 1 per 464 persons. **Infant mortality** (per 1,000 live births): 11.

Education: Free and compulsory: ages 6-14. **Literacy** (1995): 79%.

Major International Organizations: UN (FAO, IBRD, ILO, IMF, IMO, WHO, WTrO), AL, OPEC.

Embassy: 2940 Tilden St. NW 20008; 966-0702.

Website: http://www.kuwait.info.nw.dc.us/main.htm

Kuwait is ruled by the Al-Sabah dynasty, founded 1759. Britain ran foreign relations and defense from 1899 until independence in 1961. The majority of the population is non-Kuwaiti, with many Palestinians, and cannot vote.

Oil is the fiscal mainstay, providing most of Kuwait's income. Oil pays for free medical care, education, and social security. There are no taxes, except customs duties.

Kuwaiti oil tankers came under frequent attack by Iran because of Kuwait's support of Iraq in the Iran-Iraq War. In July 1987, U.S. Navy warships began escorting Kuwaiti tankers in the Persian Gulf.

Kuwait was attacked and overrun by Iraqi forces Aug. 2, 1990. The emir and senior members of the ruling family fled to Saudi Arabia to establish a government in exile. On Aug. 28, Iraq announced that Kuwait was its 19th province. Following several weeks of aerial attacks on Iraq and Iraqi forces in Kuwait, a U.S.-led coalition began a ground attack Feb. 23, 1991. By Feb. 27, Iraqi forces were routed and Kuwait liberated. Following liberation, there were reports of abuse of Palestinians and others suspected of collaborating with Iraqi occupiers. Kuwait spent more than $5 billion to repair oil installations damaged during 1990-91.

Former U.S. Pres. George Bush visited Kuwait, Apr. 14-16, 1993, and was honored as the leader of the Persian Gulf War alliance that expelled Iraqi troops. Kuwaiti authorities arrested 14 Iraqis and Kuwaitis for allegedly plotting to assassinate Bush during his visit; 13 were convicted and sentenced to prison or death, June 4, 1994.

Kyrgyzstan

Republic of Kyrgyzstan

People: Population: 4,522,281. **Age distrib. (%):** <15: 35.8; 65+: 6.2. **Pop density:** 59 per sq. mi. **Urban:** 39%. **Ethnic groups:** Kyrgyz 52%, Russian 22%, Uzbek 13%. **Principal languages:** Kyrgyz, Russian (both official). **Chief religion:** Predominantly Sunni Muslim.

Geography: Area: 76,641 sq. mi. **Location:** In Central Asia. **Neighbors:** Kazakhstan on N, China on E, Uzbekistan on W, Tajikistan on S. **Capital:** Bishkek (1996 est.) 589,800.

Government: Type: Republic. **Head of state:** Pres. Askar Akayev; b Nov. 10, 1944; in office: Oct. 28, 1990. **Head of**

government: Prime Min. Kubanychbek Zhumaliyev; in office: Mar. 25, 1988. **Local divisions:** 6 oblasts, 1 city. **Defense:** 2.6% of GNP. **Active troop strength:** 7,000.

Economy: Industries: Textiles, mining, small machinery. **Chief crops:** Tobacco, cotton, fruits. **Minerals:** Gold, coal, oil. **Crude oil reserves** (1997): 40 mil bbls. **Arable land:** 7%. **Livestock** (1997): chickens: 1.90 mil; sheep: 3.55 mil; cattle: 847,600; goats: 171,000. **Electricity prod.** (1996): 13.5 bil kWh. **Labor force:** 40% agric. & forestry; 19% ind. & const.

Finance: Monetary unit: Som (Aug. 1998: 20.40 = $1 U.S.). **Gross domestic prod.** (1996 est.): $5.8 bil. **Per capita GDP:** $1,290. **Imports** (1996): $890 mil; partners: Kazakhstan 22%, Russia 22%, Uzbekistan 17%. **Exports** (1996): $506 mil; partners: Russia 26%, China 17%, Uzbekistan 17%. **International reserves less gold** (June 1998): $147.4 mil. **Gold:** 83,100 oz t. **Consumer prices** (change in 1997): 25.5%. **Tourism:** $4 mil.

Transport: Railroad: Length: 229.8 mi. **Motor vehicles in use:** 164,000 passenger cars. **Civil aviation:** 388.4 mil passenger-mi; 2 airports. **Chief port:** Ysyk-Kol.

Communications: Telephones: 1 per 13 persons. **Daily newspaper circ.:** 11 per 1,000 pop.

Health: Life expectancy at birth: 59.5 male; 68.3 female. **Birth rate** (per 1,000 pop.): 22. **Death rate** (per 1,000 pop.): 9. **Natural increase:** 1.34%. **Hospital beds** (1995): 1 per 111 persons. **Physicians** (1995): 1 per 303 persons. **Infant mortality** (per 1,000 live births): 75.

Education: Compulsory: ages 6-15. **Literacy** (1993): 97%.

Major International Organizations: UN (FAO, IBRD, ILO, IMF, WHO), CIS, OSCE.

Embassy: 1732 Wisconsin Ave. NW, 20007; 338-5141.

The region was inhabited around the 13th century by the Kyrgyz. It was annexed to Russia 1864. After 1917, it was nominally a Kara-Kyrgyz autonomous area, which was reorganized 1926, and made a constituent republic of the USSR in 1936. Kyrgyzstan declared independence Aug. 31, 1991. It became an independent state when the USSR disbanded Dec. 26, 1991. A constitution was adopted May 5, 1993. Reelected Dec. 24, 1995, Pres. Askar Akayev gained approval by referendum of a constitutional amendment expanding his presidential powers, Feb. 10, 1996.

Laos

Lao People's Democratic Republic

People: Population: 5,260,842. **Age distrib.** (%): <15: 45.2; 65+: 3.2. **Pop. density:** 58 per sq. mi. **Urban:** 21%. **Ethnic groups:** Lao Loum 68%, Lao Theung 22%, Lao Soung (includes Hmong and Yao) 9%. **Principal languages:** Lao (official), French, English. **Chief religions:** Buddhism 60%, animist and other 40%.

Geography: Area: 91,428 sq. mi. **Location:** In Indochina Peninsula in SE Asia. **Neighbors:** Myanmar and China on N, Vietnam on E, Cambodia on S, Thailand on W. **Topography:** Landlocked, dominated by jungle. High mountains along eastern border are the source of the E-W rivers slicing across the country to the Mekong R., which defines most of the western border. **Capital:** Vientiane (1996 met. est.): 531,800.

Government: Type: Communist. **Head of state:** Pres. Khamtai Siphandon; b Feb. 8, 1924; in office: Feb. 24, 1998. **Head of government:** Prime Min. Sisavat Keobounphan; in office: Feb. 24, 1998. **Local divisions:** 16 provinces, 1 municipality, 1 special zone. **Defense:** 4.1% of GDP. **Active troop strength:** 37,000.

Economy: Industries: Wood products, mining. **Chief crops:** Sweet potatoes, corn, cotton, vegetables, coffee. **Minerals:** Gypsum, tin, gold. **Arable land:** 3%. **Livestock** (1997): chickens: 11.66 mil; pigs: 1.78 mil; buffalo: 1.20 mil; cattle: 1.19 mil; goats: 160,000. **Electricity prod.** (1996): 900 mil kWh. **Labor force:** 80% agric.

Finance: Monetary unit: Kip (Sept. 1998: 2,,602.00 = $1 U.S.). **Gross domestic product** (1996 est.): $5.7 bil. **Per capita GDP:** $1,150. **Imports** (1996 est.): $570 mil; partners: Thailand 45%. **Exports** (1996 est.): $240 mil; partners: Vietnam 49%, Thailand 30%. **National budget** (1996) est.: $379 mil. **International reserves less gold** (June 1998): $130.79 mil. **Gold:** 17,100 oz t. **Tourism:** $54 mil.

Transport: Motor vehicles in use: 9,000 passenger cars, 9,000 comm. vehicles. **Civil aviation:** 29.8 mil passenger-mi. 11 airports.

Communications: Television sets: 17 per 1,000 pop. **Radios:** 116 per 1,000 pop. **Telephones:** 1 per 239 persons.

Health: Life expectancy at birth: 52.1 male; 55.3 female. **Births** (per 1,000 pop.): 41. **Deaths** (per 1,000 pop.): 13. **Natural increase:** 2.76%. **Infant mortality** (per 1,000 live births): 92.

Education: Compulsory for 5 years between ages 6-15. **Literacy** (1995): 57%.

Major International Organizations: UN (FAO, IBRD, ILO, IMF, WHO).

Embassy: 2222 S St. NW 20008; 332-6416.

Website: http://www.laoembassy.com/discover/index.htm

Laos became a French protectorate in 1893, but regained independence as a constitutional monarchy July 19, 1949.

Conflicts among neutralist, Communist, and conservative factions created a chaotic political situation. Armed conflict increased after 1960.

The 3 factions formed a coalition government in June 1962, with neutralist Prince Souvanna Phouma as premier. A 14-nation conference in Geneva signed agreements, 1962, guaranteeing neutrality and independence. By 1964 the Pathet Lao had withdrawn from the coalition, and, with aid from North Vietnamese troops, renewed sporadic attacks. U.S. planes bombed the Ho Chi Minh trail, supply line from North Vietnam to Communist forces in Laos and South Vietnam.

In 1970 the U.S. stepped up air support and military aid. After Pathet Lao military gains, Souvanna Phouma in May 1975 ordered government troops to cease fighting; the Pathet Lao took control. The Lao People's Democratic Republic was proclaimed Dec. 3, 1975.

From the mid-1970s through the 1980s, the Laotian government relied on Vietnam for military and financial aid. Since easing its foreign investment laws in 1988, Laos has attracted more than $5 billion from Thailand, the U.S., and other nations. Laos was admitted to ASEAN on July 23, 1997.

Latvia

Republic of Latvia

People: Population: 2,385,396. **Age distrib.** (%): <15: 18.7. 65+: 14.9. **Pop density:** 96 per sq. mi. **Urban:** 73%. **Ethnic groups:** Latvian 52%, Russian 34%. **Principal languages:** Latvian (official), Lithuanian, Russian. **Chief religions:** Lutheran, Roman Catholic, Russian Orthodox.

Geography: Area: 24,749 sq. mi. **Location:** E Europe, on the Baltic Sea. **Neighbors:** Estonia on N, Lithuania and Belarus on S, Russia on E. **Capital:** Riga: 921,000.*

Government: Type: Republic. **Head of state:** Pres. Guntis Ulmanis; b Sept 13, 1939; in office: July 7, 1993. **Head of government:** Prime Min. Guntars Krasts; b Oct. 16, 1957; in office: July 28, 1997. **Local divisions:** 26 counties, 7 municipalities. **Defense:** 3.5% of GDP. **Active troop strength:** 8,000.

Economy: Industries: Machinery, vehicles, railway cars. **Chief crops:** Grains, sugar beets, potatoes. **Arable land:** 27%. **Livestock** (1997): chickens: 3.00 mil; cattle: 509,400; pigs: 459,600. **Fish catch** (1996): 142,644 metric tons. **Electricity prod.** (1996): 3.2 bil kWh. **Labor force:** 41% ind.; 16% agric. & forestry.

Finance: Monetary unit: Lat (Sept. 1998: 0.60 = $1 U.S.). **Gross domestic product** (1996 est.): $9.4 bil. **Per capita GDP:** $3,800. **Imports** (1996): $2.4 bil; partners: Russia 30%, Germany 14%. **Exports** (1996): $1.6 bil; partners: Russia 23%, Germany 14%. **International reserves less gold** (June 1998): $805.07 mil. **Gold:** 249,300 oz t. **Consumer prices** (change in 1997): 8.4%. **Tourism:** $163 mil.

Transport: Railroad: Length: 1,497.9 mi. **Motor vehicles in use:** 252,000 passenger cars, 74,000 comm. vehicles. **Civil aviation:** 216.6 mil passenger-mi; 1 airport. **Chief port:** Riga.

Communications: Television sets: 452 per 1,000 pop. **Radios:** 560 per 1,000 pop. **Telephones:** 1 per 3.6 persons. **Daily newspaper circ.:** 235 per 1,000 pop.

Health: Life expectancy at birth: 61.0 male, 73.5 female. **Births** (per 1,000 pop.): 8. **Deaths** (per 1,000 pop.): 16. **Natural increase:** –0.76%. **Hospital beds** (1995): 1 per 90 persons. **Physicians** (1995): 1 per 298 persons. **Infant mortality rates** (per 1,000 live births): 17.

Education: Compulsory: ages 7-16. **Literacy** (1989): 100%.

Major International Organizations: UN (FAO, IBRD, ILO, IMF, IMO, WHO), OSCE.

Embassy: 4325 17th St. NW 20011; 726-8213.

Websites: http://www.seas.gwu.edu/guest/latvia
http://www.csb.lv

Prior to 1918, Latvia was occupied by the Russians and Germans. It was an independent republic, 1918-39. The Aug. 1939 Soviet-German agreement assigned Latvia to the Soviet sphere of influence. It was officially accepted as part of the USSR on Aug. 5, 1940. It was overrun by the German army in 1941, but retaken in 1945.

During an abortive Soviet coup, Latvia declared independence, Aug. 21, 1991. The Soviet Union recognized Latvia's independence in Sept. 1991. The last Russian troops in Latvia withdrew by Aug. 31, 1994. Responding to international pressure, Latvian voters on Oct. 3, 1998, eased citizenship laws that had discriminated against some 500,000 ethnic Russians.

Lebanon

Republic of Lebanon

People: Population: 3,505,794. **Age distrib.** (%): <15: 29.8; 65+: 6.4. **Pop. density:** 873 per sq. mi. **Urban:** 88%. **Ethnic groups:** Arab 95%, Armenian 4%. **Principal languages:** Arabic, French (both official). **Chief religions:** Islam 70%, Christian 30%.

Geography: Area: 4,015 sq. mi. **Location:** In Middle East, on E end of Mediterranean Sea. **Neighbors:** Syria on E, Israel on S. **Topography:** There is a narrow coastal strip, and 2 mountain ranges running N-S enclosing the fertile Beqaa Valley. The Litani R. runs S through the valley, turning W to empty into the Mediterranean. **Capital:** Beirut: 1,826,000*.

Government: Type: Republic. **Head of state:** Pres. Elias Hrawi; b 1926; in office: Nov. 24, 1989. **Head of government:** Prime Min. Rafiq al-Hariri; b 1944; in office: Oct. 31, 1992. **Local divisions:** 5 governorates. **Defense:** 4.4% of GDP. **Active troop strength:** 48,900.

Economy: Industries: Banking, food products, textiles, cement, oil refining. **Chief crops:** Citrus, olives, tobacco, potatoes, vegetables. **Minerals:** Limestone, iron. **Arable land:** 21%. **Livestock** (1997): chickens: 28.00 mil; goats: 435,000; sheep: 250,000. **Electricity prod.** (1996): 5.7 bil kWh. **Labor force:** 60% services, 28% industry; 12% agric.

Finance: Monetary unit: Pound (Sept. 1998: 1,511.75 = $1 U.S.). **Gross domestic product** (1996 est.): $13 bil. **Per capita GDP:** $3,400. **Imports** (1996 est.): $7 bil; partners: Italy 19%, France 13%, U.S. 12%. **Exports** (1996 est.): $1.0 bil; partners: Saudi Arabia 13%, Switzerland 12%, U.A.E. 11%. **Tourism:** $719 mil. **National budget** (1995 est): $3.9 bil. **International reserves less gold** (June 1998): $6.17 bil. **Gold:** 9.22 mil oz t.

Transport: Railroad: Length: 137.9 mi. **Motor vehicles in use:** 1.1 mil passenger cars, 83,000 comm. vehicles. **Civil aviation:** 1.15 bil passenger-mi; 1 airport. **Chief ports:** Beirut, Tripoli, Sidon.

Communications: Television sets: 291 per 1,000 pop. **Radios:** 608 per 1,000 pop. **Telephones:** 1 per 12 persons. **Newspaper circ.:** 172 per 1,000 pop.

Health: Life expectancy at birth: 68.1 male; 73.3 female. **Births** (per 1,000 pop.): 23. **Deaths** (per 1,000 pop.): 7. **Natural increase:** 1.62%. **Hospital beds** (1995): 1 per 319 persons. **Physicians** (1995): 1 per 529 persons. **Infant mortality** (per 1,000 live births): 32.

Education: Literacy (1995): 92%.

Major International Organizations: UN (FAO, IBRD, ILO, IMF, IMO, WHO), AL.

Embassy: 2560 28th St. NW 20008; 939-6300.

Website: http://www.erols.com/lebanon/stat.htm

Formed from 5 former Turkish Empire districts, Lebanon became an independent state Sept. 1, 1920, administered under French mandate 1920-41. French troops withdrew in 1946.

Under the 1943 National Covenant, all public positions were divided among the various religious communities, with Christians in the majority. By the 1970s, Muslims became the majority and demanded a larger political and economic role.

U.S. Marines intervened, May-Oct. 1958, during a Syrian-aided revolt. Continued raids against Israeli civilians, 1970-75, brought Israeli attacks against guerrilla camps and villages. Israeli troops occupied S Lebanon, Mar. 1978, and again in Apr. 1980.

An estimated 60,000 were killed and billions of dollars in damage inflicted in a 1975-76 civil war. Palestinian units and leftist Muslims fought against the Maronite militia, the Phalange, and other Christians. Several Arab countries provided political and arms support to the various factions, while Israel aided Christian forces. Up to 15,000 Syrian troops intervened in 1976 to fight Palestinian groups. A cease-fire was mainly policed by Syria.

New clashes between Syrian troops and Christian forces erupted, Apr. 1, 1981. By Apr. 22, fighting had also broken out between two Muslim factions. In July, Israeli air raids on Beirut killed or wounded some 800 persons.

Israeli forces invaded Lebanon June 6, 1982, in a coordinated land, sea, and air attack aimed at crushing strongholds of the Palestine Liberation Organization (PLO). Israeli and Syrian forces engaged in the Bekaa Valley. By June 14, Israeli troops had encircled Beirut. On Aug. 21, the PLO evacuated west Beirut after massive Israeli bombings there. Israeli troops entered west Beirut following the Sept. 14 assassination of newly elected Lebanese Pres. Bashir Gemayel. On Sept. 16, Lebanese Christian troops entered 2 refugee camps and massacred hundreds of Palestinian refugees. An agreement May 17, 1983, between Lebanon, Israel, and the U.S. (but not Syria) provided for the withdrawal of Israeli troops; at least 30,000 Syrian troops remained in Lebanon, and Israeli forces continued to occupy a "security zone" in the south.

In 1983, terrorist bombings became a way of life in Beirut as some 50 people were killed in an explosion at the U.S. Embassy, Apr. 18; 241 U.S. servicemen and 58 French soldiers died in separate Muslim suicide attacks, Oct. 23.

Kidnapping of foreign nationals by Islamic militants became common in the 1980s. U.S., British, French, and Soviet citizens were victims. All were released by 1992.

A treaty signed May 22, 1991, between Lebanon and Syria recognized Lebanon as a separate state for the first time since the 2 countries gained independence in 1943.

Israeli forces conducted air raids and artillery strikes against guerrilla bases and villages in S Lebanon, causing over 200,000 to flee their homes July 25-29, 1993. Some 500,000 civilians fled their homes in Apr. 1996 when Israel again struck suspected guerrilla bases in the south. Pope John Paul II visited Lebanon May 10-11, 1997. During May-June 1998 the nation held its 1st municipal elections in 35 years.

Lesotho

Kingdom of Lesotho

People: Population: 2,089,829. **Age distrib.** (%): <15: 40.2; 65+: 4.6. **Pop. density:** 178 per sq. mi. **Urban:** 25%. **Ethnic groups:** Sotho 99.7%. **Principal languages:** English, Sesotho (both official). **Chief religions:** Christian 80%, indigenous beliefs 20%.

Geography: Area: 11,718 sq. mi. **Location:** In southern Africa. **Neighbors:** Completely surrounded by Republic of South Africa. **Topography:** Landlocked and mountainous, altitudes from 5,000 to 11,000 ft. **Capital:** Maseru (1995 est.): 400,200.

Government: Type: Modified constitutional monarchy. **Head of state:** King Letsie III; b July 17, 1963; in office: Feb. 7, 1996. **Head of government:** Pakalitha Mosisili; in office: May 29, 1998. **Local divisions:** 10 districts. **Defense:** 5.0% of GNP. **Active troop strength:** 2,000.

Economy: Industries: Food processing, textiles. **Chief crops:** Corn, grains, peas, beans. **Other resources:** Diamonds. **Arable land:** 10%. **Livestock** (1997): chickens: 1.50 mil; sheep: 1.20 mil; goats: 750,000; cattle: 590,000. **Labor force:** 86% subsistence agric.

Finance: Monetary unit: Maloti (Sept. 1998: 6.23 = $1 U.S.). **Gross domestic product** (1996 est.): $3.7 bil. **Per capita GDP:** $1,860. **Imports** (1996 est.): $1.1 bil; partners: South Africa 83%. **Exports** (1996 est.): $218 mil; partners: South Africa 46%. **Tourism:** $20 mil. **National budget** (FY 1994-95): $400 mil. **International reserves less gold** (Mar. 1998): $604.59 mil. **Consumer prices** (change in 1997): 9.3%.

Transport: Railroad: Length: 1.6 mi. **Motor vehicles in use:** 5,000 passenger cars, 18,000 comm. vehicles. **Civil aviation:** 3.9 mil passenger-mi, 1 airport.

Communications: Television sets: 6.7 per 1,000 pop. **Radios:** 558 per 1,000 pop. **Telephones:** 1 per 111 persons. **Daily newspaper circ.:** 7.4 per 1,000 pop.

Health: Life expectancy at birth: 52.2 male; 55.8 female. **Births** (per 1,000 pop.): 32. **Deaths** (per 1,000 pop.): 13. **Natural increase:** 1.91%. **Hospital beds** (1992): 1 per 765 persons. **Physicians** (1993): 1 per 14,306 persons. **Infant mortality** 78.

Education: Free and compulsory: ages 6-13. **Literacy** (1995): 71%.

Major International Organizations: UN (FOA, IBRD, ILO, IMF, WHO, WTrO), the Commonwealth, OAU.

Embassy: 2511 Massachusetts Ave. NW 20008; 797-5533.

Lesotho (once called Basutoland) became a British protectorate in 1868 when Chief Moshesh sought protection against the Boers. Independence came Oct. 4, 1966. Elections were suspended in 1970. Most of Lesotho's GNP is provided by citizens working in South Africa. Livestock raising is the chief industry; diamonds are the chief export.

South Africa imposed a blockade, Jan. 1, 1986, because Lesotho had given sanctuary to anti-apartheid groups. The blockade sparked a Jan. 20 military coup, and was lifted, Jan. 25, when the new leaders agreed to expel the rebels.

(continued on p. 817)

PEACE IN NORTHERN IRELAND?

© 1998 PETER TURNLEY/BLACK STAR

AP/WIDE WORLD PHOTOS

AP/WIDE WORLD PHOTOS

Hopes for peace in Northern Ireland were revived when political leaders meeting in Belfast approved a groundbreaking settlement, Apr. 10. At top, a Belfast resident walks past a peace mural; above left, Irish Prime Minister Bertie Ahern (left) and British Prime Minister Tony Blair shake hands after the accord, also strongly endorsed by voters in referenda May 22. Nevertheless, terrorist violence continued; above right, police inspect debris from an Aug. 15 bombing in Omagh, the worst single act of violence in 3 decades; 29 people, mostly women and children, were killed.

WORLD EVENTS

© RAMAN/ACTION PRESS/SABA

India shocked much of the world when it set off 5 underground nuclear devices, May 11 and 13, in the desert. Pakistan conducted its own tests 2 weeks later. The actions of the governments were popular at home; above, demonstrators in New Delhi welcome the tests.

Cuban leader Fidel Castro greets Pope John Paul II after the pontiff said Mass before at least 250,000 in Havana's Plaza of the Revolution, Jan. 25. During his historic 5-day visit to the Communist state, the pope condemned human rights violations by Cuba but also called for an end to U.S. sanctions.

AP/WIDE WORLD PHOTOS

AP/WIDE WORLD PHOTOS

JOHNSON/GAMMA-LIAISON

Pres. Bill Clinton, escorted by Chinese Pres. Jiang Zemin, arrives in Beijing June 25 (left), in the first visit to China by a U.S. president since the 1989 Tiananmen Square demonstrations. Above, Clinton joins students at an Internet cafe in Shanghai.

NATION/SIPA PRESS

© DUDMAN/SYGMA

Pol Pot, the Khmer Rouge leader blamed for over a million deaths during his rule in Cambodia (1975-79), died Apr. 15. At left, he is cremated by dissident Khmer Rouge captors who had held him in the jungle since 1997. Above, Pol Pot in 1979.

SUVOROV/SEL/SIPA PRESS

Russians line up at a Moscow bank in late August, as the ruble collapsed and prices soared. The economic crisis put mounting political pressure on ailing Russian Pres. Boris Yeltsin.

AP/WIDE WORLD PHOTOS

AP/WIDE WORLD PHOTOS

University students hurl stones at Indonesian riot police during a protest east of the capital, May 13. Escalating riots over Pres. Suharto's handling of the country's economic crisis led to hundreds of deaths and induced Suharto (inset) to resign on May 21, ending his 32 years of autocratic rule over the world's 4th-most populous nation.

Arts and Entertainment

AP/WIDE WORLD PHOTOS/20th CENTURY FOX

Leonardo DiCaprio and Kate Winslet soared to stardom in the romantic blockbuster *Titanic,* which won 11 Oscars in 1998, including best picture, and grossed $1.8 billion by September.

In 1998, Helen Hunt won a best actress Oscar, and a Golden Globe award, for her performance in the film *As Good As It Gets;* she also won an Emmy for her starring role in the TV sitcom *Mad About You.*

AP/WIDE WORLD PHOTOS

PHOTOFEST

Saving Private Ryan won acclaim for its realistic portrayal of battle in World War II. Shown here (left to right) are Tom Hanks, Matt Damon, and Edward Burns, three of the film's stars.

JOAN MARCUS

The Broadway production of *The Lion King* won 6 Tonys in 1998, including best musical and best scenic design; the director, Julie Taymor, earned Tonys both for directing and for her creative costumes.

The last episode of *Seinfeld*—one of the most popular TV sitcoms ever—was aired on May 14. In it, the characters played by (from right) Michael Richards, Jason Alexander, Julia Louis-Dreyfus, and Jerry Seinfeld went on trial and ended up in jail.

AP/WIDE WORLD PHOTOS/NBC

The popular TV series *Ally McBeal* starred Calista Flockhart in the title role; she is shown here with Gil Bellows, playing a fellow lawyer she was once in love with.

PHOTOFEST/© FOX BROADCASTING

© REX USA LTD.

© M. EVANS/SYGMA

Show-biz legend Frank Sinatra, who died May 14 at age 82, started out as a crooner in the late 1930s and was still wowing audiences in the 1980s (left) and beyond; he also appeared in 58 films, including *Pal Joey* (far left).

SPORTS HIGHLIGHTS

Veteran Denver Broncos quarterback John Elway (7) pitches the ball to running back Terrell Davis (30) in Super Bowl XXXII against the Green Bay Packers, Jan. 25, 1998, in San Diego. The Broncos upset the Packers, 31-24, for their first Super Bowl win in 4 tries.

AP/WIDE WORLD PHOTOS

Chicago Bulls guard Michael Jordan (23), named MVP in the NBA Finals for a record 6th time, shoots over the Utah Jazz's Shandon Anderson in Game 6, June 14 in Salt Lake City. The Bulls beat the Jazz, 4 games to 2, for their 6th NBA title in 8 years.

AP/WIDE WORLD PHOTOS

SYGMA/TEMPSPORT/C. LIEWIG

French soccer midfielder Zinedine Zidane on the attack in the 1998 World Cup final against Brazil, July 12, in St.-Denis, France. France upset Brazil, the defending champ, 3-0, to win the tournament, for the first time ever.

On Sept. 8, St. Louis Cardinals slugger Mark McGwire hit his 62nd home run of the season (left) to break the record set by Roger Maris in 1961. Five days later, Chicago Cubs slugger Sammy Sosa hit number 62 to tie McGwire (at right, Sosa watches his homer leave the park). In the home run race that followed, McGwire came out on top, ending the season with a record 70 homers, as against 66 for Sosa.

AP/WIDE WORLD PHOTOS

AP/WIDE WORLD PHOTOS

AP/WIDE WORLD PHOTOS

Detroit Red Wings star Steve Yzerman (below) takes a shot on goal in Game 2 of the 1998 Stanley Cup Finals. The Red Wings swept the Washington Capitals to win their 2d Stanley Cup in a row; Yzerman was named playoffs MVP.

AP/WIDE WORLD PHOTOS

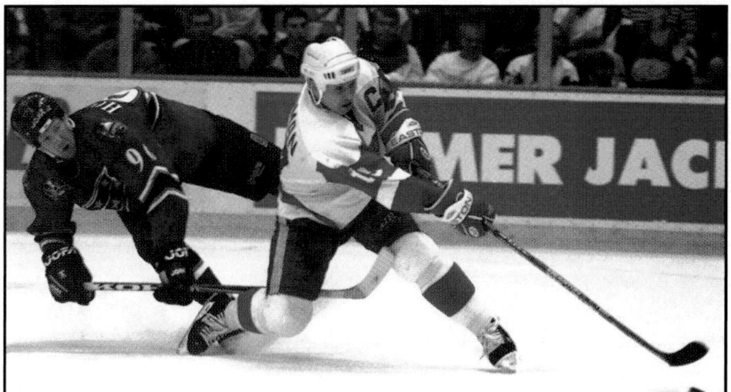

Women's NCAA Final Four MVP Chamique Holdsclaw of Tennessee leaps over her Louisiana Tech foes to score in the championship game, Mar. 29 in Kansas City. Tennessee won the game, 93-75, to take its 6th national title, and 3rd in a row.

WINTER OLYMPICS

After the favored Michelle Kwan skated a nearly flawless long program, another U.S. prodigy, 15-year-old Tara Lipinski, turned in an even more impressive performance to take the gold medal for figure skating at Nagano, Feb. 20.

JAMIE SQUIRE/ALLSPORT

SCHAUN BOTTERILL/ALLSPORT

While the highly favored U.S. men's hockey team had only a 1-3 record in the Winter Olympics at Nagano, Japan, the U.S. women's team went undefeated, surging to a 3-1 victory over Canada Feb. 17, for the first-ever Olympic championship in women's hockey. Above, Shelley Looney scores the 2d goal in the game, off Canadian goalie Manon Rheaume.

AP/WIDE WORLD PHOTOS

Austria's Hermann Maier makes a turn in the men's super giant slalom, Feb. 19, on Mount Higashidate in Japan. Maier, who went on to take the gold in this event and in the giant slalom, had emerged from a spectacular crash 3 days earlier with no serious injuries.

In Mar. 1990, King Moshoeshoe was exiled by the military government. Letsie III became king Nov. 12. In Mar. 1993, Ntsu Mokhehle, a civilian, was elected prime minister, ending 23 years of military rule. After a series of violent disturbances, the king dismissed the Mokhele government Aug. 17, 1994; constitutional rule was restored Sept. 14. Letsie abdicated and Moshoeshoe was reinstated Jan. 25, 1995.

Moshoeshoe died in an automobile accident, Jan. 15, 1996. Letsie was reinstated Feb. 7; his formal coronation was Oct. 31, 1997. South Africa and Botswana sent troops Sept. 22, 1998, to help suppress violent antigovernment protests. In Oct. 1998 the government and opposition agreed on a transitional structure plan with new elections in 18 months.

Liberia

Republic of Liberia

People: Population: 2,771,901. **Age distrib.** (%): <15: 44.7; 65+: 3.5. **Pop. density:** 72 per sq. mi. **Urban:** 46%. **Ethnic groups:** Indigenous tribes 95%, Americo-Liberians 5%. **Principal languages:** English (official), tribal languages. **Chief religions:** Traditional beliefs 70%, Muslim 20%, Christian 10%.

Geography: Area: 38,250 sq. mi. **Location:** On SW coast of W Africa. **Neighbors:** Sierra Leone on W, Guinea on N, Côte d'Ivoire on E. **Topography:** Marshy Atlantic coastline rises to low mountains and plateaus in the forested interior; 6 major rivers flow in parallel courses to the ocean. **Capital:** Monrovia: 962,000*.

Government: Type: Republic. **Head of state:** Pres. Charles Taylor; b Jan. 29, 1948; in office: Aug. 2, 1997. **Local divisions:** 13 counties. **Defense:** 3.3% of GDP. **Active troop strength:** 22,000.

Economy: Industries: Food processing, mining. **Chief crops:** Rice, cassava, coffee, cocoa, sugar. **Minerals:** Iron, diamonds, gold. **Other resources:** Rubber, timber. **Arable land:** 1%. **Livestock** (1997): chickens: 3.50 mil; goats: 220,000; sheep: 210,000; pigs: 120,000. **Electricity prod.** (1996): 480 mil kWh. **Labor force:** 71% agric.; 11% serv.

Finance: Monetary unit: Dollar (Sept. 1998: 1.00 = $1 U.S.). **Gross domestic product** (1995 est.): $2.4 bil. **Per capita GDP:** $1,100. **Imports** (1995): $5.8 bil; partners: Japan 33%; S. Korea 20%; Italy 9%. **Exports** (1995): $667 mil; partners: Belg.-Lux. 57%; Ukraine 12%. **National budget** (1994 est.): $285 mil.

Transport: Railroad: Length: 304.3 mi. **Motor vehicles in use:** 17,400 passenger cars, 10,700 comm. vehicles. **Civil aviation:** 4.3 mil passenger-mi; 1 airport. **Chief ports:** Monrovia, Buchanan, Greenville.

Communications: Television sets: 20 per 1,000 pop. **Radios:** 263 per 1,000 pop. **Telephones:** 1 per 625 persons. **Daily newspaper circ.:** 15 per 1,000 pop.

Health: Life expectancy at birth: 56.8 male; 62.2 female. **Births** (per 1,000 pop.): 42. **Deaths** (per 1,000 pop.): 11. **Natural increase:** 3.06%. **Physicians** (1992): 1 per 8,333 persons. **Infant mortality** (per 1,000 live births): 103.

Education: Free and compulsory: ages 7-16. **Literacy** (1995): 38%.

Major International Organizations: UN and most of its specialized agencies, OAU.

Embassy: 5201 16th St. NW 20011; 723-0437.

Liberia was founded in 1822 by U.S. black freedmen who settled at Monrovia with the aid of colonization societies. It became a republic July 26, 1847, with a constitution modeled on that of the U.S. Descendants of freedmen dominated politics.

Charging rampant corruption, an Army Redemption Council of enlisted men staged a bloody predawn coup, April 12, 1980, in which Pres. Tolbert was killed and replaced as head of state by Sgt. Samuel Doe. Doe was chosen president in a disputed election, and survived a subsequent coup, in 1985.

A civil war began Dec. 1989. Rebel forces seeking to depose Pres. Doe made major territorial gains and advanced on the capital, June 1990. In Sept., Doe was captured and put to death. Despite the introduction of peacekeeping forces from several countries, factional fighting intensified, and a series of cease-fires failed. A transitional Council of State was instituted Sept. 1, 1995. Factional fighting flared up again in Apr. 1996, devastating Monrovia.

On Sept. 3, 1996, Ruth Perry became modern Africa's first female head of state, leading another transitional government. By then, the civil war had claimed more than 150,000 lives and uprooted over half the population.

Former rebel leader Charles Taylor was elected president July 19, 1997, in Liberia's 1st national election in 12 years.

Libya

Socialist People's Libyan Arab Jamahiriya

People: Population: 5,690,727. **Age distrib.** (%): <15: 48.3; 65+: 2.9. **Pop. density:** 8 per sq. mi. **Urban:** 86%. **Ethnic groups:** Arab-Berber 97%. **Principal language:** Arabic (official), Italian, English. **Chief religion:** Sunni Muslim 97%.

Geography: Area: 679,358 sq. mi. **Location:** On Mediterranean coast of N Africa. **Neighbors:** Tunisia, Algeria on W; Niger, Chad on S; Sudan, Egypt on E. **Topography:** Desert and semidesert regions cover 92% of the land, with low mountains in N, higher mountains in S, and a narrow coastal zone. **Capital:** Tripoli: 1,681,000*.

Government: Type: Islamic Arabic Socialist "Mass-State." **Leader:** Col. Muammar al-Qaddafi; b Sept. 1942; in power: Sept. 1969. **Local divisions:** 13 regions subdivided into about 1500 communes. **Defense:** 5.1% of GDP. **Active troop strength:** 65,000.

Economy: Industries: Oil, food processing, textiles. **Chief crops:** Dates, olives, citrus, barley, wheat. **Minerals:** Gypsum, oil, gas. **Crude oil reserves** (1997): 29.5 bil bbls. **Arable land:** 1%. **Livestock** (1997): chickens: 17.00 mil; sheep: 4.50 mil; goats: 800,000; cattle: 160,000. **Electricity prod.** (1996): 17 bil kWh. **Labor force:** 31% ind.; 27% services; 24% govt.; 18% agric.

Finance: Monetary unit: Dinar (Sept. 1998: 1.00 = $1 U.S.). **Gross domestic product** (1995 est.): $34.5 bil. **Per capita GDP:** $6,570. **Imports** (1995 est.): $7.3 bil; partners: Italy 22%, Germany 14%. **Exports** (1995 est.): $8.4 bil; partners: Italy 41%, Germany 18%, Spain 10%. **Tourism:** $6 mil. **National budget** (1995 est.): $14.9 bil.

Transport: Motor vehicles in use: 592,000 passenger cars, 312,000 comm. vehicles. **Civil aviation:** 256.1 mil passenger-mi. **Chief ports:** Tripoli, Banghazi.

Communications: Television sets: 105 per 1,000 pop. **Radios:** 191 per 1,000 pop. **Telephones:** 1 per 17 persons. **Daily newspaper circ.:** 15 per 1,000 pop.

Health: Life expectancy at birth: 63.2 male; 67.8 female. **Births** (per 1,000 pop.): 44. **Deaths** (per 1,000 pop.): 7. **Natural increase:** 3.68%. **Infant mortality** (per 1,000 live births): 56.

Education: Compulsory: ages 6-15. **Literacy** (1995): 76%.

Major International Organizations: UN (FAO, IBRD, ILO, IMF, IMO, WHO), AL, OAU, OPEC.

First settled by Berbers, Libya was ruled in succession by Carthage, Rome, the Vandals, and the Ottomans. Italy ruled from 1912, and Britain and France after WW II. Libya became an independent constitutional monarchy Jan. 2, 1952. In 1969 a junta led by Col. Muammar al-Qaddafi seized power.

Libya and Egypt fought several air and land battles along their border in July 1977. Chad charged Libya with military occupation of its uranium-rich northern region in 1977. Libyan troops were driven from their last major stronghold by Chad forces in 1987, leaving over $1 billion in military equipment behind.

Libya reportedly helped arm violent revolutionary groups in Egypt and Sudan and aided terrorists of various nationalities.

On Jan. 7, 1986, the U.S. imposed economic sanctions against Libya, ordered all Americans to leave that country, and froze all Libyan assets in the U.S. The U.S. commenced flight operations over the Gulf of Sidra, Jan. 27, and a U.S. Navy task force began conducting exercises in the Gulf, Mar. 23. When Libya fired antiaircraft missiles at American warplanes, the U.S. responded by sinking 2 Libyan ships and bombing a missile site in Libya. The U.S. withdrew from the Gulf, Mar. 27.

The U.S. accused Qaddafi of having ordered the Apr. 5, 1986, bombing of a West Berlin discotheque, which killed 3, including a U.S. serviceman. In response, the U.S. sent warplanes to attack terrorist-related targets in Tripoli and Banghazi, Libya, Apr. 14.

The UN imposed limited sanctions, Apr. 15, 1992, for Libya's failure to extradite 2 agents linked to the 1988 bombing of Pan American World Airways Flight 103 over Lockerbie, Scotland, and 4 others linked to an airplane bombing over Niger. Sanctions were tightened Dec. 1, 1993. In 1996 the U.S. authorized sanctions on foreign firms that invest in Libya.

Liechtenstein

Principality of Liechtenstein

People: Population: 31,717. **Age distrib.** (%): <15: 18.9; 65+: 11.0. **Pop. density:** 511 per sq. mi. **Urban:** 21%. **Ethnic groups:** Alemannic 88%. **Principal languages:** German (official), Alemannic dialect. **Chief religions:** Roman Catholic 80%, Protestant 7%.

Geography: Area: 62 sq. mi. **Location:** Central Europe, in the Alps. **Neighbors:** Switzerland on W, Austria on E. **Topography:** The Rhine Valley occupies one-third of the country, the Alps cover the rest. **Capital:** Vaduz (1997 est.): 5,017.

Government: Type: Hereditary constitutional monarchy. **Head of state:** Prince Hans-Adam II; b Feb 14, 1945; in office: Nov. 13, 1989. **Head of government:** Mario Frick; b May 8, 1965; in office: Dec. 15, 1993. **Local divisions:** 11 communes.

Economy: Industries: Precision instruments, electronics, textiles, ceramics. **Chief crops:** Grain, corn, potatoes. **Arable land:** 25%. **Labor force:** 53% services; 45% industry, trade, constr.

Finance: Monetary unit: Swiss Franc (Sept. 1998: 1.42 = $1 U.S.). **Gross domestic product** (1996 est.): $713 mil. **Per capita GDP:** $23,000. **Imports** (1994): $852.3 mil. **Exports** (1994): $2.14 bil; partners: Switzerland 16%. **National budget** (1996 est.): $435 mil.

Transport: Railroad: Length: 11.5 mi.

Communications: Television sets: 371 per 1,000 pop. **Radios:** 384 per 1,000 pop. **Telephones:** 1 per 1.6 persons. **Daily newspaper circ.:** 564 per 1,000 pop.

Health: Life expectancy at birth: 75.5 male; 80.5 female. **Births** (per 1,000 pop.): 13. **Deaths** (per 1,000 pop.): 7. **Natural increase:** 0.53%. **Physicians** (1995): 1 per 962 persons. **Infant mortality** (per 1,000 live births): 5.

Education: Compulsory: ages 7-16. **Literacy** (1997): 100%.

Major International Organizations: UN (WTrO), EFTA, OSCE.

Liechtenstein became sovereign in 1806. Austria administered Liechtenstein's ports up to 1920; Switzerland has administered its postal services since 1921. Liechtenstein is united with Switzerland by a customs and monetary union. Taxes are low; many international corporations have headquarters there. Foreign workers comprise a third of the population.

Lithuania

Republic of Lithuania

People: Population: 3,600,158. **Age distrib.** (%): <15: 20.5; 65+: 13.0. **Pop. density:** 143 per sq. mi. **Urban:** 73%. **Ethnic groups:** Lithuanian 80%, Russian 9%, Polish 8%. **Principal languages:** Lithuanian (official), Polish, Russian. **Chief religions:** Primarily Roman Catholic.

Geography: Area: 25,174 sq. mi. **Location:** In E Europe, on SE coast of Baltic. **Neighbors:** Latvia on N, Belarus on E, S, Poland and Russia on W. **Capital:** Vilnius. **Cities** (1996 est.): Vilnius 573,200; Kaunas 410,800.

Government: Type: Republic. **Head of state:** Pres. Valdas Adamkus; b Nov. 3, 1926; in office: Feb. 26, 1998. **Head of government:** Prime Min. Gediminas Vagnorius; b June 10, 1957; in office: Nov. 28, 1996. **Local divisions:** 10 regions. **Defense:** 4.3% of GDP. **Active troop strength:** 5,100.

Economy: Industries: Machinery, shipbuilding, textiles. **Chief crops:** Sugar beets, grain, potatoes, vegetables. **Crude oil reserves** (1997): 12 mil bbls. **Arable land:** 35%. **Livestock** (1997): chickens: 7.60 mil; pigs: 1.13 mil; cattle: 980,000. **Electricity prod.** (1996): 14.5 bil kWh. **Labor force:** 22% agric., forestry; 18% manuf., mining.

Finance: Monetary unit: Litas (Sept. 1998: 4.00 = $1 U.S.). **Gross domestic product** (1996 est.): $14.1 bil. **Per capita GDP:** $3,870. **Imports** (1996 est.): $4.56 bil; partners: Russia 31%; Germany 15%. **Exports** (1996 est.): $3.3 bil; partners: Russia 20%; Germany 14%. **Tourism:** $360 mil. **National budget** (1995): $1.5 bil. **International reserves less gold** (June 1998): $1.11 bil. **Gold:** 186,400 oz t. **Consumer prices** (change in 1997): 8.9%.

Transport: Railroad: Length: 1,802 mi. **Motor vehicles in use:** 653,000 passenger cars, 111,000 comm. vehicles. **Civil aviation:** 188.8 mil passenger-mi; 3 airports. **Chief port:** Klaipeda.

Communications: Television sets: 364 per 1,000 pop. **Radios:** 404 per 1,000 pop. **Telephones:** 1 per 3.9 persons. **Daily newspaper circ.:** 136 per 1,000 pop.

Health: Life expectancy at birth: 62.8 male; 75.2 female. **Births** (per 1,000 pop.): 11. **Deaths** (per 1,000 pop.): 13. **Natural increase:** –0.24%. **Hospital beds** (1995): 1 per 92 persons. **Physicians** (1995): 1 per 252 persons. **Infant mortality** (per 1,000 live births): 15.

Education: Free and compulsory: ages 7-16. Literacy (1989): 98%.

Major International Organizations: UN (FAO, IBRD, ILO, IMF, IMO, WHO), OSCE.

Embassy: 2622 16th St. NW 20009; 234-5860.

Website: http://www.std.lt

Lithuania was occupied by the German army, 1914-18. It was annexed by the Soviet Russian army, but the Soviets were overthrown, 1919. Lithuania was a democratic republic until 1926, when the regime was ousted by a coup. In 1939 the Soviet-German treaty assigned most of Lithuania to the Soviet sphere of influence. Lithuania was annexed by the USSR Aug. 3, 1940.

Lithuania formally declared its independence from the Soviet Union Mar. 11, 1990. During an abortive Soviet coup in Aug., the Western nations recognized Lithuania's independence, which was ratified by the Soviet Union in Sept. 1991.

The last Russian troops withdrew on Aug. 31, 1993. Lithuania applied to join the European Union, Dec. 8, 1995. The conservative Homeland Union defeated the former Communists in parliamentary elections Oct. 20 and Nov. 10, 1996. A Lithuanian-American, Valdas Adamkus, won the presidency in a runoff election Jan. 4, 1998.

Luxembourg

Grand Duchy of Luxembourg

People: Population: 425,017. **Age distrib.** (%): <15: 18.2; 65+: 14.8. **Pop. density:** 385 per sq. mi. **Urban:** 90%. **Ethnic groups:** Mixture of French and Germans predominates. **Principal languages:** French, German, Luxembourgisch, English. **Chief religion:** Roman Catholic 97%.

Geography: Area: 1,103 sq. mi. **Location:** In W Europe. **Neighbors:** Belgium on W, France on S, Germany on E. **Topography:** Heavy forests (Ardennes) cover N, S is a low, open plateau. **Capital:** Luxembourg (1997 est.): 78,300.

Government: Type: Constitutional monarchy. **Head of state:** Grand Duke Jean; b Jan. 5, 1921; in office: Nov. 12, 1964. **Head of government:** Prime Min. Jean-Claude Juncker; b Dec. 9, 1954; in office: Jan. 19, 1995. **Local divisions:** 3 districts. **Defense:** 0.7% of GDP. **Active troop strength:** 800.

Economy: Industries: Steel, chemicals, food processing, tires, banking, engineering, metal products. **Chief crops:** Grains, potatoes, wine grapes. **Arable land:** 24%. **Electricity prod.** (1996): 381 mil kWh. **Labor force:** 60% services; 37% ind.; 3% agric.

Finance: Monetary unit: Franc (Sept. 1998: 35.74 = $1 U.S.). **Gross domestic product** (1995 est.): $10 bil. **Per capita GDP:** $24,500. **Imports** (1995 est.) $9.1 mil; partners: Belgium 38%; Germany 25%. **Exports** (1995 est.): $7.3 mil; partners: Germany 28%; France 18%. **Tourism:** $297 mil. **National budget** (1997 est.): $5.44 bil. **International reserves less gold** (Apr. 1998): $77.17 mil. **Gold:** 305,000 oz t. **Consumer prices** (change in 1997): 1.4%.

Transport: Railroad: Length: 170.8 mi. **Motor vehicles in use:** 231,666 passenger cars, 16,665 comm. vehicles. **Civil aviation:** 261.4 mil passenger-mi; 1 airport. **Chief port:** Mertert.

Communications: Television sets: 384 per 1,000 pop. **Radios:** 586 per 1,000 pop. **Telephones:** 1 per 1.8 persons. **Daily newspaper circ.:** 381 per 1,000 pop.

Health: Life expectancy at birth: 74.4 male; 80.7 female. **Births** (per 1,000 pop.): 11. **Deaths** (per 1,000 pop.): 9. **Natural increase:** 0.18%. **Hospital beds** (1994): 1 per 92 persons. **Physicians** (1995): 1 per 454 persons. **Infant mortality** (per 1,000 live births): 5.

Education: Compulsory: ages 6-15. **Literacy** (1995): 100%.

Major International Organizations: UN (FAO, IBRD, ILO, IMF, IMO, WHO, WTrO), EU, NATO, OECD, OSCE.

Embassy: 2200 Massachusetts Ave. NW 20008; 265-4171.

Luxembourg, founded about 963, was ruled by Burgundy, Spain, Austria, and France from 1448 to 1815. It left the Germanic Confederation in 1866. Overrun by Germany in 2 world wars, Luxembourg ended its neutrality in 1948, when a customs union with Belgium and Netherlands was adopted.

Macedonia

Former Yugoslav Republic of Macedonia

People: Population: 2,009,387. **Age distrib.** (%): <15: 23.6; 65+: 9.4. **Pop. density:** 205 per sq. mi. **Urban:** 60%. **Ethnic groups:** Macedonian 65%, Albanian 22%. **Principal languages:** Macedonian (official), Albanian, Serbo-Croatian. **Chief religions:** Eastern Orthodox 67%, Muslim 30%.

Geography: Area: 9,781 sq. mi. **Location:** In SE Europe. **Neighbors:** Bulgaria on E, Greece on S, Albania on W, Serbia on N. **Capital:** Skopje (1994 cen.): 541,280.

Government: Type: Republic. **Head of state:** Pres. Kiro Gligorov; b May 3, 1917; in office: Jan. 27, 1991. **Head of government:** Prime Min. Branko Crvenkovski; b Oct. 12, 1962; in office: Sept. 4, 1992. **Local divisions:** 123 communities. **Defense:** 9.2% of GDP. **Active troop strength:** 10,400.

Economy: Industries: Mining, textiles. **Chief crops:** Wheat, rice, cotton, tobacco. **Minerals:** Chromium, lead, zinc. **Arable land:** 24%. **Livestock** (1997): chickens: 3.36 mil; sheep: 1.81 mil; cattle: 294,600; pigs: 192,400. **Electricity prod.** (1996): 6.1 bil kWh. **Labor force:** 23% manuf. & mining; 12% services.

Finance: Monetary unit: Dinar (Sept. 1998: 54.29 = $1 U.S.). **Gross domestic product** (1996 est.): $2.0 bil. **Per capita GDP:** $960. **Imports** (1996 est.): $1.4 bil; partners: Germany 15%. **Exports** (1996 est.): $900 mil; Germany 13%. **National budget** (1996 est.): $1.0 bil. **International reserves less gold** (May 1998): $236.88 mil. **Gold:** 82,000.

Transport: Railroad: Length: 573 mi. **Motor vehicles in use:** 263,000 passenger cars, 23,000 comm. vehicles. **Civil aviation:** 254.3 mil passenger-mi; 2 airports.

Communications: Television sets: 179 per 1,000 pop. **Radios:** 179 per 1,000 pop. **Telephones:** 1 per 6.1 persons. **Daily newspaper circ.:** 21 per 1,000 pop.

Health: Life expectancy at birth: 70.7 male; 75.0 female. **Births** (per 1,000 pop.): 16. **Deaths** (per 1,000 pop.): 8. **Natural increase:** 0.76%. **Hospital beds** (1994): 1 per 195 persons. **Physicians** (1994): 1 per 437 persons. **Infant mortality** (per 1,000 live births): 19.

Education: Free and compulsory: ages 7-15. **Literacy** (1996): 89%.

Major International Organizations: UN (FAO, IBRD, ILO, IMF, IMO, WHO), OSCE.

Embassy: 3050 K St. NW 20007; 337-3063.

Macedonia, as part of a larger region also called Macedonia, was ruled by Muslim Turks from 1389 to 1912, when native Greeks, Bulgarians, and Slavs won independence. Serbia received the largest part of the territory, with the rest going to Greece and Bulgaria. In 1913, the area was incorporated into Serbia, which in 1918 became part of the Kingdom of Serbs, Croats, and Slovenes (later Yugoslavia). In 1946, Macedonia became a constituent republic of Yugoslavia.

Macedonia declared its independence Sept. 8, 1991, and was admitted to the UN under a provisional name in 1993. A UN force, which included several hundred U.S. troops, was deployed there to deter the warring factions in Bosnia from carrying their dispute into other areas of the Balkans.

In Feb. 1994 both Russia and the U.S. recognized Macedonia. Greece, which objected to Macedonia's use of what it considered a Hellenic name and symbols, imposed a trade blockade on the landlocked nation; the 2 countries agreed to normalize relations Sept. 13, 1995. A car bombing, Oct. 3, seriously injured Pres. Kiro Gligorov. Macedonia and Yugoslavia signed a treaty normalizing relations Apr. 8, 1996.

Madagascar

Republic of Madagascar

People: Population: 14,462,509. **Age distrib.** (%): <15: 44.7; 65+: 3.3. **Pop. density:** 64 per sq. mi. **Urban:** 27%. **Ethnic groups:** 18 Malayo-Indonesian tribes (Merina 26%), with Arab and African presence. **Principal languages:** Malagasy, French (both official). **Chief religions:** Indigenous beliefs 52%, Christian 41%, Muslim 7%.

Geography: Area: 226,656 sq. mi. **Location:** In the Indian O., off the SE coast of Africa. **Neighbors:** Comoro Isls. to NW, Mozambique to W. **Topography:** Humid coastal strip in the E, fertile valleys in the mountainous center plateau region, and a wider coastal strip on the W. **Capital:** Antananarivo: 876,000*.

Government: Type: Republic. **Head of state:** Pres. Didier Ratsiraka; b Nov. 4, 1936; in office: Jan. 31, 1997. **Head of government:** Tantely Andrianarivo; in office: July 23, 1998. **Local divisions:** 6 provinces. **Defense:** 0.8% of GDP. **Active troop strength:** 21,000.

Economy: Industries: Meat processing, textiles. **Chief crops:** Coffee, cloves, vanilla beans, rice, sugar, cassava, peanuts. **Minerals:** Chromite, graphite, coal, bauxite. **Arable land:** 4%. **Livestock** (1997): chickens: 16.50 mil; cattle: 10.33 mil; pigs: 1.66 mil; goats: 1.33 mil; sheep: 760,000. **Fish catch** (1996): 113,015 metric tons. **Electricity prod.** (1996): 595 mil kWh. **Labor force:** 86% agric.

Finance: Monetary unit: Franc (Sept. 1998: 5,400.00 = $1 U.S.). **Gross domestic product** (1996 est.): $12.1 bil. **Per capita GDP:** $880. **Imports** (1996 est.): $612 mil; partners: France 40%. **Exports** (1996 est.): $493 mil; partners: France 41%. **Tourism:** $67 mil. **National budget** (1991): $265 mil. **International reserves less gold** (June 1998): $246.6 mil. **Consumer prices** (change in 1997): 4.5%.

Transport: Railroad: Length: 640 mi. **Motor vehicles in use:** 58,100 passenger cars, 15,860 comm. vehicles. **Civil aviation:** 409.2 mil passenger-mi; 44 airports. **Chief ports:** Toamasina, Antsiranana, Mahajanga, Toliara.

Communications: Television sets: 20 per 1,000 pop. **Radios:** 193 per 1,000 pop. **Telephones:** 1 per 413 persons.

Health: Life expectancy at birth: 51.7 male; 54.1 female. **Births** (per 1,000 pop.): 42. **Deaths** (per 1,000 pop.): 14. **Natural increase:** 2.81%. **Infant mortality** (per 1,000 live births): 91.

Education: Compulsory for 5 years between ages 6 and 13. **Literacy** (1995): 46%.

Major International Organizations: UN (FAO, IBRD, ILO, IMF, IMO, WHO, WTrO), OAU.

Embassy: 2374 Massachusetts Ave. NW 20008; 265-5525.

Website: http://www3.itu.ch/missions/Madagascar

Madagascar was settled 2,000 years ago by Malayan-Indonesian people, whose descendants still predominate. A unified kingdom ruled the 18th and 19th centuries. The island became a French protectorate, 1885, and a colony 1896. Independence came June 26, 1960.

Discontent with inflation and French domination led to a coup in 1972. The new regime nationalized French-owned financial interests, closed French bases and a U.S. space-tracking station, and obtained Chinese aid. The government conducted a program of arrests, expulsion of foreigners, and repression of strikes, 1979.

In 1990, Madagascar ended a ban on multiparty politics that had been in place since 1975. Albert Zafy was elected president in 1993, ending the 17-year rule of Adm. Didier Ratsiraka. After Zafy was impeached by the legislature, Madagascar's constitutional court removed him from office, Sept. 5, 1996. Prime Min. Norbert Ratsirahonana then became interim president pending national elections, Nov. 3 and Dec. 29, in which Ratsiraka edged Zafy.

Malawi

Republic of Malawi

People: Population: 9,840,474. **Age distrib.** (%): <15: 45.5; 65+: 2.7. **Pop. density:** 215 per sq. mi. **Urban:** 14%. **Ethnic groups:** Chewa, Nyanja, Lomwe, other Bantu tribes. **Principal languages:** English, Chichewa (both official). **Chief religions:** Protestant 55%, Muslim 20%, Roman Catholic 20%.

Geography: Area: 45,745 sq. mi. **Location:** In SE Africa. **Neighbors:** Zambia on W, Mozambique on S and E, Tanzania on N. **Topography:** Malawi stretches 560 mi. N-S along Lake Malawi (Lake Nyasa), most of which belongs to Malawi. High plateaus and mountains line the Rift Valley the length of the nation. **Capital:** Lilongwe. **Cities** (1994 est.): Blantyre 446,800; Lilongwe 395,500.

Government: Type: Multiparty democracy. **Head of state and government:** Pres. Bakili Muluzi; b Mar. 17, 1943; in office: May 21, 1994. **Local divisions:** 24 districts. **Defense:** 1.2% of GNP. **Active troop strength:** 9,800.

Economy: Industries: Agricultural processing, cement. **Chief crops:** Tea, tobacco, sugar, cotton, corn, potatoes. **Arable land:** 18%. **Livestock** (1997): chickens: 14.20 mil; goats: 1.26 mil; cattle: 710,000; pigs: 230,000; sheep: 101,000. **Fish catch** (1996): 63,569 metric tons. **Electricity prod.** (1996): 800 mil kWh. **Labor force:** 86% agric.

Finance: Monetary unit: Kwacha (Sept. 1998: 39.21 = $1 U.S.). **Gross domestic product** (1996 est.): $7.5 bil. **Per capita GDP:** $800. **Imports** (1995 est.): $348 mil; partners: South Africa 44%. **Exports** (1995 est.): $431 mil; partners: South Africa 16%, Germany 15%. **Tourism:** $7 mil. **National budget** (1993): $674 mil. **International reserves less gold** (June 1998): $191.02 mil. **Gold:** 13,000 oz t.

Transport: Railroad: Length: 490 mi. **Motor vehicles in use:** 25,400 passenger cars, 28,900 comm. vehicles. **Civil aviation:** 71.7 mil passenger-mi; 5 airports.

Communications: Radios: 112 per 1,000 pop. **Telephones:** 1 per 283 persons.

Health: Life expectancy at birth: 36.6 male; 36.5 female. **Births** (per 1,000 pop.): 40. **Deaths** (per 1,000 pop.): 24.

Natural increase: 1.6%. **Infant mortality** (per 1,000 live births): 134.

Education: Compulsory: ages 6-14. **Literacy** (1995): 56%.

Major International Organizations: UN (FAO, IBRD, ILO, IMF, IMO, WHO, WTrO), the Commonwealth, OAU.

Embassy: 2408 Massachusetts Ave. NW 20008; 797-1007.

Bantus came to the land in the 16th century, Arab slavers in the 19th. The area became the British protectorate Nyasaland in 1891. It became independent July 6, 1964, and a republic in 1966. After 3 decades as a one-party state under Pres. Hastings Kamuzu Banda, Malawi adopted a new constitution and, in multiparty elections held May 17, 1994, chose a new leader, Bakili Muluzi. Banda was acquitted, Dec. 23, 1995, of complicity in the deaths of 4 political opponents in 1983; he died Nov. 25, 1997.

Malaysia

People: Population: 20,932,901. **Age distrib.** (%): <15: 35.7; 65+: 3.9. **Pop. density:** 164 per sq. mi. **Urban:** 54%. **Ethnic groups:** Malay and other indigenous 58%, Chinese 26%, Indian 7%. **Principal languages:** Malay (official), English, Chinese dialects. Indian languages. **Chief religions:** Muslim, Hindu, Buddhist, Christian.

Geography: Area: 127,316 sq. mi. **Location:** On the SE tip of Asia, plus the N coast of the island of Borneo. **Neighbors:** Thailand on N, Indonesia on S. **Topography:** Most of W Malaysia is covered by tropical jungle, including the central mountain range that runs N-S through the peninsula. The western coast is marshy, the eastern, sandy. E Malaysia has a wide, swampy coastal plain, with interior jungles and mountains. **Capital:** Kuala Lumpur: 1,236,000*.

Government: Type: Federal parliamentary democracy with a constitutional monarch. **Head of state:** Paramount Ruler Tuanku Ja'afar ibni Al-Marhum Tuanku Abdul Rahman; b July 19, 1922; in office: Apr. 26, 1994. **Head of government:** Prime Min. Datuk Seri Mahathir bin Mohamad; b Dec. 20, 1925; in office: July 16, 1981. **Local divisions:** 13 states, 2 federal territories. **Defense:** 4.2% of GDP. **Active troop strength:** 114,500 troops.

Economy: Industries: Rubber goods, logging, electronics, petroleum production. **Chief crops:** Palm oil (world's leading producer), rice, pepper. **Minerals:** Tin (a leading producer), oil, bauxite, cooper, iron. **Crude oil reserves** (1997): 3.9 bil bbls. **Other resources:** Rubber, timber. **Arable land:** 3%. **Livestock** (1997): chickens: 110.00 mil; pigs: 3.40 mil; cattle: 725,000; goats: 320,000; sheep: 255,000; buffalo: 150,000. **Fish catch** (1996): 1.13 mil metric tons. **Electricity prod.** (1996): 48 bil kWh. **Labor force:** 29% services and trade; 25% manuf.; 21% agric.

Finance: Monetary unit: Ringgit (Sept. 1998: 3.80 = $1 U.S.). **Gross domestic product** (1996 est.): $214.7 bil. **Per capita GDP:** $10,750. **Imports** (1996): $83.2 bil; partners: Japan 27%, U.S. 16%, Singapore 12%. **Exports** (1996): $84.6 bil; partners: U.S. 21%, Singapore 20%. **Tourism:** $3.85 bil. **National budget** (1996 est.): $22.0 bil. **International reserves less gold** (May 1998): $19.72 bil. **Gold:** 2.37 mil oz t. **Consumer prices** (change in 1997): 2.7%.

Transport: Railroad: Length: 1,121.5 mi. **Motor vehicles in use:** 2.95 mil passenger cars, 38,965 comm. vehicles. **Civil aviation:** 16.68 bil passenger-mi; 39 airports. **Chief ports:** Kuantan, Kelang, Kota Kinabalu, Kuching.

Communications: Television sets: 454 per 1,000 pop. **Radios:** 449 per 1,000 pop. **Telephones:** 1 per 6.0 persons. **Daily newspaper circ.:** 139 per 1,000 pop.

Health: Life expectancy at birth: 67.4 male; 73.6 female. **Births** (per 1,000 pop.): 27. **Deaths** (per 1,000 pop.): 5. **Natural increase:** 2.11%. **Hospital beds** (1995): 1 per 507 persons. **Physicians** (1995): 1 per 2,153 persons. **Infant mortality** (per 1,000 live births): 22.

Education: Free and compulsory: ages 6-16. **Literacy** (1995): 83%.

Major International Organizations: UN (FAO, IBRD, ILO, IMF, IMO, WHO, WTrO), APEC, ASEAN, the Commonwealth.

Embassy: 2401 Massachusetts Ave. NW 20008; 328-2700.

Website: http://www.jaring.my

European traders appeared in the 16th century; Britain established control in 1867. Malaysia was created Sept. 16, 1963. It included Malaya (which had become independent in 1957 after the suppression of Communist rebels), plus the formerly British Singapore, Sabah (N Borneo), and Sarawak (NW Borneo). Singapore was separated in 1965, in order to end tensions between Chinese, the majority in Singapore, and Malays in control of the Malaysian government.

A monarch is elected by a council of hereditary rulers of the Malayan states every 5 years.

Abundant natural resources have bolstered prosperity, and foreign investment has aided industrialization. Work on a new federal capital at Putrajaya, south of Kuala Lumpur, began in 1995. However, sagging stock and currency prices forced the postponement of major development projects in Sept. 1997.

As the recession deepened and political unrest grew, Prime Min. Mahathir bin Mohamad imposed new currency controls and fired his popular deputy prime minister, Anwar bin Ibrahim, Sept. 2, 1998. Anwar, who then called for Mahathir's resignation, was arrested Sept. 20.

Maldives

Republic of Maldives

People: Population: 290,211. **Age distrib.** (%): <15: 47.2; 65+: 3.1. **Pop. density:** 2,501 per sq. mi. **Urban:** 27%. **Ethnic groups:** Sinhalese, Dravidian, Arab, African. **Principal languages:** Divehi (Sinhalese dialect; official), English. **Chief religion:** Sunni Muslim.

Geography: Area: 116 sq. mi. **Location:** In the Indian O., SW of India. **Neighbors:** Nearest is India on N. **Topography:** 19 atolls with 1,190 islands, 198 inhabited. None of the islands are over 5 sq. mi. in area, and all are nearly flat. **Capital:** Male (1995 est.): 62,973.

Government: Type: Republic. **Head of state:** Pres. Maumoon Abdul Gayoom; b Dec. 29, 1937; in office: Nov. 11, 1978. **Local divisions:** 20 atolls and Male.

Economy: Industries: Fish processing, tourism. **Chief crops:** Coconuts, corn, sweet potatoes. **Arable land:** 10%. **Fish catch** (1996): 105,558 metric tons. **Electricity prod.** (1996): 60 mil kWh. **Labor force:** 25% fishing & agric.; 21% manuf. and const.; 16% trade.

Finance: Monetary unit: Rufiyaa (Sept. 1998: 11.77 = $1 U.S.). **Gross domestic product** (1995 est.): $423 mil. **Per capita GDP:** $1,620. **Imports** (1995 est.): $268 mil; partners: Singapore 32%. **Exports** (1995 est.): $50 mil; partners: UK 22%, Sri Lanka 18%. **Tourism:** $287 mil. **National budget** (1995 est.): $141 mil. **International reserves less gold** (June 1998): $114.82 mil. **Consumer prices** (change in 1997): 7.6%.

Transport: Civil aviation: 156.4 mil passenger-mi; 5 airports. **Chief port:** Male.

Communications: Television sets: 19 per 1,000 pop. **Radios:** 96 per 1,000 pop. **Telephones:** 1 per 18 persons.

Health: Life expectancy at birth: 65.9 male; 69.4 female. **Births** (per 1,000 pop.): 40. **Deaths** (per 1,000 pop.): 6. **Natural increase:** 3.42%. **Hospital beds** (1995): 1 per 1,192 persons. **Physicians** (1996): 1 per 2,587 persons. **Infant mortality** (per 1,000 live births): 41.

Education: Literacy (1995): 93%.

Major International Organizations: UN (FAO, IBRD, IMF, IMO, WHO, WTrO), the Commonwealth.

Website: http://www.undp.org:81/missions/maldives/maldives.htm

The islands had been a British protectorate since 1887. The country became independent July 26, 1965. Long a sultanate, the Maldives became a republic in 1968. Natural resources and tourism are being developed; however, the Maldives remains one of the world's poorest countries.

Mali

Republic of Mali

People: Population: 10,108,569. **Age distrib.** (%): <15: 47.4; 65+: 3.2. **Pop. density:** 21 per sq. mi. **Urban:** 28%. **Ethnic groups:** Mande (Bambara, Malinke, Sarakole) 50%, Peul 17%, Voltaic 12%, Tuareg and Moor 10%, Songhai 6%. **Principal languages:** French (official), Bambara, numerous African languages. **Chief religions:** Muslim 90%, indigenous beliefs 9%.

Geography: Area: 482,077 sq. mi. **Location:** In the interior of W Africa. **Neighbors:** Mauritania, Senegal on W; Guinea, Côte d'Ivoire, Burkina Faso on S; Niger on E; Algeria on N. **Topography:** A landlocked grassy plain in the upper basins of the Senegal and Niger rivers, extending N into the Sahara. **Capital:** Bamako: 919,000*.

Government: Type: Republic. **Head of state:** Pres. Alpha Oumar Konare; b Feb. 2, 1946; in office: June 8, 1992. **Head of government:** Prime Min. Ibrahim Boubakar Keita; b Jan. 29, 1945; in office: Feb. 4, 1994. **Local divisions:** 8 regions, 1 capital district. **Defense:** 1.8% of GDP. **Active troop strength:** 7,400.

Economy: Chief crops: Millet, rice, peanuts, cotton. **Minerals:** Gold, phosphates, kaolin. **Arable land:** 2%. **Livestock** (1997): chickens: 24.00 mil; goats: 8.55 mil; cattle: 5.73 mil; sheep: 5.95 mil. **Fish catch** (1996): 111,910 metric tons. **Electricity prod.** (1996): 288 mil kWh. **Labor force:** 80% agric.; 19% services.

Finance: Monetary unit: CFA Franc (Sept. 1998: 580.94 = $1 U.S.). **Gross domestic product** (1995 est.): $5.8 bil. **Per capita GDP:** $600. **Imports** (1994): $422 mil; partners: Côte d'Ivoire 27%, France 17%. **Exports** (1994): $320 mil; partners: China 13%. **Tourism:** $21 mil. **National budget** (1997 est.): $770 mil. **International reserves less gold** (Mar. 1998): $408.6 mil. **Gold:** 19,000 oz t. **Consumer prices** (change in 1997): -0.4%.

Transport: Railroad: Length: 398.1 mi. **Motor vehicles in use:** 24,700 passenger cars, 17,100 comm. vehicles. **Civil aviation:** 139.6 mil passenger-mi; 9 airports. **Chief port:** Koulikoro.

Communications: Television sets: 12 per 1,000 pop. **Radios:** 168 per 1,000 pop. **Telephones:** 1 per 573 persons.

Health: Life expectancy at birth: 45.7 male; 48.4 female. **Births** (per 1,000 pop.): 50. **Deaths** (per 1,000 pop.): 19. **Natural increase:** 3.08%. **Physicians** (1993): 1 per 18,376 persons. **Infant mortality** (per 1,000 live births): 122.

Education: Free and compulsory: ages 7-16. **Literacy** (1995): 31%.

Major International Organizations: UN and most of its specialized agencies, OAU.

Embassy: 2130 R St. NW 20008; 332-2249.

Website: http://www.undp.org/undp/fomli

Until the 15th century the area was part of the great Mali Empire. Timbuktu (Tombouctou) was a center of Islamic study. French rule was secured, 1898. The Sudanese Rep. and Senegal became independent as the Mali Federation June 20, 1960, but Senegal withdrew, and the Sudanese Rep. was renamed Mali.

Mali signed economic agreements with France and, in 1963, with Senegal. In 1968, a coup ended the socialist regime. Famine struck in 1973-74, killing as many as 100,000 people. Drought conditions returned in the 1980s.

The military, Mar. 26, 1991, overthrew the government of Pres. Amadou Toumani Traoré, who had been in power since 1968. Oumar Konare, a coup leader, was elected president, Apr. 26, 1992. A peace accord between the government and a Tuareg rebel group was signed in June 1994. Konare and his party won a series of flawed elections, Apr.-Aug. 1997.

Malta

Republic of Malta

People: Population: 379,563. **Age distrib.** (%): <15: 20.8; 65+: 11.6. **Pop. density:** 3,061 per sq. mi. **Urban:** 90%. **Ethnic group:** Maltese. **Principal languages:** Maltese, English (both official). **Chief religion:** Roman Catholic 98%.

Geography: Area: 124 sq. mi. **Location:** In center of Mediterranean Sea. **Neighbors:** Nearest is Italy on N. **Topography:** Island of Malta is 95 sq. mi.; other islands in the group: Gozo, 26 sq. mi.; Comino, 1 sq. mi. The coastline is heavily indented. Low hills cover the interior. **Capital:** Valletta (1996 est.): 9,128.

Government: Type: Parliamentary democracy. **Head of state:** Pres. Ugo Mifsud Bonnici; b Nov. 8, 1932; in office: Apr. 4, 1994. **Head of government:** Prime Min. Edward Fenech-Adami; b Feb. 7, 1934; in office: Sept. 6, 1998. **Local divisions:** 3 regions comprising 67 localities. **Defense:** 1.1% of GDP. **Active troop strength:** 2,000.

Economy: Industries: Tourism, electronics, construction, textiles, food & beverages. **Chief crops:** Potatoes, cauliflower, melons, tomatoes. **Arable land:** 38%. **Livestock** (1997): chickens: 820,000. **Electricity prod.** (1996): 1.4 bil kWh. **Labor force:** 37% pub. svces; 28% services; 25% manuf. & const.

Finance: Monetary unit: Lira (Sept. 1998: 2.60 = $1 U.S.). **Gross domestic product** (1996 est.): $4.7 bil. **Per capita GDP:** $12,600. **Imports** (1995): $3.0 bil; partners: Italy 27%, Germany 14%, UK 13%. **Exports** (1995): $1.9 bil; partners: Italy 32%, Germany 16%. **Tourism:** $647 mil. **National budget** (1996 est.): $1.69 bil. **International reserves less gold** (Nov. 1997): $1.49 bil. **Gold:** 11,000 oz t. **Consumer prices** (change in 1997): 3.3%.

Transport: Motor vehicles in use: 122,100 passenger cars, 19,100 comm. vehicles. **Civil aviation:** 1.03 bil passenger-mi; 1 airport. **Chief port:** Valletta.

Communications: Television sets: 739 per 1,000 pop. **Radios:** 525 per 1,000 pop. **Telephones:** 1 per 2.2 persons. **Daily newspaper circ.:** 145 per 1,000 pop.

Health: Life expectancy at birth: 75.3 male; 80.1 female. **Births** (per 1,000 pop.): 12. **Deaths** (per 1,000 pop.): 7. **Natural increase:** 0.44%. **Hospital beds** (1996): 1 per 174 persons. **Physicians** (1996): 1 per 403 persons. **Infant mortality** (per 1,000 live births): 8.

Education: Free and compulsory: ages 5-16. **Literacy** (1995): 91%.

Major International Organizations: UN (FAO, IBRD, ILO, IMF, IMO, WHO, WTrO), the Commonwealth, OSCE.

Embassy: 2017 Connecticut Ave. NW 20008; 462-3611.

Website:http://www.magnet.mt/home/cos

Malta was ruled by Phoenicians, Romans, Arabs, Normans, the Knights of Malta, France, and Britain (since 1814). It became independent Sept. 21, 1964. Malta became a republic in 1974. The withdrawal of the last British sailors, Apr. 1, 1979, ended 179 years of British military presence on the island. From 1971 to 1987, Malta was governed by the socialist Labor Party; it returned to office Oct. 1996-Sept. 1998 after an interlude of Nationalist Party government.

Marshall Islands

Republic of the Marshall Islands

People: Population: 63,031. **Age. distrib.** (%): <15: 50.0; 65+: 2.3. **Pop. density:** 900 per sq. mi. **Urban:** 70%. **Ethnic groups:** Micronesian. **Principal languages:** English (official), Marshallese, Japanese. **Chief religion:** Protestant 63%.

Geography: Area: 70 sq. mi. **Location:** In N Pacific Ocean; composed of two 800-mi-long parallel chains of coral atolls. **Neighbors:** Nearest are Micronesia to W, Nauru and Kiribati to S. **Capital:** Majuro (1995 est.) 28,000.

Government: Type: Republic. **Head of state:** Pres. Imata Kabua; b May 20, 1943; in office: Jan. 22, 1997. **Local divisions:** 24 localities.

Economy: Agriculture and tourism are mainstays.

Finance: Monetary unit: U.S. Dollar. **Gross domestic product** (1995 est.): $94 mil. **Per capita GDP:** $1,680. **Imports** (1995): $70 mil. **Exports** (1995): $21 mil. **Tourism:** $4 mil.

Transport: Civil aviation: 28.1 mil passenger-mi; 25 airports. **Chief port:** Majuro.

Communications: Telephones: 1 per 18 persons.

Health: Life expectancy at birth: 62.9 male; 66.1 female. **Births** (per 1,000 pop.): 45. **Deaths** (per 1,000 pop.): 7. **Natural increase:** 3.85%. **Hospital beds** (1995): 1 per 515 persons. **Physicians** (1995): 1 per 3,269 persons. **Infant mortality** (per 1,000 live births): 45.

Education: Compulsory: ages 6-14. **Literacy** (1994): 93%.

Major International Organizations: UN (IBRD, IMF, WHO).

Embassy: 2433 Massachusetts Ave. NW 20008; 234-5414.

The Marshall Islands were a German possession until World War I and were administered by Japan between the World Wars. After WW II, they were administered as part of the UN Trust Territory of the Pacific Islands by the U.S.

The Marshall Islands secured international recognition as an independent nation on Sept. 17, 1991. Amata Kabua, the islands' first and only president since 1979, died Dec. 19, 1996. His cousin Imata Kabua was elected Jan. 13, 1997.

Mauritania

Islamic Republic of Mauritania

People: Population: 2,511,473. **Age distrib.** (%): <15: 46.5; 65+: 2.4. **Pop. density:** 6 per sq. mi. **Urban:** 53%. **Ethnic groups:** Mixed Maur/black 40%, Maur 30%, black 30%. **Principal languages:** Hasaniya Arabic, Wolof (both official), Pular, Soninke. **Chief religion:** Muslim 100%.

Geography: Area: 397,953 sq. mi. **Location:** In NW Africa. **Neighbors:** Morocco on N, Algeria and Mali on E, Senegal on S. **Topography:** The fertile Senegal R. valley in the S gives way to a wide central region of sandy plains and scrub trees. The N is arid and extends into the Sahara. **Capital:** Nouakchott (1995 est.): 735,000.

Government: Type: Islamic republic. **Head of state:** Pres. Maaouya Ould Sidi Ahmed Taya; b 1943; in office: Apr. 18, 1992. **Head of government:** Prime Min. Mohamed Lamine Ould Guig; in office: Dec. 18, 1997. **Local divisions:** 12 regions, 1 capital district. **Defense:** 2.9% of GDP. **Active troop strength:** 15,700.

Economy: Industries: Fish processing, iron mining. **Chief crops:** Dates, grain. **Minerals:** Iron ore, gypsum. **Livestock** (1997): chickens: 3.90 mil; sheep: 6.20 mil; goats: 4.13 mil; cattle: 1.31 mil. **Fish catch** (1996): 85,000 metric tons. **Electricity prod.** (1996): 150 mil kWh. **Labor force:** 39% agric.; 15% services; 13% trade & finance.

Finance: Monetary unit: Ouguiya (Sept. 1998: 203.07 = $1 U.S.). **Gross domestic product** (1995 est.): $2.8 bil. **Per capita GDP:** $1,200. **Imports** (1995 est.): $365 mil; partners: Algeria 15%. **Exports** (1995 est.): $483 mil; partners: Japan 27%. **National budget** (1995): $269 mil. **International reserves less gold** (June 1998): $195.4 mil. **Gold:** 12,000 oz t. **Consumer prices** (change in 1997): 4.6%. **Tourism:** $11 mil.

Transport: Railroad: Length: 437.2 mi. **Motor vehicles in use:** 17,300 passenger cars, 9,210 comm. vehicles. **Civil aviation:** 190.1 mil passenger-mi; 9 airports. **Chief ports:** Nouakchott, Nouadhibou.

Communications: Radios: 428 per 1,000 pop. **Telephones:** 1 per 246 persons.

Health: Life expectancy at birth: 47.0 male; 53.1 female. **Births** (per 1,000 pop.): 44. **Deaths** (per 1,000 pop.): 15. **Natural increase:** 2.99%. **Physicians** (1994): 1 per 11,085 persons. **Infant mortality** (per 1,000 live births 1997): 78.

Education: Compulsory: ages 6-12. **Literacy** (1995): 38%.

Major International Organizations: UN (FAO, IBRD, ILO, IMF, IMO, WHO, WTrO), AL, OAU.

Embassy: 2129 Leroy Pl. NW 20008; 232-5700.

Website: http://www.embassy.org/mauritania

Mauritania was a French protectorate from 1903. It became independent Nov. 28, 1960 and annexed the south of former Spanish Sahara (now Western Sahara) in 1976. Saharan guerrillas of the Polisario Front stepped up attacks in 1977; 8,000 Moroccan troops and French bomber raids aided the government. Mauritania signed a peace treaty with the Polisario Front, 1979, resumed diplomatic relations with Algeria while breaking a defense treaty with Morocco, and renounced sovereignty over its share of Western Sahara. Opposition parties were legalized and a new constitution approved in 1991.

Although slavery has been repeatedly abolished, most recently in 1980, an estimated 90,000 Mauritanians continue to live under conditions of servitude.

Mauritius

Republic of Mauritius

People: Population: 1,168,256. **Age distrib.** (%): <15: 26.4; 65+: 5.9. **Pop. density:** 1,483 per sq. mi. **Urban:** 41%. **Ethnic groups:** Indo-Mauritian 68%, Creole 27%. **Principal languages:** English (official), French, Creole, Hindi, Bojpoori. **Chief religions:** Hindu 52%, Christian 28%, Muslim 17%.

Geography: Area: 788 sq. mi. **Location:** In the Indian O., 500 mi. E of Madagascar. **Neighbors:** Nearest is Madagascar to W. **Topography:** A volcanic island nearly surrounded by coral reefs. A central plateau is encircled by mountain peaks. **Capital:** Port Louis (1995 est.): 145,584.

Government: Type: Republic. **Head of state:** Pres. Cassam Uteem; b Mar. 22, 1941; in office: June 30, 1992. **Head of government:** Prime Min. Navin Ramgoolam; b July 14, 1947; in office: Dec. 22, 1995. **Local divisions:** 9 districts, 3 dependencies. **Defense:** 2.3% of GDP. **Active troop strength:** 1,300.

Economy: Industries: Tourism, textiles, food processing. **Chief crops:** Sugarcane, tea. **Arable land:** 49%. **Livestock** (1997): chickens: 3.20 mil. **Electricity prod.** (1996): 1.1 bil kWh. **Labor force:** 37% const. & ind.; 24% services; 15% agric. & fishing.

Finance: Monetary unit: Rupee (Sept. 1998: 24.60 = $1 U.S.). **Gross domestic product** (1996 est.): $11.7 bil. **Per capita GDP:** $10,300. **Imports** (1995): $1.98 bil; partners: France 20%. **Exports** (1995): $1.57 bil; partners: UK 34%, France 21%, U.S. 15%. **Tourism:** $504 mil. **National budget** (FY 1994-95 est.): $550 mil. **International reserves less gold** (June 1998): $634.9 mil. **Gold:** 62,000 oz t. **Consumer prices** (change in 1997): 6.8%.

Transport: Motor vehicles in use: 69,945 passenger cars, 12,328 comm. vehicles. **Civil aviation:** 2.18 bil passenger-mi; 1 airport. **Chief port:** Port Louis.

Communications: Television sets: 150 per 1,000 pop. **Radios:** 353 per 1,000 pop. **Telephones:** 1 per 7.6 persons. **Daily newspaper circ.:** 49 per 1,000 pop.

Health: Life expectancy at birth: 67.1 male; 74.7 female. **Births** (per 1,000 pop.): 19. **Deaths** (per 1,000 pop.): 7. **Natural increase:** 1.20%. **Hospital beds** (1995): 1 per 351 persons. **Physicians** (1995): 1 per 1,182 persons. **Infant mortality** (per 1,000 live births): 17.

Education: Compulsory: ages 5-12. **Literacy** (1995): 83%.

Major International Organizations: UN and all of its specialized agencies, the Commonwealth, OAU.

Embassy: 4301 Connecticut Ave. NW, Suite 441, 20008; 244-1491.

Mauritius was uninhabited when settled in 1638 by the Dutch, who introduced sugarcane. France took over in 1721, bringing African slaves. Britain ruled from 1810 to Mar. 12, 1968, bringing Indian workers for the sugar plantations.

Mauritius formally severed its association with the British crown Mar. 12, 1992.

Mexico

United Mexican States

People: Population: 98,552,776. **Age distrib.** (%): <15: 35.6; 65+: 4.1. **Pop. density:** 130 per sq. mi. **Urban:** 74%. **Ethnic groups:** Mestizo 60%, Amerindian 30%, Caucasian 9%. **Principal languages:** Spanish (official), Mayan dialects. **Chief religions:** Roman Catholic 89%, Protestant 6%.

Geography: Area: 756,066 sq. mi. **Location:** In southern North America. **Neighbors:** U.S. on N, Guatemala and Belize on S. **Topography:** The Sierra Madre Occidental Mts. run NW-SE near the west coast; the Sierra Madre Oriental Mts. run near the Gulf of Mexico. They join S of Mexico City. Between the 2 ranges lies the dry central plateau, 5,000 to 8,000 ft. alt., rising toward the S, with temperate vegetation. Coastal lowlands are tropical. About 45% of land is arid. **Capital:** Mexico City. **Cities:** Mexico City 16,562,000; Guadalajara 3,430,000*.

Government: Type: Federal republic. **Head of state:** Pres. Ernesto Zedillo Ponce de León; b Dec. 27, 1951; in office: Dec. 1, 1994. **Local divisions:** 31 states, 1 federal district. **Defense:** 0.8% of GDP. **Active troop strength:** 175,000.

Economy: Industries: Steel, food & beverages, chemicals, consumer durables, textiles, tourism. **Chief crops:** Cotton, coffee, wheat, rice, beans, vegetables, corn. **Minerals:** Silver, lead, zinc, gold, oil, gas, copper. **Crude oil reserves** (1997): 40 bil bbls. **Arable land:** 12%. **Livestock** (1997): chickens: 393.00 mil; cattle: 26.90 mil; pigs: 15.02 mil; goats: 10.40 mil; sheep: 5.99 mil. **Fish catch** (1996): 1.42 mil metric tons. **Electricity prod.** (1996): 154.4 bil kWh. **Labor force:** 32% services; 28% agric.; 15% commerce; 11% manuf.

Finance: Monetary unit: New Peso (Sept. 1998: 9.98 = $1 U.S.). **Gross domestic product** (1996 est.): $777.3 bil. **Per capita GDP:** $8,100. **Imports** (1996 est.): $88.5 bil; partners: U.S. 75%. **Exports** (1996 est.): $95.0 bil; partners: U.S. 80%. **Tourism:** $7.59 bil. **National budget** (1996 est.): $74 bil. **International reserves less gold** (June 1998): $30.65 bil. **Gold:** 256,000 oz t. **Consumer prices** (change in 1997): 20.6%.

Transport: Railroad: Length: 16,543 mi. **Motor vehicles in use:** 8.2 mil passenger cars, 4.03 mil comm. vehicles. **Civil aviation:** 12.19 bil passenger-mi; 83 airports. **Chief ports:** Coatzacoalcos, Mazatlan, Tampico, Veracruz.

Communications: Television sets: 192 per 1,000 pop. **Radios:** 227 per 1,000 pop. **Telephones:** 1 per 10 persons. **Daily newspaper circ.:** 115 per 1,000 pop.

Health: Life expectancy at birth: 68.6 male; 74.8 female. **Births** (per 1,000 pop.): 25. **Deaths** (per 1,000 pop.): 5. **Natural increase:** 2.06%. **Hospital beds** (1994): 1 per 1,196 persons. **Physicians** (1994): 1 per 613 persons. **Infant mortality** (per 1,000 live births): 26.

Education: Free and compulsory: ages 6-12. **Literacy** (1995): 90%.

Major International Organizations: UN (FAO, IBRD, ILO, IMF, IMO, WHO, WTrO), OAS, OECD.

Embassy: 1911 Pennsylvania Ave. NW 20006; 728-1600.

Website: http://www.inegi.gob.mx/homeing/homeinegi/homeing.html

Mexico was the site of advanced Indian civilizations. The Mayas, an agricultural people, moved up from Yucatan, built immense stone pyramids, invented a calendar. The Toltecs were overcome by the Aztecs, who founded Tenochtitlan AD 1325, now Mexico City. Hernando Cortes, Spanish conquistador, destroyed the Aztec empire, 1519-21.

After 3 centuries of Spanish rule the people rose, under Fr. Miguel Hidalgo y Costilla, 1810, Fr. Morelos y Payon, 1812, and Gen. Agustin Iturbide, who made himself emperor as Agustin I, 1821. A republic was declared in 1823.

Mexican territory extended into the present American Southwest and California until Texas revolted and established a republic in 1836; the Mexican legislature refused recognition but was unable to enforce its authority there. After numerous clashes, the U.S.-Mexican War, 1846-48, resulted in the loss by Mexico of the lands north of the Rio Grande.

French arms supported an Austrian archduke on the throne of Mexico as Maximilian I, 1864-67, but pressure from the U.S. forced France to withdraw. Dictatorial rule by Porfirio Diaz, president 1877-80, 1884-1911, led to a period of rebellion and factional fighting. A new constitution, Feb. 5, 1917, brought social reform.

The Institutional Revolutionary Party (PRI) dominated politics from 1929 until the late 1990s. Radical opposition, including some guerrilla activity, was contained by strong measures. Some gains in agriculture, industry, and social services were achieved, but much of the work force remained jobless or underemployed. Although prospects brightened with the discovery of vast oil reserves, inflation and a drop in world oil prices aggravated Mexico's economic problems in the 1980s.

Mexico reached agreement with the U.S. and Canada on the North American Free Trade Agreement (NAFTA) Aug. 12, 1992; it took effect Jan. 1, 1994.

Guerrillas of the Zapatista National Liberation Army (EZLN) launched an uprising, Jan. 1, 1994, in southern Mexico. A tentative peace accord was reached Mar. 2. The presidential candidate of the governing PRI, Luis Donaldo Colosio Murrieta, was assassinated at a political rally in Tijuana, Mar. 23. The new PRI candidate, Ernesto Zedillo Ponce de León, won election Aug. 21 and was inaugurated Dec. 1, 1994.

An austerity plan and pledges of aid from the U.S. saved Mexico's currency from collapse in early 1995. Popular Revolutionary Army guerrillas launched coordinated attacks on government targets in Aug. 1996. In elections July 6, 1997, the PRI failed to win a congressional majority for the first time since 1929. An armed gang massacred 45 peasants in Chiapas on Dec. 22, 1997.

Micronesia

Federated States of Micronesia

People: Population: 129,658. **Pop. density:** 478 per sq. mi. **Urban:** 28%. **Ethnic groups:** 9 ethnic Micronesian and Polynesian groups. **Principal languages:** English (official), Trukese, Pohnpeian. **Chief religions:** Roman Catholic 50%, Protestant 47%.

Geography: Area: 271 sq. mi. **Location:** Consists of 607 islands in the W Pacific Ocean. **Capital:** Palikir, on Pohnpei (1994 island pop.) 33,372.

Government: Type: Republic. **Head of state:** Jacob Nena; b Oct. 10, 1941; in office: May 8, 1997. **Local divisions:** 4 states.

Economy: Industries: Tourism, fish processing. **Chief crops:** Tropical fruits, vegetables, black, pepper.

Finance: Monetary unit: U.S. Dollar. **Gross domestic product** (1994 est.): $205 mil. **Per capita GDP:** $1,700. **Imports** (1994 est.): $141.1 mil; partners: U.S. 56%, Japan 32%. **Exports** (1994 est.): $29.1 mil; partners: Japan 80%, U.S. 9%. **Tourism:** $2.12 bil.

Transport: 4 airports.

Communications: Television sets: 19 per 1,000 pop. **Radios:** 664 per 1,000 pop. **Telephones:** 1 per 14 persons.

Health: Life expectancy at birth: 66.4 male; 70.3 female. **Births** (per 1,000 pop.): 28. **Deaths** (per 1,000 pop.): 6. **Natural increase:** 2.15%. **Hospital beds** (1993): 1 per 318 persons. **Physicians** (1993): 1 per 2,069 persons. **Infant mortality** (per 1,000 live births): 35.

Education: Compulsory: ages 6-14. **Literacy** (1991): 90%.

Major International Organizations: UN (IBRD, IMF, WHO).

Embassy: 1725 N St. NW 20036; 223-4383.

The Federated States of Micronesia, formerly known as the Caroline Islands, was ruled successively by Spain, Germany, Japan, and the U.S. It was internationally recognized as an independent nation Sept. 17, 1991.

Moldova

Republic of Moldova

People: Population: 4,457,729. **Age distrib.** (%): <15: 25.1; 65+: 9.7. **Pop. density:** 343 per sq. mi. **Urban:** 52%. **Ethnic groups:** Moldovan/Romanian 65%, Ukrainian 14%, Russian 13%. **Principal languages:** Moldovan (official), Russian. **Chief religion:** Eastern Orthodox 99%.

Geography: Area: 13,012 sq. mi. **Location:** In E Europe. **Neighbors:** Romania on W; Ukraine on N, E, and S. **Capital:** Chisinau 765,000*.

Government: Type: Republic. **Head of state:** Pres. Petru Lucinschi; b Jan. 27, 1940; in office: Jan. 15, 1997. **Head of government:** Prime Min. Ion Clubuc; b 1943; in office: Jan. 24, 1997. **Local divisions:** 21 cities and towns, 48 urban settlements, more than 1,600 villages. **Defense:** 4.2% of GDP. **Active troop strength:** 11,900.

Economy: Industries: Food processing, machinery, textiles. **Chief crops:** Grain, wine grapes. **Minerals:** Lignite, gypsum. **Arable land:** 53%. **Livestock** (1997): chickens: 13.00 mil; sheep: 1.26 mil; pigs: 950,100; cattle: 646,300; goats: 108,200. **Electricity prod.** (1996): 8.3 bil kWh. **Labor force:** 40% agric.; 12% industry.

Finance: Monetary unit: Leu (Aug. 1998: 4.69 = $1 U.S.). **Gross domestic product** (1996 est.): $10.8 bil. **Per capita GDP:** $2,400. **Imports** (1996): $1.05 bil; partners: Russia 32%, Ukraine 26%. **Exports** (1996): $775 mil; partners: Russia 47%. **International reserves less gold** (Mar. 1998): $324.73 mil. **Consumer price** (change in 1997): 11.0%. **Tourism:** $34 mil.

Transport: Railroad: Length: 746 mi. **Motor vehicles in use:** 169,000 passenger cars, 71,000 comm. vehicles. **Civil aviation:** 149.0 mil passenger-mi; 1 airport.

Communications: Television sets: 30 per 1,000 pop. **Radios:** 209 per 1,000 pop. **Telephones:** 1 per 7.7 persons. **Daily newspaper circ.:** 24 per 1,000 pop.

Health: Life expectancy at birth: 59.6 male; 69.3 female. **Births** (per 1,000 pop.): 14. **Deaths** (per 1,000 pop.): 12. **Natural increase:** 0.19%. **Hospital beds** (1995): 1 per 82 persons. **Physicians** (1995): 1 per 250 persons. **Infant mortality** (per 1,000 live births): 44.

Education: Compulsory: ages 7-16. **Literacy** (1995): 96%.

Major International Organizations: UN (FAO, IBRD, ILO, IMF, WHO), CIS, OSCE.

Embassy: 2101 S St. NW 20008; 667-1130.

Website: http://www.moldova1.net/english/default.asp

In 1918, Romania annexed all of Bessarabia that Russia had acquired from Turkey in 1812 by the Treaty of Bucharest. In 1924, the Soviet Union established the Moldavian Autonomous Soviet Socialist Republic on the eastern bank of the Dniester. It was merged with the Romanian-speaking districts of Bessarabia in 1940 to form the Moldavian SSR.

During World War II, Romania, allied with Germany, occupied the area. It was recaptured by the USSR in 1944. Moldova declared independence Aug. 27, 1991. It became an independent state when the USSR disbanded Dec. 26, 1991.

Fighting erupted Mar. 1992 in the Dnestr (Dniester) region between Moldovan security forces and Slavic separatists—ethnic Russians and ethnic Ukrainians—who feared Moldova would merge with neighboring Romania. In a plebiscite on Mar. 6, 1994, voters in Moldova supported independence, without unification with Romania.

Defying the Moldovan government, voters in the breakaway Dnestr region held legislative elections and approved a separatist constitution Dec. 24, 1995. Petru Lucinschi, a former Communist, won a presidential runoff election Dec. 1, 1996. A peace accord with Dnestr separatists was signed in Moscow May 8, 1997. The Communists won the most seats in parliamentary elections Mar. 22, 1998, but a coalition of three center-right parties formed the government.

Monaco

Principality of Monaco

People: Population: 32,035. **Age distrib.** (%): <15: 16.8; 65+: 19.5. **Pop. density:** 16,428 per sq. mi. **Urban:** 100%. **Ethnic groups:** French 47%, Italian 16%, Monegasque 16%. **Principal languages:** French (official), English, Italian, Monegasque. **Chief religion:** Roman Catholic 95%.

Geography: Area: 1.18 sq. mi. **Location:** On the NW Mediterranean coast. **Neighbors:** France to W, N, E. **Topography:** Monaco-Ville sits atop a high promontory, the rest of the principality rises from the port up the hillside. **Capital:** Monaco.

Government: Type: Constitutional monarchy. **Head of state:** Prince Rainier III; b May 31, 1923; in office: May 9, 1949. **Head of government:** Min. of State Michel Lévêque; in office: Feb. 3, 1997. **Local divisions:** 4 quarters.

Economy: Industries: Tourism, gambling, chemicals, precision instruments.

Finance: Monetary unit: French Franc (Sept. 1998: 5.81 = $1 U.S.) or Monegasque Franc. **Gross domestic product**

(1996 est.): $800 mil. **Per capita GDP:** $25,000. **National budget** (1994 est.): $570 mil.

Transport: Railroad: Length: 1.1 mi. **Motor vehicles in use:** 17,000 passenger cars, 4,000 comm. vehicles. **Civil aviation:** 820,000 passenger-mi; 1 airport. **Chief port:** Monaco.

Communications: Television sets: 690 per 1,000 pop. **Radios:** 941 per 1,000 pop.

Health: Life expectancy at birth: 74.8 male; 82.2 female. **Births** (per 1,000 pop.): 11. **Deaths** (per 1,000 pop.): 12. **Natural increase:** –0.12%. **Infant mortality** (per 1,000 live births): 7.

Education: Compulsory: ages 6-16.

Major International Organizations: UN (IMO, WHO), OSCE.

An independent principality for over 300 years, Monaco has belonged to the House of Grimaldi since 1297, except during the French Revolution. It was placed under the protectorate of Sardinia in 1815, and under France, 1861. The Prince of Monaco was an absolute ruler until the 1911 constitution. Monaco was admitted to the UN on May 28, 1993.

Monaco's fame as a tourist resort is widespread. It is noted for its mild climate, magnificent scenery, and elegant casinos.

Mongolia

People: Population: 2,578,530. **Age distrib.** (%): <15: 36.9; 65+: 3.7. **Pop. density:** 4 per sq. mi. **Urban:** 61%. **Ethnic groups:** Mongol 90%. **Principal language:** Khalkha Mongol (official). **Chief religion:** Mostly Tibetan Buddhist.

Geography: Area: 604,247 sq. mi. **Location:** In E Central Asia. **Neighbors:** Russia on N, China on E, W, and S. **Topography:** Mostly a high plateau with mountains, salt lakes, and vast grasslands. Arid lands in the S are part of the Gobi Desert. **Capital:** Ulaanbaatar. **Cities** (1997 est.): 627,300.

Government: Type: Republic. **Head of state:** Pres. Natsagiyn Bagabandi; b Apr. 22, 1950; in office: June 20, 1997. **Head of government:** Tsakhiagiyn Elbegdorj; b 1963; in office: Apr. 23, 1998 (resigned: July 24). **Local divisions:** 18 provinces, 3 municipalities. **Defense:** 1.7% of GNP. **Active troop strength:** 21,000.

Economy: Industries: Food processing, mining, construction materials. **Chief crops:** Grain, potatoes. **Minerals:** Coal, oil, tungsten, copper, molybdenum, gold, tin. **Arable land:** 1%. **Livestock** (1997): sheep: 13.56 mil; goats: 9.13 mil; cattle: 3.48 mil. **Electricity prod.** (1996): 2.3 bil kWh. **Labor force:** 40% agric.; 13% services; 12% manuf. & mining.

Finance: Monetary unit: Tugrik (Sept. 1998: 817.61 = $1 U.S.). **Gross domestic product** (1996 est.): $5.1 bil. **Per capita GDP:** $2,060. **Imports** (1996): $438.3 mil; partners: Russia 34%, Japan 18%. **Exports** (1996): $422.9 mil; partners: Switzerland 25%; Russia 21%. **National budget** (1995 est.): $1.3 bil. **International reserves less gold** (June 1998): $95.80 mil. **Gold:** 1,000 oz t. **Consumer prices** (change in 1997): 44.6%. **Tourism:** $22 mil.

Transport: Railroad: Length: 1,294 mi. **Motor vehicles in use:** 21,000 passenger cars, 27,000 comm. vehicles. **Civil aviation:** 326.1 mil passenger-mi; 1 airport.

Communications: Television sets: 60.7 per 1,000 pop. **Radios:** 74 per 1,000 pop. **Telephones:** 1 per 31 persons. **Daily newspaper circ.:** 92 per 1,000 pop.

Health: Life expectancy at birth: 59.4 male; 63.6 female. **Births** (per 1,000 pop.): 24. **Deaths** (per 1,000 pop.): 8. **Natural increase:** 1.54%. **Hospital beds** (1993): 1 per 101 persons. **Physicians** (1993): 1 per 401 persons. **Infant mortality** (per 1,000 live births): 66.

Education: Compulsory: ages 6-16. **Literacy** (1991): 83%.

Major International Organizations: UN (FAO, IBRD, ILO, IMF, WHO, WTrO).

Embassy: 2833 M St. NW 20007; 333-7117.

Website: http://www.MongoliaOnline.mn/english

One of the world's oldest countries, Mongolia reached the zenith of its power in the 13th century when Genghis Khan and his successors conquered all of China and extended their influence as far west as Hungary and Poland. In later centuries, the empire dissolved and Mongolia became a province of China.

With the advent of the 1911 Chinese revolution, Mongolia, with Russian backing, declared its independence. A Communist regime was established July 11, 1921.

In 1990, the Mongolian Communist Party yielded its monopoly on power but won election in July. A new constitution took effect Feb. 12, 1992. A democratic alliance won legislative elections, June 30, 1996. Natsagiyn Bagabandi, a former Communist, won the presidential election of May 18, 1997. A protracted political crisis took a violent turn Oct. 2, 1998, with the murder of Sanjaasuregiyn Zorig, a popular cabinet member seeking to become prime minister.

Morocco

Kingdom of Morocco

People: Population: 29,114,497. **Age distrib.** (%): <15: 36.4; 65+: 4.5. **Pop. density:** 164 per sq. mi. **Urban:** 53%. **Ethnic groups:** Arab-Berber 99%. **Principal languages:** Arabic (official), Berber dialects. **Chief religion:** Sunni Muslim 99%.

Geography: Area: 177,117 sq. mi. **Location:** On NW coast of Africa. **Neighbors:** Western Sahara on S, Algeria on E. **Topography:** Consists of 5 natural regions: mountain ranges (Riff in the N, Middle Atlas, Upper Atlas, and Anti-Atlas); rich plains in the W; alluvial plains in SW; well-cultivated plateaus in the center; a pre-Sahara arid zone extending from SE. **Capital:** Rabat. **Cities:** Casablanca 3,101,000; Rabat 1,293,000*.

Government: Type: Constitutional monarchy. **Head of state:** King Hassan II; b July 9, 1929; in office: Mar. 3, 1961. **Head of government:** Prime Min. Abdellatif Filali; b Jan. 26, 1928; in office: May 25, 1994. **Local divisions:** 7 regions. **Defense:** 4.3% of GDP. **Active troop strength:** 194,000.

Economy: Industries: Food processing, textiles, leather goods, mining, tourism. **Chief crops:** Grain, citrus, grapes, olives. **Minerals:** Phosphates, iron ore, manganese, lead, zinc. **Crude oil reserves** (1997): 2.0 mil bbls. **Arable land:** 21%. **Livestock** (1997): chickens: 100.00 mil; sheep: 17.58 mil; goats: 5.03 mil; cattle: 2.59 mil. **Fish catch** (1996): 637,793 metric tons. **Electricity prod.** (1996): 11.5 bil kWh. **Labor force:** 35% services; 34% agric.; 31% mining, manuf., & const.

Finance: Monetary unit: Dirham (Sept. 1998: 9.49 = $1 U.S.). **Gross domestic product** (1996 est.): $97.6 bil. **Per capita GDP:** $3,260. **Imports** (1996 est.): $9.8 bil; partners: France 22%, Spain 9%. **Exports** (1996 est.): $7.7 bil; partners: France 30%, Spain 9%. **Tourism:** $1.20 bil. **National budget** (1996 est.): $10.75 bil. **International reserves less gold** (June 1998): $4.11 bil. **Gold:** 704,000 oz t. **Consumer prices** (change in 1997): 0.9%.

Transport: Railroad: Length: 1,099 mi. **Motor vehicles in use:** 1.01 mil passenger cars, 325,075 comm. vehicles. **Civil aviation:** 2.90 bil passenger-mi; 11 airports. **Chief ports:** Tangier, Casablanca, Kenitra.

Communications: Television sets: 927 per 1,000 pop. **Radios:** 222 per 1,000 pop. **Telephones:** 1 per 23 persons. **Daily newspaper circ.:** 14.5 per 1,000 pop.

Health: Life expectancy at birth: 66.5 male; 70.6 female. **Births** (per 1,000 pop.): 26. **Deaths** (per 1,000 pop.): 6. **Natural increase:** 2.01%. **Hospital beds** (1994): 1 per 978 persons. **Physicians** (1994): 1 per 2,923 persons. **Infant mortality** (per 1,000 live births): 53.

Education: Compulsory: ages 7-13. **Literacy** (1995): 44%.

Major International Organizations: UN (FAO, IBRD, ILO, IMF, IMO, WHO, WTrO), AL.

Embassy: 1601 21st St. NW 20009; 462-7979.

Berbers were the original inhabitants, followed by Carthaginians and Romans. Arabs conquered in 683. In the 11th and 12th centuries, a Berber empire ruled all NW Africa and most of Spain from Morocco.

Part of Morocco came under Spanish rule in the 19th century; France controlled the rest in the early 20th. Tribal uprisings lasted from 1911 to 1933. The country became independent Mar. 2, 1956. Tangier, an internationalized seaport, was turned over to Morocco, 1956. Ifni, a Spanish enclave, was ceded in 1969. Morocco annexed the disputed territory of Western Sahara during the second half of the 1970s.

King Hassan II has ruled Morocco since 1961. Political reforms in the 1990s included the establishment of a bicameral legislature in 1997.

Western Sahara

Western Sahara, formerly the protectorate of Spanish Sahara, is bounded the N by Morocco, the NE by Algeria, the E and S by Mauritania, and on the W by the Atlantic Ocean. Phosphates are the major resource. Population (1997 est.): 228,138; capital: Laayoune (El Aaiun). Area: 102,700 sq mi.

Spain withdrew from its protectorate in Feb. 1996. On Apr. 14, 1976, Morocco annexed over 70,000 sq. mi, with the remainder annexed by Mauritania. A guerrilla movement, the Polisario Front, which had proclaimed the region independent Feb. 27, launched attacks with Algerian support. After Mauritania signed a treaty with Polisario on Aug. 5, 1979, Morocco occupied Mauritania's portion of Western Sahara.

After years of bitter fighting, Morocco controlled the main urban areas, but Polisario guerrillas moved freely in the vast, sparsely populated deserts. The 2 sides implemented a cease-fire in 1991, when a UN peacekeeping force was deployed. A UN-sponsored referendum on self-determination for Western Sahara has been repeatedly postponed.

Mozambique

Republic of Mozambique

People: Population: 18,641,469. **Age distrib.** (%): <15: 44.9; 65+: 2.3. **Pop. density:** 60 per sq. mi. **Urban:** 35%. **Ethnic groups:** Indigenous tribal groups. **Principal languages:** Portuguese (official), indigenous dialects. **Chief religions:** Indigenous beliefs 50%, Christian 30%, Muslim 20%.

Geography: Area: 309,494 sq. mi. **Location:** On SE coast of Africa. **Neighbors:** Tanzania on N; Malawi, Zambia, Zimbabwe on W; South Africa, Swaziland on S. **Topography:** Coastal lowlands comprise nearly half the country with plateaus rising in steps to the mountains along the western border. **Capital:** Maputo: 2,212,000*.

Government: Type: Republic. **Head of state:** Pres. Joaquim Chissano; b Oct. 22, 1939; in office: Oct. 19, 1986. **Head of government:** Prime Min. Pascoal Mocumbi; b Apr. 10, 1941; in office: Dec. 21, 1994. **Local divisions:** 10 provinces and the capital. **Defense:** 3.7% of GDP. **Active troop strength:** 11,000.

Economy: Industries: Chemicals, petroleum products, textiles. **Chief crops:** Cashews, cotton, sugar, corn, tea. **Minerals:** Coal, titanium. **Arable land:** 4%. **Livestock** (1997): chickens: 23.00 mil; cattle: 1.29 mil; goats: 386,000; pigs: 175,000; sheep: 122,000. **Fish catch** (1996): 34,915 metric tons. **Electricity prod.** (1996): 550 mil kWh. **Labor force:** 80% agric.

Finance: Monetary unit: Metical (Sept. 1998: 11,495.00 = $1 U.S.). **Gross domestic product** (1995 est.): $12.2 bil. **Per capita GDP:** $670. **Imports** (1995): $784 mil; partners: South Africa 44%. **Exports** (1995): $169 mil; partners: Spain 22%, South Africa 22%. **National budget** (1992 est.): $607 mil. **International reserves less gold** (Apr. 1998): $534.22 mil. **Consumer prices** (change in 1997): 5.5%.

Transport: Railroad: Length: 1,944.4 mi. **Motor vehicles in use:** 67,600 passenger cars, 21,200 comm. vehicles. **Civil aviation:** 161.4 mil passenger-mi; 7 airports. **Chief ports:** Maputo, Beira, Nacala, Inhambane.

Communications: Television sets: 3.5 per 1,000 pop. **Radios:** 38 per 1,000 pop. **Telephones:** 1 per 291 persons.

Health: Life expectancy at birth: 44.2 male; 46.6 female. **Births** (per 1,000 pop.): 44. **Deaths** (per 1,000 pop.): 18. **Natural increase:** 2.57%. **Hospital beds** (1993): 1 per 1,133 persons. **Physicians** (1993): 1 per 131,991 persons. **Infant mortality** (per 1,000 live births): 120.

Education: Compulsory: ages 7-14. **Literacy** (1995): 40%.

Major International Organizations: UN (FAO, IBRD, ILO, IMF, IMO, WHO, WTrO), the Commonwealth, OAU.

Embassy: 1990 M St. NW, Suite 570, 20036; 293-7146.

Website: http://www.mbendi.co.za/cymzcy.htm

The first Portuguese post on the Mozambique coast was established in 1505, on the trade route to the East. Mozambique became independent June 25, 1975, after a ten-year war against Portuguese colonial domination. The 1974 revolution in Portugal had paved the way for the orderly transfer of power to Frelimo (Front for the Liberation of Mozambique). Frelimo took over local administration Sept. 20, 1974, although opposed, in part violently, by some blacks and whites.

The new government, led by Maoist Pres. Samora Machel, provided for a gradual transition to a Communist system. Economic problems included the emigration of most of the country's whites, a politically untenable economic dependence on white-ruled South Africa, and a large external debt.

In the 1980s, severe drought and civil war caused famine and heavy loss of life. Pres. Machel was killed in a plane crash just inside the South African border, Oct. 19, 1986.

The ruling party formally abandoned Marxist-Leninism in 1989, and a new constitution, effective Nov. 30, 1990, provided for multiparty elections and a free-market economy.

On Oct. 4, 1992, a peace agreement was signed aimed at ending hostilities between the government and the rebel Mozambique National Resistance (MNR). Elections took place Oct. 27-28, 1994. Repatriation of 1.7 million Mozambican refugees officially ended June 1995.

Myanmar (*formerly* Burma)

Union of Myanmar

People: Population: 47,305,319. **Age distrib.** (%): <15: 36.5; 65+: 4.2. **Pop. density:** 181 per sq. mi. **Urban:** 26%. **Ethnic groups:** Burman 68%, Shan 9%, Karen 7%, Rakhine 4%. **Principal language:** Burmese (official). **Chief religions:** Buddhist 89%, Christian 4%, Muslim 4%.

Geography: Area: 261,969 sq. mi. **Location:** Between S and SE Asia, on Bay of Bengal. **Neighbors:** Bangladesh, India on W; China, Laos, Thailand on E. **Topography:** Mountains surround Myanmar on W, N, and E, and dense forests cover much of the nation. N-S rivers provide habitable valleys and communications, especially the Irrawaddy, navigable for 900 miles. The country has a tropical monsoon climate. **Capital:** Yangon (Rangoon) 3,873,000*.

Government: Type: Military. **Head of state and government:** Gen. Than Shwe; b 1933; in office: Apr. 24, 1992. **Local divisions:** 7 states and 7 divisions. **Defense:** 7.6% of GDP. **Active troop strength:** 321,000.

Economy: Industries: Mining, textiles, footwear, wood products, agric. processing. **Chief crops:** Rice, sugarcane, corn, pulses. **Minerals:** Oil, lead, copper, tin, tungsten, precious stones. **Crude oil reserves** (1997): 50 mil bbls. **Other resources:** Rubber, teakwood. **Arable land:** 15%. **Livestock** (1997): chickens: 33.07 mil; cattle: 10.30 mil; pigs: 3.36 mil; buffalo: 2.30 mil; goats: 1.27 mil; sheep: 356,700. **Fish catch** (1996): 804,830 metric tons. **Electricity prod.** (1996): 3.8 bil kWh. **Labor force:** 67% agric.; 10% trade.

Finance: Monetary unit: Kyat (Sept. 1998: 6.41 = $1 U.S.). **Gross domestic product** (1996 est.): $51.5 bil. **Per capita GDP:** $1,120. **Imports** (1996 est.): $2.0 bil; partners: Japan 24%, Singapore 15%. **Exports** (1996 est.): $1.1 bil; partners: Indonesia 16%, Singapore 16%. **Tourism:** $32 mil. **National budget** (1995 est.): $10 bil. **International reserves less gold** (Feb. 1998): $238.9 mil. **Gold:** 231,000 oz t. **Consumer prices** (change in 1997): 29.7%.

Transport: Railroad: Length: 3,144 mi. **Motor vehicles in use:** 35,000 passenger cars, 34,000 comm. vehicles. **Civil aviation:** 91.4 mil passenger-mi; 19 airports. **Chief ports:** Yangôn, Bassein, Moulmein.

Communications: Television sets: 22 per 1,000 pop. **Radios:** 72 per 1,000 pop. **Telephones:** 1 per 317 persons. **Daily newspaper circ.:** 23 per 1,000 pop.

Health: Life expectancy at birth: 53.0 male; 56.1 female. **Births** (per 1,000 pop.): 29. **Deaths** (per 1,000 pop.): 13. **Natural increase:** 1.65%. **Hospital beds** (1993-94): 1 per 1,586 persons. **Physicians** (1993-94): 1 per 3,554 persons. **Infant mortality** (per 1,000 live births): 78.

Education: Free and compulsory: ages 5-10. **Literacy** (1995): 83%.

Major International Organizations: UN (FAO, IBRD, ILO, IMF, IMO, WHO, WTrO), ASEAN.

Embassy: 2300 S St. NW 20008; 332-9044.

Website: http://www.myanmar.com/e-index.html

The Burmese arrived from Tibet before the 9th century, displacing earlier cultures, and a Buddhist monarchy was established by the 11th. Burma was conquered by the Mongol dynasty of China in 1272, then ruled by Shans as a Chinese tributary, until the 16th century.

Britain subjugated Burma in 3 wars, 1824-84, and ruled the country as part of India until 1937, when it became self-governing. Independence outside the Commonwealth was achieved Jan. 4, 1948.

Gen. Ne Win dominated politics from 1962 to 1988, first as military ruler then as constitutional president. His regime drove Indians from the civil service and Chinese from commerce. Economic socialization was advanced, isolation from foreign countries enforced. In 1987 Burma, once the richest nation in SE Asia, was granted less-developed status by the UN.

Ne Win resigned July 1988, following waves of antigovernment riots. Rioting and street violence continued, and in Sept. the military seized power, under Gen. Saw Maung. In 1989 the country's name was changed to Myanmar.

The first free multiparty elections in 30 years took place May 27, 1990, with the main opposition party winning a decisive victory, but the military refused to hand over power. A key opposition leader, Aung San Suu Kyi, awarded the Nobel Peace Prize in 1991, was held under house arrest from July 20, 1989, to July 10, 1995; after her release, the military government continued to restrict her activities and to harass and imprison her supporters. New U.S. economic sanctions took effect on May 21, 1997. Myanmar was admitted to ASEAN July 23, 1997.

Namibia

Republic of Namibia

People: Population: 1,622,328. **Age distrib.** (%): <15: 44.2; 65+: 4.0. **Pop density:** 5 per sq. mi. **Urban:** 37%. **Ethnic groups:** Ovambo 50%, Kavangos 9%, Herero 7%, Damara 7%. **Principal languages:** Afrikaans, English (official), German, indigenous languages. **Chief religions:** Lutheran 50%, other Christian 30%.

Geography: Area: 318,694 sq. mi. **Location:** In S Africa on the coast of the Atlantic Ocean. **Neighbors:** Angola on N, Botswana on E, South Africa on S. **Capital:** Windhoek (1995 est.): 190,000.

Government: Type: Republic. **Head of state:** Pres. Sam Nujoma; b May 12, 1929; in office: Mar. 21, 1990. **Head of government:** Prime Min. Hage Geingob; b Aug. 3, 1941; in office: Mar. 21, 1990. **Local divisions:** 13 regions. **Defense:** 3.0% of GDP. **Active troop strength:** 8,100.

Economy: Mining accounts for almost 25% of GDP. **Minerals:** Diamonds, copper, gold, tin, lead, uranium. **Arable land:** 1%. **Livestock** (1997): chickens: 2.40 mil; sheep: 2.43 mil; cattle: 2.06 mil; goats: 1.82 mil. **Fish catch** (1996): 266,980 metric tons. **Labor force:** 49% agric., 25% ind. & commerce.

Finance: Monetary unit: Rand (Sept. 1998: 6.23 = $1 U.S.). **Gross domestic product** (1996 est.): $6.2 bil. **Per capital GDP:** $3,700. **Imports** (1996 est.): $1.55 bil; partners: South Africa 85%. **Exports** (1996 est.): $1.45 bil; partners: UK 35%, South Africa 27%. **Tourism:** $210 mil. **National budget** (FY 1996-97 est.): $1.2 bil. **International reserves less gold** (Mar. 1998): $257.27 mil. **Consumer prices** (change in 1997): 8.8%.

Transport: Railroad: Length: 1,479.2 mi. **Motor vehicles in use:** 62,500 passenger cars, 66,500 comm. vehicles. **Civil aviation:** 552.4 mil passenger-mi; 11 airports. **Chief ports:** Luderitz, Walvis Bay.

Communications: Television sets: 27.6 per 1,000 pop. **Radios:** 152 per 1,000 pop. **Telephones:** 1 per 20 persons.

Health: Life expectancy at birth: 41.7 male; 41.2 female. **Births** (per 1,000 pop.): 36. **Deaths** (per 1,000 pop.): 20. **Natural increase:** 1.60%. **Physicians** (1992): 1 per 4,594 persons. **Infant mortality** (per 1,000 live births): 67.

Education: Compulsory: ages 6-16. **Literacy** (1993): 76%.

Major International Organizations: UN (FAO, IBRD, ILO, IMF, IMO, WHO, WTrO), the Commonwealth, OAU.

Embassy: 1605 New Hampshire Ave. NW 20009; 986-0540.

Namibia was declared a protectorate by Germany in 1890 and officially called South-West Africa. South Africa seized the territory from Germany in 1915 during World War I; the League of Nations gave South Africa a mandate over the territory in 1920. In 1966, the Marxist South-West Africa People's Organization (SWAPO) launched a guerrilla war for independence. The UN General Assembly gave the area the name Namibia in 1968.

After many years of guerrilla warfare and failed diplomatic efforts, South Africa, Angola, and Cuba signed a U.S.-mediated agreement Dec. 22, 1988, to end South African administration of Namibia and provide for a cease-fire and transition to independence, in accordance with a 1978 UN plan. A separate accord between Cuba and Angola provided for a phased withdrawal of Cuban troops from Namibia. A constitution providing for multiparty government was adopted Feb. 9, 1990, and Namibia became an independent nation Mar. 21.

Walvis Bay, the principal deepwater port, had been turned over to South African administration in 1922. It remained in South African hands after independence, but South Africa turned control of the port back to Namibia, as of Mar. 1, 1994.

Nauru

Republic of Nauru

People: Population: 10,501. **Pop. density:** 500 per sq. mi. **Urban:** 100%. **Ethnic groups:** Nauruan 58%, other Pacific Islander 26%, Chinese 8%, European 8%. **Principal languages:** Nauruan (official), English. **Chief religion:** Predominantly Christian.

Geography: Area: 21 sq. mi. **Location:** In W Pacific O. just S of the Equator. **Neighbors:** Nearest is Kiribati to E. **Topography:** Mostly a plateau bearing high-grade phosphate deposits, surrounded by a sandy shore and coral reef in concentric rings. **Capital:** Govt. offices in Yaren district.

Government: Type: Republic. **Head of state and government:** Pres. Bernard Dowiyogo; in office: June 18, 1998. **Local divisions:** 14 districts.

Economy: Phosphate mining. **Electricity prod.** (1996): 32 mil kWh.

Finance: Monetary unit: Australian Dollar (Sept. 1998: 1.73 = $1 U.S.). **Gross domestic product** (1993): $100 mil. **GDP per capita:** $10,000. **National budget** (FY1995-96): $64.8 mil.

Transport: Civil aviation: 150.9 mil passenger-mi.

Communications: Radios: 385 per 1,000 pop.

Health: Life expectancy at birth: 64.3 male; 69.2 female. **Births** (per 1,000 pop.): 18. **Deaths** (per 1,000 pop.): 5. **Natural increase:** 1.29%. **Infant mortality** (per 1,000 live births): 41.

Education: Free and compulsory: ages 6-16. **Literacy** (1995): 99%.

Major International Organizations: UN (WHO).

The island was discovered in 1798 by the British but was formally annexed to the German Empire in 1886. After World War I, Nauru became a League of Nations mandate administered by Australia. During World War II the Japanese occupied the island and shipped 1,200 Nauruans to the fortress island of Truk as slave laborers.

In 1947 Nauru was made a UN trust territory, administered by Australia. It became an independent republic Jan. 31, 1968.

Phosphate exports have provided Nauru with per capita revenues that are among the highest in the Third World. Phosphate reserves, however, are expected to be depleted by 2000, and environmental damage from strip-mining has been severe.

Nepal

Kingdom of Nepal

People: Population: 23,698,421. **Age distrib.** (%): <15: 44.2; 65+: 4.0. **Pop. density:** 417 per sq. mi. **Urban:** 11%. **Ethnic groups:** Newars, Indians, Tibetans, Gunings, Sherpas, others. **Principal languages:** Nepali (official), many dialects. **Chief religions:** Hindu (official) 90%, Buddhist 5%, Muslim 3%.

Geography: Area: 56,827 sq. mi. **Location:** Astride the Himalaya Mts. **Neighbors:** China on N, India on S. **Topography:** The Himalayas stretch across the N, the hill country with its fertile valleys extends across the center, while the S border region is part of the flat, subtropical Ganges Plain. **Capital:** Kathmandu. **Cities** (1993 met. est.): Kathmandu 535,000; Lalitpur 190,000; Biratnagar 132,000.

Government: Type: Constitutional monarchy. **Head of state:** King Birendra Bir Bikram Shah Dev; b Dec. 28, 1945; in office: Jan. 31, 1972. **Head of government:** Prime Min. Girija Prasad Koirala; b 1925; in office: Apr. 15, 1998. **Local divisions:** 5 regions subdivided into 14 zones. **Defense:** 0.9% of GDP. **Active troop strength:** 43,000.

Economy: Industries: Sugar and jute mills, tourism. **Chief crops:** Sugar, rice, grain. **Minerals:** Quartz. **Other resources:** Forests, hydroelectric power. **Arable land:** 17%. **Livestock** (1997): chickens: 15.58 mil; cattle: 7.02 mil; goats: 5.92 mil; buffalo: 3.36 mil; sheep: 869,600; pigs: 723,600. **Electricity prod.** (1996): 1.0 bil kWh. **Labor force:** 93% agric.

Finance: Monetary unit: Rupee (Sept. 1998: 68.33 = $1 U.S.). **Gross domestic product** (1996 est.): $26.5 bil. **Per capita GDP:** $1,200. **Imports** (1996 est.): $1.3 bil; partners: India 41%, Singapore 32%, Japan 16%. **Exports** (1996 est.): $343 mil; partners: Germany 46%, U.S. 36%. **Tourism:** $164 mil. **National budget** (FY 1994-95): $1.05 bil. **International reserves less gold** (Nov. 1997): $632.3 mil. **Gold:** 153,000 oz t. **Consumer prices** (change in 1997): 2.9%.

Transport: Railroad: Length: 62.7 mi. **Civil aviation:** 563.9 mil passenger-mi; 24 airports.

Communications: Television sets: 12 per 1,000 pop. **Radios:** 30 per 1,000 pop. **Telephones:** 1 per 276 persons.

Health: Life expectancy at birth: 58.0 male; 57.7 female. **Births** (per 1,000 pop.): 36. **Deaths** (per 1,000 pop.): 10. **Natural increase:** 2.52%. **Hospital beds** (1995): 1 per 6,387 persons. **Physicians** (1995): 1 per 13,777 persons. **Infant mortality** (per 1,000 live births): 76.

Education: Free and compulsory: ages 6-11. **Literacy** (1995): 27%.

Major International Organizations: UN (FAO, IBRD, ILO, IMF, IMO, WHO).

Embassy: 2131 Leroy Pl. NW 20008; 667-4550.

Website: http://www.info-nepal.com

Nepal was originally a group of petty principalities, the inhabitants of one of which, the Gurkhas, became dominant about 1769. In 1951 King Tribhubana Bir Bikram, member of the Shah family, ended the system of rule by hereditary premiers of the Ranas family, who had kept the kings virtual prisoners, and established a cabinet system of government.

Virtually closed to the outside world for centuries, Nepal is now linked to India and Pakistan by roads and air service and to Tibet by road. Polygamy, child marriage, and the caste system were officially abolished in 1963.

The government announced the legalization of political parties in 1990. Elections on Nov. 15, 1994, led to the installation of Nepal's first Communist government, which held power until a no-confidence vote Sept. 10, 1995.

Netherlands

Kingdom of the Netherlands

People: Population: 15,731,112. **Age distrib.** (%): <15: 18.3; 65+: 13.5. **Pop. density:** 981 per sq. mi. **Urban:** 89%. **Ethnic groups:** Dutch 96%. **Principal language:** Dutch (official). **Chief religions:** Roman Catholic 34%, Protestant 25%.

Geography: Area: 16,033 sq. mi. **Location:** In NW Europe on North Sea. **Neighbors:** Germany on E, Belgium on S. **Topography:** The land is flat, an average alt. of 37 ft. above sea level, with much land below sea level reclaimed and protected by some 1,500 miles of dikes. Since 1920 the government has been draining the IJsselmeer, formerly the Zuider Zee. **Capital:** Amsterdam. **Cities** (1996 est.): Amsterdam 718,119; Rotterdam 592,745; The Hague 442,503.

Government: Type: Parliamentary democracy under a constitutional monarch. **Head of state:** Queen Beatrix; b Jan. 31, 1938; in office: Apr. 30, 1980. **Head of government:** Prime Min. Wim Kok; b Sept. 29, 1938; in office: Aug. 22, 1994. **Seat of govt.:** The Hague. **Local divisions:** 12 provinces. **Defense:** 2.1% of GDP. **Active troop strength:** 63,100.

Economy: Industries: Metals, machinery, chemicals, oil refining, diamond cutting, microelectronics, tourism. **Chief crops:** Grains, potatoes, sugar beets, vegetables, fruits, flowers. **Minerals:** Natural gas, oil. **Crude oil reserves** (1997): 113 mil bbls. **Arable land:** 27%. **Livestock** (1997): chickens: 89.56; pigs: 14.25 mil; cattle: 4.37 mil; sheep: 1.67 mil. **Fish catch** (1996): 363,283 metric tons. **Electricity prod.** (1996): 79.8 bil kWh. **Labor force:** 73% services; 23% manuf. & constr.; 4% agric.

Finance: Monetary unit: Guilder (Sept. 1998: 1.95 = $1 U.S.). **Gross domestic product** (1996 est.): $317.8 bil. **Per capita GDP:** $20,500. **Imports** (1996): $159.7 bil; partners: Germany 24%, Belgium-Lux. 12%. **Exports** (1996): $176.2 bil; partners: Germany 29%, Belgium-Lux. 13%. **Tourism:** $6.60 bil. **National budget** (1996 est.): $118.9 bil. **International reserves less gold** (June 1998): $22.78 bil. **Gold:** 27.07 mil oz t. **Consumer prices** (change in 1997): 2.2%.

Transport: Railroad: Length: 1,702 mi. **Motor vehicles in use:** 5.74 mil passenger cars, 680,000 comm. vehicles. **Civil aviation:** 38.75 bil passenger-mi; 6 airports. **Chief ports:** Rotterdam, Amsterdam, IJmuiden.

Communications: Television sets: 495 per 1,000 pop. **Radios:** 877 per 1,000 pop. **Telephones:** 1 per 1.9 persons. **Daily newspaper circ.:** 299 per 1,000 pop.

Health: Life expectancy at birth: 75.1 male; 81.0 female. **Births** (per 1,000 pop.): 12. **Deaths** (per 1,000 pop.): 9. **Natural increase:** 0.29%. **Hospital beds** (1995): 1 per 181 persons. **Physicians** (1995): 1 per 412 persons. **Infant mortality** (per 1,000 live births): 5.

Education: Compulsory: ages 5-18. **Literacy** (1995): 100%.

Major International Organizations: UN and all of its specialized agencies, EU, NATO, OECD, OSCE.

Embassy: 4200 Linnean Ave. NW 20008; 244-5300.

Website: http://www.cbs.nl/indexeng.htm

Julius Caesar conquered the region in 55 BC, when it was inhabited by Celtic and Germanic tribes.

After the empire of Charlemagne fell apart, the Netherlands (Holland, Belgium, Flanders) split among counts, dukes, and bishops, passed to Burgundy and thence to Charles V of Spain. His son, Philip II, tried to check the Dutch drive toward political freedom and Protestantism (1568-1573). William the Silent, prince of Orange, led a confederation of the northern provinces, called Estates, in the Union of Utrecht, 1579. The Estates retained individual sovereignty, but were represented jointly in the States-General, a body that had control of foreign affairs and defense. In 1581 they repudiated allegiance to Spain. The rise of the Dutch republic to naval, economic, and artistic eminence came in the 17th century.

The United Dutch Republic ended 1795 when the French formed the Batavian Republic. Napoleon made his brother Louis king of Holland, 1806; Louis abdicated 1810 when Napoleon annexed Holland. In 1813 the French were expelled. In 1815 the Congress of Vienna formed a kingdom of the Netherlands, including Belgium, under William I. In 1830, the Belgians seceded and formed a separate kingdom.

The constitution, promulgated 1814, and subsequently revised, provides for a hereditary constitutional monarchy.

The Netherlands maintained its neutrality in World War I, but was invaded and brutally occupied by Germany, 1940-45.

In 1949, after several years of fighting, the Netherlands granted independence to Indonesia. In 1963, West New Guinea (now Irian Jaya) was turned over to Indonesia. Immigration from former Dutch colonies has been substantial.

Although the Netherlands is heavily industrialized, its small farms export large quantities of pork and dairy foods. Rotterdam, located along the principal mouth of the Rhine, is one of the world's leading cargo ports. Canals, extending over 3,400 miles, are important in transportation.

Netherlands Dependencies

The **Netherlands Antilles,** constitutionally on a level of equality with the Netherlands homeland within the kingdom, consist of 2 groups of islands in the West Indies. **Curaçao** and **Bonaire** are near the coast of Venezuela; **St. Eustatius, Saba,** and the southern part of **St. Maarten** are SE of Puerto Rico. The northern two-thirds of St. Maarten belongs to French Guadeloupe; the French call the island St. Martin. Total area of the 2 groups is 309 sq. mi., including Bonaire 111, Curaçao 171, St. Eustatius 8, Saba 5, St. Maarten (Dutch part) 13. St. Maarten suffered extensive damage from Hurricane Luis, Sept. 1995. Total pop. of the Netherlands Antilles (1998 est.) was 205,693. Willemstad, on Curaçao, is the capital. The principal industry is the refining of crude oil from Venezuela. Tourism is also an important industry, as is shipbuilding.

Aruba, about 26 mi. W of Curaçao, was separated from the Netherlands Antilles on Jan. 1, 1986; it is an autonomous member of the Netherlands, the same status as the Netherland Antilles. Area 75 sq. mi.; pop. (1998 est.) 68,325; capital Oranjestad. Chief industries are oil refining and tourism.

New Zealand

People: Population: 3,625,388. **Age distrib.** (%): <15: 23.0; 65+: 11.6. **Pop. density:** 35 per sq. mi. **Urban:** 86%. **Ethnic groups:** European 88%, Maori 9%. **Principal languages:** English (official), Maori. **Chief religions:** Anglican 24%, Presbyterian 18%, Roman Catholic 15%.

Geography: Area: 103,737 sq. mi. **Location:** In SW Pacific O. **Neighbors:** Nearest are Australia on W, Fiji and Tonga on N. **Topography:** Each of the 2 main islands (North and South Isls.) is mainly hilly and mountainous. The east coasts consist of fertile plains, especially the broad Canterbury Plains on South Isl. A volcanic plateau is in center of North Isl. South Isl. has glaciers and 15 peaks over 10,000 ft. **Capital:** Wellington. **Cities** (1996): Auckland 353,670; Christchurch 313,969; Wellington 158,275.

Government: Type: Parliamentary democracy. **Head of state:** Queen Elizabeth II, represented by Gov.-Gen. Sir Michael Hardie Boys; b Oct. 6, 1931; in office: Mar. 21, 1996. **Head of government:** Prime Min. Jenny Shipley; b 1952; in office: Dec. 8, 1997. **Local divisions:** 9 districts, 3 town districts. **Defense:** 1.3% of GDP. **Active troop strength:** 9,900.

Economy: Industries: Food processing, textiles, machinery, fish, forest prods. **Chief crops:** Grains, potatoes, fruits. **Minerals:** Gold, gas, iron, coal. **Crude oil reserves** (1997): 145 mil bbls. **Other resources:** Wool, timber. **Arable land:** 9%. **Livestock** (1997): chickens: 12.00 mil; sheep: 47.39 mil; cattle: 8.95 mil; pigs: 400,000; goats: 228,000. **Fish catch** (1996): 421,104 metric tons. **Electricity prod.** (1996): 35.5 bil kWh. **Labor force:** 65% services, 25% ind.; 10% agric.

Finance: Monetary unit: Dollar (Sept. 1998: 2.00 = $1 U.S.). **Gross domestic product** (1996 est.): $65.6 bil. **Per capita GDP:** $18,500. **Imports** (1995): $14 bil; partners: Australia 21%, U.S. 18%, Japan 16%. **Exports** (1995): $13.7 bil; partners: Australia 19%, Japan 15%; U.S. 12%. **Tourism:** $2.51 bil. **National budget** (FY 1995-96): $20.3 bil. **International reserves less gold** (May 1998): $4.19 bil. **Consumer prices** (change in 1997): 1.2%.

Transport: Railroad: Length: 2,467.2 mi. **Motor vehicles in use:** 1.70 mil passenger cars; 363,612 comm. vehicles. **Civil aviation:** 13.69 bil passenger-mi; 36 airports. **Chief ports:** Auckland, Christchurch, Wellington, Dunedin, Tauranga.

Communications: Television sets: 514 per 1,000 pop. **Radios:** 997 per 1,000 pop. **Daily newspaper circ.:** 239 per 1,000 pop.

Health: Life expectancy at birth: 74.4 male; 80.9 female. **Births** (per 1,000 pop.): 15. **Deaths** (per 1,000 pop.): 8. **Natural increase:** 0.73%. **Hospital beds** (1996): 1 per 164 persons. **Physicians** (1996): 1 per 318 persons. **Infant mortality** (per 1,000 live births): 6.

Education: Free and compulsory: ages 6-16. **Literacy** (1997): 100%.

Major International Organizations: UN (FAO, IBRD, ILO, IMF, IMO, WHO, WTrO), APEC, the Commonwealth, OECD.

Embassy: 37 Observatory Cir. NW 20008; 328-4800.

Website: http://www.stats.govt.nz/statsweb.nsf

The Maoris, a Polynesian group from the eastern Pacific, reached New Zealand before and during the 14th century. The first European to sight New Zealand was Dutch navigator Abel Janszoon Tasman, but Maoris refused to allow him to land. British Capt. James Cook explored the coasts, 1769-1770.

British sovereignty was proclaimed in 1840, with organized settlement beginning in the same year. Representative institutions were granted in 1853. Maori Wars ended in 1870 with British victory. The colony became a dominion in 1907, and is an independent member of the Commonwealth.

A progressive tradition in politics dates back to the 19th century, when New Zealand was internationally known for social experimentation; much of the nation's economy has been deregulated in recent years. The National Party, led by Jim Bolger, won general elections in 1990 and 1993. After inconclusive elections, Oct. 12, 1996, Bolger remained as prime minister, heading a National/New Zealand First party coalition. When Bolger lost the support of his own party, Jenny Shipley became the nation's first female prime minister, Dec. 8, 1997.

The native Maoris number about 525,000. Six of 120 members of the House of Representatives are elected directly by the Maori people.

New Zealand comprises **North Island,** 44,702 sq. mi.; **South Island,** 58,384 sq. mi.; **Stewart Island,** 674 sq. mi.; **Chatham Islands,** 372 sq. mi.; and several groups of smaller islands.

In 1965, the **Cook Islands** (pop., 1998 est., 19,989; area 93 sq. mi.), located halfway between New Zealand and Hawaii, became self-governing although New Zealand retains responsibility for defense and foreign affairs. **Niue** attained the same status in 1974; it lies 400 mi. to W (pop., 1995 est., 1,800; area 100 sq. mi.). **Tokelau** (pop., 1995 est., 1,500; area 4 sq. mi.) comprises 3 atolls 300 mi. N of Samoa.

Ross Dependency, administered by New Zealand since 1923, comprises 160,000 sq. mi. of Antarctic territory.

Nicaragua

Republic of Nicaragua

People: Population: 4,583,379. **Age distrib.** (%): <15: 44.0; 65+: 2.7. **Pop. density:** 90 per sq. mi. **Urban:** 63%. **Ethnic groups:** Mestizo 69%, white 17%, black 9%, Amerindian 5%. **Principal languages:** Spanish (official). **Chief religion:** Roman Catholic 95%.

Geography: Area: 50,893 sq. mi. **Location:** In Central America. **Neighbors:** Honduras on N, Costa Rica on S. **Topography:** Both Caribbean and Pacific coasts are over 200 mi. long. The Cordillera Mts., with many volcanic peaks, run NW-SE through the middle of the country. Between this and a volcanic range to the E lie Lakes Managua and Nicaragua. **Capital:** Managua 1,124,000*.

Government: Type: Republic. **Head of state and government:** Pres. Arnoldo Alemán Lacayo; b Jan. 23, 1946; in office Jan. 10, 1997. **Local divisions:** 15 departments, 2 autonomous regions. **Defense:** 1.5% of GDP. **Active troop strength:** 17,000.

Economy: Industries: Oil refining, food processing, chemicals, textiles. **Chief crops:** Bananas, cotton, citrus, coffee, sugar, corn, rice. **Minerals:** Gold, silver, copper, tungsten. **Other resources:** Forests, seafood. **Arable land:** 9%. **Livestock** (1997): chickens: 7.90 mil; cattle: 1.71 mil; pigs: 420,000. **Electricity prod.** (1996): 1.7 bil kWh. **Labor force:** 30% agric., forestry; 43% services; 13% trade; 11% manuf.

Finance: Monetary unit: Gold Cordoba (Sept. 1998: 10.76 = $1 U.S.). **Gross domestic product** (1996 est.): $7.7 bil. **Per capita GDP:** $1,800. **Imports** (1996): $1.19 bil partners: U.S. 25%, Venezuela 12%. **Exports** (1996): $607 mil; partners: U.S. 43%, Germany 13%. **Tourism:** $78 mil. **National budget** (1996 est.): $551 mil. **International reserves less gold** (Apr. 1998): $371.72 mil. **Consumer prices** (change in 1997): 11.6%.

Transport: Motor vehicles in use: 72,413 passenger cars, 72,227 comm. vehicles. **Civil aviation:** 52.8 mil passenger-mi; 10 airports. **Chief ports:** Corinto, Puerto Sandino, San Juan del Sur.

Communications: Television sets: 48 per 1,000 pop. **Radios:** 206 per 1,000 pop. **Telephones:** 1 per 43 persons. **Daily newspaper circ.:** 31 per 1,000 pop.

Health: Life expectancy at birth: 64.3 male; 69.1 female. **Births** (per 1,000 pop.): 36. **Deaths** (per 1,000 pop.): 6. **Natural increase:** 3.02%. **Hospital beds** (1994): 1 per 914 persons. **Physicians** (1994): 1 per 1,566 persons. **Infant mortality** (per 1,000 live births): 42.

Education: Free and compulsory: ages 7-13. **Literacy** (1995): 66%.

Major International Organizations: UN and most of its specialized agencies, OAS.

Embassy: 1627 New Hampshire Ave. NW 20009; 939-6570.

Nicaragua, inhabited by various Indian tribes, was conquered by Spain in 1552. After gaining independence from Spain, 1821, Nicaragua was united for a short period with Mexico, then with the United Provinces of Central America, finally becoming an independent republic, 1838.

U.S. Marines occupied the country at times in the early 20th century, the last time from 1926 to 1933.

Gen. Anastasio Somoza Debayle was elected president in 1967. He resigned in 1972, but was re-elected president in 1974. Martial law was imposed in Dec. 1974, after officials were kidnapped by the Marxist Sandinista guerrillas. Violent opposition spread to nearly all classes in 1978; nationwide strikes called against the government touched off a civil war, which ended when Somoza fled Nicaragua and the Sandinistas took control of Managua. in July 1979. Somoza was assassinated in Paraguay, Sept. 17, 1980.

Relations with the U.S. were strained as a result of Nicaragua's aid to leftist guerrillas in El Salvador and U.S. backing of anti-Sandinista contra guerrilla groups. In 1983 the contras launched a major offensive; the Sandinistas imposed rule by decree. In 1985 the U.S. House rejected Pres. Reagan's request for military aid to the contras. The subsequent diversion of funds to the contras from the proceeds of a secret arms sale to Iran caused a major scandal in the U.S.

In a stunning upset, Violeta Barrios de Chamorro defeated Sandinista leader Daniel Ortega Saavedra in national elections, Feb. 25, 1990. Arnoldo Alemán Lacayo, a conservative former mayor of Managua, defeated Ortega in the presidential election of Oct. 20, 1996.

Niger

Republic of Niger

People: Population: 9,671,848. **Age distrib.** (%): <15: 48.1; 65+: 2.3. **Pop. density:** 19 per sq. mi. **Urban:** 19%. **Ethnic groups:** Hausa 56%, Djerma 22%, Fula 9%, Tuareg 8%. **Principal languages:** French (official), Hausa, Djerma. **Chief religion:** Muslim 80%.

Geography: Area: 496,900 sq. mi. **Location:** In the interior of N Africa. **Neighbors:** Libya, Algeria on N; Mali, Burkina Faso on W; Benin, Nigeria on S; Chad on E. **Topography:** Mostly arid desert and mountains. A narrow savanna in the S and the Niger R. basin in the SW contain most of the population. **Capital:** Niamey (1994 est.): 420,000.

Government: Type: Republic. **Head of state:** Pres. Ibrahim Bare Mainassara; b 1949; in office: Jan. 27, 1996. **Head of government:** Prime Min. Ibrahim Hassane Mayaki; in office: Nov. 27, 1997. **Local divisions:** 7 departments, 1 capital district. **Defense:** 0.9% of GDP. **Active troop strength:** 5,300.

Economy: Chief crops: Peanuts, cowpeas, cotton. **Minerals:** Uranium, coal, iron. **Arable land:** 3%. **Livestock** (1997): chickens: 20.00 mil; goats: 6.15 mil; sheep: 4.10 mil; cattle: 2.09 mil. **Electricity prod.** (1996): 170 mil kWh. **Labor force:** 76% agric.

Finance: Monetary unit: CFA Franc (Sept. 1998: 580.94 = $1 U.S.). **Gross domestic product** (1996 est.): $5.9 bil. **Per capita GDP:** $640. **Imports** (1995 est.): $307 mil; partners: France 23%. **Exports** (1995 est.): $247 mil; partners: France 77%. **Tourism:** $18 mil. **National budget** (1997 est.): $387 mil. **International reserves less gold** (Mar. 1998): $25.3 mil. **Gold:** 11,000 oz t. **Consumer prices** (change in 1997): 2.9%.

Transport: Motor vehicles in use: 37,500 passenger cars, 14,100 comm. vehicles. **Civil aviation:** 139.6 mil passenger-mi; 6 airports.

Communications: Television sets: 2.8 per 1,000 pop. **Radios:** 48 per 1,000 pop. **Telephones:** 1 per 677 persons.

Health: Life expectancy at birth: 41.8 male; 41.2 female. **Births** (per 1,000 pop.): 53. **Deaths** (per 1,000 pop.): 23. **Natural increase:** 2.96%. **Physicians** (1993): 1 per 35,141 persons. **Infant mortality** (per 1,000 live births): 114.

Education: Free and compulsory: ages 7-15. **Literacy** (1995): 14%.

Major International Organizations: UN (FAO, IBRD, ILO, IMF, WHO, WTrO), OAU.

Embassy: 2204 R St. NW 20008; 483-4224.

Niger was part of ancient and medieval African empires. European explorers reached the area in the late 18th century. The French colony of Niger was established 1900-22, after the defeat of Tuareg fighters, who had invaded the area from the N a century before. The country became independent Aug. 3, 1960. The next year it signed a bilateral agreement with France.

In 1993, Niger held its first free and open elections since independence; an opposition leader, Mahamane Ousmane, won the presidency. A peace accord Apr. 24, 1995, ended a Tuareg rebellion that began in 1990. A coup, Jan. 27, 1996, followed by a disputed presidential election in July, left the military in control of Niger. Citing an alleged plot to assassinate Pres. Mainassara, authorities arrested opposition leaders Jan. 2, 1998.

Nigeria

Federal Republic of Nigeria

People: Population: 110,532,242. **Age distrib.** (%): <15: 44.8; 65+: 2.9. **Pop. density:** 310 per sq. mi. **Urban:** 40%. **Ethnic groups:** Hausa 21%, Yoruba 21%, Ibo 18%, Fulani 11%. **Principal languages:** English (official), Hausa, Yoruba, Ibo. **Chief religions:** Muslim (in N) 50%, Christian (in S) 40%.

Geography: Area: 356,668 sq. mi. **Location:** On the S coast of W Africa. **Neighbors:** Benin on W, Niger on N, Chad and Cameroon on E. **Topography:** 4 E-W regions divide Nigeria: a coastal mangrove swamp 10-60 mi. wide, a tropical rain forest 50-100 mi. wide, a plateau of savanna and open woodland, and semidesert in the N. **Capital:** Abuja. **Cities:** Lagos 10,287,000; Ibadan 1,484,000*.

Government: Type: In transition. **Head of state and government:** Pres. Gen. Abdulsalam Abubakar; b June 13, 1942; in office: June 9, 1998. **Local divisions:** 36 states, 1 capital territory. **Defense:** 3.5% of GDP. **Active troop strength:** 77,100.

Economy: Industries: Crude oil (98% of exports; Africa's leading producer), mining, food processing, textiles. **Chief crops:** Cocoa (main export crop), palm products, corn, rice, yams, cassava. **Minerals:** Oil, gas, coal, iron, limestone, columbite, tin. **Crude oil reserves** (1997): 17 bil bbls. **Other resources:** Timber, rubber, hides. **Arable land:** 33%. **Livestock** (1997): chickens: 126.00 mil; goats: 24.50 mil; cattle: 19.61 mil; sheep: 14.00 mil; pigs: 7.60 mil. **Fish catch** (1996): 237,611 metric tons. **Electricity prod.** (1996): 13.8 bil kWh. **Labor force:** 54% agric.; 19% ind., commerce, serv.; 15% govt.

Finance: Monetary unit: Naira (Sept. 1998: 21.89 = $1 U.S.). **Gross domestic product** (1996 est.): $143.5 bil. **Per capita GDP:** $1,380. **Imports** (1995): $10.0 bil; partners: EU 50%, U.S. 13%. **Exports** (1995): $11.6 bil; partners: U.S. 52%, EU 34%. **Tourism:** $86 mil. **National budget** (1995 est.): $16.0 bil. **International reserves less gold** (Dec. 1996): $4.08 bil. **Gold:** 687,000 oz t. **Consumer prices** (change in 1997): 8.2%.

Transport: Railroad: Length: 2,178 mi. **Motor vehicles in use:** 589,600 passenger cars, 363,900 comm. vehicles. **Civil aviation:** 169.3 mil passenger-mi; 12 airports. **Chief ports:** Port Harcourt, Lagos, Warri, Calabar.

Communications: Television sets: 38 per 1,000 pop. **Radios:** 170 per 1,000 pop. **Telephones:** 1 per 275 persons. **Daily newspaper circ.:** 18 per 1,000 pop.

Health: Life expectancy at birth: 52.7 male; 54.5 female. **Births** (per 1,000 pop.): 42. **Deaths** (per 1,000 pop.): 13. **Natural increase:** 2.93%. **Hospital beds** (1994): 1 per 1,070 persons. **Physicians** (1994): 1 per 4,496 persons. **Infant mortality** (per 1,000 live births): 71.

Education: Free and compulsory: ages 6-15. **Literacy** (1995): 57%.

Major International Organizations: UN (FAO, IBRD, ILO, IMF, IMO, WHO, WTrO), the Commonwealth (suspended Nov. 1995), OAU, OPEC.

Embassy: 1333 16th St. NW 20036; 986-8400.

Early cultures in Nigeria date back to at least 700 BC. From the 12th to the 14th centuries, more advanced cultures developed in the Yoruba area, at Ife, and in the north, where Muslim influence prevailed.

Portuguese and British slavers appeared from the 15th-16th centuries. Britain seized Lagos, 1861, and gradually extended control inland until 1900. Nigeria became independent Oct. 1, 1960, and a republic Oct. 1, 1963.

On May 30, 1967, the Eastern Region seceded, proclaiming itself the Republic of Biafra, plunging the country into civil war. Casualties in the war were estimated at over 1 million, including many "Biafrans" (mostly Ibos) who died of starvation despite international efforts to provide relief. The secessionists, after steadily losing ground, capitulated Jan. 12, 1970.

Nigeria emerged as one of the world's leading oil exporters in the 1970s, but much of the revenue has been squandered through corruption and mismanagement.

After 13 years of military rule, the nation made a peaceful return to civilian government, Oct. 1979. Military rule resumed, Dec. 31, 1983; a second coup came in 1985.

Headed by Gen. Ibrahim Babangida, the military regime held elections June 12, 1993, but annulled the vote June 23 when it appeared that Moshood Abiola would win. Riots followed and many were killed. Babangida resigned and appointed a civilian to head an interim government, Aug, 26, but that government was ousted Nov. 17 in a coup led by Gen. Sani Abacha. On June 11, 1994, Abiola declared himself president; he was jailed June 23.

The execution, Nov. 10, 1995, of Ogoni playwright and environmentalist Ken Saro-Wiwa and 8 associates, accused in connection with the deaths of 4 political opponents, led to international sanctions against Nigeria, including suspension of its Commonwealth membership.

Abacha's brutal rule ended June 8, 1998, when he died of an apparent heart attack. Abiola died in prison July 7, as Abacha's successor, Gen. Abdulsalam Abubakar, was reportedly preparing to free him; Abiola's death (also apparently of natural causes) sparked riots in Lagos and other cities. On July 20, Abubakar promised early elections and a return to civilian rule within a year. An oil fire caused by a ruptured pipeline in S. Nigeria, Oct. 17, killed at least 700 people who were scavenging for fuel.

Norway

Kingdom of Norway

People: Population: 4,419,955. **Age distrib.** (%): <15: 19.6; 65+: 15.7. **Pop. density:** 35 per sq. mi. **Urban:** 73%. **Ethnic groups:** Germanic (Nordic, Alpine, Baltic), Lapps (minority). **Principal languages:** Norwegian (official). **Chief religion:** Evangelical Lutheran 88%.

Geography: Area: 125,181 sq. mi. **Location:** W part of Scandinavian peninsula in NW Europe (extends farther north than any European land). **Neighbors:** Sweden, Finland, Russia on E. **Topography:** A highly indented coast is lined with tens of thousands of islands. Mountains and plateaus cover most of the country, which is only 25% forested. **Capital:** Oslo. **Cities** (1997 met. est.): Oslo 493,973; Bergen 224,130.

Government: Type: Hereditary constitutional monarchy. **Head of state:** King Harald V; b Feb. 21, 1937; in office: Jan. 17, 1991. **Head of government:** Prime Min. Kjell Magne Bondevik; b Sept. 3, 1947; in office: Oct. 17, 1997. **Local divisions:** 19 provinces. **Defense:** 2.4% of GDP. **Active troop strength:** 30,000.

Economy: Industries: Wood & paper prods., shipbuilding, metals, chemicals, food processing, fish, oil, gas. **Chief crops:** Grains, oats. **Minerals:** Oil, gas, copper, pyrites, nickel, iron, zinc, lead. **Crude oil reserves** (1997): 10 bil bbls. **Other resources:** Fish, livestock. **Arable land:** 3%. **Livestock** (1997): chickens: 3.66 mil; sheep: 2.52 mil; cattle: 998,400; pigs: 768,400. **Fish catch** (1996): 2.64 mil metric tons. **Electricity prod.** (1996): 103.4 bil kWh. **Labor force:** 71% services; 23% industry.

Finance: Monetary unit: Krone (Sept. 1998: 7.73 = $1 U.S.). **Gross domestic product** (1996 est.): $114.1 bil. **Per capita GDP:** $26,200. **Imports** (1995): $32.7 bil; partners: EU 71%. **Exports** (1995): $41.7 bil; partners: EU 77%. **Tourism:** $2.50 bil. **National budget** (1994 est.): $53 bil. **International reserves less gold** (June 1998): $23.72 bil. **Gold:** 1.18 mil oz t. **Consumer prices** (change in 1997): 2.6%.

Transport: Railroad: Length: 2,500.8 mi. **Motor vehicles in use:** 1.66 mil passenger cars, 392,087 comm. vehicles. **Civil aviation:** 5.39 bil passenger-mi; 50 airports. **Chief ports:** Bergen, Stavanger, Oslo, Kristiansand.

Communications: Television sets: 459 per 1,000 pop. **Radios:** 763 per 1,000 pop. **Telephones:** 1 per 1.8 persons. **Daily newspaper circ.:** 498 per 1,000 pop.

Health: Life expectancy at birth: 75.4 male; 81.2 female. **Births** (per 1,000 pop.): 13. **Deaths** (per 1,000 pop.): 10. **Natural increase:** 0.27%. **Hospital beds** (1994): 1 per 197 persons. **Physicians** (1996): 1 per 285 persons. **Infant mortality** (per 1,000 live births): 5.

Education: Compulsory: ages 6-16. **Literacy** (1994): 100%.

Major International Organizations: UN and all of its specialized agencies, EFTA, NATO, OECD, OSCE.

Embassy: 2720 34th St. NW 20008; 333-6000.

Website: http://www.ssb.no/www-open/english

The first ruler of Norway was Harald the Fairhaired, who came to power in AD 872. Between 800 and 1000, Norway's Vikings raided and occupied widely dispersed parts of Europe.

The country was united with Denmark 1381-1814, and with Sweden, 1814-1905. In 1905, the country became independent with Prince Charles of Denmark as king.

Norway remained neutral during World War I. Germany attacked Norway Apr. 9, 1940, and held it until liberation May 8, 1945. The country abandoned its neutrality after the war, and joined NATO. In a referendum Nov. 28, 1994, Norwegian voters rejected European Union membership.

Abundant hydroelectric resources provided the base for industrialization, giving Norway one of the highest living standards in the world. The country is a leading producer and exporter of crude oil, with extensive reserves in the North Sea. Norway's merchant marine is one of the world's largest.

Svalbard is a group of mountainous islands in the Arctic O., area 23,957 sq. mi., pop. (1997 est.) 3,231. The largest, Spitsbergen (formerly called West Spitsbergen), 15,060 sq. mi., seat of the governor, is about 370 mi. N of Norway. By a treaty signed in Paris, 1920, major European powers recognized the sovereignty of Norway, which incorporated it in 1925.

Jan Mayen, area 144 sq. mi., is a volcanic island located about 565 mi. WNW of Norway; it was annexed in 1929.

Oman

Sultanate of Oman

People: Population: 2,363,591. **Age distrib.** (%): <15: 40.5; 65+: 2.3. **Pop. density:** 20 per sq. mi. **Urban:** 78%. **Ethnic groups:** Omani Arab 74%, Indian 13. **Principal languages:** Arabic (official). **Chief religion:** Ibadhi Muslim 75%.

Geography: Area: 118,150 sq. mi. **Location:** On SE coast of Arabian peninsula. **Neighbors:** United Arab Emirates, Saudi Arabia, Yemen on W. **Topography:** Oman has a narrow coastal plain up to 10 mi. wide, a range of barren mountains reaching 9,900 ft., and a wide, stony, mostly waterless plateau, avg. alt. 1,000 ft. Also, an exclave at the tip of the Musandam peninsula controls access to the Persian Gulf. **Capital:** Muscat (1993): 51,969.

Government: Type: Absolute monarchy. **Head of state and government:** Sultan Qabus bin Said; b Nov. 18, 1942; in office: July 23, 1970. **Local divisions:** 59 wilayats. **Defense:** 15.6% of GDP. **Active troop strength:** 43,500.

Economy: Industries: Oil, gas, construction. **Chief crops:** Dates, limes, vegetables, alfalfa, bananas. **Minerals:** Oil (78% of exports). **Livestock** (1997): chickens: 3.00 mil; goats: 725,000; cattle: 146,000; sheep: 155,000. **Crude oil reserves** (1997): 5.2 bil bbls. **Electricity prod.** (1996): 8.0 bil kWh. **Labor force:** 37% agric.

Finance: Monetary unit: Rial Omani (Sept. 1998: 0.39 = $1 U.S.). **Gross domestic product** (1996 est.): $20.8 bil. **Per capita GDP:** $9,500. **Imports** (1996 est.): $5.5 bil; partners: UAE 25%, Japan 16%, UK 16%. **Exports** (1996 est.): $7.2 bil; partners: Japan 32%, South Korea 16%. **Tourism:** $101 mil. **National budget** (1995 est.): $5.6 bil. **International reserves less gold** (June 1998): $1.09 bil. **Gold:** 291,000 oz t.

Transport: Motor vehicles in use: 202,741 passenger cars, 90,689 comm. vehicles. **Civil aviation:** 2.04 bil passenger-mi; 6 airports. **Chief ports:** Matrah, Mina' al Fahl.

Communications: Television sets: 711 per 1,000 pop. **Radios:** 426 per 1,000 pop. **Telephones:** 1 per 13 persons.

Health: Life expectancy at birth: 69.0 male; 73.1 female. **Births** (per 1,000 pop.): 38. **Deaths** (per 1,000 pop.): 4. **Natural increase:** 3.35%. **Hospital beds** (1995): 1 per 478 persons. **Physicians** (1995): 1 per 852 persons. **Infant mortality** (per 1,000 live births): 26.

Education: Literacy (1993): 59%.

Major International Organizations: UN (FAO, IBRD, ILO, IMF, IMO, WHO), AL.

Embassy: 2535 Belmont Rd. NW 20008; 387-1980.

Oman was originally called Muscat and Oman. A long history of rule by other lands, including Portugal in the 16th century, ended with the ouster of the Persians in 1744. By the early 19th century, Muscat and Oman was one of the most important countries in the region, controlling much of the Persian and Pakistan coasts, and ruling far-away Zanzibar, which was separated in 1861 under British mediation.

British influence was confirmed in a 1951 treaty, and Britain helped suppress an uprising by traditionally rebellious interior tribes against control by Muscat in the 1950s.

On July 23, 1970, Sultan Said bin Taimur was overthrown by his son, who changed the nation's name to Sultanate of Oman.

Oil is the major source of income.

Oman opened its air bases to Western forces following the Iraqi invasion of Kuwait on Aug. 2, 1990.

Pakistan

Islamic Republic of Pakistan

People: Population: 135,135,195. **Age distrib.** (%): <15: 41.8; 65+: 4.0. **Pop. density:** 440 per sq. mi. **Urban:** 35%. **Ethnic groups:** Punjabi, Sindhi, Pashtun (Pathan), Baloch. **Principal languages:** Urdu, English (both official), Punjabi, Sindhi, Pashtu. **Chief religions:** Sunni Muslim 77%, Shi'a Muslim 20%.

Geography: Area: 307,374 sq. mi. **Location:** In W part of South Asia. **Neighbors:** Iran on W, Afghanistan and China on N, India on E. **Topography:** The Indus R. rises in the Hindu Kush and Himalaya Mts. in the N (highest is K2, or Godwin Austen, 28,250 ft., 2d highest in world), then flows over 1,000 mi. through fertile valley and empties into Arabian Sea. Thar Desert, Eastern Plains flank Indus Valley. **Capital:** Islamabad. **Cities:** Karachi 9,733,000; Lahore 5,012,000; Faisalabad 1,845,000*.

Government: Type: Republic. **Head of state:** Pres. Muhammad Rafiq Tarar; b Nov. 2, 1929; in office: Jan. 1, 1998. **Head of government:** Prime Min. Nawaz Sharif; b Dec. 25, 1949; in office: Feb. 17, 1997. **Local divisions:** 4 provinces and 1 capital territory, plus federally administered tribal areas. **Defense:** 5.7% of GDP. **Active troop strength:** 587,000.

Economy: Industries: Textiles, food processing, beverages. **Chief crops:** Rice, wheat, cotton. **Minerals:** Natural gas. **Crude oil reserves** (1997): 208 mil bbls. **Arable land:** 23%. **Livestock** (1997): chickens: 110.00 mil; goats: 47.62 mil; sheep: 30.53 mil; buffalo: 20.73 mil; cattle: 17.92 mil. **Fish catch** (1996): 5,374 metric tons. **Electricity prod.** (1996): 59.3 bil kWh. **Labor force:** 47% agric.; 17% mining & manuf.; 17% services.

Finance: Monetary unit: Rupee (Sept. 1998: 53.70 = $1 U.S.). **Gross domestic product** (1996 est.): $296.5 bil. **Per capita GDP:** $2,300. **Imports** (FY1995-96): $12.0 bil; partners: Japan 9%, Malaysia 9%, U.S. 9%. **Exports** (FY1995-96): $8.3 bil; partners: U.S. 17%. **Tourism:** $117 mil. **National budget** (FY 1995-96 est.): $14.0 bil. **International reserves less gold** (June 1998): $844 mil. **Gold:** 2.07 mil oz t. **Consumer prices** (change in 1997): 11.4%.

Transport: Railroad: Length: 5,453 mi. **Motor vehicles in use:** 800,000 passenger cars, 300,000 comm. vehicles. **Civil aviation:** 6.57 bil passenger-mi; 35 airports. **Chief port:** Karachi.

Communications: Television sets: 16 per 1,000 pop. **Radios:** 76 per 1,000 pop. **Telephones:** 1 per 61 persons. **Daily newspaper circ.:** 22 per 1,000 pop.

Health: Life expectancy at birth: 58.2 male; 60.0 female. **Births** (per 1,000 pop.): 34. **Deaths** (per 1,000 pop.): 11. **Natural increase:** 2.37%. **Hospital beds** (1995): 1 per 1,517 persons. **Physicians** (1995): 1 per 1,863 persons. **Infant mortality** (per 1,000 live births): 93.

Education: Literacy (1995): 38%.

Major International Organizations: UN (FAO, IBRD, ILO, IMF, IMO, WHO, WTrO), the Commonwealth.

Embassy: 2315 Massachusetts Ave. NW 20008; 939-6200.

Website: http://www.pak.gov.pk

Present-day Pakistan shares the 5,000-year history of the India-Pakistan subcontinent. At present-day Harappa and Mohenjo Daro, the Indus Valley Civilization, with large cities and elaborate irrigation systems, flourished c. 4,000-2,500 BC.

Aryan invaders from the NW conquered the region around 1,500 BC, forging a Hindu civilization that dominated Pakistan as well as India for 2,000 years.

Beginning with the Persians in the 6th century BC, and continuing with Alexander the Great and with the Sassanians, successive nations to the west ruled or influenced Pakistan. The first Arab invasion, AD 712, introduced Islam. Under the Mogul empire (1526-1857), Muslims ruled most of India, yielding to British encroachment and resurgent Hindus.

After World War I the Muslims of British India began agitation for minority rights in elections. Muhammad Ali Jinnah (1876-1948) was the principal architect of Pakistan. A leader of the Muslim League from 1916, he worked for dominion status for India; from 1940 he advocated a separate Muslim state.

When the British withdrew Aug. 14, 1947, the Islamic majority areas of India acquired self-government as Pakistan, with dominion status in the Commonwealth. Pakistan was divided into 2 sections, West Pakistan and East Pakistan. The 2 areas were nearly 1,000 mi. apart on opposite sides of India. Pakistan became a republic in 1956.

In Oct. 1958, Gen. Mohammad Ayub Khan took power in a coup. He was elected president in 1960, reelected in 1965. He resigned Mar. 25, 1969, after several months of violent rioting and unrest, most of it in East Pakistan, which demanded autonomy. The government was turned over to Gen. Agha Mohammad Yahya Khan and martial law was declared.

The Awami League, which sought regional autonomy for East Pakistan, won a majority in Dec. 1970 elections to a constituent assembly. In March 1971 Yahya postponed the assembly. Rioting and strikes broke out in the East.

On Mar. 25, 1971, government troops launched attacks in the East. The Easterners, aided by India, proclaimed the independent nation of Bangladesh. In months of widespread fighting, countless thousands were killed. Some 10 million Easterners fled into India.

Full-scale war between India and Pakistan had spread to both the East and West fronts by Dec. 3. Pakistan troops in the East surrendered Dec. 16; Pakistan agreed to a cease-fire in the West Dec. 17. On July 3, 1972, Pakistan and India signed a pact agreeing to withdraw troops from their borders and seek peaceful solutions to all problems.

Zulfikar Ali Bhutto, leader of the Pakistan People's Party, which had won the most West Pakistan votes in the Dec. 1970 elections, became president Dec. 20.

Bhutto was overthrown in a military coup July 1977. Convicted of complicity in a 1974 political murder, he was executed Apr. 4, 1979. More than 3 million Afghan refugees flooded into Pakistan after the USSR invaded Afghanistan Dec. 1979; more than 1 million remained in the late 1990s.

Pres. Mohammad Zia ul-Haq was killed when his plane exploded in Aug. 1988. Following Nov. elections, Benazir Bhutto, daughter of Zulfikar Ali Bhutto, was named prime minister, becoming the first woman leader of a Muslim nation. She was accused of corruption and dismissed by the president, Aug. 1990; her party was soundly defeated in Oct. 1990 elections, and Nawaz Sharif became prime minister. She regained power after elections in Oct. 1993. Opposition to Bhutto centered around Karachi, which was crippled by violent strikes and ethnic clashes during 1995 and 1996. Accusing the Bhutto government of corruption and mismanagement, Pres. Farooq Leghari appointed a caretaker prime minister Nov. 5, 1996. Elections on Feb. 3, 1997, gave Sharif a parliamentary majority.

Responding to nuclear weapons tests by India, Pakistan conducted its own tests, May 28-30, 1998; the U.S. imposed economic sanctions on both countries.

Palau

Republic of Palau

People: Population: 18,110. **Pop. density:** 96 per sq. mi. **Urban:** 72%. **Ethnic groups:** Polynesian, Malayan, Melanesian. **Principal languages:** English (official), Palauan, Sonsorolese, Angaur, Japanese, Tobi (all official within certain states). **Chief religions:** Roman Catholic, Protestant, Modekngei.

Geography: Area: 188 sq. mi. **Location:** Archipelago (26 islands, more than 300 islets) in the W Pacific Ocean, about 530 mi SE of the Philippines. **Neighbors:** Micronesia to E, Indonesia to S. **Capital:** Koror (1995) 12,000. (Note: a new capital is being built in Babelthuap.)

Government: Type: Republic. **Head of state:** Pres. Kuniwo Nakamura; in office: Jan. 1, 1993. **Local divisions:** 16 states.

Economy: Industries: Tourism, fish. **Chief crops:** Coconuts, copra, cassava, sweet potatoes.

Finance: Monetary unit: U.S. Dollar. **Gross domestic product** (1994 est.): $81.8 mil. **Per capita GDP:** $5,000.

Communications: Television sets: 98 per 1,000 pop. **Radios:** 550 per 1,000 pop.

Health: Life expectancy at birth: 64.5 male; 70.8 female. **Births** (per 1,000 pop.): 21. **Deaths** (per 1,000 pop.): 8. **Natural increase:** 1.34%. **Infant mortality (per 1,000 live births):** 19.

Education: Compulsory: ages 6-14. **Literacy** (1990): 98%.

Major International Organizations: UN (WHO).

Embassy: 2000 L St. NW, Suite 407, 20036; 452-6814.

Website: http://www.visit-palau.com

Spain acquired the Palau Islands in 1886 and sold them to Germany in 1899. Japan seized them in 1914. American forces occupied the islands in 1944; in 1947, they became part of the U.S.-administered UN Trust Territory of the Pacific Islands. In 1981 Palau became an autonomous republic; in 1993 the republic ratified a compact of free association with the U.S., which provides financial aid in return for U.S. use of Palauan military facilities over 15 years. Palau became an independent nation on Oct. 1, 1994.

Panama

Republic of Panama

People: Population: 2,735,943. **Age distrib.** (%): <15: 27.4; 65+: 4.9. **Pop. density:** 91 per sq. mi. **Urban:** 56%. **Ethnic groups:** Mestizo 70%, West Indian 14%, white 10%, Amerindian 6%. **Principal languages:** Spanish (official), English. **Chief religions:** Roman Catholic 85%, Protestant 15%.

Geography: Area: 30,193 sq. mi. **Location:** In Central America. **Neighbors:** Costa Rica on W, Colombia on E. **Topography:** 2 mountain ranges run the length of the isthmus. Tropical rain forests cover the Caribbean coast and eastern Panama. **Capital:** Panama City: 967,000*.

Government: Type: Constitutional republic. **Head of state and government:** Pres. Ernesto Pérez Balladares; b June 29, 1946; in office: Sept. 1, 1994. **Local divisions:** 9 provinces, 3 territories. **Defense:** 1.4% of GDP. **Active troop strength:** 11,800 est.

Economy: Industries: Oil refining, international banking, construction. **Chief crops:** Bananas, rice, corn, sugar. **Minerals:** Copper. **Other resources:** Forests (mahogany), shrimp. **Arable land:** 7%. **Livestock** (1997): chickens: 9.46 mil; cattle: 1.44 mil; pigs: 244,000. **Electricity prod.** (1996): 3.6 bil kWh. **Labor force:** 32% govt. & community services; 27% agric. & fishing.

Finance: Monetary unit: Balboa (Sept. 1998: 1.00 = $1 U.S.). **Gross domestic product** (1996 est.): $14.0 bil. **Per capita GDP:** $5,300. **Imports** (1996 est.): $2.51 bil; partners: U.S. 40%. **Exports** (1996 est.): $570 mil; partners: U.S. 39%. **Tourism:** $374 mil. **National budget** (1995): $1.86 bil. **International reserves less gold** (June 1998): $1.33 bil. **Consumer prices** (change in 1997): 1.3%.

Transport: Railroad: Length: 220.5 mi. **Motor vehicles in use:** 144,000 passenger cars, 82,800 comm. vehicles. **Civil aviation:** 541.2 mil passenger-mi; 10 airports. **Chief ports:** Balboa, Cristobal.

Communications: Television sets: 13 per 1,000 pop. **Radios:** 5.1 per 1,000 pop. **Telephones:** 1 per 8.8 persons. **Daily newspaper circ.:** 62 per 1,000 pop.

Health: Life expectancy at birth: 71.7 male; 77.3 female. **Births** (per 1,000 pop.): 22. **Deaths** (per 1,000 pop.): 5. **Natural increase:** 1.69%. **Hospital beds** (1995): 1 per 369 persons. **Physicians** (1995): 1 per 856 persons. **Infant mortality** (per 1,000 live births): 24.

Education: Free and compulsory for 6 years between ages 6-15. **Literacy** (1995): 91%.

Major International Organizations: UN (FAO, IBRD, ILO, IMF, IMO, WHO), OAS.

Embassy: 2862 McGill Terrace NW 20008; 483-1407.

The coast of Panama was sighted by Rodrigo de Bastidas, sailing with Columbus for Spain in 1501, and was visited by Columbus in 1502. Vasco Nunez de Balboa crossed the isthmus and "discovered" the Pacific Ocean, Sept. 13, 1513. Spanish colonies were ravaged by Francis Drake, 1572-95, and Henry Morgan, 1668-71. Morgan destroyed the old city of Panama which had been founded in 1519. Freed from Spain, Panama joined Colombia in 1821.

Panama declared its independence from Colombia Nov. 3, 1903, with U.S. recognition. In support of Panama, U.S. naval forces deterred action by Colombia. Panama granted use, occupation, and control of the Canal Zone to the U.S. by treaty, ratified Feb. 26, 1904. In 1978, a new treaty provided for a gradual takeover by Panama of the canal, and withdrawal of U.S. troops, to be completed by 1999. U.S. payments were substantially increased in the interim.

President Delvalle was ousted by the National Assembly, Feb. 26, 1988, after he tried to fire the head of the Panama Defense Forces, Gen. Manuel Antonio Noriega. Noriega had been indicted by 2 U.S. federal grand juries on drug charges. A general strike followed. Despite U.S.-imposed economic sanctions Noriega remained in power. Voters went to the polls to elect a new president May 7, 1989. Noriega claimed victory, but foreign observers said that the opposition had won overwhelmingly. The government voided the election May 10, charging foreign interference. A coup against Noriega failed Oct. 3.

U.S. troops invaded Panama Dec. 20, 1989, following a series of incidents, including the killing of a U.S. Marine by Panamanian soldiers. The operation had as its chief objective the capture of Noriega. He took refuge in the Vatican diplomatic mission, but surrendered to U.S. officials Jan. 3, 1990. He was convicted of racketeering and drug trafficking in a U.S. District Court in Miami, FL, Apr. 9, 1992.

On Aug. 30, 1998, voters rejected a constitutional change that would have allowed Pres. Ernesto Pérez Balladares to run for reelection in 1999.

Papua New Guinea

Independent State of Papua New Guinea

People: Population: 4,599,785. **Age distrib.** (%): <15: 39.7; 65+: 3.0. **Pop. density:** 26 per sq. mi. **Urban:** 16%. **Ethnic groups:** Papuan, Melanesian. **Principal languages:** English (official), Motu, 700+ indigenous dialects. **Chief religions:** Indigenous beliefs 34%, Roman Catholic 22%, Lutheran 16%.

Geography: Area: 178,703 sq. mi. **Location:** SE Asia, occupying E half of island of New Guinea and about 600 nearby islands. **Neighbors:** Indonesia (West Irian) on W, Australia on S. **Topography:** Thickly forested mts. cover much of the center of the country, with lowlands along the coasts. Included are some islands of Bismarck and Solomon groups, such as the Admiralty Isls., New Ireland, New Britain, and Bougainville. **Capital:** Port Moresby. **Cities** (1991): Port Moresby 192,000; Lae 80,700.

Government: Type: Parliamentary democracy. **Head of state:** Queen Elizabeth II, represented by Gov-Gen. Silas Atopare; in office: Nov. 1997. **Head of government:** Prime Min. Bill Skate; b 1953; in office: July 22, 1997. **Local divisions:** 20 provinces. **Defense:** 1.5% of GDP. **Active troop strength:** 3,700.

Economy: Chief crops: Coffee, coconuts, cocoa. **Minerals:** Gold, copper, silver. **Crude oil reserves** (1997): 325 mil bbls. **Livestock** (1997): chickens: 3.30 mil; pigs: 1.06 mil; cattle: 105,000. **Electricity prod.** (1996): 1.7 bil kWh. **Labor force:** 64% agric.

Finance: Monetary unit: Kina (Sept. 1998: 2.25 = $1 U.S.). **Gross domestic product** (1996 est.): $10.7 bil. **Per capita GDP:** $2,400. **Imports** (1995 est.): $1.3 bil; partners: Australia 52%. **Exports** (1995 est.): $2.7 bil; partners: Australia 30%; Japan 24%. **Tourism:** $72 mil. **National budget** (1997 est.): $1.35 bil. **International reserves less gold** (Mar. 1998): $185.85 mil. **Gold:** 63,000 oz t. **Consumer prices** (change in 1997): 3.9%.

Transport: Motor vehicles in use: 21,600 passenger cars, 77,700 comm. vehicles. **Civil aviation:** 515.4 mil passenger-mi. **Chief ports:** Port Moresby, Lae.

Communications: Television sets: 23 per 1,000 pop. **Radios:** 68 per 1,000 pop. **Telephones:** 1 per 99 persons. **Daily newspaper circ.:** 15 per 1,000 pop.

Health: Life expectancy at birth: 57.2 male; 59.0 female. **Births** (per 1,000 pop.): 32. **Deaths** (per 1,000 pop.): 10. **Natural increase:** 2.27%. **Physicians** (1993): 1 per 5,584 persons. **Infant mortality** (per 1,000 live births): 57.

Education: Literacy (1995): 72%.

Major International Organizations: UN (FAO, IBRD, ILO, IMF, IMO, WHO, WTrO), the Commonwealth, APEC.

Embassy: 1615 New Hampshire Ave. NW 20009; 745-3680.

Human remains have been found in the interior of New Guinea dating back at least 10,000 years and possibly much earlier. Successive waves of peoples probably entered the country from Asia through Indonesia. Europeans visited in the 15th century, but actual land claims did not begin until the 19th century, when the Dutch took control of the island's western half.

The southern half of eastern New Guinea was first claimed by Britain in 1884, and transferred to Australia in 1905. The northern half was claimed by Germany in 1884, but captured in World War I by Australia, which was first granted a League of Nations mandate and then a UN trusteeship over the area. The 2 territories were administered jointly after 1949, were given self-government Dec. 1, 1973, and became independent Sept. 16, 1975.

The indigenous population consists of a huge number of tribes, many living in almost complete isolation with mutually unintelligible languages. Secessionist rebels have clashed with government forces on Bougainville since 1988; a truce signed Oct. 10, 1997, brought a halt to the fighting, which had claimed an estimated 20,000 lives.

The country suffered from a severe drought in 1997. A tsunami killed at least 3,000 people July 17, 1998.

Paraguay

Republic of Paraguay

People: Population: 5,291,020. **Age distrib.** (%): <15: 39.5; 65+: 4.6. **Pop. density:** 34 per sq. mi. **Urban:** 53%. **Ethnic groups:** Mestizo 95%, white & Amerindian 5%. **Principal languages:** Spanish (official), Guarani. **Chief religion:** Roman Catholic 90%.

Geography: Area: 157,046 sq. mi. **Location:** Landlocked country in central South America. **Neighbors:** Bolivia on N, Argentina on S, Brazil on E. **Topography:** Paraguay R. bisects the country. To E are fertile plains, wooded slopes, grasslands. To W is the Gran Chaco plain, with marshes and scrub trees. Extreme W is arid. **Capital:** Asunción 1,081,000*.

Government: Type: Republic. **Head of state:** Pres. Raúl Cubas Grau; b Aug. 23, 1943; in office: Aug. 15, 1998. **Local divisions:** 18 departments and capital city. **Defense:** 1.3% of GDP. **Active troop strength:** 20,200.

Economy: Industries: Food processing, textiles, cement. **Chief crops:** Corn, cotton, soybeans, sugarcane. **Minerals:** Iron, manganese, limestone. **Other resources:** Forests. **Arable land:** 6%. **Livestock** (1997): chickens: 14.84 mil; cattle: 9.79 mil; pigs: 2.53 mil; sheep: 387,000; goats: 123,000. **Electricity prod.** (1996): 45.0 bil kWh. **Labor force:** 45% agric.

Finance: Monetary unit: Guarani (Sept. 1998: 2,825.00 = $1 U.S.). **Gross domestic product** (1996 est.): $17.7 bil. **Per capita GDP:** $3,200. **Imports** (1995): $2.87 bil; partners: Brazil 30%, EU 20%, U.S. 18%. **Exports** (1995): $819.5 mil; partners: EU 37%, Brazil 25%. **Tourism:** $759 mil. **National budget** (1995 est.): $1.66 bil. **International reserves less gold** (June 1998): $652.68 mil. **Gold:** 35,000 oz t. **Consumer prices** (change in 1997): 7.0%.

Transport: Railroad: Length: 274 mi. **Motor vehicles in use:** 71,000 passenger cars, 50,000 comm. vehicles. **Civil aviation:** 294.5 mil passenger-mi; 5 airports. **Chief port:** Asunción.

Communications: Television sets: 144 per 1,000 pop. **Radios:** 141 per 1,000 pop. **Telephones:** 1 per 30 persons. **Daily newspaper circ.:** 40 per 1,000 pop.

Health: Life expectancy at birth: 70.3 male; 74.3 female. **Births** (per 1,000 pop.): 32. **Deaths** (per 1,000 pop.): 5. **Natural increase:** 2.69%. **Hospital beds** (1993): 1 per 864 persons. **Physicians** (1993): 1 per 1,406 persons. **Infant mortality** (per 1,000 live births): 37.

Education: Compulsory: ages 6-12. **Literacy** (1995): 92%.

Major International Organizations: UN (FAO, IBRD, ILO, IMF, IMO, WHO, WTrO), OAS.

Embassy: 2400 Massachusetts Ave. NW 20008; 483-6960.

The Guarani Indians were settled farmers speaking a common language before the arrival of Europeans.

Visited by Sebastian Cabot in 1527 and settled as a Spanish possession in 1535, Paraguay gained its independence from Spain in 1811. It lost much of its territory to Brazil, Uruguay, and Argentina in the War of the Triple Alliance, 1865-1870. Large areas were won from Bolivia in the Chaco War, 1932-35.

Gen. Alfredo Stroessner, who had ruled since 1954, was ousted in a military coup led by Gen. Andrés Rodríguez on Feb. 3, 1989. Rodríguez was elected president May 1. Juan Carlos Wasmosy was elected president May 9, 1993, becoming the nation's first civilian head of state in many years.

A prolonged power struggle involving a popular military leader, Gen. Lino César Oviedo, who was accused of insubordination, culminated in his surrender Dec. 12, 1997. He was freed Aug. 18, 1998, following the inauguration of Pres. Raúl Cubas Grau, Oviedo's successor as Colorado Party nominee.

Peru

Republic of Peru

People: Population: 26,111,110. **Age distrib.** (%): <15: 35.7; 65+: 4.5. **Pop. density:** 53 per sq. mi. **Urban:** 71%. **Ethnic groups:** Amerindian 45%, mestizo 37%, white 15%. **Principal languages:** Spanish, Quechua (both official), Aymara. **Chief religion:** Predominantly Roman Catholic.

Geography: Area: 496,223 sq. mi. **Location:** On the Pacific coast of South America. **Neighbors:** Ecuador, Colombia on N; Brazil, Bolivia on E; Chile on S. **Topography:** An arid coastal strip, 10 to 100 mi. wide, supports much of the population thanks to widespread irrigation. The Andes cover 27% of land area. The uplands are well-watered, as are the eastern slopes reaching the Amazon basin, which covers half the country with its forests and jungles. **Capital:** Lima. **Cities** (1993 met. est.): Lima 6,742,576; Arequipa 981,272; Callao 684,135.

Government: Type: Republic. **Head of state:** Pres. Alberto Fujimori; b July 28, 1938; in office: July 28, 1990. **Head of government:** Prime Min. Alberto Pandolfi Arbulu; b Aug. 20, 1940; in office: Aug. 21, 1998. **Local divisions:** 24 departments, 1 constitutional province. **Defense:** 1.9% of GDP. **Active troop strength:** 125,000.

Economy: Industries: Fishing, mining, food processing, textiles. **Chief crops:** Cotton, sugar, coffee, rice. **Minerals:** Copper, silver, gold, iron, oil. **Crude oil reserves** (1997): 800 mil bbls. **Other resources:** Wool, sardines. **Arable land:** 3%. **Livestock** (1997): chickens: 81.97 mil; sheep: 13.11 mil; cattle: 4.56 mil; pigs: 2.48 mil; goats: 2.05 mil. **Fish catch** (1996): 9.52 mil metric tons. **Electricity prod.** (1996): 16.2 bil kWh. **Labor force:** 44% govt., other services; 33% agric.; 19% ind.

Finance: Monetary unit: New Sol (Sept. 1998: 3.03 = $1 U.S.). **Gross domestic product** (1996 est.): $92.0 bil. **Per capita GDP:** $3,800. **Imports** (1996): $7.5 bil; partners: U.S. 21%. **Exports** (1996): $6.0 bil; partners: U.S. 19%, Japan 9%. **Tourism:** $682 mil. **National budget** (1996 est.): $9.3 bil. **International reserves less gold** (May 1998): $10.96 bil. **Gold:** 1.12 mil oz t. **Consumer prices** (change in 1997): 8.6%.

Transport: Railroad: Length: 1,318 mi. **Motor vehicles in use:** 500,000 passenger cars, 275,000 comm. vehicles. **Civil aviation:** 1.64 bil passenger-mi; 27 airports. **Chief ports:** Callao, Chimbote, Salaverry.

Communications: Television sets: 85 per 1,000 pop. **Radios:** 221 per 1,000 pop. **Telephones:** 1 per 21 persons. **Daily newspaper circ.:** 87 per 1,000 pop.

Health: Life expectancy at birth: 67.8 male; 72.3 female. **Births** (per 1,000 pop.): 27. **Deaths** (per 1,000 pop.): 6. **Natural increase:** 2.09%. **Hospital beds** (1992): 1 per 509 persons. **Physicians** (1992): 1 per 1,116 persons. **Infant mortality** (per 1,000 live births): 43.

Education: Free and compulsory: ages 6-11. **Literacy** (1995): 89%.

Major International Organizations: UN and all of its specialized agencies, OAS.

Embassy: 1700 Massachusetts Ave. NW 20036; 833-9860.

The powerful Inca empire had its seat at Cuzco in the Andes and covered most of Peru, Bolivia, and Ecuador, as well as parts of Colombia, Chile, and Argentina. Building on the achievements of 800 years of Andean civilization, the Incas had a high level of skill in architecture, engineering, textiles, and social organization.

A civil war had weakened the empire when Francisco Pizarro, Spanish conquistador, began raiding Peru for its wealth, 1532. In 1533 he seized the ruling Inca, Atahualpa, filled a room with gold as a ransom, then executed him and enslaved the natives.

Lima was the seat of Spanish viceroys until the Argentine liberator, José de San Martin, captured it in 1821; Spanish forces were ultimately routed by Simón Bolívar, 1824.

On Oct. 3, 1968, a military coup ousted Pres. Fernando Belaunde Terry. In 1968-74, the military government started socialist programs. Food shortages, escalating foreign debt, and strikes led to another coup, Aug. 29, 1976.

After 12 years of military rule, Peru returned to democratic leadership in 1980 but was plagued by economic problems and by leftist Shining Path (Sendero Luminoso) guerrillas.

Pres. Alberto Fujimori, elected in June 1990, dissolved the National Congress, suspended parts of the constitution, and initiated press censorship, Apr. 5, 1992. The leader of Shining Path was captured Sept. 12.

With the economy booming and signs of significant progress in curtailing guerrilla activity, Fujimori won reelection Apr. 9, 1995. Repressive antiterrorism tactics, however, drew international criticism. On Dec. 17, 1996, leftist Tupac Amaru guerrillas infiltrated a reception at the Japanese ambassador's residence in Lima and took hundreds of hostages, most of whom were later released. Peruvian soldiers stormed the embassy Apr. 22, 1997, rescuing 71 of the remaining hostages; 1 hostage, 2 soldiers, and all 14 guerrillas were killed.

Philippines

Republic of the Philippines

People: Population: 77,725,862. **Age distrib.** (%): <15: 37.6; 65+: 3.6. **Pop. density:** 671 per sq. mi. **Urban:** 55%. **Ethnic groups:** Christian Malay 92%, Muslim Malay 4%. **Principal languages:** Pilipino, English (both official). **Chief religions:** Roman Catholic 83%, Protestant 9%, Muslim 5%.

Geography: Area: 115,830 sq. mi. **Location:** An archipelago off the SE coast of Asia. **Neighbors:** Nearest are Malaysia and Indonesia on S, Taiwan on N. **Topography:** The country consists of some 7,100 islands stretching 1,100 mi. N-S. About 95% of area and population are on 11 largest islands, which are mountainous, except for the heavily indented coastlines and for the central plain on Luzon. **Capital:** Manila. **Cities** (1994): Manila 8,594,150; Quezon City 1,676,644.

Government: Type: Republic. **Head of state:** Pres. Joseph Ejercito Estrada; b Apr. 19, 1937; in office: June 30, 1998. **Local divisions:** 16 regions subdivided into 76 provinces, 61 chartered cities. **Defense:** 2.0% of GNP. **Active troop strength:** 107,500.

Economy: Industries: Food processing, textiles, chemicals, pharmaceuticals, wood prods. **Chief crops:** Sugar, rice, corn, pineapples, coconuts. **Minerals:** Cobalt, copper, gold, nickel, silver, oil. **Other resources:** Forests (46% of area). **Crude oil reserves** (1997): 213 mil bbls. **Arable land:** 19%. **Livestock** (1997): chickens: 134.96 mil; buffalo: 2.97 mil; pigs: 9.75 mil; goats: 6.50 mil; cattle: 2.27 mil. **Fish catch** (1996): 1.79 mil metric tons. **Electricity prod.** (1996): 32.2 bil kWh. **Labor force:** 43% agric.; 23% services; 18% gov't services; 16% ind. and comm.

Finance: Monetary unit: Peso (Sept. 1998: 43.45 = $1 U.S.). **Gross domestic product** (1996 est.): $194.2 bil. **Per capita GDP:** $2,600. **Imports** (1996): $33.3 bil; partners: Japan 22%, U.S. 18%. **Exports** (1996): $20.5 bil; partners: U.S. 36%, Japan 16%. **Tourism:** $2.83 bil. **National budget** (1996 est.): $16.5 bil. **International reserves less gold** (Apr. 1998): $9.28 bil. **Gold:** 5.06 mil oz t. **Consumer prices** (change in 1997): 5.1%.

Transport: Railroad: Length: 557 mi. **Motor vehicles in use:** 702,578 passenger cars, 1.35 mil comm. vehicles. **Civil aviation:** 9.40 bil passenger-mi; 21 airports. **Chief ports:** Cebu, Manila, Iloilo, Davao.

Communications: Television sets: 125 per 1,000 pop. **Radios:** 116 per 1,000 pop. **Telephones:** 1 per 48 persons. **Daily newspaper circ.:** 65 per 1,000 pop.

Health: Life expectancy at birth: 63.6 male; 69.3 female. **Births** (per 1,000 pop.): 28. **Deaths** (per 1,000 pop.): 7. **Natural increase:** 2.19%. **Hospital beds** (1993): 1 per 860 persons. **Physicians** (1993): 1 per 849 persons. **Infant mortality** (per 1,000 live births): 35.

Education: Free and compulsory: ages 7-12. **Literacy** (1995): 95%.

Major International Organizations: UN (FAO, IBRD, ILO, IMF, IMO, WHO, WTrO), ASEAN.

Embassy: 1600 Massachusetts Ave. NW 20036; 467-9300.

Website: http://www.census.gov.ph

The Malay peoples of the Philippine Islands, whose ancestors probably migrated from Southeast Asia, were mostly hunters, fishers, and unsettled cultivators.

The archipelago was visited by Magellan, 1521. The Spanish founded Manila, 1571. The islands, named for King Philip II of Spain, were ceded by Spain to the U.S. for $20 million, 1898, following the Spanish-American War. U.S. troops suppressed a guerrilla uprising in a brutal 6-year war, 1899-1905.

Japan attacked the Philippines Dec. 8, 1941, and occupied the islands during WW II. On July 4, 1946, independence was proclaimed in accordance with an act passed by the U.S. Congress in 1934. A republic was established.

On Sept. 21, 1972, Pres. Ferdinand Marcos declared martial law. Marcos proclaimed a new constitution, Jan. 17, 1973, with himself as president. His wife, Imelda, received wide powers in 1978 to supervise planning and development. Political corruption was widespread. Martial law was lifted Jan. 17, 1981, but Marcos retained broad emergency powers. He was reelected in June to a new 6-year term as president.

The assassination of prominent opposition leader Benigno S. Aquino Jr., Aug. 21, 1983, sparked demonstrations calling for the resignation of Marcos. After a bitter presidential campaign, amid allegations of widespread election fraud, Marcos was declared the victor Feb. 16, 1986, over Corazon Aquino, widow of the slain opposition leader. With his support collapsing, Marcos fled the country Feb. 25.

Recognized as president by the U.S. and other nations, Aquino was plagued by a weak economy, widespread poverty, Communist and Muslim insurgencies, and lukewarm military support. Rebel troops seized military bases and TV stations and bombed the presidential palace, Dec. 1, 1989. Government forces defeated the attempted coup aided by air cover provided by U.S. F-4s. Aquino endorsed Fidel Ramos in the May 1992 presidential election, which he won.

The U.S. vacated the Subic Bay Naval Station at the end of 1992, ending its long military presence in the Philippines.

The government signed a cease-fire agreement, Jan. 30, 1994, with Muslim separatist guerrillas, but some rebels refused to abide by the accord. A new treaty providing for expansion and development of an autonomous Muslim region on Mindanao was signed Sept. 2, 1996, formally ending a rebellion that had claimed more than 120,000 lives since 1972.

Running as a populist, Joseph (Erap) Estrada, a former movie actor, won the presidential election of May 11, 1998.

Poland

Republic of Poland

People: Population: 38,606,922. **Age distrib.** (%): <15: 20.6; 65+: 11.8. **Pop. density:** 320 per sq. mi. **Urban:** 64%. **Ethnic groups:** Polish 98%. **Principal language:** Polish (official). **Chief religion:** Roman Catholic 95%.

Geography: Area: 120,727 sq. mi. **Location:** On the Baltic Sea in E central Europe. **Neighbors:** Germany on W; Czech Rep., Slovakia on S; Lithuania, Belarus, Ukraine on E; Russia on N. **Topography:** Mostly lowlands forming part of the Northern European Plain. The Carpathian Mts. along the S border rise to 8,200 ft. **Capital:** Warsaw. **Cities:** Katowice 3,425,000; Warsaw 2,219,000; Lodz 1,041,000*.

Government: Type: Republic. **Head of state:** Pres. Aleksander Kwasniewski; b Nov. 15, 1954; in office: Dec. 23, 1995. **Head of government:** Prime Min. Jerzy Buzek; b July 3, 1940; in office: Oct. 31, 1997. **Local divisions:** 49 provinces. **Defense:** 2.8% of GDP. **Active troop strength:** 248,500.

Economy: Industries: Shipbuilding, chemicals, metals, machinery, food processing. **Chief crops:** Grains, potatoes, vegetables. **Minerals:** Coal, copper, silver, lead, sulfur, natural gas. **Crude oil reserves** (1997): 40.0 mil bbls. **Arable land:** 47%. **Livestock** (1997): chickens: 53.29 mil; pigs: 18.13 mil; cattle: 7.31 mil; sheep: 490,800. **Fish catch** (1996): 341,899 metric tons. **Electricity prod.** (1996): 134.7 bil kWh. **Labor force:** 32% ind. & constr.; 28% agric.

Finance: Monetary unit: Zloty (Sept. 1998: 3.62 = $1 U.S.). **Gross domestic product** (1996 est.): $246.3 bil. **Per capita GDP:** $6,400. **Imports** (1995): $34.6 bil; partners: Germany 28%. **Exports** (1995): $30.9 bil; partners: Germany 36%. **Tourism:** $8.70 bil. **National budget** (1996 est.): $40.6 bil. **International reserves less gold** (June 1998): $24.28 bil. **Gold:** 3.30 mil oz t. **Consumer prices** (change in 1997): 15.9%.

Transport: Railroad: Length: 14,904 mi. **Motor vehicles in use:** 7.52 mil passenger cars, 1.55 mil comm. vehicles. **Civil aviation:** 2.43 bil passenger-mi; 8 airports. **Chief ports:** Gdansk, Gdynia, Szczecin.

Communications: Television sets: 249.9 per 1,000 pop. **Radios:** 263.3 per 1,000 pop. **Telephones:** 1 per 6.7 persons. **Daily newspaper circ.:** 140 per 1,000 pop.

Health: Life expectancy at birth: 68.6 male; 77.2 female. **Births** (per 1,000 pop.): 10. **Deaths** (per 1,000 pop.): 10. **Natural increase:** 0.00%. **Hospital beds** (1996): 1 per 180 persons. **Physicians** (1996): 1 per 436 persons. **Infant mortality** (per 1,000 live births): 13.

Education: Free and compulsory: ages 7-14. **Literacy** (1994): 99%.

Major International Organizations: UN (FAO, IBRD, ILO, IMF, IMO, WHO, WTrO), OECD, OSCE.

Embassy: 2640 16th St. NW 20009; 234-3800.

Website: http://www.polishworld.com

Slavic tribes in the area were converted to Latin Christianity in the 10th century. Poland was a great power from the 14th to the 17th centuries. In 3 partitions (1772, 1793, 1795) it was apportioned among Prussia, Russia, and Austria. Overrun by the Austro-German armies in World War I, it declared its independence on Nov. 11, 1918, and was recognized as independent by the Treaty of Versailles, June 28, 1919. Large territories to the east were taken in a war with Russia, 1921.

Germany and the USSR invaded Poland Sept. 1-27, 1939, and divided the country. During the war, some 6 million Polish citizens, half of them Jews, were killed by the Nazis. With Germany's defeat, a Polish government-in-exile in London was recognized by the U.S., but the USSR pressed the claims of a rival group. The election of 1947 was completely dominated by the Communists.

In compensation for 69,860 sq. mi. ceded to the USSR, 1945, Poland received approx. 40,000 sq. mi. of German territory E of the Oder-Neisse line comprising Silesia, Pomerania, West Prussia, and part of East Prussia.

In 12 years of rule by Stalinists, large estates were abolished, industries nationalized, schools secularized, and Roman Catholic prelates jailed. Farm production fell off. Harsh working conditions caused a riot in Poznan, June 28-29, 1956. A new Politburo, committed to a more independent Polish Communism, was named Oct. 1956, with Wladyslaw Gomulka as first secretary of the party. Collectivization of farms was ended. Gomulka agreed to permit religious liberty and religious publications, provided the church kept out of politics.

In Dec. 1970 workers in port cities rioted because of price rises and new incentive wage rules. On Dec. 20 Gomulka resigned as party leader; he was succeeded by Edward Gierek. The rules were dropped and price rises revoked.

After 2 months of labor turmoil had crippled the country, the Polish government, Aug. 30, 1980, met the demands of striking workers at the Lenin Shipyard, Gdansk. Among the 21 concessions granted were the right to form independent trade unions and the right to strike. By 1981, 9.5 mil workers had joined the independent trade union (Solidarity). Solidarity leaders proposed, Dec. 12, a nationwide referendum on establishing a non-Communist government if the government failed to agree to a series of demands.

Spurred by fear of Soviet intervention, the government, Dec. 13, imposed martial law. Lech Walesa and other Solidarity leaders were arrested. The U.S. imposed sanctions, which were lifted when martial law was suspended Dec. 1982

On Apr. 5, 1989, an accord was reached between the government and opposition factions on political and economic reforms, including free elections. Candidates endorsed by Solidarity swept the parliamentary elections, June 4. Lech Walesa became president Dec. 22, 1990.

A radical economic program designed to transform the economy into a free-market system led to inflation and unemployment. In Sept. 1993, former Communists and other leftists won a majority in the lower house of Parliament. Walesa lost to a former Communist, Aleksander Kwasniewski, in a presidential runoff election, Nov. 19, 1995.

A new constitution was approved by referendum May 25, 1997. On July 8, Poland was invited to become a full member of NATO within 2 years. Flooding in July caused more than $1 billion in property damage. Solidarity won parliamentary elections held Sept. 21, 1997.

Portugal

Portuguese Republic

People: Population: 9,927,556. **Age distrib.** (%): <15: 17.3; 65+: 15.1. **Pop. density:** 278 per sq. mi. **Urban:** 36%. **Ethnic groups:** Homogeneous Mediterranean stock, small African minority. **Principal languages:** Portuguese (official). **Chief religion:** Roman Catholic 97%.

Geography: Area: 35,672 sq. mi., incl. the Azores and Madeira Islands. **Location:** At SW extreme of Europe. **Neighbors:** Spain on N, E. **Topography:** Portugal N of Tajus R., which bisects the country NE-SW, is mountainous, cool and rainy. To the S there are drier, rolling plains, and a warm climate. **Capital:** Lisbon. **Cities** (1993 met. est.): Lisbon 2,048,000; Porto 1,652,000.

Government: Type: Republic. **Head of state:** Pres. Jorge Sampaio; b Sept. 18, 1939; in office: Mar. 9, 1996. **Head of government:** Prime Min. Antonio Guterres; b Apr. 30, 1949; in office: Oct. 30, 1995. **Local divisions:** 18 districts, 2 autonomous regions. **Defense:** 2.8% of GDP. **Active troop strength:** 54,200.

Economy: Industries: Textiles, footwear, cork, chemicals, fish canning, wine, paper. **Chief crops:** Grains, potatoes, grapes, olives. **Minerals:** Tungsten, uranium, iron. **Other resources:** Forests (world leader in cork production). **Arable land:** 26%. **Livestock** (1997): chickens: 27.00 mil; sheep: 6.30 mil; pigs: 2.34 mil; cattle: 1.31 mil; goats: 820,000. **Fish catch** (1996): 260,185 metric tons. **Electricity prod.** (1996): 32.8 bil kWh. **Labor force:** 55% services; 24% manuf.; 11% agric., fish.

Finance: Monetary unit: Escudo (Sept. 1998: 177.75 = $1 U.S.). **Gross domestic product** (1996 est.): $122.1 bil. **Per capita GDP:** $12,400. **Imports** (1996): $34.2 bil; partners: EU 72%. **Exports** (1996): $25.8 bil; partners: EU 80%. **Tourism:** $4.35 bil. **National budget** (1996 est.): $52 bil. **International reserves less gold** (May, 1998): $15.46 bil. **Gold:** 16.07 mil oz t. **Consumer prices** (change in 1997): 2.2%.

Transport: Railroad: Length: 1,905.2 mi. **Motor vehicles in use:** 2.75 mil passenger cars, 930,700 comm. vehicles. **Civil aviation:** 5.23 bil passenger-mi; 16 airports. **Chief ports:** Lisbon, Setubal, Leixoes.

Communications: Television sets: 333 per 1,000 pop. **Radios:** 280 per 1,000 pop. **Telephones:** 1 per 2.8 persons. **Daily newspaper circ.:** 47 per 1,000 pop.

Health: Life expectancy at birth: 72.3 male; 79.3 female. **Births** (per 1,000 pop.): 11. **Deaths** (per 1,000 pop.): 10. **Natural increase:** 0.04%. **Hospital beds** (1996): 1 per 253 persons. **Physicians** (1996): 1 per 332 persons. **Infant mortality** (per 1,000 live births): 7.

Education: Free and compulsory: ages 6-15. **Literacy** (1995): 90%.

Major International Organizations: UN (FAO, IBRD, ILO, IMF, IMO, WHO, WTrO), EU, NATO, OECD, OSCE.

Embassy: 2125 Kalorama Rd. NW 20008; 328-8610.

Website: http://infoline.ine.pt/si/english/port.html

Portugal, an independent state since the 12th century, was a kingdom until a revolution in 1910 drove out King Manoel II and a republic was proclaimed.

From 1932 a strong, repressive government was headed by Premier Antonio de Oliveira Salazar. Illness forced his retirement in Sept. 1968.

On Apr. 25, 1974, the government was seized by a military junta led by Gen. Antonio de Spinola, who became president. The new government reached agreements providing independence for Guinea-Bissau, Mozambique, Cape Verde Islands, Angola, and São Tomé and Príncipe. Banks, insurance companies, and other industries were nationalized.

Parliament approved, June 1, 1989, a package of reforms that did away with the socialist economy and created a "democratic" economy, denationalizing industries.

Azores Islands, in the Atlantic, 740 mi. W of Portugal, have an area of 868 sq. mi. and a pop. (1993 est.) of 238,000. A 1951 agreement gave the U.S. rights to use defense facilities in the Azores. The **Madeira Islands,** 350 mi. off the NW coast of Africa, have an area of 306 sq. mi. and a pop. (1993 est.) of 254,000. Both groups were offered partial autonomy in 1976.

Macau, area of 6 sq. mi., is an enclave, a peninsula and 2 small islands, at the mouth of the Xi (Pearl) R. in China. Portugal granted broad autonomy in 1976. In 1987, Portugal and China agreed Macau would revert to China Dec. 20, 1999. Macau, like Hong Kong, was guaranteed 50 years of noninterference in its way of life and capitalist system. Pop. (1998 est.): 429,152.

Qatar

State of Qatar

People: Population: 697,126. **Age distrib.** (%): <15: 27.4; 65+: 2.0. **Pop. density:** 158 per sq. mi. **Urban:** 92%. **Ethnic groups:** Arab 40%, Pakistani 18%, Indian 18%, Iranian 10%. **Principal languages:** Arabic (official), English. **Chief religion:** Muslim 95%.

Geography: Area: 4,416 sq. mi. **Location:** Middle East, occupying peninsula on W coast of Persian Gulf. **Neighbors:** Saudi Arabia on S. **Topography:** Mostly a flat desert, with some limestone ridges; vegetation of any kind is scarce. **Capital:** Doha (1993 est.): 339,471.

Government: Type: Traditional monarchy. **Head of state:** Emir Hamad bin Khalifa ath-Thani; b 1950; in office: June 27, 1995. **Head of government:** Prime Min. Abdullah bin Khalifa ath-Thani; in office: Oct. 29, 1996. **Local divisions:** 9 municipalities. **Defense:** 10.2% of GDP. **Active troop strength:** 11,800.

Economy: Industries: Oil production and refining, natural gas. **Crude oil reserves** (1997): 3.7 bil bbls. **Livestock** (1997): chickens: chickens: 3.85 mil; sheep: 199,700; goats: 172,100. **Electricity prod.** (1996): 5.2 bil kWh. **Labor force:** 51% serv.; 25% manuf. & constr.

Finance: Monetary unit: Riyal (Sept. 1998: 3.64 = $1 U.S.). **Gross domestic product** (1996 est.): $11.7 bil. **Per capita GDP:** $21,300. **Imports** (1996 est.): $4.4 bil; partners: Italy 16%, Germany 11%. Japan 10%. **Exports** (1996 est.): $4 bil; partners: Japan 54%. **National budget** (FY 1996-97): $3.8 bil. **Gold** (Apr. 1998): 54,000 oz t.

Transport: Motor vehicles in use: 96,800 passenger cars, 85,600 comm. vehicles. **Civil aviation:** 1.71 bil passenger-mi; 1 airport. **Chief ports:** Doha, Umm Said.

Communications: Television sets: 451 per 1,000 pop. **Radios:** 322 per 1,000 pop. **Telephones:** 1 per 4.5 persons. **Daily newspaper circ.:** 143 per 1,000 pop.

Health: Life expectancy at birth: 71.4 male; 76.5 female. **Births** (per 1,000 pop.): 17. **Deaths** (per 1,000 pop.): 4. **Natural increase:** 1.34%. **Hospital beds** (1994): 1 per 509 persons. **Physicians** (1994): 1 per 793 persons. **Infant mortality** (per 1,000 live births): 18.

Education: Literacy (1995): 79%.

Major International Organizations: UN (FAO, IBRD, ILO, IMF, IMO, WHO, WTrO), AL, OPEC.

Embassy: 4200 Wisconsin Ave. NW 20016; 274-1600.

Website: http://www.mofa.gov.qa

Qatar was under Bahrain's control until the Ottoman Turks took power, 1872 to 1915. In a treaty signed 1916, Qatar gave Great Britain responsibility for its defense and foreign relations. After Britain announced it would remove its military forces from the Persian Gulf area by the end of 1971, Qatar sought a federation with other British-protected states in the area; this failed and Qatar declared itself independent, Sept. 1, 1971. Crown Prince Hamad bin Khalifa ath-Thani ousted his father, Emir Khalifa bin Hamad ath-Thani, June 27, 1995.

Oil and natural gas revenues give Qatar a per capita income among the world's highest.

Romania

People: Population: 22,395,848. **Age distrib.** (%): <15: 19.0; 65+: 13.0. **Pop. density:** 244 per sq. mi. **Urban:** 56%. **Ethnic groups:** Romanian 89%, Hungarian 9%. **Principal languages:** Romanian (official), Hungarian, German. **Chief religions:** Romanian Orthodox 70%, Roman Catholic 6%, Protestant 6%.

Geography: Area: 91,699 sq. mi. **Location:** SE Europe, on the Black Sea. **Neighbors:** Moldova on E, Ukraine on N, Hungary and Yugoslavia on W, Bulgaria on S. **Topography:** The Carpathian Mts. encase the north-central Transylvanian plateau. There are wide plains S and E of the mountains, through which flow the lower reaches of the rivers of the Danube system. **Capital:** Bucharest. **Cities** (1994 met. est.): Bucharest 2,339,156; Iasi 815,368; Constanta 747,441.

Government: Type: Republic. **Head of state:** Pres. Emil Constantinescu; b Nov. 19, 1939; in office: Nov. 29, 1996. **Head of government:** Prime Min. Radu Vasile; b Oct. 10, 1942; in office: Apr. 2, 1998. **Local divisions:** 40 counties, 1 municipality. **Defense:** 2.3% of GDP. **Active troop strength:** 228,400.

Economy: Industries: Mining, construction materials, metals, machinery, oil products, chemicals, food processing. **Chief crops:** Grains, grapes, sugar beets, potatoes. **Minerals:** Oil, gas, coal, iron. **Crude oil reserves** (1997): 1.6 bil bbls. **Other resources:** Timber. **Arable land:** 41%. **Livestock** (1997): chickens: 78.48 mil; sheep: 9.66 mil; pigs: 8.23 mil; cattle: 3.43 mil; goats: 654,000. **Fish catch** (1996): 18,259 metric tons. **Electricity prod.** (1996): 59.2 bil kWh. **Labor force:** 36% agric.; 29% industry.

Finance: Monetary unit: Leu (Sept. 1998: 8,948.00 = $1 U.S.). **Gross domestic product** (1996 est.): $113.2 bil. **Per capita GDP:** $5,200. **Imports** (1996 est.): $9.38 bil; partners: Germany 17%, Russia 13%. **Exports** (1996 est.): $7.7 bil; partners: Germany 18%, Italy 16%. **Tourism:** $550 mil. **National budget** (1996 est.): $7.3 bil. **International reserves less gold** (May 1998): $3.24 bil. **Gold:** $3.12 mil oz t. **Consumer prices** (change in 1997): 154.8%.

Transport: Railroad: Length: 7,063.3 mi. **Motor vehicles in use:** 2.39 mil passenger cars; 513,312 comm. vehicles. **Civil aviation:** 1.13 bil passenger-mi; 8 airports. **Chief ports:** Constanta, Braila.

Communications: Television sets: 201 per 1,000 pop. **Radios:** 198 per 1,000 pop. **Telephones:** 1 per 7.6 persons. **Daily newspaper circ.:** 297 per 1,000 pop.

Health: Life expectancy at birth: 66.7 male; 74.5 female. **Births** (per 1,000 pop.): 9. **Deaths** (per 1,000 pop.): 12. **Natural increase:** –0.23%. **Hospital beds** (1992): 1 per 105 persons. **Physicians** (1993): 1 per 565 persons. **Infant mortality** (per 1,000 live births): 19.

Education: Compulsory: ages 6-16. **Literacy** (1992): 97%.

Major International Organizations: UN (FAO, IBRD, ILO, IMF, IMO, WHO, WTrO), OSCE.

Embassy: 1607 23d St. NW 20008; 332-4846.

Website: http://www.embassy.org/romania

Romania's earliest known people merged with invading Proto-Thracians, preceding by centuries the Dacians. The Dacian kingdom was occupied by Rome, AD 106-271; people and language were Romanized. The principalities of Wallachia and Moldavia, dominated by Turkey, were united in 1859, became Romania in 1861. In 1877 Romania proclaimed independence from Turkey, and became an independent state by the Treaty of Berlin, 1878; a kingdom under Carol I, 1881; and a constitutional monarchy with a bicameral legislature, 1886.

Romania helped Russia in its war with Turkey, 1877-78. After World War I it acquired Bessarabia, Bukovina, Transylvania, and Banat. In 1940 it ceded Bessarabia and Northern Bukovina to the USSR, part of southern Dobrudja to Bulgaria, and northern Transylvania to Hungary.

In 1941, Prem. Marshal Ion Antonescu led Romania in support of Germany against the USSR. In 1944 he was overthrown by King Michael and Romania joined the Allies.

After occupation by Soviet troops a People's Republic was proclaimed, Dec. 30, 1947; Michael was forced to abdicate.

On Aug. 22, 1965, a new constitution proclaimed Romania a Socialist Republic. Pres. Nicolae Ceausescu maintained an independent course in foreign affairs, but his domestic policies were repressive. All industry was state-owned, and state farms and cooperatives owned almost all arable land.

On Dec. 16, 1989, security forces opened fire on antigovernment demonstrators in Timisoara; hundreds were buried in mass graves. Ceausescu declared a state of emergency as protests spread to other cities. On Dec. 21, in Bucharest, security forces fired on protesters. Army units joined the rebellion, Dec. 22, and a group known as the Council of National Salvation announced that it had overthrown the government. Fierce fighting took place between the army, which backed the new government, and forces loyal to Ceausescu.

Ceausescu and his wife were captured and, following a trial in which they were found guilty of genocide, were executed Dec. 25, 1989. Former Communists dominated the government in succeeding years. A new constitution providing for a multiparty system took effect Dec. 8, 1991. Many of Romania's state-owned companies were privatized in 1996. The former Communists were swept from power in elections Nov. 3 and 17, 1996.

Russia

Russian Federation

People: Population: 146,861,022. **Age distrib.** (%): <15: 19.7; 65+: 12.5. **Pop. density:** 22 per sq. mi. **Urban:** 76%. **Ethnic groups:** Russian 82%, Tatar 4%. **Principal languages:** Russian (official), many others. **Chief religions:** Russian Orthodox, Muslim, others.

Geography: Area: 6,592,735 sq. mi., more than 76% of the total area of the former USSR and the largest country in the world. **Location:** Stretches from E Europe across N Asia to the Pacific O. **Neighbors:** Finland, Norway, Estonia, Latvia, Belarus, Ukraine on W; Georgia, Azerbaijan, Kazakhstan, China, Mongolia, North Korea on S; Kaliningrad exclave bordered by Poland on the S, Lithuania on the N and E. **Topography:** Russia contains every type of climate except the distinctly tropical, and has a varied topography. The European portion is a low plain, grassy in S, wooded in N, with Ural Mts. on the E, and Caucasus Mts. on the S. Urals stretch N-S for 2,500 mi. The Asiatic portion is also a vast plain, with mountains on the S and in the E; tundra covers extreme N, with forest belt below; plains, marshes are in W, desert in SW. **Capital:** Moscow. **Cities:** Moscow 9,269,000; St. Petersburg 5,132,000; Novosibirsk 1,476,000*.

Government: Type: Federation. **Head of state:** Pres. Boris Yeltsin; b Feb. 1, 1931; in office: July 10, 1991. **Head of government:** Prime Min. Yevgeny Primakov; b Oct. 29, 1929; in office: Sept. 11, 1998. **Local divisions:** 21 autonomous republics, 49 oblasts, 6 krays, 10 autonomous okrugs, 1 autonomous oblast; 2 autonomous cities. **Defense:** 6.5% of GDP. **Active troop strength:** 1.270 mil.

Economy: Industries: Steel, machinery, machine tools, vehicles, chemicals, mining, footwear, textiles, appliances, paper. **Chief crops:** Grains, sugar beets, potatoes, vegetables, sunflowers. **Minerals:** Manganese, mercury, potash, bauxite, cobalt, chromium, copper, coal, gold, lead, molybdenum, nickel, phosphates, silver, tin, tungsten, zinc, oil, gas, iron, potassium. **Crude oil reserves** (1997): 48.6 bil bbls. (all former USSR). **Other resources:** Forests. **Arable land:** 8%. **Livestock** (1997): chickens: 415.00 mil; cattle: 35.80 mil; sheep: 21.71 mil; pigs: 19.50 mil; goats: 1.89 mil. **Fish catch** (1996): 4.68 mil metric tons. **Electricity prod.** (1996): 805.6 bil kWh. **Labor force:** 24% mining & manuf.; 23% services; 14% agric.

Finance: Monetary unit: Ruble (Aug. 1998: 9.00 = $1 U.S. NOTE: On Jan 1, 1998, Russia eliminated 3 digits from the ruble.) **Gross domestic product** (1996 est.): $767 bil. **Per capita GDP:** $5,200. **Imports** (1996): $59.8 bil; partners: Germany 12%, U.S. 5%. **Exports** (1996): $88.3 bil; partners: Germany 8%, China 6%. **Tourism:** $6.67 bil. **National budget** (1996): $56.6 bil. **International reserves less gold** (May 1998): $9.63 bil. **Gold:** 16.67 mil oz t. **Consumer prices** (change in 1997): 14.6%.

Transport: Railroad: Length: 94,400 mi. **Motor vehicles in use:** 13.71 mil passenger cars, 9.86 mil comm. vehicles. **Civil aviation:** 32.73 bil passenger-mi; 75 airports. **Chief ports:** St. Petersburg, Murmansk, Arkhangelsk.

Communications: Television sets: 379 per 1,000 pop. **Radios:** 341 per 1,000 pop. **Telephones:** 1 per 5.9 persons. **Daily newspaper circ.:** 267 per 1,000 pop.

Health: Life expectancy at birth: 58.6 male; 71.6 female. **Births** (per 1,000 pop.): 10. **Deaths** (per 1,000 pop.): 15. **Natural increase:** –0.53%. **Hospital beds** (1995): 1 per 80 persons. **Physicians** (1995): 1 per 235 persons. **Infant mortality** (per 1,000 live births): 23.

Education: Free and compulsory: ages 7-17. **Literacy** (1995): 99%.

Major International Organizations: UN (IBRD, ILO, IMF, IMO, WHO), CIS, OSCE.

Embassy: 2650 Wisconsin Ave. NW 20007; 298-5700.

Website: http://www.undp.org/missions/russianfed

History. Slavic tribes began migrating into Russia from the W in the 5th century AD. The first Russian state, founded by Scandinavian chieftains, was established in the 9th century, centering in Novgorod and Kiev. In the 13th century the Mongols overran the country. It recovered under the grand dukes and princes of Muscovy, or Moscow, and by 1480 freed itself from the Mongols. Ivan the Terrible was the first to be formally proclaimed Tsar (1547). Peter the Great (1682-1725) extended the domain and, in 1721, founded the Russian Empire.

Western ideas and the beginnings of modernization spread through the huge Russian empire in the 19th and early 20th centuries. But political evolution failed to keep pace.

Military reverses in the 1905 war with Japan and in World War I led to the breakdown of the Tsarist regime. The 1917 Revolution began in March with a series of sporadic strikes for higher wages by factory workers. A provisional democratic government under Prince Georgi Lvov was established but was quickly followed in May by the second provisional government, led by Alexander Kerensky. The Kerensky government and the freely-elected Constituent Assembly were overthrown in a Communist coup led by Vladimir Ilyich Lenin Nov. 7.

Soviet Union

Lenin's death Jan. 21, 1924, resulted in an internal power struggle from which Joseph Stalin eventually emerged on top. Stalin secured his position at first by exiling opponents, but from the 1930s to 1953, he resorted to a series of "purge" trials, mass executions, and mass exiles to work camps. These measures resulted in millions of deaths, according to most estimates.

Germany and the Soviet Union signed a non-aggression pact Aug. 1939; Germany launched a massive invasion of the Soviet Union, June 1941. Notable heroic episode was the "900 days" siege of Leningrad (now St. Petersburg), lasting to Jan. 1944, and causing a million deaths; the city was never taken. Russian winter counterthrusts, 1941-42 and 1942-43, stopped the German advance. Turning point was the failure of German troops to take and hold Stalingrad (now Volgograd), Sept. 1942 to Feb. 1943. With British and U.S. Lend-Lease aid and sustaining great casualties, the Russians drove the German forces from eastern Europe and the Balkans in the next 2 years.

After Stalin died, Mar. 5, 1953, Nikita Khrushchev was elected first secretary of the Central Committee. In 1956 he condemned Stalin. "De-Stalinization" of the country was begun.

Under Khrushchev the open antagonism of Poles and Hungarians toward domination by Moscow was brutally suppressed in 1956. He advocated peaceful co-existence with the capitalist countries, but continued arming the Soviet Union with nuclear weapons. He aided the Cuban revolution under Fidel Castro but withdrew Soviet missiles from Cuba during confrontation by U.S. Pres. Kennedy, Sept.-Oct. 1962. Khrushchev was suddenly deposed, Oct. 1964, and replaced by Leonid I. Brezhnev.

In Aug. 1968 Russian, Polish, East German, Hungarian, and Bulgarian military forces invaded Czechoslovakia to put a curb on liberalization policies of the Czech government.

Massive Soviet military aid to North Vietnam in the late 1960s and early 1970s helped assure Communist victories throughout Indo-China. Soviet arms aid and advisers were sent to several African countries in the 1970s.

In Dec. 1979, Soviet forces entered Afghanistan to support that government against rebels. In Apr. 1988, the Soviets agreed to withdraw their troops, ending a futile 8-year war.

Mikhail Gorbachev was chosen gen. secy. of the Communist Party, Mar. 1985. He held 4 summit meetings with U.S. Pres. Ronald Reagan. In 1987, in Washington, a treaty was signed eliminating intermediate-range nuclear missiles from Europe.

In 1987, Gorbachev initiated a program of reforms, including expanded freedoms and the democratization of the political process, through openness (*glasnost*) and restructuring (*perestroika*). The reforms were opposed by some Eastern bloc countries and many old-line Communists in the USSR. Gorbachev faced economic problems as well as ethnic and nationalist unrest in the republics.

When an apparent coup against Gorbachev became known on Aug. 19, 1991, the pres. of the Russian Republic, Boris Yeltsin, denounced it and called for a general strike. Some 50,000 demonstrated at the Russian Parliament in support of Yeltsin. By Aug. 21, the coup had failed and Gorbachev was restored as president. On Aug. 24, Gorbachev resigned as leader of the Communist Party. Several republics declared their independence, including Russia, Ukraine, and Kazakhstan. On Aug. 29, the Soviet Parliament voted to suspend all activities of the Communist Party.

The Soviet Union officially broke up Dec. 26, 1991, one day after Gorbachev resigned. The Soviet hammer and sickle flying over the Kremlin was lowered and replaced by the flag of Russia, ending the domination of the Communist Party over all areas of national life since 1917.

Russian Federation

In a first major step in radical economic reform, Russia eliminated state subsidies of most goods and services, Jan. 1992. The effect was to allow prices to soar far beyond the means of ordinary workers. In June, Pres. Yeltsin and U.S. Pres. George Bush agreed to massive arms reductions.

Russia launched a drive to privatize thousands of large and medium-sized state-owned enterprises in 1993. Yeltsin narrowly survived an impeachment vote by the Congress of People's Deputies, Mar. 28. He received strong support from voters in a referendum Apr. 25, but he continued to face a legislature dominated by conservatives and former Communists.

On Sept. 21, 1993, Yeltsin called early elections and dissolved Parliament, which in turn declared him deposed. Anti-Yeltsin legislators then barricaded themselves in the Parliament building. On Oct. 3, anti-Yeltsin forces attacked some facilities in Moscow and broke into the Parliament building. Yeltsin ordered the army to attack and seize the building. About 140 people were killed in the fighting, according to medical authorities. More than 150 were arrested.

In elections Dec. 12, 1993, a Yeltsin-supported constitution was approved, but ultranationalists and Communist hard-liners made strong showings in legislative contests. In Dec. 1994 the Russian government sent troops into the breakaway republic of Chechnya. Grozny, the Chechen capital, fell in Feb. 1995 after heavy fighting, but Chechen rebels continued to resist.

Communists made further gains in parliamentary elections Dec. 17, 1995. Despite poor health, Yeltsin won a presidential runoff election over a Communist opponent, July 3, 1996. On Aug. 14, after rebels embarrassed the Russian military by retaking Grozny, Yeltsin gave his security chief, Alexander Lebed, broad powers to negotiate an end to the Chechnya war. Lebed and Chechen leaders signed a peace accord Aug. 31. On Oct. 17, Yeltsin dismissed Lebed for insubordination. Yeltsin survived quintuple-bypass heart surgery Nov. 5.

Russian troops remaining in Chechnya were pulled out Jan. 1997. A revitalized Yeltsin revamped his cabinet in Mar. to strengthen the hand of reformers. On May 27, he signed a "founding act" increasing cooperation with NATO and paving the way for NATO to admit Eastern European nations.

Russia's economic crisis deepened throughout 1998; in Aug. the ruble plummeted and the country defaulted on its debt. Yeltsin dismissed Prime Min. Viktor Chernomyrdin on Mar. 23 and Chernomyrdin's successor, Sergei Kiriyenko, on Aug. 23. Each move triggered a confrontation with parliament. Yevgeny Primakov became premier Sept. 11, 1998.

Rwanda

Republic of Rwanda

People: Population: 7,956,172. **Age distrib.** (%): <15: 44.7; 65+: 2.8. **Pop. density:** 782 per sq. mi. **Urban:** 6%. **Ethnic groups:** Hutu 80%, Tutsi 19%, Twa (Pygmy) 1%. **Principal languages:** French, Kinyarwanda (both official). **Chief religions:** Roman Catholic 65%, indigenous beliefs 25%.

Geography: Area: 10,170 sq. mi. **Location:** In E central Africa. **Neighbors:** Uganda on N, Congo-(formerly Zaire) on W, Burundi on S, Tanzania on E. **Topography:** Grassy uplands and hills cover most of the country, with a chain of volcanoes in the NW. The source of the Nile R. has been located in the headwaters of the Kagera (Akagera) R., SW of Kigali. **Capital:** Kigali (1993): 234,500.

Government: Type: Republic. **Head of state:** Pres. Pasteur Bizimungu; b 1950; in office: July 19, 1994. **Head of government:** Prime Min. Pierre Celestin Rwigema; in office: Aug. 31, 1995. **Local divisions:** 12 prefectures, 154 communes. **Defense:** 6.3% of GDP. **Active troop strength:** 33,000.

Economy: Industries: Mining, cement. **Chief crops:** Coffee, tea, pyrethrum, bananas. **Minerals:** Tin, gold, wolframite. **Arable land:** 35%. **Livestock** (1997): chickens: 1.40 mil; goats: 920,000; cattle: 465,000; sheep 250,000. **Electricity prod.** (1996): 164 mil kWh. **Labor force:** 93% agric.

Finance: Monetary unit: Franc (Sept. 1998: 3125.40 = $1 U.S.). **Gross domestic product** (1995 est.): $3.8 bil. **Per capita GDP:** $400. **Imports** (1995 est.): $237.3 mil; partners: Belg.-Lux. 17%, Kenya 13%. **Exports** (1995 est.): $51.2 mil; partners: Germany 21%, Netherlands 19%. **Tourism:** $1 mil. **National budget** (1992 est.): $453.7 mil. **International reserves less gold** (June 1998): $149.51 mil. **Consumer prices** (change in 1997): 11.5%.

Transport: Motor vehicles in use: 11,900 passenger cars, 15,900 comm. vehicles. **Civil aviation:** 1.2 mil passenger-mi; 2 airports. **Chief ports:** Gisenyi, Cyangugu.

Communications: Radios: 78.4 per 1,000 pop. **Telephones:** 1 per 530 persons.

Health: Life expectancy at birth: 41.5 male; 42.4 female. **Births** (per 1,000 pop.): 39. **Deaths** (per 1,000 pop.): 19. **Natural increase:** 2.00%. **Physicians** (1992): 1 per 50,000 persons. **Infant mortality** (per 1,000 live births): 113.

Education: Compulsory: ages 7-14. **Literacy** (1995): 60%.

Major International Organizations: UN (FAO, IBRD, ILO, IMF, WHO, WTrO), OAU.

Embassy: 2141 Wisconsin Ave NW 20007; 232-2882.

For centuries, the Tutsi (an extremely tall people) dominated the Hutu (90% of the population). A civil war broke out in 1959 and Tutsi power was ended. Many Tutsi went into exile. A referendum in 1961 abolished the monarchic system. Rwanda, which had been part of the Belgian UN trusteeship of Rwanda-Urundi, became independent July 1, 1962.

In 1963 Tutsi exiles invaded in an unsuccessful coup; a large-scale massacre of Tutsi followed. Rivalries among Hutu led to a bloodless coup July 1973 in which Juvénal Habyarimana took power. After an invasion and coup attempt by Tutsi exiles in 1990, a multiparty democracy was established.

Renewed ethnic strife led to an Aug. 1993 peace accord between the government and rebels of the Tutsi-led Rwandan Patriotic Front (RPF). But after Habyarimana and the president of Burundi were killed Apr. 6, 1994, in a suspicious plane crash, massive violence broke out. At least 500,000 died in massacres, mainly of Tutsi by Hutu militias, and in civil warfare as the RPF sought power. About 2 million Tutsi and Hutu fled to camps in Zaire (now Congo) and other countries, where many died of cholera and other natural causes. French troops under a UN mandate moved into SW Rwanda June 23 to establish a so-called safe zone. The RPF claimed victory, installing a government in July led by a moderate Hutu president. French troops pulled out Aug. 22. A UN peacekeeping mission ended Mar. 8, 1996, but the Rwandan government and a UN-sponsored tribunal in Tanzania continued to gather evidence against those responsible for genocide. More than 1 million refugees (mostly Hutu) flooded back to Rwanda from Tanzania and Zaire in Nov. and Dec. 1996.

Firing squads in Rwanda on Apr. 24, 1998, executed 22 people convicted of genocide. Former Prime Min. Jean Kambanda pleaded guilty May 1 before the UN tribunal and received a life sentence Sept. 4.

Saint Kitts and Nevis

Federation of Saint Kitts and Nevis

People: Population: 42,291. **Age distrib.** (%):<15: 33.3; 65+: 6.2. **Pop. density:** 407 per sq. mi. **Urban:** 34%. **Ethnic groups:** Black African 95%. **Principal language:** English (official). **Chief religion:** Protestant 85%.

Geography: Area: 104 sq. mi. **Location:** In the N part of the Leeward group of the Lesser Antilles in the E Caribbean Sea. **Neighbors:** Antigua and Barbuda to E. **Capital:** Basseterre (1994 est.): 12,600.

Government: Type: Constitutional monarchy. **Head of state:** Queen Elizabeth II, represented by Gov-Gen. Sir Cuthbert M. Sebastian; b Oct. 22, 1921; in office: Jan. 1, 1996. **Head of government:** Prime Min. Denzil Llewellyn Douglas; b Jan. 14, 1953; in office: July 3, 1995. **Local divisions:** 14 parishes.

Economy: Industries: Sugar (main industry), tourism. **Arable land:** 22%. **Electricity prod.** (1996): 81 mil kWh. **Labor force:** 69% services; 31% manuf.

Finance: Monetary unit: East Caribbean Dollar (Sept. 1998: 2.70 = $1 U.S.). **Gross domestic product** (1996 est.): $235 mil. **Per capita GDP:** $5,700. **Tourism:** $68 mil. **National budget:** (1996 est.) $100 mil. **International reserves less gold** (Mar 1998): $34.75 mil. **Consumer prices** (change in 1997): 8.6%.

Transport: Civil aviation: 2 airports. **Chief ports:** Basseterre, Charlestown.

Communications: Television sets: 241 per 1,000 pop. **Radios:** 659 per 1,000 pop. **Telephones:** 1 per 2.8 persons.

Health: Life expectancy at birth: 64.5 male; 70.8 female. **Births** (per 1,000 pop.): 23. **Deaths** (per 1,000 pop.): 9. **Natural increase:** 1.44%. **Hospital beds** (1995): 1 per 142 persons. **Physicians** (1995): 1 per 1,057 persons. **Infant mortality** (per 1,000 live births): 18.

Education: Compulsory for 12 years between ages 5-17. **Literacy** (1992): 90%.

Major International Organizations: UN (FAO, IBRD, ILO, IMF, WHO, WTrO), Caricom, the Commonwealth, OAS, OECS.

Embassy: 3216 New Mexico Ave., NW 20016; 686-2636.

St. Kitts (formerly St. Christopher; known by the natives as Liamuiga) and Nevis were reached (and named) by Columbus in 1493. They were settled by Britain in 1623, but ownership was disputed with France until 1713. They were part of the Leeward Islands Federation, 1871-1956, and the Federation of the West Indies, 1958-62. The colony achieved self-government as an Associated State of the UK in 1967, and became fully independent Sept. 19, 1983. A secession referendum on Nevis, Aug. 10, 1998, fell short of the two-thirds majority required.

Saint Lucia

People: Population: 152,335. **Age distrib.** (%): <15: 34.1; 65+: 5.4. **Urban:** 37%. **Pop. density:** 637 per sq. mi. **Ethnic groups:** Black 90%. **Principal languages:** English (official), French patois. **Chief religions:** Roman Catholic 90%, Protestant 7%.

Geography: Area: 239 sq. mi. **Location:** In E Caribbean, 2d largest of the Windward Isls. **Neighbors:** Martinique to N, St. Vincent to S. **Topography:** Mountainous, volcanic in origin; Soufriere, a volcanic crater, in the S. Wooded mountains run N-S to Mt. Gimie, 3,145 ft., with streams through fertile valleys. **Capital:** Castries (1992 met. est.): 13,615.

Government: Type: Parliamentary democracy. **Head of state:** Queen Elizabeth II, represented by Gov.-Gen. Calliopa Pearlette Louisy; b June 8, 1946; in office: Sept. 17, 1997. **Head of government:** Prime Min. Kenny Anthony; b Jan. 8, 1951; in office: May 24, 1997. **Local divisions:** 11 parishes.

Economy: Industries: Clothing, beverages, tourism, manufacturing. **Chief crops:** Bananas, coconuts, cocoa, citrus. **Other resources:** Forests. **Arable land:** 8%. **Livestock** (1997): chickens: 260,000. **Electricity prod.** (1996): 110 mil kWh. **Labor force:** 43% agric.; 39% services; 18% ind. & commerce.

Finance: Monetary unit: East Caribbean Dollar (Sept. 1998: 2.70 = $1 U.S.). **Gross domestic product** (1996 est.): $695 mil. **Per capita GDP:** $4,400. **Imports** (1995): $270.5 mil; partners: U.S. 34%, UK 14%. **Exports** (1995): $104.1 mil; partners: UK 56%, U.S. 22%. **Tourism:** $270 mil. **International reserves less gold** (Mar. 1998): $63.16 mil.

Transport: Motor vehicles in use: 10,000 passenger cars, 9,100 comm. vehicles. **Civil aviation:** 2 airports. **Chief ports:** Castries, Vieux Fort.

Communications: Television sets: 172 per 1,000 pop. **Radios:** 619 per 1,000 pop. **Telephones:** 1 per 5.4 persons.

Health: Life expectancy at birth: 67.9 male; 75.5 female. **Births** (per 1,000 pop.): 22. **Deaths** (per 1,000 pop.): 6. **Natural increase:** 1.68%. **Hospital beds** (1995): 1 per 269 persons. **Physicians** (1995): 1 per 2,159 persons. **Infant mortality** (per 1,000 live births): 17.

Education: Compulsory: ages 5-15. **Literacy** (1993): 80%.

Major International Organizations: UN (FAO, IBRD, ILO, IMF, IMO, WHO, WTrO), Caricom, the Commonwealth, OAS, OECS.

Embassy: 3216 New Mexico Ave. NW 20016; 364-6792.

St. Lucia was ceded to Britain by France at the Treaty of Paris, 1814. Self-government was granted with the West Indies Act, 1967. Independence was attained Feb. 22, 1979.

Saint Vincent and the Grenadines

People: Population: 119,818. **Pop. density:** 799 per sq. mi. **Urban:** 50%. **Ethnic groups:** Black 82%, mixed 14%. **Principal languages:** English (official), French patois. **Chief religions:** Anglican, Methodist, Roman Catholic.

Geography: Area: 150 sq. mi. **Location:** In the E Caribbean, St. Vincent (133 sq. mi.) and the northern islets of the Grenadines form a part of the Windward chain. **Neighbors:** St. Lucia to N, Barbados to E, Grenada to S. **Topography:** St. Vincent is volcanic, with a ridge of thickly wooded mountains running its length. **Capital:** Kingstown (1994): 15,924.

Government: Type: Constitutional monarchy. **Head of state:** Queen Elizabeth II, represented by Gov.-Gen. Sir Charles James Antrobus; b May 14, 1933; in office: June 1, 1996. **Head of government:** Prime Min. Sir James Fitz-Allen Mitchell; b May 15, 1931; in office: July 30, 1984. **Local divisions:** 6 parishes.

Economy: Industries: Agriculture, tourism. **Chief crops:** Bananas, coconuts. **Arable land:** 10%. **Livestock** (1997): chickens: 200,000. **Electricity prod.** (1996): 62 mil kWh. **Labor force:** 20% agric; 19% services.

Finance: Monetary unit: East Caribbean Dollar (Sept. 1998: 2.70 = $1 U.S.). **Gross domestic product** (1996 est.): $259 mil. **Per capita GDP:** $2,190. **Tourism:** $65 mil. **National budget** (1996 est.): $118 mil. **International reserves less gold** (Mar. 1998): $30.96 mil. **Consumer prices** (change in 1997): 0.4%.

Transport: Motor vehicles in use: 5,000 passenger cars, 3,200 comm. vehicles. **Civil aviation:** 5 airports. **Chief port:** Kingstown.

Communications: Television sets: 161 per 1,000 pop. **Radios:** 591 per 1,000 pop. **Telephones:** 1 per 6.1 persons.

Health: Life expectancy at birth: 72.0 male; 75.1 female. **Births** (per 1,000 pop.): 19. **Deaths** (per 1,000 pop.): 5. **Natural increase:** 1.35%. **Hospital beds** (1995): 1 per 248 persons. **Physicians** (1992): 1 per 2,000 persons. **Infant mortality** (per 1,000 live births): 16.

Education: Literacy (1994): 82%.

Major International Organizations: UN (FAO, IBRD, ILO, IMF, IMO, WHO, WTrO), Caricom, the Commonwealth, OAS, OECS.

Embassy: 3216 New Mexico Ave. NW 20016; 364-6730.

Website: http://www.heraldsvg.com

Columbus landed on St. Vincent on Jan. 22, 1498 (St. Vincent's Day). Britain and France both laid claim to the island in the 17th and 18th centuries; the Treaty of Versailles, 1783, finally ceded it to Britain. Associated State status was granted 1969; independence was attained Oct. 27, 1979.

Samoa (*formerly* Western Samoa)

Independent State of Samoa

People: Population: 224,713. **Age distrib.** (%): <15: 39.4; 65+: 4.1. **Pop. density:** 204 per sq. mi. **Urban:** 21%. **Ethnic groups:** Samoan (Polynesian) 93%, Euronesian (mixed) 7%, **Principal languages:** Samoan, English (both official). **Chief religion:** Christian 99.7%.

Geography: Area: 1,104 sq. mi. **Location:** In the S Pacific O. **Neighbors:** Nearest are Fiji to SW, Tonga to S. **Topography:** Main islands, Savaii (659 sq. mi.) and Upolu (432 sq. mi.), both ruggedly mountainous, and small islands Manono and Apolima. **Capital:** Apia (1995 est.): 33,000.

Government: Type: Constitutional monarchy. **Head of state:** Malietoa Tanumafili II; b Jan. 4, 1913; in office: Jan. 1, 1962. **Head of government:** Prime Min. Tofilau Eti Alesana; b June 4, 1924; in office: Apr. 11, 1988. **Local divisions:** 11 districts.

Economy: Industries: Timber, tourism. **Chief crops:** Coconuts, yams, bananas. **Other resources:** Hardwoods, fish. **Arable land:** 10%. **Livestock** (1997): chickens: 350,000; pigs: 178,800. **Electricity prod.** (1996): 65 mil kWh. **Labor force:** 65% agric.; 30% services; 5% industry.

Finance: Monetary unit: Tala (Sept. 1998: 3.08 = $1 U.S.). **Gross domestic product** (1995 est.): $415 mil. **Per capita GDP:** $1,900. **Imports** (1995): $91.0 mil; partners: NZ 37%.

Exports (1995): $8.7 mil; partners: NZ 44%; Australia 22%. **National budget** (FY1996-97): $128.0 mil. **Tourism:** $40 mil. **International reserves less gold** (May 1998): $59.15 mil. **Consumer prices** (change in 1997): 10.5%.

Transport: Motor vehicles in use: 1,200 passenger cars, 1,400 comm. vehicles. **Civil aviation:** 3 airports. **Chief ports:** Apia, Asau.

Communications: Television sets: 30 per 1,000 pop. **Radios:** 448 per 1,000 pop. **Telephones:** 1 per 22 persons.

Health: Life expectancy at birth: 67.1 male; 72.0 female. **Births** (per 1,000 pop.): 30. **Deaths** (per 1,000 pop.): 6. **Natural increase:** 2.41%. **Hospital beds** (1991): 1 per 255 persons. **Physicians** (1992): 1 per 2,682 persons. **Infant mortality** (per 1,000 live births): 32.

Education: Free and compulsory: ages 6-16. **Literacy** (1989): 100%.

Major International Organizations: UN (FAO, IBRD, IMF, IMO, WHO), the Commonwealth.

Embassy: 820 2d Ave., Suite 800D, New York, NY 10017; (212) 599-6196.

Samoa (formerly known as Western Samoa to distinguish it from American Samoa, a small U.S. territory) was a German colony, 1899 to 1914, when New Zealand landed troops and took over. It became a New Zealand mandate under the League of Nations and, in 1945, a New Zealand UN Trusteeship.

An elected local government took office in Oct. 1959, and the country became fully independent Jan. 1, 1962.

San Marino

Most Serene Republic of San Marino

People: Population: 24,894. **Age distrib.** (%): <15: 16.1; 65+: 16.6. **Pop. density:** 1,082 per sq. mi. **Urban:** 95%. **Ethnic groups:** Sammarinese 75%, Italian 23%. **Principal language:** Italian. **Chief religion:** Predominantly Roman Catholic.

Geography: Area: 23 sq. mi. **Location:** In N central Italy near Adriatic coast. **Neighbors:** Completely surrounded by Italy. **Topography:** The country lies on the slopes of Mt. Titano. **Capital:** San Marino. **Cities** (1996 est.): Serravalle/Dogano 7,904; San Marino 4,357.

Government: Type: Republic. **Head of state:** Two co-regents appt. every 6 months. **Local divisions:** 9 castelli. **Defense:** 1% of GDP.

Economy: Industries: Tourism, woolen goods, wine, cement, ceramics. **Chief crops:** Wheat, grapes, corn. **Arable land:** 17%.

Finance: Monetary unit: Italian Lira (Sept. 1998: 1710.20 = $1 US). **Gross domestic product** (1994 est.): $408.0 mil. **Per capita GDP:** $16,900. **National budget** (1995 est.): $320 mil.

Transport: Motor vehicles in use: 24,408 passenger cars, 3,955 comm. vehicles.

Communications: Radios: 514 per 1,000 pop. **Telephones:** 1 per 1.6 persons.

Health: Life expectancy at birth: 77.5 male; 85.3 female. **Births** (per 1,000 pop.): 11. **Deaths** (per 1,000 pop.): 8. **Natural increase:** 0.24%. **Infant mortality** (per 1,000 live births): 5.

Education: Compulsory: ages 6-13. **Literacy** (1997): 99%.

Major International Organizations: UN (ILO, IMF, WHO), OSCE.

San Marino claims to be the oldest state in Europe and to have been founded in the 4th century. A Communist-led coalition ruled 1947-57; a similar coalition ruled 1978-86. It has had a treaty of friendship with Italy since 1862.

São Tomé and Príncipe

Democratic Republic of São Tomé and Príncipe

People: Population: 150,123. **Age distrib.** (%): <15: 47.5; 65+: 4.1. **Pop. density:** 405 per sq. mi. **Urban:** 44%. **Ethnic groups:** Mestico (Portuguese-African), African minority (Angola, Mozambique immigrants). **Principal language:** Portuguese (official). **Chief religions:** Roman Catholic, Protestant.

Geography: Area: 371 sq. mi. **Location:** In the Gulf of Guinea about 125 miles off W central Africa. **Neighbors:** Gabon, Equatorial Guinea to E. **Topography:** São Tomé and Príncipe islands, part of an extinct volcano chain, are both covered by lush forests and croplands. **Capital:** São Tomé (1993 est.): 43,000.

Government: Type: Republic. **Head of state:** Pres. Miguel Trovoada; b Dec. 27, 1936; in office: Apr. 3, 1991. **Head of government:** Prime Min. Raul Bragança Neto; in office: Nov. 19, 1996. **Local divisions:** 7 districts.

Economy: Chief crops: Cocoa, coconut products. **Arable land:** 2%. **Livestock** (1997): chickens: 270,000. **Electricity prod.** (1996): 15 mil kWh.

Finance: Monetary unit: Dobra (Sept. 1998: 2,390.00 = $1 U.S.). **Gross domestic product** (1995 est.): $149 mil. **Per capita GDP:** $1,000. **Imports** (1995 est.): $26.2 mil; partners: Portugal 32%; France 17%. **Exports** (1995 est.): $7.8 mil; partners: Netherlands 76%. **International reserves less gold** (June 1998): $7.51 mil. **Tourism:** $2 mil.

Transport: Civil aviation: 5.4 mil passenger-mi; 2 airports. **Chief ports:** São Tomé, Santo Antonio.

Communications: Television sets: 154 per 1,000 pop. **Radios:** 232 per 1,000 pop. **Telephone:** 1 per 52 persons.

Health: Life expectancy at birth: 62.9 male; 65.9 female. **Births** (per 1,000 pop.): 43. **Deaths** (per 1,000 pop.): 8. **Natural increase:** 3.52%. **Infant mortality** (per 1,000 live births): 55.

Education: Compulsory for 4 years between ages 7-14. **Literacy** (1991): 73%.

Major International Organizations: UN (FAO, IBRD, ILO, IMF, IMO, WHO), OAU.

The islands were discovered in 1471 by the Portuguese, who brought the first settlers—convicts and exiled Jews. Sugar planting was replaced by the slave trade as the chief economic activity until coffee and cocoa were introduced in the 19th century.

Portugal agreed, 1974, to turn the colony over to the Gabon-based Movement for the Liberation of São Tomé and Príncipe, which proclaimed as first president its East German-trained leader, Manuel Pinto da Costa. Independence came July 12, 1975. Democratic reforms were instituted in 1987. In 1991 Miguel Trovoada won the first free presidential election following da Costa's withdrawal. A military coup that ousted Trovoada Aug. 15, 1995, was reversed a week later after Angolan mediation. Trovoada defeated da Costa in a presidential runoff election, July 21, 1996.

Saudi Arabia

Kingdom of Saudi Arabia

People: Population: 20,785,955. **Age distrib.** (%): <15: 43.0; 65+: 2.4. **Pop. density:** 24 per sq. mi. **Urban:** 84%. **Ethnic groups:** Arab 90%, Afro-Asian 10%. **Principal language:** Arabic (official). **Chief religion:** Muslim 100%.

Geography: Area: 864,000 sq. mi. **Location:** Occupies most of Arabian Peninsula in Mid-East. **Neighbors:** Kuwait, Iraq, Jordan on N; Yemen, Oman on S; United Arab Emirates, Qatar on E. **Topography:** Bordered by Red Sea on the W. The highlands on W, up to 9,000 ft., slope as an arid, barren desert to the Persian Gulf on the E. **Capital:** Riyadh. **Cities:** Riyadh 2,619,000; Jeddah 1,492,000; Mecca 777,000*.

Government: Type: Monarchy with council of ministers. **Head of state and government:** King Fahd ibn Abdul Aziz; b 1923; in office: June 13, 1982 (prime min. since 1982). **Local divisions:** 13 provinces. **Defense:** 12.8% of GDP. **Active troop strength:** 162,500.

Economy: Industries: Oil, oil products. **Chief crops:** Dates, wheat, barley, citrus. **Minerals:** Oil, gas, gold, copper, iron. **Crude oil reserves** (1997): 260 bil bbls. **Arable land:** 2%. **Livestock** (1997): chickens: 95.00 mil; sheep: 8.04 mil; goats: 4.40 mil; cattle: 180,000. **Electricity prod.** (1996): 95 bil kWh. **Labor force:** 40% govt.; 25% industry & oil; 30% services; 5% agric.

Finance: Monetary unit: Riyal (Sept. 1998: 3.75 = $1 U.S.). **Gross domestic product** (1996 est.): $205.6 bil. **Per capita GDP:** $10,600. **Imports** (1996 est.): $25.5 bil; partners: U.S. 21%, UK 9%. **Exports** (1996 est.): $53.1 bil; partners: Japan 18%, U.S. 15%. **Tourism:** $1.42 bil. **National budget** (1997 est.): $48.3 bil. **International reserves less gold** (June 1998): $7.62 bil. **Gold:** 4.60 mil oz t. **Consumer prices** (change in 1997): 0.1%.

Transport: Railroad: Length: 863.2 mi. **Motor vehicles in use:** 1.71 mil passenger cars, 1.17 mil comm. vehicles. **Civil aviation:** 11.79 bil passenger-mi; 25 airports. **Chief ports:** Jeddah, Ad Dammam.

Communications: Television sets: 257 per 1,000 pop. **Radios:** 213 per 1,000 pop. **Telephones:** 1 per 10 persons. **Daily newspaper circ.:** 54 per 1,000 pop.

Health: Life expectancy at birth: 68.2 male; 72.0 female. **Births** (per 1,000 pop.): 38. **Deaths** (per 1,000 pop.): 5. **Natural increase:** 3.26%. **Hospital beds** (1995): 1 per 427 persons. **Physicians** (1995): 1 per 590 persons. **Infant mortality** (per 1,000 live births): 41.

Education: Literacy (1995): 63%.

Major International Organizations: UN (FAO, IBRD, ILO, IMF, IMO, WHO), AL, OPEC.

Embassy: 601 New Hampshire Ave. NW 20037; 342-3800.

Before Muhammad, Arabia was divided among numerous warring tribes and small kingdoms and was at times dominated by larger Arabian and non-Arabian kingdoms. It was united for the first time by Muhammad, in the early 7th century AD. His successors conquered the entire Near East and North Africa, bringing Islam and the Arabic language. But Arabia itself soon returned to its former status.

Nejd, in central Arabia, long an independent state and center of the Wahhabi sect, fell under Turkish rule in the 18th century. In 1913 Ibn Saud, founder of the Saudi dynasty, overthrew the Turks and captured the Turkish province of Hasa in E Arabia; he took the Hejaz region in W Arabia in 1925 and most of Asir, in SW Arabia, by 1926. The discovery of oil in the 1930s transformed the new country.

Ibn Saud reigned until his death, Nov. 1953. Subsequent kings have been sons of Ibn Saud. The king exercises authority together with a Council of Ministers. The Islamic religious code is the law of the land. Alcohol and public entertainments are restricted, and women have an inferior legal status. There is no constitution and no parliament, although a Consultative Council was established by the king in 1993.

Saudi Arabia has often allied itself with the U.S. and other Western nations, and billions of dollars of advanced arms have been purchased from Britain, France, and the U.S.; however, Western support for Israel has often strained relations. Saudi units fought against Israel in the 1948 and 1973 Arab-Israeli wars. Beginning with the 1967 Arab-Israeli war, Saudi Arabia provided large annual financial gifts to Egypt; aid was later extended to Syria, Jordan, and Palestinian groups, as well as to other Islamic countries.

King Faisal played a leading role in the 1973-74 Arab oil embargo against the U.S. and other nations. Crown Prince Khalid was proclaimed king on Mar. 25, 1975, after the assassination of Faisal. Fahd became king on June 13, 1982, following Khalid's death.

The Hejaz contains the holy cities of Islam—Medina, where the Mosque of the Prophet enshrines the tomb of Muhammad, and Mecca, his birthplace. More than 2 million Muslims make pilgrimage to Mecca annually. In 1987, Iranians making a pilgrimage to Mecca clashed with anti-Iranian pilgrims and Saudi police; more than 400 were killed. Some 1,426 Muslim pilgrims died July 2, 1990, in a stampede in a pedestrian tunnel leading to Mecca. Nearly 300 pilgrims were killed in a stampede in Mecca, May 26, 1994. More than 340 pilgrims died in a tent fire near Mecca, Apr. 15, 1997.

Following Iraq's attack on Kuwait, Aug. 2, 1990, Saudi Arabia accepted the Kuwait royal family and more than 400,000 Kuwaiti refugees. King Fahd invited Western and Arab troops to deploy on its soil in support of Saudi defense forces. During the Persian Gulf War, 28 U.S. soldiers were killed when an Iraqi missile hit their barracks in Dhahran, Feb. 25, 1991. The nation's northern Gulf coastline suffered severe pollution as a result of Iraqi sabotage of the Kuwaiti oil fields. Islamic extremists were blamed for truck bombs that killed 7 (5 from the U.S.) at a military training center in Riyadh, Nov. 13, 1995, and 19 Americans at a base in Dhahran, June 25, 1996. U.S. officials repeatedly chided the Saudi government for failing to cooperate fully in the investigation.

With King Fahd ailing, his half-brother, Crown Prince Abdullah, has taken a leading role in recent years.

Senegal

Republic of Senegal

People: Population: 9,723,149. **Age distrib.** (%): <15: 48.1; 65+: 2.8. **Pop. density:** 128 per sq. mi. **Urban:** 44%. **Ethnic groups:** Wolof 36%, Fulani 17%, Serer 17%, Diola 9%, Toucouleur 9%, Mandingo 9%. **Principal languages:** French (official), Wolof, Pulaar, Diola, Mandingo. **Chief religions:** Muslim 92%, indigenous beliefs 6%, Christian 2%.

Geography: Area: 75,749 sq. mi. **Location:** At W extreme of Africa. **Neighbors:** Mauritania on N, Mali on E, Guinea and Guinea-Bissau on S; surrounds Gambia on three sides. **Topography:** Low rolling plains cover most of Senegal, rising somewhat in the SE. Swamp and jungles are in SW. **Capital:** Dakar: 768,000*.

Government: Type: Republic. **Head of state:** Pres. Abdou Diouf; b Sept. 7, 1935; in office: Jan. 1, 1981. **Head of government:** Prime Min. Mamadou Lamine Loum; in office: July 3, 1998. **Local divisions:** 10 regions. **Defense:** 1.7% of GDP. **Active troop strength:** 13,400.

Economy: Industries: Food processing, fishing. **Chief crops:** Peanuts, millet, rice. **Minerals:** Phosphates, iron. **Arable land:** 12%. **Livestock** (1997): chickens: 44.10 mil; sheep: 4.24 mil; goats: 3.57 mil; cattle: 2.91 mil; pigs: 320,000. **Fish catch** (1996): 436,259 metric tons. **Electricity prod.** (1996): 730 mil kWh. **Labor force:** 65% subsistence agric.

Finance: Monetary unit: CFA Franc (Sept. 1998: 580.94 = $1 U.S.). **Gross domestic product** (1996 est.): $15.6 bil. **Per capita GDP:** $1,700. **Imports** (1995): $1.22 bil; partners: France 30%. **Exports** (1995): $968 mil; partners: France 30%. **Tourism:** $160 mil. **National budget** (1996): $779.1 mil. **International reserves less gold** (Mar. 1998): $386.7 mil. **Gold:** 29,000 oz t. **Consumer prices** (change in 1997): 1.7%.

Transport: Railroad: Length: 561.4 mi. **Motor vehicles in use:** 110,000 passenger cars, 50,000 comm. vehicles. **Civil aviation:** 153.7 mil passenger-mi; 7 airports. **Chief ports:** Dakar, Saint-Louis.

Communications: Television sets: 6.9 per 1,000 pop. **Radios:** 93 per 1,000 pop. **Telephones:** 1 per 102 persons.

Health: Life expectancy at birth: 54.6 male; 60.3 female. **Births** (per 1,000 pop.): 44. **Deaths** (per 1,000 pop.): 11. **Natural increase:** 3.33%. **Hospital beds** (1992): 1 per 1,041 persons. **Physicians** (1992): 1 per 14,825 persons. **Infant mortality** (per 1,000 live births): 61.

Education: Compulsory: ages 7-13. **Literacy** (1995): 33%.

Major International Organizations: UN and all of its specialized agencies, OAU.

Embassy: 2112 Wyoming Ave. NW 20008; 234-0540.

Portuguese settlers arrived in the 15th century, but French control grew from the 17th century. The last independent Muslim state was subdued in 1893. Dakar became the capital of French West Africa.

Independence as part, along with the Sudanese Rep., of the Mali Federation, came June 20, 1960. Senegal withdrew Aug. 20. French political and economic influence remained strong.

Senegal, Dec. 17, 1981, signed an agreement with The Gambia for confederation of the 2 countries, without loss of individual sovereignty, under the name of Senegambia. The confederation collapsed in 1989, although in 1991 the 2 nations signed a friendship and cooperation treaty.

Separatists in Casamance Province of S Senegal have clashed with government forces since 1982. Senegal sent troops in June 1998 to help the Guinea-Bissau government suppress an army uprising.

Seychelles

Republic of Seychelles

People: Population: 78,641. **Age distrib.** (%): <15: 29.9; 65+: 6.3. **Pop. density:** 447 per sq. mi. **Urban:** 55%. **Ethnic groups:** Seychellois (mixture of Asians, Africans, and French). **Principal languages:** English, French (both official), Creole. **Chief religions:** Roman Catholic 90%, Anglican 8%.

Geography: Area: 176 sq. mi. **Location:** In the Indian O. 700 miles NE of Madagascar. **Neighbors:** Nearest are Madagascar on SW, Somalia on NW. **Topography:** A group of 86 islands, about half of them composed of coral, the other half granite, the latter predominantly mountainous. **Capital:** Victoria (1993 est.): 25,000.

Government: Type: Republic. **Head of state:** Pres. France-Albert René, b. Nov. 16, 1935; in office: June 5, 1977. **Local divisions:** 23 districts. **Defense:** 3.1% of GDP. **Active troop strength:** 300.

Economy: Industries: Tourism, food processing, fishing. **Chief crops:** Coconuts, cinnamon, vanilla. **Arable land:** 2%. **Livestock** (1997): chickens: 500,000. **Electricity prod.** (1996): 125 mil kWh. **Labor force:** 31% industry & comm.; 21% services; 20% govt.; 12% agric.

Finance: Monetary unit: Rupee (Sept. 1998: 5.20 = $1 U.S.). **Gross domestic product** (1995 est.): $450 mil. **Per capita GDP:** $6,000. **Imports** (1995): $238 mil; partners: U.S. 27%; UK 11%. **Exports** (1995): $56.1 mil; partners: France 43%; UK 22%. **Tourism:** $122 mil. **National budget** (1994 est.): $241 mil. **International reserves less gold** (May 1998): $29.56 mil. **Consumer prices** (change in 1997): 0.6%.

Transport: Motor vehicles in use: 6,620 passenger cars, 1,880 comm. vehicles. **Civil aviation:** 486.8 mil passenger-mi; 2 airports. **Chief port:** Victoria.

Communications: Television sets: 173.4 per 1,000 pop. **Radios:** 667 per 1,000 pop. **Telephones:** 1 per 5.6 persons. **Daily newspaper circ.:** 41 per 1,000 pop.

Health: Life expectancy at birth: 66.1 male; 75.5 female. **Births** (per 1,000 pop.): 20. **Deaths** (per 1,000 pop.): 7. **Natural increase:** 1.31%. **Hospital beds** (1996): 1 per 184 persons. **Physicians** (1996): 1 per 906 persons. **Infant mortality** (per 1,000 live births): 17.

Education: Free and compulsory: ages 6-15. **Literacy** (1995): 84%.

Major International Organizations: UN (FAO, IBRD, ILO, IMF, IMO, WHO), the Commonwealth, OAU.

Embassy: 820 2d Ave., Suite 900F, New York, NY 10017; 212-972-1785.

The islands were occupied by France in 1768, and seized by Britain in 1794. Ruled as part of Mauritius from 1814, the Seychelles became a separate colony in 1903. The ruling party had opposed independence as impractical, but pressure from the OAU and the UN became irresistible, and independence was declared June 29, 1976. The first president was ousted in a coup a year later by a socialist leader. A new constitution, approved June 1993, provided for a multiparty state.

Sierra Leone

Republic of Sierra Leone

People: Population: 5,080,004. **Age distrib.** (%): <15: 45.2; 65+: 3.1. **Pop. density:** 183 per sq. mi. **Urban:** 34%. **Ethnic groups:** Temne 30%, Mende 30%, other tribes 39%. **Principal languages:** English (official), Mende, Temne, Krio. **Chief religions:** Muslim 60%, indigenous beliefs 30%, Christian 10%.

Geography: Area: 27,699 sq. mi. **Location:** On W coast of W Africa. **Neighbors:** Guinea on N and E, Liberia on S. **Topography:** The heavily-indented, 210-mi. coastline has mangrove swamps. Behind are wooded hills, rising to a plateau and mountains in the E. **Capital:** Freetown. (1990 est.) 669,000.

Government: Type: Republic. **Head of state:** Ahmad Tejan Kabbah; b Feb. 16, 1932; in office: Mar. 10, 1998. **Local divisions:** 3 provinces, 1 area. **Defense:** 5.9% of GDP. **Active troop strength:** 14,200.

Economy: Industries: Mining, light manufacturing. **Chief crops:** Cocoa, coffee, palm kernels, rice. **Minerals:** Diamonds, titanium, bauxite. **Arable land:** 7%. **Livestock** (1997): chickens: 6.00 mil; cattle: 400,000; sheep: 350,000; goats: 190,000. **Fish catch** (1996): 61,330 metric tons. **Electricity prod.** (1996): 230 mil kWh. **Labor force:** 62% agric.; 38% ind. & serv.

Finance: Monetary unit: Leone (Sept. 1998: 1,550.00 = $1 U.S.). **Gross domestic product** (1996 est.): $4.7 bil. **Per capita GDP:** $980. **Imports** (1995): $140 mil; partners: U.S. 43%. **Exports** (1995): $39.3 mil; partners: U.S. 45%, UK 17%. **Tourism:** $10 mil. **National budget** (FY1994-95 est.): $128 mil. **International reserves less gold** (May 1998): $32.2 mil. **Consumer prices** (change in 1997): 23.2%.

Transport: Railroad: Length: 52.2 mi. **Motor vehicles in use:** 20,860 passenger cars, 21,074 comm. vehicles. **Civil aviation:** 14.9 mil passenger-mi; 1 airport. **Chief ports:** Freetown, Bonthe.

Communications: Radios: 72 per 1,000 pop. **Telephones:** 1 per 271 persons.

Health: Life expectancy at birth: 45.6 male; 51.7 female. **Births** (per 1,000 pop.): 46. **Deaths** (per 1,000 pop.): 17. **Natural increase:** 2.89%. **Physicians** (1992): 1 per 10,832 persons. **Infant mortality** (per 1,000 live births): 129.

Education: Literacy (1995): 31%.

Major International Organizations: UN (FAO, IBRD, ILO, IMF, IMO, WHO, WTrO), the Commonwealth, OAU.

Embassy: 1701 19th St. NW 20009; 939-9261.

Website: http://www.Sierra-Leone.org

Freetown was founded in 1787 by the British government as a haven for freed slaves. Their descendants, known as Creoles, number more than 60,000.

Successive steps toward independence followed the 1951 constitution. Ten years later, full independence arrived Apr. 27, 1961. Sierra Leone declared itself a republic on Apr. 19, 1971. A one-party state approved by referendum in 1978 brought political stability, but mismanagement and corruption plagued the economy.

Mutinous soldiers ousted Pres. Joseph Momoh Apr. 30, 1992. Another coup, Jan. 16, 1996, paved the way for multiparty elections and a return to civilian rule. A peace accord which was signed on Nov. 30 with the Revolutionary United Front ended a civil war that had taken more than 10,000 lives in 5 years.

A coup on May 25, 1997, was met with widespread international opposition. Armed intervention by Nigeria restored Pres. Ahmad Tejan Kabbah to power on Mar. 10, 1998, but rebels loyal to the former military regime mounted a guerrilla counteroffensive.

Singapore

Republic of Singapore

People: Population: 3,490,356. **Age distrib.** (%): <15: 21.4; 65+: 6.8. **Pop. density:** 13,961 per sq. mi. **Urban:** 100%. **Ethnic groups:** Chinese 76%, Malay 15%, Indian 6%. **Principal languages:** Chinese, Malay, Tamil, English (all official). **Chief religions:** Buddhist 32%, Taoist 22%, Muslim 15%, Christian 13%, Hindu 3%.

Geography: Area: 250 sq. mi. **Location:** Off tip of Malayan Peninsula in SE Asia. **Neighbors:** Nearest are Malaysia on N, Indonesia on S. **Topography:** Singapore is a flat, formerly swampy island. The nation includes 40 nearby islets. **Capital:** Singapore 3,327,000*.

Government: Type: Republic. **Head of state:** Pres. Ong Teng Cheong; b Jan 22, 1936; in office: Sept. 2, 1993. **Head of government:** Prime Min. Goh Chok Tong; b May 20, 1941; in office: Nov. 28, 1990. **Defense:** 5.5% of GDP. **Active troop strength:** 53,900.

Economy: Industries: Oil refining, electronics, banking, food and rubber processing, biotechnology. **Chief crops:** Copra, fruit, vegetables. **Arable land:** 2%. **Livestock** (1997): chickens: 2.00 mil; pigs: 190,000. **Fish catch** (1996): 9,943 metric tons. **Electricity prod.** (1996): 21 bil kWh. **Labor force:** 34% finance, business, other serv.; 26% manuf.; 23% commerce.

Finance: Monetary unit: Dollar (Sept. 1998: 1.76 = $1 U.S.). **Gross domestic product** (1996 est.): $72.2 bil. **Per capita GDP:** $21,200. **Imports** (1996 est.): $151.1 bil; partners: Japan 21%, Malaysia 15%, U.S. 15%. **Exports** (1996 est.): $144.8 bil; partners: Malaysia 19%, U.S. 18%. **Tourism:** $7.99 bil. **National budget** (FY 1996-97 est.): $13.5 bil. **International reserves** (May 1998): $71.86 bil. **Consumer prices** (change in 1997): 2.0%.

Transport: Railroad: Length: 52 mi. **Motor vehicles in use:** 382,724 passenger cars, 154,093 comm. vehicles. **Civil aviation:** 33.31 bil passenger-mi; 1 airport. **Chief port:** Singapore.

Communications: Television sets: 218 per 1,000 pop. **Radios:** 270 per 1,000 pop. **Telephones:** 1 per 2.1 persons. **Daily newspaper circ.:** 340 per 1,000 pop.

Health: Life expectancy at birth: 75.5 male; 81.8 female. **Births** (per 1,000 pop.): 14. **Deaths** (per 1,000 pop.): 5. **Natural increase:** 0.91%. **Hospital beds** (1996): 1 per 285 persons. **Physicians** (1996): 1 per 661 persons. **Infant mortality** (per 1,000 live births): 4.

Education: Literacy (1995): 91%.

Major International Organizations: UN (IBRD, ILO, IMF, IMO, WHO, WTrO), the Commonwealth, APEC, ASEAN.

Embassy: 3501 International Pl. NW 20008; 537-3100.

Website: http://www.singstat.gov.sg

Founded in 1819 by Sir Thomas Stamford Raffles, Singapore was a British colony until 1959, when it became autonomous within the Commonwealth. On Sept. 16, 1963, it joined with Malaya, Sarawak, and Sabah to form the Federation of Malaysia. Tensions between Malayans, dominant in the federation, and ethnic Chinese, dominant in Singapore, led to an accord under which Singapore became a separate nation, Aug. 9, 1965.

Singapore is one of the world's largest ports. Standards in health, education, and housing are generally high. International banking has grown rapidly in recent years. The government, dominated by a single party, has taken strong actions to suppress dissent.

Slovakia

Slovak Republic

People: Population: 5,392,982. **Age distrib.** (%): <15: 20.7; 65+: 11.3. **Pop. density:** 286 per sq. mi. **Urban:** 59%. **Ethnic groups:** Slovak 86%, Hungarian 11%. **Principal languages:** Slovak (official), Hungarian. **Chief religions:** Roman Catholic 60%, Protestant 8%.

Geography: Area: 18,859 sq. mi. **Location:** In E central Europe. **Neighbors:** Poland on N, Hungary on S, Austria and Czech Rep. on W, Ukraine on E. **Topography:** Mountains (Carpathians) in N, fertile Danube plane in S. **Capital:** Bratislava. **Cities** (1996 est.): Bratislava 452,053; Kosice 240,915.

Government: Type: Republic. **Head of state:** Vacant. **Head of government:** Prime Min. Vladimir Meciar; b July 26, 1942; in office: Dec. 13, 1994. **Local divisions:** 8 regions, 79 districts. **Defense:** 2.6% of GDP. **Active troop strength:** 42,600.

Economy: Industries: Metal products, food and beverages, oil, chemicals. **Chief crops:** Grains, potatoes, sugar beets, hops, fruit. **Minerals:** Coal, iron, copper. **Crude oil reserves** (1997): 9.0 mil bbls. **Arable land:** 31%. **Livestock** (1997): chickens: 13.67 mil; pigs: 1.99 mil; cattle: 892,000; sheep: 418,800. **Electricity prod.** (1996): 25.8 bil kWh. **Labor force:** 30% ind.; 9% agric.; 8% constr.

Finance: Monetary unit: Koruna (Sept. 1998: 35.02 = $1 U.S.). **Gross domestic product** (1996 est.): $42.8 bil. **Per capita GDP:** $8,000. **Imports** (1996): $9.6 bil; partners: Czech Rep. 28%. **Exports** (1996): $8.1 bil; partners: Czech Rep. 35%. **Tourism:** $535 mil. **International reserves less gold** (May 1998): 3.67 bil. **Gold:** 1.29 mil oz t. **Consumer prices** (change in 1997): 6.1%.

Transport: Railroad: Length: 2,272.9 mi. **Motor vehicles in use:** 994,000 passenger cars, 94,000 comm. vehicles. **Civil aviation:** 49.4 mil passenger-mi; 2 airports. **Chief ports:** Bratislava, Komarno.

Communications: Television sets: 216 per 1,000 pop. **Telephones:** 1 per 4.8 persons. **Daily newspaper circ.:** 256 per 1,000 pop.

Health: Life expectancy at birth: 69.4 male; 77.2 female. **Births** (per 1,000 pop.): 10. **Deaths** (per 1,000 pop.): 9. **Natural increase:** 0.05%. **Hospital beds** (1995): 1 per 86 persons. **Physicians** (1995): 1 per 381 persons. **Infant mortality** (per 1,000 live births): 10.

Education: Compulsory: ages 6-14. **Literacy** (1994): 100%.

Major International Organizations: UN (FAO, IBRD, ILO, IMF, IMO, WHO, WTrO), OSCE.

Embassy: 2201 Wisconsin Ave. NW 20007; 965-5160.

Website: http://www.slovakemb.com/index.html

Slovakia was originally settled by Illyrian, Celtic, and Germanic tribes and was incorporated into Great Moravia in the 9th century. It became part of Hungary in the 11th century. Overrun by Czech Hussites in the 15th century, it was restored to Hungarian rule in 1526. The Slovaks disassociated themselves from Hungary after World War I and joined the Czechs of Bohemia to form the Republic of Czechoslovakia, Oct. 28, 1918.

Germany invaded Czechoslovakia, 1939, and declared Slovakia independent. Slovakia rejoined Czechoslovakia in 1945.

Czechoslovakia split into 2 separate states—the Czech Republic and Slovakia—on Jan. 1, 1993. Slovakia, with its less developed economy, applied to join the European Union in 1995. A prolonged parliamentary standoff left the country without a president for much of 1998. Prime Min. Vladimir Meciar, a nationalist, suffered a setback in elections Sept. 25-26.

Slovenia

Republic of Slovenia

People: Population: 1,971,739. **Age distrib.** (%): <15: 16.7; 65+: 13.4. **Pop. density:** 252 per sq. mi. **Urban:** 52%. **Ethnic groups:** Slovene 91%, Croat 3%. **Principal languages:** Slovenian (official), Serbo-Croatian. **Chief religion:** Roman Catholic 71%.

Geography: Area: 7,821 sq. mi. **Location:** In SE Europe. **Neighbors:** Italy on W, Austria on N, Hungary on NE, Croatia on SE, S. **Topography:** Mostly hilly; 42% of the land is forested. **Capital:** Ljubljana (1996 est.): 269,621.

Government: Type: Republic. **Head of state:** Pres. Milan Kucan; b Jan. 14, 1941; in office: Apr. 1990. **Head of government:** Prime Min. Janez Drnovsek; b May 1950; in office: May 14, 1992. **Local divisions:** 136 municipalities, 11 urban municipalities. **Defense:** 1.8% of GDP. **Active troop strength:** 9,600.

Economy: Industries: Metallurgy, electronics, vehicles. **Minerals:** Coal, lead, zinc, mercury. **Chief crops:** Potatoes, hops, wheat. **Arable land:** 12%. **Livestock** (1997): chickens: 8.55 mil; pigs: 559,500; cattle: 484,300. **Electricity prod.** (1996): 12.1 bil kWh. **Labor force:** 25% mining & manuf.; 15% services.

Finance: Monetary unit: Tolar (Sept. 1998: 165.18 = $1 U.S.). **Gross domestic product** (1996 est.): $24 bil. **Per capita GDP:** $12,300. **Imports** (1996): $9.5 bil; partners: Germany 22%, Italy 17%. **Exports** (1996): $8.3 bil; partners: Germany 29%, former Yugoslavia 17%. **Tourism:** $1.28 bil. **International reserves less gold** (May 1998): $4.05 bil. **Gold:** 3,000 oz t. **Consumer prices** (change in 1997): 9.1%.

Transport: Railroad: Length: 745.8 mi. **Motor vehicles in use:** 657,000 passenger cars, 37,000 comm. vehicles. **Civil aviation:** 235.7 mil passenger-mi; 1 airport. **Chief ports:** Izola, Koper, Piran.

Communications: Television sets: 374 per 1,000 pop. **Radios:** 317 per 1,000 pop. **Telephones:** 1 per 3.2 persons. **Daily newspaper circ.:** 181 per 1,000 pop.

Health: Life expectancy at birth: 71.5 male; 79.0 female. **Births** (per 1,000 pop.): 9. **Deaths** (per 1,000 pop.): 10. **Natural increase:** –0.10%. **Hospital beds** (1995): 1 per 173 persons. **Physicians** (1995): 1 per 858 persons. **Infant mortality** (per 1,000 live births): 5.

Education: Free and compulsory: ages 6-15. **Literacy** (1993): 99%.

Major International Organizations: UN (FAO, IBRD, ILO, IMF, IMO, WHO, WTrO), OSCE.

Embassy: 1525 New Hampshire Ave. NW 20036; 667-5363.

The Slovenes settled in their current territory during the period from the 6th to the 8th century. They fell under German domination as early as the 9th century. Modern Slovenian political history began after 1848 when the Slovenes, who were divided among several Austrian provinces, began their struggle for political and national unification. In 1918 a majority of Slovenes became part of the Kingdom of Serbs, Croats, and Slovenes, later renamed Yugoslavia.

Slovenia declared independence June 25, 1991, and joined the UN May 22, 1992. Linked by trade with the European Union, Slovenia applied for full membership June 10, 1996.

Solomon Islands

People: Population: 441,039. **Age distrib.** (%): <15: 45.1; 65+: 3.0. **Pop. density:** 40 per sq. mi. **Urban:** 18%. **Ethnic groups:** Melanesian 93%, Polynesian 4%. **Principal languages:** English (official); Melanesian, Papuan, Polynesian languages. **Chief religions:** Anglican 34%, Roman Catholic 19%, Baptist 17%, other Christian 26%.

Geography: Area: 10,985 sq. mi. **Location:** Melanesian Archipelago in the W Pacific O. **Neighbors:** Nearest is Papua New Guinea to W. **Topography:** 10 large volcanic and rugged islands and 4 groups of smaller ones. **Capital:** Honiara (1996 est.): 43,643.

Government: Type: Parliamentary democracy within the Commonwealth of Nations. **Head of state:** Queen Elizabeth II, represented by Gov.-Gen. Moses Pitakaka; in office: June 1994. **Head of government:** Prime Min. Bartholomew Ulufa'alu; in office: Aug. 27, 1997. **Local divisions:** 9 provinces and Honiara.

Economy: Industries: Copra, tuna. **Chief crops:** Coconuts, rice, cocoa, beans. **Minerals:** Gold, bauxite. **Other resources:** Forests. **Arable land:** 1%. **Livestock** (1997): chickens: 145,000. **Fish catch** (1996): 53,275 metric tons. **Electricity prod.** (1996): 30 mil kWh. **Labor force:** 42% services; 24% agric., forestry, fishing.

Finance: Monetary unit: Dollar (Sept. 1998: 4.89 = $1 U.S.). **Gross domestic product** (1996 est.): $1.2 bil. **Per capita GDP:** $3,000. **Imports** (1995 est.): $152 mil; partners: Australia 34%, Japan 16%. **Exports** (1995 est.): $170 mil; partners: Japan 39%, UK 23%. **International reserves less gold** (Mar. 1998): $31.41 mil. **Consumer prices:** (change in 1997): 8.1%. **Tourism:** $13 mil.

Transport: Civil aviation: 46.0 mil passenger-mi; 21 airports.

Communications: Radios: 96 per 1,000 pop. **Telephones:** 1 per 58 persons.

Health: Life expectancy at birth: 69.3 male; 74.4 female. **Births** (per 1,000 pop.): 37. **Deaths** (per 1,000 pop.): 4. **Natural increase:** 3.24%. **Infant mortality** (per 1,000 live births): 24.

Education: Literacy (1994): 54%.

Major International Organizations: UN (FAO, IBRD, ILO, IMF, IMO, WHO, WTrO), the Commonwealth.
Embassy: 820 Second Ave., Suite 800, New York, NY 10017; (212) 599-6193.

The Solomon Islands were sighted in 1568 by an expedition from Peru. Britain established a protectorate in the 1890s over most of the group, inhabited by Melanesians. The islands saw major World War II battles. Self-government came Jan. 2, 1976, and independence was formally attained July 7, 1978.

Somalia

People: Population: 6,841,695. **Age distrib.** (%): <15: 44.2; 65+: 2.9. **Pop. density:** 28 per sq. mi. **Urban:** 26%. **Ethnic groups:** Somali 85%, Bantu, Arab. **Principal languages:** Somali (official), Arabic, Italian, English. **Chief religion:** Sunni Muslim.

Geography: Area: 246,201 sq. mi. **Location:** Occupies the eastern horn of Africa. **Neighbors:** Djibouti, Ethiopia, Kenya on W. **Topography:** The coastline extends for 1,700 mi. Hills cover the N; the center and S are flat. **Capital:** Mogadishu 997,000*.

Government: Type: In transition. **Local divisions:** 18 regions. **Defense:** 4.8% of GDP. **Active troop strength:** 225,000.

Economy: Chief crops: Sugar, bananas, sorghum, corn, mangoes. **Minerals:** Iron, tin, gypsum, bauxite, uranium. **Arable land:** 2%. **Livestock** (1997): chickens: 3.00 mil; sheep: 13.50 mil; goats: 12.50 mil; cattle: 5.20 mil. **Fish catch** (1996): 15,000 metric tons. **Electricity prod.** (1996): 258 mil kWh. **Labor force:** 71% nomadic agric; 29% industry & services.

Finance: Monetary unit: Shilling (Sept. 1998: 2,620.00 = $1 U.S.). **Gross domestic product** (1995 est.): $3.6 bil. **Per capita GDP**: $500. **Imports** (1994 est.): $269 mil; partners: Kenya 24%, Djibouti 18%. **Exports** (1994 est.): $130 mil; partners: Saudi Arabia 57%.

Transport: Motor vehicles in use: 10,000 passenger cars, 10,000 comm. vehicles. **Civil aviation:** 86.9 mil passenger-mi. **Chief ports:** Mogadishu, Berbera.

Communications: Radios: 45 per 1,000 pop. **Telephones:** 1 per 605 persons.

Health: Life expectancy at birth: 44.7 male; 47.9 female. **Births** (per 1,000 pop.): 47. **Deaths** (per 1,000 pop.): 19. **Natural increase:** 2.83%. **Infant mortality** (per 1,000 live births): 126.

Education: Free and compulsory: ages 6-14. **Literacy** (1990): 24%.

Major International Organizations: UN (FAO, IBRD, ILO, IMF, IMO, WHO), AL, OAU.

Website: http://gaia.info.usaid.gov/horn/somalia/somalia.html

British Somaliland (present-day N Somalia) was formed in the 19th century, as was Italian Somaliland (now central and S Somalia). Italy lost its African colonies in World War II. In 1949, the UN approved eventual independence for the former Italian colony (designated the UN Trust Territory of Somalia) after a 10-year period under Italian administration.

British Somaliland gained independence, June 26, 1960, and by prearrangement, merged July 1 with the trust territory of Somalia to create the independent Somali Republic (Somalia).

On Oct. 16, 1969, Pres. Abdi Rashid Ali Shirmarke was assassinated. On Oct. 21, a military group led by Maj. Gen. Muhammad Siad Barre seized power. In 1970, Barre declared the country a socialist state—the Somali Democratic Republic.

Somalia has laid claim to Ogaden, the huge eastern region of Ethiopia, peopled mostly by Somalis. Ethiopia battled Somali rebels in 1977. Some 11,000 Cuban troops with Soviet arms defeated Somali army troops and ethnic Somali rebels in Ethiopia, 1978. As many as 1.5 million refugees entered Somalia. Guerrilla fighting in Ogaden continued until 1988, when a peace agreement was reached with Ethiopia.

The civil war intensified again and Barre was forced to flee the capital, Jan. 1991. Fighting between rival factions caused 40,000 casualties in 1991 and 1992, and by mid-1992 the civil war, drought, and banditry combined to produce a famine that threatened some 1.5 million people with starvation.

In Dec. 1992 the UN accepted a U.S. offer of troops to safeguard food delivery to the starving. The UN took control of the multinational relief effort from the U.S. May 4, 1993. While the operation helped alleviate the famine, efforts to reestablish order foundered, and there were significant U.S. and other casualties. The U.S. withdrew its peacekeeping forces Mar. 25, 1994. When the last UN troops pulled out Mar. 3, 1995, Mogadishu had no functioning central government, and armed factions controlled different regions.

South Africa

Republic of South Africa

People: Population: 42,834,520. **Age distrib.** (%): <15: 34.7; 65+: 4.5. **Pop. density:** 91 per sq. mi. **Urban:** 50%. **Ethnic groups:** Black 75%, white 14%, colored 9%. **Principal languages:** 11 official languages incl. Afrikaans, English, Ndebele, Sotho. **Chief religions:** Christian 68%; traditional, animistic 29%.

Geography: Area: 471,008 sq. mi. **Location:** At the southern extreme of Africa. **Neighbors:** Namibia, Botswana, Zimbabwe on N; Mozambique, Swaziland on E; surrounds Lesotho. **Topography:** The large interior plateau reaches close to the country's 2,700-mi. coastline. There are few major rivers or lakes; rainfall is sparse in W, more plentiful in E. **Capitals:** Cape Town (legislative), Pretoria (executive), and Bloemfontein (judicial). **Cities** Cape Town 2,727,000; Johannesburg 2,172,000; Pretoria 1,314,000*.

Government: Type: Republic. **Head of state:** Pres. Nelson Mandela; b July 18, 1918; in office: May 10, 1994. **Local divisions:** 9 provinces. **Defense:** 1.8% of GDP. **Active troop strength:** 137,900.

Economy: Industries: Mining, steel, chemicals, vehicles, machinery, textiles. **Chief crops:** Corn, wheat, vegetables, sugar, fruit. **Minerals:** Platinum, chromium, antimony, coal, iron, manganese, nickel, phosphates, tin, uranium, gem diamonds, copper, vanadium; world's largest producer of gold (approx. 30% of total world prod.) **Crude oil reserves** (1997): 29 mil bbls. **Other resources:** Wool, dairy products. **Arable land:** 10%. **Livestock** (1997): chickens: 59.00 mil; sheep: 29.19 mil; cattle: 13.67 mil; goats: 6.64 mil; pigs: 1.62 mil. **Fish catch** (1996): 436,279 metric tons. **Electricity prod.** (1996): 187.0 bil kWh. **Labor force:** 35% services; 30% agric.; 20% ind.

Finance: Monetary unit: Rand (Sept. 1998: 6.23 = $1 U.S.). **Gross domestic product** (1996 est.): $227 bil. **Per capita GDP** $5,400. **Imports** (1996): $26.9 bil; partners: Germany 16%, UK 12%, U.S. 11%. **Exports** (1996): $29.2 bil; partners: Italy 8%, Japan 7%. **Tourism:** $2.26 bil. **National budget** (FY 1994-95 est.): $38 bil. **International reserves less gold** (May 1998): $5.29 bil. **Gold:** 4.09 mil oz t. **Consumer prices** (change in 1997): 8.5%.

Transport: Railroad: Length: 13,418 mi. **Motor vehicles in use:** 4.12 mil passenger cars, 2.16 mil comm. vehicles. **Civil aviation:** 9.91 bil passenger-mi; 24 airports. **Chief ports:** Durban, Cape Town, East London, Port Elizabeth.

Communications: Television sets: 84 per 1,000 pop. **Radios:** 268 per 1,000 pop. **Telephones:** 1 per 11 persons. **Daily newspaper circ.:** 29 per 1,000 pop.

Health: Life expectancy at birth: 53.6 male; 57.8 female. **Births** (per 1,000 pop.): 26. **Deaths** (per 1,000 pop.): 12. **Natural increase:** 1.42%. **Hospital beds** (1995): 1 per 239 persons. **Physicians** (1994): 1 per 1,529 persons. **Infant mortality** (per 1,000 live births): 52.

Education: Compulsory: ages 7-16. **Literacy** (1995): 82%.

Major International Organizations: UN (FAO, IBRD, ILO, IMF, IMO, WHO, WTrO), the Commonwealth, OAU.

Embassy: 3051 Massachusetts Ave. NW 20008; 232-4400.

Website: http://www.css.gov.za/index.htm

Bushmen and Hottentots were the original inhabitants. Bantus, including Zulu, Xhosa, Swazi, and Sotho, had occupied the area from NE to S South Africa before the 17th century.

The Cape of Good Hope area was settled by Dutch, beginning in the 17th century. Britain seized the Cape in 1806. Many Dutch trekked north and founded 2 republics, Transvaal and Orange Free State. Diamonds were discovered, 1867, and gold, 1886. The Dutch (Boers) resented encroachments by the British and others; the Anglo-Boer War followed, 1899-1902. Britain won and, effective May 31, 1910, created the Union of South Africa, incorporating 2 British colonies (Cape and Natal) with Transvaal and Orange Free State. After a referendum, the Union became the Republic of South Africa, May 31, 1961, and withdrew from the Commonwealth.

With the election victory of Daniel Malan's National Party in 1948, the policy of separate development of the races, or apartheid, already existing unofficially, became official. Under apartheid, blacks were severely restricted to certain occupations, and paid far lower wages than whites for similar work. Only whites could vote or run for public office. Persons of Asian Indian ancestry and those of mixed race (Coloureds) had limited political rights. In 1959 the government passed acts providing for the eventual creation of several Bantu nations, or Bantustans, on 13% of the country's land area. Most black leaders opposed the plan.

Protests against apartheid were brutally suppressed. At Sharpeville on Mar. 21, 1960, 69 black protesters were killed by government troops. At least 600 persons, mostly Bantus, were killed in 1976 riots protesting apartheid. In 1981, South Africa launched military operations in Angola and Mozambique to combat guerrilla groups. South African troops attacked the South West African People's Organization (SWAPO) guerrillas in Angola, Mar. 1982. South Africa and Mozambique signed a nonaggression pact in 1984.

A new constitution was approved by referendum, Nov. 1983, extending the parliamentary franchise to the Coloured and Asian minorities. Laws banning interracial sex and marriage were repealed in 1985.

In 1986, Nobel Peace Prize winner Bishop Desmond Tutu called for Western nations to apply sanctions against South Africa to force an end to apartheid. Pres. P. W. Botha announced in Apr. the end to the nation's system of racial pass laws and offered blacks an advisory role in government. On May 19, South Africa attacked 3 neighboring countries—Zimbabwe, Botswana, Zambia—to strike at guerrilla strongholds of the black nationalist African National Congress (ANC). A nationwide state of emergency was declared June 12, giving almost unlimited power to the security forces.

Some 2 million South African black workers staged a massive strike, June 6-8, 1988. Pres. Botha, head of the government since 1978, resigned Aug. 14, 1989, and was replaced by F. W. de Klerk. In 1990 the government lifted its ban on the ANC. Black nationalist leader Nelson Mandela was freed Feb. 11 after more than 27 years in prison. In Feb. 1991, Pres. de Klerk announced plans to end all apartheid laws.

In 1993 negotiators agreed on basic principles for a new democratic constitution. South Africa's partially self-governing black territories, or "homelands," were dissolved and incorporated into a national system of 9 provinces.

In elections Apr. 26-29, 1994, the ANC won 62.7% of the vote, making Mandela president. The National Party won 20.4%. The Inkatha Freedom Party won 10.5% and control of the legislature in a mainly Zulu province. Fighting between the ANC and Inkatha (aided, during the apartheid era, by South African defense forces) has killed more than 14,000 people in the Zulu region since the mid-1980s.

In 1995, Mandela appointed a truth commission, led by Desmond Tutu, to document human rights abuses under apartheid. A post-apartheid constitution, modified to meet the objections of the Constitutional Court, became law Dec. 10, 1996, with provisions to take effect over a 3-year period.

Spain

Kingdom of Spain

People: Population: 39,133,996. **Age distrib.** (%): <15: 15.2; 65+: 16.3. **Pop. density:** 200 per sq. mi. **Urban:** 77%. **Ethnic groups:** Mix of Mediterranean and Nordic types. **Principal languages:** Castilian Spanish (official), Catalan, Galician, Basque. **Chief religion:** Roman Catholic 99%.

Geography: Area: 195,364 sq. mi. **Location:** In SW Europe. **Neighbors:** Portugal on W, France on N. **Topography:** The interior is a high, arid plateau broken by mountain ranges and river valleys. The NW is heavily watered, the S has lowlands and a Mediterranean climate. **Capital:** Madrid. **Cities:** Madrid 4,072,000; Barcelona 2,819,000; Valencia 751,000*.

Government: Type: Constitutional monarchy. **Head of state:** King Juan Carlos I de Borbon y Borbon, b. Jan. 5, 1938; in office: Nov. 22, 1975. **Head of government:** Prime Min. José María Aznar; b Feb. 25, 1953; in office: May 5, 1996. **Local divisions:** 17 automonous communities. **Defense:** 1.5% of GDP. **Active troop strength:** 206,800.

Economy: Industries: Machinery, metals, textiles, shoes, vehicles, processed foods, tourism. **Chief crops:** Grains, olives, grapes, citrus, vegetables. **Minerals:** Lignite, uranium, lead, iron, copper, zinc, coal. **Crude oil reserves** (1997): 30 mil bbls. **Other resources:** Forests. **Arable land:** 30%. **Livestock** (1997): chickens: 126.00 mil; sheep: 21.83 mil; pigs: 18.65 mil; cattle: 5.91 mil; goats: 2.14 mil. **Fish catch** (1996): 1.06 mil metric tons. **Electricity prod.** (1996): 163.5 bil kWh. **Labor force:** 62% serv.; 29% manuf., mining, const.; 9% agric.

Finance: Monetary unit: Peseta (Sept. 1998: 147.17 = $1 U.S.). **Gross domestic product** (1996 est.): $593 bil. **Per capita GDP:** $15,300. **Imports** (1995): $118.3 bil; partners: EU 66%. **Exports** (1995): $94.5 bil; partners: EU 72%. **Tourism:** $26.59 bil. **National budget** (1995): $139 bil. **International reserves less gold** (June 1998): $67.16 bil. **Gold:** 15.63 mil oz t. **Consumer prices** (change in 1997): 2.0%.

Transport: Railroad: Length: 8,252 mi. **Motor vehicles in use:** 14.75 mil passenger cars, 3.20 mil comm. vehicles. **Civil aviation:** 21.18 bil passenger-mi; 25 airports. **Chief ports:** Barcelona, Bilbao, Valencia, Cartagena.

Communications: Television sets: 490 per 1,000 pop. **Radios:** 306 per 1,000 pop. **Telephones:** 1 per 2.6 persons. **Daily newspaper circ.:** 104 per 1,000 pop.

Health: Life expectancy at birth: 73.8 male; 81.6 female. **Births** (per 1,000 pop.): 10. **Deaths** (per 1,000 pop.): 10. **Natural increase:** 0.01%. **Hospital beds** (1994): 1 per 234 persons. **Physicians** (1995): 1 per 241 persons. **Infant mortality** (per 1,000 live births): 7.

Education: Free and compulsory: ages 6-16. **Literacy** (1995): 97%.

Major International Organizations: UN and all of its specialized agencies, EU, NATO, OECD, OSCE.

Embassy: 2375 Pennsylvania Ave. NW 20037; 452-0100.

Website: http://www.DocuWeb.ca/SiSpain

Initially settled by Iberians, Basques, and Celts, Spain was successively ruled (wholly or in part) by Carthage, Rome, and the Visigoths. Muslims invaded Iberia from North Africa in 711. Reconquest of the peninsula by Christians from the N laid the foundations of modern Spain. In 1469 the kingdoms of Aragon and Castile were united by the marriage of Ferdinand II and Isabella I. Moorish rule ended with the fall of the kingdom of Granada, 1492. Spain's large Jewish community was expelled the same year.

Spain obtained a colonial empire with the "discovery" of America by Columbus, 1492, the conquest of Mexico by Cortes, and Peru by Pizarro. It also controlled the Netherlands and parts of Italy and Germany. Spain lost its American colonies in the early 19th century. It lost Cuba, the Philippines, and Puerto Rico during the Spanish-American War, 1898.

Primo de Rivera became dictator in 1923. King Alfonso XIII revoked the dictatorship, 1930, but was forced to leave the country in 1931. A republic was proclaimed, which disestablished the church, curtailed its privileges, and secularized education. During 1936-39 a Popular Front composed of socialists, Communists, republicans, and anarchists governed Spain.

Army officers under Francisco Franco revolted against the government, 1936. In a destructive 3-year war, in which some one million died, Franco received massive help and troops from Italy and Germany, while the USSR, France, and Mexico supported the republic. The war ended Mar. 28, 1939. Franco was named caudillo, leader of the nation. Spain was officially neutral in World War II, but its cordial relations with fascist countries caused its exclusion from the UN until 1955.

In July 1969, Franco and the Cortes (Parliament) designated Prince Juan Carlos as the future king and chief of state. After Franco's death, Nov. 20, 1975, Juan Carlos was sworn in as king. In free elections June 1977, moderates and democratic socialists emerged as the largest parties.

In 1981 a coup attempt by right-wing military officers was thwarted by the king. The Socialist Workers' Party, under Felipe Gonzâlez Márquez, won 4 consecutive general elections, from 1982 to 1993, but lost to a coalition of conservative and regional parties in the election of Mar. 3, 1996.

Catalonia and the Basque country were granted autonomy, Jan. 1980, following overwhelming approval in home-rule referendums. Basque extremists, however, have pushed for independence. The militant Basque separatist group ETA proclaimed an indefinite cease-fire as of Sept. 18, 1998.

The **Balearic Islands** in the W Mediterranean, 1,927 sq. mi., are a province of Spain; they include **Majorca** (Mallorca; capital Palma de Mallorca), **Minorca, Cabrera, Ibiza,** and **Formentera.** The **Canary Islands,** 2,807 sq. mi., in the Atlantic W of Morocco, form 2 provinces, and include the islands of **Tenerife, Palma, Gomera, Hierro, Grand Canary, Fuerteventura,** and **Lanzarote;** Las Palmas and Santa Cruz are thriving ports. **Ceuta** and **Melilla,** small Spanish enclaves on Morocco's Mediterranean coast, gained limited autonomy in Sept. 1994.

Spain has sought the return of Gibraltar, in British hands since 1704.

Sri Lanka

Democratic Socialist Republic of Sri Lanka

People: Population: 18,933,558. **Age distrib.** (%): <15: 27.6; 65+: 6.3. **Pop. density:** 747 per sq. mi. **Urban:** 22%. **Ethnic groups:** Sinhalese 74%, Tamil 18%, Moor 7%, others. **Principal languages:** Sinhala, Tamil (both official), English. **Chief religions:** Buddhist 69%, Hindu 15%, Christian 8%, Muslim 8%.

Geography: Area: 25,332 sq. mi. **Location:** In Indian O. off SE coast of India. **Neighbors:** India on NW. **Topography:** The coastal area and the northern half are flat; the S-central area is hilly and mountainous. **Capital:** Colombo (1995): 1.3 mil.

Government: Type: Republic. **Head of state:** Pres. Chandrika Bandaranaike Kumaratunga; b June 29, 1945; in office: Nov. 12, 1994. **Head of government:** Prime Min. Sirimavo Bandaranaike; b Apr. 17, 1916; in office: Nov. 14, 1994. **Local divisions:** 25 administrative districts. **Defense:** 6.5% of GDP. **Active troop strength:** 115,000.

Economy: Industries: Clothing, agric. processing, oil refining, textiles. **Chief crops:** Tea, coconuts, rice, sugar. **Minerals:** Graphite, limestone, gems, phosphates. **Other resources:** Forests, rubber. **Arable land:** 14%. **Livestock** (1997): chickens: 9.30 mil; cattle: 1.64 mil; goats: 535,200; buffalo: 760,900. **Fish catch** (1996): 225,000 metric tons. **Electricity prod.** (1996): 5.1 bil kWh. **Labor force:** 42% agric.; 40% services.

Finance: Monetary unit: Rupee (Sept. 1998: 66.23 = $1 U.S.). **Gross domestic product** (1996 est.): $69.7 bil. **Per capita GDP:** $3,760. **Imports** (1996 est.): $5 bil; partners: Japan 11%, India 9%. **Exports** (1996 est.): $4 bil; partners: U.S. 35%, UK 9%. **Tourism:** $212 mil. **National budget** (1997): $4.2 bil. **International reserves less gold** (June 1998): $1.86 bil. **Gold:** 63,000 oz t. **Consumer prices** (change in 1997): 9.6%.

Transport: Railroad: Length: 921.6 mi. **Motor vehicles in use:** 220,000 passenger cars, 248,900 comm. vehicles. **Civil aviation:** 2.37 bil passenger-mi; 1 airport. **Chief ports:** Colombo, Trincomalee, Galle.

Communications: Television sets: 39 per 1,000 pop. **Radios:** 182 per 1,000 pop. **Telephones:** 1 per 90 persons.

Health: Life expectancy at birth: 69.8 male; 75.4 female. **Births** (per 1,000 pop.): 18. **Deaths** (per 1,000 pop.): 6. **Natural increase:** 1.24%. **Hospital beds** (1993): 1 per 360 persons. **Physicians** (1993): 1 per 4,745 persons. **Infant mortality** (per 1,000 live births): 16.

Education: Free and compulsory: ages 5-12. **Literacy** (1995): 88%.

Major International Organizations: UN (FAO, IBRD, ILO, IMF, IMO, WHO, WTrO), the Commonwealth.

Embassy: 2148 Wyoming Ave. NW 20008; 483-4025.

The island was known to the ancient world as Taprobane (Greek for copper-colored) and later as Serendip (from Arabic). Colonists from N India subdued the indigenous Veddahs about 543 BC; their descendants, the Buddhist Sinhalese, still form most of the population. Hindu descendants of Tamil immigrants from S India account for about one-fifth of the population.

Parts were occupied by the Portuguese in 1505 and by the Dutch in 1658. The British seized the island in 1796. As Ceylon it became an independent member of the Commonwealth in 1948. Ceylon became the Republic of Sri Lanka May 22, 1972.

Prime Min. W. R. D. Bandaranaike was assassinated Sept. 25, 1959. In new elections, the Freedom Party was victorious under Mrs. Sirimavo Bandaranaike, widow of the former prime minister. After May 1970 elections, Mrs. Bandaranaike became prime minister again. In 1971 the nation suffered economic problems and terrorist activities by ultra-leftists, thousands of whom were executed. Massive land reform and nationalization of foreign-owned plantations were undertaken in the mid-1970s. Mrs. Bandaranaike was ousted in 1977 elections. Presidential powers were increased in 1978 in an effort to restore stability.

Tensions between the Sinhalese and Tamil separatists erupted into violence in the early 1980s. More than 54,000 have died in the civil war, which continued in the late 1990s.

Pres. Ranasinghe Premadasa was assassinated May 1, 1993, by a Tamil rebel. Mrs. Bandaranaike's daughter, Chandrika Bandaranaike Kumaratunga, became prime minister after the Aug. 16, 1994, general elections. Elected president Nov. 9, Kumaratunga appointed her mother prime minister.

Sudan

Republic of the Sudan

People: Population: 33,550,552. **Age distrib.** (%): <15: 45.4; 65+: 2.2. **Pop. density:** 35 per sq. mi. **Urban:** 32%. **Ethnic groups:** Black 52%, Arab 39%, Beja 6%. **Principal languages:** Arabic (official), Nubian, Ta Bedawie. **Chief religions:** Sunni Muslim 70%, indigenous beliefs 25%.

Geography: Area: 967,493 sq. mi., the largest country in Africa. **Location:** At the E end of Sahara desert zone. **Neighbors:** Egypt on N; Libya, Chad, Central African Republic on W; Congo (formerly Zaire), Uganda, Kenya on S; Ethiopia, Eritrea on E. **Topography:** The N consists of the Libyan Desert in the W, and the mountainous Nubia Desert in E, with narrow Nile valley between. The center contains large, fertile, rainy areas with fields, pasture, and forest. The S has rich soil, heavy rain. **Capital:** Khartoum 2,249,000*.

Government: Type: Republic with strong military influence. **Head of state and government:** Pres. Gen. Omar Hassan Ahmad Al-Bashir; b Jan. 1, 1944; in office: June 30, 1989. **Local divisions:** 26 states. **Defense:** 4.3% of GDP. **Active troop strength:** 89,000.

Economy: Industries: Cotton ginning, textiles, cement. **Chief crops:** Gum arabic, sorghum, cotton (main export), wheat. **Minerals:** Chromium, copper. **Crude oil reserves** (1997): 262 mil bbls. **Arable land:** 5%. **Livestock** (1997): chickens: 40.00 mil; sheep: 24.50 mil; cattle: 22.25 mil; goats: 16.90 mil. **Electricity prod.** (1996): 1.3 bil kWh. **Labor force:** 80% agric.; 10% ind. & comm.; 6% govt.

Finance: Monetary unit: Pound (Sept. 1998: 1,826.00 = $1 U.S.), Dinar (June 1996: 182.60 = $1 U.S.). **Gross domestic product** (1996 est.): $26.6 bil. **Per capita GDP:** $860. **Imports** 1996 est.): $1 bil; partners: EU 29%, U.S. 18%. **Exports** (1996 est.): $500 mil; partners: Egypt 33%, Saudi Arabia 17%. **Tourism:** $8 mil. **National budget** (1995 est.): $1.06 bil. **International reserves less gold** (Apr. 1998): $81.9 mil.

Transport: Railroad: Length: 2,960 mi. **Motor vehicles in use:** 35,000 passenger cars, 40,000 comm. vehicles. **Civil aviation:** 403.7 mil passenger-mi; 3 airports. **Chief port:** Port Sudan.

Communications: Television sets: 8.2 per 1,000 pop. **Radios:** 182 per 1,000 pop. **Telephones:** 1 per 376 persons. **Daily newspaper circ.:** 21 per 1,000 pop.

Health: Life expectancy at birth: 55.0 male; 57.0 female. **Births** (per 1,000 pop.): 40. **Deaths** (per 1,000 pop.): 11. **Natural increase:** 2.91%. **Physicians** (1994): 1 per 11,300 persons. **Infant mortality** (per 1,000 live births): 73.

Education: Literacy (1995): 46%.

Major International Organizations: UN (FAO, IBRD, ILO, IMF, IMO, WHO), AL, OAU.

Embassy: 2210 Massachusetts Ave. NW 20008; 338-8565.

Website: http://www.sudan.net

Northern Sudan, ancient Nubia, was settled by Egyptians in antiquity. The population was converted to Coptic Christianity in the 6th century. Arab conquests brought Islam in the 15th century.

In the 1820s Egypt took over Sudan, defeating the last of earlier empires, including the Fung. In the 1880s a revolution was led by Muhammad Ahmad, who called himself the Mahdi (leader of the faithful), and his followers, the dervishes.

In 1898 an Anglo-Egyptian force crushed the Mahdi's successors. In 1951 the Egyptian Parliament abrogated its 1899 and 1936 treaties with Great Britain and amended its constitution to provide for a separate Sudanese constitution. Sudan voted for complete independence as a parliamentary government effective Jan. 1, 1956.

In 1969, a Revolutionary Council took power, but a civilian premier and cabinet were appointed; the government announced it would create a socialist state.

Economic problems plagued the nation in the 1980s and 1990s, aggravated by civil war and influxes of refugees from neighboring countries. After 16 years in power, Pres. Jaafar al-Nimeiry was overthrown in a bloodless military coup, Apr. 6, 1985. Sudan held its first democratic parliamentary elections in 18 years in 1986, but the elected government was overthrown in a bloodless coup June 30, 1989.

In the mid-1980s, rebels in the south (populated largely by black Christians and followers of tribal religions) took up arms against government domination by northern Sudan, mostly Arab-Muslim. War and related famine cost at least 1.5 million lives and displaced millions of southerners by the late 1990s. In 1993, Amnesty International accused Sudan of "ethnic cleansing" against the Nuba people in the South.

Egypt publicly blamed Sudan for an attempted assassination of Egyptian Pres. Hosni Mubarak in Ethiopia, June 26, 1995. Opposition groups boycotted elections Mar. 1996.

A new constitution based on Islamic law took effect June 30, 1998. On Aug. 20, in retaliation for bombings in Kenya and Tanzania, U.S. missiles destroyed a Khartoum pharmaceutical plant the U.S. claimed was associated with terrorist activities.

Suriname

Republic of Suriname

People: Population: 427,980. **Age distrib.** (%): <15: 33.3; 65+: 5.2. **Pop. density:** 7 per sq. mi. **Urban:** 50%. **Ethnic groups:** Hindustani 37%, Creole 31%, Javanese 15%. **Principal languages:** Dutch (official), Sranang Tongo, English, Hindustani. **Chief religions:** Hindu 27%, Protestant 25%, Roman Catholic 23%, Muslim 20%.

Geography: Area: 63,039 sq. mi. **Location:** On N shore of South America. **Neighbors:** Guyana on W, Brazil on S, French Guiana on E. **Topography:** A flat Atlantic coast, where dikes permit agriculture. Inland is a forest belt; to the S, largely unexplored hills cover 75% of the country. **Capital:** Paramaribo (1993 est.): 200,970.

Government: Type: Republic. **Head of state and government:** Pres. Jules Wijdenbosch; b May 2, 1941; in office: Sept. 14, 1996. **Local divisions:** 10 districts. **Defense:** 3.5% of GDP. **Active troop strength:** 1,800.

Economy: Industries: Aluminum, mining, food processing. **Chief crops:** Rice, bananas, palm kernels. **Minerals:** Bauxite, iron. **Crude oil reserves** (1997): 74.0 mil bbls. **Other resources:** Forests, fish, shrimp. **Livestock** (1997): chickens: 2.70 mil. **Electricity prod.** (1996): 1.6 bil kWh. **Labor force:** 39% public admin. & defense; 20% agric. & forestry.

Finance: Monetary unit: Guilder (Sept. 1998: 401.00 = $1 U.S.). **Gross domestic product** (1996 est.): $1.4 bil. **Per capita GDP:** $3,150. **Imports** (1995 est.): $418 mil; partners: U.S. 40%, Netherlands 24%. **Exports** (1995 est.): $432 mil; partners: Norway 33%, Netherlands 26%, U.S. 13%. **Tourism:** $17 mil. **National budget** (1995 est.): $174 mil. **International reserves less gold** (Mar. 1998): $101.36 mil. **Gold:** 218,000 oz t. **Consumer prices** (change in 1997): –7.1%.

Transport: Railroad: Length: 187 mi. **Motor vehicles in use:** 46,408 passenger cars, 19,255 comm. vehicles. **Civil aviation:** 548.6 mil passenger-mi; 3 airports. **Chief ports:** Paramaribo, Nieuw Nickerie.

Communications: Television sets: 146 per 1,000 pop. **Radios:** 719 per 1,000 pop. **Telephones:** 1 per 7.7 persons. **Daily newspaper circ.:** 107 per 1,000 pop.

Health: Life expectancy at birth: 68.1 male; 73.3 female. **Births** (per 1,000 pop.): 22. **Deaths** (per 1,000 pop.): 6. **Natural increase:** 1.67%. **Infant mortality** (per 1,000 live births): 27.

Education: Free and compulsory: ages 6-16. **Literacy** (1995): 93%.

Major International Organizations: UN (FAO, IBRD, ILO, IMF, IMO, WHO, WTrO), Caricom, OAS.

Embassy: 4301 Connecticut Ave. NW 20008; 244-7488.

The Netherlands acquired Suriname in 1667 from Britain, in exchange for New Netherlands (New York). The 1954 Dutch constitution raised the colony to a level of equality with the Netherlands and the Netherlands Antilles. Independence was granted Nov. 25, 1975, despite objections from East Indians. Some 40% of the population (mostly East Indians) immigrated to the Netherlands in the months before independence.

The National Military Council took control of the government, Feb. 1982. Civilian rule was restored in 1987, but political turmoil continued until 1992, disrupting the nation's economy.

Swaziland

Kingdom of Swaziland

People: Population: 966,462. **Age distrib.** (%): <15: 46.4; 65+: 2.5. **Pop. density:** 144 per sq. mi. **Urban:** 32%. **Ethnic groups:** African 97%, European 3%. **Principal languages:** siSwati, English (both official). **Chief religions:** Christian 60%, indigenous beliefs 40%.

Geography: Area: 6,703 sq. mi. **Location:** In southern Africa, near Indian O. coast. **Neighbors:** South Africa on N, W, S; Mozambique on E. **Topography:** The country descends from W-E in broad belts, becoming more arid in the low veld region, then rising to a plateau in the E. **Capital:** Mbabane (1990 est.) 47,000.

Government: Type: Constitutional monarchy. **Head of state:** King Mswati 3d; b 1968; in office: Apr. 25, 1986. **Head of government:** Prime Min. Barnabas Sibusiso Dlamini; in office: July 26, 1996. **Local divisions:** 4 districts.

Economy: Industries: Wood pulp, mining. **Chief crops:** Sugar, corn, cotton, rice, pineapples, sugar, tobacco, citrus. **Minerals:** Asbestos, clay, coal. **Other resources:** Forests. **Arable land:** 11%. **Livestock** (1997): chickens: 990,000; cattle: 650,000; goats: 440,000. **Electricity prod.** (1996): 415 mil kWh.

Finance: Monetary unit: Lilangeni (Sept. 1998: 6.23 = $1 U.S.). **Gross domestic product** (1996 est.): $3.8 bil. **Per capita GDP:** $3,800. **Imports** (1996): $831 mil; partners: South Africa 88%. **Exports** (1996): $700 mil; partners: South Africa 58%. **Tourism:** $37 mil. **National budget** (1995-96): $413 mil. **International reserves less gold** (June 1998): $326.88 mil. **Consumer prices** (change in 1997): 12.2%.

Transport: Railroad: Length: 184.4 mi. **Motor vehicles in use:** 28,523 passenger cars, 8,232 comm. vehicles. **Civil aviation:** 35.3 mil passenger-mi; 1 airport.

Communications: Television sets: 96 per 1,000 pop. **Radios:** 129 per 1,000 pop. **Telephones:** 1 per 48 persons.

Health: Life expectancy at birth: 37.3 male; 39.8 female. **Births** (per 1,000 pop.): 41. **Deaths** (per 1,000 pop.): 21. **Natural increase:** 1.96%. **Infant mortality rate** (per 1,000 live births): 103.

Education: Literacy (1995): 77%.

Major International Organizations: UN (FAO, IBRD, ILO, IMF, WHO, WTrO), the Commonwealth, OAU.

Embassy: 3400 International Dr. NW 20008; 362-6683.

Website: http://www.realnet.co.sz

The royal house of Swaziland traces back 400 years, and is one of Africa's last ruling dynasties. The Swazis, a Bantu people, were driven to Swaziland from lands to the N by the Zulus in 1820. Their autonomy was later guaranteed by Britain and Transvaal (later part of South Africa), with Britain assuming control after 1903. Independence came Sept. 6, 1968. In 1973 the king repealed the constitution and assumed full powers.

A new constitution banning political parties took effect Oct. 13, 1978. As Swaziland slowly moved toward political reform, student and labor unrest grew in the mid-1990s.

Sweden

Kingdom of Sweden

People: Population: 8,886,738. **Age distrib.** (%): <15: 18.7; 65+: 17.4. **Pop. density:** 51 per sq. mi. **Urban:** 83%. **Ethnic groups:** Swedish 89%, Finnish 2%. **Principal language:** Swedish. **Chief religion:** Evangelical Lutheran 94%.

Geography: Area: 173,731 sq. mi. **Location:** On Scandinavian Peninsula in N Europe. **Neighbors:** Norway on W, Denmark on S (across Kattegat), Finland on E. **Topography:** Mountains along NW border cover 25% of Sweden, flat or rolling terrain covers the central and southern areas, which include several large lakes. **Capital:** Stockholm. **Cities:** Stockholm 1,545,000; Göteborg 751,000*.

Government: Type: Constitutional monarchy. **Head of state:** King Carl XVI Gustaf; b Apr. 30, 1946; in office: Sept. 19, 1973. **Head of government:** Prime Min. Goran Persson; b June 20, 1949; in office: Mar. 22, 1996. **Local divisions:** 24 counties subdivided into 288 municipalities. **Defense:** 2.9% of GDP. **Active troop strength:** 62,600.

Economy: Industries: Steel, precision equipment, vehicles, processed foods, paper. **Chief crops:** Grains, potatoes, sugar beets. **Minerals:** Zinc, iron, lead, copper, silver. **Other resources:** Forests (half the country); yield about 17% of exports. **Arable land:** 7%. **Livestock** (1997): chickens: 11.00 mil; pigs: 2.34 mil; cattle: 1.78 mil; sheep: 470,000. **Fish catch** (1996): 370,881 metric tons. **Electricity prod.** (1996): 135.2 bil kWh. **Labor force:** 38% social & personal services; 21% manuf. & mining.

Finance: Monetary unit: Krona (Sept. 1998: 7.88 = $1 U.S.). **Gross domestic product** (1996 est.): $184.3 bil. **Per capita GDP:** $20,800. **Imports** (1995): $64.4 bil; partners: EU 63%. **Exports** (1995): $79.9 bil; partners: EU 59%. **Tourism:** $3.79 bil. **National budget** (FY 1995-96): $146.1 bil. **International reserves less gold** (June 1998): $12.65 bil. **Gold:** 4.72 mil oz t. **Consumer prices** (change in 1997): 0.5%.

Transport: Railroad: Length: 6,744 mi. **Motor vehicles in use:** 3.65 mil passenger cars, 326,504 comm. vehicles. **Civil aviation:** 5.54 bil passenger-mi; 48 airports. **Chief ports:** Göteborg, Stockholm, Malmö.

Communications: Television sets: 476 per 1,000 pop. **Radios:** 844 per 1,000 pop. **Telephones:** 1 per 1.5 persons. **Daily newspaper circ.:** 515 per 1,000 pop.

Health: Life expectancy at birth: 76.5 male; 82.0 female. **Births** (per 1,000 pop.): 12. **Deaths** (per 1,000 pop.): 11. **Natural increase:** 0.09%. **Hospital beds** (1995): 1 per 194 persons. **Physicians** (1995): 1 per 384 persons. **Infant mortality** (per 1,000 live births): 4.

Education: Compulsory: ages 6-15. **Literacy** (1995): 100%.
Major International Organizations: UN and all of its specialized agencies, EU, OECD, OSCE.
Embassy: 1501 M St. NW 20005; 467-2600.
Website: http://www.scb.se/scbeng/keyeng.htm

The Swedes have lived in present-day Sweden for at least 5,000 years, longer than nearly any other European people. Gothic tribes from Sweden played a major role in the disintegration of the Roman Empire. Other Swedes helped create the first Russian state in the 9th century.

The Swedes were Christianized from the 11th century, and a strong centralized monarchy developed. A parliament, the Riksdag, was first called in 1435, the earliest parliament on the European continent, with all classes of society represented.

Swedish independence from rule by Danish kings (dating from 1397) was secured by Gustavus I in a revolt, 1521-23; he built up the government and military and established the Lutheran Church. In the 17th century Sweden was a major European power, gaining most of the Baltic seacoast, but its international position subsequently declined.

The Napoleonic wars, 1799-1815, in which Sweden acquired Norway (it became independent 1905), were the last in which Sweden participated. Armed neutrality was maintained in both world wars.

More than 4 decades of Social Democratic rule ended in the 1976 parliamentary elections; the party returned to power in the 1982 elections. After Prime Min. Olof Palme was shot to death in Stockholm, Feb. 28, 1986, Ingvar Carlsson took office. Carl Bildt, a non-Socialist, became prime minister Oct. 1991, with a mandate to restore Sweden's economic competitiveness. The Social Democrats returned to power following 1994 elections.

Swedish voters approved membership in the European Union Nov. 13, 1994, and Sweden entered the EU as of Jan. 1, 1995. Carlsson retired and was succeeded by Goran Persson in Mar. 1996. Persson forged a coalition with the Left and Green parties after his Social Democrats lost ground in elections Sept. 20, 1998.

Switzerland

Swiss Confederation

People: Population: 7,260,357. **Age distrib.** (%): <15: 17.3; 65+: 14.9. **Pop. density:** 455 per sq. mi. **Urban:** 61%. **Ethnic groups:** German 65%, French 18%, Italian 10%, Romansch 1%. **Principal languages:** German, French, Italian, Romansch (all official). **Chief religions:** Roman Catholic 47%, Protestant 40%.

Geography: Area: 15,942 sq. mi. **Location:** In the Alps Mts. in central Europe. **Neighbors:** France on W, Italy on S, Austria on E, Germany on N. **Topography:** The Alps cover 60% of the land area; the Jura, near France, 10%. Running between, from NE to SW, are midlands, 30%. **Capitals:** Bern (administrative), Lausanne (judicial). **Cities** (1996 est.): Zurich 343,869; Basel 174,007; Geneva 173,549; Bern 127,469.

Government: Type: Federal republic. **Head of government:** The president is elected by the Federal Assembly to a nonrenewable 1-year term. **Local divisions:** 20 full cantons, 6 half cantons. **Defense:** 1.6% of GDP. **Active troop strength:** 27,300.

Economy: Industries: Machinery, chemicals, precision instruments, watches, textiles, foodstuffs (cheese, chocolate), banking, tourism. **Minerals:** Salt. **Other resources:** Hydropower potential, timber. **Arable land:** 10%. **Livestock** (1997): chickens: 6.25 mil; cattle: 1.76 mil; pigs: 1.55 mil; sheep: 441,600. **Electricity prod.** (1996): 54.8 bil kWh. **Labor force:** 67% serv.; 29% manuf. & const.

Finance: Monetary unit: Franc (Sept. 1998: 1.42 = $1 U.S.). **Gross domestic product** (1996 est.): $161.3 bil. **Per capita GDP:** $22,600. **Imports** (1995): $80.05 bil; partners: EU 80%. **Exports** (1995): $81.35 bil; partners: EU 62%. **Tourism:** $7.96 bil. **National budget** (1995): $36.9 bil. **International reserves less gold** (June 1998): $34.83 bil. **Gold:** 83.28 mil oz t. **Consumer prices** (change in 1997): 0.5%.

Transport: Railroad: Length: 3,125 mi. **Motor vehicles in use:** 3.27 mil passenger cars, 300,681 comm. vehicles. **Civil aviation:** 13.83 bil passenger-mi; 5 airports. **Chief port:** Basel.

Communications: Television sets: 370 per 1,000 pop. **Radios:** 791 per 1,000 pop. **Telephones:** 1 per 1.6 persons. **Daily newspaper circ.:** 418 per 1,000 pop.

Health: Life expectancy at birth: 75.7 male; 82.2 female. **Births** (per 1,000 pop.): 11. **Deaths** (per 1,000 pop.): 9. **Natural increase:** 0.18%. **Hospital beds** (1994): 1 per 144 persons. **Physicians** (1994): 1 per 592 persons. **Infant mortality** (per 1,000 live births): 5.

Education: Compulsory: ages 7-16. **Literacy** (1994): 100%.
Major International Organizations: Many UN specialized agencies (though not a member), EFTA, OECD, OSCE.
Embassy: 2900 Cathedral Ave. NW 20008; 745-7900.
Websites: http://www.swissembassy.org.uk
http://www.admin.ch/bfs/eindex.htm

Switzerland, the former Roman province of Helvetia, traces its modern history to 1291, when 3 cantons created a defensive league. Other cantons were subsequently admitted to the Swiss Confederation, which obtained its independence from the Holy Roman Empire through the Peace of Westphalia (1648). The cantons were joined under a federal constitution in 1848, with large powers of local control retained by each.

Switzerland has maintained an armed neutrality since 1815, and has not been involved in a foreign war since 1515. It is the seat of many UN and other international agencies.

Switzerland is a world banking center. In an effort to crack down on criminal transactions, the nation's strict bank-secrecy rules have been eased since 1990. Stung by charges that assets seized by the Nazis and deposited in Swiss banks in World War II had not been properly returned, the government announced, March 5, 1997, a $4.7 billion fund to compensate victims of the Holocaust and other catastrophies. Swiss banks agreed Aug. 12, 1998, to pay $1.25 billion in reparations.

Syria

Syrian Arab Republic

People: Population: 16,673,282. **Age distrib.** (%): <15: 46.1; 65+: 2.9. **Pop. density:** 233 per sq. mi. **Urban:** 53%. **Ethnic groups:** Arab 90%. **Principal languages:** Arabic (official), Kurdish, Armenian. **Chief religions:** Sunni Muslim 74%, other Muslims 16%, Christian 10%.

Geography: Area: 71,498 sq. mi. **Location:** Middle East, at E end of Mediterranean Sea. **Neighbors:** Lebanon and Israel on W, Jordan on S, Iraq on E, Turkey on N. **Topography:** Syria has a short Mediterranean coastline, then stretches E and S with fertile lowlands and plains, alternating with mountains and large desert areas. **Capital:** Damascus. **Cities:** Damascus 2,036,000; Aleppo 1,840,000*.

Government: Type: Republic (under military regime). **Head of state:** Pres. Hafez al-Assad; b Mar. 1930; in office: Feb. 22, 1971. **Head of government:** Prime Min. Mahmud Zubi; in office: Nov. 1, 1987. **Local divisions:** 14 provinces. **Defense:** 4.8% of GDP. **Active troop strength:** 421,000.

Economy: Industries: Oil prods., textiles, food processing, tobacco, phosphate mining. **Chief crops:** Cotton, grains, lentils, chickpeas. **Minerals:** Oil, phosphates, iron, gypsum. **Crude oil reserves** (1997): 2.5 bil bbls. **Other resources:** Wool, dairy prods. **Arable land:** 28%. **Livestock** (1997): chickens: 18.83 mil; sheep: 13.83 mil; goats: 1.10 mil; cattle: 856,700. **Electricity prod.** (1996): 19.3 bil kWh. **Labor force:** 40% agric.; 40% services; 20% ind.

Finance: Monetary unit: Pound (Sept. 1998: 46.25 = $1 U.S.). **Gross domestic product** (1996 est.): $98.3 bil. **Per capita GDP:** $6,300. **Imports** (1996 est.): $5.24 bil; partners: EU 33%. **Exports** (1996 est.): $4.4 bil; partners: EU 57%. **Tourism:** $1.25 bil. **National budget** (1995 est.): $3.7 bil. **Gold:** 833,000 oz t. **Consumer prices** (change in 1997): 1.9%.

Transport: Railroad: Length: 1,097 mi. **Motor vehicles in use:** 134,000 passenger cars, 218,900 comm. vehicles. **Civil aviation:** 663.1 mil passenger-mi; 5 airports. **Chief ports:** Latakia, Tartus.

Communications: Television sets: 49 per 1,000 pop. **Radios:** 211 per 1,000 pop. **Telephones:** 1 per 16 persons. **Daily newspaper circ.:** 19 per 1,000 pop.

Health: Life expectancy at birth: 66.5 male; 69.1 female. **Births** (per 1,000 pop.): 38. **Deaths** (per 1,000 pop.): 6. **Natural increase:** 3.23%. **Hospital beds** (1995): 1 per 832 persons. **Physicians** (1995): 1 per 953 persons. **Infant mortality** (per 1,000 live births): 38.

Education: Compulsory: ages 6-12. **Literacy** (1995): 79%.
Major International Organizations: UN (FAO, IBRD, ILO, IMF, IMO, WHO), AL.
Embassy: 2215 Wyoming Ave. NW 20008; 232-6313.

Syria contains some of the most ancient remains of civilization. It was the center of the Seleucid empire, but later became absorbed in the Roman and Arab empires. Ottoman rule prevailed for 4 centuries, until the end of World War I.

The state of Syria was formed from former Turkish districts, separated by the Treaty of Sevres, 1920, and divided into the states of Syria and Greater Lebanon. Both were administered under a French League of Nations mandate 1920-1941.

Syria was proclaimed a republic by the occupying French Sept. 16, 1941, and exercised full independence Apr. 17, 1946. Syria joined the Arab invasion of Israel in 1948.

Syria joined Egypt Feb. 1958 in the United Arab Republic but seceded Sept. 1961. The Socialist Baath party and military leaders seized power Mar. 1963. The Baath, a pan-Arab organization, became the only legal party. The government has been dominated by the Alawite minority.

In the Arab-Israeli war of June 1967, Israel seized and occupied the Golan Heights, from which Syria had shelled Israeli settlements. On Oct. 6, 1973, Syria joined Egypt in an attack on Israel. Arab oil states agreed in 1974 to give Syria $1 billion a year to aid anti-Israel moves. Some 30,000 Syrian troops entered Lebanon in 1976 to mediate in a civil war. They fought Palestinian guerrillas and, later, Christian militiamen. Syrian troops again battled Christian forces in Lebanon, Apr. 1981.

Following Israel's invasion of Lebanon, June 6, 1982, Israeli planes destroyed 17 Syrian antiaircraft missile batteries in the Bekaa Valley, June 9. Some 25 Syrian planes were downed during the engagement. Israel and Syria agreed to a cease-fire June 11. In 1983, Syria backed the PLO rebels who ousted Yasir Arafat's forces from Tripoli.

Syria's role in promoting international terrorism led to the breaking of diplomatic relations with Great Britain and to limited sanctions by the European Community in 1986.

Syria condemned the Aug. 1990 Iraqi invasion of Kuwait and sent troops to help Allied forces in the Gulf War. In 1991, Syria accepted U.S. proposals for the terms of an Arab-Israeli peace conference. Syria subsequently participated in negotiations with Israel, but progress toward peace was slow. Turkey has accused Syria of aiding Kurdish separatists.

Taiwan

Republic of China

People: Population: 21,908,135. **Age distrib.** (%): <15: 22.4; 65+: 8.2. **Pop. density:** 1,568 per sq. mi. **Urban:** 75%. **Ethnic groups:** Taiwanese 84%, mainland Chinese 14%. **Principal languages:** Mandarin Chinese (official), Taiwanese. **Chief religions:** Buddhist, Taoist, Confucian 93%; Christian 5%.

Geography: Area: 13,969 sq. mi. **Location:** Off SE coast of China, between East and South China seas. **Neighbors:** Nearest is China. **Topography:** A mountain range forms the backbone of the island; the eastern half is very steep and craggy, the western slope is flat, fertile, and well cultivated. **Capital:** Taipei. **Cities** (1997 est.): Taipei 2,595,699; Kaohsiung 1,434,907; Taichung 881,870.

Government: Type: Democracy. **Head of state and Nationalist Party chmn.:** Pres. Lee Teng-hui; b Jan. 15, 1923; in office: Jan. 13, 1988. **Head of government:** Prime Min. Vincent Siew; b Jan. 3, 1939, in office: Aug. 28, 1997. **Local divisions:** 16 counties, 5 municipalities, 2 special municipalities (Taipei, Kaohsiung). **Defense:** 4.9% of GDP. **Active troop strength:** 376,000.

Economy: Industries: Textiles, clothing, electronics, processed foods, chemicals. **Chief crops:** Vegetables, rice, fruit, tea. **Minerals:** Coal, limestone, marble. **Arable land:** 24%. **Livestock** (1995): pigs: 10.5 mil. **Fish catch** (1996): 967,483 metric tons. **Electricity prod.** (1996): 135.0 bil kWh. **Labor force:** 52% services; 38% ind. & comm.; 10% agric.

Finance: Monetary unit: New Taiwan Dollar (Sept. 1998: 34.77 = $1 U.S.). **Gross domestic product** (1996 est.): $315 bil. **Per capita GDP:** $14,700. **Imports** (1996): $102.4 bil; partners: Japan 30%, U.S. 22%. **Exports** (1996): $116 bil; partners: U.S. 27%, Hong Kong 22%, EU 15%. **Tourism:** $3.71 bil. **National budget** (1996 est.): $79.5 bil.

Transport: Railroad: Length: 2,410 mi. **Motor vehicles in use:** 4.30 mil passenger cars, 925,000 comm. vehicles. **Civil aviation:** 22.8 bil passenger-mi; 13 airports. **Chief ports:** Kaohsiung, Chilung (Keelung), Hualien, Taichung.

Communications: Television sets: 327 per 1,000 pop. **Radios:** 402 per 1,000 pop. **Telephones:** 1 per 2.3 persons.

Health: Life expectancy at birth: 73.8 male; 80.1 female. **Births** (per 1,000 pop.): 15. **Deaths** (per 1,000 pop.): 5. **Natural increase:** 0.94%. **Hospital beds** (1995): 1 per 189 persons. **Physicians** (1995): 1 per 867 persons. **Infant mortality** (per 1,000 live births): 6.

Education: Free and compulsory: ages 6-15. **Literacy** (1995): 94%.

Major International Organizations: APEC.

Large-scale Chinese immigration began in the 17th century. The island came under mainland control after an interval of Dutch rule, 1620-62. Taiwan (also called Formosa) was ruled by Japan 1895-1945. Two million Kuomintang supporters fled to Taiwan in 1949. Both the Taipei and Beijing governments consider Taiwan an integral part of China. Taiwan has resisted Beijing's efforts at reunification, including military pressure, but economic ties with the mainland expanded in the 1990s.

The U.S., upon its recognition of the People's Republic of China, Dec. 15, 1978, severed diplomatic ties with Taiwan. The U.S. and Taiwan maintain contact via quasi-official agencies.

Land reform, government planning, U.S. aid and investment, and free universal education have brought huge advances in industry, agriculture, and living standards. In 1987 martial law was lifted after 38 years, and in 1991 the 43-year period of emergency rule ended. Taiwan held its first direct presidential election Mar. 23, 1996. The ruling Nationalist Party has faced increasing challenge from opposition parties.

Taiwan has one of the world's strongest economies and is among the 10 leading capital exporters.

The **Penghu Isls.** (Pescadores), 49 sq. mi., pop. (1996 est.) 90,142, lie between Taiwan and the mainland. **Quemoy** and **Matsu,** pop. (1996 est.) 53,286, lie just off the mainland.

Tajikistan

Republic of Tajikistan

People: Population: 6,020,095. **Age distrib.** (%): <15: 41.4; 65+: 4.6. **Pop. density:** 109 per sq. mi. **Urban:** 32%. **Ethnic groups:** Tajik 65%, Uzbek 25%. **Principal languages:** Tajik (official), Russian. **Chief religion:** Sunni Muslim 80%.

Geography: Area: 55,251 sq. mi. **Location:** Central Asia. **Neighbors:** Uzbekistan on N and W, Kyrgyzstan on N, China on E, Afghanistan on S. **Topography:** Mountainous region that contains the Pamirs, Trans-Alai mountain system. **Capital:** Dushanbe (1994 est.): 524,000.

Government: Type: Republic. **Head of state:** Pres. Imomali Rakhmonov; b Oct. 5, 1952; in office: Nov. 16, 1994. **Head of government:** Yakhyo Azimov; b Dec. 4, 1947; in office: Feb. 8, 1996. **Local divisions:** 2 viloyats, 1 autonomous viloyat. **Defense:** 11.0% of GDP. **Active troop strength:** 7,000.

Economy: Industries: Aluminum, cement, mining. **Chief crops:** Cotton, grains, fruits, vegetables. **Minerals:** Coal, lead, zinc. **Crude oil reserves** (1997): 12.0 mil bbls. **Arable land:** 6%. **Livestock** (1997): chickens: 1.20 mil; sheep: 1.50 mil; cattle: 870,000; goats: 596,000. **Electricity prod.** (1996): 13.6 bil kWh. **Labor force:** 52% agric. & forestry; 31% serv.; 17% manuf., mining, const.

Finance: Monetary unit: Ruble (Aug. 1997: 830 = $1 U.S.). **Gross domestic product** (1996 est.): $5.4 bil. **Per capita GDP:** $920. **Imports** (1996 est.): $657 mil; partners: Uzbekistan 34%, Russia 25%. **Exports** (1996 est.): $768 mil; partners: Russia 42%, Uzbekistan 21%.

Transport: Railroad: Length: 294.5 mi. **Motor vehicles in use:** 185,000 passenger cars, 3,600 comm. vehicles. **Civil aviation:** 1.13 bil passenger-mi; 1 airport.

Communications: Television sets: 259 per 1,000 pop. **Telephones:** 1 per 22 persons. **Daily newspaper circ.:** 14 per 1,000 pop.

Health: Life expectancy at birth: 61.4 male; 67.8 female. **Births** (per 1,000 pop.): 28. **Deaths** (per 1,000 pop.): 8. **Natural increase:** 1.99%. **Hospital beds** (1995): 1 per 115 persons. **Physicians** (1995): 1 per 443 persons. **Infant mortality** (per 1,000 live births): 112.

Education: Compulsory for 9 years between ages 7-17. **Literacy** (1995): 100%.

Major International Organizations: UN (FAO, IBRD, ILO, IMF, WHO), CIS, OSCE.

Website: http://www.undp.org/undp/rbec/nhdr/1996/tajikistan

There were settled societies in the region from about 3000 BC. Throughout history, it has undergone invasions by Iranians (Arabs who converted the population to Islam), Mongols, Uzbeks, Afghans, and Russians. The USSR gained control of the region 1918-25. In 1924, the Tajik ASSR was created within the Uzbek SSR. The Tajik SSR was proclaimed in 1929.

Tajikistan declared independence Sept. 9, 1991. It became an independent state when the Soviet Union disbanded Dec. 26, 1991. Conservative Communist Pres. Rakhmon Nabiyev was forced to resign, Sept. 1992, by a coalition of Islamic, nationalist, and Western-oriented parties.

Factional fighting led to the installation of a pro-Communist regime, Jan. 1993. A new constitution establishing a presidential system was approved by referendum Nov. 6, 1994. Clashes between Muslim rebels, reportedly armed by Afghanistan, and troops loyal to the government and supported by Russia, claimed at least 30,000 lives by mid-1997, despite a series of peace accords.

Tanzania

United Republic of Tanzania

People: Population: 30,608,769. **Age distrib.** (%): <15: 44.6; 65+: 2.9. **Pop. density:** 84 per sq. mi. **Urban:** 25%. **Ethnic groups:** African 99%. **Principal languages:** Swahili, English (both official), many others. **Chief religions:** Christian 45%, Muslim 35%, indigenous beliefs 20%.

Geography: Area: 364,899 sq. mi. **Location:** On coast of E Africa. **Neighbors:** Kenya, Uganda on N; Rwanda, Burundi, Congo (formerly Zaire) on W; Zambia, Malawi, Mozambique on S. **Topography:** Hot, arid central plateau, surrounded by the lake region in the W, temperate highlands in N and S, the coastal plains. Mt. Kilimanjaro, 19,340 ft., is highest in Africa. **Capital:** Dar-es-Salaam (capital is being moved to Dodoma). **Cities:** Dar-es-Salaam 1,747,000*.

Government: Type: Republic. **Head of state:** Pres. Benjamin William Mkapa; b Nov. 12, 1938; in office: Nov. 23, 1995. **Head of government:** Prime Min. Frederick Sumaye; in office: Nov. 28, 1995. **Local divisions:** 25 regions. **Defense:** 2.5% of GDP. **Active troop strength:** 34,600.

Economy: Industries: Agricultural processing, mining, textiles. **Chief crops:** Sisal, cotton, coffee, tea, tobacco, corn, spices. **Minerals:** Tin, phospates, diamonds, gold. **Other resources:** Pyrethrum (insecticide made from chrysanthemums). **Arable land:** 3%. **Livestock** (1997): chickens: 26.00 mil; cattle: 13.37 mil; goats: 9.68 mil; sheep: 3.96 mil; pigs: 335,000. **Fish catch** (1996): 356,617 metric tons. **Electricity prod.** (1996): 1.8 bil kWh. **Labor force:** 90% agric.; 10% ind. & comm.

Finance: Monetary unit: Shilling (Sept. 1998: 667.00 = $1 U.S.). **Gross domestic product** (1995 est.): $18.9 bil. **Per capita GDP:** $650. **Imports** (1995): $1.69 bil; partners: UK 10%, Kensa 9%. **Exports** (1995): $679 mil; partners: Germany 10%, Japan 9%. **Tourism:** $360 mil. **International reserves less gold** (May 1998): $567.8 mil. **Consumer prices** (change in 1997): 16.1%.

Transport: Railroad: Length: 2,216.3 mi. **Motor vehicles in use:** 55,000 passenger cars; 78,800 comm. vehicles. **Civil aviation:** 117.9 mil passenger-mi; 11 airports. **Chief ports:** Dar-es-Salaam, Mtwara, Tanga.

Communications: Television sets: 2.8 per 1,000 pop. **Radios:** 20 per 1,000 pop. **Telephones:** 1 per 328 persons.

Health: Life expectancy at birth: 44.2 male; 48.6 female. **Births** (per 1,000 pop.): 41. **Deaths** (per 1,000 pop.): 17. **Natural increase:** 2.40%. **Hospital beds** (1993): 1 per 2,000 persons. **Physicians** (1993): 1 per 20,511 persons. **Infant mortality** (per 1,000 live births): 97.

Education: Free and compulsory: ages 7-14. **Literacy** (1995): 68%.

Major International Organizations: UN and all of its specialized agencies, the Commonwealth, OAU.

Embassy: 2139 R St. NW 20008; 939-6125.

The Republic of Tanganyika in E Africa and the island Republic of Zanzibar, off the coast of Tanganyika, both of which had recently gained independence, joined into a single nation, the United Republic of Tanzania, Apr. 26, 1964. Zanzibar retains internal self-government.

Until resigning as president in 1985, Julius K. Nyerere, a former Tanganyikan independence leader, dominated Tanzania's politics, which emphasized government planning and control of the economy, with single-party rule. In 1992 the constitution was amended to establish a multiparty system. Privatization of the economy was undertaken in the 1990s.

At least 500 people died when an overcrowded Tanzanian ferry sank in Lake Victoria, May 21, 1996. About 460,000 Rwandan refugees, mostly Hutu, returned from Tanzania to Rwanda in Dec. 1996. A bomb at the U.S. embassy in Dar-es-Salaam, Aug. 7, 1998, killed 11 people and injured at least 70 others; the U.S. blamed the attack on Islamic terrorists associated with a wealthy Saudi businessman, Osama bin Laden.

Tanganyika. Arab colonization and slaving began in the 8th century AD; Portuguese sailors explored the coast by about 1500. Other Europeans followed.

In 1885 Germany established German East Africa of which Tanganyika formed the bulk. It became a League of Nations mandate and, after 1946, a UN trust territory, both under Britain. It became independent Dec. 9, 1961, and a republic within the Commonwealth a year later.

Zanzibar, the Isle of Cloves, lies 23 mi. off mainland Tanzania; area 640 sq. mi. and pop. (1995 est.) 456,934. The island of **Pemba,** 25 mi. to the NE, area 380 sq. mi. and pop. (1995 est.) 322,466, is included in the administration.

Chief industry is cloves and clove oil production, of which Zanzibar and Pemba produce most of the world's supply.

Zanzibar was for centuries the center for Arab slave traders. Portugal ruled the region for 2 centuries until ousted by Arabs around 1700. Zanzibar became a British Protectorate in 1890; independence came Dec. 10, 1963. Revolutionary forces overthrew the Sultan Jan. 12, 1964. The new government ousted Western diplomats and newsmen, slaughtered thousands of Arabs, and nationalized farms. Union with Tanganyika followed.

Thailand

Kingdom of Thailand

People: Population: 60,037,366. **Age distrib.** (%): <15: 24.3; 65+: 6.0. **Pop. density:** 303 per sq. mi. **Urban:** 20%. **Ethnic groups:** Thai 75%, Chinese 14%. **Principal languages:** Thai (official), English. **Chief religions:** Buddhist 95%, Muslim 4%.

Geography: Area: 198,455 sq. mi. **Location:** On Indochinese and Malayan peninsulas in SE Asia. **Neighbors:** Myanmar on W and N, Laos on N, Cambodia on E, Malaysia on S. **Topography:** A plateau dominates the NE third of Thailand, dropping to the fertile alluvial valley of the Chao Phraya R. in the center. Forested mountains are in the N, with narrow fertile valleys. The S peninsula region is covered by rain forests. **Capital:** Bangkok 6,547,000*.

Government: Type: Constitutional monarchy. **Head of state:** King Bhumibol Adulyadej; b Dec. 5, 1927; in office: June 9, 1946. **Head of government:** Prime Min. Chuan Leekpai; b July 28, 1938; in office: Nov. 9, 1997. **Local divisions:** 76 provinces. **Defense:** 2.5% of GDP. **Active troop strength:** 254,000.

Economy: Industries: Textiles, agric. processing, tourism. **Chief crops:** Rice (world's largest exporter), corn, cassava, sugarcane. **Minerals:** Tin, tungsten, diamonds, gas. **Crude oil reserves** (1997): 295 mil bbls. **Other resources:** Forests, rubber, seafood (world's largest exporter of farmed shrimp). **Arable land:** 34%. **Livestock** (1997): chickens: 135.00 mil; cattle: 7.50 mil; buffalo: 4.20 mil; pigs: 4.21 mil; goats: 120,000. **Fish catch** (1996): 3.14 mil metric tons. **Electricity prod.** (1996): 82.0 bil kWh. **Labor force:** 43% agric.; 38% ind. & comm.; 13% serv. & govt.

Finance: Monetary unit: Baht (Sept. 1998: 40.73 = $1 U.S.). **Gross domestic product** (1996 est.): $455.7 bil. **Per capita GDP:** $7,700. **Imports** (1996): $72.4 bil; partners: Japan 30%, U.S. 12%. **Exports** (1996): $57.3 bil; partners: U.S. 21%, Japan 17%. **Tourism:** $8.70 bil. **National budget** (FY 1994-95): $28.4 bil. **International reserves less gold** (May 1998): $26.66 bil. **Gold:** 2.47 mil oz t. **Consumer prices** (change in 1997): 5.6%.

Transport: Railroad: Length: 2,471 mi. **Motor vehicles in use:** 1.55 mil passenger cars, 4.15 mil comm. vehicles. **Civil aviation:** 18.51 bil passenger-mi; 25 airports. **Chief ports:** Bangkok, Sattahip.

Communication: Television sets: 56 per 1,000 pop. **Radios:** 167 per 1,000 pop. **Telephones:** 1 per 17 persons. **Daily newspaper circ.:** 47 per 1,000 pop.

Health: Life expectancy at birth: 65.4 male; 72.8 female. **Births** (per 1,000 pop.): 17. **Deaths** (per 1,000 pop.): 7. **Natural increase:** 0.97%. **Physicians** (1994): 1 per 4,165 persons. **Infant mortality** (per 1,000 live births): 31.

Education: Compulsory: ages 6-15. **Literacy** (1995): 94%.

Major International Organizations: UN (FAO, IBRD, ILO, IMF, IMO, WHO, WTrO), ASEAN, APEC.

Embassy: 1024 Wisconsin Ave. NW 20007; 944-3600.

Thais began migrating from southern China during the 11th century. A unified Thai kingdom was established in 1350

Thailand, known as Siam until 1939, is the only country in SE Asia never taken over by a European power, thanks to King Mongkut and his son King Chulalongkorn. Ruling successively from 1851 to 1910, they modernized the country and signed trade treaties with Britain and France. A bloodless revolution in 1932 limited the monarchy. Thailand was an ally of Japan during World War II and of the U.S. during the postwar period.

The military took over the government in a bloody 1976 coup. Kriangsak Chomanan, prime minister, resigned Feb. 1980 because of soaring inflation, oil price increases, labor unrest, and growing crime. Vietnamese troops crossed the border but were repulsed by Thai forces in the 1980s.

Chatichai Choonhavan was chosen prime minister in a democratic election, Aug. 1988. In Feb. 1991, the military ousted Choonhavan in a bloodless coup. A violent crackdown on street demonstrations in May 1992 led to more than 50 deaths. AIDS reached epidemic proportions in Thailand in the mid-1990s.

A steep downturn in the economy forced Thailand to seek more than $15 billion in emergency international loans in Aug. 1997. A new constitution won legislative approval Sept. 27. As Thailand's economic crisis deepened, Chuan Leekpai became prime minister Nov. 9, 1997 and began implementing financial reforms.

Togo

Republic of Togo

People: Population: 4,905,827. **Age distrib.** (%): <15: 48.3; 65+: 2.2. **Pop. density:** 224 per sq. mi. **Urban:** 31%. **Ethnic groups:** Ewe, Mina, Kabye, 34 other tribes. **Principal languages:** French (official), Ewe, Mina, Dagomba, Kabye. **Chief religions:** Indigenous beliefs 70%, Christian 20%, Muslim 10%.

Geography: Area: 21,927 sq. mi. **Location:** On S coast of W Africa. **Neighbors:** Ghana on W, Burkina Faso on N, Benin on E. **Topography:** A range of hills running SW-NE splits Togo into 2 savanna plains regions. **Capital:** Lomé (1990 met. est.): 513,000.

Government: Type: Republic. **Head of state:** Pres. Gnassingbé Eyadéma; b Dec. 26, 1937; in office: Apr. 14, 1967. **Head of government:** Prime Min. Kwassi Klutsé; b July 29, 1945; in office: Aug. 20, 1996. **Local divisions:** 5 regions. **Defense:** 2.5% of GDP. **Active troop strength:** 7,000.

Economy: Industries: Textiles, handicrafts, agric. processing. **Chief crops:** Coffee, cocoa, yams, cotton, millet, rice. **Minerals:** Phosphates, limestone, marble. **Arable land:** 38%. **Livestock** (1997): chickens: 6.45 mil; goats: 1.70 mil; sheep: 1.38 mil; pigs: 850,000; cattle: 264,000. **Electricity prod.** (1996): 88 mil kWh. **Labor force:** 68% agric., 21% services, 12% mining, manuf., const.

Finance: Monetary unit: CFA Franc (Sept. 1998: 580.94 = $1 U.S.). **Gross domestic product** (1996 est.): $4.45 bil. **Per capita GDP:** $970. **Imports** (1996 est.): $350 mil; partners: Ghana 17%, China 13%, France 13%. **Exports** (1996): $265 mil; partners: Canada 9%, U.S. 8%. **Tourism:** $13 mil. **National budget** (1997 est.): $262 mil. **International reserves less gold** (Mar. 1998): $104.4 mil. **Gold:** 13,000 oz t. **Consumer prices** (change in 1997): 4.7%.

Transport: Railroad: Length: 245 mi. **Motor vehicles in use:** 74,662 passenger cars, 34,605 comm. vehicles. **Civil aviation:** 139.6 mil passenger-mi; 2 airports. **Chief port:** Lomé.

Communications: Television sets: 36 per 1,000 pop. **Radios:** 212 per 1,000 pop. **Telephones:** 1 per 191 persons.

Health: Life expectancy at birth: 56.5 male; 61.1 female. **Births** (per 1,000 pop.): 45. **Deaths** (per 1,000 pop.): 10. **Natural increase:** 3.52%. **Infant mortality** (per 1,000 live births): 80.

Education: Compulsory: ages 6-12. **Literacy** (1995): 52%.

Major International Organizations: UN (FAO, IBRD, ILO, IMF, IMO, WHO, WTrO), OAU.

Embassy: 2208 Massachusetts Ave. NW 20008; 234-4212.

The Ewe arrived in southern Togo several centuries ago. The country later became a major source of slaves. Germany took control in 1884. France and Britain administered Togoland as UN trusteeships. The French sector became the republic of Togo Apr. 27, 1960.

The population is divided between Bantus in the S and Hamitic tribes in the N. Togo has actively promoted regional integration, as a means of stimulating the economy.

In Jan. 1993 police fired on antigovernment demonstrators, killing at least 22. Some 25,000 people fled to Ghana and Benin as a result of civil unrest. In Jan. 1994 at least 40 people were killed when gunmen reportedly attacked an army base. Further violence marred Togo's 1st multiparty legislative elections, held Feb. 1994. In office since 1967, Pres. Gnassingbé Eyadéma was reelected June 21, 1998, in a vote that was disputed as in previous elections.

Tonga

Kingdom of Tonga

Pule'anga Fakatu'i 'o Tonga

People: Population: 108,207. **Pop. density:** 374 per sq. mi. **Urban:** 42%. **Ethnic groups:** Polynesian. **Principal languages:** Tongan, English (both official). **Chief religions:** Free Wesleyan 44%, Roman Catholic 16%.

Geography: Area: 289 sq. mi. **Location:** In western South Pacific O. **Neighbors:** Nearest are Fiji to W, Samoa to NE. **Topography:** Tonga comprises 170 volcanic and coral islands, 36 inhabited. **Capital:** Nuku'alofa (1990 est.): 34,000.

Government: Type: Constitutional monarchy. **Head of state:** King Taufa'ahau Tupou IV; b July 4, 1918; in office: Dec. 16, 1965. **Head of Government:** Prime Min. Baron Vaea; b 1921; in office: Aug. 22, 1991. **Local divisions:** 5 divisions, 23 districts.

Economy: Industries: Tourism, fishing. **Chief crops:** Coconuts, copra, bananas, vanilla beans. **Arable land:** 24%. **Livestock** (1997): chickens: 270,000. **Electricity prod.** (1996): 30 mil kWh. **Labor force:** 70% agric.

Finance: Monetary unit: Pa'anga (Sept. 1998: 1.59 = $1 U.S.). **Gross domestic product** (FY1995-96 est.): $228 mil. **Per capita GDP:** $2,140. **Imports** (1995): $80.3 mil; partners: N.Z. 38%, Australia 28%. **Exports** (1995): $15.25 mil; partners: Japan 59%. **Tourism:** $14 mil. **International reserves less gold** (May 1998): $18.25 mil. **Consumer prices** (change in 1997): 2.1%.

Transport: Motor vehicles in use: 3,400 passenger cars, 3,900 comm. vehicles. **Civil aviation:** 7.1 mil passenger-mi; 6 airports. **Chief port:** Nuku'alofa.

Communications: Television sets: 20 per 1,000 pop. **Radios:** 397 per 1,000 pop. **Telephones:** 1 per 15 persons.

Health: Life expectancy at birth: 67.5 male; 72.0 female. **Births** (per 1,000 pop.): 26. **Deaths** (per 1,000 pop.): 6. **Natural increase:** 2.04%. **Hospital beds** (1992): 1 per 320 persons. **Physicians** (1993): 1 per 2,201 persons. **Infant mortality** (per 1,000 live births): 39.

Education: Free and compulsory: ages 5-14. **Literacy** (1992): 93%.

Major International Organizations: FAO, IBRD, IMF, WHO, WTrO, the Commonwealth.

The islands were first visited by the Dutch in the early 17th century. A series of civil wars ended in 1845 with establishment of the Tupou dynasty. In 1900 Tonga became a British protectorate. On June 4, 1970, Tonga became independent and a member of the Commonwealth.

Trinidad and Tobago

Republic of Trinidad and Tobago

People: Population: 1,116,595. **Age distrib.** (%): <15: 28.0; 65+: 7.3. **Pop. density:** 564 per sq. mi. **Urban:** 72%. **Ethnic groups:** Black 43%, East Indian 40%, mixed 14%. **Principal languages:** English (official), Hindi, French, Spanish. **Chief religions:** Roman Catholic 32%, Protestant 28%, Hindu 24%.

Geography: Area: 1,981 sq. mi. **Location:** In Caribbean, off E coast of Venezuela. **Neighbors:** Nearest is Venezuela to SW. **Topography:** Three low mountain ranges cross Trinidad E-W, with a well-watered plain between N and central ranges. Parts of E and W coasts are swamps. Tobago, 116 sq. mi., lies 20 mi. NE. **Capital:** Port-of-Spain (1995 est.): 52,000.

Government: Type: Parliamentary democracy. **Head of state:** Pres. Arthur N. R. Robinson; b Dec. 16, 1926; in office: Mar. 19, 1997. **Head of government:** Prime Min. Basdeo Panday; b May 25, 1933; in office: Nov. 9, 1995. **Local divisions:** 7 counties, 4 municipalities, and Tobago. **Defense:** 1.1% of GDP. **Active troop strength:** 2,100.

Economy: Industries: Oil products, chemicals, tourism. **Chief crops:** Sugar, cocoa, coffee, citrus, rice. **Minerals:** Asphalt, oil, gas. **Crude oil reserves** (1997): 551 mil bbls. **Arable land:** 15%. **Livestock** (1997): chickens: 11.50 mil. **Electricity prod.** (1996): 4.0 bil kWh. **Labor force:** 62% services; 11% agric.

Finance: Monetary unit: Dollar (Sept. 1998: 6.24 = $1 U.S.). **Gross domestic product** (1996 est.): $17.1 bil. **Per capita GDP:** $13,500. **Imports** (1996): $1.8 bil; partners: U.S. 48%. **Exports** (1996): $2.3 bil; partners: U.S. 48%. **Tourism:** $108 mil. **National budget** (1996 est.): $1.61 bil. **International reserves less gold** (June 1998): $702.6 mil. **Gold:** 58,000 oz t. **Consumer prices** (change in 1997): 3.4%.

Transport: Motor vehicles in use: 128,000 passenger cars, 27,000 comm. vehicles. **Civil aviation:** 1.65 bil passenger-mi; 2 airports. **Chief ports:** Port-of-Spain, Scarborough.

Communications: Television sets: 198 per 1,000 pop. **Radios:** 433 per 1,000 pop. **Telephones:** 1 per 6.2 persons. **Daily newspaper circ.:** 139 per 1,000 pop.

Health: Life expectancy at birth: 68.1 male; 73.0 female. **Births** (per 1,000 pop.): 15. **Deaths** (per 1,000 pop.): 8. **Natural increase:** 0.69%. **Hospital beds** (1992): 1 per 340 persons. **Physicians** (1993): 1 per 1,191 persons. **Infant mortality** (per 1,000 live births): 19.

Education: Free and compulsory: ages 5-12. **Literacy** (1995): 98%.

Major International Organizations: UN (FAO, IBRD, ILO, IMF, IMO, WHO, WTrO), Caricom, the Commonwealth, OAS.

Embassy: 1708 Massachusetts Ave. NW 20036; 467-6490.

Columbus sighted Trinidad in 1498. A British possession since 1802, Trinidad and Tobago won independence Aug. 31, 1962. It became a republic in 1976.

The nation is one of the most prosperous in the Caribbean. Oil production has increased with offshore finds. Middle Eastern oil is refined and exported, mostly to the U.S.

In July 1990, some 120 Muslim extremists captured the Parliament building and TV station and took about 50 hostages, including Prime Min. Arthur N. R. Robinson, who was beaten, shot in the legs, and tied to explosives. After a 6-day siege, the rebels surrendered.

Basdeo Panday, the country's first prime minister of East Indian ancestry, took office Nov. 9, 1995. Robinson became president on Mar. 19, 1997.

Tunisia

Republic of Tunisia

People: Population: 9,380,404. **Age distrib.** (%) <15: 31.6; 65+: 5.8. **Pop. density:** 149 per sq. mi. **Urban:** 63%. **Ethnic groups:** Arab-Berber 98%. **Principal languages:** Arabic (official), French. **Chief religion:** Muslim 98%.

Geography: Area: 63,170 sq. mi. **Location:** On N coast of Africa. **Neighbors:** Algeria on W, Libya on E. **Topography:** The N is wooded and fertile. The central coastal plains are given to grazing and orchards. The S is arid, approaching Sahara Desert. **Capital:** Tunis: 1,722,000*.

Government: Type: Republic. **Head of state:** Pres. Gen. Zine al-Abidine Ben Ali; b Sept 3, 1936; in office: Nov. 7, 1987. **Head of government:** Prime Min. Hamed Karoui; b Dec. 30, 1927; in office: Sept. 27, 1989. **Local divisions:** 23 governorates. **Defense:** 2.0% of GDP. **Active troop strength:** 35,000.

Economy: Industries: Food processing, textiles, oil products, mining, tourism. **Chief crops:** Grains, dates, olives, sugar beets, grapes. **Minerals:** Phosphates, iron, oil, lead, zinc. **Crude oil reserves** (1997): 308 mil bbls. **Arable land:** 19%. **Livestock** (1997): chickens: 35.57 mil; sheep: 6.29 mil; goats: 1.26 mil; cattle: 701,390. **Fish catch** (1996): 83,567 metric tons. **Electricity prod.** (1996): 7.5 bil kWh. **Labor force:** 55% services; 23% industry; 22% agric.

Finance: Monetary unit: Dinar (Sept. 1998: 1.13 = $1 U.S.). **Gross domestic product** (1996 est.): $43.3 bil. **Per capita GDP:** $4,800. **Imports** (1996 est.): $7.7 bil; partners: EU 70%. **Exports** (1996 est.): $5.7 bil; partners: EU 75%. **Tourism:** $1.54 bil. **National budget** (1996 est.): $7.2 bil. **International reserves less gold** (Jan. 1998): $1.57 bil. **Gold:** 217,000 oz t. **Consumer prices** (change in 1997): 3.7%.

Transport: Railroad: Length: 1,337 mi. **Motor vehicles in use:** 248,000 passenger cars, 283,000 comm. vehicles. **Civil aviation:** 1.32 bil passenger-mi; 5 airports. **Chief ports:** Tunis, Sfax, Bizerte.

Communications: Television sets: 156 per 1,000 pop. **Radios:** 188 per 1,000 pop. **Telephones:** 1 per 17 persons. **Daily newspaper circ.:** 45 per 1,000 pop.

Health: Life expectancy at birth: 71.7 male; 74.6 female. **Births** (per 1,000 pop.): 20. **Deaths** (per 1,000 pop.): 5. **Natural increase:** 1.50%. **Hospital beds** (1994): 1 per 556 persons. **Physicians** (1994): 1 per 1,640 persons. **Infant mortality** (per 1,000 live births): 33.

Education: Compulsory: ages 6-16. **Literacy** (1995): 67%.

Major International Organizations: UN (FAO, IBRD, ILO, IMF, IMO, WHO, WTrO), AL, OAU.

Embassy: 1515 Massachusetts Ave. NW 20005; 862-1850.

Website: http://www.tunisiaonline.com

Site of ancient Carthage and a former Barbary state under the suzerainty of Turkey, Tunisia became a protectorate of France under a treaty signed May 12, 1881. The nation became independent Mar. 20, 1956, and ended the monarchy the following year. Habib Bourguiba, an independence leader, served as president until 1987, when he was deposed by his prime minister, Zine al-Abidine Ben Ali.

Tunisia has actively repressed Islamic fundamentalism.

Turkey

Republic of Turkey

People: Population: 64,566,511. **Age distrib.** (%): <15: 30.9; 65+: 5.7. **Pop. density:** 214 per sq. mi. **Urban:** 71%. **Ethnic groups:** Turk 80%, Kurd 20%. **Principal languages:** Turkish (official), Kurdish, Arabic. **Chief religion:** Muslim 100%.

Geography: Area: 301,382 sq. mi. **Location:** Occupies Asia Minor, stretches into continental Europe; borders on Mediterranean and Black seas. **Neighbors:** Bulgaria, Greece on W; Georgia, Armenia on N; Iran on E; Iraq, Syria on S. **Topography:** Central Turkey has wide plateaus, with hot, dry summers and cold winters. High mountains ring the interior on all but W, with more than 20 peaks over 10,000 ft. Rolling plains are in W; mild, fertile coastal plains are in S, W. **Capital:** Ankara. **Cities:** Istanbul 7,911,000; Ankara 2,846,000; Izmir 2,052,000*.

Government: Type: Republic. **Head of state:** Pres. Suleyman Demirel; b 1924; in office: May 16, 1993. **Head of government:** Prime Min. Mesut Yilmaz; b 1947; in office: July 12, 1997. **Local divisions:** 79 provinces. **Defense:** 3.9% of GDP. **Active troop strength:** 525,000.

Economy: Industries: Textiles, steel, mining, processed foods. **Chief crops:** Tobacco, grains, cotton, pulses, citrus, olives, sugar beets. **Minerals:** Antimony, chromium, mercury, copper, coal. **Crude oil reserves** (1997): 331 mil bbls. **Other resources:** Wool, forests. **Arable land:** 32%. **Livestock** (1997): chickens: 152.96 mil; sheep: 33.07 mil; cattle: 11.79 mil; goats: 8.95 mil; buffalo: 255,000. **Fish catch** (1996): 521,655 metric tons. **Electricity prod.** (1996): 91.2 bil kWh. **Labor force:** 47% agric.; 33% serv.; 20% ind.

Finance: Monetary unit: Lira (Sept. 1998: 277,882.50 = $1 U.S.). **Gross domestic product** (1996 est.): $379.1 bil. **Per capita GDP:** $6,100. **Imports** (1996 est.): $42 bil; partners: Germany 16%, U.S. 10%. **Exports** (1996 est.): $22 bil; partners: Germany 23%. **Tourism:** $7.00 bil. **National budget** (1996): $50.8 bil. **International reserves less gold** (June 1998): $26.46 bil. **Gold:** 3.75 mil oz t. **Consumer prices** (change in 1997): 85.7%.

Transport: Railroad: Length: 5,252 mi. **Motor vehicles in use:** 3.27 mil passenger cars, 1.05 mil comm. vehicles. **Civil aviation:** 6.80 bil passenger-mi; 26 airports. **Chief ports:** Istanbul, Izmir, Mersin.

Communications: Television sets: 171 per 1,000 pop. **Radios:** 141 per 1,000 pop. **Telephones:** 1 per 4.7 persons. **Daily newspaper circ:** 44 per 1,000 pop.

Health: Life expectancy at birth: 70.4 male; 75.4 female. **Births** (per 1,000 pop.): 21. **Deaths** (per 1,000 pop.): 5. **Natural increase:** 1.60%. **Hospital beds** (1994): 1 per 450 persons. **Physicians** (1995): 1 per 1,200 persons. **Infant mortality** (per 1,000 live births): 38.

Education: Free and compulsory: ages 6-14. **Literacy** (1995): 82%.

Major International Organizations: UN (FAO, IBRD, ILO, IMF, IMO, WHO, WTrO), NATO, OECD, OSCE.

Embassy: 1714 Massachusetts Ave. NW 20036; 659-8200.

Website: http://www.turkey.org

Ancient inhabitants of Turkey were among the world's first agriculturalists. Such civilizations as the Hittite, Phrygian, and Lydian flourished in Asiatic Turkey (Asia Minor), as did much of Greek civilization. After the fall of Rome in the 5th century, Constantinople (now Istanbul) was the capital of the Byzantine Empire for 1,000 years. It fell in 1453 to Ottoman Turks, who ruled a vast empire for over 400 years.

Just before World War I, Turkey, or the Ottoman Empire, ruled what is now Syria, Lebanon, Iraq, Jordan, Israel, Saudi Arabia, Yemen, and islands in the Aegean Sea.

Turkey joined Germany and Austria in World War I, and its defeat resulted in the loss of much territory and the fall of the sultanate. A republic was declared Oct. 29, 1923, with Mustafa Kemal (later Kemal Ataturk) as its first president. Ataturk led Turkey until his death in 1938. The Caliphate (spiritual leadership of Islam) was renounced in 1924.

Long embroiled with Greece over Cyprus, off Turkey's south coast, Turkey invaded the island July 20, 1974, after Greek officers seized the Cypriot government as a step toward unification with Greece. Turkey sought a new government for Cyprus, with Greek Cypriot and Turkish Cypriot zones. In reaction to Turkey's moves, the U.S. cut off military aid in 1975. Turkey, in turn, suspended the use of most U.S. bases. Aid was restored in 1978. There was a military takeover, Sept. 12, 1980.

Religious and ethnic tensions and active left and right extremists have caused endemic violence. Martial law, imposed in 1978, was lifted in 1984. The military formally transferred power to an elected Parliament in 1983.

Turkey was a member of the Allied forces that ousted Iraq from Kuwait, 1991. In the aftermath of the war, millions of Kurdish refugees fled to Turkey's border to escape Iraqi forces. The Turkish government mounted sporadic offensives against separatist Kurds in this border area and in N Iraq, causing heavy casualties among guerrillas and civilians.

Kurdish militants, demanding an independent state for the Kurds, raided Turkish diplomatic missions in some 25 Western European cities June 24, 1993. Tansu Ciller officially became Turkey's first woman prime minister July 5, 1993. The Welfare Party, an Islamic group, gained strength in the 1990s but was unable to form a government until June 1996, when it came to power in coalition with Ciller's True Path Party.

The pro-Islamic government resigned June 18, 1997, under pressure from the military. The European Union rebuffed Turkey's membership bid Dec. 12, 1997. The military stepped up its campaign against Islamic fundamentalism in 1998.

Turkmenistan

Republic of Turkmenistan

People: Population: 4,297,629. **Age distrib.** (%): <15: 38.6; 65+: 4.2. **Pop. density:** 23 per sq. mi. **Urban:** 45%. **Ethnic groups:** Turkmen 77%, Uzbek 9%, Russian 7%. **Principal languages:** Turkmen (official), Russian, Uzbek. **Chief religions:** Muslim 89%, Eastern Orthodox 9%.

Geography: Area: 188,455 sq. mi. **Neighbors:** Kazakhstan on N, Uzbekistan on N and E, Afghanistan and Iran on S. **Topography:** The Kara Kum Desert occupies 80% of the area. Bordered on W by Caspian Sea. **Capital:** Ashgabat (1995 est.): 536,000.

Government: Type: Republic. **Head of state:** Pres. Saparmurad Niyazov; b Feb. 18, 1940; in office: Oct. 27, 1990. **Local divisions:** 5 regions. **Defense:** 2.8% of GDP. **Active troop strength:** 18,000.

Economy: Industries: Oil, natural gas, food processing, textiles. **Chief crops:** Grain, cotton. **Minerals:** Coal, sulfur, oils, salt. **Crude oil reserves** (1997): 546 mil bbls. **Arable land:** 3%. **Livestock** (1997): chickens: 3.00 mil; sheep: 5.40 mil; cattle: 959,000; goats: 375,000. **Electricity prod.** (1996): 9.5 bil kWh. **Labor force:** 43% agric. & forestry; 20% ind. & constr.

Finance: Monetary unit: Manat (Aug. 1998: 5,250.00 = $1 U.S.). **Gross domestic product** (1996 est.): $11.8 bil. **Per capita GDP:** $2,840. **Imports** (1996 est): $1.3 bil, excl. former Soviet Union. **Exports** (1996 est.): $1.8 bil, excl. former Soviet Union. **Tourism:** $7 mil.

Transport: Railroad: Length: 1,316.5 mi. **Civil aviation:** 678.8 mil passenger-mi; 1 airport. **Chief port:** Turkmenbashi.

Communications: Television sets: 189 per 1,000 pop. **Radios:** 189 per 1,000 pop. **Telephones:** 1 per 14 persons.

Health: Life expectancy at birth: 57.7 male; 65.1 female. **Births** (per 1,000 pop.): 26. **Deaths** (per 1,000 pop.): 9. **Natural increase:** 1.75%. **Hospital beds** (1995): 1 per 97 persons. **Physicians** (1995): 1 per 330 persons. **Infant mortality** (per 1,000 live births): 73.

Education: Literacy (1995): 100%.

Major International Organizations: UN (FAO, IBRD, ILO, IMF, IMO, WHO), CIS, OSCE.

Embassy: 2207 Massachusetts Ave., NW 20008; 588-1500.

Website: http://www.undp.org/undp/rbec/nhdr/1996/turkmenistan

The region has been inhabited by Turkic tribes since the 10th century. It became part of Russian Turkestan in 1881, and a constituent republic of the USSR in 1925. Turkmenistan declared independence Oct. 27, 1991, and became an independent state when the USSR disbanded Dec. 26, 1991.

Extensive oil and gas reserves place Turkmenistan in a more favorable economic position than other former Soviet republics. A new rail line linking Iran and Turkmenistan was inaugurated May 13, 1996. Political power centered around the former Communist Party apparatus, and Pres. Saparmurad Niyazov became the object of a personality cult.

Tuvalu

People: Population: 10,444. **Age distrib.** (%): <15: 35.2; 65+: 4.7. **Pop. density:** 1,044 per sq. mi. **Urban:** 48%. **Ethnic group:** Polynesian 96%. **Principal languages:** Tuvaluan, English. **Chief religion:** Church of Tuvalu (Congregationalist) 97%.

Geography: Area: 10 sq. mi. **Location:** 9 islands forming a NW-SE chain 360 mi. long in the SW Pacific O. **Neighbors:** Nearest are Kiribati to N, Fiji to S. **Topography:** The islands are all low-lying atolls, nowhere rising more than 15 ft. above sea level, composed of coral reefs. **Capital:** Funafuti Atoll (1995 est.): 4,000.

Government: Head of state: Queen Elizabeth II, represented by Gov.-Gen. Tulaga Manuella; in office: June 1994. **Head of government:** Prime Min. Bikenibeu Paeniu; in office: Dec. 23, 1996.

Economy: Industries: Copra fishing, tourism. **Chief crops:** Coconuts.

Finance: Monetary unit: Australian Dollar (Sept. 1998: 1.73 = $1 US). **Gross domestic product** (1995 est.): $7.8 mil. **Per capita GDP:** $800.

Communications: Radio: 320 per 1,000 pop.

Transport: Civil aviation: 1 airport. **Chief port:** Funafuti.

Health: Life expectancy at birth: 62.7 male; 65.1 female. **Births** (per 1,000 pop.): 23. **Deaths** (per 1,000 pop.): 9. **Natural increase:** 1.40%. **Physicians** (1993): 1 per 1,152 persons. **Infant mortality** (per 1,000 live births): 26.

Education: Compulsory: ages 7-15. **Literacy** (1990): 95%.

Major International Organizations: WHO, the Commonwealth.

Website: http://www.emulateme.com/tuvalu.htm

The Ellice Islands separated from the British Gilbert and Ellice Islands Colony in 1975 and became Tuvalu; independence came Oct. 1, 1978.

Uganda

Republic of Uganda

People: Population: 22,167,195. **Age distrib.** (%): <15: 51.1; 65+: 2.2. **Pop. density:** 238 per sq. mi. **Urban:** 13%. **Ethnic groups:** Baganda 17%, Karamojong 12%, many others. **Principal languages:** English (official), Luganda, Swahili. **Chief religions:** Protestant 33%, Roman Catholic 33%, indigenous beliefs 18%, Muslim 16%.

Geography: Area: 93,070 sq. mi. **Location:** In E Central Africa. **Neighbors:** Sudan on N, Congo (formerly Zaire) on W, Rwanda and Tanzania on S, Kenya on E. **Topography:** Most of Uganda is a high plateau 3,000-6,000 ft. high, with high Ruwenzori range in W (Mt. Margherita 16,750 ft.), volcanoes in SW; NE is arid, W and SW rainy. Lakes Victoria, Edward, Albert form much of borders. **Capital:** Kampala: 954,000*.

Government: Type: Republic. **Head of state:** Pres. Yoweri Kaguta Museveni; b Mar. 1944; in office: Jan. 29, 1986. **Head of government:** Prime Min. Kintu Musoke; b May 8, 1938; in office: Nov. 18, 1994. **Local divisions:** 39 districts. **Defense:** 2.4% of budget. **Active troop strength:** 50,000.

Economy: Industries: Brewing, textiles, cement. **Chief crops:** Coffee, cotton, tea, corn, tobacco. **Minerals:** Copper, cobalt. **Arable land:** 25%. **Livestock** (1997): chickens: 22.42 mil; cattle: 5.36 mil; goats: 3.59 mil; sheep: 1.95 mil; pigs: 940,000. **Fish catch** (1996): 195,088 metric tons. **Electricity prod.** (1996): 787 mil kWh. **Labor force:** 86% agric.

Finance: Monetary unit: Shilling (Sept. 1998: 1,233.50 = $1 U.S.). **Gross domestic product** (1995 est.): $16.8 bil. **Per capita GDP:** $900. **Imports** (FY1994-95): $1.18 bil; partners: Kenya 26%, UK 12%. **Exports** (FY1994-95): $555 mil; partners: Spain 23%, France 14%, Germany 14%. **Tourism:** $103 mil. **National budget** (1994-95 est.): $1.07 bil. **International reserves less gold** (Mar. 1998): $688.8 mil. **Consumer prices** (change in 1997): 7.0%.

Transport: Railroad: Length: 770.7 mi. **Motor vehicles in use:** 24,400 passenger cars, 26,600 comm. vehicles. **Civil aviation:** 68.3 mil passenger-mi; 1 airport. **Chief ports:** Entebbe, Jinja.

Communications: Television sets: 27 per 1,000 pop. **Radios:** 485 per 1,000 pop. **Telephones:** 1 per 440 persons.

Health: Life expectancy at birth: 41.8 male; 43.4 female. **Births** (per 1,000 pop.): 49. **Deaths** (per 1,000 pop.): 19. **Natural increase:** 3.03%. **Infant mortality** (per 1,000 live births): 93.

Education: Literacy (1995): 62%.

Major International Organizations: UN (FAO, IBRD, ILO, IMF, WHO, WTrO), the Commonwealth, OAU.

Embassy: 5911 16th St. NW 20011; 726-7100.

Website: http://www.nic.ug

Britain obtained a protectorate over Uganda in 1894. The country became independent Oct. 9, 1962, and a republic within the Commonwealth a year later. In 1967, the traditional kingdoms, including the powerful Buganda state, were abolished and the central government strengthened.

Gen. Idi Amin seized power from Prime Min. Milton Obote in 1971. During his eight years of dictatorial rule, he was responsible for the deaths of up to 300,000 of his opponents. In 1972 he expelled nearly all of Uganda's 45,000 Asians. Amin was named president for life in 1976. Tanzanian troops and Ugandan exiles and rebels ousted Amin, Apr. 11, 1979.

Obote held the presidency from Dec. 1980 until his ouster in a military coup July 27, 1985. Guerrilla war and rampant human rights abuses plagued Uganda under Obote's regime.

Conditions improved after Yoweri Museveni took power in Jan. 1986. In 1993 the government authorized restoration of the Buganda and other monarchies, but only for ceremonial purposes. Under a new constitution ratified Oct. 1995, nonparty presidential and legislative elections were held in 1996.

Ukraine

People: Population: 50,125,108. **Age distrib.** (%): <15: 19.0; 65+: 14.0. **Pop. density:** 215 per sq. mi. **Urban:** 71%. **Ethnic groups:** Ukrainian 73%, Russian 22%. **Principal languages:** Ukrainian (official), Russian. **Chief religions:** Mostly Ukrainian Orthodox, some Ukrainian Catholic.

Geography: Area: 233,089 sq. mi. **Location:** In E Europe. **Neighbors:** Belarus on N; Russia on NE and E; Moldova and Romania on SW; Hungary, Slovakia, and Poland on W. **Topography:** Part of the E European plain. Mountainous areas include the Carpathians in the SW and Crimean chain in the S. Arable black soil constitutes a large part of the country. **Capital:** Kiev. **Cities:** Kiev (Kyiv) 2,812,000; Kharkov 1,681,000; Dnipropetrovsk 1,231,000*.

Government: Type: Constitutional republic. **Head of state:** Pres. Leonid Danylovich Kuchma; b Aug. 9, 1938; in office: July 19, 1994. **Head of government:** Prime Min. Valery Pustovoitenko; b Feb. 23, 1947; in office: July 16, 1997. **Local divisions:** 24 oblasts, 2 municipalities, 1 autonomous republic. **Defense:** 3.0% of GDP. **Active troop strength:** 400,800.

Economy: Industries: Chemicals, machinery, food processing. **Chief crops:** Grains, sugar beets, vegetables. **Minerals:** Iron, manganese, coal, gas, oil, sulfur, nickel, salt. **Other resources:** Forests. **Crude oil reserves** (1997): 395 mil bbls. **Arable land:** 58%. **Livestock** (1997): chickens: 105.00 mil; cattle: 15.31 mil; pigs: 11.24 mil; sheep: 2.19 mil; goats: 854,000. **Fish catch** (1996): 417,118 metric tons. **Electricity prod.** (1996): 200.5 bil kWh. **Labor force:** 33% ind. & constr.; 21% agric. & forestry.

Finance: Monetary unit: Hryvnya (Sept. 1998: 2.95 = $1 U.S.). **Gross domestic product** (1996 est.): $161.1 bil. **Per capita GDP:** $3,170. **Imports** (1996 est.): $19.4 bil; partners: Russia 43%. **Exports** (1996 est.): $18.6 bil; partners: Russia 40%. **Tourism:** $205 mil. **International reserves less gold** (May 1998): $2.04 bil. **Gold:** 71,900 oz t. **Consumer prices** (change in 1997): 15.9%.

Transport: Railroad: Length: 14,100 mi. **Motor vehicles in use:** 4.5 mil passenger cars. **Civil aviation:** 1.11 bil passenger-mi; 12 airports. **Chief ports:** Odesa, Kiev, Berdiansk.

Communications: Television sets: 233 per 1,000 pop. **Radios:** 346 per 1,000 pop. **Telephones:** 1 per 6.2 persons. **Daily newspaper circ.:** 118 per 1,000 pop.

Health: Life expectancy at birth: 60.1 male; 71.9 female. **Births** (per 1,000 pop.): 10. **Deaths** (per 1,000 pop.): 16. **Natural increase:** –0.68%. **Hospital beds** (1995): 1 per 81 persons. **Physicians** (1995): 1 per 224 persons. **Infant mortality** (per 1,000 live births): 22.

Education: Compulsory: ages 7-15. **Literacy** (1995): 99%.

Major International Organizations: UN (IBRD, ILO, IMF, IMO, WHO), CIS, OSCE.

Embassy: 3350 M St. NW 20007; 333-0606.

Website: http://www.rada.kiev.ua

Trypilians flourished along the Dnieper River, Ukraine's main artery, from 6000-1000 BC. Ukrainians' Slavic ancestors inhabited modern Ukrainian territory well before the first century AD.

In the 9th century, the princes of Kiev established a strong state called Kievan Rus, which included much of present-day Ukraine. A strong dynasty was established, with ties to virtually all major European royal families. St. Vladimir the Great, ruler of Kievan Rus, accepted Christianity as the national faith in 988. At the crossroads of European trade routes, Kievan Rus reached its zenith under Yaroslav the Wise (1019-1054). Internal conflicts led to the disintegration of the Ukrainian state by the 13th century. Mongol rule was supplanted by Poland and Lithuania in the 14th and 15th centuries. The N Black Sea coast and Crimea came under the control of the Turks in 1478.

Ukrainian Cossacks, starting in the late 16th century, waged numerous wars of liberation against the occupiers of Ukraine: Russia, Poland, and Turkey. By the late 18th century, Ukrainian independence was lost. Ukraine's neighbors once again divided its territory. At the turn of the 19th century, Ukraine was occupied by Russia and Austria-Hungary.

An independent Ukrainian National Republic was proclaimed on January 22, 1918. In 1921, Ukraine's neighbors occupied and divided Ukrainian territory. In 1922, Ukraine became a constituent republic of the USSR as the Ukrainian SSR. In 1932-33, the Soviet government engineered a man-made famine in eastern Ukraine, resulting in the deaths of 7-10 million Ukrainians.

In March 1939, independent Carpatho-Ukraine was the first European state to wage war against Nazi-led aggression in the region. During World War II the Ukrainian nationalist underground and its Ukrainian Insurgent Army (UPA) fought both Nazi German and Soviet forces. The restoration of Ukrainian independence was declared on June 30, 1941. Over 5 million Ukrainians lost their lives during the war. With the reoccupation of Ukraine by Soviet troops in 1944 came a renewed wave of mass arrests, executions, and deportations of Ukrainians.

The world's worst nuclear power plant disaster occurred in Chernobyl, Ukraine, in April 1986.

Ukrainian independence was restored in Dec. 1991 with the dissolution of the Soviet Union. In the post-Soviet period Ukraine was burdened with a deteriorating economy.

Following a 1994 accord with Russia and the U.S., Ukraine's large nuclear arsenal was transferred to Russia for destruction. A new constitution legalizing private property and establishing Ukrainian as the sole official language was approved by parliament June 29, 1996. In May 1997, Russia and Ukraine resolved disputes over the Black Sea fleet and the future of Sevastopol and signed a long-delayed treaty of friendship.

United Arab Emirates

People: Population: 2,303,088. **Age distrib.** (%): <15: 31.7; 65+: 1.9. **Pop. density:** 72 per sq. mi. **Urban:** 84%. **Ethnic groups:** Arab, Iranian, Pakistani, Indian. **Principal languages:** Arabic (official), Persian, English, Hindi, Urdu. **Chief religions:** Muslim 96%, Christian, Hindu.

Geography: Area: 32,000 sq. mi. **Location:** Middle East, on the S shore of the Persian Gulf. **Neighbors:** Saudi Arabia on W and S, Oman on E. **Topography:** A barren, flat coastal plain gives way to uninhabited sand dunes on the S. Hajar Mts. are on E. **Capital:** Abu Dhabi: 799,000*.

Government: Type: Federation of emirates. **Head of state:** Pres. Zaid ibn Sultan an-Nahayan; b. 1923; in office: Dec. 2, 1971. **Head of government:** Prime Min. Sheik Maktum ibn Rashid al-Maktum; in office: Nov. 20, 1990. **Local divisions:** 7 autonomous emirates: Abu Dhabi, Ajman, Dubai, Fujaira, Ras al-Khaimah, Sharjah, Umm al-Qaiwain. **Defense:** 5.2% of GDP. **Active troop strength:** 64,500.

Economy: Chief crops: Vegetables, dates. **Minerals:** Oil, natural gas. **Crude oil reserves** (1997): 98 bil bbls. **Livestock** (1997): chickens: 10.70 mil; goats: 990,000; sheep: 385,000. **Electricity prod.** (1996): 18 bil kWh. **Labor force:** 56% ind. and commerce; 38% serv; 6% agric.

Finance: Monetary unit: Dirham (Sept. 1998: 3.67 = $1 U.S.). **Gross domestic product** (1996 est.): $72.9 bil. **Per capita GDP:** $23,800. **Imports** (1996 est.): $22.3 bil; partners: Japan 9%, UK 8%, U.S. 8%. **Exports** (1996 est.): $31.3 bil; partners: Japan 38%. **National budget** (1997 est.): $5.4 bil. **International reserves less gold** (May 1998): $8.69 bil. **Gold:** 795,000 oz t.

Transport: Motor vehicles in use: 320,000 passenger cars, 80,000 comm. vehicles. **Civil aviation:** 7.05 bil passenger-mi; 6 airports. **Chief ports:** Dubai, Abu Dhabi.

Communications: Television sets: 18 per 1,000 pop. **Radios:** 206 per 1,000 pop. **Telephones:** 1 per 3.5 persons. **Daily newspaper circ.:** 135 per 1,000 pop.

Health: Life expectancy at birth: 73.5 male; 76.4 female. **Births** (per 1,000 pop.): 19. **Deaths** (per 1,000 pop.): 3. **Natural increase:** 1.56%. **Hospital beds** (1994): 1 per 360 persons. **Physicians** (1994): 1 per 545 persons. **Infant mortality** (per 1,000 live births): 15.

Education: Compulsory: ages 6-12. **Literacy** (1995): 79%.

Major International Organizations: UN (FAO, IBRD, ILO, IMF, IMO, WHO, WTrO), AL, OPEC.

Embassy: 3000 K St. NW, Suite 600, 20007; 338-6500.

The 7 "Trucial Sheikdoms" gave Britain control of defense and foreign relations in the 19th century. They merged to become an independent state Dec. 2, 1971.

The Abu Dhabi Petroleum Co. was fully nationalized in 1975. Oil revenues have given the UAE one of the highest per capita GDPs in the world. International banking has grown in recent years.

United Kingdom

United Kingdom of Great Britain and Northern Ireland

People: Population: 58,970,119. **Age distrib.** (%): <15: 19.3; 65+: 15.7. **Pop. density:** 624 per sq. mi. **Urban:** 89%. **Ethnic groups:** English 81.5%, Scottish 9.6%, Irish 2.4%, Welsh 1.9%, Ulster 1.8%; West Indian, Indian, Pakistani, others 2.8%. **Principal languages:** English, Welsh, Scottish, Gaelic. **Chief religions:** Anglican, Roman Catholic, other Christian, Muslim.

Geography: Area: 94,525 sq. mi. **Location:** Off the NW coast of Europe, across English Channel, Strait of Dover, and North Sea. **Neighbors:** Ireland to W, France to SE. **Topography:** England is mostly rolling land, rising to Uplands of southern Scotland; Lowlands are in center of Scotland, granite Highlands are in N. Coast is heavily indented, especially on W. British Isles have milder climate than N Europe due to the Gulf Stream and ample rainfall. Severn, 220 mi., and Thames, 215 mi., are longest rivers. **Capital:** London. **Cities:** London 7,640,000; Birmingham 2,271,000; Manchester 2,252,000; Leeds 1,433,000; Liverpool 877,000*.

Government: Type: Constitutional monarchy. **Head of state:** Queen Elizabeth II; b Apr. 21, 1926; in office: Feb. 6, 1952. **Head of government:** Prime Min. Tony Blair; b May 6, 1953; in office: May 2, 1997. **Local divisions:** England: Greater London, 9 other metropolitian areas, 35 county councils, 2 unitary councils; Wales: 22 unitary councils; Scotland: 29 unitary councils; Northern Ireland: 26 districts. **Defense:** 3.0% of GDP. **Active troop strength:** 226,000.

Economy: Industries: Steel, metals, vehicles, shipbuilding, banking, textiles, chemicals, electronics, aircraft, machinery, distilling. **Chief crops:** Cereals, oilseeds, potatoes, vegetables. **Minerals:** Coal, tin, oil, gas, limestone, iron, salt, clay. **Crude oil reserves** (1997): 5.0 bil bbls. **Arable land:** 25%. **Livestock** (1997): chickens: 130.94 mil; sheep: 42.56 mil; cattle: 11.61 mil; pigs: 7.99 mil. **Fish catch** (1996): 867,773 metric tons. **Electricity prod.** (1996): 309.7 bil kWh. **Labor force:** 63% services; 25% manuf. & constr.; 9% govt.

Finance: Monetary unit: Pound (Sept. 1998: 1.68 = $1 U.S.). **Gross domestic product** (1996 est.): $1.15 tril. **Per capita GDP:** $20,400. **Imports** (1995): $258.8 bil; partners: EU 55%, U.S. 12%. **Exports** (1995): $240.4 bil; partners: EU 56%, U.S. 13%. **Tourism:** $20.57 bil. **National budget** (FY 1995-96 est.): $474.9 bil. **International reserves less gold** (Mar. 1998): $30.14 bil. **Gold:** 18.42 mil oz t. **Consumer prices** (change in 1997): 3.1%.

Transport: Railroad: Length: 10,905.4 mi. **Motor vehicles in use:** 24.86 mil passenger cars, 3.62 mil comm. vehicles. **Civil aviation:** 104.07 bil passenger-mi; 57 airports. **Chief ports:** London, Liverpool, Southampton, Cardiff, Belfast.

Communications: Television sets: 612 per 1,000 pop. **Radios:** 1,194 per 1,000 pop. **Daily newspaper circ.:** 383 per 1,000 pop.

Health: Life expectancy at birth: 74.6 male; 80.0 female. **Births:** (per 1,000 pop.): 12. **Deaths:** (per 1,000 pop.): 11. **Natural increase:** 0.13%. **Hospital beds** (1993): 1 per 205 persons. **Physicians** (1993): 1 per 629 persons. **Infant mortality** (per 1,000 live births): 6.

Education: Compulsory: ages 5-16. **Literacy** (1993): 100%.

Major International Organizations: UN and all of its specialized agencies, the Commonwealth, EU, NATO, OECD, OSCE.

Embassy: 3100 Massachusetts Ave. NW 20008; 588-6500.

Website: http://www.ons.gov.uk/ons.htm

The United Kingdom of Great Britain and Northern Ireland comprises England, Wales, Scotland, and Northern Ireland.

Queen and Royal Family. The ruling sovereign is Elizabeth II of the House of Windsor, b Apr. 21, 1926, elder daughter of King George VI. She succeeded to the throne Feb. 6, 1952, and was crowned June 2, 1953. She was married Nov. 20, 1947, to Lt. Philip Mountbatten, b June 10, 1921, former Prince of Greece. He was created Duke of Edinburgh, and given the title H.R.H., Nov. 19, 1947; he was named Prince of the United Kingdom and Northern Ireland Feb. 22, 1957. Prince Charles Philip Arthur George, b Nov. 14, 1948, is the Prince of Wales and heir apparent. His 2d son, William Philip Arthur Louis, b June 21, 1982, is second in line to the throne.

Parliament is the legislative body for the UK, with certain powers over dependent units. It consists of 2 houses: The **House of Lords** (1997) includes 762 hereditary and 409 life peers and peeresses, 26 Lords of Appeal, 2 archbishops and 24 bishops of the Church of England. Total membership is 1,223. The **House of Commons** has 659 members, elected by direct ballot and divided as follows: England 529; Wales 40; Scotland 72; Northern Ireland 18.

Resources and Industries. Great Britain's major occupations are manufacturing and trade. Metals and metal-using industries contribute more than 50% of exports. Of about 60 million acres of land in England, Wales, and Scotland, 46 million are farmed, of which 17 million are arable, the rest pastures.

Large oil and gas fields have been found in the North Sea. Commercial oil production began in 1975. There are large deposits of coal.

Britain imports all of its cotton, rubber, sulphur, about 80% of its wool, half of its food and iron ore, also certain amounts of paper, tobacco, chemicals. Manufactured goods made from these basic materials have been exported since the industrial age began. Main exports are machinery, chemicals, woolen and synthetic textiles, clothing, autos and trucks, iron and steel, locomotives, ships, jet aircraft, farm machinery, drugs, radio, TV, radar and navigation equipment, scientific instruments, arms, whisky.

Religion and Education. The Church of England is Protestant Episcopal. The queen is its temporal head, with rights of appointments to archbishoprics, bishoprics, and other offices. There are 2 provinces, Canterbury and York, each headed by an archbishop. The most famous church is Westminster Abbey (1050-1760), site of coronations, tombs of Elizabeth I, Mary, Queen of Scots, kings, poets, and of the Unknown Warrior.

The most celebrated British universities are Oxford and Cambridge, each dating to the 13th century. There are about 70 other universities.

History. Britain was part of the continent of Europe until about 6,000 BC, but migration across the English Channel continued long afterward. Celts arrived 2,500 to 3,000 years ago. Their language survives in Welsh, and Gaelic enclaves.

England was added to the Roman Empire in AD 43. After the withdrawal of Roman legions in 410, waves of Jutes, Angles, and Saxons arrived from German lands. They contended with Danish raiders for control from the 8th through 11th centuries. The last successful invasion was by French speaking Normans in 1066, who united the country with their dominions in France.

Opposition by nobles to royal authority forced King John to sign the Magna Carta in 1215, a guarantee of rights and the rule of law. In the ensuing decades, the foundations of the parliamentary system were laid.

English dynastic claims to large parts of France led to the Hundred Years War, 1338-1453, and the defeat of England. A long civil war, the War of the Roses, lasted 1455-85, and ended with the establishment of the powerful Tudor monarchy. A distinct English civilization flourished. The economy prospered over long periods of domestic peace unmatched in continental Europe. Religious independence was secured when the Church of England was separated from the authority of the pope in 1534.

Under Queen Elizabeth I, England became a major naval power, leading to the founding of colonies in the new world and the expansion of trade with Europe and the Orient. Scotland was united with England when James VI of Scotland was crowned James I of England in 1603.

A struggle between Parliament and the Stuart kings led to a bloody civil war, 1642-49, and the establishment of a republic under the Puritan Oliver Cromwell. The monarchy was restored in 1660, but the "Glorious Revolution" of 1688 confirmed the sovereignty of Parliament: a Bill of Rights was granted 1689.

In the 18th century, parliamentary rule was strengthened. Technological and entrepreneurial innovations led to the Industrial Revolution. The 13 North American colonies were lost, but replaced by growing empires in Canada and India. Britain's role in the defeat of Napoleon, 1815, strengthened its position as the leading world power.

The extension of the franchise in 1832 and 1867, the formation of trade unions, and the development of universal public education were among the drastic social changes that accompanied the spread of industrialization and urbanization in the 19th century. Large parts of Africa and Asia were added to the empire during the reign of Queen Victoria, 1837-1901.

Though victorious in World War I, Britain suffered huge casualties and economic dislocation. Ireland became independent in 1921, and independence movements became active in India and other colonies. The country suffered major bombing damage in World War II, but held out against Germany singlehandedly for a year after France fell in 1940.

Industrial growth continued in the postwar period, but Britain lost its leadership position to other powers. Labor governments passed socialist programs nationalizing some basic industries and expanding social security. Prime Min. Margaret Thatcher's Conservative government, however, tried to increase the role of private enterprise. In 1987, Thatcher became the first British leader in 160 years to be elected to a 3d consecutive term as prime minister. Falling on unpopular times, she resigned as prime minister in Nov. 1990. Her successor, John Major, led Conservatives to an upset victory at the polls, Apr. 9, 1992.

The UK supported the UN resolutions against Iraq and sent military forces to the Persian Gulf War.

The Channel Tunnel linking Britain to the Continent was officially inaugurated May 6, 1994. Britain's relations with the European Union were frayed in 1996 when the EU banned British beef because of the threat of "mad cow" disease.

On May 1, 1997, the Labour Party swept into power in a landslide victory, the largest of any party since 1935. Labour Party leader Tony Blair, 43, became Britain's youngest prime minister since 1812. Diana, Princess of Wales, the divorced wife of Prince Charles and the mother of Prince William, died in a car crash in Paris, Aug. 31, and received an elaborate funeral in London, Sept. 6.

Wales

The Principality of Wales in western Britain has an area of 8,019 sq. mi. and a population (1992 est.) of 2,899,000. Cardiff is the capital, pop. (1994 est.) 299,000.

Less than 20% of Wales residents speak English and Welsh; about 32,000 speak Welsh solely. A 1979 referendum rejected, 4-1, the creation of an elected Welsh assembly; a similar proposal passed by a thin margin on Sept. 18, 1997.

Early Anglo-Saxon invaders drove Celtic peoples into the mountains of Wales, terming them Waelise (Welsh, or foreign). There they developed a distinct nationality. Members of the ruling house of Gwynedd in the 13th century fought England but were crushed, 1283. Edward of Caernarvon, son of Edward I of England, was created Prince of Wales, 1301.

Scotland

Scotland, a kingdom now united with England and Wales in Great Britain, occupies the northern 37% of the main British island, and the Hebrides, Orkney, Shetland, and smaller islands. Length 275 mi., breadth approx. 150 mi., area 30,418 sq. mi., population (1992 est.) 5,111,000.

The Lowlands, a belt of land approximately 60 mi. wide from the Firth of Clyde to the Firth of Forth, divide the farming region of the Southern Uplands from the granite Highlands of the North; they contain 75% of the population and most of the industry. The Highlands, famous for hunting and fishing, have been opened to industry by many hydroelectric power stations.

Edinburgh, pop. (1994 est.) 442,000, is the capital. Glasgow, pop. (1994 est.) 681,000, is Britain's greatest industrial center. It is a shipbuilding complex on the Clyde and an ocean port. Aberdeen, pop. (1994 est.) 218,000, NE of Edinburgh, is a major port, center of granite industry, fish-processing, and North Sea oil exploration. Dundee, pop. (1993 est.) 170,000, NE of Edinburgh, is an industrial and fish-processing center. About 90,000 persons speak Gaelic as well as English.

History. Scotland was called Caledonia by the Romans who battled early Celtic tribes and occupied southern areas from the 1st to the 4th centuries. Missionaries from Britain introduced Christianity in the 4th century; St. Columba, an Irish monk, converted most of Scotland in the 6th century.

The Kingdom of Scotland was founded in 1018. William Wallace and Robert Bruce both defeated English armies 1297 and 1314, respectively.

In 1603 James VI of Scotland, son of Mary, Queen of Scots, succeeded to the throne of England as James I, and effected the Union of the Crowns. In 1707 Scotland received representation in the British Parliament, resulting from the union of former separate Parliaments. Its executive in the British cabinet is the Secretary of State for Scotland. The growing Scottish National Party urges independence. A 1979 referendum on the creation of an elected Scottish assembly was defeated, but a proposal to create a regional legislature with limited taxing authority passed by an overwhelming margin, Sept. 11, 1997.

Memorials of Robert Burns, Sir Walter Scott, John Knox, and Mary, Queen of Scots, draw many tourists, as do the beauties of the Trossachs, Loch Katrine, Loch Lomond, and abbey ruins.

Industries. Engineering products are the most important industry, with growing emphasis on office machinery, autos, electronics, and other consumer goods. Oil has been discovered offshore in the North Sea, stimulating on-shore support industries.

Scotland produces fine woolens, worsteds, tweeds, silks, fine linens, and jute. It is known for its special breeds of cattle and sheep. Fisheries have large hauls of herring, cod, whiting. Whisky is the biggest export.

The Hebrides are a group of c. 500 islands, 100 inhabited, off the W coast. The Inner Hebrides include **Skye, Mull,** and **Iona,** the last famous for the arrival of St. Columba, AD 563. The Outer Hebrides include **Lewis** and **Harris.** Industries include sheep raising and weaving. The **Orkney Islands,** c. 90, are to the NE. The capital is Kirkwall, on Pomona Isl. Fish curing, sheep raising, and weaving are occupations. NE of the Orkneys are the 200 **Shetland Islands,** 24 inhabited, home of Shetland pony. The Orkneys and Shetlands are centers for the North Sea oil industry.

Northern Ireland

Northern Ireland was constituted in 1920 from 6 of the 9 counties of Ulster, the NE corner of Ireland. Area 5,452 sq. mi., pop. (1996 est.) 1,663,300, capital and chief industrial center, Belfast, pop. (1995 est.) 296,700.

Industries. Shipbuilding, including large tankers, has long been an important industry, centered in Belfast, the largest port. Linen manufacture is also important, along with apparel, rope, and twine. Growing diversification has added engineering products, synthetic fibers, and electronics. There are large numbers of cattle, hogs, and sheep. Potatoes, poultry, and dairy foods are also produced.

Government. An act of the British Parliament, 1920, divided Northern from Southern Ireland, each with a parliament and government. When Ireland became a dominion, 1921, and later a republic, Northern Ireland chose to remain a part of the United Kingdom. It elects 18 members to the British House of Commons.

During 1968-69, large demonstrations were conducted by Roman Catholics who charged they were discriminated against in voting rights, housing, and employment. The Catholics, a minority comprising about a third of the population, demanded abolition of property qualifications for voting in local elections. Violence and terrorism intensified, involving branches of the Irish Republican Army (outlawed in the Irish Republic), Protestant groups, police, and British troops.

A succession of Northern Ireland prime ministers pressed reform programs but failed to satisfy extremists on both sides. Between 1969 and 1994 more than 3,000 were killed in sectarian violence, many in England itself. Britain suspended the Northern Ireland parliament Mar. 30, 1972, and imposed direct British rule. A coalition government was formed in 1973 when moderates won election to a new one-house Assembly. But a Protestant general strike overthrew the government in 1974 and direct rule was resumed.

The agony of Northern Ireland was dramatized in 1981 by the deaths of 10 Irish nationalist hunger strikers in Maze Prison near Belfast. In 1985 the Hillsborough agreement gave the Rep. of Ireland a voice in the governing of Northern Ireland; the accord was strongly opposed by Ulster loyalists. On Dec. 12, 1993, Britain and Ireland announced a declaration of principles to resolve the Northern Ireland conflict.

On Aug. 31, 1994, the IRA announced a cease-fire, saying it would rely on political means to achieve its objectives; the IRA resumed its terrorist tactics on Feb. 9, 1996. Reinstatement of the IRA cease-fire as of July 20, 1997, led to the resumption of peace talks Sept. 15.

A settlement reached on Good Friday, April 10, 1998, provided for restoration of home rule and election of a 108-member assembly with safeguards for minority rights. Both Ireland and Great Britain agreed to give up their constitutional claims on Northern Ireland. The accord was approved May 22 by voters in Northern Ireland and the Irish Republic, and elections to the assembly were held June 25. IRA dissidents seeking to derail the agreement were responsible for a bomb at Omagh Aug. 15 that killed 29 people and injured over 330.

Education and Religion. Northern Ireland is about 58% Protestant, 42% Roman Catholic. Education is compulsory between the ages of 5 and 16 years.

Channel Islands

The Channel Islands, area 75 sq. mi., pop. (1997 est.) 152,241, off the NW coast of France, the only parts of the one-time Dukedom of Normandy belonging to England, are Jersey, Guernsey and the dependencies of Guernsey — Alderney, Brechou, Great Sark, Little Sark, Herm, Jethou and Lihou. Jersey and Guernsey have separate legal existences and lieutenant governors named by the Crown. The islands were the only British soil occupied by German troops in World War II.

Isle of Man

The Isle of Man, area 227 sq. mi., pop. (1997 est.) 74,504, is in the Irish Sea, 20 mi. from Scotland, 30 mi. from Cumberland. It is rich in lead and iron. The island has its own laws and a lieutenant governor appointed by the Crown. The Tynwald (legislature) consists of the Legislative Council, partly elected, and House of Keys, elected. Capital: Douglas. Farming, tourism, and fishing (kippers, scallops) are chief occupations. Man is famous for the Manx tailless cat.

Gibraltar

Gibraltar, a dependency on the southern coast of Spain, guards the entrance to the Mediterranean. The Rock has been in British possession since 1704. The Rock is 2.75 mi. long, 3/4 of a mi. wide and 1,396 ft. in height; a narrow isthmus connects it with the mainland. Pop. (1998 est.) 29,045.

Gibraltar has historically been an object of contention between Britain and Spain. Residents voted with near unanimity to remain under British rule, in a 1967 referendum held in pursuance of a UN resolution on decolonization. A new constitution, May 30, 1969, increased Gibraltarian control of domestic affairs (the UK continues to handle defense and internal security matters). Following a 1984 agreement between Britain and Spain, the border, closed by Spain in 1969, was fully reopened in Feb. 1985. A UN General Assembly resolution requested Britain to end Gibraltar's colonial status by Oct. 1, 1996. No settlement has been reached.

British West Indies

Swinging in a vast arc from the coast of Venezuela NE, then N and NW toward Puerto Rico are the Leeward Islands, forming a coral and volcanic barrier sheltering the Caribbean from the open Atlantic. Many of the islands are self-governing British possessions. Universal suffrage was instituted 1951-54; ministerial systems were set up 1956-1960.

The **Leeward Islands** still associated with the UK are **Montserrat**, area 32 sq. mi., pop. (1998 est.) 12,828, capital Plymouth; the **British Virgin Islands,** 59 sq. mi., pop. (1997 est.) 13,368, capital Road Town; and **Anguilla**, the most northerly of the Leeward Islands, 60 sq. mi., pop. (1998 est.) 11,147, capital The Valley. Montserrat has been devastated by the Soufrière Hills volcano, which began erupting July 18, 1995.

The three **Cayman Islands,** a dependency, lie S of Cuba, NW of Jamaica. Pop. (1998 est.) 37,716, most of it on Grand Cayman. It is a free port; in the 1970s Grand Cayman became a tax-free refuge for foreign funds and branches of many Western banks were opened there. Total area 102 sq. mi., capital Georgetown.

The **Turks and Caicos Islands** are a dependency at the SE end of the Bahama Islands. Of about 30 islands, only 6 are inhabited; area 193 sq. mi., pop. (1998 est.) 16,249; capital Grand Turk. Salt, shellfish, and conch shells are the main exports.

Bermuda

Bermuda is a British dependency governed by a royal governor and an assembly, dating from 1620, the oldest legislative body among British dependencies. Capital is Hamilton.

It is a group of about 150 small islands of coral formation, 20 inhabited, comprising 20.6 sq. mi. in the western Atlantic, 580 mi. E of North Carolina. Pop. (1998 est.) 62,009 (about 61% of African descent). Pop. density is high.

The U.S. maintains a NASA tracking facility; a U.S. naval air base was closed in 1995.

Tourism is the major industry; Bermuda boasts many resort hotels. The government raises most revenue from import duties. Exports: petroleum products, medicine. In a referendum Aug. 15, 1995, voters rejected independence by nearly a 3-to-1 majority.

South Atlantic

The **Falkland Islands,** a dependency, lie 300 mi. E of the Strait of Magellan at the southern end of South America.

The Falklands or Islas Malvinas include 2 large islands and about 200 smaller ones, area 4,700 sq. mi., pop. (1995 est.) 2,317, capital Stanley. The licensing of foreign fishing vessels has become the major source of revenue. Sheep-grazing is a main industry; wool is the principal export. There are indications of large oil and gas deposits. The islands are also claimed by Argentina, though 97% of inhabitants are of British origin. Argentina invaded the islands Apr. 2, 1982. The British responded by sending a task force to the area, landing their main force on the Falklands, May 21, and forcing an Argentine surrender at Port Stanley, June 14.

British Antarctic Territory, south of 60° S lat., formerly a dependency of the Falkland Isls., was made a separate colony in 1962 and includes the **South Shetland Islands,** the **South Orkneys**, and the Antarctic Peninsula. A chain of meteorological stations is maintained.

South Georgia and the South Sandwich Islands, formerly administered by the Falklands Isls., became a separate dependency in 1985. South Georgia, 1,450 sq. mi., with no permanent population, is about 800 mi. SE of the Falklands; the South Sandwich Isls., 130 sq. mi., are uninhabited, about 470 mi. SE of South Georgia.

St. Helena, an island 1,200 mi. off the W coast of Africa and 1,800 mi. E of South America, 47 sq. mi. and pop. (1997 est.) 6,803. Flax, lace, and rope-making are the chief industries. After Napoleon Bonaparte was defeated at Waterloo the Allies exiled him to St. Helena, where he lived from Oct. 16, 1815, to his death, May 5, 1821. Capital is Jamestown.

Tristan da Cunha is the principal of a group of islands of volcanic origin, total area 40 sq. mi., halfway between the Cape of Good Hope and South America. A volcanic peak 6,760 ft. high erupted in 1961. The 262 inhabitants were removed to England, but most returned in 1963. The islands are dependencies of St. Helena. Pop. (1993) 300.

Ascension is an island of volcanic origin, 34 sq. mi. in area, 700 mi. NW of St. Helena, through which it is administered. It is a communications relay center for Britain, and has a U.S. satellite tracking center. Pop. (1993) was 1,117, half of them communications workers. The island is noted for sea turtles.

Hong Kong (*See* China)

British Indian Ocean Territory

Formed Nov. 1965, embracing islands formerly dependencies of Mauritius or Seychelles: the Chagos Archipelago (including Diego Garcia), Aldabra, Farquhar, and Des Roches. The latter 3 were transferred to Seychelles, which became independent in 1976. Area 23 sq. mi. No permanent civilian population remains; the U.K. and the U.S. maintain a military presence.

Pacific Ocean

Pitcairn Island is in the Pacific, halfway between South America and Australia. The island was discovered in 1767 by Philip Carteret but was not inhabited until 23 years later when the mutineers of the *Bounty* landed there. The area is 1.7 sq. mi. and 1995 pop. was 54. It is a British dependency and is administered by a British High Commissioner in New Zealand and a local Council. The uninhabited islands of **Henderson, Ducie,** and **Oeno** are in the Pitcairn group.

United States

United States of America

People: Population: 270,311,758 (incl. 50 states & Dist. of Columbia). (**Note:** U.S. pop. figures may differ elsewhere in *The World Almanac.*) **Age distrib.** (%): <15: 21.6; 65+: 12.7. **Pop. density:** 74 per sq. mi. **Urban:** 76%.

Geography: Area: 3,675,031 sq. mi. (incl. 50 states and DC). **Topography:** Vast central plain, mountains in west, hills and low mountains in east. **Capital:** Washington, D.C.

Government: Federal republic, strong democratic tradition. **Head of state:** Pres. Bill Clinton; b Aug. 19, 1946; in office: Jan. 20, 1993. **Local divisions:** 50 states and Dist. of Columbia. **Defense:** 3.6% of GDP. **Active troop strength:** 1.484 mil.

Economy: Minerals: Coal, copper, lead, molybdenum, phosphates, uranium, bauxite, gold, iron, mercury, nickel, potash, silver, tungsten, zinc. **Crude oil reserves** (1997)**:** 22.0 bil bbls. **Other resources:** forests. **Arable land:** 19%. **Livestock** (1997): chickens: 1.55 bil; cattle: 101.46 mil; pigs: 56.17 mil; sheep: 7.94 mil; goats: 1.40 mil. **Fish catch** (1996): 5 mil metric tons. **Electricity prod.** (1996): 3.4 tril kWh.

Finance: Gross domestic product (1997): $8.11 tril. **Per capita GDP:** $28,600. **Imports** (1995): $771 bil; partners: Canada 20%, Western Europe 18%, Japan 17%. **Exports** (1995): $584.7 bil; partners: Canada 22%, Western Europe 21%, Japan 11%. **Tourism:** $75.06 bil. **International reserves less gold** (June 1998): $60.11 bil. **Gold:** 261.68 mil oz t. **Consumer prices** (change in 1997): 2.3%.

Transport: Railroad: Length: 149,040.0 mi. **Motor vehicles in use:** 129.73 mil passenger cars, 76.64 mil comm. vehicles. **Civil aviation:** 571.21 bil passenger-mi; 834 airports.

Communications: Television sets: 776 per 1,000 pop. **Radios:** 2,122 per 1,000 pop. **Daily newspaper circ.:** 238 per 1,000 pop.

Health: Life expectancy at birth: 72.9 male; 79.6 female. **Births** (per 1,000 pop.): 14. **Deaths** (per 1,000 pop.): 9. **Natural increase:** 0.56%. **Hospital beds** (1995): 1 per 243 persons. **Physicians** (1995): 1 per 365 persons. **Infant mortality** (per 1,000 live births): 6.

Education: Free and compulsory: ages 7-16. **Literacy** (1994): 97%.

Major International Organizations: UN (FAO, IBRD, ILO, IMF, IMO, WHO, WTrO), APEC, NATO, OAS, OECD, OSCE.

Websites: http://www.census.gov
http://www.whitehouse.gov

Uruguay

Oriental Republic of Uruguay

People: Population: 3,284,841. **Age distrib.** (%): <15: 24.1; 65+: 12.9. **Pop. density:** 48 per sq. mi. **Urban:** 91%. **Ethnic groups:** White 88%, mestizo 8%, black 4%. **Principal language:** Spanish (official). **Chief religion:** Roman Catholic 66%.

Geography: Area: 68,039 sq. mi. **Location:** In southern South America, on the Atlantic O. **Neighbors:** Argentina on W, Brazil on N. **Topography:** Uruguay is composed of rolling, grassy plains and hills, well watered by rivers flowing W to Uruguay R. **Capital:** Montevideo: 1,325,000*.

Government: Type: Republic. **Head of state:** Pres. Julio María Sanguinetti Cairolo; b Jan. 6, 1936; in office: Mar. 1, 1995. **Local divisions:** 19 departments. **Defense:** 2.3% of GDP. **Active troop strength:** 25,600.

Economy: Industries: Meat packing, wool and hides, textiles, wine, oil refining. **Chief crops:** Corn, wheat, sorghum, rice. **Arable land:** 8%. **Livestock** (1997): chickens: 11.50 mil; sheep: 19.77 mil; cattle: 10.81 mil; pigs: 270,000. **Fish catch** (1996): 123,361 metric tons. **Electricity prod.** (1996): 8.4 bil kWh.

Labor force 33% serv.; 25% govt.; 19% manuf.; 12% comm.; 11% agric.

Finance: Monetary unit: Peso (Sept. 1998: 10.74 = $1 U.S.). **Gross domestic product** (1996 est.): $26 bil. **Per capita GDP:** $8,000. **Imports** (1996): $3.3 bil; partners: Brazil 22%, Argentina 21%. **Exports** (1996): $24 bil; partners: Brazil 35%, Argentina 11%. **Tourism:** $759 mil. **National budget** (1994 est.): $3.37 bil. **International reserves less gold** (Apr. 1998): $1.86 bil. **Gold:** 1.77 mil oz t. **Consumer prices** (change in 1997): 19.8%

Transport: Railroad: Length: 1,285.5 mi. **Motor vehicles in use:** 475,000 passenger cars, 50,000 comm. vehicles. **Civil aviation:** 397.4 mil passenger-mi; 1 airport. **Chief port:** Montevideo.

Communications: Television sets: 191 per 1,000 pop. **Radios:** 586 per 1,000 pop. **Telephones:** 1 per 5.1 persons. **Daily newspaper circ.:** 241 per 1,000 pop.

Health: Life expectancy at birth: 72.4 male; 78.8 female. **Births** (per 1,000 pop.): 17. **Deaths** (per 1,000 pop.): 9. **Natural increase:** 0.80%. **Physicians** (1994): 1 per 282 persons. **Infant mortality** (per 1,000 live births): 14.

Education: Free and compulsory for 6 years between ages 6-14. **Literacy** (1995): 97%.

Major International Organizations: UN (FAO, IBRD, ILO, IMF, IMO, WHO, WTrO), OAS.

Embassy: 2715 M St. NW 20007; 331-1313.

Website: http://www.embassy.org/uruguay

Spanish settlers began to supplant the indigenous Charrua Indians in 1624. Portuguese from Brazil arrived later, but Uruguay was attached to the Spanish Viceroyalty of Rio de la Plata in the 18th century. Rebels fought against Spain beginning in 1810. An independent republic was declared Aug. 25, 1825.

Terrorist activities led Pres. Juan María Bordaberry to agree to military control of his administration Feb. 1973. In June he abolished Congress and set up a Council of State in its place. Bordaberry was removed by the military in a 1976 coup. Civilian government was restored in 1985.

Socialist measures were adopted in the early 1900s, and the state retains a dominant role in the power, telephone, railroad, cement, oil-refining, and other industries. Uruguay's standard of living remains one of the highest in South America, and political and labor conditions among the freest.

Uzbekistan

Republic of Uzbekistan

People: Population: 23,784,321. **Age distrib.** (%): <15: 38.0; 65+: 4.7. **Pop. density:** 138 per sq. mi. **Urban:** 41%. **Ethnic groups:** Uzbek 80%, Russian 6%, Tajik 5%. **Principal languages:** Uzbek (official), Russian. **Chief religions:** Muslim (mostly Sunni) 88%, Eastern Orthodox 9%.

Geography: Area: 172,741 sq. mi. **Location:** Central Asia. **Neighbors:** Kazakhstan on N and W, Kyrgyzstan and Tajikistan on E, Afghanistan and Turkmenistan on S. **Topography:** Mostly plains and desert. **Capital:** Tashkent 2,282,000*.

Government: Type: Republic. **Head of state:** Pres. Islam A. Karimov; b Jan. 30, 1938; in office: Mar. 24, 1990. **Head of government:** Prime Min. Utkir Sultanov; b July 14, 1939; in office: Dec. 21, 1995. **Local divisions:** 12 regions, 1 autonomous republic, 1 city. **Defense:** 3.8% of GDP. **Active troop strength:** 30,000.

Economy: Industries: Machinery, food processing, natural gas, textiles. **Chief crops:** Vegetables, cotton, fruits, grain. **Minerals:** Gas, oil, coal, gold, copper. **Crude oil reserves** (1997): 594 mil bbls. **Arable land:** 9%. **Livestock** (1997): chickens: 13.00 mil; sheep: 8.00 mil; cattle: 5.00 mil; goats: 900,000; pigs: 200,000. **Electricity prod.** (1996): 43.0 bil kWh. **Labor force:** 44% agric. & forestry; 20% ind. & constr.

Finance: Monetary unit: Som (Aug. 1998: 102.30 = $1 U.S.). **Gross domestic product** (1996 est.): $57 bil. **Per capita GDP:** $2,430. **Imports** (1996): $3.2 bil; partners: Russia 25%, Korea 12%. **Exports** (1996): $3.2 bil; partners: Russia 22%, Italy 9%.

Transport: Railroad: Length: 2,100 mi. **Motor vehicles in use:** 865,000 passenger cars, 14,500 comm. vehicles. **Civil aviation:** 2.15 bil passenger-mi; 9 airports. **Chief port:** Termiz.

Communications: Television sets: 176 per 1,000 pop. **Telephones:** 1 per 13 persons.

Health: Life expectancy at birth: 60.5 male; 67.9 female. **Births** (per 1,000 pop.): 24. **Deaths** (per 1,000 pop.): 8. **Natural increase:** 1.60%. **Hospital beds** (1995): 1 per 120 persons. **Physicians** (1995): 1 per 302 persons. **Infant mortality** (per 1,000 live births): 71.

Education: Compulsory: ages 6-14. **Literacy** (1993): 97%.

Major International Organizations: UN (IBRD, ILO, IMF, WHO), CIS, OSCE.

Embassy: 1746 Massachusetts Ave. NW 20036; 887-5300.

Website: http://www.gov.uz

The region was overrun by the Mongols under Genghis Khan in 1220. In the 14th century, Uzbekistan became the center of a native empire—that of the Timurids. In later centuries Muslim feudal states emerged. Russian military conquest began in the 19th century.

The Uzbek SSR became a Soviet Union republic in 1925. Uzbekistan declared independence Aug. 29, 1991. It became an independent republic when the Soviet Union disbanded Dec. 26, 1991. Subsequently, the government of Uzbekistan was dominated by former Communists.

Vanuatu

Republic of Vanuatu

People: Population: 185,204. **Age distrib.** (%): <15: 39.1; 65+: 3.0. **Pop. density:** 39 per sq. mi. **Urban:** 19%. **Ethnic groups:** Melanesian 94%, French 4%. **Principal languages:** French, English, Bislama (all official). **Chief religions:** Presbyterian 37%, Anglican 15%, Catholic 15%, other Christian 10%, indigenous beliefs 8%.

Geography: Area: 4,707 sq. mi. **Location:** SW Pacific, 1,200 mi. NE of Brisbane, Australia. **Neighbors:** Fiji to E, Solomon Isls. to NW. **Topography:** Dense forest with narrow coastal strips of cultivated land. **Capital:** Port-Vila (1996 est.): 31,800.

Government: Type: Republic. **Head of state:** Pres. Jean-Marie Leye; b 1932; in office: Mar. 2, 1994. **Head of government:** Prime Min. Donald Kalpokas; in office: Mar. 30, 1998. **Local divisions:** 6 provinces.

Economy: Industries: Fish-freezing, meat canneries, wood processing. **Chief crops:** Copra, coconuts, cocoa, coffee. **Minerals:** Manganese. **Arable land:** 2%. **Other resources:** Forests, cattle. **Fish catch** (1996): 2,729 metric tons. **Livestock** (1997): chickens: 320,000; cattle: 151,000. **Electricity prod.** (1996): 30 mil kWh.

Finance: Monetary unit: Vatu (Sept. 1998): 132.50 = $1 U.S.). **Gross domestic product** (1995 est.): $219 mil. **Per**

capita GDP: $1,230. **Imports** (1995 est.): $93 mil; partners: Australia 41%, France 15%. **Exports** (1995): $28 mil; partners: EU 32%, Japan 29%. **Tourism:** $51 mil. **National budget** (1994 est.): $76.1 mil. **International reserves less gold** (June 1998): $25.11 mil. **Consumer prices** (change in 1997): 2.8%.

Transport: Motor vehicles in use: 4,000 passenger cars, 2,500 comm. vehicles. **Civil aviation:** 93.2 mil passenger-mi.

Communications: Radios: 319 per 1,000 pop. **Telephones:** 1 per 40 persons.

Health: Life expectancy at birth: 59.0 male; 63.1 female. **Births** (per 1,000 pop.): 29. **Deaths** (per 1,000 pop.): 8. **Natural increase:** 2.07%. **Hospital beds** (1995): 1 per 450 persons. **Physicians** (1995): 1 per 14,025 persons. **Infant mortality** (per 1,000 live births): 61.

Education: Literacy (1997): 36%.

Major International Organizations: UN (FAO, IBRD, IMF, IMO, WHO), the Commonwealth.

The Anglo-French condominium of the New Hebrides, administered jointly by France and Great Britain since 1906, became the independent Republic of Vanuatu on July 30, 1980.

Vatican City (The Holy See)

People: Population: 840. **Urban:** 100%. **Ethnic groups:** Italian, Swiss. **Principal languages:** Italian, Latin. **Chief religion:** Roman Catholic.

Geography: Area: 108.7 acres. **Location:** In Rome, Italy. **Neighbors:** Completely surrounded by Italy.

Monetary unit: Vatican Lira, Italian Lira (equal value) (Sept. 1998: 1,710.20 = $1 US).

Apostolic Nunciature in U.S.: 3339 Massachusetts Ave. NW 20008; 333-7121.

The popes for many centuries, with brief interruptions, held temporal sovereignty over mid-Italy (the so-called Papal States), comprising an area of some 16,000 sq. mi., with a population in the 19th century of more than 3 million. This territory was incorporated in the new Kingdom of Italy, the sovereignty of the pope being confined to the palaces of the Vatican and the Lateran in Rome and the villa of Castel Gandolfo, by an Italian law, May 13, 1871. This law also guaranteed to the pope and his successors a yearly indemnity of over $620,000. The allowance, however, remained unclaimed.

A Treaty of Conciliation, a concordat, and a financial convention were signed Feb. 11, 1929, by Cardinal Gasparri and Premier Mussolini. The documents established the independent state of Vatican City and gave the Roman Catholic church special status in Italy. The treaty (Lateran Agreement) was made part of the Constitution of Italy (Article 7) in 1947. Italy and the Vatican signed an agreement in 1984 on revisions of the concordat; the accord eliminated Roman Catholicism as the state religion and ended required religious education in Italian schools.

Vatican City includes St. Peter's, the Vatican Palace and Museum covering over 13 acres, the Vatican gardens, and neighboring buildings between Viale Vaticano and the church. Thirteen buildings in Rome, outside the boundaries, enjoy extraterritorial rights; these buildings house congregations or officers necessary for the administration of the Holy See.

The legal system is based on the code of canon law, the apostolic constitutions, and laws especially promulgated for the Vatican City by the pope. The Secretariat of State represents the Holy See in its diplomatic relations. By the Treaty of Conciliation the pope is pledged to a perpetual neutrality unless his mediation is specifically requested. This, however, does not prevent the defense of the Church whenever it is persecuted.

The present sovereign of the State of Vatican City is the Supreme Pontiff John Paul II, Karol Wojtyla, born in Wadowice, Poland, May 18, 1920, elected Oct. 16, 1978 (the first non-Italian to be elected pope in 456 years).

The U.S. restored formal relations in 1984 after the U.S. Congress repealed an 1867 ban on diplomatic relations with the Vatican. The Vatican and Israel agreed to establish formal relations Dec. 30, 1993.

Venezuela

Republic of Venezuela

People: Population: 22,803,409. **Age distrib.** (%): <15: 33.8; 65+: 4.5. **Pop. density:** 65 per sq. mi. **Urban:** 86%. **Ethnic groups:** Mestizo 67%, white (Spanish, Portuguese, Italian) 21%, black 10%, Amerindian 2%. **Principal language:** Spanish (official). **Chief religion:** Roman Catholic 96%.

Geography: Area: 352,143 sq. mi. **Location:** On Caribbean coast of South America. **Neighbors:** Colombia on W, Brazil on S, Guyana on E. **Topography:** Flat coastal plain and Orinoco Delta are bordered by Andes Mts. and hills. Plains, called llanos, extend between mountains and Orinoco. Guiana Highlands and plains are S of Orinoco, which stretches 1,600 mi. and drains 80% of Venezuela. **Capital:** Caracas. **Cities:** Caracas 3,007,000; Maracaibo 1,603,000; Valencia 1,462,000*.

Government: Type: Federal republic. **Head of state:** Pres. Rafael Caldera; b Jan. 24, 1916; in office: Feb. 2, 1994. **Local divisions:** 22 states, 1 federal district (Caracas), 1 federal dependency (72 islands). **Defense:** 1.2% of GDP. **Active troop strength:** 46,000.

Economy: Industries: Iron mining, steel, oil products, textiles. **Chief crops:** Rice, corn, sorghum, bananas, sugar. **Minerals:** Oil, gas, aluminum, iron (extensive reserves and production), gold. **Crude oil reserves** (1997): 71.9 bil bbls. **Arable land:** 4%. **Livestock** (1997): chickens: 140.00 mil; cattle: 15.05 mil; goats: 3.10 mil; pigs: 3.60 mil; sheep: 1.20 mil. **Fish catch** (1996): 484,529 metric tons. **Electricity prod.** (1996): 73.0 bil kWh. **Labor force:** 64% services; 23% ind.; 13% agric.

Finance: Monetary unit: Bolivar (Sept. 1998: 582.50 = $1 U.S.). **Gross domestic product** (1996 est.): $197 bil. **Per capita GDP:** $9,000. **Imports** (1996 est.): $10.2 bil; partners: U.S. 40%. **Exports** (1996 est.): $22.8 bil; partners: U.S. & Puerto Rico 55%. **Tourism:** $1.06 bil. **National budget** (1996 est.): $11.48 bil. **International reserves less gold** (June 1998): $12.56 bil. **Gold:** 9.82 mil oz t. **Consumer prices** (change in 1997): 50.0%.

Transport: Railroad: Length: 390 mi. **Motor vehicles in use:** 1.50 mil passenger cars, 525,000 comm. vehicles. **Civil aviation:** 3.60 bil passenger-mi; 20 airports. **Chief ports:** Maracaibo, La Guaira, Puerto Cabello.

Communications: Television sets: 183 per 1,000 pop. **Radios:** 372 per 1,000 pop. **Telephones:** 1 per 9.0 persons. **Daily newspaper circ.:** 215 per 1,000 pop.

Health: Life expectancy at birth: 69.7 male; 75.9 female. **Births** (per 1,000 pop.): 23. **Deaths** (per 1,000 pop.): 5. **Natural increase:** 1.80%. **Hospital beds** (1992): 1 per 382 persons. **Infant mortality** (per 1,000 live births): 28.

Education: Free and compulsory: ages 5-15. **Literacy** (1995): 91%.

Major International Organizations: UN (FAO, IBRD, ILO, IMF, IMO, WHO, WTrO), OAS, OPEC.

Embassy: 1099 30th St. NW 20007; 342-2214.

Website: http://www.embassy.org/embassies/ve.html

Columbus first set foot on the South American continent on the peninsula of Paria, Aug. 1498. Alonso de Ojeda, 1499, was the first European to see Lake Maracaibo. He called the land Venezuela, or Little Venice, because the Indians had houses on stilts. Spain dominated Venezuela until Simón Bolívar's victory near Carabobo in June 1821. The republic was formed after secession from the Colombian Federation in 1830.

Military strongmen ruled Venezuela for most of the 20th century. They promoted the oil industry; some social reforms were implemented. Since 1959, the country has had democratically elected governments.

Venezuela helped found the Organization of Petroleum Exporting Countries (OPEC). The government, Jan. 1, 1976, nationalized the oil industry with compensation. Oil accounts for most of Venezuela's export earnings; the economy suffered a severe cash crisis in the 1980s and 1990s as a result of depressed oil revenues. Government attempts to reduce dependence on oil have met with limited success.

A coup attempt, led by midlevel military officers, was thwarted by loyalist troops Feb. 4, 1992. A second coup attempt was thwarted in Nov. Pres. Carlos Andrés Pérez was removed from office on corruption charges, May 1993; he was convicted, May 1996, of mismanaging a $17 million secret government security fund. Citing an economic crisis, Pres. Rafael Caldera, a populist elected Dec. 5, 1993, suspended many civil liberties June 27, 1994; constitutional rights were restored in most regions July 6, 1995.

Vietnam

Socialist Republic of Vietnam

People: Population: 76,236,259. **Age distrib.** (%): <15: 34.6; 65+: 5.3. **Pop. density:** 599 per sq. mi. **Urban:** 19%. **Ethnic groups:** Vietnamese 85-90%, Chinese 3%, Muong, Tai, Meo, Khmer, Man, Cham. **Principal languages:** Vietnamese (official), French, Chinese. **Chief religions:** Mainly Buddhist and Taoist; also Roman Catholic, indigenous beliefs.

Geography: Area: 127,243 sq. mi. **Location:** SE Asia, on the E coast of the Indochinese Peninsula. **Neighbors:** China on N, Laos and Cambodia on W. **Topography:** Vietnam is long and narrow, with a 1,400-mi. coast. About 22% of country is readily arable, including the densely settled Red R. valley in the N, narrow coastal plains in center, and the wide, often marshy Mekong R. Delta in the S. The rest consists of semi-arid plateaus and barren mountains, with some stretches of tropical rain forest. **Capital:** Hanoi. **Cities:** Ho Chi Minh City 3,521,000; Hanoi 1,236,000*.

Government: Type: Communist. **Head of state:** Pres. Tran Duc Luong; b May 1937; in office: Sept. 24, 1997. **Head of government:** Prime Min. Phan Van Khai; b Dec. 1933; in office: Sept. 25, 1997. **Local divisions:** 7 regions comprising 60 provinces and 1 municipality. **Defense:** 4.0% of GDP. **Active troop strength:** 572,000.

Economy: Industries: Food processing, textiles, chemical fertilizer. **Chief crops:** Rice, potatoes, soybeans, coffee, tea, corn. **Minerals:** Phosphates, coal, gas, manganese, bauxite, chromate, oil. **Crude oil reserves** (1997): 600 mil bbls. **Other resources:** Forests. **Arable land:** 17%. **Livestock** (1997): chickens: 100.00 mil; pigs: 17.50 mil; cattle: 3.80 mil; buffalo: 2.95 mil; goats: 514,000. **Fish catch** (1996): 811,000 mil metric tons. **Electricity prod.** (1996): 14.9 bil kWh. **Labor force:** 72% agric., forestry, fishing.

Finance: Monetary unit: Dong (Sept. 1998: 13,907.50 = $1 U.S.). **Gross domestic product** (1996 est.): $108.7 bil. **Per capita GDP:** $1,470. **Imports** (1996 est.): $11.1 bil; partners: Singapore 14%, N.& S. Korea 13%. **Exports** (1996): $7.1 bil. partners: Japan 26%, **Tourism:** $88 mil. **National budget** (1995 est.): $5 bil.

Transport: Railroad: Length: 1,619 mi. **Motor vehicles in use:** 79,079 passenger cars, 97,104 comm. vehicles. **Civil aviation:** 1.83 bil passenger-mi; 12 airports. **Chief ports:** Ho Chi Minh City, Haiphong, Da Nang.

Communications: Television sets: 43 per 1,000 pop. **Radios:** 106 per 1,000 pop. **Telephones:** 1 per 95 persons. **Daily newspaper circ.:** 8 per 1,000 pop.

Health: Life expectancy at birth: 65.4 male; 70.3 female. **Births** (per 1,000 pop.): 22. **Deaths** (per 1,000 pop.): 7. **Natural increase:** 1.49%. **Hospital beds** (1994): 1 per 380 persons. **Physicians** (1994): 1 per 2,444 persons. **Infant mortality** (per 1,000 live births): 36.

Education: Compulsory: ages 6-11. **Literacy** (1995): 94%.

Major International Organizations: UN (FAO, IBRD, ILO, IMF, IMO, WHO), ASEAN.

Embassy: 1233 20th St. NW 20036; 861-0737.

Website: http://www.batin.com.vn

Vietnam's recorded history began in Tonkin before the Christian era. Settled by Viets from central China, Vietnam was held by China, 111 BC-AD 939, and was a vassal state during subsequent periods. Vietnam defeated the armies of Kublai Khan, 1288. Conquest by France began in 1858 and ended in 1884 with the protectorates of Tonkin and Annam in the N and the colony of Cochin-China in the S.

Japan occupied Vietnam in 1940; nationalist aims gathered force. A number of groups formed the Vietminh (Independence) League, headed by Ho Chi Minh, Communist guerrilla leader. In Aug. 1945 the Vietminh forced out Bao Dai, former emperor of Annam, head of a Japan-sponsored regime. France, seeking to reestablish colonial control, battled Communist and nationalist forces, 1946-1954, and was defeated at Dienbienphu, May 8, 1954. Meanwhile, on July 1, 1949, Bao Dai had formed a State of Vietnam, with himself as chief of state, with French approval. China backed Ho Chi Minh.

A cease-fire signed in Geneva July 21, 1954, provided for a buffer zone, withdrawal of French troops from the North, and elections to determine the country's future. Under the agreement the Communists gained control of territory north of the 17th parallel, with its capital at Hanoi and Ho Chi Minh as president. South Vietnam came to comprise the 39 southern provinces. Some 900,000 North Vietnamese fled to South Vietnam.

On Oct. 26, 1955, Ngo Dinh Diem, premier of the interim government of South Vietnam, proclaimed the Republic of Vietnam and became its first president.

The North adopted a constitution Dec. 31, 1959, based on Communist principles and calling for reunification of all Vietnam. North Vietnam sought to take over South Vietnam beginning in 1954. Fighting persisted from 1956, with the Communist Vietcong, aided by North Vietnam, pressing war in the South. Northern aid to Vietcong guerrillas was intensified in 1959, and large-scale troop infiltration began in 1964, with Soviet and Chinese arms assistance. Large Northern forces were stationed in border areas of Laos and Cambodia.

A serious political conflict arose in the South in 1963 when Buddhists denounced authoritarianism and brutality. This paved the way for a military coup Nov. 1-2, 1963, which overthrew Diem. Several other military coups followed.

In 1964, the U.S. began air strikes against North Vietnam. Beginning in 1965, the raids were stepped up and U.S. troops became combatants. U.S. troop strength in Vietnam, which reached a high of 543,400 in Apr. 1969, was ordered reduced by President Nixon in a series of withdrawals, beginning in June 1969. U.S. bombings were resumed in 1972-73.

A cease-fire agreement was signed in Paris Jan. 27, 1973 by the U.S., North and South Vietnam, and the Vietcong. It was never implemented.

North Vietnamese forces launched attacks against remaining government outposts in the Central Highlands in the first months of 1975. Government retreats turned into a rout, and the Saigon regime surrendered April 30. North Vietnam assumed control, and began transforming society along Communist lines.

The war's toll included—Combat deaths: U.S. 47,369; South Vietnam more than 200,000; other allied forces 5,225. Total U.S. fatalities numbered more than 58,000. Vietnamese civilian casualties were more than a million. Displaced war refugees in South Vietnam totaled more than 6.5 million.

The country was officially reunited July 2, 1976. The Northern capital, flag, anthem, emblem, and currency were applied to the new state. Nearly all major government posts went to officials of the former Northern government.

Heavy fighting with Cambodia took place, 1977-80, amid mutual charges of aggression and atrocities against civilians. Increasing numbers of Vietnamese civilians, ethnic Chinese, escaped the country, via the sea or the overland route across Cambodia. Vietnam launched an offensive against Cambodian refugee strongholds along the Thai-Cambodian border in 1985; they also engaged Thai troops.

Relations with China soured as 140,000 ethnic Chinese left Vietnam charging discrimination; China cut off economic aid. Reacting to Vietnam's invasion of Cambodia, China attacked 4 Vietnamese border provinces, Feb. 1979.

Vietnam announced reforms aimed at reducing central control of the economy in 1987, as many of the old revolutionary followers of Ho Chi Minh were removed from office.

Citing Vietnamese cooperation in returning remains of U.S. soldiers killed in the Vietnam War, the U.S. announced an end, Feb. 3, 1994, to a 19-year-old U.S. embargo on trade with Vietnam. The U.S. extended full diplomatic recognition to Vietnam July 11, 1995. The Communist Party replaced the country's ill and aging leadership in Sept. 1997.

Western Samoa

(See Samoa)

Yemen

Republic of Yemen

People: Population: 16,387,963. **Age distrib.** (%): <15: 48.1; 65+: 3.3. **Pop. density:** 79 per sq. mi. **Urban:** 34%. **Ethnic groups:** Predominantly Arab, some Afro-Arab, South Asian. **Principal language:** Arabic (official). **Chief religions:** Mostly Muslim (Sha'fi-Sunni, Zaydi-Shi'a).

Geography: Area: 207,286 sq. mi. **Location:** Middle East, on the S coast of the Arabian Peninsula. **Neighbors:** Saudi Arabia on N, Oman on the E. **Topography:** A sandy coastal strip leads to well-watered fertile mountains in interior. **Capital:** Sanaa. **Cities:** (1995 est.) Sanaa 972,000; Aden 562,000.

Government: Type: Republic. **Head of state:** Pres. Ali Abdullah Saleh; b. 1942; in office: July 17, 1978. **Head of government:** Prime Min. Abdel Karim al Iriani; in office: May 14, 1998. **Local divisions:** 17 governorates, Sanaa. **Defense:** 3.7% of GDP. **Active troop strength:** 42,000.

Economy: Industries: Oil, food processing. **Chief crops:** Grains, fruits, qat, coffee, cotton. **Minerals:** Oil, salt. **Crude oil reserves** (1997): 4 bil bbls. **Arable land:** 3%. **Livestock** (1997): chickens: 25.20 mil; sheep: 4.27 mil; goats: 3.88 mil; cattle: 1.20 mil. **Fish catch** (1996): 103,743 metric tons. **Electricity prod.** (1996): 1.9 bil kWh.

Finance: Monetary unit: Rial (Sept. 1998: 130.99 = $1 U.S.). **Gross domestic product** (1996 est.): $39.1 bil. **Per capita GDP:** $2,900. **Imports** (1996 est.): $2.2 bil; partners: UAE 14%, Saudi Arabia 10%. **Exports** (1996 est.): $2.5 bil; partners: China 23%, S. Korea 19%. **Tourism:** $69 mil. **National budget** (1996 est.): $3.1 bil. **International reserves**

less gold (Nov. 1997): $1.18 bil. **Gold:** 50,000 oz t. **Consumer prices** (change in 1997): 5.4%.

Transport: Motor vehicles in use: 229,084 passenger cars, 282,615 comm. vehicles. **Civil aviation:** 527.4 mil passenger-mi; 11 airports. **Chief ports:** Al Hudaydah, Al Mukalla, Aden.

Communications: Television sets: 6.5 per 1,000 pop. **Radios:** 43 per 1,000 pop. **Telephones:** 1 per 81 persons.

Health: Life expectancy at birth: 57.7 male; 61.3 female. **Births** (per 1,000 pop.): 43. **Deaths** (per 1,000 pop.): 10. **Natural increase:** 3.31%. **Hospital beds** (1995): 1 per 1,582 persons. **Physicians** (1995): 1 per 4,530 persons. **Infant mortality** (per 1,000 live births): 72.

Education: Compulsory: ages 6-15. **Literacy** (1994): 43%.

Major International Organizations: UN (FAO, IBRD, ILO, IMF, IMO, WHO), AL.

Embassy: 2600 Virginia Ave. NW 20037; 965-4760.

Website: http://www.nusacc.org/yemen

Yemen's territory once was part of the ancient Kingdom of Sheba, or Saba, a prosperous link in trade between Africa and India. The Bible speaks of its gold, spices, and precious stones as gifts borne by the Queen of Sheba to King Solomon.

Yemen became independent in 1918, after years of Ottoman Turkish rule, but remained politically and economically backward. Imam Ahmed ruled 1948-1962. Army officers headed by Brig. Gen. Abdullah al-Salal declared the country to be the Yemen Arab Republic.

The Imam Ahmed's heir, the Imam Mohamad al-Badr, fled to the mountains where tribesmen joined royalist forces; internal warfare between them and the republican forces continued. About 150,000 people died in the fighting.

There was a bloodless coup Nov. 5, 1967. In April 1970 hostilities ended with an agreement between Yemen and Saudi Arabia. On June 13, 1974, an army group, led by Col. Ibrahim al-Hamidi, seized the government. He was killed in 1977.

Meanwhile, South Yemen won independence from Britain in 1967, formed out of the British colony of Aden and the British protectorate of South Arabia. It became the Arab world's only Marxist state, taking the name People's Democratic Republic of Yemen in 1970 and signing a friendship treaty with the USSR in 1979 that allowed for the stationing of Soviet troops.

More than 300,000 Yemenis fled from the south to the north after independence, contributing to 2 decades of hostility between the 2 states that flared into warfare twice in the 1970s.

An Arab League-sponsored agreement between North and South Yemen on unification of the 2 countries was signed Mar. 29, 1979. An agreement providing for widespread political and economic cooperation was signed in 1988.

The 2 countries were formally united May 21, 1990, but regional clan-based rivalries led to full-scale civil war in 1994. Secessionists declared a breakaway state in S Yemen, May 21, 1994, but northern troops captured the former southern capital of Aden in July.

A new constitution was approved Sept. 28. Parliamentary elections were held Apr. 27, 1997.

A dispute between Yemen and Eritrea over the Hanish Isls. in the Red Sea, which led to armed clashes in 1995, was resolved by arbitration in 1998.

Yugoslavia

Federal Republic of Yugoslavia

People: Population: 11,206,039. **Age distrib.** (%): <15: 21.2; 65+: 11.7. **Pop. density:** 284 per sq. mi. **Urban:** 57%. **Ethnic groups:** Serbian 63%, Albanian 14%, Montenegrin 6%. **Principal languages:** Serbo-Croatian (official) 95%, Albanian 5%. **Chief religions:** Orthodox 65%, Muslim 19%, Roman Catholic 4%.

Geography: Area: 39,517 sq. mi. **Location:** On the Balkan Peninsula in SE Europe. Present-day Yugoslavia consists of the former republics of Serbia and Montenegro. **Neighbors:** Croatia, Bosnia and Herzegovina on W; Hungary on N; Romania, Bulgaria on E; Albania, Macedonia on S. **Capital:** Belgrade 1,204,000*.

Government: Type: Republic. **Head of state:** Pres. Slobodan Milosevic; in office: Dec. 29, 1997. **Head of government:** Prime Min. Momir Bulatovic; b Sept. 21, 1956; in office: May 19, 1998. **Local divisions:** 2 republics, 2 autonomous provinces. **Defense:** 8.7% of GDP. **Active troop strength:** 113,900.

Economy: Industries: Steel, machinery, consumer goods, mining, electronics. **Chief crops:** Cereals, fruits, vegetables. **Minerals:** Oil, gas, coal, antimony, lead, nickel, gold, copper, chrome. **Livestock** (1997): chickens: 24.29 mil; pigs: 4.22 mil; sheep: 2.57 mil; cattle: 1.90 mil; goats: 293,000. **Labor force:** 41% ind.; 35% services.

Finance: Monetary unit: New Dinar (Sept. 1998: 10.49 = $1 U.S.). **Gross domestic product** (1995 est.): $20.6 bil. **Per capita GDP:** $1,900. **Imports** (1995 est.): $2.4 bil; partners: Germany 13%, Italy 11%. **Exports** (1995 est.): $1.4 bil; partners: Macedonia 12%, Russia 9%. **Tourism:** $42 mil.

Transport: Railroad: Length: 2,505 mi. **Motor vehicles in use:** 1.00 mil passenger cars, 331,000 comm. vehicles. **Civil aviation:** 93 mil passenger-mi; 4 airports. **Chief ports:** Bar, Novi Sad.

Communications: Television sets: 27 per 1,000 pop. **Radios:** 118 per 1,000 pop. **Telephones:** 1 per 5.2 persons. **Daily newspaper circ.:** 256 per 1,000 pop.

Health: Life expectancy at birth: 71.8 male; 77.9 female. **Births** (per 1,000 pop.): 14. **Deaths** (per 1,000 pop.): 10. **Natural increase:** 0.46%. **Hospital beds** (1995): 1 per 188 persons. **Physicians** (1995): 1 per 495 persons. **Infant mortality** (per 1,000 live births): 14.

Education: Free and compulsory: ages 7-15. **Literacy** (1995): 98%.

Major International Organizations: Currently suspended from UN and its agencies.

Embassy: 2410 California St. NW 20008; 462-6566.

Website: http://www.gov.yu

Serbia, which had since 1389 been a vassal principality of Turkey, was established as an independent kingdom by the Treaty of Berlin, 1878. Montenegro, independent since 1389, also obtained international recognition in 1878. After the Balkan wars, Serbia's boundaries were enlarged by the annexation of Old Serbia and Macedonia, 1913.

When the Austro-Hungarian empire collapsed after World War I, the Kingdom of Serbs, Croats, and Slovenes was formed from the former provinces of Croatia, Dalmatia, Bosnia, Herzegovina, Slovenia, Vojvodina, and the independent state of Montenegro The name became Yugoslavia in 1929.

Nazi Germany invaded in 1941. Many Yugoslav partisan troops continued to operate. Among these were the Chetniks led by Draja Mikhailovich, who fought other partisans led by Josip Broz, known as Marshal Tito. Tito, backed by the USSR and Britain from 1943, was in control by the time the Germans had been driven from Yugoslavia in 1945. Mikhailovich was executed July 17, 1946, by the Tito regime.

A constituent assembly proclaimed Yugoslavia a republic Nov. 29, 1945. It became a federal republic Jan. 31, 1946, with Tito, a Communist, heading the government. Tito rejected Stalin's policy of dictating to all Communist nations, and he accepted economic and military aid from the West.

Pres. Tito died May 4, 1980. After his death, Yugoslavia was governed by a collective presidency, with a rotating succession. On Jan. 22, 1990, the Communist Party renounced its leading role in society.

Croatia and Slovenia formally declared independence June 25, 1991. In Croatia, fighting began between Croats and ethnic Serbs. Serbia sent arms and medical supplies to the Serb rebels in Croatia. Croatian forces clashed with Yugoslav army units and their Serb supporters.

The republics of Serbia and Montenegro proclaimed a new "Federal Republic of Yugoslavia" Apr. 17, 1992. Serbia, under Pres. Slobodan Milosevic, was the main arms supplier to ethnic Serb fighters in Bosnia and Herzegovina. The UN imposed sanctions May 30 on the newly reconstituted Yugoslavia as a means of ending the bloodshed in Bosnia.

A peace agreement initialed in Dayton, Ohio, Nov. 21, 1995, was signed in Paris, Dec. 14, by Milosevic and leaders of Bosnia and Croatia. In May 1996, a UN tribunal in the Netherlands began trying suspected war criminals from the former Yugoslavia. The UN lifted sanctions against Yugoslavia Oct. 1, 1996, after elections were held in Bosnia. Mass protests erupted when Milosevic refused to accept opposition victories in local elections Nov. 17; non-Communist governments took office in Belgrade and other cities in Feb. 1997. Barred from running for a 3d term as Serbian president, Milosevic had himself inaugurated as president of Yugoslavia on July 23, 1997.

Kosovo: An area in southern Serbia (4,203 sq. mi.), with a population of about 2,000,000, mostly Albanians. The capital is Pristina. Revoking provincial autonomy, Serbia began ruling Kosovo by force in 1989. Albanian secessionists proclaimed an independent Republic of Kosovo in July 1990. Guerrilla attacks by the Kosovo Liberation Army in 1997 brought a ferocious counteroffensive by Serbian authorities. Fearful that the Serbs were employing "ethnic cleansing" tactics, as they had in Bosnia, the U.S. and its NATO allies sought to pressure the Yugoslav government in 1998. Under threat of imminent NATO air strikes, Pres. Slobodan Milosevic agreed Oct. 13 to a troop pullout and refugee resettlement plan to be monitored by 2,000 unarmed OSCE "verifiers."

Vojvodina: An area in northern Serbia (8,304 sq. mi.), with a population of about 2,000,000, mostly Serbian. The capital is Novi Sad.

Zaire

See Congo (formerly *Zaire*)

Zambia

Republic of Zambia

People: Population: 9,460,736. **Age distrib.** (%): <15: 49.2; 65+: 2.5. **Pop. density:** 33 per sq. mi. **Urban:** 43%. **Ethnic groups:** African 99%, European 1%. **Principal languages:** English (official), Bantu dialects. **Chief religions:** Christian 50-75%, Hindu and Muslim 24-49%.

Geography: Area: 290,583 sq. mi. **Location:** In S central Africa. **Neighbors:** Congo (formerly Zaire) on N; Tanzania, Malawi, Mozambique on E; Zimbabwe, Namibia on S; Angola on W. **Topography:** Zambia is mostly high plateau country covered with thick forests, and drained by several important rivers, including the Zambezi. **Capital:** Lusaka 1,317,000*.

Government: Type: Republic. **Head of state:** Pres. Frederick Chiluba; b Apr. 30, 1943; in office: Nov. 2, 1991. **Local divisions:** 9 provinces. **Defense:** 1.8% of GDP. **Active troop strength:** 21,600.

Economy: Chief crops: Corn, cassava, sorghum, sugar. **Minerals:** Cobalt, copper, zinc, emeralds, gold, lead, silver, uranium, coal. **Arable land:** 7%. **Livestock** (1997): chickens: 20.00 mil; cattle: 2.60 mil; goats: 580,000; pigs: 290,000. **Fish catch** (1996): 61,562 metric tons. **Electricity prod.** (1996): 7.8 bil kWh. **Labor force:** 85% agric.

Finance: Monetary unit: Kwacha (Sept. 1998: 2,012.50 = $1 U.S.). **Gross domestic product** (1996 est.): $9.7 bil. **Per capita GDP:** $1,060. **Imports** (1996 est.): $990 mil; South Africa 28%, UK 11%. **Exports** (1996 est.): $975 mil; partners: Japan 18%, Saudi Arabia 13%. **Tourism:** $65 mil. **National budget** (1995 est.): $835 mil. **International reserves less gold** (Feb. 1998): $185.1 mil. **Consumer prices** (change in 1997): 24.8%.

Transport: Railroad: Length: 791 mi. **Motor vehicles in use:** 142,000 passenger cars, 73,500 comm. vehicles. **Civil aviation:** 265.8 mil passenger-mi; 4 airports. **Chief port:** Mpulungu.

Communications: Television sets: 32 per 1,000 pop. **Radios:** 99 per 1,000 pop. **Telephones:** 1 per 123 persons. **Daily newspaper circ.:** 13 per 1,000 pop.

Health: Life expectancy at birth: 36.8 male; 37.3 female. **Births** (per 1,000 pop.): 45. **Deaths** (per 1,000 pop.): 23. **Natural increase:** 2.21%. **Physicians** (1993): 1 per 10,917 persons. **Infant mortality** (per 1,000 live births): 93.

Education: Compulsory: ages 7-14. **Literacy** (1995): 78%.

Major International Organizations: UN (FAO, IBRD, ILO, IMF, WHO, WTrO), the Commonwealth, OAU.

Embassy: 2419 Massachusetts Ave. NW 20008; 265-9717.

Website: http://www.zamnet.zm

As Northern Rhodesia, the country was under the administration of the South Africa Company, 1889 until 1924, when the office of governor was established, and, subsequently, a legislature. The country became an independent republic within the Commonwealth Oct. 24, 1964.

After the white government of Rhodesia (now Zimbabwe) declared its independence from Britain Nov. 11, 1965, relations between Zambia and Rhodesia became strained.

As part of a program of government participation in major industries, a government corporation in 1970 took over 51% of the ownership of 2 foreign-owned copper-mining companies. Privately-held land and other enterprises were nationalized in 1975. In the 1980s and 1990s lowered copper prices hurt the economy and severe drought caused famine.

Food riots erupted in June 1990, as the nation suffered its worst violence since independence. Elections held Oct. 1991 brought an end to one-party rule. The new government sought to sell state enterprises, including the copper industry. Pres. Frederick Chiluba won reelection Nov. 18, 1996, but international observers cited harassment of opposition parties. A coup attempt was suppressed Oct. 28, 1997.

According to UN estmates, the AIDS epidemic had orphaned nearly 500,000 children in Zambia by the late 1990s.

Zimbabwe

Republic of Zimbabwe

People: Population: 11,044,147. **Age distrib.** (%): <15: 43.8; 65+: 2.6. **Pop. density:** 73 per sq. mi. **Urban:** 33%. **Ethnic groups:** Shona 71%, Ndebele 16%. **Principal languages:** English (official), Shona, Sindebele. **Chief religions:** Syncretic (Christian-indigenous mix) 50%, Christian 25%, indigenous beliefs 24%.

Geography: Area: 150,803 sq. mi. **Location:** In southern Africa. **Neighbors:** Zambia on N, Botswana on W, South Africa on S, Mozambique on E. **Topography:** Zimbabwe is high plateau country, rising to mountains on eastern border, sloping down on the other borders. **Capital:** Harare 1,410,000*.

Government: Type: Republic. **Head of state:** Pres. Robert Mugabe; b Feb. 21, 1924; in office: Jan. 1, 1988. **Local divisions:** 8 provinces, 2 cities. **Defense:** 3.9% of GDP. **Active troop strength:** 43,000.

Economy: Industries: Clothing, mining, steel, chemicals. **Chief crops:** Tobacco, sugar, cotton, wheat, corn. **Minerals:** Chromium, gold, nickel, asbestos, copper, iron, coal. **Arable land:** 7%. **Livestock** (1997): chickens: 15.50 mil; cattle: 5.40 mil; goats: 2.70 mil; sheep: 530,000; pigs: 270,000. **Electricity prod.** (1996): 8.6 bil kWh. **Labor force:** 70% agric.; 22% serv. & transport; 8% ind.

Finance: Monetary unit: Dollar (Sept. 1998: 23.50 = $1 U.S.). **Gross domestic product** (1996 est.): $26.4 bil. **Per capita GDP:** $2,340. **Imports** (1996 est.): $2.2 bil; partners: South Africa 41%. **Exports** (1996 est.): $2.4 bil; partners: South Africa 14%, UK 10%. **Tourism:** $250 mil. **National budget** (FY 1996-97): $2.9 bil. **International reserves less gold** (June 1998): $154.1 mil. **Gold:** 650,000 oz t. **Consumer prices** (change in 1997): 18.3%.

Transport: Railroad: Length: 1,713.3 mi. **Motor vehicles in use:** 250,000 passenger cars, 108,000 comm. vehicles. **Civil aviation:** 547.1 mil passenger-mi; 7 airports. **Chief ports:** Binga, Kariba.

Communications: Television sets: 12 per 1,000 pop. **Radios:** 113 per 1,000 pop. **Telephones:** 1 per 71 persons. **Daily newspaper circ.:** 17 per 1,000 pop.

Health: Life expectancy at birth: 39.1 male; 39.2 female. **Births** (per 1,000 pop.): 31. **Deaths** (per 1,000 pop.): 20. **Natural increase:** 1.12%. **Hospital beds** (1996): 1 per 501 persons. **Physicians** (1993): 1 per 6,909 persons. **Infant mortality** (per 1,000 live births): 62.

Education: Compulsory: ages 6-13. **Literacy** (1995): 85%.

Major International Organizations: UN (FAO, IBRD, ILO, IMF, WHO, WTrO), the Commonwealth, OAU.

Embassy: 1608 New Hampshire Ave. NW 20009; 332-7100.

Britain took over the area as Southern Rhodesia in 1923 from the British South Africa Co. (which, under Cecil Rhodes, had conquered it by 1897) and granted internal self-government. Under a 1961 constitution, voting was restricted to keep whites in power. On Nov. 11, 1965, Prime Min. Ian D. Smith announced his country's unilateral declaration of independence.

Britain termed the act illegal and demanded that the country (known as Rhodesia until 1980) broaden voting rights to provide for eventual rule by the black African majority. The UN imposed sanctions and, in May 1968, a trade embargo.

Intermittent negotiations between the government and various black nationalist groups failed to prevent increasing guerrilla warfare. An "internal settlement" signed Mar. 1978 in which Smith and 3 popular black leaders would share control of the government until a transfer of power to the black majority was rejected by guerrilla leaders.

In the country's first universal-franchise election, Apr. 21, 1979, Bishop Abel Muzorewa's United African National Council gained a bare majority of the black-dominated Parliament. A cease-fire was accepted by all parties, Dec. 5. Independence as Zimbabwe was finally achieved Apr. 18, 1980.

On Mar. 6, 1992, Pres. Robert Mugabe declared a national disaster because of drought and appealed to foreign donors for food, money, and medicine, An economic adjustment program caused widespread hardship. Mugabe was reelected Mar. 1996 after opposition candidates withdrew.

An estimated 1 mil Zimbabweans have HIV, the virus that causes AIDS.

Area and Population of the World

Source: Bureau of the Census, U.S. Dept. of Commerce; prior to 1950, Rand McNally & Co.

Continent or Region	AREA (1,000 sq. mi.)	% of Earth	POPULATION (est., in thousands) 1650	1750	1850	1900	1950	1980	1998	% World Total, 1998
North America	9,400	16.2	5,000	5,000	39,000	106,000	221,000	372,000	301,000	5.1
South America	6,900	11.9	8,000	7,000	20,000	38,000	111,000	242,000	508,000	8.6
Europe	3,800	6.6	100,000	140,000	265,000	400,000	392,000	484,000	508,000	8.6
Asia	17,400	30.1	335,000	476,000	754,000	932,000	1,411,000	2,601,000	3,528,000	59.5
Africa	11,700	20.2	100,000	95,000	95,000	118,000	229,000	470,000	761,000	12.8
Former USSR	—	—	—	—	—	—	180,000	266,000	291,000	4.9
Oceania, incl. Australia	3,300	5.7	2,000	2,000	2,000	6,000	12,000	23,000	30,000	0.5
Antarctica	5,400	9.3	Uninhabited							
WORLD	**57,900**	—	**550,000**	**725,000**	**1,175,000**	**1,600,000**	**2,556,000**	**4,458,000**	**5,927,000**	—

Note: Figures may not add to total because of independent rounding.

Leading Countries in Population and Area, 1998

China had the highest population in the world, with an estimated 1.2 billion inhabitants in mid-1998, one-fifth of the world's total population. India had some 984 million people and was expected to reach 1 billion by the end of the decade. The United States had the world's third-largest population, with about 270 million, followed by Indonesia, Brazil, and Russia. Russia is the largest country in land area, with over 6.5 million square miles, followed by Canada, China, the United States, and Brazil.

Population of the World's Largest Cities

Source: United Nations, Dept. for Economic and Social Information and Policy Analysis

The figures given here are United Nations estimates and projections, as revised in 1996, for "urban agglomerations"—that is, contiguous densely populated urban areas, not demarcated by administrative boundaries. These figures may not correspond to figures for cities in other parts of *The World Almanac*.

Rank	City, Country	Pop. (thousands) 1995	Pop. (thousands, projected) 2015	Annual growth rate (percent) 1990-1995	Percentage increase for: 1975-1995	1995-2015	Pop. of city as percentage of: Total pop.[1]	Urban pop.[2]
1.	Tokyo, Japan	26,959	28,887	1.45	36.36	7.15	21.56	27.62
2.	Mexico City, Mexico	16,562	19,180	1.81	47.40	15.81	18.17	24.75
3.	Sao Paulo, Brazil	16,533	20,320	1.84	64.56	22.91	10.40	13.27
4.	New York City, U.S.	16,332	17,602	0.34	2.85	7.78	6.11	8.03
5.	Mumbai (Bombay), India	15,138	26,218	4.24	120.79	73.19	1.63	6.08
6.	Shanghai, China	13,584	17,969	0.36	18.71	32.28	1.11	3.68
7.	Los Angeles, U.S.	12,410	14,217	1.60	39.03	14.56	4.65	6.10
8.	Calcutta, India	11,923	17,305	1.81	51.15	45.14	1.28	4.79
9.	Buenos Aires, Argentina	11,802	13,856	1.15	29.07	17.40	33.95	38.54
10.	Seoul, South Korea	11,609	12,980	1.92	70.52	11.81	25.85	31.81
11.	Beijing, China	11,299	15,572	0.87	32.23	37.82	0.93	3.06
12.	Osaka, Japan	10,609	10,609	0.23	7.77	0.00	8.48	10.87
13.	Lagos, Nigeria	10,287	24,640	5.68	211.73	139.53	9.21	23.28
14.	Rio de Janeiro, Brazil	10,181	11,860	1.00	29.63	16.49	6.40	8.17
15.	Delhi, India	9,948	16,860	3.85	124.76	69.48	1.07	4.0

(1) Denotes percentage of the total population of the country in which the city is located. (2) Denotes percentage of the total urban population of the country in which the city is located.

Current Population and Projections for All Countries: 1998, 2025, and 2050

Source: Bureau of the Census, U.S. Dept. of Commerce

(midyear figures, in thousands)

COUNTRY	1998	2025	2050
Afghanistan	24,792	48,045	76,231
Albania	3,331	4,306	4,609
Algeria	30,481	47,676	58,880
Andorra	65	88	69
Angola	10,865	21,598	34,465
Antigua and Barbuda	64	65	51
Argentina	36,265	48,351	56,258
Armenia	3,422	3,434	3,428
Australia	18,613	22,191	22,846
Austria	8,134	7,822	6,136
Azerbaijan	7,856	9,429	10,585
Bahamas	280	369	404
Bahrain	616	923	1,098
Bangladesh	127,567	180,673	211,082
Barbados	259	279	266
Belarus	10,409	10,248	9,100
Belgium	10,175	9,533	7,609
Belize	230	383	489
Benin	6,101	13,541	22,171
Bhutan	1,908	3,341	4,935
Bolivia	7,826	12,007	15,240
Bosnia and Herzegovina	3,366	3,471	2,833
Botswana	1,448	1,634	2,146
Brazil	169,807	209,587	228,145
Brunei	315	530	704
Bulgaria	8,240	7,292	5,905
Burkina Faso	11,266	21,360	34,956
Burundi	5,537	10,469	17,304
Cambodia	11,340	21,434	35,065
Cameroon	15,029	29,108	48,606
Canada	30,675	37,987	40,491
Cape Verde	400	532	545
Central African Republic	3,376	5,545	7,915
Chad	7,360	14,360	22,504

COUNTRY	1998	2025	2050
Chile	14,788	18,681	19,453
China	1,236,915	1,407,739	1,322,435
Colombia	38,581	58,287	73,349
Comoros	546	1,160	1,953
Congo (formerly Zaire)	2,658	105,737	184,456
Congo Republic	49,001	4,246	6,081
Costa Rica	3,605	5,327	6,321
Côte d'Ivoire	15,446	27,840	44,509
Croatia	4,672	4,348	3,486
Cuba	11,051	11,722	10,594
Cyprus	749	870	878
Czech Republic	10,286	10,128	8,626
Denmark	5,334	5,334	4,476
Djibouti	441	841	1,329
Dominica	66	67	69
Dominican Republic	7,999	11,781	14,586
Ecuador	12,337	17,800	21,059
Egypt	66,050	97,431	117,121
El Salvador	5,752	8,382	10,814
Equatorial Guinea	454	876	1,394
Eritrea	3,842	8,438	13,736
Estonia	1,421	1,237	1,047
Ethiopia	58,390	98,763	159,170
Fiji	803	1,085	1,285
Finland	5,149	5,009	4,170
France	58,805	57,806	48,219
Gabon	1,208	1,800	2,518
Gambia, The	1,292	2,678	4,038
Georgia	5,109	4,718	4,365
Germany	82,079	75,372	57,429
Ghana	18,497	28,191	34,324
Greece	10,662	10,473	8,362
Grenada	96	154	210
Guatemala	12,008	22,344	32,185
Guinea	7,477	13,135	20,034
Guinea-Bissau	1,206	2,102	2,970
Guyana	708	710	726
Haiti	6,781	10,171	12,746
Honduras	5,862	8,612	11,001
Hungary	10,208	9,374	7,684
Iceland	271	298	279
India	984,004	1,415,274	1,706,951
Indonesia	212,942	287,985	330,566
Iran	68,960	111,891	142,336
Iraq	21,722	44,146	65,529
Ireland	3,619	3,913	3,600
Israel	5,644	7,778	8,961
Italy	56,783	50,352	38,290
Jamaica	2,635	3,355	3,712
Japan	125,932	119,865	101,334
Jordan	4,435	8,223	11,303
Kazakhstan	16,847	18,565	20,426
Kenya	28,337	34,774	43,852
Kiribati	84	99	100
Korea, North	21,234	25,485	25,930
Korea, South	46,417	54,256	52,625
Kuwait	1,913	3,559	4,159
Kyrgyzstan	4,522	6,066	7,394
Laos	5,261	9,805	13,844
Latvia	2,385	1,965	1,659
Lebanon	3,506	4,831	5,598
Lesotho	2,090	2,724	3,533
Liberia	2,772	6,524	10,992
Libya	5,691	14,185	26,625
Liechtenstein	32	36	31
Lithuania	3,600	3,417	3,063
Luxembourg	425	447	360
Macedonia	2,009	2,171	1,977
Madagascar	14,463	29,306	48,327
Malawi	9,840	12,475	16,884
Malaysia	20,933	34,248	47,289
Maldives	290	623	949
Mali	10,109	22,647	40,433
Malta	380	391	325
Marshall Islands	63	171	348
Mauritania	2,511	5,446	9,329
Mauritius	1,168	1,488	1,614
Mexico	98,553	141,593	167,479
Micronesia	130	143	143
Moldova	4,458	4,830	4,811
Monaco	32	34	34
Mongolia	2,579	3,555	4,057
Morocco	29,114	43,228	52,069
Mozambique	18,641	33,308	47,805

COUNTRY	1998	2025	2050
Myanmar	47,305	68,107	87,778
Namibia	1,622	2,310	3,757
Nauru	11	12	12
Nepal	23,698	42,576	60,661
Netherlands	15,731	15,852	12,974
New Zealand	3,625	4,445	4,561
Nicaragua	4,583	8,112	10,817
Niger	9,672	20,424	33,896
Nigeria	110,532	203,423	337,591
Norway	4,420	4,592	4,012
Oman	2,364	5,307	8,453
Pakistan	135,135	211,675	260,247
Palau	18	24	26
Panama	2,736	3,796	4,418
Papua New Guinea	4,600	7,597	10,049
Paraguay	5,291	9,929	15,001
Peru	26,111	39,158	47,855
Philippines	77,726	120,519	150,272
Poland	38,607	40,117	36,465
Portugal	9,928	9,012	7,256
Qatar	697	1,208	1,348
Romania	22,396	21,417	18,483
Russia	146,861	138,842	121,777
Rwanda	7,956	12,159	19,607
Saint Kitts and Nevis	42	60	69
Saint Lucia	152	203	224
Saint Vincent and the Grenadines	120	151	163
Samoa (formerly Western Samoa)	225	367	471
San Marino	25	27	27
São Tomé and Príncipe	150	331	518
Saudi Arabia	20,786	50,374	97,120
Senegal	9,723	22,456	39,690
Seychelles	79	91	95
Sierra Leone	5,080	11,010	18,369
Singapore	3,490	4,231	4,161
Slovakia	5,393	5,718	5,215
Slovenia	1,972	1,864	1,484
Solomon Islands	441	840	1,158
Somalia	6,842	15,192	26,243
South Africa	42,835	49,851	58,972
Spain	39,134	36,841	29,405
Sri Lanka	18,934	24,088	26,146
Sudan	33,551	64,757	93,625
Suriname	428	460	380
Swaziland	966	1,589	3,059
Sweden	8,887	9,158	8,052
Switzerland	7,260	7,064	5,614
Syria	16,673	31,684	43,463
Taiwan	21,908	25,897	25,189
Tajikistan	6,020	9,634	13,261
Tanzania	30,609	50,661	76,500
Thailand	60,037	70,316	69,741
Togo	4,906	11,712	20,725
Tonga	108	133	156
Trinidad and Tobago	1,117	1,083	1,057
Tunisia	9,380	12,760	14,399
Turkey	64,567	89,727	103,649
Turkmenistan	4,298	6,514	8,422
Tuvalu	10	15	20
Uganda	22,167	49,181	91,398
Ukraine	50,125	45,096	39,096
United Arab Emirates	2,303	3,444	4,057
United Kingdom	58,970	59,985	54,116
United States	270,312	335,360	394,241
Uruguay	3,285	3,916	4,256
Uzbekistan	23,784	34,348	42,762
Vanuatu	185	282	347
Venezuela	22,803	32,474	37,773
Vietnam	76,236	103,909	119,464
Yemen	16,388	40,439	76,008
Yugoslavia	11,206	11,244	9,798
Zambia	9,461	16,156	26,967
Zimbabwe	11,044	12,366	16,064
REGIONS			
Asia	3,527,969	4,702,882	5,327,982
Africa	760,771	1,323,381	2,028,488
Europe	508,285	491,202	407,688
South America	507,551	695,481	813,357
North America	301,115	373,494	434,873
Former Soviet Union	291,117	298,344	291,196
Oceania, incl. Australia	29,659	38,504	42,816
WORLD[1]	**5,926,467**	**7,923,288**	**9,346,399**

(1) Figures may not add to total because of rounding and exclusion of certain pseudo-national entities.

Estimated HIV Infection and Reported AIDS Cases

Source: UNAIDS, Joint United Nations Program on HIV/AIDS

Studies, primarily in industrialized nations, have indicated that about 60% of adults infected by the human immunodeficiency virus (HIV) will develop acquired immune deficiency syndrome (AIDS) within 12-13 years of becoming infected; progression of the disease might be more rapid in developing countries. It is expected that the vast majority of HIV-infected persons will eventually develop AIDS. Survival after the onset of AIDS is estimated by UNAIDS to be about 3 years, on the average, in industrialized countries and less than 1 year in developing countries. About 75-85% of adult HIV infections worldwide have been transmitted through unprotected sexual intercourse. The number of people living with HIV/AIDS worldwide as of Dec. 1997, was an estimated 30.6 million. This figure includes 29.4 million adults (3 out of 5 were male) and about 1.1 million children (under 15 years old). The virus continues to spread with great rapidity, causing almost 16,000 new infections daily. UNAIDS estimates that more than 5.8 million new HIV infections occurred in 1997 and that 2.3 million people died that year, including 460,000 children. Since the start of the global epidemic in the late 1970s, about 11.7 million people have died, including 2.7 million children.

Estimated Current and Cumulative HIV/AIDS Cases by Region, Dec. 1997

Region	Current cases[1]	Percent of adults[2]
Sub-Saharan Africa	21,000,000	71
South/Southeast Asia	5,800,000	20
Latin America	1,300,000	4
North America	860,000	3
Western Europe	480,000	2
East Asia/Pacific	420,000	1
Caribbean	310,000	1
North Africa/Middle East	210,000	—
Eastern Europe/ Central Asia	190,000	—
Australasia	12,000	—
WORLD	**30,600,000**	**100[3]**

(1) Adults and children living with HIV/AIDS. (2) Percentage of total number of adults worldwide living with HIV. (3) Details do not add to total because of rounding. Dash (—) means less than 1%.

The World's Refugees

Source: *World Refugee Survey 1998,* U.S. Committee for Refugees, a nonprofit corp. These estimates are conservative. The refugees in this table include only those considered in need of protection and/or assistance and generally do not include those who have achieved permanent resettlement.

(as of Dec. 31, 1997; only countries estimated to host 50,000 or more refugees are listed)

Place of asylum	Origin of Most	Number
Total Africa		**2,944,000**
Algeria	Western Sahara, Mali, Niger	104,000[1]
Congo[2]	Angola, Sudan, Congo Rep., Rwanda, Burundi, Uganda	256,000[1]
Côte d'Ivoire	Liberia	202,000
Ethiopia	Somalia, Sudan	313,000[1]
Guinea	Liberia, Sierra Leone	430,000[1]
Kenya	Somalia, Sudan	196,000[1]
Liberia	Sierra Leone	100,000[1]
Sudan	Eritrea, Ethiopia	365,000[1]
Tanzania	Burundi, Congo[2]	295,000[1]
Uganda	Sudan, Congo[2], Rwanda	185,000
Zambia	Angola, Congo[2]	118,000[1]
Total Americas and the Caribbean		**616,000**
United States	Cuba, various other	491,000
Total East Asia and the Pacific		**535,000**
China	Vietnam	281,800[1]
Thailand	Myanmar, Cambodia, Laos	205,600
Total Europe and Former Soviet Republics		**2,022,000**
Armenia	Azerbaijan	219,150[1]
Azerbaijan	Armenia, Uzbekistan, Georgia	244,100[1]
Croatia	Bosnia and Herzegovina	50,000
Germany	Bosnia and Herzegovina, other	277,000[1]
Netherlands	Bosnia and Herzegovina, other	64,200
Russia	Former USSR, other	324,000[1]
United Kingdom	Bosnia and Herzegovina, other	58,100[1]
Yugoslavia[3]	Croatia, Bosnia and Herzegovina	550,000[1]
Total Middle East		**5,708,000**
Gaza Strip	Palestinians	748,000
Iran	Afghanistan, Iraq	1,900,000[1]
Iraq	Palestinians, Iran, Turkey	110,000
Jordan	Palestinians	1,413,800
Kuwait	Palestinians, Iraq	90,000
Lebanon	Palestinians, other	362,300
Saudi Arabia	Palestinians, Iraq	116,750
Syria	Palestinians	361,000
West Bank	Palestinians	543,000
Yemen	Somalia, Palestinians	64,900
Total South and Central Asia		**1,743,000**
India	Tibet, Sri Lanka, Bangladesh, Myanmar	323,500[1]
Nepal	Bhutan, Tibet	116,000
Pakistan	Afghanistan, India, other	1,215,650[1]
TOTAL REFUGEES		**13,568,000**

(1) Significant variance among sources in number reported. (2) Formerly Zaire. (3) Serbia/Montenegro.

Principal Sources of Refugees

Palestinians	3,743,000[1]
Afghanistan	2,622,000[1]
Bosnia and Herzegovina	559,000[1]
Iraq	526,000[1]
Somalia	486,000[1]
Liberia	475,000[1]
Sudan	353,000
Croatia	335,000[1]
Eritrea	323,000[1]
Sierra Leone	297,000[1]
Vietnam	281,000
Burundi	248,000[1]
Angola	223,000[1]
Azerbaijan	218,000[1]
Myanmar	215,000[1]
Armenia	188,000[1]
Congo (formerly Zaire)	132,000
Tibet	128,000
Bhutan	113,000[1]
Sri Lanka	100,000[1]
Western Sahara	86,000[1]

(1) Significant variance among sources in number reported.

U.S. Immigration Law

Source: Immigration and Naturalization Service, U.S. Dept. of Justice

Most U.S. regulations affecting immigration were modified in the Immigration and Nationality Act of 1952, which has been amended several times since then. Major amendments were made through the Immigration Act of 1990, which was signed by Pres. George Bush on Nov. 29, 1990. New provisions enacted in Sept. 1996 focused extensively on illegal immigration, as did legislation enacted in Nov. 1997. The 1996 legislation also changed rules for the sponsorship of legal immigrants. Provisions enacted in Oct. 1998 increased visa allowances for skilled workers above limits shown below.

The Immigration Act of 1990 raised the number of numerically limited immigrants entering the U.S. annually during fiscal year 1992-94 to 700,000 immigrants (excluding refugees whose admission numbers are announced annually and others not subject to limitation). Beginning in fiscal year 1995, the number dropped from 700,000 to 675,000, subject to adjustment based largely on the number of visas that had been issued in the previous year.

In fiscal year 1997, 226,000 visas were allowed for family immigrants, 140,000 for employment-based immigrants, 55,000 for "diversity immigrants."

Immediate Relatives (Family Immigrants)

Fiscal year 1992-94: 465,000 minus the number of "immediate relatives" admitted the previous fiscal year, plus any numbers unused by the employment-based preference system. During this period, the number of family-sponsored visas could not fall below 226,000. If visa availability dipped below this new floor, the shortfall was made up from the category below.

During this period, 55,000 additional visas were made available to the spouses and children of aliens legalized under the Immigration Reform and Control Act (IRCA) of 1986.

Fiscal year 1995 and beyond: 480,000 minus the number of "immediate relatives" admitted during the previous fiscal year, plus any unused numbers under the employment-based preference system. Family-sponsored visas cannot drop below 226,000.

Family Preference System

First preference—unmarried sons and daughters of U.S. citizens: 23,400 visas in FY 1997 plus unused visas from the 4th preference.

Second preference—spouses and unmarried children of Lawful Permanent Residents (LPRs): 114,200 visas, plus any visas available above the floor of 226,000 family preference visas, plus any unused visas from the previous preference.

The category is subdivided as follows: A minimum of 77% of the visas allocated to the category goes to the spouses and minor children of LPRs; 75% of the visas are issued without regard to per country ceilings, in the order in which the petitions were filed. A maximum of 23% of the category visa allocation goes to the unmarried sons and daughters of LPRs. This group of visas continues to be subject to per country ceilings.

Third preference—married sons and daughters of U.S. citizens; 23,400 visas plus unused visas from all earlier preferences.

Fourth preference—brothers and sisters of U.S. citizens: 65,000 plus unused visas from all earlier preferences.

Employment-Based Immigrants

The law allows a total of 140,000 plus, beginning in fiscal year 1994, any unused numbers under the family-sponsored system. These visas are distributed as follows:

First preference—Priority Workers—28.6% of the employment-based limit plus visas unused by the 4th and 5th employment-based preferences—"investors" and "special immigrants." The category is subdivided as follows: (1) extraordinary ability, demonstrated by sustained national or international acclaim, in the sciences, arts, education, business, and athletics; no U.S. employer required; (2) professors and researchers, seeking to enter in senior positions; U.S. employer required; (3) executives and managers of multinationals—requires one year of prior service with the firm during the preceding 3 years; the terms are extensively defined; U.S. employer required.

Second preference—Professionals with advanced degrees and aliens of exceptional ability—28.6% of the employment-based limit plus any unused "priority worker" visas. A U.S. employer and labor certification are required—although the Attorney General can waive both requirements. Members of the professions with advanced degrees or exceptional ability in the sciences, arts, or business. The possession of a degree, certificate, or license is not by itself considered sufficient evidence of exceptional ability.

Third preference—Skilled workers, professionals, and "other workers"—40,000 visas plus any visas unused by the 2 previous categories. Requires a U.S. employer and labor certification. Skilled workers must be in an occupation that requires at least 2 years training or experience. Professionals need a bachelor's degree. "Other workers" refers to unskilled workers. Their numbers are limited to visas per year.

Fourth preference—Special immigrants—7.1% of the employment-based limit. This category includes ministers of religion, foreign medical graduates, employees of the U.S. government abroad including certain employees of the U.S. mission in Hong Kong who file for admission as special immigrants before Jan. 1, 2002, retired employees of international organizations, etc.

Fifth preference—7.1% of the employment-based limit—7,000 for investors of $1 million in urban areas and 3,000 for investors of no less than $500,000 in rural or high-unemployment areas. The attorney general may increase the required investment amount up to $3 million for high employment areas. Investment must create employment for at least 10 U.S. workers.

Diversity Immigrant (DV) Category

Since FY 1995, the Immigration and Nationality Act has allowed 55,000 immigrant visas each fiscal year, distributed by lottery, to provide immigration opportunities for persons from countries other than the principal sources of immigration. DV visas are divided among six geographic regions. The allotment of FY 2000 visa numbers for each region had yet to be determined as of Oct. 15, 1998. Not more than 3,500 visas may be provided to immigrants from any one country.

The Nicaraguan and Central American Relief Act (NCARA) passed by Congress in Nov. 1997 stipulates that 5,000 of the 55,000 annually allocated diversity visas will be made available under the NCARA program.

The FY 2000 DV registration mail-in was held Oct. 1-31, 1998. During this one-month period, the National Visa Center in Portsmouth, NH, expected to receive between 6 to 7 million qualified entries. An estimated 1.5 million entries were expected to be disqualified for not providing the requested information or following published guidelines. Winners of visas will be notified between Apr. and July 1999.

In order to issue all 50,000 visas in FY 2000, the National Visa Center planned to register about 100,000 persons, both principal applicants and their spouses and children. Those selected would receive instructions on how to apply for an immigrant visa. During the visa interview, applicants must provide proof of a high school education or its equivalent, or must show two years of work experience within the past 5 years in an occupation which requires at least 2 years of training or experience. Those selected need to act on their immigrant visa applications quickly. As soon as the 50,000 visas are issued, the program for FY 2000 ends.

Sponsorship of Immigrants

Under the 1996 immigration law, sponsors of an immigrant entering the country as an immediate relative or as an employment-based immigrant who will be employed by either a relative or a relative's company must earn at least 125% of the poverty level. If the sponsor does not earn enough, a cosponsor may be found who will accept joint responsibility for the immigrant. Persons who are active members of the U.S. armed forces need earn only 100% of the poverty level to be accepted as sponsors.

The sponsor must sign a legally binding affidavit of support for an immigrant, which would be enforceable until the immigrant either became a citizen or worked and paid taxes for 40 quarters as determined by the Social Security Administration.

Naturalization: How to Become an American Citizen

Source: Federal Statutes

A person who desires to be naturalized as a citizen of the United States may obtain the necessary application form as well as detailed information from the nearest office of the Immigration and Naturalization Service or from the clerk of a court handling naturalization cases.

An applicant must be at least 18 years old and must have been a lawful resident of the U.S. continuously for 5 years. For husbands and wives of U.S. citizens the period is 3 years in most instances. Special provisions apply to certain veterans of the armed forces.

An applicant must have been physically present in the country for at least half of the required 5 years' residence and must:

(1) demonstrate an understanding of the English language, including an ability to read, write, and speak words in ordinary usage in English (persons physically unable to do so and persons who, on the examination date, are over 55 years of age and have been lawful permanent residents of the United States for 15 years or more, or who are over 50 and have been residents 20 or more years, are exempt);

(2) have been a person of good moral character, attached to the principles of the Constitution, and well disposed to the good order and happiness of the United States for 5 years just before filing the petition or for whatever other period of residence is required in the particular case and continue to be such a person; and

(3) demonstrate a knowledge and understanding of the fundamentals of the history, and the principles and form of government, of the United States. This can be done at private, designated testing entities or at the interview before an immigration examiner.

At the interview the applicant may be represented by a lawyer or social service agency. If action is favorable, there is a swearing in ceremony. The following oath of allegiance is administered:

I hereby declare, on oath, that I absolutely and entirely renounce and abjure all allegiance and fidelity to any foreign prince, potentate, state or sovereignty, to whom or which I have heretofore been a subject or citizen; that I will support and defend the Constitution and laws of the United States of America against all enemies, foreign and domestic; that I will bear true faith and allegiance to the same; that I will bear arms on behalf of the United States when required by the law; that I will perform noncombatant service in the armed forces of the United States when required by the law; that I will perform work of national importance under civilian direction when required by the law; and that I take this obligation freely without any mental reservation or purpose of evasion; so help me God.

Major International Organizations

Asia-Pacific Economic Cooperation Group (APEC), founded Nov. 1989 as a forum to further cooperation on trade and investment between nations of the region and the rest of the world. Members in 1998 were Australia, Brunei, Canada, Chile, China, Indonesia, Japan, Malaysia, Mexico, New Zealand, Papua New Guinea, Philippines, Singapore, South Korea, Taiwan, Thailand, and the United States. Headquarters: Singapore. Website: http://www.apecsec.org.sg

Association of Southeast Asian Nations (ASEAN), formed Aug. 1967 to promote economic, social, and cultural cooperation and development among states of the Southeast Asian region. Members in 1998 were Brunei, Cambodia, Indonesia, Laos, Malaysia, Myanmar, Philippines, Singapore, Thailand, and Vietnam. Annual ministerial meetings set policy; the organization has a central Secretariat and specialized intergovernmental committees. Headquarters: Jakarta. Website: http://www.asean.or.id

Caribbean Community and Common Market (CARICOM), established July 4, 1973. Its aim is to further cooperation in economics, health, education, culture, science and technology, and tax administration, as well as the coordination of foreign policy. Member in 1998 were Antigua and Barbuda, Bahamas (Community only), Barbados, Belize, Dominica, Haiti (provisional), Grenada, Guyana, Jamaica, Montserrat, Saint Kitts and Nevis, Saint Lucia, Saint Vincent and the Grenadines, Suriname, and Trinidad and Tobago. Headquarters: Georgetown, Guyana. Website: http://www.caricom.org

Commonwealth of Independent States (CIS), created Dec. 1991 upon the disbanding of the Soviet Union. An alliance of independent states, it is made up of former Soviet constituent republics. Members in 1998 were 12 of the 15: Armenia, Azerbaijan, Belarus, Georgia, Kazakhstan, Kyrgyzstan, Moldova, Russia, Tajikistan, Turkmenistan, Ukraine, and Uzbekistan. Policy is set through coordinating bodies such as a Council of Heads of State and Council of Heads of Government. Capital of the commonwealth: Minsk, Belarus.

The Commonwealth, originally called the British Commonwealth of Nations, then the Commonwealth of Nations; an association of nations and dependencies that were once parts of the former British Empire. The British monarch is the symbolic head of the Commonwealth.

There are 53 self-governing independent nations in the Commonwealth, plus various colonies and protectorates. As of 1998, members included United Kingdom and 15 other nations recognizing the British monarch, represented by a governor-general, as their head of state: Antigua and Barbuda, Australia, Bahamas, Barbados, Belize, Canada, Grenada, Jamaica, New Zealand, Papua New Guinea, Saint Kitts and Nevis, Saint Lucia, Saint Vincent and the Grenadines, Solomon Islands, and Tuvalu (special member). Also members were 38 countries with their own heads of state: Bangladesh, Botswana, Brunei, Cameroon, Cyprus, Dominica, The Gambia, Ghana, Guyana, India, Kenya, Kiribati, Lesotho, Malawi, Malaysia, Maldives, Malta, Mauritius, Mozambique, Namibia, Nauru (special member), Nigeria (suspended Nov. 1995), Pakistan, Samoa, Seychelles, Sierra Leone, Singapore, South Africa, Sri Lanka, Swaziland, Tanzania, Tonga, Trinidad and Tobago, Tuvalu (special member), Uganda, Vanuatu, Zambia, and Zimbabwe.

The Commonwealth facilitates consultation among members through meetings of prime ministers and finance ministers and through a permanent Secretariat. Headquarters: London.

European Free Trade Association (EFTA), created May 3, 1960, to promote expansion of free trade. By Dec. 31, 1966, tariffs and quotas between member nations had been eliminated. Members entered into free trade agreements with the EU in 1972 and 1973. In 1992 the EFTA and EU agreed to create a single market—with free flow of goods, services, capital, and labor—among nations of the 2 organizations. Members in 1998 were Iceland, Liechtenstein, Norway, and Switzerland. Many former EFTA members are now EU members. Headquarters: Geneva. Website: http://www.efta.int/structure/main/index.html

European Union (EU)—known as the European Community (EC) until 1994—the collective designation of 3 organizations with common membership: the European Economic Community (Common Market), the European Coal and Steel Community, and the European Atomic Energy Community (Euratom). The 15 full members in 1998 were Austria, Belgium, Denmark, Finland, France, Germany, Greece, Ireland, Italy, Luxembourg, Netherlands, Portugal, Spain, Sweden, and United Kingdom. Austria, Finland, and Sweden entered the EU on Jan. 1, 1995. Some 70 nations in Africa, the Caribbean, and the Pacific are affiliated under the Lomé Convention. Website: http://europa.eu.int/index.htm

A merger of the 3 communities' executives went into effect July 1, 1967, though the component organizations date back to 1951 and 1958. The Council of Ministers, European Commission, European Parliament, and European Court of Justice comprise the permanent structure. The EU aims to integrate the economies, coordinate social developments, and bring about political union of the member states. Effective Dec. 31, 1992, there are no restrictions on the movement of goods, services, capital, workers, and tourists within the EU. There are also common agricultural, fisheries, and nuclear research policies.

Leaders of member nations (12 at the time) met Dec. 9-11, 1991, in Maastricht, the Netherlands. Treaties and accompanying protocols agreed upon by the leaders committed the organization to launching a common currency (the euro) for at least some nations by 1999 (Britain and, later, Denmark and Sweden "opted out" of joining); sought to establish common foreign policies; laid the groundwork for a common defense policy; expanded the policy issues in which the organization would have a voice; gave the organization a leading role in social policy (Britain was not included in this plan); pledged increased aid for the 4 poorest member nations—Ireland, Greece, Spain, and Portugal; and slightly increased the powers of the 567-member European Parliament.

The treaties went into effect Nov. 1, 1993, following ratification by all 12 members.

In May 1998 it was announced that all member countries that had chosen to participate had met the criteria for adoption of the euro, except Greece. In June 1998 the European Central Bank was established.

Group of Eight (G-8), established Sept. 22, 1985; organization of 7 major industrial democracies (Canada, France, Germany, Italy, Japan, United Kingdom, and United States) and (later) Russia, meeting periodically to discuss world economic and other issues. At its annual economic summit in May 1998, the name was formally changed to G-8 from G-7. The original 7 are still free to meet without Russia on some issues, especially those relating to global finance.

International Criminal Police Organization (Interpol), created June 13, 1956, to promote mutual assistance among all police authorities within the limits of the law existing in the different countries. There were 177 members (independent nations), plus 14 subbureaus (dependencies) in 1998.

League of Arab States (Arab League), created Mar. 22, 1945. The League promotes economic, social, political, and military cooperation, mediates disputes, and represents Arab states in certain international negotiations. Members in 1998 were Algeria, Bahrain, Comoros, Djibouti, Egypt, Iraq, Jordan, Kuwait, Lebanon, Libya, Mauritania, Morocco, Oman, Palestine (considered an independent state by the League), Qatar, Saudi Arabia, Somalia, Sudan, Syria, Tunisia, United Arab Emirates, and Yemen. Headquarters: Cairo.

North Atlantic Treaty Organization (NATO), created by treaty (signed Apr. 4, 1949; in effect Aug. 24, 1949). Members in 1998 were Belgium, Canada, Denmark, France, Germany, Greece, Iceland, Italy, Luxembourg, Netherlands, Norway, Portugal, Spain, Turkey, United Kingdom, and United States. Members agreed to settle disputes by peaceful means, develop their individual and collective capacity to resist armed attack, to regard an attack on one as an attack on all, and take necessary action to repel an attack under Article 51 of the UN Charter. Website: http://www.nato.int

The NATO structure consists of a Council, the Defense Planning Committee, the Military Committee (consisting of 2 commands: Allied Command Europe, Allied Command Atlantic), Nuclear Planning Group, and Canada-U.S. Regional Planning Group. France detached itself from the military command structure in 1966.

With the dissolution of the Soviet Union and the end of the cold war in the early 1990s, members sought to modify the NATO mission, putting greater stress on political action and creating a rapid deployment force to react to local crises. By the mid-1990s, 27 nations, including Russia and other former

Soviet republics, had joined with NATO in the so-called Partnership for Peace (PfP; drafted Dec. 1993), which provided for limited joint military exercises, peace-keeping missions, and information exchange. NATO has proceeded cautiously toward extending full membership to former Eastern bloc nations. On July 8, 1997, 3 former Warsaw Pact members, Hungary, Poland, and the Czech Republic, were invited to join NATO, with formal accession taking place in 1999 after ratification by NATO member states.

In Dec. 1995, a NATO-led multinational force was deployed to help keep the peace in Bosnia and Herzegovina. Headquarters: Brussels.

Organization of African Unity (OAU), formed May 25, 1963, by 32 African countries (53 members in 1997) to promote peace and security as well as economic and social development. It holds annual conferences of heads of state. Headquarters: Addis Ababa, Ethiopia.

Organization of American States (OAS), formed in Bogotá, Colombia, Apr. 30, 1948. It has a Permanent Council, Inter-American Council for Integral Development, Juridical Committee, and Commission on Human Rights. The Permanent Council can call meetings of foreign ministers to deal with urgent security matters. A General Assembly meets annually. There are 35 members: Antigua and Barbuda, Argentina, Bahamas, Barbados, Belize, Bolivia, Brazil, Canada, Chile, Colombia, Costa Rica, Cuba, Dominica, Dominican Republic, Ecuador, El Salvador, Grenada, Guatemala, Guyana, Haiti, Honduras, Jamaica, Mexico, Nicaragua, Panama, Paraguay, Peru, Saint Kitts and Nevis, Saint Lucia, Saint Vincent and the Grenadines, Suriname, Trinidad and Tobago, United States, Uruguay, and Venezuela. In 1962, the OAS suspended Cuba from participation in OAS activities but not from OAS membership. Headquarters: Washington, DC. Website: http://www.oas.org

Organization for Economic Cooperation and Development (OECD), established Sept. 30, 1961, to promote the economic and social welfare of member countries and to stimulate efforts on behalf of developing nations. The OECD also collects and disseminates economic and environmental information. Members in 1998 were Australia, Austria, Belgium, Canada, Czech Republic, Denmark, Finland, France, Germany, Greece, Hungary, Iceland, Ireland, Italy, Japan, Luxembourg, Mexico, Netherlands, New Zealand, Norway, Poland, Portugal, South Korea, Spain, Sweden, Switzerland, Turkey, United Kingdom, and the United States. Headquarters: Paris. Website: http://www.oecd.org

Organization of Petroleum Exporting Countries (OPEC), created Sept. 14, 1960. The group attempts to set world oil prices by controlling oil production. It also pursues members' interests in trade and development dealings with industrialized oil-consuming nations. Members in 1998 were Algeria, Indonesia, Iran, Iraq, Kuwait, Libya, Nigeria, Qatar, Saudi Arabia, United Arab Emirates, and Venezuela. Headquarters: Vienna. Website: http://www.opec.org

Organization for Security and Cooperation in Europe (OSCE), established in 1972 as the Conference on Security and Cooperation in Europe; current name adopted Jan. 1, 1995. The group, formed by NATO and Warsaw Pact members, is interested in furthering East-West relations through a commitment to nonaggression and human rights as well as cooperation in economics, science and technology, cultural exchange, and environmental protection.

There were 55 member states in 1998. Headquarters: Vienna. Website: http://www.osce.org

United Nations

The 53d regular session of United Nations General Assembly opened in Sept. 1997.

UN headquarters is in New York, NY, between First Ave. and Roosevelt Drive and E. 42d St. and E. 48th St. The General Assembly Bldg., Secretariat, Conference and Library bldgs. are interconnected.

Some 53,300 people work in the UN system, which includes the Secretariat and 30 other organizations.

The UN has a post office originating its own stamps.

Proposals to establish an organization of nations for maintenance of world peace led to the United Nations Conference on International Organization at San Francisco, Apr. 25-June 26, 1945, where the charter of the United Nations was drawn up. It was signed June 26 by 50 nations, and by Poland, one of the original 51 UN members, on Oct. 15, 1945. The charter came into effect Oct. 24, 1945, upon ratification by the permanent members of the Security Council and a majority of other signatories.

Purposes: To maintain international peace and security; to develop friendly relations among nations; to achieve international cooperation in solving economic, social, cultural, and humanitarian problems and in promoting respect for human rights and fundamental freedoms; to be a center for harmonizing the actions of nations in attaining these common ends.

Visitors to the UN: Headquarters is open to the public every day of the year except Christmas and New Year's Day. Guided tours are given approximately every half hour from 9:15 AM to 4:45 PM daily, except on weekends during January and February. Groups of 12 or more persons should write to the Group Program Unit, Public Services Section, Room GA-63, United Nations, New York, NY 10017, or telephone (212) 963-4440. Children under 5 are not permitted on tours.

Roster of the United Nations

The 185 members of the United Nations, with the years in which they became members; as of Sept. 1998

Member	Year	Member	Year	Member	Year	Member	Year
Afghanistan	1946	Burundi	1962	Equatorial Guinea	1968	Israel	1949
Albania	1955	Cambodia[1]	1955	Eritrea	1993	Italy	1955
Algeria	1962	Cameroon	1960	Estonia	1991	Jamaica	1962
Andorra	1993	Canada	1945	Ethiopia	1945	Japan	1956
Angola	1976	Cape Verde	1975	Fiji	1970	Jordan	1955
Antigua and Barbuda	1981	Central African Republic	1960	Finland	1955	Kazakhstan	1992
Argentina	1945	Chad	1960	France	1945	Kenya	1963
Armenia	1992	Chile	1945	Gabon	1960	Korea, North	1991
Australia	1945	China[2]	1945	Gambia, The	1965	Korea, South	1991
Austria	1955	Colombia	1945	Georgia	1992	Kuwait	1963
Azerbaijan	1992	Comoros	1975	Germany	1973	Kyrgyzstan	1992
Bahamas	1973	Congo, Democratic Republic of the (Zaire)	1960	Ghana	1957	Laos	1955
Bahrain	1971	Congo, Republic of the	1960	Greece	1945	Latvia	1991
Bangladesh	1974	Costa Rica	1945	Grenada	1974	Lebanon	1945
Barbados	1966	Côte d'Ivoire	1960	Guatemala	1945	Lesotho	1966
Belarus	1945	Croatia	1992	Guinea	1958	Liberia	1945
Belgium	1945	Cuba	1945	Guinea-Bissau	1974	Libya	1955
Belize	1981	Cyprus	1960	Guyana	1966	Liechtenstein	1990
Benin	1960	Czech Republic[3]	1993	Haiti	1945	Lithuania	1991
Bhutan	1971	Denmark	1945	Honduras	1945	Luxembourg	1945
Bolivia	1945	Djibouti	1977	Hungary	1955	Macedonia[6]	1993
Bosnia and Herzegovina	1992	Dominica	1978	Iceland	1946	Madagascar	1960
Botswana	1966	Dominican Republic	1945	India	1945	Malawi	1964
Brazil	1945	Ecuador	1945	Indonesia[5]	1950	Malaysia[7]	1957
Brunei	1984	Egypt[4]	1945	Iran	1945	Maldives	1965
Bulgaria	1955	El Salvador	1945	Iraq	1945	Mali	1960
Burkina Faso	1960			Ireland	1955	Malta	1964

Member	Year	Member	Year	Member	Year	Member	Year
Marshall Islands	1991	Pakistan	1947	São Tomé and Príncipe	1975	Thailand	1946
Mauritania	1961	Palau	1994	Saudi Arabia	1945	Togo	1960
Mauritius	1968	Panama	1945	Senegal	1960	Trinidad and Tobago	1962
Mexico	1945	Papua New Guinea	1975	Seychelles	1976	Tunisia	1956
Micronesia	1991	Paraguay	1945	Sierra Leone	1961	Turkey	1945
Moldova	1992	Peru	1945	Singapore[7]	1965	Turkmenistan	1992
Monaco	1993	Philippines	1945	Slovakia[3]	1993	Uganda	1962
Mongolia	1961	Poland	1945	Slovenia	1992	Ukraine	1945
Morocco	1956	Portugal	1955	Solomon Islands	1978	United Arab Emirates	1971
Mozambique	1975	Qatar	1971	Somalia	1960	United Kingdom	1945
Myanmar (Burma)	1948	Romania	1955	South Africa[9]	1945	United States	1945
Namibia	1990	Russia[8]	1945	Spain	1955	Uruguay	1945
Nepal	1955	Rwanda	1962	Sri Lanka	1955	Uzbekistan	1992
Netherlands	1945	Saint Kitts and Nevis	1983	Sudan	1956	Vanuatu	1981
New Zealand	1945	Saint Lucia	1979	Suriname	1975	Venezuela	1945
Nicaragua	1945	Saint Vincent and		Swaziland	1968	Vietnam	1977
Niger	1960	the Grenadines	1980	Sweden	1946	Yemen[11]	1947
Nigeria	1960	Samoa (formerly West-		Syria[4]	1945	Yugoslavia[12]	1945
Norway	1945	ern Samoa)	1976	Tajikistan	1992	Zambia	1964
Oman	1971	San Marino	1992	Tanzania[10]	1961	Zimbabwe	1980

(1) Cambodia's seat in the General Assembly was declared vacant in Sept. 1997, after a dispute over which faction should be seated, following a July 1997 coup. (2) The General Assembly voted in 1971 to expel the Chinese government on Taiwan and admit the Beijing government in its place. (3) Czechoslovakia, which split into the separate nations of the Czech Republic and Slovakia on Jan. 1, 1993, was a UN member from 1945 to 1992. (4) Egypt and Syria were original members of the UN. In 1958, the United Arab Republic was established by a union of Egypt and Syria and continued as a single member of the UN. In 1961, Syria resumed its separate membership. (5) Indonesia withdrew from the UN in 1965 and rejoined in 1966. (6) Admitted under the provisional name of The Former Yugoslav Republic of Macedonia. (7) Malaya joined the UN in 1957. In 1963, its name was changed to Malaysia following the accession of Singapore, Sabah, and Sarawak. Singapore became an independent UN member in 1965. (8) The Union of Soviet Socialist Republics was an original member of the UN from 1945. After the USSR's dissolution in 1991, Russia informed the UN it would be continuing the USSR's membership in the Security Council and all other UN organs with the support of the Commonwealth of Independent States (comprised of most of the former Soviet republics). (9) In 1994, the General Assembly accepted the credentials of the South African delegation, which had been rejected for 24 years because of the country's former apartheid policies. (10) Tanganyika was a member of the UN from 1961 and Zanzibar was a member from 1963. Following the ratification in 1964 of Articles of Union between Tanganyika and Zanzibar, the United Republic of Tanganyika and Zanzibar continued as a single member of the UN, later changing its name to United Republic of Tanzania. (11) The Yemen Arab Republic was admitted in 1947; the People's Republic of Yemen, in 1967. The two nations merged in 1990. (12) The Socialist Federal Republic of Yugoslavia became a member in 1945. After four of its six republics (Bosnia and Herzegovina, Croatia, Macedonia, and Slovenia) declared independence in 1991-92, the two remaining republics, Montenegro and Serbia, reconstituted themselves as the Federal Republic of Yugoslavia, which assumed Yugoslavia's UN seat Apr. 8, 1992. In Sept. 1992, the General Assembly decided the Federal Republic of Yugoslavia should apply for membership as it could not automatically take the seat of the former Yugoslavia. **Note:** The following sovereign countries are not members of the United Nations: China (Taiwan), Kiribati, Nauru, Switzerland, Tonga, Tuvalu, Vatican City (Holy See).

United Nations Secretaries General

Year	Secretary, Nation	Year	Secretary, Nation	Year	Secretary, Nation
1946	Trygve Lie, Norway	1972	Kurt Waldheim, Austria	1992	Boutros Boutros-Ghali, Egypt
1953	Dag Hammarskjold, Sweden	1982	Javier Perez de Cuellar, Peru	1997	Kofi Annan, Ghana
1961	U Thant, Burma				

U.S. Representatives to the United Nations

The U.S. Representative to the United Nations is the Chief of the U.S. Mission to the United Nations in New York and holds the rank and status of Ambassador Extraordinary and Plenipotentiary (A.E.P.).

Year	Representative	Year	Representative	Year	Representative
1946	Edward R. Stettinius, Jr.	1968	James Russell Wiggins	1981	Jeane J. Kirkpatrick
1946	Herschel V. Johnson (act.)	1969	Charles W. Yost	1985	Vernon A. Walters
1947	Warren R. Austin	1971	George Bush	1989	Thomas R. Pickering
1953	Henry Cabot Lodge, Jr.	1973	John A. Scali	1992	Edward J. Perkins
1960	James J. Wadsworth	1975	Daniel P. Moynihan	1993	Madeleine K. Albright
1961	Adlai E. Stevenson	1976	William W. Scranton	1997	Bill Richardson
1965	Arthur J. Goldberg	1977	Andrew Young	1998	A. Peter Burleigh (deputy representative; acting)
1968	George W. Ball	1979	Donald McHenry		

Organization of the United Nations

The text of the UN Charter may be obtained from the Public Inquiries Unit, Department of Public Information, United Nations, New York, NY 10017. (212) 963-4475.

General Assembly. The General Assembly is composed of representatives of all the member nations. Each nation is entitled to one vote.

The General Assembly meets in regular annual sessions and in special session when necessary. Special sessions are convoked by the secretary general at the request of the Security Council or of a majority of the members of the UN.

On important questions a two-thirds majority of members present and voting is required; on other questions a simple majority is sufficient.

The General Assembly must approve the UN budget and apportion expenses among members. A member in arrears can lose its vote if the amount of arrears equals or exceeds the amount of the contributions due for the preceding 2 full years.

Security Council. The Security Council consists of 15 members, 5 with permanent seats. The remaining 10 are elected for 2-year terms by the General Assembly; they are not eligible for immediate reelection.

Permanent members of the Council are: China, France, Russia, United Kingdom, and the United States.

Nonpermanent members are: (with terms expiring Dec. 31, 1998) Costa Rica, Japan, Kenya, Portugal, and Sweden; and (with terms expiring Dec. 31, 1999) Bahrain, Brazil, Gabon, Gambia, and Slovenia.

The Security Council has the primary responsibility within the UN for maintaining international peace and security. The Council may investigate any dispute that threatens international peace and security.

Any member of the UN at UN headquarters may, if invited by the Council, participate in its discussions and a nation not a member of the UN may appear if it is a party to a dispute.

Decisions on procedural questions are made by an affirmative vote of 9 members. On all other matters the affirmative vote of 9 members must include the concurring votes of all permanent members; it is this clause which gives rise to the so-called veto power of permanent members. A party to a dispute must refrain from voting.

The Security Council directs the various peacekeeping forces deployed throughout the world.

Economic and Social Council. The Economic and Social Council consists of 54 members elected by the General Assembly for 3-year terms. The council is responsible for carrying out UN functions with regard to international economic, social, cultural, educational, health, and related matters. It meets once a year.

Trusteeship Council. The administration of trust territories was under UN supervision; however, all 11 Trust Territories have attained their right to self-determination. The work of the Council has, therefore, been suspended.

Secretariat. The Secretary General is the chief administrative officer of the UN. He may bring to the attention of the Security Council any matter that threatens international peace. He reports to the General Assembly.

Budget: The General Assembly approved a total budget for 1997-98 of $2.61 billion.

International Court of Justice (World Court). The International Court of Justice is the principal judicial organ of the United Nations. All members are *ipso facto* parties to the statute of the Court. Other states may become parties to the Court's statute.

The Court has jurisdiction over cases which the parties submit to it and matters especially provided for in the charter or in treaties. The Court gives advisory opinions and renders judgments. Its decisions are binding only between parties concerned and in respect to a particular dispute. If any party to a case fails to heed a judgment, the other party may have recourse to the Security Council.

The 15 judges are elected for 9-year terms by the General Assembly and the Security Council. Retiring judges are eligible for reelection. The Court remains permanently in session, except during vacations. All questions are decided by majority. The International Court of Justice sits in The Hague, Netherlands.

Selected Specialized and Related Agencies

These agencies are autonomous, with their own memberships and organs, and have a functional relationship or working agreement with the UN (headquarters), except for UNICEF and UNHCR, which report directly to the Economic and Social Council and to the General Assembly.

Food and Agriculture Organization (FAO), aims to increase production from farms, forests, and fisheries; improve food distribution and marketing, nutrition, and the living conditions of rural people. (Viale delle Terme di Caracalla, 00100 Rome, Italy.)

International Atomic Energy Agency (IAEA), aims to promote the safe, peaceful uses of atomic energy. (Vienna International Centre, PO Box 100, A-1400, Vienna, Austria.)

International Bank for Reconstruction and Development (IBRD) (World Bank), provides loans and technical assistance for projects in developing member countries; encourages cofinancing for projects from other public and private sources. The IBRD has 4 affiliates: (1) The **International Development Association (IDA)** provides funds for development projects on concessionary terms to the poorer developing member countries. (2) The **International Finance Corporation (IFC)** promotes the growth of the private sector in developing member countries; encourages the development of local capital markets; stimulates the international flow of private capital. (3) The **Multilateral Investment Guarantee Agency (MIGA)** promotes private investment in developing countries; guarantees investments to protect investors from noncommercial risks, such as nationalization; advises governments on attracting private investment. (4) The **International Center for Settlement of Investment Disputes (ICSID)** provides conciliation and arbitration services for disputes between foreign investors and host governments which arise out of an investment. (1818 H St., NW, Washington, DC 20433.)

International Civil Aviation Org. (ICAO), promotes international civil aviation standards and regulations. (999 University St., Montreal, Quebec, Canada H3C 5H7.)

International Fund for Agricultural Development (IFAD), aims to mobilize funds for agricultural and rural projects in developing countries. (107 Via del Seratico, 00142 Rome, Italy.)

International Labor Org. (ILO), aims to promote employment; improve labor conditions and living standards. (4 route de Morillons, CH-1211 Geneva 22, Switzerland.)

International Maritime Org. (IMO), aims to promote cooperation on technical matters affecting international shipping. (4 Albert Embankment, London SE1 7SR, England.)

International Monetary Fund (IMF), aims to promote international monetary cooperation and currency stabilization and expansion of international trade. (700 19th St., NW, Washington, DC 20431.)

International Telecommunication Union (ITU), establishes international regulations for radio, telegraph, telephone, and space radio-communications, allocates radio frequencies. (Place des Nations, 1211 Geneva 20, Switzerland.)

United Nations Children's Fund (UNICEF), provides financial aid and development assistance to programs for children and mothers in developing countries. (3 UN Plaza, New York, NY 10017.)

United Nations Educational, Scientific, and Cultural Org. (UNESCO), aims to promote collaboration among nations through education, science, and culture. (7 Place de Fontenoy, 75352 Paris 07SP, France.)

United Nations High Commissioner for Refugees (UNHCR), provides essential assistance for refugees. (Place des Nations, 1211 Geneva 10, Switzerland.)

Universal Postal Union (UPU), aims to perfect postal services and promote international collaboration. (Weltpoststrasse 4, 3000 Berne, 15 Switzerland.)

World Health Org. (WHO), aims to aid the attainment of the highest possible level of health. (1211 Geneva 27, Switzerland.)

World Intellectual Property Org. (WIPO), seeks to protect, through international cooperation, literary, industrial, scientific, and artistic works. (34, Chemin des Colom Bettes, 1211 Geneva, Switzerland.)

World Meteorological Org. (WMO), aims to coordinate and improve world meteorological work. (41, Avenue Giuseppe-Motta, Case Postale 2300, 1211 Geneva 2, Switzerland.)

World Trade Org. (WTrO), replacing the General Agreement on Tariffs and Trade (GATT), is the major body overseeing international trade. The WTrO administers trade agreements and treaties, examines the trade regimes of members, keeps track of various trade measures and statistics, and attempts to settle trade disputes. (Centre William Rappard, 154 rue de Lausanne, 1211 Geneva 21, Switzerland.)

Geneva Conventions

The Geneva Conventions are 4 international treaties governing the protection of civilians in time of war, the treatment of prisoners of war, and the care of the wounded and sick in the armed forces. The first convention, covering the sick and wounded, was concluded in Geneva, Switzerland, in 1864; it was amended and expanded in 1906. A third convention, in 1929, covered prisoners of war. Outrage at the treatment of prisoners and civilians during World War II by some belligerents, notably Germany and Japan, prompted the conclusion, in Aug. 1949, of 4 new conventions. Three of these restated and strengthened the previous conventions, and the fourth codified general principles of international law governing the treatment of civilians in wartime.

The 1949 convention for civilians provided for special safeguards for the following: wounded persons, children under 15, pregnant women, and the elderly. Discrimination was forbidden on racial, religious, national, or political grounds. Torture, collective punishment, reprisals, the unwarranted destruction of property, and the forced use of civilians for an occupier's armed forces were also prohibited.

Also included in the new 1949 treaties was a pledge to treat prisoners humanely, feed them adequately, and deliver relief supplies to them. They were not to be forced to disclose more than minimal information.

Most countries have formally accepted all or most of the humanitarian conventions as binding. A nation is not free to withdraw its ratification of the conventions during wartime. However, there is no permanent machinery in place to apprehend, try, or punish violators.

Ambassadors and Envoys

"Envoys from the United States" as of Aug. 1998. "Envoys to the United States" as of Sept. 1998. The address of U.S. embassies abroad is the appropriate foreign capital. The U.S. does not have diplomatic relations with the following countries: Cuba[1], Iran[2], Iraq[3], Libya[4], Liechtenstein, North Korea, and Taiwan[5]. There are informal relations with Bhutan.

COUNTRIES	ENVOYS FROM U.S.	ENVOYS TO U.S.
Afghanistan	None	Yar Mohammad Mohabbat, Chargé
Albania	Marisa R. Lino, Amb.	Petrit Bushati, Amb.
Algeria	Cameron R. Hume, Amb.	Ramtane Lamamra, Amb.
Andorra	Edward L. Romero, Amb.	Juli Minoves Triquell, Amb.
Angola	Donald K. Steinberg, Amb.	Antonio dos Santos Franca, Amb.
Antigua & Barbuda	Vacancy	Lionel A. Hurst, Amb.
Argentina	Vacancy	Diego Ramiro Guelar, Amb.
Armenia	Michael Craig Lemmon, Amb.	Rouben Robert Shugarian, Amb.
Australia	Genta Hawkins Holmes, Amb.	Andrew S. Peacock, Amb.
Austria	Kathryn Walt Hall, Amb.	Helmut Tuerk, Amb.
Azerbaijan	Stanley Tuemler Escudero, Amb.	Hafiz Mir Jalal Oglu Pashayev, Amb.
Bahamas	Sidney Williams, Amb.	Arlington Griffith Butler, Amb.
Bahrain	Johnny Young, Amb.	Muhammad Abdul Ghaffar, Amb.
Bangladesh	John C. Holzman, Amb.	K.M. Shehabuddin, Amb.
Barbados	Vacancy	Courtney N. M. Blackman, Amb.
Belarus	Daniel W. Speckhard, Amb.	Valery V. Tsepkalo, Amb.
Belgium	Paul L. Cejas, Amb.	Alexis Reyn, Amb.
Belize	Carolyn Curiel, Amb.	James S. Murphy, Amb.
Benin	John M. Yates, Amb.	Lucien Tonoukouin, Amb.
Bolivia	Donna Jean Hrinak, Amb.	Marcelo Perez Monasterios, Amb.
Bosnia and Herzegovina	Richard D. Kauzlarich, Amb.	Sven Alkalaj, Amb.
Botswana	Robert Krueger, Amb.	Archibald Mooketsa Mogwe, Amb.
Brazil	Melvyn Levitsky, Amb.	Paulo Tarso Flecha de Lima, Amb.
Brunei	Glen R. Rase, Amb.	Pengiran Anak Dato Puteh, Amb.
Bulgaria	Avis T. Bohlen, Amb.	Philip Dimitrov Dimitrov, Amb.
Burkina Faso	Sharon P. Wilkinson, Amb.	Bruno Zidouemba, Amb.
Burundi	Morris N. Hughes Jr., Amb.	Thomas Ndikumana, Chargé
Cambodia	Kenneth M. Quinn, Amb.	Huoth Var, Amb.
Cameroon	Charles H. Twining, Amb.	Jerome Mendouga, Amb.
Canada	Gordon Giffin, Amb.	Raymond A. J. Chretien, Amb.
Cape Verde	Lawrence N. Benedict, Amb.	Manuel De Matos, Chargé
Central African Republic	Vacant, Amb.	Henry Koba, Amb.
Chad	David C. Halsted, Amb.	Ahmat Mahamat-Saleh, Amb.
Chile	John O'Leary, Amb.	Daniel G. Carvallo, Chargé
China	Jim Sasser, Amb.	Li Zhao Xing, Amb.
Colombia	Curtis Warren Kammen, Amb.	Juan Carlos Esguerra, Amb.
Comoros	Harold W. Geisel, Amb.	Ahmed Djabir, Amb.
Congo, Dem. Rep. of the (formerly Zaire)	Daniel H. Simpson, Amb.	Faida Mitifu, Chargé
Congo Republic	Aubrey Hooks, Amb.	Serge Mombouli, Chargé
Costa Rica	Thomas J. Dodd, Amb.	Jaime Daremblum, Amb.
Côte d'Ivoire	Lannon Walker, Amb.	Koffi Moise Koumoue, Amb.
Croatia	William D. Montgomery, Amb.	Miomir Zuzul, Amb.
Cyprus	Kenneth C. Brill, Amb.	Erato Kozakou-Markoullis, Amb.
Czech Republic	Jenonne R. Walker, Amb.	Alexandr Vondra, Amb.
Denmark	Edward E. Elson, Amb.	K. Erik Tygesen, Amb.
Djibouti	Lange Schermerhorn*	Roble Olhaye, Amb.
Dominica	Jeanette W. Hyde, Amb.	Nicholas J.O. Liverpool
Dominican Republic	Vacant.	Bernardo Vega, Amb.
Ecuador	Leslie M. Alexander, Amb.	Alberto F. Maspons, Amb.
Egypt	Daniel C. Kurtzer, Amb.	Ahmed Maher El Sayed, Amb.
El Salvador	Anne W. Patterson, Amb.	Rene A. Leon, Amb.
Equatorial Guinea	Charles H. Twining, Amb.	Pastor Micha Ondo Bile, Amb.
Eritrea	William D. clarke, Amb.	Semere Russon, Amb.
Estonia	Vacant.	Grigore-Kalev Stoicescu, Amb.
Ethiopia	David H. Shinn, Amb.	Berhane Gebre-Christos, Amb.
Fiji	Vacant.	Napolioni Masirewa, Amb.
Finland	Eric S. Edelman, Amb.	Jaakko Laajava, Amb.
France	Felix Rohatyn, Amb.	Francois V. Bujon, Amb.
Gabon	Elizabeth Raspolic, Amb.	Paul Boundoukou-Latha, Amb.
Gambia, The	Gearge W. B. Haley, Amb.	Crispin Grey Johnson, Amb.
Georgia	Kenneth S. Yalowitz, Amb.	Tedo Japaridze, Amb.
Germany	John Kornblum, Amb.	Juergen Chrobog, Amb.
Ghana	Edward Brynn, Amb.	Kobina Arthur Koomson, Amb.
Greece	R. Nicholas Burns, Amb.	Alexandre Philon, Amb.
Grenada	Vacant.	Denis G. Antoine, Amb.
Guatemala	Donald J. Planty, Amb.	William Howard Stixrud Herrera, Amb.
Guinea	Tibor P. Nagy Jr., Amb.	Mohamed Aly Thiam, Amb.
Guinea-Bissau	Peggy Blackford, Amb.	Mario Lopes da Rosa, Amb.
Guyana	James Mack, Amb.	Mohammed Ali Odeen Ishmael, Amb.
Haiti	Timothy M. Carney, Amb.	Louis Harold Joseph, Chargé
Honduras	James F. Creagan, Amb.	Edgardo Dumas, Amb.
Hungary	Peter F. Tufo, Amb.	Gyorgy Banlaki, Amb.
Iceland	Day Olin Mount, Amb.	Jon Baldvin Hannibalsson, Amb.
India	Richard F. Celeste, Amb.	Naresh Chandra, Amb.
Indonesia	J. Stapleton Roy, Amb.	Dorodjatun Kuntjoro Jakti, Amb.
Ireland	Jean Kennedy Smith, Amb.	Sean O'Huiginn, Amb.
Israel	Edward S. Walker, Amb.	Zalman Shoval, Amb.
Italy	Thomas M. Foglietta, Amb.	Ferdinando Salleo, Amb.
Jamaica	Stanley L. McLelland, Amb.	Richard Leighton Bernal, Amb.
Japan	Tom Foley*	Kunihiko Saito, Amb.
Jordan	William J. Burns, Amb.	Marwan Jamil Muasher, Amb.
Kazakhstan	A. Elizabeth Jones, Amb.	Bolat K. Nurgaliyev, Amb.
Kenya	Prudence Bushnell, Amb.	Samson Kipkoech Chemai, Amb.

COUNTRIES	ENVOYS FROM U.S.	ENVOYS TO U.S.
Kiribati	Joan M. Plaisted, Amb.	None
Korea, South	Steven Bosworth*	Lee Hong Koo, Amb.
Kuwait	James A. Larocco, Amb.	Mohammed Sabah Al-Salim Al-Sabah, Amb.
Kyrgyzstan	Anne Marie Sigmund, Amb	Almas Chukin, Chargé
Laos	Wendy Jean Chamberlin, Amb.	Vang Rattanavong, Amb.
Latvia	Larry C. Napper, Amb..	Ojars Eriks Kalnins, Amb.
Lebanon	Richard H. Jones, Amb.	Mohamad Baha Chatah, Amb.
Lesotho	Katherine Peterson, Amb..	Eunice M. Bulane, Amb.
Liberia	William B. Milam, Chargé	Rachel Diggs, Amb.
Lithuania	Keith Smith, Amb.	Stasys Sakalauskas, Amb.
Luxembourg	Clay Constantinou, Amb.	Arlette Conzemius, Amb.
Macedonia	Christopher R. Hill, Amb.	Lubica Z. Acevska, Amb.
Madagascar	Shirley Elizabeth Barnes, Amb.	Biclair Henri G. Andrianantoandro, Chargé
Malawi	Amelia E. Shippy, Amb.	Willie Chokani, Amb.
Malaysia	John R. Malott, Amb..	Dato Dali Mahmud Hashim, Amb.
Maldives	Shaun E. Donnelly, Amb.	None
Mali	David P. Rawson, Amb.	Cheick Oumar Diarrah, Amb.
Malta	Katheryn L. H. Proffitt, Amb.	Mark Anthony Micallef, Amb.
Marshall Islands	Joan M. Plaisted, Amb.	Banny de Brum, Amb.
Mauritania	Timberlake Foster, Amb.	Ahmed Ould Sid Ahmed, Amb.
Mauritius	Harold W. Geisel, Amb..	Chitmansing Jesseramsing, Amb.
Mexico	Jeffrey Davidow	Jesus Reyes Heroles, Amb.
Micronesia	Vacancy	Jesse B. Marehalau, Amb.
Moldova	Rudolf Vilem Perina, Amb.	Vlad Spanu, Chargé.
Mongolia	Alphonse F. LaPorta*	Jalbuu Choinhor, Chargé
Morocco	Edward M. Gabriel, Amb..	Mohamed Benaissa, Amb.
Mozambique	Brian Dean Curran*	Marcos G. Namashulua, Amb.
Myanmar	Kent M.Wiedemann, Chargé	Tin Winn, Amb.
Namibia	George F. Ward Jr., Amb.	Veiccoh K. Nghiwete, Amb.
Nauru	Vacant	None
Nepal	Ralph Frank, Amb.	Damodar Prasad Guatam, Amb.
Netherlands	Cynthia P. Schneider, Amb.	Joris M. Vos, Amb.
New Zealand	Josiah Horton Beeman, Amb.	James Brendan Bolger, Amb.
Nicaragua	Lino Gutierrez, Amb.	Francisco Aguirre Sacasa, Amb.
Niger	Charles O. Cecil, Amb.	Joseph Diatta, Amb.
Nigeria	William H. Twaddell, Amb.	Wakili Hassan Adamu, Amb.
Norway	David B. Hermelin, Amb..	Tom Eric Vraalsen, Amb.
Oman	Frances D. Cook, Amb.	Abdulla Moh'd. Aqeel Al-Dhahab, Amb.
Pakistan	Thomas W. Simons Jr., Amb.	Riaz H. Khokhar, Amb.
Palau	Thomas C. Hubbard, Amb.	Hersey Kyota, Amb.
Panama	William J. Hughes, Amb.	Eloy Alfaro, Amb.
Papua New Guinea	Arma Jane Karaer, Amb.	Nagora Bogan, Amb.
Paraguay	Maura Harty, Amb.	Elianne Cibils, Chargé
Peru	Dennis C. Jett, Amb.	Ricardo V. Luna, Amb.
Philippines	Thomas C. Hubbard, Amb.	Raul Chaves Rabe, Amb.
Poland	Daniel Fried, Amb.	Jerzy Kozminski, Amb.
Portugal	Gerald S. McGowan, Amb.	Fernando Andresen Guimaraes, Amb.
Qatar	Patrick N. Theros, Amb.	Saad Mohamed Al Kobaisi, Amb.
Romania	James C. Rosapepe, Amb..	Mircea Dan Geoana, Amb.
Russia	James F. Collins, Amb.	Yuli M. Vorontsov, Amb.
Rwanda	Robert E. Gribbin III, Amb.	Theogene N. Rudasingwa, Amb.
St. Kitts & Nevis	Vacant	Osbert W. Liburd, Amb.
St. Lucia	Vacant	Sonia Merlyn Johnny, Amb.
St. Vincent and the Grenadines	Vacant	Kingsley C.A. Layne, Amb.
Samoa (formerly Western Samoa)	Josiah Horton Beeman, Amb.	Tuiloma Neroni Slade, Amb.
São Tomé and Príncipe	Elizabeth Raspolic, Amb.	Vacancy
Saudi Arabia	Wyche Fowler Jr., Amb.	Prince Bandar Bin Sultan, Amb.
Senegal	Dane Farnsworth Smith Jr., Amb.	Mamadou Mansour Seck, Amb.
Seychelles	Harold W. Geisel, Amb..	Claude Sylvestre Anthony Morel, Amb.
Sierra Leone	John L. Hirsch, Amb..	John Ernest Leigh, Amb.
Singapore	Steven J. Green, Amb.	Heng-Chee Chan, Amb.
Slovakia	Ralph R. Johnson, Amb..	Branislav Lichardus, Amb.
Slovenia	Nancy H. Ely-Raphel, Amb.	Dimitrij Rupel, Amb.
Solomon Islands	Arma Jane Karaer, Amb.	Rex Stephen Horoi, Amb.
South Africa	James A. Joseph, Amb.	Franklin Sonn, Amb.
Spain	Edward L. Romero, Amb.	Antonio Oyarzabal, Amb.
Sri Lanka	Shaun E. Donnelly, Amb..	Warnasena Rasaputram, Amb.
Sudan	Vacant	Mahdi Ibrahim Mohamed, Amb.
Suriname	Dennis K. Hays, Amb.	Arnold T. Halfhide, Amb.
Swaziland	Alan R. McKee, Amb.	Mary M. Kanya, Amb.
Sweden	Lyndon L. Olson, Jr., Amb.	Rolf Ekeus, Amb.
Switzerland	Madeleine May Kunin, Amb.	Alfred Defago, Amb.
Syria	Ryan C. Crocker, Amb.	Walid Al-Moualem, Amb.
Tajikistan	R. Grant Smith, Amb.	None
Tanzania	Charles R. Stith, Amb.	Mustafa Salim Nyang'anyi, Amb.
Thailand	William H. Itoh, Amb.	Nitya Pibulsonggram, Amb.
Togo	Brenda Schoonover, Amb.	Akoussouleou Bodjona, Amb.
Tonga	Vacant	Akosita Fineanganofo, Amb.
Trinidad and Tobago	Edward E. Shumaker, III, Amb..	Michael Arneaud, Amb.
Tunisia	Robin L. Raphel, Amb.	Noureddine Mejdoub, Amb.
Turkey	Mark Parris*	Baki Ilkin, Amb.
Turkmenistan	Michael W. Cotter, Amb.	Halil Ugur, Amb.
Tuvalu	Vacant	None
Uganda	Nancy Jo Powell, Amb.	Edith Grace Ssempala, Amb.
Ukraine	Steven K. Pifer, Amb.	Yuri M. Shcherbak, Amb.
United Arab Emirates	David C. Litt, Amb.	Mohammad bin Hussain Al-Shaali, Amb.
United Kingdom	Philip Lader, Amb.	Christopher Meyer, Amb.
Uruguay	Christopher C. Ashby, Amb..	Alvaro Mario Diez de Medina, Amb.
Uzbekistan	Joseph A. Presel, Amb.	Sodiq Safaev, Amb.

COUNTRIES	ENVOYS FROM U.S.	ENVOYS TO U.S.
Vanuatu	Arma Jane Karaer, Amb.	None
Vatican City (The Holy See)	Corinne C. Boggs, Amb.	Most Rev. Agostino Cacciavillan, Pro-Nuncio
Venezuela	John F. Maisto, Amb..	Pedro Luis Echeverria, Amb.
Vietnam	Pete Peterson, Amb..	Bang Le, Amb.
Yemen	David G. Newton, Amb..	Abdulwahab A. Al-Hajjri, Amb.
Yugoslavia	Richard M. Miles, Chargé	Nebojsa Vujovic, Chargé
Zambia	Arlene Render, Amb.	Dunstan Weston Kamana, Amb.
Zimbabwe	Tom McDonald, Amb..	Amos Bernard Muvengwa Midzi, Amb.

Special Missions: U.S. Mission to NATO, Brussels—Robert E. Hunter, A.E.P.; U.S. Mission to the European Union, Brussels—A. Vernon Weaver, A.E.P.; U.S. Mission to the UN, New York—Bill Richardson, A.E.P.; U.S. Mission to the European Office of the UN, Geneva—Vacant; U.S. Mission to the OECD, Paris—David L. Aaron, Amb.; U.S. Mission to the Organization of American States, Washington—Harriet C. Babbitt, Amb.; U.S. Mission to the Vienna Office of the UN—John B. Ritch III, Amb.

(1) Relations severed in 1961; limited ties restored in 1977. (2) U.S. severed relations in Apr. 1980. (3) Operations temporarily suspended. (4) Embassy closed in May 1980. U.S. closed the Libyan mission in May 1981. (5) Relations severed in 1978; unofficial relations are maintained. *Ambassador designate.

Codes for International Direct Dial Calling From the U.S.

Station-to-station: 011 + country code (as shown) + city code (if required) + local number.
Person-to-person (operator-assisted, collect calls, credit card calls, and calls billed to another number): 01 + country code (below) + city code (if required) + local number.
For countries or territories not listed, contact your long distance company.
For area codes within the United States, see page 747 in the Consumer Information section.

Country/Territory	Code	Country/Territory	Code	Country/Territory	Code	Country/Territory	Code
Afghanistan	93	Cape Verde	238	Israel	972	Poland	48
Albania	355	Cayman Islands	345 *	Italy	39	Portugal	351
Algeria	213	Central African Rep.	236	Jamaica	876 *	Puerto Rico	787 *
American Samoa	684	Chad	235	Japan	81	Qatar	974
Andorra	33	Chile	56	Jordan	962	Romania	40
Angola	244	China	86	Kazakhstan	7	Russia	7
Anguilla	264 *	Colombia	57	Kenya	254	Rwanda	250
Antarctica (Scott		Comoros	269	Kiribati	686	St. Kitts & Nevis	869 *
Base)	672	Congo (formerly		Korea, North	850	St. Lucia	758 *
Antigua & Barbuda	268 *	Zaire)	243	Korea, South	82	St. Vincent & the	
Argentina	54	Congo Republic	242	Kuwait	965	Grenadines	809 *
Armenia	374	Costa Rica	506	Kyrgyzstan	7	Samoa (formerly	
Aruba	297	Côte d'Ivoire	225	Laos	856	Western Samoa)	685
Ascension Island	247	Croatia	385	Latvia	371	San Marino	378
Australia	61	Cuba	53	Lebanon	961	São Tomé & Príncipe	239
Austria	43	Cyprus	357	Lesotho	266	Saudi Arabia	966
Azerbaijan	994	Czech Republic	42	Liberia	231	Senegal	221
Bahamas	242	Denmark	45	Libya	218	Seychelles	248
Bahrain	973	Djibouti	253	Liechtenstein	41	Sierra Leone	232
Bangladesh	880	Dominica	767 *	Lithuania	370	Singapore	65
Barbados	246 *	Dominican Republic	809 *	Luxembourg	352	Slovakia	42
Belarus	375	Ecuador	593	Macao	853	Slovenia	386
Belgium	32	Egypt	20	Macedonia	389	Solomon Islands	677
Belize	501	El Salvador	503	Madagascar	261	Somalia	252
Benin	229	Equatorial Guinea	240	Malawi	265	South Africa	27
Bermuda	441 *	Eritrea	291	Malaysia	60	Spain	34
Bhutan	975	Estonia	372	Maldives	960	Sri Lanka	94
Bolivia	591	Ethiopia	251	Mali	223	Sudan	249
Bosnia & Herze-		Falkland Islands	500	Malta	356	Suriname	597
govina	387	Fiji	679	Marshall Islands	692	Swaziland	268
Botswana	267	Finland	358	Martinique	596	Sweden	46
Brazil	55	France	33	Mauritania	222	Switzerland	41
Brunei	673	French Antilles	596	Mauritius	230	Syria	963
Bulgaria	359	French Guiana	594	Mexico	52	Taiwan	886
Burkina Faso	226	French Polynesia	689	Micronesia	691	Tajikistan	7
Burundi	257	Gabon	241	Moldova	373	Tanzania	255
Cambodia	855	Gambia, The	220	Monaco	377	Thailand	66
Cameroon	237	Georgia	995	Mongolia	976	Togo	228
Canada		Germany	49	Montserrat	664 *	Tonga	676
Alberta	403 *	Ghana	233	Morocco	21	Trinidad & Tobago	868 *
British Columbia	250 *	Gibraltar	350	Mozambique	258	Tunisia	216
Vancouver	604 *	Greece	30	Myanmar	95	Turkey	90
Manitoba	204 *	Greenland	299	Namibia	264	Turkmenistan	7
New Brunswick	506 *	Grenada	473 *	Nauru	674	Turks & Caicos Isls.	649 *
Newfoundland	709 *	Guadeloupe	590	Nepal	977	Tuvalu	688
NW Territories	604 *	Guam	671 *	Netherlands	31	Uganda	256
Nova Scotia	902 *	Guantanamo Bay	53	New Caledonia	687	Ukraine	380
Ontario		Guatemala	502	New Zealand	64	United Arab Emirates	971
London	519 *	Guinea	224	Nicaragua	505	United Kingdom	44
North Bay	705 *	Guinea-Bissau	245	Niger	227	Uruguay	598
Ottawa	613 *	Guyana	592	Nigeria	234	Uzbekistan	7
Thunder Bay	807 *	Haiti	509	N. Mariana Isls.	670 *	Vanuatu	678
Toronto Metro	416 *	Honduras	504	Norway	47	Vatican City	379
Toronto Vicinity	905 *	Hong Kong	852	Oman	968	Venezuela	58
Prince Edward Isl.	902 *	Hungary	36	Pakistan	92	Vietnam	84
Quebec		Iceland	354	Palau	680	Virgin Islands, British	284 *
Montreal	514 *	India	91	Panama	507	Virgin Islands, U.S.	340 *
Quebec City	418 *	Indonesia	62	Papua New Guinea	675	Yemen	967
Sherbrooke	819 *	Iran	98	Paraguay	595	Yugoslavia	381
Saskatchewan	306 *	Iraq	964	Peru	51	Zambia	260
Yukon Territory	403 *	Ireland	353	Philippines	63	Zimbabwe	263

* These numbers are area codes. Follow Domestic Dialing instructions: dial "1" + area code + number you are calling.

VITAL STATISTICS

Annual Report for the Year 1997

Source: National Center for Health Statistics, U.S. Dept. of Health and Human Services

Highlights

Provisional data for 1997 reported by the National Center for Health Statistics show that the U.S. infant mortality rate reached a record low (7.1 infant deaths per 1,000 live births). Life expectancy reached an all-time high of 76.5 years. Marriage and divorce rates both increased, and the rate of natural increase declined slightly.

Births

An estimated 3,894,970 babies were born in the U.S. in 1997, an increase of less than 1% from the 3,891,494 births in 1996. The birthrate was lower than the rate for the preceding year (14.6 per 1,000 population as compared to 14.7). The fertility rate (the number of live births per 1,000 women aged 15-44 years) for 1997 was 65.26, slightly lower than the rate for 1996 (65.34).

Deaths

The provisional number of deaths during 1997 was 2,314,738, less than 1% greater than in the previous year (2,314,690). The death rate of 864.9 deaths per 100,000 population was slightly lower than the 1996 death rate of 872.5. The record-low infant mortality rate of 7.1 infant deaths per 1,000 live births was 3% lower than the rate of 7.3 for 1996.

Natural Increase

As a result of natural increase alone, the excess of births over deaths, an estimated 1,580,232 persons were added to the population in 1997. The rate was 5.90 per 1,000 population, slightly lower than for 1996 (5.95), and the lowest since 1976 (5.8). The nearly steady rate of natural increase was due to similar slight declines in the birth and death rates.

Marriages

An estimated 2,384,000 marriages were performed in 1997, nearly 2% more than in 1996 (2,344,000). The marriage rate for 1997 (8.9 per 1,000 population) was 1% higher than in 1996 (8.8), the lowest decline in rate of marriages since 1963.

Divorces

About 1,163,000 divorces were granted in the U.S. in 1997, 1% greater than the number for 1996 (1,150,000), but 4% fewer than the all-time high of 1,215,000 in 1992. The divorce rate per 1,000 population in 1997 (4.35) was slightly higher than the rate for 1996 (4.34), the lowest divorce rate in over 2 decades.

Births and Deaths in the U.S.

Source: National Center for Health Statistics, U.S. Dept. of Health and Human Services

	BIRTHS		DEATHS	
Year	Total number	Rate	Total number	Rate
1960	4,257,850	23.7	1,711,982	9.5
1970	3,731,386	18.4	1,921,031	9.5
1980	3,612,258	15.9	1,989,841	8.7
1990	4,158,212	16.7	2,148,463	8.6
1991	4,110,907	16.3	2,169,518	8.6
1992	4,065,014	15.9	2,175,613	8.5
1993	4,000,240	15.5	2,268,000	8.8
1994	3,952,767	15.2	2,278,994	8.8
1995	3,899,589	14.8	2,312,132	8.8
1996	3,891,494	14.7	2,314,690	8.7
1997 (P)	3,894,970	14.6	2,314,738	8.6

(P) = provisional data. **Note:** Refers only to events occurring within the U.S. Excludes fetal deaths. Rates per 1,000 population; enumerated as of Apr. 1 for 1960 and 1970; estimated as of July 1 for all other years. Beginning 1970 excludes births and deaths occurring to nonresidents of the U.S. Data include revisions.

MILLENNIUM FACT BOX

U.S. Death Rates for Selected Causes

Source: National Center for Health Statistics, Centers for Disease Control and Prevention

Since 1900, cardiovascular disease has generally remained the number-one killer in the U.S. The death rate for cancer has slowly climbed, while death rates for influenza and pneumonia and for tuberculosis have decreased and approached zero. One prominent feature is the extremely high death rate for influenza in 1918, reflecting an influenza epidemic in which about 500,000 Americans died from the disease.

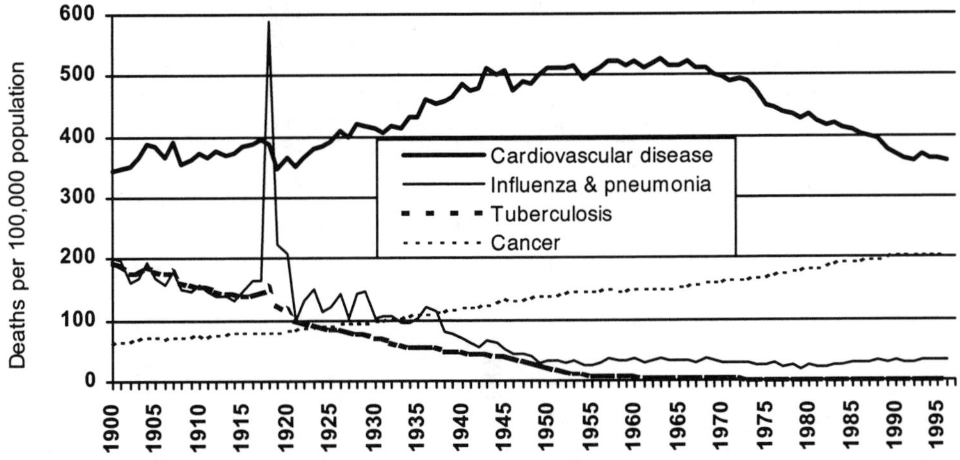

Births and Deaths, by States and Regions, 1996-97

Source: National Center for Health Statistics, U.S. Dept. of Health and Human Services

Area	LIVE BIRTHS 1996 Number	1996 Rate	1997 Number	1997 Rate	DEATHS 1996 Number	1996 Rate	1997 Number	1997 Rate
New England	**171,393**	**12.8**	**172,126**	**12.9**	**119,119**	**8.9**	**116,718**	**8.7**
Maine	13,718	11.0	13,524	10.9	11,035	8.9	11,075	8.9
New Hampshire	14,125	12.2	14,456	12.3	9,114	7.8	9,488	8.1
Vermont	6,773	11.5	6,691	11.4	4,885	8.3	5,272	9.0
Massachusetts	80,165	13.2	82,311	13.5	55,328	9.1	52,101	8.5
Rhode Island	12,601	12.7	12,355	12.5	9,574	9.7	9,784	9.9
Connecticut	44,011	13.4	42,789	13.1	29,183	8.9	28,998	8.9
Middle Atlantic	**535,193**	**14.0**	**537,939**	**14.1**	**364,233**	**9.5**	**361,153**	**9.5**
New York	271,569	14.9	282,389	15.6	162,875	9.0	161,159	8.9
New Jersey	113,713	14.2	113,235	14.1	71,895	9.0	72,102	9.0
Pennsylvania	149,911	12.4	142,315	11.8	129,463	10.7	127,892	10.6
East North Central	**624,455**	**14.3**	**601,719**	**13.7**	**394,908**	**9.1**	**383,605**	**8.7**
Ohio	152,233	13.6	151,879	13.6	105,213	9.4	105,446	9.4
Indiana	83,417	14.3	69,218	11.8	54,321	9.3	47,043	8.0
Illinois	184,526	15.6	180,621	15.2	106,355	9.0	102,480	8.6
Michigan	137,518	14.3	133,627	13.7	83,972	8.8	83,534	8.5
Wisconsin	66,761	12.9	66,374	12.8	45,047	8.7	45,102	8.7
West North Central	**253,702**	**13.7**	**255,580**	**13.8**	**168,223**	**9.1**	**170,204**	**9.2**
Minnesota	63,657	13.7	64,633	13.8	36,804	7.9	37,207	7.9
Iowa	34,838	12.2	36,868	12.9	26,315	9.2	26,179	9.2
Missouri	73,132	13.6	74,538	13.8	53,697	10.0	54,543	10.1
North Dakota	8,396	13.0	8,326	13.0	5,753	8.9	6,027	9.4
South Dakota	10,081	13.8	10,138	13.7	6,314	8.6	6,992	9.5
Nebraska	23,355	14.1	23,243	14.0	15,472	9.4	15,248	9.2
Kansas	40,243	15.6	37,834	14.6	23,868	9.3	24,008	9.3
South Atlantic	**658,995**	**13.8**	**661,656**	**13.7**	**440,186**	**9.2**	**440,432**	**9.1**
Delaware	10,142	14.0	10,135	13.9	6,443	8.9	6,424	8.8
Maryland	71,042	14.0	66,253	13.0	41,965	8.3	40,472	7.9
District of Columbia	8,240	15.2	8,327	15.7	6,317	11.6	5,984	11.3
Virginia	89,149	13.4	88,669	13.2	52,847	7.9	53,261	7.9
West Virginia	19,621	10.7	20,466	11.3	19,106	10.5	20,870	11.5
North Carolina	106,261	14.5	105,766	14.2	66,357	9.1	66,101	8.9
South Carolina	50,568	13.7	51,252	13.6	34,603	9.4	32,998	8.8
Georgia	114,603	15.6	118,365	15.8	58,802	8.0	59,314	7.9
Florida	189,369	13.2	192,423	13.1	153,746	10.7	155,008	10.6
East South Central	**229,159**	**14.2**	**230,843**	**14.1**	**156,908**	**9.7**	**160,352**	**9.8**
Kentucky	52,545	13.5	52,696	13.5	37,550	9.7	38,256	9.8
Tennessee	73,658	13.8	74,755	13.9	49,934	9.4	52,113	9.7
Alabama	61,514	14.4	60,921	14.1	42,668	10.0	42,704	9.9
Mississippi	41,442	15.3	42,471	15.6	26,756	9.9	27,279	10.0
West South Central	**462,216**	**15.8**	**465,914**	**15.7**	**235,560**	**8.0**	**230,942**	**7.8**
Arkansas	35,876	14.3	36,985	14.7	25,666	10.2	25,545	10.1
Louisiana	66,291	15.2	64,199	14.8	40,460	9.3	37,660	8.7
Oklahoma	45,151	13.7	47,985	14.5	33,224	10.1	33,687	10.2
Texas	314,898	16.5	316,745	16.3	136,210	7.1	134,050	6.9
Mountain	**254,829**	**15.8**	**270,129**	**16.4**	**121,162**	**7.5**	**120,632**	**7.3**
Montana	10,797	12.3	10,463	11.9	7,710	8.8	7,697	8.8
Idaho	18,868	15.9	17,979	14.9	8,685	7.3	9,014	7.4
Wyoming	6,198	12.9	6,387	13.3	3,610	7.5	3,737	7.8
Colorado	47,610	12.5	52,050	13.4	25,853	6.8	25,640	6.6
New Mexico	27,173	15.9	26,571	15.4	12,325	7.2	12,788	7.4
Arizona	79,530	18.0	86,032	18.9	39,005	8.8	37,334	8.2
Utah	41,214	20.6	43,670	21.2	11,077	5.5	11,437	5.6
Nevada	23,439	14.6	26,977	16.1	12,897	8.0	12,985	7.7
Pacific	**694,680**	**16.4**	**674,380**	**15.7**	**310,475**	**7.3**	**309,909**	**7.2**
Washington	79,808	14.4	79,529	14.2	39,493	7.1	42,952	7.7
Oregon	43,798	13.7	43,394	13.4	28,293	8.8	28,634	8.8
California	542,553	17.0	524,618	16.3	232,266	7.3	228,131	7.1
Alaska	10,176	16.8	9,710	15.9	2,562	4.2	2,465	4.0
Hawaii	18,345	15.5	17,129	14.4	7,861	6.6	7,727	6.5

Note: Data are provisional estimates, reported by state of residence. Figures include revisions, and so may differ from those previously published. Rates for births and deaths are per 1,000 population.

Birth Rates; Fertility Rates by Age of Mother, 1950-97

Source: National Center for Health Statistics, U.S. Dept. of Health and Human Services

	Birth rate[1]	Fertility rate[2]	AGE OF MOTHER: 10-14 years	15-19 years: Total 15-19	15-17 years	18-19 years	20-24 years	25-29 years	30-34 years	35-39 years	40-44 years	45-49 years
			Live births per 1,000 women by age group									
1950	24.1	106.2	1.0	81.6	40.7	132.7	196.6	166.1	103.7	52.9	15.1	1.2
1960	23.7	118.0	0.8	89.1	43.9	166.7	258.1	197.4	112.7	56.2	15.5	0.9
1970	18.4	87.9	1.2	68.3	38.8	114.7	167.8	145.1	73.3	31.7	8.1	0.5
1980	15.9	68.4	1.1	53.0	32.5	82.1	115.1	112.9	61.9	19.8	3.9	0.2
1990	16.7	70.9	1.4	59.9	37.5	88.6	116.5	120.2	80.8	31.7	5.5	0.2
1991	16.3	69.6	1.4	62.1	38.7	94.4	115.7	118.2	79.5	32.0	5.5	0.2
1992	15.9	68.9	1.4	60.7	37.8	94.5	114.6	117.4	80.2	32.5	5.9	0.3
1993	15.5	67.6	1.4	59.6	37.8	92.1	112.6	115.5	80.8	32.9	6.1	0.3
1994	15.2	66.7	1.4	58.9	37.6	91.5	111.1	113.9	81.5	33.7	6.4	0.3
1995	14.8	65.6	1.3	56.8	36.0	89.1	109.8	112.2	82.5	34.3	6.6	0.3
1996	14.7	65.3	1.2	54.4	33.8	86.0	110.4	113.1	83.9	35.3	6.8	0.3
1997P	14.6	65.3	1.2	52.9	32.6	84.4	110.9	114.3	85.4	36.0	6.9	0.3

P= preliminary data. (1) Live births per 1,000 population. (2) Live births per 1,000 women 15-44 years of age.

Years of Life Expected at Birth, 1900-97

Source: National Center for Health Statistics

Year[1]	ALL RACES Total	ALL RACES Male	ALL RACES Female	WHITE Total	WHITE Male	WHITE Female	BLACK AND OTHER Total	BLACK AND OTHER Male	BLACK AND OTHER Female
1900	47.3	46.3	48.3	47.6	46.6	48.7	33.0	32.5	33.5
1910	50.0	48.4	51.8	50.3	48.6	52.0	35.6	33.8	37.5
1920	54.1	53.6	54.6	54.9	54.4	55.6	45.3	45.5	45.2
1930	59.7	58.1	61.6	61.4	59.7	63.5	48.1	47.3	49.2
1940	62.9	60.8	65.2	64.2	62.1	66.6	53.1	51.5	54.9
1950	68.2	65.6	71.1	69.1	66.5	72.2	60.8	59.1	62.9
1960	69.7	66.6	73.1	70.6	67.4	74.1	63.6	61.1	66.3
1965	70.2	66.8	73.7	71.0	67.6	74.7	64.1	61.1	67.4
1970	70.8	67.1	74.7	71.7	68.0	75.6	65.3	61.3	69.4
1975	72.6	68.8	76.6	73.4	69.5	77.3	68.0	63.7	72.4
1980	73.7	70.0	77.5	74.4	70.7	78.1	69.5	65.3	73.6
1981	74.2	70.4	77.8	74.8	71.1	78.4	70.3	66.2	74.4
1982	74.5	70.9	78.1	75.1	71.5	78.7	70.9	66.8	74.9
1983	74.6	71.0	78.1	75.2	71.7	78.7	70.9	67.0	74.7
1984	74.7	71.2	78.2	75.3	71.8	78.7	71.1	67.2	74.9
1985	74.7	71.2	78.2	75.3	71.9	78.7	67.0	64.8	69.3
1986	74.8	71.3	78.3	75.4	72.0	78.8	70.9	66.8	74.9
1987	75.0	71.5	78.4	75.6	72.2	78.9	66.9	65.0	69.1
1988	74.9	71.5	78.3	75.6	72.3	78.9	70.8	66.7	74.8
1989	75.1	71.7	78.5	75.9	72.5	79.2	70.9	66.7	74.9
1990	75.4	71.8	78.8	76.1	72.9	79.4	71.2	67.0	75.2
1991	75.5	72.0	78.9	76.3	72.9	79.2	71.5	67.4	75.5
1992	75.5	72.1	78.9	76.4	73.0	79.5	71.7	67.5	75.8
1993	75.5	72.1	78.9	76.3	73.0	79.5	71.5	67.4	75.5
1994	75.7	72.4	79.0	76.5	73.3	79.6	71.7	67.5	75.8
1995	75.8	72.5	78.9	76.5	73.4	79.6	71.9	67.9	75.7
1996	76.1	73.1	79.1	76.8	73.9	79.7	72.6	68.9	76.1
1997[P]	76.5	73.6	79.2	77.1	74.3	79.8	73.4	69.9	76.7

P = preliminary. (1) Data prior to 1940 for death-registration states only.

U.S. Infant Mortality Rates, by Race and Sex, 1960-97

Source: National Center for Health Statistics, U.S. Dept. of Health and Human Services

Year	ALL RACES Both sexes	ALL RACES Male	ALL RACES Female	WHITES Both sexes	WHITES Male	WHITES Female	BLACKS Both sexes	BLACKS Male	BLACKS Female
1960	26.0	29.3	22.6	22.9	26.0	19.6	44.3	49.1	39.4
1970	20.0	22.4	17.5	17.8	20.0	15.4	32.6	36.2	29.0
1980	12.6	13.9	11.2	11.0	12.3	9.6	21.4	23.3	19.4
1981	11.9	13.1	10.7	10.5	11.7	9.2	20.0	21.7	18.3
1982	11.5	12.8	10.2	10.1	11.2	8.9	19.6	21.5	17.7
1983	11.2	12.3	10.0	9.7	10.8	8.6	19.2	21.1	17.2
1984	10.8	11.9	9.6	9.4	10.5	8.3	18.4	19.8	16.9
1985	10.6	11.9	9.3	9.3	10.6	8.0	18.2	19.9	16.5
1986	10.4	11.5	9.1	8.9	10.0	7.8	18.0	20.0	16.0
1987	10.1	11.2	8.9	8.6	9.6	7.6	17.9	19.6	16.0
1988	10.0	11.0	8.9	8.5	9.5	7.4	17.6	19.0	16.1
1989	9.8	10.8	8.8	8.1	9.0	7.1	18.6	20.0	17.2
1990	9.2	10.3	8.1	7.6	8.5	6.6	18.0	19.6	16.2
1991	8.9	10.0	7.8	7.3	8.3	6.3	17.6	19.4	15.7
1992	8.5	9.4	7.6	6.9	7.7	6.1	16.8	18.4	15.3
1993	8.4	9.3	7.4	6.8	7.6	6.0	16.5	18.3	14.7
1994	8.0	8.8	7.2	6.6	7.2	5.9	15.8	17.5	14.1
1995	7.6	8.3	6.8	6.3	7.0	5.6	15.1	16.3	13.9
1996	7.3	8.0	6.6	6.1	6.7	5.4	14.7	16.0	13.3
1997[1]	7.1	NA	NA	6.0	NA	NA	13.7	NA	NA

Note: Rates per 1,000 live births. NA = Not available. (1) Preliminary data.

U.S. Infant Deaths and Infant Mortality Rates, for Selected Causes, 1996-97

Source: National Center for Health Statistics, U.S. Dept. of Health and Human Services

Age and cause of death	1997[1] Number	1997[1] Rate[2]	1996 Number	1996 Rate[2]
Total, under 1 year	**27,692**	**711.0**	**28,487**	**732.0**
Under 28 days	18,153	466.1	18,572	477.2
28 days to 11 months	9,538	244.9	9,915	247.8
Certain gastrointestinal diseases	272	7.0	289	7.4
Pneumonia and influenza	397	10.2	496	12.7
Congenital anomalies	6,063	155.7	6,381	164.0
Disorders relating to short gestation and unspecified low birthweight	3,727	95.7	3,902	100.3
Birth trauma	201	5.2	166	4.3
Intrauterine hypoxia and birth asphyxia	456	11.7	428	11.0
Respiratory distress syndrome	1,262	32.4	1,362	35.0
Other conditions originating around the time of birth	6,920	177.7	7,097	182.4
Sudden infant death syndrome	2,705	69.4	3,050	78.4
All other causes	5,688	146.0	5,316	136.6

Note: Because of rounding of estimates, figures may not add to totals. (1) Data are preliminary. (2) Rates per 100,000 live births.

The 10 Leading Causes of Death, 1997[1]

Source: National Center for Health Statistics, U.S. Dept. of Health and Human Services

Rank	Cause of death	Number	Death rate[2]	Percentage of total deaths
	ALL CAUSES	**2,314,729**	**864.9**	**100.0**
1.	Heart disease	725,790	271.2	31.4
2.	Cancer	537,390	200.8	23.2
3.	Stroke	159,877	59.7	6.9
4.	Chronic obstructive lung diseases and allied conditions	110,637	41.3	4.8
5.	Accidents and adverse effects	92,191	34.4	4.0
	Motor vehicle accidents	42,420	15.8	1.8
	All other accidents and adverse effects	49,772	18.6	2.2
6.	Pneumonia and influenza	88,383	33.0	3.8
7.	Diabetes mellitus	62,332	23.3	2.7
8.	Suicide	29,725	11.1	1.3
9.	Kidney disease	25,570	9.6	1.1
10.	Chronic liver disease and cirrhosis	24,765	9.3	1.1

(1) Figures are based on weighted data rounded to the nearest individual. Data are preliminary and may vary somewhat from other sources. (2) Per 100,000 population.

Suicides in the U.S. by Age, Race, and Sex, 1996

Source: National Center for Health Statistics, U.S. Dept. of Health and Human Services

	All ages	1-14 yrs.	15-24 yrs.	25-34 yrs.	35-44 yrs.	45-54 yrs.	55-64 yrs.	65-74 yrs.	75-84 yrs.	85 yrs. & over	Age not stated
All races, both sexes[1]	**30,903**	**302**	**4,358**	**5,861**	**6,741**	**4,837**	**2,925**	**2,806**	**2,290**	**759**	**24**
Male	24,998	225	3,724	4,848	5,300	3,684	2,306	2,307	1,945	641	18
Female	5,905	77	634	1,013	1,441	1,153	619	499	345	118	6
White, both sexes	**27,856**	**248**	**3,639**	**5,009**	**6,102**	**4,509**	**2,737**	**2,651**	**2,205**	**737**	**19**
Male	22,547	182	3,109	4,146	4,789	3,440	2,166	2,195	1,880	627	13
Female	5,309	66	530	863	1,313	1,069	571	456	325	110	6
Black, both sexes	**2,164**	**36**	**523**	**590**	**476**	**236**	**128**	**108**	**50**	**14**	**3**
Male	1,820	28	461	503	397	184	108	87	39	10	3
Female	344	8	62	87	79	52	20	21	11	4	(—)

(—) = Data represent zero. **Note:** Data are provisional, estimated from a 10% sample of deaths. Because of rounding of estimates, figures may not add to totals. (1) "All races" includes races other than white and black.

U.S. Abortion Patients, by Selected Characteristics

Source: Alan Guttmacher Institute, New York, NY

Characteristic	% distribution: Abortion patients	% distribution: All women 15-44[1]
Age group[2]		
15-17	8.8	8.8
18-19	11.5	5.7
20-24	32.8	15.2
25-29	21.4	16.1
30-34	14.4	18.8
35-39	7.5	18.6
40 years and older	2.3	16.8
Race		
White	61.3	81.2
Black	31.1	14.0
Other	7.6	4.9
Ethnicity		
Hispanic	20.2	10.6
Non-Hispanic	79.8	89.4
Marital status		
Married	18.4	49.9
Separated	7.2	3.3
Divorced	9.4	8.6
Widowed	0.5	0.7
Never married	64.4	37.5
Cohabiting		
Yes	20.2	5.8
No/married	79.8	94.2
Number of live births		
0	45.4	41.2
1	24.7	18.2
2	17.8	23.8
3	7.7	11.1
4 or more	4.4	5.8
Region of residence		
Metropolitan	88.5	79.6
Nonmetropolitan	11.5	20.4

Characteristic	% distribution: Abortion patients	% distribution: All women 15-44[1]
Religion[3]		
Protestant	37.4	53.9
Catholic	31.3	30.9
Jewish	1.3	1.2
Other	6.3	8.1
None	23.7	5.0
Born again/Evangelical		
Yes	18.0	46.0
No	82.0	54.0
Education		
8th grade or less	4.2	4.7
9th-11th grade	16.9	16.4
H.S. graduate or GED	30.4	30.1
Some college or associate's degree	34.9	30.0
College graduate	13.7	16.8
Enrolled in school		
Yes	30.3	24.6
No	69.7	75.4
Currently employed		
Yes	66.2	65.6
No	33.8	34.4
Family income		
Less than $15,000	28.7	15.4
$15,000-$29,999	19.5	20.6
$30,000-$59,999	38.0	35.9
$60,000 or greater	13.8	23.1
Medicaid coverage		
Yes	26.5	12.9
No	73.5	87.1
Intend more children		
Yes	66.0	47.8
No	34.0	52.2

Note: Percents may not add to 100 because of rounding. (1) Data for 1994 except Medicaid status (1993), religion (1993-95), and childbearing intention (1990 intention by age, applied to 1994 population). (2) Not included are patients under the age of 15, who make up 1.2%. (3) Based on women 18-44 years of age.

Contraceptive Use in the U.S., 1995

Source: National Center for Health Statistics, U.S. Dept. of Health and Human Services

	AGE IN YEARS						
	15-44	**15-19**	**20-24**	**25-29**	**30-34**	**35-39**	**40-44**
	Number in thousands						
All women	**60,201**	**8,961**	**9,041**	**9,693**	**11,065**	**11,211**	**10,230**
	Percent distribution						
Using contraception	64.2	29.8	63.4	69.3	72.7	72.9	71.5
Female sterilization	17.8	0.1	2.5	11.8	21.4	29.8	35.6
Male sterilization	7.0	—	0.7	3.1	7.6	13.6	14.5
Pill	17.3	13.0	33.1	27.0	20.7	8.1	4.2
Implant	0.9	0.8	2.4	1.4	0.5	0.2	0.1
Injectable	1.9	2.9	3.9	2.9	1.3	0.8	0.2
Intrauterine device (IUD)	0.5	—	0.2	0.5	0.6	0.7	0.9
Diaphragm	1.2	0.0	0.4	0.6	1.7	2.2	1.9
Condom	13.1	10.9	16.7	16.8	13.4	12.3	8.8
Female condom	0.0	—	0.1	—	—	—	—
Periodic abstinence	1.5	0.4	0.6	1.2	2.3	2.1	1.8
Natural family planning	0.2	—	0.1	0.2	0.3	0.4	0.2
Withdrawal	2.0	1.2	2.1	2.6	2.1	2.3	1.4
Other methods[1]	1.0	0.3	0.9	1.2	1.3	0.9	1.8

(1) Includes morning-after pill, foam, cervical cap, Today sponge, suppository, jelly or cream (without diaphragm), and other methods not shown separately.

U.S. Median Age at First Marriage, 1900-97

Source: Bureau of the Census, U.S. Dept. of Commerce

Year[1]	Men	Women	Year[1]	Men	Women	Year[1]	Men	Women
1997	26.8	25.0	1990	26.1	23.9	1955	22.6	20.2
1996	27.1	24.8	1985	25.5	23.3	1950	22.8	20.3
1995	26.9	24.5	1980	24.7	22.0	1940	24.3	21.5
1994	26.7	24.5	1975	23.5	21.1	1930	24.3	21.3
1993	26.5	24.5	1970	23.2	20.8	1920	24.6	21.2
1992	26.5	24.4	1965	22.8	20.6	1910	25.1	21.6
1991	26.3	24.1	1960	22.8	20.3	1900	25.9	21.9

(1) Figures after 1940 based on Current Population Survey data; figures for 1900-40 based on decennial censuses.

Interracial Married Couples in the U.S., 1960-97

Source: Bureau of the Census, U.S. Dept. of Commerce; numbers in thousands

		INTERRACIAL MARRIED COUPLES				
			Black/White			
Year[1]	**TOTAL MARRIED COUPLES**	**Total interrac.**	**Black husband/ White wife**	**White husband/ Black wife**	**White/ Other race[2]**	**Black/ Other race[2]**
1997	54,666	1,264	201	110	896	57
1996	54,664	1,260	220	117	884	39
1995	54,937	1,392	206	122	988	76
1994	54,251	1,283	196	100	909	78
1993	54,199	1,195	182	60	920	33
1992	53,512	1,161	163	83	883	32
1991	53,227	994	156	75	720	43
1990	53,256	964	150	61	720	33
1980	49,714	651	122	45	450	34
1970	44,598	310	41	24	233	12
1960	40,491	149	25	26	90	7

(1) Data from Mar. of year, except for 1970 and 1960, which are from decennial census. (2) Any race other than White or Black.

Cigarette Use in the U.S., 1985-97

Source: Substance Abuse and Mental Health Services Administration (SAMHSA), U.S. Dept. of Health and Human Services

(percentage reporting use in the month prior to the survey; figures exclude persons under age 12)

Characteristic	**1985**	**1995**	**1996**	**1997**
TOTAL	**38.7**	**28.8**	**28.9**	**29.6**
Sex				
Male	43.4	31.0	31.1	31.2
Female	34.5	26.8	26.7	28.2
Race/Ethnicity				
White	38.9	29.7	29.8	30.5
Black	38.0	28.1	30.4	29.8
Hispanic	40.0	24.7	24.7	27.4
Other	(1)	23.5	17.2	18.8

Characteristic	**1985**	**1995**	**1996**	**1997**
Age group				
12-17	29.4	20.2	18.3	19.9
18-25	47.4	35.3	38.3	40.6
26-34	45.7	34.7	35.0	33.7
35 and older	35.5	27.2	27.0	27.9
Education[2]				
Non-high school graduate	37.3	36.5	36.5	40.0
High school graduate	37.0	34.8	36.8	36.1
Some college	32.6	30.8	27.5	29.5
College graduate	23.0	16.7	17.5	17.1

(1) No estimate reported. (2) Estimates for Education are for persons aged 18 and older.

Drug Use in the General U.S. Population

Source: Substance Abuse and Mental Health Services Administration (SAMHSA), U.S. Dept. of Health and Human Services

According to the Substance Abuse and Mental Health Services Administration's 1997 National Household Survey on Drug Abuse, an estimated 77 mil Americans 12 years of age and older (36%) had used an illicit drug at least once during their lifetimes, 11% used one during the previous year, and 6% used one in the month before the survey was conducted. Among those 25 years of age and under, an estimated 1.6 mil used cocaine (including crack) and 9.7 mil used marijuana at least once within the previous year. Among those 26 years of age and over, 2.6 mil used cocaine (including crack) and 9.7 mil used marijuana at least once within the previous year.

The Substance Abuse and Mental Health Services Administration's Drug Abuse Warning Network (DAWN) reported an estimated 487,600 drug-related episodes in hospital emergency departments nationwide in 1996. The number of these drug-related episodes decreased 6% from 517,800 in 1995.

Drug Use: America's Middle and High School Students

Source: *Monitoring the Future,* Univ. of Michigan Inst. for Social Research and National Inst. on Drug Abuse

Drug use among American young people showed signs of leveling off in 1997, according to the University of Michigan's 23d annual survey of high school seniors and 7th annual survey of 8th and 10th graders. For the 1st time in 6 years, use of marijuana and total use of illicit drugs among 8th graders declined, although the proportion of 8th graders taking illicit drugs in the 12 months prior to the survey (22%) was still double the 1991 level (11%). The proportion of 10th graders using illicit drugs in the prior 12 months has nearly doubled (from 21% to 39%) since 1991, and among 12th graders the proportion increased by nearly half (from 29% to 42%).

Marijuana remained the most commonly used illegal drug among the 3 grade levels. In 1997, the proportion of students that reported using marijuana in the past year declined to just below 18% of 8th graders. Marijuana use rose to 35% of 10th graders and 39% of 12th graders. Use of marijuana on a daily basis decreased (to 1.1%) among 8th graders but increased in the higher grades. About 1 in 17 high school seniors (5.8%) and 1 in 27 10th graders (3.7%) were daily users.

Use of LSD and other hallucinogens leveled off in all 3 grades, while use of stimulants leveled off among 8th and 10th graders; use of stimulants by seniors showed an increase. The use of inhalants among the 3 grade levels continued the decline that began in 1996. Although heroin use remained rather low, levels of use in 1997 increased slightly for 10th and 12th graders; use by 8th graders decreased slightly. The use of alcohol remained high but stable for all grade levels in 1997.

Prevalence of cigarette smoking rose again for seniors in 1997, but use decreased among 8th and 10th graders. About 9% of 8th graders, 18% of 10th graders, and 25% of 12th graders reported having smoked daily during the 30 days before they responded to the survey.

In 1997, about 16,000 seniors, 16,000 10th graders, and 19,000 8th graders participated in the survey; in all, students were surveyed from 429 public and private secondary schools. It should be noted that the surveys missed the 3-6% of a class group that drops out of school early and the 9-17% who are absentees. These populations have higher rates of drug use overall.

Drug Use: America's High School Seniors, 1975-97

Source: *Monitoring the Future,* Univ. of Michigan Inst. for Social Research and National Inst. on Drug Abuse

	PERCENTAGE EVER USED											
	Class of 1975	Class of 1980	Class of 1985	Class of 1990	Class of 1991	Class of 1992	Class of 1993	Class of 1994	Class of 1995	Class of 1996	Class of 1997	'96-'97 change
Marijuana/hashish	47.3	60.3	54.2	40.7	36.7	32.6	35.3	38.2	41.7	44.9	49.6	+4.7
Inhalants	NA	11.9	15.4	18.0	17.6	16.6	17.4	17.7	17.4	16.6	16.1	–0.5
Inhalants adjusted[1]	NA	17.3	18.1	18.5	18.0	17.0	17.7	18.3	17.8	17.5	16.9	–0.6
Amyl & butyl nitrites	NA	11.1	7.9	2.1	1.6	1.5	1.4	1.7	1.5	1.8	2.0	+0.2
Hallucinogens	16.3	13.3	10.3	9.4	9.6	9.2	10.9	11.4	12.7	14.0	15.1	+1.1
Hallucinogens adjusted[2]	NA	15.6	12.1	9.7	10.0	9.4	11.3	11.7	13.1	14.5	15.4	+0.9
LSD	11.3	9.3	7.5	8.7	8.8	8.6	10.3	10.5	11.7	12.6	13.6	+1.0
PCP	NA	9.6	4.9	2.8	2.9	2.4	2.9	2.8	2.7	4.0	3.9	–0.1
Cocaine	9.0	15.7	17.3	9.4	7.8	6.1	6.1	5.9	6.0	7.1	8.7	+1.6
Crack	NA	NA	NA	3.5	3.1	2.6	2.6	3.0	3.0	3.3	3.9	+0.6
Heroin[3]	2.2	1.1	1.2	1.3	0.9	1.2	1.1	1.2	1.6	1.8	2.1	+0.3
Other opiates[4]	9.0	9.8	10.2	8.3	6.6	6.1	6.4	6.6	7.2	8.2	9.7	+1.5
Stimulants[4,5]	22.3	26.4	26.2	17.5	15.4	13.9	15.1	15.7	15.3	15.3	16.5	+1.2
Sedatives[4]	18.2	14.9	11.8	7.5	6.7	6.1	6.4	7.3	7.6	8.2	8.7	+0.5
Barbiturates[4]	16.9	11.0	9.2	6.8	6.2	5.5	6.3	7.0	7.4	7.6	8.1	+0.5
Methaqualone[4]	8.1	9.5	6.7	2.3	1.3	1.6	0.8	1.4	1.2	2.0	1.7	–0.3
Tranquilizers[4]	17.0	15.2	11.9	7.2	7.2	6.0	6.4	6.6	7.1	7.2	7.8	+0.6
Alcohol	90.4	93.2	92.2	89.5	88.0	87.5	87.0	80.4[6]	80.7[6]	79.2[6]	81.7[6]	+2.5
Cigarettes	73.6	71.0	68.8	64.4	63.1	61.8	61.9	62.0	64.2	63.5	65.4	+1.9

NA=Not available. (1) Adjusted for underreporting of amyl and butyl nitrites. (2) Adjusted for underreporting of PCP. (3) Reflects use with or without injection. (4) Includes only drug use that was not under a doctor's orders. (5) Adjusted for overreporting of the nonprescription stimulants. (6) Data for 1994, 1995, 1996, and 1997 are not directly comparable to prior years.

Alcohol Use by 8th and 12th Graders, 1980-97

Source: *Monitoring the Future*, Univ. of Michigan Inst. for Social Research and National Inst. on Drug Abuse

	1980	1986	1987	1988	1989	1990	1991	1992	1993	1994	1995	1996	1997
Alcohol[1]	Percent using in the month before the survey												
All 12th graders	72.0	65.3	66.4	63.9	60.0	57.1	54.0	51.3	48.6	50.1	51.3	50.8	52.7
Male	77.4	69.0	69.9	68.0	65.1	61.3	58.4	55.8	54.2	55.5	55.7	54.8	56.2
Female	66.8	61.9	63.1	59.9	54.9	52.3	49.0	46.8	43.4	45.2	47.0	46.9	48.9
White	75.8	70.2	71.8	69.5	65.3	62.2	57.7	56.0	53.4	54.8	54.8	54.7	57.9
Black	47.7	40.4	38.5	40.9	38.1	32.9	34.4	29.5	35.1	33.1	37.4	35.7	33.1
All 8th graders	—	—	—	—	—	—	25.1	26.1	24.3	25.5	24.6	26.2	24.5
Male	—	—	—	—	—	—	26.3	26.3	25.3	26.5	25.0	26.6	25.2
Female	—	—	—	—	—	—	23.8	25.9	28.7	24.7	24.0	25.8	23.9
White	—	—	—	—	—	—	26.0	27.3	25.1	25.4	25.4	27.7	25.7
Black	—	—	—	—	—	—	17.8	19.2	17.7	20.2	17.3	19.0	16.9
Heavy alcohol[2]	Percent in the 2 weeks before the survey												
All 12th graders	41.2	36.8	37.5	34.7	33.0	32.2	29.8	27.9	27.5	28.2	29.8	30.2	31.3
Male	52.1	46.1	46.1	43.0	41.2	39.1	37.8	35.6	34.6	37.0	36.9	37.0	37.9
Female	30.5	28.1	29.2	26.5	24.9	24.4	21.2	20.3	20.7	20.2	23.0	23.5	24.4
White	44.6	40.5	41.2	38.8	36.9	36.2	32.9	31.3	31.3	31.7	32.9	34.0	36.1
Black	17.0	16.1	15.5	14.9	16.6	11.6	11.8	10.8	14.6	14.2	15.5	15.1	12.0
All 8th graders	—	—	—	—	—	—	12.9	13.4	13.5	14.5	14.5	15.6	14.5
Male	—	—	—	—	—	—	14.3	13.9	14.8	16.0	15.1	16.5	15.3
Female	—	—	—	—	—	—	11.4	12.8	12.3	13.0	13.9	14.5	13.5
White	—	—	—	—	—	—	12.6	12.9	12.4	13.4	14.5	15.7	14.6
Black	—	—	—	—	—	—	9.9	9.3	11.9	11.8	10.0	10.9	8.8

(—) = Data not available. **Note**: *Monitoring the Future* study excludes high school dropouts (about 3-6% of the class group, according to a 1996 report) and absentees (about 16-17% of 12th graders and about 9-10% of 8th graders). High school dropouts and absentees have higher alcohol usage than those included in the survey. (1) In 1993 the alcohol question was changed to indicate that a "drink" meant "more than a few sips." (2) Five or more drinks in a row at least once in the prior 2-week period.

Principal Types of Accidental Deaths in the U.S., 1970-97

Source: National Safety Council

Year	Motor vehicle	Falls	Poison (solid, liquid)	Drowning	Fires, burns	Ingestion of food, object	Firearms	Poison (gases)
1970	54,633	16,926	3,679	7,860	6,718	2,753	2,406	1,620
1980	53,172	13,294	3,089	7,257	5,822	3,249	1,955	1,242
1985	45,901	12,001	4,091	5,316	4,938	3,551	1,649	1,079
1990	46,814	12,313	5,055	4,685	4,175	3,303	1,416	748
1991	43,536	12,662	5,698	4,818	4,120	3,240	1,441	736
1992	40,982	12,646	6,449	3,542	3,958	3,182	1,409	633
1993	41,893	13,141	7,877	3,807	3,900	3,160	1,521	660
1994	42,524	13,450	8,309	3,942	3,986	3,065	1,356	685
1995	43,363	13,600	9,400	4,300	3,800	2,900	1,200	600
1996	43,300	14,100	9,800	3,900	3,200	3,000	1,400	600
1997	43,200	14,900	8,600	4,000	3,700	3,300	1,500	700
Death rates per 100,000 population								
1970	26.8	8.3	1.8	3.9	3.3	1.4	1.2	0.8
1980	23.4	5.9	1.4	3.2	2.6	1.4	0.9	0.5
1985	19.3	5.0	1.7	2.2	2.1	1.5	0.7	0.5
1990	18.8	4.9	2.0	1.9	1.7	1.3	0.6	0.3
1991	17.3	5.0	2.3	1.8	1.6	1.3	0.6	0.3
1992	16.1	5.0	2.5	1.4	1.6	1.2	0.6	0.2
1993	16.3	5.1	3.1	1.5	1.5	1.2	0.6	0.3
1994	16.3	5.2	3.2	1.5	1.5	1.2	0.5	0.3
1995	16.5	5.2	3.6	1.6	1.4	1.1	0.5	0.2
1996	16.3	5.3	3.7	1.5	1.7	1.1	0.5	0.2
1997	16.1	5.6	3.2	1.5	1.4	1.2	0.6	0.3

Note: There were 13,900 other accidental deaths in 1997; the most frequently occurring types were medical and surgical complications, machinery, air transport, water transport (except drownings), mechanical suffocation, and excessive cold.

U.S. Motor Vehicle Accidents

Source: National Safety Council

Motor vehicle deaths in the U.S. in 1997 were virtually unchanged from levels in 1996. Of the 181,700,000 licensed drivers in 1997, about 91.4 mil (50.3%) were men and 90.3 mil (49.7%) were women.

Male drivers were involved in more fatal accidents than female drivers in 1997. About 43,600 men and 16,100 women drivers were involved in fatal accidents.

About 14.3 mil male drivers and 9.6 mil female drivers were involved in all types of accidents in 1997. However, since males account for about 63% of the miles driven each year, according to the latest estimates, and females for 37%, women have higher accident involvement rates. At least part of the difference in accident involvement rates between men and women may be due to differences in the time, place, and circumstance of driving experienced by both groups of drivers. Accident rates were 90 per 10 million miles driven for men and 103 per 10 million miles driven for women.

About 41% of all traffic fatalities in 1996 involved an intoxicated or alcohol-impaired driver or nonoccupant. Of these 17,126 alcohol-related traffic fatalities, an estimated 13,395 occurred in accidents in which a driver or nonoccupant was intoxicated, and the remainder involved a driver or nonoccupant who had been drinking but was not legally intoxicated. Alcohol was also a factor in about 7% of all traffic accidents, both fatal and nonfatal, in 1996. In 1986 alcohol-related fatalities accounted for 52% of all traffic deaths.

	Death total 1997	Percentage change from 1996	Death rate 1997[1]
All motor vehicle accidents	43,200	(2)	16.1
Collision between motor vehicles	21,300	+9	8.0
Collision with fixed object	10,800	−12	4.0
Pedestrian accidents	5,700	−2	2.1
Noncollision accidents	4,200	−7	1.67
Collision with pedalcycle	700	0	0.3
Collision with railroad train	400	0	0.1
Other collision (animal, animal-drawn vehicles)	100	0	(3)

(1) Deaths per 100,000 population. (2) Change was less than 0.05%. (3) Death rate was less than 0.05.

Improper Driving Reported in Accidents, 1996-97

Source: National Safety Council

Type	Percentage of fatal accidents 1996	Percentage of fatal accidents 1997	Percentage of injury accidents 1996	Percentage of injury accidents 1997	Percentage of all accidents 1996	Percentage of all accidents 1997
Improper driving	**69.1**	**64.6**	**87.1**	**73.8**	**87.4**	**66.1**
Speed too fast or unsafe	17.6	16.8	13.5	13.2	14.3	11.0
Right of way	15.7	15.0	29.1	22.2	23.6	16.8
Failed to yield	10.1	10.1	20.2	15.9	17.2	12.7
Passed stop sign	2.1	3.1	1.3	2.3	1.2	1.5
Disregarded signal	3.5	1.8	7.6	4.0	5.2	2.6
Drove left of center	8.1	7.5	2.3	2.1	2.1	1.5
Improper overtaking	1.2	1.1	1.1	0.8	1.2	1.1
Made improper turn	4.1	3.7	4.1	3.6	5.7	4.0
Followed too closely	0.9	1.2	9.9	11.3	9.6	10.6
Other improper driving	21.5	19.3	27.1	20.6	30.9	21.1
No improper driving stated	**30.9**	**35.4**	**12.9**	**26.2**	**12.6**	**33.9**

Note: Based on reports from 12 state traffic authorities. When a driver was under the influence of alcohol or drugs, the accident was considered a result of the driver's physical condition—not a driving error. For this reason, accidents in which the driver was reported to be under the influence are classified under "no improper driving."

Deaths in the U.S. Involving Firearms, by Age, 1995

Source: National Safety Council

	All ages	Under 5	5-14	15-24	25-44	45-64	65-74	75 & over
Total firearms deaths[1]	**35,673**	**105**	**747**	**9,699**	**14,185**	**6,137**	**2,417**	**2,383**
Male	30.448	63	575	8,651	11,850	5,067	2,104	2,138
Female	5,225	42	172	1,048	2,335	1,070	313	245
Accidents	**1,225**	**20**	**161**	**423**	**386**	**147**	**52**	**36**
Male	1,055	14	136	392	313	120	49	31
Female	170	6	25	31	73	27	3	5
Suicides	**18,503**	**0**	**184**	**3,068**	**6,673**	**4,314**	**2,085**	**2,179**
Male	16,060	0	137	2,729	5,686	3,629	1,863	2,016
Female	2,443	0	47	339	987	685	222	163
Homicides	**15,551**	**82**	**380**	**6,044**	**6,995**	**1,628**	**269**	**153**
Male	13,021	47	285	5,384	5,760	1,285	183	77
Female	2,530	35	95	660	1,235	343	86	76
Undetermined[2]	**394**	**3**	**22**	**164**	**131**	**48**	**11**	**15**
Male	312	2	17	146	91	33	9	14
Female	82	1	5	18	40	15	2	1

(1) Figures exclude firearms deaths by legal intervention. These deaths totaled 284 in 1995. (2) "Undetermined" means that the intention involved (whether accident, suicide, or homicide) could not be determined.

Home Accident Deaths in the U.S., 1950-97

Source: National Safety Council

Year	Total	Falls	Poison (solid, liquid)	Fires, burns[1]	Suffoc., ingesting object	Firearms	Suffoc., mechan-ical	Poison (gases)	All other
1950	29,000	14,800	1,300	5,000	(2)	950	1,600	1,250	4,100
1960	28,000	12,300	1,350	6,350	1,850	1,200	1,500	900	2,550
1970	27,000	9,700	3,000	5,600	1,800[3]	1,400[3]	1,100[3]	1,100	3,300[3]
1980	22,800	7,100	2,500	4,800	2,000	1,100	500	700	4,100[4]
1990	21,500	6,700	4,000	3,400	2,300	800	600	500	3,200
1991	22,100	6,900	4,500	3,400	2,200	800	700	500	3,100
1992	24,000	7,700	4,800	3,700	1,500	1,000	700	400	4,200
1993	26,100	7,900	6,000	3,700	1,700	1,100	700	500	4,500
1994	26,300	8,100	6,300	3,700	1,600	900	800	500	4,400
1995[5]	27,200	8,400	6,600	3,500	1,500	900	800	400	5,100
1996[5]	27,500	8.700	7,000	3,000	1,600	1,000	700	400	5,100
1997	28,400	9,200	6,700	3,300	1,600	1,000	900	400	5,300

(1) Includes deaths resulting from conflagration, regardless of nature of injury. (2) Included under "All other" category. (3) Data for this year and subsequent years not comparable with data from previous years because of classification changes. (4) Includes about 1,000 deaths attributed to summer heat wave. (5) Revised figures. The National Safety Council adopted the count from the Bureau of Labor Statistics Census of Fatal Occupational Injuries for all work-related unintentional injuries, retroactive to 1992 data. (6) Data for 1997 are preliminary.

Worldwide Airline Fatalities, 1980-97

Source: National Safety Council

Year	Aircraft accidents[1]	Passenger deaths	Death rate[2]	Year	Aircraft accidents[1]	Passenger deaths	Death rate[2]
1980	22	814	0.14	1989	27	817	0.08
1981	21	362	0.06	1990	22	440	0.04
1982	26	764	0.13	1991	25	510	0.05
1983	20	809	0.13	1992	25	990	0.09
1984	16	223	0.03	1993	31	801	0.07
1985	22	1,066	0.15	1994	24	732	0.06
1986	17	331	0.04	1995	22	557	0.04
1987	24	890	0.10	1996	22	1,132	0.08
1988	25	699	0.08	1997[3]	25	854	0.05

(1) Those involving one or more passenger fatalities only. (2) Passenger deaths per 100 mil passenger mi. (3) Preliminary figures.

Cost of Unintentional Injuries in the U.S., 1997

Source: National Safety Council, estimates

The cost of. . .	is equivalent to. . .
. . .all injuries ($478.3 bil)	64 cents of every dollar paid in 1997 federal personal income taxes, *or* 62 cents of every dollar spent on food in the U.S. in 1997.
. . .motor vehicle accidents ($200.3 bil)	purchasing 760 gallons of gasoline per registered vehicle in the U.S., *or* more than 12 times greater than the combined profits reported by General Motors, Ford, and Chrysler in 1997.
. . .work injuries ($127.7 bil)	38 cents of every dollar of 1997 corporate dividends to stockholders, *or* 17 cents of every dollar of 1997 pre-tax corporate profits.
. . .home injuries ($99.9 bil)	an $88,100 rebate on each new single-family home built in 1997, *or* 48 cents of every dollar of property taxes paid in 1997.
. . .public injuries[1] ($66.1 bil)	a $7.0 million grant to each public library in the U.S., *or* an $82,900 bonus for each police officer and firefighter.

(1) Any injuries that occur in public places or places used in a public way and not involving motor vehicles.

U.S. Fires, 1997

Source: National Fire Protection Assn.

Fires

- Public fire departments responded to 1,795,000 fires in 1997, a decrease of 9% from 1996.
- There were 552,000 structure fires in 1997, a decrease of 5% from the 1996 figure.
- 74% of all structure fires, or 406,500 fires, occurred in residential properties.
- There were 397,000 vehicle fires in 1997, a decrease of 4% from the previous year.
- There were 846,000 fires in outside properties, a significant decrease of 14% from 1996.
- The South had the highest fire incident rate in the country, with 7.8 fires per 1,000 population.

Civilian deaths

- There were 4,050 civilian fire deaths in 1997, a significant decrease of 20% from 1996.
- The number of deaths from fire in the home decreased by 17%, to 3,360.
- About 83% of all fire deaths occurred in the home.
- The South and the Northeast had the highest regional fire death rate, with 17.5 civilian deaths per million population.
- Nationwide, someone died in a fire every 130 minutes.

Civilian injuries

- There were an estimated 23,750 civilian fire injuries in 1997, a decrease of 7% from 1996. This estimate is traditionally low because of underreporting of civilian fire injuries to the fire service.
- Residential properties were the site of 17,775 civilian fire injuries, or 75% of injuries overall; 2,600 injuries, or 11%, occurred in nonresidential structure fires.
- The Northeast had the highest regional injury rate in the U.S., with 109.9 civilian injuries per million population. The next highest rate was in the North Central region, with 96.6 injuries per million.
- Nationwide, a civilian was injured in a fire every 22 minutes.

Property damage

- Property damage resulting from fires decreased in 1997 by 9%, to an estimated $8.525 billion.
- Structure fires resulted in 83% of all property damage, or $7.087 billion.
- 65% of all structure property loss occurred in residential properties, accounting for $4.585 billion.
- The South had the highest property loss rate in the U.S.—about $35.70 per person—followed by the North Central region, with $32.30 per person, and the Northeast, with $31.20 per person.

Incendiary and suspicious fires

- About 14% of all structure fires, or an estimated 78,500 fires, were deliberately set or are suspected of having been deliberately set. This represents a decrease of 8% from 1996.
- Incendiary or suspicious structure fires resulted in 445 civilian deaths, a decrease of 14% from the previous year. Incendiary or suspicious fires caused $1.309 billion in property damage, or 19% of all property loss from structure fires.
- The number of vehicle fires of incendiary or suspicious origin in 1997 was 47,500, virtually no change from 1996. They caused an estimated $214 million in property damage, a 6% increase from the year before.

Physicians by Age, Sex, and Specialty, 1997

Source: American Medical Assn., as of Dec. 31, 1997

	Total Physicians[1]		Under 35 yrs		35-44 yrs		45-54 yrs		55-64 yrs	
	Male	Female	Male	Female	Male	Female	Male	Female	Male	Female
All Specialties	**590,011**	**166,699**	**84,445**	**49,395**	**152,210**	**61,192**	**142,314**	**33,180**	**92,260**	**12,022**
Aerospace Medicine	548	38	53	8	155	17	145	10	98	2
Allergy & Immunology	3,024	748	136	84	759	309	960	239	688	69
Anesthesiology	27,023	6,707	3,970	1,352	10,905	2,727	6,536	1,582	3,569	776
Cardiovascular Disease	17,939	1,348	1,502	233	6,166	652	5,665	332	3,006	94
Child Psychiatry	3,425	2,195	240	267	949	843	1,082	650	722	269
Colon/Rectal Surgery	974	59	974	10	325	36	322	11	162	2
Dermatology	6,328	2,734	671	753	1,477	1,199	2,028	558	1,373	167
Diagnostic Radiology	16,258	3,859	3,059	1,130	5,443	1,694	4,740	820	2,324	173
Emergency Medicine	16,943	3,662	3,325	1,164	5,740	1,497	5,727	781	1,444	169
Family Practice	48,193	16,416	7,597	5,842	16,159	6,797	13,792	2,828	5,265	656
Forensic Pathology	380	134	16	5	101	61	114	38	84	20
Gastroenterology	8,963	763	834	156	3,276	396	3,034	173	1,336	32
General Practice	14,370	2,465	195	69	1,061	502	2,586	797	3,501	583
General Preventive Med.	1,040	510	79	67	303	229	290	136	188	44
General Surgery	37,181	3,754	7,834	1,834	8,731	1,257	8,303	522	7,049	97
Internal Medicine	95,859	32,576	21,140	11,799	29,220	12,838	24,901	5,864	11,968	1,473
Medical Genetics	147	103	10	4	36	47	58	33	32	14
Neurological Surgery	4,696	217	717	71	1,266	98	1,117	41	1,059	5
Neurology	9,429	2,285	1,023	474	3,056	1,003	3,046	586	1,596	170
Nuclear Medicine	1,173	261	75	29	270	98	365	79	305	41
Obstetrics/Gynecology	26,725	12,532	2,975	4,454	6,327	4,857	7,773	2,202	5,864	749
Occupational Medicine	2,565	484	37	22	522	212	744	156	494	58
Ophthalmology	15,432	2,390	1,806	649	4,211	1,063	4,137	489	3,496	136
Orthopedic Surgery	22,132	755	3,640	267	6,415	320	5,718	132	4,354	21
Otolaryngology	8,348	748	1,286	269	2,232	329	2,080	122	1,925	18
Pathology-Anat./Clin.	13,069	5,167	1,355	993	3,291	1,952	3,452	1,319	2,932	633
Pediatric Cardiology	1,033	329	107	76	374	138	273	61	179	35
Pediatrics	29,794	25,633	5,208	8,488	8,478	9,338	8,227	5,214	4,721	1,890
Physical Med./Rehab.	3,987	1,863	754	445	1,568	684	871	447	436	187
Plastic Surgery	5,452	529	345	85	1,755	262	1,713	131	1,199	35
Psychiatry	28,159	10,905	2,236	1,723	6,049	3,852	7,643	2,982	6,384	1,401
Public Health	1,237	433	8	5	167	106	321	119	301	80
Pulmonary Diseases	6,088	671	241	90	2,127	347	2,491	162	874	42
Radiation Oncology	2,880	817	377	184	1,005	317	754	218	508	75
Radiology	7,129	1,013	371	96	1,240	366	1,490	303	2,496	173
Thoracic Surgery	256	13	89	5	164	8	2	0	1	0
Urological Surgery	9,764	264	1,167	94	2,479	125	2,647	35	2,418	7
Other	5,219	949	201	63	779	261	1,244	260	1,311	180
Unspecified	9,792	5,268	6,654	3,934	1,941	958	633	259	256	67

(1) Includes physicians 65 and older, those living in U.S. possessions, "Not Classified," "Inactive," and "Address Unknown."

U.S. Health Expenditures, 1965-96

Source: *Health, United States, 1998,* National Center for Health Statistics, U.S. Dept. of Health and Human Services

Type of expenditure	1965	1970	1975	1980	1985	1990	1993	1994	1995	1996
					Amount in billions					
TOTAL	**$41.1**	**$73.2**	**$130.7**	**$247.3**	**$428.7**	**$699.5**	**$895.1**	**$945.7**	**$991.4**	**$1,035.1**
					Percent distribution					
Health services & supplies	**91.6**	**92.7**	**93.6**	**95.3**	**96.2**	**96.5**	**96.8**	**96.8**	**96.9**	**97.0**
Personal health care	85.5	87.1	87.6	87.8	87.8	87.9	87.9	87.6	87.7	87.6
Hospital care	34.1	38.2	40.2	41.5	39.3	36.7	36.1	35.5	35.0	34.6
Physician services	19.9	18.5	18.3	18.3	19.5	20.9	20.5	20.1	19.8	19.5
Dentist services	6.8	6.4	6.1	5.4	5.0	4.5	4.4	4.4	4.5	4.6
Nursing home care	3.6	5.8	6.6	7.1	7.2	7.3	7.4	7.5	7.6	7.6
Other professional services	2.1	1.9	2.1	2.6	3.9	5.0	5.2	5.3	5.5	5.6
Home health care	0.2	0.3	0.5	1.0	1.3	1.9	2.6	2.7	2.9	2.9
Drugs & other medical nondurables	14.3	12.0	10.0	8.7	8.6	8.6	8.4	8.4	8.6	8.8
Vision products & other medical durables	2.4	2.2	2.0	1.5	1.6	1.5	1.4	1.3	1.3	1.3
Other personal health care	2.0	1.8	1.9	1.6	1.4	1.6	2.0	2.3	2.5	2.7
Program administration & net cost of health insurance	4.7	3.7	3.8	4.8	5.7	5.8	6.0	6.2	6.1	5.9
Government public health activities[1]	1.5	1.8	2.2	2.7	2.7	2.8	2.8	3.0	3.2	3.4
Research & construction	**8.4**	**7.3**	**6.4**	**4.7**	**3.8**	**3.5**	**3.2**	**3.2**	**3.1**	**3.0**
Noncommercial research	3.7	2.7	2.5	2.2	1.8	1.7	1.6	1.7	1.7	1.6
Construction	4.7	4.6	3.9	2.5	2.0	1.8	1.6	1.5	1.4	1.4
					Average annual % change from previous year shown					
All expenditures	**—**	**12.2**	**12.3**	**13.6**	**11.6**	**10.3**	**8.6**	**5.6**	**4.8**	**4.4**
Health services & supplies	**—**	**12.5**	**12.5**	**14.0**	**11.8**	**10.4**	**8.7**	**5.7**	**5.0**	**4.5**
Personal health care	—	12.7	12.4	13.6	11.6	10.3	8.6	5.3	4.9	4.4
Hospital care	—	14.8	13.4	14.3	10.4	8.8	8.0	3.9	3.3	3.4
Physician services	—	10.6	12.0	13.6	13.1	11.8	7.8	3.7	3.1	2.9
Dentist services	—	10.8	11.2	10.9	10.2	7.8	7.4	6.6	7.3	6.4
Nursing home care	—	23.4	15.5	15.3	11.7	10.7	9.2	6.8	6.2	4.3
Other professional services	—	10.2	14.2	18.4	21.2	15.8	10.1	8.8	7.9	6.8
Home health care	—	19.7	23.2	30.7	18.9	18.4	20.3	12.2	10.9	6.2
Drugs & other medical nondurables	—	8.4	8.1	10.7	11.4	10.1	8.0	5.2	6.8	7.7
Vision products & other medical durables	—	10.2	9.5	8.1	12.4	9.2	5.6	1.5	4.9	1.4
Other personal health care	—	9.5	13.8	10.2	8.8	12.9	17.0	21.8	15.4	9.4
Program administration & net cost of health insurance	—	7.1	12.5	19.3	15.4	10.9	9.8	8.2	3.3	1.2
Government public health activities[1]	—	17.0	16.8	18.1	11.5	11.0	8.9	12.5	10.7	12.5
Research & construction	**—**	**9.2**	**9.4**	**6.8**	**7.1**	**8.4**	**5.8**	**5.1**	**0.8**	**2.6**
Noncommercial research	—	5.1	11.2	10.4	7.5	9.3	5.9	9.6	5.0	1.9
Construction	—	12.1	8.3	4.1	6.7	7.6	5.7	0.5	–3.8	3.4

Note: Numbers may not add to totals because of rounding. (1) Includes personal care services delivered by government public health agencies.

Ownership of Life Insurance in the U.S. and Assets of U.S. Life Insurance Companies, 1940-97

Source: American Council of Life Insurance

(amounts in millions)

	PURCHASES OF LIFE INSURANCE				INSURANCE IN FORCE					
Year	Ordinary	Group	Industrial	Total	Ordinary	Group	Industrial	Credit	Total	Assets
1940	$6,689	$691	$3,350	$10,730	$79,346	$14,938	$20,866	$380	$115,530	$30,802
1950	17,326	6,068	5,402	28,796	149,116	47,793	33,415	3,844	234,168	64,020
1960	52,883	14,645	6,880	74,408	341,881	175,903	39,563	29,101	586,448	119,576
1970	122,820	63,690[1]	6,612	193,122[1]	734,730	551,357	38,644	77,392	1,402,123	207,254
1975	188,003	95,190[1]	6,729	289,922[1]	1,083,421	904,695	39,423	112,032	2,139,571	289,304
1980	385,575	183,418	3,609	572,602	1,760,474	1,579,355	35,994	165,215	3,541,038	479,210
1985	910,944	319,503[2]	722	1,231,169[2]	3,247,289	2,561,595	28,250	215,973	6,053,107	825,901
1990	1,069,660	459,271	220	1,529,151	5,366,982	3,753,506	24,071	248,038	9,392,597	1,408,208
1991	1,041,508	573,953[1]	198	1,615,659[1]	5,677,777	4,057,606	22,475	228,478	9,986,336	1,551,201
1992	1,048,135	440,143	222	1,488,500	5,941,810	4,240,919	20,973	202,090	10,405,792	1,664,531
1993	1,101,327	576,823	149	1,678,299	6,428,434	4,456,338	20,451	199,518	11,104,741	1,839,127
1994	1,050,930	560,232	257	1,611,419	6,407,399	4,441,730	18,947	189,398	11,057,474	1,942,273
1995	1,004,677	537,828	156	1,542,661	6,815,630	4,603,297	18,134	201,083	11,638,144	2,143,544
1996	1,035,205	614,565	130	1,649,901	7,294,079	5,066,621	18,064	210,746	12,589,510	2,327,924
1997	1,142,274	688,589	128	1,830,991	7,688,940	5,276,782	17,991	212,255	13,195,968	2,579,078

(1) Includes Servicemen's Group Life Insurance, which amounted to $17.1 billion in 1970, $1.7 billion in 1975, and $166.7 billion in 1991. (2) Includes Federal Employees' Group Life Insurance of $10.8 billion.

Health Insurance Coverage,[1] by State, 1996-97

Source: Bureau of the Census, U.S. Dept. of Commerce, Mar. 1998 Current Population Survey; in thousands

STATE	Total population, 1997	Not covered, 1997	% not covered, 1997	% not covered, 1996	STATE	Total population, 1997	Not covered, 1997	% not covered, 1997	% not covered, 1996
AL	4,247	659	15.5	12.9	MT	894	174	19.5	13.6
AK	641	116	18.1	13.5	NE	1,662	180	10.8	11.4
AZ	4,655	1,141	24.5	24.1	NV	1,724	301	17.5	15.6
AR	2,622	639	24.4	21.7	NH	1,200	141	11.8	9.5
CA	32,987	7,095	21.5	20.1	NJ	7,977	1,320	16.5	16.7
CO	3,929	592	15.1	16.6	NM	1,827	413	22.6	22.3
CT	3,299	395	12.0	11.0	NY	18,143	3,174	17.5	17.0
DE	750	98	13.1	13.4	NC	7,352	1,141	15.5	16.0
DC	518	84	16.2	14.8	ND	639	97	15.2	9.8
FL	14,399	2,817	19.6	18.9	OH	11,230	1,297	11.5	11.5
GA	7,647	1,344	17.6	17.8	OK	3,338	593	17.8	17.0
HI	1,183	89	7.5	8.6	OR	3,298	440	13.3	15.3
ID	1,257	223	17.7	16.5	PA	11,922	1,209	10.1	9.5
IL	12,098	1,506	12.4	11.3	RI	944	96	10.2	9.9
IN	5,865	669	11.4	10.6	SC	3,815	640	16.8	17.1
IA	2,830	340	12.0	11.6	SD	712	84	11.8	9.5
KS	2,590	304	11.7	11.4	TN	5,542	756	13.6	15.2
KY	3,922	587	15.0	15.4	TX	19,751	4,836	24.5	24.3
LA	4,250	827	14.9	20.9	UT	2,085	280	13.4	12.0
ME	1,225	182	14.9	12.1	VT	581	55	9.5	11.1
MD	5,057	677	13.4	11.4	VA	6,752	854	12.6	12.5
MA	6,004	755	12.6	12.4	WA	5,748	655	11.4	13.5
MI	9,794	1,133	11.6	8.9	WV	1,747	300	17.2	14.9
MN	4,767	438	9.2	10.2	WI	5,126	409	8.0	8.4
MS	2,737	550	20.1	18.5	WY	491	76	15.5	13.5
MO	5,322	669	12.6	13.2	**TOTAL U.S.**	**269,094**	**43,448**	**16.1**	**15.6**

(1) For all ages, including those 65 or over, an age group largely covered by Medicare.

Persons Not Covered by Health Insurance, by Selected Characteristics, 1997

Source: Bureau of the Census, U.S. Dept. of Commerce, Mar. 1998 Current Population Survey; in thousands

	Number	Percent
TOTAL NOT COVERED	43,448	16.1
Sex		
Male	23,130	17.6
Female	20,319	14.8
Age		
Under 18 years	10,743	15.0
18 to 24 years	7,582	30.1
25 to 34 years	9,162	23.3
35 to 44 years	7,699	17.3
45 to 64 years	7,928	14.1
65 years and over	333	1.0
Nativity		
Native	34,444	14.2
Foreign-born	9,003	34.3
Naturalized citizen	1,798	18.5
Not a citizen	7,206	43.6
Race and Hispanic origin		
White	33,242	15.0
White, not of Hispanic origin	23,135	12.0
Black	7,432	21.5
Asian or Pacific Islander	2,172	20.7
Hispanic origin[1]	10,534	34.2
Education[2]		
No high school diploma	9,189	26.1
High school graduate, no college	12,204	18.5
Some college, no degree	5,974	15.6
Associate degree	1,726	12.3
Bachelor's degree or higher	3,611	8.2
Work experience[3]		
Worked during year	24,572	18.1
Worked full-time	18,698	16.8
Worked part-time	5,874	24.1
Did not work	7,800	26.2
Household income		
Less than $25,000	18,361	25.4
$25,000-$49,999	14,527	18.1
$50,000-$74,999	5,678	10.1
$75,000 or more	4,882	8.1

(1) Persons of Hispanic origin may be of any race. (2) Persons aged 18 years and over. (3) Persons aged 18-64.

Health Coverage for Persons Under 65, by Characteristics, 1984, 1994-96

Source: *Health, United States, 1998,* National Center for Health Statistics, U.S. Dept. of Health and Human Services

	PRIVATE INSURANCE				MEDICAID[1]				NOT COVERED[2]			
	1984	1994	1995	1996[3]	1984	1994	1995	1996[3]	1984	1994	1995	1996[3]
	Percent of each population group											
Age												
Under 18 years	72.6	63.8	65.7	66.4	11.9	20.0	20.6	20.1	13.9	15.3	13.6	13.4
18-44 years	76.5	69.8	71.2	70.6	5.1	7.3	7.4	7.3	17.1	21.9	20.5	21.2
45-64 years	83.3	80.3	80.4	79.5	3.4	4.5	5.3	5.2	9.6	12.0	11.0	12.1
Race and Hispanic origin[4]												
White, non-Hispanic	82.3	77.3	78.6	78.5	4.0	7.1	7.5	7.5	11.6	14.2	12.7	12.9
Black, non-Hispanic	58.5	51.9	54.6	55.4	20.8	27.0	26.7	24.2	19.2	19.1	17.8	18.9
All Hispanic	56.3	48.6	47.3	47.5	13.1	19.6	21.2	20.1	29.0	31.4	30.8	31.6
Percent of poverty level[4]												
Below 100%	32.4	21.3	21.9	20.0	32.1	45.0	46.9	46.8	34.0	32.7	30.9	32.7
100-149%	62.4	46.8	47.8	47.1	7.7	16.0	18.4	17.2	26.4	34.0	31.2	32.8
150-199%	77.7	65.7	66.5	67.9	3.3	5.9	7.7	7.7	16.7	24.9	22.8	22.5
200% or more	91.7	88.9	89.3	89.5	0.6	1.4	1.6	1.6	5.6	8.4	7.8	7.4
Geographic region[4]												
Northeast	80.1	74.8	75.1	74.9	9.4	12.0	12.5	12.3	9.8	13.3	12.7	13.2
Midwest	80.4	77.2	77.2	78.4	7.9	10.4	11.0	9.4	10.9	11.9	11.8	11.9
South	74.0	65.0	66.7	65.9	5.5	11.3	11.6	12.0	17.4	20.9	19.1	19.7
West	71.8	65.2	67.9	67.1	7.5	12.6	13.2	13.4	17.6	20.2	17.3	18.1

Note: Data based on household interviews of a sample of the civilian noninstitutionalized population. Percents do not add to 100 because other types of health insurance (e.g., Medicare, military) are not shown and persons with both private insurance and Medicaid appear in both columns. (1) Includes Medicaid or other public assistance. In 1996, the age-adjusted percent of the population under 65 covered by Medicaid was 11.3%; 0.4% were covered by public assistance. (2) Includes persons not covered by private insurance, Medicaid or other public assistance, Medicare, or military plans. (3) Preliminary data. (4) Age adjusted.

Enrollment in Health Maintenance Organizations (HMOs), 1976-97

Source: *Health, United States, 1998,* National Center for Health Statistics, U.S. Dept. of Health and Human Services

	1976	1980	1985[1]	1990	1991	1992	1993	1994	1995	1996	1997
				Number of enrolled in millions							
TOTAL	**6.0**	**9.1**	**21.0**	**33.0**	**34.0**	**36.1**	**38.4**	**45.1**	**50.9**	**59.1**	**66.8**
Model type[2]											
Individual practice association[3]	0.4	1.7	6.4	13.7	13.6	14.7	15.3	17.8	20.1	26.0	26.7
Group[4]	5.6	7.4	14.6	19.3	17.1	16.5	15.4	13.9	13.3	14.1	11.0
Mixed	—	—	—	—	3.3	4.9	7.7	13.4	17.6	19.0	29.0
Federal program[5]											
Medicaid[6]	—	0.3	0.6	1.2	1.4	1.7	1.7	2.6	3.5	4.7	5.5
Medicare	—	0.4	1.1	1.8	2.0	2.2	2.2	2.5	2.9	3.7	4.8
				Percent of population enrolled in HMOs							
TOTAL	**2.8**	**4.0**	**8.9**	**13.4**	**13.6**	**14.3**	**15.1**	**17.3**	**19.4**	**22.3**	**25.2**
Geographic region											
Northeast	2.0	3.1	7.9	14.6	15.4	16.1	18.0	20.8	24.4	25.9	32.4
Midwest	1.5	2.8	9.7	12.6	12.7	12.8	13.2	15.2	16.4	18.8	19.5
South	0.4	0.8	3.8	7.1	7.1	7.8	8.4	10.2	12.4	15.2	17.9
West	9.7	12.2	17.3	23.2	23.8	24.7	25.1	27.4	28.6	33.2	36.4

— = Not available. **Note:** Data as of June 30 in 1976-80, Dec. 31 in 1985, Jan. 1 in 1990-97. Medicaid enrollment in 1990 as of June 30. HMOs in Guam not included prior to 1995. Open-ended enrollment in HMO plans, amounting to 7.8 million on Jan. 1, 1997, included from 1994 onwards. (1) Increases partly due to changes in reporting methods. (2) In 1976, 11 HMOs with 35,000 enrollment did not report model type. In 1997, 11 HMOs with 153,000 enrollment did not report model type. (3) This type of HMO contracts with an association of physicians from various settings (a mixture of solo and group practices) to provide health services. (4) Group includes staff, group, and network model types. (5) Enrollment by Medicaid or Medicare beneficiaries, where the Medicaid or Medicare program contracts directly with the HMO to pay the premium. (6) Data for 1990 and later include enrollment in managed-care health insuring organizations.

Physician Contacts Per Person, by Selected Characteristics, 1987-95

Source: *Health, United States, 1998,* National Center for Health Statistics, U.S. Dept. of Health and Human Services

	1987	1988	1989	1990	1991	1992	1993	1994	1995
TOTAL[1,2]	**5.4**	**5.3**	**5.3**	**5.5**	**5.6**	**5.9**	**6.0**	**6.0**	**5.8**
Age									
Under 15 years	4.5	4.6	4.6	4.5	4.7	4.6	4.9	4.6	4.5
Under 5 years	6.7	7.0	6.7	6.9	7.1	6.9	7.2	6.8	6.5
5-14 years	3.3	3.3	3.5	3.2	3.4	3.4	3.6	3.4	3.4
15-44 years	4.6	4.7	4.6	4.8	4.7	5.0	5.0	5.0	4.8
45-64 years	6.4	6.1	6.1	6.4	6.6	7.2	7.1	7.3	7.1
65 years and over	8.9	8.7	8.9	9.2	10.4	10.6	10.9	11.3	11.1
65-74 years	8.4	8.4	8.2	8.5	9.2	9.7	9.9	10.3	9.8
75 years and over	9.7	9.2	9.9	10.1	12.3	12.1	12.3	12.7	12.9
Sex									
Male[1]	4.6	4.6	4.8	4.7	4.9	5.1	5.2	5.2	4.9
Female[1]	6.0	6.0	5.9	6.1	6.3	6.6	6.7	6.7	6.5
Race									
White[1]	5.5	5.5	5.5	5.6	5.8	6.0	6.0	6.1	5.9
Black[1]	5.1	4.8	4.9	5.1	5.2	5.9	6.0	5.7	5.5
Family income[1,3]									
Less than $15,000	6.8	6.2	6.3	6.3	6.8	7.3	7.3	7.6	7.4
$15,000-$24,999	5.6	5.3	5.2	5.6	5.6	6.0	5.7	5.9	6.1
$25,000-$34,999	5.2	5.0	5.5	5.2	5.5	5.7	6.0	5.8	5.3
$35,000-$49,999	5.2	5.5	5.2	5.7	5.8	5.9	6.0	6.2	5.7
$50,000 or more	5.4	5.5	6.0	5.6	5.8	5.8	5.8	6.0	5.6
Geographic region[1]									
Northeast	5.2	5.0	5.3	5.2	5.4	5.9	5.9	5.9	5.6
Midwest	5.6	5.4	5.4	5.3	5.8	5.9	6.2	6.0	5.8
South	5.1	5.2	5.3	5.6	5.5	5.8	5.7	5.6	5.8
West	5.5	5.9	5.5	5.6	5.9	6.1	6.0	6.4	5.8
Location of residence[1]									
Within MSA	5.5	5.5	5.4	5.6	5.8	6.0	6.1	6.0	5.9
Outside MSA	4.8	4.9	5.2	4.9	5.1	5.6	5.6	5.7	5.3

MSA = metropolitan statistical area. **Note:** Data based on household interviews of a sample of the civilian noninstitutionalized population. (1) Age adjusted. (2) Includes all races whether shown separately or not, and unknown family income. (3) The family income categories listed are for 1995. The 5 income categories for 1987 are: less than $10,000; $10,000-$14,999; $15,000-$19,999; $20,000-$34,999; and $35,000 or more. Income categories for 1988 are: less than $13,000; $13,000-$18,999; $19,000-$24,999; $25,000-$44,999; and $45,000 or more. In 1989-94, the 2 lowest income categories are: less than $14,000 and $14,000-24,999; the 3 higher income categories are as shown.

Top 20 Reasons Given by Patients for Emergency Room Visits, 1996

Source: National Center for Health Statistics, U.S. Dept. of Health and Human Services

Principal reason for visit	No. of visits (1,000)	Percent of total
ALL VISITS	**90,347**	**100**
Stomach and abdominal pain, cramps, and spasms	5,108	5.7
Chest pain and related symptoms	4,661	5.2
Fever	4,125	4.6
Headache, pain in head	2,374	2.6
Injury—upper extremity	2,350	2.6
Shortness of breath	2,322	2.6
Back symptoms	2,029	2.2
Cough	1,931	2.1
Pain, site not referable to a specific body system	1,913	2.1
Symptoms referable to throat	1,874	2.1
Vomiting	1,870	2.1
Earache or ear infection	1,699	1.9
Labored or difficult breathing (dyspnea)	1,542	1.7
Laceration and cuts—facial area	1,505	1.7
Injury, other and unspecified type—head, neck, and face	1,442	1.6
Motor vehicle accident, type of injury unspecified	1,312	1.5
Vertigo—dizziness	1,309	1.4
Hand and finger injury	1,226	1.4
Skin rash	1,161	1.3
Lower back symptoms	1,136	1.3
All other reasons	47,458	52.5

Top 20 Reasons Given by Patients for Physicians' Office Visits, 1996

Source: National Center for Health Statistics, U.S. Dept. of Health and Human Services

Principal reason for visit	NUMBER OF VISITS (1,000)	PERCENTAGE DISTRIBUTION Total	Female	Male
ALL VISITS	**734,493**	**100.0**	**100.0**	**100.0**
General medical examination	50,669	6.9	7.4	6.2
Progress visit, not otherwise specified	28,804	3.9	3.6	4.4
Routine prenatal examination	23,948	3.3	5.5	—
Cough	22,800	3.1	3.0	3.3
Postoperative visit	18,663	2.5	2.6	2.4
Symptoms referable to throat	17,967	2.4	2.2	2.8
Well-baby examination	15,236	2.1	1.8	2.4
Skin rash	11,997	1.6	1.6	1.6
Stomach pain, cramps, and spasms	11,721	1.6	1.7	1.4
Back symptoms	11,438	1.6	1.5	1.7
Earache or ear infection	11,321	1.5	1.5	1.7
Nasal congestion	11,245	1.5	1.4	1.7
Fever	10,719	1.5	1.1	2.0
Vision dysfunctions	10,410	1.4	1.5	1.4
Knee symptoms	9,822	1.3	1.2	1.5
Hypertension	9,719	1.3	1.2	1.5
Blood pressure test	8,554	1.2	1.0	1.3
Chest pain and related symptoms	8,190	1.1	1.0	1.3
Depression	8,169	1.1	1.2	1.0
Headache, pain in head	8,126	1.1	1.2	0.9
All other reasons	424,975	57.9	56.8	59.5

Drugs Most Frequently Prescribed in Physicians' Offices, 1996

Source: National Center for Health Statistics, U.S. Dept. of Health and Human Services; *Physicians' Desk Reference*; in thousands

RANK	Name of drug (principal generic substance)[1]	Times prescribed	Therapeutic use
1.	Amoxicillin	15,963	Antibiotic
2.	Tylenol (acetaminophen)	12,690	Analgesic (for pain relief)
3.	Amoxil (amoxicillin)	11,317	Antibiotic
4.	Lasix (furosemide)	11,128	Diuretic, antihypertensive
5.	Premarin (estrogens)	11,040	Estrogen replacement therapy
6.	Synthroid (levothyroxine)	9,847	Thyroid hormone therapy
7.	A.S.A. (aspirin)	9,007	Analgesic (for pain relief)
8.	Motrin (ibuprofen)	8,250	Anti-inflammatory agent
8.	Prednisone	8,250	Steroid replacement therapy, anti-inflammatory agent
10.	Proventil (albuterol)	8,177	Bronchodilator
11.	Claritin (loratadine)	8,028	Antihistamine
12.	Keflex (cephalexin)	8,014	Antibiotic
13.	Lanoxin (digoxin)	7,684	For congestive heart failure, irregular heartbeat
14.	Prenatal vitamins	7,311	Vitamins, minerals
15.	Poliomyelitis vaccine	7,145	Immunization
16.	Prilosec (omeprazole)	6,821	For duodenal or gastric ulcer
17.	Prozac (fluoxetine hydrochloride)	6,613	Antidepressant
18.	Zantac (ranitidine)	6,352	For duodenal or gastric ulcer
19.	Vasotec (enalapril)	6,268	Antihypertensive
20.	Ibuprofen	6,074	Anti-inflammatory agent
	ALL OTHER	**807,739**	

(1) The trade or generic name used by the physician on the prescription or other medical records. The use of trade names is for identification only and does not imply endorsement by the Public Health Service or the U.S. Dept. of Health and Human Services.

Hospitals and Nursing Homes in the U.S., 1996

Source: *1998 Hospital Statistics*, Healthcare InfoSource, Inc., a subsidiary of the American Hospital Association, copyright 1998; *Health, United States, 1998*

STATE	Hospitals[1]	% of beds occupied[2]	Nursing homes	% of beds occupied	STATE	Hospitals[1]	% of beds occupied[2]	Nursing homes	% of beds occupied
AL	129	57.8	223	90.9	MT	65	66.9	103	86.0
AK	27	56.7	NA	NA	NE	99	55.4	236	87.3
AZ	92	59.7	162	77.4	NV	35	62.4	45	88.5
AR	95	56.7	282	65.9	NH	38	59.8	81	91.5
CA	493	58.9	1,422	77.6	NJ	105	70.3	332	92.1
CO	86	57.0	223	86.9	NM	61	57.8	86	84.3
CT	51	71.6	263	93.4	NY	282	76.6	658	94.6
DE	14	79.0	42	80.0	NC	150	67.4	400	93.8
DC	17	75.9	NA	NA	ND	50	62.4	88	95.5
FL	267	57.6	706	83.7	OH	192	57.4	1,020	69.0
GA	199	60.0	359	91.6	OK	145	52.8	430	74.9
HI	29	76.9	NA	NA	OR	69	51.8	164	81.2
ID	48	55.8	83	78.7	PA	274	67.3	784	90.2
IL	238	58.7	861	78.7	RI	17	67.2	99	93.1
IN	140	56.7	576	73.2	SC	91	63.2	171	87.9
IA	127	57.0	472	66.4	SD	59	64.7	115	94.0
KS	151	51.6	432	81.0	TN	145	60.3	348	89.9
KY	130	57.5	314	87.2	TX	515	54.6	1,312	70.6
LA	167	53.1	346	81.3	UT	51	50.4	96	80.1
ME	44	64.5	136	88.3	VT	17	74.0	45	95.9
MD	84	68.0	256	85.6	VA	127	62.5	279	91.1
MA	138	67.4	567	89.8	WA	103	54.8	285	84.5
MI	178	63.8	447	86.7	WV	69	59.1	139	93.2
MN	151	65.4	457	92.4	WI	146	58.1	423	90.1
MS	112	61.6	204	92.7	WY	31	52.3	38	83.9
MO	152	56.3	598	73.3	**U.S.**	**6,295**	**61.6**	**17,208**	**82.7**[3]

NA = Not available. (1) Community hospitals. (2) Data exclude hospital units of institutions, facilities for the mentally retarded, and alcoholism and chemical dependency hospitals. (3) Does not include data for the District of Columbia, Alaska, and Hawaii.

Estimated New Cancer Cases and Deaths, by Sex, for Leading Sites, 1998

Source: American Cancer Society

The estimates of expected new cases are offered as a rough guide only. They exclude basal and squamous cell skin cancers and in situ carcinomas except urinary bladder. Carcinoma in situ of the breast accounts for about 36,900 new cases annually, and melanoma carcinoma in situ accounts for about 21,100 new cases annually. About 1,000,000 basal and squamous cell skin cancers occur annually. About 1,900 nonmelanoma skin cancer deaths are included among the deaths in all sites expected in 1998.

Estimated New Cases

Both sexes		Women		Men	
Prostate	184,500	Breast	178,700	Prostate	184,500
Breast	180,300	Lung	80,100	Lung	91,400
Lung	171,500	Colorectal	67,000	Colorectal	64,600
Colorectal	131,600	Endometrium (uterus)	36,100	Urinary bladder	39,500
Non-Hodgkin's lymphoma	55,400	Ovary	25,400	Non-Hodgkin's lymphoma	31,100
ALL SITES	**1,228,600**	**ALL SITES**	**600,700**	**ALL SITES**	**627,900**

Estimated Deaths

Both sexes		Women		Men	
Lung	160,100	Lung	67,000	Lung	93,100
Colorectal	56,500	Breast	43,500	Prostate	39,200
Breast	43,900	Colorectal	28,600	Colorectal	27,900
Prostate	39,200	Pancreas	14,900	Pancreas	14,000
Pancreas	28,900	Ovary	14,500	Non-Hodgkin's lymphoma	13,000
ALL SITES	**564,800**	**ALL SITES**	**270,600**	**ALL SITES**	**294,200**

Trends in Cancer Death Rates, 1972-74 and 1992-94

Source: American Cancer Society

SITES	Sex	Death rate[1] 1972-74	Death rate[1] 1992-94	Percentage change	Number of deaths 1974	Number of deaths 1994
Brain	Male	4.7	5.1	9	4,740	6,702
	Female	3.2	3.5	9	3,659	5,611
Breast	Male	0.3	0.3	0	292	364
	Female	26.9	25.9	–4	32,132	43,644
Cervix (uterus)	Female	5.3	2.9	–45	5,963	4,602
Colon and rectum	Male	25.4	22.1	–13	23,853	28,471
	Female	19.8	14.9	–25	25,440	28,936
Endometrium (uterus)	Female	4.6	3.4	–26	5,603	6,163
Esophagus	Male	5.1	6.3	24	4,917	8,191
	Female	1.4	1.5	7	1,735	2,626
Hodgkin's disease	Male	1.7	0.6	–65	1,588	773
	Female	1.0	0.4	–60	1,087	667
Leukemia	Male	8.8	8.4	–5	8,231	10,948
	Female	5.2	4.9	–6	6,344	8,885
Lung	Male	62.9	72.3	15	61,507	91,825
	Female	13.5	33.4	147	17,213	57,535
Melanoma	Male	2.1	3.1	48	2,201	4,117
	Female	1.3	1.5	15	1,534	2,563
Non-Hodgkin's lymphoma	Male	5.8	8.2	41	5,686	11,280
	Female	4.0	5.4	35	4,933	10,528
Ovary	Female	8.5	7.7	–9	10,203	13,500
Pancreas	Male	11.0	10.0	–9	10,208	12,920
	Female	6.7	7.3	9	8,688	13,914
Prostate	Male	21.6	26.6	23	19,184	34,902
Stomach	Male	10.1	6.3	–38	9,159	8,039
	Female	4.8	2.9	–40	6,012	5,531
Urinary bladder	Male	7.3	5.7	–22	6,651	7,457
	Female	2.2	1.7	–23	2,926	3,713
ALL SITES	**Male**	**206.2**	**217.3**	**5**	**195,873**	**280,465**
	Female	**132.1**	**141.8**	**7**	**163,088**	**253,845**

Note: Even though some death rates declined or remained stable, the number of deaths increased because the population over 65 has become larger and older. From 1974 to 1994, the population increased 22%, while the population aged 65 and older increased 50%. (1) Death rates are per 100,000 persons and were adjusted to the age distribution of the 1970 U.S. census population.

Cardiovascular Diseases Statistical Summary, 1996

Source: American Heart Association

Prevalence — 58,800,000[1] Americans had one or more forms of heart and blood vessel disease in 1996.

- high blood pressure — 50,000,000
- coronary heart disease — 12,000,000[1]
- stroke — 4,400,000
- rheumatic heart disease — 2,000,000

Hypertension (high blood pressure) afflicts 50,000,000 Americans age 6 and above, including 1 in 4 adults.

Mortality — 959,227 in 1996 (41.4% of all deaths).

- Someone died from cardiovascular disease every 33 seconds in the U.S. in 1996.

Congenital or inborn heart defects —

- Mortality from such heart defects was 4,820 in 1996.

Coronary heart disease (heart attack and angina pectoris) — caused 476,124 deaths in 1996.

- 12,000,000[1] Americans had a history of heart attack and/or angina pectoris.
- As many as 1,100,000[1] Americans had heart attacks in 1996, about one-third of them fatal.

Stroke — killed about 159,942 Americans in 1996.

Rheumatic heart disease — killed 5,006 in 1996.

(1) Estimate is based on new methodology and therefore not directly comparable to past years.

AIDS Deaths and New AIDS Cases in the U.S., 1985-97

Source: *Health, United States, 1998; HIV/AIDS Surveillance Report,* Vol. 9, No. 2, covering through 1997; National Center for Health Statistics, U.S. Dept. of Health and Human Services

	All years[1]	1985	1990	1992	1993	1994	1995	1996	1997[2]
TOTAL DEATHS	**385,968**	**6,854**	**31,145**	**40,674**	**44,108**	**48,110**	**47,858**	**34,557**	**14,185[3]**
				NEW AIDS CASES					
TOTAL NEW CASES	**592,144**	**8,161**	**41,569**	**45,771**	**102,211**	**77,237**	**71,039**	**66,659**	**30,153**
Male									
All males, 13 years and older	**496,642**	**7,509**	**36,314**	**39,069**	**85,393**	**62,935**	**57,231**	**52,781**	**23,336**
White, not Hispanic	256,246	4,756	20,894	20,832	43,346	29,556	26,260	23,270	9,164
Black, not Hispanic	160,859	1,707	10,276	12,158	28,368	22,471	21,027	20,144	9,656
Hispanic	73,718	990	4,769	5,624	12,641	10,111	9,198	8,622	4,138
American Indian[4]	1,390	7	80	104	309	205	198	169	83
Asian or Pacific Islander[5]	3,831	49	265	295	660	527	486	478	198
13-19 years	1,769	28	108	91	362	226	229	202	108
20-29 years	83,548	1,505	6,951	6,495	14,653	9,689	8,434	7,085	3,011
30-39 years	227,984	3,585	16,727	17,879	38,941	28,996	25,904	23,954	10,468
40-49 years	130,444	1,636	8,865	10,303	22,909	17,259	16,335	15,540	6,931
50-59 years	39,074	596	2,652	3,067	6,428	5,066	4,749	4,463	2,094
60 years and over	13,823	159	1,011	1,234	2,100	1,699	1,580	1,537	724
Female									
All females, 13 years and older	**87,976**	**524**	**4,532**	**5,953**	**15,947**	**13,330**	**13,061**	**13,222**	**6,551**
White, not Hispanic	21,311	141	1,225	1,468	4,048	3,090	3,067	2,875	1,327
Black, not Hispanic	51,352	280	2,542	3,408	9,104	7,861	7,637	8,119	4,083
Hispanic	14,470	100	733	1,014	2,627	2,283	2,237	2,077	1,061
American Indian[4]	261	2	8	19	61	41	38	43	16
Asian or Pacific Islander[5]	476	1	19	39	97	49	72	80	34
13-19 years	1,055	4	65	56	198	174	155	176	89
20-29 years	19,820	178	1,118	1,386	3,726	2,945	2,684	2,684	1,266
30-39 years	40,442	233	2,078	2,731	7,528	6,007	5,987	5,927	2,934
40-49 years	18,690	45	780	1,234	3,215	3,088	3,082	3,274	1,665
50-59 years	5,130	26	272	337	850	771	816	836	418
60 years and over	2,839	38	219	209	430	345	337	325	179
Children									
All children, under 13 years	**7,526**	**128**	**723**	**749**	**871**	**972**	**747**	**656**	**266**
White, not Hispanic	1,399	26	159	128	151	143	117	96	35
Black, not Hispanic	4,579	84	387	485	535	633	483	427	178
Hispanic	1,465	18	168	129	175	181	136	127	51
American Indian[4]	26	–	5	3	3	2	2	3	1
Asian or Pacific Islander[5]	41	–	4	2	4	11	5	1	–
Under 1 year	3,029	63	315	329	351	350	271	219	85
1-12 years	4,497	65	408	420	520	622	476	437	181

Note: The definition of AIDS cases for reporting purposes was expanded in 1985, 1987, and 1993, as more was learned about the spectrum of human immunodeficiency virus-associated diseases. Data exclude residents of U.S. territories. Figures are updated periodically because of reporting delays. (1) Revised figures; includes cases and deaths prior to 1985 and for years not shown. (2) Jan.-June 1997 only, unless otherwise noted. (3) Jan.-Dec. 1997. (4) Includes Aleut and Eskimo. (5) Includes Chinese, Japanese, Filipino, Hawaiian and part-Hawaiian, and other Asian or Pacific Islander.

New AIDS Cases in the U.S., 1985-97, by Transmission Category

Source: *Health, United States, 1998,* CDC, National Center for HIV, STD, and TB Prevention, Div. of HIV/AIDS Prevention

TRANSMISSION CATEGORY	All years[1]	1985	1990	1992	1993	1994	1995	1996	1997[2]
All males, 13 years and older	**496,642**	**7,509**	**36,314**	**39,069**	**85,393**	**62,935**	**57,231**	**52,781**	**23,336**
Men who have sex with men	295,355	5,357	23,826	24,467	49,600	35,291	30,939	27,316	10,625
Injecting drug use	105,175	1,101	6,956	8,038	20,100	15,162	13,319	11,718	5,158
Men who have sex with men and injecting drug use	37,514	655	2,804	3,168	7,210	4,443	3,742	3,044	1,147
Hemophilia/coagulation disorder	4,325	68	333	324	1,048	478	420	300	99
Heterosexual contact[3]	17,048	32	720	1,234	2,991	2,798	2,756	3,088	1,468
Sex with injecting drug user	6,455	25	459	624	1,172	920	871	811	348
Transfusion[4]	4,537	103	452	346	606	374	346	282	113
Undetermined[5]	32,688	193	1,223	1,492	3,838	4,389	5,709	7,033	4,726
All females, 13 years and older	**87,976**	**524**	**4,532**	**5,953**	**15,947**	**13,330**	**13,061**	**13,222**	**6,551**
Injecting drug use	39,392	286	2,324	2,965	8,024	5,892	5,264	4,687	2,088
Hemophilia/coagulation disorder	183	3	15	10	32	27	23	21	8
Heterosexual contact[3]	33,308	119	1,541	2,289	6,063	5,442	5,356	5,521	2,375
Sex with injecting drug user	14,659	82	1,036	1,318	2,766	2,024	1,867	1,836	659
Transfusion[4]	3,323	63	336	256	491	314	276	266	98
Undetermined[5]	11,770	53	316	433	1,337	1,655	2,142	2,727	1,982

Note: The definition of AIDS cases for reporting purposes was expanded in 1985, 1987, and 1993, as more was learned about the spectrum of human immunodeficiency virus-associated diseases. Data exclude residents of U.S. territories. Figures are updated periodically because of reporting delays. (1) Includes cases prior to 1985 and for years not shown. (2) Jan.-June 1997 only. (3) Includes persons who have had heterosexual contact with a person with human immunodeficiency virus (HIV) infection or at risk of HIV infection. (4) Receipt of blood transfusion, blood components, or tissue. (5) Includes persons for whom risk information is incomplete, persons still under investigation, men reported only to have had heterosexual contact with prostitutes, and interviewed persons for whom no specific risk is identified.

CRIME

Crime in U.S. Down Overall in 1996

Serious crimes reported to law enforcement agencies in the United States decreased 3% in 1996 compared with 1995, according to *Uniform Crime Reports* figures released by the Federal Bureau of Investigation (latest data available as of Oct. 31, 1998). The decrease continued the trend of recent years; overall crime was down 1% in 1995, 1% in 1994, 2% in 1993, and 3% in 1992.

Serious crime is measured by the Crime Index, which includes 4 violent and 4 property crimes. Violent crime dropped 7% in 1996, and property crime, 2%.

All 4 violent crimes in the Crime Index decreased. Murder fell 9%, robbery decreased by 8%, aggravated assault declined 6%, and forcible rape dropped by 2%.

In the property-crime category, motor vehicle theft was down 5% in 1996, burglary fell 4%, and larceny-theft decreased by 1%. Sufficient data were not available to estimate totals for arson.

Declines in overall Crime Index totals occurred in 3 regions (8% in the West, 7% in the Northeast, and 1% in the Midwest); crime in the South increased by 1%.

Cities with more than 1 million inhabitants showed the largest decline in reported crime between 1995 and 1996—6%. Cities with populations from 250,000 to 499,999, those with 100,000 to 249,999, and those with 50,000 to 99,999 inhabitants experienced a 4% decrease. Crime data for 1995 and 1996 show that suburban counties experienced a 4% decrease in their crime level, while rural counties reported a 2% decline.

U.S. Crime Index Trends

Source: FBI, *Uniform Crime Reports,* 1996

(percentage change 1996 over 1995, offenses known to the police)

	No. of agencies[1]	Pop. (thousands)	Crime Index (total)	Violent crime[3]	Property crime[4]	Murder	Forcible rape	Robbery	Aggravated assault	Burglary	Larceny/theft	Motor vehicle theft
TOTAL U.S.		**220,886**	**–3**	**–7**	**–2**	**–9**	**–2**	**–8**	**–6**	**–4**	**–1**	**–5**
Cities[2]:												
Over 1,000,000	10	22,285	–6	–8	–5	–13	–1	–10	–7	–7	–4	–7
500,000 to 999,999	17	10,967	–3	–5	–2	–3	–5	–5	–4	–3	–2	–2
250,000 to 499,999	37	13,423	–4	–7	–3	–13	–2	–8	–7	–4	–2	–7
100,000 to 249,999	147	21,674	–4	–7	–4	–12	–4	–8	–7	–5	–2	–7
50,000 to 99,999	320	21,769	–4	–8	–4	–8	+1	–8	–9	–5	–3	–4
25,000 to 49,999	590	20,446	–2	–6	–2	–6	–1	–6	–6	–4	–1	–4
10,000 to 24,999	1,436	22,582	–1	–5	0	–10	+1	–1	–7	–2	0	0
Under 10,000	5,228	18,434	–1	–6	–1	–1	–2	–3	–8	–1	0	0
Counties[2]:												
Suburban	1,108	46,151	–4	–8	–3	–9	–6	–6	–9	–6	–2	–6
Rural[5]	2,127	23,155	–2	–5	–2	–6	–6	–2	–5	–3	–1	0
Areas[2]:												
Suburban area[6]	5,452	87,516	–3	–7	–3	–8	–4	–5	–8	–5	–1	–5

(1) Law-enforcement agencies. (2) For these categories, index trend figures are based on data from approximately 83% of agencies that reported for both 1995 and 1996. (3) Violent crimes are murder, forcible rape, robbery, and aggravated assault. (4) Property crimes are burglary, larceny-theft, and motor vehicle theft. Data for property crime of arson are not included. (5) Includes state police agencies with no county breakdowns. (6) Includes suburban city and county law enforcement agencies within metropolitan areas but not central cities. Suburban cities and counties are also included in other groups.

Crime Index Trends by Geographic Region

Source: FBI, *Uniform Crime Reports,* 1996

(percentage change 1996 over 1995, offenses known to the police)

	Crime Index (total)	Violent crime	Property crime[1]	Murder	Forcible rape	Robbery	Aggravated assault	Burglary	Larceny -theft	Motor vehicle theft
TOTAL U.S.	**–3**	**–7**	**–2**	**–9**	**–2**	**–8**	**–6**	**–4**	**–1**	**–5**
Northeast	–7	–9	–6	–13	0	–11	–8	–9	–5	–8
Midwest	–1	–8	0	–7	–5	–9	–7	–2	0	–1
South	+1	–3	+2	–7	0	–3	–3	+1	+2	0
West	–8	–9	–7	–13	–3	–8	–10	–8	–6	12

(1) Data for arson not included.

Crime Index Trends, 1993-96

Source: FBI, *Uniform Crime Reports,* 1996

(percentage change over previous year, offenses known to police)

Year	Crime Index (total)	Violent crime	Property crime[1]	Murder	Forcible rape	Robbery	Aggravated assault	Burglary	Larceny-theft	Motor vehicle theft
1992	–3	+1	–4	–4	+2	–2	+3	–6	–3	–3
1993	–2	0	–2	+3	–4	–2	+1	–5	–1	–3
1994	–1	–3	–1	–5	–4	–6	–1	–4	+1	–2
1995	–1	–1	–1	–7	–6	–7	–3	–5	+1	–5
1996	–3	–7	–2	–9	–2	–8	–6	–4	–1	–5

(1) Data for arson not included.

Crime in the U.S., 1977-96

Source: FBI, *Uniform Crime Reports*, 1996

Population[1]	Crime Index (total)[2]	Violent crime	Property crime[3]	Murder and non-negligent man-slaughter	Forcible rape	Robbery	Burglary	Larceny-theft
				NUMBER OF REPORTED OFFENSES				
Population by year								
1977–216,332,000	10,984,500	1,029,580	9,955,000	19,120	63,500	412,610	3,071,500	5,905,700
1978–218,059,000	11,209,000	1,085,550	10,123,400	19,560	67,610	426,930	3,128,300	5,991,000
1979–220,099,000	12,249,500	1,208,030	11,041,500	21,460	76,390	480,700	3,327,700	6,601,000
1980–225,349,264	13,408,300	1,344,520	12,063,700	23,040	82,990	565,840	3,795,200	7,136,900
1981–229,146,000	13,423,800	1,361,820	12,061,900	22,520	82,500	592,910	3,779,700	7,194,400
1982–231,534,000	12,974,400	1,322,390	11,652,000	21,010	78,770	553,130	3,447,100	7,142,500
1983–233,981,000	12,108,600	1,258,090	10,850,500	19,310	78,920	506,570	3,129,900	6,712,800
1984–236,158,000	11,881,800	1,273,280	10,608,500	18,690	84,230	485,010	2,984,400	6,591,900
1985–238,740,000	12,431,400	1,328,800	11,102,600	18,980	88,670	497,870	3,073,300	6,926,400
1986–241,077,000	13,211,900	1,489,170	11,722,700	20,610	91,460	542,780	3,241,400	7,257,200
1987–243,400,000	13,508,700	1,484,000	12,024,700	20,100	91,110	517,700	3,236,200	7,499,900
1988–245,807,000	13,923,100	1,566,220	12,356,900	20,680	92,490	542,970	3,218,100	7,705,900
1989–248,239,000	14,251,400	1,646,040	12,605,400	21,500	94,500	578,330	3,168,200	7,872,400
1990–248,709,873	14,475,600	1,820,130	12,655,500	23,440	102,560	639,270	3,073,900	7,945,700
1991–252,177,000	14,872,900	1,911,770	12,961,100	24,700	106,590	687,730	3,157,200	8,142,200
1992–255,082,000	14,438,200	1,932,270	12,505,900	23,760	109,060	672,480	2,979,900	7,915,200
1993–257,908,000	14,144,800	1,926,020	12,218,800	24,530	106,010	659,870	2,834,800	7,820,900
1994–260,341,000	13,989,500	1,857,670	12,131,900	23,330	102,220	618,950	2,712,800	7,879,800
1995–262,755,000[4]	13,862,700	1,798,790	12,063,900	21,610	97,470	580,510	2,593,800	7,997,700
1996–265,284,000	13,473,600	1,682,280	11,791,300	19,650	95,770	537,050	2,501,500	7,894,600
				PERCENT CHANGE: NUMBER OF OFFENSES				
1996/1995	–2.8	–6.5	–2.3	–9.1	–1.7	–7.5	–3.6	–1.3
1996/1992	–6.7	–12.9	–5.7	–17.3	–12.2	–20.1	–16.1	–0.3
1996/1987	–0.3	+13.4	–1.9	–2.2	+5.1	+3.7	–22.7	+5.3
				RATE PER 100,000 INHABITANTS				
Year								
1977	5,077.6	475.9	4,601.7	8.8	29.4	190.7	1,419.8	2,729.9
1978	5,140.3	497.8	4,642.5	9.0	31.0	195.8	1,434.6	2,747.4
1979	5,565.5	548.9	5,016.6	9.7	34.7	218.4	1,511.9	2,999.1
1980	5,950.0	596.6	5,353.3	10.2	36.8	251.1	1,684.1	3,167.0
1981	5,858.2	594.3	5,263.9	9.8	36.0	258.7	1,649.5	3,139.7
1982	5,603.6	571.1	5,032.5	9.1	34.0	238.9	1,488.8	3,084.8
1983	5,175.0	537.7	4,637.4	8.3	33.7	216.5	1,337.7	2,868.9
1984	5,031.3	539.2	4,492.1	7.9	35.7	205.4	1,263.7	2,791.3
1985	5,207.1	556.6	4,650.5	7.9	37.1	208.5	1,287.3	2,901.2
1986	5,480.4	617.7	4,862.6	8.6	37.9	225.1	1,344.6	3,010.3
1987	5,550.0	609.7	4,940.3	8.3	37.4	212.7	1,329.6	3,081.3
1988	5,664.2	637.2	5,027.1	8.4	37.6	220.9	1,309.2	3,134.9
1989	5,741.0	663.1	5,077.9	8.7	38.1	233.0	1,276.3	3,171.3
1990	5,820.3	731.8	5,088.5	9.4	41.2	257.0	1,235.9	3,194.8
1991	5,897.8	758.1	5,139.7	9.8	42.3	272.7	1,252.0	3,228.8
1992	5,660.2	757.5	4,902.7	9.3	42.8	263.6	1,168.2	3,103.0
1993	5,484.4	746.8	4,737.6	9.5	41.1	255.9	1,099.2	3,032.4
1994	5,373.5	713.6	4,660.0	9.0	39.3	237.7	1,042.0	3,026.7
1995[4]	5,275.9	684.6	4,591.3	8.2	37.1	220.9	987.1	3,043.8
1996	5,078.9	634.1	4,444.8	7.4	36.1	202.4	943.0	2,975.9
				PERCENT CHANGE: RATE PER 100,000 INHABITANTS				
1996/1995	–3.7	–7.4	–3.2	–9.8	–2.7	–8.4	–4.5	–2.2
1996/1992	–10.3	–16.3	–9.3	–20.4	–15.7	–23.2	–19.3	–4.1
1996/1987	–8.5	+4.0	–10.0	–10.8	–3.5	–4.8	–29.1	–3.4

Note: All rates were calculated on the offenses before rounding. (1) Populations are Bureau of the Census provisional estimates as of July 1, except 1980 and 1990, which are the decennial census counts. (2) Because of rounding, violent and property crime may not add to total. Not all categories of violent and property crime appear separately. (3) Data for arson not included. (4) The 1995 figures have been adjusted.

Law Enforcement Officers

Source: FBI, *Uniform Crime Reports*, 1996

The U.S. law enforcement community employed an average of 2.4 full-time officers for every 1,000 inhabitants as of Oct. 31, 1996. Including full-time civilians, the overall law enforcement employee rate was 3.3 per 1,000 inhabitants, according to 13,025 city, county, and state police agencies. These agencies collectively offered law enforcement service covering a population of about 265 million, employing 595,170 officers and 234,668 civilians.

The law enforcement employee average for all cities nationwide was 3.0 per 1,000 inhabitants. The highest city law enforcement employee average was 4.0 per 1,000 inhabitants, in cities with populations of 250,000 or more. Rural and suburban counties averaged full-time law enforcement employee rates of 4.3 and 3.8 per 1,000 population, respectively.

Regionally, the law enforcement employee rate was 3.4 in the Northeast and the South, 2.7 in the Midwest, and 2.5 in the West.

Nationally, males constituted 90 percent of all sworn employees. Ninety-three percent of the officers in rural counties were males, and in suburban counties males accounted for 88 percent.

Civilians made up 28 percent of the total U.S. law enforcement employee force. They represented 22 percent of the police employees in cities, 37 percent of those in rural counties, and 38 percent in suburban counties.

Fifty-five law enforcement officers were feloniously slain in the line of duty in 1996, 19 fewer than in 1995. Another 45 officers were killed as a result of accidents occurring while performing official duties.

Crime Rates by Region, Geographic Division, and State, 1996

Source: FBI, *Uniform Crime Reports*, 1996

(rate per 100,000 population)

	Total rate	Violent crime[1]	Property crime[2]	Murder	Rape	Robbery	Aggravated assault	Burglary	Larceny-theft	Motor vehicle theft
U.S. TOTAL	**5,078.9**	**634.1**	**4,444.8**	**7.4**	**36.1**	**202.4**	**388.2**	**943.0**	**2,975.9**	**525.9**
Northeast	**3,898.7**	**555.4**	**3,343.3**	**5.4**	**24.9**	**232.2**	**293.0**	**691.2**	**2,180.5**	**471.6**
New England	**3,777.9**	**447.1**	**3,330.9**	**3.0**	**27.2**	**111.3**	**305.6**	**726.1**	**2,176.2**	**428.6**
Connecticut	4,227.7	412.0	3,815.6	4.8	23.1	169.6	214.6	842.2	2,484.1	489.4
Maine	3,394.1	124.9	3,269.2	2.0	20.9	23.5	78.5	748.4	2,377.9	142.9
Massachusetts	3,837.1	642.2	3,194.9	2.6	29.0	127.7	482.9	704.1	1,962.6	528.2
New Hampshire	2,823.5	118.2	2,705.3	1.7	34.8	27.3	54.4	435.7	2,118.0	151.6
Rhode Island	3,993.5	347.2	3,646.4	2.5	29.0	83.2	232.4	821.7	2,360.3	464.3
Vermont	3,002.9	121.2	2,881.7	1.9	27.0	15.4	76.9	673.0	2,058.4	150.3
Middle Atlantic	**3,940.9**	**593.3**	**3,347.6**	**6.2**	**24.1**	**274.4**	**288.6**	**679.0**	**2,182.1**	**486.6**
New Jersey	4,332.9	531.5	3,801.4	4.2	24.7	235.8	266.7	791.9	2,428.2	581.3
New York	4,132.3	727.0	3,405.3	7.4	23.0	340.0	356.7	713.9	2,197.0	494.4
Pennsylvania	3,392.5	432.5	2,960.1	5.7	25.3	201.1	200.4	551.4	1,996.5	412.2
Midwest	**4,664.0**	**536.6**	**4,127.5**	**6.4**	**38.1**	**161.3**	**330.8**	**817.3**	**2,867.3**	**442.8**
East North Central	**4,765.6**	**592.1**	**4,173.5**	**7.0**	**39.5**	**184.8**	**360.9**	**833.6**	**2,850.5**	**489.5**
Illinois	5,315.8	886.2	4,429.6	10.0	34.2	279.4	562.6	913.2	3,026.2	490.2
Indiana	4,498.2	537.0	3,961.2	7.2	34.1	124.1	371.6	783.8	2,752.6	424.9
Michigan	5,117.5	635.3	4,482.2	7.5	57.0	176.2	394.6	895.4	2,886.3	700.5
Ohio	4,455.7	428.7	4,027.0	4.8	41.3	164.1	218.4	835.4	2,784.1	407.5
Wisconsin	3,821.4	252.7	3,568.7	4.0	21.0	96.6	131.1	588.3	2,634.5	345.9
West North Central	**4,424.1**	**405.5**	**4,018.6**	**4.8**	**34.9**	**105.9**	**259.8**	**778.9**	**2,907.0**	**332.8**
Iowa	3,648.9	272.5	3,376.4	1.9	19.7	45.1	205.9	664.6	2,520.8	191.1
Kansas	4,681.7	413.8	4,268.0	6.6	42.6	96.3	268.3	981.3	3,038.3	248.4
Minnesota	4,463.1	338.8	4,124.3	3.6	50.0	115.6	169.7	762.5	2,977.1	384.8
Missouri	5,084.0	590.9	4,493.0	8.1	29.2	170.6	383.1	894.2	3,151.1	447.7
Nebraska	4,436.6	434.7	4,001.8	2.9	27.1	63.7	341.1	614.5	3,045.7	341.6
North Dakota	2,669.1	84.0	2,585.1	2.2	24.1	11.0	46.7	309.2	2,085.9	190.1
South Dakota	2,969.9	177.2	2,792.8	1.2	41.0	18.9	116.1	557.0	2,121.9	113.9
South	**5,727.0**	**706.8**	**5,020.2**	**9.0**	**40.4**	**203.3**	**454.1**	**1,128.5**	**3,368.2**	**523.5**
South Atlantic	**6,081.8**	**777.8**	**5,304.0**	**8.9**	**39.3**	**234.6**	**494.9**	**1,180.8**	**3,574.0**	**549.1**
Delaware	4,894.9	668.3	4,226.6	4.3	62.6	179.9	421.5	804.1	2,988.3	434.2
District of Columbia	11,896.7	2,469.8	9,426.9	73.1	47.9	1,186.7	1,162.1	1,809.9	5,779.9	1,837.0
Florida	7,497.4	1,051.0	6,446.3	7.5	52.1	289.2	702.2	1,521.2	4,204.5	720.6
Georgia	6,309.7	638.7	5,671.0	8.6	32.1	205.4	392.8	1,114.8	3,927.7	628.5
Maryland	6,061.9	931.2	5,130.7	11.6	37.6	393.2	488.8	992.3	3,427.0	711.4
North Carolina	5,526.2	588.1	4,938.1	8.5	31.3	163.9	384.5	1,345.6	3,257.0	335.5
South Carolina	6,214.1	996.9	5,217.2	9.0	49.2	172.0	766.7	1,283.8	3,505.0	428.5
Virginia	3,968.3	341.3	3,627.0	7.5	26.7	122.6	184.5	588.1	2,760.1	278.8
West Virginia	2,483.4	210.1	2,273.3	3.8	19.6	40.4	146.3	546.5	1,549.8	176.9
East South Central	**4,580.3**	**562.2**	**4,018.1**	**9.1**	**37.6**	**162.5**	**353.0**	**1,001.7**	**2,585.7**	**430.6**
Alabama	4,820.1	565.4	4,254.7	10.4	32.7	166.7	355.6	1,002.1	2,886.7	365.8
Kentucky	3,166.3	320.5	2,845.8	5.9	31.7	93.8	189.2	688.4	1,896.3	261.1
Mississippi	4,522.9	488.3	4,034.6	11.1	36.1	134.2	306.8	1,132.4	2,551.5	350.8
Tennessee	5,449.3	774.0	4,675.4	9.5	46.5	223.7	494.3	1,163.5	2,864.8	647.1
West South Central	**5,783.9**	**671.1**	**5,112.8**	**9.2**	**43.6**	**174.9**	**443.5**	**1,113.5**	**3,466.0**	**533.3**
Arkansas	4,699.2	524.3	4,174.9	8.7	41.7	114.1	359.8	953.2	2,908.8	312.9
Louisiana	6,838.8	929.1	5,909.7	17.5	41.5	276.6	593.5	1,295.8	3,982.3	631.6
Oklahoma	5,652.9	597.1	5,055.8	6.8	46.8	106.6	436.9	1,255.6	3,317.4	482.9
Texas	5,708.9	644.4	5,064.5	7.7	43.8	171.5	421.4	1,068.5	3,447.4	548.6
West	**5,528.5**	**691.5**	**4,837.0**	**7.7**	**37.1**	**218.6**	**428.2**	**1,003.0**	**3,168.2**	**665.8**
Mountain	**5,863.9**	**516.6**	**5,347.3**	**7.0**	**41.1**	**129.5**	**339.0**	**1,034.2**	**3,747.7**	**565.4**
Arizona	7,067.0	631.5	6,435.5	8.5	31.2	167.8	424.0	1,256.3	4,252.5	926.7
Colorado	5,118.5	404.5	4,714.0	4.7	46.2	98.2	255.4	900.8	3,415.5	397.8
Idaho	4,012.5	267.2	3,745.3	3.6	26.3	20.3	217.0	709.1	2,848.8	187.5
Montana	4,493.6	161.0	4,332.7	3.9	27.1	29.7	100.3	558.4	3,518.5	255.7
Nevada	5,992.0	811.3	5,180.7	13.7	53.4	307.6	436.6	1,220.1	3,262.3	698.3
New Mexico	6,602.3	840.6	5,761.7	11.5	63.5	162.4	603.2	1,376.9	3,802.6	582.2
Utah	5,985.9	331.9	5,654.0	3.2	41.8	68.9	218.1	848.3	4,377.1	428.6
Wyoming	4,254.1	249.7	4,004.4	3.3	29.1	20.4	196.9	662.0	3,203.3	139.1
Pacific	**5,400.8**	**758.0**	**4,642.9**	**8.0**	**35.5**	**252.4**	**462.1**	**991.1**	**2,947.8**	**704.0**
Alaska	5,450.4	727.7	4,722.7	7.4	65.6	117.0	537.7	843.2	3,386.7	492.9
California	5,207.8	862.7	4,345.1	9.1	32.1	295.6	525.8	979.4	2,605.1	760.6
Hawaii	6,584.5	280.6	6,304.0	3.4	27.5	135.6	114.0	1,079.5	4,620.0	604.5
Oregon	5,996.6	463.1	5,533.6	4.0	39.7	122.2	297.2	988.3	4,014.3	531.0
Washington	5,909.4	431.2	5,478.2	4.6	51.1	119.0	256.4	1,057.5	3,898.5	522.2

Note: Offense totals are based on all reporting agencies and estimates for unreported areas. Totals may not add because of rounding. (1) Violent crimes are murder, forcible rape, robbery, and aggravated assault. (2) Property crimes are burglary, larceny-theft, and motor vehicle theft. Data are not included for the property crime of arson.

State and Federal Prison Population; Death Penalty[1]

Source: Bureau of Justice Statistics, U.S. Dept. of Justice

The total number of prisoners under the jurisdiction of federal or state adult correctional authorities was at a record high of 1,244,554 at year-end 1997. Overall, the nation's prison population grew 5.2%, which was less than the average annual growth of 7.0% since 1990. In absolute numbers, prison growth during 1997 was equivalent to 1,177 more inmates per week, up from 1,106 per week in 1996. At midyear 1997 (the latest available data), state and federal prisons housed two-thirds of the incarcerated population (1,158,763 out of 1,725,842). Jails, which are locally operated and typically hold persons awaiting trial and those with sentences of a year or less, held the other third. Relative to the number of U.S. residents, the rate of incarceration in prisons was 445 sentenced inmates per 100,000 residents, up from 292 in 1990 (1 in every 117 men and 1 in every 1,852 women were sentenced prisoners).

	SENTENCED TO MORE THAN 1 YEAR			DEATH PENALTY, 1996		
	Advance[2] 1997	Final[3] 1996	% change 1996–97	Under sentence of death	Executions	Death penalty
U.S. TOTAL	**1,197,590**	**1,138,984**	**5.1**	**3,219**	**45**	**—**
Federal institutions	**94,987**	**88,815**	**6.9**	**11**	**0**	**Yes**
State institutions	**1,102,603**	**1,050,169**	**5.0**	**3,208**	**45**	**38**
Northeast	**163,836**	**161,324**	**1.6**	**218**	**0**	**—**
Connecticut	13,005	12,465	4.3	4	0	Yes
Maine	1,542	1,351	14.1	—	—	No
Massachusetts	10,847	10,880	−0.3	—	—	No
New Hampshire	2,164	2,062	4.9	0	0	Yes
New Jersey	28,361	27,490	3.2	11	0	Yes
New York	70,026	69,709	0.5	0	0	Yes
Pennsylvania	34,963	34,535	1.2	203	0	Yes
Rhode Island	2,100	2,031	3.4	—	—	No
Vermont	828	801	3.4	—	—	No
Midwest	**216,391**	**203,701**	**6.2**	**481**	**9**	**—**
Illinois	40,788	38,852	5.0	161	1	Yes
Indiana	17,730	16,791	5.6	45	1	Yes
Iowa	6,938	6,342	9.4	—	—	No
Kansas	7,911	7,756	2.0	0	0	Yes
Michigan	44,771	42,349	5.7	—	—	No
Minnesota	5,306	5,158	2.9	—	—	No
Missouri	23,980	22,003	9.0	93	6	Yes
Nebraska	3,329	3,223	3.3	11	1	Yes
North Dakota	715	650	10.0	—	—	No
Ohio	48,002	46,174	4.0	170	0	Yes
South Dakota	2,239	2,063	8.5	1	0	Yes
Wisconsin	14,682	12,340	19.0	—	—	No
South	**480,061**	**458,671**	**4.7**	**1,779**	**29**	**—**
Alabama	21,680	21,108	2.7	151	1	Yes
Arkansas	9,936	8,992	10.5	40	1	Yes
Delaware	3,264	3,119	4.6	11	3	Yes
District of Columbia	8,814	8,668	1.7	—	—	No
Florida	64,540	63,746	1.2	373	2	Yes
Georgia	35,722	34,328	4.1	96	2	Yes
Kentucky	14,600	12,910	13.1	29	0	Yes
Louisiana	29,265	26,779	9.3	63	1	Yes
Maryland	21,088	20,980	0.5	19	0	Yes
Mississippi	14,548	13,143	10.7	57	0	Yes
North Carolina	27,726	27,751	-0.1	161	0	Yes
Oklahoma	20,542	19,593	4.8	133	2	Yes
South Carolina	20,264	19,758	2.6	68	6	Yes
Tennessee	16,659	15,626	6.6	91	0	Yes
Texas	140,729	132,383	6.3	438	3	Yes
Virginia	27,524	27,062	1.7	49	8	Yes
West Virginia	3,160	2,725	16.0	—	—	No
West	**242,315**	**226,473**	**7.0**	**730**	**7**	**—**
Alaska	2,571	2,335	10.1	—	—	No
Arizona	22,353	21,523	3.9	121	2	Yes
California	154,368	142,865	8.1	454	2	Yes
Colorado	13,461	12,438	8.2	5	0	Yes
Hawaii	3,424	2,954	15.9	—	—	No
Idaho	3,946	3,832	3.0	18	0	Yes
Montana	2,242	2,293	−2.2	7	0	Yes
Nevada	8,884	8,439	5.3	81	1	Yes
New Mexico	4,450	4,506	−1.2	4	0	Yes
Oregon	7,589	7,316	3.7	20	1	Yes
Utah	4,263	3,946	8.0	9	1	Yes
Washington	13,198	12,527	5.4	11	0	Yes
Wyoming	1,566	1,499	4.5	0	0	Yes

(1) All information applies to Dec. 31 of the year indicated. (2) The advance count of prisoners is conducted in Jan. and may be revised. (3) Revised from previous tabulations.

Sentences vs. Time Served for Selected Crimes

Source: Bureau of Justice Statistics, *Prison Sentences and Time Served for Violence,* Apr. 1995

The following is a comparison of the average maximum sentence lengths (excluding both life and death sentences) and the actual time served for selected state-court convictions.

Type of offense	Average sentence	Avg. time served[1]
All violent	7 years, 5 months	3 years, 7 months
Homicide	12 years, 5 months	5 years, 11 months
Rape	9 years, 9 months	5 years, 5 months
Kidnapping	8 years, 8 months	4 years, 4 months
Robbery	7 years, 11 months	3 years, 8 months
Sexual assault	6 years	2 years, 11 months
Assault	5 years, 1 month	2 years, 5 months
Other	5 years	2 years, 4 months

(1) Includes jail credit and prison time.

Prison Situation Among the States and in the Federal System, 1997

Source: *Prisoners in 1997,* Bureau of Justice Statistics, U.S. Dept. of Justice; year-end 1997.

10 largest prison populations, 1997	Number of inmates	10 highest incarceration rates, 1997	Prisoners per 100,000 residents[1]	10 largest % increases in prison population: 1996-97	% increase	1992-97	% increase
California	157,547	Texas	717	Hawaii	23.4	West Virginia	89.5
Texas	140,729	Louisiana	672	West Virginia	15.4	Wisconsin	79.2
Federal system	112,973	Oklahoma	617	Alaska	13.6	Texas	75.3
New York	70,026	South Carolina	536	Maine	13.6	Idaho	74.9
Florida	64,565	Mississippi	531	Vermont	13.5	Mississippi	73.5
Ohio	48,002	Nevada	518	Kentucky	13.1	Hawaii	69.1
Michigan	44,771	Alabama	500	Wisconsin	13.0	North Dakota	67.1
Illinois	40,788	Arizona	484	Mississippi	11.5	Utah	58.7
Georgia	36,450	California	475	North Dakota	10.4	North Carolina	54.7
Pennsylvania	34,964	Georgia	472	Iowa	9.4	Iowa	53.6

(1) Prisoners with sentences of more than 1 year. The Federal Bureau of Prisons and the District of Columbia are excluded.

Executions, by State and Method, 1977-96

Source: Bureau of Justice Statistics, *Capital Punishment 1996,* Dec. 1997

		METHOD OF EXECUTION				
	No.	Lethal injection	Electrocution	Lethal gas	Firing squad	Hanging
TOTAL U.S.	**358**	**216**	**128**	**9**	**2**	**3**
Texas	107	107	—	—	—	—
Florida	38	—	38	—	—	—
Virginia	37	13	24	—	—	—
Louisiana	23	3	20	—	—	—
Missouri	23	23	—	—	—	—
Georgia	22	—	22	—	—	—
Alabama	13	—	13	—	—	—
Arkansas	12	11	1	—	—	—
South Carolina	11	6	5	—	—	—
Delaware	8	7	—	—	—	1
Illinois	8	8	—	—	—	—
North Carolina	8	7	—	1	—	—
Oklahoma	8	8	—	—	—	—
Arizona	6	5	—	1	—	—
Nevada	6	5	—	1	—	—
Utah	5	3	—	—	2	—
California	4	2	—	2	—	—
Indiana	4	1	3	—	—	—
Mississippi	4	—	—	4	—	—
Nebraska	2	—	2	—	—	—
Pennsylvania	2	2	—	—	—	—
Washington	2	—	—	—	—	2
Idaho	1	1	—	—	—	—
Maryland	1	1	—	—	—	—
Montana	1	1	—	—	—	—
Oregon	1	1	—	—	—	—
Wyoming	1	1	—	—	—	—

Note: This table shows execution methods used since 1977. Lethal injection was used in 60% of the executions carried out. Eleven states—Arizona, Arkansas, California, Delaware, Indiana, Louisiana, Nevada, North Carolina, South Carolina, Utah, and Virginia—have employed 2 methods.

Total Estimated Arrests,[1] 1996

Source: FBI, *Uniform Crime Reports*, 1996

TOTAL[2]	**15,168,100**
Murder and nonnegligent manslaughter	19,020
Forcible rape	33,050
Robbery	156,270
Aggravated assault	521,570
Burglary	364,800
Larceny–theft	1,486,300
Motor vehicle theft	175,400
Arson	19,000
Violent crimes[3]	**729,900**
Property crime[4]	**2,045,600**
Crime Index total[2, 5]	**2,775,500**
Other assaults	1,329,000
Forgery and counterfeiting	121,600
Fraud	465,000
Embezzlement	15,700
Stolen property: buying, receiving, possessing	151,100
Vandalism	320,900
Weapons: carrying, possessing, etc.	216,200
Prostitution and commercialized vice	99,000
Sex offenses (except forcible rape and prostitution)	95,800
Drug abuse violations	1,506,200
Gambling	21,000
Offenses against family and children	149,800
Driving under the influence	1,467,300
Liquor laws	677,400
Drunkenness	718,700
Disorderly conduct	842,600
Vagrancy	27,800
All other offenses	3,786,700
Suspicion (not included in totals)	4,900
Curfew and loitering law violations	185,100
Runaways	195,700

(1) Arrest totals are based on all reporting agencies and estimates for unreported areas. (2) Because of rounding, figures may not add to totals. (3) Violent crimes are murder, forcible rape, robbery, and aggravated assault. (4) Property crimes are burglary, larceny-theft, motor vehicle theft, and arson. (5) Includes arson.

Federal Bureau of Investigation

The Federal Bureau of Investigation was created July 26, 1908, and was referred to as Office of Chief Examiner. It became the Bureau of Investigation (Mar. 16, 1909), United States Bureau of Investigation (July 1, 1932), Division of Investigation (Aug. 10, 1933), and Federal Bureau of Investigation (July 1, 1935).

Director	Assumed office
Stanley W. Finch	July 26, 1908
A(lexander) Bruce Bielaski	Apr. 30, 1912
William E. Allen, act.	Feb. 10, 1919
William J. Flynn	July 1, 1919
William J. Burns	Aug. 22, 1921
J. Edgar Hoover, act.	May 10, 1924
J. Edgar Hoover	Dec. 10, 1924
L. Patrick Gray, act.	May 3, 1972
William D. Ruckelshaus, act.	Apr. 27, 1973
Clarence M. Kelley	July 9, 1973
William H. Webster	Feb. 23, 1978
John E. Otto, act.	May 26, 1987
William S. Sessions	Nov. 2, 1987
Floyd I. Clarke, act.	July 19, 1993
Louis J. Freeh	Sept. 1, 1993

SPORTS

25 Most Dramatic Sports Events of the 20th Century

By Bob Costas

Bob Costas, broadcaster with NBC Sports since 1979, has covered every major sport. He has won 12 Emmy Awards—including 8 as Outstanding Sports Broadcaster—and has been named 7 times as National Sportscaster of the Year. His recent activities have included hosting the Summer Olympics at Atlanta and doing play-by-play for the baseball playoffs.

The World Almanac asked Bob Costas to pick out what he believed to be the 25 "most dramatic sports events of the 20th century." His response follows.

I have been asked to do the impossible—list the 25 most dramatic sports events of this century. Believe me, I know that many worthy moments didn't make the cut. Still, it was helpful to make the distinction between *most dramatic* and *most significant*. Jackie Robinson's breaking major league baseball's color barrier may have been the most significant sports event of the century, but that particular day was not as dramatic as it was significant. Roger Bannister running the first 4-minute mile, or Wilt Chamberlain scoring 100 points in a single game, are great achievements, but the settings and circumstances made them (in my judgment at least) less dramatic than the events listed here. So with that in mind, here are my admittedly debatable Top 25, in chronological order:

1. **1927—Dempsey-Tunney long-count fight.** Gene Tunney retains the heavyweight title, defeating the great Jack Dempsey despite being knocked down in the 7th round. Tunney was on the canvas for more than 10 seconds, as the referee delayed his count while Dempsey found his way to a neutral corner.

2. **1936—Jesse Owens.** The track great wins 4 gold medals at the Berlin Olympics. A dramatic rebuke to Hitler's doctrine of Aryan supremacy.

3. **1938—Joe Louis knocks out Max Schmeling.** With World War II on the horizon, and nationalistic passions running high, Louis avenges an earlier defeat with a decisive 1st-round K.O. of the German contender.

4. **1951—Bobby Thompson's home run beats the Brooklyn Dodgers.** "The Giants win the pennant!" "The Giants win the pennant!"

5. **1956—Don Larsen's perfect game in the World Series,** for the Yankees. Unlikely and unforgettable.

6. **1958—Colts defeat Giants for NFL title,** 23-17. A thrilling 1st overtime in league history establishes the NFL as big time.

7. **1960—Bill Mazeroski's homer** in the bottom of the 9th wins Game 7 of the World Series for the Pirates over the mighty Yankees. The blast caps a wild 10-9 win, in a series loaded with excitement.

8. **1967—Ice Bowl.** With the temperature at 13 below zero, and the wind chill at God knows what, the Packers score with 16 seconds left, to win a brutal test of wills with the Dallas Cowboys, 21-17, and go to the Super Bowl.

9. **1968—Bob Beamon long jumps 29 feet, 2½ inches,** at the Mexico City Olympics. The startling leap breaks the existing record by nearly 2 feet.

10. **1969—Joe Namath** guarantees victory, and he and the AFL's Jets deliver, shocking the NFL's Baltimore Colts, 16-7, in Super Bowl III. The win by the Jets, who were 18-point underdogs, establishes the younger league's credibility.

11. **1971—Ali-Frazier I.** Banned from the ring for over 3 years, Muhammad Ali returns to try to reclaim his title. Each man enters the ring unbeaten—each with a rightful claim to greatness. In an atmosphere brimming with racial and political overtones, Joe Frazier knocks Ali down in the 15th and prevails, in a unanimous decision at Madison Square Garden.

12. **1971—Thanksgiving Day: Nebraska 35, Oklahoma 31.** The Cornhuskers' Johnny Rodgers runs wild as Nebraska wins an epic battle between two of that generation's best college football teams.

13. **1973—Secretariat** all but laps the field in the Belmont, completing a Triple Crown run that suggests he may be the greatest thoroughbred in history.

14. **1975—Game 6 of a classic World Series** between Boston and Cincinnati is decided on Carlton Fisk's 12th-inning home run for the Red Sox. Though the Reds win Game 7 the next night, Fisk's homer at Fenway Park symbolizes the series.

15. **1979—Bird/Magic.** Larry Bird's undefeated Indiana State Sycamores are beaten in the NCAA title game by Magic Johnson's Michigan State Spartans, the first of many matchups that would define an era in basketball, as Bird and Johnson took their rivalry to the NBA, for a number of dramatic games that could also have made this list.

16. **1980—Miracle on ice.** The United States hockey team somehow upsets the seemingly invincible Soviet Union, 4-3, and goes on to win the gold medal at the Lake Placid Olympics.

17. **1980—Wimbledon men's final.** Bjorn Borg wins his 5th title in a row, but his marathon victory over young John McEnroe pushes both men to the limit.

18. **1982—Montana to Clark.** Joe Montana's last-minute touchdown throw and the leaping catch by Dwight Clark sends San Francisco to the Super Bowl, with a win over Dallas, 28-27. Probably the best remembered of countless plays and drives that made the cool and resourceful Montana a legend.

19. **1986—At age 46, Jack Nicklaus** wins his 6th Masters title.

20. **1986—Game 6 of the World Series.** Mookie Wilson's grounder in the bottom of the 10th eludes the Red Sox's Bill Buckner, and the unfathomable has occurred. The Red Sox, ahead by 2, with 2 outs and nobody on, have lost. They would lead Game 7, 3-0, and lose that, too. Last Red Sox world title: 1918 and counting.

21. **1988—World Series Game 1.** In the bottom of the 9th at Dodger Stadium, a hobbling Kirk Gibson pinch hits a 2-out, 2-run homer off the nearly untouchable Dennis Eckersley, for a 5-4 win over Oakland, launching the Dodgers to their upset series win over the heavily-favored A's.

22. **1996—Atlanta Olympics.** Michael Johnson blazes to victory in record-shattering 200-meter time, completing an unprecedented double in the men's 200 and 400.

23. **1997—Tiger Woods,** in a nearly perfect performance, breaks the Masters Tournament record and becomes the 1st African American winner of the fabled and once restrictive tournament.

24. **1998—There are several Michael Jordan moments** (dating back to the early 80s) that could be chosen. We'll go with this one: M.J.'s jumper with 5 seconds to go wins Game 6, 87-86, and the NBA title for the Bulls over the Jazz. Chosen because it might represent the dramatic conclusion of the Bulls dynasty.

25. **1998—En route to the mind-boggling total of 70,** Mark McGwire's 62d homer unites baseball's present and past. In the sport most reliant upon history and tradition, McGwire's respect for the previous record holder, Roger Maris, and his graciousness toward Maris's family and his own present rival, Sammy Sosa, made this moment touching and poignant, as well as dramatic.

Ten Most Dramatic Sports Events of 1998

By the editors of *The World Almanac*

In one of the most historic major league baseball seasons of all time, Mark McGwire of the St. Louis Cardinals hit his record-breaking 62d home run, Sept. 8, in only the team's 145th game of the season. McGwire had been in a race with Sammy Sosa of the Chicago Cubs to break Roger Maris's 37-year-old season record of 61 home runs (set in 1961). Sosa had hit 20 homers in June (the most in any one month), heating up the race. McGwire ended the season with 70 home runs (4 in the final 2 games); Sosa ended up with 66.

The XVIII Winter Olympic Games, held in Nagano, Japan, Feb. 7-22, included snowboarding, curling, and women's hockey for the first time. The Games' heroes included Japanese ski-jumper Masahiko "Happy" Harada, who vindicated himself for his failure in the 1994 Olympics with a record jump; Tara Lipinski, of the U.S., who became the youngest figure skater to win a gold; Norwegian cross-country skier Bjoern Daehlie, winning his record 8th Winter gold; and Austrian skier Hermann Maier, "The Herminator," coming back from a devastating crash to win 2 gold medals. Five new world records were set in speedskating using the advanced technology of the "clap skate."

On July 12, France upset the defending champions, Brazil, with a 3-0 victory in Saint-Denis, France, to win the 16th World Cup of soccer. It was the first World Cup win for France and the first time a host nation had won since Argentina in 1978. France went undefeated in the month-long tournament, scoring the most goals (15) and allowing the fewest (2). Midfielder Zinedine Zidane scored his first 2 goals of the Cup tournament in the first half of the final.

The New York Yankees won an unprecedented 24th World Series title, finishing off a 4-game sweep of the San Diego Padres, 3-0, on Oct. 21 at Qualcomm Stadium in San Diego. Yankee 3d-baseman Scott Brosius was named Series MVP. The Yankees also won an AL-record 114 regular-season games, including the 15th perfect game in major league baseball's history, by David Wells on May 17.

Michael Jordan and the Chicago Bulls secured their claim as the basketball team of the 90s, perhaps the best ever, by winning their 6th NBA Championship in 8 years. The Bulls defeated the Utah Jazz, 87-86, in Salt Lake City, June 14, to wrap up the title, 4 games to 2. Michael Jordan got his record 6th NBA Finals MVP award and surpassed Kareem Abdul-Jabbar as the leading playoff scorer, with 5,987 playoff points.

After 3 unsuccessful Super Bowl appearances, Denver Broncos quarterback John Elway, Jan. 25, led his team to victory in Super Bowl XXXII at Qualcomm Stadium in San Diego, CA. The victory not only snapped Denver's 4-game losing streak in the Super Bowl but also gave the AFC its first Super Bowl title in 13 years. The Broncos became only the 2d wildcard team to win the Super Bowl. Denver running back Terrell Davis, although he missed the 2d quarter, rushed for a Super Bowl record 3 touchdowns and was named the game's MVP.

The Detroit Red Wings swept their 2d straight Stanley Cup finals by defeating the Washington Capitals, 4-1, on June 16 at the MCI Center in Washington, DC. The win was the 8th career Stanley Cup championship for coach Scotty Bowman. After the game, Steve Yzerman, the Wings' captain and the playoff MVP, presented the Cup to his former teammate Vladimir Konstantinov, who was in a wheelchair because of injuries he had suffered the year before in a limousine accident.

The Tennessee Lady Vols won their 3d straight NCAA women's basketball title, Mar. 29, by defeating the Louisiana Tech Lady Techsters, 93-75, in Kansas City, MO. The Lady Vols went 39-0 for the year, and Chamique Holdsclaw was named the tournament's MVP for the 2d straight year. In the NCAA men's tournament the Kentucky Wildcats came back from a 10-point halftime deficit, Mar. 30, to beat the Utah Runnin' Utes, 78-69, in San Antonio, TX. It was Kentucky's 7th national title, and their comeback was the biggest ever in the national championship game.

Jeff Gordon needed only a 40th-place finish in the ACDelco 400 in Rockingham, NC, Nov. 1, to win his 3d Winston Cup championship in 4 years. Instead he would finish 1st, despite a 15-second penalty, and wrap up the title in winning style. Gordon joined only 6 other drivers to win 3 or more championships and, at age 27, became the youngest driver to do so. As of Nov. 1, Gordon had won 12 of the Winston Cup races and was only the 2d driver to win the points championship before the last race of the season.

In her first full season on the LPGA Tour, 20-year-old Korean golf sensation Se Ri Pak became the youngest winner of the LPGA Championship, May 17, in Wilmington, DE. On July 6, Pak won a sudden-death playoff in Kohler, WI, to also become the youngest golfer ever to win the U.S. Women's Open.

Winter Olympic Games

Sites of Winter Olympic Games

1924 Chamonix, France	**1948** St. Moritz, Switzerland	**1968** Grenoble, France	**1988** Calgary, Alberta
1928 St. Moritz, Switzerland	**1952** Oslo, Norway	**1972** Sapporo, Japan	**1992** Albertville, France
1932 Lake Placid, New York	**1956** Cortina d'Ampezzo, Italy	**1976** Innsbruck, Austria	**1994** Lillehammer, Norway
1936 Garmisch-Partenkirchen, Germany	**1960** Squaw Valley, California	**1980** Lake Placid, New York	**1998** Nagano, Japan
	1964 Innsbruck, Austria	**1984** Sarajevo, Yugoslavia	**2002** Salt Lake City, Utah

Winter Olympic Games in 1998

Nagano, Japan, Feb. 7-22, 1998

With Emperor Akihito and Empress Michiko and a crowd of 50,000 in attendance, a ritual performed by sumo wrestlers to cast off evil spirits, and the lighting of the Olympic torch by skater Midori Ito, the 1998 Winter Olympic Games got underway Feb. 7, 1998, in Nagano, Japan. Over 2,400 athletes from 72 nations cheered loudly as they anticipated the competition of the next 2 weeks. Change was in the air, as snowboarding and curling made their Olympic debuts. Some events were delayed by rain and snow, but the Olympic spirit was never extinguished; the XVIII Winter Olympics were a big success—though the weather delays, a 14-hour time difference, and some disappointing U.S. performances helped depress TV ratings and interest in the U.S.

The first gold medal for the host nation came Feb. 10, when Hiroyasu Shimizu won the men's 500-meter speedskating event. Shimizu set an Olympic record on his 2d run with a time of 35.59 seconds. The Japanese ski jumping team won 4 medals, including a gold in the team event led by Masashiko "Happy" Harada. Harada proved to be a fan favorite and redeemed himself for his failure at Lillehammer in 1994, which had cost his team a gold. His teammate, Kazuyoshi Funaki, won a gold and a silver medal in individual events. In other performance highlights, Hermann Maier won the gold for Austria in both the giant and the super giant slalom, after recovering from a horrifying crash in the downhill; cross-country skier Bjoern Daehlie won 3 golds and 1 silver for Norway, giving him an unprecedented 12 total and 8 gold Winter Olympic medals for his career. Larissa Lazutina, a Russian cross-country skier, won 5 medals, including 3 gold, to become the leading multi-medalist at Nagano. The Czech Republic, led by Dominik Hasek, captured the gold in men's hockey; the U.S. women's hockey team went undefeated and upset Team Canada for the gold in the event's inaugural year; U.S. skater Tara Lipinski, 15, nailed her long program to become the youngest Olympic figure-skating gold medalist; her U.S. rival Michelle Kwan, unbeatable in the short program, was a close 2d.

Germany won the most medals, 29, and the most gold medals, 12. The U.S. finished 6th in the medal count, with 13 (6 gold), trailing Germany, Norway (25), Russia (18), Austria (17), and Canada (15).

Final Medal Standings

	Gold	Silver	Bronze	Total
Germany	12	9	8	**29**
Norway	10	10	5	**25**
Russia	9	6	3	**18**
Austria	3	5	9	**17**
Canada	6	5	4	**15**
U.S.	6	3	4	**13**
Finland	2	4	6	**12**
Netherlands	5	4	2	**11**
Japan	5	1	4	**10**
Italy	2	6	2	**10**
France	2	1	5	**8**
China	0	6	2	**8**
Switzerland	2	2	3	**7**
Korea	3	1	2	**6**
Czech Republic	1	1	1	**3**
Sweden	0	2	1	**3**
Belarus	0	0	2	**2**
Kazakhstan	0	0	2	**2**
Bulgaria	1	0	0	**1**
Denmark	0	1	0	**1**
Ukraine	0	1	0	**1**
Australia	0	0	1	**1**
Belgium	0	0	1	**1**
Great Britain	0	0	1	**1**
TOTAL	**69**	**68**	**68**	**205**

1998 Winter Olympics Medal Winners

(G = Gold, S = Silver, B = Bronze)

Alpine Skiing

MEN

Downhill—G-Jean-Luc Cretier, France; S-Lasse Kjus, Norway; B-Hannes Trinki, Austria.

Super Giant Slalom—G-Hermann Maier, Austria; S-Didier Cuche, Switzerland; S-Hans Knauss, Austria.

Giant Slalom—G-Hermann Maier, Austria; S-Stefan Eberharter, Austria; B-Michael von Gruenigen, Switzerland.

Slalom—G-Hans-Petter Buraas, Norway; S-Ole Christian Furuseth, Norway; B-Thomas Sykora, Austria.

Combined—G-Mario Reiter, Austria; S-Lasse Kjus, Norway; B-Christian Mayer, Austria.

WOMEN

Downhill—G-Katja Seizinger, Germany; S-Pernilla Wiberg, Sweden; B-Florence Masnada, France.

Super Giant Slalom—G-Picabo Street, U.S.; S-Michaela Dorfmeister, Austria; B-Alexandra Meissnitzer, Austria.

Giant Slalom—G-Deborah Compagnoni, Italy; S-Alexandra Meissnitzer, Austria; B-Katja Seizinger, Germany.

Slalom—G-Hilde Gerg, Germany; S-Deborah Compagnoni, Italy; B-Zali Steggall, Australia.

Combined—G-Katja Seizinger, Germany; S-Martina Ertl, Germany; B-Hilde Gerg, Germany.

Biathlon

MEN

10KM—G-Ole Einar Bjoerndalen, Norway; S-Frode Andresen, Norway; B-Ville Raikkonen, Finland.

20KM—G-Halvard Hanevold, Norway; S-Pier Alberto Carrara, Italy; B-Aleksei Aidarov, Belarus.

30KM Relay—G-Germany; S-Norway; B-Russia.

WOMEN

7.5KM—G-Galina Koukleva, Russia; S-Ursula Disl, Germany; B-Katrin Apel, Germany.

15KM—G-Ekaterina Dafovska, Bulgaria; S-Elena Petrova, Ukraine; B-Ursula Disl, Germany.

30KM Relay—G-Germany; S-Russia; B-Norway.

Bobsledding

4-Man Bob—G-Germany 2; S-Switzerland 1; B-Great Britain 1 and France 1 (tie).

2-Man Bob—G-Canada 1; G-Italy 1; B-Germany 1.

Curling

Men—G-Switzerland; S-Canada; B-Norway.

Women—G-Canada; S-Denmark; B-Sweden.

Figure Skating

Men's Singles—G-Ilia Kulik, Russia; S-Elvis Stojko, Canada; B-Philippe Candeloro, France.

Women's Singles—G-Tara Lipinski, U.S.; S-Michelle Kwan, U.S.; B-Lu Chen, China.

Pairs—G-Oksana Kazakova & Artur Dmitriev, Russia; S-Elena Berezhnaya & Anton Sikharulidze, Russia; B-Mandy Wotzel & Ingo Steuer, Germany.

Ice Dancing—G-Pasha Grishuk & Evgeny Platov, Russia; S-Angelika Krylova & Olig Ovsyannikov, Russia; B-Marina Anissina & Gwendal Peizerat, France.

Freestyle Skiing

Men's Moguls—G-Jonny Moseley, U.S.; S-Janne Lahtela, Finland; B-Sami Mustonen, Finland.

Men's Aerials—G-Eric Bergoust, U.S.; S-Sebastien Foucras, France; B-Dmitri Dashchinsky, Belarus.

Women's Moguls—G-Tae Satoya, Japan; S-Tatjana Mittermayer, Germany; B-Kari Traa, Norway.

Women's Aerials—G-Nikki Stone, U.S.; S-Nannan Xu, China; B-Colette Brand, Switzerland.

Ice Hockey

Men's—G-Czech Republic; S-Russia; B-Finland.

Women's—G-U.S.; S-Canada; B-Finland.

Luge

Men's Singles—G-Georg Hackl, Germany; S-Armin Zoeggeler, Italy; B-Jens Mueller, Germany.

Men's Doubles—G-Stefan Krausse and Jan Behrendt, Germany; S-Chris Thorpe and Gordy Sheer, U.S.; B-Mark Grimmette and Brian Martin, U.S.

Women's Singles—G-Silke Kraushaar, Germany; S-Barbara Niedernhuber, Germany; B-Angelika Neuner, Austria.

Nordic Skiing

Cross-Country Events

MEN

10KM—G-Bjoern Daehlie, Norway; S-Markus Gandler, Austria; B-Mika Myllylae, Finland.

15KM—G-Thomas Alsgaard, Norway; S-Bjoern Daehlie, Norway; B-Vladimir Smirnov, Kazakhstan.

30KM—G-Mika Myllylae, Finland; S-Erling Jevne, Norway; B-Silvio Fauner, Italy.

50KM—G-Bjoern Daehlie, Norway; S-Niklas Jonsson, Sweden; B-Christian Hoffmann, Austria.

40KM Relay—G-Norway; S-Italy; B-Finland.

WOMEN

5KM—G-Larissa Lazutina, Russia; S-Katerina Neumannova, Czech Republic; B-Benter Martinesen, Norway.

10KM—G-Larissa Lazutina, Russia; S-Olga Danilova, Russia; B-Katerina Neumannova, Czech Republic.

15KM—G-Olga Danilova, Russia; S-Larissa Lazutina, Russia; B-Anita Moen-Guidon, Norway.

30KM—G-Julija Tchepalova, Russia; S-Stefania Belmondo, Italy; B-Larissa Lazutina, Russia.

20KM Relay—G-Russia; S-Norway; B-Italy.

Combined Cross-Country & Jumping Events (Men)

Nordic Combined—G-Bjarte Engen Vik, Norway; S-Samppa Lajunen, Finland; B-Valerij Stoljarov, Russia.
Team Nordic Combined—G-Norway; S-Finland; B-France.

Ski Jumping (Men)

90M (Normal hill)—G-Jani Soininen, Finland; S-Kazuyoshi Funaki, Japan; B-Andreas Widhoelzl, Austria.
120M (Large hill)—G-Kazuyoshi Funaki, Japan; S-Jani Soininen, Finland; B-Masahiko Harada, Japan.
Team 120M—G-Japan; S-Germany; B-Austria.

Snowboarding

Men's Giant Slalom—G-Ross Rebagliati, Canada; S-Thomas Prugger, Italy; B-Ueli Kestenholz, Switzerland.
Men's Halfpipe—G-Gian Simmen, Switzerland; S-Daniel Franck, Norway; B-Ross Powers, U.S.
Women's Giant Slalom—G-Karine Ruby, France; S-Heidi Renoth, Germany; B-Brigitte Koeck, Austria.
Women's Halfpipe—G-Nicola Thost, Germany; S-Stine Brun Kjeldaas, Norway; B-Shannon Dunn, U.S.

Speed Skating

MEN

500M—G-Hiroyasu Shimizu, Japan; S-Jeremy Wotherspoon, Canada; B-Kevin Overland, Canada.
1,000M—G-Ids Postma, Netherlands; S-Jan Bos, Netherlands; B-Hiroyasu Shimizu, Japan.
1,500M—G-Aadne Sondral, Norway; S-Ids Postma, Netherlands; B-Rintje Ritsma, Netherlands.
5,000M—G-Gianni Romme, Netherlands; S-Rintje Ritsma, Netherlands; B-Bart Veldkamp, Belgium.
10,000M—G-Gianni Romme, Netherlands; S-Bob de Jong, Netherlands; B-Rintje Ritsma, Netherlands.

WOMEN

500M—G-Catriona LeMay-Doan, Canada; S-Susan Auch, Canada; B-Tomomi Okazaki, Japan.
1,000M—G-Marianne Timmer, Netherlands; S-Chris Witty, U.S.; B-Catriona LeMay-Doan, Canada.
1,500M—G-Marianne Timmer, Netherlands; S-Gunda Niemann-Stirnemann, Germany; B-Chris Witty, U.S.
3,000M—G-Gunda Niemann-Stirnemann, Germany; S-Claudia Pechstein, Germany; B-Anna Friesinger, Germany.
5,000M—G-Claudia Pechstein, Germany; S-Gunda Niemann-Stirnemann, Germany; B-Lyudmila Prokasheva, Kazakhstan.

Short-Track Speed Skating

Men's 500M—G-Takafumi Nishitani, Japan; S-Yulong An, China; B-Hitoshi Uematsu, Japan.
Men's 1,000M—G-Dong-Sung Kim, Korea; S-Jiajun Li, China; B-Eric Bedard, Canada.
Men's 5,000M Relay—G-Canada; S-Korea; B-China.
Women's 500M—G-Annie Perreault, Canada; S-Yang Yang, China; B-Chun Lee-Kyung, Korea.
Women's 1,000M—G-Chun Lee-Kyung, Korea; S-Yang S. Yang, China; B-Won Hye-Kyung, Korea.
Women's 3,000M Relay—G-Korea; S-China; B-Canada.

Winter Olympic Games Champions, 1924-1998

In 1992, the Unified Team represented the former Soviet republics of Russia, Ukraine, Belarus, Kazakhstan, and Uzbekistan.

Alpine Skiing

	Men's Downhill	Time
1948	Henri Oreiller, France	2:55.0
1952	Zeno Colo, Italy	2:30.8
1956	Anton Sailer, Austria	2:52.2
1960	Jean Vuarnet, France	2:06.0
1964	Egon Zimmermann, Austria	2:18.16
1968	Jean-Claude Killy, France	1:59.85
1972	Bernhard Russi, Switzerland	1:51.43
1976	Franz Klammer, Austria	1:45.73
1980	Leonhard Stock, Austria	1:45.50
1984	Bill Johnson, U.S.	1:45:59
1988	Pirmin Zurbriggen, Switzerland	1:59.63
1992	Patrick Ortlieb, Austria	1:50.37
1994	Tommy Moe, U.S.	1:45.75
1998	Jean-Luc Cretier, France	1:50.11

	Men's Super Giant Slalom	Time
1988	Franck Piccard, France	1:39.66
1992	Kjetil-Andre Aamodt, Norway	1:13.04
1994	Markus Wasmeier, Germany	1:32.53
1998	Hermann Maier, Austria	1:34.82

	Men's Giant Slalom	Time
1952	Stein Eriksen, Norway	2:25.0
1956	Anton Sailer, Austria	3:00.1
1960	Roger Staub, Switzerland	1:48.3
1964	Francois Bonlieu, France	1:46.71
1968	Jean-Claude Killy, France	3:29.28
1972	Gustavo Thoeni, Italy	3:09.62
1976	Heini Hemmi, Switzerland	3:26.97
1980	Ingemar Stenmark, Sweden	2:40.74
1984	Max Julen, Switzerland	2:41.18
1988	Alberto Tomba, Italy	2:06:37
1992	Alberto Tomba, Italy	2:06.98
1994	Markus Wasmeier, Germany	2:52.46
1998	Hermann Maier, Austria	2:38.51

	Men's Slalom	Time
1948	Edi Reinalter, Switzerland	2:10.3
1952	Othmar Schneider, Austria	2:00.0
1956	Anton Sailer, Austria	3:14.7
1960	Ernst Hinterseer, Austria	2:08.9
1964	Josef Stiegler, Austria	2:11.13
1968	Jean-Claude Killy, France	1:39.73
1972	Francisco Fernandez Ochoa, Spain	1:49.27
1976	Piero Gros, Italy	2:03.29
1980	Ingemar Stenmark, Sweden	1:44.26
1984	Phil Mahre, U.S.	1:39.41
1988	Alberto Tomba, Italy	1:39.47
1992	Finn Christian Jagge, Norway	1:44.39
1994	Thomas Stangassinger, Austria	2:02.02
1998	Hans-Petter Buraas, Norway	1:49.31

	Men's Combined	Time
1988	Hubert Strolz, Austria	36.55 (pts.)
1992	Josef Polig, Italy	14.58 (pts.)
1994	Lasse Kjus, Norway	3:17.53
1998	Mario Reiter, Austria	3:08.06

	Women's Downhill	Time
1948	Hedi Schlunegger, Switzerland	2:28.3
1952	Trude Jochum-Beiser, Austria	1:47.1
1956	Madeleine Berthod, Switzerland	1:40.7
1960	Heidi Biebl, Germany	1:37.6
1964	Christl Haas, Austria	1:55.39
1968	Olga Pall, Austria	1:40.87
1972	Marie Therese Nadig, Switzerland	1:36.68
1976	Rosi Mittermaier, W. Germany	1:46.16
1980	Annemarie Proell Moser, Austria	1:37.52
1984	Michela Figini, Switzerland	1:13.36
1988	Marina Kiehl, W. Germany	1:25.86
1992	Kerrin Lee-Gartner, Canada	1:52.55
1994	Katja Seizinger, Germany	1:35.93
1998	Katja Seizinger, Germany	1:28.89

	Women's Super Giant Slalom	Time
1988	Sigrid Wolf, Austria	1:19.03
1992	Deborah Compagnoni, Italy	1:21.22
1994	Diann Roffe-Steinrotter, U.S.	1:22.15
1998	Picabo Street, U.S.	1:18.02

	Women's Giant Slalom	Time
1952	Andrea Mead Lawrence, U.S.	2:06.8
1956	Ossi Reichert, Germany	1:56.5
1960	Yvonne Ruegg, Switzerland	1:39.9
1964	Marielle Goitschel, France	1:52.24
1968	Nancy Greene, Canada	1:51.97
1972	Marie Therese Nadig, Switzerland	1:29.90
1976	Kathy Kreiner, Canada	1:29.13
1980	Hanni Wenzel, Liechtenstein (2 runs)	2:41.66
1984	Debbie Armstrong, U.S.	2:20.98
1988	Vreni Schneider, Switzerland	2:06.49
1992	Pernilla Wiberg, Sweden	2:12.74
1994	Deborah Compagnoni, Italy	2:30.97
1998	Deborah Compagnoni, Italy	2:50.59

	Women's Slalom	Time
1948	Gretchen Fraser, U.S.	1:57.2
1952	Andrea Mead Lawrence, U.S.	2:10.6
1956	Renee Colliard, Switzerland	1:52.3
1960	Anne Heggtveigt, Canada	1:49.6
1964	Christine Goitschel, France	1:29.86
1968	Marielle Goitschel, France	1:25.86
1972	Barbara Cochran, U.S.	1:31.24

1976	Rosi Mittermaier, W. Germany	1:30.54
1980	Hanni Wenzel, Liechtenstein	1:25.09
1984	Paoletta Magoni, Italy	1:36.47
1988	Vreni Schneider, Switzerland	1:36.69
1992	Petra Kronberger, Austria	1:32.68
1994	Vreni Schneider, Switzerland	1:56.01
1998	Hilde Gerg, Germany	1:32.40

	Women's Combined	Time
1988	Anita Wachter, Austria	29.25 (pts.)
1992	Petra Kronberger, Austria	2.55 (pts.)
1994	Pernilla Wiberg, Sweden	3:05.16
1998	Katja Seizinger, Germany	2:40.74

Biathlon

	Men's 10 Kilometers	Time
1980	Frank Ullrich, E. Germany	32:10.69
1984	Eirik Kvalfoss, Norway	30:53.80
1988	Frank-Peter Roetsch, E. Germany	25:08.10
1992	Mark Kirchner, Germany	26:02.30
1994	Serguei Tchepikov, Russia	28:07.00
1998	Ole Einar Bjoerndalen, Norway	27:16.20

	Men's 20 Kilometers	Time
1960	Klas Lestander, Sweden	1:33:21.6
1964	Vladimir Melanin, USSR	1:20:26.8
1968	Magnar Solberg, Norway	1:13:45.9
1972	Magnar Solberg, Norway	1:15:55.50
1976	Nikolai Kruglov, USSR	1:14:12.26
1980	Anatoly Aljabiev, USSR	1:08:16.31
1984	Peter Angerer, W. Germany	1:11:52.7
1988	Frank-Peter Roetsch, E. Germany	0:56:33.33
1992	Yevgeny Redkine, Unified Team	0:57:34.4
1994	Serguei Tarasov, Russia	0:57:25.3
1998	Halvard Hanevold, Norway	0:56:16.4

	Men's 30-Kilometer Relay	Time
1968	USSR, Norway, Sweden (40 km)	2:13:02.4
1972	USSR, Finland, E. Germany (40 km)	1:51:44.92
1976	USSR, Finland, E. Germany (40 km)	1:57:55.64
1980	USSR, E. Germany, W. Germany	1:34:03.27
1984	USSR, Norway, W. Germany	1:38:51.70
1988	USSR, W. Germany, Italy	1:22:30.00
1992	Germany, Unified Team, Sweden	1:24:43.50
1994	Germany, Russia, France	1:30:22.1
1998	Germany, Norway, Russia	1:19:43.3

	Women's 7.5 Kilometers	Time
1992	Anfissa Restsova, Unified Team	24:29.20
1994	Myriam Bedard, Canada	26:08.8
1998	Galina Koukleva, Russia	23:08.0

	Women's 15 Kilometers	Time
1992	Antje Misersky, Germany	51:47.2
1994	Myriam Bedard, Canada	52:06.6
1998	Ekaterina Dafovska, Bulgaria	54:52.0

	Women's 22.5-Kilometer Relay	Time
1992	France, Germany, Unified Team	1:15:55.6

	Women's 30-Kilometer Relay	Time
1994	Russia, Germany, France	1:47:19.5
1998	Germany, Russia, Norway	1:40:13.6

Bobsledding

(Driver in parentheses)

	4-Man Bob	Time
1924	Switzerland (Eduard Scherrer)	5:45.54
1928	United States (William Fiske) (5-man)	3:20.50
1932	United States (William Fiske)	7:53.68
1936	Switzerland (Pierre Musy)	5:19.85
1948	United States (Francis Tyler)	5:20.10
1952	Germany (Andreas Ostler)	5:07.84
1956	Switzerland (Franz Kapus)	5:10.44
1964	Canada (Victor Emery)	4:14.46
1968	Italy (Eugenio Monti) (2 races)	2:17.39
1972		4:43.07
1976	E. Germany (Meinhard Nehmer)	3:40.43
1980	E. Germany (Meinhard Nehmer)	3:59.92
1984	E. Germany (Wolfgang Hoppe)	3:20.22
1988	Switzerland (Ekkehard Fasser)	3:47.51
1992	Austria (Ingo Appelt)	3:53.90
1994	Germany (Wolfgang Hoppe)	3:27.28
1998	Germany-2 (Christoph Langen)	2:39.41

	2-Man Bob	Time
1932	United States (Hubert Stevens)	8:14.74
1936	United States (Ivan Brown)	5:29.29
1948	Switzerland (F. Endrich)	5:29.20
1952	Germany (Andreas Ostler)	5:24.54
1956	Italy (Dalla Costa)	5:30.14
1964	Great Britain (Anthony Nash)	4:21.90
1968	Italy (Eugenio Monti)	4:41.54
1972	W. Germany (Wolfgang Zimmerer)	4:57.07
1976	E. Germany (Meinhard Nehmer)	3:44.42
1980	Switzerland (Erich Schaerer)	4:09.36
1984	E. Germany (Wolfgang Hoppe)	3:25.56
1988	USSR (Janis Kipours)	3:54.19
1992	Switzerland (Gustav Weber)	4:03.26
1994	Switzerland (Gustav Weber)	3:30.81
1998	Canada (Pierre Lueders), Italy (Guenther Huber) (tie)	3:37.24

Curling

MEN

1998	Switzerland, Canada, Norway

WOMEN

1998	Canada, Denmark, Sweden.

Figure Skating

Men's Singles

1908#	Ulrich Salchow, Sweden
1920#	Gillis Grafstrom, Sweden
1924	Gillis Grafstrom, Sweden
1928	Gillis Grafstrom, Sweden
1932	Karl Schaefer, Austria
1936	Karl Schaefer, Austria
1948	Richard Button, U.S.
1952	Richard Button, U.S.
1956	Hayes Alan Jenkins, U.S.
1960	David W. Jenkins, U.S.
1964	Manfred Schnelldorfer, Germany
1968	Wolfgang Schwartz, Austria
1972	Ondrej Nepela, Czechoslovakia
1976	John Curry, Great Britain
1980	Robin Cousins, Great Britain
1984	Scott Hamilton, U.S.
1988	Brian Boitano, U.S.
1992	Viktor Petrenko, Unified Team
1994	Aleksei Urmanov, Russia
1998	Ilya Kulik, Russia

(#) Event was held at Summer Olympics.

Women's Singles

1908#	Madge Syers, Great Britain
1920#	Magda Julin-Mauroy, Sweden
1924	Herma von Szabo-Planck, Austria
1928	Sonja Henie, Norway
1932	Sonja Henie, Norway
1936	Sonja Henie, Norway
1948	Barbara Ann Scott, Canada
1952	Jeanette Altwegg, Great Britain
1956	Tenley Albright, U.S.
1960	Carol Heiss, U.S.
1964	Sjoukje Dijkstra, Netherlands
1968	Peggy Fleming, U.S.
1972	Beatrix Schuba, Austria
1976	Dorothy Hamill, U.S.
1980	Anett Poetzsch, E. Germany
1984	Katarina Witt, E. Germany
1988	Katarina Witt, E. Germany
1992	Kristi Yamaguchi, U.S.
1994	Oksana Baiul, Ukraine
1998	Tara Lipinski, U.S.

(#) Event was held at Summer Olympics.

Pairs

1908#	Anna Hubler & Heinrich Burger, Germany
1920#	Ludovika & Walter Jakobsson, Finland
1924	Helene Engelman & Alfred Berger, Austria
1928	Andree Joly & Pierre Brunet, France
1932	Andree Joly & Pierre Brunet, France
1936	Maxi Herber & Ernst Baier, Germany
1948	Micheline Lannoy & Pierre Baugniet, Belgium
1952	Ria and Paul Falk, Germany
1956	Elisabeth Schwartz & Kurt Oppelt, Austria
1960	Barbara Wagner & Robert Paul, Canada
1964	Ludmila Beloussova & Oleg Protopopov, USSR
1968	Ludmila Beloussova & Oleg Protopopov, USSR
1972	Irina Rodnina & Alexei Ulanov, USSR
1976	Irina Rodnina & Aleksandr Zaitzev, USSR
1980	Irina Rodnina & Aleksandr Zaitzev, USSR
1984	Elena Valova & Oleg Vassiliev, USSR
1988	Ekaterina Gordeeva & Sergei Grinkov, USSR
1992	Natalia Mishkutienok & Artur Dimitriev, Unified Team
1994	Ekaterina Gordeeva & Sergei Grinkov, Russia
1998	Oksana Kazakova & Artur Dmitriev, Russia

(#) Event was held at Summer Olympics.

Ice Dancing

1976	Ludmila Pakhomova & Aleksandr Gorschkov, USSR
1980	Natalya Linichuk & Gennadi Karponosov, USSR
1984	Jayne Torvill & Christopher Dean, Great Britain
1988	Natalia Bestemianova & Andrei Bukin, USSR
1992	Marina Klimova & Sergei Ponomarenko, Unified Team
1994	Pasha Grishuk & Evgeny Platov, Russia
1998	Pasha Grishuk & Evgeny Platov, Russia

Freestyle Skiing

Men's Moguls		Points
1992	Edgar Grospiron, France	25.81
1994	Jean-Luc Brassard, Canada	27.24
1998	Jonny Moseley, U.S.	26.93

Men's Aerials		Points
1994	Andreas Schoenbaechler, Switzerland	234.67
1998	Eric Bergoust, U.S.	255.64

Women's Moguls		Points
1992	Donna Weinbrecht, U.S.	23.69
1994	Stine Lise Hattestad, Norway	25.97
1998	Tae Satoya, Japan	25.06

Women's Aerials		Points
1994	Lina Tcherjazova, Uzbekistan	166.84
1998	Nikki Stone, U.S.	193.00

Ice Hockey

MEN

1920#	Canada, U.S., Czechoslovakia
1924	Canada, U.S., Great Britain
1928	Canada, Sweden, Switzerland
1932	Canada, U.S., Germany
1936	Great Britain, Canada, U.S.
1948	Canada, Czechoslovakia, Switzerland
1952	Canada, U.S., Sweden
1956	USSR, U.S., Canada
1960	U.S., Canada, USSR
1964	USSR, Sweden, Czechoslovakia
1968	USSR, Czechoslovakia, Canada
1972	USSR, U.S., Czechoslovakia
1976	USSR, Czechoslovakia, W. Germany
1980	U.S., USSR, Sweden
1984	USSR, Czechoslovakia, Sweden
1988	USSR, Finland, Sweden
1992	Unified Team, Canada, Czechoslovakia
1994	Sweden, Canada, Finland
1998	Czech Republic, Russia, Finland

(#) Event was held at Summer Olympics.

WOMEN

1998	U.S., Canada, Finland

Luge

Men's Singles		Time
1964	Thomas Keohler, E. Germany	3:26.77
1968	Manfred Schmid, Austria	2:52.48
1972	Wolfgang Scheidel, E. Germany	3:27.58
1976	Detlef Guenther, E. Germany	3:27.688
1980	Bernhard Glass, E. Germany	2:54.796
1984	Paul Hildgartner, Italy	3:04.258
1988	Jens Mueller, E. Germany	3:05.548
1992	Georg Hackl, Germany	3:02.363
1994	Georg Hackl, Germany	3:21.571
1998	Georg Hackl, Germany	3:18.436

Men's Doubles		Time
1964	Austria	1:41.62
1968	E. Germany	1:35.85
1972	Italy, E. Germany (tie)	1:28.35
1976	E. Germany	1:25.604
1980	E. Germany	1:19.331
1984	W. Germany	1:23.620
1988	E. Germany	1:31.940
1992	Germany	1:32.053
1994	Italy	1:36.720
1998	Germany	1:41.105

Women's Singles		Time
1964	Ortun Enderlein, Germany	3:24.67
1968	Erica Lechner, Italy	2:28.66
1972	Anna M. Muller, E. Germany	2:59.18
1976	Margit Schumann, E. Germany	2:50.621
1980	Vera Zozulya, USSR	2:36.537
1984	Steffi Martin, E. Germany	2:46.570
1988	Steffi Walter, E. Germany	3:03.973
1992	Doris Neuner, Austria	3:06.696
1994	Gerda Weissensteiner, Italy	3:15.517
1998	Silke Kraushaar, Germany	3:23.779

Nordic Skiing

Cross-Country Events

Men's 10 Kilometers (6.2 miles)		Time
1992	Vegard Ulvang, Norway	27:36.0
1994	Bjoern Daehlie, Norway	24:20.1
1998	Bjoern Daehlie, Norway	27:24.5

Men's 15 Kilometers (9.3 miles)		Time
1924	Thorleif Haug, Norway	1:14:31
1928	Johan Grottumsbraaten, Norway	1:37:01
1932	Sven Utterstrom, Sweden	1:23:07
1936	Erik-August Larsson, Sweden	1:14:38
1948	Martin Lundstrom, Sweden	1:13:50
1952	Hallgeir Brenden, Norway	1:01:34
1956	Hallgeir Brenden, Norway	0:49:39.0
1960	Haakon Brusveen, Norway	0:51:55.5
1964	Eero Maentyranta, Finland	0:50:54.1
1968	Harald Groenningen, Norway	0:47:54.2
1972	Sven-Ake Lundback, Sweden	0:45:28.24
1976	Nikolai Balukov, USSR	0:43:58.47
1980	Thomas Wassberg, Sweden	0:41:57.63
1984	Gunde Svan, Sweden	0:41:25.6
1988	Mikhail Deviatiarov, USSR	0:41:18.9
1992	Bjoern Daehlie, Norway	0:38:01.9
1994	Bjoern Daehlie, Norway	0:35:48.8
1998	Thomas Alsgaard, Norway	1:07:01.7

(Note: approx. 18-km course 1924-1952)

Men's 30 Kilometers (18.6 miles)		Time
1956	Veikko Hakulinen, Finland	1:44:06.0
1960	Sixten Jernberg, Sweden	1:51:03.9
1964	Eero Maentyranta, Finland	1:30:50.7
1968	Franco Nones, Italy	1:35:39.2
1972	Vyacheslav Vedenine, USSR	1:36:31.15
1976	Sergei Saveliev, USSR	1:30:29.38
1980	Nikolai Zimyatov, USSR	1:27:02.80
1984	Nikolai Zimyatov, USSR	1:28:56.3
1988	Aleksei Prokourorov, USSR	1:24:26.3
1992	Vegard Ulvang, Norway	1:22:27.8
1994	Thomas Alsgaard, Norway	1:12:26.4
1998	Mika Myllylae, Finland	1:33:55.8

Men's 50 Kilometers (31.2 miles)		Time
1924	Thorleif Haug, Norway	3:44:32.0
1928	Per Erik Hedlund, Sweden	4:52:03.0
1932	Veli Saarinen, Finland	4:28:00.0
1936	Elis Wiklund, Sweden	3:30:11.0
1948	Nils Karlsson, Sweden	3:47:48.0
1952	Veikko Hakulinen, Finland	3:33:33.0
1956	Sixten Jernberg, Sweden	2:50:27.0
1960	Kalevi Hamalainen, Finland	2:59:06.3
1964	Sixten Jernberg, Sweden	2:43:52.6
1968	Ole Ellefsaeter, Norway	2:28:45.8
1972	Paal Tyldum, Norway	2:43:14.75
1976	Ivar Formo, Norway	2:37:30.05
1980	Nikolai Zimyatov, USSR	2:27:24.60
1984	Thomas Wassberg, Sweden	2:15:55.8
1988	Gunde Svan, Sweden	2:04:30.9
1992	Bjoern Daehlie, Norway	2:03:41.5
1994	Vladimir Smirnov, Kazakhstan	2:07:20.3
1998	Bjoern Daehlie, Norway	2:05:08.2

Men's 40-Kilometer Relay		Time
1936	Finland, Norway, Sweden	2:41:33.0
1948	Sweden, Finland, Norway	2:32:08.0
1952	Finland, Norway, Sweden	2:20:16.0
1956	USSR, Finland, Sweden	2:15:30.0
1960	Finland, Norway, USSR	2:18:45.6
1964	Sweden, Finland, USSR	2:18:34.6
1968	Norway, Sweden, Finland	2:08:33.5
1972	USSR, Norway, Switzerland	2:04:47.94
1976	Finland, Norway, USSR	2:07:59.72
1980	USSR, Norway, Finland	1:57:03.46
1984	Sweden, USSR, Finland	1:55:06.30
1988	Sweden, USSR, Czechoslovakia	1:43:58.60
1992	Norway, Italy, Finland	1:39:26.00
1994	Italy, Norway, Finland	1:41:15.00
1998	Norway, Italy, Finland	1:40:55.70

Women's 5 Kilometers (approx. 3.1 miles)		Time
1964	Claudia Boyarskikh, USSR	17:50.5
1968	Toini Gustafsson, Sweden	16:45.2
1972	Galina Koulacova, USSR	17:00.50
1976	Helena Takalo, Finland	15:48.69
1980	Raisa Smetanina, USSR	15:06.92
1984	Marja-Liisa Haemaelainen, Finland	17:04.0
1988	Marjo Matikainen, Finland	15:04.0
1992	Marjut Lukkarinen, Finland	14:13.8
1994	Ljubov Egorova, Russia	14:08.8
1998	Larissa Lazutina, Russia	17:37.9

Women's 10 Kilometers (6.2 miles)		Time
1952	Lydia Wideman, Finland	41:40.0
1956	Lyubov Kosyreva, USSR	38:11.0
1960	Maria Gusakova, USSR	39:46.6
1964	Claudia Boyarskikh, USSR	40:24.3
1968	Toini Gustafsson, Sweden	36:46.5
1972	Galina Koulacova, USSR	34:17.82
1976	Raisa Smetanina, USSR	30:13.41
1980	Barbara Petzold, E. Germany	30:31.54
1984	Marja-Liisa Haemaelainen, Finland	31:44.2

1988	Vida Ventsene, USSR	30:08.3
1992	Lyubov Egorova, Unified Team	25:53.7
1994	Lyubov Egorova, Russia	27:30.1
1998	Larissa Lazutina, Russia	46.06.9

	Women's 15 Kilometers (9.3 miles)	Time
1992	Lyubov Egorova, Unified Team	42:20.8
1994	Manuela Di Centa, Italy	39:44.5
1998	Olga Danilova, Russia	46:55.4

	Women's 30 Kilometers (18.6 miles)	Time
1992	Stefania Belmondo, Italy	1:22:30.1
1994	Manuela Di Centa, Italy	1:25:41.6
1998	Julija Tchepalova, Russia	1:22:01.5

	Women's 20-Kilometer Relay	Time
1956	Finland, USSR, Sweden (15 km)	1:09:01.0
1960	Sweden, USSR, Finland (15 km)	1:04:21.4
1964	USSR, Sweden, Finland (15 km)	0:59:20.2
1968	Norway, Sweden, USSR (15 km)	0:57:30.0
1972	USSR, Finland, Norway (15 km)	0:48:46.15
1976	USSR, Finland, E. Germany	1:07:49.75
1980	E. Germany, USSR, Norway	1:02:11.1
1984	Norway, Czechoslovakia, Finland	1:06:49.7
1988	USSR, Norway, Finland	0:59:51.1
1992	United Team, Norway, Italy	0:59:34.8
1994	Russia, Norway, Italy	0:57:12.5
1998	Russia, Norway, Italy	0:55:13.5

Combined Cross-Country & Jumping (Men)

	Nordic Combined*
1924	Thorleif Haug, Norway
1928	Johan Grottumsbraaten, Norway
1932	Johan Grottumsbraaten, Norway
1936	Oddbjorn Hagen, Norway
1948	Heikki Hasu, Finland
1952	Simon Slattvik, Norway
1956	Sverre Stenersen, Norway
1960	Georg Thoma, W. Germany
1964	Tormod Knutsen, Norway
1968	Franz Keller, W. Germany
1972	Ulrich Wehling, E. Germany
1976	Ulrich Wehling, E. Germany
1980	Ulrich Wehling, E. Germany
1984	Tom Sandberg, Norway
1988	Hippolyt Kempf, Switzerland
1992	Fabrice Guy, France
1994	Fred Barre Lundberg, Norway
1998	Bjarte Engen Vik, Norway

	Team Nordic Combined*
1988	W. Germany, Switzerland, Austria
1992	Japan, Norway, Austria
1994	Japan, Norway, Switzerland
1998	Norway, Finland, France

*Medals based on combination of points for jumping events and time for cross-country events.

Ski Jumping (Men)

	Normal Hill	Points
1964	Veikko Kankkonen, Finland	229.9
1968	Jiri Raska, Czechoslovakia	216.5
1972	Yukio Kasaya, Japan	244.2
1976	Hans-Georg Aschenbach, E. Germany	252.0
1980	Toni Innauer, Austria	266.3
1984	Jens Weissflog, E. Germany	215.2
1988	Matti Nykaenen, Finland	230.5
1992	Ernst Vettori, Austria	222.8
1994	Espen Bredesen, Norway	282.0
1998	Jani Soininen, Finland	234.5

	Large Hill	Points
1924	Jacob Tullin Thams, Norway	18.960
1928	Alfred Andersen, Norway	19.208
1932	Birger Ruud, Norway	228.1
1936	Birger Ruud, Norway	232.0
1948	Petter Hugsted, Norway	228.1
1952	Arnfinn Bergmann, Norway	226.0
1956	Antti Hyvarinen, Finland	227.0
1960	Helmut Recknagel, E. Germany	227.2
1964	Toralf Engan, Norway	230.7
1968	Vladimir Beloussov, USSR	231.3
1972	Wojciech Fortuna, Poland	219.9
1976	Karl Schnabl, Austria	234.8
1980	Jouko Tormanen, Finland	271.0
1984	Matti Nykaenen, Finland	231.2
1988	Matti Nykaenen, Finland	224.0
1992	Toni Nieminen, Finland	239.5
1994	Jens Weissflog, Germany	274.5
1998	Kazuyoshi Funaki, Japan	272.3

	Team Large Hill	Points
1988	Finland, Yugoslavia, Norway	634.4
1992	Finland, Austria, Czechoslovakia	644.4
1994	Germany, Japan, Austria	970.1
1998	Japan, Germany, Austria	933.0

Snowboarding

	Men's Giant Slalom	Time
1998	Ross Rebagliati, Canada	2:03.96

	Men's Halfpipe	Points
1998	Gian Simmen, Switzerland	85.2

	Women's Giant Slalom	Time
1998	Karine Ruby, France	2:17.34

	Women's Halfpipe	Points
1998	Nicola Thost, Germany	74.6

Speed Skating

	Men's 500 Meters	Time*
1924	Charles Jewtraw, U.S.	0:44.0
1928	Thunberg, Finland & Evensen, Norway (tie)	0:43.4
1932	John A. Shea, U.S.	0:43.4
1936	Ivar Ballangrud, Norway	0:43.4
1948	Finn Helgesen, Norway	0:43.1
1952	Kenneth Henry, U.S.	0:43.2
1956	Evgeniy Grishin, USSR	0:40.2
1960	Evgeniy Grishin, USSR	0:40.2
1964	Terry McDermott, U.S.	0:40.1
1968	Erhard Keller, W. Germany	0:40.3
1972	Erhard Keller, W. Germany	0:39.44
1976	Evgeny Kulikov, USSR	0:39.17
1980	Eric Heiden, U.S.	0:38.03
1984	Sergei Fokichev, USSR	0:38.19
1988	Uwe-Jens Mey, E. Germany	0:36.45
1992	Uwe-Jens Mey, Germany	0:37.14
1994	Aleksandr Golubev, Russia	0:36.33
1998	Hiroyasu Shimizu, Japan	0:35.59

*Better time of two runs. Medals based on combined times.

	Men's 1,000 Meters	Time
1976	Peter Mueller, U.S.	1:19.32
1980	Eric Heiden, U.S.	1:15.18
1984	Gaetan Boucher, Canada	1:15.80
1988	Nikolai Guiliaev, USSR	1:13.03
1992	Olaf Zinke, Germany	1:14.85
1994	Dan Jansen, U.S.	1:12.43
1998	Ids Postma, Netherlands	1:10.64

	Men's 1,500 Meters	Time
1924	Clas Thunberg, Finland	2:20.8
1928	Clas Thunberg, Finland	2:21.1
1932	John A. Shea, U.S.	2:57.5
1936	Charles Mathiesen, Norway	2:19.2
1948	Sverre Farstad, Norway	2:17.6
1952	Hjalmar Andersen, Norway	2:20.4
1956	Grishin, & Mikhailov, both USSR (tie)	2:08.6
1960	Aas, Norway & Grishin, USSR (tie)	2:10.4
1964	Ants Anston, USSR	2:10.3
1968	Cornetis Verkerk, Netherlands	2:03.4
1972	Ard Schenk, Netherlands	2:02.96
1976	Jan Egil Storholt, Norway	1:59.38
1980	Eric Heiden, U.S.	1:55.44
1984	Gaetan Boucher, Canada	1:58.36
1988	Andre Hoffmann, E. Germany	1:52.06
1992	Johann Koss, Norway	1:54.81
1994	Johann Koss, Norway	1:51.29
1998	Aadne Sondral, Norway	1:47.87

	Men's 5,000 Meters	Time
1924	Clas Thunberg, Finland	8:39.0
1928	Ivar Ballangrud, Norway	8:50.5
1932	Irving Jaffee, U.S.	9:40.8
1936	Ivar Ballangrud, Norway	8:19.6
1948	Reidar Liaklev, Norway	8:29.4
1952	Hjalmar Andersen, Norway	8:10.6
1956	Boris Shilkov, USSR	7:48.7
1960	Viktor Kosichkin, USSR	7:51.3
1964	Knut Johannesen, Norway	7:38.4
1968	F. Anton Maier, Norway	7:22.4
1972	Ard Schenk, Netherlands	7:23.61
1976	Sten Stensen, Norway	7:24.48
1980	Eric Heiden, U.S.	7:02.29
1984	Sven Tomas Gustafson, Sweden	7:12.28
1988	Tomas Gustafson, Sweden	6:44.63
1992	Geir Karlstad, Norway	6:59.97
1994	Johann Koss, Norway	6:34.96
1998	Gianni Romme, Netherlands	6:22.20

	Men's 10,000 Meters	Time
1924	Julius Skutnabb, Finland	18:04.8
1928	Event not held because of thawing of ice	
1932	Irving Jaffee, U.S.	19:13.6

(continued)

1936	Ivar Ballangrud, Norway	17:24.3
1948	Ake Seyffarth, Sweden	17:26.3
1952	Hjalmar Andersen, Norway	16:45.8
1956	Sigvard Ericsson, Sweden	16:35.9
1960	Knut Johannesen, Norway	15:46.6
1964	Jonny Nilsson, Sweden	15:50.1
1968	Jonny Hoeglin, Sweden	15:23.6
1972	Ard Schenk, Netherlands	15:01.35
1976	Piet Kleine, Netherlands	14:50.59
1980	Eric Heiden, U.S.	14:28.13
1984	Igor Malkov, USSR	14:39.90
1988	Tomas Gustafson, Sweden	13:48.20
1992	Bart Veldkamp, Netherlands	14:12.12
1994	Johann Koss, Norway	13:30.55
1998	Gianni Romme, Netherlands	13:15.33

	Women's 500 Meters	Time*
1960	Helga Haase, Germany	0:45.9
1964	Lydia Skoblikova, USSR	0:45.0
1968	Ludmila Titova, USSR	0:46.1
1972	Anne Henning, U.S.	0:43.33
1976	Sheila Young, U.S.	0:42.76
1980	Karin Enke, E. Germany	0:41.78
1984	Christa Rothenburger, E. Germany	0:41.02
1988	Bonnie Blair, U.S.	0:39.10
1992	Bonnie Blair, U.S.	0:40.33
1994	Bonnie Blair, U.S.	0:39.25
1998	Catriona LeMay-Doan, Canada	0:38.21

* Better time of two runs. Medals based on combined times.

	Women's 1,000 Meters	Time
1960	Klara Guseva, USSR	1:34.1
1964	Lydia Skoblikova, USSR	1:33.2
1968	Carolina Geijssen, Netherlands	1:32.6
1972	Monika Pflug, W. Germany	1:31.40
1976	Tatiana Averina, USSR	1:28.43
1980	Natalya Petruseva, USSR	1:24.10
1984	Karin Enke, E. Germany	1:21.61
1988	Christa Rothenburger, E. Germany	1:17.65
1992	Bonnie Blair, U.S.	1:21.90
1994	Bonnie Blair, U.S.	1:18.74
1998	Marianne Timmer, Netherlands	1:16.51

	Women's 1,500 Meters	Time
1960	Lydia Skoblikova, USSR	2:52.2
1964	Lydia Skoblikova, USSR	2:22.6
1968	Kaija Mustonen, Finland	2:22.4
1972	Dianne Holum, U.S.	2:20.85
1976	Galina Stepanskaya, USSR	2:16.58
1980	Anne Borckink, Netherlands	2:10.95
1984	Karin Enke, E. Germany	2:03.42
1988	Yvonne van Gennip, Netherlands	2:00.68
1992	Jacqueline Boerner, Germany	2:05.87
1994	Emese Hunyady, Austria	2:02.19
1998	Marianne Timmer, Netherlands	1:57.58

	Women's 3,000 Meters	Time
1960	Lydia Skoblikova, USSR	5:14.3
1964	Lydia Skoblikova, USSR	5:14.9
1968	Johanna Schut, Netherlands	4:56.2
1972	Christina Baas-Kaiser, Netherlands	4:52.14
1976	Tatiana Averina, USSR	4:45.19
1980	Bjoerg Eva Jensen, Norway	4:32.13
1984	Andrea Schoene, E. Germany	4:24.79
1988	Yvonne van Gennip, Netherlands	4:11.94
1992	Gunda Niemann, Germany	4:19.90
1994	Svetlana Bazhanova, Russia	4:17.43
1998	Gunda Niemann-Stirnemann, Germany	4:07.29

	Women's 5,000 Meters	Time
1988	Yvonne van Gennip, Netherlands	7:14.13
1992	Gunda Niemann, Germany	7:31.57
1994	Claudia Pechstein, Germany	7:14.37
1998	Claudia Pechstein, Germany	6:59.61

Short-Track Speed Skating

	Men's 500 Meters	Time
1998	Takafumi Nishitani, Japan	42.862

	Men's 1,000 Meters	Time
1992	Kim Ki-Hoon, S. Korea	1:30.76
1994	Kim Ki-Hoon, S. Korea	1:34.57
1998	Dong-Sung Kim, S. Korea	1:32.375

	Men's 5,000-Meter Relay	Time
1992	S. Korea, Canada, Japan	7:14.02
1994	Italy, U.S., Australia	7:11.74
1998	Canada, S. Korea, China	7:06.075

	Women's 500 Meters	Time
1992	Cathy Turner, U.S.	47:04
1994	Cathy Turner, U.S.	45.98
1998	Annie Perreault, Canada	46.568

	Women's 1,000-Meters	Time
1998	Chun Lee-Kyung, S. Korea	1:42.776

	Women's 3,000-Meter Relay	Time
1992	Canada, U.S., Unified Team	4:36.62
1994	S. Korea, Canada, U.S.	4:26.64
1998	S. Korea, China, Canada	4:16.26

History of the Olympic Games

The modern Olympic Games, first held in Athens, Greece, in 1896, were the result of efforts by Baron Pierre de Coubertin, a French educator, to promote interest in education and culture and to foster better international understanding through love of athletics. His source of inspiration was the ancient Greek Olympic Games, most notable of the 4 Panhellenic celebrations. The games were combined patriotic, religious, and athletic festivals held every 4 years. The first such recorded festival was held in 776 BC, the date from which the Greeks began to keep their calendar by "Olympiads," or 4-year spans between the games. The first Olympiad is said to have consisted merely of a 200-yd foot race near the small city of Olympia, but the games gained in scope and became demonstrations of national pride. Only Greek citizens—amateurs—could participate. Winners received laurel, wild olive, and palm wreaths and were accorded special privileges. Under the Roman emperors, the games deteriorated into professional carnivals and circuses. Emperor Theodosius banned them in AD 394.

Baron de Coubertin enlisted 13 nations to send athletes to the first modern Olympics in 1896; now athletes from nearly 200 nations and territories compete in the Summer Olympics. The Winter Olympic Games were started in 1924.

Olympic Information

Symbol: Five rings or circles, linked together to represent the sporting friendship of all peoples. The rings also symbolize 5 geographic areas—Europe, Asia, Africa, Australia, and America. Each ring is a different color—blue, yellow, black, green, and red.

Flag: The symbol of the 5 rings on a plain white background.

Motto: "Citius, Altius, Fortius." Latin meaning "swifter, higher, stronger."

Creed: "The most important thing in the Olympic Games is not to win but to take part, just as the most important thing in life is not the triumph but the struggle. The essential thing is not to have conquered but to have fought well."

Oath: "In the name of all competitors I promise that we will take part in these Olympic Games, respecting and abiding by the rules which govern them, in the true spirit of sportsmanship for the glory of sport and the honor of our teams."

Flame: Symbolizes the continuity between the ancient and modern Games. The modern version of the flame was adopted in 1936. The torch used to kindle the flame is first lit by the sun's rays at Olympia, Greece, and then carried to the site of the Games by relays of runners. Ships and planes are used when necessary.

Paralympics

The first Olympic games for the disabled were held in Rome after the 1960 Summer Olympic Games; use of the name "paralympic" began with the 1964 games in Tokyo. The Paralympics are held by the Olympic host country in the same year and usually in the same city or venue. A goal of the Paralympics is to provide elite competition to athletes with functional disabilities that prevent their involvement in the Olympics. In 1976 the first Winter Paralympic Games were held, in Ornskoldsvik, Sweden.

The VII Paralympic Winter Games, the first to take place outside Europe, were held Mar. 5-Mar. 14, 1998, in Nagano, Japan. The games featured 571 athletes from 32 nations competing for medals in over 30 events in the following sports: Alpine skiing, cross-country skiing, biathlon, ice sledge racing, and ice sledge hockey.

Summer Olympic Games in 1996

Atlanta, GA, U.S., July 19-Aug. 4, 1996

On July 19, 1996, former boxing great Muhammad Ali lit the flame inaugurating the Centennial Olympic Games, the 26th Olympiad. About 10,750 athletes gathered for 17 days to compete for medals in a record 271 events; athletes from 197 nations and territories participated (25 more than in any previous Olympics). A bomb attack, July 27, at Centennial Olympic Park led to 2 deaths and injured more than 100, casting a somber mood on the 2d week of the games—still, the spirit of competition prevailed.

Outstanding athletes and teams included: Kerri Strug, who ignored an ankle injury to lead the U.S. women's gymnastics team to a gold medal; the U.S. women's basketball, softball, and soccer teams; the U.S. men's basketball team (Dream Team), who again breezed to a gold; U.S. runner Michael Johnson, who won the 200 and 400 meters; France's Marie-Jose Perec, winner of the women's 200 and 400 meters; Canada's Donovan Bailey, who set a world record in the 100-meter run; Dan O'Brien of the U.S., who won the decathlon, after not even qualifying for the 1992 Olympics; U.S. swimmer Amy Van Dyken, who won 4 golds; Ireland's Michelle Smith, winner of 3 gold medals in swimming; China's Fu Mingxia, who swept both women's diving events; marathon runner Josia Thugwane, South Africa's first black gold medalist; Russian Aleksandr Karelin, who won his 3d straight gold in Greco-Roman wrestling's super-heavyweight class; and Carl Lewis of the U.S., who won his 4th consecutive gold in the long jump.

The U.S. won the most medals, 101, and the most gold medals, 44. Germany finished 2d in the medal count with 65, while Russia was 3d in total medals with 63, and 2d in gold medals with 26.

Final Medal Standings

Country	G	S	B	T
United States	44	32	25	**101**
Germany	20	18	27	**65**
Russia	26	21	16	**63**
China	16	22	12	**50**
Australia	9	9	23	**41**
France	15	7	15	**37**
Italy	13	10	12	**35**
South Korea	7	15	5	**27**
Cuba	9	8	8	**25**
Ukraine	9	2	12	**23**
Canada	3	11	8	**22**
Hungary	7	4	10	**21**
Romania	4	7	9	**20**
Netherlands	4	5	10	**19**
Poland	7	5	5	**17**
Spain	5	6	6	**17**
Bulgaria	3	7	5	**15**
Brazil	3	3	9	**15**
Great Britain	1	8	6	**15**
Belarus	1	6	8	**15**
Japan	3	6	5	**14**
Czech Rep.	4	3	4	**11**
Kazakhstan	3	4	4	**11**
Greece	4	4	0	**8**
Sweden	2	4	2	**8**
Kenya	1	4	3	**8**
Switzerland	4	3	0	**7**

Country	G	S	B	T
Norway	2	2	3	**7**
Denmark	4	1	1	**6**
Turkey	4	1	1	**6**
New Zealand	3	2	1	**6**
Belgium	2	2	2	**6**
Nigeria	2	1	3	**6**
Jamaica	1	3	2	**6**
South Africa	3	1	1	**5**
North Korea	2	1	2	**5**
Ireland	3	0	1	**4**
Finland	1	2	1	**4**
Indonesia	1	1	2	**4**
Yugoslavia	1	1	2	**4**
Algeria	2	0	1	**3**
Ethiopia	2	0	1	**3**
Iran	1	1	1	**3**
Slovakia	1	1	1	**3**
Argentina	0	2	1	**3**
Austria	0	1	2	**3**
Armenia	1	1	0	**2**
Croatia	1	1	0	**2**
Portugal	1	0	1	**2**
Thailand	1	0	1	**2**
Namibia	0	2	0	**2**
Slovenia	0	2	0	**2**
Malaysia	0	1	1	**2**
Moldova	0	1	1	**2**

Country	G	S	B	T
Uzbekistan	0	1	1	**2**
Georgia	0	0	2	**2**
Morocco	0	0	2	**2**
Trinidad & Tobago	0	0	2	**2**
Burundi	1	0	0	**1**
Costa Rica	1	0	0	**1**
Ecuador	1	0	0	**1**
Hong Kong	1	0	0	**1**
Syria	1	0	0	**1**
Azerbaijan	0	1	0	**1**
Bahamas	0	1	0	**1**
Latvia	0	1	0	**1**
Philippines	0	1	0	**1**
Taiwan	0	1	0	**1**
Tonga	0	1	0	**1**
Zambia	0	1	0	**1**
India	0	0	1	**1**
Israel	0	0	1	**1**
Lithuania	0	0	1	**1**
Mexico	0	0	1	**1**
Mongolia	0	0	1	**1**
Mozambique	0	0	1	**1**
Puerto Rico	0	0	1	**1**
Tunisia	0	0	1	**1**
Uganda	0	0	1	**1**

Sites of Summer Olympic Games

1896	Athens, Greece
1900	Paris, France
1904	St. Louis, U.S.
1906*	Athens, Greece
1908	London, England
1912	Stockholm, Sweden
1920	Antwerp, Belgium
1924	Paris, France
1928	Amsterdam, Netherlands
1932	Los Angeles, U.S.
1936	Berlin, Germany
1948	London, England
1952	Helsinki, Finland
1956	Melbourne, Australia
1960	Rome, Italy
1964	Tokyo, Japan
1968	Mexico City, Mexico
1972	Munich, W. Germany
1976	Montreal, Canada
1980	Moscow, USSR
1984	Los Angeles, U.S.
1988	Seoul, South Korea
1992	Barcelona, Spain
1996	Atlanta, U.S.
2000	Sydney, Australia
2004	Athens, Greece

*Games not recognized by International Olympic Committee. Games 6 (1916), 12 (1940), and 13 (1944) were not celebrated.

Summer Olympic Games Champions, 1896-1996

(*indicates Olympic record)

The 1980 games were boycotted by 62 nations, including the U.S. The 1984 games were boycotted by the USSR and by most Eastern bloc nations. East and West Germany competed separately 1968-88. The 1992 Unified Team consisted of 12 former Soviet republics. The 1992 Independent Olympic Participants (I.O.P.) were athletes from Serbia, Montenegro, and Macedonia.

Track and Field — Men

100-Meter Run

1896	Thomas Burke, United States	12s
1900	Francis W. Jarvis, United States	11.0s
1904	Archie Hahn, United States	11.0s
1908	Reginald Walker, South Africa	10.8s
1912	Ralph Craig, United States	10.8s
1920	Charles Paddock, United States	10.8s
1924	Harold Abrahams, Great Britain	10.6s
1928	Percy Williams, Canada	10.8s
1932	Eddie Tolan, United States	10.3s
1936	Jesse Owens, United States	10.3s
1948	Harrison Dillard, United States	10.3s
1952	Lindy Remigino, United States	10.4s
1956	Bobby Morrow, United States	10.5s
1960	Armin Hary, Germany	10.2s
1964	Bob Hayes, United States	10.0s
1968	Jim Hines, United States	9.95s
1972	Valery Borzov, USSR	10.14s
1976	Hasely Crawford, Trinidad	10.06s
1980	Allan Wells, Great Britain	10.25s
1984	Carl Lewis, United States	9.99s
1988	Carl Lewis, United States	9.92s
1992	Linford Christie, Great Britain	9.96s
1996	Donovan Bailey, Canada	9.84s*

200-Meter Run

1900	Walter Tewksbury, United States	22.2s
1904	Archie Hahn, United States	21.6s
1908	Robert Kerr, Canada	22.6s
1912	Ralph Craig, United States	21.7s
1920	Allan Woodring, United States	22s
1924	Jackson Scholz, United States	21.6s
1928	Percy Williams, Canada	21.8s
1932	Eddie Tolan, United States	21.2s
1936	Jesse Owens, United States	20.7s
1948	Mel Patton, United States	21.1s
1952	Andrew Stanfield, United States	20.7s
1956	Bobby Morrow, United States	20.6s
1960	Livio Berruti, Italy	20.5s
1964	Henry Carr, United States	20.3s

(continued)

1968	Tommie Smith, United States	19.83s
1972	Valeri Borzov, USSR	20.00s
1976	Donald Quarrie, Jamaica	20.23s
1980	Pietro Mennea, Italy	20.19s
1984	Carl Lewis, United States	19.80s
1988	Joe DeLoach, United States	19.75s
1992	Mike Marsh, United States	20.01s
1996	Michael Johnson, United States	19.32s*

400-Meter Run

1896	Thomas Burke, United States	54.2s
1900	Maxey Long, United States	49.4s
1904	Harry Hillman, United States	49.2s
1908	Wyndham Halswelle, Great Britain, walkover	50s
1912	Charles Reidpath, United States	48.2s
1920	Bevil Rudd, South Africa	49.6s
1924	Eric Liddell, Great Britain	47.6s
1928	Ray Barbuti, United States	47.8s
1932	William Carr, United States	46.2s
1936	Archie Williams, United States	46.5s
1948	Arthur Wint, Jamaica	46.2s
1952	George Rhoden, Jamaica	45.9s
1956	Charles Jenkins, United States	46.7s
1960	Otis Davis, United States	44.9s
1964	Michael Larrabee, United States	45.1s
1968	Lee Evans, United States	43.8s
1972	Vincent Matthews, United States	44.66s
1976	Alberto Juantorena, Cuba	44.26s
1980	Viktor Markin, USSR	44.60s
1984	Alonzo Babers, United States	44.27s
1988	Steven Lewis, United States	43.87s
1992	Quincy Watts, United States	43.50s
1996	Michael Johnson, United States	43.49s*

800-Meter Run

1896	Edwin Flack, Australia	2m. 11s
1900	Alfred Tysoe, Great Britain	2m. 1.2s
1904	James Lightbody, United States	1m. 56s
1908	Mel Sheppard, United States	1m. 52.8s
1912	James Meredith, United States	1m. 51.9s
1920	Albert Hill, Great Britain	1m. 53.4s
1924	Douglas Lowe, Great Britain	1m. 52.4s
1928	Douglas Lowe, Great Britain	1m. 51.8s
1932	Thomas Hampson, Great Britain	1m. 49.8s
1936	John Woodruff, United States	1m. 52.9s
1948	Mal Whitfield, United States	1m. 49.2s
1952	Mal Whitfield, United States	1m. 49.2s
1956	Thomas Courtney, United States	1m. 47.7s
1960	Peter Snell, New Zealand	1m. 46.3s
1964	Peter Snell, New Zealand	1m. 45.1s
1968	Ralph Doubell, Australia	1m. 44.3s
1972	Dave Wottle, United States	1m. 45.9s
1976	Alberto Juantorena, Cuba	1m. 43.50s
1980	Steve Ovett, Great Britain	1m. 45.40s
1984	Joaquim Cruz, Brazil	1m. 43.00s
1988	Paul Ereng, Kenya	1m. 43.45s
1992	William Tanui, Kenya	1m. 43.66s
1996	Vebjoern Rodal, Norway	1m. 42.58s*

1,500-Meter Run

1896	Edwin Flack, Australia	4m. 33.2s
1900	Charles Bennett, Great Britain	4m. 6.2s
1904	James Lightbody, United States	4m. 5.4s
1908	Mel Sheppard, United States	4m. 3.4s
1912	Arnold Jackson, Great Britain	3m. 56.8s
1920	Albert Hill, Great Britain	4m. 1.8s
1924	Paavo Nurmi, Finland	3m. 53.6s
1928	Harry Larva, Finland	3m. 53.2s
1932	Luigi Beccali, Italy	3m. 51.2s
1936	Jack Lovelock, New Zealand	3m. 47.8s
1948	Henri Eriksson, Sweden	3m. 49.8s
1952	Joseph Barthel, Luxembourg	3m. 45.2s
1956	Ron Delany, Ireland	3m. 41.2s
1960	Herb Elliott, Australia	3m. 35.6s
1964	Peter Snell, New Zealand	3m. 38.1s
1968	Kipchoge Keino, Kenya	3m. 34.9s
1972	Pekka Vasala, Finland	3m. 36.3s
1976	John Walker, New Zealand	3m. 39.17s
1980	Sebastian Coe, Great Britain	3m. 38.4s
1984	Sebastian Coe, Great Britain	3m. 32.53s*
1988	Peter Rono, Kenya	3m. 35.96s
1992	Fermin Cacho Ruiz, Spain	3m. 40.12s
1996	Noureddine Morceli, Algeria	3m. 35.78s

5,000-Meter Run

1912	Hannes Kolehmainen, Finland	14m. 36.6s
1920	Joseph Guillemot, France	14m. 55.6s
1924	Paavo Nurmi, Finland	14m. 31.2s
1928	Willie Ritola, Finland	14m. 38s
1932	Lauri Lehtinen, Finland	14m. 30s
1936	Gunnar Hockert, Finland	14m. 22.2s
1948	Gaston Reiff, Belgium	14m. 17.6s
1952	Emil Zatopek, Czechoslovakia	14m. 6.6s
1956	Vladimir Kuts, USSR	13m. 39.6s
1960	Murray Halberg, New Zealand	13m. 43.4s
1964	Bob Schul, United States	13m. 48.8s
1968	Mohamed Gammoudi, Tunisia	14m. 05.0s
1972	Lasse Viren, Finland	13m. 26.4s
1976	Lasse Viren, Finland	13m. 24.76s
1980	Miruts Yifter, Ethiopia	13m. 21.0s
1984	Said Aouita, Morocco	13m. 05.59s*
1988	John Ngugi, Kenya	13m. 11.70s
1992	Dieter Baumann, Germany	13m. 12.52s
1996	Venuste Niyongabo, Burundi	13m. 07.96s

10,000-Meter Run

1912	Hannes Kolehmainen, Finland	31m. 20.8s
1920	Paavo Nurmi, Finland	31m. 45.8s
1924	Willie Ritola, Finland	30m. 23.2s
1928	Paavo Nurmi, Finland	30m. 18.8s
1932	Janusz Kusocinski, Poland	30m. 11.4s
1936	Ilmari Salminen, Finland	30m. 15.4s
1948	Emil Zatopek, Czechoslovakia	29m. 59.6s
1952	Emil Zatopek, Czechoslovakia	29m. 17.0s
1956	Vladimir Kuts, USSR	28m. 45.6s
1960	Pyotr Bolotnikov, USSR	28m. 32.2s
1964	Billy Mills, United States	28m. 24.4s
1968	Naftali Temu, Kenya	29m. 27.4s
1972	Lasse Viren, Finland	27m. 38.4s
1976	Lasse Viren, Finland	27m. 40.38s
1980	Miruts Yifter, Ethiopia	27m. 42.7s
1984	Alberto Cova, Italy	27m. 47.54s
1988	Brahim Boutaib, Morocco	27m. 21.46s
1992	Khalid Skah, Morocco	27m. 46.70s
1996	Haile Gebrselassie, Ethiopia	27m. 07.34s*

110-Meter Hurdles

1896	Thomas Curtis, United States	17.6s
1900	Alvin Kraenzlein, United States	15.4s
1904	Frederick Schule, United States	16s
1908	Forrest Smithson, United States	15s
1912	Frederick Kelly, United States	15.1s
1920	Earl Thomson, Canada	14.8s
1924	Daniel Kinsey, United States	15s
1928	Sydney Atkinson, South Africa	14.8s
1932	George Saling, United States	14.6s
1936	Forrest Towns, United States	14.2s
1948	William Porter, United States	13.9s
1952	Harrison Dillard, United States	13.7s
1956	Lee Calhoun, United States	13.5s
1960	Lee Calhoun, United States	13.8s
1964	Hayes Jones, United States	13.6s
1968	Willie Davenport, United States	13.3s
1972	Rod Milburn, United States	13.24s
1976	Guy Drut, France	13.30s
1980	Thomas Munkelt, E. Germany	13. 39s
1984	Roger Kingdom, United States	13.20s
1988	Roger Kingdom, United States	12.98s
1992	Mark McCoy, Canada	13.12s
1996	Allen Johnson, United States	12.95s*

400-Meter Hurdles

1900	J.W.B. Tewksbury, United States	57.6s
1904	Harry Hillman, United States	53s
1908	Charles Bacon, United States	55s
1920	Frank Loomis, United States	54s
1924	F. Morgan Taylor, United States	52.6s
1928	Lord Burghley, Great Britain	53.4s
1932	Robert Tisdall, Ireland	51.7s
1936	Glenn Hardin, United States	52.4s
1948	Roy Cochran, United States	51.1s
1952	Charles Moore, United States	50.8s
1956	Glenn Davis, United States	50.1s
1960	Glenn Davis, United States	49.3s
1964	Rex Cawley, United States	49.6s
1968	Dave Hemery, Great Britain	48.12s
1972	John Akii-Bua, Uganda	47.82s
1976	Edwin Moses, United States	47.64s
1980	Volker Beck, E. Germany	48.70s
1984	Edwin Moses, United States	47.75s
1988	Andre Phillips, United States	47.19s
1992	Kevin Young, United States	46.78s*
1996	Derrick Adkins, United States	47.54s

400-Meter Relay

1912	Great Britain	42.4s
1920	United States	42.2s
1924	United States	41s
1928	United States	41s
1932	United States	40s
1936	United States	39.8s
1948	United States	40.6s
1952	United States	40.1s

1956	United States	39.5s
1960	Germany (U.S. disqualified)	39.5s
1964	United States	39.0s
1968	United States	38.2s
1972	United States	38.19s
1976	United States	38.33s
1980	USSR	38.26s
1984	United States	37.83s
1988	USSR (U.S. disqualified)	38.19s
1992	United States	37.40s*
1996	Canada	37.69s

1,600-Meter Relay

1908	United States	3m. 29.4s
1912	United States	3m. 16.6s
1920	Great Britain	3m. 22.2s
1924	United States	3m. 16s
1928	United States	3m. 14.2s
1932	United States	3m. 8.2s
1936	Great Britain	3m. 9s
1948	United States	3m. 10.4s
1952	Jamaica	3m. 03.9s
1956	United States	3m. 04.8s
1960	United States	3m. 02.2s
1964	United States	3m. 00.7s
1968	United States	2m. 56.16s
1972	Kenya	2m. 59.8s
1976	United States	2m. 58.65s
1980	USSR	3m. 01.1s
1984	United States	2m. 57.91s
1988	United States	2m. 56.16s
1992	United States	2m. 55.74s*
1996	United States	2m. 55.99s

3,000-Meter Steeplechase

1920	Percy Hodge, Great Britain	10m. 0.4s
1924	Willie Ritola, Finland	9m. 33.6s
1928	Toivo Loukola, Finland	9m. 21.8s
1932	Volmari Iso-Hollo, Finland (About 3,450 m; extra lap by error.)	10m. 33.4s
1936	Volmari Iso-Hollo, Finland	9m. 3.8s
1948	Thore Sjoestrand, Sweden	9m. 4.6s
1952	Horace Ashenfelter, United States	8m. 45.4s
1956	Chris Brasher, Great Britain	8m. 41.2s
1960	Zdzislaw Krzyszkowiak, Poland	8m. 34.2s
1964	Gaston Roelants, Belgium	8m. 30.8s
1968	Amos Biwott, Kenya	8m. 51s
1972	Kipchoge Keino, Kenya	8m. 23.6s
1976	Anders Garderud, Sweden	8m. 08.2s
1980	Bronislaw Malinowski, Poland	8m. 09.7s
1984	Julius Korir, Kenya	8m. 11.8s
1988	Julius Kariuki, Kenya	8m. 05.51s*
1992	Matthew Birir, Kenya	8m. 08.84s
1996	Joseph Keter, Kenya	8m. 07.12s

20-Kilometer Walk

1956	Leonid Spirin, USSR	1h. 31m. 27.4s
1960	Vladimir Golubnichy, USSR	1h. 33m. 7.2s
1964	Kenneth Mathews, Great Britain	1h. 29m. 34.0s
1968	Vladimir Golubnichy, USSR	1h. 33m. 58.4s
1972	Peter Frenkel, E. Germany	1h. 26m. 42.4s
1976	Daniel Bautista, Mexico	1h. 24m. 40.6s
1980	Maurizio Damilano, Italy	1h. 23m. 35.5s
1984	Ernesto Canto, Mexico	1h. 23m. 13.0s
1988	Josef Pribilinec, Czechoslovakia	1h. 19m. 57.0s*
1992	Daniel Plaza Montero, Spain	1h. 21m. 45.0s
1996	Jefferson Perez, Ecuador	1h. 20m.7s

50-Kilometer Walk

1932	Thomas W. Green, Great Britain	4h. 50m. 10s
1936	Harold Whitlock, Great Britain	4h. 30m. 41.4s
1948	John Ljunggren, Sweden	4h. 41m. 52s
1952	Giuseppe Dordoni, Italy	4h. 28m. 07.8s
1956	Norman Read, New Zealand	4h. 30m. 42.8s
1960	Donald Thompson, Great Britain	4h. 25m. 30s
1964	Abdon Pamich, Italy	4h. 11m. 12.4s
1968	Christoph Hohne, E. Germany	4h. 20m. 13.6s
1972	Bern Kannenberg, W. Germany	3h. 56m. 11.6s
1980	Hartwig Gauter, E. Germany	3h. 49m. 24.0s
1984	Raul Gonzalez, Mexico	3h. 47m. 26.0s
1988	Vayachselav Ivanenko, USSR	3h. 38m. 29.0s*
1992	Andrei Perlov, Unified Team	3h. 50m. 13.0s
1996	Robert Korzeniowski, Poland	3h. 43m. 30s

Marathon

1896	Spiridon Loues, Greece	2h. 58m. 50s
1900	Michel Theato, France	2h. 59m. 45s
1904	Thomas Hicks, United States	3h. 28m. 63s
1908	John J. Hayes, United States	2h. 55m. 18.4s
1912	Kenneth McArthur, South Africa	2h. 36m. 54.8s
1920	Hannes Kolehmainen, Finland	2h. 32m. 35.8s
1924	Albin Stenroos, Finland	2h. 41m. 22.6s
1928	A.B. El Ouafi, France	2h. 32m. 57s
1932	Juan Zabala, Argentina	2h. 31m. 36s
1936	Kijung Son, Japan (Korean)	2h. 29m. 19.2s
1948	Delfo Cabrera, Argentina	2h. 34m. 51.6s
1952	Emil Zatopek, Czechoslovakia	2h. 23m. 03.2s
1956	Alain Mimoun, France	2h. 25m.
1960	Abebe Bikila, Ethiopia	2h. 15m. 16.2s
1964	Abebe Bikila, Ethiopia	2h. 12m. 11.2s
1968	Mamo Wolde, Ethiopia	2h. 20m. 26.4s
1972	Frank Shorter, United States	2h. 12m. 19.8s
1976	Waldemar Cierpinski, E. Germany	2h. 09m. 55s
1980	Waldemar Cierpinski, E. Germany	2h. 11m. 03s
1984	Carlos Lopes, Portugal	2h. 09m. 21s*
1988	Gelindo Bordin, Italy	2h. 10m. 32s
1992	Hwang Young-Cho, S. Korea	2h. 13m. 23s
1996	Josia Thugwane, South Africa	2h. 12m. 36s

High Jump

1896	Ellery Clark, United States	1.81m.
1900	Irving Baxter, United States	1.90m.
1904	Samuel Jones, United States	1.80m.
1908	Harry Porter, United States	1.905m.
1912	Alma Richards, United States	1.93m.
1920	Richmond Landon, United States	1.935m.
1924	Harold Osborn, United States	1.98m.
1928	Robert W. King, United States	1.94m.
1932	Duncan McNaughton, Canada	1.97m.
1936	Cornelius Johnson, United States	2.03m.
1948	John L. Winter, Australia	1.98m.
1952	Walter Davis, United States	2.04m.
1956	Charles Dumas, United States	2.12m.
1960	Robert Shavlakadze, USSR	2.16m.
1964	Valery Brumel, USSR	2.18m.
1968	Dick Fosbury, United States	2.24m.
1972	Juri Tarmak, USSR	2.23m.
1976	Jacek Wszola, Poland	2.25m.
1980	Gerd Wessig, E. Germany	2.36m.
1984	Dietmar Mogenburg, W. Germany	2.35m.
1988	Hennady Avdeyenko, USSR	2.38m.
1992	Javier Sotomayor Sanabria, Cuba	2.34m.
1996	Charles Austin, United States	2.39m.*

Long Jump

1896	Ellery Clark, United States	6.35m.
1900	Alvin Kraenzlein, United States	7.18m.
1904	Meyer Prinstein, United States	7.34m.
1908	Frank Irons, United States	7.48m.
1912	Albert Gutterson, United States	7.60m.
1920	William Petterssen (Bjorneman), Sweden	7.15m.
1924	William DeHart Hubbard, United States	7.44m.
1928	Edward B. Hamm, United States	7.73m.
1932	Edward Gordon, United States	7.64m.
1936	Jesse Owens, United States	8.06m.
1948	Willie Steele, United States	7.82m.
1952	Jerome Biffle, United States	7.57m.
1956	Gregory Bell, United States	7.83m.
1960	Ralph Boston, United States	8.12m.
1964	Lynn Davies, Great Britain	8.07m.
1968	Bob Beamon, United States	8.90m.*
1972	Randy Williams, United States	8.24m.
1976	Arnie Robinson, United States	8.35m.
1980	Lutz Dombrowski, E. Germany	8.54m.
1984	Carl Lewis, United States	8.54m.
1988	Carl Lewis, United States	8.72m.
1992	Carl Lewis, United States	8.67m.
1996	Carl Lewis, United States	8.50m.

Triple Jump

1896	James Connolly, United States	13.71m.
1900	Meyer Prinstein, United States	14.47m.
1904	Meyer Prinstein, United States	14.35m.
1908	Timothy Ahearne, Great Britain, Ireland	14.92m.
1912	Gustaf Lindblom, Sweden	14.76m.
1920	Vilho Tuulos, Finland	14.50m.
1924	Anthony Winter, Australia	15.525m.
1928	Mikio Oda, Japan	15.21m.
1932	Chuhei Nambu, Japan	15.72m.
1936	Naoto Tajima, Japan	16.00m.
1948	Arne Ahman, Sweden	15.40m.
1952	Adhemar Ferreira da Silva, Brazil	16.22m.
1956	Adhemar Ferreira da Silva, Brazil	16.35m.
1960	Jozef Schmidt, Poland	16.81m.
1964	Jozef Schmidt, Poland	16.85m.
1968	Viktor Saneyev, USSR	17.39m.
1972	Viktor Saneyev, USSR	17.35m.
1976	Viktor Saneyev, USSR	17.29m.
1980	Jaak Uudmae, USSR	17.35m.
1984	Al Joyner, United States	17.26m.
1988	Khristo Markov, Bulgaria	17.61m.
1992	Mike Conley, United States	18.17m.
1996	Kenny Harrison, United States	8.90m.*

Discus Throw

1896	Robert Garrett, United States	29.15m.
1900	Rudolf Bauer, Hungary	36.04m.
1904	Martin Sheridan, United States	39.28m.
1908	Martin Sheridan, United States	40.89m.
1912	Armas Taipale, Finland	45.21m.
1920	Elmer Niklander, Finland	44.685m.
1924	Clarence Houser, United States	46.15m.
1928	Clarence Houser, United States	47.32m.
1932	John Anderson, United States	49.49m.
1936	Ken Carpenter, United States	50.48m.
1948	Adolfo Consolini, Italy	52.78m.
1952	Sim Iness, United States	55.03m.
1956	Al Oerter, United States	56.36m.
1960	Al Oerter, United States	59.18m.
1964	Al Oerter, United States	61.00m.
1968	Al Oerter, United States	64.78m.
1972	Ludvik Danek, Czechoslovakia	64.40m.
1976	Mac Wilkins, United States	67.50m.
1980	Viktor Rashchupkin, USSR	66.64m.
1984	Rolf Dannenberg, W. Germany	66.60m.
1988	Jurgen Schult, E. Germany	68.82m.
1992	Romas Ubartas, Lithuania	65.12m.
1996	Lars Riedel, Germany	69.40m.*

Hammer Throw

1900	John Flanagan, United States	49.73m.
1904	John Flanagan, United States	51.23m.
1908	John Flanagan, United States	51.92m.
1912	Matt McGrath, United States	54.74m.
1920	Pat Ryan, United States	52.875m.
1924	Fred Tootell, United States	53.295m.
1928	Patrick O'Callaghan, Ireland	51.39m.
1932	Patrick O'Callaghan, Ireland	53.92m.
1936	Karl Hein, Germany	56.49m.
1948	Imre Nemeth, Hungary	56.07m.
1952	Jozsef Csermak, Hungary	60.34m.
1956	Harold Connolly, United States	63.19m.
1960	Vasily Rudenkov, USSR	67.10m.
1964	Romuald Klim, USSR	69.74m.
1968	Gyula Zsivotsky, Hungary	73.36m.
1972	Anatoly Bondarchuk, USSR	75.50m.
1976	Yuri Syedykh, USSR	77.52m.
1980	Yuri Syedykh, USSR	81.80m.
1984	Juha Tiainen, Finland	78.08m.
1988	Sergei Litvinov, USSR	84.80m.*
1992	Andrey Abduvaliyev, Unified Team	82.54m.
1996	Balazs Kiss, Hungary	81.24m.

Javelin Throw

1908	Erik Lemming, Sweden	54.825m.
1912	Erik Lemming, Sweden	60.64m.
1920	Jonni Myyra, Finland	64.78m.
1924	Jonni Myyra, Finland	62.96m.
1928	Eric Lundkvist, Sweden	66.60m.
1932	Matti Jarvinen, Finland	72.71m.
1936	Gerhard Stoeck, Germany	71.84m.
1948	Kai Tapio Rautavaara, Finland	69.77m.
1952	Cy Young, United States	73.78m.
1956	Egil Danielson, Norway	85.71m.
1960	Viktor Tsybulenko, USSR	84.64m.
1964	Pauli Nevala, Finland	82.66m.
1968	Janis Lusis, USSR	90.10m.
1972	Klaus Wolfermann, W. Germany	90.48m.
1976	Miklos Nemeth, Hungary	94.58m.
1980	Dainis Kula, USSR	91.20m.
1984	Arto Haerkoenen, Finland	86.76m.
1988	Tapio Korjus, Finland	84.28m.
1992	Jan Zelezny, Czechoslovakia	89.66m.*(a)
1996	Jan Zelezny, Czech Republic	88.16m.

(a) New records were kept after javelin was modified in 1986.

Pole Vault

1896	William Welles Hoyt, United States	3.30m.
1900	Irving Baxter, United States	3.30m.
1904	Charles Dvorak, United States	3.50m.
1908	A. C. Gilbert, United States Edward Cooke Jr., United States	3.71m.
1912	Harry Babcock, United States	3.95m.
1920	Frank Foss, United States	4.09m.
1924	Lee Barnes, United States	3.95m.
1928	Sabin W. Carr, United States	4.20m.
1932	William Miller, United States	4.31m.
1936	Earle Meadows, United States	4.35m.
1948	Guinn Smith, United States	4.30m.
1952	Robert Richards, United States	4.55m.
1956	Robert Richards, United States	4.56m.
1960	Don Bragg, United States	4.70m.
1964	Fred Hansen, United States	5.10m.
1968	Bob Seagren, United States	5.40m.
1972	Wolfgang Nordwig, E. Germany	5.50m.
1976	Tadeusz Slusarski, Poland	5.50m.
1980	Wladyslaw Kozakiewicz, Poland	5.78m.
1984	Pierre Quinon, France	5.75m.
1988	Sergei Bubka, USSR	5.90m.
1992	Maksim Tarassov, Unified Team	5.80m.
1996	Jean Galfione, France	5.92m.*

16-lb. Shot Put

1896	Robert Garrett, United States	11.22m.
1900	Richard Sheldon, United States	14.10m.
1904	Ralph Rose, United States	14.21m.
1908	Ralph Rose, United States	14.21m.
1912	Pat McDonald, United States	15.34m.
1920	Ville Porhola, Finland	14.81m.
1924	L. Clarence Houser, United States	14.99m.
1928	John Kuck, United States	15.87m.
1932	Leo Sexton, United States	16.00m.
1936	Hans Woellke, Germany	16.20m.
1948	Wilbur Thompson, United States	17.12m.
1952	W. Parry O'Brien, United States	17.41m.
1956	W. Parry O'Brien, United States	18.57m.
1960	William Nieder, United States	19.68m.
1964	Dallas Long, United States	20.33m.
1968	Randy Matson, United States	20.54m.
1972	Wladyslaw Komar, Poland	21.18m.
1976	Udo Beyer, E. Germany	21.05m.
1980	Vladimir Kyselyov, USSR	21.35m.
1984	Alessandro Andrei, Italy	21.26m.
1988	Ulf Timmermann, E. Germany	22.47m.*
1992	Michael Stulce, United States	21.70m.
1996	Randy Barnes, United States	21.62m.

Decathlon

1912	Hugo Wieslander, Sweden	7,724.49 pts.(a)
1920	Helge Lovland, Norway	6,804.35 pts.
1924	Harold Osborn, United States	7,710.77 pts.
1928	Paavo Yrjola, Finland	8,053.29 pts.
1932	James Bausch, United States	8,462.23 pts.
1936	Glenn Morris, United States	7,900 pts.
1948	Robert Mathias, United States	7,139 pts.
1952	Robert Mathias, United States	7,887 pts.
1956	Milton Campbell, United States	7,937 pts.
1960	Rafer Johnson, United States	8,392 pts.
1964	Willi Holdorf, Germany	7,887 pts.(b)
1968	Bill Toomey, United States	8,193 pts.
1972	Nikolai Avilov, USSR	8,454 pts.
1976	Bruce Jenner, United States	8,617 pts.
1980	Daley Thompson, Great Britain	8,495 pts.
1984	Daley Thompson, Great Britain	8,798 pts.*(c)
1988	Christian Schenk, E. Germany	8,488 pts.
1992	Robert Zmelik, Czechoslovakia	8,611 pts.
1996	Dan O'Brien, United States	8,824 pts.

(a) Jim Thorpe of the U.S. won the 1912 Decathlon with 8,413 pts. but was disqualified and had to return his medals because he had played professional baseball prior to the Olympic games. The medals were restored posthumously in 1982. (b) Former point systems used prior to 1964. (c) Scoring change effective Apr. 1985; Thompson's readjusted score is 8,847 pts.

Track and Field—Women

100-Meter Run

1928	Elizabeth Robinson, United States	12.2s
1932	Stella Walsh, Poland (a)	11.9s
1936	Helen Stephens, United States	11.5s
1948	Francina Blankers-Koen, Netherlands	11.9s
1952	Marjorie Jackson, Australia	11.5s
1956	Betty Cuthbert, Australia	11.5s
1960	Wilma Rudolph, United States	11.0s
1964	Wyomia Tyus, United States	11.4s
1968	Wyomia Tyus, United States	11.0s
1972	Renate Stecher, E. Germany	11.07s
1976	Annegret Richter, W. Germany	11.08s
1980	Lyudmila Kondratyeva, USSR	11.6s
1984	Evelyn Ashford, United States	10.97s
1988	Florence Griffith-Joyner, United States	10.54s*
1992	Gail Devers, United States	10.82s
1996	Gail Devers, United States	10.94s

(a) A 1980 autopsy determined that Walsh was a man.

200-Meter Run

1948	Francina Blankers-Koen, Netherlands	24.4s
1952	Marjorie Jackson, Australia	23.7s
1956	Betty Cuthbert, Australia	23.4s
1960	Wilma Rudolph, United States	24.0s
1964	Edith McGuire, United States	23.0s
1968	Irena Szewinska, Poland	22.5s
1972	Renate Stecher, E. Germany	22.40s

1976 Barbel Eckert, E. Germany 22.37s
1980 Barbel Wockel, E. Germany 22.03s
1984 Valerie Brisco-Hooks, United States 21.81s
1988 Florence Griffith-Joyner, United States 21.34s*
1992 Gwen Torrence, United States 21.81s
1996 Marie-Jose Perec, France 22.12s

400-Meter Run

1964 Betty Cuthbert, Australia 52s
1968 Colette Besson, France 52s
1972 Monika Zehrt, E. Germany 51.08s
1976 Irena Szewinska, Poland 49.29s
1980 Marita Koch, E. Germany 48.88s
1984 Valerie Brisco-Hooks, United States 48.83s
1988 Olga Bryzgina, USSR 48.65s
1992 Marie-Jose Perec, France 48.83s
1996 Marie-Jose Perec, France 48.25s*

800-Meter Run

1928 Lina Radke, Germany 2m. 16.8s
1960 Ludmila Shevtsova, USSR 2m. 4.3s
1964 Ann Packer, Great Britain 2m. 1.1s
1968 Madeline Manning, United States 2m. 0.9s
1972 Hildegard Falck, W. Germany 1m. 58.6s
1976 Tatyana Kazankina, USSR 1m. 54.94s
1980 Nadezhda Olizayrenko, USSR 1m. 53.5s*
1984 Doina Melinte, Romania 1m. 57.6s
1988 Sigrun Wodars, E. Germany 1m. 56.10s
1992 Ellen Van Langen, Netherlands 1m. 55.54s
1996 Svetlana Masterkova, Russia 1m. 57.73s

1,500-Meter Run

1972 Lyudmila Bragina, USSR 4m. 01.4s
1976 Tatyana Kazankina, USSR 4m. 05.48s
1980 Tatyana Kazankina, USSR 3m. 56.6s
1984 Gabriella Dorio, Italy 4m. 03.25s
1988 Paula Ivan, Romania 3m. 53.96s*
1992 Hassiba Boulmerka, Algeria 3m. 55.30s
1996 Svetlana Masterkova, Russia 4m. 00.83s

3,000-Meter Run

1984 Maricica Puica, Romania 8m. 35.96s
1988 Tatyana Samolenko, USSR 8m. 26.53s*
1992 Elena Romanova, Unified Team 8m. 46.04s

5,000-Meter Run

1996 Wang Junxia, China 14m. 59.88s*

10,000-Meter Run

1988 Olga Boldarenko, USSR 31m. 44.69s
1992 Derartu Tulu, Ethiopia 31m. 06.02s
1996 Fernanda Ribeiro, Portugal 31m. 01.63s*

100-Meter Hurdles

1972 Annelie Ehrhardt, E. Germany 12.59s
1976 Johanna Schaller, E. Germany 12.77s
1980 Vera Komisova, USSR 12.56s
1984 Benita Brown-Fitzgerald, United States 12.84s
1988 Jordanka Donkova, Bulgaria 12.38s*
1992 Paraskevi Patoulidou, Greece 12.64s
1996 Ludmila Enquist, Sweden 12.58s

400-Meter Hurdles

1984 Nawal el Moutawakii, Morocco 54.61s
1988 Debra Flintoff-King, Australia 53.17s
1992 Sally Gunnell, Great Britain 53.23s
1996 Deon Hemmings, Jamaica 52.82s*

400-Meter Relay

1928 Canada 48.4s
1932 United States 46.9s
1936 United States 46.9s
1948 Netherlands 47.5s
1952 United States 45.9s
1956 Australia 44.5s
1960 United States 44.5s
1964 Poland 43.6s
1968 United States 42.8s
1972 West Germany 42.81s
1976 East Germany 42.55s
1980 East Germany 41.60s*
1984 United States 41.65s
1988 United States 41.98s
1992 United States 42.11s
1996 United States 41.95s

1,600-Meter Relay

1972 East Germany 3m. 23s
1976 East Germany 3m. 19.23s
1980 USSR 3m. 20.02s
1984 United States 3m. 18.29s
1988 USSR . . . . 3 m. 15.18s*
1992 Unified Team 3m. 20.20s
1996 United States 3m. 20.91s

10 Kilometer Walk

1992 Chen Yueling, China 44m. 32s
1996 Elena Nikolayeva, Russia 41m. 49s*

Marathon

1984 Joan Benoit, United States 2h. 24m. 52s*
1988 Rosa Mota, Portugal 2h. 25m. 40s
1992 Valentina Yegorova, Unified Team 2h. 32m. 41s
1996 Fatuma Roba, Ethiopia 2h. 26m. 05s

High Jump

1928 Ethel Catherwood, Canada . . . . 1.59m.
1932 Jean Shiley, United States . . . . 1.657m.
1936 Ibolya Csak, Hungary . . . . 1.60m.
1948 Alice Coachman, United States . . . . 1.68m.
1952 Esther Brand, South Africa . . . . 1.67m.
1956 Mildred L. McDaniel, United States . . . . 1.76m.
1960 Iolanda Balas, Romania . . . . 1.85m.
1964 Iolanda Balas, Romania . . . . 1.90m.
1968 Miloslava Reskova, Czechoslovakia . . . . 1.82m.
1972 Ulrike Meyfarth, W. Germany . . . . 1.92m.
1976 Rosemarie Ackermann, E. Germany . . . . 1.93m.
1980 Sara Simeoni, Italy . . . . 1.97m.
1984 Ulrike Meyfarth, W. Germany . . . . 2.02m.
1988 Louise Ritter, United States . . . . 2.03m.
1992 Heike Henkel, Germany . . . . 2.02m.
1996 Stefka Kostadinova, Bulgaria . . . . 2.05m.*

Long Jump

1948 Olga Gyarmati, Hungary . . . . 5.695m.
1952 Yvette Williams, New Zealand . . . . 6.24m.
1956 Elzbieta Krzeskinska, Poland . . . . 6.35m.
1960 Vira Krepkina, USSR . . . . 6.37m.
1964 Mary Rand, Great Britain . . . . 6.76m.
1968 Viorica Viscopoleanu, Romania . . . . 6.82m.
1972 Heidemarie Rosendahl, W. Germany . . . . 6.78m.
1976 Angela Voigt, E. Germany . . . . 6.72m.
1980 Tatyana Kolpakova, USSR . . . . 7.06m.
1984 Anisoara Cusmir-Stanciu, Romania . . . . 6.96m.
1988 Jackie Joyner-Kersee, United States . . . . 7.40m.*
1992 Heike Drechsler, Germany . . . . 7.14m.
1996 Chioma Ajunwa, Nigeria . . . . 8.50m.

Triple Jump

1996 Inessa Kravets, Ukraine . . . . 15.33m.*

Discus Throw

1928 Halina Konopacka, Poland . . . . 39.62m.
1932 Lillian Copeland, United States . . . . 40.58m.
1936 Gisela Mauermayer, Germany . . . . 47.63m.
1948 Micheline Ostermeyer, France . . . . 41.92m.
1952 Nina Romaschkova, USSR . . . . 51.42m.
1956 Olga Fikotova, Czechoslovakia . . . . 53.69m.
1960 Nina Ponomareva, USSR . . . . 55.10m.
1964 Tamara Press, USSR . . . . 57.27m.
1968 Lia Manoliu, Romania . . . . 58.28m.
1972 Faina Melnik, USSR . . . . 66.62m.
1976 Evelin Schlaak, E. Germany . . . . 69.00m.
1980 Evelin Jahl, E. Germany . . . . 69.96m.
1984 Ria Stalman, Netherlands . . . . 65.36m.
1988 Martina Hellmann, E. Germany . . . . 72.30m.*
1992 Maritza Marten Garcia, Cuba . . . . 70.06m.
1996 Ilke Wyludda, Germany . . . . 69.66m.

Javelin Throw

1932 "Babe" Didrikson, United States . . . . 43.68m.
1936 Tilly Fleischer, Germany . . . . 45.18m.
1948 Herma Bauma, Austria . . . . 45.57m.
1952 Dana Zatopkova, Czechoslovakia . . . . 50.47m.
1956 Inese Jaunzeme, USSR . . . . 53.86m.
1960 Elvira Ozolina, USSR . . . . 55.98m.
1964 Mihaela Penes, Romania . . . . 60.54m.
1968 Angela Nemeth, Hungary . . . . 60.36m.
1972 Ruth Fuchs, E. Germany . . . . 63.88m.
1976 Ruth Fuchs, E. Germany . . . . 65.94m.
1980 Maria Colon Ruenes, Cuba . . . . 68.40m.
1984 Tessa Sanderson, Great Britain . . . . 69.56m.
1988 Petra Felke, E. Germany . . . . 74.68m.*
1992 Silke Renke, Germany . . . . 68.34m.
1996 Heli Rantanen, Finland . . . . 67.94m.

Shot Put (8 lb., 13 oz.)

1948 Micheline Ostermeyer, France . . . . 13.75m.
1952 Galina Zybina, USSR . . . . 15.28m.
1956 Tamara Tyshkyevich, USSR . . . . 16.59m.
1960 Tamara Press, USSR . . . . 17.32m.
1964 Tamara Press, USSR . . . . 18.14m.
1968 Margitta Gummel, E. Germany . . . . 19.61m.
1972 Nadezhda Chizova, USSR . . . . 21.03m.
1976 Ivanka Hristova, Bulgaria . . . . 21.16m.
1980 Ilona Slupianek, E. Germany . . . . 22.41m.*

(continued)

Shot Put (continued)

1984	Claudia Losch, W. Germany	20.48m.
1988	Natalya Lisovskaya, USSR	22.24m.
1992	Svetlana Krivelyova, Unified Team	21.06m.
1996	Astrid Kumbernuss, Germany	20.56m.

Heptathlon

1984	Glynis Nunn, Australia	6,390 pts.
1988	Jackie Joyner-Kersee, United States	7,215 pts.*
1992	Jackie Joyner-Kersee, United States	7,044 pts.
1996	Ghada Shouaa, Syria	6,780 pts.

Swimming and Diving—Men

50-Meter Freestyle

1988	Matt Biondi, U.S.	22.14
1992	Aleksandr Popov, Unified Team	21.91*
1996	Aleksandr Popov, Russia	22.13

100-Meter Freestyle

1896	Alfred Hajos, Hungary	1:22.2
1904	Zoltan de Halmay, Hungary (100 yards)	1:02.8
1908	Charles Daniels, U.S.	1:05.6
1912	Duke P. Kahanamoku, U.S.	1:03.4
1920	Duke P. Kahanamoku, U.S.	1:01.4
1924	John Weissmuller, U.S.	59.0
1928	John Weissmuller, U.S.	58.6
1932	Yasuji Miyazaki, Japan	58.2
1936	Ferenc Csik, Hungary	57.6
1948	Wally Ris, U.S.	57.3
1952	Clark Scholes, U.S.	57.4
1956	Jon Henricks, Australia	55.4
1960	John Devitt, Australia	55.2
1964	Don Schollander, U.S.	53.4
1968	Mike Wenden, Australia	52.2
1972	Mark Spitz, U.S.	51.22
1976	Jim Montgomery, U.S.	49.99
1980	Jorg Woithe, E. Germany	50.40
1984	Rowdy Gaines, U.S.	49.80
1988	Matt Biondi, U.S.	48.63*
1992	Aleksandr Popov, Unified Team	49.02
1996	Aleksandr Popov, Russia	48.74

200-Meter Freestyle

1968	Mike Wenden, Australia	1:55.2
1972	Mark Spitz, U.S.	1:52.78
1976	Bruce Furniss, U.S.	1:50.29
1980	Sergei Kopliakov, USSR	1:49.81
1984	Michael Gross, W. Germany	1:47.44
1988	Duncan Armstrong, Australia	1:47.25
1992	Yevgeny Sadovyi, Unified Team	1:46.70*
1996	Danyon Loader, New Zealand	1:47.63

400-Meter Freestyle

1904	C. M. Daniels, U.S. (440 yards)	6:16.2
1908	Henry Taylor, Great Britain	5:36.8
1912	George Hodgson, Canada	5:24.4
1920	Norman Ross, U.S.	5:26.8
1924	John Weissmuller, U.S.	5:04.2
1928	Albert Zorilla, Argentina	5:01.6
1932	Clarence Crabbe, U.S.	4:48.4
1936	Jack Medica, U.S.	4:44.5
1948	William Smith, U.S.	4:41.0
1952	Jean Boiteux, France	4:30.7
1956	Murray Rose, Australia	4:27.3
1960	Murray Rose, Australia	4:18.3
1964	Don Schollander, U.S.	4:12.2
1968	Mike Burton, U.S.	4:09.0
1972	Brad Cooper, Australia	4:00.27
1976	Brian Goodell, U.S.	3:51.93
1980	Vladimir Salnikov, USSR	3:51.31
1984	George DiCarlo, U.S.	3:51.23
1988	Ewe Dassler, E. Germany	3:46.95
1992	Yevgeny Sadovyi, Unified Team	3:45.00*
1996	Danyon Loader, New Zealand	3:47.97

1,500-Meter Freestyle

1908	Henry Taylor, Great Britain	22:48.4
1912	George Hodgson, Canada	22:00.0
1920	Norman Ross, U.S.	22:23.2
1924	Andrew Charlton, Australia	20:06.6
1928	Arne Borg, Sweden	19:51.8
1932	Kusuo Kitamura, Japan	19:12.4
1936	Noboru Terada, Japan	19:13.7
1948	James McLane, U.S.	19:18.5
1952	Ford Konno, U.S.	18:30.3
1956	Murray Rose, Australia	17:58.9
1960	Jon Konrads, Australia	17:19.6
1964	Robert Windle, Australia	17:01.7
1968	Mike Burton, U.S.	16:38.9
1972	Mike Burton, U.S.	15:52.58
1976	Brian Goodell, U.S.	15:02.40
1980	Vladimir Salnikov, USSR	14:58.27
1984	Michael O'Brien, U.S.	15:05.20
1988	Vladimir Salnikov, USSR	15:00.40
1992	Kieren Perkins, Australia	14:43.48*
1996	Kieren Perkins, Australia	14:56.40

100-Meter Backstroke

1904	Walter Brack, Germany (100 yds.)	1:16.8
1908	Arno Bieberstein, Germany	1:24.6
1912	Harry Hebner, U.S.	1:21.2
1920	Warren Kealoha, U.S.	1:15.2
1924	Warren Kealoha, U.S.	1:13.2
1928	George Kojac, U.S.	1:08.2
1932	Masaji Kiyokawa, Japan	1:08.6
1936	Adolph Kiefer, U.S.	1:05.9
1948	Allen Stack, U.S.	1:06.4
1952	Yoshi Oyakawa, U.S.	1:05.4
1956	David Thiele, Australia	1:02.2
1960	David Thiele, Australia	1:01.9
1968	Roland Matthes, E. Germany	58.7
1972	Roland Matthes, E. Germany	56.58
1976	John Naber, U.S.	55.49
1980	Bengt Baron, Sweden	56.33
1984	Rick Carey, U.S.	55.79
1988	Daichi Suzuki, Japan	55.05
1992	Mark Tewksbury, Canada	53.98*
1996	Jeff Rouse, U.S.	54.10

200-Meter Backstroke

1964	Jed Graef, U.S.	2:10.3
1968	Roland Matthes, E. Germany	2:09.6
1972	Roland Matthes, E. Germany	2:02.82
1976	John Naber, U.S.	1:59.19
1980	Sandor Wladar, Hungary	2:01.93
1984	Rick Carey, U.S.	2:00.23
1988	Igor Polianski, USSR	1:59.37
1992	Martin Lopez-Zubero, Spain	1:58.47*
1996	Brad Bridgewater, U.S.	1:58.54

100-Meter Breaststroke

1968	Don McKenzie, U.S.	1:07.7
1972	Nobutaka Taguchi, Japan	1:04.94
1976	John Hencken, U.S.	1:03.11
1980	Duncan Goodhew, Great Britain	1:03.44
1984	Steve Lundquist, U.S.	1:01.65
1988	Adrian Moorhouse, Great Britain	1:02.04
1992	Nelson Diebel, U.S.	1:01.50
1996	Fred Deburghgraeve, Belgium	1:00.60*

200-Meter Breaststroke

1908	Frederick Holman, Great Britain	3:09.2
1912	Walter Bathe, Germany	3:01.8
1920	Haken Malmroth, Sweden	3:04.4
1924	Robert Skelton, U.S.	2:56.6
1928	Yoshiyuki Tsuruta, Japan	2:48.8
1932	Yoshiyuki Tsuruta, Japan	2:45.4
1936	Tetsuo Hamuro, Japan	2:41.5
1948	Joseph Verdeur, U.S.	2:39.3
1952	John Davies, Australia	2:34.4
1956	Masura Furukawa, Japan	2:34.7
1960	William Mulliken, U.S.	2:37.4
1964	Ian O'Brien, Australia	2:27.8
1968	Felipe Munoz, Mexico	2:28.7
1972	John Hencken, U.S.	2:21.55
1976	David Wilkie, Great Britain	2:15.11
1980	Robertas Zhulpa, USSR	2:15.85
1984	Victor Davis, Canada	2:13.34
1988	Jozsef Szabo, Hungary	2:13.52
1992	Mike Barrowman, U.S.	2:10.16*
1996	Norbert Rozsa, Hungary	2:12.57

100-Meter Butterfly

1968	Doug Russell, U.S.	55.9
1972	Mark Spitz, U.S.	54.27
1976	Matt Vogel, U.S.	54.35
1980	Par Arvidsson, Sweden	54.92
1984	Michael Gross, W. Germany	53.08
1988	Anthony Nesty, Suriname	53.00
1992	Pablo Morales, U.S.	53.32
1996	Denis Pankratov, Russia	52.27*

200-Meter Butterfly

1956	William Yorzyk, U.S.	2:19.3
1960	Michael Troy, U.S.	2:12.8
1964	Kevin J. Berry, Australia	2:06.6
1968	Carl Robie, U.S.	2:08.7
1972	Mark Spitz, U.S.	2:00.70
1976	Mike Bruner, U.S.	1:59.23
1980	Sergei Fesenko, USSR	1:59.76

1984	Jon Sieben, Australia	1:57.04
1988	Michael Gross, W. Germany	1:56.94
1992	Mel Stewart, U.S.	1:56.26*
1996	Denis Pankratov, Russia	1:56.51

200-Meter Individual Medley

1968	Charles Hickcox, U.S.	2:12.0
1972	Gunnar Larsson, Sweden	2:07.17
1984	Alex Baumann, Canada	2:01.42
1988	Tamas Darnyi, Hungary	2:00.17
1992	Tamas Darnyi, Hungary	2:00.76
1996	Attila Czene, Hungary	1:59.91*

400-Meter Individual Medley

1964	Dick Roth, U.S.	4:45.4
1968	Charles Hickcox, U.S.	4:48.4
1972	Gunnar Larsson, Sweden	4:31.98
1976	Rod Strachan, U.S.	4:23.68
1980	Aleksandr Sidorenko, USSR	4:22.89
1984	Alex Baumann, Canada	4:17.41
1988	Tamas Darnyi, Hungary	4:14.75
1992	Tamas Darnyi, Hungary	4:14.23*
1996	Tom Dolan, U.S.	4:14.90

400-Meter Freestyle Relay

1964	United States	3:31.2
1968	United States	3:31.7
1972	United States	3:26.42
1984	United States	3:19.03
1988	United States	3:16.53
1992	United States	3:16.74
1996	United States	3:15.41*

800-Meter Freestyle Relay

1908	Great Britain	10:55.6
1912	Australia	10:11.6
1920	United States	10:04.4
1924	United States	9:53.4
1928	United States	9:36.2
1932	Japan	8:58.4
1936	Japan	8:51.5
1948	United States	8:46.0
1952	United States	8:31.1
1956	Australia	8:23.6
1960	United States	8:10.2
1964	United States	7:52.1
1968	United States	7:52.33
1972	United States	7:35.78
1976	United States	7:23.22
1980	USSR	7:23.50
1984	United States	7:15.69
1988	United States	7:12.51
1992	Unified Team	7:11.95*
1996	United States	7:14.84

400-Meter Medley Relay

1960	United States	4:05.4
1964	United States	3:58.4
1968	United States	3:54.9
1972	United States	3:48.16
1976	United States	3:42.22
1980	Australia	3:45.70
1984	United States	3:39.30
1988	United States	3:36.93
1992	United States	3:36.93
1996	United States	3:34.84*

Springboard Diving

		Points
1908	Albert Zurner, Germany	85.5
1912	Paul Guenther, Germany	79.23
1920	Louis Kuehn, U.S	675.40
1924	Albert White, U.S.	97.46
1928	Pete Desjardins, U.S.	185.04
1932	Michael Galitzen, U.S.	161.38
1936	Richard Degener, U.S.	163.57
1948	Bruce Harlan, U.S.	163.64
1952	David Browning, U.S.	205.29
1956	Robert Clotworthy, U.S.	159.56
1960	Gary Tobian, U.S.	170.00
1964	Kenneth Sitzberger, U.S.	159.90
1968	Bernie Wrightson, U.S.	170.15
1972	Vladimir Vasin, USSR	594.09
1976	Phil Boggs, U.S.	619.52
1980	Aleksandr Portnov, USSR	905.02
1984	Greg Louganis, U.S.	754.41
1988	Greg Louganis, U.S.	730.80
1992	Mark Lenzi, U.S.	676.53
1996	Xiong Ni, China	701.46

Platform Diving

		Points
1904	Dr. G.E. Sheldon, U.S.	12.75
1908	Hjalmar Johansson, Sweden	83.75
1912	Erik Adlerz, Sweden	73.94
1920	Clarence Pinkston, U.S.	100.67
1924	Albert White, U.S.	97.46
1928	Pete Desjardins, U.S.	98.74
1932	Harold Smith, U.S.	124.80
1936	Marshall Wayne, U.S.	113.58
1948	Sammy Lee, U.S.	130.05
1952	Sammy Lee, U.S.	156.28
1956	Joaquin Capilla, Mexico	152.44
1960	Robert Webster, U.S.	165.56
1964	Robert Webster, U.S.	148.58
1968	Klaus Dibiasi, Italy	164.18
1972	Klaus Dibiasi, Italy	504.12
1976	Klaus Dibiasi, Italy	600.51
1980	Falk Hoffmann, E. Germany	835.65
1984	Greg Louganis, U.S.	710.91
1988	Greg Louganis, U.S.	638.61
1992	Sun Shuwei, China	677.31
1996	Dmitri Sautin, Russia	692.34

Swimming and Diving—Women

50-Meter Freestyle

1988	Kristin Otto, E. Germany	25.49
1992	Yang Wenyi, China	24.76*
1996	Amy Van Dyken, U.S.	24.87

100-Meter Freestyle

1912	Fanny Durack, Australia	1:22.2
1920	Ethelda Bleibtrey, U.S.	1:13.6
1924	Ethel Lackie, U.S.	1:12.4
1928	Albina Osipowich, U.S.	1:11.0
1932	Helene Madison, U.S.	1:06.8
1936	Hendrika Mastenbroek, Holland	1:05.9
1948	Greta Andersen, Denmark	1:06.3
1952	Katalin Szoke, Hungary	1:06.8
1956	Dawn Fraser, Australia	1:02.0
1960	Dawn Fraser, Australia	1:01.2
1964	Dawn Fraser, Australia	59.5
1968	Jan Henne, U.S.	1:00.0
1972	Sandra Neilson, U.S.	58.59
1976	Kornelia Ender, E. Germany	55.65
1980	Barbara Krause, E. Germany	54.79
1984	(tie) Carrie Steinseifer, U.S.	55.92
	Nancy Hogshead, U.S.	55.92
1988	Kristin Otto, E. Germany	54.93
1992	Zhuang Yong, China	54.64
1996	Li Jingyi, China	54.50*

200-Meter Freestyle

1968	Debbie Meyer, U.S.	2:10.5
1972	Shane Gould, Australia	2:03.56
1976	Kornelia Ender, E. Germany	1:59.26
1980	Barbara Krause, E. Germany	1:58.33
1984	Mary Wayte, U.S.	1:59.23
1988	Heike Friedrich, E. Germany	1:57.65*
1992	Nicole Haislett, U.S.	1:57.90
1996	Claudia Poll, Costa Rica	1:58.16

400-Meter Freestyle

1924	Martha Norelius, U.S	.6:02.2
1928	Martha Norelius, U.S.	5:42.8
1932	Helene Madison, U.S.	5:28.5
1936	Hendrika Mastenbroek, Netherlands	5:26.4
1948	Ann Curtis, U.S.	5:17.8
1952	Valerie Gyenge, Hungary	5:12.1
1956	Lorraine Crapp, Australia	4:54.6
1960	Susan Chris von Saltza, U.S.	4:50.6
1964	Virginia Duenkel, U.S.	4:43.3
1968	Debbie Meyer, U.S.	4:31.8
1972	Shane Gould, Australia	4:19.44
1976	Petra Thuemer, E. Germany	4:09.89
1980	Ines Diers, E. Germany	4:08.76
1984	Tiffany Cohen, U.S.	4:07.10
1988	Janet Evans, U.S.	4:03.85*
1992	Dagmar Hase, Germany	4:07.18
1996	Michelle Smith, Ireland	4:07.25

800-Meter Freestyle

1968	Debbie Meyer, U.S.	9:24.0
1972	Keena Rothhammer, U.S.	8:53.68
1976	Petra Thuemer, E. Germany	8:37.14
1980	Michelle Ford, Australia	8:28.90
1984	Tiffany Cohen, U.S.	8:24.95
1988	Janet Evans, U.S.	8:20.20*
1992	Janet Evans, U.S.	8:25.52
1996	Brooke Bennett, U.S.	8:27.89

100-Meter Backstroke

1924	Sybil Bauer, U.S.	1:23.2
1928	Marie Braun, Netherlands	1:22.0
1932	Eleanor Holm, U.S.	1:19.4
1936	Dina Senff, Netherlands	1:18.9
1948	Karen Harup, Denmark	1:14.4
1952	Joan Harrison, South Africa	1:14.3
1956	Judy Grinham, Great Britain	1:12.9
1960	Lynn Burke, U.S.	1:09.3
1964	Cathy Ferguson, U.S.	1:07.7
1968	Kaye Hall, U.S.	1:06.2
1972	Melissa Belote, U.S.	1:05.78
1976	Ulrike Richter, E. Germany	1:01.83
1980	Rica Reinisch, E. Germany	1:00.86
1984	Theresa Andrews, U.S.	1:02.55
1988	Kristin Otto, E. Germany	1:00.89
1992	Krisztina Egerszegi, Hungary	1:00.68*
1996	Beth Botsford, U.S.	1:01.19

200-Meter Backstroke

1968	Pokey Watson, U.S.	2:24.8
1972	Melissa Belote, U.S.	2:19.19
1976	Ulrike Richter, E. Germany	2:13.43
1980	Rica Reinisch, E. Germany	2:11.77
1984	Jolanda De Rover, Netherlands	2:12.38
1988	Krisztina Egerszegi, Hungary	2:09.29
1992	Krisztina Egerszegi, Hungary	2:07.06*
1996	Krisztina Egerszegi, Hungary	2:07.83

100-Meter Breaststroke

1968	Djurdjica Bjedov, Yugoslavia	1:15.8
1972	Cathy Carr, U.S.	1:13.58
1976	Hannelore Anke, E. Germany	1:11:16
1980	Ute Geweniger, E. Germany	1:10.22
1984	Petra Van Staveren, Netherlands	1:09.88
1988	Tania Dangalakova, Bulgaria	1:07.95
1992	Elena Roudkovskaia, Unified Team	1:08.00
1996	Penny Heyns, South Africa	1:07.73*

200-Meter Breaststroke

1924	Lucy Morton, Great Britain	3:33.2
1928	Hilde Schrader, Germany	3:12.6
1932	Clare Dennis, Australia	3:06.3
1936	Hideko Maehata, Japan	3:03.6
1948	Nelly Van Vliet, Netherlands	2:57.2
1952	Eva Szekely, Hungary	2:51.7
1956	Ursula Happe, Germany	2:53.1
1960	Anita Lonsbrough, Great Britain	2:49.5
1964	Galina Prozumenschikova, USSR	2:46.4
1968	Sharon Wichman, U.S.	2:44.4
1972	Beverly Whitfield, Australia	2:41.71
1976	Marina Koshevaia, USSR	2:33.35
1980	Lina Kachushite, USSR	2:29.54
1984	Anne Ottenbrite, Canada	2:30.38
1988	Silke Hoerner, E. Germany	2:26.71
1992	Kyoko Iwasaki, Japan	2:26.65
1996	Penny Heyns, South Africa	2:25.41*

100-Meter Butterfly

1956	Shelley Mann, U.S.	1:11.0
1960	Carolyn Schuler, U.S.	1:09.5
1964	Sharon Stouder, U.S.	1:04.7
1968	Lynn McClements, Australia	1:05.5
1972	Mayumi Aoki, Japan	1:03.34
1976	Kornelia Ender, E. Germany	1:00.13
1980	Caren Metschuck, E. Germany	1:00.42
1984	Mary T. Meagher, U.S.	59.26
1988	Kristin Otto, E. Germany	59.00
1992	Qian Hong, China	58.62*
1996	Amy Van Dyken, U.S.	59.13

200-Meter Butterfly

1968	Ada Kok, Netherlands	2:24.7
1972	Karen Moe, U.S.	2:15.57
1976	Andrea Pollack, E. Germany	2:11.41
1980	Ines Geissler, E. Germany	2:10.44
1984	Mary T. Meagher, U.S.	2:06.90*
1988	Kathleen Nord, E. Germany	2:09.51
1992	Summer Sanders, U.S.	2:08.67
1996	Susan O'Neill, Australia	2:07.76

200-Meter Individual Medley

1968	Claudia Kolb, U.S.	2:24.7
1972	Shane Gould, Australia	2:23.07
1984	Tracy Caulkins, U.S.	2:12.64
1988	Daniela Hunger, E. Germany	2:12.59
1992	Lin Li, China	2:11.65*
1996	Michelle Smith, Ireland	2:13.93

400-Meter Individual Medley

1964	Donna de Varona, U.S.	5:18.7
1968	Claudia Kolb, U.S.	5:08.5
1972	Gail Neall, Australia	5:02.97
1976	Ulrike Tauber, E. Germany	4:42.77
1980	Petra Schneider, E. Germany	4:36.29*
1984	Tracy Caulkins, U.S.	4:39.24
1988	Janet Evans, U.S.	4:37.76
1992	Krisztina Egerszegi, Hungary	4:36.54
1996	Michelle Smith, Ireland	4:39.18

400-Meter Freestyle Relay

1912	Great Britain	5:52.8
1920	United States	5:11.6
1924	United States	4:58.8
1928	United States	4:47.6
1932	United States	4:38.0
1936	Netherlands	4:36.0
1948	United States	4:29.2
1952	Hungary	4:24.4
1956	Australia	4:17.1
1960	United States	4:08.9
1964	United States	4:03.8
1968	United States	4:02.5
1972	United States	3:55.19
1976	United States	3:44.82
1980	East Germany	3:42.71
1984	United States	3:43.43
1988	East Germany	3:40.63
1992	United States	3:39.46
1996	United States	3:39.29*

800-Meter Freestyle Relay

1996	United States	7:59.87*

400-Meter Medley Relay

1960	United States	4:41.1
1964	United States	4:33.9
1968	United States	4:28.3
1972	United States	4:20.75
1976	East Germany	4:07.95
1980	East Germany	4:06.67
1984	United States	4:08.34
1988	East Germany	4:03.74
1992	United States	4:02.54*
1996	United States	4:02.88

Springboard Diving

		Points
1920	Aileen Riggin, U.S.	539.90
1924	Elizabeth Becker, U.S.	474.50
1928	Helen Meany, U.S.	78.62
1932	Georgia Coleman U.S.	87.52
1936	Marjorie Gestring, U.S.	89.27
1948	Victoria M. Draves, U.S.	108.74
1952	Patricia McCormick, U.S.	147.30
1956	Patricia McCormick, U.S.	142.36
1960	Ingrid Kramer, Germany	155.81
1964	Ingrid Engel-Kramer, Germany	145.00
1968	Sue Gossick, U.S.	150.77
1972	Micki King, U.S.	450.03
1976	Jenni Chandler, U.S.	506.19
1980	Irina Kalinina, USSR	725.91
1984	Sylvie Bernier, Canada	530.70
1988	Gao Min, China	580.23
1992	Gao Min, China	572.40
1996	Fu Mingxia, China	547.68

Platform Diving

		Points
1912	Greta Johansson, Sweden	39.90
1920	Stefani Fryland-Clausen, Denmark	34.60
1924	Caroline Smith, U.S.	33.20
1928	Elizabeth B. Pinkston, U.S.	31.60
1932	Dorothy Poynton, U.S.	40.26
1936	Dorothy Poynton Hill, U.S.	33.93
1948	Victoria M. Draves, U.S.	68.87
1952	Patricia McCormick, U.S.	79.37
1956	Patricia McCormick, U.S.	84.85
1960	Ingrid Kramer, Germany	91.28
1964	Lesley Bush, U.S.	99.80
1968	Milena Duchkova, Czech.	109.59
1972	Ulrika Knape, Sweden	390.00
1976	Elena Vaytsekhouskaya, USSR	406.59
1980	Martina Jaschke, E. Germany	596.25
1984	Zhou Jihong, China	435.51
1988	Xu Yanmei, China	445.20
1992	Fu Mingxia, China	461.43
1996	Fu Mingxia, China	521.58

Boxing

Light Flyweight (106 lbs)
1968 Francisco Rodriguez, Venezuela
1972 Gyorgy Gedo, Hungary
1976 Jorge Hernandez, Cuba
1980 Shamil Sabyrov, USSR
1984 Paul Gonzalez, U.S.
1988 Ivailo Hristov, Bulgaria
1992 Rogelio Marcelo, Cuba
1996 Daniel Petrov, Bulgaria

Flyweight (112 lbs)
1904 George Finnegan, U.S.
1920 William Di Gennara, U.S.
1924 Fidel LaBarba, U.S.
1928 Antal Kocsis, Hungary
1932 Istvan Enekes, Hungary
1936 Willi Kaiser, Germany
1948 Pascual Perez, Argentina
1952 Nathan Brooks, U.S.
1956 Terence Spinks, Great Britain
1960 GyulaTorok, Hungary
1964 Fernando Atzori, Italy
1968 Ricardo Delgado, Mexico
1972 Georgi Kostadinov, Bulgaria
1976 Leo Randolph, U.S.
1980 Peter Lessov, Bulgaria
1984 Steve McCrory, U.S.
1988 Kim Kwang Sun, S. Korea
1992 Su Choi Choi, N. Korea
1996 Maikro Romero, Cuba

Bantamweight (119 lbs)
1904 Oliver Kirk, U.S.
1908 A. Henry Thomas, Great Britain
1920 Clarence Walker, South Africa
1924 William Smith, South Africa
1928 Vittorio Tamagnini, Italy
1932 Horace Gwynne, Canada
1936 Ulderico Sergo, Italy
1948 Tibor Csik, Hungary
1952 Pentti Hamalainen, Finland
1956 Wolfgang Behrendt, E. Germany
1960 Oleg Grigoryev, USSR
1964 Takao Sakurai, Japan
1968 Valery Sokolov, USSR
1972 Orlando Martinez, Cuba
1976 Yong-Jo Gu, N. Korea
1980 Juan Hernandez, Cuba
1984 Maurizio Stecca, Italy
1988 Kennedy McKinney, U.S.
1992 Joel Casamayor, Cuba
1996 Istvan Kovacs, Hungary

Featherweight (126 lbs)
1904 Oliver Kirk, U.S.
1908 Richard Gunn, Great Britain
1920 Paul Fritsch, France
1924 John Fields, U.S.
1928 Lambertus van Klaveren, Netherlands
1932 Carmelo Robledo, Argentina
1936 Oscar Casanovas, Argentina
1948 Ernesto Formenti, Italy
1952 Jan Zachara, Czechoslavakia
1956 Vladimir Safronov, USSR
1960 Francesco Musso, Italy
1964 Stanislav Stephashkin, USSR
1968 Antonin Roldan, Mexico
1972 Boris Kousnetsov, USSR
1976 Angel Herrera, Cuba
1980 Rudi Fink, E. Germany
1984 Meldrick Taylor, U.S.
1988 Giovanni Parisi, Italy
1992 Andreas Tews, Germany
1996 Somluck Kamsing, Thailand

Lightweight (132 lbs)
1904 Harry Spanger, U.S.
1908 Frederick Grace, Great Britain
1920 Samuel Mosberg, U.S.
1924 Hans Nielsen, Denmark
1928 Carlo Orlandi, Italy
1932 Lawrence Stevens, South Africa
1936 Imre Harangi, Hungary
1948 Gerald Dreyer, South Africa
1952 Aureliano Bolognesi, Italy
1956 Richard McTaggart, Great Britain
1960 Kazimierz Pazdzior, Poland
1964 Jozef Grudzien, Poland
1968 Ronald Harris, U.S.
1972 Jan Szczepanski, Poland
1976 Howard Davis, U.S.
1980 Angel Herrera, Cuba
1984 Pernell Whitaker, U.S.
1988 Andreas Zuelow, E. Germany
1992 Oscar De La Hoya, U.S.
1996 Hocine Soltani, Algeria

Light Welterweight (140 lbs)
1952 Charles Adkins, U.S.
1956 Vladimir Yengibaryan, USSR
1960 Bohumil Nemecek, Czechoslavakia
1964 Jerzy Kulej, Poland
1968 Jerzy Kulej, Poland
1972 Ray Seales, U.S.
1976 Ray Leonard, U.S.
1980 Patrizio Oliva, Italy
1984 Jerry Page, U.S.
1988 Viatcheslav Janovski, USSR
1992 Hector Vinent, Cuba
1996 Hector Vinent, Cuba

Welterweight (147 lbs)
1904 Albert Young, U.S.
1920 Albert Schneider, Canada
1924 Jean Delarge, Belgium
1928 Edward Morgan, New Zealand
1932 Edward Flynn, U.S.
1936 Sten Suvio, Finland
1948 Julius Torma, Czechoslavakia
1952 Zygmunt Chychia, Poland
1956 Nicolae Linca, Romania
1960 Giovanni Benvenuti, Italy
1964 Marian Kasprzyk, Poland
1968 Manfred Wolke, E. Germany
1972 Emilio Correa, Cuba
1976 Jochen Bachfeld, E. Germany
1980 Andres Aldama, Cuba
1984 Mark Breland, U.S.
1988 Robert Wangila, Kenya
1992 Michael Carruth, Ireland
1996 Oleg Saitov, Russia

Light Middleweight (157 lbs)
1952 Laszlo Papp, Hungary
1956 Laszlo Papp, Hungary
1960 Wilbert McClure, U.S.
1964 Boris Lagutin, USSR
1968 Boris Lagutin, USSR
1972 Dieter Kottysch, W. Germany
1976 Jerzy Rybicki, Poland
1980 Armando Martinez, Cuba
1984 Frank Tate, U.S.
1988 Park Si Hun, S. Korea
1992 Juan Lemus, Cuba
1996 David Reid, U.S.

Middleweight (165 lbs)
1904 Charles Mayer, U.S.
1908 John Douglas, Great Britain
1920 Harry Mallin, Great Britain
1924 Harry Mallin, Great Britain
1928 Piero Toscani, Italy
1932 Carmen Barth, U.S.
1936 Jean Despeaux, France
1948 Laszlo Papp, Hungary
1952 Floyd Patterson, U.S.
1956 Gennady Schatkov, USSR
1960 Edward Crook, U.S.
1964 Valery Popenchenko, USSR
1968 Christopher Finnegan, Great Britain
1972 Vyacheslav Lemechev, USSR
1976 Michael Spinks, U.S.
1980 Jose Gomez, Cuba
1984 Joon-Sup Shin, S. Korea
1988 Henry Maske, E. Germany
1992 Ariel Hernandez, Cuba
1996 Ariel Hernandez, Cuba

Light Heavyweight (179 lbs)
1920 Edward Eagan, U.S.
1924 Harry Mitchell, Great Britain
1928 Victor Avendano, Argentina
1932 David Carstens, South Africa
1936 Roger Michelot, France
1948 George Hunter, South Africa
1952 Norvel Lee, U.S.
1956 James Boyd, U.S.
1960 Cassius Clay, U.S.
1964 Cosimo Pinto, Italy
1968 Dan Poznyak, USSR
1972 Mate Parlov, Yugoslavia
1976 Leon Spinks, U.S.
1980 Slobodan Kacar, Yugoslavia
1984 Anton Josipovic, Yugoslavia
1988 Andrew Maynard, U.S.
1992 Torsten May, Germany
1996 Vassili Jirov, Kazakhstan

Heavyweight (201 lbs)
1984 Henry Tillman, U.S.
1988 Ray Mercer, U.S.
1992 Felix Savon, Cuba
1996 Felix Savon, Cuba

Super Heavyweight (Unlimited)
(known as heavyweight, 1904-80)
1904 Samuel Berger, U.S.
1908 Albert Oldham, Great Britain
1920 Ronald Rawson, Great Britain
1924 Otto von Porat, Norway
1928 Arturo Rodriguez Jurado, Argentina
1932 Santiago Lovell, Argentina
1936 Herbert Runge, Germany
1948 Rafael Inglesias, Argentina
1952 H. Edward Sanders, U.S.
1956 T. Peter Rademacher, U.S.
1960 Franco De Piccoli, Italy
1964 Joe Frazier, U.S.
1968 George Foreman, U.S.
1972 Teofilo Stevenson, Cuba
1976 Teofilo Stevenson, Cuba
1980 Teofilo Stevenson, Cuba
1984 Tyrell Biggs, U.S.
1988 Lennox Lewis, Canada
1992 Roberto Balado, Cuba
1996 Vladimir Klitchko, Ukraine

Other Summer Olympics Gold Medal Winners in 1996

Archery
Men's 70-Meter Individual—Justin Huish, U.S.
Men's Team—U.S.
Women's 70-Meter Individual—Kim Kyung Wook, S. Korea
Women's Team—S. Korea

Badminton
Men's Singles—Poul-Erik Hoyer-Larsen, Denmark
Men's Doubles—Rexy Mainaky & Ricky Subagja, Indonesia
Women's Singles—Bang Soo Hyun, S. Korea
Women's Doubles—Ge Fei & Gu Jun, China
Mixed Doubles—Gil Young Ah & Kim Dong Moon, S. Korea

Baseball
G-Cuba; S-Japan; B-U.S.

Basketball
Men—G-U.S.; S-Yugoslavia; B-Lithuania.
Women—G-U.S.; S-Brazil; B-Australia.

Beach Volleyball
Men—Karch Kiraly & Kent Steffes, U.S.
Women—Jackie Silva & Sandra Pires, Brazil

(continued)

Canoe/Kayak

Men

Kayak Slalom—Oliver Fix, Germany
Kayak 500M Singles—Antonio Rossi, Italy
Kayak 500M Doubles—Kay Bluhm & Torsten Gutsche, Germany
Kayak 1,000M Singles—Knut Holmann, Norway
Kayak 1,000M Doubles—Antonio Rossi & Daniele Scarpa, Italy
Kayak 1,000M Fours—G-Germany; S-Hungary; B-Russia
Canoe Slalom Singles—Michal Martikan, Slovakia
Canoe Slalom Doubles—France
Canoe 500M Singles—Martin Doktor, Czech Rep.
Canoe 500M Doubles—Csaba Horvath & Gyorgy Kolonics, Hungary
Canoe 1,000M Singles—Martin Doktor, Czech Rep.
Canoe 1,000M Doubles—Andreas Dittmer & Gunar Kirchbach, Germany

Women

Kayak Slalom—Stepnka Hilgertova, Czech Rep.
Kayak 500M Singles—Rita Koban, Hungary
Kayak 500M Doubles—Agneta Andersson & Susanne Gunnarsson, Sweden
Kayak 500M Fours—G-Germany; S-Switzerland; B-Sweden

Cycling

Men

Individual Road Race—Pascal Richard, Switzerland
Sprint—Jens Fiedler, Germany
Individual Points Race—Silvio Martinello, Italy
4KM Team Pursuit—G-France; S-Russia; B-Australia
4KM Individual Pursuit—Andrea Collinelli, Italy
1KM Time Trial—Florian Rousseau, France
Individual Time Trial—Miguel Indurain, Spain
Cross-Country—Bart Jan Brentjens, Netherlands

Women

Individual Road Race—Jeannie Longo-Ciprelli, France
Sprint—Felicia Ballanger, France
Individual Points Race—Nathalie Lancien, France
Individual Pursuit—Antonella Bellutti, Italy
Individual Time Trial—Zulfiya Zabirova, Russia
Cross-Country—Paola Pezzo, Italy

Equestrian

Individual Three-Day Event—Blyth Tait, New Zealand
Team Three-Day Event—Australia
Individual Dressage—Isabell Werth, Germany
Team Dressage—Germany
Individual Jumping—Ulrich Kirchoff, Germany
Team Jumping—Germany

Fencing

Men

Individual Foil—Alessandro Puccini, Italy
Team Foil—Russia
Individual Saber—Stanislas Pozdnyakov, Russia
Team Saber—Russia
Individual Épée—Aleksandr Beketov, Russia
Team Épée—Italy

Women

Individual Foil—Laura Badea, Romania
Team Foil—Italy
Individual Épée—Laura Flessel, France
Team Épée—France

Field Hockey

Men—G-Netherlands; S-Spain; B-Australia
Women—G-Australia; S-S. Korea; B-Netherlands

Gymnastics

Men

Floor Exercise—Ioannis Melissanidis, Greece
Horizontal Bar—Andreas Wecker, Germany
Parallel Bars—Rustam Sharipov, Ukraine
Pommel Horse—Li Donghua, Switzerland
Rings—Yuri Chechi, Italy
Vault—Aleksei Nemov, Russia
Individual All-Around—Li Xiaoshuang, China
Team—G-Russia; S-China; B-Ukraine.

Women

Balance Beam—Shannon Miller, U.S.
Floor Exercise—Lilia Podkopayeva, Ukraine
Uneven Bars—Svetlana Chorkina, Russia
Vault—Simona Amanar, Romania
Individual All-Around—Lilia Podkopayeva, Ukraine
Team—G-U.S.; S-Russia; B-Romania.

Rhythmic Gymnastics

Individual All-Around—Yekaterina Serebryanskaya, Ukraine
Team—G-Spain; S-Bulgaria; B-Russia

Judo

Men

132 Pounds—Tadahiro Nomura, Japan
143 Pounds—Udo Quellmalz, Germany
157 Pounds—Kenzo Nakamura, Japan
172 Pounds—Djamel Bouras, France
190 Pounds—Jeon Ki Young, S. Korea
209 Pounds—Pawel Nastula, Poland
Heavyweight—David Douillet, France

Women

106 Pounds—Kye Sun Hi, N. Korea
115 Pounds—Marie-Claire Restoux, France
123 Pounds—Driulis Gonzalez, Cuba
134 Pounds—Yuko Emoto, Japan
146 Pounds—Cho Min Sun, S. Korea
159 Pounds—Ulla Werbrouck, Belgium
Over 159 Pounds—Sun Fuming, China

Modern Pentathlon

Aleksandr Parygin, Kazakhstan

Rowing

Men

Single Sculls—Xeno Müller, Switzerland
Double Sculls—Italy
Lightweight Double Sculls—Switzerland
Quadruple Sculls—Germany
Coxless Pairs—Great Britain
Coxless Fours—Australia
Lightweight Coxless Fours—Denmark
Coxed Eights—Netherlands

Women

Single Sculls—Yekaterina Khodotovich, Belarus
Double Sculls—Canada
Lightweight Double Sculls—Romania
Quadruple Sculls—Germany
Coxless Pairs—Australia
Coxed Eights—Romania

Shooting

Men

Air Pistol—Roberto Di Donna, Italy
Trap—Michael Diamond, Australia
Air Rifle—Artem Khadzhibekov, Russia
Free Pistol—Boris Kokorev, Russia
Double Trap—Russell Mark, Australia
Rapid Fire Pistol—Ralf Schumann, Germany
Rifle Prone—Christian Klees, Germany
Running Game Target—Yang Ling, China
Three-Position Rifle—Jean-Pierre Amat, France
Skeet—Ennio Falco, Italy

Women

Air Pistol—Olga Klochneva, Russia
Three-Position Rifle—Aleksandra Ivosev, Yugoslavia
Double Trap—Kim Rhode, U.S.
Sport Pistol—Li Duihong, China
Air Rifle—Renata Mauer, Poland

Soccer

Men—G-Nigeria; S-Argentina; B-Brazil
Women—G-U.S.; S-China; B-Norway

Softball

G-U.S.; S-China; B-Australia

Synchronized Swimming

G-U.S.; S-Canada; B-Japan

Table Tennis

Men's Singles—Liu Guoliang, China
Men's Doubles—Kong Linghui & Liu Guoliang, China
Women's Singles—Deng Yaping, China
Women's Doubles—Deng Yaping & Qiao Hong, China

Team Handball

Men—G-Croatia; S-Sweden; B-Spain
Women—G-Denmark; S- S. Korea; B-Hungary

Tennis

Men's Singles—Andre Agassi, U.S.
Men's Doubles—Todd Woodbridge & Mark Woodforde, Australia
Women's Singles—Lindsay Davenport, U.S.
Women's Doubles—Gigi Fernandez & Mary Joe Fernandez, U.S.

Volleyball

Men—G-Netherlands; S-Italy; B-Yugoslavia
Women—G-Cuba; S-China; B- Brazil

Water Polo

G-Spain; S-Croatia; B- Italy

Weight Lifting

119 Pounds—Halil Mutlu, Turkey
130 Pounds—Tang Ningsheng, China
141 Pounds—Naim Suleymanoglu, Turkey
154 Pounds—Zhan Xugang, China
161½ Pounds—Pablo Lara, Cuba
183 Pounds—Pyrros Dimas, Greece
200½ Pounds—Aleksei Petrov, Russia
218 Pounds— Akakide Kakhiashvilis, Greece
238 Pounds—Timur Taimazov, Ukraine
Over 238 Pounds—Andrei Chemerkin, Russia

Wrestling

Freestyle

105½ Pounds—Kim Il, N. Korea
114½ Pounds—Valentin Jordanov, Bulgaria
125½ Pounds—Kendall Cross, U.S.
136½ Pounds—Tom Brands, U.S.
149½ Pounds—Vadim Bogiev, Russia
163 Pounds—Bouvaisa Satiev, Russia
180½ Pounds—Khadzhimurad Magomedov, Russia
198 Pounds—Rasul Khadem, Iran
220 Pounds—Kurt Angle, U.S.
286 Pounds—Mahmut Demir, Turkey

Greco-Roman

105½ Pounds—Sim Kwan Ho, S. Korea
114½ Pounds—Armen Nazaryan, Armenia
125½ Pounds—Yuri Melnichenko, Kazakhstan
136½ Pounds—Wlodzimierz Zwadzki, Poland
149½ Pounds—Ryszard Wolny, Poland
163 Pounds—Feliberto Ascuy Aguilera, Cuba
180½ Pounds—Hamza Yerlikiya, Turkey
198 Pounds—Vyacheslav Oleynyk, Ukraine
220 Pounds—Andrzej Wronski, Poland
286 Pounds—Aleksandr Karelin, Russia

Yachting

Open

Laser—Robert Scheidt, Brazil
Soling—G-Germany; S-Russia; B-U.S.
Star—G-Brazil; S-Sweden; B-Australia
Tornado—G-Spain; S-Australia; B-Brazil

Men

Finn—Mateusz Kusznierewicz, Poland
Mistral—Nikolaos Kaklamanakis, Greece
470—G-Ukraine; S-Great Britain; B-Portugal

Women

Europe—Kristine Rough, Denmark
Mistral—Lee Lai-Shan, Hong Kong
470—G-Spain; S-Japan; B-Ukraine.

TRACK AND FIELD

World Track and Field Records

As of mid-Oct. 1998

The International Amateur Atheletic Federation, the world body of track and field, recognizes only records in metric distances, except for the mile.

Men's Records

Running

Event	Record	Holder	Country	Date	Where made
100 meters	**9.84 s.**	Donovan Bailey	Canada	July 27, 1996	Atlanta, GA
200 meters	**19.32 s.**	Michael Johnson	U.S.	Aug. 1, 1996	Atlanta, GA
400 meters	**43.29 s.**	Harry "Butch" Reynolds	U.S.	Aug. 17, 1988	Zurich
800 meters	**1 m., 41.11 s.**	Wilson Kipketer	Denmark	Aug. 24, 1997	Cologne, Germany
1,000 meters	**2 m., 12.18 s.**	Sebastian Coe	Gr. Britain	July 11, 1981	Oslo
1,500 meters	**3 m., 26.00 s.**	Hicham El Guerrouj	Morocco	July 14, 1998	Rome
1 mile	**3 m., 44.39 s.**	Noureddine Morceli	Algeria	Sept. 5, 1993	Rieti, Italy
2,000 meters	**4 m., 47.88 s.**	Noureddine Morceli	Algeria	July 3, 1995	Paris
3,000 meters	**7 m., 20.67 s.**	Daniel Komen	Kenya	Sept. 1, 1996	Rieti, Italy
5,000 meters	**12 m., 39.36 s.**	Haile Gebreselassie	Ethiopia	June 13, 1998	Helsinki, Finland
10,000 meters	**26 m., 22.75 s.**	Haile Gebreselassie	Ethiopia	June 1,1998	Hengelo, Netherlands
20,000 meters	**56 m., 55.6 s.**	Arturo Barrios	Mexico	Mar. 30, 1991	La Fleche, France
25,000 meters	**1 hr., 13 m., 55.8 s.**	Toshihiko Seko	Japan	Mar. 22, 1981	Christchurch, New Zealand
3,000 meter stpl.	**7 m., 55.72 s.**	Bernard Barmasai	Kenya	Aug. 24, 1997	Cologne, Germany
Marathon	**2 hr., 6 m., 05 s.**	Ronaldo da Costa	Brazil	Sept. 20, 1998	Berlin

Hurdles

Event	Record	Holder	Country	Date	Where made
110 meters	**12.91 s.**	Colin Jackson	Gr. Britain	Aug. 20, 1993	Stuttgart, Germany
400 meters	**46.78 s.**	Kevin Young	U.S.	Aug. 6, 1992	Barcelona

Relay Races

Event	Record	Holder	Country	Date	Where made
400 mtrs. (4x100)	**37.40 s.**	(Marsh, Burrell, Mitchell, Lewis)	U.S.	Aug. 8, 1992	Barcelona
		(Drummond, Cason, Mitchell, Burrell)	U.S.	Aug. 21, 1993	Stuttgart, Germany
800 mtrs. (4×200)	**1 m., 18.68 s.**	(Marsh, Burrell, Heard, Lewis)	U.S.	Apr. 17, 1994	Walnut, CA
1,600 mtrs. (4×400)	**2 m., 54.20 s.**	(Young, Pettigrew, Washington, Johnson)	U.S.	July 22, 1998	Long Island, NY
3,200 mtrs. (4×800)	**7 m., 03.89 s.**	(Elliott, Cook, Cram, Coe)	Gr. Britain	Aug. 30, 1982	London

Field Events

Event	Record	Holder	Country	Date	Where made
High jump	**2.45m**	Javier Sotomayor	Cuba	July 27, 1993	Salamanca, Spain
Long jump	**8.95m**	Mike Powell	U.S.	Aug. 30, 1991	Tokyo
Triple jump	**18.29m**	Jonathan Edwards	Gr. Britain	Aug. 7, 1995	Göteborg, Sweden
Pole vault	**6.14m**	Sergei Bubka	Ukraine	July 31, 1994	Sestriere, Italy
16-lb. shot put	**23.12m**	Randy Barnes	U.S.	May 20, 1990	Los Angeles, CA
Discus	**74.08m**	Juergen Schult	E. Germany	June 6, 1986	Neubrandenburg, Germany
Javelin	**98.48m**	Jan Zelezny	Czech Rep.	May 25, 1996	Jena, Germany
16-lb. hammer	**86.74m**	Yuri Sedykh	USSR	Aug. 30, 1986	Stuttgart, W. Germany
Decathlon	**8,891 pts.**	Dan O'Brien	U.S.	Sept. 4-5, 1992	Talence, France

Women's Records

Running

Event	Record	Holder	Country	Date	Where made
100 meters	**10.49 s.**	Florence Griffith Joyner	U.S.	July 16, 1988	Indianapolis, IN
200 meters	**21.34 s.**	Florence Griffith Joyner	U.S.	Sept. 29, 1988	Seoul
400 meters	**47.60 s.**	Marita Koch	E. Germany	Oct. 6, 1985	Canberra, Australia
800 meters	**1 m., 53.28 s.**	Jarmila Kratochvilova	Czechoslovakia	July 26, 1983	Munich
1,000 meters	**2 m., 28.98 s.**	Svetlana Masterkova	Russia	Aug. 23, 1996	Brussels

(continued)

Event	Record	Holder	Country	Date	Where made
1,500 meters	**3 m., 50.46 s.**	Qu Yunxia	China	Sept. 11, 1993	Beijing
1 mile	**4 m., 12.56 s.**	Svetlana Masterkova	Russia	Aug. 14, 1996	Zurich
2,000 meters	**5 m., 25.36 s.**	Sonia O'Sullivan	Ireland	July 8, 1994	Edinburgh
3,000 meters	**8 m., 06.11 s.**	Wang Junxia	China	Sept. 13, 1993	Beijing
5,000 meters	**14 m., 28.09 s.**	Jiang Bo	China	Oct. 23, 1997	Shanghai
10,000 meters	**29 m., 31.78 s.**	Wang Junxia	China	Sept. 8, 1993	Beijing
Marathon	**2 h., 21 m., 06 s.**	Ingrid Kristiansen	Norway	Apr. 21, 1985	London
		Hurdles			
100 meters	**12.21 s.**	Yordanka Donkova	Bulgaria	Aug. 20, 1988	Bulgaria
400 meters	**52.61 s.**	Kim Batten	U.S.	Aug. 11, 1995	Göteborg, Sweden
		Field Events			
High jump	**2.09m**	Stefka Kostadinova	Bulgaria	Aug. 30, 1987	Rome
Long jump	**7.52m**	Galina Chistyakova	USSR	June 11, 1988	Leningrad
Triple jump	**15.50m**	Inessa Kravets	Ukraine	Aug. 10, 1995	Göteborg, Sweden
Pole vault	**4.59m**	Emma George	Australia	Mar. 21, 1998	Brisbane
Shot put	**22.63m**	Natalya Lisovskaya	USSR	June 7, 1987	Moscow
Discus	**76.80m**	Gabriele Reinsch	E. Germany	July 9, 1988	Neubrandenburg, Germany
Hammer	**73.14m**	Mihaela Melinte	Romania	July 16, 1998	Polana Brasov
Javelin	**80.00m**	Petra Felke	E. Germany	Sept. 9, 1988	Potsdam, Germany
Heptathlon	**7,291 pts.**	Jackie Joyner-Kersee	U.S.	Sept. 23-24, 1988	Seoul
		Relay Races			
400 mtrs. (4×100)	**41.37 s.**	(Gladisch, Rieger, Auerswald, Goehr)	E. Germany	Oct. 6, 1985	Canberra, Australia
800 mtrs. (4×200)	**1 m., 28.15 s.**	(Goehr, Mueller, Woeckel, Koch)	E. Germany	Aug. 9, 1980	Jena, E. Germany
1,600 mtrs. (4×400)	**3 m., 15.17 s.**	(Ledovskaya, Nazarova, Pinigina, Bryzgina)	USSR	Oct. 1, 1988	Seoul
3,200 mtrs. (4×800)	**7 m., 50.17 s.**	(Olizarenko, Gurina, Borisova, Podyalovskaya)	USSR	Aug. 5, 1984	Moscow

World Track and Field Indoor Records

As of mid-Oct. 1998

The International Amateur Athletic Federation began recognizing world indoor track and field records as official on Jan. 1, 1987. World indoor bests set prior to Jan. 1, 1987, are subject to approval as world records providing they meet the prescribed IAAF world records criteria, including drug testing. To be accepted as a world indoor record, a performance must meet the same criteria as a world record outdoors, except that a track performance cannot be set on an indoor track larger than 200 meters.

Men's Records

Event	Record	Holder	Country	Date	Where made
50 meters	**5.56**	Donovan Bailey	Canada	Feb. 9, 1996	Reno, NV
60 meters	**6.39**	Maurice Greene	U.S.	Feb. 3, 1998	Madrid
200 meters	**19.92**	Frankie Fredericks	Namibia	Feb. 18, 1996	Lievin, France
400 meters	**44.63**	Michael Johnson	U.S.	Mar. 4, 1995	Atlanta, GA
800 meters	**1:42.67**	Wilson Kipketer	Denmark	Mar. 9, 1997	Paris
1,000 meters	**2:15.26**	Noureddine Morceli	Algeria	Feb. 22, 1992	Birmingham, England
1,500 meters	**3:31.18**	Hicham el-Guerrouj	Morocco	Feb. 2, 1997	Stuttgart, Germany
1 mile	**3:48.45**	Hicham el-Guerrouj	Morocco	Feb. 12, 1997	Ghent, Belgium
3,000 meters	**7:24.90**	Daniel Komen	Kenya	Feb. 6, 1998	Budapest
5,000 meters	**12:51.84**	Daniel Komen	Kenya	Feb. 19, 1997	Stockholm
50-meter hurdles	**6.25**	Mark McKoy	Canada	Mar. 5, 1986	Kobe, Japan
60-meter hurdles	**7.30**	Colin Jackson	Gr. Britain	Mar. 6, 1994	Sindelfingen, Germany
High jump	**2.43m**	Javier Sotomayor	Cuba	Mar. 4, 1989	Budapest
Pole vault	**6.15m**	Sergei Bubka	Ukraine	Feb. 21, 1993	Donyetsk, Ukraine
Long jump	**8.79m**	Carl Lewis	U.S.	Jan. 27, 1984	New York, NY
Triple jump	**17.83**	Eliecer Urrutia	Cuba	Mar. 1, 1997	Sindelfingen, Germany
Shot put	**22.66m**	Randy Barnes	U.S.	Jan. 20, 1989	Los Angeles, CA

Women's Records

Event	Record	Holder	Country	Date	Where made
50 meters	**5.96**	Irina Privalova	Russia	Feb. 9, 1995	Madrid
60 meters	**6.92**	Irina Privalova	Russia	Feb. 9, 1995	Madrid
		Irina Privalova	Russia	Feb. 11, 1993	Madrid
200 meters	**21.87**	Merlene Ottey	Jamaica	Feb. 13, 1993	Lievin, France
400 meters	**49.59**	Jarmila Kratochvilova	Czechoslovakia	Mar. 7, 1982	Milan, Italy
800 meters	**1:56.36**	Maria Mutola	Mozambique	Feb. 22, 1998	Levin, France
1,000 meters	**2:31.23**	Maria Mutola	Mozambique	Feb. 25, 1996	Stockholm
1,500 meters	**4:00.27**	Doina Melinte	Romania	Feb. 9, 1990	E. Rutherford, NJ
1 mile	**4:17.14**	Doina Melinte	Romania	Feb. 9, 1990	E. Rutherford, NJ
3,000 meters	**8:33.82**	Elly van Hulst	Netherlands	Mar. 4, 1989	Budapest
5,000 meters	**15:03.17**	Liz McColgan	Gr. Britain	Feb. 22, 1992	Birmingham, England
50-meter hurdles	**6.58**	Cornelia Oschkenat	E. Germany	Feb. 20, 1988	Berlin
60-meter hurdles	**7.69**	Lyudmila Narozhilenko	USSR	Feb 4, 1990	Chelyabinsk, USSR
High jump	**2.07m**	Heike Henkel	Germany	Feb. 8, 1992	Karlsruhe, Germany
Pole vault	**4.48m**	Daniela Bartova	Czech Republic	Mar. 8, 1998	Sindelfingen, Germany
		Stacy Dragila	U.S.	Mar. 8, 1998	Sindelfingen, Germany
Long jump	**7.37m**	Heike Drechsler	E. Germany	Feb. 13, 1988	Vienna
Triple jump	**15.16m**	Ashia Hansen	Gr. Britain	Feb. 28, 1998	Valencia
Shot put	**22.50m**	Helena Fibingerova	Czechoslovakia	Feb. 19, 1977	Czechoslovakia

GYMNASTICS

World Gymnastics Championships in 1997

On Sept. 5, Svetlana Khorkina of Russia won the women's all-around title at the World Gymnastics Championship, held in Lausanne, Switzerland, with a score of 38.636. Ivan Ivankov of Belarus won the men's all-around title with a score of 56.887.

NATIONAL FOOTBALL LEAGUE

NFL 1997-98: AFC Wins One, 2,000-Yard Man, Browns Will Return

The Denver Broncos, led by John Elway and Terrell Davis, won Super Bowl XXXII on Jan. 25, 1998, becoming the first AFC team to do so in 14 years. Detroit Lions running back Barry Sanders rushed for 2,053 yards, making him only the third player ever to reach that plateau in a season. Cleveland was awarded an expansion team that will begin play in the 1999 season. In 1996, the original Cleveland Browns moved to Baltimore and became the Ravens; the new Cleveland team will again be known as the Browns and will play in a brand new stadium. Future Hall of Fame running back Marcus Allen retired at the end of the season to pursue a broadcasting career. Allen played for the Oakland/Los Angeles Raiders and the Kansas City Chiefs during his 16-year career and holds the career record for rushing touchdowns (123).

Final 1997 Standings

American Football Conference

Eastern Division

	W	L	T	Pct.	Pts.	Opp.
New England	10	6	0	.625	369	289
Miami*	9	7	0	.563	339	327
N.Y. Jets	9	7	0	.563	348	287
Buffalo	6	10	0	.375	255	367
Indianapolis	3	13	0	.188	313	401

Central Division

	W	L	T	Pct.	Pts.	Opp.
Pittsburgh	11	5	0	.688	372	307
Jacksonville*	11	5	0	.688	394	318
Tennessee	8	8	0	.500	333	310
Cincinnati	7	9	0	.438	355	405
Baltimore	6	9	1	.406	326	345

Western Division

	W	L	T	Pct.	Pts.	Opp.
Kansas City	13	3	0	.813	375	232
Denver*	12	4	0	.750	472	287
Seattle	8	8	0	.500	365	362
Oakland	4	12	0	.250	324	419
San Diego	4	12	0	.250	266	425

National Football Conference

Eastern Division

	W	L	T	Pct.	Pts.	Opp.
N.Y. Giants	10	5	1	.656	307	265
Washington	8	7	1	.531	327	289
Philadelphia	6	9	1	.406	317	372
Dallas	6	10	0	.375	304	314
Arizona	4	12	0	.250	283	379

Central Division

	W	L	T	Pct.	Pts.	Opp.
Green Bay	13	3	0	.813	422	282
Tampa Bay*	10	6	0	.625	299	263
Detroit*	9	7	0	.563	379	306
Minnesota*	9	7	0	.563	354	359
Chicago	4	12	0	.250	263	421

Western Division

	W	L	T	Pct.	Pts.	Opp.
San Francisco	13	3	0	.813	375	265
Atlanta	7	9	0	.438	320	361
Carolina	7	9	0	.438	265	314
New Orleans	6	10	0	.375	237	327
St. Louis	5	11	0	.313	299	359

* Wild card team.

AFC Playoffs—Denver 42, Jacksonville 17; New England 17, Miami 3; Pittsburgh 7, New England 6; Denver 14, Kansas City 10; Denver 24, Pittsburgh 21.
NFC Playoffs—Minnesota 23, N.Y. Giants 22; Tampa Bay 20, Detroit 10; San Francisco 38, Minnesota 22; Green Bay 21, Tampa Bay 7; Green Bay 23, San Francisco 10.
Super Bowl—Denver 31, Green Bay 24.

National Football League Champions

Year	East Winner (W-L-T)	West Winner (W-L-T)	Playoff
1933	New York Giants (11-3-0)	Chicago Bears (10-2-1)	Chicago Bears 23, New York 21
1934	New York Giants (8-5-0)	Chicago Bears (13-0-0)	New York 30, Chicago Bears 13
1935	New York Giants (9-3-0)	Detroit Lions (7-3-2)	Detroit 26, New York 7
1936	Boston Redskins (7-5-0)	Green Bay Packers (10-1-1)	Green Bay 21, Boston 6
1937	Washington Redskins (8-3-0)	Chicago Bears (9-1-1)	Washington 28, Chicago Bears 21
1938	New York Giants (8-2-1)	Green Bay Packers (8-3-0)	New York 23, Green Bay 17
1939	New York Giants (9-1-1)	Green Bay Packers (9-2-0)	Green Bay 27, New York 0
1940	Washington Redskins (9-2-0)	Chicago Bears (8-3-0)	Chicago Bears 73, Washington 0
1941	New York Giants (8-3-0)	Chicago Bears (10-1-1)(a)	Chicago Bears 37, New York 9
1942	Washington Redskins (10-1-1)	Chicago Bears (11-0-0)	Washington 14, Chicago Bears 6
1943	Washington Redskins (6-3-1)(a)	Chicago Bears (8-1-1)	Chicago Bears, 41, Washington 21
1944	New York Giants (8-1-1)	Green Bay Packers (8-2-0)	Green Bay 14, New York 7
1945	Washington Redskins (8-2-0)	Cleveland Rams (9-1-0)	Cleveland 15, Washington 14
1946	New York Giants (7-3-1)	Chicago Bears (8-2-1)	Chicago Bears 24, New York 14
1947	Philadelphia Eagles (8-4-0)(a)	Chicago Cardinals (9-3-0)	Chicago Cardinals 28, Philadelphia 21
1948	Philadelphia Eagles (9-2-1)	Chicago Cardinals (11-1-0)	Philadelphia 7, Chicago Cardinals 0
1949	Philadelphia Eagles (11-1-0)	Los Angeles Rams (8-2-2)	Philadelphia 14, Los Angeles 0
1950	Cleveland Browns (10-2-0)(a)	Los Angeles Rams (9-3-0)(a)	Cleveland 30, Los Angeles 28
1951	Cleveland Browns (11-1-0)	Los Angeles Rams (8-4-0)	Los Angeles 24, Cleveland 17
1952	Cleveland Browns (8-4-0)	Detroit Lions (9-3-0)(a)	Detroit 17, Cleveland 7
1953	Cleveland Browns (11-1-0)	Detroit Lions (10-2-0)	Detroit 17, Cleveland 16
1954	Cleveland Browns (9-3-0)	Detroit Lions (9-2-1)	Cleveland 56, Detroit 10
1955	Cleveland Browns (9-2-1)	Los Angeles Rams (8-3-1)	Cleveland 38, Los Angeles 14
1956	New York Giants (8-3-1)	Chicago Bears (9-2-1)	New York 47, Chicago Bears 7
1957	Cleveland Browns (9-2-1)	Detroit Lions (8-4-0)(a)	Detroit 59, Cleveland 14
1958	New York Giants (9-3-0)(a)	Baltimore Colts (9-3-0)	Baltimore 23, New York 17(b)
1959	New York Giants (10-2-0)	Baltimore Colts (9-3-0)	Baltimore 31, New York 16
1960	Philadelphia Eagles (10-2-0)	Green Bay Packers (8-4-0)	Philadelphia 17, Green Bay 13
1961	New York Giants (10-3-1)	Green Bay Packers (11-3-0)	Green Bay 37, New York 0
1962	New York Giants (12-2-0)	Green Bay Packers (13-1-0)	Green Bay 16, New York 7
1963	New York Giants (11-3-0)	Chicago Bears (11-1-2)	Chicago 14, New York 10
1964	Cleveland Browns (10-3-1)	Baltimore Colts (12-2-0)	Cleveland 27, Baltimore 0
1965	Cleveland Browns (11-3-0)	Green Bay Packers (10-3-1)(a)	Green Bay 23, Cleveland 12
1966	Dallas Cowboys (10-3-1)	Green Bay Packers (12-2-0)	Green Bay 34, Dallas 27

(a) Won divisional playoff. (b) Won at 8:15 of sudden death overtime period.

Year	Conference	Division	Winner (W-L-T)	Playoffs(c)
1967	East	Century	Cleveland Browns (9-5-0)	Dallas 52, Cleveland 14
		Capitol	Dallas Cowboys (9-5-0)	
	West	Central	Green Bay Packers (9-4-1)	Green Bay 28, Los Angeles 7
		Coastal	Los Angeles Rams (11-1-2)(a)	Green Bay 21, Dallas 17
1968	East	Century	Cleveland Browns (10-4-0)	Cleveland 31, Dallas 20
		Capitol	Dallas Cowboys (12-2-0)	
	West	Central	Minnesota Vikings (8-6-0)	Baltimore 24, Minnesota 14
		Coastal	Baltimore Colts (13-1-0)	Baltimore 34, Cleveland 0
1969	East	Century	Cleveland Browns (10-3-1)	Cleveland 38, Dallas 14
		Capitol	Dallas Cowboys (11-2-1)	
	West	Central	Minnesota Vikings (12-2-0)	Minnesota 23, Los Angeles 20
		Coastal	Los Angeles Rams (11-3-0)	Minnesota 27, Cleveland 7
1970	American	Eastern	Baltimore Colts (11-2-1)	Baltimore 17, Cincinnati 0
		Central	Cincinnati Bengals (8-6-0)	Oakland 21, Miami* 14
		Western	Oakland Raiders (8-4-2)	Baltimore 27, Oakland 17
	National	Eastern	Dallas Cowboys (10-4-0)	Dallas 5, Detroit* 0
		Central	Minnesota Vikings (12-2-0)	San Francisco 17, Minnesota 14
		Western	San Francisco 49ers (10-3-1)	Dallas 17, San Francisco 10
1971	American	Eastern	Miami Dolphins (10-3-1)	Miami 27, Kansas City* 24
		Central	Cleveland Browns (9-5-0)	Baltimore 20, Cleveland 3
		Western	Kansas City Chiefs(10-3-1)	Miami 21, Baltimore 0
	National	Eastern	Dallas Cowboys (11-3-0)	Dallas 20, Minnesota 12
		Central	Minnesota Vikings (11-3-0)	San Francisco 24, Washington* 20
		Western	San Francisco 49ers (9-5-0)	Dallas 14, San Francisco 3
1972	American	Eastern	Miami Dolphins (14-0-0)	Miami 20, Cleveland* 14
		Central	Pittsburgh Steelers (11-3-0)	Pittsburgh 13, Oakland 7
		Western	Oakland Raiders (10-3-1)	Miami 21, Pittsburgh 17
	National	Eastern	Washington Redskins (11-3-0)	Washington 16, Green Bay 3
		Central	Green Bay Packers (10-4-0)	Dallas* 30, San Francisco 28
		Western	San Francisco 49ers (8-5-1)	Washington 26, Dallas* 3
1973	American	Eastern	Miami Dolphins (12-2-0)	Miami 34, Cincinnati 16
		Central	Cincinnati Bengals (10-4-0)	Oakland 33, Pittsburgh* 14
		Western	Oakland Raiders (9-4-1)	Miami 27, Oakland 10
	National	Eastern	Dallas Cowboys (10-4-0)	Dallas 27, Los Angeles 16
		Central	Minnesota Vikings (12-2-0)	Minnesota 27, Washington* 20
		Western	Los Angeles Rams (12-2-0)	Minnesota 27, Dallas 10
1974	American	Eastern	Miami Dolphins (11-3-0)	Oakland 28, Miami 26
		Central	Pittsburgh Steelers (10-3-1)	Pittsburgh 32, Buffalo* 14
		Western	Oakland Raiders (12-2-0)	Pittsburgh 24, Oakland 13
	National	Eastern	St. Louis Cardinals (10-4-0)	Minnesota 30, St. Louis 14
		Central	Minnesota Vikings (10-4-0)	Los Angeles 19, Washington* 10
		Western	Los Angeles Rams (10-4-0)	Minnesota 14, Los Angeles 10
1975	American	Eastern	Baltimore Colts (10-4-0)	Pittsburgh 28, Baltimore 10
		Central	Pittsburgh Steelers (12-2-0)	Oakland 31, Cincinnati* 28
		Western	Oakland Raiders (11-3-0)	Pittsburgh 16, Oakland 10
	National	Eastern	St. Louis Cardinals (11-3-0)	Dallas* 17, Minnesota 14
		Central	Minnesota Vikings (12-2-0)	Los Angeles 35, St. Louis 23
		Western	Los Angeles Rams (12-2-0)	Dallas* 37, Los Angeles 7
1976	American	Eastern	Baltimore Colts (11-3-0)	Pittsburgh 40, Baltimore 14
		Central	Pittsburgh Steelers (10-4-0)	Oakland 24, New England* 21
		Western	Oakland Raiders (13-1-0)	Oakland 24, Pittsburgh 7
	National	Eastern	Dallas Cowboys (11-3-0)	Minnesota 35, Washington* 20
		Central	Minnesota Vikings (11-2-1)	Los Angeles 14, Dallas 12
		Western	Los Angeles Rams (10-3-1)	Minnesota 24, Los Angeles 13
1977	American	Eastern	Baltimore Colts (10-4-0)	Oakland* 37, Baltimore 31
		Central	Pittsburgh Steelers (9-5-0)	Denver 34, Pittsburgh 21
		Western	Denver Broncos (12-2-0)	Denver 20, Oakland* 17
	National	Eastern	Dallas Cowboys (12-2-0)	Dallas 37, Chicago* 7
		Central	Minnesota Vikings (9-5-0)	Minnesota 14, Los Angeles 7
		Western	Los Angeles Rams (10-4-0)	Dallas 23, Minnesota 6
1978	American	Eastern	New England Patriots (11-5-0)	Pittsburgh 33, Denver 10
		Central	Pittsburgh Steelers (14-2-0)	Houston* 31, New England 14
		Western	Denver Broncos (10-6-0)	Pittsburgh 34, Houston* 5
	National	Eastern	Dallas Cowboys (12-4-0)	Dallas 27, Atlanta* 20
		Central	Minnesota Vikings (8-7-1)	Los Angeles 34, Minnesota 10
		Western	Los Angeles Rams (12-4-0)	Dallas 28, Los Angeles 0
1979	American	Eastern	Miami Dolphins (10-6-0)	Houston* 17, San Diego 14
		Central	Pittsburgh Steelers (12-4-0)	Pittsburgh 34, Miami 14
		Western	San Diego Chargers (12-4-0)	Pittsburgh 27, Houston* 13
	National	Eastern	Dallas Cowboys (11-5-0)	Tampa Bay 24, Philadelphia* 17
		Central	Tampa Bay Buccaneers (10-6-0)	Los Angeles 21, Dallas 19
		Western	Los Angeles Rams (9-7-0)	Los Angeles 9, Tampa Bay 0
1980	American	Eastern	Buffalo Bills (11-5-0)	San Diego 20, Buffalo 14
		Central	Cleveland Browns (11-5-0)	Oakland* 14, Cleveland 12
		Western	San Diego Chargers (11-5-0)	Oakland* 34, San Diego 27
	National	Eastern	Philadelphia Eagles (12-4-0)	Philadelphia 31, Minnesota 16
		Central	Minnesota Vikings (9-7-0)	Dallas* 30, Atlanta 27
		Western	Atlanta Falcons (12-4-0)	Philadelphia 20, Dallas* 7
1981	American	Eastern	Miami Dolphins (11-4-1)	San Diego 41, Miami 38
		Central	Cincinnati Bengals (12-4-0)	Cincinnati 28, Buffalo* 21
		Western	San Diego Chargers (10-6-0)	Cincinnati 27, San Diego 7
	National	Eastern	Dallas Cowboys (12-4-0)	Dallas 38, Tampa Bay 0
		Central	Tampa Bay Buccaneers (9-7-0)	San Francisco 38, N.Y. Giants* 24
		Western	San Francisco 49ers (13-3-0)	San Francisco 28, Dallas 27

1982(d)	American		Los Angeles Raiders (8-1-0)	Strike-shortened season (see
	National		Washington Redskins (8-1-0)	playoff results after footnote)
1983	American	Eastern	Miami Dolphins (12-4-0)	Seattle* 27, Miami 20
		Central	Pittsburgh Steelers (10-6-0)	L.A. Raiders 38, Pittsburgh 10
		Western	Los Angeles Raiders (12-4-0)	L.A. Raiders 30, Seattle* 14
	National	Eastern	Washington Redskins (14-2-0)	Washington 51, L.A. Rams* 7
		Central	Detroit Lions (9-7-0)	San Francisco 24, Detroit 23
		Western	San Francisico 49ers (10-6-0)	Washington 24, San Francisco 21
1984	American	Eastern	Miami Dolphins (14-2-0)	Miami 31, Seattle* 10
		Central	Pittsburgh Steelers (9-7-0)	Pittsburgh 24, Denver 17
		Western	Denver Broncos (13-3-0)	Miami 45, Pittsburgh 28
	National	Eastern	Washington Redskins (11-5-0)	Chicago 23, Washington 19
		Central	Chicago Bears (10-6-0)	San Francisco 21, N.Y. Giants* 10
		Western	San Francisco 49ers (15-1-0)	San Francisco 23, Chicago 0
1985	American	Eastern	Miami Dolphins (12-4-0)	New England* 27, L.A. Raiders 20
		Central	Cleveland Browns (8-8-0)	Miami 24, Cleveland 21
		Western	Los Angeles Raiders (12-4-0)	New England* 31, Miami 14
	National	Eastern	Dallas Cowboys (10-6-0)	Chicago 21, N.Y. Giants* 0
		Central	Chicago Bears (15-1-0)	L.A. Rams 20, Dallas 0
		Western	Los Angeles Rams (11-5-0)	Chicago 24, L.A. Rams 0
1986	American	Eastern	New England Patriots (11-5-0)	Denver 22, New England 17
		Central	Cleveland Browns (12-4-0)	Cleveland 23, N.Y. Jets* 20
		Western	Denver Broncos (11-5-0)	Denver 23, Cleveland 20
	National	Eastern	New York Giants (14-2-0)	N.Y. Giants 49, San Francisco 3
		Central	Chicago Bears (14-2-0)	Washington* 27, Chicago 13
		Western	San Francisco 49ers (10-5-1)	N.Y. Giants 17, Washington* 0
1987	American	Eastern	Indianapolis Colts (9-6-0)	Cleveland 38, Indianapolis 21
		Central	Cleveland Browns (10-5-0)	Denver 34, Houston* 10
		Western	Denver Broncos (10-4-1)	Denver 38, Cleveland 33
	National	Eastern	Washington Redskins (11-4-0)	Washington 21, Chicago 17
		Central	Chicago Bears (11-4-0)	Minnesota* 36, San Francisco 24
		Western	San Francisco 49ers (13-2-0)	Washington 17, Minnesota* 10
1988	American	Eastern	Buffalo Bills (12-4-0)	Buffalo 17, Houston* 10
		Central	Cincinnati Bengals (12-4-0)	Cincinnati 21, Seattle 13
		Western	Seattle Seahawks (9-7-0)	Cincinnati 21, Buffalo 10
	National	Eastern	Philadelphia Eagles (10-6-0)	Chicago 20, Philadelphia 12
		Central	Chicago Bears (12-4-0)	San Francisco 34, Minnesota* 9
		Western	San Francisco 49ers (10-6-0)	San Francisco 28, Chicago 3
1989	American	Eastern	Buffalo Bills (9-7-0)	Cleveland 34, Buffalo 30
		Central	Cleveland Browns (9-6-1)	Denver 24, Pittsburgh* 23
		Western	Denver Broncos (11-5-0)	Denver 37, Cleveland 21
	National	Eastern	New York Giants (12-4-0)	San Francisco 41, Minnesota 13
		Central	Minnesota Vikings (10-6-0)	L.A. Rams* 19, N.Y. Giants 13
		Western	San Francisco 49ers (14-2-0)	San Francisco 30, L.A. Rams* 3
1990	American	Eastern	Buffalo Bills (13-3-0)	L.A. Raiders 20, Cincinnati 10
		Central	Cincinnati Bengals (9-7-0)	Buffalo 44, Miami* 34
		Western	Los Angeles Raiders (12-4-0)	Buffalo 51, L.A. Raiders 3
	National	Eastern	New York Giants (13-3-0)	San Francisco 28, Washington* 10
		Central	Chicago Bears (11-5-0)	N.Y. Giants 31, Chicago 3
		Western	San Francisco 49ers (14-2-0)	N.Y. Giants 15, San Francisco 13
1991	American	Eastern	Buffalo Bills (13-3-0)	Denver 26, Houston 24
		Central	Houston Oilers (11-5-0)	Buffalo 37, Kansas City* 14
		Western	Denver Broncos (12-4-0)	Buffalo 10, Denver 7
	National	Eastern	Washington Redskins (14-2-0)	Washington 24, Atlanta* 7
		Central	Detroit Lions (12-4-0)	Detroit 38, Dallas* 6
		Western	New Orleans Saints (11-5-0)	Washington 41, Detroit 10
1992	American	Eastern	Miami Dolphins (11-5-0)	Miami 31, San Diego 0
		Central	Pittsburgh Steelers (11-5-0)	Buffalo* 24, Pittsburgh 3
		Western	San Diego Chargers (11-5-0)	Buffalo* 29, Miami 10
	National	Eastern	Dallas Cowboys (13-3-0)	Dallas 34, Philadelphia* 10
		Central	Minnesota Vikings (11-5-0)	San Francisco 20, Washington* 13
		Western	San Francisco 49ers (14-2-0)	Dallas 30, San Francisco 20
1993	American	Eastern	Buffalo Bills (12-4-0)	Buffalo 29, L.A. Raiders* 23
		Central	Houston Oilers (12-4-0)	Kansas City 28, Houston 20
		Western	Kansas City Chiefs (11-5-0)	Buffalo 30, Kansas City 13
	National	Eastern	Dallas Cowboys (12-4-0)	Dallas 27, Green Bay* 17
		Central	Detroit Lions (10-6-0)	San Francisco 44, N.Y. Giants* 3
		Western	San Francisco 49ers (10-6-0)	Dallas 38, San Francisco 21
1994	American	Eastern	Miami Dolphins (10-6-0)	Pittsburgh 29, Cleveland* 9
		Central	Pittsburgh Steelers (12-4-0)	San Diego 22, Miami 21
		Western	San Diego Chargers (11-5-0)	San Diego 17, Pittsburgh 13
	National	Eastern	Dallas Cowboys (12-4-0)	San Francisco 44, Chicago* 15
		Central	Minnesota Vikings (10-6-0)	Dallas 35, Green Bay* 9
		Western	San Francisco 49ers (13-3-0)	San Francisco 38, Dallas 28
1995	American	Eastern	Buffalo Bills (10-6-0)	Indianapolis* 10, Kansas City 7
		Central	Pittsburgh Steelers (11-5-0)	Pittsburgh 40, Buffalo 21
		Western	Kansas City Chiefs (13-3-0)	Pittsburgh 20, Indianapolis* 16
	National	Eastern	Dallas Cowboys (12-4-0)	Dallas 30, Philadelphia* 11
		Central	Green Bay Packers (11-5-0)	Green Bay 27, San Francisco 17
		Western	San Francisco 49ers (11-5-0)	Dallas 38, Green Bay 27
1996	American	Eastern	New England Patriots (11-5-0)	Jacksonville* 30, Denver 27
		Central	Pittsburgh Steelers (10-6-0)	New England 28, Pittsburgh 3
		Western	Denver Broncos (13-3-0)	New England 20, Jacksonville* 6
	National	Eastern	Dallas Cowboys (10-6-0)	Green Bay 35, San Francisco* 14
		Central	Green Bay Packers (13-3-0)	Carolina 26, Dallas 17
		Western	Carolina Panthers (12-4-0)	Green Bay 30, Carolina 13

(continued)

National Football League Champions *(continued)*

1997	American	Eastern	New England Patriots (10-6-0)	Pittsburgh 7, New England 6
		Central	Pittsburgh Steelers (11-5-0)	Denver* 14, Kansas City 10
		Western	Kansas City Chiefs (13-3-0)	Denver* 24, Pittsburgh 21
	National	Eastern	New York Giants (10-5-1)	San Francisco 38, Minnesota* 22
		Central	Green Bay Packers (13-3-0)	Green Bay 21, Tampa Bay* 7
		Western	San Francisco 49ers (13-3-0)	Green Bay 23, San Francisco 10

*Wild card team. (c) From 1978 on, only the final 2 conference playoff rounds are shown. (d) A strike shortened the 1982 season from 16 to 9 games. The top 8 teams in each conference played in a tournament to determine the conference champion. See below.

AFC playoffs—Miami 28, New England 13; L.A. Raiders 27, Cleveland 10; N.Y. Jets 44, Cincinnati 17; San Diego 31, Pittsburgh 28; N.Y. Jets 17, L.A. Raiders 14; Miami 34, San Diego 13; Miami 14, N.Y. Jets 0. **NFC playoffs**—Washington 31, Detroit 7; Green Bay 41, St. Louis 16; Dallas 30, Tampa Bay 17; Minnesota 30, Atlanta 24; Washington 21, Minnesota 7; Dallas 37, Green Bay 26; Washington 31, Dallas 17. **AFC Champion**—Miami Dolphins. **NFC Champion**—Washington Redskins.

Denver Broncos Defeat Green Bay Packers in Super Bowl XXXII

The Denver Broncos defeated the Green Bay Packers, Jan. 25, 1998, in San Diego, CA. The Broncos, only the second wild card team ever to win a Super Bowl, pulled off a stunning upset, defeating the Packers, 31-24. The victory marked the first Super Bowl win for Denver, which had come up empty in their four previous Super Bowl appearances. Denver running back Terrell Davis rushed for 157 yards and three touchdowns and was named the Super Bowl MVP.

Score by Quarters

Green Bay	7	7	3	7—24
Denver	7	10	7	7—31

Scoring

Green Bay—Freeman 22 yd. pass from Favre (Longwell kick)
Denver—Davis 1 yd. run (Elam kick)
Denver—Elway 1 yd. run (Elam kick)
Denver—Elam 51 yd. field goal
Green Bay—Chmura 6 yd. pass from Favre (Longwell kick)
Green Bay—Longwell 27 yd. field goal
Denver—Davis 1 yd. run (Elam kick)
Green Bay—Freeman 13 yd. pass from Favre (Longwell kick)
Denver—Davis 1 yd. run (Elam kick)

Individual Statistics

Rushing — Green Bay, Levens 19-90, Brooks 1-5. Denver, Davis 30-157, Elway 5-17, Hebron 3-3, Griffith 1-2.

Passing — Green Bay, Favre 25-42-1-256. Denver, Elway 12-22-1-123.

Receiving — Green Bay, Freeman 9-126, Levens 6-56, Chmura 4-43, Brooks 3-16, Henderson 2-9, Mickens 1-6. Denver, Sharpe 5-38, McCaffrey 2-45, Davis 2-8, Griffith 1-23, Hebron 1-5, Carswell 1-4.

Team Statistics

	Green Bay	Denver
First downs	21	21
Total yards	350	302
Rushes-yards	20-95	39-179
Passing yards, net	255	123
Punt returns-yards	0-0	0-0
Kickoff returns-yards	6-104	5-95
Interception returns-yards	1-17	1-0
Comp.-att.-int.	25-42-1	12-22-1
Field goals made-attempts	1-1	1-1
Sacked-yards lost	1-1	0-0
Punts-average	4-35.5	4-36.5
Fumbles-lost	2-2	1-1
Penalties-yards	9-59	7-65
Time of possession	27:35	32:25

Attendance—68,912. Time—3:25.

Super Bowls

	Year	Winner	Loser	Winning coach	Site
I	1967	Green Bay Packers, 35	Kansas City Chiefs, 10	Vince Lombardi	Los Angeles Coliseum, CA
II	1968	Green Bay Packers, 33	Oakland Raiders, 14	Vince Lombardi	Orange Bowl, Miami, FL
III	1969	New York Jets, 16	Baltimore Colts, 7	Weeb Ewbank	Orange Bowl, Miami, FL
IV	1970	Kansas City Chiefs, 23	Minnesota Vikings, 7	Hank Stram	Tulane Stadium, New Orleans, LA
V	1971	Baltimore Colts, 16	Dallas Cowboys, 13	Don McCafferty	Orange Bowl, Miami, FL
VI	1972	Dallas Cowboys, 24	Miami Dolphins, 3	Tom Landry	Tulane Stadium, New Orleans, LA
VII	1973	Miami Dolphins, 14	Washington Redskins, 7	Don Shula	Los Angeles Coliseum, CA
VIII	1974	Miami Dolphins, 24	Minnesota Vikings, 7	Don Shula	Rice Stadium, Houston, TX
IX	1975	Pittsburgh Steelers, 16	Minnesota Vikings, 6	Chuck Noll	Tulane Stadium, New Orleans, LA
X	1976	Pittsburgh Steelers, 21	Dallas Cowboys, 17	Chuck Noll	Orange Bowl, Miami, FL
XI	1977	Oakland Raiders, 32	Minnesota Vikings, 14	John Madden	Rose Bowl, Pasadena, CA
XII	1978	Dallas Cowboys, 27	Denver Broncos, 10	Tom Landry	Superdome, New Orleans, LA
XIII	1979	Pittsburgh Steelers, 35	Dallas Cowboys, 31	Chuck Noll	Orange Bowl, Miami, FL
XIV	1980	Pittsburgh Steelers, 31	Los Angeles Rams, 19	Chuck Noll	Rose Bowl, Pasadena, CA
XV	1981	Oakland Raiders, 27	Philadelphia Eagles, 10	Tom Flores	Superdome, New Orleans, LA
XVI	1982	San Francisco 49ers, 26	Cincinnati Bengals, 21	Bill Walsh	Silverdome, Pontiac, MI
XVII	1983	Washington Redskins, 27	Miami Dolphins, 17	Joe Gibbs	Rose Bowl, Pasadena, CA
XVIII	1984	Los Angeles Raiders, 38	Washington Redskins, 9	Tom Flores	Tampa Stadium, FL
XIX	1985	San Francisco 49ers, 38	Miami Dolphins, 16	Bill Walsh	Stanford Stadium, Palo Alto, CA
XX	1986	Chicago Bears, 46	New England Patriots, 10	Mike Ditka	Superdome, New Orleans, LA
XXI	1987	New York Giants, 39	Denver Broncos, 20	Bill Parcells	Rose Bowl, Pasadena, CA
XXII	1988	Washington Redskins, 42	Denver Broncos, 10	Joe Gibbs	San Diego Stadium, CA
XXIII	1989	San Francisco 49ers, 20	Cincinnati Bengals, 16	Bill Walsh	Joe Robbie Stadium, Miami, FL
XXIV	1990	San Francisco 49ers, 55	Denver Broncos, 10	George Seifert	Superdome, New Orleans, LA
XXV	1991	New York Giants, 20	Buffalo Bills, 19	Bill Parcells	Tampa Stadium, FL
XXVI	1992	Washington Redskins, 37	Buffalo Bills, 24	Joe Gibbs	Metrodome, Minneapolis, MN
XXVII	1993	Dallas Cowboys, 52	Buffalo Bills, 17	Jimmy Johnson	Rose Bowl, Pasadena, CA
XXVIII	1994	Dallas Cowboys, 30	Buffalo Bills, 13	Jimmy Johnson	Georgia Dome, Atlanta, GA
XXIX	1995	San Francisco 49ers, 49	San Diego Chargers, 26	George Seifert	Joe Robbie Stadium, Miami, FL
XXX	1996	Dallas Cowboys, 27	Pittsburgh Steelers, 17	Barry Switzer	Sun Devil Stadium, Tempe, AZ
XXXI	1997	Green Bay Packers, 35	New England Patriots, 21	Mike Holmgren	Superdome, New Orleans, LA
XXXII	1998	Denver Broncos, 31	Green Bay Packers, 24	Mike Shanahan	Qualcomm Stadium, San Diego, CA

Super Bowl MVPs

1967 Bart Starr, Green Bay
1968 Bart Starr, Green Bay
1969 Joe Namath, N.Y. Jets
1970 Len Dawson, Kansas City
1971 Chuck Howley, Dallas
1972 Roger Staubach, Dallas
1973 Jake Scott, Miami
1974 Larry Csonka, Miami
1975 Franco Harris, Pittsburgh
1976 Lynn Swann, Pittsburgh
1977 Fred Biletnikoff, Oakland
1978 Randy White, Harvey Martin, Dallas
1979 Terry Bradshaw, Pittsburgh
1980 Terry Bradshaw, Pittsburgh
1981 Jim Plunkett, Oakland
1982 Joe Montana, San Francisco
1983 John Riggins, Washington
1984 Marcus Allen, L.A. Raiders
1985 Joe Montana, San Francisco
1986 Richard Dent, Chicago
1987 Phil Simms, N.Y. Giants
1988 Doug Williams, Washington
1989 Jerry Rice, San Francisco
1990 Joe Montana, San Francisco
1991 Ottis Anderson, N.Y. Giants
1992 Mark Rypien, Washington
1993 Troy Aikman, Dallas
1994 Emmitt Smith, Dallas
1995 Steve Young, San Francisco
1996 Larry Brown, Dallas
1997 Desmond Howard, Green Bay
1998 Terrell Davis, Denver

American Football Conference Leaders

(American Football League, 1960-69)

Passing[1]

Player, team	Att	Com	YG	TD	Year
Jack Kemp, L.A. Chargers	406	211	3,018	20	**1960**
George Blanda, Houston	362	187	3,330	36	**1961**
Len Dawson, Dallas Texans	310	189	2,759	29	**1962**
Tobin Rote, San Diego	286	170	2,510	20	**1963**
Len Dawson, Kansas City	354	199	2,879	30	**1964**
John Hadl, San Diego	348	174	2,798	20	**1965**
Len Dawson, Kansas City	284	159	2,527	26	**1966**
Daryle Lamonica, Oakland	425	220	3,228	30	**1967**
Len Dawson, Kansas City	224	131	2,109	17	**1968**
Greg Cook, Cincinnati	197	106	1,854	15	**1969**
Daryle Lamonica, Oakland	356	179	2,516	22	**1970**
Bob Griese, Miami	263	145	2,089	19	**1971**
Earl Morrall, Miami	150	83	1,360	11	**1972**
Ken Stabler, Oakland	260	163	1,997	14	**1973**
Ken Anderson, Cincinnati	328	213	2,667	18	**1974**
Ken Anderson, Cincinnati	377	228	3,169	21	**1975**
Ken Stabler, Oakland	291	194	2,737	27	**1976**
Bob Griese, Miami	307	180	2,252	22	**1977**
Terry Bradshaw, Pittsburgh	368	207	2,915	28	**1978**
Dan Fouts, San Diego	530	332	4,082	24	**1979**
Brian Sipe, Cleveland	554	337	4,132	30	**1980**
Ken Anderson, Cincinnati	479	300	3,754	29	**1981**
Ken Anderson, Cincinnati	309	218	2,495	12	**1982**
Dan Marino, Miami	296	173	2,210	20	**1983**
Dan Marino, Miami	564	362	5,084	48	**1984**
Ken O'Brien, N.Y. Jets	488	297	3,888	25	**1985**
Dan Marino, Miami	623	378	4,746	44	**1986**
Bernie Kosar, Cleveland	389	241	3,033	22	**1987**
Boomer Esiason, Cincinnati	388	223	3,572	28	**1988**
Boomer Esiason, Cincinnati	455	258	3,525	28	**1989**
Jim Kelly, Buffalo	346	219	2,829	24	**1990**
Jim Kelly, Buffalo	474	304	3,844	33	**1991**
Warren Moon, Houston	346	224	2,521	18	**1992**
John Elway, Denver	551	348	4,030	25	**1993**
Dan Marino, Miami	615	385	4,453	30	**1994**
Jim Harbaugh, Indianapolis	314	200	2,575	17	**1995**
John Elway, Denver	466	287	3,328	26	**1996**
Mark Brunell, Jacksonville	435	264	3,281	18	**1997**

Pass-Receiving

Year	Player, team	Ct	YG	TD
1960	Lionel Taylor, Denver	92	1,235	12
1961	Lionel Taylor, Denver	100	1,176	4
1962	Lionel Taylor, Denver	77	908	4
1963	Lionel Taylor, Denver	78	1,101	10
1964	Charley Hennigan, Houston	101	1,546	8
1965	Lionel Taylor, Denver	85	1,131	6
1966	Lance Alworth, San Diego	73	1,383	13
1967	George Sauer, N.Y. Jets	75	1,189	6
1968	Lance Alworth, San Diego	68	1,312	10
1969	Lance Alworth, San Diego	64	1,003	4
1970	Marlin Briscoe, Buffalo	57	1,036	8
1971	Fred Biletnikoff, Oakland	61	929	9
1972	Fred Biletnikoff, Oakland	58	802	7
1973	Fred Willis, Houston	57	371	1
1974	Lydell Mitchell, Baltimore Colts	72	544	2
1975	Reggie Rucker, Cleveland	60	770	3
	Lydell Mitchell, Baltimore Colts	60	554	4
1976	MacArthur Lane, Kansas City	66	686	1
1977	Lydell Mitchell, Baltimore Colts	71	620	4
1978	Steve Largent, Seattle	71	1,168	8
1979	Joe Washington, Baltimore Colts	82	750	3
1980	Kellen Winslow, San Diego	89	1,290	9
1981	Kellen Winslow, San Diego	88	1,075	10
1982	Kellen Winslow, San Diego	54	721	6
1983	Todd Christensen, L.A. Raiders	92	1,247	12
1984	Ozzie Newsome, Cleveland	89	1,001	5
1985	Lionel James, San Diego	86	1,027	6
1986	Todd Christensen, L.A. Raiders	95	1,153	8
1987	Al Toon, N.Y. Jets	68	976	5
1988	Al Toon, N.Y. Jets	93	1,067	5
1989	Andre Reed, Buffalo	88	1,312	9
1990	Haywood Jeffires, Houston	74	1,048	8
	Drew Hill, Houston	74	1,019	5
1991	Haywood Jeffires, Houston	100	1,181	7
1992	Haywood Jeffires, Houston	90	913	9
1993	Reggie Langhorne, Indianapolis	85	1,038	3
1994	Ben Coates, New England	96	1,174	7
1995	Carl Pickens, Cincinnati	99	1,234	17
1996	Carl Pickens, Cincinnati	100	1,180	12
1997	Tim Brown, Oakland	104	1,408	5

Scoring

Player, team	TD	PAT	FG	Pts	Year
Gene Mingo, Denver	6	33	18	123	**1960**
Gino Cappelletti, Boston	8	48	17	147	**1961**
Gene Mingo, Denver	4	32	27	137	**1962**
Gino Cappelletti, Boston	2	35	22	113	**1963**
Gino Cappelletti, Boston	7	36	25	155	**1964**
Gino Cappelletti, Boston	9	27	17	132	**1965**
Gino Cappelletti, Boston	6	35	16	119	**1966**
George Blanda, Oakland	0	56	20	116	**1967**
Jim Turner, N.Y. Jets	0	43	34	145	**1968**
Jim Turner, N.Y. Jets	0	33	32	129	**1969**
Jan Stenerud, Kansas City	0	26	30	116	**1970**
Garo Yepremian, Miami	0	33	28	117	**1971**
Bobby Howfield, N.Y. Jets	0	40	27	121	**1972**
Roy Gerela, Pittsburgh	0	36	29	123	**1973**
Roy Gerela, Pittsburgh	0	33	20	93	**1974**
O.J. Simpson, Buffalo	23	0	0	138	**1975**
Toni Linhart, Baltimore Colts	0	49	20	109	**1976**
Errol Mann, Oakland	0	39	20	99	**1977**
Pat Leahy, N.Y. Jets	0	41	22	107	**1978**
John Smith, New England	0	46	23	115	**1979**
John Smith, New England	0	51	26	129	**1980**
Jim Breech, Cincinnati	0	49	22	115	**1981**
Nick Lowery, Kansas City	0	37	26	115	
Marcus Allen, L.A. Raiders	14	0	0	84	**1982**
Gary Anderson, Pittsburgh	0	38	27	119	**1983**
Gary Anderson, Pittsburgh	0	45	24	117	**1984**
Gary Anderson, Pittsburgh	0	40	33	139	**1985**
Tony Franklin, New England	0	44	32	140	**1986**
Jim Breech, Cincinnati	0	25	24	97	**1987**
Scott Norwood, Buffalo	0	33	32	129	**1988**
David Treadwell, Denver	0	39	27	120	**1989**
Nick Lowery, Kansas City	0	37	34	139	**1990**
Pete Stoyanovich, Miami	0	28	31	121	**1991**
Pete Stoyanovich, Miami	0	34	30	124	**1992**
Jeff Jaeger, L.A. Raiders	0	27	35	132	**1993**
John Carney, San Diego	0	33	34	135	**1994**
Norm Johnson, Pittsburgh	0	39	34	141	**1995**
Cary Blanchard, Indianapolis	0	27	36	135	**1996**
Mike Hollis, Jacksonville	0	41	31	134	**1997**

Rushing

Year	Player, team	Yds	Att	TD
1960	Abner Haynes, Dallas Texans	875	156	9
1961	Billy Cannon, Houston	948	200	6
1962	Cookie Gilchrest, Buffalo	1,096	214	13
1963	Clem Daniels, Oakland	1,099	215	3
1964	Cookie Gilchrest, Buffalo	981	230	6
1965	Paul Lowe, San Diego	1,121	222	7
1966	Jim Nance, Boston	1,458	299	11
1967	Jim Nance, Boston	1,216	269	7
1968	Paul Robinson, Cincinnati	1,023	238	8
1969	Dick Post, San Diego	873	182	6
1970	Floyd Little, Denver	901	209	3
1971	Floyd Little, Denver	1,133	284	6
1972	O.J. Simpson, Buffalo	1,251	292	6
1973	O.J. Simpson, Buffalo	2,003	332	12
1974	Otis Armstrong, Denver	1,407	263	9
1975	O.J. Simpson, Buffalo	1,817	329	16
1976	O.J. Simpson, Buffalo	1,503	290	8
1977	Mark van Eeghen, Oakland	1,273	324	7
1978	Earl Campbell, Houston	1,450	302	13
1979	Earl Campbell, Houston	1,697	368	19
1980	Earl Campbell, Houston	1,934	373	13
1981	Earl Campbell, Houston	1,376	361	10
1982	Freeman McNeil, N.Y. Jets	786	151	6
1983	Curt Warner, Seattle	1,446	335	13
1984	Earnest Jackson, San Diego	1,179	296	8
1985	Marcus Allen, L.A. Raiders	1,759	380	11
1986	Curt Warner, Seattle	1,481	319	13
1987	Eric Dickerson, L.A. Rams-Ind.	1,288*	283	6
1988	Eric Dickerson, Indianapolis	1,659	388	14
1989	Christian Okoye, Kansas City	1,480	370	12
1990	Thurman Thomas, Buffalo	1,297	271	11
1991	Thurman Thomas, Buffalo	1,407	288	7
1992	Barry Foster, Pittsburgh	1,690	390	11
1993	Thurman Thomas, Buffalo	1,315	355	6
1994	Chris Warren, Seattle	1,545	333	9
1995	Curtis Martin, New England	1,487	368	14
1996	Terrell Davis, Denver	1,538	345	13
1997	Terrell Davis, Denver	1,750	369	15

*Includes 277 yards after being traded to NFC; 1,011 yards led AFC. (1) Based on quarterback ranking points.

National Football Conference Leaders

(National Football League, 1960-69)

Passing[1]

Player, team	Att	Com	YG	TD	Year
Milt Plum, Cleveland	250	151	2,297	21	**1960**
Milt Plum, Cleveland	302	177	2,416	18	**1961**
Bart Starr, Green Bay	285	178	2,438	12	**1962**
Y.A. Tittle, N.Y. Giants	367	221	3,145	36	**1963**
Bart Starr, Green Bay	272	163	2,144	15	**1964**
Rudy Bukich, Chicago	312	176	2,641	20	**1965**
Bart Starr, Green Bay	251	156	2,257	14	**1966**
Sonny Jurgensen, Washington	508	288	3,747	31	**1967**
Earl Morrall, Baltimore Colts	317	182	2,909	26	**1968**
Sonny Jurgensen, Washington	442	274	3,102	22	**1969**
John Brodie, San Francisco	378	223	2,941	24	**1970**
Roger Staubach, Dallas	211	126	1,882	15	**1971**
Norm Snead, N.Y. Giants	325	196	2,307	17	**1972**
Roger Staubach, Dallas	286	179	2,428	23	**1973**
Sonny Jurgensen, Washington	167	107	1,185	11	**1974**
Fran Tarkenton, Minnesota	425	273	2,994	25	**1975**
James Harris, L.A. Rams	158	91	1,460	8	**1976**
Roger Staubach, Dallas	361	210	2,620	18	**1977**
Roger Staubach, Dallas	413	231	3,190	25	**1978**
Roger Staubach, Dallas	461	267	3,586	27	**1979**
Ron Jaworski, Philadelphia	451	257	3,529	27	**1980**
Joe Montana, San Francisco	488	311	3,565	19	**1981**
Joe Thiesmann, Washington	252	161	2,033	13	**1982**
Steve Bartkowski, Atlanta	432	274	3,167	22	**1983**
Joe Montana, San Francisco	432	279	3,630	28	**1984**
Joe Montana, San Francisco	494	303	3,653	27	**1985**
Tommy Kramer, Minnesota	372	208	3,000	24	**1986**
Joe Montana, San Francisco	398	266	3,054	31	**1987**
Wade Wilson, Minnesota	332	204	2,746	15	**1988**
Joe Montana, San Francisco	386	271	3,521	26	**1989**
Phil Simms, N.Y. Giants	311	184	2,284	15	**1990**
Steve Young, San Francisco	279	180	2,517	17	**1991**
Steve Young, San Francisco	402	268	3,465	25	**1992**
Steve Young, San Francisco	462	314	4,023	29	**1993**
Steve Young, San Francisco	461	324	3,969	35	**1994**
Brett Favre, Green Bay	570	359	4,413	38	**1995**
Steve Young, San Francisco	316	214	2,410	14	**1996**
Steve Young, San Francisco	356	241	3,029	19	**1997**

Pass-Receiving

Year	Player, team	Ct	YG	TD
1960	Raymond Berry, Baltimore Colts	74	1,298	10
1961	Jim Phillips, L.A. Rams	78	1,092	5
1962	Bobby Mitchell, Washington	72	1,384	11
1963	Bobby Joe Conrad, St.L. Cardinals	73	967	10
1964	Johnny Morris, Chicago	93	1,200	10
1965	Dave Parks, San Francisco	80	1,344	12
1966	Charley Taylor, Washington	72	1,119	12
1967	Charley Taylor, Washington	70	990	9
1968	Clifton McNeil, San Francisco	71	994	7
1969	Dan Abramowicz, New Orleans	73	1,015	7
1970	Dick Gordon, Chicago	71	1,026	13
1971	Bob Tucker, N.Y. Giants	59	791	4
1972	Harold Jackson, Philadelphia	62	1,048	4
1973	Harold Carmichael, Philadelphia	67	1,116	9
1974	Charles Young, Philadelphia	63	696	3
1975	Chuck Foreman, Minnesota	73	691	9
1976	Drew Pearson, Dallas	58	806	6
1977	Ahmad Rashad, Minnesota	51	681	2
1978	Rickey Young, Minnesota	88	704	5
1979	Ahmad Rashad, Minnesota	80	1,156	9
1980	Earl Cooper, San Francisco	83	567	4
1981	Dwight Clark, San Francisco	85	1,105	4
1982	Dwight Clark, San Francisco	60	913	5
1983	Roy Green, St. Louis Cardinals	78	1,227	14
	Charlie Brown, Washington	78	1,225	8
	Earnest Gray, N.Y. Giants	78	1,139	5
1984	Art Monk, Washington	106	1,372	7
1985	Roger Craig, San Francisco	92	1,016	6
1986	Jerry Rice, San Francisco	86	1,570	15
1987	J.T. Smith, St. Louis Cardinals	91	1,117	8
1988	Henry Ellard, L.A. Rams	86	1,414	10
1989	Sterling Sharpe, Green Bay	90	1,423	12
1990	Jerry Rice, San Francisco	100	1,502	13
1991	Michael Irvin, Dallas	93	1,523	8
1992	Sterling Sharpe, Green Bay	108	1,461	13
1993	Sterling Sharpe, Green Bay	112	1,274	11
1994	Cris Carter, Minnesota	122	1,256	7
1995	Herman Moore, Detroit	123	1,686	14
1996	Jerry Rice, San Francisco	108	1,254	8
1997	Herman Moore, Detroit	104	1,293	8

Scoring

Player, team	TD	PAT	FG	Pts	Year
Paul Hornung, Green Bay	15	41	15	176	**1960**
Paul Hornung, Green Bay	10	41	15	146	**1961**
Jim Taylor, Green Bay	19	0	0	114	**1962**
Don Chandler, N.Y. Giants	0	52	18	106	**1963**
Lenny Moore, Baltimore Colts	20	0	0	120	**1964**
Gale Sayers, Chicago	22	0	0	132	**1965**
Bruce Gossett, L.A. Rams	0	29	28	113	**1966**
Jim Bakken, St. Louis Cardinals	0	36	27	117	**1967**
Leroy Kelly, Cleveland	20	0	0	120	**1968**
Fred Cox, Minnesota	0	43	26	121	**1969**
Fred Cox, Minnesota	0	35	30	125	**1970**
Curt Knight, Washington	0	27	29	114	**1971**
Chester Marcol, Green Bay	0	29	33	128	**1972**
David Ray, L.A. Rams	0	40	30	130	**1973**
Chester Marcol, Green Bay	0	19	25	94	**1974**
Chuck Foreman, Minnesota	22	0	0	132	**1975**
Mark Moseley, Washington	0	31	22	97	**1976**
Walter Payton, Chicago	16	0	0	96	**1977**
Frank Corral, L.A. Rams	0	31	29	118	**1978**
Mark Moseley, Washington	0	39	25	114	**1979**
Ed Murray, Detroit	0	35	27	116	**1980**
Ed Murray, Detroit	0	46	25	121	**1981**
Rafael Septien, Dallas	0	40	27	121	
Wendell Tyler, L.A. Rams	13	0	0	78	**1982**
Mark Moseley, Washington	0	62	33	161	**1983**
Ray Wersching, San Francisco	0	56	25	131	**1984**
Kevin Butler, Chicago	0	51	31	144	**1985**
Kevin Butler, Chicago	0	36	28	120	**1986**
Jerry Rice, San Francisco	23	0	0	138	**1987**
Mike Cofer, San Francisco	0	40	27	121	**1988**
Mike Cofer, San Francisco	0	49	29	136	**1989**
Chip Lohmiller, Washington	0	41	30	131	**1990**
Chip Lohmiller, Washington	0	56	31	149	**1991**
Morten Andersen, New Orleans	0	33	29	120	**1992**
Chip Lohmiller, Washington	0	30	30	120	
Jason Hanson, Detroit	0	28	34	130	**1993**
Fuad Reveiz, Minnesota	0	30	34	132	**1994**
Emmitt Smith, Dallas	22	0	0	132	
Emmitt Smith, Dallas	25	0	0	150	**1995**
John Kasay, Carolina	0	34	37	145	**1996**
Richie Cunningham, Dallas	0	24	34	126	**1997**

Rushing

Year	Player, team	Yds	Att	TD
1960	Jim Brown, Cleveland	1,257	215	9
1961	Jim Brown, Cleveland	1,408	305	8
1962	Jim Taylor, Green Bay	1,474	272	19
1963	Jim Brown, Cleveland	1,863	291	12
1964	Jim Brown, Cleveland	1,446	280	7
1965	Jim Brown, Cleveland	1,544	289	17
1966	Gale Sayers, Chicago	1,231	229	8
1967	Leroy Kelly, Cleveland	1,205	235	11
1968	Leroy Kelly, Cleveland	1,239	248	16
1969	Gale Sayers, Chicago	1,032	236	8
1970	Larry Brown, Washington	1,125	237	5
1971	John Brockington, Green Bay	1,105	216	4
1972	Larry Brown, Washington	1,216	285	8
1973	John Brockington, Green Bay	1,144	265	3
1974	Lawrence McCutcheon, L.A. Rams	1,109	236	3
1975	Jim Otis, St. Louis Cardinals	1,076	269	5
1976	Walter Payton, Chicago	1,390	311	13
1977	Walter Payton, Chicago	1,852	339	14
1978	Walter Payton, Chicago	1,395	333	11
1979	Walter Payton, Chicago	1,610	369	14
1980	Walter Payton, Chicago	1,460	317	6
1981	George Rogers, New Orleans	1,674	378	13
1982	Tony Dorsett, Dallas	745	177	5
1983	Eric Dickerson, L.A. Rams	1,808	390	18
1984	Eric Dickerson, L.A. Rams	2,105	379	14
1985	Gerald Riggs, Atlanta	1,719	397	10
1986	Eric Dickerson, L.A. Rams	1,821	404	11
1987	Charles White, L.A. Rams	1,374	324	11
1988	Herschel Walker, Dallas	1,514	361	5
1989	Barry Sanders, Detroit	1,470	280	14
1990	Barry Sanders, Detroit	1,304	255	13
1991	Emmitt Smith, Dallas	1,563	365	12
1992	Emmitt Smith, Dallas	1,713	373	18
1993	Emmitt Smith, Dallas	1,486	283	9
1994	Barry Sanders, Detroit	1,883	331	7
1995	Emmitt Smith, Dallas	1,773	377	25
1996	Barry Sanders, Detroit	1,553	307	11
1997	Barry Sanders, Detroit	2,053	335	11

(1) Based on quarterback ranking points.

1997 NFL Individual Leaders

American Football Conference

Passing

	Att	Comp	Pct comp	Yds	Avg gain	Long	TD	Pct TD	Int	Rating points
Mark Brunell, Jacksonville	455	264	60.7	3,281	7.54	75	18	4.1	7	91.2
Jeff George, Oakland	521	290	55.7	3,917	7.52	76	29	5.6	9	91.2
Drew Bledsoe, New England	522	314	60.2	3,706	7.10	76	28	5.4	15	87.7
John Elway, Denver	502	280	55.8	3,635	7.24	78	27	5.4	11	87.5
Jim Harbaugh, Indianapolis	309	189	61.2	2,060	6.67	58	10	3.2	4	86.2
Warren Moon, Seattle	528	313	59.3	3,678	6.97	60td	25	4.7	16	83.7
Dan Marino, Miami	548	319	58.2	3,780	6.90	55	16	2.9	11	80.7
Neil O'Donnell, N.Y. Jets	460	259	56.3	2,796	6.08	70	17	3.7	7	80.3
Elvis Grbac, Kansas City	314	179	57.0	1,943	6.19	55td	11	3.5	6	79.1
Jeff Blake, Cincinnati	317	184	58.0	2,125	6.70	50td	10	2.5	7	77.6
Vinny Testaverde, Baltimore	470	271	57.7	2,971	6.32	54td	18	3.8	15	75.9
Cordell Stewart, Pittsburgh	440	236	53.6	3,020	6.86	69td	21	4.8	17	75.2

Rushing

	Att	Yds	Avg	Long	TD
Terrell Davis, Denver	369	1,750	4.7	50td	15
Jerome Bettis, Pittsburgh	375	1,665	4.4	34	7
Eddie George, Houston	357	1,399	3.9	30	6
Napoleon Kaufman, Oakland	272	1,294	4.8	83td	6
Curtis Martin, New England	274	1,160	4.2	70td	4
Corey Dillon, Cincinnati	233	1,129	4.8	71td	10
Adrian Murrell, N.Y. Jets	300	1,086	3.6	43td	7
Marshall Faulk, Indianapolis	264	1,054	4.0	45	7
Gary Brown, San Diego	253	945	3.7	32	4
Karim Abdul-Jabbar, Miami	283	892	3.2	22	15

Pass Receiving

	No.	Yds	Avg	Long	TD
Tim Brown, Oakland	104	1,408	13.5	59td	5
Keenan McCardell, Jacksonville	85	1,164	13.7	60	5
Jimmy Smith, Jacksonville	82	1,324	16.1	75	4
Yancey Thigpen, Pittsburgh	79	1,398	17.7	69td	7
O. J. McDuffie, Miami	76	943	12.4	55	1
Marvin Harrison, Indianapolis	73	866	11.9	44	6
Shannon Sharpe, Denver	72	1,107	15.4	68td	3
Andre Rison, Kansas City	72	1,092	15.2	45	7
Joey Galloway, Seattle	72	1,049	14.6	53td	12
Rod Smith, Denver	70	1,180	16.9	78	12

Scoring—Non-Kickers

	TD	Rush	Pass	2 Pt	Pts
Karim Abdul-Jabbar	16	15	1	0	96
Terrell Davis, Denver	15	15	0	3	96
Joey Galloway, Seattle	12	0	12	0	72
James Jett, Oakland	12	0	12	0	72
Rod Smith, Denver	12	0	12	0	72

Scoring—Kickers

	PAT	FG	Long	Pts
Mike Hollis, Jacksonville	41/41	31/36	52	134
Jason Elam, Denver	46/46	26/36	53	124
John Hall, N.Y. Jets	36/36	28/41	55	120
Cary Blanchard, Indianapolis	21/21	32/41	50	117
Olindo Mare, Miami	33/33	28/36	50	117
Adam Vinatieri, New England	40/40	25/29	52	115
Al Del Greco, Tennessee	32/32	27/35	52	113
Pete Stoyanovich, Kansas City	35/36	26/27	54	113
Matt Stover, Baltimore	32/32	26/34	49	110
Greg Davis, Min.-San Diego	31/32	26/34	45	109

Interceptions

	No.	Yds	Avg	Long	TD
Mark McMillan, Kansas City	8	274	34.3	87td	3
Darryl Williams, Seattle	8	172	21.5	44td	1
Otis Smith, N.Y. Jets	6	158	26.3	51td	3
Willie Clay, New England	6	109	18.2	53td	1
Marcus Robertson, Tennessee	5	127	25.4	48	0
Darryl Lewis, Tennessee	5	115	23.0	47td	1
Deon Figures, Jacksonville	5	48	9.6	32	0

Kickoff Returns

	No.	Yds	Avg	Long	TD
Aaron Glenn, N.Y. Jets	28	741	26.5	96td	1
Tamarick Vanover, Kansas City	50	1,283	25.7	94td	1
Dave Megget, New England	33	816	24.7	61	0
Will Blackwell, Pittsburgh	32	791	24.7	97td	1
Irving Spikes, Miami	24	565	23.5	48	0
Vaughn Hebron, Denver	43	1,009	23.5	46	0

Punt Returns

	No.	Yds	Avg	Long	TD
Jermaine Lewis, Baltimore	28	437	15.6	89td	2
Darrien Gordon, San Diego	40	543	13.6	94td	3
Leon Johnson, N.Y. Jets	51	619	12.1	66td	1
Reggie Barlow, Jacksonville	36	412	11.4	52	0
Tamarick Vanover, Kansas City	35	383	10.9	82td	1
Eric Metcalf, San Diego	45	489	10.9	85td	3

Punting

	No.	Yds	Long	Avg
Tom Tupa, New England	78	3,569	73	45.8
Chris Gardocki, Indianapolis	67	3,034	72	45.3
Leo Araguz, Oakland	93	4,189	63	45.0
Bryan Barker, Jacksonville	66	2,964	64	44.9
Darren Bennett, San Diego	89	3,972	66	44.6

Sacks

	No.
Bruce Smith, Buffalo	14.0
Mike Sinclair, Seattle	12.0
Peter Boulware, Baltimore	11.5
Dan Footman, Indianapolis	10.5
Dan Williams, Kansas City	10.5
Bryce Paup, Buffalo	9.5
Derrick Thomas, Kansas City	9.5

National Football Conference

Passing

	Att	Comp	Pct comp	Yds	Avg gain	Long	TD	Pct TD	Int	Rating points
Steve Young, San Francisco	356	241	67.7	3,029	8.51	82	19	5.3	6	104.7
Chris Chandler, Atlanta	342	202	59.1	2,692	7.87	56	20	5.8	7	95.1
Brett Favre, Green Bay	513	304	59.3	3,867	7.54	74	35	6.8	16	92.6
Brad Johnson, Minnesota	452	275	60.8	3,036	6.72	56	20	4.4	12	84.5
Bobby Hoying, Philadelphia	225	128	56.9	1,573	6.99	72td	11	4.9	6	83.8
Trent Dilfer, Tampa Bay	386	217	56.2	2,555	6.62	59td	21	5.4	11	82.8
Scott Mitchell, Detroit	509	293	57.6	3,484	6.84	79	19	3.7	14	79.6
Troy Aikman, Dallas	518	292	56.4	3,283	6.34	64td	19	3.7	12	78.0
Erik Kramer, Chicago	477	275	57.7	3,011	6.31	78td	14	2.9	14	74.0
Ty Detmer, Philadelphia	244	134	54.9	1,567	6.42	57	7	2.9	6	73.9
Gus Frerotte, Washington	402	204	50.7	2,682	6.67	52	17	4.2	12	73.8
Jake Plummer, Arizona	296	157	53.0	2,203	7.44	70td	15	5.1	15	73.1

Rushing

	Att	Yds	Avg	Long	TD
Barry Sanders, Detroit	335	2,053	6.1	82td	11
Dorsey Levens, Green Bay	329	1,435	4.4	52td	7
Robert Smith, Minnesota	232	1,266	5.5	78td	6
Ricky Watters, Philadelphia	285	1,110	3.9	28	7
Emmitt Smith, Dallas	261	1,074	4.1	44	4
Raymont Harris, Chicago	275	1,033	3.8	68td	10
Garrison Hearst, San Francisco	234	1,019	4.4	51	4
Jamal Anderson, Atlanta	290	1,002	3.5	39	7
Warrick Dunn, Tampa Bay	224	978	4.4	76	4
Fred Lane, Carolina	182	809	4.4	50	7

Receiving

	No.	Yds	Avg	Long	TD
Herman Moore, Detroit	104	1,293	12.4	79	8
Rob Moore, Arizona	97	1,584	16.3	47td	8
Cris Carter, Minnesota	89	1,069	12.0	43	13
Irving Fryar, Philadelphia	86	1,316	15.3	72td	6
Antonio Freeman, Green Bay	81	1,243	15.3	58td	12
Johnnie Morton, Detroit	80	1,057	13.2	73td	6
Michael Irvin, Dallas	75	1,180	15.7	55	9
Frank Sanders, Arizona	75	1,017	13.6	70td	4
Jake Reed, Minnesota	68	1,138	16.7	56	6
Bert Emanuel, Atlanta	65	991	15.2	56	9

Scoring—Non-Kickers

	TD	Rush	Pass	2 Pt	Pts
Cris Carter, Minnesota	13	0	13	3	84
Barry Sanders, Detroit	14	11	3	0	84
Dorsey Levens, Green Bay	12	7	5	1	74
Antonio Freeman, Green Bay	12	0	12	0	72
Mike Alstott, Tampa Bay	10	7	3	0	60
Jamal Anderson, Atlanta	10	7	3	0	60
Raymont Harris, Chicago	10	10	0	0	60

Scoring—Kickers

	PAT	FG	Long	Pts
Richie Cunningham, Dallas	24/24	34/37	53	126
Gary Anderson, San Francisco	38/38	29/36	51	125
Ryan Longwell, Green Bay	48/48	24/30	50	120
Jason Hanson, Detroit	39/40	26/29	55	117
Jeff Wilkins, St. Louis	32/32	25/37	52	107

Interceptions

	No.	Yds	Avg	Long	TD
Ryan McNeil, St. Louis	9	127	14.1	75td	1
Keith Lyle, St. Louis	8	102	12.8	39	0
Merton Hanks, San Francisco	6	103	17.2	55td	1
Aeneas Williams, Arizona	6	95	15.8	42td	2
Jason Sehorn, N.Y. Giants	6	74	12.3	41	1

Kickoff Returns

	No.	Yds	Avg	Long	TD
Michael Bates, Carolina	47	1,281	27.3	56	0
Eric Guliford, New Orleans	43	1,128	26.2	102td	1
Kevin Williams, Arizona	59	1,458	24.7	63	0
Byron Hanspard, Atlanta	40	987	24.7	99td	2
Duce Staley, Philadelphia	47	1,139	24.2	57	0

Punt Returns

	No.	Yds	Avg	Long	TD
David Palmer, Minnesota	34	444	13.1	57	0
Karl Williams, Tampa Bay	46	597	13.0	63	1
Deion Sanders, Dallas	33	407	12.3	83td	1
Brian Mitchell, Washington	38	442	11.6	63td	1
Kevin Williams, Arizona	40	462	11.6	50	0

Punting

	No.	Yds	Long	Avg
Mark Royals, New Orleans	88	4,038	66	45.9
Matt Turk, Washington	84	3,788	62	45.1
Craig Hentrich, Green Bay	75	3,378	65	45.0
Jeff Feagles, Arizona	91	4,028	62	44.3
Mitch Berger, Minnesota	73	3,133	65	42.9
Mike Horan, St. Louis	53	2,272	60	42.9

Sacks

	No.
John Randle, Minnesota	15.5
Dana Stubblefield, San Francisco	15.0
Michael Strahan, N.Y. Giants	14.0
Robert Porcher, Detroit	12.5
Chris Doleman, San Francisco	12.0
Chuck Smith, Atlanta	12.0

NFL MVP, Defensive Player of the Year, and Rookie of the Year

The Most Valuable Player is one of many awards given out annually by the Associated Press. The George Halas Trophy is awarded to the outstanding defensive player as chosen by a panel of sports experts. Rookie of the Year is one of many awards given out annually by *The Sporting News*. Many other organizations give out annual awards honoring the NFL's finest players.

Most Valuable Player

1957 Jim Brown, Cleveland
1958 Gino Marchetti, Baltimore Colts
1959 Charley Conerly, N.Y. Giants
1960 Norm Van Brocklin, Philadelphia; Joe Schmidt, Detroit
1961 Paul Hornung, Green Bay
1962 Jim Taylor, Green Bay
1963 Y.A. Tittle, N.Y. Giants
1964 John Unitas, Baltimore Colts
1965 Jim Brown, Cleveland
1966 Bart Starr, Green Bay
1967 John Unitas, Baltimore Colts
1968 Earl Morrall, Baltimore Colts
1969 Roman Gabriel, L.A. Rams
1970 John Brodie, San Francisco
1971 Alan Page, Minnesota
1972 Larry Brown, Washington
1973 O.J. Simpson, Buffalo
1974 Ken Stabler, Oakland
1975 Fran Tarkenton, Minnesota
1976 Bert Jones, Baltimore
1977 Walter Payton, Chicago
1978 Terry Bradshaw, Pittsburgh
1979 Earl Campbell, Houston
1980 Brian Sipe, Cleveland
1981 Ken Anderson, Cincinnati
1982 Mark Moseley, Washington
1983 Joe Theismann, Washington
1984 Dan Marino, Miami
1985 Marcus Allen, L.A. Raiders
1986 Lawrence Taylor, N.Y. Giants
1987 John Elway, Denver
1988 Boomer Esiason, Cincinnati
1989 Joe Montana, San Francisco
1990 Joe Montana, San Francisco
1991 Thurman Thomas, Buffalo
1992 Steve Young, San Francisco
1993 Emmitt Smith, Dallas
1994 Steve Young, San Francisco
1995 Brett Favre, Green Bay
1996 Brett Favre, Green Bay
1997 (tie) Brett Favre, Green Bay; Barry Sanders, Detroit

Defensive Player of the Year

1966 Larry Wilson, St. Louis
1967 Deacon Jones, Los Angeles
1968 Deacon Jones, Los Angeles
1969 Dick Butkus, Chicago
1970 Dick Butkus, Chicago
1971 Carl Eller, Minnesota
1972 Joe Greene, Pittsburgh
1973 Alan Page, Minnesota
1974 Joe Greene, Pittsburgh
1975 Curley Culp, Houston
1976 Jerry Sherk, Cleveland
1977 Harvey Martin, Dallas
1978 Randy Gradishar, Denver
1979 Lee Roy Selmon, Tampa Bay
1980 Lester Hayes, Oakland
1981 Joe Klecko, N.Y. Jets
1982 Mark Gastineau, N.Y. Jets
1983 Jack Lambert, Pittsburgh
1984 Mike Haynes, L.A. Raiders
1985 Howie Long, L.A. Raiders; Andre Tippett, New England
1986 Lawrence Taylor, N.Y. Giants
1987 Reggie White, Philadelphia
1988 Mike Singletary, Chicago
1989 Tim Harris, Green Bay
1990 Bruce Smith, Buffalo
1991 Pat Swilling, New Orleans
1992 Junior Seau, San Diego
1993 Bruce Smith, Buffalo
1994 Deion Sanders, San Francisco
1995 Bryce Paup, Buffalo
1996 Bruce Smith, Buffalo
1997 Dana Stubblefield, San Francisco

Rookie of the Year

1964 Charley Taylor, Washington
1965 Gale Sayers, Chicago
1966 Tommy Nobis, Atlanta
1967 Mel Farr, Detroit
1968 Earl McCullouch, Detroit
1969 Calvin Hill, Dallas
1970 NFC: Bruce Taylor, San Francisco; AFC: Dennis Shaw, Buffalo
1971 NFC: John Brockington, Green Bay; AFC: Jim Plunkett, New England
1972 NFC: Chester Marcol, Green Bay; AFC: Franco Harris, Pittsburgh
1973 NFC: Chuck Foreman, Minnesota; AFC: Boobie Clark, Cincinnati
1974 NFC: Wilbur Jackson, San Francisco; AFC: Don Woods, San Diego
1975 NFC: Steve Bartkowski, Atlanta; AFC: Robert Brazile, Houston
1976 NFC: Sammy White, Minnesota; AFC: Mike Haynes, New England
1977 NFC: Tony Dorsett, Dallas; AFC: A. J. Duhe, Miami
1978 NFC: Al Baker, Detroit; AFC: Earl Campbell, Houston
1979 NFC: Ottis Anderson, St. Louis; AFC: Jerry Butler, Buffalo
1980 Billy Sims, Detroit
1981 George Rogers, New Orleans
1982 Marcus Allen, L.A. Raiders
1983 Dan Marino, Miami
1984 Louis Lipps, Pittsburgh
1985 Eddie Brown, Cincinnati
1986 Rueben Mayes, New Orleans
1987 Robert Awalt, St. Louis
1988 Keith Jackson, Philadelphia
1989 Barry Sanders, Detroit
1990 Richmond Webb, Miami
1991 Mike Croel, Denver
1992 Santana Dotson, Tampa Bay
1993 Jerome Bettis, L.A. Rams
1994 Marshall Faulk, Indianapolis
1995 Curtis Martin, New England
1996 Eddie George, Houston
1997 Warrick Dunn, Tampa Bay

Number One NFL Draft Choices, 1936-98

Year	Team	Player, Pos., College
1936	Philadelphia	Jay Berwanger, HB, Chicago
1937	Philadelphia	Sam Francis, FB, Nebraska
1938	Cleveland Rams	Corbett Davis, FB, Indiana
1939	Chicago Cards	Ki Aldrich, C, TCU
1940	Chicago Cards	George Cafego, HB, Tennessee
1941	Chicago Bears	Tom Harmon, HB, Michigan
1942	Pittsburgh	Bill Dudley, HB, Virginia
1943	Detroit	Frank Sinkwich, HB, Georgia
1944	Boston Yanks	Angelo Bertelli, QB, Notre Dame
1945	Chicago Cards	Charley Trippi, HB, Georgia
1946	Boston Yanks	Frank Dancewicz, QB, Notre Dame
1947	Chicago Bears	Bob Fenimore, HB, Okla. A&M
1948	Washington	Harry Gilmer, QB, Alabama
1949	Philadelphia	Chuck Bednarik, C, Penn
1950	Detroit	Leon Hart, E, Notre Dame
1951	N.Y. Giants	Kyle Rote, HB, SMU
1952	L.A. Rams	Bill Wade, QB, Vanderbilt
1953	San Francisco	Harry Babcock, E, Georgia
1954	Cleveland	Bobby Garrett, QB, Stanford
1955	Baltimore Colts	George Shaw, QB, Oregon
1956	Pittsburgh	Gary Glick, DB, Col. A&M
1957	Green Bay	Paul Hornung, QB, Notre Dame
1958	Chicago Cards	King Hill, QB, Rice
1959	Green Bay	Randy Duncan, QB, Iowa
1960	L.A. Rams	Billy Cannon, HB, LSU
1961	Minnesota	Tommy Mason, HB, Tulane
1962	Washington	Ernie Davis, HB, Syracuse
1963	L.A. Rams	Terry Baker, QB, Oregon St.
1964	San Francisco	Dave Parks, E, Texas Tech
1965	N.Y. Giants	Tucker Frederickson, HB, Auburn
1966	Atlanta	Tommy Nobis, LB, Texas
1967	Baltimore Colts	Bubba Smith, DT, Michigan St.
1968	Minnesota	Ron Yary, T, USC
1969	Buffalo	O.J. Simpson, RB, USC
1970	Pittsburgh	Terry Bradshaw, QB, La.Tech
1971	New England	Jim Plunkett, QB, Stanford
1972	Buffalo	Walt Patulski, DE, Notre Dame
1973	Houston	John Matuszak, DE, Tampa
1974	Dallas	Ed "Too Tall" Jones, DE, Tenn. St.
1975	Atlanta	Steve Bartkowski, QB, Cal.
1976	Tampa Bay	Lee Roy Selmon, DE, Oklahoma
1977	Tampa Bay	Ricky Bell, RB, USC
1978	Houston	Earl Campbell, RB, Texas
1979	Buffalo	Tom Cousineau, LB, Ohio St.
1980	Detroit	Billy Sims, RB, Oklahoma
1981	New Orleans	George Rogers, RB, S.Carolina
1982	New England	Kenneth Sims, DT, Texas
1983	Baltimore Colts	John Elway, QB, Stanford
1984	New England	Irving Fryar, WR, Nebraska
1985	Buffalo	Bruce Smith, DE, Va.Tech
1986	Tampa Bay	Bo Jackson, RB, Auburn
1987	Tampa Bay	Vinny Testaverde, QB, Miami (FL)
1988	Atlanta	Aundray Bruce, LB, Auburn
1989	Dallas	Troy Aikman, QB, UCLA
1990	Indianapolis	Jeff George, QB, Illinois
1991	Dallas	Russell Maryland, DL, Miami (FL)
1992	Indianapolis	Steve Emtman, DL, Washington
1993	New England	Drew Bledsoe, QB, Washington St.
1994	Cincinnati	Dan Wilkinson, DT, Ohio St.
1995	Cincinnati	Ki-Jana Carter, RB, Penn State
1996	N.Y. Jets	Keyshawn Johnson, WR, USC
1997	St. Louis	Orlando Pace, T, Ohio St.
1998	Indianapolis	Peyton Manning, QB, Tennessee

First-Round Selections in the 1998 NFL Draft

Team	Player	Pos	College
1. Indianapolis	Peyton Manning	QB	Tennessee
2. San Diego[1]	Ryan Leaf	QB	Washington St.
3. Arizona[2]	Andre Wadsworth	DL	Florida St.
4. Oakland	Charles Woodson	DB	Michigan
5. Chicago	Curtis Enis	RB	Penn St.
6. St. Louis	Grant Wistrom	DL	Nebraska
7. New Orleans	Kyle Turley	OL	San Diego St.
8. Dallas	Greg Ellis	DL	North Carolina
9. Jacksonville[3]	Fred Taylor	RB	Florida
10. Baltimore	Duane Starks	DB	Miami (FL)
11. Philadelphia	Tra Thomas	OL	Florida St.
12. Atlanta	Keith Brooking	LB	Georgia Tech
13. Cincinnati	Takeo Spikes	LB	Auburn
14. Carolina	Jason Peter	DL	Nebraska
15. Seattle	Anthony Simmons	LB	Clemson
16. Tennessee	Kevin Dyson	WR	Utah
17. Cincinnati[4]	Brian Simmons	LB	North Carolina
18. New England[5]	Robert Edwards	RB	Georgia
19. Green Bay[6]	Vonnie Holliday	DL	North Carolina
20. Detroit	Terry Fair	DB	Tennessee
21. Minnesota	Randy Moss	WR	Marshall
22. New England	Tebucky Jones	DB	Syracuse
23. Oakland[7]	Damon Collins	OL	Florida
24. N.Y. Giants	Shaun Williams	DB	U.C.L.A.
25. Jacksonville	Donovin Darius	DB	Syracuse
26. Pittsburgh	Alan Faneca	OL	Louisiana St.
27. Kansas City	Victor Riley	OL	Auburn
28. San Francisco	R.W. McQuarters	DB	Oklahoma St.
29. Miami[8]	John Avery	RB	Mississippi
30. Denver	Marcus Nash	WR	Tennessee

(1) From Arizona. (2) From San Diego. (3) From Buffalo. (4) From Washington. (5) From N.Y. Jets. (6) From Miami. (7) From Tampa Bay. (8) From Green Bay.

NFL Head Coaches at Start of 1998 Season

AFC

Baltimore—Ted Marchibroda
Buffalo—Wade Phillips
Cincinnati—Bruce Coslet
Denver—Mike Shanahan
Indianapolis—Jim Mora
Jacksonville—Tom Coughlin
Kansas City—Marty Schottenheimer
Miami—Jimmy Johnson
New England—Pete Carroll
N.Y. Jets—Bill Parcells
Oakland—Jon Gruden
Pittsburgh—Bill Cowher
San Diego—Kevin Gilbride
Seattle—Dennis Erickson
Tennessee—Jeff Fisher

NFC

Arizona—Vince Tobin
Atlanta—Dan Reeves
Carolina—Dom Capers
Chicago—Dave Wannstedt
Dallas—Chan Gailey
Detroit—Bobby Ross
Green Bay—Mike Holmgren
Minnesota—Dennis Green
New Orleans—Mike Ditka
N.Y. Giants—Jim Fassel
Philadelphia—Ray Rhodes
St. Louis—Dick Vermeil
San Francisco—Steve Mariucci
Tampa Bay—Tony Dungy
Washington—Norv Turner

All-Time NFL Coaching Victories

(at end of 1997 season; *active through 1997)

			Regular Season				Career			
Coach	Years	Teams	W	L	T	Pct	W	L	T	Pct
Don Shula	33	Colts, Dolphins	328	156	6	.676	347	173	6	.665
George Halas	40	Bears	318	148	31	.671	324	151	31	.671
Tom Landry	29	Cowboys	250	162	6	.605	270	178	6	.601
Curly Lambeau	33	Packers, Cardinals, Redskins	226	132	22	.624	229	134	22	.623
Chuck Noll	23	Steelers	193	148	1	.566	209	156	1	.572
Chuck Knox	22	Rams, Bills, Seahawks	186	147	1	.558	193	158	1	.550
Paul Brown	21	Browns, Bengals	166	100	6	.621	170	109	6	.607
Bud Grant	18	Vikings	158	96	5	.620	168	108	5	.607
Dan Reeves*	17	Broncos, Giants, Falcons	148	115	1	.563	156	122	1	.561
Steve Owen	23	Giants	153	100	17	.598	155	108	17	.584
Marv Levy*	17	Chiefs, Bills	143	112	0	.561	154	120	0	.562
M. Schottenheimer*	14	Browns, Chiefs	138	76	1	.644	143	87	1	.621
Joe Gibbs	12	Redskins	124	60	0	.674	140	65	0	.683
Hank Stram	17	Chiefs, Saints	131	97	10	.571	136	100	10	.573
Weeb Ewbank	20	Colts, Jets	130	129	7	.502	134	130	7	.507
Bill Parcells*	13	Giants, Patriots, Jets	118	88	1	.572	128	93	1	.579
Sid Gillman	18	Rams, Chargers, Oilers	122	99	7	.550	123	104	7	.541
George Allen	12	Rams, Redskins	116	47	5	.705	120	54	5	.684
Mike Ditka*	12	Bears, Saints	112	72	0	.609	118	78	0	.602
Don Coryell	14	Cardinals, Chargers	111	83	1	.572	114	89	1	.561

American Football League Champions

Year	Eastern Division	Western Division	Playoff
1960	Houston Oilers (10-4-0)	Los Angeles Chargers (10-4-0)	Houston 24, Los Angeles 16
1961	Houston Oilers (10-3-1)	San Diego Chargers (12-2-0)	Houston 10, San Diego 3
1962	Houston Oilers (11-3-0)	Dallas Texans (11-3-0)	Dallas 20, Houston 17 (2 overtimes)
1963	Boston Patriots (7-6-1)(a)	San Diego Chargers (11-3-0)	San Diego 51, Boston 10
1964	Buffalo Bills (12-2-0)	San Diego Chargers (8-5-1)	Buffalo 20, San Diego 7
1965	Buffalo Bills (10-3-1)	San Diego Chargers (9-2-3)	Buffalo 23, San Diego 0
1966	Buffalo Bills (9-4-1)	Kansas City Chiefs (11-2-1)	Kansas City 31, Buffalo 7
1967	Houston Oilers (9-4-1)	Oakland Raiders (13-1-0)	Oakland 40, Houston 7
1968	New York Jets (11-3-0)	Oakland Raiders (12-2-0)(b)	New York 27, Oakland 23
1969	New York Jets (10-4-0)	Oakland Raiders (12-1-1)	Kansas City 17, Oakland 7(c)

(a) Defeated Buffalo Bills in divisional playoff. (b) Defeated Kansas City Chiefs in divisional playoff. (c) Kansas City Chiefs defeated New York Jets and Oakland Raiders defeated Houston Oilers in divisional playoffs.

Pro Football Hall of Fame, Canton, Ohio

(Asterisks indicate 1998 inductees.)

Herb Adderley
Lance Alworth
Doug Atkins
Morris "Red" Badgro
Lem Barney
Cliff Battles
Sammy Baugh
Chuck Bednarik
Bert Bell
Bobby Bell
Raymond Berry
Charles Bidwill
Fred Biletnikoff
George Blanda
Mel Blount
Terry Bradshaw
Jim Brown
Paul Brown
Roosevelt Brown
Willie Brown
Buck Buchanan
Dick Butkus
Earl Campbell
Tony Canadeo
Joe Carr
Guy Chamberlin
Jack Christiansen
Earl "Dutch" Clark
George Connor
Jim Conzelman
Lou Creekmur
Larry Csonka
Al Davis
Willie Davis
Len Dawson
Dan Dierdorf
Mike Ditka
Art Donovan
Tony Dorsett
John "Paddy" Driscoll
Bill Dudley
Glen "Turk" Edwards
Weeb Ewbank
Tom Fears
Jim Finks
Ray Flaherty
Len Ford
Dr. Daniel Fortmann
Dan Fouts
Frank Gatski
Bill George
Joe Gibbs
Frank Gifford
Sid Gillman
Otto Graham
Red Grange
Bud Grant
Joe Greene
Forrest Gregg
Bob Griese
Lou Groza
Joe Guyon
George Halas
Jack Ham
John Hannah
Franco Harris
Mike Haynes
Ed Healey
Mel Hein
Ted Hendricks
Wilbur "Pete" Henry
Arnold Herber
Bill Hewitt
Clarke Hinkle
Elroy "Crazylegs" Hirsch
Paul Hornung
Ken Houston
Cal Hubbard
Sam Huff
Lamar Hunt
Don Hutson
Jimmy Johnson
John Henry Johnson
Charlie Joiner
David "Deacon" Jones
Stan Jones
Henry Jordan
Sonny Jurgensen
Leroy Kelly
Walt Kiesling
Frank "Bruiser" Kinard
Paul Krause*
Earl "Curly" Lambeau
Jack Lambert
Tom Landry
Dick "Night Train" Lane
Jim Langer
Willie Lanier
Steve Largent
Yale Lary
Dante Lavelli
Bobby Layne
Alphonse "Tuffy" Leemans
Bob Lilly
Larry Little
Vince Lombardi
Sid Luckman
Roy "Link" Lyman
John Mackey
Tim Mara
Wellington Mara
Gino Marchetti
George Preston Marshall
Ollie Matson
Don Maynard
George McAfee
Mike McCormack
Tommy McDonald*
Hugh McElhenny
Johnny "Blood" McNally
Mike Michalske
Wayne Millner
Bobby Mitchell
Ron Mix
Lenny Moore
Marion Motley
Anthony Munoz*
George Musso
Bronko Nagurski
Joe Namath
Earle "Greasy" Neale
Ernie Nevers
Ray Nitschke
Chuck Noll
Leo Nomellini
Merlin Olsen
Jim Otto
Steve Owen
Alan Page
Clarence "Ace" Parker
Jim Parker
Walter Payton
Joe Perry
Pete Pihos
Hugh "Shorty" Ray
Dan Reeves
Mel Renfro
John Riggins
Jim Ringo
Andy Robustelli
Art Rooney
Pete Rozelle
Bob St. Clair
Gale Sayers
Joe Schmidt
Tex Schramm
Lee Roy Selmon
Art Shell
Don Shula
O.J. Simpson
Mike Singletary*
Jackie Smith
Bart Starr
Roger Staubach
Ernie Stautner
Jan Stenerud
Dwight Stephenson*
Ken Strong
Joe Stydahar
Fran Tarkenton
Charley Taylor
Jim Taylor
Jim Thorpe
Y.A. Tittle
George Trafton
Charley Trippi
Emlen Tunnell
Clyde "Bulldog" Turner
Johnny Unitas
Gene Upshaw
Norm Van Brocklin
Steve Van Buren
Doak Walker
Bill Walsh
Paul Warfield
Bob Waterfield
Mike Webster
Arnie Weinmeister
Randy White
Bill Willis
Larry Wilson
Kellen Winslow
Alex Wojciechowicz
Willie Wood

NFL Stadiums

Team—Stadium, Location, Turf (Year Built)	Capacity
Bears—Soldier Field, Chicago, IL, G (1924)	66,944
Bengals—Cinergy Field[1], Cincinnati, OH, A (1970)	60,389
Bills—Rich Stad., Buffalo, NY, A (1973)	80,024
Broncos—Denver Mile High Stad., CO, G (1948)	76,282
Buccaneers—Raymond James Stad., Tampa, FL, G (1998)	65,000
Cardinals—Sun Devil Stad., Tempe, AZ, G (1958)	73,273
Chargers—Qualcomm Stad.[2], San Diego, CA, G (1967)	71,000
Chiefs—Arrowhead Stad., Kansas City, MO, G (1972)	79,409
Colts—RCA Dome, Indianapolis, IN, A (1983)	60,599
Cowboys—Texas Stad., Irving, TX, A (1971)	65,675
Dolphins—Pro Player Stad.[3], Miami, FL, G (1987)	75,192
Eagles—Veterans Stad., Philadelphia, PA, A (1971)	65,352
Falcons—Georgia Dome, Atlanta, GA, A (1992)	71,228
49ers—3Com Park[4], San Francisco, CA, G (1960)	70,140
Giants—Giants Stad.[5], E. Rutherford, NJ, A (1976)	78,148
Jaguars—ALLTEL Stad.[6], Jacksonville, FL, G (1995)	73,000
Jets—Giants Stad.[5], E. Rutherford, NJ, A (1976)	77,803
Lions—Pontiac Silverdome, MI, A (1975)	80,368
Oilers—Vanderbilt Stadium, Nashville, TN, A (1922)	41,448
Packers—Lambeau Field, Green Bay, WI, G (1957)	60,790
Panthers—Ericsson Stad.[7], Charlotte, NC, G (1996)	75,248
Patriots—Foxboro Stad., MA, G (1971)	60,292
Raiders—Oakland-Alameda Cty. Coliseum, CA, G (1966)	63,026
Rams—Trans World Dome, St. Louis, MO, A (1995)	66,000
Ravens—Ravens Stad. at Camden Yards, Baltimore, MD, SG (1998)	68,400
Redskins—Jack Kent Cooke Stad., Raljon, MD, G (1997)	78,600
Saints—Louisiana Superdome, New Orleans, A (1975)	69,420
Seahawks—Kingdome, Seattle, WA, A (1976)	66,400
Steelers—Three Rivers Stad., Pittsburgh, PA, A (1970)	59,600
Vikings—Hubert H. Humphrey Metrodome, Minneapolis, MN, A (1982)	64,182

G=Grass. A=Artificial turf. SG=SportGrass (hybrid of artificial and natural turf). Stad.=Stadium. (1) Formerly Riverfront Stadium. (2) Formerly San Diego Jack Murphy Stadium. (3) Formerly Joe Robbie Stadium. (4) Formerly Candlestick Park; full name: 3Com Park at Candlestick Point. (5) Although Giants and Jets both play at Giants Stadium, extra seating is made available for Giants games. (6) Formerly Jacksonville Municipal Stadium. (7) Formerly Carolinas Stadium.

Future Sites of the Super Bowl

No.	Site	Date
XXXIII	Pro Player Stadium, Miami, FL	Jan. 31, 1999
XXXIV	Georgia Dome, Atlanta, GA	Jan. 30, 2000
XXXV	Raymond James Stadium, Tampa, FL	Jan. 28, 2001
XXXVI	Louisiana Superdome, New Orleans, LA	Jan. 27, 2002

All-Time Professional (NFL and AFL) Football Records

(at end of 1997 season; *active through 1997)

Leading Lifetime Scorers

Player	League	Yrs	TD	PAT	FG	Total	Player	League	Yrs	TD	PAT	FG	Total
George Blanda	AFL-NFL	26	9	943	335	2,002	Mark Moseley	NFL	16	0	482	300	1,382
Nick Lowery	NFL	18	0	562	383	1,711	Jim Bakken	NFL	17	0	534	282	1,380
Jan Stenerud	AFL-NFL	19	0	580	373	1,699	Fred Cox	NFL	15	0	519	282	1,365
Gary Anderson*	NFL	16	0	526	385	1,681	Lou Groza	NFL	17	1	641	234	1,365
Morten Andersen*	NFL	16	0	507	378	1,641	Jim Breech	NFL	14	0	517	243	1,246
Norm Johnson*	NFL	16	0	592	322	1,558	Al Del Greco*	NFL	14	0	435	263	1,224
Eddie Murray	NFL	19	0	521	337	1,532	Chris Bahr	NFL	14	0	490	241	1,213
Pat Leahy	NFL	18	0	558	304	1,470	Kevin Butler*	NFL	13	0	413	265	1,208
Jim Turner	AFL-NFL	16	1	521	304	1,439	Gino Cappelletti	AFL-NFL	11	42	342	176	1,130
Matt Bahr	NFL	17	0	522	300	1,422	Ray Wersching	NFL	15	0	456	222	1,122

Note: Cappelletti's total includes 4 two-point conversions.

Leading Lifetime Touchdown Scorers

Player	League	Yrs	Rush	Rec	Tot. Ret	Tot. TDs	Player	League	Yrs	Rush	Rec	Tot. Ret	Tot. TDs
Jerry Rice*	NFL	13	10	155	1	166	Franco Harris	NFL	13	91	9	0	100
Marcus Allen*	NFL	16	123	21	1	145	Eric Dickerson	NFL	11	90	6	0	96
Jim Brown	NFL	9	106	20	0	126	Jim Taylor	NFL	10	83	10	0	93
Walter Payton	NFL	13	110	15	0	125	Tony Dorsett	NFL	12	77	13	1	91
Emmit Smith*	NFL	8	112	7	0	119	Bobby Mitchell	NFL	11	18	65	8	91
John Riggins	NFL	14	104	12	0	116	Cris Carter*	NFL	11	0	89	1	90
Lenny Moore	NFL	12	63	48	2	113	Leroy Kelly	NFL	10	74	13	3	90
Don Hutson	NFL	11	3	99	3	105	Charley Taylor	NFL	13	11	79	0	90
Barry Sanders*	NFL	9	95	10	0	105	Don Maynard	AFL-NFL	15	0	88	0	88
Steve Largent	NFL	14	1	100	0	101	Lance Alworth	AFL-NFL	11	2	85	0	87

Most Points, Season — 176, Paul Hornung, Green Bay Packers, 1960 (15 TDs, 41 PATs, 15 FGs).
Most Points, Game — 40, Ernie Nevers, Chicago Cardinals vs. Chicago Bears, Nov. 28, 1929 (6 TDs, 4 PATs).
Most Touchdowns, Season — 25, Emmitt Smith, Dallas Cowboys, 1995 (25 rushing).
Most Touchdowns, Game — 6, Ernie Nevers, Chicago Cardinals vs. Chicago Bears, Nov. 28, 1929 (6 rushing); Dub Jones, Cleveland Browns vs. Chicago Bears, Nov. 25, 1951 (4 rushing, 2 pass receptions); Gale Sayers, Chicago Bears vs. San Francisco 49ers, Dec. 12, 1965 (4 rushing, 1 pass reception, 1 punt return).
Most Points After Touchdown, Season — 66, Uwe von Schamann, Miami Dolphins, 1984.
Most Consecutive Points After Touchdown — 234, Tommy Davis, San Francisco 49ers, 1959-69.
Most Field Goals, Career — 385, Gary Anderson, Pittsburgh Steelers-Philadelphia Eagles-San Francisco 49ers, 1982-97.
Most Field Goals, Season — 37, John Kasay, Carolina Panthers, 1996.
Most Field Goals, Game — 7, Jim Bakken, St. Louis Cardinals vs. Pittsburgh Steelers, Sept. 24, 1967; Rich Karlis, Minnesota vs. L.A. Rams, Nov. 5, 1989 (OT); Chris Boniol, Dallas vs. Green Bay, Nov. 18, 1996.
Longest Field Goal — 63 yds., Tom Dempsey, New Orleans Saints vs. Detroit Lions, Nov. 8, 1970.

Leading Lifetime Rushers

(ranked by rushing yards)

Player	League	Yrs	Att	Yards	Avg	Player	League	Yrs	Att	Yards	Avg
Walter Payton	NFL	13	3,838	16,726	4.4	Emmitt Smith*	NFL	8	2,595	11,234	4.3
Barry Sanders*	NFL	9	2,719	13,778	5.1	Ottis Anderson	NFL	14	2,562	10,273	4.0
Eric Dickerson	NFL	11	2,996	13,259	4.4	Earl Campbell	NFL	8	2,187	9,407	4.3
Tony Dorsett	NFL	12	2,936	12,739	4.3	Jim Taylor	NFL	10	1,941	8,597	4.4
Jim Brown	NFL	9	2,359	12,312	5.2	Joe Perry	NFL	14	1,737	8,378	4.8
Marcus Allen*	NFL	16	3,022	12,243	4.1	Earnest Byner*	NFL	14	2,095	8,261	3.9
Franco Harris	NFL	13	2,949	12,120	4.1	Herschel Walker*	NFL	12	1,954	8,225	4.2
Thurman Thomas*	NFL	10	2,720	11,405	4.2	Roger Craig	NFL	11	1,991	8,189	4.1
John Riggins	NFL	14	2,916	11,352	3.9	Gerald Riggs	NFL	10	1,989	8,188	4.1
O.J. Simpson	AFL-NFL	11	2,404	11,236	4.7	Larry Csonka	AFL-NFL	11	1,891	8,081	4.3

Most Yards Gained, Season — 2,105, Eric Dickerson, Los Angeles Rams, 1984.
Most Yards Gained, Game — 275, Walter Payton, Chicago Bears vs. Minnesota Vikings, Nov. 20, 1977.
Most Touchdowns Rushing, Career — 123, Marcus Allen, Los Angeles Raiders-Kansas City Chiefs, 1982-97.
Most Touchdowns Rushing, Season — 25, Emmitt Smith, Dallas Cowboys, 1995.
Most Touchdowns Rushing, Game — 6, Ernie Nevers, Chicago Cardinals vs. Chicago Bears, Nov. 28, 1929.
Most Rushing Attempts, Game — 45, Jamie Morris, Washington Redskins vs. Cincinnati Bengals, Dec. 17, 1988 (overtime).
Longest Run From Scrimmage — 99 yds., Tony Dorsett, Dallas Cowboys vs. Minnesota Vikings, Jan. 3, 1983 (touchdown).

Defensive Records

Most Interceptions, Career — 81, Paul Krause, Washington Redskins-Minnesota Vikings, 1964-79.
Most Interceptions, Season — 14, Dick "Night Train" Lane, Los Angeles Rams, 1952.
Most Touchdowns, Career — 9, Ken Houston, Houston Oilers-Washington Redskins, 1967-80.
Most Touchdowns, Season — 4, Ken Houston, Houston Oilers, 1971; Jim Kearney, Kansas City Chiefs, 1972; Eric Allen, Philadelphia Eagles, 1993.
Most Sacks, Career (Since 1982) — 176.5, Reggie White, Philadelphia Eagles-Green Bay Packers, 1985-97.
Most Sacks, Season (Since 1982) — 22, Mark Gastineau, New York Jets, 1984.
Most Sacks, Game (Since 1982) — 7, Derrick Thomas, Kansas City Chiefs vs. Seattle Seahawks, Nov. 11, 1990.

Leading Lifetime Receivers

(ranked by number of completions)

Player	League	Yrs	No.	Yds	Avg
Jerry Rice*	NFL	13	1,057	16,455	15.6
Art Monk	NFL	16	940	12,721	13.5
Andre Reed*	NFL	13	826	11,764	14.2
Steve Largent	NFL	14	819	13,089	16.0
Henry Ellard*	NFL	15	807	13,662	16.9
James Lofton	NFL	16	764	14,004	18.3
Cris Carter*	NFL	11	756	9,436	12.5
Charlie Joiner	AFL-NFL	18	750	12,146	16.2
Irving Fryar*	NFL	14	736	11,427	15.5
Gary Clark	NFL	11	699	10,856	15.5
Michael Irvin*	NFL	10	666	10,680	16.0
Ozzie Newsome	NFL	13	662	7,980	12.1
Charley Taylor	NFL	13	649	9,110	14.0
Andre Rison*	NFL	9	641	8,839	13.8
Drew Hill	NFL	14	634	9,831	15.5
Don Maynard	AFL-NFL	15	633	11,834	18.7
Raymond Berry	NFL	13	631	9,275	14.7
Tim Brown*	NFL	10	599	8,588	14.3
Anthony Miller*	NFL	10	595	9,148	15.4
Sterling Sharpe	NFL	7	595	8,134	13.7

Most Yards Gained, Career — 16,455, Jerry Rice, San Francisco 49ers, 1985-97.
Most Yards Gained, Season — 1,848, Jerry Rice, San Francisco 49ers, 1995.
Most Yards Gained, Game — 336, Willie "Flipper" Anderson, Los Angeles Rams vs. New Orleans, Nov. 26, 1989 (overtime).
Most Pass Receptions, Season — 123, Herman Moore, Detroit Lions, 1995.
Most Pass Receptions, Game — 18, Tom Fears, Los Angeles Rams vs. Green Bay Packers, Dec. 3, 1950 (189 yards).
Most Touchdown Passes, Career — 155, Jerry Rice, San Francisco 49ers, 1985-97.
Most Touchdown Passes, Season — 22, Jerry Rice, San Francisco 49ers, 1987.
Most Touchdown Passes, Game — 5, Bob Shaw, Chicago Cardinals vs. Baltimore Colts, Oct. 2, 1950; Kellen Winslow, San Diego Chargers vs. Oakland Raiders, Nov. 22, 1981; Jerry Rice, San Francisco 49ers vs. Atlanta Falcons, Oct. 14, 1990.

Leading Lifetime Passers

(minimum 1,500 attempts; ranked by quarterback rating points)

Player	League	Yrs	Att	Comp	Yds	Pts[1]
Steve Young*	NFL	13	3,548	2,300	28,508	97.0
Joe Montana	NFL	15	5,391	3,409	40,551	92.3
Brett Favre*	NFL	7	3,206	1,971	22,591	89.3
Dan Marino*	NFL	15	7,452	4,453	55,416	87.8
Jim Kelly	NFL	11	4,779	2,874	35,467	84.4
Roger Staubach	NFL	11	2,958	1,685	22,700	83.4
Neil Lomax	NFL	8	3,153	1,817	22,771	82.7
Sonny Jurgensen	NFL	18	4,262	2,433	32,224	82.6
Len Dawson	NFL-AFL	19	3,741	2,136	28,711	82.6
Troy Aikman*	NFL	9	3,696	2,292	26,016	82.3
Ken Anderson	NFL	16	4,475	2,654	32,838	81.9
Bernie Kosar	NFL	12	3,365	1,994	23,301	81.8
Danny White	NFL	13	2,950	1,761	21,959	81.7
Dave Krieg*	NFL	18	5,290	3,093	37,948	81.5
Warren Moon*	NFL	14	6,528	3,827	47,465	81.2
Boomer Esiason	NFL	14	5,205	2,969	37,920	81.1
Jeff Hostetler*	NFL	14	2,338	1,357	16,430	80.5
Neil O'Donnell*	NFL	8	2,519	1,438	16,810	80.5
Bart Starr	NFL	16	3,149	1,808	24,718	80.5
Ken O'Brien	NFL	10	3,602	2,110	25,094	80.4

[1]Rating points based on performances in the following categories: Percentage of completions, percentage of touchdown passes, percentage of interceptions, and average gain per pass attempt.

Most Yards Gained, Career — 55,416, Dan Marino, Miami Dolphins, 1983-97.
Most Yards Gained, Season — 5,084, Dan Marino, Miami Dolphins, 1984.
Most Yards Gained, Game — 554, Norm Van Brocklin, Los Angeles Rams vs. New York Yanks, Sept. 18, 1951 (27 completions in 41 attempts).
Most Touchdowns Passing, Career — 385, Dan Marino, Miami Dolphins, 1983-97.
Most Touchdowns Passing, Season — 48, Dan Marino, Miami Dolphins, 1984.
Most Touchdowns Passing, Game — 7, Sid Luckman, Chicago Bears vs. New York Giants, Nov. 14, 1943; Adrian Burk, Philadelphia Eagles vs. Washington Redskins, Oct. 17, 1954; George Blanda, Houston Oilers vs. New York Titans, Nov. 19, 1961; Y.A. Tittle, New York Giants vs. Washington Redskins, Oct. 28, 1962; Joe Kapp, Minnesota Vikings vs. Baltimore Colts, Sept. 28, 1969.
Most Passes Completed, Career — 4,453, Dan Marino, Miami Dolphins, 1983-97.
Most Passes Completed, Season — 404, Warren Moon, Houston Oilers, 1991.
Most Passes Completed, Game — 45, Drew Bledsoe, New England Patriots vs. Minnesota Vikings, Nov. 13, 1994 (overtime).

The Sporting News 1998 NFL All-Pro Team

Offense—QB: Brett Favre, Green Bay. RB: Barry Sanders, Detroit; Terrell Davis, Denver. WR: Herman Moore, Detroit; Tim Brown, Oakland. TE: Shannon Sharpe, Denver. T: Tony Boselli, Jacksonville; Jonathan Odgen, Baltimore. G: Larry Allen, Dallas; Randall McDaniel, Minnesota. C: Dermontti Dawson, Pittsburgh. **Defense**—LB: Jessie Armstead, N.Y. Giants; Levon Kirkland, Pittsburgh; John Mobley, Denver. DE: Bruce Smith, Buffalo; Michael Strahan, N.Y. Giants. DT: Dana Stubblefield, San Francisco; John Randle, Minnesota. CB: Deion Sanders, Dallas; Aeneas Williams, Arizona. S: LeRoy Butler, Green Bay; Carnell Lake, Pittsburgh. **Special Teams**—K: Richie Cunningham, Dallas. P: Matt Turk, Washington. PR: Darrien Gordon, Denver. KR: Michael Bates, Carolina.

RODEO

Pro Rodeo Cowboy All-Around Champions, 1978-97

Year	Winner	Money won
1978	Tom Ferguson, Miami, OK	$103,734
1979	Tom Ferguson, Miami, OK	96,272
1980	Paul Tierney, Rapid City, SD	105,568
1981	Jimmie Cooper, Monument, NM	105,862
1982	Chris Lybbert, Coyote, CA	123,709
1983	Roy Cooper, Durant, OK	153,391
1984	Dee Pickett, Caldwell, ID	122,618
1985	Lewis Feild, Elk Ridge, UT	130,347
1986	Lewis Feild, Elk Ridge, UT	166,042
1987	Lewis Feild, Elk Ridge, UT	144,335
1988	Dave Appleton, Arlington, TX	$121,546
1989	Ty Murray, Odessa, TX	134,806
1990	Ty Murray, Stephenville, TX	213,772
1991	Ty Murray, Stephenville, TX	244,230
1992	Ty Murray, Stephenville, TX	225,992
1993	Ty Murray, Stephenville, TX	297,896
1994	Ty Murray, Stephenville, TX	246,170
1995	Joe Beaver, Huntsville, TX	141,753
1996	Joe Beaver, Huntsville, TX	166,103
1997	Dan Mortensen, Manhattan, MT	184,559

CANADIAN FOOTBALL LEAGUE

Grey Cup Championship Game, 1954-97

1954 Edmonton Eskimos 26, Montreal Alouettes 25
1955 Edmonton Eskimos 34, Montreal Alouettes 19
1956 Edmonton Eskimos 50, Montreal Alouettes 27
1957 Hamilton Tiger-Cats 32, Winnipeg Blue Bombers 7
1958 Winnipeg Blue Bombers 35, Hamilton Tiger-Cats 28
1959 Winnipeg Blue Bombers 21, Hamilton Tiger-Cats 7
1960 Ottawa Rough Riders 16, Edmonton Eskimos 6
1961 Winnipeg Blue Bombers 21, Hamilton Tiger-Cats 14
1962 Winnipeg Blue Bombers 28, Hamilton Tiger-Cats 27
1963 Hamilton Tiger-Cats 21, British Columbia Lions 10
1964 British Columbia Lions 34, Hamilton Tiger-Cats 24
1965 Hamilton Tiger-Cats 22, Winnipeg Blue Bombers 16
1966 Saskatchewan Roughriders 29, Ottawa Rough Riders 14
1967 Hamilton Tiger-Cats 24, Saskatchewan Roughriders 1
1968 Ottawa Rough Riders 24, Calgary Stampeders 21
1969 Ottawa Rough Riders 29, Saskatchewan Roughriders 11
1970 Montreal Alouettes 23, Calgary Stampeders 10
1971 Calgary Stampeders 14, Toronto Argonauts 11
1972 Hamilton Tiger-Cats 13, Saskatchewan Roughriders 10
1973 Ottawa Rough Riders 22, Edmonton Eskimos 18
1974 Montreal Alouettes 20, Edmonton Eskimos 7
1975 Edmonton Eskimos 9, Montreal Alouettes 8
1976 Ottawa Rough Riders 23, Saskatchewan Roughriders 20
1977 Montreal Alouettes 41, Edmonton Eskimos 6
1978 Edmonton Eskimos 20, Montreal Alouettes 13
1979 Edmonton Eskimos 17, Montreal Alouettes 9
1980 Edmonton Eskimos 48, Hamilton Tiger-Cats 10
1981 Edmonton Eskimos 26, Ottawa Rough Riders 23
1982 Edmonton Eskimos 32, Toronto Argonauts 16
1983 Toronto Argonauts 18, British Columbia Lions 17
1984 Winnipeg Blue Bombers 47, Hamilton Tiger-Cats 17
1985 British Columbia Lions 37, Hamilton Tiger-Cats 24
1986 Hamilton Tiger-Cats 39, Edmonton Eskimos 15
1987 Edmonton Eskimos 38, Toronto Argonauts 36
1988 Winnipeg Blue Bombers 22, British Columbia Lions 21
1989 Saskatchewan Roughriders 43, Hamilton Tiger-Cats 40
1990 Winnipeg Blue Bombers 50, Edmonton Eskimos 11
1991 Toronto Argonauts 36, Calgary Stampeders 21
1992 Calgary Stampeders 24, Winnipeg Blue Bombers 10
1993 Edmonton Eskimos 33, Winnipeg Blue Bombers 23
1994 British Columbia Lions 26, Baltimore Football Club* 23
1995 Baltimore Stallions 37, Calgary Stampeders 20
1996 Toronto Argonauts 43, Edmonton Eskimos 37
1997 Toronto Argonauts 47, Saskatchewan Roughriders 23

*Later Baltimore Stallions.

1997 CFL Review: Toronto Repeats, Flutie MVP Again, Smith Sets Cup Record

The 1997 season was the first season played under the new 8-team alignment that featured 4 teams in both divisions; the Winnipeg Blue Bombers became part of the Eastern Division before the start of the season. In the Grey Cup, the Toronto Argonauts repeated as champions, defeating the Saskatchewan Roughriders, 47-23. Doug Flutie threw for 3 touchdowns and ran for another as he picked up his 2d MVP in a row. Adrion Smith of Toronto also set a Grey Cup record when he returned the 2d-half kickoff 95 yards for a touchdown.

1997 Final Standings

Western Division	W	L	T	Pct	PF	PA
Edmonton Eskimos	12	6	0	.667	479	400
Calgary Stampeders	10	8	0	.556	519	443
Saskatchewan Roughriders	8	10	0	.444	413	479
British Columbia Lions	8	10	0	.444	429	536

Eastern Division	W	L	T	Pct	PF	PA
Toronto Argonauts	15	3	0	.833	660	327
Montreal Alouettes	13	5	0	.722	509	532
Winnipeg Blue Bombers	4	14	0	.222	443	548
Hamilton Tiger-Cats	2	16	0	.111	362	549

1997 Playoff Results

Divisional Semifinals—Montreal 45, British Columbia 35; Saskatchewan 33, Calgary 30
Divisional Finals—Toronto 37, Montreal 30; Saskatchewan 31, Edmonton 30
Grey Cup—(Nov. 16, 1997, at Commonwealth Stadium, Edmonton, Alberta) Toronto 47, Saskatchewan 23

All-Time CFL Records

(through 1997 season; *active during 1997)

Longest Run—The Canadian Football League features 3 downs, 12 players on a side, and a field that is 110 yards long. George Dixon of the Montreal Alouettes made full use of the field with a 109-yard run against Ottawa on Sept. 2, 1963. Willie Fleming of the British Columbia Lions did the same against Edmonton on Oct. 17, 1964.

Leading Lifetime Rushers

	Yrs	No	Yds	Avg	Long	TDs
George Reed, Sask.	13	3,243	16,116	5.0	71	134
Johnny Bright, Calg.-Edm.	13	1,969	10,909	5.5	90	69
Normie Kwong, Calg.-Edm.	13	1,745	9,022	5.2	60	78
Leo Lewis, Wpg.	11	1,351	8,861	6.6	92	48
Dave Thelen, Ott.-Tor.	9	1,530	8,463	5.5	77	47
*Damon Allen, Edm.-Ott.-Ham.-Mps.-B.C.	13	1,071	7,612	7.1	51	64
*Tracy Ham, Edm.-Tor.-Balt./Mtl.	11	960	7,454	7.8	80	58
Jim Evenson, B.C.-Ott.	7	1,460	7,060	4.8	68	37
Earl Lunsford, Calg.	6	1,199	6,994	5.8	85	55
Dick Shatto, Tor.	12	1,322	6,958	5.3	67	39

Leading Lifetime Passers

	Yrs	Att	Comp	Yds	Pct	Avg	Long	TDs
Ron Lancaster, Ott.-Sask.	19	6,233	3,384	50,535	54.3	14.9	102	333
Matt Dunigan, Edm.-B.C.-Tor.-Wpg.-Bhm.-Ham.	14	5,476	3,057	43,857	55.8	14.3	89	306
*Doug Flutie, B.C.-Calg.-Tor.	8	4,854	2,975	41,355	61.3	13.9	106	270
Tom Clements, Ott.-Sask.-Ham.-Wpg.	12	4,657	2,807	39,041	60.3	13.9	105	252
*Damon Allen, Edm.-Ott.-Ham.-Mps.-B.C.	13	4,955	2,667	38,211	53.8	14.3	102	215
*Tracy Ham, Edm.-Tor-Balt.-Mtl.	10	4,405	2,364	36,092	53.7	15.3	85	252
Kent Austin, Sask.-B.C.-Tor.-Wpg.	10	4,700	2,709	36,030	57.6	13.3	107	198
Dieter Brock, Wpg.-Ham.	11	4,535	2,602	34,830	57.4	13.4	98	210
Tom Burgess, Ott.-Sask.-Wpg.	10	4,034	2,118	30,308	52.5	14.3	104	190
Sam Etcheverry, Mtl.	7	2,829	1,630	25,582	57.6	15.7	109	183

Leading Lifetime Receivers

	Yrs	No	Yds	Avg	Long	TDs
Ray Elgaard, Sask.	14	830	13,198	15.9	81	78
Brian Kelly, Edm.	9	575	11,169	19.4	97	97
*Allen Pitts, Calg.	8	696	11,025	15.8	87	90
Tom Scott, Wpg.-Edm.-Calg.	11	649	10,837	16.7	98	88
*Don Narcisse, Sask.	11	777	10,551	13.5	77	67
Tommy Joe Coffey, Edm.-Ham.-Tor.	14	650	10,320	15.9	83	63
*Earl Winfield, Ham.	11	573	10,119	17.7	81	75
Tony Gabriel, Ham.-Ott.	11	614	9,832	16.0	80	69
Rocky DiPietro, Ham.	14	706	9,762	13.8	80	45
Terry Evanshen, Mtl.-Calg.-Ham.-Tor.	14	600	9,697	16.2	109	80

COLLEGE FOOTBALL

National College Football Champions, 1936-97

The unofficial national champion as selected each year by the AP poll of writers and the USA Today/ESPN (until 1991, UPI; 1991-1996 USA Today/CNN) poll of coaches. When the polls disagree, both teams are listed. The AP poll originated in 1936, and the UPI poll in 1950.

1936 Minnesota
1937 Pittsburgh
1938 Texas Christian
1939 Texas A&M
1940 Minnesota
1941 Minnesota
1942 Ohio St.
1943 Notre Dame
1944 Army
1945 Army
1946 Notre Dame
1947 Notre Dame
1948 Michigan
1949 Notre Dame
1950 Oklahoma
1951 Tennessee
1952 Michigan St.
1953 Maryland
1954 Ohio St., UCLA
1955 Oklahoma
1956 Oklahoma
1957 Auburn, Ohio St.
1958 Louisiana St.
1959 Syracuse
1960 Minnesota
1961 Alabama
1962 Southern Cal
1963 Texas
1964 Alabama
1965 Alabama, Mich. St.
1966 Notre Dame
1967 Southern Cal
1968 Ohio St.
1969 Texas
1970 Nebraska, Texas
1971 Nebraska
1972 Southern Cal
1973 Notre Dame, Alabama
1974 Oklahoma, Southern Cal
1975 Oklahoma
1976 Pittsburgh
1977 Notre Dame
1978 Alabama, Southern Cal
1979 Alabama
1980 Georgia
1981 Clemson
1982 Penn St.
1983 Miami (FL)
1984 Brigham Young
1985 Oklahoma
1986 Penn St.
1987 Miami (FL)
1988 Notre Dame
1989 Miami (FL)
1990 Colorado, Georgia Tech
1991 Miami (FL), Washington
1992 Alabama
1993 Florida St.
1994 Nebraska
1995 Nebraska
1996 Florida
1997 Michigan, Nebraska

1997 Final Associated Press and USA Today/ESPN NCAA Football Polls

Associated Press

Rank	Team[1]	Rank	Team[1]	Rank	Team[1]	Rank	Team[1]
1.	Michigan (12-0)	8.	Kansas St. (11-1)	14.	Arizona St. (9-3)	20.	Texas A&M (9-4)
2.	Nebraska (13-0)	9.	Washington St. (10-2)	15.	Purdue (9-3)	21.	Syracuse (9-4)
3.	Florida St. (11-1)	10.	Georgia (10-2)	16.	Penn St. (9-3)	22.	Mississippi (8-4)
4.	Florida (10-2)	11.	Auburn (10-3)	17.	Colorado St. (11-2)	23.	Missouri (7-5)
5.	UCLA (10-2)	12.	Ohio St. (10-3)	18.	Washington (8-4)	24.	Oklahoma St. (8-4)
6.	North Carolina (11-1)	13.	LSU (9-3)	19.	So. Mississippi (9-3)	25.	Georgia Tech (7-5)
7.	Tennessee (11-2)						

USA Today/ESPN

Rank	Team[1]	Rank	Team[1]	Rank	Team[1]	Rank	Team[1]
1.	Nebraska	8.	Tennessee	14.	Arizona St.	20.	Syracuse
2.	Michigan	9.	Washington St.	15.	Purdue	21.	Texas A&M
3.	Florida St.	10.	Georgia	16.	Colorado St.	22.	Mississippi
4.	North Carolina	11.	Auburn	17.	Penn St.	23.	Missouri
5.	UCLA	12.	Ohio St.	18.	Washington	24.	Oklahoma St.
6.	Florida	13.	LSU	19.	So. Mississippi	25.	Air Force (10-3)
7.	Kansas St.						

(1) Team records include bowl games. Won-loss records for teams (except Air Force) in USA Today/ESPN poll are under AP poll.

Annual Results of Major Bowl Games

(Dates indicate year the game was played; bowl games are generally played in late December or early January.)

Rose Bowl, Pasadena, CA

1902 (Jan.) Michigan 49, Stanford 0
1916 Washington St. 14, Brown 0
1917 Oregon 14, Pennsylvania 0
1918 Service teams
1919 Service teams
1920 Harvard 7, Oregon 6
1921 California 28, Ohio St. 0
1922 Wash. & Jeff. 0, California 0
1923 Southern Cal 14, Penn St. 3
1924 Navy 14, Washington 14
1925 Notre Dame 27, Stanford 10
1926 Alabama 20, Washington 19
1927 Alabama 7, Stanford 7
1928 Stanford 7, Pittsburgh 6
1929 Georgia Tech 8, California 7
1930 Southern Cal 47, Pittsburgh 14
1931 Alabama 24, Wash. St. 0
1932 Southern Cal 21, Tulane 12
1933 Southern Cal 35, Pittsburgh 0
1934 Columbia 7, Stanford 0
1935 Alabama 29, Stanford 13
1936 Stanford 7, SMU 0
1937 Pittsburgh 21, Washington 0
1938 California 13, Alabama 0
1939 Southern Cal 7, Duke 3
1940 Southern Cal 14, Tennessee 0
1941 Stanford 21, Nebraska 13
1942* Oregon St. 20, Duke 16
*Played at Durham, NC.
1943 Georgia 9, UCLA 0
1944 Southern Cal 29, Washington 0
1945 Southern Cal 25, Tennessee 0
1946 Alabama 34, Southern Cal 14
1947 Illinois 45, UCLA 14
1948 Michigan 49, Southern Cal 0
1949 Northwestern 20, California 14
1950 Ohio St. 17, California 14
1951 Michigan 14, California 6
1952 Illinois 40, Stanford 7
1953 Southern Cal 7, Wisconsin 0
1954 Mich. St. 28, UCLA 20
1955 Ohio St. 20, Southern Cal 7
1956 Mich. St. 17, UCLA 14
1957 Iowa 35, Oregon St. 19
1958 Ohio St. 10, Oregon 7
1959 Iowa 38, California 12
1960 Washington 44, Wisconsin 8
1961 Washington 17, Minnesota 7
1962 Minnesota 21, UCLA 3
1963 Southern Cal 42, Wisconsin 37
1964 Illinois 17, Washington 7
1965 Michigan 34, Oregon St. 7
1966 UCLA 14, Mich. St. 12
1967 Purdue 14, Southern Cal 13
1968 Southern Cal 14, Indiana 3
1969 Ohio St. 27, Southern Cal 16
1970 Southern Cal 10, Michigan 3
1971 Stanford 27, Ohio St. 17
1972 Stanford 13, Michigan 12
1973 Southern Cal 42, Ohio St. 17
1974 Ohio St. 42, Southern Cal 21
1975 Southern Cal 18, Ohio St. 17
1976 UCLA 23, Ohio St. 10
1977 Southern Cal 14, Michigan 6
1978 Washington 27, Michigan 20
1979 Southern Cal 17, Michigan 10
1980 Southern Cal 17, Ohio St. 16
1981 Michigan 23, Washington 6
1982 Washington 28, Iowa 0
1983 UCLA 24, Michigan 14
1984 UCLA 45, Illinois 9
1985 Southern Cal 20, Ohio St. 17
1986 UCLA 45, Iowa 28
1987 Arizona St. 22, Michigan 15
1988 Mich. St. 20, Southern Cal 17
1989 Michigan 22, Southern Cal 14
1990 Southern Cal 17, Michigan 10
1991 Washington 46, Iowa 34
1992 Washington 34, Michigan 14
1993 Michigan 38, Washington 31
1994 Wisconsin 21, UCLA 16
1995 Penn St. 38, Oregon 20
1996 Southern Cal 41, Northwestern 32
1997 Ohio St. 20, Arizona St. 17
1998 Michigan 21, Washington St. 16

Orange Bowl, Miami, FL

1935 (Jan.) Bucknell 26, Miami (FL) 0
1936 Catholic U. 20, Mississippi 19
1937 Duquesne 13, Mississippi St. 12
1938 Auburn 6, Michigan St. 0
1939 Tennessee 17, Oklahoma 0
1940 Georgia Tech 21, Missouri 7
1941 Mississippi St. 14, Georgetown 7
1942 Georgia 40, TCU 26
1943 Alabama 37, Boston Coll. 21
1944 LSU 19, Texas A&M 14
1945 Tulsa 26, Georgia Tech 12
1946 Miami (FL) 13, Holy Cross 6
1947 Rice 8, Tennessee 0
1948 Georgia Tech 20, Kansas 14
1949 Texas 41, Georgia 28
1950 Santa Clara 21, Kentucky 13
1951 Clemson 15, Miami (FL) 14
1952 Georgia Tech 17, Baylor 14
1953 Alabama 61, Syracuse 6
1954 Oklahoma 7, Maryland 0
1955 Duke 34, Nebraska 7

1956 Oklahoma 20, Maryland 6
1957 Colorado 27, Clemson 21
1958 Oklahoma 48, Duke 21
1959 Oklahoma 21, Syracuse 6
1960 Georgia 14, Missouri 0
1961 Missouri 21, Navy 14
1962 LSU 25, Colorado 7
1963 Alabama 17, Oklahoma 0
1964 Nebraska 13, Auburn 7
1965 Texas 21, Alabama 17
1966 Alabama 39, Nebraska 28
1967 Florida 27, Georgia Tech 12
1968 Oklahoma 26, Tennessee 24
1969 Penn St. 15, Kansas 14
1970 Penn St. 10, Missouri 3
1971 Nebraska 17, LSU 12
1972 Nebraska 38, Alabama 6
1973 Nebraska 40, Notre Dame 6
1974 Penn St. 16, LSU 9
1975 Notre Dame 13, Alabama 11
1976 Oklahoma 14, Michigan 6
1977 Ohio St. 27, Colorado 10
1978 Arkansas 31, Oklahoma 6
1979 Oklahoma 31, Nebraska 24
1980 Oklahoma 24, Florida St. 7
1981 Oklahoma 18, Florida St. 17
1982 Clemson 22, Nebraska 15
1983 Nebraska 21, LSU 20
1984 Miami (FL) 31, Nebraska 30
1985 Washington 28, Oklahoma 17
1986 Oklahoma 25, Penn St. 10
1987 Oklahoma 42, Arkansas 8
1988 Miami (FL) 20, Oklahoma 14
1989 Miami (FL) 23, Nebraska 3
1990 Notre Dame 21, Colorado 6
1991 Colorado 10, Notre Dame 9
1992 Miami (FL) 22, Nebraska 0
1993 Florida St. 27, Nebraska 14
1994 Florida St. 18, Nebraska 16
1995 Nebraska 24, Miami (FL) 17
1996 Florida St. 31, Notre Dame 26
1996 (Dec.) Nebraska 41, Virginia Tech 21
1998 (Jan.) Nebraska 42, Tennessee 17

Sugar Bowl, New Orleans, LA

1935 (Jan.) Tulane 20, Temple 14
1936 TCU 3, LSU 2
1937 Santa Clara 21, LSU 14
1938 Santa Clara 6, LSU 0
1939 TCU 15, Carnegie Tech 7
1940 Texas A&M 14, Tulane 13
1941 Boston Col. 19, Tennessee 13
1942 Fordham 2, Missouri 0
1943 Tennessee 14, Tulsa 7
1944 Georgia Tech 20, Tulsa 18
1945 Duke 29, Alabama 26
1946 Oklahoma A&M 33, St. Mary's 13
1947 Georgia 20, N. Carolina 10
1948 Texas 27, Alabama 7
1949 Oklahoma 14, N. Carolina 6
1950 Oklahoma 35, LSU 0
1951 Kentucky 13, Oklahoma 7
1952 Maryland 28, Tennessee 13
1953 Georgia Tech 24, Mississippi 7
1954 Georgia Tech 42, West Virginia 19
1955 Navy 21, Mississippi 0
1956 Georgia Tech 7, Pittsburgh 0
1957 Baylor 13, Tennessee 7
1958 Mississippi 39, Texas 7
1959 LSU 7, Clemson 0
1960 Mississippi 21, LSU 0
1961 Mississippi 14, Rice 6
1962 Alabama 10, Arkansas 3
1963 Mississippi 17, Arkansas 13
1964 Alabama 12, Mississippi 7
1965 LSU 13, Syracuse 10
1966 Missouri 20, Florida 18
1967 Alabama 34, Nebraska 7
1968 LSU 20, Wyoming 13
1969 Arkansas 16, Georgia 2
1970 Mississippi 27, Arkansas 22
1971 Tennessee 34, Air Force 13
1972 Oklahoma 40, Auburn 22
1972* (Dec.) Oklahoma 14, Penn St. 0
1973 Notre Dame 24, Alabama 23
1974 Nebraska 13, Florida 10
1975 Alabama 13, Penn St. 6
1977 (Jan.) Pittsburgh 27, Georgia 3
1978 Alabama 35, Ohio St. 6
1979 Alabama 14, Penn St. 7
1980 Alabama 24, Arkansas 9
1981 Georgia 17, Notre Dame 10
1982 Pittsburgh 24, Georgia 20
1983 Penn St. 27, Georgia 23
1984 Auburn 9, Michigan 7
1985 Nebraska 28, LSU 10
1986 Tennessee 35, Miami (FL) 7
1987 Nebraska 30, LSU 15
1988 Syracuse 16, Auburn 16
1989 Florida St. 13, Auburn 7
1990 Miami (FL) 33, Alabama 25
1991 Tennessee 23, Virginia 22
1992 Notre Dame 39, Florida 28
1993 Alabama 34, Miami (FL) 13
1994 Florida 41, West Virginia 7
1995 Florida St. 23, Florida 17
1995 (Dec.) Virginia Tech 28, Texas 10
1997 (Jan.) Florida 52, Florida St. 20
1998 Florida St. 31, Ohio St. 14

* Penn St. awarded game by forfeit.

Fiesta Bowl, Tempe, AZ

1971 (Dec.) Arizona St. 45, Florida St. 38
1972 Arizona St. 49, Missouri 35
1973 Arizona St. 28, Pittsburgh 7
1974 Okla. St. 16, Brigham Young 6
1975 Arizona St. 17, Nebraska 14
1976 Oklahoma 41, Wyoming 7
1977 Penn St. 42, Arizona St. 30
1978 UCLA 10, Arkansas 10
1979 Pittsburgh 16, Arizona 10
1980 Penn St. 31, Ohio St. 19
1982 (Jan.) Penn St. 26, USC 10
1983 Arizona St. 32, Oklahoma 21
1984 Ohio St. 28, Pittsburgh 23
1985 UCLA 39, Miami (FL) 37
1986 Michigan 27, Nebraska 23
1987 Penn St. 14, Miami (FL) 10
1988 Florida St. 31, Nebraska 28
1989 Notre Dame 34, W. Virginia 21
1990 Florida St. 41, Nebraska 17
1991 Louisville 34, Alabama 7
1992 Penn St. 42, Tennessee 17
1993 Syracuse 26, Colorado 22
1994 Arizona 29, Miami (FL) 0
1995 Colorado 41, Notre Dame 24
1996 Nebraska 62, Florida 24
1997 Penn St. 38, Texas 15
1997 (Dec.) Kansas St. 35, Syracuse 18

Cotton Bowl, Dallas, TX

1937 (Jan.) TCU 16, Marquette 6
1938 Rice 28, Colorado 14
1939 St. Mary's 20, Texas Tech 13
1940 Clemson 6, Boston Coll. 3
1941 Texas A&M 13, Fordham 12
1942 Alabama 29, Texas A&M 21
1943 Texas 14, Georgia Tech 7
1944 Randolph Field 7, Texas 7
1945 Oklahoma A&M 34, TCU 0
1946 Texas 40, Missouri 27
1947 Arkansas 0, LSU 0
1948 SMU 13, Penn St. 13
1949 SMU 21, Oregon 13
1950 Rice 27, North Carolina 13
1951 Tennessee 20, Texas 14
1952 Kentucky 20, TCU 7
1953 Texas 16, Tennessee 0
1954 Rice 28, Alabama 6
1955 Georgia Tech 14, Arkansas 6
1956 Mississippi 14, TCU 13
1957 TCU 28, Syracuse 27
1958 Navy 20, Rice 7
1959 TCU 0, Air Force 0
1960 Syracuse 23, Texas 14
1961 Duke 7, Arkansas 6
1962 Texas 12, Mississippi 7
1963 LSU 13, Texas 0
1964 Texas 28, Navy 6
1965 Arkansas 10, Nebraska 7
1966 LSU 14, Arkansas 7
1966 (Dec.) Georgia 24, SMU 9
1968 (Jan.) Texas A&M 20, Alabama 16
1969 Texas 36, Tennessee 13
1970 Texas 21, Notre Dame 17
1971 Notre Dame 24, Texas 11
1972 Penn St. 30, Texas 6
1973 Texas 17, Alabama 13
1974 Nebraska 19, Texas 3
1975 Penn St. 41, Baylor 20
1976 Arkansas 31, Georgia 10
1977 Houston 30, Maryland 21
1978 Notre Dame 38, Texas 10
1979 Notre Dame 35, Houston 34
1980 Houston 17, Nebraska 14
1981 Alabama 30, Baylor 2
1982 Texas 14, Alabama 12
1983 SMU 7, Pittsburgh 3
1984 Georgia 10, Texas 9
1985 Boston Coll. 45, Houston 28
1986 Texas A&M 36, Auburn 16
1987 Ohio St. 28, Texas A&M 12
1988 Texas A&M 35, Notre Dame 10
1989 UCLA 17, Arkansas 3
1990 Tennessee 31, Arkansas 27
1991 Miami (FL) 46, Texas 3
1992 Florida St. 10, Texas A&M 2
1993 Notre Dame 28, Texas A&M 3
1994 Notre Dame 24, Texas A&M 21
1995 Southern Cal. 55, Tex. Tech 14
1996 Colorado 38, Oregon 6
1997 Brigham Young 19, Kansas St. 15
1998 UCLA 29, Texas A&M 23

Sun Bowl, El Paso, TX (John Hancock Bowl, 1989-93)

1936 (Jan.) Hardin-Simmons 14, New Mexico St. 14
1937 Hardin-Simmons 34, Texas Mines 6
1938 West Virginia 7, Texas Tech 6
1939 Utah 26, New Mexico 0
1940 Catholic U. 0, Arizona St. 0
1941 Western Reserve 26, Arizona St. 13
1942 Tulsa 6, Texas Tech 0
1943 2d Air Force 13, Hardin-Simmons 7
1944 Southwestern (TX) 7, New Mexico 0
1945 Southwestern (TX) 35, U. of Mexico 0
1946 New Mexico 34, Denver 24
1947 Cincinnati 18, Virginia Tech 6
1948 Miami (OH) 13, Texas Tech 12
1949 West Virginia 21, Texas Mines 12
1950 Texas Western 33, Georgetown 20
1951 West Texas St. 14, Cincinnati 13
1952 Texas Tech 25, Pacific (CA) 14
1953 Pacific (CA) 26, S. Mississippi 7
1954 Texas Western 37, S. Miss. 14
1955 Texas Western 47, Florida St. 20
1956 Wyoming 21, Texas Tech 14
1957 Geo. Washington 13, Texas Western 0
1958 Louisville 34, Drake 20
1958 (Dec.) Wyoming 14, Hardin-Simmons 6
1959 New Mexico St. 28, N. Texas St. 8
1960 New Mexico St. 20, Utah St. 13
1961 Villanova 17, Wichita 9
1962 West Texas St. 15, Ohio U. 14
1963 Oregon 21, SMU 14
1964 Georgia 7, Texas Tech 0
1965 Texas Western 13, TCU 12
1966 Wyoming 28, Florida St. 20
1967 UTEP 14, Mississippi 7
1968 Auburn 34, Arizona 10
1969 Nebraska 45, Georgia 6

(continued)

Sun Bowl *(continued)*

1970 Georgia Tech. 17, Texas Tech 9
1971 LSU 33, Iowa St. 15
1972 North Carolina 32, Texas Tech 28
1973 Missouri 34, Auburn 17
1974 Mississippi St. 26, North Carolina 24
1975 Pittsburgh 33, Kansas 19
1977 (Jan.) Texas A&M 37, Florida 14
1977 (Dec.) Stanford 24, LSU 14
1978 Texas 42, Maryland 0
1979 Washington 14, Texas 7
1980 Nebraska 31, Mississippi St. 17
1981 Oklahoma 40, Houston 14
1982 North Carolina 26, Texas 10
1983 Alabama 28, SMU 7
1984 Maryland 28, Tennessee 27
1985 Georgia 13, Arizona 13
1986 Alabama 28, Washington 6
1987 Oklahoma St. 35, West Virginia 33
1988 Alabama 29, Army 28
1989 Pittsburgh 31, Texas A&M 28
1990 Michigan St. 17, USC 16
1991 UCLA 6, Illinois 3
1992 Baylor 20, Arizona 15
1993 Oklahoma 41, Texas Tech 10
1994 Texas 35, North Carolina 31
1995 Iowa 38, Washington 18
1996 Stanford 38, Michigan St. 0
1997 Arizona St. 17, Iowa 7

Gator Bowl, Jacksonville, FL

1946 (Jan.) Wake Forest 26, S. Carolina 14
1947 Oklahoma 34, N. Carolina St. 13
1948 Maryland 20, Georgia 20
1949 Clemson 24, Missouri 23
1950 Maryland 20, Missouri 7
1951 Wyoming 20, Washington & Lee 7
1952 Miami (FL) 14, Clemson 0
1953 Florida 14, Tulsa 13
1954 Texas Tech 35, Auburn 13
1954 (Dec.) Auburn 33, Baylor 13
1955 Vanderbilt 25, Auburn 13
1956 Georgia Tech 21, Pittsburgh 14
1957 Tennessee 3, Texas A&M 0
1958 Mississippi 7, Florida 3
1960 (Jan.) Arkansas 14, Georgia Tech 7
1960 (Dec.) Florida 13, Baylor 12
1961 Penn St. 30, Georgia Tech 15
1962 Florida 17, Penn St. 7
1963 N. Carolina 35, Air Force 0
1965 (Jan.) Florida St. 36, Okla.19
1965 (Dec.) Georgia Tech 31, Texas Tech 21
1966 Tennessee 18, Syracuse 12
1967 Penn St. 17, Florida St. 17
1968 Missouri 35, Alabama 10
1969 Florida 14, Tennessee 13
1971 (Jan.) Auburn 35, Mississippi 28
1971 (Dec.) Georgia 7, N. Carolina 3
1972 Auburn 24, Colorado 3
1973 Texas Tech 28, Tenn. 19
1974 Auburn 27, Texas 3
1975 Maryland 13, Florida 0
1976 Notre Dame 20, Penn St. 9
1977 Pittsburgh 34, Clemson 3
1978 Clemson 17, Ohio St. 15
1979 N. Carolina 17, Michigan 15
1980 Pittsburgh 37, S. Carolina 9
1981 N. Carolina 31, Arkansas 27
1982 Florida St. 31, West Virginia 12
1983 Florida 14, Iowa 6
1984 Oklahoma St. 21, S. Carolina 14
1985 Florida St. 34, Oklahoma St. 23
1986 Clemson 27, Stanford 21
1987 LSU 30, S. Carolina 13
1989 (Jan.) Georgia 34, Michigan St. 27
1989 (Dec.) Clemson 27, W. Virginia 7
1991 (Jan.) Michigan 35, Mississippi 3
1991 (Dec.) Oklahoma 48, Virginia 14
1992 Florida 27, N. Carolina St. 10
1993 Alabama 24, N. Carolina 10
1994 Tennessee 45, Virginia Tech 23
1996 (Jan.) Syracuse 41, Clemson 0
1997 N. Carolina 20, W. Virginia 13
1998 N. Carolina 42, Virginia Tech 3

Outback Bowl, Tampa, FL (Hall of Fame Bowl Until 1996)

1986 (Dec.) Boston College 27, Georgia 24
1988 (Jan.) Michigan 28, Alabama 24
1989 Syracuse 23, LSU 10
1990 Auburn 31, Ohio St. 14
1991 Clemson 30, Illinois 0
1992 Syracuse 24, Ohio St. 17
1993 Tennessee 38, Boston College 23
1994 Michigan 42, N. Carolina St. 7
1995 Wisconsin 34, Duke 20
1996 Penn St. 43, Auburn 14
1997 Alabama 17, Michigan 14
1998 Georgia 33, Wisconsin 6

Liberty Bowl, Memphis, TN

1959 (Dec.) Penn St. 7, Alabama 0
1960 Penn St. 41, Oregon 12
1961 Syracuse 15, Miami (FL) 14
1962 Oregon St. 6, Villanova 0
1963 Mississippi St. 16, N. Carolina St. 12
1964 Utah 32, West Virginia 6
1965 Mississippi 13, Auburn 7
1966 Miami (FL) 14, Virginia Tech 7
1967 N. Carolina St. 14, Georgia 7
1968 Mississippi 34, Virginia Tech 17
1969 Colorado 47, Alabama 33
1970 Tulane 17, Colorado 3
1971 Tennessee 14, Arkansas 13
1972 Georgia Tech 31, Iowa St. 30
1973 N. Carolina St. 31, Kansas 18
1974 Tennessee 7, Maryland 3
1975 USC 20, Texas A&M 0
1976 Alabama 36, UCLA 6
1977 Nebraska 21, N. Carolina 17
1978 Missouri 20, LSU 15
1979 Penn St. 9, Tulane 6
1980 Purdue 28, Missouri 25
1981 Ohio St. 31, Navy 28
1982 Alabama 21, Illinois 15
1983 Notre Dame 19, Boston Coll. 18
1984 Auburn 21, Arkansas 15
1985 Baylor 21, LSU 7
1986 Tennessee 21, Minnesota 14
1987 Georgia 20, Arkansas 17
1988 Indiana 34, S. Carolina 10
1989 Mississippi 42, Air Force 29
1990 Air Force 23, Ohio St. 11
1991 Air Force 38, Mississippi St. 15
1992 Mississippi 13, Air Force 0
1993 Louisville 18, Michigan St. 7
1994 Illinois 30, East Carolina 0
1995 East Carolina 19, Stanford 13
1996 Syracuse 30, Houston 17
1997 So. Mississippi 41, Pittsburgh 7

Insight.com Bowl, Tucson, AZ (Copper Bowl Until 1997)

1989 (Dec.) Arizona 17, N. Carolina St. 10
1990 California 17, Wyoming 15
1991 Indiana 24, Baylor 0
1992 Washington St. 31, Utah 28
1993 Kansas St. 52, Wyoming 17
1994 Brigham Young 31, Oklahoma 6
1995 Texas Tech 55, Air Force 41
1996 Wisconsin 38, Utah 10
1997 Arizona 20, New Mexico 14

Independence Bowl, Shreveport, LA

1976 (Dec.)McNeese St. 20, Tulsa 16
1977 Louisiana Tech 24, Louisville 14
1978 E. Carolina 35, Louisiana Tech 13
1979 Syracuse 31, McNeese St. 7
1980 So. Mississippi 16, McNeese St. 14
1981 Texas A&M 33, Oklahoma St. 16
1982 Wisconsin 14, Kansas St. 3
1983 Air Force 9, Mississippi 3
1984 Air Force 23, Virginia Tech 7
1985 Minnesota 20, Clemson 13
1986 Mississippi 20, Texas Tech 17
1987 Washington 24, Tulane 12
1988 So. Mississippi 38, UTEP 18
1989 Oregon 27, Tulsa 24
1990 Louisiana Tech 34, Maryland 34
1991 Georgia 24, Arkansas 15
1992 Wake Forest 39, Oregon 35
1993 Virginia Tech 45, Indiana 20
1994 Virginia 20, Texas Christian 10
1995 LSU 45, Michigan St. 26
1996 Auburn 32, Army 29
1997 LSU 27, Notre Dame 9

Florida Citrus Bowl, Orlando, FL (Tangerine Bowl Until 1983)

1947 (Jan.) Catawba 31, Maryville 6
1948 Catawba 7, Marshall 0
1949 Murray St. 21, Sul Ross St. 21
1950 St. Vincent 7, Emory & Henry 6
1951 Morris Harvey 35, Emory & Henry 14
1952 Stetson 35, Arkansas St. 20
1953 East Texas St. 33, Tenn. Tech 0
1954 East Texas St. 7, Arkansas St. 7
1955 Neb.-Omaha 7, E. Kentucky 6
1956 Juniata 6, Missouri Valley 6
1957 West Texas St. 20, So. Miss. 13
1958 East Texas St. 10, So. Miss. 9
1958 (Dec.) East Texas St. 26, Missouri Valley 7
1960 (Jan.) Middle Tennessee 21, Presbyterian 12
1960 (Dec.) Citadel 27, Tenn. Tech 0
1961 Lamar 21, Middle Tennessee 14
1962 Houston 49, Miami (OH) 21
1963 Western Ky. 27, Coast Guard 0
1964 E. Carolina 14, Massachusetts 13
1965 E. Carolina 31, Maine 0
1966 Morgan St. 14, West Chester 6
1967 Tenn.-Martin 25, West Chester 8
1968 Richmond 49, Ohio U. 42
1969 Toledo 56, Davidson 33
1970 Toledo 40, William & Mary 12
1971 Toledo 28, Richmond 3
1972 Tampa 21, Kent St. 18
1973 Miami (OH) 16, Florida 7
1974 Miami (OH) 21, Georgia 10
1975 Miami (OH) 20, S. Carolina 7
1976 Okla. St. 49, Brigham Young 21
1977 Florida St. 40, Texas Tech 17
1978 N. Carolina St. 30, Pittsburgh 17
1979 LSU 34, Wake Forest 10
1980 Florida 35, Maryland 20
1981 Missouri 19, So. Mississippi 17
1982 Auburn 33, Boston College 26
1983 Tennessee 30, Maryland 23
1984 Georgia 17, Florida St. 17
1985 Ohio St. 10, Brigham Young 7
1987 (Jan.) Auburn 16, USC 7
1988 Clemson 35, Penn St. 10
1989 Clemson 13, Oklahoma 6
1990 Illinois 31, Virginia 21
1991 Georgia Tech 45, Nebraska 21
1992 California 37, Clemson 13
1993 Georgia 21, Ohio St. 14
1994 Penn St. 31, Tennessee 13
1995 Alabama 24, Ohio St. 17
1996 Tennessee 20, Ohio St. 14
1997 Tennessee 48, Northwestern 28
1998 Florida 21, Penn St. 6

Peach Bowl, Atlanta, GA

1968 (Dec.) LSU 31, Florida St. 27
1969 W. Virginia 14, S. Carolina 3
1970 Arizona St. 48, N. Carolina 26
1971 Mississippi 41, Georgia Tech 18
1972 N. Carolina St. 49, W. Virginia 13
1973 Georgia 17, Maryland 16
1974 Vanderbilt 6, Texas Tech 6
1975 W. Virginia 13, N. Carolina St. 10
1976 Kentucky 21, N. Carolina 0
1977 N. Carolina St. 24, Iowa St. 14
1978 Purdue 41, Georgia Tech. 21
1979 Baylor 24, Clemson 18
1981 (Jan.) Miami (FL) 20, Virginia Tech 10
1981 (Dec.) W. Virginia 26, Florida 6
1982 Iowa 28, Tennessee 22
1983 Florida St. 28, N. Carolina 3
1984 Virginia 27, Purdue 22
1985 Army 31, Illinois 29
1986 Va. Tech 25, N. Carolina St. 24
1988 (Jan.) Tennessee 28, Indiana 22
1988 (Dec.) N. Carolina St. 28, Iowa 23
1989 Syracuse 19, Georgia 18
1990 Auburn 27, Indiana 23
1992 (Jan.) E. Carolina 37, N. Carolina St. 34
1993 N. Carolina 21, Mississippi St. 17
1993 (Dec.) Clemson 14, Kentucky 13
1995 (Jan.) N. Carolina St. 28, Mississippi St. 24
1995 (Dec.) Virginia 34, Georgia 27
1996 LSU 10, Clemson 7
1998 (Jan.) Auburn 21, Clemson 17

Holiday Bowl, San Diego, CA

1978 (Dec.) Navy 23, Brigham Young 16
1979 Indiana 38, Brigham Young 37
1980 Brigham Young 46, SMU 45
1981 Brigham Young 38, Washington St. 36
1982 Ohio St. 47, Brigham Young 17
1983 Brigham Young 21, Missouri 17
1984 Brigham Young 24, Michigan 17
1985 Arkansas 18, Arizona St. 17
1986 Iowa 39, San Diego St. 38
1987 Iowa 20, Wyoming 19
1988 Oklahoma St. 62, Wyoming 14
1989 Penn St. 50, Brigham Young 39
1990 Texas A&M 65, Brigham Young 14
1991 Iowa 13, Brigham Young 13
1992 Hawaii 27, Illinois 17
1993 Ohio St. 28, Brigham Young 21
1994 Michigan 24, Colorado St. 14
1995 Kansas St. 54, Colorado St. 21
1996 Colorado 33, Washington 21
1997 Colorado St. 35, Missouri 24

Aloha Bowl, Honolulu, HI

1982 (Dec.) Washington 21, Md. 20
1983 Penn St. 13, Washington 10
1984 SMU 27, Notre Dame 20
1985 Alabama 24, USC 3
1986 Arizona 30, North Carolina 21
1987 UCLA 20, Florida 16
1988 Washington St. 24, Houston 22
1989 Michigan St. 33, Hawaii 13
1990 Syracuse 28, Arizona 0
1991 Georgia Tech 18, Stanford 17
1992 Kansas 23, Brigham Young 20
1993 Colorado 41, Fresno St. 30
1994 Boston Coll. 12, Kansas St. 7
1995 Kansas 51, UCLA 30
1996 Navy 42, California 38
1997 Washington 51, Michigan St. 23

Carquest Bowl, Miami, FL (Blockbuster Bowl Until 1993)

1990 (Dec.) Florida St. 24, Penn St. 17
1991 Alabama 30, Colorado 25
1993 (Jan.) Stanford 24, Penn St. 3
1994 Boston Coll. 31, Virginia 13
1995 S. Carolina 24, W. Virginia 21
1995 (Dec.) N. Carolina 20, Arkansas 10
1996 Miami (FL) 31, Virginia 21
1997 Georgia Tech 35, W. Virginia 30

Las Vegas Bowl, Las Vegas, NV

1992 (Dec.) Bowling Green 35, Nevada 34
1993 Utah St. 42, Ball St. 33
1994 UNLV 52, Central Michigan 24
1995 Toledo 40, Nevada 37 (OT)
1996 Nevada 18, Ball St. 15
1997 Oregon 41, Air Force 13

Alamo Bowl, San Antonio, TX

1993 (Dec.) California 37, Iowa 3
1994 Washington St. 10, Baylor 3
1995 Texas A&M 22, Michigan 20
1996 Iowa 27, Texas Tech 0
1997 Purdue 33, Oklahoma St. 20

Motor City Bowl, Pontiac, MI

1997 (Dec.) Mississippi 34, Marshall 31

Humanitarian Bowl, Boise, ID

1997 (Dec.) Cincinnati 35, Utah St. 19

Selected College Division I Football Teams

(1997 record does not include bowl games or Division I-AA playoff games; coaches at the start of 1998 season)

Team	Nickname	Team colors	Conference	Coach	1997 record (W-L)
Air Force	Falcons	Blue & silver	Western Athletic	Fisher DeBerry	10-2
Akron	Zips	Blue & gold	Mid-American	Lee Owens	2-9
Alabama	Crimson Tide	Crimson & white	Southeastern	Mike DuBose	4-7
Arizona	Wildcats	Cardinal & navy	Pacific Ten	Dick Tomey	6-5
Arizona State	Sun Devils	Maroon & gold	Pacific Ten	Bruce Snyder	8-3
Arkansas	Razorbacks	Cardinal & white	Southeastern	Houston Nutt	4-7
Arkansas State	Indians	Scarlet & black	Independent	Joe Hollis	2-9
Army	Cadets, Black Knights	Black, gold, gray	Independent	Bob Sutton	4-7
Auburn	Tigers	Burnt orange & navy	Southeastern	Terry Bowden	9-3
Ball State	Cardinals	Cardinal & white	Mid-American	Bill Lynch	5-6
Baylor	Bears	Green & gold	Big Twelve	Dave Roberts	2-9
Boston College	Eagles	Maroon & gold	Big East	Tom O'Brien	4-7
Bowling Green	Falcons	Orange & brown	Mid-American	Gary Blackney	3-8
Brigham Young (BYU)	Cougars	Royal blue & white	Western Athletic	LaVell Edwards	6-5
Brown	Bears	Brown, cardinal, white	Ivy League	Phil Estes	6-4
California	Golden Bears	Blue & gold	Pacific Ten	Tom Holmoe	3-8
Central Michigan	Chippewas	Maroon & gold	Mid-American	Dick Flynn	2-9
Cincinnati	Bearcats	Red & black	Conference USA	Rick Minter	7-4
Citadel	Bulldogs	Blue & white	Southern	Don Powers	6-5
Clemson	Tigers	Purple & orange	Atlantic Coast	Tommy West	7-4
Colgate	Red Raiders	Maroon, gray, & white	Patriot League	Dick Biddle	7-4
Colorado	Golden Buffaloes	Silver, gold, & black	Big Twelve	Rick Neuheisel	5-6
Colorado State	Rams	Green & gold	Western Athletic	Sonny Lubick	10-2
Columbia	Lions	Columbia blue & white	Ivy League	Ray Tellier	3-7
Connecticut	Huskies	Blue & white	Atlantic Ten	Skip Holtz	7-4
Cornell	Big Red	Carnelian & white	Ivy League	Peter Mangurian	5-5
Dartmouth	Big Green	Dartmouth green & white	Ivy League	John Lyons	8-2
Delaware	Fightin' Blue Hens	Blue & gold	Atlantic Ten	Harold Raymond	10-1
Delaware State	Hornets	Red & blue	Mid-Eastern Athletic	John McKenzie	3-8
Duke	Blue Devils	Royal blue & white	Atlantic Coast	Fred Goldsmith	2-9
East Carolina	Pirates	Purple & gold	Conference USA	Steve Logan	5-6
East Tennessee State	Buccaneers	Blue & gold	Southern	Paul Hamilton	7-4
Eastern Illinois	Panthers	Blue & gray	Ohio Valley	Bob Spoo	8-3

(continued)

Team	Nickname	Team colors	Conference	Coach	1997 record (W-L)
Eastern Kentucky	Colonels	Maroon & white	Ohio Valley	Roy Kidd	8-3
Eastern Michigan	Eagles	Dark green & white	Mid-American	Rick Rasnick	4-7
Eastern Washington	Eagles	Red & white	Big Sky	Mike Kramer	10-1
Florida	Gators	Orange & blue	Southeastern	Steve Spurrier	9-2
Florida A&M	Rattlers	Orange & green	Mid-Eastern Athletic	Billy Joe	9-2
Florida State	Seminoles	Garnet & gold	Atlantic Coast	Bobby Bowden	10-1
Fresno State	Bulldogs	Cardinal & blue	Western Athletic	Pat Hill	6-6
Furman	Paladins	Purple & white	Southern	Bobby Johnson	7-4
Georgia	Bulldogs	Red & black	Southeastern	Jim Donnan	9-2
Georgia Southern	Eagles	Blue & white	Southern	Paul Johnson	9-2
Georgia Tech	Yellow Jackets	Old gold & white	Atlantic Coast	George O'Leary	6-5
Grambling	Tigers	Black & gold	Southwestern	Doug Williams	3-8
Harvard	Crimson	Crimson, black, white	Ivy League	Tim Murphy	9-1
Hawaii	Rainbows	Green & white	Western Athletic	Fred vonAppen	3-9
Holy Cross	Crusaders	Royal purple	Patriot League	Dan Allen	3-8
Houston	Cougars	Scarlet & white	Conference USA	Kim Helton	3-8
Howard	Bison	Blue, white & red	Mid-Eastern Athletic	Steve Wilson	7-4
Idaho	Vandals	Silver & gold	Big West	Chris Tormey	5-6
Idaho State	Bengals	Orange & black	Big Sky	Tom Walsh	3-8
Illinois	Fighting Illini	Orange & blue	Big Ten	Ron Turner	0-11
Illinois State	Redbirds	Red & white	Gateway	Todd Berry	2-9
Indiana	Hoosiers	Cream & crimson	Big Ten	Cam Cameron	2-9
Indiana State	Sycamores	Blue & white	Gateway	Tim McGuire	3-8
Iowa	Hawkeyes	Old gold & black	Big Ten	Hayden Fry	7-4
Iowa State	Cyclones	Cardinal & gold	Big Twelve	Dan McCarney	1-10
Jackson State	Tigers	Blue & white	Southwestern	James Carson	9-2
James Madison	Dukes	Purple & gold	Atlantic Ten	Alex Wood	5-6
Kansas	Jayhawks	Crimson & blue	Big Twelve	Terry Allen	5-6
Kansas State	Wildcats	Purple & white	Big Twelve	Bill Snyder	10-1
Kent	Golden Flashes	Navy blue & gold	Mid-American	Dean Pees	3-8
Kentucky	Wildcats	Blue & white	Southeastern	Hal Mumme	5-6
Lafayette	Leopards	Maroon & white	Patriot League	Bill Russo	3-8
Lehigh	Mountain Hawks	Brown & white	Patriot League	Kevin Higgins	4-7
Liberty	Flames	Red, white, blue	Independent	Sam Rutigliano	9-2
Louisiana State (LSU)	Fighting Tigers	Purple & gold	Southeastern	Gerry DiNardo	8-3
Louisiana Tech	Bulldogs	Red & blue	Independent	Gary Crowton	9-2
Louisville	Cardinals	Red, black, white	Conference USA	John L. Smith	1-10
Maine	Black Bears	Blue & white	Atlantic Ten	Jack Cosgrove	5-6
Marshall	Thundering Herd	Green & white	Mid-American	Bob Pruett	10-2
Maryland	Terrapins	Red, white, black, gold	Atlantic Coast	Ron Vanderlinden	2-9
Massachusetts	Minutemen	Maroon & white	Atlantic Ten	Mark Whipple	2-9
McNeese State	Cowboys	Blue & gold	Southland	Bobby Keasler	10-1
Memphis	Tigers	Blue & gray	Conference USA	Rip Scherer	4-7
Miami (Florida)	Hurricanes	Orange, green, white	Big East	Butch Davis	5-6
Miami (Ohio)	RedHawks	Red & white	Mid-American	Randy Walker	8-3
Michigan	Wolverines	Maize & blue	Big Ten	Lloyd Carr	11-0
Michigan State	Spartans	Green & white	Big Ten	Nick Saban	7-4
Middle Tennessee St.	Blue Raiders	Blue & white	Ohio Valley	Boots Donnelly	4-6
Minnesota	Golden Gophers	Maroon & gold	Big Ten	Glen Mason	3-9
Mississippi	Rebels	Cardinal red & navy	Southeastern	Tommy Tuberville	7-4
Mississippi State	Bulldogs	Maroon & white	Southeastern	Jackie Sherrill	7-4
Mississippi Valley	Delta Devils	Green & white	Southwestern	Larry Dorsey	4-6
Missouri	Tigers	Old gold & black	Big Twelve	Larry Smith	7-4
Montana	Grizzlies	Copper, silver, gold	Big Sky	Mick Dennehy	8-3
Montana State	Bobcats	Blue & gold	Big Sky	Cliff Hysell	6-5
Morehead State	Eagles	Blue & gold	Independent	Matt Ballard	7-3
Morgan State	Bears	Blue & orange	Mid-Eastern Athletic	Stump Mitchell	3-7
Murray State	Racers	Blue & gold	Ohio Valley	Denver Johnson	7-4
Navy	Midshipmen	Navy blue & gold	Independent	Charlie Weatherbie	7-4
Nebraska	Cornhuskers	Scarlet & cream	Big Twelve	Frank Solich	12-0
Nevada	Wolf Pack	Silver & blue	Big West	Jeff Tisdel	5-6
Nev.-Las Vegas (UNLV)	Rebels	Scarlet & gray	Western Athletic	Jeff Horton	3-8
New Hampshire	Wildcats	Blue & white	Atlantic Ten	Bill Bowes	5-6
New Mexico	Lobos	Cherry & silver	Western Athletic	Rocky Long	9-3
New Mexico State	Aggies	Crimson & white	Big West	Tony Samuel	2-9
Nicholls St.	Colonels	Red & gray	Southland	Darren Barbier	5-6
North Carolina	Tar Heels	Carolina blue & white	Atlantic Coast	Carl Torbush	10-1
North Carolina A & T	Aggies	Blue & gold	Mid-Eastern Athletic	Bill Hayes	7-4
North Carolina State	Wolfpack	Red & white	Atlantic Coast	Mike O'Cain	6-5
North Texas	Mean Green Eagles	Green & white	Big West	Darrell Dickey	4-7
Northeast Louisiana	Indians	Maroon & gold	Independent	Ed Zaunbrecher	5-7
Northeastern	Huskies	Red & black	Atlantic Ten	Barry Gallup	8-3
Northern Arizona	Lumberjacks	Blue & gold	Big Sky	Jerome Souers	6-5
Northern Illinois	Huskies	Cardinal & black	Mid-American	Joe Novak	0-11
Northern Iowa	Panthers	Purple & old gold	Gateway	Mike Dunbar	7-4
Northwestern	Wildcats	Purple & white	Big Ten	Gary Barnett	5-7
Northwestern State	Demons	Purple, white, & burnt orange	Southland	Sam Goodwin	8-3
Notre Dame	Fighting Irish	Gold & blue	Independent	Bob Davie	7-5
Ohio	Bobcats	Ohio green & white	Mid-American	Jim Grobe	8-3
Ohio State	Buckeyes	Scarlet & gray	Big Ten	John Cooper	10-2
Oklahoma	Sooners	Crimson & cream	Big Twelve	John Blake	4-8
Oklahoma State	Cowboys	Orange & black	Big Twelve	Bob Simmons	8-3
Oregon	Ducks	Green & yellow	Pacific Ten	Mike Bellotti	6-5
Oregon State	Beavers	Orange & black	Pacific Ten	Mike Riley	3-8
Penn State	Nittany Lions	Blue & white	Big Ten	Joe Paterno	9-2

(continued)

Team	Nickname	Team colors	Conference	Coach	1997 record (W-L)
Pennsylvania	Quakers	Red & blue	Ivy League	Al Bagnoli	6-4
Pittsburgh	Panthers	Blue & gold	Big East	Walt Harris	6-5
Princeton	Tigers	Orange & black	Ivy League	Steve Tosches	5-5
Purdue	Boilermakers	Old gold & black	Big Ten	Joe Tiller	8-3
Rhode Island	Rams	Light & dark blue, white	Atlantic Ten	Floyd Keith	2-9
Rice	Owls	Blue & gray	Western Athletic	Ken Hatfield	7-4
Richmond	Spiders	Red & blue	Atlantic Ten	Jim Reid	6-5
Rutgers	Scarlet Knights	Scarlet	Big East	Terry Shea	0-11
Sam Houston State	Bearkats	Orange & white	Southland	Ron Randleman	5-6
Samford	Bulldogs	Crimson & blue	Independent	Pete Hurt	7-4
San Diego State	Aztecs	Scarlet & black	Western Athletic	Ted Tollner	5-7
San Jose State	Spartans	Gold, white, blue	Western Athletic	Dave Baldwin	4-7
South Carolina	Fighting Gamecocks	Garnet & black	Southeastern	Brad Scott	5-6
South Carolina State	Bulldogs	Garnet & blue	Mid-Eastern Athletic	Willie E. Jeffries	9-2
SE Missouri State	Indians	Red & black	Ohio Valley	John Mumford	4-7
Southern California (USC)	Trojans	Cardinal & gold	Pacific Ten	Paul Hackett	6-5
Southern Illinois	Salukis	Maroon & white	Gateway	Jan Quarless	3-8
Southern Methodist (SMU)	Mustangs	Red & blue	Western Athletic	Mike Cavan	6-5
Southern Mississippi	Golden Eagles	Black & gold	Conference USA	Jeff Bower	8-3
SW Missouri State	Bears	Maroon & white	Gateway	Del Miller	5-6
SW Texas State	Bobcats	Maroon & gold	Southland	Bob DeBesse	5-6
SW Louisiana	Ragin' Cajuns	Vermilion & white	Independent	Nelson Stokley	1-10
Stanford	Cardinal	Cardinal & white	Pacific Ten	Tyrone Willingham	5-6
Stephen F. Austin State	Lumberjacks	Purple & white	Southland	John Pearce	8-3
Syracuse	Orangemen	Orange	Big East	Paul Pasqualoni	9-3
Temple	Owls	Cherry & white	Big East	Bobby Wallace	3-8
Tennessee	Volunteers	Orange & white	Southeastern	Phillip Fulmer	11-1
Tennessee-Chattanooga	Mocs	Navy blue & gold	Southern	Buddy Green	7-4
Tennessee-Martin	Skyhawks	Orange, white, blue	Ohio Valley	Jim Marshall	1-10
Tennessee State	Tigers	Royal blue & white	Ohio Valley	L. C. Cole	4-7
Tennessee Tech	Golden Eagles	Purple & gold	Ohio Valley	Mike Hennigan	6-5
Texas	Longhorns	Burnt orange & white	Big Twelve	Mack Brown	4-7
Texas A & M	Aggies	Maroon & white	Big Twelve	R. C. Slocum	9-3
Texas Christian (TCU)	Horned Frogs	Purple & white	Western Athletic	Dennis Franchione	1-10
Texas Southern	Tigers	Maroon & gray	Southwestern	Bill Thomas	5-6
Texas Tech	Red Raiders	Scarlet & black	Big Twelve	Spike Dykes	6-5
Toledo	Rockets	Blue & gold	Mid-American	Gary Pinkel	9-3
Troy State	Trojans	Cardinal, gray, black	Southland	Larry Blakeney	5-6
Tulane	Green Wave	Olive green & sky blue	Conference USA	Tommy Bowden	7-4
Tulsa	Golden Hurricane	Blue & gold	Western Athletic	David Rader	2-9
UCLA	Bruins	Blue & gold	Pacific Ten	Bob Toledo	9-2
Utah	Utes	Crimson & white	Western Athletic	Ron McBride	6-5
Utah State	Aggies	Navy blue & white	Big West	Dave Arslanian	6-5
UTEP (Texas-El Paso)	Miners	Orange, blue, white	Western Athletic	Charlie Bailey	4-7
Vanderbilt	Commodores	Black & gold	Southeastern	Woody Widenhofer	3-8
Villanova	Wildcats	Blue & white	Atlantic Ten	Andy Talley	11-0
Virginia	Cavaliers	Orange & blue	Atlantic Coast	George Welsh	7-4
Virginia Military Inst. (VMI)	Keydets	Red, white & yellow	Southern	Ted Cain	0-11
Virginia Tech	Gobblers, Hokies	Orange & maroon	Big East	Frank Beamer	7-4
Wake Forest	Demon Deacons	Old gold & black	Atlantic Coast	Jim Caldwell	5-6
Washington	Huskies	Purple & gold	Pacific Ten	Jim Lambright	7-4
Washington State	Cougars	Crimson & gray	Pacific Ten	Mike Price	10-1
Weber State	Wildcats	Royal purple & white	Big Sky	Jerry Graybeal	6-5
West Virginia	Mountaineers	Old gold & blue	Big East	Don Nehlen	7-4
Western Carolina	Catamounts	Purple & gold	Southern	Bill Bleil	3-8
Western Illinois	Leathernecks	Purple & gold	Gateway	Randy Ball	10-1
Western Kentucky	Hilltoppers	Red & white	Independent	Jack Harbaugh	9-1
Western Michigan	Broncos	Brown & gold	Mid-American	Gary Darnell	8-3
William & Mary	Tribe	Green, gold, silver	Atlantic Ten	Jimmye Laycock	7-4
Wisconsin	Badgers	Cardinal & white	Big Ten	Barry Alvarez	8-4
Wyoming	Cowboys	Brown & yellow	Western Athletic	Dana Dimel	7-6
Yale	Bulldogs, Elis	Yale blue & white	Ivy League	Jack Siedlecki	1-9
Youngstown State	Penguins	Red & white	Gateway	Jim Tressel	9-2

Heisman Trophy Winners

Awarded annually to the nation's outstanding college football player by the Downtown Athletic Club.

1935 Jay Berwanger, Chicago, HB
1936 Larry Kelley, Yale, E
1937 Clinton Frank, Yale, HB
1938 David O'Brien, Texas Christian, QB
1939 Nile Kinnick, Iowa, HB
1940 Tom Harmon, Michigan, HB
1941 Bruce Smith, Minnesota, HB
1942 Frank Sinkwich, Georgia, HB
1943 Angelo Bertelli, Notre Dame, QB
1944 Leslie Horvath, Ohio St., QB
1945 Felix Blanchard, Army, FB
1946 Glenn Davis, Army, HB
1947 John Lujack, Notre Dame, QB
1948 Doak Walker, SMU, HB
1949 Leon Hart, Notre Dame, E
1950 Vic Janowicz, Ohio St., HB
1951 Richard Kazmaier, Princeton, HB
1952 Billy Vessels, Oklahoma, HB
1953 John Lattner, Notre Dame, HB
1954 Alan Ameche, Wisconsin, FB
1955 Howard Cassady, Ohio St., HB
1956 Paul Hornung, Notre Dame, QB
1957 John Crow, Texas A & M, HB
1958 Pete Dawkins, Army, HB
1959 Billy Cannon, LSU, HB
1960 Joe Bellino, Navy, HB
1961 Ernest Davis, Syracuse, HB
1962 Terry Baker, Oregon St., QB
1963 Roger Staubach, Navy, QB
1964 John Huarte, Notre Dame, QB
1965 Mike Garrett, USC, HB
1966 Steve Spurrier, Florida, QB
1967 Gary Beban, UCLA, QB
1968 O. J. Simpson, USC, RB
1969 Steve Owens, Oklahoma, RB
1970 Jim Plunkett, Stanford, QB
1971 Pat Sullivan, Auburn, QB
1972 Johnny Rodgers, Nebraska, RB-WR
1973 John Cappelletti, Penn St., RB
1974 Archie Griffin, Ohio St., RB
1975 Archie Griffin, Ohio St., RB
1976 Tony Dorsett, Pittsburgh, RB
1977 Earl Campbell, Texas, RB
1978 Billy Sims, Oklahoma, RB
1979 Charles White, USC, RB
1980 George Rogers, S. Carolina, RB
1981 Marcus Allen, USC, RB
1982 Herschel Walker, Georgia, RB
1983 Mike Rozier, Nebraska, RB
1984 Doug Flutie, Boston College, QB
1985 Bo Jackson, Auburn, RB
1986 Vinny Testaverde, Miami, QB
1987 Tim Brown, Notre Dame, WR
1988 Barry Sanders, Oklahoma St., RB
1989 Andre Ware, Houston, QB
1990 Ty Detmer, BYU, QB
1991 Desmond Howard, Michigan, WR
1992 Gino Torretta, Miami, QB
1993 Charlie Ward, Florida St., QB
1994 Rashaan Salaam, Colorado, RB
1995 Eddie George, Ohio St., RB
1996 Danny Wuerffel, Florida, QB
1997 Charles Woodson, Michigan, CB

Outland Award Winners

Honoring the outstanding interior lineman selected by the Football Writers Association of America.

1946 George Connor, Notre Dame, T
1947 Joe Steffy, Army, G
1948 Bill Fischer, Notre Dame, G
1949 Ed Bagdon, Michigan St., G
1950 Bob Gain, Kentucky, T
1951 Jim Weatherall, Oklahoma, T
1952 Dick Modzelewski, Maryland, T
1953 J. D. Roberts, Oklahoma, G
1954 Bill Brooks, Arkansas, G
1955 Calvin Jones, Iowa, G
1956 Jim Parker, Ohio St., G
1957 Alex Karras, Iowa, T
1958 Zeke Smith, Auburn, G
1959 Mike McGee, Duke, T
1960 Tom Brown, Minnesota, G
1961 Merlin Olsen, Utah St., T
1962 Bobby Bell, Minnesota, T
1963 Scott Appleton, Texas, T
1964 Steve Delong, Tennessee, T
1965 Tommy Nobis, Texas, G
1966 Loyd Phillips, Arkansas, T
1967 Ron Yary, Southern Cal, T
1968 Bill Stanfill, Georgia, T
1969 Mike Reid, Penn St., DT
1970 Jim Stillwagon, Ohio St., MG
1971 Larry Jacobson, Nebraska, DT
1972 Rich Glover, Nebraska, MG
1973 John Hicks, Ohio St., OT
1974 Randy White, Maryland, DE
1975 Lee Roy Selmon, Oklahoma, DT
1976 Ross Browner, Notre Dame, DE
1977 Brad Shearer, Texas, DT
1978 Greg Roberts, Oklahoma, G
1979 Jim Ritcher, North Carolina St., C
1980 Mark May, Pittsburgh, OT
1981 Dave Rimington, Nebraska, C
1982 Dave Rimington, Nebraska, C
1983 Dean Steinkuhler, Nebraska, G
1984 Bruce Smith, Virginia Tech, DT
1985 Mike Ruth, Boston College, NG
1986 Jason Buck, BYU, DT
1987 Chad Hennings, Air Force, DT
1988 Tracy Rocker, Auburn, DT
1989 Mohammed Elewonibi, BYU, G
1990 Russell Maryland, Miami (FL), DT
1991 Steve Emtman, Washington, DT
1992 Will Shields, Nebraska, G
1993 Rob Waldrop, Arizona, NG
1994 Zach Wiegert, Nebraska, OT
1995 Jonathan Ogden, UCLA, OT
1996 Orlando Pace, Ohio St., OT
1997 Aaron Taylor, Nebraska, OT

All-Time Division I-A Percentage Leaders

(Classified as Division I-A for the last 10 years; record includes bowl games; ties computed as half won and half lost)

						Bowl Games**		
	Years	Won	Lost	Tied	Pct.	W	L	T
Notre Dame	109	753	228	42	.757	13	9	0
Michigan	118	776	254	36	.745	14	15	0
Alabama*	103	717	260	43	.724	28	17	3
Ohio St.	108	700	275	53	.707	13	17	0
Oklahoma	103	677	267	53	.706	20	11	1
Texas	105	717	291	33	.705	17	18	2
Nebraska	108	722	292	40	.704	18	18	0
USC	105	659	270	54	.698	25	13	0
Penn St.	111	715	299	41	.697	21	11	2
Tennessee*	101	677	285	52	.693	21	17	0
Florida St. *	51	358	181	17	.659	16	8	2
Washington*	108	593	325	50	.638	13	10	1
Central Michigan	97	500	280	36	.635	0	2	0
Miami (OH) *	109	574	322	44	.634	5	2	0
LSU	104	603	341	47	632	14	16	1
Arizona St	85	473	272	24	.631	10	6	1
Army	108	611	348	51	.630	2	2	0
Georgia	104	616	351	54	.630	16	14	3
Auburn*	105	593	347	47	.625	14	10	2
Colorado	108	593	359	36	.618	9	12	0
Miami (FL)	71	443	274	19	.615	11	11	0
Florida	91	535	338	40	.608	12	13	0
Texas A&M	103	583	374	48	.604	12	11	0
Syracuse	108	617	397	49	.603	10	7	1
UCLA	79	464	299	37	.603	11	9	1

*Includes games that were forfeited or changed by action of NCAA Council and/or Committee on Infractions. **Includes major bowl games only; that is, those where team's opponent was classified as a major college team that season or at the time of the bowl game.

College Football Coach of the Year

The Division I-A Coach of the Year has been selected by the American Football Coaches Assn. since 1935 and selected by the Football Writers Assn. of America since 1957. When polls disagree, both winners are indicated.

1935 Lynn Waldorf, Northwestern
1936 Dick Harlow, Harvard
1937 Edward Mylin, Lafayette
1938 Bill Kern, Carnegie Tech
1939 Eddie Anderson, Iowa
1940 Clark Shaughnessy, Stanford
1941 Frank Leahy, Notre Dame
1942 Bill Alexander, Georgia Tech
1943 Amos Alonzo Stagg, Pacific
1944 Carroll Widdoes, Ohio St.
1945 Bo McMillin, Indiana
1946 Earl "Red" Blaik, Army
1947 Fritz Crisler, Michigan
1948 Bennie Oosterbaan, Michigan
1949 Bud Wilkinson, Oklahoma
1950 Charlie Caldwell, Princeton
1951 Chuck Taylor, Stanford
1952 Biggie Munn, Michigan St.
1953 Jim Tatum, Maryland
1954 Henry "Red" Sanders, UCLA
1955 Duffy Daugherty, Michigan St.
1956 Bowden Wyatt, Tennessee
1957 Woody Hayes, Ohio St.
1958 Paul Dietzel, LSU
1959 Ben Schwartzwalder, Syracuse
1960 Murray Warmath, Minnesota
1961 Paul "Bear" Bryant, Ala. (AFCA); Darrell Royal, Texas (FWAA)
1962 John McKay, USC
1963 Darrell Royal, Texas
1964 Ara Parseghian, Notre Dame, & Frank Broyles, Arkansas (AFCA); Ara Parseghian (FWAA)
1965 Tommy Prothro, UCLA (AFCA); Duffy Daugherty, Mich. St. (FWAA)
1966 Tom Cahill, Army
1967 John Pont, Indiana
1968 Joe Paterno, Penn St. (AFCA); Woody Hayes, Ohio St. (FWAA)
1969 Bo Schembechler, Michigan
1970 Charles McClendon, LSU, & Darrell Royal, Texas (AFCA); Alex Agase, Northwestern (FWAA)
1971 Paul "Bear" Bryant, Alabama (AFCA); Bob Devaney, Nebraska (FWAA)
1972 John McKay, USC
1973 Paul "Bear" Bryant, Alabama (AFCA); Johnny Majors, Pittsburgh (FWAA)
1974 Grant Teaff, Baylor
1975 Frank Kush, Arizona St. (AFCA); Woody Hayes, Ohio St. (FWAA)
1976 Johnny Majors, Pittsburgh
1977 Don James, Washington (AFCA); Lou Holtz, Arkansas (FWAA)
1978 Joe Paterno, Penn St.
1979 Earle Bruce, Ohio St.
1980 Vince Dooley, Georgia
1981 Danny Ford, Clemson
1982 Joe Paterno, Penn St.
1983 Ken Hatfield, Air Force (AFCA); Howard Schnellenberger, Miami (FL) (FWAA)
1984 LaVell Edwards, Brigham Young
1985 Fisher De Berry, Air Force
1986 Joe Paterno, Penn St.
1987 Dick MacPherson, Syracuse
1988 Don Nehlen, W. Virginia (AFCA); Lou Holtz, Notre Dame (FWAA)
1989 Bill McCartney, Colorado
1990 Bobby Ross, Georgia Tech
1991 Don James, Washington
1992 Gene Stallings, Alabama
1993 Barry Alvarez, Wisconsin (AFCA); Terry Bowden, Auburn (FWAA)
1994 Tom Osborne, Nebraska (AFCA) Rich Brooks, Oregon (FWAA)
1995 Gary Barnett, Northwestern
1996 Bruce Snyder, Arizona St.
1997 Mike Price, Washington St.

All-Time Division I-A Coaching Victories (Including Bowl Games)

Paul "Bear" Bryant	323
Glenn "Pop" Warner	319
Amos Alonzo Stagg	314
*Joe Paterno	298
*Bobby Bowden	281
*Tom Osborne	255
Woody Hayes	238
Bo Schembechler	234
*LaVell Edwards	234
*Hayden Fry	229
Lou Holtz	216
Jess Neely	207
Warren Woodson	203
Eddie Anderson	201
Vince Dooley	201
Jim Sweeney	200
Dana X. Bible	198
Dan McGugin	197
Fielding Yost	196
Howard Jones	194
John Vaught	190
John Heisman	185
Johnny Majors	185
Darrell Royal	184
*Don Nehlen	183
Gil Dobie	180
Carl Snavely	180
Jerry Claiborne	179
Ben Schwartzwalder	178
Frank Kush	176
Don James	176
Ralph Jordan	176

Coaches active in 1997 are denoted by an asterisk (*). Eddie Robinson of Grambling State Univ. (Div. I-AA) holds the record for most college football victories, with 408 at the end of the 1997 season; Robinson retired after the 1997 season.

Selected College Football Conference Champions

Atlantic Coast

1980	North Carolina
1981	Clemson
1982	Clemson
1983	Maryland
1984	Maryland
1985	Maryland
1986	Clemson
1987	Clemson
1988	Clemson
1989	Virginia, Duke
1990	Georgia Tech
1991	Clemson
1992	Florida St.
1993	Florida St.
1994	Florida St.
1995	Virginia, Florida St.
1996	Florida St.
1997	Florida St.

Ivy Group

1980	Yale
1981	Yale, Dartmouth
1982	Harvard, Dartmouth, Penn
1983	Harvard, Penn
1984	Penn
1985	Penn
1986	Penn
1987	Harvard
1988	Penn, Cornell
1989	Yale, Princeton
1990	Cornell, Dartmouth
1991	Dartmouth
1992	Dartmouth, Princeton
1993	Penn
1994	Penn
1995	Princeton
1996	Dartmouth
1997	Harvard

Big Eight*

1980	Oklahoma
1981	Nebraska
1982	Nebraska
1983	Nebraska
1984	Nebraska, Oklahoma
1985	Oklahoma
1986	Oklahoma
1987	Oklahoma
1988	Nebraska
1989	Colorado
1990	Colorado
1991	Nebraska, Colorado
1992	Nebraska
1993	Nebraska
1994	Nebraska
1995	Nebraska

Big Ten

1980	Michigan
1981	Iowa, Ohio St.
1982	Michigan
1983	Illinois
1984	Ohio St.
1985	Iowa
1986	Michigan, Ohio St.
1987	Michigan St.
1988	Michigan
1989	Michigan
1990	Iowa, Ill., Mich., Mich. St.
1991	Michigan
1992	Michigan
1993	Ohio St., Wisconsin
1994	Penn St.
1995	Northwestern
1996	Ohio St., Northwestern
1997	Michigan

Mid-American Athletic

1980	Central Michigan
1981	Toledo
1982	Bowling Green
1983	Northern Illinois
1984	Toledo
1985	Bowling Green
1986	Miami (OH)
1987	E. Michigan
1988	W. Michigan
1989	Ball St.
1990	Central Michigan
1991	Bowling Green
1992	Bowling Green
1993	Ball St.
1994	Central Michigan
1995	Toledo
1996	Ball St.
1997	Marshall, Toledo

Southern

1980	Furman
1981	Furman
1982	Furman
1983	Furman
1984	Tenn.-Chattanooga
1985	Furman
1986	Appalachian St.
1987	Appalachian St.
1988	Marshall, Furman
1989	Furman
1990	Furman
1991	Appalachian St.
1992	Citadel
1993	Georgia Southern
1994	Marshall
1995	Appalachian St.
1996	Marshall
1997	Georgia Southern

Southeastern

1980	Georgia
1981	Georgia, Alabama
1982	Georgia
1983	Auburn
1984	Florida (title vacated)
1985	Tennessee
1986	LSU
1987	Auburn
1988	Auburn, LSU
1989	Ala., Tenn., Auburn
1990	Tennessee
1991	Florida
1992	Alabama
1993	Florida
1994	Florida
1995	Florida
1996	Florida
1997	Tennessee

Southwest*

1980	Baylor
1981	Texas
1982	SMU
1983	Texas
1984	SMU, Houston
1985	Texas A&M
1986	Texas A&M
1987	Texas A&M
1988	Arkansas
1989	Arkansas
1990	Texas
1991	Texas A&M
1992	Texas A&M
1993	Texas A&M
1994	Baylor, Rice, Texas, Texas Christian, Texas Tech
1995	Texas

Pacific Ten

1980	Washington
1981	Washington
1982	UCLA
1983	UCLA
1984	USC
1985	UCLA
1986	Arizona St.
1987	UCLA, USC
1988	USC
1989	USC
1990	Washington
1991	Washington
1992	Washington, Stanford
1993	UCLA, Arizona, USC
1994	Oregon
1995	USC, Washington
1996	Arizona St.
1997	Washington St., UCLA

Big East

1991	Miami (FL), Syracuse
1992	Miami (FL)
1993	West Virginia
1994	Miami (FL)
1995	Virginia Tech, Miami (FL)
1996	Virginia Tech, Miami (FL), Syracuse
1997	Syracuse

Western Athletic

1980	Brigham Young (BYU)
1981	Brigham Young
1982	Brigham Young
1983	Brigham Young
1984	Brigham Young
1985	Brigham Young, Air Force
1986	San Diego St.
1987	Wyoming
1988	Wyoming
1989	Brigham Young
1990	Brigham Young
1991	Brigham Young
1992	Hawaii, Brigham Young, Fresno St.
1993	Wyoming, Fresno St., BYU
1994	Colorado St.
1995	Colorado St., Air Force, Utah, BYU
1996	Brigham Young
1997	Colorado St.

Big 12*

1996	Texas
1997	Nebraska

Big West

1980	Long Beach St.
1981	San Jose St.
1982	Fresno St.
1983	Cal St.-Fullerton
1984	Cal St.-Fullerton
1985	Fresno St.
1986	San Jose St.
1987	San Jose St.
1988	Fresno St.
1989	Fresno St.
1990	San Jose St.
1991	San Jose St., Fresno St.
1992	Nevada
1993	SW Louisiana, Utah St.
1994	Nevada, SW Louisiana, UNLV
1995	Nevada
1996	Nevada, Utah St.
1997	Nevada, Utah St.

Conference USA

1996	So. Mississippi, Houston
1997	So. Mississippi

(*) After the 1995 season, the Big Eight and Southwest conferences disbanded. In 1996 all former Big Eight Conference teams joined with 4 of the 8 Southwest Conference teams to form the Big 12 Conference.

NATIONAL HOCKEY LEAGUE

1997-98 NHL Review: Olympic Domination, Nashville in Hunt, Detroit Repeats

Players from the National Hockey League participated in the Olympics for the first time as the league shut down from Feb. 8 to Feb. 24 during the 1998 season. Dominik Hasek of the Buffalo Sabres established himself as one of the world's top goaltenders by leading the Czech Republic to a gold medal. In June, Hasek was awarded both the Hart Trophy (MVP) and Vezina Trophy (for Outstanding Goaltender), becoming the first player ever to win both awards in back-to-back seasons. The Nashville Predators, the first of 4 expansion teams to be added to the NHL through the year 2002, officially became the league's 27th franchise, May 5, 1998. The Predators held their expansion draft on June 26, 1998. Wayne Gretzky, the NHL's most prolific scorer, was voted the top player by *The Hockey News* poll naming the top 50 players of all time. The Detroit Red Wings, led by Steve Yzerman, repeated as Stanley Cup champions by sweeping the Washington Capitals in the final round of the playoffs.

Final Standings 1997-98

(playoff seeding in parentheses; in each conference the two division winners automatically get the number 1 and 2 seeds)

Eastern Conference

Northeast Division

	W	L	T	GF	GA	Pts
Pittsburgh (2)	40	24	18	228	188	98
Boston (5)	39	30	13	221	194	91
Buffalo (6)	36	29	17	211	187	89
Montreal (7)	37	32	13	235	208	87
Ottawa (8)	34	33	15	193	200	83
Carolina	33	41	8	200	219	74

Atlantic Division

	W	L	T	GF	GA	Pts
New Jersey (1)	48	23	11	225	166	107
Philadelphia (3)	42	29	11	242	193	95
Washington (4)	40	30	12	220	201	92
N.Y. Islanders	30	41	11	212	225	71
N.Y. Rangers	25	39	18	197	231	68
Florida	24	43	15	203	256	63
Tampa Bay	17	55	10	151	269	44

Western Conference

Central Division

	W	L	T	GF	GA	Pts
Dallas (1)	49	22	11	242	167	109
Detroit (3)	44	23	15	250	196	103
St. Louis (4)	45	29	8	256	204	98
Phoenix (6)	35	35	12	224	227	82
Chicago	30	39	13	192	199	73
Toronto	30	43	9	194	237	69

Pacific Division

	W	L	T	GF	GA	Pts
Colorado (2)	39	26	17	231	205	95
Los Angeles (5)	38	33	11	227	225	87
Edmonton (7)	35	37	10	215	224	80
San Jose (8)	34	38	10	210	216	78
Calgary	26	41	15	217	252	67
Anaheim	26	43	13	205	261	65
Vancouver	25	43	14	224	273	64

Stanley Cup Playoff Results

Eastern Conference

Ottawa defeated New Jersey 4 games to 2
Montreal defeated Pittsburgh 4 games to 2
Buffalo defeated Philadelphia 4 games to 1
Washington defeated Boston 4 games to 2
Washington defeated Ottawa 4 games to 1
Buffalo defeated Montreal 4 games to 0
Washington defeated Buffalo 4 games to 2

Western Conference

Dallas defeated San Jose 4 games to 2
Edmonton defeated Colorado 4 games to 3
Detroit defeated Phoenix 4 games to 2
St. Louis defeated Los Angeles 4 games to 0
Dallas defeated Edmonton 4 games to 1
Detroit defeated St. Louis 4 games to 2
Detroit defeated Dallas 4 games to 2

Finals

Detroit defeated Washington 4 games to 0 [2-1, 5-4 (OT), 2-1, 4-1]

Stanley Cup Champions Since 1927

Year	Champion	Coach	Final opponent
1927	Ottawa	Dave Gill	Boston
1928	N.Y. Rangers	Lester Patrick	Montreal
1929	Boston	Cy Denneny	N.Y. Rangers
1930	Montreal	Cecil Hart	Boston
1931	Montreal	Cecil Hart	Chicago
1932	Toronto	Dick Irvin	N.Y. Rangers
1933	N.Y. Rangers	Lester Patrick	Toronto
1934	Chicago	Tommy Gorman	Detroit
1935	Montreal Maroons	Tommy Gorman	Toronto
1936	Detroit	Jack Adams	Toronto
1937	Detroit	Jack Adams	N.Y. Rangers
1938	Chicago	Bill Stewart	Toronto
1939	Boston	Art Ross	Toronto
1940	N.Y. Rangers	Frank Boucher	Toronto
1941	Boston	Cooney Weiland	Detroit
1942	Toronto	Hap Day	Detroit
1943	Detroit	Jack Adams	Boston
1944	Montreal	Dick Irvin	Chicago
1945	Toronto	Hap Day	Detroit
1946	Montreal	Dick Irvin	Boston
1947	Toronto	Hap Day	Montreal
1948	Toronto	Hap Day	Detroit
1949	Toronto	Hap Day	Detroit
1950	Detroit	Tommy Ivan	N.Y. Rangers
1951	Toronto	Joe Primeau	Montreal
1952	Detroit	Tommy Ivan	Montreal
1953	Montreal	Dick Irvin	Boston
1954	Detroit	Tommy Ivan	Montreal
1955	Detroit	Jimmy Skinner	Montreal
1956	Montreal	Toe Blake	Detroit
1957	Montreal	Toe Blake	Boston
1958	Montreal	Toe Blake	Boston
1959	Montreal	Toe Blake	Toronto
1960	Montreal	Toe Blake	Toronto
1961	Chicago	Rudy Pilous	Detroit
1962	Toronto	Punch Imlach	Chicago
1963	Toronto	Punch Imlach	Detroit
1964	Toronto	Punch Imlach	Detroit
1965	Montreal	Toe Blake	Chicago
1966	Montreal	Toe Blake	Detroit
1967	Toronto	Punch Imlach	Montreal
1968	Montreal	Toe Blake	St. Louis
1969	Montreal	Claude Ruel	St. Louis
1970	Boston	Harry Sinden	St. Louis
1971	Montreal	Al MacNeil	Chicago
1972	Boston	Tom Johnson	N.Y. Rangers
1973	Montreal	Scotty Bowman	Chicago
1974	Philadelphia	Fred Shero	Boston
1975	Philadelphia	Fred Shero	Buffalo
1976	Montreal	Scotty Bowman	Philadelphia
1977	Montreal	Scotty Bowman	Boston
1978	Montreal	Scotty Bowman	Boston
1979	Montreal	Scotty Bowman	N.Y. Rangers
1980	N.Y. Islanders	Al Arbour	Philadelphia
1981	N.Y. Islanders	Al Arbour	Minnesota
1982	N.Y. Islanders	Al Arbour	Vancouver
1983	N.Y. Islanders	Al Arbour	Edmonton
1984	Edmonton	Glen Sather	N.Y. Islanders
1985	Edmonton	Glen Sather	Philadelphia
1986	Montreal	Jean Perron	Calgary
1987	Edmonton	Glen Sather	Philadelphia
1988	Edmonton	Glen Sather	Boston
1989	Calgary	Terry Crisp	Montreal
1990	Edmonton	John Muckler	Boston
1991	Pittsburgh	Bob Johnson	Minnesota
1992	Pittsburgh	Scotty Bowman	Chicago
1993	Montreal	Jacques Demers	Los Angeles
1994	N.Y. Rangers	Mike Keenan	Vancouver
1995	New Jersey	Jacques Lemaire	Detroit
1996	Colorado	Marc Crawford	Florida
1997	Detroit	Scotty Bowman	Philadelphia
1998	Detroit	Scotty Bowman	Washington

Individual Leaders, 1997-98

Points

Jaromir Jagr, Pittsburgh, 102; Peter Forsberg, Colorado, 91; Pavel Bure, Vancouver, 90; Wayne Gretzky, N.Y. Rangers, 90; John LeClair, Philadelphia, 87; Zigmund Palffy, N.Y. Islanders, 87; Ron Francis, Pittsburgh, 87.

Goals

Peter Bondra, Washington, 52; Teemu Selanne, Anaheim, 52; Pavel Bure, Vancouver, 51; John LeClair, Philadelphia, 51; Zigmund Palffy, N.Y. Islanders, 45.

Assists

Wayne Gretzky, N.Y. Rangers, 67; Jaromir Jagr, Pittsburgh, 67; Peter Forsberg, Colorado, 66; Ron Francis, Pittsburgh, 62; Jozef Stumpel, Los Angeles, 58; Adam Oates, Washington, 58.

Power-play goals

Zigmund Palffy, N.Y. Islanders, 17; John LeClair, Philadelphia, 16; Brendan Shanahan, Detroit, 15; Stu Barnes, Pittsburgh, 15; Shane Corson, Montreal, 14; Joe Nieuwendyk, Dallas, 14.

Shorthanded goals

Pavel Bure, Vancouver, 6; Jeff Friesen, San Jose, 6; Peter Bondra, Washington, 5; Bob Corkum, Phoenix, 5; Mike Modano, Dallas, 5; Michael Peca, 5.

Shooting percentage

(minimum 82 shots)

Mike Sillinger, Van.-Phi., 21.9; Jason Allison, Boston, 20.9; Dmitri Khristich, Boston, 20.1; Teemu Selanne, Anaheim, 19.4; Joe Nieuwendyk, Dallas, 19.2.

Plus/Minus

Chris Pronger, St, Louis, 47; Larry Murphy, Detroit, 35; Jason Allison, Boston, 33; Randy McKay, New Jersey, 30; John LeClair, Philadelphia, 30.

Penalty minutes

Donald Brashear, Vancouver, 372; Tie Domi, Toronto, 365; Krzysztof Oliwa, New Jersey, 295; Paul Laus, Florida, 293; Richard Pilon, New York Islanders, 291.

Goaltending Leaders

(minimum 25 games)

Goals against average

Ed Belfour, Dallas, 1.88; Martin Brodeur, New Jersey, 1.89; Tom Barrasso, Pittsburgh, 2.07; Dominik Hasek, Buffalo, 2.09; Ron Hextall, Philadelphia, 2.17; Trevor Kidd, Carolina 2.17.

Wins

Martin Brodeur, New Jersey, 41; Ed Belfour, Dallas, 37; Dominik Hasek, Buffalo, 33; Olaf Kolzig, Washington, 33; Chris Osgood, Detroit, 33.

Save percentage

Dominik Hasek, Buffalo, .932; Tom Barrasso, Pittsburgh, .922; Trevor Kidd, Carolina, .922; Olaf Kolzig, Washington, .920, Martin Brodeur, New Jersey, .917, Jeff Hackett, Chicago, .917.

Shutouts

Dominik Hasek, Buffalo, 13; Martin Brodeur, New Jersey, 10; Ed Belfour, Dallas, 9; Jeff Hackett, Chicago, 8; Curtis Joseph, Edmonton, 8.

Individual Scoring, 1997-98

(40 or more games played; *played for more than one team during 1997-98; g = denotes goalie; E = even)

Mighty Ducks of Anaheim

	GP	G	A	Pts	PIM	+/–
Teemu Selanne	73	52	34	86	30	12
Steve Rucchin	72	17	36	53	13	8
Travis Green*	76	19	23	42	82	–29
Scott Young	73	13	20	33	22	–13
Paul Kariya	22	17	14	31	23	12
Matt Cullen	61	6	21	27	23	–4
Tomas Sandstrom	77	9	8	17	64	–25
Ted Drury	73	6	10	16	82	–10
Ruslan Salei	66	5	10	15	70	7
Dave Karpa	78	1	11	12	217	–3
Jason Marshall	72	3	6	9	189	–8
Jamie Pushor*	64	2	7	9	81	3
Jeremy Stevenson	45	3	5	8	101	–4
Drew Bannister*	61	0	8	8	89	–9
Pavel Trnka	48	3	4	7	40	–4
Doug Houda*	55	2	4	6	99	–11
Mukhail Shtalenkov (g)	40	0	1	1	0	—
Guy Hebert (g)	46	0	1	1	4	—

Coach—Pierre Page

Boston Bruins

	GP	G	A	Pts	PIM	+/–
Jason Allison	81	33	50	83	60	33
Dmitri Khristich	82	29	37	66	42	25
Ray Bourque	82	13	35	48	80	2
Sergei Samsonov	81	22	25	47	8	9
Steve Heinz	61	26	20	46	54	8
Anson Carter	78	16	27	43	31	7
Ted Donato	79	16	23	39	54	6
Tim Taylor	79	20	11	31	57	–16
Rob Dimaio	79	10	17	27	82	–13
Per Axellson	82	8	19	27	38	–14
Kyle McLaren	66	5	20	25	56	13
Grant Ledyard*	71	4	20	24	20	–4
Dave Ellet	82	3	20	23	67	3
Mike Sullivan	77	5	13	18	34	–1
Don Sweeney	59	1	15	16	24	12
Darren Van Impe*	69	3	11	14	40	–6
Joe Thornton	55	3	4	7	19	–6
Hal Gill	68	2	4	6	47	4
Dean Malkoc	40	1	0	1	86	–12
Ken Baumgartner	82	0	1	1	199	–14
Byron Dafoe (g)	65	0	3	3	2	—

Coach—Pat Burns

Buffalo Sabres

	GP	G	A	Pts	PIM	+/–
Miroslav Satan	79	22	24	46	34	2
Alexei Zhitnik	78	15	30	45	102	19
Donald Audette	75	24	20	44	59	10
Michael Peca	61	18	22	40	57	12
Brian Holzinger	69	14	21	35	36	–2
Jason Woolley	71	9	26	35	35	8
Derek Plante	72	13	21	34	26	8
Michal Grosek	67	10	20	30	60	9
Geoff Sanderson*	75	11	18	29	38	1
Matthew Barnaby	72	5	20	25	289	8
Curtis Brown	63	12	12	24	34	11
Dixon Ward	71	10	13	23	42	9
Darryl Shannon	76	3	19	22	56	26
Richard Smehlik	72	3	17	20	62	11
Jay McKee	56	1	13	14	42	–1
Wayne Primeau	69	6	6	12	87	9
Paul Kruse*	74	7	2	9	187	–11
Mike Wilson	66	4	4	8	48	13
Rob Ray	63	2	4	6	234	2
Bob Boughner	69	1	3	4	165	5
Dominik Hasek (g)	72	0	2	2	12	—

Coach—Lindy Ruff

Calgary Flames

	GP	G	A	Pts	PIM	+/–
Theoren Fleury	82	27	51	78	197	E
Cory Stillman	72	27	22	49	40	–9
Marty McInnis	75	19	25	44	34	1
Andrew Cassels	81	17	27	44	32	–7
German Titov	68	18	22	40	38	–1
Valeri Bure*	66	12	26	38	35	–5
Michael Nylander	68	13	23	36	24	10
Jarome Iginla	70	13	19	32	29	–10
Derek Morris	82	9	20	29	88	1
Cale Hulse	79	5	22	27	169	1
Jason Wiemer*	79	12	10	22	160	–10
Tommy Albelin	69	2	17	19	32	9
James Patrick	60	6	11	17	26	–2
Jim Dowd	48	6	8	14	12	10
Joel Bouchard	44	5	7	12	57	E
Jamie Allison	43	3	8	11	104	3
Ed Ward	64	4	5	9	122	–1
Chris Dingman	70	3	3	6	149	–11
Todd Simpson	53	1	5	6	109	–10
Rick Tabaracci (g)	42	0	1	1	14	—

Coach—Brian Sutter

Carolina Hurricanes

	GP	G	A	Pts	PIM	+/–
Keith Primeau	81	26	37	63	110	19
Sami Kapanen	81	26	37	63	16	9
Gary Roberts	61	20	29	49	103	3
Nelson Emerson	81	21	24	45	50	–17
Jeff O'Neill	74	19	20	39	67	–8
Ray Sheppard*	71	18	19	37	23	–11
Robert Kron	81	16	20	36	12	–8
Martin Gelinas*	64	16	18	34	40	–5
Steve Chiasson	66	7	27	34	65	–2
Glen Wesley	82	6	19	25	36	7
Kevin Dineen	54	7	16	23	105	–7
Paul Ranheim	73	5	9	14	28	–11
Curtis Leschyshyn	73	2	10	12	45	–2
Adam Burt	76	1	11	12	106	–6
Stephen Leach	45	4	5	9	42	–19
Kent Manderville	77	4	4	8	31	–6
Kevin Haller	65	3	5	8	94	–5
Stu Grimson	82	3	4	7	204	E
Sean Hill*	55	1	6	7	54	–5
Steven Rice	47	2	4	6	38	–16
Trevor Kidd (g)	47	0	0	0	2	—

Coach—Paul Maurice

Chicago Blackhawks

	GP	G	A	Pts	PIM	+/–
Tony Amonte	82	31	42	73	66	21
Alexei Zhamnov	70	21	28	49	61	16
Eric Daze	80	31	11	42	22	4
Gary Suter	73	14	28	42	74	1
Chris Chelios	81	3	39	42	151	–7
Greg Johnson*	74	12	22	34	40	–2
Jeff Shantz	61	11	20	31	36	E
Sergei Krivokrasov	58	10	13	23	33	–1
Eric Weinrich	82	2	21	23	106	10
Ethan Moreau	54	9	9	18	73	E
Steve Dubinsky	82	5	13	18	57	–6
James Black	52	10	5	15	8	–8
Jean-Yves Leroux	66	6	7	13	55	–2
Jay More*	58	5	7	12	61	7
Christian Laflamme	72	0	11	11	59	14
Brent Sutter	52	2	6	8	28	–6
Reid Simpson*	44	3	2	5	118	–3
Cam Russell	41	1	1	2	79	3
Trent Yawney	45	1	0	1	76	–5
Jeff Hackett (g)	58	0	0	0	8	—

Coach—Craig Hartsburg

Colorado Avalanche

	GP	G	A	Pts	PIM	+/–
Peter Forsberg	72	25	66	91	94	6
Valeri Kamensky	75	26	40	66	60	–2
Joe Sakic	64	27	36	63	50	E
Claude Lemieux	78	26	27	53	115	–7
Sandis Ozolinsh	66	13	38	51	65	–12
Adam Deadmarsh	73	22	21	43	125	E
Eric Lacroix	82	16	15	31	84	E
Uwe Krupp	78	9	22	31	38	21
Rene Corbet	68	16	12	28	133	8
Stephane Yelle	81	7	15	22	48	–10
Jarri Kurri	70	5	17	22	12	6
Tom Fitzgerald*	80	12	6	18	79	–4
Shean Donovan*	67	8	10	18	70	6
Adam Foote	77	3	14	17	124	–3
Eric Messier	62	4	12	16	20	4
Jon Klemm	67	6	8	14	30	–3
Alexei Gusarov	72	4	10	14	42	9
Jeff Odgers	68	5	8	13	213	5
Warren Rychel*	71	5	6	11	221	–11
Sylvain Lefebvre	81	0	10	10	48	2
Aaron Miller	55	2	2	4	51	E
Francois Leroux	50	1	2	3	140	–3
Patrick Roy (g)	65	0	3	3	39	—

Coach—Marc Crawford

Dallas Stars

	GP	G	A	Pts	PIM	+/–
Joe Nieuwendyk	73	39	30	69	30	16
Mike Modano	52	21	38	59	32	25
Pat Verbeek	82	31	26	57	170	15
Sergei Zubov	73	10	47	57	16	16
Jamie Lagenbrunner	81	23	29	52	61	9
Darryl Sydor	79	11	35	46	51	17
Jere Lehtinen	72	23	19	42	20	19
Greg Adams	49	14	18	32	20	11
Derian Hatcher	70	6	25	31	132	9
Guy Carbonneau	77	7	17	24	40	3
Shawn Chambers	57	2	22	24	26	11
Mike Keane*	83	10	13	23	52	–12
Benoit Hogue	53	6	16	22	35	7
Todd Harvey	59	9	10	19	104	5
Grant Marshall	72	9	10	19	96	2
Dave Reid	65	6	12	18	14	–15
Richard Matvichuk	74	3	15	18	63	7
Brian Skrudland*	72	7	6	13	49	–6
Bob Bassen	58	3	4	7	57	–4
Craig Ludwig	80	0	7	7	131	21
Craig Muni	40	1	1	2	25	E
Ed Belfour (g)	61	0	0	0	18	—

Coach—Ken Hitchcock

Detroit Red Wings

	GP	G	A	Pts	PIM	+/–
Steve Yzerman	75	24	45	69	46	3
Nicklas Lidstrom	80	17	42	59	18	22
Brendan Shanahan	75	28	29	57	154	6
Vyacheslav Kozlov	80	25	27	52	46	14
Larry Murphy	82	11	41	52	37	35
Igor Larionov	69	8	39	47	40	14
Dmitri Mironov*	77	8	35	43	119	–7
Doug Brown	80	19	23	42	12	17
Darren McCarty	71	15	22	37	157	E
Martin Lapointe	79	15	19	34	106	E
Brent Gilchrist	61	13	14	27	40	4
Kirk Maltby	65	14	9	23	89	11
Kris Draper	64	13	10	23	45	5
Tomas Holmstrom	57	5	17	22	44	6
Anders Eriksson	66	7	14	21	32	21
Mathieu Dadenault	68	5	12	17	43	5
Viacheslav Fetisov	58	2	12	14	72	4
Michael Knuble	53	7	6	13	16	2
Bob Rouse	71	1	11	12	57	–9
Joey Kocur	63	6	5	11	92	7
Aaron Ward	52	5	5	10	47	–1
Jamie Macoun*	74	0	7	7	65	–17
Chris Osgood (g)	64	0	0	0	31	—

Coach—Scotty Bowman

Edmonton Oilers

	GP	G	A	Pts	PIM	+/–
Doug Weight	79	26	44	70	69	1
Dean McAmmond	77	19	31	50	46	9
Boris Mironov	81	16	30	46	100	–8
Janne Niinimaa*	77	4	39	43	62	13
Roman Hamrlik*	78	9	32	41	70	–15
Bill Guerin*	59	18	21	39	93	1
Todd Marchant	76	14	21	35	71	9
Ryan Smyth	65	20	13	33	44	–24
Tony Hrkac*	49	13	14	27	10	3
Mats Lingren	82	13	13	26	42	E
Andrei Kovalenko	59	6	17	23	28	–14
Kelly Buchberger	82	6	17	23	122	–10
Valeri Zelepukin*	68	4	18	22	89	–2
Rem Murray	61	9	9	18	39	–9
Mike Grier	66	9	6	15	73	–3
Greg De Vries	65	7	4	11	80	–17
Bobby Dollas*	52	2	6	8	49	–6
Drake Berehowsky	67	1	6	7	169	1
Curtis Joseph (g)	71	0	2	2	4	—

Coach—Ron Low

Florida Panthers

	GP	G	A	Pts	PIM	+/–
Ray Whitney*	77	33	32	65	28	9
Dave Gagner	78	20	28	48	55	–21
Robert Svehla	79	9	34	43	113	–3
Scott Mellanby	79	15	24	39	127	–14
Radek Dvorak	64	12	24	36	33	–1
Dino Ciccarelli*	62	16	17	33	70	–16
Viktor Kozlov*	64	17	13	30	16	–3
Kirk Muller	70	8	21	29	54	–14
Bill Lindsay	82	12	16	28	80	–2
Ed Jovanovski	81	9	14	23	158	–12
David Nemirovsky	41	9	12	21	8	–3
Steve Washburn	58	11	8	19	32	–6
Gord Murphy	79	6	11	17	46	–3
Jeff Norton*	56	4	13	17	44	–32
Chris Wells	61	5	10	15	47	4
Paul Laus	77	0	11	11	293	–5
Terry Carkner	74	1	7	8	63	6
Rhett Warrener	79	0	4	4	99	–16
Kirk McLean* (g)	44	0	1	1	0	—
John Vanbiesbrouck (g)	60	0	3	3	6	—

Coach—Doug MacLean, Bryan Murray

Los Angeles Kings

	GP	G	A	Pts	PIM	+/–
Jozef Stumpel	77	21	58	79	53	17
Glen Murray	81	29	31	60	54	6
Vladimir Tsyplakov	73	18	34	52	18	15
Rob Blake	81	23	27	50	94	–3
Yanic Perreault	79	28	20	48	32	6
Luc Robitaille	57	16	24	40	66	5
Craig Johnson	74	17	21	38	42	9
Gary Galley	74	9	28	37	63	–5
Sandy Moger	62	11	13	24	70	4
Ian Laperriere	77	6	15	21	131	E
Russ Courtnall	58	12	6	18	27	–2
Sean O'Donnell	80	2	15	17	179	7
Philippe Boucher	45	6	10	16	49	6
Ray Ferraro	40	6	9	15	42	–10
Mattias Norstrom	73	1	12	13	90	14
Dan Bylsma	65	3	9	12	33	9
Steve McKenna	62	4	4	8	150	–9
Doug Zmolek	46	0	8	8	111	E
Aki Berg	72	0	8	8	61	3
Matt Johnson	66	2	4	6	249	–8
Stephane Fiset (g)	60	0	1	1	8	—

Coach—Larry Robinson

Montreal Canadiens

	GP	G	A	Pts	PIM	+/–
Mark Recchi	82	32	42	74	51	11
Vincent Damphousse	76	18	41	59	58	14
Saku Koivu	69	14	43	57	48	8
Shane Corson	62	21	34	55	108	2
Martin Rucinsky	78	21	32	53	84	13
Vladimir Malakhov	74	13	31	44	70	16
Brian Savage	64	26	17	43	36	11
Patrice Brisebois	79	10	27	37	67	16
Dave Manson	81	4	30	34	122	22
Benoit Brunet	68	12	20	32	61	11
Jonas Hoglund*	78	12	13	25	22	–7
Marc Bureau	74	13	6	19	12	E
Patrick Poulin*	78	6	13	19	27	–4
Stephane Quintal	71	6	10	16	97	–13
Scott Thornton	67	6	9	15	158	E
Zarley Zalapski*	63	3	12	15	63	–13
Sebastien Bordeleau	53	6	8	14	36	5
Turner Stevenson	63	4	6	10	110	–8
Igor Ulanov*	49	2	8	10	97	–7
Peter Popovic	69	2	6	8	38	–6
Craig Rivet	61	0	2	2	93	–3
Brett Clark	41	1	0	1	20	–3
Mick Vukota*	64	1	0	1	192	–4
Andy Moog (g)	42	0	0	0	4	—
Jocelyn Thibault (g)	47	0	2	2	0	—

Coach—Alain Vigneault

New Jersey Devils

	GP	G	A	Pts	PIM	+/–
Bobby Holik	82	29	36	65	100	23
Scott Niedermayer	81	14	43	57	27	5
Doug Gilmour	63	13	40	53	68	10
Randy McKay	74	24	24	48	86	30
Dave Andreychuk	75	14	34	48	26	19
Patrick Elias	74	18	19	37	28	18
Petr Sykora	58	16	20	36	22	E
Jason Arnott*	70	10	23	33	99	–24
Brian Rolston	76	16	14	30	16	7
Denis Pederson	80	15	13	28	97	–6
Scott Stevens	80	4	22	26	80	19
Steve Thomas	55	14	10	24	32	4
Lyle Odelein	79	4	19	23	171	11
Doug Bodger*	77	9	11	20	57	–1
Bob Carpenter	66	9	9	18	22	–4
Sheldon Souray	60	3	7	10	85	18
Kevin Dean	50	1	8	9	12	12
Brad Bombadir	43	1	5	6	8	11
Krzysztof Oliwa	73	2	3	5	295	3
Martin Brodeur (g)	70	3	3	3	10	—

Coach—Jacques Lemaire

New York Islanders

	GP	G	A	Pts	PIM	+/–
Zigmund Palffy	82	45	42	87	34	–2
Robert Reichel	82	25	40	65	32	–11
Bryan Berard	75	14	32	46	59	–32
Bryan Smolinski	81	13	30	43	34	–16
Kenny Jonsson	81	14	26	40	58	–2
Jason Dawe*	81	20	19	39	42	8
Trevor Linden*	67	17	21	38	82	–14
Tom Chorske	82	12	23	35	39	7
Sergei Nemchinov	74	10	19	29	24	3
Mariusz Czerkawski	68	12	13	25	23	11
Joe Sacco*	80	11	14	25	34	E
J.J. Daigneault*	71	2	21	23	49	–9
Claude Lapointe	78	10	10	20	47	–9
Scott Lachance	63	2	11	13	45	–11
Mike Hough	74	5	7	12	27	–4
Richard Pilon	76	0	7	7	291	1
Gino Odjick*	48	3	2	5	212	–2
Tommy Salo (g)	62	0	1	1	0	—

Coach—Rick Bowness, Mike Milbury

New York Rangers

	GP	G	A	Pts	PIM	+/–
Wayne Gretzky	82	23	67	90	28	–11
Pat Lafontaine	67	23	39	62	36	–16
Alexei Kovalev	73	23	30	53	44	–22
Brian Leetch	76	17	33	50	32	–36
Niklas Sundstrom	70	19	28	47	24	E
Kevin Stevens	80	14	27	41	130	–7
Adam Graves	72	23	12	35	41	–30
Tim Sweeney	56	11	18	29	26	7
Bruce Driver	75	5	15	20	46	–3
Ulf Samuelsson	73	3	9	12	122	1
Bob Errey*	71	2	9	11	53	2
Harry York*	60	4	6	10	31	–1
Alexander Karpovtsev	47	3	7	10	38	–1
Bill Berg	67	1	9	10	55	–15
Jeff Finley	63	1	6	7	55	–3
Darren Langdon	70	3	3	6	197	E
Jeff Beukeboom	63	0	5	5	195	–25
Mike Richter (g)	72	0	1	1	2	—

Coach—Colin Campbell, John Muckler

Ottawa Senators

	GP	G	A	Pts	PIM	+/–
Alexei Yashin	82	33	39	72	24	6
Shawn McEachern	81	24	24	48	42	1
Daniel Alfredsson	55	17	28	45	18	7
Igor Kravchuk	81	8	27	35	8	–19
Andreas Dackell	82	15	18	33	24	–11
Magnus Arvedson	61	11	15	26	36	2
Vaclav Prospal*	56	6	19	25	21	–11
Sergei Zholtok	78	10	13	23	16	–7
Wade Redden	80	8	14	22	27	17
Janne Laukkenen	60	4	17	21	64	–15
Denny Lambert	72	9	10	19	250	4
Shaun Van Allen	80	4	15	19	48	4
Pat Falloon*	58	8	10	18	16	–8
Bruce Gardiner	55	7	11	18	50	2
Radek Bonk	65	7	9	16	16	–13
Chris Phillips	72	5	11	16	38	2
Jason York	73	3	13	16	62	8
Randy Cunneyworth	71	2	11	13	63	–14
Chris Murray*	53	5	4	9	118	3
Lance Pitlick	69	2	7	9	50	8
Stanislav Neckar	60	2	2	4	31	–14
Ron Tugnutt (g)	42	0	0	0	0	—
Damian Rhodes (g)	50	0	1	1	0	—

Coach—Jacques Martin

Philadelphia Flyers

	GP	G	A	Pts	PIM	+/–
John LeClair	82	51	36	87	32	30
Rod Brind'Amour	82	36	38	74	54	–2
Eric Lindros	63	30	41	71	134	14
Chris Gratton	82	22	40	62	159	11
Alexandre Daigle*	75	16	26	42	14	–8
Trent Klatt	82	14	28	42	16	2
Mike Sillinger*	75	21	20	41	50	–11
Danius Zubrus	69	8	25	33	42	29
Eric Desjardins	77	6	27	33	36	11
Daniel McGillis*	80	11	20	31	109	–21
Paul Coffey	57	2	27	29	30	3
Shjon Podein	82	11	13	24	53	8
Colin Forbes	63	12	7	19	59	2
Chris Therien	78	3	16	19	80	5
Petr Svoboda	56	3	15	18	83	19
Dave Babych*	53	0	9	9	49	–9
Joel Otto	68	3	4	7	78	–2
Luke Richardson	81	2	3	5	139	7
Daniel Lacroix	56	1	4	5	135	E
Kjell Samuelsson	49	0	3	3	28	9
Dan Kordic	61	1	1	2	210	–4
Sean Burke* (g)	52	0	2	2	20	—
Ron Hextall (g)	46	0	0	0	10	—

Coach—Wayne Cashman, Roger Neilson

Phoenix Coyotes

	GP	G	A	Pts	PIM	+/–
Keith Tkachuk	69	40	26	66	147	9
Jeremy Roenick	79	24	32	56	103	5
Cliff Ronning	80	11	44	55	36	5
Craig Janney	68	10	43	53	12	5
Teppo Numminen	82	11	40	51	30	25
Rick Tocchet	68	26	19	45	157	1
Dallas Drake	60	11	29	40	71	17
Mike Gartner	60	12	15	27	24	–4
Keith Carney*	80	3	19	22	91	–2
Bob Corkum	76	12	9	21	28	–7
Oleg Tverdovsky	46	7	12	19	12	1
Gerald Diduck	78	8	10	18	118	14
Brad Isbister	66	9	8	17	102	4
John Slaney	55	3	14	17	24	–3
Darrin Shannon	58	2	12	14	26	4
Mark Janssens*	74	5	7	12	154	–21
Juha Ylonen	55	1	11	12	10	–3
Mike Stapleton	64	5	5	10	36	–4
Norm Maciver	41	2	6	8	38	–11
Jim McKenzie	64	3	4	7	146	–7
Murray Baron	45	1	5	6	106	–10
Jim Cummins*	75	0	2	2	225	–16
Nikolai Khabibulin (g)	70	0	2	2	22	—

Coach—Jim Schoenfeld

Pittsburgh Penguins

	GP	G	A	Pts	PIM	+/–
Jaromir Jagr	77	35	67	102	64	17
Ron Francis	81	25	62	87	20	12
Stu Barnes	78	30	35	65	30	15
Kevin Hatcher	74	19	29	48	66	–3
Martin Straka	75	19	23	42	28	–1
Rob Brown	82	15	25	40	59	–1
Fredrik Olausson	76	6	27	33	42	13
Alexei Morozov	76	13	13	26	8	–4
Ed Olczyk	56	11	11	22	35	–9
Robert Lang*	54	9	13	22	16	7
Sean Pronger*	67	6	15	21	32	–10
Alex Hicks	58	7	13	20	54	4
Brad Werenka	71	3	15	18	46	15
Jiri Slegr	73	5	12	17	109	10
Andreas Johansson	50	5	10	15	20	4
Darius Kasparaitis	81	4	8	12	127	3
Chris Ferraro	46	3	4	7	43	–2
Tyler Wright	82	3	4	7	112	–3
Chris Tamer	79	0	7	7	181	4
Tom Barrasso (g)	63	0	2	2	14	—

Coach—Kevin Constantine

St. Louis Blues

	GP	G	A	Pts	PIM	+/–
Brett Hull	66	27	45	72	26	–1
Pierre Turgeon	60	22	46	68	24	13
Geoff Courtnall	79	31	31	62	94	12
Steve Duchesne	80	14	42	56	32	9
Pavol Demitra	61	22	30	52	22	11
Al MacInnis	71	19	30	49	80	6
Craig Conroy	81	14	29	43	46	20
Jim Campbell	76	22	19	41	55	E
Chris Pronger	81	9	27	36	180	47
Todd Gill*	75	13	17	30	41	–11
Scott Pellerin	80	8	21	29	62	14
Blair Atcheynum	61	11	15	26	10	5
Terry Yake	65	10	15	25	38	1
Darren Turcotte	62	12	6	18	26	6
Pascal Rheaume	48	6	9	15	35	4
Mike Eastwood*	58	6	5	11	22	–2
Chris McAlpine	54	3	7	10	36	14
Marc Bergevin	81	3	7	10	90	–2
Rudy Poeschek	50	1	7	8	64	–5
Kelly Chase	67	4	3	7	231	10
Jamie Rivers	59	2	4	6	36	5
Tony Twist	60	1	1	2	105	–4
Grant Fuhr (g)	58	0	2	2	6	—

Coach—Joel Quenneville

San Jose Sharks

	GP	G	A	Pts	PIM	+/–
Jeff Friesen	79	31	32	63	40	8
John Maclean*	77	16	27	43	42	–6
Owen Nolan	75	14	27	41	144	–2
Patrick Marleau	74	13	19	32	14	5
Bill Houlder	82	7	25	32	48	13
Marco Sturm	74	10	20	30	40	–2
Stephane Matteau	73	15	14	29	60	4
Murray Craven	67	12	17	29	25	4
Bernie Nicholls	60	6	22	28	26	–4
Mike Ricci*	65	9	18	27	32	–4
Tony Granato	59	16	9	25	70	3
Marcus Ragnarsson	79	5	20	25	65	–11
Mike Rathje	81	3	12	15	59	–4
Andrei Zyuzin	56	6	7	13	66	8
Bryan Marchment*	61	2	11	13	144	–3
Shawn Burr	42	6	6	12	50	2
Marty McSorley	56	2	10	12	140	10
Ron Sutter	57	2	7	9	22	–2
Dave Lowry*	57	4	4	8	53	–1
Mike Vernon (g)	62	0	2	2	24	—

Coach—Darryl Sutter

Tampa Bay Lightning

	GP	G	A	Pts	PIM	+/–
Paul Ysebaert	82	13	27	40	32	–43
Mikael Renberg	68	16	22	38	34	–37
Alexander Selivanov	70	16	19	35	85	–38
Stephane Richer*	40	14	15	29	41	–6
Rob Zamuner	77	14	12	26	41	–31
Daymond Langkow	68	8	14	22	62	–9
Darcy Tucker*	74	7	13	20	146	–14
Sandy McCarthy*	66	8	10	18	241	–19
Mikael Andersson	72	6	11	17	29	–4
Karl Dykhuis	78	5	9	14	110	–8
Cory Cross	74	3	6	9	77	–24
Jody Hull*	49	4	4	8	8	3
Yves Racine	60	0	8	8	41	–23
Steve Kelly*	43	2	3	5	23	–13
Andrei Nazarov*	54	2	2	4	170	–13
Louie DeBrusk	54	1	2	3	166	–2
Mark Fitzpatrick* (g)	46	0	1	1	16	—

Coach—Terry Crisp, Rick Paterson, Jacques Demers

Toronto Maple Leafs

	GP	G	A	Pts	PIM	+/–
Mats Sundin	82	33	41	74	49	–3
Mike Johnson	82	15	32	47	24	–4
Derek King	77	21	25	46	43	–7
Igor Korolev	78	17	22	39	22	–18
Mathieu Schneider	76	11	26	37	44	–12
Fredrik Modin	74	16	16	32	32	–5
Sergei Berezin	68	16	15	31	10	–3
Steve Sullivan	63	10	18	28	40	–8
Sylvain Cote*	71	4	21	25	42	–3
Wendel Clark	47	12	7	19	80	–21
Alyn McCauley	60	6	10	16	6	–7
Jason Smith	81	3	13	16	100	–5
Tie Domi	80	4	10	14	365	–5
Todd Warriner	45	5	8	13	20	5
Darby Hendrickson	80	8	4	12	67	–20
Dimitri Yushkevich	72	0	12	12	78	–13
Rob Zettler	59	0	7	7	108	–8
Kris King	82	3	3	6	199	–13
Felix Potvin (g)	67	0	0	0	8	—

Coach—Mike Murphy

Vancouver Canucks

	GP	G	A	Pts	PIM	+/–
Pavel Bure	82	51	39	90	48	5
Mark Messier	82	22	38	60	58	–10
Alexander Mogilny	51	18	27	45	36	–6
Markus Naslund	76	14	20	34	56	5
Todd Bertuzzi*	74	13	20	33	121	–17
Jyrki Lumme	74	9	21	30	34	–25
Mattias Ohlund	77	7	23	30	76	3
Bret Hedican	71	3	24	27	79	3
Brian Noonan	82	10	15	25	62	–19
Dave Scratchard	76	13	11	24	165	–4
Bryan McCabe*	82	4	20	24	209	19
Brad May*	63	13	10	23	154	2
Donald Brashear	77	9	9	18	372	–9
Scott Walker	59	3	10	13	164	–8
Steve Staios	77	3	4	7	134	–3
Jamie Huscroft*	51	0	4	4	177	–2
Arturs Irbe (g)	41	0	0	0	2	—
Garth Snow* (g)	41	0	0	0	22	—

Coach—Tom Renney, Mike Keenan

Washington Capitals

	GP	G	A	Pts	PIM	+/–
Peter Bondra	76	52	26	78	44	14
Adam Oates	82	18	58	76	36	6
Calle Johansson	73	15	20	35	30	–11
Steve Konowalchuk	80	10	24	34	80	9
Joe Juneau	56	9	22	31	26	–8
Phil Housley	64	6	25	31	24	–10
Jeff Brown*	60	4	24	28	32	5
Richard Zednik	65	17	9	26	28	–2
Dale Hunter	82	8	18	26	103	1
Sergei Gonchar	72	5	16	21	66	2
Esa Tikkanen*	48	3	18	21	18	–11
Mark Tinordi	47	8	9	17	39	9
Jan Bulis	48	5	11	16	18	–5
Craig Berube	74	6	9	15	189	–3
Kelly Miller	76	7	7	14	41	–2
Todd Krygier	45	2	12	14	30	–3
Jeff Toms*	46	4	6	10	15	–17
Joe Reekie	68	2	8	10	70	15
Brendan Witt	64	1	7	8	112	–11
Ken Klee	51	4	2	6	46	–3
Olaf Kolzig (g)	64	0	1	1	12	—

Coach—Ron Wilson

Individual Goaltending, 1997-98

(25 or more games played; ranked by goals against average)

Player	GP	GAA	W	L	T	SO	SV%
Belfour, Dal.	61	1.88	37	12	10	9	.916
Brodeur, N.J.	70	1.89	43	17	8	10	.917
Barrasso, Pit.	63	2.07	31	14	13	7	.922
Hasek, Buf.	72	2.09	33	23	13	13	.932
McLennan, St. L.	30	2.17	16	8	2	2	.903
Hextall, Phi.	46	2.17	21	17	7	4	.911
Kidd, Car.	47	2.17	21	21	3	3	.922
Hackett, Chi.	58	2.20	21	25	11	8	.917
Kolzig, Was.	64	2.20	33	18	10	5	.920
Osgood, Det.	64	2.21	33	20	11	6	.913
Dafoe, Bos.	65	2.24	30	25	9	6	.914
Tugnutt, Ott.	42	2.25	15	14	8	3	.905
Rhodes, Ott.	50	2.34	19	19	7	5	.907
Roy, Col.	65	2.39	31	19	13	4	.916
Vernon, S.J.	62	2.46	30	22	8	5	.896
Thibault, Mon.	47	2.47	19	15	8	2	.902
Moog, Mon.	42	2.49	18	17	5	3	.905
Fuhr, St.L.	58	2.53	29	21	6	3	.898
Snow, Phi., Van.	41	2.59	17	15	4	1	.901
Joseph, Edm.	71	2.63	29	31	9	8	.905
Salo, N.Y.I.	62	2.64	23	29	5	4	.906
Richter, N.Y.R.	72	2.66	21	31	15	0	.903
Fiset, L.A.	60	2.71	26	25	8	2	.909
Puppa, T.B.	26	2.72	5	14	6	0	.900
Irbe, Van.	41	2.73	14	11	6	2	.907
Potvin, Tor.	67	2.73	26	33	7	5	.906
Khabibulin, Pho.	70	2.74	30	28	10	4	.900
Hrudey, S.J.	28	2.74	4	16	2	1	.897
Vanbiesbrouck, Fla.	60	2.87	18	29	11	4	.899
Tabaracci, T.B	42	2.88	13	22	6	0	.893
Hebert, Ana.	46	2.93	13	24	6	3	.903
Burke, Car.-Van.-Phi.	52	2.95	16	23	9	2	.896
Roloson, Cgy.	39	2.99	11	16	8	0	.890
Fitzpatrick, Fla., T.B.	46	3.12	9	31	3	2	.892
Shtalenkov, Ana.	40	3.22	13	18	5	1	.893
McLean, Van.-Car.-Fla.	44	3.54	14	21	5	1	.881

All-Time Leading Scorers

Player	Goals	Assists	Points
Wayne Gretzky*	885	1,910	2,795
Gordie Howe	801	1,049	1,850
Marcel Dionne	731	1,040	1,771
Mark Messier*	597	1,015	1,612
Phil Esposito	717	873	1,590
Mario Lemieux	613	881	1,494
Paul Coffey*	383	1,090	1,473
Stan Mikita	541	926	1,467
Ron Francis*	428	1,006	1,434
Bryan Trottier	524	901	1,425
Ray Bourque*	375	1,036	1,411
Dale Hawerchuk	518	891	1,409
Steve Yzerman*	563	846	1,409
Jari Kurri*	601	797	1,398
John Bucyk	556	813	1,369
Guy Lafleur	560	793	1,353
Denis Savard	473	865	1,338
Mike Gartner*	708	627	1,335
Gilbert Perreault	512	814	1,326
Alex Delvecchio	456	825	1,281

Note: Through end of 1997-98 season.* Active at end of 1997-98 season.

Most NHL Goals in a Season

Player	Team	Season	Goals
Wayne Gretzky	Edmonton	1981-82	92
Wayne Gretzky	Edmonton	1983-84	87
Brett Hull	St. Louis	1990-91	86
Mario Lemieux	Pittsburgh	1988-89	85
Phil Esposito	Boston	1970-71	76
Alexander Mogilny	Buffalo	1992-93	76
Teemu Selanne	Winnipeg	1992-93	76
Wayne Gretzky	Edmonton	1984-85	73
Brett Hull	St. Louis	1989-90	72
Wayne Gretzky	Edmonton	1982-83	71
Jari Kurri	Edmonton	1984-85	71
Bret Hull	St. Louis	1991-92	70
Mario Lemieux	Pittsburgh	1987-88	70
Bernie Nicholls	Los Angeles	1988-89	70
Mike Bossy	N.Y. Islanders	1978-79	69
Mario Lemieux	Pittsburgh	1992-93	69
Mario Lemieux	Pittsburgh	1995-96	69
Mike Bossy	N.Y. Islanders	1980-81	68
Phil Esposito	Boston	1973-74	68
Jari Kurri	Edmonton	1985-86	68

Art Ross Trophy (Leading Scorer)

1927 Bill Cook, N.Y. Rangers
1928 Howie Morenz, Montreal
1929 Ace Bailey, Toronto
1930 Cooney Weiland, Boston
1931 Howie Morenz, Montreal
1932 Harvey Jackson, Toronto
1933 Bill Cook, N.Y. Rangers
1934 Charlie Conacher, Toronto
1935 Charlie Conacher, Toronto
1936 Dave Schriner, N.Y. Americans
1937 Dave Schriner, N.Y. Americans
1938 Gordie Drillon, Toronto
1939 Toe Blake, Montreal
1940 Milt Schmidt, Boston
1941 Bill Cowley, Boston
1942 Bryan Hextall, N.Y. Rangers
1943 Doug Bentley, Chicago
1944 Herbie Cain, Boston
1945 Elmer Lach, Montreal
1946 Max Bentley, Chicago
1947 Max Bentley, Chicago
1948 Elmer Lach, Montreal
1949 Roy Conacher, Chicago
1950 Ted Lindsay, Detroit
1951 Gordie Howe, Detroit
1952 Gordie Howe, Detroit
1953 Gordie Howe, Detroit
1954 Gordie Howe, Detroit
1955 Bernie Geoffrion, Montreal
1956 Jean Beliveau, Montreal
1957 Gordie Howe, Detroit
1958 Dickie Moore, Montreal
1959 Dickie Moore, Montreal
1960 Bobby Hull, Chicago
1961 Bernie Geoffrion, Montreal
1962 Bobby Hull, Chicago
1963 Gordie Howe, Detroit
1964 Stan Mikita, Chicago
1965 Stan Mikita, Chicago
1966 Bobby Hull, Chicago
1967 Stan Mikita, Chicago
1968 Stan Mikita, Chicago
1969 Phil Esposito, Boston
1970 Bobby Orr, Boston
1971 Phil Esposito, Boston
1972 Phil Esposito, Boston
1973 Phil Esposito, Boston
1974 Phil Esposito, Boston
1975 Bobby Orr, Boston
1976 Guy Lafleur, Montreal
1977 Guy Lafleur, Montreal
1978 Guy Lafleur, Montreal
1979 Bryan Trottier, N.Y. Islanders
1980 Marcel Dionne, Los Angeles
1981 Wayne Gretzky, Edmonton
1982 Wayne Gretzky, Edmonton
1983 Wayne Gretzky, Edmonton
1984 Wayne Gretzky, Edmonton
1985 Wayne Gretzky, Edmonton
1986 Wayne Gretzky, Edmonton
1987 Wayne Gretzky, Edmonton
1988 Mario Lemieux, Pittsburgh
1989 Mario Lemieux, Pittsburgh
1990 Wayne Gretzky, Los Angeles
1991 Wayne Gretzky, Los Angeles
1992 Mario Lemieux, Pittsburgh
1993 Mario Lemieux, Pittsburgh
1994 Wayne Gretzky, Los Angeles
1995 Jaromir Jagr, Pittsburgh
1996 Mario Lemieux, Pittsburgh
1997 Mario Lemieux, Pittsburgh
1998 Jaromir Jagr, Pittsburgh

James Norris Memorial Trophy (Outstanding Defenseman)

1954 Red Kelly, Detroit
1955 Doug Harvey, Montreal
1956 Doug Harvey, Montreal
1957 Doug Harvey, Montreal
1958 Doug Harvey, Montreal
1959 Tom Johnson, Montreal
1960 Doug Harvey, Montreal
1961 Doug Harvey, Montreal
1962 Doug Harvey, N.Y. Rangers
1963 Pierre Pilote, Chicago
1964 Pierre Pilote, Chicago
1965 Pierre Pilote, Chicago
1966 Jacques Laperriere, Montreal
1967 Harry Howell, N.Y. Rangers
1968 Bobby Orr, Boston
1969 Bobby Orr, Boston
1970 Bobby Orr, Boston
1971 Bobby Orr, Boston
1972 Bobby Orr, Boston
1973 Bobby Orr, Boston
1974 Bobby Orr, Boston
1975 Bobby Orr, Boston
1976 Denis Potvin, N.Y. Islanders
1977 Larry Robinson, Montreal
1978 Denis Potvin, N.Y. Islanders
1979 Denis Potvin, N.Y. Islanders
1980 Larry Robinson, Montreal
1981 Randy Carlyle, Pittsburgh
1982 Doug Wilson, Chicago
1983 Rod Langway, Washington
1984 Rod Langway, Washington
1985 Paul Coffey, Edmonton
1986 Paul Coffey, Edmonton
1987 Ray Bourque, Boston
1988 Ray Bourque, Boston
1989 Chris Chelios, Montreal
1990 Ray Bourque, Boston
1991 Ray Bourque, Boston
1992 Brian Leetch, N.Y. Rangers
1993 Chris Chelios, Chicago
1994 Ray Bourque, Boston
1995 Paul Coffey, Detroit
1996 Chris Chelios, Chicago
1997 Brian Leetch, N.Y. Rangers
1998 Rob Blake, Los Angeles

Vezina Trophy (Outstanding Goalie)*

1927 George Hainsworth, Montreal
1928 George Hainsworth, Montreal
1929 George Hainsworth, Montreal
1930 Tiny Thompson, Boston
1931 Roy Worters, N.Y. Americans
1932 Charlie Gardiner, Chicago
1933 Tiny Thompson, Boston
1934 Charlie Gardiner, Chicago
1935 Lorne Chabot, Chicago
1936 Tiny Thompson, Boston
1937 Normie Smith, Detroit
1938 Tiny Thompson, Boston
1939 Frank Brimsek, Boston
1940 Dave Kerr, N.Y. Rangers
1941 Turk Broda, Toronto
1942 Frank Brimsek, Boston
1943 Johnny Mowers, Detroit
1944 Bill Durnan, Montreal
1945 Bill Durnan, Montreal
1946 Bill Durnan, Montreal
1947 Bill Durnan, Montreal
1948 Turk Broda, Toronto
1949 Bill Durnan, Montreal
1950 Bill Durnan, Montreal
1951 Al Rollins, Toronto
1952 Terry Sawchuk, Detroit
1953 Terry Sawchuk, Detroit
1954 Harry Lumley, Toronto
1955 Terry Sawchuk, Detroit
1956 Jacques Plante, Montreal
1957 Jacques Plante, Montreal
1958 Jacques Plante, Montreal
1959 Jacques Plante, Montreal
1960 Jacques Plante, Montreal
1961 John Bower, Toronto
1962 Jacques Plante, Montreal
1963 Glenn Hall, Chicago
1964 Charlie Hodge, Montreal
1965 Sawchuk, Bower, Toronto
1966 Worsley, Hodge, Montreal
1967 Hall, DeJordy, Chicago
1968 Worsley, Vachon, Montreal
1969 Hall, Plante, St. Louis
1970 Tony Esposito, Chicago
1971 Giacomin, Villemure, N.Y. Rangers
1972 Esposito, Smith, Chicago
1973 Ken Dryden, Montreal
1974 Bernie Parent, Philadelphia; Tony Esposito, Chicago
1975 Bernie Parent, Philadelphia
1976 Ken Dryden, Montreal
1977 Dryden, Larocque, Montreal
1978 Dryden, Larocque, Montreal
1979 Dryden, Larocque, Montreal
1980 Sauve, Edwards, Buffalo
1981 Sevigny, Larocque, Herron, Montreal
1982 Bill Smith, N.Y. Islanders
1983 Pete Peeters, Boston
1984 Tom Barrasso, Buffalo
1985 Pelle Lindbergh, Philadelphia
1986 John Vanbiesbrouck, N.Y. Rangers
1987 Ron Hextall, Philadelphia
1988 Grant Fuhr, Edmonton
1989 Patrick Roy, Montreal
1990 Patrick Roy, Montreal
1991 Ed Belfour, Chicago
1992 Patrick Roy, Montreal
1993 Ed Belfour, Chicago
1994 Dominik Hasek, Buffalo
1995 Dominik Hasek, Buffalo
1996 Jim Carey, Washington
1997 Dominik Hasek, Buffalo
1998 Dominik Hasek, Buffalo

*Before 1982, awarded to the goalie or goalies who played a minimum of 25 games for the team that allowed the fewest goals; since 1982, awarded to the outstanding goalie.

Calder Memorial Trophy (Rookie of the Year)

1933 Carl Voss, Detroit
1934 Russ Blinco, Montreal Maroons
1935 Dave Schriner, N.Y. Americans
1936 Mike Karakas, Chicago
1937 Syl Apps, Toronto
1938 Cully Dahlstrom, Chicago
1939 Frank Brimsek, Boston
1940 Kilby Macdonald, N.Y. Rangers
1941 John Quilty, Montreal
1942 Grant Warwick, N.Y. Rangers
1943 Gaye Stewart, Toronto
1944 Gus Bodnar, Toronto
1945 Frank McCool, Toronto
1946 Edgar Laprade, N.Y. Rangers
1947 Howie Meeker, Toronto
1948 Jim McFadden, Detroit
1949 Pentti Lund, N.Y. Rangers
1950 Jack Gelineau, Boston
1951 Terry Sawchuk, Detroit
1952 Bernie Geoffrion, Montreal
1953 Gump Worsley, N.Y. Rangers
1954 Camille Henry, N.Y. Rangers
1955 Ed Litzenberger, Chicago
1956 Glenn Hall, Detroit
1957 Larry Regan, Boston
1958 Frank Mahovlich, Toronto
1959 Ralph Backstrom, Montreal
1960 Bill Hay, Chicago
1961 Dave Keon, Toronto
1962 Bobby Rousseau, Montreal
1963 Kent Douglas, Toronto
1964 Jacques Laperriere, Montreal
1965 Roger Crozier, Detroit
1966 Brit Selby, Toronto
1967 Bobby Orr, Boston
1968 Derek Sanderson, Boston
1969 Danny Grant, Minnesota
1970 Tony Esposito, Chicago
1971 Gilbert Perreault, Buffalo
1972 Ken Dryden, Montreal
1973 Steve Vickers, N.Y. Rangers
1974 Denis Potvin, N.Y. Islanders
1975 Eric Vail, Atlanta
1976 Bryan Trottier, N.Y. Islanders
1977 Willi Plett, Atlanta
1978 Mike Bossy, N.Y. Islanders
1979 Bobby Smith, Minnesota
1980 Ray Bourque, Boston
1981 Peter Stastny, Quebec
1982 Dale Hawerchuk, Winnipeg
1983 Steve Larmer, Chicago
1984 Tom Barrasso, Buffalo
1985 Mario Lemieux, Pittsburgh
1986 Gary Suter, Calgary
1987 Luc Robitaille, Los Angeles
1988 Joe Nieuwendyk, Calgary
1989 Brian Leetch, N.Y. Rangers
1990 Sergei Makarov, Calgary
1991 Ed Belfour, Chicago
1992 Pavel Bure, Vancouver
1993 Teemu Selanne, Winnipeg
1994 Martin Brodeur, New Jersey
1995 Peter Forsberg, Quebec
1996 Daniel Alfredsson, Ottawa
1997 Bryan Berard, N.Y. Islanders
1998 Sergei Samsonov, Boston

Lady Byng Memorial Trophy (Most Gentlemanly Player)

1925 Frank Nighbor, Ottawa
1926 Frank Nighbor, Ottawa
1927 Billy Burch, N.Y. Americans
1928 Frank Boucher, N.Y. Rangers
1929 Frank Boucher, N.Y. Rangers
1930 Frank Boucher, N.Y. Rangers
1931 Frank Boucher, N.Y. Rangers
1932 Joe Primeau, Toronto
1933 Frank Boucher, N.Y. Rangers
1934 Frank Boucher, N.Y. Rangers
1935 Frank Boucher, N.Y. Rangers
1936 Doc Romnes, Chicago
1937 Marty Barry, Detroit
1938 Gordie Drillon, Toronto
1939 Clint Smith, N.Y. Rangers
1940 Bobby Bauer, Boston
1941 Bobby Bauer, Boston
1942 Syl Apps, Toronto
1943 Max Bentley, Chicago
1944 Clint Smith, Chicago
1945 Bill Mosienko, Chicago
1946 Toe Blake, Montreal
1947 Bobby Bauer, Boston
1948 Buddy O'Connor, N.Y. Rangers
1949 Bill Quackenbush, Detroit
1950 Edgar Laprade, N.Y. Rangers
1951 Red Kelly, Detroit
1952 Sid Smith, Toronto
1953 Red Kelly, Detroit
1954 Red Kelly, Detroit
1955 Sid Smith, Toronto
1956 Earl Reibel, Detroit
1957 Andy Hebenton, N.Y. Rangers
1958 Camille Henry, N.Y. Rangers
1959 Alex Delvecchio, Detroit
1960 Don McKenney, Boston
1961 Red Kelly, Toronto
1962 Dave Keon, Toronto
1963 Dave Keon, Toronto
1964 Ken Wharram, Chicago
1965 Bobby Hull, Chicago
1966 Alex Delvecchio, Detroit
1967 Stan Mikita, Chicago
1968 Stan Mikita, Chicago
1969 Alex Delvecchio, Detroit

1970	Phil Goyette, St. Louis
1971	John Bucyk, Boston
1972	Jean Ratelle, N.Y. Rangers
1973	Gil Perreault, Buffalo
1974	John Bucyk, Boston
1975	Marcel Dionne, Detroit
1976	Jean Ratelle, N.Y.R.-Boston
1977	Marcel Dionne, Los Angeles
1978	Butch Goring, Los Angeles
1979	Bob MacMillan, Atlanta
1980	Wayne Gretzky, Edmonton
1981	Rick Kehoe, Pittsburgh
1982	Rick Middleton, Boston
1983	Mike Bossy, N.Y. Islanders
1984	Mike Bossy, N.Y. Islanders
1985	Jari Kurri, Edmonton
1986	Mike Bossy, N.Y. Islanders
1987	Joe Mullen, Calgary
1988	Mats Naslund, Montreal
1989	Joe Mullen, Calgary
1990	Brett Hull, St. Louis
1991	Wayne Gretzky, Los Angeles
1992	Wayne Gretzky, Los Angeles
1993	Pierre Turgeon, N.Y. Islanders
1994	Wayne Gretzky, Los Angeles
1995	Ron Francis, Pittsburgh
1996	Paul Kariya, Anaheim
1997	Paul Kariya, Anaheim
1998	Ron Francis, Pittsburgh

Frank J. Selke Trophy (Best Defensive Forward)

1978	Bob Gainey, Montreal
1979	Bob Gainey, Montreal
1980	Bob Gainey, Montreal
1981	Bob Gainey, Montreal
1982	Steve Kasper, Boston
1983	Bobby Clarke, Philadelphia
1984	Doug Jarvis, Washington
1985	Craig Ramsay, Buffalo
1986	Troy Murray, Chicago
1987	Dave Poulin, Philadelphia
1988	Guy Carbonneau, Montreal
1989	Guy Carbonneau, Montreal
1990	Rick Meagher, St. Louis
1991	Dirk Graham, Chicago
1992	Guy Carbonneau, Montreal
1993	Doug Gilmour, Toronto
1994	Sergei Fedorov, Detroit
1995	Ron Francis, Pittsburgh
1996	Sergei Federov, Detroit
1997	Michael Peca, Buffalo
1998	Jere Lehtinen, Dallas

Hart Memorial Trophy (MVP)

1927	Herb Gardiner, Montreal
1928	Howie Morenz, Montreal
1929	Roy Worters, N.Y. Americans
1930	Nels Stewart, Montreal Maroons
1931	Howie Morenz, Montreal
1932	Howie Morenz, Montreal
1933	Eddie Shore, Boston
1934	Aurel Joliat, Montreal
1935	Eddie Shore, Boston
1936	Eddie Shore, Boston
1937	Babe Siebert, Montreal
1938	Eddie Shore, Boston
1939	Toe Blake, Montreal
1940	Ebbie Goodfellow, Detroit
1941	Bill Cowley, Boston
1942	Tom Anderson, N.Y. Americans
1943	Bill Cowley, Boston
1944	Babe Pratt, Toronto
1945	Elmer Lach, Montreal
1946	Max Bentley, Chicago
1947	Maurice Richard, Montreal
1948	Buddy O'Connor, N.Y. Rangers
1949	Sid Abel, Detroit
1950	Chuck Rayner, N.Y. Rangers
1951	Milt Schmidt, Boston
1952	Gordie Howe, Detroit
1953	Gordie Howe, Detroit
1954	Al Rollins, Chicago
1955	Ted Kennedy, Toronto
1956	Jean Beliveau, Montreal
1957	Gordie Howe, Detroit
1958	Gordie Howe, Detroit
1959	Andy Bathgate, N.Y. Rangers
1960	Gordie Howe, Detroit
1961	Bernie Geoffrion, Montreal
1962	Jacques Plante, Montreal
1963	Gordie Howe, Detroit
1964	Jean Beliveau, Montreal
1965	Bobby Hull, Chicago
1966	Bobby Hull, Chicago
1967	Stan Mikita, Chicago
1968	Stan Mikita, Chicago
1969	Phil Esposito, Boston
1970	Bobby Orr, Boston
1971	Bobby Orr, Boston
1972	Bobby Orr, Boston
1973	Bobby Clarke, Philadelphia
1974	Phil Esposito, Boston
1975	Bobby Clarke, Philadelphia
1976	Bobby Clarke, Philadelphia
1977	Guy Lafleur, Montreal
1978	Guy Lafleur, Montreal
1979	Bryan Trottier, N.Y. Islanders
1980	Wayne Gretzky, Edmonton
1981	Wayne Gretzky, Edmonton
1982	Wayne Gretzky, Edmonton
1983	Wayne Gretzky, Edmonton
1984	Wayne Gretzky, Edmonton
1985	Wayne Gretzky, Edmonton
1986	Wayne Gretzky, Edmonton
1987	Wayne Gretzky, Edmonton
1988	Mario Lemieux, Pittsburgh
1989	Wayne Gretzky, Los Angeles
1990	Mark Messier, Edmonton
1991	Brett Hull, St. Louis
1992	Mark Messier, N.Y. Rangers
1993	Mario Lemieux, Pittsburgh
1994	Sergei Fedorov, Detroit
1995	Eric Lindros, Philadelphia
1996	Mario Lemieux, Pittsburgh
1997	Dominik Hasek, Buffalo
1998	Dominik Hasek, Buffalo

Conn Smythe Trophy (MVP in Playoffs)

1965	Jean Beliveau, Montreal
1966	Roger Crozier, Detroit
1967	Dave Keon, Toronto
1968	Glenn Hall, St. Louis
1969	Serge Savard, Montreal
1970	Bobby Orr, Boston
1971	Ken Dryden, Montreal
1972	Bobby Orr, Boston
1973	Yvan Cournoyer, Montreal
1974	Bernie Parent, Philadelphia
1975	Bernie Parent, Philadelphia
1976	Reg Leach, Philadelphia
1977	Guy Lafleur, Montreal
1978	Larry Robinson, Montreal
1979	Bob Gainey, Montreal
1980	Bryan Trottier, N.Y. Islanders
1981	Butch Goring, N.Y. Islanders
1982	Mike Bossy, N.Y. Islanders
1983	Billy Smith, N.Y. Islanders
1984	Mark Messier, Edmonton
1985	Wayne Gretzky, Edmonton
1986	Patrick Roy, Montreal
1987	Ron Hextall, Philadelphia
1988	Wayne Gretzky, Edmonton
1989	Al MacInnis, Calgary
1990	Bill Ranford, Edmonton
1991	Mario Lemieux, Pittsburgh
1992	Mario Lemieux, Pittsburgh
1993	Patrick Roy, Montreal
1994	Brian Leetch, N.Y. Rangers
1995	Claude Lemieux, New Jersey
1996	Joe Sakic, Colorado
1997	Mike Vernon, Detroit
1998	Steve Yzerman, Detroit

Hockey Hall of Fame, Toronto, Ontario

(1998 inductees have an asterisk*)

PLAYERS

Abel, Sid
Adams, Jack
Apps, Syl
Armstrong, George
Bailey, Ace
Bain, Dan
Baker, Hobey
Barber, Bill
Barry, Marty
Bathgate, Andy
Bauer, Bobby
Beliveau, Jean
Benedict, Clint
Bentley, Doug
Bentley, Max
Blake, Toe
Boivin, Leo
Boon, Dickie
Bossy, Mike
Bouchard, Butch
Boucher, Frank
Boucher, George
Bower, Johnny
Bowie, Dubbie
Brimsek, Frank
Broadbent, Punch
Broda, Turk
Bucyk, John
Burch, Billy
Cameron, Harry
Cheevers, Gerry
Clancy, King
Clapper, Dit
Clarke, Bobby
Cleghorn, Sprague
Colville, Neil
Conacher, Charlie
Conacher, Lionel
Conacher, Roy*
Connell, Alex
Cook, Bill
Cook, Bun
Coulter, Art
Cournoyer, Yvan
Cowley, Bill
Crawford, Rusty
Darragh, Jack
Davidson, Scotty
Day, Hap
Delvecchio, Alex
Denneny, Cy
Dionne, Marcel
Drillon, Gordie
Drinkwater, Graham
Dryden, Ken
Dumart, Woody
Dunderdale, Tommy
Durnan, Bill
Dutton, Red
Dye, Babe
Esposito, Phil
Esposito, Tony
Farrel, Arthur
Flaman, Fernie
Foyston, Frank
Fredrickson, Frank
Gadsby, Bill
Gainey, Bob
Gardiner, Chuck
Gardiner, Herb
Gardiner, Jimmy
Geoffrion, Bernie
Gerard, Eddie
Giacomin, Eddie
Gilbert, Rod
Gilmour, Billy
Goheen, Moose
Goodfellow, Ebbie
Goulet, Michel*
Grant, Mike
Green, Shorty
Griffis, Si
Hainsworth, George
Hall, Glenn
Hall, Joe
Harvey, Doug
Hay, George
Hern, Riley
Hextall, Bryan
Holmes, Hap
Hooper, Tom
Horner, Red
Horton, Tim
Howe, Gordie
Howe, Syd
Howell, Harry
Hull, Bobby
Hutton, Bouse
Hyland, Harry
Irvin, Dick
Jackson, Busher
Johnson, Ching
Johnson, Ernie
Johnson, Tom
Joliat, Aurel
Keats, Duke
Kelly, Red
Kennedy, Ted
Keon, Dave
Lach, Elmer
Lafleur, Guy
Lalonde, Newsy
Laperriere, Jacques
Lapointe, Guy
Laprade, Edgar
Laviolette, Jack
LeSueur, Percy
Lehman, Hughie
Lemaire, Jacques
Lemieux, Mario
Lewis, Herbie
Lindsay, Ted
Lumley, Harry
MacKay, Mickey

Mahovlich, Frank
Malone, Joe
Mantha, Sylvio
Marshall, Jack
Maxwell, Fred
McDonald, Lanny
McGee, Frank
McGimsie, Billy
McNamara, George
Mikita, Stan
Moore, Dickie
Moran, Paddy
Morenz, Howie
Mosienko, Bill
Nighbor, Frank
Noble, Reg
O'Connor, Buddy
Oliver, Harry
Olmstead, Bert
Orr, Bobby
Parent, Bernie
Park, Brad
Patrick, Lester
Patrick, Lynn
Perreault, Gilbert
Phillips, Tom
Pilote, Pierre
Pitre, Didier
Plante, Jacques
Potvin, Denis
Pratt, Babe
Primeau, Joe
Pronovost, Marcel
Pulford, Bob
Pulford, Harvey
Quackenbush, Bill
Rankin, Frank
Ratelle, Jean
Rayner, Chuck
Reardon, Kenny
Richard, Henri
Richard, Maurice
Richardson, George
Roberts, Gordie
Robinson, Larry
Ross, Art
Russel, Blair
Russell, Ernie
Ruttan, Jack
Salming, Borje
Savard, Serge
Sawchuk, Terry
Scanlan, Fred
Schmidt, Milt
Schriner, Sweeney
Seibert, Earl
Seibert, Oliver
Shore, Eddie
Shutt, Steve
Siebert, Babe
Simpson, Joe
Sittler, Darryl
Smith, Alf
Smith, Billy
Smith, Clint
Smith, Hooley
Smith, Tommy
Stanley, Allan
Stanley, Barney
Stastny, Peter*
Stewart, Jack
Stewart, Nels
Stuart, Bruce
Stuart, Hod
Taylor, Cyclone
Thompson, Tiny
Tretiak, Vladislav
Trihey, Harry
Trottier, Bryan
Ullman, Norm
Vezina, Georges
Walker, Jack
Walsh, Marty
Watson, Harry (Moose)
Watson, Harry Percival
Weiland, Cooney
Westwick, Harry
Whitcroft, Fred
Wilson, Phat
Worsley, Gump
Worters, Roy

BUILDERS

Adams, Charles
Adams, Weston
Ahearn, Bunny
Ahearn, Frank
Allan, Sir Montagu
Allen, Keith
Arbour, Al
Ballard, Harold
Bauer, Father David
Bickell, J.P.
Bowman, Scotty
Brown, George
Brown, Walter
Buckland, Frank
Butterfield, Jack
Calder, Frank
Campbell, Angus
Campbell, Clarence
Cattarinich, Joseph
Dandurand, Leo
Dilio, Frank
Dudley, George
Dunn, James
Francis, Emile
Gibson, Jack
Gorman, Tommy
Griffiths, Frank
Hanley, Bill
Hay, Charles
Hendy, Jim
Hewitt, Foster
Hewitt, William
Hume, Fred
Imlach, Punch
Ivan, Tommy
Jennings, William
Johnson, Bob
Juckes, Gordon
Kilpatrick, John
Knox, Seymour
LeBel, Robert
Leader, Al
Lockhart, Thomas
Loicq, Paul
Mariucci, John
Mathers, Frank
McLaughlin, Frederic
Milford, Jake
Molson, Sen. Hartland
Murray, Pere Athol*
Nelson, Francis
Norris, Bruce
Norris, James
Norris, James Sr.
Northey, William
O'Brien, J. Ambrose
O'Neill, Brian Francis
Page, Frederick
Patrick, Frank
Pickard, Allan
Pilous, Rudy
Poile, Bud
Pollock, Sam
Raymond, Sen. Donat
Robertson, John Ross
Robinson, Claude
Ross, Phillip
Sabetzki, Gunther
Sather, Glen
Selke, Frank
Sinden, Harry
Smith, Frank
Smythe, Conn
Snider, Ed
Stanley, Lord (of Preston)
Sutherland, Capt. James T.
Tarasov, Anatoli
Torrey, Bill
Turner, Lloyd
Tutt, William
Voss, Carl
Waghorne, Fred
Wirtz, Arthur
Wirtz, Bill
Ziegler, John A., Jr.

REFEREES AND LINESMEN

Armstrong, Neil
Ashley, John
Chadwick, Bill
D'Amico, John
Elliott, Chaucer
Hayes, George
Hewiston, Bobby
Ion, Mickey
Pavelich, Matt
Rodden, Mike
Smeaton, Cooper
Storey, Red
Udvari, Frank

NCAA HOCKEY CHAMPIONS

1948	Michigan	1961	Denver	1974	Minnesota	1987	North Dakota
1949	Boston College	1962	Michigan Tech	1975	Michigan Tech	1988	Lake Superior St.
1950	Colorado College	1963	North Dakota	1976	Minnesota	1989	Harvard
1951	Michigan	1964	Michigan	1977	Wisconsin	1990	Wisconsin
1952	Michigan	1965	Michigan Tech	1978	Boston Univ.	1991	N. Michigan
1953	Michigan	1966	Michigan State	1979	Minnesota	1992	Lake Superior St.
1954	RPI	1967	Cornell	1980	North Dakota	1993	Maine
1955	Michigan	1968	Denver	1981	Wisconsin	1994	Lake Superior St.
1956	Michigan	1969	Denver	1982	North Dakota	1995	Boston Univ.
1957	Colorado College	1970	Cornell	1983	Wisconsin	1996	Michigan
1958	Denver	1971	Boston Univ.	1984	Bowling Green	1997	North Dakota
1959	North Dakota	1972	Boston Univ.	1985	RPI	1998	Michigan
1960	Denver	1973	Wisconsin	1986	Michigan State		

LACROSSE

Lacrosse Champions in 1998

World Lacrosse Championship (1998; held every 4 years)—Baltimore, Maryland, USA, July 24: U.S. 15, Canada 14 (OT).

U.S. Club Lacrosse Association Championship—Baltimore, MD, June 14: Long Island-Hofstra 18, New York Athletic Club 10.

National Lacrosse League Championship—Baltimore, MD, April 26, 28: Philadelphia defeated Baltimore 2 games to 0 (16-12, 17-12).

NCAA Division I Championship—Piscataway, NJ, May 25: Princeton 15, Maryland 5.

NCAA Division II Championship—Piscataway, NJ, May 24: Adelphi 18, C.W. Post 6.

NCAA Division III Championship—Piscataway, NJ, May 24: Washington College 16, Nazareth 10.

NCAA Division I All-Star Game—Rochester, NY, June 13: South 19, North 18.

National Junior College Championship—Essex, MD, May 10: Anne Arundel C.C. 17, Herkimer C.C. 13.

Women's World Cup (1997; held every 4 years)—Edogaua, Japan, May 4: USA 3, Australia 2 (OT).

NCAA Women's Division I Championship—Baltimore, MD, May 17: Maryland 11, Virginia 5.

NCAA Women's Division III Championship—Baltimore, MD, May 17: College of New Jersey 12, Williams 11 (OT).

NCAA I All America Team

Attack: Jon Hess, Princeton; Jesse Hubbard, Princeton; Casey Powell, Syracuse; Michael Watson, Virginia.

Midfield: Scott Diggs, Duke; Mark Frye, Loyola; A.J. Haugen, Johns Hopkins; Josh Sims, Princeton.

Defense: Christian Cook, Princeton; Rob Doerr, Johns Hopkins; Jamie Hanford, Loyola.

Goal: Brian Carcaterra, Johns Hopkins.

Coach of the Year: John Hind, Butler.

NCAA Division I Lacrosse Champions

Year	Champion	Year	Champion	Year	Champion	Year	Champion
1971	Cornell	1978	Johns Hopkins	1985	Johns Hopkins	1992	Princeton
1972	Virginia	1979	Johns Hopkins	1986	North Carolina	1993	Syracuse
1973	Maryland	1980	Johns Hopkins	1987	Johns Hopkins	1994	Princeton
1974	Johns Hopkins	1981	North Carolina	1988	Syracuse	1995	Syracuse
1975	Maryland	1982	North Carolina	1989	Syracuse	1996	Princeton
1976	Cornell	1983	Syracuse	1990	vacated	1997	Princeton
1977	Cornell	1984	Johns Hopkins	1991	North Carolina	1998	Princeton

THOROUGHBRED RACING

Triple Crown Winners

Since 1920, colts have carried 126 lb. in triple crown events; fillies, 121 lb.
(Kentucky Derby, Preakness, and Belmont Stakes)

Year	Horse	Jockey	Trainer
1919	Sir Barton	J. Loftus	H. G. Bedwell
1930	Gallant Fox	E. Sande	J. Fitzsimmons
1935	Omaha	W. Sanders	J. Fitzsimmons
1937	War Admiral	C. Kurtsinger	G. Conway
1941	Whirlaway	E. Arcaro	B. A. Jones
1943	Count Fleet	J. Longden	G. D. Cameron
1946	Assault	W. Mehrtens	M. Hirsch
1948	Citation	E. Arcaro	H. A. Jones
1973	Secretariat	R. Turcotte	L. Laurin
1977	Seattle Slew	J. Cruguet	W. H. Turner Jr.
1978	Affirmed	S. Cauthen	L. S. Barrera

Kentucky Derby

Churchill Downs, Louisville, KY; inaug. 1875; distance 1-1/4 mi; 1-1/2 mi until 1896. 3-year-olds.
Best time: 1:59.2, by Secretariat, 1973; 1998 time: 2:02.38.

Year	Winner	
1875	Aristides	O. Lewis
1876	Vagrant	R. Swim
1877	Baden Baden	W. Walker
1878	Day Star	J. Carter
1879	Lord Murphy	C. Schauer
1880	Fonso	G. Lewis
1881	Hindoo	J. McLaughlin
1882	Apollo	B. Hurd
1883	Leonatus	W. Donohue
1884	Buchanan	I. Murphy
1885	Joe Cotton	E. Henderson
1886	Ben Ali	P. Duffy
1887	Montrose	I. Lewis
1888	Macbeth II	G. Covington
1889	Spokane	T. Kiley
1890	Riley	I. Murphy
1891	Kingman	I. Murphy
1892	Azra	A. Clayton
1893	Lookout	E. Kunze
1894	Chant	F. Goodale
1895	Halma	J. Perkins
1896	Ben Brush	W. Simms
1897	Typhoon II	F. Garner
1898	Plaudit	W. Simms
1899	Manuel	F. Taral
1900	Lieut. Gibson	J. Boland
1901	His Eminence	J. Winkfield
1902	Alan-a-Dale	J. Winkfield
1903	Judge Himes	H. Booker
1904	Elwood	F. Prior
1905	Agile	J. Martin
1906	Sir Huon	R. Troxler
1907	Pink Star	A. Minder
1908	Stone Street	A. Pickens
1909	Wintergreen	V. Powers
1910	Donau	F. Herbert
1911	Meridian	G. Archibald
1912	Worth	C.H. Shilling
1913	Donerail	R. Goose
1914	Old Rosebud	J. McCabe
1915	Regret*	J. Notter
1916	George Smith	J. Loftus
1917	Omar Khayyam	C. Borel
1918	Exterminator	W. Knapp
1919	Sir Barton	J. Loftus
1920	Paul Jones	T. Rice
1921	Behave Yourself	C. Thompson
1922	Morvich	A. Johnson
1923	Zev	E. Sande
1924	Black Gold	J. D. Mooney
1925	Flying Ebony	E. Sande
1926	Bubbling Over	A. Johnson
1927	Whiskery	L. McAtee
1928	Reigh Count	C. Lang
1929	Clyde Van Dusen	L. McAtee
1930	Gallant Fox	E. Sande
1931	Twenty Grand	C. Kurtsinger
1932	Burgoo King	E. James
1933	Brokers Tip	D. Meade
1934	Cavalcade	M. Garner
1935	Omaha	W. Saunders
1936	Bold Venture	I. Hanford
1937	War Admiral	C. Kurtsinger
1938	Lawrin	E. Arcaro
1939	Johnstown	J. Stout
1940	Gallahadion	C. Bierman
1941	Whirlaway	E. Arcaro
1942	Shut Out	W. D. Wright
1943	Count Fleet	J. Longden
1944	Pensive	C. McCreary
1945	Hoop, Jr.	E. Arcaro
1946	Assault	W. Mehrtens
1947	Jet Pilot	E. Guerin
1948	Citation	E. Arcaro
1949	Ponder	S. Brooks
1950	Middleground	W. Boland
1951	Count Turf	C. McCreary
1952	Hill Gail	E. Arcaro
1953	Dark Star	H. Moreno
1954	Determine	R. York
1955	Swaps	W. Shoemaker
1956	Needles	D. Erb
1957	Iron Liege	W. Hartack
1958	Tim Tam	I. Valenzuela
1959	Tomy Lee	W. Shoemaker
1960	Venetian Way	W. Hartack
1961	Carry Back	J. Sellers
1962	Decidedly	W. Hartack
1963	Chateaugay	B. Baeza
1964	Northern Dancer	W. Hartack
1965	Lucky Debonair	W. Shoemaker
1966	Kauai King	D. Brumfield
1967	Proud Clarion	R. Ussery
1968	Dancer's Image#	R. Ussery
1969	Majestic Prince	W. Hartack
1970	Dust Commander	M. Manganello
1971	Canonero II	G. Avila
1972	Riva Ridge	R. Turcotte
1973	Secretariat	R. Turcotte
1974	Cannonade	A. Cordero
1975	Foolish Pleasure	J. Vasquez
1976	Bold Forbes	A. Cordero
1977	Seattle Slew	J. Cruguet
1978	Affirmed	S. Cauthen
1979	Spectacular Bid	R. Franklin
1980	Genuine Risk*	J. Vasquez
1981	Pleasant Colony	J. Velasquez
1982	Gato del Sol	E. Delahoussaye
1983	Sunny's Halo	E. Delahoussaye
1984	Swale	L. Pincay
1985	Spend a Buck	A. Cordero
1986	Ferdinand	W. Shoemaker
1987	Alysheba	C. McCarron
1988	Winning Colors*	G. Stevens
1989	Sunday Silence	P. Valenzuela
1990	Unbridled	C. Perret
1991	Strike the Gold	C. Antley
1992	Lil E. Tee	P. Day
1993	Sea Hero	J. Bailey
1994	Go for Gin	C. McCarron
1995	Thunder Gulch	G. Stevens
1996	Grindstone	J. Bailey
1997	Silver Charm	G. Stevens
1998	Real Quiet	K. Desormeaux

*Regret, Genuine Risk, and Winning Colors are the only fillies to have won the Derby. # Dancer's Image was disqualified from purse money after tests disclosed that he had run with a pain-killing drug, phenylbutazone, in his system. All wagers were paid on Dancer's Image. Forward Pass was awarded first place money.

The Kentucky Derby has been won 5 times by 2 jockeys: Eddie Arcaro, 1938, 1941, 1945, 1948, and 1952; and Bill Hartack, 1957, 1960, 1962, 1964, and 1969. It was won 4 times by Willie Shoemaker, 1955, 1959, 1965, and 1986; and 3 times by each of 4 jockeys: Isaac Murphy, 1884, 1890, and 1891; Earle Sande, 1923, 1925, and 1930; Angel Cordero, 1974, 1976, and 1985; and Gary Stevens, 1988, 1995, and 1997.

Preakness

Pimlico, Baltimore, MD; inaug. 1873; distance 1-3/16 mi. 3-year-olds. Best time: 1:53.2, by Tank's Prospect (1985) and Louis Quatorze (1996); 1998 time: 1:54.75.

Year	Winner	Jockey
1873	Survivor	G. Barbee
1874	Culpepper	M. Donohue
1875	Tom Ochiltree	L. Hughes
1876	Shirley	G. Barbee
1877	Cloverbrook	C. Holloway
1878	Duke of Magenta	C. Holloway
1879	Harold	L. Hughes
1880	Grenada	L. Hughes
1881	Saunterer	W. Costello
1882	Vanguard	W. Costello
1883	Jacobus	G. Barbee
1884	Knight of Ellerslie	S. H. Fisher
1885	Tecumseh	J. McLaughlin
1886	The Bard	S. H. Fisher
1887	Dunboyne	W. Donohue
1888	Refund	F. Littlefield
1889	Buddhist	G. Anderson
1890	Montague	W. Martin
1894	Assignee	F. Taral
1895	Belmar	F. Taral
1896	Margrave	H. Griffin
1897	Paul Kauvar	C. Thorpe
1898	Sly Fox	W. Simms
1899	Half Time	R. Clawson
1900	Hindus	H. Spencer
1901	The Parader	F. Landry
1902	Old England	L. Jackson
1903	Flocarline	W. Gannon
1904	Bryn Mawr	E. Hildebrand
1905	Cairngorm	W. Davis
1906	Whimsical	W. Miller
1907	Don Enrique	G. Mountain
1908	Royal Tourist	E. Dugan
1909	Effendi	W. Doyle
1910	Layminster	R. Estep
1911	Watervale	E. Dugan
1912	Colonel Holloway	C. Turner
1913	Buskin	J. Butwell
1914	Holiday	A. Schuttinger
1915	Rhine Maiden	D. Hoffman
1916	Damrosch	L. McAtee
1917	Kalitan	E. Haynes
1918	War Cloud	J. Loftus
	Jack Hare, Jr.	C. Peak
1919	Sir Barton	J. Loftus
1920	Man o' War	C. Kummer
1921	Broomspun	F. Coltiletti
1922	Pillory	L. Morris
1923	Vigil	B. Marinelli
1924	Nellie Morse	J. Merimee
1925	Coventry	C. Kummer
1926	Display	J. Malben
1927	Bostonian	A. Abel
1928	Victorian	R. Workman

(continued)

Year	Winner	Jockey
1929	Dr. Freeland	L. Schaefer
1930	Gallant Fox	E. Sande
1931	Mate	G. Ellis
1932	Burgoo King	E. James
1933	Head Play	C. Kurtsinger
1934	High Quest	R. Jones
1935	Omaha	W. Saunders
1936	Bold Venture	G. Woolf
1937	War Admiral	C. Kurtsinger
1938	Dauber	M. Peters
1939	Challedon	G. Seabo
1940	Bimelech	F.A. Smith
1941	Whirlaway	E. Arcaro
1942	Alsab	B. James
1943	Count Fleet	J. Longden
1944	Pensive	C. McCreary
1945	Polynesian	W.D. Wright
1946	Assault	W. Mehrtens
1947	Faultless	D. Dodson
1948	Citation	E. Arcaro
1949	Capot	T. Atkinson
1950	Hill Prince	E. Arcaro
1951	Bold	E. Arcaro
1952	Blue Man	C. McCreary
1953	Native Dancer	E. Guerin
1954	Hasty Road	J. Adams
1955	Nashua	E. Arcaro
1956	Fabius	W. Hartack
1957	Bold Ruler	E. Arcaro
1958	Tim Tam	I. Valenzuela
1959	Royal Orbit	W. Harmatz
1960	Bally Ache	R. Ussery
1961	Carry Back	J. Sellers
1962	Greek Money	J.L. Rotz
1963	Candy Spots	W. Shoemaker
1964	Northern Dancer	W. Hartack
1965	Tom Rolfe	R. Turcotte
1966	Kauai King	D. Brumfield
1967	Damascus	W. Shoemaker
1968	Forward Pass	I. Valenzuela
1969	Majestic Prince	W. Hartack
1970	Personality	E. Belmonte
1971	Canonero II	G. Avila
1972	Bee Bee Bee	E. Nelson
1973	Secretariat	R. Turcotte
1974	Little Current	M. Rivera
1975	Master Derby	D. McHargue
1976	Elocutionist	J. Lively
1977	Seattle Slew	J. Cruguet
1978	Affirmed	S. Cauthen
1979	Spectacular Bid	R. Franklin
1980	Codex	A. Cordero
1981	Pleasant Colony	J. Velasquez
1982	Aloma's Ruler	J. Kaenel
1983	Deputed Testamony	D. Miller
1984	Gate Dancer	A. Cordero
1985	Tank's Prospect	P. Day
1986	Snow Chief	A. Solis
1987	Alysheba	C. McCarron
1988	Risen Star	E. Delahoussaye
1989	Sunday Silence	P. Valenzuela
1990	Summer Squall	P. Day
1991	Hansel	J. Bailey
1992	Pine Bluff	C. McCarron
1993	Prairie Bayou	M. Smith
1994	Tabasco Cat	P. Day
1995	Timber Country	P. Day
1996	Louis Quatorze	P. Day
1997	Silver Charm	G. Stevens
1998	Real Quiet	K. Desormeaux

Belmont Stakes

Belmont Park, Elmont, NY; inaug. 1867; distance 1-1/2 mi. 3-year-olds. Best time: 2:24, Secretariat, 1973; 1998 time: 2:29.16.

Year	Winner	Jockey
1867	Ruthless	J. Gilpatrick
1868	General Duke	R. Swim
1869	Fenian	C. Miller
1870	Kingfisher	W. Dick
1871	Harry Bassett	W. Miller
1872	Joe Daniels	J. Rowe
1873	Springbok	J. Rowe
1874	Saxon	G. Barbee
1875	Calvin	R. Swim
1876	Algerine	W. Donohue
1877	Cloverbrook	C. Holloway
1878	Duke of Magenta	L. Hughes
1879	Spendthrift	S. Evans
1880	Grenada	L. Hughes
1881	Saunterer	T. Costello
1882	Forester	J. McLaughlin
1883	George Kinney	J. McLaughlin
1884	Panique	J. McLaughlin
1885	Tyrant	P. Duffy
1886	Inspector B.	J. McLaughlin
1887	Hanover	J. McLaughlin
1888	Sir Dixon	J. McLaughlin
1889	Eric	W. Hayward
1890	Burlington	S. Barnes
1891	Foxford	E. Garrison
1892	Patron	W. Hayward
1893	Comanche	W. Simms
1894	Henry of Navarre	W. Simms
1895	Belmar	F. Taral
1896	Hastings	H. Griffin
1897	Scottish Chieftain	J. Scherrer
1898	Bowling Brook	F. Littlefield
1899	Jean Bereaud	R. R. Clawson
1900	Ildrim	N. Turner
1901	Commando	H. Spencer
1902	Masterman	J. Bullman
1903	Africander	J. Bullman
1904	Delhi	G. Odom
1905	Tanya	E. Hildebrand
1906	Burgomaster	L. Lyne
1907	Peter Pan	G. Mountain
1908	Colin	J. Notter
1909	Joe Madden	E. Dugan
1910	Sweep	J. Butwell
1913	Prince Eugene	R. Troxler
1914	Luke McLuke	M. Buxton
1915	The Finn	G. Byrne
1916	Friar Rock	E. Haynes
1917	Hourless	J. Butwell
1918	Johren	F. Robinson
1919	Sir Barton	J. Loftus
1920	Man o' War	C. Kummer
1921	Grey Lag	E. Sande
1922	Pillory	C. H. Miller
1923	Zev	E. Sande
1924	Mad Play	E. Sande
1925	American Flag	A. Johnson
1926	Crusader	A. Johnson
1927	Chance Shot	E. Sande
1928	Vito	C. Kummer
1929	Blue Larkspur	M. Garner
1930	Gallant Fox	E. Sande
1931	Twenty Grand	C. Kurtsinger
1932	Faireno	T. Malley
1933	Hurryoff	M. Garner
1934	Peace Chance	W. D. Wright
1935	Omaha	W. Saunders
1936	Granville	J. Stout
1937	War Admiral	C. Kurtsinger
1938	Pasteurized	J. Stout
1939	Johnstown	J. Stout
1940	Bimelech	F. A. Smith
1941	Whirlaway	E. Arcaro
1942	Shut Out	E. Arcaro
1943	Count Fleet	J. Longden
1944	Bounding Home	G. L. Smith
1945	Pavot	E. Arcaro
1946	Assault	W. Mehrtens
1947	Phalanx	R. Donoso
1948	Citation	E. Arcaro
1949	Capot	T. Atkinson
1950	Middleground	W. Boland
1951	Counterpoint	D. Gorman
1952	One Count	E. Arcaro
1953	Native Dancer	E. Guerin
1954	High Gun	E. Guerin
1955	Nashua	E. Arcaro
1956	Needles	D. Erb
1957	Gallant Man	W. Shoemaker
1958	Cavan	P. Anderson
1959	Sword Dancer	W. Shoemaker
1960	Celtic Ash	W. Hartack
1961	Sherluck	B. Baeza
1962	Jaipur	W. Shoemaker
1963	Chateaugay	B. Baeza
1964	Quadrangle	M. Ycaza
1965	Hail to All	J. Sellers
1966	Amberoid	W. Boland
1967	Damascus	W. Shoemaker
1968	Stage Door Johnny	H. Gustines
1969	Arts and Letters	B. Baeza
1970	High Echelon	J. L. Rotz
1971	Pass Catcher	W. Blum
1972	Riva Ridge	R. Turcotte
1973	Secretariat	R. Turcotte
1974	Little Current	M. Rivera
1975	Avatar	W. Shoemaker
1976	Bold Forbes	A. Cordero
1977	Seattle Slew	J. Cruguet
1978	Affirmed	S. Cauthen
1979	Coastal	R. Hernandez
1980	Temperence Hill	E. Maple
1981	Summing	G. Martens
1982	Conquistador Cielo	L. Pincay
1983	Caveat	L. Pincay
1984	Swale	L. Pincay
1985	Creme Fraiche	E. Maple
1986	Danzig Connection	C. McCarron
1987	Bet Twice	C. Perret
1988	Risen Star	E. Delahoussaye
1989	Easy Goer	P. Day
1990	Go and Go	M. Kinane
1991	Hansel	J. Bailey
1992	A.P. Indy	E. Delahoussaye
1993	Colonial Affair	J. Krone
1994	Tabasco Cat	P. Day
1995	Thunder Gulch	G. Stevens
1996	Editor's Note	R. Douglas
1997	Touch Gold	C. McCarron
1998	Victory Gallop	G. Stevens

Annual Leading Jockey—Money Won[1]

Year	Jockey	Dollars
1957	Bill Hartack	$3,060,501
1958	Willie Shoemaker	2,961,693
1959	Willie Shoemaker	2,843,133
1960	Willie Shoemaker	2,123,961
1961	Willie Shoemaker	2,690,819
1962	Willie Shoemaker	2,916,844
1963	Willie Shoemaker	2,526,925
1964	Willie Shoemaker	2,649,553
1965	Braulio Baeza	2,582,702
1966	Braulio Baeza	2,951,022
1967	Braulio Baeza	3,088,888
1968	Braulio Baeza	2,835,108
1969	Jorge Velasquez	2,542,315
1970	Laffit Pincay, Jr.	2,626,526
1971	Laffit Pincay, Jr.	$3,784,377
1972	Laffit Pincay, Jr.	3,225,827
1973	Laffit Pincay, Jr.	4,093,492
1974	Laffit Pincay, Jr.	4,251,060
1975	Braulio Baeza	3,695,198
1976	Angel Cordero, Jr.	4,709,500
1977	Steve Cauthen	6,151,750
1978	Darrel McHargue	6,029,885
1979	Laffit Pincay, Jr.	8,193,535
1980	Chris McCarron	7,663,300
1981	Chris McCarron	8,397,604
1982	Angel Cordero, Jr.	9,483,590
1983	Angel Cordero, Jr.	10,116,697
1984	Chris McCarron	12,045,813
1985	Laffit Pincay, Jr.	$13,353,299
1986	Jose Santos	11,329,297
1987	Jose Santos	12,375,433
1988	Jose Santos	14,877,298
1989	Jose Santos	13,838,389
1990	Gary Stevens	13,881,198
1991	Chris McCarron	14,441,083
1992	Kent Desormeaux	14,193,006
1993	Mike Smith	14,024,815
1994	Mike Smith	15,979,820
1995	Jerry Bailey	16,311,876
1996	Jerry Bailey	19,465,376
1997	Jerry Bailey	18,320,743

(1) Total earnings for all horses that jockey raced in year listed; does not reflect jockey's earnings.

Breeders' Cup

The Breeders' Cup was inaugurated in 1984 and consists of 7 races at one track on one day late in the year to determine Thoroughbred racing's champion contenders. It has been held at the following locations:

1984	Hollywood Park, CA
1985	Aqueduct Racetrack, NY
1986	Santa Anita Park, CA
1987	Hollywood Park, CA
1988	Churchill Downs, KY
1989	Gulfstream Park, FL
1990	Belmont Park, NY
1991	Churchill Downs, KY
1992	Gulfstream Park, FL
1993	Santa Anita Park, CA
1994	Churchill Downs, KY
1995	Belmont Park, NY
1996	Woodbine Racetrack, Ontario
1997	Hollywood Park, CA

Juvenile

Distances: 1 mi 1984-85, 1987; 1-1/16 mi 1986 and since 1988

Year		Jockey
1984	Chief's Crown	D. MacBeth
1985	Tasso	L. Pincay, Jr.
1986	Capote	L. Pincay, Jr.
1987	Success Express	J. Santos
1988	Is It True	L. Pincay, Jr.
1989	Rhythm	C. Perret
1990	Fly So Free	J. Santos
1991	Arazi	P. Valenzuela
1992	Gilded Time	C. McCarron
1993	Brocco	G. Stevens
1994	Timber Country	P. Day
1995	Unbridled's Song	M. Smith
1996	Boston Harbor	J. Bailey
1997	Favorite Trick	P. Day

Juvenile Fillies

Distances: 1 mi 1984-85, 1987; 1-1/16 mi 1986 and since 1988

Year		Jockey
1984	*Outstandingly	W. Guerra
1985	Twilight Ridge	J. Velasquez
1986	Brave Raj	P. Valenzuela
1987	Epitome	P. Day
1988	Open Mind	A. Cordero, Jr.
1989	Go for Wand	R. Romero
1990	Meadow Star	J. Santos
1991	Pleasant Stage	E. Delahoussaye
1992	Eliza	P. Valenzuela
1993	Phone Chatter	L. Pincay, Jr.
1994	Flanders	P. Day
1995	My Flag	J. Bailey
1996	Storm Song	C. Perret
1997	Countess Diana	S. Sellers

*By disqualification.

Sprint

Distance: 6 furlongs

Year		Jockey
1984	Eillo	C. Perret
1985	Precisionist	C. McCarron
1986	Smile	J. Vasquez
1987	Very Subtle	P. Valenzuela
1988	Gulch	A. Cordero, Jr.
1989	Dancing Spree	A. Cordero, Jr.
1990	Safely Kept	C. Perret
1991	Sheikh Albadou	P. Eddery
1992	Thirty Slews	E. Delahoussaye
1993	Cardmania	E. Delahoussaye
1994	Cherokee Run	M. Smith
1995	Desert Stormer	K. Desormeaux
1996	Lit De Justice	C. Nakatani
1997	Elmhurst	C. Nakatani

Mile

Year		Jockey
1984	Royal Heroine	F. Toro
1985	Cozzene	W. Guerra
1986	Last Tycoon	Y. St.-Martin
1987	Miesque	F. Head
1988	Miesque	F. Head
1989	Steinlen	J. Santos
1990	Royal Academy	L. Piggott
1991	Opening Verse	P. Valenzuela
1992	Lure	M. Smith
1993	Lure	M. Smith
1994	Barathea	L. Dettori
1995	Ridgewood Pearl	J. Murtagh
1996	Da Hoss	G. Stevens
1997	Spinning World	C. Asmussan

Distaff

Distances: 1-1/4 mi 1984-87; 1-1/8 mi since 1988

Year		Jockey
1984	Princess Rooney	E. Delahoussaye
1985	Life's Magic	A. Cordero, Jr.
1986	Lady's Secret	P. Day
1987	Sacahuista	R. Romero
1988	Personal Ensign	R. Romero
1989	Bayakoa	L. Pincay, Jr.
1990	Bayakoa	L. Pincay, Jr.
1991	Dance Smartly	P. Day
1992	Paseana	C. McCarron
1993	Hollywood Wildcat	E. Delahoussaye
1994	One Dreamer	G. Stevens
1995	Inside Information	M. Smith
1996	Jewel Princess	C. Nakatani
1997	Ajina	M. Smith

Turf

Distance: 1-1/2 mi

Year		Jockey
1984	Lashkari	Y. St.-Martin
1985	Pebbles	P. Eddery
1986	Manila	J. Santos
1987	Theatrical	P. Day
1988	Great Communicator	R. Sibille
1989	Prized	E. Delahoussaye
1990	In The Wings	G. Stevens
1991	Miss Alleged	E. Legrix
1992	Fraise	P. Valenzuela
1993	Kotashaan	K. Desormeaux
1994	Tikkanen	M. Smith
1995	Northern Spur	C. McCarron
1996	Pilsudski	W. Swinburn
1997	Chief Bearhart	J. Santos

Classic

Distance: 1-1/4 mi

Year		Jockey
1984	Wild Again	P. Day
1985	Proud Truth	J. Velasquez
1986	Skywalker	L. Pincay, Jr.
1987	Ferdinand	W. Shoemaker
1988	Alysheba	C. McCarron
1989	Sunday Silence	C. McCarron
1990	Unbridled	P. Day
1991	Black Tie Affair	J. Bailey
1992	A.P. Indy	E. Delahoussaye
1993	Arcangues	J. Bailey
1994	Concern	J. Bailey
1995	Cigar	J. Bailey
1996	Alphabet Soup	C. McCarron
1997	Skip Away	M. Smith

Eclipse Awards

The Eclipse Awards, honoring the Horse of the Year and other champions of the sport, began in 1971 and are sponsored by the *Daily Racing Form*, the Thoroughbred Racing Associations, and the National Turf Writers Assn. Prior to 1971, the DRF (1936-70) and the TRA (1950-70) issued separate selections for Horse of the Year.

Eclipse Awards for 1997

Horse of the Year—Favorite Trick
2-year-old colt or gelding—Favorite Trick
2-year-old filly—Countess Diana
3-year-old colt or gelding—Silver Charm
3-year-old filly—Ajina
Older male (4-year-olds & up)—Skip Away
Older female (4-year-olds & up)—Hidden Lake
Male turf horse—Chief Bearhart
Turf filly or mare—Ryafan
Sprinter—Smoke Glacken
Steeplechase horse—Lonesome Glory
Trainer—Bob Baffert
Jockey—Jerry Bailey
Apprentice jockey—Philip Teator and Roberto Rosado
Breeder—Golden Eagle Farm
Owner—Carolyn Hine

Horse of the Year

1936	Granville
1937	War Admiral
1938	Seabiscuit
1939	Challedon
1940	Challedon
1941	Whirlaway
1942	Whirlaway
1943	Count Fleet
1944	Twilight Tear
1945	Busher
1946	Assault
1947	Armed
1948	Citation
1949	Capot
1950	Hill Prince
1951	Counterpoint
1952	One Count (DRF)
	Native Dancer (TRA)
1953	Tom Fool
1954	Native Dancer
1955	Nashua
1956	Swaps
1957	Bold Ruler (DRF)
	Dedicate (TRA)
1958	Round Table
1959	Sword Dancer
1960	Kelso
1961	Kelso
1962	Kelso
1963	Kelso
1964	Kelso
1965	Roman Brother (DRF)
	Moccasin (TRA)
1966	Buckpasser
1967	Damascus
1968	Dr. Fager
1969	Arts and Letters
1970	Fort Marcy (DRF)
	Personality (TRA)
1971	Ack Ack
1972	Secretariat
1973	Secretariat
1974	Forego
1975	Forego
1976	Forego
1977	Seattle Slew
1978	Affirmed
1979	Affirmed
1980	Spectacular Bid
1981	John Henry
1982	Conquistador Cielo
1983	All Along
1984	John Henry
1985	Spend A Buck
1986	Lady's Secret
1987	Ferdinand
1988	Alysheba
1989	Sunday Silence
1990	Criminal Type
1991	Black Tie Affair
1992	A.P. Indy
1993	Kotashaan
1994	Holy Bull
1995	Cigar
1996	Cigar
1997	Favorite Trick

HARNESS RACING

Harness Horse of the Year

(Chosen by the U.S. Trotting Assn. and the U.S. Harness Writers Assn.)

1947	Victory Song
1948	Rodney
1949	Good Time
1950	Proximity
1951	Pronto Don
1952	Good Time
1953	Hi Lo's Forbes
1954	Stenographer
1955	Scott Frost
1956	Scott Frost
1957	Torpid
1958	Emily's Pride
1959	Bye Bye Byrd
1960	Adios Butler
1961	Adios Butler
1962	Su Mac Lad
1963	Speedy Scot
1964	Bret Hanover
1965	Bret Hanover
1966	Bret Hanover
1967	Nevele Pride
1968	Nevele Pride
1969	Nevele Pride
1970	Fresh Yankee
1971	Albatross
1972	Albatross
1973	Sir Dalrae
1974	Delmonica Hanover
1975	Savoir
1976	Keystone Ore
1977	Green Speed
1978	Abercrombie
1979	Niatross
1980	Niatross
1981	Fan Hanover
1982	Cam Fella
1983	Cam Fella
1984	Fancy Crown
1985	Nihilator
1986	Forrest Skipper
1987	Mack Lobell
1988	Mack Lobell
1989	Matt's Scooter
1990	Beach Towel
1991	Precious Bunny
1992	Artsplace
1993	Staying Together
1994	Cam's Card Shark
1995	CR Kay Suzie
1996	Continentalvictory
1997	Malabar Man

The Hambletonian (3-year-old trotters)

Year	Winner	Driver
1965	Egyptian Candor	Del Cameron
1966	Kerry Way	Frank Ervin
1967	Speedy Streak	Del Cameron
1968	Nevele Pride	Stanley Dancer
1969	Lindy's Pride	Howard Beissinger
1970	Timothy T	John Simpson, Sr.
1971	Speedy Crown	Howard Beissinger
1972	Super Bowl	Stanley Dancer
1973	Flirth	Ralph Baldwin
1974	Christopher T	Bill Haughton
1975	Bonefish	Stanley Dancer
1976	Steve Lobell	Bill Haughton
1977	Green Speed	Bill Haughton
1978	Speedy Somolli	Howard Beissinger
1979	Legend Hanover	George Sholty
1980	Burgomeister	Bill Haughton
1981	Shiaway St. Pat	Ray Remmen
1982	Speed Bowl	Tommy Haughton
1983	Duenna	Stanley Dancer
1984	Historic Freight	Ben Webster
1985	Prakas	Bill O'Donnell
1986	Nuclear Kosmos	Ulf Thoresen
1987	Mack Lobell	John Campbell
1988	Armbro Goal	John Campbell
1989	Park Avenue Joe	Ron Waples
1990	Harmonious	John Campbell
1991	Giant Victory	Jack Moiseyev
1992	Alf Palema	Mickey McNicholl
1993	American Winner	Ron Pierce
1994	Victory Dream	Michel Lachance
1995	Tagliabue	John Campbell
1996	Continentalvictory	Michel Lachance
1997	Malabar Man	Malvern Burroughs
1998	Muscles Yankee	John Campbell

BOWLING

Professional Bowlers Association

Hall of Fame

(1998 inductees have an asterisk)

PERFORMANCE

Bill Allen
Glenn Allison
Earl Anthony
Barry Asher
Mike Aulby
Ray Bluth
Roy Buckley
Nelson Burton, Jr.
Don Carter
Pat Colwell
Steve Cook
Dave Davis
Gary Dickinson
Mike Durbin
Buzz Fazio
Dave Ferraro
Skee Foremsky
Jim Godman
Johnny Guenther
Billy Hardwick
Tommy Hudson
Dave Husted
Don Johnson
Joe Joseph
Larry Laub
Mike Limongello
Don McCune
Mike McGrath
Amleto Monacelli
David Ozio
George Pappas
Johnny Petraglia
Dick Ritger
Mark Roth
Jim St. John
Carmen Salvino
Ernie Schlegel
*Teata Semiz
Bob Strampe
Harry Smith
Dave Soutar
Jim Stefanich
Brian Voss
Wayne Webb
Dick Weber
*Pete Weber
Billy Welu
Walter Ray Williams, Jr.
Wayne Zahn

MERITORIOUS SERVICE

Joe Antenora
John Archibald
Chuck Clemens
Eddie Elias
Frank Esposito
Dick Evans
Raymond Firestone
E. A. "Bud" Fisher
Lou Frantz
Harry Golden
Ted Hoffman, Jr.
John Jowdy
Joe Kelley
Larry Lichstein
Steve Nagy
Chuck Pezzano
Jack Reichert
Joe Richards
Chris Schenkel
Lorraine Stilzlein
Al Thompson
Roger Zeller

Tournament of Champions

Year	Winner
1965	Billy Hardwick
1966	Wayne Zahn
1967	Jim Stefanich
1968	Dave Davis
1969	Jim Godman
1970	Don Johnson
1971	Johnny Petraglia
1972	Mike Durbin
1973	Jim Godman
1974	Earl Anthony
1975	Dave Davis
1976	Marshall Holman
1977	Mike Berlin
1978	Earl Anthony
1979	George Pappas
1980	Wayne Webb
1981	Steve Cook
1982	Mike Durbin
1983	Joe Berardi
1984	Mike Durbin
1985	Mark Williams
1986	Marshall Holman
1987	Pete Weber
1988	Mark Williams
1989	Del Ballard, Jr.
1990	Dave Ferraro
1991	David Ozio
1992	Marc McDowell
1993	George Branham, 3d
1994	Norm Duke
1996	Dave D'Entremont
1997	John Gant

PBA Leading Money Winners

Total winnings are from PBA, ABC Masters, and BPAA All-Star tournaments only and do not include numerous other tournaments or earnings from special television shows and matches.

Year	Bowler	Amount	Year	Bowler	Amount	Year	Bowler	Amount
1962	Don Carter	$49,972	1974	Earl Anthony	$99,585	1986	Walter Ray Williams, Jr.	$145,550
1963	Dick Weber	46,333	1975	Earl Anthony	107,585	1987	Pete Weber	175,491
1964	Bob Strampe	33,592	1976	Earl Anthony	110,833	1988	Brian Voss	225,485
1965	Dick Weber	47,674	1977	Mark Roth	105,583	1989	Mike Aulby	298,237
1966	Wayne Zahn	54,720	1978	Mark Roth	134,500	1990	Amleto Monacelli	204,775
1967	Dave Davis	54,165	1979	Mark Roth	124,517	1991	David Ozio	225,585
1968	Jim Stefanich	67,377	1980	Wayne Webb	116,700	1992	Marc McDowell	174,215
1969	Billy Hardwick	64,160	1981	Earl Anthony	164,735	1993	Walter Ray Williams, Jr.	296,370
1970	Mike McGrath	52,049	1982	Earl Anthony	134,760	1994	Norm Duke	273,753
1971	Johnny Petraglia	85,065	1983	Earl Anthony	135,605	1995	Mike Aulby	219,792
1972	Don Johnson	56,648	1984	Mark Roth	158,712	1996	Walter Ray Williams, Jr.	241,330
1973	Don McCune	69,000	1985	Mike Aulby	201,200	1997	Walter Ray Williams, Jr.	240,544

Leading PBA Averages by Year

Year	Bowler	Average	Year	Bowler	Average	Year	Bowler	Average
1962	Don Carter	212.844	1974	Earl Anthony	219.394	1986	John Gant	214.378
1963	Billy Hardwick	210.346	1975	Earl Anthony	219.060	1987	Marshall Holman	216.801
1964	Ray Bluth	210.512	1976	Mark Roth	215.970	1988	Mark Roth	218.036
1965	Dick Weber	211.895	1977	Mark Roth	218.174	1989	Pete Weber	215.432
1966	Wayne Zahn	208.663	1978	Mark Roth	219.834	1990	Amleto Monacelli	218.158
1967	Wayne Zahn	212.342	1979	Mark Roth	221.662	1991	Norm Duke	218.208
1968	Jim Stefanich	211.895	1980	Earl Anthony	218.535	1992	Dave Ferraro	219.702
1969	Bill Hardwick	212.957	1981	Mark Roth	216.699	1993	Walter Ray Williams, Jr.	222.980
1970	Nelson Burton, Jr.	214.908	1982	Marshall Holman	212.844	1994	Norm Duke	222.830
1971	Don Johnson	213.977	1983	Earl Anthony	216.645	1995	Mike Aulby	225.490
1972	Don Johnson	215.290	1984	Marshall Holman	213.911	1996	Walter Ray Williams, Jr.	225.370
1973	Earl Anthony	215.799	1985	Mark Baker	213.718	1997	Walter Ray Williams, Jr.	222.008

American Bowling Congress

ABC Masters Tournament Champions

Year	Winner	Year	Winner	Year	Winner
1980	Neil Burton, St. Louis, MO	1986	Mark Fahy, Chicago, IL	1992	Ken Johnson, N. Richmond Hills, TX
1981	Randy Lightfoot, St. Charles, MO	1987	Rick Steelsmith, Wichita, KS	1993	Norm Duke, Oklahoma City, OK
1982	Joe Berardi, Brooklyn, NY	1988	Del Ballard, Jr., Richardson, TX	1994	Steve Fehr, Cincinnati, OH
1983	Mike Lastowski, Havre de Grace, MD	1989	Mike Aulby, Indianapolis, IN	1995	Mike Aulby, Indianapolis, IN
1984	Earl Anthony, Dublin, CA	1990	Chris Warren, Dallas, TX	1996	Ernie Schlegel, Vancouver, WA
1985	Steve Wunderlich, St. Louis, MO	1991	Doug Kent, Canandaigua, NY	1997	Jason Queen, Decatur, IL
				1998	Mike Aulby, Indianapolis, IN

Champions in 1998

Singles Event—John Gaines, Davidsonville, MD
Doubles Event—Keith Klenck, Chicago, IL and Rick O'Hara, Prospect, IL
All Events—Chris Barnes, Wichita, KS
Regular Team—Drillings Amoco, Milwaukee, WI
Booster Team—Earth Service Inc., Gowen, MI

Most Sanctioned 300 Games

Bowler	Games
Bob Learn, Jr., Erie, PA	55
Joe Jimenez, Saginaw, MI	53
Jim Johnson, Jr., Wilmington, DE.	53
Mike Whalin, Cincinnati, OH	53
Jeff Jensen, Wichita, KS	50
Robert Faragon, Albany, NY	46
Bob Buckery, McAdoo, PA	45
Jerry Kessler, Dayton, OH	43
Ralph Burley, Jr., Dayton, OH	42
Dave Frascatore, Amsterdam, NY	41
John Wilcox, Jr., Lewisburg, PA	39
John Delp III, West Lawn, PA	38
Ken Hall, Schenectady, NY	38
Bob Johnson, Dayton, OH	38
Jason Hurd, Tulare, CA	37
Keith Bruening, St. Charles, MO	36
Steve Gehringer, Reading, PA	36
Jim Ewald, Jr., Louisville, KY	35
Eric Roddy, New Orleans, LA	35
Alan Hulsizer, Reading, PA	35
Doug Spicer, W. Bloomfield, MI	34
Randy Choat, Granite City, IL	33
Ron Woolet, Louisville, KY	33
John Chako, Jr., Larksville, PA	32
Woody Crist, Williamsport, PA	32
Richard (Skip) Vigars	32
Ron Bohnert, Cincinnati, OH	30
Mitch Jabczenski, Detroit, MI	29
Steve Levering, Landisville, PA	29
Jerome Penxa, Detroit, MI	29
Mark Stibora, Cleveland, OH	29
Anthony Juliano, Margate, FL	28
Michael Weston, Bay City, MI	28
Tim Zelger, Red Lion, PA	28
Lennie Boresch Jr., Kenosha, WI	27
Paul Cannon, Binghamton, NY	27
Kevin Lickers, Wilkes-Barre, PA	27
Elvin Mesger, Sullivan, MO	27
Dave Soutar, Kansas City, MO	27
Mark Crawford, Red Lion, PA	26

Women's International Bowling Congress

Champions in 1998

Queens Tournament—Lynda Norry, Wichita, KS
Singles Event—Nellie Glandon, London, ON
All Events—Liz Johnson, Niagra Falls, NY
Doubles Event—Lynda Norry, Wichita, KS and Kendra Cameron, Gambrills, MD
Team—Bowlers Choice Pro Shop, Skaneateles, NY

Most Sanctioned 300 Games

Bowler	Games
Tish Johnson, Panorama City, CA	27
Vicki Fischel, Wheat Ridge, CO	21
Jeanne Naccarato, Tacoma, WA	21
Aleta Sill, Dearborn, MI	21
Leanne Barrette, Youkon, OK	19
Cheryl Daniels, Detroit, MI	16
Cindy Coburn-Carroll, Tonawanda, NY	14
Betty Morris, Stockton, CA	13
Donna Adamek, Apple Valley, CA	11
Robin Romeo, Van Nuys, CA	9

FIGURE SKATING

U.S. Champions MEN	U.S. Champions WOMEN	YEAR	World Champions MEN	World Champions WOMEN
Dick Button	Tenley Albright	**1952**	Dick Button, U.S.	Jacqueline du Bief, France
Hayes Jenkins	Tenley Albright	**1953**	Hayes Jenkins, U.S.	Tenley Albright, U.S.
Hayes Jenkins	Tenley Albright	**1954**	Hayes Jenkins, U.S.	Gundi Busch, W. Germany
Hayes Jenkins	Tenley Albright	**1955**	Hayes Jenkins, U.S.	Tenley Albright, U.S.
Hayes Jenkins	Tenley Albright	**1956**	Hayes Jenkins, U.S.	Carol Heiss, U.S.
Dave Jenkins	Carol Heiss	**1957**	Dave Jenkins, U.S.	Carol Heiss, U.S.
Dave Jenkins	Carol Heiss	**1958**	Dave Jenkins, U.S.	Carol Heiss, U.S.
Dave Jenkins	Carol Heiss	**1959**	Dave Jenkins, U.S.	Carol Heiss, U.S.
Dave Jenkins	Carol Heiss	**1960**	Alain Giletti, France	Carol Heiss, U.S.
Bradley Lord	Laurence Owen	**1961**	none	none
Monty Hoyt	Barbara Roles Pursley	**1962**	Don Jackson, Canada	Sjoukje Dijkstra, Netherlands
Tommy Litz	Lorraine Hanlon	**1963**	Don McPherson, Canada	Sjoukje Dijkstra, Netherlands
Scott Allen	Peggy Fleming	**1964**	Manfred Schnelldorfer, W. Germany	Sjoukje Dijkstra, Netherlands
Gary Visconti	Peggy Fleming	**1965**	Alain Calmat, France	Petra Burka, Canada
Scott Allen	Peggy Fleming	**1966**	Emmerich Danzer, Austria	Peggy Fleming, U.S.
Gary Visconti	Peggy Fleming	**1967**	Emmerich Danzer, Austria	Peggy Fleming, U.S.
Tim Wood	Peggy Fleming	**1968**	Emmerich Danzer, Austria	Peggy Fleming, U.S.
Tim Wood	Janet Lynn	**1969**	Tim Wood, U.S.	Gabriele Seyfert, E. Germany
Tim Wood	Janet Lynn	**1970**	Tim Wood, U.S.	Gabriele Seyfert, E. Germany
John Misha Petkevich	Janet Lynn	**1971**	Ondrej Nepela, Czechoslovakia	Beatrix Schuba, Austria
Ken Shelley	Janet Lynn	**1972**	Ondrej Nepela, Czechoslovakia	Beatrix Schuba, Austria
Gordon McKellen, Jr.	Janet Lynn	**1973**	Ondrej Nepela, Czechoslovakia	Karen Magnussen, Canada
Gordon McKellen, Jr.	Dorothy Hamill	**1974**	Jan Hoffmann, E. Germany	Christine Errath, E. Germany
Gordon McKellen, Jr.	Dorothy Hamill	**1975**	Sergei Volkov, USSR	Dianne de Leeuw, Neth.-U.S.
Terry Kubicka	Dorothy Hamill	**1976**	John Curry, Gr. Britain	Dorothy Hamill, U.S.
Charles Tickner	Linda Fratianne	**1977**	Vladimir Kovalev, USSR	Linda Fratianne, U.S.
Charles Tickner	Linda Fratianne	**1978**	Charles Tickner, U.S.	Anett Poetzsch, E. Germany
Charles Tickner	Linda Fratianne	**1979**	Vladimir Kovalev, USSR	Linda Fratianne, U.S.
Charles Tickner	Linda Fratianne	**1980**	Jan Hoffmann, E. Germany	Anett Poetzsch, E. Germany
Scott Hamilton	Elaine Zayak	**1981**	Scott Hamilton, U.S.	Denise Biellmann, Switzerland
Scott Hamilton	Rosalynn Sumners	**1982**	Scott Hamilton, U.S.	Elaine Zayak, U.S.
Scott Hamilton	Rosalynn Sumners	**1983**	Scott Hamilton, U.S.	Rosalynn Sumners, U.S.
Scott Hamilton	Rosalynn Sumners	**1984**	Scott Hamilton, U.S.	Katarina Witt, E. Germany
Brian Boitano	Tiffany Chin	**1985**	Aleksandr Fadeev, USSR	Katarina Witt, E. Germany
Brian Boitano	Debi Thomas	**1986**	Brian Boitano, U.S.	Debi Thomas, U.S.
Brian Boitano	Jill Trenary	**1987**	Brian Orser, Canada	Katarina Witt, E. Germany
Brian Boitano	Debi Thomas	**1988**	Brian Boitano, U.S.	Katarina Witt, E. Germany
Christopher Bowman	Jill Trenary	**1989**	Kurt Browning, Canada	Midori Ito, Japan
Todd Eldredge	Jill Trenary	**1990**	Kurt Browning, Canada	Jill Trenary, U.S.
Todd Eldredge	Tonya Harding	**1991**	Kurt Browning, Canada	Kristi Yamaguchi, U.S.
Christopher Bowman	Kristi Yamaguchi	**1992**	Viktor Petrenko, Ukraine	Kristi Yamaguchi, U.S.
Scott Davis	Nancy Kerrigan	**1993**	Kurt Browning, Canada	Oksana Baiul, Ukraine
Scott Davis	vacant[1]	**1994**	Elvis Stojko, Canada	Yuka Sato, Japan
Todd Eldredge	Nicole Bobek	**1995**	Elvis Stojko, Canada	Chen Lu, China
Rudy Galindo	Michelle Kwan	**1996**	Todd Eldredge, U.S.	Michelle Kwan, U.S.
Todd Eldredge	Tara Lipinski	**1997**	Elvis Stojko, Canada	Tara Lipinski, U.S.
Todd Eldredge	Michelle Kwan	**1998**	Alexei Yagudin, Russia	Michelle Kwan, U.S.

(1) Tonya Harding was stripped of title.

JAMES E. SULLIVAN MEMORIAL TROPHY WINNERS

The James E. Sullivan Memorial Trophy, named after the former president of the AAU and inaugurated in 1930, is awarded annually by the AAU to the athlete who "by his or her performance, example and influence as an amateur, has done the most during the year to advance the cause of sportsmanship."

Year	Winner	Sport
1930	Bobby Jones	Golf
1931	Barney Berlinger	Track
1932	Jim Bausch	Track
1933	Glenn Cunningham	Track
1934	Bill Bonthron	Track
1935	Lawson Little	Golf
1936	Glenn Morris	Track
1937	Don Budge	Tennis
1938	Don Lash	Track
1939	Joe Burk	Rowing
1940	Greg Rice	Track
1941	Leslie MacMitchell	Track
1942	Cornelius Warmerdam	Track
1943	Gilbert Dodds	Track
1944	Ann Curtis	Swimming
1945	Doc Blanchard	Football
1946	Arnold Tucker	Football
1947	John Kelly, Jr.	Rowing
1948	Robert Mathias	Track
1949	Dick Button	Skating
1950	Fred Wilt	Track
1951	Rev. Robert Richards	Track
1952	Horace Ashenfelter	Track
1953	Dr. Sammy Lee	Diving
1954	Mal Whitfield	Track
1955	Harrison Dillard	Track
1956	Patricia McCormick	Diving
1957	Bobby Joe Morrow	Track
1958	Glenn Davis	Track
1959	Parry O'Brien	Track
1960	Rafer Johnson	Track
1961	Wilma Rudolph Ward	Track
1962	James Beatty	Track
1963	John Pennel	Track
1964	Don Schollander	Swimming
1965	Bill Bradley	Basketball
1966	Jim Ryun	Track
1967	Randy Matson	Track
1968	Debbie Meyer	Swimming
1969	Bill Toomey	Track
1970	John Kinsella	Swimming
1971	Mark Spitz	Swimming
1972	Frank Shorter	Track
1973	Bill Walton	Basketball
1974	Rick Wohlhutter	Track
1975	Tim Shaw	Swimming
1976	Bruce Jenner	Track
1977	John Naber	Swimming
1978	Tracy Caulkins	Swimming
1979	Kurt Thomas	Gymnastics
1980	Eric Heiden	Speed Skating
1981	Carl Lewis	Track
1982	Mary Decker	Track
1983	Edwin Moses	Track
1984	Greg Louganis	Diving
1985	Joan Benoit Samuelson	Marathon
1986	Jackie Joyner-Kersee	Track
1987	Jim Abbott	Baseball
1988	Florence Griffith Joyner	Track
1989	Janet Evans	Swimming
1990	John Smith	Wrestling
1991	Mike Powell	Track
1992	Bonnie Blair	Speed Skating
1993	Charlie Ward	Football, Basketball
1994	Dan Jansen	Speed Skating
1995	Bruce Baumgartner	Wrestling
1996	Michael Johnson	Track
1997	Peyton Manning	Football

DIRECTORY OF SPORTS ORGANIZATIONS

Major League Baseball

Website: http://www.majorleaguebaseball.com
Note: Teams and leagues as of 1998 season.

Commissioner's Office
350 Park Ave.
New York, NY 10022

American League

American League Office
350 Park Ave.
New York, NY 10022

Anaheim Angels
PO Box 2000
Anaheim, CA 92803

Baltimore Orioles
333 W. Camden St.
Baltimore, MD 21201

Boston Red Sox
4 Yawkey Way
Boston, MA 02215

Chicago White Sox
333 W. 35th St.
Chicago, IL 60616

Cleveland Indians
2401 Ontario St.
Cleveland, OH 44115

Detroit Tigers
2121 Trumbull Ave.
Detroit, MI 48216

Kansas City Royals
P.O. Box 419969
Kansas City, MO 64141

Minnesota Twins
34 Kirby Puckett Place
Minneapolis, MN 55415

New York Yankees
Yankee Stadium
Bronx, NY 10451

Oakland Athletics
Oakland Coliseum
Oakland, CA 94621

Seattle Mariners
PO Box 4100
Seattle, WA 98104

Tampa Bay Devil Rays
One Tropicana Dr.
St. Petersburg, FL 33705

Texas Rangers
PO Box 90111
Arlington, TX 76004

Toronto Blue Jays
1 Blue Jays Way, #3200
Toronto, Ont. M5V 1J1

National League

National League Office
350 Park Ave.
New York, NY 10022

Arizona Diamondbacks
PO Box 2095
Phoenix, AZ 85001

Atlanta Braves
PO Box 4064
Atlanta, GA 30302

Chicago Cubs
1060 W. Addison St.
Chicago, IL 60613

Cincinnati Reds
100 Cinergy Field
Cincinnati, OH 45202

Colorado Rockies
2001 Blake St.
Denver, CO 80205

Florida Marlins
2267 NW 199th St.
Miami, FL 33056

Houston Astros
PO Box 288
Houston, TX 77001

Los Angeles Dodgers
1000 Elysian Park Ave.
Los Angeles, CA 90012

Milwaukee Brewers
P.O. Box 3099
Milwaukee, WI 53201

Montreal Expos
PO Box 500, Station M
Montreal, Que. H1V 3P2

New York Mets
Shea Stadium
Flushing, NY 11368

Philadelphia Phillies
PO Box 7575
Philadelphia, PA 19101

Pittsburgh Pirates
PO Box 7000
Pittsburgh, PA 15212

St. Louis Cardinals
250 Stadium Plaza
St. Louis, MO 63102

San Diego Padres
PO Box 2000
San Diego, CA 92112

San Francisco Giants
3Com Park at Candlestick Pt.
San Francisco, CA 94124

National Basketball Association

Website: http://www.nba.com

League Office
645 5th Ave.
New York, NY 10022

Atlanta Hawks
One CNN Center, Ste. 405
Atlanta, GA 30303

Boston Celtics
151 Merrimac St.
Boston, MA 02114

Charlotte Hornets
100 Hive Dr.
Charlotte, NC 28217

Chicago Bulls
1901 W. Madison St.
Chicago, IL 60612

Cleveland Cavaliers
1 Center Court
Cleveland, OH 44115

Dallas Mavericks
777 Sports St.
Dallas, TX 75207

Denver Nuggets
1635 Clay St.
Denver, CO 80204

Detroit Pistons
Two Championship Dr.
Auburn Hills, MI 48326

Golden State Warriors
1011 Broadway
Oakland, CA 94607

Houston Rockets
Two Greenway Plaza, Ste. 400
Houston, TX 77046

Indiana Pacers
300 E. Market St.
Indianapolis, IN 46204

Los Angeles Clippers
3939 S. Figueroa St.
Los Angeles, CA 90037

Los Angeles Lakers
3900 W. Manchester Blvd.
P.O. Box 10
Inglewood, CA 90306

Miami Heat
SunTrust Intl. Center
One SE 3d Ave., Ste. 2300
Miami, FL 33131

Milwaukee Bucks
1001 N. 4th St.
Milwaukee, WI 53203

Minnesota Timberwolves
600 1st Ave. North
Minneapolis, MN 55403

New Jersey Nets
Nets Champion Center
390 Murray Hill Parkway
E. Rutherford, NJ 07073

New York Knickerbockers
Two Pennsylvania Plaza
New York, NY 10121

Orlando Magic
Two Magic Place
8701 Maitland Summit Blvd.
Orlando, FL 32801

Philadelphia 76ers
First Union Center
3601 S. Broad St.
Philadelphia, PA 19148

Phoenix Suns
201 E. Jefferson
Phoenix, AZ 85004

Portland Trail Blazers
One Center Ct., Ste. 200
Portland, OR 97227

Sacramento Kings
One Sports Parkway
Sacramento, CA 95834

San Antonio Spurs
100 Montana St.
San Antonio, TX 78203

Seattle SuperSonics
190 Queen Anne Ave. N
Suite 200
Seattle, WA 98109

Toronto Raptors[1]
20 Bay St., Ste. 1702
Toronto, Ont. M5J 2N8

Utah Jazz
301 W. South Temple
Salt Lake City, UT 84101

Vancouver Grizzlies
800 Griffiths Way
Vancouver, B.C. V6B 6G1

Washington Wizards
718 7th St., NW
Washington, DC 20004

(1) 40 Bay Street, Suite 300, Toronto, Ontario, M5J 2X2, as of Feb. 1999.

National Hockey League

Website: http://www.nhl.com

League Headquarters
1251 Ave. of the Americas
New York, NY 10020-1198

Mighty Ducks of Anaheim
2695 E. Katella Ave.
Anaheim, CA 92803

Boston Bruins
One FleetCenter, Ste. 250
Boston, MA 02114

Buffalo Sabres
Marine Midland Arena
One Seymour H. Knox III Plaza
Buffalo, NY 14203

Calgary Flames
PO Box 1540, Station M
Calgary, Alta. T2P 3B9

Carolina Hurricanes
5000 Aerial Ctr., Ste. 100
Morrisville, NC 27560

Chicago Blackhawks
1901 W. Madison St.
Chicago, IL 60612

Colorado Avalanche
1635 Clay St.
Denver, CO 80204

Dallas Stars
211 Cowboys Parkway
Irving, TX 75063

Detroit Red Wings
600 Civic Center Dr.
Detroit, MI 48226

Edmonton Oilers
Edmonton Coliseum
Edmonton, Alta. T5B 4M9

Florida Panthers
100 NE Third Ave.
Fort Lauderdale, FL 33301

(continued)

National Hockey League *(continued)*

Los Angeles Kings
3900 W. Manchester Blvd.
Inglewood, CA 90305

Montreal Canadiens
1260 rue de La Gauchetiere Ouest
Montreal, Que. H3B 5E8

Nashville Predators
501 Broadway
Nashville, TN 37215

New Jersey Devils
PO Box 504
E. Rutherford, NJ 07073

New York Islanders
Nassau Veterans Memorial Coliseum
Uniondale, NY 11553

New York Rangers
Two Pennsylvania Plaza
New York, NY 10121

Ottawa Senators
1000 Palladium Dr.
Kanata, Ont. K2V 1A5

Philadelphia Flyers
First Union Center
3601 South Broad St.
Philadelphia, PA 19148

Phoenix Coyotes
Cellular One Ice Den
9375 E. Bell Rd.
Scottsdale, AZ 85260

Pittsburgh Penguins
66 Mario Lemieux Place
Pittsburgh, PA 15219

St. Louis Blues
1401 Clark Ave.
St. Louis, MO 63103

San Jose Sharks
525 W. Santa Clara St.
San Jose, CA 95113

Tampa Bay Lightning
401 Channelside Dr.
Tampa, FL 33602

Toronto Maple Leafs
60 Carlton St.
Toronto, Ont. M5B 1L1

Vancouver Canucks
800 Griffiths Way
Vancouver, B.C. V6B 6G1

Washington Capitals
601 F St. NW
Washington, DC 20041

National Football League

Website: http://www.nfl.com

League Office
280 Park Avenue
New York, NY 10017

Arizona Cardinals
PO Box 888
Phoenix, AZ 85001

Atlanta Falcons
One Falcon Place
Suwanee, GA 30024

Baltimore Ravens
11001 Owings Mills Blvd.
Owings Mills, MD 21117

Buffalo Bills
One Bills Drive
Orchard Park, NY 14127

Carolina Panthers
800 S. Mint St.
Charlotte, NC 28202

Chicago Bears
1000 Football Dr.
Lake Forest, IL 60045

Cincinnati Bengals
One Bengals Dr.
Cincinnati, OH 45204

Dallas Cowboys
One Cowboys Parkway
Irving, TX 75063

Denver Broncos
13655 Broncos Parkway
Englewood, CO 80112

Detroit Lions
1200 Featherstone Rd.
Pontiac, MI 48342

Green Bay Packers
1265 Lombardi Ave.
Green Bay, WI 54304

Indianapolis Colts
PO Box 535000
Indianapolis, IN 46253

Jacksonville Jaguars
One ALLTELL Stadium Place
Jacksonville, FL 32202

Kansas City Chiefs
One Arrowhead Drive
Kansas City, MO 64129

Miami Dolphins
7500 SW 30th St.
Davie, FL 33314

Minnesota Vikings
9520 Viking Dr.
Eden Prairie, MN 55344

New England Patriots
60 Washington St.
Foxboro, MA 02035

New Orleans Saints
5800 Airline Drive
Metairie, LA 70003

New York Giants
Giants Stadium
E. Rutherford, NJ 07073

New York Jets
1000 Fulton Ave.
Hempstead, NY 11550

Oakland Raiders
1220 Harbor Bay Parkway
Alameda, CA 94502

Philadelphia Eagles
3501 S. Broad St.
Philadelphia, PA 19148

Pittsburgh Steelers
300 Stadium Circle
Pittsburgh, PA 15212

St. Louis Rams
One Rams Way
St. Louis County, MO 63045

San Diego Chargers
PO Box 609609
San Diego, CA 92160

San Francisco 49ers
4949 Centennial Blvd.
Santa Clara, CA 95054

Seattle Seahawks
11220 NE 53d St.
Kirkland, WA 98033

Tampa Bay Buccaneers
One Buccaneer Place
Tampa, FL 33607

Tennessee Oilers
7640 Hwy 70 South
Nashville, TN 37221

Washington Redskins
PO Box 17247
Washington, DC 20041

Other Sports Organizations

Amateur Athletic Union
PO Box 10000
Lake Buena Vista, FL 32830
http://www.aausports.org

Amateur Softball Assn.
2801 NE 50th St.
Oklahoma City, OK 73111
http://www.softball.org

American Basketball League
1900 Embarcadero Rd., Ste. 110
Palo Alto, CA 94303
http://www.abl.com

American Horse Shows Assn.
220 E. 42d St.
New York, NY 10017
http://www.ahsa.org

American Kennel Club
51 Madison Ave.
New York, NY 10010
http://www.akc.org

Canadian Football League
110 Eglinton Ave. W
Toronto, Ont. M4R 1A3
http://www.cfla.ca

CART
755 W. Big Beaver Rd.
Troy, MI 48084
http://www.cart.com

Intl. Game Fish Assn.
1301 E. Atlantic Blvd.
Pompano Beach, FL 33060
http://www.igfa.org

LPGA
100 International Golf Dr.
Daytona Beach, FL 32124
http://www.lpga.com

Little League Baseball
PO Box 3485
Williamsport, PA 17701
http://www.littleleague.org

Major League Soccer
110 E. 42d St., Ste. 1000
New York, NY 10017
http://www.mlsnet.com

NASCAR
1801 Intl. Speedway Blvd.
Daytona Beach, FL 32120
http://www.nascar.com

NCAA
6201 College Blvd.
Overland Park, KS 66211
http://www.ncaa.org

National Rifle Assn.
11250 Waples Mill Rd.
Fairfax, VA 22030
http://www.nra.org

Pro Bowlers Assn.
PO Box 5118
Akron, OH 44334
http://www.pbatour.com

PGA
100 Ave. of the Champions
Palm Beach Gardens, FL 33410
http://www.pgaonline.com

Pro Rodeo Cowboys Assn.
101 Pro Rodeo Dr.
Colorado Springs, CO 80919
http://www.prorodeo.com

Special Olympics
1325 G St., NW, Ste. 500
Washington, DC 20005
http://www.specialolympics.org

Thoroughbred Racing Assns.
420 Fair Hill Dr.
Elkton, MD 21921
http://www.traofna.com

USA Track & Field
1 RCA Dome, Ste. 140
Indianapolis, IN 46225
http://www.usatf.org

U.S. Auto Club
4910 W. 16th St.
Speedway, IN 46224

U.S. Figure Skating Assn.
20 First St.
Colorado Springs, CO 80906
http://www.usfsa.org

U.S. Olympic Committee
One Olympic Plaza
Colorado Springs, CO 80909
http:www.olympics-usa.org

U.S. Skiing Assn.
PO Box 100
Park City, UT 84060
http://www.usskiteam.com

U.S. Soccer Federation
1801 S. Prairie Ave.
Chicago, IL 60616
http://www.us-soccer.com

USA Swimming
One Olympic Plaza
Colorado Springs, CO 80909
http://www.usa-swimming.org

U.S. Tennis Assn.
70 W. Red Oak Lane
White Plains, NY 10604
http://www.usta.com

U.S. Trotting Assn.
750 Michigan Ave.
Columbus, OH 43215
http://www.ustrotting.com

WNBA
645 5th Ave.
New York, NY 10022
http://www.wnba.com

NCAA WRESTLING CHAMPIONS

Year	Champion	Year	Champion	Year	Champion	Year	Champion	Year	Champion
1964	Oklahoma State	1971	Oklahoma State	1978	Iowa	1985	Iowa	1992	Iowa
1965	Iowa State	1972	Iowa State	1979	Iowa	1986	Iowa	1993	Iowa
1966	Oklahoma State	1973	Iowa State	1980	Iowa	1987	Iowa State	1994	Oklahoma State
1967	Michigan State	1974	Oklahoma	1981	Iowa	1988	Arizona State	1995	Iowa
1968	Oklahoma State	1975	Iowa	1982	Iowa	1989	Oklahoma State	1996	Iowa
1969	Iowa State	1976	Iowa	1983	Iowa	1990	Oklahoma State	1997	Iowa
1970	Iowa State	1977	Iowa State	1984	Iowa	1991	Iowa	1998	Iowa

SWIMMING

World Swimming Records

(As of Oct. 1998)

Men's Records

Distance	Time	Holder	Country	Where made	Date
Freestyle					
50 meters	**0:21.81**	Tom Jager	U.S.	Nashville, TN	Mar. 24, 1990
100 meters	**0:48.21**	Alexander Popov	Russia	Monte Carlo	June 18, 1994
200 meters	**1:46.69**	Giorgio Lamberti	Italy	Bonn	Aug. 15, 1989
400 meters	**3:43.80**	Kieren Perkins	Australia	Rome	Sept. 9, 1994
800 meters	**7:46.00**	Kieren Perkins	Australia	Victoria, Canada	Aug. 24, 1994
1,500 meters	**14:41.66**	Kieren Perkins	Australia	Victoria, Canada	Aug. 24, 1994
Breaststroke					
50 meters[1]	**0:27.61**	Alexander Dzhaburiya	Ukraine	Kharkov	Apr. 27, 1996
100 meters	**1:00.60**	Fred DeBurghgraeve	Belguim	Atlanta, GA	July 20, 1996
200 meters	**2:10.16**	Mike Barrowman	U.S.	Barcelona	July 29, 1992
Butterfly					
50 meters[1]	**0:23.68**	Denis Pankratov	Russia	Mulhouse	Aug. 10, 1996
100 meters	**0:52.15**	Michael Klim	Australia	Brisbane, Australia	Oct. 9, 1997
200 meters	**1:55.22**	Denis Pankratov	Russia	Canet, France	June 14, 1995
Backstroke					
50 meters[1]	**0:25.13**	Jeff Rouse	U.S.	Edinburgh	Apr. 9, 1993
100 meters	**0:53.86**	Jeff Rouse	U.S.	Barcelona	July 29, 1992
200 meters	**1:56.57**	Martin Lopez-Zubero	Spain	Tuscaloosa, AL	Nov. 23, 1991
Individual Medley					
200 meters	**1:58.16**	Jani Sievinen	Finland	Rome	Sept. 11, 1994
400 meters	**4:12.30**	Tom Dolan	U.S.	Rome	Sept. 6, 1994
Freestyle Relays					
400 m. (4×100)	**3:15.11**	(Fox, Hudepohl, Olsen, Hall)	U.S.	Atlanta, GA	Aug. 12, 1995
800 m. (4×200)	**7:11.95**	(Lepikov, Pychenko, Taianovitch, Sadovyi)	Unified Team	Barcelona	July 27, 1992
Medley Relay					
400 m. (4×100)	**3:34.84**	(Rouse, Linn, Henderson, Hall Jr.)	U.S.	Atlanta, GA	July 26, 1996

Women's Records

Distance	Time	Holder	Country	Where made	Date
Freestyle					
50 meters	**0:24.51**	Jingyi Le	China	Rome	Sept. 11, 1994
100 meters	**0:54.01**	Jingyi Le	China	Rome	Sept. 5, 1994
200 meters	**1:56.78**	Franziska Van Almsick	Germany	Rome	Sept. 6, 1994
400 meters	**4:03.85**	Janet Evans	U.S.	Seoul	Sept. 22, 1988
800 meters	**8:16.22**	Janet Evans	U.S.	Tokyo	Aug. 20, 1989
1,500 meters	**15:52.10**	Janet Evans	U.S.	Orlando, FL	Mar. 26, 1988
Breaststroke					
50 meters	**0:30.95**	Penny Heyns	South Africa	Long Island, NY	Aug. 1, 1998
100 meters	**1:07.02**	Penny Heyns	South Africa	Atlanta, GA	July 21, 1996
200 meters	**2:24.76**	Rebecca Brown	Australia	Queensland, Australia	Mar. 16, 1994
Butterfly					
50 meters[1]	**0:26.55**	Amy Van Dyken	U.S.	Phoenix, AZ	May 17, 1996
100 meters	**0:57.93**	Mary T. Meagher	U.S.	Brown Deer, WI.	Aug. 16, 1981
200 meters	**2:05.96**	Mary T. Meagher	U.S.	Brown Deer, WI.	Aug. 13, 1981
Backstroke					
50 meters[1]	**0:29.00**	Sandra Volker	Germany	Monte Carlo	May 24, 1997
100 meters	**1:00.16**	Cihong He	China	Rome	Sept. 10, 1994
200 meters	**2:06.62**	Krisztina Egerszegi	Hungary	Athens	Aug. 25, 1991
Individual Medley					
200 meters	**2:09.72**	Yanyan Wu	China	Shanghai	Oct. 17, 1997
400 meters	**4:34.79**	Yan Chen	China	Shanghai	Oct. 17, 1997
Freestyle Relays					
400 m. (4×100)	**3:37.91**	(Jingyi Le, Shan Ying, Ying Le, Lu Bin)	China	Rome	Sept. 7, 1994
800 m. (4×200)	**7:55.47**	(Stellmach, Strauss, Mohring, Friedrich)	E. Germany	Strasbourg, France	Aug. 18, 1987
Medley Relay					
400 m. (4×100)	**4:01.67**	(Cihong He, Guohong Dai, Limin Liu, Jingyi Le)	China	Rome	Sept. 10, 1994

(1) A "world best" only, not an official world record. In 1998 FINA (Federation Internationale de Natation Amateur) began to ratify new times in the 50-meter breaststroke, backstroke, and butterfly. When an existing "world best" is verified to have been bettered, the new time becomes an official world record.

NATIONAL BASKETBALL ASSOCIATION

Bulls Run, Bird Soars, Duncan Is Top Rookie, New Season on Hold

In the 1997-98 season the Chicago Bulls captured yet another championship, and Michael Jordan won his 10th scoring title and 5th regular season MVP award. Newly elected Hall of Famer Larry Bird proved he could coach, too, as he led the Indiana Pacers deep into the playoffs and was named Coach of the Year. The number-one draft pick in 1997, Tim Duncan of the San Antonio Spurs, had a spectacular season and easily won Rookie of the Year honors. Future Hall of Famer Clyde Drexler retired at season's end to coach at the Univ. of Houston. In fall 1998 the 1998-99 season did not begin as scheduled because of a labor dispute between the NBA and the players' union. This was the first time in the league's 52-year history that a season was deferred or interrupted by a strike or, in this case, a lockout.

Final Standings, 1997-98 Season

(playoff seeding in parentheses; in each conference the two division winners automatically get the number 1 and 2 seeds)

Eastern Conference

Atlantic Division

	W	L	Pct	GB
Miami (2)	55	27	.671	—
New York (7)	43	39	.524	12
New Jersey (8)	43	39	.524	12
Washington	42	40	.512	13
Orlando	41	41	.500	14
Boston	36	46	.439	19
Philadelphia	31	51	.378	24

Central Division

	W	L	Pct	GB
Chicago (1)	62	20	.756	—
Indiana (3)	58	24	.707	4
Charlotte (4)	51	31	.622	11
Atlanta (5)	50	32	.610	12
Cleveland (6)	47	35	.573	15
Detroit	37	45	.451	25
Milwaukee	36	46	.439	26
Toronto	16	66	.195	46

Western Conference

Midwest Division

	W	L	Pct	GB
Utah (1)	62	20	.756	—
San Antonio (5)	56	26	.683	6
Minnesota (7)	45	37	.549	17
Houston (8)	41	41	.500	21
Dallas	20	62	.244	42
Vancouver	19	63	.232	43
Denver	11	71	.134	51

Pacific Division

	W	L	Pct	GB
Seattle (2)	61	21	.744	—
L.A. Lakers (3)	61	21	.744	—
Phoenix (4)	56	26	.683	5
Portland (6)	46	36	.561	15
Sacramento	27	55	.329	34
Golden State	19	63	.232	42
L.A. Clippers	17	65	.207	44

NBA Regular Season Individual Highs in 1997-98

Most minutes played, game — 61: Brian Grant, Portland v. Phoenix, Nov. 14 (4 OT).

Most points, game — 56: Karl Malone, Utah v. Golden State, April 7.

Most field goals made, game — 21: Antoine Walker, Boston at Washington, Jan. 7.

Most field goal attempts, game — 39: Michael Jordan, Chicago v. San Antonio, Nov. 3 (2 OT).

Most 3-pt. field goals made, game — 9: 3 times, most recently by John Starks, NY v. Milwaukee, Jan. 29 (1 OT).

Most 3-pt. field goal attempts, game — 14: 4 times, most recently by Chuck Person, San Antonio at Vancouver, Dec. 30.

Most free throws made, game — 22: Michael Jordan, Chicago v. New York, Apr. 18.

Most rebounds, game — 29: Dennis Rodman, Chicago v. Atlanta, Dec. 27.

Most assists, game — 20: 4 times, most recently by Rod Strickland, Washington at Golden State, Feb. 10.

Most steals, game — 10: Mookie Blaylock, Atlanta v. Philadelphia, April 14.

Most blocked shots, game — 13: Shawn Bradley, Dallas v. Portland, April 7.

Most minutes played, season — 3,394: Michael Finley, Dallas.

Most offensive rebounds, season — 443: Jayson Williams, New Jersey.

Most defensive rebounds, season — 780: Dennis Rodman, Chicago.

1998 NBA Playoff Results

Eastern Conference

Chicago defeated New Jersey 3 games to 0
New York defeated Miami 3 games to 2
Indiana defeated Cleveland 3 games to 1
Charlotte defeated Atlanta 3 games to 1
Chicago defeated Charlotte 4 games to 1
Indiana defeated New York 4 games to 1
Chicago defeated Indiana 4 games to 3

Western Conference

Utah defeated Houston 3 games to 2
Seattle defeated Minnesota 3 games to 2
L.A. Lakers defeated Portland 3 games to 1
San Antonio defeated Phoenix 3 games to 1
Utah defeated San Antonio 4 games to 1
L.A. Lakers defeated Seattle 4 games to 1
Utah defeated L.A. Lakers 4 games to 0

Championship

Chicago defeated Utah 4 games to 2 [85-88 (OT), 93-88, 96-54, 86-82, 81-83, 87-86]

The Chicago Bulls dominate the 1990s as they win their 6th NBA Championship

In June 1998, the Chicago Bulls defeated the Utah Jazz 4 games to 2 to win their 6th NBA Championship. The series was a rematch of the 1997 finals and once again saw Chicago come out on top in 6 games. Chicago's 6 championships were all won in the past 8 years as Chicago won 3 titles in a row 2 times (1991, 1992, 1993 and 1996, 1997, 1998). Michael Jordan was named the NBA Finals MVP a record 6th time, making him the MVP in all 6 championship finals for the Bulls.

Chicago Bulls

	FG A-M	FT A-M	Reb O-T	Ast	Avg
Michael Jordan	164-70	70-57	9-24	14	33.5
Scottie Pippen	83-34	24-20	17-41	29	15.7
Toni Kukoc	76-38	13-8	10-28	16	15.2
Ron Harper	33-12	12-7	3-27	17	5.3
Luc Longley	27-12	8-6	11-29	9	5.0
Steve Kerr	20-7	4-4	1-2	15	3.8
Scott Burrell	22-9	3-2	0-15	0	3.5
Dennis Rodman	13-6	12-8	20-50	6	3.3
Bill Wennington	5-2	0-0	0-3	1	1.3
Jud Buechler	5-3	0-0	1-2	2	1.3
Dickey Simpkins	2-1	2-0	1-3	1	1.0
Randy Brown	3-1	0-0	0-2	0	1.0

Utah Jazz

	FG A-M	FT A-M	Reb O-T	Ast	Avg
Karl Malone	119-60	38-30	21-63	23	25.0
Jeff Hornacek	56-23	18-15	1-16	16	10.7
John Stockton	49-24	11-8	1-15	52	9.7
Bryon Russell	44-18	16-11	4-30	8	8.8
Shandon Anderson	34-17	11-9	6-16	2	7.3
Howard Eisley	32-12	3-3	2-12	23	4.7
Chris Morris	28-11	6-4	2-15	3	4.3
Antoine Carr	22-11	4-3	5-12	0	4.2
Adam Keefe	14-6	4-2	9-17	1	2.8
Greg Ostertag	12-5	1-1	5-16	0	2.2
Greg Foster	15-4	0-0	5-14	0	1.3
Jacque Vaughn	6-0	0-0	0-2	0	0.0

NBA Finals MVP

1969 Jerry West, Los Angeles
1970 Willis Reed, New York
1971 Lew Alcindor (Kareem Abdul-Jabbar), Milwaukee
1972 Wilt Chamberlain, Los Angeles
1973 Willis Reed, New York
1974 John Havlicek, Boston
1975 Rick Barry, Golden State
1976 Jo Jo White, Boston
1977 Bill Walton, Portland
1978 Wes Unseld, Washington
1979 Dennis Johnson, Seattle
1980 Magic Johnson, Los Angeles
1981 Cedric Maxwell, Boston
1982 Magic Johnson, Los Angeles
1983 Moses Malone, Philadelphia
1984 Larry Bird, Boston
1985 Kareem Abdul-Jabbar, L.A. Lakers
1986 Larry Bird, Boston
1987 Magic Johnson, L.A. Lakers
1988 James Worthy, L.A. Lakers
1989 Joe Dumars, Detroit
1990 Isiah Thomas, Detroit
1991 Michael Jordan, Chicago
1992 Michael Jordan, Chicago
1993 Michael Jordan, Chicago
1994 Hakeem Olajuwon, Houston
1995 Hakeem Olajuwon, Houston
1996 Michael Jordan, Chicago
1997 Michael Jordan, Chicago
1998 Michael Jordan, Chicago

NBA Scoring Leaders

Year	Scoring champion	Pts	Avg
1947	Joe Fulks, Philadelphia	1,389	23.2
1948	Max Zaslofsky, Chicago	1,007	21.0
1949	George Mikan, Minneapolis	1,698	28.3
1950	George Mikan, Minneapolis	1,865	27.4
1951	George Mikan, Minneapolis	1,932	28.4
1952	Paul Arizin, Philadelphia	1,674	25.4
1953	Neil Johnston, Philadelphia	1,564	22.3
1954	Neil Johnston, Philadelphia	1,759	24.4
1955	Neil Johnston, Philadelphia	1,631	22.7
1956	Bob Pettit, St. Louis	1,849	25.7
1957	Paul Arizin, Philadelphia	1,817	25.6
1958	George Yardley, Detroit	2,001	27.8
1959	Bob Pettit, St. Louis	2,105	29.2
1960	Wilt Chamberlain, Philadelphia	2,707	37.9
1961	Wilt Chamberlain, Philadelphia	3,033	38.4
1962	Wilt Chamberlain, Philadelphia	4,029	50.4
1963	Wilt Chamberlain, San Francisco	3,586	44.8
1964	Wilt Chamberlain, San Francisco	2,948	36.5
1965	Wilt Chamberlain, San Francisco, Philadelphia	2,534	34.7
1966	Wilt Chamberlain, Philadelphia	2,649	33.5
1967	Rick Barry, San Francisco	2,775	35.6
1968	Dave Bing, Detroit	2,142	27.1
1969	Elvin Hayes, San Diego	2,327	28.4
1970	Jerry West, Los Angeles	2,309	31.2
1971	Lew Alcindor (Kareem Abdul-Jabbar), Milwaukee	2,596	31.7
1972	Kareem Abdul-Jabbar, Milwaukee	2,822	34.8
1973	Nate Archibald, Kans. City-Omaha	2,719	34.0
1974	Bob McAdoo, Buffalo	2,261	30.6
1975	Bob McAdoo, Buffalo	2,831	34.5
1976	Bob McAdoo, Buffalo	2,427	31.1
1977	Pete Maravich, New Orleans	2,273	31.1
1978	George Gervin, San Antonio	2,232	27.2
1979	George Gervin, San Antonio	2,365	29.6
1980	George Gervin, San Antonio	2,585	33.1
1981	Adrian Dantley, Utah	2,452	30.7
1982	George Gervin, San Antonio	2,551	32.3
1983	Alex English, Denver	2,326	28.4
1984	Adrian Dantley, Utah	2,418	30.6
1985	Bernard King, New York	1,809	32.9
1986	Dominique Wilkins, Atlanta	2,366	30.3
1987	Michael Jordan, Chicago	3,041	37.1
1988	Michael Jordan, Chicago	2,868	35.0
1989	Michael Jordan, Chicago	2,633	32.5
1990	Michael Jordan, Chicago	2,753	33.6
1991	Michael Jordan, Chicago	2,580	31.5
1992	Michael Jordan, Chicago	2,404	30.1
1993	Michael Jordan, Chicago	2,541	32.6
1994	David Robinson, San Antonio	2,383	29.8
1995	Shaquille O'Neal, Orlando	2,315	29.3
1996	Michael Jordan, Chicago	2,465	30.4
1997	Michael Jordan, Chicago	2,431	29.6
1998	Michael Jordan, Chicago	2,357	28.7

NBA Most Valuable Player

1956 Bob Pettit, St. Louis
1957 Bob Cousy, Boston
1958 Bill Russell, Boston
1959 Bob Pettit, St. Louis
1960 Wilt Chamberlain, Philadelphia
1961 Bill Russell, Boston
1962 Bill Russell, Boston
1963 Bill Russell, Boston
1964 Oscar Robertson, Cincinnati
1965 Bill Russell, Boston
1966 Wilt Chamberlain, Philadelphia
1967 Wilt Chamberlain, Philadelphia
1968 Wilt Chamberlain, Philadelphia
1969 Wes Unseld, Baltimore
1970 Willis Reed, New York
1971 Lew Alcindor (Kareem Abdul-Jabbar), Milwaukee
1972 Kareem Abdul-Jabbar, Milwaukee
1973 Dave Cowens, Boston
1974 Kareem Abdul-Jabbar, Milwaukee
1975 Bob McAdoo, Buffalo
1976 Kareem Abdul-Jabbar, Los Angeles
1977 Kareem Abdul-Jabbar, Los Angeles
1978 Bill Walton, Portland
1979 Moses Malone, Houston
1980 Kareem Abdul-Jabbar, Los Angeles
1981 Julius Erving, Philadelphia
1982 Moses Malone, Houston
1983 Moses Malone, Philadelphia
1984 Larry Bird, Boston
1985 Larry Bird, Boston
1986 Larry Bird, Boston
1987 Magic Johnson, L.A. Lakers
1988 Michael Jordan, Chicago
1989 Magic Johnson, L.A. Lakers
1990 Magic Johnson, L.A. Lakers
1991 Michael Jordan, Chicago
1992 Michael Jordan, Chicago
1993 Charles Barkley, Phoenix
1994 Hakeem Olajuwon, Houston
1995 David Robinson, San Antonio
1996 Michael Jordan, Chicago
1997 Karl Malone, Utah
1998 Michael Jordan, Chicago

NBA Champions, 1947-98

	Regular season		Playoffs		
Year	Eastern Conference	Western Conference	Winner	Coach	Runner-up
1947	Washington Capitols	Chicago Stags	Philadelphia	Ed Gottlieb	Chicago
1948	Philadelphia Warriors	St. Louis Bombers	Baltimore	Buddy Jeannette	Philadelphia
1949	Washington Capitols	Rochester	Minneapolis	John Kundla	Washington
1950	Syracuse	Minneapolis	Minneapolis	John Kundla	Syracuse
1951	Philadelphia Warriors	Minneapolis	Rochester	Lester Harrison	New York
1952	Syracuse	Rochester	Minneapolis	John Kundla	New York
1953	New York	Minneapolis	Minneapolis	John Kundla	New York
1954	New York	Minneapolis	Minneapolis	John Kundla	Syracuse
1955	Syracuse	Ft. Wayne	Syracuse	Al Cervi	Ft. Wayne
1956	Philadelphia Warriors	Ft. Wayne	Philadelphia	George Senesky	Ft. Wayne
1957	Boston	St. Louis	Boston	Red Auerbach	St. Louis
1958	Boston	St. Louis	St. Louis	Alex Hannum	Boston
1959	Boston	St. Louis	Boston	Red Auerbach	Minneapolis
1960	Boston	St. Louis	Boston	Red Auerbach	St. Louis
1961	Boston	St. Louis	Boston	Red Auerbach	St. Louis
1962	Boston	Los Angeles	Boston	Red Auerbach	Los Angeles

	Regular season		Playoffs		
Year	Eastern Conference	Western Conference	Winner	Coach	Runner-up
1963	Boston	Los Angeles	Boston	Red Auerbach	Los Angeles
1964	Boston	San Francisco	Boston	Red Auerbach	San Francisco
1965	Boston	Los Angeles	Boston	Red Auerbach	Los Angeles
1966	Philadelphia	Los Angeles	Boston	Red Auerbach	Los Angeles
1967	Philadelphia	San Francisco	Philadelphia	Alex Hannum	San Francisco
1968	Philadelphia	St. Louis	Boston	Bill Russell	Los Angeles
1969	Baltimore	Los Angeles	Boston	Bill Russell	Los Angeles
1970	New York	Atlanta	New York	Red Holzman	Los Angeles

Year	Atlantic	Central	Midwest	Pacific	Winner	Coach	Runner-up
1971	New York	Baltimore	Milwaukee	Los Angeles	Milwaukee	Larry Costello	Baltimore
1972	Boston	Baltimore	Milwaukee	Los Angeles	Los Angeles	Bill Sharman	New York
1973	Boston	Baltimore	Milwaukee	Los Angeles	New York	Red Holzman	Los Angeles
1974	Boston	Capital	Milwaukee	Los Angeles	Boston	Tom Heinsohn	Milwaukee
1975	Boston	Washington	Chicago	Golden State	Golden State	Al Attles	Washington
1976	Boston	Cleveland	Milwaukee	Golden State	Boston	Tom Heinsohn	Phoenix
1977	Philadelphia	Houston	Denver	Los Angeles	Portland	Jack Ramsay	Philadelphia
1978	Philadelphia	San Antonio	Denver	Portland	Washington	Dick Motta	Seattle
1979	Washington	San Antonio	Kansas City	Seattle	Seattle	Len Wilkens	Washington
1980	Boston	Atlanta	Milwaukee	Los Angeles	Los Angeles	Paul Westhead	Philadelphia
1981	Boston	Milwaukee	San Antonio	Phoenix	Boston	Bill Fitch	Houston
1982	Boston	Milwaukee	San Antonio	Los Angeles	Los Angeles	Pat Riley	Philadelphia
1983	Philadelphia	Milwaukee	San Antonio	Los Angeles	Philadelphia	Billy Cunningham	Los Angeles
1984	Boston	Milwaukee	Utah	Los Angeles	Boston	K.C. Jones	Los Angeles
1985	Boston	Milwaukee	Denver	L.A. Lakers	L.A. Lakers	Pat Riley	Boston
1986	Boston	Milwaukee	Houston	L.A. Lakers	Boston	K.C. Jones	Houston
1987	Boston	Atlanta	Dallas	L.A. Lakers	L.A. Lakers	Pat Riley	Boston
1988	Boston	Detroit	Denver	L.A. Lakers	L.A. Lakers	Pat Riley	Detroit
1989	New York	Detroit	Utah	L.A. Lakers	Detroit	Chuck Daly	L.A. Lakers
1990	Philadelphia	Detroit	San Antonio	L.A. Lakers	Detroit	Chuck Daly	Portland
1991	Boston	Chicago	San Antonio	Portland	Chicago	Phil Jackson	L.A. Lakers
1992	Boston	Chicago	Utah	Portland	Chicago	Phil Jackson	Portland
1993	New York	Chicago	Houston	Phoenix	Chicago	Phil Jackson	Phoenix
1994	New York	Atlanta	Houston	Seattle	Houston	Rudy Tomjanovich	New York
1995	Orlando	Indiana	San Antonio	Phoenix	Houston	Rudy Tomjanovich	Orlando
1996	Orlando	Chicago	San Antonio	Seattle	Chicago	Phil Jackson	Seattle
1997	Miami	Chicago	Utah	Seattle	Chicago	Phil Jackson	Utah
1998	Miami	Chicago	Utah	L.A. Lakers	Chicago	Phil Jackson	Utah

NBA Coach of the Year, 1963-98

1963 Harry Gallatin, St. Louis Hawks
1964 Alex Hannum, San Francisco Warriors
1965 Red Auerbach, Boston Celtics
1966 Dolph Schayes, Philadelphia 76ers
1967 Johnny Kerr, Chicago Bulls
1968 Richie Guerin, St. Louis Hawks
1969 Gene Shue, Baltimore Bullets
1970 Red Holzman, New York Knicks
1971 Dick Motta, Chicago Bulls
1972 Bill Sharman, Los Angeles Lakers
1973 Tom Heinsohn, Boston Celtics
1974 Ray Scott, Detroit Pistons
1975 Phil Johnson, Kansas City-Omaha Kings
1976 Bill Fitch, Cleveland Cavaliers
1977 Tom Nissalke, Houston Rockets
1978 Hubie Brown, Atlanta Hawks
1979 Cotton Fitzsimmons, Kansas City Kings
1980 Bill Fitch, Boston Celtics
1981 Jack McKinney, Indiana Pacers
1982 Gene Shue, Washington Bullets
1983 Don Nelson, Milwaukee Bucks
1984 Frank Layden, Utah Jazz
1985 Don Nelson, Milwaukee Bucks
1986 Mike Fratello, Atlanta Hawks
1987 Mike Schuler, Portland Trail Blazers
1988 Doug Moe, Denver Nuggets
1989 Cotton Fitzsimmons, Phoenix Suns
1990 Pat Riley, Los Angeles Lakers
1991 Don Chaney, Houston Rockets
1992 Don Nelson, Golden State Warriors
1993 Pat Riley, New York Knicks
1994 Lenny Wilkens, Atlanta Hawks
1995 Del Harris, Los Angeles Lakers
1996 Phil Jackson, Chicago Bulls
1997 Pat Riley, Miami Heat
1998 Larry Bird, Indiana Pacers

NBA All-League and All-Defensive Teams, 1997-98

All-League Team			All-Defensive Team	
First team	Second team	Position	First team	Second team
Karl Malone, Utah	Grant Hill, Detroit	Forward	Scottie Pippen, Chicago	Tim Duncan, San Antonio
Tim Duncan, San Antonio	Vin Baker, Seattle	Forward	Karl Malone, Utah	Charles Oakley, N.Y. Knicks
Shaquille O'Neal, L.A. Lakers	David Robinson, San Antonio	Center	Dikembe Mutombo, Atlanta	David Robinson, San Antonio
Michael Jordan, Chicago	Tim Hardaway, Miami	Guard	Michael Jordan, Chicago	Mookie Blaylock, Atlanta
Gary Payton, Seattle	Rod Strickland, Washington	Guard	Gary Payton, Seattle	Eddie Jones, L.A. Lakers

NBA Statistical Leaders, 1997-98

Scoring Average
(Minimum 70 games or 1,400 pts)

	G	FG	FT	Pts	Avg
Jordan, Chicago	82	881	565	2,357	28.7
O'Neal, L.A. Lakers	60	670	359	1,699	28.3
Malone, Utah	81	780	628	2,190	27.0
Richmond, Sacramento	70	543	407	1,623	23.2
Walker, Boston	82	722	305	1,840	22.4
Abdur-Rahim, Vancouver	82	653	502	1,829	22.3
Rice, Charlotte	82	634	428	1,826	22.3
Iverson, Philadelphia	80	649	390	1,758	22.0
Webber, Washington	71	647	196	1,555	21.9
Robinson, San Antonio	73	544	485	1,574	21.6

Rebounds per Game
(Minimum 70 games or 800 rebounds)

	G	Off	Def	Tot	Avg
Rodman, Chicago	80	421	780	1,201	15.0
Williams, New Jersey	65	443	440	883	13.6
Duncan, San Antonio	82	274	703	977	11.9
Mutombo, Atlanta	82	276	656	932	11.4
Robinson, San Antonio	73	239	536	775	10.6
Malone, Utah	81	189	645	834	10.3
Mason, Charlotte	81	177	649	826	10.2
Walker, Boston	82	270	566	836	10.2
Sabonis, Portland	73	149	580	729	10.0
Garnett, Minnesota	82	222	564	786	9.6

Field Goal Percentage
(Minimum 300 field goals made)

	FGM	FGA	Pct
O'Neal, L.A. Lakers	670	1147	.584
Outlaw, Orlando	301	543	.554
Mourning, Miami	403	732	.551
Duncan, San Antonio	706	1,287	.549
Baker, Seattle	631	1,164	.542
Mutombo, Atlanta	399	743	.537
McDyess, Phoenix	497	927	.536
Wallace, Portland	466	875	.533
Malone, Utah	780	1,472	.530
Reeves, Vancouver	492	941	.523

Free Throw Percentage
(Minimum 125 free throws made)

	FTM	FTA	Pct
Mullin, Indiana	154	164	.939
Hornacek, Utah	285	322	.885
Allen, Milwaukee	342	391	.875
Anderson, Cleveland	275	315	.873
Johnson, Phoenix	162	186	.871
Murray, Washington	182	209	.871
Hawkins, Seattle	177	204	.868
Miller, Indiana	382	440	.868
Laettner, Atlanta	306	354	.864
Richmond, Sacramento	407	471	.864

3-Point Field Goal Percentage
(Minimum 55 goals made)

	FG	FGA	Pct
Ellis, Seattle	127	274	.464
Hornacek, Utah	56	127	.441
Mullin, Indiana	107	243	.440
Davis, Dallas	101	230	.439
Kerr, Chicago	57	130	.438
Rice, Charlotte	130	300	.433
Person, Cleveland	192	447	.430
Miller, Indiana	164	382	.429
Curry, Charlotte	61	145	.421
Recasner, Atlanta	62	148	.419

Assists per Game
(Minimum 70 games or 400 assists)

	G	No	Avg
Strickland, Washington	76	801	10.5
Kidd, Phoenix	82	745	9.1
Jackson, Indiana	82	713	8.7
Marbury, Minnesota	82	704	8.6
Stockton, Utah	64	543	8.5
Hardaway, Miami	81	672	8.3
Payton, Seattle	82	679	8.3
Knight, Cleveland	80	656	8.2
Stoudamire, Portland	71	580	8.2
Cassell, New Jersey	75	603	8.0

Steals per Game
(Minimum 70 games or 125 steals)

	G	No	Avg
Blaylock, Atlanta	70	183	2.61
Knight, Cleveland	80	196	2.45
Christie, Toronto	78	190	2.44
Payton, Seattle	82	185	2.26
Iverson, Philadelphia	80	176	2.20
Jones, L.A. Lakers	80	160	2.00
Kidd, Phoenix	82	162	1.98
Gill, New Jersey	81	156	1.93
Drexler, Houston	70	126	1.80
Hawkins, Seattle	82	148	1.80

Blocked Shots per Game
(Minimum 70 games or 100 blocked shots)

	G	Blk	Avg
Camby, Toronto	63	230	3.65
Mutombo, Atlanta	82	277	3.38
Bradley, Dallas	64	214	3.34
Ratliff, Philadelphia	82	258	3.15
Robinson, San Antonio	73	192	2.63
Duncan, San Antonio	82	206	2.51
Stewart, Sacramento	81	195	2.41
O'Neal, L.A. Lakers	60	144	2.40
Mourning, Miami	58	130	2.24
Outlaw Orlando	82	181	2.21

NBA Rookie of the Year

Year	Player
1953	Don Meineke, Ft. Wayne
1954	Ray Felix, Baltimore
1955	Bob Pettit, Milwaukee
1956	Maurice Stokes, Rochester
1957	Tom Heinsohn, Boston
1958	Woody Sauldsberry, Philadelphia
1959	Elgin Baylor, Minneapolis
1960	Wilt Chamberlain, Philadelphia
1961	Oscar Robertson, Cincinnati
1962	Walt Bellamy, Chicago
1963	Terry Dischinger, Chicago
1964	Jerry Lucas, Cincinnati
1965	Willis Reed, New York
1966	Rick Barry, San Francisco
1967	Dave Bing, Detroit
1968	Earl Monroe, Baltimore
1969	Wes Unseld, Baltimore
1970	Lew Alcindor, Milwaukee
1971	Dave Cowens, Boston; Geoff Petrie, Portland (tie)
1972	Sidney Wicks, Portland
1973	Bob McAdoo, Buffalo
1974	Ernie DiGregorio, Buffalo
1975	Keith Wilkes, Golden State
1976	Alvan Adams, Phoenix
1977	Adrian Dantley, Buffalo
1978	Walter Davis, Phoenix
1979	Phil Ford, Kansas City
1980	Larry Bird, Boston
1981	Darrell Griffith, Utah
1982	Buck Williams, New Jersey
1983	Terry Cummings, San Diego
1984	Ralph Sampson, Houston
1985	Michael Jordan, Chicago
1986	Patrick Ewing, New York
1987	Chuck Person, Indiana
1988	Mark Jackson, New York
1989	Mitch Richmond, Golden State
1990	David Robinson, San Antonio
1991	Derrick Coleman, New Jersey
1992	Larry Johnson, Charlotte
1993	Shaquille O'Neal, Orlando
1994	Chris Webber, Golden State
1995	Grant Hill, Detroit; Jason Kidd, Dallas (tie)
1996	Damon Stoudamire, Toronto
1997	Allen Iverson, Philadelphia
1998	Tim Duncan, San Antonio

NBA Individual Statistics, 1997-98

(more than 600 minutes played; *played for more than one team during 1997-98)

Atlanta Hawks

	Min	FG%	FT%	Reb	Ast	Pts	Avg
Smith	2,857	.444	.855	309	292	1,464	20.1
Henderson	2,000	.485	.652	442	73	986	14.3
Laettner	2,282	.485	.864	487	190	1,020	13.8
Mutombo	2,917	.537	.670	932	82	1,101	13.4
Blaylock	2,700	.392	.709	341	469	921	13.2
Corbin	2,699	.439	.789	362	173	806	10.2
Recasner	1,454	.456	.937	142	117	548	9.3
Brown	1,202	.433	.724	183	55	387	5.0

Coach—Lenny Wilkens

Boston Celtics

	Min	FG%	FT%	Reb	Ast	Pts	Avg
Walker	3,268	.423	.645	836	273	1,840	22.4
Mercer	2,662	.450	.839	280	176	1,221	15.3
Anderson*	1,858	.398	.789	173	345	746	12.2
Barros	1,686	.461	.847	153	286	784	9.8
McCarty	2,340	.404	.742	364	177	788	9.6
Knight	1,503	.441	.786	365	104	482	6.5
Bowen	1,305	.409	.623	174	81	340	5.6
Declercq	1,523	.497	.601	392	59	439	5.4
Tabak*	984	.467	.377	212	48	307	5.4
Edney	623	.431	.793	55	139	277	5.3
Minor	1,126	.436	.686	150	88	345	5.0

Coach—Rick Pitino

Charlotte Hornets

	Min	FG%	FT%	Reb	Ast	Pts	Avg
Rice	3,295	.457	.849	353	182	1,826	22.3
Wesley	2,845	.443	.795	213	529	1,054	13.0
Mason	3,148	.509	.649	826	342	1,039	12.8
Geiger	1,839	.505	.712	521	78	885	11.3
Divac	1,805	.498	.691	518	172	667	10.4
Phills	1,887	.446	.757	216	187	642	10.4
Curry	971	.447	.788	101	69	490	9.4
Maxwell*	636	.399	.800	57	52	291	6.9
Reid	1,109	.459	.730	210	51	384	4.9
Armstrong*	831	.493	.840	76	150	261	4.0
Beck	738	.459	.729	90	98	191	3.2

Coach—Dave Cowens

Chicago Bulls

	Min	FG%	FT%	Reb	Ast	Pts	Avg
Jordan	3,181	.465	.784	475	283	2,357	28.7
Pippen	1,652	.447	.777	227	254	841	19.1
Kukoc	2,235	.455	.708	327	314	984	13.3
Longley	1,703	.455	.736	341	161	663	11.4
Harper	2,284	.441	.750	290	241	764	9.3
Kerr	1,119	.454	.918	77	96	376	7.5
Burrell	1,096	.424	.734	198	65	416	5.2
Rodman	2,856	.431	.550	1,201	230	375	4.7
Brown	1,147	.384	.718	94	151	288	4.1
Buechler	608	.483	.500	77	49	198	2.7

Coach—Phil Jackson

Cleveland Cavaliers

	Min	FG%	FT%	Reb	Ast	Pts	Avg
Kemp	2,769	.445	.727	745	197	1,442	18.0
Person	3,198	.460	.776	363	188	1,204	14.7
Ilgauskas	2,379	.518	.762	723	71	1,139	13.9
Anderson	1,839	.408	.873	187	227	770	11.7
Henderson	2,527	.480	.716	325	168	832	10.1
Knight	2,483	.441	.801	253	656	723	9.0
Potapenko	1,412	.480	.708	313	57	570	7.1
Sura	942	.377	.565	94	171	267	5.8
Ferry	1,034	.395	.800	114	59	291	4.2

Coach—Mike Fratello

Dallas Mavericks

	Min	FG%	FT%	Reb	Ast	Pts	Avg
Finley	3,394	.449	.784	438	405	1,763	21.5
Bradley	1,822	.422	.722	518	60	731	11.4
Ceballos*	990	.492	.738	221	60	536	11.4
Davis	2,378	.456	.836	169	157	898	11.1
Walker	1,027	.486	.546	302	24	365	8.9
Reeves	1,950	.418	.775	185	230	717	8.7
Strickland	1,505	.357	.774	161	167	511	7.6
Green	2,649	.453	.716	668	123	600	7.3
Respert*	911	.444	.787	100	61	339	5.9
Antsey	680	.398	.716	157	35	240	5.9
Muursepp	603	.435	.761	114	30	233	5.7

Coach—Jim Cleamons, Don Nelson

Denver Nuggets

	Min	FG%	FT%	Reb	Ast	Pts	Avg
Newman	2,176	.431	.820	141	138	1,089	14.7
L. Ellis	2,575	.407	.805	544	213	1,083	14.3
Jackson	2,042	.392	.814	302	317	790	11.6
Fortson	1,811	.452	.776	448	76	816	10.2
Goldwire	2,212	.423	.806	147	277	751	9.2
Battie	1,506	.446	.702	351	60	544	8.4
Alexander*	1,298	.428	.784	146	209	488	8.1
Washington	1,539	.404	.783	127	78	511	7.7
Stith	718	.333	.872	65	50	235	7.6
Garrett	2,632	.428	.648	644	90	598	7.3
Wolf	621	.331	.500	126	30	87	1.5

Coach—Bill Hanzlik

Detroit Pistons

	Min	FG%	FT%	Reb	Ast	Pts	Avg
Hill	3,294	.452	.740	623	551	1,712	21.1
B. Williams	2,619	.511	.707	695	94	1,261	16.2
Stack-house*	2,545	.435	.787	266	241	1,249	15.8
Dumars	2,326	.416	.825	104	253	943	13.1
Hunter	2,505	.383	.740	247	224	862	12.1
Sealy	1,641	.428	.824	219	100	591	7.7
J. Williams	1,305	.524	.651	379	48	410	5.3
Long	739	.427	.719	150	25	141	3.5
Reid	994	.534	.704	175	26	238	3.5
Montross*	691	.424	.400	199	11	138	2.9
Mahorn	707	.457	.676	195	15	141	2.4

Coach—Doug Collins, Alvin Gentry

Golden State Warriors

	Min	FG%	FT%	Reb	Ast	Pts	Avg
Jackson*	3,046	.430	.812	400	381	1,242	15.7
Marshall	2,611	.413	.731	628	159	1,123	15.4
Dampier	2,656	.445	.669	715	94	971	11.8
Delk*	1,681	.393	.735	172	172	781	10.1
Weather-spoon*	2,325	.441	.722	594	89	736	9.3
Coles	1,471	.379	.886	123	248	423	8.0
Caffey*	1,423	.485	.655	344	67	583	7.3
Bogues*	1,570	.437	.897	132	331	347	5.7
Fuller	613	.420	.688	196	10	227	4.0
Foyle	656	.406	.435	184	14	165	3.0
Spencer	813	.457	.557	226	17	162	2.4

Coach—P.J. Carlesimo

Houston Rockets

	Min	FG%	FT%	Reb	Ast	Pts	Avg
Drexler	2,473	.427	.801	346	382	1,287	18.4
Olajuwon	1,633	.483	.755	460	143	772	16.4
Willis	2,528	.510	.793	679	78	1,305	16.1
Barkley	2,243	.485	.746	794	217	1,036	15.2
Maloney	2,217	.408	.833	142	219	669	8.6
Johnson	1,490	.417	.831	153	88	633	8.4
Elie	1,988	.452	.833	156	221	612	8.4
Bullard	1,190	.450	.741	146	60	466	7.0
Harrington	903	.485	.754	207	24	350	6.0
Rhodes	1,070	.367	.617	70	110	337	5.8
Price	1,332	.413	.786	107	192	406	5.6

Coach—Rudy Tomjanovich

Indiana Pacers

	Min	FG%	FT%	Reb	Ast	Pts	Avg
Miller	2,795	.477	.868	232	171	1,578	19.5
Smits	2,085	.495	.783	505	101	1,216	16.7
Mullin	2,177	.481	.939	249	186	927	11.3
A. Davis	2,191	.481	.696	560	61	785	9.6
Rose	1,706	.478	.728	195	155	771	9.4
Jackson	2,413	.416	.761	322	713	678	8.3
D. Davis	2,174	.548	.465	611	70	626	8.0
Best	1,547	.419	.855	122	281	535	6.5
McKey	1,316	.459	.714	211	88	359	6.3
Hoiberg	874	.383	.855	123	45	261	4.0

Coach—Larry Bird

Los Angeles Clippers

	Min	FG%	FT%	Reb	Ast	Pts	Avg
Murray	2,579	.481	.748	484	142	1,220	15.4
Rogers	2,499	.456	.686	424	202	1,149	15.1
Austin*	2,266	.466	.669	557	175	1,055	13.5
Taylor	1,513	.476	.709	296	53	815	11.5
Piatkowski	1,740	.452	.824	236	85	760	11.3
Martin	2,299	.377	.848	164	331	841	10.3
Wright	2,067	.445	.659	606	55	623	9.0
Robinson	1,231	.389	.720	111	135	541	7.7
Richardson	1,252	.372	.698	96	226	289	4.2
Closs	740	.449	.597	168	19	232	4.0
Vrankovic	996	.425	.569	263	36	195	3.0

Coach—Bill Fitch

Los Angeles Lakers

	Min	FG%	FT%	Reb	Ast	Pts	Avg
O'Neal	2175	.584	.527	681	142	1,699	28.3
Jones	2910	.484	.765	302	246	1,349	16.9
Bryant	2056	.428	.794	242	199	1,220	15.4
Van Exel	2053	.419	.791	194	442	881	13.8
Fox	2709	.471	.743	358	276	983	12.0
Campbell	1784	.463	.693	455	78	816	10.1
Horry	2192	.476	.692	542	163	536	7.4
Fisher	1760	.434	.757	193	333	474	5.8
Blount	1029	.572	.500	298	37	253	3.6

Coach—Del Harris

Miami Heat

	Min	FG%	FT%	Reb	Ast	Pts	Avg
Mourning	1,939	.551	.665	558	52	1,115	19.2
Hardaway	3,031	.431	.781	299	672	1,528	18.9
Mashburn	1,729	.435	.797	236	132	723	15.1
Lenard	2,621	.425	.788	292	180	1,020	12.6
Barry*	1,600	.421	.858	171	153	631	10.9
Brown	2,362	.471	.766	635	103	707	9.6
Majerle	1,928	.419	.784	268	157	519	7.2
Strickland	847	.539	.720	213	26	349	6.8
Murdock	1,395	.422	.801	156	219	507	6.2
Mills	782	.393	.758	152	39	212	4.2
Askins	681	.320	.632	101	29	111	2.4

Coach—Pat Riley

Milwaukee Bucks

	Min	FG%	FT%	Reb	Ast	Pts	Avg
Robinson	2,294	.470	.808	307	158	1,308	23.4
Allen	3,287	.428	.875	405	356	1,602	19.5
Brandon	1,784	.464	.846	176	387	841	16.8
Gilliam	2,114	.484	.802	439	104	921	11.2
Hill	2,064	.498	.608	608	88	571	10.0
Johnson	2,261	.537	.601	685	59	649	8.0
Perry	1,752	.430	.844	108	230	591	7.3
Curry	1,978	.469	.835	98	137	543	6.6
Lang	692	.378	.772	153	16	152	2.7

Coach—Chris Ford

Minnesota Timberwolves

	Min	FG%	FT%	Reb	Ast	Pts	Avg
Gugliotta	1,582	.502	.821	356	167	823	20.1
Garnett	3,222	.491	.738	786	348	1,518	18.5
Marbury	3,112	.415	.731	230	704	1,450	17.7
Mitchell	2,239	.464	.832	385	107	1,000	12.3
Peeler*	1,193	.452	.766	123	137	469	12.3
Carr	1,165	.420	.848	155	85	504	9.9
Porter	1,786	.449	.856	168	271	777	9.5
Parks	1,703	.499	.651	437	53	558	7.1
Roberts	1,328	.495	.481	363	27	457	6.2
Hammonds	1,140	.516	.697	271	36	346	6.1
West	688	.374	.725	82	45	157	4.1

Coach—Flip Saunders

New Jersey Nets

	Min	FG%	FT%	Reb	Ast	Pts	Avg
Van Horn	2,325	.426	.846	408	106	1,219	19.7
Cassell	2,606	.441	.860	228	603	1,471	19.6
Kittles	2,814	.440	.808	362	176	1,328	17.2
Gill	2,733	.429	.688	391	200	1,087	13.4
Seikaly*	1,636	.432	.741	393	77	746	13.3
J. Williams	2,343	.498	.666	883	67	837	12.9
Gatling	1,359	.455	.600	334	53	656	11.5
Douglas	1,699	.495	.669	135	319	639	8.0
Evans*	893	.394	.807	137	55	321	4.5
Harris	671	.390	.745	52	42	191	3.8
Cage	1,201	.512	.556	308	32	106	1.3

Coach—John Calipari

New York Knickerbockers

	Min	FG%	FT%	Reb	Ast	Pts	Avg
Ewing	848	.504	.720	265	28	540	20.8
Houston	2,848	.447	.851	274	212	1,509	18.4
Johnson	2,412	.485	.756	401	150	1,087	15.5
Starks	2,188	.393	.787	230	219	1,059	12.9
Mills	2,183	.433	.804	408	133	776	9.7
Oakley	2,734	.440	.851	724	201	711	9.0
Ward	2,317	.455	.805	274	466	642	7.8
Cummings*	1,185	.467	.684	283	47	467	6.3
Childs	1,599	.421	.825	162	268	429	6.3
Williams	738	.503	.732	183	21	202	4.9
Dudley	858	.406	.446	275	21	157	3.1

Coach—Jeff Van Gundy

Orlando Magic

	Min	FG%	FT%	Reb	Ast	Pts	Avg
A. Hardaway	625	.377	.763	76	68	311	16.4
Anderson	1,701	.455	.638	297	119	890	15.3
Strong	1,638	.420	.781	427	51	736	12.7
Grant	2,803	.459	.678	618	172	921	12.1
Outlaw	2,953	.554	.575	637	216	783	9.5
Price	1,430	.431	.845	129	297	597	9.5
Armstrong	1,236	.411	.854	159	236	442	9.2
Harper	1,761	.417	.696	103	233	566	8.6
Schayes	1,272	.418	.807	242	44	406	5.5
Benoit*	1,123	.373	.824	203	25	420	5.5
Wilkins	1,252	.325	.704	90	78	380	5.3

Coach—Chuck Daly

Philadelphia 76ers

	Min	FG%	FT%	Reb	Ast	Pts	Avg
Iverson	3,150	.461	.729	296	494	1,758	22.0
Coleman	2,135	.411	.772	587	145	1,040	17.6
Smith*	2,344	.434	.775	471	94	1,155	14.6
Thomas	1,779	.447	.740	288	90	845	11.0
Ratliff*	2,447	.513	.701	547	57	809	9.9
Shaw*	1,530	.345	.692	215	261	372	6.3
McKie*	1,813	.365	.764	231	175	332	4.1
Williams	801	.437	.810	211	29	237	4.1
Davis	906	.447	.634	158	73	282	4.0
Snow*	918	.429	.690	81	177	209	3.3

Coach—Larry Brown

Phoenix Suns

	Min	FG%	FT%	Reb	Ast	Pts	Avg
Chapman	2,263	.427	.781	173	203	1,082	15.9
McDyess	2,441	.536	.702	613	106	1,225	15.1
Robinson	2,359	.479	.689	410	170	1,133	14.2
Manning	1,794	.516	.739	392	139	947	13.5
Kidd	3,118	.416	.799	510	745	954	11.6
Scott*	2,290	.397	.808	247	153	888	11.0
Johnson	1,290	.447	.871	164	245	476	9.5
Nash	1,664	.459	.860	160	262	691	9.1
McCloud	1,213	.405	.765	218	84	456	7.2
Bryant	1,110	.484	.768	244	46	291	4.2
Williams	1,333	.470	.699	312	49	255	3.6

Coach—Danny Ainge

Portland Trail Blazers

	Min	FG%	FT%	Reb	Ast	Pts	Avg
Rider	2,786	.423	.828	346	231	1,458	19.7
Stoudamire*	2,839	.411	.829	298	580	1,225	17.3
Sabonis	2,333	.493	.798	729	218	1,167	16.0
Wallace	2,896	.533	.662	478	195	1,124	14.6
Grant	1,921	.508	.750	555	86	737	12.1
Williams*	1,470	.386	.864	200	122	608	10.3
Augmon	1,445	.414	.603	235	88	403	5.7
O'Neal	808	.485	.506	201	17	269	4.5
Brunson	622	.348	.677	56	100	162	4.3
Cato	1,007	.428	.688	252	23	282	3.8

Coach—Mike Dunleavy

Sacramento Kings

	Min	FG%	FT%	Reb	Ast	Pts	Avg
Richmond	2,569	.445	.864	229	279	1,623	23.2
Williamson	2,819	.495	.630	446	230	1,401	17.7
Owens	2,348	.464	.589	582	219	818	10.5
Thorpe*	2,197	.471	.683	537	222	752	10.2
Funderburke	1,094	.490	.679	234	63	493	9.5
Polynice	1,458	.459	.452	439	107	550	7.9
Johnson	2,266	.371	.727	171	329	574	7.5
Abdul-Wahad	959	.403	.672	116	51	376	6.4
Dehere	1,410	.399	.798	106	196	489	6.4
Stewart	1,761	.480	.458	536	61	375	4.6
Hendrickson	737	.389	.825	143	41	163	3.4

Coach—Eddie Jordan

San Antonio Spurs

	Min	FG%	FT%	Reb	Ast	Pts	Avg
Robinson	2,457	.511	.735	775	199	1,574	21.6
Duncan	3,204	.549	.662	977	224	1,731	21.1
Johnson	2,674	.478	.726	150	591	766	10.2
Del Negro	1,721	.441	.796	152	183	513	9.5
Elliott	1,012	.403	.718	124	62	334	9.3
Jackson	2,226	.394	.797	210	156	722	8.8
Person	1,455	.359	.757	204	86	409	6.7
Williams	1,314	.448	.670	179	89	453	6.3
Perdue	1,491	.549	.526	535	57	394	5.0
Geary	685	.331	.500	67	74	152	2.5

Coach—Gregg Popovich

Seattle SuperSonics

	Min	FG%	FT%	Reb	Ast	Pts	Avg
Baker	2,944	.542	.591	656	152	1,574	19.2
Payton	3,145	.453	.744	376	679	1,571	19.2
Schrempf	2,742	.487	.844	554	341	1,232	15.8
Ellis	1,939	.497	.782	184	89	934	11.8
Hawkins	2,597	.440	.868	334	221	862	10.5
Perkins	1,675	.416	.789	255	113	580	7.2
Kersey	717	.416	.600	135	44	234	6.3
Anthony	1,021	.430	.663	111	205	419	5.2
Williams	757	.523	.776	147	14	296	4.6
McIlvaine	1,211	.453	.556	259	19	247	3.2

Coach—George Karl

Toronto Raptors

	Min	FG%	FT%	Reb	Ast	Pts	Avg
Christie	2,939	.428	.829	404	282	1,287	16.5
Wallace	2,361	.478	.717	373	110	1,147	14.0
Camby	2,002	.412	.611	466	111	765	12.1
Trent	1,360	.477	.679	338	72	630	11.7
Billups*	2,216	.374	.850	190	314	893	11.2
Brown	1,719	.438	.817	152	154	658	9.1
Slater	1,662	.460	.630	305	74	625	8.0
McGrady	1,179	.450	.712	269	98	451	7.0
Miller	1,628	.461	.604	400	196	401	6.3
Williams*	1,071	.443	.722	81	103	324	6.0

Coach—Darrell Walker, Butch Carter

Utah Jazz

	Min	FG%	FT%	Reb	Ast	Pts	Avg
Malone	3,030	.530	.761	834	316	2,190	27.0
Hornacek	2,460	.482	.885	270	349	1,139	14.2
Stockton	1,858	.528	.827	166	543	770	12.0
Russell	2,219	.430	.766	326	101	738	9.0
Anderson	1,602	.538	.735	227	89	681	8.3
Keefe	2,047	.540	.810	438	89	620	7.8
Eisley	1,726	.441	.852	166	346	633	7.7
Carr	1,086	.465	.776	131	48	378	5.7
Foster	1,446	.445	.770	273	51	441	5.7
Ostertag	1,288	.481	.479	374	25	297	4.7

Coach—Jerry Sloan

Vancouver Grizzlies

	Min	FG%	FT%	Reb	Ast	Pts	Avg
Abdur-Rahim	2,950	.485	.784	581	213	1,829	22.3
Reeves	2,527	.523	.706	585	155	1,207	16.3
Mack	1,414	.397	.805	133	101	616	10.8
Edwards	1,968	.439	.837	217	201	872	10.8
Daniels	1,956	.416	.659	143	334	579	7.8
Lynch	1,493	.481	.703	362	122	616	7.5
Massenburg	894	.479	.730	232	21	396	6.5
Smith*	1,053	.479	.631	306	88	251	5.2
Chilcutt	1,420	.435	.661	306	104	405	4.9
Mayberry	1,835	.375	.745	114	349	363	4.6
Hurley*	875	.391	.776	66	177	250	4.1

Coach—Brian Hill

Washington Wizards

	Min	FG%	FT%	Reb	Ast	Pts	Avg
Webber	2,809	.482	.589	674	273	1,555	21.9
Howard	2,559	.467	.721	449	208	1,184	18.5
Strickland	3,020	.434	.726	405	801	1,349	17.8
Murray	2,227	.446	.871	277	84	1,238	15.1
Cheaney	2,841	.457	.647	324	173	1,050	12.8
Whitney	1,073	.355	.915	115	196	422	5.1
Davis	1,705	.496	.580	480	30	323	4.4
Wallace	1,124	.518	.357	324	18	205	3.1
Grant	895	.383	.633	168	39	170	2.6
Ham	635	.529	.473	131	16	145	2.0

Coach—Bernie Bickerstaff

1998 NBA Player Draft, First-Round Picks

(held June 24, 1998)

	Team	Player, College
1.	L.A. Clippers	Michael Olowokandi, C, Pacific
2.	Vancouver	Mike Bibby, G, Arizona
3.	Denver	Raef LaFrentz, F, Kansas
4.	Toronto	Antawn Jamison[1], F, North Carolina
5.	Golden State	Vince Carter[2], G/F, North Carolina
6.	Dallas	Robert Traylor[3], F, Michigan
7.	Sacramento	Jason Williams, G, Florida
8.	Philadelphia	Larry Hughes, G, St. Louis
9.	Milwaukee	Dirk Nowitzki[4], F, DJK Wurzburg (Ger.)
10.	Boston	Paul Pierce, F, Kansas
11.	Detroit	Bonzi Wells, G/F, Ball State
12.	Orlando	Michael Doleac, C, Utah
13.	Orlando[5]	Keon Clark, C/F, UNLV
14.	Houston	Michael Dickerson, G, Arizona
15.	Orlando[6]	Matt Harpring, F, Georgia Tech
16.	Houston[7]	Bryce Drew, G, Valparaiso
17.	Minnesota	Radoslav Nesterovic, C, Kinder Bologna (Italy)
18.	Houston[8]	Mirsad Turkcan, F, Efes Pilsen (Turkey)
19.	Milwaukee[9]	Pat Garrity[10], F, Notre Dame
20.	Atlanta	Roshown McLeod, F, Duke
21.	Charlotte	Ricky Davis, F, Iowa
22.	L.A. Clippers[11]	Brian Skinner, C/F, Baylor
23.	Denver[12]	Tyronn Lue[13], G, Nebraska
24.	San Antonio	Felipe Lopez[14], G, St. John's
25.	Indiana	Al Harrington, F, St. Patrick's (High School), Elizabeth, NJ
26.	L.A. Lakers	Sam Jacobson, G/F, Minnesota
27.	Seattle	Vladimir Stepania, C, Union Olimpija Ljubljana (Slovenia)
28.	Chicago	Corey Benjamin, G, Oregon State
29.	Utah	Nazr Mohammed[15], C, Kentucky

(1) Traded to Golden State. (2) Traded to Toronto. (3) Traded to Milwaukee. (4) Traded to Dallas. (5) From Washington. (6) From New Jersey. (7) From New York through Toronto. (8) From Portland through Toronto. (9) From Cleveland. (10) Traded to Dallas, then to Phoenix. (11) From Miami. (12) From Phoenix. (13) Traded to L.A. Lakers. (14) Traded to Vancouver. (15) Traded to Philadelphia.

Number-One First-Round NBA Draft Picks, 1966-98

Year	Team	Player, college
1966	New York	Cazzie Russell, Michigan
1967	Detroit	Jimmy Walker, Providence
1968	Houston	Elvin Hayes, Houston
1969	Milwaukee	Lew Alcindor[1], UCLA
1970	Detroit	Bob Lanier, St. Bonaventure
1971	Cleveland	Austin Carr, Notre Dame
1972	Portland	LaRue Martin, Loyola-Chicago
1973	Philadelphia	Doug Collins, Illinois St.
1974	Portland	Bill Walton, UCLA
1975	Atlanta	David Thompson[2], N.C. State
1976	Houston	John Lucas, Maryland
1977	Milwaukee	Kent Benson, Indiana
1978	Portland	Mychal Thompson, Minnesota
1979	L.A. Lakers	Magic Johnson, Michigan St.
1980	Golden State	Joe Barry Carroll, Purdue
1981	Dallas	Mark Aguirre, DePaul
1982	L.A. Lakers	James Worthy, North Carolina
1983	Houston	Ralph Sampson, Virginia
1984	Houston	Akeem Olajuwon, Houston
1985	New York	Patrick Ewing, Georgetown
1986	Cleveland	Brad Daugherty, North Carolina
1987	San Antonio	David Robinson, Navy
1988	L.A. Clippers	Danny Manning, Kansas
1989	Sacramento	Pervis Ellison, Louisville
1990	New Jersey	Derrick Coleman, Syracuse
1991	Charlotte	Larry Johnson, UNLV
1992	Orlando	Shaquille O'Neal, LSU
1993	Orlando	Chris Webber[3], Michigan
1994	Milwaukee	Glenn Robinson, Purdue
1995	Golden State	Joe Smith, Maryland
1996	Philadelphia	Allen Iverson, Georgetown
1997	San Antonio	Tim Duncan, Wake Forest
1998	L.A. Clippers	Michael Olowokandi, Pacific

(1) Later Kareem Abdul-Jabbar. (2) Signed with Denver of the ABA. (3) Traded to Golden State.

All-Time NBA Statistical Leaders

(At the start of the 1998-98 season. *Player active in 1997-98 season.)

Scoring Average

(Minimum 400 games or 10,000 pts)

	G	Pts.	Avg
*Michael Jordan	930	29,277	31.5
Wilt Chamberlain	1,045	31,419	30.1
Elgin Baylor	846	23,149	27.4
*Shaquille O'Neal	406	11,054	27.2
Jerry West	932	25,192	27.0
Bob Pettit	792	20,880	26.4
*Karl Malone	1,061	27,782	26.2
George Gervin	791	20,708	26.2
Oscar Robertson	1,040	26,710	25.7
Dominique Wilkins	1,047	26,534	25.3

Field Goal Percentage

(Minimum 2,000 field goals made)

	FGA	FGM	Pct.
Artis Gilmore	9,570	5,732	.599
*Mark West	4,285	2,501	.584
*Shaquille O'Neal	7,660	4,430	.578
Steve Johnson	4,965	2,841	.572
Darryl Dawkins	6,079	3,477	.572
James Donaldson	5,442	3,105	.571
Jeff Ruland	3,734	2,105	.564
Kareem Abdul-Jabbar	28,307	15,837	.559
Kevin McHale	12,334	6,830	.554
Bobby Jones	6,199	3,412	.550
Dale Davis	3,757	2,067	.550

Free Throw Percentage

(Minimum 1,200 free throws made)

	FTA	FTM	Pct.
*Mark Price	2,362	2,135	.904
Rick Barry	4,243	3,818	.900
Calvin Murphy	3,864	3,445	.892
Scott Skiles	1,741	1,548	.889
Larry Bird	4,471	3,960	.886
Bill Sharman	3,559	3,143	.883
*Reggie Miller	5,037	4,416	.877
*Ricky Pierce	3,871	3,389	.875
*Jeff Hornacek	3,070	2,677	.872
Kiki Vandeweghe	3,997	3,484	.872

Points

Kareem Abdul-Jabbar	38,387
Wilt Chamberlain	31,419
*Michael Jordan	29,277
*Karl Malone	27,782
Moses Malone	27,409
Elvin Hayes	27,313
Oscar Robertson	26,710
Dominique Wilkins	26,534
John Havlicek	26,395
Alex English	25,613

Games Played

Robert Parish	1,611
Kareem Abdul-Jabbar	1,560
Moses Malone	1,329
*Buck Williams	1,307
Elvin Hayes	1,303
John Havlicek	1,270
Paul Silas	1,254
*Eddie Johnson	1,196
Alex English	1,193
James Edwards	1,168

Assists

*John Stockton	12,713
Magic Johnson	10,141
Oscar Robertson	9,887
Isiah Thomas	9,061
*Mark Jackson	7,538
Maurice Cheeks	7,392
Lenny Wilkens	7,211
Bob Cousy	6,955
Guy Rodgers	6,917
*Kevin Johnson	6,687

Field Goals Made

Kareem Abdul-Jabbar	15,837
Wilt Chamberlain	12,681
Elvin Hayes	10,976
*Michael Jordan	10,962
Alex English	10,659
John Havlicek	10,513
*Karl Malone	10,290
Dominique Wilkins	9,913
*Hakeem Olajuwon	9,706
Robert Parish	9,614

Rebounds

Wilt Chamberlain	23,924
Bill Russell	21,620
Kareem Abdul-Jabbar	17,440
Elvin Hayes	16,279
Moses Malone	16,212
Robert Parish	14,715
Nate Thurmond	14,464
Walt Bellamy	14,241
Wes Unseld	13,769
*Buck Williams	13,017

Basketball Hall of Fame, Springfield, MA

PLAYERS
Abdul-Jabbar, Kareem
Archibald, Nate
Arizin, Paul
Barlow, Thomas
Barry, Rick
Baylor, Elgin
Beckman, John
Bellamy, Walt
Belov, Sergei
Bing, Dave
*Bird, Larry
Blazejowski, Carol
Borgmann, Bennie
Bradley, Bill
Brennan, Joseph
Cervi, Al
Chamberlain, Wilt
Cooper, Charles
Cosic, Kresimir
Cousy, Bob
Cowens, Dave
Crawford, Joan
Cunningham, Billy
Curry, Denise
Davies, Bob
DeBernardi, Forrest
DeBusschere, Dave
Denhart, Dutch
Donovan, Anne
Endacott, Paul
English, Alex
Erving, Julius (Dr. J)
Foster, Bud
Frazier, Walt
Friedman, Max
Fulks, Joe
Gale, Lauren
Gallatin, Harry
Gates, Pop
Gervin, George
Gola, Tom
Goodrich, Gail
Greer, Hal
Gruenig, Ace
Hagan, Cliff
Hanson, Victor
Harris-Stewart, Luisa
Havlicek, John
Hawkins, Connie
Hayes, Elvin
*Haynes, Marques
Heinsohn, Tom
Holman, Nat
Houbregs, Bob
Howell, Bailey
Hyatt, Chuck
Issel, Dan
Jeannette, Buddy
Johnson, William
Johnston, Neil
Jones, K.C.
Jones, Sam
Krause, Moose
Kurland, Bob
Lanier, Bob
Lapchick, Joe
Lieberman-Cline, Nancy
Lovellette, Clyde
Lucas, Jerry
Luisetti, Hank
Macauley, Ed
Maravich, Pete
Martin, Slater
McCracken, Branch
McCracken, Jack
McDermott, Bobby
McGuire, Dick
Meyers, Ann
Mikan, George
Mikkelsen, Vern
Miller, Cheryl
Monroe, Earl
Murphy, Calvin
Murphy, Stretch
Page, Pat
Pettit, Bob
Phillip, Andy
Pollard, Jim
Ramsey, Frank
Reed, Willis
Risen, Arnie*
Robertson, Oscar
Roosma, John S.
Russell, Bill
Russell, Honey
Schayes, Adolph
Schmidt, Ernest
Schommer, John
Sedran, Barney
Semjonova, Uljana
Sharman, Bill
Steinmetz, Christian
Thompson, Cat
Thompson, David
Thurmond, Nate
Twyman, Jack
Unseld, Wes
Vandivier, Fuzzy
Wachter, Edward
Walton, Bill
Wanzer, Bobby
West, Jerry
White, Nera
Wilkens, Lenny
Wooden, John
Yardley, George

COACHES
Allen, Forrest (Phog)
Anderson, Harold
Auerbach, Red
Barry, Sam
Blood, Ernest
Cann, Howard
Carlson, Dr. H. C.
Carnesecca, Lou
Carnevale, Ben
Carril, Pete
Case, Everett
*Conradt, Jody
Crum, Denny
Daly, Chuck
Dean, Everett
Diaz-Miguel, Antonio
Diddle, Edgar
Drake, Bruce
Gaines, Clarence
Gardner, Jack
Gill, Slats
Gomelsky, Aleksandr
*Hannum, Alex
Harshman, Marv
Haskins, Don
Hickey, Edgar
Hobson, Howard
Holzman, Red
Iba, Hank
Julian, Alvin
Keaney, Frank
Keogan, George
Knight, Bob
Kundla, John
Lambert, Ward
Litwack, Harry
Loeffler, Kenneth
Lonborg, Dutch
McCutchan, Arad
McGuire, Al
McGuire, Frank
McLendon, John
Meanwell, Dr. W. E.
Meyer, Ray
Miller, Ralph
Newell, Pete
*Nikolic, Aleksandar
Ramsay, Jack
Rubini, Cesare
Rupp, Adolph
Sachs, Leonard
Shelton, Everett
Smith, Dean
Taylor, Fred
Wade, Margaret
Watts, Stan
*Wilkens, Lenny
Wooden, John
Woolpert, Phil

REFEREES
Enright, James
Hepbron, George
Hoyt, George
Kennedy, Matthew
Leith, Lloyd
Mihalik, Red
Nucatola, John
Quigley, Ernest
Shirley, J. Dallas
Strom, Earl
Tobey, David
Walsh, David

CONTRIBUTORS
Abbott, Senda B.
Bee, Clair
Brown, Walter
Bunn, John
Douglas, Bob
Duer, Al O.
Fagan, Cliff
Fisher, Harry
Fleisher, Larry
Gottlieb, Edward
Gulick, Dr. L. H.
Harrison, Lester
Hepp, Dr. Ferenc
Hickox, Edward
Hinkle, Tony
Irish, Ned
Jones, R. W.
Kennedy, Walter
Liston, Emil
Mokray, Bill
Morgan, Ralph
Morgenweck, Frank
Naismith, Dr. James
O'Brien, John
O'Brien, Larry
Olsen, Harold
Podoloff, Maurice
Porter, H. V.
Reid, William
Ripley, Elmer
St. John, Lynn
Saperstein, Abe
Schabinger, Arthur
Stagg, Amos Alonzo
Stankovich, Boris
Steitz, Edward
Taylor, Chuck
Teague, Bertha
Tower, Oswald
Trester, Arthur
Wells, Clifford
Wilke, Lou

TEAMS
First Team
Original Celtics
Buffalo Germans
NY Renaissance

* 1998 inductee

All-Time NBA Coaching Victories

(At the start of the 1998-99 season. *Active through 1997-98 season.)

Coach	W-L	Pct.
*Lenny Wilkens	1,120-908	.552
*Bill Fitch	944-1,106	.460
Red Auerbach	938-479	.662
Dick Motta	935-1,017	.479
*Pat Riley	914-387	.703
*Don Nelson	867-679	.561
Jack Ramsay	864-783	525
Cotton Fitzsimmons	832-775	.518
Gene Shue	784-861	.477
John MacLeod	707-657	.518
Red Holzman	696-604	.535
*Larry Brown	655-531	.552
*Jerry Sloan	639-379	.628
Doug Moe	628-529	.543
*Chuck Daly	605-420	.590
Alvin Attles	557-518	.518
*Mike Fratello	550-437	.557
*Del Harris	550-451	.549
*Phil Jackson	545-193	.738
K.C. Jones	522-252	.674
*George Karl	503-326	.607
Kevin Loughery	474-662	.417
Alex Hannum	471-412	.533
Billy Cunningham	454-196	.698
Larry Costello	430-300	.589
Tom Heinsohn	427-263	.619
John Kundla	423-302	.583
Rick Adelman	357-252	.586
Hubie Brown	341-410	.454
Bill Russell	341-290	.540
Bill Sharman	333-240	.581
Jim Lynam	328-392	.456

NBA Home Courts

Team	Name (built)	Capacity
Atlanta	Georgia Dome (1997)	21,570/34,821
	Georgia Tech (1956)	9,300
Boston	FleetCenter (1995)	18,624
Charlotte	Charlotte Coliseum (1988)	24,042
Chicago	United Center (1994)	21,711
Cleveland	Gund Arena (1994)	20,562
Dallas	Reunion Arena (1980)	18,042
Denver	McNichols Sports Arena (1975)	17,171
Detroit	Palace of Auburn Hills (1988)	22,076
Golden State	Arena in Oakland (1997)	19,200
Houston	Compaq Center (1975)	16,285
Indiana	Market Square Arena (1974)	16,530
L.A. Clippers	L.A. Memorial Sports Arena (1959)	16,021
	Arrowhead Pond of Anaheim (1992)	18,211
L.A. Lakers	The Great Western Forum (1967)	17,505
Miami	Miami Arena (1988)	15,200
Milwaukee	Bradley Center (1988)	18,717
Minnesota	Target Center (1990)	19,006
New Jersey	Continental Airlines Arena (1981)	20,049
New York	Madison Square Garden (1968)	19,763
Orlando	Orlando Arena (1989)	17,248
Philadelphia	First Union Center (1996)	20,444
Phoenix	America West Arena (1992)	19,023
Portland	The Rose Garden (1995)	19,980
Sacramento	ARCO Arena (1988)	17,317
San Antonio	Alamodome (1993)	20,557/34,215
Seattle	KeyArena (1995)	17,072
Toronto	SkyDome (1989)	20,125/35,000
	Air Canada Centre (to open Feb. 1999)	19,500
Utah	Delta Center (1991)	19,911
Vancouver	Bear Country at GM Place (1995)	19,193
Washington	MCI Center (1998)	20,674

WOMEN'S PROFESSIONAL BASKETBALL

Women's National Basketball Association

The Women's National Basketball Association (WNBA), generated even more enthusiasm in its second season, as attendance rose 12% from its inaugural season in 1997. On June 11, 1998, the season began with 10 teams, including the expansion Washington Mystics and Detroit Shock. The regular season ended Aug. 19, 1998, and on Sept. 1, the Houston Comets won the deciding game of the championship series against the Phoenix Mercury to repeat as WNBA champions.

The league has plans to expand yet again before the 1999 season. Teams were awarded to Orlando and Minnesota, as both entries surpassed the required 5,000 season-ticket deposits before the Sept. 1, 1998, deadline.

WNBA Final Standings, 1998 Season

Eastern Conference

	W	L	Pct	GB
Cleveland Rockers	20	10	.667	—
Charlotte Sting	18	12	.600	2
New York Liberty	18	12	.600	2
Detroit Shock	17	13	.567	3
Washington Mystics	3	27	.100	17

Western Conference

	W	L	Pct	GB
Houston Comets	27	3	.900	—
Phoenix Mercury	19	11	.633	8
Los Angeles Sparks	12	18	.400	15
Sacramento Monarchs	8	22	.267	19
Utah Starzz	8	22	.267	19

WNBA Playoff Semifinals

Houston defeated Charlotte 2 games to 0
Phoenix defeated Cleveland 2 games to 1

WNBA Championship

Houston defeated Phoenix 2 games to 1 [51-54, 74-69 (OT), 80-71]

WNBA Individual Highs and Awards in 1998

Most minutes played — 1,080: Ticha Penicheiro, Sacramento.
Most points — 680: Cynthia Cooper, Houston.
Most points per game — 22.7: Cynthia Cooper, Houston.
Highest field goal percentage — .547: Isabelle Fijalkowski, Cleveland.
Highest 3-point field goal percentage — .452: Eva Nemcova, Cleveland.
Highest free throw percentage — .923: Sandy Brondello, Detroit.
Most rebounds — 301: Cindy Brown, Detroit.
Most rebounds per game — 10.2: Lisa Leslie, Los Angeles.
Most assists — 224: Ticha Penicheiro, Sacramento.
Most assists per game — 7.5: Ticha Penicheiro, Sacramento.
Most steals — 100: Teresa Weatherspoon, New York.
Most blocked shots — 114: Malgorzata Dydek, Utah.

MVP — Cynthia Cooper, Houston.
Coach of the year — Van Chancellor, Houston.
Rookie of the year — Tracy Reid, Charlotte.
Defensive player of the year — Teresa Weatherspoon, New York.
MVP, Championship series — Cynthia Cooper, Houston.

American Basketball League

The ABL's 1997-98 season opened on Oct. 12, 1997, with 9 teams, including the expansion Long Beach StingRays, playing a 44-game schedule. In March, the Columbus Quest erased a 2-games-to-none deficit to defeat the Long Beach StingRays 3 games to 2 and capture their 2d straight championship (Mar. 15) in only the 2d year of the league's existence. Valerie Still of Columbus won her 2d Championship Series MVP award. Two teams, the Atlanta Glory and Long Beach StingRays, disbanded before the start of the 1998-99 season.

The ABL was scheduled to open its third season on Nov. 5, 1998, with 9 teams, including two expansion franchises, the Chicago Condors and the Nashville Noise. The regular season was scheduled to end on Mar. 25, 1999.

ABL Final Standings, 1997-98 Season

East

	W	L	Pct	GB
Columbus Quest	36	8	.818	—
New England Blizzard	24	20	.545	12
Atlanta Glory	15	29	.341	21
Philadelphia Rage	13	31	.295	23

West

	W	L	Pct	GB
Portland Power	27	17	.610	—
Long Beach StingRays	26	18	.591	1
San Jose Lasers	21	23	.477	6
Colorado Xplosion	21	23	.477	6
Seattle Reign	15	29	.341	12

ABL First Round Playoffs

San Jose defeated New England 2 games to 0; Long Beach defeated Colorado 2 games to 1

ABL Playoff Semifinals

Long Beach defeated Portland 2 games to 0; Columbus defeated San Jose 2 games to 0

ABL Championship Series

Columbus defeated Long Beach 3 games to 2

ABL Individual Highs and Awards in 1997-98

Most points — 964: Natalie Williams, Portland.
Highest field goal percentage — .580: Clarisse Machanguana, San Jose.
Highest 3-point field goal percentage — .466: Crystal Robinson, Colorado.
Highest free throw percentage — .897: Shelley Sandie, San Jose.
Most rebounds — 508: Natalie Williams, Portland.
Most assists — 293: Teresa Edwards, Atlanta.
Most steals — 138: Yolanda Griffith, Long Beach.
Most blocked shots — 64: Kara Wolters, New England.
MVP — Natalie Williams, Portland.
Coach of the year — Linn Dunn, Portland.
Rookie of the year — Shalonda Enis, Seattle.
Defensive player of the year — Yolanda Griffith, Long Beach.
MVP, Championship series — Valerie Still, Columbus.

COLLEGE BASKETBALL

Final NCAA Division I Conference Standing, 1997-98

(*conference tournament champion)

America East

	Conference W	Conference L	Full Season W	Full Season L
Delaware*	12	6	20	10
Boston U.	12	6	19	11
Hofstra	11	7	19	12
Vermont	11	7	16	11
Hartford	11	7	15	12
Drexel	10	8	13	15
Northeastern	9	9	14	14
New Hampshire	6	12	10	17
Towson	4	14	8	20
Maine	4	14	7	20

Atlantic Coast

	Conference W	Conference L	Full Season W	Full Season L
Duke	15	1	32	4
North Carolina*	13	3	34	4
Maryland	10	6	21	11
Clemson	7	9	18	14
Wake Forest	7	9	16	14
Georgia Tech	6	10	19	14
Florida St.	6	10	18	14
North Carolina St.	5	11	17	15
Virginia	3	13	11	19

Atlantic 10

	Conference W	Conference L	Full Season W	Full Season L
Eastern Division				
Temple	13	3	21	9
Rhode Island	12	4	25	9
Massachusetts	12	4	21	11
St. Bonaventure	6	10	17	15
St. Joseph's (PA)	3	13	11	17
Fordham	2	14	6	21
Western Division				
Xavier (OH)*	11	5	22	8
George Washington	11	5	24	9
Dayton	11	5	21	12
Virginia Tech	5	11	10	17
Duquesne	5	11	11	19
La Salle	5	11	9	18

Big East

	Conference W	Conference L	Full Season W	Full Season L
Big East 7				
Syracuse	12	6	26	9
Miami (FL)	11	7	18	10
Seton Hall	9	9	15	15
Providence	7	11	13	16
Georgetown	6	12	16	15
Rutgers	6	12	14	15
Pittsburgh	6	12	11	16
Big East 6				
Connecticut*	15	3	32	5
St. John's (NY)	13	5	22	10
West Virginia	11	7	24	9
Villanova	8	10	12	17
Notre Dame	7	11	13	14
Boston College	6	12	15	16

Big Sky

	Conference W	Conference L	Full Season W	Full Season L
Northern Arizona*	13	3	21	8
Weber St.	12	4	14	13
E. Washington	10	6	16	11
Portland St.[2]	10	6	15	12
Montana St.	9	7	19	11
Montana	9	7	16	14
Cal. St. Northridge	7	9	12	16
Idaho St.	2	14	6	20
Cal. St. Sacramento	0	16	1	25

Big South

	Conference W	Conference L	Full Season W	Full Season L
N.C.-Asheville	11	1	19	9
Radford*	10	2	20	10
Univ.of Maryland Balt. County	6	6	14	14
Liberty	5	7	11	17
Coastal Carolina	4	8	8	19
Winthrop	4	8	7	20
Charleston So.	2	10	5	22

Big Ten

	Conference W	Conference L	Full Season W	Full Season L
Michigan St.	13	3	22	8
Illinois	13	3	23	10
Purdue	12	4	28	8
Michigan*	11	5	25	9
Iowa	9	7	20	11
Indiana	9	7	20	12
Penn St.	8	8	19	13
Minnesota	6	10	20	15
Wisconsin	3	13	12	19
Northwestern	3	13	10	17
Ohio St.	1	15	8	22

Big 12

	Conference W	Conference L	Full Season W	Full Season L
Kansas*	15	1	35	4
Oklahoma St.	11	5	22	7
Oklahoma	11	5	22	11
Nebraska	10	6	20	12
Missouri	8	8	17	15
Baylor	8	8	14	14
Kansas St.	7	9	17	12
Colorado	7	9	13	14
Texas Tech	7	9	13	14
Texas	6	10	14	17
Iowa St.	5	11	12	18
Texas A&M	1	15	7	20

Big West

	Conference W	Conference L	Full Season W	Full Season L
Eastern Division				
Utah St.*	13	3	25	8
Nevada	11	5	16	12
Boise St.	9	7	17	13
Idaho	9	7	15	12
New Mexico St.	8	8	18	12
North Texas	4	12	5	21
Western Division				
Pacific (CA)	14	2	23	10
Cal. Poly SLO	7	9	14	14
Cal. St. Fullerton	6	10	12	16
UC Irvine	6	10	9	18
Long Beach St.	5	11	10	19
UC Santa Barbara	4	12	7	19

Colonial Athletic Association

	Conference W	Conference L	Full Season W	Full Season L
William & Mary	13	3	20	7
N.C.-Wilmington	13	3	20	11
Richmond*	12	4	23	8
Old Dominion	8	8	12	16
James Madison	6	10	11	16
George Mason	6	10	9	18
East Carolina	5	11	10	17
American	5	11	9	19
Va. Commonwealth	4	12	9	19

Conference USA

	Conference W	Conference L	Full Season W	Full Season L
American				
Cincinnati*	14	2	27	6
N.C.-Charlotte	13	3	20	11
St. Louis	11	5	22	11
Marquette	8	8	20	11
Louisville	5	11	12	20
DePaul	3	13	7	23
National				
Memphis	12	4	17	12
Ala.-Birmingham	10	6	21	12
S. Mississippi	9	7	22	11
South Florida	7	9	17	13
Houston	2	14	9	20
Tulane	2	14	7	22

Ivy Group[1]

	Conference W	Conference L	Full Season W	Full Season L
Princeton	13	0	27	2
Pennsylvania	10	3	17	12
Yale	7	7	12	14
Harvard	6	8	13	13
Columbia	6	8	11	15
Cornell	6	8	9	17
Dartmouth	4	10	7	19
Brown	3	11	6	20

Metro Atlantic Athletic

	Conference W	Conference L	Full Season W	Full Season L
Iona*	15	3	27	6
Rider	12	6	18	10
Siena	10	8	17	12
Niagara	10	8	14	13
Canisius	9	9	13	14
Loyola (MD)	9	9	12	16
Fairfield	7	11	12	15
Manhattan	7	11	12	17
Marist	7	11	11	17
St. Peter's	4	14	8	19

Mid-American

	Conference W	Conference L	Full Season W	Full Season L
East				
Akron	13	5	17	10
Miami (OH)	9	9	17	12
Kent	9	9	13	17
Marshall	7	11	11	16
Bowling Green	7	11	10	16
Ohio	3	15	5	21
West				
Ball St.	14	4	21	8
Western Michigan	14	4	21	8
Eastern Michigan*	13	5	20	10
Toledo	10	8	15	12
Northern Illinois	6	12	10	16
Central Michigan	3	15	5	21

Mid-Continent

	Conference W	Conference L	Full Season W	Full Season L
Valparaiso*	13	3	23	10
Oral Roberts	12	4	19	12
Youngstown St.	11	5	20	9
Western Illinois	11	5	16	11
Buffalo	9	7	15	13
Mo.-Kansas City	7	9	9	18
Southern Utah	4	12	7	20
Northeastern Illinois	3	13	6	19
Chicago St.	2	14	2	25

Mid-Eastern Athletic

	Conference W	Conference L	Full Season W	Full Season L
Coppin St.	17	1	21	8
South Carolina St.*	16	2	22	8
Hampton	11	7	14	12
Morgan St.	11	7	12	16
Florida A&M	8	10	11	17
Delaware St.	7	11	9	18
Md.-East. Shore	7	11	9	18
North Carolina A&T	7	11	8	19
Howard	5	13	8	20
Bethune-Cookman	1	17	1	26
Norfolk St.[3]	—	—	6	21

Midwestern Collegiate

	Conference W	Conference L	Full Season W	Full Season L
Detroit	12	2	25	6
Ill.-Chicago	12	2	22	6
Butler*	8	6	22	11
Wis.-Green Bay	7	7	17	12
Loyola (IL)	6	8	15	15
Cleveland St.	6	8	12	15
Wright St.	3	11	10	18
Wis.-Milwaukee	2	12	3	24

Missouri Valley

	Conference W	Conference L	Full Season W	Full Season L
Illinois St.*	16	2	25	6
Creighton	12	6	18	10
Wichita St.	11	7	16	15
Southwest Mo. St.	11	7	16	16
Indiana St.	10	8	16	11
Bradley	9	9	15	14
Evansville	9	9	15	15
Southern Illinois	8	10	14	18
Northern Iowa	4	14	10	17
Drake	0	18	3	24

Northeast

	Conference W	Conference L	Full Season W	Full Season L
LIU-Brooklyn	14	2	21	11
Fairleigh Dickinson*	13	3	23	7
St. Francis (PA)	10	6	17	10
St. Francis (NY)	10	6	15	12
Mt. St. Mary's (MD)	8	8	13	15
Wagner	7	9	13	16
Robert Morris	4	12	8	19
Central Conn. St.	3	13	4	22
Monmouth (NJ)	3	13	4	23

Ohio Valley

	Conference W	Conference L	Full Season W	Full Season L
Murray St.*	16	2	29	4
Eastern Illinois	13	5	16	11
Middle Tenn. St.	12	6	19	9
Austin Peay	11	7	17	11
Southeast Mo. St.	10	8	14	13
Tennessee St.	8	10	13	16
Eastern Kentucky	8	10	10	17
Tennessee Tech.	5	13	9	21
Tennessee-Martin	5	13	7	20
Morehead St.	2	16	3	23

Pacific-10[1]

	Conference W	Conference L	Full Season W	Full Season L
Arizona	17	1	30	5
Stanford	15	3	30	5
UCLA	12	6	24	9
Washington	11	7	20	10
Arizona St.	8	10	18	14
Oregon	8	10	13	14
California	8	10	12	15
USC	5	13	9	19
Oregon St.	3	15	13	17
Washington St.	3	15	10	19

Patriot League

	Conference W	Conference L	Full Season W	Full Season L
Lafayette	10	2	19	9
Navy*	10	2	19	11
Bucknell	8	4	13	15
Colgate	5	7	10	18
Lehigh	4	8	10	17
Holy Cross	3	9	7	20
Army	2	10	8	19

Southeastern

	Conference W	Conference L	Full Season W	Full Season L
Eastern Division				
Kentucky*	14	2	35	4
South Carolina	11	5	23	8
Tennessee	9	7	20	9
Vanderbilt	7	9	20	13
Georgia	7	9	20	15
Florida	6	10	14	15
Western Division				
Mississippi	12	4	22	7
Arkansas	11	5	24	9
Auburn	7	9	16	14
Alabama	6	10	15	16
Mississippi St.	4	12	15	15
LSU	2	14	9	18

Southern

	Conference W	Conference L	Full Season W	Full Season L
North				
Appalachian St.	13	2	21	8
Davidson*	13	2	20	10
VMI	8	7	14	13
Western Carolina	6	9	12	15
East Tennessee St.	6	9	11	16
N.C.-Greensboro	6	9	9	19
South				
Tenn.-Chattanooga	7	7	13	15
Citadel	6	8	15	13
Wofford	6	8	9	18
Furman	5	9	9	20
Georgia Southern	4	10	10	18

Southland

	Conference W	Conference L	Full Season W	Full Season L
Nicholls St.*	15	1	19	10
Southwest Tex. St.	10	6	17	11
Texas-San Antonio	10	6	16	11
Northwestern St.	10	6	13	14
Northeast Lousiana	8	8	13	16
Texas-Arlington	8	8	13	16
Sam Houston St.	7	9	9	17
Stephen F. Austin	6	10	10	16
McNeese St.	4	12	7	19
Southeastern La.	2	14	6	20

Southwestern Athletic

	Conference W	Conference L	Full Season W	Full Season L
Texas Southern	12	4	15	16
Jackson St.	11	5	14	13
Grambling	10	6	16	12
Southern University	10	6	14	13
Alcorn St.	8	8	12	15
Prairie View*	6	10	13	17
Alabama St.	6	10	11	17
Mississippi Val.	6	10	6	21
Arkansas-Pine Bluff[2]	3	13	4	23

Sun Belt

	Conference W	Conference L	Full Season W	Full Season L
South Alabama*	14	4	21	7
Arkansas St.	14	4	20	9
Southwestern La.	12	6	18	13
Ark.-Little Rock	10	8	15	13
New Orleans	9	9	15	12
Louisiana Tech.	9	9	12	15
Lamar	7	11	15	14
Western Kentucky	6	12	10	19
Jacksonville	6	12	8	19
Tex.-Pan American	3	15	3	24

Trans America Athletic

	Conference W	Conference L	Full Season W	Full Season L
East				
Charleston (SC)*	14	2	24	6
Florida Intl.	13	3	21	8
Central Florida	11	5	17	11
Stetson	8	8	11	15
Florida Atlantic	5	11	5	22
Campbell	4	12	10	17
West				
Georgia St.	11	5	16	12
Samford	9	7	14	13
Centenary (LA)	8	8	10	20
Jacksonville St.	6	10	12	14
Troy St.	5	11	7	20
Mercer	2	14	5	21

West Coast

	Conference W	Conference L	Full Season W	Full Season L
Gonzaga	10	4	24	10
Pepperdine	9	5	17	10
Santa Clara	8	6	18	10
San Francisco*	7	7	19	11
Portland	7	7	14	13
St. Mary's (CA)	7	7	11	15
San Diego	5	9	14	14
Loyola Marymount	3	11	7	20

Western Athletic

	Conference W	Conference L	Full Season W	Full Season L
Pacific				
Texas Christian	14	0	27	6
Fresno St.	10	4	21	13
Tulsa	9	5	19	12
Hawaii	8	6	21	9
Southern Methodist	6	8	18	10
San Diego St.	5	9	13	15
Rice	3	11	6	22
San Jose St.	1	13	3	23
Mountain				
Utah	12	2	30	4
New Mexico	11	3	24	8
Wyoming	9	5	19	9
Colorado St.	8	6	20	9
UNLV*	7	7	20	13
Brigham Young	4	10	9	21
UTEP	3	11	12	14
Air Force	2	12	10	16

(1) Conference does not hold a tournament. (2) Not Division I. (3) First year as Division I; not eligible for conference tournament.

All-Time Winningest College Teams by Percentage

School	Years	Won	Lost	Pct.
Kentucky	95	1,720	529	.765
North Carolina	88	1,709	599	.740
UNLV	40	831	307	.730
Kansas	100	1,665	714	.700
UCLA	79	1,423	612	.699
St. John's (NY)	91	1,554	706	.688
Syracuse	97	1,477	692	.681
Duke	93	1,548	753	.673
Western Kentucky	79	1,366	669	.671
Arkansas	75	1,292	671	.658
Utah	90	1,376	732	.653
Indiana	98	1,430	767	.651
Louisville	84	1,337	716	.651
Temple	102	1,496	813	.648
Notre Dame	93	1,427	776	.648
DePaul	75	1,182	641	.648
Purdue	100	1,383	758	.646
Illinois	93	1,344	746	.643
New Orleans	29	530	294	.643
Weber State	36	654	364	.642

Major College Basketball Tournaments

The National Invitation Tournament (NIT), first played in 1938, is the nation's oldest basketball tournament. The first National Collegiate Athletic Association (NCAA) national championship tournament was played a year later. Selections for both tournaments are made in Mar., with the NCAA selecting first from among the top Division I teams.

National Invitation Tournament Champions

Year	Champion
1938	Temple
1939	Long Island Univ.
1940	Colorado
1941	Long Island Univ.
1942	West Virginia
1943	St. John's
1944	St. John's
1945	De Paul
1946	Kentucky
1947	Utah
1948	St. Louis
1949	San Francisco
1950	CCNY
1951	Brigham Young
1952	LaSalle
1953	Seton Hall
1954	Holy Cross
1955	Duquesne
1956	Louisville
1957	Bradley
1958	Xavier (Ohio)
1959	St. John's
1960	Bradley
1961	Providence
1962	Dayton
1963	Providence
1964	Bradley
1965	St. John's
1966	Brigham Young
1967	Southern Illinois
1968	Dayton
1969	Temple
1970	Marquette
1971	North Carolina
1972	Maryland
1973	Virginia Tech
1974	Purdue
1975	Princeton
1976	Kentucky
1977	St. Bonaventure
1978	Texas
1979	Indiana
1980	Virginia
1981	Tulsa
1982	Bradley
1983	Fresno State
1984	Michigan
1985	UCLA
1986	Ohio State
1987	Southern Mississippi
1988	Connecticut
1989	St. John's
1990	Vanderbilt
1991	Stanford
1992	Virginia
1993	Minnesota
1994	Villanova
1995	Virginia Tech
1996	Nebraska
1997	Michigan
1998	Minnesota

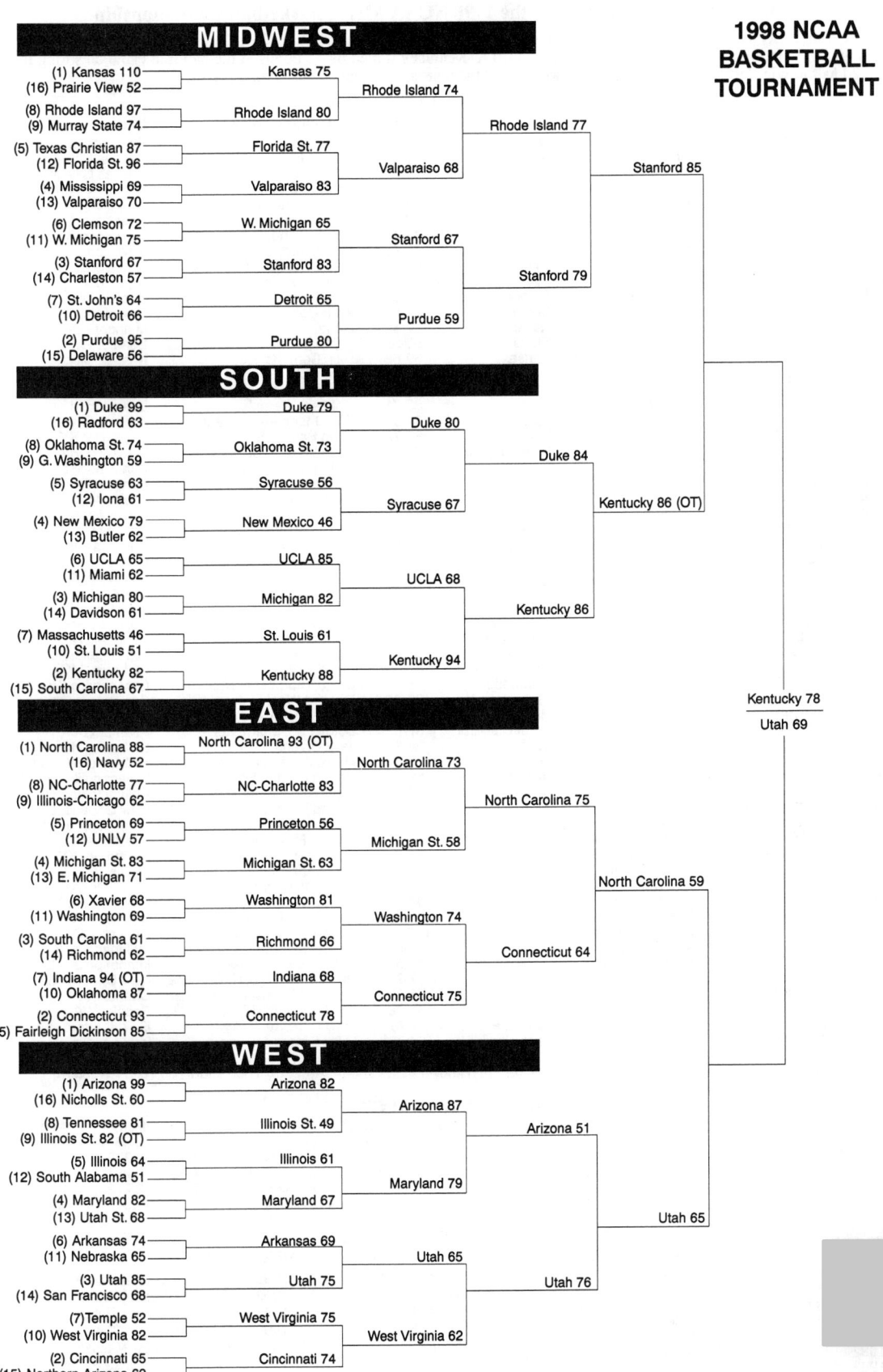

1998 NCAA BASKETBALL TOURNAMENT

MIDWEST

First round
- (1) Kansas 110, (16) Prairie View 52
- (8) Rhode Island 97, (9) Murray State 74
- (5) Texas Christian 87, (12) Florida St. 96
- (4) Mississippi 69, (13) Valparaiso 70
- (6) Clemson 72, (11) W. Michigan 75
- (3) Stanford 67, (14) Charleston 57
- (7) St. John's 64, (10) Detroit 66
- (2) Purdue 95, (15) Delaware 56

Second round
- Kansas 75, Rhode Island 80
- Florida St. 77, Valparaiso 83
- W. Michigan 65, Stanford 83
- Detroit 65, Purdue 80

Regional semifinals
- Rhode Island 74, Valparaiso 68
- Stanford 67, Purdue 59

Regional final
- Rhode Island 77, Stanford 79

SOUTH

First round
- (1) Duke 99, (16) Radford 63
- (8) Oklahoma St. 74, (9) G. Washington 59
- (5) Syracuse 63, (12) Iona 61
- (4) New Mexico 79, (13) Butler 62
- (6) UCLA 65, (11) Miami 62
- (3) Michigan 80, (14) Davidson 61
- (7) Massachusetts 46, (10) St. Louis 51
- (2) Kentucky 82, (15) South Carolina 67

Second round
- Duke 79, Oklahoma St. 73
- Syracuse 56, New Mexico 46
- UCLA 85, Michigan 82
- St. Louis 61, Kentucky 88

Regional semifinals
- Duke 80, Syracuse 67
- UCLA 68, Kentucky 94

Regional final
- Duke 84, Kentucky 86

EAST

First round
- (1) North Carolina 88, (16) Navy 52
- (8) NC-Charlotte 77, (9) Illinois-Chicago 62
- (5) Princeton 69, (12) UNLV 57
- (4) Michigan St. 83, (13) E. Michigan 71
- (6) Xavier 68, (11) Washington 69
- (3) South Carolina 61, (14) Richmond 62
- (7) Indiana 94 (OT), (10) Oklahoma 87
- (2) Connecticut 93, (15) Fairleigh Dickinson 85

Second round
- North Carolina 93 (OT), NC-Charlotte 83
- Princeton 56, Michigan St. 63
- Washington 81, Richmond 66
- Indiana 68, Connecticut 78

Regional semifinals
- North Carolina 73, Michigan St. 58
- Washington 74, Connecticut 75

Regional final
- North Carolina 75, Connecticut 64

WEST

First round
- (1) Arizona 99, (16) Nicholls St. 60
- (8) Tennessee 81, (9) Illinois St. 82 (OT)
- (5) Illinois 64, (12) South Alabama 51
- (4) Maryland 82, (13) Utah St. 68
- (6) Arkansas 74, (11) Nebraska 65
- (3) Utah 85, (14) San Francisco 68
- (7) Temple 52, (10) West Virginia 82
- (2) Cincinnati 65, (15) Northern Arizona 62

Second round
- Arizona 82, Illinois St. 49
- Illinois 61, Maryland 67
- Arkansas 69, Utah 75
- West Virginia 75, Cincinnati 74

Regional semifinals
- Arizona 87, Maryland 79
- Utah 65, West Virginia 62

Regional final
- Arizona 51, Utah 76

Final Four

Semifinals
- Stanford 85, Kentucky 86 (OT)
- North Carolina 59, Utah 65

Championship
- Kentucky 78
- Utah 69

Kentucky Defeats Utah to Win the 1998 NCAA Men's Basketball Championship

The University of Kentucky Wildcats defeated the Utah Utes, 78-69, to capture their 2nd NCAA men's basketball championship in three years, Mar. 30, at San Antonio, TX. Kentucky trailed by 10 points at the half, but came on strong in the 2d half to win. Jeff Sheppard of Kentucky was named the tournament's most outstanding player.

NCAA Division I Champions

Year	Champion	Coach	Final opponent	Score	Outstanding player	Site
1939	Oregon	Howard Hobson	Ohio St.	46-33	None	Evanston, IL
1940	Indiana	Branch McCracken	Kansas	60-42	Marvin Huffman, Indiana	Kansas City, MO
1941	Wisconsin	Harold Foster	Washington St.	39-34	John Kotz, Wisconsin	Kansas City, MO
1942	Stanford	Everett Dean	Dartmouth	53-38	Howard Dallmar, Stanford	Kansas City, MO
1943	Wyoming	Everett Shelton	Georgetown	46-34	Ken Sailors, Wyoming	New York, NY
1944	Utah	Vadal Peterson	Dartmouth	42-40[1]	Arnold Ferrin, Utah	New York, NY
1945	Oklahoma St.[2]	Henry Iba	NYU	49-45	Bob Kurland, Oklahoma St.	New York, NY
1946	Oklahoma St.[2]	Henry Iba	North Carolina	43-40	Bob Kurland, Oklahoma St.	New York, NY
1947	Holy Cross	Alvin Julian	Oklahoma	58-47	George Kaftan, Holy Cross	New York, NY
1948	Kentucky	Adolph Rupp	Baylor	58-42	Alex Groza, Kentucky	New York, NY
1949	Kentucky	Adolph Rupp	Oklahoma St.	46-36	Alex Groza, Kentucky	Seattle, WA
1950	CCNY	Nat Holman	Bradley	71-68	Irwin Dambrot, CCNY	New York, NY
1951	Kentucky	Adolph Rupp	Kansas St.	68-58	None	Minneapolis, MN
1952	Kansas	Forrest Allen	St. John's	80-63	Clyde Lovellette, Kansas	Seattle, WA
1953	Indiana	Branch McCracken	Kansas	69-68	B.H. Born, Kansas	Kansas City, MO
1954	La Salle	Kenneth Loeffler	Bradley	92-76	Tom Gola, La Salle	Kansas City, MO
1955	San Francisco	Phil Woolpert	LaSalle	77-63	Bill Russell, San Francisco	Kansas City, MO
1956	San Francisco	Phil Woolpert	Iowa	83-71	Hal Lear, Temple	Evanston, IL
1957	North Carolina	Frank McGuire	Kansas	54-53[1]	Wilt Chamberlain, Kansas	Kansas City, MO
1958	Kentucky	Adolph Rupp	Seattle	84-72	Elgin Baylor, Seattle	Louisville, KY
1959	California	Pete Newell	West Virginia	71-70	Jerry West, West Virginia	Louisville, KY
1960	Ohio St.	Fred Taylor	California	75-55	Jerry Lucas, Ohio St.	San Francisco, CA
1961	Cincinnati	Edwin Jucker	Ohio St.	70-65[1]	Jerry Lucas, Ohio St.	Kansas City, MO
1962	Cincinnati	Edwin Jucker	Ohio St.	71-59	Paul Hogue, Cincinnati	Louisville, KY
1963	Loyola (IL)	George Ireland	Cincinnati	60-58[1]	Art Heyman, Duke	Louisville, KY
1964	UCLA	John Wooden	Duke	98-83	Walt Hazzard, UCLA	Kansas City, MO
1965	UCLA	John Wooden	Michigan	91-80	Bill Bradley, Princeton	Portland, OR
1966	Texas-El Paso[3]	Don Haskins	Kentucky	72-65	Jerry Chambers, Utah	College Park, MD
1967	UCLA	John Wooden	Dayton	79-64	Lew Alcindor, UCLA	Louisville, KY
1968	UCLA	John Wooden	North Carolina	78-55	Lew Alcindor, UCLA	Los Angeles, CA
1969	UCLA	John Wooden	Purdue	92-72	Lew Alcindor, UCLA	Louisville, KY
1970	UCLA	John Wooden	Jacksonville	80-69	Sidney Wicks, UCLA	College Park, MD
1971	UCLA	John Wooden	Villanova*	68-62	Howard Porter, Villanova*	Houston, TX
1972	UCLA	John Wooden	Florida St.	81-76	Bill Walton, UCLA	Los Angeles, CA
1973	UCLA	John Wooden	Memphis St.	87-66	Bill Walton, UCLA	St. Louis, MO
1974	North Carolina St.	Norm Sloan	Marquette	76-64	David Thompson, N.C. St.	Greensboro, NC
1975	UCLA	John Wooden	Kentucky	92-85	Richard Washington, UCLA	San Diego, CA
1976	Indiana	Bob Knight	Michigan	86-68	Kent Benson, Indiana	Philadelphia, PA
1977	Marquette	Al McGuire	North Carolina	67-59	Butch Lee, Marquette	Atlanta, GA
1978	Kentucky	Joe Hall	Duke	94-88	Jack Givens, Kentucky	St. Louis, MO
1979	Michigan St.	Jud Heathcote	Indiana St.	75-64	Magic Johnson, Michigan St.	Salt Lake City, UT
1980	Louisville	Denny Crum	UCLA*	59-54	Darrell Griffith, Louisville	Indianapolis, IN
1981	Indiana	Bob Knight	North Carolina	63-50	Isiah Thomas, Indiana	Philadelphia, PA
1982	North Carolina	Dean Smith	Georgetown	63-62	James Worthy, N. Carolina	New Orleans, LA
1983	North Carolina St.	Jim Valvano	Houston	54-52	Hakeem Olajuwon, Houston	Albuquerque, NM
1984	Georgetown	John Thompson	Houston	84-75	Patrick Ewing, Georgetown	Seattle, WA
1985	Villanova	Rollie Massimino	Georgetown	66-64	Ed Pinckney, Villanova	Lexington, KY
1986	Louisville	Denny Crum	Duke	72-69	Pervis Ellison, Louisville	Dallas, TX
1987	Indiana	Bob Knight	Syracuse	74-73	Keith Smart, Indiana	New Orleans, LA
1988	Kansas	Larry Brown	Oklahoma	83-79	Danny Manning, Kansas	Kansas City, MO
1989	Michigan	Steve Fisher	Seton Hall	80-79[1]	Glen Rice, Michigan	Seattle, WA
1990	UNLV	Jerry Tarkanian	Duke	103-73	Anderson Hunt, UNLV	Denver, CO
1991	Duke	Mike Krzyzewski	Kansas	72-65	Christian Laettner, Duke	Indianapolis, IN
1992	Duke	Mike Krzyzewski	Michigan	71-51	Bobby Hurley, Duke	Minneapolis, MN
1993	North Carolina	Dean Smith	Michigan	77-71	Donald Williams, N. Carolina	New Orleans, LA
1994	Arkansas	Nolan Richardson	Duke	76-72	Corliss Williamson, Arkansas	Charlotte, NC
1995	UCLA	Jim Harrick	Arkansas	89-78	Ed O'Bannon, UCLA	Seattle, WA
1996	Kentucky	Rick Pitino	Syracuse	76-67	Tony Delk, Kentucky	E. Rutherford, NJ
1997	Arizona	Lute Olson	Kentucky	84-79[1]	Miles Simon, Arizona	Indianapolis, IN
1998	Kentucky	Tubby Smith	Utah	78-69	Jeff Sheppard, Kentucky	San Antonio, TX

*Declared ineligible after the tournament. (1) Overtime. (2) Then known as Oklahoma A&M. (3) Then known as Texas Western.

Top Career Scorers

Player, school	Years	Points	Avg.	Player, school	Years	Points	Avg.
Pete Maravich, LSU	1968-70	3,667	44.2	Frank Selvy, Furman	1952-54	2,538	32.5
Austin Carr, Notre Dame	1969-71	2,560	34.6	Rick Mount, Purdue	1968-70	2,323	32.3
Oscar Robertson, Cincinnati	1958-60	2,973	33.8	Darrell Floyd, Furman	1954-56	2,281	32.1
Calvin Murphy, Niagara	1968-70	2,548	33.1	Nick Werkman, Seton Hall	1962-64	2,273	32.0
Dwight Lamar, SW Louisiana	1972-73	1,862	32.7	Willie Humes, Idaho State	1970-71	1,510	31.5

John R. Wooden Award

Awarded to the nation's outstanding college basketball player by the Los Angeles Athletic Club.

1977	Marques Johnson, UCLA	1985	Chris Mullin, St. John's	1992	Christian Laettner, Duke
1978	Phil Ford, North Carolina	1986	Walter Berry, St. John's	1993	Calbert Cheaney, Indiana
1979	Larry Bird, Indiana State	1987	David Robinson, Navy	1994	Glenn Robinson, Purdue
1980	Darrell Griffith, Louisville	1988	Danny Manning, Kansas	1995	Ed O'Bannon, UCLA
1981	Danny Ainge, Brigham Young	1989	Sean Elliott, Arizona	1996	Marcus Camby, Massachusetts
1982	Ralph Sampson, Virginia	1990	Lionel Simmons, La Salle	1997	Tim Duncan, Wake Forest
1983	Ralph Sampson, Virginia	1991	Larry Johnson, UNLV	1998	Antawn Jamison, North Carolina
1984	Michael Jordan, North Carolina				

Selected Division I Basketball Coaches in 1998[1]

College	Coach	College	Coach	College	Coach
Akron	Dan Hipsher	Indiana St.	Royce Waltman	Rice	Willis Wilson
Alabama	Mark Gottfried	Iowa	Tom Davis	Richmond	John Beilein
Alabama-Birmingham	Murry Bartow	Iowa St.	Larry Eustachy	Rutgers	Kevin Bannon
American	Art Perry	James Madison	Sherman Dillard	St. Bonaventure	Jim Baron
Arizona	Lute Olson	Kansas	Roy Williams	St. John's (NY)	Mike Jarvis
Arizona St.	Rob Evans	Kansas St.	Tom Asbury	St. Joseph's (PA)	Phil Martelli
Arkansas	Nolan Richardson	Kent	Gary Waters	St. Louis	Charlie Spoonhour
Army	Pat Harris	Kentucky	Tubby Smith	St. Mary's (CA)	Dave Bollwinkel
Auburn	Cliff Ellis	Long Beach St.	Wayne Morgan	St. Peter's	Rodger Blind
Austin Peay	Dave Loos	LSU	John Brady	San Diego	Brad Holland
Ball St.	Ray McCallum	Louisville	Denny Crum	San Diego St.	Fred Trenkle
Baylor	Harry Miller	Loyola (IL)	Larry Farmer	San Francisco	Phil Mathews
Boise St.	Rod Jensen	Loyola Marymount	Charles Bradley	San Jose St.	Phil Johnson
Boston College	Jim O'Brien	Manhattan	John Leonard	Santa Clara	Dick Davey
Bowling Green	Dan Dakich	Marquette	Mike Deane	Seton Hall	Tommy Amaker
Bradley	Jim Molinari	Maryland	Gary Williams	South Carolina	Eddie Fogler
Brigham Young	Steve Cleveland	Massachusetts	James "Bruiser" Flint	South Florida	Seth Greenberg
Brown	Frank Dobbs	Memphis	Tic Price	SE Missouri St.	Gary Garner
Butler	Barry Collier	Miami (FL)	Leonard Hamilton	USC	Henry Bibby
California	Ben Braun	Miami (OH)	Charlie Coles	Southern Illinois	Bruce Weber
Cal. St. Fullerton	Bob Hawking	Michigan	To be announced	SMU	Mike Dement
UC Irvine	Pat Douglas	Michigan St.	Tom Izzo	Southern Mississippi	James Green
UC Santa Barbara	Bob Williams	Middle Tenn. St.	Randy Wiel	SW Missouri St.	Steve Alford
Central Michigan	Jay Smith	Minnesota	Clem Haskins	Stanford	Mike Montgomery
Cincinnati	Bob Huggins	Mississippi	Roderick Barnes	Syracuse	Jim Boeheim
Clemson	Larry Shyatt	Mississippi St.	Rick Stansbury	Temple	John Chaney
Cleveland St.	Rollie Massimino	Missouri	Norm Stewart	Tennessee	Jerry Green
Colgate	Emmett Davis	Montana	Don Holst	Tennessee St.	Frankie Allen
Colorado	Ricardo Patton	Montana St.	Mick Durham	Tennessee Tech	Jeff Lebo
Colorado St.	Ritchie McKay	Morehead St.	Kyle Macy	Tenn.-Chattanooga	Henry Dickerson
Columbia	Armond Hill	Mt. St. Mary's (MD)	Jim Phelan	Tennessee-Martin	Calvin C. Luther
Connecticut	Jim Calhoun	Murray St.	Tevester Anderson	Texas	Rick Barnes
Cornell	Scott Thompson	Nebraska	Danny Nee	Texas A&M	Melvin Watkins
Creighton	Dana Altman	Nevada	Pat Foster	Texas Christian	Billy Tubbs
Dartmouth	Dave Faucher	UNLV	Bill Bayno	Texas-Arlington	Eddie McCarter
Dayton	Oliver Purnell	New Mexico	Dave Bliss	UTEP	Don Haskins
DePaul	Pat Kennedy	New Mexico St.	Lou Henson	Texas Southern	Robert Moreland
Detroit	Perry Watson	Nicholls St.	Rickey Broussard	Toledo	Stan Joplin
Drake	Kurt Kanaskie	North Carolina	Bill Guthridge	Tulane	Perry Clark
Drexel	Bill Herrion	North Carolina A&T	Roy Thomas	Tulsa	Bill Self
Duke	Mike Krzyzewski	North Carolina St.	Herb Sendek	UCLA	Steve Lavin
E. Carolina	Joe Dooley	N.C.-Charlotte	Bobby Lutz	Utah	Rick Majerus
E. Illinois	Rick Samuels	N.C.-Greensboro	Randy Peele	Utah St.	Stew Morrill
E. Kentucky	Scott Perry	N.C.-Wilmington	Jerry Wainwright	Valparaiso	Homer Drew
E. Michigan	Milton Barnes	N. Arizona	Ben Howland	Vanderbilt	Jan van Breda Kolff
E. Washington	Steve Aggers	N. Illinois	Brian Hammel	Villanova	Steve Lappas
Evansville	Jim Crews	N. Iowa	Sam Weaver	Virginia	Pete Gillen
Florida	Billy Donovan	Northwestern	Kevin O'Neill	Va. Commonwealth	Mack McCarthy
Florida International	Shakey Rodriquez	Notre Dame	John MacLeod	Virginia Tech	Bobby Hussey
Florida St.	Steve Robinson	Ohio	Larry Hunter	Wake Forest	Dave Odom
Fresno St.	Jerry Tarkanian	Ohio St.	Jim O'Brien	Washington	Bob Bender
George Mason	Jim Larranaga	Oklahoma	Kelvin Sampson	Washington St.	Kevin Eastman
Geo. Washington	Tom Penders	Oklahoma St.	Eddie Sutton	Weber St.	Ron Abegglen
Georgetown	John Thompson	Old Dominion	Jeff Capel	West Virginia	Gale Catlett
Georgia	Ron Jirsa	Oregon	Ernie Kent	W. Illinois	Jim Kerwin
Georgia Tech	Bobby Cremins	Oregon St.	Eddie Payne	W. Kentucky	Dennis Felton
Gonzaga	Dan Monson	Pacific (CA)	Bob Thomason	W. Michigan	Bob Donewald
Harvard	Frank Sullivan	Pennsylvania	Fran Dunphy	Wichita St.	Randy Smithson
Hawaii	Riley Wallace	Penn St.	Jerry Dunn	William & Mary	Charlie Woollum
Houston	Clyde Drexler	Pepperdine	Lorenzo Romar	Wisconsin	Dick Bennett
Idaho	David Farrar	Pittsburgh	Ralph Willard	Wis.-Green Bay	Mike Heideman
Idaho St.	Doug Oliver	Portland	Rob Chavez	Wright St.	Ed Schilling
Illinois	Lon Kruger	Princeton	Bill Carmody	Wyoming	Steve McClain
Illinois-Chicago	Jimmy Collins	Providence	Tim Welsh	Xavier (OH)	Skip Prosser
Illinois St.	Kevin Stallings	Purdue	Gene Keady	Yale	Dick Kuchen
Indiana	Bob Knight	Rhode Island	Jim Harrick		

(1) As of mid-Oct.

Most Coaching Victories in the NCAA Tournament Through 1998

Coach, school(s), years	Wins	Tournaments
Dean Smith, North Carolina, 1967-97	65	27
John Wooden, UCLA, 1950-75	47	16
Mike Krzyzewski, Duke, 1984-98	43	14
Denny Crum, Louisville, 1972-97	42	21
Bob Knight, Indiana, 1973-98	41	22
John Thompson, Georgetown, 1975-97	34	20
Lute Olson, Iowa and Arizona, 1979-98	31	19
Jerry Tarkanian, Long Beach State and UNLV, 1970-91	31	13
Adolph Rupp, Kentucky, 1942-72	30	20
Jim Boeheim, Syracuse, 1977-98	29	18

Women's College Basketball

Tennessee Defeats Louisiana Tech, Winning Its Third Straight NCAA Women's Championship

The University of Tennessee Lady Volunteers beat the Louisiana Tech Lady Techsters, 93-75, to win their 3d consecutive NCAA Division I Women's Basketball Championship, Mar. 29, 1998, in Kansas City, MO. The victory capped the only undefeated season for a women's team in college basketball history, and it also gave Tennessee a record 6 national championships in the last 12 years. Chamique Holdsclaw, as she had so often in the regular season, dominated the game; she was named the tournament's most outstanding player for the 2d time in 2 years.

NCAA Division I Women's Champions

Year	Champion	Coach	Final opponent	Score	Outstanding player	Site
1982	Louisiana Tech	Sonja Hogg	Cheyney	76-62	Janice Lawrence, La. Tech	Norfolk, VA
1983	USC	Linda Sharp	Louisiana Tech	69-67	Cheryl Miller, USC	Norfolk, VA
1984	USC	Linda Sharp	Tennessee	72-61	Cheryl Miller, USC	Los Angeles, CA
1985	Old Dominion	Marianne Stanley	Georgia	70-65	Tracy Claxton, Old Dominion	Austin, TX
1986	Texas	Jody Conradt	USC	97-81	Clarissa Davis, Texas	Lexington, KY
1987	Tennessee	Pat Summitt	Louisiana Tech	67-44	Tonya Edwards, Tennessee	Austin, TX
1988	Louisiana Tech	Leon Barmore	Auburn	56-54	Erica Westbrooks, La. Tech	Tacoma, WA
1989	Tennessee	Pat Summitt	Auburn	76-60	Bridgette Gordon, Tennessee	Tacoma, WA
1990	Stanford	Tara VanDerveer	Auburn	88-81	Jennifer Azzi, Stanford	Knoxville, TN
1991	Tennessee	Pat Summitt	Virginia	70-67*	Dawn Staley, Virginia	New Orleans, LA
1992	Stanford	Tara VanDerveer	W. Kentucky	78-62	Molly Goodenbour, Stanford	Los Angeles, CA
1993	Texas Tech	Marsha Sharp	Ohio St.	84-82	Sheryl Swoopes, Texas Tech	Atlanta, GA
1994	North Carolina	Sylvia Hatchell	Louisiana Tech	60-59	Charlotte Smith, North Carolina	Richmond, VA
1995	Connecticut	Geno Auriemma	Tennessee	70-64	Rebecca Lobo, Connecticut	Minneapolis, MN
1996	Tennessee	Pat Summitt	Georgia	83-65	Michelle Marciniak, Tennessee	Charlotte, NC
1997	Tennessee	Pat Summitt	Old Dominion	68-59	Chamique Holdsclaw, Tennessee	Cincinnati, OH
1998	Tennessee	Pat Summitt	Louisiana Tech	93-75	Chamique Holdsclaw, Tennessee	Kansas City, MO

* Overtime.

Wade Trophy

Awarded by National Assn. for Girls and Women in Sport for academics, community service, and player performance.

Year	Player, school
1978	Carol Blazejowski, Montclair St.
1979	Nancy Lieberman, Old Dominion
1980	Nancy Lieberman, Old Dominion
1981	Lynette Woodard, Kansas
1982	Pam Kelly, Louisiana Tech
1983	LaTaunya Pollard, Long Beach St.
1984	Janice Lawrence, Louisiana Tech
1985	Cheryl Miller, USC
1986	Kamie Ethridge, Texas
1987	Shelly Pennefeather, Villanova
1988	Teresa Weatherspoon, Louisiana Tech
1989	Clarissa Davis, Texas
1990	Jennifer Azzi, Stanford
1991	Daedra Charles, Tennessee
1992	Susan Robinson, Penn St.
1993	Karen Jennings, Nebraska
1994	Carol Ann Shudlick, Minnesota
1995	Rebecca Lobo, Connecticut
1996	Jennifer Rizzotti, Connecticut
1997	DeLisha Milton, Florida
1998	Chamique Holdsclaw, Tennessee

Top Women's Career Scorers

(Minimum 1,500 points; ranked by average)

Player, school	Years	Points	Avg.
Patricia Hoskins, Mississippi Valley State	1985-89	3,122	28.4
Sandra Hodge, New Orleans	1981-84	2,860	26.7
Lorri Bauman, Drake	1981-84	3,115	26.0
Andrea Congreaves, Mercer	1989-93	2,796	25.9
Cindy Blodgett, Maine	1994-98	3,005	25.5
Valorie Whiteside, Appalachian State	1984-88	2,944	25.4
Joyce Walker, LSU	1981-84	2,906	24.8
Tarcha Hollis, Grambling	1988-91	2,058	24.2
Korie Hlede, Duquesne	1994-98	2,631	24.1
Karen Pelphrey, Marshall	1983-86	2,746	24.1

SKIING

World Cup Alpine Champions

Men

Year	Champion
1967	Jean Claude Killy, France
1968	Jean Claude Killy, France
1969	Karl Schranz, Austria
1970	Karl Schranz, Austria
1971	Gustavo Thoeni, Italy
1972	Gustavo Thoeni, Italy
1973	Gustavo Thoeni, Italy
1974	Piero Gros, Italy
1975	Gustavo Thoeni, Italy
1976	Ingemar Stenmark, Sweden
1977	Ingemar Stenmark, Sweden
1978	Ingemar Stenmark, Sweden
1979	Peter Luescher, Switzerland
1980	Andreas Wenzel, Liechtenstein
1981	Phil Mahre, U.S.
1982	Phil Mahre, U.S.
1983	Phil Mahre, U.S.
1984	Pirmin Zurbriggen, Switzerland
1985	Marc Girardelli, Luxembourg
1986	Marc Girardelli, Luxembourg
1987	Pirmin Zurbriggen, Switzerland
1988	Pirmin Zurbriggen, Switzerland
1989	Marc Girardelli, Luxembourg
1990	Pirmin Zurbriggen, Switzerland
1991	Marc Girardelli, Luxembourg
1992	Paul Accola, Switzerland
1993	Marc Girardelli, Luxembourg
1994	Kjetil Andre Aamodt, Norway
1995	Alberto Tomba, Italy
1996	Lasse Kjus, Norway
1997	Luc Alphand, France
1998	Hermann Maier, Austria

Women

Year	Champion
1967	Nancy Greene, Canada
1968	Nancy Greene, Canada
1969	Gertrud Gabl, Austria
1970	Michele Jacot, France
1971	Annemarie Proell, Austria
1972	Annemarie Proell, Austria
1973	Annemarie Proell, Austria
1974	Annemarie Proell, Austria
1975	Annemarie Proell, Austria
1976	Rose Mittermaier, W. Germany
1977	Lise-Marie Morerod, Switzerland
1978	Hanni Wenzel, Liechtenstein
1979	Annemarie Proell Moser, Austria
1980	Hanni Wenzel, Liechtenstein
1981	Marie-Theres Nadig, Switzerland
1982	Erika Hess, Switzerland
1983	Tamara McKinney, U.S.
1984	Erika Hess, Switzerland
1985	Michela Figini, Switzerland
1986	Maria Walliser, Switzerland
1987	Maria Walliser, Switzerland
1988	Michela Figini, Switzerland
1989	Vreni Schneider, Switzerland
1990	Petra Kronberger, Austria
1991	Petra Kronberger, Austria
1992	Petra Kronberger, Austria
1993	Anita Wachter, Austria
1994	Vreni Schneider, Switzerland
1995	Vreni Schneider, Switzerland
1996	Katja Seizinger, Germany
1997	Pernilla Wiberg, Sweden
1998	Katja Seizinger, Germany

FISHING

Selected IGFA Saltwater & Freshwater All-Tackle World Records

Source: International Game Fish Association; records confirmed to Oct. 15, 1998

Saltwater Fish Records

Species	Weight	Where caught	Date	Angler
Albacore	88 lbs. 2 oz.	Gran Canaria, Canary Islands	Nov. 19, 1977	Siegfried Dickemann
Amberjack, greater	155 lbs. 10 oz.	Challenger Bank, Bermuda	June 24, 1981	Joseph Dawson
Barracuda, great	85 lbs.	Christmas Island, Kiribati	Apr. 11, 1992	John W. Helfrich
Barracuda, Mexican	21 lbs.	Phantom Isle, Costa Rica	Mar. 27, 1987	E. Greg Kent
Barracuda, Pacific	7 lbs. 11 oz.	Catalina Island, CA	May 22, 1994	Jim Kingsmill
Bass, barred sand	13 lbs. 3 oz.	Huntington Beach, CA	Aug. 29, 1988	Robert Halal
Bass, black sea	9 lbs. 8 oz.	Virginia Beach, VA	Jan. 9, 1987	Joe Mizelle Jr.
		Virginia Beach, VA	Dec. 22, 1990	Jack G. Stallings
Bass, giant sea	563 lbs. 8 oz.	Anacaba Island, CA	Aug. 20, 1968	James D. McAdam Jr.
Bass, redeye	8 lbs. 12 oz.	Apalachicola River, FL	Jan. 28, 1995	Carl W. Davis
Bass, striped	78 lbs. 8 oz.	Atlantic City, NJ	Sept. 21, 1982	Albert R. McReynolds
Bluefish	31 lbs. 12 oz.	Hatteras Inlet, NC	Jan. 30, 1972	James M. Hussey
Bonefish	19 lbs.	Zululand, South Africa	May 26, 1962	Brian W. Batchelor
Bonito, Atlantic	18 lbs. 4 oz.	Faial Island, Azores	July 8, 1953	D. Gama Higgs
Bonito, Pacific	14 lbs. 12 oz.	San Benitos Island, Mexico	Oct. 12, 1980	Jerome H. Rilling
Cabezon	23 lbs.	Juan De Fuca Strait, WA	Aug. 4, 1990	Wesley S. Hunter
Cobia	135 lbs. 9 oz.	Shark Bay, Australia	July 9, 1985	Peter W. Goulding
Cod, Atlantic	98 lbs. 12 oz.	Isle of Shoals, NH	June 8, 1969	Alphonse J. Bielevich
Cod, Pacific	32 lbs.	Unalaska Bay, AK	June 29, 1997	Donald Boston
Conger	133 lbs. 4 oz.	Berry Head, S. Devon, England	June 5, 1995	Vic Evans
Dolphin	88 lbs.	Exuma, Bahamas	May 5, 1998	Richard D. Evans
Drum, black	113 lbs. 1 oz.	Lewes, DE	Sept. 15, 1975	Gerald M. Townsend
Drum, red	94 lbs. 2 oz.	Avon, NC	Nov. 7, 1984	David G. Deuel
Eel, American	9 lbs. 4 oz.	Cape May, NJ	Nov. 9, 1995	Jeff Pennick
Eel, marbled	36 lbs. 1 oz.	Hazelmere Dam, South Africa	June 10, 1984	Ferdie Van Nooten
Flounder, southern	20 lbs. 9 oz.	Nassau Sound, FL	Dec. 23, 1983	Larenza W. Mungin
Flounder, summer	22 lbs. 7 oz.	Montauk, NY	Sept. 15, 1975	Charles Nappi
Grouper, Warsaw	436 lbs. 12 oz.	Gulf of Mexico, Destin, FL	Dec. 22, 1985	Steve Haeusler
Halibut, Atlantic	255 lbs. 4 oz.	Gloucester, MA	July 28, 1989	Sonny Manley
Halibut, California	53 lbs. 4 oz.	Santa Rosa Island, CA	July 7, 1988	Russell J. Harmon
Halibut, Pacific	459 lbs.	Dutch Harbor, AK	June 11, 1996	Jack Tragis
Jack, crevalle	57 lbs. 14 oz.	Southwest Pass, LA	Aug. 15, 1997	Leon D. Richard
Jack, horse-eye	24 lbs. 8 oz.	Miami, FL	Dec. 20, 1982	Tito Schnau
Jack, Pacific crevalle	31 lbs.	Playa Zancudo, Costa Rica	Dec. 17, 1997	Roy Ventura Roig
Jewfish	680 lbs.	Fernandina Beach, FL	May 20, 1961	Lynn Joyner
Kawakawa	29 lbs.	Clarion Island, Mexico	Dec. 17, 1986	Ronald Nakamura
Lingcod	69 lbs.	Langara Island, British Columbia	June 16, 1992	Murray M. Romer
Mackerel, cero	17 lbs. 2 oz.	Islamorada, FL	Apr. 5, 1986	G. Michael Mills
Mackerel, king	90 lbs.	Key West, FL	Feb. 16, 1976	Norton I. Thomton
Mackerel, Spanish	13 lbs.	Ocracoke Inlet, NC	Nov. 4, 1987	Robert Cranton
Marlin, Atlantic blue	1,402 lbs. 2 oz.	Vitoria, Brazil	Feb. 29, 1992	Paulo Roberto A. Amorim
Marlin, black	1,560 lbs.	Cabo Blanco, Peru	Aug. 4, 1953	Alfred C. Glassell Jr.
Marlin, Pacific blue	1,376 lbs.	Kaaiwi Pt., Kona, HI	May 31, 1982	Jay W. deBeaubien
Marlin, striped	494 lbs.	Tutukaka, New Zealand	Jan. 16, 1986	Bill Boniface
Marlin, white	181 lbs. 14 oz.	Vitoria, Brazil	Dec. 8, 1979	Evandro Luiz Coser
Permit	56 lbs. 2 oz.	Ft. Lauderdale, FL	June 30, 1997	Thomas Sebestyen
Pollack, European	27 lbs. 6 oz.	Salcombe, Devon, England	Jan. 16, 1986	Robert Samuel Milkins
Pollock	50 lbs.	Saltraumen, Norway	Nov. 30, 1995	Thor-Magnus Lekang
Pompano, African	50 lbs. 8 oz.	Daytona Beach, FL	Apr. 21, 1990	Tom Sargent
Roosterfish	114 lbs.	La Paz, Baja Cal., Mexico	June 1, 1960	Abe Sackheim
Runner, blue	11 lbs. 2 oz.	Dauphin Isl., AL	June 28, 1997	Stacey Michelle Morien
Runner, rainbow	37 lbs. 9 oz.	Clarion Island, Mexico	Nov. 21, 1991	Tom Pfleger
Sailfish, Atlantic	141 lbs. 1 oz.	Luanda, Angola	Feb. 19, 1994	Alfredo de Sousa Neves
Sailfish, Pacific	221 lbs.	Santa Cruz Island, Ecuador	Feb. 12, 1947	C. W. Stewart
Seabass, white	83 lbs. 12 oz.	San Felipe, Mexico	Mar. 31, 1953	L. C. Baumgardner
Seatrout, spotted	17 lbs. 7 oz.	Ft. Pierce, FL	May 11, 1995	Graig F. Carson
Shark, bigeye thresher	802 lbs.	Tutukaka, New Zealand	Feb. 8, 1981	Dianne North
Shark, bignose	369 lbs. 14 oz.	Markham R., Papua New Guinea	Oct. 23, 1993	Lester J. Rohrlach
Shark, blue	454 lbs.	Martha's Vineyard, MA	July 19, 1996	Pete Bergin
Shark, great hammerhead	991 lbs.	Sarasota, FL	May 30, 1982	Allen Ogle
Shark, Greenland	1,708 lbs. 9 oz.	Trondheimsfjord, Norway	Oct. 18, 1987	Terje Nordtvedt
Shark, porbeagle	507 lbs.	Caithness, Scotland	Mar. 9, 1993	Christopher Bennet
Shark, shortfin mako	1,115 lbs.	Black River, Mauritius	Nov. 16, 1988	Patrick Guillanton
Shark, tiger	1,780 lbs.	Cherry Grove, SC	June 14, 1964	Walter Maxwell
Shark, white	2,664 lbs.	Ceduna, S.A., Australia	Apr. 21, 1959	Alfred Dean
Sheepshead	21 lbs. 4 oz.	New Orleans, LA	Apr. 16, 1982	Wayne Deselle
Skipjack, black	26 lbs.	Thetis Bank, Baja Cal., Mexico	Oct. 23, 1991	Clifford Hamaishi
Snapper, cubera	121 lbs. 8 oz.	Cameron, LA	July 5, 1982	Mike Hebert
Snapper, red	50 lbs. 4 oz.	Gulf of Mexico, LA	June 23, 1996	Capt. Doc Kennedy
Snook, common	53 lbs. 10 oz.	Parismina Ranch, Costa Rica	Oct. 18, 1978	Gilbert Ponzi
Spearfish, Mediterranean	90 lbs. 13 oz.	Madeira Island, Portugal	June 2, 1980	Joseph Larkin
Swordfish	1,182 lbs.	Iquique, Chile	May 7, 1953	L. Marron
Tarpon	283 lbs. 4 oz.	Sherbro Island, Sierra Leone	Apr. 16, 1991	Yvon Sebag
Tautog	25 lbs.	Ocean City, NJ	Jan. 20, 1998	Anthony R. Monica
Trevally, bigeye	31 lbs. 8 oz.	Poivre Isl., Seychelles	April 23, 1997	Les Sampson
Trevally, giant	145 lbs. 8 oz.	Makena, Maui, HI	Mar. 28, 1991	Russell Mori
Tuna, Atlantic bigeye	392 lbs. 6 oz.	Gran Canaria, Spain	July 15, 1996	Dieter Vogel
Tuna, blackfin	45 lbs. 8 oz.	Key West, FL	May 4, 1996	Sam J. Burnett
Tuna, bluefin	1,496 lbs.	Aulds Cove, Nova Scotia	Oct. 26, 1979	Ken Fraser

(continued)

Species	Weight	Where caught	Date	Angler
Tuna, longtail	79 lbs. 2 oz.	Montague Isl., N.S.W., Australia	Apr. 12, 1982	Tim Simpson
Tuna, Pacific bigeye	435 lbs.	Cabo Blanco, Peru	Apr. 17, 1957	Dr. Russel V. A. Lee
Tuna, skipjack	45 lbs. 4 oz.	Flathead Bank, Baja Cal., Mexico	Nov. 16, 1996	Brian Evans
Tuna, southern bluefin	348 lbs. 5 oz.	Whakatane, New Zealand	Jan. 16, 1981	Rex Wood
Tuna, yellowfin	388 lbs. 12 oz.	San Benedicto Island, Mexico	Apr. 1, 1977	Curt Wiesenhutter
Tunny, little	35 lbs. 2 oz.	Cap de Garde, Algeria	Dec. 14, 1988	Jean Yves Chatard
Wahoo	158 lbs. 8 oz.	Baja California, Mexico	June 10, 1996	Keith Winter
Weakfish	19 lbs. 2 oz.	Jones Beach Inlet, NY	Oct. 11, 1984	Dennis Roger Rooney
		Delaware Bay, DE	May 20, 1989	William E. Thomas
Yellowtail, California	79 lbs. 4 oz.	Alijos Rocks, Baja Cal., Mexico	July 2, 1991	Robert I. Welker
Yellowtail, southern	114 lbs. 10 oz.	Tauranga, New Zealand	Feb. 5, 1984	Mike Godfrey

Freshwater Fish Records

Species	Weight	Where caught	Date	Angler
Barramundi	63 lbs. 2 oz.	Normah River, Australia	Apr. 28, 1991	Scott Barnsley
Bass, largemouth	22 lbs. 4 oz.	Montgomery Lake, GA	June 2, 1932	George W. Perry
Bass, rock	3 lbs.	York River, Ontario	Aug. 1, 1974	Peter Gulgin
Bass, smallmouth	10 lbs. 14 oz.	Dale Hollow Lake, TN	Apr. 24, 1969	John T. Gorman
Bass, white	6 lbs. 13 oz.	Lake Orange, VA	July 31, 1989	Ronald L. Sprouse
Bass, whiterock	27 lbs. 5 oz.	Greers Ferry Lake, AR	April 24, 1997	Jerald C. Shaum
Bass, yellow	2 lbs. 9 oz.	Waverly, TN	Feb. 27, 1998	John T. Chappell
Bluegill	4 lbs. 12 oz.	Ketona Lake, AL	Apr. 9, 1950	T. S. Hudson
Bowfin	21 lbs. 8 oz.	Florence, SC	Jan. 29, 1980	Robert L. Harmon
Buffalo, bigmouth	70 lbs. 5 oz.	Bussey Brake, Bastrop, LA	Apr. 21, 1980	Delbert Sisk
Buffalo, black	55 lbs. 8 oz.	Cherokee Lake, TN	May 3, 1984	Edward H. McLain
Buffalo, smallmouth	82 lbs. 3 oz.	Athens Lake, AR	June 6, 1993	Randy Collins
Bullhead, brown	5 lbs. 11 oz.	Cedar Creek, FL	Mar. 28, 1995	Robert Bengis
Bullhead, yellow	4 lbs. 4 oz.	Mormon Lake, AZ	May 11, 1984	Emily Williams
Burbot	18 lbs. 11 oz.	Angenmanalren, Sweden	Oct. 22, 1996	Margit Agren
Carp, common	75 lbs. 11 oz.	Lac de St. Cassien, France	May 21, 1987	Leo van der Gugten
Catfish, blue	111 lbs.	Wheeler Reservoir, Tenn. R.	July 5, 1996	William P. McKinley
Catfish, channel	58 lbs.	Santee-Cooper Res., SC	July 7, 1964	W. B. Whaley
Catfish, flathead	123 lbs. 9 oz.	Independence, KS	May 14, 1998	Ken Paulie
Catfish, white	18 lbs. 14 oz.	Withlacoochee River, FL	Sept. 21, 1991	Jim Miller
Char, Arctic	32 lbs. 9 oz.	Tree River, Canada	July 30, 1981	Jeffrey L. Ward
Crappie, white	5 lbs. 3 oz.	Enid Dam, MS	July 31, 1957	Fred L. Bright
Dolly Varden	18 lbs. 9 oz.	Mashutuk River, AK	July 13, 1993	Richard B. Evans
Dorado	51 lbs. 5 oz.	Toledo (Corrientes), Argentina	Sept. 27, 1984	Armando Giudice
Drum, freshwater	54 lbs. 8 oz.	Nickajack Lake, TN	Apr. 20, 1972	Benny E. Hull
Gar, alligator	279 lbs.	Rio Grande, TX	Dec. 2, 1951	Bill Valverde
Gar, Florida	21 lbs. 3 oz.	Boca Raton, FL	June 3, 1981	Jeff Sabol
Gar, longnose	50 lbs. 5 oz.	Trinity River, TX	July 30, 1954	Townsend Miller
Gar, shortnose	5 lbs. 12 oz.	Rend Lake, IL	July 6, 1995	Donna K. Willmert
Gar, spotted	9 lbs. 12 oz.	Lake Mexia, TX	Apr. 7, 1994	Rick Rivard
Grayling, Arctic	5 lbs. 15 oz.	Katseyedie River, N.W.T.	Aug. 16, 1967	Jeanne P. Branson
Inconnu	53 lbs.	Pah River, AK	Aug. 20, 1986	Lawrence E. Hudnall
Kokanee	9 lbs. 6 oz.	Okanagan Lake, Vernon, B.C.	June 18, 1988	Norm Kuhn
Muskellunge	67 lbs. 8 oz.	Lake Court Oreilles, WI	July 24, 1949	Cal Johnson
Muskellunge, tiger	51 lbs. 3 oz.	Lac Vieux-Desert, WI-MI	July 16, 1919	John Knobla
Perch, Nile	213 lbs.	Lake Nassar, Egypt	Dec. 18, 1997	Adrian Brayshaw
Perch, white	4 lbs. 12 oz.	Messalonskee Lake, ME	June 4, 1949	Mrs. Earl Small
Perch, yellow	4 lbs. 3 oz.	Bordentown, NJ	May, 1865	Dr. C. C. Abbot
Pickerel, chain	9 lbs. 6 oz.	Homerville, GA	Feb. 17, 1961	Baxley McQuaig Jr.
Pike, northern	55 lbs. 1 oz.	Lake of Grefeern, W. Germany	Oct. 16, 1986	Lothar Louis
Redhorse, greater	9 lbs. 3 oz.	Salmon River, Pulaski, NY	May 11, 1985	Jason Wilson
Redhorse, silver	11 lbs. 7 oz.	Plum Creek, WI	May 29, 1985	Neal Long
Salmon, Atlantic	79 lbs. 2 oz.	Tana River, Norway	1928	Henrik Henriksen
Salmon, chinook	97 lbs. 4 oz.	Kenai River, AK	May 17, 1985	Les Anderson
Salmon, chum	35 lbs.	Edye Pass, BC	July 11, 1995	Todd A. Johansson
Salmon, coho	33 lbs. 4 oz.	Salmon River, Pulaski, NY	Sept. 27, 1989	Jerry Lifton
Salmon, pink	13 lbs. 1 oz.	St. Mary's River, Ontario	Sept. 23, 1992	Ray Higaki
Salmon, sockeye	15 lbs. 3 oz.	Kenai River, AK	Aug. 9, 1987	Stan Roach
Sauger	8 lbs. 12 oz.	Lake Sakakawea, ND	Oct. 6, 1971	Mike Fischer
Shad, American	11 lbs. 4 oz.	Connecticut River, MA	May 19, 1986	Bob Thibodo
Sturgeon, beluga	224 lbs. 13 oz.	Guryev, Kazakhstan	May 3, 1993	Merete Lehne
Sturgeon, white	468 lbs.	Benicia, CA	July 9, 1983	Joey Pallotta 3d
Sunfish, green	2 lbs. 2 oz.	Stockton Lake, MO	June 18, 1971	Paul M. Dilley
Sunfish, redbreast	1 lb. 12 oz.	Suwannee River, FL	May 29, 1984	Alvin Buchanan
Sunfish, redear	5 lbs. 3 oz.	Sacramento, CA	June 27, 1994	Anthony H. White Sr.
Tigerfish, giant	97 lbs.	Zaire River, Kinshasa, Zaire	July 9, 1988	Raymond Houtmans
Tilapia	6 lbs. 5 oz.	Lake Aranal, Costa Rica	Feb. 10, 1995	Marvin C. Smith
Trout, Apache	5 lb. 3 oz.	Apache Res., AZ	May 29, 1991	John Baldwin
Trout, brook	14 lbs. 8 oz.	Nipigon River, Ontario	July 1916	Dr. W. J. Cook
Trout, brown	40 lbs. 4 oz.	Little Red River, AR	May 9, 1992	Howard L. "Rip" Collins
Trout, bull	32 lbs.	Lake Pend Oreille, ID	Oct. 27, 1949	N. L. Higgins
Trout, cutthroat	41 lbs.	Pyramid Lake, NV	Dec. 1925	John Skimmerhorn
Trout, golden	11 lbs.	Cooks Lake, WY	Aug. 5, 1948	Charles S. Reed
Trout, lake	72 lbs.	Great Bear Lake, N.W.T.	Aug. 10, 1995	Lloyd E. Bull
Trout, rainbow	42 lbs. 2 oz.	Bell Island, AK	June 22, 1970	David Robert White
Trout, tiger	20 lbs. 13 oz.	Lake Michigan, WI	Aug. 12, 1978	Pete M. Friedland
Walleye	25 lbs.	Old Hickory Lake, TN	Aug. 2, 1960	Mabry Harper
Warmouth	2 lbs. 7 oz.	Yellow River, Holt, FL	Oct. 19, 1985	Tony D. Dempsey
Whitefish, lake	14 lbs. 6 oz.	Meaford, Ontario	May 21, 1984	Dennis Laycock
Whitefish, mountain	5 lbs. 8 oz.	Elbow River, Calgary, AB	Aug. 1, 1995	Randy G. Woo
Whitefish, round	6 lbs.	Putahow River, Manitoba	June 14, 1984	Allen Ristori
Zander	25 lbs. 2 oz.	Trosa, Sweden	June 12, 1986	Harry Lee Tennison

GOLF

United States Open Winners

Year[1]	Winner	Year[1]	Winner	Year[1]	Winner	Year[1]	Winner
1903	Willie Anderson	1928	John Farrell	1955	Jack Fleck	1977	Hubert Green
1904	Willie Anderson	1929	Bobby Jones*	1956	Cary Middlecoff	1978	Andy North
1905	Willie Anderson	1930	Bobby Jones*	1957	Dick Mayer	1979	Hale Irwin
1906	Alex Smith	1931	Wm. Burke	1958	Tommy Bolt	1980	Jack Nicklaus
1907	Alex Ross	1932	Gene Sarazen	1959	Billy Casper	1981	David Graham
1908	Fred McLeod	1933	John Goodman*	1960	Arnold Palmer	1982	Tom Watson
1909	George Sargent	1934	Olin Dutra	1961	Gene Littler	1983	Larry Nelson
1910	Alex Smith	1935	Sam Parks, Jr.	1962	Jack Nicklaus	1984	Fuzzy Zoeller
1911	John McDermott	1936	Tony Manero	1963	Julius Boros	1985	Andy North
1912	John McDermott	1937	Ralph Guldahl	1964	Ken Venturi	1986	Ray Floyd
1913	Francis Ouimet*	1938	Ralph Guldahl	1965	Gary Player	1987	Scott Simpson
1914	Walter Hagen	1939	Byron Nelson	1966	Billy Casper	1988	Curtis Strange
1915	Jerome Travers*	1940	Lawson Little	1967	Jack Nicklaus	1989	Curtis Strange
1916	Chick Evans*	1941	Craig Wood	1968	Lee Trevino	1990	Hale Irwin
1919	Walter Hagen	1946	Lloyd Mangrum	1969	Orville Moody	1991	Payne Stewart
1920	Edward Ray	1947	L. Worsham	1970	Tony Jacklin	1992	Tom Kite
1921	Jim Barnes	1948	Ben Hogan	1971	Lee Trevino	1993	Lee Janzen
1922	Gene Sarazen	1949	Cary Middlecoff	1972	Jack Nicklaus	1994	Ernie Els
1923	Bobby Jones*	1950	Ben Hogan	1973	Johnny Miller	1995	Corey Pavin
1924	Cyril Walker	1951	Ben Hogan	1974	Hale Irwin	1996	Steve Jones
1925	Willie MacFarlane	1952	Julius Boros	1975	Lou Graham	1997	Ernie Els
1926	Bobby Jones*	1953	Ben Hogan	1976	Jerry Pate	1998	Lee Janzen
1927	Tommy Armour	1954	Ed Furgol				

* Amateur. (1) 1917-18 and 1942-45 not played.

Professional Golfers' Association Championship Winners

Year[1]	Winner	Year[1]	Winner	Year[1]	Winner	Year[1]	Winner
1922	Gene Sarazen	1941	Victor Ghezzi	1961	Jerry Barber	1980	Jack Nicklaus
1923	Gene Sarazen	1942	Sam Snead	1962	Gary Player	1981	Larry Nelson
1924	Walter Hagen	1944	Bob Hamilton	1963	Jack Nicklaus	1982	Ray Floyd
1925	Walter Hagen	1945	Byron Nelson	1964	Bob Nichols	1983	Hal Sutton
1926	Walter Hagen	1946	Ben Hogan	1965	Dave Marr	1984	Lee Trevino
1927	Walter Hagen	1947	Jim Ferrier	1966	Al Geiberger	1985	Hubert Green
1928	Leo Diegel	1948	Ben Hogan	1967	Don January	1986	Bob Tway
1929	Leo Diegel	1949	Sam Snead	1968	Julius Boros	1987	Larry Nelson
1930	Tommy Armour	1950	Chandler Harper	1969	Ray Floyd	1988	Jeff Sluman
1931	Tom Creavy	1951	Sam Snead	1970	Dave Stockton	1989	Payne Stewart
1932	Olin Dutra	1952	James Turnesa	1971	Jack Nicklaus	1990	Wayne Grady
1933	Gene Sarazen	1953	Walter Burkemo	1972	Gary Player	1991	John Daly
1934	Paul Runyan	1954	Melvin Harbert	1973	Jack Nicklaus	1992	Nick Price
1935	Johnny Revolta	1955	Doug Ford	1974	Lee Trevino	1993	Paul Azinger
1936	Denny Shute	1956	Jack Burke	1975	Jack Nicklaus	1994	Nick Price
1937	Denny Shute	1957	Lionel Hebert	1976	Dave Stockton	1995	Steve Elkington
1938	Paul Runyan	1958	Dow Finsterwald	1977	Lanny Wadkins	1996	Mark Brooks
1939	Henry Picard	1959	Bob Rosburg	1978	John Mahaffey	1997	Davis Love III
1940	Byron Nelson	1960	Jay Hebert	1979	David Graham	1998	Vijay Singh

(1) 1943 not played.

Masters Golf Tournament Winners

Year[1]	Winner	Year[1]	Winner	Year[1]	Winner	Year[1]	Winner
1934	Horton Smith	1953	Ben Hogan	1969	George Archer	1984	Ben Crenshaw
1935	Gene Sarazen	1954	Sam Snead	1970	Billy Casper	1985	Bernhard Langer
1936	Horton Smith	1955	Cary Middlecoff	1971	Charles Coody	1986	Jack Nicklaus
1937	Byron Nelson	1956	Jack Burke	1972	Jack Nicklaus	1987	Larry Mize
1938	Henry Picard	1957	Doug Ford	1973	Tommy Aaron	1988	Sandy Lyle
1939	Ralph Guldahl	1958	Arnold Palmer	1974	Gary Player	1989	Nick Faldo
1940	Jimmy Demaret	1959	Art Wall Jr.	1975	Jack Nicklaus	1990	Nick Faldo
1941	Craig Wood	1960	Arnold Palmer	1976	Ray Floyd	1991	Ian Woosnam
1942	Byron Nelson	1961	Gary Player	1977	Tom Watson	1992	Fred Couples
1946	Herman Keiser	1962	Arnold Palmer	1978	Gary Player	1993	Bernhard Langer
1947	Jimmy Demaret	1963	Jack Nicklaus	1979	Fuzzy Zoeller	1994	Jose Maria Olazabal
1948	Claude Harmon	1964	Arnold Palmer	1980	Seve Ballesteros	1995	Ben Crenshaw
1949	Sam Snead	1965	Jack Nicklaus	1981	Tom Watson	1996	Nick Faldo
1950	Jimmy Demaret	1966	Jack Nicklaus	1982	Craig Stadler	1997	Tiger Woods
1951	Ben Hogan	1967	Gay Brewer, Jr.	1983	Seve Ballesteros	1998	Mark O'Meara
1952	Sam Snead	1968	Bob Goalby				

(1) 1943-45 not played.

British Open Winners

Year[1]	Winner	Year[1]	Winner	Year[1]	Winner	Year[1]	Winner
1931	Tommy Armour	1953	Ben Hogan	1969	Tony Jacklin	1984	Seve Ballesteros
1932	Gene Sarazen	1954	Peter Thomson	1970	Jack Nicklaus	1985	Sandy Lyle
1933	Denny Shute	1955	Peter Thomson	1971	Lee Trevino	1986	Greg Norman
1934	Henry Cotton	1956	Peter Thomson	1972	Lee Trevino	1987	Nick Faldo
1935	Alf Perry	1957	Bobby Locke	1973	Tom Weiskopf	1988	Seve Ballesteros
1936	Alf Padgham	1958	Peter Thomson	1974	Gary Player	1989	Mark Calcavecchia
1937	T.H. Cotton	1959	Gary Player	1975	Tom Watson	1990	Nick Faldo
1938	R.A. Whitcombe	1960	Kel Nagle	1976	Johnny Miller	1991	Ian Baker-Finch
1939	Richard Burton	1961	Arnold Palmer	1977	Tom Watson	1992	Nick Faldo
1946	Sam Snead	1962	Arnold Palmer	1978	Jack Nicklaus	1993	Greg Norman
1947	Fred Daly	1963	Bob Charles	1979	Seve Ballesteros	1994	Nick Price
1948	Henry Cotton	1964	Tony Lema	1980	Tom Watson	1995	John Daly
1949	Bobby Locke	1965	Peter Thomson	1981	Bill Rogers	1996	Tom Lehman
1950	Bobby Locke	1966	Jack Nicklaus	1982	Tom Watson	1997	Justin Leonard
1951	Max Faulkner	1967	Roberto de Vicenzo	1983	Tom Watson	1998	Mark O'Meara
1952	Bobby Locke	1968	Gary Player				

(1) 1940-45 not played.

Professional Golf Tournaments in 1998

(through Nov. 1)

Men

Date	Event	Winner	Score	Prize
Jan. 11	Mercedes Championships, Carlsbad, CA	Phil Mickelson	271	$306,000
Jan. 18	Bob Hope Chrysler Classic, Indian Wells, CA	Fred Couples	*332	414,000
Jan. 25	Phoenix Open, Scottsdale, AZ	Jesper Parnevik	269	450,000
Feb. 8	Buick Invitational La Jolla, CA	Scott Simpson	*#204	378,000
Feb. 15	United Airlines Hawaiian Open, Honolulu, HI	John Huston	T260	324,000
Feb. 22	Tucson Chrysler Classic, Tucson, AZ	David Duval	269	360,000
Mar. 1	Nissan Open, Valencia, CA	Billy Mayfair	*272	378,000
Mar. 8	Doral-Ryder Open, Miami, FL	Michael Bradley	278	360,000
Mar. 15	Honda Classic, Coral Springs, FL	Mark Calcavecchia	270	324,000
Mar. 22	Bay Hill Invitational, Orlando, FL	Ernie Els	274	360,000
Mar. 29	THE PLAYERS Championship, Ponte Vedra, FL	Justin Leonard	278	720,000
Apr. 5	Entergy Classic, New Orleans, LA	Lee Westwood	273	306,000
Apr. 12	The Masters, Augusta, GA	Mark O'Meara	279	576,000
Apr. 19	MCI Classic, Hilton Head Island, SC	Davis Love III	266	342,000
Apr. 26	Greater Greensboro Chrysler Classic, Greensboro, NC	Trevor Dodds	*276	396,000
May 3	Shell Houston Open, The Woodlands, TX	David Duval	276	360,000
May 10	BellSouth Classic, Duluth, GA	Tiger Woods	271	324,000
May 17	GTE Byron Nelson Classic, Irving, TX	John Cook	265	450,000
May 24	MasterCard Colonial, Fort Worth, TX	Tom Watson	265	414,000
May 31	Memorial Tournament, Dublin, OH	Fred Couples	271	396,000
June 7	Kemper Open, Potomac, MD	Stuart Appleby	274	360,000
June 14	Buick Classic, Rye, NY	J.P. Hayes	*#201	324,000
June 21	U.S. Open Championship, San Francisco, CA	Lee Janzen	280	535,000
June 28	Motorola Western Open, LeMont, IL	Joe Durant	271	396,000
July 5	Canon Greater Hartford Open, Cromwell, CT	Olin Browne	*266	360,000
July 12	Quad City Classic, Coal Valley, IL	Steve Jones	263	279,000
July 19	British Open, Southport, England	Mark O'Meara	*280	492,000
July 19	Deposit Guaranty Golf Classic, Madison, MS	Fred Funk	270	216,000
July 26	CVC Charity Classic, Sutton, MA	Steve Pate	269	270,000
Aug. 2	FedEx St. Jude Classic, Memphis, TN	Nick Price	*268	324,000
Aug. 9	Buick Open, Grand Blanc, MI	Billy Mayfair	271	324,000
Aug. 16	PGA Championship, Redmond, WA	Vijay Singh	271	540,000
Aug. 17[1]	AT&T Pebble Beach Pro-Am, Pebble Beach, CA	Phil Mickelson	#202	450,000
Aug. 23	Sprint International, Castle Rock, CO	Vijay Singh	47 points	360,000
Aug. 30	NEC World Series of Golf, Akron, OH	David Duvall	269	405,000
Aug. 30	Greater Vancouver Open, Surrey, British Columbia	Brandel Chamblee	265	360,000
Sept. 6	Greater Milwaukee Open, Milwaukee, WI	Jeff Sluman	265	324,000
Sept. 13	Bell Canadian Open, Oakville, Ontario	Billy Andrade	*275	396,000
Sept. 20	B.C. Open, Endicott, NY	Chris Perry	273	270,000
Sept. 27	Westin Texas Open at La Cantera, San Antonio, TX	Hal Sutton	270	306,000
Oct. 4	Buick Challenge, Pine Mountain, GA	Steve Elkington	*267	270,000
Oct. 11	Michelob Championship at Kingsmill, Williamsburg, VA	David Duval	268	342,000
Oct. 18	Las Vegas Invitational, Las Vegas, NV	Jim Furyk	335	360,000
Oct. 25	Natl. Car rental Classic at Walt Disney World Resort, Lake Buena Vista, FL	John Huston	272	360,000
Nov. 1	The Tour Championship, Atlanta, GA	Hal Sutton	*274	720,000

Women

Date	Event	Winner	Score	Prize
Jan. 18	HealthSouth Inaugural, Orlando, FL	Kelly Robbins	209	$90,000
Jan. 25	The Office Depot, West Palm Beach, FL	Helen Alfredsson	277	90,000
Feb. 15	Los Angeles Women's Championship, Glendale, CA	Dale Eggeling	*#141	97,500
Feb. 21	Cup Noodles Hawaiian Ladies Open, Kapolei, HI	Wendy Ward	*204	97,500
Mar. 1	Australian Ladies Masters, Queensland, Australia	Karrie Webb	272	105,000
Mar. 15	Welch's/Circle K Championship, Tucson, AZ	Helen Alfredsson	274	75,000
Mar. 22	Standard Register PING, Phoenix, AZ	Liselotte Neumann	*279	127,500
Mar. 29	Nabisco Dinah Shore Classic, Rancho Mirage, CA	Pat Hurst	281	150,000
Apr. 5	Longs Drugs Challenge, Lincoln, CA	Donna Andrews	278	90,000
Apr. 19	City of Hope Myrtle Beach Classic, Murrels Inlet, SC	Karrie Webb	269	90,000
Apr. 26	Chick-fil-A Charity Championship, Stockbridge, GA	Liselotte Neumann	202	105,000
May 3	Mercury Titleholders Championship, Daytona Beach, FL	Danielle Ammaccapane	276	150,000
May 10	Sara Lee Classic, Old Hickory, TN	Barb Mucha	*205	112,500
May 17	McDonald's LPGA Championship, Wilmington, DE	Se Ri Pak	273	195,000
May 24	LPGA Corning Classic, Corning, NY	Tammie Green	268	105,000
May 24	JCPenney LPGA Skins Game, Frisco, TX	Laura Davies	10 skins	270,000
May 31	Wegman's Rochester International, Pittsford, NY	Rosie Jones	279	105,000
June 7	Michelob Light Classic, St. Louis, MO	Annika Sorenstam	*208	90,000
June 14	Oldsmobile Classic, East Lansing, MI	Lisa Walters	265	97,500
June 21	Friendly's Classic, Agawam, MA	Amy Fruhwirth	280	90,000
June 28	ShopRite LPGA Classic, Atlantic City, NJ	Annika Sorenstam	196	150,000
July 5	U.S. Women's Open, Kohler, WI	Se Ri Pak	*290	232,500
July 12	Jamie Farr Kroger Classic, Sylvania, OH	Se Ri Pak	261	120,000
July 19	JAL Big Apple Classic, New Rochelle, NY	Annika Sorenstam	265	116,250
July 26	Giant Eagle LPGA Classic, Warren, OH	Se Ri Pak	201	120,000
Aug. 2	du Maurier Classic, Windsor, Ontario	Brandie Burton	270	180,000
Aug. 9	Star Bank LPGA Classic, Beavercreek, OH	Meg Mallon	*199	90,000
Aug. 16	Weetabix Women's British Open, Lancashire, England	Sherri Steinhauer	292	162,000
Aug. 23	Rainbow Foods LPGA Classic, Maple Grove, MN	Hiromi Kobayashi	*206	90,000
Aug. 30	State Farm Rail Classic, Springfield, IL	Pearl Sinn	200	105,000
Sept. 6	The Safeway LPGA Classic, Portland, OR	Danielle Ammaccapane	204	90,000
Sept. 13	SAFECO Classic, Kent, WA	Annika Sorenstam	273	90,000
Sept. 20	Solheim Cup, Dublin, OH	United States	16-12	—
Sept. 27	First Union Betsy King Classic, Kutztown, PA	Rachel Hetherington	*274	97,500
Oct. 11	Lifetime's AFLAC Tournament of Champions, Opelika, AL	Kelly Robbins	276	122,000
Oct. 25	Samsung World Championship of Women's Golf, The Villages, FL	Juli Inkster	275	122,000
Nov. 1	Nichirei International, Tsukuba, Japan	United States LPGA	24-12	450,000

* Won playoff. (#) Shortened because of weather. (T) Tournament record. (1) Started play Jan. 29-Feb. 1, finished Aug. 17.

U.S. Women's Open Golf Champions

Year	Winner	Year	Winner	Year	Winner	Year	Winner
1948	"Babe" Zaharias	1961	Mickey Wright	1974	Sandra Haynie	1987	Laura Davies
1949	Louise Suggs	1962	Murle Lindstrom	1975	Sandra Palmer	1988	Liselotte Neumann
1950	"Babe" Zaharias	1963	Mary Mills	1976	JoAnne Carner	1989	Betsy King
1951	Betsy Rawls	1964	Mickey Wright	1977	Hollis Stacy	1990	Betsy King
1952	Louise Suggs	1965	Carol Mann	1978	Hollis Stacy	1991	Meg Mallon
1953	Betsy Rawls	1966	Sandra Spuzich	1979	Jerilyn Britz	1992	Patty Sheehan
1954	"Babe" Zaharias	1967	Catherine Lacoste*	1980	Amy Alcott	1993	Lauri Merten
1955	Fay Crocker	1968	Susie Maxwell Berning	1981	Pat Bradley	1994	Patty Sheehan
1956	Mrs. K. Cornelius	1969	Donna Caponi	1982	Janet Alex	1995	Annika Sorenstam
1957	Betsy Rawls	1970	Donna Caponi	1983	Jan Stephenson	1996	Annika Sorenstam
1958	Mickey Wright	1971	JoAnne Carner	1984	Hollis Stacy	1997	Alison Nicholas
1959	Mickey Wright	1972	Susie Maxwell Berning	1985	Kathy Baker	1998	Se Ri Pak
1960	Betsy Rawls	1973	Susie Maxwell Berning	1986	Jane Geddes		

*Amateur

PGA Leading Money Winners

Year	Player	Dollars	Year	Player	Dollars	Year	Player	Dollars
1946	Ben Hogan	$42,556	1964	Jack Nicklaus	$113,284	1981	Tom Kite	$375,699
1947	Jimmy Demaret	27,936	1965	Jack Nicklaus	140,752	1982	Craig Stadler	446,462
1948	Ben Hogan	36,812	1966	Billy Casper	121,944	1983	Hal Sutton	426,668
1949	Sam Snead	31,593	1967	Jack Nicklaus	188,988	1984	Tom Watson	476,260
1950	Sam Snead	35,758	1968	Billy Casper	205,168	1985	Curtis Strange	542,321
1951	Lloyd Mangrum	26,088	1969	Frank Beard	175,223	1986	Greg Norman	653,296
1952	Julius Boros	37,032	1970	Lee Trevino	157,037	1987	Curtis Strange	925,941
1953	Lew Worsham	34,002	1971	Jack Nicklaus	244,490	1988	Curtis Strange	1,147,644
1954	Bob Toski	65,819	1972	Jack Nicklaus	320,542	1989	Tom Kite	1,395,278
1955	Julius Boros	65,121	1973	Jack Nicklaus	308,362	1990	Greg Norman	1,165,477
1956	Ted Kroll	72,835	1974	Johnny Miller	353,201	1991	Corey Pavin	979,430
1957	Dick Mayer	65,835	1975	Jack Nicklaus	323,149	1992	Fred Couples	1,344,188
1958	Arnold Palmer	42,407	1976	Jack Nicklaus	266,438	1993	Nick Price	1,478,557
1959	Art Wall, Jr.	53,167	1977	Tom Watson	310,653	1994	Nick Price	1,499,927
1960	Arnold Palmer	75,262	1978	Tom Watson	362,429	1995	Greg Norman	1,654,959
1961	Gary Player	64,540	1979	Tom Watson	462,636	1996	Tom Lehman	1,780,159
1962	Arnold Palmer	81,448	1980	Tom Watson	530,808	1997	Tiger Woods	2,066,833
1963	Arnold Palmer	128,230						

LPGA Leading Money Winners

Year	Player	Dollars	Year	Player	Dollars	Year	Player	Dollars
1954	Patty Berg	$16,011	1969	Carol Mann	$49,152	1984	Betsy King	$266,771
1955	Patty Berg	16,492	1970	Kathy Whitworth	30,235	1985	Nancy Lopez	416,472
1956	Marlene Hagge	20,235	1971	Kathy Whitworth	41,181	1986	Pat Bradley	492,021
1957	Patty Berg	16,272	1972	Kathy Whitworth	65,063	1987	Ayako Okamoto	466,034
1958	Beverly Hanson	12,629	1973	Kathy Whitworth	82,854	1988	Sherri Turner	347,255
1959	Betsy Rawls	26,774	1974	JoAnne Carner	87,094	1989	Betsy King	654,132
1960	Louise Suggs	16,892	1975	Sandra Palmer	94,805	1990	Beth Daniel	863,578
1961	Mickey Wright	22,236	1976	Judy Rankin	150,734	1991	Pat Bradley	763,118
1962	Mickey Wright	21,641	1977	Judy Rankin	122,890	1992	Dottie Mochrie	693,335
1963	Mickey Wright	31,269	1978	Nancy Lopez	189,813	1993	Betsy King	595,992
1964	Mickey Wright	29,800	1979	Nancy Lopez	215,987	1994	Laura Davies	687,201
1965	Kathy Whitworth	28,658	1980	Beth Daniel	231,000	1995	Annika Sorenstam	666,533
1966	Kathy Whitworth	33,517	1981	Beth Daniel	206,977	1996	Karrie Webb	1,002,000
1967	Kathy Whitworth	32,937	1982	JoAnne Carner	310,399	1997	Annika Sorenstam	1,236,789
1968	Kathy Whitworth	48,379	1983	JoAnne Carner	291,404			

RIFLE AND PISTOL INDIVIDUAL CHAMPIONSHIP

Source: National Rifle Association

National Outdoor Rifle and Pistol Championships in 1998

Pistol—SSGT Brian Zinz, USMC, Chesterfield, MT, 2635-135X
Civilian Pistol—Jerry Chaney, Lily, KY, 2629-117X
Woman Pistol—SFC Ruby Fox, USA, Parker, AZ, 2548-76X
Smallbore Rifle Prone—Cory Brunetti, Easton, CT, 6387-475X
Civilian Smallbore Rifle Prone— Cory Brunetti, Easton, CT, 6387-475X
Woman Smallbore Rifle Prone—Carolyn D. Millard-Sparks, Dunwoody, GA, 6383-492X
Smallbore Rifle NRA 3-Position—SGT Troy A. Bassham, USA, Phenix City, AL, 2295-85X
Civilian Smallbore Rifle NRA 3-Position—Shane Barnhart, Ashley, OH, 2287-97X
Woman Smallbore Rifle NRA 3-Position—Emily Caruso, Fairfield, CT, 2261-68X
High Power Rifle—Nancy H. Tompkins-Gallagher, Prescott, AZ, 2378-94X
Civilian High Power Rifle— Nancy H. Tompkins-Gallagher, Prescott, AZ, 2378-94X
Woman High Power Rifle—Nancy H. Tompkins-Gallagher, Prescott, AZ, 2378-94X
High Power Rifle Long Range—Michelle M. Gallagher, Prescott, AZ, 1446-79X
Woman High Power Rifle Long Range—Michelle M. Gallagher, Prescott, AZ, 1446-79X

National Indoor Rifle and Pistol Championships in 1998

Smallbore Rifle 4-Position—Steve Goff, Columbus, GA, 800
Woman Smallbore Rifle 4-Position—Vickie J. Parker, Marlborough, NH, 791
Smallbore Rifle NRA 3-Position—Steve Goff, Columbus, GA, 1188
Woman Smallbore Rifle NRA 3-Position—Katherine M. Delgrosso, Salem, OR, 1163
International Smallbore Rifle—SGT Troy A. Bassham, USA, Phenix City, AL, 1187
Woman International Smallbore Rifle—Elizabeth J. Bourland, Wichita Falls, TX, 1178
Air Rifle—SGT Troy A. Bassham, USA, Phenix City, AL, 1187
Woman Air Rifle—Crystal D. Hamilton, Prosperity, PA, 584
Conventional Pistol—Robert A. Larson, St. Ignatius, MT, 886
Woman Conventional Pistol—Marilyn Brown, Plainwell, MI, 872
International Free Pistol—Richard L. Eddler, Lower Burrell, PA, 558
Woman International Free Pistol—Jeanice Naulty, Birdsboro, PA, 482
International Standard Pistol—Eric A. Weeldreyer, Kalamazoo, MI, 573
Woman International Standard Pistol—Jeanice Naulty, Birdsboro, PA, 539
Air Pistol—Jeffrey C. Shivers, Erie, PA, 573
Woman Air Pistol—Susan E. McConnell, Clifton Park, NY, 554

NRA Bianchi Cup National Action Pistol Championships in 1998

Action Pistol—Doug Koenig, Albertis, PA, 1920-180X
Woman Action Pistol—Anita Mackiewicz, Victoria, Australia, 1914-148X
Junior Action Pistol—Alex Burridge, Port Noarlunga, Australia, 1920-156X

Notable Sports Personalities

Henry (Hank) Aaron, b. 1934: Milwaukee-Atlanta outfielder hit record 755 home runs, led NL 4 times; record 2,297 RBIs.
Kareem Abdul-Jabbar, b. 1947: Milwaukee, L.A. Lakers center; MVP 6 times; all-time leading NBA scorer.
Troy Aikman, b. 1966: quarterback led Dallas Cowboys to Super Bowl wins in 1993-94, 1996; Super Bowl MVP, 1993.
Grover Cleveland Alexander (1887-1950): pitcher; won 374 NL games; pitched 16 shutouts, 1916.
Muhammad Ali, b. 1942: 3-time heavyweight champion.
Mario Andretti, b. 1940: won Indy 500, 1969; Grand Prix champ, 1978.
Eddie Arcaro, (1916-97): only jockey to win racing's Triple Crown twice, 1941,1948; rode 4,779 winners in his career.
Henry Armstrong (1912-1988): boxer held feather-, welter-, lightweight titles simultaneously, 1937-38.
Arthur Ashe (1943-1993): U.S. singles champ, 1968; Wimbledon champ, 1975.
Red Auerbach, b. 1917: coached Boston Celtics to 9 NBA championships.
Donovan Bailey, b. 1967: Canadian Olympic gold medalist in 100 meters (set world record), 1996.
Ernie Banks, b. 1931: Chicago Cubs slugger hit 512 NL homers; twice MVP.
Roger Bannister, b. 1929: Briton ran first sub 4-minute mile, May 6, 1954.
Rick Barry, b. 1944: NBA scoring leader, 1967; ABA, 1969.
Sammy Baugh, b. 1914: Washington Redskins quarterback held numerous records upon retirement after 16 pro seasons.
Elgin Baylor, b. 1934: L.A. Lakers forward; 1st team all-star 10 times.
Boris Becker, b. 1967: German tennis star; won U.S. Open 1989; Wimbledon champ 3 times.
Jean Beliveau, b. 1931: Montreal Canadiens center scored 507 goals; twice MVP.
Johnny Bench, b. 1947: Cincinnati Reds catcher; MVP twice; led league in home runs twice, RBIs 3 times.
Patty Berg, b. 1918: won more than 80 golf tournaments; AP Woman Athlete-of-the-Year 3 times.
Yogi Berra, b. 1925: N.Y. Yankees catcher; MVP 3 times; played in 14 World Series.
Matt Biondi, b. 1965: swimmer won 5 gold medals at 1988 Olympics.
Larry Bird, b. 1956: Boston Celtics forward; chosen MVP 1984-86; 1998 coach of the year with Indiana Pacers.
George Blanda, b. 1927: quarterback, kicker; 26 years as active player, scoring record 2,002 points.
Wade Boggs, b. 1958: AL batting champ, 1983, 1985-88.
Barry Bonds, b. 1964: outfielder was NL MVP 1990, 1992-93; only player in 400 home runs/400 stolen bases club.
Bjorn Borg, b. 1956: led Sweden to first Davis Cup, 1975; Wimbledon champion 5 times.
Mike Bossy, b. 1957; N.Y. Islanders right wing scored more than 50 goals 8 times.
Ray Bourque, b. 1960: Boston Bruins defenseman won Norris Trophy 5 times.
Terry Bradshaw, b. 1948; Pittsburgh Steelers quarterback led team to 4 Super Bowl titles.
George Brett, b. 1953: Kansas City Royals infielder led AL in batting, 1976, 1980, 1990; MVP, 1980.
Lou Brock, b. 1939: St. Louis Cardinals outfielder stole NL record 118 bases, 1974; led NL 8 times.
Jim Brown, b. 1936: Cleveland Browns fullback ran for 12,312 career yards; MVP 3 times.
Paul Brown (1908-1991), football owner, coach; led Cleveland Browns to 3 NFL championships.
Paul "Bear" Bryant (1913-1983), college football coach with 323 victories.
Sergei Bubka, b. 1963: Ukrainian pole vaulter; first to clear 20 feet; gold medal, 1988 Olympics.
Maria Bueno, b. 1939: U.S. singles champ 4 times; Wimbledon champ 3 times.
Dick Butkus, b. 1942: Chicago Bears linebacker twice chosen best NFL defensive player.
Dick Button, b. 1929: figure skater won 1948, 1952 Olympic gold medals; world titlist, 1948-52.
Roy Campanella (1921-1993): Brooklyn Dodgers catcher; MVP 3 times.
Earl Campbell, b. 1955: NFL running back; MVP 1978-80.
Rod Carew, b. 1945: AL infielder; won 7 batting titles; MVP, 1977.
Steve Carlton, b. 1944: NL pitcher won 20 games 5 times, Cy Young award 4 times.
Billy Casper, b. 1931: PGA Player-of-the-Year 3 times; U.S. Open champ twice.
Wilt Chamberlain, b. 1936: center was NBA leading scorer 7 times; MVP 4 times; scored 100 pts. in a game, 1962.
Bobby Clarke, b. 1949: Philadelphia Flyers center led team to 2 Stanley Cup championships; MVP 3 times.
Roger Clemens, b. 1962: AL pitcher; AL MVP 1986; first AL pitcher to win Cy Young 4 times, 1986, 1987, 1991, 1997; twice struck out record 20 batters in a game.
Roberto Clemente (1934-1972): Pittsburgh Pirates outfielder won 4 batting titles; MVP, 1966.
Ty Cobb (1886-1961): Detroit Tigers outfielder had record .367 lifetime batting average, 12 batting titles.
Sebastian Coe, b. 1956: Briton won Olympic 1,500-meter run, 1980, 1984.
Nadia Comaneci, b. 1961: Romanian gymnast won 3 gold medals, achieved 7 perfect scores, 1976 Olympics.
Maureen Connolly (1934-1969): won tennis "grand slam," 1953; AP Woman-Athlete-of-the-Year 3 times.
Jimmy Connors, b. 1952: U.S. singles champ 5 times; Wimbledon champ twice.
James J. Corbett (1866-1933): heavyweight champion, 1892-97; credited with being the first "scientific" boxer.
Angel Cordero, b. 1942: leading money winner, 1976, 1982-83; rode 3 Kentucky Derby winners.
Margaret Smith Court, b. 1942: Australian tennis great won 24 grand slam events.
Bob Cousy, b. 1928: Boston Celtics guard led team to 6 NBA championships; MVP, 1957.
Bjoern Daehlie, b. 1967: Norwegian cross-country skier; won record 8 Winter Olympic gold medals.
Dizzy Dean (1911-1974): colorful pitcher for St. Louis Cardinals "Gashouse Gang" in the '30s; MVP, 1934.
Oscar De La Hoya, b. 1972: boxer won lightweight title, 1995; super lightweight title, 1996; welterweight title, 1997.
Jack Dempsey (1895-1983): heavyweight champ, 1919-26.
Gail Devers, b. 1966: sprinter won Olympic gold medals in 100-meter run, 1992, 1996.
Eric Dickerson, b. 1960: running back ran for NFL record 2,105 yds., 1984; led NFC 3 times, AFC twice.
Joe DiMaggio, b. 1914: N.Y. Yankees outfielder hit safely in record 56 consecutive games, 1941; AL MVP 3 times.
Dale Earnhardt, b. 1951: auto racer was NASCAR Winston Cup champion 7 times.
Stefan Edberg, b. 1966: U.S. singles champ, 1991, 1992; Wimbledon champ, 1988, 1990.
Gertrude Ederle, b. 1906: first woman to swim English Channel, broke existing men's record, 1926.
John Elway, b. 1960: quarterback led Denver Broncos to Super Bowl win, 1998; regular-season MVP, 1987.
Julius Erving, b. 1950: MVP and leading scorer in ABA 3 times; NBA MVP, 1981.
Phil Esposito, b. 1942: NHL scoring leader 5 times.
Janet Evans, b. 1971: swimmer won 3 Olympic gold medals, 1988, 1 in 1992.
Chris Evert, b. 1954: U.S. Open tennis champ 6 times, Wimbledon champ 3 times.
Ray Ewry (1873-1937): track-and-field star won 8 gold medals, 1900, 1904, and 1908 Olympics.
Nick Faldo, 1957: won Masters, British Open 3 times each.
Juan Fangio (1911-1995): World Grand Prix champion 5 times.
Brett Favre, b. 1969: quarterback led Green Bay Packers to Super Bowl win, 1997; NFL regular-season MVP, 1995, 1996; co-MVP, 1997.
Bob Feller, b. 1918: Cleveland Indians pitcher won 266 games; pitched 3 no-hitters, 12 one-hitters.
Peggy Fleming, b. 1948: world figure skating champion, 1966-68; gold medalist, 1968 Olympics.
Whitey Ford, b. 1928: N.Y. Yankees pitcher won record 10 World Series games.
George Foreman, b. 1949: heavyweight champion, 1973-74, 1994-95; at 45, the oldest to win a heavyweight title.
Dick Fosbury, b. 1947: high jumper won 1968 Olympic gold medal; developed the "Fosbury Flop."
Jimmie Foxx (1907-1967): Red Sox, Athletics slugger; MVP 3 times; triple crown, 1933.
A.J. Foyt, b. 1935: won Indy 500 4 times; U.S. Auto Club champ 7 times.
Joe Frazier, b. 1944: heavyweight champion, 1970-73.
Lou Gehrig (1903-1941): N.Y. Yankees 1st baseman; MVP, 1927, 1936; triple crown, 1934; AL record 184 RBIs, 1931.
George Gervin, b. 1952: top NBA scorer, 1978-80, 1982.
Althea Gibson, b. 1927: twice U.S. and Wimbledon singles champ.
Bob Gibson, b. 1935: St. Louis Cardinals pitcher won Cy Young award twice; struck out 3,117 batters.
Marc Girardelli, b. 1963: Luxembourg skier won 5 World Cup titles.
Jeff Gordon, b. 1971: race car driver, youngest in modern era to win NASCAR Winston Cup, 1995; also won, 1997, 1998.
Steffi Graf, b. 1969: German won tennis "grand slam," 1988; U.S. champ 5 times; Wimbledon champ 7 times.
Otto Graham, b. 1921: Cleveland Browns quarterback; all-pro 4 times.

Red Grange (1903-1991): All-America at Univ. of Illinois, 1923-25; played for Chicago Bears, 1925-35.
Joe Greene, b. 1946: Pittsburgh Steelers lineman; twice NFL outstanding defensive player.
Wayne Gretzky, b. 1961: leading scorer in NHL history; MVP, 1980-87, 1989.
Ken Griffey Jr., b. 1969: Seattle Mariner outfielder led AL in home runs, 1994, 1997, 1998; 1997 AL MVP; 9 gold gloves.
Florence Griffith Joyner, (1959-98): sprinter won 3 gold medals at 1988 Olympics; Olympic record for 100m.
Lefty Grove (1900-1975): pitcher won 300 AL games; 20-game winner 8 times.
Tony Gwynn, b. 1960: 8-time NL batting champ, 1984, 1987-89, 1994-97.
Walter Hagen (1892-1969): won PGA championship 5 times; British Open 4 times.
George Halas (1895-1983): founder-coach of Chicago Bears; won 5 NFL championships.
Scott Hamilton, b. 1958: U.S. and world figure skating champion, 1981-84; Olympic gold medalist, 1984.
Bill Hartack, b. 1932: jockey rode 5 Kentucky Derby winners.
Dominik Hasek, b. 1965: Buffalo Sabres goalie won Vezina Trophy, 1994, 1995, 1997, 1998; NHL MVP, 1997, 1998.
John Havlicek, b. 1940: Boston Celtics forward scored more than 26,000 NBA points.
Rickey Henderson, b. 1958; outfielder stole record 130 bases, 1982; record lifetime steals; AL MVP, 1990.
Sonja Henie (1912-1969): world champion figure skater, 1927-36; Olympic gold medalist, 1928, 1932, 1936.
Martina Hingis, b. 1980: youngest woman to hold No. 1 tennis ranking; won Australian Open, Wimbledon, U.S. Open, 1997.
Ben Hogan (1912-1997): won 4 U.S. Open championships, 2 PGA, 2 Masters.
Evander Holyfield, b. 1962: 3-time heavyweight champion.
Rogers Hornsby (1896-1963): NL 2d baseman batted record .424 in 1924; twice won triple crown; batting leader, 1920-25.
Paul Hornung, b. 1935: Green Bay Packers runner-placekicker scored record 176 points, 1960.
Gordie Howe, b. 1928: hockey forward; NHL MVP 6 times; scored 801 goals in 26 NHL seasons.
Carl Hubbell (1903-1988): N.Y. Giants pitcher; 20-game winner 5 consecutive years, 1933-37.
Bobby Hull, b. 1939: NHL all-star 10 times; MVP, 1965-66.
Brett Hull, b. 1964: St. Louis Blues forward led NHL in goals, 1990-92; MVP, 1991.
Catfish Hunter, b. 1946: pitched perfect game, 1968; 20-game winner 5 times.
Don Hutson (1913-1997): Green Bay Packers receiver caught 99 NFL touchdown passes.
Reggie Jackson, b. 1946: slugger led AL in home runs 4 times; MVP, 1973; hit 5 World Series home runs, 1977.
Earvin (Magic) Johnson, b. 1959: NBA MVP, 1987, 1989, 1990; Playoff MVP, 1980, 1982, 1987; 2d in career assists.
Jack Johnson (1878-1946): heavyweight champion, 1910-15.
Michael Johnson, b. 1967: won Olympic gold medals in 200-meter (shattered world record) and 400-meter run, 1996.
Walter Johnson (1887-1946): Washington Senators pitcher won 416 games; record 110 shutouts.
Bobby Jones (1902-1971): won "grand slam of golf" 1930; U.S. Amateur champ 5 times, U.S. Open champ 4 times.
Michael Jordan, b. 1963: NBA leading scorer, 1987-93, 1996-98; MVP, 1988, 1991-92, 1996, 1998; Playoff MVP, 1991-93, 1996-98.
Jackie Joyner-Kersee, b. 1962: Olympic gold medalist in heptathlon, 1988, 1992.
Duke Kahanamoku (1890-1968): swimmer won 1912, 1920 Olympic gold medals in 100-meter freestyle; surfing pioneer.
Harmon Killebrew, b. 1936: Minnesota Twins slugger led AL in home runs 6 times; 573 lifetime.
Jean Claude Killy, b. 1943: French skier won 3 1968 Olympic gold medals.
Ralph Kiner, b. 1922: Pittsburgh Pirates slugger led NL in home runs 7 consecutive years, 1946-52.
Billie Jean King, b. 1943: U.S. singles champ 4 times; Wimbledon champ 6 times.
Bob Knight, b. 1940: Indiana U. basketball coach led team to NCAA championships, 1976, 1981, 1987.
Olga Korbut, b. 1955: Soviet gymnast won 3 1972 Olympic golds.
Sandy Koufax, b. 1935: Dodgers pitcher won Cy Young award 3 times; lowest ERA in NL, 1962-66; pitched 4 no-hitters, one a perfect game.
Guy Lafleur, b. 1951: forward led NHL in scoring 3 times; MVP, 1977, 1978.
Tom Landry, b. 1924: Dallas Cowboys head coach, 1960-88.
Rod Laver, b. 1938: Australian won tennis "grand slam" twice, 1962, 1969; Wimbledon champ 4 times.
Mario Lemieux, b. 1965: 6-time NHL leading scorer; MVP, 1988, 1993, 1996; Playoff MVP, 1991-92.
Ivan Lendl, b. 1960: U.S. Open tennis champ, 1985-87.
Sugar Ray Leonard, b. 1956: boxer held titles in 5 different weight classes.
Carl Lewis, b. 1961: track-and-field star won 9 Olympic gold medals in sprinting and the long jump.
Tara Lipinski, b. 1982: youngest figure skater to win U.S. and world championships, 1997, and Winter Olympic gold medal, 1998.
Vince Lombardi (1913-1970): Green Bay Packers coach led team to 5 NFL championships and 2 Super Bowl victories.
Greg Louganis, b. 1960: won Olympic gold medals in both springboard and platform diving, 1984, 1988.
Joe Louis (1914-1981): heavyweight champion, 1937-49.
Sid Luckman (1916-1998): Chicago Bears quarterback, led team to 4 NFL championships; MVP, 1943.
Connie Mack (1862-1956): Philadelphia Athletics manager, 1901-50; won 9 pennants, 5 championships.
Greg Maddux, b. 1966: NL pitcher won 4 consecutive Cy Young awards, 1992-95.
Karl Malone, b. 1963: Utah Jazz forward was MVP, 1997; 11-time All-Star; 25,000+ career points.
Moses Malone, b. 1955: NBA center, MVP, 1979, 1982-83.
Mickey Mantle (1931-1995): N.Y. Yankees outfielder; triple crown, 1956; 18 World Series home runs; MVP 3 times.
Pete Maravich (1948-1988): guard scored NCAA record 44.2 ppg during collegiate career; led NBA in scoring, 1977.
Rocky Marciano (1923-1969): heavyweight champion, 1952-56; retired undefeated.
Dan Marino, b. 1961: Miami Dolphins quarterback passed for NFL record 5,084 yds and 48 touchdowns, 1984; holds career NFL records for touchdowns, yds passing, completions.
Roger Maris (1934-1985): N.Y. Yankees outfielder hit AL record 61 home runs, 1961; MVP, 1960 and 1961.
Eddie Mathews, b. 1931: Milwaukee-Atlanta 3d baseman hit 512 career home runs.
Christy Mathewson (1880-1925): N.Y. Giants pitcher won 373 games.
Bob Mathias, b. 1930: decathlon gold medalist, 1948, 1952.
Willie Mays, b. 1931: N.Y.-S.F. Giants center fielder hit 660 home runs, led NL 4 times; had 3,283 hits; twice MVP.
Willie McCovey, b. 1938: S.F. Giants slugger hit 521 home runs; led NL 3 times; MVP, 1969.
John McEnroe, b. 1959: U.S. Open tennis champ, 1979-81, 1984; Wimbledon champ, 1981, 1983-84.
John McGraw (1873-1934): N.Y. Giants manager led team to 10 pennants, 3 championships.
Mark McGwire, b. 1963: 1st baseman hit a major league record 70 home runs in 1998; 50 or more home runs, 1996-98.
Mark Messier, b. 1961: center chosen NHL MVP, 1990 and 1992; Conn Smythe Trophy, 1984.
George Mikan, b. 1924: Minn. Lakers center considered the best basketball player of the first half of the century.
Stan Mikita, b. 1940: Chicago Black Hawks center led NHL in scoring 4 times; MVP twice.
Joe Montana, b. 1956: S.F. 49ers quarterback was Super Bowl MVP, 1982, 1985, 1990.
Archie Moore, b. 1913: light-heavyweight champion, 1952-62.
Howie Morenz (1902-1937): Montreal Canadiens forward considered the best hockey player of first half of the century.
Eddie Murray, b. 1956: durable slugger was 3d player to combine 3,000+ hits with 500+ home runs.
Stan Musial, b. 1920: St. Louis Cardinals star won 7 NL batting titles; MVP 3 times.
Bronko Nagurski (1908-1990): Chicago Bears fullback and tackle; gained more than 4,000 yds. rushing.
Joe Namath, b. 1943: N.Y. Jets quarterback was Super Bowl MVP, 1969.
Martina Navratilova, b. 1956: Wimbledon champ 9 times, U.S. champ 1983-84, 1986-87.
Byron Nelson, b. 1912: won 11 consecutive golf tournaments in 1945; twice Masters and PGA titlist.
Ernie Nevers (1903-1976): Stanford star selected the best college fullback to play between 1919-69.
John Newcombe, b. 1943: Australian twice U.S. Open tennis champ; Wimbledon titlist 3 times.
Jack Nicklaus, b. 1940: PGA Player-of-the-Year, 1967, 1972; leading money winner 8 times; won Masters 6 times.
Chuck Noll, b. 1931: coach led Pittsburgh Steelers to 4 Super Bowl titles.
Paavo Nurmi (1897-1973): Finnish distance runner won 6 Olympic gold medals, 1920, 1924, 1928.
Al Oerter, b. 1936: discus thrower won gold medal at 4 consecutive Olympics, 1956-68.
Hakeem Olajuwon, b. 1963: Houston Rockets center was NBA MVP, 1994, Playoffs MVP, 1994-95; career leader in blocked shots.
Shaquille O'Neal, b. 1972: NBA center was rookie of the year, 1993; scoring leader, 1995.
Bobby Orr, b. 1948: Boston Bruins defenseman; Norris Trophy 8 times; led NHL in scoring twice, assists 5 times.

Mel Ott (1909-1958): N.Y. Giants outfielder hit 511 home runs; led NL 6 times.
Jesse Owens (1913-1980): track and field star won 4 1936 Olympic gold medals.
Satchel Paige (1906-1982): pitcher starred in Negro leagues, 1924-48; entered major leagues at age 42.
Se Ri Pak, b. 1977: youngest winner ever (at 20) of LPGA Championship and of U.S. Women's Open, 1998.
Arnold Palmer, b. 1929: golf's first $1 million winner; won 4 Masters, 2 British Opens.
Jim Palmer, b. 1945: Baltimore Orioles pitcher; Cy Young award 3 times; 20-game winner 8 times.
Joe Paterno, b. 1926: winningest active NCAA football coach; led Penn St. to 2 national titles, 1982, 1986.
Floyd Patterson, b. 1935: twice heavyweight champion.
Walter Payton, b. 1954: Chicago Bears running back has most rushing yards in NFL history; top NFC rusher, 1976-80.
Pele, b. 1940: Brazilian soccer star scored 1,281 goals during 22-year career.
Bob Pettit, b. 1932: first NBA player to score 20,000 points; twice NBA scoring leader.
Richard Petty, b. 1937: NASCAR national champ 7 times; 7-time Daytona 500 winner.
Laffit Pincay Jr., b. 1946: leading money-winning jockey, 1970-74, 1979, 1985.
Jacques Plante (1929-1986): goalie, 7 Vezina trophies; first goalie to wear a mask in a game.
Kirby Puckett, b. 1961: Minn. Twins outfielder won AL batting title, 1989; led AL in hits, 1987-89, 1992; RBIs, 1994.
Willis Reed, b. 1942: N.Y. Knicks center; MVP, 1970; Playoff MVP, 1970, 1973.
Jerry Rice, b. 1962: S.F. 49ers receiver; Super Bowl MVP, 1989; NFL record for career touchdowns, receptions.
Maurice Richard, b. 1921: Montreal Canadiens forward scored 544 regular season goals, 82 playoff goals.
Branch Rickey (1881-1965): executive helped break baseball's color barrier, 1947; initiated farm system, 1919.
Pat Riley, b. 1945: coached L.A. Lakers to 4 NBA titles.
Cal Ripken Jr., b. 1960: Baltimore Orioles shortstop; AL MVP 1983, 1991; most consecutive games played, 2,632.
Oscar Robertson, b. 1938: guard averaged career 25.7 points per game; 3d most career assists; MVP, 1964.
Brooks Robinson, b. 1937: Baltimore Orioles 3d baseman played in 4 World Series; MVP, 1964; 16 gold gloves.
Frank Robinson, b. 1935: slugger was MVP in both NL and AL; triple crown, 1966; 586 lifetime home runs; first black manager in majors.
Jackie Robinson (1919-1972): broke baseball's color barrier with Brooklyn Dodgers, 1947; MVP, 1949.
Sugar Ray Robinson (1920-1989): middleweight champion 5 times, welterweight champion.
Knute Rockne (1888-1931): Notre Dame football coach, 1918-31; revolutionized game by stressing forward pass.
Dennis Rodman, b. 1961: eccentric forward led NBA in rebounding 1991-98.
Pete Rose, b. 1941: won 3 NL batting titles; hit safely in 44 consecutive games, 1978; has most career hits, 4,256.
Patrick Roy, b. 1965: Montreal-Colorado goalie was 3-time Vezina Trophy winner, Playoffs MVP, 1993.
Wilma Rudolph (1940-1994): sprinter won 3 1960 Olympic gold medals.
Adolph Rupp (1901-77): winningest NCAA basketball coach; led Kentucky to 4 national titles, 1948-49, 1951, 1958.
Bill Russell, b. 1934: Boston Celtics center led team to 11 NBA titles; MVP 5 times; first black coach of major pro sports team.
Babe Ruth (1895-1948): N.Y. Yankees outfielder hit 60 home runs, 1927; 714 lifetime; led AL 12 times.
Johnny Rutherford, b. 1938: auto racer won 3 Indy 500s.
Nolan Ryan, b. 1947: pitcher struck out record 383 batters, 1973; record 5,714 career; pitched record 7 no-hitters; won 324 major league games.
Pete Sampras, b. 1971: tennis star won U.S. Open 4 times, Wimbledon 5 times.
Barry Sanders, b. 1968: rushed for 2,053 yards in 1997; led NFL in rushing, 1990, 1994, 1996, 1997.
Gene Sarazen, b. 1902: won PGA championship 3 times, U.S. Open twice; developer of sand wedge.
Gale Sayers, b. 1943: Chicago Bears back twice led NFL in rushing.
Mike Schmidt, b. 1949: Phillies 3d baseman led NL in home runs 8 times; 548 lifetime; NL MVP, 1980, 1981, 1986.
Tom Seaver, b. 1944: pitcher won NL Cy Young award 3 times; won 311 major league games.
Monica Seles, b. 1973; U.S. Open tennis champ, 1991, 1992.
Willie Shoemaker, b. 1931: jockey rode 4 Kentucky Derby and 5 Belmont Stakes winners; leading career money winner.
Eddie Shore (1902-1985): Boston Bruins defenseman; MVP 4 times, first-team all-star 7 times.
Don Shula, b. 1930: all-time winningest NFL coach.
Al Simmons (1902-1956): AL outfielder batted .334 lifetime.
O.J. Simpson, b. 1947: running back rushed for 2,003 yds., 1973; AFC leading rusher 4 times.
George Sisler (1893-1973): St. Louis Browns 1st baseman had record 257 hits, 1920; batted .340 lifetime.
Dean Smith, b. 1931: North Carolina basketball coach has most career NCAA Division I victories.
Emmitt Smith, b. 1969: Dallas Cowboys running back led NFL in rushing, 1991-93, 1995; NFL and Super Bowl MVP, 1993; record 25 rushing touchdowns, 1995.
Lee Smith, b. 1957: relief pitcher, all-time saves leader, 478.
Sam Snead, b. 1912: PGA and Masters champ 3 times each.
Sammy Sosa, b. 1968: Chicago Cubs outfielder who hit 66 home runs, led NL in RBI, 1998.
Warren Spahn, b. 1921: pitcher won 363 NL games; 20-game winner 13 times; Cy Young award, 1957.
Tris Speaker (1885-1958): AL outfielder batted .344 over 22 seasons; hit record 793 career doubles.
Mark Spitz, b. 1950: swimmer won 7 1972 Olympic gold medals.
Amos Alonzo Stagg (1862-1965): coached Univ. of Chicago football team for 41 years, including 5 undefeated seasons; introduced huddle, man-in-motion, and end-around play.
Bart Starr, b. 1934: Green Bay Packers quarterback led team to 5 NFL titles and 2 Super Bowl victories.
Roger Staubach, b. 1942: Dallas Cowboys quarterback; leading NFC passer 5 times.
Casey Stengel (1890-1975): managed Yankees to 10 pennants, 7 championships, 1949-60.
Jackie Stewart, b. 1939: Scot auto racer retired with 27 Grand Prix victories.
John Stockton, b. 1962: Utah Jazz guard is NBA career leader in assists, steals; NBA assists leader, 1988-96.
John L. Sullivan (1858-1918): last bareknuckle heavyweight champion, 1882-1892.
Fran Tarkenton, b. 1940: quarterback is 2d in career touchdown passes.
Lawrence Taylor, b. 1959; linebacker led N.Y. Giants to 2 Super Bowl titles; played in 10 Pro Bowls.
Frank Thomas, b. 1968: Chicago White Sox 1st baseman was AL MVP, 1993-94; won AL batting title, 1997.
Jim Thorpe (1888-1953): football All-America, 1911, 1912; won pentathlon and decathlon, 1912 Olympics.
Bill Tilden (1893-1953): U.S. singles champ 7 times; played on 11 Davis Cup teams.
Y.A. Tittle, b. 1926: N.Y. Giants quarterback; MVP, 1961, 1963.
Lee Trevino, b. 1939: golfer won U.S., British Open twice.
Bryan Trottier, b. 1956: center played on 6 Stanley Cup championship teams.
Wyomia Tyus, b. 1945: sprinter won 1964, 1968 Olympic 100-meter dash.
Johnny Unitas, b. 1933: Baltimore Colts quarterback passed for more than 40,000 yds; MVP, 1957, 1967.
Al Unser, b. 1939: Indy 500 winner 4 times.
Bobby Unser, b. 1934: Indy 500 winner 3 times.
Norm Van Brocklin (1926-1983): quarterback passed for game record 554 yds., 1951; MVP, 1960.
Honus Wagner (1874-1955): Pittsburgh Pirates shortstop won 8 NL batting titles.
Tom Watson, b. 1949: golfer won British Open 5 times.
Johnny Weissmuller (1903-1984): swimmer won 52 national championships, 5 Olympic gold medals; set 67 world records.
Jerry West, b. 1938: L.A. Lakers guard had career average 27 points per game; first team all-star 10 times.
Reggie White, b. 1961: defensive end, all-time NFL sack leader.
Kathy Whitworth, b. 1939: women's golf leading money winner 8 times; first woman to earn more than $300,000.
Lenny Wilkens, b. 1937: winningest coach in NBA history.
Ted Williams, b. 1918: Boston Red Sox outfielder won 6 batting titles, two triple crowns; hit .406 in 1941.
Helen Wills Moody (1905-98): tennis star won U.S. Open 7 times, Wimbledon 8 times.
Katarina Witt, b. 1965: German figure skater; won Olympic gold medal, 1984, 1988.
John Wooden, b. 1910: coached UCLA basketball team to 10 national championships.
Tiger Woods, b. 1975: only golfer to win 3 consecutive U.S. Amateur titles, 1994-96; won Masters, 1997.
Mickey Wright, b. 1935: won LPGA championship 4 times, Vare Trophy 5 times; twice AP Woman-Athlete-of-the-Year.
Carl Yastrzemski, b. 1939: Boston Red Sox slugger won 3 batting titles; triple crown, 1967.
Cy Young (1867-1955): pitcher won record 511 games.
Steve Young, b. 1961: San Francisco 49ers quarterback led NFL in passing, 1991-94, 1996, 1997; Super Bowl MVP, 1995.
Babe Didrikson Zaharias (1914-1956): track star won 2 1932 Olympic gold medals; won numerous golf tournaments.

TENNIS

U.S. Open Champions, 1925-98

Men's Singles

Year	Champion	Final opponent
1925	Bill Tilden	William Johnston
1926	Rene Lacoste	Jean Borotra
1927	Rene Lacoste	Bill Tilden
1928	Henri Cochet	Francis Hunter
1929	Bill Tilden	Francis Hunter
1930	John Doeg	Francis Shields
1931	H. Ellsworth Vines	George Lott
1932	H. Ellsworth Vines	Henri Cochet
1933	Fred Perry	John Crawford
1934	Fred Perry	Wilmer Allison
1935	Wilmer Allison	Sidney Wood
1936	Fred Perry	Don Budge
1937	Don Budge	Baron G. von Cramm
1938	Don Budge	C. Gene Mako
1939	Robert Riggs	S. Welby Van Horn
1940	Don McNeill	Robert Riggs
1941	Robert Riggs	F. L. Kovacs
1942	F. R. Schroeder Jr.	Frank Parker
1943	Joseph Hunt	Jack Kramer
1944	Frank Parker	William Talbert
1945	Frank Parker	William Talbert
1946	Jack Kramer	Thomas Brown Jr.
1947	Jack Kramer	Frank Parker
1948	Pancho Gonzales	Eric Sturgess
1949	Pancho Gonzales	F. R. Schroeder Jr.
1950	Arthur Larsen	Herbert Flam
1951	Frank Sedgman	E. Victor Seixas Jr.
1952	Frank Sedgman	Gardnar Mulloy
1953	Tony Trabert	E. Victor Seixas Jr.
1954	E. Victor Seixas Jr.	Rex Hartwig
1955	Tony Trabert	Ken Rosewall
1956	Ken Rosewall	Lewis Hoad
1957	Malcolm Anderson	Ashley Cooper
1958	Ashley Cooper	Malcolm Anderson
1959	Neale A. Fraser	Alejandro Olmedo
1960	Neale A. Fraser	Rod Laver
1961	Roy Emerson	Rod Laver
1962	Rod Laver	Roy Emerson
1963	Rafael Osuna	F. A. Froehling 3d
1964	Roy Emerson	Fred Stolle
1965	Manuel Santana	Cliff Drysdale
1966	Fred Stolle	John Newcombe
1967	John Newcombe	Clark Graebner
1968	Arthur Ashe	Tom Okker
1969	Rod Laver	Tony Roche
1970	Ken Rosewall	Tony Roche
1971	Stan Smith	Jan Kodes
1972	Ilie Nastase	Arthur Ashe
1973	John Newcombe	Jan Kodes
1974	Jimmy Connors	Ken Rosewall
1975	Manuel Orantes	Jimmy Connors
1976	Jimmy Connors	Bjorn Borg
1977	Guillermo Vilas	Jimmy Connors
1978	Jimmy Connors	Bjorn Borg
1979	John McEnroe	Vitas Gerulaitis
1980	John McEnroe	Bjorn Borg
1981	John McEnroe	Bjorn Borg
1982	Jimmy Connors	Ivan Lendl
1983	Jimmy Connors	Ivan Lendl
1984	John McEnroe	Ivan Lendl
1985	Ivan Lendl	John McEnroe
1986	Ivan Lendl	Miloslav Mecir
1987	Ivan Lendl	Mats Wilander
1988	Mats Wilander	Ivan Lendl
1989	Boris Becker	Ivan Lendl
1990	Pete Sampras	Andre Agassi
1991	Stefan Edberg	Jim Courier
1992	Stefan Edberg	Pete Sampras
1993	Pete Sampras	Cedric Pioline
1994	Andre Agassi	Michael Stich
1995	Pete Sampras	Andre Agassi
1996	Pete Sampras	Michael Chang
1997	Patrick Rafter	Greg Rusedski
1998	Patrick Rafter	Mark Philippoussis

Women's Singles

Year	Champion	Final opponent
1925	Helen Willis	Kathleen McKane
1926	Molla B. Mallory	Elizabeth Ryan
1927	Helen Wills	Betty Nuthall
1928	Helen Wills	Helen Jacobs
1929	Helen Wills	M. Watson
1930	Betty Nuthall	L. A. Harper
1931	Helen Wills Moody	E. B. Whittingstall
1932	Helen Jacobs	Carolin A. Babcock
1933	Helen Jacobs	Helen Wills Moody
1934	Helen Jacobs	Sarah H. Palfrey
1935	Helen Jacobs	Sarah Palfrey Fabyan
1936	Alice Marble	Helen Jacobs
1937	Anita Lizana	Jadwiga Jedrzejowska
1938	Alice Marble	Nancye Wynne
1939	Alice Marble	Helen Jacobs
1940	Alice Marble	Helen Jacobs
1941	Sarah Palfrey Cooke	Pauline Betz
1942	Pauline Betz	Louise Brough
1943	Pauline Betz	Louise Brough
1944	Pauline Betz	Margaret Osborne
1945	Sarah Palfrey Cooke	Pauline Betz
1946	Pauline Betz	Doris Hart
1947	Louise Brough	Margaret Osborne
1948	Margaret Osborne duPont	Louise Brough
1949	Margaret Osborne duPont	Doris Hart
1950	Margaret Osborne duPont	Doris Hart
1951	Maureen Connolly	Shirley Fry
1952	Maureen Connolly	Doris Hart
1953	Maureen Connolly	Doris Hart
1954	Doris Hart	Louise Brough
1955	Doris Hart	Patricia Ward
1956	Shirley Fry	Althea Gibson
1957	Althea Gibson	Louise Brough
1958	Althea Gibson	Darlene Hard
1959	Maria Bueno	Christine Truman
1960	Darlene Hard	Maria Bueno
1961	Darlene Hard	Ann Haydon
1962	Margaret Smith	Darlene Hard
1963	Maria Bueno	Margaret Smith
1964	Maria Bueno	Carole Graebner
1965	Margaret Smith	Billie Jean Moffitt
1966	Maria Bueno	Nancy Richey
1967	Billie Jean King	Ann Haydon Jones
1968	Virginia Wade	Billie Jean King
1969	Margaret Smith Court	Nancy Richey
1970	Margaret Smith Court	Rosemary Casals
1971	Billie Jean King	Rosemary Casals
1972	Billie Jean King	Kerry Melville
1973	Margaret Smith Court	Evonne Goolagong
1974	Billie Jean King	Evonne Goolagong
1975	Chris Evert	Evonne Goolagong
1976	Chris Evert	Evonne Goolagong
1977	Chris Evert	Wendy Turnbull
1978	Chris Evert	Pam Shriver
1979	Tracy Austin	Chris Evert Lloyd
1980	Chris Evert Lloyd	Hana Mandlikova
1981	Tracy Austin	Martina Navratilova
1982	Chris Evert Lloyd	Hana Mandlikova
1983	Martina Navratilova	Chris Evert Lloyd
1984	Martina Navratilova	Chris Evert Lloyd
1985	Hana Mandlikova	Martina Navratilova
1986	Martina Navratilova	Helena Sukova
1987	Martina Navratilova	Steffi Graf
1988	Steffi Graf	Gabriela Sabatini
1989	Steffi Graf	Martina Navratilova
1990	Gabriela Sabatini	Steffi Graf
1991	Monica Seles	Martina Navratilova
1992	Monica Seles	Arantxa Sanchez Vicario
1993	Steffi Graf	Helena Sukova
1994	Arantxa Sanchez Vicario	Steffi Graf
1995	Steffi Graf	Monica Seles
1996	Steffi Graf	Monica Seles
1997	Martina Hingis	Venus Williams
1998	Lindsay Davenport	Martina Hingis

All-England Champions, Wimbledon, 1925-98

Men's Singles

Year	Champion	Final opponent	Year	Champion	Final opponent
1925	Rene Lacoste	Jean Borotra	1965	Roy Emerson	Fred Stolle
1926	Jean Borotra	Howard Kinsey	1966	Manuel Santana	Dennis Ralston
1927	Henri Cochet	Jean Borotra	1967	John Newcombe	Wilhelm Bungert
1928	Rene Lacoste	Henri Cochet	1968	Rod Laver	Tony Roche
1929	Henri Cochet	Jean Borotra	1969	Rod Laver	John Newcombe
1930	Bill Tilden	Wilmer Allison	1970	John Newcombe	Ken Rosewall
1931	Sidney B. Wood	Francis X. Shields	1971	John Newcombe	Stan Smith
1932	Ellsworth Vines	Henry Austin	1972	Stan Smith	Ilie Nastase
1933	Jack Crawford	Ellsworth Vines	1973	Jan Kodes	Alex Metreveli
1934	Fred Perry	Jack Crawford	1974	Jimmy Connors	Ken Rosewall
1935	Fred Perry	Gottfried von Cramm	1975	Arthur Ashe	Jimmy Connors
1936	Fred Perry	Gottfried von Cramm	1976	Bjorn Borg	Ilie Nastase
1937	Donald Budge	Gottfried von Cramm	1977	Bjorn Borg	Jimmy Connors
1938	Donald Budge	Henry Austin	1978	Bjorn Borg	Jimmy Connors
1939	Bobby Riggs	Elwood Cooke	1979	Bjorn Borg	Roscoe Tanner
1940-45	Not held	Not held	1980	Bjorn Borg	John McEnroe
1946	Yvon Petra	Geoff E. Brown	1981	John McEnroe	Bjorn Borg
1947	Jack Kramer	Tom P. Brown	1982	Jimmy Connors	John McEnroe
1948	Bob Falkenburg	John Bromwich	1983	John McEnroe	Chris Lewis
1949	Ted Schroeder	Jaroslav Drobny	1984	John McEnroe	Jimmy Connors
1950	Budge Patty	Frank Sedgman	1985	Boris Becker	Kevin Curren
1951	Dick Savitt	Ken McGregor	1986	Boris Becker	Ivan Lendl
1952	Frank Sedgman	Jaroslav Drobny	1987	Pat Cash	Ivan Lendl
1953	Vic Seixas	Kurt Nielsen	1988	Stefan Edberg	Boris Becker
1954	Jaroslav Drobny	Ken Rosewall	1989	Boris Becker	Stefan Edberg
1955	Tony Trabert	Kurt Nielsen	1990	Stefan Edberg	Boris Becker
1956	Lew Hoad	Ken Rosewall	1991	Michael Stich	Boris Becker
1957	Lew Hoad	Ashley Cooper	1992	Andre Agassi	Goran Ivanisevic
1958	Ashley Cooper	Neale Fraser	1993	Pete Sampras	Jim Courier
1959	Alex Olmedo	Rod Laver	1994	Pete Sampras	Goran Ivanisevic
1960	Neale Fraser	Rod Laver	1995	Pete Sampras	Boris Becker
1961	Rod Laver	Chuck McKinley	1996	Richard Krajicek	MaliVai Washington
1962	Rod Laver	Martin Mulligan	1997	Pete Sampras	Cedric Pioline
1963	Chuck McKinley	Fred Stolle	1998	Pete Sampras	Goran Ivanisevic
1964	Roy Emerson	Fred Stolle			

Women's Singles

Year	Champion	Final Opponent	Year	Champion	Final Opponent
1925	Suzanne Lenglen	Joan Fry	1964	Maria Bueno	Margaret Smith
1926	Kathleen McKane Godfree	Lili de Alvarez	1965	Margaret Smith	Maria Bueno
			1966	Billie Jean King	Maria Bueno
1927	Helen Wills	Lili de Alvarez	1967	Billie Jean King	Ann Haydon Jones
1928	Helen Wills	Lili de Alvarez	1968	Billie Jean King	Judy Tegart
1929	Helen Wills	Helen Jacobs	1969	Ann Haydon-Jones	Billie Jean King
1930	Helen Wills Moody	Elizabeth Ryan	1970	Margaret Smith Court	Billie Jean King
1931	Cilly Aussem	Hilde Kranwinkel	1971	Evonne Goolagong	Margaret Smith Court
1932	Helen Wills Moody	Helen Jacobs	1972	Billie Jean King	Evonne Goolagong
1933	Helen Wills Moody	Dorothy Round	1973	Billie Jean King	Chris Evert
1934	Dorothy Round	Helen Jacobs	1974	Chris Evert	Olga Morozova
1935	Helen Wills Moody	Helen Jacobs	1975	Billie Jean King	Evonne Goolagong Cawley
1936	Helen Jacobs	Hilde Kranwinkel Sperling	1976	Chris Evert	Evonne Goolagong Cawley
1937	Dorothy Round	Jadwiga Jedrzejowska	1977	Virginia Wade	Betty Stove
1938	Helen Wills Moody	Helen Jacobs	1978	Martina Navratilova	Chris Evert
1939	Alice Marble	Kay Stammers	1979	Martina Navratilova	Chris Evert Lloyd
1940-45	Not held	Not held	1980	Evonne Goolagong	Chris Evert Lloyd
1946	Pauline Betz	Louise Brough	1981	Chris Evert Lloyd	Hana Mandlikova
1947	Margaret Osborne	Doris Hart	1982	Martina Navratilova	Chris Evert Lloyd
1948	Louise Brough	Doris Hart	1983	Martina Navratilova	Andrea Jaeger
1949	Louise Brough	Margaret Osborne duPont	1984	Martina Navratilova	Chris Evert Lloyd
1950	Louise Brough	Margaret Osborne duPont	1985	Martina Navratilova	Chris Evert Lloyd
1951	Doris Hart	Shirley Fry	1986	Martina Navratilova	Hana Mandlikova
1952	Maureen Connolly	Louise Brough	1987	Martina Navratilova	Steffi Graf
1953	Maureen Connolly	Doris Hart	1988	Steffi Graf	Martina Navratilova
1954	Maureen Connolly	Louise Brough	1989	Steffi Graf	Martina Navratilova
1955	Louise Brough	Beverly Fleitz	1990	Martina Navratilova	Zina Garrison
1956	Shirley Fry	Angela Buxton	1991	Steffi Graf	Gabriela Sabatini
1957	Althea Gibson	Darlene Hard	1992	Steffi Graf	Monica Seles
1958	Althea Gibson	Angela Mortimer	1993	Steffi Graf	Jana Novotna
1959	Maria Bueno	Darlene Hard	1994	Conchita Martinez	Martina Navratilova
1960	Maria Bueno	Sandra Reynolds	1995	Steffi Graf	Arantxa Sánchez Vicario
1961	Angela Mortimer	Christine Truman	1996	Steffi Graf	Arantxa Sánchez Vicario
1962	Karen Hantze-Susman	Vera Sukova	1997	Martina Hingis	Jana Novotna
1963	Margaret Smith	Billie Jean Moffitt	1998	Jana Novotna	Nathalie Tauziat

Davis Cup Challenge Round, 1900-97

Year	Result	Year	Result	Year	Result
1900	United States 3, British Isles 0	1933	Great Britain 3, France 2	1968	United States 4, Australia
1901	Not held	1934	Great Britain 4, United States 1	1969	United States 5, Romania 0
1902	United States 3, British Isles 2	1935	Great Britain 5, United States 0	1970	United States 5, W. Germany 0
1903	British Isles 4, United States 1	1936	Great Britain 3, Australia 2	1971	United States 3, Romania 2
1904	British Isles 5, Belgium 0	1937	United States 4, Great Britain 1	1972	United States 3, Romania 2
1905	British Isles 5, United States 0	1938	United States 3, Australia 2	1973	Australia 5, United States 0
1906	British Isles 5, United States 0	1939	Australia 3, United States 2	1974	South Africa (default by India)
1907	Australia 3, British Isles 2	1940-45	Not held	1975	Sweden 3, Czechoslovakia 2
1908	Australasia 3, United States 2	1946	United States 5, Australia 0	1976	Italy 4, Chile 1
1909	Australasia 5, United States 0	1947	United States 4, Australia 1	1977	Australia 3, Italy 1
1910	Not held	1948	United States 5, Australia 0	1978	United States 4, Great Britain 1
1911	Australasia 5, United States 0	1949	United States 4, Australia 1	1979	United States 5, Italy 0
1912	British Isles 3, Australasia 2	1950	Australia 4, United States 1	1980	Czechoslovakia 4, Italy 1
1913	United States 3, British Isles 2	1951	Australia 3, United States 2	1981	United States 3, Argentina 1
1914	Australasia 3, United States 2	1952	Australia 4, United States 1	1982	United States 4, France, 1
1915-18	Not held	1953	Australia 3, United States 2	1983	Australia 3, Sweden 2
1919	Australasia 4, British Isles 1	1954	United States 3, Australia 2	1984	Sweden 4, United States 1
1920	United States 5, Australasia 0	1955	Australia 5, United States 0	1985	Sweden 3, W. Germany 2
1921	United States 5, Japan 0	1956	Australia 5, United States 0	1986	Australia 3, Sweden 2
1922	United States 4, Australasia 1	1957	Australia 3, United States 2	1987	Sweden 5, India 0
1923	United States 4, Australasia 1	1958	United States 3, Australia 2	1988	W. Germany 4, Sweden 1
1924	United States 5, Australasia 0	1959	Australia 3, United States 2	1989	W. Germany 3, Sweden 2
1925	United States 5, France 0	1960	Australia 4, Italy 1	1990	United States 3, Australia 2
1926	United States 4, France 1	1961	Australia 5, Italy 0	1991	France 3, United States 1
1927	France 3, United States 2	1962	Australia 5, Mexico 0	1992	United States 3, Switzerland 1
1928	France 4, United States 1	1963	United States 3, Australia 2	1993	Germany 4, Australia 1
1929	France 3, United States 2	1964	Australia 3, United States 2	1994	Sweden 4, Russia 1
1930	France 4, United States 1	1965	Australia 4, Spain 1	1995	United States 3, Russia 2
1931	France 3, Great Britain 2	1966	Australia 4, India 1	1996	France 3, Sweden 2
1932	France 3, United States 2	1967	Australia 4, Spain 1	1997	Sweden 5, United States 0

French Open Singles Champions, 1968-98

Men's Singles

Year	Champion	Final Opponent	Year	Champion	Final Opponent
1968	Ken Rosewall	Rod Laver	1984	Ivan Lendl	John McEnroe
1969	Rod Laver	Ken Rosewall	1985	Mats Wilander	Ivan Lendl
1970	Jan Kodes	Zeljko Franulovic	1986	Ivan Lendl	Mikael Pernfors
1971	Jan Kodes	Ilie Nastase	1987	Ivan Lendl	Mats Wilander
1972	Andres Gimeno	Patrick Proisy	1988	Mats Wilander	Henri Leconte
1973	Ilie Nastase	Nikki Pilic	1989	Michael Chang	Stefan Edberg
1974	Bjorn Borg	Manuel Orantes	1990	Andres Gomez	Andre Agassi
1975	Bjorn Borg	Guillermo Vilas	1991	Jim Courier	Andre Agassi
1976	Adriano Panatta	Harold Solomon	1992	Jim Courier	Petr Korda
1977	Guillermo Vilas	Brian Gottfried	1993	Sergi Bruguera	Jim Courier
1978	Bjorn Borg	Guillermo Vilas	1994	Sergi Bruguera	Alberto Berasategui
1979	Bjorn Borg	Victor Pecci	1995	Thomas Muster	Michael Chang
1980	Bjorn Borg	Vitas Gerulaitis	1996	Yevgeny Kafelnikov	Michael Stich
1981	Bjorn Borg	Ivan Lendl	1997	Gustavo Kuerten	Sergei Bruguera
1982	Mats Wilander	Guillermo Vilas	1998	Carlos Moya	Alex Corretja
1983	Yannick Noah	Mats Wilander			

Women's Singles

Year	Champion	Final Opponent	Year	Champion	Final Opponent
1968	Nancy Richey	Ann Jones	1984	Martina Navratilova	Chris Evert Lloyd
1969	Margaret Smith Court	Ann Jones	1985	Chris Evert Lloyd	Martina Navratilova
1970	Margaret Smith Court	Helga Niessen	1986	Chris Evert Lloyd	Martina Navratilova
1971	Evonne Goolagong	Helen Gourlay	1987	Steffi Graf	Martina Navratilova
1972	Billie Jean King	Evonne Goolagong	1988	Steffi Graf	Natalia Zvereva
1973	Margaret Smith Court	Chris Evert	1989	Arantxa Sánchez Vicario	Steffi Graf
1974	Chris Evert	Olga Morozova	1990	Monica Seles	Steffi Graf
1975	Chris Evert	Martina Navratilova	1991	Monica Seles	Arantxa Sánchez Vicario
1976	Sue Barker	Renata Tomanova	1992	Monica Seles	Steffi Graf
1977	Mima Jausovec	Florenza Mihai	1993	Steffi Graf	Mary Joe Fernandez
1978	Virginia Ruzici	Mima Jausovec	1994	Arantxa Sánchez Vicario	Mary Pierce
1979	Chris Evert Lloyd	Wendy Turnbull	1995	Steffi Graf	Arantxa Sánchez Vicario
1980	Chris Evert Lloyd	Virginia Ruzici	1996	Steffi Graf	Arantxa Sánchez Vicario
1981	Hana Mandlikova	Sylvia Hanika	1997	Iva Majoli	Martina Hingis
1982	Martina Navratilova	Andrea Jaeger	1998	Arantxa Sánchez Vicario	Monica Seles
1983	Chris Evert Lloyd	Mima Jausovec			

Australian Open Singles Champions, 1969-98

Men's Singles

Year	Champion	Final Opponent	Year	Champion	Final Opponent
1969	Rod Laver	Andres Gimeno	1974	Jimmy Connors	Phil Dent
1970	Arthur Ashe	Dick Crealy	1975	John Newcombe	Jimmy Connors
1971	Ken Rosewall	Arthur Ashe	1976	Mark Edmondson	John Newcombe
1972	Ken Rosewall	Mal Anderson	1977*	Roscoe Tanner	Guillermo Vilas
1973	John Newcombe	Onny Parun		Vitas Gerulaitis	John Lloyd

(continued)

Australian Open *(continued)*

1978	Guillermo Vilas	John Marks	1989	Ivan Lendl	Miloslav Mecir
1979	Guillermo Vilas	John Sadri	1990	Ivan Lendl	Stefan Edberg
1980	Brian Teacher	Kim Warwick	1991	Boris Becker	Ivan Lendl
1981	Johan Kriek	Steve Denton	1992	Jim Courier	Stefan Edberg
1982	Johan Kriek	Steve Denton	1993	Jim Courier	Stefan Edberg
1983	Mats Wilander	Ivan Lendl	1994	Pete Sampras	Todd Martin
1984	Mats Wilander	Kevin Curren	1995	Andre Agassi	Pete Sampras
1985	Stefan Edberg	Mats Wilander	1996	Boris Becker	Michael Chang
1986**	—	—	1997	Pete Sampras	Carlos Moya
1987	Stefan Edberg	Pat Cash	1998	Petr Korda	Marcelo Rios
1988	Mats Wilander	Pat Cash			

Women's Singles

Year	Champion	Final Opponent	Year	Champion	Final Opponent
1969	Margaret Smith Court	Billie Jean King	1984	Chris Evert Lloyd	Helena Sukova
1970	Margaret Smith Court	Kerry Melville Reid	1985	Martina Navratilova	Chris Evert Lloyd
1971	Margaret Smith Court	Evonne Goolagong	1986**	—	—
1972	Virginia Wade	Evonne Goolagong	1987	Hana Mandlikova	Martina Navratilova
1973	Margaret Smith Court	Evonne Goolagong	1988	Steffi Graf	Chris Evert
1974	Evonne Goolagong	Chris Evert	1989	Steffi Graf	Helena Sukova
1975	Evonne Goolagong	Martina Navratilova	1990	Steffi Graf	Mary Joe Fernandez
1976	Evonne Goolagong	Renata Tomanova	1991	Monica Seles	Jana Novotna
1977*	Kerry Reid	Dianne Balestrat	1992	Monica Seles	Mary Joe Fernandez
	Evonne Goolagong	Helen Gourlay	1993	Monica Seles	Steffi Graf
1978	Chris O'Neill	Betsy Nagelsen	1994	Steffi Graf	Arantxa Sánchez Vicario
1979	Barbara Jordan	Sharon Walsh	1995	Mary Pierce	Arantxa Sánchez Vicario
1980	Hana Mandlikova	Wendy Turnbull	1996	Monica Seles	Anke Huber
1981	Martina Navratilova	Chris Evert Lloyd	1997	Martina Hingis	Mary Pierce
1982	Chris Evert Lloyd	Martina Navratilova	1998	Martina Hingis	Conchita Martínez
1983	Martina Navratilova	Kathy Jordan			

* Two tournaments were held in 1977 (Jan. & Dec.). ** Tournament was moved forward to Jan. 1987, so no championship was decided in 1986.

AUTO RACING

Indianapolis 500 Winners

Year	Winner, Car (Chassis-Engine)	MPH[1]	Year	Winner, Car (Chassis-Engine)	MPH[1]
1911	Ray Harroun, Marmon	74.602	1958	Jimmy Bryan, Salih-Offy	133.791
1912	Joe Dawson, National	78.719	1959	Rodger Ward, Watson-Offy	135.857
1913	Jules Goux, Peugeot	75.933	1960	Jim Rathmann, Watson-Offy	138.767
1914	Rene Thomas, Delage	82.474	1961	A.J. Foyt Jr., Trevis-Offy	139.130
1915	Ralph DePalma, Mercedes	89.840	1962	Rodger Ward, Watson-Offy	140.293
1916	Dario Resta, Peugeot	84.001	1963	Parnelli Jones, Watson-Offy	143.137
1917-18	Not held		1964	A.J. Foyt Jr., Watson-Offy	147.350
1919	Howdy Wilcox, Peugeot	88.050	1965	Jim Clark, Lotus-Ford	150.686
1920	Gaston Chevrolet, Frontenac	88.618	1966	Graham Hill, Lola-Ford	144.317
1921	Tommy Milton, Frontenac	89.621	1967	A.J. Foyt Jr., Coyote-Ford	151.207
1922	Jimmy Murphy, Duesenberg-Miller	94.484	1968	Bobby Unser, Eagle-Offy	152.882
1923	Tommy Milton, Miller	90.954	1969	Mario Andretti, Hawk-Ford	156.867
1924	L.L. Corum-Joe Boyer, Duesenberg	98.234	1970	Al Unser, P.J. Colt-Ford	155.749
1925	Peter DePaolo, Duesenberg	101.127	1971	Al Unser, P.J. Colt-Ford	157.735
1926	Frank Lockhart, Miller	95.904	1972	Mark Donohue, McLaren-Offy	162.962
1927	George Souders, Duesenberg	97.545	1973	Gordon Johncock, Eagle-Offy	159.036
1928	Louie Meyer, Miller	99.482	1974	Johnny Rutherford, McLaren-Offy	158.589
1929	Ray Keech, Miller	97.585	1975	Bobby Unser, Eagle-Offy	149.213
1930	Billy Arnold, Summers-Miller	100.448	1976	Johnny Rutherford, McLaren-Offy	148.725
1931	Louis Schneider, Stevens-Miller	96.629	1977	A.J. Foyt Jr., Coyote-Foyt	161.331
1932	Fred Frame, Wetteroth-Miller	104.144	1978	Al Unser, Lola-Cosworth	161.363
1933	Louie Meyer, Miller	104.162	1979	Rick Mears, Penske-Cosworth	158.899
1934	Bill Cummings, Miller	104.863	1980	Johnny Rutherford, Chaparral-Cosworth	142.862
1935	Kelly Petillo, Wetteroth-Offy	106.240	1981	Bobby Unser, Penske-Cosworth	139.084
1936	Louie Meyer, Stevens-Miller	109.069	1982	Gordon Johncock, Wildcat-Cosworth	162.029
1937	Wilbur Shaw, Shaw-Offy	113.580	1983	Tom Sneva, March-Cosworth	162.117
1938	Floyd Roberts, Wetteroth-Miller	117.200	1984	Rick Mears, March-Cosworth	163.612
1939	Wilbur Shaw, Maserati	115.035	1985	Danny Sullivan, March-Cosworth	152.982
1940	Wilbur Shaw, Maserati	114.277	1986	Bobby Rahal, March-Cosworth	170.722
1941	Floyd Davis-Mauri Rose, Wetteroth-Offy	115.117	1987	Al Unser, March-Cosworth	162.175
1942-45	Not held		1988	Rick Mears, Penske-Chevy Indy V8	144.809
1946	George Robson, Adams-Sparks	114.820	1989	Emerson Fittipaldi, Penske-Chevy Indy V8	167.581
1947	Mauri Rose, Deidt-Offy	116.338	1990	Arie Luyendyk, Lola-Chevy Indy V8	185.981*
1948	Mauri Rose, Deidt-Offy	119.814	1991	Rick Mears, Penske-Chevy Indy V8	176.457
1949	Bill Holland, Deidt-Offy	121.327	1992	Al Unser Jr., Galmer-Chevy Indy V8A	134.477
1950	Johnnie Parsons, Kurtis-Offy	124.002	1993	Emerson Fittipaldi, Penske-Chevy Indy V8C	157.207
1951	Lee Wallard, Kurtis-Offy	126.244	1994	Al Unser Jr., Penske-Mercedes Benz	160.872
1952	Troy Ruttman, Kuzma-Offy	128.922	1995	Jacques Villeneuve, Reynard-Ford Cosworth XB	153.616
1953	Bill Vukovich, KK500A-Offy	128.740	1996	Buddy Lazier, Reynard-Ford Cosworth	147.956
1954	Bill Vukovich, KK500A-Offy	130.840	1997	Arie Luyendyk, G Force-Aurora	145.827
1955	Bob Sweikert, KK500C-Offy	128.213	1998	Eddie Cheever, Dallara-Aurora	145.155
1956	Pat Flaherty, Watson-Offy	128.490			
1957	Sam Hanks, Salih-Offy	135.601			

*Race record. **Note:** The race was less than 500 mi in the following years: 1916 (300 mi), 1926 (400 mi), 1950 (345 mi), 1973 (332.5 mi), 1975 (435 mi), 1976 (255 mi). (1) Average speed.

FedEx Championship Series PPG Cup Winners

(U.S. Auto Club Champions prior to 1979; Championship Auto Racing Teams [CART] Champions, 1979-98)

Year	Driver	Year	Driver	Year	Driver	Year	Driver
1960	A. J. Foyt	1970	Al Unser	1980	Johnny Rutherford	1990	Al Unser Jr.
1961	A. J. Foyt	1971	Joe Leonard	1981	Rick Mears	1991	Michael Andretti
1962	Rodger Ward	1972	Joe Leonard	1982	Rick Mears	1992	Bobby Rahal
1963	A. J. Foyt	1973	Roger McCluskey	1983	Al Unser	1993	Nigel Mansell
1964	A. J. Foyt	1974	Bobby Unser	1984	Mario Andretti	1994	Al Unser Jr.
1965	Mario Andretti	1975	A. J. Foyt	1985	Al Unser	1995	Jacques Villeneuve
1966	Mario Andretti	1976	Gordon Johncock	1986	Bobby Rahal	1996	Jimmy Vasser
1967	A. J. Foyt	1977	Tom Sneva	1987	Bobby Rahal	1997	Alex Zanardi
1968	Bobby Unser	1978	Tom Sneva	1988	Danny Sullivan	1998	Alex Zanardi
1969	Mario Andretti	1979	Rick Mears	1989	Emerson Fittipaldi		

Notable One-Mile Land Speed Records

Andy Green, a Royal Air Force pilot, broke the sound barrier and set the first supersonic world speed record on land, Oct. 15, 1997, in Black Rock Desert, NV. Green, driving a car built by Richard Noble, had 2 runs at an average speed of 763.035 mph, as calculated according to the rules of the Federation Internationale Automobiliste (FIA). This record and speed exceeded the speed of sound, calculated at 751.251 mph for this time. On Sept. 25, Green had set a new world mark at 714.144 mph, which eclipsed the old record of 633.468 mph. Both 1997 records were recorded by the United States Auto Club and recognized by the FIA.

Date	Driver	Car	MPH
1/26/06	Marriott	Stanley (Steam)	127.659
3/16/10	Oldfield	Benz	131.724
4/23/11	Burman	Benz	141.732
2/12/19	DePalma	Packard	149.875
4/27/20	Milton	Dusenberg	155.046
4/28/26	Parry-Thomas	Thomas Spl.	170.624
3/29/27	Seagrave	Sunbeam	203.790
4/22/28	Keech	White Triplex	207.552
3/11/29	Seagrave	Irving-Napier	231.446
2/5/31	Campbell	Napier-Campbell	246.086
2/24/32	Campbell	Napier-Campbell	253.96
2/22/33	Campbell	Napier-Campbell	272.109
9/3/35	Campbell	Bluebird Special	301.13
11/19/37	Eyston	Thunderbolt 1	311.42
9/16/38	Eyston	Thunderbolt 1	357.5
8/23/39	Cobb	Railton	368.9
9/16/47	Cobb	Railton-Mobil	394.2
8/5/63	Breedlove	Spirit of America	407.45
10/27/64	Arfons	Green Monster	536.71
11/15/65	Breedlove	Spirit of America	600.601
10/23/70	Gabelich	Blue Flame	622.407
10/9/79	Barrett	Budweiser Rocket	638.637*
10/4/83	Noble	Thrust 2	633.468
9/25/97	Green	Thrust SSC	714.144
10/15/97	Green	Thrust SSC	763.035

*Not recognized as official by sanctioning bodies.

24 Hours of Le Mans Race in 1998

Alan McNish (Britain), Laurent Aiello (France), and Stephane Ortelli (France) drove their Porsche GT One to victory in the 1998 "24 Hours of Le Mans" race, June 7, 1998. They traveled 2,972 miles at an average of 124.577 mph.

World Grand Prix Champions, 1951-98

Year	Driver	Year	Driver	Year	Driver
1951	Juan Fangio, Argentina	1967	Denis Hulme, New Zealand	1983	Nelson Piquet, Brazil
1952	Alberto Ascari, Italy	1968	Graham Hill, England	1984	Niki Lauda, Austria
1953	Alberto Ascari, Italy	1969	Jackie Stewart, Scotland	1985	Alain Prost, France
1954	Juan Fangio, Argentina	1970	Jochen Rindt, Austria	1986	Alain Prost, France
1955	Juan Fangio, Argentina	1971	Jackie Stewart, Scotland	1987	Nelson Piquet, Brazil
1956	Juan Fangio, Argentina	1972	Emerson Fittipaldi, Brazil	1988	Ayrton Senna, Brazil
1957	Juan Fangio, Argentina	1973	Jackie Stewart, Scotland	1989	Alain Prost, France
1958	Mike Hawthorne, England	1974	Emerson Fittipaldi, Brazil	1990	Ayrton Senna, Brazil
1959	Jack Brabham, Australia	1975	Niki Lauda, Austria	1991	Ayrton Senna, Brazil
1960	Jack Brabham, Australia	1976	James Hunt, England	1992	Nigel Mansell, Britain
1961	Phil Hill, United States	1977	Niki Lauda, Austria	1993	Alain Prost, France
1962	Graham Hill, England	1978	Mario Andretti, United States	1994	Michael Schumacher, Germany
1963	Jim Clark, Scotland	1979	Jody Scheckter, South Africa	1995	Michael Schumacher, Germany
1964	John Surtees, England	1980	Alan Jones, Australia	1996	Damon Hill, England
1965	Jim Clark, Scotland	1981	Nelson Piquet, Brazil	1997	Jacques Villeneuve, Canada
1966	Jack Brabham, Australia	1982	Keke Rosberg, Finland	1998	Mika Hakkinen, Finland

Grand Prix Races for Formula 1 Cars in 1998

Date	Grand Prix	Winner, car
3/8	Australian	Mika Hakkinen, McLaren-Mercedes
3/29	Brazilian	Mika Hakkinen, McLaren-Mercedes
4/12	Argentine	Michael Schumacher, Ferrari
4/26	San Marino	David Coulthard, McLaren-Mercedes
5/10	Spanish	Mika Hakkinen, McLaren-Mercedes
5/24	Monaco	Mika Hakkinen, McLaren-Mercedes
6/7	Canadian	Michael Schumacher, Ferrari
6/28	French	Michael Schumacher, Ferrari
7/12	British	Michael Schumacher, Ferrari
7/26	Austrian	Mika Hakkinen, McLaren-Mercedes
8/2	German	Mika Hakkinen, McLaren-Mercedes
8/16	Hungary	Michael Schumacher, Ferrari
8/30	Belgian	Damon Hill, Jordan-Mugen Honda
9/13	Italian	Michael Schumacher, Ferrari
9/27	Luxembourg	Mika Hakkinen, McLaren-Mercedes
11/1	Japanese	Mika Hakkinen, McLaren-Mercedes

NASCAR Racing

Winston Cup Champions, 1949-98

Year	Driver	Year	Driver	Year	Driver	Year	Driver
1949	Red Byron	1962	Joe Weatherly	1975	Richard Petty	1987	Dale Earnhardt
1950	Bill Rexford	1963	Joe Weatherly	1976	Cale Yarborough	1988	Bill Elliott
1951	Herb Thomas	1964	Richard Petty	1977	Cale Yarborough	1989	Rusty Wallace
1952	Tim Flock	1965	Ned Jarrett	1978	Cale Yarborough	1990	Dale Earnhardt
1953	Herb Thomas	1966	David Pearson	1979	Richard Petty	1991	Dale Earnhardt
1954	Lee Petty	1967	Richard Petty	1980	Dale Earnhardt	1992	Alan Kulwicki
1955	Tim Flock	1968	David Pearson	1981	Darrell Waltrip	1993	Dale Earnhardt
1956	Buck Baker	1969	David Pearson	1982	Darrell Waltrip	1994	Dale Earnhardt
1957	Buck Baker	1970	Bobby Isaac	1983	Bobby Allison	1995	Jeff Gordon
1958	Lee Petty	1971	Richard Petty	1984	Terry Labonte	1996	Terry Labonte
1959	Lee Petty	1972	Richard Petty	1985	Darrell Waltrip	1997	Jeff Gordon
1960	Rex White	1973	Benny Parsons	1986	Dale Earnhardt	1998	Jeff Gordon
1961	Ned Jarrett	1974	Richard Petty				

Daytona 500 Winners, 1959-98

Year	Driver, car	Avg. MPH	Year	Driver, car	Avg. MPH
1959	Lee Petty, Oldsmobile	135.521	1979	Richard Petty, Oldsmobile	143.977
1960	Junior Johnson, Chevrolet	124.740	1980	Buddy Baker, Oldsmobile	177.602
1961	Marvin Panch, Pontiac	149.601	1981	Richard Petty, Buick	169.651
1962	Fireball Roberts, Pontiac	152.529	1982	Bobby Allison, Buick	153.991
1963	Tiny Lund, Ford	151.566	1983	Cale Yarborough, Pontiac	155.979
1964	Richard Petty, Plymouth	154.334	1984	Cale Yarborough, Chevrolet	150.994
1965	Fred Lorenzen, Ford (a)	141.539	1985	Bill Elliott, Ford	172.265
1966	Richard Petty, Plymouth (b)	160.627	1986	Geoff Bodine, Chevrolet	148.124
1967	Mario Andretti, Ford	146.926	1987	Bill Elliott, Ford	176.263
1968	Cale Yarborough, Mercury	143.251	1988	Bobby Allison, Buick	137.531
1969	Lee Roy Yarborough, Ford	160.875	1989	Darrell Waltrip, Chevrolet	148.466
1970	Pete Hamilton, Plymouth	149.601	1990	Derrike Cope, Chevrolet	165.761
1971	Richard Petty, Plymouth	144.456	1991	Ernie Irvan, Chevrolet	148.148
1972	A. J. Foyt, Mercury	161.550	1992	Davey Allison, Ford	160.256
1973	Richard Petty, Dodge	157.205	1993	Dale Jarrett, Chevrolet	154.972
1974	Richard Petty, Dodge (c)	140.894	1994	Sterling Marlin, Chevrolet	156.931
1975	Benny Parsons, Chevrolet	153.649	1995	Sterling Marlin, Chevrolet	141.710
1976	David Pearson, Mercury	152.181	1996	Dale Jarrett, Ford	154.308
1977	Cale Yarborough, Chevrolet	153.218	1997	Jeff Gordon, Chevrolet	148.295
1978	Bobby Allison, Ford	159.730	1998	Dale Earnhardt, Chevrolet	172.712

(a) 322.5 mi. (b) 495 mi. (c) 450 mi.

Winston Cup Series Races in 1998

(through Nov. 1)

Date	Race, site	Winner	Car	Prize
Feb. 15	Daytona 500, Daytona Beach, FL	Dale Earnhardt	Chevrolet	$1,059,105
Feb. 22	GM Goodwrench Service Plus 400, Rockingham, NC	Jeff Gordon	Chevrolet	90,090
Mar. 1	Las Vegas 400, Las Vegas, NV	Mark Martin	Ford	313,900
Mar. 9#	PRIMESTAR 500, Atlanta, GA	Bobby Labonte	Pontiac	106,800
Mar. 22	TranSouth Financial 400, Darlington, SC	Dale Jarrett	Ford	110,035
Mar. 29	Food City 500, Bristol, TN	Jeff Gordon	Chevrolet	90,860
Apr. 5	Texas 500, Fort Worth, TX	Mark Martin	Ford	356,850
Apr. 20#	Goody's Headache Powder 500, Martinsville, VA	Bobby Hamilton	Chevrolet	227,025[1]
Apr. 26	DieHard 500, Talladega, AL	Bobby Labonte	Pontiac	141,870
May 3	California 500 presented by NAPA , Fontana, CA	Mark Martin	Ford	141,375
May 16	*The Winston, Concord, NC	Mark Martin	Ford	257,500
May 24	Coca-Cola 600, Concord, NC	Jeff Gordon	Chevrolet	346,500
May 31	MBNA Platinum 400, Dover, DE	Dale Jarrett	Ford	89,950
June 6	Pontiac Excitement 400, Richmond, VA	Terry Labonte	Chevrolet	99,975
June 14	Miller Lite 400, Brooklyn, MI	Mark Martin	Ford	92,375
June 21	Pocono 500, Pocono, PA	Jeremy Mayfield	Ford	111,580
June 28	Save Mart/Kragen 350, Sonoma, CA	Jeff Gordon	Chevrolet	160,675
July 12	Jiffy Lube 300, Loudon, NH	Jeff Burton	Ford	128,575
July 26	Pennsylvania 500, Long Pond, PA	Jeff Gordon	Chevrolet	165,495
Aug. 2	Brickyard 400, Indianapolis, IN	Jeff Gordon	Chevrolet	1,637,625[2]
Aug. 9	The Bud at The Glen, Watkins Glen, NY	Jeff Gordon	Chevrolet	152,970
Aug. 16	Pepsi 400 presented by DeVilbiss , Brooklyn, MI	Jeff Gordon	Chevrolet	120,302
Aug. 22	Goody's Headache Powder 500, Bristol, TN	Mark Martin	Ford	80,315
Aug. 30	Farm Aid on CMT 300, Loudon, NH	Jeff Gordon	Chevrolet	205,400
Sept. 6	Pepsi Southern 500, Darlington, SC	Jeff Gordon	Chevrolet	134,655
Sept. 12	Exide NASCAR Select Batteries 400, Richmond, VA	Jeff Burton	Ford	108,495
Sept. 20	MBNA Gold 400, Dover, DE	Mark Martin	Ford	126,130
Sept. 27	NAPA AutoCare 500, Martinsville, VA	Ricky Rudd	Ford	102,575
Oct. 4	UAW-GM Quality 500, Concord, NC	Mark Martin	Ford	151,950
Oct. 11	Winston 500, Talladega, AL	Dale Jarrett	Ford	1,110,125[2]
Oct. 17[3]	Pepsi 400, Daytona Beach, FL	Jeff Gordon	Chevrolet	184,325
Oct. 25	Dura-Lube 500, Phoenix, AZ	Rusty Wallace	Ford	78,005
Nov. 1	AC Delco 400, Rockingham, NC	Jeff Gordon	Chevrolet	111,575

# Denotes rain delayed event. * Denotes nonpoint event. (1) Includes 76 Challenge bonus of $106,400. (2) Includes $1,000,000 bonus. (3)The Pepsi 400 at Daytona Beach, FL, was moved from July 4 to Oct. 17 because of Florida fires.

BOXING

Champions by Classes

There are many governing bodies in boxing, including the World Boxing Council, World Boxing Assn., International Boxing Federation, World Boxing Org., U.S. Boxing Assn., North American Boxing Federation, and European Boxing Union. Others are recognized by TV networks and the print media. All the governing bodies have their own champions and assorted boxing divisions. The following are the recognized champions— as of Nov. 1, 1998—in the principal divisions of the WBC, WBA, and IBF.

Class, Weight limit	WBC	WBA	IBF
Heavyweight	Lennox Lewis, U.K.	Evander Holyfield, U.S.	Evander Holyfield, U.S.
Cruiserweight (190 lb)	Juan Carlos Gomez, Cuba	Fabrice Tiozzo, France	Arthur Williams, U.S.
Light Heavyweight (175 lb)	Roy Jones Jr., U.S.	Roy Jones Jr., U.S.	Reggie Johnson, U.S.
Super Middleweight (168 lb)	Richie Woodhall, U.K.	Frank Liles, U.S.	Sven Ottke, Germany
Middleweight (160 lb)	Hassine Cherifi, France	William Joppy, U.S.	Bernard Hopkins, U.S.
Jr. Middleweight (154 lb)	Keith Mullings, U.S.	Laurent Boudouani, France	Luis "Yori Boy" Campas, Mexico
Welterweight (147 lb)	Oscar de la Hoya, U.S.	James Page, U.S.	Felix Trinidad, Puerto Rico
Jr. Welterweight (140 lb)	Vacant	Sharmba Mitchell, U.S.	Vince Phillips, U.S.
Lightweight (135 lb)	Cesar Bazan, Mexico	Jean Baptiste Mendy, France	Shane Mosely, U.S.
Jr. Lightweight (130 lb)	Floyd Mayweather Jr., U.S.	Takanori Hatakeyama, Japan	Roberto Garcia, U.S.
Featherweight (126 lb)	Luisito Espinoza, Philippines	Antonio Ceremeno, Venezuela	Manuel Medina, Mexico
Jr. Featherweight (122 lb)	Erik Morales, Mexico	Enrique Sanchez, Mexico	Vuyani Bungu, South Africa
Bantamweight (118 lb)	Joichiro Tatsuyoshi, Japan	Nana Konadu, Ghana	Tim Austin, U.S.
Jr. Bantamweight (115 lb)	In-joo Cho, S. Korea	Satoshi Iida, Japan	Johnny Tapia, U.S.
Flyweight (112 lb)	Chatchai Sasakul, Thailand	Hugo Soto, Argentina	Mark Johnson, U.S.
Jr. Flyweight (108 lb)	Saman Sorjaturong, Thailand	Pichitnoi C. Siriwat, Thailand	Vacant
Strawweight (105 lb)	Ricardo Lopez, Mexico	Rosendo Alvarez, Nicaragua	Zolani Petelo, South Africa

Ring Champions by Years

(*abandoned the title or was stripped of it; IBF champions listed only for heavyweight division)

Heavyweights

1882-1892	John L. Sullivan (a)
1892-1897	James J. Corbett (b)
1897-1899	Robert Fitzsimmons
1899-1905	James J. Jeffries* (c)
1905-1906	Marvin Hart
1906-1908	Tommy Burns
1908-1915	Jack Johnson
1915-1919	Jess Willard
1919-1926	Jack Dempsey
1926-1928	Gene Tunney*
1928-1930	Vacant
1930-1932	Max Schmeling
1932-1933	Jack Sharkey
1933-1934	Primo Carnera
1934-1935	Max Baer
1935-1937	James J. Braddock
1937-1949	Joe Louis*
1949-1951	Ezzard Charles
1951-1952	Joe Walcott
1952-1956	Rocky Marciano*
1956-1959	Floyd Patterson
1959-1960	Ingemar Johansson
1960-1962	Floyd Patterson
1962-1964	Sonny Liston
1964-1967	Cassius Clay* (Muhammad Ali) (d)
1970-1973	Joe Frazier
1973-1974	George Foreman
1974-1978	Muhammad Ali
1978	Leon Spinks (WBC*, WBA) (e); Ken Norton (WBC); Larry Holmes (WBC); Muhammad Ali* (WBA)
1978-1983	Larry Holmes* (WBC) (f)
1979-1980	John Tate (WBA)
1980-1982	Mike Weaver (WBA)
1982-1983	Michael Dokes (WBA)
1983	Gerrie Coetzee (WBA); Larry Holmes (IBF) (f)
1984	Tim Witherspoon (WBC); Pinklon Thomas (WBC); Greg Page (WBA)
1985-1986	Tony Tubbs (WBA)
1985-1987	Michael Spinks* (IBF)
1986	Tim Witherspoon (WBA); Trevor Berbick (WBC); Mike Tyson (WBC); James "Bonecrusher" Smith (WBA)
1986-1987	James "Bonecrusher" Smith (WBA)
1987	Mike Tyson (WBC, WBA); Tony Tucker (IBF)
1987-1990	Mike Tyson (WBC, WBA, IBF)
1990	James "Buster" Douglas (WBA, WBC, IBF)
1990-1992	Evander Holyfield (WBA, WBC, IBF)
1992-1993	Riddick Bowe (WBA, IBF, WBC*)
1992-1994	Lennox Lewis (WBC)
1993-1994	Evander Holyfield (WBA, IBF)
1994	Michael Moorer (WBA, IBF); Oliver McCall (WBC); George Foreman (WBA*, IBF*)
1995	Bruce Seldon (WBA); Frank Bruno (WBC); Frans Botha* (IBF)
1996	Mike Tyson (WBC*, WBA); Michael Moorer (IBF); Evander Holyfield (WBA)
1997	Lennox Lewis (WBC), Evander Holyfield (IBF)

(a) London Prize Ring (bare knuckle champion). (b) First Marquis of Queensberry champion. (c) Jeffries abandoned the title (1905) and designated Marvin Hart and Jack Root as logical contenders. Hart defeated Root in 12 rounds (1905) and in turn was defeated by Tommy Burns (1906), who laid claim to the title. Jack Johnson defeated Burns (1908) and was recognized as champion. Johnson clinched the title by defeating Jeffries in an attempted comeback (1910). (d) Title declared vacant by the WBA and other groups in 1967 after Ali's refusal to fulfill his military obligation. Joe Frazier was recognized as champion by 6 states, Mexico, and South America. Jimmy Ellis was declared champion by the WBA. Frazier KOd Ellis, Feb. 16, 1970. (e) After Spinks defeated Ali, the WBC recognized Ken Norton as champion. Ali defeated Spinks in a 1978 rematch to win the WBA title and then retired in 1979. (f) Holmes relinquished the WBC title in Dec. 1983 and began fighting as champion of the newly formed IBF.

Light Heavyweights

1903	Jack Root, George Gardner
1903-1905	Bob Fitzsimmons
1905-1912	Philadelphia Jack O'Brien*
1912-1916	Jack Dillon
1916-1920	Battling Levinsky
1920-1922	George Carpentier
1922-1923	Battling Siki
1923-1925	Mike McTigue
1925-1926	Paul Berlenbach
1926-1927	Jack Delaney*
1927-1929	Tommy Loughran*
1930-1934	Maxey Rosenbloom
1934-1935	Bob Olin
1935-1939	John Henry Lewis*
1939	Melio Bettina
1939-1941	Billy Conn*
1941	Anton Christoforidis (won NBA title)
1941-1948	Gus Lesnevich, Freddie Mills
1948-1950	Freddie Mills
1950-1952	Joey Maxim
1952-1960	Archie Moore
1961-1962	Vacant
1962-1963	Harold Johnson
1963-1965	Willie Pastrano
1965-1966	Jose Torres
1966-1968	Dick Tiger
1968-1974	Bob Foster*
1974-1977	John Conteh (WBC); Victor Galindez (WBA)
1977-1978	Miguel Cuello (WBC)
1978	Mike Rossman (WBA); Mate Parlov (WBC); Marvin Johnson (WBC)
1979	Matthew Saad Muhammad (WBC); Victor Galindez (WBA); Marvin Johnson (WBA)
1980	Eddie Mustafa Muhammad (WBA)
1981	Michael Spinks (WBA); Dwight Braxton (WBC)
1983-1985	Michael Spinks*
1985	J. B. Williamson (WBC)
1986	Marvin Johnson (WBA); Dennis Andries (WBC)
1987	Thomas Hearns* (WBC); Leslie Stewart (WBA); Virgil Hill (WBA); Don Lalonde (WBC)
1988	Ray Leonard* (WBC)
1989	Dennis Andries (WBC); Jeff Harding (WBC)

(continued)

1990	Dennis Andries (WBC)
1991	Thomas Hearns (WBA); Jeff Harding (WBC)
1992	Iran Barkley* (WBA); Virgil Hill (WBA)
1994-1995	Mike McCallum (WBC)
1995-1996	Fabrice Tiozzo* (WBC)
1996-1997	Roy Jones Jr. (WBC)
1997	Montell Griffin (WBC); Darius Michalczewski* (WBA); Roy Jones Jr. (WBC); Lou Del Valle (WBA)
1998	Roy Jones Jr. (WBA)

Middleweights

1884-1891	Jack "Nonpareil" Dempsey
1891-1897	Bob Fitzsimmons*
1897-1907	Tommy Ryan*
1907-1908	Stanley Ketchel, Billy Papke
1908-1910	Stanley Ketchel
1911-1913	vacant
1913	Frank Klaus; George Chip
1914-1917	Al McCoy
1917-1920	Mike O'Dowd
1920-1923	Johnny Wilson
1923-1926	Harry Greb
1926-1931	Tiger Flowers; Mickey Walker
1931-1932	Gorilla Jones (NBA)
1932-1937	Marcel Thil
1938	Al Hostak (NBA); Solly Krieger (NBA)
1939-1940	Al Hostak (NBA)
1941-1947	Tony Zale
1947-1948	Rocky Graziano
1948	Tony Zale; Marcel Cerdan
1949-1951	Jake LaMotta
1951	Ray Robinson; Randy Turpin; Ray Robinson*
1953-1955	Carl (Bobo) Olson
1955-1957	Ray Robinson
1957	Gene Fullmer; Ray Robinson; Carmen Basilio
1958	Ray Robinson
1959	Gene Fullmer (NBA); Ray Robinson (NY)
1960	Gene Fullmer (NBA); Paul Pender (NY and MA)
1961	Gene Fullmer (NBA); Terry Downes (NY, MA, Europe)
1962	Gene Fullmer; Dick Tiger (NBA); Paul Pender (NY and MA)*
1963	Dick Tiger (universal)
1963-1965	Joey Giardello
1965-1966	Dick Tiger
1966-1967	Emile Griffith
1967	Nino Benvenuti
1967-1968	Emile Griffith
1968-1970	Nino Benvenuti
1970-1977	Carlos Monzon*
1977-1978	Rodrigo Valdez
1978-1979	Hugo Corro
1979-1980	Vito Antuofermo
1980	Alan Minter; Marvin Hagler
1987	Ray Leonard* (WBC); Thomas Hearns (WBC); Sumbu Kalambay (WBA)
1988-1989	Iran Barkley (WBC)
1989	Mike McCallum* (WBA); Roberto Duran (WBC)
1991-1993	Julian Jackson (WBC)
1992-1993	Reggie Johnson (WBA)
1993	Gerald McClellan (WBC); John David Jackson* (WBA)
1994-1995	Jorge Castro (WBA)
1995	Julian Jackson (WBC); Quincy Taylor (WBC); Shinji Takehara (WBA)
1996	Keith Holmes (WBC); William Joppy (WBA)
1997	Julio Cesar Green (WBA)
1998	William Joppy (WBA), Hassine Cherifi (WBC)

Welterweights

1892-1894	Mysterious Billy Smith
1894-1896	Tommy Ryan
1896	Kid McCoy*
1900	Rube Ferns; Matty Matthews
1901	Rube Ferns
1901-1904	Joe Walcott
1904-1906	Dixie Kid; Joe Walcott; Honey Mellody
1907-1911	Mike Sullivan
1911-1915	Vacant
1915-1919	Ted Lewis
1919-1922	Jack Britton
1922-1926	Mickey Walker
1926	Pete Latzo
1927-1929	Joe Dundee
1929	Jackie Fields
1930	Jack Thompson; Tommy Freeman
1931	Tommy Freeman; Jack Thompson; Lou Brouillard
1932	Jackie Fields
1933	Young Corbett; Jimmy McLarnin
1934	Barney Ross; Jimmy McLarnin
1935-1938	Barney Ross
1938-1940	Henry Armstrong
1940-1941	Fritzie Zivic
1941-1946	Fred Cochrane
1946	Marty Servo*; Ray Robinson (a)
1946-1950	Ray Robinson*
1951	Johnny Bratton (NBA)
1951-1954	Kid Gavilan
1954-1955	Johnny Saxton
1955	Tony De Marco; Carmen Basilio
1956	Carmen Basilio; Johnny Saxton; Carmen Basilio
1957	Carmen Basilio*
1958-1960	Virgil Akins, Don Jordan
1960	Benny Paret
1961	Emile Griffith; Benny Paret
1962	Emile Griffith
1963	Luis Rodriguez; Emile Griffith
1964-1966	Emile Griffith*
1966-1969	Curtis Cokes
1969-1970	Jose Napoles; Billy Backus
1971-1975	Jose Napoles
1975-1976	John Stracey (WBC); Angel Espada (WBA)
1976-1979	Carlos Palomino (WBC); Jose Cuevas (WBA)
1979	Wilfredo Benitez (WBC); Sugar Ray Leonard (WBC)
1980	Roberto Duran (WBC); Thomas Hearns (WBA); Sugar Ray Leonard (WBC)
1981-1982	Sugar Ray Leonard*
1983-1985	Donald Curry (WBA); Milton McCrory (WBC)
1985-1986	Donald Curry
1986-1987	Lloyd Honeyghan (WBC)
1987	Mark Breland (WBA); Marlon Starling (WBA); Jorge Vaca (WBC).
1988-1989	Tomas Molinares (WBA); Lloyd Honeyghan (WBC)
1989-1990	Marlon Starling (WBC); Mark Breland (WBA)
1990-1991	Maurice Blocker (WBC); Aaron Davis (WBA)
1991	Meldrick Taylor (WBA); Simon Brown (WBC); Buddy McGirt (WBC)
1992-1994	Crisanto Espana (WBA)
1993-1997	Pernell Whitaker (WBC)
1994	Ike Quartey (WBA)
1997	Oscar De La Hoya (WBC)
1998	James Page (WBA)

(a) Robinson gained the title by defeating Tommy Bell in an elimination agreed to by the New York Commission and the NBA. Both claimed Robinson waived his title when he won the middleweight crown from LaMotta in 1951.

Lightweights

1896-1899	Kid Lavigne
1899-1902	Frank Erne
1902-1908	Joe Gans
1908-1910	Battling Nelson
1910-1912	Ad Wolgast
1912-1914	Willie Ritchie
1914-1917	Freddie Welsh
1917-1925	Benny Leonard*
1925	Jimmy Goodrich; Rocky Kansas
1926-1930	Sammy Mandell
1930	Al Singer; Tony Canzoneri
1930-1933	Tony Canzoneri
1933-1935	Barney Ross*
1935-1936	Tony Canzoneri
1936-1938	Lou Ambers
1938	Henry Armstrong
1939	Lou Ambers
1940	Lew Jenkins
1941-1943	Sammy Angott
1944	S. Angott (NBA); J. Zurita (NBA)
1945-1951	Ike Williams (NBA: later universal)
1951-1952	James Carter
1952	Lauro Salas; James Carter
1953-1954	James Carter
1954	Paddy De Marco; James Carter
1955	James Carter; Bud Smith
1956	Bud Smith; Joe Brown
1956-1962	Joe Brown
1962-1965	Carlos Ortiz
1965	Ismael Laguna
1965-1968	Carlos Ortiz
1968-1969	Teo Cruz
1969-1970	Mando Ramos
1970	Ismael Laguna; Ken Buchanan (WBA)
1971	Mando Ramos (WBC); Pedro Carrasco (WBC)
1972-1979	Roberto Duran* (WBA)
1972	Pedro Carrasco; Mando Ramos; Chango Carmona; Rodolfo Gonzalez (all WBC)
1974-1976	Guts Ishimatsu (WBC)
1976-1977	Esteban De Jesus (WBC)
1979	Jim Watt (WBC); Ernesto Espana (WBA)
1980	Hilmer Kenty (WBA)
1981	Alexis Arguello (WBC); Sean O'Grady (WBA); Arturo Frias (WBA)
1982-1984	Ray Mancini (WBA)

1983-1984	Edwin Rosario (WBC)
1984	Livingstone Bramble (WBA); Jose Luis Ramirez (WBC)
1985-1986	Hector (Macho) Camacho (WBC)
1986	Edwin Rosario (WBA); Jose Luis Ramirez (WBC)
1987-1989	Julio Cesar Chavez (WBA)
1989-1990	Edwin Rosario (WBA); Pernell Whitaker (WBC)
1990	Juan Nazario (WBA)
1990-1992	Pernell Whitaker*
1992	Joey Gamache (WBA); Tony Lopez (WBA)
1992-1996	Miguel Angel Gonzalez* (WBC)
1993	Dingaan Thobela (WBA); Orzubek Nazarov (WBA)
1996-1997	Jean-Baptiste Mendy (WBC)
1997	Steve Johnston (WBC)
1998	Jean-Baptiste Mendy (WBA), Cesar Bazan (WBC)

Featherweights

1892-1900	George Dixon (disputed)
1900-1901	Terry McGovern; Young Corbett*
1901-1912	Abe Attell
1912-1923	Johnny Kilbane
1923	Eugene Criqui; Johnny Dundee
1923-1925	Johnny Dundee*
1925-1927	Kid Kaplan*
1927-1928	Benny Bass; Tony Canzoneri
1928-1929	Andre Routis
1929-1932	Battling Battalino*
1932-1934	Tommy Paul (NBA)
1933-1936	Freddie Miller
1936-1937	Petey Sarron
1937-1938	Henry Armstrong*
1938-1940	Joey Archibald (a)
1940-1941	Harry Jeffra
1942-1948	Willie Pep
1948-1949	Sandy Saddler
1949-1950	Willie Pep
1950-1957	Sandy Saddler*
1957-1959	Hogan (Kid) Bassey
1959-1963	Davey Moore
1963-1964	Sugar Ramos
1964-1967	Vicente Saldivar*
1968-1971	Paul Rojas (WBA); Sho Saijo (WBA)
1971-1972	Antonio Gomez (WBA); Kuniaki Shibada (WBC)
1972	Ernesto Marcel* (WBA); Clemente Sanchez* (WBC); Jose Legra (WBC)
1973-1974	Eder Jofre (WBC)
1974	Ruben Olivares (WBA); Alexis Arguello (WBA); Bobby Chacon (WBC)
1975	Ruben Olivares (WBC); David Kotey (WBC)
1976-1980	Danny Lopez (WBC)
1977-1978	Rafael Ortega (WBA)
1978	Cecilio Lastra (WBA); Eusebio Pedrosa (WBA)
1980-1982	Salvador Sanchez (WBC)
1982-1984	Juan LaPorte (WBC)
1984	Wilfredo Gomez (WBC); Azumah Nelson (WBC)
1985-1986	Barry McGuigan (WBA)
1986-1987	Steve Cruz (WBA)
1987-1991	Antonio Esparragoza (WBA)
1988-1990	Jeff Fenech (WBC)
1990-1991	Marcos Villasana (WBC)
1991-1993	Park Yung Kyun (WBA); Paul Hodkinson (WBC)
1993	Goyo Vargas (WBC); Kevin Kelley (WBC); Eloy Rojas (WBA)
1995	Alejandro Gonzalez (WBC); Manuel Medina (WBC); Luisito Espinosa (WBC)
1996-1997	Wilfredo Vasquez (WBA)
1998	Antonio Ceremeno (WBA)

(a) After Petey Scalzo knocked out Archibald in an overweight match and was refused a title bout, the NBA named Scalzo champion. NBA title succession: Scalzo, 1938-1941; Richard Lemos, 1941; Jackie Wilson, 1941-1943; Jackie Callura, 1943; Phil Terranova, 1943-1944; Sal Bartolo, 1944-1946.

History of Heavyweight Championship Bouts

(bouts in which title changed hands)

1889—July 8—John L. Sullivan def. Jake Kilrain, 75, Richburg, MS. (Last championship bare knuckles bout.)

1892—Sept. 7—James J. Corbett def. John L. Sullivan, 21, New Orleans. (Big gloves used for first time.)

1897—Bob Fitzsimmons def. James J. Corbett, 14, Carson City, NV.

1899—June 9—James J. Jeffries def. Bob Fitzsimmons, 11, Coney Island, NY. (Jeffries retired as champion in 1905.)

1905—July 3—Marvin Hart KOd Jack Root, 12, Reno, NV. (Jeffries refereed and presented the title to the victor. Jack O'Brien also claimed the title.)

1906—Feb. 23—Tommy Burns def. Marvin Hart, 20, Los Angeles.

1908—Dec. 26—Jack Johnson KOd Tommy Burns, 14, Sydney, Australia. (Police halted contest.)

1915—April 5—Jess Willard KOd Jack Johnson, 26, Havana, Cuba.

1919—July 4—Jack Dempsey KOd Jess Willard, Toledo, OH. (Willard failed to answer bell for 4th round.)

1926—Sept. 23—Gene Tunney def. Jack Dempsey, 10, Philadelphia. (Tunney retired as champion in 1928.)

1930—June 12—Max Schmeling def. Jack Sharkey, 4, New York. (Sharkey fouled Schmeling in a bout generally considered to have resulted in the election of a successor to Tunney.)

1932—June 21—Jack Sharkey def. Max Schmeling, 15, NY.

1933—June 29—Primo Carnera KOd Jack Sharkey, 6, NY.

1934—June 14—Max Baer KOd Primo Carnera, 11, NY.

1935—June 13—James J. Braddock def. Max Baer, 15, NY.

1937—June 22—Joe Louis KOd James J. Braddock, 8, Chicago. (Louis retired as champion in 1949.)

1949—June 22—Ezzard Charles def. Joe Walcott, 15, Chicago; NBA recognition only.

1951—July 18—Joe Walcott KOd Ezzard Charles, 7, Pittsburgh.

1952—Sept. 23—Rocky Marciano KOd Joe Walcott, 13, Philadelphia. (Marciano retired as champion in 1956.)

1956—Nov. 30—Floyd Patterson KOd Archie Moore, 5, Chicago.

1959—June 26—Ingemar Johansson KOd Floyd Patterson, 3, New York.

1960—June 20—Floyd Patterson KOd Ingemar Johansson, 5, New York. (Patterson was 1st heavyweight to regain title.)

1962—Sept. 25—Sonny Liston KOd Floyd Patterson, 1, Chicago.

1964—Feb. 25—Cassius Clay (Muhammad Ali) KOd Sonny Liston, 7, Miami Beach, FL. (In 1967, Ali was stripped of his title by the WBA and others for refusing military service.)

1970—Feb. 16—Joe Frazier KOd Jimmy Ellis, 5, New York. (Frazier def. Ali in 15 rounds, Mar. 8, 1971, in New York.)

1973—Jan. 22—George Foreman KOd Joe Frazier, 2, Kingston, Jamaica.

1974—Oct. 30—Muhammad Ali KOd George Foreman, 8, Zaire.

1978—Feb. 15—Leon Spinks def. Muhammad Ali, 15, Las Vegas. (WBC recognized Ken Norton as champion after Spinks refused to fight him before his rematch with Ali.)

1978—June 9—(WBC) Larry Holmes def. Ken Norton, 15, Las Vegas. (Holmes gave up title in Dec. 1983.)

1978—Sept. 15—(WBA) Muhammad Ali def. Leon Spinks, 15, New Orleans. (Ali retired as champion in 1979.)

1979—Oct. 20—(WBA) John Tate def. Gerrie Coetzee, 15, Pretoria, South Africa.

1980—Mar. 31—(WBA) Mike Weaver KOd John Tate, 15, Knoxville, TN.

1982—Dec. 10—(WBA) Michael Dokes KOd Mike Weaver, 1, Las Vegas.

1983—Sept. 23—(WBA) Gerrie Coetzee KOd Michael Dokes, 10, Richfield, OH.

1983—In Dec., Larry Holmes relinquished the WBC title and was named champion of the newly formed IBF.

1984—Mar. 9—(WBC) Tim Witherspoon def. Greg Page, 12, Las Vegas.

1984—Aug. 31—(WBC) Pinklon Thomas def. Tim Witherspoon, 12, Las Vegas.

1984—Dec. 2—(WBA) Greg Page KOd Gerrie Coetzee, 8, Sun City, Bophuthatswana.

1985—Apr. 29—(WBA) Tony Tubbs def. Greg Page, 15, Buffalo, NY.

1985—Sept. 21—(IBF) Michael Spinks def. Larry Holmes, 15, Las Vegas. (Spinks relinquished title in Feb. 1987.)

1986—Jan. 17—(WBA) Tim Witherspoon def. Tony Tubbs, 15, Atlanta, GA.

1986—Mar. 23—(WBC) Trevor Berbick def. Pinklon Thomas, 12, Miami.

1986—Nov. 22—(WBC) Mike Tyson KOd Trevor Berbick, 2, Las Vegas.

1986—Dec. 12—(WBA) James "Bonecrusher" Smith KOd Tim Witherspoon, 1, New York.

1987—Mar. 7—(WBA, WBC) Mike Tyson def. James "Bonecrusher" Smith, 12, Las Vegas.

1987—May 30—(IBF) Tony Tucker KO'd James "Buster" Douglas, 10, Las Vegas.

1987—Aug. 1—(WBA, WBC, IBF) Mike Tyson def. Tony Tucker, 12, Las Vegas. (Tyson became undisputed champion.)

1990—Feb. 11—(WBA, WBC, IBF) James "Buster" Douglas KOd Mike Tyson, 10, Tokyo.

1990—Oct. 25—(WBA, WBC, IBF) Evander Holyfield KOd James "Buster" Douglas, 3, Las Vegas.

1992—Nov. 13—(WBA, WBC, IBF) Riddick Bowe def. Evander Holyfield, 12, Las Vegas. (Lennox Lewis was later named WBC champion when Bowe refused to fight him.)

1993—Nov. 6—(WBA, IBF) Evander Holyfield def. Riddick Bowe, 12, Las Vegas.

(continued)

1994—Apr. 22—(WBA, IBF) Michael Moorer def. Evander Holyfield, 12, Las Vegas.

1994—Sept. 24—(WBC) Oliver McCall KOd Lennox Lewis, 2, London.

1994—Nov. 5—(WBA, IBF) George Foreman KOd Michael Moorer, 10, Las Vegas. (In Mar. 1995, Foreman was stripped of the WBA title. In June, Foreman relinquished the IBF title.)

1995—Sept. 2—(WBC) Frank Bruno def. Oliver McCall, 12, London.

1995—Dec. 9—(IBF) Frans Botha def. Axel Schulz, 12, Las Vegas. (Botha was subsequently stripped of title.)

1996—Mar. 16—(WBC) Mike Tyson KOd Frank Bruno, 3, Las Vegas.

1996—June 22—(IBF) Michael Moorer def. Axel Schulz, 12, Dortmund, Germany.

1996—Sept. 7—(WBA, WBC) Mike Tyson KOd Bruce Seldon, 1, Las Vegas. (Tyson was subsequently stripped of the WBC title.)

1996—Nov. 9—(WBA) Evander Holyfield KOd Mike Tyson, 11, Las Vegas.

1997—Feb. 7—(WBC) Lennox Lewis KOd Oliver McCall, 5, Las Vegas.

1997—Nov. 8—(IBF) Evander Holyfield def. Michael Moorer, 8, Las Vegas.

YACHTING

The America's Cup

In the 1995 America's Cup match, the New Zealand yacht *Black Magic 1* defeated the U.S. yacht *Young America* 5-0 in the waters off San Diego, CA. It was only the 2d time since 1851 (the 1st since 1983) that the U.S. lost the Cup. *Black Magic 1* was skippered by Russell Coutts. The next competition was scheduled for 1999-2000 in New Zealand.

Competition for the America's Cup grew out of the first contest to establish a world yachting championship, one of the carnival features of the London Exposition of 1851. The race, open to all classes of yachts from all over the world, covered a 60-mile course around the Isle of Wight; the prize was a cup worth about $500, donated by the Royal Yacht Squadron of England, known as the "America's Cup" because it was first won by the U.S. yacht *America*.

Winners of the America's Cup

1851	America
1870	Magic defeated Cambria, England, (1-0)
1871	Columbia (first three races) and Sappho (last two races) defeated Livonia, England, (4-1)
1876	Madeline defeated Countess of Dufferin, Canada, (2-0)
1881	Mischief defeated Atalanta, Canada, (2-0)
1885	Puritan defeated Genesta, England, (2-0)
1886	Mayflower defeated Galatea, England, (2-0)
1887	Volunteer defeated Thistle, Scotland, (2-0)
1893	Vigilant defeated Valkyrie II, England, (3-0)
1895	Defender defeated Valkyrie III, England, (3-0)
1899	Columbia defeated Shamrock, England, (3-0)
1901	Columbia defeated Shamrock II, England, (3-0)
1903	Reliance defeated Shamrock III, England, (3-0)
1920	Resolute defeated Shamrock IV, England, (3-2)
1930	Enterprise defeated Shamrock V, England, (4-0)
1934	Rainbow defeated Endeavour, England, (4-2)
1937	Ranger defeated Endeavour II, England, (4-0)
1958	Columbia defeated Sceptre, England, (4-0)
1962	Weatherly defeated Gretel, Australia, (4-1)
1964	Constellation defeated Sovereign, England, (4-0)
1967	Intrepid defeated Dame Pattie, Australia, (4-0)
1970	Intrepid defeated Gretel II, Australia, (4-1)
1974	Courageous defeated Southern Cross, Australia, (4-0)
1977	Courageous defeated Australia, Australia, (4-0)
1980	Freedom defeated Australia, Australia, (4-1)
1983	Australia II, Australia, defeated Liberty, (4-3)
1987	Stars & Stripes defeated Kookaburra III, Australia, (4-0)
1988	Stars & Stripes defeated New Zealand, New Zealand, (2-0)
1992	America³ defeated Il Moro di Venezia, Italy, (4-1)
1995	Black Magic 1, New Zealand, defeated Young America, (5-0)

POWER BOATING

American Power Boat Assn. Gold Cup Champions

Year	Boat	Driver
1979	Atlas Van Lines	Bill Muncey
1980	Miss Budweiser	Dean Chenoweth
1981	Miss Budweiser	Dean Chenoweth
1982	Atlas Van Lines	Chip Hanauer
1983	Atlas Van Lines	Chip Hanauer
1984	Atlas Van Lines	Chip Hanauer
1985	Miller American	Chip Hanauer
1986	Miller American	Chip Hanauer
1987	Miller American	Chip Hanauer
1988	Circus Circus	Chip Hanauer
1989	Miss Budweiser	Tom D'Eath
1990	Miss Budweiser	Tom D'Eath
1991	Winston Eagle	Mark Tate
1992	Miss Budweiser	Chip Hanauer
1993	Miss Budweiser	Chip Hanauer
1994	Smokin' Joe's	Mark Tate
1995	Miss Budweiser	Chip Hanauer
1996	Pico American Dream	Dave Villwock
1997	Miss Budweiser	Dave Villwock
1998	Miss Budweiser	Dave Villwock

DOGS

Westminster Kennel Club

Year	Best-in-show	Breed	Owner(s)
1989	Ch. Royal Tudor's Wild As The Wind	Doberman	Sue & Art Kemp, Richard & Carolyn Vida, Beth Wilhite
1990	Ch. Wendessa Crown Prince	Pekingese	Ed Jenner
1991	Ch. Whisperwind on a Carousel	Poodle	Joan & Frederick Hartsock
1992	Ch. Registry's Lonesome Dove	Fox Terrier	Marion & Sam Lawrence
1993	Ch. Salilyn's Condor	English Springer Spaniel	Donna & Roger Herzig
1994	Ch. Chidley Willum	Norwich Terrier	Ruth Cooper & Patricia Lussier
1995	Ch. Gaelforce Post Script	Scottish Terrier	Dr. Vandra Huber & Dr. Joe Kinnarney
1996	Ch. Clussexx Country Sunrise	Clumber Spaniel	Judith & Richard Zaleski
1997	Ch. Parsifal Di Casa Netzer	Standard Schnauzer	Rita Holloway & Gabrio Del Torre
1998	Ch. Fairewood Frolic	Norwich Terrier	Sandina Kennels

Iditarod Trail Sled Dog Race in 1998

Jeff King won the 1998 Iditarod Trail Sled Dog Race, Mar. 17, with a time of 9 days, 5 hours, 52 minutes. For winning the 1,100-mile race from Anchorage to Nome, AK, King received $51,000 in prize money, as well as a truck. It was King's third Iditarod victory. DeeDee Jonrowe, a fan favorite, finished second.

CYCLING

Tour de France in 1998

On Aug. 2, Marco Pantani of Italy won the Tour de France. He completed the 21-stage, 2,455-mile (3,950-km) race in 92 hr., 49 min., 46 sec. The previous year's winner, Jan Ullrich, finished 2d, 3 hr., 21 min. off the lead. Pantani's victory ended a tainted Tour that included 2 riders' strikes, 6 team withdrawals, and expulsion of the Festina team (from France). After members of this team were found to have used drugs to enhance their performances, authorities tested other racers. Teams from Spain and Italy protested and withdrew. The race almost came to a halt, and its future seemed in jeopardy. French governing officials planned to implement new drug enforcement laws before the 1999 race.

BASEBALL

1998: McGwire Swats 70 HRs; "The Streak" Ends; Welcome Arizona, Tampa Bay

The 1998 season was particularly exciting and eventful for Major League Baseball. First and foremost, the race between the St. Louis Cardinals' Mark McGwire and the Chicago Cubs' Sammy Sosa to break Roger Maris's single-season home run record captivated the country. McGwire finished with an unbelievable 70 to Sosa's 66, both eclipsing Maris's 1961 mark of 61. McGwire became the first player to hit 50 or more homers in 3 consecutive seasons (52 in 1996, 58 in 1997); he also set the NL record for walks (162). Among other milestones: Cubs rookie pitcher Kerry Wood tied Roger Clemens's record—and set the NL record—for most strikeouts in a game (20); New York Yankees pitcher David Wells threw the 9th perfect game in AL history; Cal Ripken Jr. ended his consecutive-games-played streak at 2,632, more than 3 years after breaking Lou Gehrig's record; and the San Francisco Giants' Barry Bonds became the first player to both hit more than 400 homers and steal more than 400 bases in a career. Finally, the Yankees set an AL record for wins (114) en route to their record 35th pennant and 24th world championship; including the post-season, they won 125 games and lost only 50. Two expansion teams entered the majors: the Tampa Bay Devil Rays joined the AL East, and the Arizona Diamondbacks joined the NL West. For scheduling reasons, the Milwaukee Brewers moved from the AL Central to the NL Central (leaving the AL with 14 teams, and the NL with 16), and the Detroit Tigers moved to the AL Central so that the AL East could accommodate Tampa Bay.

Major League Pennant Winners, 1901–1968

	National League						American League				
Year	Winner	Won	Lost	Pct	Manager	Year	Winner	Won	Lost	Pct	Manager
1901	Pittsburgh	90	49	.647	Clarke	1901	Chicago	83	53	.610	Griffith
1902	Pittsburgh	103	36	.741	Clarke	1902	Philadelphia	83	53	.610	Mack
1903	Pittsburgh	91	49	.650	Clarke	1903	Boston	91	47	.659	Collins
1904	New York	106	47	.693	McGraw	1904	Boston	95	59	.617	Collins
1905	New York	105	48	.686	McGraw	1905	Philadelphia	92	56	.622	Mack
1906	Chicago	116	36	.763	Chance	1906	Chicago	93	58	.616	Jones
1907	Chicago	107	45	.704	Chance	1907	Detroit	92	58	.613	Jennings
1908	Chicago	99	55	.643	Chance	1908	Detroit	90	63	.588	Jennings
1909	Pittsburgh	110	42	.724	Clarke	1909	Detroit	98	54	.645	Jennings
1910	Chicago	104	50	.675	Chance	1910	Philadelphia	102	48	.680	Mack
1911	New York	99	54	.647	McGraw	1911	Philadelphia	101	50	.669	Mack
1912	New York	103	48	.682	McGraw	1912	Boston	105	47	.691	Stahl
1913	New York	101	51	.664	McGraw	1913	Philadelphia	96	57	.627	Mack
1914	Boston	94	59	.614	Stallings	1914	Philadelphia	99	53	.651	Mack
1915	Philadelphia	90	62	.592	Moran	1915	Boston	101	50	.669	Carrigan
1916	Brooklyn	94	60	.610	Robinson	1916	Boston	91	63	.591	Carrigan
1917	New York	98	56	.636	McGraw	1917	Chicago	100	54	.649	Rowland
1918	Chicago	84	45	.651	Mitchell	1918	Boston	75	51	.595	Barrow
1919	Cincinnati	96	44	.686	Moran	1919	Chicago	88	52	.629	Gleason
1920	Brooklyn	93	60	.604	Robinson	1920	Cleveland	98	56	.636	Speaker
1921	New York	94	56	.614	McGraw	1921	New York	98	55	.641	Huggins
1922	New York	93	61	.604	McGraw	1922	New York	94	60	.610	Huggins
1923	New York	95	58	.621	McGraw	1923	New York	98	54	.645	Huggins
1924	New York	93	60	.608	McGraw	1924	Washington	92	62	.597	Harris
1925	Pittsburgh	95	58	.621	McKechnie	1925	Washington	96	55	.636	Harris
1926	St. Louis	89	65	.578	Hornsby	1926	New York	91	63	.591	Huggins
1927	Pittsburgh	94	60	.610	Bush	1927	New York	110	44	.714	Huggins
1928	St. Louis	95	59	.617	McKechnie	1928	New York	101	53	.656	Huggins
1929	Chicago	98	54	.645	McCarthy	1929	Philadelphia	104	46	.693	Mack
1930	St. Louis	92	62	.597	Street	1930	Philadelphia	102	52	.662	Mack
1931	St. Louis	101	53	.656	Street	1931	Philadelphia	107	45	.704	Mack
1932	Chicago	90	64	.584	Grimm	1932	New York	107	47	.695	McCarthy
1933	New York	91	61	.599	Terry	1933	Washington	99	53	.651	Cronin
1934	St. Louis	95	58	.621	Frisch	1934	Detroit	101	53	.656	Cochrane
1935	Chicago	100	54	.649	Grimm	1935	Detroit	93	58	.616	Cochrane
1936	New York	91	62	.597	Terry	1936	New York	102	51	.667	McCarthy
1937	New York	95	57	.625	Terry	1937	New York	102	52	.662	McCarthy
1938	Chicago	89	63	.586	Hartnett	1938	New York	99	53	.651	McCarthy
1939	Cincinnati	97	57	.630	McKechnie	1939	New York	106	45	.702	McCarthy
1940	Cincinnati	100	53	.654	McKechnie	1940	Detroit	90	64	.584	Baker
1941	Brooklyn	100	54	.649	Durocher	1941	New York	101	53	.656	McCarthy
1942	St. Louis	106	48	.688	Southworth	1942	New York	103	51	.669	McCarthy
1943	St. Louis	105	49	.682	Southworth	1943	New York	98	56	.636	McCarthy
1944	St. Louis	105	49	.682	Southworth	1944	St. Louis	89	65	.578	Sewell
1945	Chicago	98	56	.636	Grimm	1945	Detroit	88	65	.575	O'Neill
1946	St. Louis	98	58	.628	Dyer	1946	Boston	104	50	.675	Cronin
1947	Brooklyn	94	60	.610	Shotton	1947	New York	97	57	.630	Harris
1948	Boston	91	62	.595	Southworth	1948	Cleveland	97	58	.626	Boudreau
1949	Brooklyn	97	57	.630	Shotton	1949	New York	97	57	.630	Stengel
1950	Philadelphia	91	63	.591	Sawyer	1950	New York	98	56	.636	Stengel
1951	New York	98	59	.624	Durocher	1951	New York	98	56	.636	Stengel
1952	Brooklyn	96	57	.627	Dressen	1952	New York	95	59	.617	Stengel
1953	Brooklyn	105	49	.682	Dressen	1953	New York	99	52	.656	Stengel
1954	New York	97	57	.630	Durocher	1954	Cleveland	111	43	.721	Lopez
1955	Brooklyn	98	55	.641	Alston	1955	New York	96	58	.623	Stengel
1956	Brooklyn	93	61	.604	Alston	1956	New York	97	57	.630	Stengel
1957	Milwaukee	95	59	.617	Haney	1957	New York	98	56	.636	Stengel
1958	Milwaukee	92	62	.597	Haney	1958	New York	92	62	.597	Stengel
1959	Los Angeles	88	68	.564	Alston	1959	Chicago	94	60	.610	Lopez
1960	Pittsburgh	95	59	.617	Murtaugh	1960	New York	97	57	.630	Stengel
1961	Cincinnati	93	61	.604	Hutchinson	1961	New York	109	53	.673	Houk
1962	San Francisco	103	62	.624	Dark	1962	New York	96	66	.593	Houk
1963	Los Angeles	99	63	.611	Alston	1963	New York	104	57	.646	Houk
1964	St. Louis	93	69	.574	Keane	1964	New York	99	63	.611	Berra
1965	Los Angeles	97	65	.599	Alston	1965	Minnesota	102	60	.630	Mele
1966	Los Angeles	95	67	.586	Alston	1966	Baltimore	97	63	.606	Bauer
1967	St. Louis	101	60	.627	Schoendienst	1967	Boston	92	70	.568	Williams
1968	St. Louis	97	65	.599	Schoendienst	1968	Detroit	103	59	.636	Smith

Major League Pennant Winners, 1969-1998

National League

	East					West					Pennant
Year	Winner	W	L	Pct	Manager	Winner	W	L	Pct	Manager	Winner
1969	N.Y. Mets	100	62	.617	Hodges	Atlanta	93	69	.574	Harris	New York
1970	Pittsburgh	89	73	.549	Murtaugh	Cincinnati	102	60	.630	Anderson	Cincinnati
1971	Pittsburgh	97	65	.599	Murtaugh	San Francisco	90	72	.556	Fox	Pittsburgh
1972	Pittsburgh	96	59	.619	Virdon	Cincinnati	95	59	.617	Anderson	Cincinnati
1973	N.Y. Mets	82	79	.509	Berra	Cincinnati	99	63	.611	Anderson	New York
1974	Pittsburgh	88	74	.543	Murtaugh	Los Angeles	102	60	.630	Alston	Los Angeles
1975	Pittsburgh	92	69	.571	Murtaugh	Cincinnati	108	54	.667	Anderson	Cincinnati
1976	Philadelphia	101	61	.623	Ozark	Cincinnati	102	60	.630	Anderson	Cincinnati
1977	Philadelphia	101	61	.623	Ozark	Los Angeles	98	64	.605	Lasorda	Los Angeles
1978	Philadelphia	90	72	.556	Ozark	Los Angeles	95	67	.586	Lasorda	Los Angeles
1979	Pittsburgh	98	64	.605	Tanner	Cincinnati	90	71	.559	McNamara	Pittsburgh
1980	Philadelphia	91	71	.562	Green	Houston	93	70	.571	Virdon	Philadelphia
1981(a)	Philadelphia	34	21	.618	Green	Los Angeles	36	21	.632	Lasorda	(c)
1981(b)	Montreal	30	23	.566	Williams, Fanning	Houston	33	20	.623	Virdon	Los Angeles
1982	St. Louis	92	70	.568	Herzog	Atlanta	89	73	.549	Torre	St. Louis
1983	Philadelphia	90	72	.556	Corrales, Owens	Los Angeles	91	71	.562	Lasorda	Philadelphia
1984	Chicago	96	65	.596	Frey	San Diego	92	70	.568	Williams	San Diego
1985	St. Louis	101	61	.623	Herzog	Los Angeles	95	67	.586	Lasorda	St. Louis
1986	N.Y. Mets	108	54	.667	Johnson	Houston	96	66	.593	Lanier	New York
1987	St. Louis	95	67	.586	Herzog	San Francisco	90	72	.556	Craig	St. Louis
1988	N.Y. Mets	100	60	.625	Johnson	Los Angeles	94	67	.584	Lasorda	Los Angeles
1989	Chicago	93	69	.571	Zimmer	San Francisco	92	70	.568	Craig	San Francisco
1990	Pittsburgh	95	67	.586	Leyland	Cincinnati	91	71	.562	Piniella	Cincinnati
1991	Pittsburgh	98	64	.605	Leyland	Atlanta	94	68	.580	Cox	Atlanta
1992	Pittsburgh	96	66	.593	Leyland	Atlanta	98	64	.605	Cox	Atlanta
1993	Philadelphia	97	65	.599	Fregosi	Atlanta	104	58	.642	Cox	Philadelphia

Year(d)	Division	Winner	W	L	Pct.	Manager	Playoffs	Pennant Winner
1995	East	Atlanta	90	54	.625	Cox	Atlanta 3, Colorado* 1	Atlanta
	Central	Cincinnati	85	59	.590	Johnson	Cincinnati 3, Los Angeles 0	
	West	Los Angeles	78	66	.542	Lasorda	Atlanta 4, Cincinnati 0	
1996	East	Atlanta	96	66	.593	Cox	Atlanta 3, Los Angeles* 0	Atlanta
	Central	St. Louis	88	74	.543	La Russa	St. Louis 3, San Diego 0	
	West	San Diego	91	71	.562	Bochy	Atlanta 4, St. Louis 3	
1997	East	Atlanta	101	61	.623	Cox	Atlanta 3, Houston 0	Florida* (e)
	Central	Houston	84	78	.519	Dierker	Florida* 3, San Francisco 0	
	West	San Francisco	90	72	.556	Baker	Florida* 4, Atlanta 2	
1998	East	Atlanta	106	56	.654	Cox	Atlanta 3, Chicago* 0	San Diego
	Central	Houston	102	60	.630	Dierker	San Diego 3, Houston 1	
	West	San Diego	97	64	.602	Bochy	San Diego 4, Atlanta 2	

American League

	East					West					Pennant
Year	Winner	W	L	Pct	Manager	Winner	W	L	Pct	Manager	Winner
1969	Baltimore	109	53	.673	Weaver	Minnesota	97	65	.599	Martin	Baltimore
1970	Baltimore	108	54	.667	Weaver	Minnesota	98	64	.605	Rigney	Baltimore
1971	Baltimore	101	57	.639	Weaver	Oakland	101	60	.627	Williams	Baltimore
1972	Detroit	86	70	.551	Martin	Oakland	93	62	.600	Williams	Oakland
1973	Baltimore	97	65	.599	Weaver	Oakland	94	68	.580	Williams	Oakland
1974	Baltimore	91	71	.562	Weaver	Oakland	90	72	.556	Dark	Oakland
1975	Boston	95	65	.594	Johnson	Oakland	98	64	.605	Dark	Boston
1976	New York	97	62	.610	Martin	Kansas City	90	72	.556	Herzog	New York
1977	New York	100	62	.617	Martin	Kansas City	102	60	.630	Herzog	New York
1978	New York	100	63	.613	Martin, Lemon	Kansas City	92	70	.568	Herzog	New York
1979	Baltimore	102	57	.642	Weaver	California	88	74	.543	Fregosi	Baltimore
1980	New York	103	59	.636	Howser	Kansas City	97	65	.599	Frey	Kansas City
1981(a)	New York	34	22	.607	Michael	Oakland	37	23	.617	Martin	(c)
1981(b)	Milwaukee	31	22	.585	Rodgers	Kansas City	30	23	.566	Frey, Howser	New York
1982	Milwaukee	95	67	.586	Rodgers, Kuenn	California	93	69	.574	Mauch	Milwaukee
1983	Baltimore	98	64	.605	Altobelli	Chicago	99	63	.611	La Russa	Baltimore
1984	Detroit	104	58	.642	Anderson	Kansas City	84	78	.519	Howser	Detroit
1985	Toronto	99	62	.615	Cox	Kansas City	91	71	.562	Howser	Kansas City
1986	Boston	95	66	.590	McNamara	California	92	70	.568	Mauch	Boston
1987	Detroit	98	64	.605	Anderson	Minnesota	85	77	.525	Kelly	Minnesota
1988	Boston	89	73	.549	McNamara, Morgan	Oakland	104	58	.642	La Russa	Oakland
1989	Toronto	89	73	.549	Williams, Gaston	Oakland	99	63	.611	La Russa	Oakland
1990	Boston	88	74	.543	Morgan	Oakland	103	59	.636	La Russa	Oakland
1991	Toronto	91	71	.562	Gaston	Minnesota	95	67	.586	Kelly	Minnesota
1992	Toronto	96	66	.593	Gaston	Oakland	96	66	.593	La Russa	Toronto
1993	Toronto	95	67	.586	Gaston	Chicago	94	68	.580	Lamont	Toronto

Year(d)	Division	Winner	W	L	Pct.	Manager	Playoffs	Pennant Winner
1995	East	Boston	86	58	.597	Kennedy	Cleveland 3, Boston 0	Cleveland
	Central	Cleveland	100	44	.694	Hargrove	Seattle 3, New York* 2	
	West	Seattle	79	66	.545	Piniella	Cleveland 4, Seattle 2	
1996	East	New York	92	70	.568	Torre	Baltimore* 3, Cleveland 1	New York
	Central	Cleveland	99	62	.615	Hargrove	New York 3, Texas 1	
	West	Texas	90	72	.556	Oates	New York 4, Baltimore* 1	
1997	East	Baltimore	98	64	.605	Johnson	Baltimore 3, Seattle 1	Cleveland
	Central	Cleveland	86	75	.534	Hargrove	Cleveland 3, New York* 2	
	West	Seattle	90	72	.556	Piniella	Cleveland 4, Baltimore 2	
1998	East	New York	114	48	.704	Torre	New York 3, Texas 0	New York
	Central	Cleveland	89	73	.549	Hargrove	Cleveland 3, Boston* 1	
	West	Texas	88	74	.543	Oates	New York 4, Cleveland 2	

*Wild card team. (a) First half. (b) Second half. (c) Montreal, L.A., N.Y. Yankees, and Oakland won the divisional playoffs. (d) In Aug. 1994, a players' strike began that caused the cancellation of the remainder of the season, the playoffs, and the World Series. At the time of the strike, division leaders were: in the NL, Montreal in the East, Cincinnati in the Central, and LA in the West; in the AL, NY in the East, Chicago in the Central, and Texas in the West. (e) Florida manager: Jim Leyland.

The Rawlings Gold Glove Awards in 1998

National League

Greg Maddux, Atlanta, pitcher
Charles Johnson[1], Los Angeles, catcher
J. T. Snow, San Francisco, first base
Bret Boone, Cincinnati, second base
Scott Rolen, Philadelphia, third base
Rey Ordonez, New York, shortstop
Barry Bonds, San Francisco, outfield
Andruw Jones, Atlanta, outfield
Larry Walker, Colorado, outfield
(1) Also played for Florida.

American League

Mike Mussina, Baltimore, pitcher
Ivan Rodriguez, Texas, catcher
Rafael Palmeiro, Baltimore, first base
Roberto Alomar, Baltimore, second base
Robin Ventura, Chicago, third base
Omar Vizquel, Cleveland, shortstop
Jim Edmonds, Anaheim, outfield
Ken Griffey Jr., Seattle, outfield
Bernie Williams, New York, outfield

The following are the players at each position who have won the most Gold Gloves since the award was instituted in 1957.

Pitcher:	Jim Kaat	16
	Bob Gibson	9
	Greg Maddux	9
Catcher:	Johnny Bench	10
	Bob Boone	7
	Ivan Rodriguez	7
First base:	Keith Hernandez	11
	Don Mattingly	9
Second base:	Ryne Sandberg	9
	Bill Mazeroski	8
	Frank White	8
Third base:	Brooks Robinson	16
	Mike Schmidt	10
Shortstop:	Ozzie Smith	13
	Luis Aparicio	9
Outfield:	Roberto Clemente	12
	Willie Mays	12
	Al Kaline	10
	Ken Griffey Jr.	9

Home Run Leaders

Note: Asterisk (*) indicates the all-time single-season record for each league.

National League

Year	Player, Team	HR
1901	Sam Crawford, Cincinnati	16
1902	Thomas Leach, Pittsburgh	6
1903	James Sheckard, Brooklyn	9
1904	Harry Lumley, Brooklyn	9
1905	Fred Odwell, Cincinnati	9
1906	Timothy Jordan, Brooklyn	12
1907	David Brain, Boston	10
1908	Timothy Jordan, Brooklyn	12
1909	Red Murray, New York	7
1910	Fred Beck, Boston; Frank Schulte, Chicago	10
1911	Frank Schulte, Chicago	21
1912	Henry Zimmerman, Chicago	14
1913	Gavvy Cravath, Philadelphia	19
1914	Gavvy Cravath, Philadelphia	19
1915	Gavvy Cravath, Philadelphia	24
1916	Dave Robertson, N.Y.; Fred (Cy) Williams, Chi.	12
1917	Dave Robertson, N.Y.; Gavvy Cravath, Phi.	12
1918	Gavvy Cravath, Philadelphia	8
1919	Gavvy Cravath, Philadelphia	12
1920	Cy Williams, Philadelphia	15
1921	George Kelly, New York	23
1922	Rogers Hornsby, St. Louis	42
1923	Cy Williams, Philadelphia	41
1924	Jacques Fournier, Brooklyn	27
1925	Rogers Hornsby, St. Louis	39
1926	Hack Wilson, Chicago	21
1927	Hack Wilson, Chicago; Cy Williams, Philadelphia	30
1928	Hack Wilson, Chicago; Jim Bottomley, St. Louis	31
1929	Chuck Klein, Philadelphia	43
1930	Hack Wilson, Chicago	56
1931	Chuck Klein, Philadelphia	31
1932	Chuck Klein, Philadelphia; Mel Ott, New York	38
1933	Chuck Klein, Philadelphia	28
1934	Rip Collins, St. Louis; Mel Ott, New York	35
1935	Walter Berger, Boston	34
1936	Mel Ott, New York	33
1937	Mel Ott, New York; Joe Medwick, St. Louis	31
1938	Mel Ott, New York	36
1939	John Mize, St. Louis	28
1940	John Mize, St. Louis	43
1941	Dolph Camilli, Brooklyn	34
1942	Mel Ott, New York	30
1943	Bill Nicholson, Chicago	29
1944	Bill Nicholson, Chicago	33
1945	Tommy Holmes, Boston	28
1946	Ralph Kiner, Pittsburgh	23
1947	Ralph Kiner, Pittsburgh; John Mize, New York	51
1948	Ralph Kiner, Pittsburgh; John Mize, New York	40
1949	Ralph Kiner, Pittsburgh	54
1950	Ralph Kiner, Pittsburgh	47
1951	Ralph Kiner, Pittsburgh	42
1952	Ralph Kiner, Pittsburgh; Hank Sauer, Chicago	37
1953	Ed Mathews, Milwaukee	47
1954	Ted Kluszewski, Cincinnati	49
1955	Willie Mays, New York	51
1956	Duke Snider, Brooklyn	43
1957	Hank Aaron, Milwaukee	44
1958	Ernie Banks, Chicago	47
1959	Ed Mathews, Milwaukee	46
1960	Ernie Banks, Chicago	41
1961	Orlando Cepeda, San Francisco	46
1962	Willie Mays, San Francisco	49
1963	Hank Aaron, Milwaukee; Willie McCovey, S.F.	44
1964	Willie Mays, San Francisco	47

American League

Year	Player, Team	HR
1901	Napoleon Lajoie, Philadelphia	13
1902	Socks Seybold, Philadelphia	16
1903	Buck Freeman, Boston	13
1904	Harry Davis, Philadelphia	10
1905	Harry Davis, Philadelphia	8
1906	Harry Davis, Philadelphia	12
1907	Harry Davis, Philadelphia	8
1908	Sam Crawford, Detroit	7
1909	Ty Cobb, Detroit	9
1910	Jake Stahl, Boston	10
1911	J. Franklin Baker, Philadelphia	9
1912	J. Franklin Baker, Philadelphia; Tris Speaker, Boston	10
1913	J. Franklin Baker, Philadelphia	13
1914	J. Franklin Baker, Philadelphia	9
1915	Robert Roth, Chicago-Cleveland	7
1916	Wally Pipp, New York	12
1917	Wally Pipp, New York	9
1918	Babe Ruth, Boston; Tilly Walker, Philadelphia	11
1919	Babe Ruth, Boston	29
1920	Babe Ruth, New York	54
1921	Babe Ruth, New York	59
1922	Ken Williams, St. Louis	39
1923	Babe Ruth, New York	41
1924	Babe Ruth, New York	46
1925	Bob Meusel, New York	33
1926	Babe Ruth, New York	47
1927	Babe Ruth, New York	60
1928	Babe Ruth, New York	54
1929	Babe Ruth, New York	46
1930	Babe Ruth, New York	49
1931	Babe Ruth, Lou Gehrig, both New York	46
1932	Jimmie Foxx, Philadelphia	58
1933	Jimmie Foxx, Philadelphia	48
1934	Lou Gehrig, New York	49
1935	Jimmie Foxx, Philadelphia; Hank Greenberg, Detroit	36
1936	Lou Gehrig, New York	49
1937	Joe DiMaggio, New York	46
1938	Hank Greenberg, Detroit	58
1939	Jimmie Foxx, Boston	35
1940	Hank Greenberg, Detroit	41
1941	Ted Williams, Boston	37
1942	Ted Williams, Boston	36
1943	Rudy York, Detroit	34
1944	Nick Etten, New York	22
1945	Vern Stephens, St. Louis	24
1946	Hank Greenberg, Detroit	44
1947	Ted Williams, Boston	32
1948	Joe DiMaggio, New York	39
1949	Ted Williams, Boston	43
1950	Al Rosen, Cleveland	37
1951	Gus Zernial, Chicago-Philadelphia	33
1952	Larry Doby, Cleveland	32
1953	Al Rosen, Cleveland	43
1954	Larry Doby, Cleveland	32
1955	Mickey Mantle, New York	37
1956	Mickey Mantle, New York	52
1957	Roy Sievers, Washington	42
1958	Mickey Mantle, New York	42
1959	Rocky Colavito, Cleve.; Harmon Killebrew, Wash.	42
1960	Mickey Mantle, New York	40
1961	Roger Maris, New York	*61
1962	Harmon Killebrew, Minnesota	48
1963	Harmon Killebrew, Minnesota	45
1964	Harmon Killebrew, Minnesota	49

(continued)

National League

Year	Player, Team	HR
1965	Willie Mays, San Francisco	52
1966	Hank Aaron, Atlanta	44
1967	Hank Aaron, Atlanta	39
1968	Willie McCovey, San Francisco	36
1969	Willie McCovey, San Francisco	45
1970	Johnny Bench, Cincinnati	45
1971	Willie Stargell, Pittsburgh	48
1972	Johnny Bench, Cincinnati	40
1973	Willie Stargell, Pittsburgh	44
1974	Mike Schmidt, Philadelphia	36
1975	Mike Schmidt, Philadelphia	38
1976	Mike Schmidt, Philadelphia	38
1977	George Foster, Cincinnati	52
1978	George Foster, Cincinnati	40
1979	Dave Kingman, Chicago	48
1980	Mike Schmidt, Philadelphia	48
1981	Mike Schmidt, Philadelphia	31
1982	Dave Kingman, New York	37
1983	Mike Schmidt, Philadelphia	40
1984	Mike Schmidt, Phi.; Dale Murphy, Atlanta	36
1985	Dale Murphy, Atlanta	37
1986	Mike Schmidt, Philadelphia	37
1987	Andre Dawson, Chicago	49
1988	Darryl Strawberry, New York	39
1989	Kevin Mitchell, San Francisco	47
1990	Ryne Sandberg, Chicago	40
1991	Howard Johnson, New York	38
1992	Fred McGriff, San Diego	35
1993	Barry Bonds, San Francisco	46
1994	Matt Williams, San Francisco	43
1995	Dante Bichette, Colorado	40
1996	Andres Galarraga, Colorado	47
1997[1]	Larry Walker, Colorado	49
1998	Mark McGwire, St. Louis	*70

American League

Year	Player, Team	HR
1965	Tony Conigliaro, Boston	32
1966	Frank Robinson, Baltimore	49
1967	Carl Yastrzemski, Boston; Harmon Killebrew, Minn.	44
1968	Frank Howard, Washington	44
1969	Harmon Killebrew, Minnesota	49
1970	Frank Howard, Washington	44
1971	Bill Melton, Chicago	33
1972	Dick Allen, Chicago	37
1973	Reggie Jackson, Oakland	32
1974	Dick Allen, Chicago	32
1975	George Scott, Milwaukee; Reggie Jackson, Oakland	36
1976	Graig Nettles, New York	32
1977	Jim Rice, Boston	39
1978	Jim Rice, Boston	46
1979	Gorman Thomas, Milwaukee	45
1980	Reggie Jackson, New York; Ben Oglivie, Milwaukee	41
1981	Bobby Grich, California; Tony Armas, Oakland; Dwight Evans, Boston; Eddie Murray, Baltimore	22
1982	Gorman Thomas, Milwaukee; Reggie Jackson, Cal.	39
1983	Jim Rice, Boston	39
1984	Tony Armas, Boston	43
1985	Darrell Evans, Detroit	40
1986	Jesse Barfield, Toronto	40
1987	Mark McGwire, Oakland	49
1988	Jose Canseco, Oakland	42
1989	Fred McGriff, Toronto	36
1990	Cecil Fielder, Detroit	51
1991	Cecil Fielder, Detroit; Jose Canseco, Oakland	44
1992	Juan Gonzalez, Texas	43
1993	Juan Gonzalez, Texas	46
1994	Ken Griffey Jr., Seattle	40
1995	Albert Belle, Cleveland	50
1996	Mark McGwire, Oakland	52
1997[1]	Ken Griffey Jr., Seattle	56
1998	Ken Griffey Jr., Seattle	56

(1) In 1997, Mark McGwire led the Major Leagues with 58 home runs, splitting time between the Oakland Athletics (AL), 34, and the St. Louis Cardinals (NL), 24.

Runs Batted In Leaders

Note: Asterisk (*) indicates the all-time single-season record for each league.

National League

Year	Player, Team	RBI
1907	Sherwood Magee, Philadelphia	85
1908	Honus Wager, Pittsburgh	109
1909	Honus Wager, Pittsburgh	100
1910	Sherwood Magee, Philadelphia	123
1911	Frank Schulte, Chicago	121
1912	Henry Zimmerman, Chicago	103
1913	Gavvy Cravath, Philadelphia	128
1914	Sherwood Magee, Philadelphia	103
1915	Gavvy Cravath, Philadelphia	115
1916	Henry Zimmerman, Chicago-NewYork	83
1917	Henry Zimmerman, New York	102
1918	Sherwood Magee, Philadelphia	76
1919	Hi Myers, Boston	73
1920	George Kelly, N.Y.; Rogers Hornsby, St. Louis	94
1921	Rogers Hornsby, St. Louis	126
1922	Rogers Hornsby, St. Louis	152
1923	Emil Meusel, New York	125
1924	George Kelly, New York	136
1925	Rogers Hornsby, St. Louis	143
1926	Jim Bottomley, St. Louis	120
1927	Paul Waner, Pittsburgh	131
1928	Jim Bottomley, St. Louis	136
1929	Hack Wilson, Chicago	159
1930	Hack Wilson, Chicago	*190
1931	Chuck Klein, Philadelphia	121
1932	Don Hurst, Philadelphia	143
1933	Chuck Klein, Philadelphia	120
1934	Mel Ott, New York	135
1935	Walter Berger, Boston	130
1936	Joe Medwick, St. Louis	138
1937	Joe Medwick, St. Louis	154
1938	Joe Medwick, St. Louis	122
1939	Frank McCormick, Cincinnati	128
1940	John Mize, St. Louis	137
1941	Adolph Camilli, Brooklyn	120
1942	John Mize, New York	110
1943	Bill Nicholson, Chicago	128
1944	Bill Nicholson, Chicago	122
1945	Dixie Walker, Brooklyn	124
1946	Enos Slaughter, St. Louis	130
1947	John Mize, New York	138

American League

Year	Player, Team	RBI
1907	Ty Cobb, Detroit	116
1908	Ty Cobb, Detroit	108
1909	Ty Cobb, Detroit	107
1910	Sam Crawford, Detroit	120
1911	Ty Cobb, Detroit	144
1912	J. Franklin Baker, Philadelphia	133
1913	J. Franklin Baker, Philadelphia	126
1914	Sam Crawford, Detroit	104
1915	Sam Crawford, Detroit; Robert Veach, Detroit	112
1916	Del Pratt, St. Louis	103
1917	Robert Veach, Detroit	103
1918	Robert Veach, Detroit	78
1919	Babe Ruth, Boston	114
1920	Babe Ruth, New York	137
1921	Babe Ruth, New York	171
1922	Ken Williams, St. Louis	155
1923	Babe Ruth, New York	131
1924	Goose Goslin, Washington	129
1925	Bob Meusel, New York	138
1926	Babe Ruth, New York	145
1927	Lou Gehrig, New York	175
1928	Babe Ruth, New York; Lou Gehrig, New York	142
1929	Al Simmons, Philadelphia	157
1930	Lou Gehrig, New York	174
1931	Lou Gehrig, New York	*184
1932	Jimmie Foxx, Philadelphia	169
1933	Jimmie Foxx, Philadelphia	163
1934	Lou Gehrig, New York	165
1935	Hank Greenberg, Detroit	170
1936	Hal Trosky, Cleveland	162
1937	Hank Greenberg, Detroit	183
1938	Jimmie Foxx, Boston	175
1939	Ted Williams, Boston	145
1940	Hank Greenberg, Detroit	150
1941	Joe DiMaggio, New York	125
1942	Ted Williams, Boston	137
1943	Rudy York, Detroit	118
1944	Vern Stephens, St. Louis	109
1945	Nick Etten, New York	111
1946	Hank Greenberg, Detroit	127
1947	Ted Williams, Boston	114

National League

Year	Player, Team	RBI
1948	Stan Musial, St. Louis	131
1949	Ralph Kiner, Pittsburgh	127
1950	Del Ennis, Philadelphia	126
1951	Monte Irvin, New York	121
1952	Hank Sauer, Chicago	121
1953	Roy Campanella, Brooklyn	142
1954	Ted Kluszewski, Cincinnati	141
1955	Duke Snider, Brooklyn	136
1956	Stan Musial, St. Louis	109
1957	Hank Aaron, Milwaukee	132
1958	Ernie Banks, Chicago	129
1959	Ernie Banks, Chicago	143
1960	Hank Aaron, Milwaukee	126
1961	Orlando Cepeda, San Francisco	142
1962	Tommy Davis, Los Angeles	153
1963	Hank Aaron, Milwaukee	130
1964	Ken Boyer, St. Louis	119
1965	Deron Johnson, Cincinnati	130
1966	Hank Aaron, Atlanta	127
1967	Orlando Cepeda, St. Louis	111
1968	Willie McCovey, San Francisco	105
1969	Willie McCovey, San Francisco	126
1970	Johnny Bench, Cincinnati	148
1971	Joe Torre, St. Louis	137
1972	Johnny Bench, Cincinnati	125
1973	Willie Stargell, Pittsburgh	119
1974	Johnny Bench, Cincinnati	129
1975	Greg Luzinski, Philadelphia	120
1976	George Foster, Cincinnati	121
1977	George Foster, Cincinnati	149
1978	George Foster, Cincinnati	120
1979	Dave Winfield, San Diego	118
1980	Mike Schmidt, Philadelphia	121
1981	Mike Schmidt, Philadelphia	91
1982	Dale Murphy, Atlanta; Al Oliver, Montreal	109
1983	Dale Murphy, Atlanta	121
1984	Gary Carter, Montreal; Mike Schmidt, Phi.	106
1985	Dave Parker, Cincinnati	125
1986	Mike Schmidt, Philadelphia	119
1987	Andre Dawson, Chicago	137
1988	Will Clark, San Francisco	109
1989	Kevin Mitchell, San Francisco	125
1990	Matt Williams, San Francisco	122
1991	Howard Johnson, New York	117
1992	Darren Daulton, Philadelphia	109
1993	Barry Bonds, San Francisco	123
1994	Jeff Bagwell, Houston	116
1995	Dante Bichette, Colorado	128
1996	Andres Galarraga, Colorado	150
1997	Andres Galarraga, Colorado	140
1998	Sammy Sosa, Chicago	158

American League

Year	Player, Team	RBI
1948	Joe DiMaggio, New York	155
1949	Ted Williams, Bos.; Vern Stephens, Bos.	159
1950	Walt Dropo, Bos.; Vern Stephens, Bos.	144
1951	Gus Zernial, Chicago-Philadelphia	129
1952	Al Rosen, Cleveland	105
1953	Al Rosen, Cleveland	145
1954	Larry Doby, Cleveland	126
1955	Ray Boone, Detroit; Jackie Jensen, Boston	116
1956	Mickey Mantle, New York	130
1957	Roy Sievers, Washington	114
1958	Jackie Jensen, Boston	122
1959	Jackie Jensen, Boston	112
1960	Roger Maris, New York	112
1961	Roger Maris, New York	142
1962	Harmon Killebrew, Minnesota	126
1963	Dick Stuart, Boston	118
1964	Brooks Robinson, Baltimore	118
1965	Rocky Colavito, Cleveland	108
1966	Frank Robinson, Baltimore	122
1967	Carl Yastrzemski, Boston	121
1968	Ken Harrelson, Boston	109
1969	Harmon Killebrew, Minnesota	140
1970	Frank Howard, Washington	126
1971	Harmon Killebrew, Minnesota	119
1972	Dick Allen, Chicago	113
1973	Reggie Jackson, Oakland	117
1974	Jeff Burroughs, Texas	118
1975	George Scott, Milwaukee	109
1976	Lee May, Baltimore	109
1977	Larry Hisle, Minnesota	119
1978	Jim Rice, Boston	139
1979	Don Baylor, California	139
1980	Cecil Cooper, Milwaukee	122
1981	Eddie Murray, Baltimore	78
1982	Hal McRae, Kansas City	133
1983	Cecil Cooper, Milwaukee; Jim Rice, Boston	126
1984	Tony Armas, Boston	123
1985	Don Mattingly, New York	145
1986	Joe Carter, Cleveland	121
1987	George Bell, Toronto	134
1988	Jose Canseco, Oakland	124
1989	Ruben Sierra, Texas	119
1990	Cecil Fielder, Detroit	132
1991	Cecil Fielder, Detroit	133
1992	Cecil Fielder, Detroit	124
1993	Albert Belle, Cleveland	129
1994	Kirby Puckett, Minnesota	112
1995	Albert Belle, Cleveland; Mo Vaughn, Boston	126
1996	Albert Belle, Cleveland	148
1997	Ken Griffey Jr., Seattle	147
1998	Juan Gonzalez, Texas	157

Batting Champions

Note: Asterisk (*) indicates the all-time single-season record for each league.

National League

Year	Player	Club	Avg.
1901	Jesse C. Burkett	St. Louis	**.382**
1902	Clarence Beaumont	Pittsburgh	**.357**
1903	Honus Wagner	Pittsburgh	**.355**
1904	Honus Wagner	Pittsburgh	**.349**
1905	James Seymour	Cincinnati	**.377**
1906	Honus Wagner	Pittsburgh	**.339**
1907	Honus Wagner	Pittsburgh	**.350**
1908	Honus Wagner	Pittsburgh	**.354**
1909	Honus Wagner	Pittsburgh	**.339**
1910	Sherwood Magee	Philadelphia	**.331**
1911	Honus Wagner	Pittsburgh	**.334**
1912	Henry Zimmerman	Chicago	**.372**
1913	Jacob Daubert	Brooklyn	**.350**
1914	Jacob Daubert	Brooklyn	**.329**
1915	Larry Doyle	New York	**.320**
1916	Hal Chase	Cincinnati	**.339**
1917	Edd Roush	Cincinnati	**.341**
1918	Zach Wheat	Brooklyn	**.335**
1919	Edd Roush	Cincinnati	**.321**
1920	Rogers Hornsby	St. Louis	**.370**
1921	Rogers Hornsby	St. Louis	**.397**
1922	Rogers Hornsby	St. Louis	**.401**

American League

Year	Player	Club	Avg.
1901	Napoleon Lajoie	Philadelphia	***.422**
1902	Ed Delahanty	Washington	**.376**
1903	Napoleon Lajoie	Cleveland	**.355**
1904	Napoleon Lajoie	Cleveland	**.381**
1905	Elmer Flick	Cleveland	**.306**
1906	George Stone	St. Louis	**.358**
1907	Ty Cobb	Detroit	**.350**
1908	Ty Cobb	Detroit	**.324**
1909	Ty Cobb	Detroit	**.377**
1910[1]	Ty Cobb	Detroit	**.385**
1911	Ty Cobb	Detroit	**.420**
1912	Ty Cobb	Detroit	**.410**
1913	Ty Cobb	Detroit	**.390**
1914	Ty Cobb	Detroit	**.368**
1915	Ty Cobb	Detroit	**.369**
1916	Tris Speaker	Cleveland	**.386**
1917	Ty Cobb	Detroit	**.383**
1918	Ty Cobb	Detroit	**.382**
1919	Ty Cobb	Detroit	**.384**
1920	George Sisler	St. Louis	**.407**
1921	Harry Heilmann	Detroit	**.394**
1922	George Sisler	St. Louis	**.420**

(continued)

National League				American League			
Year	Player	Club	Avg.	Year	Player	Club	Avg.
1923	Rogers Hornsby	St. Louis	**.384**	1923	Harry Heilmann	Detroit	**.403**
1924	Rogers Hornsby	St. Louis	***.424**	1924	Babe Ruth	New York	**.378**
1925	Rogers Hornsby	St. Louis	**.403**	1925	Harry Heilmann	Detroit	**.393**
1926	Eugene Hargrave	Cincinnati	**.353**	1926	Henry Manush	Detroit	**.378**
1927	Paul Waner	Pittsburgh	**.380**	1927	Harry Heilmann	Detroit	**.398**
1928	Rogers Hornsby	Boston	**.387**	1928	Goose Goslin	Washington	**.379**
1929	Lefty O'Doul	Philadelphia	**.398**	1929	Lew Fonseca	Cleveland	**.369**
1930	Bill Terry	New York	**.401**	1930	Al Simmons	Philadelphia	**.381**
1931	Chick Hafey	St. Louis	**.349**	1931	Al Simmons	Philadelphia	**.390**
1932	Lefty O'Doul	Brooklyn	**.368**	1932	Dale Alexander	Detroit-Boston	**.367**
1933	Chuck Klein	Philadelphia	**.368**	1933	Jimmie Foxx	Philadelphia	**.356**
1934	Paul Waner	Pittsburgh	**.362**	1934	Lou Gehrig	New York	**.363**
1935	Arky Vaughan	Pittsburgh	**.385**	1935	Buddy Myer	Washington	**.349**
1936	Paul Waner	Pittsburgh	**.373**	1936	Luke Appling	Chicago	**.388**
1937	Joe Medwick	St. Louis	**.374**	1937	Charlie Gehringer	Detroit	**.371**
1938	Ernie Lombardi	Cincinnati	**.342**	1938	Jimmie Foxx	Boston	**.349**
1939	John Mize	St. Louis	**.349**	1939	Joe DiMaggio	New York	**.381**
1940	Debs Garms	Pittsburgh	**.355**	1940	Joe DiMaggio	New York	**.352**
1941	Pete Reiser	Brooklyn	**.343**	1941	Ted Williams	Boston	**.406**
1942	Ernie Lombardi	Boston	**.330**	1942	Ted Williams	Boston	**.356**
1943	Stan Musial	St. Louis	**.357**	1943	Luke Appling	Chicago	**.328**
1944	Dixie Walker	Brooklyn	**.357**	1944	Lou Boudreau	Cleveland	**.327**
1945	Phil Cavarretta	Chicago	**.355**	1945	George Stirnweiss	New York	**.309**
1946	Stan Musial	St. Louis	**.365**	1946	Mickey Vernon	Washington	**.353**
1947	Harry Walker	St.L.-Phi.	**.363**	1947	Ted Williams	Boston	**.343**
1948	Stan Musial	St. Louis	**.376**	1948	Ted Williams	Boston	**.369**
1949	Jackie Robinson	Brooklyn	**.342**	1949	George Kell	Detroit	**.343**
1950	Stan Musial	St. Louis	**.346**	1950	Billy Goodman	Boston	**.354**
1951	Stan Musial	St. Louis	**.355**	1951	Ferris Fain	Philadelphia	**.344**
1952	Stan Musial	St. Louis	**.336**	1952	Ferris Fain	Philadelphia	**.327**
1953	Carl Furillo	Brooklyn	**.344**	1953	Mickey Vernon	Washington	**.337**
1954	Willie Mays	New York	**.345**	1954	Roberto Avila	Cleveland	**.341**
1955	Richie Ashburn	Philadelphia	**.338**	1955	Al Kaline	Detroit	**.340**
1956	Hank Aaron	Milwaukee	**.328**	1956	Mickey Mantle	New York	**.353**
1957	Stan Musial	St. Louis	**.351**	1957	Ted Williams	Boston	**.388**
1958	Richie Ashburn	Philadelphia	**.350**	1958	Ted Williams	Boston	**.328**
1959	Hank Aaron	Milwaukee	**.355**	1959	Harvey Kuenn	Detroit	**.353**
1960	Dick Groat	Pittsburgh	**.325**	1960	Pete Runnels	Boston	**.320**
1961	Roberto Clemente	Pittsburgh	**.351**	1961	Norm Cash	Detroit	**.361**
1962	Tommy Davis	Los Angeles	**.346**	1962	Pete Runnels	Boston	**.326**
1963	Tommy Davis	Los Angeles	**.326**	1963	Carl Yastrzemski	Boston	**.321**
1964	Roberto Clemente	Pittsburgh	**.339**	1964	Tony Oliva	Minnesota	**.323**
1965	Roberto Clemente	Pittsburgh	**.329**	1965	Tony Oliva	Minnesota	**.321**
1966	Matty Alou	Pittsburgh	**.342**	1966	Frank Robinson	Baltimore	**.316**
1967	Roberto Clemente	Pittsburgh	**.357**	1967	Carl Yastrzemski	Boston	**.326**
1968	Pete Rose	Cincinnati	**.335**	1968	Carl Yastrzemski	Boston	**.301**
1969	Pete Rose	Cincinnati	**.348**	1969	Rod Carew	Minnesota	**.332**
1970	Rico Carty	Atlanta	**.366**	1970	Alex Johnson	California	**.329**
1971	Joe Torre	St. Louis	**.363**	1971	Tony Oliva	Minnesota	**.337**
1972	Billy Williams	Chicago	**.333**	1972	Rod Carew	Minnesota	**.318**
1973	Pete Rose	Cincinnati	**.338**	1973	Rod Carew	Minnesota	**.350**
1974	Ralph Garr	Atlanta	**.353**	1974	Rod Carew	Minnesota	**.364**
1975	Bill Madlock	Chicago	**.354**	1975	Rod Carew	Minnesota	**.359**
1976	Bill Madlock	Chicago	**.339**	1976	George Brett	Kansas City	**.333**
1977	Dave Parker	Pittsburgh	**.338**	1977	Rod Carew	Minnesota	**.388**
1978	Dave Parker	Pittsburgh	**.334**	1978	Rod Carew	Minnesota	**.333**
1979	Keith Hernandez	St. Louis	**.344**	1979	Fred Lynn	Boston	**.333**
1980	Bill Buckner	Chicago	**.324**	1980	George Brett	Kansas City	**.390**
1981	Bill Madlock	Pittsburgh	**.341**	1981	Carney Lansford	Boston	**.336**
1982	Al Oliver	Montreal	**.331**	1982	Willie Wilson	Kansas City	**.332**
1983	Bill Madlock	Pittsburgh	**.323**	1983	Wade Boggs	Boston	**.361**
1984	Tony Gwynn	San Diego	**.351**	1984	Don Mattingly	New York	**.343**
1985	Willie McGee	St. Louis	**.353**	1985	Wade Boggs	Boston	**.368**
1986	Tim Raines	Montreal	**.334**	1986	Wade Boggs	Boston	**.357**
1987	Tony Gwynn	San Diego	**.370**	1987	Wade Boggs	Boston	**.363**
1988	Tony Gwynn	San Diego	**.313**	1988	Wade Boggs	Boston	**.366**
1989	Tony Gwynn	San Diego	**.336**	1989	Kirby Puckett	Minnesota	**.339**
1990	Willie McGee	St. Louis	**.335**	1990	George Brett	Kansas City	**.329**
1991	Terry Pendleton	Atlanta	**.319**	1991	Julio Franco	Texas	**.341**
1992	Gary Sheffield	San Diego	**.330**	1992	Edgar Martinez	Seattle	**.343**
1993	Andres Galarraga	Colorado	**.370**	1993	John Olerud	Toronto	**.363**
1994	Tony Gwynn	San Diego	**.394**	1994	Paul O'Neill	New York	**.359**
1995	Tony Gwynn	San Diego	**.368**	1995	Edgar Martinez	Seattle	**.356**
1996	Tony Gwynn	San Diego	**.353**	1996	Alex Rodriguez	Seattle	**.358**
1997	Tony Gwynn	San Diego	**.372**	1997	Frank Thomas	Chicago	**.347**
1998	Larry Walker	Colorado	**.363**	1998	Bernie Williams	New York	**.339**

(1) Some baseball researchers have concluded that Ty Cobb actually hit .382 in 1910 while Napoleon Lajoie, Cleveland, hit .383.

Cy Young Award Winners

Year	Player, Team
1956	Don Newcombe, Dodgers
1957	Warren Spahn, Braves
1958	Bob Turley, Yankees
1959	Early Wynn, White Sox
1960	Vernon Law, Pirates
1961	Whitey Ford, Yankees
1962	Don Drysdale, Dodgers
1963	Sandy Koufax, Dodgers
1964	Dean Chance, Angels
1965	Sandy Koufax, Dodgers
1966	Sandy Koufax, Dodgers
1967	(NL) Mike McCormick, Giants
	(AL) Jim Lonborg, Red Sox
1968	(NL) Bob Gibson, Cardinals
	(AL) Dennis McLain, Tigers
1969	(NL) Tom Seaver, Mets
	(AL) (tie) Dennis McLain, Tigers
	Mike Cuellar, Orioles
1970	(NL) Bob Gibson, Cardinals
	(AL) Jim Perry, Twins
1971	(NL) Ferguson Jenkins, Cubs
	(AL) Vida Blue, A's
1972	(NL) Steve Carlton, Phillies
	(AL) Gaylord Perry, Indians
1973	(NL) Tom Seaver, Mets
	(AL) Jim Palmer, Orioles
1974	(NL) Mike Marshall, Dodgers
	(AL) Jim (Catfish) Hunter, A's
1975	(NL) Tom Seaver, Mets
	(AL) Jim Palmer, Orioles
1976	(NL) Randy Jones, Padres
	(AL) Jim Palmer, Orioles
1977	(NL) Steve Carlton, Phillies
	(AL) Sparky Lyle, Yankees
1978	(NL) Gaylord Perry, Padres
	(AL) Ron Guidry, Yankees
1979	(NL) Bruce Sutter, Cubs
	(AL) Mike Flanagan, Orioles
1980	(NL) Steve Carlton, Phillies
	(AL) Steve Stone, Orioles
1981	(NL) Fernando Valenzuela, Dodgers
	(AL) Rollie Fingers, Brewers
1982	(NL) Steve Carlton, Phillies
	(AL) Pete Vuckovich, Brewers
1983	(NL) John Denny, Phillies
	(AL) LaMarr Hoyt, White Sox
1984	(NL) Rick Sutcliffe, Cubs
	(AL) Willie Hernandez, Tigers
1985	(NL) Dwight Gooden, Mets
	(AL) Bret Saberhagen, Royals
1986	(NL) Mike Scott, Astros
	(AL) Roger Clemens, Red Sox
1987	(NL) Steve Bedrosian, Phillies
	(AL) Roger Clemens, Red Sox
1988	(NL) Orel Hershiser, Dodgers
	(AL) Frank Viola, Twins
1989	(NL) Mark Davis, Padres
	(AL) Bret Saberhagan, Royals
1990	(NL) Doug Drabek, Pirates
	(AL) Bob Welch, A's
1991	(NL) Tom Glavine, Braves
	(AL) Roger Clemens, Red Sox
1992	(NL) Greg Maddux, Cubs
	(AL) Dennis Eckersley, A's
1993	(NL) Greg Maddux, Braves
	(AL) Jack McDowell, White Sox
1994	(NL) Greg Maddux, Braves
	(AL) David Cone, Royals
1995	(NL) Greg Maddux, Braves
	(AL) Randy Johnson, Mariners
1996	(NL) John Smoltz, Braves
	(AL) Pat Hentgen, Blue Jays
1997	(NL) Pedro Martinez, Expos
	(AL) Roger Clemens, Blue Jays

Most Valuable Player

National League

Year	Player, team
1931	Frank Frisch, St. Louis
1932	Chuck Klein, Philadelphia
1933	Carl Hubbell, New York
1934	Dizzy Dean, St. Louis
1935	Gabby Hartnett, Chicago
1936	Carl Hubbell, New York
1937	Joe Medwick, St. Louis
1938	Ernie Lombardi, Cincinnati
1939	Bucky Walters, Cincinnati
1940	Frank McCormick, Cincinnati
1941	Dolph Camilli, Brooklyn
1942	Mort Cooper, St. Louis
1943	Stan Musial, St. Louis
1944	Martin Marion, St. Louis
1945	Phil Cavarretta, Chicago
1946	Stan Musial, St. Louis
1947	Bob Elliott, Boston
1948	Stan Musial, St. Louis
1949	Jackie Robinson, Brooklyn
1950	Jim Konstanty, Philadelphia
1951	Roy Campanella, Brooklyn
1952	Hank Sauer, Chicago
1953	Roy Campanella, Brooklyn
1954	Willie Mays, New York
1955	Roy Campanella, Brooklyn
1956	Don Newcombe, Brooklyn
1957	Hank Aaron, Milwaukee
1958	Ernie Banks, Chicago
1959	Ernie Banks, Chicago
1960	Dick Groat, Pittsburgh
1961	Frank Robinson, Cincinnati
1962	Maury Wills, Los Angeles
1963	Sandy Koufax, Los Angeles
1964	Ken Boyer, St. Louis
1965	Willie Mays, San Francisco
1966	Roberto Clemente, Pittsburgh
1967	Orlando Cepeda, St. Louis
1968	Bob Gibson, St. Louis
1969	Willie McCovey, San Francisco
1970	Johnny Bench, Cincinnati
1971	Joe Torre, St. Louis
1972	Johnny Bench, Cincinnati
1973	Pete Rose, Cincinnati
1974	Steve Garvey, Los Angeles
1975	Joe Morgan, Cincinnati
1976	Joe Morgan, Cincinnati
1977	George Foster, Cincinnati
1978	Dave Parker, Pittsburgh
1979	Willie Stargell, Pittsburgh
(tie)	Keith Hernandez, St. Louis
1980	Mike Schmidt, Philadelphia
1981	Mike Schmidt, Philadelphia
1982	Dale Murphy, Atlanta
1983	Dale Murphy, Atlanta
1984	Ryne Sandberg, Chicago
1985	Willie McGee, St. Louis
1986	Mike Schmidt, Philadelphia
1987	Andre Dawson, Chicago
1988	Kirk Gibson, Los Angeles
1989	Kevin Mitchell, San Francisco
1990	Barry Bonds, Pittsburgh
1991	Terry Pendleton, Atlanta
1992	Barry Bonds, Pittsburgh
1993	Barry Bonds, San Francisco
1994	Jeff Bagwell, Houston
1995	Barry Larkin, Cincinnati
1996	Ken Caminiti, San Diego
1997	Larry Walker, Colorado

American League

Year	Player, team
1931	Lefty Grove, Philadelphia
1932	Jimmie Foxx, Philadelphia
1933	Jimmie Foxx, Philadelphia
1934	Mickey Cochrane, Detroit
1935	Hank Greenberg, Detroit
1936	Lou Gehrig, New York
1937	Charley Gehringer, Detroit
1938	Jimmie Foxx, Boston
1939	Joe DiMaggio, New York
1940	Hank Greenberg, Detroit
1941	Joe DiMaggio, New York
1942	Joe Gordon, New York
1943	Spurgeon Chandler, New York
1944	Hal Newhouser, Detroit
1945	Hal Newhouser, Detroit
1946	Ted Williams, Boston
1947	Joe DiMaggio, New York
1948	Lou Boudreau, Cleveland
1949	Ted Williams, Boston
1950	Phil Rizzuto, New York
1951	Yogi Berra, New York
1952	Bobby Shantz, Philadelphia
1953	Al Rosen, Cleveland
1954	Yogi Berra, New York
1955	Yogi Berra, New York
1956	Mickey Mantle, New York
1957	Mickey Mantle, New York
1958	Jackie Jensen, Boston
1959	Nellie Fox, Chicago
1960	Roger Maris, New York
1961	Roger Maris, New York
1962	Mickey Mantle, New York
1963	Elston Howard, New York
1964	Brooks Robinson, Baltimore
1965	Zoilo Versalles, Minnesota
1966	Frank Robinson, Baltimore
1967	Carl Yastrzemski, Boston
1968	Denny McLain, Detroit
1969	Harmon Killebrew, Minnesota
1970	John (Boog) Powell, Baltimore
1971	Vida Blue, Oakland
1972	Dick Allen, Chicago
1973	Reggie Jackson, Oakland
1974	Jeff Burroughs, Texas
1975	Fred Lynn, Boston
1976	Thurman Munson, New York
1977	Rod Carew, Minnesota
1978	Jim Rice, Boston
1979	Don Baylor, California
1980	George Brett, Kansas City
1981	Rollie Fingers, Milwaukee
1982	Robin Yount, Milwaukee
1983	Cal Ripken, Jr., Baltimore
1984	Willie Hernandez, Detroit
1985	Don Mattingly, New York
1986	Roger Clemens, Boston
1987	George Bell, Toronto
1988	Jose Canseco, Oakland
1989	Robin Yount, Milwaukee
1990	Rickey Henderson, Oakland
1991	Cal Ripken, Jr., Baltimore
1992	Dennis Eckersley, Oakland
1993	Frank Thomas, Chicago
1994	Frank Thomas, Chicago
1995	Mo Vaughn, Boston
1996	Juan Gonzalez, Texas
1997	Ken Griffey Jr., Seattle

Rookie of the Year

1947—Combined selection—Jackie Robinson, Brooklyn, 1b; 1948—Combined selection—Alvin Dark, Boston, N.L., ss

National League

Year	Player, team
1949	Don Newcombe, Brooklyn, p
1950	Sam Jethroe, Boston, of
1951	Willie Mays, New York, of
1952	Joe Black, Brooklyn, p
1953	Jim Gilliam, Brooklyn, 2b
1954	Wally Moon, St. Louis, of
1955	Bill Virdon, St. Louis, of
1956	Frank Robinson, Cincinnati, of
1957	Jack Sanford, Philadelphia, p
1958	Orlando Cepeda, S.F., 1b
1959	Willie McCovey, S.F., 1b
1960	Frank Howard, Los Angeles, of
1961	Billy Williams, Chicago, of
1962	Ken Hubbs, Chicago, 2b
1963	Pete Rose, Cincinnati, 2b
1964	Richie Allen, Philadelphia, 3b
1965	Jim Lefebvre, Los Angeles, 2b
1966	Tommy Helms, Cincinnati, 2b
1967	Tom Seaver, New York, p
1968	Johnny Bench, Cincinnati, c
1969	Ted Sizemore, Los Angeles, 2b
1970	Carl Morton, Montreal, p
1971	Earl Williams, Atlanta, c
1972	Jon Matlack, New York, p
1973	Gary Matthews, S.F., of
1974	Bake McBride, St. Louis, of
1975	John Montefusco, S.F., p
1976	Butch Metzger, San Diego, p
(tie)	Pat Zachry, Cincinnati, p
1977	Andre Dawson, Montreal, of
1978	Bob Horner, Atlanta, 3b
1979	Rick Sutcliffe, Los Angeles, p
1980	Steve Howe, Los Angeles, p
1981	Fernando Valenzuela, Los Angeles, p
1982	Steve Sax, Los Angeles, 2b
1983	Darryl Strawberry, New York, of
1984	Dwight Gooden, New York, p
1985	Vince Coleman, St. Louis, of
1986	Todd Worrell, St. Louis, p
1987	Benito Santiago, San Diego, c
1988	Chris Sabo, Cincinnati, 3b
1989	Jerome Walton, Chicago, of
1990	Dave Justice, Atlanta, 1b
1991	Jeff Bagwell, Houston, 1b
1992	Eric Karros, Los Angeles, 1b
1993	Mike Piazza, Los Angeles, c
1994	Raul Mondesi, Los Angeles, of
1995	Hideo Nomo, Los Angeles, p
1996	Todd Hollandsworth, Los Angeles, of
1997	Scot Rolen, Philadelphia, 3b

American League

1949	Roy Sievers, St. Louis, of
1950	Walt Dropo, Boston, 1b
1951	Gil McDougald, New York, 3b
1952	Harry Byrd, Philadelphia, p
1953	Harvey Kuenn, Detroit, ss
1954	Bob Grim, New York, p
1955	Herb Score, Cleveland, p
1956	Luis Aparicio, Chicago, ss
1957	Tony Kubek, New York, if-of
1958	Albie Pearson, Washington, of
1959	Bob Allison, Washington, of
1960	Ron Hansen, Baltimore, ss
1961	Don Schwall, Boston, p
1962	Tom Tresh, New York, if-of
1963	Gary Peters, Chicago, p
1964	Tony Oliva, Minnesota, of
1965	Curt Blefary, Baltimore, of
1966	Tommie Agee, Chicago, of
1967	Rod Carew, Minnesota, 2b
1968	Stan Bahnsen, New York, p
1969	Lou Piniella, Kansas City, of
1970	Thurman Munson, New York, c
1971	Chris Chambliss, Cleveland, 1b
1972	Carlton Fisk, Boston, c
1973	Al Bumbry, Baltimore, of
1974	Mike Hargrove, Texas, 1b
1975	Fred Lynn, Boston, of
1976	Mark Fidrych, Detroit, p
1977	Eddie Murray, Baltimore, dh
1978	Lou Whitaker, Detroit, 2b
1979	John Castino, Minnesota, 3b
(tie)	Alfredo Griffin, Toronto, ss
1980	Joe Charboneau, Cleveland, of
1981	Dave Righetti, New York, p
1982	Cal Ripken, Jr., Baltimore, ss
1983	Ron Kittle, Chicago, of
1984	Alvin Davis, Seattle, 1b
1985	Ozzie Guillen, Chicago, ss
1986	Jose Canseco, Oakland, of
1987	Mark McGwire, Oakland, 1b
1988	Walt Weiss, Oakland, ss
1989	Gregg Olson, Baltimore, p
1990	Sandy Alomar, Jr., Cleveland, c
1991	Chuck Knoblauch, Minnesota, 2b
1992	Pat Listach, Milwaukee, ss
1993	Tim Salmon, California, of
1994	Bob Hamelin, Kansas City, dh
1995	Marty Cordova, Minnesota, of
1996	Derek Jeter, New York, ss
1997	Nomar Garciaparra, Boston, ss

National League Final Standings, 1998

Eastern Division

	W	L	Pct.	GB	Home	vs. East	vs. Central	vs. West	vs. AL
Atlanta	106	56	.654	—	56-25	30-18	34-20	33-11	9-7
New York	88	74	.543	18	47-34	22-26	33-21	24-20	9-7
Philadelphia	75	87	.463	31	40-41	21-27	29-25	18-26	7-9
Montreal	65	97	.401	41	39-42	26-22	13-41	20-24	6-10
Florida	54	108	.333	52	31-50	21-27	12-42	13-31	8-8

Central Division

	W	L	Pct.	GB	Home	vs. East	vs. Central	vs. West	vs. AL
Houston	102	60	.630	—	55-26	30-15	38-18	24-23	10-4
Chicago*[1]	90	73	.552	12½	51-31	27-18	28-28	30-19	5-8
St. Louis	83	79	.512	19	48-34	23-22	30-26	26-22	4-9
Cincinnati	77	85	.475	25	39-42	26-19	27-29	17-31	7-6
Milwaukee	74	88	.457	28	38-43	22-23	22-34	22-25	8-6
Pittsburgh	69	93	.426	33	40-40	21-24	23-33	19-29	6-7

Western Division

	W	L	Pct.	GB	Home	vs. East	vs. Central	vs. West	vs. AL
San Diego	98	64	.605	—	54-27	26-18	35-22	31-17	6-7
San Francisco[1]	89	74	.546	9½	49-32	28-16	31-27	22-26	8-5
Los Angeles	83	79	.512	15	48-33	19-25	31-26	25-23	8-5
Colorado	77	85	.475	21	42-39	24-20	25-33	24-24	4-8
Arizona	65	97	.401	33	34-47	15-29	27-30	18-30	5-8

*Wild card team. (1) Chicago beat San Francisco (5-3) in a one game playoff to win the wild card spot.

National League Playoff Results, 1998

Division Series

Atlanta defeated Chicago 3 games to 0 (7-1, 2-1 [10], 6-2)
San Diego defeated Houston 3 games to 1 (2-1, 4-5, 2-1, 6-1)

Championship Series

San Diego defeated Atlanta 4 games to 2 (3-2 [10], 3-0, 4-1, 3-8, 6-7, 5-0)

National League Statistics, 1998

(Individual Statistics: Batting—at least 150 at-bats; Pitching—at least 70 innings or 10 saves; *traded within NL during season; entry includes statistics for more than 1 team; # traded to or from AL during season; entry includes only NL stats)

Team Batting

	Avg	AB	R	H	HR	RBI
Colorado	.291	5,632	826	1,640	183	791
Houston	.280	5,641	874	1,578	166	818
San Francisco	.274	5,628	845	1,540	161	800
Atlanta	.272	5,484	826	1,489	215	794
Chicago	.264	5,649	831	1,494	212	788
Philadelphia	.264	5,617	713	1,482	126	672
Cincinnati	.262	5,496	750	1,441	138	723
Milwaukee	.260	5,541	707	1,439	152	673
New York	.259	5,510	706	1,425	136	671
St. Louis	.258	5,593	810	1,444	223	781
Pittsburgh	.254	5,493	650	1,395	107	613
San Diego	.253	5,490	749	1,390	167	715
Los Angeles	.252	5,459	669	1,374	159	630
Montreal	.249	5,418	644	1,348	147	602
Florida	.248	5,558	667	1,381	114	621
Arizona	.246	5,491	665	1,353	159	621

Team Pitching

	ERA	IP	H	BB	SO	Sv
Atlanta	3.25	1,438.2	1,291	467	1,232	45
Houston	3.50	1,471.1	1,435	465	1,187	44
San Diego	3.63	1,454.2	1,384	501	1,217	59
New York	3.76	1,458.0	1,381	532	1,129	46
Los Angeles	3.81	1,447.1	1,332	587	1,178	47
Pittsburgh	3.91	1,449.0	1,433	530	1,112	41
San Francisco	4.18	1,477.0	1,457	562	1,089	44
St. Louis	4.31	1,469.2	1,513	558	972	44
Montreal	4.38	1,427.0	1,448	533	1,017	39
Cincinnati	4.44	1,441.1	1,400	573	1,098	42
Chicago	4.47	1,477.1	1,528	575	1,207	56
Milwaukee	4.63	1,451.0	1,538	550	1,063	39
Arizona	4.63	1,432.1	1,463	489	908	37
Philadelphia	4.64	1,463.0	1,476	544	1,176	32
Colorado	4.99	1,432.2	1,583	562	951	36
Florida	5.18	1,449.2	1,617	715	1,016	24

Arizona Diamondbacks

Batting	AB	R	H	HR	RBI	SB	AVG
Miller	168	17	48	3	14	1	.286
White	563	84	157	22	85	22	.279
Fox	502	67	139	9	44	14	.277
Batista	293	46	80	18	41	1	.273
Lee	562	71	151	22	72	8	.269
Williams	510	72	136	20	71	5	.267
Dellucci	416	43	108	5	51	3	.260
Stinnett	274	35	71	11	34	0	.259
Bell	549	79	138	20	67	3	.251
*Gilkey	365	41	85	5	33	9	.233
Brede	212	23	48	2	17	1	.226
Garcia	333	39	74	9	43	5	.222
Benitez	206	17	41	9	30	2	.199

Pitching	W	L	ERA	IP	H	BB	SO	Sv
Daal	8	12	2.88	162.2	146	51	132	0
Olson	3	4	3.01	68.2	56	25	55	30
*Telemaco	7	10	3.93	148.2	150	46	78	0
Benes	14	13	3.97	231.1	221	74	164	0
Anderson	12	13	4.33	208.0	221	24	95	0
Sodowsky	3	6	5.68	77.2	86	39	42	0

Manager—Buck Showalter

Atlanta Braves

Batting	AB	R	H	HR	RBI	SB	AVG
C. Jones	601	123	188	34	107	16	.313
*Colbrunn	166	18	51	3	23	4	.307
Williams	266	46	81	10	44	11	.305
Galarraga	555	103	169	44	121	7	.305
Lopez	489	73	139	34	106	5	.284
Weiss	347	64	97	0	27	7	.280
#Guillen	264	35	73	1	22	1	.277
Klesko	427	69	117	18	70	5	.274
A. Jones	582	89	158	31	90	27	.271
Lockhart	366	50	94	9	37	2	.257
Tucker	414	54	101	13	46	8	.244
Graffanino	289	32	61	5	22	1	.211

Pitching	W	L	ERA	IP	H	BB	SO	Sv
Maddux	18	9	2.22	251.0	201	45	204	0
Glavine	20	6	2.47	229.1	202	74	157	0
Lightenberg	3	2	2.71	73.0	51	24	79	30
Smoltz	17	3	2.90	167.2	145	44	173	0
Neagle	16	11	3.55	210.1	196	60	165	0
Millwood	17	8	4.08	174.1	175	56	163	0
Martinez	4	6	4.45	91.0	109	19	62	2

Manager—Bobby Cox

Chicago Cubs

Batting	AB	R	H	HR	RBI	SB	AVG
Grace	595	92	184	17	89	4	.309
Sosa	643	134	198	66	158	18	.308
Morandini	582	93	172	8	53	13	.296
Brown	347	56	101	14	48	4	.291
*Gaetti	434	60	122	19	70	1	.281
Johnson	304	51	85	2	21	10	.280
Houston	255	26	65	9	33	2	.255
Hernandez	488	76	124	23	75	4	.254
Rodriguez	415	56	104	31	85	1	.251
Alexander	264	34	60	5	25	4	.227
Servais	325	35	72	7	36	1	.222
Blauser	361	49	79	4	26	2	.219

Pitching	W	L	ERA	IP	H	BB	SO	Sv
Mulholland	6	5	2.89	112.0	100	39	72	3
Beck	3	4	3.02	80.1	86	20	81	51
Wood	13	6	3.40	166.2	117	85	233	0
Adams	7	7	4.33	72.2	72	41	73	1
Trachsel	15	8	4.46	208.0	204	84	149	0
Clark	9	14	4.84	213.2	236	48	161	0
Tapani	19	9	4.85	219.0	244	62	136	0
Gonzalez	7	7	5.32	110.0	124	41	70	0

Manager—Jim Riggleman

Cincinnati Reds

Batting	AB	R	H	HR	RBI	SB	AVG
Young	536	81	166	14	83	2	.310
Larkin	538	93	166	17	72	26	.309
A. Boone	181	24	51	2	28	6	.282
Taubensee	431	61	120	11	72	1	.278
Casey	302	44	82	7	52	1	.272
#Greene	356	57	96	14	49	6	.270
Sanders	481	83	129	14	59	20	.268
B. Boone	583	76	155	24	95	6	.266
Stynes	347	52	88	6	27	15	.254
Perez	172	20	41	4	30	0	.238
*Konerko	217	21	47	7	29	0	.217
Nunnally	174	29	36	7	20	3	.207

Pitching	W	L	ERA	IP	H	BB	SO	Sv
Harnisch	14	7	3.14	209.0	176	64	157	0
Graves	2	1	3.32	81.1	76	28	44	8
Parris	6	5	3.73	99.0	89	32	77	0
White	5	5	4.01	98.2	86	27	83	9
Tomko	13	12	4.44	210.2	198	64	162	0
Remlinger	8	15	4.82	164.1	164	87	144	0
Sullivan	5	5	5.21	102.0	98	36	86	1
Winchester	3	6	5.81	79.0	101	27	40	0

Manager—Jack McKeon

Colorado Rockies

Batting	AB	R	H	HR	RBI	SB	AVG
Walker	454	113	165	23	67	14	.363
Bichette	662	97	219	22	122	14	.331
Castilla	645	108	206	46	144	5	.319
Helton	530	78	167	25	97	3	.315
*Hamilton	561	95	173	6	51	13	.308
Reed	259	43	75	9	39	0	.290
Lansing	584	73	161	12	66	10	.276
Perez	647	80	177	9	59	5	.274
Manwaring	291	30	72	2	26	1	.247
Goodwin	159	27	39	1	6	5	.245

Pitching	W	L	ERA	IP	H	BB	SO	Sv
Veres	3	1	2.83	76.1	67	27	74	8
DeJean	3	1	3.03	74.1	78	24	27	2
Dipoto	3	4	3.53	71.1	61	25	49	19
Laskanic	6	4	4.40	75.2	75	40	55	2
Thomson	8	11	4.81	161.0	174	49	106	0
Kile	13	17	5.20	230.1	257	96	158	0
Jones	7	8	5.22	141.1	153	66	109	0
Wright	9	14	5.67	206.1	235	95	86	0
Astacio	13	14	6.23	209.1	245	74	170	0

Manager—Don Baylor

Florida Marlins

Batting	AB	R	H	HR	RBI	SB	AVG
Berg	182	18	57	2	21	3	.313
Renteria	517	79	146	3	31	41	.282
Floyd	588	85	166	22	90	27	.282
Kotsay	578	72	161	11	68	10	.279
#*Zeile	392	59	108	13	66	3	.276
Cangelosi	171	19	43	1	10	2	.251
Dunwoody	434	53	109	5	28	5	.251
Counsell	335	43	84	4	40	3	.251
Jackson	260	26	65	5	31	1	.250
Lee	454	62	106	17	74	5	.233
*Orie	379	47	83	8	38	2	.219
Castillo	153	21	31	1	10	3	.203
Zaun	298	19	56	5	29	5	.188

Pitching	W	L	ERA	IP	H	BB	SO	Sv
Darensbourg	0	7	3.68	71.0	52	30	74	1
*Edmondson	4	4	3.91	76.0	76	37	40	0
Alfonseca	4	6	4.08	70.2	75	33	46	8
Ojala	2	7	4.25	125.0	128	59	75	0
Sanchez	7	9	4.47	173.0	178	91	137	0
Hernandez	10	12	4.72	234.1	265	104	162	0
Meadows	11	13	5.21	174.1	222	46	88	0
Larkin	3	8	9.64	74.2	101	55	43	0

Manager—Jim Leyland

Houston Astros

Batting	AB	R	H	HR	RBI	SB	AVG
Biggio	646	123	210	20	88	50	.325
Berry	299	48	94	13	52	3	.314
Bell	630	111	198	22	108	13	.314
Alou	584	104	182	38	124	11	.312
Bagwell	540	124	164	34	111	19	.304
Hidalgo	211	31	64	7	35	3	.303
Everett	467	72	138	15	76	14	.296
Spiers	384	66	105	4	43	11	.273
Ausmus	412	62	111	6	45	10	.269
Gutierrez	491	55	128	2	46	13	.261
Eusebio	182	13	46	1	36	1	.253
Bogar	156	12	24	1	8	2	.154

Pitching	W	L	ERA	IP	H	BB	SO	Sv
#Johnson	10	1	1.28	84.1	57	26	116	0
Wagner	4	3	2.70	60.0	46	25	97	30
Henry	8	2	3.04	71.0	55	35	59	2
*Powell	7	7	3.33	70.1	58	37	62	7
Hampton	11	7	3.36	211.2	227	81	137	0
Reynolds	19	8	3.51	233.1	257	53	209	0
Lima	16	8	3.70	233.1	229	32	169	0
Bergman	12	9	3.72	172.0	183	42	100	0
#Schourek	7	6	4.50	80.0	82	36	59	0

Manager—Larry Dierker

Los Angeles Dodgers

Batting	AB	R	H	HR	RBI	SB	AVG
*Sheffield	437	73	132	22	85	22	.302
Hubbard	208	29	62	7	18	9	.298
Karros	507	59	150	23	87	7	.296
Young	452	78	129	8	43	42	.285
Mondesi	580	85	162	30	90	16	.279
*Grudzielanek	589	62	160	10	62	18	.272
Hollandsworth	175	23	47	3	20	4	.269
Vizcaino	237	30	62	3	29	7	.262
*Bonilla	333	39	83	11	45	1	.249
Cedeno	240	33	58	2	17	8	.242
Luke	237	34	56	12	34	2	.236
*Johnson	459	44	100	19	58	0	.218
Beltre	195	18	42	7	22	3	.215
*Eisenreich	191	21	41	1	13	6	.215
Castro	220	25	43	2	14	0	.195

Pitching	W	L	ERA	IP	H	BB	SO	Sv
*Shaw	3	8	2.12	85.0	75	19	55	48
Radinsky	6	6	2.63	61.2	63	20	45	13
*Bohanon	7	11	2.67	151.2	121	57	111	0
Martinez	7	3	2.83	101.2	76	41	91	0
*Perez	11	14	3.59	241.0	244	63	128	0
Park	15	9	3.71	220.2	199	97	191	0
Valdes	11	10	3.98	174.0	171	66	122	0
Dreifort	8	12	4.00	180.0	171	57	168	0
*Mlicki	8	7	4.57	181.1	188	63	117	0

Manager—Bill Russell; Glenn Hoffman

Milwaukee Brewers

Batting	AB	R	H	HR	RBI	SB	AVG
Cirillo	604	97	194	14	68	10	.321
Loretta	434	55	137	6	54	9	.316
Vina	637	101	198	7	45	22	.311
Grissom	542	57	147	10	60	13	.271
Nilsson	309	39	83	12	56	2	.269
Burnitz	609	92	160	38	125	7	.263
Jackson	204	20	49	4	20	1	.240
Matheny	320	24	76	6	27	1	.238
Newfield	186	15	44	3	25	0	.237
Hughes	218	28	50	9	29	1	.229
Jenkins	262	33	60	9	28	1	.229
Valentin	428	65	96	16	49	10	.224
Jaha	216	29	45	7	38	1	.208

Pitching	W	L	ERA	IP	H	BB	SO	SV
Wickman	6	9	3.72	82.1	79	39	71	25
Woodard	10	12	4.18	165.2	170	33	135	0
Karl	10	11	4.40	192.1	219	66	102	0
Patrick	4	1	4.69	78.2	83	29	49	0
Eldred	4	8	4.80	133.0	157	61	86	0
*Weathers	6	5	4.91	110.0	130	41	94	0
Woodall	7	9	4.96	138.0	145	47	85	0
*Pulsipher	3	4	5.10	72.1	86	31	51	0
#Jones	3	4	5.17	54.0	65	11	43	12
#Juden	7	11	5.53	138.1	149	66	109	0

Manager—Phil Garner

Montreal Expos

Batting	AB	R	H	HR	RBI	SB	AVG
V. Guerrero	623	108	202	38	109	11	.324
White	357	54	107	17	58	16	.300
*W. Guerrero	402	50	114	2	27	8	.284
Cabrera	261	44	73	3	22	6	.280
Fullmer	505	58	138	13	73	6	.273
May	180	13	43	5	15	0	.239
Andrews	492	48	117	25	69	1	.238
Widger	417	36	97	15	53	6	.233
Vidro	205	24	45	0	18	2	.220
Jones	212	30	46	1	15	16	.217
Santangelo	383	53	82	4	23	7	.214
McGuire	210	17	39	1	10	0	.186

Pitching	W	L	ERA	IP	H	BB	SO	Sv
Urbina	6	3	1.30	69.1	37	33	94	34
Kline	3	6	2.76	71.2	62	41	76	1
Hermanson	14	11	3.13	187.0	163	56	154	0
Batista	3	5	3.80	135.0	141	65	92	0
Telford	3	6	3.86	91.0	85	36	59	1
Pavano	6	9	4.21	134.2	130	43	83	0
Bennett	5	5	5.50	91.2	97	45	59	1
Vazquez	5	15	6.06	172.1	196	68	139	0

Manager—Felipe Alou

New York Mets

Batting	AB	R	H	HR	RBI	SB	AVG
Olerud	557	91	197	22	93	2	.354
*Piazza	561	88	184	32	111	1	.328
*#Allensworth	287	39	83	5	28	8	.289
Alfonso	557	94	155	17	78	8	.278
M. Franco	161	20	44	1	13	0	.273
Baerga	511	46	136	7	53	0	.266
McRae	552	79	146	21	79	20	.264
*Harris	290	30	75	6	27	6	.259
Huskey	369	43	93	13	59	7	.252
Lopez	266	37	67	2	22	2	.252
Ordonez	505	46	124	1	42	3	.246
#Phillips	188	25	42	3	14	1	.223
*Fabregas	183	11	36	2	20	0	.197

Pitching	W	L	ERA	IP	H	BB	SO	Sv
Leiter	17	6	2.47	193.0	151	71	174	0
Wendell	5	1	2.93	76.2	62	33	58	4
Reed	16	11	3.48	212.1	208	29	153	0
J. Franco	0	8	3.62	64.2	66	29	59	38
Yoshii	6	8	3.93	171.2	166	53	117	0
Jones	9	9	4.05	195.1	192	53	115	0
*Nomo	6	12	4.92	157.1	130	94	167	0
*Blair	5	16	4.98	175.1	188	61	92	0

Manager—Bobby Valentine

Philadelphia Phillies

Batting	AB	R	H	HR	RBI	SB	AVG
Sefcik	169	27	53	3	20	4	.314
Abreu	497	68	155	17	74	19	.312
#Jeffries	483	65	142	8	48	11	.294
Rolen	601	120	174	31	110	14	.290
Glanville	678	106	189	8	49	23	.279
Jordan	250	23	69	2	27	0	.276
Brogna	565	77	150	20	104	7	.265
Lieberthal	313	39	80	8	45	2	.256
Lewis	518	52	129	9	54	3	.249
Relaford	494	45	121	5	41	9	.245
Estalella	165	16	31	8	20	0	.188

Pitching	W	L	ERA	IP	H	BB	SO	Sv
Schilling	15	14	3.25	268.2	236	61	300	0
Spradin	4	4	3.53	81.2	63	20	76	1
Leiter	7	5	3.55	88.2	67	47	84	23
Gomes	9	6	4.24	93.1	94	35	86	1
Portugal	10	5	4.44	166.1	186	32	104	0
Green	6	12	5.03	159.1	142	85	113	0
Beech	3	9	5.15	117.0	126	63	113	0
Grace	4	7	5.48	90.1	116	30	46	0
Loewer	7	8	6.09	122.2	154	39	58	0

Manager—Terry Francona

Pittsburgh Pirates

Batting	AB	R	H	HR	RBI	SB	AVG
Kendall	535	95	175	12	75	26	.327
A. Brown	152	20	43	0	5	4	.283
Womack	655	85	185	3	45	58	.282
Young	592	88	160	27	108	15	.270
Guillenl	573	60	153	14	84	3	.267
Ward	282	33	74	9	46	5	.262
Garcia	172	27	44	9	26	0	.256
M. Martinez	180	21	45	6	24	0	.250
Collier	334	30	82	2	34	2	.246
Martin	440	57	105	12	47	20	.239
Ramirez	251	23	59	6	24	0	.235
Polovich	212	18	40	0	14	4	.189
Strange	185	9	32	0	14	1	.173

Pitching	W	L	ERA	IP	H	BB	SO	Sv
Rincon	0	2	2.91	65.0	50	29	64	14
Cordova	13	14	3.31	220.1	204	69	157	0
Loiselle	2	7	3.44	55.0	56	36	48	19
Peters	8	10	3.47	148.0	142	55	103	1
Schmidt	11	14	4.07	214.1	228	71	158	0
Lieber	8	14	4.11	171.0	182	40	138	1
Silva	6	7	4.40	100.1	104	30	64	0
#Loiaza	6	5	4.52	91.2	96	30	53	0
Dessens	2	6	5.67	74.2	90	25	43	0

Manager—Gene Lamont

St. Louis Cardinals

Batting	AB	R	H	HR	RBI	SB	AVG
Jordan	564	100	178	25	91	17	.316
McGwire	509	130	152	70	147	1	.299
Lankford	533	94	156	31	105	26	.293
DeShields	420	74	122	7	44	26	.290
#Tatis	202	28	58	8	26	7	.287
McGee	269	27	68	3	34	7	.253
Mabry	377	41	94	9	46	0	.249
Marrero	254	28	62	4	20	6	.244
Gant	383	60	92	26	67	8	.240
#Clayton	355	59	83	4	29	19	.234
Lampkin	216	25	50	6	28	3	.231
Pagnozzi	160	7	35	1	10	0	.219
Kelly	153	18	33	4	14	5	.216
Ordaz	153	9	31	0	8	2	.203

Pitching	W	L	ERA	IP	H	BB	SO	Sv
Morris	7	5	2.53	113.2	101	42	79	0
Acevedo	8	3	2.56	98.1	83	29	56	15
#Stottlemyre	9	9	3.51	161.1	146	51	147	0
Osborne	5	4	4.09	83.2	84	22	60	0
Frascatore	3	4	4.14	95.2	95	36	49	0
Brantley	0	5	4.44	50.2	40	18	48	14
Bottenfield	4	6	4.44	133.2	128	57	98	4
Petkovsek	7	4	4.77	105.2	131	36	55	0
Mercker	11	11	5.07	161.2	199	53	72	0
Aybar	6	6	5.98	81.1	90	42	57	0

Manager—Tony La Russa

San Diego Padres

Batting	AB	R	H	HR	RBI	SB	AVG
Gwynn	461	65	148	16	69	3	.321
Joyner	439	58	131	12	80	1	.298
Vaughn	573	112	156	50	119	11	.272
Gomez	449	55	120	4	39	1	.267
Veras	517	79	138	6	45	24	.267
Hernandez	390	34	102	9	52	2	.262
Caminiti	452	87	114	29	82	6	.252
Finley	619	92	154	14	67	12	.249
Myers	171	19	42	4	20	0	.246
Sheets	194	31	47	7	29	7	.242
Sweeney	192	17	45	2	15	1	.234
Rivera	172	31	36	6	29	5	.209

Pitching	W	L	ERA	IP	H	BB	SO	Sv
Hoffman	4	2	1.48	3.0	41	21	86	53
Brown	18	7	2.38	257.0	225	49	257	0
Wall	5	4	2.43	70.1	50	32	56	1
Miceli	10	5	3.22	72.2	64	27	70	2
Ashby	17	9	3.34	226.2	223	58	151	0
Hitchcock	9	7	3.93	176.1	169	48	158	1
Hamilton	13	13	4.27	217.1	220	106	147	0
Boehringer	5	2	4.36	76.1	75	45	67	0
Langston	4	6	5.86	81.1	107	41	56	0

Manager—Bruce Bochy

San Francisco Giants

Batting	AB	R	H	HR	RBI	SB	AVG
Benard	286	41	92	3	36	11	.322
Bonds	552	120	167	37	122	28	.303
Kent	526	94	156	31	128	9	.297
Mueller	534	93	157	9	59	3	.294
*Burks	504	76	147	21	76	11	.292
Javier	417	63	121	4	49	21	.290
Hayes	329	39	94	12	62	2	.286
Sanchez	316	44	90	2	30	0	.285
Mayne	275	26	75	3	32	2	.273
Aurilia	413	54	110	9	49	3	.266
Snow	435	65	108	15	79	1	.248
Johnson	308	34	73	13	34	0	.237

Pitching	W	L	ERA	IP	H	BB	SO	Sv
Nen	7	7	1.52	88.2	59	25	110	40
Johnstone	6	5	3.07	88.0	72	38	86	0
Tavarez	5	3	3.80	85.1	96	36	52	1
Gardner	13	6	4.33	212.0	203	65	151	0
Rueter	16	9	4.36	187.2	193	57	102	0
Hershiser	11	10	4.41	202.0	200	85	126	0
Ortiz	4	4	4.99	88.1	90	46	75	0
Estes	7	12	5.06	149.1	150	80	136	0
Darwin	8	10	5.51	148.2	176	49	81	0

Manager—Dusty Baker

American League Final Standings, 1998

Eastern Division

	W	L	Pct.	GB	Home	vs. East	vs. Central	vs. West	vs. NL
New York	114	48	.704	—	62-19	33-15	39-15	29-15	13-3
Boston*	92	70	.568	22	51-30	25-23	31-23	27-17	9-7
Toronto	88	74	.543	26	51-30	27-21	28-26	24-20	9-7
Baltimore	79	83	.488	35	42-39	19-29	29-25	26-18	5-11
Tampa Bay	63	99	.389	51	33-48	16-32	22-32	20-24	5-11

Central Division

	W	L	Pct.	GB	Home	vs. East	vs. Central	vs. West	vs. NL
Cleveland	89	73	.549	—	46-35	27-27	29-19	23-21	10-6
Chicago	80	82	.494	9½	44-37	28-26	26-22	19-25	7-9
Kansas City	72	89	.447	16½	29-51	23-31	21-27	19-24	9-7
Minnesota	70	92	.432	19	35-46	25-30	20-27	18-26	7-9
Detroit	65	97	.401	24	32-49	19-35	23-25	16-28	7-9

Western Division

	W	L	Pct.	GB	Home	vs. East	vs. Central	vs. West	vs. NL
Texas	88	74	.543	—	49-33	27-28	33-22	20-16	8-8
Anaheim	85	77	.525	3	42-39	27-28	29-26	19-17	10-6
Seattle	76	85	.472	11½	42-39	22-33	32-22	15-21	7-9
Oakland	74	88	.457	14	39-42	18-37	30-25	18-18	8-8

*Wild card team.

American League Playoff Results, 1998

Division Series

New York defeated Texas 3 games to 0 (2-0, 3-1, 4-0)
Cleveland defeated Boston 3 games to 1 (3-11, 9-5, 4-3, 2-1)

Championship Series

New York defeated Cleveland 4 games to 2 (7-2, 1-4 [12], 1-6, 4-0, 5-3, 9-5)

American League Statistics, 1998

(Individual Statistics: Batting—at least 150 at-bats; Pitching—at least 70 innings or 10 saves; *traded within AL during season, entry includes statistics for more than one team; # traded to or from NL during season, entry includes only AL stats)

Team Batting

	Avg	AB	R	H	HR	RBI
Texas	.289	5,672	940	1,637	201	894
New York	.288	5,643	965	1,625	207	907
Boston	.280	5,601	876	1,568	205	827
Seattle	.276	5,628	859	1,553	234	822
Baltimore	.273	5,565	817	1,520	214	783
Cleveland	.272	5,616	850	1,530	198	811
Anaheim	.272	5,630	787	1,530	147	739
Chicago	.271	5,585	861	1,516	198	806
Minnesota	.266	5,641	734	1,499	115	691
Toronto	.266	5,580	816	1,482	221	776
Detroit	.264	5,664	722	1,494	165	691
Kansas City	.263	5,546	714	1,459	134	686
Tampa Bay	.261	5,555	620	1,450	111	579
Oakland	.257	5,490	804	1,413	149	755

Team Pitching

	ERA	IP	H	BB	SO	Sv
New York	3.82	1,456.2	1,357	466	1,080	48
Boston	4.18	1,436.0	1,406	504	1,025	53
Toronto	4.28	1,465.0	1,443	587	1,154	47
Tampa Bay	4.35	1,443.0	1,425	643	1,008	28
Cleveland	4.44	1,460.0	1,552	563	1,037	47
Anaheim	4.49	1,444.0	1,481	630	1,091	52
Baltimore	4.74	1,431.1	1,505	535	1,065	37
Minnesota	4.75	1,447.2	1,622	458	952	42
Oakland	4.81	1,434.0	1,555	529	922	39
Detroit	4.93	1,446.1	1,551	595	947	32
Seattle	4.93	1,424.1	1,530	528	1,156	31
Texas	4.99	1,431.1	1,624	519	994	46
Kansas City	5.15	1,436.1	1,590	568	999	46
Chicago	5.22	1,438.2	1,569	580	911	42

Anaheim Angels

Batting	AB	R	H	HR	RBI	SB	AVG
Palmeiro	165	28	53	0	21	5	.321
Edmonds	599	115	184	25	91	7	.307
Salmon	463	84	139	26	88	0	.300
Erstad	537	84	159	19	82	20	.296
Anderson	622	62	183	15	79	8	.294
DiSarcina	551	73	158	3	56	11	.287
Velarde	188	29	49	4	26	7	.261
Walbeck	338	41	87	6	46	1	.257
*O'Brien	175	13	45	4	18	0	.257
Baughman	196	24	50	1	20	10	.255
*Kreuter	252	27	63	2	33	1	.250
Hollins	363	60	88	11	39	11	.242
Nevin	237	27	54	8	27	0	.228
Glaus	165	19	36	1	23	1	.218
Martin	195	20	42	1	13	3	.215

Pitching	W	L	ERA	IP	H	BB	SO	Sv
Hasegawa	8	3	3.14	97.1	86	32	73	5
Finley	11	9	3.39	223.1	210	109	212	0
Percival	2	7	3.65	66.2	45	37	87	42
Olivares	9	9	4.03	183.0	189	91	112	0
DeLucia	2	6	4.27	71.2	56	46	73	3
Sparks	9	4	4.34	128.2	130	58	90	0
Washburn	6	3	4.62	74.0	70	27	48	0
Hill	9	6	4.98	103.0	123	47	57	0
McDowell	5	3	5.09	76.0	96	19	45	0
Watson	6	7	6.04	92.1	122	34	64	0
Dickson	10	10	6.05	122.0	147	41	61	0

Manager—Terry Collins

Baltimore Orioles

Batting	AB	R	H	HR	RBI	SB	AVG
Davis	452	81	148	28	89	7	.327
Baines	293	40	88	9	57	0	.300
Palmeiro	619	98	183	43	121	11	.296
Webster	309	37	88	10	46	0	.285
Alomar	588	86	166	14	56	18	.282
Surhoff	573	79	160	22	92	9	.279
#Hammonds	171	36	46	6	28	7	.269
Ripken	601	65	163	14	61	0	.271
Hoiles	267	36	70	15	56	0	.262
Bordick	465	59	121	13	51	6	.260
#Carter	283	36	70	11	34	3	.247
Anderson	479	84	113	18	51	21	.236

Pitching	W	L	ERA	IP	H	BB	SO	Sv
Mussina	13	10	3.49	206.1	189	41	175	0
Rhodes	4	4	3.51	77.0	65	34	83	4
Mills	3	4	3.74	77.0	55	50	57	2
Benitez	5	6	3.82	68.1	48	39	87	22
Erickson	16	13	4.01	251.1	284	69	186	0
Key	6	3	4.20	79.1	77	23	53	0
*Guzman	10	16	4.35	211.0	193	98	168	0
Johns	3	3	4.57	86.2	108	32	34	1
Ponson	8	9	5.27	135.0	157	42	85	0
Drabek	6	11	7.29	108.2	138	29	55	0

Manager—Ray Miller

Boston Red Sox

Batting	AB	R	H	HR	RBI	SB	AVG
Vaughn	609	107	205	40	115	0	.337
Garciaparra	604	111	195	35	122	12	.323
Jefferson	196	24	60	8	31	0	.306
Buford	216	37	61	10	42	5	.282
Bragg	409	51	114	8	57	5	.279
Hatteberg	359	46	99	12	43	0	.276
Benjamin	349	46	95	4	39	3	.272
O'Leary	611	95	165	23	83	2	.270
Lewis	585	95	157	8	63	29	.268
*Stanley	497	74	127	29	79	3	.256
Varitek	221	31	56	7	33	2	.253
Valentin	588	113	145	23	73	4	.247

Pitching	W	L	ERA	IP	H	BB	SO	Sv
Gordon	7	4	2.72	79.1	55	25	78	46
Martinez	19	7	2.89	233.2	188	67	251	0
*Swindell	5	6	3.59	90.1	92	31	63	2
Saberhagen	15	8	3.96	175.0	181	29	100	0
Lowe	3	9	4.02	123.0	126	42	77	0
Wakefield	17	8	4.58	216.0	211	79	146	0
Avery	10	7	5.02	123.2	128	64	57	0
Wasdin	6	4	5.25	96.0	111	27	59	0

Manager—Jimy Williams

Chicago White Sox

Batting	AB	R	H	HR	RBI	SB	AVG
Belle	609	113	200	49	152	6	.328
Caruso	523	81	160	5	55	22	.306
Durham	635	126	181	19	67	36	.285
Ordonez	535	70	151	14	65	9	.282
Abbott	244	33	68	12	41	3	.279
Cordero	341	58	91	13	49	2	.267
Thomas	585	109	155	29	109	7	.265
Ventura	590	84	155	21	91	1	.263
Norton	299	38	71	9	36	3	.237
Cameron	396	53	83	8	43	27	.210

Pitching	W	L	ERA	IP	H	BB	SO	Sv
Simas	4	3	3.57	70.2	54	22	56	18
Snyder	7	2	4.80	86.1	96	23	52	0
Sirotka	14	15	5.06	211.2	255	47	128	0
Parque	7	5	5.10	113.0	135	49	77	0
Castillo	6	4	5.11	100.1	94	35	64	0

Pitching	W	L	ERA	IP	H	BB	SO	Sv
Baldwin	13	6	5.32	159.0	176	60	108	0
Eyre	3	8	5.38	107.0	114	64	73	0
Navarro	8	16	6.36	172.2	223	77	71	1
#Bere	3	7	6.45	83.2	98	58	53	0

Manager—Jerry Manuel

Cleveland Indians

Batting	AB	R	H	HR	RBI	SB	AVG
Sexson	174	28	54	11	35	1	.310
Ramirez	571	108	168	45	145	5	.294
Thome	440	89	129	30	85	1	.293
Vizquel	576	86	166	2	50	37	.288
Fryman	557	74	160	28	96	10	.287
Whiten	226	31	64	6	29	2	.283
Lofton	600	101	169	12	64	54	.282
Justice	540	94	151	21	88	9	.280
*Cora	602	111	166	6	32	15	.276
Giles	350	56	94	16	66	10	.269
Borders	160	12	38	0	6	0	.238
Alomar	409	45	96	6	44	0	.235
*Fielder	416	49	97	17	68	0	.233

Pitching	W	L	ERA	IP	H	BB	SO	Sv
Jackson	1	1	1.55	64.0	43	13	55	40
Colon	14	9	3.71	204.0	205	79	158	0
Gooden	8	6	3.76	134.0	135	51	83	0
Burba	15	10	4.11	203.2	210	69	132	0
Wright	12	10	4.72	192.2	207	87	140	0
Nagy	15	10	5.22	210.1	250	66	120	0

Manager—Mike Hargrove

Detroit Tigers

Batting	AB	R	H	HR	RBI	SB	AVG
Encarnacion	164	30	54	7	21	7	.329
Clark	602	84	175	34	103	3	.291
Higginson	612	92	174	25	85	3	.284
Catalanotto	213	23	60	6	25	3	.282
Bako	305	23	83	3	30	1	.272
Easley	594	84	161	27	100	15	.271
Gonzalez	547	84	146	23	71	12	.267
Cruz	454	52	118	5	45	3	.260
Randa	460	56	117	9	50	8	.254
Hunter	595	67	151	4	36	42	.254
Alvarez	199	16	46	5	29	1	.231
*Berroa	191	23	43	1	13	1	.225

Pitching	W	L	ERA	IP	H	BB	SO	Sv
Moehler	14	13	3.90	221.1	220	56	123	0
Thompson	11	15	4.05	222.0	227	79	149	0
Florie	8	9	4.80	133.0	141	59	97	0
Jones	1	4	4.97	63.1	58	36	57	28
Greisinger	6	9	5.12	130.0	142	48	66	0
Powell	3	8	6.35	83.2	101	36	46	0
Castillo	3	9	6.83	116.0	150	44	81	1

Manager—Buddy Bell; Larry Parrish

Kansas City Royals

Batting	AB	R	H	HR	RBI	SB	AVG
Offerman	607	102	191	7	66	45	.315
Morris	472	50	146	1	40	1	.309
Palmer	572	84	159	34	119	8	.278
*Mack	209	31	58	6	29	8	.278
Damon	642	104	178	18	66	26	.277
King	486	83	128	24	93	10	.263
Sweeney	282	32	73	8	35	2	.259
Pendleton	237	17	61	3	29	1	.257
Conine	309	30	79	8	43	3	.256
Sutton	310	29	76	5	42	3	.245
Lopez	206	18	50	1	15	5	.243
Dye	214	24	50	5	23	2	.234
Fasano	216	21	49	8	31	1	.227
Halter	204	17	45	2	13	2	.221

Pitching	W	L	ERA	IP	H	BB	SO	Sv
Service	6	4	3.48	82.2	70	34	95	4
Belcher	14	14	4.27	234.0	247	73	130	0
Rosado	8	11	4.69	174.2	180	57	135	1
Montgomery	2	5	4.98	56.0	58	22	54	36
Pichardo	7	8	5.13	112.1	126	43	55	1
Rapp	12	13	5.30	188.1	208	107	132	0
Rusch	6	15	5.88	154.2	191	50	94	1
#Haney	6	6	7.03	97.1	125	36	51	0

Manager—Tony Muser

Minnesota Twins

Batting	AB	R	H	HR	RBI	SB	AVG
Walker	528	85	167	12	62	19	.316
Nixon	448	71	133	1	20	37	.297
Molitor	502	75	141	4	69	9	.281
Lawton	557	91	155	21	77	16	.278
*#Merced	213	22	59	5	35	1	.277
Ortiz	278	47	77	9	46	1	.277
Coomer	529	54	146	15	72	2	.276
Meares	543	56	141	9	70	7	.260
Ochoa	249	35	64	2	25	6	.257
Cordova	438	52	111	10	69	3	.253
Gates	333	31	83	3	42	3	.249
Steinbach	422	45	102	14	54	0	.242
Hocking	198	32	40	3	15	2	.202
Valentin	162	11	32	3	18	0	.198

Pitching	W	L	ERA	IP	H	BB	SO	Sv
Morgan	4	2	3.49	98.0	108	24	50	0
Trombley	6	5	3.63	96.2	90	41	89	1
Aguilera	4	9	4.24	74.1	75	15	57	38
Radke	12	14	4.30	213.2	238	43	146	0
Tewksbury	7	13	4.79	148.1	174	20	60	0
Hawkins	7	14	5.25	190.1	227	61	105	0
Milton	8	14	5.64	172.1	195	70	107	0
Serafini	7	4	6.48	75.0	95	29	46	0
Rodriguez	4	6	6.56	70.0	88	30	62	0

Manager—Tom Kelly

New York Yankees

Batting	AB	R	H	HR	RBI	SB	AVG
Williams	499	101	169	26	97	15	.339
Jeter	626	127	203	19	84	30	.324
O'Neill	602	95	191	24	116	15	.317
Brosius	530	86	159	19	98	11	.300
Raines	321	53	93	5	47	8	.290
Martinez	531	92	149	28	123	2	.281
Girardi	254	31	70	3	31	2	.276
Posada	358	56	96	17	63	0	.268
Knoblauch	603	117	160	17	64	31	.265
Srawberry	295	44	73	24	57	8	.247
Curtis	456	79	111	10	56	21	.243

Pitching	W	L	ERA	IP	H	BB	SO	Sv
Rivera	3	0	1.91	61.1	48	17	36	36
Hernandez	12	4	3.13	141.0	113	52	131	0
Mendoza	10	2	3.25	130.1	131	30	56	1
Wells	18	4	3.49	214.1	195	29	163	0
Cone	20	7	3.55	207.2	186	59	209	0
Irabu	13	9	4.06	173.0	148	76	126	0
Pettitte	16	11	4.24	216.1	226	87	146	0
Stanton	4	1	5.47	79.0	71	26	69	6

Manager—Joe Torre

Oakland Athletics

Batting	AB	R	H	HR	RBI	SB	AVG
Giambi	562	92	166	27	110	2	.295
Stairs	523	88	154	26	106	8	.294
Grieve	583	94	168	18	89	2	.288
*Roberts	295	45	79	1	24	16	.268
Spiezio	406	54	105	9	50	1	.259
Christensen	370	56	95	5	40	5	.257
McDonald	175	25	44	1	16	10	.251
*MacFarlane	218	29	53	7	34	1	.243
Blowers	409	56	97	11	71	1	.237
Henderson	542	101	128	14	57	66	.236
Tejada	365	53	85	11	45	5	.233
Hinch	337	34	78	9	35	3	.231
Bournigal	209	23	47	1	19	6	.225
*Sprague	469	57	104	20	58	1	.222

Pitching	W	L	ERA	IP	H	BB	SO	Sv
Rogers	16	8	3.17	238.2	215	67	138	0
Taylor	4	9	3.58	73.0	71	22	58	33
Matthews	7	4	4.58	72.2	71	29	53	1
Candiotti	11	16	4.84	201.0	222	63	98	0
Haynes	11	9	5.09	194.1	229	88	134	0
*Worrell	2	7	5.24	103.0	106	29	82	0
Oquist	7	11	6.22	175.0	210	57	112	0
Stein	5	9	6.37	117.1	117	71	89	0

Manager—Art Howe

Seattle Mariners

Batting	AB	R	H	HR	RBI	SB	AVG
Martinez	556	86	179	29	102	1	.322
Rodriguez	686	123	213	42	124	46	.310
Segui	522	79	159	19	84	3	.305
#Hill	259	37	75	12	33	1	.290
Griffey	633	120	180	56	146	20	.284
*#Bell	420	48	115	10	49	0	.274
Davis	502	68	130	20	82	4	.259
Wilson	325	39	82	9	44	2	.252
Buhner	244	33	59	15	45	0	.242
Monohan	211	17	51	4	28	1	.242
Ducey	217	30	52	5	23	4	.240
*Oliver	240	20	54	6	32	1	.225

Pitching	W	L	ERA	IP	H	BB	SO	Sv
Timlin	3	3	2.95	79.1	78	16	60	19
Moyer	15	9	3.53	234.1	234	42	158	0
Fassero	13	12	3.97	224.2	223	66	176	0
#Johnson	9	10	4.33	160.0	146	60	213	0
McCarthy	1	2	5.01	23.1	18	17	25	0
Swift	11	9	5.85	144.2	183	51	77	0
Cloude	8	10	6.37	155.1	187	80	114	0
Spoljaric	4	6	6.48	83.1	85	55	89	0
Ayala	1	10	7.29	75.1	100	26	68	8

Manager—Lou Piniella

Tampa Bay Devil Rays

Batting	AB	R	H	HR	RBI	SB	AVG
Ledesma	299	30	97	0	29	9	.324
McCracken	614	77	179	7	59	19	.292
Trammell	199	28	57	12	35	0	.286
McGriff	564	73	160	19	81	7	.284
Boggs	435	51	122	7	52	3	.280
Winn	338	51	94	1	17	26	.278
Smith	370	44	102	11	55	5	.276
Cairo	515	49	138	5	46	19	.268
Martinez	309	31	79	3	20	8	.256
Kelly	279	39	67	10	33	13	.240
DiFelice	248	17	57	3	23	0	.230
Butler	217	25	49	7	20	4	.226
Sorrento	435	40	98	17	57	2	.225
Stocker	336	37	70	6	25	5	.208
Flaherty	304	21	63	3	24	0	.207

Pitching	W	L	ERA	IP	H	BB	SO	Sv
Lopez	7	4	2.60	79.2	73	32	62	1
Mecir	7	2	3.11	84.0	68	33	77	0
Arrojo	14	12	3.56	202.0	195	65	152	0
Yan	5	4	3.86	88.2	78	41	77	1
Hernandez	2	6	4.04	71.1	55	41	55	26
Saunders	6	15	4.12	192.1	191	111	172	0
*Santana	5	6	4.39	145.2	151	62	61	0
Alvarez	6	14	4.73	142.2	130	68	107	0

Pitching	W	L	ERA	IP	H	BB	SO	Sv
Rekar	2	8	4.98	86.2	95	21	55	0
Springer	3	11	5.45	115.2	120	60	46	0

Manager—Larry Rothschild

Texas Rangers

Batting	AB	R	H	HR	RBI	SB	AVG
Kelly	257	48	83	16	46	0	.323
Rodriguez	579	88	186	21	91	9	.321
Gonzalez	606	110	193	45	157	2	.318
Greer	598	107	183	16	108	2	.306
Clark	554	98	169	23	102	1	.305
Simms	186	36	55	16	46	0	.296
Goodwin	520	102	151	2	33	38	.290
#Clayton	186	30	53	5	24	5	.285
Alicea	259	51	71	6	33	4	.274
#Tatis	330	41	89	3	32	6	.270
Stevens	344	52	91	20	59	0	.265
#Zeile	180	26	47	6	28	1	.261
McLemore	461	79	114	5	53	12	.247

Pitching	W	L	ERA	IP	H	BB	SO	Sv
Wetteland	3	1	2.03	62.0	47	14	72	42
Crabtree	6	1	3.59	85.1	86	35	60	0
Sele	19	11	4.23	212.2	239	84	167	0
Helling	20	7	4.41	216.1	209	78	164	0
Burkett	9	13	5.68	195.0	230	46	131	0
#Loaiza	3	6	5.90	79.1	103	22	55	0
#Oliver	6	7	6.53	103.1	140	43	58	0

Manager—Johnny Oates

Toronto Blue Jays

Batting	AB	R	H	HR	RBI	SB	AVG
Fernandez	486	71	156	9	72	13	.321
Delgado	530	94	155	38	115	3	.292
Fletcher	407	37	115	9	52	0	.283
Stewart	516	90	144	12	55	51	.279
Green	630	106	175	35	100	35	.278
Grebeck	301	33	77	2	27	2	.256
Cruz	352	55	89	11	42	11	.253
Gonzalez	568	70	136	13	51	21	.239
Canseco	583	98	138	46	107	29	.237

Pitching	W	L	ERA	IP	H	BB	SO	Sv
Quantrill	3	4	2.59	80.0	88	22	59	7
Clemens	20	6	2.65	234.2	169	88	271	0
Escobar	7	3	3.73	79.2	72	35	72	0
Carpenter	12	7	4.37	175.0	177	61	136	0
#Myers	3	4	4.46	42.1	44	19	32	28
Williams	10	9	4.46	209.2	196	81	151	0
Hentgen	12	11	5.17	177.2	208	69	94	0

Manager—Tim Johnson

National Baseball Hall of Fame and Museum, Cooperstown, NY[1]

#Aaron, Hank
Alexander, Grover Cleveland
Alston, Walt
Anson, Cap
Aparicio, Luis
Appling, Luke
Ashburn, Richie
Averill, Earl
Baker, Home Run
Bancroft, Dave
#Banks, Ernie
Barlick, Al
Barrow, Edward G.
Beckley, Jake
Bell, Cool Papa
#Bench, Johnny
Bender, Chief
Berra, Yogi
Bottomley, Jim
Boudreau, Lou
Bresnahan, Roger
#Brock, Lou
Brouthers, Dan
Brown, Mordecai (Three Finger)
Bulkeley, Morgan C.
Bunning, Jim
Burkett, Jesse C.
Campanella, Roy
#Carew, Rod
Carey, Max
#Carlton, Steve
Cartwright, Alexander
Chadwick, Henry
Chance, Frank
Chandler, Happy
Charleston, Oscar
Chesbro, John
Clarke, Fred
Clarkson, John
Clemente, Roberto
Cobb, Ty[2]
Cochrane, Mickey
Collins, Eddie
Collins, James
Combs, Earle
Comiskey, Charles A.
Conlan, Jocko
Connolly, Thomas H.
Connor, Roger
Coveleski, Stan
Crawford, Sam
Cronin, Joe
Cummings, Candy
Cuyler, Kiki
Dandridge, Ray
*Davis, George "Gorgeous"
Day, Leon
Dean, Dizzy
Delahanty, Ed
Dickey, Bill
DiHigo, Martin
DiMaggio, Joe
*Doby, Larry
Doerr, Bobby
Drysdale, Don
Duffy, Hugh
Durocher, Leo
Evans, Billy
Evers, John
Ewing, Buck
Faber, Urban
#Feller, Bob
Ferrell, Rick
Fingers, Rollie
Flick, Elmer H.
Ford, Whitey
Foster, Andrew (Rube)
Foster, Bill
Fox, Nellie
Foxx, Jimmie
Frick, Ford
Frisch, Frank
Galvin, Pud
Gehrig, Lou
Gehringer, Charles
#Gibson, Bob
Gibson, Josh
Giles, Warren
Gomez, Lefty
Goslin, Goose
Greenberg, Hank
Griffith, Clark
Grimes, Burleigh
Grove, Lefty
Hafey, Chick
Haines, Jesee
Hamilton, Bill
Hanlon, Ned
Harridge, Will
Harris, Bucky
Hartnett, Gabby
Heilmann, Harry
Herman, Billy
Hooper, Harry
Hornsby, Rogers
Hoyt, Waite
Hubbard, Cal
Hubbell, Carl
Huggins, Miller
Hulbert, William
Hunter, Catfish
Irvin, Monte
#Jackson, Reggie
Jackson, Travis
Jenkins, Ferguson
Jennings, Hugh
Johnson, Byron
Johnson, William (Judy)
Johnson, Walter[2]
Joss, Addie
#Kaline, Al
Keefe, Timothy
Keeler, William
Kell, George
Kelley, Joe
Kelly, George
Kelly, King
Killebrew, Harmon
Kiner, Ralph
Klein, Chuck
Klem, Bill
#Koufax, Sandy
Lajoie, Napoleon
Landis, Kenesaw M.
Lasorda, Tom
Lazzeri, Tony
Lemon, Bob
Leonard, Buck
Lindstrom, Fred
Lloyd, Pop
Lombardi, Ernie
Lopez, Al
Lyons, Ted
Mack, Connie
MacPhail, Larry
*MacPhail, Lee
#Mantle, Mickey
Manush, Henry
Maranville, Rabbit
Marichal, Juan
Marquard, Rube
Mathews, Eddie
Mathewson, Christy[2]
#Mays, Willie

McCarthy, Joe
McCarthy, Thomas
#McCovey, Willie
McGinnity, Joe
McGowan, Bill
McGraw, John
McKechnie, Bill
Medwick, Joe
Mize, Johnny
#Morgan, Joe
#Musial, Stan
Newhouser, Hal
Nichols, Kid
Niekro, Phil
O'Rourke, James
Ott, Mel
Paige, Satchel
#Palmer, Jim
Pennock, Herb
Perry, Gaylord
Plank, Ed
Radbourn, Charlie
Reese, Pee Wee
Rice, Sam
Rickey, Branch
Rixey, Eppa
Rizzuto, Phil (Scooter)
Roberts, Robin
#Robinson, Brooks
#Robinson, Frank
#Robinson, Jackie
Robinson, Wilbert
*Rogan, Joe "Bullet"
Roush, Edd
Ruffing, Red
Rusie, Amos
Ruth, Babe[2]
Schalk, Ray
#Schmidt, Mike
Schoendienst, Red
#Seaver, Tom
Sewell, Joe
Simmons, Al
Sisler, George
Slaughter, Enos
Snider, Duke
#Spahn, Warren
Spalding, Albert
Speaker, Tris
#Stargell, Willie
Stengel, Casey
*Sutton, Don
Terry, Bill
Thompson, Sam
Tinker, Joe
Traynor, Pie
Vance, Dazzy
Vaughan, Arky
Veeck, Bill
Waddell, Rube
Wagner, Honus[2]
Wallace, Roderick
Walsh, Ed
Waner, Lloyd
Waner, Paul
Ward, John
Weaver, Earl
Weiss, George
Welch, Mickey
Wells, Willie
Wheat, Zach
Wilhelm, Hoyt
Williams, Billy
#Williams, Ted
Williams, Vic
Wilson, Hack
Wright, George
Wright, Harry
Wynn, Early
#Yastrzemski, Carl
Yawkey, Tom
Young, Cy
Youngs, Ross

(1) Player must generally be retired for five complete seasons before being eligible for induction. (2) Players inducted in 1936 (the first year the Hall of Fame began). # Denotes players chosen in first year of Hall of Fame eligibility. * Denotes 1998 inductees. Note: Four players, Babe Ruth (1936), Lou Gehrig (1939), Joe DiMaggio (1955), and Roberto Clemente (1973), were inducted less than five years after retirement or, in Clemente's case, death.

All-Star Baseball Games, 1933-1998

Year	Winner, Score	Host team
1933*	American, 4-2	Chicago (AL)
1934*	American, 9-7	New York (NL)
1935*	American, 4-1	Cleveland
1936*	National, 4-3	Boston (NL)
1937*	American, 8-3	Washington
1938*	National, 4-1	Cincinnati
1939*	American, 3-1	New York (AL)
1940*	National, 4-0	St. Louis (NL)
1941*	American, 7-5	Detroit
1942*	American, 3-1	New York (NL)
1943	American, 5-3	Philadelphia (AL)
1944	National, 7-1	Pittsburgh
1945	(Not played)	
1946*	American, 12-0	Boston (AL)
1947*	American, 2-1	Chicago (NL)
1948*	American, 5-2	St. Louis (AL)
1949*	American, 11-7	Brooklyn
1950*	National, 4-3[1]	Chicago (AL)
1951*	National, 8-3	Detroit
1952*	National, 3-2	Philadelphia (NL)
1953*	National, 5-1	Cincinnati
1954*	American, 11-9	Cleveland
1955*	National, 6-5[2]	Milwaukee
1956*	National, 7-3	Washington
1957*	American, 6-5	St. Louis
1958*	American, 4-3	Baltimore
1959*	National, 5-4	Pittsburgh
1959*	American, 5-3	Los Angeles
1960*	National, 5-3	Kansas City
1960*	National, 6-0	New York (AL)
1961*	National, 5-4[3]	San Francisco
1961*	Called–rain, 1-1	Boston
1962*	National, 3-1[3]	Washington
1962*	American, 9-4	Chicago (NL)
1963*	National, 5-3	Cleveland
1964*	National, 7-4	New York (NL)
1965*	National, 6-5	Minnesota
1966*	National, 2-1[3]	St. Louis
1967*	National, 2-1[4]	California
1968	National, 1-0	Houston
1969*	National, 9-3	Washington
1970	National, 5-4[2]	Cincinnati
1971	American, 6-4	Detroit
1972	National, 4-3[3]	Atlanta
1973	National, 7-1	Kansas City
1974	National, 7-2	Pittsburgh
1975	National, 6-3	Milwaukee
1976	National, 7-1	Philadelphia
1977	National, 7-5	New York (AL)
1978	National, 7-3	San Diego
1979	National, 7-6	Seattle
1980	National, 4-2	Los Angeles
1981	National, 5-4	Cleveland
1982	National, 4-1	Montreal
1983	American, 13-3	Chicago (AL)
1984	National, 3-1	San Francisco
1985	National, 6-1	Minnesota
1986	American, 3-2	Houston
1987	National, 2-0[5]	Oakland
1988	American, 2-1	Cincinnati
1989	American, 5-3	California
1990	American, 2-0	Chicago (NL)
1991	American, 4-2	Toronto
1992	American, 13-6	San Diego
1993	American, 9-3	Baltimore
1994	National, 8-7[3]	Pittsburgh
1995	National, 3-2	Texas
1996	National, 6-0	Philadelphia
1997	American, 3-1	Cleveland
1998	American, 13-8	Colorado

*Denotes day game. (1) 14 innings. (2) 12 innings. (3) 10 innings. (4) 15 innings. (5) 13 innings.

Major League Leaders in 1998

American League

Batting

B. Williams, New York, .339; M. Vaughn, Boston, .337; A. Belle, Chicago, .328; E. Davis, Baltimore, .327; D. Jeter, New York, .324.

Runs

D. Jeter, New York, 127; R. Durham, Chicago, 126; A. Rodriguez, Seattle, 123; K. Griffey Jr., Seattle, 120; C. Knoblauch, New York, 117.

Runs Batted In

J. Gonzalez, Texas, 157; A. Belle, 152; K. Griffey Jr., Seattle, 146; M. Ramirez, Cleveland, 145; A. Rodriguez, Seattle, 124.

Hits

A. Rodriguez, Seattle, 213; M. Vaughn, Boston, 205; D. Jeter, New York, 203; A. Belle, Chicago, 200; N. Garciaparra, Boston, 195.

Doubles

J. Gonzalez, Texas, 50; A. Belle, Chicago, 48; E. Martinez, Seattle, 46; J. Valentin, Boston, 44; C. Delgado, Toronto, 43.

Triples

J. Offerman, Kansas City, 13; J. Damon, Kansas City, 10; R. Winn, Tampa Bay, 9; R. Durham, Chicago, 8; D. Jeter, New York, 8; N. Garciaparra, Boston, 8; T. O'Leary, Boston, 8.

Home Runs

K. Griffey Jr., Seattle, 56; A. Belle, Chicago, 49; J. Canseco, Toronto, 46; J. Gonzalez, Texas, 45; M. Ramirez, Cleveland, 45.

Stolen Bases

R. Henderson, Oakland, 66; K. Lofton, Cleveland, 54; S. Stewart, Toronto, 51; A. Rodriguez, Seattle, 46; J. Offerman, Kansas City, 45.

Pitching (Most wins: W-L, ERA, Pct.)

R. Clemens, Toronto, 20-6, 2.65, .769; D. Cone, New York, 20-7, 3.55, .741; Rick Helling, Texas, 20-7, 4.41, .741; Pedro Martinez, Boston, 19-7, 2.89, .731; Aaron Sele, Texas, 19-11, 4.23, .633.

Strikeouts[1]

R. Clemens, Toronto, 271; P. Martinez, Boston, 251; R. Johnson, Seattle, 213; C. Finley, Anaheim, 212; D. Cone, New York, 209.

Saves

T. Gordon, Boston, 46; T. Percival, Anaheim, 42; J. Wetteland, Texas, 42; M. Johnson, Cleveland, 40; R. Aguilera, Minnesota, 38.

National League

Batting

L. Walker, Colorado, .363; J. Olerud, New York, .354; D. Bichette, Colorado, .331; M. Piazza, New York, .328; J. Kendall, Pittsburgh, .327.

Runs

S. Sosa, Chicago, 134; M. McGwire, St. Louis, 130; J. Bagwell, Houston, 124; C. Biggio, Houston, 123; C. Jones, Atlanta, 123.

Runs Batted In

S. Sosa, Chicago, 158; M. McGwire, St. Louis, 147; V. Castilla, Colorado, 144; J. Kent, San Francisco, 128; J. Burnitz, Milwaukee, 125.

Hits

D. Bichette, Colorado, 219; C. Biggio, Houston, 210; V. Castilla, Colorado, 206; V. Guerrero, Montreal, 202; D. Bell, Houston, 198; S. Sosa, Chicago, 198; F. Vina, Milwaukee, 198.

Doubles

C. Biggio, Houston, 51; D. Bichette, Colorado, 48; D. Young, Cincinnati, 48; L. Walker, Colorado, 46; Cliff Floyd, Florida, 45; Scott Rolen, Philadelphia, 45. *(continued)*

Triples

D. Dellucci, Arizona, 12; B. Larkin, Cincinnati, 10; N. Perez, Colorado, 9; W. Guerrero, Montreal, 9; A. Jones, Atlanta, 8; D. DeShields, St. Louis, 8; K. Garcia, Arizona, 8.

Home Runs

M. McGwire, St. Louis, 70; S. Sosa, Chicago, 66; G. Vaughn, San Diego, 50; V. Castilla, Colorado, 46; A. Galarraga, Atlanta, 44.

Stolen Bases

T. Womack, Pittsburgh, 58; C. Biggio, Houston, 50; E. Young, Los Angeles, 42; E. Renteria, Florida, 41; B. Bonds, San Francisco, 28.

Pitching (Most wins: W-L, ERA, Pct.)

T. Glavine, Atlanta, 20-6, 2.47, .769; S. Reynolds, Houston, 19-8, 3.51, .704; K. Tapani, Chicago, 19-9, 4.85, .679; G. Maddux, Atlanta, 18-9, 2.22, .667; K. Brown, San Diego, 18-7, 2.38, .720.

Strikeouts[1]

C. Schilling, Philadelphia, 300; K. Brown, San Diego, 257; K. Wood, Chicago, 233; S. Reynolds, Houston, 209; G. Maddux, Atlanta, 204.

Saves

T. Hoffman, San Diego, 53; R. Beck, Chicago, 51; J. Shaw, Los Angeles, 48; R. Nen, San Francisco, 40; J. Franco, New York, 38.

(1) Randy Johnson led the Major Leagues with 329 total strikeouts, 213 for the Seattle Mariners (AL), 116 for the Houston Astros (NL).

Mark McGwire vs. Sammy Sosa: The 1998 Home Run Race

In the year's most riveting sports story, St. Louis Cardinals slugger Mark McGwire smashed 70 home runs and the Chicago Cubs' Sammy Sosa blasted 66, both shattering Roger Maris's single-season record of 61, which Maris set as a New York Yankee in 1961. The story had the country captivated for most of the summer, as the 2 sluggers sent balls flying out of the park in unequaled numbers. On Sept. 8 in St. Louis's Busch Stadium, in the 4th inning, Big Mac rifled a shot to left field off Cubs pitcher Steve Trachsel, just clearing the fence for his record-breaking 62d homer. The ball traveled a mere 341 feet, his shortest home run of the season. McGwire was greeted at home plate by his son, and got an enormous cheer from the fans and players and a hug from Sosa, who was in the outfield. Maris's children were in the stands, and McGwire made his way up to them to hug them as well and express his respect for the man whose record he'd broken. Sosa hit his 62d homer 5 days later, on Sept. 13.

McGwire jumped off to a fast start during 1998, with 27 home runs by the end of May, but after Sosa launched a record 20 dingers in June, the race was on! Big Mac seemed to always be a step ahead of Swingin' Sammy, but on Aug. 10, Sosa tied things up when he hit his 46th homer. Sosa would pull into a tie for the home run lead a total of 8 times during the season, and even surpassed McGwire briefly on 2 occasions. On Friday night, Sept. 25, during the last weekend of the season, Sosa pulled ahead of McGwire when he hit his 66th homer, but 45 minutes later Mac tied things up again. Then, McGwire added an exclamation point to cap a remarkable season, when he smacked 2 home runs in each of the last 2 games. The 70th homer came Sept. 27, in the 7th inning off Carl Pavano of the Montreal Expos.

Home Run Comparisons—McGwire '98, Sosa '98, Maris '61, Ruth '27

Player, year	Month-by-Month Home Run Breakdown													
	Mar.	Apr.	May	Jun.	Jul.	Aug.	Sept.	Oct.	Tot.	GP	AB	AB/HR	Avg.	RBI
Mark McGwire, 1998	1	10	16	10	8	10	15	0	70	155	509	7.27	.299	147
Sammy Sosa, 1998	0	6	7	20*	9	13	11	0	66	159	643	9.74	.308	158
Roger Maris, 1961	0	1	11	15	13	11	9	1	61	161	590	9.67	.269	142
Babe Ruth, 1927	0	4	12	9	9	9	17	0	60	151	540	9.00	.356	164

*Record home runs in any one month. GP=games played. AB=at bats. AB/HR=at bats per home run.

50 Home Run Club

In addition to Mark McGwire and Sammy Sosa with their amazing totals, 2 other players hit 50 or more homers—Seattle's Ken Griffey Jr. (56) and San Diego's Greg Vaughn (50), marking the first time that more than 2 players hit 50 or more in a season. The following is a list by season showing each time a player has hit 50 or more home runs in one season.

HR	Player, team	Year
70	Mark McGwire, St. Louis Cardinals	1998
66	Sammy Sosa, Chicago Cubs	1998
61	Roger Maris, New York Yankees	1961
60	Babe Ruth, New York Yankess	1927
59	Babe Ruth, New York Yankees	1921
58	Jimmie Foxx, Philadelphia Athletics	1932
58	Hank Greenberg, Detroit Tigers	1938
58	Mark McGwire, Oakland Athletics/ St. Louis Cardinals	1997
56	Hack Wilson, Chicago Cubs	1930
56	Ken Griffey Jr., Seattle Mariners	1997
56	Ken Griffey Jr., Seattle Mariners	1998
54	Babe Ruth, New York Yankees	1920
54	Babe Ruth, New York Yankees	1928
54	Ralph Kiner, Pittsburgh Pirates	1949
54	Mickey Mantle, New York Yankees	1961
52	Mickey Mantle, New York Yankees	1956
52	Willie Mays, San Francisco Giants	1965
52	George Foster, Cincinnati Reds	1977
52	Mark McGwire, Oakland Athletics	1996
51	Ralph Kiner, Pittsburgh Pirates	1947
51	Johnny Mize, New York Giants	1947
51	Willie Mays, New York Giants	1955
51	Cecil Fielder, Detroit Tigers	1990
50	Jimmie Foxx, Boston Red Sox	1938
50	Albert Belle, Cleveland Indians	1995
50	Brady Anderson, Baltimore Orioles	1996
50	Greg Vaughn, San Diego Padres	1998

Earned Run Average Leaders

National League					American League				
Year	Player, club	G	IP	ERA	Year	Player, club	G	IP	ERA
1977	John Candelaria, Pittsburgh	33	231	**2.34**	1977	Frank Tanana, California	31	241	**2.54**
1978	Craig Swan, New York	29	207	**2.43**	1978	Ron Guidry, New York	35	274	**1.74**
1979	J. R. Richard, Houston	38	292	**2.71**	1979	Ron Guidry, New York	33	236	**2.78**
1980	Don Sutton, Los Angeles	32	212	**2.21**	1980	Rudy May, New York	41	175	**2.47**
1981	Nolan Ryan, Houston	21	149	**1.69**	1981	Steve McCatty, Oakland	22	186	**2.32**
1982	Steve Rogers, Montreal	35	277	**2.40**	1982	Rick Sutcliffe, Cleveland	34	216	**2.96**
1983	Atlee Hammaker, San Francisco	23	172	**2.25**	1983	Rick Honeycutt, Texas	25	174	**2.42**
1984	Alejandro Pena, Los Angeles	28	199	**2.48**	1984	Mike Boddicker, Baltimore	34	261	**2.79**
1985	Dwight Gooden, New York	35	276	**1.53**	1985	Dave Stieb, Toronto	36	265	**2.48**
1986	Mike Scott, Houston	37	275	**2.22**	1986	Roger Clemens, Boston	33	254	**2.48**
1987	Nolan Ryan, Houston	34	211	**2.76**	1987	Jimmy Key, Toronto	36	261	**2.76**
1988	Joe Magrane, St. Louis	24	165	**2.18**	1988	Allan Anderson, Minnesota	30	202	**2.45**

National League					American League			
Year	Player, club	G	IP	ERA	Year	Player, club	G	IP	ERA

Year	Player, club (National League)	G	IP	ERA
1989	Scott Garrelts, San Francisco	30	193	**2.28**
1990	Danny Darwin, Houston	48	162	**2.21**
1991	Dennis Martinez, Montreal	31	222	**2.39**
1992	Bill Swift, San Francisco	30	164	**2.08**
1993	Greg Maddux, Atlanta	36	267	**2.36**
1994	Greg Maddux, Atlanta	25	202	**1.56**
1995	Greg Maddux, Atlanta	28	209	**1.63**
1996	Kevin Brown, Florida	32	233	**1.89**
1997	Pedro Martinez, Montreal	31	241	**1.90**
1998	Greg Maddux, Atlanta	34	251	**2.22**

Year	Player, club (American League)	G	IP	ERA
1989	Bret Saberhagen, Kansas City	36	262	**2.16**
1990	Roger Clemens, Boston	31	228	**1.93**
1991	Roger Clemens, Boston	35	271	**2.62**
1992	Roger Clemens, Boston	32	246	**2.41**
1993	Kevin Appier, Kansas City	34	238	**2.56**
1994	Steve Ontiveros, Oakland	27	115	**2.65**
1995	Randy Johnson, Seattle	30	214	**2.48**
1996	Juan Guzman, Toronto	27	187	**2.93**
1997	Roger Clemens, Toronto	34	264	**2.05**
1998	Roger Clemens, Toronto	33	234	**2.65**

ERA is computed by multiplying earned runs allowed by 9, then dividing by innings pitched.

Yankees Sweep Padres in 4 Games to Win Their 24th World Series Title

In Oct. 1998, the New York Yankees capped off a stellar year by sweeping the World Series against the San Diego Padres. It has been argued that the 1998 Yankees, who won an American League record 114 regular season games, were the best team in Major League Baseball history. In the Series, the Yankees twice rebounded from 3-run deficits to win games in late innings. Third baseman Scott Brosius had 6 RBIs in the Series, including 4 in a 5-4 come from behind victory in Game 3, and was named the Series MVP.

Game One: Yankees 9, Padres 6

San Diego	ab	r	h	bi	New York	ab	r	h	bi
Veras, 2b	4	1	1	0	Knoblauch, 2b	4	1	2	3
Gwynn, rf	4	1	3	2	Jeter, ss	4	1	1	0
Vaughn, lf	4	3	2	3	O'Neill, rf	5	0	0	0
Caminiti, 3b	3	0	0	0	Williams, cf	4	1	0	0
Leyritz, dh	4	0	0	0	Davis, dh	3	2	1	0
Joyner, 1b	3	0	0	0	Martinez, 1b	3	2	1	4
Finley, cf	4	0	1	0	Brosius, 3b	4	0	1	0
Hernandez, c	3	0	0	0	Posada, c	3	1	1	0
G. Myers, ph	1	0	0	0	Ledee, lf	3	1	2	2
Gomez, ss	3	1	1	0	**Totals**	**33**	**9**	**9**	**9**
Vander Wal, ph	1	0	0	0					
Totals	**34**	**6**	**8**	**5**					

San Diego	0	0	2	0	3	0	0	1	0—6
New York	0	2	0	0	0	0	7	0	x—9

	ip	h	r	er	bb	so
San Diego						
Brown	6.1	6	4	4	3	5
Wall L, 0-1	0	2	2	2	0	0
Langston	0.2	1	3	3	2	0
Boehringer	0.1	0	0	0	1	1
R. Myers	0.2	0	0	0	0	2
New York						
Wells W, 1-0	7	7	5	5	2	4
Nelson	0.2	1	1	0	1	1
M. Rivera S, 1	1.1	0	0	0	0	2

E - Vaughn (1), Knoblauch (1). LOB - San Diego 4, New York 7. 2B - Finley (1), Ledee (1). HR - Vaughn 2 (2), Gwynn (1), Knoblauch (1), Martinez (1). RBI - Vaughn 3 (3), Gwynn 2 (2), Ledee 2 (2), Knoblauch 3 (3), Martinez 4 (4).

How runs were scored—Two in New York second: Davis singled. Martinez walked, Davis to second. Posada walked loading the bases. Ledee doubled, Davis and Martinez scored.

Two in San Diego third: Gomez singled. Vaughn homered scoring Gomez.

Three in San Diego fifth: Veras singled. Gwynn homered, Veras scored. Vaughn homered.

Seven in New York seventh: Posada singled. Ledee walked, Posada to second. Knoblauch homered, Posada and Ledee scored. Jeter singled. Williams was intentionally walked after a wild pitch advanced Jeter to second. Davis walked to load the bases. Martinez hit a grand slam, Jeter, Williams, and Davis scored.

One in San Diego eighth: Gwynn singled. Vaughn reached first on a fielder's choice. Caminiti walked, Vaughn to second. Joyner reached first on an error, Vaughn scored.

Game Two: Yankees 9, Padres 3

San Diego	ab	r	h	bi	New York	ab	r	h	bi
Veras, 2b	5	0	1	1	Knoblauch, 2b	3	2	2	0
Gwynn, rf	4	0	1	0	Jeter, ss	5	1	2	1
Vaughn, dh	4	0	0	0	O'Neill, rf	5	1	1	0
Caminiti, 3b	5	1	1	0	Williams, cf	4	1	1	2
Joyner, 1b	2	0	0	0	Davis, dh	3	1	1	1
Leyritz, ph-1b	1	0	0	0	Bush, pr-dh	0	0	0	0
Finley, cf	4	0	0	0	Martinez, 1b	5	1	3	0
Vander Wal, lf	3	0	2	0	Brosius, 3b	5	1	3	1
Rivera, ph-lf	1	1	1	1	Posada, c	4	1	1	2
G. Myers, c	3	0	0	0	Ledee, lf	3	0	2	1
Hernandez, ph-c	1	0	1	0	**Totals**	**37**	**9**	**16**	**8**
Gomez, ss	3	1	2	0					
Sweeney, ph	1	0	1	1					
Sheets, ss	0	0	0	0					
Totals	**37**	**3**	**10**	**3**					

San Diego	0	0	0	0	1	0	0	2	0—3
New York	3	3	1	0	2	0	0	0	0—9

	ip	h	r	er	bb	so
San Diego						
Ashby L, 0-1	2.2	10	7	4	1	1
Boehringer	1.2	4	2	2	1	2
Wall	2.2	1	0	0	3	1
Miceli	1	1	0	0	2	1
New York						
Hernandez W, 1-0	7	6	1	1	3	7
Stanton	0.2	3	2	2	0	1
Nelson	1.1	1	0	0	0	2

E - Caminiti (1). LOB - San Diego 10, New York 11. 2B - Veras (1), Vander Wal (1), Caminiti (1), R. Rivera (1), Ledee (2). 3B - Gomez (1). HR - Williams (1), Posada (1). RBI - Veras (1), R. Rivera (1), Sweeney (1), Davis (1), Brosius (1), Jeter (1), Williams 2 (2), Ledee (3), Posada 2 (2). SB - Knoblauch (1). CS - Ledee (1).

How runs were scored—Three in New York first: Knoblauch walked and stole second. O'Neill reached first on a throwing error, Knoblauch scored. Williams grounded out, O'Neill to second. Davis singled, O'Neill scored. Martinez singled, Davis to third. Brosius singled, Davis scored.

Three in New York second: Ledee singled. Knoblauch singled, Ledee to second. Ledee was thrown out, and Knoblauch moved to second on a double steal attempt. Jeter singled, Knoblauch scored. Williams homered, Jeter scored.

One in New York third: Martinez singled. Brosius singled, Martinez to second. Posada grounded into a double play, Martinez to third. Ledee doubled, Martinez scored.

One in San Diego fifth: Gomez tripled. Veras doubled, Gomez scored.

Two in New York fifth: Brosius singled. Posada homered, Brosius scored.

Two in San Diego eighth: Caminiti doubled. Finley grounded out, Caminiti to third. R. Rivera doubled, Caminiti scored. Hernandez singled, R. Rivera to third. Sweeney singled, R. Rivera scored.

Game Three: Yankees 5, Padres 4

New York	ab	r	h	bi	San Diego	ab	r	h	bi
Knoblauch, 2b	4	0	1	0	Veras, 2b	3	2	1	0
Jeter, ss	4	0	1	0	Gwynn, rf	4	1	2	1
O'Neill, rf	4	1	1	0	R. Rivera, pr-rf	0	0	0	0
Williams, cf	4	0	0	0	Vaughn, lf	3	0	0	1
Martinez, 1b	3	1	0	0	Caminiti, 3b	2	0	0	1
Brosius, 3b	4	2	3	4	Joyner, 1b	3	0	0	0
Spencer, lf	3	1	1	0	Finley, cf	4	0	0	0
Ledee, ph-lf	1	0	0	0	Leyritz, c	2	0	0	0
Girardi, c	2	0	0	0	Hernandez, c	2	0	1	0
Posada, ph-c	2	0	1	0	Vander Wal, pr	0	0	0	0
Cone, p	2	0	1	0	Gomez, ss	3	0	1	0
Davis, ph	1	0	0	1	Hoffman, p	0	0	0	0
Bush, pr	0	0	0	0	Sweeney, ph	1	0	1	0
Lloyd, p	0	0	0	0	Hitchcock, p	2	1	1	0
Mendoza, p	1	0	0	0	Hamilton, p	0	0	0	0
M. Rivera, p	0	0	0	0	R. Myers, p	0	0	0	0
Totals	**35**	**5**	**9**	**5**	Sheets, ss	2	0	0	0
					Totals	**31**	**4**	**7**	**3**

New York	0	0	0	0	0	0	2	3	0—5
San Diego	0	0	0	0	0	3	0	1	0—4

	ip	h	r	er	bb	so
New York						
Cone	6	2	3	2	3	4
Lloyd	0.1	0	0	0	0	0
Mendoza W, 1-0	1	2	1	1	0	1
M. Rivera S, 2	1.2	3	0	0	0	2
San Diego						
Hitchcock	6	7	2	1	1	7
Hamilton	1	0	0	0	1	1
R. Myers	0	0	1	1	1	0
Hoffman L, 0-1	2	2	2	2	1	0

E - O'Neill (1), Caminiti (2). PB - Leyritz (1). LOB - New York 7, San Diego 5. 2B - Spencer (1), Veras (2). HR - Brosius 2 (2). RBI - Brosius 4 (5), Davis (2), Gwynn (3), Caminiti (1), Vaughn (4). SF - Caminiti (1), Vaughn (1).

How runs were scored—Three in San Diego sixth: Hitchcock singled. Veras walked, Hitchcock to second. Gwynn singled, Hitchcock scored, Veras to third. Gwynn advanced to second on throw to third. Veras scored and Gwynn moved to third on throwing error. Caminiti hit a sacrifice fly, Gwynn scored.

Two in New York seventh: Brosius homered. Spencer doubled. Spencer moved to third on passed ball. Davis reached first on an error, Spencer scored.

Three in the New York eighth: O'Neill walked. Martinez walked, O'Neill to second. Brosius homered, O'Neill and Martinez scored.

One in San Diego eighth: Veras doubled. Gwynn singled, Veras to third. Vaughn hit a sacrifice fly, Veras scored.

Game Four: Yankees 3 , Padres 0

New York	ab	r	h	bi	San Diego	ab	r	h	bi
Knoblauch, 2b	5	0	1	0	Veras, 2b	3	0	0	0
Jeter, ss	4	2	2	0	Gwynn, rf	4	0	2	0
O'Neill, rf	5	1	2	0	Vaughn, lf	4	0	0	0
Williams, cf	4	0	0	1	Caminiti, 3b	4	0	1	0
Martinez, 1b	2	0	1	0	Leyritz, 1b	3	0	0	0
Brosius, 3b	4	0	1	1	R. Rivera, cf	4	0	3	0
Ledee, lf	3	0	2	1	Hernandez, c	4	0	0	0
Girardi, c	4	0	0	0	Gomez, ss	2	0	0	0
Pettitte, p	2	0	0	0	Sweeney, ph	1	0	0	0
Nelson, p	0	0	0	0	Brown, p	2	0	1	0
M. Rivera, p	1	0	0	0	Vander Wal, ph	1	0	0	0
Totals	**34**	**3**	**9**	**3**	Miceli, p	0	0	0	0
					R. Myers, p	0	0	0	0
					Totals	**32**	**0**	**7**	**0**

New York	0	0	0	0	0	1	0	2	0	—3
San Diego	0	0	0	0	0	0	0	0	0	—0

	ip	h	r	er	bb	so
New York						
Pettitte W, 1-0	7.1	5	0	0	3	4
Nelson	0.1	0	0	0	0	1
M. Rivera S, 3	1.1	2	0	0	0	0
San Diego						
Brown L, 0-1	8	8	3	3	3	8
Miceli	0.2	1	0	0	0	0
R. Myers	0.1	0	0	0	0	0

LOB - New York 9, San Diego 8. 2B - Ledee (3), O'Neill (1), R. Rivera (2). RBI - Williams (3), Brosius (6), Ledee (4). S - Pettitte (1). SF - Ledee (1).

How runs were scored—One in New York sixth: Jeter singled. O'Neill doubled, Jeter to third. Williams grounded out, Jeter scored.

Two in New York eighth: Jeter walked. O'Neill singled, Jeter to second. Martinez was intentionally walked to load the bases. Brosius singled, Jeter scored, O'Neill to third. Ledee hit a sacrifice fly, O'Neill scored.

World Series Results, 1903-1998

1903	Boston AL 5, Pittsburgh NL 3
1904	No series
1905	New York NL 4, Philadelphia AL 1
1906	Chicago AL 4, Chicago NL 2
1907	Chicago NL 4, Detroit AL 0, 1 tie
1908	Chicago NL 4, Detroit AL 1
1909	Pittsburgh NL 4, Detroit AL 3
1910	Philadelphia AL 4, Chicago NL 1
1911	Philadelphia AL 4, New York NL 2
1912	Boston AL 4, New York NL 3, 1 tie
1913	Philadelphia AL 4, New York NL 1
1914	Boston NL 4, Philadelphia AL 0
1915	Boston AL 4, Philadelphia NL 1
1916	Boston AL 4, Brooklyn NL 1
1917	Chicago AL 4, New York NL 2
1918	Boston AL 4, Chicago NL 2
1919	Cincinnati NL 5, Chicago AL 3
1920	Cleveland AL 5, Brooklyn NL 2
1921	New York NL 5, New York AL 3
1922	New York NL 4, New York AL 0, 1 tie
1923	New York AL 4, New York NL 2
1924	Washington AL 4, New York NL 3
1925	Pittsburgh NL 4, Washington AL 3
1926	St. Louis NL 4, New York AL 3
1927	New York AL 4, Pittsburgh NL 0
1928	New York AL 4, St. Louis NL 0
1929	Philadelphia AL 4, Chicago NL 1
1930	Philadelphia AL 4, St. Louis NL 2
1931	St. Louis NL 4, Philadelphia AL 3
1932	New York AL 4, Chicago NL 0
1933	New York NL 4, Washington AL 1
1934	St. Louis NL 4, Detroit AL 3
1935	Detroit AL 4, Chicago NL 2
1936	New York AL 4, New York NL 2
1937	New York AL 4, New York NL 1
1938	New York AL 4, Chicago NL 0
1939	New York AL 4, Cincinnati NL 0
1940	Cincinnati NL 4, Detroit AL 3
1941	New York AL 4, Brooklyn NL 1
1942	St. Louis NL 4, New York AL 1
1943	New York AL 4, St. Louis NL 1
1944	St. Louis NL 4, St. Louis AL 2
1945	Detroit AL 4, Chicago NL 3
1946	St. Louis NL 4, Boston AL 3
1947	New York AL 4, Brooklyn NL 3
1948	Cleveland AL 4, Boston NL 2
1949	New York AL 4, Brooklyn NL 1
1950	New York AL 4, Philadelphia NL 0
1951	New York AL 4, New York NL 2
1952	New York AL 4, Brooklyn NL 3
1953	New York AL 4, Brooklyn NL 2
1954	New York NL 4, Cleveland AL 0
1955	Brooklyn NL 4, New York AL 3
1956	New York AL 4, Brooklyn NL 3
1957	Milwaukee NL 4, New York AL 3
1958	New York AL 4, Milwaukee NL 3
1959	Los Angeles NL 4, Chicago AL 2
1960	Pittsburgh NL 4, New York AL 3
1961	New York AL 4, Cincinnati NL 1
1962	New York AL 4, San Francisco NL 3
1963	Los Angeles NL 4, New York AL 0
1964	St. Louis NL 4, New York AL 3
1965	Los Angeles NL 4, Minnesota AL 3
1966	Baltimore AL 4, Los Angeles NL 0
1967	St. Louis NL 4, Boston AL 3
1968	Detroit AL 4, St. Louis NL 3
1969	New York NL 4, Baltimore AL 1
1970	Baltimore AL 4, Cincinnati NL 1
1971	Pittsburgh NL 4, Baltimore AL 3
1972	Oakland AL 4, Cincinnati NL 3
1973	Oakland AL 4, New York NL 3
1974	Oakland AL 4, Los Angeles NL 1
1975	Cincinnati NL 4, Boston AL 3
1976	Cincinnati NL 4, New York AL 0
1977	New York AL 4, Los Angeles NL 2
1978	New York AL 4, Los Angeles NL 2
1979	Pittsburgh NL 4, Baltimore AL 3
1980	Philadelphia NL 4, Kansas City AL 2
1981	Los Angeles NL 4, New York AL 2
1982	St. Louis NL 4, Milwaukee AL 3
1983	Baltimore AL 4, Philadelphia NL 1
1984	Detroit AL 4, San Diego NL 1
1985	Kansas City AL 4, St. Louis NL 3
1986	New York NL 4, Boston AL 3
1987	Minnesota AL 4, St. Louis NL 3
1988	Los Angeles NL 4, Oakland AL 1
1989	Oakland AL 4, San Francisco NL 0
1990	Cincinnati NL 4, Oakland AL 0
1991	Minnesota AL 4, Atlanta NL 3
1992	Toronto AL 4, Atlanta NL 2
1993	Toronto AL 4, Philadelphia NL 2
1994	No series
1995	Atlanta NL 4, Cleveland AL 2
1996	New York AL 4, Atlanta NL 2
1997	Florida NL 4, Cleveland AL 3
1998	New York AL 4, San Diego NL 0

World Series MVP

Year	player, position, team
1955	John Podres, p, Brooklyn
1956	Don Larsen, p, New York, NL
1957	Lew Burdette, p, Milwaukee, NL
1958	Bob Turley, p, NY AL
1959	Larry Sherry, p, LA
1960[1]	Bobby Richardson, 2b, NY, AL
1961	Whitey Ford, p, NY, AL
1962	Ralph Terry, p, NY, AL
1963	Sandy Koufax, p, LA
1964	Bob Gibson, p, St. Louis
1965	Sandy Koufax, p, LA
1966	Frank Robinson, of, Baltimore
1967	Bob Gibson, p, St. Louis
1968	Mickey Lolich, p, Detroit
1969	Donn Clendenon, 1b, NY, NL
1970	Brooks Robinson, 3b, Baltimore
1971	Roberto Clemente, of, Pittsburgh
1972	Gene Tenance, c, Oakland
1973	Reggie Jackson, of, Oakland
1974	Rollie Fingers, p, Oakland
1975	Pete Rose, 3b, Cincinnati
1976	Johnny Bench, c, Cincinnati
1977	Reggie Jackson, of, NY, AL
1978	Bucky Dent, ss, NY, AL
1979	Willie Stargell, 1b, Pittsburgh
1980	Mike Schmidt, 3b, Philadelphia
1981	Ron Cey, 3b, LA
	Pedro Guerrero, of, LA
	Steve Yeager, c, LA
1982	Darrell Porter, c, St. Louis
1983	Rick Dempsey, c, Baltimore
1984	Alan Trammell, ss, Detroit
1985	Bret Saberhagen, p, Kansas City
1986	Ray Knight, 3b, NY, NL
1987	Frank Viola, p, Minnesota
1988	Orel Hershiser, p, LA
1989	Dave Stewart, p, Oakland
1990	Jose Rijo, p, Cincinnati
1991	Jack Morris, p, Minnesota
1992	Pat Borders, c, Toronto
1993	Paul Molitor, dh, Toronto
1994	no series
1995	Tom Glavine, p, Atlanta
1996	John Wetteland, p, NY, AL
1997	Livan Hernandez, p, Florida
1998	Scott Brosius, 3b, NY, AL

(1) Bobby Richardson won the MVP although Pittsburgh beat New York.

All-Time Major League Leaders

(*player active at end of 1998 season)

Games

Player	Games
Pete Rose	3,562
Carl Yastrzemski	3,308
Hank Aaron	3,298
Ty Cobb	3,035
Eddie Murray	3,026
Stan Musial	3,026
Willie Mays	2,992
Dave Winfield	2,973
Rusty Staub	2,951
Brooks Robinson	2,896

At Bats

Player	At Bats
Pete Rose	14,053
Hank Aaron	12,364
Carl Yastrzemski	11,988
Ty Cobb	11,434
Eddie Murray	11,336
Robin Yount	11,008
Dave Winfield	11,003
Stan Musial	10,972
Willie Mays	10,881
Paul Molitor*	10,835

Runs Batted In

Hank Aaron	2,297
Babe Ruth	2,213
Lou Gehrig	1,995
Stan Musial	1,951
Ty Cobb	1,937
Jimmie Foxx	1,922
Eddie Murray	1,917
Willie Mays	1,903
Mel Ott	1,860
Carl Yastrzemski	1,844

Stolen Bases

Player	Stolen Bases
Rickey Henderson*	1,297
Lou Brock	938
Billy Hamilton	912
Ty Cobb	892
Tim Raines*	803
Vince Coleman	752
Eddie Collins	744
Arlie Latham	739
Max Carey	738
Honus Wagner	722

Runs

Player	Runs
Ty Cobb	2,246
Hank Aaron	2,174
Babe Ruth	2,174
Pete Rose	2,165
Willie Mays	2,062
Rickey Henderson*	2,014
Stan Musial	1,949
Lou Gehrig	1,888
Tris Speaker	1,882
Mel Ott	1,859

Strikeouts

Player	Strikeouts
Nolan Ryan	5,714
Steve Carlton	4,136
Bert Blyleven	3,701
Tom Seaver	3,640
Don Sutton	3,574
Gaylord Perry	3,534
Walter Johnson	3,509
Phil Niekro	3,342
Ferguson Jenkins	3,192
Roger Clemens*	3,153

Shutouts

Player	Shutouts
Walter Johnson	110
Grover Alexander	90
Christy Mathewson	79
Cy Young	76
Eddie Plank	69
Warren Spahn	63
Nolan Ryan	61
Tom Seaver	61
Bert Blyleven	60
Don Sutton	58

Saves

Player	Saves
Lee Smith	478
John Franco*	397
Dennis Eckersley*	390
Jeff Reardon	367
Randy Myers*	347
Rollie Fingers	341
Tom Henke	311
Rich Gossage	310
Bruce Sutter	300
Jeff Montgomery*	292

All-Time Home Run Leaders

Player	HR	Player	HR	Player	HR	Player	HR
Hank Aaron	755	Ted Williams	521	Carl Yastrzemski	452	Joe Carter*	396
Babe Ruth	714	Ernie Banks	512	Dave Kingman	442	Graig Nettles	390
Willie Mays	660	Ed Mathews	512	Andre Dawson	438	Johnny Bench	389
Frank Robinson	586	Mel Ott	511	Billy Williams	426	Dwight Evans	385
Harmon Killebrew	573	Eddie Murray	504	Darrell Evans	414	Cal Ripken Jr.*	384
Reggie Jackson	563	Lou Gehrig	493	Barry Bonds*	411	Frank Howard	382
Mike Schmidt	548	Stan Musial	475	Duke Snider	407	Jim Rice	382
Mickey Mantle	536	Willie Stargell	475	Al Kaline	399	Orlando Cepeda	379
Jimmy Foxx	534	Dave Winfield	465	Dale Murphy	398	Tony Perez	379
Willie McCovey	521	Mark McGwire*	457	Jose Canseco*	397	Norm Cash	377

Players With 3,000 Major League Hits

Player	Hits	Player	Hits	Player	Hits
Pete Rose	4,256	Honus Wagner	3,415	Paul Waner	3,152
Ty Cobb	4,189	Paul Molitor*	3,319	Robin Yount	3,142
Hank Aaron	3,771	Eddie Collins	3,315	Dave Winfield	3,110
Stan Musial	3,630	Willie Mays	3,283	Rod Carew	3,053
Tris Speaker	3,514	Eddie Murray	3,255	Lou Brock	3,023
Carl Yastrzemski	3,419	Nap Lajoie	3,242	Al Kaline	3,007
		George Brett	3,154	Roberto Clemente	3,000

Pitchers With 300 Major League Wins

Cy Young	511	Warren Spahn	363	Steve Carlton	329	Don Sutton	324	Charley Radbourn	309
Walter Johnson	417	Kid Nichols	361	John Clarkson	328	Phil Niekro	318	Mickey Welch	307
Grover Alexander	373	Pud Galvin	360	Eddie Plank	326	Gaylord Perry	314	Lefty Grove	300
Christy Mathewson	373	Tim Keefe	342	Nolan Ryan	324	Tom Seaver	311	Early Wynn	300

Baseball Stadiums[1]

National League

Team	Stadium (year opened)	Surface	Home run distances (ft.) LF	Center	RF	Seating capacity
Arizona Diamondbacks	Bank One Ballpark (1998)	Grass	328	402	335	48,500
Atlanta Braves	Turner Field (1997)	Grass	335	401	330	50,062
Chicago Cubs	Wrigley Field (1914)	Grass	355	400	353	38,902
Cincinnati Reds	Cinergy Field (1970)	Artificial	330	404	330	52,953
Colorado Rockies	Coors Field (1995)	Grass	347	415	350	50,381
Florida Marlins	Pro Player Stadium (1987)	Grass	335	410	345	42,531
Houston Astros	The Astrodome (1965)	Artificial	325	400	325	54,699
Los Angeles Dodgers	Dodger Stadium (1962)	Grass	330	395	330	56,000
Milwaukee Brewers	County Stadium (1953)	Grass	315	402	315	53,192
Montreal Expos	Olympic Stadium (1976)	Artificial	325	404	325	46,500
New York Mets	Shea Stadium (1964)	Grass	338	410	338	55,775
Philadelphia Phillies	Veterans Stadium (1971)	Artificial	330	408	330	62,409
Pittsburgh Pirates	Three Rivers Stadium (1970)	Artificial	335	400	335	47,678
St. Louis Cardinals	Busch Stadium (1966)	Grass	330	402	330	49,625
San Diego Padres	Qualcomm Stadium (1967)	Grass	327	405	327	56,133
San Francisco Giants	3Com Park at Candlestick Point (1960)	Grass	335	400	328	63,000

American League

Team	Stadium (year opened)	Surface	LF	Center	RF	Seating capacity
Anaheim Angels	Edison Intl. Field of Anaheim (1966)	Grass	333	404	333	45,050
Baltimore Orioles	Oriole Park at Camden Yards (1992)	Grass	333	400	318	48,876
Boston Red Sox	Fenway Park (1912)	Grass	315	420	302	33,871
Chicago White Sox	Comiskey Park (1991)	Grass	347	400	347	44,321
Cleveland Indians	Jacobs Field (1994)	Grass	325	405	325	43,368
Detroit Tigers	Tiger Stadium (1912)	Grass	340	440	325	46,945
Kansas City Royals	Kauffman Stadium (1973)	Grass	330	400	330	40,625
Minnesota Twins	Hubert H. Humphrey Metrodome (1982)	Artificial	343	408	327	48,678
New York Yankees	Yankee Stadium (1923)	Grass	312	410	310	55,070
Oakland A's	Oakland Coliseum (1968)	Grass	330	400	330	43,662
Seattle Mariners	The Kingdome (1976)	Artificial	331	405	312	59,084
Tampa Bay Devil Rays	Tropicana Field (1990)	Grass	315	410	322	45,200
Texas Rangers	The Ballpark in Arlington (1994)	Grass	332	400	325	49,166
Toronto Blue Jays	SkyDome (1989)	Artificial	328	400	328	50,516

(1) As of 1998 season.

Cal Ripken, Jr., Ends His Consecutive Games Streak at 2,632

On Sept. 19, 1998, Baltimore Orioles third baseman Cal Ripken, Jr., played in his 2,632d consecutive game. The following night, he sat the game out, thereby ending the longest consecutive games streak in baseball history. More than 3 years earlier, on Sept. 6, 1995, Ripken played in his 2,131st consecutive game to break Lou Gehrig's "unbreakable record," which had stood for over 56 years. Here is a comparison of some of their statistics during their respective streaks:

Cal Ripken, Jr.		Lou Gehrig
May 30, 1982	Streak began	June 1, 1925
September 19, 1998	Streak ended	April 30, 1939
2,632	Consecutive games played	2,130
10,221	At bats	7,938
2,832	Hits	2,700
381	Home Runs	492
1,494	Runs Batted In	1,984
.277	Batting Average	.340

Major League Franchise Shifts and Additions

1953—Boston Braves (NL) became Milwaukee Braves.
1954—St. Louis Browns (AL) became Baltimore Orioles.
1955—Philadelphia Athletics (AL) became Kansas City Athletics.
1958—New York Giants (NL) became San Francisco Giants.
1958—Brooklyn Dodgers (NL) became Los Angeles Dodgers.
1961—Washington Senators (AL) became Minnesota Twins.
1961—Los Angeles Angels (renamed California Angels in 1965 and Anaheim Angels in 1997) enfranchised by the American League.
1961—Washington Senators enfranchised by the American League (a new team, replacing the former Washington club, whose franchise was moved to Minneapolis-St. Paul).
1962—Houston Colt .45's (renamed the Houston Astros in 1965) enfranchised by the National League.
1962—New York Mets enfranchised by the National League.
1966—Milwaukee Braves (NL) became Atlanta Braves.
1968—Kansas City Athletics (AL) became Oakland Athletics.
1969—Kansas City Royals and Seattle Pilots enfranchised by the American League; Montreal Expos and San Diego Padres enfranchised by the National League.
1970—Seattle Pilots became Milwaukee Brewers.
1971—Washington Senators became Texas Rangers (Dallas-Fort Worth area).
1977—Toronto Blue Jays and Seattle Mariners enfranchised by the American League.
1993—Colorado Rockies (Denver) and Florida Marlins (Miami) enfranchised by the National League.
1998—Tampa Bay Devil Rays began play in the American League; Arizona Diamondbacks (Phoenix) began play in the National League (both teams enfranchised in 1995). Milwaukee Brewers moved from the AL to the NL.

NCAA Baseball Champions

1960	Minnesota	1970	USC	1980	Arizona	1990	Georgia
1961	USC	1971	USC	1981	Arizona St.	1991	LSU
1962	Michigan	1972	USC	1982	Miami (FL)	1992	Pepperdine
1963	USC	1973	USC	1983	Texas	1993	LSU
1964	Minnesota	1974	USC	1984	Cal. St.-Fullerton	1994	Oklahoma
1965	Arizona St.	1975	Texas	1985	Miami (FL)	1995	Cal. St.-Fullerton
1966	Ohio St.	1976	Arizona	1986	Arizona	1996	LSU
1967	Arizona St.	1977	Arizona St.	1987	Stanford	1997	LSU
1968	USC	1978	USC	1988	Stanford	1998	USC
1969	Arizona St.	1979	Cal. St.-Fullerton	1989	Wichita St.		

Little League World Series

The Little League World Series is played annually in Williamsport, PA. The team from Toms River, NJ, won the 1998 Little League World Series by defeating the team from Japan, 12-9, on Aug. 29. It was the 4th time that a team from New Jersey ever won the title, but only the first time since 1993 that a team from the U.S. had done so. Toms River, labeled the "Beast from the East" by its fans, had beaten Greenville, NC (Aug. 27), 5-2, to win the U.S. Championship.

Year	Winning / Losing Team	Score
1947	Williamsport, PA; Lock Haven, PA	16-7
1948	Lock Haven, PA; St. Petersburg, FL	6-5
1949	Hammonton, NJ; Pensacola, FL	5-0
1950	Houston, TX; Bridgeport, CT	2-1
1951	Stamford, CT; Austin, TX	3-0
1952	Norwalk, CT; Monongahela, PA	4-3
1953	Birmingham, AL; Schenectady, NY	1-0
1954	Schenectady, NY; Colton, CA	7-5
1955	Morrisville, PA; Merchantville, NJ	4-3
1956	Roswell, NM; Delaware, NJ	3-1
1957	Mexico; La Mesa, CA	4-0
1958	Mexico; Kankakee, IL	10-1
1959	Hamtramck, MI; Auburn, CA	12-0
1960	Levittown, PA; Ft. Worth, TX	5-0
1961	El Cajon, CA; El Campo, TX	4-2
1962	San Jose, CA; Kankakee, IL	3-0
1963	Granada Hills, CA; Stratford, CT	2-1
1964	Staten Island, NY; Mexico	4-0
1965	Windsor Locks, CT; Ontario, Canada	3-1
1966	Houston, TX; W. New York, NJ	8-2
1967	Tokyo, Japan; Chicago, IL	4-1
1968	Osaka, Japan; Richmond, VA	1-0
1969	Taiwan; Santa Clara, CA	5-0
1970	Wayne, NJ; Campbell, CA	2-0
1971	Taiwan; Gary, IN	12-3
1972	Taiwan; Hammond, IN	6-0
1973	Taiwan; Tucson, AZ	12-0
1974	Taiwan; Red Bluff, CA	12-1
1975	Lakewood, NJ; Tampa, FL	4-3
1976	Tokyo, Japan; Campbell, CA	10-3
1977	Taiwan; El Cajon, CA	7-2
1978	Taiwan; Danville, CA	11-1
1979	Taiwan; Campbell, CA	2-1
1980	Taiwan; Tampa, FL	4-3
1981	Taiwan; Tampa, FL	4-2
1982	Kirkland, WA; Taiwan	6-0
1983	Marietta, GA; Dominican Rep.	3-1
1984	South Korea; Altamonte Springs, FL	6-2
1985	South Korea; Mexico	7-1
1986	Taiwan; Tucson, AZ	12-0
1987	Chinese Taipei; Irvine, CA	21-1
1988	Chinese Taipei; Pearl City, HI	10-0
1989	Trumbull, CT; Chinese Taipei	5-2
1990	Chinese Taipei; Shippensburg, PA	9-0
1991	Chinese Taipei; Danville, CA	11-0
1992	Long Beach, CA; Philippines	6-0
1993	Long Beach, CA; Panama	3-2
1994	Venezuela; Northridge, CA	4-3
1995	Taiwan; Spring, TX	17-3
1996	Taiwan; Cranston, RI	13-3
1997	Mexico; Mission Viejo, CA	5-4
1998	Toms River, NJ; Japan	12-9

SPECIAL OLYMPICS

Special Olympics is an international program of year-round sports training and athletic competition for children and adults with mental retardation. All 50 U.S. states, Washington, DC, and Guam have chapter offices. In addition, there are accredited Special Olympics programs in nearly 150 countries. Persons wishing to volunteer or find out more about Special Olympics can contact Special Olympics International Headquarters, 1325 G St. NW, Suite 500, Washington, DC 20005, or access the Special Olympics website at http://www.specialolympics.org

1997 Special Olympic World Winter Games/1999 Special Olympic World Summer Games

The 6th Special Olympic World Winter Games were held Feb. 2-8, 1997, in Toronto and Collingwood, Ont., Canada. Nearly 2,000 athletes from 75 countries participated, along with approx. 500 coaches, 1,500 volunteers, and 2,000 family and friends. Athletes competed in Alpine Skiing, Cross-Country Skiing, Floor Hockey, Figure Skating, Speed Skating, and Snow-Shoeing (the last not official).

The 10th Special Olympic World Summer Games were scheduled to be held June 26-July 4, 1999, in Raleigh-Durham/Chapel Hill, NC. Over 7,000 athletes and coaches from 150 countries were expected to participate, competing in 19 sports.

CHESS

World Chess Champions

Source: U.S. Chess Federation

Official world champions since the title was first used are as follows:

1866-1894	Wilhelm Steinitz, Austria
1894-1921	Emanuel Lasker, Germany
1921-1927	Jose R. Capablanca, Cuba
1927-1935	Alexander A. Alekhine, France
1935-1937	Max Euwe, Netherlands
1937-1946	Alexander A. Alekhine, France (a)
1948-1957	Mikhail Botvinnik, USSR
1957-1958	Vassily Smyslov, USSR
1958-1959	Mikhail Botvinnik, USSR
1960-1961	Mikhail Tal, USSR
1961-1963	Mikhail Botvinnik, USSR
1963-1969	Tigran Petrosian, USSR
1969-1972	Boris Spassky, USSR
1972-1975	Bobby Fischer, U.S. (b)
1975-1985	Anatoly Karpov, USSR
1985-1993	Garry Kasparov, USSR/Russia (c)
1993-	Garry Kasparov, Russia (PCA)
1993-	Anatoly Karpov, Russia (FIDE)

(a) After Alekhine died in 1946, the title was vacant until 1948, when Botvinnik won the 1st championship match sanctioned by the International Chess Federation (FIDE). (b) Defaulted championship after refusal to accept FIDE rules for a championship match, Apr. 1975. (c) Kasparov broke with FIDE, Feb. 26, 1993. FIDE stripped Kasparov of his title Mar. 23. Kasparov defeated Nigel Short of Great Britain in a world championship match played Sept.-Oct. 1993 under the auspices of a new organization the two had founded, the Professional Chess Association (PCA). FIDE held a championship match between Anatoly Karpov (Russia) and Jan Timman (the Netherlands), which Karpov won in Nov. 1993. **Recent matches:** In Feb. 1996, Kasparov defeated Deep Blue (3 wins, 1 loss, 2 draws), a computer designed by IBM, in the 1st multigame regulation match between a world chess champion and a computer. In a May 1997 rematch, however, Kasparov was soundly defeated by the computer; he scored 1 win, 2 losses, 3 draws. Karpov successfully defended the FIDE title in June-July 1996 against 1991 U.S. chess champion Gata Kamsky of New York City, 10½ to 7½. **Further information:** More information on chess and chess champions may be accessed on the U.S. Chess Federation's Internet site: http://www.uschess.org

NEW YORK CITY MARATHON

John Kagwe of Kenya won his 2d New York City Marathon in a row on Nov. 1, 1998, with a time of 2 hrs., 8 mins., 45 secs. He beat the 2d-place finisher, fellow Kenyan Joseph Chebet, by 3 secs., the 2d-closest finish in the race's 29-yr. history. Franca Fiacconi of Italy was the women's winner, finishing in 2 hrs., 25 mins., 17 secs.

BOSTON MARATHON

Moses Tanui of Kenya won the 102d Boston Marathon, Apr. 20, 1998, with a time of 2 hrs., 7 mins., 34 secs. Fatuma Roba of Ethiopia was the women's winner for the 2d time in 2 years, with a time of 2 hrs., 23 mins., 21 secs.

MILLENNIUM FACT BOX

World's Oldest Annual Marathon

The Boston Marathon, originally the Boston Athletic Association Road Race, is the world's oldest annual marathon; it dates back to Apr. 19 (Patriots' Day), 1897, and was inspired by the first modern Olympic marathon, held in 1896 in Athens, Greece. Later marathons were also held on Patriots' Day (or in some cases, the day after), which in 1969 was changed to the 3d Monday in April. Only 15 runners participated in the first Boston Marathon (10 finished), which covered 24.5 miles and was won by John J. McDermott in a time of 2 hrs., 55 mins., 10 secs. McDermott walked for parts of the last mile; he still holds the record for largest margin of victory—6 mins., 52 secs. Some later highlights in the history of the marathon follow:

1918—Because of World War I, a military relay was run instead of the usual race; a team from Camp Devens in Ayer, MA, won with a time of 2:24:53.

1921—New Jersey plumber Frank Zuna became the first runner to break the 2-hr., 20-min. mark with a time of 2:18:57.

1927—The course was lengthened to 26 miles, 385 yards, to meet an Olympic standard set in 1924. The standard was based on a decision to have runners in the 1908 Olympic marathon travel this distance, from Windsor Castle to the front of the Royal Box at White City Stadium in London.

1939—Ellison "Tarzan" Brown won his 2d Boston Marathon in a time of 2:28:51, the first finish under 2 hrs., 30 mins., since the course was lengthened.

1967—Kathrine Switzer got into the race by entering herself as K. Switzer, and became the first woman to finish.

1969—The race topped the 1,000-runner mark, with 1,342 runners. This was the last time the marathon was open to all; after 1969, runners had to qualify for entry.

1972—Women were officially sanctioned for the race, and New Yorker Nina Kuscsik became the first official women's winner, with a time of 3:10:26.

1975—Boston's Bill Rodgers became the first runner to break the 2 hr., 10 min. mark, with a time of 2:09:55. The Boston Marathon officially recognized Bob Hall as the first wheelchair participant.

1994—Cosmas Ndeti of Kenya finished the race in 2:07:15, and Uta Pippig of Germany finished in 2:21:45, setting men's and women's records that still stand.

1996—For the 100th running of the Boston Marathon it was decided to have an open division, with a limited number of entrants admitted without having to qualify. A record 38,708 runners participated in the race.

1998—The marathon was covered by more than 1,400 media members, representing more than 300 outlets and 12 countries.

SOCCER

1998 World Cup

In 1998, France became the first host country since 1978 to win the World Cup, defeating Brazil 3-0, July 12. It was the 2d time the event was held in France; the first time was in 1938. France and Brazil were the only 2 teams in the 1998 World Cup that did not have to qualify for the tournament, because they had automatic bids—France because it was the host country, and Brazil because it was the defending champion. The 2002 World Cup was scheduled to be held jointly in Japan and South Korea.

Teams from over 172 nations played matches in 1996 and 1997 to earn a berth in the 1998 World Cup, and of them 30 qualified. Those 30 teams, plus Brazil and France, played in a preliminary round-robin tournament to determine the 16 teams that would reach the final elimination round. France went undefeated in the tournament, and Zinedine Zidane scored 2 1st-half goals in the final, providing more than enough scoring for the host team to capture the cup.

First Round Results

Group A

COUNTRY	W	T	L	GF	GA	Pts
Brazil	2	0	1	6	3	6
Norway	1	2	0	5	4	5
Morocco	1	1	1	5	5	4
Scotland	0	1	2	2	6	1

Group B

COUNTRY	W	T	L	GF	GA	Pts
Italy	2	1	0	7	3	7
Chile	0	3	0	4	4	3
Austria	0	2	1	3	4	2
Cameroon	0	2	1	2	5	2

Group C

COUNTRY	W	T	L	GF	GA	Pts
France	3	0	0	9	1	9
Demark	1	1	1	3	3	4
South Africa	0	2	1	3	6	2
Saudi Arabia	0	1	2	2	7	1

Group D

COUNTRY	W	T	L	GF	GA	Pts
Nigeria	2	0	1	5	5	6
Paraguay	1	2	0	3	1	5
Spain	1	1	1	8	4	4
Bulgaria	0	1	2	1	7	1

Group E

COUNTRY	W	T	L	GF	GA	Pts
Netherlands	1	2	0	7	2	5
Mexico	1	2	0	7	5	5
Belgium	0	3	0	3	3	3
South Korea	0	1	2	2	9	1

Group F

COUNTRY	W	T	L	GF	GA	Pts
Germany	2	1	0	6	2	7
Yugoslavia	2	1	0	4	2	7
Iran	1	0	2	2	4	3
United States	0	0	3	1	5	0

Group G

COUNTRY	W	T	L	GF	GA	Pts
Romania	2	1	0	4	2	7
England	2	0	1	5	2	6
Colombia	1	0	2	1	3	3
Tunisia	0	1	2	1	4	1

Group H

COUNTRY	W	T	L	GF	GA	Pts
Argentina	3	0	0	7	0	9
Croatia	2	0	1	4	2	6
Jamaica	1	0	2	3	9	3
Japan	0	0	3	1	4	0

Final Round Results

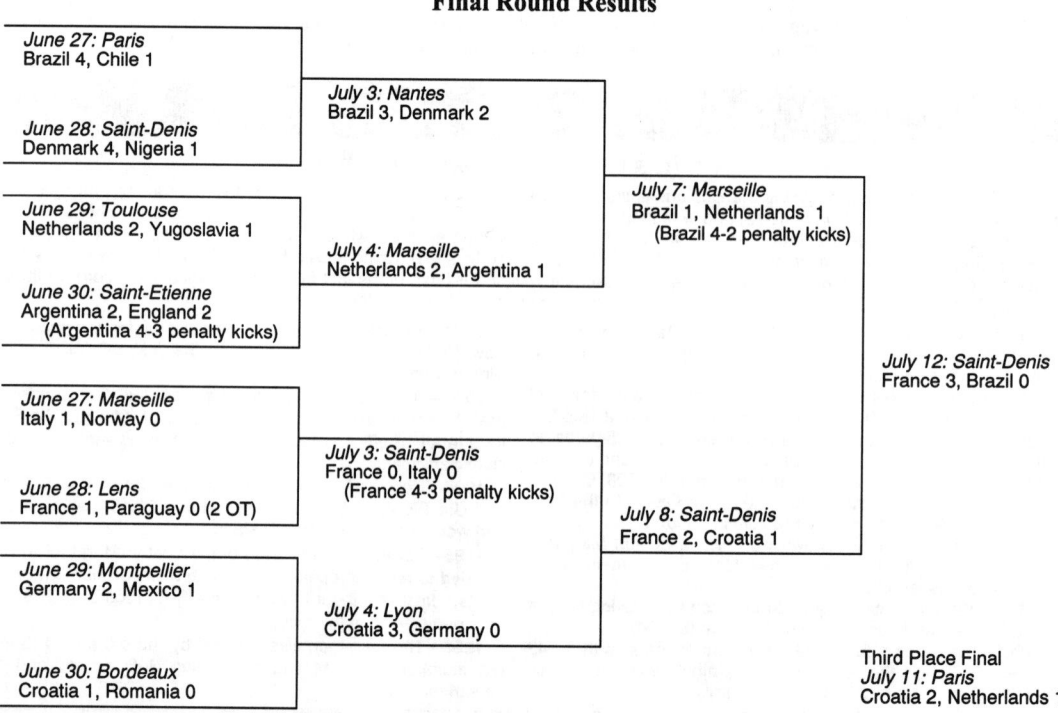

June 27: Paris
Brazil 4, Chile 1

June 28: Saint-Denis
Denmark 4, Nigeria 1

June 29: Toulouse
Netherlands 2, Yugoslavia 1

June 30: Saint-Etienne
Argentina 2, England 2
(Argentina 4-3 penalty kicks)

June 27: Marseille
Italy 1, Norway 0

June 28: Lens
France 1, Paraguay 0 (2 OT)

June 29: Montpellier
Germany 2, Mexico 1

June 30: Bordeaux
Croatia 1, Romania 0

July 3: Nantes
Brazil 3, Denmark 2

July 4: Marseille
Netherlands 2, Argentina 1

July 3: Saint-Denis
France 0, Italy 0
(France 4-3 penalty kicks)

July 4: Lyon
Croatia 3, Germany 0

July 7: Marseille
Brazil 1, Netherlands 1
(Brazil 4-2 penalty kicks)

July 8: Saint-Denis
France 2, Croatia 1

July 12: Saint-Denis
France 3, Brazil 0

Third Place Final
July 11: Paris
Croatia 2, Netherlands 1

The World Cup, 1930-98

Year	Winner	Final opponent	Site	Year	Winner	Final opponent	Site
1930	Uruguay	Argentina	Uruguay	1970	Brazil	Italy	Mexico
1934	Italy	Czechoslovakia	Italy	1974	W. Germany	Netherlands	W. Germany
1938	Italy	Hungary	France	1978	Argentina	Netherlands	Argentina
1950	Uruguay	Brazil	Brazil	1982	Italy	W. Germany	Spain
1954	W. Germany	Hungary	Switzerland	1986	Argentina	W. Germany	Mexico
1958	Brazil	Sweden	Sweden	1990	W. Germany	Argentina	Italy
1962	Brazil	Czechoslovakia	Chile	1994	Brazil	Italy	U.S.
1966	England	W. Germany	England	1998	France	Brazil	France

Major League Soccer

The 1998 Major League Soccer (MLS) season included 2 expansion teams, the Miami Fusion and the Chicago Fire. It was the 3d season for the league, which has gained in popularity throughout the U.S. On Oct. 25, 1998, the Chicago Fire upset the Washington D.C. United to win the 3d MLS Cup; the United had won the 2 previous cups.

1998 Final Standings

Eastern Conference

	W	So	L	GF	GA	Pts
Washington D.C. United	24	7	8	74	48	58
Columbus Crew	15	0	17	67	56	45
NY/NJ MetroStars	15	3	17	54	63	39
Miami Fusion	15	5	17	46	68	35
Tampa Bay Mutiny	12	1	20	46	57	34
New England Revolution	11	2	21	53	66	29

Western Conference

	W	So	L	GF	GA	Pts
Los Angeles Galaxy	24	2	8	85	44	68
Chicago Fire	20	2	12	62	45	56
Colorado Rapids	16	2	16	62	69	44
Dallas Burn	15	4	17	43	59	37
San Jose Clash	13	3	19	48	60	33
Kansas City Wizards	12	2	20	45	50	32

Note: 3 points for a regulation-time win, 1 point for a shootout win. So= shootout win.

1998 MLS Individual Statistical Leaders

Leading Scorers (2 points for a goal, 1 point for an assist)

	Name	Team	Games	Goals	Assists	Points
1.	John Stern	Columbus	27	26	5	57
2.	Cobi Jones	Los Angeles	24	19	13	51
3.	Welton	Los Angeles	31	17	11	45
4.	Roy Lassiter	Washington D.C.	31	18	8	44
5.	Raul Diaz Arce	New England	32	18	8	44
6.	Jaime Moreno	Washington D.C.	31	16	11	43
7.	Mauricio Cienfuegos	Los Angeles	30	13	16	42
8.	Marco Etcheverry	Washington D.C.	29	10	19	39
9.	Ronald Cerritos	San Jose	31	13	12	38
10.	Eduardo Hurtado	New York/New Jersey	29	11	15	37

Goalkeeping Leaders (minimum 1,395 minutes)

	Name	Team	Games	Minutes	Shots[1]	Saves	GA	GAA	Wins	Losses
1.	Zach Thornton	Chicago	25	2,076	118	85	27	1.17	16	8
2.	Kevin Hartman	Los Angeles	29	2,544	146	103	39	1.38	22	7
3.	Scott Garlick	Washington D.C.	25	2,205	129	88	35	1.43	19	5
4.	Mike Ammann	Kansas City	27	2,430	134	85	42	1.56	11	16
5.	David Kramer	San Jose	24	2,125	132	82	39	1.65	10	14
6.	Thomas Ravelli	Tampa Bay	23	2,053	179	131	38	1.67	7	13
7.	Juergen Sommer	Columbus	21	1,890	143	106	35	1.67	11	10
8.	Mark Dodd	Dallas	25	2,205	182	134	42	1.71	11	13
9.	Marcus Hahnemann	Colorado	28	2,520	200	138	52	1.86	16	12
10.	Jeff Cassar	Miami	21	1,890	151	107	41	1.95	12	9

Note: GA = goals against; GAA = goals against average. (1) Not shots on goal; includes shots over the goal or just past the post.

1998 MLS Awards

MVP: Marco Etcheverry, Washington DC
Defender of the year: Lubos Kubik, Chicago
Coach of the year: Bob Bradley, Chicago
Goalkeeper of the year: Zach Thornton, Chicago
Rookie of the year: Ben Olsen, Washington DC
Goal of the year: Brian McBride, Columbus Crew (v. Chicago, July 9 at Ohio Stadium)
Referee of the year: Paul Tamberino
Fair play, individual: Thomas Dooley, Columbus Crew
Fair play, team: Kansas City Wizards

1998 MLS Playoff Results

Eastern Conference

Columbus defeated N.Y/N.J. 2 games to 0
Washington D.C. defeated Miami 2 games to 0
Washington D.C. defeated Columbus 2 games to 1

Western Conference

Los Angeles defeated Dallas 2 games to 0
Chicago defeated Colorado 2 games to 0
Chicago defeated Los Angeles 2 games to 0

1998 MLS Cup

(Oct. 25, 1998 at the Rose Bowl, Pasadena, CA)
Chicago Fire 2, Washington D.C. United 0

QUICK REFERENCE INDEX

QUICK REFERENCE SPORTS INDEX

For complete Index, see pages 4-32.

DUE	RETURNED	DUE	RETURNED
1.		13.	
2.		14.	
3.		15.	
4.		16.	
5.		17.	
6.		18.	
7.		19.	
8.		20.	
9.		21.	
10.		22.	
11.		23.	
12.		24.	